THE OFFICIAL® 2008 PRICE GUIDE TO FOOTBALL CARDS

DR. JAMES BECKETT

TWENTY-SEVENTH EDITION

HOUSE OF COLLECTIBLES
Random House Reference • New York

House of Collectibles and colophon
are trademarks of Random House, Inc.

www.houseofcollectibles.com

Published by:
House of Collectibles
Random House Reference
New York, New York

Distributed by The Random House Information Group,
a division of Random House, Inc.,
New York, and simultaneously in Canada by
Random House of Canada Limited, Toronto.
Random House is a registered trademark of Random House, Inc.

www.randomhouse.com

Manufactured in the United States of America

ISSN: 0748-1365

ISBN: 978-0-375-72238-7

10 9 8 7 6 5 4 3 2 1

Twenty-Seventh Edition: August 2007

Table of Contents

Table of Contents

Table of Contents

Table of Contents

Table of Contents

Table of Contents

Table of Contents

Table of Contents

About the Author

Jim Beckett, the leading authority on sports card values in the United States, maintains a wide range of activities in the world of sports. He possesses one of the finest collections of sportscards and autographs in the world, has made numerous appearances on radio and television, and has been frequently cited in many national publications. He was awarded the first "Special Achievement Award for Contributions to the Hobby" by the National Sports Collectors Convention in 1980, the "Jock-Jaspersen Award for Hobby Dedication" in 1983, and the "Buck Barker, Spirit of the Hobby Award" in 1991.

Dr. Beckett is the author of *Beckett Baseball Card Price Guide, The Official Price Guide to Baseball Cards, The Sport Americana Price Guide to Baseball Collectibles, Beckett Almanac of Baseball Cards and Collectibles, The Sport Americana Baseball Memorabilia and Autograph Price Guide, Beckett Football Card Price Guide, The Official Price Guide to Football Cards, Beckett Hockey Card Price Guide and Alphabetical Checklist, Beckett Basketball Card Price Guide, The Official Price Guide to Basketball Cards,* and *Beckett Baseball Card Alphabetical Checklist.* In addition, he is the founder and publisher, of sports collectible magazines: *Beckett Baseball, Beckett Basketball Beckett Football, Beckett Hockey,* and *Beckett Racing.*

Jim Beckett received his Ph.D. in Statistics from Southern Methodist University in 1975. Prior to starting Beckett Publications in 1984, Dr. Beckett served as an Associate Professor of Statistics at Bowling Green State University and as a Vice President of a consulting firm in Dallas, Texas. He currently resides in Dallas.

How to Use This Book

Isn't it great? Every year this book gets better with all the new sets coming out. But even more exciting is that every year there are more attractive choices and, subsequently, more interest in the cards we love so much. This edition has been enhanced and expanded from the previous edition. The cards you collect —who appears on them, what they look like, where they are from, and (most important to most of you) what their current values are—are enumerated within. Many of the features contained in the other *Beckett Price Guides* have been incorporated into this volume since condition-grading, terminology, and many other aspects of collecting are common to the card hobby in general. We hope you find the book both interesting and useful in your collecting pursuits.

The Beckett Guide has been successful where other attempts have failed because it is complete, current, and valid. This price guide contains not just one, but two prices by condition for all the football cards listed. These account for most of the football cards in existence. The prices were added to the card lists just prior to printing and reflect not the author's opinions or desires but the going retail prices for each card, based on the marketplace (sports memorabilia conventions and shows, sportscard shops, hobby papers, current mail-order catalogs, Internet sales, auction results, and other firsthand reporting of actually realized prices).

What is the best price guide available on the market today? Of course card sellers will prefer the price guide with the highest prices, while card buyers will naturally prefer the one with the lowest prices. Accuracy, however, is the true test. Use the price guide used by more collectors and dealers than all the others combined. Look for the Beckett name. I won't put my name on anything I won't stake my reputation on. Not the lowest and not the highest—but the most accurate, with integrity.

To facilitate your use of this book, read the complete introductory section on the following pages before going to the pricing pages. Every collectible field has its own terminology; we've tried to capture most of these terms and definitions in our glossary. Please read carefully the section on grading and the condition of your cards, as you will not be able to determine which price column is appropriate for a given card without first knowing its condition.

Prices in This Guide

Prices found in this guide reflect current retail rates just prior to the printing of this book. They do not reflect the for-sale prices of the author, the publisher, the distributors, the advertisers, or any card dealers associated with this guide. No one is obligated in any way to buy, sell, or trade his or her cards based on these prices. The price listings were compiled by the author from actual buy/sell transactions at sports conventions, sportscard shops, buy/sell advertisements in the hobby papers, for-sale prices from dealer catalogs and price lists, and discussions with leading hobbyists in the U.S. and Canada. All prices are in U.S. dollars.

Acknowledgments

A great deal of diligence, hard work, and dedicated effort went into this year's volume. The high standards to which we hold ourselves, however, could not have been met without the expert input and generous amount of time contributed by many people. Our sincere thanks are extended to each and every one of you.

A list of these invaluable contributors appears after the Price Guide section.

Introduction

Welcome to the exciting world of sportscard collecting, one of America's most popular avocations. You have made a good choice in buying this book, since it will open up to you the entire panorama of this field in the simplest, most concise way.

The growth of *Beckett Baseball, Beckett Basketball, Beckett Football, Beckett Hockey,* and *Beckett Racing* is an indication of the unprecedented popularity of sportscards. Founded in 1984 by Dr. James Beckett, *Beckett Baseball* contains the most extensive and accepted monthly price guide, collectible glossy superstar covers, colorful feature articles, "Hot List," Convention Calendar, tips for beginners, "Readers Write" letters to and responses from the editor, information on errors and varieties, autograph collecting tips, and profiles of the sport's hottest stars. Published every month, *Beckett Baseball* is the hobby's largest paid circulation periodical. The other five magazines were built on the success of Baseball.

So collecting sportscards—while still pursued as a hobby with youthful exuberance by kids in the neighborhood—has also taken on the trappings of an industry, with thousands of full- and part-time card dealers, as well as vendors of supplies, clubs, and conventions. In fact, each year since 1980 thousands of hobbyists have assembled for a National Sports Collectors Convention, at which hundreds of dealers have displayed their wares, seminars have been conducted, autographs penned by sports notables, and millions of cards changed hands. The Beckett Guide is the best annual guide available to the exciting world of football cards. Read it and use it. May your enjoyment and your card collection increase in the coming months and years.

How to Collect

Each collection is personal and reflects the individuality of its owner. There are no set rules on how to collect cards. Since card collecting is a hobby or leisure pastime, what you collect, how much you collect, and how much time and money you spend collecting are entirely up to you. The funds you have available for collecting and your own personal taste should determine how you collect. The information and ideas presented here are intended to help you get the most enjoyment from this hobby.

It is impossible to collect every card ever produced. Therefore, beginners as well as intermediate and advanced collectors usually specialize in some way. One of the reasons this hobby is popular is that individual collectors can define and tailor their collecting methods to match their own tastes. To give you some ideas of the various approaches to collecting, we will list some of the more popular areas of specialization.

Many collectors select complete sets from particular years. For example, they may concentrate on assembling complete sets from all the years since their birth or since they became avid sports fans. They may try to collect a card for every player during that specified period of time. Many others wish to acquire only certain players. Usually such players are the superstars of the sport, but occasionally collectors will specialize in all the cards of players who attended a particular college or came from a certain town. Some collectors are only interested in the first cards or Rookie Cards of certain players.

Another fun way to collect cards is by team. Most fans have a favorite team, and it is natural for that loyalty to be translated into a desire for cards of the players on that favorite team. For most of the recent years, team sets (all the cards from a given team for that year) are readily available at a reasonable price. See Beckett.com for searchable player checklists.

Obtaining Cards

Several avenues are open to card collectors. Cards still can be purchased in the traditional way: by the pack at the local discount, grocery, or convenience store. But there are also thousands of card shops across the country that specialize in selling cards individually or by the pack, box, or set. Another alternative is the thousands of card shows held each month around the country, which feature anywhere from five to 800 tables of sports cards and memorabilia for sale.

For many years, it has been possible to purchase complete sets of cards through mail-order advertisers found in traditional sports media publications, such as *The Sporting News, Football Digest, Street & Smith* yearbooks, and others. These sets also are advertised in the card collecting periodicals. Many collectors will begin by subscribing to at least one of the hobby periodicals, all with good up-to-date information. Another way of obtaining cards and information is through Beckett's Web site, www.beckett.com.

Most serious card collectors obtain old (and new) cards from one or more of several main sources: (1) trading or buying from other collectors or dealers; (2) responding to sale or auction ads in the hobby publications; (3) buying at a local hobby store; (4) attending sports collectibles shows or conventions; and/or (5) purchasing cards over the Internet.

We advise that you try all four methods since each has its own distinct advantages: (1) trading is a great way to make new friends; (2) hobby periodicals help you keep up with what's going on in the hobby (including when and where the conventions are happening); (3) stores provide the opportunity to enjoy personalized service and consider a great diversity of material in a relaxed sports-oriented atmosphere; (4) shows allow you to choose from multiple dealers and thousands of cards under one roof in a competitive situation; and (5) the Internet allows you to purchase cards in a convenient manner from almost anywhere in the world.

Preserving Your Cards

Cards are fragile. They must be handled properly in order to retain their value. Careless handling can easily result in creased or bent cards. It is, however, not recommended that tweezers or tongs be used to pick up your cards since such utensils might mar or indent card surfaces and thus reduce those cards' conditions and values. In general, your cards should be handled directly as little as possible. This is sometimes easier to say than to do.

Although there are still many who use custom boxes, storage trays, or even shoe boxes, plastic sheets are the preferred method of many collectors for storing cards. A collection stored in plastic pages in a three-ring album allows you to view your collection at any time without the need to touch the card itself. Cards can also be kept in single holders (of various types and thicknesses) designed for the enjoyment of each card individually. For a large collection, some collectors may use a combination of the above methods. When purchasing plastic sheets for your cards, be sure that you find the pocket size that fits the cards snugly. Don't put your 1951 Bowman in a sheet designed to fit 1981 Topps.

Most hobby and collectibles shops and virtually all collectors' conventions will have these plastic pages available in quantity for the various sizes offered, or you can purchase them directly from the advertisers in this book. Also, remember that pocket size isn't the only factor to consider when looking for plastic sheets. Other factors such as safety, economy, appearance, availability, or personal preference also may indicate which types of sheets a collector may want to buy.

Damp, sunny, and/or hot conditions. No, this is not a weather forecast, but rather three elements to avoid in extremes if you are interested in preserving your collection. Too much (or too little) humidity can cause gradual deterioration of a card. Direct, bright sun (or fluorescent light) over time will bleach out the color of a card. Extreme heat accelerates the decomposition of the card. On the other hand, many cards have lasted more than 50 years without much scientific intervention. So be cautious, even if the above factors typically present a problem only when present in the extreme. It never hurts to be prudent.

Collecting vs. Investing

Collecting individual players and collecting complete sets are both popular vehicles for investment and speculation. Most investors and speculators stock up on complete sets or on quantities of players they think have good investment potential.

There is obviously no guarantee in this book, or anywhere else for that matter, that cards will outperform the stock market or other investment alternatives in the future. After all, football cards do not pay quarterly dividends and cards cannot be sold at their "current values" as easily as stocks or bonds.

Nevertheless, investors have noticed a favorable long-term trend in the past performance of sports collectibles, and certain cards and sets have outperformed just about any other investment in some years. Many hobbyists maintain that the best investment is and always will be the building of a collection, which traditionally has held up better than outright speculation.

Some of the obvious questions are Which cards? When to buy? When to sell? The best investment you can make is in your own education. The more you know about your collection and the hobby, the more informed decisions you will be able to make. We're not selling investment tips. We're selling information about the current value of football cards. It's up to you to use that information to your best advantage.

Terminology

Each hobby has its own language to describe its area of interest. The terminology traditionally used for trading cards is derived from the American Card Catalog, published in 1960 by Nostalgia Press. That catalog, written by Jefferson Burdick (who is called the "Father of Card Collecting" for his pioneering work), uses letter and number designations for each separate set of cards. The letter used in the ACC designation refers to the generic type of card. While both sport and non-sport issues are classified in the ACC, we shall confine ourselves to the sport issues. The following list defines the letters and their meanings as used by the American Card Catalog, as applied to football cards:

(none) or **N** - 19th Century U.S. Tobacco
F - Food Inserts
H - Advertising
M - Periodicals
N - 19th Century U.S. Tobacco
PC - Postcards
R - Recent Candy and Gum Cards, 1930 to Present
UO - Gas and Oil Inserts
V - Canadian Candy
W - Exhibits, Strip Cards, Team Cards

Following the letter prefix and an optional hyphen are one-, two-, or three-digit numbers, R(-)999. These typically represent the company or entity issuing the cards. In several cases, the ACC number is extended by an additional hyphen and another one- or two-digit numerical suffix. For example, the 1957 Topps regular-series football card issue carries an ACC designation of R415-5. The "R" indicates a Candy or Gum card produced since 1930. The "415" is the ACC designation for the 1957 regular issue (Topps fifth football set).

Like other traditional methods of identification, this system provides order to the process of cataloging cards; however, most serious collectors learn the ACC designation of the popular sets by repetition and familiarity, rather than by attempting to "figure out" what they might or should be. From 1948 forward, collectors and dealers commonly refer to all sets by their year, maker, type of issue, and any other distinguishing characteristic. For example, such a characteristic could be an unusual issue or one of several regular issues put out by a specific maker in a single year. Regional issues are usually referred to by year, maker, and sometimes by title or theme of the set.

Glossary/Legend

Our glossary defines terms frequently used in the card collecting hobby. Many of these terms are also common to other types of sports memorabilia collecting. Some terms may have several meanings, depending on use and context.

ACC - Acronym for American Card Catalog.

ACETATE - A transparent plastic.

AFC - American Football Conference.

AFL - American Football League.

AS - All-Star.

ATG - All Time Great card.

AU(TO) - An autographed card.

BRICK - A group or "lot" of cards, usually 50 or more having common characteristics, that is intended to be bought, sold, or traded as a unit.

C - Center.

CB - Cornerback.

CFL - Canadian Football League.

CL - Checklist card. A card that lists in order the cards and players in the set or series. Older checklist cards in mint condition that have not been checked off are very desirable and command large premiums.

CO - Coach card.

COLLECTOR ISSUE - A set produced for the sake of the card itself, with no product or service sponsor. It derives its name from the fact that most of these sets are produced for sale directly to the hobby market.

COMBINATION CARD - A single card depicting two or more players (not including team cards).

COMMON CARD - The typical card of any set; it has no premium value accruing from subject matter, numerical scarcity, popular demand, or anomaly.

CONVENTION - A large gathering of dealers and collectors at a single location for the purpose of buying, selling, and sometimes trading sports memorabilia items. Conventions are open to the public and sometimes also feature autograph guests, door prizes, films, contests, etc. More commonly called "shows."

COR - Corrected card. A version of an error card that was fixed by the manufacturer.

DB - Defensive back.

DIE-CUT - A card with its stock partially cut. In some cases, after removal or appropriate folding, the remaining part of the card can be made to stand up.

DISC - A circular-shaped card.

DISPLAY SHEET - A clear, plastic page that is punched for insertion into a binder (with standard three-ring spacing) containing pockets for displaying cards. Many different styles of sheets exist with pockets of varying sizes to hold the many differing card formats. The vast majority of current cards measure 2-1/2 by 3-1/2 inches and fit in nine-pocket sheets.

DP - Double Print. A card that was printed in approximately double the quantity compared to other cards in the same series, or draft pick card.

DT - Defensive tackle or Dream Team.

DUFEX - A method of card manufacturing technology patented by Pinnacle Brands, Inc. It involves a refractive quality to a card with a foil coating.

EMBOSSED - A raised surface; features of a card that are projected from a flat background.

ERR - Error card. A card with erroneous information, spelling, or depiction on either side of the card. Most errors are never corrected by the producing card company.

ETCHED - Impressions within the surface of a card.

EXHIBIT - The generic name given to thick-stock, postcard-size cards with single-color, obverse pictures. The name is derived from the Exhibit Supply Co. of Chicago, the principal manufacturer of this type of card. These are also known as Arcade cards since they were found in many arcades.

FB - Fullback.

FDP - First (round) draft pick.

FG - Field goal.

FOIL - A special type of sticker with a metallic-looking surface.

FULL-BLEED - A borderless card; a card containing a photo that encompasses the entire card.

FULL SHEET - A complete sheet of cards that has not been cut into individual cards by the manufacturer. Also called an uncut sheet.

G - Guard.

GLOSS - A card with luster; a shiny finish as in a card with UV coating.

HIGH NUMBER - The cards in the last series of number, in a year in which such higher-numbered cards were printed or distributed in significantly lesser amount than the lower-numbered cards. The high-number designation refers to a scarcity of the high-numbered cards.

HL - Highlight card, for example from the 1978 Topps subset.

HOF - Hall of Fame, or Hall of Famer (also abbreviated HOFer).

HOLOGRAM - A three-dimensional photographic image.

HOR - Horizontal pose on a card as opposed to the standard vertical orientation found on most cards.

IA - In Action card. A special type of card depicting a player in an action photo, such as the 1982 Topps cards.

IL - Inside linebacker.

INSERT - A card of a different type, e.g., a poster, or any other sports collectible contained and sold in the same package along with a card or cards of a major set.

INTERACTIVE - A concept that involves collector participation.

K - Kicker.

KARAT - A unit of measure for the fineness of gold; i.e., 24K.

KP - Kid Picture card.

LAYERING - The separation or peeling of one or more layers of the card stock, usually at the corner of the card. Also see the Condition Guide.

LB - Linebacker.

LID - A circular-shaped card (possibly with tab) that forms the top of the container for the product being promoted.

LL - League leader card. A card depicting the leader or leaders in a specific statistical category from the previous season. Not to be confused with team leader (TL).

LOGO - NFLPA logo on card.

MAJOR SET - A set produced by a national manufacturer of cards, containing a large number of cards. Usually 100 or more different cards comprise a major set.

MEM - Memorial.

METALLIC - A glossy design that enhances card features.

MINI - A small card or stamp (specifically the 1969 Topps Four-in-One football inserts or the 1987 Topps mini football set issued for the United Kingdom).

MVP - Most Valuable Player.

NFLPA - National Football League Players Association.

NO LOGO - No NFLPA logo on card.

NO TR - No trade reference on card.

NPO - No position.

NT - Nose tackle.

OFF - Officials cards.

O-ROY - Offensive Rookie of the Year.

OT - Offensive tackle.

P - Punter.

P1 - First Printing.

P2 - Second Printing.

PACKS - A means with which cards are issued in terms of pack type (wax, cello, foil, rack, etc.) and channels of distribution (hobby, retail, etc.).

PANEL - An extended card that is composed of multiple individual cards.

PARALLEL - A card that is similar in design to its counterpart from a basic set, but offers a distinguishing quality.

PB - Pro Bowl.

PLATINUM - A metallic element used in the process of creating a glossy card.

POY - Player of the Year.

PREMIUM - A card, sometimes on photographic stock, that is purchased or obtained in conjunction with (or redeemed for) another card or product. This term applies mainly to older products, as newer cards distributed in this manner are generally lumped together as peripheral sets.

PREMIUM CARDS - A class of products introduced recently, intended to have higher quality card stock and photography than regular cards, but more limited production and higher cost. Defining what is and isn't a premium card is somewhat subjective.

PRISMATIC/PRISM - A glossy or bright design that refracts or disperses light.

PROMOTIONAL SET - A set, usually containing a small number of cards, issued by a national card producer and distributed in limited quantities or to a select group of people, such as major show attendees or dealers with wholesale accounts. Presumably, the purpose of a promo set is to stir up demand for an upcoming set. Also called a preview, prototype, or test set.

QB - Quarterback.

RARE - A card or series of cards of very limited availability. Unfortunately, "rare" is a subjective term sometimes used indiscriminately. Using the strict definitions, rare cards are harder to obtain than scarce cards.

RB - Record Breaker card or running back.

RC - Rookie Card. A player's first appearance on a regular issue card from one of the major card companies. With a few exceptions, each player has only one RC in any given set. A Rookie Card typically cannot be an All-Star, Highlight, In Action, league leader, Super Action, or team leader card. It can, however, be a coach card or draft pick card.

REDEMPTION - A program established by manufacturers that allows collectors to mail in a special card (usually a random insert) in return for special cards, sets, or other prizes not available through conventional channels.

REFRACTORS - A card that features a design element which enhances (distorts) its color/appearance through deflecting light.

REGIONAL - A card issued and distributed only in a limited geographical area of the country. The producer may or may not be a major, national producer of trading cards. The key is whether the set was distributed nationally in any form or not.

REPLICA - An identical copy or reproduction.

RET - Retired.

REV NEG - Reversed or flopped photo side of the card. This is a major type of error card, but only some are corrected.

ROY - Rookie of the Year.

S - Safety.

SB - Super Bowl.

SCARCE - A card or series of cards of limited availability. This subjective term is sometimes used indiscriminately to promote or hype value. Using strict definitions, scarce cards are easier to obtain than rare cards.

SEMI-HIGH - A card from the next-to-last series of a sequentially issued set. It has more value than an average card and generally less value than a high number. A card is not called a semi-high unless its next-to-last series has an additional premium attached to it.

SERIES - The entire set of cards issued by a particular producer in a particular year, e.g., the 1978 Topps series. Also, within a particular set, series can refer to a group of (consecutively numbered) cards printed at the same time, e.g., the first series of the 1948 Leaf set (#1 through #49).

SET - One each of an entire run of cards of the same type, produced by a particular manufacturer during a single season. In other words, if you have a complete set of 1975 Topps football cards, then you have every card from #1 up to and including #528; i.e., all the different cards that were produced.

SHEEN - Brightness or luster emitted by a card.

SKIP-NUMBERED - A set that has many unissued card numbers between the lowest number in the set and the highest number in the set, e.g., the 1949 Leaf football set contains 49 cards skip-numbered from number 1 to number 144. A major set in which a few numbers were not printed is not considered to be skip-numbered.

SP - Single or Short Print. A card which was printed in lesser quantity compared to the other cards in the same series (also see DP). This term can only be used in a relative sense and in reference to one particular set. For instance, the 1989 Pro Set Pete Rozelle SP is less common than the other cards in that set, but it isn't necessarily scarcer than regular cards of any other set.

SPECIAL CARD - A card that portrays something other than a single player or team; for example, the 1990 Fleer Joe Montana/Jerry Rice Super Bowl

MVPs card #397.

SR - Super Rookie.

STAMP - Adhesive-backed papers depicting a player. The stamp may be individual or in a sheet of many stamps. Moisture must be applied to the adhesive in order for the stamp to be attached to another surface.

STAR CARD - A card that portrays a player of some repute, usually determined by his ability, but sometimes referring to sheer popularity.

STICKER - A card-like item with a removable layer that can be affixed to another surface. Example: 1983 Topps inserts.

STOCK - The cardboard or paper on which the card is printed.

SUPERIMPOSED - To be affixed on top of something, i.e., a player photo over a solid background.

SUPERSTAR CARD - A card that portrays a superstar, e.g., a Hall of Fame member or a player whose current performance may eventually warrant serious Hall of Fame consideration.

TAB - A card portion set off from the rest of the card, usually with perforations, that may be removed without damaging the central character or event depicted by the card.

TC - Team card or team checklist card.

TEAM CARD - A card that depicts an entire team.

THREE-DIMENSIONAL (3D) - A visual image that provides an illusion of depth and perspective.

TL - Team leader card or Top Leader.

TOPICAL - A subset or group of cards that have a common theme, i.e., MVP award winners.

TR - Trade reference on card.

TRANSPARENT - Clear, see-through.

TRIMMED - A card cut down from its original size. Trimmed cards are undesirable to most collectors, and are therefore less valuable than otherwise identical, untrimmed cards. Also see the Condition Guide.

UER - Uncorrected error card.

USFL - United States Football League.

UV - Ultraviolet, a glossy coating used in producing cards.

VAR - Variation card. One of two or more cards from the same series, with the same card number (or player with identical pose, if the series is unnumbered) differing from one another in some aspect, from the printing, stock, or other feature of the card. This is often caused when the manufacturer of the cards notices an error in a particular card, corrects the error and then resumes the print run. In this case there will be two versions or variations of the same card. Sometimes one of the variations is relatively scarce. Variations also can result from accidental or deliberate design changes, information updates, photo substitutions, etc.

VERT - Vertical pose on a card.

WFL - World Football League.

WLAF - World League of American Football.

WR - Wide receiver.

XRC - Extended Rookie Card. A player's first appearance on a card, but issued in a set that was not distributed nationally or in packs. In football sets, this term generally refers to the 1984 and 1985 Topps USFL sets.

Understanding Card Values

Determining Value

Why are some cards more valuable than others? Obviously, the economic laws of supply and demand are applicable to card collecting just as they are to any other field where a commodity is bought, sold, or traded in a free, unregulated market.

Supply (the number of cards available on the market) is less than the total number of cards originally produced since attrition diminishes that original quantity. Each year a percentage of cards is typically thrown away, destroyed, or otherwise lost to collectors. This percentage is much, much smaller today than it was in the past because more and more people have become increasingly aware of the value of their cards.

For those who collect only mint condition cards, the supply of older cards can be quite small indeed. Until recently, collectors were not so conscious of the need to preserve the condition of their cards. For this reason, it is difficult to know exactly how many 1962 Topps are currently available, mint or otherwise. It is generally accepted that there are fewer 1962 Topps available than 1972, 1982, or 1992 Topps cards. If demand were equal for each of these sets, the law of supply and demand would increase the price for the least available sets.

Demand, however, is never equal for all sets, so price correlations can be complicated. The demand for a card is influenced by many factors. These include: (1) the age of the card; (2) the number of cards printed; (3) the player(s) portrayed on the card; (4) the attractiveness and popularity of the set; and (5) the physical condition of the card.

In general, (1) the older the card, (2) the fewer the number of the cards printed, (3) the more famous, popular, and talented the player, (4) the more attractive and popular the set, and (5) the better the condition of the card, the higher the value of the card will be. There are exceptions to all but one of these factors: the condition of the card. Given two cards similar in all respects except condition, the one in the better condition will always be valued higher.

While those guidelines help to establish the value of a card, the countless exceptions and peculiarities make any simple, direct mathematical formula to determine card values impossible.

Regional Variation

Since the market varies from region to region, card prices of local players may be higher. This is known as a regional premium. How significant the premium is—and if there is any premium at all—depends on the local popularity of the team and the player.

The largest regional premiums usually do not apply to superstars, who often are so well known nationwide that the prices of their key cards are too high for local dealers to realize a premium.

Lesser stars often command the strongest premiums. Their popularity is concentrated in their home region, creating local demand that greatly exceeds overall demand.

Regional premiums can apply to popular retired players and sometimes can be found in the areas where the players grew up or starred in college.

A regional discount is the converse of a regional premium. Regional discounts occur when a player has been so popular in his region for so long that local collectors and dealers have accumulated quantities of his cards. The abundant supply may make the cards available in that area at the lowest prices anywhere.

Set Prices

A somewhat paradoxical situation exists in the price of a complete set vs. the combined cost of the individual cards in the set. In nearly every case, the sum of the prices for the individual cards is higher than the cost for the complete set. This is prevalent especially in the cards of the past few years. The reasons for this apparent anomaly stem from the habits of collectors and from the carrying costs to dealers. Today, each card in a set normally is produced in the same quantity as all others in its set.

Many collectors pick up only stars, superstars, and particular teams. As a result, the dealer is left with a shortage of certain player cards and an abundance of others. He therefore incurs an expense in simply "carrying" these less desirable cards in stock. On the other hand, if he sells a complete set, he gets rid of large numbers of cards at one time. For this reason, he generally is willing to receive less money for a complete set. By doing this, he recovers all of his costs and also makes a profit.

Set prices do not include rare card varieties, unless specifically stated. Of course, the prices for sets do include one example of each type for the given set, but this is the least expensive variety.

Scarce Series

Scarce series occur because cards issued before 1973 were made available to the public each year in several series of finite numbers of cards, rather than all cards of the set being available for purchase at one time. At some point during the season, interest in current year cards waned. Consequently, the manufacturers produced smaller numbers of these later-series cards. Nearly all nationwide issues from post World War II manufacturers (1948 to 1972) exhibit these series variations.

In the past, Topps, for example, may have issued series consisting of many different numbers of cards, including 55, 66, 80, 88, 110, and others. However, after 1968, the sheet size generally has been 132. Despite Topps' standardization of the sheet size, the company double-printed one sheet in 1983 and possibly in 1984 and 1985, too. This was apparently an effort to induce collectors to buy more packs.

We are always looking for information or photographs of printing sheets of cards for research. Each year, we try to update the hobby's knowledge of distribution anomalies. Please let us know at the address in this book if you have firsthand knowledge that would be helpful in this pursuit.

Grading Your Cards

Each hobby has its own grading terminology—stamps, coins, comic books, record collecting, etc. Collectors of sports cards are no exception. The one invariable criterion for determining the value of a card is its condition: the better the condition of the card, the more valuable it is. Condition grading, however, is subjective. Individual card dealers and collectors differ in the strictness of their grading, but the stated condition of a card should be determined without regard to whether it is being bought or sold.

No allowance is made for age. A 1952 card is judged by the same standards as a 1992 card. But there are specific sets and cards that are condition-sensitive because of their border color, consistently poor centering, etc. Such cards and sets sometimes command premiums above the listed percentages in mint condition.

Centering

Current centering terminology uses numbers representing the percentage of border on either side of the main design. Obviously, centering is diminished in importance for borderless cards such as Stadium Club.

Slightly Off-Center (60/40) - A slightly off-center card is one that upon close inspection is found to have one border bigger than the opposite border.

This degree once was offensive only to purists, but now some hobbyists try to avoid cards that are anything other than perfectly centered.

Off-Center (70/30) - An off-center card has one border that is noticeably more than twice as wide as the opposite border.

Badly Off-Center (80/20 or worse) - A badly off-center card has virtually no border on one side of the card.

Miscut - A miscut card actually shows part of the adjacent card in its larger border and consequently a corresponding amount of its card is cut off.

Corner Wear

Corner wear is the most scrutinized grading criteria in the hobby. These are the major categories of corner wear:

Corner with a slight touch of wear - The corner still is sharp, but there is a slight touch of wear showing. On a dark-bordered card, this shows as a dot of white.

Fuzzy corner - The corner still comes to a point, but the point has just begun to fray. A slightly "dinged" corner is considered the same as a fuzzy corner.

Slightly rounded corner - The fraying of the corner has increased to where there is only a hint of a point. Mild layering may be evident. A "dinged" corner is considered the same as a slightly rounded corner.

Rounded corner - The point is completely gone. Some layering is noticeable.

Badly rounded corner - The corner is completely round and rough. Severe layering is evident.

Creases

A third common defect is the crease. The degree of creasing in a card is difficult to show in a drawing or picture. On giving the specific condition of an expensive card for sale, the seller should note any creases additionally. Creases can be categorized as to severity according to the following scale.

Light Crease - A light crease is a crease that is barely noticeable upon close inspection. In fact, when cards are in plastic sheets or holders, a light crease may not be seen (until the card is taken out of the holder). A light crease on the front is much more serious than a light crease on the card back only.

Medium Crease - A medium crease is noticeable when held and studied at arm's length by the naked eye, but does not overly detract from the appearance of the card. It is an obvious crease, but not one that breaks the picture surface of the card.

Heavy Crease - A heavy crease is one that has torn or broken through the card's picture surface, e.g., puts a tear in the photo surface.

Alterations

Deceptive Trimming - This occurs when someone alters the card in order (1) to shave off edge wear, (2) to improve the sharpness of the corners, or (3) to improve centering. Obviously their objective is to falsely increase the perceived value of the card to an unsuspecting buyer. The shrinkage usually is evident only if the trimmed card is compared to an adjacent full-sized card or if the trimmed card is itself measured.

Obvious Trimming - Obvious trimming is noticeable and unfortunate. It is usually performed by non-collectors who give no thought to the present or future value of their cards.

Deceptively Retouched Borders - This occurs when the borders (especially on those cards with dark borders) are touched up on the edges and corners with magic marker or crayons of appropriate color in order to make the card appear to be mint.

Categorization of Defects

Miscellaneous Flaws

The following are common minor flaws that, depending on severity, lower a card's condition by one to four grades and often render it no better than excellent-mint: bubbles (lumps in surface), gum and wax stains, diamond cutting (slanted borders), notching, off-centered backs, paper wrinkles, scratched-off cartoons or puzzles on back, rubber band marks, scratches, surface impressions, and warping.

The following are common serious flaws that, depending on severity, lower a card's condition at least four grades and often render it no better than good: chemical or sun fading, erasure marks, mildew, miscutting (severe off-centering), holes, bleached or retouched borders, tape marks, tears, trimming, water or coffee stains, and writing.

Condition Guide

Grades

Mint (Mt) - A card with no flaws or wear. The card has four perfect corners, 55/45 or better centering from top to bottom and from left to right, original gloss, smooth edges, and original color borders. A mint card does not have print spots, color, or focus imperfections.

Near Mint-Mint (NrMt-Mt) - A card with one minor flaw. Any one of the following would lower a mint card to near mint-mint: one corner with a slight touch of wear, barely noticeable print spots, color or focus imperfections. The card must have 60/40 or better centering in both directions, original gloss, smooth edges, and original color borders.

Near Mint (NrMt) - A card with one minor flaw. Any one of the following would lower a mint card to near mint: one fuzzy corner or two to four corners with slight touches of wear, 70/30 to 60/40 centering, slightly rough edges, minor print spots, color or focus imperfections. The card must have original gloss and original color borders.

Excellent-Mint (ExMt) - A card with two or three fuzzy, but not rounded, corners and centering no worse than 80/20. The card may have no more than two of the following: slightly rough edges, very slightly discolored borders, minor print spots, color or focus imperfections. The card must have original gloss.

Excellent (Ex) - A card with four fuzzy but definitely not rounded corners and centering no worse than 80/20. The card may have a small amount of original gloss lost, rough edges, slightly discolored borders and minor print spots, color or focus imperfections.

Very Good (Vg) - A card that has been handled but not abused: slightly rounded corners with slight layering, slight notching on edges, a significant amount of gloss lost from the surface but no scuffing and moderate discoloration of borders. The card may have a few light creases.

Good (G), Fair (F), Poor (P) - A well-worn, mishandled, or abused card: badly rounded and layered corners, scuffing, most or all original gloss missing, seriously discolored borders, moderate or heavy creases, and one or more serious flaws. The grade of good, fair, or poor depends on the severity of wear and flaws. Good, fair, and poor cards generally are used only as fillers.

The most widely used grades are defined above. Obviously, many cards will not perfectly fit one of the definitions.

Therefore, categories between the major grades known as in-between grades are used, such as good to very good (G-Vg), very good to excellent (VgEx), and excellent-mint to near mint (ExMt-NrMt). Such grades indicate a card with all qualities of the lower category but with at least a few qualities of the higher category.

The Beckett Guide lists each card and set in three grades, with the middle grade valued at about 40%–45% of the top grade, and the bottom grade valued at about 10%–15% of the top grade.

The value of cards that fall between the listed columns can also be calculated using a percentage of the top grade. For example, a card that falls between the top and middle grades (Ex, ExMt, or NrMt in most cases) will generally be valued at anywhere from 50% to 90% of the top grade.

Similarly, a card that falls between the middle and bottom grades (G-Vg, Vg, or VgEx in most cases) will generally be valued at anywhere from 20% to 40% of the top grade.

There are also cases where cards are in better condition than the top grade or worse than the bottom grade. Cards that grade worse than the lowest grade are generally valued at 5%–10% of the top grade.

When a card exceeds the top grade by one—such as NrMt-Mt when the top grade is NrMt, or Mint when the top grade is NrMt-Mt—a premium of up to 50% is possible, with 10%–20% the usual norm.

When a card exceeds the top grade by two—such as Mint when the top grade is NrMt, or NrMt-Mt when the top grade is ExMt—a premium of 25%–50% is the usual norm. But certain condition-sensitive cards or sets, particularly those from the pre-war era, can bring premiums of up to 100% or even more.

Unopened packs, boxes, and factory-collated sets are considered mint in their unknown (and presumed perfect) state. Once opened, however, each card can be graded (and valued) in its own right by taking into account any defects that may be present in spite of the fact that the card has never been handled.

Selling Your Cards

Just about every collector sells cards or will sell cards eventually. Someday you may be interested in selling your duplicates or maybe even your whole collection. You may sell to other collectors, friends, or dealers. You may even sell cards you purchased from a certain dealer back to that same dealer. In any event, it helps to know some of the mechanics of the typical transaction between buyer and seller.

Dealers will buy cards in order to resell them to other collectors who are interested in the cards. Dealers will always pay a higher percentage for items that (in their opinion) can be resold quickly, and a much lower percentage for those items that are perceived as having low demand and hence are slow moving. In either case, dealers must buy at a price that allows for the expense of doing business and a margin for profit.

If you have cards for sale, the best advice we can give is that you get several offers for your cards—either from card shops or at a card show—and take the best offer, all things considered. Note, the "best" offer may not be the one for the highest amount. And remember, if a dealer really wants your cards, he won't let you get away without making his best competitive offer. Another alternative is to place your cards in an auction as one or several lots.

Many people think nothing of going into a department store and paying $15 for an item of clothing for which the store paid $5. But if you were selling your $15 card to a dealer and he offered you $5 for it, you might think his markup unreasonable. To complete the analogy, most department stores (and card dealers) that consistently pay $10 for $15 items eventually go out of business.

Centering

Well-Centered

Slightly Off-Centered

Off-Centered

Badly Off-Centered

Miscut

An exception is when the dealer has lined up a willing buyer for the item(s) you are attempting to sell, or if the cards are so hot that it's likely he'll have to hold the cards for only a short period of time.

In those cases, an offer of up to 75% of book value still will allow the dealer to make a reasonable profit considering the short time he will need to hold the merchandise. In general, however, most cards and collections will bring offers in the range of 25% to 50% of retail price. Also consider that most material from the past five to 20 years is plentiful. If that's what you're selling, don't be surprised if your best offer is well below that range.

Interesting Notes

The first card numerically of an issue is the single card most likely to obtain excessive wear. Consequently, you typically will find the price on the #1 card (in NrMt or mint condition) somewhat higher than might otherwise be the case. Similarly, but to a lesser extent (because normally the less important, reverse side of the card is the one exposed), the last card numerically in an issue also is prone to abnormal wear. This extra wear and tear occurs because the first and last cards are exposed to the elements (human element included) more than any other cards. They are generally end cards in any brick formations, rubber bandings, stackings on wet surfaces, and like activities.

Sports cards have no intrinsic value. The value of a card, like the value of other collectibles, can be determined only by you and your enjoyment in viewing and possessing these cardboard treasures.

Remember, the buyer ultimately determines the price of each card. You are the determining price factor because you have the ability to say "No" to the price of any card by not exchanging your hard-earned money for a given card. When the cost of a trading card exceeds the enjoyment you will receive from it, your answer should be "No." We assess and report the prices. You set them!

We are always interested in receiving the price input of collectors and dealers from around the country. We happily credit major contributors. We welcome your opinions, since your contributions assist us in ensuring a better guide each year. If you would like to join our survey list for the next editions of this book and others authored by Dr. Beckett, please send your name and address to Pricing-Input, 4635 McEwen DR. Dallas, Texas 75244-5308.

History of Football Cards

Until the 1930s, the only set devoted exclusively to football players was the Mayo N302 set. The first bubblegum issue dedicated entirely to football players did not appear until the National Chicle issue of 1935. Before this, athletes from several sports were pictured in the multi-sport Goudey Sport Kings issue of 1933. In that set, football was represented by three legends whose fame has not diminished through the years: Red Grange, Knute Rockne, and Jim Thorpe.

But it was not until 1948, and the post-war bubblegum boom, that the next football issues appeared. Bowman and Leaf Gum companies both issued football card sets in that year. From this point on, football cards have been issued annually by one company or another up to the present time, with Topps being the only major card producer until 1989, when Pro Set and Score debuted and sparked a football card boom.

Football cards depicting players from the Canadian Football League (CFL) did not appear until Parkhurst issued a 100-card set in 1952. Four years later, Parkhurst issued another CFL set with 50 small cards this time. Topps began issuing CFL sets in 1958 and continued annually until 1965, although from 1961 to 1965 these cards were printed in Canada by O-Pee-Chee. Post

Corner Wear

The partial cards here have been photographed at 300%. This was done in order to magnify each card's corner wear to such a degree that differences could be shown on a printed page.

This 1985 Topps Fred Quillan card has a fuzzy corner. Notice the extremely slight fraying on the corner.

This 1985 Topps Fred Smerlas card has a slightly rounded corner. Notice that there is no longer a sharp corner but heavy wear.

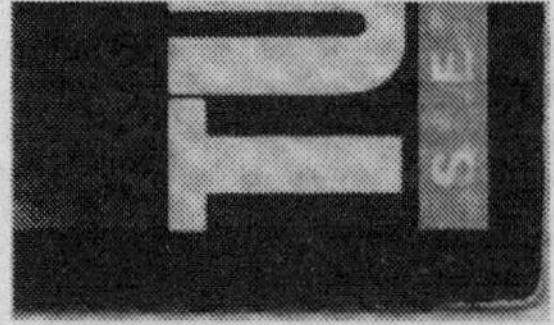

This 1985 Topps Daryl Turner card has a rounded corner evident by the lack of a sharp point and heavy wear on both edges.

This 1985 Topps Kim Bokamper card displays a badly rounded corner. Notice a large portion of missing cardboard accompanied by heavy wear and excessive fraying.

This 1985 Topps Neil O'Donaghue card displays creases of varying degrees. Light creases (left side of the card) may not break the card's surface, while heavy creases (right side) will.

Cereal issued two CFL sets in 1962 and 1963; these cards formed the backs of boxes of Post Cereals distributed in Canada. The O-Pee-Chee company, which has maintained a working relationship with the Topps Gum Company, issued four CFL sets in the years 1968, 1970, 1971, and 1972. Since 1981, the JOGO Novelties Company has been producing a number of CFL sets depicting past and present players.

Returning to American football issues, Bowman resumed its football cards (by then with full-color fronts) from 1950 to 1955. The company twice increased the size of its card during that period. Bowman was unopposed during most of the early 1950s as the sole producer of cards featuring pro football players.

Topps issued its first football card set in 1950 with a group of very small, felt-back cards. In 1951 Topps issued what is referred to as the "Magic Football Card" set. This set of 75 has a scratch-off section on the back which answers a football quiz. Topps did not issue another football set until 1955 when its All-American Football set paid tribute to past college football greats. In January 1956, Topps Gum Company (of Brooklyn) purchased the Bowman Company (of Philadelphia).

After the purchase, Topps issued sets of National Football League (NFL) players up until 1963. The 1961 Topps football set also included American Football League (AFL) players in the high-number series (133–198). Topps sets from 1964 to 1967 contained AFL players only. From 1968 to the present, Topps has issued a major set of football cards each year.

When the AFL was founded in 1960, Fleer produced a 132-card set of AFL players and coaches. In 1961, Fleer issued a 220-card set (even larger than the Topps issue of that year) featuring players from both the NFL and AFL. Apparently, for that one year, Topps and Fleer tested a reciprocal arrangement, trading the card printing rights to each other's contracted players. The 1962 and 1963 Fleer sets feature only AFL players. Both sets are relatively small at 88 cards each.

Post Cereal issued a 200-card set of National League football players in 1962 which contains numerous scarcities, namely those players appearing on unpopular varieties of Post Cereal. From 1964 to 1967 the Philadelphia Gum Company issued four 198-card NFL player sets.

In 1984 and 1985, Topps produced a set for the now defunct United States Football League, in addition to its annual NFL set. The 1984 set in particular is quite scarce, due to both low distribution and the high demand for the extended Rookie Cards of current NFL superstars Jim Kelly and Reggie White, among others.

In 1986, McDonald's Restaurants generated the most excitement in football cards in many years. McDonald's created a nationwide football card promotion in which customers could receive a card or two per food purchase, upon request. However, the cards distributed were only of the local team, or of the "McDonald's All-Stars" for areas not near NFL cities. Also, each set was produced with four possible color tabs: blue, black, gold, and green. The tab color distributed depended on the week of the promotion. In general, cards with blue tabs are the scarcest, although for some teams the cards with black tabs are the hardest to find. The tabs were intended to be scratched off and removed by customers to be redeemed for food and other prizes, but among collectors, cards with scratched or removed tabs are categorized as having a major defect, and therefore are valued considerably less.

The entire set, including four color tabs for all 29 subsets, totals over 2,800 different cards. The hoopla over the McDonald's cards fell off precipitously after 1988 as collector interest shifted to the new 1989 Score and Pro

Set issues.

The popularity of football cards has continued to grow since 1986. Topps introduced "Super Rookie" cards in 1987. Card companies other than Topps noticed the burgeoning interest in football cards, resulting in the two landmark 1989 football sets: a 330-card Score issue, and a 440-card Pro Set release. Score later produced a self-contained 110-card supplemental set, while Pro Set printed 100 Series II cards and a 21-card "Final Update" set. Topps, Pro Set, and Score all improved card quality and increased the size of their sets for 1990. That season also marked Fleer's return to football cards and Action Packed's first major set.

In 1991 Pacific, Pro Line, Upper Deck, and Wild Card joined a market that is now at least as competitive as the baseball card market. And the premium card trend that began in baseball cards spilled over to the gridiron in the form of Fleer Ultra, Pro Set Platinum, Score Pinnacle, and Topps Stadium Club sets.

The year 1992 brought even more growth with the debuts of All World, Collectors Edge, GameDay, Playoff, Pro Set Power, SkyBox Impact, and SkyBox Primetime.

The football card market stabilized somewhat in 1993 thanks to an agreement between the long-feuding NFL licensing bodies, NFL Properties and the NFL Players Association. Also helping the stabilization was the emergence of several promising rookies, including Drew Bledsoe, Jerome Bettis, and Rick Mirer. Limited production became the industry buzzword in sports cards, and football was no exception. The result was the success of three new product lines: 1993 Playoff Contenders, 1993 Select, and 1993 SP.

The year 1994 brought further stabilization and limited production. Pro Set and Wild Card dropped out, while no new card companies joined the ranks. However, several new NFL sets were added to the mix by existing manufacturers: Classic NFL Experience, Collector's Choice, Excalibur, Finest, and Sportflics. The new trend centered around multi-level parallel sets and interactive game inserts with parallel prizes. Another strong rookie crop and reported production cutbacks contributed to strong football card sales throughout 1994.

The football card market continued to grow between 1995 and 1998. Many new sets were released by the major manufacturers and a few new players entered the hobby. Companies continued to push the limits of printing technology with issues printed on plastic, leather, cloth, and various metals. Rookie Cards once more came into vogue and the "1-of-1" insert card was born. There are more choices than ever before for the football card collector; most like it that way. In the last couple of years, more changes have occurred in the football card market. The Rookie Card popularity continued but with a twist. Since 1998, many Rookie Cards have been sequentially numbered and/or printed in a shorter supply than other cards in the set they are in.

Also, many companies have begun to issue "game-worn jerseys" or certified autographed cards of leading players, both active and retired.

In addition, graded cards, old and new, have revitalized the card market. Many collectors and dealers have discovered a variety of internet websites for buying and selling cards such as eBay and Beckett.com.

The trend towards short printed Rookie Cards as well as a growing use of memorabilia on cards continued through the 2001 seasons.

Many of the key Rookie Cards are now issued with some combination of either an autograph, uniform swatch, or even both. In addition, the print run of many of these is smaller each and every year.

In addition, a significant amount of the autographs are no longer actually signed on the cards but are signed on stickers which are then affixed to a card.

One after-effect of all this emphasis on Rookie and Memorabilia cards is that many supposed "second-tier" players just do not have many cards issued. The most notable example for 2001 card season was that Tom Brady (who quarterbacked the Patriots to a Super Bowl championship) had less than five cards issued in more than 50 sets.

The 2002 football card season saw an increase in the number of memorabilia cards being issued, and a slight decrease in the number of certified autograph cards being released. Michael Vick was at the forefront of a strong collecting season, as he and several other young players look to establish themselves in the market, as many of the NFL's superstars grow older and near retirement.

While some collectors are frustrated by the changing hobby, others are thrilled because there are more choices than ever for the football card collector—and many of the collectors like it that way.

Additional Reading

Each year Beckett Media produces comprehensive annual price guides for each of the four major sports: *Beckett Baseball Card Price Guide, Beckett Football Card Price Guide, Beckett Basketball Card Price Guide*, and *Beckett Hockey Card Price Guide*. The aim of these annual guides is to provide information and accurate pricing on a wide array of sports cards, ranging from main issues by the major card manufacturers to various regional, promotional, and food issues. Also, other alphabetical checklists, such as *The Beckett Baseball Card Alphabetical*, *The Beckett Football Card Alphabetical, The Beckett Basketball Card Alphabetical,* and *The Beckett Hockey Card Price Guide and Alphabetical*, are published to assist the collector in identifying all the cards of any particular player. Our Web site Beckett.com was created to allow our readers with Internet access an avenue for buying and selling cards as well as participating in online auctions and interactive price guides. The seasoned collector will find these tools valuable sources of information that will enable him to pursue his hobby interests.

In addition, abridged editions of the Beckett Price Guides have been published for each of the three major sports as part of the House of Collectibles series: *The Official Price Guide to Baseball Cards, The Official Price Guide to Football Cards,* and *The Official Price Guide to Basketball Cards.* Published in a convenient mass-market paperback format, these price guides provide information and accurate pricing on all the important issues by the major card manufacturers.

1995 Absolute

❑ COMPLETE SET (200) 20.00 7.50
❑ 1 John Elway 2.00 .75
❑ 2 Reggie White .40 .15
❑ 3 Errict Rhett .20 .07
❑ 4 Deion Sanders .50 .20
❑ 5 Rocket Ismail .20 .07
❑ 6 Jerome Bettis .40 .15
❑ 7 Randall Cunningham .40 .15
❑ 8 Mario Bates .20 .07
❑ 9 Dave Brown .20 .07
❑ 10 Stan Humphries .20 .07
❑ 11 Drew Bledsoe .60 .25
❑ 12 Neil O'Donnell .20 .07
❑ 13 Dan Marino 2.00 .75
❑ 14 Larry Centers .20 .07
❑ 15 Craig Heyward .20 .07
❑ 16 Bruce Smith .40 .15
❑ 17 Erik Kramer .10 .02
❑ 18 Jeff Blake RC 1.00 .40
❑ 19 Vinny Testaverde .20 .07
❑ 20 Barry Sanders 1.50 .60
❑ 21 Boomer Esiason .20 .07
❑ 22 Emmitt Smith 1.50 .60
❑ 23 Warren Moon .20 .07
❑ 24 Junior Seau .40 .15
❑ 25 Heath Shuler .20 .07
❑ 26 Jackie Harris .10 .02
❑ 27 Terance Mathis .20 .07
❑ 28 Raymont Harris .10 .02
❑ 29 Jim Kelly .40 .15
❑ 30 Dan Wilkinson .20 .07
❑ 31 Herman Moore .40 .15
❑ 32 Shannon Sharpe .20 .07
❑ 33 Antonio Langham .10 .02
❑ 34 Charles Haley .20 .07
❑ 35 Brett Favre 2.00 .75
❑ 36 Marshall Faulk 1.25 .50
❑ 37 Neil Smith .20 .07
❑ 38 Harvey Williams .10 .02
❑ 39 Johnny Bailey .10 .02
❑ 40 O.J. McDuffie .40 .15
❑ 41 David Palmer .20 .07
❑ 42 Willie McGinest .20 .07
❑ 43 Quinn Early .20 .07
❑ 44 Johnny Johnson .10 .02
❑ 45 Derek Brown TE .10 .02
❑ 46 Charlie Garner .40 .15
❑ 47 Byron Bam Morris .10 .02
❑ 48 Natrone Means .20 .07
❑ 49 Ken Norton Jr. .20 .07
❑ 50 Troy Aikman 1.00 .40
❑ 51 Reggie Brooks .20 .07
❑ 52 Trent Dilfer .40 .15
❑ 53 Cortez Kennedy .20 .07
❑ 54 Chuck Levy .10 .02
❑ 55 Jeff George .20 .07
❑ 56 Steve Young .75 .30
❑ 57 Lewis Tillman .10 .02
❑ 58 Carl Pickens .20 .07
❑ 59 Jake Reed .20 .07
❑ 60 Jay Novacek .20 .07
❑ 61 Greg Hill .20 .07
❑ 62 James Jett .20 .07
❑ 63 Terry Kirby .20 .07
❑ 64 Qadry Ismail .20 .07
❑ 65 Ben Coates .20 .07
❑ 66 Kevin Greene .20 .07
❑ 67 Bryant Young .20 .07
❑ 68 Brian Mitchell .10 .02
❑ 69 Steve Walsh .10 .02
❑ 70 Darnay Scott .20 .07
❑ 71 Daryl Johnston .20 .07
❑ 72 Glyn Milburn .10 .02
❑ 73 Tim Brown .40 .15
❑ 74 Isaac Bruce .75 .30
❑ 75 Bernie Parmalee .20 .07
❑ 76 Terry Allen .20 .07
❑ 77 Jim Everett .10 .02
❑ 78 Thomas Lewis .20 .07
❑ 79 Vaughn Hebron .10 .02
❑ 80 Rod Woodson .20 .07
❑ 81 Rick Mirer .20 .07
❑ 82 Dana Stubblefield .20 .07
❑ 83 Bert Emanuel .40 .15
❑ 84 Andre Reed .20 .07
❑ 85 Jeff Graham .10 .02
❑ 86 Johnnie Morton .20 .07
❑ 87 LeShon Johnson .20 .07
❑ 88 Michael Irvin .40 .15
❑ 89 Derrick Alexander WR .40 .15
❑ 90 Lake Dawson .20 .07
❑ 91 Cody Carlson .10 .02
❑ 92 Chris Warren .20 .07
❑ 93 William Floyd .20 .07
❑ 94 Charles Johnson .20 .07
❑ 95 Roosevelt Potts .10 .02
❑ 96 Cris Carter .40 .15
❑ 97 Aaron Glenn .10 .02
❑ 98 Curtis Conway .40 .15
❑ 99 Kevin Williams WR .20 .07
❑ 100 Jerry Rice 1.00 .40
❑ 101 Frank Reich .10 .02
❑ 102 Harold Green .10 .02
❑ 103 Russell Copeland .10 .02
❑ 104 Rob Moore .20 .07
❑ 105 Edgar Bennett .20 .07
❑ 106 Darren Carrington .10 .02
❑ 107 Tommy Maddox .40 .15
❑ 108 Dave Meggett .10 .02
❑ 109 Fred Barnett .20 .07
❑ 110 Mark Seay .20 .07
❑ 111 Gus Frerotte .20 .07
❑ 112 Brent Jones .10 .02
❑ 113 Chris Miller .10 .02
❑ 114 Cedric Tillman .10 .02
❑ 115 Mark Ingram .10 .02
❑ 116 Eric Turner .10 .02
❑ 117 Mark Carrier WR .20 .07
❑ 118 Garrison Hearst .40 .15
❑ 119 Craig Erickson .10 .02
❑ 120 Derek Russell .10 .02
❑ 121 Mike Sherrard .10 .02
❑ 122 Horace Copeland .10 .02
❑ 123 Jack Trudeau .10 .02
❑ 124 Leroy Hoard .10 .02
❑ 125 Gary Brown .10 .02
❑ 126 Mel Gray .10 .02
❑ 127 Steve Beuerlein .20 .07
❑ 128 Marcus Allen .40 .15
❑ 129 Irving Fryar .20 .07
❑ 130 Marion Butts .10 .02
❑ 131 Ricky Watters .20 .07
❑ 132 Tony Martin .20 .07
❑ 133 Lawrence Dawsey .10 .02
❑ 134 Ronnie Harmon .10 .02
❑ 135 Herschel Walker .20 .07
❑ 136 Michael Haynes .20 .07
❑ 137 Eric Green .10 .02
❑ 138 Steve Bono .20 .07
❑ 139 Jamir Miller .10 .02
❑ 140 Rod Smith DB .20 .07
❑ 141 Andre Rison .20 .07
❑ 142 Eric Metcalf .20 .07
❑ 143 Michael Timpson .10 .02
❑ 144 Cornelius Bennett .20 .07
❑ 145 Sean Dawkins .20 .07
❑ 146 Scott Mitchell .20 .07
❑ 147 Ray Childress .10 .02
❑ 148 Jim Harbaugh .20 .07
❑ 149 Reggie Cobb .10 .02
❑ 150 Willie Roaf .10 .02
❑ 151 Stevie Anderson .10 .02
❑ 152 Barry Foster .20 .07
❑ 153 Joe Montana 2.00 .75
❑ 154 David Klingler .20 .07
❑ 155 Chris Chandler .20 .07
❑ 156 Carnell Lake .10 .02
❑ 157 Calvin Williams .20 .07
❑ 158 Kenneth Davis .10 .02
❑ 159 Tydus Winans .10 .02
❑ 160 Sam Adams .10 .02
❑ 161 Ronald Moore .10 .02
❑ 162 Vincent Brisby .10 .02
❑ 163 Alvin Harper .10 .02
❑ 164 Jake Reed .20 .07
❑ 165 Jeff Hostetler .20 .07
❑ 166 Mark Brunell .60 .25
❑ 167 Leonard Russell .10 .02
❑ 168 Greg Truitt .10 .02
❑ 169 Pete Metzelaars .10 .02
❑ 170 Dave Krieg .10 .02
❑ 171 Lorenzo White .10 .02
❑ 172 Robert Brooks .40 .15
❑ 173 Willie Davis .20 .07
❑ 174 Irving Spikes .20 .07
❑ 175 Rodney Hampton .20 .07
❑ 176 Erric Pegram .20 .07
❑ 177 Brian Blades .20 .07
❑ 178 Shawn Jefferson .10 .02
❑ 179 Tyrone Poole RC .40 .15
❑ 180 Rob Johnson RC 1.50 .60
❑ 181 Ki-Jana Carter RC .40 .15
❑ 182 Steve McNair RC 5.00 2.00
❑ 183 Michael Westbrook RC .40 .15
❑ 184 Kerry Collins RC 2.50 1.00
❑ 185 Kevin Carter RC .40 .15
❑ 186 Tony Boselli RC .40 .15
❑ 187 Joey Galloway RC 2.50 1.00
❑ 188 Kyle Brady RC .40 .15
❑ 189 J.J. Stokes RC .40 .15
❑ 190 Warren Sapp RC 2.50 1.00
❑ 191 Tyrone Wheatley RC 1.50 .60
❑ 192 Napoleon Kaufman RC 2.00 .75
❑ 193 James O. Stewart RC 1.50 .60
❑ 194 Rashaan Salaam RC .20 .07
❑ 195 Ray Zellars RC .20 .07
❑ 196 Todd Collins RC .20 .07
❑ 197 Sherman Williams RC .10 .02
❑ 198 Frank Sanders RC .40 .15
❑ 199 Terrell Fletcher RC .10 .02
❑ 200 Chad May RC .10 .02
❑ DP1G Tony Boselli Draft Gold 3.00 1.50
❑ DP1S Tony Boselli Draft Silver 2.00 .75
❑ DP2G Kerry Collins Draft Gold 5.00 2.00
❑ DP2S Kerry Collins Draft Silver 5.00 2.00

1996 Absolute

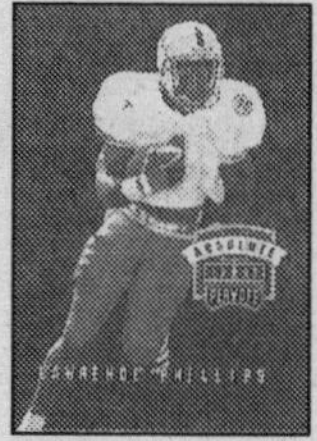

❑ COMPLETE SET (200) 60.00 25.00
❑ COMP.RED SET (100) 15.00 6.00
❑ 1 Jim Kelly .60 .25
❑ 2 Michael Irvin .60 .25
❑ 3 Jim Harbaugh .30 .10
❑ 4 Warren Moon .30 .10
❑ 5 Rick Mirer .30 .10
❑ 6 Drew Bledsoe 1.00 .40
❑ 7 Steve Young 1.25 .50
❑ 8 Junior Seau .60 .25
❑ 9 Sherman Williams .15 .05
❑ 10 Jay Novacek .15 .05
❑ 11 Bill Brooks .15 .05
❑ 12 Steve Bono .15 .05
❑ 13 Leroy Hoard .15 .05
❑ 14 Willie Jackson .30 .10
❑ 15 Irving Fryar .30 .10
❑ 16 Tony McGee .15 .05
❑ 17 Neil O'Donnell .30 .10
❑ 18 Fred Barnett .15 .05
❑ 19 Erric Pegram .15 .05
❑ 20 Derrick Moore .15 .05
❑ 21 Johnnie Morton .30 .10
❑ 22 James Jett .30 .10

❑ 23	Tim Brown	.60	.25
❑ 24	Kevin Miniefield	.15	.05
❑ 25	Jim McMahon	.30	.10
❑ 26	Brian Blades	.15	.05
❑ 27	Henry Ellard	.15	.05
❑ 28	Calvin Williams	.15	.05
❑ 29	Chris Chandler	.30	.10
❑ 30	Rod Woodson	.30	.10
❑ 31	Ronnie Harmon	.15	.05
❑ 32	Brent Jones	.15	.05
❑ 33	Qadry Ismail	.30	.10
❑ 34	Steve Tasker	.15	.05
❑ 35	Eric Green	.15	.05
❑ 36	Brian Mitchell	.15	.05
❑ 37	Herschel Walker	.30	.10
❑ 38	Sean Dawkins	.15	.05
❑ 39	Bryce Paup	.15	.05
❑ 40	Dorsey Levens	.60	.25
❑ 41	Andre Rison	.30	.10
❑ 42	Lamont Warren	.15	.05
❑ 43	Earnest Byner	.15	.05
❑ 44	Bobby Engram RC	.60	.25
❑ 45	Simeon Rice RC	1.50	.60
❑ 46	Michael Jackson	.30	.10
❑ 47	Marvin Harrison RC	4.00	1.50
❑ 48	Thurman Thomas	.60	.25
❑ 49	Charles Haley	.30	.10
❑ 50	Rob Moore	.30	.10
❑ 51	Bryan Cox	.15	.05
❑ 52	Horace Copeland	.15	.05
❑ 53	Rodney Peete	.15	.05
❑ 54	Jeff Graham	.15	.05
❑ 55	Charles Johnson	.15	.05
❑ 56	Natrone Means	.30	.10
❑ 57	Terrell Fletcher	.15	.05
❑ 58	Eric Bieniemy	.15	.05
❑ 59	Karim Abdul-Jabbar RC	.60	.25
❑ 60	Quinn Early	.15	.05
❑ 61	Mark Bruener	.15	.05
❑ 62	Shawn Jefferson	.15	.05
❑ 63	Vinny Testaverde	.30	.10
❑ 64	Derrick Mayes RC	.60	.25
❑ 65	Mario Bates	.30	.10
❑ 66	J.J. Birden	.15	.05
❑ 67	Eddie Kennison RC	.60	.25
❑ 68	Steve Walsh	.15	.05
❑ 69	Mark Chmura	.30	.10
❑ 70	Mike Sherrard	.15	.05
❑ 71	Boomer Esiason	.30	.10
❑ 72	Alex Van Dyke RC	.30	.10
❑ 73	Jake Reed	.30	.10
❑ 74	Jackie Harris	.15	.05
❑ 75	Mark Rypien	.15	.05
❑ 76	Chris Calloway	.15	.05
❑ 77	Amani Toomer RC	1.50	.60
❑ 78	Terrell Davis	3.00	1.25
❑ 79	Rocket Ismail	.15	.05
❑ 80	Derek Loville	.15	.05
❑ 81	Ben Coates	.30	.10
❑ 82	Kyle Brady	.15	.05
❑ 83	Willie Green	.15	.05
❑ 84	Randall Cunningham	.60	.25
❑ 85	Amp Lee	.15	.05
❑ 86	Bert Emanuel	.30	.10
❑ 87	Jason Dunn RC	.30	.10
❑ 88	Michael Haynes	.15	.05
❑ 89	Robert Green	.15	.05
❑ 90	Willie Davis	.15	.05
❑ 91	O.J. McDuffie	.30	.10
❑ 92	Harold Green	.15	.05
❑ 93	Ken Dilger	.30	.10
❑ 94	Brett Perriman	.15	.05
❑ 95	Eric Zeier	.15	.05
❑ 96	Jerome Bettis	.60	.25
❑ 97	Rickey Dudley RC	.60	.25
❑ 98	Darnay Scott	.30	.10
❑ 99	Mark Brunell	1.00	.40
❑ 100	Christian Fauria	.15	.05
❑ 101	Jeff Blake	1.50	.60
❑ 102	Troy Aikman	4.00	1.50
❑ 103	John Elway	8.00	3.00
❑ 104	Barry Sanders	6.00	2.50
❑ 105	Curtis Conway	1.50	.60
❑ 106	Wayne Chrebet	2.00	.75
❑ 107	Lake Dawson	.75	.30
❑ 108	Jerry Rice	4.00	1.50
❑ 109	Kevin Williams	.25	.08
❑ 110	Zack Crockett	.25	.08
❑ 111	Vincent Brisby	.25	.08
❑ 112	Rodney Thomas	.25	.08
❑ 113	Rodney Hampton	.75	.30
❑ 114	Adrian Murrell	.30	.10
❑ 115	Bruce Smith	1.50	.60
❑ 116	Napoleon Kaufman	1.50	.60
❑ 117	Byron Bam Morris	.25	.08
❑ 118	Anthony Miller	.75	.30
❑ 119	Aaron Hayden RC	.75	.30
❑ 120	Joey Galloway	.60	.25
❑ 121	Trent Dilfer	.75	.30
❑ 122	Stoney Case	.25	.08
❑ 123	Tamarick Vanover	.30	.10
❑ 124	Eric Metcalf	.75	.30
❑ 125	Marcus Allen	1.50	.60
❑ 126	James O. Stewart	.75	.30
❑ 127	Charlie Garner	.75	.30
❑ 128	Yancey Thigpen	.75	.30
❑ 129	William Floyd	.75	.30
❑ 130	Terry Allen	.75	.30
❑ 131	Robert Smith	.75	.30
❑ 132	Todd Kinchen	.25	.08
❑ 133	Gus Frerotte	.75	.30
❑ 134	Frank Sanders	.75	.30
❑ 135	Scott Mitchell	.75	.30
❑ 136	Greg Hill	.75	.30
❑ 137	Edgar Bennett	.75	.30
❑ 138	Alvin Harper	.25	.08
❑ 139	Reggie White	1.50	.60
❑ 140	Craig Heyward	.25	.08
❑ 141	Todd Collins	.75	.30
❑ 142	Ernie Mills	.25	.08
❑ 143	Keyshawn Johnson RC	2.50	1.00
❑ 144	Mark Carrier WR	.25	.08
❑ 145	Robert Brooks	1.50	.60
❑ 146	Bernie Parmalee	.25	.08
❑ 147	Carl Pickens	.75	.30
❑ 148	Kevin Hardy RC	1.50	.60
❑ 149	Jonathan Ogden RC	1.50	.60
❑ 150	Lawrence Phillips RC	1.50	.60
❑ 151	Emmitt Smith	10.00	4.00
❑ 152	Brett Favre	12.00	5.00
❑ 153	Dan Marino	12.00	5.00
❑ 154	Jim Everett	.60	.25
❑ 155	Dave Brown	1.25	.50
❑ 156	Jeff Hostetler	1.25	.50
❑ 157	Heath Shuler	1.25	.50
❑ 158	Daryl Johnston	1.25	.50
❑ 159	Terance Mathis	1.25	.50
❑ 160	Curtis Martin	5.00	2.00
❑ 161	Ray Zellars	.60	.25
❑ 162	Ricky Watters	1.25	.50
❑ 163	Chris Warren	1.25	.50
❑ 164	Larry Centers	1.25	.50
❑ 165	Steve McNair	5.00	2.00
❑ 166	Terry Kirby	1.25	.50
❑ 167	Rob Johnson	2.50	1.00
❑ 168	Dave Meggett	.60	.25
❑ 169	Antonio Freeman	.60	.25
❑ 170	Marshall Faulk	4.00	1.50
❑ 171	Andre Hastings	.15	.05
❑ 172	Stan Humphries	1.25	.50
❑ 173	Errict Rhett	1.25	.50
❑ 174	Michael Westbrook	2.50	1.00
❑ 175	Deion Sanders	4.00	1.50
❑ 176	Jeff George	1.25	.50
❑ 177	Cris Carter	2.50	1.00
❑ 178	Chris Sanders	1.25	.50
❑ 179	Ki-Jana Carter	1.25	.50
❑ 180	Kordell Stewart	2.50	1.00
❑ 181	Isaac Bruce	2.50	1.00
❑ 182	Terry Glenn RC	5.00	2.00
❑ 183	Garrison Hearst	1.25	.50
❑ 184	Erik Kramer	.60	.25
❑ 185	Leeland McElroy RC	1.25	.50
❑ 186	Rashaan Salaam	1.25	.50
❑ 187	Kimble Anders	.60	.25
❑ 188	Chad May	.60	.25
❑ 189	Tony Martin	1.25	.50
❑ 190	J.J. Stokes	2.50	1.00
❑ 191	Darick Holmes	.60	.25
❑ 192	Eric Moulds RC	6.00	2.50
❑ 193	Shannon Sharpe	1.25	.50
❑ 194	Tim Biakabutuka RC	2.50	1.00
❑ 195	Eddie George RC	6.00	2.50
❑ 196	Mike Alstott RC	5.00	2.00
❑ 197	Kerry Collins	2.50	1.00
❑ 198	Harvey Williams	.60	.25
❑ 199	Herman Moore	1.25	.50
❑ 200	Tyrone Wheatley	1.25	.50

1997 Absolute

❑	COMPLETE SET (200)	80.00	30.00
❑	COMP.GREEN SET (100)	25.00	10.00
❑ 1	Marcus Allen	.50	.20
❑ 2	Eric Bieniemy	.20	.07
❑ 3	Jason Dunn	.20	.07
❑ 4	Jim Harbaugh	.30	.10
❑ 5	Michael Westbrook	.30	.10
❑ 6	Tiki Barber RC	4.00	1.50
❑ 7	Frank Reich	.20	.07
❑ 8	Irving Fryar	.30	.10
❑ 9	Courtney Hawkins	.20	.07
❑ 10	Eric Zeier	.30	.10
❑ 11	Kent Graham	.20	.07
❑ 12	Trent Dilfer	.50	.20
❑ 13	Neil O'Donnell	.30	.10
❑ 14	Reidel Anthony RC	.50	.20
❑ 15	Jeff Hostetler	.20	.07
❑ 16	Lawrence Phillips	.20	.07
❑ 17	Dave Brown	.20	.07
❑ 18	Mike Tomczak	.20	.07
❑ 19	Jake Reed	.30	.10
❑ 20	Anthony Miller	.20	.07
❑ 21	Eric Metcalf	.30	.10
❑ 22	Sedrick Shaw RC	.30	.10
❑ 23	Anthony Johnson	.20	.07
❑ 24	Mario Bates	.20	.07
❑ 25	Dorsey Levens	.50	.20
❑ 26	Stan Humphries	.30	.10
❑ 27	Ben Coates	.30	.10
❑ 28	Tyrone Wheatley	.30	.10
❑ 29	Adrian Murrell	.30	.10
❑ 30	William Henderson	.30	.10
❑ 31	Warrick Dunn RC	2.00	.75
❑ 32	LeShon Johnson	.20	.07
❑ 33	James O.Stewart	.30	.10
❑ 34	Edgar Bennett	.30	.10
❑ 35	Raymont Harris	.20	.07
❑ 36	LeRoy Butler	.20	.07
❑ 37	Darren Woodson	.20	.07
❑ 38	Darnell Autry RC	.30	.10
❑ 39	Johnnie Morton	.30	.10
❑ 40	William Floyd	.30	.10
❑ 41	Terrell Fletcher	.20	.07
❑ 42	Leonard Russell	.20	.07
❑ 43	Henry Ellard	.20	.07
❑ 44	Terrell Owens	.50	.20
❑ 45	John Friesz	.20	.07
❑ 46	Antowain Smith RC	1.50	.60
❑ 47	Charles Johnson	.30	.10
❑ 48	Rickey Dudley	.30	.10
❑ 49	Lake Dawson	.20	.07
❑ 50	Bert Emanuel	.30	.10
❑ 51	Zach Thomas	.50	.20
❑ 52	Earnest Byner	.20	.07
❑ 53	Yatil Green RC	.30	.10
❑ 54	Chris Spielman	.20	.07
❑ 55	Muhsin Muhammad	.30	.10
❑ 56	Bobby Engram	.30	.10
❑ 57	Eric Bjornson	.20	.07
❑ 58	Willie Green	.20	.07
❑ 59	Derrick Mayes	.30	.10
❑ 60	Chris Sanders	.20	.07
❑ 61	Jimmy Smith	.30	.10
❑ 62	Tony Gonzalez RC	2.00	.75
❑ 63	Rich Gannon	.50	.20
❑ 64	Stanley Pritchett	.20	.07
❑ 65	Brad Johnson	.50	.20
❑ 66	Rodney Peete	.20	.07
❑ 67	Sam Gash	.20	.07
❑ 68	Chris Calloway	.20	.07

❑ 69	Chris T. Jones	.20	.07
❑ 70	Will Blackwell RC	.30	.10
❑ 71	Mark Bruener	.20	.07
❑ 72	Terry Kirby	.30	.10
❑ 73	Brian Blades	.20	.07
❑ 74	Craig Heyward	.20	.07
❑ 75	Jamie Asher	.20	.07
❑ 76	Terance Mathis	.30	.10
❑ 77	Troy Davis RC	.30	.10
❑ 78	Bruce Smith	.30	.10
❑ 79	Simeon Rice	.30	.10
❑ 80	Fred Barnett	.20	.07
❑ 81	Tim Brown	.50	.20
❑ 82	James Jett	.30	.10
❑ 83	Mark Carrier WR	.20	.07
❑ 84	Shawn Jefferson	.20	.07
❑ 85	Ken Dilger	.20	.07
❑ 86	Rae Carruth RC	.20	.07
❑ 87	Keenan McCardell	.30	.10
❑ 88	Michael Irvin	.50	.20
❑ 89	Mark Chmura	.30	.10
❑ 90	Derrick Alexander WR	.30	.10
❑ 91	Andre Reed	.30	.10
❑ 92	Ed McCaffrey	.30	.10
❑ 93	Erik Kramer	.20	.07
❑ 94	Albert Connell RC	.50	.20
❑ 95	Frank Wycheck	.20	.07
❑ 96	Zack Crockett	.20	.07
❑ 97	Jim Everett	.20	.07
❑ 98	Michael Haynes	.20	.07
❑ 99	Jeff Graham	.20	.07
❑ 100	Brent Jones	.30	.10
❑ 101	Troy Aikman	3.00	1.25
❑ 102	Byron Hanspard RC	.30	.10
❑ 103	Robert Brooks	1.25	.50
❑ 104	Karim Abdul-Jabbar	1.25	.50
❑ 105	Drew Bledsoe	1.50	.60
❑ 106	Napoleon Kaufman	1.25	.50
❑ 107	Steve Young	2.00	.75
❑ 108	Leeland McElroy	.20	.07
❑ 109	Jamal Anderson	.50	.20
❑ 110	David LaFleur RC	.50	.20
❑ 111	Vinny Testaverde	.75	.30
❑ 112	Eric Moulds	1.25	.50
❑ 113	Tim Biakabutuka	1.25	.50
❑ 114	Rick Mirer	.50	.20
❑ 115	Jeff Blake	1.25	.50
❑ 116	Jim Schwantz RC	.50	.20
❑ 117	Herman Moore	.75	.30
❑ 118	Ike Hilliard RC	2.50	1.00
❑ 119	Reggie White	1.25	.50
❑ 120	Steve McNair	2.00	.75
❑ 121	Marshall Faulk	2.00	.75
❑ 122	Natrone Means	.75	.30
❑ 123	Greg Hill	.75	.30
❑ 124	O.J. McDuffie	.75	.30
❑ 125	Robert Smith	.75	.30
❑ 126	Bryant Westbrook RC	1.25	.50
❑ 127	Ray Zellars	.50	.20
❑ 128	Rodney Hampton	.75	.30
❑ 129	Wayne Chrebet	.50	.20
❑ 130	Desmond Howard	.75	.30
❑ 131	Ty Detmer	.75	.30
❑ 132	Erric Pegram	.50	.20
❑ 133	Yancey Thigpen	.75	.30
❑ 134	Danny Wuerffel RC	.50	.20
❑ 135	Charlie Jones	.50	.20
❑ 136	Chris Warren	.75	.30
❑ 137	Isaac Bruce	1.25	.50
❑ 138	Errict Rhett	.75	.30
❑ 139	Gus Frerotte	1.25	.50
❑ 140	Frank Sanders	.75	.30
❑ 141	Todd Collins	.75	.30
❑ 142	Jake Plummer RC	12.00	5.00
❑ 143	Darnay Scott	.75	.30
❑ 144	Rashaan Salaam	1.25	.50
❑ 145	Terrell Davis	2.00	.75
❑ 146	Scott Mitchell	.75	.30
❑ 147	Junior Seau	1.25	.50
❑ 148	Warren Moon	.75	.30
❑ 149	Wesley Walls	.50	.20
❑ 150	Daryl Johnston	.75	.30
❑ 151	Brett Favre	12.00	5.00
❑ 152	Emmitt Smith	10.00	4.00
❑ 153	Dan Marino	12.00	5.00
❑ 154	Larry Centers	1.25	.50
❑ 155	Michael Jackson	1.25	.50
❑ 156	Kerry Collins	.50	.20
❑ 157	Curtis Conway	1.25	.50
❑ 158	Peter Boulware RC	2.00	.75
❑ 159	Carl Pickens	1.25	.50
❑ 160	Shannon Sharpe	1.25	.50
❑ 161	Brett Perriman	.75	.30
❑ 162	Eddie George	2.00	.75
❑ 163	Mark Brunell	4.00	1.50
❑ 164	Tamarick Vanover	1.25	.50
❑ 165	Cris Carter	2.00	.75
❑ 166	Corey Dillon RC	15.00	6.00
❑ 167	Curtis Martin	4.00	1.50
❑ 168	Amani Toomer	1.25	.50
❑ 169	Jeff George	1.25	.50
❑ 170	Kordell Stewart	2.00	.75
❑ 171	Garrison Hearst	1.25	.50
❑ 172	Tony Banks	1.25	.50
❑ 173	Mike Alstott	2.00	.75
❑ 174	Jim Druckenmiller RC	.30	.10
❑ 175	Chris Chandler	1.25	.50
❑ 176	Byron Bam Morris	.75	.30
❑ 177	Billy Joe Hobert	1.25	.50
❑ 178	Ernie Mills	.75	.30
❑ 179	Ki-Jana Carter	.75	.30
❑ 180	Deion Sanders	2.00	.75
❑ 181	Ricky Watters	1.25	.50
❑ 182	Shawn Springs RC	2.00	.75
❑ 183	Barry Sanders	10.00	4.00
❑ 184	Antonio Freeman	2.00	.75
❑ 185	Marvin Harrison	2.00	.75
❑ 186	Elvis Grbac	1.25	.50
❑ 187	Terry Glenn	2.00	.75
❑ 188	Willie Roaf	.75	.30
❑ 189	Keyshawn Johnson	2.00	.75
❑ 190	Orlando Pace RC	2.00	.75
❑ 191	Jerome Bettis	2.00	.75
❑ 192	Tony Martin	1.25	.50
❑ 193	Jerry Rice	6.00	2.50
❑ 194	Joey Galloway	1.25	.50
❑ 195	Terry Allen	2.00	.75
❑ 196	Eddie Kennison	1.25	.50
❑ 197	Thurman Thomas	2.00	.75
❑ 198	Darrell Russell RC	.75	.30
❑ 199	Rob Moore	1.25	.50
❑ 200	John Elway	12.00	5.00

1998 Absolute Hobby

❑	COMPLETE SET (200)	100.00	40.00
❑ 1	John Elway	10.00	4.00
❑ 2	Marcus Nash RC	1.50	.60
❑ 3	Brian Griese RC	6.00	2.50
❑ 4	Terrell Davis	2.50	1.00
❑ 5	Rod Smith WR	1.50	.60
❑ 6	Shannon Sharpe	1.50	.60
❑ 7	Ed McCaffrey	1.50	.60
❑ 8	Brett Favre	10.00	4.00
❑ 9	Dorsey Levens	2.50	1.00
❑ 10	Derrick Mayes	1.50	.60
❑ 11	Antonio Freeman	2.50	1.00
❑ 12	Robert Brooks	1.50	.60
❑ 13	Mark Chmura	1.50	.60
❑ 14	Reggie White	2.50	1.00
❑ 15	Kordell Stewart	2.50	1.00
❑ 16	Hines Ward RC	12.00	6.00
❑ 17	Jerome Bettis	2.50	1.00
❑ 18	Charles Johnson	1.00	.40
❑ 19	Courtney Hawkins	1.00	.40
❑ 20	Will Blackwell	1.00	.40
❑ 21	Mark Bruener	1.00	.40
❑ 22	Steve Young	4.00	1.50
❑ 23	Jim Druckenmiller	1.00	.40
❑ 24	Garrison Hearst	2.50	1.00
❑ 25	R.W. McQuarters RC	2.50	1.00
❑ 26	Marc Edwards	1.00	.40
❑ 27	Irv Smith	1.00	.40
❑ 28	Jerry Rice	5.00	2.00
❑ 29	Terrell Owens	2.50	1.00
❑ 30	J.J. Stokes	1.50	.60
❑ 31	Elvis Grbac	1.50	.60
❑ 32	Rashaan Shehee RC	2.50	1.00
❑ 33	Donnell Bennett	1.00	.40
❑ 34	Kimble Anders	1.50	.60
❑ 35	Ted Popson	1.00	.40
❑ 36	Derrick Alexander WR	1.50	.60
❑ 37	Tony Gonzalez	2.50	1.00
❑ 38	Andre Rison	1.50	.60
❑ 39	Brad Johnson	2.50	1.00
❑ 40	Randy Moss RC	20.00	7.50
❑ 41	Robert Smith	2.50	1.00
❑ 42	Leroy Hoard	1.00	.40
❑ 43	Cris Carter	2.50	1.00
❑ 44	Jake Reed	1.50	.60
❑ 45	Drew Bledsoe	4.00	1.50
❑ 46	Tony Simmons RC	2.50	1.00
❑ 47	Chris Floyd RC	1.50	.60
❑ 48	Robert Edwards RC	2.50	1.00
❑ 49	Shawn Jefferson	1.00	.40
❑ 50	Ben Coates	1.50	.60
❑ 51	Terry Glenn	2.50	1.00
❑ 52	Trent Dilfer	2.50	1.00
❑ 53	Jacquez Green RC	2.50	1.00
❑ 54	Warrick Dunn	2.50	1.00
❑ 55	Mike Alstott	2.50	1.00
❑ 56	Reidel Anthony	1.50	.60
❑ 57	Bert Emanuel	1.50	.60
❑ 58	Warren Sapp	1.50	.60
❑ 59	Charlie Batch RC	3.00	1.25
❑ 60	Germane Crowell RC	2.50	1.00
❑ 61	Scott Mitchell	1.50	.60
❑ 62	Barry Sanders	8.00	3.00
❑ 63	Tommy Vardell	1.00	.40
❑ 64	Herman Moore	1.50	.60
❑ 65	Johnnie Morton	1.50	.60
❑ 66	Mark Brunell	2.50	1.00
❑ 67	Jonathan Quinn RC	3.00	1.25
❑ 68	Fred Taylor RC	5.00	2.00
❑ 69	James Stewart	1.50	.60
❑ 70	Jimmy Smith	1.50	.60
❑ 71	Damon Jones	1.00	.40
❑ 72	Keenan McCardell	1.50	.60
❑ 73	Dan Marino	10.00	4.00
❑ 74	Larry Shannon RC	1.50	.60
❑ 75	John Avery RC	2.50	1.00
❑ 76	Troy Drayton	1.00	.40
❑ 77	Stanley Pritchett	1.00	.40
❑ 78	Karim Abdul-Jabbar	2.50	1.00
❑ 79	O.J. McDuffie	1.50	.60
❑ 80	Yatil Green	1.00	.40
❑ 81	Danny Kanell	1.50	.60
❑ 82	Tiki Barber	2.50	1.00
❑ 83	Tyrone Wheatley	1.50	.60
❑ 84	Charles Way	1.00	.40
❑ 85	Gary Brown	1.00	.40
❑ 86	Brian Alford RC	1.50	.60
❑ 87	Joe Jurevicius RC	3.00	1.25
❑ 88	Ike Hilliard	1.50	.60
❑ 89	Troy Aikman	5.00	2.00
❑ 90	Deion Sanders	2.50	1.00
❑ 91	Emmitt Smith	8.00	3.00
❑ 92	Chris Warren	1.50	.60
❑ 93	Daryl Johnston	1.50	.60
❑ 94	Michael Irvin	2.50	1.00
❑ 95	David LaFleur	1.00	.40
❑ 96	Kevin Dyson RC	3.00	1.25
❑ 97	Steve McNair	2.50	1.00
❑ 98	Eddie George	2.50	1.00
❑ 99	Yancey Thigpen	1.00	.40
❑ 100	Frank Wycheck	1.00	.40
❑ 101	Glenn Foley	1.50	.60
❑ 102	Vinny Testaverde	1.50	.60
❑ 103	Keyshawn Johnson	2.50	1.00
❑ 104	Curtis Martin	2.50	1.00
❑ 105	Keith Byars	1.00	.40
❑ 106	Scott Frost RC	1.50	.60
❑ 107	Wayne Chrebet	2.50	1.00
❑ 108	Warren Moon	2.50	1.00
❑ 109	Ahman Green RC	15.00	6.00
❑ 110	Steve Broussard	1.00	.40
❑ 111	Ricky Watters	1.50	.60
❑ 112	Joey Galloway	1.50	.60
❑ 113	Mike Pritchard	1.00	.40
❑ 114	Brian Blades	1.00	.40
❑ 115	Gus Frerotte	1.00	.40

❑	116 Skip Hicks RC	2.50	1.00
❑	117 Terry Allen	2.50	1.00
❑	118 Michael Westbrook	1.50	.60
❑	119 Jamie Asher	1.00	.40
❑	120 Leslie Shepherd	1.00	.40
❑	121 Jeff Blake	1.50	.60
❑	122 Corey Dillon	2.50	1.00
❑	123 Carl Pickens	1.50	.60
❑	124 Tony McGee	1.00	.40
❑	125 Darnay Scott	1.50	.60
❑	126 Kerry Collins	1.50	.60
❑	127 Fred Lane	1.00	.40
❑	128 William Floyd	1.00	.40
❑	129 Rae Carruth	1.00	.40
❑	130 Wesley Walls	1.50	.60
❑	131 Muhsin Muhammad	1.50	.60
❑	132 Jake Plummer	2.50	1.00
❑	133 Adrian Murrell	1.50	.60
❑	134 Michael Pittman RC	4.00	2.00
❑	135 Larry Centers	1.00	.40
❑	136 Frank Sanders	1.50	.60
❑	137 Rob Moore	1.50	.60
❑	138 Andre Wadsworth RC	2.50	1.00
❑	139 Mario Bates	1.50	.60
❑	140 Chris Chandler	1.50	.60
❑	141 Byron Hanspard	1.00	.40
❑	142 Jamal Anderson	2.50	1.00
❑	143 Terance Mathis	1.50	.60
❑	144 O.J. Santiago	1.00	.40
❑	145 Tony Martin	1.50	.60
❑	146 Jammi German RC	1.50	.60
❑	147 Jim Harbaugh	1.50	.60
❑	148 Errict Rhett	1.50	.60
❑	149 Michael Jackson	1.00	.40
❑	150 Pat Johnson RC	2.50	1.00
❑	151 Eric Green	1.00	.40
❑	152 Doug Flutie	2.50	1.00
❑	153 Rob Johnson	1.50	.60
❑	154 Antowain Smith	2.50	1.00
❑	155 Bruce Smith	1.50	.60
❑	156 Eric Moulds	2.50	1.00
❑	157 Andre Reed	1.50	.60
❑	158 Erik Kramer	1.00	.40
❑	159 Darnell Autry	1.00	.40
❑	160 Edgar Bennett	1.00	.40
❑	161 Curtis Enis RC	1.50	.60
❑	162 Curtis Conway	1.50	.60
❑	163 E.G. Green RC	2.50	1.00
❑	164 Jerome Pathon RC	3.00	1.25
❑	165 Peyton Manning RC	30.00	12.50
❑	166 Marshall Faulk	3.00	1.25
❑	167 Zack Crockett	1.00	.40
❑	168 Ken Dilger	1.00	.40
❑	169 Marvin Harrison	2.50	1.00
❑	170 Danny Wuerffel	1.50	.60
❑	171 Lamar Smith	1.50	.60
❑	172 Ray Zellars	1.00	.40
❑	173 Qadry Ismail	1.50	.60
❑	174 Sean Dawkins	1.00	.40
❑	175 Andre Hastings	1.00	.40
❑	176 Jeff George	1.50	.60
❑	177 Charles Woodson RC	4.00	1.50
❑	178 Napoleon Kaufman	2.50	1.00
❑	179 Jon Ritchie RC	2.50	1.00
❑	180 Desmond Howard	1.50	.60
❑	181 Tim Brown	2.50	1.00
❑	182 James Jett	1.50	.60
❑	183 Rickey Dudley	1.00	.40
❑	184 Bobby Hoying	1.50	.60
❑	185 Rodney Peete	1.00	.40
❑	186 Charlie Garner	1.50	.60
❑	187 Irving Fryar	1.50	.60
❑	188 Chris T. Jones	1.00	.40
❑	189 Jason Dunn	1.00	.40
❑	190 Tony Banks	1.50	.60
❑	191 Robert Holcombe RC	2.50	1.00
❑	192 Craig Heyward	1.00	.40
❑	193 Isaac Bruce	2.50	1.00
❑	194 Az-Zahir Hakim RC	3.00	1.25
❑	195 Eddie Kennison	1.50	.60
❑	196 Mikhael Ricks RC	2.50	1.00
❑	197 Ryan Leaf RC	3.00	1.25
❑	198 Natrone Means	1.50	.60
❑	199 Junior Seau	2.50	1.00
❑	200 Freddie Jones	1.00	.40

1999 Absolute EXP

❑	COMPLETE SET (200)	50.00	25.00
❑	1 Tim Couch RC	1.25	.50
❑	2 Donovan McNabb RC	6.00	2.50
❑	3 Akili Smith RC	.75	.30
❑	4 Edgerrin James RC	5.00	2.00
❑	5 Ricky Williams RC	2.50	1.00
❑	6 Torry Holt RC	3.00	1.25
❑	7 Champ Bailey RC	1.50	.60
❑	8 David Boston RC	1.25	.50
❑	9 Chris Claiborne RC	.50	.20
❑	10 Chris McAlister RC	.75	.30
❑	11 Daunte Culpepper RC	5.00	2.00
❑	12 Cade McNown RC	.75	.30
❑	13 Troy Edwards RC	.75	.30
❑	14 Kevin Johnson RC	1.25	.50
❑	15 James Johnson RC	.75	.30
❑	16 Rob Konrad RC	1.25	.50
❑	17 Jim Kleinsasser RC	1.25	.50
❑	18 Kevin Faulk RC	1.25	.50
❑	19 Joe Montgomery RC	.75	.30
❑	20 Shaun King RC	.75	.30
❑	21 Peerless Price RC	1.25	.50
❑	22 Mike Cloud RC	.75	.30
❑	23 Jermaine Fazande RC	.75	.30
❑	24 D'Wayne Bates RC	.75	.30
❑	25 Brock Huard RC	1.25	.50
❑	26 Marty Booker RC	1.25	.50
❑	27 Karsten Bailey RC	.75	.30
❑	28 Shawn Bryson RC	1.25	.50
❑	29 Jeff Paulk RC	.50	.20
❑	30 Sedrick Irvin RC	.50	.20
❑	31 Craig Yeast RC	.75	.30
❑	32 Joe Germaine RC	.75	.30
❑	33 Dameane Douglas RC	1.25	.50
❑	34 Brandon Stokley RC	1.50	.60
❑	35 Larry Parker RC	1.25	.50
❑	36 Wane McGarity RC	.50	.20
❑	37 Na Brown RC	.75	.30
❑	38 Cecil Collins RC	.50	.20
❑	39 Darrin Chiaverini RC	.75	.30
❑	40 Madre Hill RC	.50	.20
❑	41 Adrian Murrell	.50	.20
❑	42 Jake Plummer	.50	.20
❑	43 Frank Sanders	.50	.20
❑	44 Rob Moore	.50	.20
❑	45 Andre Wadsworth	.30	.10
❑	46 Simeon Rice	.50	.20
❑	47 Eric Swann	.30	.10
❑	48 Terance Mathis	.50	.20
❑	49 Tim Dwight	.75	.30
❑	50 Jamal Anderson	.75	.30
❑	51 Chris Chandler	.50	.20
❑	52 Chris Calloway	.30	.10
❑	53 O.J. Santiago	.30	.10
❑	54 Jermaine Lewis	.50	.20
❑	55 Priest Holmes	1.25	.50
❑	56 Scott Mitchell	.30	.10
❑	57 Tony Banks	.50	.20
❑	58 Rod Woodson	.50	.20
❑	59 Andre Reed	.50	.20
❑	60 Thurman Thomas	.50	.20
❑	61 Bruce Smith	.50	.20
❑	62 Rob Johnson	.50	.20
❑	63 Eric Moulds	.75	.30
❑	64 Doug Flutie	.75	.30
❑	65 Antowain Smith	.75	.30
❑	66 Tim Biakabutuka	.50	.20
❑	67 Muhsin Muhammad	.50	.20
❑	68 Steve Beuerlein	.30	.10
❑	69 Bobby Engram	.50	.20
❑	70 Curtis Conway	.50	.20
❑	71 Curtis Enis	.30	.10
❑	72 Edgar Bennett	.30	.10
❑	73 Jeff Blake	.50	.20
❑	74 Darnay Scott	.30	.10
❑	75 Carl Pickens	.50	.20
❑	76 Corey Dillon	.75	.30
❑	77 Ty Detmer	.50	.20
❑	78 Leslie Shepherd	.30	.10
❑	79 Sedrick Shaw	.30	.10
❑	80 Rocket Ismail	.50	.20
❑	81 Emmitt Smith	1.50	.60
❑	82 Michael Irvin	.50	.20
❑	83 Troy Aikman	1.50	.60
❑	84 Deion Sanders	.75	.30
❑	85 Darren Woodson	.30	.10
❑	86 Chris Warren	.30	.10
❑	87 John Elway	2.50	1.00
❑	88 Brian Griese	.75	.30
❑	89 Shannon Sharpe	.50	.20
❑	90 Terrell Davis	.75	.30
❑	91 Bubby Brister	.30	.10
❑	92 Ed McCaffrey	.50	.20
❑	93 Rod Smith	.50	.20
❑	94 Germane Crowell	.30	.10
❑	95 Johnnie Morton	.50	.20
❑	96 Barry Sanders	2.50	1.00
❑	97 Herman Moore	.50	.20
❑	98 Charlie Batch	.75	.30
❑	99 Mark Chmura	.30	.10
❑	100 Derrick Mayes	.30	.10
❑	101 Dorsey Levens	.75	.30
❑	102 Brett Favre	2.50	1.00
❑	103 Antonio Freeman	.75	.30
❑	104 Robert Brooks	.50	.20
❑	105 Desmond Howard	.50	.20
❑	106 Jerome Pathon	.30	.10
❑	107 Marvin Harrison	.75	.30
❑	108 Peyton Manning	2.50	1.00
❑	109 E.G. Green	.30	.10
❑	110 Tavian Banks	.30	.10
❑	111 Keenan McCardell	.50	.20
❑	112 Jimmy Smith	.50	.20
❑	113 Mark Brunell	.75	.30
❑	114 Fred Taylor	.75	.30
❑	115 Byron Bam Morris	.30	.10
❑	116 Andre Rison	.50	.20
❑	117 Elvis Grbac	.50	.20
❑	118 Warren Moon	.75	.30
❑	119 Tony Gonzalez	.75	.30
❑	120 Derrick Alexander WR	.50	.20
❑	121 Rashaan Shehee	.30	.10
❑	122 Zach Thomas	.75	.30
❑	123 Oronde Gadsden	.50	.20
❑	124 Dan Marino	2.50	1.00
❑	125 Karim Abdul-Jabbar	.50	.20
❑	126 O.J. McDuffie	.50	.20
❑	127 Jake Reed	.50	.20
❑	128 John Randle	.50	.20
❑	129 Randy Moss	2.00	.75
❑	130 Cris Carter	.75	.30
❑	131 Randall Cunningham	.75	.30
❑	132 Robert Smith	.75	.30
❑	133 Terry Glenn	.75	.30
❑	134 Ben Coates	.50	.20
❑	135 Drew Bledsoe	1.00	.40
❑	136 Ty Law	.50	.20
❑	137 Tony Simmons	.30	.10
❑	138 Eddie Kennison	.50	.20
❑	139 Cam Cleeland	.30	.10
❑	140 Ike Hilliard	.30	.10
❑	141 Joe Jurevicius	.50	.20
❑	142 Gary Brown	.30	.10
❑	143 Kerry Collins	.50	.20
❑	144 Tiki Barber	.75	.30
❑	145 Jason Sehorn	.30	.10
❑	146 Dedric Ward	.30	.10
❑	147 Vinny Testaverde	.50	.20
❑	148 Wayne Chrebet	.50	.20
❑	149 Curtis Martin	.75	.30
❑	150 Keyshawn Johnson	.75	.30
❑	151 James Jett	.50	.20
❑	152 Napoleon Kaufman	.75	.30
❑	153 Tim Brown	.75	.30
❑	154 Charles Woodson	.75	.30
❑	155 Rickey Dudley	.30	.10
❑	156 Charles Johnson	.30	.10
❑	157 Duce Staley	.75	.30
❑	158 Chris Fuamatu-Ma'afala	.30	.10
❑	159 Jerome Bettis	.75	.30
❑	160 Kordell Stewart	.50	.20
❑	161 Levon Kirkland	.30	.10
❑	162 Hines Ward	.75	.30

❑ 163 Mikhael Ricks .30 .10
❑ 164 Natrone Means .50 .20
❑ 165 Ryan Leaf .75 .30
❑ 166 Jim Harbaugh .50 .20
❑ 167 Junior Seau .75 .30
❑ 168 Steve Young 1.00 .40
❑ 169 J.J. Stokes .50 .20
❑ 170 Terrell Owens .75 .30
❑ 171 Jerry Rice 1.50 .60
❑ 172 Garrison Hearst .50 .20
❑ 173 Ricky Watters .50 .20
❑ 174 Jon Kitna .75 .30
❑ 175 Joey Galloway .50 .20
❑ 176 Ahman Green .75 .30
❑ 177 Isaac Bruce .75 .30
❑ 178 Marshall Faulk 1.00 .40
❑ 179 Trent Green .75 .30
❑ 180 Amp Lee .30 .10
❑ 181 Greg Hill .30 .10
❑ 182 Warren Sapp .30 .10
❑ 183 Hardy Nickerson .30 .10
❑ 184 Trent Dilfer .50 .20
❑ 185 Reidel Anthony .50 .20
❑ 186 Jacquez Green .30 .10
❑ 187 Warrick Dunn .75 .30
❑ 188 Mike Alstott .75 .30
❑ 189 Kevin Dyson .50 .20
❑ 190 Eddie George .75 .30
❑ 191 Yancey Thigpen .30 .10
❑ 192 Steve McNair .75 .30
❑ 193 Chris Sanders .30 .10
❑ 194 Frank Wycheck .30 .10
❑ 195 Darrell Green .30 .10
❑ 196 Stephen Alexander .30 .10
❑ 197 Albert Connell .30 .10
❑ 198 Michael Westbrook .50 .20
❑ 199 Brad Johnson .75 .30
❑ 200 Skip Hicks .30 .10

1999 Absolute SSD

❑ COMPLETE SET (200) 250.00 125.00
❑ 1 Rob Moore 1.25 .50
❑ 2 Frank Sanders 1.25 .50
❑ 3 Jake Plummer 1.25 .50
❑ 4 Adrian Murrell 1.25 .50
❑ 5 Chris Chandler 1.25 .50
❑ 6 Jamal Anderson 2.00 .75
❑ 7 Tim Dwight 2.00 .75
❑ 8 Terance Mathis 1.25 .50
❑ 9 Priest Holmes 3.00 1.25
❑ 10 Jermaine Lewis 1.25 .50
❑ 11 Antowain Smith 2.00 .75
❑ 12 Doug Flutie 2.00 .75
❑ 13 Eric Moulds 2.00 .75
❑ 14 Muhsin Muhammad 1.25 .50
❑ 15 Tim Biakabutuka 1.25 .50
❑ 16 Curtis Enis .75 .30
❑ 17 Curtis Conway 1.25 .50
❑ 18 Bobby Engram 1.25 .50
❑ 19 Corey Dillon 2.00 .75
❑ 20 Carl Pickens 1.25 .50
❑ 21 Darnay Scott .75 .30
❑ 22 Sedrick Shaw .75 .30
❑ 23 Leslie Shepherd .75 .30
❑ 24 Ty Detmer 1.25 .50
❑ 25 Deion Sanders 2.00 .75
❑ 26 Troy Aikman 4.00 1.50
❑ 27 Michael Irvin 1.25 .50
❑ 28 Emmitt Smith 4.00 1.50
❑ 29 Rocket Ismail 1.25 .50
❑ 30 Rod Smith WR 1.25 .50
❑ 31 Ed McCaffrey 1.25 .50
❑ 32 Bubby Brister .75 .30
❑ 33 Terrell Davis 2.00 .75
❑ 34 Shannon Sharpe 1.25 .50
❑ 35 Brian Griese 2.00 .75
❑ 36 John Elway 6.00 2.50
❑ 37 Charlie Batch 2.00 .75
❑ 38 Herman Moore 1.25 .50
❑ 39 Barry Sanders 6.00 2.50
❑ 40 Johnnie Morton 1.25 .50
❑ 41 Antonio Freeman 2.00 .75
❑ 42 Brett Favre 6.00 2.50
❑ 43 Dorsey Levens 2.00 .75
❑ 44 Derrick Mayes 1.25 .50
❑ 45 Mark Chmura .75 .30
❑ 46 Peyton Manning 6.00 2.50
❑ 47 Marvin Harrison 2.00 .75
❑ 48 Jerome Pathon .75 .30
❑ 49 Fred Taylor 2.00 .75
❑ 50 Mark Brunell 2.00 .75
❑ 51 Jimmy Smith 1.25 .50
❑ 52 Keenan McCardell 1.25 .50
❑ 53 Elvis Grbac 1.25 .50
❑ 54 Andre Rison 1.25 .50
❑ 55 Byron Bam Morris .75 .30
❑ 56 O.J. McDuffie 1.25 .50
❑ 57 Karim Abdul-Jabbar 1.25 .50
❑ 58 Dan Marino 6.00 2.50
❑ 59 Oronde Gadsden 1.25 .50
❑ 60 Robert Smith 2.00 .75
❑ 61 Randall Cunningham 2.00 .75
❑ 62 Cris Carter 2.00 .75
❑ 63 Randy Moss 5.00 2.00
❑ 64 Drew Bledsoe 2.50 1.00
❑ 65 Ben Coates 1.25 .50
❑ 66 Terry Glenn 2.00 .75
❑ 67 Cam Cleeland .75 .30
❑ 68 Eddie Kennison 1.25 .50
❑ 69 Kerry Collins 1.25 .50
❑ 70 Gary Brown .75 .30
❑ 71 Joe Jurevicius 1.25 .50
❑ 72 Ike Hilliard .75 .30
❑ 73 Keyshawn Johnson 2.00 .75
❑ 74 Curtis Martin 2.00 .75
❑ 75 Wayne Chrebet 1.25 .50
❑ 76 Tim Brown 2.00 .75
❑ 77 Napoleon Kaufman 2.00 .75
❑ 78 James Jett 1.25 .50
❑ 79 Duce Staley 2.00 .75
❑ 80 Charles Johnson .75 .30
❑ 81 Kordell Stewart 1.25 .50
❑ 82 Jerome Bettis 2.00 .75
❑ 83 Chris Fuamatu-Ma'afala .75 .30
❑ 84 Jim Harbaugh 1.25 .50
❑ 85 Ryan Leaf 2.00 .75
❑ 86 Natrone Means 1.25 .50
❑ 87 Mikhael Ricks .75 .30
❑ 88 Garrison Hearst 1.25 .50
❑ 89 Jerry Rice 4.00 1.50
❑ 90 Terrell Owens 2.00 .75
❑ 91 J.J. Stokes 1.25 .50
❑ 92 Steve Young 2.50 1.00
❑ 93 Joey Galloway 1.25 .50
❑ 94 Jon Kitna 2.00 .75
❑ 95 Ricky Watters 1.25 .50
❑ 96 Trent Green 2.00 .75
❑ 97 Marshall Faulk 2.50 1.00
❑ 98 Isaac Bruce 2.00 .75
❑ 99 Mike Alstott 2.00 .75
❑ 100 Warrick Dunn 2.00 .75
❑ 101 Jacquez Green .75 .30
❑ 102 Reidel Anthony 1.25 .50
❑ 103 Trent Dilfer 1.25 .50
❑ 104 Steve McNair 2.00 .75
❑ 105 Yancey Thigpen .75 .30
❑ 106 Eddie George 2.00 .75
❑ 107 Kevin Dyson 1.25 .50
❑ 108 Skip Hicks .75 .30
❑ 109 Brad Johnson 2.00 .75
❑ 110 Michael Westbrook 1.25 .50
❑ 111 Thurman Thomas CA 4.00 1.50
❑ 112 Andre Reed CA 4.00 1.50
❑ 113 Emmitt Smith CA 10.00 4.00
❑ 114 Troy Aikman CA 10.00 4.00
❑ 115 Deion Sanders CA 5.00 2.00
❑ 116 John Elway CA 15.00 6.00
❑ 117 Terrell Davis CA 5.00 2.00
❑ 118 Barry Sanders CA 15.00 6.00
❑ 119 Brett Favre CA 15.00 6.00
❑ 120 Warren Moon CA 5.00 2.00
❑ 121 Dan Marino CA 15.00 6.00
❑ 122 Cris Carter CA 5.00 2.00
❑ 124 Tim Brown CA 5.00 2.00
❑ 125 Jerome Bettis CA 4.00 1.50
❑ 126 Junior Seau CA 5.00 2.00
❑ 127 Jerry Rice CA 10.00 4.00
❑ 127 Vinny Testaverde CA 4.00 1.50
❑ 128 Steve Young CA 6.00 2.50
❑ 129 Eddie George CA 5.00 2.00
❑ 130 Cardinals CL 3.00 1.25
❑ 131 Falcons CL 3.00 1.25
❑ 132 Ravens CL 8.00 3.00
❑ 133 Bills CL 6.00 2.50
❑ 134 Panthers CL 3.00 1.25
❑ 135 Bears CL 4.00 1.50
❑ 136 Bengals CL 3.00 1.25
❑ 137 Browns CL 8.00 3.00
❑ 138 Cowboys CL 8.00 3.00
❑ 139 Broncos CL 8.00 3.00
❑ 140 Lions CL 8.00 3.00
❑ 141 Packers CL 8.00 3.00
❑ 142 Colts CL 8.00 3.00
❑ 143 Jaguars CL 4.00 1.50
❑ 144 Chiefs CL 3.00 1.25
❑ 145 Dolphins CL 3.00 1.25
❑ 146 Vikings CL 8.00 3.00
❑ 147 Patriots CL 3.00 1.25
❑ 148 Saints CL 8.00 3.00
❑ 149 Giants CL 3.00 1.25
❑ 150 Jets CL 4.00 1.50
❑ 151 Raiders CL 4.00 1.50
❑ 152 Eagles CL 4.00 1.50
❑ 153 Steelers CL 3.00 1.25
❑ 154 Chargers CL 8.00 3.00
❑ 155 49ers CL 8.00 3.00
❑ 156 Seahawks CL 3.00 1.25
❑ 157 Rams CL 4.00 1.50
❑ 158 Buccaneers CL 3.00 1.25
❑ 159 Titans CL 4.00 1.50
❑ 160 Redskins CL 3.00 1.25
❑ 161 Tim Couch RC 2.50 1.00
❑ 162 Donovan McNabb RC 12.00 5.00
❑ 163 Akili Smith RC 4.00 1.50
❑ 164 Edgerrin James RC 10.00 4.00
❑ 165 Ricky Williams RC 5.00 2.00
❑ 166 Torry Holt RC 6.00 2.50
❑ 167 Champ Bailey RC 3.00 1.25
❑ 168 David Boston RC 5.00 2.00
❑ 169 Chris Claiborne RC 1.00 .40
❑ 170 Chris McAlister RC 1.50 .60
❑ 171 Daunte Culpepper RC 10.00 4.00
❑ 172 Cade McNown RC 1.50 .60
❑ 173 Troy Edwards RC 1.50 .60
❑ 174 Kevin Johnson RC 2.50 1.00
❑ 175 James Johnson RC 1.50 .60
❑ 176 Rob Konrad RC 2.50 1.00
❑ 177 Jim Kleinsasser RC 2.50 1.00
❑ 178 Kevin Faulk RC 2.50 1.00
❑ 179 Joe Montgomery RC 1.50 .60
❑ 180 Shaun King RC 1.50 .60
❑ 181 Peerless Price RC 2.50 1.00
❑ 182 Mike Cloud RC 1.50 .60
❑ 183 Jermaine Fazande RC 1.50 .60
❑ 184 D'Wayne Bates RC 1.50 .60
❑ 185 Brock Huard RC 2.50 1.00
❑ 186 Marty Booker RC 2.50 1.00
❑ 187 Karsten Bailey RC 1.50 .60
❑ 188 Shawn Bryson RC 2.50 1.00
❑ 189 Jeff Paulk RC 1.00 .40
❑ 190 Sedrick Irvin RC 1.00 .40
❑ 191 Craig Yeast RC 1.50 .60
❑ 192 Joe Germaine RC 1.50 .60
❑ 193 Dameane Douglas RC 2.50 1.00
❑ 194 Brandon Stokley RC 3.00 1.25
❑ 195 Larry Parker RC 2.50 1.00
❑ 196 Wane McGarity RC 1.00 .40
❑ 197 Na Brown RC 1.50 .60
❑ 198 Cecil Collins RC 1.00 .40
❑ 199 Darrin Chiaverini RC 1.50 .60
❑ 200 Madre Hill RC 1.00 .40

2000 Absolute

❑ COMPLETE SET (250) 250.00 125.00
❑ COMP.SET w/o SP's (150) 20.00 7.50
❑ 1 Frank Sanders .50 .20
❑ 2 Rob Moore .50 .20
❑ 3 Jake Plummer .50 .20
❑ 4 David Boston .75 .30
❑ 5 Chris Chandler .50 .20

❑ 6 Tim Dwight .75 .30
❑ 7 Terance Mathis .50 .20
❑ 8 Jamal Anderson .75 .30
❑ 9 Priest Holmes 1.00 .40
❑ 10 Tony Banks .50 .20
❑ 11 Jermaine Lewis .30 .10
❑ 12 Qadry Ismail .50 .20
❑ 13 Brandon Stokley .50 .20
❑ 14 Shannon Sharpe .50 .20
❑ 15 Trent Dilfer .50 .20
❑ 16 Eric Moulds .75 .30
❑ 17 Doug Flutie .75 .30
❑ 18 Antowain Smith .50 .20
❑ 19 Jonathan Linton .30 .10
❑ 20 Peerless Price .50 .20
❑ 21 Rob Johnson .50 .20
❑ 22 Muhsin Muhammad .50 .20
❑ 23 Wesley Walls .30 .10
❑ 24 Tim Biakabutuka .50 .20
❑ 25 Steve Beuerlein .50 .20
❑ 26 Patrick Jeffers .75 .30
❑ 27 Natrone Means .30 .10
❑ 28 Curtis Enis .30 .10
❑ 29 Bobby Engram .50 .20
❑ 30 Marcus Robinson .75 .30
❑ 31 Marty Booker .50 .20
❑ 32 Cade McNown .30 .10
❑ 33 Darnay Scott .50 .20
❑ 34 Carl Pickens .50 .20
❑ 35 Corey Dillon .75 .30
❑ 36 Akili Smith .30 .10
❑ 37 Michael Basnight .30 .10
❑ 38 Karim Abdul-Jabbar .50 .20
❑ 39 Tim Couch .50 .20
❑ 40 Kevin Johnson .75 .30
❑ 41 Darrin Chiaverini .30 .10
❑ 42 Errict Rhett .50 .20
❑ 43 Emmitt Smith 1.50 .60
❑ 44 Michael Irvin .50 .20
❑ 45 Rocket Ismail .50 .20
❑ 46 Troy Aikman 1.50 .60
❑ 47 Jason Tucker .30 .10
❑ 48 Randall Cunningham .75 .30
❑ 49 Joey Galloway .50 .20
❑ 50 Ed McCaffrey .75 .30
❑ 51 Rod Smith .50 .20
❑ 52 Brian Griese .75 .30
❑ 53 John Elway 2.50 1.00
❑ 54 Terrell Davis .75 .30
❑ 55 Olandis Gary .75 .30
❑ 56 Johnnie Morton .50 .20
❑ 57 Charlie Batch .75 .30
❑ 58 Barry Sanders 2.00 .75
❑ 59 Germane Crowell .30 .10
❑ 60 Herman Moore .50 .20
❑ 61 James Stewart .50 .20
❑ 62 Corey Bradford .30 .10
❑ 63 Dorsey Levens .50 .20
❑ 64 Antonio Freeman .75 .30
❑ 65 Brett Favre 2.50 1.00
❑ 66 Bill Schroeder .50 .20
❑ 67 Marvin Harrison .75 .30
❑ 68 Peyton Manning 1.50 .60
❑ 69 Terrence Wilkins .30 .10
❑ 70 Edgerrin James 1.25 .50
❑ 71 Keenan McCardell .50 .20
❑ 72 Mark Brunell .75 .30
❑ 73 Fred Taylor .75 .30
❑ 74 Jimmy Smith .50 .20
❑ 75 Elvis Grbac .50 .20
❑ 76 Tony Gonzalez .50 .20
❑ 77 Donnell Bennett .30 .10
❑ 78 Warren Moon .75 .30
❑ 79 Kimble Anders .30 .10
❑ 80 Dan Marino 2.50 1.00
❑ 81 O.J. McDuffie .50 .20
❑ 82 Tony Martin .50 .20
❑ 83 James Johnson .30 .10
❑ 84 Thurman Thomas .50 .20
❑ 85 Randy Moss 1.25 .50
❑ 86 Cris Carter .75 .30
❑ 87 Robert Smith .75 .30
❑ 88 Daunte Culpepper 1.00 .40
❑ 89 Terry Glenn .50 .20
❑ 90 Drew Bledsoe 1.00 .40
❑ 91 Kevin Faulk .50 .20
❑ 92 Ricky Williams .75 .30
❑ 93 Jeff Blake .50 .20
❑ 94 Jake Reed .50 .20
❑ 95 Amani Toomer .50 .20
❑ 96 Kerry Collins .50 .20
❑ 97 Tiki Barber .75 .30
❑ 98 Ike Hilliard .50 .20
❑ 99 Curtis Martin .75 .30
❑ 100 Vinny Testaverde .50 .20
❑ 101 Wayne Chrebet .50 .20
❑ 102 Ray Lucas .50 .20
❑ 103 Tyrone Wheatley .50 .20
❑ 104 Napoleon Kaufman .50 .20
❑ 105 Tim Brown .75 .30
❑ 106 Rich Gannon .75 .30
❑ 107 Duce Staley .75 .30
❑ 108 Donovan McNabb 1.25 .50
❑ 109 Kordell Stewart .50 .20
❑ 110 Jerome Bettis .75 .30
❑ 111 Troy Edwards .30 .10
❑ 112 Junior Seau .75 .30
❑ 113 Jim Harbaugh .50 .20
❑ 114 Ryan Leaf .50 .20
❑ 115 Jermaine Fazande .30 .10
❑ 116 Curtis Conway .50 .20
❑ 117 Terrell Owens .75 .30
❑ 118 Charlie Garner .50 .20
❑ 119 Jerry Rice 1.50 .60
❑ 120 Steve Young 1.00 .40
❑ 121 Jeff Garcia .75 .30
❑ 122 Derrick Mayes .50 .20
❑ 123 Ricky Watters .50 .20
❑ 124 Jon Kitna .75 .30
❑ 125 Sean Dawkins .30 .10
❑ 126 Az-Zahir Hakim .50 .20
❑ 127 Isaac Bruce .75 .30
❑ 128 Marshall Faulk 1.00 .40
❑ 129 Trent Green .75 .30
❑ 130 Kurt Warner 1.50 .60
❑ 131 Torry Holt .75 .30
❑ 132 Jacquez Green .30 .10
❑ 133 Warren Sapp .50 .20
❑ 134 Mike Alstott .75 .30
❑ 135 Warrick Dunn .75 .30
❑ 136 Shaun King .30 .10
❑ 137 Keyshawn Johnson .75 .30
❑ 138 Eddie George .75 .30
❑ 139 Yancey Thigpen .30 .10
❑ 140 Steve McNair .75 .30
❑ 141 Kevin Dyson .50 .20
❑ 142 Frank Wycheck .30 .10
❑ 143 Jevon Kearse .75 .30
❑ 144 Stephen Davis .75 .30
❑ 145 Brad Johnson .75 .30
❑ 146 Michael Westbrook .50 .20
❑ 147 Albert Connell .30 .10
❑ 148 Bruce Smith .50 .20
❑ 149 Jeff George .50 .20
❑ 150 Deion Sanders .75 .30
❑ 151 Peter Warrick RC 4.00 1.50
❑ 152 Courtney Brown RC 4.00 1.50
❑ 153 Plaxico Burress RC 8.00 3.00
❑ 154 Corey Simon RC 4.00 1.50
❑ 155 Thomas Jones RC 6.00 2.50
❑ 156 Travis Taylor RC 4.00 1.50
❑ 157 Shaun Alexander RC 15.00 6.00
❑ 158 Chris Redman RC 3.00 1.25
❑ 159 Chad Pennington RC 10.00 4.00
❑ 160 Jamal Lewis RC 10.00 4.00
❑ 161 Brian Urlacher RC 20.00 7.50
❑ 162 Bubba Franks RC 4.00 1.50
❑ 163 Dez White RC 4.00 1.50
❑ 164 Ahmed Plummer RC 4.00 1.50
❑ 165 Ron Dayne RC 4.00 1.50
❑ 166 Shaun Ellis RC 4.00 1.50
❑ 167 Sylvester Morris RC .50 .20
❑ 168 Deltha O'Neal RC 4.00 1.50
❑ 169 R.Jay Soward RC 3.00 1.25
❑ 170 Sherrod Gideon RC 2.00 .75
❑ 171 John Abraham RC 4.00 1.50
❑ 172 Travis Prentice RC 3.00 1.25
❑ 173 Darrell Jackson RC 8.00 3.00
❑ 174 Giovanni Carmazzi RC 2.00 .75
❑ 175 Anthony Lucas RC 2.00 .75
❑ 176 Danny Farmer RC 3.00 1.25
❑ 177 Dennis Northcutt RC 4.00 1.50
❑ 178 Troy Walters RC 4.00 1.50
❑ 179 Laveranues Coles RC 5.00 2.00
❑ 180 Kwame Cavil RC 2.00 .75
❑ 181 Tee Martin RC 4.00 1.50
❑ 182 J.R. Redmond RC 3.00 1.25
❑ 183 Tim Rattay RC 4.00 1.50
❑ 184 Jerry Porter RC 5.00 2.00
❑ 185 Sebastian Janikowski RC 4.00 1.50
❑ 186 Michael Wiley RC 3.00 1.25
❑ 187 Reuben Droughns RC 5.00 2.00
❑ 188 Trung Canidate RC 3.00 1.25
❑ 189 Shyrone Stith RC 3.00 1.25
❑ 190 Ian Gold RC 3.00 1.25
❑ 191 Hank Poteat RC 3.00 1.25
❑ 192 Darren Howard RC 3.00 1.25
❑ 193 Rob Morris RC 3.00 1.25
❑ 194 Marc Bulger RC 8.00 3.00
❑ 195 Tom Brady RC 40.00 20.00
❑ 196 Doug Johnson RC 4.00 1.50
❑ 197 Todd Husak RC 4.00 1.50
❑ 198 Gari Scott RC 2.00 .75
❑ 199 Erron Kinney RC 4.00 1.50
❑ 200 Nate Webster RC 2.00 .75
❑ 201 Anthony Becht RC 4.00 1.50
❑ 202 Sammy Morris RC 3.00 1.25
❑ 203 Rondell Mealey RC 2.00 .75
❑ 204 Doug Chapman RC 3.00 1.25
❑ 205 Rogers Beckett RC 3.00 1.25
❑ 206 Ron Dugans RC 2.00 .75
❑ 207 Deon Dyer RC 3.00 1.25
❑ 208 Marcus Knight RC 3.00 1.25
❑ 209 Thomas Hamner RC 2.00 .75
❑ 210 Joe Hamilton RC 3.00 1.25
❑ 211 Todd Pinkston RC 4.00 1.50
❑ 212 Chris Cole RC 3.00 1.25
❑ 213 Ron Dixon RC 3.00 1.25
❑ 214 JaJuan Dawson RC 2.00 .75
❑ 215 Terrelle Smith RC 3.00 1.25
❑ 216 Curtis Keaton RC 3.00 1.25
❑ 217 Keith Bulluck RC 4.00 1.50
❑ 218 John Engelberger RC 3.00 1.25
❑ 219 Raynoch Thompson RC 3.00 1.25
❑ 220 Cornelius Griffin RC 3.00 1.25
❑ 221 William Bartee RC 3.00 1.25
❑ 222 Fred Robbins RC 2.00 .75
❑ 223 Dwayne Goodrich RC 2.00 .75
❑ 224 Deon Grant RC 3.00 1.25
❑ 225 Jacoby Shepherd RC 3.00 1.25
❑ 226 Ben Kelly RC 2.00 .75
❑ 227 Corey Moore RC 2.00 .75
❑ 228 Aaron Shea RC 3.00 1.25
❑ 229 Trevor Gaylor RC 3.00 1.25
❑ 230 Frank Moreau RC 3.00 1.25
❑ 231 Avion Black RC 3.00 1.25
❑ 232 Paul Smith RC 3.00 1.25
❑ 233 Dante Hall RC 8.00 3.00
❑ 234 Muneer Moore RC 2.00 .75
❑ 235 James Whalen RC 2.00 .75
❑ 236 Chad Morton RC 4.00 1.50
❑ 237 Frank Murphy RC 2.00 .75
❑ 238 Mareno Philyaw RC 2.00 .75
❑ 239 James Williams RC 3.00 1.25
❑ 240 Mike Anderson RC 5.00 2.00
❑ 241 Jarious Jackson RC 3.00 1.25
❑ 242 Demario Brown RC 2.00 .75
❑ 243 Chris Coleman RC 4.00 1.50
❑ 244 Rashard Anderson RC 3.00 1.25
❑ 245 John Jones RC 3.00 1.25
❑ 246 Erik Flowers RC 3.00 1.25
❑ 247 JaJuan Seider RC 2.00 .75
❑ 248 Leon Murray RC 2.00 .75
❑ 249 Bashir Yamini RC 2.00 .75
❑ 250 Na'il Diggs RC 3.00 1.25

2001 Absolute Memorabilia

❑ COMP.SET w/o SP's (100) 30.00 12.50
❑ 1 David Boston 1.25 .50

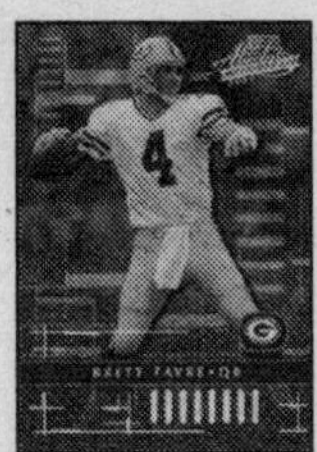

❑ 2 Jake Plummer .75 .30
❑ 3 Thomas Jones .75 .30
❑ 4 Jamal Anderson 1.25 .50
❑ 5 Chris Redman .50 .20
❑ 6 Jamal Lewis 2.00 .75
❑ 7 Qadry Ismail .75 .30
❑ 8 Ray Lewis 1.25 .50
❑ 9 Shannon Sharpe .75 .30
❑ 10 Travis Taylor .75 .30
❑ 11 Trent Dilfer .75 .30
❑ 12 Elvis Grbac .75 .30
❑ 13 Eric Moulds .75 .30
❑ 14 Rob Johnson .75 .30
❑ 15 Muhsin Muhammad .75 .30
❑ 16 Brian Urlacher 2.00 .75
❑ 17 Cade McNown .50 .20
❑ 18 Marcus Robinson 1.25 .50
❑ 19 Akili Smith .50 .20
❑ 20 Corey Dillon 1.25 .50
❑ 21 Peter Warrick 1.25 .50
❑ 22 Courtney Brown .75 .30
❑ 23 Tim Couch .75 .30
❑ 24 Emmitt Smith 2.50 1.00
❑ 25 Troy Aikman 2.00 .75
❑ 26 Brian Griese 1.25 .50
❑ 27 Ed McCaffrey 1.25 .50
❑ 28 John Elway 4.00 1.50
❑ 29 Mike Anderson 1.25 .50
❑ 30 Rod Smith .75 .30
❑ 31 Terrell Davis 1.25 .50
❑ 32 Barry Sanders 2.50 1.00
❑ 33 James Stewart .75 .30
❑ 34 Ahman Green 1.25 .50
❑ 35 Antonio Freeman 1.25 .50
❑ 36 Brett Favre 4.00 1.50
❑ 37 Edgerrin James 1.50 .60
❑ 38 Marvin Harrison 1.25 .50
❑ 39 Peyton Manning 3.00 1.25
❑ 40 Fred Taylor 1.25 .50
❑ 41 Jimmy Smith .75 .30
❑ 42 Keenan McCardell .50 .20
❑ 43 Mark Brunell 1.25 .50
❑ 44 Sylvester Morris .50 .20
❑ 45 Tony Gonzalez .75 .30
❑ 46 Dan Marino 4.00 1.50
❑ 47 Jay Fiedler 1.25 .50
❑ 48 Lamar Smith .75 .30
❑ 49 Cris Carter 1.25 .50
❑ 50 Daunte Culpepper 1.25 .50
❑ 51 Randy Moss 2.50 1.00
❑ 52 Drew Bledsoe 1.50 .60
❑ 53 Terry Glenn .75 .30
❑ 54 Aaron Brooks 1.25 .50
❑ 55 Joe Horn .75 .30
❑ 56 Ricky Williams 1.25 .50
❑ 57 Amani Toomer .75 .30
❑ 58 Ike Hilliard .75 .30
❑ 59 Kerry Collins .75 .30
❑ 60 Ron Dayne 1.25 .50
❑ 61 Tiki Barber 1.25 .50
❑ 62 Chad Pennington 2.00 .75
❑ 63 Curtis Martin 1.25 .50
❑ 64 Laveranues Coles 1.25 .50
❑ 65 Vinny Testaverde .75 .30
❑ 66 Wayne Chrebet .75 .30
❑ 67 Charles Woodson .75 .30
❑ 68 Rich Gannon 1.25 .50
❑ 69 Tim Brown 1.25 .50
❑ 70 Tyrone Wheatley .75 .30
❑ 71 Corey Simon .75 .30
❑ 72 Donovan McNabb 1.50 .60
❑ 73 Duce Staley 1.25 .50
❑ 74 Jerome Bettis 1.25 .50
❑ 75 Plaxico Burress 1.25 .50
❑ 76 Doug Flutie 1.25 .50
❑ 77 Junior Seau 1.25 .50
❑ 78 Charlie Garner .75 .30
❑ 79 Jeff Garcia 1.25 .50
❑ 80 Jerry Rice 2.50 1.00
❑ 81 Steve Young 1.25 .50
❑ 82 Terrell Owens 1.25 .50
❑ 83 Darrell Jackson 1.25 .50
❑ 84 Ricky Watters .50 .20
❑ 85 Shaun Alexander 1.50 .60
❑ 86 Isaac Bruce 1.25 .50
❑ 87 Kurt Warner 2.50 1.00
❑ 88 Marshall Faulk 1.50 .60
❑ 89 Torry Holt 1.25 .50
❑ 90 Brad Johnson 1.25 .50
❑ 91 Keyshawn Johnson 1.25 .50
❑ 92 Mike Alstott 1.25 .50
❑ 93 Shaun King .50 .20
❑ 94 Warren Sapp .75 .30
❑ 95 Warrick Dunn 1.25 .50
❑ 96 Eddie George 1.25 .50
❑ 97 Jevon Kearse .75 .30
❑ 98 Steve McNair 1.25 .50
❑ 99 Jeff George .75 .30
❑ 100 Stephen Davis 1.25 .50
❑ 101 Jason McKinley RC 4.00 1.50
❑ 102 Bobby Newcombe RC 4.00 1.50
❑ 103 Cedrick Wilson RC 6.00 2.50
❑ 104 Ken-Yon Rambo RC 4.00 1.50
❑ 105 Kevin Kasper RC 6.00 2.50
❑ 106 Jamal Reynolds RC 6.00 2.50
❑ 107 Scotty Anderson RC 4.00 1.50
❑ 108 T.J. Houshmandzadeh RC 8.00 3.00
❑ 109 Chris Taylor RC 4.00 1.50
❑ 110 Vinny Sutherland RC 4.00 1.50
❑ 111 Jabari Holloway RC 4.00 1.50
❑ 112 Shad Meier RC 4.00 1.50
❑ 113 Correll Buckhalter RC 8.00 3.00
❑ 114 Dan Alexander RC 6.00 2.50
❑ 115 David Allen RC 4.00 1.50
❑ 116 LaMont Jordan RC 12.00 5.00
❑ 117 Nate Clements RC 6.00 2.50
❑ 118 Reggie White RC 4.00 1.50
❑ 119 Javon Green RC 4.00 1.50
❑ 120 Shaun Rogers RC 6.00 2.50
❑ 121 Heath Evans RC 4.00 1.50
❑ 122 Moran Norris RC 2.50 1.00
❑ 123 Ben Leard RC 4.00 1.50
❑ 124 David Rivers RC 4.00 1.50
❑ 125 A.J. Feeley RC 6.00 2.50
❑ 126 Boo Williams RC 4.00 1.50
❑ 127 Ronney Daniels RC 2.50 1.00
❑ 128 Alge Crumpler RC 8.00 4.00
❑ 129 Todd Heap RC 6.00 2.50
❑ 130 Tim Hasselbeck RC 6.00 2.50
❑ 131 Josh Booty RC 6.00 2.50
❑ 132 Jamie Winborn RC 4.00 1.50
❑ 133 Brian Allen RC 2.50 1.00
❑ 134 Sedrick Hodge RC 2.50 1.00
❑ 135 Tommy Polley RC 6.00 2.50
❑ 136 Torrance Marshall RC 6.00 2.50
❑ 137 Damione Lewis RC 4.00 1.50
❑ 138 Marcus Stroud RC 6.00 2.50
❑ 139 Aaron Schobel RC 6.00 2.50
❑ 140 DeLawrence Grant RC 2.50 1.00
❑ 141 Fred Smoot RC 6.00 2.50
❑ 142 Jamar Fletcher RC 4.00 1.50
❑ 143 Ken Lucas RC 4.00 1.50
❑ 144 Will Allen RC 4.00 1.50
❑ 145 Adam Archuleta RC 6.00 2.50
❑ 146 Derrick Gibson RC 4.00 1.50
❑ 147 Jarrod Cooper RC 6.00 2.50
❑ 148 Eddie Berlin RC 4.00 1.50
❑ 149 Steve Smith RC 15.00 7.50
❑ 150 Willie Middlebrooks RC 4.00 1.50
❑ 151 Michael Vick RPM RC 60.00 25.00
❑ 152 Drew Brees RPM RC 50.00 20.00
❑ 153 Chris Weinke RPM RC 15.00 6.00
❑ 154 Mar Tuiasosopo RPM RC 15.00 6.00
❑ 155 Mike McMahon RPM RC 15.00 6.00
❑ 156 Deuce McAllister RPM RC 30.00 12.50
❑ 157 Leonard Davis RPM RC 10.00 4.00
❑ 158 LaD Tomlinson RPM RC 80.00 40.00
❑ 159 Anthony Thomas RPM RC 15.00 6.00
❑ 160 Travis Henry RPM RC 25.00 10.00
❑ 161 James Jackson RPM RC 15.00 6.00
❑ 162 Michael Bennett RPM RC 15.00 6.00
❑ 163 Kevan Barlow RPM RC 15.00 6.00
❑ 164 Travis Minor RPM RC 10.00 4.00
❑ 165 David Terrell RPM RC 15.00 6.00
❑ 166 Santana Moss RPM RC 25.00 10.00
❑ 167 Rod Gardner RPM RC 15.00 6.00
❑ 168 Quincy Morgan RPM RC 15.00 6.00
❑ 169 Freddie Mitchell RPM RC 15.00 6.00
❑ 170 Reggie Wayne RPM RC 30.00 12.50
❑ 171 Koren Robinson RPM RC 15.00 6.00
❑ 172 Chad Johnson RPM RC 40.00 15.00
❑ 173 Chris Chambers RPM RC 25.00 10.00
❑ 174 Josh Heupel RPM RC 15.00 6.00
❑ 175 Andre Carter RPM RC 15.00 6.00
❑ 176 Justin Smith RPM RC 15.00 6.00
❑ 177 Richard Seymour RPM RC 15.00 6.00
❑ 178 Dan Morgan RPM RC 15.00 6.00
❑ 179 Gerard Warren RPM RC 15.00 6.00
❑ 180 Robert Ferguson RPM RC 15.00 6.00
❑ 181 Sage Rosenfels RPM RC 15.00 6.00
❑ 182 Rudi Johnson RPM RC 30.00 12.50
❑ 183 Snoop Minnis RPM RC 10.00 4.00
❑ 184 Jesse Palmer RPM RC 15.00 6.00
❑ 185 Quincy Carter RPM RC 15.00 6.00

2002 Absolute Memorabilia

❑ COMP.SET w/o SP's (150) 30.00 12.50
❑ 1 Aaron Brooks 1.25 .50
❑ 2 Ahman Green 1.25 .50
❑ 3 Alge Crumpler .75 .30
❑ 4 Amani Toomer .75 .30
❑ 5 Andre Carter .50 .20
❑ 6 Anthony Thomas .75 .30
❑ 7 Antonio Freeman 1.25 .50
❑ 8 Antowain Smith .75 .30
❑ 9 Az-Zahir Hakim .50 .20
❑ 10 Bill Schroeder .75 .30
❑ 11 Brad Johnson .75 .30
❑ 12 Brett Favre 3.00 1.25
❑ 13 Brian Griese 1.25 .50
❑ 14 Brian Urlacher 2.00 .75
❑ 15 Chad Johnson 1.25 .50
❑ 16 Chad Pennington 1.50 .60
❑ 17 Champ Bailey .75 .30
❑ 18 Charles Woodson .75 .30
❑ 19 Charlie Batch .75 .30
❑ 20 Charlie Garner .75 .30
❑ 21 Chris Chambers 1.25 .50
❑ 22 Chris Redman .50 .20
❑ 23 Chris Weinke .75 .30
❑ 24 Corey Dillon .75 .30
❑ 25 Correll Buckhalter .75 .30
❑ 26 Cris Carter 1.25 .50
❑ 27 Curtis Martin 1.25 .50
❑ 28 Darnay Scott .75 .30
❑ 29 Darrell Jackson .75 .30
❑ 30 Daunte Culpepper 1.25 .50
❑ 31 David Boston 1.25 .50
❑ 32 David Terrell 1.25 .50
❑ 33 Derrick Alexander .75 .30
❑ 34 Derrick Mason .75 .30
❑ 35 Deuce McAllister 1.50 .60
❑ 36 Dominic Rhodes 1.25 .50
❑ 37 Donald Hayes .50 .20
❑ 38 Donovan McNabb 1.50 .60
❑ 39 Doug Flutie 1.25 .50
❑ 40 Drew Bledsoe 1.50 .60
❑ 41 Drew Brees 1.25 .50
❑ 42 Duce Staley 1.25 .50
❑ 43 Ed McCaffrey 1.25 .50
❑ 44 Eddie George 1.25 .50

❑ 45 Edgerrin James 1.50 .60
❑ 46 Elvis Joseph .50 .20
❑ 47 Emmitt Smith 3.00 1.25
❑ 48 Eric Moulds .75 .30
❑ 49 Frank Sanders .50 .20
❑ 50 Fred Taylor 1.25 .50
❑ 51 Freddie Mitchell .75 .30
❑ 52 Garrison Hearst .75 .30
❑ 53 Gerard Warren .50 .20
❑ 54 Germane Crowell .50 .20
❑ 55 Isaac Bruce 1.25 .50
❑ 56 Jake Plummer .75 .30
❑ 57 Jamal Anderson .75 .30
❑ 58 Jamal Lewis 1.25 .50
❑ 59 James Allen .75 .30
❑ 60 James Jackson .50 .20
❑ 61 James Stewart .75 .30
❑ 62 Jason Brookins .50 .20
❑ 63 Jay Fiedler .75 .30
❑ 64 Jeff Garcia 1.25 .50
❑ 65 Jerome Bettis 1.25 .50
❑ 66 Jerry Rice 2.50 1.00
❑ 67 Jevon Kearse .75 .30
❑ 68 Jim Miller .50 .20
❑ 69 Jimmy Smith .75 .30
❑ 70 Joe Horn .75 .30
❑ 71 Joey Galloway .75 .30
❑ 72 Jon Kitna .75 .30
❑ 73 Junior Seau 1.25 .50
❑ 74 Keenan McCardell .50 .20
❑ 75 Kendrell Bell 1.25 .50
❑ 76 Kerry Collins .75 .30
❑ 77 Kevan Barlow .75 .30
❑ 78 Kevin Dyson .75 .30
❑ 79 Kevin Johnson .75 .30
❑ 80 Kevin Kasper .50 .20
❑ 81 Keyshawn Johnson 1.25 .50
❑ 82 Kordell Stewart .75 .30
❑ 83 Koren Robinson .75 .30
❑ 84 Kurt Warner 1.25 .50
❑ 85 LaDainian Tomlinson 2.50 1.00
❑ 86 Lamar Smith .75 .30
❑ 87 Laveranues Coles .75 .30
❑ 88 MarTay Jenkins .50 .20
❑ 89 Mark Brunell 1.25 .50
❑ 90 Marshall Faulk 1.25 .50
❑ 91 Marty Booker .75 .30
❑ 92 Marvin Harrison 1.25 .50
❑ 93 Snoop Minnis .50 .20
❑ 94 Michael Bennett .75 .30
❑ 95 Michael Strahan .75 .30
❑ 96 Michael Vick 4.00 1.50
❑ 97 Mike Alstott 1.25 .50
❑ 98 Mike Anderson 1.25 .50
❑ 99 Mike McMahon 1.25 .50
❑ 100 Muhsin Muhammad .75 .30
❑ 101 Nate Clements .50 .20
❑ 102 Oronde Gadsden .75 .30
❑ 103 Peter Warrick .75 .30
❑ 104 Peyton Manning 2.50 1.00
❑ 105 Plaxico Burress .75 .30
❑ 106 Priest Holmes 1.50 .60
❑ 107 Quincy Carter .75 .30
❑ 108 Quincy Morgan .75 .30
❑ 109 Rocket Ismail .75 .30
❑ 110 Randy Moss 2.50 1.00
❑ 111 Ray Lewis 1.25 .50
❑ 112 Reggie Wayne 1.25 .50
❑ 113 Rich Gannon 1.25 .50
❑ 114 Rickey Dudley .50 .20
❑ 115 Ricky Watters .75 .30
❑ 116 Ricky Williams 1.25 .50
❑ 117 Rod Gardner .75 .30
❑ 118 Rod Smith .75 .30
❑ 119 Robert Ferguson .50 .20
❑ 120 Santana Moss 1.25 .50
❑ 121 Shaun Alexander 1.50 .60
❑ 122 Stephen Davis .75 .30
❑ 123 Steve McNair 1.25 .50
❑ 124 Steve Smith 1.25 .50
❑ 125 Terrell Davis 1.25 .50
❑ 126 Terrell Owens 1.25 .50
❑ 127 Terry Glenn .75 .30
❑ 128 Thomas Jones .75 .30
❑ 129 Tiki Barber 1.25 .50
❑ 130 Tim Brown 1.25 .50
❑ 131 Tim Couch .75 .30
❑ 132 Todd Heap .75 .30
❑ 133 Todd Pinkston .75 .30
❑ 134 Tom Brady 3.00 1.25
❑ 135 Tony Boselli .50 .20
❑ 136 Tony Gonzalez .75 .30
❑ 137 Torry Holt 1.25 .50
❑ 138 Travis Henry 1.25 .50
❑ 139 Travis Taylor .75 .30
❑ 140 Trent Dilfer .75 .30
❑ 141 Trent Green .75 .30
❑ 142 Troy Brown .75 .30
❑ 143 Troy Hambrick .50 .20
❑ 144 Trung Canidate .75 .30
❑ 145 Vinny Testaverde .75 .30
❑ 146 Warren Sapp .75 .30
❑ 147 Warrick Dunn 1.25 .50
❑ 148 Wayne Chrebet .75 .30
❑ 149 Wesley Walls .50 .20
❑ 150 Zach Thomas 1.25 .50
❑ 151 Quentin Jammer RC 6.00 2.50
❑ 152 Randy Fasani RC 5.00 2.00
❑ 153 Kurt Kittner RC 5.00 2.00
❑ 154 Chad Hutchinson RC 5.00 2.00
❑ 155 Major Applewhite RC 6.00 2.50
❑ 156 Wes Pate RC 3.00 1.25
❑ 157 J.T. O'Sullivan RC 5.00 2.00
❑ 158 Ryan Denney RC 5.00 2.00
❑ 159 Ronald Curry RC 6.00 2.50
❑ 160 Lamar Gordon RC 6.00 2.50
❑ 161 Brian Westbrook RC 10.00 4.00
❑ 162 Jonathan Wells RC 6.00 2.50
❑ 163 Ricky Williams RC 5.00 2.00
❑ 164 Verron Haynes RC 6.00 2.50
❑ 165 Josh Scobey RC 6.00 2.50
❑ 166 Larry Ned RC 5.00 2.00
❑ 167 Adrian Peterson RC 6.00 2.50
❑ 168 Chester Taylor RC 12.00 5.00
❑ 169 Luke Staley RC 5.00 2.00
❑ 170 Damien Anderson RC 5.00 2.00
❑ 171 Lee Mays RC 5.00 2.00
❑ 172 Deion Branch RC 12.00 5.00
❑ 173 Terry Charles RC 5.00 2.00
❑ 174 Woody Dantzler RC 5.00 2.00
❑ 175 Jason McAddley RC 5.00 2.00
❑ 176 Kelly Campbell RC 5.00 2.00
❑ 177 Freddie Milons RC 5.00 2.00
❑ 178 Kahlil Hill RC 5.00 2.00
❑ 179 Brian Poli-Dixon RC 5.00 2.00
❑ 180 Mike Echols RC 3.00 1.25
❑ 181 Pete Rebstock RC 3.00 1.25
❑ 182 Dwight Freeney RC 10.00 4.00
❑ 183 Bryan Thomas RC 5.00 2.00
❑ 184 Charles Grant RC 6.00 2.50
❑ 185 Kalimba Edwards RC 6.00 2.50
❑ 186 Ryan Sims RC 6.00 2.50
❑ 187 John Henderson RC 6.00 2.50
❑ 188 Wendell Bryant RC 3.00 1.25
❑ 189 Albert Haynesworth RC 5.00 2.00
❑ 190 Larry Tripplett RC 3.00 1.25
❑ 191 Phillip Buchanon RC 6.00 2.50
❑ 192 Lito Sheppard RC 6.00 2.50
❑ 193 Mike Rumph RC 6.00 2.50
❑ 194 Levar Fisher RC 3.00 1.25
❑ 195 Ed Reed RC 10.00 4.00
❑ 196 Rocky Calmus RC 6.00 2.50
❑ 197 Michael Lewis RC 6.00 2.50
❑ 198 Napoleon Harris RC 6.00 2.50
❑ 199 Robert Thomas RC 6.00 2.50
❑ 200 Anthony Weaver RC 5.00 2.00
❑ 201 Ladell Betts RPM RC 12.00 6.00
❑ 202 Antonio Bryant RPM RC 12.00 6.00
❑ 203 Reche Caldwell RPM RC 12.00 6.00
❑ 204 David Carr RPM RC 25.00 10.00
❑ 205 Tim Carter RPM RC 6.00 3.00
❑ 206 Eric Crouch RPM RC 12.00 6.00
❑ 207 Rohan Davey RPM RC 12.00 6.00
❑ 208 Andre Davis RPM RC 6.00 3.00
❑ 209 T.J. Duckett RPM RC 15.00 6.00
❑ 210 DeShaun Foster RPM RC 12.00 6.00
❑ 211 Jabar Gaffney RPM RC 12.00 6.00
❑ 212 Daniel Graham RPM RC 12.00 6.00
❑ 213 William Green RPM RC 12.00 6.00
❑ 214 Joey Harrington RPM RC 15.00 6.00
❑ 215 David Garrard RPM RC 8.00 3.00
❑ 216 Ron Johnson RPM RC 6.00 3.00
❑ 217 Ashley Lelie RPM RC 25.00 10.00
❑ 218 Josh McCown RPM RC 15.00 6.00
❑ 219 Maurice Morris RPM RC 12.00 6.00
❑ 220 Julius Peppers RPM RC 25.00 12.50
❑ 221 Clinton Portis RPM RC 30.00 12.50
❑ 222 Patrick Ramsey RPM RC 15.00 6.00
❑ 223 Antwaan Randle El RPM RC 15.00 6.00
❑ 224 Josh Reed RPM RC 12.00 6.00
❑ 225 Cliff Russell RPM RC 6.00 3.00
❑ 226 Jeremy Shockey RPM RC 30.00 12.50
❑ 227 Donte Stallworth RPM RC 25.00 10.00
❑ 228 Travis Stephens RPM RC 6.00 3.00
❑ 229 Javon Walker RPM RC 25.00 12.50
❑ 230 Marquise Walker RPM RC 6.00 3.00
❑ 231 Roy Williams RPM RC 30.00 12.50
❑ 232 Mike Williams RPM RC 6.00 3.00

2003 Absolute Memorabilia

❑ COMP.SET w/o SP's (100) 25.00 10.00
❑ 1 Jamal Lewis 1.25 .50
❑ 2 Ray Lewis 1.25 .50
❑ 3 Todd Heap .75 .30
❑ 4 Drew Bledsoe 1.25 .50
❑ 5 Travis Henry .75 .30
❑ 6 Peerless Price .75 .30
❑ 7 Corey Dillon .75 .30
❑ 8 Chad Johnson 1.25 .50
❑ 9 Tim Couch .50 .20
❑ 10 William Green .75 .30
❑ 11 Andre Davis .50 .20
❑ 12 Brian Griese 1.25 .50
❑ 13 Ashley Lelie 1.25 .50
❑ 14 Clinton Portis 2.00 .75
❑ 15 Rod Smith .75 .30
❑ 16 David Carr 2.00 .75
❑ 17 Corey Bradford .50 .20
❑ 18 Jonathan Wells .50 .20
❑ 19 Peyton Manning 2.00 .75
❑ 20 Edgerrin James 1.25 .50
❑ 21 Marvin Harrison 1.25 .50
❑ 22 Mark Brunell .75 .30
❑ 23 Fred Taylor 1.25 .50
❑ 24 Jimmy Smith .75 .30
❑ 25 Trent Green .75 .30
❑ 26 Priest Holmes 1.50 .60
❑ 27 Tony Gonzalez .75 .30
❑ 28 Jay Fiedler .75 .30
❑ 29 Ricky Williams 1.25 .50
❑ 30 Chris Chambers 1.25 .50
❑ 31 Zach Thomas 1.25 .50
❑ 32 Tom Brady 3.00 1.25
❑ 33 Troy Brown .75 .30
❑ 34 Antowain Smith .75 .30
❑ 35 Chad Pennington 1.50 .60
❑ 36 Curtis Martin 1.25 .50
❑ 37 Laveranues Coles .75 .30
❑ 38 Rich Gannon .75 .30
❑ 39 Charlie Garner .50 .20
❑ 40 Jerry Rice 2.50 1.00
❑ 41 Tim Brown 1.25 .50
❑ 42 Tommy Maddox 1.25 .50
❑ 43 Jerome Bettis 1.25 .50
❑ 44 Plaxico Burress .75 .30
❑ 45 Hines Ward 1.25 .50
❑ 46 Drew Brees 1.25 .50
❑ 47 LaDainian Tomlinson 1.25 .50
❑ 48 Junior Seau 1.25 .50
❑ 49 Steve McNair 1.25 .50
❑ 50 Eddie George .75 .30
❑ 51 Jevon Kearse .75 .30
❑ 52 Jake Plummer .75 .30
❑ 53 David Boston .75 .30
❑ 54 Marcel Shipp .75 .30
❑ 55 Michael Vick 3.00 1.25
❑ 56 T.J. Duckett .75 .30
❑ 57 Warrick Dunn .75 .30

❑ 58 Muhsin Muhammad .75 .30
❑ 59 Julius Peppers 1.25 .50
❑ 60 Steve Smith 1.25 .50
❑ 61 Anthony Thomas .75 .30
❑ 62 Brian Urlacher 2.00 .75
❑ 63 Marty Booker .75 .30
❑ 64 Antonio Bryant .75 .30
❑ 65 Chad Hutchinson .50 .20
❑ 66 Roy Williams 1.25 .50
❑ 67 Emmitt Smith 3.00 1.25
❑ 68 Joey Harrington 2.00 .75
❑ 69 James Stewart .75 .30
❑ 70 Az-Zahir Hakim .50 .20
❑ 71 Brett Favre 3.00 1.25
❑ 72 Ahman Green 1.25 .50
❑ 73 Donald Driver .75 .30
❑ 74 Daunte Culpepper 1.25 .50
❑ 75 Randy Moss 2.00 .75
❑ 76 Michael Bennett .75 .30
❑ 77 Aaron Brooks 1.25 .50
❑ 78 Deuce McAllister 1.25 .50
❑ 79 Donte Stallworth 1.25 .50
❑ 80 Tiki Barber 1.25 .50
❑ 81 Kerry Collins .75 .30
❑ 82 Jeremy Shockey 2.00 .75
❑ 83 Donovan McNabb 1.50 .60
❑ 84 Duce Staley .75 .30
❑ 85 Antonio Freeman .75 .30
❑ 86 Jeff Garcia 1.25 .50
❑ 87 Terrell Owens 1.25 .50
❑ 88 Garrison Hearst .75 .30
❑ 89 Matt Hasselbeck .75 .30
❑ 90 Koren Robinson .75 .30
❑ 91 Shaun Alexander 1.25 .50
❑ 92 Kurt Warner 1.25 .50
❑ 93 Marshall Faulk 1.25 .50
❑ 94 Isaac Bruce 1.25 .50
❑ 95 Brad Johnson .75 .30
❑ 96 Keyshawn Johnson 1.25 .50
❑ 97 Warren Sapp .75 .30
❑ 98 Patrick Ramsey 1.25 .50
❑ 99 Rod Gardner .75 .30
❑ 100 Stephen Davis .75 .30
❑ 101 Jason Gesser RC 6.00 2.50
❑ 102 Brandon Lloyd RC 6.00 2.50
❑ 103 Ken Dorsey RC 6.00 2.50
❑ 104 Avon Cobourne RC 3.00 1.25
❑ 105 Cecil Sapp RC 5.00 2.00
❑ 106 Derek Watson RC 5.00 2.00
❑ 107 Dwone Hicks RC 3.00 1.25
❑ 108 Earnest Graham RC 5.00 2.00
❑ 109 LaBrandon Toefield RC 6.00 2.50
❑ 110 Quentin Griffin RC 6.00 2.50
❑ 111 Sultan McCullough RC 5.00 2.00
❑ 112 Lee Suggs RC 6.00 2.50
❑ 113 Talman Gardner RC 6.00 2.50
❑ 114 Arnaz Battle RC 6.00 2.50
❑ 115 Billy McMullen RC 5.00 2.00
❑ 116 Doug Gabriel RC 6.00 2.50
❑ 117 Justin Gage RC 6.00 2.50
❑ 118 Kareem Kelly RC 5.00 2.00
❑ 119 Paul Arnold RC 5.00 2.00
❑ 120 Sam Aiken RC 5.00 2.00
❑ 121 Shaun McDonald RC 6.00 2.50
❑ 122 Terrence Edwards 5.00 2.00
❑ 123 Walter Young RC 3.00 1.25
❑ 124 Ryan Hoag RC 3.00 1.25
❑ 125 Jason Witten RC 12.00 5.00
❑ 126 Bennie Joppru RC 6.00 2.50
❑ 127 George Wrighster RC 5.00 2.00
❑ 128 L.J. Smith RC 6.00 2.50
❑ 129 Robert Johnson RC 3.00 1.25
❑ 130 Chris Kelsay RC 6.00 2.50
❑ 131 Cory Redding RC 5.00 2.00
❑ 132 DeWayne White RC 5.00 2.00
❑ 133 Kenny Peterson RC 5.00 2.00
❑ 134 Jerome McDougle RC 6.00 2.50
❑ 135 Michael Haynes RC 6.00 2.50
❑ 136 Jimmy Kennedy RC 6.00 2.50
❑ 137 Kevin Williams RC 6.00 2.50
❑ 138 Johnathan Sullivan RC 5.00 2.00
❑ 139 Rien Long RC 3.00 1.25
❑ 140 Ty Warren RC 6.00 2.50
❑ 141 William Joseph RC 6.00 2.50
❑ 142 E.J. Henderson RC 6.00 2.50
❑ 143 Boss Bailey RC 6.00 2.50
❑ 144 Dennis Weathersby RC 3.00 1.25
❑ 145 Chris Simms RC 10.00 4.00
❑ 146 Rashean Mathis RC 5.00 2.00
❑ 147 Charles Rogers RC 6.00 2.50
❑ 148 Andre Woolfolk RC 6.00 2.50
❑ 149 Troy Polamalu RC 25.00 12.50
❑ 150 Mike Doss RC 6.00 2.50
❑ 151 Carson Palmer RPM RC 40.00 20.00
❑ 152 Byron Leftwich RPM RC 30.00 12.50
❑ 153 Kyle Boller RPM RC 12.00 5.00
❑ 154 Rex Grossman RPM RC 30.00 15.00
❑ 155 Dave Ragone RPM RC 12.00 5.00
❑ 156 Kliff Kingsbury RPM RC 10.00 4.00
❑ 157 Seneca Wallace RPM RC 12.00 5.00
❑ 158 Larry Johnson RPM RC 40.00 20.00
❑ 159 Willis McGahee RPM RC 25.00 12.50
❑ 160 Justin Fargas RPM RC 12.00 5.00
❑ 161 Onterrio Smith RPM RC 12.00 5.00
❑ 162 Chris Brown RPM RC 12.00 5.00
❑ 163 Musa Smith RPM RC 12.00 5.00
❑ 164 Artose Pinner RPM RC 12.00 5.00
❑ 165 Andre Johnson RPM RC 20.00 7.50
❑ 166 Kelley Washington RPM RC 12.005.00
❑ 167 Taylor Jacobs RPM RC 10.00 4.00
❑ 168 Bryant Johnson RPM RC 12.00 5.00
❑ 169 Tyrone Calico RPM RC 12.00 5.00
❑ 170 Anquan Boldin RPM RC 25.00 10.00
❑ 171 Bethel Johnson RPM RC 12.00 5.00
❑ 172 Nate Burleson RPM RC 12.00 5.00
❑ 173 Kevin Curtis RPM RC 12.00 5.00
❑ 174 Dallas Clark RPM RC 12.00 5.00
❑ 175 Teyo Johnson RPM RC 12.00 5.00
❑ 176 Terrell Suggs RPM RC 20.00 7.50
❑ 177 DeWayne Robertson RPM RC 12.00 5.00
❑ 178 Brian St.Pierre RPM RC 12.00 5.00
❑ 179 Terence Newman RPM RC 20.007.50
❑ 180 Marcus Trufant RPM RC 12.00 5.00

2004 Absolute Memorabilia

❑ COMP.SET w/o SP's (150) 80.00 40.00
❑ 151-233 PRINT RUN 750 SER.#'d SETS
❑ UNPRICED SPECTRUM PLATINUM #'d TO 1
❑ 1 Anquan Boldin 3.00 1.25
❑ 2 Emmitt Smith 6.00 2.50
❑ 3 Josh McCown 2.00 .75
❑ 4 Marcel Shipp 2.00 .75
❑ 5 Michael Vick 6.00 2.50
❑ 6 Peerless Price 2.00 .75
❑ 7 T.J. Duckett 2.00 .75
❑ 8 Warrick Dunn 2.00 .75
❑ 9 Jamal Lewis 3.00 1.25
❑ 10 Kyle Boller 3.00 1.25
❑ 11 Ray Lewis 3.00 1.25
❑ 12 Terrell Suggs 2.00 .75
❑ 13 Drew Bledsoe 3.00 1.25
❑ 14 Eric Moulds 2.00 .75
❑ 15 Josh Reed 1.25 .50
❑ 16 Travis Henry 2.00 .75
❑ 17 DeShaun Foster 2.00 .75
❑ 18 Jake Delhomme 3.00 1.25
❑ 19 Julius Peppers 3.00 1.25
❑ 20 Muhsin Muhammad 2.00 .75
❑ 21 Stephen Davis 2.00 .75
❑ 22 Steve Smith 3.00 1.25
❑ 23 Anthony Thomas 2.00 .75
❑ 24 Brian Urlacher 4.00 1.50
❑ 25 Marty Booker 2.00 .75
❑ 26 Rex Grossman 3.00 1.25
❑ 27 Carson Palmer 4.00 1.50
❑ 28 Chad Johnson 3.00 1.25
❑ 29 Corey Dillon 2.00 .75
❑ 30 Peter Warrick 2.00 .75
❑ 31 Rudi Johnson 2.00 .75
❑ 32 Andre Davis 1.25 .50
❑ 33 Dennis Northcutt 1.25 .50
❑ 34 Lee Suggs 3.00 1.25
❑ 35 Tim Couch 1.25 .50
❑ 36 Jeff Garcia 3.00 1.25
❑ 37 William Green 2.00 .75
❑ 38 Antonio Bryant 2.00 .75
❑ 39 Quincy Carter 2.00 .75
❑ 40 Roy Williams S 2.00 .75
❑ 41 Terence Newman 2.00 .75
❑ 42 Keyshawn Johnson 2.00 .75
❑ 43 Garrison Hearst 2.00 .75
❑ 44 Champ Bailey 2.00 .75
❑ 45 Ashley Lelie 2.00 .75
❑ 46 Jake Plummer 2.00 .75
❑ 47 Rod Smith 2.00 .75
❑ 48 Shannon Sharpe 2.00 .75
❑ 49 Charles Rogers 2.00 .75
❑ 50 Joey Harrington 3.00 1.25
❑ 51 Ahman Green 3.00 1.25
❑ 52 Brett Favre 8.00 3.00
❑ 53 Donald Driver 2.00 .75
❑ 54 Javon Walker 2.00 .75
❑ 55 Robert Ferguson 1.25 .50
❑ 56 Andre Johnson 3.00 1.25
❑ 57 David Carr 3.00 1.25
❑ 58 Domanick Davis 3.00 1.25
❑ 59 Edgerrin James 3.00 1.25
❑ 60 Marvin Harrison 3.00 1.25
❑ 61 Peyton Manning 5.00 2.00
❑ 62 Reggie Wayne 2.00 .75
❑ 63 Byron Leftwich 4.00 1.50
❑ 64 Fred Taylor 2.00 .75
❑ 65 Jimmy Smith 2.00 .75
❑ 66 Dante Hall 3.00 1.25
❑ 67 Priest Holmes 4.00 1.50
❑ 68 Tony Gonzalez 2.00 .75
❑ 69 Trent Green 2.00 .75
❑ 70 Chris Chambers 2.00 .75
❑ 71 Jay Fiedler 1.25 .50
❑ 72 David Boston 2.00 .75
❑ 73 Ricky Williams 3.00 1.25
❑ 74 Zach Thomas 3.00 1.25
❑ 75 Daunte Culpepper 3.00 1.25
❑ 76 Michael Bennett 2.00 .75
❑ 77 Moe Williams 1.25 .50
❑ 78 Randy Moss 4.00 1.50
❑ 79 David Givens 2.00 .75
❑ 80 Deion Branch 3.00 1.25
❑ 81 Kevin Faulk 1.25 .50
❑ 82 Richard Seymour 1.25 .50
❑ 83 Tom Brady 8.00 3.00
❑ 84 Troy Brown 2.00 .75
❑ 85 Ty Law 2.00 .75
❑ 86 Aaron Brooks 2.00 .75
❑ 87 Deuce McAllister 3.00 1.25
❑ 88 Donte Stallworth 2.00 .75
❑ 89 Joe Horn 2.00 .75
❑ 90 Amani Toomer 2.00 .75
❑ 91 Jeremy Shockey 3.00 1.25
❑ 92 Kerry Collins 2.00 .75
❑ 93 Michael Strahan 2.00 .75
❑ 94 Tiki Barber 3.00 1.25
❑ 95 Chad Pennington 3.00 1.25
❑ 96 Curtis Martin 3.00 1.25
❑ 97 Santana Moss 2.00 .75
❑ 98 Wayne Chrebet 2.00 .75
❑ 99 Justin McCareins 1.25 .50
❑ 100 Charles Woodson 2.00 .75
❑ 101 Jerry Porter 2.00 .75
❑ 102 Jerry Rice 6.00 2.50
❑ 103 Rich Gannon 2.00 .75
❑ 104 Tim Brown 3.00 1.25
❑ 105 Warren Sapp 2.00 .75
❑ 106 A.J. Feeley 3.00 1.25
❑ 107 Brian Westbrook 2.00 .75
❑ 108 Correll Buckhalter 2.00 .75
❑ 109 Donovan McNabb 4.00 1.50
❑ 110 Freddie Mitchell 2.00 .75
❑ 111 Terrell Owens 3.00 1.25
❑ 112 Jevon Kearse 2.00 .75
❑ 113 Todd Pinkston 1.25 .50
❑ 114 Antwaan Randle El 3.00 1.25
❑ 115 Hines Ward 3.00 1.25
❑ 116 Jerome Bettis 3.00 1.25
❑ 117 Kendrell Bell 2.00 .75
❑ 118 Plaxico Burress 2.00 .75
❑ 119 Tommy Maddox 2.00 .75
❑ 120 Duce Staley 2.00 .75

❑ 121 Drew Brees 3.00 1.25
❑ 122 LaDainian Tomlinson 4.00 1.50
❑ 123 Kevan Barlow 2.00 .75
❑ 124 Tai Streets 1.25 .50
❑ 125 Tim Rattay 1.25 .50
❑ 126 Darrell Jackson 2.00 .75
❑ 127 Koren Robinson 2.00 .75
❑ 128 Matt Hasselbeck 2.00 .75
❑ 129 Shaun Alexander 3.00 1.25
❑ 130 Isaac Bruce 2.00 .75
❑ 131 Kurt Warner 3.00 1.25
❑ 132 Marc Bulger 3.00 1.25
❑ 133 Marshall Faulk 3.00 1.25
❑ 134 Torry Holt 3.00 1.25
❑ 135 Derrick Brooks 2.00 .75
❑ 136 Keenan McCardell 1.25 .50
❑ 137 Mike Alstott 2.00 .75
❑ 138 Thomas Jones 2.00 .75
❑ 139 Charlie Garner 2.00 .75
❑ 140 Derrick Mason 2.00 .75
❑ 141 Drew Bennett 2.00 .75
❑ 142 Eddie George 2.00 .75
❑ 143 Keith Bulluck 1.25 .50
❑ 144 Steve McNair 3.00 1.25
❑ 145 LaVar Arrington 6.00 2.50
❑ 146 Laveranues Coles 2.00 .75
❑ 147 Patrick Ramsey 2.00 .75
❑ 148 Rod Gardner 2.00 .75
❑ 149 Clinton Portis 3.00 1.25
❑ 150 Mark Brunell 2.00 .75
❑ 151 Craig Krenzel AU RC EXCH 15.00 7.50
❑ 152 Andy Hall AU RC EXCH 12.00 6.00
❑ 153 Josh Harris RC 6.00 2.50
❑ 154 Jim Sorgi AU RC 15.00 7.50
❑ 155 Jeff Smoker AU RC 15.00 7.50
❑ 156 John Navarre AU RC EXCH 15.00 7.50
❑ 157 Jared Lorenzen AU RC 12.00 6.00
❑ 158 Cody Pickett AU RC 15.00 7.50
❑ 159 Casey Bramlet RC 5.00 2.00
❑ 160 Matt Mauck AU RC 15.00 7.50
❑ 161 B.J. Symons AU RC 15.00 7.50
❑ 162 Bradlee Van Pelt RC 10.00 4.00
❑ 163 Ryan Dinwiddie RC 5.00 2.00
❑ 164 Michael Turner RC 8.00 3.00
❑ 165 Drew Henson RC 6.00 2.50
❑ 166 Troy Fleming RC 5.00 2.00
❑ 167 Adimchinobe Echemandu RC 5.00 2.00
❑ 168 Quincy Wilson RC 5.00 2.00
❑ 169 Derrick Ward RC 3.00 1.25
❑ 170 Bruce Perry RC 6.00 2.50
❑ 171 Brandon Miree RC 5.00 2.00
❑ 172 Jarrett Payton AU RC 12.00 5.00
❑ 173 Ran Carthon RC 5.00 2.00
❑ 174 Carlos Francis AU RC EXCH 12.00 6.00
❑ 175 Samie Parker RC 6.00 2.50
❑ 176 Jerricho Cotchery RC 6.00 2.50
❑ 177 Ernest Wilford RC 6.00 2.50
❑ 178 Johnnie Morant RC 6.00 2.50
❑ 179 Maurice Mann AU RC 15.00 7.50
❑ 180 D.J. Hackett RC 5.00 2.00
❑ 181 Drew Carter RC 6.00 2.50
❑ 182 P.K. Sam RC 5.00 2.00
❑ 183 Jamaar Taylor RC 6.00 2.50
❑ 184 Ryan Krause RC 5.00 2.00
❑ 185 Triandos Luke RC 6.00 2.50
❑ 186 Jeris McIntyre RC 5.00 2.00
❑ 187 Clarence Moore AU RC 15.00 7.50
❑ 188 Mark Jones RC 5.00 2.00
❑ 189 Sloan Thomas AU RC 12.00 6.00
❑ 190 Sean Taylor RC 6.00 2.50
❑ 191 Derek Abney RC 6.00 2.50
❑ 192 Jonathan Vilma RC 6.00 2.50
❑ 193 Tommie Harris RC 6.00 2.50
❑ 194 D.J. Williams RC 6.00 2.50
❑ 195 Will Smith RC 6.00 2.50
❑ 196 Kenechi Udeze RC 6.00 2.50
❑ 197 Vince Wilfork RC 6.00 2.50
❑ 198 Ahmad Carroll RC 6.00 2.50
❑ 199 Jason Babin RC 6.00 2.50
❑ 200 Chris Gamble RC 6.00 2.50
❑ 201 Larry Fitzgerald RPM RC 25.00 10.00
❑ 202 DeAngelo Hall RPM RC 10.00 4.00
❑ 203 Matt Schaub RPM RC 25.00 10.00
❑ 204 Michael Jenkins RPM AU RC 25.00 10.00
❑ 205 Devard Darling RPM AU RC 25.00 10.00
❑ 206 J.P. Losman RPM RC 15.00 6.00
❑ 207 Lee Evans RPM RC 10.00 4.00
❑ 208 Keary Colbert RPM AU RC 30.00 15.00
❑ 209 Bernard Berrian RPM AU RC 30.00 12.50
❑ 210 Chris Perry RPM RC 12.00 5.00
❑ 211 Kellen Winslow RPM RC 15.00 6.00
❑ 212 Luke McCown RPM RC 8.00 3.00
❑ 213 Julius Jones RPM RC 25.00 10.00
❑ 214 Darius Watts RPM RC 8.00 3.00
❑ 215 Tatum Bell RPM AU RC 40.00 20.00
❑ 216 Kevin Jones RPM RC 20.00 8.00
❑ 217 Roy Williams RPM RC 20.00 7.50
❑ 218 Dunta Robinson RPM RC 8.00 3.00
❑ 219 Greg Jones RPM AU RC 25.00 12.50
❑ 220 Reggie Williams RPM RC 10.00 4.00
❑ 221 Mewelde Moore RPM RC 10.00 4.00
❑ 222 Ben Watson RPM RC 8.00 3.00
❑ 223 Cedric Cobbs RPM RC 15.00 7.50
❑ 224 Dev Henderson RPM AU RC 25.00 10.00
❑ 225 Eli Manning RPM RC 50.00 20.00
❑ 226 Robert Gallery RPM RC 8.00 3.00
❑ 228 Philip Rivers RPM RC 25.00 12.50
❑ 229 Derrick Hamilton RPM RC 6.00 2.50
❑ 230 Rashaun Woods RPM RC 8.00 3.00
❑ 231 Steven Jackson RPM RC 25.00 10.00
❑ 232 Michael Clayton RPM RC 15.00 6.00
❑ 233 Ben Troupe RPM RC 8.00 3.00
❑ 227 Roethlisberger RPM RC 60.00 35.00

2005 Absolute Memorabilia

❑ 151-205 PRINT RUN 999 SER.#'d SETS
❑ 206-234 PRINT RUN 750 SER.#'d SETS
❑ UNPRICED PLATINUM PRINT RUN 1 SET
❑ HOBBY PRINTED ON HOLOFOIL STOCK
❑ 1 Anquan Boldin 2.00 .75
❑ 2 Kurt Warner 2.00 .75
❑ 3 Josh McCown 2.00 .75
❑ 4 Larry Fitzgerald 3.00 1.25
❑ 5 Alge Crumpler 2.00 .75
❑ 6 Michael Vick 5.00 2.00
❑ 7 Peerless Price 1.50 .60
❑ 8 T.J. Duckett 2.00 .75
❑ 9 Warrick Dunn 2.00 .75
❑ 10 Deion Sanders 3.00 1.25
❑ 11 Derrick Mason 2.00 .75
❑ 12 Ed Reed 2.00 .75
❑ 13 Jamal Lewis 3.00 1.25
❑ 14 Kyle Boller 2.00 .75
❑ 15 Ray Lewis 3.00 1.25
❑ 16 Todd Heap 2.00 .75
❑ 17 Eric Moulds 2.00 .75
❑ 18 J.P. Losman 3.00 1.25
❑ 19 Lee Evans 2.00 .75
❑ 20 Travis Henry 2.00 .75
❑ 21 Willis McGahee 3.00 1.25
❑ 22 DeShaun Foster 2.00 .75
❑ 23 Jake Delhomme 3.00 1.25
❑ 24 Julius Peppers 2.00 .75
❑ 25 Keary Colbert 2.00 .75
❑ 26 Stephen Davis 2.00 .75
❑ 27 Steve Smith 2.00 .75
❑ 28 Brian Urlacher 3.00 1.25
❑ 29 Muhsin Muhammad 2.00 .75
❑ 30 Thomas Jones 2.00 .75
❑ 31 Rex Grossman 2.00 .75
❑ 32 Carson Palmer 3.00 1.25
❑ 33 Chad Johnson 3.00 1.25
❑ 34 Peter Warrick 1.50 .60
❑ 35 Rudi Johnson 2.00 .75
❑ 36 T.J. Houshmandzadeh 1.50 .60
❑ 37 Antonio Bryant 1.50 .60
❑ 38 Dennis Northcutt 1.50 .60
❑ 39 Trent Dilfer 2.00 .75
❑ 40 Kellen Winslow 3.00 1.25
❑ 41 Lee Suggs 2.00 .75
❑ 42 Reuben Droughns 2.00 .75
❑ 43 Drew Bledsoe 3.00 1.25
❑ 44 Jason Witten 2.00 .75
❑ 45 Julius Jones 4.00 1.50
❑ 46 Keyshawn Johnson 2.00 .75
❑ 47 Terence Newman 1.50 .60
❑ 48 Roy Williams S 2.00 .75
❑ 49 Jake Plummer 2.00 .75
❑ 50 Rod Smith 2.00 .75
❑ 51 Ashley Lelie 2.00 .75
❑ 52 Tatum Bell 2.00 .75
❑ 53 Charles Rogers 2.00 .75
❑ 54 Joey Harrington 3.00 1.25
❑ 55 Kevin Jones 3.00 1.25
❑ 56 Roy Williams WR 3.00 1.25
❑ 57 Ahman Green 3.00 1.25
❑ 58 Brett Favre 8.00 3.00
❑ 59 Donald Driver 2.00 .75
❑ 60 Javon Walker 2.00 .75
❑ 61 Andre Johnson 2.00 .75
❑ 62 David Carr 3.00 1.25
❑ 63 Domanick Davis 2.00 .75
❑ 64 Brandon Stokley 2.00 .75
❑ 65 Dallas Clark 1.50 .60
❑ 66 Edgerrin James 3.00 1.25
❑ 67 Marvin Harrison 3.00 1.25
❑ 68 Peyton Manning 5.00 2.00
❑ 69 Reggie Wayne 2.00 .75
❑ 70 Reggie Williams 2.00 .75
❑ 71 Byron Leftwich 3.00 1.25
❑ 72 Fred Taylor 2.00 .75
❑ 73 Jimmy Smith 2.00 .75
❑ 74 Priest Holmes 3.00 1.25
❑ 75 Tony Gonzalez 2.00 .75
❑ 76 Dante Hall 2.00 .75
❑ 77 Trent Green 2.00 .75
❑ 78 Eddie Kennison 1.50 .60
❑ 79 A.J. Feeley 2.00 .75
❑ 80 Chris Chambers 2.00 .75
❑ 81 Zach Thomas 3.00 1.25
❑ 82 Junior Seau 2.00 .75
❑ 83 Marty Booker 2.00 .75
❑ 84 Daunte Culpepper 3.00 1.25
❑ 85 Nate Burleson 2.00 .75
❑ 86 Michael Bennett 2.00 .75
❑ 87 Onterrio Smith 2.00 .75
❑ 88 Corey Dillon 2.00 .75
❑ 89 Deion Branch 2.00 .75
❑ 90 Tom Brady 8.00 3.00
❑ 91 Troy Brown 2.00 .75
❑ 92 Tedy Bruschi 2.00 .75
❑ 93 Aaron Brooks 2.00 .75
❑ 94 Donte Stallworth 2.00 .75
❑ 95 Joe Horn 2.00 .75
❑ 96 Deuce McAllister 3.00 1.25
❑ 97 Amani Toomer 2.00 .75
❑ 98 Plaxico Burress 2.00 .75
❑ 99 Jeremy Shockey 3.00 1.25
❑ 100 Eli Manning 6.00 2.50
❑ 101 Tiki Barber 3.00 1.25
❑ 102 Chad Pennington 3.00 1.25
❑ 103 Laveranues Coles 2.00 .75
❑ 104 Curtis Martin 3.00 1.25
❑ 105 Justin McCareins 1.50 .60
❑ 106 Wayne Chrebet 2.00 .75
❑ 107 Jerry Porter 2.00 .75
❑ 108 LaMont Jordan 3.00 1.25
❑ 109 Randy Moss 3.00 1.25
❑ 110 Kerry Collins 2.00 .75
❑ 111 Charles Woodson 2.00 .75
❑ 112 Brian Westbrook 2.00 .75
❑ 113 Donovan McNabb 4.00 1.50
❑ 114 Jevon Kearse 2.00 .75
❑ 115 Terrell Owens 3.00 1.25
❑ 116 Ben Roethlisberger 8.00 3.00
❑ 117 Hines Ward 3.00 1.25
❑ 118 Duce Staley 2.00 .75
❑ 119 Jerome Bettis 3.00 1.25
❑ 120 Antonio Gates 3.00 1.25
❑ 121 Eric Parker 1.50 .60
❑ 122 Keenan McCardell 1.50 .60
❑ 123 Drew Brees 3.00 1.25
❑ 124 LaDainian Tomlinson 4.00 1.50
❑ 125 Brandon Lloyd 1.50 .60
❑ 126 Kevan Barlow 2.00 .75
❑ 127 Tim Rattay 1.50 .60
❑ 128 Koren Robinson 2.00 .75
❑ 129 Darrell Jackson 2.00 .75

❑	130	Jerry Rice	6.00	2.50
❑	131	Matt Hasselbeck	2.00	.75
❑	132	Shaun Alexander	4.00	1.25
❑	133	Isaac Bruce	2.00	.75
❑	134	Marc Bulger	3.00	1.25
❑	135	Marshall Faulk	3.00	1.25
❑	136	Steven Jackson	4.00	1.50
❑	137	Torry Holt	3.00	1.25
❑	138	Brian Griese	2.00	.75
❑	139	Michael Clayton	3.00	1.25
❑	140	Michael Pittman	1.50	.60
❑	141	Mike Alstott	2.00	.75
❑	142	Chris Brown	2.00	.75
❑	143	Drew Bennett	2.00	.75
❑	144	Steve McNair	3.00	1.25
❑	145	Clinton Portis	3.00	1.25
❑	146	LaVar Arrington	3.00	1.25
❑	147	Santana Moss	2.00	.75
❑	148	Patrick Ramsey	2.00	.75
❑	149	Rod Gardner	2.00	.75
❑	150	Sean Taylor	2.00	.75
❑	151	DeMarcus Ware RC	10.00	4.00
❑	152	Shawne Merriman RC	10.00	4.00
❑	153	Thomas Davis RC	6.00	2.50
❑	154	Derrick Johnson RC	10.00	4.00
❑	155	Travis Johnson RC	5.00	2.00
❑	156	David Pollack RC	6.00	2.50
❑	157	Erasmus James RC	6.00	2.50
❑	158	Marcus Spears RC	6.00	2.50
❑	159	Fabian Washington RC	6.00	2.50
❑	160	Marlin Jackson RC	6.00	2.50
❑	161	Cedric Benson RC	12.00	5.00
❑	162	Matt Roth RC	6.00	2.50
❑	163	Dan Cody RC	6.00	2.50
❑	164	Bryant McFadden RC	6.00	2.50
❑	165	Chris Henry RC	6.00	2.50
❑	166	Brandon Jones RC	6.00	2.50
❑	167	Marion Barber RC	10.00	4.00
❑	168	Brandon Jacobs RC	8.00	3.00
❑	169	Jerome Mathis RC	6.00	2.50
❑	170	Craphonso Thorpe RC	5.00	2.00
❑	171	Alvin Pearman RC	6.00	2.50
❑	172	Darren Sproles RC	6.00	2.50
❑	173	Fred Gibson RC	5.00	2.00
❑	174	Roydell Williams RC	6.00	2.50
❑	175	Airese Currie RC	6.00	2.50
❑	176	Damien Nash RC	5.00	2.00
❑	177	Dan Orlovsky RC	8.00	3.00
❑	178	Adrian McPherson RC	6.00	2.50
❑	179	Larry Brackins RC	3.00	1.25
❑	180	Aaron Rodgers RC	20.00	8.00
❑	181	Cedric Houston RC	6.00	2.50
❑	182	Mike Williams	12.00	5.00
❑	183	Heath Miller RC	15.00	6.00
❑	184	Dante Ridgeway RC	5.00	2.00
❑	185	Craig Bragg RC	5.00	2.00
❑	186	Deandra Cobb RC	5.00	2.00
❑	187	Derek Anderson RC	6.00	2.50
❑	188	Paris Warren RC	5.00	2.00
❑	189	David Greene RC	6.00	2.50
❑	190	Lionel Gates RC	5.00	2.00
❑	191	Anthony Davis RC	5.00	2.00
❑	192	Noah Herron RC	6.00	2.50
❑	193	Ryan Fitzpatrick RC	10.00	4.00
❑	194	J.R. Russell RC	5.00	2.00
❑	195	Jason White RC	6.00	2.50
❑	196	Kay-Jay Harris RC	5.00	2.00
❑	197	Steve Savoy RC	3.00	1.25
❑	198	T.A. McLendon RC	3.00	1.25
❑	199	Taylor Stubblefield RC	3.00	1.25
❑	200	Josh Davis RC	5.00	2.00
❑	201	Shaun Cody RC	6.00	2.50
❑	202	Rasheed Marshall RC	6.00	2.50
❑	203	Chad Owens RC	6.00	2.50
❑	204	Tab Perry RC	6.00	2.50
❑	205	James Kilian RC	6.00	2.50
❑	206	Adam Jones RPM RC	10.00	4.00
❑	207	Alex Smith QB RPM RC	30.00	12.50
❑	208	Antrel Rolle RPM RC	10.00	4.00
❑	209	Andrew Walter RPM RC	15.00	6.00
❑	210	Braylon Edwards RPM RC	30.00	12.50
❑	211	Cadillac Williams RPM RC	40.00	15.00
❑	212	Carlos Rogers RPM RC	12.00	5.00
❑	213	Charlie Frye RPM RC	20.00	10.00
❑	214	Ciatrick Fason RPM RC	10.00	4.00
❑	215	Courtney Roby RPM RC	10.00	4.00
❑	216	Eric Shelton RPM RC	10.00	4.00
❑	217	Frank Gore RPM RC	20.00	10.00
❑	218	J.J. Arrington RPM RC	15.00	6.00
❑	219	Kyle Orton RPM RC	15.00	6.00
❑	220	Jason Campbell RPM RC	15.00	6.00
❑	221	Mark Bradley RPM RC	10.00	4.00
❑	222	Mark Clayton RPM RC	12.00	5.00
❑	223	Matt Jones RPM RC	25.00	10.00
❑	224	Maurice Clarett RPM	10.00	4.00
❑	225	Reggie Brown RPM RC	10.00	4.00
❑	226	Ronnie Brown RPM RC	30.00	12.50
❑	227	Roddy White RPM RC	10.00	4.00
❑	228	Ryan Moats RPM RC	10.00	4.00
❑	229	Roscoe Parrish RPM RC	10.00	4.00
❑	230	Stefan LeFors RPM RC	10.00	4.00
❑	231	Terrence Murphy RPM RC	10.00	4.00
❑	232	Troy Williamson RPM RC	20.00	8.00
❑	233	Vernand Morency RPM RC	10.00	4.00
❑	234	Vincent Jackson RPM RC	10.00	4.00

2005 Absolute Memorabilia Retail

❑ COMPLETE SET (150) 30.00 15.00
❑ *VETERANS: .1X TO .25X BASIC CARDS
❑ *ROOKIES 151-205: .2X TO .5X BASIC CARDS
❑ RETAIL PRINTED ON WHITE STOCK

2006 Absolute Memorabilia

❑	1	Anquan Boldin	2.00	.75
❑	2	J.J. Arrington	2.00	.75
❑	3	Kurt Warner	2.00	.75
❑	4	Larry Fitzgerald	3.00	1.25
❑	5	Marcel Shipp	1.50	.60
❑	6	Alge Crumpler	2.00	.75
❑	7	Michael Jenkins	2.00	.75
❑	8	Michael Vick	4.00	1.50
❑	9	T.J. Duckett	2.00	.75
❑	10	Warrick Dunn	2.00	.75
❑	11	Derrick Mason	1.50	.60
❑	12	Jamal Lewis	2.00	.75
❑	13	Kyle Boller	1.50	.60
❑	14	Mark Clayton	2.00	.75
❑	15	Ray Lewis	3.00	1.25
❑	16	Todd Heap	2.00	.75
❑	17	Eric Moulds	2.00	.75
❑	18	J.P. Losman	2.00	.75
❑	19	Josh Reed	1.50	.60
❑	20	Lee Evans	2.00	.75
❑	21	Willis McGahee	3.00	1.25
❑	22	DeShaun Foster	2.00	.75
❑	23	Jake Delhomme	2.00	.75
❑	24	Julius Peppers	2.00	.75
❑	25	Keary Colbert	1.50	.60
❑	26	Stephen Davis	2.00	.75
❑	27	Steve Smith	3.00	1.25
❑	28	Brian Urlacher	3.00	1.25
❑	29	Cedric Benson	3.00	1.25
❑	30	Rex Grossman	3.00	1.25
❑	31	Thomas Jones	2.00	.75
❑	32	Muhsin Muhammad	2.00	.75
❑	33	Carson Palmer	3.00	1.25
❑	34	Chad Johnson	2.00	.75
❑	35	Rudi Johnson	2.00	.75
❑	36	T.J. Houshmandzadeh	2.00	.75
❑	37	Charlie Frye	2.00	.75
❑	38	Dennis Northcutt	1.50	.60
❑	39	Reuben Droughns	2.00	.75
❑	40	Braylon Edwards	3.00	1.25
❑	41	Drew Bledsoe	3.00	1.25
❑	42	Jason Witten	2.00	.75
❑	43	Julius Jones	3.00	1.25
❑	44	Keyshawn Johnson	2.00	.75
❑	45	Roy Williams S	2.00	.75
❑	46	Terry Glenn	2.00	.75
❑	47	Ashley Lelie	2.00	.75
❑	48	Jake Plummer	2.00	.75
❑	49	Rod Smith	2.00	.75
❑	50	Tatum Bell	2.00	.75
❑	51	Mike Anderson	2.00	.75
❑	52	Joey Harrington	2.00	.75
❑	53	Kevin Jones	3.00	1.25
❑	54	Mike Williams	3.00	1.25
❑	55	Roy Williams WR	3.00	1.25
❑	56	Marcus Pollard	1.50	.60
❑	57	Aaron Rodgers	3.00	1.25
❑	58	Brett Favre	6.00	2.50
❑	59	Donald Driver	2.00	.75
❑	60	Javon Walker	2.00	.75
❑	61	Samkon Gado	3.00	1.25
❑	62	Bubba Franks	1.50	.60
❑	63	Andre Johnson	2.00	.75
❑	64	Corey Bradford	1.50	.60
❑	65	David Carr	2.00	.75
❑	66	Domanick Davis	2.00	.75
❑	67	Jabar Gaffney	1.50	.60
❑	68	Edgerrin James	3.00	1.25
❑	69	Dallas Clark	1.50	.60
❑	70	Marvin Harrison	3.00	1.25
❑	71	Peyton Manning	5.00	2.00
❑	72	Reggie Wayne	2.00	.75
❑	73	Brandon Stokley	2.00	.75
❑	74	Byron Leftwich	2.00	.75
❑	75	Fred Taylor	2.00	.75
❑	76	Jimmy Smith	2.00	.75
❑	77	Matt Jones	3.00	1.25
❑	78	Ernest Wilford	1.50	.60
❑	79	Larry Johnson	4.00	1.50
❑	80	Tony Gonzalez	2.00	.75
❑	81	Trent Green	2.00	.75
❑	82	Eddie Kennison	1.50	.60
❑	83	Dante Hall	2.00	.75
❑	84	Chris Chambers	2.00	.75
❑	85	Randy McMichael	1.50	.60
❑	86	Terrell Owens	3.00	1.25
❑	87	Ronnie Brown	3.00	1.25
❑	88	Zach Thomas	3.00	1.25
❑	89	Marty Booker	1.50	.60
❑	90	Daunte Culpepper	3.00	1.25
❑	91	Mewelde Moore	1.50	.60
❑	92	Nate Burleson	2.00	.75
❑	93	Troy Williamson	2.00	.75
❑	94	Corey Dillon	2.00	.75
❑	95	David Givens	2.00	.75
❑	96	Deion Branch	2.00	.75
❑	97	Tedy Bruschi	3.00	1.25
❑	98	Tom Brady	5.00	2.00
❑	99	Aaron Brooks	2.00	.75
❑	100	Deuce McAllister	2.00	.75
❑	101	Donte Stallworth	2.00	.75
❑	102	Joe Horn	2.00	.75
❑	103	Eli Manning	4.00	1.50
❑	104	Jeremy Shockey	3.00	1.25
❑	105	Plaxico Burress	2.00	.75
❑	106	Tiki Barber	3.00	1.25
❑	107	Chad Pennington	2.00	.75
❑	108	Curtis Martin	3.00	1.25
❑	109	Laveranues Coles	2.00	.75
❑	110	Justin McCareins	1.50	.60
❑	111	Kerry Collins	2.00	.75
❑	112	LaMont Jordan	2.00	.75
❑	113	Randy Moss	3.00	1.25
❑	114	Jerry Porter	2.00	.75
❑	115	Brian Westbrook	2.00	.75
❑	116	Donovan McNabb	3.00	1.25
❑	117	Reggie Brown	2.00	.75
❑	118	Ryan Moats	1.50	.60
❑	119	Antwaan Randle El	2.00	.75
❑	120	Ben Roethlisberger	5.00	2.00
❑	121	Willie Parker	4.00	1.50
❑	122	Hines Ward	3.00	1.25
❑	123	Antonio Gates	3.00	1.25
❑	124	Drew Brees	3.00	1.25
❑	125	Keenan McCardell	1.50	.60
❑	126	LaDainian Tomlinson	4.00	1.50
❑	127	Alex Smith QB	4.00	1.50
❑	128	Brandon Lloyd	2.00	.75
❑	129	Frank Gore	3.00	1.25
❑	130	Kevan Barlow	2.00	.75
❑	131	Darrell Jackson	2.00	.75
❑	132	Joe Jurevicius	2.00	.75
❑	133	Matt Hasselbeck	2.00	.75

❑ 134 Shaun Alexander	3.00	1.25
❑ 135 Isaac Bruce	2.00	.75
❑ 136 Marc Bulger	2.00	.75
❑ 137 Steven Jackson	3.00	1.25
❑ 138 Torry Holt	2.00	.75
❑ 139 Cadillac Williams	3.00	1.25
❑ 140 Chris Simms	2.00	.75
❑ 141 Joey Galloway	2.00	.75
❑ 142 Michael Clayton	2.00	.75
❑ 143 Chris Brown	2.00	.75
❑ 144 Drew Bennett	1.50	.60
❑ 145 Steve McNair	2.00	.75
❑ 146 Tyrone Calico	1.50	.60
❑ 147 Clinton Portis	3.00	1.25
❑ 148 LaVar Arrington	3.00	1.25
❑ 149 Mark Brunell	2.00	.75
❑ 150 Santana Moss	2.00	.75
❑ 151 Greg Jennings RC	10.00	4.00
❑ 152 Joseph Addai RC	20.00	8.00
❑ 153 Erik Meyer RC	5.00	2.00
❑ 154 Drew Olson RC	5.00	2.00
❑ 155 Darrell Hackney RC	5.00	2.00
❑ 156 Paul Pinegar RC	5.00	2.00
❑ 157 Brandon Kirsch RC	6.00	2.50
❑ 158 Andre Hall RC	5.00	2.00
❑ 159 Taurean Henderson RC	6.00	2.50
❑ 160 Derrick Ross RC	5.00	2.00
❑ 161 Mike Bell RC	10.00	4.00
❑ 162 Wendell Mathis RC	5.00	2.00
❑ 163 Gerald Riggs RC	6.00	2.50
❑ 164 John David Washington RC	5.00	2.00
❑ 165 Devin Aromashodu RC	5.00	2.00
❑ 166 Ben Obomanu RC	5.00	2.00
❑ 167 David Anderson RC	5.00	2.00
❑ 168 Marques Colston RC	25.00	10.00
❑ 169 Kevin McMahan RC	5.00	2.00
❑ 170 Miles Austin RC	5.00	2.00
❑ 171 Martin Nance RC	5.00	2.00
❑ 172 Greg Lee RC	5.00	2.00
❑ 173 Hank Baskett RC	6.00	2.50
❑ 174 Anthony Mix RC	5.00	2.00
❑ 175 D'Brickashaw Ferguson RC	6.00	2.50
❑ 176 Kamerion Wimbley RC	6.00	2.50
❑ 177 Tamba Hali RC	6.00	2.50
❑ 178 Mathias Kiwanuka RC	8.00	3.00
❑ 179 Brodrick Bunkley RC	6.00	2.50
❑ 180 John McCargo RC	5.00	2.00
❑ 181 Claude Wroten RC	3.00	1.25
❑ 182 Gabe Watson RC	5.00	2.00
❑ 183 D'Qwell Jackson RC	5.00	2.00
❑ 184 Abdul Hodge RC	6.00	2.50
❑ 185 Ernie Sims RC	8.00	3.00
❑ 186 Chad Greenway RC	6.00	2.50
❑ 187 Bobby Carpenter RC	6.00	2.50
❑ 188 Manny Lawson RC	6.00	2.50
❑ 189 DeMeco Ryans RC	8.00	3.00
❑ 190 Rocky McIntosh RC	6.00	2.50
❑ 191 Thomas Howard RC	6.00	2.50
❑ 192 Jon Alston RC	6.00	2.50
❑ 193 A.J. Nicholson RC	3.00	1.25
❑ 194 Tye Hill RC	6.00	2.50
❑ 195 Antonio Cromartie RC	6.00	2.50
❑ 196 Johnathan Joseph RC	5.00	2.00
❑ 197 Kelly Jennings RC	6.00	2.50
❑ 198 Jimmy Williams RC	6.00	2.50
❑ 199 Ashton Youboty RC	6.00	2.50
❑ 200 Alan Zemaitis RC	6.00	2.50
❑ 201 Anwar Phillips RC	5.00	2.00
❑ 202 Jason Allen RC	6.00	2.50
❑ 203 Cedric Griffin RC	5.00	2.00
❑ 204 Ko Simpson RC	5.00	2.00
❑ 205 Pat Watkins RC	6.00	2.50
❑ 206 Donte Whitner RC	6.00	2.50
❑ 207 Bernard Pollard RC	5.00	2.00
❑ 208 Darnell Bing RC	6.00	2.50
❑ 209 De'Arrius Howard RC	6.00	2.50
❑ 210 Ethan Kilmer RC	6.00	2.50
❑ 211 Bennie Brazell RC	5.00	2.00
❑ 212 Haloti Ngata RC	6.00	2.50
❑ 213 Jeremy Bloom RC	5.00	2.00
❑ 214 Jay Cutler RC	25.00	10.00
❑ 215 Marcus Vick RC	5.00	2.00
❑ 216 Roman Harper RC	5.00	2.00
❑ 217 Anthony Smith RC	8.00	3.00
❑ 218 Daniel Bullocks RC	6.00	2.50
❑ 219 Eric Smith RC	5.00	2.00
❑ 220 Dusty Dvoracek RC	6.00	2.50
❑ 221 Brodie Croyle AU RC	30.00	12.00
❑ 222 Ingle Martin AU RC	15.00	6.00
❑ 223 Reggie McNeal AU RC	12.00	5.00
❑ 224 Bruce Gradkowski AU RC	40.00	15.00
❑ 225 D.J. Shockley AU RC	15.00	6.00
❑ 226 P.J. Daniels AU RC	12.00	5.00
❑ 227 Marques Hagans AU RC	12.00	5.00
❑ 228 Jerome Harrison RC	12.00	5.00
❑ 229 Wali Lundy AU RC	15.00	6.00
❑ 230 Cedric Humes AU RC	15.00	6.00
❑ 231 Quinton Ganther AU RC	12.00	5.00
❑ 232 Garrett Mills AU RC	15.00	6.00
❑ 233 Anthony Fasano AU RC	15.00	6.00
❑ 234 Tony Scheffler AU RC	15.00	6.00
❑ 235 Leonard Pope AU RC	15.00	6.00
❑ 236 David Thomas AU RC	15.00	6.00
❑ 237 Dominique Byrd AU RC	12.00	5.00
❑ 238 Jai Lewis AU/299 RC	12.00	5.00
❑ 239 Devin Hester AU RC	40.00	20.00
❑ 240 Willie Reid AU RC	15.00	6.00
❑ 241 Brad Smith AU RC	15.00	6.00
❑ 242 Cory Rodgers AU RC	15.00	6.00
❑ 243 Skyler Green AU RC	15.00	6.00
❑ 244 Domenik Hixon AU RC	12.00	5.00
❑ 245 Mike Hass AU RC	15.00	6.00
❑ 246 Jonathan Orr AU/299 RC	12.00	5.00
❑ 247 Delanie Walker AU/299 RC	12.00	5.00
❑ 248 Adam Jennings AU/299 RC	12.00	5.00
❑ 249 Jeff Webb AU/299 RC	12.00	5.00
❑ 250 Todd Watkins AU RC	12.00	5.00
❑ 251 Chad Jackson RPM RC	15.00	6.00
❑ 252 Laurence Maroney RPM RC	25.00	10.00
❑ 253 Tarvaris Jackson RPM RC	15.00	6.00
❑ 254 Michael Huff RPM RC	12.00	5.00
❑ 255 Mario Williams RPM RC	15.00	6.00
❑ 256 Marcedes Lewis RPM RC	10.00	4.00
❑ 257 Maurice Drew RPM RC	25.00	10.00
❑ 258 Vince Young RPM RC	40.00	15.00
❑ 259 LenDale White RPM RC	20.00	8.00
❑ 260 Reggie Bush RPM RC	60.00	25.00
❑ 261 Matt Leinart RPM RC	40.00	15.00
❑ 262 Michael Robinson RPM RC	15.00	6.00
❑ 263 Vernon Davis RPM RC	20.00	8.00
❑ 264 Brandon Williams RPM RC	10.00	4.00
❑ 265 Derek Hagan RPM RC	10.00	4.00
❑ 266 Jason Avant RPM RC	10.00	4.00
❑ 267 Brandon Marshall RPM RC	10.00	4.00
❑ 268 Omar Jacobs RPM RC	8.00	3.00
❑ 269 Santonio Holmes RPM RC	20.00	8.00
❑ 270 Jerious Norwood RPM RC	15.00	6.00
❑ 271 Demetrius Williams RPM RC	12.00	5.00
❑ 272 Sinorice Moss RPM RC	12.00	5.00
❑ 273 Leon Washington RPM RC	15.00	6.00
❑ 274 Kellen Clemens RPM RC	12.00	5.00
❑ 275 A.J. Hawk RPM RC	20.00	8.00
❑ 276 Maurice Stovall RPM RC	10.00	4.00
❑ 277 DeAngelo Williams RPM RC	25.00	10.00
❑ 278 Charlie Whitehurst RPM RC	12.00	5.00
❑ 279 Travis Wilson RPM RC	10.00	4.00
❑ 280 Joe Klopfenstein RPM RC	8.00	3.00
❑ 281 Brian Calhoun RPM RC	10.00	4.00

1995 Action Packed Rookies/Stars

❑ COMPLETE SET (105)	20.00	7.50
❑ 1 Steve Young	1.25	.50
❑ 2 Steve Bono	.25	.08
❑ 3 Natrone Means	.25	.08
❑ 4 Steve Beuerlein	.25	.08
❑ 5 Neil O'Donnell	.25	.08
❑ 6 Marshall Faulk	2.00	.75
❑ 7 Ricky Watters	.25	.08
❑ 8 Gary Brown	.10	.02
❑ 9 Jeff Hostetler	.25	.08
❑ 10 Robert Brooks	.50	.20
❑ 11 Johnny Mitchell	.10	.02
❑ 12 Barry Sanders	2.50	1.00
❑ 13 Dave Brown	.25	.08
❑ 14 John Elway	3.00	1.25
❑ 15 Garrison Hearst	.50	.20
❑ 16 Jim Everett	.10	.02
❑ 17 Michael Irvin	.50	.20
❑ 18 Dan Marino	3.00	1.25
❑ 19 Jeff George	.25	.08
❑ 20 Ben Coates	.25	.08
❑ 21 Charles Johnson	.25	.08
❑ 22 Carl Pickens	.25	.08
❑ 23 Deion Sanders	1.00	.40
❑ 24 Errict Rhett	.25	.08
❑ 25 Steve Walsh	.10	.02
❑ 26 Bruce Smith	.50	.20
❑ 27 Andre Rison	.25	.08
❑ 28 Warren Moon	.25	.08
❑ 29 Terry Allen	.25	.08
❑ 30 Desmond Howard	.25	.08
❑ 31 Shannon Sharpe	.25	.08
❑ 32 Dave Krieg	.10	.02
❑ 33 Byron Bam Morris	.10	.02
❑ 34 Rodney Hampton	.25	.08
❑ 35 Scott Mitchell	.25	.08
❑ 36 Alvin Harper	.10	.02
❑ 37 Robert Smith	.50	.20
❑ 38 Troy Aikman	1.50	.60
❑ 39 William Floyd	.25	.08
❑ 40 Randall Cunningham	.50	.20
❑ 41 Mario Bates	.25	.08
❑ 42 Reggie White	.50	.20
❑ 43 Chris Chandler	.25	.08
❑ 44 Erik Kramer	.10	.02
❑ 45 Emmitt Smith	2.50	1.00
❑ 46 Irving Fryar	.25	.08
❑ 47 Jeff Blake RC	.75	.30
❑ 48 Drew Bledsoe	1.00	.40
❑ 49 Anthony Miller	.25	.08
❑ 50 Marcus Allen	.50	.20
❑ 51 Leroy Hoard	.10	.02
❑ 52 Stan Humphries	.25	.08
❑ 53 Eric Green	.10	.02
❑ 54 Herschel Walker	.25	.08
❑ 55 Junior Seau	.50	.20
❑ 56 Terance Mathis	.25	.08
❑ 57 Boomer Esiason	.25	.08
❑ 58 Lorenzo White	.10	.02
❑ 59 Tim Brown	.50	.20
❑ 60 Brett Favre	3.00	1.25
❑ 61 Craig Erickson	.10	.02
❑ 62 Rod Woodson	.25	.08
❑ 63 Frank Reich	.10	.02
❑ 64 Cris Carter	.50	.20
❑ 65 Jerry Rice	1.50	.60
❑ 66 Greg Hill	.25	.08
❑ 67 Andre Reed	.25	.08
❑ 68 Trent Dilfer	.50	.20
❑ 69 Eric Metcalf	.25	.08
❑ 70 Jim Kelly	.50	.20
❑ 71 Herman Moore	.50	.20
❑ 72 Vinny Testaverde	.25	.08
❑ 73 Jeff Graham	.10	.02
❑ 74 Edgar Bennett	.25	.08
❑ 75 Jerome Bettis	.50	.20
❑ 76 Heath Shuler	.25	.08
❑ 77 Chris Warren	.25	.08
❑ 78 Reggie Brooks	.25	.08
❑ 79 Rick Mirer	.25	.08
❑ 80 Chris Miller	.10	.02
❑ 81 Napoleon Kaufman RC	1.25	.50
❑ 82 Christian Fauria RC	.25	.08
❑ 83 Todd Collins RC	.25	.08
❑ 84 J.J. Stokes RC	.50	.20
❑ 85 Mark Bruener RC	.25	.08
❑ 86 Frank Sanders RC	.50	.20
❑ 87 Chad May RC	.10	.02
❑ 88 Kordell Stewart RC	1.50	.60
❑ 89 Ki-Jana Carter RC	.50	.20
❑ 90 Curtis Martin RC	3.00	1.25
❑ 91 Sherman Williams RC	.10	.02
❑ 92 Terrell Davis RC	2.50	1.00
❑ 93 Chris Sanders RC	.25	.08
❑ 94 Kyle Brady RC	.50	.20
❑ 95 Tyrone Wheatley RC	1.25	.50
❑ 96 Rodney Thomas RC	.25	.08
❑ 97 James O. Stewart RC	1.25	.50

❑ 98 Kerry Collins RC	1.50	.60
❑ 99 Rashaan Salaam RC	.25	.08
❑ 100 Stoney Case RC	.10	.02
❑ 101 Steve McNair RC	3.00	1.25
❑ 102 Joey Galloway RC	1.50	.60
❑ 103 Michael Westbrook RC	.50	.20
❑ 104 Eric Zeier RC	.50	.20
❑ 105 Ray Zellars RC	.25	.08

2002 Atomic

❑ COMP.SET w/o SP's (100)	50.00	20.00
❑ 1 David Boston	2.00	.75
❑ 2 Thomas Jones	1.25	.50
❑ 3 Jake Plummer	1.25	.50
❑ 4 Jamal Anderson	1.25	.50
❑ 5 Warrick Dunn	2.00	.75
❑ 6 Michael Vick	6.00	2.50
❑ 7 Jamal Lewis	2.00	.75
❑ 8 Chris Redman	.75	.30
❑ 9 Travis Taylor	1.25	.50
❑ 10 Travis Henry	2.00	.75
❑ 11 Eric Moulds	1.25	.50
❑ 12 Peerless Price	1.25	.50
❑ 13 Muhsin Muhammad	1.25	.50
❑ 14 Lamar Smith	1.25	.50
❑ 15 Chris Weinke	1.25	.50
❑ 16 Marty Booker	.75	.30
❑ 17 Jim Miller	.75	.30
❑ 18 Anthony Thomas	1.25	.50
❑ 19 Corey Dillon	1.25	.50
❑ 20 Jon Kitna	1.25	.50
❑ 21 Peter Warrick	1.25	.50
❑ 22 Tim Couch	1.25	.50
❑ 23 Kevin Johnson	1.25	.50
❑ 24 Quincy Morgan	.75	.30
❑ 25 Quincy Carter	1.25	.50
❑ 26 Joey Galloway	1.25	.50
❑ 27 Emmitt Smith	5.00	2.00
❑ 28 Terrell Davis	2.00	.75
❑ 29 Brian Griese	2.00	.75
❑ 30 Ed McCaffrey	2.00	.75
❑ 31 Rod Smith	1.25	.50
❑ 32 Scotty Anderson	.75	.30
❑ 33 Az-Zahir Hakim	.75	.30
❑ 34 Mike McMahon	2.00	.75
❑ 35 Brett Favre	5.00	2.00
❑ 36 Terry Glenn	1.25	.50
❑ 37 Ahman Green	2.00	.75
❑ 38 James Allen	1.25	.50
❑ 39 Corey Bradford	.75	.30
❑ 40 Jermaine Lewis	.75	.30
❑ 41 Marvin Harrison	2.00	.75
❑ 42 Edgerrin James	2.50	1.00
❑ 43 Peyton Manning	4.00	1.50
❑ 44 Mark Brunell	2.00	.75
❑ 45 Jimmy Smith	1.25	.50
❑ 46 Fred Taylor	2.00	.75
❑ 47 Tony Gonzalez	1.25	.50
❑ 48 Trent Green	1.25	.50
❑ 49 Priest Holmes	2.50	1.00
❑ 50 Chris Chambers	2.00	.75
❑ 51 Jay Fiedler	1.25	.50
❑ 52 Ricky Williams	2.00	.75
❑ 53 Michael Bennett	1.25	.50
❑ 54 Daunte Culpepper	2.00	.75
❑ 55 Randy Moss	4.00	1.50
❑ 56 Tom Brady	5.00	2.00
❑ 57 Troy Brown	1.25	.50
❑ 58 Antowain Smith	1.25	.50
❑ 59 Aaron Brooks	2.00	.75
❑ 60 Joe Horn	1.25	.50
❑ 61 Deuce McAllister	2.50	1.00
❑ 62 Tiki Barber	2.00	.75
❑ 63 Kerry Collins	1.25	.50
❑ 64 Ron Dayne	1.25	.50
❑ 65 Wayne Chrebet	1.25	.50
❑ 66 Curtis Martin	2.00	.75
❑ 67 Vinny Testaverde	1.25	.50
❑ 68 Tim Brown	2.00	.75
❑ 69 Rich Gannon	2.00	.75
❑ 70 Charlie Garner	1.25	.50
❑ 71 Jerry Rice	4.00	1.50
❑ 72 Correll Buckhalter	1.25	.50
❑ 73 Donovan McNabb	2.50	1.00
❑ 74 Duce Staley	2.00	.75
❑ 75 Jerome Bettis	2.00	.75
❑ 76 Kordell Stewart	1.25	.50
❑ 77 Hines Ward	2.00	.75
❑ 78 Isaac Bruce	2.00	.75
❑ 79 Marshall Faulk	2.00	.75
❑ 80 Torry Holt	2.00	.75
❑ 81 Kurt Warner	2.00	.75
❑ 82 Drew Brees	2.00	.75
❑ 83 Tim Dwight	1.25	.50
❑ 84 Doug Flutie	2.00	.75
❑ 85 LaDainian Tomlinson	3.00	1.25
❑ 86 Jeff Garcia	2.00	.75
❑ 87 Garrison Hearst	1.25	.50
❑ 88 Terrell Owens	2.00	.75
❑ 89 Shaun Alexander	2.50	1.00
❑ 90 Trent Dilfer	1.25	.50
❑ 91 Darrell Jackson	1.25	.50
❑ 92 Mike Alstott	2.00	.75
❑ 93 Brad Johnson	1.25	.50
❑ 94 Keyshawn Johnson	2.00	.75
❑ 95 Eddie George	2.00	.75
❑ 96 Derrick Mason	1.25	.50
❑ 97 Steve McNair	2.00	.75
❑ 98 Stephen Davis	1.25	.50
❑ 99 Rod Gardner	1.25	.50
❑ 100 Jacquez Green	.75	.30
❑ 101 Damien Anderson RC	6.00	2.50
❑ 102 Ladell Betts RC	8.00	3.00
❑ 103 Antonio Bryant RC	8.00	3.00
❑ 104 Reche Caldwell RC	8.00	3.00
❑ 105 Kelly Campbell RC	6.00	2.50
❑ 106 David Carr RC	20.00	7.50
❑ 107 Rohan Davey RC	8.00	3.00
❑ 108 Andre Davis RC	6.00	2.50
❑ 109 T.J. Duckett RC	10.00	4.00
❑ 110 DeShaun Foster RC	8.00	3.00
❑ 111 David Garrard RC	8.00	3.00
❑ 112 Lamar Gordon RC	8.00	3.00
❑ 113 William Green RC	8.00	3.00
❑ 114 Joey Harrington RC	12.00	5.00
❑ 115 Kurt Kittner RC	6.00	2.50
❑ 116 Ashley Lelie RC	15.00	6.00
❑ 117 Josh McCown RC	10.00	4.00
❑ 118 Clinton Portis RC	25.00	10.00
❑ 119 Patrick Ramsey RC	10.00	4.00
❑ 120 Antwaan Randle El RC	12.00	5.00
❑ 121 Josh Reed RC	8.00	3.00
❑ 122 Luke Staley RC	6.00	2.50
❑ 123 Donte Stallworth RC	15.00	6.00
❑ 124 Marquise Walker RC	6.00	2.50
❑ 125 Brian Westbrook RC	12.00	5.00
❑ 126 Jason McAddley RC	6.00	2.50
❑ 127 Josh Scobey RC	8.00	3.00
❑ 128 Kahlil Hill RC	6.00	2.50
❑ 129 Ron Johnson RC	6.00	2.50
❑ 130 Julius Peppers RC	15.00	6.00
❑ 131 Adrian Peterson RC	8.00	3.00
❑ 132 Woody Dantzler RC	6.00	2.50
❑ 133 Roy Williams RC	20.00	10.00
❑ 134 Najeh Davenport RC	8.00	3.00
❑ 135 Javon Walker RC	15.00	6.00
❑ 136 Jabar Gaffney RC	8.00	3.00
❑ 137 John Henderson RC	8.00	3.00
❑ 138 Leonard Henry RC	6.00	2.50
❑ 139 Daniel Graham RC	8.00	3.00
❑ 140 Jeremy Shockey RC	25.00	10.00
❑ 141 Ronald Curry RC	8.00	3.00
❑ 142 Napoleon Harris RC	8.00	3.00
❑ 143 Freddie Milons RC	6.00	2.50
❑ 144 Lito Sheppard RC	8.00	3.00
❑ 145 Eric Crouch RC	8.00	3.00
❑ 146 Robert Thomas RC	8.00	3.00
❑ 147 Quentin Jammer RC	8.00	3.00
❑ 148 Maurice Morris RC	8.00	3.00
❑ 149 Travis Stephens RC	6.00	2.50
❑ 150 Cliff Russell RC	6.00	2.50
❑ 151 Dameon Hunter RC	4.00	1.50
❑ 152 Javin Hunter RC	4.00	1.50
❑ 153 Tellis Redmon RC	6.00	2.50
❑ 154 Chester Taylor RC	15.00	6.00
❑ 155 Randy Fasani RC	6.00	2.50
❑ 156 Jamin Elliott RC	4.00	1.50
❑ 157 Chad Hutchinson RC	6.00	2.50
❑ 158 Eddie Drummond RC	6.00	2.50
❑ 159 Craig Nall RC	8.00	3.00
❑ 160 Jarrod Baxter RC	6.00	2.50
❑ 161 Jonathan Wells RC	8.00	3.00
❑ 162 Shaun Hill RC	8.00	3.00
❑ 163 Deion Branch RC	15.00	6.00
❑ 164 J.T. O'Sullivan RC	6.00	2.50
❑ 165 Tim Carter RC	6.00	2.50
❑ 166 Daryl Jones RC	6.00	2.50
❑ 167 Lee Mays RC	10.00	4.00
❑ 168 Seth Burford RC	6.00	2.50
❑ 169 Brandon Doman RC	6.00	2.50
❑ 170 Jerramy Stevens RC	8.00	3.00

1998 Aurora

❑ COMPLETE SET (200)	60.00	30.00
❑ 1 Rob Moore	.60	.25
❑ 2 Jake Plummer	1.00	.40
❑ 3 Frank Sanders	.60	.25
❑ 4 Eric Swann	.40	.15
❑ 5 Jamal Anderson	1.00	.40
❑ 6 Chris Chandler	.60	.25
❑ 7 Byron Hanspard	.40	.15
❑ 8 Terance Mathis	.60	.25
❑ 9 O.J. Santiago	.40	.15
❑ 10 Chuck Smith	.40	.15
❑ 11 Jessie Tuggle	.40	.15
❑ 12 Jay Graham	.40	.15
❑ 13 Jim Harbaugh	.60	.25
❑ 14 Michael Jackson	.40	.15
❑ 15 Pat Johnson RC	1.50	.60
❑ 16 Jermaine Lewis	.60	.25
❑ 17 Errict Rhett	.60	.25
❑ 18 Rod Woodson	.60	.25
❑ 19 Quinn Early	.40	.15
❑ 20 Andre Reed	.60	.25
❑ 21 Antowain Smith	1.00	.40
❑ 22 Bruce Smith	.60	.25
❑ 23 Thurman Thomas	1.00	.40
❑ 24 Ted Washington	.40	.15
❑ 25 Michael Bates	.40	.15
❑ 26 Rae Carruth	.40	.15
❑ 27 Kerry Collins	.60	.25
❑ 28 Fred Lane	.40	.15
❑ 29 Wesley Walls	.60	.25
❑ 30 Edgar Bennett	.40	.15
❑ 31 Curtis Conway	.60	.25
❑ 32 Curtis Enis RC	1.00	.40
❑ 33 Walt Harris	.40	.15
❑ 34 Erik Kramer	.40	.15
❑ 35 Barry Minter	.40	.15
❑ 36 Jeff Blake	.60	.25
❑ 37 Corey Dillon	1.00	.40
❑ 38 Carl Pickens	.60	.25
❑ 39 Darnay Scott	.60	.25
❑ 40 Troy Aikman	2.00	.75
❑ 41 Michael Irvin	1.00	.40
❑ 42 Deion Sanders	1.00	.40
❑ 43 Emmitt Smith	3.00	1.50
❑ 44 Chris Warren	.60	.25
❑ 45 Terrell Davis	1.00	.40
❑ 46 John Elway	4.00	1.50
❑ 47 Brian Griese RC	4.00	1.50
❑ 48 Ed McCaffrey	.60	.25
❑ 49 John Mobley	.40	.15

❑ 50 Shannon Sharpe .60 .25
❑ 51 Neil Smith .60 .25
❑ 52 Rod Smith WR .60 .25
❑ 53 Stephen Boyd .40 .15
❑ 54 Scott Mitchell .60 .25
❑ 55 Herman Moore .60 .25
❑ 56 Johnnie Morton .60 .25
❑ 57 Robert Porcher .40 .15
❑ 58 Barry Sanders 3.00 1.25
❑ 59 Robert Brooks .60 .25
❑ 60 Mark Chmura .60 .25
❑ 61 Brett Favre 4.00 2.00
❑ 62 Antonio Freeman 1.00 .40
❑ 63 Vonnie Holliday RC 1.50 .60
❑ 64 Dorsey Levens 1.00 .40
❑ 65 Ross Verba .40 .15
❑ 66 Reggie White 1.00 .40
❑ 67 Elijah Alexander .40 .15
❑ 68 Ken Dilger .40 .15
❑ 69 Marshall Faulk 1.25 .50
❑ 70 Marvin Harrison 1.00 .40
❑ 71 Peyton Manning RC 20.00 7.50
❑ 72 Bryan Barker .40 .15
❑ 73 Mark Brunell 1.00 .40
❑ 74 Keenan McCardell .60 .25
❑ 75 Jimmy Smith .60 .25
❑ 76 James Stewart .60 .25
❑ 77 Derrick Alexander WR .60 .25
❑ 78 Kimble Anders .60 .25
❑ 79 Donnell Bennett .40 .15
❑ 80 Elvis Grbac .60 .25
❑ 81 Andre Rison .60 .25
❑ 82 Rashaan Shehee RC 1.50 .60
❑ 83 Derrick Thomas 1.00 .40
❑ 84 Karim Abdul-Jabbar 1.00 .40
❑ 85 Trace Armstrong .40 .15
❑ 86 Charles Jordan .40 .15
❑ 87 Dan Marino 4.00 1.50
❑ 88 O.J. McDuffie .60 .25
❑ 89 Zach Thomas 1.00 .40
❑ 90 Cris Carter 1.00 .40
❑ 91 Charles Evans .40 .15
❑ 92 Andrew Glover .40 .15
❑ 93 Brad Johnson 1.00 .40
❑ 94 Randy Moss RC 12.00 5.00
❑ 95 John Randle .60 .25
❑ 96 Jake Reed .60 .25
❑ 97 Robert Smith 1.00 .40
❑ 98 Bruce Armstrong .40 .15
❑ 99 Drew Bledsoe 1.50 .60
❑ 100 Ben Coates .60 .25
❑ 101 Robert Edwards RC 1.50 .60
❑ 102 Terry Glenn 1.00 .40
❑ 103 Willie McGinest .40 .15
❑ 104 Sedrick Shaw .40 .15
❑ 105 Tony Simmons RC 1.50 .60
❑ 106 Chris Slade .40 .15
❑ 107 Billy Joe Hobert .40 .15
❑ 108 Qadry Ismail .60 .25
❑ 109 Heath Shuler .40 .15
❑ 110 Lamar Smith .60 .25
❑ 111 Ray Zellars .40 .15
❑ 112 Tiki Barber 1.00 .40
❑ 113 Chris Calloway .40 .15
❑ 114 Ike Hilliard .60 .25
❑ 115 Joe Jurevicius RC 2.00 .75
❑ 116 Danny Kanell .60 .25
❑ 117 Amani Toomer .60 .25
❑ 118 Charles Way .40 .15
❑ 119 Tyrone Wheatley .60 .25
❑ 120 Wayne Chrebet 1.00 .40
❑ 121 John Elliott .40 .15
❑ 122 Glenn Foley .60 .25
❑ 123 Scott Frost RC .40 .15
❑ 124 Aaron Glenn .40 .15
❑ 125 Keyshawn Johnson 1.00 .40
❑ 126 Curtis Martin 1.00 .40
❑ 127 Vinny Testaverde .60 .25
❑ 128 Tim Brown 1.00 .40
❑ 129 Rickey Dudley .40 .15
❑ 130 Jeff George .60 .25
❑ 131 James Jett .60 .25
❑ 132 Napoleon Kaufman 1.00 .40
❑ 133 Darrell Russell .40 .15
❑ 134 Charles Woodson RC 2.50 1.00
❑ 135 James Darling RC .40 .15
❑ 136 Koy Detmer 1.00 .40
❑ 137 Irving Fryar .60 .25
❑ 138 Charlie Garner .60 .25
❑ 139 Bobby Hoying .60 .25
❑ 140 Chad Lewis .60 .25
❑ 141 Duce Staley 1.25 .50
❑ 142 Kevin Turner .40 .15
❑ 143 Jerome Bettis 1.00 .40
❑ 144 Will Blackwell .40 .15
❑ 145 Mark Bruener .40 .15
❑ 146 Dermontti Dawson .40 .15
❑ 147 Charles Johnson .40 .15
❑ 148 Levon Kirkland .40 .15
❑ 149 Tim Lester .40 .15
❑ 150 Kordell Stewart 1.00 .40
❑ 151 Tony Banks .60 .25
❑ 152 Isaac Bruce 1.00 .40
❑ 153 Robert Holcombe RC 1.50 .60
❑ 154 Eddie Kennison .60 .25
❑ 155 Amp Lee .40 .15
❑ 156 Jerald Moore .40 .15
❑ 157 Charlie Jones .40 .15
❑ 158 Freddie Jones .40 .15
❑ 159 Ryan Leaf RC 2.00 .75
❑ 160 Natrone Means .60 .25
❑ 161 Junior Seau 1.00 .40
❑ 162 Bryan Still .40 .15
❑ 163 Marc Edwards .40 .15
❑ 164 Merton Hanks .40 .15
❑ 165 Garrison Hearst 1.00 .40
❑ 166 Terrell Owens 1.00 .40
❑ 167 Jerry Rice 2.00 .75
❑ 168 J.J. Stokes .60 .25
❑ 169 Bryant Young .40 .15
❑ 170 Steve Young 1.25 .50
❑ 171 Chad Brown .40 .15
❑ 172 Joey Galloway .60 .25
❑ 173 Walter Jones .40 .15
❑ 174 Cortez Kennedy .40 .15
❑ 175 Jon Kitna 1.00 .40
❑ 176 James McKnight 1.00 .40
❑ 177 Warren Moon 1.00 .40
❑ 178 Michael Sinclair .40 .15
❑ 179 Mike Alstott 1.00 .40
❑ 180 Reidel Anthony .60 .25
❑ 181 Derrick Brooks 1.00 .40
❑ 182 Trent Dilfer 1.00 .40
❑ 183 Warrick Dunn 1.00 .40
❑ 184 Hardy Nickerson .40 .15
❑ 185 Warren Sapp .60 .25
❑ 186 Willie Davis .40 .15
❑ 187 Eddie George 1.00 .40
❑ 188 Steve McNair 1.00 .40
❑ 189 Jon Runyan .40 .15
❑ 190 Chris Sanders .40 .15
❑ 191 Frank Wycheck .40 .15
❑ 192 Stephen Alexander RC 1.50 .60
❑ 193 Terry Allen 1.00 .40
❑ 194 Stephen Davis .40 .15
❑ 195 Cris Dishman .40 .15
❑ 196 Gus Frerotte .40 .15
❑ 197 Darrell Green .60 .25
❑ 198 Skip Hicks RC 1.50 .60
❑ 199 Dana Stubblefield .40 .15
❑ 200 Michael Westbrook .60 .25
❑ S1 Warrick Dunn Sample 1.00 .40

1999 Aurora

❑ COMPLETE SET (150) 40.00 15.00
❑ 1 David Boston RC 1.50 .60
❑ 2 Larry Centers .25 .08
❑ 3 Rob Moore .40 .15
❑ 4 Adrian Murrell .40 .15
❑ 5 Jake Plummer .40 .15
❑ 6 Jamal Anderson .60 .25
❑ 7 Chris Chandler .40 .15
❑ 8 Tim Dwight .60 .25
❑ 9 Terance Mathis .40 .15
❑ 10 O.J. Santiago .25 .08
❑ 11 Priest Holmes 1.00 .40
❑ 12 Michael Jackson .25 .08
❑ 13 Jermaine Lewis .40 .15
❑ 14 Ray Lewis .60 .25
❑ 15 Michael McCrary .25 .08
❑ 16 Doug Flutie .60 .25
❑ 17 Eric Moulds .60 .25
❑ 18 Peerless Price RC 1.50 .60
❑ 19 Antowain Smith .60 .25
❑ 20 Bruce Smith .40 .15
❑ 21 Steve Beuerlein .40 .15
❑ 22 Tim Biakabutuka .40 .15
❑ 23 Kevin Greene .25 .08
❑ 24 Muhsin Muhammad .40 .15
❑ 25 Wesley Walls .40 .15
❑ 26 Curtis Conway .40 .15
❑ 27 Bobby Engram .40 .15
❑ 28 Curtis Enis .25 .08
❑ 29 Erik Kramer .25 .08
❑ 30 Cade McNown RC 1.25 .50
❑ 31 Jeff Blake .40 .15
❑ 32 Corey Dillon .60 .25
❑ 33 Carl Pickens .40 .15
❑ 34 Darnay Scott .25 .08
❑ 35 Akili Smith RC 1.25 .50
❑ 36 Tim Couch RC 1.50 .60
❑ 37 Ty Detmer .40 .15
❑ 38 Kevin Johnson RC 1.50 .60
❑ 39 Terry Kirby .25 .08
❑ 40 Troy Aikman 1.25 .50
❑ 41 Michael Irvin .40 .15
❑ 42 Rocket Ismail .40 .15
❑ 43 Deion Sanders .60 .25
❑ 44 Emmitt Smith 1.25 .50
❑ 45 Bubby Brister .25 .08
❑ 46 Terrell Davis .60 .25
❑ 47 Brian Griese .60 .25
❑ 48 Ed McCaffrey .40 .15
❑ 49 Shannon Sharpe .40 .15
❑ 50 Rod Smith .40 .15
❑ 51 Charlie Batch .60 .25
❑ 52 Sedrick Irvin RC .25 .08
❑ 53 Herman Moore .40 .15
❑ 54 Johnnie Morton .40 .15
❑ 55 Barry Sanders 2.00 .75
❑ 56 Robert Brooks .40 .15
❑ 57 Brett Favre 2.00 .75
❑ 58 Antonio Freeman .60 .25
❑ 59 Dorsey Levens .60 .25
❑ 60 Derrick Mayes .25 .08
❑ 61 Marvin Harrison .60 .25
❑ 62 Edgerrin James RC 6.00 2.50
❑ 63 Peyton Manning 2.00 .75
❑ 64 Jerome Pathon .25 .08
❑ 65 Tavian Banks .25 .08
❑ 66 Mark Brunell .60 .25
❑ 67 Keenan McCardell .40 .15
❑ 68 Jimmy Smith .40 .15
❑ 69 Fred Taylor .60 .25
❑ 70 Derrick Alexander .40 .15
❑ 71 Kimble Anders .40 .15
❑ 72 Mike Cloud RC 1.25 .50
❑ 73 Elvis Grbac .40 .15
❑ 74 Andre Rison .40 .15
❑ 75 Karim Abdul-Jabbar .40 .15
❑ 76 James Johnson RC 1.25 .50
❑ 77 Dan Marino 2.00 .75
❑ 78 O.J. McDuffie .40 .15
❑ 79 Lamar Thomas .25 .08
❑ 80 Cris Carter .60 .25
❑ 81 Daunte Culpepper RC 6.00 2.50
❑ 82 Randall Cunningham .60 .25
❑ 83 Randy Moss 1.50 .60
❑ 84 John Randle .40 .15
❑ 85 Robert Smith .60 .25
❑ 86 Drew Bledsoe .75 .30
❑ 87 Ben Coates .40 .15
❑ 88 Kevin Faulk RC 1.50 .60
❑ 89 Terry Glenn .60 .25
❑ 90 Ty Law .40 .15
❑ 91 Cam Cleeland .25 .08
❑ 92 Andre Hastings .25 .08
❑ 93 Billy Joe Hobert .25 .08
❑ 94 Ricky Williams RC 3.00 1.25
❑ 95 Tiki Barber .60 .25

❑ 96 Kent Graham	.25	.08
❑ 97 Ike Hilliard	.25	.08
❑ 98 Charles Way	.25	.08
❑ 99 Wayne Chrebet	.40	.15
❑ 100 Keyshawn Johnson	.60	.25
❑ 101 Curtis Martin	.60	.25
❑ 102 Vinny Testaverde	.40	.15
❑ 103 Dedric Ward	.25	.08
❑ 104 Tim Brown	.60	.25
❑ 105 Rickey Dudley	.25	.08
❑ 106 James Jett	.40	.15
❑ 107 Napoleon Kaufman	.60	.25
❑ 108 Charles Woodson	.60	.25
❑ 109 Jeff Graham	.25	.08
❑ 110 Charles Johnson	.25	.08
❑ 111 Donovan McNabb RC	8.00	3.00
❑ 112 Duce Staley	.60	.25
❑ 113 Jerome Bettis	.60	.25
❑ 114 Troy Edwards RC	1.25	.50
❑ 115 Courtney Hawkins	.25	.08
❑ 116 Kordell Stewart	.40	.15
❑ 117 Amos Zereoue RC	1.50	.60
❑ 118 Isaac Bruce	.60	.25
❑ 119 Marshall Faulk	.75	.30
❑ 120 Joe Germaine RC	1.25	.50
❑ 121 Torry Holt RC	4.00	1.50
❑ 122 Amp Lee	.25	.08
❑ 123 Charlie Jones	.25	.08
❑ 124 Ryan Leaf	.60	.25
❑ 125 Natrone Means	.40	.15
❑ 126 Junior Seau	.60	.25
❑ 127 Garrison Hearst	.40	.15
❑ 128 Terrell Owens	.60	.25
❑ 129 Jerry Rice	1.25	.50
❑ 130 J.J. Stokes	.40	.15
❑ 131 Steve Young	.75	.30
❑ 132 Chad Brown	.25	.08
❑ 133 Joey Galloway	.40	.15
❑ 134 Brock Huard RC	1.50	.60
❑ 135 Jon Kitna	.60	.25
❑ 136 Ricky Watters	.40	.15
❑ 137 Mike Alstott	.60	.25
❑ 138 Reidel Anthony	.40	.15
❑ 139 Trent Dilfer	.40	.15
❑ 140 Warrick Dunn	.60	.25
❑ 141 Jacquez Green	.25	.08
❑ 142 Shaun King RC	1.25	.50
❑ 143 Eddie George	.60	.25
❑ 144 Steve McNair	.60	.25
❑ 145 Yancey Thigpen	.25	.08
❑ 146 Frank Wycheck	.25	.08
❑ 147 Champ Bailey RC	2.00	.75
❑ 148 Skip Hicks	.25	.08
❑ 149 Brad Johnson	.60	.25
❑ 150 Michael Westbrook	.40	.15
❑ AU1 T.Owens AUTO/197	40.00	20.00

2000 Aurora

❑ COMPLETE SET (150)	30.00	12.50
❑ 1 David Boston	.60	.25
❑ 2 Thomas Jones RC	1.50	.60
❑ 3 Rob Moore	.40	.15
❑ 4 Jake Plummer	.40	.15
❑ 5 Frank Sanders	.40	.15
❑ 6 Jamal Anderson	.60	.25
❑ 7 Chris Chandler	.40	.15
❑ 8 Tim Dwight	.60	.25
❑ 9 Doug Johnson RC	1.00	.40
❑ 10 Tony Banks	.40	.15
❑ 11 Qadry Ismail	.40	.15
❑ 12 Jamal Lewis RC	2.50	1.00
❑ 13 Chris Redman RC	.75	.30
❑ 14 Travis Taylor RC	1.00	.40
❑ 15 Doug Flutie	.60	.25
❑ 16 Rob Johnson	.40	.15
❑ 17 Eric Moulds	.60	.25
❑ 18 Peerless Price	.40	.15
❑ 19 Antowain Smith	.40	.15
❑ 20 Steve Beuerlein	.40	.15
❑ 21 Tim Biakabutuka	.40	.15
❑ 22 Patrick Jeffers	.60	.25
❑ 23 Muhsin Muhammad	.40	.15
❑ 24 Curtis Enis	.25	.08
❑ 25 Cade McNown	.25	.08
❑ 26 Marcus Robinson	.60	.25
❑ 27 Dez White RC	1.00	.40
❑ 28 Corey Dillon	.60	.25
❑ 29 Ron Dugans RC	.75	.30
❑ 30 Darnay Scott	.40	.15
❑ 31 Akili Smith	.25	.08
❑ 32 Peter Warrick RC	1.00	.40
❑ 33 Tim Couch	.40	.15
❑ 34 JaJuan Dawson RC	.75	.30
❑ 35 Kevin Johnson	.60	.25
❑ 36 Dennis Northcutt RC	1.00	.40
❑ 37 Travis Prentice RC	1.00	.40
❑ 38 Troy Aikman	1.25	.50
❑ 39 Rocket Ismail	.40	.15
❑ 40 Emmitt Smith	1.25	.50
❑ 41 Jason Tucker	.25	.08
❑ 42 Terrell Davis	.60	.25
❑ 43 Olandis Gary	.60	.25
❑ 44 Brian Griese	.60	.25
❑ 45 Ed McCaffrey	.60	.25
❑ 46 Rod Smith	.40	.15
❑ 47 Charlie Batch	.60	.25
❑ 48 Germane Crowell	.25	.08
❑ 49 Reuben Droughns RC	1.25	.50
❑ 50 Herman Moore	.40	.15
❑ 51 Barry Sanders	1.50	.60
❑ 52 Brett Favre	2.00	.75
❑ 53 Bubba Franks RC	1.00	.40
❑ 54 Antonio Freeman	.60	.25
❑ 55 Dorsey Levens	.40	.15
❑ 56 Bill Schroeder	.40	.15
❑ 57 Marvin Harrison	.60	.25
❑ 58 Edgerrin James	1.00	.40
❑ 59 Peyton Manning	1.50	.60
❑ 60 Terrence Wilkins	.25	.08
❑ 61 Mark Brunell	.60	.25
❑ 62 Keenan McCardell	.40	.15
❑ 63 Jimmy Smith	.40	.15
❑ 64 R.Jay Soward RC	.75	.30
❑ 65 Shyrone Stith RC	1.00	.40
❑ 66 Fred Taylor	.60	.25
❑ 67 Derrick Alexander	.40	.15
❑ 68 Donnell Bennett	.25	.08
❑ 69 Tony Gonzalez	.40	.15
❑ 70 Elvis Grbac	.40	.15
❑ 71 Sylvester Morris RC	.75	.30
❑ 72 Damon Huard	.60	.25
❑ 73 James Johnson	.25	.08
❑ 74 Dan Marino	2.00	.75
❑ 75 Tony Martin	.40	.15
❑ 76 O.J. McDuffie	.40	.15
❑ 77 Quinton Spotwood RC	.75	.30
❑ 78 Cris Carter	.60	.25
❑ 79 Daunte Culpepper	.75	.30
❑ 80 Randy Moss	1.25	.50
❑ 81 Robert Smith	.60	.25
❑ 82 Troy Walters RC	1.00	.40
❑ 83 Drew Bledsoe	.75	.30
❑ 84 Tom Brady RC	15.00	7.50
❑ 85 Kevin Faulk	.40	.15
❑ 86 Terry Glenn	.40	.15
❑ 87 J.R. Redmond RC	.75	.30
❑ 88 Marc Bulger RC	2.00	.75
❑ 89 Sherrod Gideon RC	.75	.30
❑ 90 Keith Poole	.25	.08
❑ 91 Ricky Williams	.60	.25
❑ 92 Kerry Collins	.40	.15
❑ 93 Ron Dayne RC	1.00	.40
❑ 94 Ike Hilliard	.40	.15
❑ 95 Amani Toomer	.25	.08
❑ 96 Wayne Chrebet	.40	.15
❑ 97 Laveranues Coles RC	1.25	.50
❑ 98 Curtis Martin	.60	.25
❑ 99 Chad Pennington RC	2.50	1.00
❑ 100 Vinny Testaverde	.40	.15
❑ 101 Tim Brown	.60	.25
❑ 102 Rich Gannon	.60	.25
❑ 103 Napoleon Kaufman	.40	.15
❑ 104 Jerry Porter RC	1.25	.50
❑ 105 Tyrone Wheatley	.40	.15
❑ 106 Charles Johnson	.40	.15
❑ 107 Donovan McNabb	1.00	.40
❑ 108 Todd Pinkston RC	1.00	.40
❑ 109 Duce Staley	.60	.25
❑ 110 Jerome Bettis	.60	.25
❑ 111 Plaxico Burress RC	2.00	.75
❑ 112 Troy Edwards	.25	.08
❑ 113 Richard Huntley	.25	.08
❑ 114 Tee Martin RC	1.00	.40
❑ 115 Kordell Stewart	.40	.15
❑ 116 Isaac Bruce	.60	.25
❑ 117 Trung Canidate RC	.75	.30
❑ 118 Marshall Faulk	.75	.30
❑ 119 Torry Holt	.60	.25
❑ 120 Kurt Warner	1.25	.50
❑ 121 Jermaine Fazande	.25	.08
❑ 122 Trevor Gaylor RC	.75	.30
❑ 123 Jim Harbaugh	.40	.15
❑ 124 Junior Seau	.60	.25
❑ 125 Giovanni Carmazzi RC	.75	.30
❑ 126 Charlie Garner	.40	.15
❑ 127 Terrell Owens	.60	.25
❑ 128 Jerry Rice	1.25	.50
❑ 129 J.J. Stokes	.40	.15
❑ 130 Steve Young	.75	.30
❑ 131 Shaun Alexander RC	5.00	2.00
❑ 132 Christian Fauria	.25	.08
❑ 133 Jon Kitna	.60	.25
❑ 134 Derrick Mayes	.40	.15
❑ 135 Ricky Watters	.40	.15
❑ 136 Mike Alstott	.60	.25
❑ 137 Warrick Dunn	.60	.25
❑ 138 Jacquez Green	.25	.08
❑ 139 Joe Hamilton RC	.75	.30
❑ 140 Shaun King	.25	.08
❑ 141 Eddie George	.60	.25
❑ 142 Jevon Kearse	.60	.25
❑ 143 Steve McNair	.60	.25
❑ 144 Yancey Thigpen	.25	.08
❑ 145 Frank Wycheck	.25	.08
❑ 146 Albert Connell	.25	.08
❑ 147 Stephen Davis	.60	.25
❑ 148 Todd Husak RC	1.00	.40
❑ 149 Brad Johnson	.60	.25
❑ 150 Michael Westbrook	.40	.15
❑ S1 Jon Kitna Sample	1.00	.40

2004 Bazooka

❑ COMPLETE SET (220)	50.00	20.00
❑ 1 Peyton Manning	1.25	.50
❑ 2 Rod Gardner	.50	.20
❑ 3 Marc Bulger	.75	.30
❑ 4 Champ Bailey	.50	.20
❑ 5 Moe Williams	.40	.15
❑ 6 Andre' Davis	.40	.15
❑ 7 Corey Dillon	.50	.20
❑ 8 Trent Green	.50	.20
❑ 9 Daunte Culpepper	.75	.30
❑ 10 Chad Pennington	.75	.30
❑ 11 Hines Ward	.75	.30
❑ 12 Tim Brown	.75	.30
❑ 13 Jerome Pathon	.40	.15
❑ 14 Drew Brees	.75	.30
❑ 15 Eddie George	.50	.20
❑ 16 Duce Staley	.50	.20
❑ 17 Marques Tuiasosopo	.50	.20
❑ 18 Willis McGahee	.75	.30
❑ 19 T.J. Duckett	.50	.20
❑ 20 Brian Urlacher	1.00	.40

❑	21	Ashley Lelie	.50	.20
❑	22	Robert Ferguson	.40	.15
❑	23	Tai Streets	.40	.15
❑	24	Junior Seau	.75	.30
❑	25	Priest Holmes	1.00	.40
❑	26	Ty Law	.50	.20
❑	27	Correll Buckhalter	.50	.20
❑	28	Plaxico Burress	.50	.20
❑	29	Brad Johnson	.50	.20
❑	30	Shaun Alexander	.75	.30
❑	31	Mark Brunell	.50	.20
❑	32	Julian Peterson	.40	.15
❑	33	Marcel Shipp	.50	.20
❑	34	Kyle Boller	.75	.30
❑	35	Rudi Johnson	.50	.20
❑	36	Quincy Carter	.50	.20
❑	37	Jabar Gaffney	.50	.20
❑	38	Reggie Wayne	.50	.20
❑	39	Deion Branch	.75	.30
❑	40	Terrell Owens	.75	.30
❑	41	Chris Brown	.75	.30
❑	42	Bobby Engram	.40	.15
❑	43	Josh Reed	.40	.15
❑	44	Thomas Jones	.50	.20
❑	45	Stephen Davis	.50	.20
❑	46	Mike Anderson	.50	.20
❑	47	Javon Walker	.50	.20
❑	48	Edgerrin James	.75	.30
❑	49	Randy McMichael	.40	.15
❑	50	Deuce McAllister	.75	.30
❑	51	Nate Burleson	.75	.30
❑	52	Jevon Kearse	.50	.20
❑	53	Jay Fiedler	.40	.15
❑	54	Patrick Ramsey	.50	.20
❑	55	Brian Westbrook	.50	.20
❑	56	Tyrone Calico	.50	.20
❑	57	Alge Crumpler	.50	.20
❑	58	Josh McCown	.50	.20
❑	59	Quincy Morgan	.50	.20
❑	60	Jeff Garcia	.75	.30
❑	61	Garrison Hearst	.50	.20
❑	62	Chad Johnson	.75	.30
❑	63	Byron Leftwich	1.00	.40
❑	64	Donald Driver	.50	.20
❑	65	Ricky Williams	.75	.30
❑	66	Todd Pinkston	.40	.15
❑	67	Amani Toomer	.50	.20
❑	68	David Givens	.50	.20
❑	69	Jerome Bettis	.75	.30
❑	70	Derrick Mason	.50	.20
❑	71	Darrell Jackson	.50	.20
❑	72	Kassim Osgood	.40	.15
❑	73	Todd Heap	.50	.20
❑	74	Warrick Dunn	.50	.20
❑	75	Brett Favre	2.00	.75
❑	76	Chris Chambers	.50	.20
❑	77	Fred Taylor	.50	.20
❑	78	Charles Rogers	.50	.20
❑	79	Onterrio Smith	.50	.20
❑	80	Joe Horn	.50	.20
❑	81	Justin McCareins	.40	.15
❑	82	Ike Hilliard	.40	.15
❑	83	Kevan Barlow	.50	.20
❑	84	Charlie Garner	.50	.20
❑	85	Anquan Boldin	.75	.30
❑	86	Anthony Thomas	.50	.20
❑	87	Julius Peppers	.75	.30
❑	88	Dat Nguyen	.40	.15
❑	89	Peerless Price	.50	.20
❑	90	Randy Moss	1.00	.40
❑	91	Jamie Sharper	.40	.15
❑	92	Travis Henry	.50	.20
❑	93	Terrell Suggs	.50	.20
❑	94	Joey Galloway	.50	.20
❑	95	Torry Holt	.75	.30
❑	96	Freddie Mitchell	.50	.20
❑	97	Jerry Porter	.50	.20
❑	98	Dwight Freeney	.50	.20
❑	99	Joey Harrington	.75	.30
❑	100	Michael Vick	1.50	.60
❑	101	Kelley Washington	.40	.15
❑	102	Marty Booker	.50	.20
❑	103	Tim Rattay	.40	.15
❑	104	Derrick Brooks	.50	.20
❑	105	Laveranues Coles	.50	.20
❑	106	Ray Lewis	.75	.30
❑	107	Jon Kitna	.50	.20
❑	108	Terry Glenn	.40	.15
❑	109	Steve Smith	.75	.30
❑	110	Ahman Green	.75	.30
❑	111	Andre Johnson	.75	.30
❑	112	Dallas Clark	.50	.20
❑	113	Kevin Faulk	.40	.15
❑	114	Michael Bennett	.50	.20
❑	115	Tony Gonzalez	.50	.20
❑	116	Michael Strahan	.50	.20
❑	117	Tommy Maddox	.50	.20
❑	118	Isaac Bruce	.50	.20
❑	119	Brandon Lloyd	.50	.20
❑	120	Steve McNair	.75	.30
❑	121	Keith Brooking	.40	.15
❑	122	Drew Bledsoe	.75	.30
❑	123	Peter Warrick	.50	.20
❑	124	Antonio Bryant	.50	.20
❑	125	Clinton Portis	.75	.30
❑	126	Kelly Holcomb	.50	.20
❑	127	Jake Delhomme	.75	.30
❑	128	Rod Smith	.50	.20
❑	129	Lee Suggs	.75	.30
❑	130	Domanick Davis	.75	.30
❑	131	Carson Palmer	1.00	.40
❑	132	Kerry Collins	.50	.20
❑	133	Teyo Johnson	.40	.15
❑	134	Curtis Martin	.75	.30
❑	135	Matt Hasselbeck	.50	.20
❑	136	Cedrick Wilson	.40	.15
❑	137	Eric Moulds	.50	.20
❑	138	Keyshawn Johnson	.50	.20
❑	139	Dante Hall	.75	.30
❑	140	Jamal Lewis	.75	.30
❑	141	Kelly Campbell	.40	.15
❑	142	Jeremy Shockey	.75	.30
❑	143	Jerry Rice	1.50	.60
❑	144	Kurt Warner	.75	.30
❑	145	Jake Plummer	.50	.20
❑	146	Keenan McCardell	.40	.15
❑	147	Jimmy Smith	.50	.20
❑	148	Zach Thomas	.75	.30
❑	149	Eddie Kennison	.40	.15
❑	150	Tom Brady	2.00	.75
❑	151	Donte' Stallworth	.50	.20
❑	152	John Abraham	.40	.15
❑	153	Koren Robinson	.50	.20
❑	154	Rex Grossman	.75	.30
❑	155	Donovan McNabb	1.00	.40
❑	156	David Carr	.75	.30
❑	157	David Boston	.50	.20
❑	158	Tiki Barber	.75	.30
❑	159	Santana Moss	.50	.20
❑	160	LaDainian Tomlinson	1.25	.50
❑	161	Justin Fargas	.50	.20
❑	162	Troy Brown	.50	.20
❑	163	Marshall Faulk	.75	.30
❑	164	Aaron Brooks	.50	.20
❑	165	Marvin Harrison	.75	.30
❑	166	Kevin Jones RC	4.00	1.50
❑	167	Michael Clayton RC	3.00	1.25
❑	168	Bernard Berrian RC	2.00	.75
❑	169	Ben Watson RC	1.50	.60
❑	170	Philip Rivers RC	5.00	2.00
❑	171	Vince Wilfork RC	1.50	.60
❑	172	Jason Babin RC	1.50	.60
❑	173	Marcus Tubbs RC	1.50	.60
❑	174	Sean Taylor RC	1.50	.60
❑	175	Larry Fitzgerald RC	5.00	2.00
❑	176	Craig Krenzel RC	1.50	.60
❑	177	Cedric Cobbs RC	1.50	.60
❑	178	Lee Evans RC	2.00	.75
❑	179	Johnnie Morant RC	1.50	.60
❑	180	Kellen Winslow RC	3.00	1.25
❑	181	Mewelde Moore RC	1.50	.60
❑	182	Carlos Francis RC	1.25	.50
❑	183	Josh Harris RC	1.50	.60
❑	184	Julius Jones RC	5.00	2.00
❑	185	Reggie Williams RC	2.00	.75
❑	186	DeAngelo Hall RC	2.00	.75
❑	187	D.J. Williams RC	1.50	.60
❑	188	Cody Pickett RC	1.50	.60
❑	189	Dunta Robinson RC	1.50	.60
❑	190	J.P. Losman RC	3.00	1.25
❑	191	Jonathan Vilma RC	1.50	.60
❑	192	Jerricho Cotchery RC	1.50	.60
❑	193	Keary Colbert RC	2.00	.75
❑	194	Ben Troupe RC	1.50	.60
❑	195	Drew Henson RC	1.50	.60
❑	196	Chris Gamble RC	1.50	.60
❑	197	Samie Parker RC	1.50	.60
❑	198	Tatum Bell RC	3.00	1.25
❑	199	Robert Gallery RC	1.50	.60
❑	200	Eli Manning RC	12.00	5.00
❑	201	Ahmad Carroll RC	1.50	.60
❑	202	Devery Henderson RC	1.25	.50
❑	203	Matt Schaub RC	5.00	2.00
❑	204	Greg Jones RC	1.50	.60
❑	205	Roy Williams RC	4.00	1.50
❑	206	Tommie Harris RC	1.50	.60
❑	207	Jeff Smoker RC	1.50	.60
❑	208	Kenechi Udeze RC	1.50	.60
❑	209	Derrick Hamilton RC	1.25	.50
❑	210	Ben Roethlisberger RC	20.00	10.00
❑	211	Darius Watts RC	1.50	.60
❑	212	John Navarre RC	1.50	.60
❑	213	Ernest Wilford RC	1.50	.60
❑	214	Rashaun Woods RC	1.50	.60
❑	215	Steven Jackson RC	5.00	2.00
❑	216	Michael Jenkins RC	1.50	.60
❑	217	Will Smith RC	1.50	.60
❑	218	Devard Darling RC	1.50	.60
❑	219	Chris Perry RC	2.50	1.00
❑	220	Luke McCown RC	1.50	.60

2005 Bazooka

❑		COMPLETE SET (220)	50.00	20.00
❑		COMP.SET w/o RC's (165)	25.00	10.00
❑	1	Willis McGahee	.75	.30
❑	2	Aaron Brooks	.50	.20
❑	3	Allen Rossum	.40	.15
❑	4	Brett Favre	2.00	.75
❑	5	Donovan McNabb	1.00	.40
❑	6	Torry Holt	.75	.30
❑	7	Michael Vick	1.25	.50
❑	8	David Carr	.75	.30
❑	9	Eric Moulds	.50	.20
❑	10	Chad Pennington	.75	.30
❑	11	Larry Fitzgerald	.75	.30
❑	12	Tom Brady	2.00	.75
❑	13	Derrick Brooks	.50	.20
❑	14	Brandon Stokley	.50	.20
❑	15	Justin McCareins	.40	.15
❑	16	Champ Bailey	.50	.20
❑	17	Jake Delhomme	.75	.30
❑	18	Peyton Manning	1.25	.50
❑	19	Keyshawn Johnson	.50	.20
❑	20	Daunte Culpepper	.75	.30
❑	21	Chester Taylor	.50	.20
❑	22	Kurt Warner	.50	.20
❑	23	Cedrick Wilson	.40	.15
❑	24	Brian Westbrook	.50	.20
❑	25	Rodney Harrison	.50	.20
❑	26	Clinton Portis	.75	.30
❑	27	A.J. Feeley	.50	.20
❑	28	Curtis Martin	.75	.30
❑	29	Chris Perry	.50	.20
❑	30	Randy Moss	.75	.30
❑	31	Darrell Jackson	.50	.20
❑	32	Edgerrin James	.75	.30
❑	33	Ben Roethlisberger	2.00	.75
❑	34	Kevin Jones	.75	.30
❑	35	LaMont Jordan	.75	.30
❑	36	Jerome Bettis	.75	.30
❑	37	Ahman Green	.75	.30
❑	38	Tyrone Calico	.50	.20
❑	39	Anquan Boldin	.50	.20
❑	40	Dante Hall	.50	.20
❑	41	Todd Heap	.50	.20
❑	42	Corey Dillon	.50	.20
❑	43	Julius Peppers	.50	.20
❑	44	Antonio Bryant	.40	.15
❑	45	Dunta Robinson	.50	.20
❑	46	Michael Pittman	.40	.15

❑ 47 Billy Volek .50 .20
❑ 48 Jimmy Smith .50 .20
❑ 49 Carson Palmer .75 .30
❑ 50 Derrick Blaylock .40 .15
❑ 51 Deuce McAllister .75 .30
❑ 52 Ray Lewis .75 .30
❑ 53 Chad Johnson .75 .30
❑ 54 Zach Thomas .75 .30
❑ 55 Julius Jones 1.00 .40
❑ 56 D.J. Williams .40 .15
❑ 57 Stephen Davis .50 .20
❑ 58 Greg Jones .40 .15
❑ 59 J.P. Losman .75 .30
❑ 60 Trent Green .50 .20
❑ 61 Drew Bennett .50 .20
❑ 62 Joe Horn .50 .20
❑ 63 Mewelde Moore .50 .20
❑ 64 Alge Crumpler .50 .20
❑ 65 Javon Walker .50 .20
❑ 66 Jake Plummer .50 .20
❑ 67 Aaron Stecker .40 .15
❑ 68 Keary Colbert .50 .20
❑ 69 Joey Harrington .75 .30
❑ 70 Brian Urlacher .75 .30
❑ 71 Jeremy Shockey .75 .30
❑ 72 Duce Staley .50 .20
❑ 73 Tim Rattay .40 .15
❑ 74 Jerry Porter .50 .20
❑ 75 Steven Jackson 1.00 .40
❑ 76 David Givens .50 .20
❑ 77 Byron Leftwich .75 .30
❑ 78 T.J. Duckett .50 .20
❑ 79 Jason Witten .50 .20
❑ 80 Andre Johnson .50 .20
❑ 81 Amani Toomer .50 .20
❑ 82 Kellen Winslow .75 .30
❑ 83 Kyle Boller .50 .20
❑ 84 Santana Moss .50 .20
❑ 85 Antonio Gates .75 .30
❑ 86 Lee Evans .50 .20
❑ 87 Larry Johnson .75 .30
❑ 88 Plaxico Burress .50 .20
❑ 89 Reuben Droughns .50 .20
❑ 90 Eli Manning 1.50 .60
❑ 91 Lito Sheppard .40 .15
❑ 92 DeAngelo Hall .50 .20
❑ 93 Josh McCown .50 .20
❑ 94 Eric Parker .40 .15
❑ 95 Drew Brees .75 .30
❑ 96 Fred Taylor .50 .20
❑ 97 Jonathan Vilma .50 .20
❑ 98 Michael Strahan .50 .20
❑ 99 Dwight Freeney .50 .20
❑ 100 Kerry Collins .50 .20
❑ 101 Hines Ward .75 .30
❑ 102 Lee Suggs .50 .20
❑ 103 Luke McCown .40 .15
❑ 104 Laveranues Coles .50 .20
❑ 105 LaDainian Tomlinson 1.00 .40
❑ 106 Jeff Garcia .50 .20
❑ 107 Michael Clayton .75 .30
❑ 108 DeShaun Foster .50 .20
❑ 109 Rex Grossman .50 .20
❑ 110 Priest Holmes .75 .30
❑ 111 Roy Williams WR .75 .30
❑ 112 Drew Henson .50 .20
❑ 113 Derrick Mason .50 .20
❑ 114 Michael Bennett .50 .20
❑ 115 Chris Simms .50 .20
❑ 116 Isaac Bruce .50 .20
❑ 117 Deion Branch .50 .20
❑ 118 Rudi Johnson .50 .20
❑ 119 Nate Burleson .50 .20
❑ 120 Warrick Dunn .50 .20
❑ 121 Brian Griese .50 .20
❑ 122 T.J. Houshmandzadeh .40 .15
❑ 123 Jamaar Taylor .40 .15
❑ 124 Drew Bledsoe .75 .30
❑ 125 Najeh Davenport .40 .15
❑ 126 Charles Rogers .50 .20
❑ 127 Ronald Curry .50 .20
❑ 128 Chris Brown .50 .20
❑ 129 Doug Gabriel .40 .15
❑ 130 Todd Pinkston .40 .15
❑ 131 Marc Bulger .75 .30
❑ 132 Marshall Faulk .75 .30
❑ 133 Marvin Harrison .75 .30
❑ 134 Matt Hasselbeck .50 .20
❑ 135 Tiki Barber .75 .30
❑ 136 Muhsin Muhammad .50 .20
❑ 137 Kevan Barlow .50 .20
❑ 138 Chris Chambers .50 .20
❑ 139 Donald Driver .50 .20
❑ 140 Jamal Lewis .75 .30
❑ 141 Rashaun Woods .50 .20
❑ 142 Steve McNair .75 .30
❑ 143 Reggie Wayne .50 .20
❑ 144 Jevon Kearse .50 .20
❑ 145 Domanick Davis .50 .20
❑ 146 Donte Stallworth .50 .20
❑ 147 Chris Gamble .50 .20
❑ 148 Philip Rivers .75 .30
❑ 149 Sean Taylor .50 .20
❑ 150 Antwaan Randle El .50 .20
❑ 151 Koren Robinson .50 .20
❑ 152 Tatum Bell .50 .20
❑ 153 Tony Gonzalez .50 .20
❑ 154 Reggie Williams .50 .20
❑ 155 Onterrio Smith .50 .20
❑ 156 Patrick Ramsey .50 .20
❑ 157 Thomas Jones .50 .20
❑ 158 Michael Jenkins .50 .20
❑ 159 Rod Smith .50 .20
❑ 160 Trent Dilfer .50 .20
❑ 161 Randy McMichael .40 .15
❑ 162 Terrell Owens .75 .30
❑ 163 Travis Henry .50 .20
❑ 164 Travis Taylor .40 .15
❑ 165 Shaun Alexander 1.00 .40
❑ 166 J.J. Arrington RC 2.00 .75
❑ 167 Cedric Benson RC 3.00 1.25
❑ 168 Carlos Rogers RC 2.00 .75
❑ 169 Troy Williamson RC 3.00 1.25
❑ 170 Ronnie Brown RC 6.00 2.50
❑ 171 Jason Campbell RC 2.50 1.00
❑ 172 Alvin Pearman RC 1.50 .60
❑ 173 Reggie Brown RC 1.50 .60
❑ 174 Lionel Gates RC 1.25 .50
❑ 175 Derek Anderson RC 1.50 .60
❑ 176 Craphonso Thorpe RC 1.25 .50
❑ 177 Frank Gore RC 3.00 1.25
❑ 178 David Greene RC 1.50 .60
❑ 179 Vincent Jackson RC 1.50 .60
❑ 180 Adam Jones RC 1.50 .60
❑ 181 Derrick Johnson RC 2.50 1.00
❑ 182 Stefan LeFors RC 1.50 .60
❑ 183 Heath Miller RC 4.00 1.50
❑ 184 Ryan Moats RC 1.50 .60
❑ 185 Vernand Morency RC 1.50 .60
❑ 186 Brandon Jacobs RC 2.00 .75
❑ 187 Kyle Orton RC 2.50 1.00
❑ 188 Roscoe Parrish RC 1.50 .60
❑ 189 Courtney Roby RC 1.50 .60
❑ 190 Aaron Rodgers RC 6.00 2.50
❑ 191 Marion Barber RC 2.50 1.00
❑ 192 Antrel Rolle RC 1.50 .60
❑ 193 Airese Currie RC 1.50 .60
❑ 194 Alex Smith QB RC 6.00 2.50
❑ 195 Andrew Walter RC 2.50 1.00
❑ 196 Roddy White RC 1.50 .60
❑ 197 Cadillac Williams RC 5.00 2.00
❑ 198 Mike Williams 3.00 1.25
❑ 199 Rasheed Marshall RC 1.50 .60
❑ 200 Charlie Frye RC 3.00 1.25
❑ 201 Justin Miller RC 1.25 .50
❑ 202 Fabian Washington RC 1.50 .60
❑ 203 Mark Bradley RC 1.50 .60
❑ 204 Adrian McPherson RC 1.50 .60
❑ 205 Marcus Spears RC 1.50 .60
❑ 206 Matt Jones RC 4.00 1.50
❑ 207 Darren Sproles RC 1.50 .60
❑ 208 Eric Shelton RC 1.50 .60
❑ 209 Fred Gibson RC 1.25 .50
❑ 210 Anthony Davis RC 1.25 .50
❑ 211 Mark Clayton RC 2.00 .75
❑ 212 Braylon Edwards RC 5.00 2.00
❑ 213 Ciatrick Fason RC 1.50 .60
❑ 214 DeMarcus Ware RC 2.50 1.00
❑ 215 Dan Orlovsky RC 2.00 .75
❑ 216 Maurice Clarett 1.50 .60
❑ 217 Erasmus James RC 1.50 .60
❑ 218 Chris Henry RC 1.50 .60
❑ 219 Jerome Mathis RC 1.50 .60
❑ 220 Terrence Murphy RC 1.50 .60

1948 Bowman

❑ COMPLETE SET (108) 6000.00 4500.00
❑ COMMON 1/4/7/-/-/- 20.00 12.00

❑ COMMON 2/5/8/-/-/- 25.00 15.00
❑ COMMON SP 3/6/9 /-/-/- 100.00 65.00
❑ WRAPPER (1-CENT) 250.00 150.00
❑ 1 Joe Tereshinski RC ! 150.00 80.00
❑ 2 Larry Olsonoski 25.00 15.00
❑ 3 Johnny Lujack RC SP 350.00 250.00
❑ 4 Ray Poole 20.00 12.00
❑ 5 Bill DeCorrevont RC 25.00 15.00
❑ 6 Paul Briggs SP 100.00 65.00
❑ 7 Steve Van Buren RC 200.00 125.00
❑ 8 Kenny Washington RC 60.00 40.00
❑ 9 Nolan Luhn SP 100.00 65.00
❑ 10 Chris Iversen 20.00 12.00
❑ 11 Jack Wiley 25.00 15.00
❑ 12 Charley Conerly RC SP 350.00 250.00
❑ 13 Hugh Taylor RC 25.00 15.00
❑ 14 Frank Seno 25.00 15.00
❑ 15 Gil Bouley SP 100.00 65.00
❑ 16 Tommy Thompson RC 35.00 20.00
❑ 17 Charley Trippi RC 100.00 60.00
❑ 18 Vince Banonis SP 100.00 65.00
❑ 19 Art Faircloth 20.00 12.00
❑ 20 Clyde Goodnight 25.00 15.00
❑ 21 Bill Chipley SP 100.00 65.00
❑ 22 Sammy Baugh RC 500.00 350.00
❑ 23 Don Kindt 25.00 15.00
❑ 24 John Koniszewski SP 100.00 65.00
❑ 25 Pat McHugh 20.00 12.00
❑ 26 Bob Waterfield RC 200.00 125.00
❑ 27 Tony Compagno SP 100.00 65.00
❑ 28 Paul Governali RC 25.00 15.00
❑ 29 Pat Harder RC 60.00 40.00
❑ 30 Vic Lindskog SP 100.00 65.00
❑ 31 Salvatore Rosato 20.00 12.00
❑ 32 John Mastrangelo 25.00 15.00
❑ 33 Fred Gehrke SP 100.00 65.00
❑ 34 Bosh Pritchard 20.00 12.00
❑ 35 Mike Micka 25.00 15.00
❑ 36 Bulldog Turner RC SP 250.00 160.00
❑ 37 Len Younce 20.00 12.00
❑ 38 Pat West 25.00 15.00
❑ 39 Russ Thomas SP 100.00 65.00
❑ 40 James Peebles 20.00 12.00
❑ 41 Bob Skoglund 25.00 15.00
❑ 42 Walt Stickle SP 100.00 65.00
❑ 43 Whitey Wistert RC 25.00 15.00
❑ 44 Paul Christman RC 60.00 40.00
❑ 45 Jay Rhodemyre SP 100.00 65.00
❑ 46 Tony Minisi 20.00 12.00
❑ 47 Bob Mann 25.00 15.00
❑ 48 Mal Kutner RC SP 110.00 70.00
❑ 49 Dick Poillon 20.00 12.00
❑ 50 Charles Cherundolo 25.00 15.00
❑ 51 Gerald Cowhig SP 100.00 65.00
❑ 52 Neill Armstrong RC 25.00 15.00
❑ 53 Frank Maznicki 25.00 15.00
❑ 54 John Sanchez SP 100.00 65.00
❑ 55 Frank Reagan 20.00 12.00
❑ 56 Jim Hardy 25.00 15.00
❑ 57 John Badaczewski SP 100.00 65.00
❑ 58 Robert Nussbaumer 20.00 12.00
❑ 59 Marvin Pregulman 25.00 15.00
❑ 60 Elbie Nickel RC SP 125.00 75.00
❑ 61 Alex Wojciechowicz RC 150.00 90.00
❑ 62 Walt Schlinkman 25.00 15.00
❑ 63 Pete Pihos RC SP 225.00 150.00
❑ 64 Joseph Sulaitis 20.00 12.00
❑ 65 Mike Holovak RC 50.00 30.00
❑ 66 Cy Souders SP RC 100.00 65.00
❑ 67 Paul McKee 20.00 12.00
❑ 68 Bill Moore 25.00 15.00
❑ 69 Frank Minini SP 100.00 65.00
❑ 70 Jack Ferrante 20.00 12.00
❑ 71 Les Horvath RC 50.00 35.00

❑ 72 Ted Fritsch Sr. RC SP 110.00 70.00
❑ 73 Tex Coulter RC 25.00 15.00
❑ 74 Boley Dancewicz 25.00 15.00
❑ 75 Dante Mangani SP 100.00 65.00
❑ 76 James Hefti 20.00 12.00
❑ 77 Paul Sarringhaus 25.00 15.00
❑ 78 Joe Scott SP 100.00 65.00
❑ 79 Bucko Kilroy RC 25.00 15.00
❑ 80 Bill Dudley RC 125.00 75.00
❑ 81 Mar.Goldberg RC SP 110.00 70.00
❑ 82 John Cannady 20.00 12.00
❑ 83 Perry Moss 25.00 15.00
❑ 84 Harold Crisler RC SP 110.00 70.00
❑ 85 Bill Gray 20.00 12.00
❑ 86 John Clement 25.00 15.00
❑ 87 Dan Sandifer SP 100.00 65.00
❑ 88 Ben Kish 20.00 12.00
❑ 89 Herbert Banta 25.00 15.00
❑ 90 Bill Garnaas SP 100.00 65.00
❑ 91 Jim White RC 20.00 12.00
❑ 92 Frank Barzilauskas 25.00 15.00
❑ 93 Vic Sears SP 100.00 65.00
❑ 94 John Adams 20.00 12.00
❑ 95 George McAfee RC 150.00 90.00
❑ 96 Ralph Heywood SP 100.00 65.00
❑ 97 Joe Muha 20.00 12.00
❑ 98 Fred Enke 25.00 15.00
❑ 99 Harry Gilmer RC SP 175.00 100.00
❑ 100 Bill Miklich 20.00 12.00
❑ 101 Joe Gottlieb 25.00 15.00
❑ 102 Bud Angsman RC SP 110.00 70.00
❑ 103 Tom Farmer 20.00 12.00
❑ 104 Bruce Smith RC 75.00 40.00
❑ 105 Bob Cifers SP 100.00 65.00
❑ 106 Ernie Steele 20.00 12.00
❑ 107 Sid Luckman RC 300.00 175.00
❑ 108 Buford Ray RC SP ! 400.00 250.00

1950 Bowman

❑ COMPLETE SET (144) 4000.00 3000.00
❑ WRAPPER (5-CENT) 175.00 100.00
❑ 1 Doak Walker ! 250.00 150.00
❑ 2 John Greene 25.00 18.00
❑ 3 Bob Nowasky 25.00 18.00
❑ 4 Jonathan Jenkins 25.00 18.00
❑ 5 Y.A.Tittle RC 250.00 175.00
❑ 6 Lou Groza RC 175.00 100.00
❑ 7 Alex Agase RC 30.00 20.00
❑ 8 Mac Speedie RC 50.00 30.00
❑ 9 Tony Canadeo RC 90.00 50.00
❑ 10 Larry Craig 30.00 20.00
❑ 11 Ted Fritsch Sr. 30.00 20.00
❑ 12 Joe Golding 25.00 18.00
❑ 13 Martin Ruby 25.00 18.00
❑ 14 George Taliaferro 30.00 20.00
❑ 15 Tank Younger RC 50.00 30.00
❑ 16 Glenn Davis RC 125.00 75.00
❑ 17 Bob Waterfield 125.00 75.00
❑ 18 Val Jansante 25.00 18.00
❑ 19 Joe Geri 25.00 18.00
❑ 20 Jerry Nuzum 25.00 18.00
❑ 21 Elmer Bud Angsman 25.00 18.00
❑ 22 Billy Dewell 25.00 18.00
❑ 23 Steve Van Buren 90.00 50.00
❑ 24 Cliff Patton 25.00 18.00
❑ 25 Bosh Pritchard 25.00 18.00
❑ 26 Johnny Lujack 80.00 50.00
❑ 27 Sid Luckman 125.00 75.00
❑ 28 Bulldog Turner 60.00 35.00
❑ 29 Bill Dudley 60.00 35.00
❑ 30 Hugh Taylor 30.00 20.00
❑ 31 George Thomas 25.00 18.00
❑ 32 Ray Poole 25.00 18.00
❑ 33 Travis Tidwell 25.00 18.00
❑ 34 Gail Bruce 25.00 18.00
❑ 35 Joe Perry RC 200.00 125.00
❑ 36 Frankie Albert RC 40.00 25.00
❑ 37 Bobby Layne 200.00 125.00
❑ 38 Leon Hart 40.00 25.00
❑ 39 B.Hoernschemeyer RC 30.00 20.00
❑ 40 Dick Barwegan RC 25.00 18.00
❑ 41 Adrian Burk RC 30.00 20.00
❑ 42 Barry French 25.00 18.00
❑ 43 Marion Motley RC 250.00 150.00
❑ 44 Jim Martin 30.00 20.00
❑ 45 Otto Graham RC 450.00 300.00
❑ 46 Al Baldwin 25.00 18.00
❑ 47 Larry Coutre 30.00 20.00
❑ 48 John Rauch 25.00 18.00
❑ 49 Sam Tamburo 25.00 18.00
❑ 50 Mike Swistowicz 25.00 18.00
❑ 51 Tom Fears RC 150.00 90.00
❑ 52 Elroy Hirsch RC 225.00 125.00
❑ 53 Dick Huffman 25.00 18.00
❑ 54 Bob Gage 25.00 18.00
❑ 55 Buddy Tinsley 25.00 18.00
❑ 56 Bill Blackburn 25.00 18.00
❑ 57 John Cochran 25.00 18.00
❑ 58 Bill Fischer 25.00 18.00
❑ 59 Whitey Wistert 30.00 20.00
❑ 60 Clyde Scott 25.00 18.00
❑ 61 Walter Barnes 25.00 18.00
❑ 62 Bob Perina 25.00 18.00
❑ 63 Bill Wightkin 25.00 18.00
❑ 64 Bob Goode 25.00 18.00
❑ 65 Al Demao 25.00 18.00
❑ 66 Harry Gilmer 30.00 20.00
❑ 67 Bill Austin 25.00 18.00
❑ 68 Joe Scott 25.00 18.00
❑ 69 Tex Coulter 30.00 20.00
❑ 70 Paul Salata 25.00 18.00
❑ 71 Emil Sitko RC 30.00 20.00
❑ 72 Bill Johnson C 25.00 18.00
❑ 73 Don Doll RC 25.00 18.00
❑ 74 Dan Sandifer 25.00 18.00
❑ 75 John Panelli 25.00 18.00
❑ 76 Bill Leonard 25.00 18.00
❑ 77 Bob Kelly 25.00 18.00
❑ 78 Dante Lavelli RC 150.00 90.00
❑ 79 Tony Adamle 30.00 20.00
❑ 80 Dick Wildung 25.00 18.00
❑ 81 Tobin Rote RC 50.00 30.00
❑ 82 Paul Burris 25.00 18.00
❑ 83 Lowell Tew 25.00 18.00
❑ 84 Barney Poole 25.00 18.00
❑ 85 Fred Naumetz 25.00 18.00
❑ 86 Dick Hoerner 25.00 18.00
❑ 87 Bob Reinhard 25.00 18.00
❑ 88 Howard Hartley RC 25.00 18.00
❑ 89 Darrell Hogan RC 25.00 18.00
❑ 90 Jerry Shipkey 25.00 18.00
❑ 91 Frank Tripucka 30.00 20.00
❑ 92 Buster Ramsey RC 25.00 18.00
❑ 93 Pat Harder 30.00 20.00
❑ 94 Vic Sears 25.00 18.00
❑ 95 Tommy Thompson QB 30.00 20.00
❑ 96 Bucko Kilroy 30.00 20.00
❑ 97 George Connor 50.00 30.00
❑ 98 Fred Morrison 25.00 18.00
❑ 99 Rookie 25.00 18.00
❑ 100 Sammy Baugh 250.00 150.00
❑ 101 Harry Ulinski 25.00 18.00
❑ 102 Frank Spaniel 25.00 18.00
❑ 103 Charley Conerly 90.00 50.00
❑ 104 Dick Hensley 25.00 18.00
❑ 105 Eddie Price 25.00 18.00
❑ 106 Ed Carr 25.00 18.00
❑ 107 Leo Nomellini 75.00 45.00
❑ 108 Verl Lillywhite 25.00 18.00
❑ 109 Wallace Triplett 25.00 18.00
❑ 110 Joe Watson 25.00 18.00
❑ 111 Cloyce Box RC 30.00 20.00
❑ 112 Billy Stone 25.00 18.00
❑ 113 Earl Murray 25.00 18.00
❑ 114 Chet Mutryn RC 30.00 20.00
❑ 115 Ken Carpenter 30.00 20.00
❑ 116 Lou Rymkus RC 30.00 20.00
❑ 117 Dub Jones RC 30.00 20.00
❑ 118 Clayton Tonnemaker 25.00 18.00
❑ 119 Walt Schlinkman 25.00 18.00
❑ 120 Billy Grimes 25.00 18.00
❑ 121 George Ratterman RC 30.00 20.00
❑ 122 Bob Mann 25.00 18.00
❑ 123 Buddy Young RC 40.00 25.00
❑ 124 Jack Zilly 25.00 18.00
❑ 125 Tom Kalmanir 25.00 18.00
❑ 126 Frank Sinkovitz 25.00 18.00
❑ 127 Elbert Nickel 30.00 20.00
❑ 128 Jim Finks RC 75.00 40.00
❑ 129 Charley Trippi 60.00 35.00
❑ 130 Tom Wham 25.00 18.00
❑ 131 Ventan Yablonski 25.00 18.00
❑ 132 Chuck Bednarik 125.00 75.00
❑ 133 Joe Muha 25.00 18.00
❑ 134 Pete Pihos 80.00 45.00
❑ 135 Washington Serini 25.00 18.00
❑ 136 George Gulyanics 25.00 18.00
❑ 137 Ken Kavanaugh 30.00 20.00
❑ 138 Howie Livingston 25.00 18.00
❑ 139 Joe Tereshinski 25.00 18.00
❑ 140 Jim White 25.00 18.00
❑ 141 Gene Roberts 25.00 18.00
❑ 142 Bill Swiacki 30.00 20.00
❑ 143 Norm Standlee 25.00 18.00
❑ 144 Knox Ramsey RC ! 100.00 50.00

1951 Bowman

❑ COMPLETE SET (144) 3500.00 2500.00
❑ WRAPPER (1-CENT) 250.00 150.00
❑ WRAPPER (5-CENT) 300.00 175.00
❑ 1 Weldon Humble RC ! 80.00 50.00
❑ 2 Otto Graham 200.00 125.00
❑ 3 Mac Speedie 35.00 20.00
❑ 4 Norm Van Brocklin RC 300.00 200.00
❑ 5 Woodley Lewis RC 25.00 15.00
❑ 6 Tom Fears 50.00 30.00
❑ 7 George Musacco 20.00 12.00
❑ 8 George Taliaferro 25.00 15.00
❑ 9 Barney Poole 20.00 12.00
❑ 10 Steve Van Buren 60.00 35.00
❑ 11 Whitey Wistert 25.00 15.00
❑ 12 Chuck Bednarik 80.00 50.00
❑ 13 Bulldog Turner 50.00 30.00
❑ 14 Bob Williams 20.00 12.00
❑ 15 Johnny Lujack 60.00 35.00
❑ 16 Roy Rebel Steiner 20.00 12.00
❑ 17 Jug Girard 25.00 15.00
❑ 18 Bill Neal 20.00 12.00
❑ 19 Travis Tidwell 20.00 12.00
❑ 20 Tom Landry RC 500.00 350.00
❑ 21 Arnie Weinmeister RC 60.00 35.00
❑ 22 Joe Geri 20.00 12.00
❑ 23 Bill Walsh C RC 25.00 15.00
❑ 24 Fran Rogel 20.00 12.00
❑ 25 Doak Walker 60.00 35.00
❑ 26 Leon Hart 35.00 20.00
❑ 27 Thurman McGraw 20.00 12.00
❑ 28 Buster Ramsey 20.00 12.00
❑ 29 Frank Tripucka 35.00 20.00
❑ 30 Don Paul DB 20.00 12.00
❑ 31 Alex Loyd 20.00 12.00
❑ 32 Y.A.Tittle 135.00 75.00
❑ 33 Verl Lillywhite 20.00 12.00
❑ 34 Sammy Baugh 175.00 110.00
❑ 35 Chuck Drazenovich 20.00 12.00
❑ 36 Bob Goode 20.00 12.00
❑ 37 Horace Gillom RC 25.00 15.00
❑ 38 Lou Rymkus 25.00 15.00
❑ 39 Ken Carpenter 20.00 12.00
❑ 40 Bob Waterfield 75.00 45.00
❑ 41 Vitamin Smith RC 25.00 15.00
❑ 42 Glenn Davis 60.00 35.00
❑ 43 Dan Edwards 20.00 12.00

❑ 44 John Rauch 20.00 12.00
❑ 45 Zollie Toth 20.00 12.00
❑ 46 Pete Pihos 60.00 35.00
❑ 47 Russ Craft 20.00 12.00
❑ 48 Walter Barnes 20.00 12.00
❑ 49 Fred Morrison 20.00 12.00
❑ 50 Ray Bray 20.00 12.00
❑ 51 Ed Sprinkle RC 25.00 15.00
❑ 52 Floyd Reid 20.00 12.00
❑ 53 Billy Grimes 20.00 12.00
❑ 54 Ted Fritsch Sr. 25.00 15.00
❑ 55 Al DeRogatis 25.00 15.00
❑ 56 Charley Conerly 75.00 45.00
❑ 57 Jon Baker 20.00 12.00
❑ 58 Tom McWilliams 20.00 12.00
❑ 59 Jerry Shipkey 20.00 12.00
❑ 60 Lynn Chandnois RC 25.00 15.00
❑ 61 Don Doll 20.00 12.00
❑ 62 Lou Creekmur 50.00 30.00
❑ 63 Bob Hoernschemeyer 25.00 15.00
❑ 64 Tom Wham 20.00 12.00
❑ 65 Bill Fischer 20.00 12.00
❑ 66 Robert Nussbaumer 20.00 12.00
❑ 67 Gordy Soltau RC 20.00 12.00
❑ 68 Visco Grgich 20.00 12.00
❑ 69 John Strzykalski RC 20.00 12.00
❑ 70 Pete Stout 20.00 12.00
❑ 71 Paul Lipscomb 20.00 12.00
❑ 72 Harry Gilmer 35.00 20.00
❑ 73 Dante Lavelli 50.00 30.00
❑ 74 Dub Jones 25.00 15.00
❑ 75 Lou Groza 75.00 45.00
❑ 76 Elroy Hirsch 75.00 45.00
❑ 77 Tom Kalmanir 20.00 12.00
❑ 78 Jack Zilly 20.00 12.00
❑ 79 Bruce Alford 20.00 12.00
❑ 80 Art Weiner 20.00 12.00
❑ 81 Brad Ecklund 20.00 12.00
❑ 82 Bosh Pritchard 20.00 12.00
❑ 83 John Green 20.00 12.00
❑ 84 Ebert Van Buren 20.00 12.00
❑ 85 Julie Rykovich 20.00 12.00
❑ 86 Fred Davis 20.00 12.00
❑ 87 John Hoffman RC 20.00 12.00
❑ 88 Tobin Rote 25.00 15.00
❑ 89 Paul Burris 20.00 12.00
❑ 90 Tony Canadeo 50.00 30.00
❑ 91 Emlen Tunnell RC 100.00 60.00
❑ 92 Otto Schnellbacher RC 20.00 12.00
❑ 93 Ray Poole 20.00 12.00
❑ 94 Darrell Hogan 20.00 12.00
❑ 95 Frank Sinkovitz 20.00 12.00
❑ 96 Ernie Stautner 75.00 45.00
❑ 97 Elmer Bud Angsman 20.00 12.00
❑ 98 Jack Jennings 20.00 12.00
❑ 99 Jerry Groom 20.00 12.00
❑ 100 John Prchlik 20.00 12.00
❑ 101 J. Robert Smith 20.00 12.00
❑ 102 Bobby Layne 135.00 75.00
❑ 103 Frankie Albert 35.00 20.00
❑ 104 Gail Bruce 20.00 12.00
❑ 105 Joe Perry 75.00 45.00
❑ 106 Leon Heath 20.00 12.00
❑ 107 Ed Quirk 20.00 12.00
❑ 108 Hugh Taylor 25.00 15.00
❑ 109 Marion Motley 100.00 60.00
❑ 110 Tony Adamle 20.00 12.00
❑ 111 Alex Agase 25.00 15.00
❑ 112 Tank Younger 35.00 20.00
❑ 113 Bob Boyd 20.00 12.00
❑ 114 Jerry Williams 20.00 12.00
❑ 115 Joe Golding 20.00 12.00
❑ 116 Sherman Howard 20.00 12.00
❑ 117 John Wozniak 20.00 12.00
❑ 118 Frank Reagan 20.00 12.00
❑ 119 Vic Sears 20.00 12.00
❑ 120 Clyde Scott 20.00 12.00
❑ 121 George Gulyanics 20.00 12.00
❑ 122 Bill Wightkin 20.00 12.00
❑ 123 Chuck Hunsinger 20.00 12.00
❑ 124 Jack Cloud 20.00 12.00
❑ 125 Abner Wimberly 20.00 12.00
❑ 126 Dick Wildung 20.00 12.00
❑ 127 Eddie Price 20.00 12.00
❑ 128 Joe Scott 20.00 12.00
❑ 129 Jerry Nuzum 20.00 12.00
❑ 130 Jim Finks 35.00 20.00
❑ 131 Bob Gage 20.00 12.00
❑ 132 Bill Swiacki 25.00 15.00
❑ 133 Joe Watson 20.00 12.00
❑ 134 Ollie Cline 20.00 12.00
❑ 135 Jack Lininger 20.00 12.00
❑ 136 Fran Polsfoot 20.00 12.00
❑ 137 Charley Trippi 50.00 30.00
❑ 138 Ventan Yablonski 20.00 12.00
❑ 139 Emil Sitko 20.00 12.00
❑ 140 Leo Nomellini 60.00 30.00
❑ 141 Norm Standlee 20.00 12.00
❑ 142 Eddie Saenz 20.00 12.00
❑ 143 Al Demao 20.00 12.00
❑ 144 Bill Dudley ! 150.00 75.00
❑ NNO Johnny Lujack Proof 300.00 175.00
❑ NNO Bob Gage Proof 125.00 75.00
❑ NNO Darrell Hogan Proof 125.00 75.00

1952 Bowman Large

❑ COMPLETE SET (144) 12500.00 9500.00
❑ COMMON CARD (1-72) 35.00 20.00
❑ COMMON CARD (73-144) 40.00 25.00
❑ WRAPPER (5-CENT) 60.00 30.00
❑ 1 Norm Van Brocklin SP ! 500.00 350.00
❑ 2 Otto Graham 300.00 200.00
❑ 3 Doak Walker 100.00 60.00
❑ 4 Steve Owen RC CO 80.00 50.00
❑ 5 Frankie Albert 50.00 30.00
❑ 6 Laurie Niemi 35.00 20.00
❑ 7 Chuck Hunsinger 35.00 20.00
❑ 8 Ed Modzelewski 50.00 30.00
❑ 9 Joe Spencer SP 75.00 40.00
❑ 10 Chuck Bednarik SP 300.00 200.00
❑ 11 Barney Poole 35.00 20.00
❑ 12 Charley Trippi 75.00 40.00
❑ 13 Tom Fears 75.00 40.00
❑ 14 Paul Brown RC CO 250.00 150.00
❑ 15 Leon Hart 50.00 30.00
❑ 16 Frank Gifford RC 500.00 350.00
❑ 17 Y.A.Tittle 300.00 200.00
❑ 18 Charlie Justice SP 175.00 100.00
❑ 19 George Connor SP 175.00 100.00
❑ 20 Lynn Chandnois 35.00 20.00
❑ 21 Billy Howton RC 50.00 30.00
❑ 22 Kenneth Snyder 35.00 20.00
❑ 23 Gino Marchetti RC 250.00 150.00
❑ 24 John Karras 35.00 20.00
❑ 25 Tank Younger 50.00 30.00
❑ 26 Tommy Thompson LB 35.00 20.00
❑ 27 Bob Miller SP RC! 300.00 200.00
❑ 28 Kyle Rote RC SP 175.00 100.00
❑ 29 Hugh McElhenny RC 250.00 150.00
❑ 30 Sammy Baugh 350.00 225.00
❑ 31 Jim Dooley RC 45.00 25.00
❑ 32 Ray Mathews 35.00 20.00
❑ 33 Fred Cone ·35.00 20.00
❑ 34 Al Pollard 35.00 20.00
❑ 35 Brad Ecklund 35.00 20.00
❑ 36 John Hancock RC SP! 350.00 225.00
❑ 37 Elroy Hirsch SP 200.00 125.00
❑ 38 Keever Jankovich 35.00 20.00
❑ 39 Emlen Tunnell 125.00 75.00
❑ 40 Steve Dowden 35.00 20.00
❑ 41 Claude Hipps 35.00 20.00
❑ 42 Norm Standlee 35.00 20.00
❑ 43 Dick Todd CO 35.00 20.00
❑ 44 Babe Parilli 50.00 30.00
❑ 45 Steve Van Buren SP 300.00 200.00
❑ 46 Art Donovan RC SP 350.00 250.00
❑ 47 Bill Fischer 35.00 20.00
❑ 48 George Halas RC CO 275.00 160.00
❑ 49 Jerrell Price 35.00 20.00
❑ 50 John Sandusky RC 35.00 20.00
❑ 51 Ray Beck 35.00 20.00
❑ 52 Jim Martin 45.00 25.00
❑ 53 Joe Bach CO UER 35.00 20.00
❑ 54 Glen Christian SP 75.00 40.00
❑ 55 Andy Davis SP 75.00 40.00
❑ 56 Tobin Rote 45.00 25.00
❑ 57 Wayne Millner RC CO 90.00 50.00
❑ 58 Zollie Toth 35.00 20.00
❑ 59 Jack Jennings 35.00 20.00
❑ 60 Bill McColl 35.00 20.00
❑ 61 Les Richter RC 45.00 25.00
❑ 62 Walt Michaels RC 45.00 25.00
❑ 63 Charley Conerly SP 700.00 400.00
❑ 64 Howard Hartley SP 75.00 40.00
❑ 65 Jerome Smith 35.00 20.00
❑ 66 James Clark 35.00 20.00
❑ 67 Dick Logan 35.00 20.00
❑ 68 Wayne Robinson 35.00 20.00
❑ 69 James Hammond 35.00 20.00
❑ 70 Gene Schroeder 35.00 20.00
❑ 71 Tex Coulter 45.00 25.00
❑ 72 John Schweder RC SP! 600.00 400.00
❑ 73 Vitamin Smith SP 150.00 90.00
❑ 74 Joe Campanella RC 40.00 25.00
❑ 75 Joe Kuharich RC CO 50.00 30.00
❑ 76 Herman Clark 40.00 25.00
❑ 77 Dan Edwards 40.00 25.00
❑ 78 Bobby Layne 300.00 175.00
❑ 79 Bob Hoernschemeyer 50.00 30.00
❑ 80 John Carr Blount 40.00 25.00
❑ 81 John Kastan RC SP 150.00 90.00
❑ 82 Harry Minarik RC SP 150.00 90.00
❑ 83 Joe Perry 100.00 60.00
❑ 84 Buddy Parker RC CO 50.00 30.00
❑ 85 Andy Robustelli RC 200.00 125.00
❑ 86 Dub Jones 50.00 30.00
❑ 87 Mal Cook 40.00 25.00
❑ 88 Billy Stone 40.00 25.00
❑ 89 George Taliaferro 50.00 30.00
❑ 90 Thomas Johnson RC SP 150.00 90.00
❑ 91 Leon Heath SP 100.00 60.00
❑ 92 Pete Pihos 100.00 60.00
❑ 93 Fred Benners 40.00 25.00
❑ 94 George Tarasovic 40.00 25.00
❑ 95 Buck Shaw RC CO 40.00 25.00
❑ 96 Bill Wightkin 40.00 25.00
❑ 97 John Wozniak 40.00 25.00
❑ 98 Bobby Dillon RC 50.00 30.00
❑ 99 Joe Stydahar RC SP CO! 650.00 450.00
❑ 100 Dick Alban RC SP 150.00 90.00
❑ 101 Arnie Weinmeister 60.00 35.00
❑ 102 Bobby Cross 40.00 25.00
❑ 103 Don Paul DB 40.00 25.00
❑ 104 Buddy Young 60.00 35.00
❑ 105 Lou Groza 125.00 75.00
❑ 106 Ray Pelfrey 40.00 25.00
❑ 107 Maurice Nipp 40.00 25.00
❑ 108 Hubert Johnston RC SP! 650.00 450.00
❑ 109 Vol.Quinlan RC SP 100.00 60.00
❑ 110 Jack Simmons 40.00 25.00
❑ 111 George Ratterman 50.00 30.00
❑ 112 John Badaczewski 40.00 25.00
❑ 113 Bill Reichardt 40.00 25.00
❑ 114 Art Weiner 40.00 25.00
❑ 115 Keith Flowers 40.00 25.00
❑ 116 Russ Craft 40.00 25.00
❑ 117 J.O'Donahue RC SP 150.00 90.00
❑ 118 Darrell Hogan SP 100.00 60.00
❑ 119 Frank Ziegler 40.00 25.00
❑ 120 Dan Towler 60.00 35.00
❑ 121 Fred Williams 40.00 25.00
❑ 122 Jimmy Phelan CO 40.00 25.00
❑ 123 Eddie Price 40.00 25.00
❑ 124 Chet Ostrowski 40.00 25.00
❑ 125 Leo Nomellini 100.00 60.00
❑ 126 S.Romanik RC SP! 300.00 200.00
❑ 127 Ollie Matson RC SP 300.00 200.00
❑ 128 Dante Lavelli 90.00 50.00
❑ 129 Jack Christiansen RC 175.00 100.00
❑ 130 Dom Moselle 40.00 25.00
❑ 131 John Rapacz 40.00 25.00
❑ 132 Chuck Ortmann UER 40.00 25.00
❑ 133 Bob Williams 40.00 25.00
❑ 134 Chuck Ulrich 40.00 25.00
❑ 135 Gene Ronzani CO SP RC! 650.00 450.00
❑ 136 Bert Rechichar SP 100.00 60.00
❑ 137 Bob Waterfield 125.00 75.00
❑ 138 Bobby Walston RC 50.00 30.00
❑ 139 Jerry Shipkey 40.00 25.00

❑ 140 Yale Lary RC 175.00 100.00
❑ 141 Gordy Soltau 40.00 25.00
❑ 142 Tom Landry 600.00 450.00
❑ 143 John Papit 40.00 25.00
❑ 144 Jim Lansford RC SP! 3000.00 1800.00

1952 Bowman Small

❑ COMPLETE SET (144) 5000.00 3500.00
❑ COMMON CARD (1-72) 25.00 15.00
❑ COMMON CARD (73-144) 30.00 18.00
❑ WRAPPER (1-CENT) 60.00 40.00
❑ 1 Norm Van Brocklin ! 350.00 200.00
❑ 2 Otto Graham 200.00 125.00
❑ 3 Doak Walker 60.00 35.00
❑ 4 Steve Owen RC CO 60.00 35.00
❑ 5 Frankie Albert 35.00 20.00
❑ 6 Laurie Niemi 25.00 15.00
❑ 7 Chuck Hunsinger 25.00 15.00
❑ 8 Ed Modzelewski 35.00 20.00
❑ 9 Joe Spencer 25.00 15.00
❑ 10 Chuck Bednarik 75.00 45.00
❑ 11 Barney Poole 25.00 15.00
❑ 12 Charley Trippi 60.00 35.00
❑ 13 Tom Fears 60.00 35.00
❑ 14 Paul Brown RC CO 150.00 90.00
❑ 15 Leon Hart 35.00 20.00
❑ 16 Frank Gifford RC 400.00 200.00
❑ 17 Y.A.Tittle 125.00 75.00
❑ 18 Charlie Justice 45.00 30.00
❑ 19 George Connor 35.00 20.00
❑ 20 Lynn Chandnois 25.00 15.00
❑ 21 Billy Howton RC 40.00 25.00
❑ 22 Kenneth Snyder 25.00 15.00
❑ 23 Gino Marchetti RC 125.00 75.00
❑ 24 John Karras 25.00 15.00
❑ 25 Tank Younger 35.00 20.00
❑ 26 Tommy Thompson LB 25.00 15.00
❑ 27 Bob Miller RC 25.00 15.00
❑ 28 Kyle Rote RC 50.00 30.00
❑ 29 Hugh McElhenny RC 175.00 100.00
❑ 30 Sammy Baugh 250.00 150.00
❑ 31 Jim Dooley RC 30.00 18.00
❑ 32 Ray Mathews 25.00 15.00
❑ 33 Fred Cone 25.00 15.00
❑ 34 Al Pollard 25.00 15.00
❑ 35 Brad Ecklund 25.00 15.00
❑ 36 John Lee Hancock 25.00 15.00
❑ 37 Elroy Hirsch 60.00 35.00
❑ 38 Keever Jankovich 25.00 15.00
❑ 39 Emlen Tunnell 50.00 30.00
❑ 40 Steve Dowden 25.00 15.00
❑ 41 Claude Hipps 25.00 15.00
❑ 42 Norm Standlee 25.00 15.00
❑ 43 Dick Todd CO 25.00 15.00
❑ 44 Babe Parilli 35.00 20.00
❑ 45 Steve Van Buren 75.00 40.00
❑ 46 Art Donovan RC 200.00 125.00
❑ 47 Bill Fischer 25.00 15.00
❑ 48 George Halas RC CO 250.00 150.00
❑ 49 Jerrell Price 25.00 15.00
❑ 50 John Sandusky RC 25.00 15.00
❑ 51 Ray Beck 25.00 15.00
❑ 52 Jim Martin 30.00 18.00
❑ 53 Joe Bach CO UER 25.00 15.00
❑ 54 Glen Christian 25.00 15.00
❑ 55 Andy Davis 25.00 15.00
❑ 56 Tobin Rote 30.00 18.00
❑ 57 Wayne Millner RC CO 50.00 30.00
❑ 58 Zollie Toth 25.00 15.00
❑ 59 Jack Jennings 25.00 15.00
❑ 60 Bill McColl 25.00 15.00
❑ 61 Les Richter RC 30.00 18.00
❑ 62 Walt Michaels RC 30.00 18.00
❑ 63 Charley Conerly 75.00 40.00
❑ 64 Howard Hartley 25.00 15.00
❑ 65 Jerome Smith 25.00 15.00
❑ 66 James Clark 25.00 15.00
❑ 67 Dick Logan 25.00 15.00
❑ 68 Wayne Robinson 25.00 15.00
❑ 69 James Hammond 25.00 15.00
❑ 70 Gene Schroeder 25.00 15.00
❑ 71 Tex Coulter 30.00 18.00
❑ 72 John Schweder 25.00 15.00
❑ 73 Vitamin Smith 35.00 20.00
❑ 74 Joe Campanella RC 30.00 18.00
❑ 75 Joe Kuharich RC CO 35.00 20.00
❑ 76 Herman Clark 30.00 18.00
❑ 77 Dan Edwards 30.00 18.00
❑ 78 Bobby Layne 150.00 90.00
❑ 79 Bob Hoernschemeyer 35.00 20.00
❑ 80 John Carr Blount 30.00 18.00
❑ 81 John Kastan RC 30.00 18.00
❑ 82 Harry Minarik 30.00 18.00
❑ 83 Joe Perry 75.00 40.00
❑ 84 Buddy Parker RC CO 35.00 20.00
❑ 85 Andy Robustelli RC 125.00 75.00
❑ 86 Dub Jones 35.00 20.00
❑ 87 Mal Cook 30.00 18.00
❑ 88 Billy Stone 30.00 18.00
❑ 89 George Taliaferro 35.00 20.00
❑ 90 Thomas Johnson RC 30.00 18.00
❑ 91 Leon Heath 30.00 18.00
❑ 92 Pete Pihos 50.00 35.00
❑ 93 Fred Benners 30.00 18.00
❑ 94 George Tarasovic 30.00 18.00
❑ 95 Buck Shaw RC CO 30.00 18.00
❑ 96 Bill Wightkin 30.00 18.00
❑ 97 John Wozniak 30.00 18.00
❑ 98 Bobby Dillon RC 35.00 20.00
❑ 99 Joe Stydahar RC CO 45.00 30.00
❑ 100 Dick Alban RC 30.00 18.00
❑ 101 Arnie Weinmeister 40.00 25.00
❑ 102 Bobby Cross 30.00 18.00
❑ 103 Don Paul DB 30.00 18.00
❑ 104 Buddy Young 40.00 25.00
❑ 105 Lou Groza 75.00 45.00
❑ 106 Ray Pelfrey 30.00 18.00
❑ 107 Maurice Nipp 30.00 18.00
❑ 108 Hubert Johnston 30.00 18.00
❑ 109 Volney Quinlan RC 30.00 18.00
❑ 110 Jack Simmons 30.00 18.00
❑ 111 George Ratterman 35.00 20.00
❑ 112 John Badaczewski 30.00 18.00
❑ 113 Bill Reichardt 30.00 18.00
❑ 114 Art Weiner 30.00 18.00
❑ 115 Keith Flowers 30.00 18.00
❑ 116 Russ Craft 30.00 18.00
❑ 117 Jim O'Donahue RC 30.00 18.00
❑ 118 Darrell Hogan 30.00 18.00
❑ 119 Frank Ziegler 30.00 18.00
❑ 120 Dan Towler 40.00 25.00
❑ 121 Fred Williams 30.00 18.00
❑ 122 Jimmy Phelan CO 30.00 18.00
❑ 123 Eddie Price 30.00 18.00
❑ 124 Chet Ostrowski 30.00 18.00
❑ 125 Leo Nomellini 75.00 40.00
❑ 126 Steve Romanik 30.00 18.00
❑ 127 Ollie Matson RC 125.00 75.00
❑ 128 Dante Lavelli 60.00 35.00
❑ 129 Jack Christiansen RC 80.00 50.00
❑ 130 Dom Moselle 30.00 18.00
❑ 131 John Rapacz 30.00 18.00
❑ 132 Chuck Ortmann UER 30.00 18.00
❑ 133 Bob Williams 30.00 18.00
❑ 134 Chuck Ulrich 30.00 18.00
❑ 135 Gene Ronzani RC CO 30.00 18.00
❑ 136 Bert Rechichar 35.00 20.00
❑ 137 Bob Waterfield 75.00 45.00
❑ 138 Bobby Walston RC 35.00 20.00
❑ 139 Jerry Shipkey 30.00 18.00
❑ 140 Yale Lary RC 80.00 50.00
❑ 141 Gordy Soltau 30.00 18.00
❑ 142 Tom Landry 400.00 250.00
❑ 143 John Papit 30.00 18.00
❑ 144 Jim Lansford RC ! 175.00 100.00

1953 Bowman

❑ COMPLETE SET (96) 3400.00 2200.00
❑ WRAPPER (5-CENT) 150.00 90.00
❑ 1 Eddie LeBaron RC ! 125.00 75.00
❑ 2 John Dottley 30.00 18.00

❑ 3 Babe Parilli 35.00 20.00
❑ 4 Bucko Kilroy 35.00 20.00
❑ 5 Joe Tereshinski 30.00 18.00
❑ 6 Doak Walker 75.00 45.00
❑ 7 Fran Polsfoot 30.00 18.00
❑ 8 Sisto Averno 30.00 18.00
❑ 9 Marion Motley 75.00 45.00
❑ 10 Pat Brady 30.00 18.00
❑ 11 Norm Van Brocklin 125.00 75.00
❑ 12 Bill McColl 30.00 18.00
❑ 13 Jerry Groom 30.00 18.00
❑ 14 Al Pollard 30.00 18.00
❑ 15 Dante Lavelli 50.00 30.00
❑ 16 Eddie Price 30.00 18.00
❑ 17 Charley Trippi 50.00 30.00
❑ 18 Elbert Nickel 35.00 20.00
❑ 19 George Taliaferro 35.00 20.00
❑ 20 Charley Conerly 80.00 50.00
❑ 21 Bobby Layne 125.00 75.00
❑ 22 Elroy Hirsch 100.00 60.00
❑ 23 Jim Finks 40.00 25.00
❑ 24 Chuck Bednarik 75.00 45.00
❑ 25 Kyle Rote 40.00 25.00
❑ 26 Otto Graham 175.00 100.00
❑ 27 Harry Gilmer 35.00 20.00
❑ 28 Tobin Rote 35.00 20.00
❑ 29 Billy Stone 30.00 18.00
❑ 30 Buddy Young 40.00 25.00
❑ 31 Leon Hart 40.00 25.00
❑ 32 Hugh McElhenny 75.00 45.00
❑ 33 Dale Samuels 30.00 18.00
❑ 34 Lou Creekmur 50.00 30.00
❑ 35 Tom Catlin 30.00 18.00
❑ 36 Tom Fears 60.00 35.00
❑ 37 George Connor 40.00 25.00
❑ 38 Bill Walsh C 30.00 18.00
❑ 39 Leo Sanford SP 45.00 30.00
❑ 40 Horace Gillom 35.00 20.00
❑ 41 John Schweder SP 45.00 30.00
❑ 42 Tom O'Connell 30.00 18.00
❑ 43 Frank Gifford SP 300.00 175.00
❑ 44 Frank Continetti SP 45.00 30.00
❑ 45 John Olszewski SP 45.00 30.00
❑ 46 Dub Jones 35.00 20.00
❑ 47 Don Paul LB SP 45.00 30.00
❑ 48 Gerald Weatherly 30.00 18.00
❑ 49 Fred Bruney SP 45.00 30.00
❑ 50 Jack Scarbath 30.00 18.00
❑ 51 John Karras 30.00 18.00
❑ 52 Al Conway 30.00 18.00
❑ 53 Emlen Tunnell SP 125.00 75.00
❑ 54 Gern Nagler SP 45.00 30.00
❑ 55 Kenneth Snyder SP 45.00 30.00
❑ 56 Y.A.Tittle 150.00 90.00
❑ 57 John Rapacz SP 45.00 30.00
❑ 58 Harley Sewell SP 45.00 30.00
❑ 59 Don Bingham 30.00 18.00
❑ 60 Darrell Hogan 30.00 18.00
❑ 61 Tony Curcillo 30.00 18.00
❑ 62 Ray Renfro RC SP 50.00 30.00
❑ 63 Leon Heath 30.00 18.00
❑ 64 Tex Coulter SP 45.00 30.00
❑ 65 Dewayne Douglas 30.00 18.00
❑ 66 J. Robert Smith SP 45.00 30.00
❑ 67 Bob McChesney SP 45.00 30.00
❑ 68 Dick Alban SP 45.00 30.00
❑ 69 Andy Kozar 30.00 18.00
❑ 70 Merwin Hodel SP 45.00 30.00
❑ 71 Thurman McGraw 30.00 18.00
❑ 72 Cliff Anderson 30.00 18.00
❑ 73 Pete Pihos 60.00 35.00
❑ 74 Julie Rykovich 30.00 18.00

❑ 75 John Kreamcheck SP	45.00	30.00
❑ 76 Lynn Chandnois	30.00	18.00
❑ 77 Cloyce Box SP	45.00	30.00
❑ 78 Ray Mathews	30.00	18.00
❑ 79 Bobby Walston	35.00	20.00
❑ 80 Jim Dooley	30.00	18.00
❑ 81 Pat Harder SP	45.00	30.00
❑ 82 Jerry Shipkey	30.00	18.00
❑ 83 Bobby Thomason RC	30.00	18.00
❑ 84 Hugh Taylor	35.00	20.00
❑ 85 George Ratterman	35.00	20.00
❑ 86 Don Stonesifer	30.00	18.00
❑ 87 John Williams SP RC	45.00	30.00
❑ 88 Leo Nomellini	50.00	30.00
❑ 89 Frank Ziegler	30.00	18.00
❑ 90 Don Paul DB UER	30.00	18.00
❑ 91 Tom Dublinski	30.00	18.00
❑ 92 Ken Carpenter	30.00	18.00
❑ 93 Ted Marchibroda RC	40.00	25.00
❑ 94 Chuck Drazenovich	30.00	18.00
❑ 95 Lou Groza SP	125.00	75.00
❑ 96 William Cross RC SP !	100.00	50.00

1954 Bowman

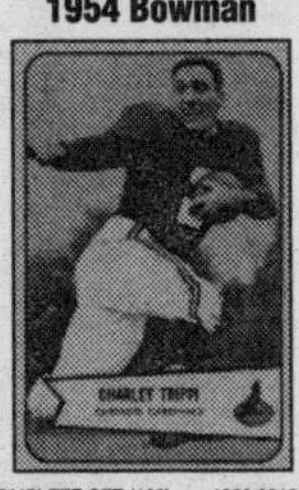

❑ COMPLETE SET (128)	1800.00	1200.00
❑ COMMON CARD (1-64)	5.00	3.00
❑ COMMON SP (65-96)	25.00	15.00
❑ COMMON CARD (97-128)	5.00	3.00
❑ WRAPPER (1-CENT)	15.00	10.00
❑ WRAPPER (5-CENT)	30.00	25.00
❑ 1 Ray Mathews !	30.00	15.00
❑ 2 John Huzvar	5.00	3.00
❑ 3 Jack Scarbath	5.00	3.00
❑ 4 Doug Atkins RC	50.00	30.00
❑ 5 Bill Stits	5.00	3.00
❑ 6 Joe Perry	30.00	18.00
❑ 7 Kyle Rote	15.00	7.50
❑ 8 Norm Van Brocklin	50.00	25.00
❑ 9 Pete Pihos	20.00	12.00
❑ 10 Babe Parilli	8.00	4.00
❑ 11 Zeke Bratkowski RC	25.00	15.00
❑ 12 Ollie Matson	25.00	15.00
❑ 13 Pat Brady	5.00	3.00
❑ 14 Fred Enke	5.00	3.00
❑ 15 Harry Ulinski	5.00	3.00
❑ 16 Bob Garrett	5.00	3.00
❑ 17 Bill Bowman	5.00	3.00
❑ 18 Leo Rucka	5.00	3.00
❑ 19 John Cannady	5.00	3.00
❑ 20 Tom Fears	25.00	15.00
❑ 21 Norm Willey	5.00	3.00
❑ 22 Floyd Reid	5.00	3.00
❑ 23 George Blanda RC	175.00	100.00
❑ 24 Don Doheney	5.00	3.00
❑ 25 John Schweder	5.00	3.00
❑ 26 Bert Rechichar	5.00	3.00
❑ 27 Harry Dowda	5.00	3.00
❑ 28 John Sandusky	5.00	3.00
❑ 29 Les Bingaman RC	15.00	7.50
❑ 30 Joe Arenas	5.00	3.00
❑ 31 Ray Wietecha RC	5.00	3.00
❑ 32 Elroy Hirsch	30.00	18.00
❑ 33 Harold Giancanelli	5.00	3.00
❑ 34 Billy Howton	8.00	4.00
❑ 35 Fred Morrison	5.00	3.00
❑ 36 Bobby Cavazos	5.00	3.00
❑ 37 Darrell Hogan	5.00	3.00
❑ 38 Buddy Young	8.00	4.00
❑ 39 Charlie Justice	20.00	12.00
❑ 40 Otto Graham	80.00	50.00
❑ 41 Doak Walker	35.00	20.00
❑ 42 Y.A.Tittle	60.00	35.00
❑ 43 Buford Long	5.00	3.00
❑ 44 Volney Quinlan	5.00	3.00
❑ 45 Bobby Thomason	5.00	3.00
❑ 46 Fred Cone	5.00	3.00
❑ 47 Gerald Weatherly	5.00	3.00
❑ 48 Don Stonesifer	5.00	3.00
❑ 49A Lynn Chandnois ERR	5.00	3.00
❑ 49B Lynn Chandnois COR	5.00	3.00
❑ 50 George Taliaferro	5.00	3.00
❑ 51 Dick Alban	5.00	3.00
❑ 52 Lou Groza	35.00	20.00
❑ 53 Bobby Layne	60.00	35.00
❑ 54 Hugh McElhenny	40.00	20.00
❑ 55 Frank Gifford	100.00	60.00
❑ 56 Leon McLaughlin	5.00	3.00
❑ 57 Chuck Bednarik	40.00	20.00
❑ 58 Art Hunter	5.00	3.00
❑ 59 Bill McColl	5.00	3.00
❑ 60 Charley Trippi	25.00	15.00
❑ 61 Jim Finks	15.00	7.50
❑ 62 Bill Lange G	5.00	3.00
❑ 63 Laurie Niemi	5.00	3.00
❑ 64 Ray Renfro	8.00	4.00
❑ 65 Dick Chapman	25.00	15.00
❑ 66 Bob Hantla	25.00	15.00
❑ 67 Ralph Starkey	25.00	15.00
❑ 68 Don Paul LB	25.00	15.00
❑ 69 Kenneth Snyder	25.00	15.00
❑ 70 Tobin Rote SP	30.00	18.00
❑ 71 Art DeCarlo	25.00	15.00
❑ 72 Tom Keane SP	25.00	15.00
❑ 73 Hugh Taylor SP	30.00	18.00
❑ 74 Warren Lahr RC SP	25.00	15.00
❑ 75 Jim Neal	25.00	15.00
❑ 76 Leo Nomellini SP	60.00	35.00
❑ 77 Dick Yelvington	25.00	15.00
❑ 78 Les Richter SP	30.00	18.00
❑ 79 Bucko Kilroy SP	30.00	18.00
❑ 80 John Martinkovic	25.00	15.00
❑ 81 Dale Dodrill RC SP	25.00	15.00
❑ 82 Ken Jackson	25.00	15.00
❑ 83 Paul Lipscomb	25.00	15.00
❑ 84 John Bauer	25.00	15.00
❑ 85 Lou Creekmur SP	50.00	30.00
❑ 86 Eddie Price	25.00	15.00
❑ 87 Kenneth Farragut	25.00	15.00
❑ 88 Dave Hanner RC SP	30.00	18.00
❑ 89 Don Boll	25.00	15.00
❑ 90 Chet Hanulak	25.00	15.00
❑ 91 Thurman McGraw	25.00	15.00
❑ 92 Don Heinrich RC SP	30.00	18.00
❑ 93 Dan McKown	25.00	15.00
❑ 94 Bob Fleck	25.00	15.00
❑ 95 Jerry Hilgenberg	25.00	15.00
❑ 96 Bill Walsh C	25.00	15.00
❑ 97A Tom Finnin ERR	60.00	35.00
❑ 97B Tom Finnan COR	8.00	4.00
❑ 98 Paul Barry	5.00	3.00
❑ 99 Chick Jagade	5.00	3.00
❑ 100 Jack Christiansen	20.00	12.00
❑ 101 Gordy Soltau	5.00	3.00
❑ 102A Emlen Tunnel ERR	20.00	12.00
❑ 102B Emlen Tunnell COR	20.00	12.00
❑ 102C Emlen Tunnell COR	20.00	12.00
❑ 103 Stan West	5.00	3.00
❑ 104 Jerry Williams	5.00	3.00
❑ 105 Veryl Switzer	5.00	3.00
❑ 106 Billy Stone	5.00	3.00
❑ 107 Jerry Watford	5.00	3.00
❑ 108 Elbert Nickel	8.00	4.00
❑ 109 Ed Sharkey	5.00	3.00
❑ 110 Steve Meilinger	5.00	3.00
❑ 111 Dante Lavelli	20.00	12.00
❑ 112 Leon Hart	15.00	7.50
❑ 113 Charley Conerly	30.00	18.00
❑ 114 Richard Lemmon	5.00	3.00
❑ 115 Al Carmichael	5.00	3.00
❑ 116 George Connor	20.00	12.00
❑ 117 John Olszewski	5.00	3.00
❑ 118 Ernie Stautner	25.00	15.00
❑ 119 Ray Smith	5.00	3.00
❑ 120 Neil Worden	5.00	3.00
❑ 121 Jim Dooley	5.00	3.00
❑ 122 Arnold Galiffa	5.00	3.00
❑ 123 Kline Gilbert	5.00	3.00
❑ 124 Bob Hoernschemeyer	8.00	4.00
❑ 125 Wilford White RC	15.00	7.50
❑ 126 Art Spinney	5.00	3.00
❑ 127 Joe Koch	5.00	3.00
❑ 128 John Lattner RC !	80.00	40.00

1955 Bowman

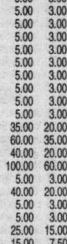

❑ COMPLETE SET (160)	1600.00	1000.00
❑ COMMON CARD (1-64)	5.00	3.00
❑ COMMON CARD (65-160)	8.00	5.00
❑ WRAPPER (1-CENT)	225.00	150.00
❑ WRAPPER (5-CENT)	100.00	60.00
❑ 1 Doak Walker !	75.00	40.00
❑ 2 Mike McCormack RC	30.00	18.00
❑ 3 John Olszewski	5.00	3.00
❑ 4 Dorne Dibble	5.00	3.00
❑ 5 Lindon Crow	5.00	3.00
❑ 6 Hugh Taylor UER	8.00	4.00
❑ 7 Frank Gifford	75.00	45.00
❑ 8 Alan Ameche RC	40.00	25.00
❑ 9 Don Stonesifer	5.00	3.00
❑ 10 Pete Pihos	15.00	7.50
❑ 11 Bill Austin	5.00	3.00
❑ 12 Dick Alban	5.00	3.00
❑ 13 Bobby Walston	8.00	4.00
❑ 14 Len Ford RC	40.00	25.00
❑ 15 Jug Girard	5.00	3.00
❑ 16 Charley Conerly	25.00	15.00
❑ 17 Volney Peters	5.00	3.00
❑ 18 Max Boydston	5.00	3.00
❑ 19 Leon Hart	12.00	6.00
❑ 20 Bert Rechichar	5.00	3.00
❑ 21 Lee Riley	5.00	3.00
❑ 22 Johnny Carson	5.00	3.00
❑ 23 Harry Thompson	5.00	3.00
❑ 24 Ray Wietecha	5.00	3.00
❑ 25 Ollie Matson	25.00	15.00
❑ 26 Eddie LeBaron	15.00	7.50
❑ 27 Jack Simmons	5.00	3.00
❑ 28 Jack Christiansen	15.00	7.50
❑ 29 Bucko Kilroy	8.00	4.00
❑ 30 Tom Keane	5.00	3.00
❑ 31 Dave Leggett	5.00	3.00
❑ 32 Norm Van Brocklin	40.00	25.00
❑ 33 Harlon Hill RC	8.00	4.00
❑ 34 Robert Haner	5.00	3.00
❑ 35 Veryl Switzer	5.00	3.00
❑ 36 Dick Stanfel RC	12.00	6.00
❑ 37 Lou Groza	25.00	15.00
❑ 38 Tank Younger	12.00	6.00
❑ 39 Dick Flanagan	5.00	3.00
❑ 40 Jim Dooley	5.00	3.00
❑ 41 Ray Collins	5.00	3.00
❑ 42 John Henry Johnson RC	40.00	25.00
❑ 43 Tom Fears	15.00	7.50
❑ 44 Joe Perry	30.00	18.00
❑ 45 Gene Brito RC	5.00	3.00
❑ 46 Bill Johnson C	5.00	3.00
❑ 47 Dan Towler	12.00	6.00
❑ 48 Dick Moegle	8.00	4.00
❑ 49 Kline Gilbert	5.00	3.00
❑ 50 Les Gobel	5.00	3.00
❑ 51 Ray Krouse RC	5.00	3.00
❑ 52 Pat Summerall RC	70.00	35.00
❑ 53 Ed Brown RC	12.00	6.00
❑ 54 Lynn Chandnois	5.00	3.00
❑ 55 Joe Heap	5.00	3.00
❑ 56 John Hoffman	5.00	3.00
❑ 57 Howard Ferguson	5.00	3.00
❑ 58 Bobby Watkins	5.00	3.00
❑ 59 Charlie Ane RC	5.00	3.00
❑ 60 Ken MacAfee E RC	8.00	4.00
❑ 61 Ralph Guglielmi RC	8.00	4.00
❑ 62 George Blanda	60.00	35.00
❑ 63 Kenneth Snyder	5.00	3.00

❑ 64 Chet Ostrowski	5.00	3.00
❑ 65 Buddy Young	15.00	7.50
❑ 66 Gordy Soltau	8.00	5.00
❑ 67 Eddie Bell	8.00	5.00
❑ 68 Ben Agajanian RC	12.00	6.00
❑ 69 Tom Dahms	8.00	5.00
❑ 70 Jim Ringo RC	50.00	30.00
❑ 71 Bobby Layne	75.00	45.00
❑ 72 Y.A.Tittle	75.00	45.00
❑ 73 Bob Gaona	8.00	5.00
❑ 74 Tobin Rote	12.00	6.00
❑ 75 Hugh McElhenny	30.00	18.00
❑ 76 John Kreamcheck	8.00	5.00
❑ 77 Al Dorow	12.00	6.00
❑ 78 Bill Wade	15.00	7.50
❑ 79 Dale Dodrill	8.00	5.00
❑ 80 Chuck Drazenovich	8.00	5.00
❑ 81 Billy Wilson RC	12.00	6.00
❑ 82 Les Richter	12.00	6.00
❑ 83 Pat Brady	8.00	5.00
❑ 84 Bob Hoernschemeyer	12.00	6.00
❑ 85 Joe Arenas	8.00	5.00
❑ 86 Len Szafaryn UER	8.00	5.00
❑ 87 Rick Casares RC	20.00	12.00
❑ 88 Leon McLaughlin	8.00	5.00
❑ 89 Charley Toogood	8.00	5.00
❑ 90 Tom Bettis	8.00	5.00
❑ 91 John Sandusky	8.00	5.00
❑ 92 Bill Wightkin	8.00	5.00
❑ 93 Darrel Brewster	8.00	5.00
❑ 94 Marion Campbell	15.00	7.50
❑ 95 Floyd Reid	8.00	5.00
❑ 96 Chick Jagade	8.00	5.00
❑ 97 George Taliaferro	8.00	5.00
❑ 98 Carlton Massey	8.00	5.00
❑ 99 Fran Rogel	8.00	5.00
❑ 100 Alex Sandusky	8.00	5.00
❑ 101 Bob St.Clair RC	35.00	20.00
❑ 102 Al Carmichael	8.00	5.00
❑ 103 Carl Taseff RC	8.00	5.00
❑ 104 Leo Nomellini	25.00	15.00
❑ 105 Tom Scott	8.00	5.00
❑ 106 Ted Marchibroda	15.00	7.50
❑ 107 Art Spinney	8.00	5.00
❑ 108 Wayne Robinson	8.00	5.00
❑ 109 Jim Ricca	8.00	5.00
❑ 110 Lou Ferry	8.00	5.00
❑ 111 Roger Zatkoff	8.00	5.00
❑ 112 Lou Creekmur	15.00	7.50
❑ 113 Kenny Konz	8.00	5.00
❑ 114 Doug Eggers	8.00	5.00
❑ 115 Bobby Thomason	8.00	5.00
❑ 116 Bill McPeak	8.00	5.00
❑ 117 William Brown	8.00	5.00
❑ 118 Royce Womble	8.00	5.00
❑ 119 Frank Gatski RC	35.00	20.00
❑ 120 Jim Finks	15.00	7.50
❑ 121 Andy Robustelli	25.00	15.00
❑ 122 Bobby Dillon	8.00	5.00
❑ 123 Leo Sanford	8.00	5.00
❑ 124 Elbert Nickel	12.00	6.00
❑ 125 Wayne Hansen	8.00	5.00
❑ 126 Buck Lansford RC	8.00	5.00
❑ 127 Gern Nagler	8.00	5.00
❑ 128 Jim Salsbury	8.00	5.00
❑ 129 Dale Atkeson RC	8.00	5.00
❑ 130 John Schweder	8.00	5.00
❑ 131 Dave Hanner	12.00	6.00
❑ 132 Eddie Price	8.00	5.00
❑ 133 Vic Janowicz	30.00	15.00
❑ 134 Ernie Stautner	25.00	15.00
❑ 135 James Parmer	8.00	5.00
❑ 136 Emlen Tunnell UER	20.00	12.00
❑ 137 Kyle Rote	15.00	7.50
❑ 138 Norm Willey	8.00	5.00
❑ 139 Charley Trippi	20.00	12.00
❑ 140 Billy Howton	12.00	6.00
❑ 141 Bobby Clatterbuck	8.00	5.00
❑ 142 Bob Boyd	8.00	5.00
❑ 143 Bob Toneff RC	12.00	6.00
❑ 144 Jerry Helluin	8.00	5.00
❑ 145 Adrian Burk	8.00	5.00
❑ 146 Walt Michaels	12.00	6.00
❑ 147 Zollie Toth	8.00	5.00
❑ 148 Frank Varrichione RC	8.00	5.00
❑ 149 Dick Bielski RC	8.00	5.00
❑ 150 George Ratterman	12.00	6.00
❑ 151 Mike Jarmoluk	8.00	5.00
❑ 152 Tom Landry	200.00	125.00
❑ 153 Ray Renfro	12.00	6.00
❑ 154 Zeke Bratkowski	12.00	6.00
❑ 155 Jerry Norton	8.00	5.00
❑ 156 Maurice Bassett	8.00	5.00
❑ 157 Volney Quinlan	8.00	5.00
❑ 158 Chuck Bednarik	30.00	18.00
❑ 159 Don Colo	8.00	5.00
❑ 160 L.G. Dupre RC !	40.00	20.00

1991 Bowman

❑ COMPLETE SET (561)	12.00	5.00
❑ COMP.FACT.SET (561)	12.00	5.00
❑ 1 Jeff George RS	.25	.08
❑ 2 Richmond Webb RS	.05	.01
❑ 3 Emmitt Smith RS	1.25	.50
❑ 4 Mark Carrier DB RS UER	.05	.01
❑ 5 Steve Christie RS	.05	.01
❑ 6 Keith Sims RS	.05	.01
❑ 7 Rob Moore RS UER	.25	.08
❑ 8 Johnny Johnson RS	.05	.01
❑ 9 Eric Green RS	.05	.01
❑ 10 Ben Smith RS	.05	.01
❑ 11 Tory Epps RS	.05	.01
❑ 12 Andre Rison	.10	.02
❑ 13 Shawn Collins	.05	.01
❑ 14 Chris Hinton	.05	.01
❑ 15 Deion Sanders	.40	.15
❑ 16 Darion Conner	.05	.01
❑ 17 Michael Haynes	.25	.08
❑ 18 Chris Miller	.10	.02
❑ 19 Jessie Tuggle	.05	.01
❑ 20 Scott Fulhage	.05	.01
❑ 21 Bill Fralic	.05	.01
❑ 22 Floyd Dixon	.05	.01
❑ 23 Oliver Barnett	.05	.01
❑ 24 Mike Rozier	.05	.01
❑ 25 Tory Epps	.05	.01
❑ 26 Tim Green	.05	.01
❑ 27 Steve Broussard	.05	.01
❑ 28 Bruce Pickens RC	.05	.01
❑ 29 Mike Pritchard RC	.25	.08
❑ 30 Andre Reed	.10	.02
❑ 31 Darryl Talley	.05	.01
❑ 32 Nate Odomes	.05	.01
❑ 33 Jamie Mueller	.05	.01
❑ 34 Leon Seals	.05	.01
❑ 35 Keith McKeller	.05	.01
❑ 36 Al Edwards	.05	.01
❑ 37 Butch Rolle	.05	.01
❑ 38 Jeff Wright RC	.05	.01
❑ 39 Will Wolford	.05	.01
❑ 40 James Williams	.05	.01
❑ 41 Kent Hull	.05	.01
❑ 42 James Lofton	.10	.02
❑ 43 Frank Reich	.10	.02
❑ 44 Bruce Smith	.25	.08
❑ 45 Thurman Thomas	.25	.08
❑ 46 Leonard Smith	.05	.01
❑ 47 Shane Conlan	.05	.01
❑ 48 Steve Tasker	.10	.02
❑ 49 Ray Bentley	.05	.01
❑ 50 Cornelius Bennett	.10	.02
❑ 51 Stan Thomas	.05	.01
❑ 52 Shaun Gayle	.05	.01
❑ 53 Wendell Davis	.05	.01
❑ 54 James Thornton	.05	.01
❑ 55 Mark Carrier DB	.10	.02
❑ 56 Richard Dent	.10	.02
❑ 57 Ron Morris	.05	.01
❑ 58 Mike Singletary	.10	.02
❑ 59 Jay Hilgenberg	.05	.01
❑ 60 Donnell Woolford	.05	.01
❑ 61 Jim Covert	.05	.01
❑ 62 Jim Harbaugh	.25	.08
❑ 63 Neal Anderson	.10	.02
❑ 64 Brad Muster	.05	.01
❑ 65 Kevin Butler	.05	.01
❑ 66 Trace Armstrong UER	.05	.01
❑ 67 Ron Cox	.05	.01
❑ 68 Peter Tom Willis	.05	.01
❑ 69 Johnny Bailey	.05	.01
❑ 70 Mark Bortz UER	.05	.01
❑ 71 Chris Zorich RC	.25	.08
❑ 72 Lamar Rogers RC	.05	.01
❑ 73 David Grant UER	.05	.01
❑ 74 Lewis Billups	.05	.01
❑ 75 Harold Green	.10	.02
❑ 76 Ickey Woods	.05	.01
❑ 77 Eddie Brown	.05	.01
❑ 78 David Fulcher	.05	.01
❑ 79 Anthony Munoz	.10	.02
❑ 80 Carl Zander	.05	.01
❑ 81 Rodney Holman	.05	.01
❑ 82 James Brooks	.10	.02
❑ 83 Tim McGee	.05	.01
❑ 84 Boomer Esiason	.10	.02
❑ 85 Leon White	.05	.01
❑ 86 James Francis UER	.05	.01
❑ 87 Mitchell Price RC	.05	.01
❑ 88 Ed King RC	.05	.01
❑ 89 Eric Turner RC	.10	.02
❑ 90 Rob Burnett RC	.10	.02
❑ 91 Leroy Hoard	.10	.02
❑ 92 Kevin Mack UER	.05	.01
❑ 93 Thane Gash UER	.05	.01
❑ 94 Gregg Rakoczy	.05	.01
❑ 95 Clay Matthews	.10	.02
❑ 96 Eric Metcalf	.10	.02
❑ 97 Stephen Braggs	.05	.01
❑ 98 Frank Minnifield	.05	.01
❑ 99 Reggie Langhorne	.05	.01
❑ 100 Mike Johnson	.05	.01
❑ 101 Brian Brennan	.05	.01
❑ 102 Anthony Pleasant	.05	.01
❑ 103 Godfrey Myles RC UER	.05	.01
❑ 104 Russell Maryland RC	.25	.08
❑ 105 James Washington RC	.05	.01
❑ 106 Nate Newton	.10	.02
❑ 107 Jimmie Jones	.05	.01
❑ 108 Jay Novacek	.25	.08
❑ 109 Alexander Wright	.05	.01
❑ 110 Jack Del Rio	.10	.02
❑ 111 Jim Jeffcoat	.05	.01
❑ 112 Mike Saxon	.05	.01
❑ 113 Troy Aikman	.75	.30
❑ 114 Issiac Holt	.05	.01
❑ 115 Ken Norton	.10	.02
❑ 116 Kelvin Martin	.05	.01
❑ 117 Emmitt Smith	2.50	1.00
❑ 118 Ken Willis	.05	.01
❑ 119 Daniel Stubbs	.05	.01
❑ 120 Michael Irvin	.25	.08
❑ 121 Danny Noonan	.05	.01
❑ 122 Alvin Harper RC	.25	.08
❑ 123 Reggie Johnson RC	.05	.01
❑ 124 Vance Johnson	.05	.01
❑ 125 Steve Atwater	.05	.01
❑ 126 Greg Kragen	.05	.01
❑ 127 John Elway	1.25	.50
❑ 128 Simon Fletcher	.05	.01
❑ 129 Wymon Henderson	.05	.01
❑ 130 Ricky Nattiel	.05	.01
❑ 131 Shannon Sharpe	.50	.20
❑ 132 Ron Holmes	.05	.01
❑ 133 Karl Mecklenburg	.05	.01
❑ 134 Bobby Humphrey	.05	.01
❑ 135 Clarence Kay	.05	.01
❑ 136 Dennis Smith	.05	.01
❑ 137 Jim Juriga	.05	.01
❑ 138 Melvin Bratton	.05	.01
❑ 139 Mark Jackson UER	.05	.01
❑ 140 Michael Brooks	.05	.01
❑ 141 Alton Montgomery	.05	.01
❑ 142 Mike Croel RC	.05	.01
❑ 143 Mel Gray	.10	.02
❑ 144 Michael Cofer	.05	.01
❑ 145 Jeff Campbell	.05	.01
❑ 146 Dan Owens	.05	.01
❑ 147 Robert Clark UER	.05	.01
❑ 148 Jim Arnold	.05	.01
❑ 149 William White	.05	.01

❑ 150 Rodney Peete .10 .02
❑ 151 Jerry Ball .05 .01
❑ 152 Bennie Blades .05 .01
❑ 153 Barry Sanders UER 1.25 .50
❑ 154 Andre Ware .10 .02
❑ 155 Lomas Brown .05 .01
❑ 156 Chris Spielman .10 .02
❑ 157 Kelvin Pritchett RC .10 .02
❑ 158 Herman Moore RC .25 .08
❑ 159 Chris Jacke .05 .01
❑ 160 Tony Mandarich .05 .01
❑ 161 Perry Kemp .05 .01
❑ 162 Johnny Holland .05 .01
❑ 163 Mark Lee .05 .01
❑ 164 Anthony Dilweg .05 .01
❑ 165 Scott Stephen RC .05 .01
❑ 166 Ed West .05 .01
❑ 167 Mark Murphy .05 .01
❑ 168 Darrell Thompson .05 .01
❑ 169 James Campen RC .05 .01
❑ 170 Jeff Query .05 .01
❑ 171 Brian Noble .05 .01
❑ 172 Sterling Sharpe UER .25 .08
❑ 173 Robert Brown .05 .01
❑ 174 Tim Harris .05 .01
❑ 175 LeRoy Butler .10 .02
❑ 176 Don Majkowski .05 .01
❑ 177 Vinnie Clark RC .05 .01
❑ 178 Esera Tuaolo RC .05 .01
❑ 179 Lorenzo White UER .05 .01
❑ 180 Warren Moon .25 .08
❑ 181 Sean Jones .10 .02
❑ 182 Curtis Duncan .05 .01
❑ 183 Al Smith .05 .01
❑ 184 Richard Johnson CB RC .05 .01
❑ 185 Tony Jones WR .05 .01
❑ 186 Bubba McDowell .05 .01
❑ 187 Bruce Matthews .10 .02
❑ 188 Ray Childress .05 .01
❑ 189 Haywood Jeffires .10 .02
❑ 190 Ernest Givins .10 .02
❑ 191 Mike Munchak .10 .02
❑ 192 Greg Montgomery .05 .01
❑ 193 Cody Carlson RC .05 .01
❑ 194 Johnny Meads .05 .01
❑ 195 Drew Hill UER .05 .01
❑ 196 Mike Dumas RC .05 .01
❑ 197 Darryll Lewis RC .10 .02
❑ 198 Rohn Stark .05 .01
❑ 199 Clarence Verdin UER .05 .01
❑ 200 Mike Prior .05 .01
❑ 201 Eugene Daniel .05 .01
❑ 202 Dean Biasucci .05 .01
❑ 203 Jeff Herrod .05 .01
❑ 204 Keith Taylor .05 .01
❑ 205 Jon Hand .05 .01
❑ 206 Pat Beach .05 .01
❑ 207 Duane Bickett .05 .01
❑ 208 Jessie Hester UER .05 .01
❑ 209 Chip Banks .05 .01
❑ 210 Ray Donaldson .05 .01
❑ 211 Bill Brooks .05 .01
❑ 212 Jeff George .25 .08
❑ 213 Tony Siragusa RC .10 .02
❑ 214 Albert Bentley .05 .01
❑ 215 Joe Valerio .05 .01
❑ 216 Chris Martin .05 .01
❑ 217 Christian Okoye .05 .01
❑ 218 Stephone Paige .05 .01
❑ 219 Percy Snow .05 .01
❑ 220 David Szott .05 .01
❑ 221 Derrick Thomas .25 .08
❑ 222 Todd McNair .05 .01
❑ 223 Albert Lewis .05 .01
❑ 224 Neil Smith .25 .08
❑ 225 Barry Word .05 .01
❑ 226 Robb Thomas .05 .01
❑ 227 John Alt .05 .01
❑ 228 Jonathan Hayes .05 .01
❑ 229 Kevin Ross .05 .01
❑ 230 Nick Lowery .05 .01
❑ 231 Tim Grunhard .05 .01
❑ 232 Dan Saleaumua .05 .01
❑ 233 Steve DeBerg .05 .01
❑ 234 Harvey Williams RC .25 .08
❑ 235 Nick Bell RC UER .05 .01
❑ 236 Mervyn Fernandez UER .05 .01
❑ 237 Howie Long .25 .08
❑ 238 Marcus Allen .25 .08
❑ 239 Eddie Anderson .05 .01
❑ 240 Ethan Horton .05 .01
❑ 241 Lionel Washington .05 .01
❑ 242 Steve Wisniewski UER .05 .01
❑ 243 Bo Jackson UER .30 .10
❑ 244 Greg Townsend .05 .01
❑ 245 Jeff Jaeger .05 .01
❑ 246 Aaron Wallace .05 .01
❑ 247 Garry Lewis .05 .01
❑ 248 Steve Smith .05 .01
❑ 249 Willie Gault UER .05 .01
❑ 250 Scott Davis .05 .01
❑ 251 Jay Schroeder .05 .01
❑ 252 Don Mosebar .05 .01
❑ 253 Todd Marinovich RC .05 .01
❑ 254 Irv Pankey .05 .01
❑ 255 Flipper Anderson .05 .01
❑ 256 Tom Newberry .05 .01
❑ 257 Kevin Greene .10 .02
❑ 258 Mike Wilcher .05 .01
❑ 259 Bern Brostek .05 .01
❑ 260 Buford McGee .05 .01
❑ 261 Cleveland Gary .05 .01
❑ 262 Jackie Slater .05 .01
❑ 263 Henry Ellard .10 .02
❑ 264 Alvin Wright .05 .01
❑ 265 Darryl Henley RC .05 .01
❑ 266 Damone Johnson RC .05 .01
❑ 267 Frank Stams .05 .01
❑ 268 Jerry Gray .05 .01
❑ 269 Jim Everett .10 .02
❑ 270 Pat Terrell .05 .01
❑ 271 Todd Lyght RC .05 .01
❑ 272 Aaron Cox .05 .01
❑ 273 Barry Sanders LL .50 .20
❑ 274 Jerry Rice LL .40 .15
❑ 275 Derrick Thomas LL .25 .08
❑ 276 Mark Carrier DB LL .10 .02
❑ 277 Warren Moon LL .25 .08
❑ 278 Randall Cunningham LL .10 .02
❑ 279 Nick Lowery LL .05 .01
❑ 280 Clarence Verdin LL .05 .01
❑ 281 Thurman Thomas LL .25 .08
❑ 282 Mike Horan LL .05 .01
❑ 283 Flipper Anderson LL .05 .01
❑ 284 John Offerdahl .05 .01
❑ 285 Dan Marino UER 1.25 .50
❑ 286 Mark Clayton .10 .02
❑ 287 Tony Paige .05 .01
❑ 288 Keith Sims .05 .01
❑ 289 Jeff Cross .05 .01
❑ 290 Pete Stoyanovich .05 .01
❑ 291 Ferrell Edmunds .05 .01
❑ 292 Reggie Roby .05 .01
❑ 293 Louis Oliver .05 .01
❑ 294 Jarvis Williams .05 .01
❑ 295 Sammie Smith .05 .01
❑ 296 Richmond Webb .05 .01
❑ 297 J.B. Brown .05 .01
❑ 298 Jim C.Jensen .05 .01
❑ 299 Mark Duper .10 .02
❑ 300 David Griggs .05 .01
❑ 301 Randal Hill RC .10 .02
❑ 302 Aaron Craver RC .05 .01
❑ 303 Keith Millard .05 .01
❑ 304 Steve Jordan .05 .01
❑ 305 Anthony Carter .10 .02
❑ 306 Mike Merriweather .05 .01
❑ 307 Audray McMillian RC UER .05 .01
❑ 308 Randall McDaniel .05 .01
❑ 309 Gary Zimmerman .05 .01
❑ 310 Carl Lee .05 .01
❑ 311 Reggie Rutland .05 .01
❑ 312 Hassan Jones .05 .01
❑ 313 Kirk Lowdermilk UER .05 .01
❑ 314 Herschel Walker .10 .02
❑ 315 Chris Doleman .05 .01
❑ 316 Joey Browner .05 .01
❑ 317 Wade Wilson .10 .02
❑ 318 Henry Thomas .05 .01
❑ 319 Rich Gannon .25 .08
❑ 320 Al Noga UER .05 .01
❑ 321 Pat Harlow RC .05 .01
❑ 322 Bruce Armstrong .05 .01
❑ 323 Maurice Hurst .05 .01
❑ 324 Brent Williams .05 .01
❑ 325 Chris Singleton .05 .01
❑ 326 Jason Staurovsky .05 .01
❑ 327 Marvin Allen .05 .01
❑ 328 Hart Lee Dykes .05 .01
❑ 329 Johnny Rembert .05 .01
❑ 330 Andre Tippett .05 .01
❑ 331 Greg McMurtry .05 .01
❑ 332 John Stephens .05 .01
❑ 333 Ray Agnew .05 .01
❑ 334 Tommy Hodson .05 .01
❑ 335 Ronnie Lippett .05 .01
❑ 336 Marv Cook .05 .01
❑ 337 Tommy Barnhardt RC .05 .01
❑ 338 Dalton Hilliard .05 .01
❑ 339 Sam Mills .05 .01
❑ 340 Morten Andersen .05 .01
❑ 341 Stan Brock .05 .01
❑ 342 Brett Maxie .05 .01
❑ 343 Steve Walsh .05 .01
❑ 344 Vaughan Johnson .05 .01
❑ 345 Rickey Jackson .05 .01
❑ 346 Renaldo Turnbull .05 .01
❑ 347 Joel Hilgenberg .05 .01
❑ 348 Toi Cook RC .05 .01
❑ 349 Robert Massey .05 .01
❑ 350 Pat Swilling .10 .02
❑ 351 Eric Martin .05 .01
❑ 352 Rueben Mayes UER .05 .01
❑ 353 Vince Buck .05 .01
❑ 354 Brett Perriman .25 .08
❑ 355 Wesley Carroll RC .05 .01
❑ 356 Jarrod Bunch RC .05 .01
❑ 357 Pepper Johnson .05 .01
❑ 358 Dave Meggett .10 .02
❑ 359 Mark Collins .05 .01
❑ 360 Sean Landeta .05 .01
❑ 361 Maurice Carthon .05 .01
❑ 362 Mike Fox UER .05 .01
❑ 363 Jeff Hostetler .10 .02
❑ 364 Phil Simms .10 .02
❑ 365 Leonard Marshall .05 .01
❑ 366 Gary Reasons .05 .01
❑ 367 Rodney Hampton .25 .08
❑ 368 Greg Jackson RC .05 .01
❑ 369 Jumbo Elliott .05 .01
❑ 370 Bob Kratch RC .05 .01
❑ 371 Lawrence Taylor .25 .08
❑ 372 Erik Howard .05 .01
❑ 373 Carl Banks .05 .01
❑ 374 Stephen Baker .05 .01
❑ 375 Mark Ingram .10 .02
❑ 376 Browning Nagle RC .05 .01
❑ 377 Jeff Lageman .05 .01
❑ 378 Ken O'Brien .05 .01
❑ 379 Al Toon .10 .02
❑ 380 Joe Prokop .05 .01
❑ 381 Tony Stargell .05 .01
❑ 382 Blair Thomas .05 .01
❑ 383 Erik McMillan .05 .01
❑ 384 Dennis Byrd .05 .01
❑ 385 Freeman McNeil .05 .01
❑ 386 Brad Baxter .05 .01
❑ 387 Mark Boyer .05 .01
❑ 388 Terance Mathis .10 .02
❑ 389 Jim Sweeney .05 .01
❑ 390 Kyle Clifton .05 .01
❑ 391 Pat Leahy .05 .01
❑ 392 Rob Moore .25 .08
❑ 393 James Hasty .05 .01
❑ 394 Blaise Bryant .05 .01
❑ 395A Jesse Campbell RC ERR 1.00 .40
❑ 395B Jesse Campbell RC COR .05 .01
❑ 396 Keith Jackson .10 .02
❑ 397 Jerome Brown .05 .01
❑ 398 Keith Byars .05 .01
❑ 399 Seth Joyner .10 .02
❑ 400 Mike Bellamy .05 .01
❑ 401 Fred Barnett .25 .08
❑ 402 Reggie Singletary RC .05 .01
❑ 403 Reggie White .25 .08
❑ 404 Randall Cunningham .25 .08
❑ 405 Byron Evans .05 .01
❑ 406 Wes Hopkins .05 .01
❑ 407 Ben Smith .05 .01
❑ 408 Roger Ruzek .05 .01
❑ 409 Eric Allen UER .05 .01
❑ 410 Anthony Toney UER .05 .01
❑ 411 Clyde Simmons .05 .01
❑ 412 Andre Waters .05 .01
❑ 413 Calvin Williams .10 .02
❑ 414 Eric Swann RC .25 .08
❑ 415 Eric Hill .05 .01

❑ 416 Tim McDonald .05 .01
❑ 417 Luis Sharpe .05 .01
❑ 418 Ernie Jones UER .05 .01
❑ 419 Ken Harvey .10 .02
❑ 420 Ricky Proehl .05 .01
❑ 421 Johnny Johnson .05 .01
❑ 422 Anthony Bell .05 .01
❑ 423 Timm Rosenbach .05 .01
❑ 424 Rich Camarillo .05 .01
❑ 425 Walter Reeves .05 .01
❑ 426 Freddie Joe Nunn .05 .01
❑ 427 Anthony Thompson UER .05 .01
❑ 428 Bill Lewis .05 .01
❑ 429 Jim Wahler RC .05 .01
❑ 430 Cedric Mack .05 .01
❑ 431 Mike Jones DE RC .05 .01
❑ 432 Ernie Mills RC .10 .02
❑ 433 Tim Worley .05 .01
❑ 434 Greg Lloyd .25 .08
❑ 435 Dermontti Dawson .05 .01
❑ 436 Louis Lipps .05 .01
❑ 437 Eric Green .05 .01
❑ 438 Donald Evans .05 .01
❑ 439 D.J. Johnson .05 .01
❑ 440 Tunch Ilkin .05 .01
❑ 441 Bubby Brister .05 .01
❑ 442 Chris Calloway .05 .01
❑ 443 David Little .05 .01
❑ 444 Thomas Everett .05 .01
❑ 445 Carnell Lake .05 .01
❑ 446 Rod Woodson .25 .08
❑ 447 Gary Anderson K .05 .01
❑ 448 Merril Hoge .05 .01
❑ 449 Gerald Williams .05 .01
❑ 450 Eric Moten RC .05 .01
❑ 451 Marion Butts .10 .02
❑ 452 Leslie O'Neal .10 .02
❑ 453 Ronnie Harmon .05 .01
❑ 454 Gill Byrd .05 .01
❑ 455 Junior Seau .25 .08
❑ 456 Nate Lewis RC .05 .01
❑ 457 Leo Goeas .05 .01
❑ 458 Burt Grossman .05 .01
❑ 459 Courtney Hall .05 .01
❑ 460 Anthony Miller .10 .02
❑ 461 Gary Plummer .05 .01
❑ 462 Billy Joe Tolliver .05 .01
❑ 463 Lee Williams .05 .01
❑ 464 Arthur Cox .05 .01
❑ 465 John Kidd UER .05 .01
❑ 466 Frank Cornish .05 .01
❑ 467 John Carney .05 .01
❑ 468 Eric Bieniemy RC .05 .01
❑ 469 Don Griffin .05 .01
❑ 470 Jerry Rice .75 .30
❑ 471 Keith DeLong .05 .01
❑ 472 John Taylor .10 .02
❑ 473 Brent Jones .25 .08
❑ 474 Pierce Holt .05 .01
❑ 475 Kevin Fagan .05 .01
❑ 476 Bill Romanowski .05 .01
❑ 477 Dexter Carter .05 .01
❑ 478 Guy McIntyre .05 .01
❑ 479 Joe Montana 1.25 .50
❑ 480 Charles Haley .10 .02
❑ 481 Mike Cofer .05 .01
❑ 482 Jesse Sapolu .05 .01
❑ 483 Eric Davis .05 .01
❑ 484 Mike Sherrard .05 .01
❑ 485 Steve Young .75 .30
❑ 486 Darryl Pollard .05 .01
❑ 487 Tom Rathman .05 .01
❑ 488 Michael Carter .05 .01
❑ 489 Ricky Watters RC 1.50 .60
❑ 490 John Johnson RC .05 .01
❑ 491 Eugene Robinson .05 .01
❑ 492 Andy Heck .05 .01
❑ 493 John L. Williams .05 .01
❑ 494 Norm Johnson .05 .01
❑ 495 David Wyman .05 .01
❑ 496 Derrick Fenner UER .05 .01
❑ 497 Rick Donnelly .05 .01
❑ 498 Tony Woods .05 .01
❑ 499 Derrick Loville RC .05 .01
❑ 500 Dave Krieg .10 .02
❑ 501 Joe Nash .05 .01
❑ 502 Brian Blades .10 .02
❑ 503 Cortez Kennedy .25 .08
❑ 504 Jeff Bryant .05 .01
❑ 505 Tommy Kane .05 .01
❑ 506 Travis McNeal .05 .01
❑ 507 Terry Wooden .05 .01
❑ 508 Chris Warren .25 .08
❑ 509A Dan McGwire RC ERR .05 .01
❑ 509B Dan McGwire RC COR .05 .01
❑ 510 Mark Robinson .05 .01
❑ 511 Ron Hall .05 .01
❑ 512 Paul Gruber .05 .01
❑ 513 Harry Hamilton .05 .01
❑ 514 Keith McCants .05 .01
❑ 515 Reggie Cobb .05 .01
❑ 516 Steve Christie UER .05 .01
❑ 517 Broderick Thomas .05 .01
❑ 518 Mark Carrier WR .25 .08
❑ 519 Vinny Testaverde .10 .02
❑ 520 Ricky Reynolds .05 .01
❑ 521 Jesse Anderson .05 .01
❑ 522 Reuben Davis .05 .01
❑ 523 Wayne Haddix .05 .01
❑ 524 Gary Anderson RB UER .05 .01
❑ 525 Bruce Hill .05 .01
❑ 526 Kevin Murphy .05 .01
❑ 527 Lawrence Dawsey RC .10 .02
❑ 528 Ricky Ervins RC .10 .02
❑ 529 Charles Mann .05 .01
❑ 530 Jim Lachey .05 .01
❑ 531 Mark Rypien UER .10 .02
❑ 532 Darrell Green .05 .01
❑ 533 Stan Humphries .25 .08
❑ 534 Jeff Bostic UER .05 .01
❑ 535 Earnest Byner .05 .01
❑ 536 Art Monk UER .10 .02
❑ 537 Don Warren .05 .01
❑ 538 Darryl Grant .05 .01
❑ 539 Wilber Marshall .05 .01
❑ 540 Kurt Gouveia RC .05 .01
❑ 541 Markus Koch .05 .01
❑ 542 Andre Collins .05 .01
❑ 543 Chip Lohmiller .05 .01
❑ 544 Alvin Walton .05 .01
❑ 545 Gary Clark .25 .08
❑ 546 Ricky Sanders .05 .01
❑ 547 Redskins vs. Eagles .05 .01
❑ 548 Bengals vs. Oilers .05 .01
❑ 549 Dolphins vs. Chiefs .05 .01
❑ 550 Bears vs. Saints UER .05 .01
❑ 551 Playoffs/Thurman Thomas .10 .02
❑ 552 49ers vs. Redskins .05 .01
❑ 553 Giants vs. Bears .05 .01
❑ 554 Playoffs/Bo Jackson .10 .02
❑ 555 AFC Championship .05 .01
❑ 556 NFC Championship .05 .01
❑ 557 Super Bowl XXV .05 .01
❑ 558 Checklist 1-140 .05 .01
❑ 559 Checklist 141-280 .05 .01
❑ 560 Checklist 281-420 UER .05 .01
❑ 561 Checklist 421-561 UER .05 .01

1992 Bowman

❑ COMPLETE SET (573) 50.00 25.00
❑ 1 Reggie White 1.00 .40
❑ 2 Johnny Meads .25 .08
❑ 3 Chip Lohmiller .25 .08
❑ 4 James Lofton .50 .20
❑ 5 Ray Horton .25 .08
❑ 6 Rich Moran .25 .08
❑ 7 Howard Cross .25 .08
❑ 8 Mike Horan .25 .08
❑ 9 Erik Kramer .50 .20
❑ 10 Steve Wisniewski .25 .08
❑ 11 Michael Haynes .50 .20
❑ 12 Donald Evans .25 .08
❑ 13 Michael Irvin FOIL 1.00 .40
❑ 14 Gary Zimmerman .25 .08
❑ 15 John Friesz .50 .20
❑ 16 Mark Carrier WR 1.00 .40
❑ 17 Mark Duper .25 .08
❑ 18 James Thornton .25 .08
❑ 19 Jon Hand .25 .08
❑ 20 Sterling Sharpe 1.00 .40
❑ 21 Jacob Green .25 .08
❑ 22 Wesley Carroll .25 .08
❑ 23 Clay Matthews .50 .20
❑ 24 Kevin Greene .50 .20
❑ 25 Brad Baxter .25 .08
❑ 26 Don Griffin .25 .08
❑ 27 Robert Delpino 1.50 .60
❑ 28 Lee Johnson .25 .08
❑ 29 Jim Wahler .25 .08
❑ 30 Leonard Russell .50 .20
❑ 31 Eric Moore .25 .08
❑ 32 Dino Hackett .25 .08
❑ 33 Simon Fletcher .25 .08
❑ 34 Al Edwards .25 .08
❑ 35 Brad Edwards .25 .08
❑ 36 James Joseph .25 .08
❑ 37 Rodney Peete .50 .20
❑ 38 Ricky Reynolds .25 .08
❑ 39 Eddie Anderson .25 .08
❑ 40 Ken Clarke .25 .08
❑ 41 Tony Bennett .50 .20
❑ 42 Larry Brown DB .25 .08
❑ 43 Ray Childress .25 .08
❑ 44 Mike Kenn .25 .08
❑ 45 Vestee Jackson .25 .08
❑ 46 Neil O'Donnell .50 .20
❑ 47 Bill Brooks .25 .08
❑ 48 Kevin Butler .25 .08
❑ 49 Joe Phillips .25 .08
❑ 50 Cortez Kennedy .50 .20
❑ 51 Rickey Jackson .25 .08
❑ 52 Vinnie Clark .25 .08
❑ 53 Michael Jackson .50 .20
❑ 54 Ernie Jones .25 .08
❑ 55 Tom Newberry .25 .08
❑ 56 Pat Harlow .25 .08
❑ 57 Craig Taylor .25 .08
❑ 58 Joe Prokop .25 .08
❑ 59 Warren Moon FOIL SP 2.00 .75
❑ 60 Jeff Lageman .25 .08
❑ 61 Neil Smith 1.00 .40
❑ 62 Jim Jeffcoat .25 .08
❑ 63 Bill Fralic .25 .08
❑ 64 Mark Schlereth RC .25 .08
❑ 65 Keith Byars .25 .08
❑ 66 Jeff Hostetler .50 .20
❑ 67 Joey Browner .25 .08
❑ 68 Bobby Hebert FOIL SP 1.50 .60
❑ 69 Keith Sims .25 .08
❑ 70 Warren Moon 1.00 .40
❑ 71 Pio Sagapolutele RC .25 .08
❑ 72 Cornelius Bennett .50 .20
❑ 73 Greg Davis .25 .08
❑ 74 Ronnie Harmon .25 .08
❑ 75 Ron Hall .25 .08
❑ 76 Howie Long 1.00 .40
❑ 77 Greg Lewis .25 .08
❑ 78 Carnell Lake .25 .08
❑ 79 Ray Crockett .25 .08
❑ 80 Tom Waddle .25 .08
❑ 81 Vincent Brown .25 .08
❑ 82 Bill Brooks .50 .20
❑ 83 John L. Williams .25 .08
❑ 84 Floyd Turner .25 .08
❑ 85 Scott Radecic .25 .08
❑ 86 Anthony Munoz .50 .20
❑ 87 Lonnie Young .25 .08
❑ 88 Dexter Carter .25 .08
❑ 89 Tony Zendejas .25 .08
❑ 90 Tim Jorden .25 .08
❑ 91 LeRoy Butler .25 .08
❑ 92 Richard Brown RC .25 .08
❑ 93 Erric Pegram .50 .20
❑ 94 Sean Landeta .25 .08
❑ 95 Clyde Simmons .25 .08
❑ 96 Martin Mayhew .25 .08
❑ 97 Jarvis Williams .25 .08
❑ 98 Barry Word .25 .08
❑ 99 John Taylor FOIL .50 .20
❑ 100 Emmitt Smith 8.00 3.00

Card	Player	Mint	Ex
❑ 101	Leon Seals	.25	.08
❑ 102	Marion Butts	.25	.08
❑ 103	Mike Merriweather	.25	.08
❑ 104	Ernest Givins	.50	.20
❑ 105	Wymon Henderson	.25	.08
❑ 106	Robert Wilson	.25	.08
❑ 107	Bobby Hebert	.25	.08
❑ 108	Terry McDaniel	.25	.08
❑ 109	Jerry Ball	.25	.08
❑ 110	John Taylor	.50	.20
❑ 111	Rob Moore	.50	.20
❑ 112	Thurman Thomas FOIL	1.00	.40
❑ 113	Checklist 1-115	.25	.08
❑ 114	Brian Blades	.50	.20
❑ 115	Larry Kelm	.25	.08
❑ 116	James Francis	.25	.08
❑ 117	Rod Woodson	1.00	.40
❑ 118	Trace Armstrong	.25	.08
❑ 119	Eugene Daniel	.25	.08
❑ 120	Andre Tippett	.25	.08
❑ 121	Chris Jacke	.25	.08
❑ 122	Jessie Tuggle	.25	.08
❑ 123	Chris Chandler	1.00	.40
❑ 124	Tim Johnson	.25	.08
❑ 125	Mark Collins	.25	.08
❑ 126	Aeneas Williams SP	1.50	.60
❑ 127	James Jones DT	.25	.08
❑ 128	George Jamison	.25	.08
❑ 129	Deron Cherry	.25	.08
❑ 130	Mark Clayton	.50	.20
❑ 131	Keith DeLong	.25	.08
❑ 132	Marcus Allen	1.00	.40
❑ 133	Joe Walter RC	.25	.08
❑ 134	Reggie Rutland	.25	.08
❑ 135	Kent Hull	.25	.08
❑ 136	Jeff Feagles	.25	.08
❑ 137	Ronnie Lott FOIL SP	2.00	.75
❑ 138	Henry Rolling	.25	.08
❑ 139	Gary Anderson RB	.25	.08
❑ 140	Morten Andersen	.25	.08
❑ 141	Cris Dishman	.25	.08
❑ 142	David Treadwell	.25	.08
❑ 143	Kevin Gogan	.25	.08
❑ 144	James Hasty	.25	.08
❑ 145	Robert Delpino	.25	.08
❑ 146	Patrick Hunter	.25	.08
❑ 147	Gary Anderson K	.25	.08
❑ 148	Chip Banks	.25	.08
❑ 149	Dan Fike	.25	.08
❑ 150	Chris Miller	.50	.20
❑ 151	Hugh Millen	.25	.08
❑ 152	Courtney Hall	.25	.08
❑ 153	Gary Clark	.50	.20
❑ 154	Michael Brooks	.25	.08
❑ 155	Jay Hilgenberg	.25	.08
❑ 156	Tim McDonald	.25	.08
❑ 157	Andre Tippett	.50	.20
❑ 158	Doug Riesenberg	.25	.08
❑ 159	Bill Maas	.25	.08
❑ 160	Fred Barnett	.50	.20
❑ 161	Pierce Holt	.25	.08
❑ 162	Brian Noble	.25	.08
❑ 163	Harold Green	.25	.08
❑ 164	Joel Hilgenberg	.25	.08
❑ 165	Mervyn Fernandez	.25	.08
❑ 166	John Offerdahl	.25	.08
❑ 167	Shane Conlan	.25	.08
❑ 168	Mark Higgs FOIL SP	1.50	.60
❑ 169	Bubba McDowell	.25	.08
❑ 170	Barry Sanders	6.00	2.50
❑ 171	Larry Roberts	.25	.08
❑ 172	Herschel Walker	.50	.20
❑ 173	Steve McMichael	.50	.20
❑ 174	Kelly Stouffer	.25	.08
❑ 175	Louis Lipps	.25	.08
❑ 176	Jim Everett	.50	.20
❑ 177	Tony Tolbert	.25	.08
❑ 178	Mike Baab	.25	.08
❑ 179	Eric Swann	.50	.20
❑ 180	Emmitt Smith FOIL SP	12.00	5.00
❑ 181	Tim Brown	1.00	.40
❑ 182	Dennis Smith	.25	.08
❑ 183	Moe Gardner	.25	.08
❑ 184	Derrick Walker	.25	.08
❑ 185	Reyna Thompson	.25	.08
❑ 186	Esera Tuaolo	.25	.08
❑ 187	Jeff Wright	.25	.08
❑ 188	Mark Rypien	.25	.08
❑ 189	Quinn Early	.50	.20
❑ 190	Christian Okoye	.25	.08
❑ 191	Keith Jackson	.50	.20
❑ 192	Doug Smith	.25	.08
❑ 193	John Elway FOIL	10.00	4.00
❑ 194	Reggie Cobb	.25	.08
❑ 195	Reggie Roby	.25	.08
❑ 196	Clarence Verdin	.25	.08
❑ 197	Jim Breech	.25	.08
❑ 198	Jim Sweeney	.25	.08
❑ 199	Marv Cook	.25	.08
❑ 200	Ronnie Lott	.50	.20
❑ 201	Mel Gray	.50	.20
❑ 202	Maury Buford	.25	.08
❑ 203	Lorenzo Lynch	.25	.08
❑ 204	Jesse Sapolu	.25	.08
❑ 205	Steve Jordan	.25	.08
❑ 206	Don Majkowski	.25	.08
❑ 207	Flipper Anderson	.25	.08
❑ 208	Ed King	.25	.08
❑ 209	Tony Woods	.25	.08
❑ 210	Ron Heller	.25	.08
❑ 211	Greg Kragen	.25	.08
❑ 212	Scott Case	.25	.08
❑ 213	Tommy Barnhardt	.25	.08
❑ 214	Charles Mann	.25	.08
❑ 215	David Griggs	.25	.08
❑ 216	Kenneth Davis FOIL SP	1.50	.60
❑ 217	Lamar Lathon	.25	.08
❑ 218	Nate Odomes	.25	.08
❑ 219	Vinny Testaverde	.50	.20
❑ 220	Rod Bernstine	.25	.08
❑ 221	Barry Sanders FOIL	10.00	4.00
❑ 222	Carlton Haselrig RC	.25	.08
❑ 223	Steve Beuerlein	.50	.20
❑ 224	John Alt	.25	.08
❑ 225	Pepper Johnson	.25	.08
❑ 226	Checklist 116-230	.25	.08
❑ 227	Irv Eatman	.25	.08
❑ 228	Greg Townsend	.25	.08
❑ 229	Mark Jackson	.25	.08
❑ 230	Robert Blackmon	.25	.08
❑ 231	Terry Allen	1.00	.40
❑ 232	Bennie Blades	.25	.08
❑ 233	Sam Mills	1.00	.40
❑ 234	Richmond Webb	.25	.08
❑ 235	Richard Dent	.50	.20
❑ 236	Alonzo Mitz RC	.25	.08
❑ 237	Steve Young	5.00	2.00
❑ 238	Pat Swilling	.25	.08
❑ 239	James Campen	.25	.08
❑ 240	Earnest Byner	.25	.08
❑ 241	Pat Terrell	.25	.08
❑ 242	Carwell Gardner	.25	.08
❑ 243	Charles McRae	.25	.08
❑ 244	Vince Newsome	.25	.08
❑ 245	Eric Hill	.25	.08
❑ 246	Steve Young FOIL	5.00	2.00
❑ 247	Nate Lewis	.25	.08
❑ 248	William Fuller	.25	.08
❑ 249	Andre Waters	.25	.08
❑ 250	Dean Biasucci	.25	.08
❑ 251	Andre Rison	.50	.20
❑ 252	Brent Williams	.25	.08
❑ 253	Todd McNair	.25	.08
❑ 254	Jeff Davidson RC	.25	.08
❑ 255	Art Monk	.50	.20
❑ 256	Kirk Lowdermilk	.25	.08
❑ 257	Bob Golic	.25	.08
❑ 258	Michael Irvin	1.00	.40
❑ 259	Eric Green	.25	.08
❑ 260	David Fulcher	.50	.20
❑ 261	Damone Johnson	.25	.08
❑ 262	Marc Spindler	.25	.08
❑ 263	Alfred Williams	.25	.08
❑ 264	Donnie Elder	.25	.08
❑ 265	Keith McKeller	.25	.08
❑ 266	Steve Bono RC	1.00	.40
❑ 267	Jumbo Elliott	.25	.08
❑ 268	Randy Hilliard RC	.25	.08
❑ 269	Rufus Porter	.25	.08
❑ 270	Neal Anderson	.25	.08
❑ 271	Dalton Hilliard	.25	.08
❑ 272	Michael Zordich RC	.25	.08
❑ 273	Cornelius Bennett FOIL	.50	.20
❑ 274	Louie Aguiar RC	.25	.08
❑ 275	Aaron Craver	.25	.08
❑ 276	Tony Bennett	.25	.08
❑ 277	Terry Wooden	.25	.08
❑ 278	Mike Munchak	.50	.20
❑ 279	Chris Hinton	.25	.08
❑ 280	John Elway	6.00	2.50
❑ 281	Randall McDaniel	.25	.08
❑ 282	Brad Baxter	.50	.20
❑ 283	Wes Hopkins	.25	.08
❑ 284	Scott Davis	.25	.08
❑ 285	Mark Tuinei	.25	.08
❑ 286	Broderick Thompson	.25	.08
❑ 287	Henry Ellard	.50	.20
❑ 288	Adrian Cooper	.25	.08
❑ 289	Don Warren	.25	.08
❑ 290	Rodney Hampton	.50	.20
❑ 291	Kevin Ross	.25	.08
❑ 292	Mark Carrier DB	.25	.08
❑ 293	Ian Beckles	.25	.08
❑ 294	Gene Atkins	.25	.08
❑ 295	Mark Rypien FOIL	.50	.20
❑ 296	Eric Metcalf	.50	.20
❑ 297	Howard Ballard	.25	.08
❑ 298	Nate Newton	.25	.08
❑ 299	Dan Owens	.25	.08
❑ 300	Tim McGee	.25	.08
❑ 301	Greg McMurtry	.25	.08
❑ 302	Walter Reeves	.25	.08
❑ 303	Jeff Herrod	.25	.08
❑ 304	Darren Comeaux	.25	.08
❑ 305	Pete Stoyanovich	.25	.08
❑ 306	Johnny Holland	.25	.08
❑ 307	Jay Novacek	.50	.20
❑ 308	Steve Broussard	.25	.08
❑ 309	Darrell Green	.25	.08
❑ 310	Sam Mills	.25	.08
❑ 311	Tim Barnett	.25	.08
❑ 312	Steve Atwater	.25	.08
❑ 313	Tom Waddle FOIL	.50	.20
❑ 314	Felix Wright	.25	.08
❑ 315	Sean Jones	.25	.08
❑ 316	Jim Harbaugh	1.00	.40
❑ 317	Eric Allen	.25	.08
❑ 318	Don Mosebar	.25	.08
❑ 319	Rob Taylor	.25	.08
❑ 320	Terance Mathis	.50	.20
❑ 321	Leroy Hoard	.50	.20
❑ 322	Kenneth Davis	.25	.08
❑ 323	Guy McIntyre	.25	.08
❑ 324	Deron Cherry	.50	.20
❑ 325	Tunch Ilkin	.25	.08
❑ 326	Willie Green	.25	.08
❑ 327	Darryl Henley	.25	.08
❑ 328	Shawn Jefferson	.25	.08
❑ 329	Greg Jackson	.25	.08
❑ 330	John Roper	.25	.08
❑ 331	Bill Lewis	.25	.08
❑ 332	Rodney Holman	.25	.08
❑ 333	Bruce Armstrong	.25	.08
❑ 334	Robb Thomas	.25	.08
❑ 335	Alvin Harper	.50	.20
❑ 336	Brian Jordan	.50	.20
❑ 337	Morten Andersen	.50	.20
❑ 338	Dermontti Dawson	.25	.08
❑ 339	Checklist 231-345	.25	.08
❑ 340	Louis Oliver	.25	.08
❑ 341	Paul McJulien RC	.25	.08
❑ 342	Karl Mecklenburg	.25	.08
❑ 343	Lawrence Dawsey	.50	.20
❑ 344	Kyle Clifton	.25	.08
❑ 345	Jeff Bostic	.25	.08
❑ 346	Cris Carter	1.50	.60
❑ 347	Al Smith	.25	.08
❑ 348	Mark Kelso	.25	.08
❑ 349	Art Monk FOIL	1.00	.40
❑ 350	Michael Carter	.25	.08
❑ 351	Ethan Horton	.25	.08
❑ 352	Andy Heck	.25	.08
❑ 353	Gill Fenerty	.25	.08
❑ 354	David Brandon RC	.25	.08
❑ 355	Anthony Johnson	1.00	.40
❑ 356	Mike Golic	.25	.08
❑ 357	Ferrell Edmunds	.25	.08
❑ 358	Dennis Gibson	.25	.08
❑ 359	Gill Byrd	.25	.08
❑ 360	Todd Lyght	.25	.08
❑ 361	Jayice Pearson RC	.25	.08
❑ 362	John Rade	.25	.08
❑ 363	Keith Van Horne	.25	.08
❑ 364	John Kasay	.25	.08
❑ 365	Broderick Thomas	1.50	.60
❑ 366	Ken Harvey	.25	.08
❑ 367	Rich Gannon	1.00	.40

❑ 368 Darrell Thompson .25 .08
❑ 369 Jon Vaughn .25 .08
❑ 370 Jesse Solomon .25 .08
❑ 371 Erik McMillan .25 .08
❑ 372 Bruce Matthews .25 .08
❑ 373 Wilber Marshall .25 .08
❑ 374 Brian Blades 1.50 .60
❑ 375 Vance Johnson .25 .08
❑ 376 Eddie Brown .25 .08
❑ 377 Don Beebe .25 .08
❑ 378 Brent Jones .50 .20
❑ 379 Matt Bahr .25 .08
❑ 380 Dwight Stone .25 .08
❑ 381 Tony Casillas .25 .08
❑ 382 Jay Schroeder .25 .08
❑ 383 Byron Evans .25 .08
❑ 384 Dan Saleaumua .25 .08
❑ 385 Wendell Davis .25 .08
❑ 386 Ron Holmes .25 .08
❑ 387 George Thomas RC .25 .08
❑ 388 Ray Berry .25 .08
❑ 389 Eric Martin .25 .08
❑ 390 Kevin Mack .25 .08
❑ 391 Natu Tuatagaloa RC .25 .08
❑ 392 Bill Romanowski .25 .08
❑ 393 Nick Bell FOIL SP 1.50 .60
❑ 394 Grant Feasel .25 .08
❑ 395 Eugene Lockhart .25 .08
❑ 396 Lorenzo White .25 .08
❑ 397 Mike Farr .25 .08
❑ 398 Eric Bieniemy .25 .08
❑ 399 Kevin Murphy .25 .08
❑ 400 Luis Sharpe .25 .08
❑ 401 Jessie Tuggle 1.50 .60
❑ 402 Cleveland Gary .25 .08
❑ 403 Tony Mandarich .25 .08
❑ 404 Bryan Cox .50 .20
❑ 405 Marvin Washington .25 .08
❑ 406 Fred Stokes .25 .08
❑ 407 Duane Bickett .25 .08
❑ 408 Leonard Marshall .25 .08
❑ 409 Barry Foster .50 .20
❑ 410 Thurman Thomas 1.00 .40
❑ 411 Willie Gault .50 .20
❑ 412 Vinson Smith RC .25 .08
❑ 413 Mark Bortz .25 .08
❑ 414 Johnny Johnson .25 .08
❑ 415 Rodney Hampton FOIL 1.00 .40
❑ 416 Steve Wallace .25 .08
❑ 417 Fuad Reveiz .25 .08
❑ 418 Derrick Thomas .50 .20
❑ 419 Jackie Harris RC 1.00 .40
❑ 420 Derek Russell .25 .08
❑ 421 David Grant .25 .08
❑ 422 Tommy Kane .25 .08
❑ 423 Stan Brock .25 .08
❑ 424 Haywood Jeffires .50 .20
❑ 425 Broderick Thomas .25 .08
❑ 426 John Kidd .25 .08
❑ 427 Shawn McCarthy RC FOIL .50 .20
❑ 428 Jim Arnold .25 .08
❑ 429 Scott Fulhage .25 .08
❑ 430 Jackie Slater .25 .08
❑ 431 Scott Galbraith RC .25 .08
❑ 432 Roger Ruzek .25 .08
❑ 433 Irving Fryar .50 .20
❑ 434A D.Thomas FOIL ERR 494 1.00 .40
❑ 434B D.Thomas FOIL COR 1.00 .40
❑ 435 D.J. Johnson .25 .08
❑ 436 Jim C.Jensen .25 .08
❑ 437 James Washington .25 .08
❑ 438 Phil Hansen .25 .08
❑ 439 Rohn Stark .25 .08
❑ 440 Jarrod Bunch .25 .08
❑ 441 Todd Marinovich .25 .08
❑ 442 Brett Perriman 1.00 .40
❑ 443 Eugene Robinson .25 .08
❑ 444 Robert Massey .25 .08
❑ 445 Nick Lowery .25 .08
❑ 446 Rickey Dixon .25 .08
❑ 447 Jim Lachey .25 .08
❑ 448 Johnny Hector .50 .20
❑ 449 Gary Plummer .25 .08
❑ 450 Robert Brown .25 .08
❑ 451 Gaston Green .25 .08
❑ 452 Checklist 346-459 .25 .08
❑ 453 Darion Conner .25 .08
❑ 454 Mike Cofer .25 .08
❑ 455 Craig Heyward .50 .20
❑ 456 Anthony Carter .50 .20
❑ 457 Pat Coleman RC .25 .08
❑ 458 Jeff Bryant .25 .08
❑ 459 Mark Gunn RC .25 .08
❑ 460 Stan Thomas .25 .08
❑ 461 Simon Fletcher 1.50 .60
❑ 462 Ray Agnew .25 .08
❑ 463 Jessie Hester .25 .08
❑ 464 Rob Burnett .25 .08
❑ 465 Mike Croel .25 .08
❑ 466 Mike Pitts .25 .08
❑ 467 Darryl Talley .25 .08
❑ 468 Rich Camarillo .25 .08
❑ 469 Reggie White FOIL 1.00 .40
❑ 470 Nick Bell .25 .08
❑ 471 Tracy Hayworth RC .25 .08
❑ 472 Eric Thomas .25 .08
❑ 473 Paul Gruber .25 .08
❑ 474 David Richards .25 .08
❑ 475 T.J. Turner .25 .08
❑ 476 Mark Ingram .25 .08
❑ 477 Tim Grunhard .25 .08
❑ 478 Marion Butts FOIL .50 .20
❑ 479 Tom Rathman .25 .08
❑ 480 Brian Mitchell .50 .20
❑ 481 Bryce Paup 1.00 .40
❑ 482 Mike Pritchard .50 .20
❑ 483 Ken Norton Jr. .50 .20
❑ 484 Roman Phifer .25 .08
❑ 485 Greg Lloyd .50 .20
❑ 486 Brett Maxie .25 .08
❑ 487 Richard Dent FOIL SP 1.50 .60
❑ 488 Curtis Duncan .25 .08
❑ 489 Chris Burkett .25 .08
❑ 490 Travis McNeal .25 .08
❑ 491 Carl Lee .25 .08
❑ 492 Clarence Kay .25 .08
❑ 493 Tom Thayer .25 .08
❑ 494 Erik Kramer FOIL SP 2.00 .75
❑ 495 Perry Kemp .25 .08
❑ 496 Jeff Jaeger .25 .08
❑ 497 Eric Sanders .25 .08
❑ 498 Burt Grossman .25 .08
❑ 499 Ben Smith .25 .08
❑ 500 Keith McCants .25 .08
❑ 501 John Stephens .25 .08
❑ 502 John Rienstra .25 .08
❑ 503 Jim Ritcher .25 .08
❑ 504 Harris Barton .25 .08
❑ 505 Andre Rison FOIL SP 2.00 .75
❑ 506 Chris Martin .25 .08
❑ 507 Freddie Joe Nunn .25 .08
❑ 508 Mark Higgs .25 .08
❑ 509 Norm Johnson .25 .08
❑ 510 Stephen Baker .25 .08
❑ 511 Ricky Sanders .25 .08
❑ 512 Ray Donaldson .25 .08
❑ 513 David Fulcher .25 .08
❑ 514 Gerald Williams .25 .08
❑ 515 Toi Cook .25 .08
❑ 516 Chris Warren 1.00 .40
❑ 517 Jeff Gossett .25 .08
❑ 518 Ken Lanier .25 .08
❑ 519 Haywood Jeffires FOIL SP 2.00 .75
❑ 520 Kevin Glover .25 .08
❑ 521 Mo Lewis .25 .08
❑ 522 Bern Brostek .25 .08
❑ 523 Bo Orlando RC .25 .08
❑ 524 Mike Saxon .25 .08
❑ 525 Seth Joyner .25 .08
❑ 526 John Carney .25 .08
❑ 527 Jeff Cross .25 .08
❑ 528 Gary Anderson K FOIL SP 1.50 .60
❑ 529 Chuck Cecil .25 .08
❑ 530 Tim Green .25 .08
❑ 531 Kevin Porter .25 .08
❑ 532 Chris Spielman .50 .20
❑ 533 Willie Drewrey .25 .08
❑ 534 Chris Singleton UER .25 .08
❑ 535 Matt Stover .25 .08
❑ 536 Andre Collins .25 .08
❑ 537 Erik Howard .25 .08
❑ 538 Steve Tasker .50 .20
❑ 539 Anthony Thompson .25 .08
❑ 540 Charles Haley .50 .20
❑ 541 Mike Merriweather .50 .20
❑ 542 Henry Thomas .25 .08
❑ 543 Scott Stephen .25 .08
❑ 544 Bruce Kozerski .25 .08
❑ 545 Tim McKyer .25 .08
❑ 546 Chris Doleman .25 .08
❑ 547 Riki Ellison .25 .08
❑ 548 Mike Prior .25 .08
❑ 549 Dwayne Harper .25 .08
❑ 550 Bubby Brister .25 .08
❑ 551 Dave Meggett .50 .20
❑ 552 Greg Montgomery .25 .08
❑ 553 Kevin Mack .50 .20
❑ 554 Mark Stepnoski .50 .20
❑ 555 Kenny Walker .25 .08
❑ 556 Eric Moten .25 .08
❑ 557 Michael Stewart .25 .08
❑ 558 Calvin Williams .50 .20
❑ 559 Johnny Hector .25 .08
❑ 560 Tony Paige .25 .08
❑ 561 Tim Newton .25 .08
❑ 562 Brad Muster .25 .08
❑ 563 Aeneas Williams .50 .20
❑ 564 Herman Moore 1.00 .40
❑ 565 Checklist 460-573 .25 .08
❑ 566 Jerome Henderson .25 .08
❑ 567 Danny Copeland .25 .08
❑ 568 Alexander Wright .50 .20
❑ 569 Tim Harris .25 .08
❑ 570 Jonathan Hayes .25 .08
❑ 571 Tony Jones T .25 .08
❑ 572 Carlton Bailey RC .25 .08
❑ 573 Vaughan Johnson .25 .08

1993 Bowman

❑ COMPLETE SET (423) 25.00 10.00
❑ 1 Troy Aikman FOIL 3.00 1.50
❑ 2 John Parrella RC .20 .07
❑ 3 Dana Stubblefield RC .75 .30
❑ 4 Mark Higgs .20 .07
❑ 5 Tom Carter RC .40 .15
❑ 6 Nate Lewis .20 .07
❑ 7 Vaughn Hebron RC .20 .07
❑ 8 Ernest Givins .40 .15
❑ 9 Vince Buck .20 .07
❑ 10 Levon Kirkland .20 .07
❑ 11 J.J. Birden .20 .07
❑ 12 Steve Jordan .20 .07
❑ 13 Simon Fletcher .20 .07
❑ 14 Willie Green .20 .07
❑ 15 Pepper Johnson .20 .07
❑ 16 Roger Harper RC .20 .07
❑ 17 Rob Moore .40 .15
❑ 18 David Lang .20 .07
❑ 19 David Klingler .20 .07
❑ 20 Garrison Hearst RC FOIL 2.00 .75
❑ 21 Anthony Johnson .40 .15
❑ 22 Eric Curry RC FOIL .40 .15
❑ 23 Nolan Harrison .20 .07
❑ 24 Earl Dotson RC .20 .07
❑ 25 Leonard Russell .40 .15
❑ 26 Doug Riesenberg .20 .07
❑ 27 Dwayne Harper .20 .07
❑ 28 Richard Dent .40 .15
❑ 29 Victor Bailey RC .20 .07
❑ 30 Junior Seau .75 .30
❑ 31 Steve Tasker .40 .15
❑ 32 Kurt Gouveia .20 .07
❑ 33 Renaldo Turnbull UER .20 .07
❑ 34 Dale Carter .20 .07
❑ 35 Russell Maryland .20 .07
❑ 36 Dana Hall .20 .07
❑ 37 Marco Coleman .20 .07
❑ 38 Greg Montgomery .20 .07
❑ 39 Deon Figures RC .20 .07
❑ 40 Troy Drayton RC .40 .15

❑ 41 Eric Metcalf .40 .15
❑ 42 Michael Husted RC .20 .07
❑ 43 Harry Newsome .20 .07
❑ 44 Kelvin Pritchett .20 .07
❑ 45 Andre Rison FOIL .75 .40
❑ 46 John Copeland RC .40 .15
❑ 47 Greg Biekert RC .20 .07
❑ 48 Johnny Johnson .20 .07
❑ 49 Chuck Cecil .20 .07
❑ 50 Rick Mirer RC FOIL 1.50 .60
❑ 51 Rod Bernstine .20 .07
❑ 52 Steve McMichael .40 .15
❑ 53 Roosevelt Potts RC .20 .07
❑ 54 Mike Sherrard .20 .07
❑ 55 Terrell Buckley .20 .07
❑ 56 Eugene Chung .20 .07
❑ 57 Kimble Anders RC .75 .30
❑ 58 Daryl Johnston .75 .30
❑ 59 Harris Barton .20 .07
❑ 60 Thurman Thomas FOIL 1.50 .60
❑ 61 Eric Martin .20 .07
❑ 62 Reggie Brooks RC FOIL .40 .15
❑ 63 Eric Bieniemy .20 .07
❑ 64 John Offerdahl .20 .07
❑ 65 Wilber Marshall .20 .07
❑ 66 Mark Carrier WR .40 .15
❑ 67 Merril Hoge .20 .07
❑ 68 Cris Carter .75 .30
❑ 69 Marty Thompson RC .20 .07
❑ 70 Randall Cunningham FOIL 1.50 .60
❑ 71 Winston Moss .20 .07
❑ 72 Doug Pelfrey RC .20 .07
❑ 73 Jackie Slater .20 .07
❑ 74 Pierce Holt .20 .07
❑ 75 Hardy Nickerson .40 .15
❑ 76 Chris Burkett .20 .07
❑ 77 Michael Brandon .20 .07
❑ 78 Tom Waddle .20 .07
❑ 79 Walter Reeves .20 .07
❑ 80 Lawrence Taylor FOIL .75 .40
❑ 81 Wayne Simmons RC .20 .07
❑ 82 Brent Williams .20 .07
❑ 83 Shannon Sharpe .75 .30
❑ 84 Robert Blackmon .20 .07
❑ 85 Keith Jackson .40 .15
❑ 86 A.J. Johnson .20 .07
❑ 87 Ryan McNeil RC .75 .30
❑ 88 Michael Dean Perry .40 .15
❑ 89 Russell Copeland RC .40 .15
❑ 90 Sam Mills .20 .07
❑ 91 Courtney Hall .20 .07
❑ 92 Gino Torretta RC .40 .15
❑ 93 Artie Smith RC .20 .07
❑ 94 David Whitmore .20 .07
❑ 95 Charles Haley .40 .15
❑ 96 Rod Woodson .75 .30
❑ 97 Lorenzo White .20 .07
❑ 98 Tom Scott OL RC .20 .07
❑ 99 Tyji Armstrong .20 .07
❑ 100 Boomer Esiason .40 .15
❑ 101 Rocket Ismail FOIL .75 .40
❑ 102 Mark Carrier DB .20 .07
❑ 103 Broderick Thompson .20 .07
❑ 104 Bob Whitfield .20 .07
❑ 105 Ben Coleman RC .20 .07
❑ 106 Jon Vaughn .20 .07
❑ 107 Marcus Buckley RC .20 .07
❑ 108 Cleveland Gary .20 .07
❑ 109 Ashley Ambrose .20 .07
❑ 110 Reggie White FOIL 1.50 .60
❑ 111 Arthur Marshall RC .20 .07
❑ 112 Greg McMurtry .20 .07
❑ 113 Mike Johnson .20 .07
❑ 114 Tim McGee .20 .07
❑ 115 John Carney .20 .07
❑ 116 Neil Smith .75 .30
❑ 117 Mark Stepnoski .20 .07
❑ 118 Don Beebe .20 .07
❑ 119 Scott Mitchell .75 .30
❑ 120 Randall McDaniel .20 .07
❑ 121 Chidi Ahanotu RC .20 .07
❑ 122 Ray Childress .20 .07
❑ 123 Tony McGee RC .40 .15
❑ 124 Marc Boutte .20 .07
❑ 125 Ronnie Lott .40 .15
❑ 126 Jason Elam RC .75 .30
❑ 127 Martin Harrison RC .20 .07
❑ 128 Leonard Renfro RC .20 .07
❑ 129 Jessie Armstead RC .40 .15
❑ 130 Quentin Coryatt .40 .15
❑ 131 Luis Sharpe .20 .07
❑ 132 Bill Maas .20 .07
❑ 133 Jesse Solomon .20 .07
❑ 134 Kevin Greene .40 .15
❑ 135 Derek Brown RC RBK .40 .15
❑ 136 Greg Townsend .20 .07
❑ 137 Neal Anderson .20 .07
❑ 138 John L. Williams .20 .07
❑ 139 Vincent Brisby RC .75 .30
❑ 140 Barry Sanders FOIL 5.00 2.00
❑ 141 Charles Mann .20 .07
❑ 142 Ken Norton .40 .15
❑ 143 Eric Moten .20 .07
❑ 144 John Alt .20 .07
❑ 145 Dan Footman RC .20 .07
❑ 146 Bill Brooks .20 .07
❑ 147 James Thornton .20 .07
❑ 148 Martin Mayhew .20 .07
❑ 149 Andy Harmon .40 .15
❑ 150 Dan Marino FOIL 6.00 2.50
❑ 151 Micheal Barrow RC .75 .30
❑ 152 Flipper Anderson .20 .07
❑ 153 Jackie Harris .20 .07
❑ 154 Todd Kelly RC .20 .07
❑ 155 Dan Williams RC .20 .07
❑ 156 Harold Green .20 .07
❑ 157 David Treadwell .20 .07
❑ 158 Chris Doleman .20 .07
❑ 159 Eric Hill .20 .07
❑ 160 Lincoln Kennedy RC .20 .07
❑ 161 Devon McDonald RC .20 .07
❑ 162 Natrone Means RC .75 .30
❑ 163 Rick Hamilton RC .20 .07
❑ 164 Kelvin Martin .20 .07
❑ 165 Jeff Hostetler .40 .15
❑ 166 Mark Brunell RC 4.00 1.50
❑ 167 Tim Barnett .20 .07
❑ 168 Ray Crockett .20 .07
❑ 169 William Perry .40 .15
❑ 170 Michael Irvin .75 .30
❑ 171 Marvin Washington .20 .07
❑ 172 Irving Fryar .40 .15
❑ 173 Scott Sisson RC .20 .07
❑ 174 Gary Anderson K .20 .07
❑ 175 Bruce Smith .75 .30
❑ 176 Clyde Simmons .20 .07
❑ 177 Russell White RC .40 .15
❑ 178 Irv Smith RC .20 .07
❑ 179 Mark Wheeler .20 .07
❑ 180 Warren Moon .75 .30
❑ 181 Del Speer RC .20 .07
❑ 182 Henry Thomas .20 .07
❑ 183 Keith Kartz .20 .07
❑ 184 Ricky Ervins .20 .07
❑ 185 Phil Simms .40 .15
❑ 186 Tim Brown .75 .30
❑ 187 Willis Peguese .20 .07
❑ 188 Rich Moran .20 .07
❑ 189 Robert Jones .20 .07
❑ 190 Craig Heyward .40 .15
❑ 191 Ricky Watters .75 .30
❑ 192 Stan Humphries .40 .15
❑ 193 Larry Webster .20 .07
❑ 194 Brad Baxter .20 .07
❑ 195 Randal Hill .20 .07
❑ 196 Robert Porcher .20 .07
❑ 197 Patrick Robinson RC .20 .07
❑ 198 Ferrell Edmunds .20 .07
❑ 199 Melvin Jenkins .20 .07
❑ 200 Joe Montana FOIL 6.00 2.50
❑ 201 Marv Cook .20 .07
❑ 202 Henry Ellard .40 .15
❑ 203 Calvin Williams .40 .15
❑ 204 Craig Erickson .40 .15
❑ 205 Steve Atwater .20 .07
❑ 206 Najee Mustafaa .20 .07
❑ 207 Darryl Talley .20 .07
❑ 208 Jarrod Bunch .20 .07
❑ 209 Tim McDonald .20 .07
❑ 210 Patrick Bates RC .20 .07
❑ 211 Sean Jones .20 .07
❑ 212 Leslie O'Neal .40 .15
❑ 213 Mike Golic .20 .07
❑ 214 Mark Clayton .20 .07
❑ 215 Leonard Marshall .20 .07
❑ 216 Curtis Conway RC 1.50 .60
❑ 217 Andre Hastings RC .40 .15
❑ 218 Barry Word .20 .07
❑ 219 Will Wolford .20 .07
❑ 220 Desmond Howard .40 .15
❑ 221 Rickey Jackson .20 .07
❑ 222 Alvin Harper .40 .15
❑ 223 William White .20 .07
❑ 224 Steve Broussard .20 .07
❑ 225 Aeneas Williams .20 .07
❑ 226 Michael Brooks .20 .07
❑ 227 Reggie Cobb .20 .07
❑ 228 Derrick Walker .20 .07
❑ 229 Marcus Allen .75 .30
❑ 230 Jerry Ball .20 .07
❑ 231 J.B. Brown .20 .07
❑ 232 Terry McDaniel .20 .07
❑ 233 LeRoy Butler .20 .07
❑ 234 Kyle Clifton .20 .07
❑ 235 Henry Jones .20 .07
❑ 236 Shane Conlan .20 .07
❑ 237 Michael Bates RC .20 .07
❑ 238 Vincent Brown .20 .07
❑ 239 William Fuller .20 .07
❑ 240 Ricardo McDonald .20 .07
❑ 241 Gary Zimmerman .20 .07
❑ 242 Fred Barnett .40 .15
❑ 243 Elvis Grbac RC 4.00 1.50
❑ 244 Myron Baker RC .20 .07
❑ 245 Steve Emtman .20 .07
❑ 246 Mike Compton RC .75 .30
❑ 247 Mark Jackson .20 .07
❑ 248 Santo Stephens RC .20 .07
❑ 249 Tommie Agee .20 .07
❑ 250 Broderick Thomas .20 .07
❑ 251 Fred Baxter RC .20 .07
❑ 252 Andre Collins .20 .07
❑ 253 Ernest Dye RC .20 .07
❑ 254 Raylee Johnson RC .40 .15
❑ 255 Rickey Dixon .20 .07
❑ 256 Ron Heller .20 .07
❑ 257 Joel Steed .20 .07
❑ 258 Everett Lindsay RC .20 .07
❑ 259 Tony Smith RB .20 .07
❑ 260 Sterling Sharpe UER .75 .30
❑ 261 Tommy Vardell .20 .07
❑ 262 Morten Andersen .20 .07
❑ 263 Eddie Robinson .20 .07
❑ 264 Jerome Bettis RC 8.00 4.00
❑ 265 Alonzo Spellman .20 .07
❑ 266 Harvey Williams .40 .15
❑ 267 Jason Belser RC .20 .07
❑ 268 Derek Russell .20 .07
❑ 269 Derrick Lassic RC .20 .07
❑ 270 Steve Young FOIL 3.00 1.50
❑ 271 Adrian Murrell RC .75 .30
❑ 272 Lewis Tillman .20 .07
❑ 273 O.J.McDuffie RC .75 .30
❑ 274 Marty Carter .20 .07
❑ 275 Ray Seals .20 .07
❑ 276 Earnest Byner .20 .07
❑ 277 Marion Butts .20 .07
❑ 278 Chris Spielman .40 .15
❑ 279 Carl Pickens .40 .15
❑ 280 Drew Bledsoe RC FOIL 6.00 2.50
❑ 281 Mark Kelso .20 .07
❑ 282 Eugene Robinson .20 .07
❑ 283 Eric Allen .20 .07
❑ 284 Ethan Horton .20 .07
❑ 285 Greg Lloyd .40 .15
❑ 286 Anthony Carter .40 .15
❑ 287 Edgar Bennett .75 .30
❑ 288 Bobby Hebert .20 .07
❑ 289 Haywood Jeffires .40 .15
❑ 290 Glyn Milburn RC .75 .30
❑ 291 Bernie Kosar .40 .15
❑ 292 Jumbo Elliott .20 .07
❑ 293 Jessie Hester .20 .07
❑ 294 Brent Jones .40 .15
❑ 295 Carl Banks .20 .07
❑ 296 Brian Washington .20 .07
❑ 297 Steve Beuerlein .40 .15
❑ 298 John Lynch RC 2.00 .75
❑ 299 Troy Vincent .20 .07
❑ 300 Emmitt Smith FOIL 5.00 2.50
❑ 301 Chris Zorich .20 .07
❑ 302 Wade Wilson .20 .07
❑ 303 Darrien Gordon RC .20 .07
❑ 304 Fred Stokes .20 .07
❑ 305 Nick Lowery .20 .07
❑ 306 Rodney Peete .20 .07
❑ 307 Chris Warren .40 .15

❑ 308 Herschel Walker	.40	.15
❑ 309 Aundray Bruce	.20	.07
❑ 310 Barry Foster FOIL	.40	.15
❑ 311 George Teague RC	.40	.15
❑ 312 Darryl Williams	.20	.07
❑ 313 Thomas Smith RC	.40	.15
❑ 314 Dennis Brown	.20	.07
❑ 315 Marvin Jones RC FOIL	.40	.15
❑ 316 Andre Tippett	.20	.07
❑ 317 Demetrius DuBose RC	.20	.07
❑ 318 Kirk Lowdermilk	.20	.07
❑ 319 Shane Dronett	.20	.07
❑ 320 Terry Kirby RC	.75	.30
❑ 321 Qadry Ismail RC	.75	.30
❑ 322 Lorenzo Lynch	.20	.07
❑ 323 Willie Drewrey	.20	.07
❑ 324 Jessie Tuggle	.20	.07
❑ 325 Leroy Hoard	.40	.15
❑ 326 Mark Collins	.20	.07
❑ 327 Darrell Green	.20	.07
❑ 328 Anthony Miller	.40	.15
❑ 329 Brad Muster	.20	.07
❑ 330 Jim Kelly FOIL	1.50	.60
❑ 331 Sean Gilbert	.40	.15
❑ 332 Tim McKyer	.20	.07
❑ 333 Scott Mersereau	.20	.07
❑ 334 Willie Davis	.75	.30
❑ 335 Brett Favre FOIL	6.00	3.00
❑ 336 Kevin Gogan	.20	.07
❑ 337 Jim Harbaugh	.75	.30
❑ 338 James Trapp RC	.20	.07
❑ 339 Pete Stoyanovich	.20	.07
❑ 340 Jerry Rice FOIL	3.00	1.50
❑ 341 Gary Anderson RB	.20	.07
❑ 342 Carlton Gray RC	.20	.07
❑ 343 Dermontti Dawson	.20	.07
❑ 344 Ray Buchanan RC	.75	.30
❑ 345 Derrick Fenner	.20	.07
❑ 346 Dennis Smith	.20	.07
❑ 347 Todd Rucci RC	.20	.07
❑ 348 Seth Joyner	.20	.07
❑ 349 Jim McMahon	.40	.15
❑ 350 Rodney Hampton	.40	.15
❑ 351 Al Smith	.20	.07
❑ 352 Steve Everitt RC	.20	.07
❑ 353 Vinnie Clark	.20	.07
❑ 354 Eric Swann	.40	.15
❑ 355 Brian Mitchell	.40	.15
❑ 356 Will Shields RC	.75	.30
❑ 357 Cornelius Bennett	.40	.15
❑ 358 Darrin Smith RC	.40	.15
❑ 359 Chris Mims	.20	.07
❑ 360 Blair Thomas	.20	.07
❑ 361 Dennis Gibson	.20	.07
❑ 362 Santana Dotson	.40	.15
❑ 363 Mark Ingram	.20	.07
❑ 364 Don Mosebar	.20	.07
❑ 365 Ty Detmer	.75	.30
❑ 366 Bob Christian RC	.20	.07
❑ 367 Adrian Hardy	.20	.07
❑ 368 Vaughan Johnson	.20	.07
❑ 369 Jim Everett	.40	.15
❑ 370 Ricky Sanders	.20	.07
❑ 371 Jonathan Hayes	.20	.07
❑ 372 Bruce Matthews	.20	.07
❑ 373 Darren Drozdov RC	.75	.30
❑ 374 Scott Brumfield RC	.20	.07
❑ 375 Cortez Kennedy	.40	.15
❑ 376 Tim Harris	.20	.07
❑ 377 Neil O'Donnell	.75	.30
❑ 378 Robert Smith RC	3.00	1.25
❑ 379 Mike Caldwell RC	.20	.07
❑ 380 Burt Grossman	.20	.07
❑ 381 Corey Miller	.20	.07
❑ 382 Kev.Williams WR FOIL RC	.40	.15
❑ 383 Ken Harvey	.20	.07
❑ 384 Greg Robinson RC	.20	.07
❑ 385 Harold Alexander RC	.20	.07
❑ 386 Andre Reed	.40	.15
❑ 387 Reggie Langhorne	.20	.07
❑ 388 Courtney Hawkins	.20	.07
❑ 389 James Hasty	.20	.07
❑ 390 Pat Swilling	.20	.07
❑ 391 Chris Slade RC	.40	.15
❑ 392 Keith Byars	.20	.07
❑ 393 Dalton Hilliard	.20	.07
❑ 394 David Williams	.20	.07
❑ 395 Terry Obee RC	.20	.07
❑ 396 Heath Sherman	.20	.07
❑ 397 John Taylor	.40	.15
❑ 398 Irv Eatman	.20	.07
❑ 399 Johnny Holland	.20	.07
❑ 400 John Elway FOIL	6.00	2.50
❑ 401 Clay Matthews	.40	.15
❑ 402 Dave Meggett	.20	.07
❑ 403 Eric Green	.20	.07
❑ 404 Bryan Cox	.20	.07
❑ 405 Jay Novacek	.40	.15
❑ 406 Kenneth Davis	.20	.07
❑ 407 Lamar Thomas RC	.20	.07
❑ 408 Lance Gunn RC	.20	.07
❑ 409 Audray McMillian	.20	.07
❑ 410 Derrick Thomas FOIL	1.50	.60
❑ 411 Rufus Porter	.20	.07
❑ 412 Coleman Rudolph RC	.20	.07
❑ 413 Mark Rypien	.20	.07
❑ 414 Duane Bickett	.20	.07
❑ 415 Chris Singleton	.20	.07
❑ 416 Mitch Lyons RC	.20	.07
❑ 417 Bill Fralic	.20	.07
❑ 418 Gary Plummer	.20	.07
❑ 419 Ricky Proehl	.20	.07
❑ 420 Howie Long	.75	.30
❑ 421 Willie Roaf RC FOIL	.75	.40
❑ 422 Checklist 1-212	.20	.07
❑ 423 Checklist 213-423	.20	.07

1994 Bowman

❑ COMPLETE SET (390)	50.00	20.00
❑ 1 Dan Wilkinson RC	.40	.15
❑ 2 Marshall Faulk RC	15.00	6.00
❑ 3 Heath Shuler RC	.75	.30
❑ 4 Willie McGinest RC	.75	.30
❑ 5 Trent Dilfer RC	3.00	1.25
❑ 6 Brent Jones	.40	.15
❑ 7 Sam Adams RC	.40	.15
❑ 8 Randy Baldwin	.20	.07
❑ 9 Jamir Miller RC	.40	.15
❑ 10 John Thierry RC	.20	.07
❑ 11 Aaron Glenn RC	.75	.30
❑ 12 Joe Johnson RC	.20	.07
❑ 13 Bernard Williams RC	.20	.07
❑ 14 Wayne Gandy RC	.20	.07
❑ 15 Aaron Taylor RC	.20	.07
❑ 16 Charles Johnson RC	.75	.30
❑ 17 Dew.Washington RC UER 309	.40	.15
❑ 18 Bernie Kosar	.40	.15
❑ 19 Johnnie Morton RC	2.50	1.00
❑ 20 Rob Fredrickson RC	.40	.15
❑ 21 Shante Carver RC	.20	.07
❑ 22 Thomas Lewis RC	.40	.15
❑ 23 Greg Hill RC	.75	.30
❑ 24 Cris Dishman	.20	.07
❑ 25 Jeff Burris RC	.40	.15
❑ 26 Isaac Davis RC	.20	.07
❑ 27 Bert Emanuel RC	.75	.30
❑ 28 Allen Aldridge RC	.20	.07
❑ 29 Kevin Lee RC	.20	.07
❑ 30 Chris Brantley RC	.20	.07
❑ 31 Rich Braham RC	.20	.07
❑ 32 Ricky Watters	.40	.15
❑ 33 Quentin Coryatt	.20	.07
❑ 34 Hardy Nickerson	.40	.15
❑ 35 Johnny Johnson	.20	.07
❑ 36 Ken Harvey	.20	.07
❑ 37 Chris Zorich	.20	.07
❑ 38 Chris Warren	.40	.15
❑ 39 David Palmer RC	.75	.30
❑ 40 Chris Miller	.20	.07
❑ 41 Ken Ruettgers	.20	.07
❑ 42 Joe Panos RC	.20	.07
❑ 43 Mario Bates RC	.75	.30
❑ 44 Harry Colon	.20	.07
❑ 45 Barry Foster	.20	.07
❑ 46 Steve Tasker	.40	.15
❑ 47 Richmond Webb	.20	.07
❑ 48 James Folston RC	.20	.07
❑ 49 Erik Williams	.20	.07
❑ 50 Rodney Hampton	.40	.15
❑ 51 Derek Russell	.20	.07
❑ 52 Greg Montgomery	.20	.07
❑ 53 Anthony Phillips	.20	.07
❑ 54 Andre Coleman RC	.20	.07
❑ 55 Gary Brown	.20	.07
❑ 56 Neil Smith	.40	.15
❑ 57 Myron Baker	.20	.07
❑ 58 Sean Dawkins RC	.75	.30
❑ 59 Marvin Washington	.20	.07
❑ 60 Steve Beuerlein	.40	.15
❑ 61 Brentson Buckner RC	.20	.07
❑ 62 William Gaines RC	.20	.07
❑ 63 LeShon Johnson RC	.40	.15
❑ 64 Errict Rhett RC	.75	.30
❑ 65 Jim Everett	.40	.15
❑ 66 Desmond Howard	.40	.15
❑ 67 Jack Del Rio	.20	.07
❑ 68 Isaac Bruce RC	12.00	6.00
❑ 69 Van Malone RC	.20	.07
❑ 70 Jim Kelly	.75	.30
❑ 71 Leon Lett	.20	.07
❑ 72 Greg Robinson	.20	.07
❑ 73 Ryan Yarborough RC	.20	.07
❑ 74 Terry Wooden	.20	.07
❑ 75 Eric Allen	.20	.07
❑ 76 Ernest Givins	.40	.15
❑ 77 Marcus Spears RC	.20	.07
❑ 78 Thomas Randolph RC	.20	.07
❑ 79 Willie Clark RC	.20	.07
❑ 80 John Elway	4.00	1.50
❑ 81 Aubrey Beavers RC	.20	.07
❑ 82 Jeff Cothran RC	.20	.07
❑ 83 Norm Johnson	.20	.07
❑ 84 Donnell Bennett RC	.75	.30
❑ 85 Phillippi Sparks	.20	.07
❑ 86 Scott Mitchell	.40	.15
❑ 87 Bucky Brooks RC	.20	.07
❑ 88 Courtney Hawkins	.20	.07
❑ 89 Kevin Greene	.40	.15
❑ 90 Doug Nussmeier RC	.20	.07
❑ 91 Floyd Turner	.20	.07
❑ 92 Anthony Newman	.20	.07
❑ 93 Vinny Testaverde	.40	.15
❑ 94 Ronnie Lott	.40	.15
❑ 95 Troy Aikman	2.00	.75
❑ 96 John Taylor	.40	.15
❑ 97 Henry Ellard	.40	.15
❑ 98 Carl Lee	.20	.07
❑ 99 Terry McDaniel	.20	.07
❑ 100 Joe Montana	4.00	1.50
❑ 101 David Klingler	.20	.07
❑ 102 Bruce Walker RC	.20	.07
❑ 103 Rick Cunningham RC	.20	.07
❑ 104 Robert Delpino	.20	.07
❑ 105 Mark Ingram	.20	.07
❑ 106 Leslie O'Neal	.20	.07
❑ 107 Darrell Thompson	.20	.07
❑ 108 Dave Meggett	.20	.07
❑ 109 Chris Gardocki	.20	.07
❑ 110 Andre Rison	.40	.15
❑ 111 Kelvin Martin	.20	.07
❑ 112 Marcus Robertson	.20	.07
❑ 113 Jason Gildon RC	3.00	1.25
❑ 114 Mel Gray	.20	.07
❑ 115 Tommy Vardell	.20	.07
❑ 116 Dexter Carter	.20	.07
❑ 117 Scottie Graham RC	.40	.15
❑ 118 Horace Copeland	.20	.07
❑ 119 Cornelius Bennett	.40	.15
❑ 120 Chris Maumalanga RC	.20	.07
❑ 121 Mo Lewis	.20	.07
❑ 122 Toby Wright RC	.20	.07
❑ 123 George Hegamin RC	.20	.07
❑ 124 Chip Lohmiller	.20	.07
❑ 125 Calvin Jones RC	.20	.07
❑ 126 Steve Shine	.20	.07
❑ 127 Chuck Levy RC	.20	.07
❑ 128 Sam Mills	.20	.07
❑ 129 Terance Mathis	.40	.15
❑ 130 Randall Cunningham	.75	.30
❑ 131 John Fina	.20	.07

❑ 132 Reggie White .75 .30
❑ 133 Tom Waddle .20 .07
❑ 134 Chris Calloway .20 .07
❑ 135 Kevin Mawae RC .75 .30
❑ 136 Lake Dawson RC .40 .15
❑ 137 Alai Kalaniubalu .20 .07
❑ 138 Tom Nalen RC .75 .30
❑ 139 Cody Carlson .20 .07
❑ 140 Dan Marino 4.00 1.50
❑ 141 Harris Barton .20 .07
❑ 142 Don Mosebar .20 .07
❑ 143 Romeo Bandison .20 .07
❑ 144 Bruce Smith .75 .30
❑ 145 Warren Moon .75 .30
❑ 146 David Lutz .20 .07
❑ 147 Dermontti Dawson .20 .07
❑ 148 Ricky Proehl .20 .07
❑ 149 Lou Benfatti RC .20 .07
❑ 150 Craig Erickson .20 .07
❑ 151 Sean Gilbert .20 .07
❑ 152 Zefross Moss .20 .07
❑ 153 Darnay Scott RC 1.25 .50
❑ 154 Courtney Hall .20 .07
❑ 155 Brian Mitchell .20 .07
❑ 156 Joe Burch RC UER 333 .20 .07
❑ 157 Terry Mickens .20 .07
❑ 158 Jay Novacek .40 .15
❑ 159 Chris Gedney .20 .07
❑ 160 Bruce Matthews .20 .07
❑ 161 Marlo Perry RC .20 .07
❑ 162 Vince Buck .20 .07
❑ 163 Michael Bates .20 .07
❑ 164 Willie Davis .40 .15
❑ 165 Mike Pritchard .20 .07
❑ 166 Doug Riesenberg .20 .07
❑ 167 Herschel Walker .40 .15
❑ 168 Tim Ruddy RC .20 .07
❑ 169 William Floyd RC .75 .30
❑ 170 John Randle .40 .15
❑ 171 Winston Moss .20 .07
❑ 172 Thurman Thomas .75 .30
❑ 173 Eric England RC .20 .07
❑ 174 Vincent Brisby .40 .15
❑ 175 Greg Lloyd .40 .15
❑ 176 Paul Gruber .20 .07
❑ 177 Brad Ottis RC .20 .07
❑ 178 George Teague .20 .07
❑ 179 Willie Jackson RC .75 .30
❑ 180 Barry Sanders 3.00 1.25
❑ 181 Brian Washington .20 .07
❑ 182 Michael Jackson .40 .15
❑ 183 Jason Mathews RC .20 .07
❑ 184 Chester McGlockton .20 .07
❑ 185 Tydus Winans RC .20 .07
❑ 186 Michael Haynes .40 .15
❑ 187 Erik Kramer .40 .15
❑ 188 Chris Doleman .20 .07
❑ 189 Haywood Jeffires .40 .15
❑ 190 Larry Whigham RC .20 .07
❑ 191 Shawn Jefferson .20 .07
❑ 192 Pete Stoyanovich .20 .07
❑ 193 Rod Bernstine .20 .07
❑ 194 William Thomas .20 .07
❑ 195 Marcus Allen .75 .30
❑ 196 Dave Brown .40 .15
❑ 197 Harold Bishop RC .20 .07
❑ 198 Lorenzo Lynch .20 .07
❑ 199 Dwight Stone .20 .07
❑ 200 Jerry Rice 2.00 .75
❑ 201 Rocket Ismail .40 .15
❑ 202 LeRoy Butler .20 .07
❑ 203 Glenn Parker .20 .07
❑ 204 Bruce Armstrong .20 .07
❑ 205 Shane Conlan .20 .07
❑ 206 Russell Maryland .20 .07
❑ 207 Herman Moore .75 .30
❑ 208 Eric Martin .20 .07
❑ 209 John Friesz .40 .15
❑ 210 Boomer Esiason .40 .15
❑ 211 Jim Harbaugh .75 .30
❑ 212 Harold Green .20 .07
❑ 213 Perry Klein RC .20 .07
❑ 214 Eric Metcalf .40 .15
❑ 215 Steve Everitt .20 .07
❑ 216 Victor Bailey .20 .07
❑ 217 Lincoln Kennedy .20 .07
❑ 218 Glyn Milburn .40 .15
❑ 219 John Copeland .20 .07
❑ 220 Drew Bledsoe 2.00 .75
❑ 221 Kevin Williams WR .40 .15
❑ 222 Roosevelt Potts .20 .07
❑ 223 Troy Drayton .20 .07
❑ 224 Terry Kirby .75 .30
❑ 225 Ronald Moore .20 .07
❑ 226 Tyrone Hughes .40 .15
❑ 227 Wayne Simmons .20 .07
❑ 228 Tony McGee .20 .07
❑ 229 Derek Brown RBK .20 .07
❑ 230 Jason Elam .40 .15
❑ 231 Qadry Ismail .75 .30
❑ 232 O.J.McDuffie .75 .30
❑ 233 Mike Caldwell .20 .07
❑ 234 Reggie Brooks .40 .15
❑ 235 Rick Mirer .75 .30
❑ 236 Steve Tovar .20 .07
❑ 237 Patrick Robinson .20 .07
❑ 238 Tom Carter .20 .07
❑ 239 Ben Coates .40 .15
❑ 240 Jerome Bettis 1.25 .50
❑ 241 Garrison Hearst .75 .30
❑ 242 Natrone Means .75 .30
❑ 243 Dana Stubblefield .40 .15
❑ 244 Willie Roaf .20 .07
❑ 245 Cortez Kennedy .40 .15
❑ 246 Todd Steussie RC .40 .15
❑ 247 Pat Coleman .20 .07
❑ 248 David Wyman .20 .07
❑ 249 Jeremy Lincoln .20 .07
❑ 250 Carlester Crumpler .20 .07
❑ 251 Dale Carter .20 .07
❑ 252 Corey Raymond RC .20 .07
❑ 253 Bryan Cox .20 .07
❑ 254 Charlie Garner RC 3.00 1.25
❑ 255 Jeff Hostetler .40 .15
❑ 256 Shane Bonham RC .20 .07
❑ 257 Thomas Everett .20 .07
❑ 258 John Jackson T .20 .07
❑ 259 Terry Irving RC .20 .07
❑ 260 Corey Sawyer .40 .15
❑ 261 Rob Waldrop .20 .07
❑ 262 Curtis Conway .75 .30
❑ 263 Winfred Tubbs RC .40 .15
❑ 264 Sean Jones .20 .07
❑ 265 James Washington .20 .07
❑ 266 Lonnie Johnson RC .20 .07
❑ 267 Rob Moore .40 .15
❑ 268 Flipper Anderson .20 .07
❑ 269 Jon Hand .20 .07
❑ 270 Joe Patton RC .20 .07
❑ 271 Howard Ballard .20 .07
❑ 272 Fernando Smith RC .20 .07
❑ 273 Jessie Tuggle .20 .07
❑ 274 John Alt .20 .07
❑ 275 Corey Miller .20 .07
❑ 276 Gus Frerotte RC .75 .30
❑ 277 Jeff Cross .20 .07
❑ 278 Kevin Smith .20 .07
❑ 279 Corey Louchiey RC .20 .07
❑ 280 Micheal Barrow .20 .07
❑ 281 Jim Flanigan RC .40 .15
❑ 282 Calvin Williams .40 .15
❑ 283 Jeff Jaeger .20 .07
❑ 284 John Reece RC .20 .07
❑ 285 Jason Hanson .20 .07
❑ 286 Kurt Haws RC .20 .07
❑ 287 Eric Davis .20 .07
❑ 288 Maurice Hurst .20 .07
❑ 289 Kirk Lowdermilk .20 .07
❑ 290 Rod Woodson .40 .15
❑ 291 Andre Reed .40 .15
❑ 292 Vince Workman .20 .07
❑ 293 Wayne Martin .20 .07
❑ 294 Keith Lyle RC .20 .07
❑ 295 Brett Favre 4.00 1.50
❑ 296 Doug Brien RC .20 .07
❑ 297 Junior Seau .75 .30
❑ 298 Randall McDaniel .20 .07
❑ 299 Johnny Mitchell .20 .07
❑ 300 Emmitt Smith 3.00 1.25
❑ 301 Michael Brooks .20 .07
❑ 302 Steve Jackson .20 .07
❑ 303 Jeff George .75 .30
❑ 304 Irving Fryar .40 .15
❑ 305 Derrick Thomas .75 .30
❑ 306 Dante Jones .20 .07
❑ 307 Darrell Green .20 .07
❑ 308 Mark Bavaro .20 .07
❑ 309 Eugene Robinson .20 .07
❑ 310 Shannon Sharpe .40 .15
❑ 311 Michael Timpson .20 .07
❑ 312 Kevin Mitchell RC .20 .07
❑ 313 Stevon Moore .20 .07
❑ 314 Eric Swann .40 .15
❑ 315 James Bostic RC .75 .30
❑ 316 Robert Brooks .75 .30
❑ 317 Pete Pierson RC .20 .07
❑ 318 Jim Sweeney .20 .07
❑ 319 Anthony Smith .20 .07
❑ 320 Rohn Stark .20 .07
❑ 321 Gary Anderson K .20 .07
❑ 322 Robert Porcher .20 .07
❑ 323 Darryl Talley .20 .07
❑ 324 Stan Humphries .40 .15
❑ 325 Shelly Hammonds RC .20 .07
❑ 326 Jim McMahon .40 .15
❑ 327 Lamont Warren RC .20 .07
❑ 328 Chris Penn RC .20 .07
❑ 329 Tony Woods .20 .07
❑ 330 Raymont Harris RC .75 .30
❑ 331 Mitch Davis RC .20 .07
❑ 332 Michael Irvin .75 .30
❑ 333 Kent Graham .40 .15
❑ 334 Brian Blades .40 .15
❑ 335 Lomas Brown .20 .07
❑ 336 Willie Drewrey .20 .07
❑ 337 Russell Freeman .20 .07
❑ 338 Eric Zomalt RC .20 .07
❑ 339 Santana Dotson .40 .15
❑ 340 Sterling Sharpe .40 .15
❑ 341 Ray Crittenden RC .20 .07
❑ 342 Perry Carter RC .20 .07
❑ 343 Austin Robbins .20 .07
❑ 344 Mike Wells DT RC .20 .07
❑ 345 Toddrick McIntosh RC .20 .07
❑ 346 Mark Carrier WR .40 .15
❑ 347 Eugene Daniel .20 .07
❑ 348 Tre Johnson RC .20 .07
❑ 349 D.J. Johnson .20 .07
❑ 350 Steve Young 1.50 .60
❑ 351 Jim Pyne RC .20 .07
❑ 352 Jocelyn Borgella RC .20 .07
❑ 353 Pat Carter .20 .07
❑ 354 Sam Rogers RC .20 .07
❑ 355 Jason Sehorn RC 1.25 .50
❑ 356 Darren Carrington .20 .07
❑ 357 Lamar Smith RC 4.00 1.50
❑ 358 James Burton RC .20 .07
❑ 359 Darrin Smith .20 .07
❑ 360 Marco Coleman .20 .07
❑ 361 Webster Slaughter .20 .07
❑ 362 Lewis Tillman .20 .07
❑ 363 David Alexander .20 .07
❑ 364 Bradford Banta RC .20 .07
❑ 365 Erric Pegram .20 .07
❑ 366 Mike Fox .20 .07
❑ 367 Jeff Lageman .20 .07
❑ 368 Kurt Gouveia .20 .07
❑ 369 Tim Brown .75 .30
❑ 370 Seth Joyner .20 .07
❑ 371 Irv Eatman .20 .07
❑ 372 Dorsey Levens RC 4.00 1.50
❑ 373 Anthony Pleasant .20 .07
❑ 374 Henry Jones .20 .07
❑ 375 Cris Carter 1.00 .40
❑ 376 Morten Andersen .20 .07
❑ 377 Neil O'Donnell .75 .30
❑ 378 Tyronne Drakeford RC .20 .07
❑ 379 John Carney .20 .07
❑ 380 Vincent Brown .20 .07
❑ 381 J.J. Birden .20 .07
❑ 382 Chris Spielman .40 .15
❑ 383 Mark Bortz .20 .07
❑ 384 Ray Childress .20 .07
❑ 385 Carlton Bailey .20 .07
❑ 386 Charles Haley .40 .15
❑ 387 Shane Dronett .20 .07
❑ 388 Jon Vaughn .20 .07
❑ 389 Checklist 1-195 .20 .07
❑ 390 Checklist 196-390 .20 .07

1995 Bowman

❑ COMPLETE SET (357) 60.00 25.00
❑ 1 Ki-Jana Carter RC .75 .30
❑ 2 Tony Boselli RC .75 .30
❑ 3 Steve McNair RC 8.00 3.00
❑ 4 Michael Westbrook RC .60 .25
❑ 5 Kerry Collins RC 4.00 1.50

❑ 6 Kevin Carter RC .75 .30
❑ 7 Mike Mamula RC .20 .05
❑ 8 Joey Galloway RC 4.00 1.50
❑ 9 Kyle Brady RC .75 .30
❑ 10 J.J. Stokes RC .75 .30
❑ 11 Derrick Alexander DE RC .20 .05
❑ 12 Warren Sapp RC 4.00 1.50
❑ 13 Mark Fields RC .75 .30
❑ 14 Ruben Brown RC .75 .30
❑ 15 Ellis Johnson RC .20 .05
❑ 16 Hugh Douglas RC .75 .30
❑ 17 Mike Pelton RC .20 .05
❑ 18 Napoleon Kaufman RC 3.00 1.25
❑ 19 James O. Stewart RC 2.50 1.00
❑ 20 Luther Elliss RC .20 .05
❑ 21 Rashaan Salaam RC .40 .15
❑ 22 Tyrone Poole RC .75 .30
❑ 23 Ty Law RC 3.00 1.25
❑ 24 Korey Stringer RC .40 .15
❑ 25 Billy Milner RC .20 .05
❑ 26 Devin Bush RC .20 .05
❑ 27 Mark Bruener RC .40 .15
❑ 28 Derrick Brooks RC 4.00 1.50
❑ 29 Blake Brockermeyer RC .20 .05
❑ 30 Alundis Brice RC .20 .05
❑ 31 Trezelle Jenkins RC .20 .05
❑ 32 Craig Newsome RC .20 .05
❑ 33 Fred Barnett .30 .10
❑ 34 Ray Childress .15 .05
❑ 35 Chris Miller .15 .05
❑ 36 Charles Haley .30 .10
❑ 37 Ray Crittenden .15 .05
❑ 38 Gus Frerotte .30 .10
❑ 39 Jeff George .30 .10
❑ 40 Dan Marino 3.00 1.25
❑ 41 Shawn Lee .15 .05
❑ 42 Herman Moore .60 .25
❑ 43 Chris Calloway .15 .05
❑ 44 Jeff Graham .15 .05
❑ 45 Ray Buchanan .15 .05
❑ 46 Doug Pelfrey .15 .05
❑ 47 Lake Dawson .30 .10
❑ 48 Glenn Parker .15 .05
❑ 49 Terry McDaniel .15 .05
❑ 50 Rod Woodson .30 .10
❑ 51 Santana Dotson .15 .05
❑ 52 Anthony Miller .30 .10
❑ 53 Bo Orlando .15 .05
❑ 54 David Palmer .30 .10
❑ 55 William Floyd .30 .10
❑ 56 Edgar Bennett .30 .10
❑ 57 Jeff Blake RC 2.50 1.00
❑ 58 Anthony Pleasant .15 .05
❑ 59 Quinn Early .30 .10
❑ 60 Bobby Houston .15 .05
❑ 61 Terrell Fletcher RC .20 .05
❑ 62 Gary Brown .15 .05
❑ 63 Dwayne Sabb .15 .05
❑ 64 Roman Phifer .15 .05
❑ 65 Sherman Williams RC .20 .05
❑ 66 Roosevelt Potts .15 .05
❑ 67 Darnay Scott .30 .10
❑ 68 Charlie Garner .60 .25
❑ 69 Bert Emanuel .60 .25
❑ 70 Herschel Walker .30 .10
❑ 71 Lorenzo Styles RC .20 .05
❑ 72 Andre Coleman .15 .05
❑ 73 Tyronne Drakeford .15 .05
❑ 74 Jay Novacek .30 .10
❑ 75 Raymont Harris .15 .05
❑ 76 Tamarick Vanover RC .75 .30
❑ 77 Tom Carter .15 .05
❑ 78 Eric Green .15 .05
❑ 79 Patrick Hunter .15 .05
❑ 80 Jeff Hostetler .30 .10
❑ 81 Robert Blackmon .15 .05
❑ 82 Anthony Cook RC .20 .05
❑ 83 Craig Erickson .15 .05
❑ 84 Glyn Milburn .15 .05
❑ 85 Greg Lloyd .30 .10
❑ 86 Brent Jones .15 .05
❑ 87 Barrett Brooks RC .20 .05
❑ 88 Alvin Harper .15 .05
❑ 89 Sean Jones .15 .05
❑ 90 Cris Carter .60 .25
❑ 91 Russell Copeland .15 .05
❑ 92 Frank Sanders RC .75 .30
❑ 93 Mo Lewis .15 .05
❑ 94 Michael Haynes .30 .10
❑ 95 Andre Rison .30 .10
❑ 96 Jesse James RC .20 .05
❑ 97 Stan Humphries .30 .10
❑ 98 James Hasty .15 .05
❑ 99 Ricardo McDonald .15 .05
❑ 100 Jerry Rice 1.50 .60
❑ 101 Chris Hudson RC .20 .05
❑ 102 Dave Meggett .15 .05
❑ 103 Brian Mitchell .15 .05
❑ 104 Mike Johnson .15 .05
❑ 105 Kordell Stewart RC 4.00 1.50
❑ 106 Michael Brooks .15 .05
❑ 107 Steve Walsh .15 .05
❑ 108 Eric Metcalf .30 .10
❑ 109 Ricky Watters .30 .10
❑ 110 Brett Favre 3.00 1.25
❑ 111 Aubrey Beavers .15 .05
❑ 112 Brian Williams LB RC .20 .05
❑ 113 Eugene Robinson .15 .05
❑ 114 Matt O'Dwyer RC .20 .05
❑ 115 Micheal Barrow .15 .05
❑ 116 Rocket Ismail .30 .10
❑ 117 Scott Gragg RC .20 .05
❑ 118 Leon Lett .15 .05
❑ 119 Reggie Roby .15 .05
❑ 120 Marshall Faulk 2.00 .75
❑ 121 Jack Jackson RC .20 .05
❑ 122 Keith Byars .15 .05
❑ 123 Eric Hill .15 .05
❑ 124 Todd Sauerbrun RC .20 .05
❑ 125 Dexter Carter .15 .05
❑ 126 Vinny Testaverde .30 .10
❑ 127 Shane Conlan .15 .05
❑ 128 Terrance Shaw RC .20 .05
❑ 129 Willie Roaf .15 .05
❑ 130 Jim Kelly .60 .25
❑ 131 Neil O'Donnell .30 .10
❑ 132 Ray McElroy RC .20 .05
❑ 133 Ed McDaniel .15 .05
❑ 134 Brian Gelzheiser RC .20 .05
❑ 135 Marcus Allen .60 .25
❑ 136 Carl Pickens .30 .10
❑ 137 Mike Verstegan RC .20 .05
❑ 138 Chris Mims .15 .05
❑ 139 Darryl Pounds RC .20 .05
❑ 140 Emmitt Smith 2.50 1.25
❑ 141 Mike Frederick RC .20 .05
❑ 142 Henry Ellard .30 .10
❑ 143 Willie McGinest .30 .10
❑ 144 Michael Roan RC .20 .05
❑ 145 Chris Spielman .30 .10
❑ 146 Darryl Talley .15 .05
❑ 147 Randall Cunningham .60 .25
❑ 148 Andrew Greene RC .20 .05
❑ 149 George Teague .15 .05
❑ 150 Tyrone Hughes .30 .10
❑ 151 Ron Davis RC .20 .05
❑ 152 Stevon Moore .15 .05
❑ 153 Merton Hanks .15 .05
❑ 154 Darren Perry .15 .05
❑ 155 Dave Brown .30 .10
❑ 156 Mike Morton RC .20 .05
❑ 157 Seth Joyner .15 .05
❑ 158 Bryan Cox .15 .05
❑ 159 Corey Fuller RC .20 .05
❑ 160 John Elway 3.00 1.25
❑ 161 Dewayne Washington .30 .10
❑ 162 Chris Warren .30 .10
❑ 163 Jeff Kopp RC .20 .05
❑ 164 Sean Dawkins .30 .10
❑ 165 Mark Carrier DB .15 .05
❑ 166 Andre Hastings .30 .10
❑ 167 Derek West RC .20 .05
❑ 168 Glenn Montgomery .15 .05
❑ 169 Trent Dilfer .60 .25
❑ 170 Rob Johnson RC 2.50 1.00
❑ 171 Todd Scott .15 .05
❑ 172 Charles Johnson .30 .10
❑ 173 Kez McCorvey RC .20 .05
❑ 174 Rob Fredrickson .15 .05
❑ 175 Corey Sawyer .15 .05
❑ 176 Brett Perriman .30 .10
❑ 177 Ken Dilger RC .75 .30
❑ 178 Dana Stubblefield .30 .10
❑ 179 Eric Allen .15 .05
❑ 180 Drew Bledsoe 1.00 .40
❑ 181 Tyrone Davis RC .20 .05
❑ 182 Reggie Brooks .30 .10
❑ 183 Dale Carter .30 .10
❑ 184 William Henderson RC 3.00 1.25
❑ 185 Reggie White .60 .25
❑ 186 Lorenzo White .15 .05
❑ 187 Leslie O'Neal .30 .10
❑ 188 Stoney Case RC .20 .05
❑ 189 Jeff Burris .15 .05
❑ 190 Leroy Hoard .15 .05
❑ 191 Thomas Randolph .15 .05
❑ 192 Rodney Thomas RC .40 .15
❑ 193 Quentin Coryatt .30 .10
❑ 194 Terry Wooden .15 .05
❑ 195 David Sloan RC .20 .05
❑ 196 Bernie Parmalee .30 .10
❑ 197 Zack Crockett RC .40 .15
❑ 198 Troy Aikman 1.50 .60
❑ 199 Bruce Smith .60 .25
❑ 200 Eric Zeier RC .75 .30
❑ 201 Anthony Smith .15 .05
❑ 202 Jake Reed .30 .10
❑ 203 Hardy Nickerson .15 .05
❑ 204 Patrick Riley RC .20 .05
❑ 205 Bruce Matthews .15 .05
❑ 206 Larry Centers .30 .10
❑ 207 Troy Drayton .15 .05
❑ 208 John Burrough RC .20 .05
❑ 209 Jason Elam .30 .10
❑ 210 Donnell Woolford .15 .05
❑ 211 Sam Shade RC .20 .05
❑ 212 Kevin Greene .30 .10
❑ 213 Ronald Moore .15 .05
❑ 214 Shane Hannah RC .20 .05
❑ 215 Jim Everett .15 .05
❑ 216 Scott Mitchell .30 .10
❑ 217 Antonio Freeman RC 3.00 1.25
❑ 218 Tony McGee .15 .05
❑ 219 Clay Matthews .30 .10
❑ 220 Neil Smith .30 .10
❑ 221 Mark Williams FOIL .40 .15
❑ 222 Derrick Graham FOIL .40 .15
❑ 223 Mike Hollis FOIL .40 .15
❑ 224 Darion Conner FOIL .40 .15
❑ 225 Steve Beuerlein FOIL .40 .15
❑ 226 Rod Smith DB FOIL .40 .15
❑ 227 James Williams LB FOIL .40 .15
❑ 228 Bob Christian FOIL .40 .15
❑ 229 Jeff Lageman FOIL .40 .15
❑ 230 Frank Reich FOIL .40 .15
❑ 231 Harry Colon FOIL .40 .15
❑ 232 Carlton Bailey FOIL .40 .15
❑ 233 Mickey Washington FOIL .40 .15
❑ 234 Shawn Bouwens FOIL .40 .15
❑ 235 Don Beebe FOIL .40 .15
❑ 236 Kelvin Pritchett FOIL .40 .15
❑ 237 Tommy Barnhardt FOIL .40 .15
❑ 238 Mike Dumas FOIL .40 .15
❑ 239 Brett Maxie FOIL .40 .15
❑ 240 Desmond Howard FOIL .40 .15
❑ 241 Sam Mills FOIL .40 .15
❑ 242 Keith Goganious FOIL .40 .15
❑ 243 Bubba McDowell FOIL .40 .15
❑ 244 Vinnie Clark FOIL .40 .15
❑ 245 Lamar Lathon FOIL .40 .15
❑ 246 Bryan Barker FOIL .40 .15
❑ 247 Darren Carrington FOIL .40 .15
❑ 248 Jay Barker RC .20 .05
❑ 249 Eric Davis .15 .05
❑ 250 Heath Shuler .30 .10
❑ 251 Donta Jones RC .20 .05
❑ 252 LeRoy Butler .15 .05
❑ 253 Michael Zordich .15 .05
❑ 254 Cortez Kennedy .30 .10
❑ 255 Brian DeMarco RC .20 .05

❑ 256 Randal Hill .15 .05
❑ 257 Michael Irvin .60 .25
❑ 258 Natrone Means .30 .10
❑ 259 Linc Harden RC .20 .05
❑ 260 Jerome Bettis .60 .25
❑ 261 Tony Bennett .15 .05
❑ 262 Dameian Jeffries RC .20 .05
❑ 263 Cornelius Bennett .30 .10
❑ 264 Chris Zorich .15 .05
❑ 265 Bobby Taylor RC .75 .30
❑ 266 Terrell Buckley .15 .05
❑ 267 Troy Dumas RC .20 .05
❑ 268 Rodney Hampton .30 .10
❑ 269 Steve Everitt .15 .05
❑ 270 Mel Gray .15 .05
❑ 271 Antonio Armstrong RC .20 .05
❑ 272 Jim Harbaugh .30 .10
❑ 273 Gary Clark .15 .05
❑ 274 Tau Pupua RC .20 .05
❑ 275 Warren Moon .30 .10
❑ 276 Corey Croom .15 .05
❑ 277 Tony Berti RC .20 .05
❑ 278 Shannon Sharpe .30 .10
❑ 279 Boomer Esiason .30 .10
❑ 280 Aeneas Williams .15 .05
❑ 281 Lethon Flowers RC .20 .05
❑ 282 Derek Brown TE .15 .05
❑ 283 Charlie Williams RC .20 .05
❑ 284 Dan Wilkinson .30 .10
❑ 285 Mike Sherrard .15 .05
❑ 286 Evan Pilgrim RC .20 .05
❑ 287 Kimble Anders .30 .10
❑ 288 Greg Jefferson RC .20 .05
❑ 289 Ken Norton .30 .10
❑ 290 Terance Mathis .30 .10
❑ 291 Torey Hunter RC .20 .05
❑ 292 Ken Harvey .15 .05
❑ 293 Irving Fryar .30 .10
❑ 294 Michael Reed RC .20 .05
❑ 295 Andre Reed .30 .10
❑ 296 Vencie Glenn .15 .05
❑ 297 Corey Swinson .15 .05
❑ 298 Harvey Williams .15 .05
❑ 299 Willie Davis .30 .10
❑ 300 Barry Sanders 2.50 1.00
❑ 301 Curtis Martin RC 8.00 3.00
❑ 302 Johnny Mitchell .15 .05
❑ 303 Daryl Johnston .30 .10
❑ 304 Lorenzo Lynch .15 .05
❑ 305 Christian Fauria RC .40 .15
❑ 306 Sean Gilbert .30 .10
❑ 307 Ray Zellars RC .40 .15
❑ 308 William Strong RC .20 .05
❑ 309 Jack Del Rio .15 .05
❑ 310 Junior Seau .60 .25
❑ 311 Justin Armour RC .20 .05
❑ 312 Eric Bjornson RC .20 .05
❑ 313 Vincent Brown .15 .05
❑ 314 Darius Holland RC .20 .05
❑ 315 Chad May RC .20 .05
❑ 316 Simon Fletcher .15 .05
❑ 317 Roell Preston RC .30 .10
❑ 318 John Thierry .15 .05
❑ 319 Orlando Thomas RC .20 .05
❑ 320 Zach Wiegert RC .20 .05
❑ 321 Derrick Alexander WR .60 .25
❑ 322 Chris Cowart RC .20 .05
❑ 323 Chris Sanders RC .40 .15
❑ 324 Robert Brooks .60 .25
❑ 325 Todd Collins RC .40 .15
❑ 326 Ken Irvin RC .20 .05
❑ 327 Erric Pegram .30 .10
❑ 328 Damien Covington RC .20 .05
❑ 329 Brendan Stai RC .20 .05
❑ 330 James A.Stewart RC .20 .05
❑ 331 Jessie Tuggle .15 .05
❑ 332 Marco Coleman .15 .05
❑ 333 Steve Young 1.25 .50
❑ 334 Greg Hill .30 .10
❑ 335 Darryl Williams .15 .05
❑ 336 Calvin Williams .30 .10
❑ 337 Cris Dishman .15 .05
❑ 338 Anthony Morgan .15 .05
❑ 339 Renaldo Turnbull .15 .05
❑ 340 Rick Mirer .30 .10
❑ 341 Tim Brown .60 .25
❑ 342 Dennis Gibson .15 .05
❑ 343 Brad Baxter .15 .05
❑ 344 Henry Jones .15 .05
❑ 345 Johnny Bailey .15 .05
❑ 346 Rocket Ismail .30 .10
❑ 347 Richmond Webb .15 .05
❑ 348 Robert Jones .15 .05
❑ 349 Garrison Hearst .60 .25
❑ 350 Errict Rhett .30 .10
❑ 351 Steve Atwater .15 .05
❑ 352 Joe Cain .15 .05
❑ 353 Ben Coates .30 .10
❑ 354 Aaron Glenn .15 .05
❑ 355 Antonio Langham .15 .05
❑ 356 Eugene Daniel .15 .05
❑ 357 Tim Bowens .15 .05

1998 Bowman

❑ COMPLETE SET (220) 50.00 20.00
❑ 1 Peyton Manning RC 25.00 12.50
❑ 2 Keith Brooking RC 1.50 .60
❑ 3 Duane Starks RC .75 .30
❑ 4 Takeo Spikes RC 1.50 .60
❑ 5 Andre Wadsworth RC 1.25 .50
❑ 6 Greg Ellis RC .75 .30
❑ 7 Brian Griese RC 3.00 1.25
❑ 8 Germane Crowell RC 1.25 .50
❑ 9 Jerome Pathon RC 1.50 .60
❑ 10 Ryan Leaf RC 1.50 .60
❑ 11 Fred Taylor RC 2.50 1.00
❑ 12 Robert Edwards RC 1.25 .50
❑ 13 Grant Wistrom RC 1.25 .50
❑ 14 Robert Holcombe RC 1.25 .50
❑ 15 Tim Dwight RC 1.50 .60
❑ 16 Jacquez Green RC 1.25 .50
❑ 17 Marcus Nash RC .75 .30
❑ 18 Jason Peter RC .75 .30
❑ 19 Anthony Simmons RC 1.25 .50
❑ 20 Curtis Enis RC .75 .30
❑ 21 John Avery RC 1.25 .50
❑ 22 Pat Johnson RC 1.25 .50
❑ 23 Joe Jurevicius RC 1.50 .60
❑ 24 Brian Simmons RC 1.25 .50
❑ 25 Kevin Dyson RC 1.50 .60
❑ 26 Skip Hicks RC 1.25 .50
❑ 27 Hines Ward RC 8.00 3.00
❑ 28 Tavian Banks RC 1.25 .50
❑ 29 Ahman Green RC 8.00 3.00
❑ 30 Tony Simmons RC 1.25 .50
❑ 31 Charles Johnson .30 .10
❑ 32 Freddie Jones .30 .10
❑ 33 Joey Galloway .50 .20
❑ 34 Tony Banks .50 .20
❑ 35 Jake Plummer .75 .30
❑ 36 Reidel Anthony .50 .20
❑ 37 Steve McNair .75 .30
❑ 38 Michael Westbrook .50 .20
❑ 39 Chris Sanders .30 .10
❑ 40 Isaac Bruce .75 .30
❑ 41 Charlie Garner .50 .20
❑ 42 Wayne Chrebet .75 .30
❑ 43 Michael Strahan .50 .20
❑ 44 Brad Johnson .75 .30
❑ 45 Mike Alstott .75 .30
❑ 46 Tony Gonzalez .75 .30
❑ 47 Johnnie Morton .50 .20
❑ 48 Darnay Scott .50 .20
❑ 49 Rae Carruth .30 .10
❑ 50 Terrell Davis .75 .30
❑ 51 Jermaine Lewis .50 .20
❑ 52 Frank Sanders .50 .20
❑ 53 Byron Hanspard .30 .10
❑ 54 Gus Frerotte .30 .10
❑ 55 Terry Glenn .75 .30
❑ 56 J.J. Stokes .50 .20
❑ 57 Will Blackwell .30 .10
❑ 58 Keyshawn Johnson .75 .30
❑ 59 Tiki Barber .75 .30
❑ 60 Dorsey Levens .75 .30
❑ 61 Zach Thomas .75 .30
❑ 62 Corey Dillon .75 .30
❑ 63 Antowain Smith .75 .30
❑ 64 Michael Sinclair .30 .10
❑ 65 Rod Smith .50 .20
❑ 66 Trent Dilfer .75 .30
❑ 67 Warren Sapp .50 .20
❑ 68 Charles Way .30 .10
❑ 69 Tamarick Vanover .30 .10
❑ 70 Drew Bledsoe 1.25 .50
❑ 71 John Mobley .30 .10
❑ 72 Kerry Collins .50 .20
❑ 73 Peter Boulware .30 .10
❑ 74 Simeon Rice .50 .20
❑ 75 Eddie George .75 .30
❑ 76 Fred Lane .30 .10
❑ 77 Jamal Anderson .75 .30
❑ 78 Antonio Freeman .75 .30
❑ 79 Jason Sehorn .50 .20
❑ 80 Curtis Martin .75 .30
❑ 81 Bobby Hoying .50 .20
❑ 82 Garrison Hearst .75 .30
❑ 83 Glenn Foley .50 .20
❑ 84 Danny Kanell .50 .20
❑ 85 Kordell Stewart .75 .30
❑ 86 O.J. McDuffie .50 .20
❑ 87 Marvin Harrison .75 .30
❑ 88 Bobby Engram .50 .20
❑ 89 Chris Slade .30 .10
❑ 90 Warrick Dunn .75 .30
❑ 91 Ricky Watters .50 .20
❑ 92 Rickey Dudley .30 .10
❑ 93 Terrell Owens .75 .30
❑ 94 Karim Abdul-Jabbar .75 .30
❑ 95 Napoleon Kaufman .75 .30
❑ 96 Darrell Green .50 .20
❑ 97 Levon Kirkland .30 .10
❑ 98 Jeff George .50 .20
❑ 99 Andre Hastings .30 .10
❑ 100 John Elway 3.00 1.25
❑ 101 John Randle .50 .20
❑ 102 Andre Rison .50 .20
❑ 103 Keenan McCardell .50 .20
❑ 104 Marshall Faulk 1.00 .40
❑ 105 Emmitt Smith 2.50 1.00
❑ 106 Robert Brooks .50 .20
❑ 107 Scott Mitchell .50 .20
❑ 108 Shannon Sharpe .50 .20
❑ 109 Deion Sanders .75 .30
❑ 110 Jerry Rice 1.50 .60
❑ 111 Erik Kramer .30 .10
❑ 112 Michael Jackson .30 .10
❑ 113 Aeneas Williams .30 .10
❑ 114 Terry Allen .75 .30
❑ 115 Steve Young 1.00 .40
❑ 116 Warren Moon .75 .30
❑ 117 Junior Seau .75 .30
❑ 118 Jerome Bettis .75 .30
❑ 119 Irving Fryar .50 .20
❑ 120 Barry Sanders 2.50 1.00
❑ 121 Tim Brown .75 .30
❑ 122 Chad Brown .30 .10
❑ 123 Ben Coates .50 .20
❑ 124 Robert Smith .75 .30
❑ 125 Brett Favre 3.00 1.25
❑ 126 Derrick Thomas .75 .30
❑ 127 Reggie White .75 .30
❑ 128 Troy Aikman 1.50 .60
❑ 129 Jeff Blake .50 .20
❑ 130 Mark Brunell .75 .30
❑ 131 Curtis Conway .50 .20
❑ 132 Wesley Walls .50 .20
❑ 133 Thurman Thomas .75 .30
❑ 134 Chris Chandler .50 .20
❑ 135 Dan Marino 3.00 1.25
❑ 136 Larry Centers .30 .10
❑ 137 Shawn Jefferson .30 .10
❑ 138 Andre Reed .50 .20
❑ 139 Jake Reed .50 .20
❑ 140 Cris Carter .75 .30
❑ 141 Elvis Grbac .50 .20
❑ 142 Mark Chmura .50 .20
❑ 143 Michael Irvin .75 .30
❑ 144 Carl Pickens .50 .20
❑ 145 Herman Moore .50 .20

❑ 146 Marvin Jones .30 .10
❑ 147 Terance Mathis .50 .20
❑ 148 Rob Moore .50 .20
❑ 149 Bruce Smith .50 .20
❑ 150 Rob Johnson CL .30 .10
❑ 151 Leslie Shepherd .30 .10
❑ 152 Chris Spielman .30 .10
❑ 153 Tony McGee .30 .10
❑ 154 Kevin Smith .30 .10
❑ 155 Bill Romanowski .30 .10
❑ 156 Stephen Boyd .30 .10
❑ 157 James Stewart .50 .20
❑ 158 Jason Taylor .50 .20
❑ 159 Troy Drayton .30 .10
❑ 160 Mark Fields .30 .10
❑ 161 Jessie Armstead .30 .10
❑ 162 James Jett .50 .20
❑ 163 Bobby Taylor .30 .10
❑ 164 Kimble Anders .50 .20
❑ 165 Jimmy Smith .50 .20
❑ 166 Quentin Coryatt .30 .10
❑ 167 Bryant Westbrook .30 .10
❑ 168 Neil Smith .50 .20
❑ 169 Darren Woodson .30 .10
❑ 170 Ray Buchanan .30 .10
❑ 171 Earl Holmes .30 .10
❑ 172 Ray Lewis .75 .30
❑ 173 Steve Broussard .30 .10
❑ 174 Derrick Brooks .75 .30
❑ 175 Ken Harvey .30 .10
❑ 176 Darryll Lewis .30 .10
❑ 177 Derrick Rodgers .30 .10
❑ 178 James McKnight .75 .30
❑ 179 Cris Dishman .30 .10
❑ 180 Hardy Nickerson .30 .10
❑ 181 Charles Woodson RC 2.00 .75
❑ 182 Randy Moss RC 10.00 4.00
❑ 183 Stephen Alexander RC 1.25 .50
❑ 184 Samari Rolle RC .75 .30
❑ 185 Jamie Duncan RC .75 .30
❑ 186 Lance Schulters RC .75 .30
❑ 187 Tony Parrish RC 1.50 .60
❑ 188 Corey Chavous RC 1.50 .60
❑ 189 Jammi German RC .75 .30
❑ 190 Sam Cowart RC 1.25 .50
❑ 191 Donald Hayes RC 1.25 .50
❑ 192 R.W. McQuarters RC 1.25 .50
❑ 193 Az-Zahir Hakim RC 1.50 .60
❑ 194 Chris Fuamatu-Ma'afala RC 1.25 .50
❑ 195 Allen Rossum RC 1.25 .50
❑ 196 Jon Ritchie RC 1.25 .50
❑ 197 Blake Spence RC .75 .30
❑ 198 Brian Alford RC .75 .30
❑ 199 Fred Weary RC .75 .30
❑ 200 Rod Rutledge RC .75 .30
❑ 201 Michael Myers RC .75 .30
❑ 202 Rashaan Shehee RC 1.25 .50
❑ 203 Donovin Darius RC 1.25 .50
❑ 204 E.G. Green RC 1.25 .50
❑ 205 Vonnie Holliday RC 1.25 .50
❑ 206 Charlie Batch RC 1.50 .60
❑ 207 Michael Pittman RC 2.00 .75
❑ 208 Artrell Hawkins RC .75 .30
❑ 209 Jonathan Quinn RC 1.50 .60
❑ 210 Kailee Wong RC .75 .30
❑ 211 DeShea Townsend RC .75 .30
❑ 212 Patrick Surtain RC 1.50 .60
❑ 213 Brian Kelly RC 1.25 .50
❑ 214 Tebucky Jones RC .75 .30
❑ 215 Pete Gonzalez RC .75 .30
❑ 216 Shaun Williams RC 1.25 .50
❑ 217 Scott Frost RC .75 .30
❑ 218 Leonard Little RC 1.50 .60
❑ 219 Alonzo Mayes RC .75 .30
❑ 220 Cordell Taylor RC .75 .30

1999 Bowman

❑ COMPLETE SET (220) 40.00 15.00
❑ 1 Dan Marino 2.50 1.00
❑ 2 Michael Westbrook .50 .20
❑ 3 Yancey Thigpen .30 .10
❑ 4 Tony Martin .50 .20
❑ 5 Michael Strahan .50 .20
❑ 6 Dedric Ward .30 .10
❑ 7 Joey Galloway .50 .20
❑ 8 Bobby Engram .50 .20
❑ 9 Frank Sanders .50 .20
❑ 10 Jake Plummer .50 .20
❑ 11 Eddie Kennison .50 .20
❑ 12 Curtis Martin .75 .30
❑ 13 Chris Spielman .30 .10
❑ 14 Trent Dilfer .50 .20
❑ 15 Tim Biakabutuka .50 .20
❑ 16 Elvis Grbac .50 .20
❑ 17 Charlie Batch .75 .30
❑ 18 Takeo Spikes .30 .10
❑ 19 Tony Banks .50 .20
❑ 20 Doug Flutie .75 .30
❑ 21 Ty Law .50 .20
❑ 22 Isaac Bruce .75 .30
❑ 23 James Jett .50 .20
❑ 24 Kent Graham .30 .10
❑ 25 Derrick Mayes .30 .10
❑ 26 Amani Toomer .30 .10
❑ 27 Ray Lewis .75 .30
❑ 28 Shawn Springs .30 .10
❑ 29 Warren Sapp .30 .10
❑ 30 Jamal Anderson .75 .30
❑ 31 Byron Bam Morris .30 .10
❑ 32 Johnnie Morton .30 .10
❑ 33 Terance Mathis .30 .10
❑ 34 Terrell Davis .75 .30
❑ 35 John Randle .50 .20
❑ 36 Vinny Testaverde .30 .10
❑ 37 Junior Seau .75 .30
❑ 38 Reidel Anthony .50 .20
❑ 39 Brad Johnson .30 .10
❑ 40 Emmitt Smith 1.50 .60
❑ 41 Mo Lewis .30 .10
❑ 42 Terry Glenn .75 .30
❑ 43 Dorsey Levens .75 .30
❑ 44 Thurman Thomas .50 .20
❑ 45 Rob Moore .50 .20
❑ 46 Corey Dillon .75 .30
❑ 47 Jessie Armstead .30 .10
❑ 48 Marshall Faulk 1.00 .40
❑ 49 Charles Woodson .30 .10
❑ 50 John Elway 2.50 1.00
❑ 51 Kevin Dyson .50 .20
❑ 52 Tony Simmons .30 .10
❑ 53 Keenan McCardell .50 .20
❑ 54 O.J. Santiago .30 .10
❑ 55 Jermaine Lewis .50 .20
❑ 56 Herman Moore .50 .20
❑ 57 Gary Brown .30 .10
❑ 58 Jim Harbaugh .50 .20
❑ 59 Mike Alstott .75 .30
❑ 60 Brett Favre 2.50 1.00
❑ 61 Tim Brown .75 .30
❑ 62 Steve McNair .75 .30
❑ 63 Ben Coates .50 .20
❑ 64 Jerome Pathon .30 .10
❑ 65 Ray Buchanan .30 .10
❑ 66 Troy Aikman 1.50 .60
❑ 67 Andre Reed .50 .20
❑ 68 Bubby Brister .30 .10
❑ 69 Karim Abdul-Jabbar .50 .20
❑ 70 Peyton Manning 2.50 1.00
❑ 71 Charles Johnson .30 .10
❑ 72 Natrone Means .50 .20
❑ 73 Michael Sinclair .30 .10
❑ 74 Skip Hicks .30 .10
❑ 75 Derrick Alexander .50 .20
❑ 76 Wayne Chrebet .50 .20
❑ 77 Rod Smith .50 .20
❑ 78 Carl Pickens .50 .20
❑ 79 Adrian Murrell .50 .20
❑ 80 Fred Taylor .75 .30
❑ 81 Eric Moulds .75 .30
❑ 82 Lawrence Phillips .50 .20
❑ 83 Marvin Harrison .75 .30
❑ 84 Cris Carter .75 .30
❑ 85 Ike Hilliard .30 .10
❑ 86 Hines Ward .75 .30
❑ 87 Terrell Owens .75 .30
❑ 88 Ricky Proehl .30 .10
❑ 89 Bert Emanuel .50 .20
❑ 90 Randy Moss 2.00 .75
❑ 91 Aaron Glenn .30 .10
❑ 92 Robert Smith .75 .30
❑ 93 Andre Hastings .30 .10
❑ 94 Jake Reed .50 .20
❑ 95 Curtis Enis .30 .10
❑ 96 Andre Wadsworth .30 .10
❑ 97 Ed McCaffrey .50 .20
❑ 98 Zach Thomas .75 .30
❑ 99 Kerry Collins .50 .20
❑ 100 Drew Bledsoe 1.00 .40
❑ 101 Germane Crowell .30 .10
❑ 102 Bryan Still .30 .10
❑ 103 Chad Brown .30 .10
❑ 104 Jacquez Green .30 .10
❑ 105 Garrison Hearst .50 .20
❑ 106 Napoleon Kaufman .75 .30
❑ 107 Ricky Watters .50 .20
❑ 108 O.J. McDuffie .50 .20
❑ 109 Keyshawn Johnson .75 .30
❑ 110 Jerome Bettis .75 .30
❑ 111 Duce Staley .75 .30
❑ 112 Curtis Conway .50 .20
❑ 113 Chris Chandler .50 .20
❑ 114 Marcus Nash .30 .10
❑ 115 Stephen Alexander .30 .10
❑ 116 Darnay Scott .30 .10
❑ 117 Bruce Smith .50 .20
❑ 118 Priest Holmes 1.25 .50
❑ 119 Mark Brunell .75 .30
❑ 120 Jerry Rice 1.50 .60
❑ 121 Randall Cunningham .75 .30
❑ 122 Scott Mitchell .30 .10
❑ 123 Antonio Freeman .75 .30
❑ 124 Kordell Stewart .50 .20
❑ 125 Jon Kitna .75 .30
❑ 126 Ahman Green .75 .30
❑ 127 Warrick Dunn .75 .30
❑ 128 Robert Brooks .50 .20
❑ 129 Derrick Thomas .75 .30
❑ 130 Steve Young 1.00 .40
❑ 131 Peter Boulware .30 .10
❑ 132 Michael Irvin .50 .20
❑ 133 Shannon Sharpe .30 .10
❑ 134 Jimmy Smith .50 .20
❑ 135 John Avery .30 .10
❑ 136 Fred Lane .30 .10
❑ 137 Trent Green .75 .30
❑ 138 Andre Rison .50 .20
❑ 139 Antowain Smith .30 .10
❑ 140 Eddie George .75 .30
❑ 141 Jeff Blake .50 .20
❑ 142 Rocket Ismail .50 .20
❑ 143 Rickey Dudley .30 .10
❑ 144 Courtney Hawkins .30 .10
❑ 145 Mikhael Ricks .30 .10
❑ 146 J.J. Stokes .50 .20
❑ 147 Levon Kirkland .30 .10
❑ 148 Deion Sanders .75 .30
❑ 149 Barry Sanders 2.50 1.00
❑ 150 Tiki Barber .75 .30
❑ 151 David Boston RC 2.00 .75
❑ 152 Chris McAlister RC 1.50 .60
❑ 153 Peerless Price RC 2.00 .75
❑ 154 D'Wayne Bates RC 1.50 .60
❑ 155 Cade McNown RC 1.50 .60
❑ 156 Akili Smith RC 1.50 .60
❑ 157 Kevin Johnson RC 2.00 .75
❑ 158 Tim Couch RC 2.00 .75
❑ 159 Sedrick Irvin RC .75 .30
❑ 160 Chris Claiborne RC .75 .30
❑ 161 Edgerrin James RC 8.00 3.00
❑ 162 Mike Cloud RC 1.50 .60
❑ 163 Cecil Collins RC .75 .30
❑ 164 James Johnson RC 1.50 .60
❑ 165 Rob Konrad RC 2.00 .75
❑ 166 Daunte Culpepper RC 8.00 3.00
❑ 167 Kevin Faulk RC 2.00 .75
❑ 168 Donovan McNabb RC 10.00 4.00
❑ 169 Troy Edwards RC 1.50 .60
❑ 170 Amos Zereoue RC 2.00 .75
❑ 171 Karsten Bailey RC 1.50 .60
❑ 172 Brock Huard RC 2.00 .75

❑ 173 Joe Germaine RC 1.50 .60
❑ 174 Torry Holt RC 5.00 2.00
❑ 175 Shaun King RC 1.50 .60
❑ 176 Jevon Kearse RC 3.00 1.25
❑ 177 Champ Bailey RC 2.50 1.00
❑ 178 Ebenezer Ekuban RC 1.50 .60
❑ 179 Andy Katzenmoyer 1.50 .60
❑ 180 Antoine Winfield RC 1.50 .60
❑ 181 Jermaine Fazande RC 1.50 .60
❑ 182 Ricky Williams RC 4.00 1.50
❑ 183 Joel Makovicka RC 2.00 .75
❑ 184 Reginald Kelly RC .75 .30
❑ 185 Brandon Stokley RC 2.50 1.00
❑ 186 L.C. Stevens RC .75 .30
❑ 187 Marty Booker RC 2.00 .75
❑ 188 Jerry Azumah 2.00 .75
❑ 189 Ted White RC .75 .30
❑ 190 Scott Covington RC 2.00 .75
❑ 191 Tim Alexander RC .75 .30
❑ 192 Darrin Chiaverini RC 1.50 .60
❑ 193 Dat Nguyen RC 2.00 .75
❑ 194 Wane McGarity RC .75 .30
❑ 195 Al Wilson RC 2.00 .75
❑ 196 Travis McGriff RC .75 .30
❑ 197 Stacey Mack RC 2.00 .75
❑ 198 Antuan Edwards RC .75 .30
❑ 199 Aaron Brooks RC 4.00 1.50
❑ 200 De'Mond Parker RC .75 .30
❑ 201 Jed Weaver RC .75 .30
❑ 202 Madre Hill RC .75 .30
❑ 203 Jim Kleinsasser RC 2.00 .75
❑ 204 Michael Bishop RC 2.00 .75
❑ 205 Michael Basnight RC .75 .30
❑ 206 Sean Bennett RC .75 .30
❑ 207 Dameane Douglas RC 1.50 .60
❑ 208 Na Brown RC 1.50 .60
❑ 209 Patrick Kerney RC 2.00 .75
❑ 210 Malcolm Johnson RC .75 .30
❑ 211 Dre Bly RC 2.00 .75
❑ 212 Terry Jackson RC 1.50 .60
❑ 213 Eugene Baker RC .75 .30
❑ 214 Autry Denson RC 1.50 .60
❑ 215 Darnell McDonald RC 1.50 .60
❑ 216 Charlie Rogers RC 1.50 .60
❑ 217 Joe Montgomery RC 1.50 .60
❑ 218 Cecil Martin RC 1.50 .60
❑ 219 Larry Parker RC 2.00 .75
❑ 220 Mike Peterson RC 2.00 .75

2000 Bowman

❑ COMPLETE SET (240) 40.00 15.00
❑ 1 Eddie George .60 .25
❑ 2 Ike Hilliard .40 .15
❑ 3 Terrell Owens .60 .25
❑ 4 James Stewart .40 .15
❑ 5 Joey Galloway .40 .15
❑ 6 Jake Reed .40 .15
❑ 7 Derrick Alexander .40 .15
❑ 8 Jeff George .40 .15
❑ 9 Kerry Collins .40 .15
❑ 10 Tony Gonzalez .40 .15
❑ 11 Marcus Robinson .60 .25
❑ 12 Charles Woodson .40 .15
❑ 13 Germane Crowell .25 .08
❑ 14 Yancey Thigpen .25 .08
❑ 15 Tony Martin .40 .15
❑ 16 Frank Sanders .40 .15
❑ 17 Napoleon Kaufman .40 .15
❑ 18 Jay Fiedler .60 .25
❑ 19 Patrick Jeffers .60 .25
❑ 20 Steve McNair .60 .25
❑ 21 Herman Moore .40 .15
❑ 22 Tim Brown .60 .25
❑ 23 Olandis Gary .60 .25
❑ 24 Corey Dillon .60 .25
❑ 25 Warren Sapp .40 .15
❑ 26 Curtis Enis .25 .08
❑ 27 Vinny Testaverde .40 .15
❑ 28 Tim Biakabutuka .40 .15
❑ 29 Kevin Johnson .60 .25
❑ 30 Charlie Batch .60 .25
❑ 31 Jermaine Fazande .25 .08
❑ 32 Shaun King .25 .08
❑ 33 Errict Rhett .40 .15
❑ 34 O.J. McDuffie .40 .15
❑ 35 Bruce Smith .40 .15
❑ 36 Antonio Freeman .60 .25
❑ 37 Tim Couch .40 .15
❑ 38 Duce Staley .60 .25
❑ 39 Jeff Blake .40 .15
❑ 40 Jim Harbaugh .40 .15
❑ 41 Jeff Graham .25 .08
❑ 42 Drew Bledsoe .75 .30
❑ 43 Mike Alstott .60 .25
❑ 44 Terance Mathis .40 .15
❑ 45 Antowain Smith .40 .15
❑ 46 Johnnie Morton .40 .15
❑ 47 Chris Chandler .40 .15
❑ 48 Keith Poole .40 .15
❑ 49 Ricky Watters .40 .15
❑ 50 Darnay Scott .40 .15
❑ 51 Damon Huard .60 .25
❑ 52 Peerless Price .40 .15
❑ 53 Brian Griese .60 .25
❑ 54 Frank Wycheck .25 .08
❑ 55 Kevin Dyson .40 .15
❑ 56 Junior Seau .60 .25
❑ 57 Curtis Conway .40 .15
❑ 58 Jamal Anderson .60 .25
❑ 59 Jim Miller .25 .08
❑ 60 Rob Johnson .25 .08
❑ 61 Mark Brunell .60 .25
❑ 62 Wayne Chrebet .40 .15
❑ 63 James Johnson .25 .08
❑ 64 Sean Dawkins .25 .08
❑ 65 Stephen Davis .60 .25
❑ 66 Daunte Culpepper .75 .30
❑ 67 Doug Flutie .60 .25
❑ 68 Pete Mitchell .25 .08
❑ 69 Bill Schroeder .40 .15
❑ 70 Terrence Wilkins .25 .08
❑ 71 Cade McNown .25 .08
❑ 72 Muhsin Muhammad .40 .15
❑ 73 E.G. Green .25 .08
❑ 74 Edgerrin James 1.00 .40
❑ 75 Troy Edwards .25 .08
❑ 76 Terry Glenn .40 .15
❑ 77 Tony Banks .40 .15
❑ 78 Derrick Mayes .40 .15
❑ 79 Curtis Martin .60 .25
❑ 80 Kordell Stewart .40 .15
❑ 81 Amani Toomer .40 .15
❑ 82 Dorsey Levens .40 .15
❑ 83 Brad Johnson .60 .25
❑ 84 Ed McCaffrey .60 .25
❑ 85 Charlie Garner .40 .15
❑ 86 Brett Favre 2.00 .75
❑ 87 J.J. Stokes .40 .15
❑ 88 Steve Young .75 .30
❑ 89 Jonathan Linton .25 .08
❑ 90 Isaac Bruce .60 .25
❑ 91 Shawn Jefferson .25 .08
❑ 92 Rod Smith .40 .15
❑ 93 Champ Bailey .40 .15
❑ 94 Ricky Williams .60 .25
❑ 95 Priest Holmes .75 .30
❑ 96 Corey Bradford .40 .15
❑ 97 Eric Moulds .60 .25
❑ 98 Warrick Dunn .60 .25
❑ 99 Jevon Kearse .60 .25
❑ 100 Albert Connell .25 .08
❑ 101 Az-Zahir Hakim .25 .08
❑ 102 Marvin Harrison .60 .25
❑ 103 Qadry Ismail .40 .15
❑ 104 Oronde Gadsden .40 .15
❑ 105 Rob Moore .40 .15
❑ 106 Marshall Faulk .75 .30
❑ 107 Steve Beuerlein .25 .08
❑ 108 Torry Holt .60 .25
❑ 109 Donovan McNabb 1.00 .40
❑ 110 Rich Gannon .60 .25
❑ 111 Jerome Bettis .60 .25
❑ 112 Peyton Manning 1.50 .60
❑ 113 Cris Carter .60 .25
❑ 114 Jake Plummer .40 .15
❑ 115 Kent Graham .25 .08
❑ 116 Keenan McCardell .40 .15
❑ 117 Tim Dwight .60 .25
❑ 118 Fred Taylor .60 .25
❑ 119 Jerry Rice 1.25 .50
❑ 120 Michael Westbrook .40 .15
❑ 121 Kurt Warner 1.25 .50
❑ 122 Jimmy Smith .40 .15
❑ 123 Emmitt Smith 1.25 .50
❑ 124 Terrell Davis .60 .25
❑ 125 Randy Moss 1.25 .50
❑ 126 Akili Smith .25 .08
❑ 127 Rocket Ismail .40 .15
❑ 128 Jon Kitna .60 .25
❑ 129 Elvis Grbac .40 .15
❑ 130 Wesley Walls .25 .08
❑ 131 Torrance Small .25 .08
❑ 132 Tyrone Wheatley .40 .15
❑ 133 Carl Pickens .40 .15
❑ 134 Zach Thomas .60 .25
❑ 135 Jacquez Green .25 .08
❑ 136 Robert Smith .60 .25
❑ 137 Keyshawn Johnson .60 .25
❑ 138 Matthew Hatchette .25 .08
❑ 139 Troy Aikman 1.25 .50
❑ 140 Charles Johnson .40 .15
❑ 141 Terry Battle EP .30 .12
❑ 142 Pepe Pearson EP RC .75 .30
❑ 143 Cory Sauter EP .30 .12
❑ 144 Brian Shay EP .30 .12
❑ 145 Marcus Crandell EP RC .50 .20
❑ 146 Danny Wuerffel EP .50 .20
❑ 147 L.C. Stevens EP .30 .12
❑ 148 Ted White EP .30 .12
❑ 149 Matt Lytle EP RC .50 .20
❑ 150 Vershan Jackson EP RC .30 .12
❑ 151 Mario Bailey EP .30 .12
❑ 152 Darryl Daniel EP RC .50 .20
❑ 153 Sean Morey EP RC .50 .20
❑ 154 Jim Kubiak EP RC .50 .20
❑ 155 Aaron Stecker EP RC .75 .30
❑ 156 Damon Dunn EP RC .50 .20
❑ 157 Kevin Daft EP .30 .12
❑ 158 Corey Thomas EP .30 .12
❑ 159 Deon Mitchell EP RC .50 .20
❑ 160 Todd Floyd EP RC .30 .12
❑ 161 Norman Miller EP RC .30 .12
❑ 162 Jeremaine Copeland EP .30 .12
❑ 163 Michael Blair EP .30 .12
❑ 164 Ron Powlus EP RC .75 .30
❑ 165 Pat Barnes EP .50 .20
❑ 166 Dez White RC 1.00 .40
❑ 167 Trung Canidate RC .75 .30
❑ 168 Thomas Jones RC 1.50 .60
❑ 169 Courtney Brown RC 1.00 .40
❑ 170 Jamal Lewis RC 2.50 1.00
❑ 171 Chris Redman RC .75 .30
❑ 172 Ron Dayne RC 1.00 .40
❑ 173 Chad Pennington RC 2.50 1.00
❑ 174 Plaxico Burress RC 2.00 .75
❑ 175 R.Jay Soward RC .75 .30
❑ 176 Travis Taylor RC 1.00 .40
■ 177 Shaun Alexander RC 5.00 2.00
❑ 178 Brian Urlacher RC 4.00 1.50
❑ 179 Danny Farmer RC .75 .30
❑ 180 Tee Martin RC 1.00 .40
❑ 181 Sylvester Morris RC .75 .30
❑ 182 Curtis Keaton RC .75 .30
❑ 183 Peter Warrick RC 1.00 .40
❑ 184 Anthony Becht RC 1.00 .40
❑ 185 Travis Prentice RC 1.00 .40
❑ 186 J.R. Redmond RC .75 .30
❑ 187 Bubba Franks RC 1.00 .40
❑ 188 Ron Dugans RC .50 .20
❑ 189 Reuben Droughns RC 1.25 .50
❑ 190 Corey Simon RC 1.00 .40
❑ 191 Joe Hamilton RC .75 .30
❑ 192 Laveranues Coles RC 1.25 .50
❑ 193 Todd Pinkston RC 1.00 .40
❑ 194 Jerry Porter RC 1.25 .50
❑ 195 Dennis Northcutt RC 1.00 .40
❑ 196 Tim Rattay RC 1.00 .40
❑ 197 Giovanni Carmazzi RC .50 .20
❑ 198 Mareno Philyaw RC .50 .20
❑ 199 Avion Black RC .75 .30

	Card	Hi	Lo
❑ 200	Chafie Fields RC	.50	.20
❑ 201	Rondell Mealey RC	.50	.20
❑ 202	Troy Walters RC	1.00	.40
❑ 203	Frank Moreau RC	.75	.30
❑ 204	Vaughn Sanders RC	.50	.20
❑ 205	Sherrod Gideon RC	.50	.20
❑ 206	Doug Chapman RC	.75	.30
❑ 207	Marcus Knight RC	.75	.30
❑ 208	Jamel White RC	.75	.30
❑ 209	Windrell Hayes RC	.75	.30
❑ 210	Reggie Jones RC	1.00	.40
❑ 211	Jarious Jackson RC	.75	.30
❑ 212	Ronney Jenkins RC	.75	.30
❑ 213	Quinton Spotwood RC	.50	.20
❑ 214	Rob Morris RC	.75	.30
❑ 215	Gari Scott RC	.50	.20
❑ 216	Kevin Thompson RC	.50	.20
❑ 217	Trevor Insley RC	.50	.20
❑ 218	Frank Murphy RC	.50	.20
❑ 219	Patrick Pass RC	.75	.30
❑ 220	Mike Anderson RC	1.25	.50
❑ 221	Derrius Thompson RC	1.00	.40
❑ 222	John Abraham RC	1.00	.40
❑ 223	Dante Hall RC	2.00	.75
❑ 224	Chad Morton RC	1.00	.40
❑ 225	Ahmed Plummer RC	1.00	.40
❑ 226	Julian Peterson RC	1.00	.40
❑ 227	Mike Green RC	.75	.30
❑ 228	Michael Wiley RC	.75	.30
❑ 229	Spergon Wynn RC	.75	.30
❑ 230	Trevor Gaylor RC	.75	.30
❑ 231	Doug Johnson RC	1.00	.40
❑ 232	Marc Bulger RC	2.00	.75
❑ 233	Ron Dixon RC	.75	.30
❑ 234	Aaron Shea RC	.75	.30
❑ 235	Thomas Hamner RC	.50	.20
❑ 236	Tom Brady RC	25.00	12.50
❑ 237	Deltha O'Neal RC	1.00	.40
❑ 238	Todd Husak RC	1.00	.40
❑ 239	Erron Kinney RC	1.00	.40
❑ 240	JaJuan Dawson RC	.50	.20

2001 Bowman

	Card	Hi	Lo
❑	COMPLETE SET (275)	70.00	35.00
❑ 1	Emmitt Smith	1.25	.50
❑ 2	James Stewart	.40	.15
❑ 3	Jeff Graham	.25	.08
❑ 4	Keyshawn Johnson	.60	.25
❑ 5	Stephen Davis	.60	.25
❑ 6	Chad Lewis	.25	.08
❑ 7	Drew Bledsoe	.75	.30
❑ 8	Fred Taylor	.60	.25
❑ 9	Mike Anderson	.60	.25
❑ 10	Tony Gonzalez	.40	.15
❑ 11	Aaron Brooks	.60	.25
❑ 12	Vinny Testaverde	.40	.15
❑ 13	Jerome Bettis	.60	.25
❑ 14	Marshall Faulk	.75	.30
❑ 15	Jeff Garcia	.60	.25
❑ 16	Terry Glenn	.40	.15
❑ 17	Jay Fiedler	.60	.25
❑ 18	Ahman Green	.60	.25
❑ 19	Cade McNown	.25	.08
❑ 20	Rob Johnson	.40	.15
❑ 21	Jamal Anderson	.60	.25
❑ 22	Corey Dillon	.60	.25
❑ 23	Jake Plummer	.40	.15
❑ 24	Rod Smith	.40	.15
❑ 25	Trent Green	.60	.25
❑ 26	Ricky Williams	.60	.25
❑ 27	Charlie Garner	.40	.15
❑ 28	Shaun Alexander	.75	.30
❑ 29	Jeff George	.40	.15
❑ 30	Torry Holt	.60	.25
❑ 31	James Thrash	.40	.15
❑ 32	Rich Gannon	.60	.25
❑ 33	Ron Dayne	.60	.25
❑ 34	Dedric Ward	.25	.08
❑ 35	Edgerrin James	.75	.30
❑ 36	Cris Carter	.60	.25
❑ 37	Derrick Mason	.40	.15
❑ 38	Brad Johnson	.60	.25
❑ 39	Charlie Batch	.60	.25
❑ 40	Joey Galloway	.40	.15
❑ 41	James Allen	.40	.15
❑ 42	Tim Biakabutuka	.40	.15
❑ 43	Ray Lewis	.60	.25
❑ 44	David Boston	.60	.25
❑ 45	Kevin Johnson	.40	.15
❑ 46	Jimmy Smith	.40	.15
❑ 47	Joe Horn	.40	.15
❑ 48	Terrell Owens	.60	.25
❑ 49	Eddie George	.60	.25
❑ 50	Brett Favre	2.00	.75
❑ 51	Wayne Chrebet	.40	.15
❑ 52	Hines Ward	.60	.25
❑ 53	Warrick Dunn	.60	.25
❑ 54	Matt Hasselbeck	.40	.15
❑ 55	Tiki Barber	.60	.25
❑ 56	Lamar Smith	.40	.15
❑ 57	Tim Couch	.40	.15
❑ 58	Eric Moulds	.40	.15
❑ 59	Shawn Jefferson	.25	.08
❑ 60	Donald Hayes	.25	.08
❑ 61	Brian Urlacher	1.00	.40
❑ 62	Steve McNair	.60	.25
❑ 63	Kurt Warner	1.25	.50
❑ 64	Tim Brown	.60	.25
❑ 65	Troy Brown	.40	.15
❑ 66	Albert Connell	.25	.08
❑ 67	Peyton Manning	1.50	.60
❑ 68	Peter Warrick	.60	.25
❑ 69	Elvis Grbac	.40	.15
❑ 70	Chris Chandler	.40	.15
❑ 71	Akili Smith	.25	.08
❑ 72	Keenan McCardell	.25	.08
❑ 73	Kerry Collins	.40	.15
❑ 74	Junior Seau	.60	.25
❑ 75	Donovan McNabb	.75	.30
❑ 76	Tony Banks	.40	.15
❑ 77	Steve Beuerlein	.25	.08
❑ 78	Daunte Culpepper	.60	.25
❑ 79	Darrell Jackson	.60	.25
❑ 80	Isaac Bruce	.60	.25
❑ 81	Tyrone Wheatley	.40	.15
❑ 82	Derrick Alexander	.40	.15
❑ 83	Germane Crowell	.25	.08
❑ 84	Jon Kitna	.40	.15
❑ 85	Jamal Lewis	1.00	.40
❑ 86	Ed McCaffrey	.60	.25
❑ 87	Mark Brunell	.60	.25
❑ 88	Jeff Blake	.40	.15
❑ 89	Duce Staley	.60	.25
❑ 90	Doug Flutie	.60	.25
❑ 91	Kordell Stewart	.40	.15
❑ 92	Randy Moss	1.25	.50
❑ 93	Marvin Harrison	.60	.25
❑ 94	Muhsin Muhammad	.40	.15
❑ 95	Brian Griese	.60	.25
❑ 96	Antonio Freeman	.60	.25
❑ 97	Amani Toomer	.40	.15
❑ 98	Oronde Gadsden	.40	.15
❑ 99	Curtis Martin	.60	.25
❑ 100	Jerry Rice	1.25	.50
❑ 101	Michael Pittman	.25	.08
❑ 102	Shannon Sharpe	.40	.15
❑ 103	Peerless Price	.40	.15
❑ 104	Bill Schroeder	.40	.15
❑ 105	Ike Hilliard	.40	.15
❑ 106	Freddie Jones	.25	.08
❑ 107	Tai Streets	.25	.08
❑ 108	Ricky Watters	.40	.15
❑ 109	Az-Zahir Hakim	.25	.08
❑ 110	Jacquez Green	.25	.08
❑ 111	Bobby Shaw	.25	.08
❑ 112	Johnnie Morton	.40	.15
❑ 113	Laveranues Coles	.60	.25
❑ 114	Chad Pennington	1.00	.40
❑ 115	Champ Bailey	.40	.15
❑ 116	Charles Woodson	.40	.15
❑ 117	Curtis Conway	.40	.15
❑ 118	Marcus Robinson	.60	.25
❑ 119	Michael Westbrook	.40	.15
❑ 120	Mike Alstott	.60	.25
❑ 121	Priest Holmes	.75	.30
❑ 122	Qadry Ismail	.40	.15
❑ 123	Rocket Ismail	.40	.15
❑ 124	Shawn Bryson	.25	.08
❑ 125	Jeff Lewis	.25	.08
❑ 126	Jeremy Mcdaniel	.25	.08
❑ 127	Terance Mathis	.25	.08
❑ 128	Travis Prentice	.25	.08
❑ 129	Warren Sapp	.40	.15
❑ 130	Jevon Kearse	.40	.15
❑ 131	George Layne RC	.75	.30
❑ 132	Correll Buckhalter RC	1.50	.60
❑ 133	Tony Stewart RC	1.25	.50
❑ 134	Chris Barnes RC	.75	.30
❑ 135	A.J. Feeley RC	1.25	.50
❑ 136	Margin Hooks RC	.50	.20
❑ 137	Anthony Henry RC	1.25	.50
❑ 138	Dwight Smith RC	.50	.20
❑ 139	Torrance Marshall RC	1.25	.50
❑ 140	Gary Baxter RC	.75	.30
❑ 141	Derek Combs RC	.75	.30
❑ 142	Marcus Bell DT RC	.75	.30
❑ 143	Delawrence Grant RC	.50	.20
❑ 144	Jameel Cook RC	.75	.30
❑ 145	Eric Downing RC	.50	.20
❑ 146	Marlon McCree RC	.75	.30
❑ 147	Tay Cody RC	.50	.20
❑ 148	Mario Monds RC	.50	.20
❑ 149	Kenny Smith RC	.75	.30
❑ 150	Sedrick Hodge RC	.50	.20
❑ 151	Marcus Stroud RC	1.25	.50
❑ 152	Steve Smith RC	3.00	1.25
❑ 153	Tyrone Robertson RC	.50	.20
❑ 154	James Reed RC	.50	.20
❑ 155	Kris Kocurek RC	.50	.20
❑ 156	Dan O'Leary RC	.75	.30
❑ 157	Harold Blackmon RC	.50	.20
❑ 158	Fred Smoot RC	1.25	.50
❑ 159	Billy Baber RC	.50	.20
❑ 160	Jarrod Cooper RC	1.25	.50
❑ 161	Travis Henry RC	2.00	.75
❑ 162	David Terrell RC	1.25	.50
❑ 163	Josh Heupel RC	1.25	.50
❑ 164	Drew Brees RC	4.00	1.50
❑ 165	T.J. Houshmandzadeh RC	1.50	.60
❑ 166	Rod Gardner RC	1.25	.50
❑ 167	Richard Seymour RC	1.25	.50
❑ 168	Koren Robinson RC	1.25	.50
❑ 169	Scotty Anderson RC	.75	.30
❑ 170	Marques Tuiasosopo RC	1.25	.50
❑ 171	John Capel RC	.75	.30
❑ 172	LaMont Jordan RC	2.50	1.00
❑ 173	James Jackson RC	1.25	.50
❑ 174	Bobby Newcombe RC	1.25	.50
❑ 175	Anthony Thomas RC	1.25	.50
❑ 176	Dan Alexander RC	1.25	.50
❑ 177	Quincy Carter RC	1.25	.50
❑ 178	Morlon Greenwood RC	.75	.30
❑ 179	Robert Ferguson RC	1.25	.50
❑ 180	Sage Rosenfels RC	1.25	.50
❑ 181	Michael Stone RC	.50	.20
❑ 182	Chris Weinke RC	1.25	.50
❑ 183	Travis Minor RC	.75	.30
❑ 184	Gerard Warren RC	1.25	.50
❑ 185	Jamar Fletcher RC	.75	.30
❑ 186	Andre Carter RC	1.25	.50
❑ 187	Deuce McAllister RC	2.50	1.00
❑ 188	Dan Morgan RC	1.25	.50
❑ 189	Todd Heap RC	1.25	.50
❑ 190	Snoop Minnis RC	.75	.30
❑ 191	Will Allen RC	.75	.30
❑ 192	Freddie Mitchell RC	1.25	.50
❑ 193	Rudi Johnson RC	2.50	1.00
❑ 194	Kevan Barlow RC	1.25	.50
❑ 195	Jamie Winborn RC	.75	.30
❑ 196	Onomo Ojo RC	.75	.30
❑ 197	Leonard Davis RC	.75	.30
❑ 198	Santana Moss RC	2.00	.75
❑ 199	Chris Chambers RC	2.00	.75
❑ 200	Michael Vick RC	6.00	2.50
❑ 201	Michael Bennett RC	1.25	.50
❑ 202	Mike McMahon RC	1.25	.50
❑ 203	Jonathan Carter RC	.75	.30
❑ 204	Jamal Reynolds RC	1.25	.50
❑ 205	Justin Smith RC	1.25	.50
❑ 206	Quincy Morgan RC	1.25	.50

❑ 207 Chad Johnson RC 3.00 1.25
❑ 208 Jesse Palmer RC 1.25 .50
❑ 209 Reggie Wayne RC 2.50 1.00
❑ 210 LaDainian Tomlinson RC 25.00 10.00
❑ 211 Andre King RC .75 .30
❑ 212 Richmond Flowers RC .75 .30
❑ 213 Derrick Blaylock RC 1.25 .50
❑ 214 Cedrick Wilson RC 1.25 .50
❑ 215 Zeke Moreno RC 1.25 .50
❑ 216 Tommy Polley RC 1.25 .50
❑ 217 Damione Lewis RC .75 .30
❑ 218 Aaron Schobel RC 1.25 .50
❑ 219 Alge Crumpler RC 1.50 .60
❑ 220 Nate Clements RC 1.25 .50
❑ 221 Quentin McCord RC .75 .30
❑ 222 Ken-Yon Rambo RC .75 .30
❑ 223 Milton Wynn RC .75 .30
❑ 224 Derrick Gibson RC .75 .30
❑ 225 Chris Taylor RC .75 .30
❑ 226 Corey Hall RC .50 .20
❑ 227 Vinny Sutherland RC .75 .30
❑ 228 Kendrell Bell RC 2.00 .75
❑ 229 Casey Hampton RC 1.25 .50
❑ 230 Demetric Evans RC .50 .20
❑ 231 Brian Allen RC .50 .20
❑ 232 Rodney Bailey RC .50 .20
❑ 233 Otis Leverette RC .50 .20
❑ 234 Ron Edwards RC .50 .20
❑ 235 Michael Jameson RC .50 .20
❑ 236 Markus Steele RC .75 .30
❑ 237 Jimmy Williams RC .50 .20
❑ 238 Roger Knight RC .50 .20
❑ 239 Randy Garner RC .50 .20
❑ 240 Raymond Perryman RC .50 .20
❑ 241 Karon Riley RC .50 .20
❑ 242 Adam Archuleta RC 1.25 .50
❑ 243 Arnold Jackson RC .75 .30
❑ 244 Ryan Pickett RC .50 .20
❑ 245 Shad Meier RC .75 .30
❑ 246 Reggie Germany RC .75 .30
❑ 247 Justin McCareins RC 1.25 .50
❑ 248 Idrees Bashir RC .50 .20
❑ 249 Josh Booty RC 1.25 .50
❑ 250 Eddie Berlin RC .75 .30
❑ 251 Heath Evans RC .75 .30
❑ 252 Alex Bannister RC .75 .30
❑ 253 Corey Alston RC .50 .20
❑ 254 Reggie White RC .75 .30
❑ 255 Orlando Huff RC .50 .20
❑ 256 Ken Lucas RC .75 .30
❑ 257 Matt Stewart RC .50 .20
❑ 258 Cedric Scott RC .75 .30
❑ 259 Ronney Daniels RC .50 .20
❑ 260 Kevin Kasper RC 1.25 .50
❑ 261 Tony Driver RC .75 .30
❑ 262 Kyle Vanden Bosch RC 1.25 .50
❑ 263 T.J. Turner RC .50 .20
❑ 264 Eric Westmoreland RC .75 .30
❑ 265 Ronald Flemons RC .50 .20
❑ 266 Eric Kelly RC .50 .20
❑ 267 Moran Norris RC .50 .20
❑ 268 Damerien McCants RC .75 .30
❑ 269 James Boyd RC .50 .20
❑ 270 Keith Adams RC .50 .20
❑ 271 Brandon Manumaleuna RC .75 .30
❑ 272 Dee Brown RC 1.25 .50
❑ 273 Ross Kolodziej RC .50 .20
❑ 274 Boo Williams RC .75 .30
❑ 275 Patrick Chukwurah RC .50 .20

2002 Bowman

❑ COMPLETE SET (275) 50.00 20.00
❑ 1 Emmitt Smith 1.50 .60
❑ 2 Drew Brees .60 .25
❑ 3 Duce Staley .60 .25
❑ 4 Curtis Martin .60 .25
❑ 5 Isaac Bruce .60 .25
❑ 6 Stephen Davis .40 .15
❑ 7 Darrell Jackson .40 .15
❑ 8 James Stewart .40 .15
❑ 9 Tim Couch .40 .15
❑ 10 Travis Henry .60 .25
❑ 11 Thomas Jones .40 .15
❑ 12 Jamal Lewis .60 .25
❑ 13 Chris Chambers .60 .25
❑ 14 Jeff Blake .40 .15
❑ 15 Plaxico Burress .60 .25
❑ 16 Michael Pittman .25 .08
❑ 17 Jeff Garcia .60 .25
❑ 18 Tim Brown .60 .25
❑ 19 Kent Graham .25 .08
❑ 20 Shannon Sharpe .40 .15
❑ 21 Corey Dillon .40 .15
❑ 22 Muhsin Muhammad .40 .15
❑ 23 Tony Gonzalez .40 .15
❑ 24 Qadry Ismail .40 .15
❑ 25 Mike McMahon .60 .25
❑ 26 Edgerrin James .75 .30
❑ 27 Daunte Culpepper .60 .25
❑ 28 Deuce McAllister .75 .30
❑ 29 Kerry Collins .40 .15
❑ 30 Eddie George .60 .25
❑ 31 Torry Holt .60 .25
❑ 32 Todd Pinkston .40 .15
❑ 33 Quincy Carter .40 .15
❑ 34 Rod Smith .40 .15
❑ 35 Michael Vick 2.00 .75
❑ 36 Jim Miller .25 .08
❑ 37 Troy Brown .40 .15
❑ 38 Wayne Chrebet .40 .15
❑ 39 Curtis Conway .25 .08
❑ 40 Reidel Anthony .25 .08
❑ 41 Mark Brunell .60 .25
❑ 42 Chris Weinke .40 .15
❑ 43 Eric Moulds .40 .15
❑ 44 Ike Hilliard .25 .08
❑ 45 Jay Fiedler .40 .15
❑ 46 Keyshawn Johnson .60 .25
❑ 47 Rod Gardner .40 .15
❑ 48 Chris Redman .25 .08
❑ 49 James Allen .40 .15
❑ 50 Kordell Stewart .40 .15
❑ 51 Priest Holmes .75 .30
❑ 52 Anthony Thomas .40 .15
❑ 53 Peter Warrick .40 .15
❑ 54 Jake Plummer .40 .15
❑ 55 Jerry Rice 1.25 .50
❑ 56 Joe Horn .40 .15
❑ 57 Derrick Mason .40 .15
❑ 58 Kurt Warner .60 .25
❑ 59 Antowain Smith .40 .15
❑ 60 Randy Moss 1.25 .50
❑ 61 Warrick Dunn .60 .25
❑ 62 Laveranues Coles .40 .15
❑ 63 LaDainian Tomlinson 1.00 .40
❑ 64 Michael Westbrook .25 .08
❑ 65 Travis Taylor .25 .08
❑ 66 Brian Griese .60 .25
❑ 67 Bill Schroeder .40 .15
❑ 68 Ahman Green .60 .25
❑ 69 Jimmy Smith .40 .15
❑ 70 Charlie Garner .40 .15
❑ 71 Terrell Owens .60 .25
❑ 72 Brad Johnson .40 .15
❑ 73 James Thrash .40 .15
❑ 74 Marvin Harrison .60 .25
❑ 75 Brett Favre 1.50 .60
❑ 76 Rocket Ismail .40 .15
❑ 77 David Boston .60 .25
❑ 78 Jermaine Lewis .25 .08
❑ 79 Aaron Brooks .60 .25
❑ 80 Shaun Alexander .75 .30
❑ 81 Steve McNair .60 .25
❑ 82 Marshall Faulk .60 .25
❑ 83 Terrell Davis .60 .25
❑ 84 Corey Bradford .25 .08
❑ 85 David Terrell .60 .25
❑ 86 Kevin Johnson .40 .15
❑ 87 Jon Kitna .40 .15
❑ 88 Az-Zahir Hakim .25 .08
❑ 89 Drew Bledsoe .75 .30
❑ 90 Garrison Hearst .40 .15
❑ 91 Doug Flutie .60 .25
❑ 92 Jerome Bettis .60 .25
❑ 93 Vinny Testaverde .40 .15
❑ 94 Tiki Barber .60 .25
❑ 95 Johnnie Morton .40 .15
❑ 96 Lamar Smith .40 .15
❑ 97 Marcus Robinson .40 .15
❑ 98 Fred Taylor .60 .25
❑ 99 Tom Brady 1.50 .60
❑ 100 Peyton Manning 1.25 .50
❑ 101 Donovan McNabb .75 .30
❑ 102 Rich Gannon .60 .25
❑ 103 Hines Ward .60 .25
❑ 104 Michael Bennett .60 .25
❑ 105 Ricky Williams .60 .25
❑ 106 Germane Crowell .25 .08
❑ 107 Joey Galloway .40 .15
❑ 108 Amani Toomer .40 .15
❑ 109 Trent Green .40 .15
❑ 110 Terry Glenn .40 .15
❑ 111 Donte Stallworth RC 3.00 1.25
❑ 112 Mike Williams RC 1.25 .50
❑ 113 Kurt Kittner RC 1.25 .50
❑ 114 Josh Reed RC 1.50 .60
❑ 115 Raonall Smith RC 1.25 .50
❑ 116 David Garrard RC 1.50 .60
❑ 117 Eric Crouch RC 1.50 .60
❑ 118 Bryan Thomas RC 1.25 .50
❑ 119 Levi Jones RC 1.25 .50
❑ 120 Andre Davis RC 1.25 .50
❑ 121 Herb Haygood RC .75 .30
❑ 122 Josh McCown RC 2.00 .75
❑ 123 Quentin Jammer RC 1.50 .60
❑ 124 Cliff Russell RC 1.25 .50
❑ 125 Jeremy Shockey RC 5.00 2.00
❑ 126 Jamin Elliott RC .75 .30
❑ 127 Roy Williams RC 4.00 1.50
❑ 128 Marquise Walker RC 1.25 .50
❑ 129 Kalimba Edwards RC 1.50 .60
❑ 130 Daniel Graham RC 1.50 .60
❑ 131 Freddie Milons RC 1.25 .50
❑ 132 Anthony Weaver RC 1.25 .50
❑ 133 Jake Schifino RC 1.25 .50
❑ 134 Antonio Bryant RC 1.50 .60
❑ 135 DeShaun Foster RC 1.50 .60
❑ 136 Antwaan Randle El RC 2.50 1.00
❑ 137 William Green RC 1.50 .60
❑ 138 Ed Reed RC 2.50 1.00
❑ 139 Maurice Morris RC 1.50 .60
❑ 140 Joey Harrington RC 2.50 1.00
❑ 141 T.J. Duckett RC 2.00 .75
❑ 142 Javon Walker RC 3.00 1.25
❑ 143 Albert Haynesworth RC 1.25 .50
❑ 144 Julius Peppers RC 3.00 1.25
❑ 145 Clinton Portis RC 5.00 2.00
❑ 146 Craig Nall RC 1.50 .60
❑ 147 Ashley Lelie RC 3.00 1.25
❑ 148 Reche Caldwell RC 1.50 .60
❑ 149 Rohan Davey RC 1.50 .60
❑ 150 Patrick Ramsey RC 2.00 .75
❑ 151 Jabar Gaffney RC 1.50 .60
❑ 152 Tank Williams RC 1.25 .50
❑ 153 Ron Johnson RC 1.25 .50
❑ 154 Ladell Betts RC 1.50 .60
❑ 155 Brian Westbrook RC 2.50 1.00
❑ 156 Jamar Martin RC 1.25 .50
❑ 157 Travis Stephens RC 1.25 .50
❑ 158 Tim Carter RC 1.25 .50
❑ 159 Darrell Hill RC 1.50 .60
❑ 160 Luke Staley RC 1.25 .50
❑ 161 Randy Fasani RC 1.25 .50
❑ 162 Matt Schobel RC 1.25 .50
❑ 163 Jon McGraw RC .75 .30
❑ 164 Dwight Freeney RC 2.50 1.00
❑ 165 Chad Hutchinson RC 1.25 .50
❑ 166 Adrian Peterson RC 1.50 .60
❑ 167 Josh Scobey RC 1.50 .60
❑ 168 Jonathan Wells RC 1.50 .60
❑ 169 Sam Simmons RC .75 .30
❑ 170 Jerramy Stevens RC 1.50 .60
❑ 171 Jason McAddley RC 1.25 .50
❑ 172 Ken Simonton RC .75 .30
❑ 173 Chester Taylor RC 3.00 1.25
❑ 174 Brandon Doman RC 1.25 .50
❑ 175 Javin Hunter RC .75 .30
❑ 176 Eddie Drummond RC 1.25 .50
❑ 177 Andre Lott RC 1.50 .60

❑ 178	Travis Fisher RC	1.50	.60
❑ 179	Jarvis Green RC	1.25	.50
❑ 180	Ross Tucker RC	.75	.30
❑ 181	Lamont Brightful RC	.75	.30
❑ 182	Rocky Calmus RC	1.50	.60
❑ 183	Wes Pate RC	.75	.30
❑ 184	Lamar Gordon RC	1.50	.60
❑ 185	Terry Jones RC	1.25	.50
❑ 186	Kyle Johnson RC	.75	.30
❑ 187	Daryl Jones RC	1.25	.50
❑ 188	Tellis Redmon RC	1.25	.50
❑ 189	Howard Green RC	.75	.30
❑ 190	Jarrod Baxter RC	1.25	.50
❑ 191	Delvon Flowers RC	1.25	.50
❑ 192	Kevin Curtis RC	.75	.30
❑ 193	Kelly Campbell RC	1.25	.50
❑ 194	Eddie Freeman RC	.75	.30
❑ 195	Atrews Bell RC	.75	.30
❑ 196	Omar Easy RC	1.50	.60
❑ 197	Jeremy Allen RC	.75	.30
❑ 198	Andra Davis RC	1.25	.50
❑ 199	Jack Brewer RC	1.25	.50
❑ 200	Mike Rumph RC	1.50	.60
❑ 201	Seth Burford RC	1.25	.50
❑ 202	Marquand Manuel RC	.75	.30
❑ 203	Marques Anderson RC	1.50	.60
❑ 204	Ben Leber RC	1.50	.60
❑ 205	Ryan Denney RC	1.25	.50
❑ 206	Justin Peelle RC	.75	.30
❑ 207	Lito Sheppard RC	1.50	.60
❑ 208	Damien Anderson RC	1.25	.50
❑ 209	Lamont Thompson RC	1.25	.50
❑ 210	David Priestley RC	1.25	.50
❑ 211	Michael Lewis RC	1.50	.60
❑ 212	Lee Mays RC	1.25	.50
❑ 213	Alan Harper RC	.75	.30
❑ 214	Verron Haynes RC	1.50	.60
❑ 215	Chris Hope RC	1.50	.60
❑ 216	David Thornton RC	.75	.30
❑ 217	Derek Ross RC	1.25	.50
❑ 218	Brett Keisel RC	4.00	1.50
❑ 219	Joseph Jefferson RC	1.25	.50
❑ 220	Andre Goodman RC	1.50	.60
❑ 221	Robert Royal RC	1.50	.60
❑ 222	Sheldon Brown RC	1.50	.60
❑ 223	DeVeren Johnson RC	1.25	.50
❑ 224	Rock Cartwright RC	2.00	.75
❑ 225	Quincy Monk RC	.75	.30
❑ 226	Nick Rogers RC	1.25	.50
❑ 227	Kendall Simmons RC	1.25	.50
❑ 228	Joe Burns RC	1.25	.50
❑ 229	Wesly Mallard RC	1.25	.50
❑ 230	Chris Cash RC	1.25	.50
❑ 231	David Givens RC	5.00	2.00
❑ 232	John Owens RC	1.25	.50
❑ 233	Jarrett Ferguson RC	1.25	.50
❑ 234	Randy McMichael RC	2.50	1.00
❑ 235	Chris Baker RC	1.25	.50
❑ 236	Rashad Bauman RC	1.25	.50
❑ 237	Matt Murphy RC	1.25	.50
❑ 238	LaVar Glover RC	.75	.30
❑ 239	Steve Bellisari RC	1.25	.50
❑ 240	Chad Williams RC	1.25	.50
❑ 241	Kevin Thomas RC	1.25	.50
❑ 242	Carlos Hall RC	1.50	.60
❑ 243	Nick Greisen RC	.75	.30
❑ 244	Justin Bannan RC	1.25	.50
❑ 245	Charles Hill RC	.75	.30
❑ 246	Mark Anelli RC	.75	.30
❑ 247	Coy Wire RC	1.50	.60
❑ 248	Darnell Sanders RC	1.25	.50
❑ 249	Larry Foote RC	4.00	1.50
❑ 250	David Carr RC	4.00	1.50
❑ 251	Ricky Williams RC	1.25	.50
❑ 252	Napoleon Harris RC	1.50	.60
❑ 253	Ennis Haywood RC	1.25	.50
❑ 254	Keyuo Craver RC	1.25	.50
❑ 255	Kahlil Hill RC	1.25	.50
❑ 256	J.T. O'Sullivan RC	1.25	.50
❑ 257	Woody Dantzler RC	1.25	.50
❑ 258	Phillip Buchanon RC	1.50	.60
❑ 259	Charles Grant RC	1.50	.60
❑ 260	Dusty Bonner RC	.75	.30
❑ 261	James Allen RC	.75	.30
❑ 262	Ronald Curry RC	1.50	.60
❑ 263	Deion Branch RC	3.00	1.25
❑ 264	Larry Ned RC	1.25	.50
❑ 265	Mel Mitchell RC	1.25	.50
❑ 266	Kendall Newson RC	.75	.30
❑ 267	Shaun Hill RC	1.50	.60
❑ 268	David Pugh RC	.75	.30
❑ 269	Dante Wesley RC	.75	.30
❑ 270	Josh Mallard RC	.75	.30
❑ 271	Akin Ayodele RC	.75	.30
❑ 272	Pete Hunter RC	1.25	.50
❑ 273	Kevin McCadam RC	1.25	.50
❑ 274	Jeff Kelly RC	1.25	.50
❑ 275	John Henderson RC	1.50	.60

2003 Bowman

❑	COMPLETE SET (273)	80.00	40.00
❑ 1	Brett Favre	2.00	.75
❑ 2	Jeremy Shockey	1.25	.50
❑ 3	Fred Taylor	.75	.30
❑ 4	Rich Gannon	.50	.20
❑ 5	Joey Galloway	.50	.20
❑ 6	Ray Lewis	.75	.30
❑ 7	Jeff Blake	.30	.10
❑ 8	Stacey Mack	.30	.10
❑ 9	Matt Hasselbeck	.50	.20
❑ 10	Laveranues Coles	.50	.20
❑ 11	Brad Johnson	.50	.20
❑ 12	Tommy Maddox	.75	.30
❑ 13	Curtis Martin	.75	.30
❑ 14	Tom Brady	2.00	.75
❑ 15	Ricky Williams	.75	.30
❑ 16	Stephen Davis	.50	.20
❑ 17	Chad Johnson	.75	.30
❑ 18	Joey Harrington	1.25	.50
❑ 19	Tony Gonzalez	.50	.20
❑ 20	Peerless Price	.50	.20
❑ 21	LaDainian Tomlinson	.75	.30
❑ 22	James Thrash	.30	.10
❑ 23	Charlie Garner	.50	.20
❑ 24	Eddie George	.50	.20
❑ 25	Terrell Owens	.75	.30
❑ 26	Brian Urlacher	1.25	.50
❑ 27	Eric Moulds	.50	.20
❑ 28	Emmitt Smith	2.00	.75
❑ 29	Tim Couch	.30	.10
❑ 30	Jake Plummer	.50	.20
❑ 31	Marvin Harrison	.75	.30
❑ 32	Chris Chambers	.75	.30
❑ 33	Tiki Barber	.75	.30
❑ 34	Kurt Warner	.75	.30
❑ 35	Michael Pittman	.30	.10
❑ 36	Kevin Dyson	.50	.20
❑ 37	Clinton Portis	1.25	.50
❑ 38	Peyton Manning	1.25	.50
❑ 39	Travis Taylor	.50	.20
❑ 40	Jeff Garcia	.75	.30
❑ 41	Patrick Ramsey	.75	.30
❑ 42	Shaun Alexander	.75	.30
❑ 43	Joe Horn	.50	.20
❑ 44	Daunte Culpepper	.75	.30
❑ 45	Travis Henry	.50	.20
❑ 46	Brian Finneran	.30	.10
❑ 47	William Green	.50	.20
❑ 48	Kordell Stewart	.50	.20
❑ 49	Reggie Wayne	.50	.20
❑ 50	Priest Holmes	1.00	.40
❑ 51	Jay Fiedler	.50	.20
❑ 52	Corey Dillon	.50	.20
❑ 53	Jamal Lewis	.75	.30
❑ 54	Mark Brunell	.50	.20
❑ 55	Santana Moss	.50	.20
❑ 56	Duce Staley	.50	.20
❑ 57	Torry Holt	.75	.30
❑ 58	Rod Gardner	.50	.20
❑ 59	Kerry Collins	.50	.20
❑ 60	Randy Moss	1.25	.50
❑ 61	Jerry Porter	.50	.20
❑ 62	Plaxico Burress	.50	.20
❑ 63	Steve McNair	.75	.30
❑ 64	Muhsin Muhammad	.50	.20
❑ 65	Drew Bledsoe	.75	.30
❑ 66	T.J. Duckett	.50	.20
❑ 67	Ahman Green	.75	.30
❑ 68	Rod Smith	.50	.20
❑ 69	Jimmy Smith	.50	.20
❑ 70	Trent Green	.50	.20
❑ 71	Tim Brown	.75	.30
❑ 72	Jerome Bettis	.75	.30
❑ 73	Isaac Bruce	.75	.30
❑ 74	Derrick Mason	.50	.20
❑ 75	Donovan McNabb	1.00	.40
❑ 76	Deuce McAllister	.75	.30
❑ 77	Zach Thomas	.75	.30
❑ 78	Garrison Hearst	.50	.20
❑ 79	Koren Robinson	.50	.20
❑ 80	Marshall Faulk	.75	.30
❑ 81	Keyshawn Johnson	.75	.30
❑ 82	Jake Delhomme	.75	.30
❑ 83	Marty Booker	.50	.20
❑ 84	James Stewart	.50	.20
❑ 85	Corey Bradford	.30	.10
❑ 86	Derrius Thompson	.30	.10
❑ 87	Edgerrin James	.75	.30
❑ 88	Darrell Jackson	.50	.20
❑ 89	Hines Ward	.75	.30
❑ 90	David Boston	.50	.20
❑ 91	Curtis Conway	.50	.20
❑ 92	David Patten	.30	.10
❑ 93	Michael Bennett	.50	.20
❑ 94	Todd Pinkston	.50	.20
❑ 95	Jerry Rice	1.50	.60
❑ 96	Jon Kitna	.50	.20
❑ 97	Ed McCaffrey	.75	.30
❑ 98	Donald Driver	.50	.20
❑ 99	Anthony Thomas	.50	.20
❑ 100	Michael Vick	2.00	.75
❑ 101	Terry Glenn	.30	.10
❑ 102	Quincy Morgan	.50	.20
❑ 103	David Carr	1.25	.50
❑ 104	Troy Brown	.50	.20
❑ 105	Aaron Brooks	.75	.30
❑ 106	Amani Toomer	.50	.20
❑ 107	Drew Brees	.75	.30
❑ 108	Chad Hutchinson	.30	.10
❑ 109	Warrick Dunn	.50	.20
❑ 110	Chad Pennington	1.00	.40
❑ 111	Carson Palmer RC	6.00	2.50
❑ 112	Brian St.Pierre RC	1.50	.60
❑ 113	Keenan Howry RC	1.50	.60
❑ 114	Sultan McCullough RC	1.25	.50
❑ 115	Terence Newman RC	3.00	1.25
❑ 116	Kelley Washington RC	1.50	.60
❑ 117	Musa Smith RC	1.50	.60
❑ 118	Kevin Williams RC	1.50	.60
❑ 119	Jordan Gross RC	1.25	.50
❑ 120	Lance Briggs RC	5.00	2.00
❑ 121	Victor Hobson RC	1.50	.60
❑ 122	Bryant Johnson RC	1.50	.60
❑ 123	Travis Anglin RC	.75	.30
❑ 124	Artose Pinner RC	1.50	.60
❑ 125	Willis McGahee RC	4.00	1.50
❑ 126	Rashean Mathis RC	1.25	.50
❑ 127	B.J. Askew RC	1.50	.60
❑ 128	DeWayne White RC	1.25	.50
❑ 129	Kevin Curtis RC	1.50	.60
❑ 130	Tyrone Calico RC	2.00	.75
❑ 131	Julian Battle RC	1.25	.50
❑ 132	Ricky Manning RC	1.50	.60
❑ 133	Cory Redding RC	1.25	.50
❑ 134	Michael Haynes RC	1.50	.60
❑ 135	Dallas Clark RC	1.50	.60
❑ 136	Shaun McDonald RC	1.50	.60
❑ 137	Marcus Trufant RC	1.50	.60
❑ 138	Kareem Kelly RC	1.25	.50
❑ 139	Sam Aiken RC	1.25	.50
❑ 140	Terrell Suggs RC	2.50	1.00
❑ 141	Gibran Hamdan RC	.75	.30
❑ 142	Bobby Wade RC	1.50	.60
❑ 143	Aaron Walker RC	1.25	.50
❑ 144	Calvin Pace RC	1.25	.50
❑ 145	Quentin Griffin RC	1.50	.60
❑ 146	Ken Dorsey RC	1.50	.60
❑ 147	Jerome McDougle RC	1.50	.60
❑ 148	Earnest Graham RC	1.25	.50
❑ 149	Rashad Moore RC	1.25	.50

❑ 150 Charles Rogers RC	1.50	.60
❑ 151 Cecil Sapp RC	1.25	.50
❑ 152 Cato June RC	2.00	.75
❑ 153 Ahmaad Galloway RC	1.25	.50
❑ 154 William Joseph RC	1.50	.60
❑ 155 Anquan Boldin RC	4.00	1.50
❑ 156 L.J. Smith RC	1.50	.60
❑ 157 Antwoine Sanders RC	.75	.30
❑ 158 Justin Griffith RC	1.25	.50
❑ 159 Kevin Garrett RC	.75	.30
❑ 160 Teyo Johnson RC	1.50	.60
❑ 161 Chris Crocker RC	1.50	.60
❑ 162 Brad Banks RC	1.25	.50
❑ 163 Justin Gage RC	1.50	.60
❑ 164 Doug Gabriel RC	1.50	.60
❑ 165 Terry Pierce RC	1.25	.50
❑ 166 Bradie James RC	1.50	.60
❑ 167 Bennie Joppru RC	1.50	.60
❑ 168 Malaefou Mackenzie RC	.75	.30
❑ 169 Terrence Edwards RC	1.25	.50
❑ 170 E.J. Henderson RC	1.50	.60
❑ 171 Tony Romo RC	30.00	15.00
❑ 172 DeWayne Robertson RC	1.50	.60
❑ 173 Dwone Hicks RC	.75	.30
❑ 174 Carl Ford RC	.75	.30
❑ 175 Byron Leftwich RC	5.00	2.00
❑ 176 Ken Hamlin RC	1.50	.60
❑ 177 Domanick Davis RC	1.50	.60
❑ 178 Adrian Madise RC	1.25	.50
❑ 179 Siddeeq Shabazz RC	.75	.30
❑ 180 Dave Ragone RC	1.50	.60
❑ 181 Mike Seidman RC	.75	.30
❑ 182 Brooks Bollinger RC	1.50	.60
❑ 183 DeAndrew Rubin RC	.75	.30
❑ 184 Mike Pinkard RC	.75	.30
❑ 185 Nate Burleson RC	1.50	.60
❑ 186 LaBrandon Toefield RC	1.50	.60
❑ 187 Angelo Crowell RC	1.25	.50
❑ 188 J.R. Tolver RC	1.25	.50
❑ 189 Osi Umenyiora RC	2.50	1.00
❑ 190 Larry Johnson RC	6.00	3.00
❑ 191 Nick Barnett RC	1.50	.60
❑ 192 Brandon Drumm RC	.75	.30
❑ 193 Rien Long RC	.75	.30
❑ 194 Zuriel Smith RC	.75	.30
❑ 195 Onterrio Smith RC	1.50	.60
❑ 196 Ronald Bellamy RC	1.25	.50
❑ 197 Kenny Peterson RC	1.25	.50
❑ 198 Charles Tillman RC	2.00	.75
❑ 199 Chaun Thompson RC	.75	.30
❑ 200 Andre Johnson RC	3.00	1.25
❑ 201 Gerald Hayes RC	.75	.30
❑ 202 Terrence Holt RC	1.25	.50
❑ 203 Ovie Mughelli RC	.75	.30
❑ 204 Talman Gardner RC	1.50	.60
❑ 205 Bethel Johnson RC	1.50	.60
❑ 206 Avon Cobourne RC	.75	.30
❑ 207 Brandon Lloyd RC	1.50	.60
❑ 208 Andre Woolfolk RC	1.50	.60
❑ 209 George Wrighster RC	1.25	.50
❑ 210 Justin Fargas RC	1.50	.60
❑ 211 Jimmy Kennedy RC	1.50	.60
❑ 212 Arnaz Battle RC	1.50	.60
❑ 213 Marquel Blackwell RC	.75	.30
❑ 214 Walter Young RC	.75	.30
❑ 215 Kliff Kingsbury RC	1.25	.50
❑ 216 Kawika Mitchell RC	1.50	.60
❑ 217 Drayton Florence RC	.75	.30
❑ 218 Jeremi Johnson RC	1.25	.50
❑ 219 Billy McMullen RC	1.25	.50
❑ 220 Lee Suggs RC	1.50	.60
❑ 221 David Kircus RC	1.50	.60
❑ 222 Rod Babers RC	1.25	.50
❑ 223 Jon Olinger RC	.75	.30
❑ 224 Ty Warren RC	1.50	.60
❑ 225 Kyle Boller RC	1.50	.60
❑ 226 Danny Curley RC	.75	.30
❑ 227 Andrew Pinnock RC	1.25	.50
❑ 228 Kirk Farmer RC	.75	.30
❑ 229 Tully Banta-Cain RC	1.25	.50
❑ 230 Alonzo Jackson RC	1.25	.50
❑ 231 Anthony Adams RC	1.25	.50
❑ 232 Trent Smith RC	1.50	.60
❑ 233 Seneca Wallace RC	1.50	.60
❑ 234 Shane Walton RC	.75	.30
❑ 235 Chris Brown RC	1.50	.60
❑ 236 Dahrran Diedrick RC	1.50	.60
❑ 237 Juston Wood RC	.75	.30
❑ 238 Mike Doss RC	1.50	.60
❑ 239 Visanthe Shiancoe RC	1.25	.50
❑ 240 Rex Grossman RC	4.00	1.50
❑ 241 David Young RC	.75	.30
❑ 242 Jimmy Wilkerson RC	1.25	.50
❑ 243 Jason Witten RC	2.50	1.00
❑ 244 Dennis Weathersby RC	.75	.30
❑ 245 Taylor Jacobs RC	1.25	.50
❑ 246 Chris Davis RC	1.25	.50
❑ 247 LaTarence Dunbar RC	1.25	.50
❑ 248 Eugene Wilson RC	1.50	.60
❑ 249 Ryan Hoag RC	.75	.30
❑ 250 Chris Simms RC	2.50	1.00
❑ 251 Ike Taylor RC	2.50	1.00
❑ 252 Brock Forsey RC	1.50	.60
❑ 253 Curt Anes RC	.75	.30
❑ 254 Taco Wallace RC	1.25	.50
❑ 255 Johnathan Sullivan RC	1.25	.50
❑ 256 David Tyree RC	1.25	.50
❑ 257 Troy Polamalu RC	12.00	6.00
❑ 258 Nate Hybl RC	1.50	.60
❑ 259 Spencer Nead RC	1.25	.50
❑ 260 Boss Bailey RC	1.50	.60
❑ 261 LaMarcus McDonald RC	.75	.30
❑ 262 Casey Moore RC	1.25	.50
❑ 263 Pisa Tinoisamoa RC	1.50	.60
❑ 264 Willie Ponder RC	.75	.30
❑ 265 Donald Lee RC	1.25	.50
❑ 266 Nnamdi Asomugha RC	1.25	.50
❑ 267 Sammy Davis RC	1.50	.60
❑ 268 Joffrey Reynolds RC	.75	.30
❑ 269 Eddie Moore RC	1.25	.50
❑ 270 Tony Hollings RC	1.50	.60
❑ 271 Nick Maddox RC	.75	.30
❑ 272 Kevin Walter RC	1.25	.50
❑ 273 Dan Klecko RC	1.50	.60
❑ 274 Antwan Peek RC	1.25	.50
❑ 275 Tyler Brayton RC	1.50	.60

2004 Bowman

❑ COMPLETE SET (275)	60.00	30.00
❑ 1 Brett Favre	2.00	.75
❑ 2 Jay Fiedler	.30	.10
❑ 3 Andre Davis	.30	.10
❑ 4 Travis Henry	.50	.20
❑ 5 Jimmy Smith	.50	.20
❑ 6 Santana Moss	.50	.20
❑ 7 Correll Buckhalter	.50	.20
❑ 8 Randy Moss	1.00	.40
❑ 9 Edgerrin James	.75	.30
❑ 10 Marc Bulger	.75	.30
❑ 11 Derrick Mason	.50	.20
❑ 12 Mark Brunell	.50	.20
❑ 13 Donte' Stallworth	.50	.20
❑ 14 Deion Branch	.75	.30
❑ 15 Jake Plummer	.50	.20
❑ 16 Steve Smith	.75	.30
❑ 17 Jon Kitna	.50	.20
❑ 18 Andre Johnson	.75	.30
❑ 19 A.J. Feeley	.75	.30
❑ 20 Drew Bledsoe	.75	.30
❑ 21 Antonio Bryant	.50	.20
❑ 22 Reggie Wayne	.50	.20
❑ 23 Thomas Jones	.50	.20
❑ 24 Alge Crumpler	.50	.20
❑ 25 Anquan Boldin	.75	.30
❑ 26 Tim Rattay	.30	.10
❑ 27 Charlie Garner	.50	.20
❑ 28 James Thrash	.30	.10
❑ 29 Koren Robinson	.50	.20
❑ 30 Terrell Owens	.75	.30
❑ 31 Amani Toomer	.50	.20
❑ 32 Kelly Campbell	.30	.10
❑ 33 Patrick Ramsey	.50	.20
❑ 34 Plaxico Burress	.50	.20
❑ 35 Chad Pennington	.75	.30
❑ 36 Fred Taylor	.50	.20
❑ 37 Domanick Davis	.75	.30
❑ 38 DeShaun Foster	.50	.20
❑ 39 T.J. Duckett	.50	.20
❑ 40 Ahman Green	.75	.30
❑ 41 Lee Suggs	.75	.30
❑ 42 Tony Gonzalez	.50	.20
❑ 43 Rich Gannon	.50	.20
❑ 44 Kevan Barlow	.50	.20
❑ 45 Torry Holt	.75	.30
❑ 46 Aaron Brooks	.50	.20
❑ 47 Tyrone Calico	.50	.20
❑ 48 Keenan McCardell	.30	.10
❑ 49 Hines Ward	.75	.30
❑ 50 LaDainian Tomlinson	1.00	.40
❑ 51 Dante Hall	.75	.30
❑ 52 Marcus Pollard	.30	.10
❑ 53 Corey Dillon	.50	.20
❑ 54 Justin McCareins	.30	.10
❑ 55 Stephen Davis	.50	.20
❑ 56 Jeff Garcia	.75	.30
❑ 57 Ashley Lelie	.50	.20
❑ 58 Javon Walker	.50	.20
❑ 59 Kyle Boller	.75	.30
❑ 60 Chad Johnson	.75	.30
❑ 61 Anthony Thomas	.50	.20
❑ 62 Byron Leftwich	1.00	.40
❑ 63 David Boston	.50	.20
❑ 64 Onterrio Smith	.50	.20
❑ 65 Deuce McAllister	.75	.30
❑ 66 Antwaan Randle El	.75	.30
❑ 67 Justin Fargas	.50	.20
❑ 68 Laveranues Coles	.50	.20
❑ 69 Quincy Morgan	.50	.20
❑ 70 Priest Holmes	1.00	.40
❑ 71 Robert Ferguson	.30	.10
❑ 72 Charles Rogers	.50	.20
❑ 73 Drew Brees	.75	.30
❑ 74 Matt Hasselbeck	.50	.20
❑ 75 Peyton Manning	1.25	.50
❑ 76 Rudi Johnson	.50	.20
❑ 77 Jake Delhomme	.75	.30
❑ 78 Tiki Barber	.75	.30
❑ 79 Brad Johnson	.50	.20
❑ 80 Steve McNair	.75	.30
❑ 81 Willis McGahee	.75	.30
❑ 82 Josh McCown	.50	.20
❑ 83 Garrison Hearst	.50	.20
❑ 84 Quincy Carter	.50	.20
❑ 85 Ricky Williams	.75	.30
❑ 86 Trent Green	.50	.20
❑ 87 Curtis Martin	.75	.30
❑ 88 Jerry Porter	.50	.20
❑ 89 Brian Westbrook	.50	.20
❑ 90 Clinton Portis	.75	.30
❑ 91 Eric Moulds	.50	.20
❑ 92 Marcel Shipp	.50	.20
❑ 93 Joey Harrington	.75	.30
❑ 94 David Carr	.75	.30
❑ 95 Marvin Harrison	.75	.30
❑ 96 Joe Horn	.50	.20
❑ 97 Chris Chambers	.50	.20
❑ 98 Darrell Jackson	.50	.20
❑ 99 Eddie George	.50	.20
❑ 100 Donovan McNabb	1.00	.40
❑ 101 Marshall Faulk	.75	.30
❑ 102 Rex Grossman	.75	.30
❑ 103 Tai Streets	.30	.10
❑ 104 Jeremy Shockey	.75	.30
❑ 105 Jamal Lewis	.75	.30
❑ 106 Tom Brady	2.00	.75
❑ 107 Shaun Alexander	.75	.30
❑ 108 Carson Palmer	1.00	.40
❑ 109 Daunte Culpepper	.75	.30
❑ 110 Michael Vick	1.50	.60
❑ 111 Eli Manning RC	12.00	5.00
❑ 112 Kevin Jones RC	4.00	1.50
❑ 113 Philip Rivers RC	5.00	2.00
❑ 114 Ben Roethlisberger RC	20.00	10.00
❑ 115 Roy Williams RC	4.00	1.50
❑ 116 Tommie Harris RC	1.50	.60
❑ 117 Vontez Duff RC	1.25	.50
❑ 118 Karlos Dansby RC	1.50	.60
❑ 119 Thomas Tapeh RC	1.25	.50
❑ 120 Matt Schaub RC	5.00	2.00
❑ 121 Dexter Reid RC	.75	.30

❑ 122	Jonathan Smith RC	1.25	.50
❑ 123	Ricardo Colclough RC	1.50	.60
❑ 124	Jeff Dugan RC	.75	.30
❑ 125	Larry Fitzgerald RC	5.00	2.00
❑ 126	Gibril Wilson RC	1.50	.60
❑ 127	Sean Taylor RC	1.50	.60
❑ 128	Marquise Hill RC	1.25	.50
❑ 129	Ernest Wilford RC	1.50	.60
❑ 130	Cedric Cobbs RC	1.50	.60
❑ 131	Rich Gardner RC	1.25	.50
❑ 132	Chris Cooley RC	1.50	.60
❑ 133	Kenechi Udeze RC	1.50	.60
❑ 134	John Navarre RC	1.50	.60
❑ 135	Ben Troupe RC	1.50	.60
❑ 136	Dave Ball RC	.75	.30
❑ 137	Antwan Odom RC	1.50	.60
❑ 138	Stuart Schweigert RC	1.50	.60
❑ 139	Derek Abney RC	1.50	.60
❑ 140	Keary Colbert RC	2.00	.75
❑ 141	Jeris McIntyre RC	1.25	.50
❑ 142	Matt Kranchick RC	1.50	.60
❑ 143	Rodney Leisle RC	.75	.30
❑ 144	Vince Wilfork RC	1.50	.60
❑ 145	Lee Evans RC	2.00	.75
❑ 146	Darnell Dockett RC	1.25	.50
❑ 147	Jeremy LeSueur RC	1.25	.50
❑ 148	Gilbert Gardner RC	1.25	.50
❑ 149	Amon Gordon RC	.75	.30
❑ 150	Darius Watts RC	1.50	.60
❑ 151	Junior Siavii RC	1.50	.60
❑ 152	Igor Olshansky RC	1.50	.60
❑ 153	Courtney Watson RC	1.50	.60
❑ 154	D.J. Williams RC	1.50	.60
❑ 155	Mewelde Moore RC	1.50	.60
❑ 156	Teddy Lehman RC	1.50	.60
❑ 157	Nathan Vasher RC	2.00	.75
❑ 158	Randy Starks RC	1.25	.50
❑ 159	Isaac Sopoaga RC	.75	.30
❑ 160	Drew Henson RC	1.50	.60
❑ 161	Erik Coleman RC	1.50	.60
❑ 162	Robert Kent RC	.75	.30
❑ 163	Jammal Lord RC	1.50	.60
❑ 164	Richard Seigler RC	1.25	.50
❑ 165	Jeff Smoker RC	1.50	.60
❑ 166	Niko Koutouvides RC	1.25	.50
❑ 167	Adimchinobe Echemandu RC	1.25	.50
❑ 168	Matt Mauck RC	1.50	.60
❑ 169	Brandon Miree RC	1.25	.50
❑ 170	Dunta Robinson RC	1.50	.60
❑ 171	B.J. Symons RC	1.50	.60
❑ 172	Courtney Anderson RC	1.25	.50
❑ 173	Bruce Perry RC	1.50	.60
❑ 174	Shaun Phillips RC	1.25	.50
❑ 175	Greg Jones RC	1.50	.60
❑ 176	Ryan Krause RC	1.25	.50
❑ 177	Charlie Anderson RC	.75	.30
❑ 178	Tank Johnson RC	1.25	.50
❑ 179	Dwan Edwards RC	.75	.30
❑ 180	Julius Jones RC	5.00	2.00
❑ 181	Chad Lavalais RC	1.25	.50
❑ 182	Tim Anderson RC	1.50	.60
❑ 183	Jarrett Payton RC	1.50	.60
❑ 184	Matt Ware RC	1.50	.60
❑ 185	DeAngelo Hall RC	2.00	.75
❑ 186	Ben Hartsock RC	1.50	.60
❑ 187	Bradlee Van Pelt RC	1.50	.60
❑ 188	Michael Boulware RC	1.50	.60
❑ 189	Keith Smith RC	1.25	.50
❑ 190	Michael Jenkins RC	1.50	.60
❑ 191	Quincy Wilson RC	1.25	.50
❑ 192	Dontarrious Thomas RC	1.50	.60
❑ 193	Sloan Thomas RC	1.25	.50
❑ 194	Tony Hargrove RC	1.25	.50
❑ 195	Ben Watson RC	1.50	.60
❑ 196	Craig Krenzel RC	1.50	.60
❑ 197	Jason Babin RC	1.50	.60
❑ 198	Jim Sorgi RC	1.50	.60
❑ 199	Triandos Luke RC	1.50	.60
❑ 200	Kellen Winslow RC	3.00	1.25
❑ 201	Patrick Crayton RC	1.50	.60
❑ 202	Michael Waddell RC	.75	.30
❑ 203	Chris Gamble RC	1.50	.60
❑ 204	Josh Harris RC	1.50	.60
❑ 205	Devard Darling RC	1.50	.60
❑ 206	Shawntae Spencer RC	1.50	.60
❑ 207	Will Smith RC	1.50	.60
❑ 208	Samie Parker RC	1.50	.60
❑ 209	Darrion Scott RC	1.50	.60
❑ 210	Chris Perry RC	2.50	1.00
❑ 211	P.K. Sam RC	1.25	.50
❑ 212	Wes Welker RC	2.00	.75
❑ 213	Ryan Dinwiddie RC	1.25	.50
❑ 214	Rod Davis RC	.75	.30
❑ 215	Casey Clausen RC	1.50	.60
❑ 216	Clarence Moore RC	1.50	.60
❑ 217	D.J. Hackett RC	1.25	.50
❑ 218	Casey Bramlet RC	1.25	.50
❑ 219	Jared Lorenzen RC	1.25	.50
❑ 220	Devery Henderson RC	1.25	.50
❑ 221	Sean Jones RC	1.25	.50
❑ 222	Maurice Mann RC	1.25	.50
❑ 223	Jared Allen RC	2.00	.75
❑ 224	Bruce Thornton RC	.75	.30
❑ 225	Tatum Bell RC	3.00	1.25
❑ 226	Leon Joe RC	.75	.30
❑ 227	Tim Euhus RC	1.50	.60
❑ 228	John Standeford RC	1.25	.50
❑ 229	Reggie Torbor RC	1.25	.50
❑ 230	Rashaun Woods RC	1.50	.60
❑ 231	Jason Shivers RC	.75	.30
❑ 232	Jason Peters RC	1.50	.60
❑ 233	Ahmad Carroll RC	1.50	.60
❑ 234	Jason David RC	1.50	.60
❑ 235	Keyaron Fox RC	1.25	.50
❑ 236	Corey Williams RC	.75	.30
❑ 237	Raheem Orr RC	.75	.30
❑ 238	Carlos Francis RC	1.25	.50
❑ 239	Von Hutchins RC	1.25	.50
❑ 240	Marcus Tubbs RC	1.50	.60
❑ 241	Daryl Smith RC	1.50	.60
❑ 242	Robert Gallery RC	1.50	.60
❑ 243	Sean Tufts RC	1.25	.50
❑ 244	Marquis Cooper RC	1.25	.50
❑ 245	Bernard Berrian RC	2.00	.75
❑ 246	Derrick Strait RC	1.50	.60
❑ 247	Travis LaBoy RC	1.50	.60
❑ 248	Johnnie Morant RC	1.50	.60
❑ 249	Caleb Miller RC	1.25	.50
❑ 250	Michael Clayton RC	3.00	1.25
❑ 251	Will Poole RC	1.50	.60
❑ 252	Andy Hall RC	1.25	.50
❑ 253	Demorrio Williams RC	1.50	.60
❑ 254	Chris Thompson RC	.75	.30
❑ 255	Derrick Hamilton RC	1.25	.50
❑ 256	Glenn Earl RC	1.25	.50
❑ 257	Jonathan Vilma RC	1.50	.60
❑ 258	Donnell Washington RC	1.50	.60
❑ 259	Drew Carter RC	1.50	.60
❑ 260	Steven Jackson RC	5.00	2.00
❑ 261	Jamaar Taylor RC	1.50	.60
❑ 262	Nate Lawrie RC	1.25	.50
❑ 263	Cody Pickett RC	1.50	.60
❑ 264	Keiwan Ratliff RC	1.25	.50
❑ 265	Luke McCown RC	1.50	.60
❑ 266	Jerricho Cotchery RC	1.50	.60
❑ 267	Joey Thomas RC	1.50	.60
❑ 268	Shawn Andrews RC	1.50	.60
❑ 269	Derrick Ward RC	.75	.30
❑ 270	Reggie Williams RC	2.00	.75
❑ 271	Rod Rutherford RC	1.25	.50
❑ 272	Michael Turner RC	2.00	.75
❑ 273	Michael Gaines RC	1.25	.50
❑ 274	Will Allen RC	1.50	.60
❑ 275	J.P. Losman RC	3.00	1.25

2005 Bowman

❑	COMP.SET w/o AU's (270)	60.00	25.00
❑ 1	Peyton Manning	1.25	.50
❑ 2	Antonio Gates	.75	.30
❑ 3	Priest Holmes	.75	.30
❑ 4	Anquan Boldin	.50	.20
❑ 5	Donovan McNabb	1.00	.40
❑ 6	Drew Bennett	.50	.20
❑ 7	Michael Vick	1.25	.50
❑ 8	David Carr	.75	.30
❑ 9	Drew Brees	.75	.30
❑ 10	Trent Green	.50	.20
❑ 11	Drew Bledsoe	.75	.30
❑ 12	Randy Moss	.75	.30
❑ 13	Terrell Owens	.75	.30
❑ 14	Donte Stallworth	.50	.20
❑ 15	Alge Crumpler	.50	.20
❑ 16	Jake Plummer	.50	.20
❑ 17	Curtis Martin	.75	.30
❑ 18	Jason Witten	.50	.20
❑ 19	Tom Brady	2.00	.75
❑ 20	Thomas Jones	.50	.20
❑ 21	Tiki Barber	.75	.30
❑ 22	Maurice Carthon CO	.50	.20
❑ 23	Rex Grossman	.50	.20
❑ 24	Brett Favre	2.00	.75
❑ 25	Marshall Faulk	.75	.30
❑ 26	LaMont Jordan	.75	.30
❑ 27	Kurt Warner	.50	.20
❑ 28	Corey Dillon	.50	.20
❑ 29	Julius Jones	1.00	.40
❑ 30	Ahman Green	.75	.30
❑ 31	Jamal Lewis	.75	.30
❑ 32	Ben Roethlisberger	2.00	.75
❑ 33	Keary Colbert	.50	.20
❑ 34	Mike Nolan CO RC	.75	.30
❑ 35	Joey Harrington	.75	.30
❑ 36	Brian Westbrook	.50	.20
❑ 37	Domanick Davis	.50	.20
❑ 38	Carson Palmer	.75	.30
❑ 39	Stephen Davis	.50	.20
❑ 40	Eli Manning	1.50	.60
❑ 41	Edgerrin James	.75	.30
❑ 42	Jonathan Vilma	.50	.20
❑ 43	Brad Childress CO RC	.50	.20
❑ 44	Willis McGahee	.75	.30
❑ 45	Steve McNair	.75	.30
❑ 46	Plaxico Burress	.50	.20
❑ 47	Rudi Johnson	.50	.20
❑ 48	Jerry Porter	.50	.20
❑ 49	Chad Pennington	.75	.30
❑ 50	Charles Rogers	.50	.20
❑ 51	Patrick Ramsey	.50	.20
❑ 52	Dwight Freeney	.50	.20
❑ 53	Brian Griese	.50	.20
❑ 54	Jerome Bettis	.75	.30
❑ 55	Tim Lewis CO	.40	.15
❑ 56	Aaron Brooks	.50	.20
❑ 57	Matt Hasselbeck	.50	.20
❑ 58	Chris Chambers	.50	.20
❑ 59	Kyle Boller	.50	.20
❑ 60	Brandon Lloyd	.40	.15
❑ 61	Marc Bulger	.75	.30
❑ 62	Isaac Bruce	.50	.20
❑ 63	Jake Delhomme	.75	.30
❑ 64	Chad Johnson	.75	.30
❑ 65	Shaun Alexander	1.00	.40
❑ 66	Kevin Jones	.75	.30
❑ 67	Eric Moulds	.50	.20
❑ 68	Laveranues Coles	.50	.20
❑ 69	A.J. Feeley	.50	.20
❑ 70	Sean Taylor	.50	.20
❑ 71	Romeo Crennel CO RC	.75	.30
❑ 72	Ashley Lelie	.50	.20
❑ 73	Nick Saban CO RC	.75	.30
❑ 74	Deuce McAllister	.75	.30
❑ 75	Kerry Collins	.50	.20
❑ 76	Chris Brown	.50	.20
❑ 77	Steven Jackson	1.00	.40
❑ 78	Nate Burleson	.50	.20
❑ 79	LaDainian Tomlinson	1.00	.40
❑ 80	Darrell Jackson	.50	.20
❑ 81	Torry Holt	.75	.30
❑ 82	Lee Suggs	.50	.20
❑ 83	Lee Evans	.50	.20
❑ 84	Santana Moss	.50	.20
❑ 85	Jeremy Shockey	.75	.30
❑ 86	Hines Ward	.75	.30
❑ 87	Muhsin Muhammad	.50	.20
❑ 88	Daunte Culpepper	.75	.30
❑ 89	Deion Branch	.50	.20
❑ 90	DeShaun Foster	.50	.20
❑ 91	Travis Henry	.50	.20
❑ 92	Jerry Rice	1.50	.60
❑ 93	Reggie Wayne	.50	.20

❑ 94 Roy Williams WR .75 .30
❑ 95 Michael Jenkins .50 .20
❑ 96 Tatum Bell .50 .20
❑ 97 Andre Johnson .50 .20
❑ 98 Dante Hall .50 .20
❑ 99 Javon Walker .50 .20
❑ 100 Larry Fitzgerald .75 .30
❑ 101 Joe Horn .50 .20
❑ 102 Marvin Harrison .75 .30
❑ 103 Fred Taylor .50 .20
❑ 104 Byron Leftwich .75 .30
❑ 105 Tony Gonzalez .50 .20
❑ 106 T.J. Houshmandzadeh .40 .15
❑ 107 J.P. Losman .75 .30
❑ 108 Michael Clayton .75 .30
❑ 109 Clinton Portis .75 .30
❑ 110 Ted Cottrell CO RC .40 .15
❑ 111 Braylon Edwards RC 5.00 2.00
❑ 112 Aaron Rodgers RC 5.00 2.00
❑ 113 Ronnie Brown RC 6.00 2.50
❑ 114 Alex Smith QB RC 6.00 2.50
❑ 115 Cadillac Williams RC 8.00 3.00
❑ 116 Ciatrick Fason RC 1.50 .60
❑ 117 Derrick Johnson RC 2.50 1.00
❑ 118 Carlos Rogers RC 2.00 .75
❑ 119 Ryan Moats RC 1.50 .60
❑ 120 Alvin Pearman RC 1.50 .60
❑ 121 Stefan LeFors RC 1.50 .60
❑ 122 Brandon Jacobs RC 2.00 .75
❑ 123 Kyle Orton RC 2.50 1.00
❑ 124 Marion Barber RC 2.50 1.00
❑ 125 Mark Bradley RC 1.50 .60
❑ 126 Travis Johnson RC 1.25 .50
❑ 127 Antrel Rolle RC 1.50 .60
❑ 128 Jason Campbell RC 2.50 1.00
❑ 129 DeMarcus Ware RC 2.50 1.00
❑ 130 Frank Gore RC 3.00 1.25
❑ 131 Justin Miller RC 1.25 .50
❑ 132 J.J. Arrington RC 2.00 .75
❑ 133 Marcus Spears RC 1.50 .60
❑ 134 Roddy White RC 1.50 .60
❑ 135 Fabian Washington RC 1.50 .60
❑ 136 Vincent Jackson RC 1.50 .60
❑ 137 Erasmus James RC 1.50 .60
❑ 138 Roscoe Parrish RC 1.50 .60
❑ 139 Airese Currie RC 1.50 .60
❑ 140 Heath Miller RC 4.00 1.50
❑ 141 Mike Patterson RC 1.50 .60
❑ 142 Troy Williamson RC 3.00 1.25
❑ 143 Terrence Murphy RC 1.50 .60
❑ 144 Dan Orlovsky RC 2.00 .75
❑ 145 Eric Shelton RC 1.50 .60
❑ 146 Thomas Davis RC 1.50 .60
❑ 147 Cedric Benson RC 3.00 1.25
❑ 148 Noah Herron RC 1.50 .60
❑ 149 Vernand Morency RC 1.50 .60
❑ 150 Darren Sproles RC 1.50 .60
❑ 151 Alex Smith TE RC 1.50 .60
❑ 152 Mark Clayton RC 2.00 .75
❑ 153 Craphonso Thorpe RC 1.25 .50
❑ 154 Mike Williams 3.00 1.25
❑ 155 Anthony Davis RC 1.25 .50
❑ 156 Charlie Frye RC 3.00 1.25
❑ 157 Fred Gibson RC 1.25 .50
❑ 158 Reggie Brown RC 1.50 .60
❑ 159 Andrew Walter RC 2.50 1.00
❑ 160 Adam Jones RC 1.50 .60
❑ 161 David Greene RC 1.50 .60
❑ 162 Maurice Clarett 1.50 .60
❑ 163 Courtney Roby RC 1.50 .60
❑ 164 Derek Anderson RC 1.50 .60
❑ 165 Matt Jones RC 4.00 1.50
❑ 166 Chris Henry RC 1.50 .60
❑ 167 Shaun Cody RC 1.50 .60
❑ 168 Khalif Barnes RC 1.25 .50
❑ 169 Matt Roth RC 1.50 .60
❑ 170 Lionel Gates RC 1.25 .50
❑ 171 Kevin Burnett RC 1.50 .60
❑ 172 Taylor Stubblefield RC .75 .30
❑ 173 Zach Tuiasosopo RC .75 .30
❑ 174 Alex Barron RC .75 .30
❑ 175 Mike Nugent RC 1.50 .60
❑ 176 Barrett Ruud RC 1.50 .60
❑ 177 Brock Berlin RC 1.25 .50
❑ 178 Kirk Morrison RC 1.50 .60
❑ 179 David Pollack RC 1.50 .60
❑ 180 Ryan Fitzpatrick RC 2.50 1.00
❑ 181 Kay-Jay Harris RC 1.25 .50
❑ 182 Dan Cody RC 1.50 .60
❑ 183 Chad Owens RC 1.50 .60
❑ 184 Stanley Wilson RC 1.25 .50
❑ 185 Rasheed Marshall RC 1.50 .60
❑ 186 Bryant McFadden RC 1.50 .60
❑ 187 Joel Dreessen RC 1.25 .50
❑ 188 Donte Nicholson RC 1.50 .60
❑ 189 Scott Starks RC 1.25 .50
❑ 190 Walter Reyes RC 1.25 .50
❑ 191 Stanford Routt RC 1.25 .50
❑ 192 Lance Mitchell RC 1.25 .50
❑ 193 Rian Wallace RC 1.25 .50
❑ 194 Timmy Chang RC 1.25 .50
❑ 195 Oshiomogho Atogwe RC 1.25 .50
❑ 196 Larry Brackins RC 1.25 .50
❑ 197 Jovan Witherspoon RC .75 .30
❑ 198 Boomer Grigsby RC 2.00 .75
❑ 199 Darryl Blackstock RC 1.25 .50
❑ 200 Jerome Mathis RC 1.50 .60
❑ 201 Ellis Hobbs RC 1.50 .60
❑ 202 Dante Ridgeway RC 1.25 .50
❑ 203 James Kilian RC 1.50 .60
❑ 204 Patrick Estes RC 1.25 .50
❑ 205 Justin Tuck RC 1.50 .60
❑ 206 Channing Crowder RC 1.50 .60
❑ 207 Dustin Fox RC 1.50 .60
❑ 208 Marlin Jackson RC 1.50 .60
❑ 209 Luis Castillo RC 1.50 .60
❑ 210 Paris Warren RC 1.25 .50
❑ 211 J.R. Russell RC 1.25 .50
❑ 212 Cedric Houston RC 1.50 .60
❑ 213 Corey Webster RC 1.50 .60
❑ 214 Craig Bragg RC 1.25 .50
❑ 215 Tab Perry RC 1.50 .60
❑ 216 Ryan Riddle RC .75 .30
❑ 217 Gino Guidugli RC .75 .30
❑ 218 Deandra Cobb RC 1.25 .50
❑ 219 Travis Daniels RC 1.25 .50
❑ 220 Marcus Maxwell RC 1.25 .50
❑ 221 Eric King RC 1.25 .50
❑ 222 Matt Cassel RC 2.50 1.00
❑ 223 Justin Green RC 1.50 .60
❑ 224 Steve Savoy RC .75 .30
❑ 225 Shawne Merriman RC 2.50 1.00
❑ 226 Damien Nash RC 1.25 .50
❑ 227 T.A. McLendon RC .75 .30
❑ 228 Vincent Fuller RC 1.25 .50
❑ 229 Jordan Beck RC 1.25 .50
❑ 230 Lofa Tatupu RC 2.00 .75
❑ 231 Will Peoples RC 1.25 .50
❑ 232 Chad Friehauf RC 1.25 .50
❑ 233 Brady Poppinga RC 1.50 .60
❑ 234 Anttaj Hawthorne RC 1.25 .50
❑ 235 Adrian McPherson RC 1.50 .60
❑ 236 Nick Collins RC 1.50 .60
❑ 237 Roydell Williams RC 1.50 .60
❑ 238 Craig Ochs RC 1.25 .50
❑ 239 Billy Bajema RC 1.25 .50
❑ 240 Jon Goldsberry RC 1.50 .60
❑ 241 Jared Newberry RC 1.25 .50
❑ 242 Odell Thurman RC 1.50 .60
❑ 243 Kelvin Hayden RC 1.25 .50
❑ 244 Jamaal Brimmer RC .75 .30
❑ 245 Jonathan Babineaux RC 1.25 .50
❑ 246 Bo Scaife RC 1.25 .50
❑ 247 Chris Spencer RC 1.50 .60
❑ 248 Manuel White RC 1.25 .50
❑ 249 Josh Davis RC 1.25 .50
❑ 250 Bryan Randall RC 1.25 .50
❑ 251 James Butler RC 1.25 .50
❑ 252 Harry Williams RC 1.25 .50
❑ 253 Leroy Hill RC 1.50 .60
❑ 254 Josh Bullocks RC 1.50 .60
❑ 255 Alfred Fincher RC 1.25 .50
❑ 256 Antonio Perkins RC 1.25 .50
❑ 257 Bobby Purify RC 1.25 .50
❑ 258 Rick Razzano RC 1.50 .60
❑ 259 Darrent Williams RC 1.50 .60
❑ 260 Darian Durant RC 1.50 .60
❑ 261 Fred Amey RC 1.25 .50
❑ 262 Ronald Bartell RC 1.25 .50
❑ 263 Kerry Rhodes RC 1.50 .60
❑ 264 Jerome Carter RC 1.25 .50
❑ 265 Marcus Randall RC 1.25 .50
❑ 266 Nehemiah Broughton RC 1.25 .50
❑ 267 Keron Henry RC .75 .30
❑ 268 Jerome Collins RC 1.25 .50
❑ 269 Trent Cole RC 1.50 .60
❑ 270 Alphonso Hodge RC .75 .30
❑ 271 Brandon Jones RC 1.50 .60
❑ 272 Chase Lyman RC 1.25 .50
❑ 273 Marviel Underwood RC 1.25 .50
❑ 274 Maurice Washington RC 1.25 .50
❑ 275 Madison Hedgecock RC 1.50 .60

1998 Bowman Chrome

❑ COMPLETE SET (220) 100.00 50.00
❑ 1 Peyton Manning RC 40.00 20.00
❑ 2 Keith Brooking RC 4.00 1.50
❑ 3 Duane Starks RC 2.00 .75
❑ 4 Takeo Spikes RC 4.00 1.50
❑ 5 Andre Wadsworth RC 3.00 1.25
❑ 6 Greg Ellis RC 2.00 .75
❑ 7 Brian Griese RC 8.00 3.00
❑ 8 Germane Crowell RC 3.00 1.25
❑ 9 Jerome Pathon RC 4.00 1.50
❑ 10 Ryan Leaf RC 4.00 1.50
❑ 11 Fred Taylor RC 6.00 2.50
❑ 12 Robert Edwards RC 3.00 1.25
❑ 13 Grant Wistrom RC 3.00 1.25
❑ 14 Robert Holcombe RC 3.00 1.25
❑ 15 Tim Dwight RC 4.00 1.50
❑ 16 Jacquez Green RC 3.00 1.25
❑ 17 Marcus Nash RC 2.00 .75
❑ 18 Jason Peter RC 2.00 .75
❑ 19 Anthony Simmons RC 3.00 1.25
❑ 20 Curtis Enis RC 2.00 .75
❑ 21 John Avery RC 3.00 1.25
❑ 22 Pat Johnson RC 3.00 1.25
❑ 23 Joe Jurevicius RC 4.00 1.50
❑ 24 Brian Simmons RC 3.00 1.25
❑ 25 Kevin Dyson RC 4.00 1.50
❑ 26 Skip Hicks RC 3.00 1.25
❑ 27 Hines Ward RC 15.00 7.50
❑ 28 Tavian Banks RC 3.00 1.25
❑ 29 Ahman Green RC 20.00 10.00
❑ 30 Tony Simmons RC 3.00 1.25
❑ 31 Charles Johnson .50 .20
❑ 32 Freddie Jones .50 .20
❑ 33 Joey Galloway .75 .30
❑ 34 Tony Banks .75 .30
❑ 35 Jake Plummer 1.25 .50
❑ 36 Reidel Anthony .75 .30
❑ 37 Steve McNair 1.25 .50
❑ 38 Michael Westbrook .75 .30
❑ 39 Chris Sanders .50 .20
❑ 40 Isaac Bruce .50 .20
❑ 41 Charlie Garner .75 .30
❑ 42 Wayne Chrebet 1.25 .50
❑ 43 Michael Strahan .75 .30
❑ 44 Brad Johnson 1.25 .50
❑ 45 Mike Alstott .50 .20
❑ 46 Tony Gonzalez 1.25 .50
❑ 47 Johnnie Morton .75 .30
❑ 48 Darnay Scott .75 .30
❑ 49 Rae Carruth .50 .20
❑ 50 Terrell Davis 1.25 .50
❑ 51 Jermaine Lewis .75 .30
❑ 52 Frank Sanders .75 .30
❑ 53 Byron Hanspard .50 .20
❑ 54 Gus Frerotte .50 .20
❑ 55 Terry Glenn 1.25 .50
❑ 56 J.J. Stokes .75 .30
❑ 57 Will Blackwell .50 .20
❑ 58 Keyshawn Johnson 1.25 .50
❑ 59 Tiki Barber 1.25 .50
❑ 60 Dorsey Levens 1.25 .50
❑ 61 Zach Thomas 1.25 .50
❑ 62 Corey Dillon 1.25 .50
❑ 63 Antowain Smith 1.25 .50
❑ 64 Michael Sinclair .50 .20
❑ 65 Rod Smith .75 .30

❑ 66	Trent Dilfer	1.25	.50
❑ 67	Warren Sapp	.75	.30
❑ 68	Charles Way	.50	.20
❑ 69	Tamarick Vanover	.50	.20
❑ 70	Drew Bledsoe	2.00	.75
❑ 71	John Mobley	.50	.20
❑ 72	Kerry Collins	.75	.30
❑ 73	Peter Boulware	.50	.20
❑ 74	Simeon Rice	.75	.30
❑ 75	Eddie George	1.25	.50
❑ 76	Fred Lane	.50	.20
❑ 77	Jamal Anderson	1.25	.50
❑ 78	Antonio Freeman	1.25	.50
❑ 79	Jason Sehorn	.75	.30
❑ 80	Curtis Martin	1.25	.50
❑ 81	Bobby Hoying	.75	.30
❑ 82	Garrison Hearst	1.25	.50
❑ 83	Glenn Foley	.75	.30
❑ 84	Danny Kanell	.75	.30
❑ 85	Kordell Stewart	1.25	.50
❑ 86	O.J. McDuffie	.75	.30
❑ 87	Marvin Harrison	1.25	.50
❑ 88	Bobby Engram	.75	.30
❑ 89	Chris Slade	.50	.20
❑ 90	Warrick Dunn	1.25	.50
❑ 91	Ricky Watters	.75	.30
❑ 92	Rickey Dudley	.50	.20
❑ 93	Terrell Owens	1.25	.50
❑ 94	Karim Abdul-Jabbar	1.25	.50
❑ 95	Napoleon Kaufman	1.25	.50
❑ 96	Darrell Green	.75	.30
❑ 97	Levon Kirkland	.50	.20
❑ 98	Jeff George	.75	.30
❑ 99	Andre Hastings	.50	.20
❑ 100	John Elway	5.00	2.00
❑ 101	John Randle	.75	.30
❑ 102	Andre Rison	.75	.30
❑ 103	Keenan McCardell	.75	.30
❑ 104	Marshall Faulk	1.50	.60
❑ 105	Emmitt Smith	4.00	1.50
❑ 106	Robert Brooks	.75	.30
❑ 107	Scott Mitchell	.75	.30
❑ 108	Shannon Sharpe	.75	.30
❑ 109	Deion Sanders	1.25	.50
❑ 110	Jerry Rice	2.50	1.00
❑ 111	Erik Kramer	.50	.20
❑ 112	Michael Jackson	.50	.20
❑ 113	Aeneas Williams	.50	.20
❑ 114	Terry Allen	1.25	.50
❑ 115	Steve Young	1.50	.60
❑ 116	Warren Moon	1.25	.50
❑ 117	Junior Seau	1.25	.50
❑ 118	Jerome Bettis	1.25	.50
❑ 119	Irving Fryar	.75	.30
❑ 120	Barry Sanders	4.00	1.50
❑ 121	Tim Brown	.50	.20
❑ 122	Chad Brown	.50	.20
❑ 123	Ben Coates	.75	.30
❑ 124	Robert Smith	1.25	.50
❑ 125	Brett Favre	5.00	2.00
❑ 126	Derrick Thomas	1.25	.50
❑ 127	Reggie White	1.25	.50
❑ 128	Troy Aikman	2.50	1.00
❑ 129	Jeff Blake	.75	.30
❑ 130	Mark Brunell	1.25	.50
❑ 131	Curtis Conway	.75	.30
❑ 132	Wesley Walls	.75	.30
❑ 133	Thurman Thomas	1.25	.50
❑ 134	Chris Chandler	.75	.30
❑ 135	Dan Marino	5.00	2.00
❑ 136	Larry Centers	.50	.20
❑ 137	Shawn Jefferson	.50	.20
❑ 138	Andre Reed	.75	.30
❑ 139	Jake Reed	.75	.30
❑ 140	Cris Carter	1.25	.50
❑ 141	Elvis Grbac	.75	.30
❑ 142	Mark Chmura	.75	.30
❑ 143	Michael Irvin	1.25	.50
❑ 144	Carl Pickens	.75	.30
❑ 145	Herman Moore	.75	.30
❑ 146	Marvin Jones	.50	.20
❑ 147	Terance Mathis	.75	.30
❑ 148	Rob Moore	.75	.30
❑ 149	Bruce Smith	.75	.30
❑ 150	Rob Johnson CL	.50	.20
❑ 151	Leslie Shepherd	.50	.20
❑ 152	Chris Spielman	.50	.20
❑ 153	Tony McGee	.50	.20
❑ 154	Kevin Smith	.50	.20
❑ 155	Bill Romanowski	.50	.20
❑ 156	Stephen Boyd	.50	.20
❑ 157	James Stewart	.75	.30
❑ 158	Jason Taylor	.75	.30
❑ 159	Troy Drayton	.50	.20
❑ 160	Mark Fields	.50	.20
❑ 161	Jessie Armstead	.50	.20
❑ 162	James Jett	.75	.30
❑ 163	Bobby Taylor	.50	.20
❑ 164	Kimble Anders	.75	.30
❑ 165	Jimmy Smith	.75	.30
❑ 166	Quentin Coryatt	.50	.20
❑ 167	Bryant Westbrook	.50	.20
❑ 168	Neil Smith	.75	.30
❑ 169	Darren Woodson	.50	.20
❑ 170	Ray Buchanan	.50	.20
❑ 171	Earl Holmes	.50	.20
❑ 172	Ray Lewis	1.25	.50
❑ 173	Steve Broussard	.50	.20
❑ 174	Derrick Brooks	1.25	.50
❑ 175	Ken Harvey	.50	.20
❑ 176	Darryll Lewis	.50	.20
❑ 177	Derrick Rodgers	.50	.20
❑ 178	James McKnight	1.25	.50
❑ 179	Cris Dishman	.50	.20
❑ 180	Hardy Nickerson	.50	.20
❑ 181	Charles Woodson RC	5.00	2.00
❑ 182	Randy Moss RC	20.00	7.50
❑ 183	Stephen Alexander RC	3.00	1.25
❑ 184	Samari Rolle RC	2.00	.75
❑ 185	Jamie Duncan RC	2.00	.75
❑ 186	Lance Schulters RC	2.00	.75
❑ 187	Tony Parrish RC	4.00	1.50
❑ 188	Corey Chavous RC	4.00	1.50
❑ 189	Jammi German RC	2.00	.75
❑ 190	Sam Cowart RC	3.00	1.25
❑ 191	Donald Hayes RC	3.00	1.25
❑ 192	R.W. McQuarters RC	3.00	1.25
❑ 193	Az-Zahir Hakim RC	4.00	1.50
❑ 194	Chris Fuamatu-Ma'afala RC	3.00	1.25
❑ 195	Allen Rossum RC	2.00	.75
❑ 196	Jon Ritchie RC	3.00	1.25
❑ 197	Blake Spence RC	2.00	.75
❑ 198	Brian Alford RC	2.00	.75
❑ 199	Fred Weary RC	2.00	.75
❑ 200	Rod Rutledge RC	2.00	.75
❑ 201	Michael Myers RC	2.00	.75
❑ 202	Rashaan Shehee RC	3.00	1.25
❑ 203	Donovin Darius RC	3.00	1.25
❑ 204	E.G. Green RC	3.00	1.25
❑ 205	Vonnie Holliday RC	3.00	1.25
❑ 206	Charlie Batch RC	4.00	1.50
❑ 207	Michael Pittman RC	4.00	1.50
❑ 208	Artrell Hawkins RC	2.00	.75
❑ 209	Jonathan Quinn RC	4.00	1.50
❑ 210	Kailee Wong RC	2.00	.75
❑ 211	Deshea Townsend RC	2.00	.75
❑ 212	Patrick Surtain RC	4.00	1.50
❑ 213	Brian Kelly RC	3.00	1.25
❑ 214	Tebucky Jones RC	2.00	.75
❑ 215	Pete Gonzalez RC	2.00	.75
❑ 216	Shaun Williams RC	3.00	1.25
❑ 217	Scott Frost RC	2.00	.75
❑ 218	Leonard Little RC	4.00	1.50
❑ 219	Alonzo Mayes RC	2.00	.75
❑ 220	Cordell Taylor RC	2.00	.75

1999 Bowman Chrome

❑	COMPLETE SET (220)	80.00	40.00
❑ 1	Dan Marino	4.00	1.50
❑ 2	Michael Westbrook	.75	.30
❑ 3	Yancey Thigpen	.50	.20
❑ 4	Tony Martin	.75	.30
❑ 5	Michael Strahan	.75	.30
❑ 6	Dedric Ward	.50	.20
❑ 7	Joey Galloway	.75	.30
❑ 8	Bobby Engram	.75	.30
❑ 9	Frank Sanders	.75	.30
❑ 10	Jake Plummer	.75	.30
❑ 11	Eddie Kennison	.75	.30
❑ 12	Curtis Martin	1.25	.50
❑ 13	Chris Spielman	.50	.20
❑ 14	Trent Dilfer	.75	.30
❑ 15	Tim Biakabutuka	.75	.30
❑ 16	Elvis Grbac	.75	.30
❑ 17	Charlie Batch	1.25	.50
❑ 18	Takeo Spikes	.50	.20
❑ 19	Tony Banks	.75	.30
❑ 20	Doug Flutie	1.25	.50
❑ 21	Ty Law	.75	.30
❑ 22	Isaac Bruce	1.25	.50
❑ 23	James Jett	.75	.30
❑ 24	Kent Graham	.50	.20
❑ 25	Derrick Mayes	.50	.20
❑ 26	Amani Toomer	.50	.20
❑ 27	Ray Lewis	1.25	.50
❑ 28	Shawn Springs	.50	.20
❑ 29	Warren Sapp	.50	.20
❑ 30	Jamal Anderson	1.25	.50
❑ 31	Byron Bam Morris	.50	.20
❑ 32	Johnnie Morton	.50	.20
❑ 33	Terance Mathis	.50	.20
❑ 34	Terrell Davis	1.25	.50
❑ 35	John Randle	.75	.30
❑ 36	Vinny Testaverde	.50	.20
❑ 37	Junior Seau	1.25	.50
❑ 38	Reidel Anthony	.75	.30
❑ 39	Brad Johnson	.50	.20
❑ 40	Emmitt Smith	2.50	1.00
❑ 41	Mo Lewis	.50	.20
❑ 42	Terry Glenn	1.25	.50
❑ 43	Dorsey Levens	1.25	.50
❑ 44	Thurman Thomas	.75	.30
❑ 45	Rob Moore	.75	.30
❑ 46	Corey Dillon	1.25	.50
❑ 47	Jessie Armstead	.50	.20
❑ 48	Marshall Faulk	1.50	.60
❑ 49	Charles Woodson	.50	.20
❑ 50	John Elway	4.00	1.50
❑ 51	Kevin Dyson	.75	.30
❑ 52	Tony Simmons	.50	.20
❑ 53	Keenan McCardell	.75	.30
❑ 54	O.J. Santiago	.50	.20
❑ 55	Jermaine Lewis	.75	.30
❑ 56	Herman Moore	.75	.30
❑ 57	Gary Brown	.50	.20
❑ 58	Jim Harbaugh	.75	.30
❑ 59	Mike Alstott	1.25	.50
❑ 60	Brett Favre	4.00	1.50
❑ 61	Tim Brown	1.25	.50
❑ 62	Steve McNair	.50	.20
❑ 63	Ben Coates	.75	.30
❑ 64	Jerome Pathon	.50	.20
❑ 65	Ray Buchanan	.50	.20
❑ 66	Troy Aikman	2.50	1.00
❑ 67	Andre Reed	.75	.30
❑ 68	Bubby Brister	.50	.20
❑ 69	Karim Abdul-Jabbar	.75	.30
❑ 70	Peyton Manning	4.00	1.50
❑ 71	Charles Johnson	.50	.20
❑ 72	Natrone Means	.75	.30
❑ 73	Michael Sinclair	.50	.20
❑ 74	Skip Hicks	.50	.20
❑ 75	Derrick Alexander	.50	.20
❑ 76	Wayne Chrebet	.75	.30
❑ 77	Rod Smith	.75	.30
❑ 78	Carl Pickens	.75	.30
❑ 79	Adrian Murrell	.75	.30
❑ 80	Fred Taylor	1.25	.50
❑ 81	Eric Moulds	1.25	.50
❑ 82	Lawrence Phillips	.75	.30
❑ 83	Marvin Harrison	1.25	.50
❑ 84	Cris Carter	1.25	.50
❑ 85	Ike Hilliard	.50	.20
❑ 86	Hines Ward	1.25	.50
❑ 87	Terrell Owens	1.25	.50
❑ 88	Ricky Proehl	.50	.20
❑ 89	Bert Emanuel	.75	.30
❑ 90	Randy Moss	3.00	1.25
❑ 91	Aaron Glenn	.50	.20
❑ 92	Robert Smith	1.25	.50

❑ 93	Andre Hastings	.50	.20
❑ 94	Jake Reed	.75	.30
❑ 95	Curtis Enis	.50	.20
❑ 96	Andre Wadsworth	.50	.20
❑ 97	Ed McCaffrey	.75	.30
❑ 98	Zach Thomas	1.25	.50
❑ 99	Kerry Collins	.75	.30
❑ 100	Drew Bledsoe	1.50	.60
❑ 101	Germane Crowell	.50	.20
❑ 102	Bryan Still	.50	.20
❑ 103	Chad Brown	.50	.20
❑ 104	Jacquez Green	.50	.20
❑ 105	Garrison Hearst	.75	.30
❑ 106	Napoleon Kaufman	1.25	.50
❑ 107	Ricky Watters	.75	.30
❑ 108	O.J. McDuffie	.75	.30
❑ 109	Keyshawn Johnson	1.25	.50
❑ 110	Jerome Bettis	1.25	.50
❑ 111	Duce Staley	1.25	.50
❑ 112	Curtis Conway	.75	.30
❑ 113	Chris Chandler	.75	.30
❑ 114	Marcus Nash	.50	.20
❑ 115	Stephen Alexander	.50	.20
❑ 116	Darnay Scott	.75	.30
❑ 117	Bruce Smith	.75	.30
❑ 118	Priest Holmes	2.00	.75
❑ 119	Mark Brunell	1.25	.50
❑ 120	Jerry Rice	2.50	1.00
❑ 121	Randall Cunningham	1.25	.50
❑ 122	Scott Mitchell	.50	.20
❑ 123	Antonio Freeman	1.25	.50
❑ 124	Kordell Stewart	.75	.30
❑ 125	Jon Kitna	1.25	.50
❑ 126	Ahman Green	1.25	.50
❑ 127	Warrick Dunn	1.25	.50
❑ 128	Robert Brooks	.75	.30
❑ 129	Derrick Thomas	1.25	.50
❑ 130	Steve Young	1.50	.60
❑ 131	Peter Boulware	.50	.20
❑ 132	Michael Irvin	.75	.30
❑ 133	Shannon Sharpe	.75	.30
❑ 134	Jimmy Smith	.75	.30
❑ 135	John Avery	.50	.20
❑ 136	Fred Lane	.50	.20
❑ 137	Trent Green	1.25	.50
❑ 138	Andre Rison	.75	.30
❑ 139	Antowain Smith	1.25	.50
❑ 140	Eddie George	1.25	.50
❑ 141	Jeff Blake	.75	.30
❑ 142	Rocket Ismail	.75	.30
❑ 143	Rickey Dudley	.50	.20
❑ 144	Courtney Hawkins	.50	.20
❑ 145	Mikhael Ricks	.50	.20
❑ 146	J.J. Stokes	.75	.30
❑ 147	Levon Kirkland	.50	.20
❑ 148	Deion Sanders	1.25	.50
❑ 149	Barry Sanders	4.00	1.50
❑ 150	Tiki Barber	1.25	.50
❑ 151	David Boston RC	2.00	.75
❑ 152	Chris McAlister RC	1.25	.50
❑ 153	Peerless Price RC	2.00	.75
❑ 154	D'Wayne Bates RC	1.25	.50
❑ 155	Cade McNown RC	1.25	.50
❑ 156	Akili Smith RC	1.25	.50
❑ 157	Kevin Johnson RC	2.00	.75
❑ 158	Tim Couch RC	2.00	.75
❑ 159	Sedrick Irvin RC	1.00	.40
❑ 160	Chris Claiborne RC	1.00	.40
❑ 161	Edgerrin James RC	10.00	4.00
❑ 162	Mike Cloud RC	1.25	.50
❑ 163	Cecil Collins RC	1.00	.40
❑ 164	James Johnson RC	1.25	.50
❑ 165	Rob Konrad RC	2.00	.75
❑ 166	Daunte Culpepper RC	10.00	4.00
❑ 167	Kevin Faulk RC	2.00	.75
❑ 168	Donovan McNabb RC	12.00	5.00
❑ 169	Troy Edwards RC	1.25	.50
❑ 170	Amos Zereoue RC	2.00	.75
❑ 171	Karsten Bailey RC	1.25	.50
❑ 172	Brock Huard RC	2.00	.75
❑ 173	Joe Germaine RC	1.25	.50
❑ 174	Torry Holt RC	6.00	2.50
❑ 175	Shaun King RC	1.25	.50
❑ 176	Jevon Kearse RC	4.00	1.50
❑ 177	Champ Bailey RC	3.00	1.25
❑ 178	Ebenezer Ekuban RC	1.25	.50
❑ 179	Andy Katzenmoyer RC	1.25	.50
❑ 180	Antoine Winfield RC	1.25	.50
❑ 181	Jermaine Fazande RC	1.25	.50
❑ 182	Ricky Williams RC	5.00	2.00
❑ 183	Joel Makovicka RC	2.00	.75
❑ 184	Reginald Kelly RC	1.25	.50
❑ 185	Brandon Stokley RC	2.50	1.00
❑ 186	L.C. Stevens RC	1.00	.40
❑ 187	Marty Booker RC	2.00	.75
❑ 188	Jerry Azumah RC	1.25	.50
❑ 189	Ted White RC	1.00	.40
❑ 190	Scott Covington RC	2.00	.75
❑ 191	Tim Alexander RC	1.00	.40
❑ 192	Darrin Chiaverini RC	1.25	.50
❑ 193	Dat Nguyen RC	2.00	.75
❑ 194	Wane McGarity RC	1.00	.40
❑ 195	Al Wilson RC	2.00	.75
❑ 196	Travis McGriff RC	1.00	.40
❑ 197	Stacey Mack RC	2.00	.75
❑ 198	Antuan Edwards RC	1.00	.40
❑ 199	Aaron Brooks RC	5.00	2.00
❑ 200	De'Mond Parker RC	1.00	.40
❑ 201	Jed Weaver RC	1.00	.40
❑ 202	Madre Hill RC	1.00	.40
❑ 203	Jim Kleinsasser RC	2.00	.75
❑ 204	Michael Bishop RC	2.00	.75
❑ 205	Michael Basnight RC	1.00	.40
❑ 206	Sean Bennett RC	1.00	.40
❑ 207	Dameane Douglas RC	1.25	.50
❑ 208	Na Brown RC	1.25	.50
❑ 209	Patrick Kerney RC	2.00	.75
❑ 210	Malcolm Johnson RC	1.00	.40
❑ 211	Dre Bly RC	2.00	.75
❑ 212	Terry Jackson RC	1.25	.50
❑ 213	Eugene Baker RC	1.00	.40
❑ 214	Autry Denson RC	1.25	.50
❑ 215	Darnell McDonald RC	1.25	.50
❑ 216	Charlie Rogers RC	1.25	.50
❑ 217	Joe Montgomery RC	1.25	.50
❑ 218	Cecil Martin RC	1.25	.50
❑ 219	Larry Parker RC	2.00	.75
❑ 220	Mike Peterson RC	1.25	.50

2000 Bowman Chrome

❑ 1	Eddie George	1.00	.40
❑ 2	Ike Hilliard	.60	.25
❑ 3	Terrell Owens	1.00	.40
❑ 4	James Stewart	.60	.25
❑ 5	Joey Galloway	.60	.25
❑ 6	Jake Reed	.40	.15
❑ 7	Derrick Alexander	.60	.25
❑ 8	Jeff George	.60	.25
❑ 9	Kerry Collins	.60	.25
❑ 10	Tony Gonzalez	.60	.25
❑ 11	Marcus Robinson	1.00	.40
❑ 12	Charles Woodson	.60	.25
❑ 13	Germane Crowell	.40	.15
❑ 14	Yancey Thigpen	.40	.15
❑ 15	Tony Martin	.40	.15
❑ 16	Frank Sanders	.60	.25
❑ 17	Napoleon Kaufman	.60	.25
❑ 18	Jay Fiedler	1.00	.40
❑ 19	Patrick Jeffers	1.00	.40
❑ 20	Steve McNair	1.00	.40
❑ 21	Herman Moore	.60	.25
❑ 22	Tim Brown	1.00	.40
❑ 23	Olandis Gary	1.00	.40
❑ 24	Corey Dillon	1.00	.40
❑ 25	Warren Sapp	.60	.25
❑ 26	Curtis Enis	.40	.15
❑ 27	Vinny Testaverde	.60	.25
❑ 28	Tim Biakabutuka	.60	.25
❑ 29	Kevin Johnson	1.00	.40
❑ 30	Charlie Batch	1.00	.40
❑ 31	Jermaine Fazande	.60	.25
❑ 32	Shaun King	.40	.15
❑ 33	Errict Rhett	.60	.25
❑ 34	O.J. McDuffie	.60	.25
❑ 35	Bruce Smith	.60	.25
❑ 36	Antonio Freeman	1.00	.40
❑ 37	Tim Couch	.60	.25
❑ 38	Duce Staley	1.00	.40
❑ 39	Jeff Blake	.60	.25
❑ 40	Jim Harbaugh	.60	.25
❑ 41	Jeff Graham	.40	.15
❑ 42	Drew Bledsoe	1.25	.50
❑ 43	Mike Alstott	1.00	.40
❑ 44	Terance Mathis	.60	.25
❑ 45	Antowain Smith	.60	.25
❑ 46	Johnnie Morton	.60	.25
❑ 47	Chris Chandler	.60	.25
❑ 48	Keith Poole	.40	.15
❑ 49	Ricky Watters	.60	.25
❑ 50	Darnay Scott	.40	.15
❑ 51	Damon Huard	.60	.25
❑ 52	Peerless Price	.60	.25
❑ 53	Brian Griese	1.00	.40
❑ 54	Frank Wycheck	.60	.25
❑ 55	Kevin Dyson	.60	.25
❑ 56	Junior Seau	1.00	.40
❑ 57	Curtis Conway	.60	.25
❑ 58	Jamal Anderson	1.00	.40
❑ 59	Jim Miller	.40	.15
❑ 60	Rob Johnson	.60	.25
❑ 61	Mark Brunell	1.00	.40
❑ 62	Wayne Chrebet	.60	.25
❑ 63	James Johnson	.40	.15
❑ 64	Sean Dawkins	.40	.15
❑ 65	Stephen Davis	1.00	.40
❑ 66	Daunte Culpepper	1.25	.50
❑ 67	Doug Flutie	1.00	.40
❑ 68	Pete Mitchell	.40	.15
❑ 69	Bill Schroeder	.40	.15
❑ 70	Terrence Wilkins	.40	.15
❑ 71	Cade McNown	.40	.15
❑ 72	Muhsin Muhammad	.60	.25
❑ 73	E.G. Green	.40	.15
❑ 74	Edgerrin James	1.50	.60
❑ 75	Troy Edwards	.40	.15
❑ 76	Terry Glenn	.60	.25
❑ 77	Tony Banks	.60	.25
❑ 78	Derrick Mayes	.60	.25
❑ 79	Curtis Martin	1.00	.40
❑ 80	Kordell Stewart	.60	.25
❑ 81	Amani Toomer	.60	.25
❑ 82	Dorsey Levens	.60	.25
❑ 83	Brad Johnson	1.00	.40
❑ 84	Ed McCaffrey	1.00	.40
❑ 85	Charlie Garner	.60	.25
❑ 86	Brett Favre	3.00	1.25
❑ 87	J.J. Stokes	.60	.25
❑ 88	Steve Young	1.25	.50
❑ 89	Jonathan Linton	.40	.15
❑ 90	Isaac Bruce	1.00	.40
❑ 91	Shawn Jefferson	.40	.15
❑ 92	Rod Smith	.60	.25
❑ 93	Champ Bailey	.60	.25
❑ 94	Ricky Williams	1.00	.40
❑ 95	Priest Holmes	1.25	.50
❑ 96	Corey Bradford	.60	.25
❑ 97	Eric Moulds	1.00	.40
❑ 98	Warrick Dunn	1.00	.40
❑ 99	Jevon Kearse	1.00	.40
❑ 100	Albert Connell	.40	.15
❑ 101	Az-Zahir Hakim	.40	.15
❑ 102	Marvin Harrison	1.00	.40
❑ 103	Qadry Ismail	.60	.25
❑ 104	Oronde Gadsden	.60	.25
❑ 105	Rob Moore	.60	.25
❑ 106	Marshall Faulk	1.50	.60
❑ 107	Steve Beuerlein	.60	.25
❑ 108	Torry Holt	1.00	.40
❑ 109	Donovan McNabb	1.50	.60
❑ 110	Rich Gannon	1.00	.40
❑ 111	Jerome Bettis	1.00	.40
❑ 112	Peyton Manning	2.50	1.00
❑ 113	Cris Carter	1.00	.40
❑ 114	Jake Plummer	.60	.25
❑ 115	Kent Graham	.40	.15
❑ 116	Keenan McCardell	.60	.25
❑ 117	Tim Dwight	1.00	.40
❑ 118	Fred Taylor	1.00	.40
❑ 119	Jerry Rice	2.00	.75
❑ 120	Michael Westbrook	.60	.25

❑ 121 Kurt Warner 2.00 .75
❑ 122 Jimmy Smith .60 .25
❑ 123 Emmitt Smith 2.00 .75
❑ 124 Terrell Davis 1.00 .40
❑ 125 Randy Moss 2.00 .75
❑ 126 Akili Smith .40 .15
❑ 127 Rocket Ismail .60 .25
❑ 128 Jon Kitna 1.00 .40
❑ 129 Elvis Grbac .60 .25
❑ 130 Wesley Walls .40 .15
❑ 131 Torrance Small .40 .15
❑ 132 Tyrone Wheatley .60 .25
❑ 133 Carl Pickens .40 .15
❑ 134 Zach Thomas 1.00 .40
❑ 135 Jacquez Green .40 .15
❑ 136 Robert Smith 1.00 .40
❑ 137 Keyshawn Johnson 1.00 .40
❑ 138 Matthew Hatchette .40 .15
❑ 139 Troy Aikman 2.00 .75
❑ 140 Charles Johnson .60 .25
❑ 141 Terry Battle EP 1.00 .40
❑ 142 Pepe Pearson EP RC 2.00 .75
❑ 143 Cory Sauter EP 1.00 .40
❑ 144 Brian Shay EP 1.00 .40
❑ 145 Marcus Crandell EP RC 1.50 .60
❑ 146 Danny Wuerffel EP 1.50 .60
❑ 147 L.C. Stevens EP 1.00 .40
❑ 148 Ted White EP 1.00 .40
❑ 149 Matt Lytle EP RC 1.50 .60
❑ 150 Vershan Jackson EP RC 1.00 .40
❑ 151 Mario Bailey EP 1.00 .40
❑ 152 Darryl Daniel EP RC 1.50 .60
❑ 153 Sean Morey EP RC 1.50 .60
❑ 154 Jim Kubiak EP RC 1.50 .60
❑ 155 Aaron Stecker EP RC 2.00 .75
❑ 156 Damon Dunn EP RC 1.50 .60
❑ 157 Kevin Daft EP 1.00 .40
❑ 158 Corey Thomas EP 1.00 .40
❑ 159 Deon Mitchell EP RC 1.50 .60
❑ 160 Todd Floyd EP RC 1.00 .40
❑ 161 Norman Miller EP RC 1.00 .40
❑ 162 Jeremaine Copeland EP 1.00 .40
❑ 163 Michael Blair EP 1.00 .40
❑ 164 Ron Powlus EP RC 2.00 .75
❑ 165 Pat Barnes EP 1.50 .60
❑ 166 Dez White RC 4.00 1.50
❑ 167 Trung Canidate SP RC 25.00 10.00
❑ 168 Thomas Jones SP RC 40.00 20.00
❑ 169 Courtney Brown SP RC 30.00 12.50
❑ 170 Jamal Lewis SP RC 50.00 20.00
❑ 171 Chris Redman SP RC 25.00 10.00
❑ 172 Ron Dayne SP RC 30.00 12.50
❑ 173 Chad Pennington SP RC 50.00 25.00
❑ 174 Plaxico Burress SP RC 60.00 25.00
❑ 175 R.Jay Soward SP RC 25.00 10.00
❑ 176 Travis Taylor SP RC 30.00 12.50
❑ 177 Shaun Alexander SP RC 80.00 40.00
❑ 178 Brian Urlacher RC 20.00 10.00
❑ 179 Danny Farmer RC 3.00 1.25
❑ 180 Tee Martin SP RC 30.00 12.50
❑ 181 Sylvester Morris SP RC 25.00 10.00
❑ 182 Curtis Keaton RC 3.00 1.25
❑ 183 Peter Warrick SP RC 30.00 12.50
❑ 184 Anthony Becht RC 4.00 1.50
❑ 185 Travis Prentice SP RC 30.00 12.50
❑ 186 J.R. Redmond SP RC 25.00 10.00
❑ 187 Bubba Franks SP RC 30.00 12.50
❑ 188 Ron Dugans SP RC 20.00 7.50
❑ 189 Reuben Droughns RC 5.00 2.00
❑ 190 Corey Simon RC 2.00 .75
❑ 191 Joe Hamilton RC 3.00 1.25
❑ 192 Laveranues Coles RC 5.00 2.00
❑ 193 Todd Pinkston SP RC 30.00 12.50
❑ 194 Jerry Porter SP RC 50.00 20.00
❑ 195 Dennis Northcutt RC 4.00 1.50
❑ 196 Tim Rattay RC 4.00 1.50
❑ 197 Giovanni Carmazzi RC 2.00 .75
❑ 198 Mareno Philyaw RC 2.00 .75
❑ 199 Avion Black RC 3.00 1.25
❑ 200 Chafie Fields RC 2.00 .75
❑ 201 Rondell Mealey RC 2.00 .75
❑ 202 Troy Walters RC 4.00 1.50
❑ 203 Frank Moreau RC 3.00 1.25
❑ 204 Vaughn Sanders RC 2.00 .75
❑ 205 Sherrod Gideon RC 2.00 .75
❑ 206 Doug Chapman RC 3.00 1.25
❑ 207 Marcus Knight RC 3.00 1.25
❑ 208 Jamel White RC 3.00 1.25
❑ 209 Windrell Hayes RC 3.00 1.25
❑ 210 Reggie Jones RC 2.00 .75
❑ 211 Jarious Jackson RC 3.00 1.25
❑ 212 Ronney Jenkins RC 3.00 1.25
❑ 213 Quinton Spotwood RC 2.00 .75
❑ 214 Rob Morris RC 3.00 1.25
❑ 215 Gari Scott RC 2.00 .75
❑ 216 Kevin Thompson RC 2.00 .75
❑ 217 Trevor Insley RC 2.00 .75
❑ 218 Frank Murphy RC 2.00 .75
❑ 219 Patrick Pass RC 3.00 1.25
❑ 220 Mike Anderson RC 2.50 1.00
❑ 221 Derrius Thompson RC 4.00 1.50
❑ 222 John Abraham RC 6.00 2.50
❑ 223 Dante Hall RC 8.00 3.00
❑ 224 Chad Morton RC 4.00 1.50
❑ 225 Ahmed Plummer RC 4.00 1.50
❑ 226 Julian Peterson RC 4.00 1.50
❑ 227 Mike Green RC 3.00 1.25
❑ 228 Michael Wiley RC 3.00 1.25
❑ 229 Spergon Wynn RC 3.00 1.25
❑ 230 Trevor Gaylor RC 3.00 1.25
❑ 231 Doug Johnson RC 4.00 1.50
❑ 232 Marc Bulger RC 8.00 3.00
❑ 233 Ron Dixon RC 3.00 1.25
❑ 234 Aaron Shea RC 1.50 .60
❑ 235 Thomas Hamner RC 2.00 .75
❑ 236 Tom Brady RC 60.00 30.00
❑ 237 Deltha O'Neal RC 4.00 1.50
❑ 238 Todd Husak RC 4.00 1.50
❑ 239 Erron Kinney RC 4.00 1.50
❑ 240 JaJuan Dawson RC 2.00 .75
❑ 241 Nick Williams 1.00 .40
❑ 242 Deon Grant RC 3.00 1.25
❑ 243 Brad Hoover RC 3.00 1.25
❑ 244 Kamil Loud .40 .15
❑ 245 Rashard Anderson RC 3.00 1.25
❑ 246 Clint Stoerner RC 1.50 .60
❑ 247 Antwan Harris RC 2.00 .75
❑ 248 Jason Webster RC 2.00 .75
❑ 249 Kevin McDougal RC 3.00 1.25
❑ 250 Tony Scott RC 2.00 .75
❑ 251 Thabiti Davis RC 2.00 .75
❑ 252 Ian Gold RC 3.00 1.25
❑ 253 Sammy Morris RC 3.00 1.25
❑ 254 Raynoch Thompson RC 3.00 1.25
❑ 255 Jeremy McDaniel 1.00 .40
❑ 256 Terrelle Smith RC 3.00 1.25
❑ 257 Deon Dyer RC 3.00 1.25
❑ 258 Na'il Diggs RC 3.00 1.25
❑ 259 Brandon Short RC 3.00 1.25
❑ 260 Mike Brown RC 8.00 3.00
❑ 261 John Engelberger RC 3.00 1.25
❑ 262 Rogers Beckett RC 3.00 1.25
❑ 263 JaJuan Seider RC 2.00 .75
❑ 264 Desmond Kitchings RC 3.00 1.25
❑ 265 Reggie Davis RC 3.00 1.25
❑ 266 Corey Moore RC 2.00 .75
❑ 267 Cornelius Griffin RC 3.00 1.25
❑ 268 Stockar McDougle RC 2.00 .75
❑ 269 James Williams RC 3.00 1.25
❑ 270 Darrell Jackson RC 6.00 2.50

2001 Bowman Chrome

❑ COMP.SET w/o SP's (110) 25.00 10.00
❑ 1 Emmitt Smith 2.00 .75
❑ 2 James Stewart .60 .25
❑ 3 Jeff Graham .40 .15
❑ 4 Keyshawn Johnson 1.00 .40
❑ 5 Stephen Davis 1.00 .40
❑ 6 Chad Lewis .40 .15
❑ 7 Drew Bledsoe 1.25 .50
❑ 8 Fred Taylor 1.00 .40
❑ 9 Mike Anderson 1.00 .40
❑ 10 Tony Gonzalez .60 .25
❑ 11 Aaron Brooks 1.00 .40
❑ 12 Vinny Testaverde .60 .25
❑ 13 Jerome Bettis 1.00 .40
❑ 14 Marshall Faulk 1.25 .50
❑ 15 Jeff Garcia 1.00 .40
❑ 16 Terry Glenn .60 .25
❑ 17 Jay Fiedler 1.00 .40
❑ 18 Ahman Green 1.00 .40
❑ 19 Cade McNown .40 .15
❑ 20 Rob Johnson .60 .25
❑ 21 Jamal Anderson 1.00 .40
❑ 22 Corey Dillon 1.00 .40
❑ 23 Jake Plummer .60 .25
❑ 24 Rod Smith .60 .25
❑ 25 Trent Green 1.00 .40
❑ 26 Ricky Williams 1.00 .40
❑ 27 Charlie Garner .60 .25
❑ 28 Shaun Alexander 1.25 .50
❑ 29 Jeff George .60 .25
❑ 30 Torry Holt 1.00 .40
❑ 31 James Thrash .60 .25
❑ 32 Rich Gannon 1.00 .40
❑ 33 Ron Dayne 1.00 .40
❑ 34 Dedric Ward .40 .15
❑ 35 Edgerrin James 1.25 .50
❑ 36 Cris Carter 1.00 .40
❑ 37 Derrick Mason .60 .25
❑ 38 Brad Johnson 1.00 .40
❑ 39 Charlie Batch 1.00 .40
❑ 40 Joey Galloway .60 .25
❑ 41 James Allen .60 .25
❑ 42 Tim Biakabutuka .60 .25
❑ 43 Ray Lewis 1.00 .40
❑ 44 David Boston 1.00 .40
❑ 45 Kevin Johnson .60 .25
❑ 46 Jimmy Smith .60 .25
❑ 47 Joe Horn .60 .25
❑ 48 Terrell Owens 1.00 .40
❑ 49 Eddie George 1.00 .40
❑ 50 Brett Favre 3.00 1.25
❑ 51 Wayne Chrebet .60 .25
❑ 52 Hines Ward 1.00 .40
❑ 53 Warrick Dunn 1.00 .40
❑ 54 Matt Hasselbeck .60 .25
❑ 55 Tiki Barber 1.00 .40
❑ 56 Lamar Smith .60 .25
❑ 57 Tim Couch .60 .25
❑ 58 Eric Moulds .60 .25
❑ 59 Shawn Jefferson .40 .15
❑ 60 Donald Hayes .40 .15
❑ 61 Brian Urlacher 1.50 .60
❑ 62 Steve McNair 1.00 .40
❑ 63 Kurt Warner 2.00 .75
❑ 64 Tim Brown 1.00 .40
❑ 65 Troy Brown .60 .25
❑ 66 Albert Connell .40 .15
❑ 67 Peyton Manning 2.50 1.00
❑ 68 Peter Warrick 1.00 .40
❑ 69 Elvis Grbac .60 .25
❑ 70 Chris Chandler .60 .25
❑ 71 Akili Smith .40 .15
❑ 72 Keenan McCardell .40 .15
❑ 73 Kerry Collins .60 .25
❑ 74 Junior Seau 1.00 .40
❑ 75 Donovan McNabb 1.25 .50
❑ 76 Tony Banks .60 .25
❑ 77 Steve Beuerlein .60 .25
❑ 78 Daunte Culpepper 1.00 .40
❑ 79 Darrell Jackson 1.00 .40
❑ 80 Isaac Bruce 1.00 .40
❑ 81 Tyrone Wheatley .60 .25
❑ 82 Derrick Alexander .60 .25
❑ 83 Germane Crowell .40 .15
❑ 84 Jon Kitna .60 .25
❑ 85 Jamal Lewis 1.50 .60
❑ 86 Ed McCaffrey 1.00 .40
❑ 87 Mark Brunell 1.00 .40
❑ 88 Jeff Blake .60 .25
❑ 89 Duce Staley 1.00 .40
❑ 90 Doug Flutie 1.00 .40
❑ 91 Kordell Stewart .60 .25
❑ 92 Randy Moss 2.00 .75
❑ 93 Marvin Harrison 1.00 .40
❑ 94 Muhsin Muhammad .60 .25
❑ 95 Brian Griese 1.00 .40
❑ 96 Antonio Freeman 1.00 .40
❑ 97 Amani Toomer .60 .25

❑ 98 Oronde Gadsden	.60	.25
❑ 99 Curtis Martin	1.00	.40
❑ 100 Jerry Rice	2.00	.75
❑ 101 Michael Pittman	.40	.15
❑ 102 Shannon Sharpe	.60	.25
❑ 103 Peerless Price	.60	.25
❑ 104 Bill Schroeder	.60	.25
❑ 105 Ike Hilliard	.60	.25
❑ 106 Freddie Jones	.40	.15
❑ 107 Tai Streets	.40	.15
❑ 108 Ricky Watters	.60	.25
❑ 109 Az-Zahir Hakim	.40	.15
❑ 110 Jacquez Green	.40	.15
❑ 111 George Layne RC	5.00	2.00
❑ 112 Correll Buckhalter RC	10.00	4.00
❑ 113 Tony Stewart RC	8.00	3.00
❑ 114 Chris Barnes RC	5.00	2.00
❑ 115 A.J. Feeley RC	8.00	3.00
❑ 116 Margin Hooks RC	3.00	1.25
❑ 117 Anthony Henry RC	8.00	3.00
❑ 118 Dwight Smith RC	3.00	1.25
❑ 119 Torrance Marshall RC	8.00	3.00
❑ 120 Gary Baxter RC	5.00	2.00
❑ 121 Derek Combs RC	5.00	2.00
❑ 122 Marcus Bell RC	5.00	2.00
❑ 123 DeLawrence Grant RC	3.00	1.25
❑ 124 Jameel Cook RC	5.00	2.00
❑ 125 Eric Downing RC	3.00	1.25
❑ 126 Marlon McCree RC	5.00	2.00
❑ 127 Tay Cody RC	3.00	1.25
❑ 128 Mario Monds RC	3.00	1.25
❑ 129 Kenny Smith RC	5.00	2.00
❑ 130 Sedrick Hodge RC	3.00	1.25
❑ 131 Marcus Stroud RC	8.00	3.00
❑ 132 Steve Smith RC	30.00	15.00
❑ 133 Tyrone Robertson RC	3.00	1.25
❑ 134 James Reed RC	3.00	1.25
❑ 135 Kris Kocurek RC	3.00	1.25
❑ 136 Dan O'Leary RC	5.00	2.00
❑ 137 Harold Blackmon RC	3.00	1.25
❑ 138 Fred Smoot RC	8.00	3.00
❑ 139 Billy Baber RC	3.00	1.25
❑ 140 Jarrod Cooper RC	8.00	3.00
❑ 141 Travis Henry RC	12.00	5.00
❑ 142 David Terrell RC	8.00	3.00
❑ 143 Josh Heupel RC	8.00	3.00
❑ 144 Drew Brees RC	40.00	20.00
❑ 145 T.J. Houshmandzadeh RC	10.00	4.00
❑ 146 Rod Gardner RC	8.00	3.00
❑ 147 Richard Seymour RC	8.00	3.00
❑ 148 Koren Robinson RC	8.00	3.00
❑ 149 Scotty Anderson RC	5.00	2.00
❑ 150 Marques Tuiasosopo RC	8.00	3.00
❑ 151 John Capel RC	5.00	2.00
❑ 152 LaMont Jordan RC	15.00	6.00
❑ 153 James Jackson RC	8.00	3.00
❑ 154 Bobby Newcombe RC	5.00	2.00
❑ 155 Anthony Thomas RC	8.00	3.00
❑ 156 Dan Alexander RC	8.00	3.00
❑ 157 Quincy Carter RC	8.00	3.00
❑ 158 Morlon Greenwood RC	5.00	2.00
❑ 159 Robert Ferguson RC	8.00	3.00
❑ 160 Sage Rosenfels RC	8.00	3.00
❑ 161 Michael Stone RC	3.00	1.25
❑ 162 Chris Weinke RC	8.00	3.00
❑ 163 Travis Minor RC	5.00	2.00
❑ 164 Gerard Warren RC	8.00	3.00
❑ 165 Jamar Fletcher RC	5.00	2.00
❑ 166 Andre Carter RC	8.00	3.00
❑ 167 Deuce McAllister RC	15.00	7.50
❑ 168 Dan Morgan RC	8.00	3.00
❑ 169 Todd Heap RC	8.00	3.00
❑ 170 Snoop Minnis RC	5.00	2.00
❑ 171 Will Allen RC	5.00	2.00
❑ 172 Freddie Mitchell RC	8.00	3.00
❑ 173 Rudi Johnson RC	15.00	6.00
❑ 174 Kevan Barlow RC	8.00	3.00
❑ 175 Jamie Winborn RC	5.00	2.00
❑ 176 Onome Ojo RC	5.00	2.00
❑ 177 Leonard Davis RC	5.00	2.00
❑ 178 Santana Moss RC	12.00	5.00
❑ 179 Chris Chambers RC	12.00	5.00
❑ 180 Michael Vick RC	60.00	30.00
❑ 181 Michael Bennett RC	8.00	3.00
❑ 182 Mike McMahon RC	8.00	3.00
❑ 183 Jonathan Carter RC	5.00	2.00
❑ 184 Jamal Reynolds RC	8.00	3.00
❑ 185 Justin Smith RC	8.00	3.00
❑ 186 Quincy Morgan RC	8.00	3.00
❑ 187 Chad Johnson RC	30.00	12.00
❑ 188 Jesse Palmer RC	8.00	3.00
❑ 189 Reggie Wayne RC	20.00	10.00
❑ 190 LaDainian Tomlinson RC	150.00	90.00
❑ 191 Andre King RC	5.00	2.00
❑ 192 Richmond Flowers RC	5.00	2.00
❑ 193 Derrick Blaylock RC	8.00	3.00
❑ 194 Cedrick Wilson RC	8.00	3.00
❑ 195 Zeke Moreno RC	8.00	3.00
❑ 196 Tommy Polley RC	8.00	3.00
❑ 197 Damione Lewis RC	5.00	2.00
❑ 198 Aaron Schobel RC	8.00	3.00
❑ 199 Alge Crumpler RC	12.00	5.00
❑ 200 Nate Clements RC	8.00	3.00
❑ 201 Quentin McCord RC	5.00	2.00
❑ 202 Ken-Yon Rambo RC	5.00	2.00
❑ 203 Milton Wynn RC	5.00	2.00
❑ 204 Derrick Gibson RC	5.00	2.00
❑ 205 Chris Taylor RC	5.00	2.00
❑ 206 Corey Hall RC	3.00	1.25
❑ 207 Vinny Sutherland RC	5.00	2.00
❑ 208 Kendrell Bell RC	12.00	5.00
❑ 209 Casey Hampton RC	8.00	3.00
❑ 210 Demetric Evans RC	3.00	1.25
❑ 211 Brian Allen RC	3.00	1.25
❑ 212 Rodney Bailey RC	3.00	1.25
❑ 213 Otis Leverette RC	3.00	1.25
❑ 214 Ron Edwards RC	3.00	1.25
❑ 215 Michael Jameson RC	3.00	1.25
❑ 216 Markus Steele RC	5.00	2.00
❑ 217 Jimmy Williams RC	3.00	1.25
❑ 218 Roger Knight RC	3.00	1.25
❑ 219 Randy Garner RC	3.00	1.25
❑ 220 Raymond Perryman RC	3.00	1.25
❑ 221 Karon Riley RC	3.00	1.25
❑ 222 Adam Archuleta RC	8.00	3.00
❑ 223 Arnold Jackson RC	5.00	2.00
❑ 224 Ryan Pickett RC	3.00	1.25
❑ 225 Shad Meier RC	5.00	2.00
❑ 226 Reggie Germany RC	5.00	2.00
❑ 227 Justin McCareins RC	8.00	3.00
❑ 228 Idrees Bashir RC	3.00	1.25
❑ 229 Josh Booty RC	8.00	3.00
❑ 230 Eddie Berlin RC	5.00	2.00
❑ 231 Heath Evans RC	5.00	2.00
❑ 232 Alex Bannister RC	5.00	2.00
❑ 233 Corey Alston RC	3.00	1.25
❑ 234 Reggie White RC	5.00	2.00
❑ 235 Orlando Huff RC	3.00	1.25
❑ 236 Ken Lucas RC	5.00	2.00
❑ 237 Matt Stewart RC	3.00	1.25
❑ 238 Cedric Scott RC	5.00	2.00
❑ 239 Ronney Daniels RC	3.00	1.25
❑ 240 Kevin Kasper RC	8.00	3.00
❑ 241 Tony Driver RC	5.00	2.00
❑ 242 Kyle Vanden Bosch RC	8.00	3.00
❑ 243 T.J. Turner RC	3.00	1.25
❑ 244 Eric Westmoreland RC	5.00	2.00
❑ 245 Ronald Flemons RC	3.00	1.25
❑ 246 Eric Kelly RC	3.00	1.25
❑ 247 Moran Norris RC	3.00	1.25
❑ 248 Damerien McCants RC	5.00	2.00
❑ 249 James Boyd RC	3.00	1.25
❑ 250 Keith Adams RC	3.00	1.25
❑ 251 Brandon Manumaleuna RC	5.00	2.00
❑ 252 Dee Brown RC	8.00	3.00
❑ 253 Ross Kolodziej RC	3.00	1.25
❑ 254 Boo Williams RC	5.00	2.00
❑ 255 Patrick Chukwurah RC	3.00	1.25

2002 Bowman Chrome

❑ COMP.SET w/o SP's (110)	25.00	10.00
❑ 1 Emmitt Smith	2.50	1.00
❑ 2 Drew Brees	1.00	.40
❑ 3 Duce Staley	1.00	.40
❑ 4 Curtis Martin	1.00	.40
❑ 5 Isaac Bruce	1.00	.40
❑ 6 Stephen Davis	.60	.25
❑ 7 Darrell Jackson	.60	.25
❑ 8 James Stewart	.60	.25
❑ 9 Tim Couch	.60	.25
❑ 10 Travis Henry	1.00	.40
❑ 11 Thomas Jones	.60	.25
❑ 12 Jamal Lewis	1.00	.40
❑ 13 Chris Chambers	1.00	.40
❑ 14 Jeff Blake	.60	.25
❑ 15 Plaxico Burress	.60	.25
❑ 16 Michael Pittman	.40	.15
❑ 17 Jeff Garcia	1.00	.40
❑ 18 Tim Brown	1.00	.40
❑ 19 Kent Graham	.40	.15
❑ 20 Shannon Sharpe	.60	.25
❑ 21 Corey Dillon	.60	.25
❑ 22 Muhsin Muhammad	.60	.25
❑ 23 Tony Gonzalez	.60	.25
❑ 24 Qadry Ismail	.60	.25
❑ 25 Mike McMahon	1.00	.40
❑ 26 Edgerrin James	1.25	.50
❑ 27 Daunte Culpepper	1.00	.40
❑ 28 Deuce McAllister	1.25	.50
❑ 29 Kerry Collins	.60	.25
❑ 30 Eddie George	1.00	.40
❑ 31 Torry Holt	1.00	.40
❑ 32 Todd Pinkston	.60	.25
❑ 33 Quincy Carter	.60	.25
❑ 34 Rod Smith	.60	.25
❑ 35 Michael Vick	3.00	1.25
❑ 36 Jim Miller	.60	.25
❑ 37 Troy Brown	.60	.25
❑ 38 Wayne Chrebet	.60	.25
❑ 39 Curtis Conway	.40	.15
❑ 40 Reidel Anthony	.40	.15
❑ 41 Mark Brunell	1.00	.40
❑ 42 Chris Weinke	.60	.25
❑ 43 Eric Moulds	.60	.25
❑ 44 Ike Hilliard	.60	.25
❑ 45 Jay Fiedler	.60	.25
❑ 46 Keyshawn Johnson	1.00	.40
❑ 47 Rod Gardner	.60	.25
❑ 48 Chris Redman	.40	.15
❑ 49 James Allen	.60	.25
❑ 50 Kordell Stewart	.60	.25
❑ 51 Priest Holmes	1.25	.50
❑ 52 Anthony Thomas	.60	.25
❑ 53 Peter Warrick	.60	.25
❑ 54 Jake Plummer	.60	.25
❑ 55 Jerry Rice	2.00	.75
❑ 56 Joe Horn	.60	.25
❑ 57 Derrick Mason	.60	.25
❑ 58 Kurt Warner	1.00	.40
❑ 59 Antowain Smith	.60	.25
❑ 60 Randy Moss	2.00	.75
❑ 61 Warrick Dunn	1.00	.40
❑ 62 Laveranues Coles	.60	.25
❑ 63 LaDainian Tomlinson	1.50	.60
❑ 64 Michael Westbrook	.60	.25
❑ 65 Travis Taylor	.60	.25
❑ 66 Brian Griese	1.00	.40
❑ 67 Bill Schroeder	.60	.25
❑ 68 Ahman Green	1.00	.40
❑ 69 Jimmy Smith	.60	.25
❑ 70 Charlie Garner	.60	.25
❑ 71 Terrell Owens	1.00	.40
❑ 72 Brad Johnson	.60	.25
❑ 73 James Thrash	.60	.25
❑ 74 Marvin Harrison	1.00	.40
❑ 75 Brett Favre	2.50	1.00
❑ 76 Rocket Ismail	.60	.25
❑ 77 David Boston	1.00	.40
❑ 78 Jermaine Lewis	.40	.15
❑ 79 Aaron Brooks	1.00	.40
❑ 80 Shaun Alexander	1.25	.50
❑ 81 Steve McNair	1.00	.40
❑ 82 Marshall Faulk	1.00	.40
❑ 83 Terrell Davis	1.00	.40
❑ 84 Corey Bradford	.40	.15
❑ 85 David Terrell	1.00	.40
❑ 86 Kevin Johnson	.60	.25
❑ 87 Jon Kitna	.60	.25
❑ 88 Az-Zahir Hakim	.40	.15

❑ 89	Drew Bledsoe	1.25	.50
❑ 90	Garrison Hearst	.60	.25
❑ 91	Doug Flutie	1.00	.40
❑ 92	Jerome Bettis	1.00	.40
❑ 93	Vinny Testaverde	.60	.25
❑ 94	Tiki Barber	1.00	.40
❑ 95	Johnnie Morton	.60	.25
❑ 96	Lamar Smith	.60	.25
❑ 97	Marcus Robinson	.60	.25
❑ 98	Fred Taylor	1.00	.40
❑ 99	Tom Brady	2.50	1.00
❑ 100	Peyton Manning	2.00	.75
❑ 101	Donovan McNabb	1.25	.50
❑ 102	Rich Gannon	1.00	.40
❑ 103	Hines Ward	1.00	.40
❑ 104	Michael Bennett	.60	.25
❑ 105	Ricky Williams	1.00	.40
❑ 106	Germane Crowell	.40	.15
❑ 107	Joey Galloway	.60	.25
❑ 108	Amani Toomer	.60	.25
❑ 109	Trent Green	.60	.25
❑ 110	Terry Glenn	.60	.25
❑ 111	Donte Stallworth RC	10.00	4.00
❑ 112	Mike Williams RC	4.00	1.50
❑ 113	Kurt Kittner RC	4.00	1.50
❑ 114	Josh Reed RC	5.00	2.00
❑ 115	Raonall Smith RC	4.00	1.50
❑ 116	David Garrard RC	5.00	2.00
❑ 117	Eric Crouch RC	5.00	2.00
❑ 118	Levi Jones RC	4.00	1.50
❑ 119	Quentin Jammer RC	5.00	2.00
❑ 120	Cliff Russell RC	4.00	1.50
❑ 121	Jamin Elliott RC	2.50	1.00
❑ 122	Roy Williams RC	12.00	5.00
❑ 123	Marquise Walker RC	4.00	1.50
❑ 124	Kalimba Edwards RC	5.00	2.00
❑ 125	Daniel Graham RC	5.00	2.00
❑ 126	Anthony Weaver RC	4.00	1.50
❑ 127	Antonio Bryant RC	5.00	2.00
❑ 128	DeShaun Foster RC	5.00	2.00
❑ 129	Antwaan Randle El RC	8.00	3.00
❑ 130	William Green RC	5.00	2.00
❑ 131	Joey Harrington RC	8.00	3.00
❑ 132	T.J. Duckett RC	6.00	2.50
❑ 133	Javon Walker RC	10.00	4.00
❑ 134	Albert Haynesworth RC	4.00	1.50
❑ 135	Julius Peppers RC	10.00	4.00
❑ 136	Clinton Portis RC	15.00	6.00
❑ 137	Ashley Lelie RC	10.00	4.00
❑ 138	Reche Caldwell RC	5.00	2.00
❑ 139	Rohan Davey RC	5.00	2.00
❑ 140	Patrick Ramsey RC	6.00	2.50
❑ 141	Ron Johnson RC	4.00	1.50
❑ 142	Jamar Martin RC	4.00	1.50
❑ 143	Travis Stephens RC	4.00	1.50
❑ 143AU	Travis Stephens AU	12.00	5.00
❑ 144	Darrell Hill RC	4.00	1.50
❑ 145	Jon McGraw RC	2.50	1.00
❑ 146	Javin Hunter RC	2.50	1.00
❑ 146AU	Javin Hunter AU	10.00	4.00
❑ 147	Eddie Drummond RC	4.00	1.50
❑ 148	Andre Lott RC	5.00	2.00
❑ 149	Travis Fisher RC	5.00	2.00
❑ 150	Lamont Brightful RC	2.50	1.00
❑ 151	Rocky Calmus RC	5.00	2.00
❑ 152	Wes Pate RC	2.50	1.00
❑ 152AU	Wes Pate AU	10.00	4.00
❑ 153	Lamar Gordon RC	5.00	2.00
❑ 154	Terry Jones RC	4.00	1.50
❑ 155	Kyle Johnson RC	2.50	1.00
❑ 155AU	Kyle Johnson AU	10.00	4.00
❑ 156	Daryl Jones RC	4.00	1.50
❑ 157	Tellis Redmon RC	4.00	1.50
❑ 158	Jarrod Baxter RC	4.00	1.50
❑ 159	Delvon Flowers RC	4.00	1.50
❑ 160	Kelly Campbell RC	4.00	1.50
❑ 161	Eddie Freeman RC	2.50	1.00
❑ 162	Atrews Bell RC	2.50	1.00
❑ 163	Omar Easy RC	5.00	2.00
❑ 164	Jeremy Allen RC	2.50	1.00
❑ 165	Andra Davis RC	4.00	1.50
❑ 166	Mike Rumph RC	5.00	2.00
❑ 167	Seth Burford RC	4.00	1.50
❑ 168	Marquand Manuel RC	2.50	1.00
❑ 169	Marques Anderson RC	5.00	2.00
❑ 170	Ben Leber RC	5.00	2.00
❑ 171	Ryan Denney RC	4.00	1.50
❑ 172	Justin Peelle RC	2.50	1.00
❑ 173	Lito Sheppard RC	5.00	2.00
❑ 174	Damien Anderson RC	4.00	1.50
❑ 175	Lamont Thompson RC	4.00	1.50
❑ 176	David Priestley RC	4.00	1.50
❑ 177	Michael Lewis RC	5.00	2.00
❑ 178	Lee Mays RC	4.00	1.50
❑ 179	Alan Harper RC	2.50	1.00
❑ 180	Verron Haynes RC	5.00	2.00
❑ 181	Chris Hope RC	5.00	2.00
❑ 182	Derek Ross RC	4.00	1.50
❑ 183	Joseph Jefferson RC	4.00	1.50
❑ 184	Carlos Hall RC	5.00	2.00
❑ 185	Robert Royal RC	5.00	2.00
❑ 186	Sheldon Brown RC	5.00	2.00
❑ 187	DeVeren Johnson RC	4.00	1.50
❑ 188	Rock Cartwright RC	6.00	2.50
❑ 189	Kendall Simmons RC	4.00	1.50
❑ 190	Joe Burns RC	4.00	1.50
❑ 191	David Givens RC	12.00	5.00
❑ 192	John Owens RC	4.00	1.50
❑ 193	Jarrett Ferguson RC	4.00	1.50
❑ 194	Randy McMichael RC	8.00	3.00
❑ 195	Chris Baker RC	4.00	1.50
❑ 196	Rashad Bauman RC	4.00	1.50
❑ 197	Matt Murphy RC	4.00	1.50
❑ 198	Steve Bellisari RC	4.00	1.50
❑ 199	Jeff Kelly RC	4.00	1.50
❑ 200	Mark Anelli RC	2.50	1.00
❑ 201	Darnell Sanders RC	4.00	1.50
❑ 202	Coy Wire RC	5.00	2.00
❑ 203	Ricky Williams RC	4.00	1.50
❑ 204	Napoleon Harris RC	5.00	2.00
❑ 205	Ennis Haywood RC	4.00	1.50
❑ 206	Keyuo Craver RC	4.00	1.50
❑ 207	Kahlil Hill RC	4.00	1.50
❑ 208	J.T. O'Sullivan RC	4.00	1.50
❑ 209	Woody Dantzler RC	4.00	1.50
❑ 210	Phillip Buchanon RC	5.00	2.00
❑ 211	Charles Grant RC	5.00	2.00
❑ 212	Dusty Bonner RC	2.50	1.00
❑ 213	James Allen RC	2.50	1.00
❑ 214	Ronald Curry RC	5.00	2.00
❑ 215	Deion Branch RC	10.00	4.00
❑ 216	Larry Ned RC	4.00	1.50
❑ 217	Kendall Newson RC	2.50	1.00
❑ 218	Shaun Hill RC	5.00	2.00
❑ 219	Akin Ayodele RC	2.50	1.00
❑ 220	John Henderson RC	5.00	2.00
❑ 221	Andre Davis AU A RC	12.00	5.00
❑ 222	Bryan Thomas AU A RC	20.00	7.50
❑ 223	Brian Westbrook AU C RC	60.00	35.00
❑ 224	Chad Hutchinson AU C RC	12.00	5.00
❑ 225	Craig Nall AU D RC	20.00	7.50
❑ 226	David Carr AU A RC	50.00	20.00
❑ 227	Dwight Freeney AU D RC	40.00	20.00
❑ 228	Adrian Peterson AU A RC	20.00	7.50
❑ 229	Randy Fasani AU E RC	12.00	5.00
❑ 230	Ed Reed AU A RC	30.00	12.00
❑ 231	Freddie Milons AU B RC	12.00	5.00
❑ 232	Herb Haygood AU E RC	10.00	4.00
❑ 233	Jabar Gaffney AU A RC	20.00	7.50
❑ 234	Josh McCown AU A RC	30.00	12.00
❑ 235	Jeremy Shockey AU A RC	100.00	50.00
❑ 236	Jake Schifino AU F RC	12.00	5.00
❑ 237	Josh Scobey AU E RC	20.00	7.50
❑ 238	Jonathan Wells AU D RC	20.00	7.50
❑ 239	Ladell Betts AU A RC	25.00	12.50
❑ 240	Luke Staley AU E RC	12.00	5.00
❑ 241	Maurice Morris AU B RC	20.00	7.50
❑ 242	Matt Schobel AU D RC	12.00	5.00
❑ 243	Sam Simmons AU C RC	10.00	4.00
❑ 244	Tim Carter AU A RC	12.00	5.00
❑ 245	Tank Williams AU E RC	12.00	5.00
❑ 246	Jerramy Stevens AU A RC	20.00	7.50
❑ 247	Jason McAddley AU C RC	12.00	5.00
❑ 248	Ken Simonton AU D RC	10.00	4.00
❑ 249	Chester Taylor AU F RC	30.00	15.00
❑ 250	Brandon Doman AU C RC	12.00	5.00

2003 Bowman Chrome

❑	COMP.SET w/o SP's (110)	25.00	10.00
❑ 1	Brett Favre	2.50	1.00
❑ 2	Jeremy Shockey	1.50	.60
❑ 3	Fred Taylor	1.00	.40
❑ 4	Rich Gannon	.60	.25
❑ 5	Joey Galloway	.60	.25
❑ 6	Ray Lewis	1.00	.40
❑ 7	Jeff Blake	.40	.15
❑ 8	Stacey Mack	.40	.15
❑ 9	Matt Hasselbeck	.60	.25
❑ 10	Laveranues Coles	.60	.25
❑ 11	Brad Johnson	.60	.25
❑ 12	Tommy Maddox	1.00	.40
❑ 13	Curtis Martin	1.00	.40
❑ 14	Tom Brady	2.50	1.00
❑ 15	Ricky Williams	1.00	.40
❑ 16	Stephen Davis	.60	.25
❑ 17	Chad Johnson	1.00	.40
❑ 18	Joey Harrington	1.50	.60
❑ 19	Tony Gonzalez	.60	.25
❑ 20	Peerless Price	.60	.25
❑ 21	LaDainian Tomlinson	1.00	.40
❑ 22	James Thrash	.60	.25
❑ 23	Charlie Garner	.60	.25
❑ 24	Eddie George	.60	.25
❑ 25	Terrell Owens	1.00	.40
❑ 26	Brian Urlacher	1.50	.60
❑ 27	Eric Moulds	.60	.25
❑ 28	Emmitt Smith	2.50	1.00
❑ 29	Tim Couch	.40	.15
❑ 30	Jake Plummer	.60	.25
❑ 31	Marvin Harrison	1.00	.40
❑ 32	Chris Chambers	1.00	.40
❑ 33	Tiki Barber	1.00	.40
❑ 34	Kurt Warner	1.00	.40
❑ 35	Michael Pittman	.40	.15
❑ 36	Kevin Dyson	.60	.25
❑ 37	Clinton Portis	1.50	.60
❑ 38	Peyton Manning	1.50	.60
❑ 39	Travis Taylor	.60	.25
❑ 40	Jeff Garcia	1.00	.40
❑ 41	Patrick Ramsey	1.00	.40
❑ 42	Shaun Alexander	1.00	.40
❑ 43	Joe Horn	.60	.25
❑ 44	Daunte Culpepper	1.00	.40
❑ 45	Travis Henry	.60	.25
❑ 46	Brian Finneran	.40	.15
❑ 47	William Green	.60	.25
❑ 48	Kordell Stewart	.60	.25
❑ 49	Reggie Wayne	.60	.25
❑ 50	Priest Holmes	1.25	.50
❑ 51	Jay Fiedler	.60	.25
❑ 52	Corey Dillon	.60	.25
❑ 53	Jamal Lewis	1.00	.40
❑ 54	Mark Brunell	.60	.25
❑ 55	Santana Moss	.60	.25
❑ 56	Duce Staley	.60	.25
❑ 57	Torry Holt	1.00	.40
❑ 58	Rod Gardner	.60	.25
❑ 59	Kerry Collins	.60	.25
❑ 60	Randy Moss	1.50	.60
❑ 61	Jerry Porter	.60	.25
❑ 62	Plaxico Burress	.60	.25
❑ 63	Steve McNair	1.00	.40
❑ 64	Muhsin Muhammad	.60	.25
❑ 65	Drew Bledsoe	1.00	.40
❑ 66	T.J. Duckett	.60	.25
❑ 67	Ahman Green	1.00	.40
❑ 68	Rod Smith	.60	.25
❑ 69	Jimmy Smith	.60	.25
❑ 70	Trent Green	.60	.25
❑ 71	Tim Brown	1.00	.40
❑ 72	Jerome Bettis	1.00	.40
❑ 73	Isaac Bruce	1.00	.40
❑ 74	Derrick Mason	.60	.25
❑ 75	Donovan McNabb	1.25	.50
❑ 76	Deuce McAllister	1.00	.40
❑ 77	Zach Thomas	1.00	.40
❑ 78	Garrison Hearst	.60	.25
❑ 79	Koren Robinson	.60	.25
❑ 80	Marshall Faulk	1.00	.40
❑ 81	Keyshawn Johnson	1.00	.40

❑ 82 Jake Delhomme 1.00 .40
❑ 83 Marty Booker .60 .25
❑ 84 James Stewart .60 .25
❑ 85 Corey Bradford .40 .15
❑ 86 Derrius Thompson .40 .15
❑ 87 Edgerrin James 1.00 .40
❑ 88 Darrell Jackson .60 .25
❑ 89 Hines Ward 1.00 .40
❑ 90 David Boston .60 .25
❑ 91 Curtis Conway .40 .15
❑ 92 David Patten .40 .15
❑ 93 Michael Bennett .60 .25
❑ 94 Todd Pinkston .60 .25
❑ 95 Jerry Rice 2.00 .75
❑ 96 Jon Kitna .60 .25
❑ 97 Ed McCaffrey 1.00 .40
❑ 98 Donald Driver .60 .25
❑ 99 Anthony Thomas .60 .25
❑ 100 Michael Vick 2.50 1.00
❑ 101 Terry Glenn .40 .15
❑ 102 Quincy Morgan .60 .25
❑ 103 David Carr 1.50 .60
❑ 104 Troy Brown .60 .25
❑ 105 Aaron Brooks 1.00 .40
❑ 106 Amani Toomer .60 .25
❑ 107 Drew Brees 1.00 .40
❑ 108 Chad Hutchinson .40 .15
❑ 109 Warrick Dunn .60 .25
❑ 110 Chad Pennington 1.25 .50
❑ 111 Brian St.Pierre RC 5.00 2.00
❑ 112 Keenan Howry RC 5.00 2.00
❑ 113 Sultan McCullough RC 4.00 1.50
❑ 114 Terence Newman RC 10.00 4.00
❑ 115 Kelley Washington RC 5.00 2.00
❑ 116 Musa Smith RC 5.00 2.00
❑ 117 Victor Hobson RC 5.00 2.00
❑ 118 Travis Anglin RC 2.50 1.00
❑ 119 Artose Pinner RC 5.00 2.00
❑ 120 Rashean Mathis RC 4.00 1.50
❑ 121 DeWayne White RC 4.00 1.50
❑ 122 Kevin Curtis RC 5.00 2.00
❑ 123 Tyrone Calico RC 6.00 2.50
❑ 124 Ricky Manning RC 5.00 2.00
❑ 125 Cory Redding RC 4.00 1.50
❑ 126 Dallas Clark RC 5.00 2.00
❑ 127 Marcus Trufant RC 5.00 2.00
❑ 128 Terrell Suggs RC 8.00 3.00
❑ 129 Aaron Walker RC 4.00 1.50
❑ 130 Calvin Pace RC 4.00 1.50
❑ 131 Ken Dorsey RC 5.00 2.00
❑ 132 Earnest Graham RC 4.00 1.50
❑ 133 Cecil Sapp RC 4.00 1.50
❑ 134 William Joseph RC 5.00 2.00
❑ 135 Anquan Boldin RC 15.00 6.00
❑ 136 Justin Griffith RC 4.00 1.50
❑ 137 Teyo Johnson RC 5.00 2.00
❑ 138 Chris Crocker RC 2.50 1.00
❑ 139 Doug Gabriel RC 6.00 2.50
❑ 140 Terry Pierce RC 4.00 1.50
❑ 141 Bradie James RC 5.00 2.00
❑ 142 Terrence Edwards RC 4.00 1.50
❑ 143 E.J. Henderson RC 5.00 2.00
❑ 144 Tony Romo RC 50.00 25.00
❑ 145 DeWayne Robertson RC 5.00 2.00
❑ 146 Dwone Hicks RC 2.50 1.00
❑ 147 Carl Ford RC 2.50 1.00
❑ 148 Ken Hamlin RC 5.00 2.00
❑ 149 Adrian Madise RC 4.00 1.50
❑ 150 Siddeeq Shabazz RC 2.50 1.00
❑ 151 Dave Ragone RC 5.00 2.00
❑ 152 Mike Seidman RC 2.50 1.00
❑ 153 DeAndrew Rubin RC 2.50 1.00
❑ 154 Mike Pinkard RC 2.50 1.00
❑ 155 Nate Burleson RC 5.00 2.00
❑ 156 Angelo Crowell RC 4.00 1.50
❑ 157 J.R. Tolver RC 4.00 1.50
❑ 158 Osi Umenyiora RC 8.00 3.00
❑ 159 Nick Barnett RC 5.00 2.00
❑ 160 Brandon Drumm RC 2.50 1.00
❑ 161 Rien Long RC 2.50 1.00
❑ 162 Zuriel Smith RC 2.50 1.00
❑ 163 Onterrio Smith RC 5.00 2.00
❑ 164 Kenny Peterson RC 4.00 1.50
❑ 165 Chaun Thompson RC 2.50 1.00
❑ 166 Terrence Holt RC 4.00 1.50
❑ 167 Ovie Mughelli RC 2.50 1.00
❑ 168 Bethel Johnson RC 5.00 2.00
❑ 169 Avon Cobourne RC 2.50 1.00
❑ 170 Andre Woolfolk RC 5.00 2.00
❑ 171 George Wrighster RC 4.00 1.50
❑ 172 Justin Fargas RC 5.00 2.00
❑ 173 Marquel Blackwell RC 2.50 1.00
❑ 174 Walter Young RC 2.50 1.00
❑ 175 Kawika Mitchell RC 5.00 2.00
❑ 176 Drayton Florence RC 2.50 1.00
❑ 177 Jeremi Johnson RC 4.00 1.50
❑ 178 Lee Suggs RC 5.00 2.00
❑ 179 David Kircus RC 5.00 2.00
❑ 180 Rex Grossman RC 15.00 6.00
❑ 180AU Rex Grossman AU B 120.00 60.00
❑ 181 Jon Olinger RC 2.50 1.00
❑ 182 Dan Curley RC 2.50 1.00
❑ 183 Andrew Pinnock RC 4.00 1.50
❑ 184 Kirk Farmer RC 2.50 1.00
❑ 185 Charles Rogers RC 5.00 2.00
❑ 186 Alonzo Jackson RC 4.00 1.50
❑ 187 Trent Smith RC 4.00 1.50
❑ 188 Seneca Wallace RC 5.00 2.00
❑ 189 Shane Walton RC 2.50 1.00
❑ 190 Chris Brown RC 5.00 2.00
❑ 191 Dahrran Diedrick RC 5.00 2.00
❑ 192 Juston Wood RC 2.50 1.00
❑ 193 Mike Doss RC 5.00 2.00
❑ 194 Visanthe Shiancoe RC 4.00 1.50
❑ 195 Andre Johnson RC 10.00 4.00
❑ 196 Dennis Weathersby RC 2.50 1.00
❑ 197 Chris Davis RC 4.00 1.50
❑ 198 LaTarence Dunbar RC 4.00 1.50
❑ 199 Eugene Wilson RC 5.00 2.00
❑ 200 Ryan Hoag RC 2.50 1.00
❑ 201 Chris Simms RC 8.00 3.00
❑ 202 Curt Anes RC 2.50 1.00
❑ 203 Taco Wallace RC 4.00 1.50
❑ 204 David Tyree RC 4.00 1.50
❑ 205 Nate Hybl RC 5.00 2.00
❑ 206 Willis McGahee RC 15.00 6.00
❑ 207 Casey Moore RC 4.00 1.50
❑ 208 Pisa Tinoisamoa RC 5.00 2.00
❑ 209 Willie Ponder RC 2.50 1.00
❑ 210 Donald Lee RC 4.00 1.50
❑ 211 Nnamdi Asomugha RC 4.00 1.50
❑ 212 Sammy Davis RC 5.00 2.00
❑ 213 Joffrey Reynolds RC 2.50 1.00
❑ 214 Eddie Moore RC 4.00 1.50
❑ 215 Tony Hollings RC 5.00 2.00
❑ 216 Nick Maddox RC 2.50 1.00
❑ 217 Kevin Walter RC 4.00 1.50
❑ 218 Dan Klecko RC 5.00 2.00
❑ 219 Antwan Peek RC 4.00 1.50
❑ 220 Tyler Brayton RC 5.00 2.00
❑ 221 Byron Leftwich AU B RC 100.00 40.00
❑ 222 Bobby Wade AU D RC 15.00 6.00
❑ 223 Jerome McDougle AU C RC 12.00 5.00
❑ 224 Michael Haynes AU D RC 12.00 5.00
❑ 225 Taylor Jacobs AU C RC 20.00 7.50
❑ 226 Shaun McDonald AU D RC 12.00 5.00
❑ 227 Bry.Johnson AU B RC EXCH
❑ 228 Talman Gardner AU D RC 12.00 5.00
❑ 229 Domanick Davis AU D RC 30.00 12.50
❑ 230 Jason Witten AU D RC 25.00 12.50
❑ 231 Kyle Boller AU B RC 30.00 15.00
❑ 232 L.J. Smith AU C RC 20.00 7.50
❑ 233 Boss Bailey AU C RC 15.00 6.00
❑ 234 Billy McMullen AU D RC 10.00 4.00
❑ 235 Larry Johnson AU B RC 250.00 125.00
❑ 236 Kareem Kelly AU E RC 10.00 4.00
❑ 237 Carson Palmer AU A RC 300.00 150.00
❑ 238 Quentin Griffin AU D RC 20.00 7.50
❑ 239 Kevin Garrett AU E RC 10.00 4.00
❑ 240 Charles Tillman AU E RC 20.00 7.50
❑ 241 Arnaz Battle AU D RC 15.00 6.00
❑ 242 Brooks Bollinger AU E RC 12.00 5.00
❑ 243 LaBrandon Toefield AU D RC 12.00 5.00
❑ 244 Sam Aiken AU D RC 10.00 4.00
❑ 245 Justin Gage AU D RC 12.00 5.00
❑ 246 Gibran Hamdan AU D RC 10.00 4.00

2004 Bowman Chrome

❑ COMP.SET w/o SP's (220) 175.00 100.00
❑ COMP.SET w/o RC's (110) 30.00 12.50
❑ ROOKIE AU/199 GROUP A ODDS 1:603
❑ ROOKIE AU GROUP B ODDS 1:1293
❑ ROOKIE AU GROUP C ODDS 1:359
❑ ROOKIE AU GROUP D ODDS 1:21
❑ 1 Brett Favre 2.50 1.00
❑ 2 Jay Fiedler .40 .15
❑ 3 Andre Davis .40 .15
❑ 4 Travis Henry .60 .25

❑ 5 Jimmy Smith .60 .25
❑ 6 Santana Moss .60 .25
❑ 7 Correll Buckhalter .60 .25
❑ 8 Randy Moss 1.25 .50
❑ 9 Edgerrin James 1.00 .40
❑ 10 Marc Bulger 1.00 .40
❑ 11 Derrick Mason .60 .25
❑ 12 Mark Brunell .60 .25
❑ 13 Donte Stallworth .60 .25
❑ 14 Deion Branch 1.00 .40
❑ 15 Jake Plummer .60 .25
❑ 16 Steve Smith 1.00 .40
❑ 17 Jon Kitna .60 .25
❑ 18 Andre Johnson 1.00 .40
❑ 19 A.J. Feeley 1.00 .40
❑ 20 Drew Bledsoe 1.00 .40
❑ 21 Antonio Bryant .60 .25
❑ 22 Reggie Wayne .60 .25
❑ 23 Thomas Jones .60 .25
❑ 24 Alge Crumpler .60 .25
❑ 25 Anquan Boldin 1.00 .40
❑ 26 Tim Rattay .40 .15
❑ 27 Charlie Garner .60 .25
❑ 28 James Thrash .40 .15
❑ 29 Koren Robinson .60 .25
❑ 30 Terrell Owens 1.00 .40
❑ 31 Amani Toomer .60 .25
❑ 32 Kelly Campbell .40 .15
❑ 33 Patrick Ramsey .60 .25
❑ 34 Plaxico Burress .60 .25
❑ 35 Chad Pennington 1.00 .40
❑ 36 Fred Taylor .60 .25
❑ 37 Domanick Davis 1.00 .40
❑ 38 DeShaun Foster .60 .25
❑ 39 T.J. Duckett .60 .25
❑ 40 Ahman Green 1.00 .40
❑ 41 Lee Suggs 1.00 .40
❑ 42 Tony Gonzalez .60 .25
❑ 43 Rich Gannon .60 .25
❑ 44 Kevan Barlow .60 .25
❑ 45 Torry Holt 1.00 .40
❑ 46 Aaron Brooks .60 .25
❑ 47 Tyrone Calico .60 .25
❑ 48 Keenan McCardell .40 .15
❑ 49 Hines Ward 1.00 .40
❑ 50 LaDainian Tomlinson 1.25 .50
❑ 51 Dante Hall 1.00 .40
❑ 52 Marcus Pollard .40 .15
❑ 53 Corey Dillon .60 .25
❑ 54 Justin McCareins .40 .15
❑ 55 Stephen Davis .60 .25
❑ 56 Jeff Garcia 1.00 .40
❑ 57 Ashley Lelie .60 .25
❑ 58 Javon Walker .60 .25
❑ 59 Kyle Boller 1.00 .40
❑ 60 Chad Johnson 1.00 .40
❑ 61 Anthony Thomas .60 .25
❑ 62 Byron Leftwich 1.25 .50
❑ 63 David Boston .60 .25
❑ 64 Onterrio Smith .60 .25
❑ 65 Deuce McAllister 1.00 .40
❑ 66 Antwaan Randle El 1.00 .40
❑ 67 Justin Fargas .60 .25
❑ 68 Laveranues Coles .60 .25
❑ 69 Quincy Morgan .60 .25
❑ 70 Priest Holmes 1.25 .50
❑ 71 Robert Ferguson .40 .15
❑ 72 Charles Rogers .60 .25
❑ 73 Drew Brees 1.00 .40
❑ 74 Matt Hasselbeck .60 .25
❑ 75 Peyton Manning 1.50 .60
❑ 76 Rudi Johnson .60 .25

❑ 77 Jake Delhomme	1.00	.40
❑ 78 Tiki Barber	1.00	.40
❑ 79 Brad Johnson	.60	.25
❑ 80 Steve McNair	1.00	.40
❑ 81 Willis McGahee	1.00	.40
❑ 82 Josh McCown	.60	.25
❑ 83 Garrison Hearst	.60	.25
❑ 84 Quincy Carter	.60	.25
❑ 85 Ricky Williams	1.00	.40
❑ 86 Trent Green	.60	.25
❑ 87 Curtis Martin	1.00	.40
❑ 88 Jerry Porter	.60	.25
❑ 89 Brian Westbrook	.60	.25
❑ 90 Clinton Portis	1.00	.40
❑ 91 Eric Moulds	.60	.25
❑ 92 Marcel Shipp	.60	.25
❑ 93 Joey Harrington	1.00	.40
❑ 94 David Carr	1.00	.40
❑ 95 Marvin Harrison	1.00	.40
❑ 96 Joe Horn	.60	.25
❑ 97 Chris Chambers	.60	.25
❑ 98 Darrell Jackson	.60	.25
❑ 99 Eddie George	.60	.25
❑ 100 Donovan McNabb	1.25	.50
❑ 101 Marshall Faulk	1.00	.40
❑ 102 Rex Grossman	1.00	.40
❑ 103 Tai Streets	.40	.15
❑ 104 Jeremy Shockey	1.00	.40
❑ 105 Jamal Lewis	1.00	.40
❑ 106 Tom Brady	2.50	1.00
❑ 107 Shaun Alexander	1.00	.40
❑ 108 Carson Palmer	1.25	.50
❑ 109 Daunte Culpepper	1.00	.40
❑ 110 Michael Vick	2.00	.75
❑ 111 Roethlis AU/199 RC	500.00	250.00
❑ 112 Tommie Harris RC	4.00	1.50
❑ 113 Thomas Tapeh RC	3.00	1.25
❑ 114 Matt Schaub RC	12.00	5.00
❑ 115 Jonathan Smith RC	3.00	1.25
❑ 116 Ricardo Colclough RC	4.00	1.50
❑ 117 Jeff Dugan RC	2.00	.75
❑ 118 Larry Fitzgerald RC	12.00	5.00
❑ 119 Gibril Wilson RC	4.00	1.50
❑ 120 Sean Taylor RC	4.00	1.50
❑ 121 Marquise Hill RC	3.00	1.25
❑ 122 Cedric Cobbs RC	4.00	1.50
❑ 123 Rich Gardner RC	3.00	1.25
❑ 124 Chris Cooley RC	4.00	1.50
❑ 125 Ben Troupe RC	4.00	1.50
❑ 126 Antwan Odom RC	4.00	1.50
❑ 127 Stuart Schweigert RC	4.00	1.50
❑ 128 Derek Abney RC	4.00	1.50
❑ 129 Keary Colbert RC	5.00	2.00
❑ 130 Jeris McIntyre RC	3.00	1.25
❑ 131 Matt Kranchick RC	4.00	1.50
❑ 132 Rodney Leisle RC	2.00	.75
❑ 133 Vince Wilfork RC	4.00	1.50
❑ 134 Darnell Dockett RC	3.00	1.25
❑ 135 Jeremy LeSueur RC	3.00	1.25
❑ 136 Gilbert Gardner RC	3.00	1.25
❑ 137 Amon Gordon RC	2.00	.75
❑ 138 Darius Watts RC	4.00	1.50
❑ 139 Junior Siavii RC	4.00	1.50
❑ 140 Igor Olshansky RC	4.00	1.50
❑ 141 Mewelde Moore RC	4.00	1.50
❑ 142 Nathan Vasher RC	5.00	2.00
❑ 143 Randy Starks RC	3.00	1.25
❑ 144 Isaac Sopoaga RC	2.00	.75
❑ 145 Drew Henson RC	4.00	1.50
❑ 146 Erik Coleman RC	4.00	1.50
❑ 147 Robert Kent RC	2.00	.75
❑ 148 Jammal Lord RC	4.00	1.50
❑ 149 Richard Seigler RC	3.00	1.25
❑ 150 Niko Koutouvides RC	3.00	1.25
❑ 151 Brandon Miree RC	3.00	1.25
❑ 152 Dunta Robinson RC	4.00	1.50
❑ 153 Courtney Anderson RC	3.00	1.25
❑ 154 Bruce Perry RC	4.00	1.50
❑ 155 Shaun Phillips RC	3.00	1.25
❑ 156 Greg Jones RC	4.00	1.50
❑ 157 Tank Johnson RC	3.00	1.25
❑ 158 Dwan Edwards RC	2.00	.75
❑ 159 Julius Jones RC	12.00	5.00
❑ 160 Chad Lavalais RC	3.00	1.25
❑ 161 Tim Anderson RC	4.00	1.50
❑ 162 Jarrett Payton RC	4.00	1.50
❑ 163 Matt Ware RC	4.00	1.50
❑ 164 DeAngelo Hall RC	5.00	2.00
❑ 165 Ben Hartsock RC	4.00	1.50
❑ 166 Keith Smith RC	3.00	1.25
❑ 167 Michael Jenkins RC	4.00	1.50
❑ 168 Quincy Wilson RC	3.00	1.25
❑ 169 Dontarrious Thomas RC	4.00	1.50
❑ 170 Tony Hargrove RC	3.00	1.25
❑ 171 Ben Watson RC	4.00	1.50
❑ 172 Triandos Luke RC	4.00	1.50
❑ 173 Kellen Winslow RC	8.00	3.00
❑ 174 Patrick Crayton RC	4.00	1.50
❑ 175 Devard Darling RC	4.00	1.50
❑ 176 Shawntae Spencer RC	4.00	1.50
❑ 177 Will Smith RC	4.00	1.50
❑ 178 Darrion Scott RC	4.00	1.50
❑ 179 Wes Welker RC	4.00	1.50
❑ 180 Ryan Dinwiddie RC	3.00	1.25
❑ 181 Rod Davis RC	2.00	.75
❑ 182 Casey Clausen RC	4.00	1.50
❑ 183 Clarence Moore RC	4.00	1.50
❑ 184 D.J. Hackett RC	3.00	1.25
❑ 185 Devery Henderson RC	3.00	1.25
❑ 186 Sean Jones RC	3.00	1.25
❑ 187 Bruce Thornton RC	2.00	.75
❑ 188 Tatum Bell RC	8.00	3.00
❑ 189 Tim Euhus RC	4.00	1.50
❑ 190 John Standeford RC	3.00	1.25
❑ 191 Reggie Torbor RC	3.00	1.25
❑ 192 Rashaun Woods RC	4.00	1.50
❑ 193 Jason Shivers RC	2.00	.75
❑ 194 Ahmad Carroll RC	4.00	1.50
❑ 195 Keyaron Fox RC	3.00	1.25
❑ 196 Von Hutchins RC	3.00	1.25
❑ 197 Marcus Tubbs RC	4.00	1.50
❑ 198 Daryl Smith RC	4.00	1.50
❑ 199 Robert Gallery RC	4.00	1.50
❑ 200 Marquis Cooper RC	3.00	1.25
❑ 201 Bernard Berrian RC	5.00	2.00
❑ 202 Derrick Strait RC	4.00	1.50
❑ 203 Travis LaBoy RC	4.00	1.50
❑ 204 Caleb Miller RC	3.00	1.25
❑ 205 Michael Clayton RC	8.00	3.00
❑ 206 Will Poole RC	4.00	1.50
❑ 207 Derrick Hamilton RC	3.00	1.25
❑ 208 Glenn Earl RC	3.00	1.25
❑ 209 Donnell Washington RC	4.00	1.50
❑ 210 Nate Lawrie RC	3.00	1.25
❑ 211 Keiwan Ratliff RC	3.00	1.25
❑ 212 Luke McCown RC	4.00	1.50
❑ 213 Joey Thomas RC	4.00	1.50
❑ 214 Shawn Andrews RC	4.00	1.50
❑ 215 Derrick Ward RC	2.00	.75
❑ 216 Reggie Williams RC	5.00	2.00
❑ 217 Rod Rutherford RC	3.00	1.25
❑ 218 Michael Gaines RC	3.00	1.25
❑ 219 Will Allen RC	4.00	1.50
❑ 220 J.P. Losman RC	8.00	3.00
❑ 221 Roy Williams AU/199 RC	150.00	75.00
❑ 222 Kevin Jones AU/199 RC	100.00	40.00
❑ 223 Philip Rivers AU/199 RC	250.00	125.00
❑ 224 Steven Jackson AU/199 RC	200.00	100.00
❑ 225 Eli Manning AU/199 RC	400.00	250.00
❑ 226 Cody Pickett AU D RC	20.00	7.50
❑ 227 P.K. Sam AU D RC	15.00	6.00
❑ 228 Maurice Mann AU D RC	15.00	6.00
❑ 229 Andy Hall AU D RC	15.00	6.00
❑ 230 Chris Perry AU D RC	20.00	7.50
❑ 231 Ernest Wilford AU C RC	20.00	7.50
❑ 232 Kenechi Udeze AU D RC	20.00	7.50
❑ 233 Michael Boulware AU D RC	20.00	7.50
❑ 234 B.J. Symons AU D RC	20.00	7.50
❑ 235 Jared Lorenzen AU D RC	15.00	6.00
❑ 236 Matt Mauck AU D RC	20.00	7.50
❑ 237 Carlos Francis AU D RC	15.00	6.00
❑ 238 Michael Turner AU D RC	50.00	30.00
❑ 239 Lee Evans AU B RC	40.00	20.00
❑ 240 Jerricho Cotchery AU D RC	20.00	7.50
❑ 241 John Navarre AU D RC	20.00	7.50
❑ 242 Jonathan Vilma AU D RC	25.00	10.00
❑ 243 Josh Harris AU D RC	20.00	7.50
❑ 244 Jeff Smoker AU C RC	20.00	7.50
❑ 245 Jamaar Taylor AU D RC	20.00	7.50

2004 Bowman Chrome Super Bowl XXXIX Unsigned Draft Picks

❑ COMPLETE SET (26)	200.00	75.00
❑ 111 Ben Roethlisberger	80.00	40.00
❑ 221 Roy Williams WR	25.00	10.00
❑ 222 Kevin Jones	25.00	10.00
❑ 223 Philip Rivers	30.00	12.50
❑ 224 Steven Jackson	30.00	12.50
❑ 225 Eli Manning	50.00	20.00
❑ 226 Cody Pickett	10.00	4.00
❑ 227 P.K. Sam	8.00	3.00
❑ 228 Maurice Mann	8.00	3.00
❑ 229 Andy Hall	8.00	3.00
❑ 230 Chris Perry	15.00	6.00
❑ 231 Ernest Wilford	10.00	4.00
❑ 232 Kenechi Udeze	10.00	4.00
❑ 233 Michael Boulware	10.00	4.00
❑ 234 B.J. Symons	10.00	4.00
❑ 235 Jared Lorenzen	8.00	3.00
❑ 236 Matt Mauck	10.00	4.00
❑ 237 Carlos Francis	8.00	3.00
❑ 238 Michael Turner	12.00	5.00
❑ 239 Lee Evans	12.00	5.00
❑ 240 Jerricho Cotchery	10.00	4.00
❑ 241 John Navarre	10.00	4.00
❑ 242 Jonathan Vilma	10.00	4.00
❑ 243 Josh Harris	10.00	4.00
❑ 244 Jeff Smoker	10.00	4.00
❑ 245 Jamaar Taylor	10.00	4.00

2005 Bowman Chrome

❑ COMP.SET w/o AU's (220)	100.00	40.00
❑ COMP.SET w/o RC's (110)	30.00	12.50
❑ ROOK.AU GROUP A ODDS 1:381 H, 1:1011 R		
❑ ROOK.AU GROUP B ODDS 1:156 H, 1:449 R		
❑ ROOK.AU GROUP C ODDS 1:318 H, 1:899 R		
❑ ROOK.AU GROUP D ODDS 1:296 H, 1:899 R		
❑ ROOK.AU GROUP E ODDS 1:281 H, 1:809 R		
❑ ROOK.AU GROUP F ODDS 1:132 H, 404 R		
❑ ROOK.AU GROUP G ODDS 1:39 H, 1:108 R		
❑ ROOKIE AU/199 ODDS 1:685 H, 1:1348 R		
❑ UNPRICED PRINT.PLATE 1/1 ODDS 1:975 H		
❑ 1 Peyton Manning	1.50	.60
❑ 2 Priest Holmes	1.00	.40
❑ 3 Anquan Boldin	.60	.25
❑ 4 Michael Vick	1.50	.60
❑ 5 Drew Brees	1.00	.40
❑ 6 Terrell Owens	1.00	.40
❑ 7 Curtis Martin	1.00	.40
❑ 8 Tom Brady	2.50	1.00
❑ 9 Maurice Carthon CO	.60	.25
❑ 10 Brett Favre	2.50	1.00
❑ 11 Marshall Faulk	1.00	.40
❑ 12 Corey Dillon	.60	.25
❑ 13 Julius Jones	1.25	.50
❑ 14 Jamal Lewis	1.00	.40
❑ 15 Keary Colbert	.60	.25
❑ 16 Joey Harrington	1.00	.40
❑ 17 Domanick Davis	.60	.25
❑ 18 Eli Manning	2.00	.75

❑ 19 Brad Childress CO .60 .25
❑ 20 Steve McNair 1.00 .40
❑ 21 Plaxico Burress .60 .25
❑ 22 Chad Pennington 1.00 .40
❑ 23 Patrick Ramsey .60 .25
❑ 24 Brian Griese .60 .25
❑ 25 Matt Hasselbeck .60 .25
❑ 26 Chris Chambers .60 .25
❑ 27 Marc Bulger 1.00 .40
❑ 28 Jake Delhomme 1.00 .40
❑ 29 Shaun Alexander 1.25 .50
❑ 30 Laveranues Coles .60 .25
❑ 31 A.J. Feeley .60 .25
❑ 32 Ashley Lelie .60 .25
❑ 33 Deuce McAllister 1.00 .40
❑ 34 Chris Brown .60 .25
❑ 35 Nate Burleson .60 .25
❑ 36 Darrell Jackson .60 .25
❑ 37 Lee Evans .60 .25
❑ 38 Jeremy Shockey 1.00 .40
❑ 39 Muhsin Muhammad .60 .25
❑ 40 Deion Branch .60 .25
❑ 41 DeShaun Foster .60 .25
❑ 42 Reggie Wayne .60 .25
❑ 43 Michael Jenkins .60 .25
❑ 44 Andre Johnson .60 .25
❑ 45 Javon Walker .60 .25
❑ 46 Joe Horn .60 .25
❑ 47 Fred Taylor .60 .25
❑ 48 Tony Gonzalez .60 .25
❑ 49 J.P. Losman 1.00 .40
❑ 50 Clinton Portis 1.00 .40
❑ 51 Randy Moss 1.00 .40
❑ 52 Jake Plummer .60 .25
❑ 53 Tiki Barber 1.00 .40
❑ 54 Edgerrin James 1.00 .40
❑ 55 Jerome Bettis 1.00 .40
❑ 56 Brandon Lloyd .50 .20
❑ 57 Romeo Crennel CO 1.00 .40
❑ 58 Antonio Gates 1.00 .40
❑ 59 Donovan McNabb 1.25 .50
❑ 60 Drew Bennett .60 .25
❑ 61 David Carr 1.00 .40
❑ 62 Trent Green .60 .25
❑ 63 Drew Bledsoe 1.00 .40
❑ 64 Donte Stallworth .60 .25
❑ 65 Alge Crumpler .60 .25
❑ 66 Jason Witten .60 .25
❑ 67 Thomas Jones .60 .25
❑ 68 Rex Grossman .60 .25
❑ 69 LaMont Jordan 1.00 .40
❑ 70 Kurt Warner .60 .25
❑ 71 Ahman Green 1.00 .40
❑ 72 Ben Roethlisberger 2.50 1.00
❑ 73 Mike Nolan CO 1.00 .40
❑ 74 Brian Westbrook .60 .25
❑ 75 Carson Palmer 1.00 .40
❑ 76 Stephen Davis .60 .25
❑ 77 Jonathan Vilma .60 .25
❑ 78 Willis McGahee 1.00 .40
❑ 79 Rudi Johnson .60 .25
❑ 80 Jerry Porter .60 .25
❑ 81 Charles Rogers .60 .25
❑ 82 Dwight Freeney .60 .25
❑ 83 Tim Lewis CO .50 .20
❑ 84 Aaron Brooks .60 .25
❑ 85 Kyle Boller .60 .25
❑ 86 Isaac Bruce .60 .25
❑ 87 Chad Johnson 1.00 .40
❑ 88 Kevin Jones 1.00 .40
❑ 89 Eric Moulds .60 .25
❑ 90 Sean Taylor .60 .25
❑ 91 Chris Perry .60 .25
❑ 92 Kerry Collins .60 .25
❑ 93 Steven Jackson 1.25 .50
❑ 94 LaDainian Tomlinson 1.25 .50
❑ 95 Torry Holt 1.00 .40
❑ 96 Lee Suggs .60 .25
❑ 97 Santana Moss .60 .25
❑ 98 Hines Ward 1.00 .40
❑ 99 Daunte Culpepper 1.00 .40
❑ 100 Travis Henry .60 .25
❑ 101 Ricky Williams .60 .25
❑ 102 Roy Williams WR 1.00 .40
❑ 103 Tatum Bell .60 .25
❑ 104 Dante Hall .60 .25
❑ 105 Larry Fitzgerald 1.00 .40
❑ 106 Marvin Harrison 1.00 .40
❑ 107 Byron Leftwich 1.00 .40
❑ 108 T.J. Houshmandzadeh .50 .20
❑ 109 Michael Clayton 1.00 .40
❑ 110 Ted Cottrell CO .50 .20
❑ 111 Carlos Rogers RC 5.00 2.00
❑ 112 Kyle Orton RC 6.00 2.50
❑ 113 Marion Barber RC 6.00 2.50
❑ 114 Mark Bradley RC 4.00 1.50
❑ 115 Travis Johnson RC 3.00 1.25
❑ 116 Antrel Rolle RC 4.00 1.50
❑ 117 Jason Campbell RC 6.00 2.50
❑ 118 Justin Miller RC 3.00 1.25
❑ 119 J.J. Arrington RC 5.00 2.00
❑ 120 Marcus Spears RC 4.00 1.50
❑ 121 Vincent Jackson RC 4.00 1.50
❑ 122 Erasmus James RC 4.00 1.50
❑ 123 Heath Miller RC 10.00 4.00
❑ 124 Eric Shelton RC 4.00 1.50
❑ 125 Cedric Benson RC 8.00 3.00
❑ 126 Mark Clayton RC 5.00 2.00
❑ 127 Anthony Davis RC 3.00 1.25
❑ 128 Charlie Frye RC 8.00 3.00
❑ 129 Fred Gibson RC 3.00 1.25
❑ 130 Reggie Brown RC 4.00 1.50
❑ 131 Andrew Walter RC 6.00 2.50
❑ 132 Adam Jones RC 4.00 1.50
❑ 133 David Greene RC 4.00 1.50
❑ 134 Maurice Clarett 4.00 1.50
❑ 135 Roscoe Parrish RC 4.00 1.50
❑ 136 Chris Henry RC 4.00 1.50
❑ 137 Mike Nugent RC 4.00 1.50
❑ 138 Kevin Burnett RC 4.00 1.50
❑ 139 Matt Roth RC 4.00 1.50
❑ 140 Barrett Ruud RC 4.00 1.50
❑ 141 Kirk Morrison RC 4.00 1.50
❑ 142 Brock Berlin RC 3.00 1.25
❑ 143 Bryant McFadden RC 4.00 1.50
❑ 144 Scott Starks RC 3.00 1.25
❑ 145 Stanford Routt RC 3.00 1.25
❑ 146 Oshiomogho Atogwe RC 3.00 1.25
❑ 147 Jovan Witherspoon RC 2.00 .75
❑ 148 Boomer Grigsby RC 5.00 2.00
❑ 149 Lance Mitchell RC 3.00 1.25
❑ 150 Darryl Blackstock RC 3.00 1.25
❑ 151 Ellis Hobbs RC 4.00 1.50
❑ 152 James Kilian RC 4.00 1.50
❑ 153 Willie Parker 10.00 4.00
❑ 154 Justin Tuck RC 4.00 1.50
❑ 155 Luis Castillo RC 4.00 1.50
❑ 156 Paris Warren RC 3.00 1.25
❑ 157 Corey Webster RC 4.00 1.50
❑ 158 Tab Perry RC 4.00 1.50
❑ 159 Rian Wallace RC 3.00 1.25
❑ 160 Joel Dreessen RC 3.00 1.25
❑ 161 Khalif Barnes RC 3.00 1.25
❑ 162 David Pollack RC 4.00 1.50
❑ 163 Zach Tuiasosopo RC 2.00 .75
❑ 164 Ryan Riddle RC 2.00 .75
❑ 165 Travis Daniels RC 3.00 1.25
❑ 166 Eric King RC 3.00 1.25
❑ 167 Justin Green RC 4.00 1.50
❑ 168 Manuel White RC 3.00 1.25
❑ 169 Jordan Beck RC 3.00 1.25
❑ 170 Lofa Tatupu RC 5.00 2.00
❑ 171 Will Peoples RC 3.00 1.25
❑ 172 Chad Friehauf RC 3.00 1.25
❑ 173 Brady Poppinga RC 4.00 1.50
❑ 174 Anttaj Hawthorne RC 3.00 1.25
❑ 175 Nick Collins RC 4.00 1.50
❑ 176 Craig Ochs RC 3.00 1.25
❑ 177 Billy Bajema RC 3.00 1.25
❑ 178 Jon Goldsberry RC 4.00 1.50
❑ 179 Jared Newberry RC 3.00 1.25
❑ 180 Odell Thurman RC 4.00 1.50
❑ 181 Kelvin Hayden RC 3.00 1.25
❑ 182 Jamaal Brimmer RC 2.00 .75
❑ 183 Jonathan Babineaux RC 3.00 1.25
❑ 184 Bo Scaife RC 3.00 1.25
❑ 185 Bryan Randall RC 3.00 1.25
❑ 186 James Butler RC 3.00 1.25
❑ 187 Harry Williams RC 3.00 1.25
❑ 188 Leroy Hill RC 4.00 1.50
❑ 189 Josh Bullocks RC 4.00 1.50
❑ 190 Alfred Fincher RC 3.00 1.25
❑ 191 Antonio Perkins RC 3.00 1.25
❑ 192 Bobby Purify RC 3.00 1.25
❑ 193 Darrent Williams RC 4.00 1.50
❑ 194 Darian Durant RC 4.00 1.50
❑ 195 Fred Amey RC 3.00 1.25
❑ 196 Ronald Bartell RC 3.00 1.25
❑ 197 Kerry Rhodes RC 4.00 1.50
❑ 198 Jerome Carter RC 3.00 1.25
❑ 199 Roddy White RC 4.00 1.50
❑ 200 Nehemiah Broughton RC 3.00 1.25
❑ 201 Keron Henry RC 2.00 .75
❑ 202 Jerome Collins RC 3.00 1.25
❑ 203 Trent Cole RC 4.00 1.50
❑ 204 Alphonso Hodge RC 2.00 .75
❑ 205 Marviel Underwood RC 3.00 1.25
❑ 206 Marlin Jackson RC 4.00 1.50
❑ 207 Madison Hedgecock RC 4.00 1.50
❑ 208 Chris Spencer RC 4.00 1.50
❑ 209 Vincent Fuller RC 3.00 1.25
❑ 210 Marcus Maxwell RC 3.00 1.25
❑ 211 Dustin Fox RC 4.00 1.50
❑ 212 Timmy Chang RC 3.00 1.25
❑ 213 Walter Reyes RC 3.00 1.25
❑ 214 Donte Nicholson RC 4.00 1.50
❑ 215 Stanley Wilson RC 3.00 1.25
❑ 216 Dan Cody RC 4.00 1.50
❑ 217 Alex Barron RC 2.00 .75
❑ 218 Taylor Stubblefield RC 2.00 .75
❑ 219 Shaun Cody RC 4.00 1.50
❑ 220 Steve Savoy RC 2.00 .75
❑ 221 Aaron Rodgers AU/199 RC 200.00 100.00
❑ 222 Alex Smith QB AU/199 RC 200.00 100.00
❑ 223 Bray.Edwards AU/199 RC 150.00 75.00
❑ 224 Cadil.Williams AU/199 RC 200.00 100.00
❑ 225 Mike Williams AU/199 80.00 40.00
❑ 226 Ronnie Brown AU/199 RC 200.00 100.00
❑ 227 T.Williamson AU/199 RC 100.00 50.00
❑ 228 Dante Ridgeway AU B RC 12.00 5.00
❑ 229 Channing Crowder AU G RC 15.00 6.00
❑ 230 Chase Lyman AU E RC 12.00 5.00
❑ 231 Courtney Roby AU F RC 15.00 6.00
❑ 232 Damien Nash AU G RC 15.00 6.00
❑ 233 Dan Orlovsky AU C RC 20.00 10.00
❑ 234 Fabian Washington AU B RC 20.00 7.50
❑ 235 Shawne Merriman AU B RC 40.00 20.00
❑ 236 Cedric Houston AU G RC 15.00 7.50
❑ 237 Alex Smith TE AU D RC 15.00 6.00
❑ 238 Brandon Jones AU B RC 15.00 6.00
❑ 239 Alvin Pearman AU G RC 15.00 6.00
❑ 240 Derek Anderson AU C RC 20.00 10.00
❑ 241 J.R. Russell AU G RC 12.00 5.00
❑ 242 Jerome Mathis AU F RC 12.00 5.00
❑ 243 Josh Davis AU A RC 15.00 6.00
❑ 244 Kay-Jay Harris AU G RC 12.00 5.00
❑ 245 Rasheed Marshall AU F RC 12.00 5.00
❑ 246 Matt Jones AU/199 RC 120.00 60.00
❑ 247 Chad Owens AU G RC 15.00 6.00
❑ 248 Larry Brackins AU A RC 15.00 6.00
❑ 249 Matt Cassel AU G RC 25.00 12.50
❑ 250 Noah Herron AU G RC 15.00 6.00
❑ 251 Roydell Williams AU G RC 15.00 6.00
❑ 252 Ryan Fitzpatrick AU F RC 25.00 10.00
❑ 253 Derrick Johnson AU E RC 25.00 10.00
❑ 254 DeMarcus Ware AU D RC 25.00 12.50
❑ 255 Brandon Jacobs AU A RC 50.00 30.00
❑ 256 Craig Bragg AU G RC 12.00 5.00
❑ 257 Ryan Moats AU G RC 25.00 12.50
❑ 258 Stefan LeFors AU G RC 15.00 6.00
❑ 259 Frank Gore AU B RC 80.00 50.00
❑ DSB Bogut/A.Smith QB AU/100 250.00 125.00

2006 Bowman Chrome

❑ 1 Devin Aromashodu RC 1.50 .60
❑ 2 Daniel Bullocks RC 2.00 .75
❑ 3 Winston Justice RC 2.00 .75
❑ 4 Lawrence Vickers RC 1.50 .60
❑ 5 Bernard Pollard RC 1.50 .60

❑ 6 Abdul Hodge RC 2.00 .75
❑ 7 Jovon Bouknight RC 1.50 .60
❑ 8 Wali Lundy RC 2.00 .75
❑ 9 Jonathan Orr RC 1.50 .60
❑ 10 Gerald Riggs RC 2.00 .75
❑ 11 Chris Gocong RC 1.50 .60
❑ 12 David Kirtman RC 1.50 .60
❑ 13 Quinn Sypniewski RC 1.50 .60
❑ 14 Richard Marshall RC 1.50 .60
❑ 15 Darryl Tapp RC 1.50 .60
❑ 16 Charles Davis RC 1.50 .60
❑ 17 Tim Massaquoi RC 1.50 .60
❑ 18 DeMario Minter RC 1.50 .60
❑ 19 Hank Baskett RC 2.00 .75
❑ 20 Andre Hall RC 1.50 .60
❑ 21 Cody Hodges RC 1.50 .60
❑ 22 Greg Lee RC 1.50 .60
❑ 23 Danieal Manning RC 2.00 .75
❑ 24 Jason Hatcher RC 1.50 .60
❑ 25 Ben Obomanu RC 1.50 .60
❑ 26 Dusty Dvoracek RC 2.00 .75
❑ 27 Domenik Hixon RC 1.50 .60
❑ 28 Josh Betts RC 1.50 .60
❑ 29 Marques Colston RC 8.00 3.00
❑ 30 P.J. Pope RC 1.50 .60
❑ 31 Gabe Watson RC 1.50 .60
❑ 32 Alan Zemaitis RC 2.00 .75
❑ 33 Jeff King RC 1.50 .60
❑ 34 Damien Rhodes RC 1.50 .60
❑ 35 Orien Harris RC 1.50 .60
❑ 36 David Anderson RC 1.50 .60
❑ 37 Garrett Mills RC 2.00 .75
❑ 38 Anthony Schlegel RC 1.50 .60
❑ 39 Omar Gaither RC 1.50 .60
❑ 40 Freddie Keiaho RC 1.50 .60
❑ 41 J.J. Outlaw RC 1.50 .60
❑ 42 Tony Scheffler RC 2.00 .75
❑ 43 Dee Webb RC 1.50 .60
❑ 44 Drew Olson RC 1.50 .60
❑ 45 Martin Nance RC 1.50 .60
❑ 46 Ko Simpson RC 1.50 .60
❑ 47 Jesse Mahelona RC 1.50 .60
❑ 48 Owen Daniels RC 2.00 .75
❑ 49 Delanie Walker RC 1.50 .60
❑ 50 Eric Smith RC 1.50 .60
❑ 51 Darrell Hackney RC 1.50 .60
❑ 52 Freddie Roach RC 1.50 .60
❑ 53 James Anderson RC 1.00 .40
❑ 54 Anthony Smith RC 2.50 1.00
❑ 55 Gerris Wilkinson RC 1.00 .40
❑ 56 Tamba Hali RC 4.00 1.50
❑ 57 Jerome Harrison RC 4.00 1.50
❑ 58 Jason Allen RC 4.00 1.50
❑ 59 Brodrick Bunkley RC 4.00 1.50
❑ 60 Bobby Carpenter RC 4.00 1.50
❑ 61 Johnathan Joseph RC 3.00 1.25
❑ 62 Travis Wilson RC 4.00 1.50
❑ 63 Reggie McNeal RC 3.00 1.25
❑ 64 Haloti Ngata RC 4.00 1.50
❑ 65 Manny Lawson RC 4.00 1.50
❑ 66 Donte Whitner RC 4.00 1.50
❑ 67 Derek Hagan RC 4.00 1.50
❑ 68 Devin Hester RC 8.00 3.00
❑ 69 Jeremy Bloom RC 3.00 1.25
❑ 70 Ashton Youboty RC 4.00 1.50
❑ 71 Kamerion Wimbley RC 4.00 1.50
❑ 72 Charlie Whitehurst RC 5.00 2.00
❑ 73 Darnell Bing RC 4.00 1.50
❑ 74 Adam Jennings RC 3.00 1.25
❑ 75 Tim Day RC 3.00 1.25
❑ 76 Jeff Webb RC 3.00 1.25
❑ 77 D.J. Shockley RC 4.00 1.50
❑ 78 Marcus Vick RC 3.00 1.25
❑ 79 Thomas Howard RC 4.00 1.50
❑ 80 Todd Watkins RC 3.00 1.25
❑ 81 Davin Joseph RC 3.00 1.25
❑ 82 Pat Watkins RC 4.00 1.50
❑ 83 Jon Alston RC 4.00 1.50
❑ 84 Ernie Sims RC 5.00 2.00
❑ 85 D'Qwell Jackson RC 3.00 1.25
❑ 86 Corey Bramlet RC 3.00 1.25
❑ 87 Antonio Cromartie RC 4.00 1.50
❑ 88 A.J. Nicholson RC 2.00 .75
❑ 89 Kevin McMahan RC 3.00 1.25
❑ 90 J.D. Runnels RC 3.00 1.25
❑ 91 Nate Salley RC 3.00 1.25
❑ 92 Matt Shelton RC 4.00 1.50
❑ 93 Brett Basanez RC 4.00 1.50
❑ 94 Rocky McIntosh RC 4.00 1.50
❑ 95 Anthony Mix RC 3.00 1.25
❑ 96 Jimmy Williams RC 4.00 1.50
❑ 97 Marcus McNeill RC 3.00 1.25
❑ 98 DeMeco Ryans RC 5.00 2.00
❑ 99 Dwayne Slay RC 3.00 1.25
❑ 100 John David Washington RC 3.00 1.25
❑ 101 P.J. Daniels RC 3.00 1.25
❑ 102 Kelly Jennings RC 4.00 1.50
❑ 103 John McCargo RC 3.00 1.25
❑ 104 Paul Pinegar RC 3.00 1.25
❑ 105 Ray Edwards RC 3.00 1.25
❑ 106 Elvis Dumervil RC 2.00 .75
❑ 107 Travis Lulay RC 3.00 1.25
❑ 108 Bennie Brazell RC 3.00 1.25
❑ 109 Dominique Byrd RC 3.00 1.25
❑ 110 Nick Mangold RC 3.00 1.25
❑ 111 Plaxico Burress .60 .25
❑ 112 Shaun Alexander 1.00 .40
❑ 113 Muhsin Muhammad .60 .25
❑ 114 Jake Plummer .60 .25
❑ 115 Deuce McAllister .60 .25
❑ 116 T.J. Houshmandzadeh .60 .25
❑ 117 Carson Palmer 1.00 .40
❑ 118 Willis McGahee 1.00 .40
❑ 119 Terrell Owens 1.00 .40
❑ 120 Fred Taylor .60 .25
❑ 121 Dante Hall .60 .25
❑ 122 Brad Johnson .60 .25
❑ 123 Reggie Wayne .60 .25
❑ 124 DeShaun Foster .60 .25
❑ 125 Tony Gonzalez .60 .25
❑ 126 Javon Walker .60 .25
❑ 127 Marc Bulger .60 .25
❑ 128 LaDainian Tomlinson 1.25 .50
❑ 129 Byron Leftwich .60 .25
❑ 130 Dwight Freeney .60 .25
❑ 131 Kevin Jones 1.00 .40
❑ 132 Hines Ward 1.00 .40
❑ 133 Randy Moss 1.00 .40
❑ 134 Edgerrin James 1.00 .40
❑ 135 Ahman Green .60 .25
❑ 136 Steven Jackson 1.00 .40
❑ 137 Ben Roethlisberger 1.50 .60
❑ 138 Daunte Culpepper 1.00 .40
❑ 139 Santana Moss .60 .25
❑ 140 Jonathan Vilma .60 .25
❑ 141 Gary Kubiak CO .60 .25
❑ 142 Marvin Harrison 1.00 .40
❑ 143 Trent Green .60 .25
❑ 144 Chris Chambers .60 .25
❑ 145 Chris Brown .60 .25
❑ 146 Eli Manning 1.25 .50
❑ 147 Corey Dillon .60 .25
❑ 148 Anquan Boldin .60 .25
❑ 149 Donovan McNabb 1.00 .40
❑ 150 Drew Bennett .50 .20
❑ 151 Jason Witten .60 .25
❑ 152 Eric Moulds .60 .25
❑ 153 Billy Volek .60 .25
❑ 154 Chris Cooley .50 .20
❑ 155 Larry Johnson 1.25 .50
❑ 156 Willie Parker 1.25 .50
❑ 157 Cadillac Williams 1.00 .40
❑ 158 Philip Rivers 1.00 .40
❑ 159 Reuben Droughns .60 .25
❑ 160 Joey Galloway .60 .25
❑ 161 Lee Evans .60 .25
❑ 162 Jamal Lewis .60 .25
❑ 163 Brett Favre 2.00 .75
❑ 164 Clinton Portis 1.00 .40
❑ 165 Rod Marinelli CO .60 .25
❑ 166 Tom Brady 1.50 .60
❑ 167 Torry Holt .60 .25
❑ 168 Rudi Johnson .60 .25
❑ 169 Priest Holmes .60 .25
❑ 170 Tatum Bell .60 .25
❑ 171 Jeremy Shockey 1.00 .40
❑ 172 Shawne Merriman .60 .25
❑ 173 Alge Crumpler .60 .25
❑ 174 Marion Barber .60 .25
❑ 175 Steve Smith 1.00 .40
❑ 176 Mike McCarthy CO .60 .25
❑ 177 David Carr .60 .25
❑ 178 Julius Jones 1.00 .40
❑ 179 Chad Johnson .60 .25
❑ 180 Curtis Martin 1.00 .40
❑ 181 Peyton Manning 1.50 .60
❑ 182 LaMont Jordan .60 .25
❑ 183 Tiki Barber 1.00 .40
❑ 184 Darrell Jackson .60 .25
❑ 185 J.P. Losman .60 .25
❑ 186 Drew Brees 1.00 .40
❑ 187 Isaac Bruce .60 .25
❑ 188 Drew Bledsoe 1.00 .40
❑ 189 Roy Williams WR 1.00 .40
❑ 190 Donte Stallworth .60 .25
❑ 191 Odell Thurman .50 .20
❑ 192 Chester Taylor .60 .25
❑ 193 Randy McMichael .50 .20
❑ 194 Larry Fitzgerald 1.00 .40
❑ 195 Charlie Frye .60 .25
❑ 196 Keary Colbert .50 .20
❑ 197 Patrick Ramsey .60 .25
❑ 198 Mark Clayton .60 .25
❑ 199 Michael Jenkins .60 .25
❑ 200 Jake Delhomme .60 .25
❑ 201 Aaron Rodgers 1.00 .40
❑ 202 Andre Johnson .60 .25
❑ 203 Matt Hasselbeck .60 .25
❑ 204 Reggie Brown .60 .25
❑ 205 Warrick Dunn .60 .25
❑ 206 Kurt Warner .60 .25
❑ 207 Antonio Gates 1.00 .40
❑ 208 Terry Glenn .60 .25
❑ 209 Steve McNair .60 .25
❑ 210 Alex Smith QB 1.25 .50
❑ 211 Joe Horn .60 .25
❑ 212 Domanick Davis .60 .25
❑ 213 Deion Branch .60 .25
❑ 214 Todd Heap .60 .25
❑ 215 Chad Pennington .60 .25
❑ 216 Brandon Lloyd .60 .25
❑ 217 Rod Smith .60 .25
❑ 218 Ronnie Brown 1.00 .40
❑ 219 Braylon Edwards 1.00 .40
❑ 220 Michael Vick 1.25 .50
❑ 221 Vince Young RC 20.00 8.00
❑ 222 Jay Cutler RC 15.00 6.00
❑ 223 Reggie Bush RC 30.00 12.50
❑ 224 Matt Leinart RC 15.00 6.00
❑ 225 Vernon Davis RC 8.00 3.00
❑ 226 A.J. Hawk RC 8.00 3.00
❑ 227 Santonio Holmes RC 8.00 3.00
❑ 228 DeAngelo Williams RC 10.00 4.00
❑ 229 LenDale White RC 8.00 3.00
❑ 230 Sinorice Moss RC 5.00 2.00
❑ 231 Joseph Addai RC 12.00 5.00
❑ 232 Mike Bell RC 6.00 2.50
❑ 233 Will Blackmon RC 3.00 1.25
❑ 234 Brian Calhoun RC 4.00 1.50
❑ 235 Kellen Clemens RC 5.00 2.00
❑ 236 Brodie Croyle RC 8.00 3.00
❑ 237 Maurice Drew RC 10.00 4.00
❑ 238 Anthony Fasano RC 4.00 1.50
❑ 239 D'Brickashaw Ferguson RC 4.00 1.50
❑ 240 Quinton Ganther RC 3.00 1.25
❑ 241 Bruce Gradkowski RC 6.00 2.50
❑ 242 Skyler Green RC 4.00 1.50
❑ 243 Chad Greenway RC 4.00 1.50
❑ 244 Marques Hagans RC 3.00 1.25
❑ 245 Michael Huff RC 5.00 2.00
❑ 246 Cedric Humes RC 4.00 1.50
❑ 247 Tarvaris Jackson RC 6.00 2.50
❑ 248 Omar Jacobs RC 3.00 1.25
❑ 249 Greg Jennings RC 6.00 2.50
❑ 250 Mathias Kiwanuka RC 5.00 2.00
❑ 251 Joe Klopfenstein RC 3.00 1.25
❑ 252 Marcedes Lewis RC 4.00 1.50
❑ 253 Brandon Marshall RC 4.00 1.50
❑ 254 Ingle Martin RC 4.00 1.50
❑ 255 Dontrell Moore RC 3.00 1.25
❑ 256 Jerious Norwood RC 6.00 2.50
❑ 257 Leonard Pope RC 4.00 1.50
❑ 258 Willie Reid RC 4.00 1.50
❑ 259 Michael Robinson RC 6.00 2.50
❑ 260 Brad Smith RC 4.00 1.50
❑ 261 Maurice Stovall RC 4.00 1.50
❑ 262 David Thomas RC 4.00 1.50
❑ 263 Leon Washington RC 6.00 2.50
❑ 264 Brandon Williams RC 4.00 1.50
❑ 265 Demetrius Williams RC 5.00 2.00
❑ 266 Tye Hill RC 4.00 1.50
❑ 267 Mike Hass RC 4.00 1.50
❑ 268 Jason Avant RC 4.00 1.50
❑ 269 Chad Jackson RC 6.00 2.50
❑ 270 Laurence Maroney RC 10.00 4.00
❑ 271 Anwar Phillips RC 3.00 1.25
❑ 272 David Kirtman RC 3.00 1.25

❑ 273 Roman Harper RC 3.00 1.25
❑ 274 Spencer Havner RC 3.00 1.25
❑ 275 Erik Meyer RC 3.00 1.25

2000 Bowman Reserve

❑ COMP.SET w/o SP's (100) 40.00 15.00
❑ 1 Chad Pennington RC 30.00 12.50
❑ 2 Shaun Alexander RC 40.00 15.00
❑ 3 Thomas Jones RC 20.00 8.00
❑ 4 Courtney Brown RC 12.00 5.00
❑ 5 Curtis Keaton RC 10.00 4.00
❑ 6 Jerry Porter RC 15.00 6.00
❑ 7 Jamal Lewis RC 30.00 12.50
❑ 8 Ron Dayne RC 12.00 5.00
❑ 9 R.Jay Soward RC 10.00 4.00
❑ 10 Tee Martin RC 12.00 5.00
❑ 11 Travis Taylor RC 12.00 5.00
❑ 12 Plaxico Burress RC 25.00 10.00
❑ 13 Giovanni Carmazzi RC 10.00 4.00
❑ 14 Sylvester Morris RC 10.00 4.00
❑ 15 Chris Redman RC 10.00 4.00
❑ 16 Trung Canidate RC 10.00 4.00
❑ 17 J.R. Redmond RC 10.00 4.00
❑ 18 Bubba Franks RC 12.00 5.00
❑ 19 Travis Prentice RC 10.00 4.00
❑ 20 Peter Warrick RC 12.00 5.00
❑ 21 Frank Sanders .75 .30
❑ 22 Edgerrin James 2.00 .75
❑ 23 Marcus Robinson 1.25 .50
❑ 24 Mike Alstott 1.25 .50
❑ 25 Jerry Rice 2.50 1.00
❑ 26 Marshall Faulk 1.50 .60
❑ 27 Brad Johnson 1.25 .50
❑ 28 Elvis Grbac .75 .30
❑ 29 Wayne Chrebet .75 .30
❑ 30 Akili Smith .50 .20
❑ 31 Rob Johnson .75 .30
❑ 32 Brett Favre 4.00 1.50
❑ 33 Ricky Williams 1.25 .50
❑ 34 Donovan McNabb 2.00 .75
❑ 35 Cris Carter 1.25 .50
❑ 36 Ricky Watters .75 .30
❑ 37 Steve McNair 2.00 .75
❑ 38 Stephen Davis 1.25 .50
❑ 39 Fred Taylor 1.25 .50
❑ 40 Rocket Ismail .75 .30
❑ 41 Terry Glenn .75 .30
❑ 42 Ed McCaffrey 1.25 .50
❑ 43 Patrick Jeffers 1.25 .50
❑ 44 Jake Plummer .75 .30
❑ 45 Doug Flutie 1.25 .50
❑ 46 Terrell Davis 1.25 .50
❑ 47 Marvin Harrison 1.25 .50
❑ 48 Amani Toomer .75 .30
❑ 49 Tyrone Wheatley .75 .30
❑ 50 Charlie Garner .75 .30
❑ 51 Jevon Kearse 1.25 .50
❑ 52 Michael Westbrook .75 .30
❑ 53 Eddie George 1.25 .50
❑ 54 Robert Smith 1.25 .50
❑ 55 Keyshawn Johnson 1.25 .50
❑ 56 Torry Holt 1.25 .50
❑ 57 Jon Kitna 1.25 .50
❑ 58 Curtis Conway .75 .30
❑ 59 Jeff Garcia 1.25 .50
❑ 60 Randy Moss 2.50 1.00
❑ 61 Jimmy Smith .75 .30
❑ 62 James Stewart .75 .30
❑ 63 Troy Aikman 2.50 1.00
❑ 64 Cade McNown .50 .20
❑ 65 Natrone Means .75 .30
❑ 66 Jamal Anderson 1.25 .50
❑ 67 Warrick Dunn 1.25 .50
❑ 68 Kordell Stewart .75 .30
❑ 69 Duce Staley 1.25 .50
❑ 70 Rich Gannon 1.25 .50
❑ 71 Curtis Martin 1.25 .50
❑ 72 Kerry Collins .75 .30
❑ 73 Jeff Blake .75 .30
❑ 74 Drew Bledsoe 1.50 .60
❑ 75 Kevin Dyson .75 .30
❑ 76 Tony Gonzalez .75 .30
❑ 77 Mark Brunell 1.25 .50
❑ 78 Peyton Manning 3.00 1.25
❑ 79 Dorsey Levens .75 .30
❑ 80 Germane Crowell .50 .20
❑ 81 Brian Griese 1.25 .50
❑ 82 Steve Beuerlein .75 .30
❑ 83 Eric Moulds 1.25 .50
❑ 84 Tony Banks .75 .30
❑ 85 Chris Chandler .75 .30
❑ 86 Isaac Bruce 1.25 .50
❑ 87 Terrell Owens 1.25 .50
❑ 88 Jerome Bettis 1.25 .50
❑ 89 Daunte Culpepper 1.50 .60
❑ 90 Emmitt Smith 2.50 1.00
❑ 91 Curtis Enis .50 .20
❑ 92 Shaun King .50 .20
❑ 93 Tim Brown 1.25 .50
❑ 94 Antonio Freeman 1.25 .50
❑ 95 Charlie Batch 1.25 .50
❑ 96 Tim Couch .75 .30
❑ 97 Corey Dillon 1.25 .50
❑ 98 Muhsin Muhammad .75 .30
❑ 99 Joey Galloway .75 .30
❑ 100 Kurt Warner 2.50 1.00
❑ 101 David Boston 1.25 .50
❑ 102 Rod Smith .50 .20
❑ 103 Derrick Mayes .75 .30
❑ 104 Tony Martin .75 .30
❑ 105 Darnay Scott .75 .30
❑ 106 Joe Horn .75 .30
❑ 107 Troy Edwards .50 .20
❑ 108 James Johnson .50 .20
❑ 109 Vinny Testaverde .75 .30
❑ 110 Qadry Ismail .75 .30
❑ 111 Andre Reed .75 .30
❑ 112 Zach Thomas 1.25 .50
❑ 113 Ike Hilliard .75 .30
❑ 114 Herman Moore .75 .30
❑ 115 Kevin Johnson 1.25 .50
❑ 116 Shawn Jefferson .50 .20
❑ 117 Terance Mathis .75 .30
❑ 118 Peerless Price .75 .30
❑ 119 Bert Emanuel .50 .20
❑ 120 Terrence Wilkins .50 .20
❑ 121 Mike Anderson RC 15.00 6.00
❑ 122 Dez White RC 12.00 5.00
❑ 123 Todd Pinkston RC 12.00 5.00
❑ 124 Reuben Droughns RC 15.00 6.00
❑ 125 Danny Farmer RC 10.00 4.00

2006 Bowman Sterling

❑ COMP.RC SET (50) 50.00 20.00
❑ 1 Jon Alston RC 3.00 1.25
❑ 2 Daniel Bullocks RC 3.00 1.25
❑ 3 Damien Rhodes RC 2.50 1.00
❑ 4 Josh Betts RC 2.50 1.00
❑ 5 Garrett Mills RC 3.00 1.25
❑ 6 Anthony Schlegel RC 2.50 1.00
❑ 7 Lawrence Vickers RC 2.50 1.00
❑ 8 Abdul Hodge RC 3.00 1.25
❑ 9 Kevin McMahan RC 2.50 1.00
❑ 10 Orien Harris RC 2.50 1.00
❑ 11 Charles Davis RC 2.50 1.00
❑ 12 Haloti Ngata RC 3.00 1.25
❑ 13 Kelly Jennings RC 3.00 1.25
❑ 14 Corey Bramlet RC 2.50 1.00
❑ 15 Manny Lawson RC 3.00 1.25
❑ 16 David Kirtman RC 2.50 1.00
❑ 17 Jeremy Bloom RC 2.50 1.00
❑ 18 Jason Allen RC 3.00 1.25
❑ 19 Owen Daniels RC 3.00 1.25
❑ 20 Ray Edwards RC 2.50 1.00
❑ 21 DeMario Minter RC 2.50 1.00
❑ 22 Ernie Sims RC 4.00 1.50
❑ 23 Jovon Bouknight RC 2.50 1.00
❑ 24 Sinorice Moss RC 4.00 1.50
❑ 25 Travis Lulay RC 2.50 1.00
❑ 26 Quinn Sypniewski RC 2.50 1.00
❑ 27 T.J. Rushing RC 1.50 .60
❑ 28 J.J. Outlaw RC 2.50 1.00
❑ 29 Donte Whitner RC 3.00 1.25
❑ 30 Freddie Keiaho RC 2.50 1.00
❑ 31 Rocky McIntosh RC 3.00 1.25
❑ 32 Tamba Hali RC 3.00 1.25
❑ 33 Johnathan Joseph RC 2.50 1.00
❑ 34 Omar Gaither RC 2.50 1.00
❑ 35 Elvis Dumervil RC 1.50 .60
❑ 36 Thomas Howard RC 3.00 1.25
❑ 37 Gabe Watson RC 2.50 1.00
❑ 38 Tony Scheffler RC 3.00 1.25
❑ 39 Tim Massaquoi RC 2.50 1.00
❑ 40 Chris Gocong RC 2.50 1.00
❑ 41 Ko Simpson RC 2.50 1.00
❑ 42 D'Qwell Jackson RC 2.50 1.00
❑ 43 James Anderson RC 1.50 .60
❑ 44 P.J. Pope RC 2.50 1.00
❑ 45 Bennie Brazell RC 2.50 1.00
❑ 46 Jeff King RC 2.50 1.00
❑ 47 Dusty Dvoracek RC 3.00 1.25
❑ 48 Dee Webb RC 2.50 1.00
❑ 49 Jimmy Williams RC 3.00 1.25
❑ 50 Danieal Manning RC 3.00 1.25
❑ AC1 Antonio Cromartie AU RC 12.00 5.00
❑ AC2 Alge Crumpler JSY 10.00 4.00
❑ AF Anthony Fasano AU RC 12.00 5.00
❑ AH1 A.J. Hawk JSY RC 15.00 6.00
❑ AH2 A.J. Hawk JSY AU 80.00 40.00
❑ AHA Andre Hall AU RC 10.00 4.00
❑ AJ Adam Jennings AU RC 10.00 4.00
❑ AW Al Wilson JSY 8.00 3.00
❑ AY Ashton Youboty AU RC 12.00 5.00
❑ AZ Alan Zemaitis AU RC 12.00 5.00
❑ BB Brett Basanez AU RC 12.00 5.00
❑ BC1 Brian Calhoun JSY RC 8.00 3.00
❑ BC2 Brian Calhoun JSY AU 15.00 6.00
❑ BCR Brodie Croyle AU RC SP 30.00 15.00
❑ BF Brett Favre JSY 25.00 10.00
❑ BG Bruce Gradkowski AU RC 30.00 12.00
❑ BM Brandon Marshall JSY RC 8.00 3.00
❑ BO Ben Obomanu AU RC 10.00 4.00
❑ BS1 Bob Sanders JSY 10.00 4.00
❑ BS2 Brad Smith AU RC SP 12.00 5.00
❑ BW1 Brandon Williams JSY RC 8.00 3.00
❑ BW2 Brandon Williams JSY AU 15.00 6.00
❑ CB1 Chris Brown JSY 8.00 3.00
❑ CB2 Chris Brown JSY AU 10.00 4.00
❑ CG Chad Greenway AU RC 12.00 5.00
❑ CH Cedric Humes AU RC 12.00 5.00
❑ CHO Cody Hodges AU RC 10.00 4.00
❑ CJ Chad Jackson JSY RC 10.00 4.00
❑ CM Curtis Martin JSY 12.00 5.00
❑ CP Carson Palmer JSY 12.00 5.00
❑ CW Charlie Whitehurst JSY RC 10.00 4.00
❑ DAN David Anderson AU RC 10.00 4.00
❑ DB1 Derrick Burgess JSY 8.00 3.00
❑ DB2 Dominique Byrd AU RC 12.00 5.00
❑ DEH Derek Hagan JSY RC 8.00 3.00
❑ DEW Demetrius Williams JSY RC 10.00 4.00
❑ DF Dwight Freeney JSY 10.00 4.00
❑ DFE D.Ferguson AU RC SP 12.00 5.00
❑ DHA Darrell Hackney AU RC SP 10.004.00
❑ DHE Devin Hester AU RC 50.00 25.00
❑ DHI Domenik Hixon AU RC 10.00 4.00
❑ DM Donovan McNabb JSY 12.00 5.00
❑ DOL Drew Olson AU RC 10.00 4.00
❑ DRY DeMeco Ryans AU RC 20.00 8.00
❑ DS1 Darren Sharper JSY 8.00 3.00
❑ DS2 D.J. Shockley AU RC 12.00 5.00
❑ DT David Thomas AU RC 12.00 5.00
❑ DW DeAngelo Williams JSY RC 20.00 8.00

❑ DWA	Delanie Walker AU RC	10.00	4.00
❑ GJ	Greg Jennings AU RC	25.00	10.00
❑ HB	Hank Baskett AU RC	15.00	6.00
❑ IM	Ingle Martin AU RC	10.00	4.00
❑ JA1	Joseph Addai AU RC	80.00	50.00
❑ JA2	Jason Avant JSY RC	8.00	3.00
❑ JD	Jake Delhomme JSY	10.00	4.00
❑ JH	Jerome Harrison AU RC	12.00	5.00
❑ JJ	Julius Jones JSY	12.00	5.00
❑ JK1	Joe Klopfenstein JSY RC	8.00	3.00
❑ JK2	Joe Klopfenstein JSY AU	12.00	5.00
❑ JL	Jamal Lewis JSY	10.00	4.00
❑ JM	Jerome Mathis JSY	8.00	3.00
❑ JN1	Jerious Norwood JSY RC	10.00	4.00
❑ JN2	Jerious Norwood AU	30.00	12.00
❑ JN3	Jerious Norwood JSY AU	40.00	15.00
❑ JO	Jonathan Orr AU RC	10.00	4.00
❑ JP	Julius Peppers JSY	10.00	4.00
❑ JS	Jeremy Shockey JSY	12.00	5.00
❑ JSM	Jimmy Smith JSY	10.00	4.00
❑ JT	Jeremiah Trotter JSY	8.00	3.00
❑ JW	Javon Walker JSY	10.00	4.00
❑ JWE	Jeff Webb AU RC	10.00	4.00
❑ KC1	Kellen Clemens JSY RC	10.00	4.00
❑ KC2	Kellen Clemens JSY AU	25.00	10.00
❑ KR	Koren Robinson JSY	10.00	4.00
❑ KW	Kamerion Wimbley AU RC	12.00	5.00
❑ LB	Lance Briggs JSY	8.00	3.00
❑ LE	Lee Evans JSY	10.00	4.00
❑ LF	Larry Fitzgerald JSY	12.00	5.00
❑ LJ	Larry Johnson JSY	15.00	6.00
❑ LM	Laurence Maroney JSY RC	20.00	8.00
❑ LN	Lorenzo Neal JSY	8.00	3.00
❑ LP	Leonard Pope AU RC SP	12.00	5.00
❑ LW	LenDale White JSY RC	12.00	5.00
❑ LWA1	Leon Washington JSY RC	12.00	5.00
❑ LWA2	Leon Washington JSY AU	25.00	10.00
❑ MB	Marion Barber JSY	10.00	4.00
❑ MBE	Mike Bell AU RC	20.00	8.00
❑ MD	Maurice Drew JSY RC	12.00	5.00
❑ MH	Marvin Harrison JSY	12.00	5.00
❑ MHA	Marques Hagans AU RC	10.00	4.00
❑ MHU	Michael Huff JSY RC	10.00	4.00
❑ MIH	Mike Hass AU RC SP	12.00	5.00
❑ MK	Mathias Kiwanuka AU RC	15.00	6.00
❑ ML	Matt Leinart JSY RC	25.00	10.00
❑ MLE	Marcedes Lewis JSY RC	8.00	3.00
❑ MN	Martin Nance AU RC	10.00	4.00
❑ MR1	Michael Robinson JSY RC	10.00	4.00
❑ MR2	Michael Robinson JSY AU	20.00	8.00
❑ MS	Michael Strahan JSY	10.00	4.00
❑ MST	Marcus Stroud JSY	8.00	3.00
❑ MST1	Maurice Stovall JSY RC	8.00	3.00
❑ MST2	Maurice Stovall AU	12.00	5.00
❑ MV	Michael Vick JSY	15.00	6.00
❑ MW1	Mario Williams JSY RC	10.00	4.00
❑ MW2	Mario Williams JSY AU	20.00	8.00
❑ OJ	Omar Jacobs JSY RC	8.00	3.00
❑ OU	Osi Umenyiora JSY	8.00	3.00
❑ PB	Plaxico Burress JSY	10.00	4.00
❑ PM	Peyton Manning JSY	20.00	8.00
❑ PP	Paul Pinegar AU RC SP	10.00	4.00
❑ QG	Quinton Ganther AU RC	10.00	4.00
❑ RB1	Reggie Bush JSY RC	40.00	15.00
❑ RB2	Reggie Bush JSY AU SP	350.00	200.00
❑ RB3	Ronnie Brown JSY	12.00	5.00
❑ RBA	Ronde Barber JSY	8.00	3.00
❑ RJ	Rudi Johnson JSY AU	20.00	8.00
❑ RM	Reggie McNeal AU RC	10.00	4.00
❑ RS	Rod Smith JSY	10.00	4.00
❑ RW	Reggie Wayne JSY	10.00	4.00
❑ RWI	Roy Williams S JSY	10.00	4.00
❑ SG	Skyler Green AU RC SP	12.00	5.00
❑ SH1	Santonio Holmes JSY RC	12.00	5.00
❑ SH2	S.Holmes JSY AU SP	60.00	30.00
❑ SMO	Santana Moss JSY	10.00	4.00
❑ SR	Shaun Rogers JSY	8.00	3.00
❑ SS	Steve Smith JSY AU SP	50.00	25.00
❑ TB	Tatum Bell JSY AU	15.00	6.00
❑ TBA	Tiki Barber JSY	12.00	5.00
❑ TG	Tony Gonzalez JSY	10.00	4.00
❑ TH	Tommie Harris JSY	8.00	3.00
❑ THO	Torry Holt JSY	10.00	4.00
❑ TJ1	Tarvaris Jackson JSY RC	10.00	4.00
❑ TJ2	Tarvaris Jackson JSY AU	40.00	20.00
❑ TW	Travis Wilson JSY RC	8.00	3.00
❑ TYH	Tye Hill AU RC	12.00	5.00
❑ VD1	Vernon Davis JSY RC	12.00	5.00
❑ VD2	Vernon Davis JSY AU SP	50.00	25.00
❑ VY1	Vince Young JSY RC	30.00	12.50
❑ VY2	Vince Young JSY AU SP	250.00	125.00
❑ WB	Will Blackmon AU RC	10.00	4.00
❑ WD	Warrick Dunn JSY	10.00	4.00
❑ WJ	Winston Justice AU RC	12.00	5.00
❑ WR	Willie Reid AU RC	12.00	5.00
❑ ZT	Zach Thomas JSY	12.00	5.00

1995 Bowman's Best

❑	COMPLETE SET (180)	100.00	40.00
❑ R1	Ki-Jana Carter RC	1.50	.60
❑ R2	Tony Boselli RC	1.50	.60
❑ R3	Steve McNair RC	15.00	6.00
❑ R4	Michael Westbrook RC	1.50	.60
❑ R5	Kerry Collins RC	6.00	2.50
❑ R6	Kevin Carter RC	1.50	.60
❑ R7	Mike Mamula RC	.40	.15
❑ R8	Joey Galloway RC	6.00	2.50
❑ R9	Kyle Brady RC	1.50	.60
❑ R10	Ray McElroy RC	.40	.15
❑ R11	Derrick Alexander DE RC	.40	.15
❑ R12	Warren Sapp RC	6.00	2.50
❑ R13	Mark Fields RC	1.50	.60
❑ R14	Ruben Brown RC	1.50	.60
❑ R15	Ellis Johnson RC	.40	.15
❑ R16	Hugh Douglas RC	1.50	.60
❑ R17	Alundis Brice RC	.40	.15
❑ R18	Napoleon Kaufman RC	5.00	2.00
❑ R19	James O. Stewart RC	3.00	1.25
❑ R20	Luther Elliss RC	.40	.15
❑ R21	Rashaan Salaam RC	.75	.30
❑ R22	Tyrone Poole RC	1.50	.60
❑ R23	Ty Law RC	4.00	1.50
❑ R24	Korey Stringer RC	.75	.30
❑ R25	Billy Milner RC	.40	.15
❑ R26	Roell Preston RC	.75	.30
❑ R27	Mark Bruener RC	.75	.30
❑ R28	Derrick Brooks RC	6.00	2.50
❑ R29	Blake Brockermeyer RC	.40	.15
❑ R30	Mike Frederick RC	.40	.15
❑ R31	Trezelle Jenkins RC	.40	.15
❑ R32	Craig Newsome RC	.40	.15
❑ R33	Matt O'Dwyer RC	.40	.15
❑ R34	Terrance Shaw RC	.40	.15
❑ R35	Anthony Cook RC	.40	.15
❑ R36	Darick Holmes RC	.75	.30
❑ R37	Cory Raymer RC	.40	.15
❑ R38	Zach Wiegert RC	.40	.15
❑ R39	Sam Shade RC	.40	.15
❑ R40	Brian DeMarco RC	.40	.15
❑ R41	Ron Davis RC	.40	.15
❑ R42	Orlando Thomas RC	.40	.15
❑ R43	Derek West RC	.40	.15
❑ R44	Ray Zellars RC	.75	.30
❑ R45	Todd Collins RC	.75	.30
❑ R46	Linc Harden RC	.40	.15
❑ R47	Frank Sanders RC	1.50	.60
❑ R48	Ken Dilger RC	1.50	.60
❑ R49	Barrett Robbins RC	.40	.15
❑ R50	Bobby Taylor RC	2.50	1.00
❑ R51	Terrell Fletcher RC	.40	.15
❑ R52	Jack Jackson RC	.40	.15
❑ R53	Jeff Kopp RC	.40	.15
❑ R54	Brendan Stai RC	.40	.15
❑ R55	Corey Fuller RC	.40	.15
❑ R56	Todd Sauerbrun RC	.40	.15
❑ R57	Dameian Jeffries RC	.40	.15
❑ R58	Troy Dumas RC	.40	.15
❑ R59	Charlie Williams RC	.40	.15
❑ R60	Kordell Stewart RC	6.00	2.50
❑ R61	Jay Barker RC	.40	.15
❑ R62	Jesse James RC	.40	.15
❑ R63	Shane Hannah RC	.40	.15
❑ R64	Rob Johnson RC	4.00	1.50
❑ R65	Darius Holland RC	.40	.15
❑ R66	William Henderson RC	5.00	2.00
❑ R67	Chris Sanders RC	.75	.30
❑ R68	Darryl Pounds RC	.40	.15
❑ R69	Melvin Tuten RC	.40	.15
❑ R70	David Sloan RC	.40	.15
❑ R71	Chris Hudson RC	.40	.15
❑ R72	William Strong RC	.40	.15
❑ R73	Brian Williams LB RC	.40	.15
❑ R74	Curtis Martin RC	15.00	6.00
❑ R75	Mike Verstegen RC	.40	.15
❑ R76	Justin Armour RC	.40	.15
❑ R77	Lorenzo Styles RC	.40	.15
❑ R78	Oliver Gibson RC	.40	.15
❑ R79	Zack Crockett RC	.75	.30
❑ R80	Tau Pupua RC	.40	.15
❑ R81	Tamarick Vanover RC	1.50	.60
❑ R82	Steve McLaughlin RC	.40	.15
❑ R83	Sean Harris RC	.40	.15
❑ R84	Eric Zeier RC	1.50	.60
❑ R85	Rodney Young RC	.40	.15
❑ R86	Chad May RC	.40	.15
❑ R87	Evan Pilgrim RC	.40	.15
❑ R88	James A.Stewart RC	.40	.15
❑ R89	Torey Hunter RC	.40	.15
❑ R90	Antonio Freeman RC	4.00	1.50
❑ V1	Rob Moore	.60	.25
❑ V2	Craig Heyward	.60	.25
❑ V3	Jim Kelly	1.25	.50
❑ V4	John Kasay	.30	.10
❑ V5	Jeff Graham	.30	.10
❑ V6	Jeff Blake RC	2.50	1.00
❑ V7	Antonio Langham	.30	.10
❑ V8	Troy Aikman	3.00	1.25
❑ V9	Simon Fletcher	.30	.10
❑ V10	Barry Sanders	5.00	2.00
❑ V11	Edgar Bennett	.60	.25
❑ V12	Ray Childress	.30	.10
❑ V13	Ray Buchanan	.30	.10
❑ V14	Desmond Howard	.60	.25
❑ V15	Dale Carter	.60	.25
❑ V16	Troy Vincent	.30	.10
❑ V17	David Palmer	.60	.25
❑ V18	Ben Coates	.60	.25
❑ V19	Derek Brown TE	.30	.10
❑ V20	Dave Brown	.60	.25
❑ V21	Mo Lewis	.30	.10
❑ V22	Harvey Williams	.30	.10
❑ V23	Randall Cunningham	1.25	.50
❑ V24	Kevin Greene	.60	.25
❑ V25	Junior Seau	1.25	.50
❑ V26	Merton Hanks	.30	.10
❑ V27	Cortez Kennedy	.60	.25
❑ V28	Troy Drayton	.30	.10
❑ V29	Hardy Nickerson	.30	.10
❑ V30	Brian Mitchell	.30	.10
❑ V31	Raymont Harris	.30	.10
❑ V32	Keith Goganious	.30	.10
❑ V33	Andre Reed	.60	.25
❑ V34	Terance Mathis	.60	.25
❑ V35	Garrison Hearst	1.25	.50
❑ V36	Glyn Milburn	.30	.10
❑ V37	Emmitt Smith	5.00	2.00
❑ V38	Vinny Testaverde	.60	.25
❑ V39	Darnay Scott	.60	.25
❑ V40	Mickey Washington	.30	.10
❑ V41	Craig Erickson	.30	.10
❑ V42	Chris Chandler	1.25	.50
❑ V43	Brett Favre	6.00	2.50
❑ V44	Scott Mitchell	.60	.25
❑ V45	Chris Slade	.30	.10
❑ V46	Warren Moon	.60	.25
❑ V47	Dan Marino	6.00	2.50
❑ V48	Greg Hill	.60	.25
❑ V49	Rocket Ismail	.60	.25
❑ V50	Bobby Houston	.30	.10
❑ V51	Rodney Hampton	.60	.25
❑ V52	Jim Everett	.30	.10
❑ V53	Rick Mirer	.60	.25
❑ V54	Steve Young	2.50	1.00
❑ V55	Dennis Gibson	.30	.10
❑ V56	Rod Woodson	.60	.25
❑ V57	Calvin Williams	.60	.25
❑ V58	Tom Carter	.30	.10
❑ V59	Trent Dilfer	1.25	.50
❑ V60	Shane Conlan	.30	.10
❑ V61	Cornelius Bennett	.60	.25

❑ V62 Eric Metcalf .60 .25
❑ V63 Frank Reich .30 .10
❑ V64 Eric Hill .30 .10
❑ V65 Erik Kramer .30 .10
❑ V66 Michael Irvin 1.25 .50
❑ V67 Tony McGee .30 .10
❑ V68 Andre Rison .60 .25
❑ V69 Shannon Sharpe .60 .25
❑ V70 Quentin Coryatt .60 .25
❑ V71 Robert Brooks 1.25 .50
❑ V72 Steve Beuerlein .60 .25
❑ V73 Herman Moore 1.25 .50
❑ V74 Jack Del Rio .30 .10
❑ V75 Dave Meggett .30 .10
❑ V76 Pete Stoyanovich .30 .10
❑ V77 Neil Smith .60 .25
❑ V78 Corey Miller .30 .10
❑ V79 Tim Brown 1.25 .50
❑ V80 Tyrone Hughes .60 .25
❑ V81 Boomer Esiason .60 .25
❑ V82 Natrone Means .60 .25
❑ V83 Chris Warren .60 .25
❑ V84 Byron Bam Morris .30 .10
❑ V85 Jerry Rice 3.00 1.25
❑ V86 Michael Zordich .30 .10
❑ V87 Errict Rhett .60 .25
❑ V88 Henry Ellard .60 .25
❑ V89 Chris Miller .30 .10
❑ V90 John Elway 6.00 2.50

1996 Bowman's Best

❑ COMPLETE SET (180) 80.00 40.00
❑ 1 Emmitt Smith 3.00 1.25
❑ 2 Kordell Stewart .75 .30
❑ 3 Mark Chmura .40 .15
❑ 4 Sean Dawkins .20 .07
❑ 5 Steve Young 1.50 .60
❑ 6 Tamarick Vanover .40 .15
❑ 7 Scott Mitchell .40 .15
❑ 8 Aaron Hayden .20 .07
❑ 9 William Thomas .20 .07
❑ 10 Dan Marino 4.00 1.50
❑ 11 Curtis Conway .75 .30
❑ 12 Steve Atwater .20 .07
❑ 13 Derrick Brooks .75 .30
❑ 14 Rick Mirer .40 .15
❑ 15 Mark Brunell 1.00 .40
❑ 16 Garrison Hearst .40 .15
❑ 17 Eric Turner .20 .07
❑ 18 Mark Carrier WR .20 .07
❑ 19 Darnay Scott .40 .15
❑ 20 Steve McNair 1.50 .60
❑ 21 Jim Everett .20 .07
❑ 22 Wayne Chrebet 1.00 .40
❑ 23 Ben Coates .40 .15
❑ 24 Harvey Williams .20 .07
❑ 25 Michael Westbrook .75 .30
❑ 26 Kevin Carter .20 .07
❑ 27 Dave Brown .20 .07
❑ 28 Jake Reed .40 .15
❑ 29 Thurman Thomas .75 .30
❑ 30 Jeff George .40 .15
❑ 31 Carnell Lake .20 .07
❑ 32 J.J. Stokes .75 .30
❑ 33 Jay Novacek .20 .07
❑ 34 Brett Perriman .20 .07
❑ 35 Robert Brooks .75 .30
❑ 36 Neil Smith .40 .15
❑ 37 Chris Zorich .20 .07
❑ 38 Micheal Barrow .20 .07
❑ 39 Quentin Coryatt .20 .07
❑ 40 Kerry Collins .75 .30
❑ 41 Aeneas Williams .20 .07
❑ 42 James O.Stewart .40 .15
❑ 43 Warren Moon .40 .15
❑ 44 Willie McGinest .20 .07
❑ 45 Rodney Hampton .40 .15
❑ 46 Jeff Hostetler .20 .07
❑ 47 Darrell Green .20 .07
❑ 48 Warren Sapp .20 .07
❑ 49 Troy Drayton .20 .07
❑ 50 Junior Seau .75 .30
❑ 51 Mike Mamula .20 .07
❑ 52 Antonio Langham .20 .07
❑ 53 Eric Metcalf .20 .07
❑ 54 Adrian Murrell .40 .15
❑ 55 Joey Galloway .75 .30
❑ 56 Anthony Miller .40 .15
❑ 57 Carl Pickens .40 .15
❑ 58 Bruce Smith .40 .15
❑ 59 Merton Hanks .20 .07
❑ 60 Troy Aikman 2.00 .75
❑ 61 Erik Kramer .20 .07
❑ 62 Tyrone Poole .20 .07
❑ 63 Michael Jackson .40 .15
❑ 64 Rob Moore .40 .15
❑ 65 Marcus Allen .75 .30
❑ 66 Orlando Thomas .20 .07
❑ 67 Dave Meggett .20 .07
❑ 68 Trent Dilfer .75 .30
❑ 69 Herman Moore .40 .15
❑ 70 Brett Favre 4.00 1.50
❑ 71 Blaine Bishop .20 .07
❑ 72 Eric Allen .20 .07
❑ 73 Bernie Parmalee .20 .07
❑ 74 Kyle Brady .20 .07
❑ 75 Terry McDaniel .20 .07
❑ 76 Rodney Peete .20 .07
❑ 77 Yancey Thigpen .40 .15
❑ 78 Stan Humphries .40 .15
❑ 79 Craig Heyward .20 .07
❑ 80 Rashaan Salaam .40 .15
❑ 81 Shannon Sharpe .40 .15
❑ 82 Jim Harbaugh .40 .15
❑ 83 Vinnie Clark .20 .07
❑ 84 Steve Bono .20 .07
❑ 85 Drew Bledsoe 1.00 .40
❑ 86 Ken Norton .20 .07
❑ 87 Brian Mitchell .20 .07
❑ 88 Hardy Nickerson .20 .07
❑ 89 Todd Lyght .20 .07
❑ 90 Barry Sanders 3.00 1.25
❑ 91 Robert Blackmon .20 .07
❑ 92 Larry Centers .40 .15
❑ 93 Jim Kelly .75 .30
❑ 94 Lamar Lathon .20 .07
❑ 95 Cris Carter .75 .30
❑ 96 Hugh Douglas .40 .15
❑ 97 Michael Strahan .40 .15
❑ 98 Lee Woodall .20 .07
❑ 99 Michael Irvin .75 .30
❑ 100 Marshall Faulk 1.00 .40
❑ 101 Terance Mathis .20 .07
❑ 102 Eric Zeier .20 .07
❑ 103 Marty Carter .20 .07
❑ 104 Steve Tovar .20 .07
❑ 105 Isaac Bruce .75 .30
❑ 106 Tony Martin .40 .15
❑ 107 Dale Carter .20 .07
❑ 108 Terry Kirby .40 .15
❑ 109 Tyrone Hughes .20 .07
❑ 110 Bryce Paup .20 .07
❑ 111 Errict Rhett .40 .15
❑ 112 Ricky Watters .40 .15
❑ 113 Chris Chandler .40 .15
❑ 114 Edgar Bennett .40 .15
❑ 115 John Elway 4.00 1.50
❑ 116 Sam Mills .20 .07
❑ 117 Seth Joyner .20 .07
❑ 118 Jeff Lageman .20 .07
❑ 119 Chris Calloway .20 .07
❑ 120 Curtis Martin 1.50 .60
❑ 121 Ken Harvey .20 .07
❑ 122 Eugene Daniel .20 .07
❑ 123 Tim Brown .75 .30
❑ 124 Mo Lewis .20 .07
❑ 125 Jeff Blake .75 .30
❑ 126 Jessie Tuggle .20 .07
❑ 127 Vinny Testaverde .40 .15
❑ 128 Chris Warren .40 .15
❑ 129 Terrell Davis 1.50 .60
❑ 130 Greg Lloyd .40 .15
❑ 131 Deion Sanders 1.00 .40
❑ 132 Derrick Thomas .75 .30
❑ 133 Darryll Lewis .20 .07
❑ 134 Reggie White .75 .30
❑ 135 Jerry Rice 2.00 .75
❑ 136 Tony Banks RC 1.00 .40
❑ 137 Derrick Mayes RC 1.00 .40
❑ 138 Leeland McElroy RC .50 .20
❑ 139 Bryan Still RC .50 .20
❑ 140 Tim Biakabutuka RC 1.00 .40
❑ 141 Rickey Dudley RC 1.00 .40
❑ 142 Tory James RC .50 .20
❑ 143 Lawyer Milloy RC 1.25 .50
❑ 144 Mike Ulufale RC .25 .08
❑ 145 Bobby Engram RC 1.00 .40
❑ 146 Willie Anderson RC .25 .08
❑ 147 Terrell Owens RC 15.00 7.50
❑ 148 Jonathan Ogden RC 1.00 .40
❑ 149 Darrius Johnson RC .25 .08
❑ 150 Kevin Hardy RC 1.00 .40
❑ 151 Simeon Rice RC 2.50 1.00
❑ 152 Alex Molden RC .25 .08
❑ 153 Cedric Jones RC .25 .08
❑ 154 Duane Clemons RC .25 .08
❑ 155 Karim Abdul-Jabbar RC 1.00 .40
❑ 156 Dedric Mathis RC .25 .08
❑ 157 John Michels RC .25 .08
❑ 158 Winslow Oliver RC .25 .08
❑ 159 Stepfret Williams RC .25 .08
❑ 160 Eddie Kennison RC 1.00 .40
❑ 161 Marcus Coleman RC .25 .08
❑ 162 Tedy Bruschi RC 25.00 10.00
❑ 163 Detron Smith RC .25 .08
❑ 164 Ray Lewis RC 25.00 12.50
❑ 165 Marvin Harrison RC 15.00 7.50
❑ 166 Je'rod Cherry RC .25 .08
❑ 167 Jerris McPhail RC .25 .08
❑ 168 Eric Moulds RC 8.00 3.00
❑ 169 Walt Harris RC .25 .08
❑ 170 Eddie George RC 8.00 3.00
❑ 171 Jermaine Lewis RC 1.00 .40
❑ 172 Jeff Lewis RC .50 .20
❑ 173 Ray Mickens RC .25 .08
❑ 174 Amani Toomer RC 5.00 2.00
❑ 175 Zach Thomas RC 3.00 1.25
❑ 176 Lawrence Phillips RC .50 .20
❑ 177 John Mobley RC .25 .08
❑ 178 Anthony Dorsett RC .25 .08
❑ 179 DeRon Jenkins .20 .07
❑ 180 Keyshawn Johnson RC 6.00 2.50

1997 Bowman's Best

❑ COMPLETE SET (125) 30.00 12.50
❑ 1 Brett Favre 4.00 1.50
❑ 2 Larry Centers .60 .25
❑ 3 Trent Dilfer 1.00 .40
❑ 4 Rodney Hampton .60 .25
❑ 5 Wesley Walls .60 .25
❑ 6 Jerome Bettis 1.00 .40
❑ 7 Keyshawn Johnson 1.00 .40
❑ 8 Keenan McCardell .60 .25
❑ 9 Terry Allen 1.00 .40
❑ 10 Troy Aikman 2.00 .75
❑ 11 Tony Banks .60 .25
❑ 12 Ty Detmer .60 .25
❑ 13 Chris Chandler .60 .25
❑ 14 Marshall Faulk 1.25 .50
❑ 15 Heath Shuler .40 .15
❑ 16 Stan Humphries .60 .25
❑ 17 Bryan Cox .40 .15
❑ 18 Chris Spielman .40 .15

❑ 19 Derrick Thomas 1.00 .40
❑ 20 Steve Young 1.25 .50
❑ 21 Desmond Howard .60 .25
❑ 22 Jeff Blake .60 .25
❑ 23 Michael Jackson .60 .25
❑ 24 Cris Carter 1.00 .40
❑ 25 Joey Galloway .60 .25
❑ 26 Simeon Rice .60 .25
❑ 27 Reggie White 1.00 .40
❑ 28 Dave Brown .40 .15
❑ 29 Mike Alstott 1.00 .40
❑ 30 Emmitt Smith 3.00 1.25
❑ 31 Anthony Johnson .40 .15
❑ 32 Mark Brunell 1.25 .50
❑ 33 Ricky Watters .60 .25
❑ 34 Terrell Davis 1.25 .50
❑ 35 Ben Coates .60 .25
❑ 36 Gus Frerotte .40 .15
❑ 37 Andre Reed .60 .25
❑ 38 Isaac Bruce 1.00 .40
❑ 39 Junior Seau 1.00 .40
❑ 40 Eddie George 1.00 .40
❑ 41 Adrian Murrell .60 .25
❑ 42 Jake Reed .60 .25
❑ 43 Karim Abdul-Jabbar .60 .25
❑ 44 Scott Mitchell .60 .25
❑ 45 Ki-Jana Carter .40 .15
❑ 46 Curtis Conway .60 .25
❑ 47 Jim Harbaugh .60 .25
❑ 48 Tim Brown 1.00 .40
❑ 49 Mario Bates .40 .15
❑ 50 Jerry Rice 2.00 .75
❑ 51 Byron Bam Morris .40 .15
❑ 52 Marcus Allen 1.00 .40
❑ 53 Errict Rhett .40 .15
❑ 54 Steve McNair 1.25 .50
❑ 55 Kerry Collins 1.00 .40
❑ 56 Bert Emanuel .60 .25
❑ 57 Curtis Martin 1.25 .50
❑ 58 Bryce Paup .40 .15
❑ 59 Brad Johnson 1.00 .40
❑ 60 John Elway 4.00 1.50
❑ 61 Natrone Means .60 .25
❑ 62 Deion Sanders 1.00 .40
❑ 63 Tony Martin .60 .25
❑ 64 Michael Westbrook .60 .25
❑ 65 Chris Calloway .40 .15
❑ 66 Antonio Freeman 1.00 .40
❑ 67 Rob Johnson 1.00 .40
❑ 68 Kent Graham .40 .15
❑ 69 O.J. McDuffie .60 .25
❑ 70 Barry Sanders 3.00 1.25
❑ 71 Chris Warren .60 .25
❑ 72 Kordell Stewart 1.00 .40
❑ 73 Thurman Thomas 1.00 .40
❑ 74 Marvin Harrison 1.00 .40
❑ 75 Carl Pickens .60 .25
❑ 76 Brent Jones .40 .15
❑ 77 Irving Fryar .60 .25
❑ 78 Neil O'Donnell .60 .25
❑ 79 Elvis Grbac .60 .25
❑ 80 Drew Bledsoe 1.25 .50
❑ 81 Shannon Sharpe .60 .25
❑ 82 Vinny Testaverde .60 .25
❑ 83 Chris Sanders .40 .15
❑ 84 Herman Moore .60 .25
❑ 85 Jeff George .60 .25
❑ 86 Bruce Smith .60 .25
❑ 87 Robert Smith .60 .25
❑ 88 Kevin Hardy .40 .15
❑ 89 Kevin Greene .60 .25
❑ 90 Dan Marino 4.00 1.50
❑ 91 Michael Irvin 1.00 .40
❑ 92 Garrison Hearst .60 .25
❑ 93 Lake Dawson .40 .15
❑ 94 Lawrence Phillips .40 .15
❑ 95 Terry Glenn 1.00 .40
❑ 96 Jake Plummer RC 6.00 2.50
❑ 97 Byron Hanspard RC .60 .25
❑ 98 Bryant Westbrook RC .40 .15
❑ 99 Troy Davis RC .60 .25
❑ 100 Danny Wuerffel RC 1.00 .40
❑ 101 Tony Gonzalez RC 4.00 1.50
❑ 102 Jim Druckenmiller RC .60 .25
❑ 103 Kevin Lockett RC .60 .25
❑ 104 Renaldo Wynn RC .40 .15
❑ 105 James Farrior RC 1.00 .40
❑ 106 Rae Carruth RC .40 .15
❑ 107 Tom Knight RC .40 .15
❑ 108 Corey Dillon RC 8.00 3.00
❑ 109 Kenny Holmes RC 1.00 .40
❑ 110 Orlando Pace RC 1.00 .40
❑ 111 Reidel Anthony RC 1.00 .40
❑ 112 Chad Scott RC .60 .25
❑ 113 Antowain Smith RC 3.00 1.25
❑ 114 David LaFleur RC .40 .15
❑ 115 Yatil Green RC .60 .25
❑ 116 Darrell Russell RC .40 .15
❑ 117 Joey Kent RC 1.00 .40
❑ 118 Darnell Autry RC .60 .25
❑ 119 Peter Boulware RC 1.00 .40
❑ 120 Shawn Springs RC .60 .25
❑ 121 Ike Hilliard RC 1.50 .60
❑ 122 Dwayne Rudd RC 1.00 .40
❑ 123 Reinard Wilson RC .60 .25
❑ 124 Michael Booker RC .40 .15
❑ 125 Warrick Dunn RC 4.00 1.50

1998 Bowman's Best

❑ COMPLETE SET (125) 80.00 30.00
❑ 1 Emmitt Smith 3.00 1.25
❑ 2 Reggie White 1.00 .40
❑ 3 Jake Plummer 1.00 .40
❑ 4 Ike Hilliard .40 .15
❑ 5 Isaac Bruce .40 .15
❑ 6 Trent Dilfer 1.00 .40
❑ 7 Ricky Watters .60 .25
❑ 8 Jeff George .60 .25
❑ 9 Wayne Chrebet 1.00 .40
❑ 10 Brett Favre 4.00 1.50
❑ 11 Terry Allen 1.00 .40
❑ 12 Bert Emanuel .40 .15
❑ 13 Andre Reed .60 .25
❑ 14 Andre Rison .60 .25
❑ 15 Jeff Blake .60 .25
❑ 16 Steve McNair 1.00 .40
❑ 17 Joey Galloway .60 .25
❑ 18 Irving Fryar .60 .25
❑ 19 Dorsey Levens 1.00 .40
❑ 20 Jerry Rice 2.00 .75
❑ 21 Kerry Collins .60 .25
❑ 22 Michael Jackson .40 .15
❑ 23 Kordell Stewart 1.00 .40
❑ 24 Junior Seau 1.00 .40
❑ 25 Jimmy Smith .60 .25
❑ 26 Michael Westbrook .60 .25
❑ 27 Eddie George 1.00 .40
❑ 28 Cris Carter 1.00 .40
❑ 29 Jason Sehorn .60 .25
❑ 30 Warrick Dunn 1.00 .40
❑ 31 Garrison Hearst 1.00 .40
❑ 32 Erik Kramer .40 .15
❑ 33 Chris Chandler .60 .25
❑ 34 Michael Irvin 1.00 .40
❑ 35 Marshall Faulk 1.25 .50
❑ 36 Warren Moon 1.00 .40
❑ 37 Rickey Dudley .40 .15
❑ 38 Drew Bledsoe 1.50 .60
❑ 39 Antowain Smith 1.00 .40
❑ 40 Terrell Davis 1.00 .40
❑ 41 Gus Frerotte .40 .15
❑ 42 Robert Brooks .60 .25
❑ 43 Tony Banks .60 .25
❑ 44 Terrell Owens 1.00 .40
❑ 45 Edgar Bennett .40 .15
❑ 46 Rob Moore .60 .25
❑ 47 J.J. Stokes .60 .25
❑ 48 Yancey Thigpen .40 .15
❑ 49 Elvis Grbac .60 .25
❑ 50 John Elway 4.00 1.50
❑ 51 Charles Johnson .40 .15
❑ 52 Karim Abdul-Jabbar 1.00 .40
❑ 53 Carl Pickens .60 .25
❑ 54 Peter Boulware .40 .15
❑ 55 Chris Warren .40 .15
❑ 56 Terance Mathis .60 .25
❑ 57 Andre Hastings .40 .15
❑ 58 Jake Reed .60 .25
❑ 59 Mike Alstott .40 .15
❑ 60 Mark Brunell 1.00 .40
❑ 61 Herman Moore .60 .25
❑ 62 Troy Aikman 2.00 .75
❑ 63 Fred Lane .40 .15
❑ 64 Rod Smith .60 .25
❑ 65 Terry Glenn 1.00 .40
❑ 66 Jerome Bettis 1.00 .40
❑ 67 Derrick Thomas 1.00 .40
❑ 68 Marvin Harrison 1.00 .40
❑ 69 Adrian Murrell .40 .15
❑ 70 Curtis Martin 1.00 .40
❑ 71 Bobby Hoying .60 .25
❑ 72 Darrell Green .60 .25
❑ 73 Sean Dawkins .40 .15
❑ 74 Robert Smith 1.00 .40
❑ 75 Antonio Freeman 1.00 .40
❑ 76 Scott Mitchell .60 .25
❑ 77 Curtis Conway .60 .25
❑ 78 Rae Carruth .40 .15
❑ 79 Jamal Anderson 1.00 .40
❑ 80 Dan Marino 4.00 1.50
❑ 81 Brad Johnson 1.00 .40
❑ 82 Danny Kanell .60 .25
❑ 83 Charlie Garner .60 .25
❑ 84 Rob Johnson .60 .25
❑ 85 Natrone Means .60 .25
❑ 86 Tim Brown 1.00 .40
❑ 87 Keyshawn Johnson 1.00 .40
❑ 88 Ben Coates .60 .25
❑ 89 Derrick Alexander .60 .25
❑ 90 Steve Young 1.25 .50
❑ 91 Shannon Sharpe .60 .25
❑ 92 Corey Dillon 1.00 .40
❑ 93 Bruce Smith .60 .25
❑ 94 Errict Rhett .60 .25
❑ 95 Jim Harbaugh .40 .15
❑ 96 Napoleon Kaufman 1.00 .40
❑ 97 Glenn Foley .60 .25
❑ 98 Tony Gonzalez 1.00 .40
❑ 99 Keenan McCardell .60 .25
❑ 100 Barry Sanders 3.00 1.25
❑ 101 Charles Woodson RC 3.00 1.25
❑ 102 Tim Dwight RC 2.50 1.00
❑ 103 Marcus Nash RC 1.25 .50
❑ 104 Joe Jurevicius RC 2.50 1.00
❑ 105 Jacquez Green RC 2.00 .75
❑ 106 Kevin Dyson RC 2.50 1.00
❑ 107 Keith Brooking RC 2.50 1.00
❑ 108 Andre Wadsworth RC 2.00 .75
❑ 109 Randy Moss RC 12.00 6.00
❑ 110 Robert Edwards RC 2.00 .75
❑ 111 Pat Johnson RC 2.00 .75
❑ 112 Peyton Manning RC 25.00 12.50
❑ 113 Duane Starks RC 1.25 .50
❑ 114 Grant Wistrom RC 2.00 .75
❑ 115 Anthony Simmons RC 2.00 .75
❑ 116 Takeo Spikes RC 2.50 1.00
❑ 117 Tony Simmons RC 2.00 .75
❑ 118 Jerome Pathon RC 2.50 1.00
❑ 119 Ryan Leaf RC 2.50 1.00
❑ 120 Skip Hicks RC 2.00 .75
❑ 121 Curtis Enis RC 1.25 .50
❑ 122 Germane Crowell RC 2.00 .75
❑ 123 John Avery RC 2.00 .75
❑ 124 Hines Ward RC 10.00 5.00
❑ 125 Fred Taylor RC 4.00 1.50

1999 Bowman's Best

❑ COMPLETE SET (133) 80.00 30.00
❑ 1 Randy Moss 2.50 1.00
❑ 2 Skip Hicks .40 .15
❑ 3 Robert Smith 1.00 .40
❑ 4 Drew Bledsoe 1.25 .50
❑ 5 Tim Brown 1.00 .40
❑ 6 Marshall Faulk 1.25 .50
❑ 7 Terance Mathis .60 .25
❑ 8 Sean Dawkins .40 .15
❑ 9 Ed McCaffrey .60 .25
❑ 10 Jamal Anderson 1.00 .40
❑ 11 Antonio Freeman 1.00 .40
❑ 12 Terry Kirby .60 .25

❑ 13	Vinny Testaverde	.60	.25
❑ 14	Eddie George	1.00	.40
❑ 15	Ricky Watters	.60	.25
❑ 16	Johnnie Morton	.60	.25
❑ 17	Natrone Means	.60	.25
❑ 18	Terry Glenn	1.00	.40
❑ 19	Michael Westbrook	.60	.25
❑ 20	Doug Flutie	1.00	.40
❑ 21	Jake Plummer	.60	.25
❑ 22	Darnay Scott	.60	.25
❑ 23	Andre Rison	.60	.25
❑ 24	Jon Kitna	1.00	.40
❑ 25	Dan Marino	3.00	1.25
❑ 26	Ike Hilliard	.60	.25
❑ 27	Warrick Dunn	1.00	.40
❑ 28	Jerome Bettis	1.00	.40
❑ 29	Curtis Conway	.60	.25
❑ 30	Emmitt Smith	2.00	.75
❑ 31	Jimmy Smith	.60	.25
❑ 32	Isaac Bruce	1.00	.40
❑ 33	Jerry Rice	2.00	.75
❑ 34	Curtis Martin	1.00	.40
❑ 35	Steve McNair	1.00	.40
❑ 36	Jeff Blake	.60	.25
❑ 37	Rob Moore	.60	.25
❑ 38	Dorsey Levens	1.00	.40
❑ 39	Terrell Davis	1.00	.40
❑ 40	John Elway	3.00	1.25
❑ 41	Trent Dilfer	.60	.25
❑ 42	Joey Galloway	.60	.25
❑ 43	Keyshawn Johnson	1.00	.40
❑ 44	O.J. McDuffie	.60	.25
❑ 45	Fred Taylor	1.00	.40
❑ 46	Andre Reed	.60	.25
❑ 47	Frank Sanders	.60	.25
❑ 48	Keenan McCardell	.60	.25
❑ 49	Elvis Grbac	.60	.25
❑ 50	Barry Sanders	3.00	1.25
❑ 51	Terrell Owens	1.00	.40
❑ 52	Trent Green	1.00	.40
❑ 53	Brad Johnson	1.00	.40
❑ 54	Rich Gannon	1.00	.40
❑ 55	Randall Cunningham	1.00	.40
❑ 56	Tony Martin	.60	.25
❑ 57	Rod Smith	.60	.25
❑ 58	Eric Moulds	1.00	.40
❑ 59	Yancey Thigpen	.40	.15
❑ 60	Brett Favre	3.00	1.25
❑ 61	Cris Carter	1.00	.40
❑ 62	Marvin Harrison	1.00	.40
❑ 63	Chris Chandler	.60	.25
❑ 64	Antowain Smith	1.00	.40
❑ 65	Carl Pickens	.60	.25
❑ 66	Shannon Sharpe	.60	.25
❑ 67	Mike Alstott	1.00	.40
❑ 68	J.J. Stokes	.60	.25
❑ 69	Ben Coates	.60	.25
❑ 70	Peyton Manning	3.00	1.25
❑ 71	Duce Staley	1.00	.40
❑ 72	Michael Irvin	.60	.25
❑ 73	Tim Biakabutuka	.60	.25
❑ 74	Priest Holmes	1.50	.60
❑ 75	Steve Young	1.25	.50
❑ 76	Jerome Pathon	.60	.25
❑ 77	Wayne Chrebet	1.00	.40
❑ 78	Bert Emanuel	.40	.15
❑ 79	Curtis Enis	.40	.15
❑ 80	Mark Brunell	1.00	.40
❑ 81	Herman Moore	.60	.25
❑ 82	Corey Dillon	1.00	.40
❑ 83	Jim Harbaugh	.60	.25
❑ 84	Gary Brown	.40	.15
❑ 85	Kordell Stewart	.60	.25
❑ 86	Garrison Hearst	.60	.25
❑ 87	Rocket Ismail	.60	.25
❑ 88	Charlie Batch	1.00	.40
❑ 89	Napoleon Kaufman	1.00	.40
❑ 90	Troy Aikman	2.00	.75
❑ 91	Brett Favre BP	1.50	.60
❑ 92	Randy Moss BP	1.25	.50
❑ 93	Terrell Davis BP	1.00	.40
❑ 94	Barry Sanders BP	1.50	.60
❑ 95	Peyton Manning BP	1.50	.60
❑ 96	Troy Edwards BP	.60	.25
❑ 97	Cade McNown BP	.60	.25
❑ 98	Edgerrin James BP	2.50	1.00
❑ 99	Torry Holt BP	1.00	.40
❑ 100	Tim Couch BP	1.00	.40
❑ 101	Chris Claiborne RC	1.00	.40
❑ 102	Brock Huard RC	2.00	.75
❑ 103	Amos Zereoue RC	2.00	.75
❑ 104	Sedrick Irvin RC	1.00	.40
❑ 105	Kevin Faulk RC	2.00	.75
❑ 106	Ebenezer Ekuban RC	1.00	.40
❑ 107	Daunte Culpepper RC	8.00	3.00
❑ 108	Rob Konrad RC	1.50	.60
❑ 109	James Johnson RC	1.50	.60
❑ 110	Kurt Warner RC	10.00	4.00
❑ 111	Mike Cloud RC	1.50	.60
❑ 112	Andy Katzenmoyer RC	1.50	.60
❑ 113	Jevon Kearse RC	3.00	1.25
❑ 114	Akili Smith RC	1.50	.60
❑ 115	Edgerrin James RC	8.00	3.00
❑ 116	Cecil Collins RC	1.00	.40
❑ 117	Chris McAlister RC	1.50	.60
❑ 118	Donovan McNabb RC	10.00	4.00
❑ 119	Kevin Johnson RC	2.00	.75
❑ 120	Torry Holt RC	5.00	2.00
❑ 121	Antoine Winfield RC	1.50	.60
❑ 122	Michael Bishop RC	2.00	.75
❑ 123	Joe Germaine RC	1.50	.60
❑ 124	David Boston RC	2.00	.75
❑ 125	D'Wayne Bates RC	1.50	.60
❑ 126	Champ Bailey RC	2.50	1.00
❑ 127	Cade McNown RC	1.50	.60
❑ 128	Shaun King RC	1.50	.60
❑ 129	Peerless Price RC	2.00	.75
❑ 130	Troy Edwards RC	1.50	.60
❑ 131	Karsten Bailey RC	1.50	.60
❑ 132	Tim Couch RC	2.00	.75
❑ 133	Ricky Williams RC	4.00	1.50
❑ C1	Rookie Class Photo	8.00	3.00

2000 Bowman's Best

❑	COMPLETE SET (150)	500.00	250.00
❑ 1	Troy Edwards	.30	.10
❑ 2	Kurt Warner	1.50	.60
❑ 3	Steve McNair	.75	.30
❑ 4	Terry Glenn	.50	.20
❑ 5	Charlie Batch	.75	.30
❑ 6	Patrick Jeffers	.75	.30
❑ 7	Jake Plummer	.50	.20
❑ 8	Derrick Alexander	.50	.20
❑ 9	Joey Galloway	.50	.20
❑ 10	Tony Banks	.50	.20
❑ 11	Robert Smith	.75	.30
❑ 12	Jerry Rice	1.50	.60
❑ 13	Jeff Garcia	.75	.30
❑ 14	Michael Westbrook	.50	.20
❑ 15	Curtis Conway	.50	.20
❑ 16	Brian Griese	.75	.30
❑ 17	Peyton Manning	2.00	.75
❑ 18	Daunte Culpepper	1.00	.40
❑ 19	Frank Sanders	.50	.20
❑ 20	Muhsin Muhammad	.50	.20
❑ 21	Corey Dillon	.75	.30
❑ 22	Brett Favre	2.50	1.00
❑ 23	Warrick Dunn	.75	.30
❑ 24	Tim Brown	.75	.30
❑ 25	Kerry Collins	.50	.20
❑ 26	Brad Johnson	.75	.30
❑ 27	Rocket Ismail	.50	.20
❑ 28	Jamal Anderson	.75	.30
❑ 29	Jimmy Smith	.50	.20
❑ 30	Torry Holt	.75	.30
❑ 31	Duce Staley	.75	.30
❑ 32	Drew Bledsoe	1.00	.40
❑ 33	Jerome Bettis	.75	.30
❑ 34	Keyshawn Johnson	.75	.30
❑ 35	Fred Taylor	.75	.30
❑ 36	Akili Smith	.30	.10
❑ 37	Rob Johnson	.50	.20
❑ 38	Elvis Grbac	.50	.20
❑ 39	Antonio Freeman	.75	.30
❑ 40	Curtis Enis	.30	.10
❑ 41	Terance Mathis	.50	.20
❑ 42	Terrell Davis	.75	.30
❑ 43	Randy Moss	1.50	.60
❑ 44	Jon Kitna	.75	.30
❑ 45	Curtis Martin	.75	.30
❑ 46	Terrell Owens	.75	.30
❑ 47	Robert Smith	.75	.30
❑ 48	Albert Connell	.30	.10
❑ 49	Edgerrin James	1.25	.50
❑ 50	Tony Gonzalez	.50	.20
❑ 51	Eric Moulds	.75	.30
❑ 52	Natrone Means	.50	.20
❑ 53	Carl Pickens	.50	.20
❑ 54	Mark Brunell	.75	.30
❑ 55	Rob Moore	.50	.20
❑ 56	Marshall Faulk	1.00	.40
❑ 57	Stephen Davis	.75	.30
❑ 58	Rich Gannon	.75	.30
❑ 59	Ricky Williams	.75	.30
❑ 60	Emmitt Smith	1.50	.60
❑ 61	Germane Crowell	.30	.10
❑ 62	Doug Flutie	.75	.30
❑ 63	O.J. McDuffie	.50	.20
❑ 64	Chris Chandler	.50	.20
❑ 65	Qadry Ismail	.50	.20
❑ 66	Tim Couch	.50	.20
❑ 67	James Stewart	.50	.20
❑ 68	Marvin Harrison	.75	.30
❑ 69	Cris Carter	.75	.30
❑ 70	Cade McNown	.30	.10
❑ 71	Marcus Robinson	.75	.30
❑ 72	Steve Beuerlein	.50	.20
❑ 73	Jevon Kearse	.75	.30
❑ 74	Eddie George	.75	.30
❑ 75	Donovan McNabb	1.25	.50
❑ 76	Jeff Blake	.50	.20
❑ 77	Wayne Chrebet	.50	.20
❑ 78	Kordell Stewart	.50	.20
❑ 79	Steve Young	1.00	.40
❑ 80	Mike Alstott	.75	.30
❑ 81	Ricky Watters	.50	.20
❑ 82	Charlie Garner	.50	.20
❑ 83	Troy Aikman	1.50	.60
❑ 84	Dorsey Levens	.50	.20
❑ 85	Ike Hilliard	.50	.20
❑ 86	Shaun King	.30	.10
❑ 87	Isaac Bruce	.75	.30
❑ 88	Tyrone Wheatley	.50	.20
❑ 89	Amani Toomer	.50	.20
❑ 90	Ed McCaffrey	.75	.30
❑ 91	E.James/M.Faulk BP	.75	.30
❑ 92	D.Bledsoe/B.Johnson BP	.75	.30
❑ 93	J.Smith/R.Moss BP	1.00	.40
❑ 94	E.George/S.Davis BP	.50	.20
❑ 95	M.Brunell/T.Aikman BP	1.00	.40
❑ 96	M.Harrison/C.Carter BP	.75	.30
❑ 97	C.Martin/E.Smith BP	1.00	.40
❑ 98	T.Brown/I.Bruce BP	.50	.20
❑ 99	F.Taylor/R.Williams BP	.75	.30
❑ 100	K.Warner/P.Manning BP	1.00	.40
❑ 101	Shaun Alexander RC	30.00	15.00
❑ 102	Thomas Jones RC	12.00	5.00
❑ 103	Courtney Brown RC	8.00	3.00
❑ 104	Curtis Keaton RC	6.00	2.50
❑ 105	Jerry Porter RC	10.00	4.00
❑ 106	Corey Simon RC	8.00	3.00
❑ 107	Dez White RC	8.00	3.00
❑ 108	Jamal Lewis RC	15.00	6.00

❑ 109 Ron Dayne RC 8.00 3.00
❑ 110 R.Jay Soward RC 6.00 2.50
❑ 111 Tee Martin RC 8.00 3.00
❑ 112 Brian Urlacher RC 25.00 10.00
❑ 113 Reuben Droughns RC 10.00 4.00
❑ 114 Travis Taylor RC 8.00 3.00
❑ 115 Plaxico Burress RC 15.00 6.00
❑ 116 Chad Pennington RC 15.00 6.00
❑ 117 Sylvester Morris RC 6.00 2.50
❑ 118 Ron Dugans RC 4.00 1.50
❑ 119 Joe Hamilton RC 6.00 2.50
❑ 120 Chris Redman RC 6.00 2.50
❑ 121 Trung Canidate RC 6.00 2.50
❑ 122 J.R. Redmond RC 6.00 2.50
❑ 123 Danny Farmer RC 6.00 2.50
❑ 124 Todd Pinkston RC 8.00 3.00
❑ 125 Dennis Northcutt RC 8.00 3.00
❑ 126 Laveranues Coles RC 10.00 4.00
❑ 127 Bubba Franks RC 8.00 3.00
❑ 128 Travis Prentice RC 6.00 2.50
❑ 129 Peter Warrick RC 8.00 3.00
❑ 130 Anthony Becht RC 8.00 3.00
❑ 131 Ike Charlton RC 4.00 1.50
❑ 132 Shaun Ellis RC 8.00 3.00
❑ 133 Sean Morey RC 6.00 2.50
❑ 134 Sebastian Janikowski RC 8.00 3.00
❑ 135 Aaron Stecker RC 8.00 3.00
❑ 136 Ronney Jenkins RC 6.00 2.50
❑ 137 Jamel White RC 6.00 2.50
❑ 138 Nick Williams 4.00 1.50
❑ 139 Andy McCullough 4.00 1.50
❑ 140 Kevin Daft 4.00 1.50
❑ 141 Thomas Hamner RC 4.00 1.50
❑ 142 Tim Rattay RC 8.00 3.00
❑ 143 Spergon Wynn RC 6.00 2.50
❑ 144 Brandon Short RC 6.00 2.50
❑ 145 Chad Morton RC 8.00 3.00
❑ 146 Gari Scott RC 4.00 1.50
❑ 147 Frank Murphy RC 4.00 1.50
❑ 148 James Williams RC 6.00 2.50
❑ 149 Windrell Hayes RC 6.00 2.50
❑ 150 Doug Johnson RC 8.00 3.00

2001 Bowman's Best

❑ COMP.SET w/o SP's (100) 20.00 7.50
❑ 1 Jerry Rice 1.50 .60
❑ 2 Doug Flutie .75 .30
❑ 3 Drew Bledsoe 1.00 .40
❑ 4 Edgerrin James 1.00 .40
❑ 5 Muhsin Muhammad .50 .20
❑ 6 Charlie Batch .75 .30
❑ 7 Marshall Faulk 1.00 .40
❑ 8 Trent Green .75 .30
❑ 9 Rich Gannon .75 .30
❑ 10 Emmitt Smith 1.50 .60
❑ 11 Steve McNair .75 .30
❑ 12 Darrell Jackson .75 .30
❑ 13 Amani Toomer .50 .20
❑ 14 Jimmy Smith .50 .20
❑ 15 Kevin Johnson .50 .20
❑ 16 Ray Lewis .75 .30
❑ 17 Peter Warrick .75 .30
❑ 18 Cris Carter .75 .30
❑ 19 Jerome Bettis .75 .30
❑ 20 Keyshawn Johnson .75 .30
❑ 21 Joey Galloway .50 .20
❑ 22 Chris Chandler .50 .20
❑ 23 Brett Favre 2.50 1.00
❑ 24 Aaron Brooks .75 .30
❑ 25 Kurt Warner 1.50 .60
❑ 26 Jeff Graham .30 .10
❑ 27 Curtis Martin .75 .30
❑ 28 Mike Anderson .75 .30
❑ 29 Eric Moulds .50 .20
❑ 30 David Boston .75 .30
❑ 31 Elvis Grbac .50 .20
❑ 32 James Stewart .50 .20
❑ 33 Randy Moss 1.50 .60
❑ 34 Donovan McNabb 1.00 .40
❑ 35 Matt Hasselbeck .50 .20
❑ 36 Stephen Davis .75 .30
❑ 37 Brad Johnson .75 .30
❑ 38 Jamal Anderson .75 .30
❑ 39 Tim Biakabutuka .50 .20
❑ 40 Antonio Freeman .75 .30
❑ 41 Mark Brunell .75 .30
❑ 42 Tiki Barber .75 .30
❑ 43 Charlie Garner .50 .20
❑ 44 Eddie George .75 .30
❑ 45 Ricky Williams .75 .30
❑ 46 Rob Johnson .50 .20
❑ 47 Jake Plummer .50 .20
❑ 48 Peyton Manning 2.00 .75
❑ 49 Lamar Smith .50 .20
❑ 50 Corey Dillon .75 .30
❑ 51 Derrick Alexander .50 .20
❑ 52 Troy Brown .50 .20
❑ 53 Wayne Chrebet .50 .20
❑ 54 Shaun Alexander 1.00 .40
❑ 55 Jeff George .50 .20
❑ 56 Tim Brown .75 .30
❑ 57 Brian Griese .75 .30
❑ 58 Cade McNown .30 .10
❑ 59 Jamal Lewis 1.25 .50
❑ 60 Germane Crowell .30 .10
❑ 61 Junior Seau .75 .30
❑ 62 Warrick Dunn .75 .30
❑ 63 Isaac Bruce .75 .30
❑ 64 Terry Glenn .50 .20
❑ 65 Fred Taylor .75 .30
❑ 66 Tim Couch .50 .20
❑ 67 Akili Smith .30 .10
❑ 68 Tony Gonzalez .50 .20
❑ 69 Kerry Collins .50 .20
❑ 70 James Thrash .50 .20
❑ 71 Terrell Owens .75 .30
❑ 72 Derrick Mason .50 .20
❑ 73 Tyrone Wheatley .50 .20
❑ 74 Oronde Gadsden .50 .20
❑ 75 Ahman Green .75 .30
❑ 76 Jon Kitna .50 .20
❑ 77 Tony Banks .50 .20
❑ 78 Marvin Harrison .75 .30
❑ 79 Daunte Culpepper .75 .30
❑ 80 Vinny Testaverde .50 .20
❑ 81 Chad Lewis .30 .10
❑ 82 Torry Holt .75 .30
❑ 83 Jeff Garcia .75 .30
❑ 84 Rod Smith .50 .20
❑ 85 Marcus Robinson .75 .30
❑ 86 Keenan McCardell .30 .10
❑ 87 Joe Horn .50 .20
❑ 88 Kordell Stewart .50 .20
❑ 89 Jay Fiedler .75 .30
❑ 90 Ed McCaffrey .75 .30
❑ 91 E.George/S.Davis .50 .20
❑ 92 P.Manning/J.Garcia 1.50 .60
❑ 93 R.Smith/T.Holt .75 .30
❑ 94 E.James/M.Faulk 1.50 .60
❑ 95 E.Grbac/D.Culpepper .75 .30
❑ 96 M.Harrison/R.Moss 1.25 .50
❑ 97 M.Anderson/E.Smith .75 .30
❑ 98 B.Griese/K.Warner 1.00 .40
❑ 99 M.Muhammad/E.McCaffrey .75 .30
❑ 100 E.Moulds/T.Owens .75 .30
❑ 101 David Terrell JSY RC 8.00 3.00
❑ 102 Kevan Barlow JSY RC 8.00 3.00
❑ 103 Quincy Morgan JSY RC 8.00 3.00
❑ 104 Chris Weinke JSY RC 8.00 3.00
❑ 105 Josh Heupel JSY RC 8.00 3.00
❑ 106 Chris Chambers JSY RC 15.00 6.00
❑ 107 Reggie Wayne JSY RC 20.00 7.50
❑ 108 Gerard Warren JSY RC 8.00 3.00
❑ 109 Freddie Mitchell JSY RC 8.00 3.00
❑ 110 Anthony Thomas JSY RC 8.00 3.00
❑ 111 Robert Ferguson JSY RC 8.00 3.00
❑ 112 Deuce McAllister JSY RC 20.00 7.50
❑ 113 Travis Henry JSY RC 15.00 6.00
❑ 114 Rod Gardner JSY RC 8.00 3.00
❑ 115 Michael Bennett JSY RC 8.00 3.00
❑ 116 Santana Moss JSY RC 15.00 6.00
❑ 117 Chad Johnson JSY RC 25.00 10.00
❑ 118 Jesse Palmer JSY RC 8.00 3.00
❑ 119 James Jackson JSY RC 8.00 3.00
❑ 120 Dan Morgan JSY RC 8.00 3.00
❑ 121 Drew Brees RC 20.00 10.00
❑ 122 Travis Minor RC 4.00 1.50
❑ 123 Quincy Carter RC 6.00 2.50
❑ 124 LaDainian Tomlinson RC 80.00 40.00
❑ 125 Michael Vick RC 40.00 15.00
❑ 126 Ryan Pickett RC 2.50 1.00
❑ 127 Mike McMahon RC 6.00 2.50
❑ 128 Alex Bannister RC 4.00 1.50
❑ 129 A.J. Feeley RC 6.00 2.50
❑ 130 Shad Meier RC 4.00 1.50
❑ 131 Jamie Winborn RC 4.00 1.50
❑ 132 Fred Smoot RC 6.00 2.50
❑ 133 Milton Wynn RC 4.00 1.50
❑ 134 Onome Ojo RC 4.00 1.50
❑ 135 Jonathan Carter RC 4.00 1.50
❑ 136 Todd Heap RC 6.00 2.50
❑ 137 Bobby Newcombe RC 4.00 1.50
❑ 138 Tony Stewart RC 6.00 2.50
❑ 139 Torrance Marshall RC 6.00 2.50
❑ 140 Jamal Reynolds RC 6.00 2.50
❑ 141 Jamar Fletcher RC 4.00 1.50
❑ 142 Richard Seymour RC 6.00 2.50
❑ 143 Tay Cody RC 2.50 1.00
❑ 144 Koren Robinson RC 6.00 2.50
❑ 145 Eddie Berlin RC 4.00 1.50
❑ 146 Damione Lewis RC 4.00 1.50
❑ 147 Marques Tuiasosopo RC 8.00 3.00
❑ 148 Snoop Minnis RC 4.00 1.50
❑ 149 Chris Barnes RC 4.00 1.50
❑ 150 Leonard Davis RC 4.00 1.50
❑ 151 Vinny Sutherland RC 4.00 1.50
❑ 152 Rudi Johnson RC 12.00 5.00
❑ 153 Derrick Gibson RC 4.00 1.50
❑ 154 Dan Alexander RC 6.00 2.50
❑ 155 Damerien McCants RC 4.00 1.50
❑ 156 Adam Archuleta RC 6.00 2.50
❑ 157 Correll Buckhalter RC 8.00 3.00
❑ 158 LaMont Jordan RC 12.00 5.00
❑ 159 Quentin McCord RC 4.00 1.50
❑ 160 Justin Smith RC 6.00 2.50
❑ 161 Nate Clements RC 6.00 2.50
❑ 162 Alge Crumpler RC 8.00 4.00
❑ 163 Dan O'Leary RC 4.00 1.50
❑ 164 Sage Rosenfels RC 8.00 3.00
❑ 165 Andre Carter RC 6.00 2.50
❑ 166 Marcus Stroud RC 6.00 2.50
❑ 167 Will Allen RC 4.00 1.50
❑ 168 Tommy Polley RC 6.00 2.50
❑ 169 Justin McCareins RC 6.00 2.50
❑ 170 Josh Booty RC 6.00 2.50

2002 Bowman's Best

❑ COMP.SET w/o SP's (90) 40.00 15.00
❑ 1 Peyton Manning 3.00 1.25
❑ 2 Chris Weinke 1.00 .40
❑ 3 Daunte Culpepper 1.50 .60
❑ 4 Deuce McAllister 2.00 .75
❑ 5 Duce Staley 1.50 .60
❑ 6 Koren Robinson 1.00 .40
❑ 7 Emmitt Smith 4.00 1.50
❑ 8 Jamal Lewis 1.50 .60
❑ 9 Jake Plummer 1.00 .40
❑ 10 Tim Brown 1.50 .60
❑ 11 LaDainian Tomlinson 2.50 1.00
❑ 12 Derrick Mason 1.00 .40
❑ 13 Keyshawn Johnson 1.50 .60
❑ 14 Priest Holmes 2.00 .75
❑ 15 Marcus Robinson 1.00 .40

#	Card	Hi	Lo
❑ 16	Drew Bledsoe	2.00	.75
❑ 17	Troy Brown	1.00	.40
❑ 18	Ahman Green	1.50	.60
❑ 19	Edgerrin James	2.00	.75
❑ 20	Hines Ward	1.50	.60
❑ 21	Marshall Faulk	1.50	.60
❑ 22	Rod Gardner	1.00	.40
❑ 23	Amani Toomer	1.00	.40
❑ 24	Ricky Williams	1.50	.60
❑ 25	Peter Warrick	1.00	.40
❑ 26	Ray Lewis	1.50	.60
❑ 27	Warrick Dunn	1.50	.60
❑ 28	Jermaine Lewis	1.00	.40
❑ 29	Mark Brunell	1.50	.60
❑ 30	Randy Moss	3.00	1.25
❑ 31	Laveranues Coles	1.00	.40
❑ 32	Kordell Stewart	1.00	.40
❑ 33	Darrell Jackson	1.00	.40
❑ 34	Jeff Garcia	1.50	.60
❑ 35	Eddie George	1.50	.60
❑ 36	Tim Dwight	1.00	.40
❑ 37	Trent Green	1.00	.40
❑ 38	Quincy Carter	1.00	.40
❑ 39	Mike McMahon	1.50	.60
❑ 40	Corey Dillon	1.00	.40
❑ 41	Corey Bradford	.60	.25
❑ 42	Aaron Brooks	1.50	.60
❑ 43	Todd Pinkston	1.00	.40
❑ 44	Isaac Bruce	1.50	.60
❑ 45	Shane Matthews	1.00	.40
❑ 46	Eric Moulds	1.00	.40
❑ 47	Anthony Thomas	1.00	.40
❑ 48	David Boston	1.50	.60
❑ 49	Kevin Johnson	1.00	.40
❑ 50	Brett Favre	4.00	1.50
❑ 51	Ron Dayne	1.00	.40
❑ 52	Donovan McNabb	2.00	.75
❑ 53	Brad Johnson	1.00	.40
❑ 54	Garrison Hearst	1.00	.40
❑ 55	Jimmy Smith	1.00	.40
❑ 56	Muhsin Muhammad	1.00	.40
❑ 57	Michael Vick	5.00	2.00
❑ 58	Kerry Collins	1.00	.40
❑ 59	Jerome Bettis	1.50	.60
❑ 60	Trent Dilfer	1.00	.40
❑ 61	Torry Holt	1.50	.60
❑ 62	Stephen Davis	1.00	.40
❑ 63	Steve McNair	1.50	.60
❑ 64	Marvin Harrison	1.50	.60
❑ 65	Zach Thomas	1.50	.60
❑ 66	Antowain Smith	1.00	.40
❑ 67	Joe Horn	1.00	.40
❑ 68	Jim Miller	1.00	.40
❑ 69	Travis Taylor	1.00	.40
❑ 70	James Allen	1.00	.40
❑ 71	Tom Brady	4.00	1.50
❑ 72	Tiki Barber	1.50	.60
❑ 73	Doug Flutie	1.50	.60
❑ 74	Rich Gannon	1.50	.60
❑ 75	Kurt Warner	1.50	.60
❑ 76	Michael Pittman	.60	.25
❑ 77	Curtis Martin	1.50	.60
❑ 78	Plaxico Burress	1.50	.60
❑ 79	Terrell Owens	1.50	.60
❑ 80	Tony Gonzalez	1.00	.40
❑ 81	Michael Bennett	1.50	.60
❑ 82	Brian Griese	1.50	.60
❑ 83	Tim Couch	1.00	.40
❑ 84	Shaun Alexander	2.00	.75
❑ 85	Drew Brees	1.50	.60
❑ 86	Vinny Testaverde	1.00	.40
❑ 87	Chris Chambers	1.50	.60
❑ 88	David Terrell	1.50	.60
❑ 89	Rod Smith	1.00	.40
❑ 90	Jerry Rice	3.00	1.25
❑ 91	David Carr JSY RC	20.00	7.50
❑ 92	Joey Harrington JSY RC	15.00	6.00
❑ 93	Marquise Walker JSY RC	6.00	2.50
❑ 94	Ladell Betts JSY RC	8.00	3.00
❑ 95	David Garrard JSY RC	10.00	4.00
❑ 96	Antwaan Randle El JSY RC	15.00	6.00
❑ 97	Antonio Bryant JSY RC	8.00	3.00
❑ 98	Eric Crouch JSY RC	8.00	3.00
❑ 99	Tim Carter JSY RC	6.00	2.50
❑ 100	William Green JSY RC	8.00	3.00
❑ 101	Rohan Davey JSY RC	8.00	3.00
❑ 102	Julius Peppers JSY RC	15.00	6.00
❑ 103	Donte Stallworth JSY RC	15.00	6.00
❑ 104	Ashley Lelie JSY RC	15.00	6.00
❑ 105	Jeremy Shockey JSY RC	25.00	10.00
❑ 106	Javon Walker JSY RC	15.00	7.50
❑ 107	Patrick Ramsey JSY RC	12.00	5.00
❑ 108	Roy Williams JSY RC	20.00	7.50
❑ 109	T.J. Duckett JSY RC	12.00	5.00
❑ 110	Jabar Gaffney JSY RC	8.00	3.00
❑ 111	Andre Davis JSY RC	6.00	2.50
❑ 112	Reche Caldwell JSY RC	8.00	3.00
❑ 113	Josh McCown JSY RC	10.00	4.00
❑ 114	Maurice Morris JSY RC	8.00	3.00
❑ 115	Ron Johnson JSY RC	6.00	2.50
❑ 116	DeShaun Foster JSY RC	8.00	3.00
❑ 117	Clinton Portis JSY RC	25.00	10.00
❑ 118	Aaron Lockett AU RC	6.00	2.50
❑ 119	Robert Thomas AU RC	12.00	5.00
❑ 121	Atrews Bell AU RC	6.00	2.50
❑ 122	Brandon Doman AU RC	10.00	4.00
❑ 124	Bryan Thomas AU RC	10.00	4.00
❑ 125	Bryant McKinnie AU RC	10.00	4.00
❑ 126	Chad Hutchinson AU RC	10.00	4.00
❑ 127	Charles Grant AU RC	12.00	5.00
❑ 128	Chester Taylor AU RC	30.00	15.00
❑ 129	Craig Nall AU RC	25.00	10.00
❑ 130	Deion Branch AU RC	40.00	15.00
❑ 131	Doug Jolley AU RC	12.00	5.00
❑ 132	Dwight Freeney AU RC	35.00	20.00
❑ 133	Ed Reed AU RC	40.00	15.00
❑ 134	Freddie Milons AU RC	10.00	4.00
❑ 135	Herb Haygood AU RC	6.00	2.50
❑ 136	J.T. O'Sullivan AU RC	10.00	4.00
❑ 137	Jake Schifino AU RC	10.00	4.00
❑ 138	Jason McAddley AU RC	10.00	4.00
❑ 139	Jeff Kelly AU RC	10.00	4.00
❑ 140	Jerramy Stevens AU RC	12.00	5.00
❑ 141	John Henderson AU RC	12.00	5.00
❑ 142	Jonathan Wells AU RC	12.00	5.00
❑ 143	Josh Scobey AU RC	12.00	5.00
❑ 144	Kelly Campbell AU RC	10.00	4.00
❑ 145	Kahlil Hill AU RC	10.00	4.00
❑ 146	Kalimba Edwards AU RC	12.00	5.00
❑ 147	Ken Simonton AU RC	6.00	2.50
❑ 148	Kurt Kittner AU RC	10.00	4.00
❑ 149	Lamar Gordon AU RC	12.00	5.00
❑ 150	Leonard Henry AU RC	10.00	4.00
❑ 151	Lito Sheppard AU RC	12.00	5.00
❑ 152	Luke Staley AU RC	10.00	4.00
❑ 153	Matt Schobel AU RC	10.00	4.00
❑ 154	Mike Rumph AU RC	12.00	5.00
❑ 155	Najeh Davenport AU RC	12.00	5.00
❑ 156	Napoleon Harris AU RC	12.00	5.00
❑ 158	Quentin Jammer AU RC	12.00	5.00
❑ 159	Randy Fasani AU RC	10.00	4.00
❑ 160	Ronald Curry AU RC	12.00	5.00
❑ 161	Ryan Sims AU RC	12.00	5.00
❑ 162	Sam Simmons AU RC	6.00	2.50
❑ 163	Seth Burford AU RC	10.00	4.00
❑ 164	Tellis Redmon AU RC	10.00	4.00
❑ 165	Terry Charles AU RC	10.00	4.00
❑ 166	Tracey Wistrom AU RC	10.00	4.00
❑ 167	Verron Haynes AU RC	20.00	7.50
❑ 168	Wes Pate AU RC	6.00	2.50
❑ 169	Wendell Bryant AU RC	6.00	2.50
❑ 170	Damien Anderson AU RC	10.00	4.00

2003 Bowman's Best

#	Card	Hi	Lo
❑	COMP.SET w/o SP's (80)	30.00	12.50
❑	ROOKIE AU STATED ODDS 1:136		
❑	CARDS 170, 175 NOT RELEASED		
❑ 1	Terrell Owens	1.50	.60
❑ 2	Peerless Price	1.00	.40
❑ 3	Joey Harrington	2.50	1.00
❑ 4	Ricky Williams	1.50	.60
❑ 5	David Boston	1.00	.40
❑ 6	Troy Brown	1.00	.40
❑ 7	Deuce McAllister	1.50	.60
❑ 8	Marvin Harrison	1.50	.60
❑ 9	Ahman Green	1.50	.60
❑ 10	Emmitt Smith	4.00	1.50
❑ 11	Brian Urlacher	2.50	1.00
❑ 12	Jamal Lewis	1.50	.60
❑ 13	Keyshawn Johnson	1.50	.60
❑ 14	Kurt Warner	1.50	.60
❑ 15	Rod Gardner	1.00	.40
❑ 16	Plaxico Burress	1.00	.40
❑ 17	Chad Pennington	2.00	.75
❑ 18	Jeremy Shockey	2.50	1.00
❑ 19	Donovan McNabb	2.00	.75
❑ 20	T.J. Duckett	1.00	.40
❑ 21	Fred Taylor	1.50	.60
❑ 22	Daunte Culpepper	1.50	.60
❑ 23	Tiki Barber	1.50	.60
❑ 24	Brian Griese	1.50	.60
❑ 25	Chad Johnson	1.50	.60
❑ 26	Julius Peppers	1.50	.60
❑ 27	Chad Hutchinson	.60	.25
❑ 28	Eddie George	1.00	.40
❑ 29	Torry Holt	1.50	.60
❑ 30	Drew Brees	1.50	.60
❑ 31	Rich Gannon	1.00	.40
❑ 32	Trent Green	1.00	.40
❑ 33	Clinton Portis	2.50	1.00
❑ 34	Tom Brady	4.00	1.50
❑ 35	Aaron Brooks	1.50	.60
❑ 36	Ray Lewis	1.50	.60
❑ 37	David Carr	2.50	1.00
❑ 38	Chris Chambers	1.50	.60
❑ 39	Brad Johnson	1.00	.40
❑ 40	Tommy Maddox	1.50	.60
❑ 41	Curtis Martin	1.50	.60
❑ 42	Travis Henry	1.00	.40
❑ 43	Brett Favre	4.00	1.50
❑ 44	Randy Moss	2.50	1.00
❑ 45	Jimmy Smith	1.00	.40
❑ 46	Joey Galloway	1.00	.40
❑ 47	Derrick Mason	1.00	.40
❑ 48	Darrell Jackson	1.00	.40
❑ 49	Curtis Conway	.60	.25
❑ 50	Michael Vick	4.00	1.50
❑ 51	Rod Smith	1.00	.40
❑ 52	Muhsin Muhammad	1.00	.40
❑ 53	Drew Bledsoe	1.50	.60
❑ 54	Michael Bennett	1.00	.40
❑ 55	Joe Horn	1.00	.40
❑ 56	Stephen Davis	1.00	.40
❑ 57	Isaac Bruce	1.50	.60
❑ 58	Shaun Alexander	1.50	.60
❑ 59	Jerry Rice	3.00	1.25
❑ 60	Peyton Manning	2.50	1.00
❑ 61	Tony Gonzalez	1.00	.40
❑ 62	Jake Plummer	1.00	.40
❑ 63	Tim Couch	.60	.25
❑ 64	Marty Booker	1.00	.40
❑ 65	Corey Dillon	1.00	.40
❑ 66	Steve McNair	1.50	.60
❑ 67	Jeff Garcia	1.50	.60
❑ 68	Hines Ward	1.50	.60
❑ 69	Laveranues Coles	1.00	.40
❑ 70	Amani Toomer	1.00	.40
❑ 71	Eric Moulds	1.00	.40
❑ 72	Donald Driver	1.00	.40
❑ 73	Jay Fiedler	1.00	.40
❑ 74	Charlie Garner	1.00	.40
❑ 75	Priest Holmes	2.00	.75
❑ 76	Edgerrin James	1.50	.60
❑ 77	Kerry Collins	1.00	.40
❑ 78	LaDainian Tomlinson	1.50	.60
❑ 79	Mark Brunell	1.00	.40
❑ 80	Marshall Faulk	1.50	.60
❑ 81	Lee Suggs RC	5.00	2.00
❑ 82	William Joseph RC	4.00	1.50
❑ 83	Brandon Lloyd RC	5.00	2.00
❑ 84	Nick Barnett RC	5.00	2.00
❑ 85	Andre Woolfolk RC	4.00	1.50
❑ 86	Jimmy Kennedy RC	4.00	1.50
❑ 87	Kliff Kingsbury RC	4.00	1.50
❑ 88	Andrew Williams RC	4.00	1.50
❑ 89	Mike Doss RC	4.00	1.50
❑ 90	Troy Polamalu RC	20.00	10.00
❑ 91	Bryant Johnson JSY RC	6.00	2.50
❑ 92	Justin Fargas JSY RC	6.00	2.50
❑ 93	Terence Newman JSY RC	12.00	6.00

❑ 94 Brian St.Pierre JSY RC 6.00 2.50
❑ 95 DeWayne Robertson JSY RC 6.00 2.50
❑ 96 Dave Ragone JSY RC 6.00 2.50
❑ 97 Teyo Johnson JSY RC 6.00 2.50
❑ 98 Bethel Johnson JSY RC 6.00 2.50
❑ 99 Tyrone Calico JSY RC 6.00 2.50
❑ 100 Carson Palmer JSY RC 25.00 12.50
❑ 101 Marcus Trufant JSY RC 6.00 2.50
❑ 102 Nate Burleson JSY RC 6.00 2.50
❑ 103 Musa Smith JSY RC 6.00 2.50
❑ 104 Anquan Boldin JSY RC 15.00 6.00
❑ 105 Chris Simms JSY RC 10.00 4.00
❑ 106 Taylor Jacobs JSY RC 6.00 2.50
❑ 107 Dallas Clark JSY RC 6.00 2.50
❑ 108 Seneca Wallace JSY RC 6.00 2.50
❑ 109 Ken Dorsey JSY RC 6.00 2.50
❑ 110 Willis McGahee JSY RC 15.00 6.00
❑ 111 Chris Brown JSY RC 6.00 2.50
❑ 112 Terrell Suggs JSY RC 10.00 4.00
❑ 113 Kelley Washington JSY RC 6.00 2.50
❑ 114 Onterrio Smith JSY RC 6.00 2.50
❑ 115 Rex Grossman JSY RC 25.00 10.00
❑ 116 LaBrandon Toefield AU RC 12.00 5.00
❑ 117 Sam Aiken AU RC 10.00 4.00
❑ 118 Malaefou Mackenzie AU RC 8.00 3.00
❑ 119 David Tyree AU RC 10.00 4.00
❑ 120 Jerome McDougle AU RC 12.00 5.00
❑ 121 DeWayne White AU RC 10.00 4.00
❑ 122 Zuriel Smith AU RC 8.00 3.00
❑ 123 Shaun McDonald AU RC 12.00 5.00
❑ 124 Andre Johnson AU/199 RC 60.00 30.00
❑ 125 Ahmaad Galloway AU RC 10.00 4.00
❑ 126 Keenan Howry AU RC 12.00 5.00
❑ 127 Kareem Kelly AU RC 10.00 4.00
❑ 128 Brooks Bollinger AU RC 12.00 5.00
❑ 129 Amaz Battle AU RC 15.00 6.00
❑ 130 Adrian Madise AU RC 10.00 4.00
❑ 131 LaTarence Dunbar AU RC 10.00 4.00
❑ 132 L.J. Smith AU RC 12.00 5.00
❑ 133 B.J. Askew AU RC 12.00 5.00
❑ 134 Michael Haynes AU RC 12.00 5.00
❑ 135 David Kircus AU RC 15.00 6.00
❑ 136 Kyle Boller AU/199 RC 40.00 20.00
❑ 137 Domanick Davis AU RC 30.00 12.50
❑ 138 Osi Umenyiora AU RC 30.00 15.00
❑ 139 Bobby Wade AU RC 12.00 5.00
❑ 140 Boss Bailey AU RC 15.00 6.00
❑ 141 Billy McMullen AU RC 10.00 4.00
❑ 142 Doug Gabriel AU RC 12.00 5.00
❑ 143 J.R. Tolver AU RC 10.00 4.00
❑ 144 Gibran Hamdan AU RC 8.00 3.00
❑ 145 Walter Young AU RC 8.00 3.00
❑ 146 Carl Ford AU RC 8.00 3.00
❑ 147 Andrew Pinnock AU RC 10.00 4.00
❑ 148 Byron Leftwich AU/199 RC 100.00 50.00
❑ 149 Ty Warren AU RC 12.00 5.00
❑ 150 Visanthe Shiancoe AU RC 10.00 4.00
❑ 151 Justin Gage AU RC 12.00 5.00
❑ 152 Brock Forsey AU RC 12.00 5.00
❑ 153 Casey Moore AU RC 10.00 4.00
❑ 154 Juston Wood AU RC 8.00 3.00
❑ 155 Aaron Walker AU RC 10.00 4.00
❑ 156 Trent Smith AU RC 12.00 5.00
❑ 157 Travis Anglin AU RC 8.00 3.00
❑ 158 Jeremi Johnson AU RC 10.00 4.00
❑ 159 Justin Griffith AU RC 10.00 4.00
❑ 160 Chris Davis AU RC 10.00 4.00
❑ 161 J.T. Wall AU RC 8.00 3.00
❑ 162 Larry Johnson AU/199 RC 175.00 100.00
❑ 163 Jon Olinger AU RC 10.00 4.00
❑ 164 Donald Lee AU RC 10.00 4.00
❑ 165 Taco Wallace AU RC 10.00 4.00
❑ 166 DeAndrew Rubin AU RC 8.00 3.00
❑ 167 Ryan Hoag AU RC 8.00 3.00
❑ 168 Kevin Williams AU RC 12.00 5.00
❑ 169 Ovie Mughelli AU RC 8.00 3.00
❑ 171 Brandon Drumm AU RC 10.00 4.00
❑ 172 Brad Banks AU RC 10.00 4.00
❑ 173 Talman Gardner AU RC 12.00 5.00
❑ 174 Jason Witten AU RC 25.00 12.50

2004 Bowman's Best

❑ COMP.SET w/o SP's (100) 50.00 25.00
❑ RC JSY GROUP A ODDS 1:130
❑ RC JSY GROUP B ODDS 1:236
❑ RC JSY GROUP C ODDS 1:86
❑ RC JSY GROUP D ODDS 1:38
❑ RC JSY GROUP E ODDS 1:31
❑ RC JSY GROUP F ODDS 1:27

❑ RC JSY GROUP G ODDS 1:50
❑ RC JSY GROUP H ODDS 1:89
❑ RC JSY GROUP I ODDS 1:29
❑ RC AU/199 STATED ODDS 1:311
❑ RC AU STATED ODDS 1:3
❑ 1 Brett Favre 4.00 1.50
❑ 2 Chris Chambers 1.00 .40
❑ 3 Kyle Boller 1.50 .60
❑ 4 Brian Urlacher 2.00 .75
❑ 5 Marvin Harrison 1.50 .60
❑ 6 Matt Hasselbeck 1.00 .40
❑ 7 Aaron Brooks 1.00 .40
❑ 8 Curtis Martin 1.50 .60
❑ 9 Keenan McCardell .60 .25
❑ 10 Terrell Owens 1.50 .60
❑ 11 Jimmy Smith 1.00 .40
❑ 12 Garrison Hearst 1.00 .40
❑ 13 Joe Horn 1.00 .40
❑ 14 David Carr 1.50 .60
❑ 15 Tom Brady 4.00 1.50
❑ 16 Shaun Alexander 1.50 .60
❑ 17 Tommy Maddox 1.00 .40
❑ 18 Tiki Barber 1.50 .60
❑ 19 Trent Green 1.00 .40
❑ 20 Anquan Boldin 1.50 .60
❑ 21 Peerless Price 1.00 .40
❑ 22 Jake Delhomme 1.50 .60
❑ 23 Eric Moulds 1.00 .40
❑ 24 Quincy Carter 1.00 .40
❑ 25 Steve McNair 1.50 .60
❑ 26 Tim Rattay .60 .25
❑ 27 Laveranues Coles 1.00 .40
❑ 28 Corey Dillon 1.00 .40
❑ 29 Byron Leftwich 2.00 .75
❑ 30 Chad Pennington 1.50 .60
❑ 31 Koren Robinson 1.00 .40
❑ 32 Plaxico Burress 1.00 .40
❑ 33 Steve Smith 1.50 .60
❑ 34 Warrick Dunn 1.00 .40
❑ 35 Jamal Lewis 1.50 .60
❑ 36 Charles Rogers 1.00 .40
❑ 37 Tony Gonzalez 1.00 .40
❑ 38 Jake Plummer 1.00 .40
❑ 39 Chad Johnson 1.50 .60
❑ 40 Peyton Manning 2.50 1.00
❑ 41 Daunte Culpepper 1.50 .60
❑ 42 Fred Taylor 1.00 .40
❑ 43 Amani Toomer 1.00 .40
❑ 44 Santana Moss 1.00 .40
❑ 45 Deuce McAllister 1.50 .60
❑ 46 Rex Grossman 1.50 .60
❑ 47 Ray Lewis 1.50 .60
❑ 48 Hines Ward 1.50 .60
❑ 49 Darrell Jackson 1.00 .40
❑ 50 Randy Moss 2.00 .75
❑ 51 Carson Palmer 2.00 .75
❑ 52 Rod Smith 1.00 .40
❑ 53 Drew Bledsoe 1.50 .60
❑ 54 Brad Johnson 1.00 .40
❑ 55 Travis Henry 1.00 .40
❑ 56 Joey Harrington 1.50 .60
❑ 57 Edgerrin James 1.50 .60
❑ 58 Kurt Warner 1.50 .60
❑ 59 Josh McCown 1.00 .40
❑ 60 Clinton Portis 1.50 .60
❑ 61 Brian Westbrook 1.00 .40
❑ 62 Marc Bulger 1.50 .60
❑ 63 Charlie Garner 1.00 .40
❑ 64 Torry Holt 1.50 .60
❑ 65 LaDainian Tomlinson 2.00 .75
❑ 66 Mark Brunell 1.00 .40
❑ 67 Derrick Mason 1.00 .40
❑ 68 Andre Johnson 1.50 .60
❑ 69 Keyshawn Johnson 1.00 .40
❑ 70 Ahman Green 1.50 .60
❑ 71 Rudi Johnson 1.00 .40
❑ 72 Stephen Davis 1.00 .40
❑ 73 Jeff Garcia 1.50 .60
❑ 74 Michael Strahan 1.00 .40
❑ 75 Michael Vick 3.00 1.25
❑ 76 Ricky Williams 1.50 .60
❑ 77 Domanick Davis 1.50 .60
❑ 78 Priest Holmes 2.00 .75
❑ 79 Marshall Faulk 1.50 .60
❑ 80 Donovan McNabb 2.00 .75
❑ 81 Dunta Robinson RC 4.00 1.50
❑ 82 Robert Gallery RC 4.00 1.50
❑ 83 Ben Troupe RC 4.00 1.50
❑ 84 Antwan Odom RC 4.00 1.50
❑ 85 Brandon Miree RC 3.00 1.25
❑ 86 Darnell Dockett RC 3.00 1.25
❑ 87 Vince Wilfork RC 4.00 1.50
❑ 88 Randy Starks RC 3.00 1.25
❑ 89 Chris Cooley RC 4.00 1.50
❑ 90 Dwan Edwards RC 2.00 .75
❑ 91 Patrick Crayton RC 4.00 1.50
❑ 92 Sean Jones RC 3.00 1.25
❑ 93 Sean Ryan RC 3.00 1.25
❑ 94 Chris Gamble RC 4.00 1.50
❑ 95 Will Smith RC 4.00 1.50
❑ 96 Sloan Thomas RC 3.00 1.25
❑ 97 Tim Euhus RC 4.00 1.50
❑ 98 Tommie Harris RC 4.00 1.50
❑ 99 Will Poole RC 4.00 1.50
❑ 100 Karlos Dansby RC 4.00 1.50
❑ 101 Bernard Berrian JSY RC D 8.00 3.00
❑ 102 DeAngelo Hall JSY RC A 8.00 3.00
❑ 103 Mewelde Moore JSY RC G 6.00 2.50
❑ 104 Rashaun Woods JSY RC G 6.00 2.50
❑ 105 Reggie Williams JSY RC 8.00 3.00
❑ 106 Derrick Hamilton JSY RC F 5.00 2.00
❑ 107 Kellen Winslow JSY RC C 12.00 5.00
❑ 108 Devard Darling JSY RC D 6.00 2.50
❑ 109 Michael Clayton JSY RC B 12.00 5.00
❑ 110 Larry Fitzgerald JSY RC E 20.00 7.50
❑ 111 Greg Jones JSY RC E 6.00 2.50
❑ 112 Chris Perry JSY RC H 12.00 5.00
❑ 113 Lee Evans JSY RC F 8.00 3.00
❑ 114 Tatum Bell JSY RC E 12.00 5.00
❑ 115 Steven Jackson JSY RC I 20.00 7.50
❑ 116 Matt Schaub JSY RC A 12.00 5.00
❑ 117 Ben Troupe JSY 6.00 2.50
❑ 118 Devery Henderson JSY RC F 5.00 2.00
❑ 119 Ben Watson JSY RC E 6.00 2.50
❑ 120 J.P. Losman JSY RC I 12.00 5.00
❑ 121 Keary Colbert JSY RC F 8.00 3.00
❑ 122 Darius Watts JSY RC C 6.00 2.50
❑ 123 Cedric Cobbs JSY RC D 6.00 2.50
❑ 124 Luke McCown JSY RC A 6.00 2.50
❑ 125 Michael Jenkins JSY RC A 6.00 2.50
❑ 126 Eli Manning AU/199 RC 200.00 100.00
❑ 127 Roy Williams AU/199 RC 100.00 50.00
❑ 128 Kevin Jones AU/199 RC 80.00 40.00
❑ 129 Philip Rivers AU/199 RC 120.00 60.00
❑ 130 Roethlis AU/199 RC 300.00 150.00
❑ 131 Carlos Francis AU RC 12.00 5.00
❑ 132 Bradlee Van Pelt AU RC 15.00 6.00
❑ 133 Michael Turner AU RC 40.00 20.00
❑ 134 Kenechi Udeze AU RC 15.00 6.00
❑ 135 Jeff Smoker AU RC 15.00 6.00
❑ 136 Josh Harris AU RC 12.00 5.00
❑ 137 Derrick Strait AU RC 12.00 5.00
❑ 138 Jonathan Vilma AU RC 20.00 7.50
❑ 139 Triandos Luke AU RC 12.00 5.00
❑ 140 Jim Sorgi AU RC 15.00 6.00
❑ 141 Ryan Krause AU RC 12.00 5.00
❑ 142 Julius Jones AU RC 80.00 40.00
❑ 143 Mark Jones AU RC 12.00 5.00
❑ 144 P.K. Sam AU RC 12.00 5.00
❑ 145 B.J. Symons AU RC 15.00 6.00
❑ 146 Adimchinobe Echemandu AU RC 12.00 5.00
❑ 147 Casey Bramlet AU RC 12.00 5.00
❑ 148 Clarence Moore AU RC 15.00 6.00
❑ 149 D.J. Williams AU RC 12.00 5.00
❑ 150 Jeris McIntyre AU RC 12.00 5.00
❑ 151 Jerricho Cotchery AU RC 15.00 6.00
❑ 152 Andy Hall AU RC 12.00 5.00
❑ 153 Samie Parker AU RC 15.00 6.00
❑ 154 Maurice Mann AU RC 12.00 5.00
❑ 155 Jonathan Smith AU RC 12.00 5.00

❑ 156 Derrick Ward AU RC 10.00 4.00
❑ 157 D.J. Hackett AU RC 12.00 5.00
❑ 158 Craig Krenzel AU RC 15.00 6.00
❑ 159 Jared Lorenzen AU RC 12.00 5.00
❑ 160 Cody Pickett AU RC 15.00 6.00
❑ 161 Jamaar Taylor AU RC 15.00 6.00
❑ 162 Michael Boulware AU RC 15.00 6.00
❑ 163 Matt Mauck AU RC 12.00 5.00
❑ 164 John Navarre AU RC 15.00 6.00
❑ 165 Ahmad Carroll AU RC 12.00 5.00
❑ 166 Bruce Perry AU RC 15.00 6.00
❑ 167 Erik Jensen AU RC 12.00 5.00
❑ 168 Matt Kranchick AU RC 15.00 6.00
❑ 169 Courtney Anderson AU RC 12.00 5.00
❑ 170 Nate Lawrie AU RC 12.00 5.00
❑ 171 Thomas Tapeh AU RC 12.00 5.00
❑ 172 Courtney Watson AU RC 15.00 6.00
❑ 173 Drew Carter AU RC 15.00 6.00
❑ 174 Ricardo Colclough AU RC 15.00 6.00
❑ 175 Dontarrious Thomas AU RC 15.00 6.00
❑ 176 Ernest Wilford AU RC 15.00 6.00
❑ 177 Quincy Wilson AU RC 12.00 5.00
❑ 178 Derek Abney AU RC 15.00 6.00
❑ 179 Jeff Dugan AU RC 10.00 4.00
❑ 180 Ben Hartsock AU RC 15.00 6.00
❑ 181 Matt Kegel AU RC 15.00 6.00
❑ 182 Derrick Knight AU RC 12.00 5.00
❑ 183 Teddy Lehman AU RC 15.00 6.00
❑ 184 Johnnie Morant AU RC 15.00 6.00
❑ 185A B.Sanders AU RC Long AU 150.00 100.00
❑ 185B B.Sanders AU RC Short AU 100.00 50.00
❑ 186 Michael Gaines AU RC 12.00 5.00
❑ 187 Daryl Smith AU RC 15.00 6.00
❑ 188 Jason Babin AU RC 15.00 6.00

2005 Bowman's Best

❑ COMP.SET w/o SPs (100) 40.00 15.00
❑ ROOKIE JSY STATED ODDS 1:14
❑ ROOKIE JSY PRINT RUN 799 SER.#'d SETS
❑ COMMON ROOKIE AU 8.00 3.00
❑ ROOKIE AU SEMISTARS 10.00 4.00
❑ ROOKIE AU UNL.STARS 12.00 5.00
❑ ROOKIE AU/999 STATED ODDS 1:8
❑ ROOKIE AU/199 STATED ODDS 1:296
❑ ROOKIE AU PRINT RUN 999 SER.#'d SETS
❑ AU EXCH EXPIRATION: 10/31/2007
❑ UNPRICED GOLD PRINT RUN 1 SET
❑ UNPRICED PRINT.PLATE PRINT RUN 1 SET
❑ 1 Tiki Barber 1.00 .40
❑ 2 Peyton Manning 2.50 1.00
❑ 3 Tony Gonzalez .60 .25
❑ 4 Terrell Owens 1.00 .40
❑ 5 Brett Favre 2.50 1.00
❑ 6 Rudi Johnson .60 .25
❑ 7 Hines Ward 1.00 .40
❑ 8 Andre Johnson .60 .25
❑ 9 Tom Brady 2.50 1.00
❑ 10 LaDainian Tomlinson 1.25 .50
❑ 11 Daunte Culpepper 1.00 .40
❑ 12 Muhsin Muhammad .60 .25
❑ 13 Dwight Freeney .60 .25
❑ 14 Curtis Martin 1.00 .40
❑ 15 Eli Manning 1.50 .60
❑ 16 Willis McGahee 1.00 .40
❑ 17 Steve McNair 1.00 .40
❑ 18 Jamal Lewis 1.00 .40
❑ 19 Reggie Wayne .60 .25
❑ 20 Trent Green .60 .25
❑ 21 Isaac Bruce .60 .25
❑ 22 Edgerrin James 1.00 .40
❑ 23 Marc Bulger 1.00 .40
❑ 24 Torry Holt 1.00 .40
❑ 25 Deuce McAllister 1.00 .40
❑ 26 Jake Plummer .60 .25
❑ 27 Randy Moss 1.00 .40
❑ 28 Drew Brees 1.00 .40
❑ 29 Ahman Green 1.00 .40
❑ 30 Marvin Harrison 1.00 .40
❑ 31 Michael Vick 1.50 .60
❑ 32 Julius Jones 1.25 .50
❑ 33 Matt Hasselbeck .60 .25
❑ 34 Priest Holmes 1.00 .40
❑ 35 Drew Bennett .60 .25
❑ 36 Donovan McNabb 1.25 .50
❑ 37 Chad Johnson 1.00 .40
❑ 38 Fred Taylor .60 .25
❑ 39 Chris Brown .60 .25
❑ 40 Jake Delhomme 1.00 .40
❑ 41 Joe Horn .60 .25
❑ 42 Chad Pennington 1.00 .40
❑ 43 Corey Dillon .60 .25
❑ 44 Byron Leftwich 1.00 .40
❑ 45 Javon Walker .60 .25
❑ 46 Ben Roethlisberger 2.50 1.00
❑ 47 Eric Moulds .60 .25
❑ 48 Domanick Davis .60 .25
❑ 49 Steven Jackson 1.25 .50
❑ 50 Shaun Alexander 1.25 .50
❑ 51 Stanford Routt RC 4.00 1.50
❑ 52 Marion Barber RC 8.00 3.00
❑ 53 Matt Roth RC 5.00 2.00
❑ 54 James Kilian RC 5.00 2.00
❑ 55 Alex Barron RC 2.50 1.00
❑ 56 Madison Hedgecock RC 5.00 2.00
❑ 57 Patrick Estes RC 4.00 1.50
❑ 58 Bryant McFadden RC 5.00 2.00
❑ 59 Dan Cody RC 5.00 2.00
❑ 60 Justin Miller RC 4.00 1.50
❑ 61 Paris Warren RC 4.00 1.50
❑ 62 Marcus Spears RC 5.00 2.00
❑ 63 Odell Thurman RC 5.00 2.00
❑ 64 Craphonso Thorpe RC 4.00 1.50
❑ 65 Dustin Fox RC 5.00 2.00
❑ 66 David Pollack RC 5.00 2.00
❑ 67 Anthony Davis RC 4.00 1.50
❑ 68 Mike Nugent RC 5.00 2.00
❑ 69 David Greene RC 5.00 2.00
❑ 70 Rick Razzano RC 5.00 2.00
❑ 70AU Rick Razzano AU 12.00 5.00
❑ 71 Mike Patterson RC 5.00 2.00
❑ 72 Derek Anderson RC 5.00 2.00
❑ 72AU Derek Anderson AU 15.00 6.00
❑ 73 Marlin Jackson RC 5.00 2.00
❑ 73AU Marlin Jackson AU 12.00 5.00
❑ 74 Boomer Grigsby RC 6.00 2.50
❑ 75 Kevin Burnett RC 5.00 2.00
❑ 76 Ryan Riddle RC 2.50 1.00
❑ 77 Brock Berlin RC 4.00 1.50
❑ 78 Khalif Barnes RC 4.00 1.50
❑ 79 Marcus Maxwell RC 4.00 1.50
❑ 80 Fred Gibson RC 4.00 1.50
❑ 81 T.A. McLendon RC 2.50 1.00
❑ 82 Kirk Morrison RC 5.00 2.00
❑ 83 Sean Considine RC 5.00 2.00
❑ 84 Luis Castillo RC 5.00 2.00
❑ 85 Darryl Blackstock RC 4.00 1.50
❑ 86 Airese Currie RC 5.00 2.00
❑ 87 Corey Webster RC 5.00 2.00
❑ 88 Kurt Campbell RC 4.00 1.50
❑ 89 Ellis Hobbs RC 5.00 2.00
❑ 90 Timmy Chang RC 4.00 1.50
❑ 91 Travis Johnson RC 4.00 1.50
❑ 92 Eric Moore RC 4.00 1.50
❑ 93 Barrett Ruud RC 5.00 2.00
❑ 94 Erasmus James RC 5.00 2.00
❑ 95 Anttaj Hawthorne RC 4.00 1.50
❑ 96 Manuel White RC 4.00 1.50
❑ 97 Rian Wallace RC 4.00 1.50
❑ 98 Justin Tuck RC 5.00 2.00
❑ 99 Travis Daniels RC 4.00 1.50
❑ 100 Donte Nicholson RC 5.00 2.00
❑ 101 Matt Jones JSY RC 15.00 6.00
❑ 102 J.J. Arrington JSY RC 10.00 4.00
❑ 103 Mark Bradley JSY RC 10.00 4.00
❑ 104 Reggie Brown JSY RC 8.00 3.00
❑ 105 Jason Campbell JSY RC 10.00 4.00
❑ 106 Maurice Clarett JSY 8.00 3.00
❑ 107 Mark Clayton JSY RC 10.00 4.00
❑ 108 Braylon Edwards JSY RC 15.00 6.00
❑ 109 Ciatrick Fason JSY RC 8.00 3.00
❑ 110 Charlie Frye JSY RC 12.00 5.00
❑ 111 Frank Gore JSY RC 12.00 5.00
❑ 112 Vincent Jackson JSY RC 8.00 3.00
❑ 113 Adam Jones JSY RC 8.00 3.00
❑ 114 Stefan LeFors JSY 8.00 3.00
❑ 114AU Stefan LeFors AU RC 12.00 5.00
❑ 115 Ryan Moats JSY 8.00 3.00
❑ 115AU Ryan Moats AU RC 20.00 7.50
❑ 116 Vernand Morency JSY RC 8.00 3.00
❑ 117 Terrence Murphy JSY RC 8.00 3.00
❑ 118 Kyle Orton JSY RC 10.00 4.00
❑ 119 Roscoe Parrish JSY RC 8.00 3.00
❑ 120 Courtney Roby JSY RC 8.00 3.00
❑ 121 Carlos Rogers JSY RC 10.00 4.00
❑ 122 Antrel Rolle JSY RC 8.00 3.00
❑ 123 Eric Shelton JSY RC 8.00 3.00
❑ 124 Andrew Walter JSY RC 10.00 4.00
❑ 125 Roddy White JSY RC 8.00 3.00
❑ 126 Cadillac Williams JSY RC 25.00 10.00
❑ 127 Troy Williamson JSY RC 12.00 5.00
❑ 128 Cedric Benson AU/199 RC 80.00 40.00
❑ 129 Aaron Rodgers AU/199 RC 100.00 50.00
❑ 130 Alex Smith QB AU/199 RC 120.00 60.00
❑ 131 Mike Williams AU/199 50.00 20.00
❑ 132 Ronnie Brown AU/199 RC 120.00 50.00
❑ 133 Adrian McPherson AU RC 15.00 6.00
❑ 134 Brandon Jacobs AU RC 30.00 12.50
❑ 135 Chad Owens AU RC 12.00 5.00
❑ 136 Chase Lyman AU RC 10.00 4.00
❑ 137 Chris Henry AU RC EXCH 12.00 5.00
❑ 138 Craig Bragg AU RC 10.00 4.00
❑ 139 Damien Nash AU RC 10.00 4.00
❑ 140 Dante Ridgeway AU RC 10.00 4.00
❑ 141 Darren Sproles AU RC 12.00 5.00
❑ 142 Deandra Cobb AU RC 10.00 4.00
❑ 143 Gino Guidugli AU RC 8.00 3.00
❑ 144 J.R. Russell AU RC 10.00 4.00
❑ 145 Jerome Mathis AU RC EXCH 12.00 5.00
❑ 146 Josh Davis AU RC 10.00 4.00
❑ 147 Kay-Jay Harris AU RC 10.00 4.00
❑ 148 Larry Brackins AU RC 10.00 4.00
❑ 149 Matt Cassel AU RC 20.00 10.00
❑ 150 Noah Herron AU RC 12.00 5.00
❑ 151 Rasheed Marshall AU RC 12.00 5.00
❑ 152 Roydell Williams AU RC 12.00 5.00
❑ 153 Ryan Fitzpatrick AU RC 25.00 10.00
❑ 154 Steve Savoy AU RC 8.00 3.00
❑ 155 Tab Perry AU RC 12.00 5.00
❑ 156 Shawne Merriman AU RC 30.00 12.50
❑ 157 Charles Frederick AU RC 10.00 4.00
❑ 158 Alvin Pearman AU RC 12.00 5.00
❑ 159 Channing Crowder AU RC 12.00 5.00
❑ 160 Fabian Washington AU RC 12.00 5.00
❑ 161 Dan Orlovsky AU RC 15.00 6.00
❑ 162 Derrick Johnson AU RC 20.00 7.50
❑ 163 Alex Smith TE AU RC 12.00 5.00
❑ 164 Cedric Houston AU RC 12.00 5.00
❑ 165 Brandon Jones AU RC 12.00 5.00
❑ 166 DeMarcus Ware AU RC 20.00 10.00
❑ 167 Lionel Gates AU RC 10.00 4.00

1994 Classic NFL Experience

❑ COMPLETE SET (100) 10.00 4.00
❑ 1 Checklist 1 .05 .01
❑ 2 Checklist 2 .05 .01
❑ 3 Bobby Hebert .05 .01
❑ 4 Eric Pegram .05 .01
❑ 5 Andre Rison .10 .02
❑ 6 Deion Sanders .40 .15
❑ 7 Cornelius Bennett .10 .02

❑ 8 Jim Kelly .20 .07
❑ 9 Andre Reed .10 .02
❑ 10 Bruce Smith .20 .07
❑ 11 Thurman Thomas .20 .07
❑ 12 Curtis Conway .20 .07
❑ 13 Jim Harbaugh .20 .07
❑ 14 John Copeland .05 .01
❑ 15 David Klingler .05 .01
❑ 16 Carl Pickens .10 .02
❑ 17 Eric Metcalf .10 .02
❑ 18 Vinny Testaverde .10 .02
❑ 19 Eric Turner .05 .01
❑ 20 Tommy Vardell .05 .01
❑ 21 Troy Aikman .75 .30
❑ 22 Michael Irvin .20 .07
❑ 23 Emmitt Smith 1.25 .50
❑ 24 Kevin Williams WR .10 .02
❑ 25 John Elway 1.50 .60
❑ 26 Glyn Milburn .10 .02
❑ 27 Shannon Sharpe .10 .02
❑ 28 Herman Moore .20 .07
❑ 29 Rodney Peete .05 .01
❑ 30 Barry Sanders 1.25 .50
❑ 31 Pat Swilling .05 .01
❑ 32 Brett Favre 1.50 .60
❑ 33 Sterling Sharpe .10 .02
❑ 34 Reggie White .20 .07
❑ 35 Haywood Jeffires .10 .02
❑ 36 Warren Moon .20 .07
❑ 37 Webster Slaughter .05 .01
❑ 38 Lorenzo White .05 .01
❑ 39 Quentin Coryatt .05 .01
❑ 40 Jeff George .20 .07
❑ 41 Roosevelt Potts .05 .01
❑ 42 Marcus Allen .20 .07
❑ 43 Joe Montana 1.50 .60
❑ 44 Neil Smith .10 .02
❑ 45 Derrick Thomas .20 .07
❑ 46 Tim Brown .20 .07
❑ 47 Jeff Hostetler .10 .02
❑ 48 Rocket Ismail .10 .02
❑ 49 Anthony Smith .05 .01
❑ 50 Jerome Bettis .40 .15
❑ 51 Jim Everett .10 .02
❑ 52 T.J.Rubley RC .05 .01
❑ 53 Keith Jackson .05 .01
❑ 54 Terry Kirby .20 .07
❑ 55 Dan Marino 1.50 .60
❑ 56 O.J.McDuffie .20 .07
❑ 57 Scott Mitchell .10 .02
❑ 58 Cris Carter .40 .15
❑ 59 Chris Doleman .05 .01
❑ 60 Robert Smith .20 .07
❑ 61 Drew Bledsoe .60 .25
❑ 62 Vincent Brisby .10 .02
❑ 63 Derek Brown RBK .05 .01
❑ 64 Willie Roaf .05 .01
❑ 65 Irv Smith .05 .01
❑ 66 Renaldo Turnbull .05 .01
❑ 67 Rodney Hampton .10 .02
❑ 68 Phil Simms .10 .02
❑ 69 Lawrence Taylor .20 .07
❑ 70 Boomer Esiason .10 .02
❑ 71 Marvin Jones .05 .01
❑ 72 Ronnie Lott .10 .02
❑ 73 Johnny Mitchell .05 .01
❑ 74 Rob Moore .10 .02
❑ 75 Victor Bailey .05 .01
❑ 76 Randall Cunningham .20 .07
❑ 77 Ken O'Brien .05 .01
❑ 78 Steve Beuerlein .10 .02
❑ 79 Garrison Hearst .20 .07
❑ 80 Ronald Moore .05 .01
❑ 81 Ricky Proehl .05 .01
❑ 82 Deon Figures .05 .01
❑ 83 Barry Foster .05 .01
❑ 84 Neil O'Donnell .20 .07
❑ 85 Rod Woodson .10 .02
❑ 86 Natrone Means .20 .07
❑ 87 Anthony Miller .10 .02
❑ 88 Junior Seau .20 .07
❑ 89 Jerry Rice .75 .30
❑ 90 Ricky Watters .10 .02
❑ 91 Steve Young .75 .30
❑ 92 Brian Blades .10 .02
❑ 93 Cortez Kennedy .10 .02
❑ 94 Rick Mirer .20 .07
❑ 95 Stan Humphries .10 .02
❑ 96 Eric Curry .05 .01
❑ 97 Craig Erickson .05 .01
❑ 98 Reggie Brooks .10 .02
❑ 99 Desmond Howard .10 .02
❑ 100 Mark Rypien .05 .01
❑ SP1 Troy Aikman/1994 40.00 15.00

1994 Collector's Choice

❑ COMPLETE SET (384) 20.00 7.50
❑ 1 Antonio Langham RC .10 .02
❑ 2 Aaron Glenn RC .25 .08
❑ 3 Sam Adams RC .10 .02
❑ 4 Dewayne Washington RC .10 .02
❑ 5 Dan Wilkinson RC .10 .02
❑ 6 Bryant Young RC .25 .08
❑ 7 Aaron Taylor RC .05 .01
❑ 8 Willie McGinest RC .25 .08
❑ 9 Trev Alberts RC .10 .02
❑ 10 Jamir Miller RC .10 .02
❑ 11 John Thierry RC .05 .01
❑ 12 Heath Shuler RC .25 .08
❑ 13 Trent Dilfer RC 1.25 .50
❑ 14 Marshall Faulk RC 5.00 2.00
❑ 15 Greg Hill RC .25 .08
❑ 16 William Floyd RC .25 .08
❑ 17 Chuck Levy RC .05 .01
❑ 18 Charlie Garner RC 1.25 .50
❑ 19 Mario Bates RC .25 .08
❑ 20 Donnell Bennett RC .25 .08
❑ 21 LeShon Johnson RC .10 .02
❑ 22 Calvin Jones RC .05 .01
❑ 23 Darnay Scott RC .50 .20
❑ 24 Charles Johnson RC .25 .08
❑ 25 Johnnie Morton RC .50 .20
❑ 26 Shante Carver RC .05 .01
❑ 27 Derrick Alexander WR RC .25 .08
❑ 28 David Palmer RC .25 .08
❑ 29 Ryan Yarborough RC .05 .01
❑ 30 Errict Rhett RC .25 .08
❑ 31 James Washington I93 .05 .01
❑ 32 Sterling Sharpe I93 .05 .01
❑ 33 Drew Bledsoe I93 .25 .08
❑ 34 Eric Allen I93 .05 .01
❑ 35 Jerome Bettis I93 .25 .08
❑ 36 Joe Montana I93 .60 .25
❑ 37 John Carney I93 .05 .01
❑ 38 Emmitt Smith I93 .50 .20
❑ 39 Chris Warren I93 .25 .08
❑ 40 Reggie Brooks I93 .05 .01
❑ 41 Gary Brown I93 .05 .01
❑ 42 Tim Brown I93 .10 .02
❑ 43 Erric Pegram I93 .05 .01
❑ 44 Ronald Moore I93 .05 .01
❑ 45 Jerry Rice I93 .40 .15
❑ 46 Ricky Watters TE .10 .02
❑ 47 Joe Montana TE .60 .25
❑ 48 Reggie Brooks TE .05 .01
❑ 49 Rick Mirer TE .25 .08
❑ 50 Rocket Ismail TE .10 .02
❑ 51 Curtis Conway TE .10 .02
❑ 52 Junior Seau TE .25 .08
❑ 53 Mark Carrier DB TE .05 .01
❑ 54 Ronnie Lott TE .10 .02
❑ 55 Marcus Allen TE .25 .08
❑ 56 Michael Irvin TE .25 .08
❑ 57 Bennie Blades .05 .01
❑ 58 Randal Hill .05 .01
❑ 59 Brian Blades .10 .02
❑ 60 Russell Maryland .05 .01
❑ 61 Jim Kelly .25 .08
❑ 62 Arthur Marshall .05 .01
❑ 63 Webster Slaughter .05 .01
❑ 64 Dave Krieg .10 .02
❑ 65 Steve Jordan .05 .01
❑ 66 Neil O'Donnell .25 .08
❑ 67 Andre Reed .10 .02
❑ 68 Mike Croel .05 .01
❑ 69 Al Smith .05 .01
❑ 70 Joe Montana 1.50 .60
❑ 71 Randall McDaniel .05 .01
❑ 72 Greg Lloyd .10 .02
❑ 73 Thomas Smith .05 .01
❑ 74 Glyn Milburn .10 .02
❑ 75 Lorenzo White .05 .01
❑ 76 Neil Smith .10 .02
❑ 77 John Randle .10 .02
❑ 78 Rod Woodson .10 .02
❑ 79 Russell Maryland .05 .01
❑ 80 Rodney Peete .05 .01
❑ 81 Jackie Harris .05 .01
❑ 82 James Jett .05 .01
❑ 83 Rodney Hampton .10 .02
❑ 84 Bill Romanowski .05 .01
❑ 85 Ken Norton Jr. .10 .02
❑ 86 Barry Sanders 1.25 .50
❑ 87 Johnny Holland .05 .01
❑ 88 Terry McDaniel .05 .01
❑ 89 Greg Jackson .05 .01
❑ 90 Dana Stubblefield .10 .02
❑ 91 Jay Novacek .10 .02
❑ 92 Chris Spielman .10 .02
❑ 93 Ken Ruettgers .05 .01
❑ 94 Greg Robinson .05 .01
❑ 95 Mark Jackson .05 .01
❑ 96 John Taylor .10 .02
❑ 97 Roger Harper .05 .01
❑ 98 Jerry Ball .05 .01
❑ 99 Keith Byars .05 .01
❑ 100 Morten Andersen .05 .01
❑ 101 Eric Allen .05 .01
❑ 102 Marion Butts .05 .01
❑ 103 Michael Haynes .10 .02
❑ 104 Rob Burnett .05 .01
❑ 105 Marco Coleman .05 .01
❑ 106 Derek Brown RBK .05 .01
❑ 107 Andy Harmon .05 .01
❑ 108 Darren Carrington .05 .01
❑ 109 Bobby Hebert .05 .01
❑ 110 Mark Carrier WR .10 .02
❑ 111 Bryan Cox .05 .01
❑ 112 Toi Cook .05 .01
❑ 113 Tim Harris .05 .01
❑ 114 John Friesz .10 .02
❑ 115 Neal Anderson .05 .01
❑ 116 Jerome Bettis .40 .15
❑ 117 Bruce Armstrong .05 .01
❑ 118 Brad Baxter .05 .01
❑ 119 Johnny Bailey .05 .01
❑ 120 Brian Blades .10 .02
❑ 121 Mark Carrier DB .05 .01
❑ 122 Shane Conlan .05 .01
❑ 123 Drew Bledsoe .60 .25
❑ 124 Chris Burkett .05 .01
❑ 125 Steve Beuerlein .10 .02
❑ 126 Ferrell Edmunds .05 .01
❑ 127 Curtis Conway .25 .08
❑ 128 Troy Drayton .05 .01
❑ 129 Vincent Brown .05 .01
❑ 130 Boomer Esiason .10 .02
❑ 131 Larry Centers .25 .08
❑ 132 Carlton Gray .05 .01
❑ 133 Chris Miller .05 .01
❑ 134 Eric Metcalf .10 .02
❑ 135 Mark Higgs .05 .01
❑ 136 Tyrone Hughes .10 .02
❑ 137 Randall Cunningham .25 .08
❑ 138 Ronnie Harmon .05 .01
❑ 139 Andre Rison .10 .02
❑ 140 Eric Turner .05 .01
❑ 141 Terry Kirby .25 .08
❑ 142 Eric Martin .05 .01
❑ 143 Seth Joyner .05 .01
❑ 144 Stan Humphries .10 .02
❑ 145 Deion Sanders .40 .15
❑ 146 Vinny Testaverde .10 .02
❑ 147 Dan Marino 1.50 .60
❑ 148 Renaldo Turnbull .05 .01
❑ 149 Herschel Walker .10 .02
❑ 150 Anthony Miller .10 .02
❑ 151 Richard Dent .10 .02
❑ 152 Jim Everett .10 .02
❑ 153 Ben Coates .10 .02

❑ 154 Jeff Lageman	.05	.01
❑ 155 Garrison Hearst	.25	.08
❑ 156 Kelvin Martin	.05	.01
❑ 157 Dante Jones	.05	.01
❑ 158 Sean Gilbert	.05	.01
❑ 159 Leonard Russell	.05	.01
❑ 160 Ronnie Lott	.10	.02
❑ 161 Randal Hill	.05	.01
❑ 162 Rick Mirer	.25	.08
❑ 163 Alonzo Spellman	.05	.01
❑ 164 Todd Lyght	.05	.01
❑ 165 Chris Slade	.05	.01
❑ 166 Johnny Mitchell	.05	.01
❑ 167 Ronald Moore	.05	.01
❑ 168 Eugene Robinson	.05	.01
❑ 169 Chris Hinton	.05	.01
❑ 170 Dan Footman	.05	.01
❑ 171 Keith Jackson	.05	.01
❑ 172 Rickey Jackson	.05	.01
❑ 173 Heath Sherman	.05	.01
❑ 174 Chris Mims	.05	.01
❑ 175 Erric Pegram	.05	.01
❑ 176 Leroy Hoard	.05	.01
❑ 177 O.J.McDuffie	.25	.08
❑ 178 Wayne Martin	.05	.01
❑ 179 Clyde Simmons	.05	.01
❑ 180 Leslie O'Neal	.05	.01
❑ 181 Mike Pritchard	.05	.01
❑ 182 Michael Jackson	.10	.02
❑ 183 Scott Mitchell	.10	.02
❑ 184 Lorenzo Neal	.05	.01
❑ 185 William Thomas	.05	.01
❑ 186 Junior Seau	.25	.08
❑ 187 Chris Gedney	.05	.01
❑ 188 Tim Lester	.05	.01
❑ 189 Sam Gash	.05	.01
❑ 190 Johnny Johnson	.05	.01
❑ 191 Chuck Cecil	.05	.01
❑ 192 Cortez Kennedy	.10	.02
❑ 193 Jim Harbaugh	.25	.08
❑ 194 Roman Phifer	.05	.01
❑ 195 Pat Harlow	.05	.01
❑ 196 Rob Moore	.10	.02
❑ 197 Gary Clark	.10	.02
❑ 198 Jon Vaughn	.05	.01
❑ 199 Craig Heyward	.10	.02
❑ 200 Michael Stewart	.05	.01
❑ 201 Greg McMurtry	.05	.01
❑ 202 Brian Washington	.05	.01
❑ 203 Ken Harvey	.05	.01
❑ 204 Chris Warren	.10	.02
❑ 205 Bruce Smith	.25	.08
❑ 206 Tom Rouen	.05	.01
❑ 207 Cris Dishman	.05	.01
❑ 208 Keith Cash	.05	.01
❑ 209 Carlos Jenkins	.05	.01
❑ 210 Levon Kirkland	.05	.01
❑ 211 Pete Metzelaars	.05	.01
❑ 212 Shannon Sharpe	.10	.02
❑ 213 Cody Carlson	.05	.01
❑ 214 Derrick Thomas	.25	.08
❑ 215 Emmitt Smith	1.25	.50
❑ 216 Robert Porcher	.05	.01
❑ 217 Sterling Sharpe	.10	.02
❑ 218 Anthony Smith	.05	.01
❑ 219 Mike Sherrard	.05	.01
❑ 220 Tom Rathman	.05	.01
❑ 221 Nate Newton	.05	.01
❑ 222 Pat Swilling	.05	.01
❑ 223 George Teague	.05	.01
❑ 224 Greg Townsend	.05	.01
❑ 225 Eric Guliford RC	.10	.02
❑ 226 Leroy Thompson	.05	.01
❑ 227 Thurman Thomas	.25	.08
❑ 228 Dan Williams	.05	.01
❑ 229 Bubba McDowell	.05	.01
❑ 230 Tracy Simien	.05	.01
❑ 231 Scottie Graham RC	.10	.02
❑ 232 Eric Green	.05	.01
❑ 233 Phil Simms	.10	.02
❑ 234 Ricky Watters	.10	.02
❑ 235 Kevin Williams WR	.10	.02
❑ 236 Brett Perriman	.10	.02
❑ 237 Reggie White	.25	.08
❑ 238 Steve Wisniewski	.05	.01
❑ 239 Mark Collins	.05	.01
❑ 240 Steve Young	.75	.30
❑ 241 Steve Tovar	.05	.01
❑ 242 Jason Belser	.05	.01
❑ 243 Ray Seals	.05	.01
❑ 244 Earnest Byner	.05	.01
❑ 245 Ricky Proehl	.05	.01
❑ 246 Rich Miano	.05	.01
❑ 247 Alfred Williams	.05	.01
❑ 248 Ray Buchanan UER	.05	.01
❑ 249 Hardy Nickerson	.10	.02
❑ 250 Brad Edwards	.05	.01
❑ 251 Jerrol Williams	.05	.01
❑ 252 Marvin Washington	.05	.01
❑ 253 Tony McGee	.05	.01
❑ 254 Jeff George	.25	.08
❑ 255 Ron Hall	.05	.01
❑ 256 Tim Johnson	.05	.01
❑ 257 Willie Roaf	.05	.01
❑ 258 Corwin Brown RC	.05	.01
❑ 259 Ricardo McDonald	.05	.01
❑ 260 Jeff Herrod	.05	.01
❑ 261 Demetrius DuBose	.05	.01
❑ 262 Ricky Sanders	.05	.01
❑ 263 John L. Williams	.05	.01
❑ 264 John Lynch	.25	.08
❑ 265 Lance Gunn	.05	.01
❑ 266 Jessie Hester	.05	.01
❑ 267 Mark Wheeler	.05	.01
❑ 268 Chip Lohmiller	.05	.01
❑ 269 Eric Swann	.10	.02
❑ 270 Byron Evans	.05	.01
❑ 271 Gary Plummer	.05	.01
❑ 272 Roger Duffy RC	.05	.01
❑ 273 Irv Smith	.05	.01
❑ 274 Todd Collins	.05	.01
❑ 275 Robert Blackmon	.05	.01
❑ 276 Reggie Roby	.05	.01
❑ 277 Russell Copeland	.05	.01
❑ 278 Simon Fletcher	.05	.01
❑ 279 Ernest Givins	.10	.02
❑ 280 Tim Barnett	.05	.01
❑ 281 Chris Doleman	.05	.01
❑ 282 Jeff Graham	.05	.01
❑ 283 Kenneth Davis	.05	.01
❑ 284 Vance Johnson	.05	.01
❑ 285 Haywood Jeffires	.10	.02
❑ 286 Todd McNair	.05	.01
❑ 287 Daryl Johnston	.10	.02
❑ 288 Ryan McNeil	.05	.01
❑ 289 Terrell Buckley	.05	.01
❑ 290 Ethan Horton	.05	.01
❑ 291 Corey Miller	.05	.01
❑ 292 Marc Logan	.05	.01
❑ 293 Lincoln Coleman RC	.05	.01
❑ 294 Derrick Moore	.05	.01
❑ 295 LeRoy Butler	.05	.01
❑ 296 Jeff Hostetler	.10	.02
❑ 297 Qadry Ismail	.25	.08
❑ 298 Andre Hastings	.10	.02
❑ 299 Henry Jones	.05	.01
❑ 300 John Elway	1.50	.60
❑ 301 Warren Moon	.25	.08
❑ 302 Willie Davis	.10	.02
❑ 303 Vencie Glenn	.05	.01
❑ 304 Kevin Greene	.10	.02
❑ 305 Marcus Buckley	.05	.01
❑ 306 Tim McDonald	.05	.01
❑ 307 Michael Irvin	.25	.08
❑ 308 Herman Moore	.25	.08
❑ 309 Brett Favre	1.50	.60
❑ 310 Rocket Ismail	.10	.02
❑ 311 Jarrod Bunch	.05	.01
❑ 312 Don Beebe	.05	.01
❑ 313 Steve Atwater	.05	.01
❑ 314 Gary Brown	.05	.01
❑ 315 Marcus Allen	.25	.08
❑ 316 Terry Allen	.10	.02
❑ 317 Chad Brown	.05	.01
❑ 318 Cornelius Bennett	.10	.02
❑ 319 Rod Bernstine	.05	.01
❑ 320 Greg Montgomery	.05	.01
❑ 321 Kimble Anders	.10	.02
❑ 322 Charles Haley	.10	.02
❑ 323 Mel Gray	.05	.01
❑ 324 Edgar Bennett	.25	.08
❑ 325 Eddie Anderson	.05	.01
❑ 326 Derek Brown TE	.05	.01
❑ 327 Steve Bono	.10	.02
❑ 328 Alvin Harper	.10	.02
❑ 329 Willie Green	.05	.01
❑ 330 Robert Brooks	.25	.08
❑ 331 Patrick Bates	.05	.01
❑ 332 Anthony Carter	.10	.02
❑ 333 Barry Foster	.05	.01
❑ 334 Bill Brooks	.05	.01
❑ 335 Jason Elam	.10	.02
❑ 336 Ray Childress	.05	.01
❑ 337 J.J. Birden	.05	.01
❑ 338 Cris Carter	.40	.15
❑ 339 Deon Figures	.05	.01
❑ 340 Carlton Bailey	.05	.01
❑ 341 Brent Jones	.10	.02
❑ 342 Troy Aikman UER	.75	.30
❑ 343 Rodney Holman	.05	.01
❑ 344 Tony Bennett	.05	.01
❑ 345 Tim Brown	.25	.08
❑ 346 Michael Brooks	.05	.01
❑ 347 Martin Harrison	.05	.01
❑ 348 Jerry Rice	.75	.30
❑ 349 John Copeland	.05	.01
❑ 350 Kerry Cash	.05	.01
❑ 351 Reggie Cobb	.05	.01
❑ 352 Brian Mitchell	.05	.01
❑ 353 Derrick Fenner	.05	.01
❑ 354 Roosevelt Potts	.05	.01
❑ 355 Courtney Hawkins	.05	.01
❑ 356 Carl Banks	.05	.01
❑ 357 Harold Green	.05	.01
❑ 358 Steve Emtman	.05	.01
❑ 359 Santana Dotson	.10	.02
❑ 360 Reggie Brooks	.10	.02
❑ 361 Terry Obee	.05	.01
❑ 362 David Klingler	.05	.01
❑ 363 Quentin Coryatt	.05	.01
❑ 364 Craig Erickson	.05	.01
❑ 365 Desmond Howard	.10	.02
❑ 366 Carl Pickens	.10	.02
❑ 367 Lawrence Dawsey	.05	.01
❑ 368 Henry Ellard	.10	.02
❑ 369 Shaun Gayle	.05	.01
❑ 370 David Lang	.05	.01
❑ 371 Anthony Johnson	.10	.02
❑ 372 Darnell Walker RC	.05	.01
❑ 373 Pepper Johnson	.05	.01
❑ 374 Kurt Gouveia	.05	.01
❑ 375 Louis Oliver	.05	.01
❑ 376 Lincoln Kennedy	.05	.01
❑ 377 Anthony Pleasant	.05	.01
❑ 378 Irving Fryar	.10	.02
❑ 379 Carolina Panthers Logo	.25	.08
❑ 380 Jacksonville Jaguars Logo	.05	.01
❑ 381 Sterling Sharpe CL UER	.10	.02
❑ 382 Dan Marino ART CL	.25	.08
❑ 383 Jerry Rice ART CL	.25	.08
❑ 384 Joe Montana ART CL	.25	.08
❑ P19 Joe Montana Promo	2.00	.75

1995 Collector's Choice

❑ COMPLETE SET (348)	20.00	10.00
❑ 1 Ki-Jana Carter RC	.25	.08
❑ 2 Tony Boselli RC	.25	.08
❑ 3 Steve McNair RC	2.50	1.00
❑ 4 Michael Westbrook RC	.25	.08
❑ 5 Kerry Collins RC	1.25	.50
❑ 6 Kevin Carter RC	.25	.08
❑ 7 Mike Mamula RC	.05	.01
❑ 8 Joey Galloway RC	1.25	.50
❑ 9 Kyle Brady RC	.25	.08
❑ 10 J.J. Stokes RC	.25	.08
❑ 11 Derrick Alexander DE RC	.05	.01
❑ 12 Warren Sapp RC	1.25	.50
❑ 13 Mark Fields RC	.25	.08
❑ 14 Tyrone Wheatley RC	1.00	.40
❑ 15 Napoleon Kaufman RC	1.00	.40

❑ 16 James O. Stewart RC 1.00 .40
❑ 17 Luther Elliss RC .05 .01
❑ 18 Rashaan Salaam RC .10 .02
❑ 19 Ty Law RC 1.25 .50
❑ 20 Mark Bruener RC .10 .02
❑ 21 Derrick Brooks RC 1.25 .50
❑ 22 Christian Fauria RC .10 .02
❑ 23 Ray Zellars RC .10 .02
❑ 24 Todd Collins RC .10 .02
❑ 25 Sherman Williams RC .05 .01
❑ 26 Frank Sanders RC .25 .08
❑ 27 Rodney Thomas RC .10 .02
❑ 28 Rob Johnson RC .75 .30
❑ 29 Steve Stenstrom RC .05 .01
❑ 30 James A.Stewart RC .05 .01
❑ 31 Barry Sanders DYK .60 .25
❑ 32 Marshall Faulk DYK .40 .15
❑ 33 Darnay Scott DYK .10 .02
❑ 34 Joe Montana DYK .60 .25
❑ 35 Michael Irvin DYK .10 .02
❑ 36 Jerry Rice DYK .40 .15
❑ 37 Errict Rhett DYK .10 .02
❑ 38 Drew Bledsoe DYK .25 .08
❑ 39 Dan Marino DYK .60 .25
❑ 40 Terance Mathis DYK .05 .01
❑ 41 Natrone Means DYK .10 .02
❑ 42 Tim Brown DYK .10 .02
❑ 43 Steve Young DYK .30 .10
❑ 44 Mel Gray DYK .05 .01
❑ 45 Jerome Bettis DYK .25 .08
❑ 46 Aeneas Williams DYK .05 .01
❑ 47 Charlie Garner DYK .10 .02
❑ 48 Deion Sanders DYK .25 .08
❑ 49 Ken Harvey DYK .05 .01
❑ 50 Emmitt Smith DYK .50 .20
❑ 51 Andre Reed .10 .02
❑ 52 Sean Dawkins .10 .02
❑ 53 Irving Fryar .10 .02
❑ 54 Vincent Brisby .05 .01
❑ 55 Rob Moore .10 .02
❑ 56 Carl Pickens .10 .02
❑ 57 Vinny Testaverde .10 .02
❑ 58 Webster Slaughter .05 .01
❑ 59 Eric Green .05 .01
❑ 60 Anthony Miller .10 .02
❑ 61 Lake Dawson .10 .02
❑ 62 Tim Brown .25 .08
❑ 63 Stan Humphries .10 .02
❑ 64 Rick Mirer .10 .02
❑ 65 Gary Clark .05 .01
❑ 66 Troy Aikman .75 .30
❑ 67 Mike Sherrard .05 .01
❑ 68 Fred Barnett .10 .02
❑ 69 Henry Ellard .10 .02
❑ 70 Terry Allen .10 .02
❑ 71 Jeff Graham .05 .01
❑ 72 Herman Moore .25 .08
❑ 73 Brett Favre 1.50 .60
❑ 74 Trent Dilfer .25 .08
❑ 75 Derek Brown RBK .05 .01
❑ 76 Andre Rison .10 .02
❑ 77 Flipper Anderson .05 .01
❑ 78 Jerry Rice .75 .30
❑ 79 Thurman Thomas .25 .08
❑ 80 Marshall Faulk 1.00 .40
❑ 81 O.J. McDuffie .25 .08
❑ 82 Ben Coates .10 .02
❑ 83 Johnny Mitchell .05 .01
❑ 84 Darnay Scott .10 .02
❑ 85 Derrick Alexander WR .25 .08
❑ 86 Micheal Barrow .05 .01
❑ 87 Charles Johnson .10 .02
❑ 88 John Elway 1.50 .60
❑ 89 Willie Davis .10 .02
❑ 90 James Jett .10 .02
❑ 91 Mark Seay .10 .02
❑ 92 Brian Blades .10 .02
❑ 93 Ricky Proehl .05 .01
❑ 94 Charles Haley .10 .02
❑ 95 Chris Calloway .05 .01
❑ 96 Calvin Williams .10 .02
❑ 97 Ethan Horton .05 .01
❑ 98 Cris Carter .25 .08
❑ 99 Curtis Conway .25 .08
❑ 100 Lomas Brown .05 .01
❑ 101 Edgar Bennett .10 .02
❑ 102 Craig Erickson .05 .01
❑ 103 Jim Everett .05 .01
❑ 104 Terance Mathis .10 .02
❑ 105 Wayne Gandy .05 .01
❑ 106 Brent Jones .05 .01
❑ 107 Bruce Smith .25 .08
❑ 108 Roosevelt Potts .05 .01
❑ 109 Dan Marino 1.50 .60
❑ 110 Michael Timpson .05 .01
❑ 111 Boomer Esiason .10 .02
❑ 112 David Klingler .10 .02
❑ 113 Eric Metcalf .10 .02
❑ 114 Lorenzo White .05 .01
❑ 115 Neil O'Donnell .10 .02
❑ 116 Shannon Sharpe .10 .02
❑ 117 Joe Montana 1.50 .60
❑ 118 Jeff Hostetler .10 .02
❑ 119 Ronnie Harmon .05 .01
❑ 120 Chris Warren .10 .02
❑ 121 Randal Hill .05 .01
❑ 122 Alvin Harper .05 .01
❑ 123 Dave Brown .10 .02
❑ 124 Randall Cunningham .25 .08
❑ 125 Heath Shuler .10 .02
❑ 126 Jake Reed .10 .02
❑ 127 Donnell Woolford .05 .01
❑ 128 Scott Mitchell .10 .02
❑ 129 Reggie White .25 .08
❑ 130 Lawrence Dawsey .05 .01
❑ 131 Michael Haynes .10 .02
❑ 132 Bert Emanuel .25 .08
❑ 133 Troy Drayton .05 .01
❑ 134 Merton Hanks .05 .01
❑ 135 Jim Kelly .25 .08
❑ 136 Tony Bennett .05 .01
❑ 137 Terry Kirby .10 .02
❑ 138 Drew Bledsoe .50 .20
❑ 139 Johnny Johnson .05 .01
❑ 140 Dan Wilkinson .10 .02
❑ 141 Leroy Hoard .05 .01
❑ 142 Gary Brown .05 .01
❑ 143 Barry Foster .10 .02
❑ 144 Shane Dronett .05 .01
❑ 145 Marcus Allen .25 .08
❑ 146 Harvey Williams .05 .01
❑ 147 Tony Martin .10 .02
❑ 148 Rod Stephens .05 .01
❑ 149 Ronald Moore .05 .01
❑ 150 Michael Irvin .25 .08
❑ 151 Rodney Hampton .10 .02
❑ 152 Herschel Walker .10 .02
❑ 153 Reggie Brooks .10 .02
❑ 154 Qadry Ismail .10 .02
❑ 155 Chris Zorich .05 .01
❑ 156 Barry Sanders 1.25 .50
❑ 157 Sean Jones .05 .01
❑ 158 Errict Rhett .10 .02
❑ 159 Tyrone Hughes .10 .02
❑ 160 Jeff George .10 .02
❑ 161 Chris Miller .05 .01
❑ 162 Steve Young .60 .25
❑ 163 Cornelius Bennett .10 .02
❑ 164 Trev Alberts .05 .01
❑ 165 J.B. Brown .05 .01
❑ 166 Marion Butts .05 .01
❑ 167 Aaron Glenn .05 .01
❑ 168 James Francis .05 .01
❑ 169 Eric Turner .05 .01
❑ 170 Darryll Lewis .05 .01
❑ 171 John L. Williams .05 .01
❑ 172 Simon Fletcher .05 .01
❑ 173 Neil Smith .10 .02
❑ 174 Chester McGlockton .10 .02
❑ 175 Natrone Means .10 .02
❑ 176 Michael Sinclair .05 .01
❑ 177 Larry Centers .10 .02
❑ 178 Daryl Johnston .10 .02
❑ 179 Dave Meggett .05 .01
❑ 180 Greg Jackson .05 .01
❑ 181 Ken Harvey .05 .01
❑ 182 Warren Moon .10 .02
❑ 183 Steve Walsh .05 .01
❑ 184 Chris Spielman .10 .02
❑ 185 Bryce Paup .10 .02
❑ 186 Courtney Hawkins .05 .01
❑ 187 Willie Roaf .05 .01
❑ 188 Chris Doleman .05 .01
❑ 189 Jerome Bettis .25 .08
❑ 190 Ricky Watters .10 .02
❑ 191 Henry Jones .05 .01
❑ 192 Quentin Coryatt .10 .02
❑ 193 Bryan Cox .05 .01
❑ 194 Kevin Turner .05 .01
❑ 195 Siupeli Malamala .05 .01
❑ 196 Louis Oliver .05 .01
❑ 197 Rob Burnett .05 .01
❑ 198 Cris Dishman .05 .01
❑ 199 Byron Bam Morris .05 .01
❑ 200 Ray Crockett .05 .01
❑ 201 Jon Vaughn .05 .01
❑ 202 Nolan Harrison .05 .01
❑ 203 Leslie O'Neal .10 .02
❑ 204 Sam Adams .05 .01
❑ 205 Eric Swann .10 .02
❑ 206 Jay Novacek .10 .02
❑ 207 Keith Hamilton .05 .01
❑ 208 Charlie Garner .25 .08
❑ 209 Tom Carter .05 .01
❑ 210 Henry Thomas .05 .01
❑ 211 Lewis Tillman .05 .01
❑ 212 Pat Swilling .05 .01
❑ 213 Terrell Buckley .05 .01
❑ 214 Hardy Nickerson .05 .01
❑ 215 Mario Bates .10 .02
❑ 216 D.J. Johnson .05 .01
❑ 217 Robert Young .05 .01
❑ 218 Dana Stubblefield .10 .02
❑ 219 Jeff Burris .05 .01
❑ 220 Floyd Turner .05 .01
❑ 221 Troy Vincent .05 .01
❑ 222 Willie McGinest .10 .02
❑ 223 James Hasty .05 .01
❑ 224 Jeff Blake RC .60 .25
❑ 225 Stevon Moore .05 .01
❑ 226 Ernest Givins .05 .01
❑ 227 Greg Lloyd .10 .02
❑ 228 Steve Atwater .05 .01
❑ 229 Dale Carter .10 .02
❑ 230 Terry McDaniel .05 .01
❑ 231 John Carney .05 .01
❑ 232 Cortez Kennedy .10 .02
❑ 233 Clyde Simmons .05 .01
❑ 234 Emmitt Smith 1.25 .50
❑ 235 Thomas Lewis .10 .02
❑ 236 William Fuller .05 .01
❑ 237 Ricky Ervins .05 .01
❑ 238 John Randle .10 .02
❑ 239 John Thierry .05 .01
❑ 240 Mel Gray .05 .01
❑ 241 George Teague .05 .01
❑ 242 Charles Wilson Bucs .05 .01
❑ 243 Joe Johnson .05 .01
❑ 244 Chuck Smith .05 .01
❑ 245 Sean Gilbert .10 .02
❑ 246 Bryant Young .10 .02
❑ 247 Bucky Brooks .05 .01
❑ 248 Ray Buchanan .05 .01
❑ 249 Tim Bowens .05 .01
❑ 250 Vincent Brown .05 .01
❑ 251 Marcus Turner .05 .01
❑ 252 Derrick Fenner .05 .01
❑ 253 Antonio Langham .05 .01
❑ 254 Cody Carlson .05 .01
❑ 255 Kevin Greene .10 .02
❑ 256 Leonard Russell .05 .01
❑ 257 Donnell Bennett .10 .02
❑ 258 Rocket Ismail .10 .02
❑ 259 Alfred Pupunu RC .05 .01
❑ 260 Eugene Robinson .05 .01
❑ 261 Seth Joyner .05 .01
❑ 262 Darren Woodson .10 .02
❑ 263 Phillippi Sparks .05 .01
❑ 264 Andy Harmon .05 .01
❑ 265 Brian Mitchell .05 .01
❑ 266 Fuad Reveiz .05 .01
❑ 267 Mark Carrier DB .05 .01
❑ 268 Johnnie Morton .10 .02
❑ 269 LeShon Johnson .10 .02
❑ 270 Eric Curry .05 .01
❑ 271 Quinn Early .10 .02
❑ 272 Elbert Shelley .05 .01
❑ 273 Roman Phifer .05 .01
❑ 274 Ken Norton Jr. .10 .02
❑ 275 Steve Tasker .10 .02
❑ 276 Jim Harbaugh .10 .02
❑ 277 Aubrey Beavers .05 .01
❑ 278 Chris Slade .05 .01
❑ 279 Mo Lewis .05 .01
❑ 280 Alfred Williams .05 .01
❑ 281 Michael Dean Perry UER .05 .01
❑ 282 Marcus Robertson .05 .01

❑ 283 Rod Woodson .10 .02
❑ 284 Glyn Milburn .05 .01
❑ 285 Greg Hill .10 .02
❑ 286 Rob Fredrickson .05 .01
❑ 287 Junior Seau .25 .08
❑ 288 Rick Tuten .05 .01
❑ 289 Aeneas Williams .05 .01
❑ 290 Darrin Smith .05 .01
❑ 291 John Booty .05 .01
❑ 292 Eric Allen .05 .01
❑ 293 Reggie Roby .05 .01
❑ 294 David Palmer .10 .02
❑ 295 Trace Armstrong .05 .01
❑ 296 Dave Krieg .05 .01
❑ 297 Robert Brooks .25 .08
❑ 298 Brad Culpepper .05 .01
❑ 299 Wayne Martin .05 .01
❑ 300 Craig Heyward .10 .02
❑ 301 Isaac Bruce .40 .15
❑ 302 Deion Sanders .40 .15
❑ 303 Matt Darby .05 .01
❑ 304 Kirk Lowdermilk .05 .01
❑ 305 Bernie Parmalee .10 .02
❑ 306 Leroy Thompson .05 .01
❑ 307 Ronnie Lott .10 .02
❑ 308 Steve Tovar .05 .01
❑ 309 Michael Jackson .10 .02
❑ 310 Al Smith .05 .01
❑ 311 Chad Brown .10 .02
❑ 312 Elijah Alexander .05 .01
❑ 313 Kimble Anders .10 .02
❑ 314 Anthony Smith .05 .01
❑ 315 Andre Coleman .05 .01
❑ 316 Terry Wooden .05 .01
❑ 317 Garrison Hearst .25 .08
❑ 318 Russell Maryland .05 .01
❑ 319 Michael Brooks .05 .01
❑ 320 Bernard Williams .05 .01
❑ 321 Andre Collins .05 .01
❑ 322 Dewayne Washington .10 .02
❑ 323 Raymont Harris .05 .01
❑ 324 Brett Perriman .10 .02
❑ 325 LeRoy Butler .05 .01
❑ 326 Santana Dotson .05 .01
❑ 327 Irv Smith .05 .01
❑ 328 Ron George .05 .01
❑ 329 Marquez Pope .05 .01
❑ 330 William Floyd .10 .02
❑ 331 Mickey Washington .05 .01
❑ 332 Keith Goganious .05 .01
❑ 333 Derek Brown TE .05 .01
❑ 334 Steve Beuerlein .10 .02
❑ 335 Reggie Cobb .05 .01
❑ 336 Jeff Lageman .05 .01
❑ 337 Kelvin Martin .05 .01
❑ 338 Darren Carrington .05 .01
❑ 339 Mark Carrier WR .10 .02
❑ 340 Willie Green .05 .01
❑ 341 Frank Reich .05 .01
❑ 342 Don Beebe .05 .01
❑ 343 Lamar Lathon .05 .01
❑ 344 Tim McKyer .05 .01
❑ 345 Pete Metzelaars .05 .01
❑ 346 Vernon Turner .05 .01
❑ 347 Dan Marino CL .25 .08
❑ 348 Joe Montana CL .25 .08
❑ PC1 Joe Montana Promo 1.00 .40
❑ P1 Joe Montana Promo 1.00 .40

1995 Collector's Choice Update

❑ COMPLETE SET (225) 15.00 7.50
❑ U1 Roell Preston RC .10 .02
❑ U2 Lorenzo Styles RC .05 .01
❑ U3 Todd Collins .25 .08
❑ U4 Darick Holmes RC .10 .02
❑ U5 Justin Armour RC .05 .01
❑ U6 Tony Cline RC .05 .01
❑ U7 Tyrone Poole .10 .02
❑ U8 Kerry Collins .25 .08
❑ U9 Sean Harris .05 .01
❑ U10 Steve Stenstrom .05 .01
❑ U11 Rashaan Salaam .10 .02
❑ U12 Ki-Jana Carter .25 .08
❑ U13 Craig Powell RC .05 .01
❑ U14 Eric Zeier RC .25 .08
❑ U15 Ernest Hunter .05 .01
❑ U16 Sherman Williams .05 .01
❑ U17 Terrell Davis RC 2.00 .75
❑ U18 Luther Elliss .05 .01
❑ U19 Craig Newsome .05 .01
❑ U20 Steve McNair 1.25 .50
❑ U21 Chris Sanders RC .10 .02
❑ U22 Rodney Thomas .10 .02
❑ U23 Ellis Johnson RC .05 .01
❑ U24 Ken Dilger RC .25 .08
❑ U25 Zack Crockett RC .10 .02
❑ U26 Tony Boselli .25 .08
❑ U27 Rob Johnson .40 .15
❑ U28 James O. Stewart .50 .20
❑ U29 Tamarick Vanover RC .25 .08
❑ U30 Napoleon Kaufman .50 .20
❑ U31 Kevin Carter .10 .02
❑ U32 Steve McLaughlin .05 .01
❑ U33 Lovell Pinkney .05 .01
❑ U34 Pete Mitchell RC .10 .02
❑ U35 James A.Stewart .05 .01
❑ U36 Chad May RC .05 .01
❑ U37 Derrick Alexander DE .05 .01
❑ U38 Curtis Martin RC 2.50 1.00
❑ U39 Will Moore RC .05 .01
❑ U40 Ty Law .50 .20
❑ U41 Ray Zellars .10 .02
❑ U42 Mark Fields .10 .02
❑ U43 Tyrone Wheatley .50 .20
❑ U44 Kyle Brady .25 .08
❑ U45 Mike Mamula .05 .01
❑ U46 Bobby Taylor RC .25 .08
❑ U47 Chris T.Jones RC .05 .01
❑ U48 Frank Sanders .10 .02
❑ U49 Stoney Case RC .05 .01
❑ U50 Mark Bruener .10 .02
❑ U51 Kordell Stewart RC 1.25 .50
❑ U52 Jimmy Oliver RC .05 .01
❑ U53 Terrance Shaw RC .05 .01
❑ U54 Terrell Fletcher RC .05 .01
❑ U55 J.J. Stokes .25 .08
❑ U56 Christian Fauria .05 .01
❑ U57 Joey Galloway .25 .08
❑ U58 Warren Sapp .25 .08
❑ U59 Derrick Brooks .60 .25
❑ U60 Michael Westbrook .25 .08
❑ U61 Emmitt Smith K .75 .30
❑ U62 Barry Sanders K .75 .30
❑ U63 Marshall Faulk K .60 .25
❑ U64 Troy Aikman K .50 .20
❑ U65 Steve Young K .40 .15
❑ U66 Junior Seau K .25 .08
❑ U67 John Elway K 1.00 .40
❑ U68 Dan Marino K 1.00 .40
❑ U69 Drew Bledsoe K .25 .08
❑ U70 Errict Rhett K .10 .02
❑ U71 Natrone Means K .10 .02
❑ U72 Deion Sanders K .30 .10
❑ U73 Brett Favre K 1.00 .40
❑ U74 Cris Carter K .25 .08
❑ U75 Ben Coates K .10 .02
❑ U76 Jerome Bettis K .25 .08
❑ U77 Reggie White K .25 .08
❑ U78 Stan Humphries K .05 .01
❑ U79 Michael Westbrook K .25 .08
❑ U80 Steve McNair K .50 .20
❑ U81 Kevin Greene K .10 .02
❑ U82 Joey Galloway K .25 .08
❑ U83 Napoleon Kaufman K .25 .08
❑ U84 Jerry Rice K .50 .20
❑ U85 Andre Rison K .10 .02
❑ U86 Eric Metcalf K .10 .02
❑ U87 Kerry Collins K .10 .02
❑ U88 Chris Warren K .10 .02
❑ U89 Irving Fryar K .10 .02
❑ U90 Michael Irvin K .25 .08
❑ U91 Don Beebe .05 .01
❑ U92 Pete Metzelaars .05 .01
❑ U93 Mark Carrier .05 .01
❑ U94 Frank Reich .05 .01
❑ U95 Randy Baldwin .05 .01
❑ U96 Bob Christian .05 .01
❑ U97 John Kasay .05 .01
❑ U98 Lamar Lathon .05 .01
❑ U99 Sam Mills .10 .02
❑ U100 Carlton Bailey .05 .01
❑ U101 Darion Conner .05 .01
❑ U102 Blake Brockermeyer .05 .01
❑ U103 Gerald Williams .05 .01
❑ U104 Willie Green .05 .01
❑ U105 Derrick Moore .05 .01
❑ U106 Desmond Howard .10 .02
❑ U107 Harry Colon .05 .01
❑ U108 Steve Beuerlein .10 .02
❑ U109 Reggie Cobb .05 .01
❑ U110 Jeff Lageman .05 .01
❑ U111 Mark Brunell 1.00 .40
❑ U112 Darren Carrington .05 .01
❑ U113 Brian DeMarco .10 .02
❑ U114 Ernest Givins .05 .01
❑ U115 Le'shai Maston .05 .01
❑ U116 Willie Jackson .10 .02
❑ U117 Keith Goganious .05 .01
❑ U118 Kelvin Pritchett .05 .01
❑ U119 Ryan Christopherson .05 .01
❑ U120 Bryan Schwartz .05 .01
❑ U121 Dave Kreig .05 .01
❑ U122 Darryl Talley .05 .01
❑ U123 Bryce Paup .10 .02
❑ U124 Anthony Johnson .10 .02
❑ U125 Eric Bieniemy .05 .01
❑ U126 Andre Rison .10 .02
❑ U127 Rodney Peete .05 .01
❑ U128 Aaron Craver .05 .01
❑ U129 Henry Thomas .05 .01
❑ U130 Antonio Freeman RC 1.00 .40
❑ U131 Chris Chandler .10 .02
❑ U132 Craig Erickson .05 .01
❑ U133 Roell Preston .10 .02
❑ U134 Brian Washington .05 .01
❑ U135 Eric Green .05 .01
❑ U136 Broderick Thomas .05 .01
❑ U137 Dave Meggett .05 .01
❑ U138 Eric Allen .05 .01
❑ U139 Herschel Walker .10 .02
❑ U140 Dexter Carter .05 .01
❑ U141 Kerry Cash .05 .01
❑ U142 Kelvin Martin .05 .01
❑ U143 Erric Pegram .10 .02
❑ U144 Bo Orlando .05 .01
❑ U145 Ricky Ervins .05 .01
❑ U146 John Friesz .10 .02
❑ U147 Alexander Wright .05 .01
❑ U148 Alvin Harper .05 .01
❑ U149 Gus Frerotte .10 .02
❑ U150 Duval Love .05 .01
❑ U151 Eric Metcalf .10 .02
❑ U152 Ruben Brown RC .25 .08
❑ U153 Marty Carter .05 .01
❑ U154 James Joseph .05 .01
❑ U155 Hugh Douglas RC .25 .08
❑ U156 Wade Wilson .05 .01
❑ U157 Britt Hager .05 .01
❑ U158 Mark Schlereth .05 .01
❑ U159 Cory Schlesinger RC UER .10 .02
❑ U160 Mark Ingram .05 .01
❑ U161 Mark Stepnoski .05 .01
❑ U162 Flipper Anderson .05 .01
❑ U163 Donta Jones .05 .01
❑ U164 James Hasty .05 .01
❑ U165 Gary Clark .05 .01
❑ U166 David Sloan RC .05 .01
❑ U167 Jeff Dellenbach .05 .01
❑ U168 Rufus Porter .05 .01
❑ U169 Mike Croel .05 .01
❑ U170 Charles Wilson Jets UER 242 .05 .01
❑ U171 Pat Swilling .05 .01
❑ U172 Kurt Gouveia .05 .01
❑ U173 Norm Johnson .05 .01
❑ U174 Shaun Gayle .05 .01
❑ U175 Marquez Pope .05 .01
❑ U176 Tyronne Stowe .05 .01
❑ U177 Anthony Parker .05 .01

❑ U178 Kenneth Gant	.05	.01
❑ U179 James Washington	.05	.01
❑ U180 Rob Moore	.10	.02
❑ U181 Alundis Brice RC	.05	.01
❑ U182 Lamont Warren	.05	.01
❑ U183 Michael Timpson	.05	.01
❑ U184 Lorenzo White	.05	.01
❑ U185 Charlie Williams RC	.05	.01
❑ U186 Ed McCaffrey	.25	.08
❑ U187 James Jones	.05	.01
❑ U188 Derrick Fenner	.05	.01
❑ U189 Mel Gray	.05	.01
❑ U190 James Williams LB	.05	.01
❑ U191 Jeff Criswell	.05	.01
❑ U192 Randal Hill	.05	.01
❑ U193 Terry Allen	.10	.02
❑ U194 Joel Smeenge	.05	.01
❑ U195 Ricky Watters	.10	.02
❑ U196 Don Sasa	.05	.01
❑ U197 Steve Bono	.10	.02
❑ U198 Steve Broussard	.05	.01
❑ U199 Carlos Jenkins	.05	.01
❑ U200 Reggie Roby	.05	.01
❑ U201 Stanley Richard	.05	.01
❑ U202 Vince Workman	.05	.01
❑ U203 Eric Guliford	.05	.01
❑ U204 Lionel Washington	.05	.01
❑ U205 Brian Williams LB	.05	.01
❑ U206 Ronnie Lott	.10	.02
❑ U207 Corey Harris	.05	.01
❑ U208 Harlon Barnett	.05	.01
❑ U209 Bubby Brister	.05	.01
❑ U210 Darren Bennett RC	.05	.01
❑ U211 Winston Moss	.05	.01
❑ U212 Leonard Russell	.05	.01
❑ U213 Ron Davis	.05	.01
❑ U214 Curtis Whitley	.05	.01
❑ U215 Webster Slaughter	.05	.01
❑ U216 Korey Stringer RC	.10	.02
❑ U217 Don Davey	.05	.01
❑ U218 Mark Rypien	.05	.01
❑ U219 Chad Cota	.05	.01
❑ U220 Tim Ruddy	.05	.01
❑ U221 Corey Fuller	.05	.01
❑ U222 Mike Dumas	.05	.01
❑ U223 Eddie Murray	.05	.01
❑ U224 Dan Marino CL	.50	.20
❑ U225 Dan Marino CL	.50	.20
❑ P1 M.Westbrook Promo	.50	.20
❑ P2 Dan Marino Promo	1.00	.40
❑ P3 Marino/West./Brown Promo	.75	.30

1996 Collector's Choice

❑ COMPLETE SET (375)	25.00	10.00
❑ COMP.FACT.SET (395)	30.00	20.00
❑ 1 Keyshawn Johnson RC	1.00	.40
❑ 2 Kevin Hardy RC	.40	.15
❑ 3 Simeon Rice RC	.75	.30
❑ 4 Jonathan Ogden RC	.40	.15
❑ 5 Cedric Jones RC	.10	.02
❑ 6 Lawrence Phillips RC	.40	.15
❑ 7 Tim Biakabutuka RC	.40	.15
❑ 8 Terry Glenn RC	1.00	.40
❑ 9 Rickey Dudley RC	.40	.15
❑ 10 Regan Upshaw RC	.10	.02
❑ 11 Walt Harris RC	.10	.02
❑ 12 Eddie George RC	1.25	.50
❑ 13 John Mobley RC	.10	.02
❑ 14 Duane Clemons RC	.10	.02
❑ 15 Marvin Harrison RC	2.50	1.00
❑ 16 Daryl Gardener RC	.10	.02
❑ 17 Pete Kendall RC	.10	.02
❑ 18 Marcus Jones RC	.10	.02
❑ 19 Eric Moulds RC	1.25	.50
❑ 20 Ray Lewis RC	2.50	1.00
❑ 21 Alex Van Dyke RC	.20	.07
❑ 22 Leeland McElroy RC	.20	.07
❑ 23 Mike Alstott RC	1.00	.40
❑ 24 Lawyer Milloy RC	.40	.15
❑ 25 Marco Battaglia RC	.10	.02
❑ 26 Je'rod Cherry RC	.10	.02
❑ 27 Israel Ifeanyi RC	.10	.02
❑ 28 Bobby Engram RC	.40	.15
❑ 29 Jason Dunn RC	.20	.07
❑ 30 Derrick Mayes RC	.40	.15
❑ 31 Stepfret Williams RC	.20	.07
❑ 32 Bobby Hoying RC	.40	.15
❑ 33 Karim Abdul-Jabbar RC	.40	.15
❑ 34 Danny Kanell RC	.40	.15
❑ 35 Chris Darkins RC	.10	.02
❑ 36 Charlie Jones RC	.40	.15
❑ 37 Tedy Bruschi RC	4.00	1.50
❑ 38 Stanley Pritchett RC	.20	.07
❑ 39 Donnie Edwards RC	.40	.15
❑ 40 Jeff Lewis RC	.20	.07
❑ 41 Stephen Davis RC	1.50	.60
❑ 42 Winslow Oliver RC	.10	.02
❑ 43 Mercury Hayes RC	.10	.02
❑ 44 Jon Runyan RC	.10	.02
❑ 45 Steve Taneyhill RC	.10	.02
❑ 46 Eric Metcalf SR	.10	.02
❑ 47 Bryce Paup SR	.10	.02
❑ 48 Kerry Collins SR	.20	.07
❑ 49 Rashaan Salaam SR	.20	.07
❑ 50 Carl Pickens SR	.20	.07
❑ 51 Emmitt Smith SR	.50	.20
❑ 52 Michael Irvin SR	.20	.07
❑ 53 Troy Aikman SR	.40	.15
❑ 54 Terrell Davis SR	.20	.07
❑ 55 John Elway SR	.75	.30
❑ 56 Herman Moore SR	.20	.07
❑ 57 Brett Favre SR	.75	.30
❑ 58 Rodney Thomas SR	.10	.02
❑ 59 Jim Harbaugh SR	.20	.07
❑ 60 Mark Brunell SR	.20	.07
❑ 61 Marcus Allen SR	.20	.07
❑ 62 Tamarick Vanover SR	.20	.07
❑ 63 Steve Bono SR	.10	.02
❑ 64 Dan Marino SR	.75	.30
❑ 65 Warren Moon SR	.10	.02
❑ 66 Curtis Martin SR	.20	.07
❑ 67 Tyrone Hughes SR	.10	.02
❑ 68 Rodney Hampton SR	.10	.02
❑ 69 Hugh Douglas SR	.10	.02
❑ 70 Tim Brown SR	.20	.07
❑ 71 Ricky Watters SR	.20	.07
❑ 72 Kordell Stewart SR	.40	.15
❑ 73 Andre Coleman SR	.10	.02
❑ 74 Jerry Rice SR	.40	.15
❑ 75 Joey Galloway SR	.20	.07
❑ 76 Isaac Bruce SR	.20	.07
❑ 77 Errict Rhett SR	.20	.07
❑ 78 Michael Westbrook SR	.10	.02
❑ 79 Brian Mitchell SR	.10	.02
❑ 80 Aeneas Williams	.10	.02
❑ 81 Andre Reed	.20	.07
❑ 82 Brett Maxie	.10	.02
❑ 83 Jim Flanigan	.10	.02
❑ 84 Jeff Blake	.40	.15
❑ 85 Mike Frederick	.10	.02
❑ 86 Michael Irvin	.40	.15
❑ 87 Aaron Craver	.10	.02
❑ 88 Barry Sanders	1.25	.50
❑ 89 Travis Jervey RC	.40	.15
❑ 90 Chris Sanders	.20	.07
❑ 91 Marshall Faulk	.40	.15
❑ 92 Bryan Schwartz	.10	.02
❑ 93 Tamarick Vanover	.20	.07
❑ 94 Troy Vincent	.10	.02
❑ 95 Robert Smith	.20	.07
❑ 96 Drew Bledsoe	.50	.20
❑ 97 Quinn Early	.10	.02
❑ 98 Wayne Chrebet	.40	.15
❑ 99 Tim Brown	.40	.15
❑ 100 Charlie Garner	.20	.07
❑ 101 Yancey Thigpen	.20	.07
❑ 102 Isaac Bruce	.40	.15
❑ 103 Natrone Means	.20	.07
❑ 104 Jerry Rice	.75	.30
❑ 105 Chris Warren	.20	.07
❑ 106 Errict Rhett	.20	.07
❑ 107 Heath Shuler	.20	.07
❑ 108 Eric Swann	.10	.02
❑ 109 Jeff George	.20	.07
❑ 110 Steve Tasker	.10	.02
❑ 111 Sam Mills	.10	.02
❑ 112 Jeff Graham	.10	.02
❑ 113 Carl Pickens	.20	.07
❑ 114 Vinny Testaverde	.20	.07
❑ 115 Emmitt Smith	1.25	.50
❑ 116 John Elway	1.50	.60
❑ 117 Henry Thomas	.10	.02
❑ 118 LeRoy Butler	.10	.02
❑ 119 Blaine Bishop	.10	.02
❑ 120 Floyd Turner	.10	.02
❑ 121 Jeff Lageman	.10	.02
❑ 122 Kimble Anders	.20	.07
❑ 123 Bryan Cox	.10	.02
❑ 124 Qadry Ismail	.20	.07
❑ 125 Ted Johnson RC	.40	.15
❑ 126 Wesley Walls	.20	.07
❑ 127 Rodney Hampton	.20	.07
❑ 128 Adrian Murrell	.20	.07
❑ 129 Daryl Hobbs RC	.10	.02
❑ 130 Ricky Watters	.20	.07
❑ 131 Carnell Lake	.10	.02
❑ 132 Toby Wright	.10	.02
❑ 133 Darren Bennett	.10	.02
❑ 134 J.J. Stokes	.40	.15
❑ 135 Eugene Robinson	.10	.02
❑ 136 Eric Curry	.10	.02
❑ 137 Tom Carter	.10	.02
❑ 138 Dave Krieg	.10	.02
❑ 139 Eric Metcalf	.10	.02
❑ 140 Bill Brooks	.10	.02
❑ 141 Pete Metzelaars	.10	.02
❑ 142 Kevin Butler	.10	.02
❑ 143 John Copeland	.10	.02
❑ 144 Keenan McCardell	.40	.15
❑ 145 Larry Brown	.10	.02
❑ 146 Jason Elam	.20	.07
❑ 147 Willie Clay	.10	.02
❑ 148 Robert Brooks	.40	.15
❑ 149 Chris Chandler	.20	.07
❑ 150 Quentin Coryatt	.10	.02
❑ 151 Pete Mitchell	.20	.07
❑ 152 Martin Bayless	.10	.02
❑ 153 Pete Stoyanovich	.10	.02
❑ 154 Cris Carter	.40	.15
❑ 155 Jimmy Hitchcock RC	.10	.02
❑ 156 Mario Bates	.20	.07
❑ 157 Mike Sherrard	.10	.02
❑ 158 Boomer Esiason	.20	.07
❑ 159 Chester McGlockton	.10	.02
❑ 160 Bobby Taylor	.10	.02
❑ 161 Kordell Stewart	.40	.15
❑ 162 Kevin Carter	.10	.02
❑ 163 Junior Seau	.40	.15
❑ 164 Derek Loville	.10	.02
❑ 165 Brian Blades	.10	.02
❑ 166 Jackie Harris	.10	.02
❑ 167 Michael Westbrook	.40	.15
❑ 168 Rob Moore	.20	.07
❑ 169 Jessie Tuggle	.10	.02
❑ 170 Darick Holmes	.10	.02
❑ 171 Tim McKyer	.10	.02
❑ 172 Erik Kramer	.10	.02
❑ 173 Harold Green	.10	.02
❑ 174 Stevon Moore	.10	.02
❑ 175 Deion Sanders	.40	.15
❑ 176 Anthony Miller	.20	.07
❑ 177 Herman Moore	.20	.07
❑ 178 Brett Favre	1.50	.60
❑ 179 Rodney Thomas	.10	.02
❑ 180 Ken Dilger	.20	.07
❑ 181 Mark Brunell	.50	.20
❑ 182 Marcus Allen	.40	.15
❑ 183 Dan Marino	1.50	.60
❑ 184 John Randle	.20	.07
❑ 185 Ben Coates	.20	.07
❑ 186 Tyrone Hughes	.10	.02
❑ 187 Dave Brown	.10	.02
❑ 188 Johnny Mitchell	.10	.02
❑ 189 Harvey Williams	.10	.02
❑ 190 Andy Harmon	.10	.02
❑ 191 Kevin Greene	.20	.07
❑ 192 D'Marco Farr	.10	.02
❑ 193 Andre Coleman	.10	.02
❑ 194 Bryant Young	.20	.07
❑ 195 Rick Mirer	.20	.07

Card	Player	Price	Price
❑ 196	Horace Copeland	.10	.02
❑ 197	Leslie Shepherd	.10	.02
❑ 198	Jamir Miller	.10	.02
❑ 199	Bert Emanuel	.20	.07
❑ 200	Steve Christie	.10	.02
❑ 201	Kerry Collins	.40	.15
❑ 202	Rashaan Salaam	.20	.07
❑ 203	Steve Tovar	.10	.02
❑ 204	Michael Jackson	.20	.07
❑ 205	Kevin Williams	.10	.02
❑ 206	Glyn Milburn	.10	.02
❑ 207	Johnnie Morton	.20	.07
❑ 208	Antonio Freeman	.40	.15
❑ 209	Cris Dishman	.10	.02
❑ 210	Ellis Johnson	.10	.02
❑ 211	Cedric Tillman	.10	.02
❑ 212	Steve Bono	.10	.02
❑ 213	Eric Green	.10	.02
❑ 214	David Palmer	.10	.02
❑ 215	Vincent Brisby	.10	.02
❑ 216	Michael Haynes	.10	.02
❑ 217	Chris Calloway	.10	.02
❑ 218	Kyle Brady	.10	.02
❑ 219	Terry McDaniel	.10	.02
❑ 220	Calvin Williams	.10	.02
❑ 221	Greg Lloyd	.20	.07
❑ 222	Jerome Bettis	.40	.15
❑ 223	Stan Humphries	.20	.07
❑ 224	Lee Woodall	.10	.02
❑ 225	Robert Blackmon	.10	.02
❑ 226	Warren Sapp	.10	.02
❑ 227	Brian Mitchell	.10	.02
❑ 228	Garrison Hearst	.20	.07
❑ 229	Terance Mathis	.10	.02
❑ 230	Bryce Paup	.10	.02
❑ 231	Derrick Moore	.10	.02
❑ 232	Curtis Conway	.40	.15
❑ 233	Darnay Scott	.20	.07
❑ 234	Andre Rison	.20	.07
❑ 235	Jay Novacek	.10	.02
❑ 236	Terrell Davis	.50	.20
❑ 237	David Sloan	.10	.02
❑ 238	Reggie White	.40	.15
❑ 239	Todd McNair	.10	.02
❑ 240	Ray Buchanan	.10	.02
❑ 241	Steve Beuerlein	.20	.07
❑ 242	Dan Saleaumua	.10	.02
❑ 243	Bernie Parmalee	.10	.02
❑ 244	Warren Moon	.20	.07
❑ 245	Ty Law	.40	.15
❑ 246	Torrance Small	.10	.02
❑ 247	Phillippi Sparks	.10	.02
❑ 248	Mo Lewis	.10	.02
❑ 249	Jeff Hostetler	.10	.02
❑ 250	Rodney Peete	.10	.02
❑ 251	Byron Bam Morris	.10	.02
❑ 252	Chris Miller	.10	.02
❑ 253	Tony Martin	.20	.07
❑ 254	Eric Davis	.10	.02
❑ 255	Joey Galloway	.40	.15
❑ 256	Derrick Brooks	.40	.15
❑ 257	Ken Harvey	.10	.02
❑ 258	Frank Sanders	.20	.07
❑ 259	Morten Andersen	.10	.02
❑ 260	Marlon Kerner	.10	.02
❑ 261	Mark Carrier WR	.10	.02
❑ 262	Mark Carrier DB	.10	.02
❑ 263	Tony McGee	.10	.02
❑ 264	Eric Zeier	.10	.02
❑ 265	Darren Woodson	.20	.07
❑ 266	Shannon Sharpe	.20	.07
❑ 267	Brett Perriman	.10	.02
❑ 268	Edgar Bennett	.20	.07
❑ 269	Darryll Lewis	.10	.02
❑ 270	Jim Harbaugh	.20	.07
❑ 271	Desmond Howard	.20	.07
❑ 272	Derrick Thomas	.40	.15
❑ 273	Irving Fryar	.20	.07
❑ 274	Jake Reed	.20	.07
❑ 275	Curtis Martin	.50	.20
❑ 276	Eric Allen	.10	.02
❑ 277	Thomas Lewis	.10	.02
❑ 278	Hugh Douglas	.20	.07
❑ 279	Pat Swilling	.10	.02
❑ 280	William Thomas	.10	.02
❑ 281	Norm Johnson	.10	.02
❑ 282	Roman Phifer	.10	.02
❑ 283	Chris Mims	.10	.02
❑ 284	Steve Young	.60	.25
❑ 285	Cortez Kennedy	.10	.02
❑ 286	Trent Dilfer	.40	.15
❑ 287	Terry Allen	.20	.07
❑ 288	Clyde Simmons	.10	.02
❑ 289	Craig Heyward	.10	.02
❑ 290	Jim Kelly	.40	.15
❑ 291	Tyrone Poole	.10	.02
❑ 292	Chris Zorich	.10	.02
❑ 293	Dan Wilkinson	.10	.02
❑ 294	Antonio Langham	.10	.02
❑ 295	Troy Aikman	.75	.30
❑ 296	Steve Atwater	.10	.02
❑ 297	Scott Mitchell	.20	.07
❑ 298	Mark Chmura	.20	.07
❑ 299	Steve McNair	.50	.20
❑ 300	Tony Bennett	.10	.02
❑ 301	Willie Jackson	.20	.07
❑ 302	Neil Smith	.20	.07
❑ 303	Terry Kirby	.20	.07
❑ 304	Orlando Thomas	.10	.02
❑ 305	Willie McGinest	.10	.02
❑ 306	Wayne Martin	.10	.02
❑ 307	Michael Brooks	.10	.02
❑ 308	Marvin Washington	.10	.02
❑ 309	Nolan Harrison	.10	.02
❑ 310	William Fuller	.10	.02
❑ 311	Willie Williams	.10	.02
❑ 312	Troy Drayton	.10	.02
❑ 313	Shawn Lee	.10	.02
❑ 314	Ken Norton	.10	.02
❑ 315	Terry Wooden	.10	.02
❑ 316	Hardy Nickerson	.10	.02
❑ 317	Gus Frerotte	.20	.07
❑ 318	Oscar McBride	.10	.02
❑ 319	Merton Hanks	.10	.02
❑ 320	Justin Armour	.10	.02
❑ 321	Willie Green	.10	.02
❑ 322	Roger Jones RC	.10	.02
❑ 323	Leroy Hoard	.10	.02
❑ 324	Chris Boniol	.10	.02
❑ 325	Jason Hanson	.10	.02
❑ 326	Sean Jones	.10	.02
❑ 327	Roosevelt Potts	.10	.02
❑ 328	Greg Hill	.20	.07
❑ 329	O.J. McDuffie	.20	.07
❑ 330	Amp Lee	.10	.02
❑ 331	Chris Slade	.10	.02
❑ 332	Jim Everett	.10	.02
❑ 333	Tyrone Wheatley	.20	.07
❑ 334	Charles Wilson	.10	.02
❑ 335	Napoleon Kaufman	.40	.15
❑ 336	Fred Barnett	.10	.02
❑ 337	Neil O'Donnell	.20	.07
❑ 338	Sean Gilbert	.10	.02
❑ 339	Aaron Hayden RC	.10	.02
❑ 340	Brent Jones	.10	.02
❑ 341	Christian Fauria	.10	.02
❑ 342	Alvin Harper	.10	.02
❑ 343	Henry Ellard	.10	.02
❑ 344	Willie Davis	.10	.02
❑ 345	Charles Haley	.20	.07
❑ 346	Chris Jacke	.10	.02
❑ 347	Allen Aldridge	.10	.02
❑ 348	Jeff Herrod	.10	.02
❑ 349	Rocket Ismail	.20	.07
❑ 350	Leslie O'Neal	.10	.02
❑ 351	Marquez Pope	.10	.02
❑ 352	Brock Marion	.10	.02
❑ 353	Ernie Mills	.10	.02
❑ 354	Larry Centers	.20	.07
❑ 355	Chris Doleman	.10	.02
❑ 356	Bruce Smith	.20	.07
❑ 357	John Kasay	.10	.02
❑ 358	Donnell Woolford	.10	.02
❑ 359	David Dunn	.10	.02
❑ 360	Eric Turner	.10	.02
❑ 361	Sherman Williams	.10	.02
❑ 362	Chris Spielman	.10	.02
❑ 363	Craig Newsome	.10	.02
❑ 364	Sean Dawkins	.10	.02
❑ 365	James O. Stewart	.20	.07
❑ 366	Dale Carter	.10	.02
❑ 367	Marco Coleman	.10	.02
❑ 368	Dave Meggett	.10	.02
❑ 369	Irv Smith	.10	.02
❑ 370	Mike Mamula	.10	.02
❑ 371	Erric Pegram	.10	.02
❑ 372	Dana Stubblefield	.20	.07
❑ 373	Terrance Shaw	.10	.02
❑ 374	Jerry Rice CL	.40	.15
❑ 375	Dan Marino CL	.40	.15
❑ P1	Jerry Rice Promo	1.00	.40
❑ P2	Dan Marino Promo	1.00	.40

1996 Collector's Choice Update

Card	Player	Price	Price
❑	COMPLETE SET (200)	15.00	7.50
❑ U1	Zach Thomas RC	.60	.25
❑ U2	Simeon Rice	.50	.20
❑ U3	Jonathan Ogden	.30	.10
❑ U4	Eric Moulds	.30	.10
❑ U5	Tim Biakabutuka	.30	.10
❑ U6	Walt Harris	.10	.02
❑ U7	Willie Anderson	.10	.02
❑ U8	Ricky Whittle	.10	.02
❑ U9	John Mobley	.10	.02
❑ U10	Reggie Brown RC	.10	.02
❑ U11	John Michels	.10	.02
❑ U12	Eddie George	.60	.25
❑ U13	Marvin Harrison	1.25	.50
❑ U14	Kevin Hardy	.20	.07
❑ U15	Kavika Pittman RC	.10	.02
❑ U16	Daryl Gardener	.10	.02
❑ U17	Duane Clemons	.10	.02
❑ U18	Terry Glenn	.30	.10
❑ U19	Alex Molden RC	.10	.02
❑ U20	Cedric Jones	.10	.02
❑ U21	Keyshawn Johnson	.50	.20
❑ U22	Rickey Dudley	.30	.10
❑ U23	Jason Dunn	.10	.02
❑ U24	Jamain Stephens	.10	.02
❑ U25	Lawrence Phillips	.30	.10
❑ U26	Bryan Still RC	.20	.07
❑ U27	Israel Ifeanyi	.10	.02
❑ U28	Pete Kendall	.10	.02
❑ U29	Regan Upshaw	.10	.02
❑ U30	Andre Johnson RC	.10	.02
❑ U31	Leeland McElroy	.10	.02
❑ U32	Ray Lewis	1.25	.50
❑ U33	Sean Moran RC	.10	.02
❑ U34	Muhsin Muhammad RC	.75	.30
❑ U35	Bobby Engram	.30	.10
❑ U36	Marco Battaglia	.10	.02
❑ U37	Stepfret Williams	.10	.02
❑ U38	Jeff Lewis	.20	.07
❑ U39	Derrick Mayes	.20	.07
❑ U40	Reggie Tongue RC	.10	.02
❑ U41	Tory James RC	.20	.07
❑ U42	Tony Banks RC	.30	.10
❑ U43	Tedy Bruschi	3.00	1.25
❑ U44	Mike Alstott	.50	.20
❑ U45	Anthony Dorsett	.10	.02
❑ U46	Tony Brackens RC	.30	.10
❑ U47	Bryant Mix	.10	.02
❑ U48	Karim Abdul-Jabbar	.30	.10
❑ U49	Moe Williams RB RC	.75	.30
❑ U50	Lawyer Milloy	.20	.07
❑ U51	Je'rod Cherry	.10	.02
❑ U52	Amani Toomer RC	1.00	.40
❑ U53	Alex Van Dyke	.20	.07
❑ U54	Lance Johnstone RC	.20	.07
❑ U55	Bobby Hoying	.30	.10
❑ U56	Jon Witman RC	.20	.07
❑ U57	Eddie Kennison RC	.30	.10
❑ U58	Brian Roche RC	.10	.02
❑ U59	Terrell Owens RC	2.50	1.00
❑ U60	Stephen Davis	.75	.30
❑ U61	Jeff George FP	.20	.07
❑ U62	Darick Holmes FP	.10	.02
❑ U63	Kerry Collins FP	.30	.10

❑ U64	Rashaan Salaam FP	.20	.07
❑ U65	Jeff Blake FP	.20	.07
❑ U66	Emmitt Smith FP	.75	.30
❑ U67	Troy Aikman FP	.50	.20
❑ U68	John Elway FP	1.00	.40
❑ U69	Terrell Davis FP	.40	.15
❑ U70	Barry Sanders FP	.75	.30
❑ U71	Herman Moore FP	.20	.07
❑ U72	Brett Favre FP	1.00	.40
❑ U73	Robert Brooks FP	.20	.07
❑ U74	Steve McNair FP	.40	.15
❑ U75	Marshall Faulk FP	.30	.10
❑ U76	Marcus Allen FP	.30	.10
❑ U77	Dan Marino FP	1.00	.40
❑ U78	Warren Moon FP	.10	.02
❑ U79	Drew Bledsoe FP	.30	.10
❑ U80	Curtis Martin FP	.40	.15
❑ U81	Mario Bates FP	.20	.07
❑ U82	Tim Brown FP	.30	.10
❑ U83	Charlie Garner FP	.20	.07
❑ U84	Kordell Stewart FP	.30	.10
❑ U85	Isaac Bruce FP	.30	.10
❑ U86	Tony Martin FP	.10	.02
❑ U87	Jerry Rice FP	.50	.20
❑ U88	J.J. Stokes FP	.30	.10
❑ U89	Joey Galloway FP	.30	.10
❑ U90	Errict Rhett FP	.20	.07
❑ U91	Mike Pritchard	.10	.02
❑ U92	Jerome Bettis	.30	.10
❑ U93	Winslow Oliver	.10	.02
❑ U94	David Klingler	.10	.02
❑ U95	Lawrence Dawsey	.10	.02
❑ U96	Charlie Jones	.20	.07
❑ U97	Dave Krieg	.10	.02
❑ U98	Chris Spielman	.10	.02
❑ U99	Stanley Pritchett	.10	.02
❑ U100	Sean Gilbert	.10	.02
❑ U101	Tommy Vardell	.10	.02
❑ U102	DeRon Jenkins	.10	.02
❑ U103	Larry Bowie	.10	.02
❑ U104	Kyle Wachholtz	.10	.02
❑ U105	Brady Smith RC	.10	.02
❑ U106	Steve Walsh	.10	.02
❑ U107	Wesley Walls	.20	.07
❑ U108	Kevin Ross	.10	.02
❑ U109	Willie Clay	.10	.02
❑ U110	Olanda Truitt	.10	.02
❑ U111	Calvin Williams	.10	.02
❑ U112	Chris Doleman	.10	.02
❑ U113	Irving Fryar	.20	.07
❑ U114	Jimmy Spencer	.10	.02
❑ U115	Reggie Barlow RC	.10	.02
❑ U116	Reggie Brown RBK RC	.10	.02
❑ U117	Dixon Edwards	.10	.02
❑ U118	Haywood Jeffires	.10	.02
❑ U119	Santana Dotson	.10	.02
❑ U120	Herschel Walker	.20	.07
❑ U121	Darryl Williams	.10	.02
❑ U122	Bryan Cox	.10	.02
❑ U123	Lamar Thomas	.10	.02
❑ U124	Hendrick Lusk	.10	.02
❑ U125	Jahine Arnold RC	.10	.02
❑ U126	Boomer Esiason	.20	.07
❑ U127	Willie Davis	.10	.02
❑ U128	Pete Stoyanovich	.10	.02
❑ U129	Bill Romanowski	.10	.02
❑ U130	Tim McKyer	.10	.02
❑ U131	Patrick Sapp	.10	.02
❑ U132	Natrone Means	.20	.07
❑ U133	Quinn Early	.10	.02
❑ U134	Leslie O'Neal	.10	.02
❑ U135	Mark Seay	.10	.02
❑ U136	Pete Metzelaars	.10	.02
❑ U137	Jay Leeuwenburg UER	.10	.02
❑ U138	Buster Owens	.10	.02
❑ U139	Todd McNair	.10	.02
❑ U140	Eugene Robinson	.10	.02
❑ U141	Sean Salisbury	.10	.02
❑ U142	Eddie Robinson	.10	.02
❑ U143	Jerris McPhail	.10	.02
❑ U144	Ray Farmer RC	.10	.02
❑ U145	Garrison Hearst	.20	.07
❑ U146	Leonard Russell	.10	.02
❑ U147	Roy Barker	.10	.02
❑ U148	Larry Brown	.10	.02
❑ U149	Webster Slaughter	.10	.02
❑ U150	Roman Oben RC	.10	.02
❑ U151	LeShon Johnson	.10	.02
❑ U152	Patrick Bates	.10	.02

❑ U153	Iheanyi Uwaezuoke RC	.30	.10
❑ U154	Scott Slutzker	.10	.02
❑ U155	John Jurkovic	.10	.02
❑ U156	Brian Milne	.10	.02
❑ U157	Mike Sherrard	.10	.02
❑ U158	Neil O'Donnell	.20	.07
❑ U159	Roger Harper	.10	.02
❑ U160	Desmond Howard	.20	.07
❑ U161	Alfred Williams	.10	.02
❑ U162	Ronnie Harmon	.10	.02
❑ U163	Sammie Burroughs RC	.10	.02
❑ U164	Keenan McCardell	.30	.10
❑ U165	Shane Dronett	.10	.02
❑ U166	Jeff Graham	.10	.02
❑ U167	Bill Brooks	.10	.02
❑ U168	Shawn Jefferson	.10	.02
❑ U169	Detron Smith	.10	.02
❑ U170	Danny Kanell	.30	.10
❑ U171	Jevon Langford	.10	.02
❑ U172	Russell Maryland	.10	.02
❑ U173	Scott Milanovich RC	.30	.10
❑ U174	Eric Davis	.10	.02
❑ U175	Ernie Conwell	.10	.02
❑ U176	Kurt Gouveia	.10	.02
❑ U177	Andre Rison	.20	.07
❑ U178	Harold Green	.10	.02
❑ U179	Frank Reich	.10	.02
❑ U180	Glyn Milburn	.10	.02
❑ U181	Nilo Silvan	.10	.02
❑ U182	Cornelius Bennett	.10	.02
❑ U183	Freddie Solomon RC	.10	.02
❑ U184	Pat Terrell	.10	.02
❑ U185	Miles Macik	.10	.02
❑ U186	Bo Orlando	.10	.02
❑ U187	Kelvin Martin	.10	.02
❑ U188	Todd Kinchen	.10	.02
❑ U189	Reggie Brooks	.10	.02
❑ U190	Steve Beuerlein	.20	.07
❑ U191	Marco Coleman	.10	.02
❑ U192	Johnny Johnson	.10	.02
❑ U193	Dedric Mathis	.10	.02
❑ U194	Leon Searcy	.10	.02
❑ U195	Kevin Greene	.20	.07
❑ U196	Daniel Stubbs	.10	.02
❑ U197	Ray Mickens	.10	.02
❑ U198	Devin Wyman	.10	.02
❑ U199	Lorenzo Lynch	.10	.02
❑ U200	Rice/Marino CL	.30	.10

1997 Collector's Choice

❑	COMPLETE SET (565)	30.00	12.50
❑	COMP.SERIES 1 (310)	20.00	7.50
❑	COMP.FACT.SER.1(330)	25.00	10.00
❑	COMP.SERIES 2 (255)	12.00	5.00
❑ 1	Orlando Pace RC	.50	.20
❑ 2	Darrell Russell RC	.20	.07
❑ 3	Shawn Springs RC	.30	.10
❑ 4	Peter Boulware RC	.50	.20
❑ 5	Bryant Westbrook RC	.20	.07
❑ 6	Tom Knight RC	.20	.07
❑ 7	Ike Hilliard RC	.75	.30
❑ 8	James Farrior RC	.50	.20
❑ 9	Chris Naeole RC	.20	.07
❑ 10	Michael Booker RC	.20	.07
❑ 11	Warrick Dunn RC	1.50	.60
❑ 12	Tony Gonzalez RC	1.50	.60
❑ 13	Reinard Wilson RC	.30	.10
❑ 14	Yatil Green RC	.30	.10
❑ 15	Reidel Anthony RC	.50	.20
❑ 16	Kenard Lang RC	.30	.10
❑ 17	Kenny Holmes RC	.50	.20
❑ 18	Tarik Glenn RC	.50	.20

❑ 19	Dwayne Rudd RC	.50	.20
❑ 20	Renaldo Wynn RC	.20	.07
❑ 21	David LaFleur RC	.20	.07
❑ 22	Antowain Smith RC	1.25	.50
❑ 23	Jim Druckenmiller RC	.30	.10
❑ 24	Rae Carruth RC	.20	.07
❑ 25	Jared Tomich RC	.20	.07
❑ 26	Chris Canty RC	.20	.07
❑ 27	Jake Plummer RC	2.50	1.00
❑ 28	Troy Davis RC	.30	.10
❑ 29	Sedrick Shaw RC	.30	.10
❑ 30	Jamie Sharper RC	.30	.10
❑ 31	Tiki Barber RC	3.00	1.25
❑ 32	Byron Hanspard RC	.30	.10
❑ 33	Darnell Autry RC	.30	.10
❑ 34	Corey Dillon RC	3.00	1.25
❑ 35	Joey Kent RC	.50	.20
❑ 36	Nathan Davis RC	.20	.07
❑ 37	Will Blackwell RC	.30	.10
❑ 38	Kim Herring RC	.20	.07
❑ 39	Pat Barnes RC	.50	.20
❑ 40	Kevin Lockett RC	.30	.10
❑ 41	Trevor Pryce RC	.50	.20
❑ 42	Matt Russell RC	.20	.07
❑ 43	Greg Jones RC	.20	.07
❑ 44	Antonio Anderson RC	.20	.07
❑ 45	George Jones RC	.30	.10
❑ 46	Steve Young NG	.50	.20
❑ 47	Jerry Rice NG	.50	.20
❑ 48	Curtis Conway NG	.20	.07
❑ 49	Jeff Blake NG	.30	.10
❑ 50	Carl Pickens NG	.30	.10
❑ 51	Bruce Smith NG	.20	.07
❑ 52	John Elway NG	1.00	.40
❑ 53	Terrell Davis NG	.50	.20
❑ 54	Shannon Sharpe NG	.20	.07
❑ 55	Junior Seau NG	.20	.07
❑ 56	Darren Bennett NG	.20	.07
❑ 57	Jim Harbaugh NG	.30	.10
❑ 58	Marshall Faulk NG	.50	.20
❑ 59	Emmitt Smith NG	.75	.30
❑ 60	Troy Aikman NG	.50	.20
❑ 61	Deion Sanders NG	.50	.20
❑ 62	Dan Marino NG	1.00	.40
❑ 63	Ricky Watters NG	.20	.07
❑ 64	Mark Brunell NG	.50	.20
❑ 65	Keenan McCardell NG	.20	.07
❑ 66	Keyshawn Johnson NG	.50	.20
❑ 67	Barry Sanders NG	.75	.30
❑ 68	Herman Moore NG	.30	.10
❑ 69	Eddie George NG	.50	.20
❑ 70	Steve McNair NG	.50	.20
❑ 71	Brett Favre NG	1.00	.40
❑ 72	Reggie White NG	.30	.10
❑ 73	Edgar Bennett NG	.20	.07
❑ 74	Kerry Collins NG	.30	.10
❑ 75	Kevin Greene NG	.20	.07
❑ 76	Drew Bledsoe NG	.30	.10
❑ 77	Terry Glenn NG	.30	.10
❑ 78	Curtis Martin NG	.50	.20
❑ 79	Jeff Hostetler NG	.20	.07
❑ 80	Napoleon Kaufman NG	.50	.20
❑ 81	Isaac Bruce NG	.50	.20
❑ 82	Terry Allen NG	.30	.10
❑ 83	Joey Galloway NG	.30	.10
❑ 84	Kordell Stewart NG	.50	.20
❑ 85	Jerome Bettis NG	.50	.20
❑ 86	Dana Stubblefield	.20	.07
❑ 87	Merton Hanks	.20	.07
❑ 88	Terrell Owens	.60	.25
❑ 89	Brent Jones	.20	.07
❑ 90	Ken Norton Jr.	.20	.07
❑ 91	Jerry Rice	1.00	.40
❑ 92	Terry Kirby	.30	.10
❑ 93	Bryant Young	.20	.07
❑ 94	Raymont Harris	.20	.07
❑ 95	Jeff Jaeger	.20	.07
❑ 96	Curtis Conway	.30	.10
❑ 97	Walt Harris	.20	.07
❑ 98	Bobby Engram	.30	.10
❑ 99	Donnell Woolford	.20	.07
❑ 100	Rashaan Salaam	.20	.07
❑ 101	Jeff Blake	.30	.10
❑ 102	Tony McGee	.20	.07
❑ 103	Ashley Ambrose	.20	.07
❑ 104	Dan Wilkinson	.20	.07
❑ 105	Jevon Langford	.20	.07
❑ 106	Darnay Scott	.30	.10
❑ 107	David Dunn	.20	.07

❑ 108 Eric Moulds .50 .20
❑ 109 Darick Holmes .20 .07
❑ 110 Thurman Thomas .50 .20
❑ 111 Quinn Early .20 .07
❑ 112 Jim Kelly .50 .20
❑ 113 Bryce Paup .20 .07
❑ 114 Bruce Smith .30 .10
❑ 115 Todd Collins .20 .07
❑ 116 Tory James .20 .07
❑ 117 Anthony Miller .20 .07
❑ 118 Terrell Davis .60 .25
❑ 119 Tyrone Braxton .20 .07
❑ 120 John Mobley .20 .07
❑ 121 Bill Romanowski .20 .07
❑ 122 Vaughn Hebron .20 .07
❑ 123 Mike Alstott .50 .20
❑ 124 Errict Rhett .20 .07
❑ 125 Trent Dilfer .50 .20
❑ 126 Courtney Hawkins .20 .07
❑ 127 Hardy Nickerson .20 .07
❑ 128 Donnie Abraham RC .50 .20
❑ 129 Regan Upshaw .20 .07
❑ 130 Kent Graham .20 .07
❑ 131 Rob Moore .30 .10
❑ 132 Simeon Rice .30 .10
❑ 133 LeShon Johnson .20 .07
❑ 134 Frank Sanders .30 .10
❑ 135 Leeland McElroy .20 .07
❑ 136 Seth Joyner .20 .07
❑ 137 Andre Coleman .20 .07
❑ 138 Stan Humphries .30 .10
❑ 139 Charlie Jones .20 .07
❑ 140 Junior Seau .50 .20
❑ 141 Rodney Harrison RC 1.00 .40
❑ 142 Darrien Gordon .20 .07
❑ 143 Terrell Fletcher .20 .07
❑ 144 Tamarick Vanover .30 .10
❑ 145 Greg Hill .20 .07
❑ 146 Marcus Allen .50 .20
❑ 147 Lake Dawson .20 .07
❑ 148 Dale Carter .20 .07
❑ 149 Kimble Anders .30 .10
❑ 150 Chris Penn .20 .07
❑ 151 Sean Dawkins .20 .07
❑ 152 Ken Dilger .20 .07
❑ 153 Marvin Harrison .50 .20
❑ 154 Jeff Herrod .20 .07
❑ 155 Jim Harbaugh .30 .10
❑ 156 Cary Blanchard .20 .07
❑ 157 Aaron Bailey .20 .07
❑ 158 Deion Sanders .50 .20
❑ 159 Jim Schwantz RC .20 .07
❑ 160 Michael Irvin .50 .20
❑ 161 Herschel Walker .30 .10
❑ 162 Emmitt Smith 1.50 .60
❑ 163 Chris Boniol .20 .07
❑ 164 Eric Bjornson .20 .07
❑ 165 Karim Abdul-Jabbar .30 .10
❑ 166 O.J. McDuffie .30 .10
❑ 167 Troy Drayton .20 .07
❑ 168 Zach Thomas .50 .20
❑ 169 Irving Spikes .20 .07
❑ 170 Shane Burton RC .30 .10
❑ 171 Stanley Pritchett .20 .07
❑ 172 Ty Detmer .30 .10
❑ 173 Chris T. Jones .20 .07
❑ 174 Troy Vincent .20 .07
❑ 175 Brian Dawkins .50 .20
❑ 176 Irving Fryar .30 .10
❑ 177 Charlie Garner .30 .10
❑ 178 Bobby Taylor .20 .07
❑ 179 Jamal Anderson .50 .20
❑ 180 Terance Mathis .30 .10
❑ 181 Craig Heyward .20 .07
❑ 182 Cornelius Bennett .20 .07
❑ 183 Jessie Tuggle .20 .07
❑ 184 Devin Bush .20 .07
❑ 185 Dave Brown .20 .07
❑ 186 Danny Kanell .20 .07
❑ 187 Rodney Hampton .30 .10
❑ 188 Tyrone Wheatley .30 .10
❑ 189 Amani Toomer .30 .10
❑ 190 Phillippi Sparks .20 .07
❑ 191 Thomas Lewis .20 .07
❑ 192 Jimmy Smith .30 .10
❑ 193 Pete Mitchell .20 .07
❑ 194 Natrone Means .30 .10
❑ 195 Mark Brunell .60 .25
❑ 196 Kevin Hardy .20 .07
❑ 197 Tony Brackens .20 .07
❑ 198 Aaron Beasley RC .20 .07
❑ 199 Chris Hudson .20 .07
❑ 200 Wayne Chrebet .50 .20
❑ 201 Keyshawn Johnson .50 .20
❑ 202 Adrian Murrell .30 .10
❑ 203 Neil O'Donnell .30 .10
❑ 204 Hugh Douglas .20 .07
❑ 205 Mo Lewis .20 .07
❑ 206 Glenn Foley .20 .07
❑ 207 Aaron Glenn .20 .07
❑ 208 Johnnie Morton .30 .10
❑ 209 Reggie Brown LB .30 .10
❑ 210 Barry Sanders 1.50 .60
❑ 211 Glyn Milburn .20 .07
❑ 212 Bennie Blades .20 .07
❑ 213 Steve McNair .60 .25
❑ 214 Frank Wycheck .20 .07
❑ 215 Chris Sanders .20 .07
❑ 216 Blaine Bishop .20 .07
❑ 217 Willie Davis .20 .07
❑ 218 Darryll Lewis .20 .07
❑ 219 Marcus Robertson .20 .07
❑ 220 Robert Brooks .30 .10
❑ 221 Antonio Freeman .50 .20
❑ 222 Keith Jackson .20 .07
❑ 223 Mark Chmura .30 .10
❑ 224 Brett Favre 2.00 .75
❑ 225 Sean Jones .20 .07
❑ 226 Reggie White .50 .20
❑ 227 LeRoy Butler .20 .07
❑ 228 Craig Newsome .20 .07
❑ 229 Wesley Walls .30 .10
❑ 230 Mark Carrier WR .20 .07
❑ 231 Muhsin Muhammad .30 .10
❑ 232 John Kasay .20 .07
❑ 233 Anthony Johnson .20 .07
❑ 234 Kerry Collins .50 .20
❑ 235 Kevin Greene .30 .10
❑ 236 Sam Mills .20 .07
❑ 237 Ben Coates .30 .10
❑ 238 Terry Glenn .50 .20
❑ 239 Willie McGinest .20 .07
❑ 240 Ted Johnson .20 .07
❑ 241 Lawyer Milloy .30 .10
❑ 242 Drew Bledsoe .60 .25
❑ 243 Willie Clay .20 .07
❑ 244 Chris Slade .20 .07
❑ 245 Tim Brown .50 .20
❑ 246 Daryl Hobbs .20 .07
❑ 247 Rickey Dudley .30 .10
❑ 248 Joe Aska .20 .07
❑ 249 Chester McGlockton .20 .07
❑ 250 Rob Fredrickson .20 .07
❑ 251 Terry McDaniel .20 .07
❑ 252 Tony Banks .30 .10
❑ 253 Lawrence Phillips .20 .07
❑ 254 Isaac Bruce .50 .20
❑ 255 Eddie Kennison .30 .10
❑ 256 Kevin Carter .20 .07
❑ 257 Roman Phifer .20 .07
❑ 258 Keith Lyle .20 .07
❑ 259 Vinny Testaverde .30 .10
❑ 260 Derrick Alexander WR .30 .10
❑ 261 Ray Lewis .75 .30
❑ 262 Jermaine Lewis .50 .20
❑ 263 Byron Bam Morris .20 .07
❑ 264 Stevon Moore .20 .07
❑ 265 Antonio Langham .20 .07
❑ 266 Brian Mitchell .20 .07
❑ 267 Henry Ellard .20 .07
❑ 268 Leslie Shepherd .20 .07
❑ 269 Michael Westbrook .30 .10
❑ 270 Jamie Asher .20 .07
❑ 271 Ken Harvey .20 .07
❑ 272 Gus Frerotte .20 .07
❑ 273 Michael Haynes .20 .07
❑ 274 Ray Zellars .20 .07
❑ 275 Jim Everett .20 .07
❑ 276 Tyrone Hughes .20 .07
❑ 277 Joe Johnson .20 .07
❑ 278 Eric Allen .20 .07
❑ 279 Brady Smith .20 .07
❑ 280 Mario Bates .20 .07
❑ 281 Torrance Small .20 .07
❑ 282 John Friesz .20 .07
❑ 283 Brian Blades .20 .07
❑ 284 Chris Warren .30 .10
❑ 285 Joey Galloway .30 .10
❑ 286 Michael Sinclair .20 .07
❑ 287 Lamar Smith .50 .20
❑ 288 Mike Pritchard .20 .07
❑ 289 Jerome Bettis .50 .20
❑ 290 Charles Johnson .30 .10
❑ 291 Mike Tomczak .20 .07
❑ 292 Levon Kirkland .20 .07
❑ 293 Carnell Lake .20 .07
❑ 294 Erric Pegram .20 .07
❑ 295 Kordell Stewart .50 .20
❑ 296 Greg Lloyd .20 .07
❑ 297 Dixon Edwards .20 .07
❑ 298 Cris Carter .50 .20
❑ 299 Brad Johnson .50 .20
❑ 300 Qadry Ismail .30 .10
❑ 301 John Randle .30 .10
❑ 302 Orlanda Thomas .20 .07
❑ 303 Dewayne Washington .20 .07
❑ 304 Jake Reed .30 .10
❑ 305 Derrick Alexander DE .20 .07
❑ 306 Eddie George CL .50 .20
❑ 307 Dan Marino CL .40 .15
❑ 308 Curtis Martin CL .30 .10
❑ 309 Troy Aikman CL .50 .20
❑ 310 Marcus Allen CL .50 .20
❑ 311 Jim Druckenmiller .20 .07
❑ 312 Greg Clark RC .20 .07
❑ 313 Darnell Autry .30 .10
❑ 314 Reinard Wilson .20 .07
❑ 315 Corey Dillon 1.25 .50
❑ 316 Antowain Smith .50 .20
❑ 317 Trevor Pryce .30 .10
❑ 318 Warrick Dunn .60 .25
❑ 319 Reidel Anthony .30 .10
❑ 320 Jake Plummer 1.00 .40
❑ 321 Tom Knight .20 .07
❑ 322 Freddie Jones RC .30 .10
❑ 323 Tony Gonzalez .60 .25
❑ 324 Pat Barnes .30 .10
❑ 325 Kevin Lockett .30 .10
❑ 326 Tarik Glenn .25 .08
❑ 327 David LaFleur .20 .07
❑ 328 Antonio Anderson .20 .07
❑ 329 Yatil Green .30 .10
❑ 330 Jason Taylor RC 1.00 .40
❑ 331 Brian Manning RC .20 .07
❑ 332 Michael Booker .20 .07
❑ 333 Byron Hanspard .30 .10
❑ 334 Ike Hilliard .50 .20
❑ 335 Tiki Barber 1.25 .50
❑ 336 Renaldo Wynn .20 .07
❑ 337 Damon Jones RC .20 .07
❑ 338 James Farrior .30 .10
❑ 339 Dedric Ward RC .30 .10
❑ 340 Bryant Westbrook .20 .07
❑ 341 Joey Kent .50 .20
❑ 342 Kenny Holmes .20 .07
❑ 343 Darren Sharper RC .50 .20
❑ 344 Rae Carruth .20 .07
❑ 345 Chris Canty .20 .07
❑ 346 Darrell Russell .20 .07
❑ 347 Orlando Pace .50 .20
❑ 348 Peter Boulware .30 .10
❑ 349 Kenard Lang .20 .07
❑ 350 Danny Wuerffel RC .50 .20
❑ 351 Troy Davis .20 .07
❑ 352 Shawn Springs .30 .10
❑ 353 Walter Jones RC .50 .20
❑ 354 Will Blackwell .20 .07
❑ 355 Dwayne Rudd .20 .07
❑ 356 49ers BB .20 .07
❑ 357 Bears BB .20 .07
❑ 358 Bengals BB .20 .07
❑ 359 Bills BB .20 .07
❑ 360 Broncos BB .30 .10
❑ 361 Buccaneers BB .20 .07
❑ 362 Cardinals BB .30 .10
❑ 363 Chargers BB .20 .07
❑ 364 Chiefs BB .30 .10
❑ 365 Colts BB .30 .10
❑ 366 Cowboys BB .20 .07
❑ 367 Dolphins BB .20 .07
❑ 368 Eagles BB .20 .07
❑ 369 Falcons BB .20 .07
❑ 370 Giants BB .20 .07
❑ 371 Jaguars BB .20 .07
❑ 372 Jets BB .20 .07
❑ 373 Lions BB .20 .07
❑ 374 Oilers BB .20 .07

	No.	Card		
❑	375	Packers BB	.50	.20
❑	376	Panthers BB	.20	.07
❑	377	Patriots BB	.20	.07
❑	378	Raiders BB	.20	.07
❑	379	Rams BB	.20	.07
❑	380	Ravens BB	.20	.07
❑	381	Redskins BB	.20	.07
❑	382	Saints BB	.20	.07
❑	383	Seahawks BB	.20	.07
❑	384	Steelers BB	.30	.10
❑	385	Vikings BB	.30	.10
❑	386	William Floyd	.30	.10
❑	387	Steve Young	.60	.25
❑	388	Lee Woodall	.20	.07
❑	389	J.J. Stokes	.30	.10
❑	390	Marc Edwards	.20	.07
❑	391	Rod Woodson	.30	.10
❑	392	Jim Schwantz	.20	.07
❑	393	Garrison Hearst	.30	.10
❑	394	Rick Mirer	.20	.07
❑	395	Alonzo Spellman	.20	.07
❑	396	Tom Carter	.20	.07
❑	397	Bryan Cox	.20	.07
❑	398	John Allred RC	.20	.07
❑	399	Ricky Proehl	.20	.07
❑	400	Tyrone Hughes	.20	.07
❑	401	Carl Pickens	.30	.10
❑	402	Tremain Mack RC	.20	.07
❑	403	Boomer Esiason	.30	.10
❑	404	Ki-Jana Carter	.20	.07
❑	405	Steve Tovar	.20	.07
❑	406	Billy Joe Hobert	.30	.10
❑	407	Andre Reed	.30	.10
❑	408	Marcellus Wiley RC	.30	.10
❑	409	Steve Tasker	.20	.07
❑	410	Chris Spielman	.20	.07
❑	411	Alfred Williams	.20	.07
❑	412	John Elway	2.00	.75
❑	413	Shannon Sharpe	.30	.10
❑	414	Steve Atwater	.20	.07
❑	415	Neil Smith	.30	.10
❑	416	Darrien Gordon	.20	.07
❑	417	Jeff Lewis	.20	.07
❑	418	Flipper Anderson	.20	.07
❑	419	Willie Green	.20	.07
❑	420	Jackie Harris	.20	.07
❑	421	Steve Walsh	.20	.07
❑	422	Anthony Parker	.20	.07
❑	423	Ronde Barber RC	1.00	.40
❑	424	Warren Sapp	.30	.10
❑	425	Aeneas Williams	.20	.07
❑	426	Larry Centers	.30	.10
❑	427	Eric Swann	.20	.07
❑	428	Kevin Williams	.20	.07
❑	429	Darren Bennett	.20	.07
❑	430	Tony Martin	.30	.10
❑	431	John Carney	.20	.07
❑	432	Jim Everett	.20	.07
❑	433	William Fuller	.20	.07
❑	434	Latario Rachal RC	.20	.07
❑	435	Erric Pegram	.20	.07
❑	436	Eric Metcalf	.30	.10
❑	437	Jerome Woods	.20	.07
❑	438	Derrick Thomas	.50	.20
❑	439	Elvis Grbac	.30	.10
❑	440	Terry Wooden	.20	.07
❑	441	Andre Rison	.30	.10
❑	442	Brett Perriman	.20	.07
❑	443	Paul Justin	.20	.07
❑	444	Robert Blackmon	.20	.07
❑	445	Carlton Gray	.20	.07
❑	446	Chris Gardocki	.20	.07
❑	447	Marshall Faulk	.60	.25
❑	448	Sammie Burroughs	.20	.07
❑	449	Quentin Coryatt	.20	.07
❑	450	Troy Aikman	1.00	.40
❑	451	Daryl Johnston	.30	.10
❑	452	Tony Tolbert	.20	.07
❑	453	Brock Marion	.20	.07
❑	454	Billy Davis RC	.20	.07
❑	455	Stepfret Williams	.20	.07
❑	456	Anthony Miller	.20	.07
❑	457	Dan Marino	2.00	.75
❑	458	Jerris McPhail	.20	.07
❑	459	Terrell Buckley	.20	.07
❑	460	Daryl Gardener	.20	.07
❑	461	George Teague	.20	.07
❑	462	Derrick Rodgers RC	.20	.07
❑	463	Fred Barnett	.20	.07
❑	464	Darrin Smith	.20	.07
❑	465	Michael Timpson	.20	.07
❑	466	Jon Harris	.20	.07
❑	467	Jason Dunn	.20	.07
❑	468	Bobby Hoying	.30	.10
❑	469	Ricky Watters	.30	.10
❑	470	Derrick Witherspoon	.20	.07
❑	471	Chris Chandler	.30	.10
❑	472	Ray Buchanan	.20	.07
❑	473	Michael Haynes	.20	.07
❑	474	O.J. Santiago RC	.30	.10
❑	475	Morten Andersen	.20	.07
❑	476	Bert Emanuel	.30	.10
❑	477	Chris Calloway	.20	.07
❑	478	Jason Sehorn	.30	.10
❑	479	John Jurkovic	.20	.07
❑	480	Keenan McCardell	.30	.10
❑	481	James O. Stewart	.30	.10
❑	482	Rob Johnson	.50	.20
❑	483	Mike Logan RC	.20	.07
❑	484	Deon Figures	.20	.07
❑	485	Kyle Brady	.20	.07
❑	486	Alex Van Dyke	.20	.07
❑	487	Jeff Graham	.20	.07
❑	488	Jason Hanson	.20	.07
❑	489	Herman Moore	.30	.10
❑	490	Scott Mitchell	.30	.10
❑	491	Tommy Vardell	.20	.07
❑	492	Derrick Mason RC	1.00	.40
❑	493	Rodney Thomas	.20	.07
❑	494	Ronnie Harmon	.20	.07
❑	495	Eddie George	.50	.20
❑	496	Edgar Bennett	.30	.10
❑	497	William Henderson	.30	.10
❑	498	Dorsey Levens	.50	.20
❑	499	Gilbert Brown	.30	.10
❑	500	Steve Bono	.30	.10
❑	501	Derrick Mayes	.30	.10
❑	502	Fred Lane RC	.30	.10
❑	503	Ernie Mills	.20	.07
❑	504	Tim Biakabutuka	.30	.10
❑	505	Michael Bates	.20	.07
❑	506	Winslow Oliver	.20	.07
❑	507	Ty Law	.30	.10
❑	508	Shawn Jefferson	.20	.07
❑	509	Vincent Brisby	.20	.07
❑	510	Henry Thomas	.20	.07
❑	511	Tedy Bruschi	1.00	.40
❑	512	Curtis Martin	.60	.25
❑	513	Jeff George	.30	.10
❑	514	Desmond Howard	.30	.10
❑	515	Napoleon Kaufman	.50	.20
❑	516	Kenny Shedd RC	.20	.07
❑	517	Russell Maryland	.20	.07
❑	518	Lance Johnstone	.20	.07
❑	519	Eric Turner	.20	.07
❑	520	Dexter McCleon RC	.20	.07
❑	521	Craig Heyward	.20	.07
❑	522	Ryan McNeil	.20	.07
❑	523	Mark Rypien	.20	.07
❑	524	Mike Jones LB	.20	.07
❑	525	Jamie Sharper	.20	.07
❑	526	Tony Siragusa	.20	.07
❑	527	Michael Jackson	.30	.10
❑	528	Floyd Turner	.20	.07
❑	529	Eric Green	.20	.07
❑	530	Michael McCrary	.20	.07
❑	531	Jay Graham RC	.30	.10
❑	532	Terry Allen	.50	.20
❑	533	Sean Gilbert	.20	.07
❑	534	Scott Turner	.20	.07
❑	535	Cris Dishman	.20	.07
❑	536	Darrell Green	.30	.10
❑	537	Stephen Davis	.50	.20
❑	538	Alvin Harper	.20	.07
❑	539	Daryl Hobbs	.20	.07
❑	540	Wayne Martin	.20	.07
❑	541	Heath Shuler	.20	.07
❑	542	Andre Hastings	.20	.07
❑	543	Jared Tomich	.20	.07
❑	544	Nicky Savoie RC	.20	.07
❑	545	Cortez Kennedy	.20	.07
❑	546	Warren Moon	.50	.20
❑	547	Chad Brown	.20	.07
❑	548	Willie Williams	.20	.07
❑	549	Bennie Blades	.20	.07
❑	550	Darren Perry	.20	.07
❑	551	Mark Bruener	.20	.07
❑	552	Yancey Thigpen	.30	.10
❑	553	Courtney Hawkins	.20	.07
❑	554	Chad Scott RC	.30	.10
❑	555	George Jones	.30	.10
❑	556	Robert Tate RC	.20	.07
❑	557	Torrian Gray RC	.20	.07
❑	558	Robert Griffith RC	.20	.07
❑	559	Leroy Hoard	.20	.07
❑	560	Robert Smith	.30	.10
❑	561	Randall Cunningham	.50	.20
❑	562	Darrell Russell CL	.20	.07
❑	563	Troy Aikman CL	.50	.20
❑	564	Dan Marino CL	.40	.15
❑	565	Jim Druckenmiller CL	.20	.07

1992 Collector's Edge

	No.	Card		
❑		COMPLETE SET (250)	25.00	12.50
❑		COMP.SERIES 1 (175)	15.00	6.00
❑		COMP.FACT.SER.1 (175)	15.00	6.00
❑		COMP.SERIES 2 (75)	10.00	5.00
❑		COMP.FACT.SER.2 (75)	12.00	5.00
❑	1	Chris Miller	.20	.07
❑	2	Steve Broussard	.10	.02
❑	3	Mike Pritchard	.20	.07
❑	4	Tim Green	.10	.02
❑	5	Andre Rison	.20	.07
❑	6	Deion Sanders	1.00	.40
❑	7	Jim Kelly	.40	.15
❑	8	James Lofton	.20	.07
❑	9	Andre Reed	.20	.07
❑	10	Bruce Smith	.40	.15
❑	11	Thurman Thomas	.40	.15
❑	12	Cornelius Bennett	.20	.07
❑	13	Jim Harbaugh	.40	.15
❑	14	William Perry	.20	.07
❑	15	Mike Singletary	.20	.07
❑	16	Mark Carrier DB	.10	.02
❑	17	Kevin Butler	.10	.02
❑	18	Tom Waddle	.10	.02
❑	19	Boomer Esiason	.20	.07
❑	20	David Fulcher	.10	.02
❑	21	Anthony Munoz	.20	.07
❑	22	Tim McGee	.10	.02
❑	23	Harold Green	.10	.02
❑	24	Rickey Dixon	.10	.02
❑	25	Bernie Kosar	.20	.07
❑	26	Michael Dean Perry	.20	.07
❑	27	Mike Baab	.10	.02
❑	28	Brian Brennan	.10	.02
❑	29	Michael Jackson	.20	.07
❑	30	Eric Metcalf	.20	.07
❑	31	Troy Aikman	2.50	1.00
❑	32	Emmitt Smith	5.00	2.50
❑	33	Michael Irvin	.40	.15
❑	34	Jay Novacek	.20	.07
❑	35	Issiac Holt	.10	.02
❑	36	Ken Norton	.20	.07
❑	37	John Elway	4.00	1.50
❑	38	Gaston Green	.10	.02
❑	39	Charles Dimry	.10	.02
❑	40	Vance Johnson	.10	.02
❑	41	Dennis Smith	.10	.02
❑	42	David Treadwell	.10	.02
❑	43	Michael Young	.10	.02
❑	44	Bennie Blades	.10	.02
❑	45	Mel Gray	.20	.07
❑	46	Andre Ware	.10	.02
❑	47	Rodney Peete	.20	.07
❑	48	Toby Caston RC	.10	.02
❑	49	Herman Moore	.40	.15
❑	50	Brian Noble	.10	.02
❑	51	Sterling Sharpe	.40	.15
❑	52	Mike Tomczak	.10	.02

❑ 53 Vinnie Clark .10 .02
❑ 54 Tony Mandarich .10 .02
❑ 55 Ed West .10 .02
❑ 56 Warren Moon .40 .15
❑ 57 Ray Childress .10 .02
❑ 58 Haywood Jeffires .20 .07
❑ 59 Al Smith .10 .02
❑ 60 Cris Dishman .10 .02
❑ 61 Ernest Givins .20 .07
❑ 62 Richard Johnson CB .10 .02
❑ 63 Eric Dickerson .20 .07
❑ 64 Jessie Hester .10 .02
❑ 65 Rohn Stark .10 .02
❑ 66 Clarence Verdin .10 .02
❑ 67 Dean Biasucci .10 .02
❑ 68 Duane Bickett .10 .02
❑ 69 Jeff George .40 .15
❑ 70 Christian Okoye .10 .02
❑ 71 Derrick Thomas .40 .15
❑ 72 Stephone Paige .10 .02
❑ 73 Dan Saleaumua .10 .02
❑ 74 Deron Cherry .10 .02
❑ 75 Kevin Ross .10 .02
❑ 76 Barry Word .10 .02
❑ 77 Ronnie Lott .20 .07
❑ 78 Greg Townsend .10 .02
❑ 79 Willie Gault .20 .07
❑ 80 Howie Long .40 .15
❑ 81 Winston Moss .10 .02
❑ 82 Steve Smith .10 .02
❑ 83 Jay Schroeder .10 .02
❑ 84 Jim Everett .20 .07
❑ 85 Flipper Anderson .10 .02
❑ 86 Henry Ellard .20 .07
❑ 87 Tony Zendejas .10 .02
❑ 88 Robert Delpino .10 .02
❑ 89 Pat Terrell .10 .02
❑ 90 Dan Marino 4.00 1.50
❑ 91 Mark Clayton .20 .07
❑ 92 Jim C.Jensen .10 .02
❑ 93 Reggie Roby .10 .02
❑ 94 Sammie Smith .10 .02
❑ 95 Tony Martin .20 .07
❑ 96 Jeff Cross .10 .02
❑ 97 Anthony Carter .20 .07
❑ 98 Chris Doleman .10 .02
❑ 99 Wade Wilson .10 .02
❑ 100 Cris Carter .75 .30
❑ 101 Mike Merriweather .10 .02
❑ 102 Gary Zimmerman .10 .02
❑ 103 Chris Singleton .10 .02
❑ 104 Bruce Armstrong .10 .02
❑ 105 Marv Cook .10 .02
❑ 106 Andre Tippett .10 .02
❑ 107 Tommy Hodson .10 .02
❑ 108 Greg McMurtry .10 .02
❑ 109 Jon Vaughn .10 .02
❑ 110 Vaughan Johnson .10 .02
❑ 111 Craig Heyward .20 .07
❑ 112 Floyd Turner .10 .02
❑ 113 Pat Swilling .10 .02
❑ 114 Rickey Jackson .10 .02
❑ 115 Steve Walsh .10 .02
❑ 116 Phil Simms .20 .07
❑ 117 Carl Banks .10 .02
❑ 118 Mark Ingram .10 .02
❑ 119 Bart Oates .10 .02
❑ 120 Lawrence Taylor .40 .15
❑ 121 Jeff Hostetler .20 .07
❑ 122 Rob Moore .20 .07
❑ 123 Ken O'Brien .10 .02
❑ 124 Bill Pickel .10 .02
❑ 125 Irv Eatman .10 .02
❑ 126 Browning Nagle .10 .02
❑ 127 Al Toon .20 .07
❑ 128 Randall Cunningham .40 .15
❑ 129 Eric Allen .10 .02
❑ 130 Mike Golic .10 .02
❑ 131 Fred Barnett .40 .15
❑ 132 Keith Byars .10 .02
❑ 133 Calvin Williams .20 .07
❑ 134 Randal Hill .10 .02
❑ 135 Ricky Proehl .10 .02
❑ 136 Lance Smith .10 .02
❑ 137 Ernie Jones .10 .02
❑ 138 Timm Rosenbach .10 .02
❑ 139 Anthony Thompson .10 .02
❑ 140 Bubby Brister .10 .02
❑ 141 Merril Hoge .10 .02
❑ 142 Louis Lipps .10 .02
❑ 143 Eric Green .10 .02
❑ 144 Gary Anderson K .10 .02
❑ 145 Neil O'Donnell .20 .07
❑ 146 Rod Bernstine .10 .02
❑ 147 John Friesz .20 .07
❑ 148 Anthony Miller .20 .07
❑ 149 Junior Seau .40 .15
❑ 150 Leslie O'Neal .20 .07
❑ 151 Nate Lewis .10 .02
❑ 152 Steve Young 2.00 .75
❑ 153 Kevin Fagan .10 .02
❑ 154 Charles Haley .20 .07
❑ 155 Tom Rathman .10 .02
❑ 156 Jerry Rice 2.50 1.00
❑ 157 John Taylor .20 .07
❑ 158 Brian Blades .20 .07
❑ 159 Patrick Hunter .10 .02
❑ 160 Cortez Kennedy .20 .07
❑ 161 Vann McElroy .10 .02
❑ 162 Dan McGwire .10 .02
❑ 163 John L. Williams .10 .02
❑ 164 Gary Anderson RB .10 .02
❑ 165 Broderick Thomas .10 .02
❑ 166 Vinny Testaverde .20 .07
❑ 167 Lawrence Dawsey .20 .07
❑ 168 Paul Gruber .10 .02
❑ 169 Keith McCants .10 .02
❑ 170 Mark Rypien .10 .02
❑ 171 Gary Clark .40 .15
❑ 172 Earnest Byner .10 .02
❑ 173 Brian Mitchell .20 .07
❑ 174 Monte Coleman .10 .02
❑ 175 Joe Jacoby .10 .02
❑ 176 Tommy Vardell RC .10 .02
❑ 177 Troy Vincent RC .10 .02
❑ 178 Robert Jones RC .10 .02
❑ 179 Marc Boutte RC .10 .02
❑ 180 Marco Coleman RC .10 .02
❑ 181 Chris Mims RC .10 .02
❑ 182 Tony Casillas .10 .02
❑ 182X Ray Roberts
Large X on front 50.00 30.00
❑ 183 Shane Dronett RC .10 .02
❑ 184 Sean Gilbert RC .20 .07
❑ 185 Siran Stacy RC .10 .02
❑ 186 Tommy Maddox RC 3.00 1.25
❑ 187 Steve Israel RC .10 .02
❑ 188 Brad Muster .10 .02
❑ 188X Casey Weldon 50.00 30.00
❑ 189 Shane Collins RC .10 .02
❑ 190 Terrell Buckley RC .10 .02
❑ 191 Eugene Chung RC .10 .02
❑ 192 Leon Searcy RC .10 .02
❑ 193 Chuck Smith RC .10 .02
❑ 194 Patrick Rowe RC .10 .02
❑ 195 Bill Johnson RC .10 .02
❑ 196 Gerald Dixon RC .10 .02
❑ 197 Robert Porcher RC .40 .15
❑ 198 Tracy Scroggins RC .10 .02
❑ 199 Jason Hanson RC .20 .07
❑ 200 Corey Harris RC .10 .02
❑ 201 Eddie Robinson RC .10 .02
❑ 202 Steve Emtman RC .10 .02
❑ 203 Ashley Ambrose RC .40 .15
❑ 204 Greg Skrepenak RC .10 .02
❑ 205 Todd Collins RC .10 .02
❑ 206 Derek Brown RC TE .10 .02
❑ 207 Kurt Barber RC .10 .02
❑ 208 Tony Sacca RC .10 .02
❑ 209 Mark Wheeler RC .10 .02
❑ 210 Kevin Smith RC DB .10 .02
❑ 211 John Fina RC .10 .02
❑ 212 Johnny Mitchell RC .10 .02
❑ 213 Dale Carter RC .20 .07
❑ 214 Bob Spitulski RC .10 .02
❑ 215 Phillippi Sparks RC .10 .02
❑ 216 Levon Kirkland RC .10 .02
❑ 217 Mike Sherrard .10 .02
❑ 218 Marquez Pope RC .10 .02
❑ 219 Courtney Hawkins RC .20 .07
❑ 220 Tyji Armstrong RC .10 .02
❑ 221 Keith Jackson .20 .07
❑ 222 Clayton Holmes RC .10 .02
❑ 223 Quentin Coryatt RC .10 .02
❑ 224 Troy Auzenne RC .10 .02
❑ 225 David Klingler RC .10 .02
❑ 226 Darryl Williams RC .10 .02
❑ 227 Carl Pickens RC .40 .15
❑ 228 Jimmy Smith RC 5.00 2.00
❑ 229 Chester McGlockton RC .20 .07
❑ 230 Robert Brooks RC 1.25 .50
❑ 231 Alonzo Spellman RC .20 .07
❑ 232 Darren Woodson RC .40 .15
❑ 233 Lewis Billups .10 .02
❑ 234 Edgar Bennett RC .40 .15
❑ 235 Vaughn Dunbar RC .10 .02
❑ 236 Steve Bono RC .40 .15
❑ 237 Clarence Kay .10 .02
❑ 238 Chris Hinton .10 .02
❑ 239 Jimmie Jones .10 .02
❑ 240 Vai Sikahema .10 .02
❑ 241 Russell Maryland .10 .02
❑ 241X Bobby Humphrey 50.00 30.00
❑ 242 Neal Anderson .10 .02
❑ 242X Mark Bavaro 50.00 30.00
❑ 243 Charles Mann .10 .02
❑ 244 Hugh Millen .10 .02
❑ 245 Roger Craig .20 .07
❑ 246 Rich Gannon .40 .15
❑ 247 Ricky Ervins .10 .02
❑ 247X Marion Butts 50.00 30.00
❑ 248 Leonard Marshall .10 .02
❑ 249 Eric Dickerson .20 .07
❑ 250 Joe Montana 4.00 1.50
❑ RL1 Ronnie Lott AU/2542 15.00 7.50
❑ RU1 Terrell Buckley Proto. 2.00 .75
❑ RU2 Tommy Maddox Proto. 5.00 2.00
❑ AU37 John Elway AU/2500 60.00 25.00
❑ AU77 Ronnie Lott AU Bonus 15.00 7.50
❑ AU123 Ken O'Brien AU/2500 8.00 3.00

1993 Collector's Edge

❑ COMPLETE SET (325) 20.00 10.00
❑ COMP.SERIES 1 (250) 10.00 5.00
❑ COMP.SERIES 2 (75) 10.00 5.00
❑ 1 Falcons Team Photo .05 .01
❑ 2 Michael Haynes .10 .02
❑ 3 Chris Miller .10 .02
❑ 4 Mike Pritchard .10 .02
❑ 5 Andre Rison .10 .02
❑ 6 Deion Sanders .50 .20
❑ 7 Chuck Smith .05 .01
❑ 8 Drew Hill .05 .01
❑ 9 Bobby Hebert .05 .01
❑ 10 Bills Team Photo .05 .01
❑ 11 Matt Darby .05 .01
❑ 12 John Fina .05 .01
❑ 13 Jim Kelly .25 .08
❑ 14 Marvcus Patton RC .10 .02
❑ 15 Andre Reed .10 .02
❑ 16 Thurman Thomas .25 .08
❑ 17 James Lofton .10 .02
❑ 18 Bruce Smith .25 .08
❑ 19 Bears Team Photo .05 .01
❑ 20 Neal Anderson .05 .01
❑ 21 Troy Auzenne .05 .01
❑ 22 Jim Harbaugh .25 .08
❑ 23 Alonzo Spellman .05 .01
❑ 24 Tom Waddle .05 .01
❑ 25 Darren Lewis .05 .01
❑ 26 Wendell Davis .05 .01
❑ 27 Will Furrer .05 .01
❑ 28 Bengals Team Photo .05 .01
❑ 29 David Klingler .05 .01
❑ 30 Ricardo McDonald .05 .01
❑ 31 Carl Pickens .10 .02
❑ 32 Harold Green .05 .01
❑ 33 Anthony Munoz .10 .02
❑ 34 Darryl Williams .05 .01
❑ 35 Browns Team Photo .05 .01

	No.	Player		
❑	36	Michael Jackson	.10	.02
❑	37	Pio Sagapolutele	.05	.01
❑	38	Tommy Vardell	.05	.01
❑	39	Bernie Kosar	.10	.02
❑	40	Michael Dean Perry	.10	.02
❑	41	Bill Johnson	.05	.01
❑	42	Vinny Testaverde	.10	.02
❑	43	Cowboys Team Photo	.05	.01
❑	44	Troy Aikman	.75	.30
❑	45	Alvin Harper	.10	.02
❑	46	Michael Irvin	.25	.08
❑	47	Russell Maryland	.05	.01
❑	48	Emmitt Smith	1.50	.60
❑	49	Kenneth Gant	.05	.01
❑	50	Jay Novacek	.10	.02
❑	51	Robert Jones	.05	.01
❑	52	Clayton Holmes	.05	.01
❑	53	Broncos Team Photo	.05	.01
❑	54	Mike Croel	.05	.01
❑	55	Shane Dronett	.05	.01
❑	56	Kenny Walker	.05	.01
❑	57	Tommy Maddox	.25	.08
❑	58	Dennis Smith	.05	.01
❑	59	John Elway	1.50	.60
❑	60	Karl Mecklenburg	.05	.01
❑	61	Steve Atwater	.05	.01
❑	62	Vance Johnson	.05	.01
❑	63	Lions Team Photo	.05	.01
❑	64	Barry Sanders	1.25	.50
❑	65	Andre Ware	.05	.01
❑	66	Pat Swilling	.05	.01
❑	67	Jason Hanson	.05	.01
❑	68	Willie Green	.05	.01
❑	69	Herman Moore	.25	.08
❑	70	Rodney Peete	.05	.01
❑	71	Erik Kramer	.10	.02
❑	72	Robert Porcher	.05	.01
❑	73	Packers Team Photo	.05	.01
❑	74	Terrell Buckley	.05	.01
❑	75	Reggie White	.25	.08
❑	76	Brett Favre	2.00	.75
❑	77	Don Majkowski	.05	.01
❑	78	Edgar Bennett	.25	.08
❑	79	Ty Detmer	.25	.08
❑	80	Sanjay Beach	.05	.01
❑	81	Sterling Sharpe	.25	.08
❑	82	Oilers Team Photo	.05	.01
❑	83	Gary Brown	.05	.01
❑	84	Ernest Givins	.10	.02
❑	85	Haywood Jeffires	.10	.02
❑	86	Corey Harris	.05	.01
❑	87	Warren Moon	.25	.08
❑	88	Eddie Robinson	.05	.01
❑	89	Lorenzo White	.05	.01
❑	90	Bo Orlando	.05	.01
❑	91	Colts Team Photo	.05	.01
❑	92	Quentin Coryatt	.10	.02
❑	93	Steve Emtman	.05	.01
❑	94	Jeff George	.25	.08
❑	95	Jessie Hester	.05	.01
❑	96	Rohn Stark	.05	.01
❑	97	Ashley Ambrose	.05	.01
❑	98	John Baylor	.05	.01
❑	99	Chiefs Team Photo	.05	.01
❑	100	Tim Barnett	.05	.01
❑	101	Derrick Thomas	.25	.08
❑	102	Barry Word	.05	.01
❑	103	Dale Carter	.05	.01
❑	104	Jayice Pearson	.05	.01
❑	105	Tracy Simien	.05	.01
❑	106	Harvey Williams	.10	.02
❑	107	Dave Krieg	.10	.02
❑	108	Christian Okoye	.05	.01
❑	109	Joe Montana	1.50	.60
❑	110	Dolphins Team Photo	.05	.01
❑	111	J.B. Brown	.05	.01
❑	112	Marco Coleman	.05	.01
❑	113	Dan Marino	1.50	.60
❑	114	Mark Clayton	.05	.01
❑	115	Mark Higgs	.05	.01
❑	116	Bryan Cox	.05	.01
❑	117	Chuck Klingbeil	.05	.01
❑	118	Troy Vincent	.05	.01
❑	119	Keith Jackson	.10	.02
❑	120	Bruce Alexander	.05	.01
❑	121	Vikings Team Photo	.05	.01
❑	122	Terry Allen	.25	.08
❑	123	Rich Gannon	.25	.08
❑	124	Todd Scott	.05	.01
❑	125	Cris Carter	.25	.08
❑	126	Sean Salisbury	.05	.01
❑	127	Jack Del Rio	.05	.01
❑	128	Chris Doleman	.05	.01
❑	129	Anthony Carter	.10	.02
❑	130	Patriots Team Photo	.05	.01
❑	131	Eugene Chung	.05	.01
❑	132	Todd Collins	.05	.01
❑	133	Tommy Hodson	.05	.01
❑	134	Leonard Russell	.10	.02
❑	135	Jon Vaughn	.05	.01
❑	136	Andre Tippett	.05	.01
❑	137	Saints Team Photo	.05	.01
❑	138	Wesley Carroll	.05	.01
❑	139	Richard Cooper	.05	.01
❑	140	Vaughn Dunbar	.05	.01
❑	141	Fred McAfee	.05	.01
❑	142	Torrance Small	.05	.01
❑	143	Steve Walsh	.05	.01
❑	144	Vaughan Johnson	.05	.01
❑	145	Giants Team Photo	.05	.01
❑	146	Jarrod Bunch	.05	.01
❑	147	Phil Simms	.10	.02
❑	148	Carl Banks	.05	.01
❑	149	Lawrence Taylor	.25	.08
❑	150	Rodney Hampton	.10	.02
❑	151	Phillippi Sparks	.05	.01
❑	152	Derek Brown TE	.05	.01
❑	153	Jets Team Photo	.05	.01
❑	154	Boomer Esiason	.10	.02
❑	155	Johnny Mitchell	.05	.01
❑	156	Rob Moore	.10	.02
❑	157	Ronnie Lott	.10	.02
❑	158	Browning Nagle	.05	.01
❑	159	Johnny Johnson	.05	.01
❑	160	Dwayne White	.05	.01
❑	161	Blair Thomas	.05	.01
❑	162	Eagles Team Photo	.05	.01
❑	163	Randall Cunningham	.25	.08
❑	164	Fred Barnett	.10	.02
❑	165	Siran Stacy	.05	.01
❑	166	Keith Byars	.05	.01
❑	167	Calvin Williams	.10	.02
❑	168	Jeff Sydner	.05	.01
❑	169	Tommy Jeter	.05	.01
❑	170	Andre Waters	.05	.01
❑	171	Phoenix Team Photo	.05	.01
❑	172	Steve Beuerlein	.10	.02
❑	173	Randal Hill	.05	.01
❑	174	Timm Rosenbach	.05	.01
❑	175	Ed Cunningham	.05	.01
❑	176	Walter Reeves	.05	.01
❑	177	Michael Zordich	.05	.01
❑	178	Gary Clark	.10	.02
❑	179	Ken Harvey	.05	.01
❑	180	Steelers Team Photo	.05	.01
❑	181	Barry Foster	.10	.02
❑	182	Neil O'Donnell	.25	.08
❑	183	Leon Searcy	.05	.01
❑	184	Bubby Brister	.05	.01
❑	185	Merril Hoge	.05	.01
❑	186	Joel Steed	.05	.01
❑	187	Raiders Team Photo	.05	.01
❑	188	Nick Bell	.05	.01
❑	189	Eric Dickerson	.10	.02
❑	190	Nolan Harrison	.05	.01
❑	191	Todd Marinovich	.05	.01
❑	192	Greg Skrepenak	.05	.01
❑	193	Howie Long	.25	.08
❑	194	Jay Schroeder	.05	.01
❑	195	Chester McGlockton	.10	.02
❑	196	Rams Team Photo	.05	.01
❑	197	Jim Everett	.10	.02
❑	198	Sean Gilbert	.10	.02
❑	199	Steve Israel	.05	.01
❑	200	Marc Boutte	.05	.01
❑	201	Joe Milinichik	.05	.01
❑	202	Henry Ellard	.10	.02
❑	203	Jackie Slater	.05	.01
❑	204	Chargers Team Photo	.05	.01
❑	205	Eric Bieniemy	.05	.01
❑	206	Marion Butts	.05	.01
❑	207	Nate Lewis	.05	.01
❑	208	Junior Seau	.25	.08
❑	209	Steve Hendrickson	.05	.01
❑	210	Chris Mims	.05	.01
❑	211	Harry Swayne	.05	.01
❑	212	Marquez Pope	.05	.01
❑	213	Donald Frank	.05	.01
❑	214	Anthony Miller	.10	.02
❑	215	Seahawks Team Photo	.05	.01
❑	216	Cortez Kennedy	.10	.02
❑	217	Dan McGwire	.05	.01
❑	218	Kelly Stouffer	.05	.01
❑	219	Chris Warren	.10	.02
❑	220	Brian Blades	.10	.02
❑	221	Rod Stephens RC	.05	.01
❑	222	49ers Team Photo	.05	.01
❑	223	Jerry Rice	1.00	.40
❑	224	Ricky Watters	.25	.08
❑	225	Steve Young	.75	.30
❑	226	Tom Rathman	.05	.01
❑	227	Dana Hall	.05	.01
❑	228	Amp Lee	.05	.01
❑	229	Brian Bollinger	.05	.01
❑	230	Keith DeLong	.05	.01
❑	231	John Taylor	.10	.02
❑	232	Buccaneers Team Photo	.05	.01
❑	233	Tyji Armstrong	.05	.01
❑	234	Lawrence Dawsey	.05	.01
❑	235	Mark Wheeler	.05	.01
❑	236	Vince Workman	.05	.01
❑	237	Reggie Cobb	.05	.01
❑	238	Tony Mayberry	.05	.01
❑	239	Marty Carter	.05	.01
❑	240	Courtney Hawkins	.05	.01
❑	241	Ray Seals	.05	.01
❑	242	Mark Carrier WR	.10	.02
❑	243	Redskins Team Photo	.05	.01
❑	244	Mark Rypien	.05	.01
❑	245	Ricky Ervins	.05	.01
❑	246	Gerald Riggs	.05	.01
❑	247	Art Monk	.10	.02
❑	248	Mark Schlereth	.05	.01
❑	249	Monte Coleman	.05	.01
❑	250	Wilber Marshall	.05	.01
❑	251	Ben Coleman RC	.05	.01
❑	252	Curtis Conway RC	.40	.15
❑	253	Ernest Dye RC	.05	.01
❑	254	Todd Kelly RC	.05	.01
❑	255	Patrick Bates RC	.05	.01
❑	256	George Teague RC	.10	.02
❑	257	Mark Brunell RC	1.50	.60
❑	258	Adrian Hardy	.05	.01
❑	259	Dana Stubblefield RC	.25	.08
❑	260	Willie Roaf RC	.10	.02
❑	261	Irv Smith RC	.05	.01
❑	262	Drew Bledsoe RC	2.50	1.00
❑	263	Dan Williams RC	.05	.01
❑	264	Jerry Ball	.05	.01
❑	265	Mark Clayton	.05	.01
❑	266	John Stephens	.05	.01
❑	267	Reggie White	.25	.08
❑	268	Jeff Hostetler	.10	.02
❑	269	Boomer Esiason	.10	.02
❑	270	Wade Wilson	.05	.01
❑	271	Steve Beuerlein	.10	.02
❑	272	Tim McDonald	.05	.01
❑	273	Craig Heyward	.10	.02
❑	274	Everson Walls	.05	.01
❑	275	Stan Humphries	.10	.02
❑	276	Carl Banks	.05	.01
❑	277	Brad Muster	.05	.01
❑	278	Tim Harris	.05	.01
❑	279	Gary Clark	.10	.02
❑	280	Joe Milinichik	.05	.01
❑	281	Leonard Marshall	.05	.01
❑	282	Joe Montana	1.50	.60
❑	283	Rod Bernstine	.05	.01
❑	284	Mark Carrier WR	.10	.02
❑	285	Michael Brooks	.05	.01
❑	286	Marvin Jones RC	.05	.01
❑	287	John Copeland RC	.10	.02
❑	288	Eric Curry RC	.05	.01
❑	289	Steve Everitt RC	.05	.01
❑	290	Tom Carter RC	.10	.02
❑	291	Deon Figures RC	.05	.01
❑	292A	Leonard Renfro RC ERR	.05	.01
❑	292B	Leonard Renfro RC COR	.05	.01
❑	293	Thomas Smith RC	.10	.02
❑	294	Carlton Gray RC	.05	.01
❑	295	Demetrius DuBose RC	.05	.01
❑	296	Coleman Rudolph RC	.05	.01
❑	297	John Parrella RC	.05	.01
❑	298	Glyn Milburn RC	.25	.08
❑	299	Reggie Brooks RC	.10	.02
❑	300	Garrison Hearst RC	.75	.30
❑	301	John Elway	1.50	.60

❑ 302 Brad Hopkins RC	.05	.01
❑ 303 Darrien Gordon RC	.05	.01
❑ 304 Robert Smith RC	1.25	.50
❑ 305 Chris Slade RC	.10	.02
❑ 306 Ryan McNeil RC	.25	.08
❑ 307 Micheal Barrow RC	.25	.08
❑ 308 Roosevelt Potts RC	.05	.01
❑ 309 Qadry Ismail RC	.25	.08
❑ 310 Reggie Freeman RC	.05	.01
❑ 311 Vincent Brisby RC	.25	.08
❑ 312 Rick Mirer RC	.25	.08
❑ 313 Billy Joe Hobert RC	.25	.08
❑ 314 Natrone Means RC	.25	.08
❑ 315 Gary Zimmerman	.05	.01
❑ 316 Bobby Hebert	.05	.01
❑ 317 Don Beebe	.05	.01
❑ 318 Wilber Marshall	.05	.01
❑ 319 Marcus Allen	.25	.08
❑ 320 Ronnie Lott	.10	.02
❑ 321 Ricky Sanders	.05	.01
❑ 322 Charles Mann	.05	.01
❑ 323 Simon Fletcher	.05	.01
❑ 324 Johnny Johnson	.05	.01
❑ 325 Gary Plummer	.05	.01
❑ 326 Panthers Insert	25.00	10.00
❑ M326 Panthers Send Away	4.00	1.50
❑ M327 Jaguars Send Away	4.00	1.50
❑ PRO1 John Elway AU/3000	60.00	30.00

1994 Collector's Edge

❑ COMPLETE SET (200)	15.00	7.50
❑ 1 Mike Pritchard	.05	.01
❑ 2 Erric Pegram	.05	.01
❑ 3 Michael Haynes	.10	.02
❑ 4 Bobby Hebert	.05	.01
❑ 5 Deion Sanders	.50	.20
❑ 6 Andre Rison	.10	.02
❑ 7 Don Beebe	.05	.01
❑ 8 Mark Kelso	.05	.01
❑ 9 Darryl Talley	.05	.01
❑ 10 Cornelius Bennett	.10	.02
❑ 11 Jim Kelly	.25	.08
❑ 12 Andre Reed	.10	.02
❑ 13 Bruce Smith	.25	.08
❑ 14 Thurman Thomas	.25	.08
❑ 15 Craig Heyward	.10	.02
❑ 16 Chris Zorich	.05	.01
❑ 17 Alonzo Spellman	.05	.01
❑ 18 Tom Waddle	.05	.01
❑ 19 Neal Anderson	.05	.01
❑ 20 Kevin Butler	.05	.01
❑ 21 Curtis Conway	.25	.08
❑ 22 Richard Dent	.10	.02
❑ 23 Jim Harbaugh	.25	.08
❑ 24 Derrick Fenner	.05	.01
❑ 25 Harold Green	.05	.01
❑ 26 David Klingler	.05	.01
❑ 27 Daniel Stubbs	.05	.01
❑ 28 Alfred Williams	.05	.01
❑ 29 John Copeland	.05	.01
❑ 30 Mark Carrier WR	.10	.02
❑ 31 Michael Jackson	.10	.02
❑ 32 Eric Metcalf	.10	.02
❑ 33 Vinny Testaverde	.10	.02
❑ 34 Tommy Vardell	.05	.01
❑ 35 Alvin Harper	.10	.02
❑ 36 Ken Norton Jr.	.10	.02
❑ 37 Tony Casillas	.05	.01
❑ 38 Leon Lett	.05	.01
❑ 39 Jay Novacek	.10	.02
❑ 40 Kevin Smith	.05	.01
❑ 41 Troy Aikman	1.00	.40
❑ 42 Michael Irvin	.25	.08
❑ 43 Russell Maryland	.05	.01
❑ 44 Emmitt Smith	1.50	.60
❑ 45 Robert Delpino	.05	.01
❑ 46 Simon Fletcher	.05	.01
❑ 47 Greg Kragen	.05	.01
❑ 48 Arthur Marshall	.05	.01
❑ 49 Steve Atwater	.05	.01
❑ 50 Rod Bernstine	.05	.01
❑ 51 John Elway	2.00	.75
❑ 52 Glyn Milburn	.10	.02
❑ 53 Shannon Sharpe	.10	.02
❑ 54 Bennie Blades	.05	.01
❑ 55 Mel Gray	.05	.01
❑ 56 Herman Moore	.25	.08
❑ 57 Pat Swilling	.05	.01
❑ 58 Chris Spielman	.10	.02
❑ 59 Rodney Peete	.05	.01
❑ 60 Andre Ware	.05	.01
❑ 61 Brett Perriman	.10	.02
❑ 62 Erik Kramer	.10	.02
❑ 63 Barry Sanders	1.50	.60
❑ 64 Mark Clayton	.05	.01
❑ 65 Chris Jacke	.05	.01
❑ 66 Terrell Buckley	.05	.01
❑ 67 Ty Detmer	.10	.02
❑ 68 Sanjay Beach	.05	.01
❑ 69 Brian Noble	.05	.01
❑ 70 Edgar Bennett	.25	.08
❑ 71 Brett Favre	2.00	.75
❑ 72 Sterling Sharpe	.10	.02
❑ 73 Reggie White	.25	.08
❑ 74 Ernest Givins	.10	.02
❑ 75 Al Del Greco	.05	.01
❑ 76 Cris Dishman	.05	.01
❑ 77 Curtis Duncan	.05	.01
❑ 78 Webster Slaughter	.05	.01
❑ 79 Spencer Tillman	.05	.01
❑ 80 Warren Moon	.25	.08
❑ 81 Wilber Marshall	.05	.01
❑ 82 Haywood Jeffires	.10	.02
❑ 83 Lorenzo White	.05	.01
❑ 84 Gary Brown	.05	.01
❑ 85 Reggie Langhorne	.05	.01
❑ 86 Dean Biasucci	.05	.01
❑ 87 Steve Emtman	.05	.01
❑ 88 Jessie Hester	.05	.01
❑ 89 Quentin Coryatt	.05	.01
❑ 90 Roosevelt Potts	.05	.01
❑ 91 Jeff George	.25	.08
❑ 92 Nick Lowery	.05	.01
❑ 93 Willie Davis	.10	.02
❑ 94 Joe Montana	2.00	.75
❑ 95 Neil Smith	.10	.02
❑ 96 Marcus Allen	.25	.08
❑ 97 Derrick Thomas	.25	.08
❑ 98 Greg Townsend	.05	.01
❑ 99 Willie Gault	.05	.01
❑ 100 Ethan Horton	.05	.01
❑ 101 Jeff Hostetler	.10	.02
❑ 102 Tim Brown	.25	.08
❑ 103 Rocket Ismail	.10	.02
❑ 104 Shane Conlan	.05	.01
❑ 105 Henry Ellard	.10	.02
❑ 106 T.J. Rubley	.05	.01
❑ 107 Sean Gilbert	.05	.01
❑ 108 Troy Drayton	.05	.01
❑ 109 Jerome Bettis	.40	.15
❑ 110 Terry Kirby	.25	.08
❑ 111 Mark Ingram	.05	.01
❑ 112 John Offerdahl	.05	.01
❑ 113 Louis Oliver	.05	.01
❑ 114 Irving Fryar	.10	.02
❑ 115 Dan Marino	2.00	.75
❑ 116 Keith Jackson	.05	.01
❑ 117 O.J.McDuffie	.25	.08
❑ 118 Jim McMahon	.10	.02
❑ 119 Sean Salisbury	.05	.01
❑ 120 Randall McDaniel	.05	.01
❑ 121 Jack Del Rio	.05	.01
❑ 122 Cris Carter	.50	.20
❑ 123 Chris Doleman	.05	.01
❑ 124 John Randle	.05	.01
❑ 125 Vincent Brisby	.10	.02
❑ 126 Greg McMurtry	.05	.01
❑ 127 Drew Bledsoe	.75	.30
❑ 128 Leonard Russell	.05	.01
❑ 129 Michael Brooks	.05	.01
❑ 130 Mark Jackson	.05	.01
❑ 131 Pepper Johnson	.05	.01
❑ 132 Doug Riesenberg	.05	.01
❑ 133 Phil Simms	.10	.02
❑ 134 Rodney Hampton	.10	.02
❑ 135 Leonard Marshall	.05	.01
❑ 136 Rob Moore	.10	.02
❑ 137 Chris Burkett	.05	.01
❑ 138 Boomer Esiason	.10	.02
❑ 139 Johnny Johnson	.05	.01
❑ 140 Ronnie Lott	.10	.02
❑ 141 Brad Muster	.05	.01
❑ 142 Renaldo Turnbull	.05	.01
❑ 143 Willie Roaf	.05	.01
❑ 144 Rickey Jackson	.05	.01
❑ 145 Morten Andersen	.05	.01
❑ 146 Vaughn Dunbar	.05	.01
❑ 147 Wade Wilson	.05	.01
❑ 148 Eric Martin	.05	.01
❑ 149 Seth Joyner	.05	.01
❑ 150 Calvin Williams	.10	.02
❑ 151 Vai Sikahema	.05	.01
❑ 152 Herschel Walker	.10	.02
❑ 153 Eric Allen	.05	.01
❑ 154 Fred Barnett	.10	.02
❑ 155 Randall Cunningham	.25	.08
❑ 156 Steve Beuerlein	.10	.02
❑ 157 Gary Clark	.10	.02
❑ 158 Anthony Edwards	.05	.01
❑ 159 Randal Hill	.05	.01
❑ 160 Freddie Joe Nunn	.05	.01
❑ 161 Garrison Hearst	.25	.08
❑ 162 Ricky Proehl	.05	.01
❑ 163 Eric Green	.05	.01
❑ 164 Levon Kirkland	.05	.01
❑ 165 Joel Steed	.05	.01
❑ 166 Deon Figures	.05	.01
❑ 167 Leroy Thompson	.05	.01
❑ 168 Barry Foster	.05	.01
❑ 169 Neil O'Donnell	.25	.08
❑ 170 Junior Seau	.25	.08
❑ 171 Leslie O'Neal	.05	.01
❑ 172 Stan Humphries	.10	.02
❑ 173 Marion Butts	.05	.01
❑ 174 Anthony Miller	.10	.02
❑ 175 Natrone Means	.25	.08
❑ 176 Odessa Turner	.05	.01
❑ 177 Dana Stubblefield	.10	.02
❑ 178 John Taylor	.10	.02
❑ 179 Ricky Watters	.10	.02
❑ 180 Steve Young	.75	.30
❑ 181 Jerry Rice	1.00	.40
❑ 182 Tom Rathman	.05	.01
❑ 183 Brian Blades	.10	.02
❑ 184 Patrick Hunter	.05	.01
❑ 185 Rick Mirer	.25	.08
❑ 186 Chris Warren	.10	.02
❑ 187 Cortez Kennedy	.10	.02
❑ 188 Reggie Cobb	.05	.01
❑ 189 Craig Erickson	.05	.01
❑ 190 Hardy Nickerson	.10	.02
❑ 191 Lawrence Dawsey	.05	.01
❑ 192 Broderick Thomas	.05	.01
❑ 193 Ricky Sanders	.05	.01
❑ 194 Carl Banks	.05	.01
❑ 195 Ricky Ervins	.05	.01
❑ 196 Darrell Green	.05	.01
❑ 197 Mark Rypien	.05	.01
❑ 198 Desmond Howard	.10	.02
❑ 199 Art Monk	.10	.02
❑ 200 Reggie Brooks	.10	.02
❑ P1 Shannon Sharpe Prototype	1.00	.40

1995 Collector's Edge

❑ COMPLETE SET (205)	20.00	10.00
❑ 1 Anthony Edwards	.05	.01
❑ 2 Garrison Hearst	.25	.08
❑ 3 Seth Joyner	.05	.01
❑ 4 Dave Krieg	.05	.01
❑ 5 Chuck Levy	.05	.01
❑ 6 Rob Moore	.10	.02
❑ 7 J.J. Birden	.05	.01
❑ 8 Jeff George	.10	.02
❑ 9 Craig Heyward	.10	.02
❑ 10 Norm Johnson	.05	.01
❑ 11 Terance Mathis	.10	.02
❑ 12 Eric Metcalf	.10	.02
❑ 13 Chuck Smith	.05	.01
❑ 14 Darryl Talley	.05	.01
❑ 15 Cornelius Bennett	.10	.02

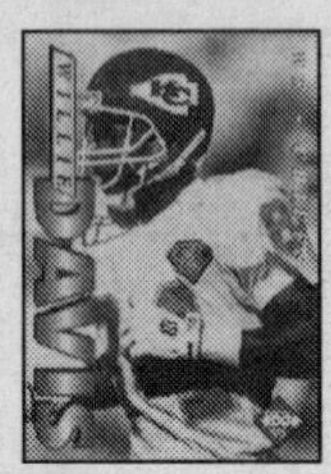

❑ 16 Steve Christie	.05	.01
❑ 17 Kenneth Davis	.05	.01
❑ 18 Phil Hansen	.05	.01
❑ 19 Jim Kelly	.25	.08
❑ 20 Bryce Paup	.10	.02
❑ 21 Andre Reed	.10	.02
❑ 22 Bruce Smith	.25	.08
❑ 23 Eric Ball	.05	.01
❑ 24 Don Beebe	.05	.01
❑ 25 Mark Carrier WR	.10	.02
❑ 26 Tim McKyer	.05	.01
❑ 27 Pete Metzelaars	.05	.01
❑ 28 Sam Mills	.10	.02
❑ 29 Jack Trudeau	.05	.01
❑ 30 Mark Carrier DB	.05	.01
❑ 31 Curtis Conway	.25	.08
❑ 32 Erik Kramer	.05	.01
❑ 33 Lewis Tillman	.05	.01
❑ 34 Michael Timpson	.05	.01
❑ 35 Steve Walsh	.05	.01
❑ 36 Chris Zorich	.05	.01
❑ 37 Jeff Blake RC	.60	.25
❑ 38 Harold Green	.05	.01
❑ 39 David Klingler	.10	.02
❑ 40 Carl Pickens	.10	.02
❑ 41 Tom Waddle	.05	.01
❑ 42 Dan Wilkinson	.10	.02
❑ 43 Leroy Hoard	.05	.01
❑ 44 Michael Jackson	.10	.02
❑ 45 Antonio Langham	.05	.01
❑ 46 Andre Rison	.10	.02
❑ 47 Vinny Testaverde	.10	.02
❑ 48 Eric Turner	.05	.01
❑ 49 Tommy Vardell	.05	.01
❑ 50 Troy Aikman	1.00	.40
❑ 51 Charles Haley	.10	.02
❑ 52 Michael Irvin	.25	.08
❑ 53 Daryl Johnston	.10	.02
❑ 54 Leon Lett	.05	.01
❑ 55 Jay Novacek	.10	.02
❑ 56 Emmitt Smith	1.50	.60
❑ 57 Kevin Williams WR	.10	.02
❑ 58 Steve Atwater	.05	.01
❑ 59 John Elway	2.00	.75
❑ 60 Simon Fletcher	.05	.01
❑ 61 Glyn Milburn	.05	.01
❑ 62 Anthony Miller	.10	.02
❑ 63 Leonard Russell	.05	.01
❑ 64 Shannon Sharpe	.10	.02
❑ 65 Scott Mitchell	.10	.02
❑ 66 Herman Moore	.25	.08
❑ 67 Johnnie Morton	.10	.02
❑ 68 Brett Perriman	.10	.02
❑ 69 Barry Sanders	1.50	.60
❑ 70 Edgar Bennett	.10	.02
❑ 71 Brett Favre	2.00	.75
❑ 72 Mark Ingram	.05	.01
❑ 73 Chris Jacke	.05	.01
❑ 74 Guy McIntyre	.05	.01
❑ 75 Reggie White	.25	.08
❑ 76 Gary Brown	.05	.01
❑ 77 Ernest Givins	.05	.01
❑ 78 Mel Gray	.05	.01
❑ 79 Haywood Jeffires	.05	.01
❑ 80 Webster Slaughter	.05	.01
❑ 81 Craig Erickson	.05	.01
❑ 82 Marshall Faulk	1.25	.50
❑ 83 Jim Harbaugh	.10	.02
❑ 84 Roosevelt Potts	.05	.01
❑ 85 Floyd Turner	.05	.01
❑ 86 Steve Beuerlein	.10	.02
❑ 87 Reggie Cobb	.05	.01
❑ 88 Jeff Lageman	.05	.01
❑ 89 Mazio Royster	.05	.01
❑ 90 Marcus Allen	.25	.08
❑ 91 Steve Bono	.10	.02
❑ 92 Willie Davis	.10	.02
❑ 93 Lake Dawson	.10	.02
❑ 94 Ronnie Lott	.10	.02
❑ 95 Eric Martin	.05	.01
❑ 96 Chris Penn	.05	.01
❑ 97 Tim Brown	.25	.08
❑ 98 Derrick Fenner	.05	.01
❑ 99 Rob Fredrickson	.05	.01
❑ 100 Nolan Harrison	.05	.01
❑ 101 Jeff Hostetler	.10	.02
❑ 102 Rocket Ismail	.10	.02
❑ 103 James Jett	.10	.02
❑ 104 Chester McGlockton	.10	.02
❑ 105 Anthony Smith	.05	.01
❑ 106 Harvey Williams	.05	.01
❑ 107 Jerome Bettis	.25	.08
❑ 108 Troy Drayton	.05	.01
❑ 109 Chris Miller	.05	.01
❑ 110 Robert Young	.05	.01
❑ 111 Keith Byars	.05	.01
❑ 112 Gary Clark	.05	.01
❑ 113 Bryan Cox	.05	.01
❑ 114 Jeff Cross	.05	.01
❑ 115 Irving Fryar	.10	.02
❑ 116 Randal Hill	.05	.01
❑ 117 Terry Kirby	.10	.02
❑ 118 Dan Marino	2.00	.75
❑ 119 O.J. McDuffie	.25	.08
❑ 120 Bernie Parmalee	.10	.02
❑ 121 Terry Allen	.10	.02
❑ 122 Cris Carter	.25	.08
❑ 123 Qadry Ismail	.10	.02
❑ 124 Warren Moon	.10	.02
❑ 125 John Randle	.10	.02
❑ 126 Jake Reed	.10	.02
❑ 127 Fuad Reveiz	.05	.01
❑ 128 Broderick Thomas	.05	.01
❑ 129 Drew Bledsoe	.60	.25
❑ 130 Vincent Brisby	.05	.01
❑ 131 Ben Coates	.10	.02
❑ 132 Dave Meggett	.05	.01
❑ 133 Chris Slade	.05	.01
❑ 134 Leroy Thompson	.05	.01
❑ 135 Eric Allen	.05	.01
❑ 136 Mario Bates	.10	.02
❑ 137 Quinn Early	.05	.01
❑ 138 Jim Everett	.05	.01
❑ 139 Michael Haynes	.10	.02
❑ 140 Torrance Small	.05	.01
❑ 141 Dave Brown	.10	.02
❑ 142 Chris Calloway	.05	.01
❑ 143 Keith Hamilton	.05	.01
❑ 144 Rodney Hampton	.10	.02
❑ 145 Mike Sherrard	.05	.01
❑ 146 David Treadwell	.05	.01
❑ 147 Herschel Walker	.10	.02
❑ 148 Boomer Esiason	.10	.02
❑ 149 Erik Howard	.05	.01
❑ 150 Johnny Johnson	.05	.01
❑ 151 Mo Lewis	.05	.01
❑ 152 Johnny Mitchell	.05	.01
❑ 153 Fred Barnett	.10	.02
❑ 154 Randall Cunningham	.25	.08
❑ 155 William Fuller	.05	.01
❑ 156 Charlie Garner	.25	.08
❑ 157 Greg Jackson	.05	.01
❑ 158 Ricky Watters	.10	.02
❑ 159 Calvin Williams	.10	.02
❑ 160 Barry Foster	.10	.02
❑ 161 Kevin Greene	.10	.02
❑ 162 Greg Lloyd	.10	.02
❑ 163 Byron Bam Morris	.05	.01
❑ 164 Neil O'Donnell	.10	.02
❑ 165 Erric Pegram	.10	.02
❑ 166 John L. Williams	.05	.01
❑ 167 Rod Woodson	.10	.02
❑ 168 John Carney	.05	.01
❑ 169 Stan Humphries	.10	.02
❑ 170 Natrone Means	.10	.02
❑ 171 Chris Mims	.05	.01
❑ 172 Leslie O'Neal	.10	.02
❑ 173 Alfred Pupunu RC	.05	.01
❑ 174 Junior Seau	.25	.08
❑ 175 Mark Seay	.10	.02
❑ 176 William Floyd	.10	.02
❑ 177 Jerry Rice	1.00	.40
❑ 178 Deion Sanders	.60	.25
❑ 179 Dana Stubblefield	.10	.02
❑ 180 John Taylor	.05	.01
❑ 181 Steve Young	.75	.30
❑ 182 Bryant Young	.10	.02
❑ 183 Brian Blades	.10	.02
❑ 184 Cortez Kennedy	.10	.02
❑ 185 Kelvin Martin	.05	.01
❑ 186 Rick Mirer	.10	.02
❑ 187 Ricky Proehl	.05	.01
❑ 188 Michael Sinclair	.05	.01
❑ 189 Chris Warren	.10	.02
❑ 190 Trent Dilfer	.25	.08
❑ 191 Alvin Harper	.05	.01
❑ 192 Jackie Harris	.05	.01
❑ 193 Hardy Nickerson	.05	.01
❑ 194 Errict Rhett	.10	.02
❑ 195 Reggie Roby	.05	.01
❑ 196 Henry Ellard	.10	.02
❑ 197 Ricky Ervins	.05	.01
❑ 198 Darrell Green	.05	.01
❑ 199 Brian Mitchell	.05	.01
❑ 200 Heath Shuler	.10	.02
❑ 201 Checklist	.05	.01
❑ 202 Checklist	.05	.01
❑ 203 Checklist	.05	.01
❑ 204 Checklist	.05	.01
❑ 205 Checklist	.05	.01
❑ P1 Natrone Means Promo	.50	.20
❑ P2 Chris Warren Promo	.50	.20

1995 Collector's Edge Instant Replay

❑ COMPLETE SET (51)	15.00	6.00
❑ 1 Jeff George	.10	.02
❑ 2 Eric Metcalf	.10	.02
❑ 3 Jim Kelly	.20	.07
❑ 4 Jeff Blake RC	.60	.25
❑ 5 Andre Rison	.10	.02
❑ 6 Troy Aikman	.75	.30
❑ 7 Michael Irvin	.20	.07
❑ 8 Emmitt Smith	1.25	.50
❑ 9 John Elway	1.50	.60
❑ 10 Terrell Davis RC	2.00	.75
❑ 11 Herman Moore	.20	.07
❑ 12 Barry Sanders	1.25	.50
❑ 13 Brett Favre	1.50	.60
❑ 14 Marshall Faulk	1.00	.40
❑ 15 Steve Beuerlein	.10	.02
❑ 16 Steve Bono	.10	.02
❑ 17 Tim Brown	.20	.07
❑ 18 Jeff Hostetler	.10	.02
❑ 19 Jerome Bettis	.20	.07
❑ 20 Dan Marino	1.50	.60
❑ 21 Cris Carter	.20	.07
❑ 22 Drew Bledsoe	.50	.20
❑ 23 Ben Coates	.10	.02
❑ 24 Randall Cunningham	.20	.07
❑ 25 Terry Kirby	.10	.02
❑ 26 Ricky Watters	.10	.02
❑ 27 Kyle Brady	.20	.07
❑ 28 Byron Bam Morris	.05	.01
❑ 29 Neil O'Donnell	.10	.02
❑ 30 Natrone Means	.10	.02
❑ 31 Junior Seau	.20	.07
❑ 32 William Floyd	.10	.02
❑ 33 Jerry Rice	.75	.30
❑ 34 Deion Sanders	.50	.20
❑ 35 Steve Young	.60	.25
❑ 36 Rick Mirer	.10	.02

❑ 37 Chris Warren .10 .02
❑ 38 Trent Dilfer .20 .07
❑ 39 Errict Rhett .10 .02
❑ 40 Heath Shuler .10 .02
❑ 41 Ki-Jana Carter RC .20 .07
❑ 42 Kerry Collins RC 1.25 .50
❑ 43 Steve McNair RC 2.50 1.00
❑ 44 Rashaan Salaam RC .10 .02
❑ 45 James O. Stewart RC 1.00 .40
❑ 46 J.J. Stokes RC .20 .07
❑ 47 Tyrone Wheatley RC 1.00 .40
❑ 48 Joey Galloway RC 1.25 .50
❑ 49 Napoleon Kaufman RC 1.00 .40
❑ 50 Michael Westbrook RC .20 .07
❑ NNO Checklist Card .05 .01

1996 Collector's Edge

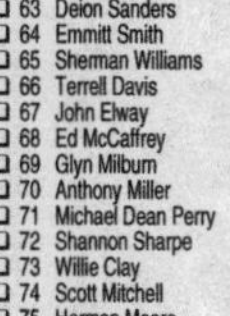

❑ COMPLETE SET (250) 20.00 8.00
❑ 1 Larry Centers .20 .07
❑ 2 Garrison Hearst .20 .07
❑ 3 Dave Krieg .10 .02
❑ 4 Rob Moore .20 .07
❑ 5 Frank Sanders .20 .07
❑ 6 Eric Swann .10 .02
❑ 7 Morten Andersen .10 .02
❑ 8 Chris Doleman .10 .02
❑ 9 Bert Emanuel .20 .07
❑ 10 Jeff George .20 .07
❑ 11 Craig Heyward .10 .02
❑ 12 Terance Mathis .10 .02
❑ 13 Clay Matthews .10 .02
❑ 14 Eric Metcalf .10 .02
❑ 15 Bill Brooks .10 .02
❑ 16 Todd Collins .20 .07
❑ 17 Russell Copeland .10 .02
❑ 18 Jim Kelly .40 .15
❑ 19 Bryce Paup .10 .02
❑ 20 Andre Reed .20 .07
❑ 21 Bruce Smith .20 .07
❑ 22 Mark Carrier WR .10 .02
❑ 23 Kerry Collins .40 .15
❑ 24 Willie Green .10 .02
❑ 25 Eric Guliford .10 .02
❑ 26 Brett Maxie .10 .02
❑ 27 Tim McKyer .10 .02
❑ 28 Derrick Moore .10 .02
❑ 29 Curtis Conway .40 .15
❑ 30 Jim Flanigan .10 .02
❑ 31 Jeff Graham .10 .02
❑ 32 Robert Green .10 .02
❑ 33 Erik Kramer .10 .02
❑ 34 Rashaan Salaam .20 .07
❑ 35 Alonzo Spellman .10 .02
❑ 36 Donnell Woolford .10 .02
❑ 37 Chris Zorich .10 .02
❑ 38 Eric Bieniemy .10 .02
❑ 39 Jeff Blake .40 .15
❑ 40 Ki-Jana Carter .20 .07
❑ 41 John Copeland .10 .02
❑ 42 Harold Green .10 .02
❑ 43 Tony McGee .10 .02
❑ 44 Carl Pickens .20 .07
❑ 45 Darnay Scott .20 .07
❑ 46 Bracy Walker RC .10 .02
❑ 47 Dan Wilkinson .10 .02
❑ 48 Rob Burnett .10 .02
❑ 49 Leroy Hoard .10 .02
❑ 50 Ernest Hunter .10 .02
❑ 51 Michael Jackson .20 .07
❑ 52 Stevon Moore .10 .02
❑ 53 Anthony Pleasant .10 .02
❑ 54 Andre Rison .20 .07
❑ 55 Vinny Testaverde .20 .07
❑ 56 Eric Zeier .10 .02
❑ 57 Troy Aikman 1.00 .40
❑ 58 Bill Bates .20 .07
❑ 59 Shante Carver .10 .02
❑ 60 Michael Irvin .40 .15
❑ 61 Daryl Johnston .20 .07
❑ 62 Jay Novacek .10 .02
❑ 63 Deion Sanders .60 .25
❑ 64 Emmitt Smith 1.50 .60
❑ 65 Sherman Williams .10 .02
❑ 66 Terrell Davis .75 .30
❑ 67 John Elway 2.00 .75
❑ 68 Ed McCaffrey .20 .07
❑ 69 Glyn Milburn .10 .02
❑ 70 Anthony Miller .20 .07
❑ 71 Michael Dean Perry .10 .02
❑ 72 Shannon Sharpe .20 .07
❑ 73 Willie Clay .10 .02
❑ 74 Scott Mitchell .20 .07
❑ 75 Herman Moore .20 .07
❑ 76 Johnnie Morton .20 .07
❑ 77 Brett Perriman .10 .02
❑ 78 Barry Sanders 1.50 .60
❑ 79 Tracy Scroggins .10 .02
❑ 80 Edgar Bennett .20 .07
❑ 81 Robert Brooks .40 .15
❑ 82 Brett Favre 2.00 .75
❑ 83 Dorsey Levens .40 .15
❑ 84 Craig Newsome .10 .02
❑ 85 Wayne Simmons .10 .02
❑ 86 Reggie White .40 .15
❑ 87 Chris Chandler .20 .07
❑ 88 Anthony Cook .10 .02
❑ 89 Mel Gray .10 .02
❑ 90 Haywood Jeffires .10 .02
❑ 91 Darryll Lewis .10 .02
❑ 92 Steve McNair .75 .30
❑ 93 Todd McNair .10 .02
❑ 94 Rodney Thomas .10 .02
❑ 95 Trev Alberts .10 .02
❑ 96 Tony Bennett .10 .02
❑ 97 Quentin Coryatt .10 .02
❑ 98 Sean Dawkins .10 .02
❑ 99 Ken Dilger .20 .07
❑ 100 Marshall Faulk .50 .20
❑ 101 Jim Harbaugh .20 .07
❑ 102 Ronald Humphrey .10 .02
❑ 103 Floyd Turner .10 .02
❑ 104 Steve Beuerlein .20 .07
❑ 105 Tony Boselli .10 .02
❑ 106 Mark Brunell .60 .25
❑ 107 Willie Jackson .20 .07
❑ 108 Jeff Lageman .10 .02
❑ 109 James O. Stewart .20 .07
❑ 110 Cedric Tillman .10 .02
❑ 111 Marcus Allen .40 .15
❑ 112 Kimble Anders .20 .07
❑ 113 Steve Bono .10 .02
❑ 114 Dale Carter .10 .02
❑ 115 Willie Davis .10 .02
❑ 116 Lake Dawson .10 .02
❑ 117 Dan Saleaumua .10 .02
❑ 118 Neil Smith .20 .07
❑ 119 Derrick Thomas .40 .15
❑ 120 Tamarick Vanover .20 .07
❑ 121 Marco Coleman .10 .02
❑ 122 Bryan Cox .10 .02
❑ 123 Steve Emtman .10 .02
❑ 124 Irving Fryar .20 .07
❑ 125 Eric Green .10 .02
❑ 126 Terry Kirby .20 .07
❑ 127 Dan Marino 2.00 .75
❑ 128 O.J. McDuffie .20 .07
❑ 129 Bernie Parmalee .10 .02
❑ 130 Troy Vincent .10 .02
❑ 131 Cris Carter .40 .15
❑ 132 Jack Del Rio .10 .02
❑ 133 Qadry Ismail .20 .07
❑ 134 Amp Lee .10 .02
❑ 135 Warren Moon .20 .07
❑ 136 John Randle .20 .07
❑ 137 Jake Reed .20 .07
❑ 138 Robert Smith .20 .07
❑ 139 Drew Bledsoe .60 .25
❑ 140 Vincent Brisby .10 .02
❑ 141 Ben Coates .20 .07
❑ 142 Curtis Martin .75 .30
❑ 143 Dave Meggett .10 .02
❑ 144 Will Moore .10 .02
❑ 145 Chris Slade .10 .02
❑ 146 Mario Bates .20 .07
❑ 147 Quinn Early .10 .02
❑ 148 Jim Everett .10 .02
❑ 149 Michael Haynes .10 .02
❑ 150 Tyrone Hughes .10 .02
❑ 151 Wayne Martin .10 .02
❑ 152 Renaldo Turnbull .10 .02
❑ 153 Dave Brown .10 .02
❑ 154 Chris Calloway .10 .02
❑ 155 Rodney Hampton .20 .07
❑ 156 Mike Sherrard .10 .02
❑ 157 Michael Strahan .20 .07
❑ 158 Herschel Walker .20 .07
❑ 159 Tyrone Wheatley .20 .07
❑ 160 Kyle Brady .10 .02
❑ 161 Wayne Chrebet .60 .25
❑ 162 Hugh Douglas .20 .07
❑ 163 Adrian Murrell .20 .07
❑ 164 Todd Scott .10 .02
❑ 165 Charles Wilson .10 .02
❑ 166 Tim Brown .40 .15
❑ 167 Aundray Bruce .10 .02
❑ 168 Andrew Glover .10 .02
❑ 169 Jeff Hostetler .10 .02
❑ 170 Napoleon Kaufman .40 .15
❑ 171 Terry McDaniel .10 .02
❑ 172 Chester McGlockton .10 .02
❑ 173 Pat Swilling .10 .02
❑ 174 Harvey Williams .10 .02
❑ 175 Fred Barnett .10 .02
❑ 176 Randall Cunningham .40 .15
❑ 177 William Fuller .10 .02
❑ 178 Charlie Garner .20 .07
❑ 179 Andy Harmon .10 .02
❑ 180 Rodney Peete .10 .02
❑ 181 Ricky Watters .20 .07
❑ 182 Calvin Williams .10 .02
❑ 183 Chad Brown .10 .02
❑ 184 Kevin Greene .20 .07
❑ 185 Greg Lloyd .20 .07
❑ 186 Byron Bam Morris .10 .02
❑ 187 Neil O'Donnell .20 .07
❑ 188 Erric Pegram .10 .02
❑ 189 Kordell Stewart .40 .15
❑ 190 Yancey Thigpen .20 .07
❑ 191 Rod Woodson .20 .07
❑ 192 Darren Bennett .10 .02
❑ 193 Ronnie Harmon .10 .02
❑ 194 Stan Humphries .20 .07
❑ 195 Tony Martin .20 .07
❑ 196 Natrone Means .20 .07
❑ 197 Leslie O'Neal .10 .02
❑ 198 Junior Seau .40 .15
❑ 199 Mark Seay .10 .02
❑ 200 William Floyd .20 .07
❑ 201 Merton Hanks .10 .02
❑ 202 Brent Jones .10 .02
❑ 203 Derek Loville .10 .02
❑ 204 Ken Norton, Jr. .10 .02
❑ 205 Gary Plummer .10 .02
❑ 206 Jerry Rice 1.00 .40
❑ 207 J.J. Stokes .40 .15
❑ 208 Dana Stubblefield .20 .07
❑ 209 John Taylor .10 .02
❑ 210 Bryant Young .20 .07
❑ 211 Steve Young .75 .30
❑ 212 Brian Blades .10 .02
❑ 213 Joey Galloway .40 .15
❑ 214 Carlton Gray .10 .02
❑ 215 Cortez Kennedy .10 .02
❑ 216 Rick Mirer .20 .07
❑ 217 Chris Warren .20 .07
❑ 218 Jerome Bettis .40 .15
❑ 219 Isaac Bruce .40 .15
❑ 220 Troy Drayton .10 .02
❑ 221 D'Marco Farr .10 .02
❑ 222 Sean Gilbert .10 .02
❑ 223 Chris Miller .10 .02
❑ 224 Roman Phifer .10 .02
❑ 225 Trent Dilfer .40 .15
❑ 226 Santana Dotson .10 .02
❑ 227 Alvin Harper .10 .02
❑ 228 Jackie Harris .10 .02
❑ 229 John Lynch .40 .15
❑ 230 Hardy Nickerson .10 .02
❑ 231 Errict Rhett .20 .07
❑ 232 Warren Sapp .10 .02

233	Terry Allen	.20	.07
234	Henry Ellard	.10	.02
235	Gus Frerotte	.20	.07
236	Ken Harvey	.10	.02
237	Brian Mitchell	.10	.02
238	Heath Shuler	.20	.07
239	James Washington	.10	.02
240	Michael Westbrook	.40	.15
241	Checklist	.10	.02
242	Checklist	.10	.02
243	Checklist	.10	.02
244	Checklist	.10	.02
245	Checklist	.10	.02
246	Checklist	.10	.02
247	Checklist	.10	.02
248	Checklist	.10	.02
249	Checklist	.10	.02
250	Checklist	.10	.02
PR1	Eddie George Promo	.50	.20

1999 Collector's Edge Advantage

	COMPLETE SET (190)	50.00	25.00
1	Larry Centers	.30	.10
2	Rob Moore	.50	.20
3	Adrian Murrell	.50	.20
4	Jake Plummer	.50	.20
5	Frank Sanders	.50	.20
6	Jamal Anderson	.75	.30
7	Chris Chandler	.50	.20
8	Tim Dwight	.75	.30
9	Tony Martin	.50	.20
10	Terance Mathis	.50	.20
11	O.J. Santiago	.30	.10
12	Jim Harbaugh	.50	.20
13	Priest Holmes	1.25	.50
14	Jermaine Lewis	.50	.20
15	Rod Woodson	.50	.20
16	Eric Zeier	.50	.20
17	Doug Flutie	.75	.30
18	Sam Gash	.30	.10
19	Rob Johnson	.50	.20
20	Eric Moulds	.75	.30
21	Andre Reed	.50	.20
22	Antowain Smith	.75	.30
23	Bruce Smith	.50	.20
24	Thurman Thomas	.50	.20
25	Steve Beuerlein	.50	.20
26	Kevin Greene	.50	.20
27	Rocket Ismail	.50	.20
28	Fred Lane	.30	.10
29	Muhsin Muhammad	.50	.20
30	Edgar Bennett	.30	.10
31	Curtis Conway	.50	.20
32	Bobby Engram	.50	.20
33	Curtis Enis	.30	.10
34	Erik Kramer	.50	.20
35	Jeff Blake	.50	.20
36	Corey Dillon	.75	.30
37	Neil O'Donnell	.50	.20
38	Carl Pickens	.50	.20
39	Takeo Spikes	.30	.10
40	Troy Aikman	1.50	.60
41	Billy Davis	.30	.10
42	Michael Irvin	.50	.20
43	Deion Sanders	.75	.30
44	Emmitt Smith	1.50	.60
45	Darren Woodson	.30	.10
46	Bubby Brister	.50	.20
47	Terrell Davis	.75	.30
48	John Elway	2.50	1.00
49	Ed McCaffrey	.50	.20
50	Bill Romanowski	.30	.10
51	Shannon Sharpe	.50	.20
52	Rod Smith	.50	.20
53	Charlie Batch	.75	.30
54	Germane Crowell	.30	.10
55	Herman Moore	.50	.20
56	Johnnie Morton	.50	.20
57	Barry Sanders	2.50	1.00
58	Robert Brooks	.50	.20
59	Brett Favre	2.50	1.00
60	Antonio Freeman	.75	.30
61	Darick Holmes	.30	.10
62	Dorsey Levens	.75	.30
63	Roell Preston	.30	.10
64	Marshall Faulk	1.00	.40
65	E.G.Green	.30	.10
66	Marvin Harrison	.75	.30
67	Peyton Manning	2.50	1.00
68	Jerome Pathon	.30	.10
69	Mark Brunell	.75	.30
70	Kevin Hardy	.30	.10
71	Keenan McCardell	.50	.20
72	Jimmy Smith	.50	.20
73	Fred Taylor	.75	.30
74	Alvis Whitted	.30	.10
75	Kimble Anders	.50	.20
76	Donnell Bennett	.30	.10
77	Rich Gannon	.75	.30
78	Elvis Grbac	.50	.20
79	Byron Bam Morris	.30	.10
80	Andre Rison	.50	.20
81	Karim Abdul-Jabbar	.50	.20
82	John Avery	.30	.10
83	Oronde Gadsden	.50	.20
84	Sam Madison	.30	.10
85	Dan Marino	2.50	1.00
86	O.J. McDuffie	.50	.20
87	Zach Thomas	.75	.30
88	Cris Carter	.75	.30
89	Randall Cunningham	.75	.30
90	Brad Johnson	.75	.30
91	Randy Moss	2.00	.75
92	John Randle	.50	.20
93	Jake Reed	.50	.20
94	Robert Smith	.75	.30
95	Drew Bledsoe	1.00	.40
96	Ben Coates	.50	.20
97	Robert Edwards	.30	.10
98	Terry Glenn	.75	.30
99	Ty Law	.50	.20
100	Cam Cleeland	.30	.10
101	Kerry Collins	.50	.20
102	Gary Brown	.30	.10
103	Kent Graham	.30	.10
104	Ike Hilliard	.50	.20
105	Joe Jurevicius	.50	.20
106	Danny Kanell	.30	.10
107	Wayne Chrebet	.50	.20
108	Aaron Glenn	.30	.10
109	Keyshawn Johnson	.75	.30
110	Curtis Martin	.75	.30
111	Vinny Testaverde	.50	.20
112	Tim Brown	.75	.30
113	Jeff George	.50	.20
114	James Jett	.50	.20
115	Napoleon Kaufman	.75	.30
116	Charles Woodson	.75	.30
117	Koy Detmer	.30	.10
118	Duce Staley	.75	.30
119	Jerome Bettis	.75	.30
120	Charles Johnson	.50	.20
121	Kordell Stewart	.50	.20
122	Tony Banks	.50	.20
123	Isaac Bruce	.75	.30
124	June Henley RC	.30	.10
125	Ryan Leaf	.75	.30
126	Natrone Means	.50	.20
127	Mikhael Ricks	.30	.10
128	Craig Whelihan	.30	.10
129	Garrison Hearst	.50	.20
130	Terrell Owens	.75	.30
131	Jerry Rice	1.50	.60
132	J.J.Stokes	.50	.20
133	Steve Young	1.00	.40
134	Joey Galloway	.50	.20
135	Ahman Green	.75	.30
136	Jon Kitna	.75	.30
137	Ricky Watters	.50	.20
138	Mike Alstott	.75	.30
139	Reidel Anthony	.50	.20
140	Trent Dilfer	.50	.20
141	Warrick Dunn	.75	.30
142	Jacquez Green	.30	.10
143	Kevin Dyson	.50	.20
144	Eddie George	.75	.30
145	Steve McNair	.75	.30
146	Yancey Thigpen	.30	.10
147	Terry Allen	.50	.20
148	Trent Green	.75	.30
149	Skip Hicks	.30	.10
150	Michael Westbrook	.50	.20
151	Rahim Abdullah RC	1.25	.50
152	Champ Bailey RC	2.00	.75
153	Marlon Barnes RC	.75	.30
154	D'Wayne Bates RC	1.25	.50
155	Michael Bishop RC	1.50	.60
156	Dre' Bly RC	1.50	.60
157	David Boston RC	1.50	.60
158	Chris Claiborne RC	.75	.30
159	Tim Couch RC	1.50	.60
160	Daunte Culpepper RC	6.00	2.50
161	Autry Denson RC	1.25	.50
162	Jared DeVries RC	1.25	.50
163	Troy Edwards RC	1.25	.50
164	Kris Farris RC	.75	.30
165	Kevin Faulk RC	1.50	.60
166	Martin Gramatica RC	.75	.30
167	Torry Holt RC	4.00	1.50
168	Brock Huard RC	1.50	.60
169	Sedrick Irvin RC	.75	.30
170	Edgerrin James RC	6.00	2.50
171	James Johnson RC	1.25	.50
172	Kevin Johnson RC	1.50	.60
173	Andy Katzenmoyer RC	1.25	.50
174	Jevon Kearse RC	2.50	1.00
175	Shaun King RC	1.25	.50
176	Rob Konrad RC	1.25	.50
177	Chris McAlister RC	1.25	.50
178	Darnell McDonald RC	1.25	.50
179	Donovan McNabb RC	8.00	3.00
180	Cade McNown RC	1.25	.50
181	Dat Nguyen RC	1.50	.60
182	Peerless Price RC	1.50	.60
183	Akili Smith RC	1.25	.50
184	Tai Streets RC	1.50	.60
185	Cuncho Brown RC UER	.75	.30
186	Ricky Williams RC	3.00	1.25
187	Craig Yeast RC	1.25	.50
188	Amos Zereoue RC	1.50	.60
189	Checklist	.30	.10
190	Checklist	.30	.10

1998 Collector's Edge First Place

	COMPLETE SET (250)	60.00	35.00
1	Karim Abdul-Jabbar	.75	.30
2	Flozell Adams RC	.60	.25
3	Troy Aikman	1.50	.60
4	Robert Smith	.75	.30
5	Stephen Alexander RC	.75	.30
6	Harold Shaw RC	.60	.25
7	Marcus Allen	.75	.30
8	Terry Allen	.75	.30
9	Mike Alstott	.75	.30
10	Jamal Anderson	.75	.30
11	Reidel Anthony	.50	.20
12	Jamie Asher	.30	.10
13	Darnell Autry	.30	.10
14	Phil Savoy RC	.75	.30

❑ 15 Jon Ritchie RC .75 .30
❑ 16 Tony Banks .50 .20
❑ 17 Tiki Barber .75 .30
❑ 18 Pat Barnes .30 .10
❑ 19 Charlie Batch RC 1.25 .50
❑ 20 Mikhael Ricks RC .75 .30
❑ 21 Jerome Bettis .75 .30
❑ 22 Tim Biakabutuka .50 .20
❑ 23 Roosevelt Blackmon RC .60 .25
❑ 24 Jeff Blake .50 .20
❑ 25 Drew Bledsoe 1.25 .50
❑ 26 Tony Boselli .30 .10
❑ 27 Peter Boulware .30 .10
❑ 28 Tony Brackens .30 .10
❑ 29 Corey Bradford RC 1.25 .50
❑ 30 Michael Pittman RC 1.50 .60
❑ 31 Keith Brooking RC 1.25 .50
❑ 32 Robert Brooks .50 .20
❑ 33 Derrick Brooks .75 .30
❑ 34 Ken Oxendine RC .60 .25
❑ 35 R.W. McQuarters RC .75 .30
❑ 36 Tim Brown .75 .30
❑ 37 Chad Brown .30 .10
❑ 38 Isaac Bruce .75 .30
❑ 39 Mark Brunell .75 .30
❑ 40 Chris Canty .30 .10
❑ 41 Mark Carrier .30 .10
❑ 42 Rae Carruth .30 .10
❑ 43 Ki-Jana Carter .30 .10
❑ 44 Cris Carter .75 .30
❑ 45 Larry Centers .30 .10
❑ 46 Corey Chavous RC 1.25 .50
❑ 47 Mark Chmura .50 .20
❑ 48 Cameron Cleeland RC .60 .25
❑ 49 Dexter Coakley .30 .10
❑ 50 Ben Coates .50 .20
❑ 51 Jonathan Linton RC .75 .30
❑ 52 Todd Collins .30 .10
❑ 53 Kerry Collins .50 .20
❑ 54 Tebucky Jones RC .60 .25
❑ 55 Curtis Conway .50 .20
❑ 56 Sam Cowart RC .75 .30
❑ 57 Bryan Cox .30 .10
❑ 58 Randall Cunningham .75 .30
❑ 59 Terrell Davis .75 .30
❑ 60 Troy Davis .30 .10
❑ 61 Pat Johnson RC .75 .30
❑ 62 Trent Dilfer .75 .30
❑ 63 Vonnie Holliday RC .75 .30
❑ 64 Corey Dillon .75 .30
❑ 65 Hugh Douglas .30 .10
❑ 66 Jim Druckenmiller .30 .10
❑ 67 Warrick Dunn .75 .30
❑ 68 Robert Edwards RC .75 .30
❑ 69 Greg Ellis RC .60 .25
❑ 70 John Elway 3.00 1.25
❑ 71 Bert Emanuel .50 .20
❑ 72 Bobby Engram .50 .20
❑ 73 Curtis Enis RC .60 .25
❑ 74 Marshall Faulk 1.00 .40
❑ 75 Brett Favre 3.00 1.25
❑ 76 Doug Flutie .75 .30
❑ 77 Glenn Foley .50 .20
❑ 78 Antonio Freeman .75 .30
❑ 79 Gus Frerotte .30 .10
❑ 80 John Friesz .30 .10
❑ 81 Irving Fryar .50 .20
❑ 82 Joey Galloway .50 .20
❑ 83 Rich Gannon .75 .30
❑ 84 Charlie Garner .50 .20
❑ 85 Jeff George .50 .20
❑ 86 Eddie George .75 .30
❑ 87 Sean Gilbert .30 .10
❑ 88 Terry Glenn .75 .30
❑ 89 Aaron Glenn .30 .10
❑ 90 Tony Gonzalez .75 .30
❑ 91 Jeff Graham .30 .10
❑ 92 Elvis Grbac .50 .20
❑ 93 Jacquez Green RC .75 .30
❑ 94 Kevin Greene .50 .20
❑ 95 Brian Griese UER RC 2.50 1.00
❑ 96 Byron Hanspard .30 .10
❑ 97 Jim Harbaugh .50 .20
❑ 98 Kevin Hardy .30 .10
❑ 99 Walt Harris .30 .10
❑ 100 Marvin Harrison .75 .30
❑ 101 Rodney Harrison .50 .20
❑ 102 Jeff Hartings .75 .30
❑ 103 Ken Harvey .30 .10
❑ 104 Garrison Hearst .75 .30
❑ 105 Ike Hilliard .50 .20
❑ 106 Jeff Hostetler .30 .10
❑ 107 Bobby Hoying .50 .20
❑ 108 Michael Jackson .30 .10
❑ 109 Anthony Johnson .30 .10
❑ 110 Brad Johnson .75 .30
❑ 111 Keyshawn Johnson .75 .30
❑ 112 Charles Johnson .30 .10
❑ 113 Daryl Johnston .50 .20
❑ 114 Chris Jones .30 .10
❑ 115 George Jones .30 .10
❑ 116 Donald Hayes RC .75 .30
❑ 117 Danny Kanell .50 .20
❑ 118 Napoleon Kaufman .75 .30
❑ 119 Cortez Kennedy .30 .10
❑ 120 Eddie Kennison .50 .20
❑ 121 Levon Kirkland .30 .10
❑ 122 Jon Kitna .75 .30
❑ 123 Erik Kramer .30 .10
❑ 124 David LaFleur .30 .10
❑ 125 Lamar Lathon .30 .10
❑ 126 Ty Law .50 .20
❑ 127 Ryan Leaf RC 1.25 .50
❑ 128 Dorsey Levens .75 .30
❑ 129 Ray Lewis .75 .30
❑ 130 Darryll Lewis .30 .10
❑ 131 Matt Hasselbeck RC 30.00 15.00
❑ 132 Greg Lloyd .30 .10
❑ 133 Kevin Lockett .30 .10
❑ 134 Keith Lyle .30 .10
❑ 135 Peyton Manning RC 15.00 6.00
❑ 136 Dan Marino 3.00 1.25
❑ 137 Wayne Martin .30 .10
❑ 138 Ahman Green RC 6.00 2.50
❑ 139 Tony Martin .50 .20
❑ 140 E.G. Green RC .75 .30
❑ 141 Derrick Mayes .50 .20
❑ 142 Ed McCaffrey .50 .20
❑ 143 Keenan McCardell .50 .20
❑ 144 O.J. McDuffie .50 .20
❑ 145 Leeland McElroy .30 .10
❑ 146 Willie McGinest .30 .10
❑ 147 Chester McGlockton .30 .10
❑ 148 Steve McNair .75 .30
❑ 149 Natrone Means .50 .20
❑ 150 Eric Metcalf .30 .10
❑ 151 Anthony Miller .30 .10
❑ 152 Rick Mirer .30 .10
❑ 153 Scott Mitchell .50 .20
❑ 154 John Mobley .30 .10
❑ 155 Warren Moon .75 .30
❑ 156 Herman Moore .50 .20
❑ 157 Randy Moss RC 10.00 4.00
❑ 158 Eric Moulds .75 .30
❑ 159 Muhsin Muhammad .50 .20
❑ 160 Adrian Murrell .50 .20
❑ 161 Marcus Nash RC .60 .25
❑ 162 Hardy Nickerson .30 .10
❑ 163 Ken Norton .30 .10
❑ 164 Neil O'Donnell .50 .20
❑ 165 Terrell Owens .75 .30
❑ 166 Orlando Pace .30 .10
❑ 167 Jammi German RC .60 .25
❑ 168 Erric Pegram .30 .10
❑ 169 Jason Peter RC .60 .25
❑ 170 Carl Pickens .50 .20
❑ 171 Jake Plummer .75 .30
❑ 172 John Randle .50 .20
❑ 173 Andre Reed .50 .20
❑ 174 Jake Reed .50 .20
❑ 175 Errict Rhett .50 .20
❑ 176 Simeon Rice .50 .20
❑ 177 Jerry Rice 1.50 .60
❑ 178 Andre Rison .50 .20
❑ 179 Darrell Russell .30 .10
❑ 180 Rashaan Salaam .30 .10
❑ 181 Deion Sanders .75 .30
❑ 182 Barry Sanders 2.50 1.00
❑ 183 Chris Sanders .30 .10
❑ 184 Warren Sapp .50 .20
❑ 185 Junior Seau .75 .30
❑ 186 Jason Sehorn .50 .20
❑ 187 Shannon Sharpe .50 .20
❑ 188 Sedrick Shaw .30 .10
❑ 189 Heath Shuler .30 .10
❑ 190 Chris Floyd RC .60 .25
❑ 191 Terry Fair RC .75 .30
❑ 192 Kevin Dyson RC 1.25 .50
❑ 193 Torrance Small .30 .10
❑ 194 Antowain Smith .75 .30
❑ 195 Bruce Smith .50 .20
❑ 196 Tarik Smith RC .75 .30
❑ 197 Emmitt Smith 2.50 1.00
❑ 198 Neil Smith .50 .20
❑ 199 Jimmy Smith .50 .20
❑ 200 Chris Spielman .30 .10
❑ 201 Danny Wuerffel .50 .20
❑ 202 Irving Spikes .30 .10
❑ 203 Shawn Springs .30 .10
❑ 204 Duane Starks RC .60 .25
❑ 205 Kordell Stewart .75 .30
❑ 206 J.J. Stokes .50 .20
❑ 207 Eric Swann .30 .10
❑ 208 Steve Tasker .30 .10
❑ 209 Tim Dwight RC 1.25 .50
❑ 210 Jason Taylor .50 .20
❑ 211 Vinny Testaverde .50 .20
❑ 212 Thurman Thomas .75 .30
❑ 213 Broderick Thomas .30 .10
❑ 214 Derrick Thomas .75 .30
❑ 215 Zach Thomas .75 .30
❑ 216 Germane Crowell RC .75 .30
❑ 217 Amani Toomer .50 .20
❑ 218 Tamarick Vanover .30 .10
❑ 219 Ross Verba .30 .10
❑ 220 Andre Wadsworth RC .75 .30
❑ 221 Ray Zellars .30 .10
❑ 222 Chris Warren .50 .20
❑ 223 Steve Young 1.00 .40
❑ 224 Tyrone Wheatley .50 .20
❑ 225 Reggie White .75 .30
❑ 226 John Avery RC .75 .30
❑ 227 Charles Woodson RC 1.50 .60
❑ 228 Takeo Spikes RC 1.25 .50
❑ 229 Bryant Young .30 .10
❑ 230 Tavian Banks RC .50 .20
❑ 231 Fred Beasley RC .60 .25
❑ 232 Chris Ruhman RC .60 .25
❑ CK1A Broncos Logo CL .10 .02
❑ CK1B Steelers Logo CL .10 .02
❑ CK2A 49ers Logo CL .10 .02
❑ CK2B Panthers Logo CL .10 .02
❑ CK3A Giants Logo CL .10 .02
❑ CK3B Packers Logo CL .10 .02
❑ CK4A Colts Logo CL .10 .02
❑ CK4B Dolphins Logo CL .10 .02
❑ CK5A Chargers Logo CL .10 .02
❑ CK5B Vikings Logo Cl .10 .02
❑ CK6A Patriots Logo Cl .10 .02
❑ CK6B Raiders Logo CL .10 .02
❑ CK7A Buccaneers Logo CL .10 .02
❑ CK7B Cowboys Logo CL .10 .02
❑ CK8A Bills Logo CL .10 .02
❑ CK8B Lions Logo CL .10 .02
❑ CK9A Chiefs Logo CL .10 .02
❑ CK9B Seahawks Logo CL .10 .02

1999 Collector's Edge First Place

❑ COMPLETE SET (200) 50.00 20.00
❑ 1 Adrian Murrell .50 .20
❑ 2 Rob Moore .50 .20
❑ 3 Jake Plummer .50 .20
❑ 4 Simeon Rice .50 .20
❑ 5 Frank Sanders .50 .20
❑ 6 Jamal Anderson .75 .30
❑ 7 Chris Calloway .30 .10
❑ 8 Chris Chandler .50 .20
❑ 9 Tim Dwight .75 .30

❑ 10 Terance Mathis .50 .20
❑ 11 Jessie Tuggle .30 .10
❑ 12 Tony Banks .50 .20
❑ 13 Priest Holmes 1.25 .50
❑ 14 Jermaine Lewis .50 .20
❑ 15 Scott Mitchell .30 .10
❑ 16 Doug Flutie .75 .30
❑ 17 Eric Moulds .75 .30
❑ 18 Andre Reed .50 .20
❑ 19 Antowain Smith .75 .30
❑ 20 Bruce Smith .50 .20
❑ 21 Thurman Thomas .50 .20
❑ 22 Steve Beuerlein .50 .20
❑ 23 Tim Biakabutuka .50 .20
❑ 24 Kevin Greene .30 .10
❑ 25 Muhsin Muhammad .50 .20
❑ 26 Edgar Bennett .30 .10
❑ 27 Curtis Conway .50 .20
❑ 28 Bobby Engram .50 .20
❑ 29 Curtis Enis .30 .10
❑ 30 Erik Kramer .30 .10
❑ 31 Jeff Blake .50 .20
❑ 32 Corey Dillon .75 .30
❑ 33 Carl Pickens .50 .20
❑ 34 Darnay Scott .30 .10
❑ 35 Takeo Spikes .30 .10
❑ 36 Ty Detmer .30 .10
❑ 37 Terry Kirby .30 .10
❑ 38 Leslie Shepherd .30 .10
❑ 39 Chris Spielman .30 .10
❑ 40 Troy Aikman 1.50 .60
❑ 41 Michael Irvin .50 .20
❑ 42 Rocket Ismail .50 .20
❑ 43 Ernie Mills .30 .10
❑ 44 Deion Sanders .75 .30
❑ 45 Emmitt Smith 1.50 .60
❑ 46 Chris Warren .30 .10
❑ 47 Bubba Brister .30 .10
❑ 48 Terrell Davis .75 .30
❑ 49 Brian Griese .75 .30
❑ 50 Ed McCaffrey .50 .20
❑ 51 Shannon Sharpe .50 .20
❑ 52 Rod Smith .50 .20
❑ 53 Charlie Batch .75 .30
❑ 54 Terry Fair .30 .10
❑ 55 Herman Moore .50 .20
❑ 56 Johnnie Morton .50 .20
❑ 57 Barry Sanders 2.50 1.00
❑ 58 Santana Dotson .30 .10
❑ 59 Brett Favre 2.50 1.00
❑ 60 Mark Chmura .30 .10
❑ 61 Antonio Freeman .75 .30
❑ 62 Dorsey Levens .75 .30
❑ 63 Derrick Mayes .50 .20
❑ 64 Marvin Harrison .75 .30
❑ 65 Peyton Manning 2.50 1.00
❑ 66 Jerome Pathon .30 .10
❑ 67 Mark Brunell .75 .30
❑ 68 Keenan McCardell .50 .20
❑ 69 Jimmy Smith .50 .20
❑ 70 Fred Taylor .75 .30
❑ 71 Derrick Alexander WR .50 .20
❑ 72 Kimble Anders .50 .20
❑ 73 Elvis Grbac .50 .20
❑ 74 Warren Moon .75 .30
❑ 75 Byron Bam Morris .30 .10
❑ 76 Andre Rison .50 .20
❑ 77 Karim Abdul-Jabbar .50 .20
❑ 78 Dan Marino 2.50 1.00
❑ 79 Tony Martin .50 .20
❑ 80 O.J. McDuffie .50 .20
❑ 81 Zach Thomas .75 .30
❑ 82 Cris Carter .75 .30
❑ 83 Randall Cunningham .75 .30
❑ 84 Jeff George .50 .20
❑ 85 Randy Moss 2.00 .75
❑ 86 Jake Reed .50 .20
❑ 87 Robert Smith .75 .30
❑ 88 Drew Bledsoe 1.00 .40
❑ 89 Ben Coates .50 .20
❑ 90 Terry Glenn .75 .30
❑ 91 Ty Law .50 .20
❑ 92 Shawn Jefferson .30 .10
❑ 93 Cameron Cleeland .30 .10
❑ 94 Andre Hastings .30 .10
❑ 95 Billy Joe Hobert .30 .10
❑ 96 Eddie Kennison .50 .20
❑ 97 Gary Brown .30 .10
❑ 98 Kerry Collins .50 .20
❑ 99 Kent Graham .30 .10
❑ 100 Ike Hilliard .30 .10
❑ 101 Joe Jurevicius .50 .20
❑ 102 Wayne Chrebet .50 .20
❑ 103 Aaron Glenn .30 .10
❑ 104 Keyshawn Johnson .75 .30
❑ 105 Mo Lewis .30 .10
❑ 106 Curtis Martin .75 .30
❑ 107 Vinny Testaverde .50 .20
❑ 108 Tim Brown .75 .30
❑ 109 Rich Gannon .75 .30
❑ 110 James Jett .50 .20
❑ 111 Napoleon Kaufman .75 .30
❑ 112 Charles Woodson .75 .30
❑ 113 Koy Detmer .30 .10
❑ 114 Charles Johnson .30 .10
❑ 115 Duce Staley .75 .30
❑ 116 Jerome Bettis .75 .30
❑ 117 Courtney Hawkins .30 .10
❑ 118 Levon Kirkland .30 .10
❑ 119 Kordell Stewart .50 .20
❑ 120 Isaac Bruce .75 .30
❑ 121 Marshall Faulk 1.00 .40
❑ 122 Trent Green .75 .30
❑ 123 Amp Lee .30 .10
❑ 124 Jim Harbaugh .50 .20
❑ 125 Bryan Still .30 .10
❑ 126 Freddie Jones .30 .10
❑ 127 Mikhael Ricks .30 .10
❑ 128 Natrone Means .50 .20
❑ 129 Junior Seau .75 .30
❑ 130 Lawrence Phillips .50 .20
❑ 131 Terrell Owens .75 .30
❑ 132 Jerry Rice 1.50 .60
❑ 133 J.J. Stokes .50 .20
❑ 134 Steve Young 1.00 .40
❑ 135 Joey Galloway .50 .20
❑ 136 Jon Kitna .75 .30
❑ 137 Ricky Watters .50 .20
❑ 138 Mike Alstott .75 .30
❑ 139 Reidel Anthony .50 .20
❑ 140 Trent Dilfer .50 .20
❑ 141 Warrick Dunn .75 .30
❑ 142 Kevin Dyson .50 .20
❑ 143 Eddie George .75 .30
❑ 144 Steve McNair .75 .30
❑ 145 Frank Wycheck .30 .10
❑ 146 Skip Hicks .30 .10
❑ 147 Brad Johnson .75 .30
❑ 148 Michael Westbrook .50 .20
❑ 149 Checklist Card .30 .10
❑ 150 Checklist Card .30 .10
❑ 151 David Boston RC 1.25 .50
❑ 152 Patrick Kerney RC 1.25 .50
❑ 153 Chris McAlister RC 1.00 .40
❑ 154 Peerless Price RC 1.25 .50
❑ 155 Antoine Winfield RC 1.00 .40
❑ 156 D'Wayne Bates RC 1.00 .40
❑ 157 Cade McNown RC 1.00 .40
❑ 158 Akili Smith RC 1.00 .40
❑ 159 Rahim Abdullah RC 1.00 .40
❑ 160 Tim Couch RC 1.25 .50
❑ 161 Kevin Johnson RC 1.25 .50
❑ 162 Ebenezer Ekuban RC 1.00 .40
❑ 163 Dat Nguyen RC 1.25 .50
❑ 164 Al Wilson RC 1.00 .40
❑ 165 Chris Claiborne RC .60 .25
❑ 166 Sedrick Irvin RC .60 .25
❑ 167 Antuan Edwards RC 1.00 .40
❑ 168 Aaron Brooks RC 2.50 1.00
❑ 169 De'Mond Parker RC .60 .25
❑ 170 Edgerrin James RC 5.00 2.00
❑ 171 Fernando Bryant RC 1.00 .40
❑ 172 Mike Cloud RC 1.00 .40
❑ 173 John Tait RC .60 .25
❑ 174 Cecil Collins RC .60 .25
❑ 175 James Johnson RC 1.00 .40
❑ 176 Rob Konrad RC 1.25 .50
❑ 177 Daunte Culpepper RC 5.00 2.00
❑ 178 Jim Kleinsasser RC 1.25 .50
❑ 179 Brock Huard RC 1.25 .50
❑ 180 Michael Bishop RC 1.25 .50
❑ 181 Kevin Faulk RC 1.25 .50
❑ 182 Andy Katzenmoyer RC 1.00 .40
❑ 183 Ricky Williams RC 2.50 1.00
❑ 184 Joe Montgomery RC 1.00 .40
❑ 185 Donovan McNabb RC 6.00 2.50
❑ 186 Troy Edwards RC 1.00 .40
❑ 187 Amos Zereoue RC 1.25 .50
❑ 188 Joe Germaine RC 1.00 .40
❑ 189 Torry Holt RC 3.00 1.25
❑ 190 Jermaine Fazande RC 1.00 .40
❑ 191 Reggie McGrew RC 1.00 .40
❑ 192 Karsten Bailey RC 1.00 .40
❑ 193 Lamar King RC .60 .25
❑ 194 Autry Denson RC 1.00 .40
❑ 195 Martin Gramatica RC .60 .25
❑ 196 Shaun King RC 1.00 .40
❑ 197 Darnell McDonald RC 1.00 .40
❑ 198 Anthony McFarland RC 1.25 .50
❑ 199 Jevon Kearse RC 2.00 .75
❑ 200 Champ Bailey RC 1.50 .60
❑ 201 Kurt Warner RC/500 100.00 40.00
❑ 201PG Kurt Warner Promo Gold 12.00 5.00
❑ 201PS Kurt Warner Promo Silver 12.00 5.00

1998 Collector's Edge Odyssey

❑ COMPLETE SET (250) 400.00 200.00
❑ 1 Terance Mathis .30 .10
❑ 2 Tony Martin .30 .10
❑ 3 Chris Chandler .30 .10
❑ 4 Jamal Anderson .50 .20
❑ 5 Jake Plummer .50 .20
❑ 6 Adrian Murrell .30 .10
❑ 7 Rob Moore .30 .10
❑ 8 Frank Sanders .30 .10
❑ 9 Larry Centers .20 .07
❑ 10 Andre Wadsworth RC 1.25 .50
❑ 11 Jim Harbaugh .30 .10
❑ 12 Errict Rhett .30 .10
❑ 13 Jermaine Lewis .30 .10
❑ 14 Michael Jackson .20 .07
❑ 15 Eric Zeier .30 .10
❑ 16 Rob Johnson .30 .10
❑ 17 Antowain Smith .50 .20
❑ 18 Andre Reed .30 .10
❑ 19 Bruce Smith .30 .10
❑ 20 Doug Flutie .50 .20
❑ 21 Thurman Thomas .50 .20
❑ 22 Kerry Collins .30 .10
❑ 23 Fred Lane .20 .07
❑ 24 Muhsin Muhammad .30 .10
❑ 25 Rae Carruth .20 .07
❑ 26 Rocket Ismail .20 .07
❑ 27 Kevin Greene .30 .10
❑ 28 Curtis Enis RC .75 .30
❑ 29 Curtis Conway .30 .10
❑ 30 Erik Kramer .20 .07
❑ 31 Edgar Bennett .20 .07
❑ 32 Neil O'Donnell .30 .10
❑ 33 Jeff Blake .30 .10
❑ 34 Carl Pickens .30 .10
❑ 35 Corey Dillon .50 .20
❑ 36 Troy Aikman 1.00 .40
❑ 37 Jason Garrett RC .20 .07
❑ 38 Emmitt Smith 1.50 .60
❑ 39 Deion Sanders .50 .20
❑ 40 Michael Irvin .50 .20
❑ 41 Chris Warren .30 .10
❑ 42 John Elway 2.00 .75
❑ 43 Terrell Davis .50 .20
❑ 44 Shannon Sharpe .30 .10
❑ 45 Rod Smith WR .30 .10
❑ 46 Marcus Nash RC .75 .30
❑ 47 Brian Griese RC 3.00 1.25
❑ 48 Barry Sanders 1.50 .60
❑ 49 Herman Moore .30 .10
❑ 50 Scott Mitchell .30 .10
❑ 51 Johnnie Morton .30 .10

❑ 52 Rashaan Shehee RC	1.25	.50
❑ 53 Charlie Batch RC	1.50	.60
❑ 54 Brett Favre	2.00	.75
❑ 55 Dorsey Levens	.50	.20
❑ 56 Antonio Freeman	.50	.20
❑ 57 Reggie White	.50	.20
❑ 58 Robert Brooks	.30	.10
❑ 59 Raymont Harris	.20	.07
❑ 60 Peyton Manning RC	15.00	6.00
❑ 61 Marshall Faulk	.60	.25
❑ 62 Jerome Pathon RC	1.50	.60
❑ 63 Marvin Harrison	.50	.20
❑ 64 Mark Brunell	.50	.20
❑ 65 Fred Taylor RC	2.50	1.00
❑ 66 Jimmy Smith	.30	.10
❑ 67 James Stewart	.30	.10
❑ 68 Keenan McCardell	.30	.10
❑ 69 Andre Rison	.30	.10
❑ 70 Elvis Grbac	.30	.10
❑ 71 Donnell Bennett	.20	.07
❑ 72 Rich Gannon	.50	.20
❑ 73 Derrick Thomas	.50	.20
❑ 74 Dan Marino	2.00	.75
❑ 75 Karim Abdul-Jabbar UER	.50	.20
❑ 76 John Avery RC UER	1.25	.50
❑ 77 O.J. McDuffie	.30	.10
❑ 78 Oronde Gadsden RC	1.50	.60
❑ 79 Zach Thomas	.50	.20
❑ 80 Randy Moss RC	10.00	4.00
❑ 81 Cris Carter	.50	.20
❑ 82 Jake Reed	.30	.10
❑ 83 Robert Smith	.50	.20
❑ 84 Brad Johnson	.50	.20
❑ 85 Drew Bledsoe	.75	.30
❑ 86 Robert Edwards RC	1.25	.50
❑ 87 Terry Glenn	.50	.20
❑ 88 Troy Brown	.30	.10
❑ 89 Shawn Jefferson	.20	.07
❑ 90 Danny Wuerffel	.30	.10
❑ 91 Dana Stubblefield	.20	.07
❑ 92 Derrick Alexander	.30	.10
❑ 93 Ray Zellars	.20	.07
❑ 94 Andre Hastings	.20	.07
❑ 95 Danny Kanell	.30	.10
❑ 96 Tiki Barber	.50	.20
❑ 97 Ike Hilliard	.30	.10
❑ 98 Charles Way	.20	.07
❑ 99 Chris Calloway	.20	.07
❑ 100 Curtis Martin	.50	.20
❑ 101 Glenn Foley	.30	.10
❑ 102 Vinny Testaverde	.30	.10
❑ 103 Keyshawn Johnson	.50	.20
❑ 104 Wayne Chrebet	.50	.20
❑ 105 Leon Johnson	.20	.07
❑ 106 Jeff George	.30	.10
❑ 107 Charles Woodson RC	2.50	1.00
❑ 108 Tim Brown	.50	.20
❑ 109 James Jett	.30	.10
❑ 110 Napoleon Kaufman	.50	.20
❑ 111 Charlie Garner	.30	.10
❑ 112 Bobby Hoying	.30	.10
❑ 113 Duce Staley	.75	.30
❑ 114 Irving Fryar	.30	.10
❑ 115 Kordell Stewart	.50	.20
❑ 116 Jerome Bettis	.50	.20
❑ 117 Charles Johnson	.20	.07
❑ 118 Randall Cunningham	.50	.20
❑ 119 Courtney Hawkins	.20	.07
❑ 120 Tony Banks	.30	.10
❑ 121 Isaac Bruce	.50	.20
❑ 122 Robert Holcombe RC	1.25	.50
❑ 123 Eddie Kennison	.30	.10
❑ 124 Ryan Leaf RC	1.50	.60
❑ 125 Mikhael Ricks RC	1.25	.50
❑ 126 Natrone Means	.30	.10
❑ 127 Junior Seau	.50	.20
❑ 128 Jerry Rice	1.00	.40
❑ 129 Terrell Owens	.50	.20
❑ 130 Garrison Hearst	.50	.20
❑ 131 Steve Young	.50	.20
❑ 132 J.J. Stokes	.30	.10
❑ 133 Warren Moon	.50	.20
❑ 134 Joey Galloway	.30	.10
❑ 135 Ricky Watters	.30	.10
❑ 136 Ahman Green RC	8.00	3.00
❑ 137 Trent Dilfer	.50	.20
❑ 138 Mike Alstott	.50	.20
❑ 139 Warrick Dunn	.50	.20
❑ 140 Reidel Anthony	.30	.10
❑ 141 Jacquez Green RC	1.25	.50
❑ 142 Steve McNair	.50	.20
❑ 143 Eddie George	.50	.20
❑ 144 Yancey Thigpen	.20	.07
❑ 145 Kevin Dyson RC	1.50	.60
❑ 146 Trent Green	.60	.25
❑ 147 Gus Frerotte	.20	.07
❑ 148 Terry Allen	.50	.20
❑ 149 Michael Westbrook	.30	.10
❑ 150 Jim Druckenmiller	.20	.07
❑ 151 Jake Plummer 2Q	.75	.30
❑ 152 Adrian Murrell 2Q	.50	.20
❑ 153 Rob Johnson 2Q	.50	.20
❑ 154 Antowain Smith 2Q	.75	.30
❑ 155 Kerry Collins 2Q	.50	.20
❑ 156 Curtis Enis 2Q	.50	.20
❑ 157 Carl Pickens 2Q	.50	.20
❑ 158 Corey Dillon 2Q	.75	.30
❑ 159 Troy Aikman 2Q	1.50	.60
❑ 160 Emmitt Smith 2Q	2.00	.75
❑ 161 Deion Sanders 2Q	.75	.30
❑ 162 Michael Irvin 2Q	.75	.30
❑ 163 John Elway 2Q	3.00	1.25
❑ 164 Terrell Davis 2Q	.75	.30
❑ 165 Shannon Sharpe 2Q	.50	.20
❑ 166 Rod Smith 2Q	.50	.20
❑ 167 Barry Sanders 2Q	2.50	1.00
❑ 168 Herman Moore 2Q	.50	.20
❑ 169 Brett Favre 2Q	3.00	1.25
❑ 170 Dorsey Levens 2Q	.75	.30
❑ 171 Antonio Freeman 2Q	.75	.30
❑ 172 Peyton Manning 2Q	12.00	5.00
❑ 173 Marshall Faulk 2Q	1.00	.40
❑ 174 Mark Brunell 2Q	.75	.30
❑ 175 Fred Taylor 2Q	3.00	1.25
❑ 176 Dan Marino 2Q	3.00	1.25
❑ 177 Randy Moss 2Q	10.00	4.00
❑ 178 Cris Carter 2Q	.75	.30
❑ 179 Drew Bledsoe 2Q	1.00	.40
❑ 180 Robert Edwards 2Q	.50	.20
❑ 181 Curtis Martin 2Q	.75	.30
❑ 182 Napoleon Kaufman 2Q	.75	.30
❑ 183 Kordell Stewart 2Q	.50	.20
❑ 184 Jerome Bettis 2Q	.75	.30
❑ 185 Tony Banks 2Q	.50	.20
❑ 186 Isaac Bruce 2Q	.75	.30
❑ 187 Ryan Leaf 2Q	.75	.30
❑ 188 Natrone Means 2Q	.50	.20
❑ 189 Jerry Rice 2Q	1.50	.60
❑ 190 Terrell Owens 2Q	.75	.30
❑ 191 Garrison Hearst 2Q	.75	.30
❑ 192 Steve Young 2Q	.75	.30
❑ 193 Warren Moon 2Q	.75	.30
❑ 194 Joey Galloway 2Q	.50	.20
❑ 195 Trent Dilfer 2Q	.75	.30
❑ 196 Mike Alstott 2Q	.75	.30
❑ 197 Warrick Dunn 2Q	.75	.30
❑ 198 Steve McNair 2Q	.75	.30
❑ 199 Eddie George 2Q	.75	.30
❑ 200 Terry Allen 2Q	.75	.30
❑ 201 Jake Plummer 3Q	1.00	.40
❑ 202 Curtis Enis 3Q	.60	.25
❑ 203 Carl Pickens 3Q	.60	.25
❑ 204 Corey Dillon 3Q	1.00	.40
❑ 205 Troy Aikman 3Q	2.00	.75
❑ 206 Emmitt Smith 3Q	3.00	1.25
❑ 207 John Elway 3Q	4.00	1.50
❑ 208 Terrell Davis 3Q	1.00	.40
❑ 209 Barry Sanders 3Q	3.00	1.25
❑ 210 Brett Favre 3Q	4.00	1.50
❑ 211 Antonio Freeman 3Q	1.00	.40
❑ 212 Peyton Manning 3Q	15.00	6.00
❑ 213 Mark Brunell 3Q	1.00	.40
❑ 214 Fred Taylor 3Q	4.00	1.50
❑ 215 Dan Marino 3Q	4.00	1.50
❑ 216 Randy Moss 3Q	12.00	5.00
❑ 217 Drew Bledsoe 3Q	1.50	.60
❑ 218 Robert Edwards 3Q	.60	.25
❑ 219 Curtis Martin 3Q	1.00	.40
❑ 220 Kordell Stewart 3Q	1.00	.40
❑ 221 Jerome Bettis 3Q	1.00	.40
❑ 222 Tony Banks 3Q	.60	.25
❑ 223 Ryan Leaf 3Q	1.00	.40
❑ 224 Jerry Rice 3Q	2.00	.75
❑ 225 Steve Young 3Q	1.00	.40
❑ 226 Warren Moon 3Q	1.00	.40
❑ 227 Trent Dilfer 3Q	1.00	.40
❑ 228 Warrick Dunn 3Q	1.00	.40
❑ 229 Steve McNair 3Q	1.00	.40
❑ 230 Eddie George 3Q	1.00	.40
❑ 231 Curtis Enis 4Q	3.00	1.25
❑ 232 Carl Pickens 4Q	3.00	1.25
❑ 233 Troy Aikman 4Q	6.00	2.50
❑ 234 Emmitt Smith 4Q	10.00	4.00
❑ 235 John Elway 4Q	12.00	5.00
❑ 236 Terrell Davis 4Q	3.00	1.25
❑ 237 Barry Sanders 4Q	10.00	4.00
❑ 238 Brett Favre 4Q	12.00	5.00
❑ 239 Peyton Manning 4Q	25.00	10.00
❑ 240 Fred Taylor 4Q	6.00	2.50
❑ 241 Dan Marino 4Q	12.00	5.00
❑ 242 Randy Moss 4Q	20.00	7.50
❑ 243 Drew Bledsoe 4Q	5.00	2.00
❑ 244 Kordell Stewart 4Q	3.00	1.25
❑ 245 Jerome Bettis 4Q	3.00	1.25
❑ 246 Ryan Leaf 4Q	3.00	1.25
❑ 247 Jerry Rice 4Q	6.00	2.50
❑ 248 Steve Young 4Q	4.00	1.50
❑ 249 Warren Moon 4Q	3.00	1.25
❑ 250 Eddie George 4Q	3.00	1.25

1999 Collector's Edge Odyssey

❑ COMPLETE SET (193)	120.00	50.00
❑ COMP.SET w/o SP's (148)	40.00	20.00
❑ 1 Checklist Card	.30	.10
❑ 2 Checklist Card	.30	.10
❑ 3 David Boston RC	1.00	.40
❑ 4 Rob Moore	.50	.20
❑ 5 Adrian Murrell	.50	.20
❑ 6 Jake Plummer	.50	.20
❑ 7 Frank Sanders	.50	.20
❑ 8 Jamal Anderson	.75	.30
❑ 9 Chris Calloway	.30	.10
❑ 10 Chris Chandler	.50	.20
❑ 11 Tim Dwight	.75	.30
❑ 12 Terance Mathis	.50	.20
❑ 13 Tony Banks	.50	.20
❑ 14 Priest Holmes	1.25	.50
❑ 15 Jermaine Lewis	.50	.20
❑ 16 Chris McAlister RC	.75	.30
❑ 17 Scott Mitchell	.50	.20
❑ 18 Doug Flutie	.75	.30
❑ 19 Eric Moulds	.75	.30
❑ 20 Peerless Price RC	1.00	.40
❑ 21 A.Smith/A.Reed SP	80.00	30.00
❑ 22 Antowain Smith	.75	.30
❑ 23 Antoine Winfield RC	.75	.30
❑ 24 Steve Beuerlein	.50	.20
❑ 25 Tim Biakabutuka	.50	.20
❑ 26 Rae Carruth	.30	.10
❑ 27 Muhsin Muhammad	.50	.20
❑ 28 D'Wayne Bates RC	.75	.30
❑ 29 Bobby Engram	.50	.20
❑ 30 Curtis Enis	.30	.10
❑ 31 Shane Matthews	.75	.30
❑ 32 Cade McNown RC	.75	.30
❑ 33 Jeff Blake	.50	.20
❑ 34 Corey Dillon	.75	.30
❑ 35 Carl Pickens	.50	.20
❑ 36 Darnay Scott	.50	.20
❑ 37 Akili Smith RC	.75	.30
❑ 38 Tim Couch RC	1.00	.40
❑ 39 Kevin Johnson RC	1.00	.40
❑ 40 Terry Kirby	.50	.20
❑ 41 Leslie Shepherd	.30	.10
❑ 42 Troy Aikman	1.50	.60
❑ 43 Michael Irvin	.50	.20
❑ 44 Rocket Ismail	.50	.20
❑ 45 Deion Sanders	.75	.30

46	Emmitt Smith	1.50	.60
47	Bubby Brister	.50	.20
48	Terrell Davis	.75	.30
49	Brian Griese	.75	.30
50	Ed McCaffrey	.50	.20
51	Shannon Sharpe	.50	.20
52	Rod Smith	.50	.20
53	Charlie Batch	.75	.30
54	Chris Claiborne RC	.75	.30
56	Herman Moore	.50	.20
57	Johnnie Morton	.50	.20
58	Ron Rivers	.30	.10
59	Brett Favre	2.50	1.00
60	Mark Chmura	.50	.20
61	Antonio Freeman	.75	.30
62	Dorsey Levens	.75	.30
63	E.G. Green	.30	.10
64	Marvin Harrison	.75	.30
65	Edgerrin James RC	4.00	1.50
66	Peyton Manning	2.50	1.00
67	Mark Brunell	.75	.30
68	Keenan McCardell	.50	.20
69	Jimmy Smith	.50	.20
70	Fred Taylor	.75	.30
71	Derrick Alexander WR	.50	.20
72	Kimble Anders	.50	.20
73	Mike Cloud RC	.75	.30
74	Elvis Grbac	.50	.20
75	Andre Rison	.50	.20
76	Karim Abdul-Jabbar	.50	.20
77	Cecil Collins RC	.50	.20
78	James Johnson RC	.75	.30
79	Rob Konrad RC	1.00	.40
80	Dan Marino	2.50	1.00
81	O.J. McDuffie	.50	.20
82	Cris Carter	.75	.30
83	Daunte Culpepper RC	4.00	1.50
84	Randall Cunningham	.75	.30
85	Randy Moss	2.00	.75
86	Jake Reed	.50	.20
87	Robert Smith	.75	.30
88	Terry Allen	.50	.20
89	Drew Bledsoe	1.00	.40
90	Ben Coates	.30	.10
91	Kevin Faulk RC	1.00	.40
92	Terry Glenn	.75	.30
93	Andy Katzenmoyer RC	.75	.30
94	Cameron Cleeland	.30	.10
95	Billy Joe Hobert	.30	.10
96	Eddie Kennison	.50	.20
97	Ricky Williams RC	2.00	.75
98	Sean Bennett RC	.50	.20
99	Gary Brown	.30	.10
100	Kerry Collins	.50	.20
101	Kent Graham	.30	.10
102	Ike Hilliard	.50	.20
103	Wayne Chrebet	.75	.30
104	Keyshawn Johnson	.75	.30
105	Curtis Martin	.75	.30
106	Rick Mirer	.30	.10
107	Tim Brown	.75	.30
108	Rich Gannon	.75	.30
109	Napoleon Kaufman	.75	.30
110	Charles Woodson	.75	.30
111	Charles Johnson	.30	.10
112	Donovan McNabb RC	5.00	2.00
113	Doug Pederson	.50	.20
114	Duce Staley	.75	.30
115	Jerome Bettis	.75	.30
116	Troy Edwards RC	.75	.30
117	Kordell Stewart	.50	.20
118	Amos Zereoue RC	1.00	.40
119	Isaac Bruce	.75	.30
120	Marshall Faulk	1.00	.40
121	Joe Germaine RC	.75	.30
122	Torry Holt RC	2.50	1.00
123	Kurt Warner RC	10.00	4.00
124	Jim Harbaugh	.50	.20
125	Erik Kramer	.30	.10
126	Natrone Means	.50	.20
127	Junior Seau	.75	.30
128	Terrell Owens	.75	.30
129	Lawrence Phillips	.50	.20
130	Jerry Rice	1.50	.60
131	J.J. Stokes	.50	.20
132	Steve Young	1.00	.40
133	Karsten Bailey RC	.75	.30
134	Joey Galloway	.50	.20
135	Brock Huard RC	1.00	.40
136	Jon Kitna	.75	.30
137	Ricky Watters	.50	.20
138	Reidel Anthony	.30	.10
139	Trent Dilfer	.50	.20
140	Warrick Dunn	.75	.30
141	Shaun King RC	.75	.30
142	Jevon Kearse RC	1.50	.60
143	Kevin Dyson	.50	.20
144	Eddie George	.75	.30
145	Steve McNair	.75	.30
146	Champ Bailey RC	1.25	.50
147	Stephen Davis	.75	.30
148	Skip Hicks	.30	.10
149	Brad Johnson	.75	.30
150	Michael Westbrook	.50	.20
151	Chris McAlister 2Q	1.00	.40
152	Peerless Price 2Q	1.25	.50
153	Antoine Winfield 2Q	1.25	.50
154	D'Wayne Bates 2Q	1.00	.40
155	Kevin Johnson 2Q	1.25	.50
156	Chris Claiborne 2Q	1.00	.40
157	Sedrick Irvin 2Q	1.00	.40
158	Mike Cloud 2Q	1.25	.50
159	Cecil Collins 2Q	1.00	.40
160	James Johnson 2Q	1.25	.50
161	Rob Konrad 2Q	1.25	.50
162	Daunte Culpepper 2Q	3.00	1.25
163	Andy Katzenmoyer 2Q	1.25	.50
164	Amos Zereoue 2Q	1.25	.50
165	Joe Germaine 2Q	1.25	.50
166	Karsten Bailey 2Q	1.25	.50
167	Brock Huard 2Q	1.25	.50
168	Shaun King 2Q	1.25	.50
169	Jevon Kearse 2Q	2.00	.75
170	Champ Bailey 2Q	1.50	.60
171	Jake Plummer 3Q	2.00	.75
172	Doug Flutie 3Q	.75	.30
173	Troy Aikman 3Q	5.00	2.00
174	Emmitt Smith 3Q	5.00	2.00
175	Terrell Davis 3Q	2.50	1.00
176	Barry Sanders 3Q	8.00	3.00
177	Brett Favre 3Q	8.00	3.00
178	Peyton Manning 3Q	8.00	3.00
179	Mark Brunell 3Q	.75	.30
180	Fred Taylor 3Q	2.50	1.00
181	Dan Marino 3Q	8.00	3.00
182	Randy Moss 3Q	6.00	2.50
183	Drew Bledsoe 3Q	3.00	1.25
184	Jerry Rice 3Q	5.00	2.00
185	Steve Young 3Q	3.00	1.25
186	David Boston 4Q	5.00	2.00
187	Cade McNown 4Q	5.00	2.00
188	Akili Smith 4Q	5.00	2.00
189	Tim Couch 4Q	5.00	2.00
190	Edgerrin James 4Q	12.00	5.00
191	Kevin Faulk 4Q	5.00	2.00
192	Ricky Williams 4Q	6.00	2.50
193	Donovan McNabb 4Q	15.00	6.00
194	Troy Edwards 4Q	5.00	2.00
195	Torry Holt 4Q	10.00	4.00

2000 Collector's Edge Odyssey

	COMPLETE SET (190)	400.00	250.00
	COMP.SET w/o SP's (100)	15.00	6.00
1	David Boston	.75	.30
2	Jake Plummer	.50	.20
3	Frank Sanders	.50	.20
4	Jamal Anderson	.75	.30
5	Chris Chandler	.50	.20
6	Terance Mathis	.50	.20
7	Tony Banks	.50	.20
8	Qadry Ismail	.50	.20
9	Doug Flutie	.75	.30
10	Rob Johnson	.50	.20
11	Eric Moulds	.75	.30
12	Peerless Price	.50	.20
13	Antowain Smith	.50	.20
14	Steve Beuerlein	.30	.10
15	Tim Biakabutuka	.50	.20
16	Muhsin Muhammad	.50	.20
17	Curtis Enis	.30	.10
18	Cade McNown	.30	.10
19	Marcus Robinson	.75	.30
20	Corey Dillon	.75	.30
21	Akili Smith	.30	.10
22	Tim Couch	.50	.20
23	Kevin Johnson	.75	.30
24	Errict Rhett	.50	.20
25	Troy Aikman	1.50	.60
26	Joey Galloway	.50	.20
27	Rocket Ismail	.50	.20
28	Emmitt Smith	1.50	.60
29	Terrell Davis	.75	.30
30	Olandis Gary	.75	.30
31	Brian Griese	.75	.30
32	Ed McCaffrey	.75	.30
33	Charlie Batch	.75	.30
34	Germane Crowell	.30	.10
35	Herman Moore	.50	.20
36	James Stewart	.50	.20
37	Brett Favre	2.50	1.00
38	Antonio Freeman	.75	.30
39	Dorsey Levens	.50	.20
40	Marvin Harrison	.75	.30
41	Edgerrin James	1.25	.50
42	Peyton Manning	2.00	.75
43	Terrence Wilkins	.30	.10
44	Mark Brunell	.75	.30
45	Keenan McCardell	.50	.20
46	Jimmy Smith	.50	.20
47	Fred Taylor	.75	.30
48	Mike Cloud	.30	.10
49	Tony Gonzalez	.50	.20
50	Elvis Grbac	.50	.20
51	Damon Huard	.75	.30
52	James Johnson	.30	.10
53	Tony Martin	.50	.20
54	Cris Carter	.75	.30
55	Daunte Culpepper	1.00	.40
56	Randy Moss	1.50	.60
57	Robert Smith	.75	.30
58	Drew Bledsoe	1.00	.40
59	Terry Glenn	.50	.20
60	Jeff Blake	.50	.20
61	Ricky Williams	.75	.30
62	Kerry Collins	.50	.20
63	Ike Hilliard	.50	.20
64	Amani Toomer	.50	.20
65	Wayne Chrebet	.50	.20
66	Curtis Martin	.75	.30
67	Vinny Testaverde	.50	.20
68	Tim Brown	.75	.30
69	Rich Gannon	.75	.30
70	Donovan McNabb	1.25	.50
71	Duce Staley	.75	.30
72	Jerome Bettis	.75	.30
73	Troy Edwards	.30	.10
74	Kordell Stewart	.50	.20
75	Isaac Bruce	.75	.30
76	Marshall Faulk	1.00	.40
77	Torry Holt	.75	.30
78	Kurt Warner	1.50	.60
79	Jermaine Fazande	.30	.10
80	Jim Harbaugh	.50	.20
81	Jeff Garcia	.75	.30
82	Charlie Garner	.50	.20
83	Terrell Owens	.75	.30
84	Jerry Rice	1.50	.60
85	Jon Kitna	.75	.30
86	Derrick Mayes	.50	.20
87	Ricky Watters	.50	.20
88	Mike Alstott	.75	.30
89	Warrick Dunn	.75	.30
90	Keyshawn Johnson	.75	.30
91	Shaun King	.30	.10
92	Kevin Dyson	.50	.20
93	Eddie George	.75	.30
94	Jevon Kearse	.75	.30
95	Steve McNair	.75	.30

❑ 96 Carl Pickens	.50	.20
❑ 97 Champ Bailey	.50	.20
❑ 98 Stephen Davis	.75	.30
❑ 99 Brad Johnson	.75	.30
❑ 100 Michael Westbrook	.50	.20
❑ 101 Thomas Jones RC	12.00	5.00
❑ 102 Doug Johnson RC	8.00	3.00
❑ 103 Mareno Philyaw RC	4.00	1.50
❑ 104 Jamal Lewis RC	20.00	7.50
❑ 105 Chris Redman RC	6.00	2.50
❑ 106 Travis Taylor RC	8.00	3.00
❑ 107 Kwame Cavil RC	4.00	1.50
❑ 108 Sammy Morris RC	6.00	2.50
❑ 109 Frank Murphy RC	4.00	1.50
❑ 110 Brian Urlacher RC	30.00	12.50
❑ 111 Dez White RC	8.00	3.00
❑ 112 Ron Dugans RC	4.00	1.50
❑ 113 Curtis Keaton RC	6.00	2.50
❑ 114 Peter Warrick RC	8.00	3.00
❑ 115 Courtney Brown RC	8.00	3.00
❑ 116 JaJuan Dawson RC	4.00	1.50
❑ 117 Dennis Northcutt RC	8.00	3.00
❑ 118 Travis Prentice RC	6.00	2.50
❑ 119 Michael Wiley RC	6.00	2.50
❑ 120 Mike Anderson RC	10.00	4.00
❑ 121 Chris Cole RC	6.00	2.50
❑ 122 Jarious Jackson RC	6.00	2.50
❑ 123 Deltha O'Neal RC	8.00	3.00
❑ 124 Reuben Droughns RC	10.00	4.00
❑ 125 Bubba Franks RC	8.00	3.00
❑ 126 Anthony Lucas RC	4.00	1.50
❑ 127 Rondell Mealey RC	4.00	1.50
❑ 128 Rob Morris RC	6.00	2.50
❑ 129 R.Jay Soward RC	6.00	2.50
❑ 130 Shyrone Stith RC	6.00	2.50
❑ 131 Frank Moreau RC	6.00	2.50
❑ 132 Sylvester Morris RC	6.00	2.50
❑ 133 Doug Chapman RC	6.00	2.50
❑ 134 J.R. Redmond RC	6.00	2.50
❑ 135 Marc Bulger RC	15.00	6.00
❑ 136 Sherrod Gideon RC	4.00	1.50
❑ 137 Terrelle Smith RC	6.00	2.50
❑ 138 Ron Dayne RC	8.00	3.00
❑ 139 Anthony Becht RC	8.00	3.00
❑ 140 Laveranues Coles RC	10.00	4.00
❑ 141 Shaun Ellis RC	8.00	3.00
❑ 142 Chad Pennington RC	20.00	7.50
❑ 143 Sebastian Janikowski RC	8.00	3.00
❑ 144 Jerry Porter RC	10.00	4.00
❑ 145 Todd Pinkston RC	8.00	3.00
❑ 146 Gari Scott RC	4.00	1.50
❑ 147 Corey Simon RC	8.00	3.00
❑ 148 Plaxico Burress RC	15.00	6.00
❑ 149 Danny Farmer RC	6.00	2.50
❑ 150 Tee Martin RC	8.00	3.00
❑ 151 Trung Canidate RC	6.00	2.50
❑ 152 Trevor Gaylor RC	6.00	2.50
❑ 153 Giovanni Carmazzi RC	4.00	1.50
❑ 154 John Engelberger RC	6.00	2.50
❑ 155 Ahmed Plummer RC	8.00	3.00
❑ 156 Tim Rattay RC	8.00	3.00
❑ 157 Shaun Alexander RC	40.00	15.00
❑ 158 Joe Hamilton RC	6.00	2.50
❑ 159 Keith Bulluck RC	8.00	3.00
❑ 160 Todd Husak RC	8.00	3.00
❑ 161 Cade McNown SV	4.00	1.50
❑ 162 Tim Couch SV	1.50	.60
❑ 163 Terrell Davis SV	1.50	.60
❑ 164 Brett Favre SV	6.00	2.50
❑ 165 Edgerrin James SV	3.00	1.25
❑ 166 Peyton Manning SV	5.00	2.00
❑ 167 Daunte Culpepper SV	2.50	1.00
❑ 168 Randy Moss SV	4.00	1.50
❑ 169 Ricky Williams SV	1.50	.60
❑ 170 Kurt Warner SV	4.00	1.50
❑ 171 Cade McNown LV	1.50	.60
❑ 172 Akili Smith LV	1.50	.60
❑ 173 Tim Couch LV	1.50	.60
❑ 174 Troy Aikman LV	4.00	1.50
❑ 175 Emmitt Smith LV	4.00	1.50
❑ 176 Terrell Davis LV	1.50	.60
❑ 177 Brett Favre LV	6.00	2.50
❑ 178 Edgerrin James LV	3.00	1.25
❑ 179 Peyton Manning LV	5.00	2.00
❑ 180 Mark Brunell LV	1.50	.60
❑ 181 Daunte Culpepper LV	2.50	1.00
❑ 182 Randy Moss LV	4.00	1.50
❑ 183 Drew Bledsoe LV	2.50	1.00
❑ 184 Ricky Williams LV	1.50	.60
❑ 185 Donovan McNabb LV	3.00	1.25
❑ 186 Torry Holt LV	1.50	.60
❑ 187 Kurt Warner LV	4.00	1.50
❑ 188 Shaun King LV	1.50	.60
❑ 189 Eddie George LV	1.50	.60
❑ 190 Steve McNair LV	1.50	.60

1996 CE President's Reserve

❑ COMPLETE SET (400)	60.00	30.00
❑ COMP.SERIES 1 (200)	30.00	15.00
❑ COMP.SERIES 2 (200)	30.00	15.00
❑ 1 Larry Centers	.50	.20
❑ 2 Frank Sanders	.50	.20
❑ 3 Clyde Simmons	.25	.08
❑ 4 Eric Swann	.50	.20
❑ 5 Morten Andersen	.25	.08
❑ 6 Lester Archambeau	.25	.08
❑ 7 J.J. Birden	.25	.08
❑ 8 Bert Emanuel	.50	.20
❑ 9 Jumpy Geathers	.25	.08
❑ 10 Jeff George	.50	.20
❑ 11 Craig Heyward	.25	.08
❑ 12 Bill Brooks	.25	.08
❑ 13 Steve Christie	.25	.08
❑ 14 Todd Collins	.50	.20
❑ 15 Darick Holmes	.25	.08
❑ 16 Andre Reed	.50	.20
❑ 17 Bryce Paup	.50	.20
❑ 18 Bruce Smith	1.00	.40
❑ 19 Blake Brockermeyer	.25	.08
❑ 20 Mark Carrier	.25	.08
❑ 21 Kerry Collins	1.00	.40
❑ 22 Darion Conner	.25	.08
❑ 23 Eric Guliford	.25	.08
❑ 24 Lamar Lathon	.25	.08
❑ 25 Derrick Moore	.25	.08
❑ 26 Frank Reich	.25	.08
❑ 27 Kevin Butler	.25	.08
❑ 28 Tony Carter RC	.25	.08
❑ 29 Curtis Conway	1.00	.40
❑ 30 Robert Green	.25	.08
❑ 31 Jay Leeuwenburg	.25	.08
❑ 32 Alonzo Spellman	.25	.08
❑ 33 Chris Zorich	.25	.08
❑ 34 Eric Bieniemy	.25	.08
❑ 35 Jeff Blake	1.00	.40
❑ 36 Tony McGee	.25	.08
❑ 37 Carl Pickens	.50	.20
❑ 38 Rob Burnett	.25	.08
❑ 39 Earnest Byner	.25	.08
❑ 40 Michael Jackson	.50	.20
❑ 41 Antonio Langham	.25	.08
❑ 42 Anthony Pleasant	.25	.08
❑ 43 Vinny Testaverde	.50	.20
❑ 44 Troy Aikman	2.50	1.25
❑ 45 Larry Allen	.25	.08
❑ 46 Bill Bates	.50	.20
❑ 47 Chris Boniol	.25	.08
❑ 48 Charles Haley	.50	.20
❑ 49 Michael Irvin	1.00	.40
❑ 50 Robert Jones	.25	.08
❑ 51 Leon Lett	.25	.08
❑ 52 Russell Maryland	.25	.08
❑ 53 Nate Newton	.25	.08
❑ 54 Deion Sanders	1.50	.60
❑ 55 Sherman Williams	.25	.08
❑ 56 Darren Woodson	.50	.20
❑ 57 Aaron Craver	.25	.08
❑ 58 Terrell Davis	2.00	.75
❑ 59 Jason Elam	.50	.20
❑ 60 Simon Fletcher	.25	.08
❑ 61 Anthony Miller	.50	.20
❑ 62 Shannon Sharpe	.50	.20
❑ 63 Tracy Scroggins	.25	.08
❑ 64 Antonio London	.25	.08
❑ 65 Scott Mitchell	.50	.20
❑ 66 Johnnie Morton	.50	.20
❑ 67 Barry Sanders	4.00	1.50
❑ 68 Edgar Bennett	.50	.20
❑ 69 Mark Chmura	.50	.20
❑ 70 Brett Favre	5.00	2.50
❑ 71 Mark Ingram	.25	.08
❑ 72 Dorsey Levens	1.00	.40
❑ 73 Wayne Simmons	.25	.08
❑ 74 Gary Brown	.25	.08
❑ 75 Anthony Cook	.25	.08
❑ 76 Al Del Greco	.25	.08
❑ 77 Haywood Jeffires	.25	.08
❑ 78 Steve McNair	2.00	.75
❑ 79 Rodney Thomas	.25	.08
❑ 80 Trev Alberts	.25	.08
❑ 81 Quentin Coryatt	.25	.08
❑ 82 Ken Dilger	.50	.20
❑ 83 Jim Harbaugh	.50	.20
❑ 84 Floyd Turner	.25	.08
❑ 85 Lamont Warren	.25	.08
❑ 86 Steve Beuerlein	.50	.20
❑ 87 Mark Brunell	1.50	.60
❑ 88 Eugene Chung	.25	.08
❑ 89 Jeff Lageman	.25	.08
❑ 90 Willie Jackson	.50	.20
❑ 91 Kimble Anders	.25	.08
❑ 92 Steve Bono	.50	.20
❑ 93 Derrick Thomas	1.00	.40
❑ 94 Willie Davis	.50	.20
❑ 95 Greg Hill	.50	.20
❑ 96 Neil Smith	.50	.20
❑ 97 Tamarick Vanover	1.00	.40
❑ 98 James Hasty	.25	.08
❑ 99 Gary Clark	.25	.08
❑ 100 Marco Coleman	.25	.08
❑ 101 Steve Emtman	.25	.08
❑ 102 Irving Fryar	.50	.20
❑ 103 Randal Hill	.25	.08
❑ 104 Terry Kirby	.50	.20
❑ 105 Dan Marino	5.00	2.00
❑ 106 Cris Carter	1.00	.40
❑ 107 Jack Del Rio	.25	.08
❑ 108 David Palmer	.50	.20
❑ 109 Jake Reed	.50	.20
❑ 110 Robert Smith	.50	.20
❑ 111 Korey Stringer	.25	.08
❑ 112 Orlando Thomas	.25	.08
❑ 113 Drew Bledsoe	1.50	.60
❑ 114 Vincent Brisby	.25	.08
❑ 115 Ted Johnson RC	1.00	.40
❑ 116 Curtis Martin	2.00	.75
❑ 117 Chris Slade	.25	.08
❑ 118 Jim Dombrowski	.25	.08
❑ 119 William Roaf	.25	.08
❑ 120 Quinn Early	.25	.08
❑ 121 Wesley Walls	.50	.20
❑ 122 Wayne Martin	.25	.08
❑ 123 Irv Smith	.25	.08
❑ 124 Torrance Small	.25	.08
❑ 125 Dave Brown	.50	.20
❑ 126 Chris Calloway	.25	.08
❑ 127 Jumbo Elliott	.25	.08
❑ 128 Rodney Hampton	.50	.20
❑ 129 Tyrone Wheatley	.50	.20
❑ 130 Kyle Brady	.50	.20
❑ 131 Hugh Douglas	.50	.20
❑ 132 Todd Scott	.25	.08
❑ 133 Adrian Murrell	.50	.20
❑ 134 Wayne Chrebet	1.50	.60
❑ 135 Aundray Bruce	.25	.08
❑ 136 Andrew Glover	.25	.08
❑ 137 Daryl Hobbs RC	.25	.08
❑ 138 Napoleon Kaufman	1.00	.40
❑ 139 Chester McGlockton	.25	.08
❑ 140 Rob Fredrickson	.25	.08
❑ 141 Guy McIntyre	.25	.08
❑ 142 Bobby Taylor	.50	.20
❑ 143 Fred Barnett	.50	.20
❑ 144 William Fuller	.25	.08
❑ 145 Rodney Peete	.25	.08
❑ 146 Daniel Stubbs	.25	.08
❑ 147 Charlie Garner	.50	.20
❑ 148 Myron Bell	.25	.08

❑ 149 Rod Woodson .50 .20
❑ 150 Charles Johnson .50 .20
❑ 151 Ernie Mills .25 .08
❑ 152 Levon Kirkland .25 .08
❑ 153 Carnell Lake .25 .08
❑ 154 Kevin Greene .50 .20
❑ 155 Neil O'Donnell .50 .20
❑ 156 Erric Pegram .50 .20
❑ 157 Ray Seals .25 .08
❑ 158 Willie Williams .25 .08
❑ 159 Kordell Stewart 1.00 .40
❑ 160 Yancey Thigpen .50 .20
❑ 161 Darren Bennett .50 .20
❑ 162 Andre Coleman .25 .08
❑ 163 Aaron Hayden RC 1.00 .40
❑ 164 Tony Martin .50 .20
❑ 165 Chris Mims .25 .08
❑ 166 Shawn Lee .25 .08
❑ 167 Junior Seau 1.00 .40
❑ 168 Merton Hanks .25 .08
❑ 169 Rickey Jackson .25 .08
❑ 170 Derek Loville .25 .08
❑ 171 Gary Plummer .25 .08
❑ 172 J.J. Stokes 1.00 .40
❑ 173 John Taylor .25 .08
❑ 174 Bryant Young .50 .20
❑ 175 Antonio Edwards RC .50 .20
❑ 176 Joey Galloway 1.00 .40
❑ 177 Carlton Gray .25 .08
❑ 178 Rick Mirer .50 .20
❑ 179 Winston Moss .25 .08
❑ 180 Jerome Bettis 1.00 .40
❑ 181 Troy Drayton .25 .08
❑ 182 Wayne Gandy .25 .08
❑ 183 Sean Gilbert .25 .08
❑ 184 Jessie Hester .25 .08
❑ 185 Sean Landeta .25 .08
❑ 186 Roman Phifer .25 .08
❑ 187 Alberto White .25 .08
❑ 188 Santana Dotson .25 .08
❑ 189 Jerry Ellison RC .25 .08
❑ 190 Jackie Harris .25 .08
❑ 191 Courtney Hawkins .25 .08
❑ 192 Horace Copeland .25 .08
❑ 193 Hardy Nickerson .25 .08
❑ 194 Warren Sapp .25 .08
❑ 195 Terry Allen .50 .20
❑ 196 Henry Ellard .50 .20
❑ 197 Gus Frerotte .50 .20
❑ 198 John Gesek .25 .08
❑ 199 Jim Lachey .25 .08
❑ 200 Brian Mitchell .25 .08
❑ 201 Garrison Hearst .50 .20
❑ 202 Dave Krieg .25 .08
❑ 203 Rob Moore .50 .20
❑ 204 Aeneas Williams .25 .08
❑ 205 Chris Doleman .25 .08
❑ 206 Terance Mathis .25 .08
❑ 207 Clay Matthews .50 .20
❑ 208 Eric Metcalf .50 .20
❑ 209 Jessie Tuggle .25 .08
❑ 210 Cornelius Bennett .50 .20
❑ 211 Ruben Brown .25 .08
❑ 212 Russell Copeland .25 .08
❑ 213 Phil Hansen .25 .08
❑ 214 Jim Kelly 1.00 .40
❑ 215 Don Beebe .25 .08
❑ 216 Willie Green .25 .08
❑ 217 Howard Griffith .25 .08
❑ 218 John Kasay .25 .08
❑ 219 Brett Maxie .25 .08
❑ 220 Tim McKyer .25 .08
❑ 221 Sam Mills .50 .20
❑ 222 Jim Flanigan .25 .08
❑ 223 Jeff Graham .25 .08
❑ 224 Erik Kramer .25 .08
❑ 225 Rashaan Salaam .50 .20
❑ 226 Steve Walsh .25 .08
❑ 227 Donnell Woolford .25 .08
❑ 228 Ki-Jana Carter .50 .20
❑ 229 John Copeland .25 .08
❑ 230 Harold Green .25 .08
❑ 231 Doug Pelfrey .25 .08
❑ 232 Darnay Scott .50 .20
❑ 233 Bracy Walker .25 .08
❑ 234 Dan Wilkinson .25 .08
❑ 235 Leroy Hoard .25 .08
❑ 236 Ernest Hunter UER .25 .08
❑ 237 Keenan McCardell 1.00 .40
❑ 238 Stevon Moore .25 .08
❑ 239 Andre Rison .50 .20
❑ 240 Eric Zeier .50 .20
❑ 241 Larry Brown .25 .08
❑ 242 Shante Carver .25 .08
❑ 243 Chad Hennings .50 .20
❑ 244 John Jett .25 .08
❑ 245 Daryl Johnston .50 .20
❑ 246 Derek Kennard .25 .08
❑ 247 Brock Marion .25 .08
❑ 248 Jay Novacek .50 .20
❑ 249 Emmitt Smith 4.00 2.00
❑ 250 Tony Tolbert .25 .08
❑ 251 Mark Tuinei .25 .08
❑ 252 Erik Williams .25 .08
❑ 253 Kevin Williams .25 .08
❑ 254 John Elway 5.00 2.00
❑ 255 Ed McCaffrey .50 .20
❑ 256 Glyn Milburn .25 .08
❑ 257 Michael Dean Perry .25 .08
❑ 258 Mike Pritchard .25 .08
❑ 259 Willie Clay .25 .08
❑ 260 Jason Hanson .25 .08
❑ 261 Herman Moore .50 .20
❑ 262 Brett Perriman .50 .20
❑ 263 Lomas Brown .25 .08
❑ 264 Chris Spielman .50 .20
❑ 265 Henry Thomas .25 .08
❑ 266 Robert Brooks 1.00 .40
❑ 267 Sean Jones .25 .08
❑ 268 John Jurkovic .25 .08
❑ 269 Anthony Morgan .25 .08
❑ 270 Craig Newsome .25 .08
❑ 271 Reggie White 1.00 .40
❑ 272 Chris Chandler .50 .20
❑ 273 Mel Gray .25 .08
❑ 274 Darryll Lewis .25 .08
❑ 275 Bruce Matthews .25 .08
❑ 276 Todd McNair .25 .08
❑ 277 Chris Sanders .50 .20
❑ 278 Mark Stepnoski .25 .08
❑ 279 Ashley Ambrose .25 .08
❑ 280 Tony Bennett .25 .08
❑ 281 Zack Crockett .25 .08
❑ 282 Sean Dawkins .25 .08
❑ 283 Marshall Faulk 1.25 .50
❑ 284 Ronald Humphrey .25 .08
❑ 285 Tony Siragusa .25 .08
❑ 286 Roosevelt Potts .25 .08
❑ 287 Bryan Barker .25 .08
❑ 288 Tony Boselli .50 .20
❑ 289 Keith Goganious .25 .08
❑ 290 Desmond Howard .50 .20
❑ 291 Don Davey .25 .08
❑ 292 Corey Mayfield .25 .08
❑ 293 James O. Stewart .50 .20
❑ 294 Cedric Tillman .25 .08
❑ 295 Marcus Allen 1.00 .40
❑ 296 Dale Carter .25 .08
❑ 297 Lake Dawson .50 .20
❑ 298 Darren Mickell .25 .08
❑ 299 Dan Saleaumua .25 .08
❑ 300 Webster Slaughter .25 .08
❑ 301 Keith Cash .25 .08
❑ 302 Bryan Cox .25 .08
❑ 303 Jeff Cross .25 .08
❑ 304 Eric Green .25 .08
❑ 305 O.J. McDuffie .50 .20
❑ 306 Bernie Parmalee .25 .08
❑ 307 Billy Milner .25 .08
❑ 308 Pete Stoyanovich .25 .08
❑ 309 Troy Vincent .25 .08
❑ 310 Qadry Ismail .50 .20
❑ 311 Amp Lee .25 .08
❑ 312 Warren Moon .50 .20
❑ 313 Scottie Graham .25 .08
❑ 314 John Randle .50 .20
❑ 315 Fuad Reveiz .25 .08
❑ 316 Broderick Thomas .25 .08
❑ 317 Ben Coates .50 .20
❑ 318 Willie McGinest .25 .08
❑ 319 Dave Meggett .25 .08
❑ 320 Will Moore .25 .08
❑ 321 Dave Wohlabaugh RC .25 .08
❑ 322 Mario Bates .50 .20
❑ 323 Jim Everett .25 .08
❑ 324 Tyrone Hughes .25 .08
❑ 325 Vaughn Dunbar .25 .08
❑ 326 Renaldo Turnbull .25 .08
❑ 327 Michael Haynes .50 .20
❑ 328 Mike Sherrard .25 .08
❑ 329 Michael Strahan .50 .20
❑ 330 Herschel Walker .50 .20
❑ 331 Charles Wilson .25 .08
❑ 332 Otis Smith RC .50 .20
❑ 333 Mo Lewis .25 .08
❑ 334 Marvin Washington .25 .08
❑ 335 Tim Brown 1.00 .40
❑ 336 Greg Skrepenak .25 .08
❑ 337 Kevin Gogan .25 .08
❑ 338 Jeff Hostetler .50 .20
❑ 339 Terry McDaniel .25 .08
❑ 340 Anthony Smith .25 .08
❑ 341 Pat Swilling .25 .08
❑ 342 Harvey Williams .25 .08
❑ 343 Tom Hutton RC .25 .08
❑ 344 Mike Mamula .25 .08
❑ 345 Randall Cunningham 1.00 .40
❑ 346 Ricky Watters .50 .20
❑ 347 Andy Harmon .25 .08
❑ 348 William Thomas .25 .08
❑ 349 Calvin Williams 1.00 .40
❑ 350 Mark Bruener .25 .08
❑ 351 Dermontti Dawson .25 .08
❑ 352 Greg Lloyd .50 .20
❑ 353 Norm Johnson .25 .08
❑ 354 Byron Bam Morris .25 .08
❑ 355 Thomas Newberry .25 .08
❑ 356 Darren Perry .25 .08
❑ 357 Rohn Stark .25 .08
❑ 358 Joel Steed .25 .08
❑ 359 Brendan Stai UER .25 .08
❑ 360 Justin Strzelczyk RC .25 .08
❑ 361 Leon Searcy .25 .08
❑ 362 Chad Brown .50 .20
❑ 363 John Carney .25 .08
❑ 364 Rodney Culver .50 .20
❑ 365 Ronnie Harmon .25 .08
❑ 366 Stan Humphries .50 .20
❑ 367 Leslie O'Neal .25 .08
❑ 368 Natrone Means .50 .20
❑ 369 Mark Seay .25 .08
❑ 370 William Floyd .50 .20
❑ 371 Brent Jones .25 .08
❑ 372 Tim McDonald .25 .08
❑ 373 Ken Norton, Jr. .50 .20
❑ 374 Jerry Rice 2.50 1.25
❑ 375 Dana Stubblefield .50 .20
❑ 376 Steve Young 2.00 .75
❑ 377 Brian Blades .50 .20
❑ 378 Cortez Kennedy .50 .20
❑ 379 Michael Sinclair .25 .08
❑ 380 Lamar Smith 1.00 .40
❑ 381 Chris Warren .50 .20
❑ 382 Johnny Bailey .25 .08
❑ 383 Isaac Bruce 1.00 .40
❑ 384 Kevin Carter .50 .20
❑ 385 Shane Conlan .25 .08
❑ 386 D'Marco Farr .25 .08
❑ 387 Todd Kinchen .25 .08
❑ 388 Chris Miller .25 .08
❑ 389 Lonnie Marts .25 .08
❑ 390 Trent Dilfer .50 .20
❑ 391 Alvin Harper .25 .08
❑ 392 John Lynch 1.00 .40
❑ 393 Errict Rhett .50 .20
❑ 394 Darnell Stephens RC .25 .08
❑ 395 Ken Harvey .25 .08
❑ 396 Eddie Murray .25 .08
❑ 397 Heath Shuler .50 .20
❑ 398 Matt Turk RC .25 .08
❑ 399 Michael Westbrook 1.00 .40
❑ 400 James Washington .25 .08

1998 CE Supreme Season Review

❑ COMPLETE SET (200) 60.00 30.00
❑ COMP.SET w/o SPs (200) 25.00 12.50
❑ 1 Larry Centers .50 .20
❑ 2 Jake Plummer 1.25 .50
❑ 3 Simeon Rice .75 .30
❑ 4 Cardinals Draft Pick .10 .02
❑ 4A Andre Wadsworth RC 1.50 .60
❑ 4B Michael Pittman RC 2.50 1.25
❑ 5 Jamal Anderson 1.25 .50
❑ 6 Bert Emanuel .75 .30
❑ 7 Byron Hanspard .50 .20
❑ 8 Falcons Draft Pick .10 .02

❑	8A	Jammi German RC	1.50	.60
❑	8B	Keith Brooking RC	2.00	.75
❑	9	Derrick Alexander WR	.75	.30
❑	10	Peter Boulware	.50	.20
❑	11	Michael Jackson	.50	.20
❑	12	Ray Lewis	1.25	.50
❑	13	Vinny Testaverde	.75	.30
❑	14	Ravens Draft Pick	.10	.02
❑	14A	Duane Starks RC	1.00	.40
❑	14B	Pat Johnson RC	1.50	.60
❑	15	Todd Collins	.50	.20
❑	16	Jim Kelly	1.25	.50
❑	17	Andre Reed	.75	.30
❑	18	Antowain Smith	1.25	.50
❑	19	Bruce Smith	.75	.30
❑	20	Thurman Thomas	1.25	.50
❑	21	Bills Draft Pick	.10	.02
❑	21A	Jonathan Linton RC	1.50	.60
❑	22	Tim Biakabutuka	.75	.30
❑	23	Rae Carruth	.50	.20
❑	24	Kerry Collins	.75	.30
❑	25	Anthony Johnson	.50	.20
❑	26	Lamar Lathon	.50	.20
❑	27	Panthers Draft Pick	.10	.02
❑	27A	Jason Peter RC	1.50	.60
❑	27B	Donald Hayes RC	1.50	.60
❑	28	Curtis Conway	.75	.30
❑	29	Bryan Cox	.50	.20
❑	30	Bobby Engram	.75	.30
❑	31	Erik Kramer	.50	.20
❑	32	Rick Mirer	.50	.20
❑	33	Rashaan Salaam	.50	.20
❑	34	Bears Draft Pick	.10	.02
❑	34A	Curtis Enis RC	1.00	.40
❑	35	Jeff Blake	.75	.30
❑	36	Ki-Jana Carter	.50	.20
❑	37	Corey Dillon	1.25	.50
❑	38	Carl Pickens	.75	.30
❑	39	Bengals Draft Pick	.10	.02
❑	39A	Takeo Spikes RC	2.00	.75
❑	39B	Brian Simmons RC	1.50	.60
❑	40	Troy Aikman	2.00	.75
❑	41	Daryl Johnston	.75	.30
❑	42	David LaFleur	.50	.20
❑	43	Anthony Miller	.50	.20
❑	44	Deion Sanders	1.25	.50
❑	45	Emmitt Smith	3.00	1.50
❑	46	Broderick Thomas	.50	.20
❑	47	Cowboys Draft Pick	.10	.02
❑	47A	Greg Ellis RC	1.00	.40
❑	48	Terrell Davis	1.25	.50
❑	49	John Elway	4.00	2.00
❑	50	Ed McCaffrey	.75	.30
❑	51	John Mobley	.50	.20
❑	52	Bill Romanowski	.50	.20
❑	53	Shannon Sharpe	.75	.30
❑	54	Neil Smith	.75	.30
❑	55	Rod Smith WR	.75	.30
❑	56	Maa Tanuvasa	.50	.20
❑	57	Broncos Draft Pick	.10	.02
❑	57A	Marcus Nash RC	1.00	.40
❑	57B	Brian Griese RC	4.00	1.50
❑	58	Scott Mitchell	.75	.30
❑	59	Herman Moore	.75	.30
❑	60	Barry Sanders	3.00	1.25
❑	61	Lions Draft Pick	.10	.02
❑	61A	Jamaal Alexander RC	1.00	.40
❑	61B	Chris Liwienski RC	1.00	.40
❑	61C	Terry Fair RC	1.50	.60
❑	61D	Germane Crowell RC	1.50	.60
❑	61E	Charlie Batch RC	2.00	.75
❑	62	Robert Brooks	.75	.30
❑	63	Mark Chmura	.75	.30
❑	64	Brett Favre	4.00	2.00
❑	65	Antonio Freeman	1.25	.50
❑	66	Dorsey Levens	1.25	.50
❑	67	Derrick Mayes	.75	.30
❑	68	Ross Verba	.50	.20
❑	69	Reggie White	1.25	.50
❑	70	Packers Draft Pick	.75	.30
❑	70A	Vonnie Holliday RC	1.50	.60
❑	70B	Roosevelt Blackmon RC	1.00	.40
❑	71	Marshall Faulk	1.50	.60
❑	72	Jim Harbaugh	.75	.30
❑	73	Marvin Harrison	1.25	.50
❑	74	Colts Draft Pick	.10	.02
❑	74A	E.G. Green RC	1.50	.60
❑	74B	Peyton Manning RC	20.00	7.50
❑	75	Tony Brackens	.50	.20
❑	76	Mark Brunell	1.25	.50
❑	77	Rob Johnson	.75	.30
❑	78	Keenan McCardell	.75	.30
❑	79	Natrone Means	.75	.30
❑	80	Jimmy Smith	.75	.30
❑	81	Jaguars Draft Pick	.10	.02
❑	81A	Tavian Banks RC	1.50	.60
❑	82	Marcus Allen	1.25	.50
❑	83	Tony Gonzalez	1.25	.50
❑	84	Elvis Grbac	.75	.30
❑	85	Derrick Thomas	1.25	.50
❑	86	Tamarick Vanover	.50	.20
❑	87	Chiefs Draft Pick	.10	.02
❑	87A	Rashaan Shehee RC	1.50	.60
❑	88	Karim Abdul-Jabbar	1.25	.50
❑	89	Fred Barnett	.50	.20
❑	90	Dan Marino	4.00	2.00
❑	91	O.J. McDuffie	.75	.30
❑	92	Brett Perriman	.50	.20
❑	93	Irving Spikes	.50	.20
❑	94	Zach Thomas	1.25	.50
❑	95	Dolphins Draft Pick	.10	.02
❑	95A	John Avery RC	1.50	.60
❑	96	Cris Carter	1.25	.50
❑	97	Brad Johnson	1.25	.50
❑	98	John Randle	.75	.30
❑	99	Jake Reed	.75	.30
❑	100	Robert Smith	1.25	.50
❑	101	Vikings Draft Pick	.10	.02
❑	101A	Randy Moss RC	12.00	5.00
❑	102	Drew Bledsoe	1.50	.60
❑	103	Chris Canty	.50	.20
❑	104	Ben Coates	.75	.30
❑	105	Terry Glenn	1.25	.50
❑	106	Curtis Martin	1.25	.50
❑	107	Willie McGinest	.50	.20
❑	108	Sedrick Shaw	.50	.20
❑	109	Patriots Draft Pick	.10	.02
❑	109A	Chris Floyd RC	1.00	.40
❑	109B	Tebucky Jones RC	1.00	.40
❑	109C	Harold Shaw RC	1.00	.40
❑	110	Mario Bates	.75	.30
❑	111	Heath Shuler	.50	.20
❑	112	Danny Wuerffel	.75	.30
❑	113	Saints Draft Pick	.10	.02
❑	113A	Cameron Cleeland RC	1.00	.40
❑	114	Ray Zellars	.50	.20
❑	115	Tiki Barber	1.25	.50
❑	116	Dave Brown	.50	.20
❑	117	Ike Hilliard	.75	.30
❑	118	Danny Kanell	.75	.30
❑	119	Jason Sehorn	.75	.30
❑	120	Amani Toomer	.75	.30
❑	121	Giants Draft Pick	.10	.02
❑	121A	Shaun Williams RC	1.50	.60
❑	121B	Joe Jurevicius RC	2.00	.75
❑	121C	Brian Alford RC	1.00	.40
❑	122	Wayne Chrebet	1.25	.50
❑	123	Hugh Douglas	.50	.20
❑	124	Jeff Graham	.50	.20
❑	125	Keyshawn Johnson	1.25	.50
❑	126	Adrian Murrell	.75	.30
❑	127	Neil O'Donnell	.75	.30
❑	128	Jets Draft Pick	.10	.02
❑	128A	Scott Frost RC	1.00	.40
❑	129	Tim Brown	1.25	.50
❑	130	Jeff George	.75	.30
❑	131	Desmond Howard	.75	.30
❑	132	Napoleon Kaufman	1.25	.50
❑	133	Darrell Russell	.50	.20
❑	134	Raiders Draft Pick	.10	.02
❑	134A	Charles Woodson RC	2.50	1.00
❑	135	Ty Detmer	.75	.30
❑	136	Irving Fryar	.75	.30
❑	137	Bobby Hoying	.75	.30
❑	138	Chris T. Jones	.50	.20
❑	139	Ricky Watters	.75	.30
❑	140	Eagles Draft Pick	.10	.02
❑	140A	Allen Rossum RC	1.00	.40
❑	141	Jerome Bettis	1.25	.50
❑	142	Charles Johnson	.50	.20
❑	143	George Jones	.50	.20
❑	144	Greg Lloyd	.50	.20
❑	145	Kordell Stewart	1.25	.50
❑	146	Yancey Thigpen	.50	.20
❑	147	Steelers Draft Pick	.10	.02
❑	147A	Chris Fuamatu-Ma'afala RC	1.50	.60
❑	148	Stan Humphries	.50	.20
❑	149	Tony Martin	.75	.30
❑	150	Eric Metcalf	.50	.20
❑	151	Junior Seau	1.25	.50
❑	152	Chargers Draft Pick	.10	.02
❑	152A	Ryan Leaf RC	2.00	.75
❑	153	Jim Druckenmiller	.50	.20
❑	154	William Floyd	.50	.20
❑	155	Kevin Greene	.75	.30
❑	156	Garrison Hearst	1.25	.50
❑	157	Ken Norton	.50	.20
❑	158	Terrell Owens	1.25	.50
❑	159	Jerry Rice	2.00	.75
❑	160	J.J. Stokes	.75	.30
❑	161	Dana Stubblefield	.50	.20
❑	162	Rod Woodson	.75	.30
❑	163	Bryant Young	.50	.20
❑	164	Steve Young	1.25	.50
❑	165	49ers Draft Pick	.50	.20
❑	165A	Fred Beasley RC	1.00	.40
❑	165B	R.W. McQuarters RC	1.50	.60
❑	165C	Chris Ruhman RC	1.00	.40
❑	166	Steve Broussard	.50	.20
❑	167	Chad Brown	.50	.20
❑	168	Joey Galloway	.75	.30
❑	169	Jon Kitna	1.25	.50
❑	170	Warren Moon	1.25	.50
❑	171	Chris Warren	.75	.30
❑	172	Seahawks Draft Pick	.10	.02
❑	172A	Ahman Green RC	10.00	4.00
❑	173	Tony Banks	.75	.30
❑	174	Isaac Bruce	1.25	.50
❑	175	Eddie Kennison	.75	.30
❑	176	Keith Lyle	.50	.20
❑	177	Lawrence Phillips	.50	.20
❑	178	Rams Draft Pick	.10	.02
❑	178A	Robert Holcombe RC	1.50	.60
❑	179	Mike Alstott	1.25	.50
❑	180	Reidel Anthony	.75	.30
❑	181	Trent Dilfer	1.25	.50
❑	182	Warrick Dunn	1.25	.50
❑	183	Hardy Nickerson	.50	.20
❑	184	Errict Rhett	.75	.30
❑	185	Warren Sapp	.75	.30
❑	186	Bucs Draft Pick	.10	.02
❑	186A	Jacquez Green RC	1.50	.60
❑	187	Eddie George	1.25	.50
❑	188	Darryll Lewis	.50	.20
❑	189	Steve McNair	1.25	.50
❑	190	Chris Sanders	.50	.20
❑	191	Oilers Draft Pick	.10	.02
❑	191A	Kevin Dyson RC	2.00	.75
❑	192	Terry Allen	1.25	.50
❑	193	Jamie Asher	.50	.20
❑	194	Stephen Davis	.50	.20
❑	195	Gus Frerotte	.50	.20
❑	196	Sean Gilbert	.50	.20
❑	197	Ken Harvey	.50	.20
❑	198	Jeff Hostetler	.50	.20
❑	199	Michael Westbrook	.75	.30
❑	200	Redskins Draft Pick	.10	.02
❑	200A	Stephen Alexander RC	1.50	.60
❑	200B	Mike Sellers RC	1.00	.40

1999 Collector's Edge Supreme

❑		COMPLETE SET (170)	250.00	100.00
❑		COMP.SET w/o #166 (169)	100.00	50.00
❑	1	Randy Moss CL	1.00	.40
❑	2	Peyton Manning CL	.75	.30
❑	3	Rob Moore	.50	.20
❑	4	Adrian Murrell	.50	.20
❑	5	Jake Plummer	.50	.20
❑	6	Andre Wadsworth	.30	.10

❑ 7 Jamal Anderson .75 .30
❑ 8 Chris Chandler .50 .20
❑ 9 Tony Martin .50 .20
❑ 10 Terence Mathis .50 .20
❑ 11 Jim Harbaugh .50 .20
❑ 12 Priest Holmes 1.25 .50
❑ 13 Jermaine Lewis .50 .20
❑ 14 Eric Zeier .30 .10
❑ 15 Doug Flutie .75 .30
❑ 16 Eric Moulds .75 .30
❑ 17 Andre Reed .50 .20
❑ 18 Antowain Smith .75 .30
❑ 19 Steve Beuerlein .30 .10
❑ 20 Kevin Greene .30 .10
❑ 21 Rocket Ismail .50 .20
❑ 22 Fred Lane .30 .10
❑ 23 Edgar Bennett .30 .10
❑ 24 Curtis Conway .50 .20
❑ 25 Curtis Enis .30 .10
❑ 26 Erik Kramer .30 .10
❑ 27 Corey Dillon .75 .30
❑ 28 Neil O'Donnell .30 .10
❑ 29 Carl Pickens .50 .20
❑ 30 Darnay Scott .30 .10
❑ 31 Troy Aikman 1.50 .60
❑ 32 Michael Irvin .50 .20
❑ 33 Deion Sanders .75 .30
❑ 34 Emmitt Smith 1.50 .60
❑ 35 Chris Warren .30 .10
❑ 36 Terrell Davis .75 .30
❑ 37 John Elway 2.50 1.00
❑ 38 Ed McCaffrey .50 .20
❑ 39 Shannon Sharpe .50 .20
❑ 40 Rod Smith .50 .20
❑ 41 Charlie Batch .75 .30
❑ 42 Herman Moore .50 .20
❑ 43 Johnnie Morton .30 .10
❑ 44 Barry Sanders 2.50 1.00
❑ 45 Robert Brooks .50 .20
❑ 46 Brett Favre 2.50 1.00
❑ 47 Antonio Freeman .75 .30
❑ 48 Darick Holmes .30 .10
❑ 49 Dorsey Levens .75 .30
❑ 50 Reggie White .30 .10
❑ 51 Marshall Faulk 1.00 .40
❑ 52 Marvin Harrison .75 .30
❑ 53 Peyton Manning 2.50 1.00
❑ 54 Jerome Pathon .30 .10
❑ 55 Tavian Banks .30 .10
❑ 56 Mark Brunell .75 .30
❑ 57 Keenan McCardell .50 .20
❑ 58 Fred Taylor .75 .30
❑ 59 Derrick Alexander .30 .10
❑ 60 Donnell Bennett .30 .10
❑ 61 Rich Gannon .75 .30
❑ 62 Andre Rison .50 .20
❑ 63 Karim Abdul-Jabbar .50 .20
❑ 64 John Avery .30 .10
❑ 65 Oronde Gadsden .50 .20
❑ 66 Dan Marino 2.50 1.00
❑ 67 O.J. McDuffie .50 .20
❑ 68 Cris Carter .75 .30
❑ 69 Randall Cunningham .75 .30
❑ 70 Brad Johnson .75 .30
❑ 71 Randy Moss 2.50 1.00
❑ 72 Jake Reed .50 .20
❑ 73 Robert Smith .75 .30
❑ 74 Drew Bledsoe 1.00 .40
❑ 75 Ben Coates .50 .20
❑ 76 Robert Edwards .30 .10
❑ 77 Terry Glenn .75 .30
❑ 78 Cameron Cleeland .30 .10
❑ 79 Kerry Collins .50 .20
❑ 80 Sean Dawkins .30 .10
❑ 81 Lamar Smith .50 .20
❑ 82 Gary Brown .30 .10
❑ 83 Chris Calloway .30 .10
❑ 84 Danny Kanell .30 .10
❑ 85 Ike Hilliard .30 .10
❑ 86 Wayne Chrebet .50 .20
❑ 87 Keyshawn Johnson .75 .30
❑ 88 Curtis Martin .75 .30
❑ 89 Vinny Testaverde .50 .20
❑ 90 Tim Brown .75 .30
❑ 91 Jeff George .50 .20
❑ 92 Napoleon Kaufman .75 .30
❑ 93 Charles Woodson .75 .30
❑ 94 Irving Fryar .50 .20
❑ 95 Bobby Hoying .50 .20
❑ 96 Duce Staley .75 .30
❑ 97 Jerome Bettis .75 .30
❑ 98 Courtney Hawkins .30 .10
❑ 99 Charles Johnson .30 .10
❑ 100 Kordell Stewart .50 .20
❑ 101 Hines Ward .75 .30
❑ 102 Tony Banks .50 .20
❑ 103 Isaac Bruce .75 .30
❑ 104 Robert Holcombe .30 .10
❑ 105 Ryan Leaf .75 .30
❑ 106 Natrone Means .50 .20
❑ 107 Mikhael Ricks .30 .10
❑ 108 Junior Seau .75 .30
❑ 109 Garrison Hearst .50 .20
❑ 110 Terrell Owens .75 .30
❑ 111 Jerry Rice 1.50 .60
❑ 112 J.J. Stokes .50 .20
❑ 113 Steve Young 1.00 .40
❑ 114 Joey Galloway .50 .20
❑ 115 Jon Kitna .75 .30
❑ 116 Warren Moon .75 .30
❑ 117 Ricky Watters .50 .20
❑ 118 Mike Alstott .75 .30
❑ 119 Reidel Anthony .50 .20
❑ 120 Warrick Dunn .75 .30
❑ 121 Trent Dilfer .50 .20
❑ 122 Jacquez Green .30 .10
❑ 123 Kevin Dyson .50 .20
❑ 124 Eddie George .75 .30
❑ 125 Steve McNair .75 .30
❑ 126 Frank Wycheck .30 .10
❑ 127 Terry Allen .50 .20
❑ 128 Trent Green .75 .30
❑ 129 Skip Hicks .30 .10
❑ 130 Michael Westbrook .50 .20
❑ 131 Rahim Abdullah RC 1.00 .40
❑ 132 Champ Bailey RC 2.00 1.00
❑ 133 Marlon Barnes RC .60 .25
❑ 134 D'Wayne Bates RC 1.00 .40
❑ 135 Michael Bishop RC 1.50 .60
❑ 136 Dre' Bly RC 1.50 .60
❑ 137 David Boston RC 1.50 .60
❑ 138 Cuncho Brown RC UER .60 .25
❑ 139 Na Brown RC 1.00 .40
❑ 140 Tony Bryant RC 1.00 .40
❑ 141 Tim Couch RC ERR 50.00 25.00
❑ 141TC Tim Couch RC COR 6.00 2.50
❑ 142 Chris Claiborne RC .60 .25
❑ 143 Daunte Culpepper RC 5.00 2.00
❑ 144 Jared DeVries RC 1.00 .40
❑ 145 Troy Edwards UER RC 1.00 .40
❑ 146 Kris Farris RC .60 .25
❑ 147 Kevin Faulk RC 1.50 .60
❑ 148 Joe Germaine RC 1.00 .40
❑ 149 Aaron Gibson RC .60 .25
❑ 150 Torry Holt RC 3.00 1.25
❑ 151 Brock Huard RC 1.50 .60
❑ 152 Sedrick Irvin RC .60 .25
❑ 153 James Johnson RC 1.00 .40
❑ 154 Kevin Johnson RC 1.50 .60
❑ 155 Andy Katzenmoyer RC 1.00 .40
❑ 156 Jevon Kearse RC 2.50 1.00
❑ 157 Shaun King RC 1.00 .40
❑ 158 Rob Konrad RC 1.00 .40
❑ 159 Chris McAlister RC 1.00 .40
❑ 160 Darnell McDonald RC 1.00 .40
❑ 161 Donovan McNabb RC 6.00 2.50
❑ 162 Cade McNown RC 1.00 .40
❑ 163 Peerless Price RC 1.50 .60
❑ 164 Akili Smith RC 1.00 .40
❑ 165 Matt Stinchcomb RC .60 .25
❑ 166A Michael Wiley 80.00 30.00
❑ 166B Edgerrin James RC 25.00 12.50
❑ 167 Ricky Williams RC 3.00 1.25
❑ 168 Antoine Winfield RC 1.00 .40
❑ 169 Craig Yeast RC 1.00 .40
❑ 170 Amos Zereoue RC 1.50 .60

2000 Collector's Edge Supreme

❑ COMPLETE SET (190) 80.00 30.00
❑ COMP.FACT.SET (190) 40.00 15.00
❑ COMP.SET w/o SP's (150) 20.00 7.50
❑ 1 David Boston .60 .25
❑ 2 Adrian Murrell .40 .15
❑ 3 Michael Pittman .25 .08
❑ 4 Jake Plummer .40 .15
❑ 5 Frank Sanders .40 .15
❑ 6 Jamal Anderson .60 .25
❑ 7 Chris Chandler .40 .15
❑ 8 Terance Mathis .40 .15
❑ 9 Justin Armour .25 .08
❑ 10 Tony Banks .40 .15
❑ 11 Qadry Ismail .40 .15
❑ 12 Errict Rhett .40 .15
❑ 13 Doug Flutie .60 .25
❑ 14 Eric Moulds .60 .25
❑ 15 Peerless Price .40 .15
❑ 16 Andre Reed .40 .15
❑ 17 Antowain Smith .40 .15
❑ 18 Steve Beuerlein .40 .15
❑ 19 Tim Biakabutuka .40 .15
❑ 20 Muhsin Muhammad .40 .15
❑ 21 Wesley Walls .25 .08
❑ 22 Bobby Engram .25 .08
❑ 23 Curtis Enis .25 .08
❑ 24 Shane Matthews .40 .15
❑ 25 Cade McNown .25 .08
❑ 26 Jim Miller .25 .08
❑ 27 Marcus Robinson .60 .25
❑ 28 Corey Dillon .60 .25
❑ 29 Carl Pickens .40 .15
❑ 30 Darnay Scott .40 .15
❑ 31 Akili Smith .25 .08
❑ 32 Karim Abdul-Jabbar .40 .15
❑ 33 Tim Couch .40 .15
❑ 34 Kevin Johnson .60 .25
❑ 35 Troy Aikman 1.25 .50
❑ 36 Michael Irvin .40 .15
❑ 37 Rocket Ismail .40 .15
❑ 38 Deion Sanders .60 .25
❑ 39 Emmitt Smith 1.25 .50
❑ 40 Terrell Davis .60 .25
❑ 41 Olandis Gary .60 .25
❑ 42 Brian Griese .60 .25
❑ 43 Ed McCaffrey .60 .25
❑ 44 Rod Smith .40 .15
❑ 45 Charlie Batch .60 .25
❑ 46 Germane Crowell .25 .08
❑ 47 Greg Hill .25 .08
❑ 48 Sedrick Irvin .25 .08
❑ 49 Herman Moore .40 .15
❑ 50 Johnnie Morton .40 .15
❑ 51 Corey Bradford .40 .15
❑ 52 Brett Favre 2.00 .75
❑ 53 Antonio Freeman .60 .25
❑ 54 Dorsey Levens .40 .15
❑ 55 Bill Schroeder .40 .15
❑ 56 E.G. Green .25 .08
❑ 57 Marvin Harrison .60 .25
❑ 58 Edgerrin James 1.00 .40
❑ 59 Peyton Manning 1.50 .60
❑ 60 Terrence Wilkins .25 .08

❑ 61 Mark Brunell .60 .25
❑ 62 Keenan McCardell .40 .15
❑ 63 Jimmy Smith .40 .15
❑ 64 James Stewart .40 .15
❑ 65 Fred Taylor .60 .25
❑ 66 Derrick Alexander .40 .15
❑ 67 Donnell Bennett .25 .08
❑ 68 Mike Cloud .25 .08
❑ 69 Tony Gonzalez .40 .15
❑ 70 Elvis Grbac .40 .15
❑ 71 Damon Huard .60 .25
❑ 72 James Johnson .25 .08
❑ 73 Rob Konrad .25 .08
❑ 74 Dan Marino 2.00 .75
❑ 75 Tony Martin .40 .15
❑ 76 O.J. McDuffie .40 .15
❑ 77 Cris Carter .60 .25
❑ 78 Daunte Culpepper .75 .30
❑ 79 Jeff George .40 .15
❑ 80 Randy Moss 1.25 .50
❑ 81 Robert Smith .60 .25
❑ 82 Terry Allen .40 .15
❑ 83 Drew Bledsoe .75 .30
❑ 84 Kevin Faulk .40 .15
❑ 85 Terry Glenn .40 .15
❑ 86 Shawn Jefferson .25 .08
❑ 87 Billy Joe Hobert .25 .08
❑ 88 Eddie Kennison .40 .15
❑ 89 Billy Joe Tolliver .25 .08
❑ 90 Ricky Williams .60 .25
❑ 91 Tiki Barber .60 .25
❑ 92 Gary Brown .25 .08
❑ 93 Kent Graham .25 .08
❑ 94 Ike Hilliard .40 .15
❑ 95 Amani Toomer .25 .08
❑ 96 Wayne Chrebet .40 .15
❑ 97 Keyshawn Johnson .60 .25
❑ 98 Ray Lucas .40 .15
❑ 99 Curtis Martin .60 .25
❑ 100 Vinny Testaverde .40 .15
❑ 101 Tim Brown .60 .25
❑ 102 Rich Gannon .60 .25
❑ 103 James Jett .25 .08
❑ 104 Napoleon Kaufman .40 .15
❑ 105 Tyrone Wheatley .40 .15
❑ 106 Charles Johnson .40 .15
❑ 107 Donovan McNabb 1.00 .40
❑ 108 Duce Staley .60 .25
❑ 109 Jerome Bettis .60 .25
❑ 110 Troy Edwards .25 .08
❑ 111 Kordell Stewart .40 .15
❑ 112 Hines Ward .60 .25
❑ 113 Isaac Bruce .60 .25
❑ 114 Marshall Faulk .75 .30
❑ 115 Az-Zahir Hakim .40 .15
❑ 116 Torry Holt .60 .25
❑ 117 Kurt Warner 1.25 .50
❑ 118 Jeff Graham .25 .08
❑ 119 Jim Harbaugh .40 .15
❑ 120 Freddie Jones .25 .08
❑ 121 Natrone Means .25 .08
❑ 122 Junior Seau .60 .25
❑ 123 Jeff Garcia .60 .25
❑ 124 Charlie Garner .40 .15
❑ 125 Terrell Owens .60 .25
❑ 126 Jerry Rice 1.25 .50
❑ 127 Steve Young .75 .30
❑ 128 Sean Dawkins .25 .08
❑ 129 Joey Galloway .40 .15
❑ 130 Jon Kitna .60 .25
❑ 131 Derrick Mayes .40 .15
❑ 132 Ricky Watters .40 .15
❑ 133 Mike Alstott .60 .25
❑ 134 Reidel Anthony .25 .08
❑ 135 Trent Dilfer .40 .15
❑ 136 Warrick Dunn .60 .25
❑ 137 Jacquez Green .25 .08
❑ 138 Shaun King .25 .08
❑ 139 Kevin Dyson .40 .15
❑ 140 Eddie George .60 .25
❑ 141 Jevon Kearse .60 .25
❑ 142 Steve McNair .60 .25
❑ 143 Yancey Thigpen .25 .08
❑ 144 Champ Bailey .40 .15
❑ 145 Albert Connell .25 .08
❑ 146 Stephen Davis .60 .25
❑ 147 Brad Johnson .60 .25
❑ 148 Michael Westbrook .40 .15
❑ 149 Checklist .25 .08
❑ 150 Checklist .25 .08
❑ 151 Sylvester Morris RC 5.00 2.00
❑ 151B LaVar Arrington SP 150.00 60.00
❑ 152 Peter Warrick RC 6.00 2.50
❑ 153 Chad Pennington RC 15.00 6.00
❑ 154 Courtney Brown RC 6.00 2.50
❑ 155 Thomas Jones RC 10.00 4.00
❑ 156 Chris Redman RC 5.00 2.00
❑ 157 R.Jay Soward RC 5.00 2.00
❑ 158 Jamal Lewis RC 15.00 6.00
❑ 159 Shaun Alexander RC 30.00 12.50
❑ 160 Travis Taylor RC 6.00 2.50
❑ 161 Ron Dayne RC 6.00 2.50
❑ 162 Travis Prentice RC 5.00 2.00
❑ 163 Plaxico Burress RC 12.00 5.00
❑ 164 J.R. Redmond RC 5.00 2.00
❑ 165 Sherrod Gideon RC 4.00 1.50
❑ 166 Dez White RC 6.00 2.50
❑ 167 Chafie Fields RC 4.00 1.50
❑ 168 Brandon Short RC 6.00 2.50
❑ 169 Reuben Droughns RC 8.00 3.00
❑ 170 Trung Canidate RC 5.00 2.00
❑ 171 Keith Bulluck RC 6.00 2.50
❑ 172 Doug Johnson RC 6.00 2.50
❑ 173 Shyrone Stith RC 6.00 2.50
❑ 174 Michael Wiley RC 5.00 2.00
❑ 175 Bubba Franks RC 6.00 2.50
❑ 176 Tom Brady RC 50.00 20.00
❑ 177 Anthony Lucas RC 6.00 2.50
❑ 178 Danny Farmer RC 5.00 2.00
❑ 179 Rob Morris RC 6.00 2.50
❑ 180 Dennis Northcutt RC 6.00 2.50
❑ 181 Troy Walters RC 6.00 2.50
❑ 182 Giovanni Carmazzi RC 4.00 1.50
❑ 183 Tee Martin RC 6.00 2.50
❑ 184 Joe Hamilton RC 5.00 2.00
❑ 185 Tim Rattay RC 6.00 2.50
❑ 186 Sebastian Janikowski RC 6.00 2.50
❑ 187 Na'il Diggs RC 5.00 2.00
❑ 188 Todd Husak RC 6.00 2.50
❑ 189 Jerry Porter RC 8.00 3.00
❑ 190 Brian Urlacher RC 25.00 10.00
❑ 59A P.Manning AUTO/300 70.00 35.00

1995 Crown Royale

❑ COMPLETE SET (144) 50.00 20.00
❑ 1 Lake Dawson .50 .20
❑ 2 Steve Beuerlein .50 .20
❑ 3 Jake Reed .50 .20
❑ 4 Jim Everett .25 .08
❑ 5 Sean Dawkins .50 .20
❑ 6 Jeff Hostetler .50 .20
❑ 7 Marshall Faulk 3.00 1.25
❑ 8 Jeff Blake RC 2.00 .75
❑ 9 Dave Brown .50 .20
❑ 10 Frank Reich .25 .08
❑ 11 Rocket Ismail .50 .20
❑ 12 Jerry Jones OWN 1.00 .40
❑ 13 Dan Marino 5.00 2.00
❑ 14 Ricky Watters .50 .20
❑ 15 Herman Moore 1.00 .40
❑ 16 Daryl Johnston .50 .20
❑ 17 Craig Erickson .25 .08
❑ 18 Alexander Wright .25 .08
❑ 19 Reggie White 1.00 .40
❑ 20 Andre Rison .50 .20
❑ 21 Fred Barnett .50 .20
❑ 22 Tyrone Wheatley RC 3.00 1.25
❑ 23 Charles Johnson .50 .20
❑ 24 Rashaan Salaam RC .50 .20
❑ 25 Mark Brunell 1.50 .60
❑ 26 Derek Loville .25 .08
❑ 27 Garrison Hearst 1.00 .40
❑ 28 Ken Norton Jr. .50 .20
❑ 29 Kerry Collins RC 4.00 1.50
❑ 30 Isaac Bruce 1.50 .60
❑ 31 Andre Reed .50 .20
❑ 32 Leon Lett .25 .08
❑ 33 Deion Sanders 1.50 .60
❑ 34 Terance Mathis .50 .20
❑ 35 Tim Bowens .25 .08
❑ 36 Shannon Sharpe .50 .20
❑ 37 Quinn Early .50 .20
❑ 38 Jerry Rice 2.50 1.00
❑ 39 Bruce Smith 1.00 .40
❑ 40 Drew Bledsoe 1.50 .60
❑ 41 Alvin Harper .25 .08
❑ 42 Jim Kelly 1.00 .40
❑ 43 Napoleon Kaufman RC 3.00 1.25
❑ 44 Errict Rhett .50 .20
❑ 45 Henry Ellard .50 .20
❑ 46 Barry Sanders 4.00 1.50
❑ 47 Vincent Brisby .25 .08
❑ 48 Chris Zorich .25 .08
❑ 49 Zack Crockett RC .50 .20
❑ 50 Haywood Jeffires .25 .08
❑ 51 Byron Bam Morris .25 .08
❑ 52 John Kasay .25 .08
❑ 53 Scott Mitchell .50 .20
❑ 54 Boomer Esiason .50 .20
❑ 55 Eric Metcalf .50 .20
❑ 56 Kevin Greene .50 .20
❑ 57 Courtney Hawkins .25 .08
❑ 58 Johnny Johnson .25 .08
❑ 59 Larry Centers .50 .20
❑ 60 Leroy Hoard .25 .08
❑ 61 Lorenzo White .25 .08
❑ 62 Chris Spielman .50 .20
❑ 63 Carl Pickens .50 .20
❑ 64 Steve Young 2.00 .75
❑ 65 Trent Dilfer 1.00 .40
❑ 66 Erik Kramer .25 .08
❑ 67 Cortez Kennedy .50 .20
❑ 68 Ray Childress .25 .08
❑ 69 Rick Mirer .50 .20
❑ 70 Kevin Williams WR .50 .20
❑ 71 Joey Galloway RC 4.00 1.50
❑ 72 Dan Wilkinson .50 .20
❑ 73 Antonio Freeman RC 3.00 1.25
❑ 74 Curtis Conway 1.00 .40
❑ 75 Troy Aikman 2.50 1.00
❑ 76 Natrone Means .50 .20
❑ 77 Jeff George .50 .20
❑ 78 Curtis Martin RC 8.00 3.00
❑ 79 William Floyd .50 .20
❑ 80 Anthony Miller .50 .20
❑ 81 Greg Hill .50 .20
❑ 82 Craig Heyward .50 .20
❑ 83 Brian Mitchell .25 .08
❑ 84 Anthony Carter .50 .20
❑ 85 Jerome Bettis 1.00 .40
❑ 86 Jim Harbaugh .50 .20
❑ 87 Harvey Williams .25 .08
❑ 88 Tony Martin .50 .20
❑ 89 Rob Moore .50 .20
❑ 90 Neil O'Donnell .50 .20
❑ 91 Cris Carter 1.00 .40
❑ 92 Warren Sapp RC 4.00 1.50
❑ 93 Terry Allen .50 .20
❑ 94 Michael Irvin 1.00 .40
❑ 95 Heath Shuler .50 .20
❑ 96 Cornelius Bennett .50 .20
❑ 97 Randy Baldwin .25 .08
❑ 98 Vince Workman .25 .08
❑ 99 Irving Fryar .50 .20
❑ 100 Randall Cunningham 1.00 .40
❑ 101 James O. Stewart RC 3.00 1.25
❑ 102 Stan Humphries .50 .20
❑ 103 Mario Bates .50 .20
❑ 104 Ben Coates .50 .20
❑ 105 Charlie Garner 1.00 .40
❑ 106 Todd Collins RC .50 .20
❑ 107 Tim Brown 1.00 .40
❑ 108 Edgar Bennett .50 .20
❑ 109 J.J. Stokes RC 1.00 .40
❑ 110 Michael Timpson .25 .08
❑ 111 Junior Seau 1.00 .40
❑ 112 Bernie Parmalee .50 .20
❑ 113 Willie McGinest .50 .20
❑ 114 David Dunn RC .25 .08
❑ 115 Kyle Brady RC 1.00 .40

❑ 116 Vinny Testaverde .50 .20
❑ 117 Ernest Givins .25 .08
❑ 118 Eric Zeier RC 1.00 .40
❑ 119 Michael Jackson .50 .20
❑ 120 Chad May RC .25 .08
❑ 121 Dave Krieg .25 .08
❑ 122 Rodney Hampton .50 .20
❑ 123 Darnay Scott .50 .20
❑ 124 Chris Miller .25 .08
❑ 125 Emmitt Smith 4.00 1.50
❑ 126 Steve McNair RC 8.00 3.00
❑ 127 Warren Moon .50 .20
❑ 128 Robert Brooks 1.00 .40
❑ 129 Bert Emanuel 1.00 .40
❑ 130 John Elway 5.00 2.00
❑ 131 Chris Warren .50 .20
❑ 132 Herschel Walker .50 .20
❑ 133 Terry Kirby .50 .20
❑ 134 Michael Westbrook RC 1.00 .40
❑ 135 Kordell Stewart RC 4.00 1.50
❑ 136 Terrell Davis RC 6.00 2.50
❑ 137 Desmond Howard .50 .20
❑ 138 Rodney Thomas RC .50 .20
❑ 139 Brett Favre 5.00 2.00
❑ 140 Ray Zellars RC .50 .20
❑ 141 Marcus Allen 1.00 .40
❑ 142 Gus Frerotte .50 .20
❑ 143 Steve Bono .50 .20
❑ 144 Aaron Craver .25 .08
❑ P144 Natrone Means P Jumbo 2.00 .75

1996 Crown Royale

❑ COMPLETE SET (144) 50.00 20.00
❑ 1 Dan Marino 5.00 2.00
❑ 2 Frank Sanders .60 .25
❑ 3 Bobby Engram RC 1.00 .40
❑ 4 Cornelius Bennett .40 .15
❑ 5 Steve Bono .40 .15
❑ 6 Aaron Hayden RC .40 .15
❑ 7 Leroy Hoard .40 .15
❑ 8 Brett Perriman .40 .15
❑ 9 Irv Smith .40 .15
❑ 10 Jim Kelly 1.00 .40
❑ 11 Rodney Thomas .40 .15
❑ 12 Eric Bieniemy .40 .15
❑ 13 Darnay Scott .60 .25
❑ 14 Ki-Jana Carter .60 .25
❑ 15 Kerry Collins 1.00 .40
❑ 16 Shannon Sharpe .60 .25
❑ 17 Michael Westbrook 1.00 .40
❑ 18 Steve McNair 2.00 .75
❑ 19 Tony Banks RC 2.00 .75
❑ 20 Rashaan Salaam .60 .25
❑ 21 Terrell Fletcher .40 .15
❑ 22 Michael Timpson .40 .15
❑ 23 Bobby Hoying RC 1.00 .40
❑ 24 Quinn Early .40 .15
❑ 25 Warren Moon .60 .25
❑ 26 Tommy Vardell .40 .15
❑ 27 Marvin Harrison RC 12.00 6.00
❑ 28 Lake Dawson .40 .15
❑ 29 Karim Abdul-Jabbar RC 2.00 .75
❑ 30 Chris Warren .60 .25
❑ 31 Heath Shuler .60 .25
❑ 32 Bert Emanuel .60 .25
❑ 33 Howard Griffith RC .60 .25
❑ 34 Alex Van Dyke RC .60 .25
❑ 35 Isaac Bruce 1.00 .40
❑ 36 Mark Brunell 1.50 .60
❑ 37 Winslow Oliver RC .60 .25
❑ 38 O.J. McDuffie .60 .25
❑ 39 Terrell Owens RC 12.00 6.00
❑ 40 Jerry Rice 2.50 1.00
❑ 41 Henry Ellard .40 .15
❑ 42 Chris Sanders .60 .25
❑ 43 Craig Heyward .40 .15
❑ 44 Eddie Kennison RC 2.00 .75
❑ 45 Terrell Davis 2.00 .75
❑ 46 Rodney Hampton .60 .25
❑ 47 Bryan Still RC .60 .25
❑ 48 Tim Brown 1.00 .40
❑ 49 Keyshawn Johnson RC 6.00 2.50
❑ 50 Barry Sanders 4.00 1.50
❑ 51 Terry Allen .60 .25
❑ 52 Sean Dawkins .40 .15
❑ 53 Bryce Paup .40 .15
❑ 54 Brett Favre 5.00 2.00
❑ 55 Deion Sanders 1.50 .60
❑ 56 Kevin Hardy RC 2.00 .75
❑ 57 Kevin Williams .40 .15
❑ 58 Jeff George .60 .25
❑ 59 Tim Biakabutuka RC 2.00 .75
❑ 60 Drew Bledsoe 1.50 .60
❑ 61 Michael Jackson .60 .25
❑ 62 James O. Stewart .60 .25
❑ 63 Mario Bates .60 .25
❑ 64 Daryl Johnston .60 .25
❑ 65 Herman Moore .60 .25
❑ 66 Ben Coates .60 .25
❑ 67 Terry Glenn RC 6.00 2.50
❑ 68 Robert Smith .60 .25
❑ 69 Irving Fryar .60 .25
❑ 70 Napoleon Kaufman 1.00 .40
❑ 71 Rickey Dudley RC 2.00 .75
❑ 72 Bernie Parmalee .40 .15
❑ 73 Kyle Brady .40 .15
❑ 74 Neil O'Donnell .60 .25
❑ 75 Lawrence Phillips RC 2.00 .75
❑ 76 Hardy Nickerson .40 .15
❑ 77 John Elway 5.00 2.00
❑ 78 Pete Mitchell .60 .25
❑ 79 Jason Dunn RC 1.25 .50
❑ 80 Reggie White 1.00 .40
❑ 81 J.J. Stokes 1.00 .40
❑ 82 Jake Reed .60 .25
❑ 83 Yancey Thigpen .60 .25
❑ 84 Jonathan Ogden RC 2.00 .75
❑ 85 Larry Centers .60 .25
❑ 86 Scott Mitchell .60 .25
❑ 87 Eric Zeier .40 .15
❑ 88 Anthony Miller .60 .25
❑ 89 Brian Blades .40 .15
❑ 90 Cris Carter 1.00 .40
❑ 91 Kordell Stewart 1.00 .40
❑ 92 Charles Way RC 1.25 .50
❑ 93 Jeff Hostetler .40 .15
❑ 94 Brad Johnson 2.00 .75
❑ 95 Marcus Allen 1.00 .40
❑ 96 Errict Rhett .60 .25
❑ 97 Stan Humphries .60 .25
❑ 98 Michael Haynes .40 .15
❑ 99 Curtis Martin 2.00 .75
❑ 100 Troy Aikman 2.50 .75
❑ 101 Earnest Byner .40 .15
❑ 102 Vincent Brisby .40 .15
❑ 103 Zack Crockett .40 .15
❑ 104 Haywood Jeffires .40 .15
❑ 105 Joey Galloway 1.00 .40
❑ 106 Carl Pickens .60 .25
❑ 107 Leeland McElroy RC 1.25 .50
❑ 108 Adrian Murrell .60 .25
❑ 109 Joe Horn RC/C 10.00 5.00
❑ 110 Steve Young 2.00 .75
❑ 111 Andre Rison .60 .25
❑ 112 Jim Everett .40 .15
❑ 113 Jamie Asher RC 1.25 .50
❑ 114 Steve Walsh .40 .15
❑ 115 Robert Brooks 1.00 .40
❑ 116 Eric Moulds RC 8.00 3.00
❑ 117 Edgar Bennett .60 .25
❑ 118 Greg Lloyd .60 .25
❑ 119 Jerris McPhail RC .60 .25
❑ 120 Marshall Faulk 1.50 .60
❑ 121 Dave Brown .40 .15
❑ 122 Harvey Williams .40 .15
❑ 123 Trent Dilfer 1.00 .40
❑ 124 Eddie George RC 8.00 3.00
❑ 125 Jeff Blake 1.00 .40
❑ 126 Mark Chmura .60 .25
❑ 127 Boomer Esiason .60 .25
❑ 128 Jim Harbaugh .60 .25
❑ 129 Bryan Cox .40 .15
❑ 130 Ricky Watters .60 .25
❑ 131 Amani Toomer RC 6.00 2.50
❑ 132 Jim Miller 1.00 .40
❑ 133 Cortez Kennedy .40 .15
❑ 134 Courtney Hawkins .40 .15
❑ 135 Junior Seau 1.00 .40
❑ 136 Tamarick Vanover .60 .25
❑ 137 Jerome Bettis 1.00 .40
❑ 138 Chris Calloway .40 .15
❑ 139 Rick Mirer .60 .25
❑ 140 Thurman Thomas 1.00 .40
❑ 141 Sheddrick Wilson RC .60 .25
❑ 142 Charlie Garner .60 .25
❑ 143 Erik Kramer .40 .15
❑ 144 Emmitt Smith 4.00 1.50

1997 Crown Royale

❑ COMPLETE SET (144) 80.00 30.00
❑ 1 Larry Centers .75 .30
❑ 2 Kent Graham .50 .20
❑ 3 LeShon Johnson .50 .20
❑ 4 Leeland McElroy .50 .20
❑ 5 Jake Plummer RC 10.00 4.00
❑ 6 Jamal Anderson 1.25 .50
❑ 7 Chris Chandler .75 .30
❑ 8 Byron Hanspard RC .75 .30
❑ 9 O.J. Santiago RC .75 .30
❑ 10 Derrick Alexander WR .75 .30
❑ 11 Jay Graham RC .75 .30
❑ 12 Michael Jackson .75 .30
❑ 13 Vinny Testaverde .75 .30
❑ 14 Todd Collins .50 .20
❑ 15 Jay Riemersma RC .50 .20
❑ 16 Antowain Smith RC 5.00 2.00
❑ 17 Steve Tasker .50 .20
❑ 18 Thurman Thomas 1.25 .50
❑ 19 Rae Carruth RC .50 .20
❑ 20 Kerry Collins 1.25 .50
❑ 21 Anthony Johnson .50 .20
❑ 22 Fred Lane RC .75 .30
❑ 23 Muhsin Muhammad .75 .30
❑ 24 Wesley Walls .75 .30
❑ 25 Darnell Autry RC .75 .30
❑ 26 Raymont Harris .50 .20
❑ 27 Erik Kramer .50 .20
❑ 28 Rick Mirer .50 .20
❑ 29 Rashaan Salaam .50 .20
❑ 30 Jeff Blake .75 .30
❑ 31 Ki-Jana Carter .50 .20
❑ 32 Corey Dillon RC 12.00 5.00
❑ 33 Carl Pickens .75 .30
❑ 34 Troy Aikman 2.50 1.00
❑ 35 Michael Irvin 1.25 .50
❑ 36 Daryl Johnston .75 .30
❑ 37 David LaFleur RC 1.25 .50
❑ 38 Deion Sanders 1.25 .50
❑ 39 Emmitt Smith 4.00 1.50
❑ 40 Terrell Davis 1.50 .60
❑ 41 John Elway 5.00 2.00
❑ 42 Ed McCaffrey .75 .30
❑ 43 Shannon Sharpe .75 .30
❑ 44 Neil Smith .75 .30
❑ 45 Scott Mitchell .75 .30
❑ 46 Herman Moore .75 .30
❑ 47 Johnnie Morton .75 .30
❑ 48 Barry Sanders 4.00 1.50
❑ 49 Robert Brooks .75 .30
❑ 50 Mark Chmura .75 .30
❑ 51 Brett Favre 5.00 2.00
❑ 52 Antonio Freeman 1.25 .50
❑ 53 Dorsey Levens 1.25 .50

❑	54 Reggie White	1.25	.50
❑	55 Ken Dilger	.50	.20
❑	56 Marshall Faulk	1.50	.60
❑	57 Jim Harbaugh	.75	.30
❑	58 Marvin Harrison	1.25	.50
❑	59 Mark Brunell	1.50	.60
❑	60 Rob Johnson	1.25	.50
❑	61 Keenan McCardell	.75	.30
❑	62 Natrone Means	.75	.30
❑	63 Jimmy Smith	.75	.30
❑	64 Marcus Allen	1.25	.50
❑	65 Tony Gonzalez RC	6.00	2.50
❑	66 Elvis Grbac	.75	.30
❑	67 Greg Hill	.50	.20
❑	68 Tamarick Vanover	.75	.30
❑	69 Karim Abdul-Jabbar	.75	.30
❑	70 Fred Barnett	.50	.20
❑	71 Dan Marino	5.00	2.00
❑	72 O.J. McDuffie	.75	.30
❑	73 Jerris McPhail	.50	.20
❑	74 Cris Carter	1.25	.50
❑	75 Randall Cunningham	1.25	.50
❑	76 Brad Johnson	1.25	.50
❑	77 Jake Reed	.75	.30
❑	78 Robert Smith	.75	.30
❑	79 Drew Bledsoe	1.50	.60
❑	80 Ben Coates	.75	.30
❑	81 Terry Glenn	1.25	.50
❑	82 Curtis Martin	1.50	.60
❑	83 Troy Davis RC	.75	.30
❑	84 Heath Shuler	.50	.20
❑	85 Irv Smith	.50	.20
❑	86 Danny Wuerffel RC	1.25	.50
❑	87 Tiki Barber RC	12.00	5.00
❑	88 Dave Brown	.50	.20
❑	89 Rodney Hampton	.75	.30
❑	90 Ike Hilliard RC	3.00	1.25
❑	91 Amani Toomer	.75	.30
❑	92 Wayne Chrebet	1.25	.50
❑	93 Keyshawn Johnson	1.25	.50
❑	94 Adrian Murrell	.75	.30
❑	95 Neil O'Donnell	.75	.30
❑	96 Dedric Ward RC	.75	.30
❑	97 Tim Brown	1.25	.50
❑	98 Jeff George	.75	.30
❑	99 Desmond Howard	.75	.30
❑	100 Napoleon Kaufman	1.25	.50
❑	101 Ty Detmer	.75	.30
❑	102 Irving Fryar	.75	.30
❑	103 Bobby Hoying	.75	.30
❑	104 Ricky Watters	.75	.30
❑	105 Jerome Bettis	1.25	.50
❑	106 Will Blackwell RC	.75	.30
❑	107 Charles Johnson	.75	.30
❑	108 George Jones RC	.75	.30
❑	109 Kordell Stewart	1.25	.50
❑	110 Tony Banks	.75	.30
❑	111 Isaac Bruce	1.25	.50
❑	112 Eddie Kennison	.75	.30
❑	113 Lawrence Phillips	.50	.20
❑	114 Jim Everett	.50	.20
❑	115 Stan Humphries	.75	.30
❑	116 Freddie Jones	.75	.30
❑	117 Tony Martin	.75	.30
❑	118 Junior Seau	1.25	.50
❑	119 Jim Druckenmiller RC	.75	.30
❑	120 Garrison Hearst	.75	.30
❑	121 Brent Jones	.50	.20
❑	122 Terrell Owens	1.50	.60
❑	123 Jerry Rice	2.50	1.00
❑	124 Steve Young	1.50	.60
❑	125 Chad Brown	.50	.20
❑	126 Joey Galloway	.75	.30
❑	127 Jon Kitna RC	6.00	2.50
❑	128 Warren Moon	1.25	.50
❑	129 Chris Warren	.75	.30
❑	130 Mike Alstott	1.25	.50
❑	131 Reidel Anthony RC	1.25	.50
❑	132 Trent Dilfer	1.25	.50
❑	133 Warrick Dunn RC	6.00	2.50
❑	134 Karl Williams RC	.75	.30
❑	135 Willie Davis	.50	.20
❑	136 Eddie George	1.25	.50
❑	137 Joey Kent RC	1.25	.50
❑	138 Steve McNair	1.50	.60
❑	139 Chris Sanders	.50	.20
❑	140 Terry Allen	1.25	.50
❑	141 Jamie Asher	.50	.20
❑	142 Stephen Davis	1.25	.50
❑	143 Henry Ellard	.50	.20
❑	144 Gus Frerotte	.50	.20
❑	S1 Mark Brunell Sample	1.00	.40

1998 Crown Royale

❑	COMPLETE SET (144)	100.00	40.00
❑	1 Larry Centers	.50	.20
❑	2 Rob Moore	.75	.30
❑	3 Adrian Murrell	.75	.30
❑	4 Jake Plummer	1.25	.50
❑	5 Jamal Anderson	1.25	.50
❑	6 Chris Chandler	.75	.30
❑	7 Tim Dwight RC	3.00	1.25
❑	8 Tony Martin	.75	.30
❑	9 Jay Graham	.50	.20
❑	10 Pat Johnson RC	2.50	1.00
❑	11 Jermaine Lewis	.75	.30
❑	12 Eric Zeier	.75	.30
❑	13 Rob Johnson	.75	.30
❑	14 Eric Moulds	1.25	.50
❑	15 Antowain Smith	1.25	.50
❑	16 Bruce Smith	.75	.30
❑	17 Steve Beuerlein	.75	.30
❑	18 Anthony Johnson	.50	.20
❑	19 Fred Lane	.50	.20
❑	20 Muhsin Muhammad	.75	.30
❑	21 Curtis Conway	.75	.30
❑	22 Curtis Enis RC	1.50	.60
❑	23 Erik Kramer	.50	.20
❑	24 Tony Parrish RC	3.00	1.25
❑	25 Corey Dillon	1.25	.50
❑	26 Neil O'Donnell	.75	.30
❑	27 Carl Pickens	.75	.30
❑	28 Takeo Spikes RC	3.00	1.25
❑	29 Troy Aikman	2.50	1.00
❑	30 Michael Irvin	1.25	.50
❑	31 Deion Sanders	1.25	.50
❑	32 Emmitt Smith	4.00	1.50
❑	33 Chris Warren	.75	.30
❑	34 Terrell Davis	1.25	.50
❑	35 John Elway	5.00	2.00
❑	36 Brian Griese RC	6.00	2.50
❑	37 Ed McCaffrey	.75	.30
❑	38 Shannon Sharpe	.75	.30
❑	39 Rod Smith WR	.75	.30
❑	40 Charlie Batch RC	3.00	1.25
❑	41 Herman Moore	.75	.30
❑	42 Johnnie Morton	.75	.30
❑	43 Barry Sanders	4.00	1.50
❑	44 Bryant Westbrook	.50	.20
❑	45 Robert Brooks	.75	.30
❑	46 Brett Favre	5.00	2.00
❑	47 Antonio Freeman	1.25	.50
❑	48 Raymont Harris	.50	.20
❑	49 Vonnie Holliday RC	2.50	1.00
❑	50 Reggie White	1.25	.50
❑	51 Marshall Faulk	1.50	.60
❑	52 E.G. Green RC	2.50	1.00
❑	53 Marvin Harrison	1.25	.50
❑	54 Peyton Manning RC	25.00	12.50
❑	55 Jerome Pathon RC	3.00	1.25
❑	56 Tavian Banks RC	.75	.30
❑	57 Mark Brunell	1.25	.50
❑	58 Keenan McCardell	.75	.30
❑	59 Jimmy Smith	.75	.30
❑	60 Fred Taylor RC	5.00	2.00
❑	61 Derrick Alexander WR	.75	.30
❑	62 Tony Gonzalez	1.25	.50
❑	63 Elvis Grbac	.75	.30
❑	64 Andre Rison	.75	.30
❑	65 Rashaan Shehee RC	2.50	1.00
❑	66 Derrick Thomas	1.25	.50
❑	67 Karim Abdul-Jabbar	1.25	.50
❑	68 John Avery RC	2.50	1.00
❑	69 Oronde Gadsden RC	3.00	1.25
❑	70 Dan Marino	5.00	2.00
❑	71 O.J. McDuffie	.75	.30
❑	72 Cris Carter	1.25	.50
❑	73 Randall Cunningham	1.25	.50
❑	74 Brad Johnson	1.25	.50
❑	75 Randy Moss RC	12.00	6.00
❑	76 John Randle	.75	.30
❑	77 Jake Reed	.75	.30
❑	78 Robert Smith	1.25	.50
❑	79 Drew Bledsoe	2.00	.75
❑	80 Robert Edwards RC	2.50	1.00
❑	81 Terry Glenn	1.25	.50
❑	82 Tebucky Jones RC	1.50	.60
❑	83 Tony Simmons RC	2.50	1.00
❑	84 Mark Fields	.50	.20
❑	85 Andre Hastings	.50	.20
❑	86 Danny Wuerffel	.75	.30
❑	87 Ray Zellars	.50	.20
❑	88 Tiki Barber	1.25	.50
❑	89 Ike Hilliard	.75	.30
❑	90 Joe Jurevicius RC	3.00	1.25
❑	91 Danny Kanell	.75	.30
❑	92 Wayne Chrebet	1.25	.50
❑	93 Glenn Foley	.75	.30
❑	94 Keyshawn Johnson	1.25	.50
❑	95 Leon Johnson	.50	.20
❑	96 Curtis Martin	1.25	.50
❑	97 Tim Brown	1.25	.50
❑	98 Jeff George	.75	.30
❑	99 Napoleon Kaufman	1.25	.50
❑	100 Jon Ritchie RC	2.50	1.00
❑	101 Charles Woodson RC	4.00	1.50
❑	102 Irving Fryar	.75	.30
❑	103 Bobby Hoying	.75	.30
❑	104 Allen Rossum RC	1.50	.60
❑	105 Duce Staley	1.50	.60
❑	106 Jerome Bettis	1.25	.50
❑	107 Chris Fuamatu-Ma'afala RC	2.50	1.00
❑	108 Charles Johnson	.50	.20
❑	109 Levon Kirkland	.50	.20
❑	110 Kordell Stewart	1.25	.50
❑	111 Hines Ward RC	10.00	5.00
❑	112 Tony Banks	.75	.30
❑	113 Tony Horne RC	1.50	.60
❑	114 Eddie Kennison	.75	.30
❑	115 Amp Lee	.50	.20
❑	116 Freddie Jones	.50	.20
❑	117 Ryan Leaf RC	3.00	1.25
❑	118 Natrone Means	.75	.30
❑	119 Mikhael Ricks RC	2.50	1.00
❑	120 Bryan Still	.50	.20
❑	121 Marc Edwards	.50	.20
❑	122 Garrison Hearst	1.25	.50
❑	123 Terrell Owens	1.25	.50
❑	124 Jerry Rice	2.50	1.00
❑	125 J.J. Stokes	.75	.30
❑	126 Steve Young	1.50	.60
❑	127 Joey Galloway	.75	.30
❑	128 Ahman Green RC	12.00	5.00
❑	129 Warren Moon	1.25	.50
❑	130 Ricky Watters	.75	.30
❑	131 Mike Alstott	1.25	.50
❑	132 Trent Dilfer	1.25	.50
❑	133 Warrick Dunn	1.25	.50
❑	134 Jacquez Green RC	2.50	1.00
❑	135 Warren Sapp	.75	.30
❑	136 Kevin Dyson RC	3.00	1.25
❑	137 Eddie George	1.25	.50
❑	138 Steve McNair	1.25	.50
❑	139 Yancey Thigpen	.50	.20
❑	140 Stephen Alexander RC	2.50	1.00
❑	141 Terry Allen	1.25	.50
❑	142 Trent Green	1.50	.60
❑	143 Skip Hicks RC	2.50	1.00
❑	144 Michael Westbrook	.75	.30

1999 Crown Royale

❑	COMPLETE SET (144)	120.00	50.00
❑	1 David Boston RC	3.00	1.25
❑	2 Chris Greisen RC	2.50	1.00
❑	3 Rob Moore	.75	.30
❑	4 Jake Plummer	.75	.30
❑	5 Frank Sanders	.75	.30
❑	6 Jamal Anderson	1.25	.50
❑	7 Chris Chandler	.75	.30
❑	8 Tim Dwight	1.25	.50

❑ 9 Byron Hanspard .50 .20
❑ 10 Stoney Case .50 .20
❑ 11 Priest Holmes 3.00 1.25
❑ 12 Jermaine Lewis .75 .30
❑ 13 Chris McAlister RC 2.50 1.00
❑ 14 Brandon Stokley RC 4.00 1.50
❑ 15 Doug Flutie 1.25 .50
❑ 16 Eric Moulds 1.25 .50
❑ 17 Peerless Price RC 3.00 1.25
❑ 18 Antowain Smith 1.25 .50
❑ 19 Steve Beuerlein .50 .20
❑ 20 Tim Biakabutuka .75 .30
❑ 21 Muhsin Muhammad .75 .30
❑ 22 Curtis Conway .75 .30
❑ 23 Curtis Enis .50 .20
❑ 24 Shane Matthews .75 .30
❑ 25 Cade McNown RC 2.50 1.00
❑ 26 Marcus Robinson 1.25 .50
❑ 27 Jeff Blake .75 .30
❑ 28 Scott Covington RC 3.00 1.25
❑ 29 Corey Dillon 1.25 .50
❑ 30 Damon Griffin RC 2.50 1.00
❑ 31 Carl Pickens .75 .30
❑ 32 Akili Smith RC 2.50 1.00
❑ 33 Tim Couch RC 3.00 1.25
❑ 34 Kevin Johnson RC 3.00 1.25
❑ 35 Terry Kirby .50 .20
❑ 36 Leslie Shepherd .50 .20
❑ 37 Troy Aikman 3.00 1.25
❑ 38 Rocket Ismail .50 .20
❑ 39 Wane McGarity RC 1.50 .60
❑ 40 Deion Sanders 1.25 .50
❑ 41 Emmitt Smith 4.00 1.50
❑ 42 Terrell Davis 1.25 .50
❑ 43 Brian Griese 1.25 .50
❑ 44 Ed McCaffrey .75 .30
❑ 45 Shannon Sharpe .75 .30
❑ 46 Rod Smith .75 .30
❑ 47 Charlie Batch 1.25 .50
❑ 48 Germane Crowell .50 .20
❑ 49 Sedrick Irvin RC 1.50 .60
❑ 50 Herman Moore .75 .30
❑ 51 Barry Sanders 5.00 2.00
❑ 52 Brett Favre 5.00 2.00
❑ 53 Antonio Freeman 1.25 .50
❑ 54 Matt Hasselbeck 1.25 .50
❑ 55 Dorsey Levens 1.25 .50
❑ 56 Basil Mitchell RC 1.50 .60
❑ 57 E.G. Green .50 .20
❑ 58 Marvin Harrison 1.25 .50
❑ 59 Edgerrin James RC 10.00 4.00
❑ 60 Peyton Manning 5.00 2.00
❑ 61 Terrence Wilkins RC 2.50 1.00
❑ 62 Mark Brunell 1.25 .50
❑ 63 Keenan McCardell .75 .30
❑ 64 Jimmy Smith .75 .30
❑ 65 Fred Taylor 1.25 .50
❑ 66 Derrick Alexander WR .75 .30
❑ 67 Elvis Grbac .75 .30
❑ 68 Warren Moon .50 .20
❑ 69 Larry Parker RC 3.00 1.25
❑ 70 Andre Rison .75 .30
❑ 71 Cecil Collins RC 1.50 .60
❑ 72 Damon Huard 1.25 .50
❑ 73 James Johnson RC 2.50 1.00
❑ 74 Rob Konrad RC 2.50 1.00
❑ 75 Dan Marino 5.00 2.00
❑ 76 O.J. McDuffie .75 .30
❑ 77 Cris Carter 1.25 .50
❑ 78 Daunte Culpepper RC 10.00 4.00
❑ 79 Randall Cunningham 1.25 .50
❑ 80 Randy Moss UER 4.00 1.50
❑ 81 Robert Smith .50 .20
❑ 82 Michael Bishop RC 3.00 1.25
❑ 83 Drew Bledsoe 2.00 .75
❑ 84 Ben Coates .75 .30
❑ 85 Kevin Faulk RC 3.00 1.25
❑ 86 Terry Glenn 1.25 .50
❑ 87 Billy Joe Hobert .50 .20
❑ 88 Eddie Kennison .75 .30
❑ 89 Keith Poole .50 .20
❑ 90 Ricky Williams RC 5.00 2.00
❑ 91 Sean Bennett RC 1.50 .60
❑ 92 Kerry Collins .75 .30
❑ 93 Pete Mitchell .50 .20
❑ 94 Amani Toomer .50 .20
❑ 95 Wayne Chrebet .75 .30
❑ 96 Keyshawn Johnson 1.25 .50
❑ 97 Curtis Martin 1.25 .50
❑ 98 Tim Brown 1.25 .50
❑ 99 Scott Dreisbach RC 2.50 1.00
❑ 100 Rich Gannon 1.25 .50
❑ 101 Napoleon Kaufman 1.25 .50
❑ 102 Tyrone Wheatley .75 .30
❑ 103 Duce Staley 1.25 .50
❑ 104 Charles Johnson .50 .20
❑ 105 Donovan McNabb RC 12.00 5.00
❑ 106 Torrance Small .50 .20
❑ 107 Jed Weaver RC 1.50 .60
❑ 108 Jerome Bettis 1.25 .50
❑ 109 Troy Edwards RC 2.50 1.00
❑ 110 Kordell Stewart .75 .30
❑ 111 Amos Zereoue RC 3.00 1.25
❑ 112 Isaac Bruce 1.25 .50
❑ 113 Marshall Faulk 2.00 .75
❑ 114 Joe Germaine RC 2.50 1.00
❑ 115 Torry Holt RC 8.00 3.00
❑ 116 Kurt Warner RC 15.00 6.00
❑ 117 Jim Harbaugh .75 .30
❑ 118 Erik Kramer .50 .20
❑ 119 Natrone Means .75 .30
❑ 120 Junior Seau 1.25 .50
❑ 121 Jeff Garcia RC 15.00 6.00
❑ 122 Terrell Owens 1.25 .50
❑ 123 Jerry Rice 4.00 1.50
❑ 124 J.J. Stokes .75 .30
❑ 125 Steve Young 2.00 .75
❑ 126 Sean Dawkins .50 .20
❑ 127 Brock Huard RC 3.00 1.25
❑ 128 Jon Kitna 1.25 .50
❑ 129 Derrick Mayes .75 .30
❑ 130 Charlie Rogers RC 1.50 .60
❑ 131 Ricky Watters .75 .30
❑ 132 Mike Alstott 1.25 .50
❑ 133 Trent Dilfer .75 .30
❑ 134 Warrick Dunn 1.25 .50
❑ 135 Eric Zeier .75 .30
❑ 136 Kevin Daft RC 2.50 1.00
❑ 137 Kevin Dyson .75 .30
❑ 138 Eddie George 1.25 .50
❑ 139 Steve McNair 1.25 .50
❑ 140 Neil O'Donnell .75 .30
❑ 141 Champ Bailey RC 4.00 1.50
❑ 142 Albert Connell .50 .20
❑ 143 Stephen Davis 1.25 .50
❑ 144 Brad Johnson 1.25 .50

2000 Crown Royale

❑ COMPLETE SET (144) 100.00 40.00
❑ 1 Rob Moore .60 .25
❑ 2 Jake Plummer .60 .25
❑ 3 Frank Sanders .60 .25
❑ 4 Jamal Anderson 1.00 .40
❑ 5 Chris Chandler .60 .25
❑ 6 Tim Dwight 1.00 .40
❑ 7 Tony Banks .60 .25
❑ 8 Priest Holmes 1.25 .50
❑ 9 Qadry Ismail .60 .25
❑ 10 Doug Flutie 1.00 .40
❑ 11 Rob Johnson .60 .25
❑ 12 Eric Moulds 1.00 .40
❑ 13 Peerless Price .60 .25
❑ 14 Steve Beuerlein .60 .25
❑ 15 Patrick Jeffers 1.00 .40
❑ 16 Muhsin Muhammad .60 .25
❑ 17 Curtis Enis .40 .15
❑ 18 Cade McNown .40 .15
❑ 19 Marcus Robinson 1.00 .40
❑ 20 Corey Dillon 1.00 .40
❑ 21 Darnay Scott .60 .25
❑ 22 Akili Smith .40 .15
❑ 23 Karim Abdul-Jabbar .60 .25
❑ 24 Tim Couch .60 .25
❑ 25 Kevin Johnson 1.00 .40
❑ 26 Troy Aikman 2.00 .75
❑ 27 Joey Galloway .60 .25
❑ 28 Emmitt Smith 2.00 .75
❑ 29 Terrell Davis 1.00 .40
❑ 30 Olandis Gary 1.00 .40
❑ 31 Brian Griese 1.00 .40
❑ 32 Ed McCaffrey 1.00 .40
❑ 33 Charlie Batch 1.00 .40
❑ 34 Herman Moore .60 .25
❑ 35 Barry Sanders 2.50 1.00
❑ 36 James Stewart .60 .25
❑ 37 Brett Favre 3.00 1.25
❑ 38 Antonio Freeman 1.00 .40
❑ 39 Dorsey Levens .60 .25
❑ 40 Marvin Harrison 1.00 .40
❑ 41 Edgerrin James 1.50 .60
❑ 42 Peyton Manning 2.50 1.00
❑ 43 Mark Brunell 1.00 .40
❑ 44 Keenan McCardell .60 .25
❑ 45 Jimmy Smith .60 .25
❑ 46 Fred Taylor 1.00 .40
❑ 47 Derrick Alexander .60 .25
❑ 48 Tony Gonzalez .60 .25
❑ 49 Elvis Grbac .60 .25
❑ 50 Damon Huard 1.00 .40
❑ 51 James Johnson .40 .15
❑ 52 Dan Marino 3.00 1.25
❑ 53 O.J. McDuffie .60 .25
❑ 54 Cris Carter 1.00 .40
❑ 55 Daunte Culpepper 1.25 .50
❑ 56 Jeff George .60 .25
❑ 57 Randy Moss 2.00 .75
❑ 58 Robert Smith 1.00 .40
❑ 59 Drew Bledsoe 1.25 .50
❑ 60 Terry Glenn .60 .25
❑ 61 Lawyer Milloy .60 .25
❑ 62 Jeff Blake .60 .25
❑ 63 Keith Poole .40 .15
❑ 64 Ricky Williams 1.00 .40
❑ 65 Kerry Collins .60 .25
❑ 66 Ike Hilliard .60 .25
❑ 67 Amani Toomer .40 .15
❑ 68 Wayne Chrebet .60 .25
❑ 69 Keyshawn Johnson 1.00 .40
❑ 70 Ray Lucas .60 .25
❑ 71 Curtis Martin 1.00 .40
❑ 72 Vinny Testaverde .60 .25
❑ 73 Tim Brown 1.00 .40
❑ 74 Rich Gannon 1.00 .40
❑ 75 Napoleon Kaufman .60 .25
❑ 76 Tyrone Wheatley .60 .25
❑ 77 Donovan McNabb 1.50 .60
❑ 78 Torrance Small .40 .15
❑ 79 Duce Staley 1.00 .40
❑ 80 Jerome Bettis 1.00 .40
❑ 81 Troy Edwards .40 .15
❑ 82 Kordell Stewart .60 .25
❑ 83 Isaac Bruce 1.00 .40
❑ 84 Marshall Faulk 1.25 .50
❑ 85 Torry Holt 1.00 .40
❑ 86 Kurt Warner 2.00 .75
❑ 87 Jim Harbaugh .60 .25
❑ 88 Jermaine Fazande .40 .15
❑ 89 Junior Seau 1.00 .40
❑ 90 Charlie Garner .60 .25
❑ 91 Terrell Owens 1.00 .40
❑ 92 Jerry Rice 2.00 .75
❑ 93 Steve Young 1.25 .50
❑ 94 Sean Dawkins .40 .15

❑ 95 Jon Kitna 1.00 .40
❑ 96 Derrick Mayes .60 .25
❑ 97 Ricky Watters .60 .25
❑ 98 Mike Alstott 1.00 .40
❑ 99 Warrick Dunn 1.00 .40
❑ 100 Jacquez Green .40 .15
❑ 101 Shaun King .40 .15
❑ 102 Kevin Dyson .60 .25
❑ 103 Eddie George 1.00 .40
❑ 104 Jevon Kearse 1.00 .40
❑ 105 Steve McNair 1.00 .40
❑ 106 Stephen Davis 1.00 .40
❑ 107 Brad Johnson 1.00 .40
❑ 108 Michael Westbrook .60 .25
❑ 109 Shaun Alexander RC 12.00 5.00
❑ 110 Tom Brady RC 30.00 12.50
❑ 111 Marc Bulger RC 5.00 2.00
❑ 112 Plaxico Burress RC 4.00 1.50
❑ 113 Giovanni Carmazzi RC 1.25 .50
❑ 114 Kwame Cavil RC 1.25 .50
❑ 115 Chris Cole RC 2.00 .75
❑ 116 Chris Coleman RC 2.50 1.00
❑ 117 Laveranues Coles RC 2.50 1.00
❑ 118 Ron Dayne RC 2.50 1.00
❑ 119 Reuben Droughns RC 3.00 1.25
❑ 120 Ron Dugans RC 1.25 .50
❑ 121 Danny Farmer RC 2.00 .75
❑ 122 Chafie Fields RC 1.25 .50
❑ 123 Joe Hamilton RC 2.00 .75
❑ 124 Todd Husak RC 2.50 1.00
❑ 125 Darrell Jackson RC 4.00 1.50
❑ 126 Thomas Jones RC 4.00 1.50
❑ 127 Jamal Lewis RC 6.00 2.50
❑ 128 Tee Martin RC 2.50 1.00
❑ 129 Rondell Mealey RC 1.25 .50
❑ 130 Sylvester Morris RC 2.00 .75
❑ 131 Chad Morton RC 2.50 1.00
❑ 132 Dennis Northcutt RC 2.50 1.00
❑ 133 Chad Pennington RC 6.00 2.50
❑ 134 Travis Prentice RC 2.00 .75
❑ 135 Tim Rattay RC 2.50 1.00
❑ 136 Chris Redman RC 2.00 .75
❑ 137 J.R. Redmond RC 2.00 .75
❑ 138 R.Jay Soward RC 2.00 .75
❑ 139 Shyrone Stith RC 2.50 1.00
❑ 140 Travis Taylor RC 2.50 1.00
❑ 141 Troy Walters RC 2.50 1.00
❑ 142 Peter Warrick RC 2.50 1.00
❑ 143 Dez White RC 2.50 1.00
❑ 144 Michael Wiley RC 2.00 .75
❑ S1 Jon Kitna Sample 2.00 .75

2001 Crown Royale

❑ COMP.SET w/o SP's (144) 25.00 10.00
❑ 1 David Boston 1.00 .40
❑ 2 Thomas Jones .60 .25
❑ 3 Rob Moore .60 .25
❑ 4 Michael Pittman .40 .15
❑ 5 Jake Plummer .60 .25
❑ 6 Jamal Anderson 1.00 .40
❑ 7 Chris Chandler .60 .25
❑ 8 Tim Dwight 1.00 .40
❑ 9 Shawn Jefferson .40 .15
❑ 10 Doug Johnson .40 .15
❑ 11 Terance Mathis .60 .25
❑ 12 Tony Banks .60 .25
❑ 13 Trent Dilfer .60 .25
❑ 14 Elvis Grbac .60 .25
❑ 15 Priest Holmes 1.25 .50
❑ 16 Qadry Ismail .60 .25
❑ 17 Jamal Lewis 1.50 .60
❑ 18 Ray Lewis 1.00 .40
❑ 19 Shannon Sharpe .60 .25
❑ 20 Shawn Bryson .40 .15
❑ 21 Rob Johnson .60 .25
❑ 22 Eric Moulds .60 .25
❑ 23 Peerless Price .60 .25
❑ 24 Antowain Smith .60 .25
❑ 25 Steve Beuerlein .60 .25
❑ 26 Tim Biakabutuka .60 .25
❑ 27 Patrick Jeffers .60 .25
❑ 28 Muhsin Muhammad .60 .25
❑ 29 James Allen .60 .25
❑ 30 Bobby Engram .40 .15
❑ 31 Cade McNown .40 .15
❑ 32 Marcus Robinson 1.00 .40
❑ 33 Brian Urlacher 1.50 .60
❑ 34 Corey Dillon 1.00 .40
❑ 35 Jon Kitna .60 .25
❑ 36 Akili Smith .40 .15
❑ 37 Peter Warrick 1.00 .40
❑ 38 Tim Couch .60 .25
❑ 39 Kevin Johnson .60 .25
❑ 40 Travis Prentice .40 .15
❑ 41 Troy Aikman 1.50 .60
❑ 42 Rocket Ismail .60 .25
❑ 43 Emmitt Smith 2.00 .75
❑ 44 Mike Anderson 1.00 .40
❑ 45 Terrell Davis 1.00 .40
❑ 46 Olandis Gary .60 .25
❑ 47 Brian Griese 1.00 .40
❑ 48 Ed McCaffrey 1.00 .40
❑ 49 Rod Smith .60 .25
❑ 50 Charlie Batch 1.00 .40
❑ 51 Herman Moore .60 .25
❑ 52 Johnnie Morton .60 .25
❑ 53 James Stewart .60 .25
❑ 54 Brett Favre 3.00 1.25
❑ 55 Antonio Freeman 1.00 .40
❑ 56 Ahman Green 1.00 .40
❑ 57 Dorsey Levens .60 .25
❑ 58 Bill Schroeder .60 .25
❑ 59 Marvin Harrison 1.00 .40
❑ 60 Edgerrin James 1.25 .50
❑ 61 Peyton Manning 2.50 1.00
❑ 62 Jerome Pathon .60 .25
❑ 63 Mark Brunell 1.00 .40
❑ 64 Keenan McCardell .40 .15
❑ 65 Jimmy Smith .60 .25
❑ 66 Fred Taylor 1.00 .40
❑ 67 Derrick Alexander .60 .25
❑ 68 Tony Gonzalez .60 .25
❑ 69 Sylvester Morris .40 .15
❑ 70 Tony Richardson .40 .15
❑ 71 Jay Fiedler 1.00 .40
❑ 72 Oronde Gadsden .60 .25
❑ 73 Tony Martin .60 .25
❑ 74 James McKnight .60 .25
❑ 75 Lamar Smith .60 .25
❑ 76 Cris Carter 1.00 .40
❑ 77 Daunte Culpepper 1.00 .40
❑ 78 Randy Moss 2.00 .75
❑ 79 Robert Smith .60 .25
❑ 80 Drew Bledsoe 1.25 .50
❑ 81 Troy Brown .60 .25
❑ 82 Kevin Faulk .60 .25
❑ 83 Terry Glenn .60 .25
❑ 84 J.R. Redmond .40 .15
❑ 85 Jeff Blake .60 .25
❑ 86 Aaron Brooks .40 .15
❑ 87 Joe Horn .60 .25
❑ 88 Ricky Williams 1.00 .40
❑ 89 Tiki Barber 1.00 .40
❑ 90 Kerry Collins .60 .25
❑ 91 Ron Dayne 1.00 .40
❑ 92 Ike Hilliard .60 .25
❑ 93 Amani Toomer .40 .15
❑ 94 Wayne Chrebet .60 .25
❑ 95 Curtis Martin 1.00 .40
❑ 96 Chad Pennington 1.50 .60
❑ 97 Vinny Testaverde .60 .25
❑ 98 Dedric Ward .40 .15
❑ 99 Tim Brown 1.00 .40
❑ 100 Rich Gannon 1.00 .40
❑ 101 Napoleon Kaufman .60 .25
❑ 102 Andre Rison .60 .25
❑ 103 Tyrone Wheatley .60 .25
❑ 104 Charles Johnson .40 .15
❑ 105 Donovan McNabb 1.25 .50
❑ 106 Torrance Small .40 .15
❑ 107 Duce Staley 1.00 .40
❑ 108 Jerome Bettis 1.00 .40
❑ 109 Plaxico Burress 1.00 .40
❑ 110 Kordell Stewart .60 .25
❑ 111 Hines Ward 1.00 .40
❑ 112 Isaac Bruce 1.00 .40
❑ 113 Marshall Faulk 1.25 .50
❑ 114 Trent Green 1.00 .40
❑ 115 Az-Zahir Hakim .40 .15
❑ 116 Torry Holt 1.00 .40
❑ 117 Kurt Warner 2.00 .75
❑ 118 Curtis Conway .60 .25
❑ 119 Doug Flutie 1.00 .40
❑ 120 Jeff Graham .40 .15
❑ 121 Junior Seau 1.00 .40
❑ 122 Jeff Garcia 1.00 .40
❑ 123 Charlie Garner .60 .25
❑ 124 Terrell Owens 1.00 .40
❑ 125 Jerry Rice 2.00 .75
❑ 126 Shaun Alexander 1.25 .50
❑ 127 Darrell Jackson 1.00 .40
❑ 128 Ricky Watters .60 .25
❑ 129 Mike Alstott 1.00 .40
❑ 130 Warrick Dunn 1.00 .40
❑ 131 Brad Johnson 1.00 .40
❑ 132 Keyshawn Johnson 1.00 .40
❑ 133 Shaun King .40 .15
❑ 134 Ryan Leaf .60 .25
❑ 135 Warren Sapp .60 .25
❑ 136 Kevin Dyson .60 .25
❑ 137 Eddie George 1.00 .40
❑ 138 Jevon Kearse .60 .25
❑ 139 Derrick Mason .60 .25
❑ 140 Steve McNair 1.00 .40
❑ 141 Stephen Davis 1.00 .40
❑ 142 Jeff George .60 .25
❑ 143 Deion Sanders 1.00 .40
❑ 144 Michael Westbrook .60 .25
❑ 145 Anthony Thomas AU/250 RC 25.00 10.00
❑ 146 Michael Vick AU/250 RC 120.00 60.00
❑ 147 Chris Chambers AU/250 RC 50.00 25.00
❑ 148 Michael Bennett AU/250 RC 20.00 8.00
❑ 149 Chris Weinke AU/250 RC 25.00 10.00
❑ 150 Drew Brees AU/250 RC 125.00 75.00
❑ 151 L.Tomlinson AU/250 RC 200.00 125.00
❑ 152 M.Tuiasosopo AU/250 RC 25.00 10.00
❑ 153 David Terrell AU/250 RC 25.00 10.00
❑ 154 Rod Gardner AU/250 RC 25.00 10.00
❑ 155 Dan Alexander/1750 RC 10.00 4.00
❑ 156 Brian Allen/1750 RC 6.00 2.50
❑ 157 David Allen/750 RC 12.00 5.00
❑ 158 Will Allen/1750 RC 6.00 2.50
❑ 159 Scotty Anderson/1000 RC 8.00 3.00
❑ 160 Adam Archuleta/1750 RC 10.00 4.00
❑ 161 Jeff Backus/1750 RC 6.00 2.50
❑ 162 Alex Bannister/1000 RC 8.00 3.00
❑ 163 Kevan Barlow/750 RC 12.00 5.00
❑ 164 Gary Baxter/1750 RC 6.00 2.50
❑ 165 Josh Booty/500 RC 20.00 7.50
❑ 166 Larry Casher/1750 RC 6.00 2.50
❑ 167 Tay Cody/1750 RC 5.00 2.00
❑ 168 Jarrod Cooper/1750 RC 10.00 4.00
❑ 169 Ennis Davis/1750 RC 5.00 2.00
❑ 170 Leonard Davis/1750 RC 6.00 2.50
❑ 171 Tony Dixon/1750 RC 8.00 3.00
❑ 172 Tony Driver/1750 RC 10.00 4.00
❑ 173 Heath Evans/1750 RC 6.00 2.50
❑ 174 Jamar Fletcher/1750 RC 6.00 2.50
❑ 175 Derrick Gibson/1750 RC 6.00 2.50
❑ 176 Morlon Greenwood/1750 RC 6.00 2.50
❑ 177 Edgerton Hartwell/1750 RC 5.00 2.00
❑ 178 Tim Hasselbeck/500 RC 20.00 7.50
❑ 179 Todd Heap/1750 RC 10.00 4.00
❑ 180 Travis Henry/750 RC 20.00 7.50
❑ 181 Josh Heupel/500 RC 20.00 7.50
❑ 182 Sedrick Hodge/1750 RC 5.00 2.00
❑ 183 Jabari Holloway/1750 RC 6.00 2.50
❑ 184 Willie Howard/1750 RC 6.00 2.50
❑ 185 Steve Hutchinson/1750 RC 6.00 2.50
❑ 186 James Jackson/750 RC 12.00 5.00
❑ 187 Chad Johnson/1000 RC 30.00 12.50
❑ 188 Rudi Johnson/750 RC 25.00 10.00
❑ 189 LaMont Jordan/750 RC 25.00 10.00
❑ 190 Ben Leard/500 RC 12.00 5.00
❑ 191 Alex Lincoln/1750 RC 6.00 2.50
❑ 192 Torrance Marshall/1750 RC 10.00 4.00
❑ 193 Deuce McAllister/750 RC 40.00 15.00
❑ 194 Jason McKinley/500 RC 12.00 5.00
❑ 195 Mike McMahon/500 RC 20.00 7.50
❑ 196 Snoop Minnis/1000 RC 8.00 3.00

❑	197	Travis Minor/750 RC	12.00	5.00
❑	198	Freddie Mitchell/1000 RC	12.00	5.00
❑	199	Zeke Moreno/1750 RC	10.00	4.00
❑	200	Quincy Morgan/1000 RC	12.00	5.00
❑	201	Santana Moss/1000 RC	20.00	7.50
❑	202	Bobby Newcombe/1000 RC	8.00	3.00
❑	203	Moran Norris/1750 RC	5.00	2.00
❑	204	Tommy Polley/1750 RC	10.00	4.00
❑	205	Ken-Yon Rambo/1000 RC	8.00	3.00
❑	206	Koren Robinson/1000 RC	12.00	5.00
❑	207	Sage Rosenfels/500 RC	20.00	7.50
❑	208	John Schlech/1750t RC	5.00	2.00
❑	209	Brandon Spoon/1750 RC	10.00	4.00
❑	210	Michael Stone/1750 RC	5.00	2.00
❑	211	Marcus Stroud/1750 RC	10.00	4.00
❑	212	Vinny Sutherland/1000 RC	8.00	3.00
❑	213	Joe Tafoya/1750 RC	5.00	2.00
❑	214	Clevan Thomas/1750 RC	5.00	2.00
❑	215	Ja'Mar Toombs/1750 RC	6.00	2.50
❑	216	Fred Wakefield/1750 RC	6.00	2.50
❑	217	Reggie Wayne/1000 RC	25.00	10.00
❑	218	Reggie White/750 RC	12.00	5.00

2002 Crown Royale

❑		COMPLETE SET (216)	200.00	100.00
❑		COMP.SET w/o SP's (144)	50.00	20.00
❑	1	David Boston	1.00	.40
❑	2	Thomas Jones	.60	.25
❑	3	Jake Plummer	.60	.25
❑	4	Frank Sanders	.40	.15
❑	5	Jamal Anderson	.60	.25
❑	6	Warrick Dunn	1.00	.40
❑	7	Brian Finneran	.40	.15
❑	8	Shawn Jefferson	.40	.15
❑	9	Michael Vick	4.00	1.50
❑	10	Jeff Blake	.60	.25
❑	11	Jamal Lewis	1.00	.40
❑	12	Ray Lewis	1.00	.40
❑	13	Chris Redman	.40	.15
❑	14	Travis Taylor	.60	.25
❑	15	Drew Bledsoe	1.50	.60
❑	16	Travis Henry	1.00	.40
❑	17	Eric Moulds	.60	.25
❑	18	Peerless Price	.60	.25
❑	19	Isaac Byrd	.40	.15
❑	20	Muhsin Muhammad	.60	.25
❑	21	Lamar Smith	.60	.25
❑	22	Chris Weinke	.60	.25
❑	23	Marty Booker	.40	.15
❑	24	Jim Miller	.40	.15
❑	25	Marcus Robinson	.60	.25
❑	26	Anthony Thomas	.60	.25
❑	27	Brian Urlacher	2.00	.75
❑	28	Corey Dillon	.60	.25
❑	29	Gus Frerotte	.40	.15
❑	30	Jon Kitna	.60	.25
❑	31	Darnay Scott	.40	.15
❑	32	Peter Warrick	.60	.25
❑	33	Tim Couch	.60	.25
❑	34	James Jackson	.40	.15
❑	35	Kevin Johnson	.60	.25
❑	36	Quincy Morgan	.40	.15
❑	37	Quincy Carter	.60	.25
❑	38	Joey Galloway	.60	.25
❑	39	Rocket Ismail	.60	.25
❑	40	Emmitt Smith	3.00	1.25
❑	41	Mike Anderson	1.00	.40
❑	42	Terrell Davis	1.00	.40
❑	43	Brian Griese	1.00	.40
❑	44	Ed McCaffrey	1.00	.40
❑	45	Rod Smith	.60	.25
❑	46	Germane Crowell	.40	.15
❑	47	Az-Zahir Hakim	.40	.15
❑	48	Mike McMahon	1.00	.40
❑	49	Bill Schroeder	.60	.25
❑	50	Brett Favre	3.00	1.25
❑	51	Bubba Franks	.60	.25
❑	52	Antonio Freeman	1.00	.40
❑	53	Terry Glenn	.60	.25
❑	54	Ahman Green	1.00	.40
❑	55	James Allen	.60	.25
❑	56	Corey Bradford	.40	.15
❑	57	Kent Graham	.40	.15
❑	58	Jermaine Lewis	.40	.15
❑	59	Marvin Harrison	1.00	.40
❑	60	Edgerrin James	1.50	.60
❑	61	Peyton Manning	2.50	1.00
❑	62	Dominic Rhodes	1.00	.40
❑	63	Reggie Wayne	1.00	.40
❑	64	Mark Brunell	1.00	.40
❑	65	Patrick Johnson	.40	.15
❑	66	Jimmy Smith	.60	.25
❑	67	Fred Taylor	1.00	.40
❑	68	Tony Gonzalez	.60	.25
❑	69	Trent Green	.60	.25
❑	70	Priest Holmes	1.50	.60
❑	71	Johnnie Morton	.60	.25
❑	72	Chris Chambers	1.00	.40
❑	73	Jay Fiedler	.60	.25
❑	74	James McKnight	.40	.15
❑	75	Ricky Williams	1.00	.40
❑	76	Derrick Alexander	.60	.25
❑	77	Michael Bennett	.60	.25
❑	78	Daunte Culpepper	1.00	.40
❑	79	Randy Moss	2.50	1.00
❑	80	Tom Brady	3.00	1.25
❑	81	Troy Brown	.60	.25
❑	82	Kevin Faulk	.60	.25
❑	83	David Patten	.40	.15
❑	84	Antowain Smith	.60	.25
❑	85	Aaron Brooks	1.00	.40
❑	86	Joe Horn	.60	.25
❑	87	Deuce McAllister	1.50	.60
❑	88	Jerome Pathon	.40	.15
❑	89	Tiki Barber	1.00	.40
❑	90	Kerry Collins	.60	.25
❑	91	Ron Dayne	.60	.25
❑	92	Ike Hilliard	.60	.25
❑	93	Michael Strahan	.60	.25
❑	94	Amani Toomer	.60	.25
❑	95	Wayne Chrebet	.60	.25
❑	96	Laveranues Coles	.60	.25
❑	97	Curtis Martin	1.00	.40
❑	98	Vinny Testaverde	.60	.25
❑	99	Tim Brown	1.00	.40
❑	100	Rich Gannon	1.00	.40
❑	101	Charlie Garner	.60	.25
❑	102	Jerry Rice	2.50	1.00
❑	103	Tyrone Wheatley	.60	.25
❑	104	Charles Woodson	.60	.25
❑	105	Donovan McNabb	1.50	.60
❑	106	Todd Pinkston	.60	.25
❑	107	Duce Staley	1.00	.40
❑	108	James Thrash	.60	.25
❑	109	Jerome Bettis	1.00	.40
❑	110	Plaxico Burress	.60	.25
❑	111	Kordell Stewart	.60	.25
❑	112	Hines Ward	1.00	.40
❑	113	Isaac Bruce	1.00	.40
❑	114	Marshall Faulk	1.00	.40
❑	115	Torry Holt	1.00	.40
❑	116	Kurt Warner	1.00	.40
❑	117	Drew Brees	1.00	.40
❑	118	Curtis Conway	.40	.15
❑	119	Tim Dwight	.60	.25
❑	120	Doug Flutie	1.00	.40
❑	121	Junior Seau	1.00	.40
❑	122	LaDainian Tomlinson	2.00	.75
❑	123	Jeff Garcia	1.00	.40
❑	124	Garrison Hearst	.60	.25
❑	125	Terrell Owens	1.00	.40
❑	126	J.J. Stokes	.40	.15
❑	127	Shaun Alexander	1.25	.50
❑	128	Trent Dilfer	.60	.25
❑	129	Darrell Jackson	.60	.25
❑	130	Koren Robinson	.60	.25
❑	131	Mike Alstott	1.00	.40
❑	132	Brad Johnson	.60	.25
❑	133	Keyshawn Johnson	1.00	.40
❑	134	Keenan McCardell	.40	.15
❑	135	Michael Pittman	.40	.15
❑	136	Warren Sapp	.60	.25
❑	137	Kevin Dyson	.60	.25
❑	138	Eddie George	1.00	.40
❑	139	Derrick Mason	.60	.25
❑	140	Steve McNair	1.00	.40
❑	141	Stephen Davis	.60	.25
❑	142	Rod Gardner	.60	.25
❑	143	Jacquez Green	.40	.15
❑	144	Shane Matthews	.40	.15
❑	145	Jason McAddley RC	2.50	1.00
❑	146	Josh McCown RC	4.00	1.50
❑	147	Josh Scobey RC	3.00	1.25
❑	148	T.J. Duckett RC	4.00	1.50
❑	149	Kahlil Hill RC	2.50	1.00
❑	150	Kurt Kittner RC	2.50	1.00
❑	151	Ron Johnson RC	2.50	1.00
❑	152	Tellis Redmon RC	2.50	1.00
❑	153	Chester Taylor RC	6.00	2.50
❑	154	Josh Reed RC	3.00	1.25
❑	155	Randy Fasani RC	2.50	1.00
❑	156	DeShaun Foster RC	3.00	1.25
❑	157	Julius Peppers RC	6.00	2.50
❑	158	Adrian Peterson RC	3.00	1.25
❑	159	Andre Davis RC	2.50	1.00
❑	160	William Green RC	3.00	1.25
❑	161	Antonio Bryant RC	3.00	1.25
❑	162	Woody Dantzler RC	2.50	1.00
❑	163	Ennis Haywood RC	2.50	1.00
❑	164	Chad Hutchinson RC	2.50	1.00
❑	165	Jamar Martin RC	2.50	1.00
❑	166	Roy Williams RC	8.00	3.00
❑	167	Herb Haygood RC	1.50	.60
❑	168	Ashley Lelie RC	6.00	2.50
❑	169	Clinton Portis RC	10.00	4.00
❑	170	Eddie Drummond RC	2.50	1.00
❑	171	Joey Harrington RC	5.00	2.00
❑	172	Luke Staley RC	2.50	1.00
❑	173	Craig Nall RC	3.00	1.25
❑	174	Javon Walker RC	6.00	2.50
❑	175	Jarrod Baxter RC	2.50	1.00
❑	176	David Carr RC	8.00	3.00
❑	177	Delvon Flowers RC	2.50	1.00
❑	178	Jabar Gaffney RC	3.00	1.25
❑	179	Jonathan Wells RC	3.00	1.25
❑	180	David Garrard RC	3.00	1.25
❑	181	John Henderson RC	3.00	1.25
❑	182	Omar Easy RC	3.00	1.25
❑	183	Leonard Henry RC	2.50	1.00
❑	184	Atrews Bell RC	1.50	.60
❑	185	Deion Branch RC	6.00	2.50
❑	186	Rohan Davey RC	3.00	1.25
❑	187	Daniel Graham RC	3.00	1.25
❑	188	Antwoine Womack RC	2.50	1.00
❑	189	J.T. O'Sullivan RC	2.50	1.00
❑	190	Donte Stallworth RC	6.00	2.50
❑	191	Tim Carter RC	2.50	1.00
❑	192	Daryl Jones RC	2.50	1.00
❑	193	Jeremy Shockey RC	10.00	4.00
❑	194	Ronald Curry RC	3.00	1.25
❑	195	Napoleon Harris RC	3.00	1.25
❑	196	Larry Ned RC	2.50	1.00
❑	197	Freddie Milons RC	2.50	1.00
❑	198	Lito Sheppard RC	3.00	1.25
❑	199	Brian Westbrook RC	5.00	2.00
❑	200	Lee Mays RC	2.50	1.00
❑	201	Antwaan Randle El RC	5.00	2.00
❑	202	Eric Crouch RC	3.00	1.25
❑	203	Lamar Gordon RC	3.00	1.25
❑	204	Robert Thomas RC	3.00	1.25
❑	205	Seth Burford RC	2.50	1.00
❑	206	Reche Caldwell RC	3.00	1.25
❑	207	Quentin Jammer RC	3.00	1.25
❑	208	Brandon Doman RC	2.50	1.00
❑	209	Maurice Morris RC	3.00	1.25
❑	210	Jerramy Stevens RC	3.00	1.25
❑	211	Travis Stephens RC	2.50	1.00
❑	212	Marquise Walker RC	2.50	1.00
❑	213	Jake Schifino RC	2.50	1.00
❑	214	Ladell Betts RC	3.00	1.25
❑	215	Patrick Ramsey RC	4.00	1.50
❑	216	Cliff Russell RC	2.50	1.00

1996 Donruss

❑		COMPLETE SET (240)	20.00	7.50
❑	1	Barry Sanders	1.50	.60
❑	2	Flipper Anderson	.10	.02
❑	3	Ben Coates	.20	.07
❑	4	Rob Johnson	.40	.15
❑	5	Rodney Hampton	.20	.07

❑ 6 Desmond Howard .20 .07
❑ 7 Craig Heyward .10 .02
❑ 8 Alvin Harper .10 .02
❑ 9 Todd Collins .20 .07
❑ 10 Ken Norton Jr. .10 .02
❑ 11 Stan Humphries .20 .07
❑ 12 Aeneas Williams .10 .02
❑ 13 Jeff Hostetler .10 .02
❑ 14 Frank Sanders .20 .07
❑ 15 J.J. Birden .10 .02
❑ 16 Bryce Paup .10 .02
❑ 17 Bill Brooks .10 .02
❑ 18 Kevin Williams .10 .02
❑ 19 Boomer Esiason .20 .07
❑ 20 O.J. McDuffie .20 .07
❑ 21 Eric Swann .10 .02
❑ 22 Neil Smith .20 .07
❑ 23 Charlie Garner .20 .07
❑ 24 Greg Lloyd .20 .07
❑ 25 Willie Jackson .20 .07
❑ 26 Shawn Jefferson .10 .02
❑ 27 Rodney Peete .10 .02
❑ 28 Michael Westbrook .40 .15
❑ 29 J.J. Stokes .40 .15
❑ 30 Troy Aikman 1.00 .40
❑ 31 Sean Dawkins .10 .02
❑ 32 Larry Centers .20 .07
❑ 33 Herschel Walker .20 .07
❑ 34 Stoney Case .10 .02
❑ 35 Kevin Greene .20 .07
❑ 36 Quinn Early .10 .02
❑ 37 Fred Barnett .10 .02
❑ 38 Andre Coleman .10 .02
❑ 39 Mark Chmura .20 .07
❑ 40 Adrian Murrell .20 .07
❑ 41 Roosevelt Potts .10 .02
❑ 42 Jay Novacek .10 .02
❑ 43 Derrick Alexander .20 .07
❑ 44 Ken Dilger .20 .07
❑ 45 Rob Moore .20 .07
❑ 46 Cris Carter .40 .15
❑ 47 Jeff Blake .40 .15
❑ 48 Derek Loville .10 .02
❑ 49 Tyrone Wheatley .20 .07
❑ 50 Terrell Fletcher .10 .02
❑ 51 Sherman Williams .10 .02
❑ 52 Justin Armour .10 .02
❑ 53 Kordell Stewart .40 .15
❑ 54 Tim Brown .40 .15
❑ 55 Kevin Carter .10 .02
❑ 56 Andre Rison .20 .07
❑ 57 James O.Stewart .20 .07
❑ 58 Brent Jones .10 .02
❑ 59 Erik Kramer .10 .02
❑ 60 Floyd Turner .10 .02
❑ 61 Ricky Watters .20 .07
❑ 62 Hardy Nickerson .10 .02
❑ 63 Aaron Craver .10 .02
❑ 64 Dave Krieg .10 .02
❑ 65 Warren Moon .20 .07
❑ 66 Wayne Chrebet .50 .20
❑ 67 Napoleon Kaufman .40 .15
❑ 68 Terance Mathis .10 .02
❑ 69 Chad May .10 .02
❑ 70 Andre Reed .20 .07
❑ 71 Reggie White .40 .15
❑ 72 Brett Favre 2.00 .75
❑ 73 Chris Zorich .10 .02
❑ 74 Kerry Collins .40 .15
❑ 75 Herman Moore .20 .07
❑ 76 Yancey Thigpen .20 .07
❑ 77 Glenn Foley .20 .07
❑ 78 Quentin Coryatt .10 .02
❑ 79 Terry Kirby .20 .07
❑ 80 Edgar Bennett .20 .07
❑ 81 Mark Brunell .60 .25
❑ 82 Heath Shuler .20 .07
❑ 83 Gus Frerotte .20 .07
❑ 84 Deion Sanders .60 .25
❑ 85 Calvin Williams .10 .02
❑ 86 Junior Seau .40 .15
❑ 87 Jim Kelly .40 .15
❑ 88 Daryl Johnston .20 .07
❑ 89 Irving Fryar .20 .07
❑ 90 Brian Blades .10 .02
❑ 91 Willie Davis .10 .02
❑ 92 Jerome Bettis .40 .15
❑ 93 Marcus Allen .40 .15
❑ 94 Jeff Graham .10 .02
❑ 95 Rick Mirer .20 .07
❑ 96 Harvey Williams .10 .02
❑ 97 Steve Atwater .10 .02
❑ 98 Carl Pickens .20 .07
❑ 99 Darick Holmes .10 .02
❑ 100 Bruce Smith .20 .07
❑ 101 Vinny Testaverde .20 .07
❑ 102 Thurman Thomas .40 .15
❑ 103 Drew Bledsoe .60 .25
❑ 104 Bernie Parmalee .10 .02
❑ 105 Greg Hill .20 .07
❑ 106 Steve McNair .75 .30
❑ 107 Andre Hastings .10 .02
❑ 108 Eric Metcalf .10 .02
❑ 109 Kimble Anders .20 .07
❑ 110 Steve Tasker .10 .02
❑ 111 Mark Carrier WR .10 .02
❑ 112 Jerry Rice 1.00 .40
❑ 113 Joey Galloway .40 .15
❑ 114 Robert Smith .20 .07
❑ 115 Hugh Douglas .20 .07
❑ 116 Willie McGinest .10 .02
❑ 117 Terrell Davis .75 .30
❑ 118 Cortez Kennedy .10 .02
❑ 119 Marshall Faulk .50 .20
❑ 120 Michael Haynes .10 .02
❑ 121 Isaac Bruce .40 .15
❑ 122 Brian Mitchell .10 .02
❑ 123 Bryan Cox .10 .02
❑ 124 Tamarick Vanover .20 .07
❑ 125 William Floyd .20 .07
❑ 126 Chris Chandler .20 .07
❑ 127 Carnell Lake .10 .02
❑ 128 Aaron Bailey .10 .02
❑ 129 Darnay Scott .20 .07
❑ 130 Darren Woodson .20 .07
❑ 131 Ernie Mills .10 .02
❑ 132 Charles Haley .20 .07
❑ 133 Rocket Ismail .10 .02
❑ 134 Bert Emanuel .20 .07
❑ 135 Lake Dawson .10 .02
❑ 136 Jake Reed .20 .07
❑ 137 Dave Brown .10 .02
❑ 138 Steve Bono .10 .02
❑ 139 Terry Allen .20 .07
❑ 140 Errict Rhett .20 .07
❑ 141 Rod Woodson .20 .07
❑ 142 Charles Johnson .10 .02
❑ 143 Emmitt Smith 1.50 .60
❑ 144 Ki-Jana Carter .20 .07
❑ 145 Garrison Hearst .20 .07
❑ 146 Rashaan Salaam .20 .07
❑ 147 Tony Boselli .10 .02
❑ 148 Derrick Thomas .40 .15
❑ 149 Mark Seay .10 .02
❑ 150 Derrick Alexander .10 .02
❑ 151 Christian Fauria .10 .02
❑ 152 Aaron Hayden .10 .02
❑ 153 Chris Warren .20 .07
❑ 154 Dave Meggett .10 .02
❑ 155 Jeff George .20 .07
❑ 156 Jackie Harris .10 .02
❑ 157 Michael Irvin .40 .15
❑ 158 Scott Mitchell .20 .07
❑ 159 Trent Dilfer .40 .15
❑ 160 Kyle Brady .10 .02
❑ 161 Dan Marino 2.00 .75
❑ 162 Curtis Martin .75 .30
❑ 163 Mario Bates .20 .07
❑ 164 Erric Pegram .10 .02
❑ 165 Eric Zeier .10 .02
❑ 166 Rodney Thomas .10 .02
❑ 167 Neil O'Donnell .20 .07
❑ 168 Warren Sapp .10 .02
❑ 169 Jim Harbaugh .20 .07
❑ 170 Henry Ellard .10 .02
❑ 171 Anthony Miller .20 .07
❑ 172 Derrick Moore .10 .02
❑ 173 John Elway 2.00 .75
❑ 174 Vincent Brisby .10 .02
❑ 175 Antonio Freeman .40 .15
❑ 176 Chris Sanders .20 .07
❑ 177 Steve Young .75 .30
❑ 178 Shannon Sharpe .20 .07
❑ 179 Brett Perriman .10 .02
❑ 180 Orlando Thomas .10 .02
❑ 181 Eric Bjornson .10 .02
❑ 182 Natrone Means .20 .07
❑ 183 Jim Everett .10 .02
❑ 184 Curtis Conway .40 .15
❑ 185 Robert Brooks .40 .15
❑ 186 Tony Martin .20 .07
❑ 187 Mark Carrier DB .10 .02
❑ 188 LeShon Johnson .10 .02
❑ 189 Bernie Kosar .10 .02
❑ 190 Ray Zellars .10 .02
❑ 191 Steve Walsh .10 .02
❑ 192 Craig Erickson .10 .02
❑ 193 Tommy Maddox .40 .15
❑ 194 Leslie O'Neal .10 .02
❑ 195 Harold Green .10 .02
❑ 196 Steve Beuerlein .20 .07
❑ 197 Ronald Moore .10 .02
❑ 198 Leslie Shepherd .10 .02
❑ 199 Leroy Hoard .10 .02
❑ 200 Michael Jackson .20 .07
❑ 201 Will Moore .10 .02
❑ 202 Ricky Ervins .10 .02
❑ 203 Keith Jennings .10 .02
❑ 204 Eric Green .10 .02
❑ 205 Mark Rypien .10 .02
❑ 206 Torrance Small .10 .02
❑ 207 Sean Gilbert .10 .02
❑ 208 Mike Alstott RC 1.00 .40
❑ 209 Willie Anderson RC .10 .02
❑ 210 Alex Molden RC .10 .02
❑ 211 Jonathan Ogden RC .40 .15
❑ 212 Stepfret Williams RC .20 .07
❑ 213 Jeff Lewis RC .20 .07
❑ 214 Regan Upshaw RC .10 .02
❑ 215 Daryl Gardener RC .10 .02
❑ 216 Danny Kanell RC .40 .15
❑ 217 John Mobley RC .10 .02
❑ 218 Reggie Brown LB RC .10 .02
❑ 219 Muhsin Muhammad RC .75 .30
❑ 220 Kevin Hardy RC .40 .15
❑ 221 Stanley Pritchett RC .20 .07
❑ 222 Cedric Jones RC .10 .02
❑ 223 Marco Battaglia RC .10 .02
❑ 224 Duane Clemons RC .10 .02
❑ 225 Jerald Moore RC .20 .07
❑ 226 Simeon Rice RC 1.00 .40
❑ 227 Chris Darkins RC .10 .02
❑ 228 Bobby Hoying RC .40 .15
❑ 229 Stephen Davis RC 1.50 .60
❑ 230 Walt Harris RC .10 .02
❑ 231 Jermane Mayberry RC .10 .02
❑ 232 Tony Brackens RC .40 .15
❑ 233 Eric Moulds RC 1.25 .50
❑ 234 Alex Van Dyke RC .20 .07
❑ 235 Marvin Harrison RC 2.50 1.00
❑ 236 Rickey Dudley RC .40 .15
❑ 237 Terrell Owens RC 2.50 1.00
❑ 238 Jerry Rice CL .40 .15
❑ 239 Dan Marino CL .40 .15
❑ 240 Emmitt Smith CL .40 .15

1997 Donruss

❑ COMPLETE SET (230) 20.00 7.50
❑ 1 Dan Marino 2.00 .75
❑ 2 Brett Favre 2.00 .75
❑ 3 Emmitt Smith 1.50 .60
❑ 4 Eddie George .50 .20
❑ 5 Karim Abdul-Jabbar .30 .10
❑ 6 Terrell Davis .60 .25
❑ 7 Curtis Martin .60 .25
❑ 8 Drew Bledsoe .60 .25
❑ 9 Jerry Rice 1.00 .40
❑ 10 Troy Aikman 1.00 .40
❑ 11 Barry Sanders 1.50 .60
❑ 12 Mark Brunell .60 .25

❑ 13	Kerry Collins	.50	.20
❑ 14	Steve Young	.60	.25
❑ 15	Kordell Stewart	.50	.20
❑ 16	Eddie Kennison	.30	.10
❑ 17	Terry Glenn	.50	.20
❑ 18	John Elway	2.00	.75
❑ 19	Joey Galloway	.30	.10
❑ 20	Deion Sanders	.50	.20
❑ 21	Keyshawn Johnson	.50	.20
❑ 22	Lawrence Phillips	.20	.07
❑ 23	Ricky Watters	.30	.10
❑ 24	Marvin Harrison	.50	.20
❑ 25	Bobby Engram	.30	.10
❑ 26	Marshall Faulk	.60	.25
❑ 27	Carl Pickens	.30	.10
❑ 28	Isaac Bruce	.50	.20
❑ 29	Herman Moore	.30	.10
❑ 30	Jerome Bettis	.50	.20
❑ 31	Rashaan Salaam	.20	.07
❑ 32	Errict Rhett	.20	.07
❑ 33	Tim Biakabutuka	.30	.10
❑ 34	Robert Brooks	.30	.10
❑ 35	Antonio Freeman	.50	.20
❑ 36	Steve McNair	.60	.25
❑ 37	Jeff Blake	.30	.10
❑ 38	Tony Banks	.30	.10
❑ 39	Terrell Owens	.60	.25
❑ 40	Eric Moulds	.50	.20
❑ 41	Leeland McElroy	.20	.07
❑ 42	Chris Sanders	.20	.07
❑ 43	Thurman Thomas	.50	.20
❑ 44	Bruce Smith	.30	.10
❑ 45	Reggie White	.50	.20
❑ 46	Chris Warren	.30	.10
❑ 47	J.J. Stokes	.30	.10
❑ 48	Ben Coates	.30	.10
❑ 49	Tim Brown	.50	.20
❑ 50	Marcus Allen	.50	.20
❑ 51	Michael Irvin	.50	.20
❑ 52	William Floyd	.30	.10
❑ 53	Ken Dilger	.20	.07
❑ 54	Bobby Taylor	.20	.07
❑ 55	Keenan McCardell	.30	.10
❑ 56	Raymont Harris	.20	.07
❑ 57	Keith Byars	.20	.07
❑ 58	O.J. McDuffie	.30	.10
❑ 59	Robert Smith	.30	.10
❑ 60	Bert Emanuel	.30	.10
❑ 61	Rick Mirer	.20	.07
❑ 62	Vinny Testaverde	.30	.10
❑ 63	Kyle Brady	.20	.07
❑ 64	Mark Bruener	.20	.07
❑ 65	Neil O'Donnell	.30	.10
❑ 66	Anthony Johnson	.20	.07
❑ 67	Ken Norton	.20	.07
❑ 68	Warren Sapp	.30	.10
❑ 69	Amani Toomer	.30	.10
❑ 70	Simeon Rice	.30	.10
❑ 71	Kevin Hardy	.20	.07
❑ 72	Junior Seau	.50	.20
❑ 73	Neil Smith	.30	.10
❑ 74	LeShon Johnson	.20	.07
❑ 75	Quinn Early	.20	.07
❑ 76	Andre Reed	.30	.10
❑ 77	Jake Reed	.30	.10
❑ 78	Elvis Grbac	.30	.10
❑ 79	Tyrone Wheatley	.30	.10
❑ 80	Adrian Murrell	.30	.10
❑ 81	Fred Barnett	.20	.07
❑ 82	Darrell Green	.30	.10
❑ 83	Stan Humphries	.30	.10
❑ 84	Troy Drayton	.20	.07
❑ 85	Steve Atwater	.20	.07
❑ 86	Quentin Coryatt	.20	.07
❑ 87	Dan Wilkinson	.20	.07
❑ 88	Scott Mitchell	.30	.10
❑ 89	Willie McGinest	.20	.07
❑ 90	Kevin Smith	.20	.07
❑ 91	Gus Frerotte	.20	.07
❑ 92	Byron Bam Morris	.20	.07
❑ 93	Darick Holmes	.20	.07
❑ 94	Zach Thomas	.50	.20
❑ 95	Tom Carter	.20	.07
❑ 96	Cortez Kennedy	.20	.07
❑ 97	Kevin Williams	.20	.07
❑ 98	Michael Haynes	.20	.07
❑ 99	Lamont Warren	.20	.07
❑ 100	Jeff Graham	.20	.07
❑ 101	Alex Van Dyke	.20	.07
❑ 102	Jim Everett	.20	.07
❑ 103	Chris Chandler	.30	.10
❑ 104	Qadry Ismail	.30	.10
❑ 105	Ray Zellars	.20	.07
❑ 106	Chris T. Jones	.20	.07
❑ 107	Charlie Garner	.30	.10
❑ 108	Bobby Hoying	.30	.10
❑ 109	Mark Chmura	.30	.10
❑ 110	Cris Carter	.50	.20
❑ 111	Darnay Scott	.30	.10
❑ 112	Anthony Miller	.20	.07
❑ 113	Desmond Howard	.30	.10
❑ 114	Terance Mathis	.30	.10
❑ 115	Rodney Hampton	.30	.10
❑ 116	Napoleon Kaufman	.50	.20
❑ 117	Jim Harbaugh	.30	.10
❑ 118	Shannon Sharpe	.30	.10
❑ 119	Irving Fryar	.30	.10
❑ 120	Garrison Hearst	.30	.10
❑ 121	Terry Allen	.50	.20
❑ 122	Larry Centers	.30	.10
❑ 123	Sean Dawkins	.20	.07
❑ 124	Jeff George	.30	.10
❑ 125	Tony Martin	.30	.10
❑ 126	Mike Alstott	.50	.20
❑ 127	Rickey Dudley	.30	.10
❑ 128	Kevin Carter	.20	.07
❑ 129	Derrick Alexander WR	.30	.10
❑ 130	Greg Lloyd	.20	.07
❑ 131	Bryce Paup	.20	.07
❑ 132	Derrick Thomas	.50	.20
❑ 133	Greg Hill	.20	.07
❑ 134	Jamal Anderson	.50	.20
❑ 135	Curtis Conway	.30	.10
❑ 136	Frank Sanders	.30	.10
❑ 137	Brett Perriman	.20	.07
❑ 138	Edgar Bennett	.30	.10
❑ 139	Wayne Chrebet	.50	.20
❑ 140	Natrone Means	.30	.10
❑ 141	Eric Metcalf	.30	.10
❑ 142	Trent Dilfer	.50	.20
❑ 143	Terry Kirby	.30	.10
❑ 144	Johnnie Morton	.30	.10
❑ 145	Dale Carter	.20	.07
❑ 146	Michael Westbrook	.30	.10
❑ 147	Stanley Pritchett	.20	.07
❑ 148	Todd Collins	.20	.07
❑ 149	Tamarick Vanover	.30	.10
❑ 150	Kevin Greene	.30	.10
❑ 151	Lamar Lathon	.20	.07
❑ 152	Muhsin Muhammad	.30	.10
❑ 153	Dorsey Levens	.50	.20
❑ 154	Rod Woodson	.30	.10
❑ 155	Brent Jones	.20	.07
❑ 156	Michael Jackson	.30	.10
❑ 157	Shawn Jefferson	.20	.07
❑ 158	Kimble Anders	.30	.10
❑ 159	Sean Gilbert	.20	.07
❑ 160	Carnell Lake	.20	.07
❑ 161	Darren Woodson	.20	.07
❑ 162	Dave Meggett	.20	.07
❑ 163	Henry Ellard	.20	.07
❑ 164	Eric Swann	.20	.07
❑ 165	Tony Boselli	.20	.07
❑ 166	Daryl Johnston	.30	.10
❑ 167	Willie Jackson	.20	.07
❑ 168	Wesley Walls	.30	.10
❑ 169	Mario Bates	.20	.07
❑ 170	Lake Dawson	.20	.07
❑ 171	Mike Mamula	.20	.07
❑ 172	Ed McCaffrey	.30	.10
❑ 173	Tony Brackens	.20	.07
❑ 174	Craig Heyward	.20	.07
❑ 175	Harvey Williams	.20	.07
❑ 176	Dave Brown	.20	.07
❑ 177	Aaron Glenn	.20	.07
❑ 178	Jeff Hostetler	.20	.07
❑ 179	Alvin Harper	.20	.07
❑ 180	Ty Detmer	.30	.10
❑ 181	James Jett	.30	.10
❑ 182	James O.Stewart	.30	.10
❑ 183	Warren Moon	.50	.20
❑ 184	Herschel Walker	.30	.10
❑ 185	Ki-Jana Carter	.20	.07
❑ 186	Leslie O'Neal	.20	.07
❑ 187	Danny Kanell	.20	.07
❑ 188	Eric Bjornson	.20	.07
❑ 189	Alex Molden	.20	.07
❑ 190	Bryant Young	.20	.07
❑ 191	Merton Hanks	.20	.07
❑ 192	Heath Shuler	.20	.07
❑ 193	Brian Blades	.20	.07
❑ 194	Steve Bono	.30	.10
❑ 195	Wayne Simmons	.20	.07
❑ 196	Warrick Dunn RC	1.50	.60
❑ 197	Peter Boulware RC	.50	.20
❑ 198	David LaFleur RC	.20	.07
❑ 199	Shawn Springs RC	.30	.10
❑ 200	Reidel Anthony RC	.50	.20
❑ 201	Jim Druckenmiller RC	.30	.10
❑ 202	Orlando Pace RC	.50	.20
❑ 203	Yatil Green RC	.30	.10
❑ 204	Bryant Westbrook RC	.20	.07
❑ 205	Tiki Barber RC	3.00	1.25
❑ 206	James Farrior RC	.50	.20
❑ 207	Rae Carruth RC	.20	.07
❑ 208	Danny Wuerffel RC	.50	.20
❑ 209	Corey Dillon RC	3.00	1.25
❑ 210	Ike Hilliard RC	.75	.30
❑ 211	Tony Gonzalez RC	1.50	.60
❑ 212	Antowain Smith RC	1.25	.50
❑ 213	Pat Barnes RC	.50	.20
❑ 214	Troy Davis RC	.30	.10
❑ 215	Byron Hanspard RC	.30	.10
❑ 216	Joey Kent RC	.50	.20
❑ 217	Jake Plummer RC	2.50	1.00
❑ 218	Kenny Holmes RC	.50	.20
❑ 219	Darnell Autry RC	.30	.10
❑ 220	Darrell Russell RC	.20	.07
❑ 221	Walter Jones RC	.50	.20
❑ 222	Dwayne Rudd RC	.50	.20
❑ 223	Tom Knight RC	.20	.07
❑ 224	Kevin Lockett RC	.30	.10
❑ 225	Will Blackwell RC	.30	.10
❑ 226	Dan Marino CL	.40	.15
❑ 227	Brett Favre CL	.40	.15
❑ 228	Emmitt Smith CL	.50	.20
❑ 229	Barry Sanders CL	.50	.20
❑ 230	Jerry Rice CL	.25	.08
❑ P1	Drew Bledsoe Promo	1.00	.40
❑ P2	Mark Brunell Promo	1.00	.40
❑ P3	Barry Sanders Promo	1.50	.60

1999 Donruss

❑	COMPLETE SET (200)	100.00	40.00
❑	COMP.SET w/o SP's (150)	20.00	10.00
❑ 1	Jake Plummer	.40	.15
❑ 2	Rob Moore	.40	.15
❑ 3	Adrian Murrell	.40	.15
❑ 4	Frank Sanders	.40	.15
❑ 5	Jamal Anderson	.60	.25
❑ 6	Tim Dwight	.40	.15
❑ 7	Terance Mathis	.40	.15
❑ 8	Chris Chandler	.40	.15

Card	Player	Hi	Lo
❑ 9	Byron Hanspard	.25	.08
❑ 10	Priest Holmes	1.00	.40
❑ 11	Jermaine Lewis	.40	.15
❑ 12	Errict Rhett	.40	.15
❑ 13	Doug Flutie	.60	.25
❑ 14	Eric Moulds	.60	.25
❑ 15	Antowain Smith	.60	.25
❑ 16	Thurman Thomas	.40	.15
❑ 17	Andre Reed	.40	.15
❑ 18	Bruce Smith	.40	.15
❑ 19	Tim Biakabutuka	.40	.15
❑ 20	Rae Carruth	.25	.08
❑ 21	Muhsin Muhammad	.40	.15
❑ 22	Curtis Enis	.25	.08
❑ 23	Curtis Conway	.40	.15
❑ 24	Bobby Engram	.40	.15
❑ 25	Corey Dillon	.60	.25
❑ 26	Carl Pickens	.40	.15
❑ 27	Jeff Blake	.40	.15
❑ 28	Darnay Scott	.40	.15
❑ 29	Ty Detmer	.40	.15
❑ 30	Leslie Shepherd	.25	.08
❑ 31	Emmitt Smith	1.25	.50
❑ 32	Troy Aikman	1.25	.50
❑ 33	Michael Irvin	.40	.15
❑ 34	Deion Sanders	.60	.25
❑ 35	Rocket Ismail	.40	.15
❑ 36	John Elway	2.00	.75
❑ 37	Terrell Davis	.60	.25
❑ 38	Ed McCaffrey	.40	.15
❑ 39	Shannon Sharpe	.40	.15
❑ 40	Rod Smith	.40	.15
❑ 41	Bubby Brister	.25	.08
❑ 42	Brian Griese	.60	.25
❑ 43	Barry Sanders	2.00	.75
❑ 44	Charlie Batch	.60	.25
❑ 45	Herman Moore	.40	.15
❑ 46	Germane Crowell	.25	.08
❑ 47	Johnnie Morton	.40	.15
❑ 48	Ron Rivers	.25	.08
❑ 49	Brett Favre	2.00	.75
❑ 50	Antonio Freeman	.60	.25
❑ 51	Dorsey Levens	.60	.25
❑ 52	Mark Chmura	.25	.08
❑ 53	Corey Bradford	.60	.25
❑ 54	Bill Schroeder	.60	.25
❑ 55	Peyton Manning	2.00	.75
❑ 56	Marvin Harrison	.60	.25
❑ 57	E.G. Green	.25	.08
❑ 58	Fred Taylor	.60	.25
❑ 59	Mark Brunell	.60	.25
❑ 60	Tavian Banks	.25	.08
❑ 61	Jimmy Smith	.40	.15
❑ 62	Keenan McCardell	.40	.15
❑ 63	Warren Moon	.60	.25
❑ 64	Derrick Alexander WR	.40	.15
❑ 65	Byron Bam Morris	.25	.08
❑ 66	Elvis Grbac	.40	.15
❑ 67	Andre Rison	.40	.15
❑ 68	Dan Marino	2.00	.75
❑ 69	Karim Abdul-Jabbar	.40	.15
❑ 70	O.J. McDuffie	.40	.15
❑ 71	Tony Martin	.25	.08
❑ 72	Randy Moss	1.50	.60
❑ 73	Cris Carter	.60	.25
❑ 74	Randall Cunningham	.60	.25
❑ 75	Robert Smith	.60	.25
❑ 76	Jeff George	.40	.15
❑ 77	Jake Reed	.40	.15
❑ 78	Terry Allen	.40	.15
❑ 79	Drew Bledsoe	.75	.30
❑ 80	Terry Glenn	.60	.25
❑ 81	Ben Coates	.40	.15
❑ 82	Tony Simmons	.25	.08
❑ 83	Cam Cleeland	.25	.08
❑ 84	Eddie Kennison	.40	.15
❑ 85	Kerry Collins	.25	.08
❑ 86	Ike Hilliard	.25	.08
❑ 87	Gary Brown	.25	.08
❑ 88	Joe Jurevicius	.40	.15
❑ 89	Kent Graham	.25	.08
❑ 90	Wayne Chrebet	.40	.15
❑ 91	Keyshawn Johnson	.60	.25
❑ 92	Curtis Martin	.60	.25
❑ 93	Vinny Testaverde	.40	.15
❑ 94	Tim Brown	.60	.25
❑ 95	Napoleon Kaufman	.60	.25
❑ 96	Charles Woodson	.60	.25
❑ 97	Tyrone Wheatley	.40	.15
❑ 98	Rich Gannon	.60	.25
❑ 99	Charles Johnson	.25	.08
❑ 100	Duce Staley	.60	.25
❑ 101	Kordell Stewart	.40	.15
❑ 102	Jerome Bettis	.60	.25
❑ 103	Hines Ward	.60	.25
❑ 104	Ryan Leaf	.60	.25
❑ 105	Natrone Means	.40	.15
❑ 106	Jim Harbaugh	.40	.15
❑ 107	Junior Seau	.60	.25
❑ 108	Mikhael Ricks	.25	.08
❑ 109	Jerry Rice	1.25	.50
❑ 110	Steve Young	.75	.30
❑ 111	Garrison Hearst	.40	.15
❑ 112	Terrell Owens	.60	.25
❑ 113	Lawrence Phillips	.40	.15
❑ 114	J.J. Stokes	.40	.15
❑ 115	Sean Dawkins	.25	.08
❑ 116	Derrick Mayes	.25	.08
❑ 117	Joey Galloway	.40	.15
❑ 118	Jon Kitna	.60	.25
❑ 119	Ahman Green	.60	.25
❑ 120	Ricky Watters	.40	.15
❑ 121	Isaac Bruce	.60	.25
❑ 122	Marshall Faulk	.75	.30
❑ 123	Az-Zahir Hakim	.25	.08
❑ 124	Warrick Dunn	.60	.25
❑ 125	Mike Alstott	.60	.25
❑ 126	Trent Dilfer	.40	.15
❑ 127	Reidel Anthony	.40	.15
❑ 128	Jacquez Green	.25	.08
❑ 129	Warren Sapp	.40	.15
❑ 130	Eddie George	.60	.25
❑ 131	Steve McNair	.60	.25
❑ 132	Kevin Dyson	.40	.15
❑ 133	Yancey Thigpen	.25	.08
❑ 134	Frank Wycheck	.25	.08
❑ 135	Stephen Davis	.60	.25
❑ 136	Brad Johnson	.60	.25
❑ 137	Skip Hicks	.25	.08
❑ 138	Michael Westbrook	.40	.15
❑ 139	Darrell Green	.25	.08
❑ 140	Albert Connell	.25	.08
❑ 141	Tim Couch RC	2.00	.75
❑ 142	Donovan McNabb RC	8.00	3.00
❑ 143	Akili Smith RC	1.50	.60
❑ 144	Edgerrin James RC	6.00	2.50
❑ 145	Ricky Williams RC	3.00	1.25
❑ 146	Torry Holt RC	4.00	1.50
❑ 147	Champ Bailey RC	2.50	1.00
❑ 148	David Boston RC	2.00	.75
❑ 149	Andy Katzenmoyer RC	1.50	.60
❑ 150	Chris McAlister RC	1.50	.60
❑ 151	Daunte Culpepper RC	6.00	2.50
❑ 152	Cade McNown RC	1.50	.60
❑ 153	Troy Edwards RC	1.50	.60
❑ 154	Kevin Johnson RC	2.00	.75
❑ 155	James Johnson RC	1.50	.60
❑ 156	Rob Konrad RC	1.50	.60
❑ 157	Jim Kleinsasser RC	2.00	.75
❑ 158	Kevin Faulk RC	2.00	.75
❑ 159	Joe Montgomery RC	1.50	.60
❑ 160	Shaun King RC	1.50	.60
❑ 161	Peerless Price RC	2.00	.75
❑ 162	Mike Cloud RC	1.50	.60
❑ 163	Jermaine Fazande RC	1.50	.60
❑ 164	D'Wayne Bates RC	1.50	.60
❑ 165	Brock Huard RC	2.00	.75
❑ 166	Marty Booker RC	2.00	.75
❑ 167	Karsten Bailey RC	1.50	.60
❑ 168	Shawn Bryson RC	2.00	.75
❑ 169	Jeff Paulk RC	1.00	.40
❑ 170	Travis McGriff RC	1.00	.40
❑ 171	Amos Zereoue RC	2.00	.75
❑ 172	Craig Yeast RC	1.50	.60
❑ 173	Joe Germaine RC	1.50	.60
❑ 174	Dameane Douglas RC	1.50	.60
❑ 175	Brandon Stokley RC	2.50	1.00
❑ 176	Larry Parker RC	2.00	.75
❑ 177	Joel Makovicka RC	2.00	.75
❑ 178	Wane McGarity RC	1.00	.40
❑ 179	Na Brown RC	1.50	.60
❑ 180	Cecil Collins RC	1.00	.40
❑ 181	Nick Williams RC	1.50	.60
❑ 182	Charlie Rogers RC	1.50	.60
❑ 183	Darrin Chiaverini RC	1.50	.60
❑ 184	Terry Jackson RC	1.50	.60
❑ 185	De'Mond Parker RC	1.00	.40
❑ 186	Sedrick Irvin RC	1.00	.40
❑ 187	MarTay Jenkins RC	2.00	.75
❑ 188	Kurt Warner RC	12.00	5.00
❑ 189	Michael Bishop RC	2.00	.75
❑ 190	Sean Bennett RC	1.00	.40
❑ 191	Jamal Anderson CL	.25	.08
❑ 192	Eric Moulds CL	.25	.08
❑ 193	Terrell Davis CL	.60	.25
❑ 194	John Elway CL	.75	.30
❑ 195	Barry Sanders CL	.75	.30
❑ 196	Peyton Manning CL	.75	.30
❑ 197	Fred Taylor CL	.60	.25
❑ 198	Dan Marino CL	.75	.30
❑ 199	Randy Moss CL	.60	.25
❑ 200	Terrell Owens CL	.40	.15

2000 Donruss

Card	Player	Hi	Lo
❑	COMPLETE SET (250)	400.00	150.00
❑ 1	Jake Plummer	.30	.10
❑ 2	Frank Sanders	.30	.10
❑ 3	Rob Moore	.30	.10
❑ 4	David Boston	.50	.20
❑ 5	Tim Dwight	.50	.20
❑ 6	Jamal Anderson	.50	.20
❑ 7	Chris Chandler	.30	.10
❑ 8	Terance Mathis	.30	.10
❑ 9	Tony Banks	.30	.10
❑ 10	Jermaine Lewis	.30	.10
❑ 11	Shannon Sharpe	.30	.10
❑ 12	Trent Dilfer	.30	.10
❑ 13	Qadry Ismail	.30	.10
❑ 14	Eric Moulds	.50	.20
❑ 15	Doug Flutie	.50	.20
❑ 16	Antowain Smith	.30	.10
❑ 17	Jonathan Linton	.20	.07
❑ 18	Peerless Price	.30	.10
❑ 19	Rob Johnson	.30	.10
❑ 20	Natrone Means	.30	.10
❑ 21	Muhsin Muhammad	.30	.10
❑ 22	Wesley Walls	.30	.10
❑ 23	Tim Biakabutuka	.30	.10
❑ 24	Steve Beuerlein	.30	.10
❑ 25	Patrick Jeffers	.50	.20
❑ 26	Curtis Enis	.20	.07
❑ 27	Cade McNown	.20	.07
❑ 28	Bobby Engram	.30	.10
❑ 29	Marcus Robinson	.50	.20
❑ 30	Marty Booker	.30	.10
❑ 31	Corey Dillon	.50	.20
❑ 32	Darnay Scott	.30	.10
❑ 33	Carl Pickens	.30	.10
❑ 34	Akili Smith	.20	.07
❑ 35	Michael Basnight	.20	.07
❑ 36	Tim Couch	.30	.10
❑ 37	Kevin Johnson	.50	.20
❑ 38	Karim Abdul-Jabbar	.30	.10
❑ 39	Errict Rhett	.30	.10
❑ 40	Darrin Chiaverini	.20	.07
❑ 41	Emmitt Smith	1.00	.40
❑ 42	Troy Aikman	1.00	.40
❑ 43	Joey Galloway	.30	.10
❑ 44	Randall Cunningham	.50	.20
❑ 45	Michael Irvin	.30	.10
❑ 46	Rocket Ismail	.30	.10
❑ 47	Jason Tucker	.20	.07
❑ 48	Terrell Davis	.50	.20
❑ 49	John Elway	1.50	.60
❑ 50	Olandis Gary	.30	.10
❑ 51	Ed McCaffrey	.50	.20
❑ 52	Rod Smith	.30	.10
❑ 53	Brian Griese	.50	.20
❑ 54	Charlie Batch	.50	.20
❑ 55	Barry Sanders	1.25	.50

❑ 56 Herman Moore .30 .10
❑ 57 Johnnie Morton .30 .10
❑ 58 Germane Crowell .20 .07
❑ 59 James Stewart .30 .10
❑ 60 Brett Favre 1.50 .60
❑ 61 Dorsey Levens .30 .10
❑ 62 Antonio Freeman .50 .20
❑ 63 Corey Bradford .30 .10
❑ 64 Bill Schroeder .30 .10
❑ 65 E.G. Green .20 .07
❑ 66 Peyton Manning 1.25 .50
❑ 67 Edgerrin James .75 .30
❑ 68 Marvin Harrison .50 .20
❑ 69 Terrence Wilkins .20 .07
❑ 70 Mark Brunell .50 .20
❑ 71 Fred Taylor .50 .20
❑ 72 Keenan McCardell .30 .10
❑ 73 Jimmy Smith .30 .10
❑ 74 Warren Moon .50 .20
❑ 75 Elvis Grbac .30 .10
❑ 76 Tony Gonzalez .30 .10
❑ 77 Dan Marino 1.50 .60
❑ 78 O.J. McDuffie .30 .10
❑ 79 Tony Martin .30 .10
❑ 80 James Johnson .20 .07
❑ 81 Thurman Thomas .30 .10
❑ 82 Randy Moss 1.00 .40
❑ 83 Daunte Culpepper .60 .25
❑ 84 Cris Carter .50 .20
❑ 85 Robert Smith .50 .20
❑ 86 John Randle .30 .10
❑ 87 Drew Bledsoe .60 .25
❑ 88 Terry Glenn .30 .10
❑ 89 Kevin Faulk .30 .10
❑ 90 Ricky Williams .50 .20
❑ 91 Jeff Blake .30 .10
❑ 92 Jake Reed .30 .10
❑ 93 Amani Toomer .30 .10
❑ 94 Kerry Collins .30 .10
❑ 95 Tiki Barber .50 .20
❑ 96 Ike Hilliard .30 .10
❑ 97 Curtis Martin .50 .20
❑ 98 Vinny Testaverde .30 .10
❑ 99 Wayne Chrebet .30 .10
❑ 100 Ray Lucas .30 .10
❑ 101 Charles Woodson .30 .10
❑ 102 Napoleon Kaufman .30 .10
❑ 103 Tim Brown .50 .20
❑ 104 Tyrone Wheatley .30 .10
❑ 105 Rich Gannon .50 .20
❑ 106 Duce Staley .50 .20
❑ 107 Donovan McNabb .75 .30
❑ 108 Amos Zereoue .50 .20
❑ 109 Kordell Stewart .30 .10
❑ 110 Jerome Bettis .50 .20
❑ 111 Troy Edwards .20 .07
❑ 112 Ryan Leaf .30 .10
❑ 113 Junior Seau .50 .20
❑ 114 Jim Harbaugh .30 .10
❑ 115 Jermaine Fazande .20 .07
❑ 116 Curtis Conway .30 .10
❑ 117 Steve Young .60 .25
❑ 118 Jerry Rice 1.00 .40
❑ 119 Terrell Owens .50 .20
❑ 120 Charlie Garner .30 .10
❑ 121 Jeff Garcia .50 .20
❑ 122 Jon Kitna .50 .20
❑ 123 Derrick Mayes .30 .10
❑ 124 Ricky Watters .30 .10
❑ 125 Kurt Warner 1.00 .40
❑ 126 Marshall Faulk .60 .25
❑ 127 Torry Holt .50 .20
❑ 128 Az-Zahir Hakim .30 .10
❑ 129 Isaac Bruce .50 .20
❑ 130 Mike Alstott .50 .20
❑ 131 Warrick Dunn .50 .20
❑ 132 Shaun King .20 .07
❑ 133 Keyshawn Johnson .50 .20
❑ 134 Jacquez Green .20 .07
❑ 135 Reidel Anthony .30 .10
❑ 136 Warren Sapp .30 .10
❑ 137 Eddie George .50 .20
❑ 138 Steve McNair .50 .20
❑ 139 Yancey Thigpen .20 .07
❑ 140 Kevin Dyson .30 .10
❑ 141 Frank Wycheck .30 .10
❑ 142 Jevon Kearse .50 .20
❑ 143 Stephen Davis .50 .20
❑ 144 Skip Hicks .20 .07
❑ 145 Brad Johnson .50 .20
❑ 146 Bruce Smith .30 .10
❑ 147 Michael Westbrook .30 .10
❑ 148 Albert Connell .20 .07
❑ 149 Jeff George .30 .10
❑ 150 Deion Sanders .50 .20
❑ 151 Courtney Brown RC 6.00 2.50
❑ 152 Corey Simon RC 6.00 2.50
❑ 153 Brian Urlacher RC 25.00 10.00
❑ 154 Shaun Ellis RC 6.00 2.50
❑ 155 John Abraham RC 6.00 2.50
❑ 156 Deltha O'Neal RC 6.00 2.50
❑ 157 Ahmed Plummer RC 6.00 2.50
❑ 158 Chris Hovan RC 5.00 2.00
❑ 159 Rob Morris RC 5.00 2.00
❑ 160 Keith Bulluck RC 6.00 2.50
❑ 161 Darren Howard RC 5.00 2.00
❑ 162 John Engelberger RC 5.00 2.00
❑ 163 Raynoch Thompson RC 5.00 2.00
❑ 164 Cornelius Griffin RC 5.00 2.00
❑ 165 William Bartee RC 5.00 2.00
❑ 166 Fred Robbins RC 3.00 1.25
❑ 167 Micheal Boireau RC 3.00 1.25
❑ 168 Brandon Short RC 5.00 2.00
❑ 169 Jacoby Shepherd RC 3.00 1.25
❑ 170 Peter Warrick RC 6.00 2.50
❑ 171 Jamal Lewis RC 15.00 6.00
❑ 172 Thomas Jones RC 10.00 4.00
❑ 173 Plaxico Burress RC 12.00 5.00
❑ 174 Travis Taylor RC 6.00 2.50
❑ 175 Ron Dayne RC 6.00 2.50
❑ 176 Bubba Franks RC 6.00 2.50
❑ 177 Sebastian Janikowski RC 6.00 2.50
❑ 178 Chad Pennington RC 15.00 6.00
❑ 179 Shaun Alexander RC 30.00 15.00
❑ 180 Sylvester Morris RC 5.00 2.00
❑ 181 Anthony Becht RC 6.00 2.50
❑ 182 R.Jay Soward RC 5.00 2.00
❑ 183 Trung Canidate RC 5.00 2.00
❑ 184 Dennis Northcutt RC 6.00 2.50
❑ 185 Todd Pinkston RC 6.00 2.50
❑ 186 Jerry Porter RC 8.00 3.00
❑ 187 Travis Prentice RC 5.00 2.00
❑ 188 Giovanni Carmazzi RC 3.00 1.25
❑ 189 Ron Dugans RC 3.00 1.25
❑ 190 Erron Kinney RC 6.00 2.50
❑ 191 Dez White RC 6.00 2.50
❑ 192 Chris Cole RC 5.00 2.00
❑ 193 Ron Dixon RC 5.00 2.00
❑ 194 Chris Redman RC 5.00 2.00
❑ 195 J.R. Redmond RC 5.00 2.00
❑ 196 Laveranues Coles RC 8.00 3.00
❑ 197 JaJuan Dawson RC 3.00 1.25
❑ 198 Darrell Jackson RC 12.00 5.00
❑ 199 Reuben Droughns RC 8.00 3.00
❑ 200 Doug Chapman RC 5.00 2.00
❑ 201 Terrelle Smith RC 5.00 2.00
❑ 202 Curtis Keaton RC 5.00 2.00
❑ 203 Gari Scott RC 3.00 1.25
❑ 204 Danny Farmer RC 5.00 2.00
❑ 205 Hank Poteat RC 5.00 2.00
❑ 206 Ben Kelly RC 3.00 1.25
❑ 207 Corey Moore RC 3.00 1.25
❑ 208 Na'il Diggs RC 5.00 2.00
❑ 209 Aaron Shea RC 5.00 2.00
❑ 210 Trevor Gaylor RC 5.00 2.00
❑ 211 Julian Peterson RC 6.00 2.50
❑ 212 Frank Moreau RC 5.00 2.00
❑ 213 Deon Dyer RC 5.00 2.00
❑ 214 Avion Black RC 5.00 2.00
❑ 215 Paul Smith RC 5.00 2.00
❑ 216 Michael Wiley RC 5.00 2.00
❑ 217 Dante Hall RC 12.00 5.00
❑ 218 Mike Brown RC 10.00 4.00
❑ 219 Sammy Morris RC 5.00 2.00
❑ 220 Billy Volek RC 10.00 4.00
❑ 221 Tee Martin RC 6.00 2.50
❑ 222 Troy Walters RC 6.00 2.50
❑ 223 Chad Morton RC 6.00 2.50
❑ 224 Erik Flowers RC 5.00 2.00
❑ 225 Ronney Jenkins RC 5.00 2.00
❑ 226 Thomas Hamner RC 3.00 1.25
❑ 227 Mareno Philyaw RC 3.00 1.25
❑ 228 James Williams RC 5.00 2.00
❑ 229 Mike Anderson RC 8.00 3.00
❑ 230 Tom Brady RC 80.00 40.00
❑ 231 Mike Green RC 5.00 2.00
❑ 232 Todd Husak RC 6.00 2.50
❑ 233 Tim Rattay RC 6.00 2.50
❑ 234 Jarious Jackson RC 5.00 2.00
❑ 235 Joe Hamilton RC 5.00 2.00
❑ 236 Shyrone Stith RC 5.00 2.00
❑ 237 Rondell Mealey RC 3.00 1.25
❑ 238 Demario Brown RC 3.00 1.25
❑ 239 Chris Coleman RC 6.00 2.50
❑ 240 Dwayne Goodrich RC 3.00 1.25
❑ 241 Drew Haddad RC 3.00 1.25
❑ 242 Doug Johnson RC 6.00 2.50
❑ 243 Windrell Hayes RC 5.00 2.00
❑ 244 Charles Lee RC 3.00 1.25
❑ 245 Kevin McDougal RC 5.00 2.00
❑ 246 Spergon Wynn RC 5.00 2.00
❑ 247 Shockmain Davis RC 3.00 1.25
❑ 248 Jamel White RC 5.00 2.00
❑ 249 Bashir Yamini RC 3.00 1.25
❑ 250 Kwame Cavil RC 3.00 1.25

2002 Donruss

❑ COMPLETE SET (300) 150.00 75.00
❑ COMP.SET w/o SP's (100) 20.00 7.50
❑ 1 Jake Plummer .30 .10
❑ 2 David Boston .50 .20
❑ 3 MarTay Jenkins .20 .07
❑ 4 Thomas Jones .30 .10
❑ 5 Frank Sanders .20 .07
❑ 6 Shawn Jefferson .20 .07
❑ 7 Alge Crumpler .30 .10
❑ 8 Michael Vick 1.50 .60
❑ 9 Jamal Anderson .30 .10
❑ 10 Warrick Dunn .50 .20
❑ 11 Peter Boulware .20 .07
❑ 12 Jamal Lewis .50 .20
❑ 13 Jeff Blake .20 .07
❑ 14 Travis Taylor .30 .10
❑ 15 Ray Lewis .50 .20
❑ 16 Todd Heap .20 .07
❑ 17 Nate Clements .20 .07
❑ 18 Alex Van Pelt .20 .07
❑ 19 Reggie Germany .20 .07
❑ 20 Larry Centers .20 .07
❑ 21 Eric Moulds .30 .10
❑ 22 Travis Henry .50 .20
❑ 23 Wesley Walls .20 .07
❑ 24 Steve Smith .50 .20
❑ 25 Lamar Smith .30 .10
❑ 26 Patrick Jeffers .20 .07
❑ 27 Chris Weinke .30 .10
❑ 28 Muhsin Muhammad .30 .10
❑ 29 Marcus Robinson .30 .10
❑ 30 Jim Miller .20 .07
❑ 31 Anthony Thomas .30 .10
❑ 32 David Terrell .50 .20
❑ 33 Brian Urlacher .75 .30
❑ 34 Marty Booker .20 .07
❑ 35 Darnay Scott .20 .07
❑ 36 Jon Kitna .30 .10
❑ 37 Chad Johnson .50 .20
❑ 38 T.J. Houshmandzadeh .30 .10
❑ 39 Corey Dillon .30 .10
❑ 40 Peter Warrick .30 .10
❑ 41 Gerard Warren .20 .07
❑ 42 Anthony Henry .20 .07
❑ 43 Quincy Morgan .20 .07
❑ 44 JaJuan Dawson .20 .07
❑ 45 Tim Couch .30 .10
❑ 46 Kevin Johnson .30 .10
❑ 47 James Jackson .20 .07
❑ 48 La'Roi Glover .20 .07
❑ 49 Anthony Wright .20 .07
❑ 50 Rocket Ismail .30 .10
❑ 51 Troy Hambrick .20 .07

❑ 52 Emmitt Smith 1.25 .50
❑ 53 Quincy Carter .30 .10
❑ 54 Joey Galloway .30 .10
❑ 55 Shannon Sharpe .30 .10
❑ 56 Kevin Kasper .20 .07
❑ 57 Olandis Gary .30 .10
❑ 58 Brian Griese .50 .20
❑ 59 Rod Smith .30 .10
❑ 60 Terrell Davis .50 .20
❑ 61 Ed McCaffrey .50 .20
❑ 62 Mike Anderson .50 .20
❑ 63 Bill Schroeder .30 .10
❑ 64 Scotty Anderson .20 .07
❑ 65 Mike McMahon .50 .20
❑ 66 James Stewart .30 .10
❑ 67 Az-Zahir Hakim .20 .07
❑ 68 Germane Crowell .20 .07
❑ 69 Kabeer Gbaja-Biamila .30 .10
❑ 70 LeRoy Butler .20 .07
❑ 71 Antonio Freeman .50 .20
❑ 72 Bubba Franks .30 .10
❑ 73 Brett Favre 1.25 .50
❑ 74 Ahman Green .50 .20
❑ 75 Terry Glenn .30 .10
❑ 76 Jamie Sharper .20 .07
❑ 77 Tony Simmons .20 .07
❑ 78 James Allen .30 .10
❑ 79 Terrence Wilkins .20 .07
❑ 80 Dominic Rhodes .50 .20
❑ 81 Qadry Ismail .30 .10
❑ 82 Peyton Manning 1.00 .40
❑ 83 Edgerrin James .60 .25
❑ 84 Marvin Harrison .50 .20
❑ 85 Reggie Wayne .50 .20
❑ 86 Fred Taylor .50 .20
❑ 87 Elvis Joseph .20 .07
❑ 88 Mark Brunell .50 .20
❑ 89 Keenan McCardell .20 .07
❑ 90 Jimmy Smith .30 .10
❑ 91 Kyle Brady .20 .07
❑ 92 Derrick Alexander .30 .10
❑ 93 Johnnie Morton .30 .10
❑ 94 Trent Green .30 .10
❑ 95 Priest Holmes .60 .25
❑ 96 Tony Gonzalez .30 .10
❑ 97 Snoop Minnis .20 .07
❑ 98 Travis Minor .20 .07
❑ 99 Oronde Gadsden .30 .10
❑ 100 Jay Fiedler .30 .10
❑ 101 Chris Chambers .50 .20
❑ 102 Ricky Williams .50 .20
❑ 103 Zach Thomas .50 .20
❑ 104 Byron Chamberlain .20 .07
❑ 105 Todd Bouman .20 .07
❑ 106 Daunte Culpepper .50 .20
❑ 107 Michael Bennett .30 .10
❑ 108 Randy Moss 1.00 .40
❑ 109 Cris Carter .50 .20
❑ 110 David Patten .20 .07
❑ 111 Donald Hayes .20 .07
❑ 112 Tom Brady 1.25 .50
❑ 113 Antowain Smith .30 .10
❑ 114 Troy Brown .30 .10
❑ 115 Drew Bledsoe .60 .25
❑ 116 Bryan Cox .20 .07
❑ 117 Boo Williams .20 .07
❑ 118 Aaron Brooks .50 .20
❑ 119 Deuce McAllister .60 .25
❑ 120 Joe Horn .30 .10
❑ 121 Amani Toomer .30 .10
❑ 122 Ron Dayne .30 .10
❑ 123 Kerry Collins .30 .10
❑ 124 Ike Hilliard .30 .10
❑ 125 Tiki Barber .50 .20
❑ 126 Michael Strahan .30 .10
❑ 127 Chad Pennington .60 .25
❑ 128 Santana Moss .50 .20
❑ 129 LaMont Jordan .50 .20
❑ 130 Curtis Martin .50 .20
❑ 131 Wayne Chrebet .30 .10
❑ 132 Laveranues Coles .30 .10
❑ 133 Vinny Testaverde .30 .10
❑ 134 Charles Woodson .30 .10
❑ 135 Tyrone Wheatley .30 .10
❑ 136 Jerry Porter .20 .07
❑ 137 Rich Gannon .50 .20
❑ 138 Charlie Garner .30 .10
❑ 139 Tim Brown .50 .20
❑ 140 Jerry Rice 1.00 .40
❑ 141 James Thrash .30 .10
❑ 142 Todd Pinkston .30 .10
❑ 143 A.J. Feeley .50 .20
❑ 144 Donovan McNabb .60 .25
❑ 145 Duce Staley .50 .20
❑ 146 Freddie Mitchell .30 .10
❑ 147 Correll Buckhalter .30 .10
❑ 148 Casey Hampton .20 .07
❑ 149 Hines Ward .50 .20
❑ 150 Chris Fuamatu-Ma'afala .20 .07
❑ 151 Jerome Bettis .50 .20
❑ 152 Kordell Stewart .30 .10
❑ 153 Plaxico Burress .30 .10
❑ 154 Kendrell Bell .50 .20
❑ 155 Trevor Gaylor .20 .07
❑ 156 Curtis Conway .20 .07
❑ 157 Doug Flutie .50 .20
❑ 158 Drew Brees .50 .20
❑ 159 LaDainian Tomlinson .75 .30
❑ 160 Junior Seau .50 .20
❑ 161 Bryant Young .20 .07
❑ 162 Andre Carter .20 .07
❑ 163 Eric Johnson .20 .07
❑ 164 Jeff Garcia .50 .20
❑ 165 Garrison Hearst .30 .10
❑ 166 Terrell Owens .50 .20
❑ 167 Kevan Barlow .30 .10
❑ 168 Levon Kirkland .20 .07
❑ 169 Ricky Watters .20 .07
❑ 170 Trent Dilfer .30 .10
❑ 171 Shaun Alexander .60 .25
❑ 172 Koren Robinson .30 .10
❑ 173 Darrell Jackson .30 .10
❑ 174 Adam Archuleta .20 .07
❑ 175 Aeneas Williams .20 .07
❑ 176 Trung Canidate .30 .10
❑ 177 Kurt Warner .50 .20
❑ 178 Marshall Faulk .50 .20
❑ 179 Torry Holt .50 .20
❑ 180 Isaac Bruce .50 .20
❑ 181 John Lynch .30 .10
❑ 182 Joe Jurevicius .20 .07
❑ 183 Brad Johnson .30 .10
❑ 184 Rob Johnson .30 .10
❑ 185 Keyshawn Johnson .50 .20
❑ 186 Mike Alstott .50 .20
❑ 187 Warren Sapp .30 .10
❑ 188 Drew Bennett .50 .20
❑ 189 Frank Wycheck .20 .07
❑ 190 Kevin Dyson .30 .10
❑ 191 Steve McNair .50 .20
❑ 192 Eddie George .50 .20
❑ 193 Jevon Kearse .30 .10
❑ 194 Derrick Mason .30 .10
❑ 195 Champ Bailey .30 .10
❑ 196 Darrell Green .20 .07
❑ 197 Bruce Smith .20 .07
❑ 198 Jacquez Green .20 .07
❑ 199 Stephen Davis .30 .10
❑ 200 Rod Gardner .30 .10
❑ 201 David Carr RC 8.00 3.00
❑ 202 Joey Harrington RC 5.00 2.00
❑ 203 Patrick Ramsey RC 4.00 1.50
❑ 204 Kurt Kittner RC 2.50 1.00
❑ 205 Rohan Davey RC 3.00 1.25
❑ 206 Josh McCown RC 4.00 1.50
❑ 207 David Garrard RC 3.00 1.25
❑ 208 Randy Fasani RC 2.50 1.00
❑ 209 Atrews Bell RC 1.50 .60
❑ 210 Brandon Doman RC 2.50 1.00
❑ 211 Eric Crouch RC 3.00 1.25
❑ 212 Woody Dantzler RC 2.50 1.00
❑ 213 Chad Hutchinson RC 2.50 1.00
❑ 214 Zak Kustok RC 3.00 1.25
❑ 215 Ronald Curry RC 3.00 1.25
❑ 216 William Green RC 3.00 1.25
❑ 217 T.J. Duckett RC 4.00 1.50
❑ 218 Clinton Portis RC 10.00 4.00
❑ 219 DeShaun Foster RC 3.00 1.25
❑ 220 Lamar Gordon RC 3.00 1.25
❑ 221 Jonathan Wells RC 3.00 1.25
❑ 222 Adrian Peterson RC 3.00 1.25
❑ 223 Ladell Betts RC 3.00 1.25
❑ 224 Maurice Morris RC 3.00 1.25
❑ 225 Brian Westbrook RC 5.00 2.00
❑ 226 Luke Staley RC 2.50 1.00
❑ 227 Travis Stephens RC 2.50 1.00
❑ 228 Craig Nall RC 3.00 1.25
❑ 229 Chester Taylor RC 6.00 2.50
❑ 230 Ken Simonton RC 1.50 .60
❑ 231 Verron Haynes RC 3.00 1.25
❑ 232 Tellis Redmon RC 2.50 1.00
❑ 233 J.T. O'Sullivan RC 2.50 1.00
❑ 234 Major Applewhite RC 3.00 1.25
❑ 235 Ricky Williams RC 2.50 1.00
❑ 236 James Mungro RC 3.00 1.25
❑ 237 Josh Scobey RC 3.00 1.25
❑ 238 Najeh Davenport RC 3.00 1.25
❑ 239 Dicenzo Miller RC 1.50 .60
❑ 240 Ennis Haywood RC 2.50 1.00
❑ 241 Jabar Gaffney RC 3.00 1.25
❑ 242 Antonio Bryant RC 3.00 1.25
❑ 243 Donte Stallworth RC 6.00 2.50
❑ 244 Josh Reed RC 3.00 1.25
❑ 245 Ashley Lelie RC 6.00 2.50
❑ 246 Reche Caldwell RC 3.00 1.25
❑ 247 Marquise Walker RC 2.50 1.00
❑ 248 Javon Walker RC 6.00 2.50
❑ 249 Andre Davis RC 2.50 1.00
❑ 250 Antwaan Randle El RC 5.00 2.00
❑ 251 Kelly Campbell RC 2.50 1.00
❑ 252 Cliff Russell RC 2.50 1.00
❑ 253 Kahlil Hill RC 2.50 1.00
❑ 254 Ron Johnson RC 2.50 1.00
❑ 255 Deion Branch RC 6.00 2.50
❑ 256 Brian Poli-Dixon RC 2.50 1.00
❑ 257 Freddie Milons RC 2.50 1.00
❑ 258 Lee Mays RC 2.50 1.00
❑ 259 Tim Carter RC 2.50 1.00
❑ 260 Terry Charles RC 2.50 1.00
❑ 261 Jamar Martin RC 2.50 1.00
❑ 262 Jason McAddley RC 2.50 1.00
❑ 263 Chris Hope RC 3.00 1.25
❑ 264 Howard Green RC 1.50 .60
❑ 265 Jeremy Shockey RC 10.00 4.00
❑ 266 Daniel Graham RC 3.00 1.25
❑ 267 Eddie Freeman RC 1.50 .60
❑ 268 Julius Peppers RC 6.00 2.50
❑ 269 Kalimba Edwards RC 3.00 1.25
❑ 270 Dwight Freeney RC 5.00 2.00
❑ 271 Dennis Johnson RC 1.50 .60
❑ 272 Alex Brown RC 3.00 1.25
❑ 273 Bryan Thomas RC 2.50 1.00
❑ 274 Bryan Fletcher RC 1.50 .60
❑ 275 Will Overstreet RC 1.50 .60
❑ 276 Ryan Denney RC 2.50 1.00
❑ 277 Charles Grant RC 3.00 1.25
❑ 278 John Henderson RC 3.00 1.25
❑ 279 Albert Haynesworth RC 2.50 1.00
❑ 280 Wendell Bryant RC 1.50 .60
❑ 281 Ryan Sims RC 3.00 1.25
❑ 282 Anthony Weaver RC 2.50 1.00
❑ 283 Larry Tripplett RC 1.50 .60
❑ 284 Alan Harper RC 1.50 .60
❑ 285 Napoleon Harris RC 3.00 1.25
❑ 286 Robert Thomas RC 3.00 1.25
❑ 287 Levar Fisher RC 1.50 .60
❑ 288 Andra Davis RC 2.50 1.00
❑ 289 Quentin Jammer RC 3.00 1.25
❑ 290 Phillip Buchanon RC 3.00 1.25
❑ 291 Keyuo Craver RC 2.50 1.00
❑ 292 Lito Sheppard RC 3.00 1.25
❑ 293 Rocky Calmus RC 3.00 1.25
❑ 294 Mike Rumph RC 3.00 1.25
❑ 295 Mike Echols RC 1.50 .60
❑ 296 Joseph Jefferson RC 2.50 1.00
❑ 297 Roy Williams RC 8.00 3.00
❑ 298 Ed Reed RC 5.00 2.00
❑ 299 Michael Lewis RC 3.00 1.25
❑ 300 Eddie Drummond RC 2.50 1.00

2001 Donruss Classics

❑ COMP.SET w/o SPs (100) 20.00 7.50
❑ 1 David Boston .75 .30
❑ 2 Jake Plummer .50 .20
❑ 3 Thomas Jones .50 .20
❑ 4 Jamal Anderson .75 .30
❑ 5 Chris Redman .30 .10
❑ 6 Elvis Grbac .50 .20
❑ 7 Jamal Lewis 1.25 .50
❑ 8 Qadry Ismail .50 .20
❑ 9 Ray Lewis .75 .30
❑ 10 Shannon Sharpe .50 .20
❑ 11 Travis Taylor .50 .20
❑ 12 Eric Moulds .50 .20
❑ 13 Rob Johnson .50 .20
❑ 14 Muhsin Muhammad .50 .20
❑ 15 Brian Urlacher 1.25 .50

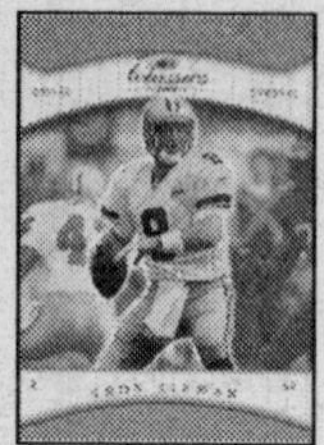

❑	16 Cade McNown	.30	.10
❑	17 Marcus Robinson	.75	.30
❑	18 Akili Smith	.30	.10
❑	19 Corey Dillon	.75	.30
❑	20 Peter Warrick	.75	.30
❑	21 Courtney Brown	.50	.20
❑	22 Tim Couch	.50	.20
❑	23 Emmitt Smith	1.50	.60
❑	24 Brian Griese	.75	.30
❑	25 Ed McCaffery	.75	.30
❑	26 Olandis Gary	.50	.20
❑	27 Mike Anderson	.75	.30
❑	28 Rod Smith	.50	.20
❑	29 Terrell Davis	.75	.30
❑	30 Charlie Batch	.75	.30
❑	31 James Stewart	.50	.20
❑	32 Ahman Green	.75	.30
❑	33 Antonio Freeman	.75	.30
❑	34 Brett Favre	2.50	1.00
❑	35 Edgerrin James	1.00	.40
❑	36 Marvin Harrison	.75	.30
❑	37 Peyton Manning	2.00	.75
❑	38 Fred Taylor	.75	.30
❑	39 Jimmy Smith	.50	.20
❑	40 Keenan McCardell	.30	.10
❑	41 Mark Brunell	.75	.30
❑	42 Sylvester Morris	.30	.10
❑	43 Tony Gonzalez	.50	.20
❑	44 Zach Thomas	.75	.30
❑	45 Jay Fiedler	.75	.30
❑	46 Lamar Smith	.50	.20
❑	47 Cris Carter	.75	.30
❑	48 Daunte Culpepper	.75	.30
❑	49 Randy Moss	1.50	.60
❑	50 Drew Bledsoe	1.00	.40
❑	51 Terry Glenn	.50	.20
❑	52 Aaron Brooks	.75	.30
❑	53 Joe Horn	.50	.20
❑	54 Ricky Williams	.75	.30
❑	55 Amani Toomer	.50	.20
❑	56 Ike Hilliard	.50	.20
❑	57 Kerry Collins	.50	.20
❑	58 Ron Dayne	.75	.30
❑	59 Tiki Barber	.75	.30
❑	60 Chad Pennington	1.25	.50
❑	61 Curtis Martin	.75	.30
❑	62 Laveranues Coles	.75	.30
❑	63 Vinny Testaverde	.50	.20
❑	64 Wayne Chrebet	.50	.20
❑	65 Charles Woodson	.50	.20
❑	66 Rich Gannon	.75	.30
❑	67 Tim Brown	.75	.30
❑	68 Tyrone Wheatley	.50	.20
❑	69 Corey Simon	.50	.20
❑	70 Donovan McNabb	1.00	.40
❑	71 Duce Staley	.75	.30
❑	72 Jerome Bettis	.75	.30
❑	73 Plaxico Burress	.75	.30
❑	74 Doug Flutie	.75	.30
❑	75 Junior Seau	.75	.30
❑	76 Jeff Garcia	.75	.30
❑	77 Jerry Rice	1.50	.60
❑	78 Giovanni Carmazzi	.30	.10
❑	79 Terrell Owens	.75	.30
❑	80 Darrell Jackson	.75	.30
❑	81 Ricky Watters	.50	.20
❑	82 Shaun Alexander	1.00	.40
❑	83 Isaac Bruce	.75	.30
❑	84 Kurt Warner	2.50	1.00
❑	85 Marshall Faulk	1.00	.40
❑	86 Torry Holt	.75	.30
❑	87 Brad Johnson	.75	.30
❑	88 Keyshawn Johnson	.75	.30
❑	89 Mike Alstott	.75	.30
❑	90 Shaun King	.30	.10
❑	91 Warren Sapp	.50	.20
❑	92 Warrick Dunn	.75	.30
❑	93 Eddie George	.75	.30
❑	94 Jevon Kearse	.50	.20
❑	95 Steve McNair	.75	.30
❑	96 Jeff George	.50	.20
❑	97 Stephen Davis	.75	.30
❑	98 Charlie Garner	.50	.20
❑	99 Trent Dilfer	.50	.20
❑	100 Troy Aikman	1.25	.50
❑	101 Michael Vick RC	30.00	12.50
❑	102 Drew Brees RC	25.00	10.00
❑	103 Chris Weinke RC	6.00	2.50
❑	104 Mike McMahon RC	6.00	2.50
❑	105 Jesse Palmer RC	6.00	2.50
❑	106 Quincy Carter RC	6.00	2.50
❑	107 Josh Heupel RC	6.00	2.50
❑	108 Tim Hasselbeck RC	6.00	2.50
❑	109 LaDainian Tomlinson RC	50.00	25.00
❑	110 Deuce McAllister RC	12.00	5.00
❑	111 Michael Bennett RC	6.00	2.50
❑	112 Anthony Thomas RC	6.00	2.50
❑	113 LaMont Jordan RC	12.00	5.00
❑	114 Travis Henry RC	10.00	4.00
❑	115 Kevan Barlow RC	6.00	2.50
❑	116 Travis Minor RC	4.00	1.50
❑	117 Rudi Johnson RC	12.00	5.00
❑	118 David Allen RC	4.00	1.50
❑	119 Heath Evans RC	4.00	1.50
❑	120 Moran Norris RC	2.50	1.00
❑	121 David Terrell RC	6.00	2.50
❑	122 Koren Robinson RC	6.00	2.50
❑	123 Rod Gardner RC	6.00	2.50
❑	124 Santana Moss RC	10.00	4.00
❑	125 Freddie Mitchell RC	6.00	2.50
❑	126 Reggie Wayne RC	12.00	5.00
❑	127 Quincy Morgan RC	6.00	2.50
❑	128 Chad Johnson RC	20.00	7.50
❑	129 Robert Ferguson RC	6.00	2.50
❑	130 Chris Chambers RC	10.00	4.00
❑	131 Snoop Minnis RC	4.00	1.50
❑	132 Eddie Berlin RC	4.00	1.50
❑	133 Alex Bannister RC	4.00	1.50
❑	134 Todd Heap RC	6.00	2.50
❑	135 Alge Crumpler RC	8.00	3.00
❑	136 Justin Smith RC	6.00	2.50
❑	137 Andre Carter RC	6.00	2.50
❑	138 Jamal Reynolds RC	6.00	2.50
❑	139 Richard Seymour RC	6.00	2.50
❑	140 Marcus Stroud RC	6.00	2.50
❑	141 Casey Hampton RC	6.00	2.50
❑	142 Gerard Warren RC	6.00	2.50
❑	143 Torrance Marshall RC	6.00	2.50
❑	144 Brian Allen RC	2.50	1.00
❑	145 Morlon Greenwood RC	4.00	1.50
❑	146 Keith Adams RC	2.50	1.00
❑	147 Will Allen RC	4.00	1.50
❑	148 Nate Clements RC	6.00	2.50
❑	149 Adam Archuleta RC	6.00	2.50
❑	150 Hakim Akbar RC	2.50	1.00
❑	151 James Lofton	1.00	.40
❑	152 Jim Kelly	2.50	1.00
❑	153 Gale Sayers	2.50	1.00
❑	154 Mike Singletary	2.00	.75
❑	155 Boomer Esiason	1.50	.60
❑	156 Charlie Joiner	1.00	.40
❑	157 Ken Anderson	1.50	.60
❑	158 Y.A. Tittle	2.00	.75
❑	159 Jim Brown	3.00	1.25
❑	160 Otto Graham	1.50	.60
❑	161 Ozzie Newsome	1.00	.40
❑	162 Drew Pearson	1.50	.60
❑	163 Lance Alworth	1.50	.60
❑	164 Roger Staubach	4.00	1.50
❑	165 Tony Dorsett	2.00	.75
❑	166 John Elway	5.00	2.00
❑	167 Barry Sanders	3.00	1.25
❑	168 Bart Starr	4.00	1.50
❑	169 Paul Hornung	2.00	.75
❑	170 Earl Campbell	2.00	.75
❑	171 Warren Moon	2.00	.75
❑	172 Johnny Unitas	3.00	1.25
❑	173 Deacon Jones	1.50	.60
❑	174 Eric Dickerson	1.50	.60
❑	175 Bob Griese	2.00	.75
❑	176 Dan Marino	5.00	2.00
❑	177 Larry Csonka	2.00	.75
❑	178 Paul Warfield	2.00	.75
❑	179 Fran Tarkenton	2.50	1.00
❑	180 Archie Manning	1.50	.60
❑	181 Frank Gifford	2.00	.75
❑	182 Lawrence Taylor	2.00	.75
❑	183 Dan Fouts	2.00	.75
❑	184 Don Maynard	1.50	.60
❑	185 Joe Namath	4.00	1.50
❑	186 Fred Biletnikoff	2.00	.75
❑	187 Marcus Allen	2.50	1.00
❑	188 Jim Plunkett	1.50	.60
❑	189 Franco Harris	2.50	1.00
❑	190 Terry Bradshaw	4.00	1.50
❑	191 Joe Montana	10.00	4.00
❑	192 Roger Craig	1.50	.60
❑	193 Steve Young	2.50	1.00
❑	194 Dwight Clark	1.50	.60
❑	195 Steve Largent	2.00	.75
❑	196 Art Monk	1.50	.60
❑	197 Charley Taylor	1.50	.60
❑	198 Joe Theismann	2.00	.75
❑	199 Sammy Baugh	2.00	.75
❑	200 Sonny Jurgensen	2.00	.75

2002 Donruss Classics

❑	COMP.SET w/o SP's (100)	20.00	7.50
❑	1 David Boston	.75	.30
❑	2 Jake Plummer	.50	.20
❑	3 Jamal Anderson	.50	.20
❑	4 Michael Vick	2.50	1.00
❑	5 Chris Weinke	.50	.20
❑	6 Muhsin Muhammad	.50	.20
❑	7 Steve Smith	.75	.30
❑	8 Anthony Thomas	.50	.20
❑	9 David Terrell	.75	.30
❑	10 Brian Urlacher	1.25	.50
❑	11 Marty Booker	.50	.20
❑	12 Quincy Carter	.50	.20
❑	13 Emmitt Smith	2.00	.75
❑	14 Mike McMahon	.75	.30
❑	15 James Stewart	.50	.20
❑	16 Brett Favre	2.00	.75
❑	17 Ahman Green	.75	.30
❑	18 Antonio Freeman	.75	.30
❑	19 Michael Bennett	.50	.20
❑	20 Randy Moss	1.50	.60
❑	21 Cris Carter	.75	.30
❑	22 Daunte Culpepper	.75	.30
❑	23 Aaron Brooks	.75	.30
❑	24 Ricky Williams	.75	.30
❑	25 Deuce McAllister	1.00	.40
❑	26 Kerry Collins	.50	.20
❑	27 Michael Strahan	.50	.20
❑	28 Donovan McNabb	1.00	.40
❑	29 Duce Staley	.75	.30
❑	30 Freddie Mitchell	.50	.20
❑	31 Correll Buckhalter	.50	.20
❑	32 Jeff Garcia	.75	.30
❑	33 Terrell Owens	.75	.30
❑	34 Garrison Hearst	.50	.20
❑	35 Marshall Faulk	.75	.30
❑	36 Isaac Bruce	.75	.30
❑	37 Kurt Warner	.75	.30
❑	38 Torry Holt	.75	.30
❑	39 Brad Johnson	.50	.20
❑	40 Keyshawn Johnson	.75	.30
❑	41 Mike Alstott	.75	.30
❑	42 Warrick Dunn	.75	.30
❑	43 Stephen Davis	.50	.20
❑	44 Rod Gardner	.50	.20
❑	45 Bruce Smith	.30	.10

❑ 46 Elvis Grbac .50 .20
❑ 47 Ray Lewis .75 .30
❑ 48 Jamal Lewis .75 .30
❑ 49 Rob Johnson .50 .20
❑ 50 Eric Moulds .50 .20
❑ 51 Travis Henry .75 .30
❑ 52 Corey Dillon .50 .20
❑ 53 Peter Warrick .50 .20
❑ 54 Tim Couch .50 .20
❑ 55 James Jackson .30 .10
❑ 56 Kevin Johnson .50 .20
❑ 57 Brian Griese .75 .30
❑ 58 Terrell Davis .75 .30
❑ 59 Rod Smith .50 .20
❑ 60 Mike Anderson .75 .30
❑ 61 Peyton Manning 1.50 .60
❑ 62 Marvin Harrison .75 .30
❑ 63 Edgerrin James 1.00 .40
❑ 64 Dominic Rhodes .75 .30
❑ 65 Mark Brunell .75 .30
❑ 66 Fred Taylor .75 .30
❑ 67 Jimmy Smith .50 .20
❑ 68 Tony Gonzalez .50 .20
❑ 69 Trent Green .50 .20
❑ 70 Priest Holmes 1.00 .40
❑ 71 Snoop Minnis .30 .10
❑ 72 Jay Fiedler .50 .20
❑ 73 Lamar Smith .50 .20
❑ 74 Chris Chambers .75 .30
❑ 75 Tom Brady 2.00 .75
❑ 76 Drew Bledsoe 1.00 .40
❑ 77 Antowain Smith .50 .20
❑ 78 Troy Brown .50 .20
❑ 79 Vinny Testaverde .50 .20
❑ 80 Curtis Martin .75 .30
❑ 81 Wayne Chrebet .50 .20
❑ 82 Laveranues Coles .50 .20
❑ 83 Tim Brown .75 .30
❑ 84 Jerry Rice 1.50 .60
❑ 85 Rich Gannon .75 .30
❑ 86 Charlie Garner .50 .20
❑ 87 Kordell Stewart .50 .20
❑ 88 Jerome Bettis .75 .30
❑ 89 Kendrell Bell .75 .30
❑ 90 Plaxico Burress .50 .20
❑ 91 Drew Brees .75 .30
❑ 92 LaDainian Tomlinson 1.25 .50
❑ 93 Doug Flutie .75 .30
❑ 94 Shaun Alexander 1.00 .40
❑ 95 Matt Hasselbeck .50 .20
❑ 96 Koren Robinson .50 .20
❑ 97 Steve McNair .75 .30
❑ 98 Eddie George .75 .30
❑ 99 Derrick Mason .50 .20
❑ 100 Jevon Kearse .50 .20
❑ 101 Joe Montana 12.00 5.00
❑ 102 Joe Namath 5.00 2.00
❑ 103 Warren Moon 3.00 1.25
❑ 104 Dan Marino 10.00 4.00
❑ 105 Steve Bartkowski 2.50 1.00
❑ 106 John Elway 10.00 4.00
❑ 107 Troy Aikman 5.00 2.00
❑ 108 Steve Young 3.00 1.25
❑ 109 Terry Bradshaw 5.00 2.00
❑ 110 Bart Starr 6.00 2.50
❑ 111 Bert Jones 1.50 .60
❑ 112 Craig Morton 2.50 1.00
❑ 113 Bob Griese 3.00 1.25
❑ 114 Dan Fouts 3.00 1.25
❑ 115 Phil Simms 2.50 1.00
❑ 116 Jim McMahon 4.00 1.50
❑ 117 Joe Theismann 3.00 1.25
❑ 118 Ken Stabler 5.00 2.00
❑ 119 Johnny Unitas 5.00 2.00
❑ 120 Roger Staubach 5.00 2.00
❑ 121 Len Dawson 3.00 1.25
❑ 122 Tony Dorsett 4.00 1.50
❑ 123 Gale Sayers 5.00 2.00
❑ 124 Jim Kelly 4.00 1.50
❑ 125 Herschel Walker 2.50 1.00
❑ 126 John Riggins 4.00 1.50
❑ 127 Eric Dickerson 2.50 1.00
❑ 128 Franco Harris 4.00 1.50
❑ 129 Earl Campbell 3.00 1.25
❑ 130 Thurman Thomas 2.50 1.00
❑ 131 Barry Sanders 5.00 2.00
❑ 132 Marcus Allen 4.00 1.50
❑ 134 Natrone Means 1.50 .60
❑ 135 Steve Largent 3.00 1.25
❑ 136 Don Maynard 2.50 1.00
❑ 137 Henry Ellard 2.50 1.00
❑ 138 Sterling Sharpe 3.00 1.25
❑ 139 Art Monk 2.50 1.00
❑ 140 Andre Reed 2.50 1.00
❑ 141 Raymond Berry 2.50 1.00
❑ 142 Ozzie Newsome 2.50 1.00
❑ 143 William Perry 2.50 1.00
❑ 144 Deacon Jones 2.50 1.00
❑ 145 Howie Long 4.00 1.50
❑ 146 L.C. Greenwood 2.50 1.00
❑ 147 Ronnie Lott 2.50 1.00
❑ 148 Dick Butkus 5.00 2.00
❑ 149 Fran Tarkenton 4.00 1.50
❑ 150 Mike Singletary 3.00 1.25
❑ 151 David Carr RC 15.00 6.00
❑ 152 Joey Harrington RC 10.00 4.00
❑ 153 Patrick Ramsey RC 8.00 3.00
❑ 154 Kurt Kittner RC 5.00 2.00
❑ 155 DeShaun Foster RC 6.00 2.50
❑ 156 William Green RC 6.00 2.50
❑ 157 Clinton Portis RC 20.00 7.50
❑ 158 T.J. Duckett RC 8.00 3.00
❑ 159 Cliff Russell RC 5.00 2.00
❑ 160 Antonio Bryant RC 6.00 2.50
❑ 161 Donte Stallworth RC 12.00 5.00
❑ 162 Reche Caldwell RC 6.00 2.50
❑ 163 Jabar Gaffney RC 6.00 2.50
❑ 164 Ashley Lelie RC 12.00 5.00
❑ 165 Andre Davis RC 5.00 2.00
❑ 166 Josh Reed RC 6.00 2.50
❑ 167 Ron Johnson RC 5.00 2.00
❑ 168 Kelly Campbell RC 5.00 2.00
❑ 169 Javon Walker RC 12.00 5.00
❑ 170 Antwaan Randle El RC 10.00 4.00
❑ 171 Marquise Walker RC 5.00 2.00
❑ 172 Jeremy Shockey RC 20.00 7.50
❑ 173 Jerramy Stevens RC 6.00 2.50
❑ 174 Daniel Graham RC 6.00 2.50
❑ 175 Julius Peppers RC 12.00 5.00
❑ 176 Kalimba Edwards RC 6.00 2.50
❑ 177 Alex Brown RC 6.00 2.50
❑ 178 Will Overstreet RC 5.00 2.00
❑ 179 Dwight Freeney RC 10.00 4.00
❑ 180 John Henderson RC 6.00 2.50
❑ 181 Ryan Sims RC 6.00 2.50
❑ 182 Albert Haynesworth RC 5.00 2.00
❑ 183 Wendell Bryant RC 3.00 1.25
❑ 184 Anthony Weaver RC 5.00 2.00
❑ 185 Napoleon Harris RC 6.00 2.50
❑ 186 Robert Thomas RC 6.00 2.50
❑ 187 Quentin Jammer RC 6.00 2.50
❑ 188 Ed Reed RC 10.00 4.00
❑ 189 Roy Williams RC 15.00 6.00
❑ 190 Phillip Buchanon RC 6.00 2.50
❑ 191 Lito Sheppard RC 6.00 2.50
❑ 192 Mike Rumph RC 6.00 2.50
❑ 193 Keyuo Craver RC 5.00 2.00
❑ 194 Randy Fasani RC 5.00 2.00
❑ 195 Rohan Davey RC 6.00 2.50
❑ 196 Chad Hutchinson RC 5.00 2.00
❑ 197 Eric Crouch RC 6.00 2.50
❑ 198 Lamar Gordon RC 6.00 2.50
❑ 199 Brian Westbrook RC 10.00 4.00
❑ 200 Adrian Peterson RC 6.00 2.50

2003 Donruss Classics

❑ COMP.SET w/o SP's (100) 20.00 7.50
❑ 1 Jake Plummer .50 .20
❑ 2 Marcel Shipp .50 .20
❑ 3 David Boston .50 .20
❑ 4 Michael Vick 2.00 .75
❑ 5 T.J. Duckett .50 .20
❑ 6 Warrick Dunn .50 .20
❑ 7 Ray Lewis .75 .30
❑ 8 Jamal Lewis .75 .30
❑ 9 Todd Heap .50 .20
❑ 10 Drew Bledsoe .75 .30
❑ 11 Travis Henry .50 .20
❑ 12 Peerless Price .50 .20
❑ 13 Eric Moulds .50 .20
❑ 14 Julius Peppers .75 .30
❑ 15 Steve Smith .75 .30
❑ 16 Lamar Smith .30 .10
❑ 17 Anthony Thomas .50 .20
❑ 18 Marty Booker .50 .20
❑ 19 Brian Urlacher 1.25 .50
❑ 20 Corey Dillon .50 .20
❑ 21 Chad Johnson .75 .30
❑ 22 Tim Couch .30 .10
❑ 23 William Green .50 .20
❑ 24 Quincy Morgan .50 .20
❑ 25 Chad Hutchinson .30 .10
❑ 26 Emmitt Smith 2.00 .75
❑ 27 Antonio Bryant .50 .20
❑ 28 Roy Williams .75 .30
❑ 29 Brian Griese .75 .30
❑ 30 Clinton Portis 1.25 .50
❑ 31 Rod Smith .50 .20
❑ 32 Ashley Lelie .75 .30
❑ 33 Joey Harrington 1.25 .50
❑ 34 James Stewart .50 .20
❑ 35 Bill Schroeder .50 .20
❑ 36 Brett Favre 2.00 .75
❑ 37 Ahman Green .75 .30
❑ 38 Donald Driver .50 .20
❑ 39 David Carr 1.25 .50
❑ 40 Jonathan Wells .30 .10
❑ 41 Corey Bradford .30 .10
❑ 42 Peyton Manning 1.25 .50
❑ 43 Edgerrin James .75 .30
❑ 44 Marvin Harrison .75 .30
❑ 45 Mark Brunell .50 .20
❑ 46 Fred Taylor .75 .30
❑ 47 Jimmy Smith .50 .20
❑ 48 Trent Green .50 .20
❑ 49 Priest Holmes 1.00 .40
❑ 50 Tony Gonzalez .50 .20
❑ 51 Ricky Williams .75 .30
❑ 52 Chris Chambers .75 .30
❑ 53 Zach Thomas .75 .30
❑ 54 Daunte Culpepper .75 .30
❑ 55 Michael Bennett .50 .20
❑ 56 Randy Moss 1.25 .50
❑ 57 Tom Brady 2.00 .75
❑ 58 Antowain Smith .50 .20
❑ 59 Troy Brown .50 .20
❑ 60 Aaron Brooks .75 .30
❑ 61 Deuce McAllister .75 .30
❑ 62 Donte Stallworth .75 .30
❑ 63 Kerry Collins .50 .20
❑ 64 Jeremy Shockey 1.25 .50
❑ 65 Amani Toomer .50 .20
❑ 66 Chad Pennington 1.00 .40
❑ 67 Curtis Martin .75 .30
❑ 68 Laveranues Coles .50 .20
❑ 69 Rich Gannon .50 .20
❑ 70 Charlie Garner .50 .20
❑ 71 Jerry Rice 1.50 .60
❑ 72 Tim Brown .75 .30
❑ 73 Donovan McNabb 1.00 .40
❑ 74 Duce Staley .50 .20
❑ 75 Todd Pinkston .50 .20
❑ 76 Tommy Maddox .75 .30
❑ 77 Jerome Bettis .75 .30
❑ 78 Plaxico Burress .50 .20
❑ 79 Hines Ward .75 .30
❑ 80 Drew Brees .75 .30
❑ 81 LaDainian Tomlinson .75 .30
❑ 82 Junior Seau .75 .30
❑ 83 Jeff Garcia .75 .30
❑ 84 Garrison Hearst .50 .20
❑ 85 Terrell Owens .75 .30
❑ 86 Matt Hasselbeck .50 .20
❑ 87 Shaun Alexander .75 .30
❑ 88 Koren Robinson .50 .20
❑ 89 Kurt Warner .75 .30
❑ 90 Marshall Faulk .75 .30
❑ 91 Isaac Bruce .75 .30
❑ 92 Brad Johnson .50 .20
❑ 93 Mike Alstott .75 .30

❑ 94 Keyshawn Johnson .75 .30
❑ 95 Steve McNair .75 .30
❑ 96 Eddie George .50 .20
❑ 97 Derrick Mason .50 .20
❑ 98 Patrick Ramsey .75 .30
❑ 99 Stephen Davis .50 .20
❑ 100 Rod Gardner .50 .20
❑ 101 Archie Manning 3.00 1.25
❑ 102 Bo Jackson 6.00 2.50
❑ 103 Bob Griese 3.00 1.25
❑ 104 Bob Lilly 2.50 1.00
❑ 105 Craig James 2.50 1.00
❑ 106 Cliff Branch 2.50 1.00
❑ 107 Dan Fouts 3.00 1.25
❑ 108 Daryl Johnston 3.00 1.25
❑ 109 Daryle Lamonica 1.50 .60
❑ 110 Dick Butkus 5.00 2.00
❑ 111 Don Maynard 2.50 1.00
❑ 112 Ed Too Tall Jones 2.50 1.00
❑ 113 Franco Harris 4.00 1.50
❑ 114 Frank Gifford 3.00 1.25
❑ 115 Fred Biletnikoff 3.00 1.25
❑ 116 Gale Sayers 5.00 2.00
❑ 117 George Blanda 3.00 1.25
❑ 118 Herman Edwards 2.50 1.00
❑ 119 Herschel Walker 2.50 1.00
❑ 120 Jack Ham 2.50 1.00
❑ 121 Jack Tatum 1.50 .60
❑ 122 Jack Youngblood 1.50 .60
❑ 123 James Lofton 1.50 .60
❑ 124 Jay Novacek 1.50 .60
❑ 125 Jim Brown 6.00 2.50
❑ 126 Jim McMahon/100* 40.00 20.00
❑ 127 Jim Plunkett 2.50 1.00
❑ 128 Jimmy Johnson/100* EXCH
❑ 129 Joe Greene 3.00 1.25
❑ 130 Joe Montana 12.00 5.00
❑ 131 John Riggins 4.00 1.50
❑ 132 John Stallworth 2.50 1.00
❑ 133 John Taylor/100* 3.00 1.25
❑ 134 Ken Stabler 5.00 2.00
❑ 135 L.C. Greenwood 2.50 1.00
❑ 136 Lance Alworth 2.50 1.00
❑ 137 Mel Blount 2.50 1.00
❑ 138 Mike Ditka/100* 5.00 2.00
❑ 139 Paul Hornung 3.00 1.25
❑ 140 Randy White 2.50 1.00
❑ 141 Raymond Berry 2.50 1.00
❑ 142 Roger Craig 2.50 1.00
❑ 143 Roger Staubach 5.00 2.00
❑ 144 Ron Jaworski 1.50 .60
❑ 145 Sammy Baugh 3.00 1.25
❑ 146 Sonny Jurgenson 2.50 1.00
❑ 147 Steve Young 3.00 1.25
❑ 148 Ted Hendricks 1.50 .60
❑ 149 Thurman Thomas 2.50 1.00
❑ 150 Tom Jackson/100* 3.00 1.25
❑ 151 Brian St.Pierre RC 6.00 2.50
❑ 152 Byron Leftwich RC 20.00 7.50
❑ 153 Carson Palmer RC 25.00 10.00
❑ 154 Chris Simms RC 10.00 4.00
❑ 155 Dave Ragone RC 6.00 2.50
❑ 156 Ken Dorsey RC 6.00 2.50
❑ 157 Kliff Kingsbury RC 5.00 2.00
❑ 158 Kyle Boller RC 6.00 2.50
❑ 159 Rex Grossman RC 20.00 7.50
❑ 160 Seneca Wallace RC 6.00 2.50
❑ 161 Jason Gesser RC 6.00 2.50
❑ 162 Artose Pinner RC 6.00 2.50
❑ 163 Avon Cobourne RC 3.00 1.25
❑ 164 Cecil Sapp RC 5.00 2.00
❑ 165 Chris Brown RC 6.00 2.50
❑ 166 Derek Watson RC 5.00 2.00
❑ 167 Domanick Davis RC 6.00 2.50
❑ 168 Dwone Hicks RC 3.00 1.25
❑ 169 Earnest Graham RC 5.00 2.00
❑ 170 Justin Fargas RC 6.00 2.50
❑ 171 Larry Johnson RC 25.00 12.50
❑ 172 Lee Suggs RC 6.00 2.50
❑ 173 Musa Smith RC 6.00 2.50
❑ 174 Onterrio Smith RC 6.00 2.50
❑ 175 Quentin Griffin RC 6.00 2.50
❑ 176 Willis McGahee RC 15.00 6.00
❑ 177 Sultan McCullough RC 5.00 2.00
❑ 178 LaBrandon Toefield RC 6.00 2.50
❑ 179 B.J. Askew RC 6.00 2.50
❑ 180 Andre Johnson RC 12.00 5.00
❑ 181 Anquan Boldin RC 15.00 6.00
❑ 182 Arnaz Battle RC 6.00 2.50
❑ 183 Bethel Johnson RC 6.00 2.50
❑ 184 Billy McMullen RC 5.00 2.00
❑ 185 Bobby Wade RC 6.00 2.50
❑ 186 Brandon Lloyd RC 6.00 2.50
❑ 187 Bryant Johnson RC 6.00 2.50
❑ 188 Charles Rogers RC 6.00 2.50
❑ 189 Doug Gabriel RC 6.00 2.50
❑ 190 Justin Gage RC 6.00 2.50
❑ 191 Kareem Kelly RC 5.00 2.00
❑ 192 Kelley Washington RC 6.00 2.50
❑ 193 Kevin Curtis RC 6.00 2.50
❑ 194 Nate Burleson RC 6.00 2.50
❑ 195 Sam Aiken RC 5.00 2.00
❑ 196 Shaun McDonald RC 6.00 2.50
❑ 197 Talman Gardner RC 6.00 2.50
❑ 198 Taylor Jacobs RC 5.00 2.00
❑ 199 Terrence Edwards RC 5.00 2.00
❑ 200 Tyrone Calico RC 6.00 2.50
❑ 201 Walter Young RC 3.00 1.25
❑ 202 Ryan Hoag/100 RC 12.00 5.00
❑ 203 Paul Arnold RC 5.00 2.00
❑ 204 Bennie Joppru RC 6.00 2.50
❑ 205 Dallas Clark RC 6.00 2.50
❑ 206 George Wrighster RC 5.00 2.00
❑ 207 Jason Witten RC 10.00 4.00
❑ 208 Mike Pinkard RC 3.00 1.25
❑ 209 Robert Johnson RC 3.00 1.25
❑ 210 Teyo Johnson RC 6.00 2.50
❑ 211 Calvin Pace RC 5.00 2.00
❑ 212 Chris Kelsay RC 6.00 2.50
❑ 213 Cory Redding RC 5.00 2.00
❑ 214 DeWayne Robertson RC 6.00 2.50
❑ 215 DeWayne White RC 5.00 2.00
❑ 216 Jerome McDougle RC 6.00 2.50
❑ 217 Kenny Peterson RC 5.00 2.00
❑ 218 Kindal Moorehead RC 5.00 2.00
❑ 219 Michael Haynes RC 6.00 2.50
❑ 220 Terrell Suggs RC 10.00 4.00
❑ 221 Tully Banta-Cain RC 5.00 2.00
❑ 222 Jimmy Kennedy RC 6.00 2.50
❑ 223 Johnathan Sullivan RC 5.00 2.00
❑ 224 Kevin Williams RC 6.00 2.50
❑ 225 Nick Eason/100 RC 12.00 5.00
❑ 226 Rien Long RC 3.00 1.25
❑ 227 Ty Warren RC 6.00 2.50
❑ 228 William Joseph RC 6.00 2.50
❑ 229 Boss Bailey RC 6.00 2.50
❑ 230 Bradie James RC 6.00 2.50
❑ 231 Victor Hobson RC 6.00 2.50
❑ 232 Clifton Smith RC 3.00 1.25
❑ 233 E.J. Henderson/100 RC 12.00 5.00
❑ 234 Gerald Hayes/100 RC 12.00 5.00
❑ 235 LaMarcus McDonald RC 3.00 1.25
❑ 236 Nick Barnett RC 6.00 2.50
❑ 237 Terry Pierce RC 5.00 2.00
❑ 238 Andre Woolfolk RC 6.00 2.50
❑ 239 Dennis Weathersby RC 3.00 1.25
❑ 240 Drayton Florence RC 3.00 1.25
❑ 241 Eugene Wilson RC 6.00 2.50
❑ 242 Marcus Trufant RC 6.00 2.50
❑ 243 Rashean Mathis RC 5.00 2.00
❑ 244 Ricky Manning RC 6.00 2.50
❑ 245 Sammy Davis/100 RC 12.00 5.00
❑ 246 Terence Newman RC 12.00 5.00
❑ 247 Julian Battle RC 5.00 2.00
❑ 248 Ken Hamlin RC 6.00 2.50
❑ 249 Mike Doss RC 6.00 2.50
❑ 250 Troy Polamalu RC 25.00 15.00

2004 Donruss Classics

❑ COMP.SET w/o SP's (100) 20.00 7.50
❑ 1 Anquan Boldin .75 .30
❑ 2 Emmitt Smith 1.50 .60
❑ 3 Michael Vick 1.50 .60
❑ 4 Peerless Price .50 .20
❑ 5 Warrick Dunn .50 .20
❑ 6 Jamal Lewis .75 .30
❑ 7 Kyle Boller .75 .30
❑ 8 Terrell Suggs .50 .20
❑ 9 Todd Heap .50 .20
❑ 10 Drew Bledsoe .75 .30
❑ 11 Travis Henry .50 .20
❑ 12 DeShaun Foster .50 .20
❑ 13 Jake Delhomme .75 .30
❑ 14 Stephen Davis .50 .20
❑ 15 Steve Smith .75 .30
❑ 16 Anthony Thomas .50 .20
❑ 17 Brian Urlacher 1.00 .40
❑ 18 Rex Grossman .75 .30
❑ 19 Chad Johnson .75 .30
❑ 20 Carson Palmer 1.00 .40
❑ 21 Rudi Johnson .50 .20
❑ 22 Andre Davis .30 .10
❑ 23 Lee Suggs .75 .30
❑ 24 Quincy Carter .50 .20
❑ 25 Roy Williams S .50 .20
❑ 26 Clinton Portis .75 .30
❑ 27 Jake Plummer .50 .20
❑ 28 Rod Smith .50 .20
❑ 29 Charles Rogers .50 .20
❑ 30 Joey Harrington .75 .30
❑ 31 Ahman Green .75 .30
❑ 32 Brett Favre 2.00 .75
❑ 33 Javon Walker .50 .20
❑ 34 Andre Johnson .75 .30
❑ 35 David Carr .75 .30
❑ 36 Domanick Davis .75 .30
❑ 37 Edgerrin James .75 .30
❑ 38 Marvin Harrison .75 .30
❑ 39 Peyton Manning 1.25 .50
❑ 40 Reggie Wayne .50 .20
❑ 41 Byron Leftwich 1.00 .40
❑ 42 Fred Taylor .50 .20
❑ 43 Jimmy Smith .50 .20
❑ 44 Priest Holmes 1.00 .40
❑ 45 Dante Hall .75 .30
❑ 46 Tony Gonzalez .50 .20
❑ 47 Trent Green .50 .20
❑ 48 Chris Chambers .50 .20
❑ 49 Ricky Williams .75 .30
❑ 50 Zach Thomas .75 .30
❑ 51 Daunte Culpepper .75 .30
❑ 52 Michael Bennett .50 .20
❑ 53 Randy Moss 1.00 .40
❑ 54 Deion Branch .75 .30
❑ 55 Adam Vinatieri .75 .30
❑ 56 Tedy Bruschi .50 .20
❑ 57 Tom Brady 2.00 .75
❑ 58 Aaron Brooks .50 .20
❑ 59 Deuce McAllister .75 .30
❑ 60 Donte' Stallworth .50 .20
❑ 61 Joe Horn .50 .20
❑ 62 Jeremy Shockey .75 .30
❑ 63 Kerry Collins .50 .20
❑ 64 Michael Strahan .50 .20
❑ 65 Tiki Barber .75 .30
❑ 66 Chad Pennington .75 .30
❑ 67 Curtis Martin .75 .30
❑ 68 Santana Moss .50 .20
❑ 69 Jerry Rice 1.50 .60
❑ 70 Charles Woodson .50 .20
❑ 71 Rod Woodson .50 .20
❑ 72 Tim Brown .75 .30
❑ 73 Brian Westbrook .50 .20
❑ 74 Correll Buckhalter .50 .20
❑ 75 Donovan McNabb 1.00 .40
❑ 76 Antwaan Randle El .75 .30
❑ 77 Hines Ward .75 .30
❑ 78 Kendrell Bell .50 .20
❑ 79 David Boston .50 .20
❑ 80 Drew Brees .75 .30
❑ 81 LaDainian Tomlinson 1.00 .40
❑ 82 Jeff Garcia .75 .30
❑ 83 Kevan Barlow .50 .20
❑ 84 Terrell Owens .75 .30
❑ 85 Koren Robinson .50 .20
❑ 86 Matt Hasselbeck .50 .20
❑ 87 Shaun Alexander .75 .30
❑ 88 Isaac Bruce .50 .20
❑ 89 Marc Bulger .75 .30
❑ 90 Marshall Faulk .75 .30

❑ 91 Torry Holt .75 .30
❑ 92 Brad Johnson .50 .20
❑ 93 Keenan McCardell .30 .10
❑ 94 Keyshawn Johnson .50 .20
❑ 95 Derrick Mason .50 .20
❑ 96 Eddie George .50 .20
❑ 97 Steve McNair .75 .30
❑ 98 LaVar Arrington 1.50 .60
❑ 99 Laveranues Coles .50 .20
❑ 100 Patrick Ramsey .50 .20
❑ 101 Archie Manning 2.00 .75
❑ 102 Bart Starr 5.00 2.00
❑ 103 Bo Jackson 4.00 1.50
❑ 104 Bob Griese 2.00 .75
❑ 105 Christian Okoye 1.00 .40
❑ 106 Daryl Johnston 2.00 .75
❑ 107 Deacon Jones 1.50 .60
❑ 108 Deion Sanders 3.00 1.25
❑ 109 Dick Butkus 3.00 1.25
❑ 110 Lynn Swann 2.50 1.00
❑ 111 Don Maynard 1.50 .60
❑ 112 Don Shula 2.00 .75
❑ 113 Franco Harris 2.50 1.00
❑ 114 Fred Biletnikoff 2.00 .75
❑ 115 Gale Sayers 2.50 1.00
❑ 116 George Blanda 2.00 .75
❑ 117 Herman Edwards 1.50 .60
❑ 118 Herschel Walker 1.50 .60
❑ 119 Jack Lambert 3.00 1.25
❑ 120 James Lofton 1.00 .40
❑ 121 Jim Plunkett 1.50 .60
❑ 122 Jim Thorpe 2.00 .75
❑ 123 Joe Greene 2.00 .75
❑ 124 John Riggins 2.50 1.00
❑ 125 L.C. Greenwood 1.50 .60
❑ 126 Larry Csonka 2.00 .75
❑ 127 Leroy Kelly 1.50 .60
❑ 128 Walter Payton 8.00 3.00
❑ 129 Marcus Allen 2.00 .75
❑ 130 Mark Bavaro 1.00 .40
❑ 131 Mel Blount 1.50 .60
❑ 132 Michael Irvin 2.00 .75
❑ 133 Mike Ditka 2.00 .75
❑ 134 Mike Singletary 2.00 .75
❑ 135 Ozzie Newsome 1.50 .60
❑ 136 Paul Hornung 2.00 .75
❑ 137 Paul Warfield 1.50 .60
❑ 138 Randall Cunningham 1.50 .60
❑ 139 Ray Nitschke 2.00 .75
❑ 140 Reggie White 2.00 .75
❑ 141 Richard Dent 1.00 .40
❑ 142 Sammy Baugh 2.00 .75
❑ 143 Sonny Jurgensen 1.50 .60
❑ 144 Sterling Sharpe 1.50 .60
❑ 145 Steve Largent 2.00 .75
❑ 146 Terrell Davis 2.00 .75
❑ 147 Terry Bradshaw 4.00 1.50
❑ 148 Thurman Thomas 1.50 .60
❑ 149 Tony Dorsett 2.00 .75
❑ 150 Warren Moon 1.50 .60
❑ 151 John Navarre RC 5.00 2.00
❑ 152 Derek Abney RC 5.00 2.00
❑ 153 Ryan Dinwiddie RC 4.00 1.50
❑ 154 Bruce Perry/100 RC 20.00 7.50
❑ 155 Adimchinobe Echemandu RC 4.00 1.50
❑ 156 Troy Fleming RC 4.00 1.50
❑ 157 Brandon Miree RC 4.00 1.50
❑ 158 Jarrett Payton RC 6.00 2.50
❑ 159 Ben Hartsock RC 5.00 2.00
❑ 160 Chris Cooley RC 5.00 2.00
❑ 161 Derrick Ward RC 2.50 1.00
❑ 162 Triandos Luke RC 5.00 2.00
❑ 163 Clarence Moore RC 5.00 2.00
❑ 164 D.J. Hackett RC 4.00 1.50
❑ 165 Mark Jones RC 4.00 1.50
❑ 166 Sloan Thomas RC 4.00 1.50
❑ 167 Jamaar Taylor RC 5.00 2.00
❑ 168 Casey Bramlet RC 4.00 1.50
❑ 169 Drew Carter RC 5.00 2.00
❑ 170 Antwan Odom RC 5.00 2.00
❑ 171 Marquise Hill RC 4.00 1.50
❑ 172 Ricardo Colclough RC 5.00 2.00
❑ 173 Keith Smith RC 4.00 1.50
❑ 174 Joey Thomas RC 5.00 2.00
❑ 175 Stuart Schweigert RC 5.00 2.00
❑ 176 Cody Pickett RC 6.00 2.50
❑ 177 B.J. Symons RC 6.00 2.50
❑ 178 Matt Mauck RC 6.00 2.50
❑ 179 Bradlee Van Pelt RC 6.00 2.50
❑ 180 Jim Sorgi RC 6.00 2.50
❑ 181 Ernest Wilford RC 6.00 2.50
❑ 182 Bernard Berrian RC 8.00 3.00
❑ 183 Darius Watts RC 6.00 2.50
❑ 184 Derrick Hamilton RC 5.00 2.00
❑ 185 Jerricho Cotchery RC 6.00 2.50
❑ 186 Jeris McIntyre RC 5.00 2.00
❑ 187 Carlos Francis RC 5.00 2.00
❑ 188 Maurice Mann RC 5.00 2.00
❑ 189 Randy Starks RC 5.00 2.00
❑ 190 Darnell Dockett RC 5.00 2.00
❑ 191 Marcus Tubbs RC 6.00 2.50
❑ 192 Daryl Smith RC 6.00 2.50
❑ 193 Karlos Dansby RC 6.00 2.50
❑ 194 Michael Boulware RC 6.00 2.50
❑ 195 Teddy Lehman RC 6.00 2.50
❑ 196 Will Poole RC 6.00 2.50
❑ 197 Derrick Strait RC 8.00 3.00
❑ 198 Ahmad Carroll RC 6.00 2.50
❑ 199 Jeremy LeSueur RC 5.00 2.00
❑ 200 Bob Sanders RC 15.00 6.00
❑ 201 J.P. Losman RC 15.00 6.00
❑ 202 Matt Schaub RC 25.00 10.00
❑ 203 Josh Harris RC 6.00 2.50
❑ 204 Luke McCown RC 6.00 2.50
❑ 205 Quincy Wilson RC 5.00 2.00
❑ 206 Michael Turner RC 6.00 2.50
❑ 207 Mewelde Moore RC 6.00 2.50
❑ 208 Cedric Cobbs RC 6.00 2.50
❑ 209 Ben Watson RC 6.00 2.50
❑ 210 Michael Jenkins RC 6.00 2.50
❑ 211 Devery Henderson RC 5.00 2.00
❑ 212 Johnnie Morant RC 6.00 2.50
❑ 213 Keary Colbert RC 8.00 3.00
❑ 214 Devard Darling RC 6.00 2.50
❑ 215 P.K. Sam RC 5.00 2.00
❑ 216 Samie Parker RC 6.00 2.50
❑ 217 Jason Babin RC 6.00 2.50
❑ 218 Tommie Harris RC 6.00 2.50
❑ 219 Vince Wilfork RC 6.00 2.50
❑ 220 Jonathan Vilma RC 6.00 2.50
❑ 221 D.J. Williams RC 6.00 2.50
❑ 222 Chris Gamble RC 6.00 2.50
❑ 223 Matt Ware RC 6.00 2.50
❑ 224 Shawntae Spencer RC 6.00 2.50
❑ 225 Sean Jones RC 5.00 2.00
❑ 226 Drew Henson RC 8.00 3.00
❑ 227 Ben Roethlisberger RC 60.00 35.00
❑ 228 Eli Manning RC 40.00 20.00
❑ 229 Philip Rivers RC 25.00 12.50
❑ 230 Steven Jackson RC 25.00 10.00
❑ 231 Kevin Jones RC 20.00 8.00
❑ 232 Chris Perry RC 12.00 5.00
❑ 233 Greg Jones RC 8.00 3.00
❑ 234 Tatum Bell RC 15.00 6.00
❑ 235 Jeff Smoker RC 8.00 3.00
❑ 236 Julius Jones RC 25.00 10.00
❑ 237 Kellen Winslow RC 15.00 6.00
❑ 238 Ben Troupe RC 8.00 3.00
❑ 239 Larry Fitzgerald RC 25.00 10.00
❑ 240 Craig Krenzel RC 8.00 3.00
❑ 241 Roy Williams RC 20.00 7.50
❑ 242 Reggie Williams RC 10.00 4.00
❑ 243 Michael Clayton RC 15.00 6.00
❑ 244 Lee Evans RC 8.00 3.00
❑ 245 Rashaun Woods RC 8.00 3.00
❑ 246 Kenechi Udeze RC 8.00 3.00
❑ 247 Will Smith RC 8.00 3.00
❑ 248 DeAngelo Hall RC 10.00 4.00
❑ 249 Dunta Robinson RC 8.00 3.00
❑ 250 Sean Taylor RC 6.00 2.50

2005 Donruss Classics

❑ COMP.SET w/o SP's (100) 20.00 7.50
❑ 101-150 LEG PRINT RUN 1000 SER.#'d SETS
❑ 151-175 PRINT RUN 1999 SER.#'d SETS
❑ 176-200 PRINT RUN 1499 SER.#'d SETS
❑ 201-225 PRINT RUN 999 SER.#'d SETS
❑ 226-250 AU PRINT RUN 499 SER.#'d SETS
❑ 1 Kurt Warner .50 .20
❑ 2 Josh McCown .50 .20
❑ 3 Larry Fitzgerald .75 .30
❑ 4 Alge Crumpler .50 .20
❑ 5 Michael Vick 1.25 .50
❑ 6 Warrick Dunn .50 .20
❑ 7 Todd Heap .50 .20
❑ 8 Jamal Lewis .75 .30
❑ 9 Kyle Boller .50 .20
❑ 10 Drew Bledsoe .75 .30
❑ 11 Lee Evans .50 .20
❑ 12 Willis McGahee .75 .30
❑ 13 Steve Smith .50 .20
❑ 14 Jake Delhomme .75 .30
❑ 15 Muhsin Muhammad .50 .20
❑ 16 Brian Urlacher .75 .30
❑ 17 Rex Grossman .50 .20
❑ 18 Thomas Jones .50 .20
❑ 19 Carson Palmer .75 .30
❑ 20 Chad Johnson .75 .30
❑ 21 Rudi Johnson .50 .20
❑ 22 Antonio Bryant .40 .15
❑ 23 Kellen Winslow Jr. .75 .30
❑ 24 Lee Suggs .50 .20
❑ 25 Julius Jones 1.00 .40
❑ 26 Keyshawn Johnson .50 .20
❑ 27 Roy Williams S .50 .20
❑ 28 Jake Plummer .50 .20
❑ 29 Rod Smith .50 .20
❑ 30 Tatum Bell .50 .20
❑ 31 Joey Harrington .75 .30
❑ 32 Kevin Jones .75 .30
❑ 33 Roy Williams WR .75 .30
❑ 34 Ahman Green .75 .30
❑ 35 Brett Favre 2.00 .75
❑ 36 Javon Walker .50 .20
❑ 37 Andre Johnson .50 .20
❑ 38 David Carr .75 .30
❑ 39 Domanick Davis .50 .20
❑ 40 Edgerrin James .75 .30
❑ 41 Marvin Harrison .75 .30
❑ 42 Peyton Manning 1.25 .50
❑ 43 Reggie Wayne .50 .20
❑ 44 Byron Leftwich .75 .30
❑ 45 Fred Taylor .50 .20
❑ 46 Jimmy Smith .50 .20
❑ 47 Priest Holmes .75 .30
❑ 48 Tony Gonzalez .50 .20
❑ 49 Trent Green .50 .20
❑ 50 A.J. Feeley .50 .20
❑ 51 Chris Chambers .50 .20
❑ 52 Zach Thomas .75 .30
❑ 53 Daunte Culpepper .75 .30
❑ 54 Michael Bennett .50 .20
❑ 55 Randy Moss .75 .30
❑ 56 Corey Dillon .50 .20
❑ 57 David Givens .50 .20
❑ 58 Tom Brady 2.00 .75
❑ 59 Aaron Brooks .50 .20
❑ 60 Deuce McAllister .75 .30
❑ 61 Joe Horn .50 .20
❑ 62 Eli Manning 1.50 .60
❑ 63 Jeremy Shockey .75 .30
❑ 64 Tiki Barber .75 .30
❑ 65 Chad Pennington .75 .30
❑ 66 Curtis Martin .75 .30
❑ 67 Santana Moss .50 .20
❑ 68 Jerry Porter .50 .20
❑ 69 Kerry Collins .50 .20
❑ 70 J.P. Losman .75 .30
❑ 71 Brian Westbrook .50 .20
❑ 72 Donovan McNabb 1.00 .40
❑ 73 Terrell Owens .75 .30
❑ 74 Ben Roethlisberger 2.00 .75
❑ 75 Duce Staley .50 .20
❑ 76 Hines Ward .75 .30
❑ 77 Jerome Bettis .75 .30
❑ 78 Antonio Gates .75 .30
❑ 79 Drew Brees .75 .30
❑ 80 LaDainian Tomlinson 1.00 .40
❑ 81 Brandon Lloyd .40 .15
❑ 82 Kevan Barlow .50 .20

- ❑ 83 Laveranues Coles .50 .20
- ❑ 84 Darrell Jackson .50 .20
- ❑ 85 Jerry Rice 1.50 .60
- ❑ 86 Matt Hasselbeck .50 .20
- ❑ 87 Shaun Alexander 1.00 .40
- ❑ 88 Isaac Bruce .50 .20
- ❑ 89 Marc Bulger .75 .30
- ❑ 90 Steven Jackson 1.00 .40
- ❑ 91 Torry Holt .75 .30
- ❑ 92 Brian Griese .50 .20
- ❑ 93 Michael Clayton .75 .30
- ❑ 94 Mike Alstott .50 .20
- ❑ 95 Chris Brown .50 .20
- ❑ 96 Drew Bennett .50 .20
- ❑ 97 Steve McNair .75 .30
- ❑ 98 Clinton Portis .75 .30
- ❑ 99 LaVar Arrington .75 .30
- ❑ 100 Patrick Ramsey .50 .20
- ❑ 101 Don Shula 3.00 1.25
- ❑ 102 James Lofton 2.50 1.00
- ❑ 103 Thurman Thomas 3.00 1.25
- ❑ 104 Gale Sayers 5.00 2.00
- ❑ 105 Mike Singletary 4.00 1.50
- ❑ 106 Boomer Esiason 3.00 1.25
- ❑ 107 Cris Collinsworth 3.00 1.25
- ❑ 108 Ickey Woods 2.50 1.00
- ❑ 109 Jim Brown 6.00 2.50
- ❑ 110 Leroy Kelly 3.00 1.25
- ❑ 111 Ozzie Newsome 3.00 1.25
- ❑ 112 Paul Warfield 3.00 1.25
- ❑ 113 Deion Sanders 4.00 1.50
- ❑ 114 Herschel Walker 3.00 1.25
- ❑ 115 Mike Ditka 4.00 1.50
- ❑ 116 Michael Irvin 4.00 1.50
- ❑ 117 Roger Staubach 6.00 2.50
- ❑ 118 Tony Dorsett 4.00 1.50
- ❑ 119 Troy Aikman 5.00 2.00
- ❑ 120 John Elway 6.00 2.50
- ❑ 121 Barry Sanders 6.00 2.50
- ❑ 122 Bart Starr 6.00 2.50
- ❑ 123 Paul Hornung 4.00 1.50
- ❑ 124 Sterling Sharpe 3.00 1.25
- ❑ 125 Warren Moon 4.00 1.50
- ❑ 126 Christian Okoye 3.00 1.25
- ❑ 127 Marcus Allen 4.00 1.50
- ❑ 128 Deacon Jones 3.00 1.25
- ❑ 129 Bob Griese 4.00 1.50
- ❑ 130 Dan Marino 8.00 3.00
- ❑ 131 Fran Tarkenton 5.00 2.00
- ❑ 132 Y.A. Tittle 4.00 1.50
- ❑ 133 Don Maynard 3.00 1.25
- ❑ 134 Joe Namath 5.00 2.00
- ❑ 135 Jim Plunkett 3.00 1.25
- ❑ 136 Bo Jackson 5.00 2.00
- ❑ 137 Herman Edwards 3.00 1.25
- ❑ 138 Randall Cunningham 3.00 1.25
- ❑ 139 Franco Harris 5.00 2.00
- ❑ 140 Jack Lambert 5.00 2.00
- ❑ 141 Joe Greene 4.00 1.50
- ❑ 142 L.C. Greenwood 3.00 1.25
- ❑ 143 Terry Bradshaw 6.00 2.50
- ❑ 144 Dan Fouts 4.00 1.50
- ❑ 145 Joe Montana 10.00 4.00
- ❑ 146 John Taylor 3.00 1.25
- ❑ 147 Roger Craig 4.00 1.50
- ❑ 148 Steve Young 5.00 2.00
- ❑ 149 Steve Largent 4.00 1.50
- ❑ 150 Sonny Jurgensen 3.00 1.25
- ❑ 151 Adam Jones RC 5.00 2.00
- ❑ 152 Antrel Rolle RC 5.00 2.00
- ❑ 153 Carlos Rogers RC 6.00 2.50
- ❑ 154 DeMarcus Ware RC 8.00 3.00
- ❑ 155 Shawne Merriman RC 8.00 3.00
- ❑ 156 Thomas Davis RC 5.00 2.00
- ❑ 157 Derrick Johnson RC 8.00 3.00
- ❑ 158 Travis Johnson RC 4.00 1.50
- ❑ 159 David Pollack RC 6.00 2.50
- ❑ 160 Erasmus James RC 6.00 2.50
- ❑ 161 Marcus Spears RC 6.00 2.50
- ❑ 162 Fabian Washington RC 5.00 2.00
- ❑ 163 Luis Castillo RC 5.00 2.00
- ❑ 164 Marlin Jackson RC 5.00 2.00
- ❑ 165 Mike Patterson RC 5.00 2.00
- ❑ 166 Brodney Pool RC 5.00 2.00
- ❑ 167 Barrett Ruud RC 5.00 2.00
- ❑ 168 Shaun Cody RC 5.00 2.00
- ❑ 169 Stanford Routt RC 4.00 1.50
- ❑ 170 Josh Bullocks RC 5.00 2.00
- ❑ 171 Kevin Burnett RC 5.00 2.00
- ❑ 172 Corey Webster RC 5.00 2.00
- ❑ 173 Lofa Tatupu RC 6.00 2.50
- ❑ 174 Justin Miller RC 4.00 1.50
- ❑ 175 Odell Thurman RC 4.00 1.50
- ❑ 176 Heath Miller RC 15.00 6.00
- ❑ 177 Vernand Morency RC 6.00 2.50
- ❑ 178 Ryan Moats RC 6.00 2.50
- ❑ 179 Courtney Roby RC 6.00 2.50
- ❑ 180 Alex Smith TE RC 6.00 2.50
- ❑ 181 Kevin Everett RC 6.00 2.50
- ❑ 182 Brandon Jones RC 6.00 2.50
- ❑ 183 Maurice Clarett 6.00 2.50
- ❑ 184 Marion Barber RC 10.00 4.00
- ❑ 185 Brandon Jacobs RC 8.00 3.00
- ❑ 186 Matt Cassel RC 15.00 6.00
- ❑ 187 Stefan LeFors RC 6.00 2.50
- ❑ 188 Alvin Pearman RC 6.00 2.50
- ❑ 189 James Kilian RC 6.00 2.50
- ❑ 190 Airese Currie RC 6.00 2.50
- ❑ 191 Damien Nash RC 5.00 2.00
- ❑ 192 Dan Orlovsky RC 8.00 3.00
- ❑ 193 Larry Brackins RC 3.00 1.25
- ❑ 194 Rasheed Marshall RC 6.00 2.50
- ❑ 195 Marcus Maxwell RC 5.00 2.00
- ❑ 196 LeRon McCoy RC 5.00 2.00
- ❑ 197 Harry Williams RC 5.00 2.00
- ❑ 198 Noah Herron RC 6.00 2.50
- ❑ 199 Tab Perry RC 6.00 2.50
- ❑ 200 Chad Owens RC 6.00 2.50
- ❑ 201 Alex Smith QB RC 25.00 10.00
- ❑ 202 Ronnie Brown RC 25.00 10.00
- ❑ 203 Braylon Edwards RC 20.00 7.50
- ❑ 204 Cedric Benson RC 12.00 5.00
- ❑ 205 Cadillac Williams RC 30.00 12.50
- ❑ 206 Troy Williamson RC 12.00 5.00
- ❑ 207 Mike Williams 12.00 5.00
- ❑ 208 Matt Jones RC 15.00 6.00
- ❑ 209 Mark Clayton RC 6.00 2.50
- ❑ 210 Aaron Rodgers RC 20.00 7.50
- ❑ 211 Jason Campbell RC 10.00 4.00
- ❑ 212 Roddy White RC 6.00 2.50
- ❑ 213 Reggie Brown RC 6.00 2.50
- ❑ 214 Mark Bradley RC 6.00 2.50
- ❑ 215 J.J. Arrington RC 8.00 3.00
- ❑ 216 Eric Shelton RC 6.00 2.50
- ❑ 217 Roscoe Parrish RC 6.00 2.50
- ❑ 218 Terrence Murphy RC 6.00 2.50
- ❑ 219 Vincent Jackson RC 6.00 2.50
- ❑ 220 Frank Gore RC 12.00 5.00
- ❑ 221 Charlie Frye RC 12.00 5.00
- ❑ 222 Andrew Walter RC 10.00 4.00
- ❑ 223 David Greene RC 6.00 2.50
- ❑ 224 Kyle Orton RC 10.00 4.00
- ❑ 225 Ciatrick Fason RC 5.00 2.00
- ❑ 226 Cedric Houston AU RC EXCH 15.00 6.00
- ❑ 227 Dante Ridgeway AU RC 12.00 5.00
- ❑ 228 Craig Bragg AU RC 12.00 5.00
- ❑ 229 Deandra Cobb AU RC 10.00 4.00
- ❑ 230 Derek Anderson AU RC 20.00 10.00
- ❑ 231 Paris Warren AU RC 12.00 5.00
- ❑ 232 Lionel Gates AU RC 12.00 5.00
- ❑ 233 Anthony Davis AU RC 12.00 5.00
- ❑ 234 Ryan Fitzpatrick AU RC 25.00 12.50
- ❑ 235 J.R. Russell AU RC 12.00 5.00
- ❑ 236 Dan Cody AU RC 15.00 6.00
- ❑ 237 Bryant McFadden AU RC 20.00 7.50
- ❑ 238 Adrian McPherson AU RC 20.00 7.50
- ❑ 239 Chris Henry AU RC 15.00 6.00
- ❑ 240 Craphonso Thorpe AU RC 12.00 5.00
- ❑ 241 Darren Sproles AU RC EXCH 15.00 6.00
- ❑ 242 Fred Gibson AU RC EXCH 12.00 5.00
- ❑ 243 Jerome Mathis AU RC 15.00 6.00
- ❑ 244 Josh Davis AU RC 12.00 5.00
- ❑ 245 Kay-Jay Harris AU RC 12.00 5.00
- ❑ 246 Matt Roth AU RC 20.00 7.50
- ❑ 247 Roydell Williams AU RC 15.00 6.00
- ❑ 248 Steve Savoy AU RC 10.00 4.00
- ❑ 249 T.A. McLendon AU RC 10.00 4.00
- ❑ 250 Taylor Stubblefield AU RC 10.00 4.00

2006 Donruss Classics

- ❑ COMP.SET w/o SP's (100) 20.00 7.50
- ❑ LEGEND PRINT RUN 1000 SER.#'d SETS
- ❑ 1 Anquan Boldin .50 .20
- ❑ 2 Kurt Warner .50 .20
- ❑ 3 Larry Fitzgerald .75 .30
- ❑ 4 Marcel Shipp .40 .15
- ❑ 5 Alge Crumpler .50 .20
- ❑ 6 Michael Vick 1.00 .40
- ❑ 7 Warrick Dunn .50 .20
- ❑ 8 Jamal Lewis .50 .20
- ❑ 9 Kyle Boller .40 .15
- ❑ 10 Eric Moulds .50 .20
- ❑ 11 J.P. Losman .50 .20
- ❑ 12 Willis McGahee .75 .30
- ❑ 13 Jake Delhomme .50 .20
- ❑ 14 Stephen Davis .50 .20
- ❑ 15 Steve Smith .75 .30
- ❑ 16 Cedric Benson .75 .30
- ❑ 17 Kyle Orton .50 .20
- ❑ 18 Muhsin Muhammad .50 .20
- ❑ 19 Thomas Jones .50 .20
- ❑ 20 Carson Palmer .75 .30
- ❑ 21 Chad Johnson .50 .20
- ❑ 22 Rudi Johnson .50 .20
- ❑ 23 T.J. Houshmandzadeh .50 .20
- ❑ 24 Braylon Edwards .75 .30
- ❑ 25 Reuben Droughns .50 .20
- ❑ 26 Trent Dilfer .50 .20
- ❑ 27 Drew Bledsoe .75 .30
- ❑ 28 Julius Jones .75 .30
- ❑ 29 Keyshawn Johnson .50 .20
- ❑ 30 Terry Glenn .50 .20
- ❑ 31 Ashley Lelie .50 .20
- ❑ 32 Jake Plummer .50 .20
- ❑ 33 Tatum Bell .50 .20
- ❑ 34 Joey Harrington .50 .20
- ❑ 35 Kevin Jones .75 .30
- ❑ 36 Roy Williams WR .75 .30
- ❑ 37 Aaron Rodgers .75 .30
- ❑ 38 Brett Favre 1.50 .60
- ❑ 39 Samkon Gado .75 .30
- ❑ 40 Andre Johnson .50 .20
- ❑ 41 David Carr .50 .20
- ❑ 42 Domanick Davis .50 .20
- ❑ 43 Edgerrin James .75 .30
- ❑ 44 Marvin Harrison .75 .30
- ❑ 45 Peyton Manning 1.25 .50
- ❑ 46 Reggie Wayne .50 .20
- ❑ 47 Byron Leftwich .50 .20
- ❑ 48 Fred Taylor .50 .20
- ❑ 49 Jimmy Smith .50 .20
- ❑ 50 Matt Jones .75 .30
- ❑ 51 Larry Johnson 1.00 .40
- ❑ 52 Tony Gonzalez .50 .20
- ❑ 53 Trent Green .50 .20
- ❑ 54 Chris Chambers .50 .20
- ❑ 55 Ricky Williams .50 .20
- ❑ 56 Ronnie Brown .75 .30
- ❑ 57 Daunte Culpepper .75 .30
- ❑ 58 Mewelde Moore .40 .15
- ❑ 59 Nate Burleson .50 .20
- ❑ 60 Corey Dillon .50 .20
- ❑ 61 Deion Branch .50 .20
- ❑ 62 Tom Brady 1.25 .50
- ❑ 63 Aaron Brooks .50 .20
- ❑ 64 Deuce McAllister .50 .20
- ❑ 65 Donte Stallworth .50 .20
- ❑ 66 Eli Manning 1.00 .40
- ❑ 67 Plaxico Burress .50 .20
- ❑ 68 Tiki Barber .75 .30
- ❑ 69 Chad Pennington .50 .20
- ❑ 70 Curtis Martin .75 .30
- ❑ 71 Laveranues Coles .50 .20
- ❑ 72 Kerry Collins .50 .20
- ❑ 73 LaMont Jordan .50 .20
- ❑ 74 Randy Moss .75 .30
- ❑ 75 Brian Westbrook .50 .20
- ❑ 76 Donovan McNabb .75 .30
- ❑ 77 Reggie Brown .50 .20
- ❑ 78 Ben Roethlisberger 1.25 .50

❑ 79 Hines Ward .75 .30
❑ 80 Willie Parker 1.00 .40
❑ 81 Antonio Gates .75 .30
❑ 82 Drew Brees .75 .30
❑ 83 LaDainian Tomlinson 1.00 .40
❑ 84 Alex Smith QB 1.00 .40
❑ 85 Frank Gore .75 .30
❑ 86 Darrell Jackson .50 .20
❑ 87 Matt Hasselbeck .50 .20
❑ 88 Shaun Alexander .75 .30
❑ 89 Marc Bulger .50 .20
❑ 90 Steven Jackson .75 .30
❑ 91 Torry Holt .50 .20
❑ 92 Cadillac Williams .75 .30
❑ 93 Joey Galloway .50 .20
❑ 94 Michael Clayton .50 .20
❑ 95 Chris Brown .50 .20
❑ 96 Steve McNair .50 .20
❑ 97 Drew Bennett .40 .15
❑ 98 Clinton Portis .75 .30
❑ 99 Mark Brunell .50 .20
❑ 100 Santana Moss .50 .20
❑ 101 Brodie Croyle/999 RC 12.00 5.00
❑ 102 Omar Jacobs/1499 RC 5.00 2.00
❑ 103 Charlie Whitehurst/999 RC 8.00 3.00
❑ 104 Tarvaris Jackson/999 RC 10.00 4.00
❑ 105 Kellen Clemens/999 RC 8.00 3.00
❑ 106 Vince Young/599 RC 40.00 20.00
❑ 107 Reggie McNeal/1499 RC 5.00 2.00
❑ 108 Marcus Vick/1499 RC 5.00 2.00
❑ 109 DonTrell Moore/1499 RC 5.00 2.00
❑ 110 Willie Reid/1499 RC 6.00 2.50
❑ 111 Matt Leinart/599 RC 30.00 12.00
❑ 112 Jay Cutler/599 RC 30.00 15.00
❑ 113 Brad Smith/1499 RC 6.00 2.50
❑ 114 Joseph Addai/599 RC 25.00 10.00
❑ 115 DeAngelo Williams/599 RC 20.00 8.00
❑ 116 Laurence Maroney/599 RC 20.00 8.00
❑ 117 Jerious Norwood/999 RC 10.00 4.00
❑ 118 Claude Wroten/1499 RC 3.00 1.25
❑ 119 Antonio Cromartie/1499 RC 6.00 2.50
❑ 120 Maurice Drew/999 RC 15.00 6.00
❑ 121 Anwar Phillips/1499 RC 5.00 2.00
❑ 122 LenDale White/599 RC 15.00 6.00
❑ 123 Reggie Bush/599 RC 50.00 20.00
❑ 124 Cedric Humes/1499 RC 6.00 2.50
❑ 125 Jerome Harrison/1499 RC 6.00 2.50
❑ 126 Brian Calhoun/999 RC 6.00 2.50
❑ 127 Joe Klopfenstein/999 RC 5.00 2.00
❑ 128 Leonard Pope/1499 RC 6.00 2.50
❑ 129 Vernon Davis/599 RC 15.00 6.00
❑ 130 Anthony Fasano/999 RC 6.00 2.50
❑ 131 Marcedes Lewis/999 RC 6.00 2.50
❑ 132 Dominique Byrd/1499 RC 5.00 2.00
❑ 133 Derek Hagan/1499 RC 6.00 2.50
❑ 134 Pat Watkins/1499 RC 6.00 2.50
❑ 135 Todd Watkins/1499 RC 5.00 2.00
❑ 136 Jeremy Bloom/1499 RC 5.00 2.00
❑ 137 Chad Jackson/599 RC 12.00 5.00
❑ 138 Devin Hester/1499 RC 12.00 5.00
❑ 139 Sinorice Moss/599 RC 10.00 4.00
❑ 140 Jason Avant/1499 RC 6.00 2.50
❑ 141 Maurice Stovall/1499 RC 6.00 2.50
❑ 142 Santonio Holmes/599 RC 15.00 6.00
❑ 143 Travis Wilson/999 RC 6.00 2.50
❑ 144 Demetrius Williams/1499 RC 8.00 3.00
❑ 145 Bernard Pollard/1499 RC 5.00 2.00
❑ 146 Michael Robinson/1499 RC 10.00 4.00
❑ 147 Brandon Marshall/1499 RC 6.00 2.50
❑ 148 Greg Jennings/999 RC 10.00 4.00
❑ 149 Brandon Williams/1499 RC 6.00 2.50
❑ 150 Jonathan Orr/1499 RC 5.00 2.00
❑ 151 David Thomas/1499 RC 6.00 2.50
❑ 152 Skyler Green/1499 RC 6.00 2.50
❑ 153 Mario Williams/499 RC 12.00 5.00
❑ 154 Ernie Sims/999 RC 8.00 3.00
❑ 155 A.J. Hawk/599 RC 15.00 6.00
❑ 156 Donte Whitner/1499 RC 6.00 2.50
❑ 157 Michael Huff/999 RC 8.00 3.00
❑ 158 Leon Washington/1499 RC 10.00 4.00
❑ 159 P.J. Daniels/1499 RC 5.00 2.00
❑ 160 Cory Rodgers/1499 RC 6.00 2.50
❑ 161 Tony Scheffler AU/499 RC 15.00 6.00
❑ 162 Paul Pinegar AU/999 RC 10.00 4.00
❑ 163 D.J. Shockley AU/599 RC 15.00 6.00
❑ 164 Ben Obomanu AU/899 RC 10.00 4.00
❑ 165 Adam Jennings AU/599 RC 12.00 5.00
❑ 166 Brandon Kirsch AU/999 RC 12.00 5.00
❑ 167 Mike Bell AU/999 RC 30.00 12.50
❑ 168 De'Arrius Howard AU/999 RC 12.00 5.00
❑ 169 Martin Nance AU/999 RC 10.00 4.00
❑ 170 Miles Austin AU/999 RC 10.00 4.00
❑ 171 Wendell Mathis AU/999 RC 10.00 4.00
❑ 172 Gerald Riggs AU/995 RC 12.00 5.00
❑ 173 Hank Baskett AU/999 RC 12.00 5.00
❑ 174 Greg Lee AU/999 RC 10.00 4.00
❑ 175 Quinton Ganther AU/799 RC 10.00 4.00
❑ 176 Garrett Mills/1499 RC 6.00 2.50
❑ 177 Jeff Webb AU/599 RC 12.00 5.00
❑ 178 Delanie Walker AU/599 RC 12.00 5.00
❑ 179 D'Brick Ferguson AU/599 RC 15.00 6.00
❑ 180 Mathias Kiwanuka AU/499 RC 20.00 8.00
❑ 181 Kamerion Wimbley AU/499 RC 15.00 6.00
❑ 182 Tamba Hali AU/499 RC 15.00 6.00
❑ 183 Brodrick Bunkley AU/499 RC 15.00 6.00
❑ 184 Gabe Watson/1499 RC 5.00 2.00
❑ 185 Haloti Ngata AU/499 RC 15.00 6.00
❑ 186 DeMeco Ryans AU/599 RC 20.00 8.00
❑ 187 A.J. Nicholson/1499 RC 3.00 1.25
❑ 188 Abdul Hodge AU/999 RC 12.00 5.00
❑ 189 Chad Greenway AU/499 RC 15.00 6.00
❑ 190 D'Qwell Jackson AU/599 RC 12.00 5.00
❑ 191 Manny Lawson AU/499 RC 15.00 6.00
❑ 192 Bobby Carpenter AU/499 RC 15.00 6.00
❑ 193 Jon Alston AU/999 RC 12.00 5.00
❑ 194 Thomas Howard AU/599 RC 15.00 6.00
❑ 195 Tye Hill AU/499 RC 15.00 6.00
❑ 196 Kelly Jennings AU/499 RC 15.00 6.00
❑ 197 Ashton Youboty AU/999 RC 12.00 5.00
❑ 198 Alan Zemaitis AU/999 RC 12.00 5.00
❑ 199 Johnathan Joseph AU/499 RC 12.00 5.00
❑ 200 Jimmy Williams AU/599 RC 15.00 6.00
❑ 201 Ko Simpson AU/999 RC 10.00 4.00
❑ 202 Jason Allen AU/499 RC 25.00 12.50
❑ 203 Darnell Bing AU/999 RC 12.00 5.00
❑ 204 Erik Meyer AU/999 RC 10.00 4.00
❑ 205 Bruce Gradkowski AU/499 RC 25.00 10.00
❑ 206 Darrell Hackney AU/999 RC 10.00 4.00
❑ 207 Derrick Ross AU/799 RC 10.00 4.00
❑ 207 Drew Olson AU/999 RC 10.00 4.00
❑ 209 Taurean Henderson AU/999 RC 12.00 5.00
❑ 210 Andre Hall AU/999 RC 10.00 4.00
❑ 211 Devin Aromashodu AU/899 RC 10.00 4.00
❑ 212 Mike Hass AU/599 RC 15.00 6.00
❑ 213 Ingle Martin AU/499 RC 15.00 6.00
❑ 214 Marques Hagans AU/499 RC 12.00 5.00
❑ 215 Wali Lundy AU/499 RC 15.00 6.00
❑ 216 Domenik Hixon AU/499 RC 12.00 5.00
❑ 217 Ethan Kilmer AU/899 RC 12.00 5.00
❑ 218 Bennie Brazell/1499 RC 5.00 2.00
❑ 219 David Anderson/1499 RC 5.00 2.00
❑ 220 Marques Colston AU/770 RC 75.00 40.00
❑ 221 Kevin McMahan AU/999 RC 10.00 4.00
❑ 222 Anthony Mix/1499 RC 5.00 2.00
❑ 223 John McCargo AU/499 RC 12.00 5.00
❑ 224 Rocky McIntosh/1499 RC 6.00 2.50
❑ 225 Cedric Griffin AU/599 RC 12.00 5.00
❑ 226 Barry Sanders 6.00 2.50
❑ 227 Bart Starr 6.00 2.50
❑ 228 Bo Jackson 5.00 2.00
❑ 229 Bob Griese 4.00 1.50
❑ 230 Bobby Layne 4.00 1.50
❑ 231 Boomer Esiason 3.00 1.25
❑ 232 Bulldog Turner 3.00 1.25
❑ 233 Dan Marino 8.00 3.00
❑ 234 Deacon Jones 3.00 1.25
❑ 235 Derrick Thomas 4.00 1.50
❑ 236 Dick Butkus 5.00 2.00
❑ 237 Don Meredith 4.00 1.50
❑ 238 Eric Dickerson 3.00 1.25
❑ 239 Fran Tarkenton 5.00 2.00
❑ 240 Fred Biletnikoff 4.00 1.50
❑ 241 Gale Sayers 5.00 2.00
❑ 242 Harvey Martin 2.50 1.00
❑ 243 Herman Edwards 3.00 1.25
❑ 244 Jack Lambert 4.00 1.50
❑ 245 Jim Brown 5.00 2.00
❑ 246 Jim Kelly 5.00 2.00
❑ 247 Jim Plunkett 3.00 1.25
❑ 248 Jim Thorpe 5.00 2.00
❑ 249 Joe Montana 8.00 3.00
❑ 250 John Elway 6.00 2.50
❑ 251 John Riggins 4.00 1.50
❑ 252 Johnny Unitas 6.00 2.50
❑ 253 Len Dawson 4.00 1.50
❑ 254 Marcus Allen 4.00 1.50
❑ 255 Mike Singletary 4.00 1.50
❑ 256 Ozzie Newsome 3.00 1.25
❑ 257 Phil Simms 3.00 1.25
❑ 258 Ray Nitschke 4.00 1.50
❑ 259 Red Grange 5.00 2.00
❑ 260 Roger Staubach 6.00 2.50
❑ 261 Ronnie Lott 3.00 1.25
❑ 262 Steve Largent 4.00 1.50
❑ 263 Terry Bradshaw 6.00 2.50
❑ 264 Troy Aikman 5.00 2.00
❑ 265 Walter Payton 8.00 3.00
❑ 266 Bill Dudley 3.00 1.25
❑ 267 Joe Perry 3.00 1.25
❑ 268 Charley Trippi 2.50 1.00
❑ 269 Paul Lowe 2.50 1.00
❑ 270 Clem Daniels 2.50 1.00
❑ 271 Ken Kavanaugh 2.50 1.00
❑ 272 Andre Reed 3.00 1.25
❑ 273 Steve Van Buren 3.00 1.25
❑ 274 Jim Taylor 4.00 1.50

1999 Donruss Elite

❑ COMPLETE SET (200) 100.00 40.00
❑ COMP.SET w/o SP's (160) 30.00 15.00
❑ 1 Warren Moon 1.25 .50
❑ 2 Terry Allen .75 .30
❑ 3 Jeff George .75 .30
❑ 4 Brett Favre 4.00 1.50
❑ 5 Rob Moore .75 .30
❑ 6 Bubby Brister .50 .20
❑ 7 John Elway 4.00 1.50
❑ 8 Troy Aikman 2.50 1.00
❑ 9 Steve McNair 1.25 .50
❑ 10 Charlie Batch 1.25 .50
❑ 11 Elvis Grbac .75 .30
❑ 12 Trent Dilfer .75 .30
❑ 13 Kerry Collins .75 .30
❑ 14 Neil O'Donnell .50 .20
❑ 15 Tony Simmons .50 .20
❑ 16 Ryan Leaf 1.25 .50
❑ 17 Bobby Hoying .75 .30
❑ 18 Marvin Harrison 1.25 .50
❑ 19 Keyshawn Johnson 1.25 .50
❑ 20 Cris Carter 1.25 .50
❑ 21 Deion Sanders 1.25 .50
❑ 22 Emmitt Smith 2.50 1.00
❑ 23 Antowain Smith 1.25 .50
❑ 24 Terry Fair .50 .20
❑ 25 Robert Holcombe .50 .20
❑ 26 Napoleon Kaufman 1.25 .50
❑ 27 Eddie George 1.25 .50
❑ 28 Corey Dillon 1.25 .50
❑ 29 Adrian Murrell .75 .30
❑ 30 Charles Way .50 .20
❑ 31 Amp Lee .50 .20
❑ 32 Ricky Watters .75 .30
❑ 33 Gary Brown .50 .20
❑ 34 Thurman Thomas .75 .30
❑ 35 Pat Johnson .50 .20
❑ 36 Jerome Bettis 1.25 .50
❑ 37 Muhsin Muhammad .75 .30
❑ 38 Kimble Anders .75 .30
❑ 39 Curtis Enis .50 .20
❑ 40 Mike Alstott 1.25 .50
❑ 41 Charles Johnson .50 .20
❑ 42 Chris Warren .50 .20
❑ 43 Tony Banks .75 .30
❑ 44 Leroy Hoard .50 .20
❑ 45 Chris Fuamatu-Ma'afala .50 .20
❑ 46 Michael Irvin 1.25 .50
❑ 47 Robert Edwards .50 .20
❑ 48 Hines Ward 1.25 .50
❑ 49 Trent Green 1.25 .50
❑ 50 Eric Zeier .50 .20

❑ 51	Sean Dawkins	.50	.20
❑ 52	Yancey Thigpen	.50	.20
❑ 53	Jacquez Green	.50	.20
❑ 54	Zach Thomas	1.25	.50
❑ 55	Junior Seau	1.25	.50
❑ 56	Darnay Scott	.50	.20
❑ 57	Kent Graham	.50	.20
❑ 58	O.J. Santiago	.50	.20
❑ 59	Tony Gonzalez	1.25	.50
❑ 60	Ty Detmer	.50	.20
❑ 61	Albert Connell	.50	.20
❑ 62	James Jett	.75	.30
❑ 63	Bert Emanuel	.75	.30
❑ 64	Derrick Alexander WR	.75	.30
❑ 65	Wesley Walls	.75	.30
❑ 66	Jake Reed	.75	.30
❑ 67	Randall Cunningham	1.25	.50
❑ 68	Leslie Shepherd	.50	.20
❑ 69	Mark Chmura	.50	.20
❑ 70	Bobby Engram	.75	.30
❑ 71	Rickey Dudley	.50	.20
❑ 72	Darick Holmes	.50	.20
❑ 73	Andre Reed	.75	.30
❑ 74	Az-Zahir Hakim	.50	.20
❑ 75	Cameron Cleeland	.50	.20
❑ 76	Lamar Thomas	.50	.20
❑ 77	Oronde Gadsden	.75	.30
❑ 78	Ben Coates	.75	.30
❑ 79	Bruce Smith	.75	.30
❑ 80	Jerry Rice	2.50	1.00
❑ 81	Tim Brown	1.25	.50
❑ 82	Michael Westbrook	.75	.30
❑ 83	J.J. Stokes	.75	.30
❑ 84	Shannon Sharpe	.75	.30
❑ 85	Reidel Anthony	.75	.30
❑ 86	Antonio Freeman	1.25	.50
❑ 87	Keenan McCardell	.75	.30
❑ 88	Terry Glenn	1.25	.50
❑ 89	Andre Rison	.75	.30
❑ 90	Neil Smith	.75	.30
❑ 91	Terrance Mathis	.75	.30
❑ 92	Rocket Ismail	.75	.30
❑ 93	Byron Bam Morris	.50	.20
❑ 94	Ike Hilliard	.50	.20
❑ 95	Eddie Kennison	.75	.30
❑ 96	Tavian Banks	.50	.20
❑ 97	Yatil Green	.50	.20
❑ 98	Frank Wycheck	.50	.20
❑ 99	Warren Sapp	.50	.20
❑ 100	Germane Crowell	.50	.20
❑ 101	Curtis Martin	2.50	1.00
❑ 102	John Avery	1.00	.40
❑ 103	Eric Moulds	2.50	1.00
❑ 104	Randy Moss	8.00	3.00
❑ 105	Terrell Owens	2.50	1.00
❑ 106	Vinny Testaverde	1.50	.60
❑ 107	Doug Flutie	1.25	.50
❑ 108	Mark Brunell	1.25	.50
❑ 109	Isaac Bruce	2.50	1.00
❑ 110	Kordell Stewart	1.50	.60
❑ 111	Drew Bledsoe	3.00	1.25
❑ 112	Chris Chandler	1.50	.60
❑ 113	Dan Marino	8.00	3.00
❑ 114	Brian Griese	2.50	1.00
❑ 115	Carl Pickens	1.50	.60
❑ 116	Jake Plummer	1.50	.60
❑ 117	Natrone Means	1.50	.60
❑ 118	Peyton Manning	10.00	4.00
❑ 119	Garrison Hearst	2.50	1.00
❑ 120	Barry Sanders	8.00	3.00
❑ 121	Steve Young	3.00	1.25
❑ 122	Rashaan Shehee	1.00	.40
❑ 123	Ed McCaffrey	1.50	.60
❑ 124	Charles Woodson	2.50	1.00
❑ 125	Dorsey Levens	2.50	1.00
❑ 126	Robert Smith	2.50	1.00
❑ 127	Greg Hill	1.00	.40
❑ 128	Fred Taylor	2.50	1.00
❑ 129	Marcus Nash	1.00	.40
❑ 130	Terrell Davis	2.50	1.00
❑ 131	Ahman Green	2.50	1.00
❑ 132	Jamal Anderson	2.50	1.00
❑ 133	Karim Abdul-Jabbar	1.50	.60
❑ 134	Jermaine Lewis	1.50	.60
❑ 135	Jerome Pathon	1.50	.60
❑ 136	Brad Johnson	2.50	1.00
❑ 137	Herman Moore	1.50	.60
❑ 138	Tim Dwight	2.50	1.00
❑ 139	Johnnie Morton	1.00	.40
❑ 140	Marshall Faulk	3.00	1.25
❑ 141	Frank Sanders	1.50	.60
❑ 142	Kevin Dyson	1.50	.60
❑ 143	Curtis Conway	1.50	.60
❑ 144	Derrick Mayes	1.00	.40
❑ 145	O.J. McDuffie	1.50	.60
❑ 146	Joe Jurevicius	1.50	.60
❑ 147	Jon Kitna	2.50	1.00
❑ 148	Joey Galloway	1.50	.60
❑ 149	Jimmy Smith	1.50	.60
❑ 150	Skip Hicks	1.00	.40
❑ 151	Rod Smith	1.50	.60
❑ 152	Duce Staley	2.50	1.00
❑ 153	James Stewart	1.00	.40
❑ 154	Rob Johnson	1.50	.60
❑ 155	Mikhael Ricks	1.00	.40
❑ 156	Wayne Chrebet	1.50	.60
❑ 157	Robert Brooks	1.50	.60
❑ 158	Tim Biakabutuka	1.50	.60
❑ 159	Priest Holmes	4.00	1.25
❑ 160	Warrick Dunn	2.50	1.00
❑ 161	Champ Bailey RC	5.00	2.00
❑ 162	D'Wayne Bates RC	2.50	1.00
❑ 163	Michael Bishop RC	3.00	1.25
❑ 164	David Boston RC	3.00	1.25
❑ 165	Na Brown RC	2.50	1.00
❑ 166	Chris Claiborne RC	1.50	.60
❑ 167	Joe Montgomery RC	2.50	1.00
❑ 168	Mike Cloud RC	2.50	1.00
❑ 169	Travis McGriff RC	1.50	.60
❑ 170	Tim Couch RC	3.00	1.25
❑ 171	Daunte Culpepper RC	12.00	5.00
❑ 172	Autry Denson RC	2.50	1.00
❑ 173	Jermaine Fazande RC	2.50	1.00
❑ 174	Troy Edwards RC	2.50	1.00
❑ 175	Kevin Faulk RC	3.00	1.25
❑ 176	Dee Miller RC	1.50	.60
❑ 177	Brock Huard RC	3.00	1.25
❑ 178	Torry Holt RC	8.00	3.00
❑ 179	Sedrick Irvin RC	1.50	.60
❑ 180	Edgerrin James RC	12.00	5.00
❑ 181	Joe Germaine RC	2.50	1.00
❑ 182	James Johnson RC	2.50	1.00
❑ 183	Kevin Johnson RC	2.50	1.00
❑ 184	Andy Katzenmoyer RC	2.50	1.00
❑ 185	Jevon Kearse RC	6.00	2.50
❑ 186	Shaun King RC	2.50	1.00
❑ 187	Rob Konrad RC	3.00	1.25
❑ 188	Jim Kleinsasser RC	3.00	1.25
❑ 189	Chris McAlister RC	2.50	1.00
❑ 190	Donovan McNabb RC	15.00	6.00
❑ 191	Cade McNown RC	2.50	1.00
❑ 192	De'Mond Parker RC	1.00	.40
❑ 193	Craig Yeast RC	2.50	1.00
❑ 194	Shawn Bryson RC	3.00	1.25
❑ 195	Peerless Price RC	3.00	1.25
❑ 196	Darnell McDonald RC	2.50	1.00
❑ 197	Akili Smith RC	1.50	.60
❑ 198	Tai Streets RC	3.00	1.25
❑ 199	Ricky Williams RC	6.00	2.50
❑ 200	Amos Zereoue RC	2.50	1.00

2000 Donruss Elite

❑	COMPLETE SET (200)	500.00	300.00
❑ 1	Jake Plummer	.50	.20
❑ 2	David Boston	.75	.30
❑ 3	Rob Moore	.50	.20
❑ 4	Chris Chandler	.50	.20
❑ 5	Tim Dwight	.75	.30
❑ 6	Terance Mathis	.50	.20
❑ 7	Jamal Anderson	.75	.30
❑ 8	Priest Holmes	1.00	.40
❑ 9	Tony Banks	.50	.20
❑ 10	Shannon Sharpe	.50	.20
❑ 11	Qadry Ismail	.50	.20
❑ 12	Eric Moulds	.75	.30
❑ 13	Doug Flutie	.75	.30
❑ 14	Antowain Smith	.50	.20
❑ 15	Peerless Price	.50	.20
❑ 16	Muhsin Muhammad	.50	.20
❑ 17	Tim Biakabutuka	.50	.20
❑ 18	Patrick Jeffers	.75	.30
❑ 19	Steve Beuerlein	.50	.20
❑ 20	Wesley Walls	.30	.10
❑ 21	Curtis Enis	.30	.10
❑ 22	Marcus Robinson	.75	.30
❑ 23	Carl Pickens	.50	.20
❑ 24	Corey Dillon	.75	.30
❑ 25	Akili Smith	.30	.10
❑ 26	Darnay Scott	.50	.20
❑ 27	Kevin Johnson	.75	.30
❑ 28	Errict Rhett	.50	.20
❑ 29	Emmitt Smith	1.50	.60
❑ 30	Deion Sanders	.75	.30
❑ 31	Troy Aikman	1.50	.60
❑ 32	Joey Galloway	.50	.20
❑ 33	Michael Irvin	.50	.20
❑ 34	Rocket Ismail	.50	.20
❑ 35	Jason Tucker	.30	.10
❑ 36	Ed McCaffrey	.75	.30
❑ 37	Rod Smith	.50	.20
❑ 38	Brian Griese	.75	.30
❑ 39	Terrell Davis	.75	.30
❑ 40	Olandis Gary	.75	.30
❑ 41	Charlie Batch	.75	.30
❑ 42	Johnnie Morton	.50	.20
❑ 43	Herman Moore	.50	.20
❑ 44	James Stewart	.50	.20
❑ 45	Dorsey Levens	.50	.20
❑ 46	Antonio Freeman	.75	.30
❑ 47	Brett Favre	2.50	1.00
❑ 48	Bill Schroeder	.50	.20
❑ 49	Peyton Manning	2.00	.75
❑ 50	Keenan McCardell	.50	.20
❑ 51	Fred Taylor	.75	.30
❑ 52	Jimmy Smith	.50	.20
❑ 53	Elvis Grbac	.50	.20
❑ 54	Tony Gonzalez	.50	.20
❑ 55	Derrick Alexander	.50	.20
❑ 56	Dan Marino	2.50	1.00
❑ 57	Tony Martin	.50	.20
❑ 58	James Johnson	.30	.10
❑ 59	Damon Huard	.75	.30
❑ 60	Thurman Thomas	.50	.20
❑ 61	Robert Smith	.75	.30
❑ 62	Randall Cunningham	.75	.30
❑ 63	Jeff George	.50	.20
❑ 64	Terry Glenn	.50	.20
❑ 65	Drew Bledsoe	1.00	.40
❑ 66	Jeff Blake	.50	.20
❑ 67	Amani Toomer	.50	.20
❑ 68	Kerry Collins	.50	.20
❑ 69	Joe Montgomery	.30	.10
❑ 70	Vinny Testaverde	.50	.20
❑ 71	Ray Lucas	.50	.20
❑ 72	Keyshawn Johnson	.75	.30
❑ 73	Wayne Chrebet	.50	.20
❑ 74	Napoleon Kaufman	.50	.20
❑ 75	Tim Brown	.75	.30
❑ 76	Rich Gannon	.75	.30
❑ 77	Duce Staley	.75	.30
❑ 78	Kordell Stewart	.50	.20
❑ 79	Jerome Bettis	.75	.30
❑ 80	Troy Edwards	.30	.10
❑ 81	Natrone Means	.30	.10
❑ 82	Curtis Conway	.50	.20
❑ 83	Jim Harbaugh	.50	.20
❑ 84	Junior Seau	.75	.30
❑ 85	Jermaine Fazande	.30	.10
❑ 86	Terrell Owens	.75	.30
❑ 87	Charlie Garner	.50	.20
❑ 88	Steve Young	1.00	.40
❑ 89	Jeff Garcia	.75	.30
❑ 90	Derrick Mayes	.50	.20
❑ 91	Ricky Watters	.50	.20
❑ 92	Az-Zahir Hakim	.50	.20
❑ 93	Torry Holt	.75	.30
❑ 94	Warren Sapp	.50	.20
❑ 95	Mike Alstott	.75	.30
❑ 96	Warrick Dunn	.75	.30
❑ 97	Kevin Dyson	.50	.20

- ❑ 98 Bruce Smith .50 .20
- ❑ 99 Albert Connell .30 .10
- ❑ 100 Michael Westbrook .50 .20
- ❑ 101 Cade McNown .30 .10
- ❑ 102 Tim Couch 2.00 .75
- ❑ 103 John Elway 6.00 2.50
- ❑ 104 Barry Sanders 5.00 2.00
- ❑ 105 Germane Crowell 1.25 .50
- ❑ 106 Marvin Harrison 2.00 .75
- ❑ 107 Edgerrin James 3.00 1.25
- ❑ 108 Mark Brunell 2.00 .75
- ❑ 109 Randy Moss 4.00 1.50
- ❑ 110 Cris Carter 2.00 .75
- ❑ 111 Daunte Culpepper 2.50 1.00
- ❑ 112 Ricky Williams .75 .30
- ❑ 113 Curtis Martin 2.00 .75
- ❑ 114 Donovan McNabb 3.00 1.25
- ❑ 115 Jerry Rice 4.00 1.50
- ❑ 116 Jon Kitna 2.00 .75
- ❑ 117 Isaac Bruce 2.00 .75
- ❑ 118 Marshall Faulk 2.50 1.00
- ❑ 119 Kurt Warner 4.00 1.50
- ❑ 120 Shaun King .30 .10
- ❑ 121 Eddie George 2.00 .75
- ❑ 122 Steve McNair 2.00 .75
- ❑ 123 Jevon Kearse 2.00 .75
- ❑ 124 Stephen Davis 2.00 .75
- ❑ 125 Brad Johnson 2.00 .75
- ❑ 126 Mike Anderson RC 2.50 1.00
- ❑ 127 Peter Warrick RC 5.00 2.00
- ❑ 128 Courtney Brown RC 2.00 .75
- ❑ 129 Plaxico Burress RC 10.00 4.00
- ❑ 130 Corey Simon RC 5.00 2.00
- ❑ 131 Thomas Jones RC 8.00 3.00
- ❑ 132 Travis Taylor RC 2.00 .75
- ❑ 133 Shaun Alexander RC 30.00 12.50
- ❑ 134 Deon Grant RC 4.00 1.50
- ❑ 135 Chris Redman RC 4.00 1.50
- ❑ 136 Chad Pennington RC 12.00 5.00
- ❑ 137 Jamal Lewis RC 12.00 5.00
- ❑ 138 Brian Urlacher RC 25.00 10.00
- ❑ 139 Keith Bulluck RC 5.00 2.00
- ❑ 140 Bubba Franks RC 5.00 2.00
- ❑ 141 Dez White RC 5.00 2.00
- ❑ 142 Na'il Diggs RC 4.00 1.50
- ❑ 143 Ahmed Plummer RC 5.00 2.00
- ❑ 144 Ron Dayne RC 5.00 2.00
- ❑ 145 Shaun Ellis RC 5.00 2.00
- ❑ 146 Sylvester Morris RC 4.00 1.50
- ❑ 147 Deltha O'Neal RC 5.00 2.00
- ❑ 148 Raynoch Thompson RC 4.00 1.50
- ❑ 149 R.Jay Soward RC 4.00 1.50
- ❑ 150 Mario Edwards RC 4.00 1.50
- ❑ 151 John Engelberger RC 4.00 1.50
- ❑ 152 Dwayne Goodrich RC 5.00 2.00
- ❑ 153 Sherrod Gideon RC 2.50 1.00
- ❑ 154 John Abraham RC 5.00 2.00
- ❑ 155 Ben Kelly RC 5.00 2.00
- ❑ 156 Travis Prentice RC 4.00 1.50
- ❑ 157 Darrell Jackson RC 10.00 4.00
- ❑ 158 Giovanni Carmazzi RC 2.50 1.00
- ❑ 159 Anthony Lucas RC 2.50 1.00
- ❑ 160 Danny Farmer RC 4.00 1.50
- ❑ 161 Dennis Northcutt RC 5.00 2.00
- ❑ 162 Troy Walters RC 5.00 2.00
- ❑ 163 Laveranues Coles RC 6.00 2.50
- ❑ 164 Tee Martin RC 5.00 2.00
- ❑ 165 J.R. Redmond RC 4.00 1.50
- ❑ 166 Tim Rattay RC 5.00 2.00
- ❑ 167 Jerry Porter RC 6.00 2.50
- ❑ 168 Sebastian Janikowski RC 5.00 2.00
- ❑ 169 Michael Wiley RC 4.00 1.50
- ❑ 170 Reuben Droughns RC 6.00 2.50
- ❑ 171 Trung Canidate RC 4.00 1.50
- ❑ 172 Shyrone Stith RC 5.00 2.00
- ❑ 173 Chris Hovan RC 4.00 1.50
- ❑ 174 Brandon Short RC 5.00 2.00
- ❑ 175 Mark Roman RC 4.00 1.50
- ❑ 176 Trevor Gaylor RC 4.00 1.50
- ❑ 177 Chris Cole RC 4.00 1.50
- ❑ 178 Hank Poteat RC 4.00 1.50
- ❑ 179 Darren Howard RC 4.00 1.50
- ❑ 180 Rob Morris RC 5.00 2.00
- ❑ 181 Spergon Wynn RC 4.00 1.50
- ❑ 182 Marc Bulger RC 10.00 5.00
- ❑ 183 Tom Brady RC 75.00 40.00
- ❑ 184 Todd Husak RC 5.00 2.00
- ❑ 185 Gari Scott RC 2.50 1.00
- ❑ 186 Erron Kinney RC 4.00 1.50
- ❑ 187 Julian Peterson RC 5.00 2.00
- ❑ 188 Sammy Morris RC 4.00 1.50
- ❑ 189 Rondell Mealey RC 2.50 1.00
- ❑ 190 Doug Chapman RC 4.00 1.50
- ❑ 191 Ron Dugans RC 2.50 1.00
- ❑ 192 Deon Dyer RC 4.00 1.50
- ❑ 193 Fred Robbins RC 2.50 1.00
- ❑ 194 Ike Charlton RC 5.00 2.00
- ❑ 195 Mareno Philyaw RC 2.50 1.00
- ❑ 196 Thomas Hamner RC 2.50 1.00
- ❑ 197 Jarious Jackson RC 4.00 1.50
- ❑ 198 Anthony Becht RC 5.00 2.00
- ❑ 199 Joe Hamilton RC 4.00 1.50
- ❑ 200 Todd Pinkston RC 5.00 2.00

2001 Donruss Elite

- ❑ COMP.SET w/o SP's (100) 20.00 7.50
- ❑ 1 David Boston .60 .25
- ❑ 2 Jake Plummer .40 .15
- ❑ 3 Thomas Jones .40 .15
- ❑ 4 Jamal Anderson .60 .25
- ❑ 5 Chris Redman .25 .08
- ❑ 6 Jamal Lewis 1.00 .40
- ❑ 7 Shannon Sharpe .40 .15
- ❑ 8 Travis Taylor .40 .15
- ❑ 9 Trent Dilfer .40 .15
- ❑ 10 Doug Flutie .60 .25
- ❑ 11 Eric Moulds .40 .15
- ❑ 12 Rob Johnson .40 .15
- ❑ 13 Muhsin Muhammad .40 .15
- ❑ 14 Steve Beuerlein .25 .08
- ❑ 15 Brian Urlacher 1.00 .40
- ❑ 16 Cade McNown .25 .08
- ❑ 17 Marcus Robinson .60 .25
- ❑ 18 Akili Smith .25 .08
- ❑ 19 Corey Dillon .60 .25
- ❑ 20 Peter Warrick .60 .25
- ❑ 21 Kevin Johnson .40 .15
- ❑ 22 Tim Couch .40 .15
- ❑ 23 Emmitt Smith 1.25 .50
- ❑ 24 Troy Aikman 1.00 .40
- ❑ 25 Brian Griese .60 .25
- ❑ 26 John Elway 2.00 .75
- ❑ 27 Mike Anderson .60 .25
- ❑ 28 Rod Smith .40 .15
- ❑ 29 Terrell Davis .60 .25
- ❑ 30 Barry Sanders 1.25 .50
- ❑ 31 Charlie Batch .60 .25
- ❑ 32 James Stewart .40 .15
- ❑ 33 Ahman Green .60 .25
- ❑ 34 Antonio Freeman .60 .25
- ❑ 35 Brett Favre 2.00 .75
- ❑ 36 Edgerrin James .75 .30
- ❑ 37 Marvin Harrison .60 .25
- ❑ 38 Peyton Manning 1.50 .60
- ❑ 39 Fred Taylor .60 .25
- ❑ 40 Jimmy Smith .40 .15
- ❑ 41 Keenan McCardell .25 .08
- ❑ 42 Mark Brunell .60 .25
- ❑ 43 Derrick Alexander .40 .15
- ❑ 44 Elvis Grbac .40 .15
- ❑ 45 Sylvester Morris .25 .08
- ❑ 46 Tony Gonzalez .40 .15
- ❑ 47 Dan Marino 2.00 .75
- ❑ 48 Jay Fiedler .60 .25
- ❑ 49 Lamar Smith .40 .15
- ❑ 50 Oronde Gadsden .40 .15
- ❑ 51 Cris Carter .60 .25
- ❑ 52 Daunte Culpepper .60 .25
- ❑ 53 Randy Moss 1.25 .50
- ❑ 54 Robert Smith .40 .15
- ❑ 55 Drew Bledsoe .75 .30
- ❑ 56 Terry Glenn .25 .08
- ❑ 57 Aaron Brooks .60 .25
- ❑ 58 Joe Horn .40 .15
- ❑ 59 Ricky Williams .60 .25
- ❑ 60 Amani Toomer .25 .08
- ❑ 61 Ike Hilliard .40 .15
- ❑ 62 Kerry Collins .40 .15
- ❑ 63 Ron Dayne .60 .25
- ❑ 64 Tiki Barber .60 .25
- ❑ 65 Chad Pennington 1.00 .40
- ❑ 66 Curtis Martin .60 .25
- ❑ 67 Vinny Testaverde .40 .15
- ❑ 68 Wayne Chrebet .40 .15
- ❑ 69 Rich Gannon .60 .25
- ❑ 70 Tim Brown .60 .25
- ❑ 71 Tyrone Wheatley .40 .15
- ❑ 72 Donovan McNabb .75 .30
- ❑ 73 Jerome Bettis .60 .25
- ❑ 74 Plaxico Burress .60 .25
- ❑ 75 Junior Seau .60 .25
- ❑ 76 Charlie Garner .40 .15
- ❑ 77 Jeff Garcia .60 .25
- ❑ 78 Jerry Rice 1.25 .50
- ❑ 79 Terrell Owens .60 .25
- ❑ 80 Darrell Jackson .60 .25
- ❑ 81 Ricky Watters .40 .15
- ❑ 82 Shaun Alexander .75 .30
- ❑ 83 Isaac Bruce .60 .25
- ❑ 84 Kurt Warner 1.25 .50
- ❑ 85 Marshall Faulk .75 .30
- ❑ 86 Torry Holt .60 .25
- ❑ 87 Trent Green .60 .25
- ❑ 88 Keyshawn Johnson .60 .25
- ❑ 89 Shaun King .25 .08
- ❑ 90 Warren Sapp .40 .15
- ❑ 91 Warrick Dunn .60 .25
- ❑ 92 Eddie George .60 .25
- ❑ 93 Jevon Kearse .40 .15
- ❑ 94 Steve McNair .60 .25
- ❑ 95 Albert Connell .25 .08
- ❑ 96 Jeff George .40 .15
- ❑ 97 Brad Johnson .60 .25
- ❑ 98 Bruce Smith .25 .08
- ❑ 99 Michael Westbrook .40 .15
- ❑ 100 Stephen Davis .60 .25
- ❑ 101 Michael Vick RC 60.00 25.00
- ❑ 102 Drew Brees RC 40.00 20.00
- ❑ 103 Chris Weinke RC 10.00 4.00
- ❑ 104 Quincy Carter RC 10.00 4.00
- ❑ 105 Sage Rosenfels RC 10.00 4.00
- ❑ 106 Josh Heupel RC 10.00 4.00
- ❑ 107 Tony Driver RC 6.00 2.50
- ❑ 108 Ben Leard RC 6.00 2.50
- ❑ 109 Marques Tuiasosopo RC 10.00 4.00
- ❑ 110 Tim Hasselbeck RC 10.00 4.00
- ❑ 111 Mike McMahon RC 10.00 4.00
- ❑ 112 Deuce McAllister RC 25.00 10.00
- ❑ 113 LaMont Jordan RC 25.00 10.00
- ❑ 114 LaDainian Tomlinson RC 100.00 60.00
- ❑ 115 James Jackson RC 10.00 4.00
- ❑ 116 Anthony Thomas RC 10.00 4.00
- ❑ 117 Travis Henry RC 15.00 6.00
- ❑ 118 DeAngelo Evans RC 6.00 2.50
- ❑ 119 Travis Minor RC 6.00 2.50
- ❑ 120 Rudi Johnson RC 25.00 12.50
- ❑ 121 Michael Bennett RC 10.00 4.00
- ❑ 122 Kevan Barlow RC 10.00 4.00
- ❑ 123 Dan Alexander RC 10.00 4.00
- ❑ 124 David Allen RC 6.00 2.50
- ❑ 125 Correll Buckhalter RC 12.00 5.00
- ❑ 126 David Rivers RC 6.00 2.50
- ❑ 127 Reggie White RC 6.00 2.50
- ❑ 128 Moran Norris RC 4.00 1.50
- ❑ 129 Ja'Mar Toombs RC 6.00 2.50
- ❑ 130 Jason McKinley RC 6.00 2.50
- ❑ 131 Scotty Anderson RC 6.00 2.50
- ❑ 132 Dustin McClintock RC 10.00 4.00
- ❑ 133 Heath Evans RC 6.00 2.50
- ❑ 134 David Terrell RC 10.00 4.00
- ❑ 135 Santana Moss RC 15.00 6.00
- ❑ 136 Rod Gardner RC 10.00 4.00
- ❑ 137 Quincy Morgan RC 10.00 4.00
- ❑ 138 Freddie Mitchell RC 10.00 4.00
- ❑ 139 Boo Williams RC 6.00 2.50
- ❑ 140 Reggie Wayne RC 25.00 10.00
- ❑ 141 Ronney Daniels RC 4.00 1.50
- ❑ 142 Bobby Newcombe RC 6.00 2.50
- ❑ 143 Reggie Germany/250 RC 12.00 5.00
- ❑ 144 Jesse Palmer RC 10.00 4.00

	No.	Player	Price	Price
❑	145	Robert Ferguson RC	10.00	4.00
❑	146	Ken-Yon Rambo RC	6.00	2.50
❑	147	Alex Bannister RC	6.00	2.50
❑	148	Koren Robinson RC	10.00	4.00
❑	149	Chad Johnson RC	30.00	12.50
❑	150	Chris Chambers RC	15.00	6.00
❑	151	Javon Green RC	6.00	2.50
❑	152	Snoop Minnis RC	6.00	2.50
❑	153	Vinny Sutherland RC	6.00	2.50
❑	154	Cedrick Wilson RC	10.00	4.00
❑	155	John Capel/250 RC	12.00	5.00
❑	156	T.J. Houshmandzadeh RC	12.00	5.00
❑	157	Todd Heap RC	10.00	4.00
❑	158	Alge Crumpler RC	15.00	6.00
❑	159	Jabari Holloway RC	6.00	2.50
❑	160	Marcellus Rivers RC	6.00	2.50
❑	161	Rashon Burns RC	4.00	1.50
❑	162	Tony Stewart RC	10.00	4.00
❑	163	Jevaris Johnson RC	4.00	1.50
❑	164	Jamal Reynolds RC	10.00	4.00
❑	165	Andre Carter RC	10.00	4.00
❑	166	David Warren RC	4.00	1.50
❑	167	Justin Smith RC	10.00	4.00
❑	168	Josh Booty RC	10.00	4.00
❑	169	Karon Riley RC	4.00	1.50
❑	170	Cedric Scott RC	4.00	1.50
❑	171	Kenny Smith RC	6.00	2.50
❑	172	Richard Seymour RC	10.00	4.00
❑	173	Willie Howard RC	6.00	2.50
❑	174	Markus Steele RC	6.00	2.50
❑	175	Marcus Stroud RC	10.00	4.00
❑	176	Damione Lewis RC	6.00	2.50
❑	177	Casey Hampton RC	10.00	4.00
❑	178	Ennis Davis RC	4.00	1.50
❑	179	Gerard Warren RC	.60	.25
❑	180	Tommy Polley RC	10.00	4.00
❑	181	Kendrell Bell/250 RC	40.00	15.00
❑	182	Dan Morgan RC	10.00	4.00
❑	183	Morlon Greenwood RC	6.00	2.50
❑	184	Quinton Caver/250	10.00	4.00
❑	185	Keith Adams RC	4.00	1.50
❑	186	Brian Allen RC	4.00	1.50
❑	187	Carlos Polk RC	4.00	1.50
❑	188	Torrance Marshall RC	10.00	4.00
❑	189	Jamie Winborn RC	6.00	2.50
❑	190	Jamar Fletcher RC	6.00	2.50
❑	191	Ken Lucas RC	6.00	2.50
❑	192	Fred Smoot RC	10.00	4.00
❑	193	Nate Clements RC	10.00	4.00
❑	194	Will Allen RC	6.00	2.50
❑	195	Willie Middlebrooks/250 RC	10.00	4.00
❑	196	Gary Baxter RC	6.00	2.50
❑	197	Derrick Gibson RC	6.00	2.50
❑	198	Robert Carswell/250 RC	10.00	4.00
❑	199	Hakim Akbar RC	4.00	1.50
❑	200	Adam Archuleta RC	10.00	4.00

2002 Donruss Elite

	No.	Player	Price	Price
❑		COMP.SET w/o SP's (100)	20.00	7.50
❑	1	Elvis Grbac	.30	.10
❑	2	Jamal Lewis	.50	.20
❑	3	Ray Lewis	.50	.20
❑	4	Travis Henry	.50	.20
❑	5	Eric Moulds	.30	.10
❑	6	Corey Dillon	.30	.10
❑	7	Peter Warrick	.30	.10
❑	8	Tim Couch	.30	.10
❑	9	James Jackson	.20	.07
❑	10	Kevin Johnson	.30	.10
❑	11	Mike Anderson	.50	.20
❑	12	Terrell Davis	.50	.20
❑	13	Brian Griese	.50	.20
❑	14	Rod Smith	.30	.10
❑	15	Marvin Harrison	.50	.20
❑	16	Reggie Wayne	.50	.20
❑	17	Dominic Rhodes	.50	.20
❑	18	Edgerrin James	.60	.25
❑	19	Mark Brunell	.50	.20
❑	20	Keenan McCardell	.20	.07
❑	21	Jimmy Smith	.30	.10
❑	22	Tony Gonzalez	.30	.10
❑	23	Trent Green	.30	.10
❑	24	Priest Holmes	.60	.25
❑	25	Snoop Minnis	.20	.07
❑	26	Chris Chambers	.50	.20
❑	27	Jay Fiedler	.30	.10
❑	28	Travis Minor	.20	.07
❑	29	Lamar Smith	.30	.10
❑	30	Tom Brady	1.25	.50
❑	31	Troy Brown	.30	.10
❑	32	Antowain Smith	.30	.10
❑	33	Laveranues Coles	.30	.10
❑	34	Curtis Martin	.50	.20
❑	35	Vinny Testaverde	.30	.10
❑	36	Wayne Chrebet	.30	.10
❑	37	Tim Brown	.50	.20
❑	38	Rich Gannon	.50	.20
❑	39	Jerry Rice	1.00	.40
❑	40	Charlie Garner	.30	.10
❑	41	Jerome Bettis	.50	.20
❑	42	Plaxico Burress	.30	.10
❑	43	Kordell Stewart	.30	.10
❑	44	Kendrell Bell	.50	.20
❑	45	Doug Flutie	.50	.20
❑	46	LaDainian Tomlinson	.75	.30
❑	47	Junior Seau	.50	.20
❑	48	Drew Brees	.50	.20
❑	49	Shaun Alexander	.60	.25
❑	50	Koren Robinson	.30	.10
❑	51	Ricky Watters	.30	.10
❑	52	Eddie George	.50	.20
❑	53	Derrick Mason	.30	.10
❑	54	Steve McNair	.50	.20
❑	55	David Boston	.50	.20
❑	56	Jake Plummer	.30	.10
❑	57	Chris Chandler	.30	.10
❑	58	Jamal Anderson	.30	.10
❑	59	Michael Vick	1.50	.60
❑	60	Wesley Walls	.20	.07
❑	61	Chris Weinke	.30	.10
❑	62	David Terrell	.50	.20
❑	63	Anthony Thomas	.30	.10
❑	64	Brian Urlacher	.75	.30
❑	65	Quincy Carter	.30	.10
❑	66	Rocket Ismail	.30	.10
❑	67	Emmitt Smith	1.25	.50
❑	68	James Stewart	.30	.10
❑	69	Germane Crowell	.20	.07
❑	70	Mike McMahon	.50	.20
❑	71	Brett Favre	1.25	.50
❑	72	Ahman Green	.50	.20
❑	73	Antonio Freeman	.50	.20
❑	74	Michael Bennett	.30	.10
❑	75	Cris Carter	.50	.20
❑	76	Daunte Culpepper	.50	.20
❑	77	Randy Moss	1.00	.40
❑	78	Aaron Brooks	.50	.20
❑	79	Deuce McAllister	.60	.25
❑	80	Ricky Williams	.50	.20
❑	81	Kerry Collins	.30	.10
❑	82	Ron Dayne	.30	.10
❑	83	Amani Toomer	.30	.10
❑	84	Correll Buckhalter	.30	.10
❑	85	James Thrash	.30	.10
❑	86	Freddie Mitchell	.30	.10
❑	87	Duce Staley	.50	.20
❑	88	Jeff Garcia	.50	.20
❑	89	Garrison Hearst	.30	.10
❑	90	Terrell Owens	.50	.20
❑	91	Isaac Bruce	.50	.20
❑	92	Marshall Faulk	.50	.20
❑	93	Torry Holt	.50	.20
❑	94	Kurt Warner	.50	.20
❑	95	Mike Alstott	.50	.20
❑	96	Brad Johnson	.30	.10
❑	97	Keyshawn Johnson	.50	.20
❑	98	Stephen Davis	.30	.10
❑	99	Rod Gardner	.30	.10
❑	100	Tony Banks	.20	.07
❑	101	David Carr RC	50.00	20.00
❑	102	Joey Harrington RC	25.00	10.00
❑	103	Rohan Davey RC	15.00	6.00
❑	104	Chad Hutchinson RC	12.00	5.00
❑	105	Patrick Ramsey RC	20.00	7.50
❑	106	Kurt Kittner RC	12.00	5.00
❑	107	Eric Crouch RC	15.00	6.00
❑	108	David Garrard RC	15.00	6.00
❑	109	Ronald Curry RC	15.00	6.00
❑	110	Zak Kustok RC	15.00	6.00
❑	111	Woody Dantzler RC	12.00	5.00
❑	112	Wes Pate RC	6.00	2.50
❑	113	Brian Westbrook RC	25.00	10.00
❑	114	Josh McCown RC	20.00	7.50
❑	115	Travis Stephens RC	12.00	5.00
❑	116	Luke Staley RC	12.00	5.00
❑	117	William Green RC	15.00	6.00
❑	118	Clinton Portis RC	50.00	20.00
❑	119	DeShaun Foster RC	15.00	6.00
❑	120	Verron Haynes RC	15.00	6.00
❑	121	T.J. Duckett RC	20.00	8.00
❑	122	Antwoine Womack RC	12.00	5.00
❑	123	Leonard Henry RC	12.00	5.00
❑	124	Lamar Gordon RC	15.00	6.00
❑	125	Adrian Peterson RC	15.00	6.00
❑	126	Chester Taylor RC	30.00	12.50
❑	127	Damien Anderson RC	12.00	5.00
❑	128	Maurice Morris RC	15.00	6.00
❑	129	Ricky Williams RC	12.00	5.00
❑	130	Terry Charles RC	12.00	5.00
❑	131	Demontray Carter RC	6.00	2.50
❑	132	Jason McAddley RC	12.00	5.00
❑	133	Ladell Betts RC	15.00	6.00
❑	134	Cortlen Johnson RC	6.00	2.50
❑	135	James Mungro RC	15.00	6.00
❑	136	Atrews Bell RC	6.00	2.50
❑	137	Josh Scobey RC	15.00	6.00
❑	138	Justin Peelle RC	6.00	2.50
❑	139	Najeh Davenport RC	15.00	6.00
❑	140	Josh Reed RC	15.00	6.00
❑	141	Marquise Walker RC	12.00	5.00
❑	142	Jabar Gaffney RC	15.00	6.00
❑	143	Antwaan Randle El RC	25.00	10.00
❑	144	Ashley Lelie RC	30.00	12.50
❑	145	Tavon Mason RC	6.00	2.50
❑	146	Antonio Bryant RC	15.00	6.00
❑	147	Javon Walker RC	30.00	12.50
❑	148	Kelly Campbell RC	12.00	5.00
❑	149	Ron Johnson RC	12.00	5.00
❑	150	Andre Davis RC	12.00	5.00
❑	151	Cliff Russell RC	12.00	5.00
❑	152	Reche Caldwell RC	15.00	6.00
❑	153	Kyle Johnson RC	6.00	2.50
❑	154	Freddie Milons RC	12.00	5.00
❑	155	Brian Poli-Dixon RC	12.00	5.00
❑	156	David Thornton RC	6.00	2.50
❑	157	Bryan Thomas RC	12.00	5.00
❑	158	Kahlil Hill RC	12.00	5.00
❑	159	Deion Branch RC	25.00	12.50
❑	160	Akin Ayodele RC	6.00	2.50
❑	161	Donte Stallworth RC	30.00	12.50
❑	162	Tim Carter RC	12.00	5.00
❑	163	Kenyon Coleman RC	6.00	2.50
❑	164	Jeremy Shockey RC	40.00	15.00
❑	165	Eddie Freeman RC	6.00	2.50
❑	166	Tracey Wistrom RC	12.00	5.00
❑	167	Daniel Graham RC	15.00	6.00
❑	168	Julius Peppers RC	30.00	12.50
❑	169	Alex Brown RC	15.00	6.00
❑	170	Dwight Freeney RC	25.00	10.00
❑	171	Kalimba Edwards RC	15.00	6.00
❑	172	Dennis Johnson RC	6.00	2.50
❑	173	Travis Fisher RC	15.00	6.00
❑	174	John Henderson RC	15.00	6.00
❑	175	Anthony Weaver RC	12.00	5.00
❑	176	Ryan Sims RC	15.00	6.00
❑	177	Alan Harper RC	6.00	2.50
❑	178	Larry Tripplett RC	6.00	2.50
❑	179	Wendell Bryant RC	6.00	2.50
❑	180	Albert Haynesworth RC	12.00	5.00
❑	181	Levar Fisher RC	6.00	2.50
❑	182	Andra Davis RC	12.00	5.00
❑	183	Joseph Jefferson RC	12.00	5.00
❑	184	Lamont Thompson RC	12.00	5.00
❑	185	Robert Thomas RC	15.00	6.00
❑	186	Michael Lewis RC	15.00	6.00
❑	187	Rocky Calmus RC	15.00	6.00
❑	188	Napoleon Harris RC	15.00	6.00
❑	189	Lito Sheppard RC	15.00	6.00
❑	190	Quentin Jammer RC	15.00	6.00
❑	191	Roy Williams RC	40.00	20.00

❑ 192 Marques Anderson RC	15.00	6.00
❑ 193 Chris Hope RC	15.00	6.00
❑ 194 Raonall Smith RC	12.00	5.00
❑ 195 Mike Rumph RC	15.00	6.00
❑ 196 James Allen RC	6.00	2.50
❑ 197 Ed Reed RC	25.00	12.50
❑ 198 Mike Williams RC	12.00	5.00
❑ 199 Phillip Buchanon RC	15.00	6.00
❑ 200 Bryant McKinnie RC	12.00	5.00

2003 Donruss Elite

❑ COMP.SET w/o SP's (100)	20.00	7.50
❑ 1 Jamal Lewis	.50	.20
❑ 2 Ray Lewis	.50	.20
❑ 3 Todd Heap	.30	.10
❑ 4 Drew Bledsoe	.50	.20
❑ 5 Travis Henry	.30	.10
❑ 6 Eric Moulds	.30	.10
❑ 7 Peerless Price	.30	.10
❑ 8 Jon Kitna	.30	.10
❑ 9 Corey Dillon	.30	.10
❑ 10 Chad Johnson	.50	.20
❑ 11 Tim Couch	.20	.08
❑ 12 William Green	.30	.10
❑ 13 Andre Davis	.20	.08
❑ 14 Brian Griese	.50	.20
❑ 15 Ashley Lelie	.50	.20
❑ 16 Clinton Portis	.75	.30
❑ 17 Rod Smith	.30	.10
❑ 18 David Carr	.75	.30
❑ 19 Jonathan Wells	.20	.08
❑ 20 Jabar Gaffney	.30	.10
❑ 21 Peyton Manning	.75	.30
❑ 22 Edgerrin James	.50	.20
❑ 23 Marvin Harrison	.50	.20
❑ 24 Mark Brunell	.30	.10
❑ 25 Jimmy Smith	.30	.10
❑ 26 Fred Taylor	.50	.20
❑ 27 Priest Holmes	.60	.25
❑ 28 Trent Green	.30	.10
❑ 29 Tony Gonzalez	.30	.10
❑ 30 Chris Chambers	.50	.20
❑ 31 Zach Thomas	.30	.10
❑ 32 Ricky Williams	.50	.20
❑ 33 Tom Brady	1.25	.50
❑ 34 Antowain Smith	.30	.10
❑ 35 Troy Brown	.30	.10
❑ 36 Chad Pennington	.60	.25
❑ 37 Curtis Martin	.50	.20
❑ 38 Laveranues Coles	.30	.10
❑ 39 Tim Brown	.50	.20
❑ 40 Rich Gannon	.30	.10
❑ 41 Jerry Rice	1.00	.40
❑ 42 Charlie Garner	.30	.10
❑ 43 Antwaan Randle El	.50	.20
❑ 44 Plaxico Burress	.30	.10
❑ 45 Tommy Maddox	.50	.20
❑ 46 Jerome Bettis	.50	.20
❑ 47 Drew Brees	.50	.20
❑ 48 LaDainian Tomlinson	.50	.20
❑ 49 Junior Seau	.50	.20
❑ 50 Eddie George	.30	.10
❑ 51 Steve McNair	.50	.20
❑ 52 Derrick Mason	.30	.10
❑ 53 David Boston	.30	.10
❑ 54 Jake Plummer	.30	.10
❑ 55 Marcel Shipp	.30	.10
❑ 56 Michael Vick	1.25	.50
❑ 57 T.J. Duckett	.30	.10
❑ 58 Warrick Dunn	.30	.10
❑ 59 Julius Peppers	.50	.20
❑ 60 Steve Smith	.50	.20
❑ 61 Muhsin Muhammad	.30	.10
❑ 62 Anthony Thomas	.30	.10
❑ 63 Brian Urlacher	.75	.30
❑ 64 Marty Booker	.30	.10
❑ 65 Chad Hutchinson	.20	.08
❑ 66 Antonio Bryant	.30	.10
❑ 67 Emmitt Smith	1.25	.50
❑ 68 Joey Harrington	.75	.30
❑ 69 Germane Crowell	.20	.08
❑ 70 James Stewart	.30	.10
❑ 71 Brett Favre	1.25	.50
❑ 72 Donald Driver	.30	.10
❑ 73 Ahman Green	.50	.20
❑ 74 Randy Moss	.75	.30
❑ 75 Michael Bennett	.30	.10
❑ 76 Daunte Culpepper	.50	.20
❑ 77 Aaron Brooks	.50	.20
❑ 78 Deuce McAllister	.50	.20
❑ 79 Donte Stallworth	.50	.20
❑ 80 Tiki Barber	.50	.20
❑ 81 Jeremy Shockey	.75	.30
❑ 82 Kerry Collins	.30	.10
❑ 83 Donovan McNabb	.60	.25
❑ 84 James Thrash	.20	.08
❑ 85 Duce Staley	.30	.10
❑ 86 Jeff Garcia	.50	.20
❑ 87 Terrell Owens	.50	.20
❑ 88 Garrison Hearst	.30	.10
❑ 89 Shaun Alexander	.50	.20
❑ 90 Darrell Jackson	.30	.10
❑ 91 Koren Robinson	.20	.08
❑ 92 Marshall Faulk	.50	.20
❑ 93 Kurt Warner	.50	.20
❑ 94 Isaac Bruce	.50	.20
❑ 95 Keyshawn Johnson	.50	.20
❑ 96 Brad Johnson	.30	.10
❑ 97 Warren Sapp	.30	.10
❑ 98 Patrick Ramsey	.50	.20
❑ 99 Rod Gardner	.30	.10
❑ 100 Stephen Davis	.30	.10
❑ 101 Brian St.Pierre RC	12.00	5.00
❑ 102 Byron Leftwich RC	40.00	15.00
❑ 103 Carson Palmer RC	50.00	20.00
❑ 104 Chris Simms RC	20.00	7.50
❑ 105 Dave Ragone RC	12.00	5.00
❑ 106 Ken Dorsey RC	12.00	5.00
❑ 107 Kliff Kingsbury RC	10.00	4.00
❑ 108 Kyle Boller RC	12.00	5.00
❑ 109 Rex Grossman RC	40.00	15.00
❑ 110 Seneca Wallace RC	12.00	5.00
❑ 111 Jason Gesser RC	12.00	5.00
❑ 112 Artose Pinner RC	12.00	5.00
❑ 113 Avon Cobourne RC	6.00	2.50
❑ 114 Cecil Sapp RC	10.00	4.00
❑ 115 Chris Brown RC	12.00	5.00
❑ 116 Derek Watson RC	10.00	4.00
❑ 117 Domanick Davis RC	12.00	5.00
❑ 118 Dwone Hicks/100 RC	30.00	15.00
❑ 119 Earnest Graham RC	10.00	4.00
❑ 120 Justin Fargas RC	12.00	5.00
❑ 121 Larry Johnson RC	50.00	25.00
❑ 122 Lee Suggs RC	12.00	5.00
❑ 123 Musa Smith RC	12.00	5.00
❑ 124 Onterrio Smith RC	12.00	5.00
❑ 125 Quentin Griffin RC	12.00	5.00
❑ 126 Willis McGahee RC	30.00	15.00
❑ 127 Sultan McCullough RC	10.00	4.00
❑ 128 LaBrandon Toefield RC	12.00	5.00
❑ 129 B.J. Askew RC	12.00	5.00
❑ 130 Andre Johnson RC	25.00	10.00
❑ 131 Anquan Boldin RC	30.00	12.50
❑ 132 Arnaz Battle RC	12.00	5.00
❑ 133 Bethel Johnson RC	12.00	5.00
❑ 134 Billy McMullen RC	10.00	4.00
❑ 135 Bobby Wade RC	12.00	5.00
❑ 136 Brandon Lloyd RC	12.00	5.00
❑ 137 Bryant Johnson RC	12.00	5.00
❑ 138 Charles Rogers RC	12.00	5.00
❑ 139 Doug Gabriel RC	12.00	5.00
❑ 140 Justin Gage RC	12.00	5.00
❑ 141 Kareem Kelly RC	10.00	4.00
❑ 142 Kelley Washington RC	12.00	5.00
❑ 143 Kevin Curtis RC	12.00	5.00
❑ 144 Nate Burleson RC	12.00	5.00
❑ 145 Sam Aiken RC	10.00	4.00
❑ 146 Shaun McDonald RC	12.00	5.00
❑ 147 Talman Gardner RC	12.00	5.00
❑ 148 Taylor Jacobs RC	10.00	4.00
❑ 149 Terrence Edwards RC	10.00	4.00
❑ 150 Tyrone Calico RC	12.00	5.00
❑ 151 Walter Young RC	6.00	2.50
❑ 152 Ryan Hoag/100 RC	30.00	15.00
❑ 153 Paul Arnold/100 RC	30.00	15.00
❑ 154 Bennie Joppru RC	12.00	5.00
❑ 155 Dallas Clark RC	12.00	5.00
❑ 156 George Wrighster RC	10.00	4.00
❑ 157 Jason Witten RC	20.00	7.50
❑ 158 Mike Pinkard RC	6.00	2.50
❑ 159 Robert Johnson/100 RC	30.00	15.00
❑ 160 Teyo Johnson RC	12.00	5.00
❑ 161 Andrew Williams RC	10.00	4.00
❑ 162 Chris Kelsay RC	12.00	5.00
❑ 163 Cory Redding RC	10.00	4.00
❑ 164 DeWayne Robertson RC	12.00	5.00
❑ 165 DeWayne White RC	10.00	4.00
❑ 166 Jerome McDougle RC	12.00	5.00
❑ 167 Kenny Peterson RC	10.00	4.00
❑ 168 Kindal Moorehead RC	10.00	4.00
❑ 169 Michael Haynes RC	12.00	5.00
❑ 170 Terrell Suggs RC	20.00	7.50
❑ 171 Tully Banta-Cain RC	10.00	4.00
❑ 172 Jimmy Kennedy RC	12.00	5.00
❑ 173 Johnathan Sullivan RC	6.00	2.50
❑ 174 Kevin Williams RC	12.00	5.00
❑ 175 Nick Eason/100 RC	30.00	15.00
❑ 176 Rien Long RC	6.00	2.50
❑ 177 Ty Warren RC	12.00	5.00
❑ 178 William Joseph RC	12.00	5.00
❑ 179 Boss Bailey RC	12.00	5.00
❑ 180 Bradie James RC	12.00	5.00
❑ 181 Victor Hobson RC	12.00	5.00
❑ 182 Clifton Smith/100 RC	30.00	15.00
❑ 183 E.J. Henderson/100 RC	30.00	15.00
❑ 184 Gerald Hayes/100 RC	30.00	15.00
❑ 185 LaM McDonald/100 RC	30.00	15.00
❑ 186 Nick Barnett RC	12.00	5.00
❑ 187 Terry Pierce RC	10.00	4.00
❑ 188 Andre Woolfolk RC	12.00	5.00
❑ 189 Dennis Weathersby RC	6.00	2.50
❑ 190 Drayton Florence/100 RC	30.00	15.00
❑ 191 Eugene Wilson RC	12.00	5.00
❑ 192 Marcus Trufant RC	12.00	5.00
❑ 193 Rashean Mathis RC	10.00	4.00
❑ 194 Ricky Manning RC	12.00	5.00
❑ 195 Sammy Davis/100 RC	30.00	15.00
❑ 196 Terence Newman RC	25.00	10.00
❑ 197 Julian Battle RC	10.00	4.00
❑ 198 Ken Hamlin RC	12.00	5.00
❑ 199 Mike Doss RC	12.00	5.00
❑ 200 Troy Polamalu/100 RC	100.00	60.00

2004 Donruss Elite

❑ COMP.SET w/o SP's (100)	20.00	7.50
❑ ROOKIE PRINT RUN 500 SER.#'d SETS		
❑ 1 Emmitt Smith	2.00	.75
❑ 2 Anquan Boldin	1.00	.40
❑ 3 Michael Vick	2.00	.75
❑ 4 Peerless Price	.60	.25
❑ 5 T.J. Duckett	.60	.25
❑ 6 Warrick Dunn	.60	.25
❑ 7 Jamal Lewis	1.00	.40
❑ 8 Kyle Boller	1.00	.40
❑ 9 Todd Heap	.60	.25
❑ 10 Ray Lewis	1.00	.40
❑ 11 Drew Bledsoe	1.00	.40
❑ 12 Eric Moulds	.60	.25
❑ 13 Travis Henry	.60	.25
❑ 14 Jake Delhomme	1.00	.40
❑ 15 Stephen Davis	.60	.25
❑ 16 Steve Smith	1.00	.40
❑ 17 Anthony Thomas	.60	.25

❑	18	Brian Urlacher	1.25	.50
❑	19	Rex Grossman	1.00	.40
❑	20	Chad Johnson	1.00	.40
❑	21	Carson Palmer	1.25	.50
❑	22	Rudi Johnson	.60	.25
❑	23	Peter Warrick	.60	.25
❑	24	Andre Davis	.40	.15
❑	25	Tim Couch	.40	.15
❑	26	Quincy Carter	.60	.25
❑	27	Roy Williams S	.60	.25
❑	28	Terence Newman	.60	.25
❑	29	Clinton Portis	1.00	.40
❑	30	Jake Plummer	.60	.25
❑	31	Rod Smith	.60	.25
❑	32	Charles Rogers	.60	.25
❑	33	Joey Harrington	1.00	.40
❑	34	Ahman Green	1.00	.40
❑	35	Brett Favre	2.50	1.00
❑	36	Javon Walker	.60	.25
❑	37	Andre Johnson	1.00	.40
❑	38	David Carr	1.00	.40
❑	39	Domanick Davis	1.00	.40
❑	40	Edgerrin James	1.00	.40
❑	41	Marvin Harrison	1.00	.40
❑	42	Peyton Manning	1.50	.60
❑	43	Reggie Wayne	.60	.25
❑	44	Byron Leftwich	1.25	.50
❑	45	Fred Taylor	.60	.25
❑	46	Jimmy Smith	.60	.25
❑	47	Priest Holmes	1.25	.50
❑	48	Tony Gonzalez	.60	.25
❑	49	Trent Green	.60	.25
❑	50	Chris Chambers	.60	.25
❑	51	Ricky Williams	1.00	.40
❑	52	Zach Thomas	1.00	.40
❑	53	Daunte Culpepper	1.00	.40
❑	54	Michael Bennett	.60	.25
❑	55	Moe Williams	.40	.15
❑	56	Randy Moss	1.25	.50
❑	57	Deion Branch	1.00	.40
❑	58	Tom Brady	2.50	1.00
❑	59	Tedy Bruschi	.60	.25
❑	60	Aaron Brooks	.60	.25
❑	61	Deuce McAllister	1.00	.40
❑	62	Joe Horn	.60	.25
❑	63	Jeremy Shockey	1.00	.40
❑	64	Kerry Collins	.60	.25
❑	65	Michael Strahan	.60	.25
❑	66	Tiki Barber	1.00	.40
❑	67	Chad Pennington	1.00	.40
❑	68	Curtis Martin	1.00	.40
❑	69	Santana Moss	.60	.25
❑	70	Jerry Porter	.60	.25
❑	71	Jerry Rice	2.00	.75
❑	72	Tim Brown	1.00	.40
❑	73	Brian Westbrook	.60	.25
❑	74	Correll Buckhalter	.60	.25
❑	75	Donovan McNabb	1.25	.50
❑	76	Hines Ward	1.00	.40
❑	77	Kendrell Bell	.60	.25
❑	78	Plaxico Burress	.60	.25
❑	79	David Boston	.60	.25
❑	80	Drew Brees	1.00	.40
❑	81	LaDainian Tomlinson	1.25	.50
❑	82	Jeff Garcia	1.00	.40
❑	83	Kevan Barlow	.60	.25
❑	84	Terrell Owens	1.00	.40
❑	85	Koren Robinson	.60	.25
❑	86	Matt Hasselbeck	.60	.25
❑	87	Shaun Alexander	1.00	.40
❑	88	Isaac Bruce	.60	.25
❑	89	Marc Bulger	1.00	.40
❑	90	Marshall Faulk	1.00	.40
❑	91	Torry Holt	1.00	.40
❑	92	Brad Johnson	.60	.25
❑	93	Derrick Brooks	.60	.25
❑	94	Keenan McCardell	.40	.15
❑	95	Derrick Mason	.60	.25
❑	96	Eddie George	.60	.25
❑	97	Steve McNair	1.00	.40
❑	98	Jevon Kearse	.60	.25
❑	99	Laveranues Coles	.60	.25
❑	100	Patrick Ramsey	.60	.25
❑	101	Adimchinobe Echemandu RC	6.00	2.50
❑	102	Ahmad Carroll RC	8.00	3.00
❑	103	Antwan Odom RC	8.00	3.00
❑	104	B.J. Johnson RC	6.00	2.50
❑	105	Ben Roethlisberger RC	80.00	50.00
❑	106	Ben Troupe RC	8.00	3.00
❑	107	Ben Watson RC	8.00	3.00
❑	108	Bernard Berrian RC	10.00	4.00
❑	109	Bob Sanders RC	20.00	8.00
❑	110	Brandon Everage RC	6.00	2.50
❑	111	Brandon Miree RC	6.00	2.50
❑	112	Carlos Francis RC	6.00	2.50
❑	113	Cedric Cobbs RC	10.00	4.00
❑	114	Chad Lavalais RC	6.00	2.50
❑	115	Chris Collins RC	6.00	2.50
❑	116	Chris Gamble RC	8.00	3.00
❑	117	Chris Perry RC	12.00	5.00
❑	118	Cody Pickett RC	8.00	3.00
❑	119	Craig Krenzel RC	8.00	3.00
❑	120	D.J. Hackett RC	6.00	2.50
❑	121	D.J. Williams RC	8.00	3.00
❑	122	Darius Watts RC	8.00	3.00
❑	123	Darnell Dockett RC	6.00	2.50
❑	124	DeAngelo Hall RC	10.00	4.00
❑	125	Derek Abney RC	8.00	3.00
❑	126	Derrick Hamilton RC	6.00	2.50
❑	127	Derrick Strait RC	8.00	3.00
❑	128	Devard Darling RC	8.00	3.00
❑	129	Devery Henderson RC	6.00	2.50
❑	130	Dontarrious Thomas RC	8.00	3.00
❑	131	Drew Henson RC	8.00	3.00
❑	132	Dunta Robinson RC	8.00	3.00
❑	133	Dwan Edwards RC	4.00	1.50
❑	134	Eli Manning RC	50.00	25.00
❑	135	Ernest Wilford RC	8.00	3.00
❑	136	Fred Russell RC	8.00	3.00
❑	137	Greg Jones RC	8.00	3.00
❑	138	Igor Olshansky RC	8.00	3.00
❑	139	J.P. Losman RC	15.00	6.00
❑	140	Jared Lorenzen RC	6.00	2.50
❑	141	Jarrett Payton RC	8.00	3.00
❑	142	Jason Babin RC	8.00	3.00
❑	143	Jason Fife RC	6.00	2.50
❑	144	Jeff Smoker RC	8.00	3.00
❑	145	Jeremy LeSueur RC	6.00	2.50
❑	146	Jerricho Cotchery RC	8.00	3.00
❑	147	John Navarre RC	8.00	3.00
❑	148	John Standeford RC	6.00	2.50
❑	149	Johnnie Morant RC	8.00	3.00
❑	150	Jonathan Vilma RC	8.00	3.00
❑	151	Josh Davis RC	6.00	2.50
❑	152	Josh Harris RC	8.00	3.00
❑	153	Julius Jones RC	25.00	10.00
❑	154	Justin Jenkins RC	6.00	2.50
❑	155	Karlos Dansby RC	8.00	3.00
❑	156	Keary Colbert RC	10.00	4.00
❑	157	Keith Smith RC	6.00	2.50
❑	158	Keiwan Ratliff RC	6.00	2.50
❑	159	Kellen Winslow RC	15.00	6.00
❑	160	Kendrick Starling RC	4.00	1.50
❑	161	Kenechi Udeze RC	8.00	3.00
❑	162	Kevin Jones RC	20.00	8.00
❑	163	Larry Fitzgerald RC	30.00	12.50
❑	164	Lee Evans RC	10.00	4.00
❑	165	Luke McCown RC	8.00	3.00
❑	166	Marquise Hill RC	6.00	2.50
❑	167	Matt Schaub RC	25.00	10.00
❑	168	Matt Ware RC	8.00	3.00
❑	169	Matt Mauck RC	8.00	3.00
❑	170	Maurice Mann RC	6.00	2.50
❑	171	Mewelde Moore RC	8.00	3.00
❑	172	Michael Boulware RC	8.00	3.00
❑	173	Michael Clayton RC	15.00	6.00
❑	174	Michael Jenkins RC	8.00	3.00
❑	175	Michael Turner RC	10.00	4.00
❑	176	B.J. Symons RC	8.00	3.00
❑	177	Nathan Vasher RC	10.00	4.00
❑	178	P.K. Sam RC	6.00	2.50
❑	179	Philip Rivers RC	25.00	12.50
❑	180	Quincy Wilson RC	6.00	2.50
❑	181	Ran Carthon RC	6.00	2.50
❑	182	Randy Starks RC	6.00	2.50
❑	183	Rashaun Woods RC	8.00	3.00
❑	184	Reggie Williams RC	10.00	4.00
❑	185	Ricardo Colclough RC	8.00	3.00
❑	186	Robert Kent RC	4.00	1.50
❑	187	Roy Williams RC	25.00	10.00
❑	188	Samie Parker RC	8.00	3.00
❑	189	Scott Rislov RC	8.00	3.00
❑	190	Sean Jones RC	6.00	2.50
❑	191	Sean Taylor RC	8.00	3.00
❑	192	Steven Jackson RC	25.00	10.00
❑	193	Stuart Schweigert RC	8.00	3.00
❑	194	Tatum Bell RC	15.00	6.00
❑	195	Teddy Lehman RC	8.00	3.00
❑	196	Tommie Harris RC	8.00	3.00
❑	197	Troy Fleming RC	6.00	2.50
❑	198	Vince Wilfork RC	8.00	3.00
❑	199	Will Poole RC	8.00	3.00
❑	200	Will Smith RC	8.00	3.00

2005 Donruss Elite

❑ COMP.SET w/o SP's (100) 20.00 7.50
❑ 101-200 PRINT RUN 499 SER.#'d SETS

❑	1	Kurt Warner	.60	.25
❑	2	Larry Fitzgerald	1.00	.40
❑	3	Anquan Boldin	.60	.25
❑	4	Emmitt Smith	2.00	.75
❑	5	Michael Vick	1.50	.60
❑	6	Warrick Dunn	.60	.25
❑	7	Alge Crumpler	.60	.25
❑	8	Jamal Lewis	1.00	.40
❑	9	Kyle Boller	.60	.25
❑	10	Ray Lewis	1.00	.40
❑	11	Drew Bledsoe	1.00	.40
❑	12	Willis McGahee	1.00	.40
❑	13	Travis Henry	.60	.25
❑	14	Eric Moulds	.60	.25
❑	15	Rex Grossman	.60	.25
❑	16	Brian Urlacher	1.00	.40
❑	17	Thomas Jones	.60	.25
❑	18	Carson Palmer	1.00	.40
❑	19	Rudi Johnson	.60	.25
❑	20	Chad Johnson	1.00	.40
❑	21	J.P. Losman	1.00	.40
❑	22	Lee Suggs	.60	.25
❑	23	Antonio Bryant	.50	.20
❑	24	Julius Jones	1.25	.50
❑	25	Roy Williams S	.60	.25
❑	26	Keyshawn Johnson	.60	.25
❑	27	Jake Plummer	.60	.25
❑	28	Tatum Bell	.60	.25
❑	29	Rod Smith	.60	.25
❑	30	Joey Harrington	1.00	.40
❑	31	Kevin Jones	1.00	.40
❑	32	Roy Williams WR	1.00	.40
❑	33	Brett Favre	2.50	1.00
❑	34	Ahman Green	1.00	.40
❑	35	Javon Walker	.60	.25
❑	36	David Carr	1.00	.40
❑	37	Andre Johnson	.60	.25
❑	38	Domanick Davis	.60	.25
❑	39	Peyton Manning	1.50	.60
❑	40	Edgerrin James	1.00	.40
❑	41	Brandon Stokley	.60	.25
❑	42	Reggie Wayne	.60	.25
❑	43	Marvin Harrison	1.00	.40
❑	44	Byron Leftwich	1.00	.40
❑	45	Jimmy Smith	.60	.25
❑	46	Fred Taylor	.60	.25
❑	47	Trent Green	.60	.25
❑	48	Priest Holmes	1.00	.40
❑	49	Tony Gonzalez	.60	.25
❑	50	A.J. Feeley	.60	.25
❑	51	Chris Chambers	.60	.25
❑	52	Daunte Culpepper	1.00	.40
❑	53	Randy Moss	1.00	.40
❑	54	Onterrio Smith	.60	.25
❑	55	Corey Dillon	.60	.25
❑	56	Tom Brady	2.50	1.00
❑	57	David Givens	.60	.25
❑	58	Aaron Brooks	.60	.25
❑	59	Deuce McAllister	1.00	.40
❑	60	Joe Horn	.60	.25
❑	61	Eli Manning	2.00	.75
❑	62	Tiki Barber	1.00	.40
❑	63	Jeremy Shockey	1.00	.40

❑ 64	Chad Pennington	1.00	.40
❑ 65	Curtis Martin	1.00	.40
❑ 66	Santana Moss	.60	.25
❑ 67	Kerry Collins	.60	.25
❑ 68	Jerry Porter	.60	.25
❑ 69	Donovan McNabb	1.25	.50
❑ 70	Terrell Owens	1.00	.40
❑ 71	Brian Westbrook	.60	.25
❑ 72	Ben Roethlisberger	2.50	1.00
❑ 73	Plaxico Burress	.60	.25
❑ 74	Hines Ward	1.00	.40
❑ 75	Jerome Bettis	1.00	.40
❑ 76	Duce Staley	.60	.25
❑ 77	Antonio Gates	1.00	.40
❑ 78	Drew Brees	1.00	.40
❑ 79	LaDainian Tomlinson	1.25	.50
❑ 80	Brandon Lloyd	.50	.20
❑ 81	Kevan Barlow	.60	.25
❑ 82	Matt Hasselbeck	.60	.25
❑ 83	Shaun Alexander	1.25	.50
❑ 84	Darrell Jackson	.60	.25
❑ 85	Jerry Rice	2.00	.75
❑ 86	Marc Bulger	1.00	.40
❑ 87	Marshall Faulk	1.00	.40
❑ 88	Steven Jackson	1.25	.50
❑ 89	Isaac Bruce	.60	.25
❑ 90	Torry Holt	1.00	.40
❑ 91	Michael Clayton	1.00	.40
❑ 92	Brian Griese	.60	.25
❑ 93	Mike Alstott	.60	.25
❑ 94	Steve McNair	1.00	.40
❑ 95	Derrick Mason	.60	.25
❑ 96	Chris Brown	.60	.25
❑ 97	Drew Bennett	.60	.25
❑ 98	Patrick Ramsey	.60	.25
❑ 99	Clinton Portis	1.00	.40
❑ 100	LaVar Arrington	1.00	.40
❑ 101	Aaron Rodgers RC	40.00	15.00
❑ 102	Adam Jones RC	10.00	4.00
❑ 103	Adrian McPherson RC	10.00	4.00
❑ 104	Alex Smith TE ERR RC	20.00	7.50
❑ 105	Alex Smith QB ERR RC	50.00	25.00
❑ 106	Alvin Pearman RC	10.00	4.00
❑ 107	Andrew Walter RC	15.00	6.00
❑ 108	Anthony Davis RC	8.00	3.00
❑ 109	Antrel Rolle RC	10.00	4.00
❑ 110	Anttaj Hawthorne RC	8.00	3.00
❑ 111	Brandon Browner RC	8.00	3.00
❑ 112	Brandon Jacobs RC	12.00	5.00
❑ 113	Braylon Edwards RC	40.00	15.00
❑ 114	Brock Berlin RC	8.00	3.00
❑ 115	Brandon Jones RC	10.00	4.00
❑ 116	Bryant McFadden RC	10.00	4.00
❑ 117	Carlos Rogers RC	12.00	5.00
❑ 118	Cadillac Williams RC	50.00	20.00
❑ 119	Cedric Benson RC	25.00	10.00
❑ 120	Cedric Houston RC	10.00	4.00
❑ 121	Channing Crowder RC	10.00	4.00
❑ 122	Charles Frederick RC	8.00	3.00
❑ 123	Charlie Frye RC	20.00	7.50
❑ 124	Chase Lyman RC	8.00	3.00
❑ 125	Chris Henry RC	10.00	4.00
❑ 126	Chris Rix RC	8.00	3.00
❑ 127	Ciatrick Fason RC	10.00	4.00
❑ 128	Corey Webster RC	10.00	4.00
❑ 129	Courtney Roby RC	10.00	4.00
❑ 130	Craig Bragg RC	8.00	3.00
❑ 131	Craphonso Thorpe RC	8.00	3.00
❑ 132	Damien Nash RC	8.00	3.00
❑ 133	Dan Cody RC	10.00	4.00
❑ 134	Dan Orlovsky RC	12.00	5.00
❑ 135	Dante Ridgeway RC	8.00	3.00
❑ 136	Darian Durant RC	10.00	4.00
❑ 137	Darren Sproles RC	10.00	4.00
❑ 138	Darryl Blackstock RC	8.00	3.00
❑ 139	David Greene RC	10.00	4.00
❑ 140	David Pollack RC	10.00	4.00
❑ 141	DeMarcus Ware RC	15.00	6.00
❑ 142	Derek Anderson RC	10.00	4.00
❑ 143	Derrick Johnson RC	15.00	6.00
❑ 144	Erasmus James RC	10.00	4.00
❑ 145	Eric Shelton RC	10.00	4.00
❑ 146	Ernest Shazor RC	10.00	4.00
❑ 147	Fabian Washington RC	10.00	4.00
❑ 148	Frank Gore UER RC	20.00	8.00
❑ 149	Fred Amey RC	8.00	3.00
❑ 150	Fred Gibson RC	8.00	3.00
❑ 151	Maurice Clarett	10.00	4.00
❑ 152	Gino Guidugli RC	5.00	2.00
❑ 153	Heath Miller RC	30.00	12.50
❑ 154	J.J. Arrington RC	12.00	5.00
❑ 155	J.R. Russell RC	8.00	3.00
❑ 156	Jason Campbell RC	15.00	6.00
❑ 157	Jason White RC	10.00	4.00
❑ 158	Jerome Mathis RC	10.00	4.00
❑ 159	Josh Bullocks RC	10.00	4.00
❑ 160	Josh Davis RC	8.00	3.00
❑ 161	Justin Miller RC	8.00	3.00
❑ 162	Justin Tuck RC	10.00	4.00
❑ 163	Kay-Jay Harris RC	8.00	3.00
❑ 164	Kevin Burnett RC	10.00	4.00
❑ 165	Kyle Orton RC	15.00	6.00
❑ 166	Larry Brackins RC	5.00	2.00
❑ 167	Marcus Spears RC	10.00	4.00
❑ 168	Marion Barber RC	15.00	6.00
❑ 169	Mark Bradley RC	10.00	4.00
❑ 170	Mark Clayton RC	12.00	5.00
❑ 171	Marlin Jackson RC	10.00	4.00
❑ 172	Matt Jones RC	30.00	12.50
❑ 173	Matt Roth RC	10.00	4.00
❑ 174	Mike Patterson RC	10.00	4.00
❑ 175	Mike Williams	30.00	12.50
❑ 176	Airese Currie RC	10.00	4.00
❑ 177	Reggie Brown RC	10.00	4.00
❑ 178	Roddy White RC	10.00	4.00
❑ 179	Ronnie Brown RC	50.00	25.00
❑ 180	Roscoe Parrish RC	10.00	4.00
❑ 181	Roydell Williams RC	10.00	4.00
❑ 182	Ryan Fitzpatrick RC	15.00	6.00
❑ 183	Rasheed Marshall RC	10.00	4.00
❑ 184	Ryan Moats RC	10.00	4.00
❑ 185	Shaun Cody RC	10.00	4.00
❑ 186	Shawne Merriman RC	15.00	6.00
❑ 187	Chad Owens RC	10.00	4.00
❑ 188	Stefan LeFors RC	10.00	4.00
❑ 189	Steve Savoy RC	5.00	2.00
❑ 190	T.A. McLendon RC	5.00	2.00
❑ 191	Tab Perry RC	10.00	4.00
❑ 192	Taylor Stubblefield RC	5.00	2.00
❑ 193	Terrence Murphy RC	10.00	4.00
❑ 194	Thomas Davis RC	10.00	4.00
❑ 195	Timmy Chang RC	8.00	3.00
❑ 196	Travis Johnson RC	8.00	3.00
❑ 197	Troy Williamson RC	25.00	10.00
❑ 198	Vernand Morency RC	10.00	4.00
❑ 199	Vincent Jackson RC	10.00	4.00
❑ 200	Walter Reyes RC	8.00	3.00

2006 Donruss Elite

❑	COMP.SET w/o RC's (100)	20.00	7.50
❑	ROOKIE PRINT RUN 599 SER.#'d SETS		
❑ 1	Anquan Boldin	.60	.25
❑ 2	Kurt Warner	.60	.25
❑ 3	Larry Fitzgerald	1.00	.40
❑ 4	Marcel Shipp	.50	.20
❑ 5	Alge Crumpler	.60	.25
❑ 6	Michael Vick	1.25	.50
❑ 7	Warrick Dunn	.60	.25
❑ 8	Derrick Mason	.50	.20
❑ 9	Jamal Lewis	.60	.25
❑ 10	Kyle Boller	.50	.20
❑ 11	J.P. Losman	.60	.25
❑ 12	Lee Evans	.60	.25
❑ 13	Willis McGahee	1.00	.40
❑ 14	Jake Delhomme	.60	.25
❑ 15	Stephen Davis	.60	.25
❑ 16	Steve Smith	1.00	.40
❑ 17	Cedric Benson	1.00	.40
❑ 18	Kyle Orton	.60	.25
❑ 19	Thomas Jones	.60	.25
❑ 20	Carson Palmer	1.00	.40
❑ 21	Chad Johnson	.60	.25
❑ 22	Rudi Johnson	.60	.25
❑ 23	Braylon Edwards	1.00	.40
❑ 24	Reuben Droughns	.60	.25
❑ 25	Trent Dilfer	.60	.25
❑ 26	Drew Bledsoe	1.00	.40
❑ 27	Julius Jones	1.00	.40
❑ 28	Keyshawn Johnson	.60	.25
❑ 29	Jake Plummer	.60	.25
❑ 30	Rod Smith	.60	.25
❑ 31	Tatum Bell	.60	.25
❑ 32	Joey Harrington	.60	.25
❑ 33	Kevin Jones	1.00	.40
❑ 34	Roy Williams WR	1.00	.40
❑ 35	Aaron Rodgers	1.00	.40
❑ 36	Brett Favre	2.00	.75
❑ 37	Ahman Green	.60	.25
❑ 38	Andre Johnson	.60	.25
❑ 39	David Carr	.60	.25
❑ 40	Domanick Davis	.60	.25
❑ 41	Edgerrin James	1.00	.40
❑ 42	Marvin Harrison	1.00	.40
❑ 43	Peyton Manning	1.50	.60
❑ 44	Byron Leftwich	.60	.25
❑ 45	Fred Taylor	.60	.25
❑ 46	Jimmy Smith	.60	.25
❑ 47	Matt Jones	1.00	.40
❑ 48	Larry Johnson	1.25	.50
❑ 49	Tony Gonzalez	.60	.25
❑ 50	Trent Green	.60	.25
❑ 51	Chris Chambers	.60	.25
❑ 52	Ricky Williams	.60	.25
❑ 53	Ronnie Brown	1.00	.40
❑ 54	Randy McMichael	.50	.20
❑ 55	Daunte Culpepper	1.00	.40
❑ 56	Mewelde Moore	.50	.20
❑ 57	Nate Burleson	.60	.25
❑ 58	Corey Dillon	.60	.25
❑ 59	Deion Branch	.60	.25
❑ 60	Tom Brady	1.50	.60
❑ 61	Aaron Brooks	.60	.25
❑ 62	Deuce McAllister	.60	.25
❑ 63	Donte Stallworth	.60	.25
❑ 64	Eli Manning	1.25	.50
❑ 65	Jeremy Shockey	1.00	.40
❑ 66	Plaxico Burress	.60	.25
❑ 67	Tiki Barber	1.00	.40
❑ 68	Chad Pennington	.60	.25
❑ 69	Curtis Martin	1.00	.40
❑ 70	Laveranues Coles	.60	.25
❑ 71	Kerry Collins	.60	.25
❑ 72	LaMont Jordan	.60	.25
❑ 73	Randy Moss	1.00	.40
❑ 74	Donovan McNabb	1.00	.40
❑ 75	Reggie Brown	.60	.25
❑ 76	Brian Westbrook	.60	.25
❑ 77	Ben Roethlisberger	1.50	.60
❑ 78	Duce Staley	.60	.25
❑ 79	Hines Ward	1.00	.40
❑ 80	Antonio Gates	1.00	.40
❑ 81	Drew Brees	1.00	.40
❑ 82	LaDainian Tomlinson	1.25	.50
❑ 83	Alex Smith QB	1.25	.50
❑ 84	Kevan Barlow	.60	.25
❑ 85	Brandon Lloyd	.60	.25
❑ 86	Darrell Jackson	.60	.25
❑ 87	Matt Hasselbeck	.60	.25
❑ 88	Shaun Alexander	1.00	.40
❑ 89	Marc Bulger	.60	.25
❑ 90	Steven Jackson	1.00	.40
❑ 91	Torry Holt	.60	.25
❑ 92	Cadillac Williams	1.00	.40
❑ 93	Joey Galloway	.60	.25
❑ 94	Michael Clayton	.60	.25
❑ 95	Chris Brown	.60	.25
❑ 96	Drew Bennett	.50	.20
❑ 97	Steve McNair	.60	.25
❑ 98	Clinton Portis	1.00	.40
❑ 99	Mark Brunell	.60	.25
❑ 100	Santana Moss	.60	.25
❑ 101	A.J. Hawk RC	25.00	10.00
❑ 102	Abdul Hodge RC	12.00	5.00
❑ 103	Adam Jennings RC	10.00	4.00
❑ 104	Alan Zemaitis RC	12.00	5.00
❑ 105	Andre Hall RC	10.00	4.00
❑ 106	Anthony Fasano RC	12.00	5.00
❑ 107	Anthony Mix RC	10.00	4.00
❑ 108	Ashton Youboty RC	12.00	5.00
❑ 109	Miles Austin RC	10.00	4.00

❑	110 Barrick Nealy RC	10.00	4.00
❑	111 Ben Obomanu RC	10.00	4.00
❑	112 Bobby Carpenter RC	12.00	5.00
❑	113 Brad Smith RC	12.00	5.00
❑	114 Brandon Kirsch RC	12.00	5.00
❑	115 Brandon Marshall RC	12.00	5.00
❑	116 Brandon Williams RC	12.00	5.00
❑	117 Brett Elliott RC	12.00	5.00
❑	118 Brian Calhoun RC	12.00	5.00
❑	119 Brodie Croyle RC	25.00	10.00
❑	120 Brodrick Bunkley RC	12.00	5.00
❑	121 Bruce Gradkowski RC	20.00	8.00
❑	122 Cedric Griffin RC	10.00	4.00
❑	123 Cedric Humes RC	12.00	5.00
❑	124 Chad Greenway RC	12.00	5.00
❑	125 Chad Jackson RC	20.00	8.00
❑	126 Charlie Whitehurst RC	15.00	6.00
❑	127 Cory Rodgers RC	12.00	5.00
❑	128 D.J. Shockley RC	12.00	5.00
❑	129 Darnell Bing RC	12.00	5.00
❑	130 Darrell Hackney RC	10.00	4.00
❑	131 David Thomas RC	12.00	5.00
❑	132 D'Brickashaw Ferguson RC	12.00	5.00
❑	133 DeAngelo Williams RC	30.00	12.00
❑	134 De'Arrius Howard RC	12.00	5.00
❑	135 Dee Webb RC	10.00	4.00
❑	136 Delanie Walker RC	10.00	4.00
❑	137 DeMeco Ryans RC	15.00	6.00
❑	138 Demetrius Williams RC	15.00	6.00
❑	139 Derek Hagan RC	12.00	5.00
❑	140 Derrick Ross RC	10.00	4.00
❑	141 Devin Aromashodu RC	10.00	4.00
❑	142 Devin Hester RC	25.00	10.00
❑	143 Dominique Byrd RC	10.00	4.00
❑	144 Donte Whitner RC	12.00	5.00
❑	145 DonTrell Moore RC	10.00	4.00
❑	146 D'Qwell Jackson RC	10.00	4.00
❑	147 Drew Olson RC	10.00	4.00
❑	148 Eric Winston RC	6.00	2.50
❑	149 Erik Meyer RC	10.00	4.00
❑	150 Ernie Sims RC	15.00	6.00
❑	151 Gabe Watson RC	10.00	4.00
❑	152 Gerald Riggs RC	12.00	5.00
❑	153 Ryan Gilbert RC	10.00	4.00
❑	154 Greg Jennings RC	20.00	8.00
❑	155 Greg Lee RC	10.00	4.00
❑	156 Haloti Ngata RC	12.00	5.00
❑	157 Hank Baskett RC	12.00	5.00
❑	158 Ingle Martin RC	12.00	5.00
❑	159 Jason Allen RC	12.00	5.00
❑	160 Jason Avant RC	12.00	5.00
❑	161 Jason Carter RC	10.00	4.00
❑	162 Jay Cutler RC	50.00	20.00
❑	163 Jeff King RC	10.00	4.00
❑	164 Jeff Webb RC	10.00	4.00
❑	165 Jeremy Bloom RC	10.00	4.00
❑	166 Jerious Norwood RC	20.00	8.00
❑	167 Jerome Harrison RC	12.00	5.00
❑	168 Jimmy Williams RC	12.00	5.00
❑	169 Joe Klopfenstein RC	10.00	4.00
❑	170 Jon Alston RC	12.00	5.00
❑	171 Johnathan Joseph RC	10.00	4.00
❑	172 Jonathan Orr RC	10.00	4.00
❑	173 Joseph Addai RC	40.00	15.00
❑	174 Kai Parham RC	12.00	5.00
❑	175 Kamerion Wimbley RC	12.00	5.00
❑	176 Kellen Clemens RC	15.00	6.00
❑	177 Kelly Jennings RC	12.00	5.00
❑	178 Kent Smith RC	12.00	5.00
❑	179 Ko Simpson RC	10.00	4.00
❑	180 Laurence Maroney RC	30.00	12.00
❑	181 Lawrence Vickers RC	10.00	4.00
❑	182 LenDale White RC	25.00	10.00
❑	183 Leon Washington RC	20.00	8.00
❑	184 Leonard Pope RC	12.00	5.00
❑	185 Manny Lawson RC	12.00	5.00
❑	186 Marcedes Lewis RC	12.00	5.00
❑	187 Marcus Vick RC	10.00	4.00
❑	188 Mario Williams RC	20.00	8.00
❑	189 Marques Colston RC	50.00	20.00
❑	190 Martin Nance RC	10.00	4.00
❑	191 Mathias Kiwanuka RC	15.00	6.00
❑	192 Matt Leinart RC	50.00	20.00
❑	193 Maurice Drew RC	30.00	12.00
❑	194 Maurice Stovall RC	12.00	5.00
❑	195 Michael Huff RC	15.00	6.00
❑	196 Michael Robinson RC	20.00	8.00
❑	197 Mike Bell RC	20.00	8.00
❑	198 Mike Hass RC	12.00	5.00
❑	199 Omar Jacobs RC	10.00	4.00
❑	200 Owen Daniels RC	12.00	5.00
❑	201 P.J. Daniels RC	10.00	4.00
❑	202 Paul Pinegar RC	10.00	4.00
❑	203 Quinton Ganther RC	10.00	4.00
❑	204 Reggie Bush RC	80.00	30.00
❑	205 Reggie McNeal RC	10.00	4.00
❑	206 Rodrique Wright RC	6.00	2.50
❑	207 Santonio Holmes RC	25.00	10.00
❑	208 Sinorice Moss RC	15.00	6.00
❑	209 Skyler Green RC	12.00	5.00
❑	210 Tamba Hali RC	12.00	5.00
❑	211 Tarvaris Jackson RC	20.00	8.00
❑	212 Taurean Henderson RC	12.00	5.00
❑	213 Terrence Whitehead RC	10.00	4.00
❑	214 Tim Day RC	10.00	4.00
❑	215 Todd Watkins RC	10.00	4.00
❑	216 Tony Scheffler RC	12.00	5.00
❑	217 Travis Lulay RC	10.00	4.00
❑	218 Travis Wilson RC	12.00	5.00
❑	219 Tye Hill RC	12.00	5.00
❑	220 Vernon Davis RC	25.00	10.00
❑	221 Vince Young RC	50.00	20.00
❑	222 Wali Lundy RC	12.00	5.00
❑	223 Wendell Mathis RC	10.00	4.00
❑	224 Willie Reid RC	12.00	5.00
❑	225 Winston Justice RC	12.00	5.00

2005 Donruss Gridiron Gear

❑	COMP.SET w/o RC's (100)	25.00	10.00
❑	101-150 PRINT RUN 399 SER.#'d SETS		
❑	1 Aaron Brooks	.60	.25
❑	2 Ahman Green	1.00	.40
❑	3 Alge Crumpler	.60	.25
❑	4 Amani Toomer	.60	.25
❑	5 Andre Johnson	.60	.25
❑	6 Anquan Boldin	.60	.25
❑	7 Antonio Gates	1.00	.40
❑	8 Antwaan Randle El	.60	.25
❑	9 Ashley Lelie	.60	.25
❑	10 Barry Sanders	4.00	1.50
❑	11 Ben Roethlisberger	2.50	1.00
❑	12 Bob Griese	2.50	1.00
❑	13 Brandon Lloyd	.60	.25
❑	14 Brett Favre	2.50	1.00
❑	15 Brian Urlacher	1.00	.40
❑	16 Brian Westbrook	.60	.25
❑	17 Byron Leftwich	1.00	.40
❑	18 Carson Palmer	1.00	.40
❑	19 Chad Johnson	.60	.25
❑	20 Chad Pennington	1.00	.40
❑	21 Champ Bailey	.60	.25
❑	22 Chris Brown	.60	.25
❑	23 Chris Chambers	.60	.25
❑	24 Clinton Portis	1.00	.40
❑	25 Corey Dillon	.60	.25
❑	26 Curtis Martin	1.00	.40
❑	27 Daunte Culpepper	1.00	.40
❑	28 David Carr	1.00	.40
❑	29 Deion Sanders	1.25	.50
❑	30 Derrick Brooks	.60	.25
❑	31 Deuce McAllister	1.00	.40
❑	32 Domanick Davis	.60	.25
❑	33 Don Maynard	.75	.30
❑	34 Donovan McNabb	1.25	.50
❑	35 Drew Bledsoe	1.00	.40
❑	36 Drew Brees	1.00	.40
❑	37 Edgerrin James	1.00	.40
❑	38 Eli Manning	2.00	.75
❑	39 Eric Moulds	.60	.25
❑	40 Fred Taylor	.60	.25
❑	41 Hines Ward	1.00	.40
❑	42 Ickey Woods	.60	.25
❑	43 Isaac Bruce	.60	.25
❑	44 J.P. Losman	1.00	.40
❑	45 Jake Delhomme	1.00	.40
❑	46 Jake Plummer	.60	.25
❑	47 Jamal Lewis	.60	.25
❑	48 Javon Walker	.60	.25
❑	49 Jeremy Shockey	1.00	.40
❑	50 Jerome Bettis	1.00	.40
❑	51 Jerry Porter	.60	.25
❑	52 Jevon Kearse	.60	.25
❑	53 Jimmy Smith	.60	.25
❑	54 Joe Namath	1.25	.50
❑	55 Joey Harrington	1.00	.40
❑	56 Josh McCown	.60	.25
❑	57 Josh Reed	.50	.20
❑	58 Julius Jones	1.25	.50
❑	59 Julius Peppers	.60	.25
❑	60 Keary Colbert	.60	.25
❑	61 Kerry Collins	.60	.25
❑	62 Kevin Jones	1.25	.50
❑	63 Kyle Boller	.60	.25
❑	64 LaDainian Tomlinson	1.25	.50
❑	65 LaMont Jordan	.60	.25
❑	66 Larry Fitzgerald	1.00	.40
❑	67 Lee Evans	.60	.25
❑	68 Marc Bulger	1.00	.40
❑	69 Marvin Harrison	1.00	.40
❑	70 Matt Hasselbeck	.60	.25
❑	71 Michael Clayton	1.00	.40
❑	72 Michael Vick	1.50	.60
❑	73 Mike Alstott	.60	.25
❑	74 Muhsin Muhammad	.60	.25
❑	75 Nate Burleson	.60	.25
❑	76 Peyton Manning	1.50	.60
❑	77 Plaxico Burress	.60	.25
❑	78 Priest Holmes	1.00	.40
❑	79 Randy Moss	1.00	.40
❑	80 Ray Lewis	1.00	.40
❑	81 Reggie Wayne	.60	.25
❑	82 Rex Grossman	1.00	.40
❑	83 Rod Smith	.60	.25
❑	84 Roy Williams S	.60	.25
❑	85 Roy Williams WR	1.00	.40
❑	86 Rudi Johnson	.60	.25
❑	87 Shaun Alexander	1.00	.40
❑	88 Sonny Jurgensen	.75	.30
❑	89 Stephen Davis	.60	.25
❑	90 Steve McNair	.60	.25
❑	91 Steve Smith	1.00	.40
❑	92 Steven Jackson	1.25	.50
❑	93 Terrell Owens	1.00	.40
❑	94 Tiki Barber	1.00	.40
❑	95 Todd Heap	.60	.25
❑	96 Tom Brady	2.00	.75
❑	97 Tony Gonzalez	.60	.25
❑	98 Torry Holt	.60	.25
❑	99 Trent Green	.60	.25
❑	100 Willis McGahee	1.00	.40
❑	101 Alex Smith QB RC	15.00	6.00
❑	102 Ronnie Brown RC	15.00	6.00
❑	103 Braylon Edwards RC	12.00	5.00
❑	104 Cedric Benson RC	8.00	3.00
❑	105 Cadillac Williams RC	20.00	8.00
❑	106 Adam Jones RC	4.00	1.50
❑	107 Troy Williamson RC	8.00	3.00
❑	108 Mike Williams	8.00	3.00
❑	109 Derrick Johnson RC	4.00	1.50
❑	110 Demarcus Ware RC	6.00	2.50
❑	111 Matt Jones RC	10.00	4.00
❑	112 Mark Clayton RC	5.00	2.00
❑	113 Aaron Rodgers RC	12.00	5.00
❑	114 Jason Campbell RC	6.00	2.50
❑	115 Roddy White RC	4.00	1.50
❑	116 Heath Miller RC	10.00	4.00
❑	117 Reggie Brown RC	4.00	1.50
❑	118 Mark Bradley RC	4.00	1.50
❑	119 J.J. Arrington RC	5.00	2.00
❑	120 Odell Thurman RC	4.00	1.50
❑	121 Roscoe Parrish RC	4.00	1.50
❑	122 Terrence Murphy RC	4.00	1.50
❑	123 Vincent Jackson RC	4.00	1.50
❑	124 Frank Gore RC	8.00	3.00
❑	125 Charlie Frye RC	8.00	3.00
❑	126 Courtney Roby RC	4.00	1.50
❑	127 Andrew Walter RC	6.00	2.50
❑	128 Vernand Morency RC	4.00	1.50

❑ 129 Ryan Moats RC 4.00 1.50
❑ 130 Chris Henry RC 4.00 1.50
❑ 131 David Greene RC 4.00 1.50
❑ 132 Brandon Jones RC 4.00 1.50
❑ 133 Kyle Orton RC 8.00 3.00
❑ 134 Marion Barber RC 6.00 2.50
❑ 135 Brandon Jacobs RC 5.00 2.00
❑ 136 Ciatrick Fason RC 4.00 1.50
❑ 137 Lofa Tatupu RC 8.00 3.00
❑ 138 Stefan LeFors RC 4.00 1.50
❑ 139 Alvin Pearman RC 4.00 1.50
❑ 140 Darren Sproles RC 4.00 1.50
❑ 141 Samkon Gado RC 40.00 20.00
❑ 142 Antrel Rolle RC 4.00 1.50
❑ 143 Maurice Clarett 4.00 1.50
❑ 144 Adrian McPherson RC 4.00 1.50
❑ 145 Eric Shelton RC 4.00 1.50
❑ 146 Bo Scaife RC 3.00 1.25
❑ 147 Carlos Rogers RC 5.00 2.00
❑ 148 Otis Amey RC 3.00 1.25
❑ 149 Alex Smith TE RC 4.00 1.50
❑ 150 Jerome Mathis RC 4.00 1.50

2006 Donruss Gridiron Gear

❑ 1 Edgerrin James 1.00 .40
❑ 2 Kurt Warner .60 .25
❑ 3 Larry Fitzgerald 1.00 .40
❑ 4 Alge Crumpler .60 .25
❑ 5 Michael Vick 1.25 .50
❑ 6 Warrick Dunn .60 .25
❑ 7 Jamal Lewis .60 .25
❑ 8 Mike Anderson .60 .25
❑ 9 Neil Rackers .50 .20
❑ 10 Derrick Mason .50 .20
❑ 11 J.P. Losman .60 .25
❑ 12 Lee Evans .60 .25
❑ 13 Willis McGahee 1.00 .40
❑ 14 DeShaun Foster .60 .25
❑ 15 Jake Delhomme .60 .25
❑ 16 Josh Brown .50 .20
❑ 17 Steve Smith 1.00 .40
❑ 18 Cedric Benson 1.00 .40
❑ 19 Rex Grossman 1.00 .40
❑ 20 Shayne Graham .50 .20
❑ 21 Carson Palmer 1.00 .40
❑ 22 Chad Johnson .60 .25
❑ 23 Rudi Johnson .60 .25
❑ 24 T.J. Houshmandzadeh .60 .25
❑ 25 Charlie Frye .60 .25
❑ 26 Lance Briggs .60 .25
❑ 27 Reuben Droughns .60 .25
❑ 28 Drew Bledsoe 1.00 .40
❑ 29 Julius Jones 1.00 .40
❑ 30 Terrell Owens 1.00 .40
❑ 31 Terry Glenn .60 .25
❑ 32 Jake Plummer .60 .25
❑ 33 Rod Smith .60 .25
❑ 34 Tatum Bell .60 .25
❑ 35 Robert Mathis .50 .20
❑ 36 Kevin Jones 1.00 .40
❑ 37 Roy Williams WR 1.00 .40
❑ 38 Ahman Green .60 .25
❑ 39 Brett Favre 2.00 .75
❑ 40 Scottie Vines .50 .20
❑ 41 Samkon Gado 1.00 .40
❑ 42 Andre Johnson .60 .25
❑ 43 David Carr .60 .25
❑ 44 Domanick Davis .60 .25
❑ 45 Marvin Harrison 1.00 .40
❑ 46 Peyton Manning 1.50 .60
❑ 47 Reggie Wayne .60 .25
❑ 48 Byron Leftwich .60 .25
❑ 49 Fred Taylor .60 .25
❑ 50 Jimmy Smith .60 .25
❑ 51 Matt Jones 1.00 .40
❑ 52 Larry Johnson 1.25 .50
❑ 53 Tony Gonzalez .60 .25
❑ 54 Trent Green .60 .25
❑ 55 Chris Chambers .60 .25
❑ 56 Daunte Culpepper 1.00 .40
❑ 57 Ronnie Brown 1.00 .40
❑ 58 Robert Pollard .50 .20
❑ 59 Mewelde Moore .50 .20
❑ 60 Chester Taylor .60 .25
❑ 61 Corey Dillon .60 .25
❑ 62 Deion Branch .60 .25
❑ 63 Tom Brady 1.50 .60
❑ 64 Deuce McAllister .60 .25
❑ 65 Drew Brees 1.00 .40
❑ 66 Donte Stallworth .60 .25
❑ 67 Eli Manning 1.25 .50
❑ 68 Jeremy Shockey 1.00 .40
❑ 69 Plaxico Burress .60 .25
❑ 70 Tiki Barber 1.00 .40
❑ 71 Chad Pennington .60 .25
❑ 72 Curtis Martin 1.00 .40
❑ 73 Laveranues Coles .60 .25
❑ 74 LaMont Jordan .60 .25
❑ 75 Randy Moss 1.00 .40
❑ 76 Aaron Brooks .60 .25
❑ 77 Brian Westbrook .60 .25
❑ 78 Donovan McNabb 1.00 .40
❑ 79 Jabar Gaffney .50 .20
❑ 80 Ben Roethlisberger 1.50 .60
❑ 81 Hines Ward 1.00 .40
❑ 82 Willie Parker 1.25 .50
❑ 83 Antonio Gates 1.00 .40
❑ 84 LaDainian Tomlinson 1.25 .50
❑ 85 Philip Rivers 1.00 .40
❑ 86 Alex Smith QB 1.25 .50
❑ 87 Edell Shepherd .50 .20
❑ 88 Kevan Barlow .60 .25
❑ 89 Darrell Jackson .60 .25
❑ 90 Matt Hasselbeck .60 .25
❑ 91 Shaun Alexander 1.00 .40
❑ 92 Marc Bulger .60 .25
❑ 93 Torry Holt .60 .25
❑ 94 Steven Jackson 1.00 .40
❑ 95 Chris Simms .60 .25
❑ 96 Cadillac Williams 1.00 .40
❑ 97 Joey Galloway .60 .25
❑ 98 Chris Brown .60 .25
❑ 99 Clinton Portis 1.00 .40
❑ 100 Santana Moss .60 .25
❑ 101 A.J. Nicholson RC 2.50 1.00
❑ 102 Abdul Hodge RC 5.00 2.00
❑ 103 Adam Jennings RC 4.00 1.50
❑ 104 Andre Hall RC 4.00 1.50
❑ 105 Anthony Fasano RC 5.00 2.00
❑ 106 Anthony Mix RC 4.00 1.50
❑ 107 Anthony Smith RC 6.00 2.50
❑ 108 Antonio Cromartie RC 5.00 2.00
❑ 109 Ashton Youboty RC 5.00 2.00
❑ 110 Ben Obomanu RC 4.00 1.50
❑ 111 Bennie Brazell RC 4.00 1.50
❑ 112 Bernard Pollard RC 4.00 1.50
❑ 113 Bobby Carpenter RC 5.00 2.00
❑ 114 Brad Smith RC 5.00 2.00
❑ 115 Brodie Croyle RC 8.00 3.00
❑ 116 Brodrick Bunkley RC 5.00 2.00
❑ 117 Bruce Gradkowski RC 8.00 3.00
❑ 118 Calvin Lowry RC 5.00 2.00
❑ 119 Cedric Griffin RC 4.00 1.50
❑ 120 Cedric Humes RC 5.00 2.00
❑ 121 Chad Greenway RC 5.00 2.00
❑ 122 Claude Wroten RC 2.50 1.00
❑ 123 Cory Rodgers RC 5.00 2.00
❑ 124 D.J. Shockley RC 5.00 2.00
❑ 125 Danieal Manning RC 5.00 2.00
❑ 126 Daniel Bullocks RC 5.00 2.00
❑ 127 Darryl Tapp RC 4.00 1.50
❑ 128 David Anderson RC 4.00 1.50
❑ 129 David Kirtman RC 4.00 1.50
❑ 130 David Pittman RC 4.00 1.50
❑ 131 David Thomas RC 5.00 2.00
❑ 132 Dawan Landry RC 8.00 3.00
❑ 133 D'Brickashaw Ferguson RC 5.00 2.00
❑ 134 Delanie Walker RC 4.00 1.50
❑ 135 DeMario Minter RC 4.00 1.50
❑ 136 DeMeco Ryans RC 6.00 2.50
❑ 137 Derrick Ross RC 4.00 1.50
❑ 138 Devin Aromashodu RC 4.00 1.50
❑ 139 Devin Hester RC 10.00 4.00
❑ 140 Domenik Hixon RC 4.00 1.50
❑ 141 Dominique Byrd RC 4.00 1.50
❑ 142 Donte Whitner RC 5.00 2.00
❑ 143 D'Qwell Jackson RC 4.00 1.50
❑ 144 Dusty Dvoracek RC 5.00 2.00
❑ 145 Erik Meyer RC 4.00 1.50
❑ 146 Ernie Sims RC 6.00 2.50
❑ 147 Ethan Kilmer RC 5.00 2.00
❑ 148 Gabe Watson RC 4.00 1.50
❑ 149 Garrett Mills RC 5.00 2.00
❑ 150 Greg Blue RC 4.00 1.50
❑ 151 Greg Jennings RC 10.00 4.00
❑ 152 Greg Lee RC 4.00 1.50
❑ 153 Haloti Ngata RC 5.00 2.00
❑ 154 Ingle Martin RC 5.00 2.00
❑ 155 Jai Lewis RC 4.00 1.50
❑ 156 Jason Allen RC 5.00 2.00
❑ 157 Jay Cutler RC 20.00 8.00
❑ 158 Jeffrey Webb RC 4.00 1.50
❑ 159 Jeremy Bloom RC 4.00 1.50
❑ 160 Jerome Harrison RC 5.00 2.00
❑ 161 Jimmy Williams RC 5.00 2.00
❑ 162 John David Washington RC 4.00 1.50
❑ 163 John McCargo RC 4.00 1.50
❑ 164 Johnathan Joseph RC 4.00 1.50
❑ 165 Jon Alston RC 5.00 2.00
❑ 166 Jonathan Orr RC 4.00 1.50
❑ 167 Joseph Addai RC 15.00 6.00
❑ 168 Kamerion Wimbley RC 5.00 2.00
❑ 169 Kelly Jennings RC 5.00 2.00
❑ 170 Ko Simpson RC 4.00 1.50
❑ 171 Leonard Pope RC 5.00 2.00
❑ 172 Manny Lawson RC 5.00 2.00
❑ 173 Marcus Maxey RC 4.00 1.50
❑ 174 Marcus Vick RC 4.00 1.50
❑ 175 Marques Hagans RC 4.00 1.50
❑ 176 Martin Nance RC 4.00 1.50
❑ 177 Mathias Kiwanuka RC 6.00 2.50
❑ 178 Mike Bell RC 8.00 3.00
❑ 179 Mike Hass RC 5.00 2.00
❑ 180 Nate Salley RC 4.00 1.50
❑ 181 Owen Daniels RC 5.00 2.00
❑ 182 P.J. Daniels RC 4.00 1.50
❑ 183 Pat Watkins RC 5.00 2.00
❑ 184 Paul Pinegar RC 4.00 1.50
❑ 185 Quinton Ganther RC 4.00 1.50
❑ 186 Reggie McNeal RC 4.00 1.50
❑ 187 Richard Marshall RC 4.00 1.50
❑ 188 Rocky McIntosh RC 5.00 2.00
❑ 189 Roman Harper RC 4.00 1.50
❑ 190 Skyler Green RC 5.00 2.00
❑ 191 Tamba Hali RC 5.00 2.00
❑ 192 Thomas Howard RC 5.00 2.00
❑ 193 Tim Jennings RC 4.00 1.50
❑ 194 Todd Watkins RC 4.00 1.50
❑ 195 Tony Scheffler RC 5.00 2.00
❑ 196 Tye Hill RC 5.00 2.00
❑ 197 Wali Lundy RC 5.00 2.00
❑ 198 Wendell Mathis RC 4.00 1.50
❑ 199 Will Blackmon RC 4.00 1.50
❑ 200 Willie Reid RC 5.00 2.00
❑ 201 Brian Calhoun JSY RC 8.00 3.00
❑ 202 Joe Klopfenstein JSY RC 8.00 3.00
❑ 203 Travis Wilson JSY RC 8.00 3.00
❑ 204 Charlie Whitehurst JSY RC 10.00 4.00
❑ 205 DeAngelo Williams JSY RC 20.00 8.00
❑ 206 Maurice Stovall JSY RC 8.00 3.00
❑ 207 A.J. Hawk JSY RC 20.00 8.00
❑ 208 Kellen Clemens JSY RC 10.00 4.00
❑ 209 Leon Washington JSY RC 10.00 4.00
❑ 210 Sinorice Moss JSY RC 10.00 4.00
❑ 211 Demetrius Williams JSY RC 10.00 4.00
❑ 212 Jerious Norwood JSY RC 10.00 4.00
❑ 213 Santonio Holmes JSY RC 12.00 5.00
❑ 214 Omar Jacobs JSY RC 8.00 3.00
❑ 215 Brandon Marshall JSY RC 8.00 3.00
❑ 216 Jason Avant JSY RC 8.00 3.00
❑ 217 Derek Hagan JSY RC 8.00 3.00
❑ 218 Brandon Williams JSY RC 8.00 3.00
❑ 219 Vernon Davis JSY RC 12.00 5.00
❑ 220 Michael Robinson JSY RC 10.00 4.00
❑ 221 Matt Leinart JSY RC 25.00 10.00
❑ 222 Reggie Bush JSY RC 50.00 20.00
❑ 223 LenDale White JSY RC 12.00 5.00
❑ 224 Vince Young JSY RC 30.00 12.00

❑ 225 Maurice Drew JSY RC	15.00	6.00
❑ 226 Marcedes Lewis JSY RC	8.00	3.00
❑ 227 Mario Williams JSY RC	10.00	4.00
❑ 228 Michael Huff JSY RC	10.00	4.00
❑ 229 Tarvaris Jackson JSY RC	10.00	4.00
❑ 230 Laurence Maroney JSY RC	20.00	8.00
❑ 231 Chad Jackson JSY RC	10.00	4.00

1997 Donruss Preferred

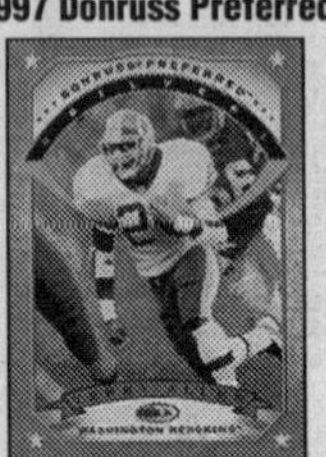

❑ COMPLETE SET (150)	300.00	150.00
❑ COMP.BRONZE SET (80)	25.00	10.00
❑ 1 Emmitt Smith P	20.00	7.50
❑ 2 Steve Young G	8.00	3.00
❑ 3 Cris Carter S	6.00	2.50
❑ 4 Tim Biakabutuka B	.60	.25
❑ 5 Brett Favre P	25.00	10.00
❑ 6 Troy Aikman G	12.00	5.00
❑ 7 Eddie Kennison S	4.00	1.50
❑ 8 Ben Coates B	.60	.25
❑ 9 Dan Marino P	25.00	10.00
❑ 10 Deion Sanders G	6.00	2.50
❑ 11 Curtis Conway S	4.00	1.50
❑ 12 Jeff George B	.60	.25
❑ 13 Barry Sanders P	20.00	7.50
❑ 14 Kerry Collins G	6.00	2.50
❑ 15 Marvin Harrison S	6.00	2.50
❑ 16 Bobby Engram B	.60	.25
❑ 17 Jerry Rice P	12.00	5.00
❑ 18 Kordell Stewart G	6.00	2.50
❑ 19 Tony Banks S	6.00	2.50
❑ 20 Jim Harbaugh B	.60	.25
❑ 21 Mark Brunell P	8.00	3.00
❑ 22 Steve McNair G	8.00	3.00
❑ 23 Terrell Owens S	8.00	3.00
❑ 24 Raymont Harris B	.40	.15
❑ 25 Curtis Martin P	8.00	3.00
❑ 26 Karim Abdul-Jabbar G	6.00	2.50
❑ 27 Joey Galloway S	4.00	1.50
❑ 28 Bobby Hoying B	.60	.25
❑ 29 Terrell Davis P	8.00	3.00
❑ 30 Terry Glenn G	4.00	1.50
❑ 31 Antonio Freeman S	6.00	2.50
❑ 32 Brad Johnson B	1.00	.40
❑ 33 Drew Bledsoe P	8.00	3.00
❑ 34 John Elway G	25.00	10.00
❑ 35 Herman Moore G	4.00	1.50
❑ 36 Robert Brooks S	4.00	1.50
❑ 37 Rod Smith B	1.00	.40
❑ 38 Eddie George P	6.00	2.50
❑ 39 Keyshawn Johnson G	6.00	2.50
❑ 40 Greg Hill S	2.50	1.00
❑ 41 Scott Mitchell B	.60	.25
❑ 42 Muhsin Muhammad B	.60	.25
❑ 43 Isaac Bruce G	6.00	2.50
❑ 44 Jeff Blake S	4.00	1.50
❑ 45 Neil O'Donnell B	.60	.25
❑ 46 Jimmy Smith B	.60	.25
❑ 47 Jerome Bettis G	6.00	2.50
❑ 48 Terry Allen S	4.00	1.50
❑ 49 Andre Reed B	.60	.25
❑ 50 Frank Sanders B	.60	.25
❑ 51 Tim Brown G	6.00	2.50
❑ 52 Thurman Thomas S	4.00	1.50
❑ 53 Heath Shuler B	.40	.15
❑ 54 Vinny Testaverde B	.60	.25
❑ 55 Marcus Allen S	6.00	2.50
❑ 56 Napoleon Kaufman B	1.00	.40
❑ 57 Derrick Alexander WR B	.60	.25
❑ 58 Carl Pickens G	4.00	1.50
❑ 59 Marshall Faulk S	8.00	3.00
❑ 60 Mike Alstott B	1.00	.40
❑ 61 Jamal Anderson B	1.00	.40
❑ 62 Ricky Watters G	4.00	1.50
❑ 63 Dorsey Levens S	6.00	2.50
❑ 64 Todd Collins B	.40	.15
❑ 65 Trent Dilfer B	1.00	.40
❑ 66 Natrone Means S	4.00	1.50
❑ 67 Gus Frerotte B	.40	.15
❑ 68 Irving Fryar B	.60	.25
❑ 69 Adrian Murrell S	4.00	1.50
❑ 70 Rodney Hampton B	.60	.25
❑ 71 Garrison Hearst B	.60	.25
❑ 72 Reggie White S	6.00	2.50
❑ 73 Anthony Johnson B	.40	.15
❑ 74 Tony Martin B	.60	.25
❑ 75 Chris Sanders S	2.50	1.00
❑ 76 O.J. McDuffie B	.60	.25
❑ 77 Leeland McElroy B	.40	.15
❑ 78 Ki-Jana Carter S	4.00	1.50
❑ 79 Anthony Miller B	.40	.15
❑ 80 Johnnie Morton B	.60	.25
❑ 81 Robert Smith S	.60	.25
❑ 82 Brett Perriman B	.40	.15
❑ 83 Errict Rhett B	.40	.15
❑ 84 Michael Irvin S	4.00	1.50
❑ 85 Darnay Scott B	.60	.25
❑ 86 Shannon Sharpe B	.60	.25
❑ 87 Lawrence Phillips S	4.00	1.50
❑ 88 Bruce Smith B	.60	.25
❑ 89 James O.Stewart B	.60	.25
❑ 90 J.J. Stokes B	.60	.25
❑ 91 Chris Warren B	.60	.25
❑ 92 Daryl Johnston B	.60	.25
❑ 93 Andre Rison B	.60	.25
❑ 94 Rashaan Salaam B	.40	.15
❑ 95 Amani Toomer B	.60	.25
❑ 96 Warrick Dunn RC G	20.00	7.50
❑ 97 Tiki Barber RC S	15.00	6.00
❑ 98 Peter Boulware RC B	1.00	.40
❑ 99 Ike Hilliard RC G	12.00	5.00
❑ 100 Antowain Smith RC S	10.00	4.00
❑ 101 Yatil Green RC S	4.00	1.50
❑ 102 Tony Gonzalez RC B	6.00	2.50
❑ 103 Reidel Anthony RC G	6.00	2.50
❑ 104 Troy Davis RC S	4.00	1.50
❑ 105 Rae Carruth RC S	2.50	1.00
❑ 106 David LaFleur RC B	.40	.15
❑ 107 Jim Druckenmiller RC G	4.00	1.50
❑ 108 Joey Kent RC S	6.00	2.50
❑ 109 Byron Hanspard RC S	4.00	1.50
❑ 110 Darrell Russell RC B	.40	.15
❑ 111 Danny Wuerffel RC S	6.00	2.50
❑ 112 Jake Plummer RC S	12.00	5.00
❑ 113 Jay Graham RC B	.60	.25
❑ 114 Corey Dillon RC S	15.00	6.00
❑ 115 Orlando Pace RC B	1.00	.40
❑ 116 Pat Barnes RC S	4.00	1.50
❑ 117 Shawn Springs RC B	.60	.25
❑ 118 Troy Aikman NT B	2.00	.75
❑ 119 Drew Bledsoe NT B	1.25	.50
❑ 120 Mark Brunell NT B	1.25	.50
❑ 121 Kerry Collins NT B	1.00	.40
❑ 122 Terrell Davis NT B	1.25	.50
❑ 123 Jerome Bettis NT B	1.00	.40
❑ 124 Brett Favre NT B	4.00	2.00
❑ 125 Eddie George NT B	1.00	.40
❑ 126 Terry Glenn NT B	1.00	.40
❑ 127 Karim Abdul-Jabbar NT B	.60	.25
❑ 128 Keyshawn Johnson NT B	1.00	.40
❑ 129 Dan Marino NT B	4.00	2.00
❑ 130 Curtis Martin NT B	1.25	.50
❑ 131 Natrone Means NT B	.60	.25
❑ 132 Herman Moore NT S	4.00	1.50
❑ 133 Jerry Rice NT B	2.00	.75
❑ 134 Barry Sanders NT B	3.00	1.25
❑ 135 Deion Sanders NT B	1.00	.40
❑ 136 Emmitt Smith NT B	3.00	1.50
❑ 137 Kordell Stewart NT B	1.00	.40
❑ 138 Steve Young NT B	1.25	.50
❑ 139 Carl Pickens NT S	4.00	1.50
❑ 140 Isaac Bruce NT S	6.00	2.50
❑ 141 Steve McNair NT S	5.00	2.00
❑ 142 John Elway NT S	10.00	5.00
❑ 143 Cris Carter NT B	.60	.25
❑ 144 Tim Brown NT B	.60	.25
❑ 145 Ricky Watters NT B	.40	.15
❑ 146 Robert Brooks NT B	.60	.25
❑ 147 Jeff Blake NT B	.60	.25
❑ 148 Tiki Barber CL B	1.50	.60
❑ 149 Jim Druckenmiller CL B	.40	.15
❑ 150 Warrick Dunn CL B	1.25	.50

1999 Donruss Preferred QBC

❑ COMPLETE SET (120)	150.00	75.00
❑ COMP.BRONZE SET (45)	25.00	12.50
❑ 1 Troy Aikman B	1.50	.60
❑ 2 Tony Banks B	.50	.20
❑ 3 Jeff Blake B	.50	.20
❑ 4 Drew Bledsoe B	1.00	.40
❑ 5 Bubby Brister B	.30	.10
❑ 6 Chris Chandler B	.50	.20
❑ 7 Kerry Collins B	.50	.20
❑ 8 Randall Cunningham B	.75	.30
❑ 9 Terrell Davis B	.75	.30
❑ 10 Trent Dilfer B	.50	.20
❑ 11 John Elway B	2.50	1.00
❑ 12 Boomer Esiason B	.30	.10
❑ 13 Jim Everett B	.30	.10
❑ 14 Brett Favre B	2.50	1.00
❑ 15 Doug Flutie B	.75	.30
❑ 16 Gus Frerotte B	.30	.10
❑ 17 Jeff George B	.50	.20
❑ 18 Elvis Grbac B	.50	.20
❑ 19 Jim Harbaugh B	.50	.20
❑ 20 Michael Irvin B	.50	.20
❑ 21 Brad Johnson B	.75	.30
❑ 22 Keyshawn Johnson B	.75	.30
❑ 23 Danny Kanell B	.30	.10
❑ 24 Jim Kelly B	.30	.10
❑ 25 Bernie Kosar B	.30	.10
❑ 26 Erik Kramer B	.30	.10
❑ 27 Ryan Leaf B	.75	.30
❑ 28 Peyton Manning B	2.50	1.00
❑ 29 Dan Marino B	2.50	1.00
❑ 30 Donovan McNabb RC B	6.00	2.50
❑ 31 Steve McNair B	.75	.30
❑ 32 Cade McNown RC B	1.00	.40
❑ 33 Scott Mitchell B	.30	.10
❑ 34 Warren Moon B	.75	.30
❑ 35 Neil O'Donnell B	.50	.20
❑ 36 Jake Plummer B	.50	.20
❑ 37 Jerry Rice B	1.50	.60
❑ 38 Barry Sanders B	2.50	1.00
❑ 39 Junior Seau B	.75	.30
❑ 40 Phil Simms B	.30	.10
❑ 41 Kordell Stewart B	.50	.20
❑ 42 Vinny Testaverde B	.50	.20
❑ 43 Ricky Williams RC B	2.50	1.00
❑ 44 Steve Young B	1.00	.40
❑ 45 Marino/Favre/Elway B	3.00	1.25
❑ 46 Troy Aikman S	2.50	1.00
❑ 47 Tony Banks S	.75	.30
❑ 48 Drew Bledsoe S	1.50	.60
❑ 49 Bubby Brister S	.50	.20
❑ 50 Chris Chandler S	.75	.30
❑ 51 Kerry Collins S	1.25	.50
❑ 52 Randall Cunningham S	1.25	.50
❑ 53 Terrell Davis S	1.25	.50
❑ 54 Trent Dilfer S	.75	.30
❑ 55 John Elway S	4.00	1.50
❑ 56 Boomer Esiason S	.75	.30
❑ 57 Brett Favre S	4.00	1.50
❑ 58 Doug Flutie S	1.25	.50
❑ 59 Elvis Grbac S	.75	.30
❑ 60 Jim Harbaugh S	.75	.30
❑ 61 Michael Irvin S	1.25	.50
❑ 62 Brad Johnson S	.75	.30
❑ 63 Keyshawn Johnson S	1.25	.50
❑ 64 Jim Kelly S	1.25	.50
❑ 65 Ryan Leaf S	.50	.20
❑ 66 Peyton Manning S	4.00	1.50
❑ 67 Dan Marino S	4.00	1.50

❑ 68 Donovan McNabb S 8.00 3.00
❑ 69 Steve McNair S 1.25 .50
❑ 70 Cade McNown S 2.00 .75
❑ 71 Warren Moon S 1.25 .50
❑ 72 Jake Plummer S .75 .30
❑ 73 Jerry Rice S 2.50 1.00
❑ 74 Barry Sanders S 4.00 1.50
❑ 75 Junior Seau S 1.25 .50
❑ 76 Phil Simms S .75 .30
❑ 77 Kordell Stewart S .75 .30
❑ 78 Vinny Testaverde S .75 .30
❑ 79 Ricky Williams S 3.00 1.25
❑ 80 Steve Young S 1.50 .60
❑ 81 Troy Aikman G 5.00 2.00
❑ 82 Drew Bledsoe G 3.00 1.25
❑ 83 Bubby Brister G 1.00 .40
❑ 84 Chris Chandler G 1.50 .60
❑ 85 Randall Cunningham G 1.50 .60
❑ 86 Terrell Davis G 2.50 1.00
❑ 87 John Elway G 8.00 3.00
❑ 88 Brett Favre G 8.00 3.00
❑ 89 Doug Flutie G 2.50 1.00
❑ 90 Brad Johnson G 1.50 .60
❑ 91 Keyshawn Johnson G 2.50 1.00
❑ 92 Ryan Leaf G 1.00 .40
❑ 93 Peyton Manning G 8.00 3.00
❑ 94 Dan Marino G 8.00 3.00
❑ 95 Donovan McNabb G 15.00 6.00
❑ 96 Steve McNair G 2.50 1.00
❑ 97 Cade McNown G 4.00 1.50
❑ 98 Warren Moon G 2.50 1.00
❑ 99 Jake Plummer G 1.50 .60
❑ 100 Jerry Rice G 5.00 2.00
❑ 101 Barry Sanders G 8.00 3.00
❑ 102 Kordell Stewart G 1.50 .60
❑ 103 Vinny Testaverde G 1.50 .60
❑ 104 Ricky Williams G 6.00 2.50
❑ 105 Steve Young G 3.00 1.25
❑ 106 Troy Aikman P 8.00 3.00
❑ 107 Drew Bledsoe P 5.00 2.00
❑ 108 Terrell Davis P 4.00 1.50
❑ 109 John Elway P 12.00 5.00
❑ 110 Brett Favre P 12.00 5.00
❑ 111 Keyshawn Johnson P 4.00 1.50
❑ 112 Peyton Manning P 12.00 5.00
❑ 113 Dan Marino P 12.00 5.00
❑ 114 Donovan McNabb P 20.00 7.50
❑ 115 Cade McNown P 5.00 2.00
❑ 116 Jake Plummer P 2.50 1.00
❑ 117 Jerry Rice P 8.00 3.00
❑ 118 Barry Sanders P 12.00 5.00
❑ 119 Kordell Stewart P 2.50 1.00
❑ 120 Ricky Williams P 8.00 3.00

2006 Donruss Threads

❑ 1 Braylon Edwards 1.00 .40
❑ 2 Jason Witten .60 .25
❑ 3 Julius Jones 1.00 .40
❑ 4 Roy Williams S .60 .25
❑ 5 Terry Glenn .60 .25
❑ 6 Ashley Lelie .60 .25
❑ 7 Kevin Jones 1.00 .40
❑ 8 Mike Williams 1.00 .40
❑ 9 Roy Williams WR 1.00 .40
❑ 10 Aaron Rodgers 1.00 .40
❑ 11 Tatum Bell .60 .25
❑ 12 Samkon Gado 1.00 .40
❑ 13 Corey Bradford .50 .20
❑ 14 Dallas Clark .50 .20
❑ 15 Matt Jones 1.00 .40
❑ 16 Larry Johnson 1.25 .50
❑ 17 Byron Leftwich .60 .25
❑ 18 Fred Taylor .60 .25
❑ 19 Anquan Boldin .60 .25
❑ 20 Kurt Warner .60 .25
❑ 21 Larry Fitzgerald 1.00 .40
❑ 22 Alge Crumpler .60 .25
❑ 23 Michael Vick 1.25 .50
❑ 24 Warrick Dunn .60 .25
❑ 25 Jamal Lewis .60 .25
❑ 26 Ray Lewis 1.00 .40
❑ 27 Eric Moulds .60 .25
❑ 28 Josh Reed .50 .20
❑ 29 Lee Evans .60 .25
❑ 30 Steve Smith 1.00 .40
❑ 31 Brian Urlacher 1.00 .40
❑ 32 Thomas Jones .60 .25
❑ 33 Chad Johnson .60 .25
❑ 34 Rudi Johnson .60 .25
❑ 35 T.J. Houshmandzadeh .60 .25
❑ 36 Reuben Droughns .60 .25
❑ 37 Drew Bledsoe 1.00 .40
❑ 38 Keyshawn Johnson .60 .25
❑ 39 Jake Plummer .60 .25
❑ 40 Rod Smith .60 .25
❑ 41 Mike Anderson .60 .25
❑ 42 Joey Harrington .60 .25
❑ 43 Brett Favre 2.00 .75
❑ 44 Donald Driver .60 .25
❑ 45 Javon Walker .60 .25
❑ 46 Andre Johnson .60 .25
❑ 47 David Carr .60 .25
❑ 48 Domanick Davis .60 .25
❑ 49 Edgerrin James 1.00 .40
❑ 50 Marvin Harrison 1.00 .40
❑ 51 Peyton Manning 1.50 .60
❑ 52 Reggie Wayne .60 .25
❑ 53 Jimmy Smith .60 .25
❑ 54 Tony Gonzalez .60 .25
❑ 55 Trent Green .60 .25
❑ 56 Eddie Kennison .50 .20
❑ 57 Chris Chambers .60 .25
❑ 58 Zach Thomas 1.00 .40
❑ 59 Daunte Culpepper 1.00 .40
❑ 60 Corey Dillon .60 .25
❑ 61 Deion Branch .60 .25
❑ 62 Tedy Bruschi 1.00 .40
❑ 63 Tom Brady 1.50 .60
❑ 64 Deuce McAllister .60 .25
❑ 65 Donte Stallworth .60 .25
❑ 66 Jeremy Shockey 1.00 .40
❑ 67 Tiki Barber 1.00 .40
❑ 68 Chad Pennington .60 .25
❑ 69 Curtis Martin 1.00 .40
❑ 70 Donovan McNabb 1.00 .40
❑ 71 Antwaan Randle El .60 .25
❑ 72 Hines Ward 1.00 .40
❑ 73 Antonio Gates 1.00 .40
❑ 74 Drew Brees 1.00 .40
❑ 75 Keenan McCardell .50 .20
❑ 76 LaDainian Tomlinson 1.25 .50
❑ 77 Alex Smith QB 1.25 .50
❑ 78 Brandon Lloyd .60 .25
❑ 79 Frank Gore 1.00 .40
❑ 80 Kevan Barlow .60 .25
❑ 81 Darrell Jackson .60 .25
❑ 82 Joe Jurevicius .60 .25
❑ 83 Matt Hasselbeck .60 .25
❑ 84 Shaun Alexander 1.00 .40
❑ 85 Shaun McDonald .50 .20
❑ 86 Marc Bulger .60 .25
❑ 87 Steven Jackson 1.00 .40
❑ 88 Torry Holt .60 .25
❑ 89 Cadillac Williams 1.00 .40
❑ 90 Chris Simms .60 .25
❑ 91 Joey Galloway .60 .25
❑ 92 Michael Clayton .60 .25
❑ 93 Chris Brown .60 .25
❑ 94 Drew Bennett .50 .20
❑ 95 Steve McNair .60 .25
❑ 96 Tyrone Calico .50 .20
❑ 97 Clinton Portis 1.00 .40
❑ 98 David Patten .50 .20
❑ 99 Mark Brunell .60 .25
❑ 100 Santana Moss .60 .25
❑ 101 Randy McMichael .50 .20
❑ 102 Ronnie Brown 1.00 .40
❑ 103 Mewelde Moore .50 .20
❑ 104 Nate Burleson .60 .25
❑ 105 Troy Williamson .60 .25
❑ 106 David Givens .60 .25
❑ 107 Aaron Brooks .60 .25
❑ 108 Laveranues Coles .60 .25
❑ 109 Justin McCareins .50 .20
❑ 110 Kerry Collins .60 .25
❑ 111 LaMont Jordan .60 .25
❑ 112 Randy Moss 1.00 .40
❑ 113 Jerry Porter .60 .25
❑ 114 Brian Westbrook .60 .25
❑ 115 Plaxico Burress .60 .25
❑ 116 Joe Horn .60 .25
❑ 117 Eli Manning 1.25 .50
❑ 118 Reggie Brown .60 .25
❑ 119 Ryan Moats .50 .20
❑ 120 Ben Roethlisberger 1.50 .60
❑ 121 Willie Parker 1.25 .50
❑ 122 Marcus Pollard .50 .20
❑ 123 Bubba Franks .50 .20
❑ 124 Jabar Gaffney .50 .20
❑ 125 Brandon Stokley .60 .25
❑ 126 Ernest Wilford .50 .20
❑ 127 Dante Hall .60 .25
❑ 128 Marty Booker .50 .20
❑ 129 Samie Parker .50 .20
❑ 130 J.J. Arrington .60 .25
❑ 131 Marcel Shipp .50 .20
❑ 132 Michael Jenkins .60 .25
❑ 133 T.J. Duckett .60 .25
❑ 134 Derrick Mason .50 .20
❑ 135 Kyle Boller .50 .20
❑ 136 Mark Clayton .60 .25
❑ 137 Willis McGahee 1.00 .40
❑ 138 DeShaun Foster .60 .25
❑ 139 Jake Delhomme .60 .25
❑ 140 Julius Peppers .60 .25
❑ 141 Keary Colbert .50 .20
❑ 142 Stephen Davis .60 .25
❑ 143 Todd Heap .60 .25
❑ 144 J.P. Losman .60 .25
❑ 145 Muhsin Muhammad .60 .25
❑ 146 Carson Palmer 1.00 .40
❑ 147 Cedric Benson 1.00 .40
❑ 148 Rex Grossman 1.00 .40
❑ 149 Charlie Frye .60 .25
❑ 150 Dennis Northcutt .50 .20
❑ 151 Mathias Kiwanuka RC 8.00 3.00
❑ 152 Ingle Martin RC 6.00 2.50
❑ 153 Reggie McNeal RC 5.00 2.00
❑ 154 Bruce Gradkowski RC 10.00 4.00
❑ 155 D.J. Shockley RC 6.00 2.50
❑ 156 Paul Pinegar RC 5.00 2.00
❑ 157 Brandon Kirsch RC 6.00 2.50
❑ 158 P.J. Daniels RC 5.00 2.00
❑ 159 Marques Hagans RC 5.00 2.00
❑ 160 Jerome Harrison RC 6.00 2.50
❑ 161 Wali Lundy RC 6.00 2.50
❑ 162 Cedric Humes RC 6.00 2.50
❑ 163 Quinton Ganther RC 5.00 2.00
❑ 164 Mike Bell RC 10.00 4.00
❑ 165 John David Washington RC 5.00 2.00
❑ 166 Anthony Fasano RC 6.00 2.50
❑ 167 Tony Scheffler RC 6.00 2.50
❑ 168 Leonard Pope RC 6.00 2.50
❑ 169 David Thomas RC 6.00 2.50
❑ 170 Dominique Byrd RC 5.00 2.00
❑ 171 Devin Hester RC 12.00 5.00
❑ 172 Willie Reid RC 6.00 2.50
❑ 173 Brad Smith RC 6.00 2.50
❑ 174 Cory Rodgers RC 6.00 2.50
❑ 175 Domenik Hixon RC 5.00 2.00
❑ 176 Jeremy Bloom RC 5.00 2.00
❑ 177 Jonathan Orr RC 5.00 2.00
❑ 178 Jeff Webb RC 5.00 2.00
❑ 179 Ethan Kilmer RC 6.00 2.50
❑ 180 Bennie Brazell RC 5.00 2.00
❑ 181 David Anderson RC 5.00 2.00
❑ 182 Kevin McMahan RC 5.00 2.00
❑ 183 Anthony Mix RC 5.00 2.00
❑ 184 D'Brickashaw Ferguson RC 6.00 2.50
❑ 185 Kamerion Wimbley RC 6.00 2.50
❑ 186 Tamba Hali RC 6.00 2.50
❑ 187 Haloti Ngata RC 6.00 2.50
❑ 188 Brodrick Bunkley RC 6.00 2.50
❑ 189 John McCargo RC 5.00 2.00
❑ 190 Claude Wroten RC 3.00 1.25
❑ 191 Gabe Watson RC 5.00 2.00
❑ 192 D'Qwell Jackson RC 5.00 2.00
❑ 193 Abdul Hodge RC 6.00 2.50
❑ 194 Ernie Sims RC 8.00 3.00
❑ 195 Chad Greenway RC 6.00 2.50

❑ 196 Bobby Carpenter RC	6.00	2.50
❑ 197 Manny Lawson RC	6.00	2.50
❑ 198 DeMeco Ryans RC	8.00	3.00
❑ 199 Rocky McIntosh RC	6.00	2.50
❑ 200 Thomas Howard RC	6.00	2.50
❑ 201 Jon Alston RC	6.00	2.50
❑ 202 A.J. Nicholson RC	3.00	1.25
❑ 203 Tye Hill RC	6.00	2.50
❑ 204 Antonio Cromartie RC	6.00	2.50
❑ 205 Johnathan Joseph RC	5.00	2.00
❑ 206 Kelly Jennings RC	6.00	2.50
❑ 207 Ashton Youboty RC	6.00	2.50
❑ 208 Alan Zemaitis RC	6.00	2.50
❑ 209 Jason Allen RC	6.00	2.50
❑ 210 Cedric Griffin RC	5.00	2.00
❑ 211 Ko Simpson RC	5.00	2.00
❑ 212 Pat Watkins RC	6.00	2.50
❑ 213 Donte Whitner RC	6.00	2.50
❑ 214 Bernard Pollard RC	5.00	2.00
❑ 215 Darnell Bing RC	6.00	2.50
❑ 216 Marcus Vick RC	5.00	2.00
❑ 217 Roman Harper RC	5.00	2.00
❑ 218 Anthony Smith RC	8.00	3.00
❑ 219 Daniel Bullocks RC	6.00	2.50
❑ 220 Eric Smith RC	5.00	2.00
❑ 221 Danieal Manning RC	6.00	2.50
❑ 222 Anthony Schlegel RC	5.00	2.00
❑ 223 Dusty Dvoracek RC	6.00	2.50
❑ 224 Darryl Tapp RC	5.00	2.00
❑ 225 Chris Gocong RC	5.00	2.00
❑ 226 Brandon Williams AU/240 RC	50.00	25.00
❑ 227 Michael Robinson AU/240 RC	80.00	40.00
❑ 228 Vernon Davis AU/100 RC	120.00	60.00
❑ 229 Brandon Marshall AU/240 RC	80.00	40.00
❑ 230 Travis Wilson AU/180 RC	60.00	30.00
❑ 231 Maurice Stovall AU/140 RC	80.00	40.00
❑ 232 Matt Leinart AU/140 RC	300.00	175.00
❑ 233 Ch.Whitehurst AU/200 RC	80.00	40.00
❑ 234 Derek Hagan AU/100 RC	60.00	30.00
❑ 235 Jason Avant AU/150 RC	50.00	20.00
❑ 236 Jerious Norwood AU/210 RC	100.00	50.00
❑ 237 Sinorice Moss AU/100 RC	80.00	40.00
❑ 238 Marcedes Lewis AU/100 RC	60.00	30.00
❑ 239 Maurice Drew AU/100 RC	150.00	75.00
❑ 240 Kellen Clemens AU/210 RC	80.00	40.00
❑ 241 Leon Washington AU/200 RC	80.00	40.00
❑ 242 Brian Calhoun AU/140 RC	60.00	30.00
❑ 243 A.J. Hawk AU/100 RC	200.00	100.00
❑ 244 DeAn.Williams AU/160 RC	150.00	75.00
❑ 245 Chad Jackson AU/140 RC	80.00	40.00
❑ 246 L.Maroney AU/140 RC	150.00	75.00
❑ 247 Michael Huff AU/100 RC	100.00	50.00
❑ 248 Joe Klopfenstein AU/240 RC	50.00	25.00
❑ 249 Dem.Williams AU/160 RC	50.00	25.00
❑ 250 Reggie Bush AU/100 RC	600.00	350.00
❑ 251 Omar Jacobs AU/120 RC	50.00	25.00
❑ 252 Santonio Holmes AU/120 RC	100.00	50.00
❑ 253 Mario Williams AU/160 RC	100.00	50.00
❑ 254 LenDale White AU/100 RC	135.00	75.00
❑ 255 Vince Young AU/100 RC	350.00	200.00
❑ 256 Tarvaris Jackson AU/210 RC	100.00	50.00
❑ 257 Jay Cutler AU/120 RC EXCH	250.00	150.00
❑ 258 Joseph Addai AU/100 RC	250.00	150.00
❑ 259 Brodie Croyle AU/120 RC	120.00	60.00
❑ 260 Greg Jennings AU/240 RC	100.00	60.00
❑ 261 Erik Meyer AU RC	10.00	4.00
❑ 262 Drew Olson AU RC	10.00	4.00
❑ 263 Darrell Hackney AU RC	10.00	4.00
❑ 264 Andre Hall AU RC	10.00	4.00
❑ 265 Taurean Henderson AU RC	12.00	5.00
❑ 266 Derrick Ross AU RC	10.00	4.00
❑ 267 De'Arrius Howard AU RC	12.00	5.00
❑ 268 Wendell Mathis AU RC	10.00	4.00
❑ 269 Gerald Riggs AU RC	12.00	5.00
❑ 270 Garrett Mills AU RC	12.00	5.00
❑ 271 Jai Lewis AU RC	10.00	4.00
❑ 272 Skyler Green AU RC	12.00	5.00
❑ 273 Mike Hass AU RC	12.00	5.00
❑ 274 Delanie Walker AU RC	10.00	4.00
❑ 275 Adam Jennings AU RC	10.00	4.00
❑ 276 Todd Watkins AU RC	10.00	4.00
❑ 277 Devin Aromashodu AU RC	10.00	4.00
❑ 278 Ben Obomanu AU RC	10.00	4.00
❑ 279 Marques Colston AU RC	60.00	35.00
❑ 280 Miles Austin AU RC	10.00	4.00
❑ 281 Martin Nance AU RC	10.00	4.00
❑ 282 Greg Lee AU RC	10.00	4.00
❑ 283 Hank Baskett AU RC	12.00	5.00
❑ 284 Jimmy Williams AU RC	12.00	5.00
❑ 285 Anwar Phillips AU RC	10.00	4.00

2002 eTopps Classic

❑ 1 Barry Sanders/3000	10.00	5.00
❑ 2 Ray Nitschke/983		
❑ 3 Dan Marino/3000	12.00	6.00
❑ 4 Chuck Bednarik/1291	8.00	4.00
❑ 5 Sammy Baugh/1259	8.00	4.00
❑ 6 Frank Gifford/1270	6.00	3.00
❑ 7 Terry Bradshaw/3000	8.00	4.00
❑ 7 Kellen Winslow/777		
❑ 8 Jim Brown/3000	8.00	4.00
❑ 9 Jim Kelly/985	12.00	6.00
❑ 10 Y.A. Tittle/1064	10.00	5.00
❑ 11 DeaconÂ Jones/865	15.00	7.50
❑ 11 Fran Tarkenton/1106	12.00	6.00
❑ 12 Joe Montana/3000	25.00	15.00
❑ 13 Joe Namath/3000	10.00	5.00
❑ 14 John Elway/2422	10.00	5.00
❑ 14 Elroy Hirsch/906	12.00	6.00
❑ 15 Norm Van Brocklin/975	15.00	7.50
❑ 19 Bubba Smith/805	12.00	6.00
❑ 20 Dan Fouts/843	15.00	7.50

2003 eTopps Classic

❑ 21 Lawrence Taylor/702		
❑ 22 Gale Sayers/947	15.00	7.50
❑ 23 Johnny Unitas/661		
❑ 24 Bo Jackson/1000	20.00	10.00
❑ 25 Walter Payton/1500		
❑ 26 Phil Simms/781		
❑ 27 Tony Dorsett/788		
❑ 28 Steve Largent/639		
❑ 29 Steve Young/592		
❑ 30 Marcus Allen/722		
❑ 31 Mike Singletary/953	15.00	7.50
❑ 32 Eric Dickerson/774		
❑ 33 Otto Graham/547		
❑ 34 Troy Aikman/587		
❑ 35 Fred Biletnikoff/450		
❑ 36 Jim Thorpe/785		
❑ 37 Ronnie Lott/711		
❑ 38 Jack Lambert/754	20.00	10.00
❑ 39 Raymond Berry/477		
❑ 40 Earl Campbell/523		

2004 eTopps Autographs

❑ 1 T.Brady 02eTop/155	225.00	125.00
❑ 2 T.Brady 03eTop/50		
❑ 3 C.Pennington 01eTop/19		
❑ 4 C.Pennington 02eTop/54		
❑ 5 C.Pennington 03eTop/27		
❑ 6 B.Roethlisberger 04eTop/150	250.00	150.00
❑ 7 B.Westbrook 02eTop/143	75.00	40.00

1997 E-X2000

❑ COMPLETE SET (60)	30.00	12.50
❑ 1 Jake Plummer RC	10.00	4.00
❑ 2 Jamal Anderson	1.50	.60
❑ 3 Rae Carruth RC	.60	.25
❑ 4 Kerry Collins	1.50	.60
❑ 5 Darnell Autry RC	1.50	.60
❑ 6 Rashaan Salaam	.60	.25
❑ 7 Troy Aikman	3.00	1.25
❑ 8 Deion Sanders	1.50	.60
❑ 9 Emmitt Smith	5.00	2.00
❑ 10 Herman Moore	1.00	.40
❑ 11 Barry Sanders	5.00	2.00
❑ 12 Mark Chmura	1.00	.40
❑ 13 Brett Favre	6.00	2.50
❑ 14 Antonio Freeman	1.50	.60
❑ 15 Reggie White	1.50	.60
❑ 16 Cris Carter	1.50	.60
❑ 17 Brad Johnson	1.50	.60
❑ 18 Troy Davis RC	1.00	.40
❑ 19 Danny Wuerffel RC	1.50	.60
❑ 20 Dave Brown	.60	.25
❑ 21 Ike Hilliard RC	3.00	1.25
❑ 22 Ty Detmer	1.00	.40
❑ 23 Ricky Watters	1.00	.40
❑ 24 Tony Banks	1.00	.40
❑ 25 Eddie Kennison	1.00	.40
❑ 26 Jim Druckenmiller RC	1.00	.40
❑ 27 Jerry Rice	3.00	1.25
❑ 28 Steve Young	2.00	.75
❑ 29 Trent Dilfer	1.50	.60
❑ 30 Warrick Dunn RC	8.00	3.00
❑ 31 Terry Allen	1.50	.60
❑ 32 Gus Frerotte	.60	.25
❑ 33 Vinny Testaverde	1.00	.40
❑ 34 Antowain Smith RC	6.00	2.50
❑ 35 Thurman Thomas	1.50	.60
❑ 36 Jeff Blake	1.00	.40
❑ 37 Carl Pickens	1.00	.40
❑ 38 Terrell Davis	2.00	.75
❑ 39 John Elway	6.00	2.50
❑ 40 Eddie George	1.50	.60
❑ 41 Steve McNair	2.00	.75
❑ 42 Marshall Faulk	2.00	.75
❑ 43 Marvin Harrison	1.50	.60
❑ 44 Mark Brunell	2.00	.75
❑ 45 Marcus Allen	1.50	.60
❑ 46 Elvis Grbac	1.00	.40
❑ 47 Karim Abdul-Jabbar	1.00	.40
❑ 48 Dan Marino	6.00	2.50
❑ 49 Drew Bledsoe	2.00	.75
❑ 50 Terry Glenn	1.50	.60
❑ 51 Curtis Martin	2.00	.75
❑ 52 Keyshawn Johnson	1.50	.60
❑ 53 Tim Brown	1.50	.60
❑ 54 Jeff George	1.00	.40
❑ 55 Jerome Bettis	1.50	.60
❑ 56 Kordell Stewart	1.50	.60
❑ 57 Stan Humphries	1.00	.40
❑ 58 Junior Seau	1.50	.60
❑ 59 Joey Galloway	1.00	.40
❑ 60 Chris Warren	1.00	.40

1998 E-X2001

❑ COMPLETE SET (60)	50.00	20.00
❑ 1 Kordell Stewart	.75	.30
❑ 2 Steve Young	1.50	.60
❑ 3 Mark Brunell	.75	.30
❑ 4 Brett Favre	5.00	2.00
❑ 5 Barry Sanders	4.00	1.50
❑ 6 Warrick Dunn	.75	.30

❑ 7 Jerry Rice 2.50 1.00
❑ 8 Dan Marino 5.00 2.00
❑ 9 Emmitt Smith 4.00 1.50
❑ 10 John Elway 5.00 2.00
❑ 11 Eddie George .75 .30
❑ 12 Jake Plummer .75 .30
❑ 13 Terrell Davis .75 .30
❑ 14 Curtis Martin .75 .30
❑ 15 Troy Aikman 2.50 1.00
❑ 16 Terry Glenn .75 .30
❑ 17 Mike Alstott .75 .30
❑ 18 Drew Bledsoe 2.00 .75
❑ 19 Keyshawn Johnson .75 .30
❑ 20 Dorsey Levens .75 .30
❑ 21 Elvis Grbac .50 .20
❑ 22 Ricky Watters .50 .20
❑ 23 Robert Smith .75 .30
❑ 24 Trent Dilfer .75 .30
❑ 25 Joey Galloway .50 .20
❑ 26 Rob Moore .50 .20
❑ 27 Steve McNair .75 .30
❑ 28 Jim Harbaugh .50 .20
❑ 29 Troy Davis .30 .10
❑ 30 Rob Johnson .50 .20
❑ 31 Shannon Sharpe .50 .20
❑ 32 Jerome Bettis .75 .30
❑ 33 Tim Brown .75 .30
❑ 34 Kerry Collins .50 .20
❑ 35 Garrison Hearst .75 .30
❑ 36 Antonio Freeman .75 .30
❑ 37 Charlie Garner .50 .20
❑ 38 Glenn Foley .50 .20
❑ 39 Yatil Green .30 .10
❑ 40 Tiki Barber .75 .30
❑ 41 Bobby Hoying .50 .20
❑ 42 Corey Dillon .75 .30
❑ 43 Antowain Smith .75 .30
❑ 44 Robert Edwards RC 2.50 1.00
❑ 45 Jammi German RC 1.50 .60
❑ 46 Ahman Green RC 12.00 5.00
❑ 47 Hines Ward RC 10.00 5.00
❑ 48 Skip Hicks RC 2.50 1.00
❑ 49 Brian Griese RC 6.00 2.50
❑ 50 Charlie Batch RC 3.00 1.25
❑ 51 Jacquez Green RC 2.50 1.00
❑ 52 John Avery RC 2.50 1.00
❑ 53 Kevin Dyson RC 3.00 1.25
❑ 54 Peyton Manning RC 25.00 12.50
❑ 55 Randy Moss RC 12.00 6.00
❑ 56 Ryan Leaf RC 3.00 1.25
❑ 57 Curtis Enis RC 1.50 .60
❑ 58 Charles Woodson RC 4.00 1.50
❑ 59 Robert Holcombe RC 2.50 1.00
❑ 60 Fred Taylor RC 5.00 2.00
❑ NNO Jake Plummer PROMO 1.00 .40
❑ NNO Checklist Card 1 .30 .10
❑ NNO Checklist Card 2 .30 .10

1999 E-X Century

❑ COMPLETE SET (90) 120.00 50.00
❑ COMP.SET w/o SP's (60) 40.00 20.00
❑ 1 Keyshawn Johnson 1.25 .50
❑ 2 Natrone Means .75 .30
❑ 3 Antonio Freeman 1.25 .50
❑ 4 Muhsin Muhammad .75 .30
❑ 5 Curtis Martin 1.25 .50
❑ 6 Chris Chandler .75 .30
❑ 7 Priest Holmes 2.00 .75
❑ 8 Vinny Testaverde .75 .30
❑ 9 Tim Brown 1.25 .50
❑ 10 Eddie George 1.25 .50
❑ 11 Brad Johnson 1.25 .50
❑ 12 Mike Alstott 1.25 .50
❑ 13 Dorsey Levens 1.25 .50
❑ 14 Jamal Anderson 1.25 .50
❑ 15 Herman Moore .75 .30
❑ 16 Brett Favre 4.00 1.50
❑ 17 John Elway 4.00 1.50
❑ 18 Steve Young 1.50 .60
❑ 19 Warrick Dunn 1.25 .50
❑ 20 Fred Taylor 1.25 .50
❑ 21 Charlie Batch 1.25 .50
❑ 22 Jimmy Smith .75 .30
❑ 23 Steve McNair 1.25 .50
❑ 24 Jerry Rice 2.50 1.00
❑ 25 Dan Marino 4.00 1.50
❑ 26 Jake Plummer .75 .30
❑ 27 Marshall Faulk 1.50 .60
❑ 28 Garrison Hearst .75 .30
❑ 29 Terrell Davis 1.25 .50
❑ 30 Barry Sanders 4.00 1.50
❑ 31 Carl Pickens .75 .30
❑ 32 Jerome Bettis 1.25 .50
❑ 33 Scott Mitchell .50 .20
❑ 34 Duce Staley 1.25 .50
❑ 35 Robert Smith 1.25 .50
❑ 36 Wayne Chrebet .75 .30
❑ 37 Steve Beuerlein .50 .20
❑ 38 Elvis Grbac .75 .30
❑ 39 Troy Aikman 2.50 1.00
❑ 40 Emmitt Smith 2.50 1.00
❑ 41 Joey Galloway .75 .30
❑ 42 Ryan Leaf 1.25 .50
❑ 43 Skip Hicks .50 .20
❑ 44 Cris Carter 1.25 .50
❑ 45 Shannon Sharpe .75 .30
❑ 46 Mark Brunell 1.25 .50
❑ 47 Kerry Collins .75 .30
❑ 48 Corey Dillon 1.25 .50
❑ 49 Kordell Stewart .75 .30
❑ 50 Randy Moss 3.00 1.25
❑ 51 Jon Kitna 1.25 .50
❑ 52 Deion Sanders 1.25 .50
❑ 53 Rod Smith .75 .30
❑ 54 Drew Bledsoe 1.50 .60
❑ 55 Terrell Owens 1.25 .50
❑ 56 Napoleon Kaufman 1.25 .50
❑ 57 Trent Green 1.25 .50
❑ 58 Ricky Watters .75 .30
❑ 59 Randall Cunningham 1.25 .50
❑ 60 Peyton Manning 4.00 1.50
❑ 61 Tim Couch RC 4.00 1.50
❑ 62 Amos Zereoue RC 4.00 1.50
❑ 63 Cade McNown RC 3.00 1.25
❑ 64 Donovan McNabb RC 15.00 6.00
❑ 65 Ricky Williams RC 6.00 2.50
❑ 66 Daunte Culpepper RC 12.00 5.00
❑ 67 Troy Edwards RC 3.00 1.25
❑ 68 Peerless Price RC 4.00 1.50
❑ 69 Edgerrin James RC 12.00 5.00
❑ 70 Champ Bailey RC 5.00 2.00
❑ 71 Akili Smith RC 3.00 1.25
❑ 72 Kevin Johnson RC 4.00 1.50
❑ 73 Cecil Collins RC 2.00 .75
❑ 74 David Boston RC 4.00 1.50
❑ 75 Torry Holt RC 10.00 4.00
❑ 76 James Johnson RC 3.00 1.25
❑ 77 Na Brown RC 3.00 1.25
❑ 78 Rob Konrad RC 3.00 1.25
❑ 79 Mike Cloud RC 3.00 1.25
❑ 80 Craig Yeast RC 3.00 1.25
❑ 81 Brock Huard RC 4.00 1.50
❑ 82 Chris McAlister RC 3.00 1.25
❑ 83 Shaun King RC 3.00 1.25
❑ 84 Wane McGarity RC 2.00 .75
❑ 85 Joe Germaine RC 3.00 1.25
❑ 86 D'Wayne Bates RC 3.00 1.25
❑ 87 Kevin Faulk RC 4.00 1.50
❑ 88 Antoine Winfield RC 3.00 1.25
❑ 89 Reginald Kelly RC 2.00 .75
❑ 90 Antuan Edwards RC 2.00 .75
❑ P1 Jake Plummer Promo 1.00 .40

2000 E-X

❑ COMPLETE SET (150) 400.00 200.00
❑ COMP.SET w/o SP's (100) 15.00 6.00
❑ 1 Tim Couch .50 .20
❑ 2 Daunte Culpepper 1.00 .40
❑ 3 Jake Reed .50 .20
❑ 4 Donovan McNabb 1.25 .50
❑ 5 Terry Glenn .50 .20

❑ 6 Vinny Testaverde .50 .20
❑ 7 Michael Westbrook .50 .20
❑ 8 Errict Rhett .50 .20
❑ 9 Joey Galloway .50 .20
❑ 10 O.J. McDuffie .50 .20
❑ 11 Rob Johnson .50 .20
❑ 12 Warren Sapp .50 .20
❑ 13 Brian Griese .75 .30
❑ 14 Derrick Mayes .50 .20
❑ 15 Ike Hilliard .50 .20
❑ 16 Kevin Dyson .50 .20
❑ 17 Shannon Sharpe .50 .20
❑ 18 Cade McNown .30 .10
❑ 19 Damon Huard .75 .30
❑ 20 James Stewart .50 .20
❑ 21 Kevin Johnson .75 .30
❑ 22 Muhsin Muhammad .50 .20
❑ 23 Shaun King .30 .10
❑ 24 Corey Dillon .75 .30
❑ 25 Fred Taylor .75 .30
❑ 26 Peyton Manning 2.00 .75
❑ 27 Steve McNair .75 .30
❑ 28 Tim Brown .75 .30
❑ 29 Brad Johnson .75 .30
❑ 30 Edgerrin James 1.25 .50
❑ 31 Germane Crowell .30 .10
❑ 32 Kordell Stewart .50 .20
❑ 33 Randy Moss 1.50 .60
❑ 34 Tony Banks .50 .20
❑ 35 Akili Smith .30 .10
❑ 36 Charlie Batch .75 .30
❑ 37 Duce Staley .75 .30
❑ 38 Jerome Bettis .75 .30
❑ 39 Rich Gannon .75 .30
❑ 40 Steve Young 1.00 .40
❑ 41 Tony Gonzalez .50 .20
❑ 42 Curtis Martin .75 .30
❑ 43 Eddie George .75 .30
❑ 44 Marshall Faulk 1.00 .40
❑ 45 Troy Edwards .30 .10
❑ 46 Curtis Enis .30 .10
❑ 47 Jake Plummer .50 .20
❑ 48 Jon Kitna .75 .30
❑ 49 Qadry Ismail .50 .20
❑ 50 Terrell Davis .75 .30
❑ 51 Troy Aikman 1.50 .60
❑ 52 Elvis Grbac .50 .20
❑ 53 Jeff Blake .50 .20
❑ 54 Kurt Warner 1.50 .60
❑ 55 Ricky Watters .50 .20
❑ 56 Torry Holt .75 .30
❑ 57 Brett Favre 2.50 1.00
❑ 58 Chris Chandler .50 .20
❑ 59 Eric Moulds .75 .30
❑ 60 Jimmy Smith .50 .20
❑ 61 Ricky Williams .75 .30
❑ 62 Antonio Freeman .75 .30
❑ 63 Curtis Conway .50 .20
❑ 64 Emmitt Smith 1.50 .60
❑ 65 Kerry Collins .50 .20
❑ 66 Marvin Harrison .75 .30
❑ 67 Tyrone Wheatley .50 .20
❑ 68 Charlie Garner .50 .20
❑ 69 Derrick Alexander .50 .20
❑ 70 Jamal Anderson .75 .30
❑ 71 Mike Alstott .75 .30
❑ 72 Ryan Leaf .50 .20
❑ 73 Tim Biakabutuka .50 .20
❑ 74 Amani Toomer .50 .20
❑ 75 Dorsey Levens .50 .20
❑ 76 Frank Sanders .50 .20
❑ 77 Junior Seau .75 .30

❑ 78	Steve Beuerlein	.30	.10
❑ 79	Wayne Chrebet	.50	.20
❑ 80	Carl Pickens	.50	.20
❑ 81	Drew Bledsoe	1.00	.40
❑ 82	Isaac Bruce	.75	.30
❑ 83	Marcus Robinson	.75	.30
❑ 84	Stephen Davis	.75	.30
❑ 85	Cris Carter	.75	.30
❑ 86	Ed McCaffrey	.75	.30
❑ 87	Jerry Rice	1.50	.60
❑ 88	Mark Brunell	.75	.30
❑ 89	Peerless Price	.50	.20
❑ 90	Terance Mathis	.50	.20
❑ 91	Tony Martin	.50	.20
❑ 92	Jevon Kearse	.75	.30
❑ 93	Robert Smith	.75	.30
❑ 94	Rob Moore	.50	.20
❑ 95	Charles Johnson	.50	.20
❑ 96	Doug Flutie	.75	.30
❑ 97	Sean Dawkins	.30	.10
❑ 98	Keenan McCardell	.50	.20
❑ 99	Bill Schroeder	.50	.20
❑ 100	Rod Smith	.50	.20
❑ 101	Peter Warrick RC	8.00	3.00
❑ 102	Corey Simon RC	8.00	3.00
❑ 103	Danny Farmer RC	6.00	2.50
❑ 104	Jamal Lewis RC	20.00	7.50
❑ 105	Jerry Porter RC	10.00	4.00
❑ 106	Joe Hamilton RC	6.00	2.50
❑ 107	Marc Bulger RC	15.00	6.00
❑ 108	R.Jay Soward RC	6.00	2.50
❑ 109	Ron Dugans RC	4.00	1.50
❑ 110	Shaun Alexander RC	40.00	15.00
❑ 111	Travis Prentice RC	6.00	2.50
❑ 112	Anthony Becht RC	8.00	3.00
❑ 113	Bubba Franks RC	8.00	3.00
❑ 114	Chris Redman RC	6.00	2.50
❑ 115	Dennis Northcutt RC	8.00	3.00
❑ 116	Dez White RC	8.00	3.00
❑ 117	Gari Scott RC	4.00	1.50
❑ 118	Mareno Philyaw RC	4.00	1.50
❑ 119	Ron Dayne RC	8.00	3.00
❑ 120	Shyrone Stith RC	6.00	2.50
❑ 121	Tee Martin RC	8.00	3.00
❑ 122	Tom Brady RC	80.00	40.00
❑ 123	Trung Canidate RC	6.00	2.50
❑ 124	Chad Pennington RC	20.00	7.50
❑ 125	Chris Cole RC	6.00	2.50
❑ 126	Courtney Brown RC	8.00	3.00
❑ 127	Doug Chapman RC	6.00	2.50
❑ 128	Giovanni Carmazzi RC	4.00	1.50
❑ 129	J.R. Redmond RC	6.00	2.50
❑ 130	Michael Wiley RC	6.00	2.50
❑ 131	Reuben Droughns RC	10.00	4.00
❑ 132	Terrelle Smith RC	6.00	2.50
❑ 133	Thomas Jones RC	12.00	5.00
❑ 134	Travis Taylor RC	8.00	3.00
❑ 135	Anthony Lucas RC	4.00	1.50
❑ 136	Curtis Keaton RC	6.00	2.50
❑ 137	Frank Moreau RC	6.00	2.50
❑ 138	Darrell Jackson RC	15.00	6.00
❑ 139	Laveranues Coles RC	10.00	4.00
❑ 140	Brian Urlacher RC	30.00	12.50
❑ 141	Plaxico Burress RC	15.00	6.00
❑ 142	Sammy Morris RC	6.00	2.50
❑ 143	Sylvester Morris RC	6.00	2.50
❑ 144	Tim Rattay RC	8.00	3.00
❑ 145	Todd Pinkston RC	8.00	3.00
❑ 146	Troy Walters RC	8.00	3.00
❑ 147	Sebastian Janikowski RC	8.00	3.00
❑ 148	JaJuan Dawson RC	4.00	1.50
❑ 149	Trevor Gaylor RC	6.00	2.50
❑ 150	Rondell Mealey RC	4.00	1.50

2001 E-X

❑	COMP.SET w/o SP's (90)	25.00	10.00
❑ 1	Jamal Anderson	.75	.30
❑ 2	Tim Couch	.50	.20
❑ 3	Jeff Garcia	.75	.30
❑ 4	Brett Favre	2.50	1.00
❑ 5	Donovan McNabb	1.00	.40
❑ 6	Kerry Collins	.50	.20
❑ 7	Doug Flutie	.75	.30
❑ 8	Steve McNair	.75	.30
❑ 9	Kordell Stewart	.50	.20
❑ 10	Daunte Culpepper	.75	.30
❑ 11	Rich Gannon	.75	.30
❑ 12	Kurt Warner	1.50	.60
❑ 13	Brian Griese	.75	.30

❑ 14	Brad Johnson	.75	.30
❑ 15	Jake Plummer	.50	.20
❑ 16	Mark Brunell	.75	.30
❑ 17	Peyton Manning	2.00	.75
❑ 18	Keyshawn Johnson	.75	.30
❑ 19	Derrick Alexander	.50	.20
❑ 20	Emmitt Smith	1.50	.60
❑ 21	Rob Johnson	.50	.20
❑ 22	Aaron Brooks	.75	.30
❑ 23	Charlie Garner	.50	.20
❑ 24	Lamar Smith	.50	.20
❑ 25	Eddie George	.75	.30
❑ 26	Marshall Faulk	1.00	.40
❑ 27	Tiki Barber	.75	.30
❑ 28	Terrell Davis	.75	.30
❑ 29	Jamal Lewis	1.25	.50
❑ 30	Edgerrin James	1.00	.40
❑ 31	Duce Staley	.75	.30
❑ 32	Ricky Williams	.75	.30
❑ 33	Dorsey Levens	.50	.20
❑ 34	Jerome Bettis	.75	.30
❑ 35	Ron Dayne	.75	.30
❑ 36	Mike Anderson	.75	.30
❑ 37	Peter Warrick	.75	.30
❑ 38	Mike Alstott	.75	.30
❑ 39	Fred Taylor	.75	.30
❑ 40	Curtis Martin	.75	.30
❑ 41	Warrick Dunn	.75	.30
❑ 42	Vinny Testaverde	.50	.20
❑ 43	Stephen Davis	.75	.30
❑ 44	Ahman Green	.75	.30
❑ 45	James Stewart	.50	.20
❑ 46	Ricky Watters	.50	.20
❑ 47	Ray Lewis	.75	.30
❑ 48	Thomas Jones	.50	.20
❑ 49	Zach Thomas	.75	.30
❑ 50	Junior Seau	.75	.30
❑ 51	Brian Urlacher	1.25	.50
❑ 52	Isaac Bruce	.75	.30
❑ 53	Corey Dillon	.75	.30
❑ 54	Cris Carter	.75	.30
❑ 55	Terrell Owens	.75	.30
❑ 56	Drew Bledsoe	1.00	.40
❑ 57	Torry Holt	.75	.30
❑ 58	Charlie Batch	.75	.30
❑ 59	Germane Crowell	.30	.10
❑ 60	Jimmy Smith	.50	.20
❑ 61	Tim Biakabutuka	.50	.20
❑ 62	Jay Fiedler	.75	.30
❑ 63	Joey Galloway	.50	.20
❑ 64	Michael Westbrook	.50	.20
❑ 65	Shaun Alexander	1.00	.40
❑ 66	Matt Hasselbeck	.50	.20
❑ 67	Elvis Grbac	.50	.20
❑ 68	Derrick Mason	.50	.20
❑ 69	Trent Green	.75	.30
❑ 70	Wayne Chrebet	.50	.20
❑ 71	Rod Smith	.50	.20
❑ 72	Jerry Rice	1.50	.60
❑ 73	Tim Brown	.75	.30
❑ 74	Shannon Sharpe	.50	.20
❑ 75	Joe Horn	.50	.20
❑ 76	Randy Moss	1.50	.60
❑ 77	Amani Toomer	.50	.20
❑ 78	Antonio Freeman	.75	.30
❑ 79	Ed McCaffrey	.75	.30
❑ 80	Marvin Harrison	.75	.30
❑ 81	Muhsin Muhammad	.50	.20
❑ 82	Chad Pennington	1.25	.50
❑ 83	Kevin Johnson	.50	.20
❑ 84	Tony Gonzalez	.50	.20
❑ 85	Terry Glenn	.50	.20
❑ 86	David Boston	.75	.30
❑ 87	Jevon Kearse	.50	.20
❑ 88	Marcus Robinson	.75	.30
❑ 89	Warren Sapp	.50	.20
❑ 90	Eric Moulds	.50	.20
❑ 91	Andre Carter/1250 RC	10.00	4.00
❑ 92	Kevan Barlow/1250 RC	10.00	4.00
❑ 93	Michael Bennett/1000 RC	10.00	4.00
❑ 94	Josh Booty/1500 RC	10.00	4.00
❑ 95	Drew Brees/1000 RC	25.00	12.50
❑ 96	Correll Buckhalter/1500 RC	12.00	5.00
❑ 97	Quincy Carter/1250 RC	10.00	4.00
❑ 98	Chris Chambers/1000 RC	15.00	6.00
❑ 99	Nick Goings/1500 RC	10.00	4.00
❑ 100	Kevin Kasper/1500 RC	10.00	4.00
❑ 101	Dave Dickenson/1500 RC	6.00	2.50
❑ 102	Robert Ferguson/1250 RC	10.00	4.00
❑ 103	Jamar Fletcher/1500 RC	6.00	2.50
❑ 104	Rod Gardner/1250 RC	10.00	4.00
❑ 105	Justin McCareins/1250 RC	10.00	4.00
❑ 106	Jason Brookins/1500 RC	10.00	4.00
❑ 107	Todd Heap/1500 RC	10.00	4.00
❑ 108	Travis Henry/1000 RC	15.00	6.00
❑ 109	Gerard Warren/1500 RC	10.00	4.00
❑ 110	James Jackson/1250 RC	10.00	4.00
❑ 111	Chad Johnson/1250 RC	25.00	10.00
❑ 112	Rudi Johnson/1500 RC	15.00	6.00
❑ 113	LaMont Jordan/1250 RC	20.00	7.50
❑ 114	Deuce McAllister/1250 RC	20.00	7.50
❑ 115	Mike McMahon/1250 RC	10.00	4.00
❑ 116	Snoop Minnis/1000 RC	6.00	2.50
❑ 117	Travis Minor/1500 RC	6.00	2.50
❑ 118	Freddie Mitchell/1000 RC	10.00	4.00
❑ 119	Quincy Morgan/1250 RC	10.00	4.00
❑ 120	Santana Moss/1250 RC	15.00	6.00
❑ 121	Cedrick Wilson/1500 RC	10.00	4.00
❑ 122	Jesse Palmer/1500 RC	10.00	4.00
❑ 123	Ken-Yon Rambo/1500 RC	6.00	2.50
❑ 124	Jamal Reynolds/1500 RC	10.00	4.00
❑ 125	Koren Robinson/1250 RC	10.00	4.00
❑ 126	Sage Rosenfels/1500 RC	10.00	4.00
❑ 127	Dan Morgan/1250 RC	10.00	4.00
❑ 128	Justin Smith/1500 RC	10.00	4.00
❑ 129	Fred Smoot/1500 RC	10.00	4.00
❑ 130	Vinny Sutherland/1500 RC	6.00	2.50
❑ 131	David Terrell/1000 RC	10.00	4.00
❑ 132	Anthony Thomas/1250 RC	10.00	4.00
❑ 133	LaDan Tomlinson/1000 RC	60.00	35.00
❑ 134	Dan Alexander/1500 RC	10.00	4.00
❑ 135	Marq Tuiasosopo/1250 RC	10.00	4.00
❑ 136	Michael Vick/1000 RC	40.00	20.00
❑ 137	Steve Smith/1250 RC	25.00	12.50
❑ 138	Reggie Wayne/1250 RC	20.00	7.50
❑ 139	Chris Weinke/1000 RC	10.00	4.00
❑ 140	Alex Bannister/1250 RC	6.00	2.50

2004 E-X

❑ UNSIGNED RC PRINT RUN 500 SER.#'d SETS

❑ 1	Travis Henry	5.00	2.00
❑ 2	Deion Sanders	6.00	2.50
❑ 3	Donovan McNabb	8.00	3.00
❑ 4	LaDainian Tomlinson	8.00	3.00
❑ 5	Shaun Alexander	6.00	2.50
❑ 6	Daunte Culpepper	6.00	2.50
❑ 7	Peyton Manning	10.00	4.00
❑ 8	Deuce McAllister	6.00	2.50
❑ 9	Marshall Faulk	6.00	2.50
❑ 10	Jamal Lewis	6.00	2.50
❑ 11	Chad Pennington	6.00	2.50
❑ 12	Clinton Portis	6.00	2.50
❑ 13	Brett Favre	15.00	6.00

	Card	Price 1	Price 2
❑	14 Anquan Boldin	6.00	2.50
❑	15 Priest Holmes	8.00	3.00
❑	16 Brian Urlacher	8.00	3.00
❑	17 David Carr	6.00	2.50
❑	18 Joey Harrington	6.00	2.50
❑	19 Tom Brady	15.00	6.00
❑	20 Michael Vick	12.00	5.00
❑	21 Jerry Rice	12.00	5.00
❑	22 Mike Alstott	5.00	2.00
❑	23 Keyshawn Johnson	5.00	2.00
❑	24 Jeremy Shockey	6.00	2.50
❑	25 Stephen Davis	5.00	2.00
❑	26 Kevan Barlow	5.00	2.00
❑	27 Carson Palmer	8.00	3.00
❑	28 Steve McNair	6.00	2.50
❑	29 Jake Plummer	5.00	2.00
❑	30 Jeff Garcia	6.00	2.50
❑	31 Byron Leftwich	8.00	3.00
❑	32 Hines Ward	6.00	2.50
❑	33 Randy Moss	8.00	3.00
❑	34 Marvin Harrison	6.00	2.50
❑	35 Terrell Owens	6.00	2.50
❑	36 Ahman Green	6.00	2.50
❑	37 Edgerrin James	6.00	2.50
❑	38 Emmitt Smith	12.00	5.00
❑	39 Torry Holt	6.00	2.50
❑	40 Drew Bledsoe	6.00	2.50
❑	42 P.Rivers JSY AU/90 RC	100.00	50.00
❑	43 Larry Fitzgerald RC	25.00	10.00
❑	44 Ro.Williams JSY AU/100 RC	80.00	30.00
❑	45 D.Henson JSY AU/95 RC	40.00	15.00
❑	46 Roethl. JSY AU/100 RC	300.00	175.00
❑	48 Kellen Winslow RC	15.00	6.00
❑	49 Chris Perry RC	12.00	5.00
❑	50 Re.Williams JSY AU/100 RC	40.00	15.00
❑	51 Steven Jackson RC	25.00	10.00
❑	52 Rashaun Woods RC	8.00	3.00
❑	53 Tatum Bell RC	15.00	6.00
❑	54 J.P. Losman RC	15.00	6.00
❑	55 Sean Taylor RC	10.00	4.00
❑	56 M.Clayton JSY AU/80 RC	60.00	25.00
❑	57 Lee Evans RC	10.00	4.00
❑	58 Julius Jones RC	25.00	10.00
❑	59 Jonathan Vilma RC	8.00	3.00
❑	60 M.Jenkins JSY AU/96 RC	30.00	12.50
❑	61 Greg Jones RC	8.00	3.00
❑	62 Will Smith RC	8.00	3.00
❑	63 Ernest Wilford RC	8.00	3.00
❑	64 Quincy Wilson RC	6.00	2.50
❑	65 Cody Pickett RC	8.00	3.00

1994 Excalibur

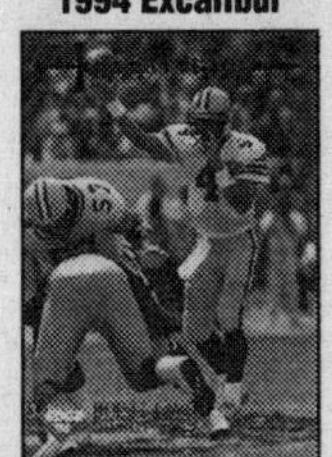

	Card	Price 1	Price 2
❑	COMPLETE SET (75)	20.00	7.50
❑	1 Bobby Hebert	.25	.08
❑	2 Deion Sanders	1.00	.40
❑	3 Andre Rison	.50	.20
❑	4 Cornelius Bennett	.50	.20
❑	5 Jim Kelly	.75	.30
❑	6 Andre Reed	.50	.20
❑	7 Bruce Smith	.75	.30
❑	8 Thurman Thomas	.75	.30
❑	9 Curtis Conway	.75	.30
❑	10 Richard Dent	.50	.20
❑	11 Jim Harbaugh	.75	.30
❑	12 Troy Aikman	2.00	.75
❑	13 Michael Irvin	.75	.30
❑	14 Russell Maryland	.25	.08
❑	15 Emmitt Smith	3.00	1.25
❑	16 Steve Atwater	.25	.08
❑	17 Rod Bernstine	.25	.08
❑	18 John Elway	4.00	1.50
❑	19 Glyn Milburn	.50	.20
❑	20 Shannon Sharpe	.50	.20
❑	21 Barry Sanders	3.00	1.25
❑	22 Edgar Bennett	.75	.30
❑	23 Brett Favre	4.00	1.50
❑	24 Sterling Sharpe	.50	.20
❑	25 Reggie White	.75	.30
❑	26 Warren Moon	.75	.30
❑	27 Wilber Marshall	.25	.08
❑	28 Haywood Jeffires	.50	.20
❑	29 Lorenzo White	.25	.08
❑	30 Quentin Coryatt	.25	.08
❑	31 Roosevelt Potts	.25	.08
❑	32 Jeff George	.75	.30
❑	33 Joe Montana	4.00	1.50
❑	34 Neil Smith	.50	.20
❑	35 Marcus Allen	.75	.30
❑	36 Derrick Thomas	.75	.30
❑	37 Jeff Hostetler	.50	.20
❑	38 Tim Brown	.75	.30
❑	39 Rocket Ismail	.50	.20
❑	40 Randall Cunningham	.75	.30
❑	41 Jerome Bettis	1.00	.40
❑	42 Dan Marino	4.00	1.50
❑	43 Keith Jackson	.25	.08
❑	44 O.J.McDuffie	.75	.30
❑	45 Drew Bledsoe	1.50	.60
❑	46 Leonard Russell	.25	.08
❑	47 Wade Wilson	.25	.08
❑	48 Eric Martin	.25	.08
❑	49 Phil Simms	.50	.20
❑	50 Gary Brown RB	.75	.30
❑	51 Rodney Hampton	.50	.20
❑	52 Boomer Esiason	.50	.20
❑	53 Johnny Johnson	.25	.08
❑	54 Ronnie Lott	.50	.20
❑	55 Fred Barnett	.50	.20
❑	56 Leroy Thompson	.25	.08
❑	57 Barry Foster	.25	.08
❑	58 Neil O'Donnell	.75	.30
❑	59 Stan Humphries	.50	.20
❑	60 Marion Butts	.25	.08
❑	61 Anthony Miller	.50	.20
❑	62 Natrone Means	.75	.30
❑	63 Dana Stubblefield	.50	.20
❑	64 John Taylor	.50	.20
❑	65 Ricky Watters	.50	.20
❑	66 Steve Young	1.50	.60
❑	67 Jerry Rice	2.00	.75
❑	68 Tom Rathman	.25	.08
❑	69 Rick Mirer	.75	.30
❑	70 Chris Warren	.50	.20
❑	71 Cortez Kennedy	.50	.20
❑	72 Mark Rypien	.25	.08
❑	73 Desmond Howard	.50	.20
❑	74 Art Monk	.50	.20
❑	75 Reggie Brooks	.50	.20

1995 Excalibur

	Card	Price 1	Price 2
❑	COMPLETE SET (150)	30.00	15.00
❑	COMP.SERIES 1 (75)	15.00	7.50
❑	COMP.SERIES 2 (75)	15.00	7.50
❑	1 Gary Clark	.15	.05
❑	2 Randal Hill	.15	.05
❑	3 Anthony Edwards	.15	.05
❑	4 Terance Mathis	.30	.10
❑	5 Erric Pegram	.30	.10
❑	6 Jeff George	.30	.10
❑	7 Pete Metzelaars	.15	.05
❑	8 Jim Kelly	.50	.20
❑	9 Andre Reed	.30	.10
❑	10 Lewis Tillman	.15	.05
❑	11 Curtis Conway	.50	.20
❑	12 Steve Walsh	.15	.05
❑	13 Derrick Fenner	.15	.05
❑	14 Harold Green	.15	.05
❑	15 Michael Jackson	.30	.10
❑	16 Eric Metcalf	.30	.10
❑	17 Antonio Langham	.15	.05
❑	18 Troy Aikman	2.00	.75
❑	19 Alvin Harper	.15	.05
❑	20 Jay Novacek	.30	.10
❑	21 John Elway	4.00	1.50
❑	22 Glyn Milburn	.15	.05
❑	23 Steve Atwater	.15	.05
❑	24 Mel Gray	.15	.05
❑	25 Herman Moore	.50	.20
❑	26 Scott Mitchell	.30	.10
❑	27 Guy McIntyre	.15	.05
❑	28 Edgar Bennett	.30	.10
❑	29 Sterling Sharpe	.30	.10
❑	30 Gary Brown	.15	.05
❑	31 Haywood Jeffires	.15	.05
❑	32 Marshall Faulk	2.50	1.00
❑	33 Roosevelt Potts	.15	.05
❑	34 Marcus Allen	.50	.20
❑	35 Willie Davis	.30	.10
❑	36 Lake Dawson	.30	.10
❑	37 Jeff Hostetler	.30	.10
❑	38 Rocket Ismail	.30	.10
❑	39 Troy Drayton	.15	.05
❑	40 Jerome Bettis	.50	.20
❑	41 Dan Marino	4.00	1.50
❑	42 Mark Ingram	.15	.05
❑	43 O.J. McDuffie	.50	.20
❑	44 Warren Moon	.30	.10
❑	45 Qadry Ismail	.30	.10
❑	46 Jake Reed	.30	.10
❑	47 Ben Coates	.30	.10
❑	48 Vincent Brisby	.15	.05
❑	49 Michael Timpson	.15	.05
❑	50 Brad Daluiso	.15	.05
❑	51 Rodney Hampton	.30	.10
❑	52 Chris Calloway	.15	.05
❑	53 Rob Moore	.30	.10
❑	54 Boomer Esiason	.30	.10
❑	55 Michael Haynes	.30	.10
❑	56 Vaughn Dunbar	.15	.05
❑	57 Calvin Williams	.30	.10
❑	58 Herschel Walker	.30	.10
❑	59 Charlie Garner	.50	.20
❑	60 Neil O'Donnell	.30	.10
❑	61 Deon Figures	.15	.05
❑	62 Byron Bam Morris	.15	.05
❑	63 Junior Seau	.50	.20
❑	64 Leslie O'Neal	.30	.10
❑	65 Natrone Means	.30	.10
❑	66 Jerry Rice	2.00	.75
❑	67 Deion Sanders	1.25	.50
❑	68 William Floyd	.30	.10
❑	69 Chris Warren	.30	.10
❑	70 Cortez Kennedy	.30	.10
❑	71 Hardy Nickerson	.15	.05
❑	72 Craig Erickson	.15	.05
❑	73 Heath Shuler	.30	.10
❑	74 Reggie Brooks	.30	.10
❑	75 Henry Ellard	.30	.10
❑	76 Garrison Hearst	.50	.20
❑	77 Steve Beuerlein	.30	.10
❑	78 Seth Joyner	.15	.05
❑	79 Andre Rison	.30	.10
❑	80 Norm Johnson	.15	.05
❑	81 Craig Heyward	.30	.10
❑	82 Darryl Talley	.15	.05
❑	83 Kenneth Davis	.15	.05
❑	84 Bruce Smith	.50	.20
❑	85 Tom Waddle	.15	.05
❑	86 Erik Kramer	.15	.05
❑	87 Carl Pickens	.30	.10
❑	88 Dan Wilkinson	.30	.10
❑	89 Jeff Blake RC	.75	.30
❑	90 Vinny Testaverde	.30	.10
❑	91 Tommy Vardell	.15	.05
❑	92 Leroy Hoard	.15	.05
❑	93 Emmitt Smith	3.00	1.25
❑	94 Michael Irvin	.50	.20
❑	95 Daryl Johnston	.30	.10
❑	96 Shannon Sharpe	.30	.10
❑	97 Anthony Miller	.30	.10
❑	98 Leonard Russell	.15	.05
❑	99 Barry Sanders	3.00	1.25
❑	100 Brett Perriman	.30	.10

❑ 101 Johnnie Morton .30 .10
❑ 102 Brett Favre 4.00 1.50
❑ 103 Bryce Paup .30 .10
❑ 104 Ernest Givins .15 .05
❑ 105 Webster Slaughter .15 .05
❑ 106 Jim Harbaugh .30 .10
❑ 107 Joe Montana 4.00 1.50
❑ 108 J.J. Birden .15 .05
❑ 109 Steve Bono .30 .10
❑ 110 James Jett .30 .10
❑ 111 Tim Brown .50 .20
❑ 112 Rob Fredrickson .15 .05
❑ 113 Chris Miller .15 .05
❑ 114 Bernie Parmalee .30 .10
❑ 115 Terry Kirby .30 .10
❑ 116 Bryan Cox .15 .05
❑ 117 Irving Fryar .30 .10
❑ 118 Terry Allen .30 .10
❑ 119 Cris Carter .50 .20
❑ 120 Fuad Reveiz .15 .05
❑ 121 Drew Bledsoe 1.25 .50
❑ 122 Greg McMurtry .15 .05
❑ 123 Dave Brown .30 .10
❑ 124 Dave Meggett .15 .05
❑ 125 Johnny Johnson .15 .05
❑ 126 Ronnie Lott .30 .10
❑ 127 Johnny Mitchell .15 .05
❑ 128 Eric Martin .15 .05
❑ 129 Jim Everett .15 .05
❑ 130 Randall Cunningham .50 .20
❑ 131 Eric Allen .15 .05
❑ 132 Fred Barnett .30 .10
❑ 133 Barry Foster .30 .10
❑ 134 Kevin Greene .30 .10
❑ 135 Eric Green .15 .05
❑ 136 Stan Humphries .30 .10
❑ 137 Mark Seay .30 .10
❑ 138 Alfred Pupunu RC .15 .05
❑ 139 Steve Young 1.50 .60
❑ 140 John Taylor .15 .05
❑ 141 Ricky Watters .30 .10
❑ 142 Brian Blades .30 .10
❑ 143 Rick Mirer .30 .10
❑ 144 Cortez Kennedy .30 .10
❑ 145 Jackie Harris .15 .05
❑ 146 Errict Rhett .30 .10
❑ 147 Trent Dilfer .50 .20
❑ 148 Brian Mitchell .15 .05
❑ 149 Ricky Ervins .15 .05
❑ 150 Darrell Green .15 .05

1997 Excalibur

❑ COMPLETE SET (150) 60.00 30.00
❑ 1 Larry Centers .75 .30
❑ 2 Leeland McElroy .50 .20
❑ 3 Simeon Rice .75 .30
❑ 4 Eric Swann .50 .20
❑ 5 Jamal Anderson 1.25 .50
❑ 6 Bert Emanuel .75 .30
❑ 7 Eric Metcalf .75 .30
❑ 8 Ray Lewis 2.00 .75
❑ 9 Derrick Alexander WR .75 .30
❑ 10 Michael Jackson .75 .30
❑ 11 Vinny Testaverde .75 .30
❑ 12 Todd Collins .50 .20
❑ 13 Jim Kelly 1.25 .50
❑ 14 Eric Moulds 1.25 .50
❑ 15 Andre Reed .75 .30
❑ 16 Bruce Smith .75 .30
❑ 17 Thurman Thomas 1.25 .50
❑ 18 Tim Biakabutuka .75 .30
❑ 19 Kerry Collins 1.25 .50
❑ 20 Kevin Greene .75 .30
❑ 21 Anthony Johnson .50 .20
❑ 22 Lamar Lathon .50 .20
❑ 23 Muhsin Muhammad .75 .30
❑ 24 Curtis Conway .75 .30
❑ 25 Bryan Cox .50 .20
❑ 26 Walt Harris .50 .20
❑ 27 Erik Kramer .50 .20
❑ 28 Rick Mirer .50 .20
❑ 29 Rashaan Salaam .50 .20
❑ 30 Jeff Blake .75 .30
❑ 31 Ki-Jana Carter .50 .20
❑ 32 Carl Pickens .75 .30
❑ 33 Troy Aikman 3.00 1.50
❑ 34 Michael Irvin 1.25 .50
❑ 35 Daryl Johnston .75 .30
❑ 36 Emmitt Smith 5.00 2.50
❑ 37 Broderick Thomas .50 .20
❑ 38 Terrell Davis 1.50 .60
❑ 39 John Elway 6.00 2.50
❑ 40 Anthony Miller .50 .20
❑ 41 John Mobley .50 .20
❑ 42 Shannon Sharpe .75 .30
❑ 43 Neil Smith .75 .30
❑ 44 Scott Mitchell .75 .30
❑ 45 Herman Moore .75 .30
❑ 46 Brett Perriman .50 .20
❑ 47 Barry Sanders 5.00 2.00
❑ 48 Edgar Bennett .75 .30
❑ 49 Robert Brooks .75 .30
❑ 50 Brett Favre 6.00 3.00
❑ 51 Antonio Freeman 1.25 .50
❑ 52 Dorsey Levens 1.25 .50
❑ 53 Reggie White 1.25 .50
❑ 54 Eddie George 1.25 .50
❑ 55 Darryll Lewis .50 .20
❑ 56 Steve McNair 1.50 .60
❑ 57 Chris Sanders .50 .20
❑ 58 Marshall Faulk 1.50 .60
❑ 59 Jim Harbaugh .75 .30
❑ 60 Marvin Harrison 1.25 .50
❑ 61 Jimmy Smith .75 .30
❑ 62 Tony Brackens .50 .20
❑ 63 Mark Brunell 1.50 .60
❑ 64 Kevin Hardy .50 .20
❑ 65 Keenan McCardell .75 .30
❑ 66 Natrone Means .75 .30
❑ 67 Marcus Allen 1.25 .50
❑ 68 Elvis Grbac .75 .30
❑ 69 Derrick Thomas 1.25 .50
❑ 70 Tamarick Vanover .75 .30
❑ 71 Karim Abdul-Jabbar .75 .30
❑ 72 Terrell Buckley .50 .20
❑ 73 Irving Fryar .75 .30
❑ 74 Dan Marino 6.00 2.50
❑ 75 O.J. McDuffie .75 .30
❑ 76 Zach Thomas 1.25 .50
❑ 77 Terry Kirby .75 .30
❑ 78 Cris Carter 1.25 .50
❑ 79 Brad Johnson 1.25 .50
❑ 80 John Randle .75 .30
❑ 81 Jake Reed .75 .30
❑ 82 Robert Smith .75 .30
❑ 83 Drew Bledsoe 1.50 .60
❑ 84 Ben Coates .75 .30
❑ 85 Terry Glenn 1.25 .50
❑ 86 Ty Law .75 .30
❑ 87 Curtis Martin 1.50 .60
❑ 88 Willie McGinest .50 .20
❑ 89 Mario Bates .50 .20
❑ 90 Jim Everett .50 .20
❑ 91 Wayne Martin .50 .20
❑ 92 Heath Shuler .50 .20
❑ 93 Torrance Small .50 .20
❑ 94 Ray Zellars .50 .20
❑ 95 Dave Brown .50 .20
❑ 96 Jason Sehorn .75 .30
❑ 97 Amani Toomer .75 .30
❑ 98 Tyrone Wheatley .75 .30
❑ 99 Hugh Douglas .50 .20
❑ 100 Aaron Glenn .50 .20
❑ 101 Jeff Graham .50 .20
❑ 102 Keyshawn Johnson 1.25 .50
❑ 103 Adrian Murrell .75 .30
❑ 104 Neil O'Donnell .75 .30
❑ 105 Tim Brown 1.25 .50
❑ 106 Jeff George .75 .30
❑ 107 Jeff Hostetler .50 .20
❑ 108 Napoleon Kaufman 1.25 .50
❑ 109 Chester McGlockton .50 .20
❑ 110 Fred Barnett .50 .20
❑ 111 Ty Detmer .75 .30
❑ 112 Chris T. Jones .50 .20
❑ 113 Ricky Watters .75 .30
❑ 114 Bobby Engram .75 .30
❑ 115 Jerome Bettis 1.25 .50
❑ 116 Charles Johnson .75 .30
❑ 117 Greg Lloyd .50 .20
❑ 118 Kordell Stewart 1.25 .50
❑ 119 Yancey Thigpen .75 .30
❑ 120 Rod Woodson .75 .30
❑ 121 Stan Humphries .75 .30
❑ 122 Tony Martin .75 .30
❑ 123 Leonard Russell .50 .20
❑ 124 Junior Seau 1.25 .50
❑ 125 Chad Brown .50 .20
❑ 126 John Friesz .50 .20
❑ 127 Joey Galloway .75 .30
❑ 128 Cortez Kennedy .50 .20
❑ 129 Warren Moon 1.25 .50
❑ 130 Chris Warren .75 .30
❑ 131 Garrison Hearst .75 .30
❑ 132 Terrell Owens 1.50 .60
❑ 133 Jerry Rice 3.00 1.50
❑ 134 Dana Stubblefield .50 .20
❑ 135 Bryant Young .50 .20
❑ 136 Steve Young 2.00 .75
❑ 137 Tony Banks .75 .30
❑ 138 Isaac Bruce 1.25 .50
❑ 139 Eddie Kennison .75 .30
❑ 140 Keith Lyle .50 .20
❑ 141 Lawrence Phillips .50 .20
❑ 142 Mike Alstott 1.25 .50
❑ 143 Hardy Nickerson .50 .20
❑ 144 Errict Rhett .50 .20
❑ 145 Warren Sapp .75 .30
❑ 146 Gus Frerotte .50 .20
❑ 147 Sean Gilbert .50 .20
❑ 148 Ken Harvey .50 .20
❑ 149 Terry Allen 1.25 .50
❑ 150 Michael Westbrook .75 .30

2005 Exquisite Collection

❑ 1-42 PRINT RUN 150 SER.#'d SETS
❑ ROOKIE AU PRINT RUN 150 SER.#'d SETS
❑ ROOKIE JSY AU PRINT RUN 199 SER.#'d SETS
❑ 1 Larry Fitzgerald 40.00 15.00
❑ 2 Michael Vick 60.00 25.00
❑ 3 Jamal Lewis 25.00 10.00
❑ 4 Ray Lewis 40.00 15.00
❑ 5 Willis McGahee 40.00 15.00
❑ 6 Jake Delhomme 40.00 15.00
❑ 7 Brian Urlacher 40.00 15.00
❑ 8 Carson Palmer 50.00 25.00
❑ 9 Julius Jones 50.00 20.00
❑ 10 Drew Bledsoe 40.00 15.00
❑ 11 Jake Plummer 25.00 10.00
❑ 12 Kevin Jones 50.00 20.00
❑ 13 Roy Williams WR 40.00 15.00
❑ 14 Ahman Green 40.00 15.00
❑ 15 Brett Favre 120.00 60.00
❑ 16 David Carr 40.00 15.00
❑ 17 Edgerrin James 40.00 15.00
❑ 18 Marvin Harrison 40.00 15.00
❑ 19 Peyton Manning 80.00 40.00
❑ 20 Byron Leftwich 40.00 15.00
❑ 21 Priest Holmes 40.00 15.00
❑ 22 Daunte Culpepper 40.00 15.00
❑ 23 Tom Brady 80.00 40.00
❑ 24 Deuce McAllister 40.00 15.00

Card	Hi	Lo
❑ 25 Eli Manning	80.00	30.00
❑ 26 Jeremy Shockey	40.00	15.00
❑ 27 Chad Pennington	40.00	15.00
❑ 28 Curtis Martin	40.00	15.00
❑ 29 Randy Moss	40.00	15.00
❑ 30 Donovan McNabb	50.00	20.00
❑ 31 Terrell Owens	40.00	15.00
❑ 32 Jerome Bettis	40.00	15.00
❑ 33 Ben Roethlisberger	100.00	40.00
❑ 34 Drew Brees	40.00	15.00
❑ 35 LaDainian Tomlinson	50.00	20.00
❑ 36 Antonio Gates	40.00	15.00
❑ 37 Shaun Alexander	40.00	15.00
❑ 38 Marc Bulger	40.00	15.00
❑ 39 Torry Holt	25.00	10.00
❑ 40 Steven Jackson	50.00	20.00
❑ 41 Steve McNair	25.00	10.00
❑ 42 Clinton Portis	40.00	15.00
❑ 43 Dan Orlovsky AU RC	80.00	50.00
❑ 44 Darren Sproles AU RC	60.00	25.00
❑ 45 Marion Barber AU RC	250.00	150.00
❑ 46 Chris Henry AU RC	120.00	60.00
❑ 47 Derek Anderson AU RC	60.00	35.00
❑ 48 Erasmus James AU RC	40.00	20.00
❑ 49 Thomas Davis AU RC	40.00	20.00
❑ 50 David Pollack AU RC	60.00	30.00
❑ 51 Fred Gibson AU RC	50.00	25.00
❑ 52 Craphonso Thorpe AU RC	40.00	20.00
❑ 53 Derrick Johnson AU RC	100.00	50.00
❑ 54 Brandon Jacobs AU RC	350.00	200.00
❑ 55 Adrian McPherson AU RC	50.00	25.00
❑ 56 Matt Cassel AU RC	100.00	50.00
❑ 57 Anthony Davis AU RC	50.00	25.00
❑ 58 Alvin Pearman AU RC	50.00	25.00
❑ 59 Brandon Jones AU RC	50.00	25.00
❑ 60 Jerome Mathis AU RC	50.00	25.00
❑ 61 Chase Lyman AU RC	30.00	15.00
❑ 62 Roydell Williams AU RC	40.00	20.00
❑ 63 DeMarcus Ware AU RC	80.00	50.00
❑ 64 Mike Patterson AU RC	40.00	20.00
❑ 65 Mike Nugent AU RC	50.00	25.00
❑ 66 Ryan Fitzpatrick AU RC	80.00	30.00
❑ 67 Barrett Ruud AU RC	50.00	25.00
❑ 68 Kevin Burnett AU RC	50.00	25.00
❑ 69 J.R. Russell AU RC	40.00	20.00
❑ 70 C.Houston AU RC EXCH	60.00	30.00
❑ 71 Marlin Jackson AU RC	50.00	25.00
❑ 72 Shawne Merriman AU RC	250.00	150.00
❑ 73 Alex Smith TE AU RC	50.00	25.00
❑ 74 Fabian Washington AU RC	50.00	25.00
❑ 75 Corey Webster AU RC	50.00	25.00
❑ 76 Larry Brackins AU RC	40.00	20.00
❑ 77 Kay-Jay Harris AU RC	40.00	20.00
❑ 78 Airese Currie AU RC	50.00	25.00
❑ 79 Taylor Stubblefield AU RC	30.00	15.00
❑ 80 James Kilian AU RC	40.00	20.00
❑ 81 Travis Johnson AU RC	30.00	15.00
❑ 82 Walter Reyes AU RC	30.00	15.00
❑ 83 Anttaj Hawthorne AU RC	40.00	20.00
❑ 84 Chad Owens AU RC	60.00	30.00
❑ 85 J.J. Arrington JSY AU RC	100.00	50.00
❑ 86 Mark Bradley JSY AU RC	100.00	50.00
❑ 87 Reggie Brown JSY AU RC	150.00	75.00
❑ 88 Jason Campbell JSY AU RC	300.00	150.00
❑ 89 Maurice Clarett JSY AU	80.00	40.00
❑ 90 Mark Clayton JSY AU RC	200.00	100.00
❑ 91 Ciatrick Fason JSY AU RC	80.00	30.00
❑ 92 Charlie Frye JSY AU RC	250.00	125.00
❑ 93 Frank Gore JSY AU RC	450.00	250.00
❑ 94 David Greene JSY AU RC	100.00	50.00
❑ 95 Vincent Jackson JSY AU RC	135.00	75.00
❑ 96 Adam Jones JSY AU RC	80.00	40.00
❑ 97 Matt Jones JSY AU RC	250.00	125.00
❑ 98 Stefan LeFors JSY AU RC	80.00	40.00
❑ 99 Heath Miller JSY AU RC	150.00	75.00
❑ 100 Ryan Moats JSY AU RC	120.00	60.00
❑ 101 Vernand Morency JSY AU RC	120.00	60.00
❑ 102 Terrence Murphy JSY AU RC	80.00	30.00
❑ 103 Kyle Orton JSY AU RC	100.00	40.00
❑ 104 Roscoe Parrish JSY AU RC	80.00	40.00
❑ 105 Courtney Roby JSY AU RC	60.00	30.00
❑ 106 Aaron Rodgers JSY AU RC	500.00	250.00
❑ 107 Carlos Rogers JSY AU RC	80.00	40.00
❑ 108 Antrel Rolle JSY AU RC	80.00	40.00
❑ 109 Eric Shelton JSY AU RC	80.00	40.00
❑ 110 Andrew Walter JSY AU RC	150.00	75.00
❑ 111 Roddy White JSY AU RC	120.00	50.00
❑ 112 T.Williamson JSY AU/99 RC	200.00	100.00
❑ 113 Mike Williams JSY AU	120.00	60.00
❑ 114 Ro.Brown JSY AU/99 RC	1200.00	600.00
❑ 115 B.Edwards JSY AU/99 RC	500.00	300.00
❑ 116 C.Benson JSY AU/99 RC	800.00	500.00
❑ 117 C.Williams JSY AU/99 RC	120.00	600.00
❑ 118 A.Smith QB JSY AU/99 RC	1200.00	700.00
❑ 120 Tyson Thompson AU RC	60.00	30.00
❑ 121 Chris Carr AU RC	40.00	15.00
❑ 122 Fred Amey AU RC	40.00	15.00
❑ 123 Brodney Pool AU RC	40.00	15.00
❑ 124 Stanford Routt AU RC	40.00	15.00
❑ 125 Justin Tuck AU RC	50.00	20.00
❑ 126 Luis Castillo AU RC	50.00	20.00
❑ 127 Kirk Morrison AU RC	50.00	20.00
❑ 128 DeAndra Cobb AU RC	40.00	15.00

1992 Finest

Card	Hi	Lo
❑ COMPLETE SET (45)	20.00	7.50
❑ 1 Neal Anderson	.50	.20
❑ 2 Cornelius Bennett	.50	.20
❑ 3 Marion Butts	.30	.10
❑ 4 Anthony Carter	.50	.20
❑ 5 Mike Croel	.30	.10
❑ 6 John Elway	5.00	2.00
❑ 7 Jim Everett	.50	.20
❑ 8 Ernest Givins	.30	.10
❑ 9 Rodney Hampton	.50	.20
❑ 10 Alvin Harper	.30	.10
❑ 11 Michael Irvin	1.00	.40
❑ 12 Rickey Jackson	.30	.10
❑ 13 Seth Joyner	.30	.10
❑ 14 James Lofton	.50	.20
❑ 15 Ronnie Lott	.50	.20
❑ 16 Eric Metcalf	.50	.20
❑ 17 Chris Miller	.50	.20
❑ 18 Art Monk	.50	.20
❑ 19 Warren Moon	1.00	.40
❑ 20 Rob Moore	.50	.20
❑ 21 Anthony Munoz	.50	.20
❑ 22 Christian Okoye	.30	.10
❑ 23 Andre Rison	.50	.20
❑ 24 Leonard Russell	.30	.10
❑ 25 Mark Rypien	.50	.20
❑ 26 Barry Sanders	5.00	2.00
❑ 27 Emmitt Smith	6.00	2.50
❑ 28 Pat Swilling	.30	.10
❑ 29 John Taylor	.50	.20
❑ 30 Derrick Thomas	1.00	.40
❑ 31 Thurman Thomas	1.00	.40
❑ 32 Reggie White	1.00	.40
❑ 33 Rod Woodson	1.00	.40
❑ 34 Edgar Bennett	.50	.20
❑ 35 Terrell Buckley	.30	.10
❑ 36 Keith Hamilton	.50	.20
❑ 37 Amp Lee	.30	.10
❑ 38 Ricardo McDonald	.30	.10
❑ 39 Chris Mims	.30	.10
❑ 40 Robert Porcher	1.00	.40
❑ 41 Leon Searcy	.30	.10
❑ 42 Siran Stacy	.30	.10
❑ 43 Tommy Vardell	.30	.10
❑ 44 Bob Whitfield	.30	.10
❑ NNO Checklist	.30	.10

1994 Finest

Card	Hi	Lo
❑ COMPLETE SET (220)	40.00	15.00
❑ 1 Emmitt Smith	6.00	2.50
❑ 2 Calvin Williams	.60	.25
❑ 3 Mark Collins	.30	.10
❑ 4 Steve McMichael	.60	.25
❑ 5 Jim Kelly	1.25	.50
❑ 6 Michael Dean Perry	.60	.25
❑ 7 Wayne Simmons	.30	.10

Card	Hi	Lo
❑ 8 Rocket Ismail	.60	.25
❑ 9 Mark Rypien	.30	.10
❑ 10 Brian Blades	.60	.25
❑ 11 Barry Word	.30	.10
❑ 12 Jerry Rice	4.00	1.50
❑ 13 Derrick Fenner	.30	.10
❑ 14 Karl Mecklenburg	.30	.10
❑ 15 Reggie Cobb	.30	.10
❑ 16 Eric Swann	.60	.25
❑ 17 Neil Smith	.60	.25
❑ 18 Barry Foster	.30	.10
❑ 19 Willie Roaf	.30	.10
❑ 20 Troy Drayton	.30	.10
❑ 21 Warren Moon	1.25	.50
❑ 22 Richmond Webb	.30	.10
❑ 23 Anthony Miller	.60	.25
❑ 24 Chris Slade	.30	.10
❑ 25 Mel Gray	.30	.10
❑ 26 Ronnie Lott	.60	.25
❑ 27 Andre Rison	.60	.25
❑ 28 Jeff George	1.25	.50
❑ 29 John Copeland	.30	.10
❑ 30 Derrick Thomas	1.25	.50
❑ 31 Sterling Sharpe	.60	.25
❑ 32 Chris Doleman	.30	.10
❑ 33 Monte Coleman	.30	.10
❑ 34 Mark Bavaro	.30	.10
❑ 35 Kevin Williams WR	.60	.25
❑ 36 Eric Metcalf	.60	.25
❑ 37 Brent Jones	.60	.25
❑ 38 Steve Tasker	.60	.25
❑ 39 Dave Meggett	.30	.10
❑ 40 Howie Long	1.25	.50
❑ 41 Rick Mirer	1.25	.50
❑ 42 Jerome Bettis	4.00	1.50
❑ 43 Marion Butts	.30	.10
❑ 44 Barry Sanders	6.00	2.50
❑ 45 Jason Elam	.60	.25
❑ 46 Broderick Thomas	.30	.10
❑ 47 Derek Brown RBK	.30	.10
❑ 48 Lorenzo White	.30	.10
❑ 49 Neil O'Donnell	1.25	.50
❑ 50 Chris Burkett	.30	.10
❑ 51 John Offerdahl	.30	.10
❑ 52 Rohn Stark	.30	.10
❑ 53 Neal Anderson	.30	.10
❑ 54 Steve Beuerlein	.60	.25
❑ 55 Bruce Armstrong	.30	.10
❑ 56 Lincoln Kennedy	.30	.10
❑ 57 Darrell Green	.30	.10
❑ 58 Ricardo McDonald	.30	.10
❑ 59 Chris Warren	.60	.25
❑ 60 Mark Jackson	.30	.10
❑ 61 Pepper Johnson	.30	.10
❑ 62 Chris Spielman	.60	.25
❑ 63 Marcus Allen	1.25	.50
❑ 64 Jim Everett	.60	.25
❑ 65 Greg Townsend	.30	.10
❑ 66 Cris Carter	1.50	.60
❑ 67 Don Beebe	.30	.10
❑ 68 Reggie Langhorne	.30	.10
❑ 69 Randall Cunningham	1.25	.50
❑ 70 Johnny Holland	.30	.10
❑ 71 Morten Andersen	.30	.10
❑ 72 Leonard Marshall	.30	.10
❑ 73 Keith Jackson	.30	.10
❑ 74 Leslie O'Neal	.30	.10
❑ 75 Hardy Nickerson	.60	.25
❑ 76 Dan Williams	.30	.10
❑ 77 Steve Young	3.00	1.25
❑ 78 Deon Figures	.30	.10
❑ 79 Michael Irvin	1.25	.50

❑ 80	Luis Sharpe	.30	.10
❑ 81	Andre Tippett	.30	.10
❑ 82	Ricky Sanders	.30	.10
❑ 83	Erric Pegram	.30	.10
❑ 84	Albert Lewis	.30	.10
❑ 85	Anthony Blaylock	.30	.10
❑ 86	Pat Swilling	.30	.10
❑ 87	Duane Bickett	.30	.10
❑ 88	Myron Guyton	.30	.10
❑ 89	Clay Matthews	.30	.10
❑ 90	Jim McMahon	.60	.25
❑ 91	Bruce Smith	1.25	.50
❑ 92	Reggie White	1.25	.50
❑ 93	Shannon Sharpe	.60	.25
❑ 94	Rickey Jackson	.30	.10
❑ 95	Ronnie Harmon	.30	.10
❑ 96	Terry McDaniel	.30	.10
❑ 97	Bryan Cox	.30	.10
❑ 98	Webster Slaughter	.30	.10
❑ 99	Boomer Esiason	.60	.25
❑ 100	Tim Krumrie	.30	.10
❑ 101	Cortez Kennedy	.60	.25
❑ 102	Henry Ellard	.60	.25
❑ 103	Clyde Simmons	.30	.10
❑ 104	Craig Erickson	.30	.10
❑ 105	Eric Green	.30	.10
❑ 106	Gary Clark	.60	.25
❑ 107	Jay Novacek	.60	.25
❑ 108	Dana Stubblefield	.60	.25
❑ 109	Mike Johnson	.30	.10
❑ 110	Ray Crockett	.30	.10
❑ 111	Leonard Russell	.30	.10
❑ 112	Robert Smith	1.25	.50
❑ 113	Art Monk	.60	.25
❑ 114	Ray Childress	.30	.10
❑ 115	O.J.McDuffie	1.25	.50
❑ 116	Tim Brown	1.25	.50
❑ 117	Kevin Ross	.30	.10
❑ 118	Richard Dent	.60	.25
❑ 119	John Elway	8.00	3.00
❑ 120	James Hasty	.30	.10
❑ 121	Gary Plummer	.30	.10
❑ 122	Pierce Holt	.30	.10
❑ 123	Eric Martin	.30	.10
❑ 124	Brett Favre	8.00	3.00
❑ 125	Cornelius Bennett	.60	.25
❑ 126	Jessie Hester	.30	.10
❑ 127	Lewis Tillman	.30	.10
❑ 128	Qadry Ismail	1.25	.50
❑ 129	Jay Schroeder	.30	.10
❑ 130	Curtis Conway	1.25	.50
❑ 131	Santana Dotson	.60	.25
❑ 132	Nick Lowery	.30	.10
❑ 133	Lomas Brown	.30	.10
❑ 134	Reggie Roby	.30	.10
❑ 135	John L. Williams	.30	.10
❑ 136	Vinny Testaverde	.60	.25
❑ 137	Seth Joyner	.30	.10
❑ 138	Ethan Horton	.30	.10
❑ 139	Jackie Slater	.30	.10
❑ 140	Rod Bernstine	.30	.10
❑ 141	Rob Moore	.60	.25
❑ 142	Dan Marino	8.00	3.00
❑ 143	Ken Harvey	.30	.10
❑ 144	Ernest Givins	.60	.25
❑ 145	Russell Maryland	.30	.10
❑ 146	Drew Bledsoe	3.00	1.25
❑ 147	Kevin Greene	.60	.25
❑ 148	Bobby Hebert	.30	.10
❑ 149	Junior Seau	1.25	.50
❑ 150	Tim McDonald	.30	.10
❑ 151	Thurman Thomas	1.25	.50
❑ 152	Phil Simms	.60	.25
❑ 153	Terrell Buckley	.30	.10
❑ 154	Sam Mills	.30	.10
❑ 155	Anthony Carter	.60	.25
❑ 156	Kelvin Martin	.30	.10
❑ 157	Shane Conlan	.30	.10
❑ 158	Irving Fryar	.60	.25
❑ 159	Demetrius DuBose	.30	.10
❑ 160	David Klingler	.30	.10
❑ 161	Herman Moore	1.25	.50
❑ 162	Jeff Hostetler	.60	.25
❑ 163	Tommy Vardell	.30	.10
❑ 164	Craig Heyward	.60	.25
❑ 165	Wilber Marshall	.30	.10
❑ 166	Quentin Coryatt	.30	.10
❑ 167	Glyn Milburn	.60	.25
❑ 168	Fred Barnett	.60	.25
❑ 169	Charles Haley	.60	.25
❑ 170	Carl Banks	.30	.10
❑ 171	Ricky Proehl	.30	.10
❑ 172	Joe Montana	8.00	3.00
❑ 173	Johnny Mitchell	.30	.10
❑ 174	Andre Reed	.60	.25
❑ 175	Marco Coleman	.30	.10
❑ 176	Vaughan Johnson	.30	.10
❑ 177	Carl Pickens	.60	.25
❑ 178	Dwight Stone	.30	.10
❑ 179	Ricky Watters	.60	.25
❑ 180	Michael Haynes	.60	.25
❑ 181	Roger Craig	.60	.25
❑ 182	Cleveland Gary	.30	.10
❑ 183	Steve Emtman	.30	.10
❑ 184	Patrick Bates	.30	.10
❑ 185	Mark Carrier WR	.60	.25
❑ 186	Brad Hopkins	.30	.10
❑ 187	Dennis Smith	.30	.10
❑ 188	Natrone Means	1.25	.50
❑ 189	Michael Jackson	.60	.25
❑ 190	Ken Norton Jr.	.60	.25
❑ 191	Carlton Gray	.30	.10
❑ 192	Edgar Bennett	1.25	.50
❑ 193	Lawrence Taylor	1.25	.50
❑ 194	Marv Cook	.30	.10
❑ 195	Eric Curry	.30	.10
❑ 196	Victor Bailey	.30	.10
❑ 197	Ryan McNeil	.30	.10
❑ 198	Rod Woodson	.60	.25
❑ 199	Earnest Byner	.30	.10
❑ 200	Marvin Jones	.30	.10
❑ 201	Thomas Smith	.30	.10
❑ 202	Troy Aikman	4.00	1.50
❑ 203	Audray McMillian	.30	.10
❑ 204	Wade Wilson	.30	.10
❑ 205	George Teague	.30	.10
❑ 206	Deion Sanders	2.00	.75
❑ 207	Will Shields	.60	.25
❑ 208	John Taylor	.60	.25
❑ 209	Jim Harbaugh	1.25	.50
❑ 210	Micheal Barrow	.30	.10
❑ 211	Harold Green	.30	.10
❑ 212	Steve Everitt	.30	.10
❑ 213	Flipper Anderson	.30	.10
❑ 214	Rodney Hampton	.60	.25
❑ 215	Steve Atwater	.30	.10
❑ 216	James Trapp	.30	.10
❑ 217	Terry Kirby	1.25	.50
❑ 218	Garrison Hearst	1.25	.50
❑ 219	Jeff Bryant	.30	.10
❑ 220	Roosevelt Potts	.30	.10

1995 Finest

❑	COMPLETE SET (275)	80.00	30.00
❑	COMP.SERIES 1 (165)	20.00	10.00
❑	COMP.SERIES 2 (110)	60.00	25.00
❑ 1	Natrone Means	.60	.25
❑ 2	Dave Meggett	.25	.08
❑ 3	Tim Bowens	.25	.08
❑ 4	Jay Novacek	.60	.25
❑ 5	Michael Jackson	.60	.25
❑ 6	Calvin Williams	.60	.25
❑ 7	Neil Smith	.60	.25
❑ 8	Chris Gardocki	.25	.08
❑ 9	Jeff Burris	.25	.08
❑ 10	Warren Moon	.60	.25
❑ 11	Gary Anderson K	.25	.08
❑ 12	Bert Emanuel	1.25	.50
❑ 13	Rick Tuten	.25	.08
❑ 14	Steve Wallace	.25	.08
❑ 15	Marion Butts	.25	.08
❑ 16	Johnnie Morton	.60	.25
❑ 17	Rob Moore	.60	.25
❑ 18	Wayne Gandy	.25	.08
❑ 19	Quentin Coryatt	.60	.25
❑ 20	Richmond Webb	.25	.08
❑ 21	Errict Rhett	.60	.25
❑ 22	Joe Johnson	.25	.08
❑ 23	Gary Brown	.25	.08
❑ 24	Jeff Hostetler	.60	.25
❑ 25	Larry Centers	.60	.25
❑ 26	Tom Carter	.25	.08
❑ 27	Steve Atwater	.25	.08
❑ 28	Doug Pelfrey	.25	.08
❑ 29	Bryce Paup	.60	.25
❑ 30	Erik Williams	.25	.08
❑ 31	Henry Jones	.25	.08
❑ 32	Stanley Richard	.25	.08
❑ 33	Marcus Allen	1.25	.50
❑ 34	Antonio Langham	.25	.08
❑ 35	Lewis Tillman	.25	.08
❑ 36	Thomas Randolph	.25	.08
❑ 37	Byron Bam Morris	.25	.08
❑ 38	David Palmer	.60	.25
❑ 39	Ricky Watters	.60	.25
❑ 40	Brett Perriman	.60	.25
❑ 41	Will Wolford	.25	.08
❑ 42	Burt Grossman	.25	.08
❑ 43	Vincent Brisby	.25	.08
❑ 44	Ronnie Lott	.60	.25
❑ 45	Brian Blades	.60	.25
❑ 46	Brent Jones	.25	.08
❑ 47	Anthony Newman	.25	.08
❑ 48	Willie Roaf	.25	.08
❑ 49	Paul Gruber	.25	.08
❑ 50	Jeff George	.60	.25
❑ 51	Jamir Miller	.25	.08
❑ 52	Anthony Miller	.60	.25
❑ 53	Darrell Green	.25	.08
❑ 54	Steve Wisniewski	.25	.08
❑ 55	Dan Wilkinson	.60	.25
❑ 56	Brett Favre	5.00	2.00
❑ 57	Leslie O'Neal	.60	.25
❑ 58	Keith Byars	.25	.08
❑ 59	James Washington	.25	.08
❑ 60	Andre Reed	.60	.25
❑ 61	Ken Norton Jr.	.60	.25
❑ 62	John Randle	.60	.25
❑ 63	Lake Dawson	.60	.25
❑ 64	Greg Montgomery	.25	.08
❑ 65	Erric Pegram	.60	.25
❑ 66	Steve Everitt	.25	.08
❑ 67	Chris Brantley	.25	.08
❑ 68	Rod Woodson	.60	.25
❑ 69	Eugene Robinson	.25	.08
❑ 70	Dave Brown	.60	.25
❑ 71	Ricky Reynolds	.25	.08
❑ 72	Rohn Stark	.25	.08
❑ 73	Randal Hill	.25	.08
❑ 74	Brian Washington	.25	.08
❑ 75	Heath Shuler	.60	.25
❑ 76	Darion Conner	.25	.08
❑ 77	Terry McDaniel	.25	.08
❑ 78	Al Del Greco	.25	.08
❑ 79	Allen Aldridge	.25	.08
❑ 80	Trace Armstrong	.25	.08
❑ 81	Darnay Scott	.60	.25
❑ 82	Charlie Garner	1.25	.50
❑ 83	Harold Bishop	.25	.08
❑ 84	Reggie White	1.25	.50
❑ 85	Shawn Jefferson	.25	.08
❑ 86	Irving Spikes	.60	.25
❑ 87	Mel Gray	.25	.08
❑ 88	D.J. Johnson	.25	.08
❑ 89	Daryl Johnston	.60	.25
❑ 90	Joe Montana	5.00	2.00
❑ 91	Michael Strahan	1.25	.50
❑ 92	Robert Blackmon	.25	.08
❑ 93	Ryan Yarborough	.60	.25
❑ 94	Terry Allen	.60	.25
❑ 95	Michael Haynes	.60	.25
❑ 96	Jim Harbaugh	.60	.25
❑ 97	Micheal Barrow	.25	.08
❑ 98	John Thierry	.25	.08
❑ 99	Seth Joyner	.25	.08
❑ 100	Deion Sanders	2.00	.75
❑ 101	Eric Turner	.25	.08
❑ 102	LeShon Johnson	.60	.25
❑ 103	John Copeland	.25	.08
❑ 104	Cornelius Bennett	.60	.25

❑ 105	Sean Gilbert	.60	.25
❑ 106	Herschel Walker	.60	.25
❑ 107	Henry Ellard	.60	.25
❑ 108	Neil O'Donnell	.60	.25
❑ 109	Charles Wilson	.25	.08
❑ 110	Willie McGinest	.60	.25
❑ 111	Tim Brown	1.25	.50
❑ 112	Simon Fletcher	.25	.08
❑ 113	Broderick Thomas	.25	.08
❑ 114	Tom Waddle	.25	.08
❑ 115	Jessie Tuggle	.25	.08
❑ 116	Maurice Hurst	.25	.08
❑ 117	Aubrey Beavers	.25	.08
❑ 118	Donnell Bennett	.60	.25
❑ 119	Shante Carver	.25	.08
❑ 120	Eric Metcalf	.60	.25
❑ 121	John Carney	.25	.08
❑ 122	Thomas Lewis	.60	.25
❑ 123	Johnny Mitchell	.25	.08
❑ 124	Trent Dilfer	1.25	.50
❑ 125	Marshall Faulk	3.00	1.25
❑ 126	Ernest Givins	.25	.08
❑ 127	Aeneas Williams	.25	.08
❑ 128	Bucky Brooks	.25	.08
❑ 129	Todd Steussie	.25	.08
❑ 130	Randall Cunningham	1.25	.50
❑ 131	Reggie Brooks	.60	.25
❑ 132	Morten Andersen	.25	.08
❑ 133	James Jett	.60	.25
❑ 134	George Teague	.25	.08
❑ 135	John Taylor	.25	.08
❑ 136	Charles Johnson	.60	.25
❑ 137	Isaac Bruce	2.50	1.00
❑ 138	Jason Elam	.60	.25
❑ 139	Carl Pickens	.60	.25
❑ 140	Chris Warren	.60	.25
❑ 141	Bruce Armstrong	.25	.08
❑ 142	Mark Carrier DB	.25	.08
❑ 143	Irving Fryar	.60	.25
❑ 144	Van Malone	.25	.08
❑ 145	Charles Haley	.60	.25
❑ 146	Chris Calloway	.25	.08
❑ 147	J.J. Birden	.25	.08
❑ 148	Tony Bennett	.25	.08
❑ 149	Lincoln Kennedy	.25	.08
❑ 150	Stan Humphries	.60	.25
❑ 151	Hardy Nickerson	.25	.08
❑ 152	Randall McDaniel	.25	.08
❑ 153	Marcus Robertson	.25	.08
❑ 154	Ronald Moore	.25	.08
❑ 155	Thurman Thomas	1.25	.50
❑ 156	Tommy Vardell	.25	.08
❑ 157	Ken Ruettgers	.25	.08
❑ 158	Rob Fredrickson	.25	.08
❑ 159	Johnny Bailey	.25	.08
❑ 160	Greg Lloyd	.60	.25
❑ 161	David Alexander	.25	.08
❑ 162	Kevin Mawae	.25	.08
❑ 163	Derek Brown RBK	.25	.08
❑ 164	William Floyd	.60	.25
❑ 165	Aaron Glenn	.25	.08
❑ 166	Joey Galloway RC	8.00	3.00
❑ 167	Troy Drayton	.25	.08
❑ 168	Dermontti Dawson	.60	.25
❑ 169	Ronald Moore	.25	.08
❑ 170	Dan Marino	5.00	2.00
❑ 171	Dennis Gibson	.25	.08
❑ 172	Raymont Harris	.25	.08
❑ 173	Shannon Sharpe	.60	.25
❑ 174	Kevin Williams	.60	.25
❑ 175	Jim Everett	.25	.08
❑ 176	Rocket Ismail	.60	.25
❑ 177	Mark Fields RC	1.25	.50
❑ 178	George Koonce	.25	.08
❑ 179	Chris Hudson	.25	.08
❑ 180	Jerry Rice	2.50	1.00
❑ 181	Dewayne Washington	.60	.25
❑ 182	Dale Carter	.60	.25
❑ 183	Pete Stoyanovich	.25	.08
❑ 184	Blake Brockermeyer	.25	.08
❑ 185	Troy Aikman	2.50	1.00
❑ 186	Jeff Blake RC	2.50	1.00
❑ 187	Troy Vincent	.25	.08
❑ 188	Lamar Lathon	.25	.08
❑ 189	Tony Boselli	1.25	.50
❑ 190	Emmitt Smith	4.00	1.50
❑ 191	Bobby Houston	.25	.08
❑ 192	Edgar Bennett	.60	.25
❑ 193	Derrick Brooks RC	8.00	3.00
❑ 194	Ricky Proehl	.25	.08
❑ 195	Rodney Hampton	.60	.25
❑ 196	Dave Krieg	.25	.08
❑ 197	Vinny Testaverde	.60	.25
❑ 198	Erik Kramer	.25	.08
❑ 199	Ben Coates	.60	.25
❑ 200	Steve Young	2.00	.75
❑ 201	Glyn Milburn	.25	.08
❑ 202	Bryan Cox	.25	.08
❑ 203	Luther Elliss	.25	.08
❑ 204	Mark McMillian	.25	.08
❑ 205	Jerome Bettis	1.25	.50
❑ 206	Craig Heyward	.60	.25
❑ 207	Ray Buchanan	.25	.08
❑ 208	Kimble Anders	.60	.25
❑ 209	Kevin Greene	.60	.25
❑ 210	Eric Allen	.25	.08
❑ 211	Ricardo McDonald	.25	.08
❑ 212	Ruben Brown RC	1.50	.60
❑ 213	Harvey Williams	.25	.08
❑ 214	Broderick Thomas	.25	.08
❑ 215	Frank Reich	.25	.08
❑ 216	Frank Sanders RC	1.50	.60
❑ 217	Craig Newsome	.25	.08
❑ 218	Merton Hanks	.25	.08
❑ 219	Chris Miller	.25	.08
❑ 220	John Elway	5.00	2.00
❑ 221	Ernest Givins	.25	.08
❑ 222	Boomer Esiason	.60	.25
❑ 223	Reggie Roby	.25	.08
❑ 224	Qadry Ismail	.60	.25
❑ 225	Ki-Jana Carter RC	1.50	.60
❑ 226	Leon Lett	.25	.08
❑ 227	Eric Hill	.25	.08
❑ 228	Scott Mitchell	.60	.25
❑ 229	Craig Erickson	.25	.08
❑ 230	Drew Bledsoe	2.00	.75
❑ 231	Sean Landeta	.25	.08
❑ 232	Barrett Brooks	.25	.08
❑ 233	Brian Mitchell	.25	.08
❑ 234	Tyrone Poole	1.25	.50
❑ 235	Desmond Howard	.60	.25
❑ 236	Wayne Simmons	.25	.08
❑ 237	Michael Westbrook RC	1.50	.60
❑ 238	Quinn Early	.60	.25
❑ 239	Willie Davis	.60	.25
❑ 240	Rashaan Salaam RC	.75	.30
❑ 241	Devin Bush	.25	.08
❑ 242	Dana Stubblefield	.60	.25
❑ 243	Dexter Carter	.25	.08
❑ 244	Shane Conlan	.25	.08
❑ 245	Keith Elias RC	.25	.08
❑ 246	Robert Brooks	1.25	.50
❑ 247	Garrison Hearst	1.25	.50
❑ 248	Eric Zeier RC	1.50	.60
❑ 249	Nate Newton	.60	.25
❑ 250	Barry Sanders	4.00	1.50
❑ 251	Dave Meggett	.25	.08
❑ 252	Courtney Hawkins	.25	.08
❑ 253	Cortez Kennedy	.60	.25
❑ 254	Mario Bates	.60	.25
❑ 255	Junior Seau	1.25	.50
❑ 256	Brian Washington	.25	.08
❑ 257	Darius Holland	.25	.08
❑ 258	Jeff Graham	.25	.08
❑ 259	Rob Moore	.60	.25
❑ 260	Andre Rison	.60	.25
❑ 261	Kerry Collins RC	8.00	3.00
❑ 262	Roosevelt Potts	.25	.08
❑ 263	Cris Carter	1.25	.50
❑ 264	Curtis Martin RC	15.00	6.00
❑ 265	Rick Mirer	.60	.25
❑ 266	Mo Lewis	.25	.08
❑ 267	Mike Sherrard	.25	.08
❑ 268	Herman Moore	1.25	.50
❑ 269	Eric Metcalf	.60	.25
❑ 270	Ray Childress	.25	.08
❑ 271	Chris Slade	.25	.08
❑ 272	Michael Irvin	1.25	.50
❑ 273	Jim Kelly	1.25	.50
❑ 274	Terance Mathis	.60	.25
❑ 275	LeRoy Butler	.25	.08

1996 Finest

❑ COMPLETE SET (359)	300.00	150.00
❑ COMP.SERIES 1 (191)	200.00	100.00
❑ COMP.SERIES 2 (168)	100.00	50.00
❑ COMP.BRONZE SER.1 (110)	40.00	15.00
❑ COMP.BRONZE SER.2 (110)	40.00	15.00

❑ B2	Jay Novacek B	.60	.25
❑ B3	Ray Buchanan B	.30	.10
❑ B5	Phil Hansen B	.30	.10
❑ B6	Mike Mamula B	.30	.10
❑ B9	Bernie Parmalee B	.30	.10
❑ B10	Herman Moore B	.60	.25
❑ B11	Shawn Jefferson B	.30	.10
❑ B12	Chris Doleman B	.30	.10
❑ B13	Erik Kramer B	.60	.25
❑ B15	Orlando Thomas B	.30	.10
❑ B16	Terrell Davis B	4.00	1.50
❑ B18	Roman Phifer B	.30	.10
❑ B19	Trent Dilfer B	.60	.25
❑ B21	Darnay Scott B	.60	.25
❑ B22	Steve McNair B	4.00	1.50
❑ B23	Lamar Lathon B	.30	.10
❑ B26	Thomas Randolph B	.30	.10
❑ B27	Michael Jackson B	.60	.25
❑ B28	Seth Joyner B	.30	.10
❑ B29	Jeff Lageman B	.30	.10
❑ B30	Darryl Williams B	.30	.10
❑ B32	Erric Pegram B	.60	.25
❑ B34	Sean Dawkins B	.60	.25
❑ B38	Dan Saleaumua B UER 28	.30	.10
❑ B39	Henry Thomas B	.30	.10
❑ B43	Pat Swilling B	.30	.10
❑ B44	Marty Carter B	.30	.10
❑ B45	Anthony Miller B	.60	.25
❑ B48	Chris Warren B	.60	.25
❑ B49	Derek Brown RBK B	.30	.10
❑ B51	Blaine Bishop B	.30	.10
❑ B52	Jake Reed B	.60	.25
❑ B55	Vencie Glenn B	.30	.10
❑ B58	Derrick Alexander WR B	.60	.25
❑ B64	Jessie Tuggle B	.30	.10
❑ B65	Terrance Shaw B	.30	.10
❑ B66	David Sloan B	.60	.25
❑ B68	Brent Jones B	.30	.10
❑ B70	William Thomas B	.30	.10
❑ B71	Robert Smith B	.60	.25
❑ B72	Wayne Simmons B	.30	.10
❑ B73	Jim Harbaugh B	.60	.25
❑ B76	Wayne Chrebet B	2.00	.75
❑ B77	Chris Hudson B	.30	.10
❑ B79	Stevon Moore B	.30	.10
❑ B80	Chris Calloway B	.30	.10
❑ B81	Tom Carter B	.30	.10
❑ B82	Dave Meggett B	.30	.10
❑ B83	Sam Mills B	.60	.25
❑ B86	Renaldo Turnbull B	.30	.10
❑ B87	Derrick Brooks B	1.00	.40
❑ B89	Eugene Robinson B	.30	.10
❑ B91	Rodney Thomas B	.30	.10
❑ B92	Dan Wilkinson B	.30	.10
❑ B93	Mark Fields B	.30	.10
❑ B94	Warren Sapp B	.30	.10
❑ B95	Curtis Martin B	4.00	1.50
❑ B97	Ray Crockett B	.30	.10
❑ B98	Ed McDaniel B	.30	.10
❑ B101	Craig Heyward B	.30	.10
❑ B102	Ellis Johnson B	.30	.10
❑ B104	O.J. McDuffie B	.60	.25
❑ B105	J.J. Stokes B	1.00	.40
❑ B106	Mo Lewis B	.30	.10
❑ B108	Rob Moore B	.60	.25
❑ B110	Tyrone Wheatley B	.60	.25
❑ B111	Ken Harvey B	.30	.10
❑ B113	Willie Green B	.30	.10
❑ B114	Willie Davis B	.60	.25
❑ B115	Andy Harmon B	.30	.10
❑ B117	Bryan Cox B	.30	.10
❑ B119	Bert Emanuel B	.60	.25

❑ B120	Greg Lloyd B	.60	.25
❑ B122	Willie Jackson B	.60	.25
❑ B123	Lorenzo Lynch B	.30	.10
❑ B124	Pepper Johnson B	.30	.10
❑ B128	Tyrone Poole B	.30	.10
❑ B129	Neil Smith B	.60	.25
❑ B130	Eddie Robinson B	.30	.10
❑ B131	Bryce Paup B	.60	.25
❑ B134	Troy Aikman B	5.00	2.00
❑ B136	Chris Sanders B	.60	.25
❑ B138	Jim Everett B	.30	.10
❑ B139	Frank Sanders B	.60	.25
❑ B141	Cortez Kennedy B	.60	.25
❑ B143	Derrick Alexander DE B	.30	.10
❑ B144	Rob Fredrickson B	.30	.10
❑ B145	Chris Zorich B	.30	.10
❑ B146	Devin Bush B	.30	.10
❑ B149	Troy Vincent B	.30	.10
❑ B151	Deion Sanders B	2.50	1.00
❑ B152	James O. Stewart B	.60	.25
❑ B156	Lawrence Dawsey B	.30	.10
❑ B157	Robert Brooks B	1.00	.40
❑ B158	Rashaan Salaam B	.60	.25
❑ B161	Tim Brown B	.60	.25
❑ B162	Brendan Stai B	.30	.10
❑ B163	Sean Gilbert B	.30	.10
❑ B169	Calvin Williams B	.60	.25
❑ B171	Ruben Brown B	.30	.10
❑ B172	Eric Green B	.30	.10
❑ B175	Jerry Rice B	5.00	2.00
❑ B176	Bruce Smith B	1.00	.40
❑ B177	Mark Bruener B	.30	.10
❑ B179	Lamont Warren B	.30	.10
❑ B180	Tamarick Vanover B	1.00	.40
❑ B182	Scott Mitchell B	.60	.25
❑ B186	Terry Wooden B	.30	.10
❑ B187	Ken Norton B	.60	.25
❑ B188	Jeff Herrod B	.30	.10
❑ B192	Gus Frerotte B	.60	.25
❑ B194	Brett Maxie B	.30	.10
❑ B198	Eddie Kennison B RC	1.25	.50
❑ B201	Marcus Jones B RC	.30	.10
❑ B202	Terry Allen B	.60	.25
❑ B203	Leroy Hoard B	.30	.10
❑ B205	Reggie White B	1.00	.40
❑ B206	Larry Centers B	.60	.25
❑ B208	Vincent Brisby B	.30	.10
❑ B209	Michael Timpson B	.30	.10
❑ B211	John Mobley B RC	.30	.10
❑ B212	Clay Matthews B	.60	.25
❑ B213	Shannon Sharpe B	.60	.25
❑ B214	Tony Bennett B	.30	.10
❑ B216	Mickey Washington B	.30	.10
❑ B217	Fred Barnett B	.60	.25
❑ B218	Michael Haynes B	.60	.25
❑ B219	Stan Humphries B	.60	.25
❑ B221	Winston Moss B	.30	.10
❑ B222	Tim Biakabutuka B RC	1.25	.50
❑ B223	Leeland McElroy B RC	.60	.25
❑ B224	Vinnie Clark B	.30	.10
❑ B225	Keyshawn Johnson B RC	5.00	2.00
❑ B228	Tony Woods B	.30	.10
❑ B231	Anthony Pleasant B	.30	.10
❑ B232	Jeff George B	.60	.25
❑ B233	Curtis Conway B	1.00	.40
❑ B235	Jeff Lewis B RC	.60	.25
❑ B236	Edgar Bennett B	.60	.25
❑ B237	Regan Upshaw B RC	.30	.10
❑ B238	William Fuller B	.30	.10
❑ B241	Willie Anderson B RC	.30	.10
❑ B242	Derrick Thomas B	1.00	.40
❑ B243	Marvin Harrison B RC	15.00	6.00
❑ B244	Darion Conner B	.30	.10
❑ B245	Antonio Langham B	.30	.10
❑ B246	Rodney Peete B	.30	.10
❑ B247	Tim McDonald B	.30	.10
❑ B248	Robert Jones B	.30	.10
❑ B251	Mark Carrier DB B	.30	.10
❑ B252	Stephen Grant B	.30	.10
❑ B254	Jeff Hostetler B	.60	.25
❑ B255	Darrell Green B	.30	.10
❑ B261	Eric Swann B	.60	.25
❑ B263	Irv Smith B	.30	.10
❑ B264	Tim McKyer B	.30	.10
❑ B266	Sean Jones B	.30	.10
❑ B271	Yancey Thigpen B	.60	.25
❑ B273	Quentin Coryatt B	.30	.10
❑ B274	Hardy Nickerson B	.30	.10
❑ B275	Ricardo McDonald B	.30	.10
❑ B277	Robert Blackmon B	.30	.10
❑ B279	Alonzo Spellman B	.30	.10
❑ B281	Rickey Dudley B RC	1.25	.50
❑ B282	Joe Cain B	.30	.10
❑ B284	John Randle B	.60	.25
❑ B286	Vinny Testaverde B	.60	.25
❑ B289	Henry Jones B	.30	.10
❑ B290	Simeon Rice B RC	3.00	1.25
❑ B295	Leslie O'Neal B	.30	.10
❑ B297	Greg Hill B	.60	.25
❑ B301	Eric Metcalf B	.60	.25
❑ B303	Jerome Woods B RC	.30	.10
❑ B306	Anthony Smith B	.30	.10
❑ B307	Darren Perry B	.30	.10
❑ B311	James Hasty B	.30	.10
❑ B312	Cris Carter B	1.00	.40
❑ B314	Lawrence Phillips B RC	.60	.25
❑ B317	Aeneas Williams B	.30	.10
❑ B318	Eric Hill B	.30	.10
❑ B319	Kevin Hardy B RC	1.25	.50
❑ B321	Chris Chandler B	.60	.25
❑ B322	Rocket Ismail B	.60	.25
❑ B323	Anthony Parker B	.30	.10
❑ B324	John Thierry B	.30	.10
❑ B325	Micheal Barrow B	.30	.10
❑ B326	Henry Ford B	.30	.10
❑ B327	Aaron Hayden B RC	.30	.10
❑ B328	Terance Mathis B	.30	.10
❑ B329	Kirk Pointer B RC	.30	.10
❑ B330	Ray Mickens B RC	.30	.10
❑ B331	Jermane Mayberry B RC	.30	.10
❑ B332	Mario Bates B	.60	.25
❑ B333	Carlton Gray B	.30	.10
❑ B334	Derek Loville B	.30	.10
❑ B335	Mike Alstott B RC	5.00	2.00
❑ B336	Eric Guliford B	.30	.10
❑ B337	Marvcus Patton B	.30	.10
❑ B338	Terrell Owens B RC	15.00	6.00
❑ B339	Lance Johnstone B RC	.60	.25
❑ B340	Lake Dawson B	.60	.25
❑ B341	Winslow Oliver B RC	.30	.10
❑ B342	Adrian Murrell B	.60	.25
❑ B343	Jason Belser B	.30	.10
❑ B344	Brian Dawkins B RC	6.00	2.50
❑ B345	Reggie Brown B RC	.30	.10
❑ B346	Shaun Gayle B	.30	.10
❑ B347	Tony Brackens B RC	1.25	.50
❑ B348	Thomas Lewis B	.30	.10
❑ B349	Kelvin Pritchett B	.30	.10
❑ B350	Bobby Engram B RC	1.25	.50
❑ B351	Moe Williams B RC	3.00	1.25
❑ B352	Thomas Smith B	.30	.10
❑ B353	Dexter Carter B	.30	.10
❑ B354	Qadry Ismail B	.60	.25
❑ B355	Marco Battaglia B RC	.30	.10
❑ B356	Levon Kirkland B	.30	.10
❑ B357	Eric Allen B	.30	.10
❑ B358	Bobby Hoying B RC	1.25	.50
❑ B359	Checklist B	.30	.10
❑ G1	Kordell Stewart G	5.00	2.00
❑ G7	Kimble Anders G	1.50	.60
❑ G8	Merton Hanks G	1.50	.60
❑ G17	Rick Mirer G	3.00	1.25
❑ G33	Craig Newsome G	1.50	.60
❑ G36	Bryce Paup G	3.00	1.25
❑ G40	Dan Marino G	20.00	7.50
❑ G42	Andre Coleman G	1.50	.60
❑ G47	Kevin Carter G	1.50	.60
❑ G60	Mark Brunell G	8.00	3.00
❑ G61	David Palmer G	3.00	1.25
❑ G75	Camell Lake G	1.50	.60
❑ G96	Joey Galloway G	5.00	2.00
❑ G112	Melvin Tuten G	1.50	.60
❑ G121	Aaron Glenn G	1.50	.60
❑ G132	Brett Favre G	20.00	7.50
❑ G133	Ken Dilger G	3.00	1.25
❑ G140	Barry Sanders G	20.00	7.50
❑ G142	Glyn Milburn G	1.50	.60
❑ G148	Brett Perriman G	3.00	1.25
❑ G160	Kerry Collins G	5.00	2.00
❑ G164	Lee Woodall G	1.50	.60
❑ G173	Marshall Faulk G	6.00	2.50
❑ G178	Troy Aikman G	12.00	5.00
❑ G190	Drew Bledsoe G	8.00	3.00
❑ G191	Checklist G	1.50	.60
❑ G193	Michael Irvin G	5.00	2.00
❑ G196	Warren Moon G	3.00	1.25
❑ G200	Steve Young G	10.00	4.00
❑ G207	Alex Van Dyke G RC	3.00	1.25
❑ G220	Cris Carter G	5.00	2.00
❑ G230	John Elway G	20.00	7.50
❑ G234	Charles Haley G	3.00	1.25
❑ G240	Jim Kelly G	5.00	2.00
❑ G250	Rodney Hampton G	3.00	1.25
❑ G256	Errict Rhett G	3.00	1.25
❑ G257	Alex Molden G	1.50	.60
❑ G260	Kevin Hardy G	3.00	1.25
❑ G267	Bryant Young G	3.00	1.25
❑ G268	Jeff Blake G	5.00	2.00
❑ G270	Keyshawn Johnson G	5.00	2.00
❑ G278	Junior Seau G	5.00	2.00
❑ G285	Terry Kirby G	3.00	1.25
❑ G293	Hugh Douglas G	3.00	1.25
❑ G296	Reggie White G	5.00	2.00
❑ G298	Elvis Grbac G	5.00	2.00
❑ G300	Emmitt Smith G	15.00	6.00
❑ G309	Ricky Watters G	3.00	1.25
❑ S4	Brett Favre S	15.00	6.00
❑ S14	Chester McGlockton S	.75	.30
❑ S20	Tyrone Hughes S	.75	.30
❑ S24	Ty Law S	3.00	1.25
❑ S25	Brian Mitchell S	.75	.30
❑ S31	Darren Woodson S	1.50	.60
❑ S35	Brian Mitchell S	.75	.30
❑ S37	Dana Stubblefield S	1.50	.60
❑ S41	Kerry Collins S	3.00	1.25
❑ S46	Orlando Thomas S	.75	.30
❑ S50	Jerry Rice S	8.00	3.00
❑ S53	Willie McGinest S	.75	.30
❑ S54	Blake Brockermeyer S	.75	.30
❑ S56	Michael Westbrook S	3.00	1.25
❑ S57	Garrison Hearst S	3.00	1.25
❑ S59	Kyle Brady S	1.50	.60
❑ S62	Tim Brown S	1.50	.60
❑ S63	Jeff Graham S	.75	.30
❑ S67	Dan Marino S	15.00	6.00
❑ S69	Tamarick Vanover S	3.00	1.25
❑ S74	Daryl Johnston S	1.50	.60
❑ S78	Frank Sanders S	1.50	.60
❑ S84	Darryll Lewis S	.75	.30
❑ S85	Carl Pickens S	1.50	.60
❑ S88	Jerome Bettis S	3.00	1.25
❑ S90	Terrell Davis S	6.00	2.50
❑ S99	Napoleon Kaufman S	3.00	1.25
❑ S100	Rashaan Salaam S	1.50	.60
❑ S103	Barry Sanders S	15.00	6.00
❑ S107	Tony Boselli S	1.50	.60
❑ S109	Eric Zeier S	1.50	.60
❑ S116	Bruce Smith S	3.00	1.25
❑ S118	Zack Crockett S	.75	.30
❑ S125	Joey Galloway S	3.00	1.25
❑ S126	Heath Shuler S	1.50	.60
❑ S127	Curtis Martin S	6.00	2.50
❑ S135	Greg Lloyd S	1.50	.60
❑ S137	Marshall Faulk S	4.00	1.50
❑ S147	Tyrone Poole S	.75	.30
❑ S150	J.J. Stokes S	3.00	1.25
❑ S153	Drew Bledsoe S	5.00	2.00
❑ S154	Terry McDaniel S	.75	.30
❑ S155	Terrell Fletcher S	.75	.30
❑ S159	Dave Brown S	.75	.30
❑ S165	Jim Harbaugh S	1.50	.60
❑ S166	Larry Brown S	.75	.30
❑ S167	Neil Smith S	1.50	.60
❑ S168	Herman Moore S	1.50	.60
❑ S170	Deion Sanders S	5.00	2.00
❑ S174	Mark Chmura S	1.50	.60
❑ S181	Chris Warren S	1.50	.60
❑ S183	Robert Brooks S	3.00	1.25
❑ S184	Steve McNair S	6.00	2.50
❑ S185	Kordell Stewart S	3.00	1.25
❑ S189	Charlie Garner S	1.50	.60
❑ S195	Harvey Williams S	.75	.30
❑ S197	Jeff George S	1.50	.60
❑ S199	Ricky Watters S	1.50	.60
❑ S204	Steve Bono S	1.50	.60
❑ S210	Jeff Blake S	3.00	1.25
❑ S215	Phillippi Sparks S	.75	.30
❑ S226	William Floyd S	1.50	.60
❑ S227	Troy Drayton S	.75	.30
❑ S229	Rodney Hampton S	1.50	.60
❑ S239	Duane Clemons S RC	.75	.30
❑ S249	Curtis Conway S	3.00	1.25
❑ S253	John Mobley S	.75	.30
❑ S258	Chris Slade S	.75	.30
❑ S259	Derrick Thomas S	3.00	1.25
❑ S262	Eric Metcalf S	1.50	.60
❑ S265	Emmitt Smith S	12.00	5.00

❑ S269 Jeff Hostetler S 1.50 .60
❑ S272 Thurman Thomas S 3.00 1.25
❑ S276 Steve Atwater S .75 .30
❑ S280 Isaac Bruce S 3.00 1.25
❑ S283 Neil O'Donnell S 1.50 .60
❑ S287 Jim Kelly S 3.00 1.25
❑ S288 Lawrence Phillips S 3.00 1.25
❑ S291 Terance Mathis S .75 .30
❑ S292 Errict Rhett S 1.50 .60
❑ S294 Santo Stephens S .75 .30
❑ S299 Walt Harris S RC .75 .30
❑ S302 Jamir Miller S .75 .30
❑ S304 Ben Coates S 1.50 .60
❑ S305 Marcus Allen S 3.00 1.25
❑ S308 Jonathan Ogden S RC 3.00 1.25
❑ S310 John Elway S 15.00 6.00
❑ S313 Irving Fryar S 1.50 .60
❑ S315 Junior Seau S 3.00 1.25
❑ S316 Alex Molden S RC .75 .30
❑ S320 Steve Young S 6.00 2.50

1997 Finest

❑ COMPLETE SET (350) 500.00 250.00
❑ COMP.SERIES 1 SET (175) 250.00 125.00
❑ COMP.SERIES 2 SET (175) 250.00 125.00
❑ COMP.BRONZE SER.1 (100) 25.00 10.00
❑ COMP.BRONZE SER.2 (100) 40.00 15.00
❑ 1 Mark Brunell B 2.00 .75
❑ 2 Chris Slade B .60 .25
❑ 3 Chris Doleman B .60 .25
❑ 4 Chris Hudson B .60 .25
❑ 5 Karim Abdul-Jabbar B 1.00 .40
❑ 6 Darren Perry B .60 .25
❑ 7 Daryl Johnston B 1.00 .40
❑ 8 Rob Moore B UER 1.00 .40
❑ 9 Robert Smith B 1.00 .40
❑ 10 Terry Allen B 1.50 .60
❑ 11 Jason Dunn B .60 .25
❑ 12 Henry Thomas B .60 .25
❑ 13 Rod Stephens B .60 .25
❑ 14 Ray Mickens B .60 .25
❑ 15 Ty Detmer B 1.00 .40
❑ 16 Fred Barnett B .60 .25
❑ 17 Derrick Alexander WR B 1.00 .40
❑ 18 Marcus Robertson B .60 .25
❑ 19 Robert Blackmon B .60 .25
❑ 20 Isaac Bruce B 1.50 .60
❑ 21 Chester McGlockton B .60 .25
❑ 22 Stan Humphries B 1.00 .40
❑ 23 Lonnie Marts B .60 .25
❑ 24 Jason Sehorn B 1.00 .40
❑ 25 Bobby Engram B UER 1.00 .40
❑ 26 Brett Perriman B UER .60 .25
❑ 27 Stevon Moore B .60 .25
❑ 28 Jamal Anderson B 1.50 .60
❑ 29 Wayne Martin B .60 .25
❑ 30 Michael Irvin B UER 1.50 .60
❑ 31 Thomas Smith B .60 .25
❑ 32 Tony Brackens B .60 .25
❑ 33 Eric Davis B .60 .25
❑ 34 James O.Stewart B 1.00 .40
❑ 35 Ki-Jana Carter B .60 .25
❑ 36 Ken Norton B .60 .25
❑ 37 William Thomas B .60 .25
❑ 38 Tim Brown B 1.50 .60
❑ 39 Lawrence Phillips B .60 .25
❑ 40 Ricky Watters B 1.00 .40
❑ 41 Tony Bennett B .60 .25
❑ 42 Jessie Armstead B .60 .25
❑ 43 Trent Dilfer B 1.50 .60
❑ 44 Rodney Hampton B 1.00 .40
❑ 45 Sam Mills B .60 .25
❑ 46 Rodney Harrison B RC 3.00 1.25
❑ 47 Rob Fredrickson B .60 .25
❑ 48 Eric Hill B .60 .25
❑ 49 Bennie Blades B .60 .25
❑ 50 Eddie George B 1.50 .60
❑ 51 Dave Brown B .60 .25
❑ 52 Raymont Harris B .60 .25
❑ 53 Steve Tovar B .60 .25
❑ 54 Thurman Thomas B 1.50 .60
❑ 55 Leeland McElroy B .60 .25
❑ 56 Brian Mitchell B UER .60 .25
❑ 57 Eric Allen B .60 .25
❑ 58 Vinny Testaverde B 1.00 .40
❑ 59 Marvin Washington B .60 .25
❑ 60 Junior Seau B 1.50 .60
❑ 61 Bert Emanuel B 1.00 .40
❑ 62 Kevin Carter B .60 .25
❑ 63 Mark Carrier DB B .60 .25
❑ 64 Andre Coleman B .60 .25
❑ 65 Chris Warren B 1.00 .40
❑ 66 Aeneas Williams B .60 .25
❑ 67 Eugene Robinson B .60 .25
❑ 68 Darren Woodson B .60 .25
❑ 69 Anthony Johnson B .60 .25
❑ 70 Terry Glenn B 1.50 .60
❑ 71 Troy Vincent B .60 .25
❑ 72 John Copeland B .60 .25
❑ 73 Warren Sapp B 1.00 .40
❑ 74 Bobby Hebert B .60 .25
❑ 75 Jeff Hostetler B .60 .25
❑ 76 Willie Davis B .60 .25
❑ 77 Mickey Washington B .60 .25
❑ 78 Cortez Kennedy B .60 .25
❑ 79 Michael Strahan B 1.00 .40
❑ 80 Jerome Bettis B 1.50 .60
❑ 81 Andre Hastings B UER .60 .25
❑ 82 Simeon Rice B 1.00 .40
❑ 83 Cornelius Bennett B .60 .25
❑ 84 Napoleon Kaufman B 1.50 .60
❑ 85 Jim Harbaugh B 1.00 .40
❑ 86 Aaron Hayden B .60 .25
❑ 87 Gus Frerotte B .60 .25
❑ 88 Jeff Blake B 1.00 .40
❑ 89 Anthony Miller B UER .60 .25
❑ 90 Deion Sanders B 1.50 .60
❑ 91 Curtis Conway B 1.00 .40
❑ 92 William Floyd B 1.00 .40
❑ 93 Eric Moulds B UER 1.50 .60
❑ 94 Mel Gray B .60 .25
❑ 95 Andre Rison B UER 1.00 .40
❑ 96 Eugene Daniel B .60 .25
❑ 97 Jason Belser B .60 .25
❑ 98 Mike Mamula B .60 .25
❑ 99 Jim Everett B .60 .25
❑ 100 Checklist B .60 .25
❑ 101 Drew Bledsoe S 4.00 1.50
❑ 102 Shannon Sharpe S 2.00 .75
❑ 103 Ken Harvey S 1.25 .50
❑ 104 Isaac Bruce S 3.00 1.25
❑ 105 Terry Allen S 3.00 1.25
❑ 106 Lawyer Milloy S 2.00 .75
❑ 107 Ashley Ambrose S 1.25 .50
❑ 108 Alfred Williams S 1.25 .50
❑ 109 Hugh Douglas S 1.25 .50
❑ 110 Junior Seau S 3.00 1.25
❑ 111 Kordell Stewart S 3.00 1.25
❑ 112 Adrian Murrell S 2.00 .75
❑ 113 Byron Bam Morris S 1.25 .50
❑ 114 Terrell Buckley S 1.25 .50
❑ 115 Dan Marino S 12.00 5.00
❑ 116 Willie Clay S 1.25 .50
❑ 117 Neil Smith S 2.00 .75
❑ 118 Blaine Bishop S 1.25 .50
❑ 119 John Mobley S 1.25 .50
❑ 120 Herman Moore S 2.00 .75
❑ 121 Keyshawn Johnson S 3.00 1.25
❑ 122 Boomer Esiason S 2.00 .75
❑ 123 Marshall Faulk S 4.00 1.50
❑ 124 Keith Jackson S 1.25 .50
❑ 125 Ricky Watters S 2.00 .75
❑ 126 Carl Pickens S 2.00 .75
❑ 127 Cris Carter S 3.00 1.25
❑ 128 Mike Alstott S 3.00 1.25
❑ 129 Simeon Rice S 2.00 .75
❑ 130 Troy Aikman S 6.00 2.50
❑ 131 Tamarick Vanover S 2.00 .75
❑ 132 Marquez Pope S 1.25 .50
❑ 133 Winslow Oliver S 1.25 .50
❑ 134 Edgar Bennett S 2.00 .75
❑ 135 Dave Meggett S 1.25 .50
❑ 136 Marcus Allen S 3.00 1.25
❑ 137 Jerry Rice S 6.00 2.50
❑ 138 Steve Atwater S 1.25 .50
❑ 139 Tim McDonald S 1.25 .50
❑ 140 Barry Sanders S 10.00 4.00
❑ 141 Eddie George S 3.00 1.25
❑ 142 Wesley Walls S 1.25 .50
❑ 143 Jerome Bettis S 3.00 1.25
❑ 144 Kevin Greene S 2.00 .75
❑ 145 Terrell Davis S 4.00 1.50
❑ 146 Gus Frerotte S 2.00 .75
❑ 147 Joey Galloway S 2.00 .75
❑ 148 Vinny Testaverde S 2.00 .75
❑ 149 Hardy Nickerson S 1.25 .50
❑ 150 Brett Favre S 12.00 5.00
❑ 151 Desmond Howard G 1.50 .60
❑ 152 Keyshawn Johnson G 5.00 2.00
❑ 153 Tony Banks G 5.00 2.00
❑ 154 Chris Spielman G 1.50 .60
❑ 155 Reggie White G 5.00 2.00
❑ 156 Zach Thomas G 5.00 2.00
❑ 157 Carl Pickens G 3.00 1.25
❑ 158 Karim Abdul-Jabbar G 5.00 2.00
❑ 159 Chad Brown G 1.50 .60
❑ 160 Kerry Collins G 5.00 2.00
❑ 161 Marvin Harrison G 5.00 2.00
❑ 162 Steve Young G 6.00 2.50
❑ 163 Deion Sanders G 5.00 2.00
❑ 164 Trent Dilfer G 5.00 2.00
❑ 165 Barry Sanders G 15.00 6.00
❑ 166 Cris Carter G 5.00 2.00
❑ 167 Keenan McCardell G 3.00 1.25
❑ 168 Terry Glenn G 5.00 2.00
❑ 169 Emmitt Smith G 15.00 6.00
❑ 170 John Elway G 20.00 7.50
❑ 171 Jerry Rice G 10.00 4.00
❑ 172 Troy Aikman G 10.00 4.00
❑ 173 Curtis Martin G 6.00 2.50
❑ 174 Darrell Green G 1.50 .60
❑ 175 Mark Brunell G 6.00 2.50
❑ 176 Corey Dillon B RC 12.00 5.00
❑ 177 Tyrone Poole B .60 .25
❑ 178 Anthony Pleasant B .60 .25
❑ 179 Frank Sanders B 1.00 .40
❑ 180 Troy Aikman B 3.00 1.50
❑ 181 Bill Romanowski B .60 .25
❑ 182 Ty Law B 1.00 .40
❑ 183 Orlando Thomas B .60 .25
❑ 184 Quentin Coryatt B .60 .25
❑ 185 Kenny Holmes RC B 1.25 .50
❑ 186 Bryant Young B .60 .25
❑ 187 Michael Sinclair B .60 .25
❑ 188 Mike Tomczak B .60 .25
❑ 189 Bobby Taylor B .60 .25
❑ 190 Brett Favre B 6.00 3.00
❑ 191 Kent Graham B .60 .25
❑ 192 Jessie Tuggle B .60 .25
❑ 193 Jimmy Smith B 1.00 .40
❑ 194 Greg Hill B .60 .25
❑ 195 Yatil Green B RC .75 .30
❑ 196 Mark Fields B .60 .25
❑ 197 Phillippi Sparks B .60 .25
❑ 198 Aaron Glenn B .60 .25
❑ 199 Pat Swilling B .60 .25
❑ 200 Barry Sanders B 5.00 2.00
❑ 201 Mark Chmura B 1.00 .40
❑ 202 Marco Coleman B .60 .25
❑ 203 Merton Hanks B .60 .25
❑ 204 Brian Blades B .60 .25
❑ 205 Errict Rhett B .60 .25
❑ 206 Henry Ellard B .60 .25
❑ 207 Andre Reed B 1.00 .40
❑ 208 Bryan Cox B .60 .25
❑ 209 Darnay Scott B 1.00 .40
❑ 210 John Elway B 6.00 3.00
❑ 211 Glyn Milburn B .60 .25
❑ 212 Don Beebe B .60 .25
❑ 213 Kevin Lockett B RC .75 .30
❑ 214 Dorsey Levens B 1.50 .60
❑ 215 Kordell Stewart B 1.50 .60
❑ 216 Larry Centers B 1.00 .40
❑ 217 Cris Carter B 1.50 .60
❑ 218 Willie McGinest B .60 .25
❑ 219 Renaldo Wynn RC B .30 .10
❑ 220 Jerry Rice B 3.00 1.50
❑ 221 Reidel Anthony B RC .75 .30
❑ 222 Mark Carrier WR B .60 .25
❑ 223 Quinn Early B .60 .25

❑ 224 Chris Sanders B .60 .25
❑ 225 Shawn Springs B RC .75 .30
❑ 226 Kevin Smith B .60 .25
❑ 227 Ben Coates B 1.00 .40
❑ 228 Tyrone Wheatley B 1.00 .40
❑ 229 Antonio Freeman B 1.50 .60
❑ 230 Dan Marino B 6.00 3.00
❑ 231 Dwayne Rudd RC B 1.25 .50
❑ 232 Leslie O'Neal B .60 .25
❑ 233 Brent Jones B .60 .25
❑ 234 Jake Plummer B RC 10.00 4.00
❑ 235 Kerry Collins B 1.50 .60
❑ 236 Rashaan Salaam B .60 .25
❑ 237 Tyrone Braxton B .60 .25
❑ 238 Herman Moore B 1.00 .40
❑ 239 Keyshawn Johnson B 1.50 .60
❑ 240 Drew Bledsoe B 2.00 .75
❑ 241 Rickey Dudley B 1.00 .40
❑ 242 Antowain Smith B RC 5.00 2.00
❑ 243 Jeff Lageman B .60 .25
❑ 244 Chris T. Jones B .60 .25
❑ 245 Steve Young B 2.00 .75
❑ 246 Eddie Robinson B .60 .25
❑ 247 Chad Cota B .60 .25
❑ 248 Michael Jackson B 1.00 .40
❑ 249 Robert Porcher B .60 .25
❑ 250 Reggie White B 1.50 .60
❑ 251 Carnell Lake B .60 .25
❑ 252 Chris Calloway B .60 .25
❑ 253 Terance Mathis B 1.00 .40
❑ 254 Carl Pickens B 1.00 .40
❑ 255 Curtis Martin B 2.00 .75
❑ 256 Jeff Graham B .60 .25
❑ 257 Regan Upshaw RC B .30 .10
❑ 258 Sean Gilbert B .60 .25
❑ 259 Will Blackwell B RC .75 .30
❑ 260 Emmitt Smith B 5.00 2.50
❑ 261 Reinard Wilson RC B .75 .30
❑ 262 Darrell Russell RC B .30 .10
❑ 263 Wayne Chrebet B 1.00 .40
❑ 264 Kevin Hardy B .60 .25
❑ 265 Shannon Sharpe B 1.00 .40
❑ 266 Harvey Williams B .60 .25
❑ 267 John Randle B 1.00 .40
❑ 268 Tim Bowens B .60 .25
❑ 269 Tony Gonzalez B RC 6.00 2.50
❑ 270 Warrick Dunn B RC 6.00 2.50
❑ 271 Sean Dawkins B .60 .25
❑ 272 Darryll Lewis B .60 .25
❑ 273 Alonzo Spellman B .60 .25
❑ 274 Mark Collins B .60 .25
❑ 275 Checklist Card B .60 .25
❑ 276 Pat Barnes S RC 2.00 .75
❑ 277 Dana Stubblefield S 2.00 .75
❑ 278 Dan Wilkinson S 1.25 .50
❑ 279 Bryce Paup S 1.25 .50
❑ 280 Kerry Collins S 3.00 1.25
❑ 281 Derrick Brooks S 3.00 1.25
❑ 282 Walter Jones S RC 3.00 1.25
❑ 283 Terry McDaniel S 1.25 .50
❑ 284 James Farrior RC S 3.00 1.25
❑ 285 Curtis Martin S 4.00 1.50
❑ 286 O.J. McDuffie S 2.00 .75
❑ 287 Natrone Means S 2.00 .75
❑ 288 Bryant Westbrook RC S 2.00 .75
❑ 289 Peter Boulware RC S 3.00 1.25
❑ 290 Emmitt Smith S 10.00 4.00
❑ 291 Joey Kent S RC 3.00 1.25
❑ 292 Eddie Kennison S 2.00 .75
❑ 293 LeRoy Butler S 1.25 .50
❑ 294 Dale Carter S 1.25 .50
❑ 295 Jim Druckenmiller S RC 2.00 .75
❑ 296 Byron Hanspard S RC 2.00 .75
❑ 297 Jeff Blake S 2.00 .75
❑ 298 Levon Kirkland S 1.25 .50
❑ 299 Michael Westbrook S 2.00 .75
❑ 300 John Elway S 12.00 5.00
❑ 301 Lamar Lathon S 1.25 .50
❑ 302 Ray Lewis S 5.00 2.00
❑ 303 Steve McNair S 4.00 1.50
❑ 304 Shawn Springs S 2.00 .75
❑ 305 Karim Abdul-Jabbar S 2.00 .75
❑ 306 Orlando Pace S RC 3.00 1.25
❑ 307 Scott Mitchell S 1.25 .50
❑ 308 Walt Harris S 1.25 .50
❑ 309 Bruce Smith S 2.00 .75
❑ 310 Reggie White S 3.00 1.25
❑ 311 Eric Swann S 1.25 .50
❑ 312 Derrick Thomas S 3.00 1.25
❑ 313 Tony Martin S 2.00 .75
❑ 314 Darrell Russell RC S 2.00 .75
❑ 315 Mark Brunell S 4.00 1.50
❑ 316 Trent Dilfer S 3.00 1.25
❑ 317 Irving Fryar S 1.25 .50
❑ 318 Amani Toomer S 2.00 .75
❑ 319 Jake Reed S 2.00 .75
❑ 320 Steve Young S 4.00 1.50
❑ 321 Troy Davis S RC 2.00 .75
❑ 322 Jim Harbaugh S 2.00 .75
❑ 323 Neil O'Donnell S 1.25 .50
❑ 324 Terry Glenn S 3.00 1.25
❑ 325 Deion Sanders S 3.00 1.25
❑ 326 Gus Frerotte G 3.00 1.25
❑ 327 Tom Knight RC G 3.00 1.25
❑ 328 Peter Boulware G 3.00 1.25
❑ 329 Jerome Bettis G 5.00 2.00
❑ 330 Orlando Pace G 5.00 2.00
❑ 331 Darnell Autry G RC 3.00 1.25
❑ 332 Ike Hilliard G RC 12.00 5.00
❑ 333 David LaFleur G RC 1.50 .60
❑ 334 Jim Harbaugh G 3.00 1.25
❑ 335 Eddie George G 5.00 2.00
❑ 336 Vinny Testaverde G 3.00 1.25
❑ 337 Terry Allen G 3.00 1.25
❑ 338 Jim Druckenmiller G 3.00 1.25
❑ 339 Ricky Watters G 3.00 1.25
❑ 340 Brett Favre G 20.00 7.50
❑ 341 Simeon Rice G 3.00 1.25
❑ 342 Shannon Sharpe G 3.00 1.25
❑ 343 Kordell Stewart G 5.00 2.00
❑ 344 Isaac Bruce G 5.00 2.00
❑ 345 Drew Bledsoe G 6.00 2.50
❑ 346 Jeff Blake G 3.00 1.25
❑ 347 Herman Moore G 3.00 1.25
❑ 348 Junior Seau G 5.00 2.00
❑ 349 Rae Carruth G RC 1.50 .60
❑ 350 Dan Marino G 20.00 7.50
❑ P5 K.Abdul-Jabbar Promo 1.50 .60
❑ P32 Tony Brackens Promo 1.50 .60
❑ P45 Sam Mills Promo 1.50 .60
❑ P70 Terry Glenn Promo 1.50 .60
❑ P87 Gus Frerotte Promo 1.50 .60

1998 Finest

❑ COMPLETE SET (270) 80.00 30.00
❑ COMP.SERIES 1 (150) 50.00 20.00
❑ COMP.SERIES 2 (120) 30.00 12.50
❑ 1 John Elway 4.00 1.50
❑ 2 Terance Mathis .60 .25
❑ 3 Jermaine Lewis .60 .25
❑ 4 Fred Lane .40 .15
❑ 5 Simeon Rice .60 .25
❑ 6 David Dunn .40 .15
❑ 7 Dexter Coakley .40 .15
❑ 8 Carl Pickens .60 .25
❑ 9 Antonio Freeman 1.00 .40
❑ 10 Herman Moore .60 .25
❑ 11 Kevin Hardy .40 .15
❑ 12 Tony Gonzalez 1.00 .40
❑ 13 O.J. McDuffie .60 .25
❑ 14 David Palmer .40 .15
❑ 15 Lawyer Milloy .60 .25
❑ 16 Danny Kanell .60 .25
❑ 17 Randal Hill .40 .15
❑ 18 Chris Slade .40 .15
❑ 19 Charlie Garner .60 .25
❑ 20 Mark Brunell 1.00 .40
❑ 21 Donnell Woolford .40 .15
❑ 22 Freddie Jones .40 .15
❑ 23 Ken Norton .40 .15
❑ 24 Tony Banks .60 .25
❑ 25 Isaac Bruce 1.00 .40
❑ 26 Willie Davis .40 .15
❑ 27 Cris Dishman .40 .15
❑ 28 Aeneas Williams .40 .15
❑ 29 Michael Booker .40 .15
❑ 30 Cris Carter 1.00 .40
❑ 31 Michael McCrary .40 .15
❑ 32 Eric Moulds 1.00 .40
❑ 33 Rae Carruth .40 .15
❑ 34 Bobby Engram .60 .25
❑ 35 Jeff Blake .60 .25
❑ 36 Deion Sanders 1.00 .40
❑ 37 Rod Smith .60 .25
❑ 38 Bryant Westbrook .40 .15
❑ 39 Mark Chmura .60 .25
❑ 40 Tim Brown 1.00 .40
❑ 41 Bobby Taylor .40 .15
❑ 42 James Stewart .60 .25
❑ 43 Kimble Anders .60 .25
❑ 44 Karim Abdul-Jabbar 1.00 .40
❑ 45 Willie McGinest .40 .15
❑ 46 Jessie Armstead .40 .15
❑ 47 Brad Johnson 1.00 .40
❑ 48 Greg Lloyd .40 .15
❑ 49 Stephen Davis .40 .15
❑ 50 Jerome Bettis 1.00 .40
❑ 51 Warren Sapp .60 .25
❑ 52 Horace Copeland .40 .15
❑ 53 Chad Brown .40 .15
❑ 54 Chris Canty .40 .15
❑ 55 Robert Smith 1.00 .40
❑ 56 Pete Mitchell .40 .15
❑ 57 Aaron Bailey .40 .15
❑ 58 Robert Porcher .40 .15
❑ 59 John Mobley .40 .15
❑ 60 Tony Martin .60 .25
❑ 61 Michael Irvin 1.00 .40
❑ 62 Charles Way .40 .15
❑ 63 Raymont Harris .40 .15
❑ 64 Chuck Smith .40 .15
❑ 65 Larry Centers .40 .15
❑ 66 Greg Hill .40 .15
❑ 67 Kenny Holmes .40 .15
❑ 68 John Lynch .60 .25
❑ 69 Michael Sinclair .40 .15
❑ 70 Steve Young 1.25 .50
❑ 71 Michael Strahan .60 .25
❑ 72 Levon Kirkland .40 .15
❑ 73 Rickey Dudley .40 .15
❑ 74 Marcus Allen 1.00 .40
❑ 75 John Randle .60 .25
❑ 76 Erik Kramer .40 .15
❑ 77 Neil Smith .60 .25
❑ 78 Byron Hanspard .40 .15
❑ 79 Quinn Early .40 .15
❑ 80 Warren Moon 1.00 .40
❑ 81 William Thomas .40 .15
❑ 82 Ben Coates .60 .25
❑ 83 Lake Dawson .40 .15
❑ 84 Steve McNair 1.00 .40
❑ 85 Gus Frerotte .40 .15
❑ 86 Rodney Harrison .60 .25
❑ 87 Reggie White 1.00 .40
❑ 88 Derrick Thomas 1.00 .40
❑ 89 Dale Carter .40 .15
❑ 90 Warrick Dunn 1.00 .40
❑ 91 Will Blackwell .40 .15
❑ 92 Troy Vincent .40 .15
❑ 93 Johnnie Morton .60 .25
❑ 94 David LaFleur .40 .15
❑ 95 Tony McGee .40 .15
❑ 96 Lonnie Johnson .40 .15
❑ 97 Thurman Thomas 1.00 .40
❑ 98 Chris Chandler .60 .25
❑ 99 Jamal Anderson 1.00 .40
❑ 100 Checklist .40 .15
❑ 101 Marshall Faulk 1.50 .60
❑ 102 Chris Calloway .40 .15
❑ 103 Chris Spielman .40 .15
❑ 104 Zach Thomas 1.00 .40
❑ 105 Jeff George .60 .25
❑ 106 Darrell Russell .40 .15
❑ 107 Darryll Lewis .40 .15
❑ 108 Reidel Anthony .60 .25
❑ 109 Terrell Owens 1.00 .40
❑ 110 Rob Moore .60 .25
❑ 111 Darrell Green .60 .25
❑ 112 Merton Hanks .40 .15
❑ 113 Shawn Jefferson .40 .15

❑ 114	Chris Sanders	.40	.15
❑ 115	Scott Mitchell	.60	.25
❑ 116	Vaughn Hebron	.40	.15
❑ 117	Ed McCaffrey	.60	.25
❑ 118	Bruce Smith	.60	.25
❑ 119	Peter Boulware	.40	.15
❑ 120	Brett Favre	4.00	1.50
❑ 121	Peyton Manning RC	30.00	15.00
❑ 122	Brian Griese RC	5.00	2.00
❑ 123	Tavian Banks RC	1.50	.60
❑ 124	Duane Starks RC	1.00	.40
❑ 125	Robert Holcombe RC	1.50	.60
❑ 126	Brian Simmons RC	1.50	.60
❑ 127	Skip Hicks RC	1.50	.60
❑ 128	Keith Brooking RC	2.50	1.00
❑ 129	Ahman Green RC	12.00	5.00
❑ 130	Jerome Pathon RC	2.50	1.00
❑ 131	Curtis Enis RC	1.00	.40
❑ 132	Grant Wistrom RC	1.50	.60
❑ 133	Germane Crowell RC	1.50	.60
❑ 134	Jacquez Green RC	1.50	.60
❑ 135	Randy Moss RC	15.00	6.00
❑ 136	Jason Peter RC	1.00	.40
❑ 137	John Avery RC	1.50	.60
❑ 138	Takeo Spikes RC	2.50	1.00
❑ 139	Pat Johnson RC	1.50	.60
❑ 140	Andre Wadsworth RC	1.50	.60
❑ 141	Fred Taylor RC	4.00	1.50
❑ 142	Charles Woodson RC	3.00	1.25
❑ 143	Marcus Nash RC	1.00	.40
❑ 144	Robert Edwards RC	1.50	.60
❑ 145	Kevin Dyson RC	2.50	1.00
❑ 146	Joe Jurevicius RC	2.50	1.00
❑ 147	Anthony Simmons RC	1.50	.60
❑ 148	Hines Ward RC	10.00	5.00
❑ 149	Greg Ellis RC	1.00	.40
❑ 150	Ryan Leaf RC	2.50	1.00
❑ 151	Jerry Rice	2.00	.75
❑ 152	Tony Martin	.60	.25
❑ 153	Checklist	.40	.15
❑ 154	Rob Johnson	.60	.25
❑ 155	Shannon Sharpe	.60	.25
❑ 156	Bert Emanuel	.60	.25
❑ 157	Eric Metcalf	.40	.15
❑ 158	Natrone Means	.60	.25
❑ 159	Derrick Alexander	.60	.25
❑ 160	Emmitt Smith	3.00	1.25
❑ 161	Jeff Burris	.40	.15
❑ 162	Chris Warren	.60	.25
❑ 163	Corey Fuller	.40	.15
❑ 164	Courtney Hawkins	.40	.15
❑ 165	James McKnight	1.00	.40
❑ 166	Shawn Springs	.40	.15
❑ 167	Wayne Martin	.40	.15
❑ 168	Michael Westbrook	.60	.25
❑ 169	Michael Jackson	.40	.15
❑ 170	Dan Marino	4.00	1.50
❑ 171	Amp Lee	.40	.15
❑ 172	James Jett	.60	.25
❑ 173	Ty Law	.60	.25
❑ 174	Kerry Collins	.60	.25
❑ 175	Robert Brooks	.60	.25
❑ 176	Blaine Bishop	.40	.15
❑ 177	Stephen Boyd	.40	.15
❑ 178	Keyshawn Johnson	1.00	.40
❑ 179	Deon Figures	.40	.15
❑ 180	Allen Aldridge	.40	.15
❑ 181	Corey Miller	.40	.15
❑ 182	Chad Lewis	.60	.25
❑ 183	Derrick Rodgers	.40	.15
❑ 184	Troy Drayton	.40	.15
❑ 185	Darren Woodson	.40	.15
❑ 186	Ken Dilger	.40	.15
❑ 187	Elvis Grbac	.60	.25
❑ 188	Terrell Fletcher	.40	.15
❑ 189	Frank Sanders	.60	.25
❑ 190	Curtis Martin	1.00	.40
❑ 191	Derrick Brooks	1.00	.40
❑ 192	Darrien Gordon	.40	.15
❑ 193	Andre Reed	.60	.25
❑ 194	Darnay Scott	.60	.25
❑ 195	Curtis Conway	.60	.25
❑ 196	Tim McDonald	.40	.15
❑ 197	Sean Dawkins	.40	.15
❑ 198	Napoleon Kaufman	1.00	.40
❑ 199	Willie Clay	.40	.15
❑ 200	Terrell Davis	1.00	.40
❑ 201	Wesley Walls	.60	.25
❑ 202	Santana Dotson	.40	.15
❑ 203	Frank Wycheck	.40	.15
❑ 204	Wayne Chrebet	1.00	.40
❑ 205	Andre Rison	.60	.25
❑ 206	Jason Sehorn	.60	.25
❑ 207	Jessie Tuggle	.40	.15
❑ 208	Kevin Turner	.40	.15
❑ 209	Jason Taylor	.60	.25
❑ 210	Yancey Thigpen	.40	.15
❑ 211	Jake Reed	.60	.25
❑ 212	Carnell Lake	.40	.15
❑ 213	Joey Galloway	.60	.25
❑ 214	Andre Hastings	.40	.15
❑ 215	Terry Allen	1.00	.40
❑ 216	Jim Harbaugh	.60	.25
❑ 217	Tony Banks	.60	.25
❑ 218	Greg Clark	.40	.15
❑ 219	Corey Dillon	1.00	.40
❑ 220	Troy Aikman	2.00	.75
❑ 221	Antowain Smith	1.00	.40
❑ 222	Steve Atwater	.40	.15
❑ 223	Trent Dilfer	1.00	.40
❑ 224	Junior Seau	1.00	.40
❑ 225	Garrison Hearst	1.00	.40
❑ 226	Eric Allen	.40	.15
❑ 227	Chad Cota	.40	.15
❑ 228	Vinny Testaverde	.60	.25
❑ 229	Duce Staley	1.25	.50
❑ 230	Drew Bledsoe	1.50	.60
❑ 231	Charles Johnson	.40	.15
❑ 232	Jake Plummer	1.00	.40
❑ 233	Errict Rhett	.60	.25
❑ 234	Doug Evans	.40	.15
❑ 235	Phillippi Sparks	.40	.15
❑ 236	Ashley Ambrose	.40	.15
❑ 237	Bryan Cox	.40	.15
❑ 238	Kevin Smith	.40	.15
❑ 239	Hardy Nickerson	.40	.15
❑ 240	Terry Glenn	1.00	.40
❑ 241	Lee Woodall	.40	.15
❑ 242	Andre Coleman	.40	.15
❑ 243	Michael Bates	.40	.15
❑ 244	Mark Fields	.40	.15
❑ 245	Eddie Kennison	.60	.25
❑ 246	Dana Stubblefield	.40	.15
❑ 247	Bobby Hoying	.60	.25
❑ 248	Mo Lewis	.40	.15
❑ 249	Derrick Mayes	.60	.25
❑ 250	Eddie George	1.00	.40
❑ 251	Mike Alstott	1.00	.40
❑ 252	J.J. Stokes	.60	.25
❑ 253	Adrian Murrell	.60	.25
❑ 254	Kevin Greene	.60	.25
❑ 255	LeRoy Butler	.40	.15
❑ 256	Glenn Foley	.60	.25
❑ 257	Jimmy Smith	.60	.25
❑ 258	Tiki Barber	1.00	.40
❑ 259	Irving Fryar	.60	.25
❑ 260	Ricky Watters	.60	.25
❑ 261	Jeff Graham	.40	.15
❑ 262	Kordell Stewart	1.00	.40
❑ 263	Rod Woodson	.60	.25
❑ 264	Leslie Shepherd	.40	.15
❑ 265	Ryan McNeil	.40	.15
❑ 266	Ike Hilliard	.60	.25
❑ 267	Keenan McCardell	.60	.25
❑ 268	Marvin Harrison	1.00	.40
❑ 269	Dorsey Levens	1.00	.40
❑ 270	Barry Sanders	3.00	1.25

1999 Finest

❑	COMPLETE SET (175)	80.00	30.00
❑	COMP.SET w/o SPs (124)	30.00	15.00
❑ 1	Peyton Manning	3.00	1.25
❑ 2	Priest Holmes	1.50	.60
❑ 3	Kordell Stewart	.60	.25
❑ 4	Shannon Sharpe	.60	.25
❑ 5	Andre Rison	.60	.25
❑ 6	Rickey Dudley	.40	.15
❑ 7	Duce Staley	1.00	.40
❑ 8	Randall Cunningham	1.00	.40
❑ 9	Warrick Dunn	1.00	.40
❑ 10	Dan Marino	3.00	1.25
❑ 11	Kevin Greene	.40	.15
❑ 12	Garrison Hearst	.60	.25
❑ 13	Eric Moulds	1.00	.40
❑ 14	Marvin Harrison	1.00	.40
❑ 15	Eddie George	1.00	.40
❑ 16	Vinny Testaverde	.60	.25
❑ 17	Brad Johnson	1.00	.40
❑ 18	Derrick Thomas	1.00	.40
❑ 19	Chris Chandler	.60	.25
❑ 20	Troy Aikman	2.00	.75
❑ 21	Terance Mathis	.60	.25
❑ 22	Terrell Owens	1.00	.40
❑ 23	Junior Seau	1.00	.40
❑ 24	Cris Carter	1.00	.40
❑ 25	Fred Taylor	1.00	.40
❑ 26	Adrian Murrell	.60	.25
❑ 27	Terry Glenn	1.00	.40
❑ 28	Rod Smith	.60	.25
❑ 29	Darnay Scott	.60	.25
❑ 30	Brett Favre	3.00	1.25
❑ 31	Cam Cleeland	.40	.15
❑ 32	Ricky Watters	.60	.25
❑ 33	Derrick Alexander	.60	.25
❑ 34	Bruce Smith	.60	.25
❑ 35	Steve McNair	1.00	.40
❑ 36	Wayne Chrebet	.60	.25
❑ 37	Herman Moore	.60	.25
❑ 38	Bert Emanuel	.60	.25
❑ 39	Michael Irvin	.60	.25
❑ 40	Steve Young	1.25	.50
❑ 41	Napoleon Kaufman	1.00	.40
❑ 42	Tim Biakabutuka	.60	.25
❑ 43	Isaac Bruce	1.00	.40
❑ 44	J.J. Stokes	.60	.25
❑ 45	Antonio Freeman	1.00	.40
❑ 46	John Randle	.60	.25
❑ 47	Frank Sanders	.60	.25
❑ 48	O.J. McDuffie	.60	.25
❑ 49	Keenan McCardell	.60	.25
❑ 50	Randy Moss	2.50	1.00
❑ 51	Ed McCaffrey	.60	.25
❑ 52	Yancey Thigpen	.40	.15
❑ 53	Curtis Conway	.60	.25
❑ 54	Mike Alstott	1.00	.40
❑ 55	Deion Sanders	1.00	.40
❑ 56	Dorsey Levens	1.00	.40
❑ 57	Joey Galloway	.60	.25
❑ 58	Natrone Means	.60	.25
❑ 59	Tim Brown	1.00	.40
❑ 60	Jerry Rice	2.00	.75
❑ 61	Robert Smith	1.00	.40
❑ 62	Carl Pickens	.60	.25
❑ 63	Ben Coates	.60	.25
❑ 64	Jerome Bettis	1.00	.40
❑ 65	Corey Dillon	1.00	.40
❑ 66	Curtis Martin	1.00	.40
❑ 67	Jimmy Smith	.60	.25
❑ 68	Keyshawn Johnson	1.00	.40
❑ 69	Charlie Batch	1.00	.40
❑ 70	Jamal Anderson	1.00	.40
❑ 71	Mark Brunell	1.00	.40
❑ 72	Antowain Smith	1.00	.40
❑ 73	Aeneas Williams	.40	.15
❑ 74	Wesley Walls	.60	.25
❑ 75	Jake Plummer	.60	.25
❑ 76	Oronde Gadsden	.60	.25
❑ 77	Gary Brown	.40	.15
❑ 78	Peter Boulware	.40	.15
❑ 79	Stephen Alexander	.40	.15
❑ 80	Barry Sanders	3.00	1.25
❑ 81	Warren Sapp	.60	.25
❑ 82	Michael Sinclair	.40	.15
❑ 83	Freddie Jones	.40	.15
❑ 84	Ike Hilliard	.40	.15
❑ 85	Jake Reed	.60	.25
❑ 86	Tim Dwight	1.00	.40
❑ 87	Johnnie Morton	.60	.25
❑ 88	Robert Brooks	.60	.25
❑ 89	Rocket Ismail	.60	.25

❑ 90 Emmitt Smith 2.00 .75
❑ 91 Ricky Proehl .40 .15
❑ 92 James Jett .60 .25
❑ 93 Karim Abdul-Jabbar .60 .25
❑ 94 Mark Chmura .40 .15
❑ 95 Andre Reed .60 .25
❑ 96 Michael Westbrook .60 .25
❑ 97 Michael Strahan .60 .25
❑ 98 Chad Brown .40 .15
❑ 99 Trent Dilfer .60 .25
❑ 100 Terrell Davis 1.00 .40
❑ 101 Aaron Glenn .40 .15
❑ 102 Skip Hicks .40 .15
❑ 103 Tony Gonzalez 1.00 .40
❑ 104 Ty Law .60 .25
❑ 105 Jermaine Lewis .60 .25
❑ 106 Ray Lewis 1.00 .40
❑ 107 Zach Thomas 1.00 .40
❑ 108 Reidel Anthony .60 .25
❑ 109 Levon Kirkland .40 .15
❑ 110 Drew Bledsoe 1.25 .50
❑ 111 Bobby Engram .60 .25
❑ 112 Jerome Pathon .40 .15
❑ 113 Muhsin Muhammad .60 .25
❑ 114 Vonnie Holliday .40 .15
❑ 115 Bill Romanowski .40 .15
❑ 116 Marshall Faulk 1.25 .50
❑ 117 Ty Detmer .60 .25
❑ 118 Mo Lewis .40 .15
❑ 119 Charles Woodson 1.00 .40
❑ 120 Doug Flutie 1.00 .40
❑ 121 Jon Kitna 1.00 .40
❑ 122 Courtney Hawkins .40 .15
❑ 123 Trent Green 1.00 .40
❑ 124 John Elway 3.00 1.25
❑ 125 Barry Sanders GM 5.00 2.00
❑ 126 Brett Favre GM 5.00 2.00
❑ 127 Curtis Martin GM 1.50 .60
❑ 128 Dan Marino GM 5.00 2.00
❑ 129 Eddie George GM 1.00 .40
❑ 130 Emmitt Smith GM 5.00 2.00
❑ 131 Jamal Anderson GM 1.50 .60
❑ 132 Jerry Rice GM 3.00 1.25
❑ 133 John Elway GM 5.00 2.00
❑ 134 Terrell Davis GM 2.50 1.00
❑ 135 Troy Aikman GM 3.00 1.25
❑ 136 Skip Hicks SN .40 .15
❑ 137 Charles Woodson SN 1.00 .40
❑ 138 Charlie Batch SN 2.50 1.00
❑ 139 Curtis Enis SN 1.50 .60
❑ 140 Fred Taylor SN 2.50 1.00
❑ 141 Jake Plummer SN 1.50 .60
❑ 142 Peyton Manning SN 5.00 2.00
❑ 143 Randy Moss SN 4.00 1.50
❑ 144 Corey Dillon SN 1.50 .60
❑ 145 Priest Holmes SN 1.50 .60
❑ 146 Warrick Dunn SN 1.50 .60
❑ 147 Jevon Kearse RC 4.00 1.50
❑ 148 Chris Claiborne RC 1.50 .60
❑ 149 Akili Smith RC 1.50 .60
❑ 150 Brock Huard RC 3.00 1.25
❑ 151 Daunte Culpepper RC 10.00 4.00
❑ 152 Edgerrin James RC 10.00 4.00
❑ 153 Cecil Collins RC 1.50 .60
❑ 154 Kevin Faulk RC 3.00 1.25
❑ 155 Amos Zereoue RC 3.00 1.25
❑ 156 James Johnson RC 2.50 1.00
❑ 157 Sedrick Irvin RC 1.50 .60
❑ 158 Ricky Williams RC 5.00 2.00
❑ 159 Mike Cloud RC 2.50 1.00
❑ 160 Chris McAlister 1.50 .60
❑ 161 Rob Konrad RC 2.50 1.00
❑ 162 Champ Bailey RC 3.00 1.25
❑ 163 Ebenezer Ekuban RC 2.50 1.00
❑ 164 Tim Couch RC 3.00 1.25
❑ 165 Cade McNown RC 2.50 1.00
❑ 166 Donovan McNabb RC 12.00 5.00
❑ 167 Joe Germaine RC 2.50 1.00
❑ 168 Shaun King RC 2.50 1.00
❑ 169 Peerless Price RC 3.00 1.25
❑ 170 Kevin Johnson RC 2.50 1.00
❑ 171 Troy Edwards RC 2.50 1.00
❑ 172 Karsten Bailey RC 2.50 1.00
❑ 173 David Boston RC 3.00 1.25
❑ 174 D'Wayne Bates RC 2.50 1.00
❑ 175 Torry Holt RC 6.00 2.50

2000 Finest

❑ COMPLETE SET (205) 400.00 150.00
❑ 1 Tim Dwight .75 .30

❑ 2 Cade McNown .30 .10
❑ 3 Drew Bledsoe 1.00 .40
❑ 4 Torry Holt .75 .30
❑ 5 Derrick Mayes .50 .20
❑ 6 Vinny Testaverde .50 .20
❑ 7 Patrick Jeffers .75 .30
❑ 8 Dorsey Levens .50 .20
❑ 9 James Johnson .30 .10
❑ 10 Champ Bailey .50 .20
❑ 11 Jeff George .50 .20
❑ 12 Shawn Jefferson .30 .10
❑ 13 Terrence Wilkins .30 .10
❑ 14 J.J. Stokes .50 .20
❑ 15 Doug Flutie .75 .30
❑ 16 Corey Dillon .75 .30
❑ 17 Rod Smith .50 .20
❑ 18 Jimmy Smith .50 .20
❑ 19 Amani Toomer .50 .20
❑ 20 Curtis Conway .50 .20
❑ 21 Brad Johnson .75 .30
❑ 22 Edgerrin James 1.25 .50
❑ 23 Derrick Alexander .50 .20
❑ 24 Terrell Owens .75 .30
❑ 25 Kurt Warner 1.50 .60
❑ 26 Frank Sanders .50 .20
❑ 27 Tony Banks .50 .20
❑ 28 Troy Aikman 1.50 .60
❑ 29 Curtis Enis .30 .10
❑ 30 Eddie George .75 .30
❑ 31 Bill Schroeder .50 .20
❑ 32 Kent Graham .30 .10
❑ 33 Mike Alstott .75 .30
❑ 34 Steve Young 1.00 .40
❑ 35 Jacquez Green .30 .10
❑ 36 Frank Wycheck .30 .10
❑ 37 Kerry Collins .50 .20
❑ 38 Stephen Davis .75 .30
❑ 39 Tony Gonzalez .50 .20
❑ 40 Tyrone Wheatley .50 .20
❑ 41 Brett Favre 2.50 1.00
❑ 42 Joey Galloway .50 .20
❑ 43 Terrell Davis .75 .30
❑ 44 Marvin Harrison .75 .30
❑ 45 Zach Thomas .75 .30
❑ 46 Jerry Rice 1.50 .60
❑ 47 Keyshawn Johnson .75 .30
❑ 48 Rob Johnson .50 .20
❑ 49 Rocket Ismail .50 .20
❑ 50 Elvis Grbac .50 .20
❑ 51 Warrick Dunn .75 .30
❑ 52 Jevon Kearse .75 .30
❑ 53 Albert Connell .30 .10
❑ 54 Muhsin Muhammad .50 .20
❑ 55 Carl Pickens .50 .20
❑ 56 Peyton Manning 2.00 .75
❑ 57 Daunte Culpepper 1.00 .40
❑ 58 Ike Hilliard .50 .20
❑ 59 Steve McNair .75 .30
❑ 60 Sean Dawkins .30 .10
❑ 61 Steve Beuerlein .50 .20
❑ 62 Priest Holmes 1.00 .40
❑ 63 Jim Harbaugh .50 .20
❑ 64 Germane Crowell .30 .10
❑ 65 Cris Carter .75 .30
❑ 66 Jamal Anderson .75 .30
❑ 67 Kevin Johnson .75 .30
❑ 68 Herman Moore .50 .20
❑ 69 Ricky Williams .75 .30
❑ 70 Rich Gannon .75 .30
❑ 71 Isaac Bruce .75 .30
❑ 72 Peerless Price .50 .20
❑ 73 Az-Zahir Hakim .50 .20
❑ 74 Mark Brunell .75 .30
❑ 75 Rob Moore .50 .20
❑ 76 Antowain Smith .50 .20
❑ 77 Tim Biakabutuka .50 .20
❑ 78 Ed McCaffrey .75 .30
❑ 79 Tony Martin .50 .20
❑ 80 Marcus Robinson .75 .30
❑ 81 Kevin Dyson .50 .20
❑ 82 Wesley Walls .30 .10
❑ 83 Chris Chandler .50 .20
❑ 84 Keenan McCardell .50 .20
❑ 85 Napoleon Kaufman .50 .20
❑ 86 Emmitt Smith 1.50 .60
❑ 87 James Stewart .50 .20
❑ 88 Tim Brown .75 .30
❑ 89 Ricky Watters .50 .20
❑ 90 Johnnie Morton .50 .20
❑ 91 Jake Plummer .50 .20
❑ 92 Olandis Gary .75 .30
❑ 93 Jerome Bettis .75 .30
❑ 94 Terry Glenn .50 .20
❑ 95 Kordell Stewart .50 .20
❑ 96 Charlie Garner .50 .20
❑ 97 Yancey Thigpen .30 .10
❑ 98 Michael Westbrook .50 .20
❑ 99 Bobby Engram .50 .20
❑ 100 Eric Moulds .75 .30
❑ 101 Darnay Scott .50 .20
❑ 102 Antonio Freeman .75 .30
❑ 103 Wayne Chrebet .50 .20
❑ 104 Akili Smith .30 .10
❑ 105 Jeff Blake .50 .20
❑ 106 Curtis Martin .75 .30
❑ 107 Errict Rhett .50 .20
❑ 108 Damon Huard .75 .30
❑ 109 Jeff Graham .30 .10
❑ 110 Terance Mathis .50 .20
❑ 111 Jon Kitna .75 .30
❑ 112 Tim Couch .50 .20
❑ 113 Fred Taylor .75 .30
❑ 114 Qadry Ismail .50 .20
❑ 115 Donovan McNabb 1.25 .50
❑ 116 Charles Johnson .50 .20
❑ 117 Troy Edwards .30 .10
❑ 118 Shaun King .30 .10
❑ 119 Charlie Batch .75 .30
❑ 120 Robert Smith .75 .30
❑ 121 Marshall Faulk 1.00 .40
❑ 122 Brian Griese .75 .30
❑ 123 O.J. McDuffie .50 .20
❑ 124 Randy Moss 1.50 .60
❑ 125 Duce Staley .75 .30
❑ 126 Peter Warrick RC 8.00 3.00
❑ 127 Dez White RC 8.00 3.00
❑ 128 Ron Dayne RC 8.00 3.00
❑ 129 J.R. Redmond RC 6.00 2.50
❑ 130 Thomas Jones RC 12.00 5.00
❑ 131 Plaxico Burress RC 15.00 6.00
❑ 132 Reuben Droughns RC 10.00 4.00
❑ 133 Shaun Alexander RC 40.00 20.00
❑ 134 Ron Dugans RC 6.00 2.50
❑ 135 Travis Prentice RC 6.00 2.50
❑ 136 Joe Hamilton RC 6.00 2.50
❑ 137 Curtis Keaton RC 6.00 2.50
❑ 138 Chris Redman RC 6.00 2.50
❑ 139 Chad Pennington RC 20.00 7.50
❑ 140 Travis Taylor RC 8.00 3.00
❑ 141 Bubba Franks RC 8.00 3.00
❑ 142 Dennis Northcutt RC 8.00 3.00
❑ 143 Jerry Porter RC 10.00 4.00
❑ 144 Sylvester Morris RC 6.00 2.50
❑ 145 Anthony Becht RC 8.00 3.00
❑ 146 Trung Canidate RC 6.00 2.50
❑ 147 Jamal Lewis RC 20.00 7.50
❑ 148 R.Jay Soward RC 6.00 2.50
❑ 149 Tee Martin RC 8.00 3.00
❑ 150 Courtney Brown RC 8.00 3.00
❑ 151 Brian Urlacher RC 30.00 12.50
❑ 152 Danny Farmer RC 6.00 2.50
❑ 153 Laveranues Coles RC 10.00 4.00
❑ 154 Todd Pinkston RC 8.00 3.00
❑ 155 Corey Simon RC 8.00 3.00
❑ 156 Spergon Wynn RC 6.00 2.50
❑ 157 Tim Rattay RC 8.00 3.00
❑ 158 Todd Husak RC 8.00 3.00
❑ 159 Aaron Shea RC 6.00 2.50
❑ 160 Giovanni Carmazzi RC 6.00 2.50
❑ 161 Trevor Gaylor RC 6.00 2.50
❑ 162 JaJuan Dawson RC 6.00 2.50

❑ 163	Jarious Jackson RC	6.00	2.50
❑ 164	Chris Samuels RC	6.00	2.50
❑ 165	Rob Morris RC	6.00	2.50
❑ 166	P.Warrick/R.Moss IF	2.00	.75
❑ 167	R.Moss/P.Warrick IF	2.00	.75
❑ 168	T.Prentice/S.Davis IF	1.50	.60
❑ 169	S.Davis/T.Prentice IF	1.50	.60
❑ 170	C.Redman/K.Warner IF	1.50	.60
❑ 171	K.Warner/C.Redman IF	1.50	.60
❑ 172	Syl.Morris/J.Smith IF	1.50	.60
❑ 173	J.Smith/Syl.Morris IF	1.50	.60
❑ 174	C.Pennington/P.Manning IF	4.00	1.50
❑ 175	P.Manning/C.Pennington IF	4.00	1.50
❑ 176	R.Soward/M.Harrison IF	1.50	.60
❑ 177	M.Harrison/R.Soward IF	1.50	.60
❑ 178	R.Dayne/J.Anderson IF	1.50	.60
❑ 179	J.Anderson/R.Dayne IF	1.50	.60
❑ 180	S.Alexander/E.George IF	4.00	1.50
❑ 181	E.George/S.Alexander IF	3.00	1.25
❑ 182	C.Brown/B.Smith IF	1.50	.60
❑ 183	B.Smith/C.Brown IF	1.50	.60
❑ 184	J.Lewis/E.James IF	3.00	1.25
❑ 185	E.James/J.Lewis IF	3.00	1.25
❑ 186	T.Canidate/E.Smith IF	3.00	1.25
❑ 187	E.Smith/T.Canidate IF	3.00	1.25
❑ 188	T.Taylor/C.Carter IF	2.00	.75
❑ 189	C.Carter/T.Taylor IF	2.00	.75
❑ 190	C.Keaton/M.Faulk IF	2.00	.75
❑ 191	M.Faulk/C.Keaton IF	2.00	.75
❑ 192	P.Burress/J.Rice IF	3.00	1.25
❑ 193	J.Rice/P.Burress IF	3.00	1.25
❑ 194	T.Jones/T.Davis IF	2.00	.75
❑ 195	T.Davis/T.Jones IF	2.00	.75
❑ 196	Peyton Manning GM	5.00	2.00
❑ 197	Randy Moss GM	4.00	1.50
❑ 198	Terrell Davis GM	1.50	.60
❑ 199	Marshall Faulk GM	2.50	1.00
❑ 200	Edgerrin James GM	4.00	1.50
❑ 201	Emmitt Smith GM	4.00	1.50
❑ 202	Ricky Williams GM	1.50	.60
❑ 203	Kurt Warner GM	3.00	1.25
❑ 204	Eddie George GM	1.50	.60
❑ 205	Brett Favre GM	6.00	2.50

2001 Finest

❑	COMP.SET w/o SP's (100)	40.00	20.00
❑ 1	Eddie George	1.25	.50
❑ 2	Jay Fiedler	1.25	.50
❑ 3	Peter Warrick	1.25	.50
❑ 4	Vinny Testaverde	.75	.30
❑ 5	Charles Johnson	.50	.20
❑ 6	Ahman Green	1.25	.50
❑ 7	Isaac Bruce	1.25	.50
❑ 8	Junior Seau	1.25	.50
❑ 9	Daunte Culpepper	1.25	.50
❑ 10	Ike Hilliard	.75	.30
❑ 11	Tony Banks	.75	.30
❑ 12	Steve Beuerlein	.75	.30
❑ 13	Jamal Anderson	1.25	.50
❑ 14	Tyrone Wheatley	.75	.30
❑ 15	Sylvester Morris	.50	.20
❑ 16	Edgerrin James	1.50	.60
❑ 17	Shaun King	.50	.20
❑ 18	Terrell Owens	1.25	.50
❑ 19	Donovan Mcnabb	1.50	.60
❑ 20	Cade Mcnown	.50	.20
❑ 21	Elvis Grbac	.75	.30
❑ 22	James Stewart	.75	.30
❑ 23	Joe Horn	.75	.30
❑ 24	Randy Moss	2.50	1.00
❑ 25	Matt Hasselbeck	.75	.30
❑ 26	Jerome Bettis	1.25	.50
❑ 27	Bill Schroeder	.75	.30
❑ 28	Jake Plummer	.75	.30
❑ 29	Rod Smith	.75	.30
❑ 30	Akili Smith	.50	.20
❑ 31	Jimmy Smith	.75	.30
❑ 32	Oronde Gadsden	.75	.30
❑ 33	Kerry Collins	.75	.30
❑ 34	Warrick Dunn	1.25	.50
❑ 35	Jeff Graham	.50	.20
❑ 36	Ray Lewis	1.25	.50
❑ 37	Joey Galloway	.75	.30
❑ 38	Tim Brown	1.25	.50
❑ 39	Derrick Alexander	.75	.30
❑ 40	Jerry Rice	2.50	1.00
❑ 41	Muhsin Muhammad	.75	.30
❑ 42	Shawn Jefferson	.50	.20
❑ 43	Curtis Martin	1.25	.50
❑ 44	Terry Glenn	.75	.30
❑ 45	Marvin Harrison	1.25	.50
❑ 46	Mike Anderson	1.25	.50
❑ 47	Stephen Davis	1.25	.50
❑ 48	Chad Lewis	.50	.20
❑ 49	Fred Taylor	1.25	.50
❑ 50	Corey Dillon	1.25	.50
❑ 51	Charlie Batch	1.25	.50
❑ 52	Kevin Johnson	.75	.30
❑ 53	Brett Favre	4.00	1.50
❑ 54	Marshall Faulk	1.50	.60
❑ 55	Kordell Stewart	.75	.30
❑ 56	Steve McNair	1.25	.50
❑ 57	Jeff Blake	.75	.30
❑ 58	Eric Moulds	.75	.30
❑ 59	Emmitt Smith	2.50	1.00
❑ 60	David Boston	1.25	.50
❑ 61	Cris Carter	1.25	.50
❑ 62	Peyton Manning	3.00	1.25
❑ 63	Keyshawn Johnson	1.25	.50
❑ 64	Doug Flutie	1.25	.50
❑ 65	Drew Bledsoe	1.50	.60
❑ 66	Ricky Williams	1.25	.50
❑ 67	Keenan Mccardell	.50	.20
❑ 68	Brian Urlacher	2.00	.75
❑ 69	Jamal Lewis	2.00	.75
❑ 70	Ed McCaffrey	1.25	.50
❑ 71	Antonio Freeman	1.25	.50
❑ 72	Darrell Jackson	1.25	.50
❑ 73	Jeff George	.75	.30
❑ 74	Chris Chandler	.75	.30
❑ 75	Germane Crowell	.50	.20
❑ 76	Tim Biakabutuka	.75	.30
❑ 77	Jon Kitna	.75	.30
❑ 78	Troy Brown	.75	.30
❑ 79	Lamar Smith	.75	.30
❑ 80	Derrick Mason	.75	.30
❑ 81	Hines Ward	1.25	.50
❑ 82	Mark Brunell	1.25	.50
❑ 83	Trent Dilfer	.75	.30
❑ 84	Tim Couch	.75	.30
❑ 85	Donald Hayes	.50	.20
❑ 86	Amani Toomer	.75	.30
❑ 87	Tony Gonzalez	.75	.30
❑ 88	Rich Gannon	1.25	.50
❑ 89	Rob Johnson	.75	.30
❑ 90	Torry Holt	1.25	.50
❑ 91	Jeff Garcia	1.25	.50
❑ 92	Kurt Warner	2.50	1.00
❑ 93	Aaron Brooks	1.25	.50
❑ 94	Brian Griese	1.25	.50
❑ 95	James Allen	.75	.30
❑ 96	Wayne Chrebet	.75	.30
❑ 97	Tiki Barber	1.25	.50
❑ 98	Brad Johnson	1.25	.50
❑ 99	Ricky Watters	.75	.30
❑ 100	Charlie Garner	.75	.30
❑ 101	Andre Carter RC	10.00	4.00
❑ 102	Dan Morgan RC	10.00	4.00
❑ 103	Gerard Warren RC	10.00	4.00
❑ 104	Jesse Palmer RC	10.00	4.00
❑ 105	Josh Heupel RC	10.00	4.00
❑ 106	Justin Smith RC	10.00	4.00
❑ 107	LaMont Jordan RC	20.00	10.00
❑ 108	Leonard Davis RC	6.00	2.50
❑ 109	Marques Tuiasosopo RC	10.00	4.00
❑ 110	Snoop Minnis RC	6.00	2.50
❑ 111	Quincy Carter RC	10.00	4.00
❑ 112	Quincy Morgan RC	10.00	4.00
❑ 113	Richard Seymour RC	10.00	4.00
❑ 114	Rudi Johnson RC	20.00	7.50
❑ 115	Sage Rosenfels RC	10.00	4.00
❑ 116	Todd Heap RC	10.00	4.00
❑ 117	Travis Minor RC	6.00	2.50
❑ 118	Will Allen RC	6.00	2.50
❑ 119	Jamal Reynolds RC	10.00	4.00
❑ 120	Scotty Anderson RC	6.00	2.50
❑ 121	Anthony Thomas RC	10.00	4.00
❑ 122	Chad Johnson RC	25.00	10.00
❑ 123	Chris Chambers RC	15.00	6.00
❑ 124	Chris Weinke RC	10.00	4.00
❑ 125	David Terrell RC	10.00	4.00
❑ 126	Deuce McAllister RC	20.00	7.50
❑ 127	Drew Brees RC	40.00	15.00
❑ 128	Freddie Mitchell RC	10.00	4.00
❑ 129	James Jackson RC	10.00	4.00
❑ 130	Kevan Barlow RC	10.00	4.00
❑ 131	Koren Robinson RC	10.00	4.00
❑ 132	LaDainian Tomlinson RC	135.00	75.00
❑ 133	Michael Bennett RC	10.00	4.00
❑ 134	Michael Vick RC	50.00	20.00
❑ 135	Mike McMahon RC	10.00	4.00
❑ 136	Reggie Wayne RC	20.00	7.50
❑ 137	Robert Ferguson RC	10.00	4.00
❑ 138	Rod Gardner RC	10.00	4.00
❑ 139	Santana Moss RC	15.00	6.00
❑ 140	Travis Henry RC	15.00	6.00

2002 Finest

❑	COMP.SET w/o SP's (62)	40.00	15.00
❑ 1	Peyton Manning	2.50	1.00
❑ 2	Troy Brown	.75	.30
❑ 3	Curtis Martin	1.25	.50
❑ 4	Kordell Stewart	.75	.30
❑ 5	Michael Pittman	.50	.20
❑ 6	Rod Gardner	.75	.30
❑ 7	Germane Crowell	.50	.20
❑ 8	Terrell Davis	1.25	.50
❑ 9	Eric Moulds	.75	.30
❑ 10	Jake Plummer	.75	.30
❑ 11	Tony Gonzalez	.75	.30
❑ 12	Ricky Williams	1.25	.50
❑ 13	Deuce McAllister	1.50	.60
❑ 14	Jerry Rice	2.50	1.00
❑ 15	Torry Holt	1.25	.50
❑ 16	Michael Vick	4.00	1.50
❑ 17	David Terrell	1.25	.50
❑ 18	Terry Glenn	.75	.30
❑ 19	Mark Brunell	1.25	.50
❑ 20	Vinny Testaverde	.75	.30
❑ 21	Jerome Bettis	1.25	.50
❑ 22	Randy Moss	2.50	1.00
❑ 23	Marvin Harrison	1.25	.50
❑ 24	Chris Weinke	.75	.30
❑ 25	Tiki Barber	1.25	.50
❑ 26	Corey Bradford	.50	.20
❑ 27	David Boston	1.25	.50
❑ 28	Emmitt Smith	3.00	1.25
❑ 29	Santana Moss	1.25	.50
❑ 30	Brian Griese	1.25	.50
❑ 31	Priest Holmes	1.50	.60
❑ 32	Rich Gannon	1.25	.50
❑ 33	Antowain Smith	.75	.30
❑ 34	Marcus Robinson	.75	.30
❑ 35	Warrick Dunn	1.25	.50
❑ 36	Daunte Culpepper	1.25	.50
❑ 37	Shaun Alexander	1.50	.60
❑ 38	Kurt Warner	1.25	.50
❑ 39	Quincy Carter	.75	.30
❑ 40	Ray Lewis	1.25	.50
❑ 41	Aaron Brooks	1.25	.50
❑ 42	Plaxico Burress	.75	.30
❑ 43	Jamal Lewis	1.25	.50
❑ 44	Ahman Green	1.25	.50

❑ 45 Rod Smith .75 .30
❑ 46 Tim Couch .75 .30
❑ 47 Muhsin Muhammad .75 .30
❑ 48 Drew Bledsoe 1.50 .60
❑ 49 Anthony Thomas .75 .30
❑ 50 Tom Brady 3.00 1.25
❑ 51 Trent Green .75 .30
❑ 52 Charlie Garner .75 .30
❑ 53 Darrell Jackson .75 .30
❑ 54 Mike McMahon 1.25 .50
❑ 55 Donovan McNabb 1.50 .60
❑ 56 Fred Taylor 1.25 .50
❑ 57 Corey Dillon .75 .30
❑ 58 Keyshawn Johnson 1.25 .50
❑ 59 Drew Brees 1.25 .50
❑ 60 Steve McNair 1.25 .50
❑ 61 Jimmy Smith .75 .30
❑ 62 Terrell Owens 1.25 .50
❑ 63 Eddie George JSY/499 20.00 7.50
❑ 64 Jeff Garcia JSY/999 15.00 6.00
❑ 65 LaDain Tomlinson JSY/999 25.00 10.00
❑ 66 Cris Carter JSY/499 20.00 7.50
❑ 67 Chris Chambers JSY/499 20.00 7.50
❑ 68 Brian Urlacher JSY/999 25.00 10.00
❑ 69 Tim Brown JSY/999 15.00 6.00
❑ 70 Marshall Faulk JSY/999 20.00 7.50
❑ 71 Stephen Davis JSY/999 12.00 5.00
❑ 72 Jevon Kearse JSY/999 12.00 5.00
❑ 73 Edgerrin James JSY/999 15.00 6.00
❑ 74 Mike Anderson JSY/999 15.00 6.00
❑ 75 Warren Sapp JSY/499 20.00 7.50
❑ 76 Brett Favre JSY/499 30.00 15.00
❑ 77 Julius Peppers RC 6.00 2.50
❑ 78 Tim Carter RC 3.00 1.25
❑ 79 Travis Stephens RC 3.00 1.25
❑ 80 Jabar Gaffney RC 4.00 1.50
❑ 81 Cliff Russell RC 3.00 1.25
❑ 82 Reche Caldwell RC 4.00 1.50
❑ 83 Maurice Morris RC 4.00 1.50
❑ 84 Antwaan Randle El RC 6.00 2.50
❑ 85 Ladell Betts RC 4.00 1.50
❑ 86 Daniel Graham RC 4.00 1.50
❑ 87 Jeremy Shockey RC 12.00 5.00
❑ 88 Mike Williams RC 3.00 1.25
❑ 89 Josh McCown RC 5.00 2.00
❑ 90 Rohan Davey RC 4.00 1.50
❑ 91 David Garrard RC 4.00 1.50
❑ 92 Dwight Freeney RC 6.00 2.50
❑ 93 Leonard Henry RC 3.00 1.25
❑ 94 Albert Haynesworth RC 3.00 1.25
❑ 95 Herb Haygood RC 2.00 .75
❑ 96 Kurt Kittner RC 3.00 1.25
❑ 97 Jason McAddley RC 3.00 1.25
❑ 98 Bryan Thomas RC 3.00 1.25
❑ 99 Wendell Bryant RC 2.00 .75
❑ 100 Mike Rumph RC 4.00 1.50
❑ 101 Chad Hutchinson RC 3.00 1.25
❑ 102 Brian Westbrook RC 6.00 2.50
❑ 103 Deion Branch RC 8.00 4.00
❑ 104 John Henderson RC 4.00 1.50
❑ 105 Jerramy Stevens RC 4.00 1.50
❑ 106 Tracey Wistrom RC 3.00 1.25
❑ 107 Phillip Buchanon RC 4.00 1.50
❑ 108 Matt Schobel RC 3.00 1.25
❑ 109 Ed Reed RC 6.00 2.50
❑ 110 Randy Fasani RC 3.00 1.25
❑ 111 Josh Scobey RC 4.00 1.50
❑ 112 Luke Staley RC 3.00 1.25
❑ 113 Anthony Weaver RC 3.00 1.25
❑ 114 Kyle Johnson RC 2.00 .75
❑ 115 David Carr AU RC 50.00 20.00
❑ 116 Joey Harrington AU RC 30.00 12.50
❑ 117 Donte Stallworth AU RC 40.00 20.00
❑ 118 Ashley Lelie AU RC 30.00 12.50
❑ 119 Patrick Ramsey AU RC 30.00 12.50
❑ 120 William Green AU RC 20.00 7.50
❑ 121 Josh Reed AU RC 20.00 7.50
❑ 122 Clinton Portis AU RC 60.00 30.00
❑ 123 Antonio Bryant AU RC 20.00 7.50
❑ 124 Javon Walker AU RC 40.00 15.00
❑ 125 Roy Williams AU RC 40.00 15.00
❑ 126 Marquise Walker AU RC 20.00 7.50
❑ 127 Quentin Jammer AU RC 20.00 7.50
❑ 128 DeShaun Foster AU RC 25.00 12.50
❑ 129 Andre Davis AU RC 20.00 7.50
❑ 130 Ron Johnson AU RC 20.00 7.50
❑ 131 Lamar Gordon AU RC 20.00 7.50
❑ 132 T.J. Duckett AU/300 RC 30.00 15.00
❑ 133 Freddie Milons AU RC 20.00 7.50
❑ 134 Eric Crouch AU RC 20.00 7.50
❑ 135 Adrian Peterson AU RC 20.00 7.50
❑ 136 Damien Anderson AU RC 20.00 7.50

2003 Finest

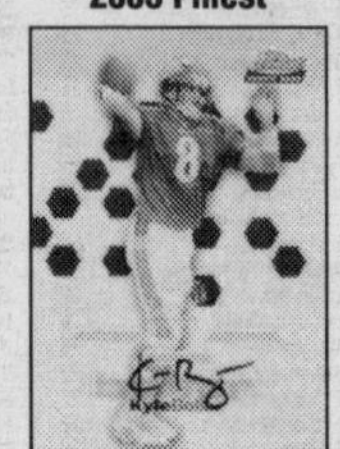

❑ COMP.SET w/o SP's (100) 50.00 20.00
❑ 101-118 GROUP A ODDS 1:171 MINI-BOXES
❑ 101-118 GROUP B ODDS 1:38 MINI-BOXES
❑ 101-118 GROUP C ODDS 1:4 MINI-BOXES
❑ ROOKIE AU/399 ODDS 1:30 MINI-BOXES
❑ ROOKIE AU/999 ODDS 1:3 MINI-BOXES
❑ 1 Chad Pennington 1.50 .60
❑ 2 Tommy Maddox 1.25 .50
❑ 3 Brett Favre 3.00 1.25
❑ 4 Eric Moulds .75 .30
❑ 5 Randy Moss 2.00 .75
❑ 6 Duce Staley .75 .30
❑ 7 Derrick Mason .75 .30
❑ 8 Shaun Alexander 1.25 .50
❑ 9 Peyton Manning 2.00 .75
❑ 10 Kerry Collins .75 .30
❑ 11 Joe Horn .75 .30
❑ 12 Laveranues Coles .75 .30
❑ 13 Marty Booker .75 .30
❑ 14 Emmitt Smith 3.00 1.25
❑ 15 Edgerrin James 1.25 .50
❑ 16 Aaron Brooks 1.25 .50
❑ 17 Curtis Martin 1.25 .50
❑ 18 Hines Ward 1.25 .50
❑ 19 Rod Smith .75 .30
❑ 20 Priest Holmes 1.50 .60
❑ 21 Jerry Rice 2.50 1.00
❑ 22 Peerless Price .75 .30
❑ 23 Mark Brunell .75 .30
❑ 24 Trent Green .75 .30
❑ 25 David Boston .75 .30
❑ 26 Chris Chambers 1.25 .50
❑ 27 Marshall Faulk 1.25 .50
❑ 28 Fred Taylor 1.25 .50
❑ 29 Tim Couch .50 .20
❑ 30 Amani Toomer .75 .30
❑ 31 Travis Henry .75 .30
❑ 32 Jeff Blake .50 .20
❑ 33 Troy Brown .75 .30
❑ 34 Charlie Garner .75 .30
❑ 35 Tom Brady 3.00 1.25
❑ 36 Warrick Dunn .75 .30
❑ 37 Plaxico Burress .75 .30
❑ 38 Marvin Harrison 1.25 .50
❑ 39 Clinton Portis 2.00 .75
❑ 40 Deuce McAllister 1.25 .50
❑ 41 Matt Hasselbeck .75 .30
❑ 42 Jeff Garcia 1.25 .50
❑ 43 David Carr 2.00 .75
❑ 44 Ahman Green 1.25 .50
❑ 45 Eddie George .75 .30
❑ 46 Drew Brees 1.25 .50
❑ 47 Tiki Barber 1.25 .50
❑ 48 Jay Fiedler .75 .30
❑ 49 Curtis Conway .75 .30
❑ 50 Steve McNair 1.25 .50
❑ 51 Donald Driver .75 .30
❑ 52 Jake Plummer .75 .30
❑ 53 Jamal Lewis 1.25 .50
❑ 54 Corey Dillon .75 .30
❑ 55 Stephen Davis .75 .30
❑ 56 Terrell Owens 1.25 .50
❑ 57 Torry Holt 1.25 .50
❑ 58 Chad Johnson 1.25 .50
❑ 59 Chad Hutchinson .50 .20
❑ 60 Kurt Warner 1.25 .50
❑ 61 Troy Polamalu RC 25.00 12.50
❑ 62 Eugene Wilson RC 3.00 1.25
❑ 63 Juston Wood RC 1.50 .60
❑ 64 Anquan Boldin RC 8.00 3.00
❑ 65 Doug Gabriel RC 3.00 1.25
❑ 66 Domanick Davis RC 3.00 1.25
❑ 67 J.R. Tolver RC 2.50 1.00
❑ 68 Jerome McDougle RC 3.00 1.25
❑ 69 Keenan Howry RC 3.00 1.25
❑ 70 Teyo Johnson RC 3.00 1.25
❑ 71 Bethel Johnson RC 3.00 1.25
❑ 72 Ken Hamlin RC 3.00 1.25
❑ 73 L.J. Smith RC 3.00 1.25
❑ 74 Rashean Mathis RC 1.50 .60
❑ 75 Arnaz Battle RC 3.00 1.25
❑ 76 B.J. Askew RC 3.00 1.25
❑ 77 Mike Doss RC 3.00 1.25
❑ 78 Kevin Curtis RC 3.00 1.25
❑ 79 Terence Newman RC 6.00 2.50
❑ 80 Shaun McDonald RC 3.00 1.25
❑ 81 Kevin Williams RC 3.00 1.25
❑ 82 Nate Burleson RC 3.00 1.25
❑ 83 Tyrone Calico RC 3.00 1.25
❑ 84 DeWayne White RC 2.50 1.00
❑ 85 Marcus Trufant RC 3.00 1.25
❑ 86 Nick Barnett RC 3.00 1.25
❑ 87 Bennie Joppru RC 3.00 1.25
❑ 88 Andre Woolfolk RC 3.00 1.25
❑ 89 Billy McMullen RC 2.50 1.00
❑ 90 Boss Bailey RC 3.00 1.25
❑ 91 William Joseph RC 3.00 1.25
❑ 92 Michael Haynes RC 3.00 1.25
❑ 93 DeWayne Robertson RC 3.00 1.25
❑ 94 LaTarence Dunbar RC 2.50 1.00
❑ 95 David Tyree RC 2.50 1.00
❑ 96 Walter Young RC 1.50 .60
❑ 97 E.J. Henderson RC 3.00 1.25
❑ 98 Ty Warren RC 3.00 1.25
❑ 99 Zuriel Smith RC 1.50 .60
❑ 100 Brock Forsey RC 3.00 1.25
❑ 101 Ricky Williams JSY C 12.00 5.00
❑ 102 Drew Bledsoe JSY C 12.00 5.00
❑ 103 Joey Harrington JSY C 15.00 6.00
❑ 104 Tim Brown JSY C 15.00 6.00
❑ 105 Brian Urlacher JSY C 20.00 7.50
❑ 106 Zach Thomas JSY C 12.00 5.00
❑ 107 Jeremy Shockey JSY C 15.00 6.00
❑ 108 Michael Strahan JSY A 12.00 5.00
❑ 109 Jason Taylor JSY C 12.00 5.00
❑ 110 Donovan McNabb JSY C 20.00 7.50
❑ 111 LaDainian Tomlinson JSY B 15.00 6.00
❑ 112 Rich Gannon JSY C 12.00 5.00
❑ 113 Brad Johnson JSY C 12.00 5.00
❑ 114 Daunte Culpepper JSY C 12.00 5.00
❑ 115 Michael Vick JSY C 25.00 10.00
❑ 116 Jimmy Smith JSY B 10.00 4.00
❑ 117 Keyshawn Johnson JSY C 12.00 5.00
❑ 118 Keith Brooking JSY C 10.00 4.00
❑ 119 Carson Palmer AU/399 RC 150.00 75.00
❑ 120 Byron Leftwich AU/399 RC 80.00 30.00
❑ 121 Chris Simms AU/399 RC 60.00 30.00
❑ 122 Kyle Boller AU/399 RC 30.00 12.50
❑ 123 Justin Fargas AU RC 15.00 6.00
❑ 124 Seneca Wallace AU RC 15.00 6.00
❑ 125 Larry Johnson AU RC 120.00 50.00
❑ 126 Kareem Kelly AU RC 15.00 6.00
❑ 127 Willis McGahee AU/399 RC 60.00 30.00
❑ 128 Kelley Washington AU RC 20.00 10.00
❑ 129 Brian St.Pierre AU RC 15.00 6.00
❑ 130 Kliff Kingsbury AU RC 15.00 6.00
❑ 131 Ken Dorsey AU RC 15.00 6.00
❑ 132 Bryant Johnson AU RC 15.00 6.00
❑ 133 Dallas Clark AU RC 15.00 6.00
❑ 134 Chris Brown AU RC 25.00 10.00
❑ 135 Taylor Jacobs AU RC 15.00 6.00
❑ 136 Artose Pinner AU RC 15.00 6.00
❑ 137 Lee Suggs AU RC 25.00 10.00
❑ 138 LaBrandon Toefield AU RC 15.00 6.00
❑ 139 Jason Witten AU RC 30.00 15.00
❑ 140 Brad Banks AU RC 15.00 6.00
❑ 141 Earnest Graham AU RC 15.00 6.00
❑ 142 Bobby Wade AU RC 15.00 6.00
❑ 143 Talman Gardner AU RC 15.00 6.00
❑ 144 Justin Gage AU RC 15.00 6.00
❑ 145 Sam Aiken AU RC 15.00 6.00
❑ 146 Musa Smith AU RC 15.00 6.00
❑ 147 Terrell Suggs AU RC 20.00 7.50
❑ 148 Brandon Lloyd AU RC 25.00 10.00
❑ 150 Rex Grossman AU RC 60.00 30.00

2004 Finest

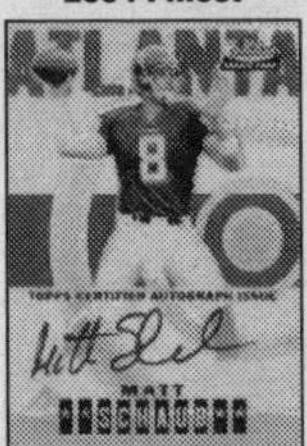

❑ COMP.SET w/o SP's (100) 40.00 15.00
❑ COMP.SET w/o RC's (60) 12.00 5.00
❑ 108-134 AU/399 RC STATED ODDS 1:120
❑ 108-134 AU/999 RC STATED ODDS 1:12
❑ 1 Steve McNair .75 .30
❑ 2 Corey Dillon .50 .20
❑ 3 Joey Harrington .75 .30
❑ 4 Travis Henry .50 .20
❑ 5 Donovan McNabb 1.00 .40
❑ 6 Jamal Lewis .75 .30
❑ 7 Jeff Garcia .75 .30
❑ 8 Fred Taylor .50 .20
❑ 9 Aaron Brooks .50 .20
❑ 10 Marc Bulger .75 .30
❑ 11 Keenan McCardell .30 .10
❑ 12 David Carr .75 .30
❑ 13 Charles Rogers .50 .20
❑ 14 Ray Lewis .75 .30
❑ 15 Priest Holmes 1.00 .40
❑ 16 Curtis Martin .75 .30
❑ 17 Plaxico Burress .50 .20
❑ 18 Shaun Alexander .75 .30
❑ 19 Brad Johnson .50 .20
❑ 20 Marvin Harrison .75 .30
❑ 21 Rod Smith .50 .20
❑ 22 Jake Delhomme .75 .30
❑ 23 Santana Moss .50 .20
❑ 24 Trent Green .50 .20
❑ 25 Michael Vick 1.50 .60
❑ 26 Tim Rattay .30 .10
❑ 27 Chris Chambers .50 .20
❑ 28 Robert Ferguson .30 .10
❑ 29 Tiki Barber .75 .30
❑ 30 Terrell Owens .75 .30
❑ 31 Marshall Faulk .75 .30
❑ 32 Quincy Carter .50 .20
❑ 33 Stephen Davis .50 .20
❑ 34 Josh McCown .50 .20
❑ 35 Jeremy Shockey .75 .30
❑ 36 Tommy Maddox .50 .20
❑ 37 Derrick Mason .50 .20
❑ 38 Kerry Collins .50 .20
❑ 39 Jimmy Smith .50 .20
❑ 40 Chad Pennington .75 .30
❑ 41 Domanick Davis .75 .30
❑ 42 Darrell Jackson .50 .20
❑ 43 Steve Smith .75 .30
❑ 44 Drew Bledsoe .75 .30
❑ 45 Deuce McAllister .75 .30
❑ 46 Jerry Porter .50 .20
❑ 47 Peerless Price .50 .20
❑ 48 Eric Moulds .50 .20
❑ 49 Garrison Hearst .50 .20
❑ 50 Brett Favre 3.00 1.25
❑ 51 Amani Toomer .50 .20
❑ 52 Andre Johnson .75 .30
❑ 53 Edgerrin James .75 .30
❑ 54 Rex Grossman .75 .30
❑ 55 Daunte Culpepper .75 .30
❑ 56 Tony Gonzalez .50 .20
❑ 57 Byron Leftwich 1.00 .40
❑ 58 Mark Brunell .50 .20
❑ 59 Laveranues Coles .50 .20
❑ 60 Matt Hasselbeck .50 .20
❑ 61 Chris Gamble RC 2.00 .75
❑ 62 Michael Turner RC 2.50 1.00
❑ 63 Julius Jones RC 8.00 3.00
❑ 64 Dunta Robinson RC 2.00 .75
❑ 65 Sean Taylor RC 2.00 .75
❑ 66 Ahmad Carroll RC 2.00 .75
❑ 67 Derrick Strait RC 2.00 .75
❑ 68 Dontarrious Thomas RC 2.00 .75
❑ 69 Jason Babin RC 2.00 .75
❑ 70 Reggie Williams RC 2.50 1.00
❑ 71 Dwan Edwards RC 1.00 .40
❑ 72 Rashaun Woods RC 2.00 .75
❑ 73 Ricardo Colclough RC 2.00 .75
❑ 74 Will Smith RC 2.00 .75
❑ 75 Kellen Winslow RC 4.00 1.50
❑ 76 Roy Williams RC 5.00 2.00
❑ 77 B.J. Symons RC 2.00 .75
❑ 78 Carlos Francis RC 1.50 .60
❑ 79 Triandos Luke RC 2.00 .75
❑ 80 Drew Henson RC 2.00 .75
❑ 81 Keiwan Ratliff RC 1.50 .60
❑ 82 Will Poole RC 2.00 .75
❑ 83 Tommie Harris RC 2.00 .75
❑ 84 Steven Jackson RC 6.00 2.50
❑ 85 Greg Jones RC 2.00 .75
❑ 86 Vince Wilfork RC 2.00 .75
❑ 87 DeAngelo Hall RC 2.50 1.00
❑ 88 Daryl Smith RC 2.00 .75
❑ 89 Teddy Lehman RC 2.00 .75
❑ 90 Casey Bramlet RC 1.50 .60
❑ 91 Marcus Tubbs RC 2.00 .75
❑ 92 Andy Hall RC 1.50 .60
❑ 93 Jim Sorgi RC 2.00 .75
❑ 94 Kenechi Udeze RC 2.00 .75
❑ 95 Darius Watts RC 2.00 .75
❑ 96 Tank Johnson RC 1.50 .60
❑ 97 Matt Mauck RC 2.00 .75
❑ 98 Bradlee Van Pelt RC 2.50 1.00
❑ 99 D.J. Williams RC 2.00 .75
❑ 100 Larry Fitzgerald RC 6.00 2.50
❑ 101 Peyton Manning JSY 15.00 6.00
❑ 102 Clinton Portis JSY 8.00 3.00
❑ 103 Chad Johnson JSY 8.00 3.00
❑ 104 Randy Moss JSY 10.00 4.00
❑ 105 Tom Brady JSY 20.00 7.50
❑ 106 LaDainian Tomlinson JSY 10.00 4.00
❑ 107 Ahman Green JSY 8.00 3.00
❑ 108 Roethlisberger AU/399 RC 250.00 125.00
❑ 109 Philip Rivers AU/399 RC 120.00 60.00
❑ 110 Eli Manning AU/399 RC 200.00 100.00
❑ 111 Kevin Jones AU/399 RC 60.00 25.00
❑ 112 Bernard Berrian AU RC 25.00 12.50
❑ 113 Jeff Smoker AU RC 15.00 6.00
❑ 114 Mewelde Moore AU RC 15.00 6.00
❑ 115 Michael Clayton AU RC 30.00 12.50
❑ 116 Jonathan Vilma AU RC 20.00 7.50
❑ 117 J Morant AU RC EXCH 15.00 6.00
❑ 118 Devard Darling AU RC 15.00 6.00
❑ 119 Cedric Cobbs AU RC 15.00 6.00
❑ 120 Chris Perry AU/399 RC 30.00 12.50
❑ 121 Ernest Wilford AU RC 15.00 6.00
❑ 122 Michael Jenkins AU RC 15.00 6.00
❑ 123 Jerricho Cotchery AU RC 15.00 6.00
❑ 124 P.K. Sam AU RC 12.00 5.00
❑ 125 Tatum Bell AU RC 30.00 12.50
❑ 126 Derrick Hamilton AU RC 12.00 5.00
❑ 127 Luke McCown AU RC 15.00 6.00
❑ 128 Devery Henderson AU RC 12.00 5.00
❑ 129 Craig Krenzel AU RC 15.00 6.00
❑ 130 J.P. Losman AU RC 30.00 12.50
❑ 131 Lee Evans AU RC 20.00 10.00
❑ 132 Matt Schaub AU RC 40.00 25.00
❑ 133 Robert Gallery AU RC 15.00 6.00
❑ 134 Keary Colbert AU RC 20.00 7.50

2005 Finest

❑ COMPLETE SET (183)
❑ UNPRICED FRAMED REF. PRINT RUN 1 SET
❑ UNPRICED FRAM.XFRAC. PRINT RUN 1 SET
❑ UNPRICED GOLD XFRAC.PRINT RUN 10 SETS
❑ UNPRICED PRINT.PLATE PRINT RUN 1 SET
❑ UNPRICED SUPERFRACTORS #'d TO 1
❑ 1 Muhsin Muhammad .50 .20
❑ 2 Kevin Jones .75 .30
❑ 3 Eli Manning 1.50 .60
❑ 4 Kevan Barlow .50 .20
❑ 5 Randy Moss .75 .30
❑ 6 Brian Griese .50 .20
❑ 7 Dante Hall .50 .20
❑ 8 Chris Brown .50 .20
❑ 9 Antonio Gates .75 .30
❑ 10 Champ Bailey .50 .20
❑ 11 Eric Moulds .50 .20
❑ 12 Ray Lewis .75 .30
❑ 13 Larry Fitzgerald .75 .30
❑ 14 Byron Leftwich .75 .30
❑ 15 Marvin Harrison .75 .30
❑ 16 Stephen Davis .50 .20
❑ 17 Laveranues Coles .50 .20
❑ 18 Shaun Alexander 1.00 .40
❑ 19 Drew Bledsoe .75 .30
❑ 20 Sean Taylor .50 .20
❑ 21 Deuce McAllister .75 .30
❑ 22 Nate Burleson .50 .20
❑ 23 A.J. Feeley .50 .20
❑ 24 Jerome Bettis .75 .30
❑ 25 Torry Holt .75 .30
❑ 26 LaDainian Tomlinson 1.00 .40
❑ 27 Travis Henry .50 .20
❑ 28 T.J. Houshmandzadeh .40 .15
❑ 29 Fred Taylor .50 .20
❑ 30 Michael Jenkins .50 .20
❑ 31 Edgerrin James .75 .30
❑ 32 Terrell Owens .75 .30
❑ 33 Jason Witten .50 .20
❑ 34 Clinton Portis .75 .30
❑ 35 Deion Branch .50 .20
❑ 36 Priest Holmes .75 .30
❑ 37 Javon Walker .50 .20
❑ 38 Rex Grossman .50 .20
❑ 39 Domanick Davis .50 .20
❑ 40 Allen Rossum .40 .15
❑ 41 Dwight Freeney .50 .20
❑ 42 Jimmy Smith .50 .20
❑ 43 Tiki Barber .75 .30
❑ 44 Steve McNair .75 .30
❑ 45 Steven Jackson 1.00 .40
❑ 46 Joe Horn .50 .20
❑ 47 Randy McMichael .40 .15
❑ 48 J.P. Losman .75 .30
❑ 49 Warrick Dunn .50 .20
❑ 50 Tatum Bell .50 .20
❑ 51 Roy Williams WR .75 .30
❑ 52 Curtis Martin .75 .30
❑ 53 Donovan McNabb 1.00 .40
❑ 54 LaMont Jordan .75 .30
❑ 55 Marc Bulger .75 .30
❑ 56 Drew Bennett .50 .20
❑ 57 Julius Jones 1.00 .40
❑ 58 Santana Moss .50 .20
❑ 59 Michael Bennett .50 .20
❑ 60 Tony Gonzalez .50 .20
❑ 61 Jamal Lewis .75 .30
❑ 62 Keary Colbert .50 .20
❑ 63 Carson Palmer .75 .30
❑ 64 Dunta Robinson .50 .20
❑ 65 Brandon Stokley .50 .20
❑ 66 Brett Favre 2.00 .75
❑ 67 Jonathan Vilma .50 .20
❑ 68 Darrell Jackson .50 .20
❑ 69 Michael Pittman .40 .15
❑ 70 Drew Brees .75 .30
❑ 71 Amani Toomer .50 .20
❑ 72 Corey Dillon .50 .20
❑ 73 Willis McGahee .75 .30
❑ 74 Michael Vick 1.25 .50
❑ 75 Chad Johnson .75 .30
❑ 76 Anquan Boldin .50 .20
❑ 77 Kerry Collins .50 .20
❑ 78 Marshall Faulk .75 .30
❑ 79 Roy Williams S .50 .20
❑ 80 Trent Green .50 .20
❑ 81 Chris Gamble .50 .20
❑ 82 Ahman Green .75 .30
❑ 83 Todd Heap .50 .20

❑ 84 Brandon Lloyd .40 .15
❑ 85 Andre Johnson .50 .20
❑ 86 Lee Suggs .50 .20
❑ 87 Plaxico Burress .50 .20
❑ 88 Hines Ward .75 .30
❑ 89 Rod Smith .50 .20
❑ 90 Joey Harrington .75 .30
❑ 91 Derrick Mason .50 .20
❑ 92 Rudi Johnson .50 .20
❑ 93 Isaac Bruce .50 .20
❑ 94 Chris Chambers .50 .20
❑ 95 Matt Hasselbeck .50 .20
❑ 96 Donte Stallworth .50 .20
❑ 97 Philip Rivers .75 .30
❑ 98 Michael Clayton .75 .30
❑ 99 Alge Crumpler .50 .20
❑ 100 Chad Pennington .75 .30
❑ 101 Brian Westbrook .50 .20
❑ 102 Daunte Culpepper .75 .30
❑ 103 Jeremy Shockey .75 .30
❑ 104 Jerry Porter .50 .20
❑ 105 Tom Brady 2.00 .75
❑ 106 Lee Evans .50 .20
❑ 107 Jake Delhomme .75 .30
❑ 108 Ben Roethlisberger 2.00 .75
❑ 109 Jake Plummer .50 .20
❑ 110 Charles Rogers .50 .20
❑ 111 Patrick Ramsey .50 .20
❑ 112 Reggie Wayne .50 .20
❑ 113 Reuben Droughns .50 .20
❑ 114 Aaron Brooks .50 .20
❑ 115 David Carr .75 .30
❑ 116 Thomas Jones .50 .20
❑ 117 Ashley Lelie .50 .20
❑ 118 Donald Driver .50 .20
❑ 119 Billy Volek .50 .20
❑ 120 Peyton Manning 1.25 .50
❑ 121 Frank Gore RC 5.00 2.00
❑ 122 Adam Jones RC 2.50 1.00
❑ 123 Antrel Rolle RC 2.50 1.00
❑ 124 Roddy White RC 2.50 1.00
❑ 125 Derrick Johnson RC 4.00 1.50
❑ 126 Troy Williamson RC 5.00 2.00
❑ 127 Maurice Clarett 2.50 1.00
❑ 128 Dan Orlovsky RC 3.00 1.25
❑ 129 Andrew Walter RC 4.00 1.50
❑ 130 Reggie Brown RC 2.50 1.00
❑ 131 Matt Jones RC 6.00 2.50
❑ 132 David Greene RC 2.50 1.00
❑ 133 Jerome Mathis RC 2.50 1.00
❑ 134 Thomas Davis RC 2.50 1.00
❑ 135 Roscoe Parrish RC 2.50 1.00
❑ 136 Ciatrick Fason RC 2.50 1.00
❑ 137 David Pollack RC 2.50 1.00
❑ 138 Kyle Orton RC 4.00 1.50
❑ 139 Heath Miller RC 6.00 2.50
❑ 140 Courtney Roby RC 2.50 1.00
❑ 141 Terrence Murphy RC 2.50 1.00
❑ 142 DeMarcus Ware RC 4.00 1.50
❑ 143 Fabian Washington RC 2.50 1.00
❑ 144 J.J. Arrington RC 3.00 1.25
❑ 145 Fred Gibson RC 2.00 .75
❑ 146 Carlos Rogers RC 3.00 1.25
❑ 147 Eric Shelton RC 2.50 1.00
❑ 148 Craphonso Thorpe RC 2.00 .75
❑ 149 Anthony Davis RC 2.00 .75
❑ 150 Marion Barber RC 4.00 1.50
❑ 151 Aaron Rodgers AU/299 RC 100.00 40.00
❑ 152 Alex Smith QB AU/299 RC 120.00 50.00
❑ 153 Braylon Edwards AU/299 RC 80.00 30.00
❑ 154 Cadillac Williams AU/299 RC 120.00 60.00
❑ 155 Cedric Benson AU/299 RC 80.00 40.00
❑ 156 Charlie Frye AU/299 RC 50.00 25.00
❑ 157 Jason Campbell AU/299 RC 60.00 30.00
❑ 158 Mark Clayton AU/299 RC 40.00 20.00
❑ 159 Mike Williams AU/299 50.00 20.00
❑ 160 Ronnie Brown AU/299 RC 120.00 50.00
❑ 161 Alex Smith TE AU RC 12.00 5.00
❑ 162 Alvin Pearman AU RC 12.00 5.00
❑ 163 Brandon Jacobs AU RC 30.00 15.00
❑ 164 Channing Crowder AU RC 12.00 5.00
❑ 165 Chris Henry AU RC 15.00 6.00
❑ 166 Courtney Roby AU RC 12.00 5.00
❑ 167 Derek Anderson AU RC 15.00 6.00
❑ 168 Mark Bradley AU RC 15.00 6.00
❑ 169 Ryan Fitzpatrick AU RC 20.00 7.50
❑ 170 Ryan Moats AU RC 20.00 7.50
❑ 171 Stefan LeFors AU RC 12.00 5.00
❑ 172 Steve Savoy AU RC 10.00 4.00
❑ 173 Tab Perry AU RC 12.00 5.00
❑ 174 Timmy Chang AU RC 15.00 6.00
❑ 175 Vincent Jackson AU RC 12.00 5.00
❑ 176 Charles Frederick AU RC 12.00 5.00
❑ 177 Kay-Jay Harris AU RC 10.00 4.00
❑ 178 Darren Sproles AU RC 12.00 5.00
❑ 179 Adrian McPherson AU RC 15.00 6.00
❑ 180 Craig Bragg AU RC 10.00 4.00
❑ 181 J.R. Russell AU RC 10.00 4.00
❑ 182 Gino Guidugli AU RC 10.00 4.00
❑ 183 Vernand Morency AU RC 12.00 5.00

2006 Finest

❑ COMP.SET w/o AU's (150) 30.00 12.50
❑ 1 Muhsin Muhammad .50 .20
❑ 2 Kevin Jones .75 .30
❑ 3 Eli Manning 1.00 .40
❑ 4 Marion Barber .50 .20
❑ 5 Randy Moss .75 .30
❑ 6 Odell Thurman .40 .15
❑ 7 Dante Hall .50 .20
❑ 8 Chris Brown .50 .20
❑ 9 Antonio Gates .75 .30
❑ 10 Champ Bailey .50 .20
❑ 11 Eric Moulds .50 .20
❑ 12 Ray Lewis .75 .30
❑ 13 Larry Fitzgerald .75 .30
❑ 14 Byron Leftwich .50 .20
❑ 15 Marvin Harrison .75 .30
❑ 16 Larry Johnson 1.00 .40
❑ 17 Steve Smith .75 .30
❑ 18 Shaun Alexander .75 .30
❑ 19 Drew Bledsoe .75 .30
❑ 20 Joey Galloway .50 .20
❑ 21 Deuce McAllister .50 .20
❑ 22 Ben Obomanu RC 3.00 1.25
❑ 23 Chester Taylor .50 .20
❑ 24 Delanie Walker RC 3.00 1.25
❑ 25 Torry Holt .50 .20
❑ 26 LaDainian Tomlinson 1.00 .40
❑ 27 Derrick Mason .40 .15
❑ 28 T.J. Houshmandzadeh .50 .20
❑ 29 Fred Taylor .50 .20
❑ 30 Michael Jenkins .50 .20
❑ 31 Edgerrin James .75 .30
❑ 32 Terrell Owens .75 .30
❑ 33 Jason Witten .50 .20
❑ 34 Clinton Portis .75 .30
❑ 35 Deion Branch .50 .20
❑ 36 Priest Holmes .50 .20
❑ 37 Quinton Ganther RC 3.00 1.25
❑ 38 Kurt Warner .50 .20
❑ 39 Domanick Davis .50 .20
❑ 40 Chris Simms .50 .20
❑ 41 Dwight Freeney .50 .20
❑ 42 Daniel Bullocks RC 4.00 1.50
❑ 43 Tiki Barber .75 .30
❑ 44 Steve McNair .50 .20
❑ 45 Steven Jackson .75 .30
❑ 46 Joe Horn .50 .20
❑ 47 Randy McMichael .40 .15
❑ 48 Cedric Humes RC 4.00 1.50
❑ 49 Warrick Dunn .50 .20
❑ 50 Tatum Bell .50 .20
❑ 51 P.J. Pope RC 3.00 1.25
❑ 52 Curtis Martin .75 .30
❑ 53 Donovan McNabb .75 .30
❑ 54 LaMont Jordan .50 .20
❑ 55 Marc Bulger .50 .20
❑ 56 Drew Bennett .40 .15
❑ 57 Julius Jones .75 .30
❑ 58 Santana Moss .50 .20
❑ 59 Ronnie Brown .75 .30
❑ 60 Tony Gonzalez .50 .20
❑ 61 Jamal Lewis .50 .20
❑ 62 D.J. Shockley RC 4.00 1.50
❑ 63 Carson Palmer .75 .30
❑ 64 Jonathan Orr RC 3.00 1.25
❑ 65 Brandon Stokley .50 .20
❑ 66 Brett Favre 1.50 .60
❑ 67 Jonathan Vilma .50 .20
❑ 68 Darrell Jackson .50 .20
❑ 69 Brian Urlacher .75 .30
❑ 70 Drew Brees .75 .30
❑ 71 Mike Williams .75 .30
❑ 72 Corey Dillon .50 .20
❑ 73 Willis McGahee .75 .30
❑ 74 Michael Vick 1.00 .40
❑ 75 Chad Johnson .50 .20
❑ 76 Anquan Boldin .50 .20
❑ 77 Shawne Merriman .50 .20
❑ 78 Willie Parker 1.00 .40
❑ 79 Roy Williams S .50 .20
❑ 80 Trent Green .50 .20
❑ 81 Chris Gamble .40 .15
❑ 82 Ahman Green .50 .20
❑ 83 Todd Heap .50 .20
❑ 84 Brett Basanez RC 4.00 1.50
❑ 85 Andre Johnson .50 .20
❑ 86 Abdul Hodge RC 4.00 1.50
❑ 87 Plaxico Burress .50 .20
❑ 88 Hines Ward .75 .30
❑ 89 Rod Smith .50 .20
❑ 90 Cadillac Williams .75 .30
❑ 91 Braylon Edwards .75 .30
❑ 92 Rudi Johnson .50 .20
❑ 93 Isaac Bruce .50 .20
❑ 94 Chris Chambers .50 .20
❑ 95 Matt Hasselbeck .50 .20
❑ 96 Donte Stallworth .50 .20
❑ 97 Philip Rivers .75 .30
❑ 98 Will Blackmon RC 3.00 1.25
❑ 99 Alge Crumpler .50 .20
❑ 100 Chad Pennington .50 .20
❑ 101 Darnell Bing RC 4.00 1.50
❑ 102 Daunte Culpepper .75 .30
❑ 103 Jeremy Shockey .75 .30
❑ 104 Jerry Porter .50 .20
❑ 105 Tom Brady 1.25 .50
❑ 106 Jeff Webb RC 3.00 1.25
❑ 107 Jake Delhomme .50 .20
❑ 108 Ben Roethlisberger 1.25 .50
❑ 109 Jake Plummer .50 .20
❑ 110 Paul Pinegar RC 3.00 1.25
❑ 111 Kevin McMahan RC 3.00 1.25
❑ 112 Reggie Wayne .50 .20
❑ 113 Bennie Brazell RC 3.00 1.25
❑ 114 Todd Watkins RC 3.00 1.25
❑ 115 David Carr .50 .20
❑ 116 Cory Rodgers RC 4.00 1.50
❑ 117 Leon Washington RC 6.00 2.50
❑ 118 Michael Strahan .50 .20
❑ 119 P.J. Daniels RC 3.00 1.25
❑ 120 Peyton Manning 1.25 .50
❑ 121 Brandon Marshall RC 4.00 1.50
❑ 122 Jerome Harrison RC 4.00 1.50
❑ 123 Mario Williams RC 6.00 2.50
❑ 124 Ernie Sims RC 5.00 2.00
❑ 125 Devin Hester RC 8.00 3.00
❑ 126 Jimmy Williams RC 4.00 1.50
❑ 127 Charlie Whitehurst RC 5.00 2.00
❑ 128 Jason Avant RC 4.00 1.50
❑ 129 Marcus Vick RC 3.00 1.25
❑ 130 Mathias Kiwanuka RC 5.00 2.00
❑ 131 Brodrick Bunkley RC 4.00 1.50
❑ 132 Reggie McNeal RC 3.00 1.25
❑ 133 Dominique Byrd RC 3.00 1.25
❑ 134 Jason Allen RC 4.00 1.50
❑ 135 D'Qwell Jackson RC 3.00 1.25
❑ 136 Donte Whitner RC 4.00 1.50
❑ 137 Willie Reid RC 4.00 1.50
❑ 138 Kamerion Wimbley RC 4.00 1.50
❑ 139 Martin Nance RC 3.00 1.25
❑ 140 Haloti Ngata RC 4.00 1.50
❑ 141 Devin Aromashodu RC 3.00 1.25
❑ 142 Jeremy Bloom RC 3.00 1.25
❑ 143 Manny Lawson RC 4.00 1.50
❑ 144 Johnathan Joseph RC 3.00 1.25
❑ 145 Brad Smith RC 4.00 1.50
❑ 146 Thomas Howard RC 4.00 1.50
❑ 147 Demetrius Williams RC 5.00 2.00

❑ 148	Antonio Cromartie RC	4.00	1.50
❑ 149	Bobby Carpenter RC	4.00	1.50
❑ 150	Tamba Hali RC	4.00	1.50
❑ 151	Reggie Bush AU/199 RC	400.00	200.00
❑ 152	Matt Leinart AU/199 RC	200.00	100.00
❑ 153	Vince Young AU/199 RC	250.00	125.00
❑ 154	Jay Cutler AU/199 RC	200.00	100.00
❑ 155	S.Holmes AU/199 RC	40.00	15.00
❑ 156	LenDale White AU/199 RC	50.00	20.00
❑ 157	DeA.Williams AU/199 RC	80.00	40.00
❑ 158	Sinorice Moss AU/199 RC	30.00	15.00
❑ 159	Vernon Davis AU/199 RC	40.00	15.00
❑ 160	Joseph Addai AU/199 RC	100.00	50.00
❑ 161	Omar Jacobs AU/199 RC	20.00	8.00
❑ 162	Chad Jackson AU/199 RC	40.00	20.00
❑ 163	Chad Greenway AU RC	12.00	5.00
❑ 164	Maurice Drew AU RC	50.00	25.00
❑ 165	D.Ferguson AU RC	12.00	5.00
❑ 166	Anthony Fasano AU RC	12.00	5.00
❑ 167	Derek Hagan AU/199 RC	20.00	8.00
❑ 168	A.J. Hawk AU/199 RC	100.00	50.00
❑ 169	David Thomas AU RC	12.00	5.00
❑ 170	Brian Calhoun AU RC	12.00	5.00
❑ 171	K.Clemens AU RC EXCH	15.00	6.00
❑ 172	Tarvaris Jackson AU RC	25.00	12.50
❑ 173	M.Stovall AU RC EXCH	12.00	5.00
❑ 174	Michael Huff AU/199 RC	8.00	3.00
❑ 175	Greg Jennings AU RC	30.00	15.00
❑ 176	Joe Klopfenstein AU RC	10.00	4.00
❑ 177	Leonard Pope AU RC	12.00	5.00
❑ 178	Michael Robinson AU RC	20.00	8.00
❑ 179	Ingle Martin AU RC	10.00	4.00
❑ 180	Wali Lundy AU RC	12.00	5.00
❑ 181	Drew Olson AU RC	10.00	4.00
❑ 182	Jerious Norwood AU RC	30.00	12.00
❑ 183	Travis Wilson AU RC	12.00	5.00
❑ 184	Tye Hill AU RC	12.00	5.00
❑ 185	Brandon Williams AU RC	12.00	5.00
❑ 186	Marques Hagans AU RC	10.00	4.00

1995 Flair

❑	COMPLETE SET (220)	30.00	12.50
❑ 1	Larry Centers	.40	.15
❑ 2	Garrison Hearst	.75	.30
❑ 3	Seth Joyner	.20	.07
❑ 4	Dave Krieg	.20	.07
❑ 5	Rob Moore	.40	.15
❑ 6	Frank Sanders RC	.75	.30
❑ 7	Eric Swann	.40	.15
❑ 8	Devin Bush	.20	.07
❑ 9	Chris Doleman	.20	.07
❑ 10	Bert Emanuel	.75	.30
❑ 11	Jeff George	.40	.15
❑ 12	Craig Heyward	.40	.15
❑ 13	Terance Mathis	.40	.15
❑ 14	Eric Metcalf	.40	.15
❑ 15	Cornelius Bennett	.40	.15
❑ 16	Jeff Burris	.20	.07
❑ 17	Todd Collins RC	.40	.15
❑ 18	Russell Copeland	.20	.07
❑ 19	Jim Kelly	.75	.30
❑ 20	Andre Reed	.40	.15
❑ 21	Bruce Smith	.75	.30
❑ 22	Don Beebe	.20	.07
❑ 23	Mark Carrier WR	.40	.15
❑ 24	Kerry Collins RC	2.00	.75
❑ 25	Barry Foster	.40	.15
❑ 26	Pete Metzelaars	.20	.07
❑ 27	Tyrone Poole	.75	.30
❑ 28	Frank Reich	.20	.07
❑ 29	Curtis Conway	.75	.30
❑ 30	Chris Gedney	.20	.07
❑ 31	Jeff Graham	.20	.07
❑ 32	Raymont Harris	.20	.07
❑ 33	Erik Kramer	.20	.07
❑ 34	Rashaan Salaam RC	.40	.15
❑ 35	Lewis Tillman	.20	.07
❑ 36	Michael Timpson	.20	.07
❑ 37	Jeff Blake RC	1.00	.40
❑ 38	Ki-Jana Carter RC	.75	.30
❑ 39	Tony McGee	.20	.07
❑ 40	Carl Pickens	.40	.15
❑ 41	Corey Sawyer	.20	.07
❑ 42	Darnay Scott	.40	.15
❑ 43	Dan Wilkinson	.40	.15
❑ 44	Derrick Alexander WR	.75	.30
❑ 45	Leroy Hoard	.20	.07
❑ 46	Michael Jackson	.40	.15
❑ 47	Antonio Langham	.20	.07
❑ 48	Andre Rison	.40	.15
❑ 49	Vinny Testaverde	.40	.15
❑ 50	Eric Turner	.20	.07
❑ 51	Troy Aikman	2.00	.75
❑ 52	Charles Haley	.40	.15
❑ 53	Michael Irvin	.75	.30
❑ 54	Daryl Johnston	.40	.15
❑ 55	Leon Lett	.20	.07
❑ 56	Jay Novacek	.40	.15
❑ 57	Emmitt Smith	3.00	1.25
❑ 58	Kevin Williams WR	.40	.15
❑ 59	Steve Atwater	.20	.07
❑ 60	Rod Bernstine	.20	.07
❑ 61	John Elway	4.00	1.50
❑ 62	Glyn Milburn	.20	.07
❑ 63	Anthony Miller	.40	.15
❑ 64	Mike Pritchard	.20	.07
❑ 65	Shannon Sharpe	.40	.15
❑ 66	Scott Mitchell	.40	.15
❑ 67	Herman Moore	.75	.30
❑ 68	Johnnie Morton	.40	.15
❑ 69	Brett Perriman	.40	.15
❑ 70	Barry Sanders	3.00	1.25
❑ 71	Chris Spielman	.40	.15
❑ 72	Edgar Bennett	.40	.15
❑ 73	Robert Brooks	.75	.30
❑ 74	Brett Favre	4.00	1.50
❑ 75	LeShon Johnson	.40	.15
❑ 76	Sean Jones	.20	.07
❑ 77	George Teague	.20	.07
❑ 78	Reggie White	.75	.30
❑ 79	Micheal Barrow	.20	.07
❑ 80	Gary Brown	.20	.07
❑ 81	Mel Gray	.20	.07
❑ 82	Haywood Jeffires	.20	.07
❑ 83	Steve McNair RC	4.00	1.50
❑ 84	Rodney Thomas RC	.40	.15
❑ 85	Trev Alberts	.20	.07
❑ 86	Flipper Anderson	.20	.07
❑ 87	Tony Bennett	.20	.07
❑ 88	Quentin Coryatt	.40	.15
❑ 89	Sean Dawkins	.40	.15
❑ 90	Craig Erickson	.20	.07
❑ 91	Marshall Faulk	2.50	1.00
❑ 92	Steve Beuerlein	.40	.15
❑ 93	Tony Boselli RC	.75	.30
❑ 94	Reggie Cobb	.20	.07
❑ 95	Ernest Givins	.20	.07
❑ 96	Desmond Howard	.40	.15
❑ 97	Jeff Lageman	.20	.07
❑ 98	James O. Stewart RC	1.50	.60
❑ 99	Marcus Allen	.75	.30
❑ 100	Steve Bono	.40	.15
❑ 101	Dale Carter	.40	.15
❑ 102	Willie Davis	.40	.15
❑ 103	Lake Dawson	.40	.15
❑ 104	Greg Hill	.40	.15
❑ 105	Neil Smith	.40	.15
❑ 106	Tim Bowens	.20	.07
❑ 107	Bryan Cox	.20	.07
❑ 108	Irving Fryar	.40	.15
❑ 109	Eric Green	.20	.07
❑ 110	Terry Kirby	.40	.15
❑ 111	Dan Marino	4.00	1.50
❑ 112	O.J. McDuffie	.75	.30
❑ 113	Bernie Parmalee	.40	.15
❑ 114	Derrick Alexander DE RC	.20	.07
❑ 115	Cris Carter	.75	.30
❑ 116	Qadry Ismail	.40	.15
❑ 117	Warren Moon	.40	.15
❑ 118	Jake Reed	.40	.15
❑ 119	Robert Smith	.75	.30
❑ 120	Dewayne Washington	.40	.15
❑ 121	Drew Bledsoe	1.25	.50
❑ 122	Vincent Brisby	.20	.07
❑ 123	Ben Coates	.40	.15
❑ 124	Curtis Martin RC	4.00	1.50
❑ 125	Willie McGinest	.40	.15
❑ 126	Dave Meggett	.20	.07
❑ 127	Chris Slade UER 126	.20	.07
❑ 128	Eric Allen	.20	.07
❑ 129	Mario Bates	.40	.15
❑ 130	Jim Everett	.20	.07
❑ 131	Michael Haynes	.40	.15
❑ 132	Tyrone Hughes	.40	.15
❑ 133	Renaldo Turnbull	.20	.07
❑ 134	Ray Zellars RC	.40	.15
❑ 135	Michael Brooks	.20	.07
❑ 136	Dave Brown	.40	.15
❑ 137	Rodney Hampton	.40	.15
❑ 138	Thomas Lewis	.40	.15
❑ 139	Mike Sherrard	.20	.07
❑ 140	Herschel Walker	.40	.15
❑ 141	Tyrone Wheatley RC	1.50	.60
❑ 142	Kyle Brady RC	.75	.30
❑ 143	Boomer Esiason	.40	.15
❑ 144	Aaron Glenn	.20	.07
❑ 145	Mo Lewis	.20	.07
❑ 146	Johnny Mitchell	.20	.07
❑ 147	Ronald Moore	.20	.07
❑ 148	Joe Aska	.40	.15
❑ 149	Tim Brown	.75	.30
❑ 150	Jeff Hostetler	.40	.15
❑ 151	Rocket Ismail	.40	.15
❑ 152	Napoleon Kaufman RC	1.50	.60
❑ 153	Chester McGlockton	.40	.15
❑ 154	Harvey Williams	.20	.07
❑ 155	Fred Barnett	.40	.15
❑ 156	Randall Cunningham	.75	.30
❑ 157	Charlie Garner	.75	.30
❑ 158	Mike Mamula RC	.20	.07
❑ 159	Kevin Turner	.20	.07
❑ 160	Ricky Watters	.40	.15
❑ 161	Calvin Williams	.40	.15
❑ 162	Mark Bruener RC	.40	.15
❑ 163	Kevin Greene	.40	.15
❑ 164	Charles Johnson	.40	.15
❑ 165	Greg Lloyd	.40	.15
❑ 166	Byron Bam Morris	.20	.07
❑ 167	Neil O'Donnell	.40	.15
❑ 168	Kordell Stewart RC	2.00	.75
❑ 169	John L. Williams	.20	.07
❑ 170	Rod Woodson	.40	.15
❑ 171	Jerome Bettis	.75	.30
❑ 172	Isaac Bruce	1.25	.50
❑ 173	Kevin Carter RC	.75	.30
❑ 174	Troy Drayton	.20	.07
❑ 175	Sean Gilbert	.40	.15
❑ 176	Carlos Jenkins	.20	.07
❑ 177	Todd Lyght	.20	.07
❑ 178	Chris Miller	.20	.07
❑ 179	Andre Coleman	.20	.07
❑ 180	Stan Humphries	.40	.15
❑ 181	Shawn Jefferson	.20	.07
❑ 182	Natrone Means	.40	.15
❑ 183	Leslie O'Neal	.40	.15
❑ 184	Junior Seau	.75	.30
❑ 185	Mark Seay	.40	.15
❑ 186	William Floyd	.40	.15
❑ 187	Merton Hanks	.20	.07
❑ 188	Brent Jones	.20	.07
❑ 189	Ken Norton	.40	.15
❑ 190	Jerry Rice	2.00	.75
❑ 191	Deion Sanders	1.00	.40
❑ 192	J.J. Stokes RC	.75	.30
❑ 193	Dana Stubblefield	.40	.15
❑ 194	Steve Young	1.50	.60
❑ 195	Sam Adams	.20	.07
❑ 196	Brian Blades	.40	.15
❑ 197	Joey Galloway RC	2.00	.75
❑ 198	Cortez Kennedy	.40	.15
❑ 199	Rick Mirer	.40	.15
❑ 200	Chris Warren	.40	.15
❑ 201	Derrick Brooks RC	2.00	.75
❑ 202	Lawrence Dawsey	.20	.07
❑ 203	Trent Dilfer	.75	.30
❑ 204	Alvin Harper	.20	.07
❑ 205	Jackie Harris	.20	.07
❑ 206	Courtney Hawkins	.20	.07
❑ 207	Hardy Nickerson	.20	.07
❑ 208	Errict Rhett	.40	.15

❑ 209 Warren Sapp RC	2.00	.75
❑ 210 Terry Allen	.40	.15
❑ 211 Tom Carter	.20	.07
❑ 212 Henry Ellard	.40	.15
❑ 213 Darrell Green	.20	.07
❑ 214 Brian Mitchell	.20	.07
❑ 215 Heath Shuler	.40	.15
❑ 216 Michael Westbrook RC	.75	.30
❑ 217 Tydus Winans	.20	.07
❑ 218 Checklist	.20	.07
❑ 219 Checklist	.20	.07
❑ 220 Checklist	.40	.15
❑ S1 Michael Irvin Sample	1.25	.50

2002 Flair

❑ COMP.SET w/o SP's (90)	25.00	10.00
❑ 1 Jeff Garcia	1.25	.50
❑ 2 Jevon Kearse	.75	.30
❑ 3 Chris Weinke	.75	.30
❑ 4 Ray Lewis	1.25	.50
❑ 5 Donovan McNabb	1.50	.60
❑ 6 Tiki Barber	1.25	.50
❑ 7 Rich Gannon	1.25	.50
❑ 8 Jamal Anderson	.75	.30
❑ 9 Curtis Martin	1.25	.50
❑ 10 Darrell Jackson	.75	.30
❑ 11 Ricky Williams	1.25	.50
❑ 12 Drew Brees	1.25	.50
❑ 13 Mark Brunell	1.25	.50
❑ 14 Johnnie Morton	.75	.30
❑ 15 Quincy Carter	.75	.30
❑ 16 Brian Urlacher	2.00	.75
❑ 17 Peerless Price	.75	.30
❑ 18 Drew Bledsoe	1.50	.60
❑ 19 Aaron Brooks	1.25	.50
❑ 20 Derrick Mason	.75	.30
❑ 21 Charlie Garner	.75	.30
❑ 22 Mike Alstott	1.25	.50
❑ 23 Freddie Mitchell	.75	.30
❑ 24 Isaac Bruce	1.25	.50
❑ 25 Hines Ward	1.25	.50
❑ 26 Doug Flutie	1.25	.50
❑ 27 Terrell Owens	1.25	.50
❑ 28 Peyton Manning	2.50	1.00
❑ 29 Ron Dayne	.75	.30
❑ 30 Peter Warrick	.75	.30
❑ 31 Randy Moss	2.50	1.00
❑ 32 Priest Holmes	1.50	.60
❑ 33 Joey Galloway	.75	.30
❑ 34 Jimmy Smith	.75	.30
❑ 35 Marvin Harrison	1.25	.50
❑ 36 Junior Seau	1.25	.50
❑ 37 Zach Thomas	1.25	.50
❑ 38 Antowain Smith	.75	.30
❑ 39 Marty Booker	.75	.30
❑ 40 Deuce McAllister	1.50	.60
❑ 41 Rod Smith	.75	.30
❑ 42 Michael Westbrook	.50	.20
❑ 43 Antonio Freeman	1.25	.50
❑ 44 Kerry Collins	.75	.30
❑ 45 Koren Robinson	.75	.30
❑ 46 Jamal Lewis	1.25	.50
❑ 47 Duce Staley	1.25	.50
❑ 48 Jerome Bettis	1.25	.50
❑ 49 David Terrell	1.25	.50
❑ 50 Daunte Culpepper	1.25	.50
❑ 51 Tim Couch	.75	.30
❑ 52 Brian Griese	1.25	.50
❑ 53 Marshall Faulk	1.25	.50
❑ 54 Brad Johnson	.75	.30
❑ 55 Eddie George	1.25	.50
❑ 56 Kurt Warner	1.25	.50
❑ 57 Steve McNair	1.25	.50
❑ 58 Stephen Davis	.75	.30
❑ 59 Corey Dillon	.75	.30
❑ 60 Troy Brown	.75	.30
❑ 61 Warrick Dunn	1.25	.50
❑ 62 Ed McCaffrey	1.25	.50
❑ 63 Amani Toomer	.75	.30
❑ 64 Rod Gardner	.75	.30
❑ 65 Mike McMahon	1.25	.50
❑ 66 Wayne Chrebet	.75	.30
❑ 67 Jake Plummer	.75	.30
❑ 68 Edgerrin James	1.50	.60
❑ 69 Eric Moulds	.75	.30
❑ 70 Tony Gonzalez	.75	.30
❑ 71 Marcus Robinson	.75	.30
❑ 72 Muhsin Muhammad	.75	.30
❑ 73 Trent Dilfer	.75	.30
❑ 74 Kevin Johnson	.75	.30
❑ 75 Fred Taylor	1.25	.50
❑ 76 Terrell Davis	1.25	.50
❑ 77 Emmitt Smith	3.00	1.25
❑ 78 Az-Zahir Hakim	.50	.20
❑ 79 Tim Brown	1.25	.50
❑ 80 Jerry Rice	2.50	1.00
❑ 81 Warren Sapp	.75	.30
❑ 82 Michael Strahan	.75	.30
❑ 83 Garrison Hearst	.75	.30
❑ 84 David Boston	1.25	.50
❑ 85 Michael Vick	4.00	1.50
❑ 86 Anthony Thomas	.75	.30
❑ 87 Ahman Green	1.25	.50
❑ 88 Chris Chambers	1.25	.50
❑ 89 Tom Brady	3.00	1.25
❑ 90 Plaxico Burress	.75	.30
❑ 91 LaDainian Tomlinson	2.00	.75
❑ 92 Shaun Alexander	1.50	.60
❑ 93 Torry Holt	1.25	.50
❑ 94 Kordell Stewart	.75	.30
❑ 95 Chad Pennington	1.50	.60
❑ 96 Chris Redman	.50	.20
❑ 97 Kendrell Bell	1.25	.50
❑ 98 Michael Bennett	.75	.30
❑ 99 Joe Horn	.75	.30
❑ 100 Brett Favre	3.00	1.25
❑ 101 David Carr RC	15.00	6.00
❑ 102 Joey Harrington RC	10.00	4.00
❑ 103 Ashley Lelie RC	12.00	5.00
❑ 104 Javon Walker RC	12.00	5.00
❑ 105 Reche Caldwell RC	6.00	2.50
❑ 106 Andre Davis RC	5.00	2.00
❑ 107 William Green RC	6.00	2.50
❑ 108 Antonio Bryant RC	6.00	2.50
❑ 109 Clinton Portis RC	20.00	7.50
❑ 110 Luke Staley RC	5.00	2.00
❑ 111 Josh Reed RC	6.00	2.50
❑ 112 Ron Johnson RC	5.00	2.00
❑ 113 Lamar Gordon RC	6.00	2.50
❑ 114 Cliff Russell RC	5.00	2.00
❑ 115 Eric Crouch RC	6.00	2.50
❑ 116 Ladell Betts RC	6.00	2.50
❑ 117 Patrick Ramsey RC	8.00	3.00
❑ 118 Adrian Peterson RC	6.00	2.50
❑ 119 DeShaun Foster RC	6.00	2.50
❑ 120 Tim Carter RC	5.00	2.00
❑ 121 Jabar Gaffney RC	6.00	2.50
❑ 122 T.J. Duckett RC	8.00	3.00
❑ 123 Julius Peppers RC	12.00	5.00
❑ 124 Rohan Davey RC	6.00	2.50
❑ 125 Antwaan Randle El RC	10.00	4.00
❑ 126 Jeremy Shockey RC	20.00	7.50
❑ 127 Donte Stallworth RC	12.00	5.00
❑ 128 Marquise Walker RC	5.00	2.00
❑ 129 Brian Westbrook RC	10.00	4.00
❑ 130 Randy Fasani RC	5.00	2.00
❑ 131 Jonathan Wells RC	6.00	2.50
❑ 132 Travis Stephens RC	5.00	2.00
❑ 133 Daniel Graham RC	6.00	2.50
❑ 134 Maurice Morris RC	6.00	2.50
❑ 135 David Garrard RC	6.00	2.50

2003 Flair

❑ COMP.SET w/o SP's (90)	25.00	10.00
❑ 1 Jamal Lewis	1.25	.50
❑ 2 Aaron Brooks	1.25	.50
❑ 3 Joey Harrington	2.00	.75
❑ 4 Brett Favre	3.00	1.25
❑ 5 Donovan McNabb	1.50	.60
❑ 6 Marcel Shipp	.75	.30
❑ 7 Michael Vick	3.00	1.25
❑ 8 David Carr	2.00	.75
❑ 9 Tommy Maddox	1.25	.50
❑ 10 Drew Brees	1.25	.50
❑ 11 Chad Pennington	1.50	.60
❑ 12 Drew Bledsoe	1.25	.50
❑ 13 Rich Gannon	.75	.30
❑ 14 Kurt Warner	1.25	.50
❑ 15 Brian Griese	1.25	.50
❑ 16 William Green	.75	.30
❑ 17 Jake Plummer	.75	.30
❑ 18 Eric Moulds	.75	.30
❑ 19 Peyton Manning	2.00	.75
❑ 20 Keyshawn Johnson	1.25	.50
❑ 21 Travis Henry	.75	.30
❑ 22 Tiki Barber	1.25	.50
❑ 23 Emmitt Smith	3.00	1.25
❑ 24 Michael Bennett	.75	.30
❑ 25 Curtis Martin	1.25	.50
❑ 26 Donald Driver	.75	.30
❑ 27 Clinton Portis	2.00	.75
❑ 28 Eddie George	.75	.30
❑ 29 Marshall Faulk	1.25	.50
❑ 30 Jeremy Shockey	2.00	.75
❑ 31 Ahman Green	1.25	.50
❑ 32 Priest Holmes	1.50	.60
❑ 33 Edgerrin James	1.25	.50
❑ 34 Plaxico Burress	.75	.30
❑ 35 Ricky Williams	1.25	.50
❑ 36 Anthony Thomas	.75	.30
❑ 37 Jerome Bettis	1.25	.50
❑ 38 Shaun Alexander	1.25	.50
❑ 39 Fred Taylor	1.25	.50
❑ 40 Isaac Bruce	1.25	.50
❑ 41 Mike Alstott	1.25	.50
❑ 42 Peerless Price	.75	.30
❑ 43 Corey Dillon	.75	.30
❑ 44 Amani Toomer	.75	.30
❑ 45 Warrick Dunn	.75	.30
❑ 46 Tim Brown	1.25	.50
❑ 47 Deuce McAllister	1.25	.50
❑ 48 Terrell Owens	1.25	.50
❑ 49 Stephen Davis	.75	.30
❑ 50 Torry Holt	1.25	.50
❑ 51 Duce Staley	.75	.30
❑ 52 Jimmy Smith	.75	.30
❑ 53 Ray Lewis	1.25	.50
❑ 54 Brian Urlacher	2.00	.75
❑ 55 Zach Thomas	1.25	.50
❑ 56 Joey Galloway	.75	.30
❑ 57 LaDainian Tomlinson	1.25	.50
❑ 58 Chris Chambers	1.25	.50
❑ 59 Ronde Barber	.50	.20
❑ 60 Randy Moss	2.00	.75
❑ 61 Tom Brady	3.00	1.25
❑ 62 Jerry Porter	.75	.30
❑ 63 Patrick Ramsey	1.25	.50
❑ 64 Derrick Mason	.75	.30
❑ 65 Daunte Culpepper	1.25	.50
❑ 66 Marty Booker	.75	.30
❑ 67 Steve McNair	1.25	.50
❑ 68 Hines Ward	1.25	.50
❑ 69 Matt Hasselbeck	.75	.30
❑ 70 Joe Horn	.75	.30
❑ 71 Mark Brunell	.75	.30
❑ 72 Laveranues Coles	.75	.30
❑ 73 Chad Hutchinson	.50	.20
❑ 74 Tony Gonzalez	.75	.30
❑ 75 Jeff Garcia	1.25	.50
❑ 76 Kendrell Bell	.75	.30
❑ 77 Kerry Collins	.75	.30
❑ 78 Warren Sapp	.75	.30
❑ 79 Tim Couch	.50	.20

❑ 80 Jerry Rice	2.50	1.00
❑ 81 Koren Robinson	.75	.30
❑ 82 Antwaan Randle El	1.25	.50
❑ 83 Donte Stallworth	1.25	.50
❑ 84 Shannon Sharpe	.75	.30
❑ 85 Chad Johnson	1.25	.50
❑ 86 Todd Heap	.75	.30
❑ 87 Rod Gardner	.75	.30
❑ 88 Marvin Harrison	1.25	.50
❑ 89 David Boston	.75	.30
❑ 90 Julius Peppers	1.25	.50
❑ 91 Byron Leftwich RC	40.00	15.00
❑ 92 Terrell Suggs RC	20.00	7.50
❑ 93 Kelley Washington RC	12.00	5.00
❑ 94 Brandon Lloyd RC	12.00	5.00
❑ 95 Kliff Kingsbury RC	10.00	4.00
❑ 96 Willis McGahee RC	30.00	12.50
❑ 97 Terence Newman RC	25.00	10.00
❑ 98 Bryant Johnson RC	12.00	5.00
❑ 99 Musa Smith RC	12.00	5.00
❑ 100 Ken Dorsey RC	12.00	5.00
❑ 101 Larry Johnson RC	50.00	25.00
❑ 102 DeWayne Robertson RC	12.00	5.00
❑ 103 Onterrio Smith RC	12.00	5.00
❑ 104 Tyrone Calico RC	15.00	6.00
❑ 105 Kareem Kelly RC	10.00	4.00
❑ 106 Chris Brown RC	12.00	5.00
❑ 107 Andrew Pinnock RC	10.00	4.00
❑ 108 Taylor Jacobs RC	10.00	4.00
❑ 109 Dallas Clark RC	12.00	5.00
❑ 110 Marcus Trufant RC	12.00	5.00
❑ 111 Charles Rogers RC	12.00	5.00
❑ 112 Lee Suggs RC	12.00	5.00
❑ 113 Rex Grossman RC	40.00	15.00
❑ 114 Doug Gabriel RC	12.00	5.00
❑ 115 Arnaz Battle RC	12.00	5.00
❑ 116 William Joseph RC	12.00	5.00
❑ 117 Justin Fargas RC	12.00	5.00
❑ 118 Anquan Boldin RC	30.00	12.50
❑ 119 Teyo Johnson RC	12.00	5.00
❑ 120 Bobby Wade RC	12.00	5.00
❑ 121 Brian St.Pierre RC	12.00	5.00
❑ 122 Carson Palmer RC	50.00	25.00
❑ 123 Kyle Boller RC	12.00	5.00
❑ 124 Andre Johnson RC	25.00	10.00
❑ 125 Dave Ragone RC	12.00	5.00
❑ 126 Chris Simms RC	20.00	7.50
❑ 127 Seneca Wallace RC	12.00	5.00
❑ 128 Justin Gage RC	12.00	5.00
❑ 129 LaBrandon Toefield RC	12.00	5.00
❑ 130 Talman Gardner RC	12.00	5.00

2004 Flair

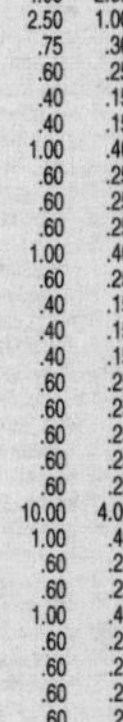

❑ COMP.SET w/o SP's (60)	40.00	20.00
❑ ROOKIE STATED ODDS 1:100 RETAIL		
❑ ROOKIE PRINT RUN 799 SER.#'d SETS		
❑ 1 Clinton Portis	2.00	.75
❑ 2 Deuce McAllister	2.00	.75
❑ 3 Marshall Faulk	2.00	.75
❑ 4 Tom Brady	5.00	2.00
❑ 5 Ahman Green	2.00	.75
❑ 6 LaDainian Tomlinson	2.50	1.00
❑ 7 Lee Suggs	2.00	.75
❑ 8 Amani Toomer	1.25	.50
❑ 9 Priest Holmes	2.50	1.00
❑ 10 Peerless Price	1.25	.50
❑ 11 Warren Sapp	1.25	.50
❑ 12 Andre Davis	.75	.30
❑ 13 Chad Pennington	2.00	.75
❑ 14 Quincy Carter	1.25	.50
❑ 15 Santana Moss	1.25	.50
❑ 16 Antonio Bryant	1.25	.50
❑ 17 Jerry Porter	1.25	.50
❑ 18 Laveranues Coles	1.25	.50
❑ 19 Daunte Culpepper	2.00	.75
❑ 20 Stephen Davis	1.25	.50
❑ 21 Rich Gannon	1.25	.50
❑ 22 Chad Johnson	2.00	.75
❑ 23 Ashley Lelie	1.25	.50
❑ 24 Ray Lewis	2.00	.75
❑ 25 Joey Harrington	2.00	.75
❑ 26 Brian Westbrook	1.25	.50
❑ 27 Marvin Harrison	2.00	.75
❑ 28 Torry Holt	2.00	.75
❑ 29 Kevan Barlow	1.25	.50
❑ 30 Peyton Manning	3.00	1.25
❑ 31 Andre Johnson	2.00	.75
❑ 32 Steve Smith	2.00	.75
❑ 33 Troy Brown	1.25	.50
❑ 34 Brian Urlacher	2.50	1.00
❑ 35 Anquan Boldin	2.00	.75
❑ 36 Matt Hasselbeck	1.25	.50
❑ 37 Edgerrin James	2.00	.75
❑ 38 Dante Hall	2.00	.75
❑ 39 Brad Johnson	1.25	.50
❑ 40 Jamal Lewis	2.00	.75
❑ 41 Rudi Johnson	1.25	.50
❑ 42 Michael Strahan	1.25	.50
❑ 43 Donovan McNabb	2.50	1.00
❑ 44 Steve McNair	2.00	.75
❑ 45 Ricky Williams	2.00	.75
❑ 46 Jake Delhomme	2.00	.75
❑ 47 Patrick Ramsey	1.25	.50
❑ 48 Randy Moss	2.50	1.00
❑ 49 David Carr	2.00	.75
❑ 50 Jeff Garcia	2.00	.75
❑ 51 Shaun Alexander	2.00	.75
❑ 52 Byron Leftwich	2.50	1.00
❑ 53 Michael Vick	4.00	1.50
❑ 54 Brett Favre	5.00	2.00
❑ 55 Hines Ward	2.00	.75
❑ 56 Chris Chambers	1.25	.50
❑ 57 Eddie George	1.25	.50
❑ 58 Eric Moulds	1.25	.50
❑ 59 Plaxico Burress	1.25	.50
❑ 60 Charles Rogers	1.25	.50
❑ 61 Eli Manning RC	25.00	10.00
❑ 62 Larry Fitzgerald RC	15.00	6.00
❑ 63 Chris Perry RC	8.00	3.00
❑ 64 Ben Roethlisberger RC	40.00	20.00
❑ 65 Roy Williams RC	12.00	5.00
❑ 66 Kellen Winslow RC	10.00	4.00
❑ 67 Steven Jackson RC	15.00	6.00
❑ 68 Kevin Jones RC	12.00	5.00
❑ 69 Reggie Williams RC	6.00	2.50
❑ 70 Michael Clayton RC	10.00	4.00
❑ 71 Rashaun Woods RC	5.00	2.00
❑ 72 Ben Troupe RC	5.00	2.00
❑ 73 Greg Jones RC	5.00	2.00
❑ 74 J.P. Losman RC	10.00	4.00
❑ 75 Philip Rivers RC	15.00	7.50
❑ 76 Michael Jenkins RC	5.00	2.00
❑ 77 Darius Watts RC	5.00	2.00
❑ 78 Michael Turner RC	6.00	2.50
❑ 79 Lee Evans RC	6.00	2.50
❑ 80 Drew Henson RC	5.00	2.00
❑ 81 Luke McCown RC	5.00	2.00
❑ 82 Julius Jones RC	15.00	6.00
❑ 83 Bernard Berrian RC	6.00	2.50
❑ 84 Keary Colbert RC	6.00	2.50
❑ 85 Tatum Bell RC	10.00	4.00

1997 Flair Showcase Row 2

❑ COMPLETE SET (120)	40.00	15.00
❑ 1 Jerry Rice	2.00	.75
❑ 2 Mark Brunell	1.25	.50
❑ 3 Eddie Kennison	.60	.25
❑ 4 Brett Favre	4.00	1.50
❑ 5 Karim Abdul-Jabbar	.60	.25
❑ 6 David LaFleur RC	.40	.15
❑ 7 John Elway	4.00	1.50
❑ 8 Troy Aikman	2.00	.75
❑ 9 Steve McNair	1.25	.50
❑ 10 Kordell Stewart	1.00	.40
❑ 11 Drew Bledsoe	1.25	.50
❑ 12 Kerry Collins	1.00	.40
❑ 13 Dan Marino	4.00	1.50
❑ 14 Steve Young	1.25	.50
❑ 15 Marvin Harrison	1.00	.40
❑ 16 Lawrence Phillips	.40	.15
❑ 17 Jeff Blake	.60	.25
❑ 18 Yatil Green RC	.60	.25
❑ 19 Jake Plummer RC	8.00	3.00
❑ 20 Barry Sanders	3.00	1.25
❑ 21 Deion Sanders	1.00	.40
❑ 22 Emmitt Smith	3.00	1.25
❑ 23 Rae Carruth RC	.40	.15
❑ 24 Chris Warren	.60	.25
❑ 25 Terry Glenn	1.00	.40
❑ 26 Jim Druckenmiller RC	.60	.25
❑ 27 Eddie George	1.00	.40
❑ 28 Curtis Martin	1.25	.50
❑ 29 Warrick Dunn RC	5.00	2.00
❑ 30 Terrell Davis	1.25	.50
❑ 31 Rashaan Salaam	.40	.15
❑ 32 Marcus Allen	1.00	.40
❑ 33 Jeff George	.60	.25
❑ 34 Thurman Thomas	1.00	.40
❑ 35 Keyshawn Johnson	1.00	.40
❑ 36 Jerome Bettis	1.00	.40
❑ 37 Larry Centers	.60	.25
❑ 38 Tony Banks	.60	.25
❑ 39 Marshall Faulk	1.25	.50
❑ 40 Mike Alstott	1.00	.40
❑ 41 Elvis Grbac	.60	.25
❑ 42 Errict Rhett	.40	.15
❑ 43 Edgar Bennett	.60	.25
❑ 44 Jim Harbaugh	.60	.25
❑ 45 Antonio Freeman	1.25	.50
❑ 46 Tiki Barber RC	10.00	4.00
❑ 47 Tim Biakabutuka	.60	.25
❑ 48 Joey Galloway	.75	.30
❑ 49 Tony Gonzalez RC	5.00	2.00
❑ 50 Keenan McCardell	.60	.25
❑ 51 Darnay Scott	.60	.25
❑ 52 Brad Johnson	1.25	.50
❑ 53 Herman Moore	.60	.25
❑ 54 Reidel Anthony RC	1.25	.50
❑ 55 Junior Seau	1.00	.40
❑ 56 Ricky Watters	.60	.25
❑ 57 Amani Toomer	.60	.25
❑ 58 Andre Reed	.60	.25
❑ 59 Antowain Smith RC	4.00	2.00
❑ 60 Ike Hilliard RC	2.50	1.00
❑ 61 Byron Hanspard RC	.75	.30
❑ 62 Robert Smith	.60	.25
❑ 63 Gus Frerotte	.40	.15
❑ 64 Charles Way	.40	.15
❑ 65 Trent Dilfer	1.00	.40
❑ 66 Adrian Murrell	.60	.25
❑ 67 Stan Humphries	.60	.25
❑ 68 Robert Brooks	.60	.25
❑ 69 Jamal Anderson	1.00	.40
❑ 70 Natrone Means	.60	.25
❑ 71 John Friesz	.40	.15
❑ 72 Ki-Jana Carter	.40	.15
❑ 73 Marc Edwards RC	.40	.15
❑ 74 Michael Westbrook	.60	.25
❑ 75 Neil O'Donnell	.60	.25
❑ 76 Scott Mitchell	.60	.25
❑ 77 Wesley Walls	.60	.25
❑ 78 Bruce Smith	.60	.25
❑ 79 Corey Dillon RC	10.00	4.00
❑ 80 Wayne Chrebet	1.00	.40
❑ 81 Tony Martin	.60	.25
❑ 82 Jimmy Smith	.60	.25
❑ 83 Terry Allen	1.00	.40
❑ 84 Shannon Sharpe	.60	.25
❑ 85 Derrick Alexander WR	.60	.25
❑ 86 Garrison Hearst	.60	.25
❑ 87 Tamarick Vanover	.60	.25
❑ 88 Michael Irvin	1.00	.40

❑ 89 Mark Chmura	.60	.25
❑ 90 Bert Emanuel	.60	.25
❑ 91 Eric Metcalf	.60	.25
❑ 92 Reggie White	1.00	.40
❑ 93 Carl Pickens	.60	.25
❑ 94 Chris Sanders	.40	.15
❑ 95 Frank Sanders	.60	.25
❑ 96 Desmond Howard	.60	.25
❑ 97 Michael Jackson	.60	.25
❑ 98 Tim Brown	1.00	.40
❑ 99 O.J. McDuffie	.60	.25
❑ 100 Mario Bates	.40	.15
❑ 101 Warren Moon	1.00	.40
❑ 102 Curtis Conway	.60	.25
❑ 103 Irving Fryar	.60	.25
❑ 104 Isaac Bruce	1.00	.40
❑ 105 Cris Carter	1.00	.40
❑ 106 Chris Chandler	.60	.25
❑ 107 Charles Johnson	.60	.25
❑ 108 Kevin Lockett RC	.60	.25
❑ 109 Rob Moore	.60	.25
❑ 110 Napoleon Kaufman	1.00	.40
❑ 111 Henry Ellard	.40	.15
❑ 112 Vinny Testaverde	.60	.25
❑ 113 Rick Mirer	.40	.15
❑ 114 Ty Detmer	.60	.25
❑ 115 Todd Collins	.40	.15
❑ 116 Jake Reed	.60	.25
❑ 117 Dave Brown	.40	.15
❑ 118 Dedric Ward RC	.60	.25
❑ 119 Heath Shuler	.40	.15
❑ 120 Ben Coates	.60	.25
❑ S1 Rae Carruth Sample	.25	.10

1998 Flair Showcase Row 3

❑ COMPLETE SET (80)	80.00	40.00
❑ 1 Brett Favre	3.00	1.25
❑ 2 Emmitt Smith	2.50	1.00
❑ 3 Peyton Manning RC	15.00	6.00
❑ 4 Mark Brunell	1.00	.40
❑ 5 Randy Moss RC	10.00	4.00
❑ 6 Jerry Rice	1.50	.60
❑ 7 John Elway	3.00	1.25
❑ 8 Troy Aikman	1.50	.60
❑ 9 Warrick Dunn	1.00	.40
❑ 10 Kordell Stewart	1.00	.40
❑ 11 Drew Bledsoe	1.25	.50
❑ 12 Eddie George	1.00	.40
❑ 13 Dan Marino	3.00	1.25
❑ 14 Antowain Smith	1.00	.40
❑ 15 Curtis Enis RC	.75	.30
❑ 16 Jake Plummer	1.00	.40
❑ 17 Steve Young	1.00	.40
❑ 18 Ryan Leaf RC	1.50	.60
❑ 19 Terrell Davis	1.00	.40
❑ 20 Barry Sanders	2.50	1.00
❑ 21 Corey Dillon	1.00	.40
❑ 22 Fred Taylor RC	2.50	1.00
❑ 23 Herman Moore	.60	.25
❑ 24 Marshall Faulk	1.25	.50
❑ 25 John Avery RC	.60	.25
❑ 26 Terry Glenn	1.00	.40
❑ 27 Keyshawn Johnson	1.00	.40
❑ 28 Charles Woodson RC	2.00	.75
❑ 29 Garrison Hearst	1.00	.40
❑ 30 Steve McNair	1.00	.40
❑ 31 Deion Sanders	1.00	.40
❑ 32 Robert Holcombe RC	.60	.25
❑ 33 Jerome Bettis	1.00	.40
❑ 34 Robert Edwards RC	1.25	.50
❑ 35 Skip Hicks RC	1.25	.50
❑ 36 Marcus Nash RC	.75	.30
❑ 37 Fred Lane	.40	.15
❑ 38 Kevin Dyson RC	1.50	.60
❑ 39 Dorsey Levens	1.00	.40
❑ 40 Jacquez Green RC	1.25	.50
❑ 41 Shannon Sharpe	.75	.30
❑ 42 Michael Irvin	1.25	.50
❑ 43 Jim Harbaugh	.75	.30
❑ 44 Curtis Martin	1.25	.50
❑ 45 Bobby Hoying	.75	.30
❑ 46 Trent Dilfer	1.25	.50
❑ 47 Yancey Thigpen	.50	.20
❑ 48 Warren Moon	1.25	.50
❑ 49 Danny Kanell	.75	.30
❑ 50 Rob Johnson	.75	.30
❑ 51 Carl Pickens	.75	.30
❑ 52 Scott Mitchell	.75	.30
❑ 53 Tim Brown	1.25	.50
❑ 54 Tony Banks	1.25	.50
❑ 55 Jamal Anderson	1.25	.50
❑ 56 Kerry Collins	.75	.30
❑ 57 Elvis Grbac	.75	.30
❑ 58 Mike Alstott	1.25	.50
❑ 59 Glenn Foley	.75	.30
❑ 60 Brad Johnson	1.25	.50
❑ 61 Robert Brooks	1.25	.50
❑ 62 Irving Fryar	1.25	.50
❑ 63 Natrone Means	1.25	.50
❑ 64 Rae Carruth	.75	.30
❑ 65 Isaac Bruce	2.00	.75
❑ 66 Andre Rison	1.25	.50
❑ 67 Jeff George	1.25	.50
❑ 68 Charles Way	.75	.30
❑ 69 Derrick Alexander	1.25	.50
❑ 70 Michael Jackson	.75	.30
❑ 71 Rob Moore	1.25	.50
❑ 72 Ricky Watters	1.25	.50
❑ 73 Curtis Conway	1.25	.50
❑ 74 Antonio Freeman	2.00	.75
❑ 75 Jimmy Smith	1.25	.50
❑ 76 Troy Davis	.75	.30
❑ 77 Robert Smith	2.00	.75
❑ 78 Terry Allen	2.00	.75
❑ 79 Joey Galloway	1.25	.50
❑ 80 Charles Johnson	.75	.30
❑ NNO Checklist Card	.40	.15

1999 Flair Showcase

❑ COMPLETE SET (192)	600.00	300.00
❑ COMP.SET w/o SPs (160)	50.00	20.00
❑ 1 Troy Aikman PW	2.00	.75
❑ 2 Jamal Anderson PW	.40	.15
❑ 3 Charlie Batch PW	1.00	.40
❑ 4 Jerome Bettis PW	.40	.15
❑ 5 Drew Bledsoe PW	1.25	.50
❑ 6 Mark Brunell PW	1.00	.40
❑ 7 Randall Cunningham PW	1.00	.40
❑ 8 Terrell Davis PW	1.00	.40
❑ 9 Corey Dillon PW	1.00	.40
❑ 10 Warrick Dunn PW	1.00	.40
❑ 11 Curtis Enis PW	.40	.15
❑ 12 Marshall Faulk PW	1.25	.50
❑ 13 Brett Favre PW	3.00	1.25
❑ 14 Doug Flutie PW	1.00	.40
❑ 15 Eddie George PW	1.00	.40
❑ 16 Brian Griese PW	1.00	.40
❑ 17 Keyshawn Johnson PW	1.00	.40
❑ 18 Peyton Manning PW	3.00	1.25
❑ 19 Dan Marino PW	3.00	1.25
❑ 20 Curtis Martin PW	1.00	.40
❑ 21 Steve McNair PW	1.00	.40
❑ 22 Randy Moss PW	2.50	1.00
❑ 23 Terrell Owens PW	1.00	.40
❑ 24 Jake Plummer PW	.60	.25
❑ 25 Jerry Rice PW	2.00	.75
❑ 26 Barry Sanders PW	3.00	1.25
❑ 27 Antowain Smith PW	1.00	.40
❑ 28 Emmitt Smith PW	2.00	.75
❑ 29 Kordell Stewart PW	.60	.25
❑ 30 J.J. Stokes PW	.60	.25
❑ 31 Fred Taylor PW	1.00	.40
❑ 32 Steve Young PW	1.25	.50
❑ 33 Troy Aikman PN	2.00	.75
❑ 34 Mike Alstott PN	1.00	.40
❑ 35 Jamal Anderson PN	1.00	.40
❑ 36 Charlie Batch PN	1.00	.40
❑ 37 Jerome Bettis PN	1.00	.40
❑ 38 Drew Bledsoe PN	1.25	.50
❑ 39 Mark Brunell PN	1.00	.40
❑ 40 Cris Carter PN	1.00	.40
❑ 41 Mark Chmura PN	.40	.15
❑ 42 Wayne Chrebet PN	.60	.25
❑ 43 Kerry Collins PN	.40	.15
❑ 44 Randall Cunningham PN	1.00	.40
❑ 45 Terrell Davis PN	1.00	.40
❑ 46 Trent Dilfer PN	.60	.25
❑ 47 Corey Dillon PN	1.00	.40
❑ 48 Warrick Dunn PN	1.00	.40
❑ 49 Kevin Dyson PN	.60	.25
❑ 50 Curtis Enis PN	.40	.15
❑ 51 Marshall Faulk PN	1.25	.50
❑ 52 Brett Favre PN	3.00	1.25
❑ 53 Doug Flutie PN	1.00	.40
❑ 54 Antonio Freeman PN	1.00	.40
❑ 55 Eddie George PN	1.00	.40
❑ 56 Terry Glenn PN	1.00	.40
❑ 57 Tony Gonzalez PN	1.00	.40
❑ 58 Elvis Grbac PN	.60	.25
❑ 59 Jacquez Green PN	.40	.15
❑ 60 Brian Griese PN	1.00	.40
❑ 61 Marvin Harrison PN	1.00	.40
❑ 62 Garrison Hearst PN	.60	.25
❑ 63 Skip Hicks PN	.40	.15
❑ 64 Priest Holmes PN	1.50	.60
❑ 65 Michael Irvin PN	.60	.25
❑ 66 Brad Johnson PN	.60	.25
❑ 67 Keyshawn Johnson PN	1.00	.40
❑ 68 Napoleon Kaufman PN	1.00	.40
❑ 69 Dorsey Levens PN	1.00	.40
❑ 70 Peyton Manning PN	3.00	1.25
❑ 71 Dan Marino PN	3.00	1.25
❑ 72 Curtis Martin PN	1.00	.40
❑ 73 Ed McCaffrey PN	.60	.25
❑ 74 Keenan McCardell PN	.60	.25
❑ 75 O.J. McDuffie PN	.60	.25
❑ 76 Steve McNair PN	1.00	.40
❑ 77 Scott Mitchell PN	.40	.15
❑ 78 Randy Moss PN	2.50	1.00
❑ 79 Eric Moulds PN	1.00	.40
❑ 80 Terrell Owens PN	1.00	.40
❑ 81 Lawrence Phillips PN	.60	.25
❑ 82 Jake Plummer PN	.60	.25
❑ 83 Jerry Rice PN	2.00	.75
❑ 84 Andre Rison PN	.60	.25
❑ 85 Barry Sanders PN	3.00	1.25
❑ 86 Shannon Sharpe PN	.60	.25
❑ 87 Antowain Smith PN	1.00	.40
❑ 88 Emmitt Smith PN	2.00	.75
❑ 89 Rod Smith PN	.60	.25
❑ 90 Duce Staley PN	1.00	.40
❑ 91 Kordell Stewart PN	.60	.25
❑ 92 J.J. Stokes PN	.60	.25
❑ 93 Fred Taylor PN	1.00	.40
❑ 94 Vinny Testaverde PN	.60	.25
❑ 95 Ricky Watters PN	.60	.25
❑ 96 Steve Young PN	1.25	.50
❑ 97 Mike Alstott	1.00	.40
❑ 98 Jamal Anderson	1.00	.40
❑ 99 Charlie Batch	1.00	.40
❑ 100 Jerome Bettis	1.00	.40
❑ 101 Tim Biakabutuka	.60	.25
❑ 102 Drew Bledsoe	1.25	.50
❑ 103 Tim Brown	1.00	.40
❑ 104 Mark Brunell	1.00	.40
❑ 105 Cris Carter	1.00	.40
❑ 106 Chris Chandler	.60	.25
❑ 107 Mark Chmura	.40	.15
❑ 108 Wayne Chrebet	.60	.25
❑ 109 Ben Coates	.60	.25
❑ 110 Kerry Collins	.60	.25

- ❑ 111 Randall Cunningham 1.00 .40
- ❑ 112 Trent Dilfer .60 .25
- ❑ 113 Corey Dillon 1.00 .40
- ❑ 114 Warrick Dunn 1.00 .40
- ❑ 115 Kevin Dyson .60 .25
- ❑ 116 Curtis Enis .40 .15
- ❑ 117 Marshall Faulk 1.25 .50
- ❑ 118 Doug Flutie 1.00 .40
- ❑ 119 Antonio Freeman 1.00 .40
- ❑ 120 Joey Galloway .60 .25
- ❑ 121 Rich Gannon 1.00 .40
- ❑ 122 Eddie George 1.00 .40
- ❑ 123 Terry Glenn 1.00 .40
- ❑ 124 Tony Gonzalez 1.00 .40
- ❑ 125 Elvis Grbac .60 .25
- ❑ 126 Jacquez Green .40 .15
- ❑ 127 Brian Griese 1.00 .40
- ❑ 128 Marvin Harrison 1.00 .40
- ❑ 129 Garrison Hearst .60 .25
- ❑ 130 Skip Hicks .40 .15
- ❑ 131 Priest Holmes 1.50 .60
- ❑ 132 Michael Irvin .60 .25
- ❑ 133 Brad Johnson .60 .25
- ❑ 134 Napoleon Kaufman 1.00 .40
- ❑ 135 Terry Kirby .40 .15
- ❑ 136 Dorsey Levens 1.00 .40
- ❑ 137 Curtis Martin 1.00 .40
- ❑ 138 Ed McCaffrey .60 .25
- ❑ 139 Keenan McCardell .60 .25
- ❑ 140 O.J. McDuffie .60 .25
- ❑ 141 Steve McNair 1.00 .40
- ❑ 142 Natrone Means .60 .25
- ❑ 143 Scott Mitchell .40 .15
- ❑ 144 Herman Moore .60 .25
- ❑ 145 Eric Moulds 1.00 .40
- ❑ 146 Terrell Owens 1.00 .40
- ❑ 147 Lawrence Phillips .60 .25
- ❑ 148 Jerry Rice 2.00 .75
- ❑ 149 Andre Rison .60 .25
- ❑ 150 Deion Sanders 1.00 .40
- ❑ 151 Shannon Sharpe .60 .25
- ❑ 152 Antowain Smith 1.00 .40
- ❑ 153 Rod Smith .60 .25
- ❑ 154 Duce Staley 1.00 .40
- ❑ 155 Kordell Stewart .60 .25
- ❑ 156 J.J. Stokes .60 .25
- ❑ 157 Vinny Testaverde .60 .25
- ❑ 158 Yancey Thigpen .40 .15
- ❑ 159 Ricky Watters .60 .25
- ❑ 160 Steve Young 1.25 .50
- ❑ 161 Troy Aikman SP 12.00 6.00
- ❑ 162 Champ Bailey RC 12.00 5.00
- ❑ 163 Karsten Bailey RC 8.00 3.00
- ❑ 164 D'Wayne Bates RC 8.00 3.00
- ❑ 165 David Boston RC 10.00 4.00
- ❑ 166 Mike Cloud RC 8.00 3.00
- ❑ 167 Cecil Collins RC 5.00 2.00
- ❑ 168 Tim Couch RC 10.00 4.00
- ❑ 169 Daunte Culpepper RC 40.00 15.00
- ❑ 170 Terrell Davis SP 6.00 2.50
- ❑ 171 Troy Edwards RC 8.00 3.00
- ❑ 172 Kevin Faulk RC 10.00 4.00
- ❑ 173 Brett Favre SP 20.00 10.00
- ❑ 174 Torry Holt RC 25.00 10.00
- ❑ 175 Sedrick Irvin RC 5.00 2.00
- ❑ 176 Edgerrin James RC 40.00 15.00
- ❑ 177 James Johnson RC 8.00 3.00
- ❑ 178 Kevin Johnson RC 10.00 4.00
- ❑ 179 Keyshawn Johnson SP 5.00 2.00
- ❑ 180 Peyton Manning SP 20.00 10.00
- ❑ 181 Dan Marino SP 20.00 10.00
- ❑ 182 Donovan McNabb RC 50.00 20.00
- ❑ 183 Cade McNown RC 8.00 3.00
- ❑ 184 Joe Montgomery RC 8.00 3.00
- ❑ 185 Randy Moss SP 15.00 6.00
- ❑ 186 Jake Plummer SP 6.00 2.50
- ❑ 187 Peerless Price RC 10.00 4.00
- ❑ 188 Barry Sanders SP 20.00 10.00
- ❑ 189 Akili Smith RC 8.00 3.00
- ❑ 190 Emmitt Smith SP 12.00 6.00
- ❑ 191 Fred Taylor SP 8.00 3.00
- ❑ 192 Ricky Williams RC 20.00 7.50
- ❑ P24 Jake Plummer PW Promo 1.00 .40
- ❑ P82 Jake Plummer PN Promo 1.00 .40
- ❑ P147 Jake Plummer Promo 1.00 .40

2006 Flair Showcase

- ❑ COMP.SET w/o SP's (100) 20.00 8.00
- ❑ 101-142 PRINT RUN 699 SER.#'d SETS

- ❑ 143-184 PRINT RUN 499 SER.#'d SETS
- ❑ 185-226 PRINT RUN 299 SER.#'d SETS
- ❑ 227-236 PRINT RUN 199 SER.#'d SETS
- ❑ 237-268 PRINT RUN 999 SER.#'d SETS
- ❑ 1 Edgerrin James .75 .30
- ❑ 2 Larry Fitzgerald .75 .30
- ❑ 3 Anquan Boldin .50 .20
- ❑ 4 Michael Vick 1.00 .40
- ❑ 5 Warrick Dunn .50 .20
- ❑ 6 Roddy White .50 .20
- ❑ 7 Steve McNair .50 .20
- ❑ 8 Jamal Lewis .50 .20
- ❑ 9 Derrick Mason .40 .15
- ❑ 10 Willis McGahee .75 .30
- ❑ 11 Lee Evans .50 .20
- ❑ 12 J.P. Losman .50 .20
- ❑ 13 Jake Delhomme .50 .20
- ❑ 14 DeShaun Foster .50 .20
- ❑ 15 Steve Smith .75 .30
- ❑ 16 Rex Grossman .75 .30
- ❑ 17 Thomas Jones .50 .20
- ❑ 18 Muhsin Muhammad .50 .20
- ❑ 19 Brian Urlacher .75 .30
- ❑ 20 Carson Palmer .75 .30
- ❑ 21 Rudi Johnson .50 .20
- ❑ 22 Chad Johnson .50 .20
- ❑ 23 Charlie Frye .50 .20
- ❑ 24 Reuben Droughns .50 .20
- ❑ 25 Braylon Edwards .75 .30
- ❑ 26 Drew Bledsoe .75 .30
- ❑ 27 Julius Jones .75 .30
- ❑ 28 Terrell Owens .75 .30
- ❑ 29 Jake Plummer .50 .20
- ❑ 30 Tatum Bell .50 .20
- ❑ 31 Javon Walker .50 .20
- ❑ 32 Kevin Jones .75 .30
- ❑ 33 Roy Williams WR .75 .30
- ❑ 34 Mike Williams .75 .30
- ❑ 35 Brett Favre 1.50 .60
- ❑ 36 Ahman Green .50 .20
- ❑ 37 Donald Driver .50 .20
- ❑ 38 David Carr .50 .20
- ❑ 39 Eric Moulds .50 .20
- ❑ 40 Andre Johnson .50 .20
- ❑ 41 Peyton Manning 1.25 .50
- ❑ 42 Marvin Harrison .75 .30
- ❑ 43 Reggie Wayne .50 .20
- ❑ 44 Byron Leftwich .50 .20
- ❑ 45 Fred Taylor .50 .20
- ❑ 46 Ernest Wilford .40 .15
- ❑ 47 Trent Green .50 .20
- ❑ 48 Larry Johnson 1.00 .40
- ❑ 49 Tony Gonzalez .50 .20
- ❑ 50 Eddie Kennison .40 .15
- ❑ 51 Daunte Culpepper .75 .30
- ❑ 52 Ronnie Brown .75 .30
- ❑ 53 Chris Chambers .50 .20
- ❑ 54 Brad Johnson .50 .20
- ❑ 55 Chester Taylor .50 .20
- ❑ 56 Troy Williamson .50 .20
- ❑ 57 Tom Brady 1.25 .50
- ❑ 58 Corey Dillon .50 .20
- ❑ 59 Troy Brown .50 .20
- ❑ 60 Drew Brees .75 .30
- ❑ 61 Deuce McAllister .50 .20
- ❑ 62 Joe Horn .50 .20
- ❑ 63 Eli Manning 1.00 .40
- ❑ 64 Tiki Barber .75 .30
- ❑ 65 Plaxico Burress .50 .20
- ❑ 66 Jeremy Shockey .75 .30
- ❑ 67 Chad Pennington .50 .20
- ❑ 68 Curtis Martin .75 .30
- ❑ 69 Laveranues Coles .50 .20
- ❑ 70 Aaron Brooks .50 .20
- ❑ 71 LaMont Jordan .50 .20
- ❑ 72 Randy Moss .75 .30
- ❑ 73 Jerry Porter .50 .20
- ❑ 74 Donovan McNabb .75 .30
- ❑ 75 Brian Westbrook .50 .20
- ❑ 76 Reggie Brown .50 .20
- ❑ 77 Ben Roethlisberger 1.25 .50
- ❑ 78 Willie Parker 1.00 .40
- ❑ 79 Hines Ward .75 .30
- ❑ 80 Philip Rivers .75 .30
- ❑ 81 LaDainian Tomlinson 1.00 .40
- ❑ 82 Antonio Gates .75 .30
- ❑ 83 Alex Smith QB 1.00 .40
- ❑ 84 Frank Gore .75 .30
- ❑ 85 Antonio Bryant .50 .20
- ❑ 86 Matt Hasselbeck .50 .20
- ❑ 87 Shaun Alexander .75 .30
- ❑ 88 Nate Burleson .50 .20
- ❑ 89 Marc Bulger .50 .20
- ❑ 90 Steven Jackson .75 .30
- ❑ 91 Torry Holt .50 .20
- ❑ 92 Chris Simms .50 .20
- ❑ 93 Cadillac Williams .75 .30
- ❑ 94 Joey Galloway .50 .20
- ❑ 95 Kerry Collins .50 .20
- ❑ 96 David Givens .50 .20
- ❑ 97 Drew Bennett .40 .15
- ❑ 98 Mark Brunell .50 .20
- ❑ 99 Clinton Portis .75 .30
- ❑ 100 Santana Moss .50 .20
- ❑ 101 Todd Watkins RC 5.00 2.00
- ❑ 102 Adam Jennings RC 5.00 2.00
- ❑ 103 David Pittman RC 5.00 2.00
- ❑ 104 Dawan Landry RC 6.00 2.50
- ❑ 105 Ko Simpson RC 5.00 2.00
- ❑ 106 James Anderson RC 3.00 1.25
- ❑ 107 Dusty Dvoracek RC 6.00 2.50
- ❑ 108 Jamar Williams RC 5.00 2.00
- ❑ 109 Bennie Brazell RC 5.00 2.00
- ❑ 110 Leon Williams RC 5.00 2.00
- ❑ 111 Lawrence Vickers RC 5.00 2.00
- ❑ 112 Elvis Dumervil RC 3.00 1.25
- ❑ 113 Domenik Hixon RC 5.00 2.00
- ❑ 114 Antoine Bethea RC 6.00 2.50
- ❑ 115 David Anderson RC 5.00 2.00
- ❑ 116 Freddie Keiaho RC 5.00 2.00
- ❑ 117 Clint Ingram RC 6.00 2.50
- ❑ 118 Jeff Webb RC 5.00 2.00
- ❑ 119 Devin Aromashodu RC 5.00 2.00
- ❑ 120 Mike Hass RC 6.00 2.50
- ❑ 121 Josh Lay RC 3.00 1.25
- ❑ 122 Marques Colston RC 25.00 10.00
- ❑ 123 Gerris Wilkinson RC 3.00 1.25
- ❑ 124 Barry Cofield RC 6.00 2.50
- ❑ 125 Guy Whimper RC 3.00 1.25
- ❑ 126 Nick Mangold RC 3.00 1.25
- ❑ 127 Anthony Schlegel RC 5.00 2.00
- ❑ 128 Eric Smith RC 5.00 2.00
- ❑ 129 Darnell Bing RC 6.00 2.50
- ❑ 130 Anthony Smith RC 8.00 3.00
- ❑ 131 Charlie Whitehurst RC 8.00 3.00
- ❑ 132 Delanie Walker RC 5.00 2.00
- ❑ 133 Marcus Hudson RC 5.00 2.00
- ❑ 134 David Kirtman RC 5.00 2.00
- ❑ 135 Victor Adeyanju RC 5.00 2.00
- ❑ 136 Davin Joseph RC 5.00 2.00
- ❑ 137 Marcus McNeill RC 5.00 2.00
- ❑ 138 Calvin Lowry RC 6.00 2.50
- ❑ 139 Stephen Tulloch RC 5.00 2.00
- ❑ 140 Tema Nande RC 5.00 2.00
- ❑ 141 Jonathan Orr RC 5.00 2.00
- ❑ 142 Jon Alston RC 6.00 2.50
- ❑ 143 Jimmy Williams RC 8.00 3.00
- ❑ 144 D.J. Shockley RC 8.00 3.00
- ❑ 145 Demetrius Williams RC 10.00 4.00
- ❑ 146 P.J. Daniels RC 6.00 2.50
- ❑ 147 Quinn Sypniewski RC 6.00 2.50
- ❑ 148 Ashton Youboty RC 8.00 3.00
- ❑ 149 Richard Marshall RC 6.00 2.50
- ❑ 150 Jeff King RC 6.00 2.50
- ❑ 151 Danieal Manning RC 8.00 3.00
- ❑ 152 Reggie McNeal RC 6.00 2.50
- ❑ 153 D'Qwell Jackson RC 6.00 2.50
- ❑ 154 Jerome Harrison RC 8.00 3.00
- ❑ 155 Skyler Green RC 8.00 3.00
- ❑ 156 Brandon Marshall RC 8.00 3.00
- ❑ 157 Daniel Bullocks RC 8.00 3.00

❑ 158 Abdul Hodge RC	8.00	3.00
❑ 159 Cory Rodgers RC	8.00	3.00
❑ 160 Ingle Martin RC	8.00	3.00
❑ 161 Stephen Gostkowski RC	6.00	2.50
❑ 162 Wali Lundy RC	8.00	3.00
❑ 163 Bernard Pollard RC	6.00	2.50
❑ 164 Marcus Vick RC	6.00	2.50
❑ 165 Cedric Griffin RC	6.00	2.50
❑ 166 Garrett Mills RC	8.00	3.00
❑ 167 Roman Harper RC	6.00	2.50
❑ 168 Brad Smith RC	8.00	3.00
❑ 169 Leon Washington RC	12.00	5.00
❑ 170 Ahmad Brooks RC	6.00	2.50
❑ 171 Thomas Howard RC	8.00	3.00
❑ 172 Jason Avant RC	8.00	3.00
❑ 173 Jeremy Bloom RC	6.00	2.50
❑ 174 Omar Jacobs RC	6.00	2.50
❑ 175 Mike Bell RC	12.00	5.00
❑ 176 Cedric Humes RC	8.00	3.00
❑ 177 Michael Robinson RC	12.00	5.00
❑ 178 Ben Obomanu RC	6.00	2.50
❑ 179 Darryl Tapp RC	6.00	2.50
❑ 180 Claude Wroten RC	4.00	1.50
❑ 181 Dominique Byrd RC	6.00	2.50
❑ 182 Marques Hagans RC	6.00	2.50
❑ 183 Bruce Gradkowski RC	12.00	5.00
❑ 184 Rocky McIntosh RC	8.00	3.00
❑ 185 Leonard Pope RC	8.00	3.00
❑ 186 Jerious Norwood RC	12.00	5.00
❑ 187 Haloti Ngata RC	8.00	3.00
❑ 188 Donte Whitner RC	8.00	3.00
❑ 189 John McCargo RC	6.00	2.50
❑ 190 Devin Hester RC	15.00	6.00
❑ 191 Johnathan Joseph RC	6.00	2.50
❑ 192 Kamerion Wimbley RC	8.00	3.00
❑ 193 Travis Wilson RC	8.00	3.00
❑ 194 Bobby Carpenter RC	8.00	3.00
❑ 195 Anthony Fasano RC	8.00	3.00
❑ 196 Tony Scheffler RC	8.00	3.00
❑ 197 Ernie Sims RC	10.00	4.00
❑ 198 Brian Calhoun RC	8.00	3.00
❑ 199 A.J. Hawk RC	15.00	6.00
❑ 200 Greg Jennings RC	15.00	6.00
❑ 201 Mario Williams RC	12.00	5.00
❑ 202 DeMeco Ryans RC	10.00	4.00
❑ 203 Marcedes Lewis RC	8.00	3.00
❑ 204 Maurice Drew RC	20.00	8.00
❑ 205 Tamba Hali RC	8.00	3.00
❑ 206 Brodie Croyle RC	12.00	5.00
❑ 207 Jason Allen RC	8.00	3.00
❑ 208 Derek Hagan RC	8.00	3.00
❑ 209 Chad Greenway RC	8.00	3.00
❑ 210 Tarvaris Jackson RC	12.00	5.00
❑ 211 Chad Jackson RC	12.00	5.00
❑ 212 David Thomas RC	8.00	3.00
❑ 213 Mathias Kiwanuka RC	10.00	4.00
❑ 214 Sinorice Moss RC	10.00	4.00
❑ 215 D'Brickashaw Ferguson RC	8.00	3.00
❑ 216 Kellen Clemens RC	10.00	4.00
❑ 217 Michael Huff RC	10.00	4.00
❑ 218 Brodrick Bunkley RC	8.00	3.00
❑ 219 Willie Reid RC	8.00	3.00
❑ 220 Antonio Cromartie RC	8.00	3.00
❑ 221 Manny Lawson RC	8.00	3.00
❑ 222 Brandon Williams RC	8.00	3.00
❑ 223 Kelly Jennings RC	8.00	3.00
❑ 224 Tye Hill RC	8.00	3.00
❑ 225 Joe Klopfenstein RC	6.00	2.50
❑ 226 Maurice Stovall RC	8.00	3.00
❑ 227 Matt Leinart RC	40.00	15.00
❑ 228 DeAngelo Williams RC	25.00	10.00
❑ 229 Jay Cutler RC	40.00	15.00
❑ 230 Joseph Addai RC	30.00	12.00
❑ 231 Laurence Maroney RC	30.00	12.00
❑ 232 Reggie Bush RC	60.00	25.00
❑ 233 Santonio Holmes RC	20.00	8.00
❑ 234 Vernon Davis RC	20.00	8.00
❑ 235 Vince Young RC	40.00	15.00
❑ 236 LenDale White RC	20.00	8.00
❑ 237 Edgerrin James	4.00	1.50
❑ 238 Michael Vick	5.00	2.00
❑ 239 Jamal Lewis	2.50	1.00
❑ 240 Willis McGahee	4.00	1.50
❑ 241 Steve Smith	4.00	1.50
❑ 242 Brian Urlacher	4.00	1.50
❑ 243 Carson Palmer	4.00	1.50
❑ 244 Charlie Frye	2.50	1.00
❑ 245 Terrell Owens	4.00	1.50
❑ 246 Jake Plummer	2.50	1.00
❑ 247 Kevin Jones	4.00	1.50
❑ 248 Brett Favre	8.00	3.00
❑ 249 David Carr	2.50	1.00
❑ 250 Peyton Manning	6.00	2.50
❑ 251 Byron Leftwich	2.50	1.00
❑ 252 Larry Johnson	5.00	2.00
❑ 253 Daunte Culpepper	4.00	1.50
❑ 254 Brad Johnson	2.50	1.00
❑ 255 Tom Brady	6.00	2.50
❑ 256 Drew Brees	4.00	1.50
❑ 257 Eli Manning	5.00	2.00
❑ 258 Curtis Martin	4.00	1.50
❑ 259 Randy Moss	4.00	1.50
❑ 260 Donovan McNabb	4.00	1.50
❑ 261 Ben Roethlisberger	6.00	2.50
❑ 262 LaDainian Tomlinson	5.00	2.00
❑ 263 Alex Smith QB	5.00	2.00
❑ 264 Shaun Alexander	4.00	1.50
❑ 265 Marc Bulger	2.50	1.00
❑ 266 Cadillac Williams	4.00	1.50
❑ 267 Drew Bennett	2.00	.75
❑ 268 Clinton Portis	4.00	1.50

1960 Fleer

❑ COMPLETE SET (132)	750.00	500.00
❑ WRAPPER (5-CENT)	25.00	20.00
❑ 1 Harvey White RC !	20.00	12.00
❑ 2 Tom Corky Tharp	3.50	2.00
❑ 3 Dan McGrew	3.50	2.00
❑ 4 Bob White	3.50	2.00
❑ 5 Dick Jamieson	3.50	2.00
❑ 6 Sam Salerno	3.50	2.00
❑ 7 Sid Gillman RC CO !	20.00	12.00
❑ 8 Ben Preston	3.50	2.00
❑ 9 George Blanch	3.50	2.00
❑ 10 Bob Stransky	3.50	2.00
❑ 11 Fran Curci	3.50	2.00
❑ 12 George Shirkey	3.50	2.00
❑ 13 Paul Larson	3.50	2.00
❑ 14 John Stolte	3.50	2.00
❑ 15 Serafino Fazio RC	5.00	2.50
❑ 16 Tom Dimitroff	3.50	2.00
❑ 17 Elbert Dubenion RC	12.00	6.00
❑ 18 Hogan Wharton	3.50	2.00
❑ 19 Tom O'Connell	3.50	2.00
❑ 20 Sammy Baugh CO	50.00	30.00
❑ 21 Tony Sardisco	3.50	2.00
❑ 22 Alan Cann	3.50	2.00
❑ 23 Mike Hudock	3.50	2.00
❑ 24 Bill Atkins	3.50	2.00
❑ 25 Charlie Jackson	3.50	2.00
❑ 26 Frank Tripucka	6.00	3.00
❑ 27 Tony Teresa	3.50	2.00
❑ 28 Joe Amstutz	3.50	2.00
❑ 29 Bob Fee RC	3.50	2.00
❑ 30 Jim Baldwin	3.50	2.00
❑ 31 Jim Yates	3.50	2.00
❑ 32 Don Flynn	3.50	2.00
❑ 33 Ken Adamson	3.50	2.00
❑ 34 Ron Drzewiecki	3.50	2.00
❑ 35 J.W. Slack	3.50	2.00
❑ 36 Bob Yates	3.50	2.00
❑ 37 Gary Cobb	3.50	2.00
❑ 38 Jacky Lee RC	5.00	2.50
❑ 39 Jack Spikes RC	5.00	2.50
❑ 40 Jim Padgett	3.50	2.00
❑ 41 Jack Larscheid UER RC	3.50	2.00
❑ 42 Bob Reifsnyder RC	3.50	2.00
❑ 43 Fran Rogel	3.50	2.00
❑ 44 Ray Moss	3.50	2.00
❑ 45 Tony Banfield RC	5.00	2.50
❑ 46 George Herring	3.50	2.00
❑ 47 Willie Smith RC	3.50	2.00
❑ 48 Buddy Allen	3.50	2.00
❑ 49 Bill Brown LB	3.50	2.00
❑ 50 Ken Ford RC	3.50	2.00
❑ 51 Billy Kinard	3.50	2.00
❑ 52 Buddy Mayfield	3.50	2.00
❑ 53 Bill Krisher	3.50	2.00
❑ 54 Frank Bernardi	3.50	2.00
❑ 55 Lou Saban RC CO	5.00	2.50
❑ 56 Gene Cockrell	3.50	2.00
❑ 57 Sam Sanders	3.50	2.00
❑ 58 George Blanda	50.00	30.00
❑ 59 Sherrill Headrick RC	5.00	2.50
❑ 60 Carl Larpenter	3.50	2.00
❑ 61 Gene Prebola	3.50	2.00
❑ 62 Dick Chorovich	3.50	2.00
❑ 63 Bob McNamara	3.50	2.00
❑ 64 Tom Saidock	3.50	2.00
❑ 65 Willie Evans	3.50	2.00
❑ 66 Billy Cannon RC UER	18.00	10.00
❑ 67 Sam McCord	3.50	2.00
❑ 68 Mike Simmons	3.50	2.00
❑ 69 Jim Swink RC	5.00	2.50
❑ 70 Don Hitt	3.50	2.00
❑ 71 Gerhard Schwedes	3.50	2.00
❑ 72 Thurlow Cooper	3.50	2.00
❑ 73 Abner Haynes RC	18.00	10.00
❑ 74 Billy Shoemake	3.50	2.00
❑ 75 Marv Lasater	3.50	2.00
❑ 76 Paul Lowe RC	15.00	7.50
❑ 77 Bruce Hartman	3.50	2.00
❑ 78 Blanche Martin	3.50	2.00
❑ 79 Gene Grabosky	3.50	2.00
❑ 80 Lou Rymkus CO	5.00	2.50
❑ 81 Chris Burford RC	8.00	4.00
❑ 82 Don Allen	3.50	2.00
❑ 83 Bob Nelson C	3.50	2.00
❑ 84 Jim Woodard	3.50	2.00
❑ 85 Tom Rychlec	3.50	2.00
❑ 86 Bob Cox	3.50	2.00
❑ 87 Jerry Cornelison	3.50	2.00
❑ 88 Jack Work	3.50	2.00
❑ 89 Sam DeLuca	3.50	2.00
❑ 90 Rommie Loudd	3.50	2.00
❑ 91 Teddy Edmondson	3.50	2.00
❑ 92 Buster Ramsey CO	3.50	2.00
❑ 93 Doug Asad	3.50	2.00
❑ 94 Jimmy Harris	3.50	2.00
❑ 95 Larry Cundiff	3.50	2.00
❑ 96 Richie Lucas RC	6.00	3.00
❑ 97 Don Norwood	3.50	2.00
❑ 98 Larry Grantham RC	5.00	2.50
❑ 99 Bill Mathis RC	6.00	3.00
❑ 100 Mel Branch RC	5.00	2.50
❑ 101 Marvin Terrell	3.50	2.00
❑ 102 Charlie Flowers	3.50	2.00
❑ 103 John McMullan	3.50	2.00
❑ 104 Charlie Kaaihue	3.50	2.00
❑ 105 Joe Schaffer	3.50	2.00
❑ 106 Al Day	3.50	2.00
❑ 107 Johnny Carson	3.50	2.00
❑ 108 Alan Goldstein	3.50	2.00
❑ 109 Doug Cline	3.50	2.00
❑ 110 Al Carmichael	3.50	2.00
❑ 111 Bob Dee	3.50	2.00
❑ 112 John Bredice	3.50	2.00
❑ 113 Don Floyd	3.50	2.00
❑ 114 Ronnie Cain	3.50	2.00
❑ 115 Stan Flowers	3.50	2.00
❑ 116 Hank Stram RC CO	40.00	25.00
❑ 117 Bob Dougherty	3.50	2.00
❑ 118 Ron Mix RC	40.00	25.00
❑ 119 Roger Ellis	3.50	2.00
❑ 120 Elvin Caldwell	3.50	2.00
❑ 121 Bill Kimber	3.50	2.00
❑ 122 Jim Matheny	3.50	2.00
❑ 123 Curley Johnson RC	3.50	2.00
❑ 124 Jack Kemp RC	175.00	90.00
❑ 125 Ed Denk	3.50	2.00
❑ 126 Jerry McFarland	3.50	2.00
❑ 127 Dan Lanphear	3.50	2.00
❑ 128 Paul Maguire RC	18.00	10.00
❑ 129 Ray Collins	3.50	2.00
❑ 130 Ron Burton RC	6.00	3.00
❑ 131 Eddie Erdelatz CO	3.50	2.00
❑ 132 Ron Beagle RC !	15.00	7.50

1961 Fleer

❑ COMPLETE SET (220)	1600.00	1000.00
❑ COMMON CARD (1-132)	4.00	2.50

❑ COMMON CARD (133-220) 6.00 3.50
❑ WRAPPER (5-CENT, SER.1) 25.00 20.00
❑ WRAPPER (5-CENT, SER.2) 30.00 25.00
❑ 1 Ed Brown ! 15.00 7.50
❑ 2 Rick Casares 6.00 3.00
❑ 3 Willie Galimore 6.00 3.00
❑ 4 Jim Dooley 4.00 2.50
❑ 5 Harlon Hill 4.00 2.50
❑ 6 Stan Jones 7.00 3.50
❑ 7 J.C. Caroline 4.00 2.50
❑ 8 Joe Fortunato 4.00 2.50
❑ 9 Doug Atkins 8.00 4.00
❑ 10 Milt Plum 6.00 3.00
❑ 11 Jim Brown 150.00 90.00
❑ 12 Bobby Mitchell 10.00 5.00
❑ 13 Ray Renfro 6.00 3.00
❑ 14 Gern Nagler 4.00 2.50
❑ 15 Jim Shofner 4.00 2.50
❑ 16 Vince Costello 4.00 2.50
❑ 17 Galen Fiss 4.00 2.50
❑ 18 Walt Michaels 6.00 3.00
❑ 19 Bob Gain 4.00 2.50
❑ 20 Mal Hammack 4.00 2.50
❑ 21 Frank Mestnik RC 4.00 2.50
❑ 22 Bobby Joe Conrad 6.00 3.00
❑ 23 John David Crow 6.00 3.00
❑ 24 Sonny Randle RC 6.00 3.00
❑ 25 Don Gillis 4.00 2.50
❑ 26 Jerry Norton 4.00 2.50
❑ 27 Bill Stacy 4.00 2.50
❑ 28 Leo Sugar 4.00 2.50
❑ 29 Frank Fuller 4.00 2.50
❑ 30 Johnny Unitas 60.00 35.00
❑ 31 Alan Ameche 7.00 3.50
❑ 32 Lenny Moore 15.00 7.50
❑ 33 Raymond Berry 15.00 7.50
❑ 34 Jim Mutscheller 4.00 2.50
❑ 35 Jim Parker 7.00 3.50
❑ 36 Bill Pellington 4.00 2.50
❑ 37 Gino Marchetti 10.00 5.00
❑ 38 Gene Lipscomb 7.00 3.50
❑ 39 Art Donovan 15.00 7.50
❑ 40 Eddie LeBaron 6.00 3.00
❑ 41 Don Meredith RC 150.00 90.00
❑ 42 Don McIlhenny 4.00 2.50
❑ 43 L.G. Dupre 4.00 2.50
❑ 44 Fred Dugan 4.00 2.50
❑ 45 Billy Howton 6.00 3.00
❑ 46 Duane Putnam 4.00 2.50
❑ 47 Gene Cronin 4.00 2.50
❑ 48 Jerry Tubbs 4.00 2.50
❑ 49 Clarence Peaks 4.00 2.50
❑ 50 Ted Dean RC 4.00 2.50
❑ 51 Tommy McDonald 8.00 4.00
❑ 52 Bill Barnes 4.00 2.50
❑ 53 Pete Retzlaff 6.00 3.00
❑ 54 Bobby Walston 4.00 2.50
❑ 55 Chuck Bednarik 12.00 6.00
❑ 56 Maxie Baughan RC 6.00 3.00
❑ 57 Bob Pellegrini 4.00 2.50
❑ 58 Jesse Richardson 4.00 2.50
❑ 59 John Brodie RC 50.00 30.00
❑ 60 J.D. Smith RB 6.00 3.00
❑ 61 Ray Norton RC 4.00 2.50
❑ 62 Monty Stickles RC 4.00 2.50
❑ 63 Bob St.Clair 7.00 3.50
❑ 64 Dave Baker 4.00 2.50
❑ 65 Abe Woodson 4.00 2.50
❑ 66 Matt Hazeltine 4.00 2.50
❑ 67 Leo Nomellini 10.00 5.00
❑ 68 Charley Conerly 10.00 5.00
❑ 69 Kyle Rote 7.00 3.50
❑ 70 Jack Stroud 4.00 2.50
❑ 71 Roosevelt Brown 7.00 3.50
❑ 72 Jim Patton 4.00 2.50
❑ 73 Erich Barnes 4.00 2.50
❑ 74 Sam Huff 15.00 7.50
❑ 75 Andy Robustelli 10.00 5.00
❑ 76 Dick Modzelewski 4.00 2.50
❑ 77 Roosevelt Grier 7.00 3.50
❑ 78 Earl Morrall 7.00 3.50
❑ 79 Jim Ninowski 4.00 2.50
❑ 80 Nick Pietrosante RC 6.00 3.00
❑ 81 Howard Cassady 6.00 3.00
❑ 82 Jim Gibbons 4.00 2.50
❑ 83 Gail Cogdill RC 6.00 3.00
❑ 84 Dick Lane 7.00 3.50
❑ 85 Yale Lary 7.00 3.50
❑ 86 Joe Schmidt 8.00 4.00
❑ 87 Darris McCord 4.00 2.50
❑ 88 Bart Starr 60.00 35.00
❑ 89 Jim Taylor 50.00 30.00
❑ 90 Paul Hornung 55.00 30.00
❑ 91 Tom Moore RC 8.00 4.00
❑ 92 Boyd Dowler RC 15.00 7.50
❑ 93 Max McGee 7.00 3.50
❑ 94 Forrest Gregg 8.00 4.00
❑ 95 Jerry Kramer 10.00 5.00
❑ 96 Jim Ringo 8.00 4.00
❑ 97 Bill Forester 6.00 3.00
❑ 98 Frank Ryan 6.00 3.00
❑ 99 Ollie Matson 12.00 6.00
❑ 100 Jon Arnett 6.00 3.00
❑ 101 Dick Bass RC 6.00 3.00
❑ 102 Jim Phillips 4.00 2.50
❑ 103 Del Shofner 6.00 3.00
❑ 104 Art Hunter 4.00 2.50
❑ 105 Lindon Crow 4.00 2.50
❑ 106 Les Richter 6.00 3.00
❑ 107 Lou Michaels 4.00 2.50
❑ 108 Ralph Guglielmi 4.00 2.50
❑ 109 Don Bosseler 4.00 2.50
❑ 110 John Olszewski 4.00 2.50
❑ 111 Bill Anderson 4.00 2.50
❑ 112 Joe Walton 4.00 2.50
❑ 113 Jim Schrader 4.00 2.50
❑ 114 Gary Glick 4.00 2.50
❑ 115 Ralph Felton 4.00 2.50
❑ 116 Bob Toneff 4.00 2.50
❑ 117 Bobby Layne 40.00 25.00
❑ 118 John Henry Johnson 7.00 3.50
❑ 119 Tom Tracy 6.00 3.00
❑ 120 Jimmy Orr RC 7.00 3.50
❑ 121 John Nisby 4.00 2.50
❑ 122 Dean Derby 4.00 2.50
❑ 123 John Reger 4.00 2.50
❑ 124 George Tarasovic 4.00 2.50
❑ 125 Ernie Stautner 10.00 5.00
❑ 126 George Shaw 4.00 2.50
❑ 127 Hugh McElhenny 12.00 6.00
❑ 128 Dick Haley 4.00 2.50
❑ 129 Dave Middleton 4.00 2.50
❑ 130 Perry Richards 4.00 2.50
❑ 131 Gene Johnson DB 4.00 2.50
❑ 132 Don Joyce ! 4.00 2.50
❑ 133 Johnny Green ! 8.00 4.00
❑ 134 Wray Carlton RC 8.00 4.00
❑ 135 Richie Lucas 8.00 4.00
❑ 136 Elbert Dubenion ! 8.00 4.00
❑ 137 Tom Rychlec 6.00 3.50
❑ 138 Mack Yoho 6.00 3.50
❑ 139 Phil Blazer 6.00 3.50
❑ 140 Dan McGrew 6.00 3.50
❑ 141 Bill Atkins 6.00 3.50
❑ 142 Archie Matsos RC 6.00 3.50
❑ 143 Gene Grabosky 6.00 3.50
❑ 144 Frank Tripucka 10.00 5.00
❑ 145 Al Carmichael 6.00 3.50
❑ 146 Bob McNamara 6.00 3.50
❑ 147 Lionel Taylor RC 15.00 7.50
❑ 148 Eldon Danenhauer 6.00 3.50
❑ 149 Willie Smith 6.00 3.50
❑ 150 Carl Larpenter 6.00 3.50
❑ 151 Ken Adamson 6.00 3.50
❑ 152 Goose Gonsoulin RC UER 10.00 5.00
❑ 153 Joe Young 6.00 3.50
❑ 154 Gordy Holz RC 6.00 3.50
❑ 155 Jack Kemp 120.00 60.00
❑ 156 Charlie Flowers 6.00 3.50
❑ 157 Paul Lowe 10.00 5.00
❑ 158 Don Norton 6.00 3.50
❑ 159 Howard Clark 6.00 3.50
❑ 160 Paul Maguire 15.00 7.50
❑ 161 Ernie Wright RC 8.00 4.00
❑ 162 Ron Mix 15.00 7.50
❑ 163 Fred Cole 6.00 3.50
❑ 164 Jim Sears 6.00 3.50
❑ 165 Volney Peters 6.00 3.50
❑ 166 George Blanda 45.00 25.00
❑ 167 Jacky Lee 8.00 4.00
❑ 168 Bob White 6.00 3.50
❑ 169 Doug Cline 6.00 3.50
❑ 170 Dave Smith RB 6.00 3.50
❑ 171 Billy Cannon 15.00 7.50
❑ 172 Bill Groman 6.00 3.50
❑ 173 Al Jamison 6.00 3.50
❑ 174 Jim Norton 6.00 3.50
❑ 175 Dennit Morris 6.00 3.50
❑ 176 Don Floyd 6.00 3.50
❑ 177 Butch Songin 6.00 3.50
❑ 178 Billy Lott 6.00 3.50
❑ 179 Ron Burton 10.00 5.00
❑ 180 Jim Colclough 6.00 3.50
❑ 181 Charley Leo 6.00 3.50
❑ 182 Walt Cudzik 6.00 3.50
❑ 183 Fred Bruney 6.00 3.50
❑ 184 Ross O'Hanley 6.00 3.50
❑ 185 Tony Sardisco 6.00 3.50
❑ 186 Harry Jacobs 6.00 3.50
❑ 187 Bob Dee 6.00 3.50
❑ 188 Tom Flores RC 30.00 15.00
❑ 189 Jack Larscheid 6.00 3.50
❑ 190 Dick Christy 6.00 3.50
❑ 191 Alan Miller RC 6.00 3.50
❑ 192 James Smith 6.00 3.50
❑ 193 Gerald Burch 6.00 3.50
❑ 194 Gene Prebola 6.00 3.50
❑ 195 Alan Goldstein 6.00 3.50
❑ 196 Don Manoukian 6.00 3.50
❑ 197 Jim Otto RC 75.00 40.00
❑ 198 Wayne Crow 6.00 3.50
❑ 199 Cotton Davidson RC 8.00 4.00
❑ 200 Randy Duncan RC 8.00 4.00
❑ 201 Jack Spikes 8.00 4.00
❑ 202 Johnny Robinson RC 15.00 7.50
❑ 203 Abner Haynes 15.00 7.50
❑ 204 Chris Burford 8.00 4.00
❑ 205 Bill Krisher 6.00 3.50
❑ 206 Marvin Terrell 6.00 3.50
❑ 207 Jimmy Harris 6.00 3.50
❑ 208 Mel Branch 8.00 4.00
❑ 209 Paul Miller 6.00 3.50
❑ 210 Al Dorow 6.00 3.50
❑ 211 Dick Jamieson 6.00 3.50
❑ 212 Pete Hart 6.00 3.50
❑ 213 Bill Shockley 6.00 3.50
❑ 214 Dewey Bohling 6.00 3.50
❑ 215 Don Maynard RC 80.00 40.00
❑ 216 Bob Mischak 6.00 3.50
❑ 217 Mike Hudock 6.00 3.50
❑ 218 Bob Reifsnyder 6.00 3.50
❑ 219 Tom Saidock 6.00 3.50
❑ 220 Sid Youngelman ! 20.00 12.00

1962 Fleer

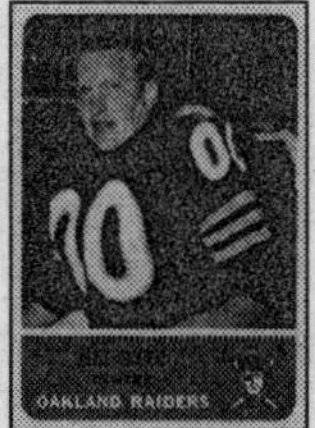

❑ COMPLETE SET (88) 900.00 500.00
❑ WRAPPER (5-CENT) 200.00 100.00
❑ 1 Billy Lott ! 16.00 8.00
❑ 2 Ron Burton 10.00 5.00
❑ 3 Gino Cappelletti RC 15.00 7.50
❑ 4 Babe Parilli 10.00 5.00
❑ 5 Jim Colclough 7.00 3.50
❑ 6 Tony Sardisco 7.00 3.50

❑ 7 Walt Cudzik	7.00	3.50
❑ 8 Bob Dee	7.00	3.50
❑ 9 Tommy Addison RC	8.00	4.00
❑ 10 Harry Jacobs	7.00	3.50
❑ 11 Ross O'Hanley	7.00	3.50
❑ 12 Art Baker	7.00	3.50
❑ 13 Johnny Green	7.00	3.50
❑ 14 Elbert Dubenion	10.00	5.00
❑ 15 Tom Rychlec	7.00	3.50
❑ 16 Billy Shaw RC	30.00	18.00
❑ 17 Ken Rice	7.00	3.50
❑ 18 Bill Atkins	7.00	3.50
❑ 19 Richie Lucas	8.00	4.00
❑ 20 Archie Matsos	7.00	3.50
❑ 21 Laverne Torczon	7.00	3.50
❑ 22 Warren Rabb	7.00	3.50
❑ 23 Jack Spikes	8.00	4.00
❑ 24 Cotton Davidson	8.00	4.00
❑ 25 Abner Haynes	15.00	7.50
❑ 26 Jimmy Saxton	7.00	3.50
❑ 27 Chris Burford	8.00	4.00
❑ 28 Bill Miller	7.00	3.50
❑ 29 Sherrill Headrick	8.00	4.00
❑ 30 E.J.Holub RC	8.00	4.00
❑ 31 Jerry Mays RC	10.00	5.00
❑ 32 Mel Branch	8.00	4.00
❑ 33 Paul Rochester RC	7.00	3.50
❑ 34 Frank Tripucka	10.00	5.00
❑ 35 Gene Mingo	7.00	3.50
❑ 36 Lionel Taylor	12.00	6.00
❑ 37 Ken Adamson	7.00	3.50
❑ 38 Eldon Danenhauer	7.00	3.50
❑ 39 Goose Gonsoulin	10.00	5.00
❑ 40 Gordy Holz	7.00	3.50
❑ 41 Bud McFadin	8.00	4.00
❑ 42 Jim Stinnette	7.00	3.50
❑ 43 Bob Hudson RC	7.00	3.50
❑ 44 George Herring	7.00	3.50
❑ 45 Charley Tolar RC	7.00	3.50
❑ 46 George Blanda	50.00	30.00
❑ 47 Billy Cannon	15.00	7.50
❑ 48 Charlie Hennigan RC	15.00	7.50
❑ 49 Bill Groman	7.00	3.50
❑ 50 Al Jamison	7.00	3.50
❑ 51 Tony Banfield	7.00	3.50
❑ 52 Jim Norton	7.00	3.50
❑ 53 Dennit Morris	7.00	3.50
❑ 54 Don Floyd	7.00	3.50
❑ 55 Ed Husmann UER	7.00	3.50
❑ 56 Robert Brooks	7.00	3.50
❑ 57 Al Dorow	7.00	3.50
❑ 58 Dick Christy	7.00	3.50
❑ 59 Don Maynard	50.00	30.00
❑ 60 Art Powell	10.00	5.00
❑ 61 Mike Hudock	7.00	3.50
❑ 62 Bill Mathis	8.00	4.00
❑ 63 Butch Songin	7.00	3.50
❑ 64 Larry Grantham	7.00	3.50
❑ 65 Nick Mumley	7.00	3.50
❑ 66 Tom Saidock	7.00	3.50
❑ 67 Alan Miller	7.00	3.50
❑ 68 Tom Flores	15.00	7.50
❑ 69 Bob Coolbaugh	7.00	3.50
❑ 70 George Fleming	7.00	3.50
❑ 71 Wayne Hawkins RC	8.00	4.00
❑ 72 Jim Otto	40.00	25.00
❑ 73 Wayne Crow	7.00	3.50
❑ 74 Fred Williamson RC	30.00	18.00
❑ 75 Tom Louderback	7.00	3.50
❑ 76 Volney Peters	7.00	3.50
❑ 77 Charley Powell	7.00	3.50
❑ 78 Don Norton	7.00	3.50
❑ 79 Jack Kemp	200.00	125.00
❑ 80 Paul Lowe	10.00	5.00
❑ 81 Dave Kocourek	7.00	3.50
❑ 82 Ron Mix	15.00	7.50
❑ 83 Ernie Wright	10.00	5.00
❑ 84 Dick Harris	7.00	3.50
❑ 85 Bill Hudson	7.00	3.50
❑ 86 Ernie Ladd RC	25.00	15.00
❑ 87 Earl Faison RC	8.00	4.00
❑ 88 Ron Nery !	18.00	9.00

1963 Fleer

❑ COMPLETE SET (88)	1800.00	1200.00
❑ WRAPPER (5-CENT)	120.00	60.00
❑ 1 Larry Garron RC !	20.00	10.00
❑ 2 Babe Parilli	10.00	5.00
❑ 3 Ron Burton	12.00	6.00

❑ 4 Jim Colclough	8.00	4.00
❑ 5 Gino Cappelletti	12.00	6.00
❑ 6 Charles Long RC SP	150.00	75.00
❑ 7 Billy Neighbors RC	8.00	4.00
❑ 8 Dick Felt	8.00	4.00
❑ 9 Tommy Addison	8.00	4.00
❑ 10 Nick Buoniconti RC	80.00	45.00
❑ 11 Larry Eisenhauer RC	8.00	4.00
❑ 12 Bill Mathis	8.00	4.00
❑ 13 Lee Grosscup RC	10.00	5.00
❑ 14 Dick Christy	8.00	4.00
❑ 15 Don Maynard	50.00	30.00
❑ 16 Alex Kroll RC	8.00	4.00
❑ 17 Bob Mischak	8.00	4.00
❑ 18 Dainard Paulson	8.00	4.00
❑ 19 Lee Riley	8.00	4.00
❑ 20 Larry Grantham	10.00	5.00
❑ 21 Hubert Bobo	8.00	4.00
❑ 22 Nick Mumley	8.00	4.00
❑ 23 Cookie Gilchrist RC	50.00	30.00
❑ 24 Jack Kemp	150.00	75.00
❑ 25 Wray Carlton	8.00	4.00
❑ 26 Elbert Dubenion	10.00	5.00
❑ 27 Ernie Warlick RC	10.00	5.00
❑ 28 Billy Shaw	15.00	7.50
❑ 29 Ken Rice	8.00	4.00
❑ 30 Booker Edgerson	8.00	4.00
❑ 31 Ray Abruzzese	8.00	4.00
❑ 32 Mike Stratton RC	15.00	7.50
❑ 33 Tom Sestak RC	10.00	5.00
❑ 34 Charley Tolar	8.00	4.00
❑ 35 Dave Smith RB	8.00	4.00
❑ 36 George Blanda	55.00	30.00
❑ 37 Billy Cannon	15.00	7.50
❑ 38 Charlie Hennigan	10.00	5.00
❑ 39 Bob Talamini RC	8.00	4.00
❑ 40 Jim Norton	8.00	4.00
❑ 41 Tony Banfield	8.00	4.00
❑ 42 Doug Cline	8.00	4.00
❑ 43 Don Floyd	8.00	4.00
❑ 44 Ed Husmann	8.00	4.00
❑ 45 Curtis McClinton RC	15.00	7.50
❑ 46 Jack Spikes	10.00	5.00
❑ 47 Len Dawson RC	200.00	125.00
❑ 48 Abner Haynes	15.00	7.50
❑ 49 Chris Burford	10.00	5.00
❑ 50 Fred Arbanas RC	12.00	6.00
❑ 51 Johnny Robinson	10.00	5.00
❑ 52 E.J. Holub	10.00	5.00
❑ 53 Sherrill Headrick	10.00	5.00
❑ 54 Mel Branch	10.00	5.00
❑ 55 Jerry Mays	10.00	5.00
❑ 56 Cotton Davidson	10.00	5.00
❑ 57 Clem Daniels RC	15.00	7.50
❑ 58 Bo Roberson RC	10.00	5.00
❑ 59 Art Powell	12.00	6.00
❑ 60 Bob Coolbaugh	8.00	4.00
❑ 61 Wayne Hawkins	8.00	4.00
❑ 62 Jim Otto	30.00	18.00
❑ 63 Fred Williamson	20.00	10.00
❑ 64 Bob Dougherty SP	120.00	60.00
❑ 65 Dalva Allen	8.00	4.00
❑ 66 Chuck McMurtry	8.00	4.00
❑ 67 Gerry McDougall RC	8.00	4.00
❑ 68 Tobin Rote	10.00	5.00
❑ 69 Paul Lowe	12.00	6.00
❑ 70 Keith Lincoln RC	40.00	25.00
❑ 71 Dave Kocourek	8.00	4.00
❑ 72 Lance Alworth RC	250.00	125.00
❑ 73 Ron Mix	25.00	15.00
❑ 74 Charley McNeil RC	8.00	4.00
❑ 75 Emil Karas	8.00	4.00
❑ 76 Ernie Ladd	20.00	10.00
❑ 77 Earl Faison	8.00	4.00
❑ 78 Jim Stinnette	8.00	4.00
❑ 79 Frank Tripucka	12.00	6.00
❑ 80 Don Stone	8.00	4.00
❑ 81 Bob Scarpitto	8.00	4.00
❑ 82 Lionel Taylor	12.00	6.00
❑ 83 Jerry Tarr	8.00	4.00
❑ 84 Eldon Danenhauer	8.00	4.00
❑ 85 Goose Gonsoulin	10.00	5.00
❑ 86 Jim Fraser	8.00	4.00
❑ 87 Chuck Gavin	8.00	4.00
❑ 88 Bud McFadin !	20.00	10.00
❑ NNO Checklist SP !	350.00	250.00

1990 Fleer

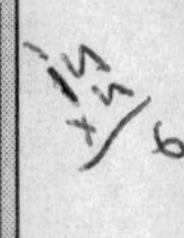

❑ COMPLETE SET (400)	10.00	4.00
❑ 1 Harris Barton	.04	.01
❑ 2 Chet Brooks	.04	.01
❑ 3 Michael Carter	.04	.01
❑ 4 Mike Cofer UER	.04	.01
❑ 5 Roger Craig	.10	.02
❑ 6 Kevin Fagan RC	.04	.01
❑ 7 Charles Haley UER	.10	.02
❑ 8 Pierce Holt RC	.04	.01
❑ 9 Ronnie Lott	.10	.02
❑ 10A Joe Montana ERR	1.25	.50
❑ 10B Joe Montana COR	1.25	.50
❑ 11 Bubba Paris	.04	.01
❑ 12 Tom Rathman	.04	.01
❑ 13 Jerry Rice	.75	.30
❑ 14 John Taylor	.25	.08
❑ 15 Keena Turner	.04	.01
❑ 16 Michael Walter	.04	.01
❑ 17 Steve Young	.50	.20
❑ 18 Steve Atwater	.04	.01
❑ 19 Tyrone Braxton	.04	.01
❑ 20 Michael Brooks RC	.04	.01
❑ 21 John Elway	1.25	.50
❑ 22 Simon Fletcher	.04	.01
❑ 23 Bobby Humphrey	.04	.01
❑ 24 Mark Jackson	.04	.01
❑ 25 Vance Johnson	.04	.01
❑ 26 Greg Kragen	.04	.01
❑ 27 Ken Lanier RC	.04	.01
❑ 28 Karl Mecklenburg	.04	.01
❑ 29 Orson Mobley RC	.04	.01
❑ 30 Steve Sewell	.04	.01
❑ 31 Dennis Smith	.04	.01
❑ 32 David Treadwell	.04	.01
❑ 33 Flipper Anderson	.04	.01
❑ 34 Greg Bell	.04	.01
❑ 35 Henry Ellard	.10	.02
❑ 36 Jim Everett	.10	.02
❑ 37 Jerry Gray	.04	.01
❑ 38 Kevin Greene	.10	.02
❑ 39 Pete Holohan	.04	.01
❑ 40 LeRoy Irvin	.04	.01
❑ 41 Mike Lansford	.04	.01
❑ 42 Buford McGee RC	.04	.01
❑ 43 Tom Newberry	.04	.01
❑ 44 Vince Newsome RC	.04	.01
❑ 45 Jackie Slater	.04	.01
❑ 46 Mike Wilcher	.04	.01
❑ 47 Matt Bahr	.04	.01
❑ 48 Brian Brennan	.04	.01
❑ 49 Thane Gash RC	.04	.01
❑ 50 Mike Johnson	.04	.01
❑ 51 Bernie Kosar	.10	.02
❑ 52 Reggie Langhorne	.04	.01
❑ 53 Tim Manoa	.04	.01
❑ 54 Clay Matthews	.10	.02

24	Bruce Kozerski	.05	.01
25	Tim McGee	.05	.01
26	Anthony Munoz	.10	.02
27	Bruce Reimers	.05	.01
28	Ickey Woods	.05	.01
29	Carl Zander	.05	.01
30	Mike Baab	.05	.01
31	Brian Brennan	.05	.01
32	Rob Burnett RC	.10	.02
33	Paul Farren	.05	.01
34	Thane Gash	.05	.01
35	David Grayson	.05	.01
36	Mike Johnson	.05	.01
37	Reggie Langhorne	.05	.01
38	Kevin Mack	.05	.01
39	Eric Metcalf	.10	.02
40	Frank Minnifield	.05	.01
41	Gregg Rakoczy	.05	.01
42	Felix Wright	.05	.01
43	Steve Atwater	.05	.01
44	Michael Brooks	.05	.01
45	John Elway	1.25	.50
46	Simon Fletcher	.05	.01
47	Bobby Humphrey	.05	.01
48	Mark Jackson	.05	.01
49	Keith Kartz	.05	.01
50	Clarence Kay	.05	.01
51	Greg Kragen	.05	.01
52	Karl Mecklenburg	.05	.01
53	Warren Powers	.05	.01
54	Dennis Smith	.05	.01
55	Jim Szymanski	.05	.01
56	David Treadwell	.05	.01
57	Michael Young	.05	.01
58	Ray Childress	.05	.01
59	Curtis Duncan	.05	.01
60	William Fuller	.10	.02
61	Ernest Givins	.10	.02
62	Drew Hill	.05	.01
63	Haywood Jeffires	.10	.02
64	Richard Johnson DB	.05	.01
65	Sean Jones	.10	.02
66	Don Maggs	.05	.01
67	Bruce Matthews	.10	.02
68	Johnny Meads	.05	.01
69	Greg Montgomery	.05	.01
70	Warren Moon	.25	.08
71	Mike Munchak	.10	.02
72	Allen Pinkett	.05	.01
73	Lorenzo White	.05	.01
74	Pat Beach	.05	.01
75	Albert Bentley	.05	.01
76	Dean Biasucci	.05	.01
77	Duane Bickett	.05	.01
78	Bill Brooks	.05	.01
79	Sam Clancy	.05	.01
80	Ray Donaldson	.05	.01
81	Jeff George	.25	.08
82	Alan Grant	.05	.01
83	Jessie Hester	.05	.01
84	Jeff Herrod	.05	.01
85	Rohn Stark	.05	.01
86	Jack Trudeau	.05	.01
87	Clarence Verdin	.05	.01
88	John Alt	.05	.01
89	Steve DeBerg	.05	.01
90	Tim Grunhard	.05	.01
91	Dino Hackett	.05	.01
92	Jonathan Hayes	.05	.01
93	Albert Lewis	.05	.01
94	Nick Lowery	.05	.01
95	Bill Maas UER	.05	.01
96	Christian Okoye	.05	.01
97	Stephone Paige	.05	.01
98	Kevin Porter	.05	.01
99	David Szott	.05	.01
100	Derrick Thomas	.25	.08
101	Barry Word FFC	.05	.01
102	Marcus Allen	.25	.08
103	Thomas Benson	.05	.01
104	Tim Brown	.25	.08
105	Riki Ellison	.05	.01
106	Mervyn Fernandez	.05	.01
107	Willie Gault	.10	.02
108	Bob Golic	.05	.01
109	Ethan Horton FFC	.05	.01
110	Bo Jackson	.30	.10
111	Howie Long	.25	.08
112	Don Mosebar	.05	.01
113	Jerry Robinson	.05	.01
114	Jay Schroeder	.05	.01
115	Steve Smith	.05	.01
116	Greg Townsend	.05	.01
117	Steve Wisniewski	.05	.01
118	Mark Clayton	.10	.02
119	Mark Duper	.10	.02
120	Ferrell Edmunds	.05	.01
121	Hugh Green	.05	.01
122	David Griggs	.05	.01
123	Jim C. Jensen	.05	.01
124	Dan Marino	1.25	.50
125	Tim McKyer	.05	.01
126	John Offerdahl	.05	.01
127	Louis Oliver	.05	.01
128	Tony Paige	.05	.01
129	Reggie Roby	.05	.01
130	Keith Sims	.05	.01
131	Sammie Smith	.05	.01
132	Pete Stoyanovich	.05	.01
133	Richmond Webb	.05	.01
134	Bruce Armstrong	.05	.01
135	Vincent Brown	.05	.01
136	Hart Lee Dykes	.05	.01
137	Irving Fryar	.10	.02
138	Tim Goad	.05	.01
139	Tommy Hodson	.05	.01
140	Maurice Hurst	.05	.01
141	Ronnie Lippett	.05	.01
142	Greg McMurtry	.05	.01
143	Ed Reynolds	.05	.01
144	John Stephens	.05	.01
145	Andre Tippett	.05	.01
146	Danny Villa	.05	.01
147	Brad Baxter	.05	.01
148	Kyle Clifton	.05	.01
149	Jeff Criswell	.05	.01
150	James Hasty	.05	.01
151	Jeff Lageman	.05	.01
152	Pat Leahy	.05	.01
153	Rob Moore	.25	.08
154	Al Toon	.10	.02
155	Gary Anderson K	.05	.01
156	Bubby Brister	.05	.01
157	Chris Calloway	.05	.01
158	Donald Evans	.05	.01
159	Eric Green	.05	.01
160	Bryan Hinkle	.05	.01
161	Merril Hoge	.05	.01
162	Tunch Ilkin	.05	.01
163	Louis Lipps	.05	.01
164	David Little	.05	.01
165	Mike Mularkey	.05	.01
166	Gerald Williams	.05	.01
167	Warren Williams	.05	.01
168	Rod Woodson	.25	.08
169	Tim Worley	.05	.01
170	Martin Bayless	.05	.01
171	Marion Butts	.10	.02
172	Gill Byrd	.05	.01
173	Frank Cornish	.05	.01
174	Arthur Cox	.05	.01
175	Burt Grossman	.05	.01
176	Anthony Miller	.10	.02
177	Leslie O'Neal	.10	.02
178	Gary Plummer	.05	.01
179	Junior Seau	.25	.08
180	Billy Joe Tolliver	.05	.01
181	Derrick Walker RC	.05	.01
182	Lee Williams	.05	.01
183	Robert Blackmon	.05	.01
184	Brian Blades	.10	.02
185	Grant Feasel	.05	.01
186	Derrick Fenner	.05	.01
187	Andy Heck	.05	.01
188	Norm Johnson	.05	.01
189	Tommy Kane	.05	.01
190	Cortez Kennedy	.25	.08
191	Dave Krieg	.10	.02
192	Travis McNeal	.05	.01
193	Eugene Robinson	.05	.01
194	Chris Warren FFC	.25	.08
195	John L. Williams	.05	.01
196	Steve Broussard	.05	.01
197	Scott Case	.05	.01
198	Shawn Collins	.05	.01
199	Darion Conner UER	.05	.01
200	Tory Epps	.05	.01
201	Bill Fralic	.05	.01
202	Michael Haynes FFC	.25	.08
203	Chris Hinton	.05	.01
204	Keith Jones	.05	.01
205	Brian Jordan	.10	.02
206	Mike Kenn	.05	.01
207	Chris Miller	.10	.02
208	Andre Rison	.10	.02
209	Mike Rozier	.05	.01
210	Deion Sanders	.40	.15
211	Gary Wilkins	.05	.01
212	Neal Anderson	.10	.02
213	Trace Armstrong	.05	.01
214	Mark Bortz	.05	.01
215	Kevin Butler	.05	.01
216	Mark Carrier DB	.10	.02
217	Wendell Davis FFC	.05	.01
218	Richard Dent	.10	.02
219	Dennis Gentry	.05	.01
220	Jim Harbaugh	.25	.08
221	Jay Hilgenberg	.05	.01
222	Steve McMichael	.10	.02
223	Ron Morris	.05	.01
224	Brad Muster	.05	.01
225	Mike Singletary	.10	.02
226	James Thornton	.05	.01
227	Tommie Agee	.05	.01
228	Troy Aikman	.75	.30
229	Jack Del Rio	.10	.02
230	Issiac Holt	.05	.01
231	Ray Horton	.05	.01
232	Jim Jeffcoat	.05	.01
233	Eugene Lockhart	.05	.01
234	Kelvin Martin	.05	.01
235	Nate Newton	.10	.02
236	Mike Saxon	.05	.01
237	Emmitt Smith	2.50	1.00
238A	Daniel Stubbs	.10	.02
238B	Daniel Stubbs	.10	.02
239	Jim Arnold	.05	.01
240	Jerry Ball	.05	.01
241	Bennie Blades	.05	.01
242	Lomas Brown	.05	.01
243	Robert Clark	.05	.01
244	Mike Cofer	.05	.01
245	Mel Gray	.10	.02
246	Rodney Peete	.10	.02
247	Barry Sanders	1.25	.50
248	Andre Ware	.10	.02
249	Matt Brock RC	.05	.01
250	Robert Brown	.05	.01
251	Anthony Dilweg	.05	.01
252	Johnny Holland	.05	.01
253	Tim Harris	.05	.01
254	Chris Jacke	.05	.01
255	Perry Kemp	.05	.01
256	Don Majkowski UER	.05	.01
257	Tony Mandarich	.05	.01
258	Mark Murphy	.05	.01
259	Brian Noble	.05	.01
260	Jeff Query	.05	.01
261	Sterling Sharpe	.25	.08
262	Ed West	.05	.01
263	Keith Woodside	.05	.01
264	Flipper Anderson	.05	.01
265	Aaron Cox	.05	.01
266	Henry Ellard	.10	.02
267	Jim Everett	.10	.02
268	Cleveland Gary	.05	.01
269	Kevin Greene	.10	.02
270	Pete Holohan	.05	.01
271	Mike Lansford	.05	.01
272	Duval Love RC	.05	.01
273	Buford McGee	.05	.01
274	Tom Newberry	.05	.01
275	Jackie Slater	.05	.01
276	Frank Stams	.05	.01
277	Alfred Anderson	.05	.01
278	Joey Browner	.05	.01
279	Anthony Carter	.10	.02
280	Chris Doleman	.05	.01
281	Rick Fenney	.05	.01
282	Rich Gannon	.25	.08
283	Hassan Jones	.05	.01
284	Steve Jordan	.05	.01
285	Carl Lee	.05	.01
286	Randall McDaniel	.05	.01
287	Keith Millard	.05	.01
288	Herschel Walker	.10	.02
289	Wade Wilson	.10	.02

290	Gary Zimmerman	.05	.01
291	Morten Andersen	.05	.01
292	Jim Dombrowski	.05	.01
293	Gill Fenerty	.05	.01
294	Craig Heyward	.10	.02
295	Dalton Hilliard	.05	.01
296	Rickey Jackson	.05	.01
297	Vaughan Johnson	.05	.01
298	Eric Martin	.05	.01
299	Robert Massey	.05	.01
300	Rueben Mayes	.05	.01
301	Sam Mills	.05	.01
302	Brett Perriman	.25	.08
303	Pat Swilling	.10	.02
304	Steve Walsh	.05	.01
305	Ottis Anderson	.10	.02
306	Matt Bahr	.05	.01
307	Mark Bavaro	.05	.01
308	Maurice Carthon	.05	.01
309	Mark Collins	.05	.01
310	John Elliott	.05	.01
311	Rodney Hampton	.25	.08
312	Jeff Hostetler	.10	.02
313	Erik Howard	.05	.01
314	Pepper Johnson	.05	.01
315	Sean Landeta	.05	.01
316	Dave Meggett	.10	.02
317	Bart Oates	.05	.01
318	Phil Simms	.10	.02
319	Lawrence Taylor	.25	.08
320	Reyna Thompson	.05	.01
321	Everson Walls	.05	.01
322	Eric Allen	.05	.01
323	Fred Barnett FFC	.25	.08
324	Jerome Brown	.05	.01
325	Keith Byars	.05	.01
326	Randall Cunningham	.25	.08
327	Byron Evans	.05	.01
328	Ron Heller	.05	.01
329	Keith Jackson	.10	.02
330	Seth Joyner	.10	.02
331	Heath Sherman	.05	.01
332	Clyde Simmons	.05	.01
333	Ben Smith	.05	.01
334	Anthony Toney	.05	.01
335	Andre Waters	.05	.01
336	Reggie White	.25	.08
337	Calvin Williams	.10	.02
338	Anthony Bell	.05	.01
339	Rich Camarillo	.05	.01
340	Roy Green	.05	.01
341	Tim Jorden RC	.05	.01
342	Cedric Mack	.05	.01
343	Dexter Manley	.05	.01
344	Freddie Joe Nunn	.05	.01
345	Ricky Proehl	.05	.01
346	Tootie Robbins	.05	.01
347	Timm Rosenbach	.05	.01
348	Luis Sharpe	.05	.01
349	Vai Sikahema	.05	.01
350	Anthony Thompson	.05	.01
351	Lonnie Young	.05	.01
352	Dexter Carter	.05	.01
353	Mike Cofer	.05	.01
354	Kevin Fagan	.05	.01
355	Don Griffin	.05	.01
356	Charles Haley UER	.10	.02
357	Pierce Holt	.05	.01
358	Brent Jones	.25	.08
359	Guy McIntyre	.05	.01
360	Joe Montana	1.25	.50
361	Darryl Pollard	.05	.01
362	Tom Rathman	.05	.01
363	Jerry Rice	.75	.30
364	Bill Romanowski	.05	.01
365	John Taylor	.10	.02
366	Steve Wallace	.10	.02
367	Steve Young	.75	.30
368	Gary Anderson RB	.05	.01
369	Ian Beckles	.05	.01
370	Mark Carrier WR	.25	.08
371	Reggie Cobb	.05	.01
372	Reuben Davis	.05	.01
373	Randy Grimes	.05	.01
374	Wayne Haddix	.05	.01
375	Ron Hall	.05	.01
376	Harry Hamilton	.05	.01
377	Bruce Hill	.05	.01
378	Keith McCants	.05	.01
379	Bruce Perkins	.05	.01
380	Vinny Testaverde UER	.10	.02
381	Broderick Thomas	.05	.01
382	Jeff Bostic	.05	.01
383	Earnest Byner	.05	.01
384	Gary Clark	.25	.08
385	Darryl Grant	.05	.01
386	Darrell Green	.05	.01
387	Stan Humphries	.25	.08
388	Jim Lachey	.05	.01
389	Charles Mann	.05	.01
390	Wilber Marshall	.05	.01
391	Art Monk	.10	.02
392	Gerald Riggs	.05	.01
393	Mark Rypien	.10	.02
394	Ricky Sanders	.05	.01
395	Don Warren	.05	.01
396	Bruce Smith HIT	.10	.02
397	Reggie White HIT	.10	.02
398	Lawrence Taylor HIT	.10	.02
399	David Fulcher HIT	.05	.01
400	Derrick Thomas HIT	.10	.02
401	Mark Carrier DB HIT	.05	.01
402	Mike Singletary HIT	.10	.02
403	Charles Haley HIT	.05	.01
404	Jeff Cross HIT	.05	.01
405	Leslie O'Neal HIT	.10	.02
406	Tim Harris HIT	.05	.01
407	Steve Atwater HIT	.05	.01
408	Joe Montana LL UER	.50	.20
409	Randall Cunningham LL	.10	.02
410	Warren Moon LL	.10	.02
411	Andre Rison LL UER 412	.10	.02
412	Haywood Jeffires LL	.10	.02
413	Stephone Paige LL	.05	.01
414	Phil Simms LL	.10	.02
415	Barry Sanders LL	.50	.20
416	Bo Jackson LL	.10	.02
417	Thurman Thomas LL	.10	.02
418	Emmitt Smith LL	1.25	.50
419	John L. Williams LL	.05	.01
420	Nick Bell RC	.05	.01
421	Eric Bieniemy RC	.05	.01
422	Mike Dumas RC UER	.05	.01
423	Russell Maryland RC	.25	.08
424	Derek Russell RC	.05	.01
425	Chris Smith RC	.05	.01
426	Mike Stonebreaker RP	.05	.01
427	Pat Tyrance RP	.05	.01
428	Kenny Walker RC	.05	.01
429	Checklist 1-108 UER	.05	.01
430	Checklist 109-216	.05	.01
431	Checklist 217-324	.05	.01
432	Checklist 325-432	.05	.01

1992 Fleer

	COMPLETE SET (480)	10.00	5.00
1	Steve Broussard	.05	.01
2	Rick Bryan	.05	.01
3	Scott Case	.05	.01
4	Tory Epps	.05	.01
5	Bill Fralic	.05	.01
6	Moe Gardner	.05	.01
7	Michael Haynes	.10	.02
8	Chris Hinton	.05	.01
9	Brian Jordan	.10	.02
10	Mike Kenn	.05	.01
11	Tim McKyer	.05	.01
12	Chris Miller	.10	.02
13	Erric Pegram	.10	.02
14	Mike Pritchard	.10	.02
15	Andre Rison	.10	.02
16	Jessie Tuggle	.05	.01
17	Carlton Bailey RC	.10	.02
18	Howard Ballard	.05	.01
19	Don Beebe	.05	.01
20	Cornelius Bennett	.10	.02
21	Shane Conlan	.05	.01
22	Kent Hull	.05	.01
23	Mark Kelso	.05	.01
24	James Lofton	.10	.02
25	Keith McKeller	.05	.01
26	Scott Norwood	.05	.01
27	Nate Odomes	.05	.01
28	Frank Reich	.10	.02
29	Jim Ritcher	.05	.01
30	Leon Seals	.05	.01
31	Darryl Talley	.05	.01
32	Steve Tasker	.10	.02
33	Thurman Thomas	.25	.08
34	Will Wolford	.05	.01
35	Neal Anderson	.05	.01
36	Trace Armstrong	.05	.01
37	Mark Carrier DB	.05	.01
38	Richard Dent	.10	.02
39	Shaun Gayle	.05	.01
40	Jim Harbaugh	.25	.08
41	Jay Hilgenberg	.05	.01
42	Darren Lewis	.05	.01
43	Steve McMichael	.10	.02
44	Brad Muster	.05	.01
45	William Perry	.10	.02
46	John Roper	.05	.01
47	Lemuel Stinson	.05	.01
48	Stan Thomas	.05	.01
49	Keith Van Horne	.05	.01
50	Tom Waddle	.05	.01
51	Donnell Woolford	.05	.01
52	Chris Zorich	.10	.02
53	Eddie Brown	.05	.01
54	James Francis	.05	.01
55	David Fulcher	.05	.01
56	David Grant	.05	.01
57	Harold Green	.05	.01
58	Rodney Holman	.05	.01
59	Lee Johnson	.05	.01
60	Tim Krumrie	.05	.01
61	Anthony Munoz	.10	.02
62	Joe Walter RC	.05	.01
63	Mike Baab	.05	.01
64	Stephen Braggs	.05	.01
65	Richard Brown RC	.05	.01
66	Dan Fike	.05	.01
67	Scott Galbraith RC	.05	.01
68	Randy Hilliard RC	.05	.01
69	Michael Jackson	.10	.02
70	Tony Jones T	.05	.01
71	Ed King	.05	.01
72	Kevin Mack	.05	.01
73	Clay Matthews	.10	.02
74	Eric Metcalf	.10	.02
75	Vince Newsome	.05	.01
76	John Rienstra	.05	.01
77	Steve Beuerlein	.10	.02
78	Larry Brown DB	.05	.01
79	Tony Casillas	.05	.01
80	Alvin Harper	.10	.02
81	Issiac Holt	.05	.01
82	Ray Horton	.05	.01
83	Michael Irvin	.25	.08
84	Daryl Johnston	.25	.08
85	Kelvin Martin	.05	.01
86	Nate Newton	.10	.02
87	Ken Norton	.10	.02
88	Jay Novacek	.10	.02
89	Emmitt Smith	1.50	.60
90	Vinson Smith RC	.05	.01
91	Mark Stepnoski	.10	.02
92	Steve Atwater	.05	.01
93	Mike Croel	.05	.01
94	John Elway	1.25	.50
95	Simon Fletcher	.05	.01
96	Gaston Green	.05	.01
97	Mark Jackson	.05	.01
98	Keith Kartz	.05	.01
99	Greg Kragen	.05	.01
100	Greg Lewis	.05	.01
101	Karl Mecklenburg	.05	.01
102	Derek Russell	.05	.01
103	Steve Sewell	.05	.01
104	Dennis Smith	.05	.01

❑ 105 David Treadwell .05 .01
❑ 106 Kenny Walker .05 .01
❑ 107 Doug Widell .05 .01
❑ 108 Michael Young .05 .01
❑ 109 Jerry Ball .05 .01
❑ 110 Bennie Blades .05 .01
❑ 111 Lomas Brown .05 .01
❑ 112 Scott Conover RC .05 .01
❑ 113 Ray Crockett .05 .01
❑ 114 Mike Farr .05 .01
❑ 115 Mel Gray .10 .02
❑ 116 Willie Green .05 .01
❑ 117 Tracy Hayworth RC .05 .01
❑ 118 Erik Kramer .10 .02
❑ 119 Herman Moore .25 .08
❑ 120 Dan Owens .05 .01
❑ 121 Rodney Peete .10 .02
❑ 122 Brett Perriman .25 .08
❑ 123 Barry Sanders 1.25 .50
❑ 124 Chris Spielman .10 .02
❑ 125 Marc Spindler .05 .01
❑ 126 Tony Bennett .05 .01
❑ 127 Matt Brock .05 .01
❑ 128 LeRoy Butler .05 .01
❑ 129 Johnny Holland .05 .01
❑ 130 Perry Kemp .05 .01
❑ 131 Don Majkowski .05 .01
❑ 132 Mark Murphy .05 .01
❑ 133 Brian Noble .05 .01
❑ 134 Bryce Paup .25 .08
❑ 135 Sterling Sharpe .25 .08
❑ 136 Scott Stephen .05 .01
❑ 137 Darrell Thompson .05 .01
❑ 138 Mike Tomczak .05 .01
❑ 139 Esera Tuaolo .05 .01
❑ 140 Keith Woodside .05 .01
❑ 141 Ray Childress .05 .01
❑ 142 Cris Dishman .05 .01
❑ 143 Curtis Duncan .05 .01
❑ 144 John Flannery .05 .01
❑ 145 William Fuller .10 .02
❑ 146 Ernest Givins .10 .02
❑ 147 Haywood Jeffires .10 .02
❑ 148 Sean Jones .10 .02
❑ 149 Lamar Lathon .05 .01
❑ 150 Bruce Matthews .05 .01
❑ 151 Bubba McDowell .05 .01
❑ 152 Johnny Meads .05 .01
❑ 153 Warren Moon .25 .08
❑ 154 Mike Munchak .10 .02
❑ 155 Al Smith .05 .01
❑ 156 Doug Smith .05 .01
❑ 157 Lorenzo White .05 .01
❑ 158 Michael Ball .05 .01
❑ 159 Chip Banks .05 .01
❑ 160 Duane Bickett .05 .01
❑ 161 Bill Brooks .05 .01
❑ 162 Ken Clark .05 .01
❑ 163 Jon Hand .05 .01
❑ 164 Jeff Herrod .05 .01
❑ 165 Jessie Hester .05 .01
❑ 166 Scott Radecic .05 .01
❑ 167 Rohn Stark .05 .01
❑ 168 Clarence Verdin .05 .01
❑ 169 John Alt .05 .01
❑ 170 Tim Barnett .05 .01
❑ 171 Tim Grunhard .05 .01
❑ 172 Dino Hackett .05 .01
❑ 173 Jonathan Hayes .05 .01
❑ 174 Bill Maas .05 .01
❑ 175 Chris Martin .05 .01
❑ 176 Christian Okoye .05 .01
❑ 177 Stephone Paige .05 .01
❑ 178 Jayice Pearson RC .05 .01
❑ 179 Kevin Porter .05 .01
❑ 180 Kevin Ross .05 .01
❑ 181 Dan Saleaumua .05 .01
❑ 182 Tracy Simien RC .05 .01
❑ 183 Neil Smith .25 .08
❑ 184 Derrick Thomas .25 .08
❑ 185 Robb Thomas .05 .01
❑ 186 Mark Vlasic .05 .01
❑ 187 Barry Word .05 .01
❑ 188 Marcus Allen .25 .08
❑ 189 Eddie Anderson .05 .01
❑ 190 Nick Bell .05 .01
❑ 191 Tim Brown .25 .08
❑ 192 Scott Davis .05 .01
❑ 193 Riki Ellison .05 .01
❑ 194 Mervyn Fernandez .05 .01
❑ 195 Willie Gault .10 .02
❑ 196 Jeff Gossett .05 .01
❑ 197 Ethan Horton .05 .01
❑ 198 Jeff Jaeger .05 .01
❑ 199 Howie Long .25 .08
❑ 200 Ronnie Lott .10 .02
❑ 201 Todd Marinovich .05 .01
❑ 202 Don Mosebar .05 .01
❑ 203 Jay Schroeder .05 .01
❑ 204 Greg Townsend .05 .01
❑ 205 Lionel Washington .05 .01
❑ 206 Steve Wisniewski .05 .01
❑ 207 Flipper Anderson .05 .01
❑ 208 Bern Brostek .05 .01
❑ 209 Robert Delpino .05 .01
❑ 210 Henry Ellard .10 .02
❑ 211 Jim Everett .10 .02
❑ 212 Cleveland Gary .05 .01
❑ 213 Kevin Greene .10 .02
❑ 214 Darryl Henley .05 .01
❑ 215 Damone Johnson .05 .01
❑ 216 Larry Kelm .05 .01
❑ 217 Todd Lyght .05 .01
❑ 218 Jackie Slater .05 .01
❑ 219 Michael Stewart .05 .01
❑ 220 Pat Terrell UER .05 .01
❑ 221 Robert Young .05 .01
❑ 222 Mark Clayton .10 .02
❑ 223 Bryan Cox .10 .02
❑ 224 Aaron Craver .05 .01
❑ 225 Jeff Cross .05 .01
❑ 226 Mark Duper .05 .01
❑ 227 Harry Galbreath .05 .01
❑ 228 David Griggs .05 .01
❑ 229 Mark Higgs .05 .01
❑ 230 Vestee Jackson .05 .01
❑ 231 John Offerdahl .05 .01
❑ 232 Louis Oliver .05 .01
❑ 233 Tony Paige .05 .01
❑ 234 Reggie Roby .05 .01
❑ 235 Sammie Smith .05 .01
❑ 236 Pete Stoyanovich .05 .01
❑ 237 Richmond Webb .05 .01
❑ 238 Terry Allen .25 .08
❑ 239 Ray Berry .05 .01
❑ 240 Joey Browner .05 .01
❑ 241 Anthony Carter .10 .02
❑ 242 Cris Carter .50 .20
❑ 243 Chris Doleman .05 .01
❑ 244 Rich Gannon .25 .08
❑ 245 Tim Irwin .05 .01
❑ 246 Steve Jordan .05 .01
❑ 247 Carl Lee .05 .01
❑ 248 Randall McDaniel .05 .01
❑ 249 Mike Merriweather .05 .01
❑ 250 Harry Newsome .05 .01
❑ 251 John Randle .10 .02
❑ 252 Henry Thomas .05 .01
❑ 253 Herschel Walker .10 .02
❑ 254 Ray Agnew .05 .01
❑ 255 Bruce Armstrong .05 .01
❑ 256 Vincent Brown .05 .01
❑ 257 Marv Cook .05 .01
❑ 258 Irving Fryar .10 .02
❑ 259 Pat Harlow .05 .01
❑ 260 Tommy Hodson .05 .01
❑ 261 Maurice Hurst .05 .01
❑ 262 Ronnie Lippett .05 .01
❑ 263 Eugene Lockhart .05 .01
❑ 264 Greg McMurtry .05 .01
❑ 265 Hugh Millen .05 .01
❑ 266 Leonard Russell .10 .02
❑ 267 Andre Tippett .05 .01
❑ 268 Brent Williams .05 .01
❑ 269 Morten Andersen .05 .01
❑ 270 Gene Atkins .05 .01
❑ 271 Wesley Carroll .05 .01
❑ 272 Jim Dombrowski .05 .01
❑ 273 Quinn Early .10 .02
❑ 274 Gill Fenerty .05 .01
❑ 275 Bobby Hebert .05 .01
❑ 276 Joel Hilgenberg .05 .01
❑ 277 Rickey Jackson .05 .01
❑ 278 Vaughan Johnson .05 .01
❑ 279 Eric Martin .05 .01
❑ 280 Brett Maxie .05 .01
❑ 281 Fred McAfee RC .05 .01
❑ 282 Sam Mills .05 .01
❑ 283 Pat Swilling .10 .02
❑ 284 Floyd Turner .05 .01
❑ 285 Steve Walsh .05 .01
❑ 286 Frank Warren .05 .01
❑ 287 Stephen Baker .05 .01
❑ 288 Maurice Carthon .05 .01
❑ 289 Mark Collins .05 .01
❑ 290 John Elliott .05 .01
❑ 291 Myron Guyton .05 .01
❑ 292 Rodney Hampton .10 .02
❑ 293 Jeff Hostetler .10 .02
❑ 294 Mark Ingram .05 .01
❑ 295 Pepper Johnson .05 .01
❑ 296 Sean Landeta .05 .01
❑ 297 Leonard Marshall .05 .01
❑ 298 Dave Meggett .10 .02
❑ 299 Bart Oates .05 .01
❑ 300 Phil Simms .10 .02
❑ 301 Reyna Thompson .05 .01
❑ 302 Lewis Tillman .05 .01
❑ 303 Brad Baxter .05 .01
❑ 304 Kyle Clifton .05 .01
❑ 305 James Hasty .05 .01
❑ 306 Joe Kelly .05 .01
❑ 307 Jeff Lageman .05 .01
❑ 308 Mo Lewis .05 .01
❑ 309 Erik McMillan .05 .01
❑ 310 Rob Moore .10 .02
❑ 311 Tony Stargell .05 .01
❑ 312 Jim Sweeney .05 .01
❑ 313 Marvin Washington .05 .01
❑ 314 Lonnie Young .05 .01
❑ 315 Eric Allen .05 .01
❑ 316 Fred Barnett .25 .08
❑ 317 Jerome Brown .05 .01
❑ 318 Keith Byars .05 .01
❑ 319 Wes Hopkins .05 .01
❑ 320 Keith Jackson .10 .02
❑ 321 James Joseph .05 .01
❑ 322 Seth Joyner .10 .02
❑ 323 Jeff Kemp .05 .01
❑ 324 Roger Ruzek .05 .01
❑ 325 Clyde Simmons .05 .01
❑ 326 William Thomas .05 .01
❑ 327 Heggie White .25 .08
❑ 328 Calvin Williams .10 .02
❑ 329 Rich Camarillo .05 .01
❑ 330 Ken Harvey .05 .01
❑ 331 Eric Hill .05 .01
❑ 332 Johnny Johnson .05 .01
❑ 333 Ernie Jones .05 .01
❑ 334 Tim Jorden .05 .01
❑ 335 Tim McDonald .05 .01
❑ 336 Freddie Joe Nunn .05 .01
❑ 337 Luis Sharpe .05 .01
❑ 338 Eric Swann .10 .02
❑ 339 Aeneas Williams .10 .02
❑ 340 Gary Anderson K .05 .01
❑ 341 Bubby Brister .05 .01
❑ 342 Adrian Cooper .05 .01
❑ 343 Barry Foster .10 .02
❑ 344 Eric Green .05 .01
❑ 345 Bryan Hinkle .05 .01
❑ 346 Tunch Ilkin .05 .01
❑ 347 Carnell Lake .05 .01
❑ 348 Louis Lipps .05 .01
❑ 349 David Little .05 .01
❑ 350 Greg Lloyd .10 .02
❑ 351 Neil O'Donnell .25 .08
❑ 352 Dwight Stone .05 .01
❑ 353 Rod Woodson .25 .08
❑ 354 Rod Bernstine .05 .01
❑ 355 Eric Bieniemy .05 .01
❑ 356 Marion Butts .05 .01
❑ 357 Gill Byrd .05 .01
❑ 358 John Friesz .10 .02
❑ 359 Burt Grossman .05 .01
❑ 360 Courtney Hall .05 .01
❑ 361 Ronnie Harmon .05 .01
❑ 362 Shawn Jefferson .05 .01
❑ 363 Nate Lewis .05 .01
❑ 364 Craig McEwen RC .05 .01
❑ 365 Eric Moten .05 .01
❑ 366 Joe Phillips .05 .01
❑ 367 Gary Plummer .05 .01
❑ 368 Henry Rolling .05 .01
❑ 369 Broderick Thompson .05 .01
❑ 370 Harris Barton .05 .01
❑ 371 Steve Bono RC .25 .08

Card	Player	Nrmt	Exc
❑ 372	Todd Bowles	.05	.01
❑ 373	Dexter Carter	.05	.01
❑ 374	Michael Carter	.05	.01
❑ 375	Mike Cofer	.05	.01
❑ 376	Keith DeLong	.05	.01
❑ 377	Charles Haley	.10	.02
❑ 378	Merton Hanks	.10	.02
❑ 379	Tim Harris	.05	.01
❑ 380	Brent Jones	.10	.02
❑ 381	Guy McIntyre	.05	.01
❑ 382	Tom Rathman	.05	.01
❑ 383	Bill Romanowski	.05	.01
❑ 384	Jesse Sapolu	.05	.01
❑ 385	John Taylor	.10	.02
❑ 386	Steve Young	.60	.25
❑ 387	Robert Blackmon	.05	.01
❑ 388	Brian Blades	.10	.02
❑ 389	Jacob Green	.05	.01
❑ 390	Dwayne Harper	.05	.01
❑ 391	Andy Heck	.05	.01
❑ 392	Tommy Kane	.05	.01
❑ 393	John Kasay	.05	.01
❑ 394	Cortez Kennedy	.10	.02
❑ 395	Bryan Millard	.05	.01
❑ 396	Rufus Porter	.05	.01
❑ 397	Eugene Robinson	.05	.01
❑ 398	John L. Williams	.05	.01
❑ 399	Terry Wooden	.05	.01
❑ 400	Gary Anderson RB	.05	.01
❑ 401	Ian Beckles	.05	.01
❑ 402	Mark Carrier WR	.10	.02
❑ 403	Reggie Cobb	.05	.01
❑ 404	Lawrence Dawsey	.10	.02
❑ 405	Ron Hall	.05	.01
❑ 406	Keith McCants	.05	.01
❑ 407	Charles McRae	.05	.01
❑ 408	Tim Newton	.05	.01
❑ 409	Jesse Solomon	.05	.01
❑ 410	Vinny Testaverde	.10	.02
❑ 411	Broderick Thomas	.05	.01
❑ 412	Robert Wilson	.05	.01
❑ 413	Jeff Bostic	.05	.01
❑ 414	Earnest Byner	.05	.01
❑ 415	Gary Clark	.25	.08
❑ 416	Andre Collins	.05	.01
❑ 417	Brad Edwards	.05	.01
❑ 418	Kurt Gouveia	.05	.01
❑ 419	Darrell Green	.05	.01
❑ 420	Joe Jacoby	.05	.01
❑ 421	Jim Lachey	.05	.01
❑ 422	Chip Lohmiller	.05	.01
❑ 423	Charles Mann	.05	.01
❑ 424	Wilber Marshall	.05	.01
❑ 425	Ron Middleton RC	.05	.01
❑ 426	Brian Mitchell	.10	.02
❑ 427	Art Monk	.10	.02
❑ 428	Mark Rypien	.05	.01
❑ 429	Ricky Sanders	.05	.01
❑ 430	Mark Schlereth RC	.05	.01
❑ 431	Fred Stokes	.05	.01
❑ 432	Edgar Bennett RC	.25	.08
❑ 433	Brian Bollinger RC	.05	.01
❑ 434	Joe Bowden RC	.05	.01
❑ 435	Terrell Buckley RC	.05	.01
❑ 436	Willie Clay RC	.05	.01
❑ 437	Steve Gordon RC	.05	.01
❑ 438	Keith Hamilton RC	.10	.02
❑ 439	Carlos Huerta	.05	.01
❑ 440	Matt LaBounty RC	.05	.01
❑ 441	Amp Lee RC	.05	.01
❑ 442	Ricardo McDonald RC	.05	.01
❑ 443	Chris Mims RC	.10	.02
❑ 444	Michael Moody RC	.05	.01
❑ 445	Patrick Rowe RC	.05	.01
❑ 446	Leon Searcy RC	.10	.02
❑ 447	Siran Stacy RC	.05	.01
❑ 448	Kevin Turner RC	.05	.01
❑ 449	Tommy Vardell RC	.10	.02
❑ 450	Bob Whitfield RC	.05	.01
❑ 451	Darryl Williams RC	.05	.01
❑ 452	Thurman Thomas LL	.10	.02
❑ 453	Emmitt Smith LL	.75	.30
❑ 454	Haywood Jeffires LL	.05	.01
❑ 455	Michael Irvin LL	.10	.02
❑ 456	Mark Clayton LL	.05	.01
❑ 457	Barry Sanders LL	.60	.25
❑ 458	Pete Stoyanovich LL	.05	.01
❑ 459	Chip Lohmiller LL	.05	.01
❑ 460	William Fuller LL	.05	.01
❑ 461	Pat Swilling LL	.05	.01
❑ 462	Ronnie Lott LL	.05	.01
❑ 463	Ray Crockett LL	.05	.01
❑ 464	Tim McKyer LL	.05	.01
❑ 465	Aeneas Williams LL	.05	.01
❑ 466	Rod Woodson LL	.10	.02
❑ 467	Mel Gray LL	.05	.01
❑ 468	Nate Lewis LL	.05	.01
❑ 469	Steve Young LL	.30	.10
❑ 470	Reggie Roby LL	.05	.01
❑ 471	John Elway PV	.60	.25
❑ 472	Ronnie Lott PV	.05	.01
❑ 473	Art Monk PV UER	.05	.01
❑ 474	Warren Moon PV	.10	.02
❑ 475	Emmitt Smith PV	.75	.30
❑ 476	Thurman Thomas PV	.10	.02
❑ 477	Checklist 1-120	.05	.01
❑ 478	Checklist 121-240	.05	.01
❑ 479	Checklist 241-360	.05	.01
❑ 480	Checklist 361-480	.05	.01

1993 Fleer

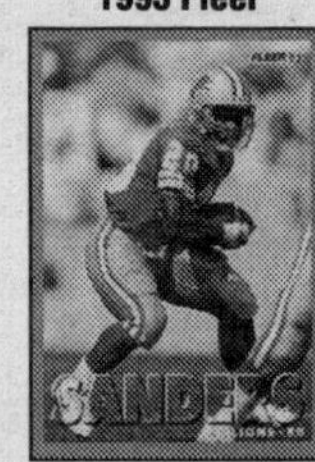

Card	Player	Nrmt	Exc
❑	COMPLETE SET (500)	20.00	10.00
❑ 1	Dan Saleaumua	.05	.01
❑ 2	Bryan Cox	.05	.01
❑ 3	Dermontti Dawson	.05	.01
❑ 4	Michael Jackson	.10	.02
❑ 5	Calvin Williams	.10	.02
❑ 6	Terry McDaniel	.05	.01
❑ 7	Jack Del Rio	.05	.01
❑ 8	Steve Atwater	.05	.01
❑ 9	Ernie Jones	.05	.01
❑ 10	Brad Muster	.05	.01
❑ 11	Harold Green	.05	.01
❑ 12	Eric Bieniemy	.05	.01
❑ 13	Eric Dorsey	.05	.01
❑ 14	Fred Barnett	.10	.02
❑ 15	Cleveland Gary	.05	.01
❑ 16	Darion Conner	.05	.01
❑ 17	Jerry Ball	.05	.01
❑ 18	Tony Casillas	.05	.01
❑ 19	Brian Blades	.10	.02
❑ 20	Tony Bennett	.05	.01
❑ 21	Reggie Cobb	.05	.01
❑ 22	Kurt Gouveia	.05	.01
❑ 23	Greg McMurtry	.05	.01
❑ 24	Kyle Clifton	.05	.01
❑ 25	Trace Armstrong	.05	.01
❑ 26	Terry Allen	.25	.08
❑ 27	Steve Bono	.10	.02
❑ 28	Barry Word	.05	.01
❑ 29	Mark Duper	.05	.01
❑ 30	Nate Newton	.10	.02
❑ 31	Will Wolford	.05	.01
❑ 32	Curtis Duncan	.05	.01
❑ 33	Nick Bell	.05	.01
❑ 34	Don Beebe	.05	.01
❑ 35	Mike Croel	.05	.01
❑ 36	Rich Camarillo	.05	.01
❑ 37	Wade Wilson	.05	.01
❑ 38	John Taylor	.10	.02
❑ 39	Marion Butts	.05	.01
❑ 40	Rodney Hampton	.10	.02
❑ 41	Seth Joyner	.05	.01
❑ 42	Wilber Marshall	.05	.01
❑ 43	Bobby Hebert	.05	.01
❑ 44	Bennie Blades	.05	.01
❑ 45	Thomas Everett	.05	.01
❑ 46	Ricky Sanders	.05	.01
❑ 47	Matt Brock	.05	.01
❑ 48	Lawrence Dawsey	.05	.01
❑ 49	Brad Edwards	.05	.01
❑ 50	Vincent Brown	.05	.01
❑ 51	Jeff Lageman	.05	.01
❑ 52	Mark Carrier DB	.05	.01
❑ 53	Cris Carter	.25	.08
❑ 54	Brent Jones	.10	.02
❑ 55	Barry Foster	.10	.02
❑ 56	Derrick Thomas	.25	.08
❑ 57	Scott Zolak	.05	.01
❑ 58	Mark Stepnoski	.05	.01
❑ 59	Eric Metcalf	.10	.02
❑ 60	Al Smith	.05	.01
❑ 61	Ronnie Harmon	.05	.01
❑ 62	Cornelius Bennett	.10	.02
❑ 63	Karl Mecklenburg	.05	.01
❑ 64	Chris Chandler	.10	.02
❑ 65	Toi Cook	.05	.01
❑ 66	Tim Krumrie	.05	.01
❑ 67	Gill Byrd	.05	.01
❑ 68	Mark Jackson	.05	.01
❑ 69	Tim Harris	.05	.01
❑ 70	Shane Conlan	.05	.01
❑ 71	Moe Gardner	.05	.01
❑ 72	Lomas Brown	.05	.01
❑ 73	Charles Haley	.10	.02
❑ 74	Mark Rypien	.05	.01
❑ 75	LeRoy Butler	.05	.01
❑ 76	Steve DeBerg	.05	.01
❑ 77	Darrell Green	.05	.01
❑ 78	Marv Cook	.05	.01
❑ 79	Chris Burkett	.05	.01
❑ 80	Richard Dent	.10	.02
❑ 81	Roger Craig	.10	.02
❑ 82	Amp Lee	.05	.01
❑ 83	Eric Green	.05	.01
❑ 84	Willie Davis	.25	.08
❑ 85	Mark Higgs	.05	.01
❑ 86	Carlton Haselrig	.05	.01
❑ 87	Tommy Vardell	.05	.01
❑ 88	Haywood Jeffires	.10	.02
❑ 89	Tim Brown	.25	.08
❑ 90	Randall McDaniel	.05	.01
❑ 91	John Elway	1.50	.60
❑ 92	Ken Harvey	.05	.01
❑ 93	Joel Hilgenberg	.05	.01
❑ 94	Steve Wallace	.05	.01
❑ 95	Stan Humphries	.10	.02
❑ 96	Greg Jackson	.05	.01
❑ 97	Clyde Simmons	.05	.01
❑ 98	Jim Everett	.10	.02
❑ 99	Michael Haynes	.10	.02
❑ 100	Mel Gray	.10	.02
❑ 101	Alvin Harper	.10	.02
❑ 102	Art Monk	.10	.02
❑ 103	Brett Favre	2.00	.75
❑ 104	Keith McCants	.05	.01
❑ 105	Charles Mann	.05	.01
❑ 106	Leonard Russell	.10	.02
❑ 107	Mo Lewis	.05	.01
❑ 108	Shaun Gayle	.05	.01
❑ 109	Chris Doleman	.05	.01
❑ 110	Tim McDonald	.05	.01
❑ 111	Louis Oliver	.05	.01
❑ 112	Greg Lloyd	.10	.02
❑ 113	Chip Banks	.05	.01
❑ 114	Sean Jones	.05	.01
❑ 115	Ethan Horton	.05	.01
❑ 116	Kenneth Davis	.05	.01
❑ 117	Simon Fletcher	.05	.01
❑ 118	Johnny Johnson	.05	.01
❑ 119	Vaughan Johnson	.05	.01
❑ 120	Derrick Fenner	.05	.01
❑ 121	Nate Lewis	.05	.01
❑ 122	Pepper Johnson	.05	.01
❑ 123	Heath Sherman	.05	.01
❑ 124	Darryl Henley	.05	.01
❑ 125	Pierce Holt	.05	.01
❑ 126	Herman Moore	.25	.08
❑ 127	Michael Irvin	.25	.08
❑ 128	Tommy Kane	.05	.01
❑ 129	Jackie Harris	.05	.01
❑ 130	Hardy Nickerson	.10	.02
❑ 131	Chip Lohmiller	.05	.01
❑ 132	Andre Tippett	.05	.01
❑ 133	Leonard Marshall	.05	.01
❑ 134	Craig Heyward	.10	.02
❑ 135	Anthony Carter	.10	.02
❑ 136	Tom Rathman	.05	.01
❑ 137	Lorenzo White	.05	.01
❑ 138	Nick Lowery	.05	.01

❑ 139 John Offerdahl .05 .01
❑ 140 Neil O'Donnell .25 .08
❑ 141 Clarence Verdin .05 .01
❑ 142 Ernest Givins .10 .02
❑ 143 Todd Marinovich .05 .01
❑ 144 Jeff Wright .05 .01
❑ 145 Michael Brooks .05 .01
❑ 146 Freddie Joe Nunn .05 .01
❑ 147 William Perry .10 .02
❑ 148 Daniel Stubbs .05 .01
❑ 149 Morten Andersen .05 .01
❑ 150 Dave Meggett .05 .01
❑ 151 Andre Waters .05 .01
❑ 152 Todd Lyght .05 .01
❑ 153 Chris Miller .10 .02
❑ 154 Rodney Peete .05 .01
❑ 155 Jim Jeffcoat .05 .01
❑ 156 Cortez Kennedy .10 .02
❑ 157 Johnny Holland .05 .01
❑ 158 Ricky Reynolds .05 .01
❑ 159 Kevin Greene .10 .02
❑ 160 Jeff Herrod .05 .01
❑ 161 Bruce Matthews .05 .01
❑ 162 Anthony Smith .05 .01
❑ 163 Henry Jones .05 .01
❑ 164 Rob Burnett .05 .01
❑ 165 Eric Swann .10 .02
❑ 166 Tom Waddle .05 .01
❑ 167 Alfred Williams .05 .01
❑ 168 Darren Carrington RC .05 .01
❑ 169 Mike Sherrard .05 .01
❑ 170 Frank Reich .10 .02
❑ 171 Anthony Newman RC .05 .01
❑ 172 Mike Pritchard .10 .02
❑ 173 Andre Ware .05 .01
❑ 174 Daryl Johnston .25 .08
❑ 175 Rufus Porter .05 .01
❑ 176 Reggie White .25 .08
❑ 177 Charles Mincy RC .05 .01
❑ 178 Pete Stoyanovich .05 .01
❑ 179 Rod Woodson .25 .08
❑ 180 Anthony Johnson .10 .02
❑ 181 Cody Carlson .05 .01
❑ 182 Gaston Green .05 .01
❑ 183 Audray McMillian .05 .01
❑ 184 Mike Johnson .05 .01
❑ 185 Aeneas Williams .05 .01
❑ 186 Jarrod Bunch .05 .01
❑ 187 Dennis Smith .05 .01
❑ 188 Quinn Early .10 .02
❑ 189 James Hasty .05 .01
❑ 190 Darryl Talley .05 .01
❑ 191 Jon Vaughn .05 .01
❑ 192 Andre Rison .10 .02
❑ 193 Kelvin Pritchett .05 .01
❑ 194 Ken Norton Jr. .10 .02
❑ 195 Chris Warren .10 .02
❑ 196 Sterling Sharpe .25 .08
❑ 197 Christian Okoye .05 .01
❑ 198 Richmond Webb .05 .01
❑ 199 James Francis .05 .01
❑ 200 Reggie Langhorne .05 .01
❑ 201 J.J. Birden .05 .01
❑ 202 Aaron Wallace .05 .01
❑ 203 Henry Thomas .05 .01
❑ 204 Clay Matthews .10 .02
❑ 205 Robert Massey .05 .01
❑ 206 Donnell Woolford .05 .01
❑ 207 Ricky Watters .25 .08
❑ 208 Wayne Martin .05 .01
❑ 209 Rob Moore .10 .02
❑ 210 Steve Tasker .10 .02
❑ 211 Jackie Slater .05 .01
❑ 212 Steve Young .75 .30
❑ 213 Barry Sanders 1.25 .50
❑ 214 Jay Novacek .10 .02
❑ 215 Eugene Robinson .05 .01
❑ 216 Duane Bickett .05 .01
❑ 217 Broderick Thomas .05 .01
❑ 218 David Fulcher .05 .01
❑ 219 Rohn Stark .05 .01
❑ 220 Warren Moon .25 .08
❑ 221 Steve Wisniewski .05 .01
❑ 222 Nate Odomes .05 .01
❑ 223 Shannon Sharpe .25 .08
❑ 224 Byron Evans .05 .01
❑ 225 Mark Collins .05 .01
❑ 226 Rod Bernstine .05 .01
❑ 227 Sam Mills .05 .01
❑ 228 Marvin Washington .05 .01
❑ 229 Thurman Thomas .25 .08
❑ 230 Brent Williams .05 .01
❑ 231 Jessie Tuggle .05 .01
❑ 232 Chris Spielman .10 .02
❑ 233 Emmitt Smith 1.50 .60
❑ 234 John L. Williams .05 .01
❑ 235 Jeff Cross .05 .01
❑ 236 Chris Doleman AW .05 .01
❑ 237 John Elway AW .75 .30
❑ 238 Barry Foster AW .05 .01
❑ 239 Cortez Kennedy AW .05 .01
❑ 240 Steve Young AW .40 .15
❑ 241 Barry Foster LL .05 .01
❑ 242 Warren Moon LL .05 .01
❑ 243 Sterling Sharpe LL .05 .01
❑ 244 Emmitt Smith LL .75 .30
❑ 245 Thurman Thomas LL .10 .02
❑ 246 Michael Irvin PV .10 .02
❑ 247 Steve Young PV .40 .15
❑ 248 Barry Foster PV .05 .01
❑ 249 Checklist .05 .01
❑ 250 Checklist .05 .01
❑ 251 Checklist .05 .01
❑ 252 Checklist .05 .01
❑ 253 Troy Aikman AW .40 .15
❑ 254 Jason Hanson AW .05 .01
❑ 255 Carl Pickens AW .10 .02
❑ 256 Santana Dotson AW .05 .01
❑ 257 Dale Carter AW .05 .01
❑ 258 Clyde Simmons LL .05 .01
❑ 259 Audray McMillian LL .05 .01
❑ 260 Henry Jones LL .05 .01
❑ 261 Deion Sanders LL .25 .08
❑ 262 Haywood Jeffires LL .05 .01
❑ 263 Deion Sanders PV .25 .08
❑ 264 Andre Reed PV .10 .02
❑ 265 Vince Workman .05 .01
❑ 266 Robert Brown .05 .01
❑ 267 Ray Agnew .05 .01
❑ 268 Ronnie Lott .10 .02
❑ 269 Wesley Carroll .05 .01
❑ 270 John Randle .10 .02
❑ 271 Rodney Culver .05 .01
❑ 272 David Alexander .05 .01
❑ 273 Troy Aikman .75 .30
❑ 274 Bernie Kosar .10 .02
❑ 275 Scott Case .05 .01
❑ 276 Dan McGwire .05 .01
❑ 277 John Alt .05 .01
❑ 278 Dan Marino 1.50 .60
❑ 279 Santana Dotson .10 .02
❑ 280 Johnny Mitchell .05 .01
❑ 281 Alonzo Spellman .05 .01
❑ 282 Adrian Cooper .05 .01
❑ 283 Gary Clark .10 .02
❑ 284 Vance Johnson .05 .01
❑ 285 Eric Martin .05 .01
❑ 286 Jesse Solomon .05 .01
❑ 287 Carl Banks .05 .01
❑ 288 Harris Barton .05 .01
❑ 289 Jim Harbaugh .25 .08
❑ 290 Bubba McDowell .05 .01
❑ 291 Anthony McDowell RC .05 .01
❑ 292 Terrell Buckley .05 .01
❑ 293 Bruce Armstrong .05 .01
❑ 294 Kurt Barber .05 .01
❑ 295 Reginald Jones .05 .01
❑ 296 Steve Jordan .05 .01
❑ 297 Kerry Cash .05 .01
❑ 298 Ray Crockett .05 .01
❑ 299 Keith Byars .05 .01
❑ 300 Russell Maryland .05 .01
❑ 301 Johnny Bailey .05 .01
❑ 302 Vinnie Clark .05 .01
❑ 303 Terry Wooden .05 .01
❑ 304 Harvey Williams .10 .02
❑ 305 Marco Coleman .05 .01
❑ 306 Mark Wheeler .05 .01
❑ 307 Greg Townsend .05 .01
❑ 308 Tim McGee .05 .01
❑ 309 Donald Evans .05 .01
❑ 310 Randal Hill .05 .01
❑ 311 Kenny Walker .05 .01
❑ 312 Dalton Hilliard .05 .01
❑ 313 Howard Ballard .05 .01
❑ 314 Phil Simms .10 .02
❑ 315 Jerry Rice 1.00 .40
❑ 316 Courtney Hall .05 .01
❑ 317 Darren Lewis .05 .01
❑ 318 Greg Montgomery .05 .01
❑ 319 Paul Gruber .05 .01
❑ 320 George Koonce RC .05 .01
❑ 321 Eugene Chung .05 .01
❑ 322 Mike Brim .05 .01
❑ 323 Patrick Hunter .05 .01
❑ 324 Todd Scott .05 .01
❑ 325 Steve Emtman .05 .01
❑ 326 Andy Harmon RC .10 .02
❑ 327 Larry Brown DB .05 .01
❑ 328 Chuck Cecil .05 .01
❑ 329 Tim McKyer .05 .01
❑ 330 Jeff Bryant .05 .01
❑ 331 Tim Barnett .05 .01
❑ 332 Irving Fryar .10 .02
❑ 333 Tyji Armstrong .05 .01
❑ 334 Brad Baxter .05 .01
❑ 335 Shane Collins .05 .01
❑ 336 Jeff Graham .10 .02
❑ 337 Ricky Proehl .05 .01
❑ 338 Tommy Maddox .25 .08
❑ 339 Jim Dombrowski .05 .01
❑ 340 Bill Brooks .05 .01
❑ 341 Dave Brown RC .25 .08
❑ 342 Eric Davis .05 .01
❑ 343 Leslie O'Neal .10 .02
❑ 344 Jim Morrissey .05 .01
❑ 345 Mike Munchak .10 .02
❑ 346 Ron Hall .05 .01
❑ 347 Brian Noble .05 .01
❑ 348 Chris Singleton .05 .01
❑ 349 Boomer Esiason .10 .02
❑ 350 Ray Roberts .05 .01
❑ 351 Gary Zimmerman .05 .01
❑ 352 Quentin Coryatt .10 .02
❑ 353 Willie Green .05 .01
❑ 354 Randall Cunningham .25 .08
❑ 355 Kevin Smith .10 .02
❑ 356 Michael Dean Perry .10 .02
❑ 357 Tim Green .05 .01
❑ 358 Dwayne Harper .05 .01
❑ 359 Dale Carter .05 .01
❑ 360 Keith Jackson .10 .02
❑ 361 Martin Mayhew .05 .01
❑ 362 Brian Washington .05 .01
❑ 363 Earnest Byner .05 .01
❑ 364 D.J. Johnson .05 .01
❑ 365 Timm Rosenbach .05 .01
❑ 366 Doug Widell .05 .01
❑ 367 Vaughn Dunbar .05 .01
❑ 368 Phil Hansen .05 .01
❑ 369 Mike Fox .05 .01
❑ 370 Dana Hall .05 .01
❑ 371 Junior Seau .25 .08
❑ 372 Steve McMichael .10 .02
❑ 373 Eddie Robinson .05 .01
❑ 374 Milton Mack RC .05 .01
❑ 375 Mike Prior .05 .01
❑ 376 Jerome Henderson .05 .01
❑ 377 Scott Mersereau .05 .01
❑ 378 Neal Anderson .05 .01
❑ 379 Harry Newsome .05 .01
❑ 380 John Baylor .05 .01
❑ 381 Bill Fralic .05 .01
❑ 382 Mark Bavaro .05 .01
❑ 383 Robert Jones .05 .01
❑ 384 Tyronne Stowe .05 .01
❑ 385 Deion Sanders .50 .20
❑ 386 Robert Blackmon .05 .01
❑ 387 Neil Smith .25 .08
❑ 388 Mark Ingram .05 .01
❑ 389 Mark Carrier WR .10 .02
❑ 390 Browning Nagle .05 .01
❑ 391 Ricky Ervins .05 .01
❑ 392 Carnell Lake .05 .01
❑ 393 Luis Sharpe .05 .01
❑ 394 Greg Kragen .05 .01
❑ 395 Tommy Barnhardt .05 .01
❑ 396 Mark Kelso .05 .01
❑ 397 Kent Graham RC .25 .08
❑ 398 Bill Romanowski .05 .01
❑ 399 Anthony Miller .10 .02
❑ 400 John Roper .05 .01
❑ 401 Lamar Rogers .05 .01
❑ 402 Troy Auzenne .05 .01
❑ 403 Webster Slaughter .05 .01
❑ 404 David Brandon .05 .01
❑ 405 Chris Hinton .05 .01

❑ 406 Andy Heck	.05	.01
❑ 407 Tracy Simien	.05	.01
❑ 408 Troy Vincent	.05	.01
❑ 409 Jason Hanson	.05	.01
❑ 410 Rod Jones CB RC	.05	.01
❑ 411 Al Noga	.05	.01
❑ 412 Ernie Mills	.05	.01
❑ 413 Willie Gault	.05	.01
❑ 414 Henry Ellard	.10	.02
❑ 415 Rickey Jackson	.05	.01
❑ 416 Bruce Smith	.25	.08
❑ 417 Derek Brown TE	.05	.01
❑ 418 Kevin Fagan	.05	.01
❑ 419 Gary Plummer	.05	.01
❑ 420 Wendell Davis	.05	.01
❑ 421 Craig Thompson	.05	.01
❑ 422 Wes Hopkins	.05	.01
❑ 423 Ray Childress	.05	.01
❑ 424 Pat Harlow	.05	.01
❑ 425 Howie Long	.25	.08
❑ 426 Shane Dronett	.05	.01
❑ 427 Sean Salisbury	.05	.01
❑ 428 Dwight Hollier RC	.05	.01
❑ 429 Brett Perriman	.25	.08
❑ 430 Donald Hollas RC	.05	.01
❑ 431 Jim Lachey	.05	.01
❑ 432 Darren Perry	.05	.01
❑ 433 Lionel Washington	.05	.01
❑ 434 Sean Gilbert	.10	.02
❑ 435 Gene Atkins	.05	.01
❑ 436 Jim Kelly	.25	.08
❑ 437 Ed McCaffrey	.25	.08
❑ 438 Don Griffin	.05	.01
❑ 439 Jerrol Williams	.05	.01
❑ 440 Bryce Paup	.10	.02
❑ 441 Darryl Williams	.05	.01
❑ 442 Vai Sikahema	.05	.01
❑ 443 Cris Dishman	.05	.01
❑ 444 Kevin Mack	.05	.01
❑ 445 Winston Moss	.05	.01
❑ 446 Tyrone Braxton	.05	.01
❑ 447 Mike Merriweather	.05	.01
❑ 448 Tony Paige	.05	.01
❑ 449 Robert Porcher	.05	.01
❑ 450 Ricardo McDonald	.05	.01
❑ 451 Danny Copeland	.05	.01
❑ 452 Tony Tolbert	.05	.01
❑ 453 Eric Dickerson	.10	.02
❑ 454 Flipper Anderson	.05	.01
❑ 455 Dave Krieg	.10	.02
❑ 456 Brad Lamb RC	.05	.01
❑ 457 Bart Oates	.05	.01
❑ 458 Guy McIntyre	.05	.01
❑ 459 Stanley Richard	.05	.01
❑ 460 Edgar Bennett	.25	.08
❑ 461 Pat Carter	.05	.01
❑ 462 Eric Allen	.05	.01
❑ 463 William Fuller	.05	.01
❑ 464 James Jones DT	.05	.01
❑ 465 Chester McGlockton	.10	.02
❑ 466 Charles Dimry	.05	.01
❑ 467 Tim Grunhard	.05	.01
❑ 468 Jarvis Williams	.05	.01
❑ 469 Tracy Scroggins	.05	.01
❑ 470 David Klingler	.05	.01
❑ 471 Andre Collins	.05	.01
❑ 472 Erik Williams	.05	.01
❑ 473 Eddie Anderson	.05	.01
❑ 474 Marc Boutte	.05	.01
❑ 475 Joe Montana	1.50	.60
❑ 476 Andre Reed	.10	.02
❑ 477 Lawrence Taylor	.25	.08
❑ 478 Jeff George	.25	.08
❑ 479 Chris Mims	.05	.01
❑ 480 Ken Ruettgers	.05	.01
❑ 481 Roman Phifer	.05	.01
❑ 482 William Thomas	.05	.01
❑ 483 Lamar Lathon	.05	.01
❑ 484 Vinny Testaverde	.10	.02
❑ 485 Mike Kenn	.05	.01
❑ 486 Greg Lewis	.05	.01
❑ 487 Chris Martin	.05	.01
❑ 488 Maurice Hurst	.05	.01
❑ 489 Pat Swilling	.05	.01
❑ 490 Carl Pickens	.10	.02
❑ 491 Tony Smith RB	.05	.01
❑ 492 James Washington	.05	.01
❑ 493 Jeff Hostetler	.10	.02
❑ 494 Jeff Chadwick	.05	.01
❑ 495 Kevin Ross	.05	.01
❑ 496 Jim Ritcher	.05	.01
❑ 497 Jessie Hester	.05	.01
❑ 498 Burt Grossman	.05	.01
❑ 499 Keith Van Horne	.05	.01
❑ 500 Gerald Robinson	.05	.01
❑ P1 Promo Panel	5.00	2.00

1994 Fleer

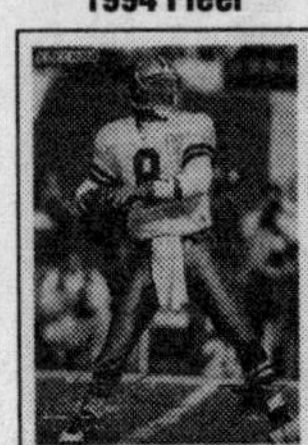

❑ COMPLETE SET (480)	20.00	10.00
❑ 1 Michael Bankston	.05	.01
❑ 2 Steve Beuerlein	.10	.02
❑ 3 John Booty	.05	.01
❑ 4 Rich Camarillo	.05	.01
❑ 5 Chuck Cecil	.05	.01
❑ 6 Larry Centers	.25	.08
❑ 7 Gary Clark	.10	.02
❑ 8 Garrison Hearst	.25	.08
❑ 9 Eric Hill	.05	.01
❑ 10 Randal Hill	.05	.01
❑ 11 Ronald Moore	.05	.01
❑ 12 Ricky Proehl	.05	.01
❑ 13 Luis Sharpe	.05	.01
❑ 14 Clyde Simmons	.05	.01
❑ 15 Tyronne Stowe	.05	.01
❑ 16 Eric Swann	.10	.02
❑ 17 Aeneas Williams	.05	.01
❑ 18 Darion Conner	.05	.01
❑ 19 Moe Gardner	.05	.01
❑ 20 Jumpy Geathers	.05	.01
❑ 21 Jeff George	.25	.08
❑ 22 Roger Harper	.05	.01
❑ 23 Bobby Hebert	.05	.01
❑ 24 Pierce Holt	.05	.01
❑ 25 D.J. Johnson	.05	.01
❑ 26 Mike Kenn	.05	.01
❑ 27 Lincoln Kennedy	.05	.01
❑ 28 Erric Pegram	.05	.01
❑ 29 Mike Pritchard	.05	.01
❑ 30 Andre Rison	.10	.02
❑ 31 Deion Sanders	.50	.20
❑ 32 Tony Smith RB	.05	.01
❑ 33 Jesse Solomon	.05	.01
❑ 34 Jessie Tuggle	.05	.01
❑ 35 Don Beebe	.05	.01
❑ 36 Cornelius Bennett	.10	.02
❑ 37 Bill Brooks	.05	.01
❑ 38 Kenneth Davis	.05	.01
❑ 39 John Fina	.05	.01
❑ 40 Phil Hansen	.05	.01
❑ 41 Kent Hull	.05	.01
❑ 42 Henry Jones	.05	.01
❑ 43 Jim Kelly	.25	.08
❑ 44 Pete Metzelaars	.05	.01
❑ 45 Marvcus Patton	.05	.01
❑ 46 Andre Reed	.10	.02
❑ 47 Frank Reich	.10	.02
❑ 48 Bruce Smith	.25	.08
❑ 49 Thomas Smith	.05	.01
❑ 50 Darryl Talley	.05	.01
❑ 51 Steve Tasker	.10	.02
❑ 52 Thurman Thomas	.25	.08
❑ 53 Jeff Wright	.05	.01
❑ 54 Neal Anderson	.05	.01
❑ 55 Trace Armstrong	.05	.01
❑ 56 Troy Auzenne	.05	.01
❑ 57 Joe Cain RC	.05	.01
❑ 58 Mark Carrier DB	.05	.01
❑ 59 Curtis Conway	.25	.08
❑ 60 Richard Dent	.10	.02
❑ 61 Shaun Gayle	.05	.01
❑ 62 Andy Heck	.05	.01
❑ 63 Dante Jones	.05	.01
❑ 64 Erik Kramer	.10	.02
❑ 65 Steve McMichael	.10	.02
❑ 66 Terry Obee	.05	.01
❑ 67 Vinson Smith	.05	.01
❑ 68 Alonzo Spellman	.05	.01
❑ 69 Tom Waddle	.05	.01
❑ 70 Donnell Woolford	.05	.01
❑ 71 Tim Worley	.05	.01
❑ 72 Chris Zorich	.05	.01
❑ 73 Mike Brim	.05	.01
❑ 74 John Copeland	.05	.01
❑ 75 Derrick Fenner	.05	.01
❑ 76 James Francis	.05	.01
❑ 77 Harold Green	.05	.01
❑ 78 Rod Jones CB	.05	.01
❑ 79 David Klingler	.05	.01
❑ 80 Bruce Kozerski	.05	.01
❑ 81 Tim Krumrie	.05	.01
❑ 82 Ricardo McDonald	.05	.01
❑ 83 Tim McGee	.05	.01
❑ 84 Tony McGee	.05	.01
❑ 85 Louis Oliver	.05	.01
❑ 86 Carl Pickens	.10	.02
❑ 87 Jeff Query	.05	.01
❑ 88 Daniel Stubbs	.05	.01
❑ 89 Steve Tovar	.05	.01
❑ 90 Alfred Williams	.05	.01
❑ 91 Darryl Williams	.05	.01
❑ 92 Rob Burnett	.05	.01
❑ 93 Mark Carrier WR	.10	.02
❑ 94 Leroy Hoard	.05	.01
❑ 95 Michael Jackson	.10	.02
❑ 96 Mike Johnson	.05	.01
❑ 97 Pepper Johnson	.05	.01
❑ 98 Tony Jones T	.05	.01
❑ 99 Clay Matthews	.05	.01
❑ 100 Eric Metcalf	.10	.02
❑ 101 Stevon Moore	.05	.01
❑ 102 Michael Dean Perry	.10	.02
❑ 103 Anthony Pleasant	.05	.01
❑ 104 Vinny Testaverde	.10	.02
❑ 105 Eric Turner	.05	.01
❑ 106 Tommy Vardell	.05	.01
❑ 107 Troy Aikman	1.00	.40
❑ 108 Larry Brown DB	.05	.01
❑ 109 Dixon Edwards	.05	.01
❑ 110 Charles Haley	.10	.02
❑ 111 Alvin Harper	.10	.02
❑ 112 Michael Irvin	.25	.08
❑ 113 Jim Jeffcoat	.05	.01
❑ 114 Daryl Johnston	.10	.02
❑ 115 Leon Lett	.05	.01
❑ 116 Russell Maryland	.05	.01
❑ 117 Nate Newton	.05	.01
❑ 118 Ken Norton Jr.	.10	.02
❑ 119 Jay Novacek	.10	.02
❑ 120 Darrin Smith	.05	.01
❑ 121 Emmitt Smith	1.50	.60
❑ 122 Kevin Smith	.05	.01
❑ 123 Mark Stepnoski	.05	.01
❑ 124 Tony Tolbert	.05	.01
❑ 125 Erik Williams	.05	.01
❑ 126 Kevin Williams WR	.10	.02
❑ 127 Darren Woodson	.10	.02
❑ 128 Steve Atwater	.05	.01
❑ 129 Rod Bernstine	.05	.01
❑ 130 Ray Crockett	.05	.01
❑ 131 Mike Croel	.05	.01
❑ 132 Robert Delpino	.05	.01
❑ 133 Shane Dronett	.05	.01
❑ 134 Jason Elam	.10	.02
❑ 135 John Elway	2.00	.75
❑ 136 Simon Fletcher	.05	.01
❑ 137 Greg Kragen	.05	.01
❑ 138 Karl Mecklenburg	.05	.01
❑ 139 Glyn Milburn	.10	.02
❑ 140 Anthony Miller	.10	.02
❑ 141 Derek Russell	.05	.01
❑ 142 Shannon Sharpe	.10	.02
❑ 143 Dennis Smith	.05	.01
❑ 144 Dan Williams	.05	.01
❑ 145 Gary Zimmerman	.05	.01
❑ 146 Bennie Blades	.05	.01
❑ 147 Lomas Brown	.05	.01
❑ 148 Bill Fralic	.05	.01
❑ 149 Mel Gray	.05	.01
❑ 150 Willie Green	.05	.01
❑ 151 Jason Hanson	.05	.01

❑ 152	Robert Massey	.05	.01
❑ 153	Ryan McNeil	.05	.01
❑ 154	Scott Mitchell	.10	.02
❑ 155	Derrick Moore	.05	.01
❑ 156	Herman Moore	.25	.08
❑ 157	Brett Perriman	.10	.02
❑ 158	Robert Porcher	.05	.01
❑ 159	Kelvin Pritchett	.05	.01
❑ 160	Barry Sanders	1.50	.60
❑ 161	Tracy Scroggins	.05	.01
❑ 162	Chris Spielman	.10	.02
❑ 163	Pat Swilling	.05	.01
❑ 164	Edgar Bennett	.25	.08
❑ 165	Robert Brooks	.25	.08
❑ 166	Terrell Buckley	.05	.01
❑ 167	LeRoy Butler	.05	.01
❑ 168	Brett Favre	2.00	.75
❑ 169	Harry Galbreath	.05	.01
❑ 170	Jackie Harris	.05	.01
❑ 171	Johnny Holland	.05	.01
❑ 172	Chris Jacke	.05	.01
❑ 173	George Koonce	.05	.01
❑ 174	Bryce Paup	.10	.02
❑ 175	Ken Ruettgers	.05	.01
❑ 176	Sterling Sharpe	.10	.02
❑ 177	Wayne Simmons	.05	.01
❑ 178	George Teague	.05	.01
❑ 179	Darrell Thompson	.05	.01
❑ 180	Reggie White	.25	.08
❑ 181	Gary Brown	.05	.01
❑ 182	Cody Carlson	.05	.01
❑ 183	Ray Childress	.05	.01
❑ 184	Cris Dishman	.05	.01
❑ 185	Ernest Givins	.10	.02
❑ 186	Haywood Jeffires	.10	.02
❑ 187	Sean Jones	.05	.01
❑ 188	Lamar Lathon	.05	.01
❑ 189	Bruce Matthews	.05	.01
❑ 190	Bubba McDowell	.05	.01
❑ 191	Glenn Montgomery	.05	.01
❑ 192	Greg Montgomery	.05	.01
❑ 193	Warren Moon	.25	.08
❑ 194	Bo Orlando	.05	.01
❑ 195	Marcus Robertson	.05	.01
❑ 196	Eddie Robinson	.05	.01
❑ 197	Webster Slaughter	.05	.01
❑ 198	Lorenzo White	.05	.01
❑ 199	John Baylor	.05	.01
❑ 200	Jason Belser	.05	.01
❑ 201	Tony Bennett	.05	.01
❑ 202	Dean Biasucci	.05	.01
❑ 203	Ray Buchanan	.05	.01
❑ 204	Kerry Cash	.05	.01
❑ 205	Quentin Coryatt	.05	.01
❑ 206	Eugene Daniel	.05	.01
❑ 207	Steve Emtman	.05	.01
❑ 208	Jon Hand	.05	.01
❑ 209	Jim Harbaugh	.25	.08
❑ 210	Jeff Herrod	.05	.01
❑ 211	Anthony Johnson	.10	.02
❑ 212	Roosevelt Potts	.05	.01
❑ 213	Rohn Stark	.05	.01
❑ 214	Will Wolford	.05	.01
❑ 215	Marcus Allen	.25	.08
❑ 216	John Alt	.05	.01
❑ 217	Kimble Anders	.10	.02
❑ 218	J.J. Birden	.05	.01
❑ 219	Dale Carter	.05	.01
❑ 220	Keith Cash	.05	.01
❑ 221	Tony Casillas	.05	.01
❑ 222	Willie Davis	.10	.02
❑ 223	Tim Grunhard	.05	.01
❑ 224	Nick Lowery	.05	.01
❑ 225	Charles Mincy	.05	.01
❑ 226	Joe Montana	2.00	.75
❑ 227	Dan Saleaumua	.05	.01
❑ 228	Tracy Simien	.05	.01
❑ 229	Neil Smith	.10	.02
❑ 230	Derrick Thomas	.25	.08
❑ 231	Eddie Anderson	.05	.01
❑ 232	Tim Brown	.25	.08
❑ 233	Nolan Harrison	.05	.01
❑ 234	Jeff Hostetler	.10	.02
❑ 235	Rocket Ismail	.10	.02
❑ 236	Jeff Jaeger	.05	.01
❑ 237	James Jett	.05	.01
❑ 238	Joe Kelly	.05	.01
❑ 239	Albert Lewis	.05	.01
❑ 240	Terry McDaniel	.05	.01
❑ 241	Chester McGlockton	.05	.01
❑ 242	Winston Moss	.05	.01
❑ 243	Gerald Perry	.05	.01
❑ 244	Greg Robinson	.05	.01
❑ 245	Anthony Smith	.05	.01
❑ 246	Steve Smith	.05	.01
❑ 247	Greg Townsend	.05	.01
❑ 248	Lionel Washington	.05	.01
❑ 249	Steve Wisniewski	.05	.01
❑ 250	Alexander Wright	.05	.01
❑ 251	Flipper Anderson	.05	.01
❑ 252	Jerome Bettis	.50	.20
❑ 253	Marc Boutte	.05	.01
❑ 254	Shane Conlan	.05	.01
❑ 255	Troy Drayton	.05	.01
❑ 256	Henry Ellard	.10	.02
❑ 257	Sean Gilbert	.05	.01
❑ 258	Nate Lewis	.05	.01
❑ 259	Todd Lyght	.05	.01
❑ 260	Chris Miller	.05	.01
❑ 261	Anthony Newman	.05	.01
❑ 262	Roman Phifer	.05	.01
❑ 263	Henry Rolling	.05	.01
❑ 264	T.J.Rubley RC	.05	.01
❑ 265	Jackie Slater	.05	.01
❑ 266	Fred Stokes	.05	.01
❑ 267	Robert Young	.05	.01
❑ 268	Gene Atkins	.05	.01
❑ 269	J.B. Brown	.05	.01
❑ 270	Keith Byars	.05	.01
❑ 271	Marco Coleman	.05	.01
❑ 272	Bryan Cox	.05	.01
❑ 273	Jeff Cross	.05	.01
❑ 274	Irving Fryar	.10	.02
❑ 275	Mark Higgs	.05	.01
❑ 276	Dwight Hollier	.05	.01
❑ 277	Mark Ingram	.05	.01
❑ 278	Keith Jackson	.05	.01
❑ 279	Terry Kirby	.25	.08
❑ 280	Bernie Kosar	.10	.02
❑ 281	Dan Marino	2.00	.75
❑ 282	O.J.McDuffie	.25	.08
❑ 283	Keith Sims	.05	.01
❑ 284	Pete Stoyanovich	.05	.01
❑ 285	Troy Vincent	.05	.01
❑ 286	Richmond Webb	.05	.01
❑ 287	Terry Allen	.10	.02
❑ 288	Anthony Carter	.10	.02
❑ 289	Cris Carter	.50	.20
❑ 290	Jack Del Rio	.05	.01
❑ 291	Chris Doleman	.05	.01
❑ 292	Vencie Glenn	.05	.01
❑ 293	Scottie Graham RC	.10	.02
❑ 294	Chris Hinton	.05	.01
❑ 295	Qadry Ismail	.25	.08
❑ 296	Carlos Jenkins	.05	.01
❑ 297	Steve Jordan	.05	.01
❑ 298	Carl Lee	.05	.01
❑ 299	Randall McDaniel	.05	.01
❑ 300	John Randle	.10	.02
❑ 301	Todd Scott	.05	.01
❑ 302	Robert Smith	.25	.08
❑ 303	Fred Strickland	.05	.01
❑ 304	Henry Thomas	.05	.01
❑ 305	Bruce Armstrong	.05	.01
❑ 306	Harlon Barnett	.05	.01
❑ 307	Drew Bledsoe	.75	.30
❑ 308	Vincent Brown	.05	.01
❑ 309	Ben Coates	.10	.02
❑ 310	Todd Collins	.05	.01
❑ 311	Myron Guyton	.05	.01
❑ 312	Pat Harlow	.05	.01
❑ 313	Maurice Hurst	.05	.01
❑ 314	Leonard Russell	.05	.01
❑ 315	Chris Slade	.05	.01
❑ 316	Michael Timpson	.05	.01
❑ 317	Andre Tippett	.05	.01
❑ 318	Morten Andersen	.05	.01
❑ 319	Derek Brown RBK	.05	.01
❑ 320	Vince Buck	.05	.01
❑ 321	Toi Cook	.05	.01
❑ 322	Quinn Early	.10	.02
❑ 323	Jim Everett	.10	.02
❑ 324	Michael Haynes	.10	.02
❑ 325	Tyrone Hughes	.10	.02
❑ 326	Rickey Jackson	.05	.01
❑ 327	Vaughan Johnson	.05	.01
❑ 328	Eric Martin	.05	.01
❑ 329	Wayne Martin	.05	.01
❑ 330	Sam Mills	.05	.01
❑ 331	Willie Roaf	.05	.01
❑ 332	Irv Smith	.05	.01
❑ 333	Keith Taylor	.05	.01
❑ 334	Renaldo Turnbull	.05	.01
❑ 335	Carlton Bailey	.05	.01
❑ 336	Michael Brooks	.05	.01
❑ 337	Jarrod Bunch	.05	.01
❑ 338	Chris Calloway	.05	.01
❑ 339	Mark Collins	.05	.01
❑ 340	Howard Cross	.05	.01
❑ 341	Stacey Dillard RC	.05	.01
❑ 342	John Elliott	.05	.01
❑ 343	Rodney Hampton	.10	.02
❑ 344	Greg Jackson	.05	.01
❑ 345	Mark Jackson	.05	.01
❑ 346	Dave Meggett	.05	.01
❑ 347	Corey Miller	.05	.01
❑ 348	Mike Sherrard	.05	.01
❑ 349	Phil Simms	.10	.02
❑ 350	Lewis Tillman	.05	.01
❑ 351	Brad Baxter	.05	.01
❑ 352	Kyle Clifton	.05	.01
❑ 353	Boomer Esiason	.10	.02
❑ 354	James Hasty	.05	.01
❑ 355	Bobby Houston	.05	.01
❑ 356	Johnny Johnson	.05	.01
❑ 357	Jeff Lageman	.05	.01
❑ 358	Mo Lewis	.05	.01
❑ 359	Ronnie Lott	.10	.02
❑ 360	Leonard Marshall	.05	.01
❑ 361	Johnny Mitchell	.05	.01
❑ 362	Rob Moore	.10	.02
❑ 363	Eric Thomas	.05	.01
❑ 364	Brian Washington	.05	.01
❑ 365	Marvin Washington	.05	.01
❑ 366	Eric Allen	.05	.01
❑ 367	Fred Barnett	.10	.02
❑ 368	Bubby Brister	.05	.01
❑ 369	Randall Cunningham	.25	.08
❑ 370	Byron Evans	.05	.01
❑ 371	William Fuller	.05	.01
❑ 372	Andy Harmon	.05	.01
❑ 373	Seth Joyner	.05	.01
❑ 374	William Perry	.10	.02
❑ 375	Leonard Renfro	.05	.01
❑ 376	Heath Sherman	.05	.01
❑ 377	Ben Smith	.05	.01
❑ 378	William Thomas	.05	.01
❑ 379	Herschel Walker	.10	.02
❑ 380	Calvin Williams	.10	.02
❑ 381	Chad Brown	.05	.01
❑ 382	Dermontti Dawson	.05	.01
❑ 383	Deon Figures	.05	.01
❑ 384	Barry Foster	.05	.01
❑ 385	Jeff Graham	.05	.01
❑ 386	Eric Green	.05	.01
❑ 387	Kevin Greene	.10	.02
❑ 388	Carlton Haselrig	.05	.01
❑ 389	Levon Kirkland	.05	.01
❑ 390	Carnell Lake	.05	.01
❑ 391	Greg Lloyd	.10	.02
❑ 392	Neil O'Donnell	.25	.08
❑ 393	Darren Perry	.05	.01
❑ 394	Dwight Stone	.05	.01
❑ 395	Leroy Thompson	.05	.01
❑ 396	Rod Woodson	.10	.02
❑ 397	Marion Butts	.05	.01
❑ 398	John Carney	.05	.01
❑ 399	Darren Carrington	.05	.01
❑ 400	Burt Grossman	.05	.01
❑ 401	Courtney Hall	.05	.01
❑ 402	Ronnie Harmon	.05	.01
❑ 403	Stan Humphries	.10	.02
❑ 404	Shawn Jefferson	.05	.01
❑ 405	Vance Johnson	.05	.01
❑ 406	Chris Mims	.05	.01
❑ 407	Leslie O'Neal	.05	.01
❑ 408	Stanley Richard	.05	.01
❑ 409	Junior Seau	.25	.08
❑ 410	Harris Barton	.05	.01
❑ 411	Dennis Brown	.05	.01
❑ 412	Eric Davis	.05	.01
❑ 413	Merton Hanks	.10	.02
❑ 414	John Johnson	.05	.01
❑ 415	Brent Jones	.10	.02
❑ 416	Marc Logan	.05	.01
❑ 417	Tim McDonald	.05	.01
❑ 418	Gary Plummer	.05	.01

❑ 419 Tom Rathman	.05	.01
❑ 420 Jerry Rice	1.00	.40
❑ 421 Bill Romanowski	.05	.01
❑ 422 Jesse Sapolu	.05	.01
❑ 423 Dana Stubblefield	.10	.02
❑ 424 John Taylor	.10	.02
❑ 425 Steve Wallace	.05	.01
❑ 426 Ted Washington	.05	.01
❑ 427 Ricky Watters	.10	.02
❑ 428 Troy Wilson RC	.05	.01
❑ 429 Steve Young	.75	.30
❑ 430 Howard Ballard	.05	.01
❑ 431 Michael Bates	.05	.01
❑ 432 Robert Blackmon	.05	.01
❑ 433 Brian Blades	.10	.02
❑ 434 Ferrell Edmunds	.05	.01
❑ 435 Carlton Gray	.05	.01
❑ 436 Patrick Hunter	.05	.01
❑ 437 Cortez Kennedy	.10	.02
❑ 438 Kelvin Martin	.05	.01
❑ 439 Rick Mirer	.25	.08
❑ 440 Nate Odomes	.05	.01
❑ 441 Ray Roberts	.05	.01
❑ 442 Eugene Robinson	.05	.01
❑ 443 Rod Stephens	.05	.01
❑ 444 Chris Warren	.10	.02
❑ 445 John L. Williams	.05	.01
❑ 446 Terry Wooden	.05	.01
❑ 447 Marty Carter	.05	.01
❑ 448 Reggie Cobb	.05	.01
❑ 449 Lawrence Dawsey	.05	.01
❑ 450 Santana Dotson	.10	.02
❑ 451 Craig Erickson	.05	.01
❑ 452 Thomas Everett	.05	.01
❑ 453 Paul Gruber	.05	.01
❑ 454 Courtney Hawkins	.05	.01
❑ 455 Martin Mayhew	.05	.01
❑ 456 Hardy Nickerson	.10	.02
❑ 457 Ricky Reynolds	.05	.01
❑ 458 Vince Workman	.05	.01
❑ 459 Reggie Brooks	.10	.02
❑ 460 Earnest Byner	.05	.01
❑ 461 Andre Collins	.05	.01
❑ 462 Brad Edwards	.05	.01
❑ 463 Kurt Gouveia	.05	.01
❑ 464 Darrell Green	.05	.01
❑ 465 Ken Harvey	.05	.01
❑ 466 Ethan Horton	.05	.01
❑ 467 A.J. Johnson	.05	.01
❑ 468 Tim Johnson	.05	.01
❑ 469 Jim Lachey	.05	.01
❑ 470 Chip Lohmiller	.05	.01
❑ 471 Art Monk	.10	.02
❑ 472 Sterling Palmer RC	.05	.01
❑ 473 Mark Rypien	.05	.01
❑ 474 Ricky Sanders	.05	.01
❑ 475 Checklist 1-106	.05	.01
❑ 476 Checklist 107-214	.05	.01
❑ 477 Checklist 215-317	.05	.01
❑ 478 Checklist 318-409	.05	.01
❑ 479 Checklist 410-480/Inserts	.05	.01
❑ 480 Inserts Checklist	.05	.01
❑ P244 Jerome Bettis Promo	1.00	.40

1995 Fleer

❑ COMPLETE SET (400)	25.00	10.00
❑ 1 Michael Bankston	.10	.02
❑ 2 Larry Centers	.20	.07
❑ 3 Gary Clark	.10	.02
❑ 4 Eric Hill	.10	.02
❑ 5 Seth Joyner	.10	.02
❑ 6 Dave Krieg	.10	.02
❑ 7 Lorenzo Lynch	.10	.02
❑ 8 Jamir Miller	.10	.02
❑ 9 Ronald Moore	.10	.02
❑ 10 Ricky Proehl	.10	.02
❑ 11 Clyde Simmons	.10	.02
❑ 12 Eric Swann	.20	.07
❑ 13 Aeneas Williams	.10	.02
❑ 14 J.J. Birden	.10	.02
❑ 15 Chris Doleman	.10	.02
❑ 16 Bert Emanuel	.30	.10
❑ 17 Jumpy Geathers	.10	.02
❑ 18 Jeff George	.20	.07
❑ 19 Roger Harper	.10	.02
❑ 20 Craig Heyward	.20	.07
❑ 21 Pierce Holt	.10	.02
❑ 22 D.J. Johnson	.10	.02
❑ 23 Terance Mathis	.20	.07
❑ 24 Clay Matthews	.20	.07
❑ 25 Andre Rison	.20	.07
❑ 26 Chuck Smith	.10	.02
❑ 27 Jessie Tuggle	.10	.02
❑ 28 Cornelius Bennett	.20	.07
❑ 29 Bucky Brooks	.10	.02
❑ 30 Jeff Burris	.10	.02
❑ 31 Russell Copeland	.10	.02
❑ 32 Matt Darby	.10	.02
❑ 33 Phil Hansen	.10	.02
❑ 34 Henry Jones	.10	.02
❑ 35 Jim Kelly	.30	.10
❑ 36 Mark Maddox RC	.10	.02
❑ 37 Bryce Paup	.20	.07
❑ 38 Andre Reed	.20	.07
❑ 39 Bruce Smith	.30	.10
❑ 40 Darryl Talley	.10	.02
❑ 41 Dewell Brewer RC	.10	.02
❑ 42 Mike Fox	.10	.02
❑ 43 Eric Guliford	.10	.02
❑ 44 Lamar Lathon	.10	.02
❑ 45 Pete Metzelaars	.10	.02
❑ 46 Sam Mills	.20	.07
❑ 47 Frank Reich	.10	.02
❑ 48 Rod Smith DB	.20	.07
❑ 49 Jack Trudeau	.10	.02
❑ 50 Trace Armstrong	.10	.02
❑ 51 Joe Cain	.10	.02
❑ 52 Mark Carrier DB	.10	.02
❑ 53 Curtis Conway	.30	.10
❑ 54 Shaun Gayle	.10	.02
❑ 55 Jeff Graham	.10	.02
❑ 56 Raymont Harris	.10	.02
❑ 57 Erik Kramer	.10	.02
❑ 58 Lewis Tillman	.10	.02
❑ 59 Tom Waddle	.10	.02
❑ 60 Steve Walsh	.10	.02
❑ 61 Donnell Woolford	.10	.02
❑ 62 Chris Zorich	.10	.02
❑ 63 Jeff Blake RC	.60	.25
❑ 64 Mike Brim	.10	.02
❑ 65 Steve Broussard	.10	.02
❑ 66 James Francis	.10	.02
❑ 67 Ricardo McDonald	.10	.02
❑ 68 Tony McGee	.10	.02
❑ 69 Darnay Scott	.20	.07
❑ 71 Steve Tovar	.10	.02
❑ 72 Dan Wilkinson	.20	.07
❑ 73 Alfred Williams	.10	.02
❑ 74 Darryl Williams	.10	.02
❑ 75 Derrick Alexander WR	.30	.10
❑ 76 Randy Baldwin	.10	.02
❑ 77 Carl Banks	.10	.02
❑ 78 Rob Burnett	.10	.02
❑ 79 Steve Everitt	.10	.02
❑ 80 Leroy Hoard	.10	.02
❑ 81 Michael Jackson	.20	.07
❑ 82 Pepper Johnson	.10	.02
❑ 83 Tony Jones T	.10	.02
❑ 84 Antonio Langham	.10	.02
❑ 85 Eric Metcalf	.20	.07
❑ 86 Stevon Moore	.10	.02
❑ 87 Anthony Pleasant	.10	.02
❑ 88 Vinny Testaverde	.20	.07
❑ 89 Eric Turner	.10	.02
❑ 90 Troy Aikman	1.00	.40
❑ 91 Charles Haley	.20	.07
❑ 92 Michael Irvin	.30	.10
❑ 93 Daryl Johnston	.20	.07
❑ 94 Robert Jones	.10	.02
❑ 95 Leon Lett	.10	.02
❑ 96 Russell Maryland	.10	.02
❑ 97 Nate Newton	.20	.07
❑ 98 Jay Novacek	.20	.07
❑ 99 Darrin Smith	.10	.02
❑ 100 Emmitt Smith	1.50	.60
❑ 101 Kevin Smith	.10	.02
❑ 102 Erik Williams	.10	.02
❑ 103 Kevin Williams WR	.20	.07
❑ 104 Darren Woodson	.20	.07
❑ 105 Elijah Alexander	.10	.02
❑ 106 Steve Atwater	.10	.02
❑ 107 Ray Crockett	.10	.02
❑ 108 Shane Dronett	.10	.02
❑ 109 Jason Elam	.20	.07
❑ 110 John Elway	2.00	.75
❑ 111 Simon Fletcher	.10	.02
❑ 112 Glyn Milburn	.10	.02
❑ 113 Anthony Miller	.20	.07
❑ 114 Michael Dean Perry	.10	.02
❑ 115 Mike Pritchard	.10	.02
❑ 116 Derek Russell	.10	.02
❑ 117 Leonard Russell	.10	.02
❑ 118 Shannon Sharpe	.20	.07
❑ 119 Gary Zimmerman	.10	.02
❑ 120 Bennie Blades	.10	.02
❑ 121 Lomas Brown	.10	.02
❑ 122 Willie Clay	.10	.02
❑ 123 Mike Johnson	.10	.02
❑ 124 Robert Massey	.10	.02
❑ 125 Scott Mitchell	.20	.07
❑ 126 Herman Moore	.30	.10
❑ 127 Brett Perriman	.20	.07
❑ 128 Robert Porcher	.10	.02
❑ 129 Barry Sanders	1.50	.60
❑ 130 Chris Spielman	.20	.07
❑ 131 Henry Thomas	.10	.02
❑ 132 Edgar Bennett	.20	.07
❑ 134 LeRoy Butler	.10	.02
❑ 135 Brett Favre	2.00	.75
❑ 136 Sean Jones	.10	.02
❑ 137 John Jurkovic	.10	.02
❑ 138 George Koonce	.10	.02
❑ 139 Wayne Simmons	.10	.02
❑ 140 George Teague	.10	.02
❑ 141 Reggie White	.30	.10
❑ 142 Micheal Barrow	.10	.02
❑ 143 Gary Brown	.10	.02
❑ 144 Cody Carlson	.10	.02
❑ 145 Ray Childress	.10	.02
❑ 146 Cris Dishman	.10	.02
❑ 147 Ernest Givins	.10	.02
❑ 148 Mel Gray	.10	.02
❑ 149 Darryll Lewis	.10	.02
❑ 150 Bruce Matthews	.10	.02
❑ 151 Marcus Robertson	.10	.02
❑ 152 Webster Slaughter	.10	.02
❑ 153 Al Smith	.10	.02
❑ 154 Mark Stepnoski	.10	.02
❑ 155 Trev Alberts	.10	.02
❑ 156 Flipper Anderson	.10	.02
❑ 157 Jason Belser	.10	.02
❑ 158 Tony Bennett	.10	.02
❑ 159 Ray Buchanan	.10	.02
❑ 160 Quentin Coryatt	.20	.07
❑ 161 Sean Dawkins	.20	.07
❑ 162 Steve Emtman	.10	.02
❑ 163 Marshall Faulk	1.25	.50
❑ 164 Stephen Grant RC	.10	.02
❑ 165 Jim Harbaugh	.20	.07
❑ 166 Jeff Herrod	.10	.02
❑ 167 Tony Siragusa	.10	.02
❑ 168 Steve Beuerlein	.20	.07
❑ 169 Darren Carrington	.10	.02
❑ 170 Reggie Cobb	.10	.02
❑ 171 Kelvin Martin	.10	.02
❑ 172 Kelvin Pritchett	.10	.02
❑ 173 Joel Smeenge	.10	.02
❑ 174 James Williams LB	.10	.02
❑ 175 Marcus Allen	.30	.10
❑ 176 Kimble Anders	.20	.07
❑ 177 Dale Carter	.20	.07
❑ 178 Mark Collins	.10	.02
❑ 179 Willie Davis	.20	.07
❑ 180 Lake Dawson	.20	.07
❑ 181 Greg Hill	.20	.07
❑ 182 Darren Mickell	.10	.02
❑ 183 Joe Montana	2.00	.75
❑ 184 Tracy Simien	.10	.02
❑ 185 Neil Smith	.20	.07
❑ 186 William White	.10	.02

❑ 187 Greg Biekert .10 .02
❑ 188 Tim Brown .30 .10
❑ 189 Rob Fredrickson .10 .02
❑ 190 Andrew Glover RC .10 .02
❑ 191 Nolan Harrison .10 .02
❑ 192 Jeff Hostetler .20 .07
❑ 193 Rocket Ismail .20 .07
❑ 194 Terry McDaniel .10 .02
❑ 195 Chester McGlockton .20 .07
❑ 196 Winston Moss .10 .02
❑ 197 Anthony Smith .10 .02
❑ 198 Harvey Williams .10 .02
❑ 199 Steve Wisniewski .10 .02
❑ 200 Johnny Bailey .10 .02
❑ 201 Jerome Bettis .30 .10
❑ 202 Isaac Bruce .50 .20
❑ 203 Shane Conlan .10 .02
❑ 204 Troy Drayton .10 .02
❑ 205 Sean Gilbert .20 .07
❑ 206 Jessie Hester .10 .02
❑ 207 Jimmie Jones .10 .02
❑ 208 Todd Lyght .10 .02
❑ 209 Chris Miller .10 .02
❑ 210 Roman Phifer .10 .02
❑ 211 Marquez Pope .10 .02
❑ 212 Robert Young .10 .02
❑ 213 Gene Atkins .10 .02
❑ 214 Aubrey Beavers .10 .02
❑ 215 Tim Bowens .10 .02
❑ 216 Bryan Cox .10 .02
❑ 217 Jeff Cross .10 .02
❑ 218 Irving Fryar .20 .07
❑ 219 Eric Green .10 .02
❑ 220 Mark Ingram .10 .02
❑ 221 Terry Kirby .20 .07
❑ 222 Dan Marino 2.00 .75
❑ 223 O.J. McDuffie .30 .10
❑ 224 Bernie Parmalee .20 .07
❑ 225 Keith Sims .10 .02
❑ 226 Irving Spikes .20 .07
❑ 227 Michael Stewart .10 .02
❑ 228 Troy Vincent .10 .02
❑ 229 Richmond Webb .10 .02
❑ 230 Terry Allen .20 .07
❑ 231 Cris Carter .30 .10
❑ 232 Jack Del Rio .10 .02
❑ 233 Vencie Glenn .10 .02
❑ 234 Qadry Ismail .20 .07
❑ 235 Carlos Jenkins .10 .02
❑ 236 Ed McDaniel .10 .02
❑ 237 Randall McDaniel .10 .02
❑ 238 Warren Moon .20 .07
❑ 239 Anthony Parker .10 .02
❑ 240 John Randle .20 .07
❑ 241 Jake Reed .20 .07
❑ 242 Fuad Reveiz .10 .02
❑ 243 Broderick Thomas .10 .02
❑ 244 Dewayne Washington .20 .07
❑ 245 Bruce Armstrong .10 .02
❑ 246 Drew Bledsoe .60 .25
❑ 247 Vincent Brisby .10 .02
❑ 248 Vincent Brown .10 .02
❑ 249 Marion Butts .10 .02
❑ 250 Ben Coates .20 .07
❑ 251 Tim Goad .10 .02
❑ 252 Myron Guyton .10 .02
❑ 253 Maurice Hurst .10 .02
❑ 254 Mike Jones .10 .02
❑ 255 Willie McGinest .20 .07
❑ 256 Dave Meggett .10 .02
❑ 257 Ricky Reynolds .10 .02
❑ 258 Chris Slade .20 .07
❑ 259 Michael Timpson .10 .02
❑ 260 Mario Bates .20 .07
❑ 261 Derek Brown RBK .10 2
❑ 262 Darion Conner .10 .02
❑ 263 Quinn Early .20 .07
❑ 264 Jim Everett .10 .02
❑ 265 Michael Haynes .20 .07
❑ 266 Tyrone Hughes .20 .07
❑ 267 Joe Johnson .10 .02
❑ 268 Wayne Martin .10 .02
❑ 269 Willie Roaf .10 .02
❑ 270 Irv Smith .10 .02
❑ 271 Jimmy Spencer .10 .02
❑ 272 Winfred Tubbs .10 .02
❑ 273 Renaldo Turnbull .10 .02
❑ 274 Michael Brooks .10 .02
❑ 275 Dave Brown .20 .07
❑ 276 Chris Calloway .10 .02
❑ 277 Jesse Campbell .10 .02
❑ 278 Howard Cross .10 .02
❑ 279 John Elliott .10 .02
❑ 280 Keith Hamilton .10 .02
❑ 281 Rodney Hampton .20 .07
❑ 282 Thomas Lewis .20 .07
❑ 283 Thomas Randolph .10 .02
❑ 284 Mike Sherrard .10 .02
❑ 285 Michael Strahan .30 .10
❑ 286 Brad Baxter .10 .02
❑ 287 Tony Casillas .10 .02
❑ 288 Kyle Clifton .10 .02
❑ 289 Boomer Esiason .20 .07
❑ 290 Aaron Glenn .10 .02
❑ 291 Bobby Houston .10 .02
❑ 292 Johnny Johnson .10 .02
❑ 293 Jeff Lageman .10 .02
❑ 294 Mo Lewis .10 .02
❑ 295 Johnny Mitchell .10 .02
❑ 296 Rob Moore .20 .07
❑ 297 Marcus Turner .10 .02
❑ 298 Marvin Washington .10 .02
❑ 299 Eric Allen .10 .02
❑ 300 Fred Barnett .20 .07
❑ 301 Randall Cunningham .30 .10
❑ 302 Byron Evans .10 .02
❑ 303 William Fuller .10 .02
❑ 304 Charlie Garner .30 .10
❑ 305 Andy Harmon .10 .02
❑ 306 Greg Jackson .10 .02
❑ 307 Bill Romanowski .10 .02
❑ 308 William Thomas .10 .02
❑ 309 Herschel Walker .20 .07
❑ 310 Calvin Williams .20 .07
❑ 311 Michael Zordich .10 .02
❑ 312 Chad Brown .20 .07
❑ 313 Dermontti Dawson .20 .07
❑ 314 Barry Foster .20 .07
❑ 315 Kevin Greene .20 .07
❑ 316 Charles Johnson .20 .07
❑ 317 Levon Kirkland .10 .02
❑ 318 Carnell Lake .10 .02
❑ 319 Greg Lloyd .20 .07
❑ 320 Byron Bam Morris .10 .02
❑ 321 Neil O'Donnell .20 .07
❑ 322 Darren Perry .10 .02
❑ 323 Ray Seals .10 .02
❑ 324 John L. Williams .10 .02
❑ 325 Rod Woodson .20 .07
❑ 326 John Carney .10 .02
❑ 327 Andre Coleman .10 .02
❑ 328 Courtney Hall .10 .02
❑ 329 Ronnie Harmon .10 .02
❑ 330 Dwayne Harper .10 .02
❑ 331 Stan Humphries .20 .07
❑ 332 Shawn Jefferson .10 .02
❑ 333 Tony Martin .20 .07
❑ 334 Natrone Means .20 .07
❑ 335 Chris Mims .10 .02
❑ 336 Leslie O'Neal .20 .07
❑ 337 Alfred Pupunu RC .10 .02
❑ 338 Junior Seau .30 .10
❑ 339 Mark Seay .20 .07
❑ 340 Eric Davis .10 .02
❑ 341 William Floyd .20 .07
❑ 342 Merton Hanks .10 .02
❑ 343 Rickey Jackson .10 .02
❑ 344 Brent Jones .10 .02
❑ 345 Tim McDonald .10 .02
❑ 346 Ken Norton Jr. .20 .07
❑ 347 Gary Plummer .10 .02
❑ 348 Jerry Rice 1.00 .40
❑ 349 Deion Sanders .40 .15
❑ 350 Jesse Sapolu .10 .02
❑ 351 Dana Stubblefield .20 .07
❑ 352 John Taylor .10 .02
❑ 353 Steve Wallace .10 .02
❑ 354 Ricky Watters .20 .07
❑ 355 Lee Woodall .10 .02
❑ 356 Bryant Young .20 .07
❑ 357 Steve Young .75 .30
❑ 358 Sam Adams .10 .02
❑ 359 Howard Ballard .10 .02
❑ 360 Robert Blackmon .10 .02
❑ 361 Brian Blades .20 .07
❑ 362 Carlton Gray .10 .02
❑ 363 Cortez Kennedy .20 .07
❑ 364 Rick Mirer .20 .07
❑ 365 Eugene Robinson .10 .02
❑ 366 Chris Warren .20 .07
❑ 367 Terry Wooden .10 .02
❑ 368 Brad Culpepper .10 .02
❑ 369 Lawrence Dawsey .10 .02
❑ 370 Trent Dilfer .30 .10
❑ 371 Santana Dotson .10 .02
❑ 372 Craig Erickson .10 .02
❑ 373 Thomas Everett .10 .02
❑ 374 Paul Gruber .10 .02
❑ 375 Alvin Harper .10 .02
❑ 376 Jackie Harris .10 .02
❑ 377 Courtney Hawkins .10 .02
❑ 378 Martin Mayhew .10 .02
❑ 379 Hardy Nickerson .10 .02
❑ 380 Errict Rhett .20 .07
❑ 381 Charles Wilson .10 .02
❑ 382 Reggie Brooks .20 .07
❑ 383 Tom Carter .10 .02
❑ 384 Andre Collins .10 .02
❑ 385 Henry Ellard .20 .07
❑ 386 Ricky Ervins .10 .02
❑ 387 Darrell Green .10 .02
❑ 388 Ken Harvey .10 .02
❑ 389 Brian Mitchell .10 .02
❑ 390 Stanley Richard .10 .02
❑ 391 Heath Shuler .20 .07
❑ 392 Rod Stephens .10 .02
❑ 393 Tyronne Stowe .10 .02
❑ 394 Tydus Winans .10 .02
❑ 395 Tony Woods .10 .02
❑ 396 Checklist .10 .02
❑ 397 Checklist .10 .02
❑ 398 Checklist .10 .02
❑ 399 Checklist .10 .02
❑ 400 Checklist .10 .02
❑ P1 Promo Panel/Bettis/Mirer/R.Brooks 2.50 1.00

1996 Fleer

❑ COMPLETE SET (200) 20.00 7.50
❑ 1 Garrison Hearst .20 .07
❑ 2 Rob Moore .20 .07
❑ 3 Frank Sanders .20 .07
❑ 4 Eric Swann .10 .02
❑ 5 Aeneas Williams .10 .02
❑ 6 Jeff George .20 .07
❑ 7 Craig Heyward .10 .02
❑ 8 Terance Mathis .10 .02
❑ 9 Eric Metcalf .10 .02
❑ 10 Michael Jackson .20 .07
❑ 11 Andre Rison .20 .07
❑ 12 Vinny Testaverde .20 .07
❑ 13 Eric Turner .10 .02
❑ 14 Darick Holmes .10 .02
❑ 15 Jim Kelly .30 .10
❑ 16 Bryce Paup .10 .02
❑ 17 Bruce Smith .20 .07
❑ 18 Thurman Thomas .30 .10
❑ 19 Kerry Collins .30 .10
❑ 20 Lamar Lathon .10 .02
❑ 21 Derrick Moore .10 .02
❑ 22 Tyrone Poole .10 .02
❑ 23 Curtis Conway .30 .10
❑ 24 Bryan Cox .10 .02
❑ 25 Erik Kramer .10 .02
❑ 26 Rashaan Salaam .20 .07
❑ 27 Jeff Blake .30 .10
❑ 28 Ki-Jana Carter .20 .07
❑ 29 Carl Pickens .20 .07
❑ 30 Darnay Scott .20 .07
❑ 31 Troy Aikman .75 .30

❑ 32 Charles Haley .20 .07
❑ 33 Michael Irvin .30 .10
❑ 34 Daryl Johnston .20 .07
❑ 35 Jay Novacek .10 .02
❑ 36 Deion Sanders .40 .15
❑ 37 Emmitt Smith 1.25 .50
❑ 38 Steve Atwater .10 .02
❑ 39 Terrell Davis .60 .25
❑ 40 John Elway 1.50 .60
❑ 41 Anthony Miller .20 .07
❑ 42 Shannon Sharpe .20 .07
❑ 43 Scott Mitchell .20 .07
❑ 44 Herman Moore .20 .07
❑ 45 Johnnie Morton .20 .07
❑ 46 Brett Perriman .10 .02
❑ 47 Barry Sanders 1.25 .50
❑ 48 Edgar Bennett .20 .07
❑ 49 Robert Brooks .30 .10
❑ 50 Mark Chmura .20 .07
❑ 51 Brett Favre 1.50 .60
❑ 52 Reggie White .30 .10
❑ 53 Mel Gray .10 .02
❑ 54 Steve McNair .60 .25
❑ 55 Chris Sanders .20 .07
❑ 56 Rodney Thomas .10 .02
❑ 57 Quentin Coryatt .10 .02
❑ 58 Sean Dawkins .10 .02
❑ 59 Ken Dilger .20 .07
❑ 60 Marshall Faulk .40 .15
❑ 61 Jim Harbaugh .20 .07
❑ 62 Tony Boselli .10 .02
❑ 63 Mark Brunell .50 .20
❑ 64 Natrone Means .20 .07
❑ 65 James O.Stewart .20 .07
❑ 66 Marcus Allen .30 .10
❑ 67 Steve Bono .10 .02
❑ 68 Neil Smith .20 .07
❑ 69 Derrick Thomas .30 .10
❑ 70 Tamarick Vanover .20 .07
❑ 71 Fred Barnett .10 .02
❑ 72 Eric Green .10 .02
❑ 73 Dan Marino 1.50 .60
❑ 74 O.J. McDuffie .20 .07
❑ 75 Bernie Parmalee .10 .02
❑ 76 Cris Carter .30 .10
❑ 77 Qadry Ismail .20 .07
❑ 78 Warren Moon .20 .07
❑ 79 Jake Reed .20 .07
❑ 80 Robert Smith .20 .07
❑ 81 Drew Bledsoe .50 .20
❑ 82 Vincent Brisby .10 .02
❑ 83 Ben Coates .20 .07
❑ 84 Curtis Martin .60 .25
❑ 85 Dave Meggett .10 .02
❑ 86 Mario Bates .20 .07
❑ 87 Jim Everett .10 .02
❑ 88 Michael Haynes .10 .02
❑ 89 Renaldo Turnbull .10 .02
❑ 90 Dave Brown .10 .02
❑ 91 Rodney Hampton .20 .07
❑ 92 Thomas Lewis .10 .02
❑ 93 Tyrone Wheatley .20 .07
❑ 94 Kyle Brady .10 .02
❑ 95 Hugh Douglas .20 .07
❑ 96 Aaron Glenn .10 .02
❑ 97 Jeff Graham .10 .02
❑ 98 Adrian Murrell .20 .07
❑ 99 Neil O'Donnell .20 .07
❑ 100 Tim Brown .30 .10
❑ 101 Jeff Hostetler .10 .02
❑ 102 Napoleon Kaufman .30 .10
❑ 103 Chester McGlockton .10 .02
❑ 104 Harvey Williams .10 .02
❑ 105 William Fuller .10 .02
❑ 106 Charlie Garner .20 .07
❑ 107 Ricky Watters .20 .07
❑ 108 Calvin Williams .10 .02
❑ 109 Jerome Bettis .30 .10
❑ 110 Greg Lloyd .20 .07
❑ 111 Byron Bam Morris .10 .02
❑ 112 Kordell Stewart .30 .10
❑ 113 Yancey Thigpen .20 .07
❑ 114 Rod Woodson .20 .07
❑ 115 Isaac Bruce .30 .10
❑ 116 Troy Drayton .10 .02
❑ 117 Leslie O'Neal .10 .02
❑ 118 Steve Walsh .10 .02
❑ 119 Marco Coleman .10 .02
❑ 120 Aaron Hayden .10 .02
❑ 121 Stan Humphries .20 .07
❑ 122 Junior Seau .30 .10
❑ 123 William Floyd .20 .07
❑ 124 Brent Jones .10 .02
❑ 125 Ken Norton .10 .02
❑ 126 Jerry Rice .75 .30
❑ 127 J.J. Stokes .30 .10
❑ 128 Steve Young .60 .25
❑ 129 Brian Blades .10 .02
❑ 130 Joey Galloway .30 .10
❑ 131 Rick Mirer .20 .07
❑ 132 Chris Warren .20 .07
❑ 133 Trent Dilfer .30 .10
❑ 134 Alvin Harper .10 .02
❑ 135 Hardy Nickerson .10 .02
❑ 136 Errict Rhett .20 .07
❑ 137 Terry Allen .20 .07
❑ 138 Henry Ellard .10 .02
❑ 139 Heath Shuler .20 .07
❑ 140 Michael Westbrook .30 .10
❑ 141 Karim Abdul-Jabbar RC .30 .10
❑ 142 Mike Alstott RC 1.00 .40
❑ 143 Marco Battaglia RC .10 .02
❑ 144 Tim Biakabutuka RC .30 .10
❑ 145 Tony Brackens RC .30 .10
❑ 146 Duane Clemons RC .10 .02
❑ 147 Ernie Conwell RC .10 .02
❑ 148 Chris Darkins RC .10 .02
❑ 149 Stephen Davis RC 1.50 .60
❑ 150 Brian Dawkins RC 1.25 .50
❑ 151 Rickey Dudley RC .30 .10
❑ 152 Jason Dunn RC .20 .07
❑ 153 Bobby Engram RC .30 .10
❑ 154 Daryl Gardener RC .10 .02
❑ 155 Eddie George RC 1.25 .50
❑ 156 Terry Glenn RC 1.00 .40
❑ 157 Kevin Hardy RC .30 .10
❑ 158 Walt Harris RC .10 .02
❑ 159 Marvin Harrison RC 2.50 1.00
❑ 160 Bobby Hoying RC .30 .10
❑ 161 Keyshawn Johnson RC 1.00 .40
❑ 162 Cedric Jones RC .10 .02
❑ 163 Marcus Jones RC .10 .02
❑ 164 Eddie Kennison RC .30 .10
❑ 165 Ray Lewis RC 2.50 1.00
❑ 166 Derrick Mayes RC .30 .10
❑ 167 Leeland McElroy RC .20 .07
❑ 168 Johnny McWilliams RC .20 .07
❑ 169 John Mobley RC .10 .02
❑ 170 Alex Molden RC .10 .02
❑ 171 Eric Moulds RC 1.25 .50
❑ 172 Muhsin Muhammad RC .75 .30
❑ 173 Jonathan Ogden RC .30 .10
❑ 174 Lawrence Phillips RC .30 .10
❑ 175 Stanley Pritchett RC .20 .07
❑ 176 Simeon Rice RC .75 .30
❑ 177 Bryan Still RC .20 .07
❑ 178 Amani Toomer RC 1.00 .40
❑ 179 Regan Upshaw RC .10 .02
❑ 180 Alex Van Dyke RC .20 .07
❑ 181 Barry Sanders PFW .60 .25
❑ 182 Marcus Allen PFW .30 .10
❑ 183 Bryce Paup PFW .10 .02
❑ 184 Jerry Rice PFW .40 .15
❑ 185 D.Howard/B.Christian PFW .20 .07
❑ 186 Leon Lett PFW .10 .02
❑ 187 Brett Favre PFW .75 .30
❑ 188 G.Lloyd/D.Thomas PFW .10 .02
❑ 189 Jeff Blake PFW .20 .07
❑ 190 Emmitt Smith PFW .60 .25
❑ 191 J.Elway/J.Hostetler PFW .40 .15
❑ 192 Chiefs PFW .10 .02
❑ 193 Marshall Faulk PFW .30 .10
❑ 194 T.Aikman/S.Young PFW .40 .15
❑ 195 Dan Marino PFW .75 .30
❑ 196 Donta Jones PFW .10 .02
❑ 197 Jim Kelly PFW .30 .10
❑ 198 Checklist .10 .02
❑ 199 Checklist .10 .02
❑ 200 Checklist .10 .02
❑ P1 Promo Sheet/WFloyd/TDil/Favre 4.00 1.50

1997 Fleer

❑ COMPLETE SET (450) 40.00 15.00
❑ 1 Mark Brunell 1.00 .40
❑ 2 Andre Reed .50 .20
❑ 3 Darrell Green .50 .20
❑ 4 Mario Bates .30 .10
❑ 5 Eddie George .75 .30
❑ 6 Cris Carter .75 .30
❑ 7 Terrell Owens 1.00 .40
❑ 8 Bill Romanowski .30 .10
❑ 9 Isaac Bruce .75 .30
❑ 10 Eric Curry .30 .10
❑ 11 Danny Kanell .30 .10
❑ 12 Ki-Jana Carter .30 .10
❑ 13 Antonio Freeman .75 .30
❑ 14 Ricky Watters .50 .20
❑ 15 Ty Law .50 .20
❑ 16 Alonzo Spellman .30 .10
❑ 17 Kordell Stewart .75 .30
❑ 18 Jerry Rice 1.50 .60
❑ 19 Derrick Alexander WR .50 .20
❑ 20 Barry Sanders 2.50 1.00
❑ 21 Keyshawn Johnson .75 .30
❑ 22 Emmitt Smith 2.50 1.00
❑ 23 Ricky Proehl .30 .10
❑ 24 Daryl Gardener .30 .10
❑ 25 Dan Saleaumua .30 .10
❑ 26 Kevin Greene .50 .20
❑ 27 Junior Seau .75 .30
❑ 28 Randall McDaniel .30 .10
❑ 29 Marshall Faulk 1.00 .40
❑ 30 Lorenzo Lynch .30 .10
❑ 31 Terance Mathis .50 .20
❑ 32 Warren Sapp .50 .20
❑ 33 Chris Sanders .30 .10
❑ 34 Tom Carter .30 .10
❑ 35 Aeneas Williams .30 .10
❑ 36 Lawrence Phillips .30 .10
❑ 37 John Elway 3.00 1.25
❑ 38 Stanley Richard .30 .10
❑ 39 Darryl Williams .30 .10
❑ 40 Phillippi Sparks .30 .10
❑ 41 Tedy Bruschi 1.50 .60
❑ 42 Merton Hanks .30 .10
❑ 43 Ray Lewis 1.25 .50
❑ 44 Erik Williams .30 .10
❑ 45 Jason Gildon .30 .10
❑ 46 George Koonce .30 .10
❑ 47 Louis Oliver .30 .10
❑ 48 Muhsin Muhammad .50 .20
❑ 49 Daryl Hobbs .30 .10
❑ 50 Terry Glenn .75 .30
❑ 51 Marvin Harrison .75 .30
❑ 52 Brian Dawkins .75 .30
❑ 53 Dale Carter .30 .10
❑ 54 Alex Molden .30 .10
❑ 55 Raymont Harris .30 .10
❑ 56 Jeff Burris .30 .10
❑ 57 Don Beebe .30 .10
❑ 58 Jamir Miller .30 .10
❑ 59 Carl Pickens .50 .20
❑ 60 Antonio London .30 .10
❑ 61 Courtney Hall .30 .10
❑ 62 Derrick Brooks .75 .30
❑ 63 Chris Boniol .30 .10
❑ 64 Jeff Lageman .30 .10
❑ 65 Roy Barker .30 .10
❑ 66 Devin Bush .30 .10
❑ 67 Aaron Glenn .30 .10
❑ 68 Wayne Simmons .30 .10
❑ 69 Steve Atwater .30 .10
❑ 70 Jimmie Jones .30 .10
❑ 71 Mark Carrier WR .30 .10
❑ 72 Chris Chandler .50 .20
❑ 73 Andy Harmon .30 .10
❑ 74 John Friesz .30 .10
❑ 75 Karim Abdul-Jabbar .50 .20
❑ 76 Levon Kirkland .30 .10
❑ 77 Torrance Small .30 .10

❑ 78	Harvey Williams	.30	.10
❑ 79	Chris Calloway	.30	.10
❑ 80	Vinny Testaverde	.50	.20
❑ 81	Bryant Young	.30	.10
❑ 82	Ray Buchanan	.30	.10
❑ 83	Robert Smith	.50	.20
❑ 84	Robert Brooks	.50	.20
❑ 85	Ray Crockett	.30	.10
❑ 86	Bennie Blades	.30	.10
❑ 87	Mark Carrier DB	.30	.10
❑ 88	Mike Tomczak	.30	.10
❑ 89	Darick Holmes	.30	.10
❑ 90	Drew Bledsoe	1.00	.40
❑ 91	Darren Woodson	.30	.10
❑ 92	Dan Wilkinson	.30	.10
❑ 93	Charles Way	.30	.10
❑ 94	Ray Farmer	.30	.10
❑ 95	Marcus Allen	.75	.30
❑ 96	Marco Coleman	.30	.10
❑ 97	Zach Thomas	.75	.30
❑ 98	Wesley Walls	.50	.20
❑ 99	Frank Wycheck	.30	.10
❑ 100	Troy Aikman	1.50	.60
❑ 101	Clyde Simmons	.30	.10
❑ 102	Courtney Hawkins	.30	.10
❑ 103	Chuck Smith	.30	.10
❑ 104	Neil O'Donnell	.50	.20
❑ 105	Kevin Carter	.30	.10
❑ 106	Chris Slade	.30	.10
❑ 107	Jessie Armstead	.30	.10
❑ 108	Sean Dawkins	.30	.10
❑ 109	Robert Blackmon	.30	.10
❑ 110	Kevin Smith	.30	.10
❑ 111	Lonnie Johnson	.30	.10
❑ 112	Craig Newsome	.30	.10
❑ 113	Jonathan Ogden	.30	.10
❑ 114	Chris Zorich	.30	.10
❑ 115	Tim Brown	.75	.30
❑ 116	Fred Barnett	.30	.10
❑ 117	Michael Haynes	.30	.10
❑ 118	Eric Hill	.30	.10
❑ 119	Ronnie Harmon	.30	.10
❑ 120	Sean Gilbert	.30	.10
❑ 121	Derrick Alexander DE	.30	.10
❑ 122	Derrick Thomas	.75	.30
❑ 123	Tyrone Wheatley	.50	.20
❑ 124	Cortez Kennedy	.30	.10
❑ 125	Jeff George	.50	.20
❑ 126	Chad Cota	.30	.10
❑ 127	Gary Zimmerman	.30	.10
❑ 128	Johnnie Morton	.50	.20
❑ 129	Chad Brown	.30	.10
❑ 130	Marvcus Patton	.30	.10
❑ 131	James O.Stewart	.50	.20
❑ 132	Terry Kirby	.50	.20
❑ 133	Chris Mims	.30	.10
❑ 134	William Thomas	.30	.10
❑ 135	Steve Tasker	.30	.10
❑ 136	Jason Belser	.30	.10
❑ 137	Bryan Cox	.30	.10
❑ 138	Jessie Tuggle	.30	.10
❑ 139	Ashley Ambrose	.30	.10
❑ 140	Mark Chmura	.50	.20
❑ 141	Jeff Hostetler	.30	.10
❑ 142	Rich Owens	.30	.10
❑ 143	Willie Davis	.30	.10
❑ 144	Hardy Nickerson	.30	.10
❑ 145	Curtis Martin	1.00	.40
❑ 146	Ken Norton	.30	.10
❑ 147	Victor Green	.30	.10
❑ 148	Anthony Miller	.30	.10
❑ 149	John Kasay	.30	.10
❑ 150	O.J. McDuffie	.50	.20
❑ 151	Darren Perry	.30	.10
❑ 152	Luther Elliss	.30	.10
❑ 153	Greg Hill	.30	.10
❑ 154	John Randle	.50	.20
❑ 155	Stephen Grant	.30	.10
❑ 156	Leon Lett	.30	.10
❑ 157	Darrien Gordon	.30	.10
❑ 158	Ray Zellars	.30	.10
❑ 159	Michael Jackson	.50	.20
❑ 160	Leslie O'Neal	.30	.10
❑ 161	Bruce Smith	.50	.20
❑ 162	Santana Dotson	.30	.10
❑ 163	Bobby Hebert	.30	.10
❑ 164	Keith Hamilton	.30	.10
❑ 165	Tony Boselli	.30	.10
❑ 166	Alfred Williams	.30	.10
❑ 167	Ty Detmer	.50	.20
❑ 168	Chester McGlockton	.30	.10
❑ 169	William Floyd	.50	.20
❑ 170	Bruce Matthews	.30	.10
❑ 171	Simeon Rice	.50	.20
❑ 172	Scott Mitchell	.50	.20
❑ 173	Ricardo McDonald	.30	.10
❑ 174	Tyrone Poole	.30	.10
❑ 175	Greg Lloyd	.30	.10
❑ 176	Bruce Armstrong	.30	.10
❑ 177	Erik Kramer	.30	.10
❑ 178	Kimble Anders	.50	.20
❑ 179	Lamar Smith	.75	.30
❑ 180	Tony Tolbert	.30	.10
❑ 181	Joe Aska	.30	.10
❑ 182	Eric Allen	.30	.10
❑ 183	Eric Turner	.30	.10
❑ 184	Brad Johnson	.75	.30
❑ 185	Tony Martin	.50	.20
❑ 186	Mike Mamula	.30	.10
❑ 187	Irving Spikes	.30	.10
❑ 188	Keith Jackson	.30	.10
❑ 189	Carlton Bailey	.30	.10
❑ 190	Tyrone Braxton	.30	.10
❑ 191	Chad Bratzke	.30	.10
❑ 192	Adrian Murrell	.50	.20
❑ 193	Roman Phifer	.30	.10
❑ 194	Todd Collins	.30	.10
❑ 195	Chris Warren	.50	.20
❑ 196	Kevin Hardy	.30	.10
❑ 197	Rick Mirer	.30	.10
❑ 198	Cornelius Bennett	.30	.10
❑ 199	Jimmy Hitchcock	.30	.10
❑ 200	Michael Irvin	.75	.30
❑ 201	Quentin Coryatt	.30	.10
❑ 202	Reggie White	.75	.30
❑ 203	Larry Centers	.50	.20
❑ 204	Rodney Thomas	.30	.10
❑ 205	Dana Stubblefield	.30	.10
❑ 206	Rod Woodson	.50	.20
❑ 207	Rhett Hall	.30	.10
❑ 208	Steve Tovar	.30	.10
❑ 209	Michael Westbrook	.50	.20
❑ 210	Steve Wisniewski	.30	.10
❑ 211	Carlester Crumpler	.30	.10
❑ 212	Elvis Grbac	.50	.20
❑ 213	Tim Bowens	.30	.10
❑ 214	Robert Porcher	.30	.10
❑ 215	John Carney	.30	.10
❑ 216	Anthony Newman	.30	.10
❑ 217	Earnest Byner	.30	.10
❑ 218	Dewayne Washington	.30	.10
❑ 219	Willie Green	.30	.10
❑ 220	Terry Allen	.75	.30
❑ 221	William Fuller	.30	.10
❑ 222	Al Del Greco	.30	.10
❑ 223	Trent Dilfer	.75	.30
❑ 224	Michael Dean Perry	.30	.10
❑ 225	Larry Allen	.30	.10
❑ 226	Mark Bruener	.30	.10
❑ 227	Clay Matthews	.30	.10
❑ 228	Reuben Brown	.30	.10
❑ 229	Edgar Bennett	.50	.20
❑ 230	Neil Smith	.50	.20
❑ 231	Ken Harvey	.30	.10
❑ 232	Kyle Brady	.30	.10
❑ 233	Corey Miller	.30	.10
❑ 234	Tony Siragusa	.30	.10
❑ 235	Todd Sauerbrun	.30	.10
❑ 236	Daniel Stubbs	.30	.10
❑ 237	Robb Thomas	.30	.10
❑ 238	Jimmy Smith	.50	.20
❑ 239	Marquez Pope	.30	.10
❑ 240	Tim Biakabutuka	.50	.20
❑ 241	Jamie Asher	.30	.10
❑ 242	Steve McNair	1.00	.40
❑ 243	Harold Green	.30	.10
❑ 244	Frank Sanders	.50	.20
❑ 245	Joe Johnson	.30	.10
❑ 246	Eric Bieniemy	.30	.10
❑ 247	Kevin Turner	.30	.10
❑ 248	Rickey Dudley	.50	.20
❑ 249	Orlando Thomas	.30	.10
❑ 250	Dan Marino	3.00	1.25
❑ 251	Deion Sanders	.75	.30
❑ 252	Dan Williams	.30	.10
❑ 253	Sam Gash	.30	.10
❑ 254	Lonnie Marts	.30	.10
❑ 255	Mo Lewis	.30	.10
❑ 256	Charles Johnson	.50	.20
❑ 257	Chris Jacke	.30	.10
❑ 258	Keenan McCardell	.50	.20
❑ 259	Donnell Woolford	.30	.10
❑ 260	Terrance Shaw	.30	.10
❑ 261	Jason Dunn	.30	.10
❑ 262	Willie McGinest	.30	.10
❑ 263	Ken Dilger	.30	.10
❑ 264	Keith Lyle	.30	.10
❑ 265	Antonio Langham	.30	.10
❑ 266	Carlton Gray	.30	.10
❑ 267	LeShon Johnson	.30	.10
❑ 268	Thurman Thomas	.75	.30
❑ 269	Jesse Campbell	.30	.10
❑ 270	Carnell Lake	.30	.10
❑ 271	Cris Dishman	.30	.10
❑ 272	Kevin Williams	.30	.10
❑ 273	Troy Brown	.50	.20
❑ 274	William Roaf	.30	.10
❑ 275	Terrell Davis	1.00	.40
❑ 276	Herman Moore	.50	.20
❑ 277	Walt Harris	.30	.10
❑ 278	Mark Collins	.30	.10
❑ 279	Bert Emanuel	.50	.20
❑ 280	Qadry Ismail	.50	.20
❑ 281	Phil Hansen	.30	.10
❑ 282	Steve Young	1.00	.40
❑ 283	Michael Sinclair	.30	.10
❑ 284	Jeff Graham	.30	.10
❑ 285	Sam Mills	.30	.10
❑ 286	Terry McDaniel	.30	.10
❑ 287	Eugene Robinson	.30	.10
❑ 288	Tony Bennett	.30	.10
❑ 289	Daryl Johnston	.50	.20
❑ 290	Eric Swann	.30	.10
❑ 291	Byron Bam Morris	.30	.10
❑ 292	Thomas Lewis	.30	.10
❑ 293	Terrell Fletcher	.30	.10
❑ 294	Gus Frerotte	.30	.10
❑ 295	Stanley Pritchett	.30	.10
❑ 296	Mike Alstott	.75	.30
❑ 297	Will Shields	.30	.10
❑ 298	Errict Rhett	.30	.10
❑ 299	Garrison Hearst	.50	.20
❑ 300	Kerry Collins	.75	.30
❑ 301	Darryll Lewis	.30	.10
❑ 302	Chris T. Jones	.30	.10
❑ 303	Yancey Thigpen	.50	.20
❑ 304	Jackie Harris	.30	.10
❑ 305	Steve Christie	.30	.10
❑ 306	Gilbert Brown	.50	.20
❑ 307	Terry Wooden	.30	.10
❑ 308	Pete Mitchell	.30	.10
❑ 309	Tim McDonald	.30	.10
❑ 310	Jake Reed	.50	.20
❑ 311	Ed McCaffrey	.50	.20
❑ 312	Chris Doleman	.30	.10
❑ 313	Eric Metcalf	.50	.20
❑ 314	Ricky Reynolds	.30	.10
❑ 315	David Sloan	.30	.10
❑ 316	Marvin Washington	.30	.10
❑ 317	Herschel Walker	.50	.20
❑ 318	Michael Timpson	.30	.10
❑ 319	Blaine Bishop	.30	.10
❑ 320	Irv Smith	.30	.10
❑ 321	Seth Joyner	.30	.10
❑ 322	Terrell Buckley	.30	.10
❑ 323	Michael Strahan	.50	.20
❑ 324	Sam Adams	.30	.10
❑ 325	Leslie Shepherd	.30	.10
❑ 326	James Jett	.50	.20
❑ 327	Anthony Pleasant	.30	.10
❑ 328	Lee Woodall	.30	.10
❑ 329	Shannon Sharpe	.50	.20
❑ 330	Jamal Anderson	.75	.30
❑ 331	Andre Hastings	.30	.10
❑ 332	Troy Vincent	.30	.10
❑ 333	Sean LaChapelle	.30	.10
❑ 334	Winslow Oliver	.30	.10
❑ 335	Sean Jones	.30	.10
❑ 336	Darnay Scott	.50	.20
❑ 337	Todd Lyght	.30	.10
❑ 338	Leonard Russell	.30	.10
❑ 339	Nate Newton	.30	.10
❑ 340	Zack Crockett	.30	.10
❑ 341	Amp Lee	.30	.10
❑ 342	Bobby Engram	.50	.20
❑ 343	Mike Hollis	.30	.10
❑ 344	Rodney Hampton	.50	.20

❑	345 Mel Gray	.30	.10
❑	346 Van Malone	.30	.10
❑	347 Aaron Craver	.30	.10
❑	348 Jim Everett	.30	.10
❑	349 Trace Armstrong	.30	.10
❑	350 Pat Swilling	.30	.10
❑	351 Brent Jones	.30	.10
❑	352 Chris Spielman	.30	.10
❑	353 Brett Perriman	.30	.10
❑	354 Brian Kinchen	.30	.10
❑	355 Joey Galloway	.50	.20
❑	356 Henry Ellard	.30	.10
❑	357 Ben Coates	.50	.20
❑	358 Dorsey Levens	.75	.30
❑	359 Charlie Garner	.50	.20
❑	360 Erric Pegram	.30	.10
❑	361 Anthony Johnson	.30	.10
❑	362 Rashaan Salaam	.30	.10
❑	363 Jeff Blake	.50	.20
❑	364 Kent Graham	.30	.10
❑	365 Broderick Thomas	.30	.10
❑	366 Richmond Webb	.30	.10
❑	367 Alfred Pupunu	.30	.10
❑	368 Mark Stepnoski	.30	.10
❑	369 David Dunn	.30	.10
❑	370 Bobby Houston	.30	.10
❑	371 Anthony Parker	.30	.10
❑	372 Quinn Early	.30	.10
❑	373 LeRoy Butler	.30	.10
❑	374 Kurt Gouveia	.30	.10
❑	375 Greg Biekert	.30	.10
❑	376 Jim Harbaugh	.50	.20
❑	377 Eric Bjornson	.30	.10
❑	378 Craig Heyward	.30	.10
❑	379 Steve Bono	.50	.20
❑	380 Tony Banks	.50	.20
❑	381 John Mobley	.30	.10
❑	382 Irving Fryar	.50	.20
❑	383 Dermontti Dawson	.30	.10
❑	384 Eric Davis	.30	.10
❑	385 Natrone Means	.50	.20
❑	386 Jason Sehorn	.50	.20
❑	387 Michael McCrary	.30	.10
❑	388 Corwin Brown	.30	.10
❑	389 Kevin Glover	.30	.10
❑	390 Jerris McPhail	.30	.10
❑	391 Bobby Taylor	.30	.10
❑	392 Tony McGee	.30	.10
❑	393 Curtis Conway	.50	.20
❑	394 Napoleon Kaufman	.75	.30
❑	395 Brian Blades	.30	.10
❑	396 Richard Dent	.30	.10
❑	397 Dave Brown	.30	.10
❑	398 Stan Humphries	.50	.20
❑	399 Stevon Moore	.30	.10
❑	400 Brett Favre	3.00	1.50
❑	401 Jerome Bettis	.75	.30
❑	402 Darrin Smith	.30	.10
❑	403 Chris Penn	.30	.10
❑	404 Rob Moore	.50	.20
❑	405 Micheal Barrow	.30	.10
❑	406 Tony Brackens	.30	.10
❑	407 Wayne Martin	.30	.10
❑	408 Warren Moon	.75	.30
❑	409 Jason Elam	.50	.20
❑	410 J.J. Birden	.30	.10
❑	411 Hugh Douglas	.30	.10
❑	412 Lamar Lathon	.30	.10
❑	413 John Kidd	.30	.10
❑	414 Bryce Paup	.30	.10
❑	415 Shawn Jefferson	.30	.10
❑	416 Leeland McElroy SS	.30	.10
❑	417 Elbert Shelley SS	.30	.10
❑	418 Jermaine Lewis SS	.50	.20
❑	419 Eric Moulds SS	.75	.30
❑	420 Michael Bates SS	.30	.10
❑	421 John Mangum SS	.30	.10
❑	422 Corey Sawyer SS	.30	.10
❑	423 Jim Schwantz SS RC	.30	.10
❑	424 Rod Smith WR SS	.75	.30
❑	425 Glyn Milburn SS	.30	.10
❑	426 Desmond Howard SS	.50	.20
❑	427 John Henry Mills SS RC	.30	.10
❑	428 Cary Blanchard SS RC	.30	.10
❑	429 Chris Hudson SS	.30	.10
❑	430 Tamarick Vanover SS	.50	.20
❑	431 Kirby Dar Dar SS RC	.50	.20
❑	432 David Palmer SS	.30	.10
❑	433 Dave Meggett SS	.30	.10
❑	434 Tyrone Hughes SS	.30	.10
❑	435 Amani Toomer SS	.50	.20
❑	436 Wayne Chrebet SS	.50	.20
❑	437 Carl Kidd RC SS	.30	.10
❑	438 Derrick Witherspoon SS	.30	.10
❑	439 Jahine Arnold SS	.30	.10
❑	440 Andre Coleman SS	.30	.10
❑	441 Jeff Wilkins SS	.30	.10
❑	442 Jay Bellamy SS RC	.30	.10
❑	443 Eddie Kennison SS	.50	.20
❑	444 Nilo Silvan SS	.30	.10
❑	445 Brian Mitchell SS	.30	.10
❑	446 Garrison Hearst CL	.50	.20
❑	447 Napoleon Kaufman CL	.75	.30
❑	448 Brian Mitchell CL	.30	.10
❑	449 Rodney Hampton CL	.30	.10
❑	450 Edgar Bennett CL	.30	.10
❑	S1 Mark Chmura Sample	1.00	.40
❑	AU1 Reggie White AUTO	125.00	75.00

2006 Fleer

❑	1 Anquan Boldin	.30	.10
❑	2 Larry Fitzgerald	.50	.20
❑	3 J.J. Arrington	.30	.10
❑	4 Michael Vick	.60	.25
❑	5 Warrick Dunn	.30	.10
❑	6 Roddy White	.30	.10
❑	7 Jamal Lewis	.30	.10
❑	8 Kyle Boller	.25	.10
❑	9 Derrick Mason	.25	.10
❑	10 Willis McGahee	.50	.20
❑	11 J.P. Losman	.30	.10
❑	12 Lee Evans	.30	.10
❑	13 Steve Smith	.50	.20
❑	14 Jake Delhomme	.30	.10
❑	15 DeShaun Foster	.30	.10
❑	16 Rex Grossman	.50	.20
❑	17 Brian Urlacher	.50	.20
❑	18 Thomas Jones	.30	.10
❑	19 Carson Palmer	.50	.20
❑	20 Chad Johnson	.30	.10
❑	21 Rudi Johnson	.30	.10
❑	22 Charlie Frye	.30	.12
❑	23 Braylon Edwards	.50	.20
❑	24 Reuben Droughns	.30	.10
❑	25 Julius Jones	.50	.20
❑	26 Drew Bledsoe	.50	.20
❑	27 Terry Glenn	.30	.10
❑	28 Jake Plummer	.30	.10
❑	29 Tatum Bell	.30	.10
❑	30 Champ Bailey	.30	.10
❑	31 Rod Smith	.30	.10
❑	32 Roy Williams WR	.50	.20
❑	33 Kevin Jones	.50	.20
❑	34 Mike Williams	.50	.20
❑	35 Brett Favre	1.00	.40
❑	36 Ahman Green	.30	.10
❑	37 Javon Walker	.30	.10
❑	38 David Carr	.30	.10
❑	39 Andre Johnson	.30	.10
❑	40 Domanick Davis	.30	.10
❑	41 Peyton Manning	.75	.30
❑	42 Edgerrin James	.50	.20
❑	43 Marvin Harrison	.50	.20
❑	44 Reggie Wayne	.30	.10
❑	45 Byron Leftwich	.30	.10
❑	46 Fred Taylor	.30	.10
❑	47 Ernest Wilford	.25	.10
❑	48 Larry Johnson	.60	.25
❑	49 Trent Green	.30	.10
❑	50 Tony Gonzalez	.30	.10
❑	51 Ronnie Brown	.50	.20
❑	52 Ricky Williams	.30	.10
❑	53 Chris Chambers	.30	.10
❑	54 Daunte Culpepper	.50	.20
❑	55 Troy Williamson	.30	.10
❑	56 Brad Johnson	.30	.10
❑	57 Tom Brady	.75	.30
❑	58 Deion Branch	.30	.10
❑	59 Corey Dillon	.30	.10
❑	60 Deuce McAllister	.30	.10
❑	61 Donte Stallworth	.30	.10
❑	62 Joe Horn	.30	.10
❑	63 Eli Manning	.60	.25
❑	64 Tiki Barber	.50	.20
❑	65 Plaxico Burress	.30	.10
❑	66 Jeremy Shockey	.50	.20
❑	67 Chad Pennington	.30	.10
❑	68 Curtis Martin	.50	.20
❑	69 Laveranues Coles	.30	.10
❑	70 Randy Moss	.50	.20
❑	71 Aaron Brooks	.30	.10
❑	72 LaMont Jordan	.30	.10
❑	73 Donovan McNabb	.50	.20
❑	74 Brian Westbrook	.30	.10
❑	75 Terrell Owens	.50	.20
❑	76 Ben Roethlisberger	.75	.30
❑	77 Hines Ward	.50	.20
❑	78 Willie Parker	.60	.25
❑	79 Heath Miller	.50	.20
❑	80 LaDainian Tomlinson	.60	.25
❑	81 Drew Brees	.50	.20
❑	82 Antonio Gates	.50	.20
❑	83 Alex Smith QB	.60	.25
❑	84 Antonio Bryant	.30	.10
❑	85 Frank Gore	.50	.20
❑	86 Shaun Alexander	.50	.20
❑	87 Matt Hasselbeck	.30	.10
❑	88 Darrell Jackson	.30	.10
❑	89 Marc Bulger	.30	.10
❑	90 Steven Jackson	.50	.20
❑	91 Torry Holt	.30	.10
❑	92 Cadillac Williams	.50	.20
❑	93 Chris Simms	.30	.10
❑	94 Joey Galloway	.30	.10
❑	95 Steve McNair	.30	.12
❑	96 Chris Brown	.30	.10
❑	97 Drew Bennett	.25	.10
❑	98 Clinton Portis	.50	.20
❑	99 Santana Moss	.30	.10
❑	100 Mark Brunell	.30	.10
❑	101 A.J. Hawk RC	4.00	1.50
❑	102 A.J. Nicholson RC	1.00	.40
❑	103 Abdul Hodge RC	2.00	.75
❑	104 Andre Hall RC	1.50	.60
❑	105 Anthony Fasano RC	2.00	.75
❑	106 Antonio Cromartie RC	2.00	.75
❑	107 Ashton Youboty RC	2.00	.75
❑	108 Bobby Carpenter RC	2.00	.75
❑	109 Brad Smith RC	2.00	.75
❑	110 Greg Jennings RC	3.00	1.25
❑	111 Brandon Williams RC	2.00	.75
❑	112 Brian Calhoun RC	2.00	.75
❑	113 Brodie Croyle RC	4.00	1.50
❑	114 Brodrick Bunkley RC	2.00	.75
❑	115 Bruce Gradkowski RC	3.00	1.25
❑	116 Chad Greenway RC	2.00	.75
❑	117 Chad Jackson RC	3.00	1.25
❑	118 Charles Davis RC	1.50	.60
❑	119 Charles Gordon RC	1.50	.60
❑	120 Charlie Whitehurst RC	2.50	1.00
❑	121 Claude Wroten RC	1.00	.40
❑	122 Cory Rodgers RC	2.00	.75
❑	123 D.J. Shockley RC	2.00	.75
❑	124 Darnell Bing RC	2.00	.75
❑	125 Darrell Hackney RC	1.50	.60
❑	126 David Thomas RC	2.00	.75
❑	127 D'Brickashaw Ferguson RC	2.00	.75
❑	128 DeAngelo Williams RC	5.00	2.00
❑	129 DeMeco Ryans RC	2.50	1.00
❑	130 Demetrius Williams RC	2.50	1.00
❑	131 Derek Hagan RC	2.00	.75
❑	132 Devin Hester RC	4.00	1.50
❑	133 Dominique Byrd RC	1.50	.60
❑	134 DonTrell Moore RC	1.50	.60
❑	135 D'Qwell Jackson RC	1.50	.60
❑	136 Drew Olson RC	1.50	.60
❑	137 Elvis Dumervil RC	1.00	.40
❑	138 Ernie Sims RC	2.50	1.00
❑	139 Garrett Mills RC	2.00	.75
❑	140 Gerald Riggs RC	2.00	.75

❑ 141 Greg Lee RC	1.50	.60
❑ 142 Haloti Ngata RC	2.00	.75
❑ 143 Hank Baskett RC	2.00	.75
❑ 144 Jason Allen RC	2.00	.75
❑ 145 Jason Avant RC	2.00	.75
❑ 146 Jay Cutler RC	8.00	3.00
❑ 147 Jeff Webb RC	1.50	.60
❑ 148 Jeremy Bloom RC	1.50	.60
❑ 149 Jerome Harrison RC	2.00	.75
❑ 150 Jimmy Williams RC	2.00	.75
❑ 151 Joe Klopfenstein RC	1.50	.60
❑ 152 Johnathan Joseph RC	1.50	.60
❑ 153 Joseph Addai RC	6.00	2.50
❑ 154 Jovon Bouknight RC	1.50	.60
❑ 155 Kai Parham RC	2.00	.75
❑ 156 Kamerion Wimbley RC	2.00	.75
❑ 157 Kellen Clemens RC	2.50	1.00
❑ 158 Kelly Jennings RC	2.00	.75
❑ 159 Ko Simpson RC	1.50	.60
❑ 160 Laurence Maroney RC	5.00	2.00
❑ 161 Lawrence Vickers RC	1.50	.60
❑ 162 LenDale White RC	4.00	1.50
❑ 163 Leon Washington RC	3.00	1.25
❑ 164 Leonard Pope RC	2.00	.75
❑ 165 Manny Lawson RC	2.00	.75
❑ 166 Marcedes Lewis RC	2.00	.75
❑ 167 Marcus McNeill RC	1.50	.60
❑ 168 Donte Whitner RC	2.00	.75
❑ 169 Mario Williams RC	3.00	1.25
❑ 170 Martin Nance RC	1.50	.60
❑ 171 Mathias Kiwanuka RC	2.50	1.00
❑ 172 Matt Bernstein RC	1.00	.40
❑ 173 Matt Leinart RC	8.00	3.00
❑ 174 Maurice Drew RC	5.00	2.00
❑ 175 Maurice Stovall RC	2.00	.75
❑ 176 Michael Huff RC	2.50	1.00
❑ 177 Michael Robinson RC	3.00	1.25
❑ 178 Mike Hass RC	2.00	.75
❑ 179 Omar Jacobs RC	1.50	.60
❑ 180 Orien Harris RC	1.50	.60
❑ 181 Owen Daniels RC	2.00	.75
❑ 182 Miles Austin RC	1.50	.60
❑ 183 Reggie Bush RC	12.00	5.00
❑ 184 Reggie McNeal RC	1.50	.60
❑ 185 Santonio Holmes RC	4.00	1.50
❑ 186 Sinorice Moss RC	2.50	1.00
❑ 187 Skyler Green RC	2.00	.75
❑ 188 Tony Scheffler RC	2.00	.75
❑ 189 Tamba Hali RC	2.00	.75
❑ 190 Tarvaris Jackson RC	3.00	1.25
❑ 191 Thomas Howard RC	2.00	.75
❑ 192 Tim Day RC	1.50	.60
❑ 193 Todd Watkins RC	1.50	.60
❑ 194 Travis Wilson RC	2.00	.75
❑ 195 Tye Hill RC	2.00	.75
❑ 196 Vernon Davis RC	4.00	1.50
❑ 197 Vince Young RC	8.00	3.00
❑ 198 Wali Lundy RC	2.00	.75
❑ 199 Will Blackmon RC	1.50	.60
❑ 200 Winston Justice RC	2.00	.75

2002 Fleer Authentix

❑ COMP.SET w/o SP's (100)	20.00	7.50
❑ 1 Jake Plummer	.60	.25
❑ 2 Chad Pennington	1.25	.50
❑ 3 Corey Bradford	.40	.15
❑ 4 Mike Anderson	1.00	.40
❑ 5 Donovan McNabb	1.25	.50
❑ 6 Brian Griese	1.00	.40
❑ 7 Keyshawn Johnson	1.00	.40
❑ 8 Michael Strahan	.60	.25
❑ 9 Rod Smith	.60	.25
❑ 10 Warren Sapp	.60	.25
❑ 11 Joe Horn	.60	.25
❑ 12 Anthony Thomas	.60	.25
❑ 13 Jeff Garcia	1.00	.40
❑ 14 Michael Bennett	.60	.25
❑ 15 Richard Huntley	.40	.15
❑ 16 Doug Flutie	1.00	.40
❑ 17 Tony Gonzalez	.60	.25
❑ 18 David Boston	1.00	.40
❑ 19 Freddie Mitchell	.60	.25
❑ 20 Terrell Davis	1.00	.40
❑ 21 Torry Holt	1.00	.40
❑ 22 Drew Bledsoe	1.25	.50
❑ 23 Peter Warrick	.60	.25
❑ 24 Darrell Jackson	.60	.25
❑ 25 Chris Chambers	1.00	.40
❑ 26 Marvin Harrison	1.00	.40
❑ 27 Warrick Dunn	1.00	.40
❑ 28 Tim Brown	1.00	.40
❑ 29 Terry Glenn	.60	.25
❑ 30 Rod Gardner	.60	.25
❑ 31 Aaron Brooks	1.00	.40
❑ 32 Johnnie Morton	.60	.25
❑ 33 Steve McNair	1.00	.40
❑ 34 Deuce McAllister	1.25	.50
❑ 35 Emmitt Smith	2.50	1.00
❑ 36 Isaac Bruce	1.00	.40
❑ 37 Cris Carter	1.00	.40
❑ 38 Marty Booker	.40	.15
❑ 39 Garrison Hearst	.60	.25
❑ 40 Jay Fiedler	.60	.25
❑ 41 Eric Moulds	.60	.25
❑ 42 Hines Ward	1.00	.40
❑ 43 Peyton Manning	2.00	.75
❑ 44 Trent Dilfer	.60	.25
❑ 45 Ricky Williams	1.00	.40
❑ 46 Quincy Carter	.60	.25
❑ 47 Kurt Warner	1.00	.40
❑ 48 Tom Brady	2.50	1.00
❑ 49 Chris Weinke	.60	.25
❑ 50 LaDainian Tomlinson	1.50	.60
❑ 51 Antowain Smith	.60	.25
❑ 52 Corey Dillon	.60	.25
❑ 53 Shaun Alexander	1.25	.50
❑ 54 Daunte Culpepper	1.00	.40
❑ 55 Ray Lewis	1.00	.40
❑ 56 Kordell Stewart	.60	.25
❑ 57 Trent Green	.60	.25
❑ 58 Chris Redman	.40	.15
❑ 59 Plaxico Burress	.60	.25
❑ 60 Fred Taylor	1.00	.40
❑ 61 Snoop Minnis	.40	.15
❑ 62 Jerry Rice	2.00	.75
❑ 63 James Allen	.60	.25
❑ 64 Peerless Price	.60	.25
❑ 65 Curtis Martin	1.00	.40
❑ 66 Mike McMahon	1.00	.40
❑ 67 Brad Johnson	.60	.25
❑ 68 Troy Brown	.60	.25
❑ 69 Jamal Lewis	1.00	.40
❑ 70 Jerome Bettis	1.00	.40
❑ 71 Dominic Rhodes	1.00	.40
❑ 72 Az-Zahir Hakim	.40	.15
❑ 73 Rich Gannon	1.00	.40
❑ 74 Ahman Green	1.00	.40
❑ 75 Eddie George	1.00	.40
❑ 76 Tim Couch	.60	.25
❑ 77 Ricky Watters	.60	.25
❑ 78 Randy Moss	2.00	.75
❑ 79 Brian Urlacher	1.50	.60
❑ 80 Terrell Owens	1.00	.40
❑ 81 Jimmy Smith	.60	.25
❑ 82 Travis Henry	1.00	.40
❑ 83 Drew Brees	1.00	.40
❑ 84 Priest Holmes	1.25	.50
❑ 85 Michael Vick	3.00	1.25
❑ 86 James Thrash	.60	.25
❑ 87 Jamie Sharper	.40	.15
❑ 88 Marcus Robinson	.60	.25
❑ 89 Laveranues Coles	.60	.25
❑ 90 Brett Favre	2.50	1.00
❑ 91 Stephen Davis	.60	.25
❑ 92 Tiki Barber	1.00	.40
❑ 93 Kevin Johnson	.60	.25
❑ 94 Marshall Faulk	1.00	.40
❑ 95 Mark Brunell	1.00	.40
❑ 96 Jamal Anderson	.60	.25
❑ 97 Duce Staley	1.00	.40
❑ 98 Edgerrin James	1.25	.50
❑ 99 Kevan Barlow	.60	.25
❑ 100 Kerry Collins	.60	.25
❑ 101 David Carr RC	20.00	7.50
❑ 102 Joey Harrington RC	12.00	5.00
❑ 103 William Green RC	8.00	3.00
❑ 104 Donte Stallworth RC	15.00	6.00
❑ 105 Ashley Lelie RC	15.00	6.00
❑ 106 Jabar Gaffney RC	8.00	3.00
❑ 107 Antonio Bryant RC	8.00	3.00
❑ 108 Josh Reed RC	8.00	3.00
❑ 109 Daniel Graham RC	8.00	3.00
❑ 110 Reche Caldwell RC	8.00	3.00
❑ 111 Jeremy Shockey RC	25.00	10.00
❑ 112 T.J. Duckett RC	10.00	4.00
❑ 113 Marquise Walker RC	6.00	2.50
❑ 114 Lamar Gordon RC	8.00	3.00
❑ 115 DeShaun Foster RC	8.00	3.00
❑ 116 Patrick Ramsey RC	10.00	4.00
❑ 117 Andre Davis RC	6.00	2.50
❑ 118 Ron Johnson RC	6.00	2.50
❑ 119 Luke Staley RC	6.00	2.50
❑ 120 Clinton Portis RC	25.00	10.00
❑ 121 Freddie Milons RC	6.00	2.50
❑ 122 Javon Walker RC	15.00	6.00
❑ 123 David Garrard RC	8.00	3.00
❑ 124 Kurt Kittner RC	6.00	2.50
❑ 125 Adrian Peterson RC	8.00	3.00
❑ 126 Roy Williams RC	20.00	10.00
❑ 127 Maurice Morris RC	8.00	3.00
❑ 128 Cliff Russell RC	6.00	2.50
❑ 129 Antwaan Randle El RC	12.00	5.00
❑ 130 Verron Haynes RC	8.00	3.00
❑ 131 Eric Crouch RC	8.00	3.00
❑ 132 Kahlil Hill RC	6.00	2.50
❑ 133 Brian Westbrook RC	12.00	5.00
❑ 134 Travis Stephens RC	6.00	2.50
❑ 135 Julius Peppers RC	15.00	6.00
❑ 136 Quentin Jammer RC	8.00	3.00
❑ 137 Rohan Davey RC	8.00	3.00
❑ 138 Ladell Betts RC	8.00	3.00
❑ 139 Tim Carter RC	6.00	2.50
❑ 140 Josh McCown RC	10.00	4.00
❑ 141 Emmitt Smith HH		
❑ 142 Quincy Carter HH		
❑ 143 Joey Galloway HH		
❑ 144 Anthony Wright HH		
❑ 145 La'Roi Glover HH		
❑ 146 Greg Ellis HH		
❑ 147 Dexter Coakley HH		
❑ 148 Dat Nguyen HH		
❑ 149 Darren Woodson HH		
❑ 150 Troy Hambrick HH		
❑ 151 Larry Allen HH		
❑ 152 Ebenezer Ekuban HH		
❑ 153 Reggie Swinton HH		
❑ 154 Michael Wiley HH		
❑ 155 Duane Hawthorne HH		
❑ 156 Brett Favre HH		
❑ 157 Ahman Green HH		
❑ 158 Terry Glenn HH		
❑ 159 Donald Driver HH		
❑ 160 Ryan Longwell HH		
❑ 161 Nate Wayne HH		
❑ 162 Darren Sharper HH		
❑ 163 Kabeer Gbaja-Biamila HH		
❑ 164 Vonnie Holliday HH		
❑ 165 Bubba Franks HH		
❑ 166 LeRoy Butler HH		
❑ 167 Dorsey Levens HH		
❑ 168 William Henderson HH		
❑ 169 Tyrone Williams HH		
❑ 170 Robert Ferguson HH		
❑ 171 Jeff Garcia HH		
❑ 172 Garrison Hearst HH		
❑ 173 Terrell Owens HH		
❑ 174 Kevan Barlow HH		
❑ 175 J.J. Stokes HH		
❑ 176 Tai Streets HH		
❑ 177 Eric Johnson HH		
❑ 178 Fred Beasley HH		
❑ 179 Tim Rattay HH		
❑ 180 Derek Smith HH XRC		
❑ 181 Zack Bronson HH		
❑ 182 Ahmed Plummer HH		
❑ 183 Bryant Young HH		
❑ 184 Vinny Sutherland HH		
❑ 185 Andre Carter HH		
❑ 186 Kordell Stewart HH		
❑ 187 Jerome Bettis HH		

❑ 188 Hines Ward HH
❑ 189 Plaxico Burress HH
❑ 190 Kendrell Bell HH
❑ 191 Amos Zereoue HH
❑ 192 Jason Gildon HH
❑ 193 Chad Scott HH
❑ 194 Joey Porter HH
❑ 195 Hank Poteat HH
❑ 196 Troy Edwards HH
❑ 197 Lee Flowers HH
❑ 198 Aaron Smith HH RC
❑ 199 Dan Kreider HH RC 30.00 12.50
❑ 200 Tommy Maddox HH
❑ 201 Jay Fiedler HH
❑ 202 Ricky Williams HH
❑ 203 Chris Chambers HH
❑ 204 Oronde Gadsden HH
❑ 205 Travis Minor HH
❑ 206 Zach Thomas HH
❑ 207 Jason Taylor HH
❑ 208 Olindo Mare HH
❑ 209 Sam Madison HH
❑ 210 Patrick Surtain HH
❑ 211 Tim Bowens HH
❑ 212 Daryl Gardener HH
❑ 213 Dedric Ward HH
❑ 214 James McKnight HH
❑ 215 Deon Dyer HH
❑ 216 Donovan McNabb HH
❑ 217 Duce Staley HH
❑ 218 James Thrash HH
❑ 219 Correll Buckhalter HH
❑ 220 Freddie Mitchell HH
❑ 221 Chad Lewis HH
❑ 222 Hugh Douglas HH
❑ 223 Brian Dawkins HH
❑ 224 David Akers HH
❑ 225 Troy Vincent HH
❑ 226 Bobby Taylor HH
❑ 227 Rod Smart HH RC
❑ 228 Todd Pinkston HH
❑ 229 Corey Simon HH
❑ 230 A.J. Feeley HH

2003 Fleer Authentix

❑ COMP.SET w/o SP's (100) 20.00 7.50
❑ 1 Donovan McNabb 1.25 .50
❑ 2 Tim Brown 1.00 .40
❑ 3 Donald Driver .60 .25
❑ 4 Eddie George .60 .25
❑ 5 Curtis Martin 1.00 .40
❑ 6 Chad Hutchinson .40 .15
❑ 7 Shaun Alexander 1.00 .40
❑ 8 Kerry Collins .60 .25
❑ 9 Trent Green .60 .25
❑ 10 Marc Bulger 1.00 .40
❑ 11 Donte Stallworth 1.00 .40
❑ 12 Julius Peppers 1.00 .40
❑ 13 Ronde Barber .40 .15
❑ 14 Jason Taylor .40 .15
❑ 15 Eric Moulds .60 .25
❑ 16 Amos Zereoue .60 .25
❑ 17 Fred Taylor 1.00 .40
❑ 18 Jake Plummer .60 .25
❑ 19 Jerry Rice 2.00 .75
❑ 20 Quincy Morgan .60 .25
❑ 21 Koren Robinson .60 .25
❑ 22 Tom Brady 2.50 1.00
❑ 23 Brian Urlacher 1.50 .60
❑ 24 Terrell Owens 1.00 .40
❑ 25 Priest Holmes 1.25 .50
❑ 26 Brett Favre 2.50 1.00
❑ 27 Derrick Mason .60 .25
❑ 28 Charlie Garner .60 .25
❑ 29 Clinton Portis 1.50 .60
❑ 30 Warren Sapp .60 .25
❑ 31 Joe Horn .60 .25
❑ 32 Michael Lewis .40 .15
❑ 33 Torry Holt 1.00 .40
❑ 34 Aaron Brooks 1.00 .40
❑ 35 William Green .60 .25
❑ 36 Matt Hasselbeck .60 .25
❑ 37 Ricky Williams 1.00 .40
❑ 38 Travis Henry .60 .25
❑ 39 Junior Seau 1.00 .40
❑ 40 Duce Staley .60 .25
❑ 41 Todd Heap .60 .25
❑ 42 Hines Ward 1.00 .40
❑ 43 David Carr 1.50 .60
❑ 44 Rod Gardner .60 .25
❑ 45 Deuce McAllister 1.00 .40
❑ 46 Chad Johnson 1.00 .40
❑ 47 Garrison Hearst .60 .25
❑ 48 Daunte Culpepper 1.00 .40
❑ 49 Ray Lewis 1.00 .40
❑ 50 Plaxico Burress .60 .25
❑ 51 Randy Moss 1.50 .60
❑ 52 Drew Bledsoe 1.00 .40
❑ 53 LaDainian Tomlinson 1.00 .40
❑ 54 Chris Chambers 1.00 .40
❑ 55 Chris Redman .40 .15
❑ 56 Jerome Bettis 1.00 .40
❑ 57 Tony Gonzalez .60 .25
❑ 58 Michael Vick 2.50 1.00
❑ 59 Tommy Maddox 1.00 .40
❑ 60 Marvin Harrison 1.00 .40
❑ 61 Stephen Davis .60 .25
❑ 62 Chad Pennington 1.25 .50
❑ 63 James Stewart .60 .25
❑ 64 Simeon Rice .60 .25
❑ 65 Jeremy Shockey 1.50 .60
❑ 66 Emmitt Smith 2.50 1.00
❑ 67 Marshall Faulk 1.00 .40
❑ 68 Troy Brown .60 .25
❑ 69 Warrick Dunn .60 .25
❑ 70 David Boston .60 .25
❑ 71 Edgerrin James 1.00 .40
❑ 72 Patrick Ramsey 1.00 .40
❑ 73 Rich Gannon .60 .25
❑ 74 Ed McCaffrey 1.00 .40
❑ 75 Kurt Warner 1.00 .40
❑ 76 Marty Booker .60 .25
❑ 77 Tai Streets .60 .25
❑ 78 Michael Bennett .60 .25
❑ 79 Peerless Price .60 .25
❑ 80 Drew Brees 1.00 .40
❑ 81 Mark Brunell .60 .25
❑ 82 Jamal Lewis 1.00 .40
❑ 83 Brad Johnson .60 .25
❑ 84 Jimmy Smith .60 .25
❑ 85 T.J. Duckett .60 .25
❑ 86 Todd Pinkston .60 .25
❑ 87 Joey Harrington 1.50 .60
❑ 88 Derrick Brooks .60 .25
❑ 89 Laveranues Coles .60 .25
❑ 90 Shannon Sharpe .60 .25
❑ 91 Keyshawn Johnson 1.00 .40
❑ 92 Tiki Barber 1.00 .40
❑ 93 Corey Dillon .60 .25
❑ 94 Jeff Garcia 1.00 .40
❑ 95 Peyton Manning 1.50 .60
❑ 96 Marcel Shipp .60 .25
❑ 97 Brian Dawkins .60 .25
❑ 98 Ahman Green 1.00 .40
❑ 99 Steve McNair 1.00 .40
❑ 100 Amani Toomer .60 .25
❑ 101 Carson Palmer RC 25.00 10.00
❑ 102 Taylor Jacobs RC 5.00 2.00
❑ 103 Kyle Boller RC 6.00 2.50
❑ 104 Anquan Boldin RC 15.00 6.00
❑ 105 Willis McGahee RC 15.00 6.00
❑ 106 Kevin Curtis RC 6.00 2.50
❑ 107 Musa Smith RC 6.00 2.50
❑ 108 Dallas Clark RC 6.00 2.50
❑ 109 Larry Johnson RC 25.00 12.50
❑ 110 Billy McMullen RC 5.00 2.00
❑ 111 B.J. Askew RC 6.00 2.50
❑ 112 Bennie Joppru RC 6.00 2.50
❑ 113 Bryant Johnson RC 6.00 2.50
❑ 114 Byron Leftwich RC 20.00 7.50
❑ 115 Onterrio Smith RC 6.00 2.50
❑ 116 Justin Fargas RC 6.00 2.50
❑ 117 Terence Newman RC 12.00 5.00
❑ 118 Andre Johnson RC 12.00 5.00
❑ 119 Rex Grossman RC 20.00 7.50
❑ 120 Tyrone Calico RC 6.00 2.50
❑ 121 Chris Simms RC 10.00 4.00
❑ 122 Kelley Washington RC 6.00 2.50
❑ 123 Dave Ragone RC 6.00 2.50
❑ 124 Teyo Johnson RC 6.00 2.50
❑ 125 Seneca Wallace RC 6.00 2.50
❑ 126 Lee Suggs RC 6.00 2.50
❑ 127 Chris Brown RC 6.00 2.50
❑ 128 L.J. Smith RC 6.00 2.50
❑ 129 Charles Rogers RC 6.00 2.50
❑ 130 Terrell Suggs RC 10.00 4.00
❑ 131 Antonio Bryant HH
❑ 132 Roy Williams HH
❑ 133 Joey Galloway HH
❑ 134 Dexter Coakley HH
❑ 135 Greg Ellis HH
❑ 136 Troy Hambrick HH
❑ 137 La'Roi Glover HH
❑ 138 Tony Fisher HH
❑ 139 Javon Walker HH
❑ 140 Robert Ferguson HH
❑ 141 Bubba Franks HH
❑ 142 Kabeer Gbaja-Biamila HH
❑ 143 Na'il Diggs HH
❑ 144 Darren Sharper HH
❑ 145 Jerry Porter HH
❑ 146 Doug Jolley HH
❑ 147 Sebastian Janikowski HH
❑ 148 Rod Woodson HH
❑ 149 Phillip Buchanon HH
❑ 150 Charles Woodson HH
❑ 151 Zack Crockett HH
❑ 152 Michael Strahan HH
❑ 153 Dhani Jones HH
❑ 154 Will Allen HH
❑ 155 Will Peterson HH
❑ 156 Ron Dixon HH
❑ 157 Mike Barrow HH
❑ 158 Ike Hilliard HH
❑ 159 Antwaan Randle El HH
❑ 160 Joey Porter HH
❑ 161 Jason Gildon HH
❑ 162 Chris Fuamatu-Ma'afala HH
❑ 163 Kendrell Bell HH
❑ 164 Chad Scott HH
❑ 165 Dan Kreider HH

2004 Fleer Authentix

❑ COMP.SET w/o SP's (100) 25.00 10.00
❑ 131-140 PRINT RUN 250 SER.#'d SETS
❑ 1 Tom Brady 2.00 .75
❑ 2 Kerry Collins .50 .20
❑ 3 Terry Glenn .30 .10
❑ 4 Eddie George .50 .20
❑ 5 Bryant Johnson .30 .10
❑ 6 Carson Palmer 1.00 .40
❑ 7 Matt Hasselbeck .50 .20
❑ 8 Randy Moss 1.00 .40
❑ 9 Chad Johnson .75 .30
❑ 10 Darrell Jackson .50 .20
❑ 11 Chris Chambers .50 .20
❑ 12 Jake Delhomme .75 .30
❑ 13 Plaxico Burress .50 .20
❑ 14 Marvin Harrison .75 .30
❑ 15 Drew Bledsoe .75 .30
❑ 16 Terrell Owens .75 .30
❑ 17 Andre Johnson .75 .30
❑ 18 Anquan Boldin .75 .30

❑ 19 Jeremy Shockey .75 .30
❑ 20 Champ Bailey .50 .20
❑ 21 Shaun Alexander .75 .30
❑ 22 DantÃ© Hall .75 .30
❑ 23 Julius Peppers .75 .30
❑ 24 Duce Staley .50 .20
❑ 25 Domanick Davis .75 .30
❑ 26 Quentin Griffin .75 .30
❑ 27 Clinton Portis .75 .30
❑ 28 Aaron Brooks .50 .20
❑ 29 Justin McCareins .30 .10
❑ 30 Joey Galloway .50 .20
❑ 31 David Boston .50 .20
❑ 32 Lee Suggs .75 .30
❑ 33 Torry Holt .75 .30
❑ 34 Daunte Culpepper .75 .30
❑ 35 Brian Urlacher 1.00 .40
❑ 36 Kevan Barlow .50 .20
❑ 37 Fred Taylor .50 .20
❑ 38 Eric Moulds .50 .20
❑ 39 Donovan McNabb 1.00 .40
❑ 40 Edgerrin James .75 .30
❑ 41 Ray Lewis .75 .30
❑ 42 Rich Gannon .50 .20
❑ 43 Joey Harrington .75 .30
❑ 44 Laveranues Coles .50 .20
❑ 45 Ricky Williams .75 .30
❑ 46 Rex Grossman .75 .30
❑ 47 Drew Brees .75 .30
❑ 48 Priest Holmes 1.00 .40
❑ 49 Travis Henry .50 .20
❑ 50 Tim Rattay .30 .10
❑ 51 Tony Gonzalez .50 .20
❑ 52 Stephen Davis .50 .20
❑ 53 Hines Ward .75 .30
❑ 54 Peyton Manning 1.25 .50
❑ 55 Peerless Price .50 .20
❑ 56 Jerry Rice 1.50 .60
❑ 57 David Carr .75 .30
❑ 58 Jamal Lewis .75 .30
❑ 59 Tim Brown .75 .30
❑ 60 Warren Sapp .50 .20
❑ 61 Tommy Maddox .50 .20
❑ 62 Joe Horn .50 .20
❑ 63 Roy Williams S .50 .20
❑ 64 Charlie Garner .50 .20
❑ 65 Deion Branch .75 .30
❑ 66 Corey Dillon .50 .20
❑ 67 Marc Bulger .75 .30
❑ 68 Trent Green .50 .20
❑ 69 Michael Vick 1.50 .60
❑ 70 Chad Pennington .75 .30
❑ 71 Charles Rogers .50 .20
❑ 72 Mark Brunell .50 .20
❑ 73 Tiki Barber .75 .30
❑ 74 Jeff Garcia .75 .30
❑ 75 Marshall Faulk .75 .30
❑ 76 DeShaun Foster .50 .20
❑ 77 LaVar Arrington 1.50 .60
❑ 78 Byron Leftwich 1.00 .40
❑ 79 Willis McGahee .75 .30
❑ 80 Brian Westbrook .50 .20
❑ 81 Ahman Green .75 .30
❑ 82 Kyle Boller .75 .30
❑ 83 Jevon Kearse .50 .20
❑ 84 Donald Driver .50 .20
❑ 85 Warrick Dunn .50 .20
❑ 86 Santana Moss .50 .20
❑ 87 Keyshawn Johnson .50 .20
❑ 88 Steve McNair .75 .30
❑ 89 Deuce McAllister .75 .30
❑ 90 A.J. Feeley .75 .30
❑ 91 Keenan McCardell .30 .10
❑ 92 Michael Bennett .50 .20
❑ 93 Terrell Suggs .50 .20
❑ 94 LaDainian Tomlinson 1.00 .40
❑ 95 Brett Favre 2.00 .75
❑ 96 Emmitt Smith 1.50 .60
❑ 97 Curtis Martin .75 .30
❑ 98 Jake Plummer .50 .20
❑ 99 Derrick Mason .50 .20
❑ 100 Ty Law .50 .20
❑ 101 Ben Troupe RC 5.00 2.00
❑ 102 DeAngelo Hall RC 6.00 2.50
❑ 103 Eli Manning RC 25.00 10.00
❑ 104 Cody Pickett RC 5.00 2.00
❑ 105 Matt Schaub RC 15.00 6.00
❑ 106 J.P. Losman RC 10.00 4.00
❑ 107 Chris Perry RC 8.00 3.00
❑ 108 Steven Jackson RC 15.00 6.00
❑ 109 Kevin Jones RC 12.00 5.00
❑ 110 Michael Turner RC 6.00 2.50
❑ 111 Philip Rivers RC 15.00 7.50
❑ 112 Quincy Wilson RC 4.00 1.50
❑ 113 Luke McCown RC 5.00 2.00
❑ 114 Greg Jones RC 5.00 2.00
❑ 115 Julius Jones RC 15.00 6.00
❑ 116 Sean Taylor RC 5.00 2.00
❑ 117 Kellen Winslow RC 10.00 4.00
❑ 118 Rashaun Woods RC 5.00 2.00
❑ 119 Ben Watson RC 5.00 2.00
❑ 120 Devery Henderson RC 4.00 1.50
❑ 121 Ernest Wilford RC 5.00 2.00
❑ 122 Michael Jenkins RC 5.00 2.00
❑ 123 Roy Williams RC 12.00 5.00
❑ 124 Lee Evans RC 6.00 2.50
❑ 125 Bernard Berrian RC 6.00 2.50
❑ 126 Mewelde Moore RC 5.00 2.00
❑ 127 Jammal Lord RC 5.00 2.00
❑ 128 Darius Watts RC 5.00 2.00
❑ 129 Derrick Hamilton RC 4.00 1.50
❑ 130 Devard Darling RC 5.00 2.00
❑ 131 A.Hall RC/Reid AU RC 20.00 7.50
❑ 132 T.Bell RC/Shanahan AU 30.00 12.50
❑ 133 D.Henson RC/Parcells AU 60.00 30.00
❑ 134 Roethlisber RC/Cowh.AU 125.00 75.00
❑ 135 Gallery RC/N.Turner AU RC 30.00 12.50
❑ 136 Cobbs RC/Belichick AU 60.00 30.00
❑ 137 Re.Williams RC/Del Rio AU 20.00 7.50
❑ 138 L.Fitzgerald RC/Green AU 30.00 12.50
❑ 139 Clayton RC/Gruden AU RC 25.00 10.00
❑ 140 K.Colbert RC/Fox AU RC 25.00 10.00
❑ 141 Najeh Davenport HT 1.00 .40
❑ 142 Javon Walker HT 1.50 .60
❑ 143 Robert Ferguson HT 1.00 .40
❑ 144 Nick Barnett HT 1.50 .60
❑ 145 Kabeer Gbaja-Biamila HT 1.50 .60
❑ 146 Terence Newman HT 1.50 .60
❑ 147 Dexter Coakley HT 1.00 .40
❑ 148 Darren Woodson HT 1.50 .60
❑ 149 Jason Witten HT 1.50 .60
❑ 150 Antonio Bryant HT 1.50 .60

2001 Fleer Authority

❑ COMP.SET w/o SP's (100) 25.00 10.00
❑ 1 Brian Urlacher 1.25 .50
❑ 2 James Stewart .50 .20
❑ 3 Lamar Smith .50 .20
❑ 4 Curtis Martin .75 .30
❑ 5 Shannon Sharpe .50 .20
❑ 6 Germane Crowell .30 .10
❑ 7 Daunte Culpepper .75 .30
❑ 8 Charlie Garner .50 .20
❑ 9 Jake Plummer .50 .20
❑ 10 Eric Moulds .50 .20
❑ 11 Brett Favre 2.50 1.00
❑ 12 Robert Smith .50 .20
❑ 13 Tim Brown .75 .30
❑ 14 David Boston .75 .30
❑ 15 Cade McNown .30 .10
❑ 16 Ahman Green .75 .30
❑ 17 Terry Glenn .50 .20
❑ 18 Wayne Chrebet .50 .20
❑ 19 Jamal Lewis 1.25 .50
❑ 20 Peter Warrick .75 .30
❑ 21 Peyton Manning 2.00 .75
❑ 22 Ricky Williams .75 .30
❑ 23 Donovan McNabb 1.00 .40
❑ 24 Isaac Bruce .75 .30
❑ 25 Tim Couch .50 .20
❑ 26 Marvin Harrison .75 .30
❑ 27 Kerry Collins .50 .20
❑ 28 Kordell Stewart .50 .20
❑ 29 Keyshawn Johnson .75 .30
❑ 30 Kevin Johnson .50 .20
❑ 31 Mark Brunell .75 .30
❑ 32 Ron Dayne .75 .30
❑ 33 Doug Flutie .75 .30
❑ 34 Warrick Dunn .75 .30
❑ 35 Emmitt Smith 1.50 .60
❑ 36 Jimmy Smith .50 .20
❑ 37 Amani Toomer .50 .20
❑ 38 Chad Pennington 1.25 .50
❑ 39 Steve McNair .75 .30
❑ 40 Brian Griese .75 .30
❑ 41 Derrick Alexander .50 .20
❑ 42 Vinny Testaverde .50 .20
❑ 43 Terrell Owens .75 .30
❑ 44 Derrick Mason .50 .20
❑ 45 Mike Anderson .75 .30
❑ 46 Michael Westbrook .50 .20
❑ 47 Rich Gannon .75 .30
❑ 48 Shaun Alexander 1.00 .40
❑ 49 Jevon Kearse .50 .20
❑ 50 Ed McCaffrey .75 .30
❑ 51 Tony Gonzalez .50 .20
❑ 52 Tyrone Wheatley .50 .20
❑ 53 Kurt Warner 1.50 .60
❑ 54 Stephen Davis .75 .30
❑ 55 Rod Smith .50 .20
❑ 56 Deion Sanders .75 .30
❑ 57 Brad Johnson .75 .30
❑ 58 Ike Hilliard .50 .20
❑ 59 Trent Green .75 .30
❑ 60 Terrell Davis .75 .30
❑ 61 Warren Sapp .50 .20
❑ 62 Marshall Faulk 1.00 .40
❑ 63 Tiki Barber .75 .30
❑ 64 Keenan McCardell .30 .10
❑ 65 Joey Galloway .50 .20
❑ 66 Frank Wycheck .30 .10
❑ 67 Ricky Watters .50 .20
❑ 68 Joe Horn .50 .20
❑ 69 Fred Taylor .75 .30
❑ 70 Troy Aikman 1.25 .50
❑ 71 Mike Alstott .75 .30
❑ 72 Matt Hasselbeck .50 .20
❑ 73 Aaron Brooks .75 .30
❑ 74 Terrence Wilkins .30 .10
❑ 75 Travis Prentice .30 .10
❑ 76 Eddie George .75 .30
❑ 77 Jeff Garcia .75 .30
❑ 78 Randy Moss 1.50 .60
❑ 79 Edgerrin James 1.00 .40
❑ 80 Corey Dillon .75 .30
❑ 81 Torry Holt .75 .30
❑ 82 Todd Pinkston .50 .20
❑ 83 Drew Bledsoe 1.00 .40
❑ 84 Antonio Freeman .75 .30
❑ 85 Marcus Robinson .75 .30
❑ 86 Muhsin Muhammad .50 .20
❑ 87 Junior Seau .75 .30
❑ 88 Zach Thomas .75 .30
❑ 89 Dorsey Levens .50 .20
❑ 90 Tim Biakabutuka .50 .20
❑ 91 Elvis Grbac .50 .20
❑ 92 Jerome Bettis .75 .30
❑ 93 Cris Carter .75 .30
❑ 94 Jerry Rice 1.50 .60
❑ 95 Rob Johnson .50 .20
❑ 96 Thomas Jones .50 .20
❑ 97 Duce Staley .75 .30
❑ 98 Ray Lucas .30 .10
❑ 99 Charlie Batch .75 .30
❑ 100 Jamal Anderson .75 .30
❑ 101 Michael Vick RC 25.00 10.00
❑ 102 Drew Brees RC 15.00 6.00
❑ 103 Andre Carter RC 5.00 2.00
❑ 104 David Terrell RC 5.00 2.00
❑ 105 Koren Robinson RC 5.00 2.00
❑ 106 Rod Gardner RC 5.00 2.00
❑ 107 Santana Moss RC 8.00 3.00
❑ 108 Deuce McAllister RC 10.00 4.00
❑ 109 Freddie Mitchell RC 5.00 2.00
❑ 110 Michael Bennett RC 5.00 2.00
❑ 111 Reggie Wayne RC 10.00 4.00
❑ 112 Todd Heap RC 5.00 2.00
❑ 113 LaDainian Tomlinson RC 40.00 25.00
❑ 114 Chad Johnson RC 12.00 5.00
❑ 115 Anthony Thomas RC 5.00 2.00

❑ 116	Robert Ferguson RC	5.00	2.00
❑ 117	LaMont Jordan RC	10.00	4.00
❑ 118	Chris Chambers RC	8.00	3.00
❑ 119	Travis Henry RC	8.00	3.00
❑ 120	Marques Tuiasosopo RC	5.00	2.00
❑ 121	James Jackson RC	5.00	2.00
❑ 122	Heath Evans RC	3.00	1.25
❑ 123	Travis Minor RC	3.00	1.25
❑ 124	Rudi Johnson RC	10.00	4.00
❑ 125	Chris Weinke RC	5.00	2.00
❑ 126	Sage Rosenfels RC	5.00	2.00
❑ 127	Fred Smoot RC	5.00	2.00
❑ 128	Correll Buckhalter RC	6.00	2.50
❑ 129	Justin McCareins RC	5.00	2.00
❑ 130	Jesse Palmer RC	5.00	2.00
❑ 131	Scotty Anderson RC	3.00	1.25
❑ 132	Kevan Barlow RC	5.00	2.00
❑ 133	John Capel RC	3.00	1.25
❑ 134	Mike McMahon RC	5.00	2.00
❑ 135	Snoop Minnis RC	3.00	1.25
❑ 136	Quincy Morgan RC	5.00	2.00
❑ 137	Vinny Sutherland RC	3.00	1.25
❑ 138	Dan Alexander RC	5.00	2.00
❑ 139	Cedrick Wilson RC	5.00	2.00
❑ 140	Josh Booty RC	5.00	2.00
❑ 141	Bobby Newcombe RC	3.00	1.25
❑ 142	Josh Heupel RC	5.00	2.00
❑ 143	Ken-Yon Rambo RC	3.00	1.25
❑ 144	Eddie Berlin RC	3.00	1.25
❑ 145	Reggie Germany RC	3.00	1.25
❑ 146	Quincy Carter RC	5.00	2.00
❑ 147	Steve Smith RC	12.00	6.00
❑ 148	Dan Morgan RC	5.00	2.00
❑ 149	Chris Barnes RC	3.00	1.25
❑ 150	Alex Bannister RC	3.00	1.25
❑ 151	A.J. Feeley RC	5.00	2.00
❑ 152	Jason Brookins RC	5.00	2.00
❑ 153	Kevin Kasper RC	5.00	2.00
❑ 154	Nick Goings RC	5.00	2.00
❑ 155	Gerard Warren RC	5.00	2.00

2003 Fleer Avant

❑	COMP.SET w/o SP's (60)	30.00	12.50
❑ 1	Priest Holmes	1.50	.60
❑ 2	Hines Ward	1.25	.50
❑ 3	Patrick Ramsey	1.25	.50
❑ 4	Deuce McAllister	1.25	.50
❑ 5	Tony Gonzalez	.75	.30
❑ 6	Daunte Culpepper	1.25	.50
❑ 7	Edgerrin James	1.25	.50
❑ 8	Jeremy Shockey	2.00	.75
❑ 9	Donovan McNabb	1.50	.60
❑ 10	Eddie George	.75	.30
❑ 11	Ray Lewis	1.25	.50
❑ 12	LaDainian Tomlinson	1.25	.50
❑ 13	Peyton Manning	2.00	.75
❑ 14	Charlie Garner	.75	.30
❑ 15	Brad Johnson	.75	.30
❑ 16	David Carr	2.00	.75
❑ 17	Jerry Rice	2.50	1.00
❑ 18	Keyshawn Johnson	1.25	.50
❑ 19	Ahman Green	1.25	.50
❑ 20	Rich Gannon	.75	.30
❑ 21	William Green	.75	.30
❑ 22	Torry Holt	1.25	.50
❑ 23	Brett Favre	3.00	1.25
❑ 24	Curtis Martin	1.25	.50
❑ 25	Derrick Brooks	.75	.30
❑ 26	Joey Harrington	2.00	.75
❑ 27	Chad Pennington	1.50	.60
❑ 28	Koren Robinson	.75	.30
❑ 29	Clinton Portis	2.00	.75
❑ 30	Michael Strahan	.75	.30
❑ 31	Marvin Harrison	1.25	.50
❑ 32	Travis Henry	.75	.30
❑ 33	Aaron Brooks	1.25	.50
❑ 34	Antwaan Randle El	1.25	.50
❑ 35	Antonio Bryant	.75	.30
❑ 36	Shaun Alexander	1.25	.50
❑ 37	Jake Plummer	.75	.30
❑ 38	Emmitt Smith	3.00	1.25
❑ 39	Plaxico Burress	.75	.30
❑ 40	Peerless Price	.75	.30
❑ 41	Drew Bledsoe	1.25	.50
❑ 42	Jeff Garcia	1.25	.50
❑ 43	Fred Taylor	1.25	.50
❑ 44	Correll Buckhalter	.75	.30
❑ 45	Steve McNair	1.25	.50
❑ 46	Stephen Davis	.75	.30
❑ 47	Terrell Owens	1.25	.50
❑ 48	Corey Dillon	.75	.30
❑ 49	Marshall Faulk	1.25	.50
❑ 50	Tom Brady	3.00	1.25
❑ 51	Tiki Barber	1.25	.50
❑ 52	Michael Vick	3.00	1.25
❑ 53	Drew Brees	1.25	.50
❑ 54	Chad Johnson	1.25	.50
❑ 55	Randy Moss	2.00	.75
❑ 56	Eric Moulds	.75	.30
❑ 57	Brian Urlacher	2.00	.75
❑ 58	Kurt Warner	1.25	.50
❑ 59	Ricky Williams	1.25	.50
❑ 60	Laveranues Coles	.75	.30
❑ 61	Carson Palmer RC	20.00	7.50
❑ 62	Charles Rogers RC	5.00	2.00
❑ 63	Andre Johnson RC	10.00	4.00
❑ 64	DeWayne Robertson RC	5.00	2.00
❑ 65	Terence Newman RC	10.00	4.00
❑ 66	Byron Leftwich RC	15.00	6.00
❑ 67	Terrell Suggs RC	8.00	3.00
❑ 68	Bryant Johnson RC	5.00	2.00
❑ 69	Kyle Boller RC	5.00	2.00
❑ 70	Rex Grossman RC	15.00	6.00
❑ 71	Willis McGahee RC	12.00	5.00
❑ 72	Dallas Clark RC	5.00	2.00
❑ 73	Larry Johnson RC	20.00	10.00
❑ 74	Bennie Joppru RC	5.00	2.00
❑ 75	Taylor Jacobs RC	4.00	1.50
❑ 76	Anquan Boldin RC	12.00	5.00
❑ 77	Tyrone Calico RC	5.00	2.00
❑ 78	L.J. Smith RC	5.00	2.00
❑ 79	Teyo Johnson RC	5.00	2.00
❑ 80	Kelley Washington RC	5.00	2.00
❑ 81	Jason Witten RC	8.00	3.00
❑ 82	Nate Burleson RC	5.00	2.00
❑ 83	Musa Smith RC	5.00	2.00
❑ 84	Tony Hollings RC	5.00	2.00
❑ 85	Chris Brown RC	5.00	2.00
❑ 86	Billy McMullen RC	4.00	1.50
❑ 87	Chris Simms RC	8.00	3.00
❑ 88	Artose Pinner RC	5.00	2.00
❑ 89	Quentin Griffin RC	5.00	2.00
❑ 90	Onterrio Smith RC	5.00	2.00

2002 Fleer Box Score

❑	COMP.SET w/o SP's (150)	25.00	10.00
❑ 1	Brian Urlacher	1.50	.60
❑ 2	Edgerrin James	1.25	.50
❑ 3	Ricky Williams	1.00	.40
❑ 4	Tim Brown	1.00	.40
❑ 5	Tim Couch	.60	.25
❑ 6	Kurt Warner	1.00	.40
❑ 7	Kendrell Bell	1.00	.40
❑ 8	Daunte Culpepper	1.00	.40
❑ 9	Anthony Thomas	.60	.25
❑ 10	Marvin Harrison	1.00	.40
❑ 11	Jerry Rice	2.00	.75
❑ 12	Eddie George	1.00	.40
❑ 13	Donovan McNabb	1.25	.50
❑ 14	Chris Chambers	1.00	.40
❑ 15	Emmitt Smith	2.50	1.00
❑ 16	David Boston	1.00	.40
❑ 17	Plaxico Burress	1.00	.40
❑ 18	Randy Moss	2.00	.75
❑ 19	Peyton Manning	2.00	.75
❑ 20	Michael Vick	3.00	1.25
❑ 21	Marshall Faulk	1.00	.40
❑ 22	Tom Brady	2.50	1.00
❑ 23	LaDainian Tomlinson	1.50	.60
❑ 24	Shaun Alexander	1.25	.50
❑ 25	Curtis Martin	1.00	.40
❑ 26	Brett Favre	2.50	1.00
❑ 27	Drew Bledsoe	1.25	.50
❑ 28	Jeff Garcia	1.00	.40
❑ 29	Terrell Davis	1.00	.40
❑ 30	Corey Dillon	.60	.25
❑ 31	Troy Brown	.60	.25
❑ 32	Drew Brees	1.00	.40
❑ 33	Jamal Lewis	1.00	.40
❑ 34	Derrick Alexander	.60	.25
❑ 35	Az-Zahir Hakim	.40	.15
❑ 36	Antowain Smith	.60	.25
❑ 37	Muhsin Muhammad	.60	.25
❑ 38	Warrick Dunn	1.00	.40
❑ 39	Curtis Conway	.40	.15
❑ 40	Antonio Freeman	1.00	.40
❑ 41	Bill Schroeder	.60	.25
❑ 42	Joe Horn	.60	.25
❑ 43	Peerless Price	.60	.25
❑ 44	Ahman Green	1.00	.40
❑ 45	Marcus Robinson	.60	.25
❑ 46	Aaron Brooks	1.00	.40
❑ 47	Cris Carter	1.00	.40
❑ 48	Tiki Barber	1.00	.40
❑ 49	Terry Glenn	.60	.25
❑ 50	Ed McCaffrey	1.00	.40
❑ 51	Darrell Jackson	.60	.25
❑ 52	Garrison Hearst	.60	.25
❑ 53	Hines Ward	1.00	.40
❑ 54	Deuce McAllister	1.25	.50
❑ 55	Rod Gardner	.60	.25
❑ 56	Amani Toomer	.60	.25
❑ 57	Thomas Jones	.60	.25
❑ 58	Travis Henry	1.00	.40
❑ 59	Koren Robinson	.60	.25
❑ 60	Travis Taylor	.60	.25
❑ 61	Ron Dayne	.60	.25
❑ 62	Robert Ferguson	.60	.25
❑ 63	Chad Pennington	1.25	.50
❑ 64	James Allen	.60	.25
❑ 65	Chris Weinke	.60	.25
❑ 66	Torry Holt	1.00	.40
❑ 67	Chris Chandler	.60	.25
❑ 68	Shane Matthews	.60	.25
❑ 69	Ike Hilliard	.60	.25
❑ 70	Charlie Garner	.60	.25
❑ 71	Laveranues Coles	.60	.25
❑ 72	Lamar Smith	.60	.25
❑ 73	Rob Johnson	.60	.25
❑ 74	Qadry Ismail	.60	.25
❑ 75	James Jackson	.60	.25
❑ 76	Wayne Chrebet	.60	.25
❑ 77	Priest Holmes	1.25	.50
❑ 78	Michael Westbrook	.40	.15
❑ 79	Michael Pittman	.40	.15
❑ 80	Derrick Mason	.60	.25
❑ 81	Dominic Rhodes	1.00	.40
❑ 82	Eric Moulds	.60	.25
❑ 83	Fred Taylor	1.00	.40
❑ 84	Corey Bradford	.40	.15
❑ 85	Steve McNair	1.00	.40
❑ 86	Tyrone Wheatley	.60	.25
❑ 87	Peter Warrick	.60	.25
❑ 88	Freddie Mitchell	.60	.25
❑ 89	Peter Boulware	.40	.15
❑ 90	Kevin Johnson	.60	.25
❑ 91	Jermaine Lewis	.40	.15
❑ 92	Joey Galloway	.60	.25
❑ 93	Stephen Davis	.60	.25
❑ 94	James Thrash	.60	.25
❑ 95	James Stewart	.60	.25
❑ 96	Quincy Morgan	.60	.25
❑ 97	Dorsey Levens	.60	.25

❑ 98 Johnnie Morton .60 .25
❑ 99 Rocket Ismail .60 .25
❑ 100 Rod Smith .60 .25
❑ 101 David Terrell 1.00 .40
❑ 102 Kordell Stewart .60 .25
❑ 103 Marty Booker .60 .25
❑ 104 Brian Griese 1.00 .40
❑ 105 Snoop Minnis .40 .15
❑ 106 Jake Plummer .60 .25
❑ 107 Keenan McCardell .40 .15
❑ 108 Duce Staley 1.00 .40
❑ 109 Isaac Bruce 1.00 .40
❑ 110 Bubba Franks .60 .25
❑ 111 Keyshawn Johnson 1.00 .40
❑ 112 Kevan Barlow .60 .25
❑ 113 Reggie Wayne 1.00 .40
❑ 114 Michael Bennett 1.00 .40
❑ 115 Santana Moss 1.00 .40
❑ 116 David Carr RC 8.00 3.00
❑ 117 Joey Harrington RC 5.00 2.00
❑ 118 Antwaan Randle El RC 4.00 1.50
❑ 119 Eric Crouch RC 2.50 1.00
❑ 120 Javon Walker RC 6.00 2.50
❑ 121 William Green RC 2.50 1.00
❑ 122 Patrick Ramsey RC 4.00 1.50
❑ 123 Clinton Portis RC 10.00 4.00
❑ 124 Andre Davis RC 2.00 .75
❑ 125 T.J. Duckett RC 4.00 1.50
❑ 126 Ladell Betts RC 2.50 1.00
❑ 127 Marquise Walker RC 2.00 .75
❑ 128 Maurice Morris RC 2.50 1.00
❑ 129 Brian Westbrook RC 5.00 2.00
❑ 130 Phillip Buchanon RC 2.50 1.00
❑ 131 Tim Carter RC 2.00 .75
❑ 132 Zak Kustok RC 2.50 1.00
❑ 133 Chester Taylor RC 4.00 1.50
❑ 134 Josh Reed RC 2.50 1.00
❑ 135 Kurt Kittner RC 2.00 .75
❑ 136 Cliff Russell RC 2.00 .75
❑ 137 Travis Fisher RC 2.50 1.00
❑ 138 Jerramy Stevens RC 2.50 1.00
❑ 139 Verron Haynes RC 2.50 1.00
❑ 140 Ricky Williams RC 2.00 .75
❑ 141 Randy McMichael RC 4.00 1.50
❑ 142 Dwight Freeney RC 3.00 1.25
❑ 143 Lito Sheppard RC 2.50 1.00
❑ 144 Mike Williams RC 2.00 .75
❑ 145 Jason McAddley RC 2.00 .75
❑ 146 Deion Branch RC 6.00 2.50
❑ 147 Daniel Graham RC 2.50 1.00
❑ 148 J.T. O'Sullivan RC 2.00 .75
❑ 149 Freddie Milons RC 2.00 .75
❑ 150 Ron Johnson RC 2.00 .75
❑ 151 Ashley Lelie RC 4.00 1.50
❑ 152 Roy Williams RC 5.00 2.00
❑ 153 Donte Stallworth RC 4.00 1.50
❑ 154 Randy Fasani RC 1.50 .60
❑ 155 Antonio Bryant RC 2.00 .75
❑ 156 Julius Peppers RC 4.00 1.50
❑ 157 Jabar Gaffney RC 2.00 .75
❑ 158 Chad Hutchinson RC 1.50 .60
❑ 159 DeShaun Foster RC 2.00 .75
❑ 160 Micah Ross RC 1.50 .60
❑ 161 Rocky Calmus RC 2.00 .75
❑ 162 Travis Stephens RC 1.50 .60
❑ 163 Quentin Jammer RC 2.00 .75
❑ 164 Napoleon Harris RC 2.00 .75
❑ 165 Jeremy Shockey RC 6.00 2.50
❑ 166 Rohan Davey RC 2.00 .75
❑ 167 Najeh Davenport RC 2.00 .75
❑ 168 Adrian Peterson RC 2.00 .75
❑ 169 Ed Reed RC 3.00 1.25
❑ 170 Ben Leber RC 2.00 .75
❑ 171 Robert Thomas RC 2.00 .75
❑ 172 Lamar Gordon RC 2.00 .75
❑ 173 Reche Caldwell RC 2.00 .75
❑ 174 Michael Lewis RC 2.00 .75
❑ 175 Ryan Sims RC 2.00 .75
❑ 176 David Garrard RC 2.00 .75
❑ 177 Jonathan Wells RC 2.00 .75
❑ 178 Albert Haynesworth RC 1.50 .60
❑ 179 Josh McCown RC 2.50 1.00
❑ 180 John Henderson RC 2.00 .75
❑ 181 Jake Plummer QBC 1.00 .40
❑ 182 Michael Vick QBC 5.00 2.00
❑ 183 Chris Redman QBC 1.00 .40
❑ 184 Drew Bledsoe QBC 2.00 .75
❑ 185 Jim Miller QBC 1.00 .40
❑ 186 Jon Kitna QBC 1.00 .40
❑ 187 Tim Couch QBC 1.00 .40
❑ 188 Quincy Carter QBC 1.00 .40
❑ 189 Brian Griese QBC 1.50 .60
❑ 190 Mike McMahon QBC 1.50 .60
❑ 191 Brett Favre QBC 4.00 1.50
❑ 192 David Carr QBC 3.00 1.25
❑ 193 Peyton Manning QBC 3.00 1.25
❑ 194 Mark Brunell QBC 1.50 .60
❑ 195 Trent Green QBC 1.00 .40
❑ 196 Jay Fiedler QBC 1.00 .40
❑ 197 Daunte Culpepper QBC 1.50 .60
❑ 198 Tom Brady QBC 4.00 1.50
❑ 199 Aaron Brooks QBC 1.50 .60
❑ 200 Kerry Collins QBC 1.00 .40
❑ 201 Vinny Testaverde QBC 1.00 .40
❑ 202 Rich Gannon QBC 1.50 .60
❑ 203 Donovan McNabb QBC 2.00 .75
❑ 204 Kordell Stewart QBC 1.00 .40
❑ 205 Doug Flutie QBC 1.50 .60
❑ 206 Jeff Garcia QBC 1.50 .60
❑ 207 Trent Dilfer QBC 1.00 .40
❑ 208 Kurt Warner QBC 1.50 .60
❑ 209 Brad Johnson QBC 1.00 .40
❑ 210 Steve McNair QBC 1.50 .60
❑ 211 Sam Madison AP .75 .30
❑ 212 Bruce Matthews AP .75 .30
❑ 213 Brett Favre AP 3.00 1.25
❑ 214 Cris Carter AP 1.25 .50
❑ 215 Michael Strahan AP .75 .30
❑ 216 Ray Lewis AP 1.25 .50
❑ 217 Randy Moss AP 2.50 1.00
❑ 218 Jerome Bettis AP 1.25 .50
❑ 219 Warren Sapp AP .75 .30
❑ 220 Junior Seau AP 1.25 .50
❑ 221 Emmitt Smith AP 3.00 1.25
❑ 222 Jimmy Smith AP .75 .30
❑ 223 Mike Alstott AP 1.25 .50
❑ 224 Zach Thomas AP 1.25 .50
❑ 225 Marshall Faulk AP 1.25 .50
❑ 226 John Lynch AP .75 .30
❑ 227 Larry Allen AP .75 .30
❑ 228 Kurt Warner AP 1.25 .50
❑ 229 Eddie George AP 1.25 .50
❑ 230 Tony Gonzalez AP .75 .30
❑ 231 Marvin Harrison AP 1.25 .50
❑ 232 Terrell Davis AP 1.25 .50
❑ 233 Peyton Manning AP 2.50 1.00
❑ 234 Terrell Owens AP 1.25 .50
❑ 235 Jevon Kearse AP .75 .30
❑ 236 Jerry Rice AP 2.50 1.00
❑ 237 Shannon Sharpe AP .75 .30
❑ 238 Rod Woodson AP .75 .30
❑ 239 Mark Brunell AP 1.25 .50
❑ 240 Tim Brown AP 1.25 .50

1998 Fleer Brilliants

❑ COMPLETE SET (150) 100.00 40.00
❑ 1 John Elway 5.00 2.00
❑ 2 Curtis Conway .75 .30
❑ 3 Danny Wuerffel .75 .30
❑ 4 Emmitt Smith 4.00 1.50
❑ 5 Marvin Harrison 1.25 .50
❑ 6 Antowain Smith 1.25 .50
❑ 7 James Stewart .75 .30
❑ 8 Junior Seau 1.25 .50
❑ 9 Herman Moore .75 .30
❑ 10 Drew Bledsoe 2.00 .75
❑ 11 Rae Carruth .50 .20
❑ 12 Trent Dilfer 1.25 .50
❑ 13 Derrick Alexander .75 .30
❑ 14 Ike Hilliard .75 .30
❑ 15 Bruce Smith .75 .30
❑ 16 Warren Moon 1.25 .50
❑ 17 Jermaine Lewis .75 .30
❑ 18 Mike Alstott 1.25 .50
❑ 19 Robert Brooks .75 .30
❑ 20 Jerome Bettis 1.25 .50
❑ 21 Brett Favre 5.00 2.00
❑ 22 Garrison Hearst 1.25 .50
❑ 23 Neil O'Donnell .75 .30
❑ 24 Joey Galloway .75 .30
❑ 25 Barry Sanders 4.00 1.50
❑ 26 Donnell Bennett .50 .20
❑ 27 Jamal Anderson 1.25 .50
❑ 28 Isaac Bruce 1.25 .50
❑ 29 Chris Chandler .75 .30
❑ 30 Kordell Stewart 1.25 .50
❑ 31 Corey Dillon 1.25 .50
❑ 32 Troy Aikman 2.50 1.00
❑ 33 Frank Sanders .75 .30
❑ 34 Cris Carter 1.25 .50
❑ 35 Greg Hill .50 .20
❑ 36 Tony Martin .75 .30
❑ 37 Shannon Sharpe .75 .30
❑ 38 Wayne Chrebet 1.25 .50
❑ 39 Trent Green 1.25 .50
❑ 40 Warrick Dunn 1.25 .50
❑ 41 Michael Irvin 1.25 .50
❑ 42 Eddie George 1.25 .50
❑ 43 Carl Pickens .75 .30
❑ 44 Wesley Walls .75 .30
❑ 45 Steve McNair 1.25 .50
❑ 46 Bert Emanuel .75 .30
❑ 47 Terry Glenn 1.25 .50
❑ 48 Elvis Grbac .75 .30
❑ 49 Charles Way .50 .20
❑ 50 Steve Young 1.50 .60
❑ 51 Deion Sanders 1.25 .50
❑ 52 Keyshawn Johnson 1.25 .50
❑ 53 Kerry Collins .75 .30
❑ 54 O.J. McDuffie .75 .30
❑ 55 Ricky Watters .75 .30
❑ 56 Derrick Thomas 1.25 .50
❑ 57 Antonio Freeman 1.25 .50
❑ 58 Jake Plummer 1.25 .50
❑ 59 Andre Reed .75 .30
❑ 60 Jerry Rice 2.50 1.00
❑ 61 Dorsey Levens 1.25 .50
❑ 62 Eddie Kennison .75 .30
❑ 63 Marshall Faulk 1.50 .60
❑ 64 Michael Jackson .50 .20
❑ 65 Karim Abdul-Jabbar 1.25 .50
❑ 66 Andre Rison .75 .30
❑ 67 Glenn Foley .75 .30
❑ 68 Jake Reed .75 .30
❑ 69 Tony Banks .75 .30
❑ 70 Dan Marino 5.00 2.00
❑ 71 Bryan Still .50 .20
❑ 72 Tim Brown 1.25 .50
❑ 73 Charles Johnson .50 .20
❑ 74 Jeff George .75 .30
❑ 75 Jimmy Smith .75 .30
❑ 76 Ben Coates .75 .30
❑ 77 Rob Moore .75 .30
❑ 78 Johnnie Morton .75 .30
❑ 79 Peter Boulware .50 .20
❑ 80 Curtis Martin 1.25 .50
❑ 81 James McKnight 1.25 .50
❑ 82 Danny Kanell .75 .30
❑ 83 Brad Johnson 1.25 .50
❑ 84 Amani Toomer .75 .30
❑ 85 Terry Allen 1.25 .50
❑ 86 Rod Smith .75 .30
❑ 87 Keenan McCardell .75 .30
❑ 88 Leslie Shepherd .50 .20
❑ 89 Irving Fryar .75 .30
❑ 90 Terrell Davis 1.25 .50
❑ 91 Robert Smith 1.25 .50
❑ 92 Duce Staley 1.50 .60
❑ 93 Rickey Dudley .50 .20
❑ 94 Bobby Hoying .75 .30
❑ 95 Terrell Owens 1.25 .50
❑ 96 Fred Lane .50 .20
❑ 97 Natrone Means .75 .30
❑ 98 Yancey Thigpen .50 .20
❑ 99 Reggie White 1.25 .50
❑ 100 Mark Brunell 1.25 .50
❑ 101 Ahman Green RC 15.00 6.00
❑ 102 Skip Hicks RC 2.50 1.00
❑ 103 Hines Ward RC 12.00 6.00
❑ 104 Marcus Nash RC 1.50 .60

❑ 105 Terry Hardy RC	1.50	.60
❑ 106 Patrick Johnson RC	2.50	1.00
❑ 107 Tremayne Stephens RC	1.50	.60
❑ 108 Joe Jurevicius RC	3.00	1.25
❑ 109 Moses Moreno RC	1.50	.60
❑ 110 Charles Woodson RC	4.00	1.50
❑ 111 Kevin Dyson RC	3.00	1.25
❑ 112 Alvis Whitted RC	2.50	1.00
❑ 113 Michael Pittman RC	4.00	2.00
❑ 114 Stephen Alexander RC	2.50	1.00
❑ 115 Tavian Banks RC	2.50	1.00
❑ 116 John Avery RC	2.50	1.00
❑ 117 Keith Brooking RC	3.00	1.25
❑ 118 Jerome Pathon RC	3.00	1.25
❑ 119 Terry Fair RC	2.50	1.00
❑ 120 Peyton Manning RC	30.00	12.50
❑ 121 R.W. McQuarters RC	2.50	1.00
❑ 122 Charlie Batch RC	3.00	1.25
❑ 123 Jonathan Quinn RC	3.00	1.25
❑ 124 Chris Fuamatu-Ma'afala RC	2.50	1.00
❑ 125 Jacquez Green RC	2.50	1.00
❑ 126 Germane Crowell RC	2.50	1.00
❑ 127 Oronde Gadsden RC	3.00	1.25
❑ 128 Koy Detmer	3.00	1.25
❑ 129 Robert Holcombe RC	2.50	1.00
❑ 130 Curtis Enis RC	1.50	.60
❑ 131 Brian Griese RC	6.00	2.50
❑ 132 Tony Simmons RC	2.50	1.00
❑ 133 Vonnie Holliday RC	2.50	1.00
❑ 134 Alonzo Mayes RC	1.50	.60
❑ 135 Jon Ritchie RC	2.50	1.00
❑ 136 Robert Edwards RC	2.50	1.00
❑ 137 Mike Vanderjagt RC	3.00	1.25
❑ 138 Jonathan Linton RC	2.50	1.00
❑ 139 Fred Taylor RC	5.00	2.00
❑ 140 Randy Moss RC	20.00	7.50
❑ 141 Rod Rutledge RC	1.50	.60
❑ 142 Andre Wadsworth RC	2.50	1.00
❑ 143 Rashaan Shehee RC	2.50	1.00
❑ 144 Shaun Williams RC	2.50	1.00
❑ 145 Mikhael Ricks RC	2.50	1.00
❑ 146 Wade Richey RC	1.50	.60
❑ 147 Carlos King RC	1.50	.60
❑ 148 Tim Dwight RC	3.00	1.25
❑ 149 Scott Frost RC	1.50	.60
❑ 150 Ryan Leaf RC	3.00	1.25

1999 Fleer Focus

❑ COMPLETE SET (175)	200.00	100.00
❑ COMP.SET w/o SP's (100)	40.00	20.00
❑ 1 Randy Moss	2.50	1.00
❑ 2 Andre Rison	.60	.25
❑ 3 Ed McCaffrey	.60	.25
❑ 4 Jerry Rice	2.00	.75
❑ 5 Tim Biakabutuka	.60	.25
❑ 6 Wayne Chrebet	.60	.25
❑ 7 Deion Sanders	1.00	.40
❑ 8 Ricky Watters	.60	.25
❑ 9 Skip Hicks	.40	.15
❑ 10 Charlie Batch	1.00	.40
❑ 11 Joey Galloway	.60	.25
❑ 12 Stephen Alexander	.40	.15
❑ 13 Curtis Conway	.60	.25
❑ 14 Garrison Hearst	.60	.25
❑ 15 Kerry Collins	.60	.25
❑ 16 Cris Carter	1.00	.40
❑ 17 Eddie George	1.00	.40
❑ 18 Eric Moulds	1.00	.40
❑ 19 Vinny Testaverde	.60	.25
❑ 20 Curtis Enis	.40	.15
❑ 21 Gary Brown	.40	.15
❑ 22 Junior Seau	1.00	.40
❑ 23 Kevin Dyson	.60	.25
❑ 24 Jeff Blake	.60	.25
❑ 25 Herman Moore	.60	.25
❑ 26 Natrone Means	.60	.25
❑ 27 Terry Glenn	1.00	.40
❑ 28 Fred Taylor	1.00	.40
❑ 29 Ben Coates	.60	.25
❑ 30 Corey Dillon	1.00	.40
❑ 31 Eddie Kennison	.60	.25
❑ 32 Byron Bam Morris	.40	.15
❑ 33 Doug Pederson	.40	.15
❑ 34 Jamal Anderson	1.00	.40
❑ 35 Michael Westbrook	.60	.25
❑ 36 Peyton Manning	3.00	1.25
❑ 37 Carl Pickens	.60	.25
❑ 38 Drew Bledsoe	1.50	.60
❑ 39 Jim Harbaugh	.60	.25
❑ 40 Kurt Warner RC	8.00	3.00
❑ 41 Mark Chmura	.40	.15
❑ 42 Hines Ward	1.00	.40
❑ 43 Terry Kirby	.40	.15
❑ 44 Brett Favre	3.00	1.25
❑ 45 Kordell Stewart	.60	.25
❑ 46 Leslie Shepherd	.40	.15
❑ 47 Marshall Faulk	1.25	.50
❑ 48 Troy Aikman	2.00	.75
❑ 49 Isaac Bruce	1.00	.40
❑ 50 Michael Irvin	.60	.25
❑ 51 Robert Smith	.60	.25
❑ 52 Dorsey Levens	1.00	.40
❑ 53 Duce Staley	1.00	.40
❑ 54 Jake Plummer	.60	.25
❑ 55 Adrian Murrell	.60	.25
❑ 56 Antonio Freeman	1.00	.40
❑ 57 Jerome Bettis	.60	.25
❑ 58 Elvis Grbac	.60	.25
❑ 59 Keyshawn Johnson	1.00	.40
❑ 60 Steve Beuerlein	.40	.15
❑ 61 Yancey Thigpen	.40	.15
❑ 62 Doug Flutie	1.00	.40
❑ 63 Jacquez Green	.40	.15
❑ 64 Jimmy Smith	.60	.25
❑ 65 Tim Brown	1.00	.40
❑ 66 Jason Sehorn	.40	.15
❑ 67 Muhsin Muhammad	.60	.25
❑ 68 Shannon Sharpe	.60	.25
❑ 69 Terrell Owens	1.00	.40
❑ 70 Keenan McCardell	.60	.25
❑ 71 Rich Gannon	1.00	.40
❑ 72 Scott Mitchell	.40	.15
❑ 73 Warrick Dunn	1.00	.40
❑ 74 Brad Johnson	.60	.25
❑ 75 Charles Johnson	.40	.15
❑ 76 Chris Chandler	.60	.25
❑ 77 Marcus Pollard	.40	.15
❑ 78 Mike Alstott	1.00	.40
❑ 79 Bubby Brister	.60	.25
❑ 80 Jon Kitna	1.00	.40
❑ 81 Randall Cunningham	1.00	.40
❑ 82 Antowain Smith	1.00	.40
❑ 83 Curtis Martin	1.00	.40
❑ 84 Steve McNair	1.00	.40
❑ 85 Tony Gonzalez	1.00	.40
❑ 86 O.J. McDuffie	.60	.25
❑ 87 Steve Young	1.25	.50
❑ 88 Terrell Davis	1.00	.40
❑ 89 Mark Brunell	1.00	.40
❑ 90 Napoleon Kaufman	1.00	.40
❑ 91 Priest Holmes	1.50	.60
❑ 92 Trent Dilfer	.60	.25
❑ 93 Brian Griese	1.00	.40
❑ 94 J.J. Stokes	.60	.25
❑ 95 Karim Abdul-Jabbar	.60	.25
❑ 96 Barry Sanders	3.00	1.25
❑ 97 Dan Marino	3.00	1.25
❑ 98 Emmitt Smith	2.00	.75
❑ 99 Marvin Harrison	1.00	.40
❑ 100 Rod Smith	.60	.25
❑ 101 Champ Bailey RC	3.00	1.25
❑ 102 Fernando Bryant RC	1.50	.60
❑ 103 Chris Claiborne RC	1.00	.40
❑ 104 Antuan Edwards RC	1.50	.60
❑ 105 Martin Gramatica RC	1.00	.40
❑ 106 Andy Katzenmoyer RC	1.50	.60
❑ 107 Jevon Kearse RC	4.00	1.50
❑ 108 Chris McAlister RC	1.50	.60
❑ 109 Al Wilson RC	1.50	.60
❑ 110 Antoine Winfield RC	1.50	.60
❑ 111 Karsten Bailey RC	3.00	1.25
❑ 112 D'Wayne Bates RC	3.00	1.25
❑ 113 Marty Booker RC	4.00	1.50
❑ 114 David Boston RC	4.00	1.50
❑ 115 Na Brown RC	3.00	1.25
❑ 116 Desmond Clark RC	4.00	1.50
❑ 117 Dameane Douglas RC	2.50	1.00
❑ 118 Donald Driver RC	8.00	3.00
❑ 119 Troy Edwards RC	3.00	1.25
❑ 120 Torry Holt RC	10.00	4.00
❑ 121 Kevin Johnson RC	4.00	1.50
❑ 122 Reginald Kelly RC	2.50	1.00
❑ 123 Jimmy Kleinsasser RC	3.00	1.25
❑ 124 Jeremy McDaniel RC	4.00	1.50
❑ 125 Darnell McDonald RC	3.00	1.25
❑ 126 Travis McGriff RC	2.50	1.00
❑ 127 Billy Miller RC	2.50	1.00
❑ 128 Dee Miller RC	2.50	1.00
❑ 129 Peerless Price RC	4.00	1.50
❑ 130 Troy Smith RC	2.50	1.00
❑ 131 Brandon Stokley RC	5.00	2.00
❑ 132 Wane McGarity RC	2.50	1.00
❑ 133 Mark Campbell RC	2.50	1.00
❑ 134 Jerame Tuman RC	4.00	1.50
❑ 135 Craig Yeast RC	3.00	1.25
❑ 136 Jerry Azumah RC	5.00	2.00
❑ 137 Marlon Barnes RC	3.00	1.25
❑ 138 Michael Basnight RC	3.00	1.25
❑ 139 Shawn Bryson RC	6.00	2.50
❑ 140 Mike Cloud RC	5.00	2.00
❑ 141 Cecil Collins RC	3.00	1.25
❑ 142 Autry Denson RC	5.00	2.00
❑ 143 Kevin Faulk RC	6.00	2.50
❑ 144 Jermaine Fazande RC	5.00	2.00
❑ 145 Jim Finn RC	3.00	1.25
❑ 146 Madre Hill RC	3.00	1.25
❑ 147 Sedrick Irvin RC	3.00	1.25
❑ 148 Terry Jackson RC	5.00	2.00
❑ 149 Edgerrin James RC	15.00	6.00
❑ 150 James Johnson RC	5.00	2.00
❑ 151 Rob Konrad RC	6.00	2.50
❑ 152 Joel Makovicka RC	6.00	2.50
❑ 153 Cecil Martin RC	6.00	2.50
❑ 154 Joe Montgomery RC	5.00	2.00
❑ 155 De'Mond Parker RC	3.00	1.25
❑ 156 Sirr Parker RC	3.00	1.25
❑ 157 Jeff Paulk RC	3.00	1.25
❑ 158 Nick Williams RC	5.00	2.00
❑ 159 Ricky Williams RC	10.00	4.00
❑ 160 Amos Zereoue RC	6.00	2.50
❑ 161 Michael Bishop RC	8.00	3.00
❑ 162 Aaron Brooks RC	12.00	5.00
❑ 163 Tim Couch RC	8.00	3.00
❑ 164 Scott Covington RC	8.00	3.00
❑ 165 Daunte Culpepper RC	20.00	7.50
❑ 166 Kevin Daft RC	6.00	2.50
❑ 167 Joe Germaine RC	6.00	2.50
❑ 168 Chris Greisen RC	6.00	2.50
❑ 169 Brock Huard RC	6.00	2.50
❑ 170 Shaun King RC	5.00	2.00
❑ 171 Cory Sauter RC	5.00	2.00
❑ 172 Donovan McNabb RC	25.00	10.00
❑ 173 Cade McNown RC	5.00	2.00
❑ 174 Chad Plummer RC	5.00	2.00
❑ 175 Akili Smith RC	1.50	.60
❑ P1 Promo Sheet	4.00	1.50
❑ P54 Jake Plummer PROMO	1.00	.40

2000 Fleer Focus

❑ COMPLETE SET (260)	400.00	200.00
❑ COMP.SET w/o SPs (200)	25.00	10.00
❑ 1 Tim Couch	.40	.15
❑ 2 Germane Crowell	.25	.08

❑ 3	Curtis Martin	.60	.25
❑ 4	Samari Rolle	.25	.08
❑ 5	Brian Griese	.60	.25
❑ 6	Kerry Collins	.40	.15
❑ 7	Jevon Kearse	.60	.25
❑ 8	Rocket Ismail	.40	.15
❑ 9	Cam Cleeland	.25	.08
❑ 10	Warrick Dunn	.60	.25
❑ 11	Carl Pickens	.40	.15
❑ 12	Cris Carter	.60	.25
❑ 13	Mike Pritchard	.25	.08
❑ 14	Corey Dillon	.60	.25
❑ 15	Randy Moss	1.25	.50
❑ 16	Derrick Mayes	.40	.15
❑ 17	Marcus Robinson	.60	.25
❑ 18	Thurman Thomas	.40	.15
❑ 19	J.J. Stokes	.40	.15
❑ 20	Muhsin Muhammad	.40	.15
❑ 21	Derrick Alexander	.40	.15
❑ 22	Curtis Conway	.40	.15
❑ 23	Qadry Ismail	.40	.15
❑ 24	Ken Dilger	.25	.08
❑ 25	Troy Edwards	.25	.08
❑ 26	Shawn Jefferson	.25	.08
❑ 27	Terrence Wilkins	.25	.08
❑ 28	Duce Staley	.60	.25
❑ 29	Aeneas Williams	.25	.08
❑ 30	Antonio Freeman	.60	.25
❑ 31	Tim Brown	.60	.25
❑ 32	Darrell Green	.25	.08
❑ 33	Herman Moore	.40	.15
❑ 34	Vinny Testaverde	.40	.15
❑ 35	Yancey Thigpen	.25	.08
❑ 36	Emmitt Smith	1.25	.50
❑ 37	Ricky Williams	.60	.25
❑ 38	Keyshawn Johnson	.60	.25
❑ 39	Eddie Kennison	.25	.08
❑ 40	Zach Thomas	.60	.25
❑ 41	Shawn Springs	.25	.08
❑ 42	Wesley Walls	.25	.08
❑ 43	Andre Rison	.40	.15
❑ 44	Jerry Rice	1.25	.50
❑ 45	Rob Johnson	.40	.15
❑ 46	Keenan McCardell	.40	.15
❑ 47	Ryan Leaf	.40	.15
❑ 48	Michael McCrary	.25	.08
❑ 49	Marvin Harrison	.60	.25
❑ 50	Donovan McNabb	1.00	.40
❑ 51	Curtis Enis	.25	.08
❑ 52	Tony Martin	.40	.15
❑ 53	Jeff Garcia	.60	.25
❑ 54	Tim Biakabutuka	.40	.15
❑ 55	Tony Gonzalez	.40	.15
❑ 56	Jim Harbaugh	.40	.15
❑ 57	Peerless Price	.40	.15
❑ 58	Fred Taylor	.60	.25
❑ 59	Kordell Stewart	.40	.15
❑ 60	Chris Chandler	.40	.15
❑ 61	Bill Schroeder	.40	.15
❑ 62	Charles Woodson	.40	.15
❑ 63	Terance Mathis	.40	.15
❑ 64	Brett Favre	2.00	.75
❑ 65	Rickey Dudley	.25	.08
❑ 66	Rob Moore	.40	.15
❑ 67	Charlie Batch	.60	.25
❑ 68	Wayne Chrebet	.40	.15
❑ 69	Jeff George	.40	.15
❑ 70	Olandis Gary	.60	.25
❑ 71	Amani Toomer	.40	.15
❑ 72	Kevin Dyson	.40	.15
❑ 73	Darrin Chiaverini	.25	.08
❑ 74	Willie McGinest	.25	.08
❑ 75	Ricky Proehl	.25	.08
❑ 76	Craig Yeast	.25	.08
❑ 77	Dwayne Rudd	.25	.08
❑ 78	Marshall Faulk	.75	.30
❑ 79	Bobby Engram	.40	.15
❑ 80	Jay Fiedler	.60	.25
❑ 81	Jon Kitna	.60	.25
❑ 82	Patrick Jeffers	.60	.25
❑ 83	James Johnson	.25	.08
❑ 84	Charlie Garner	.40	.15
❑ 85	Eric Moulds	.60	.25
❑ 86	Mark Brunell	.60	.25
❑ 87	Richard Huntley	.25	.08
❑ 88	Frank Sanders	.40	.15
❑ 89	Robert Porcher	.25	.08
❑ 90	Aaron Glenn	.25	.08
❑ 91	Stephen Davis	.60	.25
❑ 92	Ed McCaffrey	.60	.25
❑ 93	Pete Mitchell	.25	.08
❑ 94	Frank Wycheck	.25	.08
❑ 95	David LaFleur	.25	.08
❑ 96	Jake Delhomme RC	3.00	1.25
❑ 97	John Lynch	.40	.15
❑ 98	Michael Pittman	.25	.08
❑ 99	Andy Katzenmoyer	.25	.08
❑ 100	Isaac Bruce	.60	.25
❑ 101	Terry Kirby	.25	.08
❑ 102	Kevin Faulk	.40	.15
❑ 103	Kevin Carter	.40	.15
❑ 104	Darnay Scott	.40	.15
❑ 105	Robert Smith	.60	.25
❑ 106	Brian Mitchell	.25	.08
❑ 107	Shane Matthews	.25	.08
❑ 108	O.J. McDuffie	.40	.15
❑ 109	Bryant Young	.25	.08
❑ 110	Jay Riemersma	.25	.08
❑ 111	Elvis Grbac	.40	.15
❑ 112	Jermaine Fazande	.25	.08
❑ 113	Jonathan Linton	.25	.08
❑ 114	Kyle Brady	.25	.08
❑ 115	Junior Seau	.60	.25
❑ 116	Shannon Sharpe	.40	.15
❑ 117	Jerome Pathon	.40	.15
❑ 118	Jerome Bettis	.60	.25
❑ 119	O.J. Santiago	.25	.08
❑ 120	Ahman Green	.60	.25
❑ 121	Troy Vincent	.25	.08
❑ 122	David Boston	.60	.25
❑ 123	James Stewart	.40	.15
❑ 124	Ray Lucas	.40	.15
❑ 125	Brad Johnson	.60	.25
❑ 126	Rod Smith	.40	.15
❑ 127	Joe Jurevicius	.25	.08
❑ 128	Eddie George	.60	.25
❑ 129	Darren Woodson	.25	.08
❑ 130	Jake Reed	.40	.15
❑ 131	Mike Alstott	.60	.25
❑ 132	Leslie Shepherd	.25	.08
❑ 133	Terry Glenn	.40	.15
❑ 134	Az-Zahir Hakim	.40	.15
❑ 135	Alonzo Mayes	.25	.08
❑ 136	Sam Madison	.25	.08
❑ 137	Ricky Watters	.40	.15
❑ 138	Antowain Smith	.40	.15
❑ 139	Jimmy Smith	.40	.15
❑ 140	Hines Ward	.60	.25
❑ 141	Priest Holmes	.75	.30
❑ 142	Edgerrin James	1.00	.40
❑ 143	Charles Johnson	.40	.15
❑ 144	Jamal Anderson	.60	.25
❑ 145	Dorsey Levens	.40	.15
❑ 146	Rich Gannon	.60	.25
❑ 147	Champ Bailey	.40	.15
❑ 148	Bill Romanowski	.25	.08
❑ 149	Jason Sehorn	.25	.08
❑ 150	Steve McNair	.60	.25
❑ 151	Jermaine Lewis	.40	.15
❑ 152	Cornelius Bennett	.25	.08
❑ 153	Torrance Small	.25	.08
❑ 154	Tim Dwight	.60	.25
❑ 155	Corey Bradford	.40	.15
❑ 156	Napoleon Kaufman	.40	.15
❑ 157	Jake Plummer	.40	.15
❑ 158	David Sloan	.25	.08
❑ 159	Dedric Ward	.25	.08
❑ 160	Michael Westbrook	.40	.15
❑ 161	Terrell Davis	.60	.25
❑ 162	Ike Hilliard	.40	.15
❑ 163	Derrick Brooks	.60	.25
❑ 164	Greg Ellis	.25	.08
❑ 165	Keith Poole	.25	.08
❑ 166	Jacquez Green	.25	.08
❑ 167	Joey Galloway	.40	.15
❑ 168	Lawyer Milloy	.40	.15
❑ 169	Warren Sapp	.40	.15
❑ 170	Takeo Spikes	.25	.08
❑ 171	John Randle	.40	.15
❑ 172	Torry Holt	.60	.25
❑ 173	Cade McNown	.25	.08
❑ 174	Damon Huard	.60	.25
❑ 175	Terrell Owens	.60	.25
❑ 176	Steve Beuerlein	.40	.15
❑ 177	Tony Richardson RC	.40	.15
❑ 178	Jeff Graham	.40	.15
❑ 179	Doug Flutie	.60	.25
❑ 180	Kevin Hardy	.25	.08
❑ 181	Mark Bruener	.25	.08
❑ 182	Tony Banks	.40	.15
❑ 183	Peyton Manning	1.50	.60
❑ 184	Hugh Douglas	.25	.08
❑ 185	Simeon Rice	.40	.15
❑ 186	Terry Fair	.25	.08
❑ 187	James Jett	.25	.08
❑ 188	Albert Connell	.25	.08
❑ 189	Troy Aikman	1.50	.60
❑ 190	Jeff Blake	.40	.15
❑ 191	Shaun King	.25	.08
❑ 192	Kevin Johnson	.60	.25
❑ 193	Drew Bledsoe	.75	.30
❑ 194	Kurt Warner	1.25	.50
❑ 195	Akili Smith	.25	.08
❑ 196	Daunte Culpepper	.75	.30
❑ 197	Sean Dawkins	.25	.08
❑ 198	Natrone Means	.25	.08
❑ 199	Kimble Anders	.25	.08
❑ 200	Steve Young	.75	.30
❑ 201	Courtney Brown RC	4.00	1.50
❑ 202	Chris Samuels RC	3.00	1.25
❑ 203	Corey Simon RC	4.00	1.50
❑ 204	Deon Grant RC	4.00	1.50
❑ 205	Darren Howard RC	3.00	1.25
❑ 206	Rob Morris RC	4.00	1.50
❑ 207	Ahmed Plummer RC	4.00	1.50
❑ 208	Anthony Becht RC	4.00	1.50
❑ 209	Brian Urlacher RC	15.00	6.00
❑ 210	Shaun Ellis RC	4.00	1.50
❑ 211	Bubba Franks RC	4.00	1.50
❑ 212	Plaxico Burress RC	15.00	6.00
❑ 213	R.Jay Soward RC	8.00	3.00
❑ 214	Dez White RC	8.00	3.00
❑ 215	Peter Warrick RC	8.00	3.00
❑ 216	Jerry Porter RC	10.00	4.00
❑ 217	Ron Dugans RC	6.00	2.50
❑ 218	Laveranues Coles RC	10.00	4.00
❑ 219	Travis Taylor RC	8.00	3.00
❑ 220	Anthony Lucas RC	6.00	2.50
❑ 221	Sylvester Morris RC	8.00	3.00
❑ 222	Dennis Northcutt RC	8.00	3.00
❑ 223	Chafie Fields RC	6.00	2.50
❑ 224	Danny Farmer RC	8.00	3.00
❑ 225	Chris Cole RC	6.00	2.50
❑ 226	Sherrod Gideon RC	6.00	2.50
❑ 227	Todd Pinkston RC	8.00	3.00
❑ 228	Gari Scott RC	6.00	2.50
❑ 229	Darrell Jackson RC	15.00	6.00
❑ 230	JaJuan Dawson RC	6.00	2.50
❑ 231	Trevor Gaylor RC	6.00	2.50
❑ 232	Bashir Yamini RC	6.00	2.50
❑ 233	Quinton Spotwood RC	6.00	2.50
❑ 234	Michael Wiley RC	5.00	2.00
❑ 235	Ron Dayne RC	6.00	2.50
❑ 236	Thomas Jones RC	10.00	4.00
❑ 237	Jamal Lewis RC	20.00	7.50
❑ 238	Travis Prentice RC	5.00	2.00
❑ 239	J.R. Redmond RC	5.00	2.00
❑ 240	Trung Canidate RC	5.00	2.00
❑ 241	Shaun Alexander RC	40.00	15.00
❑ 242	Frank Murphy RC	4.00	1.50
❑ 243	Shyrone Stith RC	6.00	2.50
❑ 244	Rondell Mealey RC	4.00	1.50
❑ 245	Terrelle Smith RC	5.00	2.00
❑ 246	Reuben Droughns RC	8.00	3.00
❑ 247	Chad Morton RC	6.00	2.50
❑ 248	Mike Anderson RC	8.00	3.00
❑ 249	Paul Smith RC	5.00	2.00
❑ 250	Curtis Keaton RC	5.00	2.00
❑ 251	Jarious Jackson RC	6.00	2.50
❑ 252	Marc Bulger RC	10.00	4.00
❑ 253	Tee Martin RC	6.00	2.50
❑ 254	Todd Husak RC	6.00	2.50
❑ 255	Joe Hamilton RC	6.00	2.50
❑ 256	Doug Johnson RC	6.00	2.50
❑ 257	Giovanni Carmazzi RC	5.00	2.00
❑ 258	Chris Redman RC	6.00	2.50
❑ 259	Tim Rattay RC	6.00	2.50
❑ 260	Chad Pennington RC	20.00	7.50
❑ P16	Tim Couch Promo	1.00	.40

2001 Fleer Focus

❑	COMP.SET w/o SP's (180)	25.00	10.00
❑ 1	Marshall Faulk	.75	.30
❑ 2	Randy Moss	1.25	.50
❑ 3	Cade McNown	.25	.08
❑ 4	Jeff Graham	.25	.08
❑ 5	Donovan McNabb	.75	.30

6	Shannon Sharpe	.40	.15
7	Todd Pinkston	.40	.15
8	Terrence Wilkins	.25	.08
9	Michael Strahan	.40	.15
10	Rich Gannon	.60	.25
11	Germane Crowell	.25	.08
12	Warren Sapp	.40	.15
13	La'Roi Glover	.25	.08
14	Peter Warrick	.60	.25
15	Shaun Alexander	.75	.30
16	Ray Lucas	.25	.08
17	Muhsin Muhammad	.40	.15
18	Curtis Conway	.40	.15
19	R.Jay Soward	.25	.08
20	Jamal Lewis	1.00	.40
21	Tony Gonzalez	.40	.15
22	Bill Schroeder	.40	.15
23	Frank Sanders	.25	.08
24	Charles Woodson	.40	.15
25	Johnnie Morton	.40	.15
26	Frank Wycheck	.25	.08
27	Ron Dayne	.60	.25
28	Travis Prentice	.25	.08
29	Isaac Bruce	.60	.25
30	Drew Bledsoe	.75	.30
31	James Allen	.40	.15
32	Matt Hasselbeck	.40	.15
33	Zach Thomas	.60	.25
34	Shawn Bryson	.25	.08
35	Jerry Rice	1.25	.50
36	Mike Cloud	.25	.08
37	Sammy Morris	.25	.08
38	Corey Simon	.40	.15
39	Peyton Manning	1.50	.60
40	Thomas Jones	.40	.15
41	Tyrone Wheatley	.40	.15
42	Herman Moore	.40	.15
43	Jeff George	.40	.15
44	Kerry Collins	.40	.15
45	Rocket Ismail	.40	.15
46	Andre Rison	.40	.15
47	David Sloan	.25	.08
48	Michael Westbrook	.40	.15
49	Ron Dixon	.25	.08
50	Randall Cunningham	.60	.25
51	Keyshawn Johnson	.60	.25
52	Aaron Brooks	.60	.25
53	Corey Dillon	.60	.25
54	John Randle	.40	.15
55	Cris Carter	.60	.25
56	Donald Hayes	.25	.08
57	Hines Ward	.60	.25
58	Edgerrin James	.75	.30
59	Terance Mathis	.25	.08
60	Doug Johnson	.25	.08
61	Rod Smith	.40	.15
62	Kevin Dyson	.40	.15
63	Amani Toomer	.40	.15
64	Courtney Brown	.40	.15
65	Mike Alstott	.60	.25
66	Kevin Faulk	.40	.15
67	Shane Matthews	.25	.08
68	Ricky Watters	.40	.15
69	Peter Boulware	.25	.08
70	Tim Biakabutuka	.40	.15
71	Troy Aikman	1.00	.40
72	Keenan McCardell	.25	.08
73	Priest Holmes	.75	.30
74	Duce Staley	.60	.25
75	Antonio Freeman	.60	.25
76	David Boston	.60	.25
77	Chad Pennington	1.00	.40
78	Brian Griese	.60	.25
79	Stephen Davis	.60	.25
80	Curtis Martin	.60	.25
81	Tony Banks	.40	.15
82	Warrick Dunn	.60	.25
83	Willie McGinest	.25	.08
84	Marty Booker	.25	.08
85	James Williams	.25	.08
86	Oronde Gadsden	.40	.15
87	Patrick Jeffers	.40	.15
88	Junior Seau	.60	.25
89	Frank Moreau	.25	.08
90	Ray Lewis	.60	.25
91	Doug Flutie	.60	.25
92	Jimmy Smith	.40	.15
93	Qadry Ismail	.40	.15
94	Jeremiah Trotter	.40	.15
95	Dorsey Levens	.40	.15
96	Michael Pittman	.25	.08
97	Wayne Chrebet	.40	.15
98	Mike Anderson	.60	.25
99	Derrick Mason	.40	.15
100	Jason Sehorn	.25	.08
101	Kevin Johnson	.40	.15
102	Terrell Owens	.60	.25
103	Lamar Smith	.40	.15
104	Eric Moulds	.40	.15
105	Jerome Bettis	.60	.25
106	Marvin Harrison	.60	.25
107	Shawn Jefferson	.25	.08
108	Rickey Dudley	.25	.08
109	James Stewart	.40	.15
110	Bruce Smith	.25	.08
111	Matthew Hatchette	.25	.08
112	Emmitt Smith	1.25	.50
113	Steve McNair	.60	.25
114	Ricky Williams	.60	.25
115	Tim Couch	.40	.15
116	Darrell Jackson	.60	.25
117	Doug Chapman	.25	.08
118	Jeff Lewis	.25	.08
119	Freddie Jones	.25	.08
120	Sylvester Morris	.25	.08
121	Elvis Grbac	.40	.15
122	Plaxico Burress	.60	.25
123	Marcus Pollard	.25	.08
124	Chris Chandler	.40	.15
125	James Thrash	.40	.15
126	Brett Favre	2.00	.75
127	Jake Plummer	.40	.15
128	Vinny Testaverde	.40	.15
129	Terrell Davis	.60	.25
130	Jevon Kearse	.40	.15
131	Albert Connell	.25	.08
132	Dennis Northcutt	.40	.15
133	Az-Zahir Hakim	.40	.15
134	J.R. Redmond	.25	.08
135	Marcus Robinson	.60	.25
136	Eddie George	.60	.25
137	Ike Hilliard	.40	.15
138	Hugh Douglas	.25	.08
139	Kurt Warner	1.25	.50
140	Terry Glenn	.40	.15
141	Brian Urlacher	1.00	.40
142	Charlie Garner	.40	.15
143	Jay Fiedler	.60	.25
144	Rob Johnson	.40	.15
145	Kordell Stewart	.40	.15
146	Mark Brunell	.60	.25
147	Travis Taylor	.40	.15
148	Laveranues Coles	.60	.25
149	Ed McCaffrey	.60	.25
150	Jacquez Green	.25	.08
151	Joe Horn	.40	.15
152	Darnay Scott	.40	.15
153	Torry Holt	.60	.25
154	Daunte Culpepper	.60	.25
155	Wesley Walls	.25	.08
156	Jeff Garcia	.60	.25
157	Derrick Alexander	.40	.15
158	Peerless Price	.40	.15
159	Bobby Shaw	.25	.08
160	Fred Taylor	.60	.25
161	Chris Redman	.25	.08
162	Tim Brown	.60	.25
163	Charlie Batch	.60	.25
164	Champ Bailey	.40	.15
165	Tiki Barber	.60	.25
166	Joey Galloway	.40	.15
167	Brad Johnson	.60	.25
168	Jeff Blake	.40	.15
169	Jon Kitna	.40	.15
170	Trent Green	.60	.25
171	Troy Brown	.40	.15
172	Eddie Kennison	.40	.15
173	J.J. Stokes	.40	.15
174	James McKnight	.40	.15
175	Jeremy McDaniel	.25	.08
176	Richard Huntley	.25	.08
177	Kyle Brady	.25	.08
178	Jamal Anderson	.60	.25
179	Chad Lewis	.25	.08
180	Ahman Green	.60	.25
181	Michael Vick RC	20.00	8.00
182	Deuce McAllister RC	10.00	4.00
183	David Terrell RC	5.00	2.00
184	Koren Robinson RC	5.00	2.00
185	LaDainian Tomlinson RC	40.00	20.00
186	Michael Bennett RC	5.00	2.00
187	Chris Chambers RC	8.00	3.00
188	Chad Johnson RC	12.00	5.00
189	Santana Moss RC	8.00	3.00
190	Todd Heap RC	5.00	2.00
191	Freddie Mitchell RC	5.00	2.00
192	Quincy Morgan RC	5.00	2.00
193	Rod Gardner RC	5.00	2.00
194	Kevan Barlow RC	5.00	2.00
195	Drew Brees RC	15.00	6.00
196	Robert Ferguson RC	5.00	2.00
197	Ken-Yon Rambo RC	3.00	1.25
198	Travis Henry RC	8.00	3.00
199	LaMont Jordan RC	10.00	4.00
200	Chris Weinke RC	5.00	2.00
201	Sage Rosenfels RC	5.00	2.00
202	Josh Heupel RC	5.00	2.00
203	Quincy Carter RC	5.00	2.00
204	Jesse Palmer RC	5.00	2.00
205	Mike McMahon RC	5.00	2.00
206	Rudi Johnson RC	10.00	4.00
207	Anthony Thomas RC	5.00	2.00
208	James Jackson RC	5.00	2.00
209	Snoop Minnis RC	3.00	1.25
210	Derek Combs RC	3.00	1.25
211	Ronney Daniels RC	3.00	1.25
212	Alex Bannister RC	3.00	1.25
213	Cedrick Wilson RC	5.00	2.00
214	Travis Minor RC	3.00	1.25
215	Marques Tuiasosopo RC	5.00	2.00
216	Reggie Wayne RC	10.00	5.00
217	Josh Booty RC	5.00	2.00
218	Jamal Reynolds RC	5.00	2.00
219	Gerard Warren RC	5.00	2.00
220	Justin Smith RC	5.00	2.00
221	Andre Carter RC	5.00	2.00
222	Milton Wynn RC	3.00	1.25
223	Fred Smoot RC	5.00	2.00
224	Jamar Fletcher RC	3.00	1.25
225	Dan Morgan RC	5.00	2.00
226	Jonathan Carter RC	3.00	1.25
227	Correll Buckhalter RC	6.00	2.50
228	Kevin Kasper RC	5.00	2.00
229	Derrick Blaylock RC	5.00	2.00
230	Justin McCareins RC	5.00	2.00

2002 Fleer Focus JE

	COMP.SET w/o SP's (100)	20.00	7.50
1	Tom Brady	2.50	1.00
2	Curtis Martin	1.00	.40
3	Brett Favre	2.50	1.00
4	Michael Pittman	.40	.15
5	Donovan McNabb	1.25	.50

Card		
❑ 6 Quincy Carter	.60	.25
❑ 7 Trent Dilfer	.60	.25
❑ 8 Troy Brown	.60	.25
❑ 9 Ed McCaffrey	1.00	.40
❑ 10 Shaun Alexander	1.25	.50
❑ 11 Daunte Culpepper	1.00	.40
❑ 12 Marty Booker	.60	.25
❑ 13 Junior Seau	1.00	.40
❑ 14 Zach Thomas	1.00	.40
❑ 15 Muhsin Muhammad	.60	.25
❑ 16 Kordell Stewart	.60	.25
❑ 17 Jimmy Smith	.60	.25
❑ 18 David Boston	1.00	.40
❑ 19 Laveranues Coles	.60	.25
❑ 20 Emmitt Smith	2.50	1.00
❑ 21 Darrell Jackson	.60	.25
❑ 22 Charlie Garner	.60	.25
❑ 23 Marcus Robinson	.60	.25
❑ 24 Drew Brees	1.00	.40
❑ 25 Tony Gonzalez	.60	.25
❑ 26 James Allen	.60	.25
❑ 27 Steve McNair	1.00	.40
❑ 28 Kerry Collins	.60	.25
❑ 29 Az-Zahir Hakim	.40	.15
❑ 30 Marshall Faulk	1.00	.40
❑ 31 Derrick Mason	.60	.25
❑ 32 Rod Smith	.60	.25
❑ 33 Torry Holt	1.00	.40
❑ 34 Jake Plummer	.60	.25
❑ 35 Kevin Johnson	.60	.25
❑ 36 Kevan Barlow	.60	.25
❑ 37 Priest Holmes	1.25	.50
❑ 38 Anthony Thomas	.60	.25
❑ 39 Jerome Bettis	1.00	.40
❑ 40 Johnnie Morton	.60	.25
❑ 41 Eric Moulds	.60	.25
❑ 42 James Thrash	.40	.15
❑ 43 Jamie Sharper	.40	.15
❑ 44 Eddie George	1.00	.40
❑ 45 Randy Moss	2.00	.75
❑ 46 Tim Couch	.60	.25
❑ 47 Terrell Owens	1.00	.40
❑ 48 Jay Fiedler	.60	.25
❑ 49 Travis Henry	1.00	.40
❑ 50 Hines Ward	1.00	.40
❑ 51 Ricky Williams	1.00	.40
❑ 52 Brian Urlacher	1.50	.60
❑ 53 LaDainian Tomlinson	1.50	.60
❑ 54 Trent Green	.60	.25
❑ 55 Chris Redman	.40	.15
❑ 56 Deuce McAllister	1.25	.50
❑ 57 Mark Brunell	.60	.25
❑ 58 Jamal Lewis	1.00	.40
❑ 59 Freddie Mitchell	.60	.25
❑ 60 Peyton Manning	2.00	.75
❑ 61 Stephen Davis	.60	.25
❑ 62 Tiki Barber	1.00	.40
❑ 63 Terry Glenn	.60	.25
❑ 64 Keyshawn Johnson	1.00	.40
❑ 65 Aaron Brooks	1.00	.40
❑ 66 Brian Griese	1.00	.40
❑ 67 Koren Robinson	.60	.25
❑ 68 Michael Bennett	.60	.25
❑ 69 Ray Lewis	1.00	.40
❑ 70 Rich Gannon	1.00	.40
❑ 71 Marvin Harrison	1.00	.40
❑ 72 Rod Gardner	.60	.25
❑ 73 Chad Pennington	1.25	.50
❑ 74 Terrell Davis	1.00	.40
❑ 75 Isaac Bruce	1.00	.40
❑ 76 Peter Warrick	.60	.25
❑ 77 Jeff Garcia	1.00	.40
❑ 78 Chris Chambers	1.00	.40
❑ 79 Chris Weinke	.60	.25
❑ 80 Plaxico Burress	1.00	.40
❑ 81 Edgerrin James	1.25	.50
❑ 82 Drew Bledsoe	1.25	.50
❑ 83 Duce Staley	1.00	.40
❑ 84 Fred Taylor	1.00	.40
❑ 85 Warrick Dunn	1.00	.40
❑ 86 Jerry Rice	2.00	.75
❑ 87 Ahman Green	1.00	.40
❑ 88 Warren Sapp	.60	.25
❑ 89 Michael Strahan	.60	.25
❑ 90 Bill Schroeder	.60	.25
❑ 91 Kurt Warner	1.00	.40
❑ 92 Antowain Smith	.60	.25
❑ 93 Corey Dillon	.60	.25
❑ 94 Garrison Hearst	.60	.25
❑ 95 Joey Galloway	.60	.25
❑ 96 Michael Vick	3.00	1.25
❑ 97 Tim Brown	1.00	.40
❑ 98 Corey Bradford	.40	.15
❑ 99 Brad Johnson	.60	.25
❑ 100 Joe Horn	.60	.25
❑ 101 Quentin Jammer RC	4.00	1.50
❑ 102 Rohan Davey RC	4.00	1.50
❑ 103 David Garrard RC	4.00	1.50
❑ 104 Ron Johnson RC	3.00	1.25
❑ 105 Jeremy Shockey RC	12.00	5.00
❑ 106 Marquise Walker RC	3.00	1.25
❑ 107 Luke Staley RC	3.00	1.25
❑ 108 Josh Scobey RC	4.00	1.50
❑ 109 Adrian Peterson RC	5.00	2.00
❑ 110 Lito Sheppard RC	4.00	1.50
❑ 111 Daniel Graham RC	3.00	1.25
❑ 112 Ryan Sims RC	4.00	1.50
❑ 113 William Green RC	4.00	1.50
❑ 114 Ashley Lelie RC	8.00	3.00
❑ 115 Deion Branch RC	8.00	3.00
❑ 116 Omar Easy RC	4.00	1.50
❑ 117 Jake Schifino RC	3.00	1.25
❑ 118 Donte Stallworth RC	8.00	3.00
❑ 119 Craig Nall RC	4.00	1.50
❑ 120 Clinton Portis RC	12.00	5.00
❑ 121 Brandon Doman RC	3.00	1.25
❑ 122 Eric Crouch RC	4.00	1.50
❑ 123 Josh McCown RC	5.00	2.00
❑ 124 Cliff Russell RC	3.00	1.25
❑ 125 T.J. Duckett RC	5.00	2.00
❑ 126 Jason McAddley RC	3.00	1.25
❑ 127 Chad Hutchinson RC	3.00	1.25
❑ 128 Jonathan Wells RC	4.00	1.50
❑ 129 Antwaan Randle El RC	6.00	2.50
❑ 130 Terry Charles RC	3.00	1.25
❑ 131 Lamar Gordon RC	4.00	1.50
❑ 132 Antonio Bryant RC	4.00	1.50
❑ 133 Brian Westbrook RC	6.00	2.50
❑ 134 Javon Walker RC	8.00	3.00
❑ 135 J.T. O'Sullivan RC	3.00	1.25
❑ 136 Maurice Morris RC	4.00	1.50
❑ 137 Tim Carter RC	3.00	1.25
❑ 138 Antwoine Womack RC	3.00	1.25
❑ 139 Ladell Betts RC	4.00	1.50
❑ 140 Joey Harrington RC	6.00	2.50
❑ 141 Chester Taylor RC	8.00	3.00
❑ 142 David Carr RC	10.00	4.00
❑ 143 Roy Williams RC	10.00	4.00
❑ 144 Reche Caldwell RC	4.00	1.50
❑ 145 Lamont Brightful RC	2.00	.75
❑ 146 Patrick Ramsey RC	5.00	2.00
❑ 147 Travis Stephens RC	3.00	1.25
❑ 148 Andre Davis RC	3.00	1.25
❑ 149 Herb Haygood RC	2.00	.75
❑ 150 Randy Fasani RC	3.00	1.25
❑ 151 Jabar Gaffney RC	4.00	1.50
❑ 152 Kahlil Hill RC	3.00	1.25
❑ 153 Julius Peppers RC	8.00	3.00
❑ 154 Kurt Kittner RC	3.00	1.25
❑ 155 DeShaun Foster RC	4.00	1.50
❑ 156 Verron Haynes RC	4.00	1.50
❑ 157 Josh Reed RC	4.00	1.50
❑ 158 Freddie Milons RC	3.00	1.25
❑ 159 Robert Thomas RC	4.00	1.50
❑ 160 Sam Simmons RC	2.00	.75

2003 Fleer Focus

Card		
❑ COMP.SET w/o SP's (120)	25.00	10.00
❑ 1 Tony Gonzalez	.60	.25
❑ 2 Aaron Brooks	1.00	.40
❑ 3 Joey Harrington	1.50	.60
❑ 4 Brett Favre	2.50	1.00
❑ 5 Donovan McNabb	1.25	.50
❑ 6 Jerome Bettis	1.00	.40
❑ 7 Michael Vick	2.50	1.00
❑ 8 Travis Taylor	.60	.25
❑ 9 Jay Fiedler	.60	.25
❑ 10 David Boston	.60	.25
❑ 11 Peerless Price	.60	.25
❑ 12 Kevan Barlow	.60	.25
❑ 13 LaDainian Tomlinson	1.00	.40
❑ 14 Jevon Kearse	.60	.25
❑ 15 Peyton Manning	1.50	.60
❑ 16 T.J. Duckett	.60	.25
❑ 17 Drew Brees	1.00	.40
❑ 18 Brian Dawkins	.60	.25
❑ 19 Charles Woodson	.60	.25
❑ 20 Emmitt Smith	2.50	1.00
❑ 21 Joe Jurevicius	.40	.15
❑ 22 Duce Staley	.60	.25
❑ 23 Rod Gardner	.60	.25
❑ 24 Jamal Lewis	1.00	.40
❑ 25 Jeff Garcia	1.00	.40
❑ 26 Clinton Portis	1.50	.60
❑ 27 Priest Holmes	1.25	.50
❑ 28 Mike Alstott	1.00	.40
❑ 29 Shaun Alexander	1.00	.40
❑ 30 Randy Moss	1.50	.60
❑ 31 Eric Moulds	.60	.25
❑ 32 Troy Brown	.60	.25
❑ 33 Michael Bennett	.60	.25
❑ 34 Ricky Williams	1.00	.40
❑ 35 Champ Bailey	.60	.25
❑ 36 Hugh Douglas	.40	.15
❑ 37 Travis Henry	.60	.25
❑ 38 Daunte Culpepper	1.00	.40
❑ 39 Koren Robinson	.60	.25
❑ 40 Todd Heap	.60	.25
❑ 41 John Abraham	.40	.15
❑ 42 Drew Bledsoe	1.00	.40
❑ 43 Tom Brady	2.50	1.00
❑ 44 Torry Holt	1.00	.40
❑ 45 Jake Delhomme	1.00	.40
❑ 46 Joe Horn	.60	.25
❑ 47 Julius Peppers	1.00	.40
❑ 48 Ray Lewis	1.00	.40
❑ 49 Deuce McAllister	1.00	.40
❑ 50 Marshall Faulk	1.00	.40
❑ 51 Takeo Spikes	.40	.15
❑ 52 Kordell Stewart	.60	.25
❑ 53 Brian Urlacher	1.50	.60
❑ 54 Zach Thomas	1.00	.40
❑ 55 Kurt Warner	1.00	.40
❑ 56 Peter Warrick	.60	.25
❑ 57 Marty Booker	.60	.25
❑ 58 Warren Sapp	.60	.25
❑ 59 Jon Kitna	.60	.25
❑ 60 Chad Johnson	1.00	.40
❑ 61 Jeremy Shockey	1.50	.60
❑ 62 Keyshawn Johnson	1.00	.40
❑ 63 Kelly Holcomb	.60	.25
❑ 64 Corey Dillon	.60	.25
❑ 65 Tiki Barber	1.00	.40
❑ 66 Eddie George	.60	.25
❑ 67 Joey Galloway	.60	.25
❑ 68 Tim Couch	.40	.15
❑ 69 Amani Toomer	.60	.25
❑ 70 Steve McNair	1.00	.40
❑ 71 Troy Hambrick	.40	.15
❑ 72 William Green	.60	.25
❑ 73 Chad Pennington	1.25	.50
❑ 74 Laveranues Coles	.60	.25
❑ 75 Quincy Carter	.60	.25
❑ 76 Antonio Bryant	.60	.25
❑ 77 Curtis Martin	1.00	.40
❑ 78 Terrell Owens	1.00	.40
❑ 79 Patrick Ramsey	1.00	.40
❑ 80 Ashley Lelie	1.00	.40
❑ 81 Donte Stallworth	1.00	.40
❑ 82 Roy Williams	1.00	.40
❑ 83 Charlie Garner	.60	.25
❑ 84 Chris Chambers	1.00	.40
❑ 85 Warrick Dunn	.60	.25
❑ 86 Shannon Sharpe	.60	.25
❑ 87 Rod Smith	.60	.25
❑ 88 Marvin Harrison	1.00	.40
❑ 89 Rich Gannon	.60	.25
❑ 90 Stephen Davis	.60	.25
❑ 91 James Stewart	.60	.25
❑ 92 Tim Brown	1.00	.40

❑ 93	Anthony Thomas	.60	.25
❑ 94	Stacey Mack	.40	.15
❑ 95	Jake Plummer	.60	.25
❑ 96	Jerry Rice	2.00	.75
❑ 97	Quincy Morgan	.60	.25
❑ 98	Dwight Freeney	.60	.25
❑ 99	Jason Taylor	.40	.15
❑ 100	Ahman Green	1.00	.40
❑ 101	Hines Ward	1.00	.40
❑ 102	Kerry Collins	.60	.25
❑ 103	Plaxico Burress	.60	.25
❑ 104	Santana Moss	.60	.25
❑ 105	Michael Strahan	.60	.25
❑ 106	Donald Driver	.60	.25
❑ 107	Tommy Maddox	1.00	.40
❑ 108	Jerry Porter	.60	.25
❑ 109	David Carr	1.50	.60
❑ 110	Garrison Hearst	.60	.25
❑ 111	Edgerrin James	1.00	.40
❑ 112	Isaac Bruce	1.00	.40
❑ 113	Marc Bulger	1.00	.40
❑ 114	Brad Johnson	.60	.25
❑ 115	Fred Taylor	1.00	.40
❑ 116	Derrick Brooks	.60	.25
❑ 117	Jimmy Smith	.60	.25
❑ 118	Derrick Mason	.60	.25
❑ 119	Mark Brunell	.60	.25
❑ 120	Trent Green	.60	.25
❑ 121	Mike Doss RC	5.00	2.00
❑ 122	Carson Palmer RC	25.00	10.00
❑ 123	Charles Rogers RC	5.00	2.00
❑ 124	Andre Johnson RC	10.00	4.00
❑ 125	Tony Hollings RC	5.00	2.00
❑ 126	Terence Newman RC	10.00	4.00
❑ 127	Byron Leftwich RC	15.00	6.00
❑ 128	Terrell Suggs RC	8.00	3.00
❑ 129	Bryant Johnson RC	5.00	2.00
❑ 130	Kyle Boller RC	5.00	2.00
❑ 131	Rex Grossman RC	15.00	6.00
❑ 132	Willis McGahee RC	15.00	6.00
❑ 133	Dallas Clark RC	5.00	2.00
❑ 134	Bobby Wade RC	5.00	2.00
❑ 135	Tony Romo RC	40.00	20.00
❑ 136	Michael Haynes RC	5.00	2.00
❑ 137	Bethel Johnson RC	5.00	2.00
❑ 138	Anquan Boldin RC	12.00	5.00
❑ 139	Seneca Wallace RC	5.00	2.00
❑ 140	Nick Barnett RC	5.00	2.00
❑ 141	Teyo Johnson RC	5.00	2.00
❑ 142	Kelley Washington RC	5.00	2.00
❑ 143	Nate Burleson RC	5.00	2.00
❑ 144	Ken Dorsey RC	5.00	2.00
❑ 145	Dewayne White RC	4.00	1.50
❑ 146	Chris Kelsay RC	5.00	2.00
❑ 147	Dave Ragone RC	5.00	2.00
❑ 148	David Tyree RC	4.00	1.50
❑ 149	Billy McMullen RC	4.00	1.50
❑ 150	Chris Simms RC	8.00	3.00
❑ 151	Onterrio Smith RC	5.00	2.00
❑ 152	Marcus Trufant RC	5.00	2.00
❑ 153	Jason Witten RC	8.00	3.00
❑ 154	Johnathan Sullivan RC	4.00	1.50
❑ 155	Kevin Williams RC	5.00	2.00
❑ 156	Justin Fargas RC	5.00	2.00
❑ 157	Domanick Davis RC	5.00	2.00
❑ 158	LaBrandon Toefield RC	5.00	2.00
❑ 159	Shaun McDonald RC	5.00	2.00
❑ 160	Brandon Lloyd RC	5.00	2.00

2001 Fleer Game Time

❑	COMP.SET w/o SP's (110)	15.00	6.00
❑ 1	Donovan McNabb	.75	.30
❑ 2	Travis Prentice	.25	.08
❑ 3	Keenan McCardell	.25	.08
❑ 4	Kurt Warner	1.25	.50
❑ 5	Ray Lewis	.60	.25
❑ 6	Terrell Davis	.60	.25
❑ 7	Kevin Faulk	.25	.08
❑ 8	Terrell Owens	.60	.25
❑ 9	Jeff George	.40	.15
❑ 10	Dennis Northcutt	.40	.15
❑ 11	Fred Taylor	.60	.25
❑ 12	Cris Carter	.60	.25
❑ 13	Aaron Brooks	.60	.25
❑ 14	Marshall Faulk	.75	.30
❑ 15	David Boston	.60	.25
❑ 16	Rocket Ismail	.40	.15
❑ 17	Jerome Bettis	.60	.25
❑ 18	Warrick Dunn	.60	.25
❑ 19	Corey Dillon	.60	.25
❑ 20	Mark Brunell	.60	.25
❑ 21	Torry Holt	.60	.25
❑ 22	Michael McCrary	.25	.08
❑ 23	Rod Smith	.40	.15
❑ 24	Charlie Garner	.40	.15
❑ 25	Bruce Smith	.25	.08
❑ 26	Doug Johnson	.25	.08
❑ 27	Brian Griese	.60	.25
❑ 28	Jeff Garcia	.60	.25
❑ 29	Eddie George	.60	.25
❑ 30	Shawn Bryson	.25	.08
❑ 31	Marvin Harrison	.60	.25
❑ 32	Hugh Douglas	.25	.08
❑ 33	Terance Mathis	.40	.15
❑ 34	Emmitt Smith	1.25	.50
❑ 35	Lamar Smith	.40	.15
❑ 36	Junior Seau	.60	.25
❑ 37	Steve McNair	.60	.25
❑ 38	Jake Plummer	.40	.15
❑ 39	Tim Couch	.40	.15
❑ 40	Jay Fiedler	.60	.25
❑ 41	Plaxico Burress	.60	.25
❑ 42	Keyshawn Johnson	.60	.25
❑ 43	Jason Taylor	.25	.08
❑ 44	Charlie Batch	.60	.25
❑ 45	Terry Glenn	.40	.15
❑ 46	Laveranues Coles	.60	.25
❑ 47	Darrell Jackson	.60	.25
❑ 48	Jamal Lewis	1.00	.40
❑ 49	Ed McCaffrey	.60	.25
❑ 50	Vinny Testaverde	.40	.15
❑ 51	Ricky Watters	.40	.15
❑ 52	Champ Bailey	.25	.08
❑ 53	Peter Warrick	.60	.25
❑ 54	Eric Moulds	.40	.15
❑ 55	Michael Strahan	.40	.15
❑ 56	Warren Sapp	.40	.15
❑ 57	Tony Gonzalez	.40	.15
❑ 58	Kerry Collins	.40	.15
❑ 59	Shaun King	.25	.08
❑ 60	Jason Sehorn	.25	.08
❑ 61	Marcus Robinson	.60	.25
❑ 62	James Stewart	.40	.15
❑ 63	Curtis Martin	.60	.25
❑ 64	Brian Urlacher	1.00	.40
❑ 65	Germane Crowell	.25	.08
❑ 66	Wesley Walls	.25	.08
❑ 67	Antonio Freeman	.60	.25
❑ 68	Ron Dayne	.60	.25
❑ 69	Tyrone Wheatley	.40	.15
❑ 70	Zach Thomas	.60	.25
❑ 71	Shannon Sharpe	.40	.15
❑ 72	Mike Anderson	.60	.25
❑ 73	Wayne Chrebet	.40	.15
❑ 74	Shaun Alexander	.75	.30
❑ 75	Stephen Davis	.60	.25
❑ 76	Derrick Mason	.40	.15
❑ 77	Dorsey Levens	.25	.08
❑ 78	Jessie Armstead	.25	.08
❑ 79	Rich Gannon	.60	.25
❑ 80	Muhsin Muhammad	.40	.15
❑ 81	Brett Favre	2.00	.75
❑ 82	Randy Moss	1.25	.50
❑ 83	Joe Horn	.40	.15
❑ 84	Charles Woodson	.40	.15
❑ 85	Brad Hoover	.25	.08
❑ 86	Terrence Wilkins	.25	.08
❑ 87	Sylvester Morris	.25	.08
❑ 88	Tim Brown	.60	.25
❑ 89	Jamal Anderson	.60	.25
❑ 90	Joey Galloway	.40	.15
❑ 91	Drew Bledsoe	.75	.30
❑ 92	Rodney Harrison	.25	.08
❑ 93	Jevon Kearse	.40	.15
❑ 94	Rob Johnson	.40	.15
❑ 95	Edgerrin James	.75	.30
❑ 96	Thomas Jones	.40	.15
❑ 97	Courtney Brown	.40	.15
❑ 98	Jimmy Smith	.40	.15
❑ 99	Ricky Williams	.60	.25
❑ 100	Isaac Bruce	.60	.25
❑ 101	Akili Smith	.25	.08
❑ 102	Derrick Alexander	.40	.15
❑ 103	Daunte Culpepper	.60	.25
❑ 104	Amani Toomer	.25	.08
❑ 105	Mike Alstott	.60	.25
❑ 106	Sam Cowart	.25	.08
❑ 107	Peyton Manning	1.50	.60
❑ 108	Robert Smith	.40	.15
❑ 109	Duce Staley	.60	.25
❑ 110	Cade McNown	.25	.08
❑ 111	Michael Vick RC	20.00	8.00
❑ 112	David Terrell RC	4.00	1.50
❑ 113	Deuce McAllister RC	8.00	3.00
❑ 114	Koren Robinson RC	4.00	1.50
❑ 115	Rod Gardner RC	4.00	1.50
❑ 116	Chris Chambers RC	6.00	2.50
❑ 117	Santana Moss RC	6.00	2.50
❑ 118	Reggie Wayne RC	8.00	3.00
❑ 119	Quincy Morgan RC	4.00	1.50
❑ 120	Rudi Johnson RC	8.00	3.00
❑ 121	Robert Ferguson RC	4.00	1.50
❑ 122	Ja'Mar Toombs RC	2.50	1.00
❑ 123	Michael Bennett RC	4.00	1.50
❑ 124	Ronney Daniels RC	1.50	.60
❑ 125	Drew Brees RC	15.00	6.00
❑ 126	Josh Heupel RC	4.00	1.50
❑ 127	Chris Weinke RC	4.00	1.50
❑ 128	LaDainian Tomlinson RC	30.00	15.00
❑ 129	Chad Johnson RC	10.00	4.00
❑ 130	LaMont Jordan RC	8.00	3.00
❑ 131	Freddie Mitchell RC	4.00	1.50
❑ 132	Anthony Thomas RC	4.00	1.50
❑ 133	Ben Leard RC	2.50	1.00
❑ 134	Sage Rosenfels RC	4.00	1.50
❑ 135	Marques Tuiasosopo RC	4.00	1.50
❑ 136	Gerard Warren RC	4.00	1.50
❑ 137	Jamar Fletcher RC	2.50	1.00
❑ 138	Justin Smith RC	4.00	1.50
❑ 139	Dan Morgan RC	4.00	1.50
❑ 140	Jamal Reynolds RC	4.00	1.50
❑ 141	Shaun Rogers RC	4.00	1.50
❑ 142	Todd Heap RC	4.00	1.50
❑ 143	Travis Minor RC	2.50	1.00
❑ 144	Mike McMahon RC	4.00	1.50
❑ 145	Travis Henry RC	6.00	2.50
❑ 146	Kevan Barlow RC	4.00	1.50
❑ 147	Javon Green RC	2.50	1.00
❑ 148	Ken-Yon Rambo RC	2.50	1.00
❑ 149	Tim Hasselbeck RC	4.00	1.50
❑ 150	Snoop Minnis RC	2.50	1.00

2000 Fleer Gamers

❑	COMPLETE SET (150)	100.00	50.00
❑	COMP.SET w/o SPs (100)	20.00	7.50
❑ 1	Edgerrin James	1.25	.50
❑ 2	Tim Couch	.50	.20
❑ 3	Cris Carter	.75	.30
❑ 4	Rich Gannon	.75	.30
❑ 5	Akili Smith	.30	.10
❑ 6	Muhsin Muhammad	.50	.20
❑ 7	Dorsey Levens	.50	.20
❑ 8	Dedric Ward	.30	.10

❑ 9 Jevon Kearse .75 .30
❑ 10 Peerless Price .50 .20
❑ 11 Mike Alstott .75 .30
❑ 12 Michael Strahan .50 .20
❑ 13 Stephen Davis .75 .30
❑ 14 Rob Moore .50 .20
❑ 15 James Stewart .50 .20
❑ 16 Robert Smith .75 .30
❑ 17 Napoleon Kaufman .50 .20
❑ 18 Peyton Manning 2.00 .75
❑ 19 Keyshawn Johnson .75 .30
❑ 20 Tony Martin .50 .20
❑ 21 Jermaine Fazande .30 .10
❑ 22 Jamal Anderson .75 .30
❑ 23 Ed McCaffrey .75 .30
❑ 24 Drew Bledsoe 1.00 .40
❑ 25 Duce Staley .75 .30
❑ 26 Warrick Dunn .75 .30
❑ 27 Chris Chandler .50 .20
❑ 28 Olandis Gary .75 .30
❑ 29 Terry Glenn .50 .20
❑ 30 Donovan McNabb 1.25 .50
❑ 31 Torry Holt .75 .30
❑ 32 Tim Dwight .75 .30
❑ 33 Terrell Davis .75 .30
❑ 34 Tony Simmons .30 .10
❑ 35 Jerome Bettis .75 .30
❑ 36 Az-Zahir Hakim .50 .20
❑ 37 Darrin Chiaverini .30 .10
❑ 38 Fred Taylor .75 .30
❑ 39 Jon Kitna .75 .30
❑ 40 Tony Banks .50 .20
❑ 41 Brian Griese .75 .30
❑ 42 Jeff Blake .50 .20
❑ 43 Kordell Stewart .50 .20
❑ 44 Isaac Bruce .75 .30
❑ 45 Shannon Sharpe .50 .20
❑ 46 Rocket Ismail .50 .20
❑ 47 Ricky Williams .75 .30
❑ 48 Marshall Faulk 1.00 .40
❑ 49 Qadry Ismail .50 .20
❑ 50 Joey Galloway .50 .20
❑ 51 Jake Reed .50 .20
❑ 52 Kurt Warner 1.50 .60
❑ 53 Cade McNown .30 .10
❑ 54 Herman Moore .50 .20
❑ 55 Curtis Martin .75 .30
❑ 56 Steve McNair .75 .30
❑ 57 Tim Biakabutuka .50 .20
❑ 58 Brett Favre 2.50 1.00
❑ 59 Wayne Chrebet .50 .20
❑ 60 Eddie George .75 .30
❑ 61 Troy Aikman 1.50 .60
❑ 62 Jimmy Smith .50 .20
❑ 63 Derrick Mayes .50 .20
❑ 64 Emmitt Smith 1.50 .60
❑ 65 Mark Brunell .75 .30
❑ 66 Ricky Watters .50 .20
❑ 67 Marcus Robinson .75 .30
❑ 68 Randy Moss 1.50 .60
❑ 69 Troy Edwards .30 .10
❑ 70 Carl Pickens .50 .20
❑ 71 Damon Huard .75 .30
❑ 72 Mikhael Ricks .30 .10
❑ 73 David Boston .75 .30
❑ 74 Charlie Batch .75 .30
❑ 75 Randall Cunningham .75 .30
❑ 76 Tim Brown .75 .30
❑ 77 Shaun King .30 .10
❑ 78 Darnay Scott .50 .20
❑ 79 Derrick Alexander .50 .20
❑ 80 Steve Young 1.00 .40
❑ 81 Kevin Johnson .75 .30
❑ 82 Elvis Grbac .50 .20
❑ 83 Tai Streets .30 .10
❑ 84 Steve Beuerlein .50 .20
❑ 85 Antonio Freeman .75 .30
❑ 86 Vinny Testaverde .50 .20
❑ 87 Brad Johnson .75 .30
❑ 88 Curtis Enis .30 .10
❑ 89 Jay Fiedler .50 .20
❑ 90 Junior Seau .75 .30
❑ 91 Eric Moulds .75 .30
❑ 92 Jake Plummer .50 .20
❑ 93 Amani Toomer .50 .20
❑ 94 Champ Bailey .50 .20
❑ 95 Germane Crowell .30 .10
❑ 96 Tony Gonzalez .50 .20
❑ 97 Jerry Rice 1.50 .60
❑ 98 Rob Johnson .50 .20
❑ 99 Marvin Harrison .75 .30
❑ 100 Kerry Collins .50 .20
❑ 101 Thomas Jones RC 4.00 1.50
❑ 102 Jarious Jackson RC 2.00 .75
❑ 103 R.Jay Soward RC 2.00 .75
❑ 104 Trung Canidate RC 2.00 .75
❑ 105 Travis Taylor RC 2.50 1.00
❑ 106 Giovanni Carmazzi RC 2.00 .75
❑ 107 Jerry Porter RC 3.00 1.25
❑ 108 Chris Redman RC 2.00 .75
❑ 109 Tee Martin RC 2.50 1.00
❑ 110 Dez White RC 2.50 1.00
❑ 111 Danny Farmer RC 2.00 .75
❑ 112 Brian Urlacher RC 10.00 4.00
❑ 113 Reuben Droughns RC 3.00 1.25
❑ 114 Marc Bulger RC 5.00 2.00
❑ 115 Peter Warrick RC 2.50 1.00
❑ 116 Plaxico Burress RC 5.00 2.00
❑ 117 Ron Dugans RC 2.00 .75
❑ 118 Gari Scott RC 2.00 .75
❑ 119 Curtis Keaton RC 2.00 .75
❑ 120 Corey Simon RC 2.50 1.00
❑ 121 Rob Morris RC 2.00 .75
❑ 122 Chad Morton RC 2.50 1.00
❑ 123 Hank Poteat RC 2.00 .75
❑ 124 Ahmed Plummer RC 2.50 1.00
❑ 125 Bashir Yamini RC 2.00 .75
❑ 126 J.R. Redmond RC 2.00 .75
❑ 127 Travis Prentice RC 2.00 .75
❑ 128 Todd Pinkston RC 2.50 1.00
❑ 129 Courtney Brown RC 2.50 1.00
❑ 130 Laveranues Coles RC 3.00 1.25
❑ 131 Jamal Lewis RC 6.00 2.50
❑ 132 Tim Rattay RC 2.50 1.00
❑ 133 Anthony Becht RC 2.50 1.00
❑ 134 Chris Cole RC 2.00 .75
❑ 135 Ron Dayne RC 2.50 1.00
❑ 136 Sylvester Morris RC 2.00 .75
❑ 137 Joe Hamilton RC 2.00 .75
❑ 138 Dennis Northcutt RC 2.50 1.00
❑ 139 Doug Johnson RC 2.50 1.00
❑ 140 Shyrone Stith RC 2.00 .75
❑ 141 Darrell Jackson RC 5.00 2.00
❑ 142 Michael Wiley RC 2.00 .75
❑ 143 Chad Pennington RC 6.00 2.50
❑ 144 Bubba Franks RC 2.50 1.00
❑ 145 Shaun Alexander RC 12.00 5.00

2001 Fleer Genuine

❑ COMP.SET w/o SP's (125) 25.00 10.00
❑ 1 Donovan McNabb 1.25 .50
❑ 2 Daunte Culpepper 1.00 .40
❑ 3 Derrick Alexander .60 .25
❑ 4 Jessie Armstead .40 .15
❑ 5 Hines Ward 1.00 .40
❑ 6 Peter Warrick 1.00 .40
❑ 7 Jay Fiedler 1.00 .40
❑ 8 Cris Carter 1.00 .40
❑ 9 Az-Zahir Hakim .40 .15
❑ 10 Michael Westbrook .60 .25
❑ 11 Akili Smith .40 .15
❑ 12 Lamar Smith .60 .25
❑ 13 Eric Moulds .60 .25
❑ 14 Shaun Alexander 1.25 .50
❑ 15 Jeff George .60 .25
❑ 16 Brad Hoover .40 .15
❑ 17 Brian Griese 1.00 .40
❑ 18 Keenan McCardell .40 .15
❑ 19 Freddie Jones .40 .15
❑ 20 Brian Urlacher 1.50 .60
❑ 21 Thomas Jones .60 .25
❑ 22 Charlie Batch 1.00 .40
❑ 23 Aaron Brooks 1.00 .40
❑ 24 Hugh Douglas .40 .15
❑ 25 Mike Alstott 1.00 .40
❑ 26 Darrell Russell .40 .15
❑ 27 Muhsin Muhammad .60 .25
❑ 28 Rocket Ismail .60 .25
❑ 29 Fred Taylor 1.00 .40
❑ 30 Tyrone Wheatley .60 .25
❑ 31 Rodney Harrison .40 .15
❑ 32 Curtis Martin 1.00 .40
❑ 33 Jason Sehorn .40 .15
❑ 34 James McKnight .60 .25
❑ 35 Jimmy Smith .60 .25
❑ 36 Laveranues Coles 1.00 .40
❑ 37 Jeff Garcia 1.00 .40
❑ 38 Sam Cowart .40 .15
❑ 39 Joey Galloway .60 .25
❑ 40 Mark Brunell 1.00 .40
❑ 41 Vinny Testaverde .60 .25
❑ 42 Terrell Owens 1.00 .40
❑ 43 Ray Lewis 1.00 .40
❑ 44 Ahman Green 1.00 .40
❑ 45 Ron Dayne 1.00 .40
❑ 46 Samari Rolle .40 .15
❑ 47 Shawn Bryson .40 .15
❑ 48 Emmitt Smith 2.00 .75
❑ 49 Terrence Wilkins .40 .15
❑ 50 Charlie Garner .60 .25
❑ 51 Rob Johnson .60 .25
❑ 52 Courtney Brown .60 .25
❑ 53 Edgerrin James 1.25 .50
❑ 54 Kurt Warner 2.00 .75
❑ 55 Michael McCrary .40 .15
❑ 56 Dennis Northcutt .60 .25
❑ 57 Marvin Harrison 1.00 .40
❑ 58 Rich Gannon 1.00 .40
❑ 59 Marshall Faulk 1.25 .50
❑ 60 Travis Prentice .40 .15
❑ 61 Terrell Davis 1.00 .40
❑ 62 Charles Woodson .60 .25
❑ 63 Isaac Bruce 1.00 .40
❑ 64 Tim Couch .60 .25
❑ 65 Oronde Gadsden .60 .25
❑ 66 Randy Moss 2.00 .75
❑ 67 Torry Holt 1.00 .40
❑ 68 Shannon Sharpe .60 .25
❑ 69 Antonio Freeman 1.00 .40
❑ 70 Michael Strahan .60 .25
❑ 71 Jevon Kearse .60 .25
❑ 72 Jamal Lewis 1.50 .60
❑ 73 Peyton Manning 2.50 1.00
❑ 74 Amani Toomer .40 .15
❑ 75 Derrick Mason .60 .25
❑ 76 Jake Plummer .60 .25
❑ 77 Rod Smith .60 .25
❑ 78 Terry Glenn .60 .25
❑ 79 Plaxico Burress 1.00 .40
❑ 80 Warren Sapp .60 .25
❑ 81 Jamal Anderson 1.00 .40
❑ 82 James Stewart .60 .25
❑ 83 Ricky Williams 1.00 .40
❑ 84 Chad Lewis .40 .15
❑ 85 Shaun King .40 .15
❑ 86 Wesley Walls .40 .15
❑ 87 Mike Anderson 1.00 .40
❑ 88 Corey Simon .60 .25
❑ 89 Wayne Chrebet .60 .25
❑ 90 Junior Seau 1.00 .40
❑ 91 Terance Mathis .60 .25
❑ 92 Germane Crowell .40 .15
❑ 93 Joe Horn .60 .25
❑ 94 Duce Staley 1.00 .40
❑ 95 Keyshawn Johnson 1.00 .40
❑ 96 Qadry Ismail .60 .25
❑ 97 Dorsey Levens 1.00 .40
❑ 98 Kerry Collins .60 .25
❑ 99 Corey Dillon 1.00 .40
❑ 100 Zach Thomas 1.00 .40
❑ 101 Chad Pennington 1.50 .60
❑ 102 Ricky Watters .60 .25
❑ 103 Bruce Smith .40 .15
❑ 104 David Boston 1.00 .40
❑ 105 Ed McCaffrey 1.00 .40
❑ 106 Kevin Faulk 1.00 .40
❑ 107 Jerome Bettis 1.00 .40
❑ 108 Warrick Dunn 1.00 .40
❑ 109 Tim Brown 1.00 .40
❑ 110 Marcus Robinson 1.00 .40

111	Tony Gonzalez	.60	.25
112	Drew Bledsoe	1.25	.50
113	Darrell Jackson	1.00	.40
114	Stephen Davis	1.00	.40
115	Doug Johnson	.40	.15
116	Brett Favre	3.00	1.25
117	Darren Howard	.40	.15
118	Cade McNown	.40	.15
119	Steve McNair	1.00	.40
120	James Allen	.60	.25
121	Sylvester Morris	.40	.15
122	J.R. Redmond	.40	.15
123	Jacquez Green	.40	.15
124	Champ Bailey	.60	.25
125	Eddie George	1.00	.40
126	Michael Vick JSY RC	50.00	20.00
127	David Terrell JSY RC	12.00	5.00
128	Deuce McAllister JSY RC	25.00	10.00
129	Koren Robinson JSY RC	12.00	5.00
130	Rod Gardner JSY RC	12.00	5.00
131	Chris Chambers JSY RC	20.00	7.50
132	Santana Moss JSY RC	20.00	7.50
133	Reggie Wayne JSY RC	25.00	10.00
134	Quincy Morgan JSY RC	12.00	5.00
135	Rudi Johnson JSY RC	25.00	10.00
136	Robert Ferguson JSY RC	12.00	5.00
137	Todd Heap JSY RC	12.00	5.00
138	Michael Bennett JSY RC	12.00	5.00
139	Jesse Palmer JSY RC	12.00	5.00
140	Drew Brees JSY RC	40.00	15.00
141	James Jackson JSY RC	12.00	5.00
142	Chris Weinke JSY RC	12.00	5.00
143	LaDainian Tomlinson JSY RC	60.00	30.00
144	Chad Johnson JSY RC	30.00	12.50
145	Quincy Carter JSY RC	12.00	5.00
146	Freddie Mitchell JSY RC	12.00	5.00
147	Anthony Thomas JSY RC	12.00	5.00
148	Travis Henry JSY RC	20.00	7.50
149	Snoop Minnis JSY RC	12.00	5.00
150	Marques Tuiasosopo JSY RC	12.00	5.00
151	Travis Minor JSY RC	12.00	5.00
152	Mike McMahon JSY RC	12.00	5.00
153	Josh Heupel JSY RC	12.00	5.00
154	Sage Rosenfels JSY RC	12.00	5.00
155	Kevan Barlow JSY RC	12.00	5.00

2002 Fleer Genuine

	COMP.SET w/o SP's (125)	20.00	7.50
1	Brian Urlacher	1.50	.60
2	Keyshawn Johnson	1.00	.40
3	Donovan McNabb	1.25	.50
4	Tim Couch	.60	.25
5	Junior Seau	1.00	.40
6	Eric Moulds	.60	.25
7	Randy Moss	2.00	.75
8	Rod Smith	.60	.25
9	Torry Holt	1.00	.40
10	Plaxico Burress	1.00	.40
11	Kordell Stewart	.60	.25
12	Brett Favre	2.50	1.00
13	Stephen Davis	.60	.25
14	Santana Moss	1.00	.40
15	Kurt Warner	1.00	.40
16	Jake Plummer	.60	.25
17	Jimmy Smith	.60	.25
18	Quincy Carter	.60	.25
19	Marvin Harrison	1.00	.40
20	Fred Taylor	1.00	.40
21	Warren Sapp	.60	.25
22	Curtis Martin	1.00	.40
23	Isaac Bruce	1.00	.40
24	Drew Brees	1.00	.40
25	Ray Lewis	1.00	.40
26	Hines Ward	1.00	.40
27	Koren Robinson	.60	.25
28	Jevon Kearse	.60	.25
29	Jerry Rice	2.00	.75
30	Jeff Garcia	1.00	.40
31	Edgerrin James	1.25	.50
32	Warrick Dunn	1.00	.40
33	Ricky Williams	1.00	.40
34	Doug Flutie	1.00	.40
35	Brian Griese	1.00	.40
36	Chad Pennington	1.25	.50
37	Duce Staley	1.00	.40
38	Eddie George	1.00	.40
39	Daunte Culpepper	1.00	.40
40	Jerome Bettis	1.00	.40
41	Michael Vick	3.00	1.25
42	Tim Brown	1.00	.40
43	Tom Brady	2.50	1.00
44	Steve McNair	1.00	.40
45	Terrell Owens	1.00	.40
46	Corey Dillon	.60	.25
47	Peyton Manning	2.00	.75
48	Rich Gannon	1.00	.40
49	Emmitt Smith	2.50	1.00
50	David Boston	1.00	.40
51	Mark Brunell	1.00	.40
52	Ron Dayne	.60	.25
53	Wayne Chrebet	.60	.25
54	Terrell Davis	1.00	.40
55	Zach Thomas	1.00	.40
56	Kevin Johnson	.60	.25
57	Marshall Faulk	1.00	.40
58	Anthony Thomas	.60	.25
59	Deuce McAllister	1.25	.50
60	LaDainian Tomlinson	1.50	.60
61	Thomas Jones	.60	.25
62	Ahman Green	1.00	.40
63	Aaron Brooks	1.00	.40
64	Courtney Brown	.60	.25
65	Chris Chambers	1.00	.40
66	Jamal Lewis	1.00	.40
67	David Terrell	1.00	.40
68	Tony Gonzalez	.60	.25
69	Laveranues Coles	.60	.25
70	Shaun Alexander	1.25	.50
71	Chris Weinke	.60	.25
72	Antowain Smith	.60	.25
73	Rod Gardner	.60	.25
74	Mike Anderson	1.00	.40
75	Antonio Freeman	1.00	.40
76	Kevan Barlow	.60	.25
77	Jim Miller	.60	.25
78	Bill Schroeder	.60	.25
79	Joe Horn	.60	.25
80	Travis Henry	1.00	.40
81	Michael Bennett	.60	.25
82	Michael Pittman	.40	.15
83	Keenan McCardell	.40	.15
84	Amani Toomer	.60	.25
85	Peerless Price	.60	.25
86	Az-Zahir Hakim	.40	.15
87	James Thrash	.60	.25
88	Drew Bledsoe	1.25	.50
89	Mike McMahon	1.00	.40
90	Derrick Mason	.60	.25
91	Joey Galloway	.60	.25
92	Snoop Minnis	.40	.15
93	Ed McCaffrey	1.00	.40
94	Johnnie Morton	.60	.25
95	Richard Huntley	.40	.15
96	Troy Brown	.60	.25
97	Shane Matthews	.40	.15
98	Muhsin Muhammad	.60	.25
99	David Patten	.40	.15
100	Jon Kitna	.60	.25
101	Terrence Wilkins	.40	.15
102	Kerry Collins	.60	.25
103	Tiki Barber	1.00	.40
104	Fred Beasley	.40	.15
105	Trent Dilfer	.60	.25
106	Chris Redman	.40	.15
107	Jay Fiedler	.60	.25
108	Charlie Garner	.60	.25
109	Mike Alstott	1.00	.40
110	Darnay Scott	.40	.15
111	Garrison Hearst	.60	.25
112	James Jackson	.40	.15
113	Darrell Jackson	.60	.25
114	Freddie Mitchell	.60	.25
115	Brad Johnson	.60	.25
116	Olandis Gary	.60	.25
117	Priest Holmes	1.25	.50
118	Vinny Testaverde	.60	.25
119	Takeo Spikes	.40	.15
120	Marty Booker	.60	.25
121	Curtis Conway	.40	.15
122	Jacquez Green	.40	.15
123	Champ Bailey	.60	.25
124	Trent Green	.60	.25
125	Terry Glenn	.60	.25
126	Ladell Betts RC	6.00	2.50
127	DeShaun Foster RC	6.00	2.50
128	Maurice Morris RC	6.00	2.50
129	Chester Taylor RC	12.00	5.00
130	Randy McMichael RC	10.00	4.00
131	Verron Haynes RC	6.00	2.50
132	Cliff Russell RC	5.00	2.00
133	Brandon Doman RC	5.00	2.00
134	Ashley Lelie RC	12.00	5.00
135	Roy Williams RC	15.00	6.00
136	Antonio Bryant RC	6.00	2.50
137	William Green RC	6.00	2.50
138	Clinton Portis RC	20.00	7.50
139	J.T. O'Sullivan RC	5.00	2.00
140	Javon Walker RC	12.00	5.00
141	Randy Fasani RC	5.00	2.00
142	Chad Hutchinson RC	5.00	2.00
143	Ben Leber RC	6.00	2.50
144	Tim Carter RC	5.00	2.00
145	Jason McAddley RC	5.00	2.00
146	Donte Stallworth RC	12.00	5.00
147	Andre Davis RC	5.00	2.00
148	Julius Peppers RC	12.00	5.00
149	Patrick Ramsey RC	8.00	3.00
150	Deion Branch RC	12.00	5.00
151	Jonathan Wells RC	6.00	2.50
152	Jabar Gaffney RC	6.00	2.50
153	Josh McCown RC	8.00	3.00
154	Jeremy Shockey RC	20.00	7.50
155	Eric Crouch RC	6.00	2.50
156	Joey Harrington RC	10.00	4.00
157	Jerramy Stevens RC	6.00	2.50
158	T.J. Duckett RC	8.00	3.00
159	Ron Johnson RC	5.00	2.00
160	Josh Reed RC	6.00	2.50
161	Reche Caldwell RC	6.00	2.50
162	Lamar Gordon RC	6.00	2.50
163	David Garrard RC	6.00	2.50
164	Freddie Milons RC	5.00	2.00
165	Marquise Walker RC	5.00	2.00
166	Rohan Davey RC	6.00	2.50
167	Coy Wire RC	6.00	2.50
168	Quentin Jammer RC	6.00	2.50
169	Omar Easy RC	6.00	2.50
170	Kurt Kittner RC	5.00	2.00
171	Travis Stephens RC	5.00	2.00
172	David Carr RC	15.00	6.00
173	Daniel Graham RC	6.00	2.50
174	Antwaan Randle El RC	10.00	4.00
175	Brian Westbrook RC	10.00	4.00

2003 Fleer Genuine Insider

	COMP.SET w/o SP's (100)	20.00	7.50
1	Donovan McNabb	1.25	.50
2	Rich Gannon	.60	.25
3	Joey Harrington	1.50	.60
4	Eddie George	.60	.25
5	Jeremy Shockey	1.50	.60

❑ 6	Tim Couch	.40	.15
❑ 7	Shaun Alexander	1.00	.40
❑ 8	Tiki Barber	1.00	.40
❑ 9	Antonio Bryant	.60	.25
❑ 10	Marc Bulger	1.00	.40
❑ 11	Tom Brady	2.50	1.00
❑ 12	Julius Peppers	1.00	.40
❑ 13	Junior Seau	1.00	.40
❑ 14	Trent Green	.60	.25
❑ 15	Eric Moulds	.60	.25
❑ 16	Santana Moss	.60	.25
❑ 17	Hugh Douglas	.40	.15
❑ 18	Emmitt Smith	2.50	1.00
❑ 19	Tim Brown	1.00	.40
❑ 20	William Green	.60	.25
❑ 21	Koren Robinson	.60	.25
❑ 22	Randy Moss	1.50	.60
❑ 23	Anthony Thomas	.60	.25
❑ 24	Terrell Owens	1.00	.40
❑ 25	Fred Taylor	1.00	.40
❑ 26	Ahman Green	1.00	.40
❑ 27	Derrick Mason	.60	.25
❑ 28	Chad Pennington	1.25	.50
❑ 29	Shannon Sharpe	.60	.25
❑ 30	Warren Sapp	.60	.25
❑ 31	Deuce McAllister	1.00	.40
❑ 32	Rod Smith	.60	.25
❑ 33	Torry Holt	1.00	.40
❑ 34	Joe Horn	.60	.25
❑ 35	Chad Johnson	1.00	.40
❑ 36	Matt Hasselbeck	.60	.25
❑ 37	Chris Chambers	1.00	.40
❑ 38	Travis Henry	.60	.25
❑ 39	David Boston	.60	.25
❑ 40	Tony Gonzalez	.60	.25
❑ 41	Todd Heap	.60	.25
❑ 42	Hines Ward	1.00	.40
❑ 43	Brett Favre	2.50	1.00
❑ 44	Rod Gardner	.60	.25
❑ 45	Donte Stallworth	1.00	.40
❑ 46	Corey Dillon	.60	.25
❑ 47	Garrison Hearst	.60	.25
❑ 48	Ricky Williams	1.00	.40
❑ 49	Ray Lewis	1.00	.40
❑ 50	Plaxico Burress	.60	.25
❑ 51	Michael Bennett	.60	.25
❑ 52	Stephen Davis	.60	.25
❑ 53	LaDainian Tomlinson	1.00	.40
❑ 54	Priest Holmes	1.25	.50
❑ 55	Jonathan Wells	.40	.15
❑ 56	Jerome Bettis	1.00	.40
❑ 57	Jimmy Smith	.60	.25
❑ 58	Michael Vick	2.50	1.00
❑ 59	Tommy Maddox	1.00	.40
❑ 60	Edgerrin James	1.00	.40
❑ 61	Laveranues Coles	.60	.25
❑ 62	Curtis Conway	.40	.15
❑ 63	Clinton Portis	1.50	.60
❑ 64	Derrick Brooks	.60	.25
❑ 65	Amani Toomer	.60	.25
❑ 66	Roy Williams	1.00	.40
❑ 67	Marshall Faulk	1.00	.40
❑ 68	Daunte Culpepper	1.00	.40
❑ 69	Peerless Price	.60	.25
❑ 70	Marcel Shipp	.60	.25
❑ 71	David Carr	1.50	.60
❑ 72	Patrick Ramsey	1.00	.40
❑ 73	Charlie Garner	.60	.25
❑ 74	Jake Plummer	.60	.25
❑ 75	Kurt Warner	1.00	.40
❑ 76	Brian Urlacher	1.50	.60
❑ 77	Tai Streets	.40	.15
❑ 78	Jason Taylor	.40	.15
❑ 79	Drew Bledsoe	1.00	.40
❑ 80	Drew Brees	1.00	.40
❑ 81	Peyton Manning	1.50	.60
❑ 82	Jamal Lewis	1.00	.40
❑ 83	Antwaan Randle El	1.00	.40
❑ 84	Mark Brunell	.60	.25
❑ 85	Warrick Dunn	.60	.25
❑ 86	Brian Dawkins	.60	.25
❑ 87	James Stewart	.60	.25
❑ 88	Ronde Barber	.40	.15
❑ 89	Curtis Martin	1.00	.40
❑ 90	Jon Kitna	.60	.25
❑ 91	Keyshawn Johnson	1.00	.40
❑ 92	Aaron Brooks	1.00	.40
❑ 93	Marty Booker	.60	.25
❑ 94	Jeff Garcia	1.00	.40
❑ 95	Marvin Harrison	1.00	.40
❑ 96	T.J. Duckett	.60	.25
❑ 97	Jerry Rice	2.00	.75
❑ 98	Donald Driver	.60	.25
❑ 99	Steve McNair	1.00	.40
❑ 100	Kerry Collins	.60	.25
❑ 101	Carson Palmer RC	25.00	10.00
❑ 102	Kyle Boller RC	6.00	2.50
❑ 103	Willis McGahee RC	15.00	6.00
❑ 104	Larry Johnson RC	25.00	12.50
❑ 105	Bryant Johnson RC	6.00	2.50
❑ 106	Byron Leftwich RC	20.00	7.50
❑ 107	Andre Johnson RC	12.00	5.00
❑ 108	Rex Grossman RC	20.00	7.50
❑ 109	Kelley Washington RC	6.00	2.50
❑ 110	Charles Rogers RC	6.00	2.50
❑ 111	Taylor Jacobs RC	4.00	1.50
❑ 112	Sam Aiken RC	4.00	1.50
❑ 113	Dallas Clark RC	5.00	2.00
❑ 114	B.J. Askew RC	5.00	2.00
❑ 115	Quentin Griffin RC	6.00	2.50
❑ 116	Terence Newman RC	10.00	4.00
❑ 117	Chris Simms RC	8.00	3.00
❑ 118	Brandon Lloyd RC	6.00	2.50
❑ 119	Lee Suggs RC	6.00	2.50
❑ 120	L.J. Smith RC	5.00	2.00
❑ 121	Anquan Boldin RC	12.00	5.00
❑ 122	Musa Smith RC	5.00	2.00
❑ 123	Billy McMullen RC	4.00	1.50
❑ 124	Bennie Joppru RC	5.00	2.00
❑ 125	Justin Fargas RC	5.00	2.00
❑ 126	Tyrone Calico RC	6.00	2.50
❑ 127	Dave Ragone RC	5.00	2.00
❑ 128	Seneca Wallace RC	5.00	2.00
❑ 129	Chris Brown RC	6.00	2.50
❑ 130	Terrell Suggs RC	8.00	3.00
❑ 131	Bethel Johnson RC	8.00	3.00
❑ 132	Nate Burleson RC	6.00	2.50
❑ 133	Teyo Johnson RC	8.00	3.00
❑ 134	Kevin Curtis RC	8.00	3.00
❑ 135	Jason Witten RC	12.00	5.00
❑ 136	Artose Pinner RC	8.00	3.00
❑ 137	Boss Bailey RC	6.00	2.50
❑ 138	Jerome McDougle RC	8.00	3.00
❑ 139	LaBrandon Toefield RC	8.00	3.00
❑ 140	Domanick Davis RC	6.00	2.50

2004 Fleer Genuine

❑	76-100 ROOKIE PRINT RUN 500 SER.#'d SETS		
❑ 1	Anquan Boldin	1.00	.40
❑ 2	Rod Smith	.60	.25
❑ 3	Randy Moss	1.25	.50
❑ 4	Drew Brees	1.00	.40
❑ 5	Jamal Lewis	1.00	.40
❑ 6	Ahman Green	1.00	.40
❑ 7	Aaron Brooks	.60	.25
❑ 8	Torry Holt	1.00	.40
❑ 9	Steve Smith	1.00	.40
❑ 10	Marvin Harrison	1.00	.40
❑ 11	Santana Moss	.60	.25
❑ 12	Eddie George	.60	.25
❑ 13	Lee Suggs	1.00	.40
❑ 14	Randy McMichael	.40	.15
❑ 15	Hines Ward	1.00	.40
❑ 16	Drew Bledsoe	1.00	.40
❑ 17	Andre Johnson	1.00	.40
❑ 18	Jeremy Shockey	1.00	.40
❑ 19	Mike Alstott	.60	.25
❑ 20	Chad Johnson	1.00	.40
❑ 21	Priest Holmes	1.25	.50
❑ 22	Brian Westbrook	.60	.25
❑ 23	Rudi Johnson	.60	.25
❑ 24	Keyshawn Johnson	.60	.25
❑ 25	Chris Chambers	.60	.25
❑ 26	LaDainian Tomlinson	1.25	.50
❑ 27	Ray Lewis	1.00	.40
❑ 28	Brett Favre	2.50	1.00
❑ 29	Deuce McAllister	1.00	.40
❑ 30	Marshall Faulk	1.00	.40
❑ 31	Brian Urlacher	1.25	.50
❑ 32	Byron Leftwich	1.25	.50
❑ 33	Jerry Rice	2.00	.75
❑ 34	Clinton Portis	1.00	.40
❑ 35	Derrick Mason	.60	.25
❑ 36	Emmitt Smith	2.00	.75
❑ 37	Plaxico Burress	.60	.25
❑ 38	Peerless Price	.60	.25
❑ 39	Joey Harrington	1.00	.40
❑ 40	Corey Dillon	.60	.25
❑ 41	Matt Hasselbeck	.60	.25
❑ 42	Stephen Davis	.60	.25
❑ 43	Peyton Manning	1.50	.60
❑ 44	Tiki Barber	1.00	.40
❑ 45	Derrick Brooks	.60	.25
❑ 46	Jeff Garcia	1.00	.40
❑ 47	Trent Green	.60	.25
❑ 48	Donovan McNabb	1.25	.50
❑ 49	Michael Vick	2.00	.75
❑ 50	Jake Plummer	.60	.25
❑ 51	Tom Brady	2.50	1.00
❑ 52	Brandon Lloyd	.60	.25
❑ 53	Eric Moulds	.60	.25
❑ 54	David Carr	1.00	.40
❑ 55	Joe Horn	.60	.25
❑ 56	Isaac Bruce	.60	.25
❑ 57	Rex Grossman	1.00	.40
❑ 58	Fred Taylor	.60	.25
❑ 59	Rich Gannon	.60	.25
❑ 60	Laveranues Coles	.60	.25
❑ 61	T.J. Duckett	.60	.25
❑ 62	Charles Rogers	.60	.25
❑ 63	Deion Branch	1.00	.40
❑ 64	Shaun Alexander	1.00	.40
❑ 65	Jake Delhomme	1.00	.40
❑ 66	Edgerrin James	1.00	.40
❑ 67	Chad Pennington	1.00	.40
❑ 68	Steve McNair	1.00	.40
❑ 69	Carson Palmer	1.25	.50
❑ 70	Tony Gonzalez	.60	.25
❑ 71	Terrell Owens	1.00	.40
❑ 72	Josh McCown	.60	.25
❑ 73	Ashley Lelie	.60	.25
❑ 74	Daunte Culpepper	1.00	.40
❑ 75	Kevan Barlow	.60	.25
❑ 76	Eli Manning RC	20.00	7.50
❑ 77	Larry Fitzgerald RC	12.00	5.00
❑ 78	Philip Rivers RC	12.00	6.00
❑ 79	Kellen Winslow RC	8.00	3.00
❑ 80	Roy Williams RC	10.00	4.00
❑ 81	Reggie Williams RC	5.00	2.00
❑ 82	Ben Roethlisberger RC	40.00	25.00
❑ 83	Lee Evans RC	5.00	2.00
❑ 84	Michael Clayton RC	8.00	3.00
❑ 85	J.P. Losman RC	8.00	3.00
❑ 86	Steven Jackson RC	12.00	5.00
❑ 87	Chris Perry RC	6.00	2.50
❑ 88	Michael Jenkins RC	4.00	1.50
❑ 89	Kevin Jones RC	10.00	4.00
❑ 90	Rashaun Woods RC	4.00	1.50
❑ 91	Ben Watson RC	4.00	1.50
❑ 92	Ben Troupe RC	4.00	1.50
❑ 93	Tatum Bell RC	8.00	3.00
❑ 94	Julius Jones RC	12.00	5.00
❑ 95	Devery Henderson RC	3.00	1.25
❑ 96	Darius Watts RC	4.00	1.50
❑ 97	Greg Jones RC	4.00	1.50
❑ 98	Keary Colbert RC	5.00	2.00
❑ 99	Derrick Hamilton RC	3.00	1.25
❑ 100	Drew Henson RC	4.00	1.50

1997 Fleer Goudey

❑	COMPLETE SET (150)	15.00	6.00
❑ 1	Michael Jackson	.30	.10
❑ 2	Ray Lewis	.75	.30
❑ 3	Vinny Testaverde	.30	.10
❑ 4	Eric Turner	.20	.07
❑ 5	Jim Kelly	.50	.20
❑ 6	Bryce Paup	.20	.07
❑ 7	Andre Reed	.30	.10
❑ 8	Bruce Smith	.30	.10
❑ 9	Thurman Thomas	.50	.20

❑ 10 Jeff Blake .30 .10
❑ 11 Ki-Jana Carter .20 .07
❑ 12 Carl Pickens .30 .10
❑ 13 Darnay Scott .30 .10
❑ 14 Terrell Davis .60 .25
❑ 15 John Elway 2.00 .75
❑ 16 Anthony Miller .20 .07
❑ 17 John Mobley .20 .07
❑ 18 Shannon Sharpe .30 .10
❑ 19 Chris Chandler .30 .10
❑ 20 Eddie George .50 .20
❑ 21 Steve McNair .60 .25
❑ 22 Chris Sanders .20 .07
❑ 23 Quentin Coryatt .20 .07
❑ 24 Sean Dawkins .20 .07
❑ 25 Ken Dilger .20 .07
❑ 26 Marshall Faulk .60 .25
❑ 27 Jim Harbaugh .30 .10
❑ 28 Marvin Harrison .50 .20
❑ 29 Tony Brackens .20 .07
❑ 30 Mark Brunell .60 .25
❑ 31 Kevin Hardy .20 .07
❑ 32 Keenan McCardell .30 .10
❑ 33 James O.Stewart .30 .10
❑ 34 Marcus Allen .50 .20
❑ 35 Steve Bono .30 .10
❑ 36 Dale Carter .20 .07
❑ 37 Neil Smith .30 .10
❑ 38 Derrick Thomas .50 .20
❑ 39 Tamarick Vanover .30 .10
❑ 40 Karim Abdul-Jabbar .30 .10
❑ 41 Dan Marino 2.00 .75
❑ 42 O.J. McDuffie .30 .10
❑ 43 Stanley Pritchett .20 .07
❑ 44 Zach Thomas .50 .20
❑ 45 Drew Bledsoe .60 .25
❑ 46 Ben Coates .30 .10
❑ 47 Terry Glenn .50 .20
❑ 48 Shawn Jefferson .20 .07
❑ 49 Curtis Martin .60 .25
❑ 50 Dave Meggett .20 .07
❑ 51 Hugh Douglas .20 .07
❑ 52 Keyshawn Johnson .50 .20
❑ 53 Adrian Murrell .30 .10
❑ 54 Tim Brown .50 .20
❑ 55 Rickey Dudley .30 .10
❑ 56 Jeff Hostetler .20 .07
❑ 57 Napoleon Kaufman .50 .20
❑ 58 Chester McGlockton .20 .07
❑ 59 Jerome Bettis .50 .20
❑ 60 Andre Hastings .20 .07
❑ 61 Greg Lloyd .20 .07
❑ 62 Kordell Stewart .50 .20
❑ 63 Yancey Thigpen .30 .10
❑ 64 Rod Woodson .30 .10
❑ 65 Andre Coleman .20 .07
❑ 66 Stan Humphries .30 .10
❑ 67 Tony Martin .30 .10
❑ 68 Leonard Russell .20 .07
❑ 69 Junior Seau .50 .20
❑ 70 Brian Blades .20 .07
❑ 71 Joey Galloway .30 .10
❑ 72 Chris Warren .30 .10
❑ 73 Larry Centers .30 .10
❑ 74 Leeland McElroy .20 .07
❑ 75 Simeon Rice .30 .10
❑ 76 Frank Sanders .30 .10
❑ 77 Eric Swann .20 .07
❑ 78 Jamal Anderson .50 .20
❑ 79 Bert Emanuel .30 .10
❑ 80 Terance Mathis .30 .10
❑ 81 Eric Metcalf .30 .10
❑ 82 Tim Biakabutuka .30 .10
❑ 83 Kerry Collins .50 .20
❑ 84 Kevin Greene .30 .10
❑ 85 Muhsin Muhammad .30 .10
❑ 86 Wesley Walls .30 .10
❑ 87 Curtis Conway .30 .10
❑ 88 Bryan Cox .20 .07
❑ 89 Walt Harris .20 .07
❑ 90 Erik Kramer .20 .07
❑ 91 Rashaan Salaam .20 .07
❑ 92 Troy Aikman 1.00 .40
❑ 93 Michael Irvin .50 .20
❑ 94 Daryl Johnston .30 .10
❑ 95 Leon Lett .20 .07
❑ 96 Deion Sanders .50 .20
❑ 97 Emmitt Smith 1.50 .60
❑ 98 Scott Mitchell .30 .10
❑ 99 Herman Moore .30 .10
❑ 100 Johnnie Morton .30 .10
❑ 101 Brett Perriman .20 .07
❑ 102 Barry Sanders 1.50 .60
❑ 103 Edgar Bennett .30 .10
❑ 104 Robert Brooks .30 .10
❑ 105 Brett Favre 2.00 .75
❑ 106 Antonio Freeman .50 .20
❑ 107 Keith Jackson .20 .07
❑ 108 Reggie White .50 .20
❑ 109 Cris Carter .50 .20
❑ 110 Warren Moon .50 .20
❑ 111 John Randle .30 .10
❑ 112 Jake Reed .30 .10
❑ 113 Robert Smith .30 .10
❑ 114 Jim Everett .20 .07
❑ 115 Michael Haynes .20 .07
❑ 116 Alex Molden .20 .07
❑ 117 Ray Zellars .20 .07
❑ 118 Chris Calloway .20 .07
❑ 119 Rodney Hampton .30 .10
❑ 120 Phillippi Sparks .20 .07
❑ 121 Amani Toomer .30 .10
❑ 122 Ty Detmer .30 .10
❑ 123 Jason Dunn .20 .07
❑ 124 Irving Fryar .30 .10
❑ 125 Chris T. Jones .20 .07
❑ 126 Ricky Watters .30 .10
❑ 127 Tony Banks .30 .10
❑ 128 Isaac Bruce .50 .20
❑ 129 Eddie Kennison .30 .10
❑ 130 Lawrence Phillips .20 .07
❑ 131 Merton Hanks .20 .07
❑ 132 Terry Kirby .30 .10
❑ 133 Ken Norton .20 .07
❑ 134 Jerry Rice 1.00 .40
❑ 135 J.J. Stokes .30 .10
❑ 136 Steve Young .60 .25
❑ 137 Alvin Harper .20 .07
❑ 138 Jackie Harris .20 .07
❑ 139 Hardy Nickerson .20 .07
❑ 140 Errict Rhett .20 .07
❑ 141 Terry Allen .50 .20
❑ 142 Henry Ellard .20 .07
❑ 143 Gus Frerotte .20 .07
❑ 144 Brian Mitchell .20 .07
❑ 145 Michael Westbrook .30 .10
❑ 146 Chuck Bednarik .30 .10
❑ 146AU Chuck Bednarik AUTO 50.00 20.00
❑ 147 Y.A. Tittle .30 .10
❑ 147AU Y.A. Tittle AUTO 50.00 20.00
❑ 148 Checklist .20 .07
❑ 149 Checklist .20 .07
❑ 150 Checklist .20 .07
❑ P1 Brett Favre Promo 2.00 .75

1997 Fleer Goudey II

❑ COMPLETE SET (150) 20.00 7.50
❑ 1 Gale Sayers SP .50 .20
❑ 1AU Gale Sayers AUTO 100.00 40.00
❑ 1RT Gale Sayers Rare Trad. 8.00 4.00
❑ 2 Vinny Testaverde .30 .10
❑ 3 Jeff George .30 .10
❑ 4 Brett Favre 2.00 .75
❑ 5 Eddie Kennison .30 .10
❑ 6 Ken Norton .20 .07
❑ 7 John Elway 2.00 .75
❑ 8 Troy Aikman 1.00 .40
❑ 9 Steve McNair .60 .25
❑ 10 Kordell Stewart .50 .20
❑ 11 Drew Bledsoe .60 .25
❑ 12 Kerry Collins .50 .20
❑ 13 Dan Marino 2.00 .75
❑ 14 Brad Johnson .50 .20
❑ 15 Todd Collins .20 .07
❑ 16 Ki-Jana Carter .20 .07
❑ 17 Pat Barnes RC .50 .20
❑ 18 Aeneas Williams .20 .07
❑ 19 Keyshawn Johnson .50 .20
❑ 20 Barry Sanders 1.50 .60
❑ 21 Tiki Barber RC 3.00 1.25
❑ 22 Emmitt Smith 1.50 .60
❑ 23 Kevin Hardy .20 .07
❑ 24 Mario Bates .20 .07
❑ 25 Ricky Watters .30 .10
❑ 26 Chris Canty RC .20 .07
❑ 27 Eddie George .50 .20
❑ 28 Curtis Martin .60 .25
❑ 29 Adrian Murrell .30 .10
❑ 30 Terrell Davis .60 .25
❑ 31 Rashaan Salaam .20 .07
❑ 32 Marcus Allen .50 .20
❑ 33 Karim Abdul-Jabbar .50 .20
❑ 34 Thurman Thomas .50 .20
❑ 35 Marvin Harrison .50 .20
❑ 36 Jerome Bettis .50 .20
❑ 37 Larry Centers .30 .10
❑ 38 Stan Humphries .30 .10
❑ 39 Lawrence Phillips .20 .07
❑ 40 Gale Sayers SP .50 .20
❑ 40AU Gale Sayers AUTO 100.00 40.00
❑ 40RT Gale Sayers Rare Trad. 8.00 4.00
❑ 41 Henry Ellard .20 .07
❑ 42 Chris Warren .30 .10
❑ 43 Robert Brooks .30 .10
❑ 44 Sedrick Shaw RC .30 .10
❑ 45 Muhsin Muhammad .30 .10
❑ 46 Napoleon Kaufman .50 .20
❑ 47 Reidel Anthony RC .50 .20
❑ 48 Jamal Anderson .50 .20
❑ 49 Scott Mitchell .30 .10
❑ 50 Mark Brunell .60 .25
❑ 51 William Thomas .20 .07
❑ 52 Bryan Cox .20 .07
❑ 53 Carl Pickens .30 .10
❑ 54 Chris Spielman .20 .07
❑ 55 Junior Seau .50 .20
❑ 56 Hardy Nickerson .20 .07
❑ 57 Dwayne Rudd RC .50 .20
❑ 58 Peter Boulware RC .50 .20
❑ 59 Jim Druckenmiller RC .30 .10
❑ 60 Michael Westbrook .30 .10
❑ 61 Shawn Springs RC .30 .10
❑ 62 Zach Thomas .50 .20
❑ 63 David LaFleur RC .20 .07
❑ 64 Darrell Russell RC .20 .07
❑ 65 Jake Plummer RC 2.50 1.00
❑ 66 Tim Biakabutuka .30 .10
❑ 67 Tyrone Wheatley .30 .10
❑ 68 Elvis Grbac .30 .10
❑ 69 Antonio Freeman .50 .20
❑ 70 Wayne Chrebet .50 .20
❑ 71 Walter Jones RC .50 .20
❑ 72 Marshall Faulk .60 .25
❑ 73 Jason Dunn .20 .07
❑ 74 Darnay Scott .30 .10
❑ 75 Errict Rhett .20 .07
❑ 76 Orlando Pace RC .50 .20
❑ 77 Natrone Means .30 .10
❑ 78 Bruce Smith .30 .10
❑ 79 Jamie Sharper RC .30 .10
❑ 80 Jerry Rice 1.00 .40
❑ 81 Tim Brown .50 .20
❑ 82 Brian Mitchell .20 .07
❑ 83 Andre Reed .30 .10
❑ 84 Herman Moore .30 .10
❑ 85 Rob Moore .30 .10
❑ 86 Rae Carruth RC .20 .07

❑ 87 Bert Emanuel .30 .10
❑ 88 Michael Irvin .50 .20
❑ 89 Mark Chmura .30 .10
❑ 90 Tony Brackens .20 .07
❑ 91 Kevin Greene .30 .10
❑ 92 Reggie White .50 .20
❑ 93 Derrick Thomas .50 .20
❑ 94 Troy Davis RC .30 .10
❑ 95 Greg Lloyd .20 .07
❑ 96 Cortez Kennedy .20 .07
❑ 97 Simeon Rice .30 .10
❑ 98 Terrell Owens .60 .25
❑ 99 Hugh Douglas .20 .07
❑ 100 Terry Glenn .50 .20
❑ 101 Jim Harbaugh .30 .10
❑ 102 Shannon Sharpe .30 .10
❑ 103 Joey Kent RC .50 .20
❑ 104 Jeff Blake .30 .10
❑ 105 Terry Allen .50 .20
❑ 106 Cris Carter .50 .20
❑ 107 Amani Toomer .30 .10
❑ 108 Derrick Alexander WR .30 .10
❑ 109 Darnell Autry RC .30 .10
❑ 110 Irving Fryar .30 .10
❑ 111 Bryant Westbrook RC .20 .07
❑ 112 Tony Banks .30 .10
❑ 113 Michael Booker RC .20 .07
❑ 114 Yatil Green RC .30 .10
❑ 115 James Farrior RC .50 .20
❑ 116 Warrick Dunn RC 1.50 .60
❑ 117 Greg Hill .20 .07
❑ 118 Tony Martin .30 .10
❑ 119 Chris Sanders .20 .07
❑ 120 Charles Johnson .30 .10
❑ 121 John Mobley .20 .07
❑ 122 Keenan McCardell .30 .10
❑ 123 Willie McGinest .20 .07
❑ 124 O.J. McDuffie .30 .10
❑ 125 Deion Sanders .50 .20
❑ 126 Curtis Conway .30 .10
❑ 127 Desmond Howard .30 .10
❑ 128 Johnnie Morton .30 .10
❑ 129 Ike Hilliard RC .75 .30
❑ 130 Gus Frerotte .20 .07
❑ 131 Tom Knight .20 .07
❑ 132 Sean Dawkins .20 .07
❑ 133 Isaac Bruce .50 .20
❑ 134 Wesley Walls .30 .10
❑ 135 Danny Wuerffel RC .50 .20
❑ 136 Tony Gonzalez RC 1.50 .60
❑ 137 Ben Coates .30 .10
❑ 138 Joey Galloway .30 .10
❑ 139 Michael Jackson .30 .10
❑ 140 Steve Young .60 .25
❑ 141 Corey Dillon RC 3.00 1.25
❑ 142 Jake Reed .30 .10
❑ 143 Edgar Bennett .30 .10
❑ 144 Ty Detmer .30 .10
❑ 145 Darrell Green .30 .10
❑ 146 Antowain Smith RC 1.25 .50
❑ 147 Mike Alstott .50 .20
❑ 148 Checklist .20 .07
❑ 149 Checklist .20 .07
❑ 150 Gale Sayers SP .50 .20
❑ 150AU Gale Sayers AUTO 100.00 40.00
❑ 150RT Gale Sayers Rare Trad. 8.00 4.00
❑ P92 Reggie White Promo .50 .20

2004 Fleer Inscribed

❑ COMP.SET w/o SP's (75) 25.00 10.00
❑ 1 Terrell Owens 1.00 .40
❑ 2 David Carr 1.00 .40
❑ 3 Jerry Porter .60 .25
❑ 4 Charles Rogers .60 .25
❑ 5 Torry Holt 1.00 .40
❑ 6 Byron Leftwich 1.25 .50
❑ 7 Laveranues Coles .60 .25
❑ 8 Edgerrin James 1.00 .40
❑ 9 Brian Urlacher 1.25 .50
❑ 10 Hines Ward 1.00 .40
❑ 11 LaDainian Tomlinson 1.25 .50
❑ 12 Ahman Green 1.00 .40
❑ 13 Kevan Barlow .60 .25
❑ 14 Trent Green .60 .25
❑ 15 Deuce McAllister 1.00 .40
❑ 16 Lee Suggs 1.00 .40
❑ 17 Drew Brees 1.00 .40
❑ 18 Randy Moss 1.25 .50
❑ 19 Brandon Lloyd .60 .25
❑ 20 Jeff Garcia 1.00 .40
❑ 21 Roy Williams S .60 .25
❑ 22 Daunte Culpepper 1.00 .40
❑ 23 Matt Hasselbeck .60 .25
❑ 24 Keyshawn Johnson .60 .25
❑ 25 Michael Vick 2.00 .75
❑ 26 Shaun Alexander 1.00 .40
❑ 27 Chad Pennington 1.00 .40
❑ 28 Ashley Lelie .60 .25
❑ 29 Anquan Boldin 1.00 .40
❑ 30 Carson Palmer 1.25 .50
❑ 31 Jeremy Shockey 1.00 .40
❑ 32 Peerless Price .60 .25
❑ 33 Chad Johnson 1.00 .40
❑ 34 Tiki Barber 1.00 .40
❑ 35 Warrick Dunn .60 .25
❑ 36 Jamal Lewis 1.00 .40
❑ 37 Brian Westbrook .60 .25
❑ 38 Stephen Davis .60 .25
❑ 39 Steve McNair 1.00 .40
❑ 40 Donovan McNabb 1.25 .50
❑ 41 Fred Taylor .60 .25
❑ 42 Clinton Portis 1.00 .40
❑ 43 Santana Moss .60 .25
❑ 44 Rod Smith .60 .25
❑ 45 Josh McCown .60 .25
❑ 46 Ray Lewis 1.00 .40
❑ 47 Marshall Faulk 1.00 .40
❑ 48 Eric Moulds .60 .25
❑ 49 Jerry Rice 2.00 .75
❑ 50 Jake Delhomme 1.00 .40
❑ 51 Tony Gonzalez .60 .25
❑ 52 Aaron Brooks .60 .25
❑ 53 Randy McMichael .40 .15
❑ 54 David Boston .60 .25
❑ 55 Plaxico Burress .60 .25
❑ 56 Rich Gannon .60 .25
❑ 57 Brett Favre 2.50 1.00
❑ 58 Isaac Bruce .60 .25
❑ 59 Tom Brady 2.50 1.00
❑ 60 Priest Holmes 1.25 .50
❑ 61 Joe Horn .60 .25
❑ 62 Troy Brown .60 .25
❑ 63 Jake Plummer .60 .25
❑ 64 Derrick Brooks .60 .25
❑ 65 Marvin Harrison 1.00 .40
❑ 66 LaVar Arrington 2.00 .75
❑ 67 Drew Bledsoe 1.00 .40
❑ 68 Steve Smith 1.00 .40
❑ 69 Peyton Manning 1.50 .60
❑ 70 Rex Grossman 1.00 .40
❑ 71 Corey Dillon .60 .25
❑ 72 Mike Alstott .60 .25
❑ 73 Andre Johnson 1.00 .40
❑ 74 Joey Harrington 1.00 .40
❑ 75 Tyrone Calico .60 .25
❑ 76 Eli Manning RC 25.00 12.50
❑ 77 Larry Fitzgerald RC 15.00 6.00
❑ 78 Philip Rivers RC 15.00 7.50
❑ 79 Kellen Winslow RC 10.00 4.00
❑ 80 Roy Williams RC 12.00 5.00
❑ 81 Reggie Williams RC 6.00 2.50
❑ 82 Ben Roethlisberger RC 50.00 25.00
❑ 83 Lee Evans RC 6.00 2.50
❑ 84 Michael Clayton RC 10.00 4.00
❑ 85 J.P. Losman RC 10.00 4.00
❑ 86 Steven Jackson RC 15.00 6.00
❑ 87 Chris Perry RC 8.00 3.00
❑ 88 Michael Jenkins RC 5.00 2.00
❑ 89 Kevin Jones RC 12.00 5.00
❑ 90 Rashaun Woods RC 5.00 2.00
❑ 91 Ben Watson RC 5.00 2.00
❑ 92 Ben Troupe RC 5.00 2.00
❑ 93 Tatum Bell RC 10.00 4.00
❑ 94 Julius Jones RC 15.00 6.00
❑ 95 Devery Henderson RC 4.00 1.50
❑ 96 Darius Watts RC 5.00 2.00
❑ 97 Greg Jones RC 5.00 2.00
❑ 98 Keary Colbert RC 6.00 2.50
❑ 99 Derrick Hamilton RC 4.00 1.50
❑ 100 Bernard Berrian RC 6.00 2.50

2001 Fleer Legacy

❑ COMP.SET w/o SP's (90) 25.00 10.00
❑ 1 Donovan McNabb 1.25 .50
❑ 2 Doug Flutie 1.00 .40
❑ 3 Amani Toomer .60 .25
❑ 4 Jay Fiedler 1.00 .40
❑ 5 Antonio Freeman 1.00 .40
❑ 6 Jon Kitna .60 .25
❑ 7 Jake Plummer .60 .25
❑ 8 Ricky Watters .60 .25
❑ 9 Jerry Rice 2.00 .75
❑ 10 Troy Brown .60 .25
❑ 11 Jimmy Smith .60 .25
❑ 12 Edgerrin James 1.25 .50
❑ 13 Todd Pinkston .60 .25
❑ 14 Eric Moulds .60 .25
❑ 15 Stephen Davis 1.00 .40
❑ 16 Matt Hasselbeck .60 .25
❑ 17 Vinny Testaverde .60 .25
❑ 18 Priest Holmes 1.25 .50
❑ 19 Mike Anderson 1.00 .40
❑ 20 Shane Matthews .40 .15
❑ 21 Qadry Ismail .60 .25
❑ 22 Torry Holt 1.00 .40
❑ 23 Duce Staley 1.00 .40
❑ 24 Ahman Green 1.00 .40
❑ 25 Corey Dillon 1.00 .40
❑ 26 Peerless Price .60 .25
❑ 27 Steve McNair 1.00 .40
❑ 28 Junior Seau 1.00 .40
❑ 29 Doug Chapman .40 .15
❑ 30 Mark Brunell 1.00 .40
❑ 31 Joey Galloway .60 .25
❑ 32 James Allen .60 .25
❑ 33 David Boston 1.00 .40
❑ 34 Marshall Faulk 1.25 .50
❑ 35 Shaun Alexander 1.25 .50
❑ 36 Wayne Chrebet .60 .25
❑ 37 Randy Moss 2.00 .75
❑ 38 Marvin Harrison 1.00 .40
❑ 39 Tim Couch .60 .25
❑ 40 Jamal Anderson 1.00 .40
❑ 41 Warren Sapp .60 .25
❑ 42 Brad Johnson 1.00 .40
❑ 43 Kerry Collins .60 .25
❑ 44 Derrick Alexander .60 .25
❑ 45 Terrell Davis 1.00 .40
❑ 46 Tiki Barber 1.00 .40
❑ 47 Trent Green 1.00 .40
❑ 48 James Stewart .60 .25
❑ 49 Kevin Johnson .60 .25
❑ 50 Ray Lewis 1.00 .40
❑ 51 Warrick Dunn 1.00 .40
❑ 52 Tim Brown 1.00 .40
❑ 53 Daunte Culpepper 1.00 .40
❑ 54 Fred Taylor 1.00 .40
❑ 55 Brian Griese 1.00 .40
❑ 56 Wesley Walls .40 .15
❑ 57 Rob Johnson .60 .25
❑ 58 Travis Taylor .60 [illegible]
❑ 59 Jeff Garcia 1.00 [illegible]
❑ 60 Rich Gannon 1.[illegible]

61	Cris Carter	1.00	.40
62	Peyton Manning	2.50	1.00
63	Peter Warrick	1.00	.40
64	Terance Mathis	.40	.15
65	Kurt Warner	2.00	.75
66	Kordell Stewart	.60	.25
67	Aaron Brooks	1.00	.40
68	JaJuan Dawson	.40	.15
69	Elvis Grbac	.60	.25
70	Keyshawn Johnson	1.00	.40
71	Terrell Owens	1.00	.40
72	Curtis Martin	1.00	.40
73	Lamar Smith	.60	.25
74	Rod Smith	.60	.25
75	Tim Biakabutuka	.60	.25
76	Thomas Jones	.60	.25
77	Isaac Bruce	1.00	.40
78	Joe Horn	.60	.25
79	Drew Bledsoe	1.25	.50
80	Oronde Gadsden	.60	.25
81	Brett Favre	3.00	1.25
82	Emmitt Smith	2.00	.75
83	Muhsin Muhammad	.60	.25
84	Eddie George	1.00	.40
85	Jerome Bettis	1.00	.40
86	Ricky Williams	1.00	.40
87	Tony Gonzalez	.60	.25
88	Germane Crowell	.40	.15
89	Brian Urlacher	1.50	.60
90	Shawn Jefferson	.40	.15
91	Michael Vick RC	30.00	12.50
92	David Terrell RC	8.00	3.00
93	Chris Chambers RC	12.00	5.00
94	Freddie Mitchell RC	8.00	3.00
95	Drew Brees RC	25.00	10.00
96	LaMont Jordan RC	15.00	6.00
97	Quincy Carter RC	8.00	3.00
98	Anthony Thomas RC	8.00	3.00
99	LaDainian Tomlinson RC	60.00	25.00
100	Santana Moss RC	12.00	5.00
101	Rod Gardner RC	8.00	3.00
102	Nick Goings RC	8.00	3.00
103	Sage Rosenfels RC	8.00	3.00
104	Mike McMahon RC	8.00	3.00
105	Snoop Minnis RC	5.00	2.00
106	Michael Bennett RC	8.00	3.00
107	Todd Heap RC	8.00	3.00
108	Kevan Barlow RC	8.00	3.00
109	Travis Henry RC	12.00	5.00
110	Jason Brookins RC	8.00	3.00
111	Rudi Johnson RC	15.00	6.00
112	Reggie Wayne RC	15.00	6.00
113	Koren Robinson RC	8.00	3.00
114	Chad Johnson RC	20.00	7.50
115	Quincy Morgan RC	8.00	3.00
116	Robert Ferguson RC	8.00	3.00
117	Chris Weinke RC	8.00	3.00
118	Jesse Palmer RC	8.00	3.00
119	James Jackson RC	8.00	3.00
120	Deuce McAllister RC	15.00	6.00

2002 Fleer Maximum

	COMP.SET w/o SP's (250)	25.00	10.00
1	Tom Brady	2.50	1.00
2	Kurt Warner	1.00	.40
3	Mike McMahon	1.00	.40
4	Ronney Jenkins	.40	.15
5	Tyrone Wheatley	.60	.25
6	Germane Crowell	.40	.15
7	James Jackson	.40	.15
8	Eric Metcalf	.40	.15
9	Muhsin Muhammad	.60	.25
10	Tony Richardson	.40	.15
11	Wayne Chrebet	.60	.25
12	Daunte Culpepper	1.00	.40
13	Trent Dilfer	.60	.25
14	Kevin Dyson	.60	.25
15	Chris Fuamatu-Ma'afala	.40	.15
16	Dominic Rhodes	1.00	.40
17	David Terrell	1.00	.40
18	Rod Woodson	.60	.25
19	Anthony Wright	.40	.15
20	Jerome Bettis	1.00	.40
21	Kendrell Bell	1.00	.40
22	Edgerrin James	1.25	.50
23	Jamal Lewis	1.00	.40
24	Jim Miller	.40	.15
25	Warren Sapp	.60	.25
26	Clint Stoerner	.40	.15
27	Michael Strahan	.60	.25
28	Vinny Sutherland	.40	.15
29	Mike Alstott	1.00	.40
30	Jay Fiedler	.60	.25
31	Willie Jackson	.40	.15
32	Earl Little RC	1.00	.40
33	Robert Porcher	.40	.15
34	Junior Seau	1.00	.40
35	Darrick Vaughn	.40	.15
36	Wesley Walls	.40	.15
37	Michael Westbrook	.40	.15
38	Freddie Mitchell	.60	.25
39	Drew Bledsoe	1.00	.40
40	Gus Frerotte	.40	.15
41	Travis Henry	1.00	.40
42	MarTay Jenkins	.40	.15
43	Curtis Keaton	.40	.15
44	Keenan McCardell	.40	.15
45	Neil O'Donnell	.40	.15
46	Chad Pennington	1.25	.50
47	Charlie Rogers	.40	.15
48	Hines Ward	1.00	.40
49	Jason Gildon	.40	.15
50	Travis Taylor	.60	.25
51	Dre Bly	.40	.15
52	Oronde Gadsden	.60	.25
53	Danny Wuerffel	.40	.15
54	Jamir Miller	.40	.15
55	Cory Schlesinger	.40	.15
56	LaDainian Tomlinson	1.50	.60
57	Michael Vick	3.00	1.25
58	Chris Weinke	.60	.25
59	Brandon Stokley	.60	.25
60	James Allen	.60	.25
61	Correll Buckhalter	.60	.25
62	Jameel Cook	.40	.15
63	Deuce McAllister	1.25	.50
64	Travis Minor	.40	.15
65	James Stewart	.60	.25
66	Kwamie Lassiter	.40	.15
67	Jamel White	.40	.15
68	Ronde Barber	.40	.15
69	Kevan Barlow	.60	.25
70	Marty Booker	.40	.15
71	Peter Boulware	.40	.15
72	Quincy Carter	.60	.25
73	Warrick Dunn	1.00	.40
74	Brett Favre	2.50	1.00
75	Chad Lewis	.40	.15
76	Jeff Ogden	.40	.15
77	Todd Sauerbrun	.40	.15
78	Ricky Williams	1.00	.40
79	Charlie Batch	.60	.25
80	Courtney Brown	.60	.25
81	Stephen Davis	.60	.25
82	Fred Smoot	.40	.15
83	Marshall Faulk	1.00	.40
84	Doug Flutie	1.00	.40
85	Rich Gannon	1.00	.40
86	Dante Hall	1.00	.40
87	Frank Sanders	.40	.15
88	Antowain Smith	.60	.25
89	Tiki Barber	1.00	.40
90	Fred Beasley	.40	.15
91	Jason Brookins	.40	.15
92	Rocket Ismail	.60	.25
93	Bubba Franks	.60	.25
94	Joey Galloway	.60	.25
95	Keyshawn Johnson	1.00	.40
96	Donovan McNabb	1.25	.50
97	Lamar Smith	.60	.25
98	Corey Bradford	.40	.15
99	Kerry Collins	.60	.25
100	Autry Denson	.40	.15
101	Antonio Freeman	1.00	.40
102	Fred Taylor	1.00	.40
103	Troy Hambrick	.40	.15
104	Brad Johnson	.60	.25
105	Brian Mitchell	.40	.15
106	Zach Thomas	1.00	.40
107	Michael Bennett	.60	.25
108	Ron Dayne	.60	.25
109	Jeff Garcia	1.00	.40
110	Ahman Green	1.00	.40
111	Scotty Anderson	.40	.15
112	Qadry Ismail	.60	.25
113	Ed McCaffrey	1.00	.40
114	Shaun King	.40	.15
115	Duce Staley	1.00	.40
116	Travis Brown	.40	.15
117	Mark Brunell	1.00	.40
118	Chris Cole	.40	.15
119	Aaron Glenn	.60	.25
120	Darrell Jackson	.60	.25
121	Jevon Kearse	.60	.25
122	Randy Moss	2.00	.75
123	Hank Poteat	.40	.15
124	Brian Urlacher	1.50	.60
125	Mike Anderson	1.00	.40
126	David Akers	.40	.15
127	Laveranues Coles	.60	.25
128	Eddie George	1.00	.40
129	J.J. Stokes	.60	.25
130	Matt Hasselbeck	.60	.25
131	Nate Jacquet	.40	.15
132	Anthony Thomas	.60	.25
133	Terrence Wilkins	.40	.15
134	Tim Couch	.60	.25
135	Ty Detmer	.40	.15
136	Rod Gardner	.60	.25
137	Charlie Garner	.60	.25
138	Terry Glenn	.60	.25
139	Az-Zahir Hakim	.40	.15
140	Donald Hayes	.40	.15
141	Priest Holmes	1.25	.50
142	Jermaine Wiggins	.40	.15
143	Aaron Brooks	1.00	.40
144	Alge Crumpler	.60	.25
145	Benjamin Gay	.60	.25
146	Marcellus Wiley	.40	.15
147	Torry Holt	1.00	.40
148	Desmond Howard	.40	.15
149	Richard Huntley	.40	.15
150	Bryan Johnson RC	.40	.15
151	Terry Kirby	.40	.15
152	Snoop Minnis	.40	.15
153	David Boston	1.00	.40
154	Shawn Bryson	.40	.15
155	Scott Covington	.40	.15
156	Terrell Davis	1.00	.40
157	Damon Gibson	.40	.15
158	Curtis Martin	1.00	.40
159	Derrick Mason	.60	.25
160	Jacquez Green	.40	.15
161	Chad Scott	.40	.15
162	Tony Boselli	.40	.15
163	Derrick Alexander	.60	.25
164	Ian Gold	.40	.15
165	Rob Johnson	.60	.25
166	Thomas Jones	.60	.25
167	Steve Smith	1.00	.40
168	Jonathan Quinn	.40	.15
169	Mack Strong	.60	.25
170	Vinny Testaverde	.60	.25
171	Frank Wycheck	.40	.15
172	Amos Zereoue	1.00	.40
173	Chris Chambers	1.00	.40
174	Joe Horn	.60	.25
175	Kevin Johnson	.60	.25
176	Ryan McNeil	.40	.15
177	Marcus Pollard	.40	.15
178	Jerry Rice	2.00	.75
179	Jon Kitna	.60	.25
180	Maurice Smith	.60	.25
181	Jerome Pathon	.60	.25
182	Darrien Gordon	.40	.15
183	Champ Bailey	.60	.25
184	Drew Brees	1.00	.40
185	Troy Brown	.60	.25
186	Brian Griese	1.00	.40
187	Jamal Anderson	.60	.25

❑ 188	Eric Moulds	.60	.25
❑ 189	Darnay Scott	.40	.15
❑ 190	Jimmy Smith	.60	.25
❑ 191	Ricky Watters	.60	.25
❑ 192	Craig Yeast	.40	.15
❑ 193	Michael Bates	.40	.15
❑ 194	Trung Canidate	.60	.25
❑ 195	David Dunn	.40	.15
❑ 196	Tim Dwight	.60	.25
❑ 197	Trent Green	.60	.25
❑ 198	David Patten	.40	.15
❑ 199	Jake Plummer	.60	.25
❑ 200	Rod Smith	.60	.25
❑ 201	Alex Van Pelt	.60	.25
❑ 202	Peter Warrick	.60	.25
❑ 203	Shaun Alexander	1.25	.50
❑ 204	Plaxico Burress	.60	.25
❑ 205	Byron Chamberlain	.40	.15
❑ 206	Peyton Manning	2.00	.75
❑ 207	Marcus Robinson	.60	.25
❑ 208	Desmond Clark	.40	.15
❑ 209	Reggie Swinton	.40	.15
❑ 210	Amani Toomer	.60	.25
❑ 211	Karl Williams	.40	.15
❑ 212	Larry Centers	.40	.15
❑ 213	Corey Dillon	.60	.25
❑ 214	Jason Elam	.40	.15
❑ 215	Arnold Jackson	.40	.15
❑ 216	Stacey Mack	.40	.15
❑ 217	Steve McNair	1.00	.40
❑ 218	Santana Moss	1.00	.40
❑ 219	Koren Robinson	.60	.25
❑ 220	Kordell Stewart	.60	.25
❑ 221	Spergon Wynn	.40	.15
❑ 222	Todd Bouman	.40	.15
❑ 223	Marvin Harrison	1.00	.40
❑ 224	Joe Jurevicius	.40	.15
❑ 225	Terry Allen	.40	.15
❑ 226	Jermaine Lewis	.40	.15
❑ 227	Terrell Owens	1.00	.40
❑ 228	Shane Matthews	.40	.15
❑ 229	Emmitt Smith	2.50	1.00
❑ 230	Jeremiah Trotter	.40	.15
❑ 231	Tony Banks	.40	.15
❑ 232	Tim Brown	1.00	.40
❑ 233	Isaac Bruce	1.00	.40
❑ 234	Curtis Conway	.40	.15
❑ 235	Marc Edwards	.40	.15
❑ 236	Tony Gonzalez	.60	.25
❑ 237	Deltha O'Neal	.40	.15
❑ 238	Michael Pittman	.40	.15
❑ 239	Peerless Price	.60	.25
❑ 240	Takeo Spikes	.40	.15
❑ 241	Charlie Clemons RC	.40	.15
❑ 242	Garrison Hearst	.60	.25
❑ 243	Ike Hilliard	.60	.25
❑ 244	Leonard Johnson	.40	.15
❑ 245	Chris Redman	.40	.15
❑ 246	Ray Lewis	1.00	.40
❑ 247	John Lynch	.60	.25
❑ 248	Bill Schroeder	.60	.25
❑ 249	James Thrash	.60	.25
❑ 250	Chad Johnson	1.00	.40
❑ 251	David Carr RC	10.00	4.00
❑ 252	Joey Harrington RC	6.00	2.50
❑ 253	DeShaun Foster RC	4.00	1.50
❑ 254	William Green RC	4.00	1.50
❑ 255	Julius Peppers RC	8.00	3.00
❑ 256	Javon Walker RC	8.00	3.00
❑ 257	Ashley Lelie RC	8.00	3.00
❑ 258	Adrian Peterson RC	4.00	1.50
❑ 259	Patrick Ramsey RC	5.00	2.00
❑ 260	Kurt Kittner RC	3.00	1.25
❑ 261	Josh Reed RC	4.00	1.50
❑ 262	David Garrard RC	4.00	1.50
❑ 263	Reche Caldwell RC	4.00	1.50
❑ 264	Quentin Jammer RC	4.00	1.50
❑ 265	Rohan Davey RC	4.00	1.50
❑ 266	Eric Crouch RC	4.00	1.50
❑ 267	Kahlil Hill RC	3.00	1.25
❑ 268	Antwaan Randle El RC	6.00	2.50
❑ 269	Josh McCown RC	4.00	1.50
❑ 270	Maurice Morris RC	4.00	1.50
❑ 271	Jeremy Shockey RC	12.00	5.00
❑ 272	Travis Stephens RC	3.00	1.25
❑ 273	Jonathan Wells RC	4.00	1.50
❑ 274	Roy Williams RC	10.00	4.00
❑ 275	Brian Westbrook RC	6.00	2.50
❑ 276	Daniel Graham RC	4.00	1.50
❑ 277	Marquise Walker RC	3.00	1.25
❑ 278	Lamar Gordon RC	4.00	1.50
❑ 279	Jason McAddley RC	3.00	1.25
❑ 280	Jabar Gaffney RC	4.00	1.50
❑ 281	Luke Staley RC	3.00	1.25
❑ 282	Clinton Portis RC	12.00	5.00
❑ 283	Cliff Russell RC	3.00	1.25
❑ 284	Andre Davis RC	3.00	1.25
❑ 285	Ron Johnson RC	3.00	1.25
❑ 286	Ladell Betts RC	4.00	1.50
❑ 287	T.J. Duckett RC	5.00	2.00
❑ 288	Donte Stallworth RC	8.00	3.00
❑ 289	Antonio Bryant RC	4.00	1.50
❑ 290	Chad Hutchinson RC	3.00	1.25

1999 Fleer Mystique

❑	COMPLETE SET (160)	200.00	100.00
❑	COMP.SHORT SET (100)	50.00	25.00
❑ 1	Terrell Davis SP	2.00	.75
❑ 2	Jerome Bettis SP	2.00	.75
❑ 3	J.J. Stokes	.75	.30
❑ 4	Frank Wycheck	.50	.20
❑ 5	O.J. McDuffie	.75	.30
❑ 6	Johnnie Morton	.75	.30
❑ 7	Marshall Faulk SP	2.50	1.00
❑ 8	Ryan Leaf	1.25	.50
❑ 9	Sean Dawkins	.50	.20
❑ 10	Brett Favre SP	6.00	2.50
❑ 11	Steve Young SP	2.50	1.00
❑ 12	Jimmy Smith	.75	.30
❑ 13	Isaac Bruce	1.25	.50
❑ 14	Trent Dilfer	.75	.30
❑ 15	Brian Mitchell	.50	.20
❑ 16	Kordell Stewart SP	1.50	.60
❑ 17	Herman Moore	.75	.30
❑ 18	Troy Aikman SP	4.00	1.50
❑ 19	Cris Carter	1.25	.50
❑ 20	Barry Sanders SP	6.00	2.50
❑ 21	Tony Gonzalez	1.25	.50
❑ 22	Skip Hicks	.50	.20
❑ 23	Steve McNair SP	2.00	.75
❑ 24	Brad Johnson	.75	.30
❑ 25	Mark Chmura	.50	.20
❑ 26	Randall Cunningham SP	2.00	.75
❑ 27	Jerry Rice SP	4.00	1.50
❑ 28	Jamie Asher	.50	.20
❑ 29	Brian Griese SP	2.00	.75
❑ 30	Peyton Manning SP	6.00	2.50
❑ 31	Keith Poole	.50	.20
❑ 32	Wayne Chrebet	.75	.30
❑ 33	Rich Gannon	1.25	.50
❑ 34	Michael Irvin	.75	.30
❑ 35	Yancey Thigpen	.50	.20
❑ 36	Corey Dillon	1.25	.50
❑ 37	Steve Beuerlein	.50	.20
❑ 38	Terry Kirby	.50	.20
❑ 39	Jacquez Green	.50	.20
❑ 40	Mark Brunell SP	1.50	.60
❑ 41	Rickey Dudley	.50	.20
❑ 42	Shannon Sharpe	.75	.30
❑ 43	Andre Rison	.75	.30
❑ 44	Chris Chandler	.75	.30
❑ 45	Fred Taylor SP	2.00	.75
❑ 46	Kerry Collins	.75	.30
❑ 47	Antowain Smith SP	1.50	.60
❑ 48	Wesley Walls	.50	.20
❑ 49	Rob Moore	.75	.30
❑ 50	Dan Marino SP	6.00	2.50
❑ 51	Robert Smith	1.25	.50
❑ 52	Keenan McCardell	.75	.30
❑ 53	Joey Galloway	.75	.30
❑ 54	Fred Lane	.50	.20
❑ 55	Napoleon Kaufman	1.25	.50
❑ 56	Curtis Martin	1.25	.50
❑ 57	Rod Smith	.75	.30
❑ 58	Curtis Conway	.75	.30
❑ 59	Kevin Dyson	.75	.30
❑ 60	Warrick Dunn SP	2.00	.75
❑ 61	Ahman Green	1.25	.50
❑ 62	Duce Staley	1.25	.50
❑ 63	Emmitt Smith SP	4.00	1.50
❑ 64	Adrian Murrell	.75	.30
❑ 65	Dorsey Levens	1.25	.50
❑ 66	Drew Bledsoe SP	2.50	1.00
❑ 67	Ed McCaffrey	.75	.30
❑ 68	Natrone Means	.75	.30
❑ 69	Deion Sanders	1.25	.50
❑ 70	Keyshawn Johnson SP	2.00	.75
❑ 71	Antonio Freeman	1.25	.50
❑ 72	James Stewart	.75	.30
❑ 73	Ben Coates	.75	.30
❑ 74	Priest Holmes	2.00	.75
❑ 75	Jake Reed	.75	.30
❑ 76	Mike Alstott	1.25	.50
❑ 77	Vinny Testaverde	.75	.30
❑ 78	Ricky Watters	.75	.30
❑ 79	Garrison Hearst	.75	.30
❑ 80	Junior Seau	1.25	.50
❑ 81	Tim Brown	1.25	.50
❑ 82	Jamal Anderson	1.25	.50
❑ 83	Robert Brooks	.75	.30
❑ 84	Marc Edwards	.50	.20
❑ 85	Curtis Enis	.50	.20
❑ 86	Doug Flutie	1.25	.50
❑ 87	Terry Glenn	.50	.20
❑ 88	Charlie Batch SP	1.50	.60
❑ 89	Marvin Harrison	1.25	.50
❑ 90	Jake Plummer SP	1.50	.60
❑ 91	Terrell Owens	1.25	.50
❑ 92	Scott Mitchell	.50	.20
❑ 93	Tim Dwight	.75	.30
❑ 94	Eddie George SP	2.00	.75
❑ 95	Ike Hilliard	.50	.20
❑ 96	Robert Holcombe	.50	.20
❑ 97	Charles Johnson	.50	.20
❑ 98	Eric Moulds	1.25	.50
❑ 99	Michael Westbrook	.75	.30
❑ 100	Randy Moss SP	5.00	2.00
❑ 101	Tim Couch RC	6.00	2.50
❑ 102	Donovan McNabb RC	25.00	10.00
❑ 103	Akili Smith RC	3.00	1.25
❑ 104	Cade McNown RC	5.00	2.00
❑ 105	Daunte Culpepper RC	20.00	7.50
❑ 106	Ricky Williams RC	10.00	4.00
❑ 107	Edgerrin James RC	20.00	7.50
❑ 108	Kevin Faulk RC	6.00	2.50
❑ 109	Torry Holt RC	15.00	6.00
❑ 110	David Boston RC	6.00	2.50
❑ 111	Chris Claiborne RC	3.00	1.25
❑ 112	Mike Cloud RC	5.00	2.00
❑ 113	Joe Germaine RC	5.00	2.00
❑ 114	Cecil Collins RC	3.00	1.25
❑ 115	Tim Alexander RC	3.00	1.25
❑ 116	Brandon Stokley RC	8.00	3.00
❑ 117	Lamarr Glenn RC	3.00	1.25
❑ 118	Shawn Bryson RC	6.00	2.50
❑ 119	Jeff Paulk RC	3.00	1.25
❑ 120	Kevin Johnson RC	6.00	2.50
❑ 121	Charlie Rogers RC	5.00	2.00
❑ 122	Joe Montgomery RC	5.00	2.00
❑ 123	Travis McGriff RC	3.00	1.25
❑ 124	Dee Miller RC	3.00	1.25
❑ 125	Rob Konrad RC	6.00	2.50
❑ 126	Peerless Price RC	6.00	2.50
❑ 127	D'Wayne Bates RC	5.00	2.00
❑ 128	Craig Yeast RC	5.00	2.00
❑ 129	Malcolm Johnson RC	3.00	1.25
❑ 130	Brock Huard RC	6.00	2.50
❑ 131	Sedrick Irvin RC	1.50	.60
❑ 132	Troy Smith RC	3.00	1.25
❑ 133	Troy Edwards RC	5.00	2.00
❑ 134	Al Wilson RC	5.00	2.00
❑ 135	Terry Jackson RC	5.00	2.00
❑ 136	Dameane Douglas RC	5.00	2.00
❑ 137	Amos Zereoue RC	6.00	2.50
❑ 138	Shaun King RC	5.00	2.00
❑ 139	James Johnson RC	5.00	2.00
❑ 140	Jermaine Fazande RC	5.00	2.00
❑ 141	Autry Denson RC	5.00	2.00
❑ 142	Darran Hall RC	3.00	1.25
❑ 143	Na Brown RC	5.00	2.00

❑ 144 Mike Lucky RC 3.00 1.25
❑ 145 Karsten Bailey RC 5.00 2.00
❑ 146 Kevin Daft RC 5.00 2.00
❑ 147 Sean Bennett RC 3.00 1.25
❑ 148 Madre Hill RC 3.00 1.25
❑ 149 Michael Bishop RC 6.00 2.50
❑ 150 Scott Covington RC 6.00 2.50
❑ 151 Randy Moss STAR 10.00 4.00
❑ 152 Fred Taylor STAR 4.00 1.50
❑ 153 Brett Favre STAR 12.00 5.00
❑ 154 Dan Marino STAR 12.00 5.00
❑ 155 Terrell Davis STAR 4.00 1.50
❑ 156 Barry Sanders STAR 12.00 5.00
❑ 157 Emmitt Smith STAR 10.00 4.00
❑ 158 Jake Plummer STAR 3.00 1.25
❑ 159 Warrick Dunn STAR 4.00 1.50
❑ 160 Troy Aikman STAR 8.00 3.00
❑ P86 Doug Flutie Promo 1.25 .50

2000 Fleer Mystique

❑ COMPLETE SET (145) 250.00 125.00
❑ COMP.SET w/o SP's (100) 15.00 6.00
❑ 1 Tim Couch .60 .25
❑ 2 Edgerrin James 1.50 .60
❑ 3 Terrell Davis 1.25 .50
❑ 4 Eddie George 1.00 .40
❑ 5 Jevon Kearse 1.00 .40
❑ 6 Mike Alstott 1.00 .40
❑ 7 Tony Martin .60 .25
❑ 8 Jermaine Fazande .40 .15
❑ 9 Akili Smith .40 .15
❑ 10 Damon Huard 1.00 .40
❑ 11 Kordell Stewart .60 .25
❑ 12 Peyton Manning 2.50 1.00
❑ 13 Michael Westbrook .60 .25
❑ 14 Tim Biakabutuka .60 .25
❑ 15 Curtis Martin 1.00 .40
❑ 16 Shaun King .40 .15
❑ 17 Jamal Anderson 1.00 .40
❑ 18 Terry Allen .60 .25
❑ 19 Sean Dawkins .40 .15
❑ 20 Muhsin Muhammad .60 .25
❑ 21 Vinny Testaverde .60 .25
❑ 22 Warren Sapp .60 .25
❑ 23 Wesley Walls .60 .25
❑ 24 Mark Brunell 1.00 .40
❑ 25 Tim Brown 1.00 .40
❑ 26 Kevin Dyson .60 .25
❑ 27 Curtis Enis .40 .15
❑ 28 Keenan McCardell .60 .25
❑ 29 Rich Gannon 1.00 .40
❑ 30 Jermaine Lewis .60 .25
❑ 31 Johnnie Morton .60 .25
❑ 32 Kerry Collins .60 .25
❑ 33 Az-Zahir Hakim .40 .15
❑ 34 Cade McNown .40 .15
❑ 35 Jimmy Smith .60 .25
❑ 36 Tyrone Wheatley .60 .25
❑ 37 Marcus Robinson 1.00 .40
❑ 38 Fred Taylor 1.00 .40
❑ 39 Donovan McNabb 1.50 .60
❑ 40 Steve McNair 1.00 .40
❑ 41 Corey Dillon 1.00 .40
❑ 42 Tony Gonzalez .60 .25
❑ 43 Duce Staley 1.00 .40
❑ 44 Albert Connell .40 .15
❑ 45 Isaac Bruce 1.00 .40
❑ 46 Troy Aikman 2.00 .75
❑ 47 Charlie Garner .60 .25
❑ 48 Kevin Johnson 1.00 .40
❑ 49 Cris Carter 1.00 .40
❑ 50 Ryan Leaf .60 .25
❑ 51 Doug Flutie 1.00 .40
❑ 52 Brett Favre 3.00 1.25
❑ 53 Joe Montgomery .40 .15
❑ 54 Torry Holt 1.00 .40
❑ 55 Jonathan Linton .40 .15
❑ 56 Antonio Freeman 1.00 .40
❑ 57 Amani Toomer .60 .25
❑ 58 Kurt Warner 2.00 .75
❑ 59 Jake Plummer .60 .25
❑ 60 Rob Johnson .60 .25
❑ 61 Randy Moss 2.00 .75
❑ 62 Jerry Rice 2.00 .75
❑ 63 Chris Chandler .60 .25
❑ 64 Joey Galloway .60 .25
❑ 65 Olandis Gary .60 .25
❑ 66 Drew Bledsoe 1.25 .50
❑ 67 Steve Beuerlein .40 .15
❑ 68 Marvin Harrison 1.00 .40
❑ 69 Keyshawn Johnson 1.00 .40
❑ 70 Warrick Dunn 1.00 .40
❑ 71 Tim Dwight 1.00 .40
❑ 72 Brian Griese 1.00 .40
❑ 73 Terry Glenn .60 .25
❑ 74 Jon Kitna 1.00 .40
❑ 75 Qadry Ismail .60 .25
❑ 76 Germane Crowell .40 .15
❑ 77 Ricky Williams 1.00 .40
❑ 78 Marshall Faulk 1.25 .50
❑ 79 Karim Abdul-Jabbar .60 .25
❑ 80 James Johnson .40 .15
❑ 81 Hines Ward 1.00 .40
❑ 82 Frank Sanders .60 .25
❑ 83 Emmitt Smith 2.00 .75
❑ 84 Robert Smith 1.00 .40
❑ 85 Steve Young 1.25 .50
❑ 86 Darnay Scott .60 .25
❑ 87 Tamarick Vanover .40 .15
❑ 88 Troy Edwards .40 .15
❑ 89 Brad Johnson 1.00 .40
❑ 90 Tony Banks .60 .25
❑ 91 Charlie Batch 1.00 .40
❑ 92 Jeff Blake .60 .25
❑ 93 Ricky Watters .60 .25
❑ 94 Carl Pickens .60 .25
❑ 95 Elvis Grbac .60 .25
❑ 96 Jerome Bettis 1.00 .40
❑ 97 Eric Moulds 1.00 .40
❑ 98 Dorsey Levens .60 .25
❑ 99 Wayne Chrebet .60 .25
❑ 100 Stephen Davis 1.00 .40
❑ 101 Shaun Alexander RC 20.00 7.50
❑ 102 Sebastian Janikowski RC 4.00 1.50
❑ 103 Tom Brady RC 40.00 20.00
❑ 104 Courtney Brown RC 4.00 1.50
❑ 105 Marc Bulger RC 8.00 3.00
❑ 106 Plaxico Burress RC 8.00 3.00
❑ 107 Trung Canidate RC 3.00 1.25
❑ 108 Giovanni Carmazzi RC 2.00 .75
❑ 109 Trevor Gaylor RC 3.00 1.25
❑ 110 Laveranues Coles RC 5.00 2.00
❑ 111 Ron Dayne RC 4.00 1.50
❑ 112 Reuben Droughns RC 5.00 2.00
❑ 113 Danny Farmer RC 3.00 1.25
❑ 114 Chafie Fields RC 2.00 .75
❑ 115 Bubba Franks RC 4.00 1.50
❑ 116 Sherrod Gideon RC 2.00 .75
❑ 117 Joe Hamilton RC 3.00 1.25
❑ 118 Chris Cole RC 3.00 1.25
❑ 119 Darrell Jackson RC 8.00 3.00
❑ 120 Thomas Jones RC 6.00 2.50
❑ 121 Jamal Lewis RC 10.00 4.00
❑ 122 Anthony Lucas RC 2.00 .75
❑ 123 Tee Martin RC 4.00 1.50
❑ 124 Frank Murphy RC 2.00 .75
❑ 125 Rondell Mealey RC 2.00 .75
❑ 126 Sylvester Morris RC 3.00 1.25
❑ 127 Dennis Northcutt RC 4.00 1.50
❑ 128 Chad Pennington RC 10.00 4.00
❑ 129 Travis Prentice RC 3.00 1.25
❑ 130 Tim Rattay RC 4.00 1.50
❑ 131 Chris Redman RC 3.00 1.25
❑ 132 J.R. Redmond RC 3.00 1.25
❑ 133 R.Jay Soward RC 3.00 1.25
❑ 134 Quinton Spotwood RC 2.00 .75
❑ 135 Shyrone Stith RC 3.00 1.25
❑ 136 Travis Taylor RC 4.00 1.50
❑ 137 Troy Walters RC 4.00 1.50
❑ 138 Peter Warrick RC 4.00 1.50
❑ 139 Dez White RC 4.00 1.50
❑ 140 Michael Wiley RC 3.00 1.25
❑ 141 Jerry Porter RC 5.00 2.00
❑ 142 Mareno Philyaw RC 2.00 .75
❑ 143 Anthony Becht RC 4.00 1.50
❑ 144 JaJuan Dawson RC 2.00 .75
❑ 145 Ron Dugans RC 5.00 2.00

2003 Fleer Mystique

❑ COMP. SET w/o SP's (80) 30.00 12.50
❑ 1 Emmitt Smith 2.50 1.00
❑ 2 Marcel Shipp .60 .25
❑ 3 Michael Vick 2.50 1.00
❑ 4 Warrick Dunn .60 .25
❑ 5 T.J. Duckett .60 .25
❑ 6 Peerless Price .60 .25
❑ 7 Ray Lewis 1.00 .40
❑ 8 Todd Heap .60 .25
❑ 9 Jamal Lewis 1.00 .40
❑ 10 Eric Moulds .60 .25
❑ 11 Drew Bledsoe 1.00 .40
❑ 12 Travis Henry .60 .25
❑ 13 Stephen Davis .60 .25
❑ 14 Julius Peppers 1.00 .40
❑ 15 Marty Booker .60 .25
❑ 16 Brian Urlacher 1.50 .60
❑ 17 Chad Johnson 1.00 .40
❑ 18 Corey Dillon .60 .25
❑ 19 William Green .60 .25
❑ 20 Tim Couch .40 .15
❑ 21 Joey Galloway .60 .25
❑ 22 Chad Hutchinson .40 .15
❑ 23 Jake Plummer .60 .25
❑ 24 Ed McCaffrey 1.00 .40
❑ 25 Clinton Portis 1.50 .60
❑ 26 Joey Harrington 1.50 .60
❑ 27 Ahman Green 1.00 .40
❑ 28 Brett Favre 2.50 1.00
❑ 29 Jabar Gaffney .60 .25
❑ 30 David Carr 1.50 .60
❑ 31 Peyton Manning 1.50 .60
❑ 32 Marvin Harrison 1.00 .40
❑ 33 Edgerrin James 1.00 .40
❑ 34 Mark Brunell .60 .25
❑ 35 Fred Taylor 1.00 .40
❑ 36 Trent Green .60 .25
❑ 37 Priest Holmes 1.25 .50
❑ 38 Tony Gonzalez .60 .25
❑ 39 Chris Chambers 1.00 .40
❑ 40 Zach Thomas 1.00 .40
❑ 41 Ricky Williams 1.00 .40
❑ 42 Michael Bennett .60 .25
❑ 43 Daunte Culpepper 1.00 .40
❑ 44 Randy Moss 1.50 .60
❑ 45 Deion Branch 1.00 .40
❑ 46 Tom Brady 2.50 1.00
❑ 47 Aaron Brooks 1.00 .40
❑ 48 Deuce McAllister 1.00 .40
❑ 49 Joe Horn .60 .25
❑ 50 Jeremy Shockey 1.50 .60
❑ 51 Amani Toomer .60 .25
❑ 52 Tiki Barber 1.00 .40
❑ 53 Chad Pennington 1.00 .40
❑ 54 Curtis Martin 1.00 .40
❑ 55 Rich Gannon .60 .25
❑ 56 Tim Brown 1.00 .40
❑ 57 Jerry Rice 2.00 .75
❑ 58 Donovan McNabb 1.25 .50
❑ 59 Duce Staley .60 .25
❑ 60 Hines Ward 1.00 .40
❑ 61 Tommy Maddox 1.00 .40
❑ 62 Plaxico Burress .60 .25
❑ 63 Jerome Bettis 1.00 .40

64	David Boston	.60	.25
65	Drew Brees	1.00	.40
66	LaDainian Tomlinson	1.00	.40
67	Jeff Garcia	1.00	.40
68	Terrell Owens	1.00	.40
69	Koren Robinson	.60	.25
70	Shaun Alexander	1.00	.40
71	Kurt Warner	1.00	.40
72	Torry Holt	1.00	.40
73	Marshall Faulk	1.00	.40
74	Keyshawn Johnson	1.00	.40
75	Mike Alstott	1.00	.40
76	Warren Sapp	.60	.25
77	Steve McNair	1.00	.40
78	Eddie George	.60	.25
79	Patrick Ramsey	1.00	.40
80	Rod Gardner	.60	.25
81	Bennie Joppru RC	6.00	2.50
82	Musa Smith RC	6.00	2.50
83	Ken Dorsey RC	6.00	2.50
84	Billy McMullen RC	5.00	2.00
85	Bethel Johnson RC	6.00	2.50
86	Terence Newman RC	12.00	5.00
87	Jason Witten RC	10.00	4.00
88	Jimmy Kennedy RC	6.00	2.50
89	Johnathan Sullivan RC	5.00	2.00
90	Chris Simms RC	10.00	4.00
91	Brian St.Pierre RC	6.00	2.50
92	Quentin Griffin RC	6.00	2.50
93	Tyrone Calico RC	6.00	2.50
94	DeWayne Robertson RC	6.00	2.50
95	Bryant Johnson RC	6.00	2.50
96	Charles Rogers RC	6.00	2.50
97	William Joseph RC	6.00	2.50
98	Dallas Clark RC	6.00	2.50
99	Michael Haynes RC	6.00	2.50
100	Larry Johnson RC	25.00	12.50
101	Terrell Suggs RC	10.00	4.00
102	Marcus Trufant RC	6.00	2.50
103	Dave Ragone RC	6.00	2.50
104	Seneca Wallace RC	6.00	2.50
105	Willis McGahee RC	15.00	6.00
106	Andre Woolfolk RC	6.00	2.50
107	LaBrandon Toefield RC	6.00	2.50
108	Andre Johnson RC	12.00	5.00
109	Lee Suggs RC	6.00	2.50
110	Brandon Lloyd RC	6.00	2.50
111	Kyle Boller RC	6.00	2.50
112	B.J. Askew RC	6.00	2.50
113	Anquan Boldin RC	15.00	6.00
114	Kelley Washington RC	6.00	2.50
115	Kevin Williams RC	6.00	2.50
116	Kliff Kingsbury RC	5.00	2.00
117	Jerome McDougle RC	6.00	2.50
118	L.J. Smith RC	6.00	2.50
119	J.R. Tolver RC	5.00	2.00
120	Carson Palmer RC	25.00	10.00
121	Kevin Curtis RC	6.00	2.50
122	Shaun McDonald RC	6.00	2.50
123	Byron Leftwich RC	20.00	7.50
124	Bobby Wade RC	6.00	2.50
125	Nate Burleson RC	6.00	2.50
126	Justin Fargas RC	6.00	2.50
127	DeWayne White RC	5.00	2.00
128	Taylor Jacobs RC	5.00	2.00
129	Rex Grossman RC	20.00	7.50
130	Boss Bailey RC	6.00	2.50
P28	Brett Favre PROMO	2.50	1.00
P41	Ricky Williams PROMO	1.25	.50
P123	Byron Leftwich PROMO	4.00	1.50

2002 Fleer Platinum

	COMP.SET w/o SP's (230)	30.00	12.50
1	Donovan McNabb	1.25	.50
2	Tom Brady	2.50	1.00
3	Kurt Warner	1.00	.40
4	Jerry Porter	.40	.15
5	LaDainian Tomlinson	1.50	.60
6	Rod Gardner	.60	.25
7	Dorsey Levens	.60	.25
8	Drew Bledsoe	1.25	.50
9	David Terrell	1.00	.40
10	Ahman Green	1.00	.40
11	D'Wayne Bates	.40	.15
12	Wayne Chrebet	.60	.25
13	Doug Flutie	1.00	.40
14	Steve McNair	1.00	.40
15	Nate Clements	.40	.15
16	Gerard Warren	.40	.15
17	James Allen	.60	.25
18	David Patten	.40	.15
19	Jerry Rice	2.00	.75
20	Garrison Hearst	.60	.25
21	Samari Rolle	.40	.15
22	Jay Riemersma	.40	.15
23	Quincy Carter	.60	.25
24	Lamar Smith	.60	.25
25	Jacquez Green	.40	.15
26	John Abraham	.60	.25
27	Kevin Dyson	.60	.25
28	James Thrash	.60	.25
29	Todd Heap	.60	.25
30	Gus Frerotte	.40	.15
31	Terry Glenn	.60	.25
32	Mark Brunell	1.00	.40
33	Randy Moss	2.00	.75
34	John Lynch	.60	.25
35	Curtis Conway	.40	.15
36	Bill Romanowski	.40	.15
37	Thomas Jones	.60	.25
38	Dez White	.40	.15
39	Greg Ellis	.40	.15
40	Trent Green	.60	.25
41	Deuce McAllister	1.25	.50
42	Hines Ward	1.00	.40
43	Isaac Bruce	1.00	.40
44	Edgerrin James	1.25	.50
45	Chad Lewis	.40	.15
46	Ray Lewis	1.00	.40
47	Corey Dillon	.60	.25
48	Brett Favre	2.50	1.00
49	Daunte Culpepper	1.00	.40
50	Vinny Testaverde	.60	.25
51	Warren Sapp	.60	.25
52	Corey Simon	.40	.15
53	Chris McAlister	.40	.15
54	Peter Warrick	.60	.25
55	Luther Elliss	.40	.15
56	Sam Madison	.40	.15
57	Will Allen	.40	.15
58	Michael Pittman	.40	.15
59	Jamal Lewis	1.00	.40
60	Takeo Spikes	.40	.15
61	Robert Porcher	.40	.15
62	Peyton Manning	2.00	.75
63	Robert Edwards	.40	.15
64	Rob Johnson	.40	.15
65	Willie Jackson	.40	.15
66	Dan Morgan	.40	.15
67	Ian Gold	.40	.15
68	Donald Driver	.60	.25
69	Fred Taylor	1.00	.40
70	Dante Hall	1.00	.40
71	Jerome Pathon	.60	.25
72	Amos Zereoue	1.00	.40
73	Darrell Jackson	.60	.25
74	Chris Redman	.40	.15
75	Chad Johnson	1.00	.40
76	Az-Zahir Hakim	.40	.15
77	Jermaine Lewis	.40	.15
78	Zach Thomas	1.00	.40
79	Michael Strahan	.60	.25
80	Junior Seau	1.00	.40
81	Brad Johnson	.60	.25
82	Keith Brooking	.40	.15
83	Shawn Springs	.40	.15
84	Tim Couch	1.25	.50
85	Bill Schroeder	.60	.25
86	Jamie Sharper	.40	.15
87	Ricky Williams	1.00	.40
88	Ron Dayne	.60	.25
89	Brian Finneran	.40	.15
90	Kevin Johnson	.60	.25
91	Scotty Anderson	.40	.15
92	Chris Chambers	1.00	.40
93	Amani Toomer	.60	.25
94	Jeff Garcia	1.00	.40
95	Chad Brown	.40	.15
96	Rodney Peete	.60	.25
97	Dennis Northcutt	.60	.25
98	Jamel White	.40	.15
99	Patrick Johnson	.40	.15
100	Ty Law	.60	.25
101	Charles Woodson	.60	.25
102	Stephen Davis	.60	.25
103	Charlie Garner	.60	.25
104	Courtney Brown	.60	.25
105	Aaron Glenn	.40	.15
106	Antowain Smith	.60	.25
107	Tim Brown	1.00	.40
108	Shane Matthews	.40	.15
109	Warrick Dunn	1.00	.40
110	Wesley Walls	.40	.15
111	Jason Elam	.40	.15
112	Jay Fiedler	.60	.25
113	Kerry Collins	.60	.25
114	Jerome Bettis	1.00	.40
115	Koren Robinson	.60	.25
116	Patrick Kerney	.40	.15
117	Muhsin Muhammad	.60	.25
118	Mike McMahon	1.00	.40
119	Qadry Ismail	.60	.25
120	Oronde Gadsden	.60	.25
121	Tiki Barber	1.00	.40
122	Kordell Stewart	.60	.25
123	Shaun Alexander	1.25	.50
124	Jake Plummer	.60	.25
125	Marty Booker	.60	.25
126	La'Roi Glover	.40	.15
127	Marvin Harrison	1.00	.40
128	Bobby Shaw	.40	.15
129	Kevin Faulk	.60	.25
130	Drew Brees	1.00	.40
131	Marshall Faulk	1.00	.40
132	MarTay Jenkins	.40	.15
133	Anthony Thomas	.60	.25
134	Brian Griese	1.00	.40
135	Johnnie Morton	.60	.25
136	Aaron Brooks	1.00	.40
137	Ernie Conwell	.40	.15
138	Rod Smith	.60	.25
139	Antonio Freeman	1.00	.40
140	Travis Taylor	.60	.25
141	Jon Kitna	.60	.25
142	Robert Ferguson	.40	.15
143	Derrick Alexander	.60	.25
144	Laveranues Coles	.60	.25
145	Keyshawn Johnson	1.00	.40
146	Freddie Jones	.40	.15
147	Jim Miller	.40	.15
148	Mike Anderson	1.00	.40
149	Marcus Pollard	.40	.15
150	Priest Holmes	1.25	.50
151	Joe Horn	.60	.25
152	Plaxico Burress	.60	.25
153	Shannon Sharpe	.60	.25
154	Michael Vick	3.00	1.25
155	Steve Smith	1.00	.40
156	Ed McCaffrey	1.00	.40
157	Eddie Kennison	.40	.15
158	Darren Howard	.40	.15
159	Trent Dilfer	.60	.25
160	Peerless Price	.60	.25
161	Quincy Morgan	.60	.25
162	Corey Bradford	.40	.15
163	Jimmy Smith	.60	.25
164	Troy Brown	.60	.25
165	Rich Gannon	.60	.25
166	Kevan Barlow	.60	.25
167	Jevon Kearse	1.00	.40
168	David Boston	1.00	.40
169	Marcel Shipp	1.00	.40
170	Joey Galloway	.60	.25
171	Kyle Brady	.40	.15
172	Donald Hayes	.40	.15
173	Chad Scott	.40	.15
174	Torry Holt	1.00	.40
175	Champ Bailey	.60	.25
176	Travis Henry	1.00	.40
177	Troy Hambrick	.40	.15

❑ 178	Hardy Nickerson	.40	.15
❑ 179	Michael Bennett	.60	.25
❑ 180	Chad Pennington	1.25	.50
❑ 181	Eric Johnson	.40	.15
❑ 182	Derrick Mason	.40	.15
❑ 183	Kwamie Lassiter	.40	.15
❑ 184	Brian Urlacher	1.50	.60
❑ 185	Olandis Gary	.60	.25
❑ 186	Tony Gonzalez	.60	.25
❑ 187	David Sloan	.40	.15
❑ 188	Kendrell Bell	1.00	.40
❑ 189	Jamie Martin	.40	.15
❑ 190	Eric Moulds	.60	.25
❑ 191	Emmitt Smith	2.50	1.00
❑ 192	Bubba Franks	.60	.25
❑ 193	Byron Chamberlain	.40	.15
❑ 194	Santana Moss	1.00	.40
❑ 195	Dana Stubblefield	.40	.15
❑ 196	Eddie George	1.00	.40
❑ 197	Brian Dawkins	.60	.25
❑ 198	Stephen Alexander	.40	.15
❑ 199	Terrell Owens	1.00	.40
❑ 200	Curtis Martin	1.00	.40
❑ 201	Larry Izzo UH	.40	.15
❑ 202	Brian Simmons UH	.40	.15
❑ 203	Jason Fisk UH RC	.60	.25
❑ 204	Carlos Emmons UH	.40	.15
❑ 205	Justin McCareins UH	.60	.25
❑ 206	Adam Vinatieri UH	1.00	.40
❑ 207	Cornelius Griffin UH	.40	.15
❑ 208	Trevor Pryce UH	.40	.15
❑ 209	Sam Shade UH	.40	.15
❑ 210	Rod Smart UH RC	1.00	.40
❑ 211	Tony Richardson UH	.40	.15
❑ 212	Kevin Kasper UH	.40	.15
❑ 213	Rodney Harrison UH	.40	.15
❑ 214	Patrick Surtain UH	.40	.15
❑ 215	Fred Beasley UH	.40	.15
❑ 216	James Farrior UH	.40	.15
❑ 217	Rosevelt Colvin UH RC	1.00	.40
❑ 218	Anthony McFarland UH	.40	.15
❑ 219	Dat Nguyen UH	.40	.15
❑ 220	Greg Comella UH	.40	.15
❑ 221	Rob Konrad UH	.40	.15
❑ 222	London Fletcher UH	.40	.15
❑ 223	Omar Stoutmire UH	.40	.15
❑ 224	Warrick Holdman UH	.40	.15
❑ 225	Bob Christian UH	.40	.15
❑ 226	David Akers UH	.40	.15
❑ 227	Tony Brackens UH	.40	.15
❑ 228	Deon Grant UH	.40	.15
❑ 229	Olin Kreutz UH RC	1.00	.40
❑ 230	Gary Walker UH	.40	.15
❑ 231	Lito Sheppard RC	3.00	1.25
❑ 232	Kalimba Edwards RC	3.00	1.25
❑ 233	Hayden Epstein RC	2.50	1.00
❑ 234	Napoleon Harris RC	3.00	1.25
❑ 235	Josh McCown RC	4.00	1.50
❑ 236	J.T. O'Sullivan RC	2.50	1.00
❑ 237	Omar Easy RC	3.00	1.25
❑ 238	Adrian Peterson RC	3.00	1.25
❑ 239	Jarrod Baxter RC	2.50	1.00
❑ 240	John Henderson RC	3.00	1.25
❑ 241	Jon McGraw RC	1.50	.60
❑ 242	Terry Jones RC	2.50	1.00
❑ 243	Ron Johnson RC	2.50	1.00
❑ 244	Josh Reed RC	3.00	1.25
❑ 245	Jason McAddley RC	2.50	1.00
❑ 246	Sheldon Brown RC	3.00	1.25
❑ 247	Rocky Bernard RC	3.00	1.25
❑ 248	Nick Davis RC	1.50	.60
❑ 249	Robert Thomas RC	3.00	1.25
❑ 250	Rohan Davey RC	3.00	1.25
❑ 251	Seth Burford RC	2.50	1.00
❑ 252	Najeh Davenport RC	3.00	1.25
❑ 253	Verron Haynes RC	3.00	1.25
❑ 254	Tellis Redmon RC	2.50	1.00
❑ 255	Vernon Fox RC	1.50	.60
❑ 256	Willie Offord RC	2.50	1.00
❑ 257	Marquise Walker RC	2.50	1.00
❑ 258	Antonio Bryant RC	3.00	1.25
❑ 259	Andre Davis RC	2.50	1.00
❑ 260	Eddie Drummond RC	2.50	1.00
❑ 261	Marques Anderson RC	3.00	1.25
❑ 262	Charles Stackhouse RC	2.50	1.00
❑ 263	Rocky Calmus RC	3.00	1.25
❑ 264	Mike Williams RC	2.50	1.00
❑ 265	Brandon Doman RC	2.50	1.00
❑ 266	Maurice Morris RC	3.00	1.25
❑ 267	Ladell Betts RC	3.00	1.25
❑ 268	Ricky Williams RC	2.50	1.00
❑ 269	Tony Fisher RC	3.00	1.25
❑ 270	Michael Lewis RC	3.00	1.25
❑ 271	Jerramy Stevens RC	3.00	1.25
❑ 272	Reche Caldwell RC	3.00	1.25
❑ 273	Antwaan Randle El RC	5.00	2.00
❑ 274	Charles Grant RC	3.00	1.25
❑ 275	Lee Mays RC	2.50	1.00
❑ 276	Phillip Buchanon RC	3.00	1.25
❑ 277	Carlos Hall RC	3.00	1.25
❑ 278	Billy Cundiff RC	5.00	2.00
❑ 279	Saleem Rasheed RC	3.00	1.25
❑ 280	David Garrard RC	3.00	1.25
❑ 281	Preston Parsons RC	1.50	.60
❑ 282	Travis Stephens RC	2.50	1.00
❑ 283	Clinton Portis RC	10.00	4.00
❑ 284	James Mungro RC	3.00	1.25
❑ 285	Tank Williams RC	2.50	1.00
❑ 286	Ed Reed RC	5.00	3.00
❑ 287	Javon Walker RC	6.00	2.50
❑ 288	Cliff Russell RC	2.50	1.00
❑ 289	Daryl Jones RC	2.50	1.00
❑ 290	Freddie Milons RC	2.50	1.00
❑ 291	Dwight Freeney RC	8.00	3.00
❑ 292	Lamar Gordon RC	5.00	2.00
❑ 293	Donte Stallworth RC	10.00	4.00
❑ 294	Craig Nall RC	5.00	2.00
❑ 295	Coy Wire RC	5.00	2.00
❑ 296	T.J. Duckett RC	6.00	2.50
❑ 297	Jeremy Shockey RC	15.00	6.00
❑ 298	Patrick Ramsey RC	6.00	2.50
❑ 299	Chester Taylor RC	10.00	4.00
❑ 300	Tim Carter RC	4.00	1.50
❑ 301	Joey Harrington RC	12.00	5.00
❑ 302	Roy Williams RC	15.00	6.00
❑ 303	Julius Peppers RC	12.00	5.00
❑ 304	William Green RC	8.00	3.00
❑ 305	Ashley Lelie RC	12.00	5.00
❑ 306	Rock Cartwright RC	8.00	3.00
❑ 307	DeShaun Foster RC	3.00	1.25
❑ 308	Marc Boerigter RC	12.00	5.00
❑ 309	Chad Hutchinson RC	6.00	2.50
❑ 310	Daniel Graham RC	8.00	3.00
❑ 311	Ryan Sims RC	10.00	4.00
❑ 312	Kurt Kittner RC	10.00	4.00
❑ 313	Jabar Gaffney RC	10.00	4.00
❑ 314	David Carr RC	25.00	10.00
❑ 315	Brian Westbrook RC	15.00	6.00
❑ 316	Randy Fasani RC	10.00	4.00
❑ 317	Randy McMichael RC	15.00	6.00
❑ 318	Ben Leber RC	8.00	3.00
❑ 319	Jonathan Wells RC	10.00	4.00
❑ 320	Deion Branch RC	20.00	7.50

2003 Fleer Platinum

❑	COMP.SET w/o SP's (210)	30.00	12.50
❑ 1	Donovan McNabb	1.25	.50
❑ 2	Jonathan Wells	.40	.15
❑ 3	Amos Zereoue	.60	.25
❑ 4	Ray Lewis	1.00	.40
❑ 5	Trent Green	.60	.25
❑ 6	Jeff Garcia	1.00	.40
❑ 7	Marty Booker	.60	.25
❑ 8	Antowain Smith	.60	.25
❑ 9	Brad Johnson	.60	.25
❑ 10	Joey Galloway	.60	.25
❑ 11	Chad Pennington	1.25	.50
❑ 12	Patrick Ramsey	1.00	.40
❑ 13	James Stewart	.60	.25
❑ 14	Charles Woodson	.60	.25
❑ 15	Warrick Dunn	.60	.25
❑ 16	Marvin Harrison	1.00	.40
❑ 17	Jerome Bettis	1.00	.40
❑ 18	Muhsin Muhammad	.60	.25
❑ 19	Zach Thomas	1.00	.40
❑ 20	Darrell Jackson	.60	.25
❑ 21	Kelly Holcomb	.60	.25
❑ 22	Deuce McAllister	1.00	.40
❑ 23	Mike Alstott	1.00	.40
❑ 24	Kabeer Gbaja-Biamila	.60	.25
❑ 25	Todd Pinkston	.60	.25
❑ 26	Chris Redman	.40	.15
❑ 27	Jimmy Smith	.60	.25
❑ 28	Tim Dwight	.60	.25
❑ 29	Kordell Stewart	.60	.25
❑ 30	Daunte Culpepper	1.00	.40
❑ 31	Isaac Bruce	1.00	.40
❑ 32	William Green	.60	.25
❑ 33	Tiki Barber	1.00	.40
❑ 34	Jevon Kearse	.60	.25
❑ 35	Ashley Lelie	1.00	.40
❑ 36	Charlie Garner	.60	.25
❑ 37	Marcel Shipp	.60	.25
❑ 38	Corey Bradford	.40	.15
❑ 39	Hines Ward	1.00	.40
❑ 40	Josh Reed	.60	.25
❑ 41	Jay Fiedler	.60	.25
❑ 42	Matt Hasselbeck	.60	.25
❑ 43	Corey Dillon	.60	.25
❑ 44	David Patten	.40	.15
❑ 45	Warren Sapp	.60	.25
❑ 46	Chad Johnson	1.00	.40
❑ 47	Troy Brown	.60	.25
❑ 48	Keyshawn Johnson	1.00	.40
❑ 49	Roy Williams	1.00	.40
❑ 50	Curtis Martin	1.00	.40
❑ 51	Rod Gardner	.60	.25
❑ 52	David Carr	1.50	.60
❑ 53	Tommy Maddox	1.00	.40
❑ 54	Todd Heap	.60	.25
❑ 55	Hugh Douglas	.40	.15
❑ 56	Julian Peterson	.40	.15
❑ 57	Julius Peppers	1.00	.40
❑ 58	Sam Madison	.40	.15
❑ 59	Jerramy Stevens	.40	.15
❑ 60	Andre Davis	.40	.15
❑ 61	Joe Horn	.60	.25
❑ 62	Ronde Barber	.40	.15
❑ 63	Joey Harrington	1.50	.60
❑ 64	Jerry Porter	.60	.25
❑ 65	T.J. Duckett	.60	.25
❑ 66	Edgerrin James	1.00	.40
❑ 67	Joey Porter	1.00	.40
❑ 68	Brian Urlacher	1.50	.60
❑ 69	Randy Moss	1.50	.60
❑ 70	Torry Holt	1.00	.40
❑ 71	Quincy Morgan	.60	.25
❑ 72	Amani Toomer	.60	.25
❑ 73	Derrick Mason	.60	.25
❑ 74	Donald Driver	.60	.25
❑ 75	Duce Staley	.60	.25
❑ 76	Peerless Price	.60	.25
❑ 77	Mark Brunell	.60	.25
❑ 78	David Boston	.60	.25
❑ 79	Takeo Spikes	.40	.15
❑ 80	Ricky Williams	1.00	.40
❑ 81	Shaun Alexander	1.00	.40
❑ 82	Jon Kitna	.60	.25
❑ 83	Deion Branch	1.00	.40
❑ 84	Derrick Brooks	.60	.25
❑ 85	Rod Smith	.60	.25
❑ 86	Rich Gannon	.60	.25
❑ 87	Jason McAddley	.40	.15
❑ 88	Jabar Gaffney	.40	.15
❑ 89	Plaxico Burress	.60	.25
❑ 90	Troy Hambrick	.40	.15
❑ 91	Santana Moss	.60	.25
❑ 92	Champ Bailey	.60	.25
❑ 93	Bubba Franks	.60	.25
❑ 94	Brian Westbrook	.60	.25
❑ 95	Ed Reed	.60	.25
❑ 96	Priest Holmes	1.25	.50
❑ 97	Terrell Owens	1.00	.40
❑ 98	Anthony Thomas	.60	.25
❑ 99	Michael Bennett	.60	.25
❑ 100	Marshall Faulk	1.00	.40
❑ 101	Kevin Johnson	.60	.25
❑ 102	Kerry Collins	.60	.25
❑ 103	Eddie George	.60	.25
❑ 104	Shannon Sharpe	.60	.25

❑ 105 Tim Brown 1.00 .40
❑ 106 Brian Finneran .40 .15
❑ 107 Reggie Wayne .60 .25
❑ 108 Drew Brees 1.00 .40
❑ 109 Jake Delhomme 1.00 .40
❑ 110 Chris Chambers 1.00 .40
❑ 111 Maurice Morris .40 .15
❑ 112 Antonio Bryant .60 .25
❑ 113 Michael Strahan .60 .25
❑ 114 Laveranues Coles .60 .25
❑ 115 Ahman Green 1.00 .40
❑ 116 Jeff Blake .40 .15
❑ 117 Jamal Lewis 1.00 .40
❑ 118 Fred Taylor 1.00 .40
❑ 119 Marcellus Wiley .40 .15
❑ 120 Stephen Davis .60 .25
❑ 121 Randy McMichael 1.00 .40
❑ 122 Kurt Warner 1.00 .40
❑ 123 Tim Couch .40 .15
❑ 124 Aaron Brooks 1.00 .40
❑ 125 John Lynch .60 .25
❑ 126 Clinton Portis 1.50 .60
❑ 127 Wayne Chrebet .60 .25
❑ 128 Emmitt Smith 2.50 1.00
❑ 129 Aaron Glenn .40 .15
❑ 130 Antwaan Randle El 1.00 .40
❑ 131 Travis Henry .60 .25
❑ 132 Tony Gonzalez .60 .25
❑ 133 Garrison Hearst .60 .25
❑ 134 Drew Bledsoe 1.00 .40
❑ 135 Eddie Kennison .40 .15
❑ 136 Kevan Barlow .60 .25
❑ 137 David Terrell .60 .25
❑ 138 Tom Brady 2.50 1.00
❑ 139 Joe Jurevicius .40 .15
❑ 140 Terry Glenn .40 .15
❑ 141 Curtis Conway .40 .15
❑ 142 Trung Canidate .60 .25
❑ 143 Javon Walker .60 .25
❑ 144 Brian Dawkins .60 .25
❑ 145 Keith Brooking .40 .15
❑ 146 Dwight Freeney .60 .25
❑ 147 LaDainian Tomlinson 1.00 .40
❑ 148 Kevin Dyson .40 .15
❑ 149 Jason Taylor .40 .15
❑ 150 Koren Robinson .60 .25
❑ 151 Dennis Northcutt .60 .25
❑ 152 Donte Stallworth 1.00 .40
❑ 153 Steve McNair 1.00 .40
❑ 154 Ed McCaffrey 1.00 .40
❑ 155 Jerry Rice 2.00 .75
❑ 156 Travis Taylor .60 .25
❑ 157 Kyle Brady .40 .15
❑ 158 Quentin Jammer .40 .15
❑ 159 DeShaun Foster .40 .15
❑ 160 Derrius Thompson .40 .15
❑ 161 Marc Bulger 1.00 .40
❑ 162 Chad Hutchinson .40 .15
❑ 163 Jeremy Shockey 1.50 .60
❑ 164 Frank Wycheck .40 .15
❑ 165 Brett Favre 2.50 1.00
❑ 166 Phillip Buchanon .40 .15
❑ 167 Michael Vick 2.50 1.00
❑ 168 Peyton Manning 1.50 .60
❑ 169 Kendrell Bell .60 .25
❑ 170 Eric Moulds .60 .25
❑ 171 Johnnie Morton .60 .25
❑ 172 Tai Streets .40 .15
❑ 173 Ron Dugans .40 .15
❑ 174 Ty Law .60 .25
❑ 175 Simeon Rice .60 .25
❑ 176 Jake Plummer .60 .25
❑ 177 John Abraham .40 .15
❑ 178 Fred Smoot .40 .15
❑ 179 Arizona TC/Shipp .40 .15
❑ 180 Atlanta TC/Vick 1.25 .50
❑ 181 Baltimore TC/Lewis .40 .15
❑ 182 Buffalo TC/Bledsoe .60 .25
❑ 183 Carolina TC/Weinke .40 .15
❑ 184 Chicago TC/Thomas .40 .15
❑ 185 Cincinnati TC/Dillon .40 .15
❑ 186 Cleveland TC/J.White .40 .15
❑ 187 Dallas TC/Hambrick .40 .15
❑ 188 Denver TC/Wilson .40 .15
❑ 189 Detroit TC/Schlesinger .40 .15
❑ 190 Green Bay TC/Fisher .40 .15
❑ 191 Houston TC/Carr 1.00 .40
❑ 192 Indianapolis TC/Manning .60 .25
❑ 193 Jacksonville TC/Taylor .40 .15
❑ 194 Kansas City TC/Green .40 .15
❑ 195 Miami TC/Fiedler .40 .15
❑ 196 Minnesota TC/Williams .40 .15
❑ 197 New England TC/Johnson .40 .15
❑ 198 New Orleans TC/McAllister .40 .15
❑ 199 NY Giants TC/Barrow .40 .15
❑ 200 NY Jets TC/Jordan .60 .25
❑ 201 Oakland TC/Wheatley .40 .15
❑ 202 Philadelphia TC/Staley .40 .15
❑ 203 Pittsburgh TC/Maddox .40 .15
❑ 204 San Diego TC/Tomlinson .40 .15
❑ 205 San Francisco TC/Hearst .40 .15
❑ 206 Seattle TC/Hasselbeck .40 .15
❑ 207 St. Louis TC/Warner .40 .15
❑ 208 Tampa Bay TC/Stecker .40 .15
❑ 209 Tennessee TC/Smith .40 .15
❑ 210 Washington TC/Ramsey .40 .15
❑ 211 L.J. Smith RC 3.00 1.25
❑ 212 Taylor Jacobs RC 2.50 1.00
❑ 213 J.R. Tolver RC 4.00 1.50
❑ 214 Musa Smith RC 3.00 1.25
❑ 215 Bennie Joppru RC 3.00 1.25
❑ 216 Ken Dorsey RC 3.00 1.25
❑ 217 Kareem Kelly RC 2.50 1.00
❑ 218 Andre Woolfolk RC 3.00 1.25
❑ 219 Brian St.Pierre RC 3.00 1.25
❑ 220 Jerome McDougle RC 3.00 1.25
❑ 221 Avon Cobourne RC 2.50 1.00
❑ 222 William Joseph RC 3.00 1.25
❑ 223 Dallas Clark RC 5.00 2.00
❑ 224 Anquan Boldin RC 8.00 3.00
❑ 225 Mike Doss RC 3.00 1.25
❑ 226 Cecil Sapp RC 2.50 1.00
❑ 227 Domanick Davis RC 5.00 2.00
❑ 228 Brad Banks RC 2.50 1.00
❑ 229 Justin Gage RC 3.00 1.25
❑ 230 Nate Burleson RC 4.00 1.50
❑ 231 Earnest Graham RC 2.50 1.00
❑ 232 DeWayne White RC 2.50 1.00
❑ 233 Kevin Williams RC 3.00 1.25
❑ 234 Billy McMullen RC 2.50 1.00
❑ 235 Talman Gardner RC 3.00 1.25
❑ 236 Marcus Trufant RC 3.00 1.25
❑ 237 Quentin Griffin RC 3.00 1.25
❑ 238 LaBrandon Toefield RC 3.00 1.25
❑ 239 Kliff Kingsbury RC 2.50 1.00
❑ 240 Doug Gabriel RC 3.00 1.25
❑ 241 Kyle Boller RC 5.00 2.00
❑ 242 Dave Ragone RC 5.00 2.00
❑ 243 Larry Johnson RC 30.00 15.00
❑ 244 Lee Suggs RC 5.00 2.00
❑ 245 Charles Rogers RC 5.00 2.00
❑ 246 Jimmy Kennedy RC 5.00 2.00
❑ 247 Onterrio Smith RC 5.00 2.00
❑ 248 Artose Pinner RC 5.00 2.00
❑ 249 Tyrone Calico RC 6.00 2.50
❑ 250 Terence Newman RC 10.00 4.00
❑ 251 Byron Leftwich RC 25.00 10.00
❑ 252 Kelley Washington RC 6.00 2.50
❑ 253 Justin Fargas RC 5.00 2.00
❑ 254 DeWayne Robertson RC 6.00 2.50
❑ 255 Boss Bailey RC 6.00 2.50
❑ 256 Sam Aiken RC 6.00 2.50
❑ 257 Bryant Johnson RC 6.00 2.50
❑ 258 Rex Grossman RC 25.00 10.00
❑ 259 Teyo Johnson RC 6.00 2.50
❑ 260 Willis McGahee RC 20.00 7.50
❑ 261 Carson Palmer RC 30.00 12.50
❑ 262 Chris Simms RC 12.00 5.00
❑ 263 Andre Johnson RC 12.00 5.00
❑ 264 Seneca Wallace RC 8.00 3.00
❑ 265 Terrell Suggs RC 12.00 5.00
❑ 266 Chris Brown RC 6.00 2.50
❑ 267 Kevin Curtis RC 8.00 3.00
❑ 268 Brandon Lloyd RC 6.00 2.50
❑ 269 Jason Witten RC 12.00 5.00
❑ 270 Bobby Wade RC 8.00 3.00

2004 Fleer Platinum

❑ COMP.SET w/o SP's (135) 20.00 7.50
❑ 1 Joey Harrington .75 .30
❑ 2 Kyle Boller .75 .30
❑ 3 Randy McMichael .30 .10
❑ 4 David Tyree .30 .10
❑ 5 Darrell Jackson .50 .20
❑ 6 Brian Urlacher 1.00 .40
❑ 7 Ahman Green .75 .30
❑ 8 Onterrio Smith .50 .20
❑ 9 Jevon Kearse .50 .20
❑ 10 Eddie George .50 .20
❑ 11 Julius Peppers .75 .30
❑ 12 Donald Driver .50 .20
❑ 13 Randy Moss 1.00 .40
❑ 14 Brian Westbrook .50 .20
❑ 15 Derrick Brooks .50 .20
❑ 16 Jamal Lewis .75 .30
❑ 17 Artose Pinner .30 .10
❑ 18 Ricky Williams .75 .30
❑ 19 Chad Pennington .75 .30
❑ 20 Matt Hasselbeck .50 .20
❑ 21 Josh McCown .50 .20
❑ 22 Carson Palmer 1.00 .40
❑ 23 Byron Leftwich 1.00 .40
❑ 24 Tedy Bruschi .50 .20
❑ 25 Duce Staley .50 .20
❑ 26 Laveranues Coles .50 .20
❑ 27 Drew Bledsoe .75 .30
❑ 28 Shannon Sharpe .50 .20
❑ 29 A.J. Feeley .75 .30
❑ 30 Santana Moss .50 .20
❑ 31 Adam Archuleta .30 .10
❑ 32 Travis Henry .50 .20
❑ 33 Ashley Lelie .50 .20
❑ 34 Dante Hall .75 .30
❑ 35 Curtis Martin .75 .30
❑ 36 Isaac Bruce .50 .20
❑ 37 Eric Moulds .50 .20
❑ 38 Jake Plummer .50 .20
❑ 39 Trent Green .50 .20
❑ 40 Shaun Ellis .30 .10
❑ 41 Torry Holt .75 .30
❑ 42 T.J. Duckett .50 .20
❑ 43 Quincy Morgan .50 .20
❑ 44 Jabar Gaffney .50 .20
❑ 45 Tiki Barber .75 .30
❑ 46 Tim Rattay .30 .10
❑ 47 Champ Bailey .50 .20
❑ 48 Tony Gonzalez .50 .20
❑ 49 Rich Gannon .50 .20
❑ 50 Marshall Faulk .75 .30
❑ 51 Jake Delhomme .75 .30
❑ 52 Antonio Bryant .50 .20
❑ 53 Priest Holmes 1.00 .40
❑ 54 Jerry Rice 1.50 .60
❑ 55 Marc Bulger .75 .30
❑ 56 Stephen Davis .50 .20
❑ 57 Roy Williams S .50 .20
❑ 58 Willis McGahee .75 .30
❑ 59 Julian Peterson .30 .10
❑ 60 Thomas Jones .50 .20
❑ 61 Dre Bly .30 .10
❑ 62 Corey Dillon .50 .20
❑ 63 Tommy Maddox .50 .20
❑ 64 Derrick Mason .50 .20
❑ 65 Marty Booker .50 .20
❑ 66 Brett Favre 2.00 .75
❑ 67 Tom Brady 2.00 .75
❑ 68 Correll Buckhalter .50 .20
❑ 69 Steve McNair .75 .30
❑ 70 Alge Crumpler .50 .20
❑ 71 Quincy Carter .50 .20
❑ 72 Andre Johnson .75 .30
❑ 73 Jeremy Shockey .75 .30
❑ 74 Kevan Barlow .50 .20
❑ 75 Jerry Porter .50 .20
❑ 76 Ray Lewis .75 .30
❑ 77 Keyshawn Johnson .50 .20
❑ 78 Domanick Davis .75 .30
❑ 79 Michael Strahan .50 .20
❑ 80 Brandon Lloyd .50 .20
❑ 81 Anquan Boldin .75 .30

❑ 82 Chad Johnson .75 .30
❑ 83 Jimmy Smith .50 .20
❑ 84 Troy Brown .50 .20
❑ 85 Hines Ward .75 .30
❑ 86 Tyrone Calico .50 .20
❑ 87 Marcel Shipp .50 .20
❑ 88 Peter Warrick .50 .20
❑ 89 Reggie Wayne .50 .20
❑ 90 Aaron Brooks .50 .20
❑ 91 Antwaan Randle El .75 .30
❑ 92 Mark Brunell .50 .20
❑ 93 Todd Heap .50 .20
❑ 94 Charles Rogers .50 .20
❑ 95 Chris Chambers .50 .20
❑ 96 Amani Toomer .50 .20
❑ 97 Shaun Alexander .75 .30
❑ 98 Michael Vick 1.50 .60
❑ 99 Jeff Garcia .75 .30
❑ 100 Edgerrin James .75 .30
❑ 101 Deuce McAllister .75 .30
❑ 102 LaDainian Tomlinson 1.00 .40
❑ 103 Warrick Dunn .50 .20
❑ 104 Andre Davis .30 .10
❑ 105 Peyton Manning 1.25 .50
❑ 106 Boo Williams .30 .10
❑ 107 Drew Brees .75 .30
❑ 108 Rex Grossman .75 .30
❑ 109 Javon Walker .50 .20
❑ 110 Michael Bennett .50 .20
❑ 111 Terrell Owens .75 .30
❑ 112 Michael Pittman .30 .10
❑ 113 Emmitt Smith 1.50 .60
❑ 114 Rudi Johnson .50 .20
❑ 115 Fred Taylor .50 .20
❑ 116 Deion Branch .75 .30
❑ 117 Plaxico Burress .50 .20
❑ 118 Clinton Portis .75 .30
❑ 119 DeShaun Foster .50 .20
❑ 120 Najeh Davenport .30 .10
❑ 121 Daunte Culpepper .75 .30
❑ 122 Donovan McNabb 1.00 .40
❑ 123 Charles Lee .30 .10
❑ 124 Peerless Price .50 .20
❑ 125 Lee Suggs .75 .30
❑ 126 Marvin Harrison .75 .30
❑ 127 Joe Horn .50 .20
❑ 128 Antonio Gates .75 .30
❑ 129 Steve Smith .75 .30
❑ 130 David Carr .75 .30
❑ 131 Jason Taylor .30 .10
❑ 132 Phillip Buchanon .30 .10
❑ 133 Brad Johnson .50 .20
❑ 134 Takeo Spikes .30 .10
❑ 135 Koren Robinson .50 .20
❑ 136 Eli Manning RC 40.00 15.00
❑ 137 Ben Roethlisberger RC 75.00 40.00
❑ 138 Drew Henson RC 8.00 3.00
❑ 139 Kellen Winslow RC 15.00 6.00
❑ 140 Kevin Jones RC 20.00 8.00
❑ 141 Larry Fitzgerald RC 25.00 10.00
❑ 142 Roy Williams RC 20.00 7.50
❑ 143 Philip Rivers RC 25.00 10.00
❑ 144 Lee Evans RC 10.00 4.00
❑ 145 Julius Jones RC 25.00 12.50
❑ 146 Chris Perry RC 8.00 3.00
❑ 147 Michael Clayton RC 10.00 4.00
❑ 148 Sean Taylor RC 5.00 2.00
❑ 149 Reggie Williams RC 6.00 2.50
❑ 150 Steven Jackson RC 15.00 6.00
❑ 151 Tatum Bell RC 10.00 4.00
❑ 152 Keary Colbert RC 6.00 2.50
❑ 153 J.P. Losman RC 10.00 4.00
❑ 154 Devery Henderson RC 4.00 1.50
❑ 155 Ben Troupe RC 5.00 2.00
❑ 156 Luke McCown RC 4.00 1.50
❑ 157 Greg Jones RC 4.00 1.50
❑ 158 Ben Watson RC 4.00 1.50
❑ 159 Bernard Berrian RC 5.00 2.00
❑ 160 Devard Darling RC 3.00 1.25
❑ 161 Cedric Cobbs RC 4.00 1.50
❑ 162 Darius Watts RC 4.00 1.50
❑ 163 Derrick Hamilton RC 3.00 1.25
❑ 164 Matt Schaub RC 15.00 6.00
❑ 165 Mewelde Moore RC 4.00 1.50
❑ 166 Michael Jenkins RC 3.00 1.25
❑ 167 Rashaun Woods RC 4.00 1.50
❑ 168 Quincy Wilson RC 2.50 1.00
❑ 169 Jonathan Vilma RC 3.00 1.25
❑ 170 Jerricho Cotchery RC 3.00 1.25
❑ 171 John Navarre RC 3.00 1.25
❑ 172 Josh Harris RC 3.00 1.25
❑ 173 Teddy Lehman RC 3.00 1.25
❑ 174 Ernest Wilford RC 3.00 1.25
❑ 175 P.K. Sam RC 2.50 1.00
❑ 176 Jeff Smoker RC 4.00 1.50
❑ 177 Chris Gamble RC 3.00 1.25
❑ 178 Johnnie Morant RC 3.00 1.25
❑ 179 DeAngelo Hall RC 5.00 2.00
❑ 180 Vince Wilfork RC 3.00 1.25
❑ 181 Michael Turner RC 4.00 1.50
❑ 182 Robert Gallery RC 3.00 1.25
❑ 183 Ricardo Colclough RC 3.00 1.25
❑ 184 Kenechi Udeze RC 3.00 1.25
❑ 185 Dunta Robinson RC 3.00 1.25

2001 Fleer Premium

❑ COMP.SET w/o SP's (200) 25.00 10.00
❑ 1 Ricky Williams .60 .25
❑ 2 Dez White .25 .08
❑ 3 Jay Riemersma .25 .08
❑ 4 Derrick Mason .40 .15
❑ 5 Chad Lewis .25 .08
❑ 6 Shaun King .25 .08
❑ 7 Jevon Kearse .40 .15
❑ 8 Bobby Engram .25 .08
❑ 9 Warrick Dunn .60 .25
❑ 10 Randall Cunningham .60 .25
❑ 11 Stephen Alexander .25 .08
❑ 12 Jimmy Smith .40 .15
❑ 13 Az-Zahir Hakim .40 .15
❑ 14 Antonio Freeman .60 .25
❑ 15 Curtis Conway .40 .15
❑ 16 Tim Biakabutuka .40 .15
❑ 17 Peter Warrick .60 .25
❑ 18 Kurt Warner 1.25 .50
❑ 19 Brian Urlacher 1.00 .40
❑ 20 Rod Smith .40 .15
❑ 21 Frank Sanders .25 .08
❑ 22 Trevor Pryce .25 .08
❑ 23 Sammy Morris .25 .08
❑ 24 Cade McNown .25 .08
❑ 25 Keyshawn Johnson .60 .25
❑ 26 Tim Couch .40 .15
❑ 27 Dedric Ward .25 .08
❑ 28 Bill Schroeder .40 .15
❑ 29 John Randle .40 .15
❑ 30 Donovan McNabb .75 .30
❑ 31 Marvin Harrison .60 .25
❑ 32 Trent Dilfer .40 .15
❑ 33 David Boston .60 .25
❑ 34 Donnell Bennett .25 .08
❑ 35 Trace Armstrong .25 .08
❑ 36 Sam Adams .25 .08
❑ 37 Jeremiah Trotter .40 .15
❑ 38 Zach Thomas .60 .25
❑ 39 Shawn Jefferson .25 .08
❑ 40 J.J. Stokes .40 .15
❑ 41 Akili Smith .25 .08
❑ 42 Tony Siragusa .25 .08
❑ 43 William Roaf .25 .08
❑ 44 Muhsin Muhammad .40 .15
❑ 45 Terance Mathis .40 .15
❑ 46 Tee Martin .40 .15
❑ 47 Ray Lewis .60 .25
❑ 48 Matt Hasselbeck .40 .15
❑ 49 Todd Pinkston .25 .08
❑ 50 Rob Johnson .40 .15
❑ 51 Edgerrin James .75 .30
❑ 52 Rocket Ismail .40 .15
❑ 53 Trent Green .60 .25
❑ 54 Tim Dwight .60 .25
❑ 55 Anthony Becht .25 .08
❑ 56 Jessie Armstead .25 .08
❑ 57 Mike Anderson .60 .25
❑ 58 Jamal Anderson .60 .25
❑ 59 Anthony Wright .25 .08
❑ 60 Regan Upshaw .25 .08
❑ 61 John Holecek .25 .08
❑ 62 Shaun Alexander .75 .30
❑ 63 Troy Aikman 1.00 .40
❑ 64 Peter Boulware .25 .08
❑ 65 Hines Ward .60 .25
❑ 66 Michael Strahan .40 .15
❑ 67 Herman Moore .40 .15
❑ 68 Rich Gannon .60 .25
❑ 69 Ken Dilger .25 .08
❑ 70 Terrell Davis .60 .25
❑ 71 Terrence Wilkins .25 .08
❑ 72 Fred Taylor .60 .25
❑ 73 Napoleon Kaufman .25 .08
❑ 74 Tony Horne .25 .08
❑ 75 Ahman Green .60 .25
❑ 76 Jay Fiedler .60 .25
❑ 77 Albert Connell .25 .08
❑ 78 Charlie Batch .60 .25
❑ 79 James Allen .40 .15
❑ 80 Sylvester Morris .25 .08
❑ 81 Isaac Bruce .60 .25
❑ 82 Charles Woodson .40 .15
❑ 83 Lamar Smith .40 .15
❑ 84 Peyton Manning 1.50 .60
❑ 85 Sam Madison .25 .08
❑ 86 Olandis Gary .40 .15
❑ 87 Kevin Faulk .40 .15
❑ 88 Jeff Garcia .60 .25
❑ 89 JaJuan Dawson .25 .08
❑ 90 Sam Cowart .25 .08
❑ 91 David Sloan .25 .08
❑ 92 Bobby Shaw .25 .08
❑ 93 Travis Prentice .25 .08
❑ 94 Terrell Owens .60 .25
❑ 95 John Lynch .40 .15
❑ 96 Jim Harbaugh .40 .15
❑ 97 Brian Griese .60 .25
❑ 98 Jeff Graham .25 .08
❑ 99 La'Roi Glover .25 .08
❑ 100 Joey Galloway .40 .15
❑ 101 Wesley Walls .25 .08
❑ 102 Vinny Testaverde .40 .15
❑ 103 Jason Taylor .25 .08
❑ 104 Darnay Scott .25 .08
❑ 105 Samari Rolle .25 .08
❑ 106 Adrian Murrell .25 .08
❑ 107 Eric Moulds .40 .15
❑ 108 Keenan McCardell .25 .08
❑ 109 Donald Hayes .25 .08
❑ 110 Brett Favre 2.00 .75
❑ 111 Troy Edwards .25 .08
❑ 112 Ron Dayne .60 .25
❑ 113 Daunte Culpepper .60 .25
❑ 114 Chris Chandler .40 .15
❑ 115 Mark Brunell .60 .25
❑ 116 Courtney Brown .40 .15
❑ 117 Aaron Brooks .60 .25
❑ 118 Fred Beasley .25 .08
❑ 119 Mike Alstott .60 .25
❑ 120 Tyrone Wheatley .40 .15
❑ 121 R.Jay Soward .25 .08
❑ 122 Deion Sanders .60 .25
❑ 123 Jake Reed .40 .15
❑ 124 Jamal Lewis 1.00 .40
❑ 125 Tony Gonzalez .40 .15
❑ 126 Terrell Fletcher .25 .08
❑ 127 Wayne Chrebet .40 .15
❑ 128 Cris Carter .60 .25
❑ 129 Drew Bledsoe .75 .30
❑ 130 Tiki Barber .60 .25
❑ 131 Derrick Alexander .40 .15
❑ 132 Frank Wycheck .25 .08
❑ 133 Jerome Pathon .40 .15
❑ 134 Warren Sapp .40 .15
❑ 135 Joe Horn .40 .15
❑ 136 Ricky Watters .40 .15
❑ 137 Amani Toomer .40 .15
❑ 138 Bruce Smith .40 .15
❑ 139 Andre Rison .40 .15
❑ 140 J.R. Redmond .25 .08
❑ 141 Steve McNair .60 .25
❑ 142 Michael McCrary .25 .08
❑ 143 Ike Hilliard .40 .15

❑	144	Charlie Garner	.40	.15
❑	145	Mark Bruener	.25	.08
❑	146	Emmitt Smith	1.25	.50
❑	147	Darren Sharper	.25	.08
❑	148	Peerless Price	.40	.15
❑	149	Johnnie Morton	.40	.15
❑	150	Curtis Martin	.60	.25
❑	151	Joe Johnson	.25	.08
❑	152	MarTay Jenkins	.25	.08
❑	153	Priest Holmes	.75	.30
❑	154	Terry Glenn	.40	.15
❑	155	Oronde Gadsden	.40	.15
❑	156	Germane Crowell	.25	.08
❑	157	Steve Beuerlein	.25	.08
❑	158	Champ Bailey	.40	.15
❑	159	Troy Vincent	.25	.08
❑	160	James Stewart	.40	.15
❑	161	Jerry Rice	1.25	.50
❑	162	Randy Moss	1.25	.50
❑	163	Dave Moore	.25	.08
❑	164	Ed McCaffrey	.60	.25
❑	165	Thomas Jones	.40	.15
❑	166	Rickey Dudley	.25	.08
❑	167	Hugh Douglas	.25	.08
❑	168	Stephen Davis	.60	.25
❑	169	Kerry Collins	.40	.15
❑	170	Cam Cleeland	.25	.08
❑	171	Stephen Boyd	.25	.08
❑	172	Jerome Bettis	.60	.25
❑	173	Aeneas Williams	.25	.08
❑	174	Chad Pennington	1.00	.40
❑	175	Dorsey Levens	.40	.15
❑	176	Desmond Howard	.25	.08
❑	177	Torry Holt	.60	.25
❑	178	Plaxico Burress	.60	.25
❑	179	Kevin Johnson	.40	.15
❑	180	Kyle Brady	.25	.08
❑	181	Jake Plummer	.40	.15
❑	182	Brad Johnson	.60	.25
❑	183	Eddie George	.60	.25
❑	184	Corey Dillon	.60	.25
❑	185	Curtis Enis	.25	.08
❑	186	Tim Brown	.60	.25
❑	187	Tony Boselli	.25	.08
❑	188	Duce Staley	.60	.25
❑	189	Junior Seau	.60	.25
❑	190	Marshall Faulk	.75	.30
❑	191	Kordell Stewart	.40	.15
❑	192	Corey Simon	.40	.15
❑	193	Shannon Sharpe	.40	.15
❑	194	Marcus Robinson	.60	.25
❑	195	Carl Pickens	.25	.08
❑	196	Doug Flutie	.60	.25
❑	197	Freddie Jones	.25	.08
❑	198	Patrick Jeffers	.40	.15
❑	199	Shawn Bryson	.25	.08
❑	200	Kevin Dyson	.40	.15
❑	201	David Terrell RC	5.00	2.00
❑	202	Dan Morgan RC	5.00	2.00
❑	203	Chris Weinke RC	5.00	2.00
❑	204	Correll Buckhalter RC	6.00	2.50
❑	205	Chad Johnson RC	12.00	5.00
❑	206	LaDainian Tomlinson RC	40.00	25.00
❑	207	Reggie Wayne RC	10.00	4.00
❑	208	Tim Hasselbeck RC	5.00	2.00
❑	209	Michael Vick RC	20.00	8.00
❑	210	Heath Evans RC	3.00	1.25
❑	211	Damione Lewis RC	3.00	1.25
❑	212	Richard Seymour RC	5.00	2.00
❑	213	Quincy Morgan RC	5.00	2.00
❑	214	Drew Brees RC	15.00	6.00
❑	215	Freddie Mitchell RC	5.00	2.00
❑	216	Justin McCareins RC	5.00	2.00
❑	217	Mike McMahon RC	5.00	2.00
❑	218	Derrick Gibson RC	3.00	1.25
❑	219	Rudi Johnson RC	10.00	4.00
❑	220	Todd Heap RC	5.00	2.00
❑	221	Josh Booty RC	5.00	2.00
❑	222	Justin Smith RC	5.00	2.00
❑	223	Marcus Stroud RC	5.00	2.00
❑	224	Rod Gardner RC	5.00	2.00
❑	225	Vinny Sutherland RC	3.00	1.25
❑	226	Marques Tuiasosopo RC	5.00	2.00
❑	227	Anthony Thomas RC	5.00	2.00
❑	228	Bobby Newcombe RC	3.00	1.25
❑	229	Michael Bennett RC	5.00	2.00
❑	230	Snoop Minnis RC	3.00	1.25
❑	231	Travis Minor RC	3.00	1.25
❑	232	Travis Henry RC	8.00	3.00
❑	233	Kevan Barlow RC	5.00	2.00
❑	234	Gerard Warren RC	5.00	2.00
❑	235	Sage Rosenfels RC	5.00	2.00
❑	236	Chris Chambers RC	8.00	3.00
❑	237	James Jackson RC	5.00	2.00
❑	238	Deuce McAllister RC	10.00	4.00
❑	239	Koren Robinson RC	5.00	2.00
❑	240	Andre Carter RC	5.00	2.00
❑	241	Santana Moss RC	8.00	3.00
❑	242	LaMont Jordan RC	10.00	4.00
❑	243	Ken-Yon Rambo RC	3.00	1.25
❑	244	Jamal Reynolds RC	5.00	2.00
❑	245	Fred Smoot RC	5.00	2.00
❑	246	Robert Ferguson RC	5.00	2.00
❑	247	Alex Bannister RC	3.00	1.25
❑	248	Dan Alexander RC	5.00	2.00
❑	249	Nate Clements RC	5.00	2.00
❑	250	Quincy Carter RC	5.00	2.00

2002 Fleer Premium

❑		COMP.SET w/o SP's (160)	40.00	15.00
❑	1	Kevin Dyson	.60	.25
❑	2	Kerry Collins	.60	.25
❑	3	Marty Booker	.60	.25
❑	4	Curtis Conway	.40	.15
❑	5	Drew Bledsoe	1.25	.50
❑	6	Kurt Warner	1.00	.40
❑	7	Hines Ward	1.00	.40
❑	8	Terrell Owens	1.00	.40
❑	9	Todd Pinkston	.60	.25
❑	10	Eric Moulds	.60	.25
❑	11	Quincy Morgan	.40	.15
❑	12	Fred Taylor	1.00	.40
❑	13	Santana Moss	1.00	.40
❑	14	Peyton Manning	2.00	.75
❑	15	Qadry Ismail	.60	.25
❑	16	Mike McMahon	1.00	.40
❑	17	David Patten	.40	.15
❑	18	Wayne Chrebet	.60	.25
❑	19	David Terrell	1.00	.40
❑	20	Corey Bradford	.40	.15
❑	21	Derrick Mason	.60	.25
❑	22	Anthony Thomas	.60	.25
❑	23	James Allen	.60	.25
❑	24	Vinny Testaverde	.60	.25
❑	25	Trent Green	.60	.25
❑	26	Thomas Jones	.60	.25
❑	27	Rocket Ismail	.60	.25
❑	28	Duce Staley	1.00	.40
❑	29	Drew Brees	1.00	.40
❑	30	Chris Chandler	.60	.25
❑	31	Kordell Stewart	.60	.25
❑	32	Koren Robinson	.60	.25
❑	33	Jon Kitna	.60	.25
❑	34	Jamie Sharper	.40	.15
❑	35	Germane Crowell	.40	.15
❑	36	Lamar Smith	.60	.25
❑	37	LaDainian Tomlinson	1.50	.60
❑	38	Freddie Mitchell	.60	.25
❑	39	Corey Dillon	.60	.25
❑	40	Isaac Bruce	1.00	.40
❑	41	James Thrash	.60	.25
❑	42	Brian Griese	1.00	.40
❑	43	Marvin Harrison	1.00	.40
❑	44	Aaron Brooks	1.00	.40
❑	45	Rich Gannon	1.00	.40
❑	46	Mike Alstott	1.00	.40
❑	47	Shannon Sharpe	.60	.25
❑	48	Travis Henry	1.00	.40
❑	49	Keyshawn Johnson	1.00	.40
❑	50	Daunte Culpepper	1.00	.40
❑	51	James Jackson	.40	.15
❑	52	Justin McCareins	.60	.25
❑	53	Quincy Carter	.60	.25
❑	54	Stephen Davis	.60	.25
❑	55	Joey Galloway	.60	.25
❑	56	Joe Horn	.60	.25
❑	57	Plaxico Burress	.60	.25
❑	58	Brett Favre	2.50	1.00
❑	59	Brian Urlacher	1.50	.60
❑	60	David Boston	1.00	.40
❑	61	Darrell Jackson	.60	.25
❑	62	Trung Canidate	.60	.25
❑	63	Shaun Alexander	1.25	.50
❑	64	Steve McNair	1.00	.40
❑	65	Doug Flutie	1.00	.40
❑	66	LaMont Jordan	1.00	.40
❑	67	Rod Smith	.60	.25
❑	68	Marshall Faulk	1.00	.40
❑	69	Tiki Barber	1.00	.40
❑	70	James Stewart	.60	.25
❑	71	Frank Wycheck	.40	.15
❑	72	Peerless Price	.60	.25
❑	73	Derrick Alexander	.60	.25
❑	74	Charlie Garner	.60	.25
❑	75	Peter Warrick	.60	.25
❑	76	Warren Sapp	.60	.25
❑	77	Kevan Barlow	.60	.25
❑	78	Edgerrin James	1.25	.50
❑	79	Willie Jackson	.40	.15
❑	80	Keenan McCardell	.40	.15
❑	81	Bill Schroeder	.40	.15
❑	82	Curtis Martin	1.00	.40
❑	83	Torry Holt	1.00	.40
❑	84	Tony Gonzalez	.60	.25
❑	85	Jeff Garcia	1.00	.40
❑	86	Travis Taylor	.60	.25
❑	87	Johnnie Morton	.60	.25
❑	88	Tim Couch	.60	.25
❑	89	Troy Brown	.60	.25
❑	90	Emmitt Smith	2.50	1.00
❑	91	Aeneas Williams	.40	.15
❑	92	Rod Gardner	.60	.25
❑	93	Brandon Stokley	.60	.25
❑	94	Warrick Dunn	1.00	.40
❑	95	Jay Riemersma	.40	.15
❑	96	Kevin Johnson	.60	.25
❑	97	Antowain Smith	.60	.25
❑	98	James McKnight	.40	.15
❑	99	Amani Toomer	.60	.25
❑	100	Ricky Williams	1.00	.40
❑	101	Priest Holmes	1.25	.50
❑	102	Muhsin Muhammad	.60	.25
❑	103	Jake Plummer	.60	.25
❑	104	Marcus Robinson	.60	.25
❑	105	Donovan McNabb	1.25	.50
❑	106	Tom Brady	2.50	1.00
❑	107	Jimmy Smith	.60	.25
❑	108	Jamal Lewis	1.00	.40
❑	109	Antonio Freeman	1.00	.40
❑	110	Ron Dayne	.60	.25
❑	111	Tim Brown	1.00	.40
❑	112	Chris Chambers	1.00	.40
❑	113	Garrison Hearst	.60	.25
❑	114	Michael Vick	3.00	1.25
❑	115	Snoop Minnis	.40	.15
❑	116	Terrell Davis	1.00	.40
❑	117	Ahman Green	1.00	.40
❑	118	Donald Hayes	.40	.15
❑	119	Jermaine Lewis	.40	.15
❑	120	Chad Johnson	1.00	.40
❑	121	Jay Fiedler	.60	.25
❑	122	Randy Moss	2.00	.75
❑	123	Wesley Walls	.40	.15
❑	124	Eddie George	1.00	.40
❑	125	Jerry Rice	2.00	.75
❑	126	Michael Bennett	.60	.25
❑	127	Jerome Bettis	1.00	.40
❑	128	Mark Brunell	1.00	.40
❑	129	Adam Vinatieri	1.00	.40
❑	130	Ed McCaffrey	1.00	.40
❑	131	Maurice Morris RC	5.00	2.00
❑	132	Ron Johnson RC	4.00	1.50
❑	133	Antwaan Randle El RC	8.00	3.00
❑	134	Brian Westbrook RC	8.00	3.00
❑	135	Julius Peppers RC	10.00	4.00
❑	136	Travis Stephens RC	4.00	1.50
❑	137	David Carr RC	12.00	5.00
❑	138	Clinton Portis RC	15.00	6.00
❑	139	Reche Caldwell RC	5.00	2.00
❑	140	Tim Carter RC	4.00	1.50

❑ 141 Daniel Graham RC 5.00 2.00
❑ 142 Rohan Davey RC 5.00 2.00
❑ 143 T.J. Duckett RC 6.00 2.50
❑ 144 Luke Staley RC 4.00 1.50
❑ 145 Ashley Lelie RC 10.00 4.00
❑ 146 Josh Reed RC 5.00 2.00
❑ 147 Randy Fasani RC 4.00 1.50
❑ 148 Andre Davis RC 4.00 1.50
❑ 149 Joey Harrington RC 8.00 3.00
❑ 150 David Garrard RC 5.00 2.00
❑ 151 Ladell Betts RC 5.00 2.00
❑ 152 Donte Stallworth RC 10.00 4.00
❑ 153 Adrian Peterson RC 5.00 2.00
❑ 154 Lamar Gordon RC 5.00 2.00
❑ 155 Jonathan Wells RC 5.00 2.00
❑ 156 Jabar Gaffney RC 5.00 2.00
❑ 157 Patrick Ramsey RC 6.00 2.50
❑ 158 Roy Williams RC 12.00 5.00
❑ 159 Jeremy Shockey RC 15.00 6.00
❑ 160 Javon Walker RC 10.00 4.00
❑ 161 Marquise Walker RC 4.00 1.50
❑ 162 Antonio Bryant RC 5.00 2.00
❑ 163 Josh McCown RC 6.00 2.50
❑ 164 Najeh Davenport RC 5.00 2.00
❑ 165 William Green RC 5.00 2.00
❑ 166 Jerramy Stevens RC 5.00 2.00
❑ 167 DeShaun Foster RC 5.00 2.00
❑ 168 Cliff Russell RC 4.00 1.50
❑ 169 Kurt Kittner RC 4.00 1.50
❑ 170 Eric Crouch RC 5.00 2.00
❑ 171 Michael Pittman PP .40 .15
❑ 172 Darnay Scott PP .40 .15
❑ 173 Charles Woodson PP .60 .25
❑ 174 Ty Law PP .40 .15
❑ 175 Tony Boselli PP .40 .15
❑ 176 Zach Thomas PP 1.00 .40
❑ 177 Trent Dilfer PP .60 .25
❑ 178 Bubba Franks PP .60 .25
❑ 179 Laveranues Coles PP .60 .25
❑ 180 John Lynch PP .60 .25
❑ 181 Kendrell Bell PP 1.00 .40
❑ 182 Mike Anderson PP 1.00 .40
❑ 183 Amos Zereoue PP 1.00 .40
❑ 184 Michael Strahan PP .60 .25
❑ 185 Chad Lewis PP .40 .15
❑ 186 Travis Minor PP .40 .15
❑ 187 Jevon Kearse PP .60 .25
❑ 188 Darren Sharper PP .40 .15
❑ 189 Az-Zahir Hakim PP .40 .15
❑ 190 Ray Lewis PP 1.00 .40
❑ 191 Deuce McAllister PP 1.25 .50
❑ 192 Chris Weinke PP .60 .25
❑ 193 Desmond Howard PP .40 .15
❑ 194 Dominic Rhodes PP 1.00 .40
❑ 195 Joe Jurevicius PP .40 .15
❑ 196 Tim Dwight PP 1.00 .40
❑ 197 Jeff Zgonina PP .40 .15
❑ 198 Junior Seau PP 1.00 .40
❑ 199 Rosevelt Colvin PP RC 1.00 .40
❑ 200 Chad Pennington PP 1.25 .50

2000 Fleer Showcase

❑ COMP.SET w/o SP's (100) 25.00 10.00
❑ 1 Tim Couch .50 .20
❑ 2 Deion Sanders .75 .30
❑ 3 Darnay Scott .50 .20
❑ 4 Brett Favre 2.50 1.00
❑ 5 Mark Brunell .75 .30
❑ 6 Randy Moss 1.50 .60
❑ 7 Tyrone Wheatley .50 .20
❑ 8 Isaac Bruce .75 .30
❑ 9 Eddie George .75 .30
❑ 10 Troy Aikman 1.50 .60
❑ 11 Charlie Batch .75 .30
❑ 12 Marvin Harrison .75 .30
❑ 13 Terry Glenn .50 .20
❑ 14 Charles Johnson .50 .20
❑ 15 Jerry Rice 1.50 .60
❑ 16 Kurt Warner 1.50 .60
❑ 17 Kevin Johnson .75 .30
❑ 18 Jay Fiedler .75 .30
❑ 19 Vinny Testaverde .50 .20
❑ 20 Curtis Enis .30 .10
❑ 21 Elvis Grbac .50 .20
❑ 22 Kordell Stewart .50 .20
❑ 23 Jamal Anderson .75 .30
❑ 24 Dorsey Levens .50 .20
❑ 25 Derrick Mayes .50 .20
❑ 26 Marcus Robinson .75 .30
❑ 27 Cam Cleeland .30 .10
❑ 28 Charlie Garner .50 .20
❑ 29 Germane Crowell .30 .10
❑ 30 Cade McNown .30 .10
❑ 31 Tony Gonzalez .50 .20
❑ 32 Shaun King .30 .10
❑ 33 Wayne Chrebet .50 .20
❑ 34 Muhsin Muhammad .50 .20
❑ 35 Olandis Gary .75 .30
❑ 36 Ray Lewis .75 .30
❑ 37 Terrell Davis .75 .30
❑ 38 Steve Beuerlein .50 .20
❑ 39 James Stewart .50 .20
❑ 40 Jon Kitna .75 .30
❑ 41 Tim Biakabutuka .50 .20
❑ 42 Ryan Leaf .50 .20
❑ 43 Mike Alstott .75 .30
❑ 44 Yancey Thigpen .30 .10
❑ 45 Champ Bailey .50 .20
❑ 46 Peerless Price .50 .20
❑ 47 Ken Dilger .30 .10
❑ 48 Derrick Alexander .50 .20
❑ 49 Drew Bledsoe 1.00 .40
❑ 50 Jerome Bettis .75 .30
❑ 51 Jermaine Fazande .30 .10
❑ 52 Joey Galloway .50 .20
❑ 53 Jeff Blake .50 .20
❑ 54 Emmitt Smith 1.50 .60
❑ 55 Ricky Williams .75 .30
❑ 56 Marshall Faulk 1.25 .50
❑ 57 Stephen Davis .75 .30
❑ 58 Rob Johnson .50 .20
❑ 59 Brian Griese .75 .30
❑ 60 Damon Huard .75 .30
❑ 61 Jevon Kearse .75 .30
❑ 62 Doug Flutie .75 .30
❑ 63 Curtis Martin .75 .30
❑ 64 Torry Holt .75 .30
❑ 65 David Boston .75 .30
❑ 66 Cris Carter .75 .30
❑ 67 Jason Sehorn .30 .10
❑ 68 Keyshawn Johnson .75 .30
❑ 69 Chris Chandler .50 .20
❑ 70 Antonio Freeman .75 .30
❑ 71 Kerry Collins .50 .20
❑ 72 Akili Smith .30 .10
❑ 73 Troy Edwards .30 .10
❑ 74 Tim Dwight .75 .30
❑ 75 Donovan McNabb 1.25 .50
❑ 76 Tony Banks .50 .20
❑ 77 Ed McCaffrey .75 .30
❑ 78 Errict Rhett .30 .10
❑ 79 Fred Taylor .75 .30
❑ 80 Terrell Owens .75 .30
❑ 81 Steve McNair .75 .30
❑ 82 Rob Moore .50 .20
❑ 83 Jimmy Smith .50 .20
❑ 84 Daunte Culpepper 1.00 .40
❑ 85 Carl Pickens .50 .20
❑ 86 Moses Moreno .30 .10
❑ 87 Brad Johnson .75 .30
❑ 88 Jake Plummer .50 .20
❑ 89 Edgerrin James 1.25 .50
❑ 90 Zach Thomas .75 .30
❑ 91 Rich Gannon .75 .30
❑ 92 Warrick Dunn .75 .30
❑ 93 Shannon Sharpe .50 .20
❑ 94 Peyton Manning 2.00 .75
❑ 95 Keenan McCardell .50 .20
❑ 96 Tony Simmons .30 .10
❑ 97 Duce Staley .75 .30
❑ 98 Corey Dillon .75 .30
❑ 99 Tim Brown .75 .30
❑ 100 Ricky Watters .50 .20
❑ 101 Peter Warrick RC 10.00 4.00
❑ 102 Shaun Alexander RC 40.00 15.00
❑ 103 Anthony Becht RC 10.00 4.00
❑ 104 Courtney Brown RC 10.00 4.00
❑ 105 Plaxico Burress RC 20.00 7.50
❑ 106 Trung Canidate RC 8.00 3.00
❑ 107 Giovanni Carmazzi RC 8.00 3.00
❑ 108 Laveranues Coles RC 12.00 5.00
❑ 109 Ron Dayne RC 10.00 4.00
❑ 110 Reuben Droughns RC 12.00 5.00
❑ 111 Danny Farmer RC 8.00 3.00
❑ 112 Bubba Franks RC 10.00 4.00
❑ 113 Thomas Jones RC 15.00 6.00
❑ 114 Jamal Lewis RC 20.00 7.50
❑ 115 Sylvester Morris RC 8.00 3.00
❑ 116 Chad Pennington RC 20.00 7.50
❑ 117 Travis Prentice RC 8.00 3.00
❑ 118 J.R. Redmond RC 8.00 3.00
❑ 119 R.Jay Soward RC 8.00 3.00
❑ 120 Dez White RC 10.00 4.00
❑ 121 Sebastian Janikowski RC 5.00 2.00
❑ 122 Todd Pinkston RC 5.00 2.00
❑ 123 Marc Bulger RC 10.00 4.00
❑ 124 Ron Dugans RC 2.50 1.00
❑ 125 Joe Hamilton RC 4.00 1.50
❑ 126 Curtis Keaton RC 4.00 1.50
❑ 127 Tee Martin RC 5.00 2.00
❑ 128 Dennis Northcutt RC 5.00 2.00
❑ 129 Corey Simon RC 5.00 2.00
❑ 130 Chris Redman RC 4.00 1.50
❑ 131 Brian Urlacher RC 20.00 7.50
❑ 132 Travis Taylor RC 5.00 2.00
❑ 133 Michael Wiley RC 4.00 1.50
❑ 134 Tim Rattay RC 5.00 2.00
❑ 135 Jerry Porter RC 6.00 2.50
❑ 136 Tom Brady RC 80.00 40.00
❑ 137 Deon Dyer RC 4.00 1.50
❑ 138 Mareno Philyaw RC 2.50 1.00
❑ 139 Spergon Wynn RC 4.00 1.50
❑ 140 John Abraham RC 5.00 2.00
❑ 141 Ahmed Plummer RC 5.00 2.00
❑ 142 Chris Hovan RC 4.00 1.50
❑ 143 Rob Morris RC 4.00 1.50
❑ 144 Keith Bulluck RC 5.00 2.00
❑ 145 JaJuan Dawson RC 2.50 1.00
❑ 146 Chris Cole RC 4.00 1.50
❑ 147 Chafie Fields RC 2.50 1.00
❑ 148 Darrell Jackson RC 10.00 4.00
❑ 149 Marcus Knight RC 4.00 1.50
❑ 150 Gari Scott RC 2.50 1.00
❑ 151 Kwame Cavil RC 2.50 1.00
❑ 152 Frank Moreau RC 4.00 1.50
❑ 153 Doug Chapman RC 4.00 1.50
❑ 154 Erron Kinney RC 5.00 2.00
❑ 155 Ron Dixon RC 4.00 1.50
❑ 156 Ben Kelly RC 2.50 1.00
❑ 157 Bashir Yamini RC 2.50 1.00
❑ 158 Anthony Lucas RC 2.50 1.00
❑ 159 Avion Black RC 4.00 1.50
❑ 160 Ian Gold RC 4.00 1.50

2001 Fleer Showcase

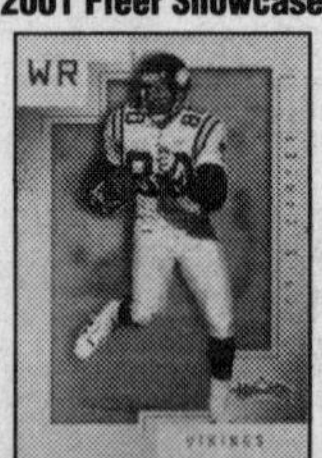

❑ COMP.SET w/o SP's (100) 25.00 10.00
❑ 1 Cris Carter 1.00 .40
❑ 2 Sylvester Morris .40 .15
❑ 3 Vinny Testaverde .60 .25
❑ 4 Jevon Kearse .60 .25
❑ 5 Terance Mathis .40 .15
❑ 6 Mike Anderson 1.00 .40
❑ 7 Aaron Brooks 1.00 .40

❑ 8 Jerry Rice 2.00 .75
❑ 9 Mike Alstott 1.00 .40
❑ 10 Jon Kitna .60 .25
❑ 11 Derrick Alexander .60 .25
❑ 12 Shaun Alexander 1.25 .50
❑ 13 Thomas Jones .60 .25
❑ 14 James Stewart .60 .25
❑ 15 Ron Dayne 1.00 .40
❑ 16 Az-Zahir Hakim .60 .25
❑ 17 Terrell Owens 1.00 .40
❑ 18 Travis Prentice .40 .15
❑ 19 Lamar Smith .60 .25
❑ 20 James Thrash .60 .25
❑ 21 Doug Flutie 1.00 .40
❑ 22 Derrick Mason .60 .25
❑ 23 Ray Lewis 1.00 .40
❑ 24 Ed McCaffrey 1.00 .40
❑ 25 Ricky Williams 1.00 .40
❑ 26 Tyrone Wheatley .60 .25
❑ 27 Chris Chandler .60 .25
❑ 28 Rod Smith .60 .25
❑ 29 Joe Horn .60 .25
❑ 30 Jerome Bettis 1.00 .40
❑ 31 Brian Urlacher 1.50 .60
❑ 32 Dorsey Levens .60 .25
❑ 33 Kordell Stewart .60 .25
❑ 34 Michael Westbrook .60 .25
❑ 35 Jamal Anderson 1.00 .40
❑ 36 Charlie Batch 1.00 .40
❑ 37 Kerry Collins .60 .25
❑ 38 Jake Plummer .60 .25
❑ 39 Robert Porcher .40 .15
❑ 40 Jason Sehorn .40 .15
❑ 41 Junior Seau 1.00 .40
❑ 42 Warren Sapp .60 .25
❑ 43 Champ Bailey .60 .25
❑ 44 Jamal Lewis 1.50 .60
❑ 45 Tony Banks .60 .25
❑ 46 Doug Chapman .40 .15
❑ 47 Stephen Davis 1.00 .40
❑ 48 Elvis Grbac .60 .25
❑ 49 Joey Galloway .60 .25
❑ 50 Terry Glenn .60 .25
❑ 51 Todd Pinkston .60 .25
❑ 52 JaJuan Dawson .40 .15
❑ 53 Zach Thomas 1.00 .40
❑ 54 Tim Couch .60 .25
❑ 55 Cade McNown .40 .15
❑ 56 Charlie Garner .60 .25
❑ 57 Jeff George .60 .25
❑ 58 Peerless Price .60 .25
❑ 59 Tony Gonzalez .60 .25
❑ 60 Rob Johnson .40 .15
❑ 61 Keenan McCardell .40 .15
❑ 62 Eric Moulds .60 .25
❑ 63 Jimmy Smith .60 .25
❑ 64 Jeff Garcia 1.00 .40
❑ 65 Rod Woodson .60 .25
❑ 66 Brian Griese 1.00 .40
❑ 67 Kevin Faulk .60 .25
❑ 68 Plaxico Burress 1.00 .40
❑ 69 Isaac Bruce 1.00 .40
❑ 70 Keyshawn Johnson 1.00 .40
❑ 71 Tim Biakabutuka .60 .25
❑ 72 Mark Brunell 1.00 .40
❑ 73 Wesley Walls .40 .15
❑ 74 Jerome Pathon .60 .25
❑ 75 Wayne Chrebet .60 .25
❑ 76 Muhsin Muhammad .60 .25
❑ 77 Marvin Harrison 1.00 .40
❑ 78 David Boston 1.00 .40
❑ 79 Germane Crowell .40 .15
❑ 80 Tiki Barber 1.00 .40
❑ 81 Laveranues Coles 1.00 .40
❑ 82 Tim Brown 1.00 .40
❑ 83 Matt Hasselbeck .60 .25
❑ 84 Brad Johnson 1.00 .40
❑ 85 Marcus Robinson 1.00 .40
❑ 86 Ahman Green 1.00 .40
❑ 87 Curtis Martin 1.00 .40
❑ 88 Peter Warrick 1.00 .40
❑ 89 Ray Lucas .40 .15
❑ 90 Duce Staley 1.00 .40
❑ 91 Darrell Jackson .40 .15
❑ 92 Steve McNair 1.00 .40
❑ 93 Rickey Dudley .40 .15
❑ 94 Jason Taylor .40 .15
❑ 95 Rich Gannon 1.00 .40
❑ 96 Torry Holt 1.00 .40
❑ 97 James Allen .60 .25
❑ 98 Antonio Freeman 1.00 .40
❑ 99 Trent Green .60 .25
❑ 100 Ricky Watters .60 .25
❑ 101 Corey Dillon AC 4.00 1.50
❑ 102 Emmitt Smith AC 8.00 3.00
❑ 103 Terrell Davis AC 4.00 1.50
❑ 104 Brett Favre AC 12.00 5.00
❑ 105 Peyton Manning AC 10.00 4.00
❑ 106 Edgerrin James AC 5.00 2.00
❑ 107 Fred Taylor AC 4.00 1.50
❑ 108 Daunte Culpepper AC 4.00 1.50
❑ 109 Randy Moss AC 8.00 3.00
❑ 110 Drew Bledsoe AC 5.00 2.00
❑ 111 Donovan McNabb AC 5.00 2.00
❑ 112 Kurt Warner AC 8.00 3.00
❑ 113 Marshall Faulk AC 5.00 2.00
❑ 114 Warrick Dunn AC 4.00 1.50
❑ 115 Eddie George AC 4.00 1.50
❑ 116 Michael Vick AC RC 60.00 30.00
❑ 117 David Terrell AC RC 15.00 6.00
❑ 118 Deuce McAllister AC RC 25.00 10.00
❑ 119 Koren Robinson AC RC 15.00 6.00
❑ 120 Rod Gardner AC RC 15.00 6.00
❑ 121 Santana Moss AC RC 25.00 10.00
❑ 122 Drew Brees AC RC 40.00 15.00
❑ 123 Chris Weinke AC RC 15.00 6.00
❑ 124 LaDainian Tomlinson AC RC 100.00 50.00
❑ 125 Freddie Mitchell AC RC 15.00 6.00
❑ 126 Chris Chambers AC RC 12.00 5.00
❑ 127 Reggie Wayne RC 15.00 6.00
❑ 128 Quincy Morgan RC 6.00 2.50
❑ 129 Rudi Johnson RC 15.00 6.00
❑ 130 Robert Ferguson RC 6.00 2.50
❑ 131 Todd Heap RC 6.00 2.50
❑ 132 Michael Bennett RC 6.00 2.50
❑ 133 Jesse Palmer RC 6.00 2.50
❑ 134 James Jackson RC 6.00 2.50
❑ 135 Chad Johnson RC 20.00 7.50
❑ 136 LaMont Jordan RC 15.00 6.00
❑ 137 Anthony Thomas RC 6.00 2.50
❑ 138 Travis Henry RC 12.00 5.00
❑ 139 Snoop Minnis RC 6.00 2.50
❑ 140 Marques Tuiasosopo RC 6.00 2.50
❑ 141 Travis Minor RC 6.00 2.50
❑ 142 Mike McMahon RC 6.00 2.50
❑ 143 Josh Heupel RC 6.00 2.50
❑ 144 Sage Rosenfels RC 6.00 2.50
❑ 145 Quincy Carter RC 6.00 2.50
❑ 146 Alge Crumpler RC 8.00 3.00
❑ 147 Kevan Barlow RC 6.00 2.50
❑ 148 Heath Evans RC 4.00 1.50
❑ 149 Correll Buckhalter RC 8.00 3.00
❑ 150 Justin McCareins RC 6.00 2.50
❑ 151 Reggie Germany RC 4.00 1.50
❑ 152 Vinny Sutherland RC 4.00 1.50
❑ 153 Scotty Anderson RC 4.00 1.50
❑ 154 Tim Hasselbeck RC 6.00 2.50
❑ 155 Alex Bannister RC 4.00 1.50
❑ 156 Andre Carter RC 6.00 2.50
❑ 157 Adam Archuleta RC 6.00 2.50
❑ 158 Ken-Yon Rambo RC 4.00 1.50
❑ 159 Gerard Warren RC 6.00 2.50
❑ 160 Justin Smith RC 6.00 2.50
❑ NNO Donovan McNabb AU/300 50.00 25.00

2002 Fleer Showcase

❑ COMP.SET w/o SP's (125) 25.00 10.00
❑ 1 Kevin Johnson .60 .25
❑ 2 Chris Walsh .40 .15
❑ 3 Vinny Testaverde .60 .25
❑ 4 Kordell Stewart .60 .25
❑ 5 Chris Redman .40 .15
❑ 6 Johnnie Morton .60 .25
❑ 7 Tony Gonzalez .60 .25
❑ 8 Torry Holt 1.00 .40
❑ 9 Champ Bailey .60 .25
❑ 10 Eric Moulds .60 .25
❑ 11 Az-Zahir Hakim .40 .15
❑ 12 Mark Brunell 1.00 .40
❑ 13 Laveranues Coles .60 .25
❑ 14 Kevan Barlow .60 .25
❑ 15 Stephen Davis .60 .25
❑ 16 Benjamin Gay .60 .25
❑ 17 Randy Moss 2.00 .75
❑ 18 Hines Ward 1.00 .40
❑ 19 Brian Urlacher 1.50 .60
❑ 20 Dominic Rhodes 1.00 .40
❑ 21 David Patten .40 .15
❑ 22 Tim Brown 1.00 .40
❑ 23 Trent Dilfer .60 .25
❑ 24 David Boston 1.00 .40
❑ 25 Quincy Carter .60 .25
❑ 26 Daunte Culpepper 1.00 .40
❑ 27 Plaxico Burress .60 .25
❑ 28 Michael Pittman .40 .15
❑ 29 Joey Galloway .60 .25
❑ 30 Jason Taylor .40 .15
❑ 31 Drew Brees 1.00 .40
❑ 32 Jamal Anderson .60 .25
❑ 33 Dat Nguyen .40 .15
❑ 34 Chris Chambers 1.00 .40
❑ 35 Tiki Barber 1.00 .40
❑ 36 LaDainian Tomlinson 1.50 .60
❑ 37 Peter Warrick .60 .25
❑ 38 Bubba Franks .60 .25
❑ 39 Joe Horn .60 .25
❑ 40 Correll Buckhalter .60 .25
❑ 41 Mike Alstott 1.00 .40
❑ 42 Brian Finneran .40 .15
❑ 43 Troy Hambrick .40 .15
❑ 44 Zach Thomas 1.00 .40
❑ 45 Kerry Collins .60 .25
❑ 46 Junior Seau 1.00 .40
❑ 47 Alvis Whitted .40 .15
❑ 48 Terrell Davis 1.00 .40
❑ 49 Ricky Williams 1.00 .40
❑ 50 Curtis Conway .40 .15
❑ 51 Travis Taylor .60 .25
❑ 52 Brian Griese 1.00 .40
❑ 53 Sylvester Morris .40 .15
❑ 54 Amani Toomer .60 .25
❑ 55 Jeff Garcia 1.00 .40
❑ 56 Michael McCrary .40 .15
❑ 57 Ahman Green 1.00 .40
❑ 58 Trent Green .60 .25
❑ 59 Trung Canidate .60 .25
❑ 60 Jamal Lewis 1.00 .40
❑ 61 Larry Foster .40 .15
❑ 62 Priest Holmes 1.25 .50
❑ 63 Isaac Bruce 1.00 .40
❑ 64 Bruce Smith .40 .15
❑ 65 Darnay Scott .40 .15
❑ 66 Terry Glenn .60 .25
❑ 67 Darren Howard .40 .15
❑ 68 Hugh Douglas .40 .15
❑ 69 Milton Wynn .40 .15
❑ 70 Tim Couch .60 .25
❑ 71 Bill Schroeder .60 .25
❑ 72 Michael Strahan .60 .25
❑ 73 James Thrash .60 .25
❑ 74 Steve McNair 1.00 .40
❑ 75 Patrick Jeffers .40 .15
❑ 76 Marcus Pollard .40 .15
❑ 77 Willie McGinest .40 .15
❑ 78 Santana Moss 1.00 .40
❑ 79 Grant Wistrom .40 .15
❑ 80 Jim Miller .40 .15
❑ 81 Marvin Harrison 1.00 .40
❑ 82 Troy Brown .60 .25
❑ 83 Rich Gannon 1.00 .40
❑ 84 Shaun Alexander 1.25 .50
❑ 85 Jake Plummer .60 .25
❑ 86 Quincy Morgan .40 .15
❑ 87 Michael Bennett .60 .25
❑ 88 Jerome Bettis 1.00 .40
❑ 89 Marty Booker .40 .15
❑ 90 Trevor Insley .40 .15
❑ 91 Adam Vinatieri 1.00 .40
❑ 92 Charles Woodson .60 .25
❑ 93 Darrell Jackson .60 .25

No.	Player	Price	Price
❑ 94	Corey Dillon	.60	.25
❑ 95	Corey Bradford	.40	.15
❑ 96	Deuce McAllister	1.25	.50
❑ 97	Todd Pinkston	.60	.25
❑ 98	Warren Sapp	.60	.25
❑ 99	Alex Van Pelt	.60	.25
❑ 100	Mike McMahon	1.00	.40
❑ 101	Fred Taylor	1.00	.40
❑ 102	Ron Dayne	.60	.25
❑ 103	Ernie Conwell	.40	.15
❑ 104	Rod Gardner	.60	.25
❑ 105	Muhsin Muhammad	.60	.25
❑ 106	Reggie Wayne	1.00	.40
❑ 107	Antowain Smith	.60	.25
❑ 108	Chad Pennington	1.25	.50
❑ 109	Koren Robinson	.60	.25
❑ 110	Travis Henry	1.00	.40
❑ 111	Ed McCaffrey	1.00	.40
❑ 112	Keenan McCardell	.40	.15
❑ 113	Curtis Martin	1.00	.40
❑ 114	Bryant Young	.40	.15
❑ 115	Derrick Mason	.60	.25
❑ 116	Anthony Thomas	.60	.25
❑ 117	Jermaine Lewis	.40	.15
❑ 118	Aaron Brooks	1.00	.40
❑ 119	Charlie Garner	.60	.25
❑ 120	Keyshawn Johnson	1.00	.40
❑ 121	Chris Weinke	.60	.25
❑ 122	Rod Smith	.60	.25
❑ 123	Jimmy Smith	.60	.25
❑ 124	Terrell Owens	1.00	.40
❑ 125	Eddie George	1.00	.40
❑ 126	Tom Brady AC	10.00	4.00
❑ 127	Donovan McNabb AC	5.00	2.00
❑ 128	Kurt Warner AC	4.00	1.50
❑ 129	Peyton Manning AC	8.00	3.00
❑ 130	Marshall Faulk AC	4.00	1.50
❑ 131	Michael Vick AC	12.00	5.00
❑ 132	Emmitt Smith AC	10.00	4.00
❑ 133	Jerry Rice AC	8.00	3.00
❑ 134	Edgerrin James AC	5.00	2.00
❑ 135	Brett Favre AC	10.00	4.00
❑ 136	David Carr AC RC	25.00	10.00
❑ 137	Joey Harrington AC RC	15.00	6.00
❑ 138	Ashley Lelie AC RC	20.00	7.50
❑ 139	William Green AC RC	12.00	5.00
❑ 140	T.J. Duckett AC RC	15.00	6.00
❑ 141	Donte Stallworth AC RC	20.00	7.50
❑ 142	Ron Johnson RC	6.00	2.50
❑ 143	Jeremy Shockey RC	25.00	10.00
❑ 144	Daniel Graham RC	8.00	3.00
❑ 145	Reche Caldwell RC	8.00	3.00
❑ 146	Antonio Bryant RC	8.00	3.00
❑ 147	DeShaun Foster RC	8.00	3.00
❑ 148	Clinton Portis RC	25.00	10.00
❑ 149	Patrick Ramsey RC	10.00	4.00
❑ 150	Lamar Gordon RC	8.00	3.00
❑ 151	Josh Reed RC	8.00	3.00
❑ 152	Ladell Betts RC	8.00	3.00
❑ 153	Kurt Kittner RC	6.00	2.50
❑ 154	Jabar Gaffney RC	8.00	3.00
❑ 155	Josh McCown RC	10.00	4.00
❑ 156	Marquise Walker RC	6.00	2.50
❑ 157	Brian Westbrook RC	12.00	5.00
❑ 158	Andre Davis RC	6.00	2.50
❑ 159	David Garrard RC	8.00	3.00
❑ 160	Cliff Russell RC	6.00	2.50
❑ 161	Julius Peppers RC	15.00	6.00
❑ 162	Adrian Peterson RC	8.00	3.00
❑ 163	Antwaan Randle El RC	12.00	5.00
❑ 164	Javon Walker RC	15.00	6.00
❑ 165	Rohan Davey RC	8.00	3.00
❑ 166	Luke Staley RC	6.00	2.50

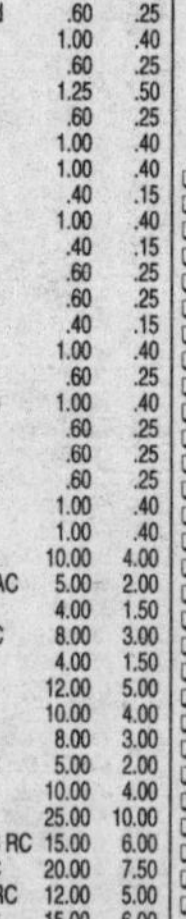

2003 Fleer Showcase

No.	Player	Price	Price
❑	COMP.SET w/o SP's (90)	25.00	10.00
❑ 1	Edgerrin James	1.00	.40
❑ 2	Donald Driver	.60	.25
❑ 3	Drew Brees	1.00	.40
❑ 4	Corey Dillon	.60	.25
❑ 5	Jerome Bettis	1.00	.40
❑ 6	Charlie Garner	.60	.25
❑ 7	Eddie George	.60	.25
❑ 8	Mark Brunell	.60	.25
❑ 9	David Boston	.60	.25
❑ 10	Todd Heap	.60	.25
❑ 11	Terrell Owens	1.00	.40
❑ 12	Tommy Maddox	1.00	.40
❑ 13	Keyshawn Johnson	1.00	.40
❑ 14	Jamal Lewis	1.00	.40
❑ 15	Zach Thomas	.60	.25
❑ 16	Isaac Bruce	1.00	.40
❑ 17	Michael Bennett	.60	.25
❑ 18	Rod Smith	.60	.25
❑ 19	Eric Moulds	.60	.25
❑ 20	T.J Duckett	.60	.25
❑ 21	Hines Ward	1.00	.40
❑ 22	Tiki Barber	1.00	.40
❑ 23	Julius Peppers	1.00	.40
❑ 24	Rich Gannon	.60	.25
❑ 25	Rod Gardner	.60	.25
❑ 26	Curtis Martin	1.00	.40
❑ 27	Donte Stallworth	1.00	.40
❑ 28	Anthony Thomas	.60	.25
❑ 29	Warren Sapp	.60	.25
❑ 30	Jake Plummer	.60	.25
❑ 31	Patrick Ramsey	1.00	.40
❑ 32	Tai Streets	.40	.15
❑ 33	Matt Hasselbeck	.60	.25
❑ 34	James Stewart	.60	.25
❑ 35	Chad Hutchinson	.40	.15
❑ 36	Hugh Douglas	.40	.15
❑ 37	Jimmy Smith	.60	.25
❑ 38	Kerry Collins	.60	.25
❑ 39	Junior Seau	1.00	.40
❑ 40	Ed McCaffrey	.60	.25
❑ 41	Marshall Faulk	1.00	.40
❑ 42	Deuce McAllister	1.00	.40
❑ 43	Drew Bledsoe	1.00	.40
❑ 44	Brian Urlacher	1.50	.60
❑ 45	William Green	.60	.25
❑ 46	Chris Chambers	1.00	.40
❑ 47	Daunte Culpepper	1.00	.40
❑ 48	Warrick Dunn	.60	.25
❑ 49	Antwaan Randle El	1.00	.40
❑ 50	Joey Harrington	1.50	.60
❑ 51	Tim Brown	1.00	.40
❑ 52	Duce Staley	.60	.25
❑ 53	Laveranues Coles	.60	.25
❑ 54	Ray Lewis	1.00	.40
❑ 55	Marvin Harrison	1.00	.40
❑ 56	Tony Gonzalez	.60	.25
❑ 57	Torry Holt	1.00	.40
❑ 58	Jeff Garcia	1.00	.40
❑ 59	Peerless Price	.60	.25
❑ 60	Marcel Shipp	.60	.25
❑ 61	Brian Finneran	.40	.15
❑ 62	Fred Taylor	1.00	.40
❑ 63	Koren Robinson	.40	.15
❑ 64	Shaun Alexander	1.00	.40
❑ 65	Plaxico Burress	.60	.25
❑ 66	Ahman Green	1.00	.40
❑ 67	Simeon Rice	.60	.25
❑ 68	Joe Horn	.60	.25
❑ 69	Steve McNair	1.00	.40
❑ 70	Amani Toomer	.60	.25
❑ 71	Kendrell Bell	.60	.25
❑ 72	Marty Booker	.60	.25
❑ 73	Stephen Davis	.60	.25
❑ 74	David Carr	1.50	.60
❑ 75	Garrison Hearst	.60	.25
❑ 76	Joey Galloway	.60	.25
❑ 77	Aaron Brooks	1.00	.40
❑ 78	Mike Alstott	1.00	.40
❑ 79	Shannon Sharpe	.60	.25
❑ 80	Derrick Mason	.60	.25
❑ 81	Tim Couch	.40	.15
❑ 82	Chad Johnson	1.00	.40
❑ 83	Jason Taylor	.40	.15
❑ 84	Travis Henry	.60	.25
❑ 85	Curtis Conway	.40	.15
❑ 86	Peyton Manning	1.50	.60
❑ 87	Kurt Warner	1.00	.40
❑ 88	LaDainian Tomlinson	1.00	.40
❑ 89	Emmitt Smith	2.50	1.00
❑ 90	Priest Holmes	1.25	.50
❑ 91	Ricky Williams AC	5.00	2.00
❑ 92	Brett Favre AC	12.00	5.00
❑ 93	Clinton Portis AC	8.00	3.00
❑ 94	Randy Moss AC	8.00	3.00
❑ 95	Tom Brady AC	12.00	5.00
❑ 96	Chad Pennington AC	8.00	3.00
❑ 97	Michael Vick AC	15.00	6.00
❑ 98	Jeremy Shockey AC	10.00	4.00
❑ 99	Donovan McNabb AC	8.00	3.00
❑ 100	Jerry Rice AC	12.00	5.00
❑ 101	Carson Palmer AC/350 RC	50.00	20.00
❑ 102	Lee Suggs AC/350 RC	12.00	5.00
❑ 103	Larry Johnson AC/350 RC	50.00	20.00
❑ 104	Taylor Jacobs AC/650 RC	5.00	2.00
❑ 105	Andre Johnson AC/350 RC	25.00	10.00
❑ 106	Justin Fargas AC/650 RC	10.00	4.00
❑ 107	Charles Rogers AC/350 RC	12.00	5.00
❑ 108	Willis McGahee AC/650 RC	25.00	10.00
❑ 109	Byron Leftwich AC/350 RC	40.00	15.00
❑ 110	Kyle Boller AC/650 RC	10.00	4.00
❑ 111	Bobby Wade RC	8.00	3.00
❑ 112	Brian St.Pierre RC	8.00	3.00
❑ 113	Doug Gabriel RC	8.00	3.00
❑ 114	Chris Brown RC	10.00	3.00
❑ 115	DeWayne Robertson RC	8.00	3.00
❑ 116	Anquan Boldin RC	20.00	7.50
❑ 117	Brandon Lloyd RC	10.00	3.00
❑ 118	Brad Banks RC	6.00	2.50
❑ 119	Dallas Clark RC	8.00	3.00
❑ 120	Artose Pinner RC	8.00	3.00
❑ 121	Dave Ragone RC	8.00	3.00
❑ 122	Arnaz Battle RC	8.00	3.00
❑ 123	Andrew Pinnock RC	6.00	2.50
❑ 124	Billy McMullen RC	6.00	2.50
❑ 125	Avon Cobourne RC	6.00	2.50
❑ 126	Terence Newman RC	15.00	6.00
❑ 127	Jimmy Kennedy RC	8.00	3.00
❑ 128	Terrell Suggs RC	12.00	5.00
❑ 129	Rex Grossman RC	25.00	10.00
❑ 130	Musa Smith RC	8.00	3.00
❑ 131	William Joseph RC	8.00	3.00
❑ 132	Tyrone Calico RC	10.00	4.00
❑ 133	Teyo Johnson RC	8.00	3.00
❑ 134	Onterrio Smith RC	8.00	3.00
❑ 135	Mike Doss RC	8.00	3.00
❑ 136	Kliff Kingsbury RC	6.00	2.50
❑ 137	Kelley Washington RC	8.00	3.00
❑ 138	Kareem Kelly RC	6.00	2.50
❑ 139	Jason Gesser RC	8.00	3.00
❑ 140	Chris Simms RC	12.00	5.00

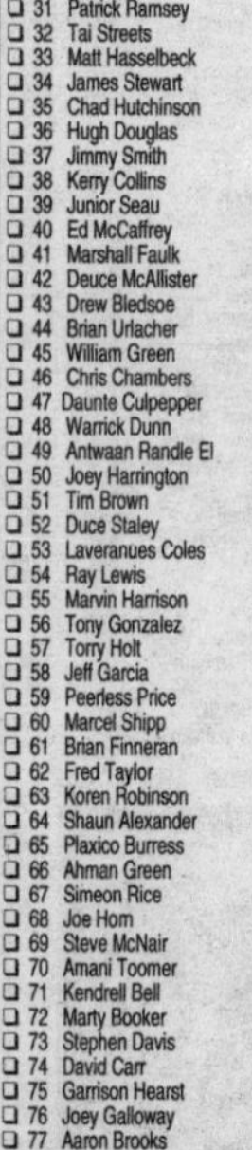

2004 Fleer Showcase

No.	Player	Price	Price
❑	COMP.SET w/o SP's (100)	25.00	10.00
❑ 1	Jamal Lewis	1.00	.40
❑ 2	Kevan Barlow	.60	.25
❑ 3	Travis Henry	.60	.25
❑ 4	Jon Kitna	.60	.25
❑ 5	David Boston	.60	.25
❑ 6	Andre Davis	.40	.15
❑ 7	Steve McNair	1.00	.40
❑ 8	Freddie Mitchell	.60	.25
❑ 9	Plaxico Burress	.60	.25
❑ 10	Jake Delhomme	1.00	.40
❑ 11	Andre Johnson	1.00	.40
❑ 12	T.J. Duckett	.60	.25
❑ 13	Ray Lewis	1.00	.40
❑ 14	Shaun Alexander	1.00	.40

❑	15 Stephen Davis	.60	.25
❑	16 Priest Holmes	1.25	.50
❑	17 Edgerrin James	1.00	.40
❑	18 Josh McCown	.60	.25
❑	19 Jerry Rice	2.00	.75
❑	20 Fred Taylor	.60	.25
❑	21 Marty Booker	.60	.25
❑	22 Eddie George	.60	.25
❑	23 Jake Plummer	.60	.25
❑	24 LaDainian Tomlinson	1.25	.50
❑	25 David Carr	1.00	.40
❑	26 Keenan McCardell	.40	.15
❑	27 Jerry Porter	.60	.25
❑	28 Drew Bledsoe	1.00	.40
❑	29 Brian Dawkins	.60	.25
❑	30 Curtis Martin	1.00	.40
❑	31 Troy Brown	.60	.25
❑	32 Peyton Manning	1.50	.60
❑	33 Clinton Portis	1.00	.40
❑	34 Brett Favre	2.50	1.00
❑	35 Joey Harrington	1.00	.40
❑	36 Tiki Barber	1.00	.40
❑	37 Hines Ward	1.00	.40
❑	38 Laveranues Coles	.60	.25
❑	39 Deuce McAllister	1.00	.40
❑	40 Kyle Boller	1.00	.40
❑	41 Jeff Garcia	1.00	.40
❑	42 Julius Peppers	1.00	.40
❑	43 Chris Chambers	.60	.25
❑	44 Willis McGahee	1.00	.40
❑	45 Michael Vick	2.00	.75
❑	46 Carson Palmer	1.25	.50
❑	47 Ricky Williams	1.00	.40
❑	48 Matt Hasselbeck	.60	.25
❑	49 Anquan Boldin	1.00	.40
❑	50 Tony Gonzalez	.60	.25
❑	51 Marvin Harrison	1.00	.40
❑	52 Santana Moss	.60	.25
❑	53 Ahman Green	1.00	.40
❑	54 Eric Moulds	.60	.25
❑	55 Byron Leftwich	1.25	.50
❑	56 Daunte Culpepper	1.00	.40
❑	57 Terrell Owens	1.00	.40
❑	58 Kerry Collins	.60	.25
❑	59 Tommy Maddox	.60	.25
❑	60 Chad Johnson	1.00	.40
❑	61 Rich Gannon	.60	.25
❑	62 Patrick Ramsey	.60	.25
❑	63 Quincy Morgan	.60	.25
❑	64 Koren Robinson	.60	.25
❑	65 Deion Branch	1.00	.40
❑	66 Rex Grossman	1.00	.40
❑	67 Damerien McCants	.40	.15
❑	68 Ashley Lelie	.60	.25
❑	69 Roy Williams S	.60	.25
❑	70 Michael Bennett	.60	.25
❑	71 Domanick Davis	1.00	.40
❑	72 Warren Sapp	.60	.25
❑	73 Randy Moss	1.25	.50
❑	74 Drew Brees	1.00	.40
❑	75 Brian Westbrook	.60	.25
❑	76 Kelly Holcomb	.60	.25
❑	77 Jason Taylor	.40	.15
❑	78 Charles Rogers	.60	.25
❑	79 Marc Bulger	1.00	.40
❑	80 Donald Driver	.60	.25
❑	81 Trent Green	.60	.25
❑	82 Peerless Price	.60	.25
❑	83 Quincy Carter	.60	.25
❑	84 Torry Holt	1.00	.40
❑	85 Derrick Mason	.60	.25
❑	86 Donte Stallworth	.60	.25
❑	87 Derrick Brooks	.60	.25
❑	88 Dre Bly	.40	.15
❑	89 Antonio Bryant	.60	.25
❑	90 DeShaun Foster	.60	.25
❑	91 Emmitt Smith	2.00	.75
❑	92 Chad Pennington	1.00	.40
❑	93 Jeremy Shockey	1.00	.40
❑	94 Aaron Brooks	.60	.25
❑	95 Marshall Faulk	1.00	.40
❑	96 Dante Hall	1.00	.40
❑	97 Brian Urlacher	1.25	.50
❑	98 Corey Dillon	.60	.25
❑	99 Donovan McNabb	1.25	.50
❑	100 Tom Brady	2.50	1.00
❑	101 Derrick Strait RC	5.00	2.00
❑	102 Michael Clayton RC	10.00	4.00
❑	103 Larry Fitzgerald RC	15.00	6.00
❑	104 Chris Gamble RC	5.00	2.00
❑	105 Devery Henderson RC	4.00	1.50
❑	106 Steven Jackson RC	15.00	6.00
❑	107 Michael Jenkins RC	5.00	2.00
❑	108 Greg Jones RC	5.00	2.00
❑	109 Kevin Jones RC	12.00	5.00
❑	110 Eli Manning RC	30.00	12.50
❑	111 Chris Perry RC	8.00	3.00
❑	112 Philip Rivers RC	15.00	7.50
❑	113 Ben Roethlisberger RC	40.00	20.00
❑	114 Bernard Berrian RC	6.00	2.50
❑	115 Sean Taylor RC	5.00	2.00
❑	116 Reggie Williams RC	6.00	2.50
❑	117 Roy Williams RC	12.00	5.00
❑	118 Kellen Winslow RC	10.00	4.00
❑	119 Rashaun Woods RC	5.00	2.00
❑	120 J.P. Losman RC	10.00	4.00
❑	121 Will Poole RC	5.00	2.00
❑	122 Will Smith RC	5.00	2.00
❑	123 Devard Darling RC	5.00	2.00
❑	124 Jonathan Vilma RC	5.00	2.00
❑	125 Drew Henson RC	5.00	2.00
❑	126 Michael Turner RC	6.00	2.50
❑	127 Lee Evans RC	6.00	2.50
❑	128 Ernest Wilford RC	5.00	2.00
❑	129 Cedric Cobbs RC	5.00	2.00
❑	130 Ricardo Colclough RC	5.00	2.00
❑	131 Ryan Dinwiddie RC	4.00	1.50
❑	132 DeAngelo Hall RC	6.00	2.50
❑	133 Cody Pickett RC	5.00	2.00
❑	134 Quincy Wilson RC	4.00	1.50
❑	135 Ahmad Carroll RC	5.00	2.00
❑	136 Robert Gallery RC	5.00	2.00
❑	137 John Navarre RC	5.00	2.00
❑	138 P.K. Sam RC	4.00	1.50
❑	139 Jeff Smoker RC	5.00	2.00
❑	140 Ben Troupe RC	5.00	2.00
❑	141 Marquise Hill RC	4.00	1.50
❑	142 D.J. Williams RC	5.00	2.00
❑	143 Tommie Harris RC	5.00	2.00
❑	144 Ben Watson RC	5.00	2.00
❑	145 Tatum Bell RC	10.00	4.00
❑	146 B.J. Symons RC	5.00	2.00
❑	147 Matt Schaub RC	15.00	6.00
❑	148 Casey Clausen RC	5.00	2.00
❑	149 Jason Fife RC	2.50	1.00
❑	150 Mike Williams No Ser.#	15.00	6.00

2004 Fleer Sweet Sigs

❑	COMP.SET w/o RC's (75)	15.00	6.00
❑	1 Brett Favre	2.00	.75
❑	2 Daunte Culpepper	.75	.30
❑	3 Marshall Faulk	.75	.30
❑	4 Ashley Lelie	.50	.20
❑	5 Rex Grossman	.75	.30
❑	6 Jeff Garcia	.75	.30
❑	7 Jake Plummer	.50	.20
❑	8 Tony Gonzalez	.50	.20
❑	9 Terrell Owens	.75	.30
❑	10 Plaxico Burress	.50	.20
❑	11 Michael Vick	1.50	.60
❑	12 Carson Palmer	1.00	.40
❑	13 Charles Rogers	.50	.20
❑	14 Corey Dillon	.50	.20
❑	15 Aaron Brooks	.50	.20
❑	16 Torry Holt	.75	.30
❑	17 Joey Galloway	.50	.20
❑	18 Mark Brunell	.50	.20
❑	19 Anquan Boldin	.75	.30
❑	20 Domanick Davis	.75	.30
❑	21 Edgerrin James	.75	.30
❑	22 Hines Ward	.75	.30
❑	23 Kyle Boller	.75	.30
❑	24 Kurt Warner	.75	.30
❑	25 Matt Hasselbeck	.50	.20
❑	26 Chris Chambers	.50	.20
❑	27 Deuce McAllister	.75	.30
❑	28 Chad Pennington	.75	.30
❑	29 Eddie George	.50	.20
❑	30 Ray Lewis	.75	.30
❑	31 Ahman Green	.75	.30
❑	32 Marvin Harrison	.75	.30
❑	33 Tiki Barber	.75	.30
❑	34 Jerry Rice	1.50	.60
❑	35 Emmitt Smith	1.50	.60
❑	36 Chad Johnson	.75	.30
❑	37 Roy Williams S	.50	.20
❑	38 Peyton Manning	1.25	.50
❑	39 Stephen Davis	.50	.20
❑	40 Jamal Lewis	.75	.30
❑	41 David Carr	.75	.30
❑	42 A.J. Feeley	.75	.30
❑	43 Jerry Porter	.50	.20
❑	44 Willis McGahee	.75	.30
❑	45 Quincy Morgan	.50	.20
❑	46 Fred Taylor	.50	.20
❑	47 Trent Green	.50	.20
❑	48 Donovan McNabb	1.00	.40
❑	49 Marc Bulger	.75	.30
❑	50 LaVar Arrington	1.50	.60
❑	51 Joey Harrington	.75	.30
❑	52 Jake Delhomme	.75	.30
❑	53 Jeremy Shockey	.75	.30
❑	54 LaDainian Tomlinson	1.00	.40
❑	55 Brian Urlacher	1.00	.40
❑	56 Rudi Johnson	.50	.20
❑	57 Shaun Alexander	.75	.30
❑	58 Charlie Garner	.50	.20
❑	59 Eric Moulds	.50	.20
❑	60 Tom Brady	2.00	.75
❑	61 Curtis Martin	.75	.30
❑	62 Koren Robinson	.50	.20
❑	63 Steve McNair	.75	.30
❑	64 Travis Henry	.50	.20
❑	65 Julius Peppers	.75	.30
❑	66 Keyshawn Johnson	.50	.20
❑	67 Andre Johnson	.75	.30
❑	68 Priest Holmes	1.00	.40
❑	69 Drew Brees	.75	.30
❑	70 Rich Gannon	.50	.20
❑	71 Randy Moss	1.00	.40
❑	72 Peerless Price	.50	.20
❑	73 Drew Bledsoe	.75	.30
❑	74 Byron Leftwich	1.00	.40
❑	75 Clinton Portis	.75	.30
❑	76 Roy Williams RC	10.00	4.00
❑	77 Eli Manning RC	25.00	10.00
❑	78 Kevin Jones RC	10.00	4.00
❑	79 Tatum Bell RC	8.00	3.00
❑	80 DeAngelo Hall RC	5.00	2.00
❑	81 Michael Clayton RC	8.00	3.00
❑	82 Rashaun Woods RC	4.00	1.50
❑	83 Darius Watts RC	4.00	1.50
❑	84 J.P. Losman RC	8.00	3.00
❑	85 Drew Henson RC	4.00	1.50
❑	86 Philip Rivers RC	12.00	6.00
❑	87 Ben Roethlisberger RC	30.00	15.00
❑	88 Larry Fitzgerald RC	12.00	5.00
❑	89 Chris Perry RC	6.00	2.50
❑	90 Devery Henderson RC	3.00	1.25
❑	91 Sean Taylor RC	4.00	1.50
❑	92 Reggie Williams RC	5.00	2.00
❑	93 Lee Evans RC	5.00	2.00
❑	94 Julius Jones RC	12.00	5.00
❑	95 Dunta Robinson RC	4.00	1.50
❑	96 Michael Jenkins RC	4.00	1.50
❑	97 Greg Jones RC	4.00	1.50
❑	98 Kellen Winslow RC	8.00	3.00
❑	99 Steven Jackson RC	12.00	5.00
❑	100 Matt Schaub RC	12.00	5.00

2002 Fleer Throwbacks

❑	COMP.SET w/o SP's (100)	30.00	12.50
❑	1 Terry Bradshaw	2.50	1.00
❑	2 Franco Harris	2.00	.75
❑	3 Y.A. Tittle	1.50	.60
❑	4 Tony Dorsett	1.50	.60
❑	5 Paul Hornung	1.50	.60
❑	6 Rocky Bleier	1.50	.60
❑	7 Archie Griffin	.75	.30
❑	8 Dwight Clark	1.25	.50

❑ 9	Bo Jackson	2.50	1.00
❑ 10	Fran Tarkenton	2.00	.75
❑ 11	Howie Long	2.00	.75
❑ 12	Bob Griese	1.50	.60
❑ 13	George Rogers	.75	.30
❑ 14	Roger Craig	1.25	.50
❑ 15	Jim Plunkett	1.25	.50
❑ 16	Eric Dickerson	1.25	.50
❑ 17	Marcus Allen	2.00	.75
❑ 18	Roger Staubach	2.50	1.00
❑ 19	Lawrence Taylor	1.50	.60
❑ 20	Joe Greene	1.50	.60
❑ 21	Earl Campbell	1.50	.60
❑ 22	Dave Casper	.75	.30
❑ 23	Charles White	.75	.30
❑ 24	Fred Biletnikoff	1.50	.60
❑ 25	Dan Pastorini	.75	.30
❑ 26	John Cappelletti	.75	.30
❑ 27	Paul Warfield	1.50	.60
❑ 28	Ozzie Newsome	1.25	.50
❑ 29	Johnny Rodgers	1.50	.60
❑ 30	William Perry	1.25	.50
❑ 31	Charley Taylor	1.25	.50
❑ 32	Deacon Jones	1.25	.50
❑ 33	Bubba Smith	1.25	.50
❑ 34	James Lofton	.75	.30
❑ 35	Mike Rozier	.75	.30
❑ 36	Ray Nitschke	1.50	.60
❑ 37	Dan Fouts	1.50	.60
❑ 38	Bob Lilly	1.25	.50
❑ 39	Ronnie Lott	1.25	.50
❑ 40	Barry Sanders	2.50	1.00
❑ 41	Troy Aikman	2.50	1.00
❑ 42	John Elway	5.00	2.00
❑ 43	Irving Fryar	.75	.30
❑ 44	Jim Kelly	2.00	.75
❑ 45	Jim McMahon	2.00	.75
❑ 46	Joe Montana	6.00	2.50
❑ 47	Warren Moon	1.50	.60
❑ 48	Jay Novacek	.75	.30
❑ 49	Mel Renfro	.75	.30
❑ 50	Mike Singletary	1.25	.50
❑ 51	Johnny Unitas	2.50	1.00
❑ 52	Steve Young	2.00	.75
❑ 53	Walter Payton	6.00	2.50
❑ 54	Dan Marino	5.00	2.00
❑ 55	Torry Holt	1.00	.40
❑ 56	Rod Smith	.60	.25
❑ 57	Priest Holmes	1.25	.50
❑ 58	Anthony Thomas	.60	.25
❑ 59	Curtis Martin	1.00	.40
❑ 60	LaDainian Tomlinson	1.50	.60
❑ 61	Antowain Smith	.60	.25
❑ 62	Terrell Owens	1.00	.40
❑ 63	Tony Gonzalez	.60	.25
❑ 64	Steve McNair	1.00	.40
❑ 65	Jerome Bettis	1.00	.40
❑ 66	Rich Gannon	1.00	.40
❑ 67	Jake Plummer	.60	.25
❑ 68	Jamal Lewis	1.00	.40
❑ 69	Drew Brees	1.50	.60
❑ 70	Jevon Kearse	.60	.25
❑ 71	Keyshawn Johnson	1.00	.40
❑ 72	Kordell Stewart	.60	.25
❑ 73	Tim Brown	1.00	.40
❑ 74	Vinny Testaverde	.60	.25
❑ 75	Tom Brady	2.50	1.00
❑ 76	Drew Bledsoe	1.25	.50
❑ 77	Stephen Davis	1.00	.40
❑ 78	Marvin Harrison	1.00	.40
❑ 79	Brian Griese	1.00	.40
❑ 80	Michael Vick	3.00	1.25
❑ 81	Emmitt Smith	2.50	1.00
❑ 82	Edgerrin James	1.25	.50
❑ 83	Mark Brunell	1.00	.40
❑ 84	Tim Couch	.60	.25
❑ 85	Randy Moss	2.00	.75
❑ 86	Brian Urlacher	1.50	.60
❑ 87	Marshall Faulk	1.00	.40
❑ 88	Corey Dillon	.60	.25
❑ 89	Eddie George	1.00	.40
❑ 90	Terrell Davis	1.00	.40
❑ 91	Brett Favre	2.50	1.00
❑ 92	Peyton Manning	2.00	.75
❑ 93	Fred Taylor	1.00	.40
❑ 94	Daunte Culpepper	1.00	.40
❑ 95	Ricky Williams	1.50	.60
❑ 96	Jerry Rice	2.00	.75
❑ 97	Donovan McNabb	1.25	.50
❑ 98	Doug Flutie	1.00	.40
❑ 99	Jeff Garcia	1.00	.40
❑ 100	Kurt Warner	1.50	.60
❑ 101	Antonio Bryant RC	2.50	1.00
❑ 102	Reche Caldwell RC	2.50	1.00
❑ 103	David Carr RC	6.00	2.50
❑ 104	Tim Carter RC	1.25	.50
❑ 105	Rohan Davey RC	2.50	1.00
❑ 106	Andre Davis RC	1.25	.50
❑ 107	T.J. Duckett RC	3.00	1.25
❑ 108	DeShaun Foster RC	2.50	1.00
❑ 109	Jabar Gaffney RC	2.50	1.00
❑ 110	William Green RC	2.50	1.00
❑ 111	Joey Harrington RC	4.00	1.50
❑ 112	Ron Johnson RC	1.25	.50
❑ 113	Ashley Lelie RC	5.00	2.00
❑ 114	Josh McCown RC	3.00	1.25
❑ 115	Julius Peppers RC	5.00	2.00
❑ 116	Clinton Portis RC	8.00	3.00
❑ 117	Patrick Ramsey RC	3.00	1.25
❑ 118	Antwaan Randle El RC	4.00	1.50
❑ 119	Josh Reed RC	2.50	1.00
❑ 120	Cliff Russell RC	1.25	.50
❑ 121	Jeremy Shockey RC	8.00	3.00
❑ 122	Donte Stallworth RC	5.00	2.00
❑ 123	Travis Stephens RC	1.25	.50
❑ 124	Javon Walker RC	5.00	2.00
❑ 125	Marquise Walker RC	1.25	.50

1998 Fleer Tradition

❑	COMPLETE SET (250)	40.00	20.00
❑ 1	Brett Favre	2.00	.75
❑ 2	Barry Sanders	1.50	.60
❑ 3	John Elway	2.00	.75
❑ 4	Emmitt Smith	1.50	.60
❑ 5	Dan Marino	2.00	.75
❑ 6	Eddie George	.50	.20
❑ 7	Jerry Rice	1.00	.40
❑ 8	Jake Plummer	.50	.20
❑ 9	Joey Galloway	.30	.10
❑ 10	Mike Alstott	.50	.20
❑ 11	Brian Mitchell	.20	.07
❑ 12	Keyshawn Johnson	.50	.20
❑ 13	Jerald Moore	.20	.07
❑ 14	Randal Hill	.20	.07
❑ 15	Byron Hanspard	.20	.07
❑ 16	Jeff George	.30	.10
❑ 17	Terry Glenn	.50	.20
❑ 18	Jerome Bettis	.50	.20
❑ 19	Curtis Conway	.30	.10
❑ 20	Fred Lane	.20	.07
❑ 21	Isaac Bruce	.50	.20
❑ 22	Tiki Barber	.50	.20
❑ 23	Bobby Hoying	.30	.10
❑ 24	Marcus Allen	.50	.20
❑ 25	Dana Stubblefield	.20	.07
❑ 26	Peter Boulware	.20	.07
❑ 27	John Randle	.30	.10
❑ 28	Jason Sehorn	.30	.10
❑ 29	Rod Smith	.30	.10
❑ 30	Michael Sinclair	.20	.07
❑ 31	Marshall Faulk	.60	.25
❑ 32	Karl Williams	.20	.07
❑ 33	Kordell Stewart	.50	.20
❑ 34	Corey Dillon	.50	.20
❑ 35	Bryant Young	.20	.07
❑ 36	Charlie Garner	.30	.10
❑ 37	Andre Reed	.30	.10
❑ 38	Ray Buchanan	.20	.07
❑ 39	Brett Perriman	.20	.07
❑ 40	Leon Lett	.20	.07
❑ 41	Keenan McCardell	.30	.10
❑ 42	Eric Swann	.20	.07
❑ 43	Leslie Shepherd	.20	.07
❑ 44	Curtis Martin	.50	.20
❑ 45	Andre Rison	.30	.10
❑ 46	Keith Lyle	.20	.07
❑ 47	Rae Carruth	.20	.07
❑ 48	William Henderson	.30	.10
❑ 49	Sean Dawkins	.20	.07
❑ 50	Terrell Davis	.50	.20
❑ 51	Tim Brown	.50	.20
❑ 52	Willie McGinest	.20	.07
❑ 53	Jermaine Lewis	.30	.10
❑ 54	Ricky Watters	.30	.10
❑ 55	Freddie Jones	.20	.07
❑ 56	Robert Smith	.50	.20
❑ 57	Reidel Anthony	.30	.10
❑ 58	James Stewart	.30	.10
❑ 59	Earl Holmes RC	.50	.20
❑ 60	Dale Carter	.20	.07
❑ 61	Michael Irvin	.50	.20
❑ 62	Jason Taylor	.30	.10
❑ 63	Eric Metcalf	.20	.07
❑ 64	LeRoy Butler	.20	.07
❑ 65	Jamal Anderson	.50	.20
❑ 66	Jamie Asher	.20	.07
❑ 67	Chris Sanders	.20	.07
❑ 68	Warren Sapp	.30	.10
❑ 69	Ray Zellars	.20	.07
❑ 70	Carl Pickens	.30	.10
❑ 71	Garrison Hearst	.50	.20
❑ 72	Eddie Kennison	.30	.10
❑ 73	John Mobley	.20	.07
❑ 74	Rob Johnson	.30	.10
❑ 75	William Thomas	.20	.07
❑ 76	Drew Bledsoe	.75	.30
❑ 77	Micheal Barrow	.20	.07
❑ 78	Jim Harbaugh	.30	.10
❑ 79	Terry McDaniel	.20	.07
❑ 80	Johnnie Morton	.30	.10
❑ 81	Danny Kanell	.30	.10
❑ 82	Larry Centers	.20	.07
❑ 83	Courtney Hawkins	.20	.07
❑ 84	Tony Brackens	.20	.07
❑ 85	Tony Gonzalez	.50	.20
❑ 86	Aaron Glenn	.20	.07
❑ 87	Cris Carter	.50	.20
❑ 88	Chuck Smith	.20	.07
❑ 89	Tamarick Vanover	.20	.07
❑ 90	Karim Abdul-Jabbar	.50	.20
❑ 91	Bryant Westbrook	.20	.07
❑ 92	Mike Pritchard	.20	.07
❑ 93	Darren Woodson	.20	.07
❑ 94	Wesley Walls	.30	.10
❑ 95	Tony Banks	.30	.10
❑ 96	Michael Westbrook	.30	.10
❑ 97	Shannon Sharpe	.30	.10
❑ 98	Jeff Blake	.30	.10
❑ 99	Terrell Owens	.50	.20
❑ 100	Warrick Dunn	.50	.20
❑ 101	Levon Kirkland	.20	.07
❑ 102	Frank Wycheck	.20	.07
❑ 103	Gus Frerotte	.20	.07
❑ 104	Simeon Rice	.30	.10
❑ 105	Shawn Jefferson	.20	.07
❑ 106	Irving Fryar	.30	.10
❑ 107	Michael McCrary	.20	.07
❑ 108	Robert Brooks	.30	.10
❑ 109	Chris Chandler	.30	.10
❑ 110	Junior Seau	.50	.20
❑ 111	O.J. McDuffie	.30	.10
❑ 112	Glenn Foley	.30	.10
❑ 113	Darryl Williams	.20	.07

❑ 114	Elvis Grbac	.30	.10
❑ 115	Napoleon Kaufman	.50	.20
❑ 116	Anthony Miller	.20	.07
❑ 117	Troy Davis	.20	.07
❑ 118	Charles Way	.20	.07
❑ 119	Scott Mitchell	.30	.10
❑ 120	Ken Harvey	.20	.07
❑ 121	Tyrone Hughes	.20	.07
❑ 122	Mark Brunell	.50	.20
❑ 123	David Palmer	.20	.07
❑ 124	Rob Moore	.30	.10
❑ 125	Kerry Collins	.30	.10
❑ 126	Will Blackwell	.20	.07
❑ 127	Ray Crockett	.20	.07
❑ 128	Leslie O'Neal	.20	.07
❑ 129	Antowain Smith	.50	.20
❑ 130	Carlester Crumpler	.20	.07
❑ 131	Michael Jackson	.20	.07
❑ 132	Trent Dilfer	.50	.20
❑ 133	Dan Williams	.20	.07
❑ 134	Dorsey Levens	.50	.20
❑ 135	Ty Law	.30	.10
❑ 136	Rickey Dudley	.20	.07
❑ 137	Jessie Tuggle	.20	.07
❑ 138	Darrien Gordon	.20	.07
❑ 139	Kevin Turner	.20	.07
❑ 140	Willie Davis	.20	.07
❑ 141	Zach Thomas	.50	.20
❑ 142	Tony McGee	.20	.07
❑ 143	Dexter Coakley	.20	.07
❑ 144	Troy Brown	.30	.10
❑ 145	Leeland McElroy	.20	.07
❑ 146	Michael Strahan	.30	.10
❑ 147	Ken Dilger	.20	.07
❑ 148	Bryce Paup	.20	.07
❑ 149	Herman Moore	.30	.10
❑ 150	Reggie White	.50	.20
❑ 151	Dewayne Washington	.20	.07
❑ 152	Natrone Means	.30	.10
❑ 153	Ben Coates	.30	.10
❑ 154	Bert Emanuel	.30	.10
❑ 155	Steve Young	.60	.25
❑ 156	Jimmy Smith	.30	.10
❑ 157	Darrell Green	.30	.10
❑ 158	Troy Aikman	1.00	.40
❑ 159	Greg Hill	.20	.07
❑ 160	Raymont Harris	.20	.07
❑ 161	Troy Drayton	.20	.07
❑ 162	Stevon Moore	.20	.07
❑ 163	Warren Moon	.50	.20
❑ 164	Wayne Martin	.20	.07
❑ 165	Jason Gildon	.20	.07
❑ 166	Chris Calloway	.20	.07
❑ 167	Aeneas Williams	.20	.07
❑ 168	Michael Bates	.20	.07
❑ 169	Hugh Douglas	.20	.07
❑ 170	Brad Johnson	.50	.20
❑ 171	Bruce Smith	.30	.10
❑ 172	Neil Smith	.30	.10
❑ 173	James McKnight	.50	.20
❑ 174	Robert Porcher	.20	.07
❑ 175	Merton Hanks	.20	.07
❑ 176	Ki-Jana Carter	.20	.07
❑ 177	Mo Lewis	.20	.07
❑ 178	Chester McGlockton	.20	.07
❑ 179	Zack Crockett	.20	.07
❑ 180	Derrick Thomas	.50	.20
❑ 181	J.J. Stokes	.30	.10
❑ 182	Derrick Rodgers	.20	.07
❑ 183	Daryl Johnston	.30	.10
❑ 184	Chris Penn	.20	.07
❑ 185	Steve Atwater	.20	.07
❑ 186	Amp Lee	.20	.07
❑ 187	Frank Sanders	.30	.10
❑ 188	Chris Slade	.20	.07
❑ 189	Mark Chmura	.30	.10
❑ 190	Kimble Anders	.30	.10
❑ 191	Charles Johnson	.20	.07
❑ 192	William Floyd	.20	.07
❑ 193	Jay Graham	.20	.07
❑ 194	Hardy Nickerson	.20	.07
❑ 195	Terry Allen	.50	.20
❑ 196	James Jett	.30	.10
❑ 197	Jessie Armstead	.20	.07
❑ 198	Yancey Thigpen	.30	.10
❑ 199	Terance Mathis	.30	.10
❑ 200	Steve McNair	.50	.20
❑ 201	Wayne Chrebet	.50	.20
❑ 202	Jamir Miller	.20	.07
❑ 203	Duce Staley	.60	.25
❑ 204	Deion Sanders	.50	.20
❑ 205	Carnell Lake	.20	.07
❑ 206	Ed McCaffrey	.30	.10
❑ 207	Shawn Springs	.20	.07
❑ 208	Tony Martin	.30	.10
❑ 209	Jerris McPhail	.20	.07
❑ 210	Darnay Scott	.30	.10
❑ 211	Jake Reed	.30	.10
❑ 212	Adrian Murrell	.30	.10
❑ 213	Quinn Early	.20	.07
❑ 214	Marvin Harrison	.50	.20
❑ 215	Ryan McNeil	.20	.07
❑ 216	Derrick Alexander	.30	.10
❑ 217	Ray Lewis	.50	.20
❑ 218	Antonio Freeman	.50	.20
❑ 219	Dwayne Rudd	.20	.07
❑ 220	Muhsin Muhammad	.30	.10
❑ 221	Kevin Hardy	.20	.07
❑ 222	Andre Hastings	.20	.07
❑ 223	John Avery RC	.75	.30
❑ 224	Keith Brooking RC	1.25	.50
❑ 225	Kevin Dyson RC	1.25	.50
❑ 226	Robert Edwards RC	.75	.30
❑ 227	Greg Ellis RC	.50	.20
❑ 228	Curtis Enis RC	.50	.20
❑ 229	Terry Fair RC	.75	.30
❑ 230	Ahman Green RC	6.00	2.50
❑ 231	Jacquez Green RC	.75	.30
❑ 232	Brian Griese RC	3.00	1.25
❑ 233	Skip Hicks RC	.75	.30
❑ 234	Ryan Leaf RC	1.25	.50
❑ 235	Peyton Manning RC	15.00	6.00
❑ 236	R.W. McQuarters RC	.75	.30
❑ 237	Randy Moss RC	8.00	3.00
❑ 238	Marcus Nash RC	.50	.20
❑ 239	Anthony Simmons RC	.75	.30
❑ 240	Brian Simmons RC	.75	.30
❑ 241	Takeo Spikes RC	1.25	.50
❑ 242	Duane Starks RC	.50	.20
❑ 243	Fred Taylor RC	2.00	.75
❑ 244	Andre Wadsworth RC	.75	.30
❑ 245	Shaun Williams RC	.75	.30
❑ 246	Grant Wistrom RC	.75	.30
❑ 247	Charles Woodson RC	1.50	.60
❑ 248	Checklist	.20	.07
❑ 249	Checklist	.20	.07
❑ 250	Checklist	.20	.07

1999 Fleer Tradition

❑ COMPLETE SET (300)		40.00	20.00
❑ 1	Randy Moss	1.25	.50
❑ 2	Peyton Manning	1.50	.60
❑ 3	Barry Sanders	1.50	.60
❑ 4	Terrell Davis	.50	.20
❑ 5	Brett Favre	1.50	.60
❑ 6	Fred Taylor	.50	.20
❑ 7	Jake Plummer	.30	.10
❑ 8	John Elway	1.50	.60
❑ 9	Emmitt Smith	1.00	.40
❑ 10	Kerry Collins	.30	.10
❑ 11	Peter Boulware	.20	.07
❑ 12	Jamal Anderson	.50	.20
❑ 13	Doug Flutie	.50	.20
❑ 14	Michael Bates	.20	.07
❑ 15	Corey Dillon	.50	.20
❑ 16	Curtis Conway	.30	.10
❑ 17	Ty Detmer	.30	.10
❑ 18	Robert Brooks	.30	.10
❑ 19	Dale Carter	.20	.07
❑ 20	Charlie Batch	.50	.20
❑ 21	Ken Dilger	.20	.07
❑ 22	Troy Aikman	1.00	.40
❑ 23	Tavian Banks	.20	.07
❑ 24	Cris Carter	.50	.20
❑ 25	Derrick Alexander WR	.30	.10
❑ 26	Chris Bordano RC	.20	.07
❑ 27	Karim Abdul-Jabbar	.30	.10
❑ 28	Jessie Armstead	.20	.07
❑ 29	Drew Bledsoe	.60	.25
❑ 30	Brian Dawkins	.50	.20
❑ 31	Wayne Chrebet	.30	.10
❑ 32	Garrison Hearst	.30	.10
❑ 33	Eric Allen	.20	.07
❑ 34	Tony Banks	.30	.10
❑ 35	Jerome Bettis	.50	.20
❑ 36	Stephen Alexander	.20	.07
❑ 37	Rodney Harrison	.20	.07
❑ 38	Mike Alstott	.50	.20
❑ 39	Chad Brown	.20	.07
❑ 40	Johnny McWilliams	.20	.07
❑ 41	Kevin Dyson	.30	.10
❑ 42	Keith Brooking	.20	.07
❑ 43	Jim Harbaugh	.30	.10
❑ 44	Bobby Engram	.30	.10
❑ 45	John Holecek	.20	.07
❑ 46	Steve Beuerlein	.20	.07
❑ 47	Tony McGee	.20	.07
❑ 48	Greg Ellis	.20	.07
❑ 49	Corey Fuller	.20	.07
❑ 50	Stephen Boyd	.20	.07
❑ 51	Marshall Faulk	.60	.25
❑ 52	LeRoy Butler	.20	.07
❑ 53	Reggie Barlow	.20	.07
❑ 54	Randall Cunningham	.50	.20
❑ 55	Aeneas Williams	.20	.07
❑ 56	Kimble Anders	.30	.10
❑ 57	Cam Cleeland	.20	.07
❑ 58	John Avery	.20	.07
❑ 59	Gary Brown	.20	.07
❑ 60	Ben Coates	.30	.10
❑ 61	Koy Detmer	.20	.07
❑ 62	Bryan Cox	.20	.07
❑ 63	Edgar Bennett	.20	.07
❑ 64	Tim Brown	.50	.20
❑ 65	Isaac Bruce	.50	.20
❑ 66	Eddie George	.50	.20
❑ 67	Reidel Anthony	.30	.10
❑ 68	Charlie Jones	.20	.07
❑ 69	Terry Allen	.30	.10
❑ 70	Joey Galloway	.30	.10
❑ 71	Jamir Miller	.20	.07
❑ 72	Will Blackwell	.20	.07
❑ 73	Ray Buchanan	.20	.07
❑ 74	Priest Holmes	.75	.30
❑ 75	Michael Irvin	.30	.10
❑ 76	Jonathan Linton	.20	.07
❑ 77	Curtis Enis	.20	.07
❑ 78	Neil O'Donnell	.30	.10
❑ 79	Tim Biakabutuka	.30	.10
❑ 80	Terry Kirby	.20	.07
❑ 81	Germane Crowell	.20	.07
❑ 82	Jason Elam	.20	.07
❑ 83	Mark Chmura	.20	.07
❑ 84	Marvin Harrison	.50	.20
❑ 85	Jimmy Hitchcock	.20	.07
❑ 86	Tony Brackens	.20	.07
❑ 87	Sean Dawkins	.20	.07
❑ 88	Tony Gonzalez	.50	.20
❑ 89	Kent Graham	.20	.07
❑ 90	Oronde Gadsden	.30	.10
❑ 91	Hugh Douglas	.20	.07
❑ 92	Robert Edwards	.20	.07
❑ 93	R.W. McQuarters	.20	.07
❑ 94	Aaron Glenn	.20	.07
❑ 95	Kevin Carter	.20	.07
❑ 96	Rickey Dudley	.20	.07
❑ 97	Derrick Brooks	.50	.20
❑ 98	Mark Bruener	.20	.07
❑ 99	Darrell Green	.20	.07
❑ 100	Jessie Tuggle	.20	.07
❑ 101	Freddie Jones	.20	.07
❑ 102	Rob Moore	.30	.10
❑ 103	Ahman Green	.50	.20
❑ 104	Chris Chandler	.30	.10
❑ 105	Steve McNair	.50	.20
❑ 106	Kevin Greene	.20	.07
❑ 107	Jermaine Lewis	.30	.10
❑ 108	Erik Kramer	.20	.07
❑ 109	Eric Moulds	.50	.20
❑ 110	Terry Fair	.20	.07

❑ 111	Carl Pickens	.30	.10
❑ 112	La'Roi Glover RC		
❑ 113	Chris Spielman	.20	.07
❑ 114	Leroy Hoard	.20	.07
❑ 115	Mark Brunell	.50	.20
❑ 116	Patrick Jeffers RC	3.00	1.50
❑ 117	Elvis Grbac	.30	.10
❑ 118	Ike Hilliard	.20	.07
❑ 119	Sam Madison	.20	.07
❑ 120	Terrell Owens	.50	.20
❑ 121	Rich Gannon	.50	.20
❑ 122	Skip Hicks	.20	.07
❑ 123	Eric Green	.20	.07
❑ 124	Trent Dilfer	.30	.10
❑ 125	Terry Glenn	.50	.20
❑ 126	Trent Green	.50	.20
❑ 127	Charles Johnson	.20	.07
❑ 128	Adrian Murrell	.30	.10
❑ 129	Jason Gildon	.20	.07
❑ 130	Tim Dwight	.50	.20
❑ 131	Ryan Leaf	.50	.20
❑ 132	Rocket Ismail	.30	.10
❑ 133	Jon Kitna	.50	.20
❑ 134	Alonzo Mayes	.20	.07
❑ 135	Yancey Thigpen	.20	.07
❑ 136	David LaFleur	.20	.07
❑ 137	Ray Lewis	.50	.20
❑ 138	Herman Moore	.30	.10
❑ 139	Brian Griese	.50	.20
❑ 140	Antonio Freeman	.50	.20
❑ 141	Darnay Scott	.20	.07
❑ 142	Ed McDaniel	.20	.07
❑ 143	Andre Reed	.30	.10
❑ 144	Andre Hastings	.20	.07
❑ 145	Chris Warren	.20	.07
❑ 146	Kevin Hardy	.20	.07
❑ 147	Joe Jurevicius	.30	.10
❑ 148	Jerome Pathon	.20	.07
❑ 149	Duce Staley	.50	.20
❑ 150	Dan Marino	1.50	.60
❑ 151	Jerry Rice	1.00	.40
❑ 152	Byron Bam Morris	.20	.07
❑ 153	Az-Zahir Hakim	.20	.07
❑ 154	Ty Law	.30	.10
❑ 155	Warrick Dunn	.50	.20
❑ 156	Keyshawn Johnson	.50	.20
❑ 157	Brian Mitchell	.20	.07
❑ 158	James Jett	.30	.10
❑ 159	Fred Lane	.20	.07
❑ 160	Courtney Hawkins	.20	.07
❑ 161	Andre Wadsworth	.20	.07
❑ 162	Natrone Means	.30	.10
❑ 163	Andrew Glover	.20	.07
❑ 164	Anthony Simmons	.20	.07
❑ 165	Leon Lett	.20	.07
❑ 166	Frank Wycheck	.20	.07
❑ 167	Barry Minter	.20	.07
❑ 168	Michael McCrary	.20	.07
❑ 169	Johnnie Morton	.30	.10
❑ 170	Jay Riemersma	.20	.07
❑ 171	Vonnie Holliday	.20	.07
❑ 172	Brian Simmons	.20	.07
❑ 173	Joe Johnson	.20	.07
❑ 174	Ed McCaffrey	.30	.10
❑ 175	Jason Sehorn	.20	.07
❑ 176	Keenan McCardell	.30	.10
❑ 177	Bobby Taylor	.20	.07
❑ 178	Andre Rison	.30	.10
❑ 179	Greg Hill	.20	.07
❑ 180	O.J. McDuffie	.30	.10
❑ 181	Darren Woodson	.20	.07
❑ 182	Willie McGinest	.20	.07
❑ 183	J.J. Stokes	.30	.10
❑ 184	Leon Johnson	.20	.07
❑ 185	Bert Emanuel	.30	.10
❑ 186	Napoleon Kaufman	.50	.20
❑ 187	Leslie Shepherd	.20	.07
❑ 188	Levon Kirkland	.20	.07
❑ 189	Simeon Rice	.30	.10
❑ 190	Mikhael Ricks	.20	.07
❑ 191	Robert Smith	.50	.20
❑ 192	Michael Sinclair	.20	.07
❑ 193	Muhsin Muhammad	.30	.10
❑ 194	Duane Starks	.20	.07
❑ 195	Terance Mathis	.30	.10
❑ 196	Antowain Smith	.50	.20
❑ 197	Tony Parrish	.20	.07
❑ 198	Takeo Spikes	.20	.07
❑ 199	Ernie Mills	.20	.07
❑ 200	John Mobley	.20	.07
❑ 202	Pete Mitchell	.20	.07
❑ 203	Darick Holmes	.20	.07
❑ 204	Derrick Thomas	.50	.20
❑ 205	David Palmer	.20	.07
❑ 206	Jason Taylor	.20	.07
❑ 207	Sammy Knight	.20	.07
❑ 208	Dwayne Rudd	.20	.07
❑ 209	Lawyer Milloy	.30	.10
❑ 210	Michael Strahan	.30	.10
❑ 211	Mo Lewis	.20	.07
❑ 212	William Thomas	.20	.07
❑ 213	Darrell Russell	.20	.07
❑ 214	Brad Johnson	.50	.20
❑ 215	Kordell Stewart	.30	.10
❑ 216	Robert Holcombe	.20	.07
❑ 217	Junior Seau	.50	.20
❑ 218	Jacquez Green	.20	.07
❑ 219	Shawn Springs	.20	.07
❑ 220	Michael Westbrook	.30	.10
❑ 221	Rod Woodson	.30	.10
❑ 222	Frank Sanders	.30	.10
❑ 223	Bruce Smith	.30	.10
❑ 224	Eugene Robinson	.20	.07
❑ 225	Bill Romanowski	.20	.07
❑ 226	Wesley Walls	.30	.10
❑ 227	Jimmy Smith	.30	.10
❑ 228	Deion Sanders	.50	.20
❑ 229	Lamar Thomas	.20	.07
❑ 230	Dorsey Levens	.50	.20
❑ 231	Tony Simmons	.20	.07
❑ 232	John Randle	.30	.10
❑ 233	Curtis Martin	.50	.20
❑ 234	Bryant Young	.20	.07
❑ 235	Charles Woodson	.50	.20
❑ 236	Charles Way	.20	.07
❑ 237	Zach Thomas	.50	.20
❑ 238	Ricky Proehl	.20	.07
❑ 239	Ricky Watters	.30	.10
❑ 240	Hardy Nickerson	.20	.07
❑ 241	Shannon Sharpe	.30	.10
❑ 242	O.J. Santiago	.20	.07
❑ 243	Vinny Testaverde	.30	.10
❑ 244	Roell Preston	.20	.07
❑ 245	James Stewart	.30	.10
❑ 246	Jake Reed	.30	.10
❑ 247	Steve Young	.60	.25
❑ 248	Shaun Williams	.20	.07
❑ 249	Rod Smith	.30	.10
❑ 250	Warren Sapp	.30	.10
❑ 251	Champ Bailey RC	1.50	.60
❑ 252	Karsten Bailey RC	.75	.30
❑ 253	D'Wayne Bates RC	.75	.30
❑ 254	Michael Bishop RC	1.25	.50
❑ 255	David Boston RC	1.25	.50
❑ 256	Na Brown RC	.75	.30
❑ 257	Fernando Bryant RC	.75	.30
❑ 258	Shawn Bryson RC	1.25	.50
❑ 259	Darrin Chiaverini RC	.75	.30
❑ 260	Chris Claiborne RC	.40	.15
❑ 261	Mike Cloud RC	.75	.30
❑ 262	Cecil Collins RC	.40	.15
❑ 263	Tim Couch RC	1.25	.50
❑ 264	Scott Covington RC	1.25	.50
❑ 265	Daunte Culpepper RC	5.00	2.00
❑ 266	Antuan Edwards RC	.40	.15
❑ 267	Troy Edwards RC	.75	.30
❑ 268	Ebenezer Ekuban RC	.75	.30
❑ 269	Kevin Faulk RC	1.25	.50
❑ 270	Jermaine Fazande RC	.75	.30
❑ 271	Joe Germaine RC	.75	.30
❑ 272	Martin Gramatica RC	.40	.15
❑ 273	Torry Holt RC	3.00	1.25
❑ 274	Brock Huard RC	1.25	.50
❑ 275	Sedrick Irvin RC	.40	.15
❑ 276	Sheldon Jackson RC	.75	.30
❑ 277	Edgerrin James RC	5.00	2.00
❑ 278	James Johnson RC	.75	.30
❑ 279	Kevin Johnson RC	1.25	.50
❑ 280	Malcolm Johnson RC	.40	.15
❑ 281	Andy Katzenmoyer RC	.75	.30
❑ 282	Jevon Kearse RC	2.00	.75
❑ 283	Patrick Kerney RC	1.25	.50
❑ 284	Shaun King RC	.75	.30
❑ 285	Jim Kleinsasser RC	1.25	.50
❑ 286	Rob Konrad RC	1.25	.50
❑ 287	Chris McAlister RC	.75	.30
❑ 288	Donovan McNabb RC	6.00	2.50
❑ 289	Cade McNown RC	.75	.30
❑ 290	Dee Miller RC	.40	.15
❑ 291	Joe Montgomery RC	.75	.30
❑ 292	De'Mond Parker RC	.40	.15
❑ 293	Peerless Price RC	1.25	.50
❑ 294	Akili Smith RC	.75	.30
❑ 295	Justin Swift RC	.40	.15
❑ 296	Jerame Tuman RC	1.25	.50
❑ 297	Ricky Williams RC	2.50	1.00
❑ 298	Antoine Winfield	.75	.30
❑ 299	Craig Yeast RC	.75	.30
❑ 300	Amos Zereoue RC	1.25	.50
❑ P6	Fred Taylor Promo	1.00	.40

2000 Fleer Tradition

❑	COMPLETE SET (400)	60.00	25.00
❑ 1	Kevin Johnson	.50	.20
❑ 2	Chris Chandler	.30	.10
❑ 3	Peerless Price	.30	.10
❑ 4	Andre Rison	.30	.10
❑ 5	Curtis Enis	.20	.07
❑ 6	Tim Couch	.30	.10
❑ 7	Brian Dawkins	.50	.20
❑ 8	Akili Smith	.20	.07
❑ 9	Kevin Faulk	.30	.10
❑ 10	Joey Galloway	.30	.10
❑ 11	Bill Romanowski	.20	.07
❑ 12	Charlie Batch	.50	.20
❑ 13	Terrence Wilkins	.20	.07
❑ 14	Kevin Hardy	.20	.07
❑ 15	Cade McNown	.20	.07
❑ 16	Elvis Grbac	.30	.10
❑ 17	Cris Carter	.50	.20
❑ 18	Willie McGinest	.20	.07
❑ 19	Michael Bishop	.20	.07
❑ 20	Lee Woodall	.20	.07
❑ 21	Jake Reed	.30	.10
❑ 22	Bryan Cox	.20	.07
❑ 23	Chris Sanders	.20	.07
❑ 24	Tavian Banks	.20	.07
❑ 25	Levon Kirkland	.20	.07
❑ 26	James Hundon	.20	.07
❑ 27	Junior Seau	.50	.20
❑ 28	Darren Woodson	.20	.07
❑ 29	Kevin Carter	.20	.07
❑ 30	Joe Jurevicius	.20	.07
❑ 31	John Lynch	.30	.10
❑ 32	Steve McNair	.50	.20
❑ 33	Jake Plummer	.30	.10
❑ 34	Antonio Freeman	.50	.20
❑ 35	Peter Boulware	.20	.07
❑ 36	Brad Johnson	.50	.20
❑ 37	Bobby Engram	.30	.10
❑ 38	David Boston	.50	.20
❑ 39	Jason Tucker	.20	.07
❑ 40	Troy Brown	.30	.10
❑ 41	Brian Griese	.50	.20
❑ 42	Dorsey Levens	.30	.10
❑ 43	Cornelius Bennett	.20	.07
❑ 44	Donovan McNabb	.75	.30
❑ 45	Rob Johnson	.30	.10
❑ 46	Robert Smith	.50	.20
❑ 47	Stanley Pritchett	.20	.07
❑ 48	Tedy Bruschi	.50	.20
❑ 49	Dan Marino	1.50	.60
❑ 50	Amani Toomer	.30	.10
❑ 51	Aaron Glenn	.20	.07
❑ 52	Rickey Dudley	.20	.07
❑ 53	Tim Brown	.50	.20
❑ 54	Jim Harbaugh	.30	.10
❑ 55	Terrell Owens	.50	.20
❑ 56	Jason Sehorn	.20	.07
❑ 57	Cortez Kennedy	.20	.07

❑ 58 London Fletcher RC .30 .10
❑ 59 Simeon Rice .30 .10
❑ 60 Shaun King .20 .07
❑ 61 Stephen Davis .50 .20
❑ 62 Andre Wadsworth .20 .07
❑ 63 Kyle Brady .20 .07
❑ 64 Priest Holmes .60 .25
❑ 65 Patrick Jeffers .50 .20
❑ 66 Barry Minter .20 .07
❑ 67 Curtis Martin .50 .20
❑ 68 Darrin Chiaverini .20 .07
❑ 69 Robert Thomas .20 .07
❑ 70 Samari Rolle .20 .07
❑ 71 Robert Porcher .20 .07
❑ 72 Jerry Rice 1.00 .40
❑ 73 Bill Schroeder .30 .10
❑ 74 Chad Bratzke .20 .07
❑ 75 Tony Brackens .20 .07
❑ 76 O.J. McDuffie .30 .10
❑ 77 John Randle .30 .10
❑ 78 Michael Pittman .20 .07
❑ 79 Drew Bledsoe .60 .25
❑ 80 Ike Hilliard .30 .10
❑ 81 Victor Green .20 .07
❑ 82 Duce Staley .50 .20
❑ 83 Bruce Smith .30 .10
❑ 84 Amos Zereoue .50 .20
❑ 85 Charlie Garner .30 .10
❑ 86 Shawn Springs .20 .07
❑ 87 Kurt Warner 1.00 .40
❑ 88 Eddie George .50 .20
❑ 89 Michael Westbrook .30 .10
❑ 90 Dexter Coakley .20 .07
❑ 91 Rob Moore .30 .10
❑ 92 Duane Starks .20 .07
❑ 93 Steve Beuerlein .30 .10
❑ 94 Marty Booker .30 .10
❑ 95 Karim Abdul-Jabbar .30 .10
❑ 96 Troy Aikman 1.00 .40
❑ 97 Germane Crowell .20 .07
❑ 98 Matt Hasselbeck .30 .10
❑ 99 E.G. Green .20 .07
❑ 100 Mark Brunell .50 .20
❑ 101 Tony Martin .30 .10
❑ 102 Darrell Green .20 .07
❑ 103 Ricky Williams .50 .20
❑ 104 Michael Strahan .30 .10
❑ 105 Vinny Testaverde .30 .10
❑ 106 Charles Johnson .30 .10
❑ 107 Hines Ward .50 .20
❑ 108 Bryant Young .20 .07
❑ 109 Mo Lewis .20 .07
❑ 110 Greg Clark .20 .07
❑ 111 Jon Kitna .50 .20
❑ 112 Jacquez Green .20 .07
❑ 113 Kevin Dyson .30 .10
❑ 114 Stephen Alexander .20 .07
❑ 115 Cam Cleeland .20 .07
❑ 116 Keith Poole .20 .07
❑ 117 Az-Zahir Hakim .30 .10
❑ 118 Tim Dwight .50 .20
❑ 119 Corey Bradford .20 .07
❑ 120 Carlos Emmons .20 .07
❑ 121 Trent Dilfer .30 .10
❑ 122 Lance Schulters .20 .07
❑ 123 Byron Hanspard .20 .07
❑ 124 Tim Biakabutuka .30 .10
❑ 125 Eddie Kennison .30 .10
❑ 126 Terry Kirby .20 .07
❑ 127 Mike McKenzie .20 .07
❑ 128 Fred Beasley .20 .07
❑ 129 Chad Brown .20 .07
❑ 130 Terrell Davis .50 .20
❑ 131 Herman Moore .30 .10
❑ 132 Vonnie Holliday .20 .07
❑ 133 Jim Miller .20 .07
❑ 134 Peyton Manning 1.25 .50
❑ 135 Derrick Alexander .30 .10
❑ 136 Oronde Gadsden .30 .10
❑ 137 Robert Griffith .20 .07
❑ 138 Troy Edwards .20 .07
❑ 139 Damon Huard .50 .20
❑ 140 Jessie Armstead .20 .07
❑ 141 Charles Woodson .30 .10
❑ 142 Troy Vincent .20 .07
❑ 143 Natrone Means .20 .07
❑ 144 Jeff Garcia .50 .20
❑ 145 Terry Glenn .30 .10
❑ 146 Marshall Faulk .60 .25
❑ 147 Pat Johnson .20 .07
❑ 148 Frank Wycheck .20 .07
❑ 149 Champ Bailey .30 .10
❑ 150 Jamal Anderson .50 .20
❑ 151 Doug Flutie .50 .20
❑ 152 Michael Bates .20 .07
❑ 153 Corey Dillon .50 .20
❑ 154 Keith McKenzie .20 .07
❑ 155 Orpheus Roye .20 .07
❑ 156 Olandis Gary .50 .20
❑ 157 Johnnie Morton .30 .10
❑ 158 Brett Favre 1.50 .60
❑ 159 Adrian Murrell .20 .07
❑ 160 Fred Taylor .50 .20
❑ 161 Tony Gonzalez .30 .10
❑ 162 Zach Thomas .50 .20
❑ 163 Randy Moss 1.00 .40
❑ 164 Marcus Robinson .50 .20
❑ 165 Tiki Barber .50 .20
❑ 166 Rich Gannon .50 .20
❑ 167 Jeremiah Trotter RC 1.50 .60
❑ 168 Jermaine Fazande .20 .07
❑ 169 Steve Young .60 .25
❑ 170 Isaac Bruce .50 .20
❑ 171 Warrick Dunn .50 .20
❑ 172 Yancey Thigpen .20 .07
❑ 173 Rod Smith .30 .10
❑ 174 Albert Connell .20 .07
❑ 175 Freddie Jones .20 .07
❑ 176 Terance Mathis .30 .10
❑ 177 Eric Moulds .50 .20
❑ 178 Brian Mitchell .20 .07
❑ 179 Wesley Walls .20 .07
❑ 180 Carl Pickens .30 .10
❑ 181 Errict Rhett .30 .10
❑ 182 Madre Hill .20 .07
❑ 183 Jason Elam .20 .07
❑ 184 Greg Ellis .20 .07
❑ 185 David Sloan .20 .07
❑ 186 Edgerrin James .75 .30
❑ 187 Jimmy Smith .30 .10
❑ 188 Tony Richardson RC .30 .10
❑ 189 James Hasty .20 .07
❑ 190 Sam Madison .20 .07
❑ 191 Tony Simmons .20 .07
❑ 192 Andre Hastings .20 .07
❑ 193 Keyshawn Johnson .50 .20
❑ 194 Na Brown .20 .07
❑ 195 Napoleon Kaufman .30 .10
❑ 196 Torrance Small .20 .07
❑ 197 Curtis Conway .30 .10
❑ 198 Jeff Graham .20 .07
❑ 199 Jason Hanson .20 .07
❑ 200 Derrick Mayes .30 .10
❑ 201 Torry Holt .50 .20
❑ 202 Warren Sapp .30 .10
❑ 203 Kimble Anders .20 .07
❑ 204 Blaine Bishop .20 .07
❑ 205 Leroy Hoard .20 .07
❑ 206 Larry Centers .20 .07
❑ 207 O.J. Santiago .20 .07
❑ 208 Antowain Smith .30 .10
❑ 209 Chuck Smith .20 .07
❑ 210 Takeo Spikes .20 .07
❑ 211 Rocket Ismail .30 .10
❑ 212 Ed McCaffrey .50 .20
❑ 213 Karsten Bailey .20 .07
❑ 214 Terry Fair .20 .07
❑ 215 Ken Dilger .20 .07
❑ 216 Jamie Martin .30 .10
❑ 217 Cris Dishman .20 .07
❑ 218 Jay Fiedler .30 .10
❑ 219 Lawyer Milloy .30 .10
❑ 220 Jake Delhomme RC 3.00 1.25
❑ 221 Wayne Chrebet .30 .10
❑ 222 Darrell Russell .20 .07
❑ 223 Christian Fauria .20 .07
❑ 224 Jerome Bettis .50 .20
❑ 225 Ryan Leaf .30 .10
❑ 226 Ricky Watters .30 .10
❑ 227 Keenan McCardell .30 .10
❑ 228 Grant Wistrom .20 .07
❑ 229 Jevon Kearse .50 .20
❑ 230 Frank Sanders .30 .10
❑ 231 Shannon Sharpe .30 .10
❑ 232 Jonathan Linton .20 .07
❑ 233 Alonzo Mayes .20 .07
❑ 234 Jason Garrett .20 .07
❑ 235 Kordell Stewart .30 .10
❑ 236 David LaFleur .20 .07
❑ 237 Kenny Bynum .20 .07
❑ 238 Byron Chamberlain .20 .07
❑ 239 Tyrone Davis .20 .07
❑ 240 Jerome Pathon .30 .10
❑ 241 Alvis Whitted .20 .07
❑ 242 Kevin Lockett .20 .07
❑ 243 Matthew Hatchette .20 .07
❑ 244 Rod Woodson .30 .10
❑ 245 Joe Horn .30 .10
❑ 246 Ronnie Powell .20 .07
❑ 247 Dedric Ward .20 .07
❑ 248 James Johnson .20 .07
❑ 249 James Jett .20 .07
❑ 250 Bobby Shaw RC .50 .20
❑ 251 J.J. Stokes .30 .10
❑ 252 Paul Shields RC .20 .07
❑ 253 Sean Dawkins .20 .07
❑ 254 Hardy Nickerson .20 .07
❑ 255 Stephen Boyd .20 .07
❑ 256 Chris Warren .20 .07
❑ 257 Kerry Collins .30 .10
❑ 258 Isaac Byrd .20 .07
❑ 259 Bobby Hoying .20 .07
❑ 260 Daunte Culpepper .60 .25
❑ 261 Moe Williams .30 .10
❑ 262 Kamil Loud .20 .07
❑ 263 Derrick Brooks .50 .20
❑ 264 Jay Riemersma .20 .07
❑ 265 Ray Lucas .30 .10
❑ 266 Jason Gildon .20 .07
❑ 267 James Stewart .30 .10
❑ 268 Marcellus Wiley .20 .07
❑ 269 Craig Yeast .20 .07
❑ 270 Michael Basnight .20 .07
❑ 271 Tyrone Wheatley .30 .10
❑ 272 Martin Gramatica .20 .07
❑ 273 Phillip Daniels RC .30 .10
❑ 274 Richard Huntley .20 .07
❑ 275 Muhsin Muhammad .30 .10
❑ 276 Todd Lyght .20 .07
❑ 277 Carlester Crumpler .20 .07
❑ 278 Jeff Lewis .20 .07
❑ 279 Jeff George .30 .10
❑ 280 Jeff Blake .30 .10
❑ 281 Michael McCrary .20 .07
❑ 282 Shawn Jefferson .20 .07
❑ 283 Mark Bruener .20 .07
❑ 284 Donnie Abraham .20 .07
❑ 285 Yatil Green .20 .07
❑ 286 Jermaine Lewis .20 .07
❑ 287 Rob Fredrickson .20 .07
❑ 288 Thurman Thomas .30 .10
❑ 289 Kent Graham .20 .07
❑ 290 Darnay Scott .30 .10
❑ 291 Tony Graziani .20 .07
❑ 292 Qadry Ismail .30 .10
❑ 293 Aeneas Williams .20 .07
❑ 294 Marvin Harrison .50 .20
❑ 295 Jimmy Hitchcock .20 .07
❑ 296 Bob Christian .20 .07
❑ 297 Pete Mitchell .20 .07
❑ 298 Mike Alstott .50 .20
❑ 299 Emmitt Smith 1.00 .40
❑ 300 Trevor Pryce .20 .07
❑ 301 Tony Banks .30 .10
❑ 302 Mikhael Ricks .20 .07
❑ 303 Randall Cunningham .50 .20
❑ 304 Thomas Jones RC 1.25 .50
❑ 305 Mark Simoneau RC .60 .25
❑ 306 Jamal Lewis RC 2.00 .75
❑ 307 Kwame Cavil RC .40 .15
❑ 308 Rashard Anderson RC .60 .25
❑ 309 Brian Urlacher RC 3.00 1.25
❑ 310 Peter Warrick RC .75 .30
❑ 311 Courtney Brown RC .75 .30
❑ 312 Michael Wiley RC .60 .25
❑ 313 Chris Cole RC .60 .25
❑ 314 Reuben Droughns RC 1.00 .40
❑ 315 Bubba Franks RC .75 .30
❑ 316 Rob Morris RC .60 .25
❑ 317 R.Jay Soward RC .60 .25
❑ 318 Sylvester Morris RC .60 .25
❑ 319 Ben Kelly RC .40 .15
❑ 320 Doug Chapman RC .60 .25
❑ 321 J.R. Redmond RC .60 .25
❑ 322 Darren Howard RC .60 .25
❑ 323 Ron Dayne RC .75 .30
❑ 324 Chad Pennington RC 2.00 .75

❑ 325 Jerry Porter RC 1.00 .40
❑ 326 Corey Simon RC .75 .30
❑ 327 Plaxico Burress RC 1.50 .60
❑ 328 Trung Canidate RC .60 .25
❑ 329 Rogers Beckett RC .60 .25
❑ 330 Giovanni Carmazzi RC .40 .15
❑ 331 Shaun Alexander RC 4.00 1.50
❑ 332 Joe Hamilton RC .60 .25
❑ 333 Keith Bulluck RC .75 .30
❑ 334 Todd Husak RC .75 .30
❑ 335 D.Walker RC/R.Thompson RC .60 .25
❑ 336 M.Philyaw RC/A.Midget RC .40 .15
❑ 337 C.Redman RC/T.Taylor RC .75 .30
❑ 338 Sam.Morris RC/A.Black RC .60 .25
❑ 339 D.Grant RC/A.McKinley RC .60 .25
❑ 340 D.White RC/F.Murphy RC .75 .30
❑ 341 C.Keaton RC/R.Dugans RC 1.00 .40
❑ 342 Prentice RC/Northcutt RC .60 .25
❑ 343 O.Grant RC/D.Goodrich RC .40 .15
❑ 344 D.O'Neal RC/I.Gold RC .75 .30
❑ 345 S.McDougle RC/B.Green RC .40 .15
❑ 346 A.Lucas RC/N.Diggs RC .60 .25
❑ 347 M.Washington RC/D.Kendra RC .60 .25
❑ 348 T.Slaughter RC/S.Stith RC .60 .25
❑ 349 W.Bartee RC/F.Moreau RC .60 .25
❑ 350 D.Dyer RC/T.Wade RC .60 .25
❑ 351 C.Hovan RC/T.Walters .75 .30
❑ 352 T.Brady RC/Stachelski RC 25.00 12.50
❑ 353 M.Bulger RC/T.Smith RC 1.50 .60
❑ 354 C.Griffin RC/R.Dixon RC .60 .25
❑ 355 L.Coles RC/A.Becht RC .75 .30
❑ 356 Janikowski RC/Lechler RC .75 .30
❑ 357 T.Pinkston RC/G.Scott RC .75 .30
❑ 358 D.Farmer RC/T.Martin RC .60 .25
❑ 359 B.Young RC/J.Shepherd RC .60 .25
❑ 360 J.Seider RC/T.Gaylor RC .60 .25
❑ 361 T.Rattay RC/C.Fields RC .75 .30
❑ 362 D.Jackson RC/J.Williams RC 1.25 .50
❑ 363 N.Webster RC/J.Whalen RC .40 .15
❑ 364 E.Kinney RC/C.Coleman RC .75 .30
❑ 365 C.Samuels RC/L.Murray RC .60 .25
❑ 366 Cardinals IA/Plummer .30 .10
❑ 367 Falcons IA/Chandlr/Andrson .30 .10
❑ 368 Ravens IA/Boulware .20 .07
❑ 369 Bills IA/Flutie .30 .10
❑ 370 Panthers IA/Beuerlein .30 .10
❑ 371 Bears IA/McNown .20 .07
❑ 372 Bengals IA/Dillon .30 .10
❑ 373 Browns IA/Couch .30 .10
❑ 374 Cowboys IA/Smith .50 .20
❑ 375 Broncos IA/Gary .30 .10
❑ 376 Lions IA/Batch .30 .10
❑ 377 Packers IA/Levens .30 .10
❑ 378 Colts IA/James .60 .25
❑ 379 Jaguars IA/Brackens .20 .07
❑ 380 Chiefs IA/Grbac .20 .07
❑ 381 Dolphins IA/Marino .75 .30
❑ 382 Vikings IA/Rob.Smith .30 .10
❑ 383 Patriots IA/Bledsoe .30 .10
❑ 384 Saints IA/Williams .50 .20
❑ 385 Giants IA/Armstead .20 .07
❑ 386 Jets IA/Martin .30 .10
❑ 387 Raiders IA/Kaufman .30 .10
❑ 388 Eagles IA/McNabb .30 .10
❑ 389 Steelers IA/Bettis .30 .10
❑ 390 Rams IA/Faulk .50 .20
❑ 391 Chargers IA/Fazande .20 .07
❑ 392 49ers IA/Garner .30 .10
❑ 393 Seahawks IA/Kennedy .20 .07
❑ 394 Buccaneers IA/Alstott .30 .10
❑ 395 Titans IA/McNair .30 .10
❑ 396 Redskins IA/S.Davis .30 .10
❑ 397 Tim Couch CL .30 .10
❑ 398 Peyton Manning CL .60 .25
❑ 399 Kurt Warner CL .50 .20
❑ 400 Randy Moss CL .50 .20

2001 Fleer Tradition

❑ COMPLETE SET (450) 40.00 20.00
❑ 1 Thomas Jones .40 .15
❑ 2 Bruce Smith .25 .08
❑ 3 Marvin Harrison .60 .25
❑ 4 Darrell Jackson .60 .25
❑ 5 Trent Green .60 .25
❑ 6 Wesley Walls .25 .08
❑ 7 Jimmy Smith .40 .15
❑ 8 Isaac Bruce .60 .25
❑ 9 Jamal Anderson .60 .25
❑ 10 Marty Booker .25 .08

❑ 11 Elvis Grbac .40 .15
❑ 12 Joe Jurevicius .25 .08
❑ 13 Reidel Anthony .25 .08
❑ 14 Darnay Scott .25 .08
❑ 15 Oronde Gadsden .40 .15
❑ 16 Shawn Bryson .25 .08
❑ 17 Jonathan Ogden .25 .08
❑ 18 Aaron Shea .25 .08
❑ 19 Randy Moss 1.25 .50
❑ 20 Eddie George .60 .25
❑ 21 Stephen Davis .60 .25
❑ 22 Emmitt Smith 1.25 .50
❑ 23 Willie McGinest .25 .08
❑ 24 Trent Dilfer .40 .15
❑ 25 Peter Boulware .25 .08
❑ 26 Rod Smith .40 .15
❑ 27 Ricky Williams .60 .25
❑ 28 Albert Connell .25 .08
❑ 29 Robert Porcher .25 .08
❑ 30 Jessie Armstead .25 .08
❑ 31 Shane Matthews .25 .08
❑ 32 Eric Moulds .40 .15
❑ 33 Kurt Schulz .25 .08
❑ 34 Richie Anderson .25 .08
❑ 35 Ron Dugans .25 .08
❑ 36 Steve Beuerlein .40 .15
❑ 37 Darren Sharper .25 .08
❑ 38 Andre Rison .40 .15
❑ 39 Courtney Brown .40 .15
❑ 40 Eddie Kennison .40 .15
❑ 41 Ken Dilger .25 .08
❑ 42 Charles Johnson .25 .08
❑ 43 Dexter Coakley .25 .08
❑ 44 Akili Smith .25 .08
❑ 45 R.Jay Soward .25 .08
❑ 46 Danny Farmer .25 .08
❑ 47 Dez White .25 .08
❑ 48 Olandis Gary .40 .15
❑ 49 Wali Rainer .25 .08
❑ 50 Derrick Alexander .40 .15
❑ 51 Donnie Abraham .25 .08
❑ 52 David Sloan .25 .08
❑ 53 Larry Allen .25 .08
❑ 54 Sam Madison .25 .08
❑ 55 Troy Edwards .25 .08
❑ 56 Ryan Longwell .25 .08
❑ 57 Brian Griese .60 .25
❑ 58 John Randle .40 .15
❑ 59 Reggie Jones .25 .08
❑ 60 Mike Peterson .25 .08
❑ 61 Bill Romanowski .25 .08
❑ 62 Kevin Faulk .40 .15
❑ 63 Tai Streets .25 .08
❑ 64 Tony Brackens .25 .08
❑ 65 James Stewart .40 .15
❑ 66 Joe Horn .40 .15
❑ 67 Kurt Warner 1.25 .50
❑ 68 Eric Hicks RC .25 .08
❑ 69 Bryan Westbrook .25 .08
❑ 70 Tiki Barber .60 .25
❑ 71 Frank Sanders .25 .08
❑ 72 Olindo Mare .25 .08
❑ 73 Bill Schroeder .40 .15
❑ 74 Anthony Becht .25 .08
❑ 75 Rob Johnson .40 .15
❑ 76 Troy Brown .40 .15
❑ 77 Chad Bratzke .25 .08
❑ 78 Rickey Dudley .25 .08
❑ 79 Doug Johnson .25 .08
❑ 80 Joe Johnson .25 .08
❑ 81 Keenan McCardell .25 .08
❑ 82 Tim Brown .60 .25
❑ 83 Blaine Bishop .25 .08
❑ 84 Ron Dixon .25 .08
❑ 85 Michael Cloud .25 .08
❑ 86 Todd Pinkston .25 .08
❑ 87 Shannon Sharpe .40 .15
❑ 88 Marvin Jones .25 .08
❑ 89 Zach Thomas .60 .25
❑ 90 Kordell Stewart .40 .15
❑ 91 Champ Bailey .40 .15
❑ 92 Jacquez Green .25 .08
❑ 93 Daunte Culpepper .60 .25
❑ 94 Freddie Jones .25 .08
❑ 95 Donald Hayes .25 .08
❑ 96 Rich Gannon .60 .25
❑ 97 Ty Law .40 .15
❑ 98 Grant Wistrom .25 .08
❑ 99 James Allen .40 .15
❑ 100 Corey Simon .40 .15
❑ 101 Jeff Blake .40 .15
❑ 102 Bryant Young .25 .08
❑ 103 Craig Yeast .25 .08
❑ 104 Bobby Shaw .25 .08
❑ 105 Kerry Collins .40 .15
❑ 106 Brock Huard .25 .08
❑ 107 JaJuan Dawson .25 .08
❑ 108 Jeff Graham .25 .08
❑ 109 Chad Pennington 1.00 .40
❑ 110 Jake Plummer .40 .15
❑ 111 James McKnight .40 .15
❑ 112 Terrell Owens .60 .25
❑ 113 Mo Lewis .25 .08
❑ 114 Jeremy McDaniel .25 .08
❑ 115 Ed McCaffrey .60 .25
❑ 116 Ricky Watters .25 .08
❑ 117 Jerry Porter .40 .15
❑ 118 Shawn Jefferson .25 .08
❑ 119 Charlie Batch .60 .25
❑ 120 Justin Watson .25 .08
❑ 121 Donovan McNabb .75 .30
❑ 122 Shaun King .25 .08
❑ 123 Brett Favre 2.00 .75
❑ 124 Ronald McKinnon .25 .08
❑ 125 Richard Huntley .25 .08
❑ 126 Ray Lewis .60 .25
❑ 127 Jerome Pathon .40 .15
❑ 128 Sam Cowart .25 .08
❑ 129 Ryan Leaf .40 .15
❑ 130 Greg Clark .25 .08
❑ 131 Tony Boselli .25 .08
❑ 132 Frank Wycheck .25 .08
❑ 133 Charlie Garner .40 .15
❑ 134 Tony Siragusa .25 .08
❑ 135 Sylvester Morris .25 .08
❑ 136 Qadry Ismail .40 .15
❑ 137 Jon Kitna .40 .15
❑ 138 James Thrash .40 .15
❑ 139 Lamar Smith .40 .15
❑ 140 Brad Johnson .60 .25
❑ 141 London Fletcher .25 .08
❑ 142 Tim Biakabutuka .40 .15
❑ 143 Ed McDaniel .25 .08
❑ 144 Tony Parrish .25 .08
❑ 145 David Boston .60 .25
❑ 146 Brian Urlacher 1.00 .40
❑ 147 Drew Bledsoe .75 .30
❑ 148 David Patten .25 .08
❑ 149 Marcellus Wiley .25 .08
❑ 150 Peter Warrick .60 .25
❑ 151 La'Roi Glover .25 .08
❑ 152 Troy Aikman 1.00 .40
❑ 153 Chris Chandler .40 .15
❑ 154 Travis Prentice .25 .08
❑ 155 Ike Hilliard .40 .15
❑ 156 John Mobley .25 .08
❑ 157 Warren Sapp .40 .15
❑ 158 Joey Galloway .40 .15
❑ 159 Laveranues Coles .60 .25
❑ 160 Germane Crowell .25 .08
❑ 161 Jamal Lewis 1.00 .40
❑ 162 Mike Anderson .60 .25
❑ 163 Charles Woodson .40 .15
❑ 164 Antonio Freeman .60 .25
❑ 165 Derrick Mason .40 .15
❑ 166 Chris Claiborne .25 .08
❑ 167 Brian Mitchell .25 .08
❑ 168 Mike Vanderjagt .25 .08
❑ 169 Rod Woodson .40 .15
❑ 170 Doug Chapman .25 .08
❑ 171 John Lynch .40 .15

❑ 172	Kevin Hardy	.25	.08
❑ 173	Sam Shade	.25	.08
❑ 174	Edgerrin James	.75	.30
❑ 175	Brian Dawkins	.40	.15
❑ 176	Donnie Edwards	.25	.08
❑ 177	Patrick Jeffers	.40	.15
❑ 178	Mark Brunell	.60	.25
❑ 179	Junior Seau	.60	.25
❑ 180	Trace Armstrong	.25	.08
❑ 181	Marcus Robinson	.60	.25
❑ 182	Tony Gonzalez	.40	.15
❑ 183	J.J. Stokes	.40	.15
❑ 184	Jake Reed	.40	.15
❑ 185	Corey Dillon	.60	.25
❑ 186	Jay Fiedler	.60	.25
❑ 187	Christian Fauria	.25	.08
❑ 188	Sammy Knight	.25	.08
❑ 189	Kevin Johnson	.40	.15
❑ 190	Matthew Hatchette	.25	.08
❑ 191	Az-Zahir Hakim	.40	.15
❑ 192	Keith Hamilton	.25	.08
❑ 193	Darren Woodson	.25	.08
❑ 194	Terry Glenn	.40	.15
❑ 195	Simeon Rice	.40	.15
❑ 196	Keyshawn Johnson	.60	.25
❑ 197	Terrell Davis	.60	.25
❑ 198	William Roaf	.25	.08
❑ 199	Doug Flutie	.60	.25
❑ 200	Kevin Carter	.25	.08
❑ 201	Stephen Boyd	.25	.08
❑ 202	Michael Strahan	.40	.15
❑ 203	Ray Buchanan	.25	.08
❑ 204	Tyrone Wheatley	.40	.15
❑ 205	Jason Hanson	.25	.08
❑ 206	Wayne Chrebet	.40	.15
❑ 207	Samari Rolle	.25	.08
❑ 208	Duce Staley	.60	.25
❑ 209	Dorsey Levens	.40	.15
❑ 210	Sebastian Janikowski	.25	.08
❑ 211	Duane Starks	.25	.08
❑ 212	Jason Gildon	.25	.08
❑ 213	Terrence Wilkins	.25	.08
❑ 214	Eric Allen	.25	.08
❑ 215	Deion Sanders	.60	.25
❑ 216	Curtis Conway	.40	.15
❑ 217	Fred Taylor	.60	.25
❑ 218	Troy Vincent	.25	.08
❑ 219	Mike Minter RC	.40	.15
❑ 220	Jeff Garcia	.60	.25
❑ 221	Tony Richardson	.25	.08
❑ 222	Jerome Bettis	.60	.25
❑ 223	Chad Morton	.25	.08
❑ 224	Tony Horne	.25	.08
❑ 225	Dave Moore	.25	.08
❑ 226	Victor Green	.25	.08
❑ 227	Chris Sanders	.25	.08
❑ 228	Marshall Faulk	.75	.30
❑ 229	Cris Carter	.60	.25
❑ 230	Rodney Harrison	.25	.08
❑ 231	Tim Couch	.40	.15
❑ 232	Antowain Smith	.40	.15
❑ 233	Lawyer Milloy	.40	.15
❑ 234	Lance Schulters	.25	.08
❑ 235	Michael Wiley	.25	.08
❑ 236	Steve McNair	.60	.25
❑ 237	Aaron Brooks	.60	.25
❑ 238	Anthony Simmons	.25	.08
❑ 239	Dwayne Carswell	.25	.08
❑ 240	Priest Holmes	.75	.30
❑ 241	Amani Toomer	.40	.15
❑ 242	Aeneas Williams	.25	.08
❑ 243	MarTay Jenkins	.25	.08
❑ 244	Jeff George	.40	.15
❑ 245	Vinny Testaverde	.40	.15
❑ 246	Peerless Price	.40	.15
❑ 247	Bubba Franks	.40	.15
❑ 248	Randall Cunningham	.60	.25
❑ 249	Aaron Glenn	.25	.08
❑ 250	Terance Mathis	.40	.15
❑ 251	Peyton Manning	1.50	.60
❑ 252	Terrell Buckley	.25	.08
❑ 253	Greg Biekert	.25	.08
❑ 254	Martin Gramatica	.25	.08
❑ 255	Kyle Brady	.25	.08
❑ 256	Johnnie Morton	.40	.15
❑ 257	Jeremiah Trotter	.40	.15
❑ 258	Travis Taylor	.40	.15
❑ 259	Frank Moreau	.25	.08
❑ 260	LeRoy Butler	.25	.08
❑ 261	Plaxico Burress	.60	.25
❑ 262	Randall Godfrey	.25	.08
❑ 263	Jason Taylor	.25	.08
❑ 264	Jeff Burris	.25	.08
❑ 265	Jim Harbaugh	.40	.15
❑ 266	Marco Coleman	.25	.08
❑ 267	Robert Smith	.40	.15
❑ 268	Mike Hollis	.25	.08
❑ 269	Jerry Rice	1.25	.50
❑ 270	Muhsin Muhammad	.40	.15
❑ 271	J.R. Redmond	.25	.08
❑ 272	Brian Walker	.25	.08
❑ 273	Orlando Pace	.25	.08
❑ 274	Cade McNown	.25	.08
❑ 275	Darren Howard	.25	.08
❑ 276	Ron Dayne	.60	.25
❑ 277	Shaun Alexander	.75	.30
❑ 278	Brandon Bennett	.25	.08
❑ 279	Jason Sehorn	.25	.08
❑ 280	Matt Hasselbeck	.40	.15
❑ 281	Michael Pittman	.25	.08
❑ 282	Dennis Northcutt	.40	.15
❑ 283	Dedric Ward	.25	.08
❑ 284	Curtis Martin	.60	.25
❑ 285	Sammy Morris	.25	.08
❑ 286	Rocket Ismail	.40	.15
❑ 287	Jon Ritchie	.25	.08
❑ 288	Shaun Ellis	.25	.08
❑ 289	Tim Dwight	.60	.25
❑ 290	Trevor Pryce	.25	.08
❑ 291	Warrick Dunn	.60	.25
❑ 292	Napoleon Kaufman	.40	.15
❑ 293	Mike Alstott	.60	.25
❑ 294	Herman Moore	.40	.15
❑ 295	Chad Lewis	.25	.08
❑ 296	Hugh Douglas	.25	.08
❑ 297	Chris Redman	.25	.08
❑ 298	Ahman Green	.60	.25
❑ 299	Hines Ward	.60	.25
❑ 300	Mark Bruener	.25	.08
❑ 301	Jevon Kearse	.40	.15
❑ 302	Jermaine Fazande	.25	.08
❑ 303	Terrell Fletcher	.25	.08
❑ 304	Torry Holt	.60	.25
❑ 305	Chris McAlister	.25	.08
❑ 306	Jason Elam	.25	.08
❑ 307	Fred Beasley	.25	.08
❑ 308	Frank Wycheck UH	.25	.08
❑ 309	Michael McCrary UH	.25	.08
❑ 310	Mark Brunell UH	.60	.25
❑ 311	Tim Couch UH	.40	.15
❑ 312	Takeo Spikes UH	.25	.08
❑ 313	Jerome Bettis UH	.40	.15
❑ 314	Zach Thomas UH	.60	.25
❑ 315	Drew Bledsoe UH	.60	.25
❑ 316	Wayne Chrebet UH	.25	.08
❑ 317	Jay Riemersma UH	.25	.08
❑ 318	Marvin Harrison UH	.40	.15
❑ 319	Ed McCaffrey UH	.40	.15
❑ 320	Tony Gonzalez UH	.25	.08
❑ 321	Tim Brown UH	.40	.15
❑ 322	Junior Seau UH	.40	.15
❑ 323	Shawn Springs UH	.25	.08
❑ 324	Troy Aikman UH	.40	.15
❑ 325	Pat Tillman UH RC	20.00	8.00
❑ 326	David Akers UH RC	.40	.15
❑ 327	Michael Strahan UH	.40	.15
❑ 328	Darrell Green UH	.25	.08
❑ 329	Kurt Warner UH	.60	.25
❑ 330	Jeff Garcia UH	.40	.15
❑ 331	Aaron Brooks UH	.40	.15
❑ 332	Jamal Anderson UH	.40	.15
❑ 333	Brad Hoover UH	.25	.08
❑ 334	Cris Carter UH	.40	.15
❑ 335	Derrick Brooks UH	.60	.25
❑ 336	Antonio Freeman UH	.40	.15
❑ 337	Luther Elliss UH	.25	.08
❑ 338	James Allen UH	.25	.08
❑ 339	Arizona Cardinals TC	.40	.15
❑ 340	Atlanta Falcons TC	.40	.15
❑ 341	Baltimore Ravens TC	.25	.08
❑ 342	Buffalo Bills TC	.25	.08
❑ 343	Carolina Panthers TC	.25	.08
❑ 344	Chicago Bears TC	.60	.25
❑ 345	Cincinnati Bengals TC	.40	.15
❑ 346	Cleveland Browns TC	.25	.08
❑ 347	Cowboys TC/Emmitt	.60	.25
❑ 348	Denver Broncos TC	.40	.15
❑ 349	Detroit Lions TC	.25	.08
❑ 350	Packers TC/Favre	1.00	.40
❑ 351	Colts TC/James	.60	.25
❑ 352	Jacksonville Jaguars TC	.60	.25
❑ 353	Kansas City Chiefs TC	.25	.08
❑ 354	Miami Dolphins TC	.40	.15
❑ 355	Minnesota Vikings TC	.60	.25
❑ 356	New England Patriots TC	.60	.25
❑ 357	New Orleans Saints TC	.40	.15
❑ 358	New York Giants TC	.40	.15
❑ 359	New York Jets TC	.40	.15
❑ 360	Oakland Raiders TC	.40	.15
❑ 361	Philadelphia Eagles TC	.60	.25
❑ 362	Pittsburgh Steelers TC	.40	.15
❑ 363	San Diego Chargers TC	.25	.08
❑ 364	San Francisco 49ers TC	.25	.08
❑ 365	Seattle Seahawks TC	.25	.08
❑ 366	Rams TC/Warner	.60	.25
❑ 367	Tampa Bay Buccaneers TC	.40	.15
❑ 368	Tennessee Titans TC	.40	.15
❑ 369	Washington Redskins TC	.40	.15
❑ 370	Buffalo Bills TL	.25	.08
❑ 371	Indianapolis Colts TL	.60	.25
❑ 372	Miami Dolphins TL	.25	.08
❑ 373	New England Patriots TL	.40	.15
❑ 374	New York Jets TL	.40	.15
❑ 375	Baltimore Ravens TL	.40	.15
❑ 376	Cincinnati Bengals TL	.25	.08
❑ 377	Cleveland Browns TL	.25	.08
❑ 378	Jacksonville Jaguars TL	.40	.15
❑ 379	Pittsburgh Steelers TL	.40	.15
❑ 380	Tennessee Titans TL	.40	.15
❑ 381	Denver Broncos TL	.40	.15
❑ 382	Kansas City Chiefs TL	.40	.15
❑ 383	Oakland Raiders TL	.40	.15
❑ 384	San Diego Chargers TL	.40	.15
❑ 385	Seattle Seahawks TL	.25	.08
❑ 386	Arizona Cardinals TL	.25	.08
❑ 387	Dallas Cowboys TL	.60	.25
❑ 388	New York Giants TL	.40	.15
❑ 389	Philadelphia Eagles TL	.40	.15
❑ 390	Washington Redskins TL	.40	.15
❑ 391	Chicago Bears TL	.25	.08
❑ 392	Detroit Lions TL	.25	.08
❑ 393	Green Bay Packers TL	.60	.25
❑ 394	Minnesota Vikings TL	.60	.25
❑ 395	Tampa Bay Buccaneers TL	.40	.15
❑ 396	Atlanta Falcons TL	.25	.08
❑ 397	Carolina Panthers TL	.25	.08
❑ 398	New Orleans Saints TL	.40	.15
❑ 399	San Francisco 49ersTL	.40	.15
❑ 400	St. Louis Rams TL	.60	.25
❑ 401	Michael Vick RC	6.00	2.50
❑ 402	Drew Brees RC	4.00	1.50
❑ 403	Michael Bennett RC	1.25	.50
❑ 404	David Terrell RC	1.25	.50
❑ 405	Deuce McAllister RC	2.50	1.00
❑ 406	Santana Moss RC	2.00	.75
❑ 407	Koren Robinson RC	1.25	.50
❑ 408	Chris Weinke RC	1.25	.50
❑ 409	Reggie Wayne RC	2.50	1.00
❑ 410	Rod Gardner RC	1.25	.50
❑ 411	James Jackson RC	1.25	.50
❑ 412	Travis Henry RC	2.00	.75
❑ 413	Josh Heupel RC	1.25	.50
❑ 414	LaDainian Tomlinson RC	15.00	7.50
❑ 415	Chad Johnson RC	3.00	1.25
❑ 416	Sage Rosenfels RC	1.25	.50
❑ 417	Quincy Morgan RC	1.25	.50
❑ 418	Ken-Yon Rambo RC	.75	.30
❑ 419	LaMont Jordan RC	2.50	1.00
❑ 420	Anthony Thomas RC	1.25	.50
❑ 421	Dave Dickenson RC	.75	.30
❑ 422	Travis Minor RC	.75	.30
❑ 423	Kevan Barlow RC	1.25	.50
❑ 424	Chris Chambers RC	2.00	.75
❑ 425	Richard Seymour RC	1.25	.50
❑ 426	Gerard Warren RC	1.25	.50
❑ 427	Jamar Fletcher RC	.75	.30
❑ 428	Freddie Mitchell RC	1.25	.50
❑ 429	Jamal Reynolds RC	1.25	.50
❑ 430	Marques Tuiasosopo RC	1.25	.50
❑ 431	Snoop Minnis RC	.75	.30
❑ 432	Mike McMahon RC	1.25	.50
❑ 433	Robert Ferguson RC	1.25	.50
❑ 434	Ronney Daniels RC	.50	.20
❑ 435	Rudi Johnson RC	2.50	1.00
❑ 436	Vinny Sutherland RC	.75	.30
❑ 437	Josh Booty RC	1.25	.50
❑ 438	Reggie White RC	.75	.30

❑	439	Todd Heap RC	1.25	.50
❑	440	Justin Smith RC	1.25	.50
❑	441	Andre Carter RC	1.25	.50
❑	442	Bobby Newcombe RC	.75	.30
❑	443	Alex Bannister RC	.75	.30
❑	444	Correll Buckhalter RC	1.50	.60
❑	445	Quincy Carter RC	1.25	.50
❑	446	Jesse Palmer RC	1.25	.50
❑	447	Heath Evans RC	.75	.30
❑	448	Dan Morgan RC	1.25	.50
❑	449	Justin McCareins RC	1.25	.50
❑	450	Alge Crumpler RC	1.50	.60

2001 Fleer Tradition Glossy

❑		COMP.SET w/o SP's (400)	40.00	20.00
❑	1	Thomas Jones	.50	.20
❑	2	Bruce Smith	.30	.10
❑	3	Marvin Harrison	.75	.30
❑	4	Darrell Jackson	.75	.30
❑	5	Trent Green	.75	.30
❑	6	Wesley Walls	.30	.10
❑	7	Jimmy Smith	.50	.20
❑	8	Isaac Bruce	.75	.30
❑	9	Jamal Anderson	.75	.30
❑	10	Marty Booker	.30	.10
❑	11	Elvis Grbac	.50	.20
❑	12	Joe Jurevicius	.30	.10
❑	13	Reidel Anthony	.30	.10
❑	14	Darnay Scott	.30	.10
❑	15	Oronde Gadsden	.50	.20
❑	16	Shawn Bryson	.30	.10
❑	17	Jonathan Ogden	.30	.10
❑	18	Aaron Shea	.30	.10
❑	19	Randy Moss	1.50	.60
❑	20	Eddie George	.75	.30
❑	21	Stephen Davis	.75	.30
❑	22	Emmitt Smith	1.50	.60
❑	23	Willie McGinest	.30	.10
❑	24	Trent Dilfer	.50	.20
❑	25	Peter Boulware	.30	.10
❑	26	Rod Smith	.50	.20
❑	27	Ricky Williams	.75	.30
❑	28	Albert Connell	.30	.10
❑	29	Robert Porcher	.30	.10
❑	30	Jessie Armstead	.30	.10
❑	31	Shane Matthews	.30	.10
❑	32	Eric Moulds	.50	.20
❑	33	Kurt Schulz	.30	.10
❑	34	Richie Anderson	.30	.10
❑	35	Ron Dugans	.30	.10
❑	36	Steve Beuerlein	.50	.20
❑	37	Darren Sharper	.30	.10
❑	38	Andre Rison	.50	.20
❑	39	Courtney Brown	.50	.20
❑	40	Eddie Kennison	.50	.20
❑	41	Ken Dilger	.30	.10
❑	42	Charles Johnson	.30	.10
❑	43	Dexter Coakley	.30	.10
❑	44	Akili Smith	.30	.10
❑	45	R.Jay Soward	.30	.10
❑	46	Danny Farmer	.30	.10
❑	47	Dez White	.30	.10
❑	48	Olandis Gary	.50	.20
❑	49	Wali Rainer	.30	.10
❑	50	Derrick Alexander	.50	.20
❑	51	Donnie Abraham	.30	.10
❑	52	David Sloan	.30	.10
❑	53	Larry Allen	.30	.10
❑	54	Sam Madison	.30	.10
❑	55	Troy Edwards	.30	.10
❑	56	Ryan Longwell	.30	.10
❑	57	Brian Griese	.75	.30
❑	58	John Randle	.50	.20
❑	59	Reggie Jones	.30	.10
❑	60	Mike Peterson	.30	.10
❑	61	Bill Romanowski	.30	.10
❑	62	Kevin Faulk	.50	.20
❑	63	Tai Streets	.30	.10
❑	64	Tony Brackens	.30	.10
❑	65	James Stewart	.50	.20
❑	66	Joe Horn	.50	.20
❑	67	Kurt Warner	1.50	.60
❑	68	Eric Hicks RC	.30	.10
❑	69	Bryan Westbrook	.30	.10
❑	70	Tiki Barber	.75	.30
❑	71	Frank Sanders	.30	.10
❑	72	Olindo Mare	.30	.10
❑	73	Bill Schroeder	.50	.20
❑	74	Anthony Becht	.30	.10
❑	75	Rob Johnson	.50	.20
❑	76	Troy Brown	.50.	.20
❑	77	Chad Bratzke	.30	.10
❑	78	Rickey Dudley	.30	.10
❑	79	Doug Johnson	.30	.10
❑	80	Joe Johnson	.30	.10
❑	81	Keenan McCardell	.30	.10
❑	82	Tim Brown	.75	.30
❑	83	Blaine Bishop	.30	.10
❑	84	Ron Dixon	.30	.10
❑	85	Michael Cloud	.30	.10
❑	86	Todd Pinkston	.30	.10
❑	87	Shannon Sharpe	.50	.20
❑	88	Marvin Jones	.30	.10
❑	89	Zach Thomas	.75	.30
❑	90	Kordell Stewart	.50	.20
❑	91	Champ Bailey	.50	.20
❑	92	Jacquez Green	.30	.10
❑	93	Daunte Culpepper	.75	.30
❑	94	Freddie Jones	.30	.10
❑	95	Donald Hayes	.30	.10
❑	96	Rich Gannon	.75	.30
❑	97	Ty Law	.50	.20
❑	98	Grant Wistrom	.30	.10
❑	99	James Allen	.50	.20
❑	100	Corey Simon	.50	.20
❑	101	Jeff Blake	.50	.20
❑	102	Bryant Young	.30	.10
❑	103	Craig Yeast	.30	.10
❑	104	Bobby Shaw	.30	.10
❑	105	Kerry Collins	.50	.20
❑	106	Brock Huard	.30	.10
❑	107	JaJuan Dawson	.30	.10
❑	108	Jeff Graham	.30	.10
❑	109	Chad Pennington	1.25	.50
❑	110	Jake Plummer	.50	.20
❑	111	James McKnight	.50	.20
❑	112	Terrell Owens	.75	.30
❑	113	Mo Lewis	.30	.10
❑	114	Jeremy McDaniel	.30	.10
❑	115	Ed McCaffrey	.75	.30
❑	116	Ricky Watters	.30	.10
❑	117	Jerry Porter	.50	.20
❑	118	Shawn Jefferson	.30	.10
❑	119	Charlie Batch	.75	.30
❑	120	Justin Watson	.30	.10
❑	121	Donovan McNabb	1.00	.40
❑	122	Shaun King	.30	.10
❑	123	Brett Favre	2.50	1.00
❑	124	Ronald McKinnon	.30	.10
❑	125	Richard Huntley	.30	.10
❑	126	Ray Lewis	.75	.30
❑	127	Jerome Pathon	.50	.20
❑	128	Sam Cowart	.30	.10
❑	129	Ryan Leaf	.50	.20
❑	130	Greg Clark	.30	.10
❑	131	Tony Boselli	.30	.10
❑	132	Frank Wycheck	.30	.10
❑	133	Charlie Garner	.50	.20
❑	134	Tony Siragusa	.30	.10
❑	135	Sylvester Morris	.30	.10
❑	136	Qadry Ismail	.50	.20
❑	137	Jon Kitna	.50	.20
❑	138	James Thrash	.50	.20
❑	139	Lamar Smith	.50	.20
❑	140	Brad Johnson	.75	.30
❑	141	London Fletcher	.30	.10
❑	142	Tim Biakabutuka	.50	.20
❑	143	Ed McDaniel	.30	.10
❑	144	Tony Parrish	.30	.10
❑	145	David Boston	.75	.30
❑	146	Brian Urlacher	1.25	.50
❑	147	Drew Bledsoe	1.00	.40
❑	148	David Patten	.30	.10
❑	149	Marcellus Wiley	.30	.10
❑	150	Peter Warrick	.75	.30
❑	151	La'Roi Glover	.30	.10
❑	152	Troy Aikman	1.25	.50
❑	153	Chris Chandler	.50	.20
❑	154	Travis Prentice	.30	.10
❑	155	Ike Hilliard	.50	.20
❑	156	John Mobley	.30	.10
❑	157	Warren Sapp	.50	.20
❑	158	Joey Galloway	.50	.20
❑	159	Laveranues Coles	.75	.30
❑	160	Germane Crowell	.30	.10
❑	161	Jamal Lewis	1.25	.50
❑	162	Mike Anderson	.75	.30
❑	163	Charles Woodson	.50	.20
❑	164	Antonio Freeman	.75	.30
❑	165	Derrick Mason	.50	.20
❑	166	Chris Claiborne	.30	.10
❑	167	Brian Mitchell	.30	.10
❑	168	Mike Vanderjagt	.30	.10
❑	169	Rod Woodson	.50	.20
❑	170	Doug Chapman	.30	.10
❑	171	John Lynch	.50	.20
❑	172	Kevin Hardy	.30	.10
❑	173	Sam Shade	.30	.10
❑	174	Edgerrin James	1.00	.40
❑	175	Brian Dawkins	.50	.20
❑	176	Donnie Edwards	.30	.10
❑	177	Patrick Jeffers	.50	.20
❑	178	Mark Brunell	.75	.30
❑	179	Junior Seau	.75	.30
❑	180	Trace Armstrong	.30	.10
❑	181	Marcus Robinson	.75	.30
❑	182	Tony Gonzalez	.50	.20
❑	183	J.J. Stokes	.50	.20
❑	184	Jake Reed	.50	.20
❑	185	Corey Dillon	.75	.30
❑	186	Jay Fiedler	.75	.30
❑	187	Christian Fauria	.30	.10
❑	188	Sammy Knight	.30	.10
❑	189	Kevin Johnson	.50	.20
❑	190	Matthew Hatchette	.30	.10
❑	191	Az-Zahir Hakim	.50	.20
❑	192	Keith Hamilton	.30	.10
❑	193	Darren Woodson	.30	.10
❑	194	Terry Glenn	.50	.20
❑	195	Simeon Rice	.50	.20
❑	196	Keyshawn Johnson	.75	.30
❑	197	Terrell Davis	.75	.30
❑	198	William Roaf	.30	.10
❑	199	Doug Flutie	.75	.30
❑	200	Kevin Carter	.30	.10
❑	201	Stephen Boyd	.30	.10
❑	202	Michael Strahan	.50	.20
❑	203	Ray Buchanan	.30	.10
❑	204	Tyrone Wheatley	.50	.20
❑	205	Jason Hanson	.30	.10
❑	206	Wayne Chrebet	.50	.20
❑	207	Samari Rolle	.30	.10
❑	208	Duce Staley	.75	.30
❑	209	Dorsey Levens	.50	.20
❑	210	Sebastian Janikowski	.30	.10
❑	211	Duane Starks	.30	.10
❑	212	Jason Gildon	.30	.10
❑	213	Terrence Wilkins	.30	.10
❑	214	Eric Allen	.30	.10
❑	215	Deion Sanders	.75	.30
❑	216	Curtis Conway	.50	.20
❑	217	Fred Taylor	.75	.30
❑	218	Troy Vincent	.30	.10
❑	219	Mike Minter	.50	.20
❑	220	Jeff Garcia	.75	.30
❑	221	Tony Richardson	.30	.10
❑	222	Jerome Bettis	.75	.30
❑	223	Chad Morton	.30	.10
❑	224	Tony Horne	.30	.10
❑	225	Dave Moore	.30	.10
❑	226	Victor Green	.30	.10
❑	227	Chris Sanders	.30	.10
❑	228	Marshall Faulk	1.00	.40
❑	229	Cris Carter	.75	.30
❑	230	Rodney Harrison	.30	.10
❑	231	Tim Couch	.50	.20
❑	232	Antowain Smith	.50	.20
❑	233	Lawyer Milloy	.50	.20

❑ 234 Lance Schulters .30 .10
❑ 235 Michael Wiley .30 .10
❑ 236 Steve McNair .75 .30
❑ 237 Aaron Brooks .75 .30
❑ 238 Anthony Simmons .30 .10
❑ 239 Dwayne Carswell .30 .10
❑ 240 Priest Holmes 1.00 .40
❑ 241 Amani Toomer .50 .20
❑ 242 Aeneas Williams .30 .10
❑ 243 MarTay Jenkins .30 .10
❑ 244 Jeff George .50 .20
❑ 245 Vinny Testaverde .50 .20
❑ 246 Peerless Price .50 .20
❑ 247 Bubba Franks .50 .20
❑ 248 Randall Cunningham .75 .30
❑ 249 Aaron Glenn .30 .10
❑ 250 Terance Mathis .50 .20
❑ 251 Peyton Manning 2.00 .75
❑ 252 Terrell Buckley .30 .10
❑ 253 Greg Biekert .30 .10
❑ 254 Martin Gramatica .30 .10
❑ 255 Kyle Brady .30 .10
❑ 256 Johnnie Morton .50 .20
❑ 257 Jeremiah Trotter .50 .20
❑ 258 Travis Taylor .50 .20
❑ 259 Frank Moreau .30 .10
❑ 260 LeRoy Butler .30 .10
❑ 261 Plaxico Burress .75 .30
❑ 262 Randall Godfrey .30 .10
❑ 263 Jason Taylor .30 .10
❑ 264 Jeff Burris .30 .10
❑ 265 Jim Harbaugh .50 .20
❑ 266 Marco Coleman .30 .10
❑ 267 Robert Smith .50 .20
❑ 268 Mike Hollis .30 .10
❑ 269 Jerry Rice 1.50 .60
❑ 270 Muhsin Muhammad .50 .20
❑ 271 J.R. Redmond .30 .10
❑ 272 Brian Walker .30 .10
❑ 273 Orlando Pace .30 .10
❑ 274 Cade McNown .30 .10
❑ 275 Darren Howard .30 .10
❑ 276 Ron Dayne .75 .30
❑ 277 Shaun Alexander 1.00 .40
❑ 278 Brandon Bennett .30 .10
❑ 279 Jason Sehorn .30 .10
❑ 280 Matt Hasselbeck .50 .20
❑ 281 Michael Pittman .30 .10
❑ 282 Dennis Northcutt .50 .20
❑ 283 Dedric Ward .30 .10
❑ 284 Curtis Martin .75 .30
❑ 285 Sammy Morris .30 .10
❑ 286 Rocket Ismail .50 .20
❑ 287 Jon Ritchie .30 .10
❑ 288 Shaun Ellis .30 .10
❑ 289 Tim Dwight .75 .30
❑ 290 Trevor Pryce .30 .10
❑ 291 Warrick Dunn .75 .30
❑ 292 Napoleon Kaufman .50 .20
❑ 293 Mike Alstott .75 .30
❑ 294 Herman Moore .50 .20
❑ 295 Chad Lewis .30 .10
❑ 296 Hugh Douglas .30 .10
❑ 297 Chris Redman .30 .10
❑ 298 Ahman Green .75 .30
❑ 299 Hines Ward .75 .30
❑ 300 Mark Bruener .30 .10
❑ 301 Jevon Kearse .50 .20
❑ 302 Jermaine Fazande .30 .10
❑ 303 Terrell Fletcher .30 .10
❑ 304 Torry Holt .75 .30
❑ 305 Chris McAlister .30 .10
❑ 306 Jason Elam .30 .10
❑ 307 Fred Beasley .30 .10
❑ 308 Frank Wycheck UH .30 .10
❑ 309 Michael McCrary UH .30 .10
❑ 310 Mark Brunell UH .75 .30
❑ 311 Tim Couch UH .50 .20
❑ 312 Takeo Spikes UH .30 .10
❑ 313 Jerome Bettis UH .50 .20
❑ 314 Zach Thomas UH .75 .30
❑ 315 Drew Bledsoe UH .75 .30
❑ 316 Wayne Chrebet UH .30 .10
❑ 317 Jay Riemersma UH .30 .10
❑ 318 Marvin Harrison UH .50 .20
❑ 319 Ed McCaffrey UH .50 .20
❑ 320 Tony Gonzalez UH .30 .10
❑ 321 Tim Brown UH .50 .20
❑ 322 Junior Seau UH .50 .20
❑ 323 Shawn Springs UH .30 .10
❑ 324 Troy Aikman UH .75 .30
❑ 325 Pat Tillman UH RC 20.00 8.00
❑ 326 David Akers UH RC .50 .20
❑ 327 Michael Strahan UH .50 .20
❑ 328 Darrell Green UH .30 .10
❑ 329 Kurt Warner UH 1.00 .40
❑ 330 Jeff Garcia UH .50 .20
❑ 331 Aaron Brooks UH .50 .20
❑ 332 Jamal Anderson UH .50 .20
❑ 333 Brad Hoover UH .30 .10
❑ 334 Cris Carter UH .50 .20
❑ 335 Derrick Brooks UH .75 .30
❑ 336 Antonio Freeman UH .50 .20
❑ 337 Luther Elliss UH .30 .10
❑ 338 James Allen UH .30 .10
❑ 339 Arizona Cardinals TC .50 .20
❑ 340 Atlanta Falcons TC .50 .20
❑ 341 Baltimore Ravens TC .30 .10
❑ 342 Buffalo Bills TC .30 .10
❑ 343 Carolina Panthers TC .30 .10
❑ 344 Chicago Bears TC .75 .30
❑ 345 Cincinnati Bengals TC .50 .20
❑ 346 Cleveland Browns TC .30 .10
❑ 347 Cowboys TC/Emmitt .75 .30
❑ 348 Denver Broncos TC .50 .20
❑ 349 Detroit Lions TC .30 .10
❑ 350 Packers TC/Favre 1.25 .50
❑ 351 Colts TC/James .75 .30
❑ 352 Jacksonville Jaguars TC .75 .30
❑ 353 Kansas City Chiefs TC .30 .10
❑ 354 Miami Dolphins TC .50 .20
❑ 355 Minnesota Vikings TC .75 .30
❑ 356 New England Patriots TC .75 .30
❑ 357 New Orleans Saints TC .50 .20
❑ 358 New York Giants TC .50 .20
❑ 359 New York Jets TC .50 .20
❑ 360 Oakland Raiders TC .50 .20
❑ 361 Philadelphia Eagles TC .75 .30
❑ 362 Pittsburgh Steelers TC .50 .20
❑ 363 San Diego Chargers TC .30 .10
❑ 364 San Francisco 49ers TC .30 .10
❑ 365 Seattle Seahawks TC .30 .10
❑ 366 Rams TC/Warner .75 .30
❑ 367 Tampa Bay Buccaneers TC .50 .20
❑ 368 Tennessee Titans TC .50 .20
❑ 369 Washington Redskins TC .50 .20
❑ 370 Buffalo Bills TL .50 .20
❑ 371 Indianapolis Colts TL .75 .30
❑ 372 Miami Dolphins TL .30 .10
❑ 373 New England Patriots TL .50 .20
❑ 374 New York Jets TL .50 .20
❑ 375 Baltimore Ravens TL .50 .20
❑ 376 Cincinnati Bengals TL .30 .10
❑ 377 Cleveland Browns TL .30 .10
❑ 378 Jacksonville Jaguars TL .50 .20
❑ 379 Pittsburgh Steelers TL .50 .20
❑ 380 Tennessee Titans TL .50 .20
❑ 381 Denver Broncos TL .50 .20
❑ 382 Kansas City Chiefs TL .50 .20
❑ 383 Oakland Raiders TL .50 .20
❑ 384 San Diego Chargers TL .50 .20
❑ 385 Seattle Seahawks TL .30 .10
❑ 386 Arizona Cardinals TL .30 .10
❑ 387 Dallas Cowboys TL .75 .30
❑ 388 New York Giants TL .50 .20
❑ 389 Philadelphia Eagles TL .50 .20
❑ 390 Washington Redskins TL .50 .20
❑ 391 Chicago Bears TL .30 .10
❑ 392 Detroit Lions TL .30 .10
❑ 393 Green Bay Packers TL .75 .30
❑ 394 Minnesota Vikings TL .75 .30
❑ 395 Tampa Bay Buccaneers TL .50 .20
❑ 396 Atlanta Falcons TL .30 .10
❑ 397 Carolina Panthers TL .30 .10
❑ 398 New Orleans Saints TL .50 .20
❑ 399 San Francisco 49ersTL .50 .20
❑ 400 St. Louis Rams TL .75 .30
❑ 401 Michael Vick RC 25.00 10.00
❑ 402 Drew Brees RC 15.00 6.00
❑ 403 Michael Bennett RC 4.00 1.50
❑ 404 David Terrell RC 4.00 1.50
❑ 405 Deuce McAllister RC 10.00 4.00
❑ 406 Santana Moss RC 8.00 3.00
❑ 407 Koren Robinson RC 4.00 1.50
❑ 408 Chris Weinke RC 4.00 1.50
❑ 409 Reggie Wayne RC 10.00 4.00
❑ 410 Rod Gardner RC 4.00 1.50
❑ 411 James Jackson RC 4.00 1.50
❑ 412 Travis Henry RC 8.00 3.00
❑ 413 Josh Heupel RC 4.00 1.50
❑ 415 Chad Johnson RC 12.00 5.00
❑ 416 Sage Rosenfels RC 4.00 1.50
❑ 417 Quincy Morgan RC 4.00 1.50
❑ 418 Ken-Yon Rambo RC 3.00 1.25
❑ 419 LaMont Jordan RC 10.00 4.00
❑ 420 Anthony Thomas RC 4.00 1.50
❑ 421 Dave Dickenson RC 3.00 1.25
❑ 422 Travis Minor RC 3.00 1.25
❑ 423 Kevan Barlow RC 4.00 1.50
❑ 424 Chris Chambers RC 8.00 3.00
❑ 425 Richard Seymour RC 4.00 1.50
❑ 426 Gerard Warren RC 4.00 1.50
❑ 427 Jamar Fletcher RC 3.00 1.25
❑ 428 Freddie Mitchell RC 4.00 1.50
❑ 429 Jamal Reynolds RC 4.00 1.50
❑ 430 Marques Tuiasosopo RC 4.00 1.50
❑ 431 Snoop Minnis RC 3.00 1.25
❑ 432 Mike McMahon RC 4.00 1.50
❑ 433 Robert Ferguson RC 4.00 1.50
❑ 434 Ronney Daniels RC 3.00 1.25
❑ 435 Rudi Johnson RC 10.00 4.00
❑ 436 Vinny Sutherland RC 3.00 1.25
❑ 437 Josh Booty RC 4.00 1.50
❑ 438 Reggie White RC 3.00 1.25
❑ 439 Todd Heap RC 4.00 1.50
❑ 440 Justin Smith RC 4.00 1.50
❑ 441 Andre Carter RC 4.00 1.50
❑ 442 Bobby Newcombe RC 3.00 1.25
❑ 443 Alex Bannister RC 3.00 1.25
❑ 444 Correll Buckhalter RC 6.00 2.50
❑ 445 Quincy Carter RC 4.00 1.50
❑ 446 Jesse Palmer RC 4.00 1.50
❑ 447 Heath Evans RC 3.00 1.25
❑ 448 Dan Morgan RC 4.00 1.50
❑ 449 Justin McCareins RC 4.00 1.50
❑ 450 Alge Crumpler RC 5.00 2.00
❑ 414 LaDainian Tomlinson RC 50.00 20.00

2002 Fleer Tradition

❑ COMPLETE SET (300) 80.00 30.00
❑ 1 Jeff Garcia .60 .25
❑ 2 Brian Simmons .25 .08
❑ 3 Kordell Stewart .40 .15
❑ 4 Chris Weinke .40 .15
❑ 5 Donovan McNabb .75 .30
❑ 6 Antoine Winfield .25 .08
❑ 7 Ray Lewis .60 .25
❑ 8 Drew Brees .60 .25
❑ 9 Frank Sanders .25 .08
❑ 10 Rich Gannon .60 .25
❑ 11 Jamal Anderson .40 .15
❑ 12 Curtis Martin .60 .25
❑ 13 Darrell Jackson .40 .15
❑ 14 Micheal Barrow .25 .08
❑ 15 Jeff Wilkins .25 .08
❑ 16 Ricky Williams .60 .25
❑ 17 Brad Johnson .40 .15
❑ 18 Tedy Bruschi .60 .25
❑ 19 Frank Wycheck .25 .08
❑ 20 Byron Chamberlain .25 .08
❑ 21 Terry Glenn .25 .08
❑ 22 James McKnight .25 .08
❑ 23 Thomas Jones .40 .15
❑ 24 Jamie Sharper .25 .08
❑ 25 Trent Green .40 .15
❑ 26 Mike Rucker RC 1.00 .40
❑ 27 Mark Brunell .60 .25
❑ 28 Takeo Spikes .25 .08
❑ 29 Dominic Rhodes .60 .25
❑ 30 Jim Miller .25 .08

❑ 31 Corey Bradford .25 .08
❑ 32 Jamir Miller .25 .08
❑ 33 Johnnie Morton .40 .15
❑ 34 Rocket Ismail .40 .15
❑ 35 Mike Anderson .60 .25
❑ 36 James Allen .40 .15
❑ 37 Quincy Carter .40 .15
❑ 38 Germane Crowell .25 .08
❑ 39 Quincy Morgan .25 .08
❑ 40 Kabeer Gbaja-Biamila .40 .15
❑ 41 Reggie Wayne .60 .25
❑ 42 Brian Urlacher 1.00 .40
❑ 43 Stacey Mack .25 .08
❑ 44 Justin Smith .25 .08
❑ 45 Snoop Minnis .25 .08
❑ 46 Donald Hayes .25 .08
❑ 47 Jay Fiedler .40 .15
❑ 48 Nate Clements .25 .08
❑ 49 Drew Bledsoe .75 .30
❑ 50 Peter Boulware .25 .08
❑ 51 Lawyer Milloy .40 .15
❑ 52 Michael Pittman .25 .08
❑ 53 Aaron Brooks .60 .25
❑ 54 Maurice Smith .40 .15
❑ 55 Ike Hilliard .40 .15
❑ 56 Derrick Mason .40 .15
❑ 57 LaMont Jordan .60 .25
❑ 58 Charlie Garner .40 .15
❑ 59 Mike Alstott .60 .25
❑ 60 Freddie Mitchell .40 .15
❑ 61 Isaac Bruce .60 .25
❑ 62 Hines Ward .60 .25
❑ 63 John Randle .25 .08
❑ 64 Doug Flutie .60 .25
❑ 65 Terrell Owens .60 .25
❑ 66 Garrison Hearst .40 .15
❑ 67 Rodney Harrison .25 .08
❑ 68 Koren Robinson .40 .15
❑ 69 Amos Zereoue .60 .25
❑ 70 Aeneas Williams .25 .08
❑ 71 Hugh Douglas .25 .08
❑ 72 Jacquez Green .25 .08
❑ 73 Sebastian Janikowski .25 .08
❑ 74 Kevin Dyson .40 .15
❑ 75 Terance Mathis .25 .08
❑ 76 Vinny Testaverde .40 .15
❑ 77 Kwamie Lassiter .25 .08
❑ 78 Ron Dayne .40 .15
❑ 79 Jonathan Ogden .25 .08
❑ 80 Charlie Clemons RC .25 .08
❑ 81 Peter Warrick .40 .15
❑ 82 Adam Vinatieri .60 .25
❑ 83 Ted Washington .25 .08
❑ 84 Randy Moss 1.25 .50
❑ 85 Rosevelt Colvin RC 1.00 .40
❑ 86 Oronde Gadsden .40 .15
❑ 87 Anthony Henry .25 .08
❑ 88 Priest Holmes .75 .30
❑ 89 Joey Galloway .40 .15
❑ 90 Jimmy Smith .40 .15
❑ 91 Bill Romanowski .25 .08
❑ 92 Chris Claiborne .40 .15
❑ 93 Marvin Harrison .60 .25
❑ 94 Vonnie Holliday .25 .08
❑ 95 Darren Sharper .25 .08
❑ 96 Chad Bratzke .25 .08
❑ 97 James Stewart .40 .15
❑ 98 Fred Taylor .60 .25
❑ 99 Jason Elam .25 .08
❑ 100 Keyshawn Johnson .60 .25
❑ 101 Dexter Coakley .25 .08
❑ 102 Zach Thomas .60 .25
❑ 103 Jamel White .25 .08
❑ 104 Antowain Smith .40 .15
❑ 105 Marty Booker .25 .08
❑ 106 Deuce McAllister .75 .30
❑ 107 Adam Archuleta .25 .08
❑ 108 Rod Smith .40 .15
❑ 109 Tony Boselli .25 .08
❑ 110 Joe Johnson .25 .08
❑ 111 Simeon Rice .40 .15
❑ 112 Cory Schlesinger .25 .08
❑ 113 La'Roi Glover .25 .08
❑ 114 Tiki Barber .60 .25
❑ 115 Michael Westbrook .25 .08
❑ 116 Antonio Freeman .60 .25
❑ 117 Kerry Collins .40 .15
❑ 118 Laveranues Coles .40 .15
❑ 119 Jay Feely .25 .08
❑ 120 Champ Bailey .40 .15
❑ 121 Peyton Manning 1.25 .50
❑ 122 Chad Pennington .75 .30
❑ 123 Anthony Dorsett .25 .08
❑ 124 Jamal Lewis .60 .25
❑ 125 Marcus Pollard .25 .08
❑ 126 Charles Woodson .40 .15
❑ 127 Duce Staley .60 .25
❑ 128 Travis Henry .60 .25
❑ 129 Tony Brackens .25 .08
❑ 130 Jeremiah Trotter .25 .08
❑ 131 Jerome Bettis .60 .25
❑ 132 Chad Johnson .60 .25
❑ 133 Lamar Smith .40 .15
❑ 134 Joey Porter .60 .25
❑ 135 Curtis Conway .25 .08
❑ 136 David Terrell .60 .25
❑ 137 Daunte Culpepper .60 .25
❑ 138 Chris Fuamatu-Ma'afala .25 .08
❑ 139 J.J. Stokes .25 .08
❑ 140 Tim Couch .40 .15
❑ 141 Ty Law .40 .15
❑ 142 Vinny Sutherland .25 .08
❑ 143 Trung Canidate .40 .15
❑ 144 Larry Allen .25 .08
❑ 145 Darren Howard .25 .08
❑ 146 Ricky Watters .40 .15
❑ 147 Grant Wistrom .25 .08
❑ 148 Brian Griese .60 .25
❑ 149 Jason Sehorn .25 .08
❑ 150 Marshall Faulk .60 .25
❑ 151 Martin Gramatica .25 .08
❑ 152 Robert Porcher .25 .08
❑ 153 Richie Anderson .25 .08
❑ 154 Derrick Brooks .60 .25
❑ 155 Jevon Kearse .40 .15
❑ 156 Bill Schroeder .40 .15
❑ 157 Marvin Jones .25 .08
❑ 158 Eddie George .60 .25
❑ 159 Keith Brooking .25 .08
❑ 160 Ryan Longwell .25 .08
❑ 161 Brian Dawkins .40 .15
❑ 162 Chris Redman .25 .08
❑ 163 Az-Zahir Hakim .25 .08
❑ 164 James Thrash .40 .15
❑ 165 Rob Johnson .40 .15
❑ 166 Hardy Nickerson .25 .08
❑ 167 Chad Scott .25 .08
❑ 168 Jon Kitna .40 .15
❑ 169 Donnie Edwards .25 .08
❑ 170 Andre Carter .25 .08
❑ 171 Warrick Holdman .25 .08
❑ 172 Jason Taylor .25 .08
❑ 173 Levon Kirkland .25 .08
❑ 174 Mike Brown .60 .25
❑ 175 David Patten .25 .08
❑ 176 Kurt Warner .60 .25
❑ 177 Fred Smoot .25 .08
❑ 178 Dat Nguyen .25 .08
❑ 179 Joe Horn .40 .15
❑ 180 John Lynch .40 .15
❑ 181 Troy Hambrick .25 .08
❑ 182 John Carney .25 .08
❑ 183 Wesley Walls .25 .08
❑ 184 Deltha O'Neal .25 .08
❑ 185 Joe Jurevicius .25 .08
❑ 186 Steve McNair .60 .25
❑ 187 Scotty Anderson .25 .08
❑ 188 John Abraham .40 .15
❑ 189 Stephen Davis .40 .15
❑ 190 Nate Wayne .25 .08
❑ 191 Corey Simon .25 .08
❑ 192 Joel Makovicka .25 .08
❑ 193 Rob Morris .25 .08
❑ 194 Correll Buckhalter .40 .15
❑ 195 Qadry Ismail .40 .15
❑ 196 Keenan McCardell .25 .08
❑ 197 Jason Gildon .25 .08
❑ 198 Peerless Price .40 .15
❑ 199 Tony Richardson .25 .08
❑ 200 Kevan Barlow .40 .15
❑ 201 Corey Dillon .40 .15
❑ 202 Sam Madison .25 .08
❑ 203 Chad Brown .25 .08
❑ 204 Dez White .25 .08
❑ 205 Troy Brown .40 .15
❑ 206 Orlando Pace .25 .08
❑ 207 Jermaine Lewis .25 .08
❑ 208 Willie Jackson .25 .08
❑ 209 Warrick Dunn .60 .25
❑ 210 James Jackson .25 .08
❑ 211 Sammy Knight .25 .08
❑ 212 Ronde Barber .25 .08
❑ 213 Ed McCaffrey .60 .25
❑ 214 Amani Toomer .40 .15
❑ 215 Rod Gardner .40 .15
❑ 216 Mike McMahon .60 .25
❑ 217 Wayne Chrebet .40 .15
❑ 218 Jake Plummer .40 .15
❑ 219 Bubba Franks .40 .15
❑ 220 Shane Lechler .40 .15
❑ 221 Travis Taylor .40 .15
❑ 222 Edgerrin James .75 .30
❑ 223 David Akers .25 .08
❑ 224 Eric Moulds .40 .15
❑ 225 Mike Vanderjagt .25 .08
❑ 226 Kendrell Bell .60 .25
❑ 227 Darnay Scott .25 .08
❑ 228 Tony Gonzalez .40 .15
❑ 229 Marcellus Wiley .25 .08
❑ 230 Marcus Robinson .40 .15
❑ 231 Muhsin Muhammad .40 .15
❑ 232 Trent Dilfer .40 .15
❑ 233 Kevin Johnson .40 .15
❑ 234 Travis Minor .25 .08
❑ 235 London Fletcher .25 .08
❑ 236 Reggie Swinton .25 .08
❑ 237 Michael Bennett .40 .15
❑ 238 Brett Favre DD 1.50 .60
❑ 239 Terrell Davis DD .60 .25
❑ 240 Emmitt Smith DD 1.50 .60
❑ 241 Shannon Sharpe DD .40 .15
❑ 242 Cris Carter DD .60 .25
❑ 243 Tim Brown DD .60 .25
❑ 244 Jerry Rice DD 1.25 .50
❑ 245 Bruce Smith DD .40 .15
❑ 246 Warren Sapp DD .40 .15
❑ 247 Michael Strahan DD .40 .15
❑ 248 Junior Seau DD .60 .25
❑ 249 Darrell Green DD .25 .08
❑ 250 Rod Woodson DD .40 .15
❑ 251 David Boston BB .60 .25
❑ 252 Michael Vick BB 2.00 .75
❑ 253 Anthony Thomas BB .40 .15
❑ 254 Ahman Green BB .60 .25
❑ 255 Chris Chambers BB .60 .25
❑ 256 Tom Brady BB 1.50 .60
❑ 257 Plaxico Burress BB .40 .15
❑ 258 LaDainian Tomlinson BB 1.00 .40
❑ 259 Shaun Alexander BB .75 .30
❑ 260 Torry Holt BB .60 .25
❑ 261 Julius Peppers RC 4.00 1.50
❑ 262 William Green RC 2.00 .75
❑ 263 Joey Harrington RC 3.00 1.25
❑ 264 Jabar Gaffney RC 2.00 .75
❑ 265 T.J. Duckett RC 2.50 1.00
❑ 266 Antwaan Randle El RC 3.00 1.25
❑ 267 Javon Walker RC 4.00 1.50
❑ 268 David Carr RC 5.00 2.00
❑ 269 DeShaun Foster RC 2.00 .75
❑ 270 Donte Stallworth RC 4.00 1.50
❑ 271 Antonio Bryant RC 2.00 .75
❑ 272 Clinton Portis RC 6.00 2.50
❑ 273 Josh Reed RC 2.00 .75
❑ 274 Ashley Lelie RC 4.00 1.50
❑ 275 Patrick Ramsey RC 2.50 1.00
❑ 276 J.Wells RC/A.Peterson RC 2.00 .75
❑ 277 Q.Jammer RC/R.Williams RC 5.00 2.00
❑ 278 J.Shockey RC/D.Graham RC 6.00 2.50
❑ 279 E.Crouch RC/Applewhite RC 2.00 .75
❑ 280 Buchanon RC/Sheppard RC 2.00 .75
❑ 281 K.Hill RC/D.Branch RC 4.00 1.50
❑ 282 R.Sims RC/W.Bryant RC 2.00 .75
❑ 283 J.Scobey RC/Westbrook RC 3.00 1.25
❑ 284 L.Betts RC/O.Easy RC 2.00 .75
❑ 285 A.Davis RC/D.Jones RC 1.50 .60
❑ 286 C.Russell RC/C.Taylor RC 3.00 1.25
❑ 287 McAddley RC/J.McCown RC 2.50 1.00
❑ 288 D.Garrard RC/R.Davey RC 2.50 1.00
❑ 289 M.Walker RC/R.Johnson RC 1.50 .60
❑ 290 L.Staley RC/L.Gordon RC 2.00 .75
❑ 291 R.Caldwell RC/L.Mays RC 2.00 .75
❑ 292 R.Thomas RC/N.Harris RC 2.00 .75
❑ 293 M.Morris RC/J.Stevens RC 2.00 .75
❑ 294 K.Kittner RC/R.Fasani RC 1.50 .60
❑ 295 R.Calmus RC/J.Schifino RC 2.00 .75
❑ 296 T.Carter RC/F.Milons RC 1.50 .60
❑ 297 Wistrom RC/Stephens RC 2.00 .75

No.	Player	Price	Price
❑ 298	M.Williams RC/D.Freeney RC	3.00	1.25
❑ 299	Hendersn RC/Hayneswrth RC	2.00	.75
❑ 300	N.Davenport RC/C.Nall RC	2.00	.75

2003 Fleer Tradition

No.	Player	Price	Price
❑	COMPLETE SET (300)	40.00	15.00
❑ 1	Aaron Glenn	.25	.08
❑ 2	Jerry Rice	1.25	.50
❑ 3	Chad Hutchinson	.25	.08
❑ 4	Kris Jenkins	.25	.08
❑ 5	Ed Reed	.40	.15
❑ 6	Ed McCaffrey	.60	.25
❑ 7	Rod Gardner	.40	.15
❑ 8	Aaron Brooks	.60	.25
❑ 9	Chad Pennington	.75	.30
❑ 10	Jevon Kearse	.40	.15
❑ 11	Kurt Warner	.60	.25
❑ 12	Eddie George	.40	.15
❑ 13	Ron Dugans	.25	.08
❑ 14	Adam Vinatieri	.60	.25
❑ 15	Jimmy Smith	.40	.15
❑ 16	Chad Johnson	.60	.25
❑ 17	Kyle Brady	.25	.08
❑ 18	Eddie Kennison	.25	.08
❑ 19	Joe Jurevicius	.25	.08
❑ 20	Ronde Barber	.25	.08
❑ 21	Adam Archuleta	.25	.08
❑ 22	Champ Bailey	.40	.15
❑ 23	Joe Horn	.40	.15
❑ 24	Ladell Betts	.40	.15
❑ 25	Edgerrin James	.60	.25
❑ 26	Rosevelt Colvin	.25	.08
❑ 27	Ahman Green	.60	.25
❑ 28	Joey Porter	.60	.25
❑ 29	Charles Woodson	.40	.15
❑ 30	Lance Schulters	.25	.08
❑ 31	Edgerton Hartwell	.25	.08
❑ 32	Joey Galloway	.40	.15
❑ 33	Roy Williams	.60	.25
❑ 34	Al Wilson	.25	.08
❑ 35	Charlie Garner	.40	.15
❑ 36	John Lynch	.25	.08
❑ 37	La'Roi Glover	.25	.08
❑ 38	Emmitt Smith	1.50	.60
❑ 39	Ryan Longwell	.25	.08
❑ 40	Alge Crumpler	.40	.15
❑ 41	John Abraham	.25	.08
❑ 42	Chris Hovan	.25	.08
❑ 43	Laveranues Coles	.40	.15
❑ 44	Eric Hicks	.25	.08
❑ 45	Johnnie Morton	.40	.15
❑ 46	Sam Madison	.25	.08
❑ 47	Amani Toomer	.40	.15
❑ 48	Chris Redman	.25	.08
❑ 49	Jon Kitna	.40	.15
❑ 50	Leonard Little	.25	.08
❑ 51	Eric Moulds	.40	.15
❑ 52	Santana Moss	.40	.15
❑ 53	Amos Zereoue	.40	.15
❑ 54	Jonathan Wells	.25	.08
❑ 55	Chris Chambers	.60	.25
❑ 56	London Fletcher	.25	.08
❑ 57	Frank Wycheck	.25	.08
❑ 58	Josh McCown	.40	.15
❑ 59	Shannon Sharpe	.25	.08
❑ 60	Andre Carter	.25	.08
❑ 61	Corey Dillon	.40	.15
❑ 62	Josh Reed	.40	.15
❑ 63	Marc Boerigter	.40	.15
❑ 64	Fred Smoot	.25	.08
❑ 65	Shaun Alexander	.60	.25
❑ 66	Andre Davis	.25	.08
❑ 67	Julian Peterson	.25	.08
❑ 68	Corey Bradford	.25	.08
❑ 69	Marc Bulger	.60	.25
❑ 70	Fred Taylor	.60	.25
❑ 71	Junior Seau	.60	.25
❑ 72	Simeon Rice	.40	.15
❑ 73	Anthony Thomas	.40	.15
❑ 74	Correll Buckhalter	.40	.15
❑ 75	Justin Smith	.25	.08
❑ 76	Marcel Shipp	.40	.15
❑ 77	Garrison Hearst	.40	.15
❑ 78	Stacey Mack	.25	.08
❑ 79	Antowain Smith	.40	.15
❑ 80	Kabeer Gbaja-Biamila	.40	.15
❑ 81	Curtis Martin	.60	.25
❑ 82	Marcellus Wiley	.25	.08
❑ 83	Gary Walker	.25	.08
❑ 84	Kalimba Edwards	.25	.08
❑ 85	Stephen Davis	.40	.15
❑ 86	Antwaan Randle El	.60	.25
❑ 87	Curtis Conway	.25	.08
❑ 88	Keith Brooking	.25	.08
❑ 89	Mark Word RC	.25	.08
❑ 90	Greg Ellis	.25	.08
❑ 91	Steve McNair	.60	.25
❑ 92	Ashley Lelie	.60	.25
❑ 93	Kelly Holcomb	.40	.15
❑ 94	Darrell Jackson	.40	.15
❑ 95	Mark Brunell	.40	.15
❑ 96	Hugh Douglas	.25	.08
❑ 97	Kendrell Bell	.40	.15
❑ 98	Steve Smith	.60	.25
❑ 99	Bill Schroeder	.40	.15
❑ 100	Darren Howard	.25	.08
❑ 101	Kevan Barlow	.40	.15
❑ 102	Marshall Faulk	.60	.25
❑ 103	Ike Hilliard	.25	.08
❑ 104	T.J. Duckett	.40	.15
❑ 105	Bobby Taylor	.25	.08
❑ 106	Kevin Carter	.25	.08
❑ 107	Darren Sharper	.25	.08
❑ 108	Marty Booker	.40	.15
❑ 109	Isaac Bruce	.60	.25
❑ 110	Kevin Hardy	.25	.08
❑ 111	Tai Streets	.25	.08
❑ 112	Brad Johnson	.40	.15
❑ 113	Daunte Culpepper	.60	.25
❑ 114	Kevin Johnson	.40	.15
❑ 115	Matt Hasselbeck	.40	.15
❑ 116	Jabar Gaffney	.40	.15
❑ 117	Takeo Spikes	.25	.08
❑ 118	Brett Favre	1.50	.60
❑ 119	Keyshawn Johnson	.60	.25
❑ 120	David Akers	.25	.08
❑ 121	Maurice Morris	.25	.08
❑ 122	Jake Delhomme	.60	.25
❑ 123	Kordell Stewart	.40	.15
❑ 124	Terrell Davis	.60	.25
❑ 125	Brian Kelly	.25	.08
❑ 126	David Terrell	.40	.15
❑ 127	Koren Robinson	.40	.15
❑ 128	Michael Strahan	.40	.15
❑ 129	Jake Plummer	.40	.15
❑ 130	Terrell Owens	.60	.25
❑ 131	Brian Urlacher	1.00	.40
❑ 132	David Patten	.25	.08
❑ 133	Michael Vick	1.50	.60
❑ 134	Jamal Lewis	.60	.25
❑ 135	Terry Glenn	.25	.08
❑ 136	Brian Simmons	.25	.08
❑ 137	David Boston	.40	.15
❑ 138	Michael Bennett	.40	.15
❑ 139	James Stewart	.40	.15
❑ 140	Tiki Barber	.60	.25
❑ 141	Brian Griese	.60	.25
❑ 142	Deion Branch	.60	.25
❑ 143	Mike Peterson	.25	.08
❑ 144	James Mungro	.25	.08
❑ 145	Tim Couch	.25	.08
❑ 146	Brian Dawkins	.40	.15
❑ 147	Dennis Northcutt	.40	.15
❑ 148	Mike Alstott	.60	.25
❑ 149	James Thrash	.25	.08
❑ 150	Tim Brown	.60	.25
❑ 151	Brian Finneran	.25	.08
❑ 152	Derrick Brooks	.40	.15
❑ 153	Muhsin Muhammad	.40	.15
❑ 154	Jason Elam	.25	.08
❑ 155	Tim Dwight	.40	.15
❑ 156	Bruce Smith	.40	.15
❑ 157	Derrick Mason	.40	.15
❑ 158	Napoleon Harris	.25	.08
❑ 159	Jason Gildon	.25	.08
❑ 160	Todd Heap	.40	.15
❑ 161	Aaron Schobel	.40	.15
❑ 162	Derrius Thompson	.25	.08
❑ 163	Nate Clements	.25	.08
❑ 164	Jason McAddley	.25	.08
❑ 165	Todd Pinkston	.40	.15
❑ 166	Bubba Franks	.40	.15
❑ 167	Deuce McAllister	.60	.25
❑ 168	Patrick Surtain	.25	.08
❑ 169	Javon Walker	.40	.15
❑ 170	Tom Brady	1.50	.60
❑ 171	Dexter Coakley	.25	.08
❑ 172	Patrick Kerney	.25	.08
❑ 173	Jay Fiedler	.40	.15
❑ 174	Tommy Maddox	.60	.25
❑ 175	Donald Driver	.40	.15
❑ 176	Patrick Ramsey	.60	.25
❑ 177	Olandis Gary	.40	.15
❑ 178	Tony Gonzalez	.40	.15
❑ 179	Donnie Edwards	.25	.08
❑ 180	Peter Boulware	.25	.08
❑ 181	Jeff Blake	.25	.08
❑ 182	Torry Holt	.60	.25
❑ 183	Donovan McNabb	.75	.30
❑ 184	Peter Warrick	.25	.08
❑ 185	Jeff Garcia	.60	.25
❑ 186	Travis Henry	.40	.15
❑ 187	Doug Jolley	.25	.08
❑ 188	Peyton Manning	1.00	.40
❑ 189	Jerome Bettis	.60	.25
❑ 190	Travis Taylor	.40	.15
❑ 191	Drew Brees	.60	.25
❑ 192	Phillip Buchanon	.25	.08
❑ 193	Jerramy Stevens	.25	.08
❑ 194	Trent Green	.40	.15
❑ 195	Duce Staley	.40	.15
❑ 196	Plaxico Burress	.40	.15
❑ 197	Jerry Porter	.40	.15
❑ 198	Trevor Pryce	.25	.08
❑ 199	Dwight Freeney	.40	.15
❑ 200	Quincy Morgan	.40	.15
❑ 201	Troy Vincent	.25	.08
❑ 202	Randy McMichael	.40	.15
❑ 203	Troy Hambrick	.25	.08
❑ 204	Randy Moss	1.00	.40
❑ 205	Troy Brown	.40	.15
❑ 206	Ray Lewis	.60	.25
❑ 207	Trung Canidate	.40	.15
❑ 208	Raynoch Thompson	.25	.08
❑ 209	Ty Law	.40	.15
❑ 210	Reggie Wayne	.40	.15
❑ 211	Warren Sapp	.40	.15
❑ 212	Richard Seymour	.25	.08
❑ 213	Warrick Dunn	.40	.15
❑ 214	Robert Ferguson	.25	.08
❑ 215	Wayne Chrebet	.40	.15
❑ 216	Rod Coleman RC	.60	.25
❑ 217	Will Allen	.25	.08
❑ 218	Rod Woodson	.40	.15
❑ 219	Zach Thomas	.60	.25
❑ 220	Rod Smith	.40	.15
❑ 221	Ricky Williams	.60	.25
❑ 222	LaDainian Tomlinson	.60	.25
❑ 223	Priest Holmes	.75	.30
❑ 224	Rich Gannon	.40	.15
❑ 225	Drew Bledsoe	.60	.25
❑ 226	Kerry Collins	.40	.15
❑ 227	Marvin Harrison	.60	.25
❑ 228	Hines Ward	.60	.25
❑ 229	Peerless Price	.40	.15
❑ 230	Jason Taylor	.25	.08
❑ 231	Jeremy Shockey	1.00	.40
❑ 232	Clinton Portis	1.00	.40
❑ 233	Antonio Bryant	.40	.15
❑ 234	Donte Stallworth	.60	.25
❑ 235	David Carr	1.00	.40
❑ 236	Joey Harrington	1.00	.40
❑ 237	William Green	.40	.15
❑ 238	Julius Peppers	.60	.25
❑ 239	Shipp/Thompson/Wilson	.25	.08
❑ 240	Vick/Dunn/Finner/Brooking	.75	.30
❑ 241	Lewis/Hartwell/Taylor/Reed	.40	.15
❑ 242	Bled/Henry/Mould/Fletch	.40	.15
❑ 243	Peppers/Smith/Muhammad	.60	.25
❑ 244	Booker/Urlacher/Thomas	.60	.25

❑ 245 Dillon/Smith/Johnson/Kitna .60 .25
❑ 246 Couch/Green/Morgan/Word .40 .15
❑ 247 Hutchinson/Galloway/Williams/Ellis .25 .08
❑ 248 Portis/Smith/Wilson .60 .25
❑ 249 Harring/Stew/Schr/Edwards .60 .25
❑ 250 Favre/Green/Driver/KGB .75 .30
❑ 251 Carr/Wells/Bradford/Glenn .60 .25
❑ 252 Mann/James/Harr/Freen .60 .25
❑ 253 Brunell/Taylor/Smith/McCree .25 .08
❑ 254 Green/Holmes/Kenn/Hicks .40 .15
❑ 255 Willms/Chamb/Thom/Tayl .60 .25
❑ 256 Culp/Benn/Moss/Williams .60 .25
❑ 257 Brady/Smith/Brown/Vina 1.00 .40
❑ 258 Brooks/McAllister/Horn/Howard .25 .08
❑ 259 Collins/Barber/Toomer/Strahan .60 .25
❑ 260 Pennington/Martin/Chrebet/Abraham .40 .15
❑ 261 Gannon/Garn/Rice/Woods .60 .25
❑ 262 McNabb/Staley/Pinkston/Taylor .40 .15
❑ 263 Maddox/Zereoue/Ward/Gildon/Porter .40 .15
❑ 264 Brees/Tomlinson/Edwards .60 .25
❑ 265 Garcia/Hearst/Owens/Carter .40 .15
❑ 266 Hasselbeck/Alexander/Robin/Tongue .25 .08
❑ 267 Bulger/Faulk/Holt/Little .60 .25
❑ 268 B.John/Key.John/S.Rice/Kelly .40 .15
❑ 269 McNair/George/Mason/Schulters .25 .08
❑ 270 Ramsey/Gardner/Smoot .25 .08
❑ 271 Carson Palmer RC 5.00 2.00
❑ 272 Kyle Boller RC 1.25 .50
❑ 273 Byron Leftwich RC 4.00 1.50
❑ 274 Willis McGahee RC 3.00 1.25
❑ 275 Larry Johnson RC 5.00 2.50
❑ 276 Charles Rogers RC 1.25 .50
❑ 277 Andre Johnson RC 2.50 1.00
❑ 278 Bryant Johnson RC 1.25 .50
❑ 279 Rex Grossman RC 4.00 1.50
❑ 280 Taylor Jacobs RC 1.00 .40
❑ 281 Rober RC/Sull RC/Will RC 1.25 .50
❑ 282 Jopp RC/Davis RC/Rag RC 1.25 .50
❑ 283 Witt RC/Clark RC/Smith RC 1.25 .50
❑ 284 Edwds RC/Smith RC/Bail RC 1.25 .50
❑ 285 SuggsRC/BrownRC/SmithRC 1.25 .50
❑ 286 Griff RC/Pinn RC/Askew RC 1.25 .50
❑ 287 Farg RC/Gabr RC/Johns RC 1.25 .50
❑ 288 Kenn RC/Joseph RC/Warr RC 1.25 .50
❑ 289 Sug RC/Hayn RC/McDo RC 2.00 .75
❑ 290 Wash RC/Curt RC/Burles RC 1.25 .50
❑ 291 Wall RC/Dors RC/Simms RC 2.00 .75
❑ 292 Wade RC/Aik RC/Gage RC 1.25 .50
❑ 293 McCull RC/Sapp RC/Grah RC 1.00 .40
❑ 294 Kelly RC/Gard RC/Tolv RC 1.00 .40
❑ 295 Johns RC/Bold RC/Calic RC 3.00 1.25
❑ 296 Lloyd RC/McM RC/McD RC 1.25 .50
❑ 297 Kels RC/White RC/Doss RC 1.25 .50
❑ 298 Newm RC/Truf RC/Wool RC 2.50 1.00
❑ 299 Kings RC/Rom RC/St.P RC 20.00 10.00
❑ 300 Pinn RC/Toef RC/Cobou RC 1.25 .50

2004 Fleer Tradition

❑ COMPLETE SET (360) 100.00 50.00
❑ COMP.SET w/o SP's (330) 30.00 15.00
❑ 1 Dolphins TL .40 .15
❑ 2 Bills TL .40 .15
❑ 3 Patriots TL .60 .25
❑ 4 Jets TL .40 .15
❑ 5 Colts TL .60 .25
❑ 6 Jaguars TL .40 .15
❑ 7 Titans TL .25 .08
❑ 8 Texans TL .40 .15
❑ 9 Raiders TL .60 .25
❑ 10 Broncos TL .40 .15
❑ 11 Chiefs TL .40 .15
❑ 12 Chargers TL .50 .20
❑ 13 Steelers TL .60 .25
❑ 14 Browns TL .25 .08
❑ 15 Bengals TL .40 .15
❑ 16 Ravens TL .40 .15
❑ 17 Eagles TL .40 .15
❑ 18 Giants TL .40 .15
❑ 19 Redskins TL .40 .15
❑ 20 Cowboys TL .40 .15
❑ 21 Vikings TL .60 .25
❑ 22 Packers TL .75 .30
❑ 23 Bears TL .60 .25
❑ 24 Lions TL .40 .15
❑ 25 49ers TL .40 .15
❑ 26 Rams TL .40 .15
❑ 27 Seahawks TL .40 .15
❑ 28 Cardinals TL .25 .08
❑ 29 Panthers TL .40 .15
❑ 30 BuccaneersTL .25 .08
❑ 31 Falcons TL .25 .08
❑ 32 Saints TL .40 .15
❑ 33 Anquan Boldin .60 .25
❑ 34 Michael Vick 1.25 .50
❑ 35 Kyle Boller .60 .25
❑ 36 Aeneas Williams .25 .08
❑ 37 Jake Delhomme .60 .25
❑ 38 Rex Grossman .60 .25
❑ 39 Carson Palmer .75 .30
❑ 40 Quincy Morgan .40 .15
❑ 41 Terry Glenn .25 .08
❑ 42 Jake Plummer .40 .15
❑ 43 Joey Harrington .60 .25
❑ 44 Brett Favre 1.50 .60
❑ 45 Jeff Garcia .60 .25
❑ 46 Peyton Manning 1.00 .40
❑ 47 Byron Leftwich .75 .30
❑ 48 Trent Green .40 .15
❑ 49 A.J. Feeley .60 .25
❑ 50 Daunte Culpepper .60 .25
❑ 51 Tom Brady 1.50 .60
❑ 52 Aaron Brooks .40 .15
❑ 53 Kerry Collins .40 .15
❑ 54 Chad Pennington .60 .25
❑ 55 Rich Gannon .40 .15
❑ 56 Donovan McNabb .75 .30
❑ 57 Tommy Maddox .40 .15
❑ 58 Drew Brees .60 .25
❑ 59 Terrell Owens .60 .25
❑ 60 Matt Hasselbeck .40 .15
❑ 61 Kurt Warner .60 .25
❑ 62 Brad Johnson .40 .15
❑ 63 Jerome Bettis .60 .25
❑ 64 Keith Bulluck .25 .08
❑ 65 Rod Gardner .40 .15
❑ 66 Eddie George .40 .15
❑ 67 Warren Sapp .40 .15
❑ 68 Marc Bulger .60 .25
❑ 69 Shaun Alexander .60 .25
❑ 70 Tai Streets .25 .08
❑ 71 LaDainian Tomlinson .75 .30
❑ 72 Steve McNair .60 .25
❑ 73 Brian Westbrook .40 .15
❑ 74 Jerry Rice 1.25 .50
❑ 75 Santana Moss .40 .15
❑ 76 Moe Williams .25 .08
❑ 77 Deuce McAllister .60 .25
❑ 78 Adam Vinatieri .60 .25
❑ 79 Randy Moss .75 .30
❑ 80 Ricky Williams .60 .25
❑ 81 Priest Holmes .75 .30
❑ 82 Jimmy Smith .40 .15
❑ 83 Edgerrin James .60 .25
❑ 84 Andre Johnson .60 .25
❑ 85 Ahman Green .60 .25
❑ 86 Charles Rogers .40 .15
❑ 87 Champ Bailey .40 .15
❑ 88 Roy Williams S .40 .15
❑ 89 Tim Couch .25 .08
❑ 90 Corey Dillon .40 .15
❑ 91 Thomas Jones .40 .15
❑ 92 Stephen Davis .40 .15
❑ 93 Travis Henry .40 .15
❑ 94 Jamal Lewis .60 .25
❑ 95 Warrick Dunn .40 .15
❑ 96 Emmitt Smith 1.25 .50
❑ 97 Mark Brunell .40 .15
❑ 98 Willis McGahee .60 .25
❑ 99 Duce Staley .40 .15
❑ 100 Lee Suggs .60 .25
❑ 101 Rod Smith .40 .15
❑ 102 Marvin Harrison .60 .25
❑ 103 Larry Johnson .75 .30
❑ 104 Michael Bennett .40 .15
❑ 105 Donte Stallworth .40 .15
❑ 106 DeShaun Foster .40 .15
❑ 107 Hines Ward .60 .25
❑ 108 T.J. Duckett .40 .15
❑ 109 Brian Urlacher .75 .30
❑ 110 Boss Bailey .40 .15
❑ 111 Tim Brown .60 .25
❑ 112 David Boston .40 .15
❑ 113 Marshall Faulk .60 .25
❑ 114 Jason Witten .40 .15
❑ 115 Richard Seymour .25 .08
❑ 116 Domanick Davis .60 .25
❑ 117 Jon Kitna .40 .15
❑ 118 Ray Lewis .60 .25
❑ 119 Tedy Bruschi .40 .15
❑ 120 Chris Chambers .40 .15
❑ 121 Freddie Mitchell .40 .15
❑ 122 Amani Toomer .40 .15
❑ 123 Curtis Martin .60 .25
❑ 124 Eric Moulds .40 .15
❑ 125 Darrell Jackson .40 .15
❑ 126 Clinton Portis .60 .25
❑ 127 Jay Fiedler .25 .08
❑ 128 Todd Heap .40 .15
❑ 129 Dexter Jackson .25 .08
❑ 130 James Jackson .25 .08
❑ 131 Shannon Sharpe .40 .15
❑ 132 Donald Driver .40 .15
❑ 133 Billy Miller .25 .08
❑ 134 Dante Hall .60 .25
❑ 135 Onterrio Smith .40 .15
❑ 136 Joe Horn .40 .15
❑ 137 Shaun Ellis .25 .08
❑ 138 L.J. Smith .40 .15
❑ 139 Jerry Porter .40 .15
❑ 140 Reggie Wayne .40 .15
❑ 141 Derrick Brooks .40 .15
❑ 142 Terrell Suggs .40 .15
❑ 143 Randy McMichael .25 .08
❑ 144 Mike Alstott .40 .15
❑ 145 Nate Poole RC .60 .25
❑ 146 Chris Brown .60 .25
❑ 147 Torry Holt .60 .25
❑ 148 Adewale Ogunleye .40 .15
❑ 149 Peter Warrick .40 .15
❑ 150 Alge Crumpler .40 .15
❑ 151 Charlie Garner .40 .15
❑ 152 Jeremy Shockey .60 .25
❑ 153 Simeon Rice .40 .15
❑ 154 Julian Peterson .25 .08
❑ 155 Patrick Ramsey .40 .15
❑ 156 Shawn Springs .25 .08
❑ 157 Marcus Stroud .25 .08
❑ 158 Keyshawn Johnson .40 .15
❑ 159 Steve Smith .60 .25
❑ 160 Ty Law .40 .15
❑ 161 Derrick Mason .40 .15
❑ 162 Josh Reed .25 .08
❑ 163 Fred Smoot .25 .08
❑ 164 Muhsin Muhammad .40 .15
❑ 165 Justin Gage .40 .15
❑ 166 Chad Johnson .60 .25
❑ 167 Dennis Northcutt .25 .08
❑ 168 Joey Galloway .40 .15
❑ 169 Ashley Lelie .40 .15
❑ 170 Casey Fitzsimmons .25 .08
❑ 171 Dwight Freeney .40 .15
❑ 172 Nick Barnett .40 .15
❑ 173 LaBrandon Toefield .25 .08
❑ 174 Jabar Gaffney .40 .15
❑ 175 Tony Gonzalez .40 .15
❑ 176 Zach Thomas .60 .25
❑ 177 Nate Burleson .60 .25
❑ 178 Deion Branch .60 .25
❑ 179 Boo Williams .25 .08
❑ 180 Michael Strahan .40 .15
❑ 181 Anthony Becht .25 .08
❑ 182 Charles Woodson .40 .15
❑ 183 Sheldon Brown .25 .08
❑ 184 Kendrell Bell .40 .15
❑ 185 Kassim Osgood .25 .08
❑ 186 Tony Parrish .25 .08
❑ 187 Marcel Shipp .40 .15
❑ 188 Bobby Engram .25 .08
❑ 189 Keith Brooking .25 .08

❑ 190	Isaac Bruce	.40	.15
❑ 191	Travis Taylor	.25	.08
❑ 192	Charles Lee	.25	.08
❑ 193	Takeo Spikes	.25	.08
❑ 194	Justin McCareins	.25	.08
❑ 195	Julius Peppers	.60	.25
❑ 196	LaVar Arrington	1.25	.50
❑ 197	Dez White	.40	.15
❑ 198	Rudi Johnson	.40	.15
❑ 199	Andre Davis	.25	.08
❑ 200	Quincy Carter	.40	.15
❑ 201	Quentin Griffin	.60	.25
❑ 202	Dallas Clark	.40	.15
❑ 203	Artose Pinner	.25	.08
❑ 204	Kevin Johnson	.25	.08
❑ 205	Kabeer Gbaja-Biamila	.40	.15
❑ 206	Marcus Coleman	.25	.08
❑ 207	Johnnie Morton	.40	.15
❑ 208	Jason Taylor	.25	.08
❑ 209	Kevin Williams	.25	.08
❑ 210	David Givens	.40	.15
❑ 211	Charles Grant	.25	.08
❑ 212	Ike Hilliard	.25	.08
❑ 213	Wayne Chrebet	.40	.15
❑ 214	Teyo Johnson	.25	.08
❑ 215	Brian Dawkins	.40	.15
❑ 216	Antwaan Randle El	.60	.25
❑ 217	Eric Parker	.25	.08
❑ 218	Josh McCown	.40	.15
❑ 219	Tim Rattay	.25	.08
❑ 220	Brian Finneran	.25	.08
❑ 221	Chad Brown	.25	.08
❑ 222	Ed Reed	.40	.15
❑ 223	Dane Looker	.40	.15
❑ 224	Aaron Schobel	.40	.15
❑ 225	Joe Jurevicius	.25	.08
❑ 226	Ricky Manning	.25	.08
❑ 227	Jevon Kearse	.40	.15
❑ 228	Laveranues Coles	.40	.15
❑ 229	Kelley Washington	.25	.08
❑ 230	William Green	.40	.15
❑ 231	Terence Newman	.40	.15
❑ 232	Bryant Johnson	.25	.08
❑ 233	Peerless Price	.40	.15
❑ 234	Peter Boulware	.40	.15
❑ 235	Drew Bledsoe	.60	.25
❑ 236	Kris Jenkins	.25	.08
❑ 237	Marty Booker	.40	.15
❑ 238	Matt Schobel	.25	.08
❑ 239	Earl Little	.25	.08
❑ 240	Antonio Bryant	.40	.15
❑ 241	Al Wilson	.25	.08
❑ 242	Dre Bly	.25	.08
❑ 243	Javon Walker	.40	.15
❑ 244	David Carr	.60	.25
❑ 245	Mike Vanderjagt	.25	.08
❑ 246	Fred Taylor	.40	.15
❑ 247	Eddie Kennison	.25	.08
❑ 248	Patrick Surtain	.25	.08
❑ 249	Jim Kleinsasser	.25	.08
❑ 250	Daniel Graham	.25	.08
❑ 251	Jerome Pathon	.25	.08
❑ 252	Tiki Barber	.60	.25
❑ 253	John Abraham	.25	.08
❑ 254	Justin Fargas	.40	.15
❑ 255	Correll Buckhalter	.40	.15
❑ 256	Plaxico Burress	.40	.15
❑ 257	Quentin Jammer	.25	.08
❑ 258	Kevan Barlow	.40	.15
❑ 259	Koren Robinson	.40	.15
❑ 260	Leonard Little	.25	.08
❑ 261	John Lynch	.40	.15
❑ 262	Tyrone Calico	.40	.15
❑ 263	Taylor Jacobs	.40	.15
❑ 264	Joey Porter	.40	.15
❑ 265	Freddie Jones	.25	.08
❑ 266	Marcus Pollard	.25	.08
❑ 267	Mike Peterson	.25	.08
❑ 268	Justin Griffith	.25	.08
❑ 269	Shawn Bryson	.25	.08
❑ 270	Will Allen	.25	.08
❑ 271	Antonio Gates	.60	.25
❑ 272	Chris McAlister	.25	.08
❑ 273	Tony Hollings	.25	.08
❑ 274	Cedrick Wilson	.25	.08
❑ 275	Adam Archuleta	.25	.08
❑ 276	London Fletcher	.25	.08
❑ 277	Drew Bennett	.40	.15
❑ 278	Rod Smart	.25	.08
❑ 279	LaMont Jordan	.60	.25
❑ 280	Jerry Azumah	.25	.08
❑ 281	Bubba Franks	.40	.15
❑ 282	Troy Edwards	.25	.08
❑ 283	Willie McGinest	.25	.08
❑ 284	Morten Andersen	.25	.08
❑ 285	Dat Nguyen	.25	.08
❑ 286	Samari Rolle	.25	.08
❑ 287	Brian Simmons	.25	.08
❑ 288	Chike Okeafor	.25	.08
❑ 289	Rodney Harrison	.25	.08
❑ 290	Jason Elam	.25	.08
❑ 291	Tim Dwight	.40	.15
❑ 292	Corey Bradford	.25	.08
❑ 293	Charles Tillman	.40	.15
❑ 294	Tim Carter	.25	.08
❑ 295	Ahmed Plummer	.25	.08
❑ 296	Troy Walters	.25	.08
❑ 297	Michael Lewis	.25	.08
❑ 298	Tory James	.25	.08
❑ 299	Doug Flutie	.60	.25
❑ 300	Az-Zahir Hakim	.25	.08
❑ 301	Itula Mili	.25	.08
❑ 302	Jamie Sharper	.25	.08
❑ 303	Vonnie Holliday	.25	.08
❑ 304	Brian Russell RC	.60	.25
❑ 305	Bryan Gilmore	.25	.08
❑ 306	Darren Sharper	.25	.08
❑ 307	Kyle Brady	.25	.08
❑ 308	David Tyree	.25	.08
❑ 309	Andre Carter	.25	.08
❑ 310	Lawyer Milloy	.40	.15
❑ 311	David Terrell	.40	.15
❑ 312	Richie Anderson	.25	.08
❑ 313	Darren Howard	.25	.08
❑ 314	Sebastian Janikowski	.25	.08
❑ 315	Kimo von Oelhoffen	.60	.25
❑ 316	Donnie Edwards	.25	.08
❑ 317	Brandon Lloyd	.40	.15
❑ 318	Robert Ferguson	.25	.08
❑ 319	Derek Smith	.25	.08
❑ 320	Anthony Thomas	.40	.15
❑ 321	Ken Hamlin	.25	.08
❑ 322	Ronde Barber	.25	.08
❑ 323	Erron Kinney	.25	.08
❑ 324	Tom Brady AW	.60	.25
❑ 325	Peyton Manning AW	.60	.25
❑ 326	Steve McNair AW	.40	.15
❑ 327	Jamal Lewis AW	.40	.15
❑ 328	Ray Lewis AW	.40	.15
❑ 329	Anquan Boldin AW	.25	.08
❑ 330	Terrell Suggs AW	.25	.08
❑ 331	Eli Manning RC	10.00	5.00
❑ 332	Larry Fitzgerald RC	6.00	2.50
❑ 333	Ben Roethlisberger RC	15.00	6.00
❑ 334	Tatum Bell RC	4.00	1.50
❑ 335	Roy Williams RC	5.00	2.00
❑ 336	Drew Henson RC	2.00	.75
❑ 337	Philip Rivers RC	6.00	2.50
❑ 338	Rashaun Woods RC	2.00	.75
❑ 339	Kevin Jones RC	5.00	2.00
❑ 340	Sean Taylor RC	2.00	.75
❑ 341	Steven Jackson RC	6.00	2.50
❑ 342	Kellen Winslow RC	4.00	1.50
❑ 343	Chris Perry RC	4.00	1.50
❑ 344	J.P. Losman RC	4.00	1.50
❑ 345	Greg Jones RC	2.00	.75
❑ 346	Reggie Williams RC	2.50	1.00
❑ 347	Michael Clayton RC	4.00	1.50
❑ 348	Jonathan Vilma RC	2.00	.75
❑ 349	Julius Jones RC	6.00	2.50
❑ 350	Michael Jenkins RC	2.00	.75
❑ 351	E.Manning/Rivers/Roethlis.	25.00	12.50
❑ 352	Fitzgerald/Re.Will/Ro.Will.	8.00	3.00
❑ 353	Evans RC/Berr.RC/Ham.RC	4.00	1.50
❑ 354	Ude.RC/Poole RC/Colb.RC	3.00	1.25
❑ 355	Gamb.RC/Rob.RC/Hall RC	3.00	1.25
❑ 356	Trou.RC/Wats.RC/Harts.RC	3.00	1.25
❑ 357	Darl.RC/Morant RC/Wilf.RC	2.50	1.00
❑ 358	McCo.RC/Pick.RC/Sch.RC	5.00	2.00
❑ 359	Bell/Turn.RC/Cobbs RC	5.00	2.00
❑ 360	Moore RC/Wils.RC/Kni.RC	3.00	1.25

2000 Greats of the Game

❑	COMP.SET w/o SP's (100)	40.00	20.00
❑ 1	Terry Bradshaw	1.50	.60
❑ 2	Paul Hornung	.60	.25
❑ 3	Tony Dorsett	.60	.25
❑ 4	L.C. Greenwood	.40	.15

❑ 5	Ozzie Newsome	.25	.08
❑ 6	Michael Irvin	.40	.15
❑ 7	Art Donovan	.40	.15
❑ 8	Don Maynard	.40	.15
❑ 9	Bobby Mitchell	.40	.15
❑ 10	Bob Lilly	.40	.15
❑ 11	Earl Morrall	.25	.08
❑ 12	Harvey Martin	.25	.08
❑ 13	Dan Fouts	.60	.25
❑ 14	Joe Theismann	.60	.25
❑ 15	Roger Staubach	1.50	.60
❑ 16	Otto Graham	.40	.15
❑ 17	Cliff Branch	.40	.15
❑ 18	Sonny Jurgensen	.60	.25
❑ 19	Eric Dickerson	.40	.15
❑ 20	Lee Roy Selmon	.25	.08
❑ 21	Roger Craig	.40	.15
❑ 22	Raymond Berry	.40	.15
❑ 23	Bob Hayes	.40	.15
❑ 24	Steve Largent	.60	.25
❑ 25	Lenny Moore	.40	.15
❑ 26	Chuck Bednarik	.40	.15
❑ 27	Ken Stabler	1.25	.50
❑ 28	William Perry	.40	.15
❑ 29	Joe Greene	.60	.25
❑ 30	Joe Namath	1.50	.60
❑ 31	Jim Kelly	.75	.30
❑ 32	Steve Young	1.25	.50
❑ 33	Randy White	.40	.15
❑ 34	Lawrence Taylor	.60	.25
❑ 35	Franco Harris	.75	.30
❑ 36	Marcus Allen	.60	.25
❑ 37	Mike Singletary	.60	.25
❑ 38	Fran Tarkenton	1.25	.50
❑ 39	Mel Renfro	.25	.08
❑ 40	Len Dawson	.60	.25
❑ 41	Carl Eller	.25	.08
❑ 42	Chuck Foreman	.25	.08
❑ 43	Gino Marchetti	.25	.08
❑ 44	Jim Marshall	.25	.08
❑ 45	Jack Ham	.40	.15
❑ 46	Mercury Morris	.25	.08
❑ 47	Anthony Munoz	.40	.15
❑ 48	Herschel Walker	.40	.15
❑ 49	Drew Pearson	.40	.15
❑ 50	John Elway	2.50	1.00
❑ 51	George Blanda	.60	.25
❑ 52	Earl Campbell	.60	.25
❑ 53	Bart Starr	2.00	.75
❑ 54	Dan Marino	2.50	1.00
❑ 55	Johnny Unitas	1.50	.60
❑ 56	Sammy Baugh	.60	.25
❑ 57	Steve Van Buren	.40	.15
❑ 58	Mel Blount	.40	.15
❑ 59	Fred Biletnikoff	.60	.25
❑ 60	John Brodie	.25	.08
❑ 61	Daryle Lamonica	.25	.08
❑ 62	James Lofton	.25	.08
❑ 63	Ronnie Lott	.40	.15
❑ 64	Gale Sayers	1.25	.50
❑ 65	Art Monk	.40	.15
❑ 66	Jim Plunkett	.40	.15
❑ 67	Charlie Joiner	.25	.08
❑ 68	Deacon Jones	.40	.15
❑ 69	Paul Warfield	.60	.25
❑ 70	Jim Otto	.25	.08
❑ 71	Billy Kilmer	.40	.15
❑ 72	Archie Manning	.40	.15
❑ 73	Alex Karras	.40	.15
❑ 74	Tom Matte	.25	.08
❑ 75	Jay Novacek	.25	.08
❑ 76	Charley Taylor	.40	.15

❑ 77 Sam Huff	.40	.15
❑ 78 Jack Lambert	.60	.25
❑ 79 Mike Ditka	.60	.25
❑ 80 Frank Gifford	.60	.25
❑ 81 Jim Thorpe	.60	.25
❑ 82 Walter Payton	3.00	1.25
❑ 83 Doak Walker	.60	.25
❑ 84 Sid Luckman	.40	.15
❑ 85 Bronko Nagurski	.60	.25
❑ 86 Alan Ameche	.25	.08
❑ 87 Merlin Olsen	.40	.15
❑ 88 Dick Butkus	1.25	.50
❑ 89 Elroy Hirsch	.40	.15
❑ 90 Max McGee	.40	.15
❑ 91 Ray Nitschke	.60	.25
❑ 92 Phil Simms	.40	.15
❑ 93 Vince Lombardi CC	1.25	.50
❑ 94 Tom Landry CC	.75	.30
❑ 95 Bill Walsh CC	.40	.15
❑ 96 Mike Ditka CC	.60	.25
❑ 97 Jimmy Johnson CC	.40	.15
❑ 98 Chuck Noll CC	.40	.15
❑ 99 Dan Reeves CC	.40	.15
❑ 100 Don Shula CC	.60	.25
❑ 101 Peter Warrick RC	8.00	3.00
❑ 102 Thomas Jones RC	12.00	5.00
❑ 103 Jamal Lewis RC	20.00	7.50
❑ 104 Chad Pennington RC	20.00	7.50
❑ 105 Chris Redman RC	6.00	2.50
❑ 106 Ron Dayne RC	8.00	3.00
❑ 107 Trung Canidate RC	6.00	2.50
❑ 108 Shaun Alexander RC	40.00	15.00
❑ 109 Plaxico Burress RC	15.00	6.00
❑ 110 J.R. Redmond RC	6.00	2.50
❑ 111 Travis Taylor RC	8.00	3.00
❑ 112 Dez White RC	8.00	3.00
❑ 113 Todd Pinkston RC	8.00	3.00
❑ 114 Laveranues Coles RC	10.00	4.00
❑ 115 Dennis Northcutt RC	8.00	3.00
❑ 116 Jerry Porter RC	10.00	4.00
❑ 117 R.Jay Soward RC	6.00	2.50
❑ 118 Sylvester Morris RC	6.00	2.50
❑ 119 Ron Dugans RC	6.00	2.50
❑ 120 Travis Prentice RC	6.00	2.50
❑ 121 Tee Martin RC	8.00	3.00
❑ 122 James Williams RC	6.00	2.50
❑ 123 Trevor Gaylor RC	6.00	2.50
❑ 124 Shyrone Stith RC	6.00	2.50
❑ 125 Frank Moreau RC	6.00	2.50
❑ 126 Kwame Cavil RC	6.00	2.50
❑ 127 Ron Dixon RC	6.00	2.50
❑ 128 Darrell Jackson RC	15.00	6.00
❑ 129 Sammy Morris RC	6.00	2.50
❑ 130 JaJuan Dawson RC	6.00	2.50
❑ 131 Doug Johnson RC	20.00	8.00
❑ 132 Brian Urlacher RC	50.00	20.00
❑ 133 Brad Hoover RC	20.00	8.00
❑ 134 Mike Anderson AUTO RC	30.00	15.00

2004 Greats of the Game

❑ COMP.SET w/o RC's (67)	40.00	15.00
❑ 1 Jim Brown	3.00	1.25
❑ 2 Jim Thorpe	2.00	.75
❑ 3 Terry Bradshaw	3.00	1.25
❑ 4 Fran Tarkenton	2.50	1.00
❑ 5 Joe Namath	3.00	1.25
❑ 6 Joe Montana	6.00	2.50
❑ 7 George Rogers	1.00	.40
❑ 8 Marcus Allen	2.00	.75
❑ 9 Walter Payton	6.00	2.50
❑ 10 Dick Butkus	3.00	1.25
❑ 11 Dan Fouts	2.00	.75
❑ 12 Kellen Winslow Sr.	1.50	.60
❑ 13 Sammy Baugh	2.00	.75
❑ 14 Bart Starr	4.00	1.50
❑ 15 Steve Young	2.50	1.00
❑ 16 Sid Luckman	2.00	.75
❑ 17 Y.A. Tittle	2.00	.75
❑ 18 Dan Marino	5.00	2.00
❑ 19 Paul Hornung	2.00	.75
❑ 20 John Elway	3.00	1.25
❑ 21 Earl Campbell	2.00	.75
❑ 22 Max McGee	1.50	.60
❑ 23 Alan Ameche	1.00	.40
❑ 24 Bronko Nagurski	2.00	.75
❑ 25 Elroy Hirsch	1.50	.60
❑ 26 Jack Lambert	2.50	1.00
❑ 27 Sam Huff	1.50	.60
❑ 28 Jay Novacek	1.50	.60
❑ 29 Roger Staubach	3.00	1.25
❑ 30 Bob Hayes	1.50	.60
❑ 31 Ken Stabler	2.50	1.00
❑ 32 Chuck Bednarik	1.50	.60
❑ 33 Ronnie Lott	2.00	.75
❑ 34 Steve Van Buren	1.50	.60
❑ 36 Gale Sayers	2.50	1.00
❑ 37 Jim Otto	1.00	.40
❑ 38 Jim Plunkett	1.50	.60
❑ 40 Don Maynard	1.50	.60
❑ 41 John Riggins	2.50	1.00
❑ 42 Billy Sims	1.50	.60
❑ 43 Franco Harris	2.50	1.00
❑ 44 Tony Dorsett	2.00	.75
❑ 45 Wilbert Montgomery	1.00	.40
❑ 46 Eric Dickerson SP	4.00	1.50
❑ 47 Jim Taylor	2.00	.75
❑ 48 George Blanda	2.00	.75
❑ 49 Cris Carter	2.00	.75
❑ 50 Mike Quick	1.00	.40
❑ 51 James Lofton	1.00	.40
❑ 52 Lawrence Taylor	2.00	.75
❑ 53 Roger Craig	2.00	.75
❑ 54 Paul Warfield	1.50	.60
❑ 55 Dan Pastorini	1.00	.40
❑ 56 Ozzie Newsome	1.50	.60
❑ 57 Charley Taylor	1.50	.60
❑ 58 Deacon Jones	1.50	.60
❑ 59 Bob Lilly	2.00	.75
❑ 60 Mike Singletary	2.00	.75
❑ 61 Warren Moon	1.50	.60
❑ 62 Charles White	1.00	.40
❑ 63 Bob Griese	2.00	.75
❑ 64 Dwight Clark	1.50	.60
❑ 65 Joe Greene	2.00	.75
❑ 66 Dave Casper	1.00	.40
❑ 67 Harold Carmichael	1.00	.40
❑ 68 Drew Pearson	1.50	.60
❑ 69 Tony Hill	1.00	.40
❑ 70 Ray Nitschke	2.00	.75
❑ 71 Eli Manning RC	20.00	10.00
❑ 72 Philip Rivers RC	12.00	5.00
❑ 73 Ben Roethlisberger RC	40.00	20.00
❑ 74 Julius Jones RC	12.00	5.00
❑ 75 Larry Fitzgerald RC	12.00	5.00
❑ 76 Steven Jackson RC	12.00	5.00
❑ 77 Kevin Jones RC	10.00	4.00
❑ 78 Tatum Bell RC	8.00	3.00
❑ 79 Rashaun Woods RC	4.00	1.50
❑ 80 Roy Williams RC	10.00	4.00
❑ 81 Lee Evans RC	5.00	2.00
❑ 82 Michael Clayton RC	8.00	3.00
❑ 83 J.P. Losman RC	8.00	3.00
❑ 84 Drew Henson RC	4.00	1.50
❑ 85 Kellen Winslow RC	8.00	3.00
❑ 86 Chris Perry RC	6.00	2.50
❑ 87 Reggie Williams RC	5.00	2.00
❑ 88 Michael Jenkins RC	4.00	1.50
❑ 89 Darius Watts RC	4.00	1.50
❑ 90 Keary Colbert RC	5.00	2.00

2002 Gridiron Kings

❑ COMPLETE SET (175)	120.00	60.00
❑ COMP.SET w/o SP"s (100)	40.00	15.00
❑ 1 David Boston	1.25	.50
❑ 2 Jake Plummer	.75	.30
■ 3 Michael Vick	4.00	1.50
❑ 4 Warrick Dunn	1.25	.50
❑ 5 Jamal Lewis	1.25	.50
❑ 6 Ray Lewis	1.25	.50
❑ 7 Drew Bledsoe	1.50	.60
❑ 8 Travis Henry	1.25	.50

❑ 9 Eric Moulds	.75	.30
❑ 10 Chris Weinke	.75	.30
❑ 11 Lamar Smith	.75	.30
❑ 12 Anthony Thomas	.75	.30
❑ 13 Chris Chandler	.75	.30
❑ 14 Brian Urlacher	2.00	.75
❑ 15 Corey Dillon	.75	.30
❑ 16 Peter Warrick	.75	.30
❑ 17 Tim Couch	.75	.30
❑ 18 James Jackson	.50	.20
❑ 19 Kevin Johnson	.75	.30
❑ 20 Quincy Carter	.75	.30
❑ 21 Emmitt Smith	3.00	1.25
❑ 22 Joey Galloway	.75	.30
❑ 23 Brian Griese	1.25	.50
❑ 24 Terrell Davis	1.25	.50
❑ 25 Ed McCaffrey	1.25	.50
❑ 26 Rod Smith	.75	.30
❑ 27 Mike McMahon	1.25	.50
❑ 28 Az-Zahir Hakim	.50	.20
❑ 29 Germane Crowell	.50	.20
❑ 30 Brett Favre	3.00	1.25
❑ 31 Terry Glenn	.75	.30
❑ 32 Ahman Green	1.25	.50
❑ 33 James Allen	.75	.30
❑ 34 Tony Simmons	.50	.20
❑ 35 Peyton Manning	2.50	1.00
❑ 36 Edgerrin James	1.50	.60
❑ 37 Marvin Harrison	1.25	.50
❑ 38 Dominic Rhodes	.75	.30
❑ 39 Mark Brunell	1.25	.50
❑ 40 Jimmy Smith	.75	.30
❑ 41 Keenan McCardell	.50	.20
❑ 42 Fred Taylor	1.25	.50
❑ 43 Priest Holmes	1.50	.60
❑ 44 Snoop Minnis	.50	.20
❑ 45 Trent Green	.75	.30
❑ 46 Tony Gonzalez	.75	.30
❑ 47 Chris Chambers	1.25	.50
❑ 48 Ricky Williams	1.25	.50
❑ 49 Jay Fiedler	.75	.30
❑ 50 Zach Thomas	1.25	.50
❑ 51 Randy Moss	2.50	1.00
❑ 52 Cris Carter	1.25	.50
❑ 53 Daunte Culpepper	1.25	.50
❑ 54 Michael Bennett	1.25	.50
❑ 55 Tom Brady	3.00	1.25
❑ 56 Antowain Smith	.75	.30
❑ 57 Troy Brown	.75	.30
❑ 58 Aaron Brooks	1.25	.50
❑ 59 Deuce McAllister	1.50	.60
❑ 60 Joe Horn	.75	.30
❑ 61 Kerry Collins	.75	.30
❑ 62 Ron Dayne	.75	.30
❑ 63 Michael Strahan	.75	.30
❑ 64 Vinny Testaverde	.75	.30
❑ 65 Curtis Martin	1.25	.50
❑ 66 Wayne Chrebet	.75	.30
❑ 67 Rich Gannon	1.25	.50
❑ 68 Tim Brown	1.25	.50
❑ 69 Jerry Rice	2.50	1.00
❑ 70 Charlie Garner	.75	.30
❑ 71 Donovan McNabb	1.50	.60
❑ 72 Duce Staley	1.25	.50
❑ 73 Freddie Mitchell	.75	.30
❑ 74 Kordell Stewart	.75	.30
❑ 75 Jerome Bettis	1.25	.50
❑ 76 Plaxico Burress	1.25	.50
❑ 77 Kendrell Bell	1.25	.50
❑ 78 LaDainian Tomlinson	2.00	.75
❑ 79 Drew Brees	1.25	.50
❑ 80 Doug Flutie	1.25	.50

❑ 81	Junior Seau	1.25	.50
❑ 82	Jeff Garcia	1.25	.50
❑ 83	Terrell Owens	1.25	.50
❑ 84	Garrison Hearst	.75	.30
❑ 85	Trent Dilfer	.75	.30
❑ 86	Shaun Alexander	1.50	.60
❑ 87	Koren Robinson	.75	.30
❑ 88	Marshall Faulk	1.25	.50
❑ 89	Kurt Warner	1.25	.50
❑ 90	Torry Holt	1.25	.50
❑ 91	Isaac Bruce	1.25	.50
❑ 92	Brad Johnson	.75	.30
❑ 93	Keyshawn Johnson	1.25	.50
❑ 94	Mike Alstott	1.25	.50
❑ 95	Warren Sapp	.75	.30
❑ 96	Steve McNair	1.25	.50
❑ 97	Eddie George	1.25	.50
❑ 98	Jevon Kearse	1.25	.50
❑ 99	Stephen Davis	.75	.30
❑ 100	Rod Gardner	.75	.30
❑ 101	David Carr RC	10.00	4.00
❑ 102	Joey Harrington RC	6.00	2.50
❑ 103	Patrick Ramsey RC	5.00	2.00
❑ 104	Josh McCown RC	5.00	2.00
❑ 105	David Garrard RC	4.00	1.50
❑ 106	Rohan Davey RC	4.00	1.50
❑ 107	Randy Fasani RC	3.00	1.25
❑ 108	Kurt Kittner RC	3.00	1.25
❑ 109	William Green RC	4.00	1.50
❑ 110	T.J. Duckett RC	5.00	2.00
❑ 111	DeShaun Foster RC	1.25	.50
❑ 112	Clinton Portis RC	12.00	5.00
❑ 113	Maurice Morris RC	4.00	1.50
❑ 114	Ladell Betts RC	4.00	1.50
❑ 115	Lamar Gordon RC	4.00	1.50
❑ 116	Brian Westbrook RC	6.00	2.50
❑ 117	Jonathan Wells RC	4.00	1.50
❑ 118	Travis Stephens RC	3.00	1.25
❑ 119	Josh Scobey RC	4.00	1.50
❑ 120	Donte Stallworth RC	8.00	3.00
❑ 121	Ashley Lelie RC	8.00	3.00
❑ 122	Javon Walker RC	8.00	3.00
❑ 123	Jabar Gaffney RC	4.00	1.50
❑ 124	Josh Reed RC	4.00	1.50
❑ 125	Tim Carter RC	3.00	1.25
❑ 126	Andre Davis RC	3.00	1.25
❑ 127	Reche Caldwell RC	4.00	1.50
❑ 128	Antwaan Randle El RC	6.00	2.50
❑ 129	Antonio Bryant RC	4.00	1.50
❑ 130	Deion Branch RC	8.00	3.00
❑ 131	Marquise Walker RC	3.00	1.25
❑ 132	Cliff Russell RC	3.00	1.25
❑ 133	Eric Crouch RC	4.00	1.50
❑ 134	Ron Johnson RC	3.00	1.25
❑ 135	Terry Charles RC	3.00	1.25
❑ 136	Jeremy Shockey RC	12.00	5.00
❑ 137	Daniel Graham RC	4.00	1.50
❑ 138	Julius Peppers RC	8.00	3.00
❑ 139	Dwight Freeney RC	6.00	2.50
❑ 140	Ryan Sims RC	4.00	1.50
❑ 141	John Henderson RC	4.00	1.50
❑ 142	Wendell Bryant RC	3.00	1.25
❑ 143	Albert Haynesworth RC	3.00	1.25
❑ 144	Quentin Jammer RC	4.00	1.50
❑ 145	Phillip Buchanon RC	4.00	1.50
❑ 146	Lito Sheppard RC	4.00	1.50
❑ 147	Roy Williams RC	10.00	4.00
❑ 148	Ed Reed RC	6.00	2.50
❑ 149	Napoleon Harris RC	4.00	1.50
❑ 150	Mike Williams RC	3.00	1.25
❑ 151	Art Monk	4.00	1.50
❑ 152	Barry Sanders	8.00	3.00
❑ 153	Bob Griese	5.00	2.00
❑ 154	Dan Marino	10.00	4.00
❑ 155	Dick Butkus	10.00	4.00
❑ 156	Earl Campbell	5.00	2.00
❑ 157	Eric Dickerson	5.00	2.00
❑ 158	Fran Tarkenton	5.00	2.00
❑ 159	Franco Harris	5.00	2.00
❑ 160	Herschel Walker	4.00	1.50
❑ 161	Joe Montana	15.00	6.00
❑ 162	Ronnie Lott	4.00	1.50
❑ 163	Joe Theismann	4.00	1.50
❑ 164	John Elway	10.00	4.00
❑ 165	John Riggins	5.00	2.00
❑ 166	Ken Stabler	6.00	2.50
❑ 167	Len Dawson	5.00	2.00
❑ 168	Marcus Allen	4.00	1.50
❑ 169	Mike Singletary	4.00	1.50
❑ 170	Roger Staubach	6.00	2.50
❑ 171	Walter Payton	12.00	5.00
❑ 172	Steve Largent	5.00	2.00
❑ 173	Terry Bradshaw	6.00	2.50
❑ 174	Thurman Thomas	4.00	1.50
❑ 175	Tony Dorsett	5.00	2.00

2003 Gridiron Kings

❑	COMPLETE SET (175)	200.00	100.00
❑	COMP.SET w/o SP's (100)	30.00	12.50
❑ 1	David Boston	.75	.30
❑ 2	Marcel Shipp	.75	.30
❑ 3	Jake Plummer	.75	.30
❑ 4	Michael Vick	3.00	1.25
❑ 5	T.J. Duckett	.75	.30
❑ 6	Warrick Dunn	.75	.30
❑ 7	Ray Lewis	1.25	.50
❑ 8	Jamal Lewis	1.25	.50
❑ 9	Todd Heap	.75	.30
❑ 10	Drew Bledsoe	1.25	.50
❑ 11	Eric Moulds	.75	.30
❑ 12	Travis Henry	.75	.30
❑ 13	Julius Peppers	1.25	.50
❑ 14	Steve Smith	1.25	.50
❑ 15	Muhsin Muhammad	.75	.30
❑ 16	Anthony Thomas	.75	.30
❑ 17	David Terrell	.75	.30
❑ 18	Brian Urlacher	2.00	.75
❑ 19	Corey Dillon	.75	.30
❑ 20	Chad Johnson	1.25	.50
❑ 21	William Green	.75	.30
❑ 22	Tim Couch	.50	.20
❑ 23	Quincy Morgan	.75	.30
❑ 24	Roy Williams	1.25	.50
❑ 25	Emmitt Smith	3.00	1.25
❑ 26	Antonio Bryant	.75	.30
❑ 27	Clinton Portis	2.00	.75
❑ 28	Ashley Lelie	1.25	.50
❑ 29	Rod Smith	.75	.30
❑ 30	Brian Griese	1.25	.50
❑ 31	Joey Harrington	2.00	.75
❑ 32	James Stewart	.75	.30
❑ 33	Az-Zahir Hakim	.50	.20
❑ 34	Brett Favre	3.00	1.25
❑ 35	Ahman Green	1.25	.50
❑ 36	Donald Driver	.75	.30
❑ 37	Javon Walker	.75	.30
❑ 38	David Carr	2.00	.75
❑ 39	Jabar Gaffney	.75	.30
❑ 40	Jonathan Wells	.50	.20
❑ 41	Edgerrin James	1.25	.50
❑ 42	Marvin Harrison	1.25	.50
❑ 43	Peyton Manning	2.00	.75
❑ 44	Mark Brunell	.75	.30
❑ 45	Jimmy Smith	.75	.30
❑ 46	Fred Taylor	1.25	.50
❑ 47	Priest Holmes	1.50	.60
❑ 48	Tony Gonzalez	.75	.30
❑ 49	Trent Green	.75	.30
❑ 50	Jay Fiedler	.75	.30
❑ 51	Chris Chambers	1.25	.50
❑ 52	Zach Thomas	1.25	.50
❑ 53	Ricky Williams	1.25	.50
❑ 54	Randy Moss	2.00	.75
❑ 55	Daunte Culpepper	1.25	.50
❑ 56	Michael Bennett	.75	.30
❑ 57	Tom Brady	3.00	1.25
❑ 58	Deion Branch	1.25	.50
❑ 59	Antowain Smith	.50	.20
❑ 60	Donte Stallworth	1.25	.50
❑ 61	Deuce McAllister	1.25	.50
❑ 62	Aaron Brooks	1.25	.50
❑ 63	Kerry Collins	.75	.30
❑ 64	Jeremy Shockey	2.00	.75
❑ 65	Tiki Barber	1.25	.50
❑ 66	Curtis Martin	1.25	.50
❑ 67	Chad Pennington	1.50	.60
❑ 68	Santana Moss	.75	.30
❑ 69	Jerry Rice	2.50	1.00
❑ 70	Rich Gannon	.75	.30
❑ 71	Tim Brown	1.25	.50
❑ 72	Charlie Garner	.75	.30
❑ 73	Donovan McNabb	1.50	.60
❑ 74	Duce Staley	.75	.30
❑ 75	Antonio Freeman	.75	.30
❑ 76	Tommy Maddox	1.25	.50
❑ 77	Jerome Bettis	1.25	.50
❑ 78	Antwaan Randle El	1.25	.50
❑ 79	Plaxico Burress	.75	.30
❑ 80	LaDainian Tomlinson	1.25	.50
❑ 81	Junior Seau	1.25	.50
❑ 82	Drew Brees	1.25	.50
❑ 83	Terrell Owens	1.25	.50
❑ 84	Jeff Garcia	1.25	.50
❑ 85	Garrison Hearst	.75	.30
❑ 86	Koren Robinson	.75	.30
❑ 87	Shaun Alexander	1.25	.50
❑ 88	Trent Dilfer	.75	.30
❑ 89	Marshall Faulk	1.25	.50
❑ 90	Kurt Warner	1.25	.50
❑ 91	Isaac Bruce	1.25	.50
❑ 92	Brad Johnson	.75	.30
❑ 93	Keyshawn Johnson	1.25	.50
❑ 94	Warren Sapp	.75	.30
❑ 95	Steve McNair	1.25	.50
❑ 96	Derrick Mason	.75	.30
❑ 97	Eddie George	.75	.30
❑ 98	Bruce Smith	.75	.30
❑ 99	Rod Gardner	.75	.30
❑ 100	Patrick Ramsey	1.25	.50
❑ 101	Carson Palmer RC	12.00	5.00
❑ 102	Byron Leftwich RC	10.00	4.00
❑ 103	Kyle Boller RC	3.00	1.25
❑ 104	Chris Simms RC	5.00	2.00
❑ 105	Dave Ragone RC	3.00	1.25
❑ 106	Rex Grossman RC	10.00	4.00
❑ 107	Brian St.Pierre RC	3.00	1.25
❑ 108	Kliff Kingsbury RC	2.50	1.00
❑ 109	Seneca Wallace RC	3.00	1.25
❑ 110	Larry Johnson RC	12.00	6.00
❑ 111	Lee Suggs RC	3.00	1.25
❑ 112	Justin Fargas RC	3.00	1.25
❑ 113	Onterrio Smith RC	3.00	1.25
❑ 114	Willis McGahee RC	8.00	3.00
❑ 115	Chris Brown RC	3.00	1.25
❑ 116	Musa Smith RC	3.00	1.25
❑ 117	Artose Pinner RC	3.00	1.25
❑ 118	Domanick Davis RC	3.00	1.25
❑ 119	Charles Rogers RC	3.00	1.25
❑ 120	Andre Johnson RC	6.00	2.50
❑ 121	Taylor Jacobs RC	2.50	1.00
❑ 122	Bryant Johnson RC	3.00	1.25
❑ 123	Kelley Washington RC	3.00	1.25
❑ 124	Brandon Lloyd RC	3.00	1.25
❑ 125	Tyrone Calico RC	3.00	1.25
❑ 126	Kevin Curtis RC	3.00	1.25
❑ 127	Bethel Johnson RC	3.00	1.25
❑ 128	Anquan Boldin RC	8.00	3.00
❑ 129	Nate Burleson RC	3.00	1.25
❑ 130	Jason Witten RC	5.00	2.00
❑ 131	Bennie Joppru RC	3.00	1.25
❑ 132	Teyo Johnson RC	3.00	1.25
❑ 133	Dallas Clark RC	3.00	1.25
❑ 134	Terrell Suggs RC	5.00	2.00
❑ 135	Chris Kelsay RC	3.00	1.25
❑ 136	Jerome McDougle RC	3.00	1.25
❑ 137	Michael Haynes RC	3.00	1.25
❑ 138	Calvin Pace RC	2.50	1.00
❑ 139	Jimmy Kennedy RC	3.00	1.25
❑ 140	Kevin Williams RC	3.00	1.25
❑ 141	DeWayne Robertson RC	3.00	1.25
❑ 142	William Joseph RC	3.00	1.25
❑ 143	Johnathan Sullivan RC	2.50	1.00
❑ 144	Boss Bailey RC	3.00	1.25
❑ 145	E.J. Henderson RC	3.00	1.25
❑ 146	Terence Newman RC	6.00	2.50
❑ 147	Marcus Trufant RC	3.00	1.25
❑ 148	Andre Woolfolk RC	3.00	1.25
❑ 149	Troy Polamalu RC	15.00	7.50
❑ 150	Mike Doss RC	3.00	1.25
❑ 151	Andre Reed	3.00	1.25

152 Bo Jackson	5.00	2.00
153 Dan Marino	10.00	4.00
154 Deacon Jones	3.00	1.25
155 Deion Sanders	4.00	1.50
156 Doak Walker	3.00	1.25
157 Don Maynard	3.00	1.25
158 Frank Gifford	3.00	1.25
159 Fred Biletnikoff	3.00	1.25
160 Gale Sayers	3.00	1.25
161 Jack Lambert	4.00	1.50
162 Jim Brown	4.00	1.50
163 Jim Kelly	5.00	2.00
164 Joe Greene	3.00	1.25
165 Joe Montana	12.00	5.00
166 John Elway	10.00	4.00
167 John Riggins	4.00	1.50
168 Johnny Unitas	3.00	1.25
169 Larry Csonka	3.00	1.25
170 Lawrence Taylor	3.00	1.25
171 Mike Ditka	3.00	1.25
172 Ozzie Newsome	3.00	1.25
173 Red Grange	3.00	1.25
174 Troy Aikman	5.00	2.00
175 Warren Moon	3.00	1.25

2001 Hot Prospects

COMP.SET w/o SP's (100)	25.00	10.00
1 Aaron Brooks	1.00	.40
2 Tim Couch	.60	.25
3 Jeff George	.60	.25
4 Brett Favre	3.00	1.25
5 Donovan McNabb	1.25	.50
6 Ray Lucas	.40	.15
7 Doug Flutie	1.00	.40
8 Mark Brunell	1.00	.40
9 Steve McNair	1.00	.40
10 Trent Green	1.00	.40
11 Daunte Culpepper	1.00	.40
12 Rich Gannon	1.00	.40
13 Kurt Warner	2.00	.75
14 Brian Griese	1.00	.40
15 Kerry Collins	.60	.25
16 Vinny Testaverde	.60	.25
17 David Boston	1.00	.40
18 Peyton Manning	2.50	1.00
19 Keyshawn Johnson	1.00	.40
20 Tim Biakabutuka	.60	.25
22 Emmitt Smith	2.00	.75
23 Terry Glenn	.60	.25
24 Tony Gonzalez	.60	.25
25 Charlie Garner	.60	.25
26 Lamar Smith	.60	.25
27 Eddie George	1.00	.40
28 Fred Taylor	1.00	.40
29 Marvin Harrison	1.00	.40
30 Terrell Davis	1.00	.40
31 Marcus Robinson	1.00	.40
32 Edgerrin James	1.25	.50
33 Ed McCaffrey	1.00	.40
34 Ricky Williams	1.00	.40
36 Jerome Bettis	1.00	.40
37 Shaun Alexander	1.25	.50
38 Mike Anderson	1.00	.40
39 Keenan McCardell	.40	.15
40 Mike Alstott	1.00	.40
41 Terrell Fletcher	.40	.15
42 Kevin Johnson	.60	.25
43 Wesley Walls	.40	.15
44 Derrick Mason	.60	.25
45 Sammy Morris	.40	.15
46 Joey Galloway	.60	.25
47 Sylvester Morris	.40	.15
48 Stephen Davis	1.00	.40
49 Terrell Owens	1.00	.40
50 Troy Edwards	.40	.15
51 Amani Toomer	.60	.25
52 Ray Lewis	1.00	.40
53 Terance Mathis	.60	.25
54 Brian Urlacher	1.50	.60
55 Junior Seau	1.00	.40
56 Rocket Ismail	.60	.25
57 Wayne Chrebet	.60	.25
58 Peter Warrick	1.00	.40
59 Andre Rison	.60	.25
60 Desmond Howard	.40	.15
61 Eric Moulds	.60	.25
62 Jerry Rice	2.00	.75
63 Stephen Alexander	.40	.15
64 Isaac Bruce	1.00	.40
65 Travis Prentice	.40	.15
66 James Stewart	.60	.25
67 Jamal Anderson	1.00	.40
68 Ricky Watters	.40	.15
69 Jamal Lewis	1.50	.60
70 Priest Holmes	1.25	.50
71 Ahman Green	1.00	.40
72 Marshall Faulk	1.25	.50
73 Warrick Dunn	1.00	.40
74 Curtis Martin	1.00	.40
75 Corey Dillon	1.00	.40
76 Ron Dayne	1.00	.40
77 Thomas Jones	.60	.25
78 Duce Staley	1.00	.40
79 Tiki Barber	1.00	.40
80 Cris Carter	1.00	.40
81 Tim Brown	1.00	.40
82 Jimmy Smith	.60	.25
83 Elvis Grbac	.60	.25
84 Randy Moss	2.00	.75
85 Tim Dwight	1.00	.40
86 Antonio Freeman	1.00	.40
87 Muhsin Muhammad	.60	.25
88 Torry Holt	1.00	.40
89 Frank Wycheck	.40	.15
90 Jake Plummer	.60	.25
91 Brad Johnson	1.00	.40
92 Chris Chandler	.60	.25
93 Drew Bledsoe	1.25	.50
94 Rob Johnson	.60	.25
95 Matt Hasselbeck	.60	.25
96 Jon Kitna	.60	.25
97 Kordell Stewart	.60	.25
98 Charlie Batch	1.00	.40
99 Cade McNown	.40	.15
100 Jeff Garcia	1.00	.40
101 Quincy Morgan RC	3.00	1.25
102 Jesse Palmer RC	3.00	1.25
103 Reggie Wayne RC	6.00	2.50
104 Deuce McAllister RC	6.00	2.50
105 Chad Johnson RC	8.00	3.00
106 Chris Weinke RC	3.00	1.25
107 Michael Bennett RC	3.00	1.25
108 Rod Gardner RC	3.00	1.25
109 Michael Vick RC	15.00	6.00
110 Anthony Thomas RC	3.00	1.25
111 Santana Moss RC	5.00	2.00
112 Kevan Barlow RC	3.00	1.25
113 Koren Robinson RC	3.00	1.25
114 Rudi Johnson RC	6.00	2.50
115 Josh Heupel RC	3.00	1.25
116 James Jackson RC	3.00	1.25
117 Freddie Mitchell RC	3.00	1.25
118 LaDainian Tomlinson RC	30.00	15.00
119 Marques Tuiasosopo RC	3.00	1.25
120 Drew Brees RC	12.00	5.00
121 David Terrell RC	3.00	1.25
122 Chris Chambers RC	5.00	2.00
123 Mike McMahon RC	3.00	1.25
124 Robert Ferguson RC	3.00	1.25
125 Justin Smith RC	3.00	1.25
126 Leonard Davis RC	2.00	.75
127 Todd Heap RC	3.00	1.25
128 Dan Morgan RC	3.00	1.25
129 Gerard Warren RC	3.00	1.25
130 Travis Henry RC	5.00	2.00
131 Travis Minor RC	2.00	.75
132 Richard Seymour RC	3.00	1.25
133 Quincy Carter RC	3.00	1.25
134 Snoop Minnis RC	2.00	.75
135 Sage Rosenfels RC	3.00	1.25
CL1 Checklist	.10	.02

2002 Hot Prospects

COMP.SET w/o SP's (80)	25.00	10.00
1 Donovan McNabb	1.50	.60
2 Drew Brees	1.25	.50
3 Curtis Martin	1.25	.50
4 Priest Holmes	1.50	.60
5 Quincy Carter	.75	.30
6 Chris Weinke	.75	.30
7 Marshall Faulk	1.25	.50
8 Jake Plummer	.75	.30
9 Tom Brady	3.00	1.25
10 Ahman Green	1.25	.50
11 Brian Urlacher	2.00	.75
12 Keyshawn Johnson	1.25	.50
13 Jerome Bettis	1.25	.50
14 Tiki Barber	1.25	.50
15 Edgerrin James	1.50	.60
16 Jamal Lewis	1.25	.50
17 Terrell Owens	1.25	.50
18 Joe Horn	.75	.30
19 Daunte Culpepper	1.25	.50
20 Terrell Davis	1.25	.50
21 Fred Taylor	1.25	.50
22 Emmitt Smith	3.00	1.25
23 Jamal Anderson	.75	.30
24 Garrison Hearst	.75	.30
25 Chad Pennington	1.50	.60
26 Michael Bennett	.75	.30
27 James Allen	.75	.30
28 Marty Booker	.50	.20
29 Warren Sapp	.75	.30
30 Jerry Rice	2.50	1.00
31 Antowain Smith	.75	.30
32 Marvin Harrison	1.25	.50
33 Tim Couch	.75	.30
34 Stephen Davis	.75	.30
35 Kordell Stewart	.75	.30
36 Tony Gonzalez	.75	.30
37 Mike McMahon	1.25	.50
38 Eric Moulds	.75	.30
39 Kurt Warner	1.25	.50
40 Ricky Williams	1.25	.50
41 Michael Strahan	.75	.30
42 Trent Green	.75	.30
43 Brian Griese	1.25	.50
44 David Boston	1.25	.50
45 LaDainian Tomlinson	2.00	.75
46 Tim Brown	1.25	.50
47 Deuce McAllister	1.50	.60
48 Jamie Sharper	.50	.20
49 Rod Gardner	.75	.30
50 Isaac Bruce	1.25	.50
51 Freddie Mitchell	.75	.30
52 Kerry Collins	.75	.30
53 Mark Brunell	1.25	.50
54 Corey Dillon	.75	.30
55 Steve McNair	1.25	.50
56 Aaron Brooks	1.25	.50
57 Chris Chambers	1.25	.50
58 Bill Schroeder	.75	.30
59 Ray Lewis	1.25	.50
60 Shaun Alexander	1.50	.60
61 Kevin Johnson	.75	.30
62 Michael Vick	4.00	1.50
63 Jeff Garcia	1.25	.50
64 Laveranues Coles	.75	.30
65 Jimmy Smith	.75	.30
66 Brett Favre	3.00	1.25
67 Anthony Thomas	.75	.30
68 Torry Holt	1.25	.50
69 Duce Staley	1.25	.50

❑ 70 Randy Moss 2.50 1.00
❑ 71 Peyton Manning 2.50 1.00
❑ 72 Peter Warrick .75 .30
❑ 73 Eddie George 1.25 .50
❑ 74 Plaxico Burress .75 .30
❑ 75 Troy Brown .75 .30
❑ 76 Rod Smith .75 .30
❑ 77 Drew Bledsoe 1.50 .60
❑ 78 Darrell Jackson .75 .30
❑ 79 Rich Gannon 1.25 .50
❑ 80 Jay Fiedler .75 .30
❑ 81 David Carr/250 RC 40.00 15.00
❑ 82 Andre Davis JSY RC 8.00 3.00
❑ 83 Daniel Graham JSY RC 10.00 4.00
❑ 84 Ron Johnson JSY RC 8.00 3.00
❑ 85 Julius Peppers JSY RC 20.00 7.50
❑ 86 Josh Reed JSY RC 10.00 4.00
❑ 87 Travis Stephens JSY RC 8.00 3.00
❑ 88 Mike Williams JSY RC 8.00 3.00
❑ 89 Antonio Bryant JSY RC 10.00 4.00
❑ 90 Eric Crouch JSY RC 10.00 4.00
❑ 91 DeShaun Foster JSY RC 10.00 4.00
❑ 92 Joey Harrington JSY RC 15.00 6.00
❑ 93 Josh McCown JSY RC 15.00 6.00
❑ 94 Patrick Ramsey JSY RC 12.00 5.00
❑ 95 Jeremy Shockey JSY RC 25.00 10.00
❑ 96 Marquise Walker JSY RC 8.00 3.00
❑ 97 Reche Caldwell JSY RC 10.00 4.00
❑ 98 Rohan Davey JSY RC 10.00 4.00
❑ 99 Jabar Gaffney JSY RC 10.00 4.00
❑ 100 David Garrard JSY RC 10.00 4.00
❑ 101 Maurice Morris JSY RC 10.00 4.00
❑ 102 Antwaan Randle El JSY RC 15.00 6.00
❑ 103 Donte Stallworth JSY RC 20.00 7.50
❑ 104 Roy Williams JSY RC 25.00 10.00
❑ 105 Ladell Betts JSY RC 10.00 4.00
❑ 106 Tim Carter JSY RC 8.00 3.00
❑ 107 T.J. Duckett JSY RC 12.00 5.00
❑ 108 William Green JSY RC 10.00 4.00
❑ 109 Ashley Lelie JSY RC 20.00 7.50
❑ 110 Clinton Portis JSY RC 25.00 10.00
❑ 111 Cliff Russell JSY RC 8.00 3.00
❑ 112 Javon Walker JSY RC 20.00 7.50

2003 Hot Prospects

❑ COMP.SET w/o SP's (80) 20.00 7.50
❑ 1 Emmitt Smith 2.50 1.00
❑ 2 Terrell Owens 1.00 .40
❑ 3 Tiki Barber 1.00 .40
❑ 4 Trent Green .60 .25
❑ 5 Quincy Morgan .60 .25
❑ 6 Eric Moulds .60 .25
❑ 7 Simeon Rice .60 .25
❑ 8 Hines Ward 1.00 .40
❑ 9 Michael Bennett .60 .25
❑ 10 Donald Driver .60 .25
❑ 11 Stephen Davis .60 .25
❑ 12 Steve McNair 1.00 .40
❑ 13 David Boston .60 .25
❑ 14 Deuce McAllister 1.00 .40
❑ 15 Marvin Harrison 1.00 .40
❑ 16 Peerless Price .60 .25
❑ 17 Matt Hasselbeck .60 .25
❑ 18 Jerry Rice 2.00 .75
❑ 19 Junior Seau 1.00 .40
❑ 20 Clinton Portis 1.50 .60
❑ 21 Fred Taylor 1.00 .40
❑ 22 William Green .60 .25
❑ 23 Warrick Dunn .60 .25
❑ 24 Koren Robinson .60 .25
❑ 25 Jeremy Shockey 1.50 .60
❑ 26 Chris Chambers 1.00 .40
❑ 27 Brett Favre 2.50 1.00
❑ 28 Julius Peppers 1.00 .40
❑ 29 Eddie George .60 .25
❑ 30 Todd Pinkston .60 .25
❑ 31 Tom Brady 2.50 1.00
❑ 32 Edgerrin James 1.00 .40
❑ 33 Chad Johnson 1.00 .40
❑ 34 Laveranues Coles .60 .25
❑ 35 LaDainian Tomlinson 1.00 .40
❑ 36 Priest Holmes 1.25 .50
❑ 37 Shannon Sharpe .60 .25
❑ 38 Jamal Lewis 1.00 .40
❑ 39 Warren Sapp .60 .25
❑ 40 Tim Brown 1.00 .40
❑ 41 Kerry Collins .60 .25
❑ 42 Jimmy Smith .60 .25
❑ 43 Chad Hutchinson .60 .25
❑ 44 Marcel Shipp .60 .25
❑ 45 Jeff Garcia 1.00 .40
❑ 46 Donovan McNabb 1.25 .50
❑ 47 Randy Moss 1.50 .60
❑ 48 Ahman Green 1.00 .40
❑ 49 Travis Henry .60 .25
❑ 50 Brad Johnson .60 .25
❑ 51 Tommy Maddox 1.00 .40
❑ 52 Aaron Brooks 1.00 .40
❑ 53 Peyton Manning 1.50 .60
❑ 54 Brian Urlacher 1.50 .60
❑ 55 Rod Gardner .60 .25
❑ 56 Chad Pennington 1.25 .50
❑ 57 Ricky Williams 1.00 .40
❑ 58 James Stewart .60 .25
❑ 59 Todd Heap .60 .25
❑ 60 Marshall Faulk 1.00 .40
❑ 61 Corey Dillon .60 .25
❑ 62 Michael Vick 2.50 1.00
❑ 63 Shaun Alexander 1.00 .40
❑ 64 Curtis Martin 1.00 .40
❑ 65 Mark Brunell .60 .25
❑ 66 Joey Harrington 1.50 .60
❑ 67 Drew Bledsoe 1.00 .40
❑ 68 Keyshawn Johnson 1.00 .40
❑ 69 Jerome Bettis 1.00 .40
❑ 70 Daunte Culpepper 1.00 .40
❑ 71 David Carr 1.50 .60
❑ 72 Marty Booker .60 .25
❑ 73 Patrick Ramsey 1.00 .40
❑ 74 Drew Brees 1.00 .40
❑ 75 Donte Stallworth 1.00 .40
❑ 76 Jake Plummer .60 .25
❑ 77 Ray Lewis 1.00 .40
❑ 78 Kurt Warner 1.00 .40
❑ 79 Rich Gannon .60 .25
❑ 80 Tony Gonzalez .60 .25
❑ 92 Dallas Clark JSY RC 10.00 4.00
❑ 93 Terence Newman JSY RC 15.00 6.00
❑ 94 Rex Grossman JSY RC 25.00 10.00
❑ 95 Kelley Washington JSY RC 10.00 4.00
❑ 96 Kyle Boller JSY RC 8.00 3.00
❑ 97 Carson Palmer JSY RC 30.00 12.50
❑ 98 Charles Rogers JSY RC 8.00 3.00
❑ 99 Chris Simms JSY RC 10.00 4.00
❑ 100 Larry Johnson JSY RC 30.00 15.00
❑ 101 Andre Johnson JSY RC 15.00 6.00
❑ 102 Taylor Jacobs JSY RC 8.00 3.00
❑ 103 Byron Leftwich JSY RC 25.00 10.00
❑ 110 Tyrone Calico RC 5.00 2.00
❑ 111 Billy McMullen RC 4.00 1.50
❑ 112 Jerome McDougle RC 5.00 2.00
❑ 113 Willis McGahee RC 12.00 5.00
❑ 114 Anquan Boldin RC 12.00 5.00
❑ 115 Artose Pinner RC 5.00 2.00
❑ 116 Kevin Williams RC 5.00 2.00
❑ 117 Bethel Johnson RC 5.00 2.00
❑ 118 Quentin Griffin RC 5.00 2.00
❑ 119 Nate Burleson RC 5.00 2.00
❑ 120 DeWayne Robertson RC 5.00 2.00

2004 Hot Prospects

❑ COMP.SET w/o SP's (70) 20.00 7.50
❑ 71-94 AU JSY RC ODDS 1:20H, 1:840R
❑ 103-112 RC PRINT RUN 1000 SER. #'d SETS
❑ 1 Donovan McNabb 1.00 .40
❑ 2 Charlie Garner .50 .20
❑ 3 Tim Rattay .30 .10
❑ 4 Drew Brees .75 .30
❑ 5 Jerry Rice 1.50 .60
❑ 6 Aaron Brooks .50 .20

❑ 7 Chris Chambers .50 .20
❑ 8 Byron Leftwich 1.00 .40
❑ 9 Andre Johnson .75 .30
❑ 10 Edgerrin James .75 .30
❑ 11 Charles Rogers .50 .20
❑ 12 Quentin Griffin .75 .30
❑ 13 Carson Palmer 1.00 .40
❑ 14 Ray Lewis .75 .30
❑ 15 Clinton Portis .75 .30
❑ 16 Marc Bulger .75 .30
❑ 17 Matt Hasselbeck .50 .20
❑ 18 Plaxico Burress .50 .20
❑ 19 Priest Holmes 1.00 .40
❑ 20 David Carr .75 .30
❑ 21 Ahman Green .75 .30
❑ 22 Roy Williams S .50 .20
❑ 23 Travis Henry .50 .20
❑ 24 Michael Vick 1.50 .60
❑ 25 Eddie George .50 .20
❑ 26 Marshall Faulk .75 .30
❑ 27 Kevan Barlow .50 .20
❑ 28 Shaun Alexander .75 .30
❑ 29 Hines Ward .75 .30
❑ 30 Anquan Boldin .75 .30
❑ 31 Chad Pennington .75 .30
❑ 32 Randy Moss 1.00 .40
❑ 33 Fred Taylor .50 .20
❑ 34 Marvin Harrison .75 .30
❑ 35 Joey Harrington .75 .30
❑ 36 Rich Gannon .50 .20
❑ 37 Deuce McAllister .75 .30
❑ 38 Deion Branch .75 .30
❑ 39 Tony Gonzalez .50 .20
❑ 40 Brett Favre 2.00 .75
❑ 41 Keyshawn Johnson .50 .20
❑ 42 Lee Suggs .75 .30
❑ 43 Jake Delhomme .75 .30
❑ 44 Rex Grossman .75 .30
❑ 45 Drew Bledsoe .75 .30
❑ 46 Warrick Dunn .50 .20
❑ 47 Steve McNair .75 .30
❑ 48 Torry Holt .75 .30
❑ 49 Brian Westbrook .50 .20
❑ 50 Santana Moss .50 .20
❑ 51 Jeremy Shockey .75 .30
❑ 52 Daunte Culpepper .75 .30
❑ 53 Jeff Garcia .75 .30
❑ 54 Stephen Davis .50 .20
❑ 55 Eric Moulds .50 .20
❑ 56 Emmitt Smith 1.50 .60
❑ 57 Keenan McCardell .30 .10
❑ 58 LaDainian Tomlinson 1.00 .40
❑ 59 Terrell Owens .75 .30
❑ 60 Curtis Martin .75 .30
❑ 61 Joe Horn .50 .20
❑ 62 Tiki Barber .75 .30
❑ 63 Tom Brady 2.00 .75
❑ 64 Ricky Williams .75 .30
❑ 65 Peyton Manning 1.25 .50
❑ 66 Jake Plummer .50 .20
❑ 67 Chad Johnson .75 .30
❑ 68 Brian Urlacher 1.00 .40
❑ 69 Jamal Lewis .75 .30
❑ 70 Laveranues Coles .50 .20
❑ 71 Tatum Bell JSY AU/350 RC 80.00 30.00
❑ 72 B.Berrian JSY AU/344 RC 50.00 25.00
❑ 73 M.Clayton JSY AU/350 RC 80.00 40.00
❑ 74 Lee Evans JSY AU/350 RC 60.00 30.00
❑ 75 Fitzgerald JSY AU/140 RC 150.00 75.00
❑ 76 Henderson JSY AU/350 RC 30.00 15.00
❑ 77 D.Henson JSY AU/331 RC 40.00 20.00
❑ 78 St.Jackson JSY AU/300 RC 125.00 75.00

❑ 79 M.Jenkins JSY AU/349 RC 40.00 15.00
❑ 80 Greg Jones JSY AU/289 RC 50.00 25.00
❑ 81 Kev.Jones JSY AU/278 RC 100.00 50.00
❑ 82 J.Losman JSY AU/350 RC 80.00 40.00
❑ 83 Eli Manning JSY AU/350 RC 250.00 125.00
❑ 84 Chris Perry JSY AU/350 RC 50.0020.00
❑ 85 Phil.Rivers JSY AU/350 RC 150.0075.00
❑ 86 Roethlis.JSY AU/150 RC 400.00 200.00
❑ 87 Reg.Williams JSY AU/350 RC 60.00 25.00
❑ 88 Ro.Williams JSY AU/350 RC 100.00 50.00
❑ 89 Kell.Winslow JSY AU/50 RC 200.00 100.00
❑ 90 R.Woods JSY AU/350 RC 40.00 20.00
❑ 91 Jul.Jones JSY AU/350 RC 120.0060.00
❑ 93 K.Colbert JSY AU/349 RC 50.00 25.00
❑ 94 M.Schaub JSY AU/120 RC 175.00 100.00
❑ 95 Cedric Cobbs JSY RC 15.00 6.00
❑ 96 Darius Watts JSY RC 15.00 6.00
❑ 97 DeAngelo Hall JSY RC 25.00 10.00
❑ 98 Derrick Hamilton JSY RC 12.00 5.00
❑ 99 Devard Darling JSY RC 15.00 6.00
❑ 100 Ben Troupe JSY RC 15.00 6.00
❑ 101 Mewelde Moore JSY RC 15.00 6.00
❑ 102 Ben Watson JSY RC 15.00 6.00
❑ 103 Sean Taylor RC 5.00 2.00
❑ 104 Ricky Ray RC 4.00 1.50
❑ 105 Carlos Francis RC 4.00 1.50
❑ 106 Samie Parker RC 5.00 2.00
❑ 107 Jerricho Cotchery RC 5.00 2.00
❑ 108 Ernest Wilford RC 5.00 2.00
❑ 109 Craig Krenzel RC 5.00 2.00
❑ 110 Robert Gallery RC 5.00 2.00
❑ 111 Dunta Robinson RC 5.00 2.00
❑ 112 Jonathan Vilma RC 5.00 2.00

1994 Images

❑ COMPLETE SET (125) 40.00 15.00
❑ 1 Emmitt Smith 3.00 1.25
❑ 2 Reggie White .75 .30
❑ 3 Michael Haynes .40 .15
❑ 4 Chris Warren .40 .15
❑ 5 Jeff George .75 .30
❑ 6 Sean Gilbert .20 .07
❑ 7 Ricky Watters .40 .15
❑ 8 Eric Metcalf .40 .15
❑ 9 Randall Cunningham .75 .30
❑ 10 Tim Brown .75 .30
❑ 11 Trent Dilfer RC 2.00 .75
❑ 12 Marshall Faulk RC 8.00 3.00
❑ 13 David Klingler .20 .07
❑ 14 Barry Foster .20 .07
❑ 15 John Elway 4.00 1.50
❑ 16 Joe Montana 4.00 1.50
❑ 17 Rodney Hampton .40 .15
❑ 18 Todd Steussie RC .40 .15
❑ 19 Bruce Smith .75 .30
❑ 20 Wayne Gandy RC .20 .07
❑ 21 Anthony Miller .40 .15
❑ 22 Reggie Brooks .40 .15
❑ 23 Johnny Johnson .20 .07
❑ 24 Byron Bam Morris RC .40 .15
❑ 25 Drew Bledsoe 2.00 .75
❑ 26 Jeff Hostetler .40 .15
❑ 27 Alvin Harper .40 .15
❑ 28 Cris Carter 1.00 .40
❑ 29 Bert Emanuel RC .75 .30
❑ 30 Errict Rhett RC .75 .30
❑ 31 Scott Mitchell .40 .15
❑ 32 Deion Sanders 1.00 .40
❑ 33 Lewis Tillman .20 .07
❑ 34 Tim Bowens RC .40 .15
❑ 35 Charles Haley .40 .15
❑ 36 Stan Humphries .40 .15
❑ 37 Haywood Jeffires .40 .15
❑ 38 Andre Reed .40 .15
❑ 39 Charles Johnson RC .75 .30
❑ 40 Ronald Moore .20 .07
❑ 41 Jim Everett .40 .15
❑ 42 Greg Hill RC .75 .30
❑ 43 Thurman Thomas .75 .30
❑ 44 Willie McGinest RC .75 .30
❑ 45 Aaron Glenn RC .75 .30
❑ 46 Erric Pegram .20 .07
❑ 47 Terry Kirby .75 .30
❑ 48 Warren Moon .75 .30
❑ 49 Clyde Simmons .20 .07
❑ 50 Eric Turner .20 .07
❑ 51 Heath Shuler RC .75 .30
❑ 52 Rickey Jackson .20 .07
❑ 53 Johnnie Morton RC 2.00 .75
❑ 54 Charlie Garner RC 2.00 .75
❑ 55 Mark Collins .20 .07
❑ 56 Mike Pritchard .20 .07
❑ 57 Bryant Young RC .75 .30
❑ 58 Joe Johnson RC .20 .07
❑ 59 Erik Kramer .40 .15
❑ 60 Barry Sanders 3.00 1.25
❑ 61 Rod Woodson .40 .15
❑ 62 Dave Brown .40 .15
❑ 63 Gary Brown .20 .07
❑ 64 Brett Favre 4.00 1.50
❑ 65 Isaac Bruce RC 6.00 2.50
❑ 66 Boomer Esiason .40 .15
❑ 67 Jim Harbaugh .75 .30
❑ 68 Jackie Harris .20 .07
❑ 69 Art Monk .40 .15
❑ 70 Jamir Miller RC .40 .15
❑ 71 Neil O'Donnell .75 .30
❑ 72 Neil Smith .40 .15
❑ 73 Junior Seau .75 .30
❑ 74 Jerome Bettis 1.25 .50
❑ 75 Bernard Williams RC .20 .07
❑ 76 Jeff Burris RC .40 .15
❑ 77 Henry Ellard .40 .15
❑ 78 Reggie Cobb .20 .07
❑ 79 Shante Carver RC .20 .07
❑ 80 Terry Allen .40 .15
❑ 81 Cortez Kennedy .40 .15
❑ 82 Trev Alberts RC .40 .15
❑ 83 Michael Irvin .75 .30
❑ 84 Herschel Walker .40 .15
❑ 85 Dan Marino 4.00 1.50
❑ 86 Dave Meggett .20 .07
❑ 87 Herman Moore .75 .30
❑ 88 Darnay Scott RC 1.00 .40
❑ 89 Dewayne Washington RC .40 .15
❑ 90 Rob Fredrickson RC .40 .15
❑ 91 Rick Mirer .75 .30
❑ 92 Thomas Lewis RC .40 .15
❑ 93 Chris Miller .20 .07
❑ 94 Marion Butts .20 .07
❑ 95 Sam Adams RC .40 .15
❑ 96 Jerry Rice 2.00 .75
❑ 97 Ben Coates .40 .15
❑ 98 David Palmer RC .75 .30
❑ 99 Antonio Langham RC .40 .15
❑ 100 Curtis Conway .75 .30
❑ 101 Derrick Thomas .75 .30
❑ 102 Ken Norton Jr. .40 .15
❑ 103 Ronnie Lott .40 .15
❑ 104 Sterling Sharpe .40 .15
❑ 105 Troy Aikman 2.00 .75
❑ 106 Shannon Sharpe .40 .15
❑ 107 Natrone Means .75 .30
❑ 108 Derek Brown RBK .20 .07
❑ 109 Dan Wilkinson RC .40 .15
❑ 110 Andre Rison .40 .15
❑ 111 Quentin Coryatt .20 .07
❑ 112 Cody Carlson .20 .07
❑ 113 William Floyd RC .75 .30
❑ 114 Marcus Allen .75 .30
❑ 115 Steve Young 1.50 .60
❑ 116 Jim Kelly .75 .30
❑ 117 LeShon Johnson RC .40 .15
❑ 118 Irving Fryar .40 .15
❑ 119 Carl Pickens .40 .15
❑ 120 Keith Jackson .20 .07
❑ 121 John Thierry RC .20 .07
❑ 122 Vinny Testaverde .40 .15
❑ 123 Derrick Alexander WR RC .75 .30
❑ 124 Seth Joyner .20 .07
❑ 125 Checklist .20 .07
❑ IF1 Emmitt Smith Promo 2.50 1.00
❑ TP1 D.Bledsoe NFL Exp/1994 50.00 25.00
❑ NNO Emmitt Smith NFL Exp. 10.00 4.00

1995 Images Limited

❑ COMPLETE SET (125) 25.00 10.00
❑ 1 Emmitt Smith 2.00 .75
❑ 2 Steve Young 1.00 .40
❑ 3 Drew Bledsoe .75 .30
❑ 4 Dan Marino 2.50 1.00
❑ 5 John Elway 2.50 1.00
❑ 6 Barry Sanders 2.00 .75
❑ 7 Brett Favre 2.50 1.00
❑ 8 Troy Aikman 1.25 .50
❑ 9 Jim Kelly .40 .15
❑ 10 Marshall Faulk 1.50 .60
❑ 11 Jerry Rice 1.25 .50
❑ 12 Warren Moon .20 .07
❑ 13 Jim Everett .10 .02
❑ 14 Rodney Hampton .20 .07
❑ 15 Jeff Hostetler .20 .07
❑ 16 Errict Rhett .20 .07
❑ 17 Jerome Bettis .40 .15
❑ 18 Byron Bam Morris .10 .02
❑ 19 Randall Cunningham .40 .15
❑ 20 Rick Mirer .20 .07
❑ 21 Natrone Means .20 .07
❑ 22 Jeff George .20 .07
❑ 23 Garrison Hearst .40 .15
❑ 24 Michael Irvin .40 .15
❑ 25 Cris Carter .40 .15
❑ 26 Irving Fryar .20 .07
❑ 27 Jeff Blake RC .75 .30
❑ 28 Bruce Smith .40 .15
❑ 29 Shannon Sharpe .20 .07
❑ 30 Steve Beuerlein .20 .07
❑ 31 Stan Humphries .20 .07
❑ 32 Chris Warren .20 .07
❑ 33 Ben Coates .20 .07
❑ 34 Boomer Esiason .20 .07
❑ 35 Trent Dilfer .40 .15
❑ 36 Chris Miller .10 .02
❑ 37 Dave Brown .20 .07
❑ 38 Herman Moore .40 .15
❑ 39 Anthony Miller .20 .07
❑ 40 Andre Reed .20 .07
❑ 41 Reggie White .40 .15
❑ 42 Darnay Scott .20 .07
❑ 43 Erik Kramer .10 .02
❑ 44 Leroy Hoard .10 .02
❑ 45 Fred Barnett .20 .07
❑ 46 Junior Seau .40 .15
❑ 47 Vinny Testaverde .20 .07
❑ 48 Gus Frerotte .20 .07
❑ 49 William Floyd .20 .07
❑ 50 Mo Lewis .10 .02
❑ 51 Tim Brown .40 .15
❑ 52 Greg Lloyd .20 .07
❑ 53 Chester McGlockton .20 .07
❑ 54 Heath Shuler .20 .07
❑ 55 Rod Woodson .20 .07
❑ 56 Don Beebe .10 .02
❑ 57 Carl Pickens .20 .07
❑ 58 Charles Haley .20 .07
❑ 59 Steve Bono .20 .07
❑ 60 Harvey Williams .10 .02
❑ 61 Greg Hill .20 .07
❑ 62 Eric Metcalf .20 .07
❑ 63 Mario Bates .20 .07
❑ 64 Terry Allen .20 .07
❑ 65 Michael Timpson .10 .02
❑ 66 Mark Stepnoski .10 .02

❑ 67	Jeff Lageman	.10	.02
❑ 68	Robert Smith	.40	.15
❑ 69	Eric Allen	.10	.02
❑ 70	Ricky Watters	.20	.07
❑ 71	Derek Loville	.10	.02
❑ 72	Bernie Parmalee	.20	.07
❑ 73	Bryce Paup	.20	.07
❑ 74	Frank Reich	.10	.02
❑ 75	Henry Thomas	.10	.02
❑ 76	Craig Erickson	.10	.02
❑ 77	Eric Green	.10	.02
❑ 78	Dave Meggett	.10	.02
❑ 79	Deion Sanders	.75	.30
❑ 80	Herschel Walker	.20	.07
❑ 81	Andre Rison	.20	.07
❑ 82	Ki-Jana Carter RC	.40	.15
❑ 83	Tony Boselli RC	.40	.15
❑ 84	Steve McNair RC	3.00	1.25
❑ 85	Michael Westbrook RC	.40	.15
❑ 86	Kerry Collins RC	1.50	.60
❑ 87	Kevin Carter RC	.40	.15
❑ 88	Warren Sapp RC	1.50	.60
❑ 89	Joey Galloway RC	1.50	.60
❑ 90	J.J. Stokes RC	.40	.15
❑ 92	Kyle Brady RC	.40	.15
❑ 93	Napoleon Kaufman RC	1.00	.40
❑ 94	Tyrone Wheatley RC	1.00	.40
❑ 95	Mike Mamula RC	.10	.02
❑ 96	Desmond Howard	.20	.07
❑ 97	James O. Stewart RC	1.00	.40
❑ 98	Craig Newsome RC	.10	.02
❑ 99	Ty Law RC	2.50	1.00
❑ 100	Ellis Johnson RC	.10	.02
❑ 101	Hugh Douglas RC	.40	.15
❑ 102	Mark Bruener RC	.20	.07
❑ 103	Tyrone Poole	.40	.15
❑ 104	Luther Elliss	.10	.02
❑ 105	Mark Fields RC	.40	.15
❑ 106	Frank Sanders RC	.40	.15
❑ 107	Rashaan Salaam RC	.20	.07
❑ 108	Craig Powell RC	.10	.02
❑ 109	Sherman Williams RC	.10	.02
❑ 110	Chad May RC	.10	.02
❑ 111	Rob Johnson RC	.75	.30
❑ 112	Todd Collins RC	.20	.07
❑ 113	Terrell Davis RC	2.50	1.00
❑ 114	Eric Zeier RC	.40	.15
❑ 115	Curtis Martin RC	3.00	1.25
❑ 116	Kordell Stewart RC	1.50	.60
❑ 117	Troy Vincent	.10	.02
❑ 118	Ray Zellars RC	.20	.07
❑ 119	Dave Krieg	.10	.02
❑ 120	Mike Sherrard	.10	.02
❑ 121	Willie Davis	.10	.02
❑ 122	Robert Brooks	.20	.07
❑ 123	Chris Sanders RC	.20	.07
❑ 124	Drew Bledsoe CL	.40	.15
❑ 125	Emmitt Smith CL	.60	.25
❑ LT1	Drew Bledsoe Promo	1.50	.60

2000 Impact

❑	COMPLETE SET (199)	30.00	12.50
❑ 1	Kurt Warner	1.00	.40
❑ 2	Dan Marino	1.50	.60
❑ 3	Sedrick Irvin	.20	.07
❑ 4	Chris Redman RC	.50	.20
❑ 5	Robert Smith	.50	.20
❑ 6	Amani Toomer	.20	.07
❑ 7	Richard Huntley	.20	.07
❑ 8	Ahman Green	.50	.20
❑ 9	Fred Lane	.20	.07
❑ 10	Eddie George	.50	.20
❑ 11	Rocket Ismail	.30	.10
❑ 12	Shannon Sharpe	.30	.10
❑ 13	Shawn Jefferson	.20	.07
❑ 14	Michael Wiley RC	.50	.20
❑ 15	Jeff Graham	.20	.07
❑ 16	Steve Beuerlein	.30	.10
❑ 17	Tim Biakabutuka	.30	.10
❑ 18	Chris Watson	.20	.07
❑ 19	Kevin Faulk	.30	.10
❑ 20	Emmitt Smith	1.00	.40
❑ 21	Plaxico Burress RC	1.25	.50
❑ 22	Hines Ward	.50	.20
❑ 23	Jacquez Green	.20	.07
❑ 24	Doug Flutie	.50	.20
❑ 25	Leslie Shepherd	.20	.07
❑ 26	Johnnie Morton	.30	.10
❑ 27	Tom Brady RC	15.00	6.00
❑ 28	Jeff George	.30	.10
❑ 29	Derrick Mason	.30	.10
❑ 30	Marshall Faulk	.75	.30
❑ 31	Derrick Mayes	.30	.10
❑ 32	Jerome Bettis	.50	.20
❑ 33	Adrian Murrell	.30	.10
❑ 34	Curtis Enis	.20	.07
❑ 35	Kimble Anders	.20	.07
❑ 36	Travis Prentice RC	.50	.20
❑ 37	Curtis Martin	.50	.20
❑ 38	Ronnie Powell	.20	.07
❑ 39	Steve Christie	.20	.07
❑ 40	Brett Favre	1.50	.60
❑ 41	Michael Bates	.20	.07
❑ 42	Rondell Mealey RC	.40	.15
❑ 43	Randall Cunningham	.50	.20
❑ 44	Kerry Collins	.30	.10
❑ 45	William Thomas	.20	.07
❑ 46	Ricky Watters	.30	.10
❑ 47	Marvin Harrison	.50	.20
❑ 48	Corey Bradford	.30	.10
❑ 49	Terry Kirby	.20	.07
❑ 50	Troy Aikman	1.00	.40
❑ 51	Cris Carter	.50	.20
❑ 52	Jamal Lewis RC	1.50	.60
❑ 53	Duce Staley	.50	.20
❑ 54	Isaac Bruce	.50	.20
❑ 55	Yancey Thigpen	.20	.07
❑ 56	R.Jay Soward RC	.50	.20
❑ 57	Jermaine Lewis	.20	.07
❑ 58	Zach Thomas	.50	.20
❑ 59	Sylvester Morris RC	.50	.20
❑ 60	Steve McNair	.50	.20
❑ 61	Tiki Barber	.50	.20
❑ 62	Torrance Small	.20	.07
❑ 63	Champ Bailey	.30	.10
❑ 64	Tim Dwight	.50	.20
❑ 65	Willie Jackson	.20	.07
❑ 66	Edgerrin James	.75	.30
❑ 67	Ron Dayne RC	.60	.25
❑ 68	Rich Gannon	.50	.20
❑ 69	Junior Seau	.50	.20
❑ 70	Warren Sapp	.30	.10
❑ 71	Rob Johnson	.30	.10
❑ 72	Antonio Freeman	.50	.20
❑ 73	O.J. McDuffie	.30	.10
❑ 74	Tamarick Vanover	.20	.07
❑ 75	Courtney Brown RC	.60	.25
❑ 76	Donovan McNabb	.75	.30
❑ 77	Az-Zahir Hakim	.30	.10
❑ 78	Albert Connell	.20	.07
❑ 79	Qadry Ismail	.30	.10
❑ 80	Terrell Davis	.50	.20
❑ 81	Dorsey Levens	.30	.10
❑ 82	Tony Martin	.30	.10
❑ 83	Laveranues Coles RC	.75	.30
❑ 84	Karim Abdul-Jabbar	.30	.10
❑ 85	Charles Johnson	.30	.10
❑ 86	Torry Holt	.50	.20
❑ 87	Stephen Davis	.50	.20
❑ 88	Tony Banks	.30	.10
❑ 89	Akili Smith	.20	.07
❑ 90	Tim Couch	.30	.10
❑ 91	Bill Schroeder	.30	.10
❑ 92	Andre Hastings	.20	.07
❑ 93	Eddie Kennison	.20	.07
❑ 94	Randy Moss	1.00	.40
❑ 95	Tony Horne	.20	.07
❑ 96	Sherrod Gideon RC	.40	.15
❑ 97	Wesley Walls	.20	.07
❑ 98	Brian Griese	.50	.20
❑ 99	Jake Delhomme RC	2.50	1.00
❑ 100	Peyton Manning	1.25	.50
❑ 101	Brad Johnson	.50	.20
❑ 102	Trung Canidate RC	.50	.20
❑ 103	Freddie Jones	.20	.07
❑ 104	Muhsin Muhammad	.30	.10
❑ 105	Eric Moulds	.50	.20
❑ 106	Ed McCaffrey	.50	.20
❑ 107	Joe Montgomery	.20	.07
❑ 108	Olandis Gary	.50	.20
❑ 109	J.J. Stokes	.20	.07
❑ 110	Ricky Williams	.50	.20
❑ 111	Jim Harbaugh	.30	.10
❑ 112	Mike Alstott	.50	.20
❑ 113	Errict Rhett	.30	.10
❑ 114	Terance Mathis	.30	.10
❑ 115	Kevin Johnson	.50	.20
❑ 116	Tremain Mack	.20	.07
❑ 117	Peter Warrick RC	.60	.25
❑ 118	Lamont Warren	.20	.07
❑ 119	Damon Huard	.50	.20
❑ 120	Cade McNown	.20	.07
❑ 121	Natrone Means	.20	.07
❑ 122	Ken Oxendine	.20	.07
❑ 123	J.R. Redmond RC	.50	.20
❑ 124	Ken Dilger	.20	.07
❑ 125	James Johnson	.20	.07
❑ 126	Napoleon Kaufman	.30	.10
❑ 127	Ryan Leaf	.30	.10
❑ 128	Michael Westbrook	.30	.10
❑ 129	Mario Bates	.20	.07
❑ 130	Jake Plummer	.30	.10
❑ 131	James Jett	.20	.07
❑ 132	Darnay Scott	.30	.10
❑ 133	Curtis Conway	.30	.10
❑ 134	Fred Taylor	.50	.20
❑ 135	Wayne Chrebet	.30	.10
❑ 136	Sean Dawkins	.20	.07
❑ 138	Keenan McCardell	.30	.10
❑ 139	Donnell Bennett	.20	.07
❑ 140	Jerry Rice	1.00	.40
❑ 141	Vinny Testaverde	.30	.10
❑ 142	Chad Pennington RC	1.50	.60
❑ 143	Jonathan Linton	.20	.07
❑ 144	Herman Moore	.30	.10
❑ 145	David Patten	.30	.10
❑ 146	Troy Edwards	.20	.07
❑ 147	Jon Kitna	.50	.20
❑ 148	Jimmy Smith	.30	.10
❑ 149	Tee Martin RC	.60	.25
❑ 150	Jevon Kearse	.50	.20
❑ 151	Frank Sanders	.20	.07
❑ 152	Marcus Robinson	.50	.20
❑ 153	Mike Hollis	.20	.07
❑ 154	Frank Wycheck	.20	.07
❑ 155	Tim Rattay RC	.60	.25
❑ 156	Dedric Ward	.20	.07
❑ 157	Terrell Owens	.50	.20
❑ 158	Chris Chandler	.30	.10
❑ 159	Damon Griffin	.20	.07
❑ 160	Mike Vanderjagt	.20	.07
❑ 161	Elvis Grbac	.20	.07
❑ 162	Rickey Dudley	.20	.07
❑ 163	Jeff Garcia	.50	.20
❑ 164	Thomas Jones RC	1.00	.40
❑ 165	Tyrone Wheatley	.30	.10
❑ 166	Rod Smith	.30	.10
❑ 167	Bubba Franks RC	.60	.25
❑ 168	Chris Warren	.20	.07
❑ 169	Anthony Lucas RC	.20	.07
❑ 170	Terry Glenn	.30	.10
❑ 171	John Carney	.20	.07
❑ 172	Warrick Dunn	.50	.20
❑ 173	Shaun Alexander RC	3.00	1.25
❑ 174	David Boston	.50	.20
❑ 175	Bobby Engram	.20	.07
❑ 176	Travis Taylor RC	.60	.25
❑ 177	Derrick Alexander	.30	.10
❑ 178	Keyshawn Johnson	.50	.20
❑ 179	Steve Young	.60	.25
❑ 180	Deion Sanders	.50	.20
❑ 181	Charlie Batch	.50	.20
❑ 182	Drew Bledsoe	.60	.25
❑ 183	Reuben Droughns RC	.75	.30
❑ 184	Ray Lucas	.30	.10
❑ 185	Shaun King	.20	.07
❑ 186	Jamal Anderson	.50	.20
❑ 187	Corey Dillon	.50	.20
❑ 188	Joe Hamilton RC	.50	.20
❑ 189	Terrence Wilkins	.20	.07

190 Mark Brunell	.50	.20
191 Tony Gonzalez	.30	.10
192 Tim Brown	.50	.20
193 Charlie Garner	.30	.10
194 Antowain Smith	.30	.10
195 David LaFleur	.20	.07
196 Germane Crowell	.20	.07
197 Terry Allen	.30	.10
198 Marc Bulger RC	1.25	.50
199 Kevin Dyson	.30	.10
200 Kordell Stewart	.30	.10

1948 Leaf

COMPLETE SET (98)	6000.00	4500.00
COMMON CARD (1-49)	30.00	20.00
COMMON CARD (50-98)	175.00	100.00
VAR (8B/12B/14B)	50.00	30.00
WRAPPER (5-CENT)	160.00	110.00
1A Sid Luckman YB RC	400.00	250.00
1B Sid Luckman WB RC	500.00	300.00
2 Steve Suhey	30.00	20.00
3A Bull.Turner RB RC	135.00	75.00
3B Bull.Turner WB RC	175.00	100.00
4 Doak Walker RC	200.00	125.00
5A Levi Jackson BJ RC	40.00	25.00
5B Levi Jackson WJ RC	50.00	30.00
6A Bobby Layne YP RC	400.00	250.00
6B Bobby Layne RP RC	500.00	300.00
7A Bill Fischer RB RC	30.00	20.00
7B Bill Fischer WB RC	40.00	25.00
8A Vince Banonis BL RC	30.00	20.00
8B Vince Banonis WL RC	50.00	30.00
8C Vince Banonis WB RC	50.00	30.00
9A Tommy Thompson YJN RC	40.00	25.00
9B Tommy Thompson BJN RC	50.00	30.00
10 Perry Moss	30.00	20.00
11 Terry Brennan RC	40.00	25.00
12A Bill Swiacki BL RC	30.00	20.00
12B Bill Swiacki WL RC	50.00	30.00
13A Johnny Lujack RC	200.00	125.00
13B Johnny Lujack RC ERR	300.00	175.00
14A Mal Kutner BL RC	30.00	20.00
14B Mal Kutner WL RC	50.00	30.00
15 Charlie Justice RC	90.00	50.00
16A Pete Pihos YJN RC	150.00	90.00
16B Pete Pihos BJN RC	175.00	100.00
17A K.Washington BL RC	55.00	35.00
17B K.Washington WL RC	80.00	50.00
18 Harry Gilmer RC	50.00	30.00
19A George McAfee RC	150.00	90.00
19B G.McAfee RC ERR	200.00	125.00
20A George Taliaferro YB RC	40.00	25.00
20B George Taliaferro WB RC	50.00	30.00
21 Paul Christman RC	50.00	30.00
22A Steve Van Buren GJ RC	250.00	150.00
22B Steve Van Buren YJ RC	300.00	175.00
23 Ken Kavanaugh RC	40.00	25.00
24A Jim Martin RB RC	40.00	25.00
24B Jim Martin WB RC	50.00	30.00
25A Bud Angsman BL RC	40.00	25.00
25B Bud Angsman WL RC	60.00	35.00
25C Bud Angsman WB RC	60.00	35.00
26A Bob Waterfield BL RC	250.00	150.00
26B Bob Waterfield WL RC	450.00	300.00
27A Fred Davis YB	30.00	20.00
27B Fred Davis WB	50.00	30.00
28A Whitey Wistert YJ RC	40.00	25.00
28B Whitey Wistert GJ RC	50.00	30.00
29 Charley Trippi RC	110.00	65.00
30 Paul Governali RC	40.00	25.00
31A Tom McWilliams MJ RC	30.00	20.00
31B Tom McWilliams RJ RC	40.00	25.00
32 Leroy Zimmerman	30.00	20.00
33 Pat Harder RC UER	55.00	30.00
34 Sammy Baugh RC	600.00	400.00
35 Ted Fritsch Sr. RC	40.00	25.00
36 Bill Dudley RC	125.00	75.00
37 George Connor RC	100.00	50.00
38 Frank Dancewicz	30.00	20.00
39 Billy Dewell	30.00	20.00
40 John Nolan	30.00	20.00
41A Harry Szulborski OP RC	30.00	20.00
41B Harry Szulborski YP RC	50.00	30.00
42 Tex Coulter RC	40.00	25.00
43A Robert Nussbaumer MJ RC	30.00	20.00
43B Robert Nussbaumer RJ RC	50.00	30.00
44 Bob Mann	30.00	20.00
45 Jim White RC	30.00	20.00
46A Jack Jacobs JN RC	30.00	20.00
46B Jack Jacobs NJN RC	40.00	25.00
47 John Clement	30.00	20.00
48 Frank Reagan	30.00	20.00
49 Frank Tripucka RC	45.00	25.00
50 John Rauch RC	175.00	100.00
51 Mike Dimitro	175.00	100.00
52A Leo Nomellini BBMJ RC	450.00	300.00
52B Leo Nomellini BBRJ RC	500.00	350.00
52C Leo Nomellini WB RC	500.00	350.00
53 Charley Conerly RC	450.00	300.00
54A Chuck Bednarik YB RC	500.00	350.00
54B Chuck Bednarik WB RC	500.00	350.00
55 Chick Jagade	175.00	100.00
56 Bob Folsom RC	200.00	125.00
57 Gene Rossides RC	200.00	125.00
58 Art Weiner	175.00	100.00
59 Alex Sarkistian	175.00	100.00
60 Dick Harris Texas	175.00	100.00
61 Len Younce	175.00	100.00
62 Gene Derricotte	175.00	100.00
63A Roy Rebel Steiner RJ RC	175.00	100.00
63B Roy Rebel Steiner WJ RC	200.00	125.00
64 Frank Seno	175.00	100.00
65 Bob Hendren RC	175.00	100.00
66A Jack Cloud BB RC	175.00	100.00
66B Jack Cloud WB RC	200.00	125.00
67 Harrell Collins	175.00	100.00
68A Clyde LeForce RB RC	175.00	100.00
68B Clyde LeForce WB RC	200.00	125.00
69 Larry Joe	175.00	100.00
70 Phil O'Reilly	175.00	100.00
71 Paul Campbell	175.00	100.00
72 Ray Evans	175.00	100.00
73A Jackie Jensen RB RC	400.00	250.00
73B Jackie Jensen WB RC	450.00	300.00
74 Russ Steger	175.00	100.00
75 Tony Minisi	175.00	100.00
76 Clayton Tonnemaker	175.00	100.00
77A George Savitsky GS RC	175.00	100.00
77B George Savitsky NGS RC	200.00	125.00
78 Clarence Self	175.00	100.00
79 Rod Franz	175.00	100.00
80A Jim Youle RC	175.00	100.00
80B Jim Youle WB RC	200.00	125.00
81A Billy Bye YPMJ RC	175.00	100.00
81B Billy Bye YPRJ RC	200.00	125.00
82 Fred Enke	175.00	100.00
83A Fred Folger GJ RC	175.00	100.00
83B Fred Folger WJ RC	200.00	125.00
84 Jug Girard RC	200.00	125.00
85 Joe Scott	175.00	100.00
86 Bob Demoss	175.00	100.00
87 Dave Templeton	175.00	100.00
88 Herb Siegert	175.00	100.00
89 Bucky O'Conner	175.00	100.00
90 Joe Whisler	175.00	100.00
91 Leon Hart RC	250.00	150.00
92 Earl Banks	175.00	100.00
93 Frank Aschenbrenner	175.00	100.00
94 John Goldsberry RC	175.00	100.00
95 Porter Payne	175.00	100.00
96 Pete Perini	175.00	100.00
97 Jay Rhodemyre	175.00	100.00
98 Al DiMarco RC !	250.00	125.00

1949 Leaf

COMPLETE SET (49)	2200.00	1500.00
WRAPPER (5-CENT)	300.00	250.00
1 Bob Hendren !	80.00	40.00
2 Joe Scott	25.00	18.00
3 Frank Reagan	25.00	18.00
4 John Rauch	25.00	18.00
7 Bill Fischer	25.00	18.00
9 Elmer Bud Angsman	35.00	25.00
10 Billy Dewell	25.00	18.00
13 Tommy Thompson QB	35.00	25.00
15 Sid Luckman	125.00	75.00
16 Charley Trippi	55.00	35.00
17 Bob Mann	25.00	18.00
19 Paul Christman	35.00	25.00
22 Bill Dudley	55.00	35.00
23 Clyde LeForce	25.00	18.00
26 Sammy Baugh	300.00	200.00
28 Pete Pihos	70.00	50.00
31 Tex Coulter	35.00	25.00
32 Mal Kutner	35.00	25.00
35 Whitey Wistert	35.00	25.00
37 Ted Fritsch Sr.	35.00	25.00
38 Vince Banonis	25.00	18.00
39 Jim White	25.00	18.00
40 George Connor	55.00	35.00
41 George McAfee	55.00	35.00
43 Frank Tripucka	45.00	30.00
47 Fred Enke	25.00	18.00
49 Charley Conerly	100.00	60.00
51 Ken Kavanaugh	35.00	25.00
52 Bob Demoss	25.00	18.00
56 Johnny Lujack	100.00	60.00
57 Jim Youle	25.00	18.00
62 Harry Gilmer	35.00	25.00
65 Robert Nussbaumer	25.00	18.00
67 Bobby Layne	200.00	125.00
70 Herb Siegert	25.00	18.00
74 Tony Minisi	25.00	18.00
79 Steve Van Buren	150.00	90.00
81 Perry Moss	25.00	18.00
89 Bob Waterfield	125.00	75.00
90 Jack Jacobs	25.00	18.00
95 Kenny Washington	45.00	30.00
101 Pat Harder UER	35.00	25.00
110 Bill Swiacki	35.00	25.00
118 Fred Davis	25.00	18.00
126 Jay Rhodemyre	25.00	18.00
127 Frank Seno	25.00	18.00
134 Chuck Bednarik	175.00	110.00
144 George Savitsky	25.00	18.00
150 Bulldog Turner !	150.00	90.00

1996 Leaf

COMPLETE SET (190)	20.00	7.50
1 Troy Aikman	1.00	.40
2 Ricky Watters	.20	.07
3 Robert Brooks	.40	.15
4 Ki-Jana Carter	.20	.07
5 Drew Bledsoe	.60	.25
6 Eric Swann	.10	.02
7 Hardy Nickerson	.10	.02
8 Tony Martin	.20	.07
9 Garrison Hearst	.20	.07
10 Bernie Parmalee	.10	.02
11 Neil Smith	.20	.07

❑ 12	Aaron Craver	.10	.02
❑ 13	Rashaan Salaam	.20	.07
❑ 14	Greg Hill	.20	.07
❑ 15	Charlie Garner	.20	.07
❑ 16	Kimble Anders	.20	.07
❑ 17	Steve McNair	.75	.30
❑ 18	Neil O'Donnell	.20	.07
❑ 19	Greg Lloyd	.20	.07
❑ 20	Warren Moon	.20	.07
❑ 21	Bernie Kosar	.10	.02
❑ 22	Derrick Thomas	.40	.15
❑ 23	Andre Hastings	.10	.02
❑ 24	Wayne Chrebet	.60	.25
❑ 25	Mark Seay	.10	.02
❑ 26	Eric Metcalf	.10	.02
❑ 27	Shawn Jefferson	.10	.02
❑ 28	Napoleon Kaufman	.40	.15
❑ 29	Steve Walsh	.10	.02
❑ 30	Derrick Alexander DE	.10	.02
❑ 31	Rodney Peete	.10	.02
❑ 32	Terance Mathis	.10	.02
❑ 33	Michael Westbrook	.40	.15
❑ 34	Kevin Carter	.10	.02
❑ 35	Aaron Hayden RC	.10	.02
❑ 36	J.J. Stokes	.40	.15
❑ 37	Andre Reed	.20	.07
❑ 38	Chris Warren	.20	.07
❑ 39	Jerry Rice	1.00	.40
❑ 40	Ben Coates	.20	.07
❑ 41	Reggie White	.40	.15
❑ 42	Joey Galloway	.40	.15
❑ 43	Sean Dawkins	.10	.02
❑ 44	Brett Favre	2.00	.75
❑ 45	Jeff George	.20	.07
❑ 46	Robert Smith	.20	.07
❑ 47	Ken Dilger	.20	.07
❑ 48	Larry Centers	.20	.07
❑ 49	Jackie Harris	.10	.02
❑ 50	Hugh Douglas	.20	.07
❑ 51	Herschel Walker	.20	.07
❑ 52	Kerry Collins	.40	.15
❑ 53	Michael Irvin	.40	.15
❑ 54	Willie McGinest	.10	.02
❑ 55	Herman Moore	.20	.07
❑ 56	Leroy Hoard	.10	.02
❑ 57	Scott Mitchell	.20	.07
❑ 58	Terrell Davis	.75	.30
❑ 59	Kevin Greene	.20	.07
❑ 60	Yancey Thigpen	.20	.07
❑ 61	Kevin Smith	.10	.02
❑ 62	Trent Dilfer	.40	.15
❑ 63	Cortez Kennedy	.10	.02
❑ 64	Carnell Lake	.10	.02
❑ 65	Quinn Early	.10	.02
❑ 66	Kyle Brady	.10	.02
❑ 67	Marshall Faulk	.50	.20
❑ 68	Fred Barnett	.10	.02
❑ 69	Quentin Coryatt	.10	.02
❑ 70	Dan Marino	2.00	.75
❑ 71	Junior Seau	.40	.15
❑ 72	Andre Coleman	.10	.02
❑ 73	Terry Kirby	.20	.07
❑ 74	Curtis Martin	.75	.30
❑ 75	Isaac Bruce	.40	.15
❑ 76	Mark Chmura	.20	.07
❑ 77	Edgar Bennett	.20	.07
❑ 78	Mario Bates	.20	.07
❑ 79	Eric Zeier	.10	.02
❑ 80	Adrian Murrell	.20	.07
❑ 81	Mark Brunell	.60	.25
❑ 82	Mark Rypien	.10	.02
❑ 83	Erric Pegram	.10	.02
❑ 84	Bryan Cox	.10	.02
❑ 85	Heath Shuler	.20	.07
❑ 86	Lake Dawson	.10	.02
❑ 87	O.J. McDuffie	.20	.07
❑ 88	Emmitt Smith	1.50	.60
❑ 89	Jim Harbaugh	.20	.07
❑ 90	Aaron Bailey	.10	.02
❑ 91	Jim Kelly	.40	.15
❑ 92	Rodney Hampton	.20	.07
❑ 93	Cris Carter	.40	.15
❑ 94	Henry Ellard	.10	.02
❑ 95	Darnay Scott	.20	.07
❑ 96	Daryl Johnston	.20	.07
❑ 97	Tamarick Vanover	.20	.07
❑ 98	Jeff Blake	.40	.15
❑ 99	Anthony Miller	.20	.07
❑ 100	Darren Woodson	.20	.07
❑ 101	Irving Fryar	.20	.07
❑ 102	Craig Heyward	.10	.02
❑ 103	Derek Loville	.10	.02
❑ 104	Ernie Mills	.10	.02
❑ 105	Brian Blades	.10	.02
❑ 106	Gus Frerotte	.20	.07
❑ 107	Alvin Harper	.10	.02
❑ 108	Tyrone Wheatley	.20	.07
❑ 109	John Elway	2.00	.75
❑ 110	Charles Haley	.20	.07
❑ 111	Terrell Fletcher	.10	.02
❑ 112	Vincent Brisby	.10	.02
❑ 113	Jerome Bettis	.40	.15
❑ 114	Barry Sanders	1.50	.60
❑ 115	Ken Norton Jr.	.10	.02
❑ 116	Sherman Williams	.10	.02
❑ 117	Antonio Freeman	.40	.15
❑ 118	Bert Emanuel	.20	.07
❑ 119	Marcus Allen	.40	.15
❑ 120	Stan Humphries	.20	.07
❑ 121	Chris Sanders	.20	.07
❑ 122	Jeff Graham	.10	.02
❑ 123	Jay Novacek	.10	.02
❑ 124	Aeneas Williams	.10	.02
❑ 125	Kordell Stewart	.40	.15
❑ 126	Steve Young	.75	.30
❑ 127	Jake Reed	.20	.07
❑ 128	Rick Mirer	.20	.07
❑ 129	Jeff Hostetler	.10	.02
❑ 130	Tim Brown	.40	.15
❑ 131	Shannon Sharpe	.20	.07
❑ 132	Dave Brown	.10	.02
❑ 133	Harvey Williams	.10	.02
❑ 134	Rodney Thomas	.10	.02
❑ 135	Frank Sanders	.20	.07
❑ 136	Brett Perriman	.10	.02
❑ 137	Steve Bono	.10	.02
❑ 138	Steve Atwater	.10	.02
❑ 139	Andre Rison	.20	.07
❑ 140	Orlando Thomas	.10	.02
❑ 141	Terry Allen	.20	.07
❑ 142	Carl Pickens	.20	.07
❑ 143	William Floyd	.20	.07
❑ 144	Bryce Paup	.10	.02
❑ 145	James O. Stewart	.20	.07
❑ 146	Eric Bjornson	.10	.02
❑ 147	Errict Rhett	.20	.07
❑ 148	Darick Holmes	.10	.02
❑ 149	Brian Mitchell	.10	.02
❑ 150	Brent Jones	.10	.02
❑ 151	Natrone Means	.20	.07
❑ 152	Rod Woodson	.20	.07
❑ 153	Bruce Smith	.20	.07
❑ 154	Deion Sanders	.60	.25
❑ 155	Kevin Williams	.10	.02
❑ 156	Erik Kramer	.10	.02
❑ 157	Jim Everett	.10	.02
❑ 158	Vinny Testaverde	.20	.07
❑ 159	Boomer Esiason	.20	.07
❑ 160	Leslie O'Neal	.10	.02
❑ 161	Curtis Conway	.40	.15
❑ 162	Thurman Thomas	.40	.15
❑ 163	Tony Brackens RC	.40	.15
❑ 164	Stepfret Williams RC	.20	.07
❑ 165	Alex Van Dyke RC	.20	.07
❑ 166	Cedric Jones RC	.10	.02
❑ 167	Stanley Pritchett RC	.20	.07
❑ 168	Willie Anderson RC	.10	.02
❑ 169	Regan Upshaw RC	.10	.02
❑ 170	Daryl Gardener RC	.10	.02
❑ 171	Alex Molden RC	.10	.02
❑ 172	John Mobley RC	.10	.02
❑ 173	Danny Kanell RC	.40	.15
❑ 174	Marco Battaglia RC	.10	.02
❑ 175	Simeon Rice RC	1.00	.40
❑ 176	Tony Banks RC	.40	.15
❑ 177	Stephen Davis RC	1.50	.60
❑ 178	Walt Harris RC	.10	.02
❑ 179	Amani Toomer RC	1.00	.40
❑ 180	Derrick Mayes RC	.40	.15
❑ 181	Jeff Lewis RC	.20	.07
❑ 182	Chris Darkins RC	.10	.02
❑ 183	Rickey Dudley RC	.40	.15
❑ 184	Jonathan Ogden RC	.40	.15
❑ 185	Mike Alstott RC	1.25	.50
❑ 186	Eric Moulds RC	1.50	.60
❑ 187	Karim Abdul-Jabbar RC	.40	.15
❑ 188	Jerry Rice CL	.40	.15
❑ 189	Dan Marino CL	.40	.15
❑ 190	Emmitt Smith CL	.40	.15

1997 Leaf

❑	COMPLETE SET (200)	25.00	10.00
❑ 1	Steve Young	.75	.30
❑ 2	Brett Favre	2.50	1.00
❑ 3	Barry Sanders	2.00	.75
❑ 4	Drew Bledsoe	.75	.30
❑ 5	Troy Aikman	1.25	.50
❑ 6	Kerry Collins	.60	.25
❑ 7	Dan Marino	2.50	1.00
❑ 8	Jerry Rice	1.25	.50
❑ 9	John Elway	2.50	1.00
❑ 10	Emmitt Smith	2.00	.75
❑ 11	Tony Banks	.40	.15
❑ 12	Gus Frerotte	.25	.08
❑ 13	Elvis Grbac	.40	.15
❑ 14	Neil O'Donnell	.40	.15
❑ 15	Michael Irvin	.60	.25
❑ 16	Marshall Faulk	.75	.30
❑ 17	Todd Collins	.25	.08
❑ 18	Scott Mitchell	.40	.15
❑ 19	Trent Dilfer	.60	.25
❑ 20	Rick Mirer	.25	.08
❑ 21	Frank Sanders	.40	.15
❑ 22	Larry Centers	.40	.15
❑ 23	Brad Johnson	.60	.25
❑ 24	Garrison Hearst	.40	.15
❑ 25	Steve McNair	.75	.30
❑ 26	Dorsey Levens	.60	.25
❑ 27	Eric Metcalf	.40	.15
❑ 28	Jeff George	.40	.15
❑ 29	Rodney Hampton	.40	.15
❑ 30	Michael Westbrook	.40	.15
❑ 31	Cris Carter	.60	.25
❑ 32	Heath Shuler	.25	.08
❑ 33	Warren Moon	.60	.25
❑ 34	Rod Woodson	.40	.15
❑ 35	Ken Dilger	.25	.08
❑ 36	Ben Coates	.40	.15
❑ 37	Andre Reed	.40	.15
❑ 38	Terrell Owens	.75	.30
❑ 39	Jeff Blake	.40	.15
❑ 40	Vinny Testaverde	.40	.15
❑ 41	Robert Brooks	.40	.15
❑ 42	Shannon Sharpe	.40	.15
❑ 43	Terry Allen	.60	.25
❑ 44	Terance Mathis	.40	.15
❑ 45	Bobby Engram	.40	.15
❑ 46	Rickey Dudley	.40	.15
❑ 47	Alex Molden	.25	.08
❑ 48	Lawrence Phillips	.25	.08
❑ 49	Curtis Martin	.75	.30
❑ 50	Jim Harbaugh	.40	.15
❑ 51	Wayne Chrebet	.60	.25
❑ 52	Quentin Coryatt	.25	.08
❑ 53	Eddie George	.60	.25
❑ 54	Michael Jackson	.40	.15
❑ 55	Greg Lloyd	.25	.08
❑ 56	Natrone Means	.40	.15
❑ 57	Marcus Allen	.60	.25
❑ 58	Desmond Howard	.40	.15
❑ 59	Stan Humphries	.40	.15
❑ 60	Reggie White	.60	.25
❑ 61	Brett Perriman	.25	.08
❑ 62	Warren Sapp	.40	.15
❑ 63	Adrian Murrell	.40	.15
❑ 64	Mark Brunell	.75	.30
❑ 65	Carl Pickens	.40	.15
❑ 66	Kordell Stewart	.60	.25
❑ 67	Ricky Watters	.40	.15

❑ 68	Tyrone Wheatley	.40	.15
❑ 69	Stanley Pritchett	.25	.08
❑ 70	Kevin Greene	.40	.15
❑ 71	Karim Abdul-Jabbar	.40	.15
❑ 72	Ki-Jana Carter	.25	.08
❑ 73	Rashaan Salaam	.25	.08
❑ 74	Simeon Rice	.40	.15
❑ 75	Napoleon Kaufman	.60	.25
❑ 76	Muhsin Muhammad	.40	.15
❑ 77	Bruce Smith	.40	.15
❑ 78	Eric Moulds	.60	.25
❑ 79	O.J. McDuffie	.40	.15
❑ 80	Danny Kanell	.25	.08
❑ 81	Harvey Williams	.25	.08
❑ 82	Greg Hill	.25	.08
❑ 83	Terrell Davis	.75	.30
❑ 84	Dan Wilkinson	.25	.08
❑ 85	Yancey Thigpen	.40	.15
❑ 86	Darrell Green	.40	.15
❑ 87	Tamarick Vanover	.40	.15
❑ 88	Mike Alstott	.60	.25
❑ 89	Johnnie Morton	.40	.15
❑ 90	Dale Carter	.25	.08
❑ 91	Jerome Bettis	.60	.25
❑ 92	James O.Stewart	.40	.15
❑ 93	Irving Fryar	.40	.15
❑ 94	Junior Seau	.60	.25
❑ 95	Sean Dawkins	.25	.08
❑ 96	J.J. Stokes	.40	.15
❑ 97	Tim Biakabutuka	.40	.15
❑ 98	Bert Emanuel	.40	.15
❑ 99	Eddie Kennison	.40	.15
❑ 100	Ray Zellars	.25	.08
❑ 101	Dave Brown	.25	.08
❑ 102	Leeland McElroy	.25	.08
❑ 103	Chris Warren	.40	.15
❑ 104	Byron Bam Morris	.25	.08
❑ 105	Thurman Thomas	.60	.25
❑ 106	Kyle Brady	.25	.08
❑ 107	Anthony Miller	.25	.08
❑ 108	Derrick Thomas	.60	.25
❑ 109	Mark Chmura	.40	.15
❑ 110	Deion Sanders	.60	.25
❑ 111	Eric Swann	.25	.08
❑ 112	Amani Toomer	.40	.15
❑ 113	Raymont Harris	.25	.08
❑ 114	Jake Reed	.40	.15
❑ 115	Bryant Young	.25	.08
❑ 116	Keenan McCardell	.40	.15
❑ 117	Herman Moore	.60	.25
❑ 118	Errict Rhett	.25	.08
❑ 119	Henry Ellard	.25	.08
❑ 120	Bobby Hoying	.40	.15
❑ 121	Robert Smith	.40	.15
❑ 122	Keyshawn Johnson	.60	.25
❑ 123	Zach Thomas	.60	.25
❑ 124	Charlie Garner	.40	.15
❑ 125	Terry Kirby	.40	.15
❑ 126	Darren Woodson	.25	.08
❑ 127	Darnay Scott	.40	.15
❑ 128	Chris Sanders	.25	.08
❑ 129	Charles Johnson	.40	.15
❑ 130	Joey Galloway	.40	.15
❑ 131	Curtis Conway	.40	.15
❑ 132	Isaac Bruce	.60	.25
❑ 133	Bobby Taylor	.25	.08
❑ 134	Jamal Anderson	.60	.25
❑ 135	Ken Norton	.25	.08
❑ 136	Darick Holmes	.25	.08
❑ 137	Tony Brackens	.25	.08
❑ 138	Tony Martin	.40	.15
❑ 139	Antonio Freeman	.60	.25
❑ 140	Neil Smith	.40	.15
❑ 141	Terry Glenn	.60	.25
❑ 142	Marvin Harrison	.60	.25
❑ 143	Daryl Johnston	.40	.15
❑ 144	Tim Brown	.60	.25
❑ 145	Kimble Anders	.40	.15
❑ 146	Derrick Alexander WR	.40	.15
❑ 147	LeShon Johnson	.25	.08
❑ 148	Anthony Johnson	.25	.08
❑ 149	Leslie Shepherd	.25	.08
❑ 150	Chris T. Jones	.25	.08
❑ 151	Edgar Bennett	.40	.15
❑ 152	Ty Detmer	.40	.15
❑ 153	Ike Hilliard RC	1.00	.40
❑ 154	Jim Druckenmiller RC	.40	.15
❑ 155	Warrick Dunn RC	2.00	.75
❑ 156	Yatil Green RC	.40	.15
❑ 157	Reidel Anthony RC	.60	.25
❑ 158	Antowain Smith RC	1.50	.60
❑ 159	Rae Carruth RC	.25	.08
❑ 160	Tiki Barber RC	4.00	1.50
❑ 161	Byron Hanspard RC	.40	.15
❑ 162	Jake Plummer RC	3.00	1.25
❑ 163	Joey Kent RC	.60	.25
❑ 164	Corey Dillon RC	4.00	1.50
❑ 165	Kevin Lockett RC	.40	.15
❑ 166	Will Blackwell RC	.40	.15
❑ 167	Troy Davis RC	.40	.15
❑ 168	James Farrior RC	.60	.25
❑ 169	Danny Wuerffel RC	.60	.25
❑ 170	Pat Barnes RC	.60	.25
❑ 171	Darnell Autry RC	.40	.15
❑ 172	Tom Knight RC	.25	.08
❑ 173	David LaFleur RC	.25	.08
❑ 174	Tony Gonzalez RC	2.00	.75
❑ 175	Kenny Holmes RC	.60	.25
❑ 176	Reinard Wilson RC	.40	.15
❑ 177	Renaldo Wynn RC	.25	.08
❑ 178	Bryant Westbrook RC	.25	.08
❑ 179	Darrell Russell RC	.25	.08
❑ 180	Orlando Pace RC	.60	.25
❑ 181	Shawn Springs RC	.40	.15
❑ 182	Peter Boulware RC	.60	.25
❑ 183	Dan Marino L	1.25	.50
❑ 184	Brett Favre L	1.25	.50
❑ 185	Emmitt Smith L	1.00	.40
❑ 186	Eddie George L	.60	.25
❑ 187	Curtis Martin L	.40	.15
❑ 188	Tim Brown L	.40	.15
❑ 189	Mark Brunell L	.60	.25
❑ 190	Isaac Bruce L	.40	.15
❑ 191	Deion Sanders L	.40	.15
❑ 192	John Elway L	1.25	.50
❑ 193	Jerry Rice L	.60	.25
❑ 194	Barry Sanders L	1.00	.40
❑ 195	Herman Moore L	.40	.15
❑ 196	Carl Pickens L	.40	.15
❑ 197	Karim Abdul-Jabbar L	.40	.15
❑ 198	Drew Bledsoe CL	.60	.25
❑ 199	Troy Aikman CL	.60	.25
❑ 200	Terrell Davis CL	.60	.25

1999 Leaf Certified

❑	COMPLETE SET (225)	200.00	100.00
❑	COMP.SET w/o RCs 175)	40.00	15.00
❑ 1	Simeon Rice	.60	.25
❑ 2	Frank Sanders	.60	.25
❑ 3	Andre Wadsworth	.40	.15
❑ 4	Larry Centers	.40	.15
❑ 5	Byron Hanspard	.40	.15
❑ 6	Terance Mathis	.60	.25
❑ 7	O.J. Santiago	.40	.15
❑ 8	Chris Calloway	.40	.15
❑ 9	Michael Jackson	.40	.15
❑ 10	Rod Woodson	.60	.25
❑ 11	Pat Johnson	.40	.15
❑ 12	Rob Johnson	.60	.25
❑ 13	Andre Reed	.60	.25
❑ 14	Tim Biakabutuka	.60	.25
❑ 15	Rae Carruth	.40	.15
❑ 16	Fred Lane	.40	.15
❑ 17	Muhsin Muhammad	.60	.25
❑ 18	Wesley Walls	.60	.25
❑ 19	Edgar Bennett	.40	.15
❑ 20	Curtis Conway	.60	.25
❑ 21	Bobby Engram	.60	.25
❑ 22	Jeff Blake	.60	.25
❑ 23	Darnay Scott	.40	.15
❑ 24	Ty Detmer	.60	.25
❑ 25	Sedrick Shaw	.40	.15
❑ 26	Leslie Shepherd	.40	.15
❑ 27	Terry Kirby	.40	.15
❑ 28	Chris Warren	.40	.15
❑ 29	Rocket Ismail	.60	.25
❑ 30	Marcus Nash	.40	.15
❑ 31	Neil Smith	.60	.25
❑ 32	Bubby Brister	.40	.15
❑ 33	Brian Griese	1.00	.40
❑ 34	Germane Crowell	.40	.15
❑ 35	Johnnie Morton	.60	.25
❑ 36	Gus Frerotte	.40	.15
❑ 37	Robert Brooks	.60	.25
❑ 38	Mark Chmura	.40	.15
❑ 39	Derrick Mayes	.40	.15
❑ 40	Jerome Pathon	.40	.15
❑ 41	Jimmy Smith	.60	.25
❑ 42	James Stewart	.60	.25
❑ 43	Tavian Banks	.40	.15
❑ 44	Derrick Alexander WR	.60	.25
❑ 45	Kimble Anders	.60	.25
❑ 46	Elvis Grbac	.60	.25
❑ 47	Derrick Thomas	1.00	.40
❑ 48	Byron Bam Morris	.40	.15
❑ 49	Tony Gonzalez	1.00	.40
❑ 50	John Avery	.40	.15
❑ 51	Tyrone Wheatley	.60	.25
❑ 52	Zach Thomas	1.00	.40
❑ 53	Lamar Thomas	.40	.15
❑ 54	Jeff George	.60	.25
❑ 55	John Randle	.60	.25
❑ 56	Jake Reed	.60	.25
❑ 57	Leroy Hoard	.40	.15
❑ 58	Robert Edwards	.40	.15
❑ 59	Ben Coates	.60	.25
❑ 60	Tony Simmons	.40	.15
❑ 61	Shawn Jefferson	.40	.15
❑ 62	Eddie Kennison	.60	.25
❑ 63	Lamar Smith	.60	.25
❑ 64	Tiki Barber	1.00	.40
❑ 65	Kerry Collins	.60	.25
❑ 66	Ike Hilliard	.40	.15
❑ 67	Gary Brown	.40	.15
❑ 68	Joe Jurevicius	.60	.25
❑ 69	Kent Graham	.40	.15
❑ 70	Dedric Ward	.40	.15
❑ 71	Terry Allen	.60	.25
❑ 72	Neil O'Donnell	.60	.25
❑ 73	Desmond Howard	.60	.25
❑ 74	James Jett	.60	.25
❑ 75	Jon Ritchie	.40	.15
❑ 76	Rickey Dudley	.40	.15
❑ 77	Charles Johnson	.40	.15
❑ 78	Chris Fuamatu-Ma'afala	.40	.15
❑ 79	Hines Ward	1.00	.40
❑ 80	Ryan Leaf	1.00	.40
❑ 81	Jim Harbaugh	.60	.25
❑ 82	Junior Seau	1.00	.40
❑ 83	Mikhael Ricks	.40	.15
❑ 84	J.J. Stokes	.60	.25
❑ 85	Ahman Green	1.00	.40
❑ 86	Tony Banks	.60	.25
❑ 87	Robert Holcombe	.40	.15
❑ 88	Az-Zahir Hakim	.40	.15
❑ 89	Greg Hill	.40	.15
❑ 90	Trent Green	1.00	.40
❑ 91	Eric Zeier	.40	.15
❑ 92	Reidel Anthony	.60	.25
❑ 93	Bert Emanuel	.60	.25
❑ 94	Warren Sapp	.40	.15
❑ 95	Kevin Dyson	.60	.25
❑ 96	Yancey Thigpen	.40	.15
❑ 97	Frank Wycheck	.40	.15
❑ 98	Michael Westbrook	.60	.25
❑ 99	Albert Connell	.40	.15
❑ 100	Darrell Green	.40	.15
❑ 101	Rob Moore	.60	.25
❑ 102	Adrian Murrell	.60	.25
❑ 103	Jake Plummer	1.00	.40
❑ 104	Chris Chandler	.60	.25
❑ 105	Jamal Anderson	1.00	.40
❑ 106	Tim Dwight	1.00	.40
❑ 107	Jermaine Lewis	1.00	.40
❑ 108	Priest Holmes	2.50	1.00
❑ 109	Bruce Smith	1.00	.40
❑ 110	Eric Moulds	1.00	.40
❑ 111	Antowain Smith	1.50	.60
❑ 112	Curtis Enis	1.00	.40
❑ 113	Corey Dillon	1.50	.60

❑ 114 Michael Irvin 1.00 .40
❑ 115 Ed McCaffrey 1.00 .40
❑ 116 Shannon Sharpe 1.00 .40
❑ 117 Terrell Davis 1.50 .60
❑ 118 Charlie Batch 1.50 .60
❑ 119 Antonio Freeman 1.00 .40
❑ 120 Dorsey Levens 1.00 .40
❑ 121 Marvin Harrison 1.50 .60
❑ 122 Peyton Manning 5.00 2.00
❑ 123 Keenan McCardell 1.00 .40
❑ 124 Fred Taylor 1.50 .60
❑ 125 Andre Rison 1.00 .40
❑ 126 O.J. McDuffie 1.00 .40
❑ 127 Karim Abdul-Jabbar 1.00 .40
❑ 128 Randy Moss 4.00 1.50
❑ 129 Terry Glenn 1.00 .40
❑ 130 Vinny Testaverde 1.00 .40
❑ 131 Keyshawn Johnson 1.00 .40
❑ 132 Curtis Martin 1.00 .40
❑ 133 Wayne Chrebet 1.00 .40
❑ 134 Napoleon Kaufman 1.00 .40
❑ 135 Charles Woodson 1.00 .40
❑ 136 Duce Staley 1.50 .60
❑ 137 Kordell Stewart 1.00 .40
❑ 138 Terrell Owens 1.50 .60
❑ 139 Ricky Watters 1.00 .40
❑ 140 Joey Galloway 1.00 .40
❑ 141 Jon Kitna 1.00 .40
❑ 142 Isaac Bruce 1.50 .60
❑ 143 Jacquez Green 1.00 .40
❑ 144 Warrick Dunn 1.00 .40
❑ 145 Mike Alstott 1.00 .40
❑ 146 Trent Dilfer 1.00 .40
❑ 147 Steve McNair 1.00 .40
❑ 148 Eddie George 1.50 .60
❑ 149 Skip Hicks 1.00 .40
❑ 150 Brad Johnson 1.50 .60
❑ 151 Doug Flutie 1.50 .60
❑ 152 Thurman Thomas 1.00 .40
❑ 153 Carl Pickens 1.00 .40
❑ 154 Emmitt Smith 5.00 2.00
❑ 155 Troy Aikman 5.00 2.00
❑ 156 Deion Sanders 1.50 .60
❑ 157 John Elway 8.00 3.00
❑ 158 Rod Smith 1.00 .40
❑ 159 Barry Sanders 8.00 3.00
❑ 160 Herman Moore 1.50 .60
❑ 161 Brett Favre 8.00 3.00
❑ 162 Mark Brunell 1.50 .60
❑ 163 Warren Moon 1.50 .60
❑ 164 Dan Marino 8.00 3.00
❑ 165 Randall Cunningham 1.50 .60
❑ 166 Robert Smith 1.50 .60
❑ 167 Cris Carter 1.50 .60
❑ 168 Drew Bledsoe 3.00 1.25
❑ 169 Tim Brown 1.50 .60
❑ 170 Jerome Bettis 1.50 .60
❑ 171 Natrone Means 1.00 .40
❑ 172 Jerry Rice 5.00 2.00
❑ 173 Steve Young 3.00 1.25
❑ 174 Garrison Hearst 1.50 .60
❑ 175 Marshall Faulk 3.00 1.25
❑ 176 David Boston RC 5.00 2.00
❑ 177 Jeff Paulk RC 2.00 .75
❑ 178 Reginald Kelly RC 2.00 .75
❑ 179 Scott Covington RC 5.00 2.00
❑ 180 Chris McAlister RC 3.00 1.25
❑ 181 Shawn Bryson RC 5.00 2.00
❑ 182 Peerless Price RC 5.00 2.00
❑ 183 Cade McNown RC 3.00 1.25
❑ 184 Michael Bishop RC 5.00 2.00
❑ 185 D'Wayne Bates RC 3.00 1.25
❑ 186 Marty Booker RC 5.00 2.00
❑ 187 Akili Smith RC 2.00 .75
❑ 188 Craig Yeast RC 3.00 1.25
❑ 189 Tim Couch RC 5.00 2.00
❑ 190 Kevin Johnson RC 5.00 2.00
❑ 191 Wane McGarity RC 2.00 .75
❑ 192 Olandis Gary RC 5.00 2.00
❑ 193 Travis McGriff RC 2.00 .75
❑ 194 Sedrick Irvin RC 2.00 .75
❑ 195 Chris Claiborne RC 2.00 .75
❑ 196 De'Mond Parker RC 2.00 .75
❑ 197 Dee Miller RC 2.00 .75
❑ 198 Edgerrin James RC 15.00 6.00
❑ 199 Mike Cloud RC 3.00 1.25
❑ 200 Larry Parker RC 5.00 2.00
❑ 201 Cecil Collins RC 2.00 .75
❑ 202 James Johnson RC 3.00 1.25
❑ 203 Rob Konrad RC 5.00 2.00
❑ 204 Daunte Culpepper RC 15.00 6.00
❑ 205 Jim Kleinsasser RC 5.00 2.00
❑ 206 Kevin Faulk RC 5.00 2.00
❑ 207 Andy Katzenmoyer RC 3.00 1.25
❑ 208 Ricky Williams RC 8.00 3.00
❑ 209 Joe Montgomery RC 3.00 1.25
❑ 210 Sean Bennett RC 2.00 .75
❑ 211 Dameane Douglas RC 5.00 2.00
❑ 212 Donovan McNabb RC 20.00 7.50
❑ 213 Na Brown RC 3.00 1.25
❑ 214 Amos Zereoue RC 5.00 2.00
❑ 215 Troy Edwards RC 3.00 1.25
❑ 216 Jermaine Fazande RC 3.00 1.25
❑ 217 Tai Streets RC 5.00 2.00
❑ 218 Brock Huard RC 5.00 2.00
❑ 219 Charlie Rogers RC 3.00 1.25
❑ 220 Karsten Bailey RC 3.00 1.25
❑ 221 Joe Germaine RC 3.00 1.25
❑ 222 Torry Holt RC 10.00 4.00
❑ 223 Shaun King RC 3.00 1.25
❑ 224 Jevon Kearse RC 8.00 3.00
❑ 225 Champ Bailey RC 6.00 2.50

2000 Leaf Certified

❑ COMP.SET w/o RC's (150) 40.00 15.00
❑ 1 Frank Sanders .40 .15
❑ 2 Rob Moore .60 .25
❑ 3 Simeon Rice .60 .25
❑ 4 David Boston 1.00 .40
❑ 5 Tim Dwight 1.00 .40
❑ 6 Jamal Anderson 1.00 .40
❑ 7 Chris Chandler .40 .15
❑ 8 Terance Mathis .60 .25
❑ 9 Priest Holmes 1.25 .50
❑ 10 Rod Woodson .60 .25
❑ 11 Tony Banks .40 .15
❑ 12 Jermaine Lewis .40 .15
❑ 13 Shannon Sharpe .40 .15
❑ 14 Qadry Ismail .60 .25
❑ 15 Doug Flutie 1.00 .40
❑ 16 Antowain Smith .60 .25
❑ 17 Peerless Price .60 .25
❑ 18 Rob Johnson .40 .15
❑ 19 Muhsin Muhammad .60 .25
❑ 20 Wesley Walls .40 .15
❑ 21 Tim Biakabutuka .40 .15
❑ 22 Steve Beuerlein .40 .15
❑ 23 Patrick Jeffers .40 .15
❑ 24 Natrone Means .40 .15
❑ 25 Curtis Enis .40 .15
❑ 26 Bobby Engram .40 .15
❑ 27 Marcus Robinson 1.00 .40
❑ 28 Eddie Kennison .40 .15
❑ 29 Marty Booker .60 .25
❑ 30 Darnay Scott .40 .15
❑ 31 Carl Pickens .40 .15
❑ 32 Karim Abdul-Jabbar .40 .15
❑ 33 Errict Rhett .40 .15
❑ 34 Darrin Chiaverini .40 .15
❑ 35 Randall Cunningham .40 .15
❑ 36 Michael Irvin .40 .15
❑ 37 Rocket Ismail .40 .15
❑ 38 Ed McCaffrey 1.00 .40
❑ 39 Rod Smith .40 .15
❑ 40 Herman Moore .60 .25
❑ 41 Johnnie Morton .40 .15
❑ 42 James Stewart .40 .15
❑ 43 Bill Schroeder .60 .25
❑ 44 Ahman Green 1.00 .40
❑ 45 Terrence Wilkins .40 .15
❑ 46 Keenan McCardell .40 .15
❑ 47 Derrick Alexander .40 .15
❑ 48 Elvis Grbac .40 .15
❑ 49 Tony Gonzalez .40 .15
❑ 50 O.J. McDuffie .40 .15
❑ 51 Tony Martin .40 .15
❑ 52 James Johnson .40 .15
❑ 53 Thurman Thomas .40 .15
❑ 54 Jay Fiedler 1.00 .40
❑ 55 Damon Huard .40 .15
❑ 56 Leroy Hoard .40 .15
❑ 57 Terry Glenn .60 .25
❑ 58 Kevin Faulk .40 .15
❑ 59 Jeff Blake .40 .15
❑ 60 Jake Reed .40 .15
❑ 61 Amani Toomer .40 .15
❑ 62 Kerry Collins .40 .15
❑ 63 Ike Hilliard .40 .15
❑ 64 Joe Montgomery .40 .15
❑ 65 Vinny Testaverde .40 .15
❑ 66 Wayne Chrebet .40 .15
❑ 67 Ray Lucas .60 .25
❑ 68 Napoleon Kaufman .60 .25
❑ 69 Charles Woodson .40 .15
❑ 70 Tyrone Wheatley .40 .15
❑ 71 Rich Gannon 1.00 .40
❑ 72 Duce Staley 1.00 .40
❑ 73 Kordell Stewart .60 .25
❑ 74 Jerome Bettis 1.00 .40
❑ 75 Troy Edwards .40 .15
❑ 76 Junior Seau 1.00 .40
❑ 77 Jim Harbaugh .40 .15
❑ 78 Curtis Conway .60 .25
❑ 79 Jermaine Fazande .40 .15
❑ 80 Terrell Owens 1.00 .40
❑ 81 Charlie Garner .60 .25
❑ 82 Garrison Hearst .40 .15
❑ 83 Jeff Garcia 1.00 .40
❑ 84 Derrick Mayes .40 .15
❑ 85 Az-Zahir Hakim .40 .15
❑ 86 Mike Alstott 1.00 .40
❑ 87 Warrick Dunn 1.00 .40
❑ 88 Jacquez Green .40 .15
❑ 89 Warren Sapp .40 .15
❑ 90 Yancey Thigpen .40 .15
❑ 91 Kevin Dyson .40 .15
❑ 92 Frank Wycheck .40 .15
❑ 93 Jevon Kearse 1.00 .40
❑ 94 Adrian Murrell .40 .15
❑ 95 Bruce Smith .40 .15
❑ 96 Michael Westbrook .40 .15
❑ 97 Albert Connell .40 .15
❑ 98 Champ Bailey .60 .25
❑ 99 Jeff George .40 .15
❑ 100 Deion Sanders 1.00 .40
❑ 101 Jake Plummer 1.00 .40
❑ 102 Eric Moulds 1.50 .60
❑ 103 Cade McNown .40 .15
❑ 104 Corey Dillon 1.50 .60
❑ 105 Akili Smith .60 .25
❑ 106 Tim Couch 1.00 .40
❑ 107 Kevin Johnson 1.50 .60
❑ 108 Emmitt Smith 3.00 1.25
❑ 109 Troy Aikman 3.00 1.25
❑ 110 Joey Galloway 1.00 .40
❑ 111 John Elway 5.00 2.00
❑ 112 Terrell Davis 1.00 .40
❑ 113 Olandis Gary 1.50 .60
❑ 114 Brian Griese 1.00 .40
❑ 115 Charlie Batch 1.50 .60
❑ 116 Barry Sanders 4.00 1.50
❑ 117 Germane Crowell .60 .25
❑ 118 Brett Favre 5.00 2.00
❑ 119 Dorsey Levens .60 .25
❑ 120 Antonio Freeman 1.50 .60
❑ 121 Peyton Manning 4.00 1.50
❑ 122 Edgerrin James 2.50 1.00
❑ 123 Marvin Harrison 1.50 .60
❑ 124 Mark Brunell 1.00 .40
❑ 125 Fred Taylor 1.00 .40
❑ 126 Jimmy Smith 1.00 .40
❑ 127 Dan Marino 5.00 2.00
❑ 128 Randy Moss 3.00 1.25
❑ 129 Daunte Culpepper 2.00 .75
❑ 130 Cris Carter 1.50 .60
❑ 131 Robert Smith 1.50 .60
❑ 132 Drew Bledsoe 2.00 .75
❑ 133 Ricky Williams 1.00 .40
❑ 134 Curtis Martin 1.50 .60
❑ 135 Tim Brown 1.50 .60

❑ 136	Donovan McNabb	2.50	1.00
❑ 137	Jerry Rice	3.00	1.25
❑ 138	Steve Young	2.00	.75
❑ 139	Jon Kitna	1.50	.60
❑ 140	Ricky Watters	.60	.25
❑ 141	Kurt Warner	3.00	1.25
❑ 142	Marshall Faulk	2.00	.75
❑ 143	Torry Holt	1.50	.60
❑ 144	Isaac Bruce	1.50	.60
❑ 145	Shaun King	.40	.15
❑ 146	Keyshawn Johnson	1.50	.60
❑ 147	Eddie George	1.00	.40
❑ 148	Steve McNair	1.50	.60
❑ 149	Stephen Davis	1.50	.60
❑ 150	Brad Johnson	1.50	.60
❑ 151	Rogers Beckett RC	4.00	1.50
❑ 152	Erik Flowers RC	4.00	1.50
❑ 153	Demario Brown RC	2.50	1.00
❑ 154	Doug Johnson RC	5.00	2.00
❑ 155	Deon Grant RC	4.00	1.50
❑ 156	Ian Gold RC	4.00	1.50
❑ 157	Brian Urlacher RC	20.00	7.50
❑ 158	Frank Murphy RC	2.50	1.00
❑ 159	James Whalen RC	2.50	1.00
❑ 160	JaJuan Dawson RC	2.50	1.00
❑ 161	William Bartee RC	4.00	1.50
❑ 162	Aaron Shea RC	1.00	.40
❑ 163	Deltha O'Neal RC	5.00	2.00
❑ 164	Jarious Jackson RC	4.00	1.50
❑ 165	Muneer Moore RC	2.50	1.00
❑ 166	Hank Poteat RC	4.00	1.50
❑ 167	Jacoby Shepherd RC	2.50	1.00
❑ 168	Ben Kelly RC	2.50	1.00
❑ 169	Orantes Grant RC	2.50	1.00
❑ 170	Chris Hovan RC	4.00	1.50
❑ 171	Leon Murray RC	2.50	1.00
❑ 172	Marc Bulger RC	10.00	4.00
❑ 173	Chad Morton RC	5.00	2.00
❑ 174	Na'il Diggs RC	4.00	1.50
❑ 175	Shaun Ellis RC	5.00	2.00
❑ 176	John Abraham RC	5.00	2.00
❑ 177	Fred Robbins RC	2.50	1.00
❑ 178	Marcus Knight RC	4.00	1.50
❑ 179	Thomas Hamner RC	2.50	1.00
❑ 180	Cornelius Griffin RC	4.00	1.50
❑ 181	Raynoch Thompson RC	4.00	1.50
❑ 182	Paul Smith RC	4.00	1.50
❑ 183	Ahmed Plummer RC	5.00	2.00
❑ 184	John Engelberger RC	4.00	1.50
❑ 185	Darren Howard RC	4.00	1.50
❑ 186	Corey Moore RC	2.50	1.00
❑ 187	Joe Hamilton RC	4.00	1.50
❑ 188	Rob Morris RC	4.00	1.50
❑ 189	Keith Bulluck RC	5.00	2.00
❑ 190	Todd Husak RC	5.00	2.00
❑ 191	Mareno Philyaw RC	3.00	1.25
❑ 192	Kwame Cavil RC	3.00	1.25
❑ 193	Sammy Morris RC	5.00	2.00
❑ 194	Avion Black RC	5.00	2.00
❑ 195	Bashir Yamini RC	3.00	1.25
❑ 196	Curtis Keaton RC	5.00	2.00
❑ 197	Mike Anderson RC	8.00	3.00
❑ 198	Bubba Franks RC	6.00	2.50
❑ 199	Anthony Lucas RC	3.00	1.25
❑ 200	Rondell Mealey RC	3.00	1.25
❑ 201	Terrelle Smith RC	5.00	2.00
❑ 202	Frank Moreau RC	5.00	2.00
❑ 203	Deon Dyer RC	5.00	2.00
❑ 204	Quinton Spotwood RC	3.00	1.25
❑ 205	Troy Walters RC	10.00	4.00
❑ 206	Doug Chapman RC	5.00	2.00
❑ 207	Tom Brady RC	80.00	40.00
❑ 208	Sherrod Gideon RC	3.00	1.25
❑ 209	Ron Dixon RC	5.00	2.00
❑ 210	Anthony Becht RC	6.00	2.50
❑ 211	James Williams RC	5.00	2.00
❑ 212	Sebastian Janikowski RC	6.00	2.50
❑ 213	Corey Simon RC	6.00	2.50
❑ 214	Gari Scott RC	3.00	1.25
❑ 215	Dante Hall RC	12.00	5.00
❑ 216	Tim Rattay RC	6.00	2.50
❑ 217	Chafie Fields RC	3.00	1.25
❑ 218	Trung Canidate RC	5.00	2.00
❑ 219	Chris Coleman RC	6.00	2.50
❑ 220	Erron Kinney RC	6.00	2.50
❑ 221	Thomas Jones RC	15.00	6.00
❑ 222	Travis Taylor RC	10.00	4.00
❑ 223	Chris Redman RC	8.00	3.00
❑ 224	Jamal Lewis RC	25.00	10.00
❑ 225	Dez White RC	10.00	4.00
❑ 226	Peter Warrick RC	10.00	4.00
❑ 227	Ron Dugans RC	8.00	3.00
❑ 228	Courtney Brown RC	10.00	4.00
❑ 229	Travis Prentice RC	8.00	3.00
❑ 230	Dennis Northcutt RC	10.00	4.00
❑ 231	Michael Wiley RC	8.00	3.00
❑ 232	Chris Cole RC	8.00	3.00
❑ 233	Reuben Droughns RC	12.00	5.00
❑ 234	R.Jay Soward RC	8.00	3.00
❑ 235	Shyrone Stith RC	8.00	3.00
❑ 236	Sylvester Morris RC	8.00	3.00
❑ 237	J.R. Redmond RC	8.00	3.00
❑ 238	Ron Dayne RC	10.00	4.00
❑ 239	Chad Pennington RC	25.00	10.00
❑ 240	Laveranues Coles RC	12.00	5.00
❑ 241	Jerry Porter RC	12.00	5.00
❑ 242	Todd Pinkston RC	10.00	4.00
❑ 243	Plaxico Burress RC	20.00	7.50
❑ 244	Danny Farmer RC	8.00	3.00
❑ 245	Tee Martin RC	10.00	4.00
❑ 246	Trevor Gaylor RC	8.00	3.00
❑ 247	Giovanni Carmazzi RC	8.00	3.00
❑ 248	Darrell Jackson RC	20.00	7.50
❑ 249	Shaun Alexander RC	50.00	20.00
❑ 250	Chris Samuels RC	8.00	3.00

2001 Leaf Certified Materials

❑	COMP.SET w/o SPs (100)	30.00	12.50
❑ 1	Aaron Brooks	1.00	.40
❑ 2	Ahman Green	1.00	.40
❑ 3	Akili Smith	.40	.15
❑ 4	Amani Toomer	.60	.25
❑ 5	Antonio Freeman	1.00	.40
❑ 6	Barry Sanders	2.00	.75
❑ 7	Brad Johnson	1.00	.40
❑ 8	Brett Favre	3.00	1.25
❑ 9	Brian Griese	1.00	.40
❑ 10	Brian Urlacher	1.50	.60
❑ 11	Bruce Smith	.40	.15
❑ 12	Cade McNown	.40	.15
❑ 13	Chad Pennington	1.50	.60
❑ 14	Charlie Batch	1.00	.40
❑ 15	Charlie Garner	.60	.25
❑ 16	Corey Dillon	1.00	.40
❑ 17	Cris Carter	1.00	.40
❑ 18	Curtis Martin	1.00	.40
❑ 19	Dan Marino	3.00	1.25
❑ 20	Darrell Jackson	.40	.15
❑ 21	Daunte Culpepper	1.00	.40
❑ 22	David Boston	1.00	.40
❑ 23	Derrick Alexander	.60	.25
❑ 24	Donovan McNabb	1.25	.50
❑ 25	Dorsey Levens	.60	.25
❑ 26	Doug Flutie	1.00	.40
❑ 27	Drew Bledsoe	1.25	.50
❑ 28	Ed McCaffrey	1.00	.40
❑ 29	Eddie George	1.00	.40
❑ 30	Edgerrin James	1.25	.50
❑ 31	Elvis Grbac	.60	.25
❑ 32	Emmitt Smith	2.00	.75
❑ 33	Eric Moulds	1.00	.40
❑ 34	Frank Wycheck	.40	.15
❑ 35	Fred Taylor	1.00	.40
❑ 36	Ike Hilliard	.60	.25
❑ 37	Isaac Bruce	1.00	.40
❑ 38	Jacquez Green	.40	.15
❑ 39	Jake Plummer	.60	.25
❑ 40	Jamal Anderson	1.00	.40
❑ 41	Jamal Lewis	1.50	.60
❑ 42	James Stewart	.60	.25
❑ 43	Jay Fiedler	1.00	.40
❑ 44	Jeff Garcia	1.00	.40
❑ 45	Jeff George	.60	.25
❑ 46	Jerome Bettis	1.00	.40
❑ 47	Jerry Rice	2.00	.75
❑ 48	Jevon Kearse	.60	.25
❑ 49	Jimmy Smith	.60	.25
❑ 50	Joe Horn	.60	.25
❑ 51	Joey Galloway	.60	.25
❑ 52	John Elway	3.00	1.25
❑ 53	Junior Seau	1.00	.40
❑ 54	Keenan McCardell	.40	.15
❑ 55	Kerry Collins	1.00	.40
❑ 56	Keyshawn Johnson	1.00	.40
❑ 57	Kurt Warner	2.00	.75
❑ 58	Lamar Smith	.60	.25
❑ 59	Laveranues Coles	1.00	.40
❑ 60	Marcus Robinson	1.00	.40
❑ 61	Mark Brunell	1.00	.40
❑ 62	Marshall Faulk	1.25	.50
❑ 63	Marvin Harrison	1.00	.40
❑ 64	Matt Hasselbeck	.60	.25
❑ 65	Mike Alstott	1.00	.40
❑ 66	Mike Anderson	1.00	.40
❑ 67	Muhsin Muhammad	.60	.25
❑ 68	Peter Warrick	1.00	.40
❑ 69	Peyton Manning	2.50	1.00
❑ 70	Plaxico Burress	1.00	.40
❑ 71	Randy Moss	2.00	.75
❑ 72	Ray Lewis	1.00	.40
❑ 73	Rich Gannon	1.00	.40
❑ 74	Ricky Watters	.60	.25
❑ 75	Ricky Williams	1.00	.40
❑ 76	Rob Johnson	1.00	.40
❑ 77	Rod Smith	.60	.25
❑ 78	Ron Dayne	1.00	.40
❑ 79	Shannon Sharpe	.60	.25
❑ 80	Shaun Alexander	1.25	.50
❑ 81	Stephen Davis	1.00	.40
❑ 82	Steve McNair	1.00	.40
❑ 83	Steve Young	1.00	.40
❑ 84	Sylvester Morris	.40	.15
❑ 85	Terrell Davis	1.00	.40
❑ 86	Terrell Owens	1.00	.40
❑ 87	Terry Glenn	.60	.25
❑ 88	Thomas Jones	.60	.25
❑ 89	Tiki Barber	1.00	.40
❑ 90	Tim Brown	1.00	.40
❑ 91	Tim Couch	.60	.25
❑ 92	Tony Gonzalez	.60	.25
❑ 93	Torry Holt	1.00	.40
❑ 94	Travis Taylor	.60	.25
❑ 95	Troy Aikman	1.50	.60
❑ 96	Tyrone Wheatley	.60	.25
❑ 97	Vinny Testaverde	.60	.25
❑ 98	Warren Sapp	.60	.25
❑ 99	Warrick Dunn	1.00	.40
❑ 100	Wayne Chrebet	.60	.25
❑ 101	Chris Taylor RC	6.00	2.50
❑ 102	Ken-Yon Rambo RC	6.00	2.50
❑ 103	Correll Buckhalter RC	12.00	5.00
❑ 104	A.J. Feeley RC	10.00	4.00
❑ 105	Josh Booty RC	10.00	4.00
❑ 106	LaMont Jordan RC	25.00	10.00
❑ 107	Alge Crumpler RC	12.00	5.00
❑ 108	Jamal Reynolds RC	10.00	4.00
❑ 109	Nate Clements RC	10.00	4.00
❑ 110	Will Allen RC	6.00	2.50
❑ 111	Santana Moss FF RC	25.00	10.00
❑ 112	Chad Johnson FF RC	40.00	15.00
❑ 113	Chris Chambers FF RC	25.00	10.00
❑ 114	David Terrell FF RC	15.00	6.00
❑ 115	Freddie Mitchell FF RC	15.00	6.00
❑ 116	Koren Robinson FF RC	15.00	6.00
❑ 117	Quincy Morgan FF RC	15.00	6.00
❑ 118	Reggie Wayne FF RC	30.00	12.50
❑ 119	Robert Ferguson FF RC	15.00	6.00
❑ 120	Rod Gardner FF RC	15.00	6.00
❑ 121	Snoop Minnis FF RC	10.00	4.00
❑ 122	Josh Heupel FF RC	15.00	6.00
❑ 123	Anthony Thomas FF RC	15.00	6.00
❑ 124	Deuce McAllister FF RC	30.00	12.50
❑ 125	James Jackson FF RC	15.00	6.00
❑ 126	Travis Minor FF RC	10.00	4.00
❑ 127	Kevan Barlow FF RC	15.00	6.00
❑ 128	LaDain Tomlinson FF RC	100.00	60.00
❑ 129	Todd Heap FF RC	15.00	6.00
❑ 130	Michael Bennett FF RC	15.00	6.00

❑ 131 Rudi Johnson FF RC 30.00 12.50
❑ 132 Travis Henry FF RC 25.00 10.00
❑ 133 Michael Vick FF RC 60.00 25.00
❑ 134 Drew Brees FF RC 50.00 25.00
❑ 135 Chris Weinke FF RC 15.00 6.00
❑ 136 Quincy Carter FF RC 15.00 6.00
❑ 137 Mike McMahon FF RC 15.00 6.00
❑ 138 Jesse Palmer FF RC 15.00 6.00
❑ 139 Marq Tuiasosopo FF RC 15.00 6.00
❑ 140 Dan Morgan FF RC 15.00 6.00
❑ 141 Gerard Warren FF RC 15.00 6.00
❑ 142 Leonard Davis FF RC 10.00 4.00
❑ 143 Andre Carter FF RC 15.00 6.00
❑ 144 Justin Smith FF RC 15.00 6.00
❑ 145 Sage Rosenfels FF RC 15.00 6.00

2002 Leaf Certified

❑ COMP.SET w/o SP's (100) 25.00 10.00
❑ 1 David Boston 1.00 .40
❑ 2 Jake Plummer .60 .25
❑ 3 Michael Vick 3.00 1.25
❑ 4 Jamal Anderson .60 .25
❑ 5 Chris Redman .40 .15
❑ 6 Ray Lewis 1.00 .40
❑ 7 Eric Moulds .60 .25
❑ 8 Travis Henry 1.00 .40
❑ 9 Nate Clements .40 .15
❑ 10 Chris Weinke .60 .25
❑ 11 Muhsin Muhammad .60 .25
❑ 12 Wesley Walls .40 .15
❑ 13 Anthony Thomas .60 .25
❑ 14 Brian Urlacher 1.50 .60
❑ 15 Dez White .40 .15
❑ 16 Corey Dillon .60 .25
❑ 17 Peter Warrick .60 .25
❑ 18 Tim Couch .60 .25
❑ 19 Kevin Johnson .60 .25
❑ 20 James Jackson .40 .15
❑ 21 Emmitt Smith 2.50 1.00
❑ 22 Quincy Carter .60 .25
❑ 23 Brian Griese 1.00 .40
❑ 24 Ed McCaffrey 1.00 .40
❑ 25 Rod Smith .60 .25
❑ 26 Terrell Davis 1.00 .40
❑ 27 Mike Anderson 1.00 .40
❑ 28 Germane Crowell .40 .15
❑ 29 James Stewart .60 .25
❑ 30 Charlie Batch .60 .25
❑ 31 Antonio Freeman 1.00 .40
❑ 32 Brett Favre 2.50 1.00
❑ 33 Ahman Green 1.00 .40
❑ 34 LeRoy Butler .40 .15
❑ 35 Edgerrin James 1.25 .50
❑ 36 Marvin Harrison 1.00 .40
❑ 37 Peyton Manning 2.00 .75
❑ 38 Fred Taylor 1.00 .40
❑ 39 Jimmy Smith .60 .25
❑ 40 Mark Brunell 1.00 .40
❑ 41 Keenan McCardell .40 .15
❑ 42 Tony Gonzalez .60 .25
❑ 43 Priest Holmes 1.25 .50
❑ 44 Jay Fiedler .60 .25
❑ 45 Chris Chambers 1.00 .40
❑ 46 Zach Thomas 1.00 .40
❑ 47 Travis Minor .40 .15
❑ 48 Cris Carter 1.00 .40
❑ 49 Daunte Culpepper 1.00 .40
❑ 50 Randy Moss 2.00 .75
❑ 51 Drew Bledsoe 1.25 .50
❑ 52 Tom Brady 2.50 1.00
❑ 53 Antowain Smith .60 .25
❑ 54 Troy Brown .40 .15
❑ 55 Aaron Brooks 1.00 .40
❑ 56 Ricky Williams 1.00 .40
❑ 57 Ron Dayne .60 .25
❑ 58 Kerry Collins .60 .25
❑ 59 Michael Strahan .60 .25
❑ 60 Amani Toomer .60 .25
❑ 61 Chad Pennington 1.25 .50
❑ 62 Curtis Martin 1.00 .40
❑ 63 Vinny Testaverde .60 .25
❑ 64 Wayne Chrebet .60 .25
❑ 65 Charles Woodson .60 .25
❑ 66 Rich Gannon 1.00 .40
❑ 67 Tim Brown 1.00 .40
❑ 68 Jerry Rice 2.00 .75
❑ 69 Tyrone Wheatley .60 .25
❑ 70 Donovan McNabb 1.25 .50
❑ 71 Duce Staley 1.00 .40
❑ 72 Todd Pinkston .60 .25
❑ 73 Correll Buckhalter .60 .25
❑ 74 Jerome Bettis 1.00 .40
❑ 75 Kordell Stewart .60 .25
❑ 76 Plaxico Burress .60 .25
❑ 77 Hines Ward 1.00 .40
❑ 78 Junior Seau 1.00 .40
❑ 79 LaDainian Tomlinson 1.50 .60
❑ 80 Doug Flutie 1.00 .40
❑ 81 Terrell Owens 1.00 .40
❑ 82 Jeff Garcia 1.00 .40
❑ 83 Ricky Watters .60 .25
❑ 84 Shaun Alexander 1.25 .50
❑ 85 Koren Robinson .60 .25
❑ 86 Isaac Bruce 1.00 .40
❑ 87 Kurt Warner 1.00 .40
❑ 88 Marshall Faulk 1.00 .40
❑ 89 Torry Holt 1.00 .40
❑ 90 Keyshawn Johnson 1.00 .40
❑ 91 Mike Alstott 1.00 .40
❑ 92 Warren Sapp .60 .25
❑ 93 Brad Johnson .60 .25
❑ 94 Eddie George 1.00 .40
❑ 95 Jevon Kearse .60 .25
❑ 96 Steve McNair 1.00 .40
❑ 97 Derrick Mason .60 .25
❑ 98 Frank Wycheck .40 .15
❑ 99 Champ Bailey .60 .25
❑ 100 Stephen Davis .60 .25
❑ 101 Ladell Betts JSY RC 8.00 3.00
❑ 102 Antonio Bryant JSY RC 8.00 3.00
❑ 103 Reche Caldwell JSY RC 8.00 3.00
❑ 104 David Carr JSY RC 20.00 7.50
❑ 105 Tim Carter JSY RC 5.00 2.00
❑ 106 Eric Crouch JSY RC 8.00 3.00
❑ 107 Rohan Davey JSY RC 8.00 3.00
❑ 108 Andre Davis JSY RC 5.00 2.00
❑ 109 T.J. Duckett JSY RC 10.00 4.00
❑ 110 DeShaun Foster JSY RC 8.00 3.00
❑ 111 Jabar Gaffney JSY RC 8.00 3.00
❑ 112 Daniel Graham JSY RC 8.00 3.00
❑ 113 William Green FB RC 8.00 3.00
❑ 114 Joey Harrington JSY RC 12.00 5.00
❑ 115 David Garrard JSY RC 10.00 4.00
❑ 116 Ron Johnson JSY RC 5.00 2.00
❑ 117 Ashley Lelie JSY RC 15.00 6.00
❑ 118 Josh McCown JSY RC 10.00 4.00
❑ 119 Maurice Morris JSY RC 8.00 3.00
❑ 120 Julius Peppers JSY RC 15.00 6.00
❑ 121 Clinton Portis JSY RC 25.00 10.00
❑ 122 Patrick Ramsey JSY RC 10.00 4.00
❑ 123 Antwaan Randle El JSY RC 12.00 5.00
❑ 124 Josh Reed JSY RC 8.00 3.00
❑ 125 Cliff Russell JSY RC 5.00 2.00
❑ 126 Jeremy Shockey JSY RC 25.00 10.00
❑ 127 Donte Stallworth JSY RC 15.00 6.00
❑ 128 Travis Stephens JSY RC 5.00 2.00
❑ 129 Javon Walker JSY RC 15.00 6.00
❑ 130 Marquise Walker JSY RC 5.00 2.00
❑ 131 Roy Williams JSY RC 20.00 7.50
❑ 132 Mike Williams JSY RC 5.00 2.00

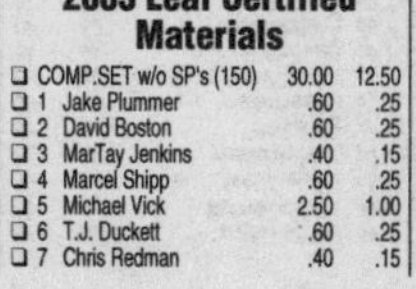

2003 Leaf Certified Materials

❑ COMP.SET w/o SP's (150) 30.00 12.50
❑ 1 Jake Plummer .60 .25
❑ 2 David Boston .60 .25
❑ 3 MarTay Jenkins .40 .15
❑ 4 Marcel Shipp .60 .25
❑ 5 Michael Vick 2.50 1.00
❑ 6 T.J. Duckett .60 .25
❑ 7 Chris Redman .40 .15

❑ 8 Ray Lewis 1.00 .40
❑ 9 Jamal Lewis 1.00 .40
❑ 10 Eric Moulds .60 .25
❑ 11 Nate Clements .40 .15
❑ 12 Travis Henry .60 .25
❑ 13 Drew Bledsoe 1.00 .40
❑ 14 Peerless Price .60 .25
❑ 15 Josh Reed .60 .25
❑ 16 Wesley Walls .40 .15
❑ 17 Muhsin Muhammad .60 .25
❑ 18 Julius Peppers 1.00 .40
❑ 19 Dez White .40 .15
❑ 20 Mike Brown .60 .25
❑ 21 Brian Urlacher 1.50 .60
❑ 22 Anthony Thomas .60 .25
❑ 23 David Terrell .60 .25
❑ 24 Corey Dillon .60 .25
❑ 25 Peter Warrick .60 .25
❑ 26 Josh McCown .60 .25
❑ 27 Dennis Northcutt .60 .25
❑ 28 Kevin Johnson .60 .25
❑ 29 Tim Couch .40 .15
❑ 30 Gerard Warren .40 .15
❑ 31 William Green .60 .25
❑ 32 Antonio Bryant .60 .25
❑ 33 Darren Woodson .40 .15
❑ 34 Emmitt Smith 2.50 1.00
❑ 35 Quincy Carter .60 .25
❑ 36 Roy Williams 1.00 .40
❑ 37 Brian Griese 1.00 .40
❑ 38 Ed McCaffrey 1.00 .40
❑ 39 Mike Anderson .60 .25
❑ 40 Rod Smith .60 .25
❑ 41 Clinton Portis 1.50 .60
❑ 42 Ashley Lelie 1.00 .40
❑ 43 Cory Schlesinger .40 .15
❑ 44 Germane Crowell .40 .15
❑ 45 James Stewart .60 .25
❑ 46 Scotty Anderson .40 .15
❑ 47 Joey Harrington 1.50 .60
❑ 48 Brett Favre 2.50 1.00
❑ 49 Terry Glenn .40 .15
❑ 50 Ahman Green 1.00 .40
❑ 51 Donald Driver .60 .25
❑ 52 Javon Walker .60 .25
❑ 53 David Carr 1.50 .60
❑ 54 Ron Dayne .40 .15
❑ 55 Terrell Davis 1.00 .40
❑ 56 Edgerrin James 1.00 .40
❑ 57 Marvin Harrison 1.00 .40
❑ 58 Peyton Manning 1.50 .60
❑ 59 Fred Taylor 1.00 .40
❑ 60 Jimmy Smith .60 .25
❑ 61 Kyle Brady .40 .15
❑ 62 Mark Brunell .60 .25
❑ 63 Tony Gonzalez .60 .25
❑ 64 Priest Holmes 1.25 .50
❑ 65 Trent Green .60 .25
❑ 66 Jason Taylor .40 .15
❑ 67 Jay Fiedler .60 .25
❑ 68 Zach Thomas 1.00 .40
❑ 69 Chris Chambers 1.00 .40
❑ 70 Ricky Williams 1.00 .40
❑ 71 Randy McMichael .60 .25
❑ 72 Daunte Culpepper 1.00 .40
❑ 73 Randy Moss 1.50 .60
❑ 74 Michael Bennett .60 .25
❑ 75 Ty Law .60 .25
❑ 76 Tom Brady 2.50 1.00
❑ 77 Troy Brown .60 .25
❑ 78 Antowain Smith .60 .25
❑ 79 Aaron Brooks 1.00 .40

❑ 80 Donte Stallworth 1.00 .40
❑ 81 Joe Horn .60 .25
❑ 82 Deuce McAllister 1.00 .40
❑ 83 Amani Toomer .60 .25
❑ 84 Kerry Collins .60 .25
❑ 85 Michael Strahan .60 .25
❑ 86 Tiki Barber 1.00 .40
❑ 87 Jeremy Shockey 1.50 .60
❑ 88 Chad Pennington 1.25 .50
❑ 89 Curtis Martin 1.00 .40
❑ 90 Laveranues Coles .60 .25
❑ 91 Vinny Testaverde .60 .25
❑ 92 Santana Moss .60 .25
❑ 93 Charles Woodson .60 .25
❑ 94 Sebastian Janikowski .40 .15
❑ 95 Tim Brown 1.00 .40
❑ 96 Rich Gannon .60 .25
❑ 97 Jerry Rice 2.00 .75
❑ 98 Donovan McNabb 1.25 .50
❑ 99 Duce Staley .60 .25
❑ 100 Todd Pinkston .40 .15
❑ 101 Chad Lewis .40 .15
❑ 102 A.J. Feeley .40 .15
❑ 103 Jerome Bettis 1.00 .40
❑ 104 Plaxico Burress .60 .25
❑ 105 Hines Ward 1.00 .40
❑ 106 Antwaan Randle El 1.00 .40
❑ 107 Kendrell Bell .60 .25
❑ 108 Junior Seau 1.00 .40
❑ 109 LaDainian Tomlinson 1.00 .40
❑ 110 Doug Flutie 1.00 .40
❑ 111 Drew Brees 1.00 .40
❑ 112 Terrell Owens 1.00 .40
❑ 113 Jeff Garcia 1.00 .40
❑ 114 Garrison Hearst .60 .25
❑ 115 Koren Robinson .60 .25
❑ 116 Shaun Alexander 1.00 .40
❑ 117 Isaac Bruce 1.00 .40
❑ 118 Kurt Warner 1.00 .40
❑ 119 Marshall Faulk 1.00 .40
❑ 120 Torry Holt 1.00 .40
❑ 121 Keyshawn Johnson 1.00 .40
❑ 122 Warren Sapp .60 .25
❑ 123 Mike Alstott 1.00 .40
❑ 124 Brad Johnson .60 .25
❑ 125 Eddie George .60 .25
❑ 126 Jevon Kearse .60 .25
❑ 127 Steve McNair 1.00 .40
❑ 128 Derrick Mason .60 .25
❑ 129 Keith Bulluck .40 .15
❑ 130 Champ Bailey .60 .25
❑ 131 Darrell Green .40 .15
❑ 132 Stephen Davis .60 .25
❑ 133 Rod Gardner .60 .25
❑ 134 Barry Sanders 2.50 1.00
❑ 135 Cris Carter 1.00 .40
❑ 136 Dan Marino 5.00 2.00
❑ 137 Deion Sanders 1.25 .50
❑ 138 Jim Kelly 2.00 .75
❑ 139 Joe Montana 6.00 2.50
❑ 140 John Elway 5.00 2.00
❑ 141 Marcus Allen 1.25 .50
❑ 142 Reggie White 1.00 .40
❑ 143 Sterling Sharpe 1.00 .40
❑ 144 Steve Young 1.50 .60
❑ 145 Thurman Thomas 1.00 .40
❑ 146 Troy Aikman 2.00 .75
❑ 147 Warren Moon 1.00 .40
❑ 148 Drew Bledsoe 1.00 .40
❑ 149 Jerry Rice 2.00 .75
❑ 150 Ricky Williams 1.00 .40
❑ 151 Carson Palmer JSY RC 30.00 12.50
❑ 152 Byron Leftwich JSY RC 25.00 10.00
❑ 153 Kyle Boller JSY RC 8.00 3.00
❑ 154 Rex Grossman JSY RC 25.00 10.00
❑ 155 Dave Ragone JSY RC 8.00 3.00
❑ 156 Kliff Kingsbury JSY RC 8.00 3.00
❑ 157 Seneca Wallace JSY RC 8.00 3.00
❑ 158 Larry Johnson JSY RC 30.00 15.00
❑ 159 Willis McGahee JSY RC 20.00 7.50
❑ 160 Justin Fargas JSY RC 8.00 3.00
❑ 161 Onterrio Smith JSY RC 8.00 3.00
❑ 162 Chris Brown JSY RC 8.00 3.00
❑ 163 Musa Smith JSY RC 8.00 3.00
❑ 164 Artose Pinner JSY RC 8.00 3.00
❑ 165 Andre Johnson JSY RC 15.00 6.00
❑ 166 Kelley Washington JSY RC 8.00 3.00
❑ 167 Taylor Jacobs JSY RC 8.00 3.00
❑ 168 Bryant Johnson JSY RC 8.00 3.00
❑ 169 Tyrone Calico JSY RC 8.00 3.00
❑ 170 Anquan Boldin JSY RC 20.00 7.50
❑ 171 Bethel Johnson JSY RC 8.00 3.00
❑ 172 Nate Burleson JSY RC 8.00 3.00
❑ 173 Kevin Curtis JSY RC 8.00 3.00
❑ 174 Dallas Clark JSY RC 8.00 3.00
❑ 175 Teyo Johnson JSY RC 8.00 3.00
❑ 176 Terrell Suggs JSY RC 12.00 5.00
❑ 177 DeWayne Robertson JSY RC 8.003.00
❑ 178 Brian St.Pierre JSY RC 8.00 3.00
❑ 179 Terence Newman JSY RC 15.00 6.00
❑ 180 Marcus Trufant JSY RC 8.00 3.00

2004 Leaf Certified Materials

❑ COMP.SET w/o SP's (150) 30.00 12.50
❑ 151-200 PRINT RUN 1000 SER.#'d SETS
❑ 201-233 PRINT RUN 1250 SER.#'d SETS
❑ UNPRICED MIRROR BLACK #'d OF 1
❑ UNPRICED MIRROR EMERALD #'d OF 5
❑ 1 Anquan Boldin 1.00 .40
❑ 2 Emmitt Smith 2.00 .75
❑ 3 Josh McCown .60 .25
❑ 4 Marcel Shipp .60 .25
❑ 5 Michael Vick 2.00 .75
❑ 6 Peerless Price .60 .25
❑ 7 T.J. Duckett .60 .25
❑ 8 Warrick Dunn .60 .25
❑ 9 Jamal Lewis 1.00 .40
❑ 10 Kyle Boller 1.00 .40
❑ 11 Ray Lewis 1.00 .40
❑ 12 Terrell Suggs .60 .25
❑ 13 Todd Heap .60 .25
❑ 14 Drew Bledsoe 1.00 .40
❑ 15 Eric Moulds .60 .25
❑ 16 Travis Henry .60 .25
❑ 17 Julius Peppers 1.00 .40
❑ 18 Muhsin Muhammad .60 .25
❑ 19 Stephen Davis .60 .25
❑ 20 Anthony Thomas .60 .25
❑ 21 Brian Urlacher 1.25 .50
❑ 22 Rex Grossman 1.00 .40
❑ 23 Chad Johnson 1.00 .40
❑ 24 Corey Dillon .60 .25
❑ 25 Peter Warrick .60 .25
❑ 26 Jeff Garcia 1.00 .40
❑ 27 Tim Couch .40 .15
❑ 28 William Green .60 .25
❑ 29 Antonio Bryant .60 .25
❑ 30 Keyshawn Johnson .60 .25
❑ 31 Quincy Carter .60 .25
❑ 32 Roy Williams S .60 .25
❑ 33 Terence Newman .60 .25
❑ 34 Ashley Lelie .60 .25
❑ 35 Ed McCaffrey .60 .25
❑ 36 Jake Plummer .60 .25
❑ 37 Mike Anderson .60 .25
❑ 38 Rod Smith .60 .25
❑ 39 Charles Rogers .60 .25
❑ 40 Joey Harrington 1.00 .40
❑ 41 Ahman Green 1.00 .40
❑ 42 Brett Favre 2.50 1.00
❑ 43 Donald Driver .60 .25
❑ 44 Javon Walker .60 .25
❑ 45 Robert Ferguson .40 .15
❑ 46 Andre Johnson 1.00 .40
❑ 47 David Carr 1.00 .40
❑ 48 Edgerrin James 1.00 .40
❑ 49 Marvin Harrison 1.00 .40
❑ 50 Peyton Manning 1.50 .60
❑ 51 Reggie Wayne .60 .25
❑ 52 Byron Leftwich 1.25 .50
❑ 53 Fred Taylor .60 .25
❑ 54 Jimmy Smith .60 .25
❑ 55 Dante Hall 1.00 .40
❑ 56 Priest Holmes 1.25 .50
❑ 57 Tony Gonzalez .60 .25
❑ 58 Trent Green .60 .25
❑ 59 A.J. Feeley 1.00 .40
❑ 60 Chris Chambers .60 .25
❑ 61 David Boston .60 .25
❑ 62 Jason Taylor .40 .15
❑ 63 Jay Fiedler .40 .15
❑ 64 Junior Seau 1.00 .40
❑ 65 Randy McMichael .40 .15
❑ 66 Ricky Williams 1.00 .40
❑ 67 Zach Thomas 1.00 .40
❑ 68 Daunte Culpepper 1.00 .40
❑ 69 Michael Bennett .60 .25
❑ 70 Randy Moss 1.25 .50
❑ 71 Tom Brady 2.50 1.00
❑ 72 Troy Brown .60 .25
❑ 73 Ty Law .60 .25
❑ 74 Aaron Brooks .60 .25
❑ 75 Deuce McAllister 1.00 .40
❑ 76 Donte Stallworth .60 .25
❑ 77 Amani Toomer .60 .25
❑ 78 Jeremy Shockey 1.00 .40
❑ 79 Kerry Collins .60 .25
❑ 80 Michael Strahan .60 .25
❑ 81 Tiki Barber 1.00 .40
❑ 82 Chad Pennington 1.00 .40
❑ 83 Curtis Martin 1.00 .40
❑ 84 Justin McCareins .40 .15
❑ 85 Santana Moss .60 .25
❑ 86 Charles Woodson .60 .25
❑ 87 Jerry Rice 2.00 .75
❑ 88 Rich Gannon .60 .25
❑ 89 Tim Brown 1.00 .40
❑ 90 Warren Sapp .60 .25
❑ 91 Correll Buckhalter .60 .25
❑ 92 Donovan McNabb 1.25 .50
❑ 93 Freddie Mitchell .60 .25
❑ 94 Jevon Kearse .60 .25
❑ 95 Terrell Owens 1.00 .40
❑ 96 Antwaan Randle El 1.00 .40
❑ 97 Duce Staley .60 .25
❑ 98 Hines Ward 1.00 .40
❑ 99 Jerome Bettis 1.00 .40
❑ 100 Plaxico Burress .60 .25
❑ 101 Doug Flutie 1.00 .40
❑ 102 LaDainian Tomlinson 1.25 .50
❑ 103 Koren Robinson .60 .25
❑ 104 Matt Hasselbeck .60 .25
❑ 105 Shaun Alexander 1.00 .40
❑ 106 Isaac Bruce .60 .25
❑ 107 Kurt Warner 1.00 .40
❑ 108 Marc Bulger 1.00 .40
❑ 109 Marshall Faulk 1.00 .40
❑ 110 Torry Holt 1.00 .40
❑ 111 Brad Johnson .60 .25
❑ 112 Mike Alstott .60 .25
❑ 113 Derrick Mason .60 .25
❑ 114 Drew Bennett .60 .25
❑ 115 Eddie George .60 .25
❑ 116 Frank Wycheck .40 .15
❑ 117 Keith Bulluck .40 .15
❑ 118 Steve McNair 1.00 .40
❑ 119 Tyrone Calico .60 .25
❑ 120 Clinton Portis 1.00 .40
❑ 121 LaVar Arrington 2.00 .75
❑ 122 Laveranues Coles .60 .25
❑ 123 Mark Brunell .60 .25
❑ 124 Patrick Ramsey .60 .25
❑ 125 Rod Gardner .60 .25
❑ 126 Jake Plummer FLB .60 .25
❑ 127 Thomas Jones FLB .60 .25
❑ 128 Priest Holmes FLB 1.25 .50
❑ 129 Jim Kelly FLB 2.00 .75
❑ 130 Doug Flutie FLB 1.00 .40
❑ 131 Walter Payton FLB 6.00 2.50
❑ 132 Troy Aikman FLB 2.50 1.00
❑ 133 John Elway FLB 4.00 1.50
❑ 134 Barry Sanders FLB 3.00 1.25
❑ 135 Mark Brunell FLB .60 .25
❑ 136 Earl Campbell FLB 1.50 .60
❑ 137 Joe Montana FLB 6.00 2.50
❑ 138 Dan Marino FLB 5.00 2.00
❑ 139 Curtis Martin FLB 1.00 .40
❑ 140 Drew Bledsoe FLB 1.00 .40

❑ 141 Ricky Williams FLB 1.00 .40
❑ 142 Junior Seau FLB 1.00 .40
❑ 143 Charlie Garner FLB .60 .25
❑ 144 Jerry Rice FLB 2.00 .75
❑ 145 Ahman Green FLB 1.00 .40
❑ 146 Jerome Bettis FLB 1.00 .40
❑ 147 Trent Green FLB .60 .25
❑ 148 Warrick Dunn FLB .60 .25
❑ 149 Deion Sanders FLB 1.50 .60
❑ 150 Stephen Davis FLB .60 .25
❑ 151 Adimchinobe Echemandu AU RC 10.00 4.00
❑ 152 Ahmad Carroll RC 6.00 2.50
❑ 153 Andy Hall AU RC 10.00 4.00
❑ 154 B.J. Johnson AU RC 10.00 4.00
❑ 155 B.J. Symons AU RC 15.00 6.00
❑ 156 Bradlee Van Pelt AU RC 20.00 8.00
❑ 157 Brandon Miree AU RC 10.00 4.00
❑ 158 Bruce Perry AU RC 15.00 6.00
❑ 159 Carlos Francis AU RC 10.00 4.00
❑ 160 Casey Bramlet AU RC 10.00 4.00
❑ 161 Chris Gamble RC 6.00 2.50
❑ 162 Clarence Moore AU RC 15.00 6.00
❑ 163 Cody Pickett AU RC 15.00 6.00
❑ 164 Craig Krenzel AU RC 15.00 6.00
❑ 165 D.J. Hackett RC 5.00 2.00
❑ 166 D.J. Williams RC 6.00 2.50
❑ 167 Derrick Ward AU RC 8.00 3.00
❑ 168 Drew Carter AU RC 15.00 6.00
❑ 169 Ernest Wilford RC 6.00 2.50
❑ 170 Drew Henson RC 6.00 2.50
❑ 171 Jamaar Taylor AU RC 15.00 6.00
❑ 172 Jared Lorenzen AU RC 10.00 4.00
❑ 173 Jarrett Payton AU RC 15.00 6.00
❑ 174 Jason Babin AU RC EXCH 15.00 6.00
❑ 175 Jeff Smoker AU RC 15.00 6.00
❑ 176 Jeris McIntyre AU RC 10.00 4.00
❑ 177 Jerricho Cotchery RC 6.00 2.50
❑ 178 Jim Sorgi AU RC 15.00 6.00
❑ 179 John Navarre AU RC 15.00 6.00
❑ 180 Patrick Crayton AU RC 15.00 6.00
❑ 181 Johnnie Morant RC 6.00 2.50
❑ 182 Sean Taylor RC 6.00 2.50
❑ 183 Jonathan Vilma RC 6.00 2.50
❑ 184 Josh Harris RC 6.00 2.50
❑ 185 Kenechi Udeze RC 8.00 3.00
❑ 186 Mark Jones AU RC 10.00 4.00
❑ 187 Matt Mauck AU RC 15.00 6.00
❑ 188 Maurice Mann AU RC 10.00 4.00
❑ 189 Michael Turner RC 8.00 3.00
❑ 190 P.K. Sam RC 5.00 2.00
❑ 191 Quincy Wilson RC 5.00 2.00
❑ 192 Ran Carthon AU RC 10.00 4.00
❑ 193 Ryan Krause AU RC 10.00 4.00
❑ 194 Samie Parker RC 6.00 2.50
❑ 195 Sloan Thomas AU RC 10.00 4.00
❑ 196 Tommie Harris RC 6.00 2.50
❑ 197 Triandos Luke AU RC 15.00 6.00
❑ 198 Troy Fleming AU RC 10.00 4.00
❑ 199 Vince Wilfork RC 6.00 2.50
❑ 200 Will Smith RC 6.00 2.50
❑ 201 Larry Fitzgerald JSY RC 20.00 7.50
❑ 202 DeAngelo Hall JSY RC 10.00 4.00
❑ 203 Matt Schaub JSY RC 20.00 7.50
❑ 204 Michael Jenkins JSY RC 8.00 3.00
❑ 205 Devard Darling JSY RC 8.00 3.00
❑ 206 J.P. Losman JSY RC 12.00 5.00
❑ 207 Lee Evans JSY RC 10.00 4.00
❑ 208 Keary Colbert JSY RC 10.00 4.00
❑ 209 Bernard Berrian JSY RC 10.00 4.00
❑ 210 Chris Perry JSY RC 10.00 4.00
❑ 211 Kellen Winslow JSY RC 12.00 5.00
❑ 212 Luke McCown JSY RC 8.00 3.00
❑ 213 Julius Jones JSY RC 20.00 7.50
❑ 214 Darius Watts JSY RC 8.00 3.00
❑ 215 Tatum Bell JSY RC 12.00 5.00
❑ 216 Kevin Jones JSY RC 15.00 6.00
❑ 217 Roy Williams JSY RC 15.00 6.00
❑ 218 Dunta Robinson JSY RC 8.00 3.00
❑ 219 Greg Jones JSY RC 10.00 4.00
❑ 220 Reggie Williams JSY RC 10.00 4.00
❑ 221 Mewelde Moore JSY RC 8.00 3.00
❑ 222 Ben Watson JSY RC 8.00 3.00
❑ 223 Cedric Cobbs JSY RC 8.00 3.00
❑ 224 Devery Henderson JSY RC 8.00 3.00
❑ 225 Eli Manning JSY RC 30.00 15.00
❑ 226 Robert Gallery JSY RC 8.00 3.00
❑ 227 Ben Roethlisberger JSY RC 50.00 25.00
❑ 228 Philip Rivers JSY RC 20.00 10.00
❑ 229 Derrick Hamilton JSY RC 8.00 3.00
❑ 230 Rashaun Woods JSY RC 8.00 3.00
❑ 231 Steven Jackson JSY RC 20.00 7.50
❑ 232 Michael Clayton JSY RC 12.00 5.00
❑ 233 Ben Troupe JSY RC 8.00 3.00

2005 Leaf Certified Materials

❑ COMPLETE SET (229)
❑ COMP.SET w/o RCs (150) 40.00 15.00
❑ 151-200 PRINT RUN 1000 SER.#'d SETS
❑ UNPRICED MIR.BLACK PRINT RUN 1 SET
❑ UNPRICED MIR.EMERALD PRINT RUN 5 SETS
❑ 1 Anquan Boldin .60 .25
❑ 2 Josh McCown .60 .25
❑ 3 Larry Fitzgerald 1.00 .40
❑ 4 Michael Vick 1.50 .60
❑ 5 Peerless Price .50 .20
❑ 6 T.J. Duckett .60 .25
❑ 7 Warrick Dunn .60 .25
❑ 8 Jamal Lewis 1.00 .40
❑ 9 Kyle Boller .60 .25
❑ 10 Todd Heap .60 .25
❑ 11 Ray Lewis 1.00 .40
❑ 12 Terrell Suggs .60 .25
❑ 13 Drew Bledsoe 1.00 .40
❑ 14 Eric Moulds .60 .25
❑ 15 J.P. Losman 1.00 .40
❑ 16 Lee Evans .60 .25
❑ 17 Willis McGahee 1.00 .40
❑ 18 DeShaun Foster .60 .25
❑ 19 Jake Delhomme 1.00 .40
❑ 20 Steve Smith .60 .25
❑ 21 Brian Urlacher 1.00 .40
❑ 22 Rex Grossman .60 .25
❑ 23 Carson Palmer 1.00 .40
❑ 24 Chad Johnson 1.00 .40
❑ 25 Rudi Johnson .60 .25
❑ 26 Kellen Winslow Jr. 1.00 .40
❑ 27 Kelly Holcomb .50 .20
❑ 28 Lee Suggs .60 .25
❑ 29 William Green .50 .20
❑ 30 Julius Jones 1.25 .50
❑ 31 Keyshawn Johnson .60 .25
❑ 32 Roy Williams S .60 .25
❑ 33 Terence Newman .50 .20
❑ 34 Ashley Lelie .60 .25
❑ 35 Champ Bailey .60 .25
❑ 36 Darius Watts .60 .25
❑ 37 Jake Plummer .60 .25
❑ 38 Tatum Bell .60 .25
❑ 39 Charles Rogers .60 .25
❑ 40 Joey Harrington 1.00 .40
❑ 41 Kevin Jones 1.00 .40
❑ 42 Roy Williams WR 1.00 .40
❑ 43 Ahman Green 1.00 .40
❑ 44 Brett Favre 2.50 1.00
❑ 45 Javon Walker .60 .25
❑ 46 Robert Ferguson .50 .20
❑ 47 Andre Johnson .60 .25
❑ 48 David Carr 1.00 .40
❑ 49 Domanick Davis .60 .25
❑ 50 Dallas Clark .50 .20
❑ 51 Edgerrin James 1.00 .40
❑ 52 Marvin Harrison 1.00 .40
❑ 53 Peyton Manning 1.50 .60
❑ 54 Reggie Wayne .60 .25
❑ 55 Byron Leftwich 1.00 .40
❑ 56 Fred Taylor .60 .25
❑ 57 Jimmy Smith .60 .25
❑ 58 Reggie Williams .60 .25
❑ 59 Priest Holmes 1.00 .40
❑ 60 Tony Gonzalez .60 .25
❑ 61 Trent Green .60 .25
❑ 62 Chris Chambers .60 .25
❑ 63 Jason Taylor .50 .20
❑ 64 Junior Seau .60 .25
❑ 65 Zach Thomas 1.00 .40
❑ 66 Daunte Culpepper 1.00 .40
❑ 67 Michael Bennett .60 .25
❑ 68 Randy Moss 1.00 .40
❑ 69 Corey Dillon .60 .25
❑ 70 Tom Brady 2.50 1.00
❑ 71 Deion Branch .60 .25
❑ 72 Aaron Brooks .60 .25
❑ 73 Deuce McAllister 1.00 .40
❑ 74 Donte Stallworth .60 .25
❑ 75 Joe Horn .60 .25
❑ 76 Eli Manning 2.00 .75
❑ 77 Jeremy Shockey 1.00 .40
❑ 78 Michael Strahan .60 .25
❑ 79 Tiki Barber 1.00 .40
❑ 80 Anthony Becht .50 .20
❑ 81 Chad Pennington 1.00 .40
❑ 82 Curtis Martin 1.00 .40
❑ 83 Justin McCareins .50 .20
❑ 84 Laveranues Coles .60 .25
❑ 85 Santana Moss .60 .25
❑ 86 Shaun Ellis .50 .20
❑ 87 Jerry Porter .60 .25
❑ 88 Brian Westbrook .60 .25
❑ 89 Chad Lewis .50 .20
❑ 90 Donovan McNabb 1.25 .50
❑ 91 Freddie Mitchell .50 .20
❑ 92 Hugh Douglas .50 .20
❑ 93 Jevon Kearse .60 .25
❑ 94 Terrell Owens 1.00 .40
❑ 95 Todd Pinkston .50 .20
❑ 96 Antwaan Randle El .60 .25
❑ 97 Ben Roethlisberger 2.50 1.00
❑ 98 Duce Staley .60 .25
❑ 99 Hines Ward 1.00 .40
❑ 100 Jerome Bettis 1.00 .40
❑ 101 Antonio Gates 1.00 .40
❑ 102 Drew Brees 1.00 .40
❑ 103 LaDainian Tomlinson 1.25 .50
❑ 104 Kevan Barlow .60 .25
❑ 105 Darrell Jackson .60 .25
❑ 106 Koren Robinson .60 .25
❑ 107 Matt Hasselbeck .60 .25
❑ 108 Shaun Alexander 1.25 .50
❑ 109 Marc Bulger 1.00 .40
❑ 110 Steven Jackson 1.25 .50
❑ 111 Torry Holt 1.00 .40
❑ 112 Michael Clayton 1.00 .40
❑ 113 Chris Brown .60 .25
❑ 114 Drew Bennett .60 .25
❑ 115 Keith Bulluck .50 .20
❑ 116 Steve McNair 1.00 .40
❑ 117 Clinton Portis 1.00 .40
❑ 118 LaVar Arrington 1.00 .40
❑ 119 John Riggins 1.25 .50
❑ 120 Sean Taylor .60 .25
❑ 121 Jake Plummer .60 .25
❑ 122 Thomas Jones .60 .25
❑ 123 Doug Flutie 1.00 .40
❑ 124 Walter Payton 4.00 1.50
❑ 125 Corey Dillon .60 .25
❑ 126 Troy Aikman 1.50 .60
❑ 127 Terrell Davis 1.25 .50
❑ 128 Marshall Faulk 1.00 .40
❑ 129 Dan Marino 3.00 1.25
❑ 130 Thurman Thomas 1.00 .40
❑ 131 Warren Moon 1.00 .40
❑ 132 Curtis Martin 1.00 .40
❑ 133 Drew Bledsoe 1.00 .40
❑ 134 Kerry Collins .60 .25
❑ 135 Keyshawn Johnson .60 .25
❑ 136 A.J. Feeley .60 .25
❑ 137 Duce Staley .60 .25
❑ 138 Junior Seau .60 .25
❑ 139 Jerry Rice 2.00 .75
❑ 140 Steve Young 1.50 .60
❑ 141 Jerome Bettis 1.00 .40
❑ 142 Kurt Warner .60 .25
❑ 143 Trent Green .60 .25
❑ 144 Keyshawn Johnson .60 .25
❑ 145 Warren Sapp .60 .25
❑ 146 Warrick Dunn .60 .25
❑ 147 Jevon Kearse .60 .25

❑ 148 Deion Sanders 1.50 .60
❑ 149 Laveranues Coles .60 .25
❑ 150 Stephen Davis .60 .25
❑ 151 Cedric Benson RC 10.00 4.00
❑ 152 Mike Williams 10.00 4.00
❑ 153 DeMarcus Ware RC 8.00 3.00
❑ 154 Shawne Merriman RC 8.00 3.00
❑ 155 Thomas Davis RC 5.00 2.00
❑ 156 Derrick Johnson RC 8.00 3.00
❑ 157 Travis Johnson RC 4.00 1.50
❑ 158 David Pollack RC 5.00 2.00
❑ 159 Erasmus James RC 5.00 2.00
❑ 160 Marcus Spears RC 5.00 2.00
❑ 161 Fabian Washington RC 5.00 2.00
❑ 162 Aaron Rodgers RC 15.00 6.00
❑ 163 Marlin Jackson RC 5.00 2.00
❑ 164 Heath Miller RC 12.00 5.00
❑ 165 Matt Roth RC 5.00 2.00
❑ 166 Dan Cody RC 5.00 2.00
❑ 167 Bryant McFadden RC 5.00 2.00
❑ 168 Chris Henry RC 5.00 2.00
❑ 169 David Greene RC 5.00 2.00
❑ 170 Brandon Jones RC 5.00 2.00
❑ 171 Marion Barber RC 8.00 3.00
❑ 172 Brandon Jacobs RC 6.00 2.50
❑ 173 Jerome Mathis RC 5.00 2.00
❑ 174 Craphonso Thorpe RC 4.00 1.50
❑ 175 Alvin Pearman RC 5.00 2.00
❑ 176 Darren Sproles RC 5.00 2.00
❑ 177 Fred Gibson RC 4.00 1.50
❑ 178 Roydell Williams RC 5.00 2.00
❑ 179 Airese Currie RC 5.00 2.00
❑ 180 Damien Nash RC 4.00 1.50
❑ 181 Dan Orlovsky RC 6.00 2.50
❑ 182 Adrian McPherson RC 5.00 2.00
❑ 183 Larry Brackins RC 4.00 1.50
❑ 184 Rasheed Marshall RC 5.00 2.00
❑ 185 Cedric Houston RC 5.00 2.00
❑ 186 Chad Owens RC 5.00 2.00
❑ 187 Tab Perry RC 5.00 2.00
❑ 188 Dante Ridgeway RC 4.00 1.50
❑ 189 Craig Bragg RC 4.00 1.50
❑ 190 Deandra Cobb RC 4.00 1.50
❑ 191 Derek Anderson RC 5.00 2.00
❑ 192 Paris Warren RC 4.00 1.50
❑ 193 Lionel Gates RC 4.00 1.50
❑ 194 Anthony Davis RC 4.00 1.50
❑ 195 Ryan Fitzpatrick RC 8.00 3.00
❑ 196 J.R. Russell RC 4.00 1.50
❑ 197 Jason White RC 5.00 2.00
❑ 198 Kay-Jay Harris RC 4.00 1.50
❑ 199 T.A. McLendon RC 3.00 1.25
❑ 200 Taylor Stubblefield RC 3.00 1.25
❑ 201 Adam Jones JSY/1499 RC 8.00 3.00
❑ 202 Alex Smith QB JSY/499 RC 30.00 12.50
❑ 203 Andrew Walter JSY/1249 RC 10.00 4.00
❑ 204 Antrel Rolle JSY/999 RC 8.00 3.00
❑ 205 Braylon Edwards JSY/499 RC 25.00 10.00
❑ 206 Cadillac Williams JSY/499 RC 40.00 15.00
❑ 207 Carlos Rogers JSY/1499 RC 10.00 4.00
❑ 208 Charlie Frye JSY/1499 RC 12.00 5.00
❑ 209 Ciatrick Fason JSY/1499 RC 8.00 3.00
❑ 210 Courtney Roby JSY/1249 RC 8.00 3.00
❑ 211 Eric Shelton JSY/999 RC 8.00 3.00
❑ 212 Frank Gore JSY/999 RC 12.00 5.00
❑ 213 J.J. Arrington JSY/499 RC 12.00 5.00
❑ 214 Kyle Orton JSY/1499 RC 10.00 4.00
❑ 215 Jason Campbell JSY/749 RC 12.00 5.00
❑ 216 Mark Bradley JSY/999 RC 8.00 3.00
❑ 217 Mark Clayton JSY/499 RC 12.00 5.00
❑ 218 Matt Jones JSY/749 RC 20.00 7.50
❑ 219 Maurice Clarett JSY/999 8.00 3.00
❑ 220 Reggie Brown JSY/999 RC 8.00 3.00
❑ 221 Roddy White JSY/749 RC 8.00 3.00
❑ 222 Ronnie Brown JSY/499 RC 30.00 12.50
❑ 223 Roscoe Parrish JSY/999 RC 8.00 3.00
❑ 224 Ryan Moats JSY/999 RC 8.00 3.00
❑ 225 Stefan LeFors JSY/1499 RC 8.00 3.00
❑ 226 Terrence Murphy JSY/1499 RC 8.00 3.00
❑ 227 Troy Williamson JSY/749 RC 12.00 5.00
❑ 228 Vernand Morency JSY/1499 RC 8.00 3.00
❑ 229 Vincent Jackson JSY/1499 RC 8.00 3.00

2006 Leaf Certified Materials

❑ COMP.SET w/o SP's (150) 40.00 15.00
❑ 1 Anquan Boldin .60 .25
❑ 2 Edgerrin James 1.00 .40
❑ 3 Kurt Warner .60 .25

❑ 4 Larry Fitzgerald 1.00 .40
❑ 5 Alge Crumpler .60 .25
❑ 6 Brian Finneran .50 .20
❑ 7 Michael Jenkins .60 .25
❑ 8 Michael Vick 1.25 .50
❑ 9 Warrick Dunn .60 .25
❑ 10 Derrick Mason .50 .20
❑ 11 Jamal Lewis .60 .25
❑ 12 Kyle Boller .50 .20
❑ 13 Todd Heap .60 .25
❑ 14 Mark Clayton .60 .25
❑ 15 Eric Moulds .60 .25
❑ 16 J.P. Losman .60 .25
❑ 17 Josh Reed .50 .20
❑ 18 Lee Evans .60 .25
❑ 19 Willis McGahee 1.00 .40
❑ 20 DeShaun Foster .60 .25
❑ 21 Jake Delhomme .60 .25
❑ 22 Stephen Davis .60 .25
❑ 23 Keary Colbert .50 .20
❑ 24 Steve Smith 1.00 .40
❑ 25 Brian Urlacher 1.00 .40
❑ 26 Cedric Benson 1.00 .40
❑ 27 Muhsin Muhammad .60 .25
❑ 28 Rex Grossman 1.00 .40
❑ 29 Thomas Jones .60 .25
❑ 30 Carson Palmer 1.00 .40
❑ 31 Chad Johnson .60 .25
❑ 32 Rudi Johnson .60 .25
❑ 33 T.J. Houshmandzadeh .60 .25
❑ 34 Charlie Frye .60 .25
❑ 35 Dennis Northcutt .50 .20
❑ 36 Braylon Edwards 1.00 .40
❑ 37 Reuben Droughns .60 .25
❑ 38 Drew Bledsoe 1.00 .40
❑ 39 Julius Jones 1.00 .40
❑ 40 Terrell Owens 1.00 .40
❑ 41 Jason Witten .60 .25
❑ 42 Terry Glenn .60 .25
❑ 43 Roy Williams S .60 .25
❑ 44 Jake Plummer .60 .25
❑ 45 Rod Smith .60 .25
❑ 46 Tatum Bell .60 .25
❑ 47 Ashley Lelie .60 .25
❑ 48 Josh McCown .60 .25
❑ 49 Kevin Jones 1.00 .40
❑ 50 Mike Williams 1.00 .40
❑ 51 Roy Williams WR 1.00 .40
❑ 52 Ahman Green .60 .25
❑ 53 Brett Favre 2.00 .75
❑ 54 Aaron Rodgers 1.00 .40
❑ 55 Samkon Gado 1.00 .40
❑ 56 Donald Driver .60 .25
❑ 57 Robert Ferguson .50 .20
❑ 58 Andre Johnson .60 .25
❑ 59 David Carr .60 .25
❑ 60 Domanick Davis .60 .25
❑ 61 Dallas Clark .50 .20
❑ 62 Marvin Harrison 1.00 .40
❑ 63 Peyton Manning 1.50 .60
❑ 64 Reggie Wayne .60 .25
❑ 65 Brandon Stokley .60 .25
❑ 66 Byron Leftwich .60 .25
❑ 67 Fred Taylor .60 .25
❑ 68 Jimmy Smith .60 .25
❑ 69 Matt Jones 1.00 .40
❑ 70 Larry Johnson 1.25 .50
❑ 71 Tony Gonzalez .60 .25
❑ 72 Trent Green .60 .25
❑ 73 Eddie Kennison .50 .20
❑ 74 Samie Parker .50 .20
❑ 75 Chris Chambers .60 .25
❑ 76 Daunte Culpepper 1.00 .40
❑ 77 Randy McMichael .50 .20
❑ 78 Ronnie Brown 1.00 .40
❑ 79 Marty Booker .50 .20
❑ 80 Zach Thomas 1.00 .40
❑ 81 Brad Johnson .60 .25
❑ 82 Mewelde Moore .50 .20
❑ 83 Nate Burleson .60 .25
❑ 84 Troy Williamson .60 .25
❑ 85 Deion Branch .60 .25
❑ 86 Tom Brady 1.50 .60
❑ 87 Corey Dillon .60 .25
❑ 88 Daniel Graham .50 .20
❑ 89 Troy Brown .60 .25
❑ 90 Deuce McAllister .60 .25
❑ 91 Donte Stallworth .60 .25
❑ 92 Drew Brees 1.00 .40
❑ 93 Joe Horn .60 .25
❑ 94 Devery Henderson .50 .20
❑ 95 Eli Manning 1.25 .50
❑ 96 Jeremy Shockey 1.00 .40
❑ 97 Plaxico Burress .60 .25
❑ 98 Amani Toomer .60 .25
❑ 99 Tiki Barber 1.00 .40
❑ 100 Chad Pennington .60 .25
❑ 101 Curtis Martin 1.00 .40
❑ 102 Laveranues Coles .60 .25
❑ 103 Justin McCareins .50 .20
❑ 104 Jerry Porter .60 .25
❑ 105 LaMont Jordan .60 .25
❑ 106 Doug Gabriel .50 .20
❑ 107 Randy Moss 1.00 .40
❑ 108 Brian Westbrook .60 .25
❑ 109 Donovan McNabb 1.00 .40
❑ 110 Reggie Brown .60 .25
❑ 111 Chad Lewis .50 .20
❑ 112 Ryan Moats .50 .20
❑ 113 Jevon Kearse .60 .25
❑ 114 Ben Roethlisberger 1.50 .60
❑ 115 Heath Miller 1.00 .40
❑ 116 Hines Ward 1.00 .40
❑ 117 Willie Parker 1.25 .50
❑ 118 Troy Polamalu 1.25 .50
❑ 119 Antonio Gates 1.00 .40
❑ 120 Eric Parker .50 .20
❑ 121 Keenan McCardell .50 .20
❑ 122 LaDainian Tomlinson 1.25 .50
❑ 123 Philip Rivers 1.00 .40
❑ 124 Alex Smith QB 1.25 .50
❑ 125 Antonio Bryant .60 .25
❑ 126 Frank Gore 1.00 .40
❑ 127 Kevan Barlow .60 .25
❑ 128 Darrell Jackson .60 .25
❑ 129 Jerramy Stevens .60 .25
❑ 130 Matt Hasselbeck .60 .25
❑ 131 Shaun Alexander 1.00 .40
❑ 132 Isaac Bruce .60 .25
❑ 133 Marc Bulger .60 .25
❑ 134 Marshall Faulk .60 .25
❑ 135 Steven Jackson 1.00 .40
❑ 136 Torry Holt .60 .25
❑ 137 Cadillac Williams 1.00 .40
❑ 138 Chris Simms .60 .25
❑ 139 Joey Galloway .60 .25
❑ 140 Michael Clayton .60 .25
❑ 141 Brandon Jones .50 .20
❑ 142 Chris Brown .60 .25
❑ 143 Drew Bennett .50 .20
❑ 144 Tyrone Calico .50 .20
❑ 145 Steve McNair .60 .25
❑ 146 Antwaan Randle El .60 .25
❑ 147 Clinton Portis 1.00 .40
❑ 148 Mark Brunell .60 .25
❑ 149 Santana Moss .60 .25
❑ 150 Jason Campbell .60 .25
❑ 151 Brodie Croyle/500 RC 12.00 5.00
❑ 152 Greg Jennings/500 RC 15.00 6.00
❑ 153 Joseph Addai/500 RC 25.00 10.00
❑ 154 Bennie Brazell/1000 RC 4.00 1.50
❑ 155 David Thomas/500 RC 8.00 3.00
❑ 156 Marques Colston/1000 RC 15.00 6.00
❑ 157 Reggie McNeal/500 RC 6.00 2.50
❑ 158 D.J. Shockley/1000 RC 5.00 2.00
❑ 159 Dominique Byrd/500 RC 6.00 2.50
❑ 160 Antonio Cromartie/1000 RC 5.00 2.00
❑ 161 Donte Whitner/1000 RC 5.00 2.00
❑ 162 Anwar Phillips/1000 RC 4.00 1.50
❑ 163 A.J. Nicholson/1000 RC 2.50 1.00
❑ 164 De'Arrius Howard/500 RC 8.00 3.00

❑ 165 Erik Meyer/500 RC 6.00 2.50
❑ 166 Darrell Hackney/1000 RC 4.00 1.50
❑ 167 Paul Pinegar/500 RC 6.00 2.50
❑ 168 Brandon Kirsch/500 RC 8.00 3.00
❑ 169 Quinton Ganther/1000 RC 4.00 1.50
❑ 170 Andre Hall/1000 RC 4.00 1.50
❑ 171 Derrick Ross/1000 RC 4.00 1.50
❑ 172 Mike Bell/1000 RC 8.00 3.00
❑ 173 Wendell Mathis/500 RC 6.00 2.50
❑ 174 Garrett Mills/500 RC 8.00 3.00
❑ 175 David Anderson/1000 RC 4.00 1.50
❑ 176 Kevin McMahan/1000 RC 4.00 1.50
❑ 177 Martin Nance/1000 RC 4.00 1.50
❑ 178 Greg Lee/500 RC 6.00 2.50
❑ 179 Anthony Mix/500 RC 6.00 2.50
❑ 180 D.Ferguson/500 RC 8.00 3.00
❑ 181 Tamba Hali/500 RC 8.00 3.00
❑ 182 Haloti Ngata/1000 RC 5.00 2.00
❑ 183 Claude Wroten/1000 RC 2.50 1.00
❑ 184 Gabe Watson/1000 RC 4.00 1.50
❑ 185 D'Qwell Jackson/1000 RC 4.00 1.50
❑ 186 Abdul Hodge/500 RC 8.00 3.00
❑ 187 Chad Greenway/500 RC 8.00 3.00
❑ 188 Bobby Carpenter/1000 RC 5.00 2.00
❑ 189 DeMeco Ryans/500 RC 10.00 4.00
❑ 190 Rocky McIntosh/500 RC 8.00 3.00
❑ 191 Thomas Howard/1000 RC 5.00 2.00
❑ 192 Jon Alston/500 RC 8.00 3.00
❑ 193 Jimmy Williams/1000 RC 5.00 2.00
❑ 194 Ashton Youboty/500 RC 8.00 3.00
❑ 195 Alan Zemaitis/1000 RC 5.00 2.00
❑ 196 Cedric Griffin/500 RC 6.00 2.50
❑ 197 Ko Simpson/1000 RC 4.00 1.50
❑ 198 Pat Watkins/500 RC 8.00 3.00
❑ 199 Bernard Pollard/1000 RC 4.00 1.50
❑ 200 Jay Cutler/500 RC 20.00 8.00
❑ 201 Chad Jackson JSY/1400 RC 10.00 4.00
❑ 202 L.Maroney JSY/550 RC 25.00 10.00
❑ 203 Tar.Jackson JSY/1400 RC 10.00 4.00
❑ 204 Michael Huff JSY/1400 RC 8.00 3.00
❑ 205 Mario Williams JSY/1400 RC 10.00 4.00
❑ 206 Mar.Lewis JSY/1400 RC 8.00 3.00
❑ 207 Maurice Drew JSY/1400 RC 15.00 6.00
❑ 208 Vince Young JSY/550 RC 25.00 10.00
❑ 209 LenDale White JSY/550 RC 12.00 5.00
❑ 210 Reggie Bush JSY/550 RC 40.00 15.00
❑ 211 Matt Leinart JSY/550 RC 25.00 10.00
❑ 212 M.Robinson JSY/1400 RC 10.00 4.00
❑ 213 Vernon Davis JSY/550 RC 15.00 6.00
❑ 214 Br.Williams JSY/1400 RC 8.00 3.00
❑ 215 Derek Hagan JSY/1400 RC 8.00 3.00
❑ 216 Jason Avant JSY/1400 RC 6.00 2.50
❑ 217 B.Marshall JSY/1400 RC 8.00 3.00
❑ 218 Omar Jacobs JSY/1400 RC 8.00 3.00
❑ 219 Santonio Holmes JSY/550 RC 15.00 6.00
❑ 220 J.Norwood JSY/1400 RC 10.00 4.00
❑ 221 Dem.Williams JSY/1400 RC 8.00 3.00
❑ 222 Sinorice Moss JSY/1400 RC 8.00 3.00
❑ 223 L.Washington JSY/1400 RC 10.00 4.00
❑ 224 Kellen Clemens JSY/900 RC 10.00 4.00
❑ 225 A.J. Hawk JSY/550 RC 20.00 8.00
❑ 226 Maurice Stovall JSY/1400 RC 8.00 3.00
❑ 227 DeA.Williams JSY/550 RC 20.00 8.00
❑ 228 C.Whitehurst JSY/1400 RC 8.00 3.00
❑ 229 Travis Wilson JSY/1400 RC 8.00 3.00
❑ 230 J.Klopfenstein JSY/1400 RC 8.00 3.00
❑ 231 Brian Calhoun JSY/1400 RC 8.00 3.00
❑ 232 Barry Sanders JSY/150 25.00 10.00
❑ 233 Jerry Rice JSY/150 20.00 8.00
❑ 234 Dan Marino JSY/150 30.00 12.00
❑ 235 Earl Campbell JSY/150 15.00 6.00
❑ 236 Jim Brown JSY/100 25.00 10.00
❑ 237 Joe Montana JSY/125 25.00 10.00
❑ 238 Troy Aikman JSY/150 20.00 8.00
❑ 239 Walter Payton JSY/100 40.00 15.00
❑ 240 Terry Bradshaw JSY/150 25.00 10.00
❑ 241 John Elway JSY/150 25.00 10.00
❑ 242 Fred Biletnikoff JSY/100 15.00 6.00
❑ 243 Lance Alworth JSY/125 15.00 6.00
❑ 244 Ronnie Lott JSY/150 15.00 6.00
❑ 245 Yale Lary JSY/125 15.00 6.00
❑ 246 Bart Starr JSY/80 30.00 12.00
❑ 247 Doak Walker JSY/75 25.00 10.00
❑ 248 Gale Sayers JSY/100 20.00 8.00
❑ 249 Bo Jackson JSY/150 15.00 6.00
❑ 250 Roger Staubach JSY/125 25.00 10.00
❑ 251 Dick Butkus JSY/150 20.00 8.00

2000 Leaf Limited

❑ COMP.SET w/o SPs (200) 120.00 60.00
❑ 1 Ben Coates .50 .20
❑ 2 Joe Horn .75 .30
❑ 3 Jonathan Linton .50 .20
❑ 4 Derrick Mason .75 .30
❑ 5 Ray Lucas .75 .30
❑ 6 Brock Huard .75 .30
❑ 7 Frank Wycheck .50 .20
❑ 8 Michael Strahan .75 .30
❑ 9 Jessie Armstead .50 .20
❑ 10 Stephen Alexander .50 .20
❑ 11 Larry Centers .50 .20
❑ 12 Michael Pittman .50 .20
❑ 13 Priest Holmes 1.50 .60
❑ 14 Jermaine Lewis .75 .30
❑ 15 Jay Riemersma .50 .20
❑ 16 Wesley Walls .50 .20
❑ 17 Curtis Enis .50 .20
❑ 18 Bobby Engram .75 .30
❑ 19 Jim Miller .50 .20
❑ 20 Eddie Kennison .75 .30
❑ 21 Errict Rhett .50 .20
❑ 22 Chris Warren .50 .20
❑ 23 Byron Chamberlain .50 .20
❑ 24 Desmond Howard .50 .20
❑ 25 Lamar Smith .75 .30
❑ 26 Robert Porcher .50 .20
❑ 27 Corey Bradford .75 .30
❑ 28 Donald Driver 1.25 .50
❑ 29 Ahman Green 1.25 .50
❑ 30 Ken Dilger .50 .20
❑ 31 James McKnight .75 .30
❑ 32 Kimble Anders .50 .20
❑ 33 Zach Thomas 1.25 .50
❑ 34 James Johnson .50 .20
❑ 35 Lawyer Milloy .75 .30
❑ 36 Ty Law .75 .30
❑ 37 Willie McGinest .50 .20
❑ 38 Jason Sehorn .75 .30
❑ 39 Andre Rison .75 .30
❑ 40 Rickey Dudley .50 .20
❑ 41 Patrick Jeffers 1.25 .50
❑ 42 Darrell Russell .50 .20
❑ 43 Charles Johnson .75 .30
❑ 44 Michael Westbrook .75 .30
❑ 45 Levon Kirkland .50 .20
❑ 46 Ryan Leaf .75 .30
❑ 47 Sean Dawkins .50 .20
❑ 48 Todd Lyght .50 .20
❑ 49 Kevin Carter .50 .20
❑ 50 Neil O'Donnell .50 .20
❑ 51 Randall Cunningham 1.50 .60
❑ 52 Oronde Gadsden 1.00 .40
❑ 53 O.J. McDuffie 1.00 .40
❑ 54 Jake Reed 1.00 .40
❑ 55 Brian Mitchell .60 .25
❑ 56 Kordell Stewart 1.00 .40
❑ 57 Derrick Mayes 1.00 .40
❑ 58 Az-Zahir Hakim .60 .25
❑ 59 Jacquez Green .60 .25
❑ 60 Andre Reed 1.00 .40
❑ 61 Deion Sanders 1.50 .60
❑ 62 Frank Sanders 1.00 .40
❑ 63 Rob Moore 1.00 .40
❑ 64 Shawn Jefferson .60 .25
❑ 65 Pat Johnson .60 .25
❑ 66 Peter Boulware .60 .25
❑ 67 Donald Hayes .60 .25
❑ 68 Marty Booker 1.00 .40
❑ 69 Leslie Shepherd .60 .25
❑ 70 Jason Tucker .60 .25
❑ 71 Johnnie Morton 1.00 .40
❑ 72 Germane Crowell .60 .25
❑ 73 Herman Moore 1.00 .40
❑ 74 Bill Schroeder 1.00 .40
❑ 75 E.G. Green .60 .25
❑ 76 Jerome Pathon 1.00 .40
❑ 77 Tony Brackens .60 .25
❑ 78 Tony Richardson RC .60 .25
❑ 79 Sam Madison .60 .25
❑ 80 Jeff George 1.00 .40
❑ 81 Matthew Hatchette .60 .25
❑ 82 Kevin Faulk 1.00 .40
❑ 83 Jeff Blake 1.00 .40
❑ 84 Ike Hilliard 1.00 .40
❑ 85 Napoleon Kaufman 1.00 .40
❑ 86 Charles Woodson 1.00 .40
❑ 87 Na Brown .60 .25
❑ 88 Hines Ward 1.50 .60
❑ 89 Troy Edwards .60 .25
❑ 90 Curtis Conway 1.00 .40
❑ 91 Junior Seau 1.50 .60
❑ 92 Jim Harbaugh 1.00 .40
❑ 93 J.J. Stokes 1.00 .40
❑ 94 Jon Kitna 1.50 .60
❑ 95 Reidel Anthony .60 .25
❑ 96 Warrick Dunn 1.50 .60
❑ 97 Carl Pickens 1.00 .40
❑ 98 Yancey Thigpen .60 .25
❑ 99 Albert Connell .60 .25
❑ 100 Irving Fryar 1.00 .40
❑ 101 Qadry Ismail 1.25 .50
❑ 102 Shannon Sharpe 1.25 .50
❑ 103 Joey Galloway 1.25 .50
❑ 104 Ed McCaffrey 2.00 .75
❑ 105 Rod Smith 1.25 .50
❑ 106 Terrell Owens 2.00 .75
❑ 107 Warren Sapp 1.25 .50
❑ 108 Jevon Kearse 2.00 .75
❑ 109 Bruce Smith 1.25 .50
❑ 110 Champ Bailey 1.25 .50
❑ 111 David Boston 2.00 .75
❑ 112 Tim Dwight 2.00 .75
❑ 113 Terance Mathis 1.25 .50
❑ 114 Tony Banks 1.25 .50
❑ 115 Shawn Bryson .75 .30
❑ 116 Peerless Price 1.25 .50
❑ 117 Muhsin Muhammad 1.25 .50
❑ 118 Tim Biakabutuka 1.25 .50
❑ 119 Steve Beuerlein 1.25 .50
❑ 120 Corey Dillon 2.00 .75
❑ 121 Kevin Johnson 2.00 .75
❑ 122 Rocket Ismail 1.25 .50
❑ 123 Charlie Batch 2.00 .75
❑ 124 James Stewart 1.25 .50
❑ 125 Terrence Wilkins .75 .30
❑ 126 Keenan McCardell 1.25 .50
❑ 127 Mark Brunell 2.00 .75
❑ 128 Fred Taylor 2.00 .75
❑ 129 Derrick Alexander 1.25 .50
❑ 130 Tony Gonzalez 1.25 .50
❑ 131 Warren Moon 2.00 .75
❑ 132 Thurman Thomas 1.25 .50
❑ 133 Tony Martin 1.25 .50
❑ 134 Jay Fiedler 2.00 .75
❑ 135 John Randle 1.25 .50
❑ 136 Troy Brown 1.25 .50
❑ 137 Amani Toomer 1.25 .50
❑ 138 Kerry Collins 1.25 .50
❑ 139 Tiki Barber 2.00 .75
❑ 140 Wayne Chrebet 1.25 .50
❑ 141 Tyrone Wheatley 1.25 .50
❑ 142 Duce Staley 2.00 .75
❑ 143 Jermaine Fazande .75 .30
❑ 144 Charlie Garner 1.25 .50
❑ 145 Torry Holt 2.00 .75
❑ 146 Mike Alstott 2.00 .75
❑ 147 Shaun King .50 .20
❑ 148 Darrell Green .75 .30
❑ 149 Brad Johnson 2.00 .75
❑ 150 Olandis Gary 2.00 .75
❑ 151 Jake Plummer 1.50 .60
❑ 152 Chris Chandler 1.50 .60
❑ 153 Jamal Anderson 2.50 1.00
❑ 154 Eric Moulds 2.50 1.00
❑ 155 Doug Flutie 2.50 1.00
❑ 156 Rob Johnson 1.50 .60
❑ 157 Marcus Robinson 2.50 1.00
❑ 158 Cade McNown 1.00 .40

- ❑ 159 Akili Smith 1.00 .40
- ❑ 160 Tim Couch 1.50 .60
- ❑ 161 Emmitt Smith 5.00 2.00
- ❑ 162 Troy Aikman 5.00 2.00
- ❑ 163 Brian Griese 2.50 1.00
- ❑ 164 John Elway 8.00 3.00
- ❑ 165 Terrell Davis 2.50 1.00
- ❑ 166 Dorsey Levens 1.50 .60
- ❑ 167 Antonio Freeman 2.50 1.00
- ❑ 168 Brett Favre 8.00 3.00
- ❑ 169 Marvin Harrison 2.50 1.00
- ❑ 170 Peyton Manning 6.00 2.50
- ❑ 171 Edgerrin James 4.00 1.50
- ❑ 172 Jimmy Smith 1.50 .60
- ❑ 173 Elvis Grbac 1.50 .60
- ❑ 174 Dan Marino 8.00 3.00
- ❑ 175 Randy Moss 5.00 2.00
- ❑ 176 Cris Carter 2.50 1.00
- ❑ 177 Robert Smith 2.50 1.00
- ❑ 178 Daunte Culpepper 3.00 1.25
- ❑ 179 Terry Glenn 1.50 .60
- ❑ 180 Drew Bledsoe 3.00 1.25
- ❑ 181 Ricky Williams 1.25 .50
- ❑ 182 Jake Delhomme RC 8.00 3.00
- ❑ 183 Curtis Martin 2.50 1.00
- ❑ 184 Vinny Testaverde 1.50 .60
- ❑ 185 Tim Brown 2.50 1.00
- ❑ 186 Rich Gannon 2.50 1.00
- ❑ 187 Donovan McNabb 3.00 1.25
- ❑ 188 Jerome Bettis 2.50 1.00
- ❑ 189 Bobby Shaw RC 2.50 1.00
- ❑ 190 Jerry Rice 5.00 2.00
- ❑ 191 Steve Young 3.00 1.25
- ❑ 192 Jeff Garcia 2.50 1.00
- ❑ 193 Ricky Watters 1.00 .40
- ❑ 194 Isaac Bruce 2.50 1.00
- ❑ 195 Marshall Faulk 3.00 1.25
- ❑ 196 Kurt Warner 5.00 2.00
- ❑ 197 Keyshawn Johnson 2.50 1.00
- ❑ 198 Eddie George 2.50 1.00
- ❑ 199 Steve McNair 2.50 1.00
- ❑ 200 Stephen Davis 2.50 1.00
- ❑ 201 Bobby Brooks RC 3.00 1.25
- ❑ 202 Cornelius Griffin RC 4.00 1.50
- ❑ 203 Danny Clark RC 4.00 1.50
- ❑ 204 Pat Dennis RC 3.00 1.25
- ❑ 205 Tommy Hendricks RC 5.00 2.00
- ❑ 206 Fred Jones RC 3.00 1.25
- ❑ 207 Isaiah Kacyvenski RC 3.00 1.25
- ❑ 208 Keith Miller RC 3.00 1.25
- ❑ 209 Andre O' Neal RC 3.00 1.25
- ❑ 210 Justin Snow RC 3.00 1.25
- ❑ 211 Armegis Spearman RC 4.00 1.50
- ❑ 212 Lester Towns RC 3.00 1.25
- ❑ 213 Antonio Wilson RC 3.00 1.25
- ❑ 214 Greg Wesley RC 5.00 2.00
- ❑ 215 Jabari Issa RC 3.00 1.25
- ❑ 216 Darwin Walker RC 3.00 1.25
- ❑ 217 Reggie Grimes RC 3.00 1.25
- ❑ 218 Rian Lindell RC 3.00 1.25
- ❑ 219 Chris Combs RC 3.00 1.25
- ❑ 220 Rashard Anderson RC 4.00 1.50
- ❑ 221 Erik Flowers RC 4.00 1.50
- ❑ 222 Corey Moore RC 3.00 1.25
- ❑ 223 Rob Meier RC 3.00 1.25
- ❑ 224 John Milem RC 3.00 1.25
- ❑ 225 Jeremiah Parker RC 3.00 1.25
- ❑ 226 Neil Rackers RC 5.00 2.00
- ❑ 227 Josh Taves RC 4.00 1.50
- ❑ 228 Mao Tosi RC 3.00 1.25
- ❑ 229 Gary Berry RC 3.00 1.25
- ❑ 230 Matt Bowen RC 3.00 1.25
- ❑ 231 Ralph Brown RC 3.00 1.25
- ❑ 232 Tony Darden RC 3.00 1.25
- ❑ 233 Arturo Freeman RC 3.00 1.25
- ❑ 234 David Gibson RC 3.00 1.25
- ❑ 235 Demario Brown RC 3.00 1.25
- ❑ 236 Deveron Harper RC 3.00 1.25
- ❑ 237 Johnnie Harris RC 3.00 1.25
- ❑ 238 Marcus Knight RC 4.00 1.50
- ❑ 239 Ronnie Heard RC 4.00 1.50
- ❑ 240 Eric Johnson RC 4.00 1.50
- ❑ 241 John Keith RC 3.00 1.25
- ❑ 242 Anthony Malbrough RC 3.00 1.25
- ❑ 243 Anthony Mitchell RC 3.00 1.25
- ❑ 244 Aric Morris RC 3.00 1.25
- ❑ 245 Bobby Myers RC 3.00 1.25
- ❑ 246 Erik Olson RC 3.00 1.25
- ❑ 247 Lewis Sanders RC 3.00 1.25
- ❑ 248 Tony Scott RC 3.00 1.25
- ❑ 249 David Terrell RC 3.00 1.25
- ❑ 250 Travares Tillman RC 3.00 1.25
- ❑ 251 David Stachelski RC 4.00 1.50
- ❑ 252 Darren Howard RC 5.00 2.00
- ❑ 253 Frank Chamberlin RC 4.00 1.50
- ❑ 254 Na'il Diggs RC 5.00 2.00
- ❑ 255 Orantes Grant RC 4.00 1.50
- ❑ 256 Barrett Green RC 4.00 1.50
- ❑ 257 Kory Minor RC 4.00 1.50
- ❑ 258 Deon Grant RC 5.00 2.00
- ❑ 259 Mark Simoneau RC 5.00 2.00
- ❑ 260 Raynoch Thompson RC 5.00 2.00
- ❑ 261 Kenyatta Wright RC 4.00 1.50
- ❑ 262 Marcus Bell LB RC 4.00 1.50
- ❑ 263 Jack Golden RC 4.00 1.50
- ❑ 264 Thomas Hamner RC 4.00 1.50
- ❑ 265 Sekou Sanyika RC 4.00 1.50
- ❑ 266 Marcus Washington RC 5.00 2.00
- ❑ 267 Tim Seder RC 5.00 2.00
- ❑ 268 Paul Edinger RC 6.00 2.50
- ❑ 269 Michael Boireau RC 4.00 1.50
- ❑ 270 Byron Frisch RC 4.00 1.50
- ❑ 271 Ketric Sanford RC 4.00 1.50
- ❑ 272 Frank Murphy RC 4.00 1.50
- ❑ 273 Robaire Smith RC 4.00 1.50
- ❑ 274 Adalius Thomas RC 10.00 4.00
- ❑ 275 William Bartee RC 5.00 2.00
- ❑ 276 Robert Bean RC 5.00 2.00
- ❑ 277 Tyrone Carter RC 6.00 2.50
- ❑ 278 Ike Charlton RC 4.00 1.50
- ❑ 279 Mario Edwards RC 5.00 2.00
- ❑ 280 Dwayne Goodrich RC 4.00 1.50
- ❑ 281 Michael Hawthorne RC 4.00 1.50
- ❑ 282 Kareem Larrimore RC 4.00 1.50
- ❑ 283 Mark Roman RC 5.00 2.00
- ❑ 284 Jacoby Shepherd RC 4.00 1.50
- ❑ 285 Jason Webster RC 4.00 1.50
- ❑ 286 Jimmy Wyrick RC 4.00 1.50
- ❑ 287 Rashidi Barnes RC 4.00 1.50
- ❑ 288 David Barrett RC 4.00 1.50
- ❑ 289 Ainsley Battles RC 4.00 1.50
- ❑ 290 Lamar Chapman RC 4.00 1.50
- ❑ 291 Todd Franz RC 4.00 1.50
- ❑ 292 Michael Green RC 4.00 1.50
- ❑ 293 Antwan Harris RC 4.00 1.50
- ❑ 294 Brandon Jennings RC 4.00 1.50
- ❑ 295 Darrick Vaughn RC 4.00 1.50
- ❑ 296 David Macklin RC 4.00 1.50
- ❑ 297 Bobby Brown RC 4.00 1.50
- ❑ 298 Reggie Stephens RC 4.00 1.50
- ❑ 299 Kenoy Kennedy RC 4.00 1.50
- ❑ 300 Raion Hill RC 4.00 1.50
- ❑ 301 Windrell Hayes RC 8.00 3.00
- ❑ 302 DaShon Polk RC 6.00 2.50
- ❑ 303 Tywan Mitchell RC 8.00 3.00
- ❑ 304 Casey Crawford RC 6.00 2.50
- ❑ 305 Hank Poteat RC 8.00 3.00
- ❑ 306 Mondriel Fulcher RC 6.00 2.50
- ❑ 307 Cory Geason RC 6.00 2.50
- ❑ 308 James Hill RC 6.00 2.50
- ❑ 309 Brian Jennings RC 6.00 2.50
- ❑ 310 John Jones RC 8.00 3.00
- ❑ 311 Anthony Lucas RC 6.00 2.50
- ❑ 312 Mike Leach RC 6.00 2.50
- ❑ 313 Dustin Lyman RC 6.00 2.50
- ❑ 314 Derek Rackley RC 6.00 2.50
- ❑ 315 Sebastian Janikowski RC 10.00 4.00
- ❑ 316 Brad St.Louis RC 6.00 2.50
- ❑ 317 Jay Tant RC 6.00 2.50
- ❑ 318 Austin Wheatley RC 6.00 2.50
- ❑ 319 Jermaine Wiggins RC 10.00 4.00
- ❑ 320 Todd Yoder RC 8.00 3.00
- ❑ 321 Deon Dyer RC 8.00 3.00
- ❑ 322 Jim Finn 6.00 2.50
- ❑ 323 Herbert Goodman RC 8.00 3.00
- ❑ 324 Mike Green RC 8.00 3.00
- ❑ 325 Dante Hall RC 20.00 7.50
- ❑ 326 Thabiti Davis RC 6.00 2.50
- ❑ 327 Kevin Houser RC 8.00 3.00
- ❑ 328 Jonas Lewis RC 6.00 2.50
- ❑ 329 Chad Morton RC 10.00 4.00
- ❑ 330 Patrick Pass RC 8.00 3.00
- ❑ 331 Maurice Smith RC 10.00 4.00
- ❑ 332 Paul Smith RC 8.00 3.00
- ❑ 333 Terrelle Smith RC 8.00 3.00
- ❑ 334 Craig Walendy RC 6.00 2.50
- ❑ 335 Jamel White RC 8.00 3.00
- ❑ 336 Jarious Jackson RC 8.00 3.00
- ❑ 337 Matt Lytle RC 8.00 3.00
- ❑ 338 Ron Powlus RC 10.00 4.00
- ❑ 339 Ian Gold RC 8.00 3.00
- ❑ 340 Brandon Short RC 8.00 3.00
- ❑ 341 T.J. Slaughter RC 6.00 2.50
- ❑ 342 Nate Webster RC 6.00 2.50
- ❑ 343 John Engelberger RC 8.00 3.00
- ❑ 344 Rogers Beckett RC 8.00 3.00
- ❑ 345 Mike Brown RC 15.00 6.00
- ❑ 346 Anthony Wright RC 12.00 5.00
- ❑ 347 Danny Farmer RC 8.00 3.00
- ❑ 348 Clint Stoerner RC 8.00 3.00
- ❑ 349 Julian Peterson RC 10.00 4.00
- ❑ 350 Ahmed Plummer RC 10.00 4.00
- ❑ 351 Avion Black RC 10.00 4.00
- ❑ 352 Kwame Cavil RC 8.00 3.00
- ❑ 353 Chris Cole RC 10.00 4.00
- ❑ 354 Chris Coleman RC 8.00 3.00
- ❑ 355 Trevor Gaylor RC 10.00 4.00
- ❑ 356 Damon Hodge RC 10.00 4.00
- ❑ 357 Darrell Jackson RC 25.00 10.00
- ❑ 358 Reggie Jones RC 8.00 3.00
- ❑ 359 Charles Lee RC 8.00 3.00
- ❑ 360 Jerry Porter RC 15.00 6.00
- ❑ 361 Bobby Shaw 10.00 4.00
- ❑ 362 Ron Dugans RC 8.00 3.00
- ❑ 363 James Williams RC 10.00 4.00
- ❑ 364 Bashir Yamini RC 8.00 3.00
- ❑ 365 Anthony Becht RC 12.00 5.00
- ❑ 366 Erron Kinney RC 12.00 5.00
- ❑ 367 Aaron Shea RC 10.00 4.00
- ❑ 368 Chris Samuels RC 10.00 4.00
- ❑ 369 Trung Canidate RC 10.00 4.00
- ❑ 370 Obafemi Ayanbadejo RC 10.00 4.00
- ❑ 371 Doug Chapman RC 10.00 4.00
- ❑ 372 Ronney Jenkins RC 10.00 4.00
- ❑ 373 Curtis Keaton RC 10.00 4.00
- ❑ 374 Kevin McDougal RC 10.00 4.00
- ❑ 375 Frank Moreau RC 10.00 4.00
- ❑ 376 Aaron Stecker RC 12.00 5.00
- ❑ 377 Shyrone Stith RC 10.00 4.00
- ❑ 378 Tom Brady RC 150.00 75.00
- ❑ 379 Giovanni Carmazzi RC 8.00 3.00
- ❑ 380 Joe Hamilton RC 10.00 4.00
- ❑ 381 Todd Husak RC 12.00 5.00
- ❑ 382 Doug Johnson RC 12.00 5.00
- ❑ 383 Tee Martin RC 12.00 5.00
- ❑ 384 Chad Pennington RC 60.00 25.00
- ❑ 385 Tim Rattay RC 12.00 5.00
- ❑ 386 Chris Redman RC 10.00 4.00
- ❑ 387 Billy Volek RC 20.00 7.50
- ❑ 388 Spergon Wynn RC 10.00 4.00
- ❑ 389 John Abraham RC 12.00 5.00
- ❑ 390 Keith Bulluck RC 12.00 5.00
- ❑ 391 Rob Morris RC 10.00 4.00
- ❑ 392 JaJuan Dawson RC 8.00 3.00
- ❑ 393 Chris Hovan RC 10.00 4.00
- ❑ 394 Shaun Ellis RC 12.00 5.00
- ❑ 395 Deltha O'Neal RC 12.00 5.00
- ❑ 396 Gari Scott RC 8.00 3.00
- ❑ 397 Dialleo Burks RC 8.00 3.00
- ❑ 398 Shockmain Davis RC 8.00 3.00
- ❑ 399 Brad Hoover RC 10.00 4.00
- ❑ 400 Brian Finneran RC 12.00 5.00
- ❑ 401 Sylvester Morris J/FB/750 RC 8.00 3.00
- ❑ 402 Denn Northcutt J/FB/500 RC 25.00 10.00
- ❑ 403 Todd Pinkston J/FB/100 RC 20.00 7.50
- ❑ 404 Larry Foster J/FB/500 RC 20.00 7.50
- ❑ 405 R.Jay Soward J/FB/1000 RC 12.00 5.00
- ❑ 406 Travis Taylor J/FB/250 RC 40.00 15.00
- ❑ 407 Peter Warrick J/FB/1000 RC 20.00 7.50
- ❑ 408 Dez White J/FB/1000 RC 20.00 7.50
- ❑ 409 Ron Dayne J/FB/1000 RC 20.00 7.50
- ❑ 410 Thomas Jones J/FB/500 RC 25.00 10.00
- ❑ 411 Jamal Lewis J/FB/1000 RC 30.00 12.50
- ❑ 412 Sammy Morris J/FB/500 RC 20.00 7.50
- ❑ 413 Travis Prentice J/FB/500 RC 20.00 7.50
- ❑ 414 J.R. Redmond J/FB/250 RC 25.00 10.00
- ❑ 415 Michael Wiley FB/1000 RC 12.00 5.00
- ❑ 416 Laver Coles J/FB/250 RC 40.00 15.00
- ❑ 417 Bubba Franks J/FB/500 RC 20.00 7.50
- ❑ 418 Mike Anderson J/FB/250 RC 40.00 20.00
- ❑ 419 Plaxico Burress J/FB/250 RC 60.00 25.00
- ❑ 420 Ron Dixon J/FB/1000 RC 12.00 5.00
- ❑ 421 Troy Walters J/FB/1000 RC 12.00 5.00
- ❑ 422 Sha Alexander J/FB/1000 RC 50.00 25.00
- ❑ 423 Brian Urlacher J/FB/1000 RC 40.00 15.00
- ❑ 424 Corey Simon J/FB/1000 RC 12.00 5.00
- ❑ 425 Courtney Brown J/FB/500 RC 25.00 10.00

2003 Leaf Limited

❑ COMP.SET w/o SP's (100)	250.00	100.00
❑ 1 Emmitt Smith	10.00	4.00
❑ 2 Michael Vick	10.00	4.00
❑ 3 Peerless Price	2.50	1.00
❑ 4 T.J. Duckett	2.50	1.00
❑ 5 Jamal Lewis	4.00	1.50
❑ 6 Drew Bledsoe	4.00	1.50
❑ 7 Eric Moulds	2.50	1.00
❑ 8 Travis Henry	2.50	1.00
❑ 9 Jim Kelly	8.00	3.00
❑ 10 Julius Peppers	4.00	1.50
❑ 11 Dick Butkus	6.00	2.50
❑ 12 Mike Singletary	4.00	1.50
❑ 13 Walter Payton	15.00	6.00
❑ 14 Anthony Thomas	2.50	1.00
❑ 15 Brian Urlacher	6.00	2.50
❑ 16 Marty Booker	2.50	1.00
❑ 17 Corey Dillon	2.50	1.00
❑ 18 Jim Thorpe	5.00	2.00
❑ 19 Jim Brown	10.00	4.00
❑ 20 Tim Couch	2.50	1.00
❑ 21 William Green	2.50	1.00
❑ 22 Deion Sanders	4.00	1.50
❑ 23 Michael Irvin	4.00	1.50
❑ 24 Roger Staubach	8.00	3.00
❑ 25 Troy Aikman	6.00	2.50
❑ 26 Tony Dorsett	6.00	2.50
❑ 27 Antonio Bryant	2.50	1.00
❑ 28 Clinton Portis	6.00	2.50
❑ 29 Jake Plummer	2.50	1.00
❑ 30 Rod Smith	2.50	1.00
❑ 31 Barry Sanders	8.00	3.00
❑ 32 Doak Walker	4.00	1.50
❑ 33 Joey Harrington	6.00	2.50
❑ 34 Bart Starr	8.00	3.00
❑ 35 Ahman Green	4.00	1.50
❑ 36 Brett Favre	10.00	4.00
❑ 37 Donald Driver	2.50	1.00
❑ 38 David Carr	6.00	2.50
❑ 39 Don Shula	5.00	2.00
❑ 40 Johnny Unitas	8.00	3.00
❑ 41 Edgerrin James	4.00	1.50
❑ 42 Marvin Harrison	4.00	1.50
❑ 43 Peyton Manning	6.00	2.50
❑ 44 Fred Taylor	4.00	1.50
❑ 45 Jimmy Smith	2.50	1.00
❑ 46 Mark Brunell	2.50	1.00
❑ 47 Marcus Allen	4.00	1.50
❑ 48 Priest Holmes	5.00	2.00
❑ 49 Tony Gonzalez	2.50	1.00
❑ 50 Trent Green	2.50	1.00
❑ 51 Dan Marino	12.00	5.00
❑ 52 Bob Griese	5.00	2.00
❑ 53 Chris Chambers	4.00	1.50
❑ 54 Ricky Williams	4.00	1.50
❑ 55 Fran Tarkenton	5.00	2.00
❑ 56 Daunte Culpepper	4.00	1.50
❑ 57 Michael Bennett	2.50	1.00
❑ 58 Randy Moss	6.00	2.50
❑ 59 Tom Brady	10.00	4.00
❑ 60 Aaron Brooks	4.00	1.50
❑ 61 Deuce McAllister	4.00	1.50
❑ 62 Donte Stallworth	4.00	1.50
❑ 63 Mark Bavaro	2.50	1.00
❑ 64 Jeremy Shockey	6.00	2.50
❑ 65 Kerry Collins	2.50	1.00
❑ 66 Tiki Barber	4.00	1.50
❑ 67 Joe Namath	8.00	3.00
❑ 68 Chad Pennington	5.00	2.00
❑ 69 Curtis Martin	4.00	1.50
❑ 70 Jerry Porter	2.50	1.00
❑ 71 Jerry Rice	8.00	3.00
❑ 72 Rich Gannon	2.50	1.00
❑ 73 Tim Brown	4.00	1.50
❑ 74 Donovan McNabb	5.00	2.00
❑ 75 Terry Bradshaw	8.00	3.00
❑ 76 Antwaan Randle El	4.00	1.50
❑ 77 Plaxico Burress	2.50	1.00
❑ 78 Tommy Maddox	4.00	1.50
❑ 79 David Boston	2.50	1.00
❑ 80 Drew Brees	4.00	1.50
❑ 81 LaDainian Tomlinson	4.00	1.50
❑ 82 Joe Montana	20.00	7.50
❑ 83 Steve Young	5.00	2.00
❑ 84 Jeff Garcia	4.00	1.50
❑ 85 Terrell Owens	4.00	1.50
❑ 86 Koren Robinson	2.50	1.00
❑ 87 Matt Hasselbeck	2.50	1.00
❑ 88 Shaun Alexander	4.00	1.50
❑ 89 Isaac Bruce	4.00	1.50
❑ 90 Kurt Warner	4.00	1.50
❑ 91 Marshall Faulk	4.00	1.50
❑ 92 Torry Holt	4.00	1.50
❑ 93 Brad Johnson	2.50	1.00
❑ 94 Keyshawn Johnson	4.00	1.50
❑ 95 Earl Campbell	4.00	1.50
❑ 96 Eddie George	2.50	1.00
❑ 97 Steve McNair	4.00	1.50
❑ 98 John Riggins	6.00	2.50
❑ 99 Laveranues Coles	2.50	1.00
❑ 100 Patrick Ramsey	4.00	1.50
❑ 101 LaTarence Dunbar RC	5.00	2.00
❑ 102 Sam Aiken RC	5.00	2.00
❑ 103 Bobby Wade RC	6.00	2.50
❑ 104 Justin Gage RC	6.00	2.50
❑ 105 Lee Suggs RC	8.00	3.00
❑ 106 Jason Witten RC	10.00	4.00
❑ 107 Quentin Griffin RC	6.00	2.50
❑ 108 Domanick Davis RC	6.00	2.50
❑ 109 LaBrandon Toefield RC	6.00	2.50
❑ 110 J.R. Tolver RC	5.00	2.00
❑ 111 Kliff Kingsbury RC	5.00	2.00
❑ 112 Talman Gardner RC	6.00	2.50
❑ 113 Teyo Johnson RC	6.00	2.50
❑ 114 Billy McMullen RC	5.00	2.00
❑ 115 L.J. Smith RC	6.00	2.50
❑ 116 Brian St.Pierre RC	6.00	2.50
❑ 117 Brandon Lloyd RC	8.00	3.00
❑ 118 Seneca Wallace RC	6.00	2.50
❑ 119 Kevin Curtis RC	6.00	2.50
❑ 120 Shaun McDonald RC	6.00	2.50
❑ 121 Terrell Suggs RC	10.00	4.00
❑ 122 Terence Newman RC	12.00	5.00
❑ 123 Tony Romo RC	50.00	25.00
❑ 124 DeWayne Robertson RC	6.00	2.50
❑ 125 Marcus Trufant RC	6.00	2.50
❑ 126 Artose Pinner AU RC	25.00	10.00
❑ 127 Bryant Johnson AU RC	25.00	10.00
❑ 128 Kelley Washington AU RC	30.00	12.50
❑ 129 Dallas Clark AU RC	25.00	10.00
❑ 130 Onterrio Smith AU RC	25.00	10.00
❑ 131 Tony Hollings AU RC	25.00	10.00
❑ 132 Tyrone Calico AU RC	25.00	10.00
❑ 133 Carson Palmer AU RC	150.00	90.00
❑ 134 Byron Leftwich AU RC	100.00	50.00
❑ 135 Rex Grossman AU RC	100.00	50.00
❑ 136 Kyle Boller AU RC	25.00	10.00
❑ 137 Chris Simms AU RC	60.00	30.00
❑ 138 Dave Ragone AU RC	25.00	10.00
❑ 139 Ken Dorsey AU RC	25.00	10.00
❑ 140 Willis McGahee AU RC	80.00	40.00
❑ 141 Larry Johnson AU RC	150.00	75.00
❑ 142 Musa Smith AU RC	25.00	10.00
❑ 143 Chris Brown AU RC	25.00	10.00
❑ 144 Charles Rogers AU RC	25.00	10.00
❑ 145 Andre Johnson AU RC	60.00	30.00
❑ 146 Taylor Jacobs AU RC	25.00	10.00
❑ 147 Anquan Boldin AU RC	80.00	40.00
❑ 148 Bethel Johnson AU RC	25.00	10.00
❑ 149 Justin Fargas AU RC	25.00	10.00
❑ 150 Nate Burleson AU RC	25.00	10.00

2004 Leaf Limited

❑ 201-233 JSY AU PRINT RUN 150 SETS
❑ EXCH EXPIRATION: 7/1/2006

❑ 1 A.J. Feeley	4.00	1.50
❑ 2 Aaron Brooks	3.00	1.25
❑ 3 Ahman Green	4.00	1.50
❑ 4 Andre Johnson	4.00	1.50

❑ 5 Anquan Boldin	4.00	1.50
❑ 6 Antwaan Randle El	4.00	1.50
❑ 7 Ashley Lelie	3.00	1.25
❑ 8 Brad Johnson	3.00	1.25
❑ 9 Brett Favre	10.00	4.00
❑ 10 Brian Urlacher	5.00	2.00
❑ 11 Brian Westbrook	3.00	1.25
❑ 12 Byron Leftwich	5.00	2.00
❑ 13 Carson Palmer	5.00	2.00
❑ 14 Chad Johnson	4.00	1.50
❑ 15 Chad Pennington	4.00	1.50
❑ 16 Charlie Garner	3.00	1.25
❑ 17 Charles Rogers	3.00	1.25
❑ 18 Chris Brown	4.00	1.50
❑ 19 Chris Chambers	3.00	1.25
❑ 20 Clinton Portis	4.00	1.50
❑ 21 Corey Dillon	3.00	1.25
❑ 22 Deion Sanders	4.00	1.50
❑ 23 Curtis Martin	4.00	1.50
❑ 24 Daunte Culpepper	4.00	1.50
❑ 25 David Terrell	3.00	1.25
❑ 26 David Carr	4.00	1.50
❑ 27 Deion Branch	4.00	1.50
❑ 28 Derrick Mason	3.00	1.25
❑ 29 DeShaun Foster	3.00	1.25
❑ 30 Deuce McAllister	4.00	1.50
❑ 31 Domanick Davis	4.00	1.50
❑ 32 Donovan McNabb	5.00	2.00
❑ 33 Donte Stallworth	3.00	1.25
❑ 34 Drew Bledsoe	4.00	1.50
❑ 35 Duce Staley	3.00	1.25
❑ 36 Eddie George	3.00	1.25
❑ 37 Edgerrin James	4.00	1.50
❑ 38 Emmitt Smith	8.00	3.00
❑ 39 Eric Moulds	3.00	1.25
❑ 40 Fred Taylor	3.00	1.25
❑ 41 Hines Ward	4.00	1.50
❑ 42 Isaac Bruce	4.00	1.50
❑ 43 Jake Delhomme	4.00	1.50
❑ 44 Jake Plummer	3.00	1.25
❑ 45 Javon Walker	3.00	1.25
❑ 46 Jeff Garcia	4.00	1.50
❑ 47 Jeremy Shockey	4.00	1.50
❑ 48 Jerome Bettis	4.00	1.50
❑ 49 Jerry Porter	3.00	1.25
❑ 50 Jerry Rice	8.00	3.00
❑ 51 Jevon Kearse	3.00	1.25
❑ 52 Jimmy Smith	3.00	1.25
❑ 53 Joe Horn	3.00	1.25
❑ 54 Joey Harrington	4.00	1.50
❑ 55 Josh McCown	3.00	1.25
❑ 56 Kevan Barlow	3.00	1.25
❑ 57 Koren Robinson	3.00	1.25
❑ 58 Kyle Boller	4.00	1.50
❑ 59 LaDainian Tomlinson	5.00	2.00
❑ 60 LaVar Arrington	8.00	3.00
❑ 61 Laveranues Coles	3.00	1.25
❑ 62 Lee Suggs	4.00	1.50
❑ 63 Marc Bulger	4.00	1.50
❑ 64 Mark Brunell	3.00	1.25
❑ 65 Marshall Faulk	4.00	1.50
❑ 66 Marvin Harrison	4.00	1.50
❑ 67 Matt Hasselbeck	3.00	1.25
❑ 68 Michael Bennett	3.00	1.25
❑ 69 Michael Strahan	3.00	1.25
❑ 70 Michael Vick	8.00	3.00
❑ 71 Peerless Price	3.00	1.25
❑ 72 Peter Warrick	3.00	1.25
❑ 73 Peyton Manning	6.00	2.50
❑ 74 Priest Holmes	5.00	2.00
❑ 75 Quentin Griffin	4.00	1.50
❑ 76 Randy Moss	5.00	2.00

- ❑ 77 Ray Lewis 4.00 1.50
- ❑ 78 Rex Grossman 4.00 1.50
- ❑ 79 Lamar Gordon 2.50 1.00
- ❑ 80 Rod Smith 3.00 1.25
- ❑ 81 Roy Williams S 3.00 1.25
- ❑ 82 Rudi Johnson 3.00 1.25
- ❑ 83 Santana Moss 3.00 1.25
- ❑ 84 Shaun Alexander 4.00 1.50
- ❑ 85 Stephen Davis 3.00 1.25
- ❑ 86 Steve McNair 4.00 1.50
- ❑ 87 Steve Smith 4.00 1.50
- ❑ 88 T.J. Duckett 3.00 1.25
- ❑ 89 Terrell Owens 4.00 1.50
- ❑ 90 Thomas Jones 3.00 1.25
- ❑ 91 Tiki Barber 4.00 1.50
- ❑ 92 Tim Brown 4.00 1.50
- ❑ 93 Tom Brady 10.00 4.00
- ❑ 94 Tony Gonzalez 3.00 1.25
- ❑ 95 Torry Holt 4.00 1.50
- ❑ 96 Travis Henry 3.00 1.25
- ❑ 97 Trent Green 3.00 1.25
- ❑ 98 Warren Sapp 3.00 1.25
- ❑ 99 William Green 3.00 1.25
- ❑ 100 Willis McGahee 4.00 1.50
- ❑ 101 Barry Sanders 8.00 3.00
- ❑ 102 Bart Starr 10.00 4.00
- ❑ 103 Bo Jackson 8.00 3.00
- ❑ 104 Bob Griese 5.00 2.00
- ❑ 105 Bronko Nagurski 5.00 2.00
- ❑ 106 Dan Marino 12.00 5.00
- ❑ 107 Deion Sanders 8.00 3.00
- ❑ 108 Dick Butkus 8.00 3.00
- ❑ 109 Doak Walker 5.00 2.00
- ❑ 110 Don Maynard 4.00 1.50
- ❑ 111 Don Shula 5.00 2.00
- ❑ 112 Earl Campbell 5.00 2.00
- ❑ 113 Fran Tarkenton 6.00 2.50
- ❑ 114 Franco Harris 6.00 2.50
- ❑ 115 Fred Biletnikoff 5.00 2.00
- ❑ 116 Gale Sayers 6.00 2.50
- ❑ 117 Herman Edwards 4.00 1.50
- ❑ 118 Jim Brown 8.00 3.00
- ❑ 119 Jim Kelly 6.00 2.50
- ❑ 120 Jim Thorpe 5.00 2.00
- ❑ 121 Jimmy Johnson 4.00 1.50
- ❑ 122 Joe Greene 5.00 2.00
- ❑ 123 Joe Montana 15.00 6.00
- ❑ 124 Joe Namath 8.00 3.00
- ❑ 125 John Elway 8.00 3.00
- ❑ 126 John Riggins 6.00 2.50
- ❑ 127 Johnny Unitas 8.00 3.00
- ❑ 128 Larry Csonka 5.00 2.00
- ❑ 129 Lawrence Taylor 5.00 2.00
- ❑ 130 Marcus Allen 5.00 2.00
- ❑ 131 Mark Bavaro 3.00 1.25
- ❑ 132 Michael Irvin 5.00 2.00
- ❑ 133 Mike Ditka 5.00 2.00
- ❑ 134 Mike Singletary 5.00 2.00
- ❑ 135 Ozzie Newsome 4.00 1.50
- ❑ 136 Paul Warfield 4.00 1.50
- ❑ 137 Randall Cunningham 4.00 1.50
- ❑ 138 Ray Nitschke 5.00 2.00
- ❑ 139 Red Grange 6.00 2.50
- ❑ 140 Reggie White 5.00 2.00
- ❑ 141 Roger Staubach 8.00 3.00
- ❑ 142 Sterling Sharpe 4.00 1.50
- ❑ 143 Steve Largent 5.00 2.00
- ❑ 144 Terrell Davis 5.00 2.00
- ❑ 145 Terry Bradshaw 8.00 3.00
- ❑ 146 Thurman Thomas 4.00 1.50
- ❑ 147 Tony Dorsett 5.00 2.00
- ❑ 148 Troy Aikman 6.00 2.50
- ❑ 149 Walter Payton 15.00 6.00
- ❑ 150 Warren Moon 4.00 1.50
- ❑ 151 Ahmad Carroll RC 10.00 4.00
- ❑ 152 Andy Hall RC 8.00 3.00
- ❑ 153 Antwan Odom RC 10.00 4.00
- ❑ 154 B.J. Symons RC 10.00 4.00
- ❑ 155 Carlos Francis RC 8.00 3.00
- ❑ 156 Casey Bramlet RC 8.00 3.00
- ❑ 157 Chris Cooley RC 10.00 4.00
- ❑ 158 Chris Gamble RC 10.00 4.00
- ❑ 159 Clarence Moore RC 10.00 4.00
- ❑ 160 Cody Pickett RC 10.00 4.00
- ❑ 161 Courtney Watson RC 10.00 4.00
- ❑ 162 Craig Krenzel RC 10.00 4.00
- ❑ 163 D.J. Hackett RC 8.00 3.00
- ❑ 164 D.J. Williams RC 10.00 4.00
- ❑ 165 Derrick Strait RC 10.00 4.00
- ❑ 166 Dontarrious Thomas RC 10.00 4.00
- ❑ 167 Drew Henson RC 10.00 4.00
- ❑ 168 Ernest Wilford RC 10.00 4.00
- ❑ 169 Jamaar Taylor RC 10.00 4.00
- ❑ 170 Jason Babin RC 10.00 4.00
- ❑ 171 Jeff Smoker RC 10.00 4.00
- ❑ 172 Jerricho Cotchery RC 10.00 4.00
- ❑ 173 Jim Sorgi RC 10.00 4.00
- ❑ 174 Joey Thomas RC 10.00 4.00
- ❑ 175 John Navarre RC 10.00 4.00
- ❑ 176 Johnnie Morant RC 10.00 4.00
- ❑ 177 Jonathan Vilma RC 10.00 4.00
- ❑ 178 Josh Harris RC 10.00 4.00
- ❑ 179 Keiwan Ratliff RC 8.00 3.00
- ❑ 180 Kenechi Udeze RC 10.00 4.00
- ❑ 181 Kris Wilson RC 10.00 4.00
- ❑ 182 Marcus Tubbs RC 10.00 4.00
- ❑ 183 Marquise Hill RC 8.00 3.00
- ❑ 184 Matt Mauck RC 10.00 4.00
- ❑ 185 Maurice Mann RC 8.00 3.00
- ❑ 186 Michael Boulware RC 10.00 4.00
- ❑ 187 Michael Turner RC 12.00 5.00
- ❑ 188 P.K. Sam RC 8.00 3.00
- ❑ 189 Patrick Crayton RC 10.00 4.00
- ❑ 190 Ricardo Colclough RC 10.00 4.00
- ❑ 191 Richard Smith RC 8.00 3.00
- ❑ 192 Samie Parker RC 10.00 4.00
- ❑ 193 Sean Taylor RC 10.00 4.00
- ❑ 194 Teddy Lehman RC 10.00 4.00
- ❑ 195 Thomas Tapeh RC 8.00 3.00
- ❑ 196 Tommie Harris RC 10.00 4.00
- ❑ 197 Triandos Luke RC 10.00 4.00
- ❑ 198 Troy Fleming RC 8.00 3.00
- ❑ 199 Vince Wilfork RC 10.00 4.00
- ❑ 200 Will Smith RC 10.00 4.00
- ❑ 201 Larry Fitzgerald JSY AU RC 100.00 60.00
- ❑ 202 DeAngelo Hall JSY AU RC 40.00 15.00
- ❑ 203 Matt Schaub JSY AU RC 100.00 50.00
- ❑ 204 Michael Jenkins JSY AU RC 30.00 12.50
- ❑ 205 Devard Darling JSY AU RC 30.00 12.50
- ❑ 206 J.P. Losman JSY AU RC 60.00 30.00
- ❑ 207 Lee Evans JSY AU RC 40.00 20.00
- ❑ 208 Keary Colbert JSY AU RC 40.00 15.00
- ❑ 209 Bernard Berrian JSY AU RC 40.00 20.00
- ❑ 210 Chris Perry JSY AU RC 50.00 20.00
- ❑ 211 K.Winslow JSY AU RC 60.00 30.00
- ❑ 212 Luke McCown JSY AU RC 30.00 12.50
- ❑ 213 Julius Jones JSY AU RC 100.00 50.00
- ❑ 214 Darius Watts JSY AU RC 30.00 12.50
- ❑ 215 Tatum Bell JSY AU RC 60.00 25.00
- ❑ 216 Kevin Jones JSY AU RC 80.00 40.00
- ❑ 217 Roy Will.WR JSY AU RC 100.00 50.00
- ❑ 218 Dunta Robinson JSY AU RC 30.00 12.50
- ❑ 219 Greg Jones JSY AU RC 40.00 15.00
- ❑ 220 Reggie Williams JSY AU RC 40.00 20.00
- ❑ 221 Mewelde Moore JSY AU RC 30.00 12.50
- ❑ 222 Ben Watson JSY AU RC 40.00 20.00
- ❑ 223 Cedric Cobbs JSY AU RC 30.00 12.50
- ❑ 224 Devery Henderson JSY AU RC 25.00 10.00
- ❑ 225 Eli Manning JSY AU RC 200.00 100.00
- ❑ 226 Robert Gallery JSY AU RC 30.00 12.50
- ❑ 227 Roethlisberger JSY AU RC 250.00 125.00
- ❑ 228 Philip Rivers JSY AU RC 150.00 75.00
- ❑ 229 Derrick Hamilton JSY AU RC 25.00 10.00
- ❑ 230 Rashaun Woods JSY AU RC 30.00 12.50
- ❑ 231 Stev.Jackson JSY AU RC 100.00 50.00
- ❑ 232 Michael Clayton JSY AU RC 60.00 25.00
- ❑ 233 Ben Troupe JSY AU RC 30.00 12.50

2005 Leaf Limited

- ❑ 1-150 PRINT RUN 599 SER.#'d SETS
- ❑ 151-200 ROOKIE PRINT RUN 250 SER.#'d SETS
- ❑ 201-229 JSY AU PRINT RUN 100 SETS
- ❑ JSY AU EXCH EXPIRATION 6/1/2007
- ❑ UNPRICED PLATINUM SER.#'d TO 1
- ❑ 1 Anquan Boldin 3.00 1.25
- ❑ 2 Kurt Warner 3.00 1.25
- ❑ 3 Larry Fitzgerald 4.00 1.50
- ❑ 4 Alge Crumpler 3.00 1.25
- ❑ 5 Michael Vick 6.00 2.50
- ❑ 6 Warrick Dunn 3.00 1.25
- ❑ 7 Jamal Lewis 4.00 1.50
- ❑ 8 Kyle Boller 3.00 1.25
- ❑ 9 Ray Lewis 4.00 1.50
- ❑ 10 Derrick Mason 3.00 1.25
- ❑ 11 J.P. Losman 4.00 1.50
- ❑ 12 Lee Evans 3.00 1.25
- ❑ 13 Willis McGahee 4.00 1.50
- ❑ 14 DeShaun Foster 3.00 1.25
- ❑ 15 Jake Delhomme 4.00 1.50
- ❑ 16 Steve Smith 3.00 1.25
- ❑ 17 Brian Urlacher 4.00 1.50
- ❑ 18 Rex Grossman 3.00 1.25
- ❑ 19 Muhsin Muhammad 3.00 1.25
- ❑ 20 Carson Palmer 4.00 1.50
- ❑ 21 Chad Johnson 4.00 1.50
- ❑ 22 Rudi Johnson 3.00 1.25
- ❑ 23 Antonio Bryant 2.50 1.00
- ❑ 24 Lee Suggs 3.00 1.25
- ❑ 25 Trent Dilfer 3.00 1.25
- ❑ 26 Drew Bledsoe 4.00 1.50
- ❑ 27 Julius Jones 5.00 2.00
- ❑ 28 Keyshawn Johnson 3.00 1.25
- ❑ 29 Roy Williams S 3.00 1.25
- ❑ 30 Ashley Lelie 3.00 1.25
- ❑ 31 Jake Plummer 3.00 1.25
- ❑ 32 Tatum Bell 3.00 1.25
- ❑ 33 Rod Smith 3.00 1.25
- ❑ 34 Joey Harrington 4.00 1.50
- ❑ 35 Kevin Jones 4.00 1.50
- ❑ 36 Roy Williams WR 4.00 1.50
- ❑ 37 Ahman Green 4.00 1.50
- ❑ 38 Brett Favre 10.00 4.00
- ❑ 39 Javon Walker 3.00 1.25
- ❑ 40 Andre Johnson 3.00 1.25
- ❑ 41 David Carr 4.00 1.50
- ❑ 42 Domanick Davis 3.00 1.25
- ❑ 43 Edgerrin James 4.00 1.50
- ❑ 44 Marvin Harrison 4.00 1.50
- ❑ 45 Peyton Manning 6.00 2.50
- ❑ 46 Reggie Wayne 3.00 1.25
- ❑ 47 Byron Leftwich 4.00 1.50
- ❑ 48 Fred Taylor 3.00 1.25
- ❑ 49 Jimmy Smith 3.00 1.25
- ❑ 50 Priest Holmes 4.00 1.50
- ❑ 51 Tony Gonzalez 3.00 1.25
- ❑ 52 Trent Green 3.00 1.25
- ❑ 53 Chris Chambers 3.00 1.25
- ❑ 54 Ricky Williams 3.00 1.25
- ❑ 55 Daunte Culpepper 4.00 1.50
- ❑ 56 Nate Burleson 3.00 1.25
- ❑ 57 Michael Bennett 3.00 1.25
- ❑ 58 Corey Dillon 3.00 1.25
- ❑ 59 Deion Branch 3.00 1.25
- ❑ 60 Tom Brady 10.00 4.00
- ❑ 61 Aaron Brooks 3.00 1.25
- ❑ 62 Deuce McAllister 4.00 1.50
- ❑ 63 Joe Horn 3.00 1.25
- ❑ 64 Eli Manning 8.00 3.00
- ❑ 65 Jeremy Shockey 4.00 1.50
- ❑ 66 Plaxico Burress 3.00 1.25
- ❑ 67 Tiki Barber 4.00 1.50
- ❑ 68 Chad Pennington 4.00 1.50
- ❑ 69 Curtis Martin 4.00 1.50
- ❑ 70 Laveranues Coles 3.00 1.25
- ❑ 71 Kerry Collins 3.00 1.25
- ❑ 72 LaMont Jordan 4.00 1.50
- ❑ 73 Randy Moss 4.00 1.50
- ❑ 74 Brian Westbrook 3.00 1.25
- ❑ 75 Donovan McNabb 5.00 2.00
- ❑ 76 Terrell Owens 4.00 1.50
- ❑ 77 Ben Roethlisberger 10.00 4.00
- ❑ 78 Duce Staley 3.00 1.25
- ❑ 79 Hines Ward 4.00 1.50
- ❑ 80 Jerome Bettis 4.00 1.50
- ❑ 81 Antonio Gates 4.00 1.50
- ❑ 82 Drew Brees 4.00 1.50
- ❑ 83 LaDainian Tomlinson 5.00 2.00
- ❑ 84 Brandon Lloyd 2.50 1.00
- ❑ 85 Kevan Barlow 3.00 1.25

❑ 86 Darrell Jackson 3.00 1.25
❑ 87 Matt Hasselbeck 3.00 1.25
❑ 88 Shaun Alexander 5.00 2.00
❑ 89 Marc Bulger 4.00 1.50
❑ 90 Steven Jackson 5.00 2.00
❑ 91 Torry Holt 4.00 1.50
❑ 92 Brian Griese 3.00 1.25
❑ 93 Michael Clayton 4.00 1.50
❑ 94 Chris Brown 3.00 1.25
❑ 95 Drew Bennett 3.00 1.25
❑ 96 Steve McNair 4.00 1.50
❑ 97 Clinton Portis 4.00 1.50
❑ 98 LaVar Arrington 4.00 1.50
❑ 99 Patrick Ramsey 3.00 1.25
❑ 100 Santana Moss 3.00 1.25
❑ 101 Barry Sanders 8.00 3.00
❑ 102 Bart Starr 8.00 3.00
❑ 103 Bo Jackson 6.00 2.50
❑ 104 Brian Piccolo 6.00 2.50
❑ 105 Bob Griese 5.00 2.00
❑ 106 Dan Fouts 5.00 2.00
❑ 107 Dan Marino 10.00 4.00
❑ 108 Deacon Jones 4.00 1.50
❑ 109 Doak Walker 5.00 2.00
❑ 110 Don Maynard 4.00 1.50
❑ 111 Don Meredith 5.00 2.00
❑ 112 Don Shula 4.00 1.50
❑ 113 Earl Campbell 5.00 2.00
❑ 114 Eric Dickerson 4.00 1.50
❑ 115 Fran Tarkenton 6.00 2.50
❑ 116 Franco Harris 6.00 2.50
❑ 117 Gale Sayers 6.00 2.50
❑ 118 Jack Lambert 6.00 2.50
❑ 119 James Lofton 3.00 1.25
❑ 120 Jim Brown 8.00 3.00
❑ 121 Jim Kelly 6.00 2.50
❑ 122 Jim Thorpe 6.00 2.50
❑ 123 Joe Greene 5.00 2.00
❑ 124 Joe Montana 12.00 5.00
❑ 125 Joe Namath 6.00 2.50
❑ 126 John Elway 8.00 3.00
❑ 127 John Riggins 5.00 2.00
❑ 128 Johnny Unitas 8.00 3.00
❑ 129 Lawrence Taylor 5.00 2.00
❑ 130 Leroy Kelly 4.00 1.50
❑ 131 Marcus Allen 5.00 2.00
❑ 132 Michael Irvin 5.00 2.00
❑ 133 Mike Ditka 5.00 2.00
❑ 134 Mike Singletary 5.00 2.00
❑ 135 Ozzie Newsome 4.00 1.50
❑ 136 Paul Hornung 5.00 2.00
❑ 137 Paul Warfield 4.00 1.50
❑ 138 Randall Cunningham 4.00 1.50
❑ 139 Red Grange 6.00 2.50
❑ 140 Roger Staubach 8.00 3.00
❑ 141 Sammy Baugh 5.00 2.00
❑ 142 Sonny Jurgensen 4.00 1.50
❑ 143 Steve Largent 5.00 2.00
❑ 144 Steve Young 6.00 2.50
❑ 145 Terrell Davis 5.00 2.00
❑ 146 Terry Bradshaw 8.00 3.00
❑ 147 Tony Dorsett 4.00 1.50
❑ 148 Troy Aikman 6.00 2.50
❑ 149 Walter Payton 10.00 4.00
❑ 150 Warren Moon 5.00 2.00
❑ 151 Aaron Rodgers RC 25.00 10.00
❑ 152 Adrian McPherson RC 8.00 3.00
❑ 153 Airese Currie RC 8.00 3.00
❑ 154 Alvin Pearman RC 8.00 3.00
❑ 155 Anthony Davis RC 6.00 2.50
❑ 156 Brandon Jacobs RC 10.00 4.00
❑ 157 Brandon Jones RC 8.00 3.00
❑ 158 Cedric Benson RC 15.00 6.00
❑ 159 Cedric Houston RC 8.00 3.00
❑ 160 Chad Owens RC 8.00 3.00
❑ 161 Chris Henry RC 8.00 3.00
❑ 162 Nate Washington RC 6.00 2.50
❑ 163 Craig Bragg RC 6.00 2.50
❑ 164 Craphonso Thorpe RC 6.00 2.50
❑ 165 Damien Nash RC 6.00 2.50
❑ 166 Dan Orlovsky RC 10.00 4.00
❑ 167 Dante Ridgeway RC 6.00 2.50
❑ 168 Darren Sproles RC 8.00 3.00
❑ 169 David Greene RC 8.00 3.00
❑ 170 David Pollack RC 8.00 3.00
❑ 171 Deandra Cobb RC 6.00 2.50
❑ 172 DeMarcus Ware RC 12.00 5.00
❑ 173 Derek Anderson RC 8.00 3.00
❑ 174 Derrick Johnson RC 12.00 5.00
❑ 175 Erasmus James RC 8.00 3.00
❑ 176 Fabian Washington RC 8.00 3.00
❑ 177 Fred Gibson RC 6.00 2.50
❑ 178 Harry Williams RC 6.00 2.50
❑ 179 Heath Miller RC 20.00 7.50
❑ 180 J.R. Russell RC 6.00 2.50
❑ 181 James Kilian RC 8.00 3.00
❑ 182 Jerome Mathis RC 8.00 3.00
❑ 183 Larry Brackins RC 4.00 1.50
❑ 184 LeRon McCoy RC 6.00 2.50
❑ 185 Lionel Gates RC 6.00 2.50
❑ 186 Marcus Spears RC 8.00 3.00
❑ 187 Marion Barber RC 12.00 5.00
❑ 188 Marlin Jackson RC 8.00 3.00
❑ 189 Matt Cassel RC 12.00 5.00
❑ 190 Mike Williams 12.00 5.00
❑ 191 Noah Herron RC 8.00 3.00
❑ 192 Paris Warren RC 6.00 2.50
❑ 193 Rasheed Marshall RC 8.00 3.00
❑ 194 Roscoe Crosby RC 6.00 2.50
❑ 195 Roydell Williams RC 8.00 3.00
❑ 196 Ryan Fitzpatrick RC 12.00 5.00
❑ 197 Shawne Merriman RC 12.00 5.00
❑ 198 Tab Perry RC 8.00 3.00
❑ 199 Thomas Davis RC 8.00 3.00
❑ 200 Travis Johnson RC 6.00 2.50
❑ 201 Adam Jones JSY AU RC 30.00 12.50
❑ 202 Alex Smith QB JSY AU RC 100.00 50.00
❑ 203 Andrew Walter JSY AU RC 40.00 15.00
❑ 204 Antrel Rolle JSY AU RC 25.00 10.00
❑ 205 Braylon Edwards JSY AU RC 60.00 30.00
❑ 206 Cadillac Williams JSY AU RC 120.00 50.00
❑ 207 Carlos Rogers JSY AU RC 30.00 15.00
❑ 208 Charlie Frye JSY AU RC 60.00 30.00
❑ 209 Ciatrick Fason JSY AU RC 25.00 10.00
❑ 210 Courtney Roby JSY AU RC 25.00 10.00
❑ 211 Eric Shelton JSY AU RC 25.00 10.00
❑ 212 Frank Gore JSY AU RC 80.00 40.00
❑ 213 J.J. Arrington JSY AU RC 40.00 20.00
❑ 214 Kyle Orton JSY AU RC 40.00 20.00
❑ 215 Jason Campbell JSY AU RC 60.00 30.00
❑ 216 Mark Bradley JSY AU RC 30.00 12.50
❑ 217 Mark Clayton JSY AU RC 30.00 12.50
❑ 218 Matt Jones JSY AU RC 60.00 35.00
❑ 219 Maurice Clarett JSY AU 25.00 10.00
❑ 220 Reggie Brown JSY AU RC 40.00 15.00
❑ 221 Ronnie Brown JSY AU RC 100.00 50.00
❑ 222 Roddy White JSY AU RC 25.00 10.00
❑ 223 Ryan Moats JSY AU RC 30.00 15.00
❑ 224 Roscoe Parrish JSY AU RC 25.00 10.00
❑ 225 Stefan LeFors JSY AU RC 25.00 10.00
❑ 226 Terrence Murphy JSY AU RC 25.00 10.00
❑ 227 Troy Williamson JSY AU RC 50.00 25.00
❑ 228 Vernand Morency JSY AU RC 20.00 7.50
❑ 229 Vincent Jackson JSY AU RC 25.00 10.00

2006 Leaf Limited

❑ 1 Alex Smith QB 5.00 2.00
❑ 2 Antonio Bryant 2.50 1.00
❑ 3 Frank Gore 4.00 1.50
❑ 4 Rex Grossman 4.00 1.50
❑ 5 Thomas Jones 2.50 1.00
❑ 6 Cedric Benson 4.00 1.50
❑ 7 Carson Palmer 4.00 1.50
❑ 8 Chad Johnson 2.50 1.00
❑ 9 Rudi Johnson 2.50 1.00
❑ 10 T.J. Houshmandzadeh 2.50 1.00
❑ 11 J.P. Losman 2.50 1.00
❑ 12 Lee Evans 2.50 1.00
❑ 13 Willis McGahee 4.00 1.50
❑ 14 Jake Plummer 2.50 1.00
❑ 15 Javon Walker 2.50 1.00
❑ 16 Rod Smith 2.50 1.00
❑ 17 Tatum Bell 2.50 1.00
❑ 18 Braylon Edwards 4.00 1.50
❑ 19 Charlie Frye 2.50 1.00
❑ 20 Reuben Droughns 2.50 1.00
❑ 21 Cadillac Williams 4.00 1.50
❑ 22 Chris Simms 2.50 1.00
❑ 23 Joey Galloway 2.50 1.00
❑ 24 Anquan Boldin 2.50 1.00
❑ 25 Edgerrin James 4.00 1.50
❑ 26 Kurt Warner 2.50 1.00
❑ 27 Larry Fitzgerald 4.00 1.50
❑ 28 Antonio Gates 4.00 1.50
❑ 29 Keenan McCardell 2.00 .75
❑ 30 LaDainian Tomlinson 5.00 2.00
❑ 31 Philip Rivers 4.00 1.50
❑ 32 Eddie Kennison 2.00 .75
❑ 33 Larry Johnson 5.00 2.00
❑ 34 Priest Holmes 2.50 1.00
❑ 35 Trent Green 2.50 1.00
❑ 36 Tony Gonzalez 2.50 1.00
❑ 37 Dallas Clark 2.00 .75
❑ 38 Marvin Harrison 4.00 1.50
❑ 39 Peyton Manning 6.00 2.50
❑ 40 Reggie Wayne 2.50 1.00
❑ 41 Drew Bledsoe 4.00 1.50
❑ 42 Julius Jones 4.00 1.50
❑ 43 Roy Williams S 2.50 1.00
❑ 44 Terrell Owens 4.00 1.50
❑ 45 Terry Glenn 2.50 1.00
❑ 46 Chris Chambers 2.50 1.00
❑ 47 Daunte Culpepper 4.00 1.50
❑ 48 Marty Booker 2.00 .75
❑ 49 Ronnie Brown 4.00 1.50
❑ 50 Brian Westbrook 2.50 1.00
❑ 51 Donovan McNabb 4.00 1.50
❑ 52 Jevon Kearse 2.50 1.00
❑ 53 Reggie Brown 2.50 1.00
❑ 54 Alge Crumpler 2.50 1.00
❑ 55 Michael Vick 5.00 2.00
❑ 56 Warrick Dunn 2.50 1.00
❑ 57 Eli Manning 5.00 2.00
❑ 58 Jeremy Shockey 4.00 1.50
❑ 59 Plaxico Burress 2.50 1.00
❑ 60 Tiki Barber 4.00 1.50
❑ 61 Byron Leftwich 2.50 1.00
❑ 62 Fred Taylor 2.50 1.00
❑ 63 Jimmy Smith 2.50 1.00
❑ 64 Matt Jones 4.00 1.50
❑ 65 Josh McCown 2.50 1.00
❑ 66 Roy Williams WR 4.00 1.50
❑ 67 Kevin Jones 4.00 1.50
❑ 68 Aaron Rodgers 4.00 1.50
❑ 69 Brett Favre 8.00 3.00
❑ 70 Robert Ferguson 2.00 .75
❑ 71 Samkon Gado 4.00 1.50
❑ 72 Ahman Green 2.50 1.00
❑ 73 DeShaun Foster 2.50 1.00
❑ 74 Jake Delhomme 2.50 1.00
❑ 75 Keary Colbert 2.00 .75
❑ 76 Steve Smith 4.00 1.50
❑ 77 Corey Dillon 2.50 1.00
❑ 78 Deion Branch 2.50 1.00
❑ 79 Tedy Bruschi 4.00 1.50
❑ 80 Tom Brady 6.00 2.50
❑ 81 Jerry Porter 2.50 1.00
❑ 82 Randy Moss 4.00 1.50
❑ 83 LaMont Jordan 2.50 1.00
❑ 84 Isaac Bruce 2.50 1.00
❑ 85 Marc Bulger 2.50 1.00
❑ 86 Steven Jackson 4.00 1.50
❑ 87 Torry Holt 2.50 1.00
❑ 88 Derrick Mason 2.00 .75
❑ 89 Mark Clayton 2.50 1.00
❑ 90 Steve McNair 2.50 1.00
❑ 91 Jamal Lewis 2.50 1.00
❑ 92 Antwaan Randle El 2.50 1.00
❑ 93 Clinton Portis 4.00 1.50
❑ 94 Santana Moss 2.50 1.00
❑ 95 Chad Pennington 2.50 1.00
❑ 96 Laveranues Coles 2.50 1.00
❑ 97 Curtis Martin 4.00 1.50
❑ 98 Mewelde Moore 2.00 .75
❑ 99 Troy Williamson 2.50 1.00
❑ 100 Brad Johnson 2.50 1.00
❑ 101 Darrell Jackson 2.50 1.00
❑ 102 Matt Hasselbeck 2.50 1.00
❑ 103 Nate Burleson 2.50 1.00
❑ 104 Shaun Alexander 4.00 1.50

❑ 105 Ben Roethlisberger	6.00	2.50
❑ 106 Hines Ward	4.00	1.50
❑ 107 Willie Parker	5.00	2.00
❑ 108 Donte Stallworth	2.50	1.00
❑ 109 Drew Brees	4.00	1.50
❑ 110 Deuce McAllister	2.50	1.00
❑ 111 Andre Johnson	2.50	1.00
❑ 112 David Carr	2.50	1.00
❑ 113 Domanick Davis	2.50	1.00
❑ 114 Eric Moulds	2.50	1.00
❑ 115 David Givens	2.50	1.00
❑ 116 Drew Bennett	2.00	.75
❑ 117 Chris Brown	2.50	1.00
❑ 118 Bob Griese	5.00	2.00
❑ 119 Daryle Lamonica	3.00	1.25
❑ 120 Dave Casper	3.00	1.25
❑ 121 Don Meredith	5.00	2.00
❑ 122 Herschel Walker	4.00	1.50
❑ 123 Jack Lambert	5.00	2.00
❑ 124 Jackie Smith	3.00	1.25
❑ 125 Jim Otto	3.00	1.25
❑ 126 John Riggins	5.00	2.00
❑ 127 John Stallworth	4.00	1.50
❑ 128 Lawrence Taylor	5.00	2.00
❑ 129 Lester Hayes	3.00	1.25
❑ 130 L.C. Greenwood	4.00	1.50
❑ 131 Paul Warfield	4.00	1.50
❑ 132 Barry Sanders	8.00	3.00
❑ 133 Bart Starr	8.00	3.00
❑ 134 Billy Sims	4.00	1.50
❑ 135 Bulldog Turner	4.00	1.50
❑ 136 Deion Sanders	6.00	2.50
❑ 137 Dutch Clark	4.00	1.50
❑ 138 Forrest Gregg	3.00	1.25
❑ 139 Gale Sayers	6.00	2.50
❑ 140 Jim Brown	6.00	2.50
❑ 141 Jim Thorpe	6.00	2.50
❑ 142 Joe Montana	10.00	4.00
❑ 143 John Elway	8.00	3.00
❑ 144 Johnny Unitas	8.00	3.00
❑ 145 Lance Alworth	4.00	1.50
❑ 146 Raymond Berry	4.00	1.50
❑ 147 Doak Walker	5.00	2.00
❑ 148 Red Grange	6.00	2.50
❑ 149 Walter Payton	10.00	4.00
❑ 150 Yale Lary	3.00	1.25
❑ 151 Adam Jennings RC	6.00	2.50
❑ 152 Alan Zemaitis RC	8.00	3.00
❑ 153 Patrick Cobbs RC	6.00	2.50
❑ 154 Anthony Schlegel RC	6.00	2.50
❑ 155 Anthony Smith RC	10.00	4.00
❑ 156 Antonio Cromartie RC	8.00	3.00
❑ 157 Ashton Youboty RC	8.00	3.00
❑ 158 Bennie Brazell RC	6.00	2.50
❑ 159 Bernard Pollard RC	6.00	2.50
❑ 160 Brodrick Bunkley RC	8.00	3.00
❑ 161 Calvin Lowry RC	8.00	3.00
❑ 162 Cedric Griffin RC	6.00	2.50
❑ 163 Cedric Humes RC	8.00	3.00
❑ 164 Charles Davis RC	6.00	2.50
❑ 165 Chris Gocong RC	6.00	2.50
❑ 166 Claude Wroten RC	4.00	1.50
❑ 167 Clint Ingram RC	8.00	3.00
❑ 168 D.J. Shockley RC	8.00	3.00
❑ 169 Danieal Manning RC	8.00	3.00
❑ 170 Daniel Bullocks RC	8.00	3.00
❑ 171 Darnell Bing RC	8.00	3.00
❑ 172 Chris Hannon RC	6.00	2.50
❑ 173 Darryl Tapp RC	6.00	2.50
❑ 174 David Anderson RC	6.00	2.50
❑ 175 David Kirtman RC	6.00	2.50
❑ 176 David Pittman RC	6.00	2.50
❑ 177 Davin Joseph RC	6.00	2.50
❑ 178 Sam Hurd RC	12.00	5.00
❑ 179 Delanie Walker RC	6.00	2.50
❑ 180 DeMeco Ryans RC	10.00	4.00
❑ 181 Derrick Ross RC	6.00	2.50
❑ 182 Devin Hester RC	15.00	6.00
❑ 183 Domenik Hixon RC	6.00	2.50
❑ 184 Dominique Byrd RC	6.00	2.50
❑ 185 Donte Whitner RC	8.00	3.00
❑ 186 D'Qwell Jackson RC	6.00	2.50
❑ 187 Dusty Dvoracek RC	8.00	3.00
❑ 188 Eric Smith RC	6.00	2.50
❑ 189 Fred Evans RC	6.00	2.50
❑ 190 Ernie Sims RC	10.00	4.00
❑ 191 Ethan Kilmer RC	8.00	3.00
❑ 192 Freddie Keiaho RC	6.00	2.50
❑ 193 Frostee Rucker RC	6.00	2.50
❑ 194 Gabe Watson RC	6.00	2.50
❑ 195 Garrett Mills RC	8.00	3.00
❑ 196 Dawan Landry RC	8.00	3.00
❑ 197 Gerris Wilkinson RC	4.00	1.50
❑ 198 Jarrad Page RC	8.00	3.00
❑ 199 Haloti Ngata RC	8.00	3.00
❑ 200 Hank Baskett RC	8.00	3.00
❑ 201 Jai Lewis RC	6.00	2.50
❑ 202 Jamar Williams RC	6.00	2.50
❑ 203 James Anderson RC	4.00	1.50
❑ 204 Jason Allen RC	8.00	3.00
❑ 205 Jason Hatcher RC	6.00	2.50
❑ 206 Chris Barclay RC	6.00	2.50
❑ 207 J.D. Runnels RC	6.00	2.50
❑ 208 Jeff King RC	6.00	2.50
❑ 209 Jeffrey Webb RC	6.00	2.50
❑ 210 Jerome Harrison RC	8.00	3.00
❑ 211 Jimmy Williams RC	8.00	3.00
❑ 212 John David Washington RC	6.00	2.50
❑ 213 Jon Alston RC	8.00	3.00
❑ 214 Johnathan Joseph RC	6.00	2.50
❑ 215 Kamerion Wimbley RC	8.00	3.00
❑ 216 Kelly Jennings RC	8.00	3.00
❑ 217 Charles Sharon RC	6.00	2.50
❑ 218 Ko Simpson RC	6.00	2.50
❑ 219 Lawrence Vickers RC	6.00	2.50
❑ 220 Leon Williams RC	6.00	2.50
❑ 221 Leonard Pope RC	8.00	3.00
❑ 222 Marques Colston RC	25.00	10.00
❑ 223 Martin Nance RC	6.00	2.50
❑ 224 Mathias Kiwanuka RC	10.00	4.00
❑ 225 Mike Bell RC	12.00	5.00
❑ 226 Mike Hass RC	8.00	3.00
❑ 227 Miles Austin RC	6.00	2.50
❑ 228 Nate Salley RC	6.00	2.50
❑ 229 Nick Mangold RC	6.00	2.50
❑ 230 Owen Daniels RC	8.00	3.00
❑ 231 Shaun Bodiford RC	6.00	2.50
❑ 232 Quinn Sypniewski RC	6.00	2.50
❑ 233 Quinton Ganther RC	6.00	2.50
❑ 234 Richard Marshall RC	6.00	2.50
❑ 235 Rocky McIntosh RC	8.00	3.00
❑ 236 Roman Harper RC	6.00	2.50
❑ 237 Stephen Tulloch RC	6.00	2.50
❑ 238 Brett Basanez RC	8.00	3.00
❑ 239 Tamba Hali RC	8.00	3.00
❑ 240 Brett Elliott RC	8.00	3.00
❑ 241 Thomas Howard RC	8.00	3.00
❑ 242 Tim Jennings RC	6.00	2.50
❑ 243 Jason Carter RC	6.00	2.50
❑ 244 Todd Watkins RC	6.00	2.50
❑ 245 Tony Scheffler RC	8.00	3.00
❑ 246 Tye Hill RC	8.00	3.00
❑ 247 Victor Adeyanju RC	6.00	2.50
❑ 248 Wendell Mathis RC	6.00	2.50
❑ 249 Will Blackmon RC	6.00	2.50
❑ 250 Willie Reid RC	8.00	3.00
❑ 251 Mario Williams JSY AU RC	30.00	12.00
❑ 252 Reggie Bush JSY AU RC	250.00	150.00
❑ 253 Vince Young JSY AU RC	150.00	75.00
❑ 254 A.J. Hawk JSY AU RC	60.00	25.00
❑ 255 Vernon Davis JSY AU RC	50.00	20.00
❑ 256 Michael Huff JSY AU RC	30.00	12.50
❑ 257 Matt Leinart JSY AU RC	135.00	75.00
❑ 258 Jay Cutler AU RC	135.00	75.00
❑ 259 L.Maroney JSY AU RC	80.00	40.00
❑ 260 Santonio Holmes JSY AU RC	40.00	15.00
❑ 261 DeA.Williams JSY AU RC	80.00	40.00
❑ 262 Marcedes Lewis JSY AU RC	25.00	12.50
❑ 263 Joseph Addai AU RC	120.00	60.00
❑ 264 Chad Jackson JSY AU RC	40.00	20.00
❑ 265 Sinorice Moss JSY AU RC	30.00	15.00
❑ 266 LenDale White JSY AU RC	40.00	20.00
❑ 267 Kellen Clemens JSY AU RC	30.00	12.50
❑ 268 Greg Jennings AU RC	30.00	15.00
❑ 269 Joe Klopfenstein JSY AU RC	20.00	8.00
❑ 270 Maurice Drew JSY AU RC	80.00	50.00
❑ 271 Tarvaris Jackson JSY AU RC	60.00	30.00
❑ 272 Brian Calhoun JSY AU RC	25.00	12.50
❑ 273 Travis Wilson JSY AU RC	25.00	12.50
❑ 274 Jerious Norwood JSY AU RC	50.00	25.00
❑ 275 C.Whitehurst JSY AU RC	30.00	15.00
❑ 276 Derek Hagan JSY AU RC	25.00	12.50
❑ 277 Brandon Williams JSY AU RC	25.00	12.50
❑ 278 Brodie Croyle AU RC	40.00	20.00
❑ 279 Maurice Stovall JSY AU RC	25.00	12.50
❑ 280 Michael Robinson JSY AU RC	30.00	15.00
❑ 281 Jason Avant JSY AU RC	25.00	12.50
❑ 282 Dem.Williams JSY AU RC	25.00	12.50
❑ 283 Leon Washington JSY AU RC	40.00	15.00
❑ 284 Brandon Marshall JSY AU RC	30.00	15.00
❑ 285 Omar Jacobs JSY AU RC	25.00	12.50
❑ 286 Anthony Fasano AU RC	25.00	12.50
❑ 287 Ingle Martin AU RC	20.00	8.00
❑ 288 Reggie McNeal AU RC	15.00	6.00
❑ 289 Brad Smith AU RC	20.00	8.00
❑ 290 Jeremy Bloom AU RC	20.00	8.00
❑ 291 Bruce Gradkowski AU RC	30.00	15.00
❑ 292 P.J. Daniels AU RC	15.00	6.00
❑ 293 Cory Rodgers AU RC	15.00	6.00
❑ 294 Skyler Green AU RC	20.00	8.00
❑ 295 Bobby Carpenter AU RC	20.00	8.00
❑ 296 Arom/Obom/Mix AU/100	25.00	12.50
❑ 297 Hodge/Greenway AU/100	40.00	20.00
❑ 298 M.Will/McCar/Lwsn AU/100	50.00	20.00
❑ 299 Fasano/Stovall AU/50	40.00	20.00
❑ 300 Hawk/Carpenter AU/50	100.00	50.00
❑ 301 Leinart/Bush/Wht AU/25	400.00	250.00
❑ 302 Young/Thomas AU/50	100.00	60.00
❑ 303 Olson/Drew/Lewis AU/100	60.00	35.00
❑ 304 Hagans/Lundy/Ferg AU/100	40.00	20.00
❑ 305 Calhn/Willms/Orr AU/100	40.00	20.00

1998 Leaf Rookies and Stars

❑ COMPLETE SET (300)	250.00	125.00
❑ 1 Keyshawn Johnson	.60	.25
❑ 2 Marvin Harrison	.60	.25
❑ 3 Eddie Kennison	.40	.15
❑ 4 Bryant Young	.25	.08
❑ 5 Darren Woodson	.25	.08
❑ 6 Tyrone Wheatley	.40	.15
❑ 7 Michael Westbrook	.40	.15
❑ 8 Charles Way	.25	.08
❑ 9 Ricky Watters	.40	.15
❑ 10 Chris Warren	.40	.15
❑ 11 Wesley Walls	.40	.15
❑ 12 Tamarick Vanover	.25	.08
❑ 13 Zach Thomas	.60	.25
❑ 14 Derrick Thomas	.60	.25
❑ 15 Yancey Thigpen	.25	.08
❑ 16 Vinny Testaverde	.40	.15
❑ 17 Dana Stubblefield	.25	.08
❑ 18 J.J. Stokes	.40	.15
❑ 19 James Stewart	.40	.15
❑ 20 Jeff George	.40	.15
❑ 21 John Randle	.40	.15
❑ 22 Gary Brown	.25	.08
❑ 23 Ed McCaffrey	.40	.15
❑ 24 James Jett	.40	.15
❑ 25 Rob Johnson	.40	.15
❑ 26 Daryl Johnston	.40	.15
❑ 27 Jermaine Lewis	.40	.15
❑ 28 Tony Martin	.40	.15
❑ 29 Derrick Mayes	.40	.15
❑ 30 Keenan McCardell	.40	.15
❑ 31 O.J. McDuffie	.40	.15
❑ 32 Chris Chandler	.40	.15
❑ 33 Doug Flutie	.60	.25
❑ 34 Scott Mitchell	.40	.15
❑ 35 Warren Moon	.60	.25
❑ 36 Rob Moore	.40	.15
❑ 37 Johnnie Morton	.40	.15
❑ 38 Neil O'Donnell	.40	.15
❑ 39 Rich Gannon	.60	.25
❑ 40 Andre Reed	.40	.15
❑ 41 Jake Reed	.40	.15
❑ 42 Errict Rhett	.40	.15
❑ 43 Simeon Rice	.40	.15
❑ 44 Andre Rison	.40	.15

❑ 45	Eric Moulds	.60	.25
❑ 46	Frank Sanders	.40	.15
❑ 47	Darnay Scott	.40	.15
❑ 48	Junior Seau	.60	.25
❑ 49	Shannon Sharpe	.40	.15
❑ 50	Bruce Smith	.40	.15
❑ 51	Jimmy Smith	.40	.15
❑ 52	Robert Smith	.60	.25
❑ 53	Derrick Alexander	.40	.15
❑ 54	Kimble Anders	.40	.15
❑ 55	Jamal Anderson	.60	.25
❑ 56	Mario Bates	.40	.15
❑ 57	Edgar Bennett	.25	.08
❑ 58	Tim Biakabutuka	.40	.15
❑ 59	Ki-Jana Carter	.25	.08
❑ 60	Larry Centers	.25	.08
❑ 61	Mark Chmura	.40	.15
❑ 62	Wayne Chrebet	.60	.25
❑ 63	Ben Coates	.40	.15
❑ 64	Curtis Conway	.40	.15
❑ 65	Randall Cunningham	.60	.25
❑ 66	Rickey Dudley	.25	.08
❑ 67	Bert Emanuel	.40	.15
❑ 68	Bobby Engram	.40	.15
❑ 69	William Floyd	.25	.08
❑ 70	Irving Fryar	.40	.15
❑ 71	Elvis Grbac	.40	.15
❑ 72	Kevin Greene	.40	.15
❑ 73	Jim Harbaugh	.40	.15
❑ 74	Raymont Harris	.25	.08
❑ 75	Garrison Hearst	.60	.25
❑ 76	Greg Hill	.25	.08
❑ 77	Desmond Howard	.40	.15
❑ 78	Bobby Hoying	.40	.15
❑ 79	Michael Jackson	.25	.08
❑ 80	Terry Allen	.60	.25
❑ 81	Jerome Bettis	.60	.25
❑ 82	Jeff Blake	.40	.15
❑ 83	Robert Brooks	.40	.15
❑ 84	Tim Brown	.60	.25
❑ 85	Isaac Bruce	.60	.25
❑ 86	Cris Carter	.60	.25
❑ 87	Ty Detmer	.40	.15
❑ 88	Trent Dilfer	.60	.25
❑ 89	Marshall Faulk	.75	.30
❑ 90	Antonio Freeman	.60	.25
❑ 91	Gus Frerotte	.25	.08
❑ 92	Joey Galloway	.40	.15
❑ 93	Michael Irvin	.60	.25
❑ 94	Brad Johnson	.60	.25
❑ 95	Danny Kanell	.40	.15
❑ 96	Napoleon Kaufman	.60	.25
❑ 97	Dorsey Levens	.60	.25
❑ 98	Natrone Means	.40	.15
❑ 99	Herman Moore	.40	.15
❑ 100	Adrian Murrell	.40	.15
❑ 101	Carl Pickens	.40	.15
❑ 102	Rod Smith	.40	.15
❑ 103	Thurman Thomas	.60	.25
❑ 104	Reggie White	.60	.25
❑ 105	Jim Druckenmiller	.25	.08
❑ 106	Antowain Smith	.60	.25
❑ 107	Reidel Anthony	.40	.15
❑ 108	Ike Hilliard	.40	.15
❑ 109	Rae Carruth	.25	.08
❑ 110	Troy Davis	.25	.08
❑ 111	Terance Mathis	.40	.15
❑ 112	Brett Favre	2.50	1.00
❑ 113	Dan Marino	2.50	1.00
❑ 114	Emmitt Smith	2.00	.75
❑ 115	Barry Sanders	2.00	.75
❑ 116	Eddie George	.60	.25
❑ 117	Drew Bledsoe	1.00	.40
❑ 118	Troy Aikman	1.25	.50
❑ 119	Terrell Davis	.60	.25
❑ 120	John Elway	2.50	1.00
❑ 121	Mark Brunell	.60	.25
❑ 122	Jerry Rice	1.25	.50
❑ 123	Kordell Stewart	.60	.25
❑ 124	Steve McNair	.60	.25
❑ 125	Curtis Martin	.60	.25
❑ 126	Steve Young	.75	.30
❑ 127	Kerry Collins	.40	.15
❑ 128	Terry Glenn	.60	.25
❑ 129	Deion Sanders	.60	.25
❑ 130	Mike Alstott	.60	.25
❑ 131	Tony Banks	.40	.15
❑ 132	Karim Abdul-Jabbar	.60	.25
❑ 133	Terrell Owens	.60	.25
❑ 134	Yatil Green	.25	.08
❑ 135	Tony Gonzalez	.60	.25
❑ 136	Byron Hanspard	.25	.08
❑ 137	David LaFleur	.25	.08
❑ 138	Danny Wuerffel	.40	.15
❑ 139	Tiki Barber	.60	.25
❑ 140	Peter Boulware	.25	.08
❑ 141	Will Blackwell	.25	.08
❑ 142	Warrick Dunn	.60	.25
❑ 143	Corey Dillon	.60	.25
❑ 144	Jake Plummer	.60	.25
❑ 145	Neil Smith	.40	.15
❑ 146	Charles Johnson	.25	.08
❑ 147	Fred Lane	.25	.08
❑ 148	Dan Wilkinson	.25	.08
❑ 149	Ken Norton Jr.	.25	.08
❑ 150	Stephen Davis	.25	.08
❑ 151	Gilbert Brown	.25	.08
❑ 152	Kenny Bynum RC	.25	.08
❑ 153	Derrick Cullors	.25	.08
❑ 154	Charlie Garner	.40	.15
❑ 155	Jeff Graham	.25	.08
❑ 156	Warren Sapp	.40	.15
❑ 157	Jerald Moore	.25	.08
❑ 158	Sean Dawkins	.25	.08
❑ 159	Charlie Jones	.25	.08
❑ 160	Kevin Lockett	.25	.08
❑ 161	James McKnight	.60	.25
❑ 162	Chris Penn	.25	.08
❑ 163	Leslie Shepherd	.25	.08
❑ 164	Karl Williams	.25	.08
❑ 165	Mark Bruener	.25	.08
❑ 166	Ernie Conwell	.25	.08
❑ 167	Ken Dilger	.25	.08
❑ 168	Troy Drayton	.25	.08
❑ 169	Freddie Jones	.25	.08
❑ 170	Dale Carter	.25	.08
❑ 171	Charles Woodson RC	8.00	3.00
❑ 172	Alonzo Mayes RC	2.50	1.00
❑ 173	Andre Wadsworth RC	4.00	1.50
❑ 174	Grant Wistrom RC	4.00	1.50
❑ 175	Greg Ellis RC	2.50	1.00
❑ 176	Chris Howard RC	2.50	1.00
❑ 177	Keith Brooking RC	6.00	2.50
❑ 178	Takeo Spikes RC	6.00	2.50
❑ 179	Anthony Simmons RC	4.00	1.50
❑ 180	Brian Simmons RC	4.00	1.50
❑ 181	Sam Cowart RC	4.00	1.50
❑ 182	Ken Oxendine RC	2.50	1.00
❑ 183	Vonnie Holliday RC	4.00	1.50
❑ 184	Terry Fair RC	4.00	1.50
❑ 185	Shaun Williams RC	4.00	1.50
❑ 186	Tremayne Stephens RC	2.50	1.00
❑ 187	Duane Starks RC	2.50	1.00
❑ 188	Jason Peter RC	2.50	1.00
❑ 189	Tebucky Jones RC	2.50	1.00
❑ 190	Donovin Darius RC	4.00	1.50
❑ 191	R.W. McQuarters RC	4.00	1.50
❑ 192	Corey Chavous RC	6.00	2.50
❑ 193	Cameron Cleeland RC	2.50	1.00
❑ 194	Stephen Alexander RC	4.00	1.50
❑ 195	Rod Rutledge RC	2.50	1.00
❑ 196	Scott Frost RC	2.50	1.00
❑ 197	Fred Beasley RC	2.50	1.00
❑ 198	Dorian Boose RC	2.50	1.00
❑ 199	Randy Moss RC	25.00	12.50
❑ 200	Jacquez Green RC	4.00	1.50
❑ 201	Marcus Nash RC	2.50	1.00
❑ 202	Hines Ward RC	25.00	12.50
❑ 203	Kevin Dyson RC	6.00	2.50
❑ 204	E.G. Green RC	4.00	1.50
❑ 205	Germane Crowell RC	4.00	1.50
❑ 206	Joe Jurevicius RC	6.00	2.50
❑ 207	Tony Simmons RC	4.00	1.50
❑ 208	Tim Dwight RC	6.00	2.50
❑ 209	Az-Zahir Hakim RC	6.00	2.50
❑ 210	Jerome Pathon RC	6.00	2.50
❑ 211	Pat Johnson RC	4.00	1.50
❑ 212	Mikhael Ricks RC	4.00	1.50
❑ 213	Donald Hayes RC	4.00	1.50
❑ 214	Jammi German RC	2.50	1.00
❑ 215	Larry Shannon RC	2.50	1.00
❑ 216	Brian Alford RC	2.50	1.00
❑ 217	Curtis Enis RC	2.50	1.00
❑ 218	Fred Taylor RC	10.00	4.00
❑ 219	Robert Edwards RC	4.00	1.50
❑ 220	Ahman Green RC	25.00	12.50
❑ 221	Tavian Banks RC	4.00	1.50
❑ 222	Skip Hicks RC	4.00	1.50
❑ 223	Robert Holcombe RC	4.00	1.50
❑ 224	John Avery RC	4.00	1.50
❑ 225	Chris Fuamatu-Ma'afala RC	4.00	1.50
❑ 226	Michael Pittman RC	8.00	4.00
❑ 227	Rashaan Shehee RC	4.00	1.50
❑ 228	Jonathan Linton RC	4.00	1.50
❑ 229	Jon Ritchie RC	4.00	1.50
❑ 230	Chris Floyd RC	2.50	1.00
❑ 231	Wilmont Perry RC	2.50	1.00
❑ 232	Raymond Priester RC	2.50	1.00
❑ 233	Peyton Manning RC	50.00	25.00
❑ 234	Ryan Leaf RC	6.00	2.50
❑ 235	Brian Griese RC	12.00	5.00
❑ 236	Jeff Ogden RC	6.00	2.50
❑ 237	Charlie Batch RC	6.00	2.50
❑ 238	Moses Moreno RC	2.50	1.00
❑ 239	Jonathan Quinn RC	6.00	2.50
❑ 240	Flozell Adams RC	2.50	1.00
❑ 241	Brett Favre PT	12.00	5.00
❑ 242	Dan Marino PT	12.00	5.00
❑ 243	Emmitt Smith PT	10.00	4.00
❑ 244	Barry Sanders PT	10.00	4.00
❑ 245	Eddie George PT	2.50	1.00
❑ 246	Drew Bledsoe PT	5.00	2.00
❑ 247	Troy Aikman PT	6.00	2.50
❑ 248	Terrell Davis PT	2.50	1.00
❑ 249	John Elway PT	12.00	5.00
❑ 250	Carl Pickens PT	2.50	1.00
❑ 251	Jerry Rice PT	6.00	2.50
❑ 252	Kordell Stewart PT	2.50	1.00
❑ 253	Steve McNair PT	2.50	1.00
❑ 254	Curtis Martin PT	2.50	1.00
❑ 255	Steve Young PT	4.00	1.50
❑ 256	Herman Moore PT	2.50	1.00
❑ 257	Dorsey Levens PT	2.50	1.00
❑ 258	Deion Sanders PT	2.50	1.00
❑ 259	Napoleon Kaufman PT	2.50	1.00
❑ 260	Warrick Dunn PT	2.50	1.00
❑ 261	Corey Dillon PT	2.50	1.00
❑ 262	Jerome Bettis PT	2.50	1.00
❑ 263	Tim Brown PT	2.50	1.00
❑ 264	Cris Carter PT	2.50	1.00
❑ 265	Antonio Freeman PT	2.50	1.00
❑ 266	Randy Moss PT	15.00	6.00
❑ 267	Curtis Enis PT	2.50	1.00
❑ 268	Fred Taylor PT	4.00	1.50
❑ 269	Robert Edwards PT	2.50	1.00
❑ 270	Peyton Manning PT	25.00	10.00
❑ 271	Barry Sanders TL	1.00	.40
❑ 272	Eddie George TL	.40	.15
❑ 273	Troy Aikman TL	.60	.25
❑ 274	Mark Brunell TL	.60	.25
❑ 275	Kordell Stewart TL	.60	.25
❑ 276	Tim Biakabutuka TL	.25	.08
❑ 277	Terry Glenn TL	.25	.08
❑ 278	Mike Alstott TL	.25	.08
❑ 279	Tony Banks TL	.25	.08
❑ 280	Karim Abdul-Jabbar TL	.25	.08
❑ 281	Terrell Owens TL	.40	.15
❑ 282	Byron Hanspard TL	.25	.08
❑ 283	Jake Plummer TL	.40	.15
❑ 284	Terry Allen TL	.25	.08
❑ 285	Jeff Blake TL	.25	.08
❑ 286	Brad Johnson TL	.25	.08
❑ 287	Danny Kanell TL	.25	.08
❑ 288	Natrone Means TL	.25	.08
❑ 289	Rod Smith TL	.25	.08
❑ 290	Thurman Thomas TL	.25	.08
❑ 291	Reggie White TL	.25	.08
❑ 292	Troy Davis TL	.25	.08
❑ 293	Curtis Conway TL	.25	.08
❑ 294	Irving Fryar TL	.25	.08
❑ 295	Jim Harbaugh TL	.25	.08
❑ 296	Andre Rison TL	.25	.08
❑ 297	Ricky Watters TL	.25	.08
❑ 298	Keyshawn Johnson TL	.25	.08
❑ 299	Jeff George TL	.25	.08
❑ 300	Marshall Faulk TL	.60	.25

1999 Leaf Rookies and Stars

❑	COMPLETE SET (300)	150.00	75.00
❑	COMP.SET w/o SP's (200)	30.00	15.00
❑ 1	Frank Sanders	.40	.15
❑ 2	Adrian Murrell	.40	.15
❑ 3	Rob Moore	.40	.15
❑ 4	Simeon Rice	.40	.15
❑ 5	Michael Pittman	.25	.08
❑ 6	Jake Plummer	.40	.15

❑ 7 Chris Chandler	.40	.15
❑ 8 Tim Dwight	.40	.15
❑ 9 Chris Calloway	.25	.08
❑ 10 Terance Mathis	.40	.15
❑ 11 Jamal Anderson	.60	.25
❑ 12 Byron Hanspard	.25	.08
❑ 13 O.J. Santiago	.25	.08
❑ 14 Ken Oxendine	.25	.08
❑ 15 Priest Holmes	1.00	.40
❑ 16 Scott Mitchell	.25	.08
❑ 17 Tony Banks	.40	.15
❑ 18 Patrick Johnson	.25	.08
❑ 19 Rod Woodson	.40	.15
❑ 20 Jermaine Lewis	.40	.15
❑ 21 Errict Rhett	.40	.15
❑ 22 Stoney Case	.25	.08
❑ 23 Andre Reed	.40	.15
❑ 24 Eric Moulds	.40	.15
❑ 25 Rob Johnson	.40	.15
❑ 26 Doug Flutie	.60	.25
❑ 27 Bruce Smith	.40	.15
❑ 28 Jay Riemersma	.25	.08
❑ 29 Antowain Smith	.25	.08
❑ 30 Thurman Thomas	.40	.15
❑ 31 Jonathan Linton	.25	.08
❑ 32 Muhsin Muhammad	.40	.15
❑ 33 Rae Carruth	.25	.08
❑ 34 Wesley Walls	.40	.15
❑ 35 Fred Lane	.25	.08
❑ 36 Kevin Greene	.25	.08
❑ 37 Tim Biakabutuka	.40	.15
❑ 38 Curtis Enis	.25	.08
❑ 39 Shane Matthews	.40	.15
❑ 40 Bobby Engram	.40	.15
❑ 41 Curtis Conway	.40	.15
❑ 42 Marcus Robinson	1.25	.50
❑ 43 Darnay Scott	.25	.08
❑ 44 Carl Pickens	.40	.15
❑ 45 Corey Dillon	.60	.25
❑ 46 Jeff Blake	.40	.15
❑ 47 Terry Kirby	.25	.08
❑ 48 Ty Detmer	.40	.15
❑ 49 Leslie Shepherd	.25	.08
❑ 50 Karim Abdul-Jabbar	.40	.15
❑ 51 Emmitt Smith	1.25	.50
❑ 52 Deion Sanders	.60	.25
❑ 53 Michael Irvin	.40	.15
❑ 54 Rocket Ismail	.40	.15
❑ 55 David LaFleur	.25	.08
❑ 56 Troy Aikman	1.25	.50
❑ 57 Ed McCaffrey	.40	.15
❑ 58 Rod Smith	.40	.15
❑ 59 Shannon Sharpe	.40	.15
❑ 60 Brian Griese	.60	.25
❑ 61 John Elway	2.00	.75
❑ 62 Bubby Brister	.25	.08
❑ 63 Neil Smith	.40	.15
❑ 64 Terrell Davis	.60	.25
❑ 65 John Avery	.25	.08
❑ 66 Derek Loville	.25	.08
❑ 67 Ron Rivers	.25	.08
❑ 68 Herman Moore	.40	.15
❑ 69 Johnnie Morton	.40	.15
❑ 70 Charlie Batch	.60	.25
❑ 71 Barry Sanders	2.00	.75
❑ 72 Germane Crowell	.25	.08
❑ 73 Greg Hill	.25	.08
❑ 74 Gus Frerotte	.40	.15
❑ 75 Corey Bradford	.25	.08
❑ 76 Dorsey Levens	.60	.25
❑ 77 Antonio Freeman	.60	.25
❑ 78 Mark Chmura	.25	.08
❑ 79 Brett Favre	2.00	.75
❑ 80 Bill Schroeder	.40	.15
❑ 81 Matt Hasselbeck	.60	.25
❑ 82 E.G. Green	.25	.08
❑ 83 Ken Dilger	.25	.08
❑ 84 Jerome Pathon	.25	.08
❑ 85 Marvin Harrison	.60	.25
❑ 86 Peyton Manning	2.00	.75
❑ 87 Tavian Banks	.25	.08
❑ 88 Keenan McCardell	.40	.15
❑ 89 Mark Brunell	.60	.25
❑ 90 Fred Taylor	.60	.25
❑ 91 Jimmy Smith	.40	.15
❑ 92 James Stewart	.40	.15
❑ 93 Kyle Brady	.25	.08
❑ 94 Derrick Thomas	.60	.25
❑ 95 Rashaan Shehee	.25	.08
❑ 96 Derrick Alexander WR	.40	.15
❑ 97 Byron Bam Morris	.25	.08
❑ 98 Andre Rison	.40	.15
❑ 99 Elvis Grbac	.40	.15
❑ 100 Tony Gonzalez	.60	.25
❑ 101 Donnell Bennett	.25	.08
❑ 102 Warren Moon	.60	.25
❑ 103 Zach Thomas	.60	.25
❑ 104 Oronde Gadsden	.40	.15
❑ 105 Dan Marino	2.00	.75
❑ 106 O.J. McDuffie	.40	.15
❑ 107 Tony Martin	.40	.15
❑ 108 Randy Moss	1.50	.60
❑ 109 Cris Carter	.60	.25
❑ 110 Robert Smith	.60	.25
❑ 111 Randall Cunningham	.60	.25
❑ 112 Jake Reed	.40	.15
❑ 113 John Randle	.40	.15
❑ 114 Leroy Hoard	.25	.08
❑ 115 Jeff George	.40	.15
❑ 116 Ty Law	.40	.15
❑ 117 Shawn Jefferson	.25	.08
❑ 118 Troy Brown	.40	.15
❑ 119 Robert Edwards	.25	.08
❑ 120 Tony Simmons	.25	.08
❑ 121 Terry Glenn	.60	.25
❑ 122 Ben Coates	.40	.15
❑ 123 Drew Bledsoe	.75	.30
❑ 124 Terry Allen	.40	.15
❑ 125 Cameron Cleeland	.25	.08
❑ 126 Eddie Kennison	.40	.15
❑ 127 Amani Toomer	.25	.08
❑ 128 Kerry Collins	.40	.15
❑ 129 Joe Jurevicius	.40	.15
❑ 130 Tiki Barber	.60	.25
❑ 131 Ike Hilliard	.25	.08
❑ 132 Michael Strahan	.40	.15
❑ 133 Gary Brown	.25	.08
❑ 134 Jason Sehorn	.25	.08
❑ 135 Curtis Martin	.60	.25
❑ 136 Vinny Testaverde	.40	.15
❑ 137 Dedric Ward	.25	.08
❑ 138 Keyshawn Johnson	.60	.25
❑ 139 Wayne Chrebet	.40	.15
❑ 140 Tyrone Wheatley	.40	.15
❑ 141 Napoleon Kaufman	.60	.25
❑ 142 Tim Brown	.60	.25
❑ 143 Rickey Dudley	.25	.08
❑ 144 Jon Ritchie	.25	.08
❑ 145 James Jett	.25	.08
❑ 146 Rich Gannon	.60	.25
❑ 147 Charles Woodson	.60	.25
❑ 148 Charles Johnson	.25	.08
❑ 149 Duce Staley	.60	.25
❑ 150 Will Blackwell	.25	.08
❑ 151 Kordell Stewart	.40	.15
❑ 152 Jerome Bettis	.60	.25
❑ 153 Hines Ward	.60	.25
❑ 154 Richard Huntley	.40	.15
❑ 155 Natrone Means	.40	.15
❑ 156 Mikhael Ricks	.25	.08
❑ 157 Junior Seau	.60	.25
❑ 158 Jim Harbaugh	.40	.15
❑ 159 Ryan Leaf	.60	.25
❑ 160 Erik Kramer	.25	.08
❑ 161 Terrell Owens	.60	.25
❑ 162 J.J. Stokes	.40	.15
❑ 163 Lawrence Phillips	.40	.15
❑ 164 Charlie Garner	.40	.15
❑ 165 Jerry Rice	1.25	.50
❑ 166 Garrison Hearst	.40	.15
❑ 167 Steve Young	.75	.30
❑ 168 Derrick Mayes	.40	.15
❑ 169 Ahman Green	.60	.25
❑ 170 Joey Galloway	.40	.15
❑ 171 Ricky Watters	.40	.15
❑ 172 Jon Kitna	.60	.25
❑ 173 Sean Dawkins	.25	.08
❑ 174 Az-Zahir Hakim	.25	.08
❑ 175 Robert Holcombe	.25	.08
❑ 176 Isaac Bruce	.60	.25
❑ 177 Amp Lee	.25	.08
❑ 178 Marshall Faulk	.75	.30
❑ 179 Trent Green	.60	.25
❑ 180 Eric Zeier	.40	.15
❑ 181 Bert Emanuel	.40	.15
❑ 182 Jacquez Green	.25	.08
❑ 183 Reidel Anthony	.40	.15
❑ 184 Warren Sapp	.25	.08
❑ 185 Mike Alstott	.60	.25
❑ 186 Warrick Dunn	.60	.25
❑ 187 Trent Dilfer	.60	.25
❑ 188 Neil O'Donnell	.40	.15
❑ 189 Eddie George	.60	.25
❑ 190 Yancey Thigpen	.25	.08
❑ 191 Steve McNair	.60	.25
❑ 192 Kevin Dyson	.40	.15
❑ 193 Frank Wycheck	.25	.08
❑ 194 Stephen Davis	.60	.25
❑ 195 Stephen Alexander	.25	.08
❑ 196 Darrell Green	.25	.08
❑ 197 Skip Hicks	.25	.08
❑ 198 Brad Johnson	.60	.25
❑ 199 Michael Westbrook	.40	.15
❑ 200 Albert Connell	.25	.08
❑ 201 David Boston RC	3.00	1.50
❑ 202 Joel Makovicka RC	3.00	1.50
❑ 203 Chris Greisen RC	2.50	1.25
❑ 204 Jeff Paulk RC	1.50	.75
❑ 205 Reginald Kelly RC	2.50	1.25
❑ 206 Chris McAlister RC	2.50	1.25
❑ 207 Brandon Stokley RC	4.00	1.50
❑ 208 Antoine Winfield RC	2.50	1.25
❑ 209 Bobby Collins RC	1.50	.75
❑ 210 Peerless Price RC	3.00	1.50
❑ 211 Shawn Bryson RC	3.00	1.50
❑ 212 Sheldon Jackson RC	2.50	1.25
❑ 213 Kamil Loud RC	1.50	.75
❑ 214 D'Wayne Bates RC	2.50	1.25
❑ 215 Jerry Azumah RC	2.50	1.25
❑ 216 Marty Booker RC	3.00	1.50
❑ 217 Cade McNown RC	2.50	1.25
❑ 218 James Allen RC	3.00	1.50
❑ 219 Nick Williams RC	2.50	1.25
❑ 220 Akili Smith RC	2.50	1.25
❑ 221 Craig Yeast RC	2.50	1.25
❑ 222 Damon Griffen RC	2.50	1.25
❑ 223 Scott Covington RC	3.00	1.50
❑ 224 Michael Basnight RC	1.50	.75
❑ 225 Ronnie Powell RC	1.50	.75
❑ 226 Rahim Abdullah RC	2.50	1.25
❑ 227 Tim Couch RC	3.00	1.50
❑ 228 Kevin Johnson RC	3.00	1.50
❑ 229 Darrin Chiaverini RC	2.50	1.25
❑ 230 Mark Campbell RC	2.50	1.25
❑ 231 Mike Lucky RC	2.50	1.25
❑ 232 Robert Thomas RC	2.50	1.25
❑ 233 Ebenezer Ekuban RC	2.50	1.25
❑ 234 Dat Nguyen RC	3.00	1.50
❑ 235 Wane McGarity RC	1.50	.75
❑ 236 Jason Tucker RC	2.50	1.25
❑ 237 Olandis Gary RC	3.00	1.50
❑ 238 Al Wilson RC	3.00	1.50
❑ 239 Travis McGriff RC	1.50	.75
❑ 240 Desmond Clark RC	3.00	1.50
❑ 241 Andre Cooper RC	1.50	.75
❑ 242 Chris Watson RC	1.50	.75
❑ 243 Sedrick Irvin RC	1.50	.75
❑ 244 Chris Claiborne RC	1.50	.75
❑ 245 Cory Sauter RC	1.50	.75
❑ 246 Brock Olivo RC	1.50	.75
❑ 247 De'Mond Parker RC	1.50	.75
❑ 248 Aaron Brooks RC	10.00	4.00
❑ 249 Antuan Edwards RC	2.50	1.25
❑ 250 Basil Mitchell RC	1.50	.75
❑ 251 Terrence Wilkins RC	2.50	1.25
❑ 252 Edgerrin James RC	15.00	6.00
❑ 253 Fernando Bryant RC	2.50	1.25
❑ 254 Mike Cloud RC	2.50	1.25
❑ 255 Larry Parker RC	3.00	1.50
❑ 256 Rob Konrad RC	3.00	1.50

❑ 257 Cecil Collins RC 1.50 .75
❑ 258 James Johnson RC 2.50 1.25
❑ 259 Jim Kleinsasser RC 3.00 1.50
❑ 260 Daunte Culpepper RC 15.00 6.00
❑ 261 Michael Bishop RC 3.00 1.50
❑ 262 Andy Katzenmoyer RC 2.50 1.25
❑ 263 Kevin Faulk RC 3.00 1.50
❑ 264 Brett Bech RC 1.50 .75
❑ 265 Ricky Williams RC 8.00 3.00
❑ 266 Sean Bennett RC 1.50 .75
❑ 267 Joe Montgomery RC 2.50 1.25
❑ 268 Dan Campbell RC 1.50 .75
❑ 269 Ray Lucas RC 3.00 1.50
❑ 270 Scott Dreisbach RC 2.50 1.25
❑ 271 Jed Weaver RC 1.50 .75
❑ 272 Dameane Douglas RC 2.50 1.25
❑ 273 Cecil Martin RC 2.50 1.25
❑ 274 Donovan McNabb RC 20.00 7.50
❑ 275 Na Brown RC 2.50 1.25
❑ 276 Jerame Tuman RC 3.00 1.50
❑ 277 Amos Zereoue RC 3.00 1.50
❑ 278 Troy Edwards RC 2.50 1.25
❑ 279 Jermaine Fazande RC 2.50 1.25
❑ 280 Steve Heiden RC 3.00 1.50
❑ 281 Jeff Garcia RC 20.00 7.50
❑ 282 Terry Jackson RC 2.50 1.25
❑ 283 Charlie Rogers RC 2.50 1.25
❑ 284 Brock Huard RC 3.00 1.50
❑ 285 Karsten Bailey RC 2.50 1.25
❑ 286 Lamar King RC 1.50 .75
❑ 287 Justin Watson RC 1.50 .75
❑ 288 Kurt Warner RC 20.00 7.50
❑ 289 Torry Holt RC 12.00 5.00
❑ 290 Joe Germaine RC 2.50 1.25
❑ 291 Dre' Bly RC 3.00 1.50
❑ 292 Martin Gramatica RC 1.50 .75
❑ 293 Rabih Abdullah RC 2.50 1.25
❑ 294 Shaun King RC 2.50 1.25
❑ 295 Anthony McFarland RC 2.50 1.25
❑ 296 Darnell McDonald RC 2.50 1.25
❑ 297 Kevin Daft RC 2.50 1.25
❑ 298 Jevon Kearse RC 8.00 3.00
❑ 299 Mike Sellers .25 .08
❑ 300 Champ Bailey RC 6.00 2.50

2000 Leaf Rookies and Stars

❑ COMP.SET w/o SP's (100) 15.00 6.00
❑ 1 Jake Plummer .40 .15
❑ 2 David Boston .60 .25
❑ 3 Tim Dwight .60 .25
❑ 4 Jamal Anderson .60 .25
❑ 5 Chris Chandler .40 .15
❑ 6 Tony Banks .40 .15
❑ 7 Qadry Ismail .40 .15
❑ 8 Eric Moulds .60 .25
❑ 9 Doug Flutie .60 .25
❑ 10 Lamar Smith .40 .15
❑ 11 Peerless Price .40 .15
❑ 12 Rob Johnson .40 .15
❑ 13 Reggie White .60 .25
❑ 14 Muhsin Muhammad .40 .15
❑ 15 Steve Beuerlein .40 .15
❑ 16 Cade McNown .25 .08
❑ 17 Derrick Alexander .40 .15
❑ 18 Marcus Robinson .60 .25
❑ 19 Corey Dillon .60 .25
❑ 20 Akili Smith .25 .08
❑ 21 Tim Couch .40 .15
❑ 22 Kevin Johnson .60 .25
❑ 23 Emmitt Smith 1.25 .50
❑ 24 Troy Aikman 1.25 .50
❑ 25 Joey Galloway .40 .15
❑ 26 Rocket Ismail .40 .15
❑ 27 John Elway 2.00 .75
❑ 28 Terrell Davis .60 .25
❑ 29 Brian Griese .60 .25
❑ 30 Olandis Gary .60 .25
❑ 31 Ed McCaffrey .60 .25
❑ 32 Rod Smith .40 .15
❑ 33 Barry Sanders 1.50 .60
❑ 34 Charlie Batch .60 .25
❑ 35 Germane Crowell .25 .08
❑ 36 James Stewart .40 .15
❑ 37 Brett Favre 2.00 .75
❑ 38 Dorsey Levens .40 .15
❑ 39 Antonio Freeman .60 .25
❑ 40 Peyton Manning 1.50 .60
❑ 41 Edgerrin James 1.00 .40
❑ 42 Marvin Harrison .60 .25
❑ 43 Fred Taylor .60 .25
❑ 44 Mark Brunell .60 .25
❑ 45 Jimmy Smith .40 .15
❑ 46 Elvis Grbac .40 .15
❑ 47 Tony Gonzalez .40 .15
❑ 48 Dan Marino 2.00 .75
❑ 49 Joe Horn .40 .15
❑ 50 Jay Fiedler .60 .25
❑ 51 James Allen .40 .15
❑ 52 Randy Moss 1.25 .50
❑ 53 Daunte Culpepper .75 .30
❑ 54 Cris Carter .60 .25
❑ 55 Robert Smith .60 .25
❑ 56 Drew Bledsoe .75 .30
❑ 57 Terry Glenn .60 .25
❑ 58 Ricky Williams .60 .25
❑ 59 Amani Toomer .40 .15
❑ 60 Kerry Collins .40 .15
❑ 61 Curtis Martin .60 .25
❑ 62 Vinny Testaverde .40 .15
❑ 63 Wayne Chrebet .40 .15
❑ 64 Tim Brown .60 .25
❑ 65 Tyrone Wheatley .40 .15
❑ 66 Rich Gannon .60 .25
❑ 67 Donovan McNabb 1.00 .40
❑ 68 Duce Staley .60 .25
❑ 69 Jerome Bettis .60 .25
❑ 70 Donald Hayes .25 .08
❑ 71 Junior Seau .60 .25
❑ 72 Jermaine Fazande .25 .08
❑ 73 Jerry Rice 1.25 .50
❑ 74 Steve Young .75 .30
❑ 75 Terrell Owens .60 .25
❑ 76 Charlie Garner .40 .15
❑ 77 Jeff Garcia .60 .25
❑ 78 Tim Biakabutuka .40 .15
❑ 79 Tiki Barber .60 .25
❑ 80 Ricky Watters .40 .15
❑ 81 Kurt Warner 1.25 .50
❑ 82 Marshall Faulk .75 .30
❑ 83 Isaac Bruce .60 .25
❑ 84 Torry Holt .60 .25
❑ 85 Mike Alstott .60 .25
❑ 86 Warrick Dunn .60 .25
❑ 87 Shaun King .25 .08
❑ 88 Keyshawn Johnson .60 .25
❑ 89 Warren Sapp .40 .15
❑ 90 Eddie George .60 .25
❑ 91 Jevon Kearse .60 .25
❑ 92 Steve McNair .60 .25
❑ 93 Carl Pickens .40 .15
❑ 94 Deion Sanders .60 .25
❑ 95 Stephen Davis .60 .25
❑ 96 Brad Johnson .60 .25
❑ 97 Bruce Smith .40 .15
❑ 98 Michael Westbrook .40 .15
❑ 99 Albert Connell .25 .08
❑ 100 Jeff George .40 .15
❑ 101 Thomas Jones RC 15.00 6.00
❑ 102 Bashir Yamini RC 5.00 2.00
❑ 103 Jamal Lewis RC 25.00 10.00
❑ 104 Travis Taylor RC 10.00 4.00
❑ 105 Chris Redman RC 8.00 3.00
❑ 106 Avion Black RC 8.00 3.00
❑ 107 Sammy Morris RC 8.00 3.00
❑ 108 Dez White RC 10.00 4.00
❑ 109 Peter Warrick RC 10.00 4.00
❑ 110 Ron Dugans RC 5.00 2.00
❑ 111 Curtis Keaton RC 8.00 3.00
❑ 112 Danny Farmer RC 8.00 3.00
❑ 113 Courtney Brown RC 10.00 4.00
❑ 114 Dennis Northcutt RC 10.00 4.00
❑ 115 Travis Prentice RC 8.00 3.00
❑ 116 JaJuan Dawson RC 5.00 2.00
❑ 117 Spergon Wynn RC 8.00 3.00
❑ 118 Michael Wiley RC 8.00 3.00
❑ 119 Chris Cole RC 8.00 3.00
❑ 120 Mike Anderson RC 12.00 5.00
❑ 121 Muneer Moore RC 5.00 2.00
❑ 122 Reuben Droughns RC 12.00 5.00
❑ 123 Bubba Franks RC 10.00 4.00
❑ 124 Anthony Lucas RC 5.00 2.00
❑ 125 Charles Lee RC 5.00 2.00
❑ 126 R.Jay Soward RC 8.00 3.00
❑ 127 Shyrone Stith RC 8.00 3.00
❑ 128 Sylvester Morris RC 8.00 3.00
❑ 129 Frank Moreau RC 8.00 3.00
❑ 130 Dante Hall RC 20.00 7.50
❑ 131 Doug Chapman RC 8.00 3.00
❑ 132 Troy Walters RC 10.00 4.00
❑ 133 J.R. Redmond RC 8.00 3.00
❑ 134 Tom Brady RC 120.00 60.00
❑ 135 Terrelle Smith RC 8.00 3.00
❑ 136 Chad Morton RC 10.00 4.00
❑ 137 Ron Dayne RC 10.00 4.00
❑ 138 Ron Dixon RC 8.00 3.00
❑ 139 Chad Pennington RC 25.00 10.00
❑ 140 Anthony Becht RC 10.00 4.00
❑ 141 Laveranues Coles RC 12.00 5.00
❑ 142 Windrell Hayes RC 8.00 3.00
❑ 143 Sebastian Janikowski RC 10.00 4.00
❑ 144 Jerry Porter RC 12.00 5.00
❑ 145 Corey Simon RC 10.00 4.00
❑ 146 Todd Pinkston RC 10.00 4.00
❑ 147 Gari Scott RC 5.00 2.00
❑ 148 Plaxico Burress RC 20.00 7.50
❑ 149 Tee Martin RC 10.00 4.00
❑ 150 Trevor Gaylor RC 8.00 3.00
❑ 151 Ronney Jenkins RC 8.00 3.00
❑ 152 Giovanni Carmazzi RC 5.00 2.00
❑ 153 Tim Rattay RC 10.00 4.00
❑ 154 Shaun Alexander RC 40.00 20.00
❑ 155 Darrell Jackson RC 15.00 6.00
❑ 156 James Williams RC 8.00 3.00
❑ 157 Trung Canidate RC 8.00 3.00
❑ 158 Joe Hamilton RC 8.00 3.00
❑ 159 Erron Kinney RC 10.00 4.00
❑ 160 Todd Husak RC 10.00 4.00
❑ 161 Raynoch Thompson RC 8.00 3.00
❑ 162 Darwin Walker RC 5.00 2.00
❑ 163 Jay Tant RC 5.00 2.00
❑ 164 Doug Johnson RC 10.00 4.00
❑ 165 Robert Bean RC 8.00 3.00
❑ 166 Mark Simoneau RC 8.00 3.00
❑ 167 John Jones RC 8.00 3.00
❑ 168 Obafemi Ayanbadejo RC 8.00 3.00
❑ 169 Mike Brown RC 15.00 6.00
❑ 170 Shockmain Davis RC 5.00 2.00
❑ 171 Erik Flowers RC 8.00 3.00
❑ 172 Corey Moore RC 5.00 2.00
❑ 173 Drew Haddad RC 5.00 2.00
❑ 174 Kwame Cavil RC 5.00 2.00
❑ 175 Pat Dennis RC 5.00 2.00
❑ 176 Rashard Anderson RC 8.00 3.00
❑ 177 Brian Finneran RC 10.00 4.00
❑ 178 Na'il Diggs RC 8.00 3.00
❑ 179 Marc Bulger RC 20.00 7.50
❑ 180 Mondriel Fulcher RC 5.00 2.00
❑ 181 Dwayne Carswell 5.00 2.00
❑ 182 Brian Urlacher RC 25.00 10.00
❑ 183 Paul Edinger RC 10.00 4.00
❑ 184 Karon Coleman RC 8.00 3.00
❑ 185 Aaron Shea RC 8.00 3.00
❑ 186 Fabien Bownes RC 5.00 2.00
❑ 187 Damon Hodge RC 8.00 3.00
❑ 188 Dwayne Goodrich RC 5.00 2.00
❑ 189 Clint Stoerner RC 8.00 3.00
❑ 190 James Whalen RC 5.00 2.00
❑ 191 Deltha O'Neal RC 10.00 4.00
❑ 192 Ian Gold RC 8.00 3.00
❑ 193 Kenoy Kennedy RC 5.00 2.00
❑ 194 Jarious Jackson RC 8.00 3.00
❑ 195 Leroy Fields RC 5.00 2.00
❑ 196 Barrett Green RC 5.00 2.00
❑ 197 Joey Jamison RC 5.00 2.00
❑ 198 Rondell Mealey RC 5.00 2.00
❑ 199 Rob Morris RC 8.00 3.00
❑ 200 Marcus Washington RC 8.00 3.00
❑ 201 Trevor Insley RC 5.00 2.00

❑ 202 Jamel White RC 8.00 3.00
❑ 203 Kevin McDougal RC 8.00 3.00
❑ 204 Ibn Green RC 5.00 2.00
❑ 205 T.J. Slaughter RC 5.00 2.00
❑ 206 Emanuel Smith RC 5.00 2.00
❑ 207 Herbert Goodman RC 8.00 3.00
❑ 208 William Bartee RC 8.00 3.00
❑ 209 Orantes Grant RC 5.00 2.00
❑ 210 Brad Hoover RC 8.00 3.00
❑ 211 Deon Dyer RC 8.00 3.00
❑ 212 Jonas Lewis RC 5.00 2.00
❑ 213 Chris Hovan RC 8.00 3.00
❑ 214 Fred Robbins RC 5.00 2.00
❑ 215 Michael Boireau RC 5.00 2.00
❑ 216 Giles Cole RC 5.00 2.00
❑ 217 Dave Stachelski RC 5.00 2.00
❑ 218 Patrick Pass RC 8.00 3.00
❑ 219 Darren Howard RC 8.00 3.00
❑ 220 Austin Wheatley RC 5.00 2.00
❑ 221 Kevin Houser RC 8.00 3.00
❑ 222 Rian Lindell RC 5.00 2.00
❑ 223 Jake Delhomme RC 50.00 25.00
❑ 224 Cornelius Griffin RC 8.00 3.00
❑ 225 Shaun Ellis RC 10.00 4.00
❑ 226 John Abraham RC 10.00 4.00
❑ 227 Travares Tillman RC 5.00 2.00
❑ 228 Julian Peterson RC 10.00 4.00
❑ 229 Marcus Knight RC 8.00 3.00
❑ 230 Thomas Hamner RC 5.00 2.00
❑ 231 Hank Poteat RC 8.00 3.00
❑ 232 Neil Rackers RC 10.00 4.00
❑ 233 Bobby Shaw RC 8.00 3.00
❑ 234 Rogers Beckett RC 8.00 3.00
❑ 235 Reggie Jones RC 5.00 2.00
❑ 236 Tim Seder RC 8.00 3.00
❑ 237 Durell Price RC 5.00 2.00
❑ 238 Ahmed Plummer RC 10.00 4.00
❑ 239 John Engelberger RC 8.00 3.00
❑ 240 Paul Smith RC 8.00 3.00
❑ 241 Chafie Fields RC 5.00 2.00
❑ 242 Kevin Feterik RC 5.00 2.00
❑ 243 Jacoby Shepherd RC 5.00 2.00
❑ 244 Nate Webster RC 5.00 2.00
❑ 245 Ketric Sanford RC 5.00 2.00
❑ 246 Tavarus Hogans RC 5.00 2.00
❑ 247 Keith Bulluck RC 10.00 4.00
❑ 248 Mike Green RC 8.00 3.00
❑ 249 Chris Coleman RC 10.00 4.00
❑ 250 Demario Brown RC 5.00 2.00
❑ 251 Billy Volek RC 15.00 6.00
❑ 252 Mareno Philyaw RC 5.00 2.00
❑ 253 Ethan Howell RC 5.00 2.00
❑ 254 Chris Samuels RC 8.00 3.00
❑ 255 Brandon Short RC 8.00 3.00
❑ 256 Maurice Smith RC 8.00 3.00
❑ 257 Frank Murphy RC 5.00 2.00
❑ 258 Darrick Vaughn RC 5.00 2.00
❑ 259 Payton Williams RC 5.00 2.00
❑ 260 JaJuan Seider RC 5.00 2.00
❑ 261 Antonio Banks EP RC 2.00 .75
❑ 262 Jonathan Brown EP RC 2.00 .75
❑ 263 Ontiwaun Carter EP RC 2.00 .75
❑ 264 Jeremaine Copeland EP 2.00 .75
❑ 265 Ralph Dawkins EP RC 3.00 1.25
❑ 266 Marques Douglas EP RC 2.00 .75
❑ 267 Kevin Drake EP RC 2.00 .75
❑ 268 Damon Dunn EP RC 3.00 1.25
❑ 269 Todd Floyd EP RC 2.00 .75
❑ 270 Tony Graziani EP 3.00 1.25
❑ 271 Derrick Ham EP RC 3.00 1.25
❑ 272 Duane Hawthorne EP RC 3.00 1.25
❑ 273 Alonzo Johnson EP RC 2.00 .75
❑ 274 Mark Kacmarynski EP RC 2.00 .75
❑ 275 Eric Kresser EP 2.00 .75
❑ 276 Jim Kubiak EP RC 3.00 1.25
❑ 277 Blaine McElmurry EP RC 2.00 .75
❑ 278 Scott Milanovich EP 3.00 1.25
❑ 279 Norman Miller EP RC 2.00 .75
❑ 280 Sean Morey EP RC 3.00 1.25
❑ 281 Jeff Ogden EP 3.00 1.25
❑ 282 Pepe Pearson EP RC 3.00 1.25
❑ 283 Ron Powlus EP RC 4.00 1.50
❑ 284 Jason Shelley EP RC 2.00 .75
❑ 285 Ben Snell EP RC 2.00 .75
❑ 286 Aaron Stecker EP RC 4.00 1.50
❑ 287 L.C. Stevens EP 2.00 .75
❑ 288 Mike Sutton EP RC 2.00 .75
❑ 289 Damian Vaughn EP RC 2.00 .75
❑ 290 Ted White EP 2.00 .75
❑ 291 Marcus Crandell EP RC 3.00 1.25
❑ 292 Darryl Daniel EP RC 3.00 1.25
❑ 293 Jesse Haynes EP 2.00 .75
❑ 294 Matt Lytle EP RC 3.00 1.25
❑ 295 Deon Mitchell EP RC 3.00 1.25
❑ 296 Kendrick Nord EP RC 2.00 .75
❑ 297 Ronnie Powell EP 2.00 .75
❑ 298 Selucio Sanford EP RC 3.00 1.25
❑ 299 Corey Thomas EP 2.00 .75
❑ 300 Vershan Jackson EP RC 2.00 .75
❑ 301 Michael Vick XRC 60.00 25.00
❑ 302 Drew Brees XRC 40.00 20.00
❑ 303 Quincy Carter XRC 12.00 5.00
❑ 304 Marques Tuiasosopa XRC 15.00 6.00
❑ 305 Chris Weinke XRC 10.00 4.00
❑ 306 LaDainian Tomlinson XRC 100.00 50.00
❑ 307 Deuce McAllister XRC 25.00 10.00
❑ 308 Michael Bennett XRC 10.00 4.00
❑ 309 Anthony Thomas XRC 10.00 4.00
❑ 310 LaMont Jordan XRC 25.00 10.00
❑ 311 David Terrell XRC 12.00 5.00
❑ 312 Koren Robinson XRC 10.00 4.00
❑ 313 Rod Gardner XRC 12.00 5.00
❑ 314 Santana Moss XRC 20.00 7.50
❑ 315 Freddie Mitchell XRC 10.00 4.00
❑ 316 Gerard Warren XRC 10.00 4.00
❑ 317 Justin Smith XRC 10.00 4.00
❑ 318 Richard Seymour XRC 20.00 7.50
❑ 319 Andre Carter XRC 10.00 4.00
❑ 320 Jamal Reynolds XRC 10.00 4.00

2001 Leaf Rookies and Stars

❑ COMP.SET w/o SP's (100) 20.00 7.50
❑ 1 Aaron Brooks .60 .25
❑ 2 Ahman Green .60 .25
❑ 3 Antonio Freeman .60 .25
❑ 4 Brad Johnson .60 .25
❑ 5 Brett Favre 2.00 .75
❑ 6 Brian Griese .60 .25
❑ 7 Brian Urlacher 1.00 .40
❑ 8 Bruce Smith .25 .08
❑ 9 Cade McNown .25 .08
❑ 10 Chad Pennington 1.00 .40
❑ 11 Champ Bailey .40 .15
❑ 12 Charles Woodson .40 .15
❑ 13 Charlie Batch .60 .25
❑ 14 Charlie Garner .40 .15
❑ 15 Corey Dillon .60 .25
❑ 16 Cris Carter .60 .25
❑ 17 Curtis Martin .60 .25
❑ 18 Dan Marino 2.50 1.00
❑ 19 Daunte Culpepper .60 .25
❑ 20 David Boston .60 .25
❑ 21 Deion Sanders .60 .25
❑ 22 Donovan McNabb .75 .30
❑ 23 Doug Flutie .60 .25
❑ 24 Drew Bledsoe .75 .30
❑ 25 Duce Staley .60 .25
❑ 26 Ed McCaffrey .60 .25
❑ 27 Eddie George .60 .25
❑ 28 Edgerrin James .75 .30
❑ 29 Elvis Grbac .40 .15
❑ 30 Emmitt Smith 1.25 .50
❑ 31 Eric Moulds .40 .15
❑ 32 Fred Taylor .60 .25
❑ 33 Germane Crowell .25 .08
❑ 34 Ike Hilliard .40 .15
❑ 35 Isaac Bruce .60 .25
❑ 36 Jake Plummer .40 .15
❑ 37 Jamal Anderson .60 .25
❑ 38 Jamal Lewis 1.00 .40
❑ 39 James Allen .40 .15
❑ 40 James Stewart .40 .15
❑ 41 Jay Fiedler .60 .25
❑ 42 Jeff Garcia .60 .25
❑ 43 Jeff George .40 .15
❑ 44 Jeff Lewis .25 .08
❑ 45 Jerome Bettis .60 .25
❑ 46 Jerry Rice 1.25 .50
❑ 47 Jevon Kearse .40 .15
❑ 48 Jimmy Smith .40 .15
❑ 49 Joey Galloway .40 .15
❑ 50 John Elway 2.50 1.00
❑ 51 Junior Seau .60 .25
❑ 52 Keenan McCardell .25 .08
❑ 53 Kerry Collins .40 .15
❑ 54 Kevin Johnson .40 .15
❑ 55 Keyshawn Johnson .60 .25
❑ 56 Kordell Stewart .40 .15
❑ 57 Kurt Warner 1.25 .50
❑ 58 Lamar Smith .40 .15
❑ 59 Marcus Robinson .60 .25
❑ 60 Mark Brunell .60 .25
❑ 61 Marshall Faulk .75 .30
❑ 62 Marvin Harrison .60 .25
❑ 63 Matt Hasselbeck .40 .15
❑ 64 Mike Alstott .60 .25
❑ 65 Mike Anderson .60 .25
❑ 66 Muhsin Muhammad .40 .15
❑ 67 Peter Warrick .60 .25
❑ 68 Peyton Manning 1.50 .60
❑ 69 Priest Holmes .75 .30
❑ 70 Randy Moss 1.25 .50
❑ 71 Ray Lewis .60 .25
❑ 72 Rich Gannon .60 .25
❑ 73 Ricky Watters .40 .15
❑ 74 Ricky Williams .60 .25
❑ 75 Rob Johnson .40 .15
❑ 76 Rod Smith .40 .15
❑ 77 Ron Dayne .60 .25
❑ 78 Shannon Sharpe .40 .15
❑ 79 Shaun Alexander .75 .30
❑ 80 Stephen Davis .60 .25
❑ 81 Steve McNair .60 .25
❑ 82 Steve Young .75 .30
❑ 83 Sylvester Morris .25 .08
❑ 84 Terrell Davis .60 .25
❑ 85 Terrell Owens .60 .25
❑ 86 Thomas Jones .40 .15
❑ 87 Tim Brown .60 .25
❑ 88 Tim Couch .40 .15
❑ 89 Tony Banks .40 .15
❑ 90 Tony Gonzalez .40 .15
❑ 91 Torry Holt .60 .25
❑ 92 Travis Taylor .40 .15
❑ 93 Trent Green .60 .25
❑ 94 Troy Aikman 1.00 .40
❑ 95 Tyrone Wheatley .40 .15
❑ 96 Vinny Testaverde .40 .15
❑ 97 Warren Sapp .40 .15
❑ 98 Warrick Dunn .60 .25
❑ 99 Wayne Chrebet .40 .15
❑ 100 Zach Thomas .60 .25
❑ 101 A.J. Feeley RC 6.00 2.50
❑ 102 Josh Booty RC 6.00 2.50
❑ 103 Roderick Robinson RC 4.00 1.50
❑ 104 Renaldo Hill RC 4.00 1.50
❑ 105 Harold Blackmon RC 2.50 1.00
❑ 106 Rudi Johnson RC 10.00 4.00
❑ 107 Curtis Fuller RC 2.50 1.00
❑ 108 Dan Alexander RC 6.00 2.50
❑ 109 Anthony Thomas RPS 6.00 2.50
❑ 110 Travis Minor RPS 3.00 1.25
❑ 111 Heath Evans RC 4.00 1.50
❑ 112 Joe Walker RC 2.50 1.00
❑ 113 Moran Norris RC 2.50 1.00
❑ 114 Quincy Carter RPS 4.00 1.50
❑ 115 Michael Vick RPS 20.00 8.00
❑ 116 Vinny Sutherland RC 4.00 1.50
❑ 117 Scotty Anderson RC 4.00 1.50
❑ 118 Eddie Berlin RC 4.00 1.50
❑ 119 Jonathan Carter RC 4.00 1.50
❑ 120 Monty Beisel RC 6.00 2.50
❑ 121 T.J. Houshmandzadeh RC 8.00 3.00
❑ 122 Rodney Bailey RC 2.50 1.00
❑ 123 Reggie Germany RC 4.00 1.50
❑ 124 Ellis Wyms RC 2.50 1.00
❑ 125 Koren Robinson RPS 6.00 2.50
❑ 126 Antonio Pierce RC 12.00 5.00

❑ 127 Arnold Jackson RC 4.00 1.50
❑ 128 Andre Rone RC 2.50 1.00
❑ 129 Richard Newsome RC 2.50 1.00
❑ 130 Ifeanyi Ohalete RC 2.50 1.00
❑ 131 Dan O'Leary RC 4.00 1.50
❑ 132 Shad Meier RC 4.00 1.50
❑ 133 Jay Feely RC 2.50 1.00
❑ 134 Brandon Manumaleuna RC 4.00 1.50
❑ 135 Riall Johnson RC 2.50 1.00
❑ 136 Snoop Minnis RPS 4.00 1.50
❑ 137 Jermaine Hampton RC 2.50 1.00
❑ 138 Johnny Huggins RC 2.50 1.00
❑ 139 Marcellus Rivers RC 4.00 1.50
❑ 140 Andre Carter RPS 6.00 2.50
❑ 141 Michael Stone RC 2.50 1.00
❑ 142 Tony Dixon RC 4.00 1.50
❑ 143 Bhawoh Jue RC 6.00 2.50
❑ 144 Will Peterson RC 4.00 1.50
❑ 145 Anthony Henry RC 6.00 2.50
❑ 146 Marques Tuiasosopo RPS 4.00 1.50
❑ 147 Reggie Swinton RC 4.00 1.50
❑ 148 Robert Carswell RC 2.50 1.00
❑ 149 Freddie Mitchell RPS 3.00 1.25
❑ 150 Idrees Bashir RC 2.50 1.00
❑ 151 James Boyd RC 2.50 1.00
❑ 152 Chris Chambers RPS 6.00 2.50
❑ 153 Aaron Schobel RC 6.00 2.50
❑ 154 Dominic Raiola RC 2.50 1.00
❑ 155 Derrick Burgess RC 6.00 2.50
❑ 156 DeLawrence Grant RC 2.50 1.00
❑ 157 Karon Riley RC 2.50 1.00
❑ 158 Cedric Scott RC 4.00 1.50
❑ 159 Patrick Washington RC 4.00 1.50
❑ 160 Eric Johnson RC 10.00 4.00
❑ 161 Tevita Ofahengaue RC 2.50 1.00
❑ 162 Chris Cooper RC 4.00 1.50
❑ 163 Fred Wakefield RC 4.00 1.50
❑ 164 Kenny Smith RC 4.00 1.50
❑ 165 Marcus Bell RC 4.00 1.50
❑ 166 Mario Fatafehi RC 4.00 1.50
❑ 167 Anthony Herron RC 2.50 1.00
❑ 168 Joe Tafoya RC 2.50 1.00
❑ 169 Morlon Greenwood RC 4.00 1.50
❑ 170 Orlando Huff RC 2.50 1.00
❑ 171 Carlos Polk RC 2.50 1.00
❑ 172 Edgerton Hartwell RC 2.50 1.00
❑ 173 Zeke Moreno RC 6.00 2.50
❑ 174 Alex Lincoln RC 4.00 1.50
❑ 175 Quinton Caver RC 4.00 1.50
❑ 176 Matt Stewart RC 2.50 1.00
❑ 177 Markus Steele RC 4.00 1.50
❑ 178 Dwight Smith RC 2.50 1.00
❑ 179 Reggie Wayne RPS 8.00 3.00
❑ 180 Jerametrius Butler RC 4.00 1.50
❑ 181 Jason Doering RC 2.50 1.00
❑ 182 John Howell RC 2.50 1.00
❑ 183 Alvin Porter RC 2.50 1.00
❑ 184 Eric Downing RC 2.50 1.00
❑ 185 John Nix RC 2.50 1.00
❑ 186 Tim Baker RC 2.50 1.00
❑ 187 Robert Garza RC 2.50 1.00
❑ 188 Randy Chevrier RC 2.50 1.00
❑ 189 Drew Brees RPS 12.00 5.00
❑ 190 Shawn Worthen RC 2.50 1.00
❑ 191 Drew Bennett RC 20.00 8.00
❑ 192 Marlon McCree RC 4.00 1.50
❑ 193 David Terrell RPS 4.00 1.50
❑ 194 Jeff Backus RC 4.00 1.50
❑ 195 Otis Leverette RC 2.50 1.00
❑ 196 Jason Glenn RC 6.00 2.50
❑ 197 Rashad Holman RC 2.50 1.00
❑ 198 T.J. Turner RC 2.50 1.00
❑ 199 Lynn Scott RC 6.00 2.50
❑ 200 Bill Gramatica RC 2.50 1.00
❑ 201 Michael Vick RC 40.00 20.00
❑ 202 Drew Brees RC 30.00 12.00
❑ 203 Quincy Carter RC 8.00 3.00
❑ 204 Jesse Palmer RC 8.00 3.00
❑ 205 Mike McMahon RC 8.00 3.00
❑ 206 Dave Dickenson RC 4.00 1.50
❑ 207 Jameel Cook RC 5.00 2.00
❑ 208 Marques Tuiasosopo RC 8.00 3.00
❑ 209 Chris Weinke RC 6.00 2.50
❑ 210 Sage Rosenfels RC 6.00 2.50
❑ 211 Josh Heupel RC 8.00 3.00
❑ 212 LaDainian Tomlinson RC 80.00 50.00
❑ 213 Michael Bennett RC 8.00 3.00
❑ 214 Anthony Thomas RC 8.00 3.00
❑ 215 Travis Henry RC 12.00 5.00
❑ 216 James Jackson RC 6.00 2.50
❑ 217 Correll Buckhalter RC 10.00 4.00
❑ 218 Derrick Blaylock RC 8.00 3.00
❑ 219 Dee Brown RC 8.00 3.00
❑ 220 LeVar Woods RC 5.00 2.00
❑ 221 Deuce McAllister RC 15.00 6.00
❑ 222 LaMont Jordan RC 15.00 6.00
❑ 223 Kevan Barlow RC 8.00 3.00
❑ 224 Travis Minor RC 5.00 2.00
❑ 225 David Terrell RC 8.00 3.00
❑ 226 Koren Robinson RC 8.00 3.00
❑ 227 Rod Gardner RC 8.00 3.00
❑ 228 Santana Moss RC 12.00 5.00
❑ 229 Freddie Mitchell RC 8.00 3.00
❑ 230 Reggie Wayne RC 1.00 6.00
❑ 231 Quincy Morgan RC 8.00 3.00
❑ 232 Chris Chambers RC 12.00 5.00
❑ 233 Steve Smith RC 20.00 10.00
❑ 234 Snoop Minnis RC 5.00 2.00
❑ 235 Justin McCareins RC 8.00 3.00
❑ 236 Onome Ojo RC 5.00 2.00
❑ 237 Damerien McCants RC 5.00 2.00
❑ 238 Mike McMahon RPS 3.00 1.25
❑ 239 Cedrick Wilson RC 8.00 3.00
❑ 240 Kevin Kasper RC 6.00 2.50
❑ 241 Chris Taylor RC 5.00 2.00
❑ 242 Ken-Yon Rambo RC 5.00 2.00
❑ 243 Richmond Flowers RC 5.00 2.00
❑ 244 Andre King RC 5.00 2.00
❑ 245 Boo Williams RC 5.00 2.00
❑ 246 Adrian Wilson RC 5.00 2.00
❑ 247 Cory Bird RC 8.00 3.00
❑ 248 Alex Bannister RC 5.00 2.00
❑ 249 Elvis Joseph RC 5.00 2.00
❑ 250 Chad Johnson RC 20.00 7.50
❑ 251 Robert Ferguson RC 8.00 3.00
❑ 252 David Martin RC 5.00 2.00
❑ 253 Quentin McCord RC 5.00 2.00
❑ 254 Todd Heap RC 8.00 3.00
❑ 255 Alge Crumpler RC 10.00 5.00
❑ 256 Nate Clements RC 8.00 3.00
❑ 257 Will Allen RC 5.00 2.00
❑ 258 Willie Middlebrooks RC 5.00 2.00
❑ 259 Fred Smoot RC 8.00 3.00
❑ 260 Andre Dyson RC 3.00 1.25
❑ 261 Gary Baxter RC 5.00 2.00
❑ 262 Jamar Fletcher RC 5.00 2.00
❑ 263 Ken Lucas RC 5.00 2.00
❑ 264 Tay Cody RC 3.00 1.25
❑ 265 Eric Kelly RC 3.00 1.25
❑ 266 Adam Archuleta RC 8.00 3.00
❑ 267 Derrick Gibson RC 5.00 2.00
❑ 268 Jarrod Cooper RC 8.00 3.00
❑ 269 Hakim Akbar RC 3.00 1.25
❑ 270 Tony Driver RC 5.00 2.00
❑ 271 Justin Smith RC 8.00 3.00
❑ 272 Andre Carter RC 8.00 3.00
❑ 273 Jamal Reynolds RC 8.00 3.00
❑ 274 Gerard Warren RC 8.00 3.00
❑ 275 Richard Seymour RC 8.00 3.00
❑ 276 Damione Lewis RC 5.00 2.00
❑ 277 Casey Hampton RC 5.00 2.00
❑ 278 Marcus Stroud RC 8.00 3.00
❑ 279 Benjamin Gay RC 6.00 2.50
❑ 280 Shaun Rogers RC 8.00 3.00
❑ 281 Dan Morgan RC 8.00 3.00
❑ 282 Kendrell Bell RC 12.00 5.00
❑ 283 Tommy Polley RC 8.00 3.00
❑ 284 Jamie Winborn RC 5.00 2.00
❑ 285 Sedrick Hodge RC 3.00 1.25
❑ 286 Torrance Marshall RC 8.00 3.00
❑ 287 Eric Westmoreland RC 5.00 2.00
❑ 288 Brian Allen RC 3.00 1.25
❑ 289 Brandon Spoon RC 8.00 3.00
❑ 290 Henry Burris RC 5.00 2.00
❑ 291 Leonard Davis RC 5.00 2.00
❑ 292 Kenyatta Walker RC 3.00 1.25
❑ 293 Cedric James RC 5.00 2.00
❑ 294 Sean Brewer RC 3.00 1.25
❑ 295 Jason Brookins RC 6.00 2.50
❑ 296 Kyle Vanden Bosch RC 8.00 3.00
❑ 297 Nick Goings RC 8.00 3.00
❑ 298 Kris Jenkins RC 8.00 3.00
❑ 299 Dominic Rhodes RC 12.00 6.00
❑ 300 Leonard Myers RC 3.00 1.25

2002 Leaf Rookies and Stars

❑ COMPLETE SET (300) 250.00 100.00
❑ COMP.SET w/o SP's (100) 25.00 10.00
❑ 1 Jake Plummer .50 .20
❑ 2 David Boston .75 .30
❑ 3 Thomas Jones .50 .20
❑ 4 Michael Vick 2.50 1.00
❑ 5 Warrick Dunn .75 .30
❑ 6 Jamal Lewis .75 .30
❑ 7 Chris Redman .30 .10
❑ 8 Ray Lewis .75 .30
❑ 9 Drew Bledsoe 1.00 .40
❑ 10 Travis Henry .75 .30
❑ 11 Eric Moulds .50 .20
❑ 12 Steve Smith .75 .30
❑ 13 Chris Weinke .50 .20
❑ 14 Lamar Smith .50 .20
❑ 15 Anthony Thomas .50 .20
❑ 16 David Terrell .75 .30
❑ 17 Brian Urlacher 1.25 .50
❑ 18 Corey Dillon .50 .20
❑ 19 Michael Westbrook .50 .20
❑ 20 Peter Warrick .50 .20
❑ 21 Tim Couch .50 .20
❑ 22 James Jackson .50 .20
❑ 23 Kevin Johnson .50 .20
❑ 24 Quincy Carter .50 .20
❑ 25 Joey Galloway .50 .20
❑ 26 Emmitt Smith 2.00 .75
❑ 27 Terrell Davis .75 .30
❑ 28 Brian Griese .75 .30
❑ 29 Ed McCaffrey .75 .30
❑ 30 Rod Smith .50 .20
❑ 31 Mike McMahon .75 .30
❑ 32 Germane Crowell .30 .10
❑ 33 Az-Zahir Hakim .30 .10
❑ 34 Terry Glenn .50 .20
❑ 35 Brett Favre 2.00 .75
❑ 36 Ahman Green .75 .30
❑ 37 James Allen .50 .20
❑ 38 Corey Bradford .30 .10
❑ 39 Peyton Manning 1.50 .60
❑ 40 Edgerrin James 1.00 .40
❑ 41 Marvin Harrison .75 .30
❑ 42 Qadry Ismail .50 .20
❑ 43 Fred Taylor .75 .30
❑ 44 Mark Brunell .75 .30
❑ 45 Jimmy Smith .50 .20
❑ 46 Priest Holmes 1.00 .40
❑ 47 Tony Gonzalez .50 .20
❑ 48 Trent Green .50 .20
❑ 49 Johnnie Morton .50 .20
❑ 50 Chris Chambers .75 .30
❑ 51 Ricky Williams .75 .30
❑ 52 Zach Thomas .75 .30
❑ 53 Randy Moss 1.50 .60
❑ 54 Michael Bennett .50 .20
❑ 55 Derrick Alexander .50 .20
❑ 56 Daunte Culpepper .75 .30
❑ 57 Tom Brady 2.00 .75
❑ 58 Troy Brown .50 .20
❑ 59 Antowain Smith .50 .20
❑ 60 Joe Horn .50 .20
❑ 61 Aaron Brooks .75 .30
❑ 62 Deuce McAllister 1.00 .40
❑ 63 Kerry Collins .50 .20
❑ 64 Amani Toomer .50 .20
❑ 65 Michael Strahan .50 .20
❑ 66 Laveranues Coles .50 .20
❑ 67 Vinny Testaverde .50 .20

Card	Hi	Lo
❑ 68 Curtis Martin	.75	.30
❑ 69 Rich Gannon	.75	.30
❑ 70 Tim Brown	.75	.30
❑ 71 Jerry Rice	1.50	.60
❑ 72 Donovan McNabb	1.00	.40
❑ 73 Freddie Mitchell	.50	.20
❑ 74 Duce Staley	.75	.30
❑ 75 Kordell Stewart	.50	.20
❑ 76 Jerome Bettis	.75	.30
❑ 77 Plaxico Burress	.50	.20
❑ 78 Drew Brees	.75	.30
❑ 79 LaDainian Tomlinson	1.25	.50
❑ 80 Junior Seau	.75	.30
❑ 81 Jeff Garcia	.75	.30
❑ 82 Garrison Hearst	.50	.20
❑ 83 Terrell Owens	.75	.30
❑ 84 Shaun Alexander	1.00	.40
❑ 85 Koren Robinson	.50	.20
❑ 86 Kurt Warner	.75	.30
❑ 87 Marshall Faulk	.75	.30
❑ 88 Isaac Bruce	.75	.30
❑ 89 Torry Holt	.75	.30
❑ 90 Rob Johnson	.50	.20
❑ 91 Brad Johnson	.50	.20
❑ 92 Keyshawn Johnson	.75	.30
❑ 93 Mike Alstott	.75	.30
❑ 94 Eddie George	.75	.30
❑ 95 Steve McNair	.75	.30
❑ 96 Derrick Mason	.50	.20
❑ 97 Jevon Kearse	.50	.20
❑ 98 Stephen Davis	.50	.20
❑ 99 Sage Rosenfels	.30	.10
❑ 100 Rod Gardner	.50	.20
❑ 101 Adrian Peterson RC	5.00	2.00
❑ 102 Nick Rolovich RC	4.00	1.50
❑ 103 Lew Thomas RC	2.50	1.00
❑ 104 David Carr RC	12.00	5.00
❑ 105 Daryl Jones RC	4.00	1.50
❑ 106 Brandon Doman RC	4.00	1.50
❑ 107 Ed Reed RC	8.00	3.00
❑ 108 Tellis Redmon RC	4.00	1.50
❑ 109 Andra Davis RC	4.00	1.50
❑ 110 Kendall Newson RC	2.50	1.00
❑ 111 Joe Burns RC	4.00	1.50
❑ 112 Maurice Morris RC	5.00	2.00
❑ 113 Craig Nall RC	5.00	2.00
❑ 114 Phillip Buchanon RC	5.00	2.00
❑ 115 Mike Echols RC	2.50	1.00
❑ 116 Terry Jones Jr. RC	4.00	1.50
❑ 117 Anthony Weaver RC	4.00	1.50
❑ 118 Jeb Putzier RC	5.00	2.00
❑ 119 Tony Fisher RC	5.00	2.00
❑ 120 Joey Harrington RC	8.00	3.00
❑ 121 Lamar Gordon RC	5.00	2.00
❑ 122 Tracey Wistrom RC	4.00	1.50
❑ 123 Ashley Lelie RC	10.00	4.00
❑ 124 Will Witherspoon RC	5.00	2.00
❑ 125 Travis Stephens RC	4.00	1.50
❑ 126 J.T. O'Sullivan RC	4.00	1.50
❑ 127 Brian Westbrook RC	8.00	3.00
❑ 128 James Mungro RC	5.00	2.00
❑ 129 Lamont Thompson RC	4.00	1.50
❑ 130 Jarrod Baxter RC	4.00	1.50
❑ 131 Andre Lott RC	5.00	2.00
❑ 132 Steve Bellisari RC	4.00	1.50
❑ 133 David Garrard RC	5.00	2.00
❑ 134 Michael Lewis RC	5.00	2.00
❑ 135 James Allen RC	2.50	1.00
❑ 136 Bryant McKinnie RC	4.00	1.50
❑ 137 Marques Anderson RC	5.00	2.00
❑ 138 Rohan Davey RC	5.00	2.00
❑ 139 Kyle Johnson RC	2.50	1.00
❑ 140 Dusty Bonner RC	2.50	1.00
❑ 141 DeShaun Foster RC	5.00	2.00
❑ 142 Chad Hutchinson RC	4.00	1.50
❑ 143 Jack Brewer RC	4.00	1.50
❑ 144 Eddie Freeman RC	2.50	1.00
❑ 145 Seth Burford RC	4.00	1.50
❑ 146 Roosevelt Williams RC	2.50	1.00
❑ 147 Jamin Elliott RC	2.50	1.00
❑ 148 Charles Grant RC	5.00	2.00
❑ 149 Jeff Kelly RC	4.00	1.50
❑ 150 Cliff Russell RC	4.00	1.50
❑ 151 Josh Scobey RC	5.00	2.00
❑ 152 Tank Williams RC	4.00	1.50
❑ 153 Larry Tripplett RC	2.50	1.00
❑ 154 Clinton Portis RC	15.00	6.00
❑ 155 Javin Hunter RC	2.50	1.00
❑ 156 Deveren Johnson RC	4.00	1.50
❑ 157 Reche Caldwell RC	5.00	2.00
❑ 158 Ronald Curry RC	5.00	2.00
❑ 159 Chris Hope RC	5.00	2.00
❑ 160 Damien Anderson RC	4.00	1.50
❑ 161 Saleem Rasheed RC	5.00	2.00
❑ 162 Albert Haynesworth RC	4.00	1.50
❑ 163 Bryan Gilmore RC	4.00	1.50
❑ 164 Wes Pate RC	2.50	1.00
❑ 165 Deion Branch RC	10.00	5.00
❑ 166 Ben Leber RC	5.00	2.00
❑ 167 Andre Davis RC	4.00	1.50
❑ 168 Darrell Hill RC	4.00	1.50
❑ 169 Rodney Wright RC	2.50	1.00
❑ 170 Demontray Carter RC	2.50	1.00
❑ 171 Zak Kustok RC	5.00	2.00
❑ 172 James Wofford RC	4.00	1.50
❑ 173 David Priestley RC	4.00	1.50
❑ 174 Donte Stallworth RC	10.00	4.00
❑ 175 Marc Boerigter RC	8.00	3.00
❑ 176 Freddie Milons RC	4.00	1.50
❑ 177 John Simon RC	4.00	1.50
❑ 178 Josh Norman RC	5.00	2.00
❑ 179 Jabar Gaffney RC	5.00	2.00
❑ 180 Doug Jolley RC	5.00	2.00
❑ 181 Preston Parsons RC	2.50	1.00
❑ 182 Chris Baker RC	4.00	1.50
❑ 183 Javon Walker RC	10.00	4.00
❑ 184 Justin Peelle RC	2.50	1.00
❑ 185 Josh Reed RC	5.00	2.00
❑ 186 Omar Easy RC	5.00	2.00
❑ 187 Jerramy Stevens RC	5.00	2.00
❑ 188 Shaun Hill RC	5.00	2.00
❑ 189 David Thornton RC	2.50	1.00
❑ 190 John Henderson RC	5.00	2.00
❑ 191 Verron Haynes RC	5.00	2.00
❑ 192 Dennis Johnson RC	2.50	1.00
❑ 193 Napoleon Harris RC	5.00	2.00
❑ 194 Jonathan Wells RC	5.00	2.00
❑ 195 Howard Green RC	2.50	1.00
❑ 196 Travis Fisher RC	5.00	2.00
❑ 197 Anton Palepoi RC	2.50	1.00
❑ 198 Ed Stansbury RC	2.50	1.00
❑ 199 Josh McCown RC	6.00	2.50
❑ 200 Alex Brown RC	5.00	2.00
❑ 201 Joseph Jefferson RC	4.00	1.50
❑ 202 Julius Peppers RC	10.00	4.00
❑ 203 Larry Ned RC	4.00	1.50
❑ 204 Rock Cartwright RC	6.00	2.50
❑ 205 Kalimba Edwards RC	5.00	2.00
❑ 206 Matt Schobel RC	4.00	1.50
❑ 207 Maurice Jackson RC	2.50	1.00
❑ 208 Kelly Campbell RC	4.00	1.50
❑ 209 Mel Mitchell RC	4.00	1.50
❑ 210 Ken Simonton RC	2.50	1.00
❑ 211 Brian Allen RC	4.00	1.50
❑ 212 Darnell Sanders RC	4.00	1.50
❑ 213 Jesse Chatman RC	5.00	2.00
❑ 214 Keyuo Craver RC	4.00	1.50
❑ 215 Chester Taylor RC	10.00	4.00
❑ 216 Kurt Kittner RC	4.00	1.50
❑ 217 Derek Ross RC	4.00	1.50
❑ 218 Charles Hill RC	2.50	1.00
❑ 219 Jarvis Green RC	4.00	1.50
❑ 220 Mike Jenkins RC	2.50	1.00
❑ 221 Robert Royal RC	5.00	2.00
❑ 222 Ladell Betts RC	5.00	2.00
❑ 223 Antwoine Womack RC	4.00	1.50
❑ 224 Raonall Smith RC	4.00	1.50
❑ 225 Charles Stackhouse RC	4.00	1.50
❑ 226 Quinn Gray RC	2.50	1.00
❑ 227 Lito Sheppard RC	5.00	2.00
❑ 228 Ryan Van Dyke RC	5.00	2.00
❑ 229 Will Overstreet RC	2.50	1.00
❑ 230 Leonard Henry RC	4.00	1.50
❑ 231 Dorsett Davis RC	2.50	1.00
❑ 232 Marquand Manuel RC	2.50	1.00
❑ 233 Luke Staley RC	4.00	1.50
❑ 234 Carlos Hall RC	5.00	2.00
❑ 235 Marcus Brady RC	4.00	1.50
❑ 236 Ryan Denney RC	4.00	1.50
❑ 237 Eric McCoo RC	2.50	1.00
❑ 238 Major Applewhite RC	5.00	2.00
❑ 239 Adam Tate RC	2.50	1.00
❑ 240 Marquise Walker RC	4.00	1.50
❑ 241 John Flowers RC	2.50	1.00
❑ 242 Levar Fisher RC	2.50	1.00
❑ 243 Ricky Williams RC	4.00	1.50
❑ 244 Mike Rumph RC	5.00	2.00
❑ 245 Delvin Joyce RC	4.00	1.50
❑ 246 Bryan Thomas RC	4.00	1.50
❑ 247 Mike Williams RC	4.00	1.50
❑ 248 Sam Brandon RC	4.00	1.50
❑ 249 Eddie Drummond RC	4.00	1.50
❑ 250 Najeh Davenport RC	5.00	2.00
❑ 251 Brian Williams RC	2.50	1.00
❑ 252 Scott Fujita RC	5.00	2.00
❑ 253 Dwight Freeney RC	8.00	3.00
❑ 254 Herb Haygood RC	2.50	1.00
❑ 255 Patrick Ramsey RC	6.00	2.50
❑ 256 Atnaf Harris RC	2.50	1.00
❑ 257 Jason McAddley RC	4.00	1.50
❑ 258 Pete Rebstock RC	2.50	1.00
❑ 259 Quentin Jammer RC	5.00	2.00
❑ 260 Luke Butkus RC	2.50	1.00
❑ 261 Jeremy Allen RC	2.50	1.00
❑ 262 Jake Schifino RC	4.00	1.50
❑ 263 Randy Fasani RC	4.00	1.50
❑ 264 Bryan Fletcher RC	2.50	1.00
❑ 265 Jeremy Shockey RC	15.00	6.00
❑ 266 Kevin Bentley RC	2.50	1.00
❑ 267 Jon McGraw RC	2.50	1.00
❑ 268 Robert Thomas RC	5.00	2.00
❑ 269 Coy Wire RC	5.00	2.00
❑ 270 Brian Poli-Dixon RC	4.00	1.50
❑ 271 Willie Offord RC	4.00	1.50
❑ 272 Rocky Calmus RC	5.00	2.00
❑ 273 Sheldon Brown RC	5.00	2.00
❑ 274 Terry Charles RC	4.00	1.50
❑ 275 Ron Johnson RC	4.00	1.50
❑ 276 Roy Williams RC	12.00	5.00
❑ 277 Sam Simmons RC	2.50	1.00
❑ 278 Andre Goodman RC	5.00	2.00
❑ 279 Ryan Sims RC	5.00	2.00
❑ 280 Antwaan Randle El RC	8.00	3.00
❑ 281 Alan Harper RC	2.50	1.00
❑ 282 Tavon Mason RC	2.50	1.00
❑ 283 Kahlil Hill RC	4.00	1.50
❑ 284 Antonio Bryant RC	5.00	2.00
❑ 285 Akin Ayodele RC	2.50	1.00
❑ 286 T.J. Duckett RC	6.00	2.50
❑ 287 Kenyon Coleman RC	2.50	1.00
❑ 288 Tim Carter RC	4.00	1.50
❑ 289 Lamont Brightful RC	2.50	1.00
❑ 290 Trev Faulk RC	2.50	1.00
❑ 291 Randy McMichael RC	8.00	3.00
❑ 292 Daniel Graham RC	5.00	2.00
❑ 293 Wendell Bryant RC	2.50	1.00
❑ 294 Jamar Martin RC	4.00	1.50
❑ 295 Chris Luzar RC	4.00	1.50
❑ 296 William Green RC	5.00	2.00
❑ 297 Lee Mays RC	4.00	1.50
❑ 298 Eric Crouch RC	5.00	2.00
❑ 299 Steve Smith RC	2.50	1.00
❑ 300 Woody Dantzler RC	4.00	1.50

2003 Leaf Rookies and Stars

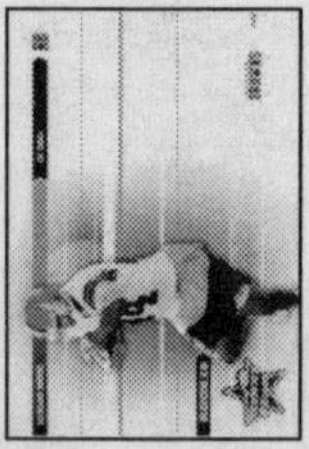

Card	Hi	Lo
❑ COMP.SET w/o SP's (100)	20.00	7.50
❑ 1 Emmitt Smith	2.00	.75
❑ 2 Michael Vick	2.00	.75
❑ 3 Peerless Price	.50	.20
❑ 4 T.J. Duckett	.50	.20
❑ 5 Warrick Dunn	.50	.20
❑ 6 Jamal Lewis	.75	.30
❑ 7 Ray Lewis	.75	.30
❑ 8 Drew Bledsoe	.75	.30
❑ 9 Eric Moulds	.50	.20
❑ 10 Josh Reed	.50	.20
❑ 11 Travis Henry	.50	.20
❑ 12 Julius Peppers	.75	.30

❑ 13 Anthony Thomas .50 .20
❑ 14 Brian Urlacher 1.25 .50
❑ 15 Marty Booker .50 .20
❑ 16 Kordell Stewart .50 .20
❑ 17 Corey Dillon .50 .20
❑ 18 Chad Johnson .75 .30
❑ 19 Tim Couch .30 .10
❑ 20 William Green .50 .20
❑ 21 Antonio Bryant .50 .20
❑ 22 Roy Williams .75 .30
❑ 23 Ashley Lelie .75 .30
❑ 24 Clinton Portis 1.25 .50
❑ 25 Ed McCaffrey .75 .30
❑ 26 Jake Plummer .50 .20
❑ 27 Rod Smith .50 .20
❑ 28 Joey Harrington 1.25 .50
❑ 29 Ahman Green .75 .30
❑ 30 Brett Favre 2.00 .75
❑ 31 Donald Driver .50 .20
❑ 32 Javon Walker .50 .20
❑ 33 David Carr 1.25 .50
❑ 34 Edgerrin James .75 .30
❑ 35 Marvin Harrison .75 .30
❑ 36 Peyton Manning 1.25 .50
❑ 37 Fred Taylor .75 .30
❑ 38 Jimmy Smith .50 .20
❑ 39 Mark Brunell .50 .20
❑ 40 Priest Holmes 1.25 .50
❑ 41 Tony Gonzalez .50 .20
❑ 42 Trent Green .50 .20
❑ 43 Chris Chambers .75 .30
❑ 44 Jay Fiedler .50 .20
❑ 45 Junior Seau .75 .30
❑ 46 Ricky Williams .75 .30
❑ 47 Zach Thomas .75 .30
❑ 48 Daunte Culpepper .75 .30
❑ 49 Michael Bennett .50 .20
❑ 50 Randy Moss 1.25 .50
❑ 51 Tom Brady 2.00 .75
❑ 52 Troy Brown .50 .20
❑ 53 Aaron Brooks .75 .30
❑ 54 Deuce McAllister .75 .30
❑ 55 Donte Stallworth .75 .30
❑ 56 Joe Horn .50 .20
❑ 57 Jeremy Shockey 1.25 .50
❑ 58 Kerry Collins .50 .20
❑ 59 Michael Strahan .50 .20
❑ 60 Tiki Barber .75 .30
❑ 61 Chad Pennington 1.00 .40
❑ 62 Curtis Martin .75 .30
❑ 63 Santana Moss .50 .20
❑ 64 Charles Woodson .50 .20
❑ 65 Jerry Rice 1.50 .60
❑ 66 Rich Gannon .50 .20
❑ 67 Tim Brown .75 .30
❑ 68 Donovan McNabb 1.00 .40
❑ 69 Antwaan Randle El .75 .30
❑ 70 Tommy Maddox .75 .30
❑ 71 Jerome Bettis .75 .30
❑ 72 Kendrell Bell .50 .20
❑ 73 Plaxico Burress .50 .20
❑ 74 David Boston .50 .20
❑ 75 Drew Brees .75 .30
❑ 76 LaDainian Tomlinson .75 .30
❑ 77 Kevan Barlow .50 .20
❑ 78 Jeff Garcia .75 .30
❑ 79 Terrell Owens .75 .30
❑ 80 Matt Hasselbeck .50 .20
❑ 81 Koren Robinson .50 .20
❑ 82 Shaun Alexander .75 .30
❑ 83 Isaac Bruce .75 .30
❑ 84 Kurt Warner .75 .30
❑ 85 Marshall Faulk .75 .30
❑ 86 Torry Holt .75 .30
❑ 87 Brad Johnson .50 .20
❑ 88 Keyshawn Johnson .75 .30
❑ 89 Mike Alstott .75 .30
❑ 90 Warren Sapp .50 .20
❑ 91 Eddie George .50 .20
❑ 92 Jevon Kearse .50 .20
❑ 93 Steve McNair .75 .30
❑ 94 Laveranues Coles .50 .20
❑ 95 Rod Gardner .50 .20
❑ 96 Patrick Ramsey .75 .30
❑ 97 Boller/Suggs/Smith CL .75 .30
❑ 98 R.Grossman/T.Jacobs CL 1.00 .40
❑ 99 A.Boldin/B.Johnson CL .75 .30
❑ 100 T.Calico/C.Brown CL .75 .30
❑ 101 Charles Tillman RC 5.00 2.00
❑ 102 Justin Griffith RC 3.00 1.25
❑ 103 Ovie Mughelli RC 2.00 .75
❑ 104 Chris Edmonds RC 2.00 .75
❑ 105 Jeremi Johnson RC 3.00 1.25
❑ 106 Malaefou MacKenzie RC 2.00 .75
❑ 107 James Lynch RC 3.00 1.25
❑ 108 B.J. Askew RC 4.00 1.50
❑ 109 Andrew Pinnock RC 3.00 1.25
❑ 110 Chris Davis RC 3.00 1.25
❑ 111 Dan Curley RC 2.00 .75
❑ 112 Lenny Walls RC 3.00 1.25
❑ 113 Travis Fisher RC 2.00 .75
❑ 114 Ahmaad Galloway RC 3.00 1.25
❑ 115 Joe Smith RC 4.00 1.50
❑ 116 Reno Mahe RC 4.00 1.50
❑ 117 Torrie Cox RC 3.00 1.25
❑ 118 Kerry Carter RC 3.00 1.25
❑ 119 Dwone Hicks RC 2.00 .75
❑ 120 Cato June RC 5.00 2.00
❑ 121 Terry Pierce RC 3.00 1.25
❑ 122 Eddie Moore RC 3.00 1.25
❑ 123 Mike Seidman RC 2.00 .75
❑ 124 Michael Nattiel RC 4.00 1.50
❑ 125 Casey Fitzsimmons RC 4.00 1.50
❑ 126 George Wrighster RC 3.00 1.25
❑ 127 Mike Pinkard RC 2.00 .75
❑ 128 Donald Lee RC 3.00 1.25
❑ 129 Sean Berton RC 2.00 .75
❑ 130 Soloman Bates RC 2.00 .75
❑ 131 Zach Hilton RC 3.00 1.25
❑ 132 Antonio Gates RC 30.00 15.00
❑ 133 Aaron Walker RC 3.00 1.25
❑ 134 Richard Angulo RC 3.00 1.25
❑ 135 Will Heller RC 3.00 1.25
❑ 136 Theo Sanders RC 2.00 .75
❑ 137 Jimmy Farris RC 3.00 1.25
❑ 138 Ryan Nece RC 4.00 1.50
❑ 139 Antonio Brown RC 2.00 .75
❑ 140 Clarence Coleman RC 2.00 .75
❑ 141 Lawrence Hamilton RC 2.00 .75
❑ 142 C.J. Jones RC 2.00 .75
❑ 143 Frisman Jackson RC 4.00 1.50
❑ 144 Antonio Chatman RC 4.00 1.50
❑ 145 Rocky Boiman RC 3.00 1.25
❑ 146 Tron LaFavor RC 2.00 .75
❑ 147 Derick Armstrong RC 4.00 1.50
❑ 148 J.J. Moses RC 3.00 1.25
❑ 149 Aaron Moorehead RC 4.00 1.50
❑ 150 Brad Pyatt RC 3.00 1.25
❑ 151 Arland Bruce RC 2.00 .75
❑ 152 Chris Horn RC 2.00 .75
❑ 153 Kareem Kelly RC 3.00 1.25
❑ 154 Talman Gardner RC 4.00 1.50
❑ 155 David Tyree RC 3.00 1.25
❑ 156 Willie Ponder RC 2.00 .75
❑ 157 Greg Lewis RC 8.00 3.00
❑ 158 Eric Parker RC 4.00 1.50
❑ 159 Kassim Osgood RC 4.00 1.50
❑ 160 Jason Willis RC 2.00 .75
❑ 161 Akbar Gbaja-Biamila RC 4.00 1.50
❑ 162 Mike Furrey RC 15.00 6.00
❑ 163 Chris Kelsay RC 4.00 1.50
❑ 164 Cory Redding RC 3.00 1.25
❑ 165 Kenny Peterson RC 3.00 1.25
❑ 166 Osi Umenyiora RC 6.00 2.50
❑ 167 Tyler Brayton RC 4.00 1.50
❑ 168 DeWayne White RC 3.00 1.25
❑ 169 Kevin Williams RC 4.00 1.50
❑ 170 Dan Klecko RC 6.00 2.50
❑ 171 Johnathan Sullivan RC 3.00 1.25
❑ 172 William Joseph RC 4.00 1.50
❑ 173 Rien Long RC 2.00 .75
❑ 174 Angelo Crowell RC 3.00 1.25
❑ 175 Chaun Thompson RC 2.00 .75
❑ 176 Bradie James RC 4.00 1.50
❑ 177 Antwan Peek RC 3.00 1.25
❑ 178 Kawika Mitchell RC 3.00 1.25
❑ 179 Cie Grant RC 4.00 1.50
❑ 180 E.J. Henderson RC 4.00 1.50
❑ 181 Victor Hobson RC 4.00 1.50
❑ 182 Alonzo Jackson RC 3.00 1.25
❑ 183 Matt Wilhelm RC 4.00 1.50
❑ 184 Pisa Tinoisamoa RC 4.00 1.50
❑ 185 Ricky Manning RC 4.00 1.50
❑ 186 Dennis Weathersby RC 2.00 .75
❑ 187 Donald Strickland RC 2.00 .75
❑ 188 Asante Samuel RC 4.00 1.50
❑ 189 Eugene Wilson RC 4.00 1.50
❑ 190 Nnamdi Asomugha RC 3.00 1.25
❑ 191 Ike Taylor RC 8.00 3.00
❑ 192 Drayton Florence RC 2.00 .75
❑ 193 DeJuan Groce RC 4.00 1.50
❑ 194 Shane Walton RC 2.00 .75
❑ 195 Terrence Holt RC 3.00 1.25
❑ 196 Rashean Mathis RC 3.00 1.25
❑ 197 Julian Battle RC 3.00 1.25
❑ 198 Hanik Milligan RC 3.00 1.25
❑ 199 Terrence Kiel RC 4.00 1.50
❑ 200 David Kircus RC 4.00 1.50
❑ 201 Lee Suggs RC 6.00 2.50
❑ 202 Charles Rogers RC 6.00 2.50
❑ 203 Brandon Lloyd RC 6.00 2.50
❑ 204 Terrence Edwards RC 5.00 2.00
❑ 205 Tony Romo RC 50.00 25.00
❑ 206 Brooks Bollinger RC 6.00 2.50
❑ 207 Jerome McDougle RC 6.00 2.50
❑ 208 Jimmy Kennedy RC 6.00 2.50
❑ 209 Ken Dorsey RC 6.00 2.50
❑ 210 Kirk Farmer RC 3.00 1.25
❑ 211 Mike Doss RC 6.00 2.50
❑ 212 Chris Simms RC 10.00 4.00
❑ 213 Cecil Sapp RC 5.00 2.00
❑ 214 Justin Gage RC 6.00 2.50
❑ 215 Sam Aiken RC 5.00 2.00
❑ 216 Doug Gabriel RC 6.00 2.50
❑ 217 Jason Witten RC 10.00 4.00
❑ 218 Bennie Joppru RC 6.00 2.50
❑ 219 Jason Gesser RC 6.00 2.50
❑ 220 Brock Forsey RC 6.00 2.50
❑ 221 Quentin Griffin RC 6.00 2.50
❑ 222 Avon Cobourne RC 3.00 1.25
❑ 223 Domanick Davis RC 6.00 2.50
❑ 224 Boss Bailey RC 6.00 2.50
❑ 225 Tony Hollings RC 6.00 2.50
❑ 226 LaBrandon Toefield RC 6.00 2.50
❑ 227 Arlen Harris RC 6.00 2.50
❑ 228 Sultan McCullough RC 5.00 2.00
❑ 229 Visanthe Shiancoe RC 5.00 2.00
❑ 230 L.J. Smith RC 6.00 2.50
❑ 231 LaTarence Dunbar RC 5.00 2.00
❑ 232 Walter Young RC 3.00 1.25
❑ 233 Bobby Wade RC 6.00 2.50
❑ 234 Zuriel Smith RC 3.00 1.25
❑ 235 Adrian Madise RC 5.00 2.00
❑ 236 Ken Hamlin RC 6.00 2.50
❑ 237 Carl Ford RC 3.00 1.25
❑ 238 Cortez Hankton RC 5.00 2.00
❑ 239 J.R. Tolver RC 5.00 2.00
❑ 240 Keenan Howry RC 6.00 2.50
❑ 241 Billy McMullen RC 5.00 2.00
❑ 242 Arnaz Battle RC 6.00 2.50
❑ 243 Shaun McDonald RC 6.00 2.50
❑ 244 Andre Woolfolk RC 6.00 2.50
❑ 245 Sammy Davis RC 6.00 2.50
❑ 246 Calvin Pace RC 5.00 2.00
❑ 247 Michael Haynes RC 6.00 2.50
❑ 248 Ty Warren RC 6.00 2.50
❑ 249 Nick Barnett RC 6.00 2.50
❑ 250 Troy Polamalu RC 30.00 15.00
❑ 251 Carson Palmer JSY RC 30.00 12.50
❑ 252 Byron Leftwich JSY RC 25.00 10.00
❑ 253 Kyle Boller JSY RC 6.00 2.50
❑ 254 Rex Grossman JSY RC 25.00 10.00
❑ 255 Dave Ragone JSY RC 6.00 2.50
❑ 256 Brian St.Pierre JSY RC 6.00 2.50
❑ 257 Kliff Kingsbury JSY RC 6.00 2.50
❑ 258 Seneca Wallace JSY RC 6.00 2.50
❑ 259 Larry Johnson JSY RC 30.00 15.00
❑ 260 Willis McGahee JSY RC 15.00 6.00
❑ 261 Justin Fargas JSY RC 6.00 2.50
❑ 262 Onterrio Smith JSY RC 6.00 2.50
❑ 263 Chris Brown JSY RC 6.00 2.50
❑ 264 Musa Smith JSY RC 6.00 2.50
❑ 265 Artose Pinner JSY RC 6.00 2.50
❑ 266 Andre Johnson JSY RC 15.00 6.00
❑ 267 Kelley Washington JSY RC 8.00 3.00
❑ 268 Taylor Jacobs JSY RC 6.00 2.50
❑ 269 Bryant Johnson JSY RC 6.00 2.50
❑ 270 Tyrone Calico JSY RC 10.00 4.00
❑ 271 Anquan Boldin JSY RC 20.00 7.50
❑ 272 Bethel Johnson JSY RC 6.00 2.50
❑ 273 Nate Burleson JSY RC 6.00 2.50
❑ 274 Kevin Curtis JSY RC 6.00 2.50
❑ 275 Dallas Clark JSY RC 6.00 2.50
❑ 276 Teyo Johnson JSY RC 6.00 2.50
❑ 277 Terrell Suggs JSY RC 10.00 4.00
❑ 278 DeWayne Robertson JSY RC 6.002.50
❑ 279 Terence Newman JSY RC 12.00 5.00

❑ 280	Marcus Trufant JSY RC	6.00	2.50
❑ 281	C.Palmer/B.Leftwich JSY	30.00	12.50
❑ 282	K.Boller/D.Ragone JSY	6.00	2.50
❑ 283	R.Grossman/B.St.Pierre JSY	25.00	10.00
❑ 284	K.Kingsbury/S.Wallace JSY	10.00	4.00
❑ 285	L.Johnson/W.McGahee JSY	30.00	12.50
❑ 286	J.Fargas/O.Smith JSY	10.00	4.00
❑ 287	C.Brown/M.Smith JSY	6.00	2.50
❑ 288	A.Pinner/A.Johnson JSY	15.00	6.00
❑ 289	K.Washington/T.Jacobs JSY	10.00	4.00
❑ 290	B.Johnson/T.Calico JSY	12.00	5.00
❑ 291	A.Boldin/B.Johnson JSY	25.00	10.00
❑ 292	N.Burleson/K.Curtis JSY	6.00	2.50
❑ 293	D.Clark/T.Johnson JSY	10.00	4.00
❑ 294	T.Suggs/D.Robertson JSY	10.00	4.00
❑ 295	T.Newman/M.Trufant JSY	12.00	5.00

2004 Leaf Rookies and Stars

❑ COMP.SET w/o SP's (200) 60.00 30.00
❑ COMP.SET w/o RC's (100) 20.00 7.50
❑ 251-283 JSY PRINT RUN 750 SER.#'d SETS
❑ 284-299 PRINT RUN 500 SER.#'d SETS

❑ 1	Anquan Boldin	.75	.30
❑ 2	Emmitt Smith	1.50	.60
❑ 3	Josh McCown	.50	.20
❑ 4	Michael Vick	1.50	.60
❑ 5	Peerless Price	.50	.20
❑ 6	T.J. Duckett	.50	.20
❑ 7	Warrick Dunn	.50	.20
❑ 8	Jamal Lewis	.75	.30
❑ 9	Kyle Boller	.75	.30
❑ 10	Ray Lewis	.75	.30
❑ 11	Drew Bledsoe	.75	.30
❑ 12	Eric Moulds	.50	.20
❑ 13	Travis Henry	.50	.20
❑ 14	Jake Delhomme	.75	.30
❑ 15	Stephen Davis	.50	.20
❑ 16	Steve Smith	.75	.30
❑ 17	Brian Urlacher	1.00	.40
❑ 18	Rex Grossman	.75	.30
❑ 19	Thomas Jones	.50	.20
❑ 20	Carson Palmer	1.00	.40
❑ 21	Chad Johnson	.75	.30
❑ 22	Rudi Johnson	.50	.20
❑ 23	Jeff Garcia	.75	.30
❑ 24	William Green	.50	.20
❑ 25	Keyshawn Johnson	.50	.20
❑ 26	Terence Newman	.50	.20
❑ 27	Roy Williams S	.50	.20
❑ 28	Jake Plummer	.50	.20
❑ 29	Quentin Griffin	.75	.30
❑ 30	Rod Smith	.50	.20
❑ 31	Charles Rogers	.50	.20
❑ 32	Joey Harrington	.75	.30
❑ 33	Ahman Green	.75	.30
❑ 34	Brett Favre	2.00	.75
❑ 35	Javon Walker	.50	.20
❑ 36	Andre Johnson	.75	.30
❑ 37	David Carr	.75	.30
❑ 38	Domanick Davis	.75	.30
❑ 39	Edgerrin James	.75	.30
❑ 40	Marvin Harrison	.75	.30
❑ 41	Peyton Manning	1.25	.50
❑ 42	Byron Leftwich	1.00	.40
❑ 43	Fred Taylor	.50	.20
❑ 44	Jimmy Smith	.50	.20
❑ 45	Priest Holmes	1.00	.40
❑ 46	Tony Gonzalez	.50	.20
❑ 47	Trent Green	.50	.20
❑ 48	A.J. Feeley	.75	.30
❑ 49	Chris Chambers	.50	.20
❑ 50	Deion Sanders	1.00	.40
❑ 51	Daunte Culpepper	.75	.30
❑ 52	Michael Bennett	.50	.20
❑ 53	Randy Moss	1.00	.40
❑ 54	Corey Dillon	.50	.20
❑ 55	Deion Branch	.75	.30
❑ 56	Tom Brady	2.00	.75
❑ 57	Aaron Brooks	.50	.20
❑ 58	Deuce McAllister	.75	.30
❑ 59	Joe Horn	.50	.20
❑ 60	Jeremy Shockey	.75	.30
❑ 61	Michael Strahan	.50	.20
❑ 62	Tiki Barber	.75	.30
❑ 63	Chad Pennington	.75	.30
❑ 64	Curtis Martin	.75	.30
❑ 65	Santana Moss	.50	.20
❑ 66	Jerry Porter	.50	.20
❑ 67	Jerry Rice	1.50	.60
❑ 68	Warren Sapp	.50	.20
❑ 69	Donovan McNabb	1.00	.40
❑ 70	Jevon Kearse	.50	.20
❑ 71	Terrell Owens	.75	.30
❑ 72	Duce Staley	.50	.20
❑ 73	Hines Ward	.75	.30
❑ 74	Jerome Bettis	.75	.30
❑ 75	LaDainian Tomlinson	1.00	.40
❑ 76	Kevan Barlow	.50	.20
❑ 77	Tim Rattay	.50	.20
❑ 78	Koren Robinson	.50	.20
❑ 79	Matt Hasselbeck	.50	.20
❑ 80	Shaun Alexander	.75	.30
❑ 81	Isaac Bruce	.50	.20
❑ 82	Marc Bulger	.75	.30
❑ 83	Marshall Faulk	.75	.30
❑ 84	Torry Holt	.75	.30
❑ 85	Brad Johnson	.50	.20
❑ 86	Derrick Brooks	.50	.20
❑ 87	Chris Brown	.75	.30
❑ 88	Derrick Mason	.50	.20
❑ 89	Eddie George	.50	.20
❑ 90	Steve McNair	.75	.30
❑ 91	Clinton Portis	.75	.30
❑ 92	LaVar Arrington	1.50	.60
❑ 93	Laveranues Coles	.50	.20
❑ 94	Mark Brunell	.50	.20
❑ 95	Hall/Schaub/Jenkins CL	.75	.30
❑ 96	Losman/L.Evans CL	1.00	.40
❑ 97	Winslow Jr./L.McCown CL	1.50	.60
❑ 98	D.Watts/T.Bell CL	.75	.30
❑ 99	K.Jones/Ro.Will. CL	1.25	.50
❑ 100	G.Jones/Re.Will. CL	.75	.30
❑ 101	Darnell Dockett RC	3.00	1.25
❑ 102	Karlos Dansby RC	4.00	1.50
❑ 103	Larry Croom RC	3.00	1.25
❑ 104	Chad Lavalais RC	3.00	1.25
❑ 105	Demorrio Williams RC	4.00	1.50
❑ 106	B.J. Sams RC	4.00	1.50
❑ 107	Dwan Edwards RC	2.00	.75
❑ 108	Jason Peters RC	4.00	1.50
❑ 109	Shaud Williams RC	3.00	1.25
❑ 110	Tim Anderson RC	4.00	1.50
❑ 111	Tim Euhus RC	4.00	1.50
❑ 112	Michael Gaines RC	3.00	1.25
❑ 113	Rod Rutherford RC	3.00	1.25
❑ 114	Leon Joe RC	2.00	.75
❑ 115	Nathan Vasher RC	5.00	2.00
❑ 116	Caleb Miller RC	3.00	1.25
❑ 117	Jamall Broussard RC	2.00	.75
❑ 118	Keiwan Ratliff RC	3.00	1.25
❑ 119	Landon Johnson RC	3.00	1.25
❑ 120	Madieu Williams RC	3.00	1.25
❑ 121	Matthias Askew RC	3.00	1.25
❑ 122	Robert Geathers RC	3.00	1.25
❑ 123	Richard Alston RC	3.00	1.25
❑ 124	Bruce Thornton RC	2.00	.75
❑ 125	Patrick Crayton RC	4.00	1.50
❑ 126	Bradlee Van Pelt RC	6.00	2.50
❑ 127	Charlie Adams RC	2.00	.75
❑ 128	Nate Jackson RC	2.00	.75
❑ 129	Roc Alexander RC	2.00	.75
❑ 130	Romar Crenshaw RC	2.00	.75
❑ 131	Keith Smith RC	3.00	1.25
❑ 132	Joey Thomas RC	4.00	1.50
❑ 133	Kelvin Kight RC	2.00	.75
❑ 134	Scott McBrien RC	4.00	1.50
❑ 135	Andrae Thurman RC	2.00	.75
❑ 136	Derick Armstrong	3.00	1.25
❑ 137	Glenn Earl RC	3.00	1.25
❑ 138	Kendrick Starling RC	2.00	.75
❑ 139	Ben Hartsock RC	4.00	1.50
❑ 140	Gilbert Gardner RC	3.00	1.25
❑ 141	Jason David RC	4.00	1.50
❑ 142	Daryl Smith RC	4.00	1.50
❑ 143	Jared Allen RC	5.00	2.00
❑ 144	Jeris McIntyre RC	3.00	1.25
❑ 145	John Booth RC	3.00	1.25
❑ 146	Jonathan Smith RC	3.00	1.25
❑ 147	Junior Siavii RC	4.00	1.50
❑ 148	Keyaron Fox RC	3.00	1.25
❑ 149	Kris Wilson RC	4.00	1.50
❑ 150	Doug Easlick RC	3.00	1.25
❑ 151	Fred Russell RC	4.00	1.50
❑ 152	Tony Bua RC	3.00	1.25
❑ 153	Will Poole RC	4.00	1.50
❑ 154	Ben Nelson RC	2.00	.75
❑ 155	Brock Lesnar RC	5.00	2.00
❑ 156	Butchie Wallace RC	3.00	1.25
❑ 157	Darrion Scott RC	4.00	1.50
❑ 158	Dontarrious Thomas RC	4.00	1.50
❑ 159	Richard Owens RC	2.00	.75
❑ 160	Rod Davis RC	2.00	.75
❑ 161	Dexter Reid RC	2.00	.75
❑ 162	Kory Chapman RC	3.00	1.25
❑ 163	Marquise Hill RC	3.00	1.25
❑ 164	Courtney Watson RC	4.00	1.50
❑ 165	Mike Karney RC	3.00	1.25
❑ 166	Gibril Wilson RC	4.00	1.50
❑ 167	Reggie Torbor RC	3.00	1.25
❑ 168	Darrell McClover RC	3.00	1.25
❑ 169	Derrick Strait RC	4.00	1.50
❑ 170	Erik Coleman RC	4.00	1.50
❑ 171	Johnathan Reese RC	2.00	.75
❑ 172	Rashad Washington RC	3.00	1.25
❑ 173	Courtney Anderson RC	3.00	1.25
❑ 174	Stuart Schweigert RC	4.00	1.50
❑ 175	J.R. Reed RC	3.00	1.25
❑ 176	Justin Jenkins RC	3.00	1.25
❑ 177	Matt Ware RC	4.00	1.50
❑ 178	Nate Lawrie RC	3.00	1.25
❑ 179	Thomas Tapeh RC	3.00	1.25
❑ 180	Matt Kranchick RC	4.00	1.50
❑ 181	Willie Parker RC	20.00	10.00
❑ 182	Igor Olshansky RC	4.00	1.50
❑ 183	Ryan Krause RC	3.00	1.25
❑ 184	Shaun Phillips RC	3.00	1.25
❑ 185	Wes Welker RC	6.00	2.50
❑ 186	Richard Seigler RC	3.00	1.25
❑ 187	Shawntae Spencer RC	4.00	1.50
❑ 188	Marcus Tubbs RC	4.00	1.50
❑ 189	Niko Koutouvides RC	3.00	1.25
❑ 190	Brandon Chillar RC	3.00	1.25
❑ 191	Tony Hargrove RC	3.00	1.25
❑ 192	Mark Jones RC	3.00	1.25
❑ 193	Marquis Cooper RC	3.00	1.25
❑ 194	Antwan Odom RC	4.00	1.50
❑ 195	Michael Waddell RC	2.00	.75
❑ 196	Randy Starks RC	3.00	1.25
❑ 197	Rich Gardner RC	3.00	1.25
❑ 198	Travis Laboy RC	4.00	1.50
❑ 199	Vick King RC	3.00	1.25
❑ 200	Chris Cooley RC	4.00	1.50
❑ 201	Adimchinobe Echemandu RC	5.00	2.00
❑ 202	Ahmad Carroll RC	6.00	2.50
❑ 203	Andy Hall RC	5.00	2.00
❑ 204	B.J. Johnson RC	5.00	2.00
❑ 205	B.J. Symons RC	6.00	2.50
❑ 206	Brandon Miree RC	5.00	2.00
❑ 207	Bruce Perry RC	6.00	2.50
❑ 208	Carlos Francis RC	5.00	2.00
❑ 209	Casey Bramlet RC	5.00	2.00
❑ 210	Chris Gamble RC	6.00	2.50
❑ 211	Clarence Moore RC	6.00	2.50
❑ 212	Cody Pickett RC	6.00	2.50
❑ 213	Craig Krenzel RC	6.00	2.50
❑ 214	D.J. Hackett RC	5.00	2.00
❑ 215	D.J. Williams RC	6.00	2.50
❑ 216	Derrick Ward RC	3.00	1.25
❑ 217	Drew Carter RC	6.00	2.50
❑ 218	Drew Henson RC	6.00	2.50
❑ 219	Ernest Wilford RC	6.00	2.50
❑ 220	Jamaar Taylor RC	6.00	2.50
❑ 221	Jared Lorenzen RC	5.00	2.00
❑ 222	Jarrett Payton RC	5.00	2.00
❑ 223	Jason Babin RC	6.00	2.50
❑ 224	Jeff Smoker RC	6.00	2.50
❑ 225	Jerricho Cotchery RC	6.00	2.50
❑ 226	Jim Sorgi RC	6.00	2.50

❑ 227 John Navarre RC 6.00 2.50
❑ 228 Johnnie Morant RC 6.00 2.50
❑ 229 Jonathan Vilma RC 6.00 2.50
❑ 230 Josh Harris RC 6.00 2.50
❑ 231 Kenechi Udeze RC 6.00 2.50
❑ 232 Matt Mauck RC 6.00 2.50
❑ 233 Maurice Mann RC 5.00 2.00
❑ 234 Michael Turner RC 8.00 3.00
❑ 235 P.K. Sam RC 5.00 2.00
❑ 236 Quincy Wilson RC 5.00 2.00
❑ 237 Ran Carthon RC 5.00 2.00
❑ 238 Ricardo Colclough RC 6.00 2.50
❑ 239 Samie Parker RC 6.00 2.50
❑ 240 Sean Jones RC 5.00 2.00
❑ 241 Sean Taylor RC 6.00 2.50
❑ 242 Sloan Thomas RC 5.00 2.00
❑ 243 Tommie Harris RC 6.00 2.50
❑ 244 Triandos Luke RC 6.00 2.50
❑ 245 Troy Fleming RC 5.00 2.00
❑ 246 Vince Wilfork RC 6.00 2.50
❑ 247 Will Smith RC 6.00 2.50
❑ 248 Michael Boulware RC 6.00 2.50
❑ 249 Richard Smith RC 5.00 2.00
❑ 250 Teddy Lehman RC 6.00 2.50
❑ 251 Larry Fitzgerald JSY RC 20.00 7.50
❑ 252 DeAngelo Hall JSY RC 10.00 4.00
❑ 253 Matt Schaub JSY RC 20.00 7.50
❑ 254 Michael Jenkins JSY RC 8.00 3.00
❑ 255 Devard Darling JSY RC 8.00 3.00
❑ 256 J.P. Losman JSY RC 12.00 5.00
❑ 257 Lee Evans JSY RC 10.00 4.00
❑ 258 Keary Colbert JSY RC 10.00 4.00
❑ 259 Bernard Berrian JSY RC 8.00 3.00
❑ 260 Chris Perry JSY RC 10.00 4.00
❑ 261 Kellen Winslow Jr. JSY RC 12.00 5.00
❑ 262 Luke McCown JSY RC 8.00 3.00
❑ 263 Julius Jones JSY RC 20.00 7.50
❑ 264 Darius Watts JSY RC 8.00 3.00
❑ 265 Tatum Bell JSY RC 12.00 5.00
❑ 266 Kevin Jones JSY RC 15.00 6.00
❑ 267 Roy Williams JSY RC 15.00 6.00
❑ 268 Dunta Robinson JSY RC 8.00 3.00
❑ 269 Greg Jones JSY RC 8.00 3.00
❑ 270 Reggie Williams JSY RC 10.00 4.00
❑ 271 Mewelde Moore JSY RC 8.00 3.00
❑ 272 Ben Watson JSY RC 8.00 3.00
❑ 273 Cedric Cobbs JSY RC 8.00 3.00
❑ 274 Devery Henderson JSY RC 6.00 2.50
❑ 275 Eli Manning JSY RC 30.00 15.00
❑ 276 Robert Gallery JSY RC 8.00 3.00
❑ 277 Ben Roethlisberger JSY RC 50.00 25.00
❑ 278 Philip Rivers JSY RC 20.00 10.00
❑ 279 Derrick Hamilton JSY RC 6.00 2.50
❑ 280 Rashaun Woods JSY RC 8.00 3.00
❑ 281 Steven Jackson JSY RC 20.00 7.50
❑ 282 Michael Clayton JSY RC 12.00 5.00
❑ 283 Ben Troupe JSY RC 8.00 3.00
❑ 284 E.Manning/Rivers JSY 30.00 15.00
❑ 285 Fitzgerald/Ro.Williams JSY 20.00 7.50
❑ 286 Winslow Jr./G.Jones JSY 12.00 5.00
❑ 287 D.Hall/D.Robinson JSY 10.00 4.00
❑ 288 Re.Williams/Darling JSY 8.00 3.00
❑ 289 Roethlisberger/Losman JSY 50.00 25.00
❑ 290 Clayton/Henderson JSY 15.00 6.00
❑ 291 S.Jackson/Perry JSY 20.00 7.50
❑ 292 L.Evans/M.Jenkins JSY 12.00 5.00
❑ 293 R.Woods/T.Bell JSY 12.00 5.00
❑ 294 K.Jones/Berrian JSY 20.00 7.50
❑ 295 Watson/Troupe JSY 8.00 3.00
❑ 296 J.Jones/M.Moore JSY 20.00 7.50
❑ 297 M.Schaub/Hamilton JSY 20.00 7.50
❑ 298 L.McCown/Watts JSY 8.00 3.00
❑ 299 Colbert/Cobbs JSY 8.00 3.00

2005 Leaf Rookies and Stars

❑ COMP.SET w/o RC's (100) 20.00 7.50
❑ 201-250 RC PRINT RUN 799 SER.#'d SETS
❑ 251-279 JSY PRINT RUN 750 SER.#'d SETS
❑ 280-293 JSY DUAL PRINT RUN 500 SER.#'d SETS
❑ 1 Anquan Boldin .50 .20
❑ 2 Kurt Warner .50 .20
❑ 3 Larry Fitzgerald .75 .30
❑ 4 Michael Vick 1.25 .50
❑ 5 T.J. Duckett .50 .20
❑ 6 Warrick Dunn .50 .20
❑ 7 Jamal Lewis .75 .30
❑ 8 Kyle Boller .50 .20
❑ 9 Ray Lewis .75 .30
❑ 10 Derrick Mason .50 .20
❑ 11 J.P. Losman .75 .30
❑ 12 Lee Evans .50 .20
❑ 13 Willis McGahee .75 .30
❑ 14 DeShaun Foster .50 .20
❑ 15 Jake Delhomme .75 .30
❑ 16 Steve Smith .50 .20
❑ 17 Brian Urlacher .75 .30
❑ 18 Rex Grossman .50 .20
❑ 19 Muhsin Muhammad .50 .20
❑ 20 Carson Palmer .75 .30
❑ 21 Chad Johnson .75 .30
❑ 22 Rudi Johnson .50 .20
❑ 23 Lee Suggs .50 .20
❑ 24 Drew Bledsoe .75 .30
❑ 25 Julius Jones 1.00 .40
❑ 26 Keyshawn Johnson .50 .20
❑ 27 Roy Williams S .50 .20
❑ 28 Ashley Lelie .50 .20
❑ 29 Jake Plummer .50 .20
❑ 30 Rod Smith .50 .20
❑ 31 Tatum Bell .50 .20
❑ 32 Joey Harrington .75 .30
❑ 33 Kevin Jones .75 .30
❑ 34 Roy Williams WR .75 .30
❑ 35 Ahman Green .75 .30
❑ 36 Brett Favre 2.00 .75
❑ 37 Javon Walker .50 .20
❑ 38 Andre Johnson .50 .20
❑ 39 David Carr .75 .30
❑ 40 Domanick Davis .50 .20
❑ 41 Edgerrin James .75 .30
❑ 42 Marvin Harrison .75 .30
❑ 43 Peyton Manning 1.25 .50
❑ 44 Reggie Wayne .50 .20
❑ 45 Byron Leftwich .75 .30
❑ 46 Fred Taylor .50 .20
❑ 47 Jimmy Smith .50 .20
❑ 48 Priest Holmes .75 .30
❑ 49 Tony Gonzalez .50 .20
❑ 50 Trent Green .50 .20
❑ 51 Chris Chambers .50 .20
❑ 52 Daunte Culpepper .75 .30
❑ 53 Michael Bennett .50 .20
❑ 54 Nate Burleson .50 .20
❑ 55 Corey Dillon .50 .20
❑ 56 Deion Branch .50 .20
❑ 57 Tom Brady 2.00 .75
❑ 58 Aaron Brooks .50 .20
❑ 59 Deuce McAllister .75 .30
❑ 60 Joe Horn .50 .20
❑ 61 Eli Manning 1.50 .60
❑ 62 Jeremy Shockey .75 .30
❑ 63 Tiki Barber .75 .30
❑ 64 Plaxico Burress .50 .20
❑ 65 Chad Pennington .75 .30
❑ 66 Curtis Martin .75 .30
❑ 67 Laveranues Coles .50 .20
❑ 68 Jerry Porter .50 .20
❑ 69 Kerry Collins .50 .20
❑ 70 LaMont Jordan .75 .30
❑ 71 Randy Moss .75 .30
❑ 72 Brian Westbrook .50 .20
❑ 73 Donovan McNabb 1.00 .40
❑ 74 Terrell Owens .75 .30
❑ 75 Ben Roethlisberger 2.00 .75
❑ 76 Duce Staley .50 .20
❑ 77 Hines Ward .75 .30
❑ 78 Jerome Bettis .75 .30
❑ 79 Antonio Gates .75 .30
❑ 80 Drew Brees .75 .30
❑ 81 LaDainian Tomlinson 1.00 .40
❑ 82 Kevan Barlow .50 .20
❑ 83 Darrell Jackson .50 .20
❑ 84 Matt Hasselbeck .50 .20
❑ 85 Shaun Alexander 1.00 .40
❑ 86 Marc Bulger .75 .30
❑ 87 Steven Jackson 1.00 .40
❑ 88 Torry Holt .75 .30
❑ 89 Brian Griese .50 .20
❑ 90 Michael Clayton .75 .30
❑ 91 Chris Brown .50 .20
❑ 92 Drew Bennett .50 .20
❑ 93 Steve McNair .75 .30
❑ 94 Clinton Portis .75 .30
❑ 95 LaVar Arrington .75 .30
❑ 96 Santana Moss .50 .20
❑ 97 A.Smith QB CL/F.Gore 4.00 1.50
❑ 98 B.Edwards CL/C.Frye 2.00 .75
❑ 99 C.Fason CL/T.Williamson 1.25 .50
❑ 100 C.Rogers CL/J.Campbell 1.00 .40
❑ 101 Travis Johnson RC 4.00 1.50
❑ 102 Alex Smith TE RC 5.00 2.00
❑ 103 Channing Crowder RC 5.00 2.00
❑ 104 Craig Bragg RC 4.00 1.50
❑ 105 Darrent Williams RC 5.00 2.00
❑ 106 Derrick Wimbush RC 5.00 2.00
❑ 107 Josh Cribbs RC 5.00 2.00
❑ 108 Luis Castillo RC 5.00 2.00
❑ 109 Matt Roth RC 5.00 2.00
❑ 110 Mike Patterson RC 5.00 2.00
❑ 111 Fred Gibson RC 4.00 1.50
❑ 112 Marcus Spears RC 5.00 2.00
❑ 113 Brodney Pool RC 5.00 2.00
❑ 114 Barrett Ruud RC 5.00 2.00
❑ 115 Stanford Routt RC 4.00 1.50
❑ 116 Josh Bullocks RC 5.00 2.00
❑ 117 Kevin Burnett RC 5.00 2.00
❑ 118 Corey Webster RC 5.00 2.00
❑ 119 Lofa Tatupu RC 6.00 2.50
❑ 120 Mike Nugent RC 5.00 2.00
❑ 121 Jim Leonhard RC 8.00 3.00
❑ 122 Ronald Bartell RC 4.00 1.50
❑ 123 Nick Collins RC 5.00 2.00
❑ 124 Justin Miller RC 4.00 1.50
❑ 125 Jonathan Babineaux RC 4.00 1.50
❑ 126 Kelvin Hayden RC 4.00 1.50
❑ 127 Matt McCoy RC 4.00 1.50
❑ 128 Oshiomogho Atogwe RC 4.00 1.50
❑ 129 Stanley Wilson RC 4.00 1.50
❑ 130 Justin Tuck RC 5.00 2.00
❑ 131 Eric Green RC 2.50 1.00
❑ 132 Karl Paymah RC 8.00 3.00
❑ 133 Kirk Morrison RC 5.00 2.00
❑ 134 Dustin Fox RC 5.00 2.00
❑ 135 Alfred Fincher RC 4.00 1.50
❑ 136 Chris Henry RC 5.00 2.00
❑ 137 Ellis Hobbs RC 5.00 2.00
❑ 138 Scott Starks RC 4.00 1.50
❑ 139 Jordan Beck RC 4.00 1.50
❑ 140 Vincent Burns RC 4.00 1.50
❑ 141 Darryl Blackstock RC 4.00 1.50
❑ 142 Domonique Foxworth RC 5.00 2.00
❑ 143 Leroy Hill RC 5.00 2.00
❑ 144 Cedric Killings RC 4.00 1.50
❑ 145 Leonard Weaver RC 4.00 1.50
❑ 146 Sean Considine RC 5.00 2.00
❑ 147 Antonio Perkins RC 4.00 1.50
❑ 148 Travis Daniels RC 4.00 1.50
❑ 149 Vincent Fuller RC 4.00 1.50
❑ 150 Manuel White RC 4.00 1.50
❑ 151 Kerry Rhodes RC 5.00 2.00
❑ 152 Brady Poppinga RC 5.00 2.00
❑ 153 Chris Canty RC 5.00 2.00
❑ 154 James Sanders RC 5.00 2.00
❑ 155 Matt Giordano RC 5.00 2.00
❑ 156 Boomer Grigsby RC 6.00 2.50
❑ 157 Donte Nicholson RC 5.00 2.00
❑ 158 Jerome Collins RC 4.00 1.50
❑ 159 Trent Cole RC 5.00 2.00
❑ 160 Alphonso Hodge RC 2.50 1.00
❑ 161 Jonathan Welsh RC 4.00 1.50
❑ 162 Adam Seward RC 6.00 2.50
❑ 163 Robert McCune RC 4.00 1.50
❑ 164 Eric King RC 4.00 1.50
❑ 165 Gerald Sensabaugh RC 8.00 3.00
❑ 166 Justin Green RC 5.00 2.00
❑ 167 Jeb Huckeba RC 5.00 2.00
❑ 168 Michael Boley RC 4.00 1.50
❑ 169 Andre Maddox RC 4.00 1.50

❑ 170 Rian Wallace RC 4.00 1.50
❑ 171 Michael Hawkins RC 4.00 1.50
❑ 172 Lance Mitchell RC 4.00 1.50
❑ 173 Ryan Claridge RC 4.00 1.50
❑ 174 James Butler RC 4.00 1.50
❑ 175 Ryan Riddle RC 2.50 1.00
❑ 176 Bo Scaife RC 4.00 1.50
❑ 177 Chris Harris RC 10.00 4.00
❑ 178 C.C. Brown RC 4.00 1.50
❑ 179 Pat Thomas RC 4.00 1.50
❑ 180 Derrick Johnson CB RC 5.00 2.00
❑ 181 Joel Dreessen RC 4.00 1.50
❑ 182 Rick Razzano RC 5.00 2.00
❑ 183 Nehemiah Broughton RC 4.00 1.50
❑ 184 Marcus Maxwell RC 4.00 1.50
❑ 185 Harry Williams RC 4.00 1.50
❑ 186 Patrick Estes RC 4.00 1.50
❑ 187 Billy Bajema RC 4.00 1.50
❑ 188 Madison Hedgecock RC 5.00 2.00
❑ 189 Manuel Wright RC 5.00 2.00
❑ 190 Roscoe Crosby RC 4.00 1.50
❑ 191 Wesley Duke RC 5.00 2.00
❑ 192 Ronnie Cruz RC 4.00 1.50
❑ 193 Adam Bergen RC 5.00 2.00
❑ 194 B.J. Ward RC 4.00 1.50
❑ 195 Stephen Spach RC 4.00 1.50
❑ 196 Marviel Underwood RC 4.00 1.50
❑ 197 John Bronson RC 4.00 1.50
❑ 198 Zak Keasey RC 5.00 2.00
❑ 199 Gregg Guenther RC 4.00 1.50
❑ 200 Jerome Carter RC 4.00 1.50
❑ 201 Aaron Rodgers RC 20.00 7.50
❑ 202 Adrian McPherson RC 6.00 2.50
❑ 203 Alvin Pearman RC 6.00 2.50
❑ 204 Airese Currie RC 6.00 2.50
❑ 205 Anthony Davis RC 5.00 2.00
❑ 206 Brandon Jacobs RC 8.00 3.00
❑ 207 Brandon Jones RC 6.00 2.50
❑ 208 Bryant McFadden RC 6.00 2.50
❑ 209 Cedric Benson RC 12.00 5.00
❑ 210 Cedric Houston RC 6.00 2.50
❑ 211 Chad Owens RC 6.00 2.50
❑ 212 Chris Henry 6.00 2.50
❑ 213 Craphonso Thorpe RC 5.00 2.00
❑ 214 Damien Nash RC 5.00 2.00
❑ 215 Dan Cody RC 6.00 2.50
❑ 216 Dan Orlovsky RC 8.00 3.00
❑ 217 Dante Ridgeway RC 5.00 2.00
❑ 218 Darren Sproles RC 6.00 2.50
❑ 219 David Greene RC 6.00 2.50
❑ 220 David Pollack RC 6.00 2.50
❑ 221 Deandra Cobb RC 5.00 2.00
❑ 222 DeMarcus Ware RC 10.00 4.00
❑ 223 Derek Anderson RC 6.00 2.50
❑ 224 Derrick Johnson RC 10.00 4.00
❑ 225 Fabian Washington RC 6.00 2.50
❑ 226 Roydell Williams RC 6.00 2.50
❑ 227 Heath Miller RC 15.00 6.00
❑ 228 J.R. Russell RC 5.00 2.00
❑ 229 James Kilian RC 6.00 2.50
❑ 230 Jerome Mathis RC 6.00 2.50
❑ 231 Larry Brackins RC 5.00 2.00
❑ 232 LeRon McCoy RC 5.00 2.00
❑ 233 Lionel Gates RC 5.00 2.00
❑ 234 Marion Barber RC 10.00 4.00
❑ 235 Marlin Jackson RC 6.00 2.50
❑ 236 Matt Cassel RC 10.00 4.00
❑ 237 Mike Williams 12.00 5.00
❑ 238 Nate Washington RC 5.00 2.00
❑ 239 Noah Herron RC 6.00 2.50
❑ 240 Fred Amey RC 5.00 2.00
❑ 241 Paris Warren RC 5.00 2.00
❑ 242 Rasheed Marshall RC 6.00 2.50
❑ 243 Ryan Fitzpatrick RC 10.00 4.00
❑ 244 Shaun Cody RC 6.00 2.50
❑ 245 Shawne Merriman RC 10.00 4.00
❑ 246 Tab Perry RC 6.00 2.50
❑ 247 Thomas Davis RC 6.00 2.50
❑ 248 Tyson Thompson RC 8.00 3.00
❑ 249 Chris Carr RC 8.00 3.00
❑ 250 Odell Thurman RC 6.00 2.50
❑ 251 Adam Jones JSY RC 8.00 3.00
❑ 252 Alex Smith QB JSY RC 20.00 7.50
❑ 253 Andrew Walter JSY RC 10.00 4.00
❑ 254 Antrel Rolle JSY RC 8.00 3.00
❑ 255 Braylon Edwards JSY RC 15.00 6.00
❑ 256 Carlos Rogers JSY RC 10.00 4.00
❑ 257 Cadillac Williams JSY RC 25.00 10.00
❑ 258 Charlie Frye JSY RC 12.00 5.00
❑ 259 Ciatrick Fason JSY RC 8.00 3.00
❑ 260 Courtney Roby JSY RC 8.00 3.00
❑ 261 Eric Shelton JSY RC 8.00 3.00
❑ 262 Frank Gore JSY RC 12.00 5.00
❑ 263 J.J. Arrington JSY RC 10.00 4.00
❑ 264 Jason Campbell JSY RC 10.00 4.00
❑ 265 Kyle Orton JSY RC 12.00 5.00
❑ 266 Mark Clayton JSY RC 10.00 4.00
❑ 267 Mark Bradley JSY RC 8.00 3.00
❑ 268 Matt Jones JSY RC 15.00 6.00
❑ 269 Maurice Clarett JSY 8.00 3.00
❑ 270 Reggie Brown JSY RC 8.00 3.00
❑ 271 Roddy White JSY RC 8.00 3.00
❑ 272 Ronnie Brown JSY RC 20.00 7.50
❑ 273 Roscoe Parrish JSY RC 6.00 2.50
❑ 274 Ryan Moats JSY RC 8.00 3.00
❑ 275 Stefan LeFors JSY RC 8.00 3.00
❑ 276 Terrence Murphy JSY RC 8.00 3.00
❑ 277 Troy Williamson JSY RC 12.00 5.00
❑ 278 Vernand Morency JSY RC 8.00 3.00
❑ 279 Vincent Jackson JSY RC 8.00 3.00
❑ 280 A.Smith QB J/J.Campbell J 25.00 10.00
❑ 281 R.Brown J/C.Williams J 30.00 12.50
❑ 282 B.Edwards J/T.Williamson J 20.00 7.50
❑ 283 A.Jones J/A.Rolle J 10.00 4.00
❑ 284 R.Parrish J/F.Gore J 15.00 6.00
❑ 285 C.Frye J/A.Walter J 15.00 6.00
❑ 286 J.Arrington J/E.Shelton J 12.00 5.00
❑ 287 C.Rogers J/K.Orton J 12.00 5.00
❑ 288 M.Clayton J/M.Bradley J 12.00 5.00
❑ 289 R.White J/Re.Brown J 10.00 4.00
❑ 290 T.Murphy J/C.Roby J 10.00 4.00
❑ 291 M.Clarett J/C.Fason J 10.00 4.00
❑ 292 R.Moats J/S.LeFors J 10.00 4.00
❑ 293 M.Jones J/V.Jackson J 15.00 6.00

2005 Leaf Rookies and Stars Longevity

❑ COMP.SET w/o RC's (100) 25.00 10.00
❑ *VETS 1-100: .6X TO 1.5X BASIC CARDS
❑ *ROOKIES 101-200: .5X TO 1.2X
❑ 101-200 PRINT RUN 999 SER.#'d SETS
❑ *ROOKIES 201-250: .4X TO 1X
❑ 201-250 PRINT RUN 599 SER.#'d SETS
❑ *ROOKIE JSYs 251-279: .4X TO 1X
❑ 251-279 JSY PRINT RUN 299 SER.#'d SETS

2006 Leaf Rookies and Stars

❑ 1 Anquan Boldin .40 .15
❑ 2 Edgerrin James .60 .25
❑ 3 Kurt Warner .40 .15
❑ 4 Larry Fitzgerald .60 .25
❑ 5 Alge Crumpler .40 .15
❑ 6 Michael Vick .75 .30
❑ 7 Warrick Dunn .40 .15
❑ 8 Derrick Mason .30 .12
❑ 9 Jamal Lewis .40 .15
❑ 10 Mike Anderson .40 .15
❑ 11 Josh Reed .30 .12
❑ 12 Lee Evans .40 .15
❑ 13 Willis McGahee .60 .25
❑ 14 DeShaun Foster .40 .15
❑ 15 Jake Delhomme .40 .15
❑ 16 Keyshawn Johnson .40 .15
❑ 17 Steve Smith .60 .25
❑ 18 Cedric Benson .60 .25
❑ 19 Muhsin Muhammad .40 .15
❑ 20 Rex Grossman .60 .25
❑ 21 Carson Palmer .60 .25
❑ 22 Chad Johnson .40 .15
❑ 23 Rudi Johnson .40 .15
❑ 24 T.J. Houshmandzadeh .40 .15
❑ 25 Charlie Frye .40 .15
❑ 26 Joe Jurevicius .40 .15
❑ 27 Reuben Droughns .40 .15
❑ 28 Drew Bledsoe .60 .25
❑ 29 Julius Jones .60 .25
❑ 30 Terrell Owens .60 .25
❑ 31 Terry Glenn .40 .15
❑ 32 Jake Plummer .40 .15
❑ 33 Rod Smith .40 .15
❑ 34 Tatum Bell .40 .15
❑ 35 Josh McCown .40 .15
❑ 36 Kevin Jones .60 .25
❑ 37 Roy Williams WR .60 .25
❑ 38 Ahman Green .40 .15
❑ 39 Brett Favre 1.25 .50
❑ 40 Donald Driver .40 .15
❑ 41 Robert Ferguson .30 .12
❑ 42 Samkon Gado .60 .25
❑ 43 Andre Johnson .40 .15
❑ 44 David Carr .40 .15
❑ 45 Domanick Davis .40 .15
❑ 46 Eric Moulds .40 .15
❑ 47 Marvin Harrison .60 .25
❑ 48 Peyton Manning 1.00 .40
❑ 49 Reggie Wayne .40 .15
❑ 50 Dallas Clark .30 .12
❑ 51 Fred Taylor .40 .15
❑ 52 Byron Leftwich .40 .15
❑ 53 Jimmy Smith .40 .15
❑ 54 Larry Johnson .75 .30
❑ 55 Tony Gonzalez .40 .15
❑ 56 Trent Green .40 .15
❑ 57 Eddie Kennison .30 .12
❑ 58 Chris Chambers .40 .15
❑ 59 Daunte Culpepper .60 .25
❑ 60 Ronnie Brown .60 .25
❑ 61 Chester Taylor .40 .15
❑ 62 Brad Johnson .40 .15
❑ 63 Deion Branch .40 .15
❑ 64 Corey Dillon .40 .15
❑ 65 Tom Brady 1.00 .40
❑ 66 Deuce McAllister .40 .15
❑ 67 Donte Stallworth .40 .15
❑ 68 Drew Brees .60 .25
❑ 69 Eli Manning .75 .30
❑ 70 Plaxico Burress .40 .15
❑ 71 Tiki Barber .60 .25
❑ 72 Chad Pennington .40 .15
❑ 73 Curtis Martin .60 .25
❑ 74 Laveranues Coles .40 .15
❑ 75 Aaron Brooks .40 .15
❑ 76 LaMont Jordan .40 .15
❑ 77 Randy Moss .60 .25
❑ 78 Brian Westbrook .40 .15
❑ 79 Donovan McNabb .60 .25
❑ 80 Jabar Gaffney .30 .12
❑ 81 Hines Ward .60 .25
❑ 82 Ben Roethlisberger 1.00 .40
❑ 83 Willie Parker .75 .30
❑ 84 Antonio Gates .60 .25
❑ 85 LaDainian Tomlinson .75 .30
❑ 86 Philip Rivers .60 .25
❑ 87 Alex Smith QB .75 .30
❑ 88 Antonio Bryant .40 .15
❑ 89 Kevan Barlow .40 .15
❑ 90 Darrell Jackson .40 .15
❑ 91 Matt Hasselbeck .40 .15
❑ 92 Shaun Alexander .60 .25
❑ 93 Torry Holt .40 .15

❑ 94 Steven Jackson .60 .25
❑ 95 Cadillac Williams .60 .25
❑ 96 Joey Galloway .40 .15
❑ 97 David Givens .40 .15
❑ 98 Drew Bennett .30 .12
❑ 99 Antwaan Randle El .40 .15
❑ 100 Clinton Portis .60 .25
❑ 101 Kamerion Wimbley RC 4.00 1.50
❑ 102 Mathias Kiwanuka RC 5.00 2.00
❑ 103 Reggie McNeal RC 3.00 1.25
❑ 104 Claude Wroten RC 2.00 .75
❑ 105 Gabe Watson RC 3.00 1.25
❑ 106 D'Qwell Jackson RC 3.00 1.25
❑ 107 Todd Watkins RC 3.00 1.25
❑ 108 Bennie Brazell RC 3.00 1.25
❑ 109 David Anderson RC 3.00 1.25
❑ 110 John David Washington RC 3.00 1.25
❑ 111 Marques Hagans RC 3.00 1.25
❑ 112 Kevin Youngblood RC 3.00 1.25
❑ 113 Ben Obomanu RC 3.00 1.25
❑ 114 Jamal Jones RC 3.00 1.25
❑ 115 Nick Mangold RC 2.00 .75
❑ 116 Davin Joseph RC 3.00 1.25
❑ 117 Erik Meyer RC 3.00 1.25
❑ 118 Taurean Henderson RC 4.00 1.50
❑ 119 A.J. Nicholson RC 2.00 .75
❑ 120 Thomas Howard RC 4.00 1.50
❑ 121 Jon Alston RC 4.00 1.50
❑ 122 Ashton Youboty RC 4.00 1.50
❑ 123 Alan Zemaitis RC 4.00 1.50
❑ 124 Lawrence Vickers RC 3.00 1.25
❑ 125 J.D. Runnels RC 3.00 1.25
❑ 126 Ray Perkins RC 3.00 1.25
❑ 127 Jeff King RC 3.00 1.25
❑ 128 Quinn Sypniewski RC 3.00 1.25
❑ 129 Jason Carter RC 3.00 1.25
❑ 130 Malcolm Floyd RC 4.00 1.50
❑ 131 Mike Jennings RC 3.00 1.25
❑ 132 Chris Gocong RC 3.00 1.25
❑ 133 Frostee Rucker RC 3.00 1.25
❑ 134 Jason Hatcher RC 3.00 1.25
❑ 135 Victor Adeyanju RC 3.00 1.25
❑ 136 Elvis Dumervil RC 2.00 .75
❑ 137 Ray Edwards RC 3.00 1.25
❑ 138 Anthony Schlegel RC 3.00 1.25
❑ 139 Freddie Keiaho RC 3.00 1.25
❑ 140 Gerris Wilkinson RC 2.00 .75
❑ 141 Leon Williams RC 3.00 1.25
❑ 142 Stephen Tulloch RC 3.00 1.25
❑ 143 Jamar Williams RC 3.00 1.25
❑ 144 Clint Ingram RC 4.00 1.50
❑ 145 James Anderson RC 2.00 .75
❑ 146 Darrell Hackney RC 3.00 1.25
❑ 147 Paul Pinegar RC 3.00 1.25
❑ 148 Brandon Kirsch RC 4.00 1.50
❑ 149 Andre Hall RC 3.00 1.25
❑ 150 De'Arrius Howard RC 4.00 1.50
❑ 151 Cedric Humes RC 4.00 1.50
❑ 152 Wendell Mathis RC 3.00 1.25
❑ 153 Gerald Riggs RC 4.00 1.50
❑ 154 Quinton Ganther RC 3.00 1.25
❑ 155 Martin Nance RC 3.00 1.25
❑ 156 Greg Lee RC 3.00 1.25
❑ 157 Jai Lewis RC 3.00 1.25
❑ 158 Cory Rodgers RC 4.00 1.50
❑ 159 Mike Espy RC 4.00 1.50
❑ 160 Chris Barclay RC 3.00 1.25
❑ 161 DeMeco Ryans RC 5.00 2.00
❑ 162 Rocky McIntosh RC 4.00 1.50
❑ 163 David Kirtman RC 3.00 1.25
❑ 164 Skyler Green RC 4.00 1.50
❑ 165 Will Blackmon RC 3.00 1.25
❑ 166 Darryl Tapp RC 3.00 1.25
❑ 167 Dusty Dvoracek RC 4.00 1.50
❑ 168 Richard Marshall RC 3.00 1.25
❑ 169 Tim Jennings RC 3.00 1.25
❑ 170 David Pittman RC 3.00 1.25
❑ 171 DeMario Minter RC 3.00 1.25
❑ 172 Marcus Maxey RC 3.00 1.25
❑ 173 Roman Harper RC 3.00 1.25
❑ 174 Anthony Smith RC 5.00 2.00
❑ 175 Nate Salley RC 3.00 1.25
❑ 176 Mike Hass RC 4.00 1.50
❑ 177 Greg Blue RC 3.00 1.25
❑ 178 Daniel Bullocks RC 4.00 1.50
❑ 179 Danieal Manning RC 4.00 1.50
❑ 180 Calvin Lowry RC 4.00 1.50
❑ 181 Eric Smith RC 3.00 1.25
❑ 182 Jimmy Williams RC 4.00 1.50
❑ 183 Cedric Griffin RC 3.00 1.25
❑ 184 Ko Simpson RC 3.00 1.25
❑ 185 Pat Watkins RC 4.00 1.50
❑ 186 Marcus Vick RC 3.00 1.25
❑ 187 Bernard Pollard RC 3.00 1.25
❑ 188 Darnell Bing RC 4.00 1.50
❑ 189 Cory Ross RC 6.00 2.50
❑ 190 Patrick Cobbs RC 4.00 1.50
❑ 191 Montell Owens RC 3.00 1.25
❑ 192 Chris Hannon RC 3.00 1.25
❑ 193 John Madsen RC 4.00 1.50
❑ 194 Shaun Bodiford RC 3.00 1.25
❑ 195 Fred Evans RC 3.00 1.25
❑ 196 Cletis Gordon RC 2.00 .75
❑ 197 Jarrad Page RC 4.00 1.50
❑ 198 Brett Elliott RC 4.00 1.50
❑ 199 Brett Basanez RC 4.00 1.50
❑ 200 Drew Olson RC 3.00 1.25
❑ 201 Jay Cutler RC 20.00 8.00
❑ 202 Brodie Croyle RC 8.00 3.00
❑ 203 Ingle Martin RC 5.00 2.00
❑ 204 Derrick Ross RC 4.00 1.50
❑ 205 Bruce Gradkowski RC 8.00 3.00
❑ 206 D.J. Shockley RC 5.00 2.00
❑ 207 Joseph Addai RC 15.00 6.00
❑ 208 P.J. Daniels RC 4.00 1.50
❑ 209 Marques Colston RC 20.00 8.00
❑ 210 Jerome Harrison RC 5.00 2.00
❑ 211 Wali Lundy RC 5.00 2.00
❑ 212 Mike Bell RC 8.00 3.00
❑ 213 Miles Austin RC 4.00 1.50
❑ 214 Anthony Fasano RC 5.00 2.00
❑ 215 Tony Scheffler RC 5.00 2.00
❑ 216 Leonard Pope RC 5.00 2.00
❑ 217 David Thomas RC 5.00 2.00
❑ 218 Dominique Byrd RC 4.00 1.50
❑ 219 Garrett Mills RC 5.00 2.00
❑ 220 Hank Baskett RC 5.00 2.00
❑ 221 Greg Jennings RC 10.00 4.00
❑ 222 Devin Hester RC 10.00 4.00
❑ 223 Willie Reid RC 5.00 2.00
❑ 224 Brad Smith RC 5.00 2.00
❑ 225 Sam Hurd RC 8.00 3.00
❑ 226 Owen Daniels RC 5.00 2.00
❑ 227 Domenik Hixon RC 4.00 1.50
❑ 228 Jeremy Bloom RC 4.00 1.50
❑ 229 Dawan Landry RC 5.00 2.00
❑ 230 Jonathan Orr RC 4.00 1.50
❑ 231 Delanie Walker RC 4.00 1.50
❑ 232 Adam Jennings RC 4.00 1.50
❑ 233 Jeffrey Webb RC 4.00 1.50
❑ 234 Ethan Kilmer RC 5.00 2.00
❑ 235 Tye Hill RC 5.00 2.00
❑ 236 Jason Allen RC 5.00 2.00
❑ 237 Antonio Cromartie RC 5.00 2.00
❑ 238 D'Brickashaw Ferguson RC 5.00 2.00
❑ 239 Tamba Hali RC 5.00 2.00
❑ 240 Haloti Ngata RC 5.00 2.00
❑ 241 Brodrick Bunkley RC 5.00 2.00
❑ 242 John McCargo RC 4.00 1.50
❑ 243 Johnathan Joseph RC 4.00 1.50
❑ 244 Kelly Jennings RC 5.00 2.00
❑ 245 Donte Whitner RC 5.00 2.00
❑ 246 Abdul Hodge RC 5.00 2.00
❑ 247 Ernie Sims RC 6.00 2.50
❑ 248 Chad Greenway RC 5.00 2.00
❑ 249 Bobby Carpenter RC 5.00 2.00
❑ 250 Manny Lawson RC 5.00 2.00
❑ 251 Matt Leinart JSY/599 RC 20.00 8.00
❑ 252 Kellen Clemens JSY RC 8.00 3.00
❑ 253 Tarvaris Jackson JSY RC 8.00 3.00
❑ 254 Charlie Whitehurst JSY RC 8.00 3.00
❑ 255 DeAn.Williams JSY/599 RC 12.00 5.00
❑ 256 Maurice Drew JSY RC 10.00 4.00
❑ 257 Brian Calhoun JSY RC 6.00 2.50
❑ 258 Jerious Norwood JSY RC 10.00 4.00
❑ 259 Vernon Davis JSY RC 10.00 4.00
❑ 260 Joe Klopfenstein JSY RC 6.00 2.50
❑ 261 Sinorice Moss JSY RC 8.00 3.00
❑ 262 Derek Hagan JSY RC 6.00 2.50
❑ 263 Brandon Williams JSY RC 6.00 2.50
❑ 264 Michael Robinson JSY RC 8.00 3.00
❑ 265 Jason Avant JSY RC 6.00 2.50
❑ 266 Brandon Marshall JSY RC 6.00 2.50
❑ 267 Demetrius Williams JSY RC 6.00 2.50
❑ 268 Mario Williams JSY RC 8.00 3.00
❑ 269 Michael Huff JSY RC 8.00 3.00
❑ 270 Chad Jackson JSY RC 8.00 3.00
❑ 271 Vince Young JSY AU/249 RC 150.00 90.00
❑ 272 Omar Jacobs JSY AU/449 RC 15.00 6.00
❑ 273 Reggie Bush JSY AU/99 RC 300.00 150.00
❑ 274 L.Maroney JSY AU/99 RC 100.00 50.00
❑ 275 LenDale White JSY AU/249 RC 40.00 15.00
❑ 276 L.Washington JSY AU/199 RC 30.00 12.00
❑ 277 M.Lewis JSY AU/449 RC 15.00 6.00
❑ 278 S.Holmes JSY AU/449 RC 40.00 15.00
❑ 279 Travis Wilson JSY AU/449 RC 12.00 5.00
❑ 280 Maurice Stovall JSY AU/99 RC 20.00 8.00
❑ 281 A.J. Hawk JSY AU/99 RC 60.00 30.00

1997 Leaf Signature

❑ COMPLETE SET (117) 150.00 90.00
❑ 1 Karim Abdul-Jabbar 2.50 1.00
❑ 2 Troy Aikman 5.00 2.00
❑ 3 Derrick Alexander WR 1.50 .60
❑ 4 Terry Allen 2.50 1.00
❑ 5 Mike Alstott 2.50 1.00
❑ 6 Jamal Anderson 2.50 1.00
❑ 7 Reidel Anthony RC 2.50 1.00
❑ 8 Darnell Autry RC 1.50 .60
❑ 9 Tony Banks 1.50 .60
❑ 10 Tiki Barber RC 10.00 4.00
❑ 11 Pat Barnes RC 2.50 1.00
❑ 12 Jerome Bettis 2.50 1.00
❑ 13 Tim Biakabutuka 1.50 .60
❑ 14 Will Blackwell RC 1.50 .60
❑ 15 Jeff Blake 1.50 .60
❑ 16 Drew Bledsoe 3.00 1.25
❑ 17 Peter Boulware RC 2.50 1.00
❑ 18 Robert Brooks 1.50 .60
❑ 19 Dave Brown 1.50 .60
❑ 20 Tim Brown 2.50 1.00
❑ 21 Isaac Bruce 2.50 1.00
❑ 22 Mark Brunell 3.00 1.25
❑ 23 Rae Carruth RC 1.00 .40
❑ 24 Ki-Jana Carter 1.00 .40
❑ 25 Cris Carter 2.50 1.00
❑ 26 Larry Centers 1.50 .60
❑ 27 Ben Coates 1.50 .60
❑ 28 Kerry Collins 2.50 1.00
❑ 29 Todd Collins 1.00 .40
❑ 30 Albert Connell RC 2.50 1.00
❑ 31 Curtis Conway 1.50 .60
❑ 32 Terrell Davis 3.00 1.25
❑ 33 Troy Davis RC 1.50 .60
❑ 34 Corey Dillon RC 10.00 4.00
❑ 35 Jim Druckenmiller RC 1.50 .60
❑ 36 Warrick Dunn RC 5.00 2.00
❑ 37 John Elway 10.00 4.00
❑ 38 Bert Emanuel 1.50 .60
❑ 39 Bobby Engram 1.50 .60
❑ 40 Boomer Esiason 1.50 .60
❑ 41 Jim Everett 1.00 .40
❑ 42 Marshall Faulk 3.00 1.25
❑ 43 Brett Favre 10.00 4.00
❑ 44 Antonio Freeman 2.50 1.00
❑ 45 Gus Frerotte 1.00 .40
❑ 46 Irving Fryar 1.50 .60
❑ 47 Joey Galloway 1.50 .60
❑ 48 Eddie George 2.50 1.00
❑ 49 Jeff George 1.50 .60
❑ 50 Tony Gonzalez RC 5.00 2.00
❑ 51 Jay Graham 1.50 .60
❑ 52 Elvis Grbac 1.50 .60
❑ 53 Darrell Green 1.50 .60
❑ 54 Yatil Green RC 1.50 .60
❑ 55 Rodney Hampton 1.50 .60
❑ 56 Byron Hanspard RC 1.50 .60
❑ 57 Jim Harbaugh 1.50 .60
❑ 58 Marvin Harrison 2.50 1.00
❑ 59 Garrison Hearst 1.50 .60

❑ 60 Greg Hill 1.00 .40
❑ 61 Ike Hilliard RC 2.50 1.00
❑ 62 Jeff Hostetler 1.00 .40
❑ 63 Brad Johnson 2.50 1.00
❑ 64 Keyshawn Johnson 2.50 1.00
❑ 65 Daryl Johnston 1.50 .60
❑ 66 Napoleon Kaufman 2.50 1.00
❑ 67 Jim Kelly 2.50 1.00
❑ 68 Eddie Kennison 1.50 .60
❑ 69 Joey Kent 2.50 1.00
❑ 70 Bernie Kosar 1.00 .40
❑ 71 Erik Kramer 1.00 .40
❑ 72 Dorsey Levens 2.50 1.00
❑ 73 Kevin Lockett RC 1.50 .60
❑ 74 Dan Marino 10.00 4.00
❑ 75 Curtis Martin 3.00 1.25
❑ 76 Tony Martin 1.50 .60
❑ 77 Leeland McElroy 1.00 .40
❑ 78 Steve McNair 3.00 1.25
❑ 79 Natrone Means 1.50 .60
❑ 80 Eric Metcalf 1.50 .60
❑ 81 Anthony Miller 1.00 .40
❑ 82 Rick Mirer 1.00 .40
❑ 83 Scott Mitchell 1.50 .60
❑ 84 Warren Moon 2.50 1.00
❑ 85 Herman Moore 1.50 .60
❑ 86 Muhsin Muhammad 1.50 .60
❑ 87 Adrian Murrell 1.50 .60
❑ 88 Neil O'Donnell 1.50 .60
❑ 89 Terrell Owens 3.00 1.25
❑ 90 Brett Perriman 1.00 .40
❑ 91 Lawrence Phillips 1.00 .40
❑ 92 Jake Plummer RC 8.00 3.00
❑ 93 Andre Reed 1.50 .60
❑ 94 Jerry Rice 5.00 2.00
❑ 95 Darrell Russell RC 1.00 .40
❑ 96 Rashaan Salaam 1.00 .40
❑ 97 Barry Sanders 8.00 3.00
❑ 98 Chris Sanders 1.00 .40
❑ 99 Deion Sanders 2.50 1.00
❑ 100 Frank Sanders 1.50 .60
❑ 101 Darnay Scott 1.50 .60
❑ 102 Junior Seau 2.50 1.00
❑ 103 Shannon Sharpe 1.50 .60
❑ 104 Sedrick Shaw RC 1.50 .60
❑ 105 Heath Shuler 1.00 .40
❑ 106 Antowain Smith RC 4.00 1.50
❑ 107 Bruce Smith 1.50 .60
❑ 108 Emmitt Smith 8.00 3.00
❑ 109 Kordell Stewart 2.50 1.00
❑ 110 J.J. Stokes 1.50 .60
❑ 111 Vinny Testaverde 1.50 .60
❑ 112 Thurman Thomas 2.50 1.00
❑ 113 Tamarick Vanover 1.50 .60
❑ 114 Herschel Walker 1.50 .60
❑ 115 Michael Westbrook 1.50 .60
❑ 116 Danny Wuerffel RC 2.50 1.00
❑ 117 Steve Young 3.00 1.25

1995 Metal

❑ COMPLETE SET (200) 20.00 7.50
❑ 1 Garrison Hearst .40 .15
❑ 2 Seth Joyner .10 .02
❑ 3 Dave Krieg .10 .02
❑ 4 Lorenzo Lynch .10 .02
❑ 5 Rob Moore .20 .07
❑ 6 Eric Swann .20 .07
❑ 7 Aeneas Williams .10 .02
❑ 8 Chris Doleman .10 .02
❑ 9 Bert Emanuel .40 .15
❑ 10 Jeff George .20 .07
❑ 11 Craig Heyward .20 .07
❑ 12 Terance Mathis .20 .07
❑ 13 Eric Metcalf .20 .07
❑ 14 Cornelius Bennett .20 .07
❑ 15 Bucky Brooks .10 .02
❑ 16 Jeff Burris .10 .02
❑ 17 Jim Kelly .40 .15
❑ 18 Andre Reed .20 .07
❑ 19 Bruce Smith .40 .15
❑ 20 Don Beebe .10 .02
❑ 21 Kerry Collins RC 1.50 .60
❑ 22 Barry Foster .20 .07
❑ 23 Lamar Lathon .10 .02
❑ 24 Sam Mills .20 .07
❑ 25 Tyrone Poole RC .40 .15
❑ 26 Frank Reich .10 .02
❑ 27 Joe Cain .10 .02
❑ 28 Curtis Conway .40 .15
❑ 29 Jeff Graham .10 .02
❑ 30 Erik Kramer .10 .02
❑ 31 Rashaan Salaam RC .20 .07
❑ 32 Lewis Tillman .10 .02
❑ 33 Chris Zorich .10 .02
❑ 34 Jeff Blake RC .75 .30
❑ 35 Ki-Jana Carter RC .40 .15
❑ 36 Carl Pickens .20 .07
❑ 37 Corey Sawyer .10 .02
❑ 38 Darnay Scott .20 .07
❑ 39 Dan Wilkinson .20 .07
❑ 40 Darryl Williams .10 .02
❑ 41 Derrick Alexander WR .40 .15
❑ 42 Leroy Hoard .10 .02
❑ 43 Michael Jackson .20 .07
❑ 44 Antonio Langham .10 .02
❑ 45 Andre Rison .20 .07
❑ 46 Vinny Testaverde .20 .07
❑ 47 Eric Turner .10 .02
❑ 48 Troy Aikman 1.00 .40
❑ 49 Charles Haley .20 .07
❑ 50 Michael Irvin .40 .15
❑ 51 Daryl Johnston .20 .07
❑ 52 Jay Novacek .20 .07
❑ 53 Emmitt Smith 1.50 .60
❑ 54 Kevin Williams WR .20 .07
❑ 55 Steve Atwater .10 .02
❑ 56 Rod Bernstine .10 .02
❑ 57 John Elway 2.00 .75
❑ 58 Glyn Milburn .10 .02
❑ 59 Anthony Miller .20 .07
❑ 60 Mike Pritchard .10 .02
❑ 61 Shannon Sharpe .20 .07
❑ 62 Mike Johnson .10 .02
❑ 63 Scott Mitchell .20 .07
❑ 64 Herman Moore .40 .15
❑ 65 Brett Perriman .20 .07
❑ 66 Barry Sanders 1.50 .60
❑ 67 Chris Spielman .20 .07
❑ 68 Edgar Bennett .20 .07
❑ 69 Robert Brooks .40 .15
❑ 70 Brett Favre 2.00 .75
❑ 71 LeShon Johnson .20 .07
❑ 72 George Koonce .10 .02
❑ 73 Reggie White .40 .15
❑ 74 Gary Brown .10 .02
❑ 75 Cris Dishman .10 .02
❑ 76 Mel Gray .10 .02
❑ 77 Steve McNair RC 3.00 1.25
❑ 78 Webster Slaughter .10 .02
❑ 79 Rodney Thomas RC .20 .07
❑ 80 Trev Alberts .10 .02
❑ 81 Quentin Coryatt .20 .07
❑ 82 Sean Dawkins .20 .07
❑ 83 Craig Erickson .10 .02
❑ 84 Marshall Faulk 1.25 .50
❑ 85 Stephen Grant RC .10 .02
❑ 86 Steve Beuerlein .20 .07
❑ 87 Tony Boselli RC .40 .15
❑ 88 Desmond Howard .20 .07
❑ 89 James O. Stewart RC 1.25 .50
❑ 90 Marcus Allen .40 .15
❑ 91 Kimble Anders .20 .07
❑ 92 Steve Bono .20 .07
❑ 93 Lake Dawson .20 .07
❑ 94 Greg Hill .20 .07
❑ 95 Neil Smith .20 .07
❑ 96 William White .10 .02
❑ 97 Tim Bowens .10 .02
❑ 98 Bryan Cox .10 .02
❑ 99 Irving Fryar .20 .07
❑ 100 Eric Green .10 .02
❑ 101 Dan Marino 2.00 .75
❑ 102 O.J. McDuffie .40 .15
❑ 103 Bernie Parmalee .20 .07
❑ 104 Cris Carter .40 .15
❑ 105 Jack Del Rio .10 .02
❑ 106 Rocket Ismail .20 .07
❑ 107 Warren Moon .20 .07
❑ 108 Jake Reed .20 .07
❑ 109 Dewayne Washington .20 .07
❑ 110 Bruce Armstrong .10 .02
❑ 111 Drew Bledsoe .60 .25
❑ 112 Vincent Brisby .10 .02
❑ 113 Ben Coates .20 .07
❑ 114 Willie McGinest .20 .07
❑ 115 Dave Meggett .10 .02
❑ 116 Chris Slade .10 .02
❑ 117 Mario Bates .20 .07
❑ 118 Quinn Early .20 .07
❑ 119 Jim Everett .10 .02
❑ 120 Michael Haynes .20 .07
❑ 121 Tyrone Hughes .20 .07
❑ 122 Renaldo Turnbull .10 .02
❑ 123 Ray Zellars RC .20 .07
❑ 124 Dave Brown .20 .07
❑ 125 Chris Calloway .10 .02
❑ 126 Rodney Hampton .20 .07
❑ 127 Thomas Lewis .20 .07
❑ 128 Phillippi Sparks .10 .02
❑ 129 Tyrone Wheatley RC 1.25 .50
❑ 130 Kyle Brady RC .40 .15
❑ 131 Boomer Esiason .20 .07
❑ 132 Aaron Glenn .10 .02
❑ 133 Bobby Houston .10 .02
❑ 134 Mo Lewis .10 .02
❑ 135 Johnny Mitchell .10 .02
❑ 136 Ronald Moore .10 .02
❑ 137 Greg Biekert .10 .02
❑ 138 Tim Brown .40 .15
❑ 139 Jeff Hostetler .20 .07
❑ 140 Rocket Ismail .20 .07
❑ 141 Napoleon Kaufman RC 1.25 .50
❑ 142 Chester McGlockton .20 .07
❑ 143 Harvey Williams .10 .02
❑ 144 Fred Barnett .20 .07
❑ 145 Randall Cunningham .40 .15
❑ 146 William Fuller .10 .02
❑ 147 Charlie Garner .40 .15
❑ 148 Andy Harmon .10 .02
❑ 149 Ricky Watters .20 .07
❑ 150 Calvin Williams .20 .07
❑ 151 Kevin Greene .20 .07
❑ 152 Charles Johnson .20 .07
❑ 153 Greg Lloyd .20 .07
❑ 154 Byron Bam Morris .10 .02
❑ 155 Neil O'Donnell .20 .07
❑ 156 Darren Perry .10 .02
❑ 157 Rod Woodson .20 .07
❑ 158 Jerome Bettis .40 .15
❑ 159 Isaac Bruce .60 .25
❑ 160 Troy Drayton .10 .02
❑ 161 Sean Gilbert .20 .07
❑ 162 Todd Lyght .10 .02
❑ 163 Chris Miller .10 .02
❑ 164 Andre Coleman .10 .02
❑ 165 Stan Humphries .20 .07
❑ 166 Shawn Jefferson .10 .02
❑ 167 Natrone Means .20 .07
❑ 168 Leslie O'Neal .20 .07
❑ 169 Junior Seau .40 .15
❑ 170 Mark Seay .20 .07
❑ 171 William Floyd .20 .07
❑ 172 Merton Hanks .10 .02
❑ 173 Brent Jones .10 .02
❑ 174 Jerry Rice 1.00 .40
❑ 175 Deion Sanders UER .60 .25
❑ 176 J.J. Stokes RC .40 .15
❑ 177 Lee Woodall .10 .02
❑ 178 Bryant Young .20 .07
❑ 179 Steve Young .75 .30
❑ 180 Brian Blades .20 .07
❑ 181 Joey Galloway RC 1.50 .60
❑ 182 Cortez Kennedy .20 .07
❑ 183 Kevin Mawae .10 .02
❑ 184 Rick Mirer .20 .07
❑ 185 Chris Warren .20 .07
❑ 186 Lawrence Dawsey .10 .02
❑ 187 Trent Dilfer .40 .15
❑ 188 Paul Gruber .10 .02
❑ 189 Hardy Nickerson .10 .02

❑ 190 Errict Rhett .20 .07
❑ 191 Warren Sapp RC 1.50 .60
❑ 192 Tom Carter .10 .02
❑ 193 Henry Ellard .20 .07
❑ 194 Darrell Green .10 .02
❑ 195 Brian Mitchell .10 .02
❑ 196 Heath Shuler .20 .07
❑ 197 Michael Westbrook RC .40 .15
❑ 198 Checklist 1-96 .10 .02
❑ 199 Checklist 97-200 .10 .02
❑ 200 Checklist Inserts .10 .02
❑ S1 Trent Dilfer Sample 1.00 .40

1996 Metal

❑ COMPLETE SET (150) 25.00 10.00
❑ 1 Garrison Hearst .20 .07
❑ 2 Rob Moore .20 .07
❑ 3 Frank Sanders .20 .07
❑ 4 Eric Swann .10 .02
❑ 5 Jeff George .20 .07
❑ 6 Craig Heyward .10 .02
❑ 7 Terance Mathis .10 .02
❑ 8 Eric Metcalf .10 .02
❑ 9 Derrick Alexander WR .20 .07
❑ 10 Andre Rison .20 .07
❑ 11 Vinny Testaverde .20 .07
❑ 12 Eric Turner .10 .02
❑ 13 Jim Kelly .40 .15
❑ 14 Bryce Paup .10 .02
❑ 15 Bruce Smith .20 .07
❑ 16 Thurman Thomas .40 .15
❑ 17 Bob Christian .10 .02
❑ 18 Kerry Collins .40 .15
❑ 19 Lamar Lathon .10 .02
❑ 20 Tyrone Poole .10 .02
❑ 21 Curtis Conway .40 .15
❑ 22 Bryan Cox .10 .02
❑ 23 Erik Kramer .10 .02
❑ 24 Rashaan Salaam .20 .07
❑ 25 Jeff Blake .40 .15
❑ 26 Ki-Jana Carter .20 .07
❑ 27 Carl Pickens .20 .07
❑ 28 Darnay Scott .20 .07
❑ 29 Troy Aikman 1.00 .40
❑ 30 Michael Irvin .40 .15
❑ 31 Daryl Johnston .20 .07
❑ 32 Deion Sanders .60 .25
❑ 33 Emmitt Smith 1.50 .60
❑ 34 Terrell Davis .75 .30
❑ 35 John Elway 2.00 .75
❑ 36 Anthony Miller .20 .07
❑ 37 Shannon Sharpe .20 .07
❑ 38 Scott Mitchell .20 .07
❑ 39 Herman Moore .20 .07
❑ 40 Brett Perriman .10 .02
❑ 41 Barry Sanders 1.50 .60
❑ 42 Edgar Bennett .20 .07
❑ 43 Robert Brooks .40 .15
❑ 44 Mark Chmura .20 .07
❑ 45 Brett Favre 2.00 .75
❑ 46 Reggie White .40 .15
❑ 47 Mel Gray .10 .02
❑ 48 Steve McNair .75 .30
❑ 49 Chris Sanders .20 .07
❑ 50 Rodney Thomas .10 .02
❑ 51 Quentin Coryatt .10 .02
❑ 52 Sean Dawkins .10 .02
❑ 53 Ken Dilger .20 .07
❑ 54 Marshall Faulk .50 .20
❑ 55 Jim Harbaugh .20 .07
❑ 56 Tony Boselli .10 .02
❑ 57 Mark Brunell .60 .25
❑ 58 Natrone Means .20 .07
❑ 59 James O.Stewart .20 .07
❑ 60 Marcus Allen .40 .15
❑ 61 Steve Bono .10 .02
❑ 62 Neil Smith .20 .07
❑ 63 Tamarick Vanover .20 .07
❑ 64 Eric Green .10 .02
❑ 65 Terry Kirby .20 .07
❑ 66 Dan Marino 2.00 .75
❑ 67 O.J. McDuffie .20 .07
❑ 68 Cris Carter .40 .15
❑ 69 Qadry Ismail .20 .07
❑ 70 Warren Moon .20 .07
❑ 71 Jake Reed .20 .07
❑ 72 Drew Bledsoe .60 .25
❑ 73 Ben Coates .20 .07
❑ 74 Curtis Martin .75 .30
❑ 75 Dave Meggett .10 .02
❑ 76 Mario Bates .20 .07
❑ 77 Jim Everett .10 .02
❑ 78 Michael Haynes .10 .02
❑ 79 Tyrone Hughes .10 .02
❑ 80 Dave Brown .10 .02
❑ 81 Rodney Hampton .20 .07
❑ 82 Thomas Lewis .10 .02
❑ 83 Tyrone Wheatley .20 .07
❑ 84 Kyle Brady .10 .02
❑ 85 Hugh Douglas .20 .07
❑ 86 Adrian Murrell .20 .07
❑ 87 Neil O'Donnell .20 .07
❑ 88 Tim Brown .40 .15
❑ 89 Jeff Hostetler .10 .02
❑ 90 Napoleon Kaufman .40 .15
❑ 91 Harvey Williams .10 .02
❑ 92 Charlie Garner .20 .07
❑ 93 Rodney Peete .10 .02
❑ 94 Ricky Watters .20 .07
❑ 95 Calvin Williams .10 .02
❑ 96 Jerome Bettis .40 .15
❑ 97 Greg Lloyd .20 .07
❑ 98 Kordell Stewart .40 .15
❑ 99 Yancey Thigpen .20 .07
❑ 100 Rod Woodson .20 .07
❑ 101 Isaac Bruce .40 .15
❑ 102 Kevin Carter .10 .02
❑ 103 Steve Walsh .10 .02
❑ 104 Aaron Hayden .10 .02
❑ 105 Stan Humphries .20 .07
❑ 106 Junior Seau .40 .15
❑ 107 William Floyd .20 .07
❑ 108 Brent Jones .10 .02
❑ 109 Jerry Rice 1.00 .40
❑ 110 J.J. Stokes .40 .15
❑ 111 Steve Young .75 .30
❑ 112 Brian Blades .10 .02
❑ 113 Joey Galloway .40 .15
❑ 114 Rick Mirer .20 .07
❑ 115 Chris Warren .20 .07
❑ 116 Trent Dilfer .40 .15
❑ 117 Alvin Harper .10 .02
❑ 118 Hardy Nickerson .10 .02
❑ 119 Errict Rhett .20 .07
❑ 120 Terry Allen .20 .07
❑ 121 Brian Mitchell .10 .02
❑ 122 Heath Shuler .20 .07
❑ 123 Michael Westbrook .40 .15
❑ 124 Karim Abdul-Jabbar RC .40 .15
❑ 125 Tim Biakabutuka RC .40 .15
❑ 126 Duane Clemons RC .10 .02
❑ 127 Stephen Davis RC 2.00 .75
❑ 128 Rickey Dudley RC .40 .15
❑ 129 Bobby Engram RC .40 .15
❑ 130 Daryl Gardener RC .10 .02
❑ 131 Eddie George RC 1.50 .60
❑ 132 Terry Glenn RC 1.25 .50
❑ 133 Kevin Hardy RC .40 .15
❑ 134 Walt Harris RC .10 .02
❑ 135 Marvin Harrison RC 3.00 1.25
❑ 136 Keyshawn Johnson RC 1.25 .50
❑ 137 Cedric Jones RC .10 .02
❑ 138 Eddie Kennison RC .40 .15
❑ 139 Sam/Sean Manuel RC .10 .02
❑ 140 Leeland McElroy RC .20 .07
❑ 141 Ray Mickens RC .10 .02
❑ 142 Jonathan Ogden RC .40 .15
❑ 143 Lawrence Phillips RC .40 .15
❑ 144 Kavika Pittman RC .10 .02
❑ 145 Simeon Rice RC 1.00 .40
❑ 146 Regan Upshaw RC .10 .02
❑ 147 Alex Van Dyke RC .20 .07
❑ 148 Stepfret Williams RC .20 .07
❑ 149 Checklist .10 .02
❑ 150 Checklist .10 .02
❑ P1 Promo Sheet 2.50 1.00

1997 Metal Universe

❑ COMPLETE SET (200) 20.00 7.50
❑ 1 Terry Glenn .50 .20
❑ 2 Terry Kirby .30 .10
❑ 3 Thomas Lewis .20 .07
❑ 4 Tim Biakabutuka .30 .10
❑ 5 Tim Brown .50 .20
❑ 6 Todd Collins .20 .07
❑ 7 Tony Banks .30 .10
❑ 8 Tony Brackens .20 .07
❑ 9 Tony Martin .30 .10
❑ 10 Trent Dilfer .50 .20
❑ 11 Troy Aikman 1.00 .40
❑ 12 Ty Detmer .30 .10
❑ 13 Tyrone Wheatley .30 .10
❑ 14 Vinny Testaverde .30 .10
❑ 15 Wayne Chrebet .50 .20
❑ 16 Wesley Walls .30 .10
❑ 17 William Floyd .30 .10
❑ 18 Willie McGinest .20 .07
❑ 19 Yancey Thigpen .30 .10
❑ 20 Zach Thomas .50 .20
❑ 21 Terry Allen .50 .20
❑ 22 Terrell Owens .60 .25
❑ 23 Terrell Davis .60 .25
❑ 24 Terance Mathis .30 .10
❑ 25 Ted Johnson .20 .07
❑ 26 Tamarick Vanover .30 .10
❑ 27 Steve Young .60 .25
❑ 28 Steve McNair .60 .25
❑ 29 Stan Humphries .30 .10
❑ 30 Simeon Rice .30 .10
❑ 31 Shannon Sharpe .30 .10
❑ 32 Sean Jones .20 .07
❑ 33 Scott Mitchell .30 .10
❑ 34 Sam Mills .20 .07
❑ 35 Rodney Hampton .30 .10
❑ 36 Rod Woodson .30 .10
❑ 37 Robert Smith .30 .10
❑ 38 Rob Moore .30 .10
❑ 39 Ricky Watters .30 .10
❑ 40 Rickey Dudley .30 .10
❑ 41 Rick Mirer .20 .07
❑ 42 Reggie White .50 .20
❑ 43 Ray Zellars .20 .07
❑ 44 Ray Lewis .75 .30
❑ 45 Rashaan Salaam .20 .07
❑ 46 Quentin Coryatt .20 .07
❑ 47 Qadry Ismail .30 .10
❑ 48 O.J. McDuffie .30 .10
❑ 49 Nilo Silvan .20 .07
❑ 50 Neil Smith .30 .10
❑ 51 Neil O'Donnell .30 .10
❑ 52 Natrone Means .30 .10
❑ 53 Napoleon Kaufman .50 .20
❑ 54 Mike Tomczak .20 .07
❑ 55 Mike Alstott .50 .20
❑ 56 Michael Westbrook .30 .10
❑ 57 Michael Jackson .30 .10
❑ 58 Michael Irvin .50 .20
❑ 59 Michael Haynes .20 .07
❑ 60 Michael Bates .20 .07
❑ 61 Mel Gray .20 .07
❑ 62 Marvin Harrison .50 .20
❑ 63 Marshall Faulk .60 .25
❑ 64 Mark Brunell .60 .25

❑ 65 Mario Bates .20 .07
❑ 66 Marcus Allen .50 .20
❑ 67 Lorenzo Neal .20 .07
❑ 68 Levon Kirkland .20 .07
❑ 69 Leonard Russell .20 .07
❑ 70 Leeland McElroy .20 .07
❑ 71 Lawyer Milloy .30 .10
❑ 72 Lawrence Phillips .20 .07
❑ 73 Larry Centers .30 .10
❑ 74 Lamar Lathon .20 .07
❑ 75 Kordell Stewart .50 .20
❑ 76 Kimble Anders .30 .10
❑ 77 Ki-Jana Carter .20 .07
❑ 78 Keyshawn Johnson .50 .20
❑ 79 Kevin Turner .20 .07
❑ 80 Jermaine Lewis .50 .20
❑ 81 Jerome Bettis .50 .20
❑ 82 Jerris McPhail .20 .07
❑ 83 Joey Galloway .30 .10
❑ 84 Jerry Rice 1.00 .40
❑ 85 Jim Everett .20 .07
❑ 86 Jimmy Smith .30 .10
❑ 87 Jim Harbaugh .30 .10
❑ 88 John Elway 2.00 .75
❑ 89 John Friesz .20 .07
❑ 90 John Mobley .20 .07
❑ 91 Johnnie Morton .30 .10
❑ 92 Junior Seau .50 .20
❑ 93 Karim Abdul-Jabbar .30 .10
❑ 94 Keenan McCardell .30 .10
❑ 95 Ken Dilger .20 .07
❑ 96 Ken Norton .20 .07
❑ 97 Kent Graham .20 .07
❑ 98 Kerry Collins .50 .20
❑ 99 Kevin Greene .30 .10
❑ 100 Kevin Hardy .20 .07
❑ 101 Jeff Lewis .20 .07
❑ 102 Jeff George .30 .10
❑ 103 Jeff Graham .20 .07
❑ 104 Jeff Blake .30 .10
❑ 105 Jason Sehorn .30 .10
❑ 106 Jason Dunn .20 .07
❑ 107 Jamie Asher .20 .07
❑ 108 Jamal Anderson .50 .20
❑ 109 Jake Reed .30 .10
❑ 110 Isaac Bruce .50 .20
❑ 111 Irving Fryar .30 .10
❑ 112 Iheanyi Uwaezuoke .20 .07
❑ 113 Hugh Douglas .20 .07
❑ 114 Herman Moore .30 .10
❑ 115 Harvey Williams .20 .07
❑ 116 Hardy Nickerson .20 .07
❑ 117 Gus Frerotte .20 .07
❑ 118 Greg Hill .20 .07
❑ 119 Glyn Milburn .20 .07
❑ 120 Frank Wycheck .20 .07
❑ 121 Frank Sanders .30 .10
❑ 122 Errict Rhett .20 .07
❑ 123 Erik Kramer .20 .07
❑ 124 Eric Moulds .50 .20
❑ 125 Eric Metcalf .30 .10
❑ 126 Emmitt Smith 1.50 .60
❑ 127 Edgar Bennett .30 .10
❑ 128 Eddie Kennison .30 .10
❑ 129 Eddie George .50 .20
❑ 130 Drew Bledsoe .60 .25
❑ 131 Dorsey Levens .50 .20
❑ 132 Desmond Howard .30 .10
❑ 133 Derrick Thomas .50 .20
❑ 134 Derrick Alexander WR .30 .10
❑ 135 Deion Sanders .50 .20
❑ 136 Dave Brown .20 .07
❑ 137 Daryl Johnston .30 .10
❑ 138 Darnay Scott .30 .10
❑ 139 Darick Holmes .20 .07
❑ 140 Dan Marino 2.00 .75
❑ 141 Curtis Martin .60 .25
❑ 142 Curtis Conway .30 .10
❑ 143 Cris Carter .50 .20
❑ 144 Chris Warren .30 .10
❑ 145 Chris T. Jones .20 .07
❑ 146 Chris Slade .20 .07
❑ 147 Chris Sanders .20 .07
❑ 148 Chester McGlockton .20 .07
❑ 149 Charlie Jones .20 .07
❑ 150 Charles Way .20 .07
❑ 151 Carl Pickens .30 .10
❑ 152 Bryan Still .20 .07
❑ 153 Bruce Smith .30 .10
❑ 154 Brian Mitchell .20 .07
❑ 155 Brett Perriman .20 .07
❑ 156 Brett Favre 2.00 .75
❑ 157 Brad Johnson .50 .20
❑ 158 Thurman Thomas .50 .20
❑ 159 Bobby Engram .30 .10
❑ 160 Bert Emanuel .30 .10
❑ 161 Ben Coates .30 .10
❑ 162 Barry Sanders 1.50 .60
❑ 163 Byron Bam Morris .20 .07
❑ 164 Ashley Ambrose .20 .07
❑ 165 Antonio Freeman .50 .20
❑ 166 Anthony Miller .20 .07
❑ 167 Anthony Johnson .20 .07
❑ 168 Andre Rison .30 .10
❑ 169 Andre Reed .30 .10
❑ 170 Alex Molden .20 .07
❑ 171 Aeneas Williams .20 .07
❑ 172 Adrian Murrell .30 .10
❑ 173 Aaron Hayden .20 .07
❑ 174 Darnell Autry RC .30 .10
❑ 175 Orlando Pace RC .50 .20
❑ 176 Darrell Russell RC .20 .07
❑ 177 Peter Boulware RC .50 .20
❑ 178 Shawn Springs RC .30 .10
❑ 179 Bryant Westbrook RC .20 .07
❑ 180 Dwayne Rudd RC .50 .20
❑ 181 Rae Carruth RC .20 .07
❑ 182 Troy Davis RC .30 .10
❑ 183 Antowain Smith RC 2.00 .75
❑ 184 James Farrior RC .50 .20
❑ 185 Walter Jones RC .50 .20
❑ 186 Sam Madison RC .50 .20
❑ 187 Tom Knight RC .20 .07
❑ 188 Reidel Anthony RC .50 .20
❑ 189 Warrick Dunn RC 2.50 1.00
❑ 190 Reinard Wilson RC .30 .10
❑ 191 Tyrus McCloud RC .20 .07
❑ 192 Michael Booker RC .20 .07
❑ 193 Tony Gonzalez RC 2.50 1.00
❑ 194 Pat Barnes RC .50 .20
❑ 195 Tiki Barber RC 5.00 2.00
❑ 196 Sedrick Shaw RC .30 .10
❑ 197 Corey Dillon RC 5.00 2.00
❑ 198 Danny Wuerffel RC .50 .20
❑ 199 Checklist (1-152) .20 .07
❑ 200 Checklist (153-200/inserts) .20 .07
❑ S1 Terrell Davis Sample 2.00 .75

1998 Metal Universe

❑ COMPLETE SET (200) 40.00 15.00
❑ 1 Jerry Rice 1.00 .40
❑ 2 Muhsin Muhammad .30 .10
❑ 3 Ed McCaffrey .30 .10
❑ 4 Brett Favre 2.00 .75
❑ 5 Troy Brown .30 .10
❑ 6 Brad Johnson .50 .20
❑ 7 John Elway 2.00 .75
❑ 8 Herman Moore .30 .10
❑ 9 O.J. McDuffie .30 .10
❑ 10 Tim Brown .50 .20
❑ 11 Byron Hanspard .20 .07
❑ 12 Rae Carruth .20 .07
❑ 13 Rod Smith WR .30 .10
❑ 14 John Randle .30 .10
❑ 15 Karim Abdul-Jabbar .50 .20
❑ 16 Bobby Hoying .30 .10
❑ 17 Steve Young .60 .25
❑ 18 Andre Hastings .20 .07
❑ 19 Chidi Ahanotu .20 .07
❑ 20 Barry Sanders 1.50 .60
❑ 21 Bruce Smith .30 .10
❑ 22 Kimble Anders .30 .10
❑ 23 Troy Davis .20 .07
❑ 24 Jamal Anderson .50 .20
❑ 25 Curtis Conway .30 .10
❑ 26 Mark Chmura .30 .10
❑ 27 Reggie White .50 .20
❑ 28 Jake Reed .30 .10
❑ 29 Willie McGinest .20 .07
❑ 30 Terrell Davis .50 .20
❑ 31 Joey Galloway .30 .10
❑ 32 Leslie Shepherd .20 .07
❑ 33 Peter Boulware .20 .07
❑ 34 Chad Lewis .30 .10
❑ 35 Marcus Allen .50 .20
❑ 36 Randal Hill .20 .07
❑ 37 Jerome Bettis .50 .20
❑ 38 William Floyd .20 .07
❑ 39 Warren Moon .50 .20
❑ 40 Mike Alstott .50 .20
❑ 41 Jay Graham .20 .07
❑ 42 Emmitt Smith 1.50 .60
❑ 43 James O. Stewart .30 .10
❑ 44 Charlie Garner .30 .10
❑ 45 Merton Hanks .20 .07
❑ 46 Shawn Springs .20 .07
❑ 47 Chris Calloway .20 .07
❑ 48 Larry Centers .20 .07
❑ 49 Michael Jackson .20 .07
❑ 50 Deion Sanders .50 .20
❑ 51 Jimmy Smith .30 .10
❑ 52 Jason Sehorn .30 .10
❑ 53 Charles Johnson .20 .07
❑ 54 Garrison Hearst .50 .20
❑ 55 Chris Warren .30 .10
❑ 56 Warren Sapp .30 .10
❑ 57 Corey Dillon .50 .20
❑ 58 Marvin Harrison .50 .20
❑ 59 Chris Sanders .20 .07
❑ 60 Jamie Asher .20 .07
❑ 61 Yancey Thigpen .20 .07
❑ 62 Freddie Jones .20 .07
❑ 63 Rob Moore .30 .10
❑ 64 Jermaine Lewis .30 .10
❑ 65 Michael Irvin .50 .20
❑ 66 Natrone Means .30 .10
❑ 67 Charles Way .20 .07
❑ 68 Terry Kirby .20 .07
❑ 69 Tony Banks .30 .10
❑ 70 Steve McNair .50 .20
❑ 71 Vinny Testaverde .30 .10
❑ 72 Dexter Coakley .20 .07
❑ 73 Keenan McCardell .30 .10
❑ 74 Glenn Foley .30 .10
❑ 75 Isaac Bruce .50 .20
❑ 76 Terry Allen .50 .20
❑ 77 Todd Collins .20 .07
❑ 78 Troy Aikman 1.00 .40
❑ 79 Damon Jones .20 .07
❑ 80 Leon Johnson .20 .07
❑ 81 James Jett .30 .10
❑ 82 Frank Wycheck .20 .07
❑ 83 Andre Reed .30 .10
❑ 84 Derrick Alexander WR .30 .10
❑ 85 Jason Taylor .30 .10
❑ 86 Wayne Chrebet .50 .20
❑ 87 Napoleon Kaufman .50 .20
❑ 88 Eddie George .50 .20
❑ 89 Ernie Conwell .20 .07
❑ 90 Antowain Smith .50 .20
❑ 91 Johnnie Morton .30 .10
❑ 92 Jerris McPhail .20 .07
❑ 93 Cris Carter .50 .20
❑ 94 Danny Kanell .30 .10
❑ 95 Stan Humphries .20 .07
❑ 96 Terrell Owens .50 .20
❑ 97 Willie Davis .20 .07
❑ 98 David Dunn .20 .07
❑ 99 Tony Brackens .20 .07
❑ 100 Kordell Stewart .50 .20
❑ 101 Rodney Thomas .20 .07
❑ 102 Keyshawn Johnson .50 .20
❑ 103 Carl Pickens .30 .10
❑ 104 Mark Brunell .50 .20
❑ 105 Jeff George .30 .10
❑ 106 Bert Emanuel .30 .10
❑ 107 Wesley Walls .30 .10
❑ 108 Bryant Westbrook .20 .07
❑ 109 Dorsey Levens .50 .20
❑ 110 Drew Bledsoe .75 .30

❑ 111 Adrian Murrell	.30	.10
❑ 112 Aeneas Williams	.20	.07
❑ 113 Raymont Harris	.20	.07
❑ 114 Tony Gonzalez	.50	.20
❑ 115 Sean Dawkins	.20	.07
❑ 116 Billy Joe Hobert	.20	.07
❑ 117 James McKnight	.50	.20
❑ 118 Reidel Anthony	.30	.10
❑ 119 Terance Mathis	.30	.10
❑ 120 Darrien Gordon	.20	.07
❑ 121 Dale Carter	.20	.07
❑ 122 Duce Staley	.60	.25
❑ 123 Jerald Moore	.20	.07
❑ 124 Eric Swann	.20	.07
❑ 125 Antonio Freeman	.50	.20
❑ 126 Chris Penn	.20	.07
❑ 127 Ken Dilger	.20	.07
❑ 128 Robert Smith	.50	.20
❑ 129 Tiki Barber	.50	.20
❑ 130 Mark Bruener	.20	.07
❑ 131 Junior Seau	.50	.20
❑ 132 Trent Dilfer	.50	.20
❑ 133 Gus Frerotte	.20	.07
❑ 134 Jake Plummer	.50	.20
❑ 135 Jeff Blake	.30	.10
❑ 136 Jim Harbaugh	.30	.10
❑ 137 Michael Strahan	.30	.10
❑ 138 Gary Brown	.20	.07
❑ 139 Tony Martin	.30	.10
❑ 140 Stephen Davis	.20	.07
❑ 141 Thurman Thomas	.50	.20
❑ 142 Scott Mitchell	.30	.10
❑ 143 Dan Marino	2.00	.75
❑ 144 David Palmer	.20	.07
❑ 145 J.J. Stokes	.30	.10
❑ 146 Chris Chandler	.30	.10
❑ 147 Darnell Autry	.20	.07
❑ 148 Robert Brooks	.30	.10
❑ 149 Derrick Mayes	.30	.10
❑ 150 Curtis Martin	.50	.20
❑ 151 Steve Broussard	.20	.07
❑ 152 Eddie Kennison	.30	.10
❑ 153 Kerry Collins	.30	.10
❑ 154 Shannon Sharpe	.30	.10
❑ 155 Andre Rison	.30	.10
❑ 156 Dwayne Rudd	.20	.07
❑ 157 Orlando Pace	.20	.07
❑ 158 Terry Glenn	.50	.20
❑ 159 Frank Sanders	.30	.10
❑ 160 Ricky Proehl	.20	.07
❑ 161 Marshall Faulk	.60	.25
❑ 162 Irving Fryar	.30	.10
❑ 163 Courtney Hawkins	.20	.07
❑ 164 Eric Metcalf	.20	.07
❑ 165 Warrick Dunn	.50	.20
❑ 166 Cris Dishman	.20	.07
❑ 167 Fred Lane	.20	.07
❑ 168 John Mobley	.20	.07
❑ 169 Elvis Grbac	.30	.10
❑ 170 Ben Coates	.30	.10
❑ 171 Rickey Dudley	.20	.07
❑ 172 Ricky Watters	.30	.10
❑ 173 Alonzo Mayes RC	.60	.25
❑ 174 Andre Wadsworth RC	1.00	.40
❑ 175 Brian Simmons RC	1.00	.40
❑ 176 Charles Woodson RC	1.50	.60
❑ 177 Curtis Enis RC	.60	.25
❑ 178 Fred Taylor RC	2.00	.75
❑ 179 Germane Crowell RC	1.00	.40
❑ 180 Greg Ellis RC	.60	.25
❑ 181 Jacquez Green RC	1.00	.40
❑ 182 Jason Peter RC	.60	.25
❑ 183 John Dutton RC	.60	.25
❑ 184 Kevin Dyson RC	1.25	.50
❑ 185 Kivuusama Mays RC	.60	.25
❑ 186 Marcus Nash RC	.60	.25
❑ 187 Michael Myers RC	.60	.25
❑ 188 Ahman Green RC	6.00	2.50
❑ 189 Peyton Manning RC	15.00	7.50
❑ 190 Randy Moss RC	6.00	3.00
❑ 191 Robert Edwards RC	1.00	.40
❑ 192 Robert Holcombe RC	1.00	.40
❑ 193 Ryan Leaf RC	1.25	.50
❑ 194 Takeo Spikes RC	1.25	.50
❑ 195 Tavian Banks RC	1.00	.40
❑ 196 Tim Dwight RC	1.25	.50
❑ 197 Vonnie Holliday RC	1.00	.40
❑ 198 Dorsey Levens CL	.20	.07
❑ 199 Jerry Rice CL	.50	.20
❑ 200 Dan Marino CL	.75	.30

1999 Metal Universe

❑ COMPLETE SET (250)	40.00	15.00
❑ 1 Eric Moulds	.50	.20
❑ 2 David Palmer	.20	.07
❑ 3 Ricky Watters	.30	.10
❑ 4 Antonio Freeman	.50	.20
❑ 5 Hugh Douglas	.20	.07
❑ 6 Johnnie Morton	.30	.10
❑ 7 Corey Fuller	.20	.07
❑ 8 J.J. Stokes	.30	.10
❑ 9 Keith Poole	.20	.07
❑ 10 Steve Beuerlein	.20	.07
❑ 11 Keenan McCardell	.30	.10
❑ 12 Carl Pickens	.30	.10
❑ 13 Mark Bruener	.20	.07
❑ 14 Warren Sapp	.30	.10
❑ 15 Rich Gannon	.50	.20
❑ 16 Bruce Smith	.30	.10
❑ 17 Mark Chmura	.20	.07
❑ 18 Drew Bledsoe	.60	.25
❑ 19 Charles Woodson	.50	.20
❑ 20 Ahman Green	.50	.20
❑ 21 Ricky Proehl	.20	.07
❑ 22 Corey Dillon	.50	.20
❑ 23 Terry Fair	.20	.07
❑ 24 Mark Brunell	.50	.20
❑ 25 Leroy Hoard	.20	.07
❑ 26 La'Roi Glover RC	.50	.20
❑ 27 Tim Brown	.50	.20
❑ 28 Kevin Turner	.20	.07
❑ 29 Terrell Owens	.50	.20
❑ 30 Mike Alstott	.50	.20
❑ 31 Rob Moore	.30	.10
❑ 32 Troy Aikman	1.00	.40
❑ 33 Derrick Alexander	.20	.07
❑ 34 Chris Calloway	.20	.07
❑ 35 Kordell Stewart	.30	.10
❑ 36 Reidel Anthony	.30	.10
❑ 37 Michael Westbrook	.30	.10
❑ 38 Ray Lewis	.50	.20
❑ 39 Alonzo Mayes	.20	.07
❑ 40 Rod Smith	.30	.10
❑ 41 Reggie Barlow	.20	.07
❑ 42 Sean Dawkins	.20	.07
❑ 43 Duce Staley	.50	.20
❑ 44 R.W. McQuarters	.20	.07
❑ 45 Robert Holcombe	.20	.07
❑ 46 Priest Holmes	.75	.30
❑ 47 Erik Kramer	.20	.07
❑ 48 Shannon Sharpe	.30	.10
❑ 49 Mike Vanderjagt	.20	.07
❑ 50 Cris Carter	.50	.20
❑ 51 Billy Joe Tolliver	.20	.07
❑ 52 Vinny Testaverde	.30	.10
❑ 53 Antonio Langham	.20	.07
❑ 54 Damon Gibson	.20	.07
❑ 55 Garrison Hearst	.30	.10
❑ 56 Brad Johnson	.50	.20
❑ 57 Randall Cunningham	.50	.20
❑ 58 Jim Harbaugh	.30	.10
❑ 59 Curtis Enis	.20	.07
❑ 60 Bill Romanowski	.20	.07
❑ 61 Marcus Pollard	.20	.07
❑ 62 Zach Thomas	.50	.20
❑ 63 Cameron Cleeland	.20	.07
❑ 64 Curtis Martin	.50	.20
❑ 65 Charlie Garner	.30	.10
❑ 66 Jerris McPhail	.20	.07
❑ 67 Jon Kitna	.50	.20
❑ 68 Chris Chandler	.30	.10
❑ 69 Emmitt Smith	1.00	.40
❑ 70 Andre Rison	.30	.10
❑ 71 Wayne Chrebet	.30	.10
❑ 72 Mikhael Ricks	.20	.07
❑ 73 Yancey Thigpen	.20	.07
❑ 74 Peter Boulware	.20	.07
❑ 75 Bobby Engram	.30	.10
❑ 76 John Mobley	.20	.07
❑ 77 Peyton Manning	1.50	.60
❑ 78 O.J. McDuffie	.30	.10
❑ 79 Tony Simmons	.20	.07
❑ 80 Mo Lewis	.20	.07
❑ 81 Bryan Still	.20	.07
❑ 82 Eugene Robinson	.20	.07
❑ 83 Curtis Conway	.30	.10
❑ 84 Ed McCaffrey	.30	.10
❑ 85 Marvin Harrison	.50	.20
❑ 86 Dan Marino	1.50	.60
❑ 87 Ty Law	.30	.10
❑ 88 Leon Johnson	.20	.07
❑ 89 Junior Seau	.50	.20
❑ 90 Terance Mathis	.30	.10
❑ 91 Wesley Walls	.30	.10
❑ 92 John Elway	1.50	.60
❑ 93 Marshall Faulk	.60	.25
❑ 94 Oronde Gadsden	.30	.10
❑ 95 Keyshawn Johnson	.50	.20
❑ 96 Muhsin Muhammad	.30	.10
❑ 97 Dorsey Levens	.50	.20
❑ 98 Shawn Jefferson	.20	.07
❑ 99 Rocket Ismail	.30	.10
❑ 100 Vonnie Holliday	.20	.07
❑ 101 Terry Glenn	.50	.20
❑ 102 Shawn Springs	.20	.07
❑ 103 Tim Dwight	.50	.20
❑ 104 Terrell Davis	.50	.20
❑ 105 Karim Abdul-Jabbar	.30	.10
❑ 106 Bryan Cox	.20	.07
❑ 107 Steve McNair	.50	.20
❑ 108 Tony Martin	.30	.10
❑ 109 Jason Elam	.20	.07
❑ 110 John Avery	.20	.07
❑ 111 Aaron Glenn	.20	.07
❑ 112 Eddie George	.50	.20
❑ 113 Larry Centers	.20	.07
❑ 114 Darnay Scott	.20	.07
❑ 115 Jimmy Smith	.30	.10
❑ 116 Tiki Barber	.50	.20
❑ 117 Charles Johnson	.20	.07
❑ 118 Mike Archie RC	.30	.10
❑ 119 Adrian Murrell	.30	.10
❑ 120 Dexter Coakley	.20	.07
❑ 121 Dale Carter	.20	.07
❑ 122 Kent Graham	.20	.07
❑ 123 Hines Ward	.50	.20
❑ 124 Greg Hill	.20	.07
❑ 125 Skip Hicks	.20	.07
❑ 126 Doug Flutie	.50	.20
❑ 127 Leslie Shepherd	.20	.07
❑ 128 Neil O'Donnell	.30	.10
❑ 129 Herman Moore	.30	.10
❑ 130 Kevin Hardy	.20	.07
❑ 131 Randy Moss	1.25	.50
❑ 132 Andre Hastings	.20	.07
❑ 133 Rickey Dudley	.20	.07
❑ 134 Jerome Bettis	.50	.20
❑ 135 Jerry Rice	1.00	.40
❑ 136 Jake Plummer	.30	.10
❑ 137 Billy Davis	.20	.07
❑ 138 Tony Gonzalez	.50	.20
❑ 139 Ike Hilliard	.20	.07
❑ 140 Freddie Jones	.20	.07
❑ 141 Isaac Bruce	.50	.20
❑ 142 Darrell Green	.20	.07
❑ 143 Trent Green	.50	.20
❑ 144 Jamal Anderson	.50	.20
❑ 145 Deion Sanders	.50	.20
❑ 146 Byron Bam Morris	.20	.07
❑ 147 Charles Way	.20	.07
❑ 148 Natrone Means	.30	.10
❑ 149 Frank Wycheck	.20	.07
❑ 150 Brett Favre	1.50	.60
❑ 151 Michael Bates	.20	.07
❑ 152 Ben Coates	.30	.10
❑ 153 Koy Detmer	.20	.07
❑ 154 Eddie Kennison	.30	.10
❑ 155 Eric Metcalf	.20	.07
❑ 156 Takeo Spikes	.20	.07

❑	157 Fred Taylor	.50	.20
❑	158 Gary Brown	.20	.07
❑	159 Levon Kirkland	.20	.07
❑	160 Trent Dilfer	.30	.10
❑	161 Antowain Smith	.50	.20
❑	162 Robert Brooks	.30	.10
❑	163 Robert Smith	.50	.20
❑	164 Napoleon Kaufman	.50	.20
❑	165 Chad Brown	.20	.07
❑	166 Warrick Dunn	.50	.20
❑	167 Joey Galloway	.30	.10
❑	168 Frank Sanders	.30	.10
❑	169 Michael Irvin	.30	.10
❑	170 Elvis Grbac	.30	.10
❑	171 Michael Strahan	.30	.10
❑	172 Ryan Leaf	.50	.20
❑	173 Stephen Alexander	.20	.07
❑	174 Andre Reed	.30	.10
❑	175 Barry Sanders	1.50	.60
❑	176 Jake Reed	.30	.10
❑	177 James Jett	.30	.10
❑	178 Steve Young	.60	.25
❑	179 Jermaine Lewis	.30	.10
❑	180 Charlie Batch	.50	.20
❑	181 Jacquez Green	.20	.07
❑	182 Kevin Dyson	.30	.10
❑	183 Roell Preston PD	.20	.07
❑	184 Randall Cunningham PD	.50	.20
❑	185 Charlie Batch PD	.50	.20
❑	186 Kordell Stewart PD	.30	.10
❑	187 Bennie Thompson PD	.20	.07
❑	188 Deion Sanders PD	.50	.20
❑	189 Jake Plummer PD	.30	.10
❑	190 Eric Moulds PD	.50	.20
❑	191 Derrick Brooks PD	.50	.20
❑	192 Steve McNair PD	.50	.20
❑	193 Ryan Leaf PD	.30	.10
❑	194 Keyshawn Johnson PD	.50	.20
❑	195 Eddie George PD	.30	.10
❑	196 Warrick Dunn PD	.50	.20
❑	197 Jessie Tuggle PD	.20	.07
❑	198 Rodney Harrison PD	.20	.07
❑	199 Vinny Testaverde PD	.30	.10
❑	200 Marshall Faulk PD	.60	.25
❑	201 Ray Buchanan PD	.20	.07
❑	202 Garrison Hearst PD	.30	.10
❑	203 John Randle PD	.30	.10
❑	204 Drew Bledsoe PD	.50	.20
❑	205 Sam Gash PD	.20	.07
❑	206 Troy Aikman PD	.50	.20
❑	207 Michael McCrary PD	.20	.07
❑	208 Chris Claiborne RC	.40	.15
❑	209 Ricky Williams RC	2.50	1.00
❑	210 Tim Couch RC	1.25	.50
❑	211 Champ Bailey RC	1.50	.60
❑	212 Torry Holt RC	3.00	1.25
❑	213 Donovan McNabb RC	6.00	2.50
❑	214 David Boston RC	1.25	.50
❑	215 Chris McAlister RC	.75	.30
❑	216 Aaron Gibson RC	.20	.07
❑	217 Daunte Culpepper RC	5.00	2.00
❑	218 Matt Stinchcomb RC	.40	.15
❑	219 Edgerrin James RC	5.00	2.00
❑	220 Jevon Kearse RC	2.00	.75
❑	221 Ebenezer Ekuban RC	.75	.30
❑	222 Kris Farris RC	.40	.15
❑	223 Chris Terry RC	.40	.15
❑	224 Cecil Collins RC	.40	.15
❑	225 Akili Smith RC	.75	.30
❑	226 Shaun King RC	.75	.30
❑	227 Rahim Abdullah RC	.75	.30
❑	228 Peerless Price RC	1.25	.50
❑	229 Antoine Winfield RC	.75	.30
❑	230 Antuan Edwards RC	.40	.15
❑	231 Rob Konrad RC	.75	.30
❑	232 Troy Edwards RC	.75	.30
❑	233 John Thornton RC	.40	.15
❑	234 Fred Vinson RC	.40	.15
❑	235 Gary Stills RC	.40	.15
❑	236 Desmond Clark RC	1.25	.50
❑	237 Lamar King RC	.40	.15
❑	238 Jared DeVries RC	.75	.30
❑	239 Martin Gramatica RC	.40	.15
❑	240 Montae Reagor RC	.40	.15
❑	241 Andy Katzenmoyer RC	.75	.30
❑	242 Rufus French RC	.40	.15
❑	243 D'Wayne Bates RC	.75	.30
❑	244 Amos Zereoue RC	1.25	.50
❑	245 Dre' Bly RC	1.25	.50
❑	246 Kevin Johnson RC	1.25	.50
❑	247 Cade McNown RC	.75	.30
❑	248 Kordell Stewart CL	.30	.10
❑	249 Deion Sanders CL	.50	.20
❑	250 Vinny Testaverde CL	.30	.10
❑	P1 Doug Flutie Promo	1.00	.40

2000 Metal

❑	COMPLETE SET (300)	80.00	40.00
❑	COMP.SET w/o SP's (250)	15.00	6.00
❑	1 Tim Couch	.30	.10
❑	2 Olandis Gary	.50	.20
❑	3 Andre Hastings	.20	.07
❑	4 Donovan McNabb	.75	.30
❑	5 Bobby Engram	.30	.10
❑	6 Bert Emanuel	.20	.07
❑	7 Levon Kirkland	.20	.07
❑	8 Chris Chandler	.30	.10
❑	9 Herman Moore	.30	.10
❑	10 Jeff Blake	.30	.10
❑	11 Cortez Kennedy	.20	.07
❑	12 Antowain Smith	.30	.10
❑	13 Marvin Harrison	.50	.20
❑	14 Bryant Young	.20	.07
❑	15 Peerless Price	.30	.10
❑	16 Peyton Manning	1.25	.50
❑	17 Darrell Russell	.20	.07
❑	18 Darrell Green	.20	.07
❑	19 James Allen	.30	.10
❑	20 Tedy Bruschi	.50	.20
❑	21 Jon Kitna	.50	.20
❑	22 Doug Flutie	.50	.20
❑	23 Bill Schroeder	.30	.10
❑	24 Curtis Martin	.50	.20
❑	25 Kevin Lockett	.20	.07
❑	26 Errict Rhett	.30	.10
❑	27 Kevin Faulk	.30	.10
❑	28 J.J. Stokes	.30	.10
❑	29 Jonathan Linton	.20	.07
❑	30 Jimmy Smith	.30	.10
❑	31 Brian Dawkins	.50	.20
❑	32 Michael Westbrook	.30	.10
❑	33 Randall Cunningham	.50	.20
❑	34 Oronde Gadsden	.30	.10
❑	35 Shawn Springs	.20	.07
❑	36 Shannon Sharpe	.30	.10
❑	37 Terrence Wilkins	.20	.07
❑	38 Aaron Glenn	.20	.07
❑	39 Torrance Small	.20	.07
❑	40 Sean Dawkins	.20	.07
❑	41 Terrell Davis	.50	.20
❑	42 Ike Hilliard	.30	.10
❑	43 Warrick Dunn	.50	.20
❑	44 Jeremiah Trotter RC	1.50	.60
❑	45 O.J. McDuffie	.30	.10
❑	46 Richard Huntley	.20	.07
❑	47 Aeneas Williams	.20	.07
❑	48 Rocket Ismail	.30	.10
❑	49 Terry Glenn	.50	.20
❑	50 Derrick Mayes	.30	.10
❑	51 Wayne Chrebet	.30	.10
❑	52 Kevin Dyson	.30	.10
❑	53 Takeo Spikes	.20	.07
❑	54 Matthew Hatchette	.20	.07
❑	55 Shawn Bryson	.20	.07
❑	56 Qadry Ismail	.30	.10
❑	57 Jerome Pathon	.30	.10
❑	58 Rich Gannon	.50	.20
❑	59 Stephen Davis	.50	.20
❑	60 Marcus Robinson	.50	.20
❑	61 Damon Huard	.50	.20
❑	62 Junior Seau	.50	.20
❑	63 Curtis Enis	.20	.07
❑	64 Tony Richardson RC	.20	.07
❑	65 Troy Edwards	.20	.07
❑	66 Robert Brooks	.30	.10
❑	67 Antonio Freeman	.50	.20
❑	68 Kerry Collins	.30	.10
❑	69 Jacquez Green	.20	.07
❑	70 Akili Smith	.20	.07
❑	71 Zach Thomas	.50	.20
❑	72 Kordell Stewart	.30	.10
❑	73 Deion Sanders	.50	.20
❑	74 David Patten	.30	.10
❑	75 Drew Bledsoe	.60	.25
❑	76 Shaun King	.20	.07
❑	77 Eddie Kennison	.30	.10
❑	78 Stacey Mack	.30	.10
❑	79 Jim Harbaugh	.30	.10
❑	80 Shawn Jefferson	.20	.07
❑	81 James Stewart	.30	.10
❑	82 Pete Mitchell	.20	.07
❑	83 Mike Alstott	.50	.20
❑	84 Marty Booker	.30	.10
❑	85 Hardy Nickerson	.20	.07
❑	86 Charles Johnson	.30	.10
❑	87 Jeff George	.30	.10
❑	88 Jermaine Lewis	.30	.10
❑	89 Edgerrin James	.75	.30
❑	90 Rickey Dudley	.20	.07
❑	91 Eddie George	.50	.20
❑	92 Darren Woodson	.20	.07
❑	93 Willie McGinest	.20	.07
❑	94 Jeff Garcia	.50	.20
❑	95 Eric Moulds	.50	.20
❑	96 Tony Brackens	.20	.07
❑	97 Charles Woodson	.30	.10
❑	98 Warren Sapp	.30	.10
❑	99 Corey Dillon	.50	.20
❑	100 Tony Martin	.30	.10
❑	101 Bruce Smith	.30	.10
❑	102 Troy Aikman	1.00	.40
❑	103 Daunte Culpepper	.60	.25
❑	104 Christian Fauria	.20	.07
❑	105 Steve Beuerlein	.30	.10
❑	106 Fred Taylor	.50	.20
❑	107 Ricky Watters	.30	.10
❑	108 Brian Mitchell	.20	.07
❑	109 Emmitt Smith	1.00	.40
❑	110 Robert Smith	.50	.20
❑	111 Jerry Rice	1.00	.40
❑	112 Priest Holmes	.60	.25
❑	113 Jay Fiedler	.50	.20
❑	114 Curtis Conway	.30	.10
❑	115 Jamal Anderson	.50	.20
❑	116 E.G. Green	.20	.07
❑	117 Kent Graham	.20	.07
❑	118 Frank Wycheck	.20	.07
❑	119 Jake Plummer	.30	.10
❑	120 Randy Moss	1.00	.40
❑	121 Charlie Garner	.30	.10
❑	122 Frank Sanders	.30	.10
❑	123 Germane Crowell	.20	.07
❑	124 Jason Sehorn	.20	.07
❑	125 Marshall Faulk	.60	.25
❑	126 David Sloan	.20	.07
❑	127 Cris Carter	.50	.20
❑	128 Robert Chancey	.20	.07
❑	129 Tony Banks	.30	.10
❑	130 Ken Dilger	.20	.07
❑	131 Dedric Ward	.20	.07
❑	132 Yancey Thigpen	.20	.07
❑	133 Jeremy McDaniel	.30	.10
❑	134 John Randle	.20	.07
❑	135 Jerome Bettis	.50	.20
❑	136 Tim Dwight	.50	.20
❑	137 Charlie Batch	.50	.20
❑	138 Mark Brunell	.50	.20
❑	139 Tyrone Wheatley	.30	.10
❑	140 Champ Bailey	.30	.10
❑	141 Brian Griese	.50	.20
❑	142 Keith Poole	.20	.07
❑	143 Kurt Warner	1.00	.40
❑	144 Tim Biakabutuka	.30	.10
❑	145 Elvis Grbac	.30	.10
❑	146 Cade McNown	.20	.07
❑	147 Albert Connell	.20	.07
❑	148 Donald Driver	.50	.20
❑	149 Donald Hayes	.20	.07
❑	150 Terrell Owens	.50	.20
❑	151 Johnnie Morton	.30	.10

❑ 152 Tiki Barber .50 .20
❑ 153 Keyshawn Johnson .50 .20
❑ 154 Carl Pickens .30 .10
❑ 155 Thurman Thomas .30 .10
❑ 156 Jeff Graham .20 .07
❑ 157 Peter Boulware .20 .07
❑ 158 Brett Favre 1.50 .60
❑ 159 Vinny Testaverde .30 .10
❑ 160 Derrick Brooks .50 .20
❑ 161 Wesley Walls .20 .07
❑ 162 Derrick Alexander .30 .10
❑ 163 Duce Staley .50 .20
❑ 164 Troy Brown .30 .10
❑ 165 Keenan McCardell .30 .10
❑ 166 James Jett .20 .07
❑ 167 Simeon Rice .30 .10
❑ 168 Rod Smith .30 .10
❑ 169 Ricky Williams .50 .20
❑ 170 Az-Zahir Hakim .20 .07
❑ 171 Muhsin Muhammad .30 .10
❑ 172 Andre Rison .30 .10
❑ 173 Tim Brown .50 .20
❑ 174 Brad Johnson .50 .20
❑ 175 Darrin Chiaverini .20 .07
❑ 176 Jake Reed .30 .10
❑ 177 Kevin Carter .20 .07
❑ 178 Jay Riemersma .20 .07
❑ 179 Tony Gonzalez .30 .10
❑ 180 Hines Ward .50 .20
❑ 181 David Boston .50 .20
❑ 182 Ed McCaffrey .50 .20
❑ 183 Amani Toomer .20 .07
❑ 184 Torry Holt .50 .20
❑ 185 Rob Johnson .30 .10
❑ 186 Kevin Hardy .20 .07
❑ 187 Napoleon Kaufman .30 .10
❑ 188 Jevon Kearse .50 .20
❑ 189 Terance Mathis .30 .10
❑ 190 Dorsey Levens .30 .10
❑ 191 Kyle Brady .20 .07
❑ 192 Steve McNair .50 .20
❑ 193 Kevin Johnson .50 .20
❑ 194 Lamar Smith .30 .10
❑ 195 Ryan Leaf .30 .10
❑ 196 Rod Woodson .30 .10
❑ 197 Corey Bradford .20 .07
❑ 198 Joe Horn .30 .10
❑ 199 Isaac Bruce .50 .20
❑ 200 S.Young/D.Marino 1.50 .60
❑ 201 DeMario Brown RC .60 .25
❑ 202 Chad Morton RC 1.25 .50
❑ 203 Quinton Spotwood RC .60 .25
❑ 204 Mike Anderson RC 1.50 .60
❑ 205 Jarious Jackson RC 1.00 .40
❑ 206 Hank Poteat RC 1.00 .40
❑ 207 Rogers Beckett RC 1.00 .40
❑ 208 Deon Dyer RC 1.00 .40
❑ 209 Charles Lee RC .60 .25
❑ 210 Barrett Green RC .60 .25
❑ 211 T.J. Slaughter RC .60 .25
❑ 212 Chris Hovan RC 1.00 .40
❑ 213 Mark Simoneau RC 1.00 .40
❑ 214 Rashard Anderson RC 1.00 .40
❑ 215 Trevor Insley RC .60 .25
❑ 216 Paul Smith RC 1.00 .40
❑ 217 Doug Johnson RC 1.25 .50
❑ 218 Dwayne Goodrich RC .60 .25
❑ 219 Julian Peterson RC 1.25 .50
❑ 220 Keith Bulluck RC 1.25 .50
❑ 221 Chris Samuels RC 1.00 .40
❑ 222 Shaun Ellis RC 1.25 .50
❑ 223 Na'il Diggs RC 1.00 .40
❑ 224 William Bartee RC 1.00 .40
❑ 225 John Abraham RC 1.25 .50
❑ 226 Trevor Gaylor RC 1.00 .40
❑ 227 Dante Hall RC 2.50 1.00
❑ 228 Marcus Knight RC 1.00 .40
❑ 229 Patrick Pass RC 1.00 .40
❑ 230 Bashir Yamini RC .60 .25
❑ 231 Deltha O'Neal RC 1.25 .50
❑ 232 Vaughn Sanders RC .60 .25
❑ 233 Todd Husak RC 1.25 .50
❑ 234 Thomas Hamner RC .60 .25
❑ 235 Chafie Fields RC .60 .25
❑ 236 Orantes Grant RC .60 .25
❑ 237 Muneer Moore RC .60 .25
❑ 238 Kwame Cavil RC .60 .25
❑ 239 Spergon Wynn RC 1.00 .40
❑ 240 Leon Murray RC .60 .25

❑ 241 Rob Morris RC 1.00 .40
❑ 242 Ben Kelly RC .60 .25
❑ 243 Darren Howard RC 1.00 .40
❑ 244 Raynoch Thompson RC 1.00 .40
❑ 245 Mike Green RC 1.00 .40
❑ 246 Sammy Morris RC 1.00 .40
❑ 247 Ahmed Plummer RC 1.25 .50
❑ 248 Ian Gold RC 1.00 .40
❑ 249 Chris Coleman RC 1.25 .50
❑ 250 Ron Dixon RC 1.00 .40
❑ 251 Peter Warrick RC 2.00 .75
❑ 252 Joe Hamilton RC 1.50 .60
❑ 253 Dennis Northcutt RC 2.00 .75
❑ 254 Laveranues Coles RC 2.50 1.00
❑ 255 Michael Wiley RC 1.00 .40
❑ 256 Plaxico Burress RC 4.00 1.50
❑ 257 Danny Farmer RC 1.50 .60
❑ 258 Aaron Shea RC 1.00 .40
❑ 259 Sebastian Janikowski RC 2.00 .75
❑ 260 Corey Simon RC 1.25 .50
❑ 261 Frank Murphy RC 1.00 .40
❑ 262 JaJuan Dawson RC 1.00 .40
❑ 263 Ron Dayne RC 2.00 .75
❑ 264 Tim Rattay RC 1.25 .50
❑ 265 Troy Walters RC 2.00 .75
❑ 266 J.R. Redmond RC 1.50 .60
❑ 267 Tom Brady RC 40.00 15.00
❑ 268 Jamal Lewis RC 5.00 2.00
❑ 269 Anthony Lucas RC 1.00 .40
❑ 270 Reuben Droughns RC 2.50 1.00
❑ 271 James Williams RC 1.50 .60
❑ 272 Shyrone Stith RC 1.50 .60
❑ 273 Jerry Porter RC 2.50 1.00
❑ 274 Brian Urlacher RC 8.00 3.00
❑ 275 Avion Black RC 1.50 .60
❑ 276 Thomas Jones RC 3.00 1.25
❑ 277 Chad Pennington RC 5.00 2.00
❑ 278 Travis Prentice RC 1.50 .60
❑ 279 Chris Redman RC 1.00 .40
❑ 280 Travis Taylor RC 1.25 .50
❑ 281 Giovanni Carmazzi RC 1.00 .40
❑ 282 Sherrod Gideon RC 1.00 .40
❑ 283 Bubba Franks RC 2.00 .75
❑ 284 Sylvester Morris RC 1.00 .40
❑ 285 Curtis Keaton RC 1.50 .60
❑ 286 Frank Moreau RC 1.50 .60
❑ 287 Terrelle Smith RC 1.50 .60
❑ 288 Shaun Alexander RC 10.00 4.00
❑ 289 Tee Martin RC 1.25 .50
❑ 290 R.Jay Soward RC 1.50 .60
❑ 291 Dez White RC 2.00 .75
❑ 292 Trung Canidate RC 1.50 .60
❑ 293 Darrell Jackson RC 4.00 1.50
❑ 294 Marc Bulger RC 4.00 1.50
❑ 295 Courtney Brown RC 1.25 .50
❑ 296 Todd Pinkston RC 2.00 .75
❑ 297 Anthony Becht RC 2.00 .75
❑ 298 Doug Chapman RC 1.50 .60
❑ 299 Gari Scott RC 1.00 .40
❑ 300 Chris Cole RC 1.50 .60

1991 Pacific

❑ COMPLETE SET (660) 15.00 7.50
❑ COMP.SERIES 1 (550) 8.00 4.00
❑ COMP.FACT.SER.1 (550) 10.00 5.00
❑ COMP.SERIES 2 (110) 8.00 4.00
❑ COMP.FACT.SER.2 (110) 12.00 6.00
❑ COMP.CHECKLIST SET (5) 15.00 7.50
❑ 1 Deion Sanders .40 .15
❑ 2 Steve Broussard .05 .01
❑ 3 Aundray Bruce .05 .01
❑ 4 Rick Bryan .05 .01

❑ 5 John Rade .05 .01
❑ 6 Scott Case .05 .01
❑ 7 Tony Casillas .05 .01
❑ 8 Shawn Collins .05 .01
❑ 9 Darion Conner .05 .01
❑ 10 Tory Epps .05 .01
❑ 11 Bill Fralic .05 .01
❑ 12 Mike Gann .05 .01
❑ 13 Tim Green UER .05 .01
❑ 14 Chris Hinton .05 .01
❑ 15 Houston Hoover UER .05 .01
❑ 16 Chris Miller .10 .02
❑ 17 Andre Rison .10 .02
❑ 18 Mike Rozier .05 .01
❑ 19 Jessie Tuggle .05 .01
❑ 20 Don Beebe .05 .01
❑ 21 Ray Bentley .05 .01
❑ 22 Shane Conlan .05 .01
❑ 23 Kent Hull .05 .01
❑ 24 Mark Kelso .05 .01
❑ 25 James Lofton UER .10 .02
❑ 26 Scott Norwood .05 .01
❑ 27 Andre Reed .10 .02
❑ 28 Leonard Smith .05 .01
❑ 29 Bruce Smith .25 .08
❑ 30 Leon Seals .05 .01
❑ 31 Darryl Talley .05 .01
❑ 32 Steve Tasker .10 .02
❑ 33 Thurman Thomas .25 .08
❑ 34 James Williams .05 .01
❑ 35 Will Wolford .05 .01
❑ 36 Frank Reich .10 .02
❑ 37 Jeff Wright RC .05 .01
❑ 38 Neal Anderson .10 .02
❑ 39 Trace Armstrong .05 .01
❑ 40 Johnny Bailey UER .05 .01
❑ 41 Mark Bortz UER .05 .01
❑ 42 Cap Boso RC .05 .01
❑ 43 Kevin Butler .05 .01
❑ 44 Mark Carrier DB .10 .02
❑ 45 Jim Covert .05 .01
❑ 46 Wendell Davis .05 .01
❑ 47 Richard Dent .10 .02
❑ 48 Shaun Gayle .05 .01
❑ 49 Jim Harbaugh .25 .08
❑ 50 Jay Hilgenberg .05 .01
❑ 51 Brad Muster .05 .01
❑ 52 William Perry .10 .02
❑ 53 Mike Singletary UER .10 .02
❑ 54 Peter Tom Willis .05 .01
❑ 55 Donnell Woolford .05 .01
❑ 56 Steve McMichael .10 .02
❑ 57 Eric Ball .05 .01
❑ 58 Lewis Billups .05 .01
❑ 59 Jim Breech .05 .01
❑ 60 James Brooks .10 .02
❑ 61 Eddie Brown .05 .01
❑ 62 Rickey Dixon .05 .01
❑ 63 Boomer Esiason .10 .02
❑ 64 James Francis .05 .01
❑ 65 David Fulcher .05 .01
❑ 66 David Grant .05 .01
❑ 67 Harold Green UER .05 .01
❑ 68 Rodney Holman .05 .01
❑ 69 Stanford Jennings .05 .01
❑ 70A Tim Krumrie ERR .50 .20
❑ 70B Tim Krumrie COR .30 .10
❑ 71 Tim McGee .05 .01
❑ 72 Anthony Munoz .10 .02
❑ 73 Mitchell Price RC .05 .01
❑ 74 Eric Thomas .05 .01
❑ 75 Ickey Woods .05 .01
❑ 76 Mike Baab .05 .01
❑ 77 Thane Gash .05 .01
❑ 78 David Grayson .05 .01
❑ 79 Mike Johnson .05 .01
❑ 80 Reggie Langhorne .05 .01
❑ 81 Kevin Mack .05 .01
❑ 82 Clay Matthews .10 .02
❑ 83A Eric Metcalf ERR .50 .20
❑ 83B Eric Metcalf COR .30 .10
❑ 84 Frank Minnifield .05 .01
❑ 85 Mike Oliphant .05 .01
❑ 86 Mike Pagel .05 .01
❑ 87 John Talley .05 .01
❑ 88 Lawyer Tillman .05 .01
❑ 89 Gregg Rakoczy UER .05 .01
❑ 90 Bryan Wagner .05 .01
❑ 91 Rob Burnett RC .10 .02

❑	92	Tommie Agee	.05	.01
❑	93	Troy Aikman UER	.75	.30
❑	94A	Bill Bates ERR	.50	.20
❑	94B	Bill Bates COR	.30	.10
❑	95	Jack Del Rio	.10	.02
❑	96	Issiac Holt UER	.05	.01
❑	97	Michael Irvin	.25	.08
❑	98	Jim Jeffcoat UER	.05	.01
❑	99	Jimmie Jones	.05	.01
❑	100	Kelvin Martin	.05	.01
❑	101	Nate Newton	.10	.02
❑	102	Danny Noonan	.05	.01
❑	103	Ken Norton Jr.	.10	.02
❑	104	Jay Novacek	.25	.08
❑	105	Mike Saxon	.05	.01
❑	106	Derrick Shepard	.05	.01
❑	107	Emmitt Smith	2.50	1.00
❑	108	Daniel Stubbs	.05	.01
❑	109	Tony Tolbert	.05	.01
❑	110	Alexander Wright	.05	.01
❑	111	Steve Atwater	.05	.01
❑	112	Melvin Bratton	.05	.01
❑	113	Tyrone Braxton UER	.05	.01
❑	114	Alphonso Carreker	.05	.01
❑	115	John Elway	1.25	.50
❑	116	Simon Fletcher	.05	.01
❑	117	Bobby Humphrey	.05	.01
❑	118	Mark Jackson	.05	.01
❑	119	Vance Johnson	.05	.01
❑	120	Greg Kragen UER	.05	.01
❑	121	Karl Mecklenburg UER	.05	.01
❑	122A	Orsen Mobley ERR	.50	.20
❑	122B	Orson Mobley COR	.10	.02
❑	123	Alton Montgomery	.05	.01
❑	124	Ricky Nattiel	.05	.01
❑	125	Steve Sewell	.05	.01
❑	126	Shannon Sharpe	.50	.20
❑	127	Dennis Smith	.05	.01
❑	128A	Andre Townsend RC ERR	.50	.20
❑	128B	Andre Townsend RC COR	.10	.02
❑	129	Mike Horan	.05	.01
❑	130	Jerry Ball	.05	.01
❑	131	Bennie Blades	.05	.01
❑	132	Lomas Brown	.05	.01
❑	133	Jeff Campbell UER	.05	.01
❑	134	Robert Clark	.05	.01
❑	135	Michael Cofer	.05	.01
❑	136	Dennis Gibson	.05	.01
❑	137	Mel Gray	.10	.02
❑	138	LeRoy Irvin UER	.05	.01
❑	139	George Jamison RC	.05	.01
❑	140	Richard Johnson	.05	.01
❑	141	Eddie Murray	.05	.01
❑	142	Dan Owens	.05	.01
❑	143	Rodney Peete	.10	.02
❑	144	Barry Sanders	1.25	.50
❑	145	Chris Spielman	.10	.02
❑	146	Marc Spindler	.05	.01
❑	147	Andre Ware	.10	.02
❑	148	William White	.05	.01
❑	149	Tony Bennett	.10	.02
❑	150	Robert Brown	.05	.01
❑	151	LeRoy Butler	.10	.02
❑	152	Anthony Dilweg	.05	.01
❑	153	Michael Haddix	.05	.01
❑	154	Ron Hallstrom	.05	.01
❑	155	Tim Harris	.05	.01
❑	156	Johnny Holland	.05	.01
❑	157	Chris Jacke	.05	.01
❑	158	Perry Kemp	.05	.01
❑	159	Mark Lee	.05	.01
❑	160	Don Majkowski	.05	.01
❑	161	Tony Mandarich UER	.05	.01
❑	162	Mark Murphy	.05	.01
❑	163	Brian Noble	.05	.01
❑	164	Shawn Patterson	.05	.01
❑	165	Jeff Query	.05	.01
❑	166	Sterling Sharpe	.25	.08
❑	167	Darrell Thompson	.05	.01
❑	168	Ed West	.05	.01
❑	169	Ray Childress UER	.05	.01
❑	170A	Cris Dishman RC ERR Chris	.10	.02
❑	170B	Cris Dishman RC ERR/COR	.10	.02
❑	170C	Cris Dishman RC COR	.10	.02
❑	171	Curtis Duncan	.05	.01
❑	172	William Fuller	.10	.02
❑	173	Ernest Givins UER	.10	.02
❑	174	Drew Hill	.05	.01
❑	175A	Haywood Jeffires ERR	.25	.08
❑	175B	Haywood Jeffires COR	.25	.08
❑	176	Sean Jones	.10	.02
❑	177	Lamar Lathon	.05	.01
❑	178	Bruce Matthews	.10	.02
❑	179	Bubba McDowell	.05	.01
❑	180	Johnny Meads	.05	.01
❑	181	Warren Moon UER	.25	.08
❑	182	Mike Munchak	.10	.02
❑	183	Allen Pinkett	.05	.01
❑	184	Dean Steinkuhler UER	.05	.01
❑	185	Lorenzo White UER	.05	.01
❑	186A	John Grimsley ERR	.50	.20
❑	186B	John Grimsley COR	.10	.02
❑	187	Pat Beach	.05	.01
❑	188	Albert Bentley	.05	.01
❑	189	Dean Biasucci	.05	.01
❑	190	Duane Bickett	.05	.01
❑	191	Bill Brooks	.05	.01
❑	192	Eugene Daniel	.05	.01
❑	193	Jeff George	.25	.08
❑	194	Jon Hand	.05	.01
❑	195	Jeff Herrod	.05	.01
❑	196A	Jessie Hester ERR Jesse	.30	.10
❑	196B	Jessie Hester ERR	.10	.02
❑	197	Mike Prior	.05	.01
❑	198	Stacey Simmons	.05	.01
❑	199	Rohn Stark	.05	.01
❑	200	Pat Tomberlin	.05	.01
❑	201	Clarence Verdin	.05	.01
❑	202	Keith Taylor	.05	.01
❑	203	Jack Trudeau	.05	.01
❑	204	Chip Banks	.05	.01
❑	205	John Alt	.05	.01
❑	206	Deron Cherry	.05	.01
❑	207	Steve DeBerg	.05	.01
❑	208	Tim Grunhard	.05	.01
❑	209	Albert Lewis	.05	.01
❑	210	Nick Lowery UER	.05	.01
❑	211	Bill Maas	.05	.01
❑	212	Chris Martin	.05	.01
❑	213	Todd McNair	.05	.01
❑	214	Christian Okoye	.05	.01
❑	215	Stephone Paige	.05	.01
❑	216	Steve Pelluer	.05	.01
❑	217	Kevin Porter	.05	.01
❑	218	Kevin Ross	.05	.01
❑	219	Dan Saleaumua	.05	.01
❑	220	Neil Smith	.25	.08
❑	221	David Szott UER	.05	.01
❑	222	Derrick Thomas	.25	.08
❑	223	Barry Word	.05	.01
❑	224	Percy Snow	.05	.01
❑	225	Marcus Allen	.25	.08
❑	226	Eddie Anderson UER	.05	.01
❑	227	Steve Beuerlein UER	.10	.02
❑	228A	Tim Brown ERR NPO	.25	.08
❑	228B	Tim Brown COR	.25	.08
❑	229	Scott Davis	.05	.01
❑	230	Mike Dyal	.05	.01
❑	231	Mervyn Fernandez UER	.05	.01
❑	232	Willie Gault UER	.05	.01
❑	233	Ethan Horton UER	.05	.01
❑	234	Bo Jackson UER	.30	.10
❑	235	Howie Long	.25	.08
❑	236	Terry McDaniel	.05	.01
❑	237	Max Montoya	.05	.01
❑	238	Don Mosebar	.05	.01
❑	239	Jay Schroeder	.05	.01
❑	240	Steve Smith	.05	.01
❑	241	Greg Townsend	.05	.01
❑	242	Aaron Wallace	.05	.01
❑	243	Lionel Washington	.05	.01
❑	244A	Steve Wisniewski ERR	.10	.02
❑	244B	Steve Wisniewski ERR/COR	.75	.30
❑	244C	Steve Wisniewski COR	.10	.02
❑	245	Flipper Anderson	.05	.01
❑	246	Latin Berry RC	.05	.01
❑	247	Robert Delpino	.05	.01
❑	248	Marcus Dupree	.05	.01
❑	249	Henry Ellard	.10	.02
❑	250	Jim Everett	.10	.02
❑	251	Cleveland Gary	.05	.01
❑	252	Jerry Gray	.05	.01
❑	253	Kevin Greene	.10	.02
❑	254	Pete Holohan UER	.05	.01
❑	255	Buford McGee	.05	.01
❑	256	Tom Newberry	.05	.01
❑	257A	Irv Pankey ERR	.50	.20
❑	257B	Irv Pankey COR	.10	.02
❑	258	Jackie Slater	.05	.01
❑	259	Doug Smith	.05	.01
❑	260	Frank Stams	.05	.01
❑	261	Michael Stewart	.05	.01
❑	262	Fred Strickland	.05	.01
❑	263	J.B. Brown UER	.05	.01
❑	264	Mark Clayton	.10	.02
❑	265	Jeff Cross	.05	.01
❑	266	Mark Dennis RC	.05	.01
❑	267	Mark Duper	.10	.02
❑	268	Ferrell Edmunds	.05	.01
❑	269	Dan Marino	1.25	.50
❑	270	John Offerdahl	.05	.01
❑	271	Louis Oliver	.05	.01
❑	272	Tony Paige	.05	.01
❑	273	Reggie Roby	.05	.01
❑	274	Sammie Smith	.05	.01
❑	275	Keith Sims	.05	.01
❑	276	Brian Sochia	.05	.01
❑	277	Pete Stoyanovich	.05	.01
❑	278	Richmond Webb	.05	.01
❑	279	Jarvis Williams	.05	.01
❑	280	Tim McKyer	.05	.01
❑	281A	Jim C. Jensen ERR	.50	.20
❑	281B	Jim C. Jensen COR	.10	.02
❑	282	Scott Secules RC	.05	.01
❑	283	Ray Berry	.05	.01
❑	284	Joey Browner UER	.05	.01
❑	285	Anthony Carter	.10	.02
❑	286A	Cris Carter ERR Chris	.50	.20
❑	286B	Cris Carter ERR/COR Chris	1.50	.60
❑	286C	Cris Carter COR	.50	.20
❑	287	Chris Doleman	.05	.01
❑	288	Mark Dusbabek UER	.05	.01
❑	289	Hassan Jones	.05	.01
❑	290	Steve Jordan	.05	.01
❑	291	Carl Lee	.05	.01
❑	292	Kirk Lowdermilk	.05	.01
❑	293	Randall McDaniel	.05	.01
❑	294	Mike Merriweather	.05	.01
❑	295A	Keith Millard UER	.20	.07
❑	295B	Keith Millard COR	2.50	1.00
❑	296	Al Noga UER	.05	.01
❑	297	Scott Studwell UER	.05	.01
❑	298	Henry Thomas	.05	.01
❑	299	Herschel Walker	.10	.02
❑	300	Gary Zimmerman	.05	.01
❑	301	Rich Gannon	.25	.08
❑	302	Wade Wilson UER	.10	.02
❑	303	Vincent Brown	.05	.01
❑	304	Marv Cook	.05	.01
❑	305	Hart Lee Dykes	.05	.01
❑	306	Irving Fryar	.10	.02
❑	307	Tommy Hodson UER	.05	.01
❑	308	Maurice Hurst	.05	.01
❑	309	Ronnie Lippett UER	.05	.01
❑	310	Fred Marion	.05	.01
❑	311	Greg McMurtry	.05	.01
❑	312	Johnny Rembert	.05	.01
❑	313	Chris Singleton	.05	.01
❑	314	Ed Reynolds	.05	.01
❑	315	Andre Tippett	.05	.01
❑	316	Garin Veris	.05	.01
❑	317	Brent Williams	.05	.01
❑	318A	John Stephens ERR	.10	.02
❑	318B	John Stephens ERR/COR	.75	.30
❑	318C	John Stephens COR	.10	.02
❑	319	Sammy Martin	.05	.01
❑	320	Bruce Armstrong	.05	.01
❑	321A	Morten Andersen ERR	.30	.10
❑	321B	Morten Andersen ERR/COR	.75	.30
❑	321C	Morten Andersen COR	.10	.02
❑	322	Gene Atkins UER	.05	.01
❑	323	Vince Buck	.05	.01
❑	324	John Fourcade	.05	.01
❑	325	Kevin Haverdink	.05	.01
❑	326	Bobby Hebert	.05	.01
❑	327	Craig Heyward	.10	.02
❑	328	Dalton Hilliard	.05	.01
❑	329	Rickey Jackson	.05	.01
❑	330A	Vaughan Johnson ERR	.20	.07
❑	330B	Vaughan Johnson COR	2.50	1.00
❑	331	Eric Martin	.05	.01
❑	332	Wayne Martin	.05	.01
❑	333	Rueben Mayes UER	.05	.01
❑	334	Sam Mills	.05	.01
❑	335	Brett Perriman	.25	.08
❑	336	Pat Swilling	.10	.02
❑	337	Renaldo Turnbull	.05	.01

❑ 338 Lonzell Hill .05 .01
❑ 339 Steve Walsh .05 .01
❑ 340 Carl Banks UER .05 .01
❑ 341 Mark Bavaro UER .05 .01
❑ 342 Maurice Carthon .05 .01
❑ 343 Pat Harlow RC .05 .01
❑ 344 Eric Dorsey .05 .01
❑ 345 John Elliott .05 .01
❑ 346 Rodney Hampton .25 .08
❑ 347 Jeff Hostetler .10 .02
❑ 348 Erik Howard UER .05 .01
❑ 349 Pepper Johnson .05 .01
❑ 350A Sean Landeta ERR .10 .02
❑ 350B Sean Landeta COR .50 .20
❑ 351 Leonard Marshall .05 .01
❑ 352 Dave Meggett .10 .02
❑ 353A Bart Oates ERR .10 .02
❑ 353B Bart Oates ERR/COR .75 .30
❑ 353C Bart Oates COR .10 .02
❑ 354 Gary Reasons .05 .01
❑ 355 Phil Simms .10 .02
❑ 356 Lawrence Taylor .25 .08
❑ 357 Reyna Thompson .05 .01
❑ 358 Brian Williams OL UER .05 .01
❑ 359 Matt Bahr .05 .01
❑ 360 Mark Ingram .10 .02
❑ 361 Brad Baxter .05 .01
❑ 362 Mark Boyer .05 .01
❑ 363 Dennis Byrd .05 .01
❑ 364 Dave Cadigan UER .05 .01
❑ 365 Kyle Clifton .05 .01
❑ 366 James Hasty .05 .01
❑ 367 Joe Kelly UER .05 .01
❑ 368 Jeff Lageman .05 .01
❑ 369 Pat Leahy UER .05 .01
❑ 370 Terance Mathis .10 .02
❑ 371 Erik McMillan .05 .01
❑ 372 Rob Moore .25 .08
❑ 373 Ken O'Brien .05 .01
❑ 374 Tony Stargell .05 .01
❑ 375 Jim Sweeney UER .05 .01
❑ 376 Al Toon .10 .02
❑ 377 Johnny Hector .05 .01
❑ 378 Jeff Criswell .05 .01
❑ 379 Mike Haight RC .05 .01
❑ 380 Troy Benson .05 .01
❑ 381 Eric Allen .05 .01
❑ 382 Fred Barnett .25 .08
❑ 383 Jerome Brown .05 .01
❑ 384 Keith Byars .05 .01
❑ 385 Randall Cunningham .25 .08
❑ 386 Byron Evans .05 .01
❑ 387 Wes Hopkins .05 .01
❑ 388 Keith Jackson .10 .02
❑ 389 Seth Joyner UER .10 .02
❑ 390 Bobby Wilson RC .05 .01
❑ 391 Heath Sherman .05 .01
❑ 392 Clyde Simmons UER .05 .01
❑ 393 Ben Smith .05 .01
❑ 394 Andre Waters .05 .01
❑ 395 Reggie White UER .25 .08
❑ 396 Calvin Williams .10 .02
❑ 397 Al Harris .05 .01
❑ 398 Anthony Toney .05 .01
❑ 399 Mike Quick .05 .01
❑ 400 Anthony Bell .05 .01
❑ 401 Rich Camarillo .05 .01
❑ 402 Roy Green .05 .01
❑ 403 Ken Harvey .10 .02
❑ 404 Eric Hill .05 .01
❑ 405 Garth Jax RC UER .05 .01
❑ 406 Ernie Jones .05 .01
❑ 407A Cedric Mack ERR .20 .07
❑ 407B Cedric Mack COR 2.50 1.00
❑ 408 Dexter Manley .05 .01
❑ 409 Tim McDonald .05 .01
❑ 410 Freddie Joe Nunn .05 .01
❑ 411 Ricky Proehl .05 .01
❑ 412 Moe Gardner RC .05 .01
❑ 413 Timm Rosenbach .05 .01
❑ 414 Luis Sharpe UER .05 .01
❑ 415 Vai Sikahema UER .05 .01
❑ 416 Anthony Thompson .05 .01
❑ 417 Ron Wolfley UER .05 .01
❑ 418 Lonnie Young .05 .01
❑ 419 Gary Anderson K .05 .01
❑ 420 Bubby Brister .05 .01
❑ 421 Thomas Everett .05 .01
❑ 422 Eric Green .05 .01
❑ 423 Delton Hall .05 .01
❑ 424 Bryan Hinkle .05 .01
❑ 425 Merril Hoge .05 .01
❑ 426 Carnell Lake .05 .01
❑ 427 Louis Lipps .05 .01
❑ 428 David Little .05 .01
❑ 429 Greg Lloyd .25 .08
❑ 430 Mike Mularkey .05 .01
❑ 431 Keith Willis UER .05 .01
❑ 432 Dwayne Woodruff .05 .01
❑ 433 Rod Woodson .25 .08
❑ 434 Tim Worley .05 .01
❑ 435 Warren Williams .05 .01
❑ 436 Terry Long UER .05 .01
❑ 437 Martin Bayless .05 .01
❑ 438 Jarrod Bunch RC .05 .01
❑ 439 Marion Butts .10 .02
❑ 440 Gill Byrd UER .05 .01
❑ 441 Arthur Cox .05 .01
❑ 442 John Friesz .25 .08
❑ 443 Leo Goeas .05 .01
❑ 444 Burt Grossman .05 .01
❑ 445 Courtney Hall UER .05 .01
❑ 446 Ronnie Harmon .05 .01
❑ 447 Nate Lewis RC .05 .01
❑ 448 Anthony Miller .10 .02
❑ 449 Leslie O'Neal .10 .02
❑ 450 Gary Plummer .05 .01
❑ 451 Junior Seau .25 .08
❑ 452 Billy Ray Smith .05 .01
❑ 453 Billy Joe Tolliver .05 .01
❑ 454 Broderick Thompson .05 .01
❑ 455 Lee Williams .05 .01
❑ 456 Michael Carter .05 .01
❑ 457 Mike Cofer .05 .01
❑ 458 Kevin Fagan .05 .01
❑ 459 Charles Haley .10 .02
❑ 460 Pierce Holt .05 .01
❑ 461 Johnnie Jackson UER RC .05 .01
❑ 462 Brent Jones .25 .08
❑ 463 Guy McIntyre .05 .01
❑ 464 Joe Montana 1.25 .50
❑ 465A Bubba Paris ERR .10 .02
❑ 465B Bubba Paris ERR/COR .50 .20
❑ 465C Bubba Paris COR .10 .02
❑ 466 Tom Rathman UER .05 .01
❑ 467 Jerry Rice UER .75 .30
❑ 468 Mike Sherrard .05 .01
❑ 469 John Taylor UER .10 .02
❑ 470 Steve Young .75 .30
❑ 471 Dennis Brown .05 .01
❑ 472 Dexter Carter .05 .01
❑ 473 Bill Romanowski .05 .01
❑ 474 Dave Waymer .05 .01
❑ 475 Robert Blackmon .05 .01
❑ 476 Derrick Fenner .05 .01
❑ 477 Nesby Glasgow UER .05 .01
❑ 478 Jacob Green .05 .01
❑ 479 Andy Heck .05 .01
❑ 480 Norm Johnson UER .05 .01
❑ 481 Tommy Kane .05 .01
❑ 482 Cortez Kennedy .25 .08
❑ 483A Dave Krieg ERR .20 .07
❑ 483B Dave Krieg COR 2.50 1.00
❑ 484 Bryan Millard .05 .01
❑ 485 Joe Nash .05 .01
❑ 486 Rufus Porter .05 .01
❑ 487 Eugene Robinson .05 .01
❑ 488 Mike Tice RC .05 .01
❑ 489 Chris Warren .25 .08
❑ 490 John L. Williams UER .05 .01
❑ 491 Terry Wooden .05 .01
❑ 492 Tony Woods .05 .01
❑ 493 Brian Blades .10 .02
❑ 494 Paul Skansi .05 .01
❑ 495 Gary Anderson RB .05 .01
❑ 496 Mark Carrier WR .25 .08
❑ 497 Chris Chandler .25 .08
❑ 498 Steve Christie .05 .01
❑ 499 Reggie Cobb .05 .01
❑ 500 Reuben Davis .05 .01
❑ 501 Willie Drewrey UER .05 .01
❑ 502 Randy Grimes .05 .01
❑ 503 Paul Gruber .05 .01
❑ 504 Wayne Haddix .05 .01
❑ 505 Ron Hall .05 .01
❑ 506 Harry Hamilton .05 .01
❑ 507 Bruce Hill .05 .01
❑ 508 Eugene Marve .05 .01
❑ 509 Keith McCants .05 .01
❑ 510 Winston Moss .05 .01
❑ 511 Kevin Murphy .05 .01
❑ 512 Mark Robinson .05 .01
❑ 513 Vinny Testaverde .10 .02
❑ 514 Broderick Thomas .05 .01
❑ 515A Jeff Bostic UER .10 .02
❑ 515B Jeff Bostic UER .10 .02
❑ 516 Todd Bowles .05 .01
❑ 517 Earnest Byner .05 .01
❑ 518 Gary Clark .25 .08
❑ 519 Craig Erickson RC .25 .08
❑ 520 Darryl Grant .05 .01
❑ 521 Darrell Green .05 .01
❑ 522 Russ Grimm .05 .01
❑ 523 Stan Humphries .25 .08
❑ 524 Joe Jacoby UER .05 .01
❑ 525 Jim Lachey .05 .01
❑ 526 Chip Lohmiller .05 .01
❑ 527 Charles Mann .05 .01
❑ 528 Wilber Marshall .05 .01
❑ 529A Art Monk .10 .02
❑ 529B Art Monk .10 .02
❑ 530 Tracy Rocker .05 .01
❑ 531 Mark Rypien .10 .02
❑ 532 Ricky Sanders UER .05 .01
❑ 533 Alvin Walton UER .05 .01
❑ 534 Todd Marinovich RC UER .05 .01
❑ 535 Mike Dumas RC .05 .01
❑ 536A Russell Maryland RC ERR .25 .08
❑ 536B Russell Maryland RC COR .25 .08
❑ 537 Eric Turner RC UER .10 .02
❑ 538 Ernie Mills RC .10 .02
❑ 539 Ed King RC .05 .01
❑ 540 Mike Stonebreaker .05 .01
❑ 541 Chris Zorich RC .25 .08
❑ 542A Mike Croel RC ERR .05 .01
❑ 542B Mike Croel RC COR .05 .01
❑ 543 Eric Moten RC .05 .01
❑ 544 Dan McGwire RC .05 .01
❑ 545 Keith Cash RC .05 .01
❑ 546 Kenny Walker RC UER .05 .01
❑ 547 Leroy Hoard UER .10 .02
❑ 548 Luis Cristobal UER .05 .01
❑ 549 Stacy Danley .05 .01
❑ 550 Todd Lyght RC .05 .01
❑ 551 Brett Favre RC 8.00 3.00
❑ 552 Mike Pritchard RC .25 .08
❑ 553 Moe Gardner .05 .01
❑ 554 Tim McKyer .05 .01
❑ 555 Erric Pegram RC .25 .08
❑ 556 Norm Johnson .05 .01
❑ 557 Bruce Pickens RC .05 .01
❑ 558 Henry Jones RC .10 .02
❑ 559 Phil Hansen RC .05 .01
❑ 560 Cornelius Bennett .10 .02
❑ 561 Stan Thomas .05 .01
❑ 562 Chris Zorich .10 .02
❑ 563 Anthony Morgan RC .05 .01
❑ 564 Darren Lewis RC .05 .01
❑ 565 Mike Stonebreaker .05 .01
❑ 566 Alfred Williams RC .05 .01
❑ 567 Lamar Rogers RC .05 .01
❑ 568 Erik Wilhelm RC UER .05 .01
❑ 569 Ed King .05 .01
❑ 570 Michael Jackson RC WR .25 .08
❑ 571 James Jones RC DT .05 .01
❑ 572 Russell Maryland .25 .08
❑ 573 Dixon Edwards RC .05 .01
❑ 574 Darrick Brownlow RC .05 .01
❑ 575 Larry Brown RC DB .10 .02
❑ 576 Mike Croel .05 .01
❑ 577 Keith Traylor RC .05 .01
❑ 578 Kenny Walker .05 .01
❑ 579 Reggie Johnson RC .05 .01
❑ 580 Herman Moore RC .25 .08
❑ 581 Kelvin Pritchett RC .10 .02
❑ 582 Kevin Scott RC .05 .01
❑ 583 Vinnie Clark RC .05 .01
❑ 584 Esera Tuaolo RC .05 .01
❑ 585 Don Davey .05 .01
❑ 586 Blair Kiel RC .05 .01
❑ 587 Mike Dumas .05 .01
❑ 588 Darryll Lewis RC .10 .02
❑ 589 John Flannery RC .05 .01
❑ 590 Kevin Donnalley RC .05 .01
❑ 591 Shane Curry .05 .01
❑ 592 Mark Vander Poel RC .05 .01
❑ 593 Dave McCloughan .05 .01

❑ 594 Mel Agee RC	.05	.01
❑ 595 Kerry Cash RC	.05	.01
❑ 596 Harvey Williams RC	.25	.08
❑ 597 Joe Valerio	.05	.01
❑ 598 Tim Barnett RC UER	.05	.01
❑ 599 Todd Marinovich	.10	.02
❑ 600 Nick Bell RC	.05	.01
❑ 601 Roger Craig	.10	.02
❑ 602 Ronnie Lott	.10	.02
❑ 603 Mike Jones RC LB	.05	.01
❑ 604 Todd Lyght	.05	.01
❑ 605 Roman Phifer RC	.05	.01
❑ 606 David Lang RC	.05	.01
❑ 607 Aaron Craver RC	.05	.01
❑ 608 Mark Higgs RC	.05	.01
❑ 609 Chris Green	.05	.01
❑ 610 Randy Baldwin RC	.05	.01
❑ 611 Pat Harlow	.05	.01
❑ 612 Leonard Russell RC	.25	.08
❑ 613 Jerome Henderson RC	.05	.01
❑ 614 Scott Zolak RC	.05	.01
❑ 615 Jon Vaughn RC	.05	.01
❑ 616 Harry Colon RC	.05	.01
❑ 617 Wesley Carroll RC	.05	.01
❑ 618 Quinn Early	.10	.02
❑ 619 Reginald Jones RC	.05	.01
❑ 620 Jarrod Bunch	.05	.01
❑ 621 Kanavis McGhee RC	.05	.01
❑ 622 Ed McCaffrey RC	2.00	.75
❑ 623 Browning Nagle RC	.05	.01
❑ 624 Mo Lewis RC	.10	.02
❑ 625 Blair Thomas	.05	.01
❑ 626 Antone Davis RC	.05	.01
❑ 627 Jim McMahon	.10	.02
❑ 628 Scott Kowalkowski RC	.05	.01
❑ 629 Brad Goebel RC	.05	.01
❑ 630 William Thomas RC	.05	.01
❑ 631 Eric Swann RC	.25	.08
❑ 632 Mike Jones DE RC	.05	.01
❑ 633 Aeneas Williams RC	.25	.08
❑ 634 Dexter Davis RC	.05	.01
❑ 635 Tom Tupa UER	.05	.01
❑ 636 Johnny Johnson	.05	.01
❑ 637 Randal Hill RC	.10	.02
❑ 638 Jeff Graham RC WR	.25	.08
❑ 639 Ernie Mills	.05	.01
❑ 640 Adrian Cooper RC	.05	.01
❑ 641 Stanley Richard RC	.05	.01
❑ 642 Eric Bieniemy RC	.05	.01
❑ 643 Eric Moten	.05	.01
❑ 644 Shawn Jefferson RC	.10	.02
❑ 645 Ted Washington RC	.05	.01
❑ 646 John Johnson RC	.05	.01
❑ 647 Dan McGwire	.05	.01
❑ 648 Doug Thomas RC	.05	.01
❑ 649 David Daniels RC	.05	.01
❑ 650 John Kasay RC	.10	.02
❑ 651 Jeff Kemp	.05	.01
❑ 652 Charles McRae RC	.05	.01
❑ 653 Lawrence Dawsey RC	.10	.02
❑ 654 Robert Wilson RC	.05	.01
❑ 655 Dexter Manley	.05	.01
❑ 656 Chuck Weatherspoon	.05	.01
❑ 657 Tim Ryan G RC	.05	.01
❑ 658 Bobby Wilson	.05	.01
❑ 659 Ricky Ervins RC	.10	.02
❑ 660 Matt Millen	.10	.02

1992 Pacific

❑ COMPLETE SET (660)	15.00	6.00
❑ COMP.FACT.SET (690)	25.00	10.00
❑ COMP.SERIES 1 (330)	8.00	3.00
❑ COMP.SERIES 2 (330)	8.00	3.00
❑ COMP.CHECKLIST SET (5)	3.00	1.50
❑ 1 Steve Broussard	.05	.01
❑ 2 Darion Conner	.05	.01
❑ 3 Tory Epps	.05	.01
❑ 4 Michael Haynes	.10	.02
❑ 5 Chris Hinton	.05	.01
❑ 6 Mike Kenn	.05	.01
❑ 7 Tim McKyer	.05	.01
❑ 8 Chris Miller	.10	.02
❑ 9 Erric Pegram	.10	.02
❑ 10 Mike Pritchard	.10	.02
❑ 11 Moe Gardner	.05	.01
❑ 12 Tim Green	.05	.01
❑ 13 Norm Johnson	.05	.01
❑ 14 Don Beebe	.05	.01
❑ 15 Cornelius Bennett	.10	.02
❑ 16 Al Edwards	.05	.01
❑ 17 Mark Kelso	.05	.01
❑ 18 James Lofton	.10	.02
❑ 19 Frank Reich	.10	.02
❑ 20 Leon Seals	.05	.01
❑ 21 Darryl Talley	.05	.01
❑ 22 Thurman Thomas	.25	.08
❑ 23 Kent Hull	.05	.01
❑ 24 Jeff Wright	.05	.01
❑ 25 Nate Odomes	.05	.01
❑ 26 Carwell Gardner	.05	.01
❑ 27 Neal Anderson	.05	.01
❑ 28 Mark Carrier DB	.05	.01
❑ 29 Johnny Bailey	.05	.01
❑ 30 Jim Harbaugh	.25	.08
❑ 31 Jay Hilgenberg	.05	.01
❑ 32 William Perry	.10	.02
❑ 33 Wendell Davis	.05	.01
❑ 34 Donnell Woolford	.05	.01
❑ 35 Keith Van Horne	.05	.01
❑ 36 Shaun Gayle	.05	.01
❑ 37 Tom Waddle	.05	.01
❑ 38 Chris Zorich	.10	.02
❑ 39 Tom Thayer	.05	.01
❑ 40 Rickey Dixon	.05	.01
❑ 41 James Francis	.05	.01
❑ 42 David Fulcher	.05	.01
❑ 43 Reggie Rembert	.05	.01
❑ 44 Anthony Munoz	.10	.02
❑ 45 Harold Green	.05	.01
❑ 46 Mitchell Price	.05	.01
❑ 47 Rodney Holman	.05	.01
❑ 48 Bruce Kozerski	.05	.01
❑ 49 Bruce Reimers	.05	.01
❑ 50 Erik Wilhelm	.05	.01
❑ 51 Harlon Barnett	.05	.01
❑ 52 Mike Johnson	.05	.01
❑ 53 Brian Brennan	.05	.01
❑ 54 Ed King	.05	.01
❑ 55 Reggie Langhorne	.05	.01
❑ 56 James Jones DT	.05	.01
❑ 57 Mike Baab	.05	.01
❑ 58 Dan Fike	.05	.01
❑ 59 Frank Minnifield	.05	.01
❑ 60 Clay Matthews	.10	.02
❑ 61 Kevin Mack	.05	.01
❑ 62 Tony Casillas	.05	.01
❑ 63 Jay Novacek	.10	.02
❑ 64 Larry Brown DB	.05	.01
❑ 65 Michael Irvin	.25	.08
❑ 66 Jack Del Rio	.05	.01
❑ 67 Ken Willis	.05	.01
❑ 68 Emmitt Smith	1.50	.60
❑ 69 Alan Veingrad	.05	.01
❑ 70 John Gesek	.05	.01
❑ 71 Steve Beuerlein	.10	.02
❑ 72 Vinson Smith RC	.05	.01
❑ 73 Steve Atwater	.05	.01
❑ 74 Mike Croel	.05	.01
❑ 75 John Elway	1.25	.50
❑ 76 Gaston Green	.05	.01
❑ 77 Mike Horan	.05	.01
❑ 78 Vance Johnson	.05	.01
❑ 79 Karl Mecklenburg	.05	.01
❑ 80 Shannon Sharpe	.25	.08
❑ 81 David Treadwell	.05	.01
❑ 82 Kenny Walker	.05	.01
❑ 83 Greg Lewis	.05	.01
❑ 84 Shawn Moore	.05	.01
❑ 85 Alton Montgomery	.05	.01
❑ 86 Michael Young	.05	.01
❑ 87 Jerry Ball	.05	.01
❑ 88 Bennie Blades	.05	.01
❑ 89 Mel Gray	.10	.02
❑ 90 Herman Moore	.25	.08
❑ 91 Erik Kramer	.10	.02
❑ 92 Willie Green	.05	.01
❑ 93 George Jamison	.05	.01
❑ 94 Chris Spielman	.10	.02
❑ 95 Kelvin Pritchett	.05	.01
❑ 96 William White	.05	.01
❑ 97 Mike Utley	.10	.02
❑ 98 Tony Bennett	.05	.01
❑ 99 LeRoy Butler	.05	.01
❑ 100 Vinnie Clark	.05	.01
❑ 101 Ron Hallstrom	.05	.01
❑ 102 Chris Jacke	.05	.01
❑ 103 Tony Mandarich	.05	.01
❑ 104 Sterling Sharpe	.25	.08
❑ 105 Don Majkowski	.05	.01
❑ 106 Johnny Holland	.05	.01
❑ 107 Esera Tuaolo	.05	.01
❑ 108 Darrell Thompson	.05	.01
❑ 109 Bubba McDowell	.05	.01
❑ 110 Curtis Duncan	.05	.01
❑ 111 Lamar Lathon	.05	.01
❑ 112 Drew Hill	.05	.01
❑ 113 Bruce Matthews	.05	.01
❑ 114 Bo Orlando RC	.05	.01
❑ 115 Don Maggs	.05	.01
❑ 116 Lorenzo White	.05	.01
❑ 117 Ernest Givins	.10	.02
❑ 118 Tony Jones WR	.05	.01
❑ 119 Dean Steinkuhler	.05	.01
❑ 120 Dean Biasucci	.05	.01
❑ 121 Duane Bickett	.05	.01
❑ 122 Bill Brooks	.05	.01
❑ 123 Ken Clark	.05	.01
❑ 124 Jessie Hester	.05	.01
❑ 125 Anthony Johnson	.10	.02
❑ 126 Chip Banks	.05	.01
❑ 127 Mike Prior	.05	.01
❑ 128 Rohn Stark	.05	.01
❑ 129 Jeff Herrod	.05	.01
❑ 130 Clarence Verdin	.05	.01
❑ 131 Tim Manoa	.05	.01
❑ 132 Brian Baldinger RC	.05	.01
❑ 133 Tim Barnett	.05	.01
❑ 134 J.J. Birden	.05	.01
❑ 135 Deron Cherry	.05	.01
❑ 136 Steve DeBerg	.05	.01
❑ 137 Nick Lowery	.05	.01
❑ 138 Todd McNair	.05	.01
❑ 139 Christian Okoye	.05	.01
❑ 140 Mark Vlasic	.05	.01
❑ 141 Dan Saleaumua	.05	.01
❑ 142 Neil Smith	.25	.08
❑ 143 Robb Thomas	.05	.01
❑ 144 Eddie Anderson	.05	.01
❑ 145 Nick Bell	.05	.01
❑ 146 Tim Brown	.25	.08
❑ 147 Roger Craig	.10	.02
❑ 148 Jeff Gossett	.05	.01
❑ 149 Ethan Horton	.05	.01
❑ 150 Jamie Holland	.05	.01
❑ 151 Jeff Jaeger	.05	.01
❑ 152 Todd Marinovich	.05	.01
❑ 153 Marcus Allen	.25	.08
❑ 154 Steve Smith	.05	.01
❑ 155 Flipper Anderson	.05	.01
❑ 156 Robert Delpino	.05	.01
❑ 157 Cleveland Gary	.05	.01
❑ 158 Kevin Greene	.10	.02
❑ 159 Dale Hatcher	.05	.01
❑ 160 Duval Love	.05	.01
❑ 161 Ron Brown	.05	.01
❑ 162 Jackie Slater	.05	.01
❑ 163 Doug Smith	.05	.01
❑ 164 Aaron Cox	.05	.01
❑ 165 Larry Kelm	.05	.01
❑ 166 Mark Clayton	.10	.02
❑ 167 Louis Oliver	.05	.01
❑ 168 Mark Higgs	.05	.01
❑ 169 Aaron Craver	.05	.01
❑ 170 Sammie Smith	.05	.01
❑ 171 Tony Paige	.05	.01
❑ 172 Jeff Cross	.05	.01
❑ 173 David Griggs	.05	.01
❑ 174 Richmond Webb	.05	.01
❑ 175 Vestee Jackson	.05	.01
❑ 176 Jim C. Jensen	.05	.01

❑ 177	Anthony Carter	.10	.02
❑ 178	Cris Carter	.50	.20
❑ 179	Chris Doleman	.05	.01
❑ 180	Rich Gannon	.25	.08
❑ 181	Al Noga	.05	.01
❑ 182	Randall McDaniel	.05	.01
❑ 183	Todd Scott	.05	.01
❑ 184	Henry Thomas	.05	.01
❑ 185	Felix Wright	.05	.01
❑ 186	Gary Zimmerman	.05	.01
❑ 187	Herschel Walker	.10	.02
❑ 188	Vincent Brown	.05	.01
❑ 189	Harry Colon	.05	.01
❑ 190	Irving Fryar	.10	.02
❑ 191	Marv Cook	.05	.01
❑ 192	Leonard Russell	.10	.02
❑ 193	Hugh Millen	.05	.01
❑ 194	Pat Harlow	.05	.01
❑ 195	Jon Vaughn	.05	.01
❑ 196	Ben Coates RC	.75	.30
❑ 197	Johnny Rembert	.05	.01
❑ 198	Greg McMurtry	.05	.01
❑ 199	Morten Andersen	.05	.01
❑ 200	Tommy Barnhardt	.05	.01
❑ 201	Bobby Hebert	.05	.01
❑ 202	Dalton Hilliard	.05	.01
❑ 203	Sam Mills	.05	.01
❑ 204	Pat Swilling	.05	.01
❑ 205	Rickey Jackson	.05	.01
❑ 206	Stan Brock	.05	.01
❑ 207	Reginald Jones	.05	.01
❑ 208	Gill Fenerty	.05	.01
❑ 209	Eric Martin	.05	.01
❑ 210	Matt Bahr	.05	.01
❑ 211	Rodney Hampton	.10	.02
❑ 212	Jeff Hostetler	.10	.02
❑ 213	Pepper Johnson	.05	.01
❑ 214	Leonard Marshall	.05	.01
❑ 215	Doug Riesenberg	.05	.01
❑ 216	Stephen Baker	.05	.01
❑ 217	Mike Fox	.05	.01
❑ 218	Bart Oates	.05	.01
❑ 219	Everson Walls	.05	.01
❑ 220	Gary Reasons	.05	.01
❑ 221	Jeff Lageman	.05	.01
❑ 222	Joe Kelly	.05	.01
❑ 223	Mo Lewis	.05	.01
❑ 224	Tony Stargell	.05	.01
❑ 225	Jim Sweeney	.05	.01
❑ 226	Freeman McNeil	.10	.02
❑ 227	Brian Washington	.05	.01
❑ 228	Johnny Hector	.05	.01
❑ 229	Terance Mathis	.10	.02
❑ 230	Rob Moore	.10	.02
❑ 231	Brad Baxter	.05	.01
❑ 232	Eric Allen	.05	.01
❑ 233	Fred Barnett	.10	.02
❑ 234	Jerome Brown	.05	.01
❑ 235	Keith Byars	.05	.01
❑ 236	William Thomas	.05	.01
❑ 237	Jessie Small	.05	.01
❑ 238	Robert Drummond	.05	.01
❑ 239	Reggie White	.25	.08
❑ 240	James Joseph	.05	.01
❑ 241	Brad Goebel	.05	.01
❑ 242	Clyde Simmons	.05	.01
❑ 243	Rich Camarillo	.05	.01
❑ 244	Ken Harvey	.05	.01
❑ 245	Garth Jax	.05	.01
❑ 246	Johnny Johnson	.05	.01
❑ 247	Mike Jones	.05	.01
❑ 248	Ernie Jones	.05	.01
❑ 249	Tom Tupa	.05	.01
❑ 250	Ron Wolfley	.05	.01
❑ 251	Luis Sharpe	.05	.01
❑ 252	Eric Swann	.10	.02
❑ 253	Anthony Thompson	.05	.01
❑ 254	Gary Anderson K	.05	.01
❑ 255	Dermontti Dawson	.05	.01
❑ 256	Jeff Graham	.25	.08
❑ 257	Eric Green	.05	.01
❑ 258	Louis Lipps	.05	.01
❑ 259	Neil O'Donnell	.10	.02
❑ 260	Rod Woodson	.25	.08
❑ 261	Dwight Stone	.05	.01
❑ 262	Aaron Jones	.05	.01
❑ 263	Keith Willis	.05	.01
❑ 264	Ernie Mills	.05	.01
❑ 265	Martin Bayless	.05	.01
❑ 266	Rod Bernstine	.05	.01
❑ 267	John Carney	.05	.01
❑ 268	John Friesz	.10	.02
❑ 269	Nate Lewis	.05	.01
❑ 270	Shawn Jefferson	.05	.01
❑ 271	Burt Grossman	.05	.01
❑ 272	Eric Moten	.05	.01
❑ 273	Gary Plummer	.05	.01
❑ 274	Henry Rolling	.05	.01
❑ 275	Steve Hendrickson RC	.05	.01
❑ 276	Michael Carter	.05	.01
❑ 277	Steve Bono RC	.25	.08
❑ 278	Dexter Carter	.05	.01
❑ 279	Mike Cofer	.05	.01
❑ 280	Charles Haley	.10	.02
❑ 281	Tom Rathman	.05	.01
❑ 282	Guy McIntyre	.05	.01
❑ 283	John Taylor	.10	.02
❑ 284	Dave Waymer	.05	.01
❑ 285	Steve Wallace	.05	.01
❑ 286	Jamie Williams	.05	.01
❑ 287	Brian Blades	.10	.02
❑ 288	Jeff Bryant	.05	.01
❑ 289	Grant Feasel	.05	.01
❑ 290	Jacob Green	.05	.01
❑ 291	Andy Heck	.05	.01
❑ 292	Kelly Stouffer	.05	.01
❑ 293	John Kasay	.05	.01
❑ 294	Cortez Kennedy	.10	.02
❑ 295	Bryan Millard	.05	.01
❑ 296	Eugene Robinson	.05	.01
❑ 297	Tony Woods	.05	.01
❑ 298	Jesse Anderson UER	.05	.01
❑ 299	Gary Anderson RB	.05	.01
❑ 300	Mark Carrier WR	.10	.02
❑ 301	Reggie Cobb	.05	.01
❑ 302	Robert Wilson	.05	.01
❑ 303	Jesse Solomon	.05	.01
❑ 304	Broderick Thomas	.05	.01
❑ 305	Lawrence Dawsey	.10	.02
❑ 306	Charles McRae	.05	.01
❑ 307	Paul Gruber	.05	.01
❑ 308	Vinny Testaverde	.10	.02
❑ 309	Brian Mitchell	.10	.02
❑ 310	Darrell Green	.05	.01
❑ 311	Art Monk	.10	.02
❑ 312	Russ Grimm	.05	.01
❑ 313	Mark Rypien	.05	.01
❑ 314	Bobby Wilson	.05	.01
❑ 315	Wilber Marshall	.05	.01
❑ 316	Gerald Riggs	.05	.01
❑ 317	Chip Lohmiller	.05	.01
❑ 318	Joe Jacoby	.05	.01
❑ 319	Martin Mayhew	.05	.01
❑ 320	Amp Lee RC	.05	.01
❑ 321	Terrell Buckley RC	.05	.01
❑ 322	Tommy Vardell RC	.05	.01
❑ 323	Ricardo McDonald RC	.05	.01
❑ 324	Joe Bowden RC	.05	.01
❑ 325	Darryl Williams RC	.05	.01
❑ 326	Carlos Huerta	.05	.01
❑ 327	Patrick Rowe RC	.05	.01
❑ 328	Siran Stacy RC	.05	.01
❑ 329	Dexter McNabb RC	.05	.01
❑ 330	Willie Clay RC	.05	.01
❑ 331	Oliver Barnett	.05	.01
❑ 332	Aundray Bruce	.05	.01
❑ 333	Ken Tippins RC	.05	.01
❑ 334	Jessie Tuggle	.05	.01
❑ 335	Brian Jordan	.10	.02
❑ 336	Andre Rison	.10	.02
❑ 337	Houston Hoover	.05	.01
❑ 338	Bill Fralic	.05	.01
❑ 339	Pat Chaffey RC	.05	.01
❑ 340	Keith Jones	.05	.01
❑ 341	Jamie Dukes RC	.05	.01
❑ 342	Chris Mohr	.05	.01
❑ 343	John Davis	.05	.01
❑ 344	Ray Bentley	.05	.01
❑ 345	Scott Norwood	.05	.01
❑ 346	Shane Conlan	.05	.01
❑ 347	Steve Tasker	.10	.02
❑ 348	Will Wolford	.05	.01
❑ 349	Gary Baldinger RC	.05	.01
❑ 350	Kirby Jackson	.05	.01
❑ 351	Jamie Mueller	.05	.01
❑ 352	Pete Metzelaars	.05	.01
❑ 353	Richard Dent	.10	.02
❑ 354	Ron Rivera	.05	.01
❑ 355	Jim Morrissey	.05	.01
❑ 356	John Roper	.05	.01
❑ 357	Steve McMichael	.10	.02
❑ 358	Ron Morris	.05	.01
❑ 359	Darren Lewis	.05	.01
❑ 360	Anthony Morgan	.05	.01
❑ 361	Stan Thomas	.05	.01
❑ 362	James Thornton	.05	.01
❑ 363	Brad Muster	.05	.01
❑ 364	Tim Krumrie	.05	.01
❑ 365	Lee Johnson	.05	.01
❑ 366	Eric Ball	.05	.01
❑ 367	Alonzo Mitz RC	.05	.01
❑ 368	David Grant	.05	.01
❑ 369	Lynn James	.05	.01
❑ 370	Lewis Billups	.05	.01
❑ 371	Jim Breech	.05	.01
❑ 372	Alfred Williams	.05	.01
❑ 373	Wayne Haddix	.05	.01
❑ 374	Tim McGee	.05	.01
❑ 375	Michael Jackson	.10	.02
❑ 376	Leroy Hoard	.10	.02
❑ 377	Tony Jones T	.05	.01
❑ 378	Vince Newsome	.05	.01
❑ 379	Todd Philcox RC	.05	.01
❑ 380	Eric Metcalf	.10	.02
❑ 381	John Rienstra	.05	.01
❑ 382	Matt Stover	.05	.01
❑ 383	Brian Hansen	.05	.01
❑ 384	Joe Morris	.05	.01
❑ 385	Anthony Pleasant	.05	.01
❑ 386	Mark Stepnoski	.05	.01
❑ 387	Erik Williams	.05	.01
❑ 388	Jimmie Jones	.05	.01
❑ 389	Kevin Gogan	.05	.01
❑ 390	Manny Hendrix RC	.05	.01
❑ 391	Issiac Holt	.05	.01
❑ 392	Ken Norton	.10	.02
❑ 393	Tommie Agee	.05	.01
❑ 394	Alvin Harper	.10	.02
❑ 395	Alexander Wright	.05	.01
❑ 396	Mike Saxon	.05	.01
❑ 397	Michael Brooks	.05	.01
❑ 398	Bobby Humphrey	.05	.01
❑ 399	Ken Lanier	.05	.01
❑ 400	Steve Sewell	.05	.01
❑ 401	Robert Perryman	.05	.01
❑ 402	Wymon Henderson	.05	.01
❑ 403	Keith Kartz	.05	.01
❑ 404	Clarence Kay	.05	.01
❑ 405	Keith Traylor	.05	.01
❑ 406	Doug Widell	.05	.01
❑ 407	Dennis Smith	.05	.01
❑ 408	Marc Spindler	.05	.01
❑ 409	Lomas Brown	.05	.01
❑ 410	Robert Clark	.05	.01
❑ 411	Eric Andolsek	.05	.01
❑ 412	Mike Farr	.05	.01
❑ 413	Ray Crockett	.05	.01
❑ 414	Jeff Campbell	.05	.01
❑ 415	Dan Owens	.05	.01
❑ 416	Jim Arnold	.05	.01
❑ 417	Barry Sanders	1.25	.50
❑ 418	Eddie Murray	.05	.01
❑ 419	Vince Workman	.05	.01
❑ 420	Ed West	.05	.01
❑ 421	Charles Wilson	.05	.01
❑ 422	Perry Kemp	.05	.01
❑ 423	Chuck Cecil	.05	.01
❑ 424	James Campen	.05	.01
❑ 425	Robert Brown	.05	.01
❑ 426	Brian Noble	.05	.01
❑ 427	Rich Moran	.05	.01
❑ 428	Vai Sikahema	.05	.01
❑ 429	Allen Rice	.05	.01
❑ 430	Haywood Jeffires	.10	.02
❑ 431	Warren Moon	.25	.08
❑ 432	Greg Montgomery	.05	.01
❑ 433	Sean Jones	.05	.01
❑ 434	Richard Johnson CB	.05	.01
❑ 435	Al Smith	.05	.01
❑ 436	Johnny Meads	.05	.01
❑ 437	William Fuller	.05	.01
❑ 438	Mike Munchak	.10	.02
❑ 439	Ray Childress	.05	.01
❑ 440	Cody Carlson	.05	.01
❑ 441	Scott Radecic	.05	.01
❑ 442	Quintus McDonald RC	.05	.01
❑ 443	Eugene Daniel	.05	.01

❑ 444 Mark Herrmann RC .05 .01
❑ 445 John Baylor RC .05 .01
❑ 446 Dave McCloughan .05 .01
❑ 447 Mark Vander Poel .05 .01
❑ 448 Randy Dixon .05 .01
❑ 449 Keith Taylor .05 .01
❑ 450 Alan Grant .05 .01
❑ 451 Tony Siragusa .05 .01
❑ 452 Rich Baldinger .05 .01
❑ 453 Derrick Thomas .25 .08
❑ 454 Bill Jones RC .05 .01
❑ 455 Troy Stradford .05 .01
❑ 456 Barry Word .05 .01
❑ 457 Tim Grunhard .05 .01
❑ 458 Chris Martin .05 .01
❑ 459 Jayice Pearson RC .05 .01
❑ 460 Dino Hackett .05 .01
❑ 461 David Lutz .05 .01
❑ 462 Albert Lewis .05 .01
❑ 463 Fred Jones RC .05 .01
❑ 464 Winston Moss .05 .01
❑ 465 Sam Graddy RC .05 .01
❑ 466 Steve Wisniewski .05 .01
❑ 467 Jay Schroeder .05 .01
❑ 468 Ronnie Lott .10 .02
❑ 469 Willie Gault .10 .02
❑ 470 Greg Townsend .05 .01
❑ 471 Max Montoya .05 .01
❑ 472 Howie Long .25 .08
❑ 473 Lionel Washington .05 .01
❑ 474 Riki Ellison .05 .01
❑ 475 Tom Newberry .05 .01
❑ 476 Damone Johnson .05 .01
❑ 477 Pat Terrell .05 .01
❑ 478 Marcus Dupree .05 .01
❑ 479 Todd Lyght .05 .01
❑ 480 Buford McGee .05 .01
❑ 481 Bern Brostek .05 .01
❑ 482 Jim Price .05 .01
❑ 483 Robert Young .05 .01
❑ 484 Tony Zendejas .05 .01
❑ 485 Robert Bailey RC .05 .01
❑ 486 Alvin Wright .05 .01
❑ 487 Pat Carter .05 .01
❑ 488 Pete Stoyanovich .05 .01
❑ 489 Reggie Roby .05 .01
❑ 490 Harry Galbreath .05 .01
❑ 491 Mike McGruder RC**/C .05 .01
❑ 492 J.B. Brown .05 .01
❑ 493 E.J. Junior .05 .01
❑ 494 Ferrell Edmunds .05 .01
❑ 495 Scott Secules .05 .01
❑ 496 Greg Baty RC .05 .01
❑ 497 Mike Iaquaniello .05 .01
❑ 498 Keith Sims .05 .01
❑ 499 John Randle .10 .02
❑ 500 Joey Browner .05 .01
❑ 501 Steve Jordan .05 .01
❑ 502 Darrin Nelson .05 .01
❑ 503 Audray McMillian .05 .01
❑ 504 Harry Newsome .05 .01
❑ 505 Hassan Jones .05 .01
❑ 506 Ray Berry .05 .01
❑ 507 Mike Merriweather .05 .01
❑ 508 Leo Lewis .05 .01
❑ 509 Tim Irwin .05 .01
❑ 510 Kirk Lowdermilk .05 .01
❑ 511 Alfred Anderson .05 .01
❑ 512 Michael Timpson RC .05 .01
❑ 513 Jerome Henderson .05 .01
❑ 514 Andre Tippett .05 .01
❑ 515 Chris Singleton .05 .01
❑ 516 John Stephens .05 .01
❑ 517 Ronnie Lippett .05 .01
❑ 518 Bruce Armstrong .05 .01
❑ 519 Marion Hobby RC .05 .01
❑ 520 Tim Goad .05 .01
❑ 521 Mickey Washington RC .05 .01
❑ 522 Fred Smerlas .05 .01
❑ 523 Wayne Martin .05 .01
❑ 524 Frank Warren .05 .01
❑ 525 Floyd Turner .05 .01
❑ 526 Wesley Carroll .05 .01
❑ 527 Gene Atkins .05 .01
❑ 528 Vaughan Johnson .05 .01
❑ 529 Hoby Brenner .05 .01
❑ 530 Renaldo Turnbull .05 .01
❑ 531 Joel Hilgenberg .05 .01
❑ 532 Craig Heyward .10 .02
❑ 533 Vince Buck .05 .01
❑ 534 Jim Dombrowski .05 .01
❑ 535 Fred McAfee RC .05 .01
❑ 536 Phil Simms .10 .02
❑ 537 Lewis Tillman .05 .01
❑ 538 John Elliott .05 .01
❑ 539 Dave Meggett .10 .02
❑ 540 Mark Collins .05 .01
❑ 541 Ottis Anderson .10 .02
❑ 542 Bobby Abrams RC .05 .01
❑ 543 Sean Landeta .05 .01
❑ 544 Brian Williams OL .05 .01
❑ 545 Erik Howard .05 .01
❑ 546 Mark Ingram .05 .01
❑ 547 Kanavis McGhee .05 .01
❑ 548 Kyle Clifton .05 .01
❑ 549 Marvin Washington .05 .01
❑ 550 Jeff Criswell .05 .01
❑ 551 Dave Cadigan .05 .01
❑ 552 Chris Burkett .05 .01
❑ 553 Erik McMillan .05 .01
❑ 554 James Hasty .05 .01
❑ 555 Louie Aguiar RC .05 .01
❑ 556 Troy Johnson RC .05 .01
❑ 557 Troy Taylor RC .05 .01
❑ 558 Pat Kelly RC .05 .01
❑ 559 Heath Sherman .05 .01
❑ 560 Roger Ruzek .05 .01
❑ 561 Andre Waters .05 .01
❑ 562 Izel Jenkins .05 .01
❑ 563 Keith Jackson .10 .02
❑ 564 Byron Evans .05 .01
❑ 565 Wes Hopkins .05 .01
❑ 566 Rich Miano .05 .01
❑ 567 Seth Joyner .05 .01
❑ 568 Thomas Sanders .05 .01
❑ 569 David Alexander .05 .01
❑ 570 Jeff Kemp .05 .01
❑ 571 Jock Jones RC .05 .01
❑ 572 Craig Patterson RC .05 .01
❑ 573 Robert Massey .05 .01
❑ 574 Bill Lewis .05 .01
❑ 575 Freddie Joe Nunn .05 .01
❑ 576 Aeneas Williams .10 .02
❑ 577 John Jackson WR .05 .01
❑ 578 Tim McDonald .05 .01
❑ 579 Michael Zordich RC .05 .01
❑ 580 Eric Hill .05 .01
❑ 581 Lorenzo Lynch .05 .01
❑ 582 Vernice Smith RC .05 .01
❑ 583 Greg Lloyd .10 .02
❑ 584 Carnell Lake .05 .01
❑ 585 Hardy Nickerson .10 .02
❑ 586 Delton Hall .05 .01
❑ 587 Gerald Williams .05 .01
❑ 588 Bryan Hinkle .05 .01
❑ 589 Barry Foster .10 .02
❑ 590 Bubby Brister .10 .02
❑ 591 Rick Strom RC .05 .01
❑ 592 David Little .05 .01
❑ 593 Leroy Thompson RC .05 .01
❑ 594 Eric Bieniemy .05 .01
❑ 595 Courtney Hall .05 .01
❑ 596 George Thornton .05 .01
❑ 597 Donnie Elder .05 .01
❑ 598 Billy Ray Smith .05 .01
❑ 599 Gill Byrd .05 .01
❑ 600 Marion Butts .05 .01
❑ 601 Ronnie Harmon .05 .01
❑ 602 Anthony Shelton .05 .01
❑ 603 Mark May .05 .01
❑ 604 Craig McEwen RC .05 .01
❑ 605 Steve Young .60 .25
❑ 606 Keith Henderson .05 .01
❑ 607 Pierce Holt .05 .01
❑ 608 Roy Foster .05 .01
❑ 609 Don Griffin .05 .01
❑ 610 Harry Sydney .05 .01
❑ 611 Todd Bowles .05 .01
❑ 612 Ted Washington .05 .01
❑ 613 Johnnie Jackson .05 .01
❑ 614 Jesse Sapolu .05 .01
❑ 615 Brent Jones .10 .02
❑ 616 Travis McNeal .05 .01
❑ 617 Darrick Brilz RC .05 .01
❑ 618 Terry Wooden .05 .01
❑ 619 Tommy Kane .05 .01
❑ 620 Nesby Glasgow .05 .01
❑ 621 Dwayne Harper .05 .01
❑ 622 Rick Tuten .05 .01
❑ 623 Chris Warren .10 .02
❑ 624 John L. Williams .05 .01
❑ 625 Rufus Porter .05 .01
❑ 626 David Daniels .05 .01
❑ 627 Keith McCants .05 .01
❑ 628 Reuben Davis .05 .01
❑ 629 Mark Royals .05 .01
❑ 630 Marty Carter RC .05 .01
❑ 631 Ian Beckles .05 .01
❑ 632 Ron Hall .05 .01
❑ 633 Eugene Marve .05 .01
❑ 634 Willie Drewrey .05 .01
❑ 635 Tom McHale RC .05 .01
❑ 636 Kevin Murphy .05 .01
❑ 637 Robert Hardy RC .05 .01
❑ 638 Ricky Sanders .05 .01
❑ 639 Gary Clark .10 .02
❑ 640 Andre Collins .05 .01
❑ 641 Brad Edwards .05 .01
❑ 642 Monte Coleman .05 .01
❑ 643 Clarence Vaughn RC .05 .01
❑ 644 Fred Stokes .05 .01
❑ 645 Charles Mann .05 .01
❑ 646 Earnest Byner .05 .01
❑ 647 Jim Lachey .05 .01
❑ 648 Jeff Bostic .05 .01
❑ 649 Chris Mims RC .05 .01
❑ 650 George Williams RC .05 .01
❑ 651 Ed Cunningham RC .05 .01
❑ 652 Tony Smith RC WR .05 .01
❑ 653 Will Furrer RC .05 .01
❑ 654 Matt Elliott RC .05 .01
❑ 655 Mike Mooney RC .05 .01
❑ 656 Eddie Blake RC .05 .01
❑ 657 Leon Searcy RC .05 .01
❑ 658 Kevin Turner RC .05 .01
❑ 659 Keith Hamilton RC .10 .02
❑ 660 Alan Haller RC .05 .01

1993 Pacific

❑ COMPLETE SET (440) 20.00 10.00
❑ 1 Emmitt Smith 1.50 .60
❑ 2 Troy Aikman .75 .30
❑ 3 Larry Brown DB .05 .01
❑ 4 Tony Casillas .05 .01
❑ 5 Thomas Everett .05 .01
❑ 6 Alvin Harper .10 .02
❑ 7 Michael Irvin .25 .08
❑ 8 Charles Haley .10 .02
❑ 9 Leon Lett RC .10 .02
❑ 10 Kevin Smith .10 .02
❑ 11 Robert Jones .05 .01
❑ 12 Jimmy Smith .25 .08
❑ 13 Derrick Gainer RC .05 .01
❑ 14 Lin Elliott .05 .01
❑ 15 William Thomas .05 .01
❑ 16 Clyde Simmons .05 .01
❑ 17 Seth Joyner .05 .01
❑ 18 Randall Cunningham .25 .08
❑ 19 Byron Evans .05 .01
❑ 20 Fred Barnett .10 .02
❑ 21 Calvin Williams .10 .02
❑ 22 James Joseph .05 .01
❑ 23 Heath Sherman .05 .01
❑ 24 Siran Stacy .05 .01
❑ 25 Andy Harmon .10 .02
❑ 26 Eric Allen .05 .01
❑ 27 Herschel Walker .10 .02
❑ 28 Vai Sikahema .05 .01
❑ 29 Earnest Byner .05 .01
❑ 30 Jeff Bostic .05 .01

	No.	Player		
❑	31	Monte Coleman	.05	.01
❑	32	Ricky Ervins	.05	.01
❑	33	Darrell Green	.05	.01
❑	34	Mark Schlereth	.05	.01
❑	35	Mark Rypien	.05	.01
❑	36	Art Monk	.10	.02
❑	37	Brian Mitchell	.10	.02
❑	38	Chip Lohmiller	.05	.01
❑	39	Charles Mann	.05	.01
❑	40	Shane Collins	.05	.01
❑	41	Jim Lachey	.05	.01
❑	42	Desmond Howard	.10	.02
❑	43	Rodney Hampton	.10	.02
❑	44	Dave Brown RC	.25	.08
❑	45	Mark Collins	.05	.01
❑	46	Jarrod Bunch	.05	.01
❑	47	William Roberts	.05	.01
❑	48	Sean Landeta	.05	.01
❑	49	Lawrence Taylor	.25	.08
❑	50	Ed McCaffrey	.25	.08
❑	51	Bart Oates	.05	.01
❑	52	Pepper Johnson	.05	.01
❑	53	Eric Dorsey	.05	.01
❑	54	Erik Howard	.05	.01
❑	55	Phil Simms	.10	.02
❑	56	Derek Brown TE	.05	.01
❑	57	Johnny Bailey	.05	.01
❑	58	Rich Camarillo	.05	.01
❑	59	Larry Centers RC	.25	.08
❑	60	Chris Chandler	.10	.02
❑	61	Randal Hill	.05	.01
❑	62	Ricky Proehl	.05	.01
❑	63	Freddie Joe Nunn	.05	.01
❑	64	Robert Massey	.05	.01
❑	65	Aeneas Williams	.05	.01
❑	66	Luis Sharpe	.05	.01
❑	67	Eric Swann	.10	.02
❑	68	Timm Rosenbach	.05	.01
❑	69	Anthony Edwards RC	.05	.01
❑	70	Greg Davis	.05	.01
❑	71	Terry Allen	.25	.08
❑	72	Anthony Carter	.10	.02
❑	73	Cris Carter	.25	.08
❑	74	Roger Craig	.10	.02
❑	75	Jack Del Rio	.05	.01
❑	76	Chris Doleman	.05	.01
❑	77	Rich Gannon	.25	.08
❑	78	Hassan Jones	.05	.01
❑	79	Steve Jordan	.05	.01
❑	80	Randall McDaniel	.05	.01
❑	81	Sean Salisbury	.05	.01
❑	82	Harry Newsome	.05	.01
❑	83	Carlos Jenkins	.05	.01
❑	84	Jake Reed	.25	.08
❑	85	Edgar Bennett	.25	.08
❑	86	Tony Bennett	.05	.01
❑	87	Terrell Buckley	.05	.01
❑	88	Ty Detmer	.25	.08
❑	89	Brett Favre	2.00	.75
❑	90	Chris Jacke	.05	.01
❑	91	Sterling Sharpe	.25	.08
❑	92	James Campen	.05	.01
❑	93	Brian Noble	.05	.01
❑	94	Lester Archambeau RC	.05	.01
❑	95	Harry Sydney	.05	.01
❑	96	Corey Harris	.05	.01
❑	97	Don Majkowski	.05	.01
❑	98	Ken Ruettgers	.05	.01
❑	99	Lomas Brown	.05	.01
❑	100	Jason Hanson	.05	.01
❑	101	Robert Porcher	.05	.01
❑	102	Chris Spielman	.10	.02
❑	103	Erik Kramer	.10	.02
❑	104	Tracy Scroggins	.05	.01
❑	105	Rodney Peete	.05	.01
❑	106	Barry Sanders	1.25	.50
❑	107	Herman Moore	.25	.08
❑	108	Brett Perriman	.25	.08
❑	109	Mel Gray	.10	.02
❑	110	Dennis Gibson	.05	.01
❑	111	Bennie Blades	.05	.01
❑	112	Andre Ware	.05	.01
❑	113	Gary Anderson RB	.05	.01
❑	114	Tyji Armstrong	.05	.01
❑	115	Reggie Cobb	.05	.01
❑	116	Marty Carter	.05	.01
❑	117	Lawrence Dawsey	.05	.01
❑	118	Steve DeBerg	.05	.01
❑	119	Ron Hall	.05	.01
❑	120	Courtney Hawkins	.05	.01
❑	121	Broderick Thomas	.05	.01
❑	122	Keith McCants	.05	.01
❑	123	Bruce Reimers	.05	.01
❑	124	Darrick Brownlow	.05	.01
❑	125	Mark Wheeler	.05	.01
❑	126	Ricky Reynolds	.05	.01
❑	127	Neal Anderson	.05	.01
❑	128	Trace Armstrong	.05	.01
❑	129	Mark Carrier DB	.05	.01
❑	130	Richard Dent	.10	.02
❑	131	Wendell Davis	.05	.01
❑	132	Darren Lewis	.05	.01
❑	133	Tom Waddle	.05	.01
❑	134	Jim Harbaugh	.25	.08
❑	135	Steve McMichael	.10	.02
❑	136	William Perry	.10	.02
❑	137	Alonzo Spellman	.05	.01
❑	138	John Roper	.05	.01
❑	139	Peter Tom Willis	.05	.01
❑	140	Dante Jones	.05	.01
❑	141	Harris Barton	.05	.01
❑	142	Michael Carter	.05	.01
❑	143	Eric Davis	.05	.01
❑	144	Dana Hall	.05	.01
❑	145	Amp Lee	.05	.01
❑	146	Don Griffin	.05	.01
❑	147	Jerry Rice	1.00	.40
❑	148	Ricky Watters	.25	.08
❑	149	Steve Young	.75	.30
❑	150	Bill Romanowski	.05	.01
❑	151	Klaus Wilmsmeyer	.05	.01
❑	152	Steve Bono	.10	.02
❑	153	Tom Rathman	.05	.01
❑	154	Odessa Turner	.05	.01
❑	155	Morten Andersen	.05	.01
❑	156	Richard Cooper	.05	.01
❑	157	Toi Cook	.05	.01
❑	158	Quinn Early	.10	.02
❑	159	Vaughn Dunbar	.05	.01
❑	160	Rickey Jackson	.05	.01
❑	161	Wayne Martin	.05	.01
❑	162	Hoby Brenner	.05	.01
❑	163	Joel Hilgenberg	.05	.01
❑	164	Mike Buck	.05	.01
❑	165	Torrance Small	.05	.01
❑	166	Eric Martin	.05	.01
❑	167	Vaughan Johnson	.05	.01
❑	168	Sam Mills	.05	.01
❑	169	Steve Broussard	.05	.01
❑	170	Darion Conner	.05	.01
❑	171	Drew Hill	.05	.01
❑	172	Chris Hinton	.05	.01
❑	173	Chris Miller	.10	.02
❑	174	Tim McKyer	.05	.01
❑	175	Norm Johnson	.05	.01
❑	176	Mike Pritchard	.10	.02
❑	177	Andre Rison	.10	.02
❑	178	Deion Sanders	.50	.20
❑	179	Tony Smith RB	.05	.01
❑	180	Bruce Pickens	.05	.01
❑	181	Michael Haynes	.10	.02
❑	182	Jessie Tuggle	.05	.01
❑	183	Marc Boutte	.05	.01
❑	184	Don Bracken	.05	.01
❑	185	Bern Brostek	.05	.01
❑	186	Henry Ellard	.10	.02
❑	187	Jim Everett	.10	.02
❑	188	Sean Gilbert	.10	.02
❑	189	Cleveland Gary	.05	.01
❑	190	Todd Kinchen	.05	.01
❑	191	Pat Terrell	.05	.01
❑	192	Jackie Slater	.05	.01
❑	193	David Lang	.05	.01
❑	194	Flipper Anderson	.05	.01
❑	195	Tony Zendejas	.05	.01
❑	196	Roman Phifer	.05	.01
❑	197	Steve Christie	.05	.01
❑	198	Cornelius Bennett	.10	.02
❑	199	Phil Hansen	.05	.01
❑	200	Don Beebe	.05	.01
❑	201	Mark Kelso	.05	.01
❑	202	Bruce Smith	.25	.08
❑	203	Darryl Talley	.05	.01
❑	204	Andre Reed	.10	.02
❑	205	Mike Lodish	.05	.01
❑	206	Jim Kelly	.25	.08
❑	207	Thurman Thomas	.25	.08
❑	208	Kenneth Davis	.05	.01
❑	209	Frank Reich	.10	.02
❑	210	Kent Hull	.05	.01
❑	211	Marco Coleman	.05	.01
❑	212	Bryan Cox	.05	.01
❑	213	Jeff Cross	.05	.01
❑	214	Mark Higgs	.05	.01
❑	215	Keith Jackson	.10	.02
❑	216	Scott Miller	.05	.01
❑	217	John Offerdahl	.05	.01
❑	218	Dan Marino	1.50	.60
❑	219	Keith Sims	.05	.01
❑	220	Chuck Klingbeil	.05	.01
❑	221	Troy Vincent	.05	.01
❑	222	Mike Williams RC WR	.05	.01
❑	223	Pete Stoyanovich	.05	.01
❑	224	J.B. Brown	.05	.01
❑	225	Ashley Ambrose	.05	.01
❑	226	Jason Belser RC	.05	.01
❑	227	Jeff George	.25	.08
❑	228	Quentin Coryatt	.10	.02
❑	229	Duane Bickett	.05	.01
❑	230	Steve Emtman	.05	.01
❑	231	Anthony Johnson	.10	.02
❑	232	Rohn Stark	.05	.01
❑	233	Jessie Hester	.05	.01
❑	234	Reggie Langhorne	.05	.01
❑	235	Clarence Verdin	.05	.01
❑	236	Dean Biasucci	.05	.01
❑	237	Jack Trudeau	.05	.01
❑	238	Tony Siragusa	.05	.01
❑	239	Chris Burkett	.05	.01
❑	240	Brad Baxter	.05	.01
❑	241	Rob Moore	.10	.02
❑	242	Browning Nagle	.05	.01
❑	243	Jim Sweeney	.05	.01
❑	244	Kurt Barber	.05	.01
❑	245	Siupeli Malamala RC	.05	.01
❑	246	Mike Brim	.05	.01
❑	247	Mo Lewis	.05	.01
❑	248	Johnny Mitchell	.05	.01
❑	249	Ken Whisenhunt RC	.30	.10
❑	250	James Hasty	.05	.01
❑	251	Kyle Clifton	.05	.01
❑	252	Terance Mathis	.10	.02
❑	253	Ray Agnew	.05	.01
❑	254	Eugene Chung	.05	.01
❑	255	Marv Cook	.05	.01
❑	256	Johnny Rembert	.05	.01
❑	257	Maurice Hurst	.05	.01
❑	258	Jon Vaughn	.05	.01
❑	259	Leonard Russell	.10	.02
❑	260	Pat Harlow	.05	.01
❑	261	Andre Tippett	.05	.01
❑	262	Michael Timpson	.05	.01
❑	263	Greg McMurtry	.05	.01
❑	264	Chris Singleton	.05	.01
❑	265	Reggie Redding RC	.05	.01
❑	266	Walter Stanley	.05	.01
❑	267	Gary Anderson K	.05	.01
❑	268	Merril Hoge	.05	.01
❑	269	Barry Foster	.10	.02
❑	270	Charles Davenport	.05	.01
❑	271	Jeff Graham	.10	.02
❑	272	Adrian Cooper	.05	.01
❑	273	David Little	.05	.01
❑	274	Neil O'Donnell	.25	.08
❑	275	Rod Woodson	.25	.08
❑	276	Ernie Mills	.05	.01
❑	277	Dwight Stone	.05	.01
❑	278	Darren Perry	.05	.01
❑	279	Dermontti Dawson	.05	.01
❑	280	Carlton Haselrig	.05	.01
❑	281	Pat Coleman	.05	.01
❑	282	Ernest Givins	.10	.02
❑	283	Warren Moon	.25	.08
❑	284	Haywood Jeffires	.10	.02
❑	285	Cody Carlson	.05	.01
❑	286	Ray Childress	.05	.01
❑	287	Bruce Matthews	.05	.01
❑	288	Webster Slaughter	.05	.01
❑	289	Bo Orlando	.05	.01
❑	290	Lorenzo White	.05	.01
❑	291	Eddie Robinson	.05	.01
❑	292	Bubba McDowell	.05	.01
❑	293	Bucky Richardson	.05	.01
❑	294	Sean Jones	.05	.01
❑	295	David Brandon	.05	.01
❑	296	Shawn Collins	.05	.01
❑	297	Lawyer Tillman	.05	.01

❑ 298 Bob Dahl .05 .01
❑ 299 Kevin Mack .05 .01
❑ 300 Bernie Kosar .10 .02
❑ 301 Tommy Vardell .05 .01
❑ 302 Jay Hilgenberg .05 .01
❑ 303 Michael Dean Perry .10 .02
❑ 304 Michael Jackson .10 .02
❑ 305 Eric Metcalf .10 .02
❑ 306 Rico Smith RC .05 .01
❑ 307 Stevon Moore RC .05 .01
❑ 308 Leroy Hoard .10 .02
❑ 309 Eric Ball .05 .01
❑ 310 Derrick Fenner .05 .01
❑ 311 James Francis .05 .01
❑ 312 Ricardo McDonald .05 .01
❑ 313 Tim Krumrie .05 .01
❑ 314 Carl Pickens .10 .02
❑ 315 David Klingler .05 .01
❑ 316 Donald Hollas RC .05 .01
❑ 317 Harold Green .05 .01
❑ 318 Daniel Stubbs .05 .01
❑ 319 Alfred Williams .05 .01
❑ 320 Darryl Williams .05 .01
❑ 321 Mike Arthur RC .05 .01
❑ 322 Leonard Wheeler .05 .01
❑ 323 Gill Byrd .05 .01
❑ 324 Eric Bieniemy .05 .01
❑ 325 Marion Butts .05 .01
❑ 326 John Carney .05 .01
❑ 327 Stan Humphries .10 .02
❑ 328 Ronnie Harmon .05 .01
❑ 329 Junior Seau .25 .08
❑ 330 Nate Lewis .05 .01
❑ 331 Harry Swayne .05 .01
❑ 332 Leslie O'Neal .10 .02
❑ 333 Eric Moten .05 .01
❑ 334 Blaise Winter RC .05 .01
❑ 335 Anthony Miller .10 .02
❑ 336 Gary Plummer .05 .01
❑ 337 Willie Davis .25 .08
❑ 338 J.J. Birden .05 .01
❑ 339 Tim Barnett .05 .01
❑ 340 Dave Krieg .10 .02
❑ 341 Barry Word .05 .01
❑ 342 Tracy Simien .05 .01
❑ 343 Christian Okoye .05 .01
❑ 344 Todd McNair .05 .01
❑ 345 Dan Saleaumua .05 .01
❑ 346 Derrick Thomas .25 .08
❑ 347 Harvey Williams .10 .02
❑ 348 Kimble Anders RC .25 .08
❑ 349 Tim Grunhard .05 .01
❑ 350 Tony Hargain RC UER .05 .01
❑ 351 Simon Fletcher .05 .01
❑ 352 John Elway 1.50 .60
❑ 353 Mike Croel .05 .01
❑ 354 Steve Atwater .05 .01
❑ 355 Tommy Maddox .25 .08
❑ 356 Karl Mecklenburg .05 .01
❑ 357 Shane Dronett .05 .01
❑ 358 Kenny Walker .05 .01
❑ 359 Reggie Rivers RC .05 .01
❑ 360 Cedric Tillman RC .05 .01
❑ 361 Arthur Marshall RC .05 .01
❑ 362 Greg Lewis .05 .01
❑ 363 Shannon Sharpe .25 .08
❑ 364 Doug Widell .05 .01
❑ 365 Todd Marinovich .05 .01
❑ 366 Nick Bell .05 .01
❑ 367 Eric Dickerson .10 .02
❑ 368 Max Montoya .05 .01
❑ 369 Winston Moss .05 .01
❑ 370 Howie Long .25 .08
❑ 371 Willie Gault .05 .01
❑ 372 Tim Brown .25 .08
❑ 373 Steve Smith .05 .01
❑ 374 Steve Wisniewski .05 .01
❑ 375 Alexander Wright .05 .01
❑ 376 Ethan Horton .05 .01
❑ 377 Napoleon McCallum .05 .01
❑ 378 Terry McDaniel .05 .01
❑ 379 Patrick Hunter .05 .01
❑ 380 Robert Blackmon .05 .01
❑ 381 John Kasay .05 .01
❑ 382 Cortez Kennedy .10 .02
❑ 383 Andy Heck .05 .01
❑ 384 Bill Hitchcock RC .05 .01
❑ 385 Rick Mirer RC .25 .08
❑ 386 Jeff Bryant .05 .01
❑ 387 Eugene Robinson .05 .01
❑ 388 John L. Williams .05 .01
❑ 389 Chris Warren .10 .02
❑ 390 Rufus Porter .05 .01
❑ 391 Joe Tofflemire RC .05 .01
❑ 392 Dan McGwire .05 .01
❑ 393 Boomer Esiason .10 .02
❑ 394 Brad Muster .05 .01
❑ 395 James Lofton .10 .02
❑ 396 Tim McGee .05 .01
❑ 397 Steve Beuerlein .10 .02
❑ 398 Gaston Green .05 .01
❑ 399 Bill Brooks .05 .01
❑ 400 Ronnie Lott .10 .02
❑ 401 Jay Schroeder .05 .01
❑ 402 Marcus Allen .25 .08
❑ 403 Kevin Greene .10 .02
❑ 404 Kirk Lowdermilk .05 .01
❑ 405 Hugh Millen .05 .01
❑ 406 Pat Swilling .05 .01
❑ 407 Bobby Hebert .05 .01
❑ 408 Carl Banks .05 .01
❑ 409 Jeff Hostetler .10 .02
❑ 410 Leonard Marshall .05 .01
❑ 411 Ken O'Brien .05 .01
❑ 412 Joe Montana 1.50 .60
❑ 413 Reggie White .25 .08
❑ 414 Gary Clark .10 .02
❑ 415 Johnny Johnson .05 .01
❑ 416 Tim McDonald .05 .01
❑ 417 Pierce Holt .05 .01
❑ 418 Gino Torretta RC .10 .02
❑ 419 Glyn Milburn RC .25 .08
❑ 420 O.J.McDuffie RC .25 .08
❑ 421 Coleman Rudolph RC .05 .01
❑ 422 Reggie Brooks RC .10 .02
❑ 423 Garrison Hearst RC .60 .25
❑ 424 Leonard Renfro RC .05 .01
❑ 425 Kevin Williams RC WR .25 .08
❑ 426 Demetrius DuBose RC .05 .01
❑ 427 Elvis Grbac RC 1.25 .50
❑ 428 Lincoln Kennedy RC .05 .01
❑ 429 Carlton Gray RC .05 .01
❑ 430 Micheal Barrow RC .25 .08
❑ 431 George Teague RC .10 .02
❑ 432 Curtis Conway RC .40 .15
❑ 433 Natrone Means RC .25 .08
❑ 434 Jerome Bettis RC 5.00 2.00
❑ 435 Drew Bledsoe RC 2.00 .75
❑ 436 Robert Smith RC 1.00 .40
❑ 437 Deon Figures RC .05 .01
❑ 438 Qadry Ismail RC .25 .08
❑ 439 Chris Slade RC .10 .02
❑ 440 Dana Stubblefield RC .25 .08

1994 Pacific

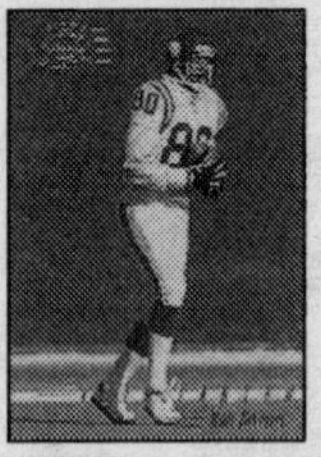

❑ COMPLETE SET (450) 30.00 15.00
❑ 1 Troy Aikman 1.00 .40
❑ 2 Charles Haley .10 .02
❑ 3 Alvin Harper .10 .02
❑ 4 Michael Irvin .25 .08
❑ 5 Jim Jeffcoat .05 .01
❑ 6 Daryl Johnston .10 .02
❑ 7 Robert Jones .05 .01
❑ 8 Brock Marion RC .25 .08
❑ 9 Russell Maryland .05 .01
❑ 10 Ken Norton .10 .02
❑ 11 Jay Novacek .10 .02
❑ 12 Emmitt Smith 1.50 .60
❑ 13 Kevin Smith .05 .01
❑ 14 Tony Tolbert .05 .01
❑ 15 Kevin Williams WR .10 .02
❑ 16 Don Beebe .05 .01
❑ 17 Cornelius Bennett .10 .02
❑ 18 Bill Brooks .05 .01
❑ 19 Steve Christie .05 .01
❑ 20 Russell Copeland .05 .01
❑ 21 Kenneth Davis .05 .01
❑ 22 Kent Hull .05 .01
❑ 23 Jim Kelly .25 .08
❑ 24 Pete Metzelaars .05 .01
❑ 25 Andre Reed .10 .02
❑ 26 Frank Reich .10 .02
❑ 27 Bruce Smith .25 .08
❑ 28 Darryl Talley .05 .01
❑ 29 Steve Tasker .10 .02
❑ 30 Thurman Thomas .25 .08
❑ 31 Steve Bono .10 .02
❑ 32 Dexter Carter .05 .01
❑ 33 Kevin Fagan .05 .01
❑ 34 Dana Hall .05 .01
❑ 35 Brent Jones .10 .02
❑ 36 Amp Lee .05 .01
❑ 37 Marc Logan .05 .01
❑ 38 Tim McDonald .05 .01
❑ 39 Guy McIntyre .05 .01
❑ 40 Tom Rathman .05 .01
❑ 41 Jerry Rice 1.00 .40
❑ 42 Dana Stubblefield .10 .02
❑ 43 Steve Wallace .05 .01
❑ 44 Ricky Watters .10 .02
❑ 45 Steve Young .75 .30
❑ 46 Marcus Allen .25 .08
❑ 47 Kimble Anders .10 .02
❑ 48 Tim Barnett .05 .01
❑ 49 J.J. Birden .05 .01
❑ 50 Dale Carter .05 .01
❑ 51 Jonathan Hayes .05 .01
❑ 52 Dave Krieg .10 .02
❑ 53 Albert Lewis .05 .01
❑ 54 Nick Lowery .05 .01
❑ 55 Joe Montana 2.00 .75
❑ 56 Neil Smith .10 .02
❑ 57 John Stephens .05 .01
❑ 58 Derrick Thomas .25 .08
❑ 59 Harvey Williams .10 .02
❑ 60 Micheal Barrow .05 .01
❑ 61 Gary Brown .05 .01
❑ 62 Cody Carlson .05 .01
❑ 63 Ray Childress .05 .01
❑ 64 Curtis Duncan .05 .01
❑ 65 Ernest Givins .10 .02
❑ 66 Haywood Jeffires .10 .02
❑ 67 Wilber Marshall .05 .01
❑ 68 Bubba McDowell .05 .01
❑ 69 Warren Moon .25 .08
❑ 70 Mike Munchak .10 .02
❑ 71 Marcus Robertson .05 .01
❑ 72 Webster Slaughter .05 .01
❑ 73 Gary Wellman RC .05 .01
❑ 74 Lorenzo White .05 .01
❑ 75 Ray Crockett .05 .01
❑ 76 Jason Hanson .05 .01
❑ 77 Rodney Holman .05 .01
❑ 78 George Jamison .05 .01
❑ 79 Erik Kramer .10 .02
❑ 80 Ryan McNeil .05 .01
❑ 81 Derrick Moore .05 .01
❑ 82 Herman Moore .25 .08
❑ 83 Rodney Peete .05 .01
❑ 84 Brett Perriman .10 .02
❑ 85 Barry Sanders 1.50 .60
❑ 86 Chris Spielman .10 .02
❑ 87 Pat Swilling .05 .01
❑ 88 Vernon Turner .05 .01
❑ 89 Andre Ware .05 .01
❑ 90 Michael Brooks .05 .01
❑ 91 Dave Brown .10 .02
❑ 92 Derek Brown TE .05 .01
❑ 93 Jarrod Bunch .05 .01
❑ 94 Chris Calloway .05 .01
❑ 95 Kent Graham .10 .02
❑ 96 Rodney Hampton .10 .02
❑ 97 Mark Jackson .05 .01
❑ 98 Ed McCaffrey .25 .08
❑ 99 Dave Meggett .05 .01
❑ 100 Aaron Pierce .05 .01
❑ 101 Mike Sherrard .05 .01
❑ 102 Phil Simms .10 .02

	Card	Player	Price 1	Price 2
❑	103	Lewis Tillman	.05	.01
❑	104	Eddie Anderson	.05	.01
❑	105	Patrick Bates	.05	.01
❑	106	Nick Bell	.05	.01
❑	107	Tim Brown	.25	.08
❑	108	Willie Gault	.05	.01
❑	109	Jeff Gossett	.05	.01
❑	110	Ethan Horton	.05	.01
❑	111	Jeff Hostetler	.10	.02
❑	112	Rocket Ismail	.10	.02
❑	113	Chester McGlockton	.05	.01
❑	114	Anthony Smith	.05	.01
❑	115	Steve Smith	.05	.01
❑	116	Greg Townsend	.05	.01
❑	117	Steve Wisniewski	.05	.01
❑	118	Alexander Wright	.05	.01
❑	119	Steve Atwater	.05	.01
❑	120	Rod Bernstine	.05	.01
❑	121	Mike Croel	.05	.01
❑	122	Shane Dronett	.05	.01
❑	123	Jason Elam	.10	.02
❑	124	John Elway	2.00	.75
❑	125	Brian Habib	.05	.01
❑	126	Rondell Jones	.05	.01
❑	127	Tommy Maddox	.25	.08
❑	128	Karl Mecklenburg	.05	.01
❑	129	Glyn Milburn	.10	.02
❑	130	Derek Russell	.05	.01
❑	131	Shannon Sharpe	.10	.02
❑	132	Dennis Smith	.05	.01
❑	133	Edgar Bennett	.25	.08
❑	134	Tony Bennett	.05	.01
❑	135	Robert Brooks	.25	.08
❑	136	Terrell Buckley	.05	.01
❑	137	LeRoy Butler	.05	.01
❑	138	Mark Clayton	.05	.01
❑	139	Ty Detmer	.10	.02
❑	140	Brett Favre	2.00	.75
❑	141	John Jurkovic RC	.10	.02
❑	142	Bryce Paup	.10	.02
❑	143	Sterling Sharpe	.10	.02
❑	144	George Teague	.05	.01
❑	145	Darrell Thompson	.05	.01
❑	146	Ed West	.05	.01
❑	147	Reggie White	.25	.08
❑	148	Terry Allen	.10	.02
❑	149	Anthony Carter	.10	.02
❑	150	Cris Carter	.50	.20
❑	151	Roger Craig	.10	.02
❑	152	Jack Del Rio	.05	.01
❑	153	Chris Doleman	.05	.01
❑	154	Scottie Graham RC	.10	.02
❑	155	Eric Guliford RC	.05	.01
❑	156	Qadry Ismail	.25	.08
❑	157	Steve Jordan	.05	.01
❑	158	Randall McDaniel	.05	.01
❑	159	Jim McMahon	.10	.02
❑	160	Audray McMillian	.05	.01
❑	161	Sean Salisbury	.05	.01
❑	162	Robert Smith	.25	.08
❑	163	Henry Thomas	.05	.01
❑	164	Gary Anderson K	.05	.01
❑	165	Deon Figures	.05	.01
❑	166	Barry Foster	.05	.01
❑	167	Jeff Graham	.05	.01
❑	168	Kevin Greene	.10	.02
❑	169	Dave Hoffman	.05	.01
❑	170	Merril Hoge	.05	.01
❑	171	Gary Jones	.05	.01
❑	172	Greg Lloyd	.10	.02
❑	173	Ernie Mills	.05	.01
❑	174	Neil O'Donnell	.25	.08
❑	175	Darren Perry	.05	.01
❑	176	Leon Searcy	.05	.01
❑	177	Leroy Thompson	.05	.01
❑	178	Willie Williams RC	.05	.01
❑	179	Rod Woodson	.10	.02
❑	180	Keith Byars	.05	.01
❑	181	Marco Coleman	.05	.01
❑	182	Bryan Cox	.05	.01
❑	183	Irving Fryar	.10	.02
❑	184	John Grimsley	.05	.01
❑	185	Mark Higgs	.05	.01
❑	186	Mark Ingram	.05	.01
❑	187	Keith Jackson	.05	.01
❑	188	Terry Kirby	.25	.08
❑	189	Dan Marino	2.00	.75
❑	190	O.J.McDuffie	.25	.08
❑	191	Scott Mitchell	.10	.02
❑	192	Pete Stoyanovich	.05	.01
❑	193	Troy Vincent	.05	.01
❑	194	Richmond Webb	.05	.01
❑	195	Brad Baxter	.05	.01
❑	196	Chris Burkett	.05	.01
❑	197	Rob Carpenter WR	.05	.01
❑	198	Boomer Esiason	.10	.02
❑	199	Johnny Johnson	.05	.01
❑	200	Jeff Lageman	.05	.01
❑	201	Mo Lewis	.05	.01
❑	202	Ronnie Lott	.10	.02
❑	203	Leonard Marshall	.05	.01
❑	204	Terance Mathis	.10	.02
❑	205	Johnny Mitchell	.05	.01
❑	206	Rob Moore	.10	.02
❑	207	Anthony Prior	.05	.01
❑	208	Blair Thomas	.05	.01
❑	209	Brian Washington	.05	.01
❑	210	Eric Bieniemy	.05	.01
❑	211	Marion Butts	.05	.01
❑	212	Gill Byrd	.05	.01
❑	213	John Carney	.05	.01
❑	214	Darren Carrington	.05	.01
❑	215	John Friesz	.10	.02
❑	216	Ronnie Harmon	.05	.01
❑	217	Stan Humphries	.10	.02
❑	218	Nate Lewis	.05	.01
❑	219	Natrone Means	.25	.08
❑	220	Anthony Miller	.10	.02
❑	221	Chris Mims	.05	.01
❑	222	Eric Moten	.05	.01
❑	223	Leslie O'Neal	.05	.01
❑	224	Junior Seau	.25	.08
❑	225	Morten Andersen	.05	.01
❑	226	Gene Atkins	.05	.01
❑	227	Derek Brown RBK	.05	.01
❑	228	Toi Cook	.05	.01
❑	229	Vaughn Dunbar	.05	.01
❑	230	Quinn Early	.10	.02
❑	231	Reggie Freeman	.05	.01
❑	232	Tyrone Hughes	.10	.02
❑	233	Rickey Jackson	.05	.01
❑	234	Eric Martin	.05	.01
❑	235	Sam Mills	.05	.01
❑	236	Brad Muster	.05	.01
❑	237	Torrance Small	.05	.01
❑	238	Irv Smith	.05	.01
❑	239	Wade Wilson	.05	.01
❑	240	Eric Allen	.05	.01
❑	241	Victor Bailey	.05	.01
❑	242	Fred Barnett	.10	.02
❑	243	Mark Bavaro	.05	.01
❑	244	Bubby Brister	.10	.02
❑	245	Randall Cunningham	.25	.08
❑	246	Antone Davis	.05	.01
❑	247	Britt Hager RC	.05	.01
❑	248	Vaughn Hebron	.05	.01
❑	249	James Joseph	.05	.01
❑	250	Seth Joyner	.05	.01
❑	251	Rich Miano	.05	.01
❑	252	Heath Sherman	.05	.01
❑	253	Clyde Simmons	.05	.01
❑	254	Herschel Walker	.10	.02
❑	255	Calvin Williams	.10	.02
❑	256	Jerry Ball	.05	.01
❑	257	Mark Carrier WR	.10	.02
❑	258	Michael Jackson	.10	.02
❑	259	Mike Johnson	.05	.01
❑	260	James Jones DT	.05	.01
❑	261	Brian Kinchen	.05	.01
❑	262	Clay Matthews	.05	.01
❑	263	Eric Metcalf	.10	.02
❑	264	Stevon Moore	.05	.01
❑	265	Michael Dean Perry	.10	.02
❑	266	Todd Philcox	.05	.01
❑	267	Anthony Pleasant	.05	.01
❑	268	Vinny Testaverde	.10	.02
❑	269	Eric Turner	.05	.01
❑	270	Tommy Vardell	.05	.01
❑	271	Neal Anderson	.05	.01
❑	272	Trace Armstrong	.05	.01
❑	273	Mark Carrier DB	.05	.01
❑	274	Bob Christian	.05	.01
❑	275	Curtis Conway	.25	.08
❑	276	Richard Dent	.10	.02
❑	277	Robert Green	.05	.01
❑	278	Jim Harbaugh	.25	.08
❑	279	Craig Heyward	.10	.02
❑	280	Terry Obee	.05	.01
❑	281	Alonzo Spellman	.05	.01
❑	282	Tom Waddle	.05	.01
❑	283	Peter Tom Willis	.05	.01
❑	284	Donnell Woolford	.05	.01
❑	285	Tim Worley	.05	.01
❑	286	Chris Zorich	.05	.01
❑	287	Steve Broussard	.05	.01
❑	288	Darion Conner	.05	.01
❑	289	Jumpy Geathers	.05	.01
❑	290	Michael Haynes	.10	.02
❑	291	Bobby Hebert	.05	.01
❑	292	Lincoln Kennedy	.05	.01
❑	293	Chris Miller	.05	.01
❑	294	David Mims RC	.05	.01
❑	295	Erric Pegram	.05	.01
❑	296	Mike Pritchard	.05	.01
❑	297	Andre Rison	.10	.02
❑	298	Deion Sanders	.50	.20
❑	299	Chuck Smith	.05	.01
❑	300	Tony Smith RB	.05	.01
❑	301	Johnny Bailey	.05	.01
❑	302	Steve Beuerlein	.10	.02
❑	303	Chuck Cecil	.05	.01
❑	304	Chris Chandler	.10	.02
❑	305	Gary Clark	.10	.02
❑	306	Rick Cunningham RC	.05	.01
❑	307	Ken Harvey	.05	.01
❑	308	Garrison Hearst	.25	.08
❑	309	Randal Hill	.05	.01
❑	310	Robert Massey	.05	.01
❑	311	Ronald Moore	.05	.01
❑	312	Ricky Proehl	.05	.01
❑	313	Eric Swann	.10	.02
❑	314	Aeneas Williams	.05	.01
❑	315	Michael Bates	.05	.01
❑	316	Brian Blades	.10	.02
❑	317	Carlton Gray	.05	.01
❑	318	Paul Green RC	.05	.01
❑	319	Patrick Hunter	.05	.01
❑	320	John Kasay	.05	.01
❑	321	Cortez Kennedy	.10	.02
❑	322	Kelvin Martin	.05	.01
❑	323	Dan McGwire	.05	.01
❑	324	Rick Mirer	.25	.08
❑	325	Eugene Robinson	.05	.01
❑	326	Rick Tuten	.05	.01
❑	327	Chris Warren	.10	.02
❑	328	John L. Williams	.05	.01
❑	329	Reggie Cobb	.05	.01
❑	330	Horace Copeland	.05	.01
❑	331	Lawrence Dawsey	.05	.01
❑	332	Santana Dotson	.10	.02
❑	333	Craig Erickson	.05	.01
❑	334	Ron Hall	.05	.01
❑	335	Courtney Hawkins	.05	.01
❑	336	Keith McCants	.05	.01
❑	337	Hardy Nickerson	.10	.02
❑	338	Mazio Royster RC	.05	.01
❑	339	Broderick Thomas	.05	.01
❑	340	Casey Weldon RC	.25	.08
❑	341	Mark Wheeler	.05	.01
❑	342	Vince Workman	.05	.01
❑	343	Flipper Anderson	.05	.01
❑	344	Jerome Bettis	.50	.20
❑	345	Richard Buchanan	.05	.01
❑	346	Shane Conlan	.05	.01
❑	347	Troy Drayton	.05	.01
❑	348	Henry Ellard	.10	.02
❑	349	Jim Everett	.10	.02
❑	350	Cleveland Gary	.05	.01
❑	351	Sean Gilbert	.05	.01
❑	352	David Lang	.05	.01
❑	353	Todd Lyght	.05	.01
❑	354	T.J. Rubley	.05	.01
❑	355	Jackie Slater	.05	.01
❑	356	Russell White	.10	.02
❑	357	Bruce Armstrong	.05	.01
❑	358	Drew Bledsoe	.75	.30
❑	359	Vincent Brisby	.10	.02
❑	360	Vincent Brown	.05	.01
❑	361	Ben Coates	.10	.02
❑	362	Marv Cook	.05	.01
❑	363	Ray Crittenden RC	.05	.01

❑ 364 Corey Croom RC .05 .01
❑ 365 Pat Harlow .05 .01
❑ 366 Dion Lambert .05 .01
❑ 367 Greg McMurtry .05 .01
❑ 368 Leonard Russell .05 .01
❑ 369 Scott Secules .05 .01
❑ 370 Chris Slade .05 .01
❑ 371 Michael Timpson .05 .01
❑ 372 Kevin Turner .05 .01
❑ 373 Ashley Ambrose .05 .01
❑ 374 Dean Biasucci .05 .01
❑ 375 Duane Bickett .05 .01
❑ 376 Quentin Coryatt .05 .01
❑ 377 Rodney Culver .05 .01
❑ 378 Sean Dawkins RC .25 .08
❑ 379 Jeff George .25 .08
❑ 380 Jeff Herrod .05 .01
❑ 381 Jessie Hester .05 .01
❑ 382 Anthony Johnson .10 .02
❑ 383 Reggie Langhorne .05 .01
❑ 384 Roosevelt Potts .05 .01
❑ 385 William Schultz RC .05 .01
❑ 386 Rohn Stark .05 .01
❑ 387 Clarence Verdin .05 .01
❑ 388 Carl Banks .05 .01
❑ 389 Reggie Brooks .10 .02
❑ 390 Earnest Byner .05 .01
❑ 391 Tom Carter .05 .01
❑ 392 Cary Conklin .05 .01
❑ 393 Pat Eilers RC .05 .01
❑ 394 Ricky Ervins .05 .01
❑ 395 Rich Gannon .25 .08
❑ 396 Darrell Green .05 .01
❑ 397 Desmond Howard .10 .02
❑ 398 Chip Lohmiller .05 .01
❑ 399 Sterling Palmer RC .05 .01
❑ 400 Mark Rypien .05 .01
❑ 401 Ricky Sanders .05 .01
❑ 402 Johnny Thomas CB .05 .01
❑ 403 John Copeland .05 .01
❑ 404 Derrick Fenner .05 .01
❑ 405 Alex Gordon .05 .01
❑ 406 Harold Green .05 .01
❑ 407 Lance Gunn .05 .01
❑ 408 David Klingler .05 .01
❑ 409 Ricardo McDonald .05 .01
❑ 410 Tim McGee .05 .01
❑ 411 Reggie Rembert .05 .01
❑ 412 Patrick Robinson .05 .01
❑ 413 Jay Schroeder .05 .01
❑ 414 Erik Wilhelm .05 .01
❑ 415 Alfred Williams .05 .01
❑ 416 Darryl Williams .05 .01
❑ 417 Sam Adams RC .10 .02
❑ 418 Mario Bates RC .25 .08
❑ 419 James Bostic RC .25 .08
❑ 420 Bucky Brooks RC .05 .01
❑ 421 Jeff Burris RC .10 .02
❑ 422 Shante Carver RC .05 .01
❑ 423 Jeff Cothran RC .05 .01
❑ 424 Lake Dawson RC .10 .02
❑ 425 Trent Dilfer RC 1.25 .50
❑ 426 Marshall Faulk RC 5.00 2.00
❑ 427 Cory Fleming RC .05 .01
❑ 428 William Floyd RC .25 .08
❑ 429 Glenn Foley RC .25 .08
❑ 430 Rob Fredrickson RC .10 .02
❑ 431 Charlie Garner RC 1.25 .50
❑ 432 Greg Hill RC .25 .08
❑ 433 Charles Johnson RC .25 .08
❑ 434 Calvin Jones RC .05 .01
❑ 435 Jimmy Klingler RC .05 .01
❑ 436 Antonio Langham RC .10 .02
❑ 437 Kevin Lee RC .05 .01
❑ 438 Chuck Levy RC .05 .01
❑ 439 Willie McGinest RC .25 .08
❑ 440 Jamir Miller RC .10 .02
❑ 441 Johnnie Morton RC .50 .20
❑ 442 David Palmer RC .25 .08
❑ 443 Errict Rhett RC .25 .08
❑ 444 Corey Sawyer RC .10 .02
❑ 445 Darnay Scott RC .50 .20
❑ 446 Heath Shuler RC .25 .08
❑ 447 Lamar Smith RC 1.25 .50
❑ 448 Dan Wilkinson RC .10 .02
❑ 449 Bernard Williams RC .05 .01
❑ 450 Bryant Young RC .25 .08
❑ P1 Sterling Sharpe Promo .75 .30

1995 Pacific

❑ COMPLETE SET (450) 25.00 10.00
❑ 1 Randy Baldwin .10 .02
❑ 2 Tommy Barnhardt .10 .02
❑ 3 Tim McKyer .10 .02
❑ 4 Sam Mills .20 .07
❑ 5 Brian O'Neal .10 .02
❑ 6 Frank Reich .10 .02
❑ 7 Jack Trudeau .10 .02
❑ 8 Vernon Turner .10 .02
❑ 9 Kerry Collins RC 1.50 .60
❑ 10 Shawn King .10 .02
❑ 11 Steve Beuerlein .20 .07
❑ 12 Derek Brown TE .10 .02
❑ 13 Reggie Clark .10 .02
❑ 14 Reggie Cobb .10 .02
❑ 15 Desmond Howard .20 .07
❑ 16 Jeff Lageman .10 .02
❑ 17 Kelvin Pritchett .10 .02
❑ 18 Cedric Tillman .10 .02
❑ 19 Tony Boselli RC .30 .10
❑ 20 James O. Stewart RC 1.25 .50
❑ 21 Eric Davis .10 .02
❑ 22 William Floyd .20 .07
❑ 23 Elvis Grbac .30 .10
❑ 24 Brent Jones .10 .02
❑ 25 Ken Norton, Jr. .20 .07
❑ 26 Bart Oates .10 .02
❑ 27 Jerry Rice 1.00 .40
❑ 28 Deion Sanders .40 .15
❑ 29 John Taylor .10 .02
❑ 30 Adam Walker RC .10 .02
❑ 31 Steve Wallace .10 .02
❑ 32 Ricky Watters .20 .07
❑ 33 Lee Woodall .10 .02
❑ 34 Bryant Young .20 .07
❑ 35 Steve Young .75 .30
❑ 36 J.J. Stokes RC .30 .10
❑ 37 Troy Aikman 1.00 .40
❑ 38 Larry Allen .20 .07
❑ 39 Chris Boniol RC .10 .02
❑ 40 Lincoln Coleman .10 .02
❑ 41 Charles Haley .20 .07
❑ 42 Alvin Harper .10 .02
❑ 43 Chad Hennings .20 .07
❑ 44 Michael Irvin .30 .10
❑ 45 Daryl Johnston .20 .07
❑ 46 Leon Lett .10 .02
❑ 47 Nate Newton .20 .07
❑ 48 Jay Novacek .20 .07
❑ 49 Emmitt Smith 1.50 .60
❑ 50 James Washington .10 .02
❑ 51 Kevin Williams .20 .07
❑ 52 Sherman Williams RC .10 .02
❑ 53 Barry Foster .20 .07
❑ 54 Eric Green .10 .02
❑ 55 Kevin Greene .20 .07
❑ 56 Andre Hastings .20 .07
❑ 57 Charles Johnson .20 .07
❑ 58 Greg Lloyd .20 .07
❑ 59 Ernie Mills .10 .02
❑ 60 Byron Bam Morris .10 .02
❑ 61 Neil O'Donnell .20 .07
❑ 62 Darren Perry .10 .02
❑ 63 Yancey Thigpen RC .20 .07
❑ 64 Mike Tomczak .10 .02
❑ 65 John L. Williams .10 .02
❑ 66 Rod Woodson .20 .07
❑ 67 Mark Bruener RC .20 .07
❑ 68 Kordell Stewart RC 1.50 .60
❑ 69 Jeff Brohm RC .10 .02
❑ 70 Andre Coleman .10 .02
❑ 71 Reuben Davis .10 .02
❑ 72 Dennis Gibson .10 .02
❑ 73 Darrien Gordon .10 .02
❑ 74 Stan Humphries .20 .07
❑ 75 Shawn Jefferson .10 .02
❑ 76 Tony Martin .20 .07
❑ 77 Natrone Means .20 .07
❑ 78 Shannon Mitchell RC .10 .02
❑ 79 Leslie O'Neal .20 .07
❑ 80 Alfred Pupunu .10 .02
❑ 81 Stanley Richard .10 .02
❑ 82 Junior Seau .30 .10
❑ 83 Mark Seay .20 .07
❑ 84 Derrick Alexander WR .30 .10
❑ 85 Carl Banks .10 .02
❑ 86 Isaac Booth .10 .02
❑ 87 Rob Burnett .10 .02
❑ 88 Earnest Byner .10 .02
❑ 89 Steve Everitt .10 .02
❑ 90 Leroy Hoard .10 .02
❑ 91 Pepper Johnson .10 .02
❑ 92 Antonio Langham .10 .02
❑ 93 Eric Metcalf .20 .07
❑ 94 Anthony Pleasant .10 .02
❑ 95 Frank Stams .10 .02
❑ 96 Vinny Testaverde .20 .07
❑ 97 Eric Turner .10 .02
❑ 98 Mike Miller RC .10 .02
❑ 99 Craig Powell RC .10 .02
❑ 100 Gene Atkins .10 .02
❑ 101 Aubrey Beavers .10 .02
❑ 102 Tim Bowens .10 .02
❑ 103 Keith Byars .10 .02
❑ 104 Bryan Cox .10 .02
❑ 105 Aaron Craver .10 .02
❑ 106 Jeff Cross .10 .02
❑ 107 Irving Fryar .20 .07
❑ 108 Dan Marino 2.00 .75
❑ 109 O.J. McDuffie .30 .10
❑ 110 Bernie Parmalee .20 .07
❑ 111 James Saxon .10 .02
❑ 112 Keith Sims .10 .02
❑ 113 Irving Spikes .20 .07
❑ 114 Pete Mitchell RC .20 .07
❑ 115 Terry Allen .20 .07
❑ 116 Cris Carter .30 .10
❑ 117 Adrian Cooper .10 .02
❑ 118 Bernard Dafney .10 .02
❑ 119 Jack Del Rio .10 .02
❑ 120 Vencie Glenn .10 .02
❑ 121 Qadry Ismail .20 .07
❑ 122 Carlos Jenkins .10 .02
❑ 123 Andrew Jordan .10 .02
❑ 124 Ed McDaniel .10 .02
❑ 125 Warren Moon .20 .07
❑ 126 David Palmer .20 .07
❑ 127 John Randle .20 .07
❑ 128 Jake Reed .20 .07
❑ 129 Derrick Alexander DE RC .10 .02
❑ 130 Chad May RC .10 .02
❑ 131 Korey Stringer RC .20 .07
❑ 132 Bruce Armstrong .10 .02
❑ 133 Drew Bledsoe .60 .25
❑ 134 Vincent Brisby .10 .02
❑ 135 Troy Brown .30 .10
❑ 136 Vincent Brown .10 .02
❑ 137 Marion Butts .10 .02
❑ 138 Ben Coates .20 .07
❑ 139 Ray Crittenden .10 .02
❑ 140 Maurice Hurst .10 .02
❑ 141 Aaron Jones .10 .02
❑ 142 Willie McGinest .20 .07
❑ 143 Marty Moore RC .30 .10
❑ 144 Mike Pitts .10 .02
❑ 145 Leroy Thompson .10 .02
❑ 146 Michael Timpson .10 .02
❑ 147 Bennie Blades .10 .02
❑ 148 Jocelyn Borgella .10 .02
❑ 149 Anthony Carter .20 .07
❑ 150 Willie Clay .10 .02
❑ 151 Mel Gray .10 .02

❑	152	Mike Johnson	.10	.02
❑	153	Dave Krieg	.10	.02
❑	154	Robert Massey	.10	.02
❑	155	Scott Mitchell	.20	.07
❑	156	Herman Moore	.30	.10
❑	157	Johnnie Morton	.20	.07
❑	158	Barry Sanders	1.50	.60
❑	159	Chris Spielman	.20	.07
❑	160	Broderick Thomas	.10	.02
❑	161	Cory Schlesinger RC	.20	.07
❑	162	Marcus Allen	.30	.10
❑	163	Donnell Bennett	.20	.07
❑	164	J.J. Birden	.10	.02
❑	165	Matt Blundin RC	.10	.02
❑	166	Steve Bono	.20	.07
❑	167	Dale Carter	.20	.07
❑	168	Lake Dawson	.20	.07
❑	169	Ron Dickerson	.10	.02
❑	170	Lin Elliott	.10	.02
❑	171	Jaime Fields	.10	.02
❑	172	Greg Hill	.20	.07
❑	173	Danan Hughes	.10	.02
❑	174	Neil Smith	.20	.07
❑	175	Steve Stenstrom RC	.10	.02
❑	176	Edgar Bennett	.20	.07
❑	177	Robert Brooks	.30	.10
❑	178	Mark Brunell	.60	.25
❑	179	Doug Evans RC	.30	.10
❑	180	Brett Favre	2.00	.75
❑	181	Corey Harris	.10	.02
❑	182	LeShon Johnson	.20	.07
❑	183	Sean Jones	.10	.02
❑	184	Lenny McGill RC	.10	.02
❑	185	Terry Mickens	.10	.02
❑	186	Sterling Sharpe	.20	.07
❑	187	Joe Sims	.10	.02
❑	188	Darrell Thompson	.10	.02
❑	189	Reggie White	.30	.10
❑	190	Craig Newsome RC	.10	.02
❑	191	Tim Brown	.30	.10
❑	192	Vince Evans	.10	.02
❑	193	Rob Fredrickson	.10	.02
❑	194	Andrew Glover RC	.10	.02
❑	195	Jeff Hostetler	.20	.07
❑	196	Rocket Ismail	.20	.07
❑	197	Jeff Jaeger	.10	.02
❑	198	James Jett	.20	.07
❑	199	Chester McGlockton	.20	.07
❑	200	Don Mosebar	.10	.02
❑	201	Tom Rathman	.10	.02
❑	202	Harvey Williams	.10	.02
❑	203	Steve Wisniewski	.10	.02
❑	204	Alexander Wright	.10	.02
❑	205	Napoleon Kaufman RC	1.25	.50
❑	206	Trace Armstrong	.10	.02
❑	207	Curtis Conway	.30	.10
❑	208	Raymont Harris	.10	.02
❑	209	Erik Kramer	.10	.02
❑	210	Nate Lewis	.10	.02
❑	211	Shane Matthews RC	.30	.10
❑	212	John Thierry	.10	.02
❑	213	Lewis Tillman	.10	.02
❑	214	Tom Waddle	.10	.02
❑	215	Steve Walsh	.10	.02
❑	216	James Williams T RC	.10	.02
❑	217	Donnell Woolford	.10	.02
❑	218	Chris Zorich	.10	.02
❑	219	Rashaan Salaam RC	.20	.07
❑	220	John Booty	.10	.02
❑	221	Michael Brooks	.10	.02
❑	222	Dave Brown	.20	.07
❑	223	Chris Calloway	.10	.02
❑	224	Gary Downs	.10	.02
❑	225	Kent Graham	.20	.07
❑	226	Keith Hamilton	.10	.02
❑	227	Rodney Hampton	.20	.07
❑	228	Brian Kozlowski	.10	.02
❑	229	Thomas Lewis	.20	.07
❑	230	Dave Meggett	.10	.02
❑	231	Aaron Pierce	.10	.02
❑	232	Mike Sherrard	.10	.02
❑	233	Phillippi Sparks	.10	.02
❑	234	Tyrone Wheatley RC	1.25	.50
❑	235	Trev Alberts	.10	.02
❑	236	Aaron Bailey RC	.10	.02
❑	237	Jason Belser	.10	.02
❑	238	Tony Bennett	.10	.02
❑	239	Kerry Cash	.10	.02
❑	240	Marshall Faulk	1.25	.50
❑	241	Stephen Grant	.10	.02
❑	242	Jeff Herrod	.10	.02
❑	243	Ronald Humphrey	.10	.02
❑	244	Kirk Lowdermilk	.10	.02
❑	245	Don Majkowski	.10	.02
❑	246	Tony McCoy	.10	.02
❑	247	Floyd Turner	.10	.02
❑	248	Lamont Warren	.10	.02
❑	249	Zack Crockett RC	.20	.07
❑	250	Michael Bankston	.10	.02
❑	251	Larry Centers	.20	.07
❑	252	Gary Clark	.10	.02
❑	253	Ed Cunningham	.10	.02
❑	254	Garrison Hearst	.30	.10
❑	255	Eric Hill	.10	.02
❑	256	Terry Irving	.10	.02
❑	257	Lorenzo Lynch	.10	.02
❑	258	Jamir Miller	.10	.02
❑	259	Ronald Moore	.10	.02
❑	260	Terry Samuels	.10	.02
❑	261	Jay Schroeder	.10	.02
❑	262	Eric Swann	.20	.07
❑	263	Aeneas Williams	.10	.02
❑	264	Frank Sanders RC	.30	.10
❑	265	Morten Andersen	.10	.02
❑	266	Mario Bates	.20	.07
❑	267	Derek Brown RBK	.10	.02
❑	268	Darion Conner	.10	.02
❑	269	Quinn Early	.20	.07
❑	270	Jim Everett	.10	.02
❑	271	Michael Haynes	.20	.07
❑	272	Wayne Martin	.10	.02
❑	273	Derrell Mitchell RC	.10	.02
❑	274	Lorenzo Neal	.10	.02
❑	275	Jimmy Spencer	.10	.02
❑	276	Winfred Tubbs	.10	.02
❑	277	Renaldo Turnbull	.10	.02
❑	278	Jeff Uhlenhake	.10	.02
❑	279	Steve Atwater	.10	.02
❑	280	Keith Burns RC	.10	.02
❑	281	Butler By'Not'e RC	.20	.07
❑	282	Jeff Campbell	.10	.02
❑	283	Derrick Clark RC	.10	.02
❑	284	Shane Dronett	.10	.02
❑	285	Jason Elam	.20	.07
❑	286	John Elway	2.00	.75
❑	287	Jerry Evans	.10	.02
❑	288	Karl Mecklenburg	.10	.02
❑	289	Glyn Milburn	.10	.02
❑	290	Anthony Miller	.20	.07
❑	291	Tom Rouen	.10	.02
❑	292	Leonard Russell	.10	.02
❑	293	Shannon Sharpe	.20	.07
❑	294	Steve Russ RC	.10	.02
❑	295	Mel Agee	.10	.02
❑	296	Lester Archambeau	.10	.02
❑	297	Bert Emanuel	.30	.10
❑	298	Jeff George	.20	.07
❑	299	Craig Heyward	.20	.07
❑	300	Bobby Hebert	.10	.02
❑	301	D.J. Johnson	.10	.02
❑	302	Mike Kenn	.10	.02
❑	303	Terance Mathis	.20	.07
❑	304	Clay Matthews	.20	.07
❑	305	Erric Pegram	.20	.07
❑	306	Andre Rison	.20	.07
❑	307	Chuck Smith	.10	.02
❑	308	Jessie Tuggle	.10	.02
❑	309	Lorenzo Styles RC	.10	.02
❑	310	Cornelius Bennett	.20	.07
❑	311	Bill Brooks	.10	.02
❑	312	Jeff Burris	.10	.02
❑	313	Carwell Gardner	.10	.02
❑	314	Kent Hull	.10	.02
❑	315	Yonel Jourdain	.10	.02
❑	316	Jim Kelly	.30	.10
❑	317	Vince Marrow	.10	.02
❑	318	Pete Metzelaars	.10	.02
❑	319	Andre Reed	.20	.07
❑	320	Kurt Schulz RC	.10	.02
❑	321	Bruce Smith	.30	.10
❑	322	Darryl Talley	.10	.02
❑	323	Matt Darby	.10	.02
❑	324	Justin Armour RC	.10	.02
❑	325	Todd Collins RC	.20	.07
❑	326	David Alexander DE	.10	.02
❑	327	Eric Allen	.10	.02
❑	328	Fred Barnett	.20	.07
❑	329	Randall Cunningham	.30	.10
❑	330	William Fuller	.10	.02
❑	331	Charlie Garner	.30	.10
❑	332	Vaughn Hebron	.10	.02
❑	333	James Joseph	.10	.02
❑	334	Bill Romanowski	.10	.02
❑	335	Ken Rose	.10	.02
❑	336	Jeff Snyder	.10	.02
❑	337	William Thomas	.10	.02
❑	338	Herschel Walker	.20	.07
❑	339	Calvin Williams	.20	.07
❑	340	Dave Barr RC	.10	.02
❑	341	Chidi Ahanotu	.10	.02
❑	342	Barney Bussey	.10	.02
❑	343	Horace Copeland	.10	.02
❑	344	Trent Dilfer	.30	.10
❑	345	Craig Erickson	.10	.02
❑	346	Paul Gruber	.10	.02
❑	347	Courtney Hawkins	.10	.02
❑	348	Lonnie Marts	.10	.02
❑	349	Martin Mayhew	.10	.02
❑	350	Hardy Nickerson	.10	.02
❑	351	Errict Rhett	.20	.07
❑	352	Lamar Thomas	.10	.02
❑	353	Charles Wilson	.10	.02
❑	354	Vince Workman	.10	.02
❑	355	Derrick Brooks RC	1.50	.60
❑	356	Warren Sapp RC	1.50	.60
❑	357	Sam Adams	.10	.02
❑	358	Michael Bates	.10	.02
❑	359	Brian Blades	.20	.07
❑	360	Carlton Gray	.10	.02
❑	361	Bill Hitchcock	.10	.02
❑	362	Cortez Kennedy	.20	.07
❑	363	Rick Mirer	.20	.07
❑	364	Eugene Robinson	.10	.02
❑	365	Michael Sinclair	.10	.02
❑	366	Steve Smith	.10	.02
❑	367	Bob Spitulski	.10	.02
❑	368	Rick Tuten	.10	.02
❑	369	Chris Warren	.20	.07
❑	370	Terrence Warren	.10	.02
❑	371	Christian Fauria RC	.20	.07
❑	372	Joey Galloway RC	1.50	.60
❑	373	Boomer Esiason	.20	.07
❑	374	Aaron Glenn	.10	.02
❑	375	Victor Green RC	.10	.02
❑	376	Johnny Johnson	.10	.02
❑	377	Mo Lewis	.10	.02
❑	378	Ronnie Lott	.20	.07
❑	379	Nick Lowery	.10	.02
❑	380	Johnny Mitchell	.10	.02
❑	381	Rob Moore	.20	.07
❑	382	Adrian Murrell	.20	.07
❑	383	Anthony Prior	.10	.02
❑	384	Brian Washington	.10	.02
❑	385	Matt Willig RC	.10	.02
❑	386	Kyle Brady RC	.30	.10
❑	387	Flipper Anderson	.10	.02
❑	388	Johnny Bailey	.10	.02
❑	389	Jerome Bettis	.30	.10
❑	390	Isaac Bruce	.50	.20
❑	391	Shane Conlan	.10	.02
❑	392	Troy Drayton	.10	.02
❑	393	D'Marco Farr	.10	.02
❑	394	Jessie Hester	.10	.02
❑	395	Todd Kinchen	.10	.02
❑	396	Ron Middleton	.10	.02
❑	397	Chris Miller	.10	.02
❑	398	Marquez Pope	.10	.02
❑	399	Robert Young	.10	.02
❑	400	Tony Zendejas	.10	.02
❑	401	Kevin Carter RC	.30	.10
❑	402	Reggie Brooks	.20	.07
❑	403	Tom Carter	.10	.02
❑	404	Andre Collins	.10	.02
❑	405	Pat Eilers	.10	.02
❑	406	Henry Ellard	.20	.07
❑	407	Ricky Ervins	.10	.02
❑	408	Gus Frerotte	.20	.07
❑	409	Ken Harvey	.10	.02
❑	410	Jim Lachey	.10	.02
❑	411	Brian Mitchell	.10	.02
❑	412	Reggie Roby	.10	.02

❑ 413	Heath Shuler	.20	.07
❑ 414	Tyronne Stowe	.10	.02
❑ 415	Tydus Winans	.10	.02
❑ 416	Cory Raymer RC	.10	.02
❑ 417	Michael Westbrook RC	.30	.10
❑ 418	Jeff Blake RC	.75	.30
❑ 419	Steve Broussard	.10	.02
❑ 420	Dave Cadigan	.10	.02
❑ 421	Jeff Cothran	.10	.02
❑ 422	Derrick Fenner	.10	.02
❑ 423	James Francis	.10	.02
❑ 424	Lee Johnson	.10	.02
❑ 425	Louis Oliver	.10	.02
❑ 426	Carl Pickens	.20	.07
❑ 427	Jeff Query	.10	.02
❑ 428	Corey Sawyer	.10	.02
❑ 429	Darnay Scott	.20	.07
❑ 430	Dan Wilkinson	.20	.07
❑ 431	Alfred Williams	.10	.02
❑ 432	Ki-Jana Carter RC	.30	.10
❑ 433	David Dunn RC	.10	.02
❑ 434	John Walsh RC	.10	.02
❑ 435	Gary Brown	.10	.02
❑ 436	Pat Carter	.10	.02
❑ 437	Ray Childress	.10	.02
❑ 438	Ernest Givins	.10	.02
❑ 439	Haywood Jeffires	.10	.02
❑ 440	Lamar Lathon	.10	.02
❑ 441	Bruce Matthews	.10	.02
❑ 442	Marcus Robertson	.10	.02
❑ 443	Eddie Robinson	.10	.02
❑ 444	Malcolm Seabron RC	.10	.02
❑ 445	Webster Slaughter	.10	.02
❑ 446	Al Smith	.10	.02
❑ 447	Billy Joe Tolliver	.10	.02
❑ 448	Lorenzo White	.10	.02
❑ 449	Steve McNair RC	3.00	1.25
❑ 450	Rodney Thomas RC	.20	.07
❑ P1	Natrone Means Promo	1.00	.40
❑ P1J	Natrone Means Promo	1.00	.40

1996 Pacific

❑	COMPLETE SET (450)	40.00	20.00
❑ 1	Jeff Feagles	.10	.02
❑ 2	Rob Moore	.20	.07
❑ 3	Clyde Simmons	.10	.02
❑ 4	Mike Buck	.10	.02
❑ 5	Aeneas Williams	.10	.02
❑ 6	Simeon Rice RC	1.00	.40
❑ 7	Garrison Hearst	.20	.07
❑ 8	Eric Swann	.10	.02
❑ 9	Dave Krieg	.10	.02
❑ 10	Leeland McElroy RC	.20	.07
❑ 11	Oscar McBride	.10	.02
❑ 12	Frank Sanders	.20	.07
❑ 13	Larry Centers	.20	.07
❑ 14	Seth Joyner	.10	.02
❑ 15	Stevie Anderson	.10	.02
❑ 16	Craig Heyward	.10	.02
❑ 17	Devin Bush	.10	.02
❑ 18	Eric Metcalf	.10	.02
❑ 19	Jeff George	.20	.07
❑ 20	Richard Huntley RC	.20	.07
❑ 21	Jamal Anderson RC	.50	.20
❑ 22	Bert Emanuel	.20	.07
❑ 23	Terance Mathis	.10	.02
❑ 24	Roman Fortin	.10	.02
❑ 25	Jessie Tuggle	.10	.02
❑ 26	Morten Andersen	.10	.02
❑ 27	Chris Doleman	.10	.02
❑ 28	D.J. Johnson	.10	.02
❑ 29	Kevin Ross	.10	.02
❑ 30	Michael Jackson	.20	.07
❑ 31	Eric Zeier	.10	.02
❑ 32	Jonathan Ogden RC	.40	.15
❑ 33	Eric Turner	.10	.02
❑ 34	Andre Rison	.20	.07
❑ 35	Lorenzo White	.10	.02
❑ 36	Earnest Byner	.10	.02
❑ 37	Derrick Alexander WR	.20	.07
❑ 38	Brian Kinchen	.10	.02
❑ 39	Anthony Pleasant	.10	.02
❑ 40	Vinny Testaverde	.20	.07
❑ 41	Pepper Johnson	.10	.02
❑ 42	Frank Hartley	.10	.02
❑ 43	Craig Powell	.10	.02
❑ 44	Leroy Hoard	.10	.02
❑ 45	Kent Hull	.10	.02
❑ 46	Bryce Paup	.10	.02
❑ 47	Andre Reed	.20	.07
❑ 48	Darick Holmes	.10	.02
❑ 49	Russell Copeland	.10	.02
❑ 50	Jerry Ostroski	.10	.02
❑ 51	Chris Green	.10	.02
❑ 52	Eric Moulds RC	1.25	.50
❑ 53	Justin Armour	.10	.02
❑ 54	Jim Kelly	.40	.15
❑ 55	Cornelius Bennett	.10	.02
❑ 56	Steve Tasker	.10	.02
❑ 57	Thurman Thomas	.40	.15
❑ 58	Bruce Smith	.20	.07
❑ 59	Todd Collins	.20	.07
❑ 60	Shawn King	.10	.02
❑ 61	Don Beebe	.10	.02
❑ 62	John Kasay	.10	.02
❑ 63	Tim McKyer	.10	.02
❑ 64	Darion Conner	.10	.02
❑ 65	Pete Metzelaars	.10	.02
❑ 66	Derrick Moore	.10	.02
❑ 67	Blake Brockermeyer	.10	.02
❑ 68	Tim Biakabutuka RC	.40	.15
❑ 69	Sam Mills	.10	.02
❑ 70	Vince Workman	.10	.02
❑ 71	Kerry Collins	.40	.15
❑ 72	Carlton Bailey	.10	.02
❑ 73	Mark Carrier WR	.10	.02
❑ 74	Donnell Woolford	.10	.02
❑ 75	Walt Harris RC	.10	.02
❑ 76	John Thierry	.10	.02
❑ 77	Al Fontenot RC	.10	.02
❑ 78	Lewis Tillman	.10	.02
❑ 79	Curtis Conway	.40	.15
❑ 80	Chris Zorich	.10	.02
❑ 81	Mark Carrier DB	.10	.02
❑ 82	Bobby Engram RC	.40	.15
❑ 83	Alonzo Spellman	.10	.02
❑ 84	Rashaan Salaam	.20	.07
❑ 85	Michael Timpson	.10	.02
❑ 86	Nate Lewis	.10	.02
❑ 87	James Williams T	.10	.02
❑ 88	Jeff Graham	.10	.02
❑ 89	Erik Kramer	.10	.02
❑ 90	Willie Anderson	.10	.02
❑ 91	Tony McGee	.10	.02
❑ 92	Marco Battaglia	.10	.02
❑ 93	Dan Wilkinson	.10	.02
❑ 94	John Walsh	.10	.02
❑ 95	Eric Bieniemy	.10	.02
❑ 96	Ricardo McDonald	.10	.02
❑ 97	Carl Pickens	.20	.07
❑ 98	Kevin Sargent	.10	.02
❑ 99	David Dunn	.10	.02
❑ 100	Jeff Blake	.40	.15
❑ 101	Harold Green	.10	.02
❑ 102	James Francis	.10	.02
❑ 103	John Copeland	.10	.02
❑ 104	Darnay Scott	.20	.07
❑ 105	Darren Woodson	.20	.07
❑ 106	Jay Novacek	.10	.02
❑ 107	Charles Haley	.20	.07
❑ 108	Mark Tuinei	.10	.02
❑ 109	Michael Irvin	.40	.15
❑ 110	Troy Aikman	1.00	.40
❑ 111	Chris Boniol	.10	.02
❑ 112	Sherman Williams	.10	.02
❑ 113	Deion Sanders	.60	.25
❑ 114	Emmitt Smith	1.50	.60
❑ 115	Eric Bjornson	.10	.02
❑ 116	Nate Newton	.10	.02
❑ 117	Larry Allen	.10	.02
❑ 118	Kevin Williams	.10	.02
❑ 119	Leon Lett	.10	.02
❑ 120	John Mobley	.10	.02
❑ 121	Anthony Miller	.20	.07
❑ 122	Brian Habib	.10	.02
❑ 123	Aaron Craver	.10	.02
❑ 124	Glyn Milburn	.10	.02
❑ 125	Shannon Sharpe	.20	.07
❑ 126	Steve Atwater	.10	.02
❑ 127	Jason Elam	.20	.07
❑ 128	John Elway	2.00	.75
❑ 129	Reggie Rivers	.10	.02
❑ 130	Mike Pritchard	.10	.02
❑ 131	Vance Johnson	.10	.02
❑ 132	Terrell Davis	.75	.30
❑ 133	Tyrone Braxton	.10	.02
❑ 134	Ed McCaffrey	.20	.07
❑ 135	Brett Perriman	.10	.02
❑ 136	Chris Spielman	.10	.02
❑ 137	Luther Elliss	.10	.02
❑ 138	Johnnie Morton	.20	.07
❑ 139	Zefross Moss	.10	.02
❑ 140	Barry Sanders	1.50	.60
❑ 141	Lomas Brown	.10	.02
❑ 142	Cory Schlesinger	.10	.02
❑ 143	Jason Hanson	.10	.02
❑ 144	Kevin Glover	.10	.02
❑ 145	Ron Rivers RC	.20	.07
❑ 146	Aubrey Matthews	.10	.02
❑ 147	Reggie Brown LB RC	.10	.02
❑ 148	Herman Moore	.20	.07
❑ 149	Scott Mitchell	.20	.07
❑ 150	Brett Favre	2.00	.75
❑ 151	Sean Jones	.10	.02
❑ 152	LeRoy Butler	.10	.02
❑ 153	Mark Chmura	.20	.07
❑ 154	Derrick Mayes RC	.40	.15
❑ 155	Mark Ingram	.10	.02
❑ 156	Antonio Freeman	.40	.15
❑ 157	Chris Darkins RC	.10	.02
❑ 158	Robert Brooks	.40	.15
❑ 159	William Henderson	.40	.15
❑ 160	George Koonce	.10	.02
❑ 161	Craig Newsome	.10	.02
❑ 162	Darius Holland	.10	.02
❑ 163	George Teague	.10	.02
❑ 164	Edgar Bennett	.20	.07
❑ 165	Reggie White	.40	.15
❑ 166	Micheal Barrow	.10	.02
❑ 167	Mel Gray	.10	.02
❑ 168	Anthony Dorsett	.10	.02
❑ 169	Roderick Lewis	.10	.02
❑ 170	Henry Ford	.10	.02
❑ 171	Mark Stepnoski	.10	.02
❑ 172	Chris Sanders	.20	.07
❑ 173	Anthony Cook	.10	.02
❑ 174	Eddie Robinson	.10	.02
❑ 175	Steve McNair	.75	.30
❑ 176	Haywood Jeffires	.10	.02
❑ 177	Eddie George RC	1.25	.50
❑ 178	Marion Butts	.10	.02
❑ 179	Malcolm Seabron	.10	.02
❑ 180	Rodney Thomas	.10	.02
❑ 181	Ken Dilger	.20	.07
❑ 182	Zack Crockett	.10	.02
❑ 183	Tony Bennett	.10	.02
❑ 184	Quentin Coryatt	.10	.02
❑ 185	Marshall Faulk	.50	.20
❑ 186	Sean Dawkins	.10	.02
❑ 187	Jim Harbaugh	.20	.07
❑ 188	Eugene Daniel	.10	.02
❑ 189	Roosevelt Potts	.10	.02
❑ 190	Lamont Warren	.10	.02
❑ 191	Will Wolford	.10	.02
❑ 192	Tony Siragusa	.10	.02
❑ 193	Aaron Bailey	.10	.02
❑ 194	Trev Alberts	.10	.02
❑ 195	Kevin Hardy	.20	.07
❑ 196	Greg Spann	.10	.02
❑ 197	Steve Beuerlein	.20	.07
❑ 198	Steve Taneyhill	.10	.02
❑ 199	Vaughn Dunbar	.10	.02
❑ 200	Mark Brunell	.60	.25

❑ 201 Bernard Carter .10 .02
❑ 202 James O. Stewart .20 .07
❑ 203 Tony Boselli .10 .02
❑ 204 Chris Doering .10 .02
❑ 205 Willie Jackson .20 .07
❑ 206 Tony Brackens RC .40 .15
❑ 207 Ernest Givins .10 .02
❑ 208 Le'Shai Maston .10 .02
❑ 209 Pete Mitchell .20 .07
❑ 210 Desmond Howard .20 .07
❑ 211 Vinnie Clark .10 .02
❑ 212 Jeff Lageman .10 .02
❑ 213 Derrick Walker .10 .02
❑ 214 Dan Saleaumua .10 .02
❑ 215 Derrick Thomas .40 .15
❑ 216 Neil Smith .20 .07
❑ 217 Willie Davis .10 .02
❑ 218 Mark Collins .10 .02
❑ 219 Lake Dawson .10 .02
❑ 220 Greg Hill .20 .07
❑ 221 Anthony Davis .10 .02
❑ 222 Kimble Anders .20 .07
❑ 223 Webster Slaughter .10 .02
❑ 224 Tamarick Vanover .20 .07
❑ 225 Marcus Allen .40 .15
❑ 226 Steve Bono .10 .02
❑ 227 Will Shields .10 .02
❑ 228 Karim Abdul-Jabbar RC .40 .15
❑ 229 Tim Bowens .10 .02
❑ 230 Keith Sims .10 .02
❑ 231 Terry Kirby .20 .07
❑ 232 Gene Atkins .10 .02
❑ 233 Dan Marino 2.00 .75
❑ 234 Richmond Webb .10 .02
❑ 235 Gary Clark .10 .02
❑ 236 O.J. McDuffie .20 .07
❑ 237 Marco Coleman .10 .02
❑ 238 Bernie Parmalee .10 .02
❑ 239 Randal Hill .10 .02
❑ 240 Bryan Cox .10 .02
❑ 241 Irving Fryar .20 .07
❑ 242 Derrick Alexander DE .10 .02
❑ 243 Qadry Ismail .20 .07
❑ 244 Warren Moon .20 .07
❑ 245 Cris Carter .40 .15
❑ 246 Chad May .10 .02
❑ 247 Robert Smith .20 .07
❑ 248 Fuad Reveiz .10 .02
❑ 249 Orlando Thomas .10 .02
❑ 250 Chris Hinton .10 .02
❑ 251 Jack Del Rio .10 .02
❑ 252 Moe Williams RB RC 1.00 .40
❑ 253 Roy Barker .10 .02
❑ 254 Jake Reed .20 .07
❑ 255 Adrian Cooper .10 .02
❑ 256 Curtis Martin .75 .30
❑ 257 Ben Coates .20 .07
❑ 258 Drew Bledsoe .60 .25
❑ 259 Maurice Hurst .10 .02
❑ 260 Troy Brown .40 .15
❑ 261 Bruce Armstrong .10 .02
❑ 262 Myron Guyton .10 .02
❑ 263 Dave Meggett .10 .02
❑ 264 Terry Glenn RC 1.00 .40
❑ 265 Chris Slade .10 .02
❑ 266 Vincent Brisby .10 .02
❑ 267 Willie McGinest .10 .02
❑ 268 Vincent Brown .10 .02
❑ 269 Will Moore .10 .02
❑ 270 Jay Barker .10 .02
❑ 271 Ray Zellars .10 .02
❑ 272 Derek Brown RBK .10 .02
❑ 273 William Roaf .10 .02
❑ 274 Quinn Early .10 .02
❑ 275 Michael Haynes .10 .02
❑ 276 Rufus Porter .10 .02
❑ 277 Renaldo Turnbull .10 .02
❑ 278 Wayne Martin .10 .02
❑ 279 Tyrone Hughes .10 .02
❑ 280 Irv Smith .10 .02
❑ 281 Eric Allen .10 .02
❑ 282 Mark Fields .10 .02
❑ 283 Mario Bates .20 .07
❑ 284 Jim Everett .10 .02
❑ 285 Vince Buck .10 .02
❑ 286 Alex Molden RC .10 .02
❑ 287 Tyrone Wheatley .20 .07
❑ 288 Chris Calloway .10 .02
❑ 289 Jessie Armstead .10 .02
❑ 290 Arthur Marshall .10 .02
❑ 291 Aaron Pierce .10 .02
❑ 292 Dave Brown .10 .02
❑ 293 Rodney Hampton .20 .07
❑ 294 Jumbo Elliott .10 .02
❑ 295 Mike Sherrard .10 .02
❑ 296 Howard Cross .10 .02
❑ 297 Michael Brooks .10 .02
❑ 298 Herschel Walker .20 .07
❑ 299 Danny Kanell RC .40 .15
❑ 300 Keith Elias .10 .02
❑ 301 Bobby Houston .10 .02
❑ 302 Dexter Carter .10 .02
❑ 303 Tony Casillas .10 .02
❑ 304 Kyle Brady .10 .02
❑ 305 Glenn Foley .20 .07
❑ 306 Ronald Moore .10 .02
❑ 307 Ryan Yarborough .10 .02
❑ 308 Aaron Glenn .10 .02
❑ 309 Adrian Murrell .20 .07
❑ 310 Boomer Esiason .20 .07
❑ 311 Kyle Clifton .10 .02
❑ 312 Wayne Chrebet .60 .25
❑ 313 Erik Howard .10 .02
❑ 314 Keyshawn Johnson RC 1.00 .40
❑ 315 Marvin Washington .10 .02
❑ 316 Johnny Mitchell .10 .02
❑ 317 Alex Van Dyke RC .20 .07
❑ 318 Billy Joe Hobert .20 .07
❑ 319 Andrew Glover .10 .02
❑ 320 Vince Evans .10 .02
❑ 321 Chester McGlockton .10 .02
❑ 322 Pat Swilling .10 .02
❑ 323 Rocket Ismail .10 .02
❑ 324 Eddie Anderson .10 .02
❑ 325 Rickey Dudley RC .40 .15
❑ 326 Steve Wisniewski .10 .02
❑ 327 Harvey Williams .10 .02
❑ 328 Napoleon Kaufman .40 .15
❑ 329 Tim Brown .40 .15
❑ 330 Jeff Hostetler .10 .02
❑ 331 Anthony Smith .10 .02
❑ 332 Terry McDaniel .10 .02
❑ 333 Charlie Garner .20 .07
❑ 334 Ricky Watters .20 .07
❑ 335 Brian Dawkins RC 1.25 .50
❑ 336 Randall Cunningham .40 .15
❑ 337 Gary Anderson .10 .02
❑ 338 Calvin Williams .10 .02
❑ 339 Chris T. Jones .20 .07
❑ 340 Bobby Hoying RC .40 .15
❑ 341 William Fuller .10 .02
❑ 342 William Thomas .10 .02
❑ 343 Mike Mamula .10 .02
❑ 344 Fred Barnett .10 .02
❑ 345 Rodney Peete .10 .02
❑ 346 Mark McMillian .10 .02
❑ 347 Bobby Taylor .10 .02
❑ 348 Yancey Thigpen .20 .07
❑ 349 Neil O'Donnell .20 .07
❑ 350 Rod Woodson .20 .07
❑ 351 Kordell Stewart .40 .15
❑ 352 Dermontti Dawson .10 .02
❑ 353 Norm Johnson .10 .02
❑ 354 Ernie Mills .10 .02
❑ 355 Byron Bam Morris .10 .02
❑ 356 Mark Bruener .10 .02
❑ 357 Kevin Greene .20 .07
❑ 358 Greg Lloyd .20 .07
❑ 359 Andre Hastings .10 .02
❑ 360 Erric Pegram .10 .02
❑ 361 Carnell Lake .10 .02
❑ 362 Dwayne Harper .10 .02
❑ 363 Ronnie Harmon .10 .02
❑ 364 Leslie O'Neal .10 .02
❑ 365 John Carney .10 .02
❑ 366 Stan Humphries .20 .07
❑ 367 Brian Roche RC .10 .02
❑ 368 Terrell Fletcher .10 .02
❑ 369 Shaun Gayle .10 .02
❑ 370 Alfred Pupunu .10 .02
❑ 371 Shawn Jefferson .10 .02
❑ 372 Junior Seau .40 .15
❑ 373 Mark Seay .10 .02
❑ 374 Aaron Hayden .10 .02
❑ 375 Tony Martin .20 .07
❑ 376 Steve Young .75 .30
❑ 377 J.J. Stokes .40 .15
❑ 378 Jerry Rice 1.00 .40
❑ 379 Derek Loville .10 .02
❑ 380 Lee Woodall .10 .02
❑ 381 Terrell Owens RC 2.50 1.00
❑ 382 Elvis Grbac .20 .07
❑ 383 Ricky Ervins .10 .02
❑ 384 Eric Davis .10 .02
❑ 385 Dana Stubblefield .20 .07
❑ 386 Gary Plummer .10 .02
❑ 387 Tim McDonald .10 .02
❑ 388 William Floyd .20 .07
❑ 389 Ken Norton Jr. .10 .02
❑ 390 Merton Hanks .10 .02
❑ 391 Bart Oates .10 .02
❑ 392 Brent Jones .10 .02
❑ 393 Steve Broussard .10 .02
❑ 394 Robert Blackmon .10 .02
❑ 395 Rick Tuten .10 .02
❑ 396 Pete Kendall .10 .02
❑ 397 John Friesz .10 .02
❑ 398 Terry Wooden .10 .02
❑ 399 Rick Mirer .20 .07
❑ 400 Chris Warren .20 .07
❑ 401 Joey Galloway .40 .15
❑ 402 Howard Ballard .10 .02
❑ 403 Jason Kyle .10 .02
❑ 404 Kevin Mawae .10 .02
❑ 405 Mack Strong .40 .15
❑ 406 Reggie Brown RBK RC .10 .02
❑ 407 Cortez Kennedy .10 .02
❑ 408 Sean Gilbert .10 .02
❑ 409 J.T. Thomas .10 .02
❑ 410 Shane Conlan .10 .02
❑ 411 Johnny Bailey .10 .02
❑ 412 Mark Rypien .10 .02
❑ 413 Leonard Russell .10 .02
❑ 414 Troy Drayton .10 .02
❑ 415 Jerome Bettis .40 .15
❑ 416 Jessie Hester .10 .02
❑ 417 Isaac Bruce .40 .15
❑ 418 Roman Phifer .10 .02
❑ 419 Todd Kinchen .10 .02
❑ 420 Alexander Wright .10 .02
❑ 421 Marcus Jones RC .10 .02
❑ 422 Horace Copeland .10 .02
❑ 423 Eric Curry .10 .02
❑ 424 Courtney Hawkins .10 .02
❑ 425 Alvin Harper .10 .02
❑ 426 Derrick Brooks .40 .15
❑ 427 Errict Rhett .20 .07
❑ 428 Trent Dilfer .40 .15
❑ 429 Hardy Nickerson .10 .02
❑ 430 Brad Culpepper .10 .02
❑ 431 Warren Sapp .10 .02
❑ 432 Reggie Roby .10 .02
❑ 433 Santana Dotson .10 .02
❑ 434 Jerry Ellison .10 .02
❑ 435 Lawrence Dawsey .10 .02
❑ 436 Heath Shuler .20 .07
❑ 437 Stanley Richard .20 .07
❑ 438 Rod Stephens .10 .02
❑ 439 Stephen Davis RC 1.50 .60
❑ 440 Terry Allen .20 .07
❑ 441 Michael Westbrook .40 .15
❑ 442 Ken Harvey .10 .02
❑ 443 Coleman Bell .10 .02
❑ 444 Marvcus Patton .10 .02
❑ 445 Gus Frerotte .20 .07
❑ 446 Leslie Shepherd .10 .02
❑ 447 Tom Carter .10 .02
❑ 448 Brian Mitchell .10 .02
❑ 449 Darrell Green .10 .02
❑ 450A Tony Woods .10 .02
❑ 450B Chris Warren Promo .50 .20
❑ CW1 Chris Warren Promo 1.00 .40

1997 Pacific

❑ COMPLETE SET (450) 30.00 15.00
❑ 1 Lomas Brown .20 .07
❑ 2 Pat Carter .20 .07
❑ 3 Larry Centers .30 .10
❑ 4 Matt Darby .20 .07
❑ 5 Marcus Dowdell .20 .07
❑ 6 Aaron Graham .20 .07

❑	7	Kent Graham	.20	.07
❑	8	LeShon Johnson	.20	.07
❑	9	Seth Joyner	.20	.07
❑	10	Leeland McElroy	.20	.07
❑	11	Rob Moore	.30	.10
❑	12	Simeon Rice	.30	.10
❑	13	Eric Swann	.20	.07
❑	14	Aeneas Williams	.20	.07
❑	15	Morten Andersen	.20	.07
❑	16	Jamal Anderson	.50	.20
❑	17	Lester Archambeau	.20	.07
❑	18	Cornelius Bennett	.20	.07
❑	19	J.J. Birden	.20	.07
❑	20	Antone Davis	.20	.07
❑	21	Bert Emanuel	.30	.10
❑	22	Travis Hall RC	.20	.07
❑	23	Bobby Hebert	.20	.07
❑	24	Craig Heyward	.20	.07
❑	25	Terance Mathis	.30	.10
❑	26	Tim McKyer	.20	.07
❑	27	Eric Metcalf	.30	.10
❑	28	Jessie Tuggle	.20	.07
❑	29	Derrick Alexander WR	.30	.10
❑	30	Orlando Brown	.20	.07
❑	31	Rob Burnett	.20	.07
❑	32	Earnest Byner	.20	.07
❑	33	Ray Ethridge	.20	.07
❑	34	Steve Everitt	.20	.07
❑	35	Carwell Gardner	.20	.07
❑	36	Michael Jackson	.30	.10
❑	37	Jermaine Lewis	.50	.20
❑	38	Stevon Moore	.20	.07
❑	39	Byron Bam Morris	.20	.07
❑	40	Jonathan Ogden	.20	.07
❑	41	Vinny Testaverde	.30	.10
❑	42	Todd Collins	.20	.07
❑	43	Russell Copeland	.20	.07
❑	44	Quinn Early	.20	.07
❑	45	John Fina	.20	.07
❑	46	Phil Hansen	.20	.07
❑	47	Eric Moulds	.50	.20
❑	48	Bryce Paup	.20	.07
❑	49	Andre Reed	.30	.10
❑	50	Kurt Schulz	.20	.07
❑	51	Bruce Smith	.30	.10
❑	52	Chris Spielman	.20	.07
❑	53	Steve Tasker	.20	.07
❑	54	Thurman Thomas	.50	.20
❑	55	Carlton Bailey	.20	.07
❑	56	Michael Bates	.20	.07
❑	57	Blake Brockermeyer	.20	.07
❑	58	Mark Carrier WR	.20	.07
❑	59	Kerry Collins	.50	.20
❑	60	Eric Davis	.20	.07
❑	61	Kevin Greene	.30	.10
❑	62	Rocket Ismail	.30	.10
❑	63	Anthony Johnson	.20	.07
❑	64	Shawn King	.20	.07
❑	65	Greg Kragen	.20	.07
❑	66	Sam Mills	.20	.07
❑	67	Tyrone Poole	.20	.07
❑	68	Wesley Walls	.30	.10
❑	69	Mark Carrier DB	.20	.07
❑	70	Curtis Conway	.30	.10
❑	71	Bobby Engram	.30	.10
❑	72	Jim Flanigan	.20	.07
❑	73	Al Fontenot	.20	.07
❑	74	Raymont Harris	.20	.07
❑	75	Walt Harris	.20	.07
❑	76	Andy Heck	.20	.07
❑	77	Dave Krieg	.20	.07
❑	78	Rashaan Salaam	.20	.07
❑	79	Vinson Smith	.20	.07
❑	80	Alonzo Spellman	.20	.07
❑	81	Michael Timpson	.20	.07
❑	82	James Williams	.20	.07
❑	83	Ashley Ambrose	.20	.07
❑	84	Eric Bieniemy	.20	.07
❑	85	Jeff Blake	.30	.10
❑	86	Ki-Jana Carter	.20	.07
❑	87	John Copeland	.20	.07
❑	88	David Dunn	.20	.07
❑	89	Jeff Hill	.20	.07
❑	90	Ricardo McDonald	.20	.07
❑	91	Tony McGee	.20	.07
❑	92	Greg Myers	.20	.07
❑	93	Carl Pickens	.30	.10
❑	94	Corey Sawyer	.20	.07
❑	95	Darnay Scott	.30	.10
❑	96	Dan Wilkinson	.20	.07
❑	97	Troy Aikman	1.00	.40
❑	98	Larry Allen	.20	.07
❑	99	Eric Bjornson	.20	.07
❑	100	Ray Donaldson	.20	.07
❑	101	Michael Irvin	.50	.20
❑	102	Daryl Johnston	.30	.10
❑	103	Nate Newton	.20	.07
❑	104	Deion Sanders	.50	.20
❑	105	Jim Schwantz RC	.20	.07
❑	106	Emmitt Smith	1.50	.60
❑	107	Broderick Thomas	.20	.07
❑	108	Tony Tolbert	.20	.07
❑	109	Erik Williams	.20	.07
❑	110	Sherman Williams	.20	.07
❑	111	Darren Woodson	.20	.07
❑	112	Steve Atwater	.20	.07
❑	113	Aaron Craver	.20	.07
❑	114	Ray Crockett	.20	.07
❑	115	Terrell Davis	.60	.25
❑	116	Jason Elam	.30	.10
❑	117	John Elway	2.00	.75
❑	118	Todd Kinchen	.20	.07
❑	119	Ed McCaffrey	.30	.10
❑	120	Anthony Miller	.20	.07
❑	121	John Mobley	.20	.07
❑	122	Michael Dean Perry	.20	.07
❑	123	Reggie Rivers	.20	.07
❑	124	Shannon Sharpe	.30	.10
❑	125	Alfred Williams	.20	.07
❑	126	Reggie Brown LB	.30	.10
❑	127	Luther Elliss	.20	.07
❑	128	Kevin Glover	.20	.07
❑	129	Jason Hanson	.20	.07
❑	130	Pepper Johnson	.20	.07
❑	131	Glyn Milburn	.20	.07
❑	132	Scott Mitchell	.30	.10
❑	133	Herman Moore	.30	.10
❑	134	Johnnie Morton	.30	.10
❑	135	Brett Perriman	.20	.07
❑	136	Robert Porcher	.20	.07
❑	137	Ron Rivers	.20	.07
❑	138	Barry Sanders	1.50	.60
❑	139	Henry Thomas	.20	.07
❑	140	Don Beebe	.20	.07
❑	141	Edgar Bennett	.30	.10
❑	142	Robert Brooks	.30	.10
❑	143	LeRoy Butler	.20	.07
❑	144	Mark Chmura	.30	.10
❑	145	Brett Favre	2.00	.75
❑	146	Antonio Freeman	.50	.20
❑	147	Chris Jacke	.20	.07
❑	148	Travis Jervey	.30	.10
❑	149	Sean Jones	.20	.07
❑	150	Dorsey Levens	.50	.20
❑	151	John Michels	.20	.07
❑	152	Craig Newsome	.20	.07
❑	153	Eugene Robinson	.20	.07
❑	154	Reggie White	.50	.20
❑	155	Micheal Barrow	.20	.07
❑	156	Blaine Bishop	.20	.07
❑	157	Chris Chandler	.30	.10
❑	158	Anthony Cook	.20	.07
❑	159	Malcolm Floyd	.20	.07
❑	160	Eddie George	.50	.20
❑	161	Roderick Lewis	.20	.07
❑	162	Steve McNair	.60	.25
❑	163	John Henry Mills RC	.20	.07
❑	164	Derek Russell	.20	.07
❑	165	Chris Sanders	.20	.07
❑	166	Mark Stepnoski	.20	.07
❑	167	Frank Wycheck	.20	.07
❑	168	Robert Young	.20	.07
❑	169	Trev Alberts	.20	.07
❑	170	Aaron Bailey	.20	.07
❑	171	Tony Bennett	.20	.07
❑	172	Ray Buchanan	.20	.07
❑	173	Quentin Coryatt	.20	.07
❑	174	Eugene Daniel	.20	.07
❑	175	Sean Dawkins	.20	.07
❑	176	Ken Dilger	.20	.07
❑	177	Marshall Faulk	.60	.25
❑	178	Jim Harbaugh	.30	.10
❑	179	Marvin Harrison	.50	.20
❑	180	Paul Justin	.20	.07
❑	181	Lamont Warren	.20	.07
❑	182	Bernard Whittington	.20	.07
❑	183	Tony Boselli	.20	.07
❑	184	Tony Brackens	.20	.07
❑	185	Mark Brunell	.60	.25
❑	186	Brian DeMarco	.20	.07
❑	187	Rich Griffith	.20	.07
❑	188	Kevin Hardy	.20	.07
❑	189	Willie Jackson	.20	.07
❑	190	Jeff Lageman	.20	.07
❑	191	Keenan McCardell	.30	.10
❑	192	Natrone Means	.30	.10
❑	193	Pete Mitchell	.20	.07
❑	194	Joel Smeenge	.20	.07
❑	195	Jimmy Smith	.30	.10
❑	196	James O.Stewart	.30	.10
❑	197	Marcus Allen	.50	.20
❑	198	John Alt	.20	.07
❑	199	Kimble Anders	.30	.10
❑	200	Steve Bono	.30	.10
❑	201	Vaughn Booker	.20	.07
❑	202	Dale Carter	.20	.07
❑	203	Mark Collins	.20	.07
❑	204	Greg Hill	.20	.07
❑	205	Joe Horn	.50	.20
❑	206	Dan Saleaumua	.20	.07
❑	207	Will Shields	.20	.07
❑	208	Neil Smith	.30	.10
❑	209	Derrick Thomas	.50	.20
❑	210	Tamarick Vanover	.30	.10
❑	211	Karim Abdul-Jabbar	.30	.10
❑	212	Fred Barnett	.20	.07
❑	213	Tim Bowens	.20	.07
❑	214	Kirby Dar Dar RC	.30	.10
❑	215	Troy Drayton	.20	.07
❑	216	Craig Erickson	.20	.07
❑	217	Daryl Gardener	.20	.07
❑	218	Randal Hill	.20	.07
❑	219	Dan Marino	2.00	.75
❑	220	O.J. McDuffie	.30	.10
❑	221	Bernie Parmalee	.20	.07
❑	222	Stanley Pritchett	.20	.07
❑	223	Daniel Stubbs	.20	.07
❑	224	Zach Thomas	.50	.20
❑	225	Derrick Alexander DE	.20	.07
❑	226	Cris Carter	.50	.20
❑	227	Jeff Christy	.20	.07
❑	228	Qadry Ismail	.30	.10
❑	229	Brad Johnson	.50	.20
❑	230	Andrew Jordan	.20	.07
❑	231	Randall McDaniel	.20	.07
❑	232	David Palmer	.20	.07
❑	233	John Randle	.30	.10
❑	234	Jake Reed	.30	.10
❑	235	Scott Sisson	.20	.07
❑	236	Korey Stringer	.20	.07
❑	237	Darryl Talley	.20	.07
❑	238	Orlando Thomas	.20	.07
❑	239	Bruce Armstrong	.20	.07
❑	240	Drew Bledsoe	.60	.25
❑	241	Willie Clay	.20	.07
❑	242	Ben Coates	.30	.10
❑	243	Ferric Collons RC	.20	.07
❑	244	Terry Glenn	.50	.20
❑	245	Jerome Henderson	.20	.07
❑	246	Shawn Jefferson	.20	.07
❑	247	Dietrich Jells	.20	.07
❑	248	Ty Law	.30	.10
❑	249	Curtis Martin	.60	.25
❑	250	Willie McGinest	.20	.07

❑ 251	Dave Meggett	.20	.07
❑ 252	Lawyer Milloy	.30	.10
❑ 253	Chris Slade	.20	.07
❑ 254	Je'rod Cherry	.20	.07
❑ 255	Jim Everett	.20	.07
❑ 256	Mark Fields	.20	.07
❑ 257	Michael Haynes	.20	.07
❑ 258	Tyrone Hughes	.20	.07
❑ 259	Haywood Jeffires	.20	.07
❑ 260	Wayne Martin	.20	.07
❑ 261	Mark McMillian	.20	.07
❑ 262	Rufus Porter	.20	.07
❑ 263	William Roaf	.20	.07
❑ 264	Torrance Small	.20	.07
❑ 265	Renaldo Turnbull	.20	.07
❑ 266	Ray Zellars	.20	.07
❑ 267	Jessie Armstead	.20	.07
❑ 268	Chad Bratzke	.20	.07
❑ 269	Dave Brown	.20	.07
❑ 270	Chris Calloway	.20	.07
❑ 271	Howard Cross	.20	.07
❑ 272	Lawrence Dawsey	.20	.07
❑ 273	Rodney Hampton	.30	.10
❑ 274	Danny Kanell	.20	.07
❑ 275	Arthur Marshall	.20	.07
❑ 276	Aaron Pierce	.20	.07
❑ 277	Phillippi Sparks	.20	.07
❑ 278	Amani Toomer	.30	.10
❑ 279	Charles Way	.20	.07
❑ 280	Richie Anderson	.30	.10
❑ 281	Fred Baxter	.20	.07
❑ 282	Wayne Chrebet	.50	.20
❑ 283	Kyle Clifton	.20	.07
❑ 284	Jumbo Elliott	.20	.07
❑ 285	Aaron Glenn	.20	.07
❑ 286	Jeff Graham	.20	.07
❑ 287	Bobby Hamilton RC	.20	.07
❑ 288	Keyshawn Johnson	.50	.20
❑ 289	Adrian Murrell	.30	.10
❑ 290	Neil O'Donnell	.30	.10
❑ 291	Webster Slaughter	.20	.07
❑ 292	Alex Van Dyke	.20	.07
❑ 293	Marvin Washington	.20	.07
❑ 294	Joe Aska	.20	.07
❑ 295	Jerry Ball	.20	.07
❑ 296	Tim Brown	.50	.20
❑ 297	Rickey Dudley	.30	.10
❑ 298	Pat Harlow	.20	.07
❑ 299	Nolan Harrison	.20	.07
❑ 300	Billy Joe Hobert	.30	.10
❑ 301	James Jett	.30	.10
❑ 302	Napoleon Kaufman	.50	.20
❑ 303	Lincoln Kennedy	.20	.07
❑ 304	Albert Lewis	.20	.07
❑ 305	Chester McGlockton	.20	.07
❑ 306	Pat Swilling	.20	.07
❑ 307	Steve Wisniewski	.20	.07
❑ 308	Darion Conner	.20	.07
❑ 309	Ty Detmer	.30	.10
❑ 310	Jason Dunn	.20	.07
❑ 311	Irving Fryar	.30	.10
❑ 312	James Fuller	.20	.07
❑ 313	William Fuller	.20	.07
❑ 314	Charlie Garner	.30	.10
❑ 315	Bobby Hoying	.30	.10
❑ 316	Tom Hutton	.20	.07
❑ 317	Chris T. Jones	.20	.07
❑ 318	Mike Mamula	.20	.07
❑ 319	Mark Seay	.20	.07
❑ 320	Bobby Taylor	.20	.07
❑ 321	Ricky Watters	.30	.10
❑ 322	Jahine Arnold	.20	.07
❑ 323	Jerome Bettis	.50	.20
❑ 324	Chad Brown	.20	.07
❑ 325	Mark Bruener	.20	.07
❑ 326	Andre Hastings	.20	.07
❑ 327	Norm Johnson	.20	.07
❑ 328	Levon Kirkland	.20	.07
❑ 329	Carnell Lake	.20	.07
❑ 330	Greg Lloyd	.20	.07
❑ 331	Ernie Mills	.20	.07
❑ 332	Orpheus Roye RC	.20	.07
❑ 333	Kordell Stewart	.50	.20
❑ 334	Yancey Thigpen	.30	.10
❑ 335	Mike Tomczak	.20	.07
❑ 336	Rod Woodson	.30	.10
❑ 337	Tony Banks	.30	.10
❑ 338	Bern Brostek	.20	.07
❑ 339	Isaac Bruce	.50	.20
❑ 340	Ernie Conwell	.20	.07
❑ 341	Keith Crawford	.20	.07
❑ 342	Wayne Gandy	.20	.07
❑ 343	Harold Green	.20	.07
❑ 344	Carlos Jenkins	.20	.07
❑ 345	Jimmie Jones	.20	.07
❑ 346	Eddie Kennison	.30	.10
❑ 347	Todd Lyght	.20	.07
❑ 348	Leslie O'Neal	.20	.07
❑ 349	Lawrence Phillips	.20	.07
❑ 350	Greg Robinson	.20	.07
❑ 351	Darren Bennett	.20	.07
❑ 352	Lewis Bush	.20	.07
❑ 353	Eric Castle	.20	.07
❑ 354	Terrell Fletcher	.20	.07
❑ 355	Darrien Gordon	.20	.07
❑ 356	Kurt Gouveia	.20	.07
❑ 357	Aaron Hayden	.20	.07
❑ 358	Stan Humphries	.30	.10
❑ 359	Tony Martin	.30	.10
❑ 360	Vaughn Parker RC	.20	.07
❑ 361	Brian Roche	.20	.07
❑ 362	Leonard Russell	.20	.07
❑ 363	Junior Seau	.50	.20
❑ 364	Roy Barker	.20	.07
❑ 365	Harris Barton	.20	.07
❑ 366	Dexter Carter	.20	.07
❑ 367	Chris Doleman	.20	.07
❑ 368	Tyronne Drakeford	.20	.07
❑ 369	Elvis Grbac	.30	.10
❑ 370	Derek Loville	.20	.07
❑ 371	Tim McDonald	.20	.07
❑ 372	Ken Norton	.20	.07
❑ 373	Terrell Owens	.60	.25
❑ 374	Gary Plummer	.20	.07
❑ 375	Jerry Rice	1.00	.40
❑ 376	Dana Stubblefield	.20	.07
❑ 377	Lee Woodall	.20	.07
❑ 378	Steve Young	.60	.25
❑ 379	Robert Blackmon	.20	.07
❑ 380	Brian Blades	.20	.07
❑ 381	Carlester Crumpler	.20	.07
❑ 382	Christian Fauria	.20	.07
❑ 383	John Friesz	.20	.07
❑ 384	Joey Galloway	.30	.10
❑ 385	Derrick Graham	.20	.07
❑ 386	Cortez Kennedy	.20	.07
❑ 387	Warren Moon	.50	.20
❑ 388	Winston Moss	.20	.07
❑ 389	Mike Pritchard	.20	.07
❑ 390	Michael Sinclair	.20	.07
❑ 391	Lamar Smith	.50	.20
❑ 392	Chris Warren	.30	.10
❑ 393	Chidi Ahanotu	.20	.07
❑ 394	Mike Alstott	.50	.20
❑ 395	Reggie Brooks	.20	.07
❑ 396	Trent Dilfer	.50	.20
❑ 397	Jerry Ellison	.20	.07
❑ 398	Paul Gruber	.20	.07
❑ 399	Alvin Harper	.20	.07
❑ 400	Courtney Hawkins	.20	.07
❑ 401	Dave Moore	.20	.07
❑ 402	Errict Rhett	.20	.07
❑ 403	Warren Sapp	.30	.10
❑ 404	Nilo Silvan	.20	.07
❑ 405	Regan Upshaw	.20	.07
❑ 406	Casey Weldon	.20	.07
❑ 407	Terry Allen	.50	.20
❑ 408	Jamie Asher	.20	.07
❑ 409	Bill Brooks	.20	.07
❑ 410	Tom Carter	.20	.07
❑ 411	Henry Ellard	.20	.07
❑ 412	Gus Frerotte	.20	.07
❑ 413	Darrell Green	.30	.10
❑ 414	Ken Harvey	.20	.07
❑ 415	Tre Johnson	.20	.07
❑ 416	Brian Mitchell	.20	.07
❑ 417	Rich Owens	.20	.07
❑ 418	Heath Shuler	.20	.07
❑ 419	Michael Westbrook	.30	.10
❑ 420	Tony Woods RC	.20	.07
❑ 421	Reidel Anthony RC	.50	.20
❑ 422	Darnell Autry RC	.30	.10
❑ 423	Tiki Barber RC	3.00	1.25
❑ 424	Pat Barnes RC	.50	.20
❑ 425	Terry Battle RC	.20	.07
❑ 426	Will Blackwell RC	.30	.10
❑ 427	Peter Boulware RC	.50	.20
❑ 428	Rae Carruth RC	.20	.07
❑ 429	Troy Davis RC	.30	.10
❑ 430	Jim Druckenmiller RC	.30	.10
❑ 431	Warrick Dunn RC	1.50	.60
❑ 432	Marc Edwards RC	.20	.07
❑ 433	James Farrior RC	.50	.20
❑ 434	Yatil Green RC	.30	.10
❑ 435	Byron Hanspard RC	.30	.10
❑ 436	Ike Hilliard RC	.75	.30
❑ 437	David LaFleur RC	.20	.07
❑ 438	Kevin Lockett RC	.30	.10
❑ 439	Sam Madison RC	.50	.20
❑ 440	Brian Manning RC	.30	.10
❑ 441	Orlando Pace RC	.50	.20
❑ 442	Jake Plummer RC	2.50	1.00
❑ 443	Chad Scott RC	.30	.10
❑ 444	Sedrick Shaw RC	.30	.10
❑ 445	Antowain Smith RC	1.25	.50
❑ 446	Shawn Springs RC	.30	.10
❑ 447	Ross Verba RC	.20	.07
❑ 448	Bryant Westbrook RC	.20	.07
❑ 449	Renaldo Wynn RC	.20	.07
❑ 450	Jimmy Johnson CO	.30	.10
❑ S1	Mark Brunell Sample	1.00	.40

1998 Pacific

❑	COMPLETE SET (450)	60.00	25.00
❑ 1	Mario Bates	.40	.15
❑ 2	Lomas Brown	.25	.08
❑ 3	Larry Centers	.25	.08
❑ 4	Chris Gedney	.25	.08
❑ 5	Terry Irving	.25	.08
❑ 6	Tom Knight	.25	.08
❑ 7	Eric Metcalf	.25	.08
❑ 8	Jamir Miller	.25	.08
❑ 9	Rob Moore	.40	.15
❑ 10	Joe Nedney	.25	.08
❑ 11	Jake Plummer	.60	.25
❑ 12	Simeon Rice	.40	.15
❑ 13	Frank Sanders	.40	.15
❑ 14	Eric Swann	.25	.08
❑ 15	Aeneas Williams	.25	.08
❑ 16	Morten Andersen	.25	.08
❑ 17	Jamal Anderson	.60	.25
❑ 18	Michael Booker	.25	.08
❑ 19	Keith Brooking RC	1.50	.60
❑ 20	Ray Buchanan	.25	.08
❑ 21	Devin Bush	.25	.08
❑ 22	Chris Chandler	.40	.15
❑ 23	Tony Graziani	.25	.08
❑ 24	Harold Green	.25	.08
❑ 25	Byron Hanspard	.25	.08
❑ 26	Todd Kinchen	.25	.08
❑ 27	Tony Martin	.40	.15
❑ 28	Terance Mathis	.40	.15
❑ 29	Eugene Robinson	.25	.08
❑ 30	O.J. Santiago	.25	.08
❑ 31	Chuck Smith	.25	.08
❑ 32	Jessie Tuggle	.25	.08
❑ 33	Bob Whitfield	.25	.08
❑ 34	Peter Boulware	.25	.08
❑ 35	Jay Graham	.25	.08
❑ 36	Eric Green	.25	.08
❑ 37	Jim Harbaugh	.40	.15
❑ 38	Michael Jackson	.25	.08
❑ 39	Jermaine Lewis	.40	.15

❑ 40	Ray Lewis	.60	.25
❑ 41	Michael McCrary	.25	.08
❑ 42	Stevon Moore	.25	.08
❑ 43	Jonathan Ogden	.25	.08
❑ 44	Errict Rhett	.40	.15
❑ 45	Matt Stover	.25	.08
❑ 46	Rod Woodson	.40	.15
❑ 47	Eric Zeier	.40	.15
❑ 48	Ruben Brown	.25	.08
❑ 49	Steve Christie	.25	.08
❑ 50	Quinn Early	.25	.08
❑ 51	John Fina	.25	.08
❑ 52	Doug Flutie	.60	.25
❑ 53	Phil Hansen	.25	.08
❑ 54	Lonnie Johnson	.25	.08
❑ 55	Rob Johnson	.40	.15
❑ 56	Henry Jones	.25	.08
❑ 57	Eric Moulds	.60	.25
❑ 58	Andre Reed	.40	.15
❑ 59	Antowain Smith	.60	.25
❑ 60	Bruce Smith	.40	.15
❑ 61	Thurman Thomas	.60	.25
❑ 62	Ted Washington	.25	.08
❑ 63	Michael Bates	.25	.08
❑ 64	Tim Biakabutuka	.40	.15
❑ 65	Blake Brockermeyer	.25	.08
❑ 66	Mark Carrier	.25	.08
❑ 67	Rae Carruth	.25	.08
❑ 68	Kerry Collins	.40	.15
❑ 69	Doug Evans	.25	.08
❑ 70	William Floyd	.25	.08
❑ 71	Sean Gilbert	.25	.08
❑ 72	Rocket Ismail	.25	.08
❑ 73	John Kasay	.25	.08
❑ 74	Fred Lane	.25	.08
❑ 75	Lamar Lathon	.25	.08
❑ 76	Muhsin Muhammad	.40	.15
❑ 77	Wesley Walls	.40	.15
❑ 78	Edgar Bennett	.25	.08
❑ 79	Tom Carter	.25	.08
❑ 80	Curtis Conway	.40	.15
❑ 81	Bobby Engram	.40	.15
❑ 82	Curtis Enis RC	.75	.30
❑ 83	Jim Flanigan	.25	.08
❑ 84	Walt Harris	.25	.08
❑ 85	Jeff Jaeger	.25	.08
❑ 86	Erik Kramer	.25	.08
❑ 87	John Mangum	.25	.08
❑ 88	Glyn Milburn	.25	.08
❑ 89	Barry Minter	.25	.08
❑ 90	Chris Penn	.25	.08
❑ 91	Todd Sauerbrun	.25	.08
❑ 92	James Williams	.25	.08
❑ 93	Ashley Ambrose	.25	.08
❑ 94	Willie Anderson	.25	.08
❑ 95	Eric Bieniemy	.25	.08
❑ 96	Jeff Blake	.40	.15
❑ 97	Ki-Jana Carter	.25	.08
❑ 98	John Copeland	.25	.08
❑ 99	Corey Dillon	.60	.25
❑ 100	Tony McGee	.25	.08
❑ 101	Neil O'Donnell	.40	.15
❑ 102	Carl Pickens	.40	.15
❑ 103	Kevin Sargent	.25	.08
❑ 104	Darnay Scott	.40	.15
❑ 105	Takeo Spikes RC	1.50	.60
❑ 106	Troy Aikman	1.25	.50
❑ 107	Larry Allen	.25	.08
❑ 108	Eric Bjornson	.25	.08
❑ 109	Billy Davis	.25	.08
❑ 110	Jason Garrett RC	.75	.30
❑ 111	Michael Irvin	.60	.25
❑ 112	Daryl Johnston	.40	.15
❑ 113	David LaFleur	.25	.08
❑ 114	Everett McIver	.25	.08
❑ 115	Ernie Mills	.25	.08
❑ 116	Nate Newton	.25	.08
❑ 117	Deion Sanders	.60	.25
❑ 118	Emmitt Smith	2.00	.75
❑ 119	Kevin Smith	.25	.08
❑ 120	Erik Williams	.25	.08
❑ 121	Steve Atwater	.25	.08
❑ 122	Tyrone Braxton	.25	.08
❑ 123	Ray Crockett	.25	.08
❑ 124	Terrell Davis	.60	.25
❑ 125	Jason Elam	.25	.08
❑ 126	John Elway	2.50	1.00
❑ 127	Willie Green	.25	.08
❑ 128	Brian Griese RC	3.00	1.25
❑ 129	Tony Jones	.25	.08
❑ 130	Ed McCaffrey	.40	.15
❑ 131	John Mobley	.25	.08
❑ 132	Tom Nalen	.25	.08
❑ 133	Marcus Nash RC	.75	.30
❑ 134	Bill Romanowski	.25	.08
❑ 135	Shannon Sharpe	.40	.15
❑ 136	Neil Smith	.40	.15
❑ 137	Rod Smith	.40	.15
❑ 138	Keith Traylor	.25	.08
❑ 139	Stephen Boyd	.25	.08
❑ 140	Mark Carrier DB	.25	.08
❑ 141	Charlie Batch RC	1.50	.60
❑ 142	Jason Hanson	.25	.08
❑ 143	Scott Mitchell	.40	.15
❑ 144	Herman Moore	.40	.15
❑ 145	Johnnie Morton	.40	.15
❑ 146	Robert Porcher	.25	.08
❑ 147	Ron Rivers	.25	.08
❑ 148	Barry Sanders	2.00	.75
❑ 149	Tracy Scroggins	.25	.08
❑ 150	David Sloan	.25	.08
❑ 151	Tommy Vardell	.25	.08
❑ 152	Kerwin Waldroup	.25	.08
❑ 153	Bryant Westbrook	.25	.08
❑ 154	Robert Brooks	.40	.15
❑ 155	Gilbert Brown	.25	.08
❑ 156	LeRoy Butler	.25	.08
❑ 157	Mark Chmura	.40	.15
❑ 158	Earl Dotson	.25	.08
❑ 159	Santana Dotson	.25	.08
❑ 160	Brett Favre	2.50	1.00
❑ 161	Antonio Freeman	.60	.25
❑ 162	Raymont Harris	.25	.08
❑ 163	William Henderson	.40	.15
❑ 164	Vonnie Holliday RC	1.25	.50
❑ 165	George Koonce	.25	.08
❑ 166	Dorsey Levens	.60	.25
❑ 167	Derrick Mayes	.40	.15
❑ 168	Craig Newsome	.25	.08
❑ 169	Ross Verba	.25	.08
❑ 170	Reggie White	.60	.25
❑ 171	Elijah Alexander	.25	.08
❑ 172	Aaron Bailey	.25	.08
❑ 173	Jason Belser	.25	.08
❑ 174	Robert Blackmon	.25	.08
❑ 175	Zack Crockett	.25	.08
❑ 176	Ken Dilger	.25	.08
❑ 177	Marshall Faulk	.75	.30
❑ 178	Tarik Glenn	.25	.08
❑ 179	Marvin Harrison	.60	.25
❑ 180	Tony Mandarich	.25	.08
❑ 181	Peyton Manning RC	15.00	6.00
❑ 182	Marcus Pollard	.25	.08
❑ 183	Lamont Warren	.25	.08
❑ 184	Tavian Banks RC	1.25	.50
❑ 185	Reggie Barlow	.25	.08
❑ 186	Tony Boselli	.25	.08
❑ 187	Tony Brackens	.25	.08
❑ 188	Mark Brunell	.60	.25
❑ 189	Kevin Hardy	.25	.08
❑ 190	Mike Hollis	.25	.08
❑ 191	Jeff Lageman	.25	.08
❑ 192	Keenan McCardell	.40	.15
❑ 193	Pete Mitchell	.25	.08
❑ 194	Bryce Paup	.25	.08
❑ 195	Leon Searcy	.25	.08
❑ 196	Jimmy Smith	.40	.15
❑ 197	James Stewart	.40	.15
❑ 198	Fred Taylor RC	2.50	1.00
❑ 199	Renaldo Wynn	.25	.08
❑ 200	Derrick Alexander WR	.40	.15
❑ 201	Kimble Anders	.40	.15
❑ 202	Donnell Bennett	.25	.08
❑ 203	Dale Carter	.25	.08
❑ 204	Anthony Davis	.25	.08
❑ 205	Rich Gannon	.60	.25
❑ 206	Tony Gonzalez	.60	.25
❑ 207	Elvis Grbac	.40	.15
❑ 208	James Hasty	.25	.08
❑ 209	Leslie O'Neal	.25	.08
❑ 210	Andre Rison	.40	.15
❑ 211	Rashaan Shehee RC	1.25	.50
❑ 212	Will Shields	.25	.08
❑ 213	Pete Stoyanovich	.25	.08
❑ 214	Derrick Thomas	.60	.25
❑ 215	Tamarick Vanover	.25	.08
❑ 216	Karim Abdul-Jabbar	.60	.25
❑ 217	Trace Armstrong	.25	.08
❑ 218	John Avery RC	1.25	.50
❑ 219	Tim Bowens	.25	.08
❑ 220	Terrell Buckley	.25	.08
❑ 221	Troy Drayton	.25	.08
❑ 222	Daryl Gardener	.25	.08
❑ 223	Damon Huard RC	8.00	3.00
❑ 224	Charles Jordan	.25	.08
❑ 225	Dan Marino	2.50	1.00
❑ 226	O.J. McDuffie	.40	.15
❑ 227	Bernie Parmalee	.25	.08
❑ 228	Stanley Pritchett	.25	.08
❑ 229	Derrick Rodgers	.25	.08
❑ 230	Lamar Thomas	.25	.08
❑ 231	Zach Thomas	.60	.25
❑ 232	Richmond Webb	.25	.08
❑ 233	Derrick Alexander DE	.25	.08
❑ 234	Jerry Ball	.25	.08
❑ 235	Cris Carter	.60	.25
❑ 236	Randall Cunningham	.60	.25
❑ 237	Charles Evans	.25	.08
❑ 238	Corey Fuller	.25	.08
❑ 239	Andrew Glover	.25	.08
❑ 240	Leroy Hoard	.25	.08
❑ 241	Brad Johnson	.60	.25
❑ 242	Ed McDaniel	.25	.08
❑ 243	Randall McDaniel	.25	.08
❑ 244	Randy Moss RC	10.00	4.00
❑ 245	John Randle	.40	.15
❑ 246	Jake Reed	.40	.15
❑ 247	Dwayne Rudd	.25	.08
❑ 248	Robert Smith	.60	.25
❑ 249	Bruce Armstrong	.25	.08
❑ 250	Drew Bledsoe	1.00	.40
❑ 251	Vincent Brisby	.25	.08
❑ 252	Tedy Bruschi	1.25	.50
❑ 253	Ben Coates	.40	.15
❑ 254	Derrick Cullors	.25	.08
❑ 255	Terry Glenn	.60	.25
❑ 256	Shawn Jefferson	.25	.08
❑ 257	Ted Johnson	.25	.08
❑ 258	Ty Law	.40	.15
❑ 259	Willie McGinest	.25	.08
❑ 260	Lawyer Milloy	.40	.15
❑ 261	Sedrick Shaw	.25	.08
❑ 262	Chris Slade	.25	.08
❑ 263	Troy Davis	.25	.08
❑ 264	Mark Fields	.25	.08
❑ 265	Andre Hastings	.25	.08
❑ 266	Billy Joe Hobert	.25	.08
❑ 267	Qadry Ismail	.40	.15
❑ 268	Tony Johnson	.25	.08
❑ 269	Sammy Knight RC	.60	.25
❑ 270	Wayne Martin	.25	.08
❑ 271	Chris Naeole	.25	.08
❑ 272	Keith Poole	.25	.08
❑ 273	William Roaf	.25	.08
❑ 274	Pio Sagapolutele	.25	.08
❑ 275	Danny Wuerffel	.40	.15
❑ 276	Ray Zellars	.25	.08
❑ 277	Jessie Armstead	.25	.08
❑ 278	Tiki Barber	.60	.25
❑ 279	Chris Calloway	.25	.08
❑ 280	Percy Ellsworth	.25	.08
❑ 281	Sam Garnes RC	.75	.30
❑ 282	Kent Graham	.25	.08
❑ 283	Ike Hilliard	.40	.15
❑ 284	Danny Kanell	.40	.15
❑ 285	Corey Miller	.25	.08
❑ 286	Phillippi Sparks	.25	.08
❑ 287	Michael Strahan	.40	.15
❑ 288	Amani Toomer	.40	.15
❑ 289	Charles Way	.25	.08
❑ 290	Tyrone Wheatley	.40	.15
❑ 291	Tito Wooten	.25	.08
❑ 292	Kyle Brady	.25	.08
❑ 293	Keith Byars	.25	.08
❑ 294	Wayne Chrebet	.60	.25
❑ 295	John Elliott	.25	.08
❑ 296	Glenn Foley	.40	.15
❑ 297	Aaron Glenn	.25	.08
❑ 298	Keyshawn Johnson	.60	.25
❑ 299	Curtis Martin	.60	.25
❑ 300	Otis Smith	.25	.08

❑ 301 Vinny Testaverde .40 .15
❑ 302 Alex Van Dyke .25 .08
❑ 303 Dedric Ward .25 .08
❑ 304 Greg Biekert .25 .08
❑ 305 Tim Brown .60 .25
❑ 306 Rickey Dudley .25 .08
❑ 307 Jeff George .40 .15
❑ 308 Pat Harlow .25 .08
❑ 309 Desmond Howard .40 .15
❑ 310 James Jett .40 .15
❑ 311 Napoleon Kaufman .60 .25
❑ 312 Lincoln Kennedy .25 .08
❑ 313 Russell Maryland .25 .08
❑ 314 Darrell Russell .25 .08
❑ 315 Eric Turner .25 .08
❑ 316 Steve Wisniewski .25 .08
❑ 317 Charles Woodson RC 2.00 .75
❑ 318 James Darling RC .75 .30
❑ 319 Jason Dunn .25 .08
❑ 320 Irving Fryar .40 .15
❑ 321 Charlie Garner .40 .15
❑ 322 Jeff Graham .25 .08
❑ 323 Bobby Hoying .40 .15
❑ 324 Chad Lewis .40 .15
❑ 325 Rodney Peete .25 .08
❑ 326 Freddie Solomon .25 .08
❑ 327 Duce Staley .75 .30
❑ 328 Bobby Taylor .25 .08
❑ 329 William Thomas .25 .08
❑ 330 Kevin Turner .25 .08
❑ 331 Troy Vincent .25 .08
❑ 332 Jerome Bettis .60 .25
❑ 333 Will Blackwell .25 .08
❑ 334 Mark Bruener .25 .08
❑ 335 Andre Coleman .25 .08
❑ 336 Dermontti Dawson .25 .08
❑ 337 Jason Gildon .25 .08
❑ 338 Courtney Hawkins .25 .08
❑ 339 Charles Johnson .25 .08
❑ 340 Levon Kirkland .25 .08
❑ 341 Carnell Lake .25 .08
❑ 342 Tim Lester .25 .08
❑ 343 Joel Steed .25 .08
❑ 344 Kordell Stewart .60 .25
❑ 345 Will Wolford .25 .08
❑ 346 Tony Banks .40 .15
❑ 347 Isaac Bruce .60 .25
❑ 348 Ernie Conwell .25 .08
❑ 349 D'Marco Farr .25 .08
❑ 350 Wayne Gandy .25 .08
❑ 351 Jerome Pathon RC 1.50 .60
❑ 352 Eddie Kennison .40 .15
❑ 353 Amp Lee .25 .08
❑ 354 Keith Lyle .25 .08
❑ 355 Ryan McNeil .25 .08
❑ 356 Jerald Moore .25 .08
❑ 357 Orlando Pace .25 .08
❑ 358 Roman Phifer .25 .08
❑ 359 David Thompson RC .75 .30
❑ 360 Darren Bennett .25 .08
❑ 361 John Carney .25 .08
❑ 362 Marco Coleman .25 .08
❑ 363 Terrell Fletcher .25 .08
❑ 364 William Fuller .25 .08
❑ 365 Charlie Jones .25 .08
❑ 366 Freddie Jones .25 .08
❑ 367 Ryan Leaf RC 1.50 .60
❑ 368 Natrone Means .40 .15
❑ 369 Junior Seau .60 .25
❑ 370 Terrance Shaw .25 .08
❑ 371 Tremayne Stephens RC .75 .30
❑ 372 Bryan Still .25 .08
❑ 373 Aaron Taylor .25 .08
❑ 374 Greg Clark .25 .08
❑ 375 Ty Detmer .40 .15
❑ 376 Jim Druckenmiller .25 .08
❑ 377 Marc Edwards .25 .08
❑ 378 Merton Hanks .25 .08
❑ 379 Garrison Hearst .60 .25
❑ 380 Chuck Levy .25 .08
❑ 381 Ken Norton .25 .08
❑ 382 Terrell Owens .60 .25
❑ 383 Marquez Pope .25 .08
❑ 384 Jerry Rice 1.25 .50
❑ 385 Irv Smith .25 .08
❑ 386 J.J. Stokes .40 .15
❑ 387 Iheanyi Uwaezuoke .25 .08
❑ 388 Bryant Young .25 .08
❑ 389 Steve Young .75 .30
❑ 390 Sam Adams .25 .08
❑ 391 Chad Brown .25 .08
❑ 392 Christian Fauria .25 .08
❑ 393 Joey Galloway .40 .15
❑ 394 Ahman Green RC 8.00 3.00
❑ 395 Walter Jones .25 .08
❑ 396 Cortez Kennedy .25 .08
❑ 397 Jon Kitna .60 .25
❑ 398 James McKnight .60 .25
❑ 399 Warren Moon .60 .25
❑ 400 Mike Pritchard .25 .08
❑ 401 Michael Sinclair .25 .08
❑ 402 Shawn Springs .25 .08
❑ 403 Ricky Watters .40 .15
❑ 404 Darryl Williams .25 .08
❑ 405 Mike Alstott .60 .25
❑ 406 Reidel Anthony .40 .15
❑ 407 Derrick Brooks .60 .25
❑ 408 Brad Culpepper .25 .08
❑ 409 Trent Dilfer .60 .25
❑ 410 Warrick Dunn .60 .25
❑ 411 Bert Emanuel .40 .15
❑ 412 Jacquez Green RC 1.25 .50
❑ 413 Paul Gruber .25 .08
❑ 414 Patrick Hape RC 1.25 .50
❑ 415 Dave Moore .25 .08
❑ 416 Hardy Nickerson .25 .08
❑ 417 Warren Sapp .40 .15
❑ 418 Robb Thomas .25 .08
❑ 419 Regan Upshaw .25 .08
❑ 420 Karl Williams .25 .08
❑ 421 Blaine Bishop .25 .08
❑ 422 Anthony Cook .25 .08
❑ 423 Willie Davis .25 .08
❑ 424 Al Del Greco .25 .08
❑ 425 Kevin Dyson .60 .25
❑ 426 Henry Ford .25 .08
❑ 427 Eddie George .60 .25
❑ 428 Jackie Harris .25 .08
❑ 429 Steve McNair .60 .25
❑ 430 Chris Sanders .25 .08
❑ 431 Mark Stepnoski .25 .08
❑ 432 Yancey Thigpen .25 .08
❑ 433 Barron Wortham .25 .08
❑ 434 Frank Wycheck .25 .08
❑ 435 Stephen Alexander RC 1.25 .50
❑ 436 Terry Allen .60 .25
❑ 437 Jamie Asher .25 .08
❑ 438 Bob Dahl .25 .08
❑ 439 Stephen Davis .25 .08
❑ 440 Cris Dishman .25 .08
❑ 441 Gus Frerotte .25 .08
❑ 442 Darrell Green .40 .15
❑ 443 Trent Green .75 .30
❑ 444 Ken Harvey .25 .08
❑ 445 Skip Hicks RC 1.25 .50
❑ 446 Jeff Hostetler .25 .08
❑ 447 Brian Mitchell .25 .08
❑ 448 Leslie Shepherd .25 .08
❑ 449 Michael Westbrook .40 .15
❑ 450 Dan Wilkinson .25 .08
❑ S1 Warrick Dunn Sample 1.00 .40

1999 Pacific

❑ COMPLETE SET (450) 80.00 30.00
❑ 1 Mario Bates .25 .08
❑ 2 Larry Centers .25 .08
❑ 3 Chris Gedney .25 .08
❑ 4 Kwamie Lassiter RC .60 .25
❑ 5 Johnny McWilliams .25 .08
❑ 6 Eric Metcalf .25 .08
❑ 7 Rob Moore .40 .15
❑ 8 Adrian Murrell .40 .15
❑ 9 Jake Plummer .40 .15
❑ 10 Simeon Rice .40 .15
❑ 11 Frank Sanders .40 .15
❑ 12 Andre Wadsworth .25 .08
❑ 13 Aeneas Williams .25 .08
❑ 14 M.Pittman/R.Anderson RC 1.25 .50
❑ 15 Morten Andersen .25 .08
❑ 16 Jamal Anderson .60 .25
❑ 17 Lester Archambeau .25 .08
❑ 18 Chris Chandler .40 .15
❑ 19 Bob Christian .25 .08
❑ 20 Steve DeBerg .25 .08
❑ 21 Tim Dwight .60 .25
❑ 22 Tony Martin .40 .15
❑ 23 Terance Mathis .40 .15
❑ 24 Eugene Robinson .25 .08
❑ 25 O.J. Santiago .25 .08
❑ 26 Chuck Smith .25 .08
❑ 27 Jessie Tuggle .25 .08
❑ 28 Jammi German/Ken Oxendine .25 .08
❑ 29 Peter Boulware .25 .08
❑ 30 Jay Graham .25 .08
❑ 31 Jim Harbaugh .40 .15
❑ 32 Priest Holmes 1.00 .40
❑ 33 Michael Jackson .25 .08
❑ 34 Jermaine Lewis .40 .15
❑ 35 Ray Lewis .60 .25
❑ 36 Michael McCrary .25 .08
❑ 37 Jonathan Ogden .25 .08
❑ 38 Errict Rhett .25 .08
❑ 39 James Roe RC 1.00 .40
❑ 40 Floyd Turner .25 .08
❑ 41 Rod Woodson .40 .15
❑ 42 Eric Zeier .25 .08
❑ 43 Wally Richardson/Patrick Johnson .25 .08
❑ 44 Ruben Brown .25 .08
❑ 45 Quinn Early .25 .08
❑ 46 Doug Flutie .60 .25
❑ 47 Sam Gash .25 .08
❑ 48 Phil Hansen .25 .08
❑ 49 Lonnie Johnson .25 .08
❑ 50 Rob Johnson .40 .15
❑ 51 Eric Moulds .60 .25
❑ 52 Andre Reed .40 .15
❑ 53 Jay Riemersma .25 .08
❑ 54 Antowain Smith .60 .25
❑ 55 Bruce Smith .40 .15
❑ 56 Thurman Thomas .40 .15
❑ 57 Ted Washington .25 .08
❑ 58 J.Linton/Kamil Loud RC 1.00 .40
❑ 59 Michael Bates .25 .08
❑ 60 Steve Beuerlein .25 .08
❑ 61 Tim Biakabutuka .40 .15
❑ 62 Mark Carrier WR .25 .08
❑ 63 Eric Davis .25 .08
❑ 64 William Floyd .25 .08
❑ 65 Sean Gilbert .25 .08
❑ 66 Kevin Greene .25 .08
❑ 67 Rocket Ismail .40 .15
❑ 68 Anthony Johnson .25 .08
❑ 69 Fred Lane .25 .08
❑ 70 Muhsin Muhammad .40 .15
❑ 71 Winslow Oliver .25 .08
❑ 72 Wesley Walls .40 .15
❑ 73 D.Craig RC/S.Matthews 1.50 .60
❑ 74 Edgar Bennett .25 .08
❑ 75 Curtis Conway .40 .15
❑ 76 Bobby Engram .40 .15
❑ 77 Curtis Enis .25 .08
❑ 78 Ty Hallock RC 1.00 .40
❑ 79 Walt Harris .25 .08
❑ 80 Jeff Jaeger .25 .08
❑ 81 Erik Kramer .25 .08
❑ 82 Glyn Milburn .25 .08
❑ 83 Chris Penn .25 .08
❑ 84 Steve Stenstrom .25 .08
❑ 85 Ryan Wetnight .25 .08
❑ 86 James Allen RC/Moreno 1.50 .60
❑ 87 Ashley Ambrose .25 .08
❑ 88 Brandon Bennett RC 1.00 .40
❑ 89 Eric Bieniemy .25 .08

❑ 90 Jeff Blake .40 .15
❑ 91 Corey Dillon .60 .25
❑ 92 Paul Justin .25 .08
❑ 93 Eric Kresser RC 1.00 .40
❑ 94 Tremain Mack .25 .08
❑ 95 Tony McGee .25 .08
❑ 96 Neil O'Donnell .40 .15
❑ 97 Carl Pickens .40 .15
❑ 98 Darnay Scott .25 .08
❑ 99 Takeo Spikes .25 .08
❑ 100 Ty Detmer .25 .08
❑ 101 Chris Gardocki .25 .08
❑ 102 Damon Gibson .25 .08
❑ 103 Antonio Langham .25 .08
❑ 104 Jerris McPhail .25 .08
❑ 105 Irv Smith .25 .08
❑ 106 Freddie Solomon .25 .08
❑ 107 S.Milanovich/Fred Brock RC 1.00 .40
❑ 108 Troy Aikman 1.25 .50
❑ 109 Larry Allen .25 .08
❑ 110 Eric Bjornson .25 .08
❑ 111 Billy Davis .25 .08
❑ 112 Michael Irvin .40 .15
❑ 113 David LaFleur .25 .08
❑ 114 Ernie Mills .25 .08
❑ 115 Nate Newton .25 .08
❑ 116 Deion Sanders .60 .25
❑ 117 Emmitt Smith 1.25 .50
❑ 118 Chris Warren .25 .08
❑ 119 Bubby Brister .40 .15
❑ 120 Terrell Davis .60 .25
❑ 121 Jason Elam .25 .08
❑ 122 John Elway 2.00 .75
❑ 123 Willie Green .25 .08
❑ 124 Howard Griffith .25 .08
❑ 125 Vaughn Hebron .25 .08
❑ 126 Ed McCaffrey .40 .15
❑ 127 John Mobley .25 .08
❑ 128 Bill Romanowski .25 .08
❑ 129 Shannon Sharpe .40 .15
❑ 130 Neil Smith .40 .15
❑ 131 Rod Smith .40 .15
❑ 132 Brian Griese/M.Nash .60 .25
❑ 133 Charlie Batch .60 .25
❑ 134 Stephen Boyd .25 .08
❑ 135 Mark Carrier DB .25 .08
❑ 136 Germane Crowell .25 .08
❑ 137 Terry Fair .25 .08
❑ 138 Jason Hanson .25 .08
❑ 139 Greg Jeffries RC 1.00 .40
❑ 140 Herman Moore .40 .15
❑ 141 Johnnie Morton .40 .15
❑ 142 Robert Porcher .25 .08
❑ 143 Ron Rivers .25 .08
❑ 144 Barry Sanders 2.00 .75
❑ 145 Tommy Vardell .25 .08
❑ 146 Bryant Westbrook .25 .08
❑ 147 Robert Brooks .40 .15
❑ 148 LeRoy Butler .25 .08
❑ 149 Mark Chmura .25 .08
❑ 150 Tyrone Davis .25 .08
❑ 151 Brett Favre 2.00 .75
❑ 152 Antonio Freeman .60 .25
❑ 153 Raymont Harris .25 .08
❑ 154 Vonnie Holliday .25 .08
❑ 155 Darick Holmes .25 .08
❑ 156 Dorsey Levens .60 .25
❑ 157 Brian Manning .25 .08
❑ 158 Derrick Mayes .25 .08
❑ 159 Roell Preston .25 .08
❑ 160 Jeff Thomason .25 .08
❑ 161 Tyrone Williams .25 .08
❑ 162 C.Bradford/Michael Blair RC 1.50 .60
❑ 163 Aaron Bailey .25 .08
❑ 164 Ken Dilger .25 .08
❑ 165 Marshall Faulk .75 .30
❑ 166 E.G. Green .25 .08
❑ 167 Marvin Harrison .60 .25
❑ 168 Craig Heyward .25 .08
❑ 169 Peyton Manning 2.00 .75
❑ 170 Jerome Pathon .40 .15
❑ 171 Marcus Pollard .25 .08
❑ 172 Torrance Small .25 .08
❑ 173 Mike Vanderjagt .25 .08
❑ 174 Lamont Warren .25 .08
❑ 175 Tavian Banks .25 .08
❑ 176 Reggie Barlow .25 .08
❑ 177 Tony Boselli .25 .08
❑ 178 Tony Brackens .25 .08
❑ 179 Mark Brunell .60 .25
❑ 180 Kevin Hardy .25 .08
❑ 181 Damon Jones .25 .08
❑ 182 Jamie Martin .60 .25
❑ 183 Keenan McCardell .40 .15
❑ 184 Pete Mitchell .25 .08
❑ 185 Bryce Paup .25 .08
❑ 186 Jimmy Smith .40 .15
❑ 187 Fred Taylor .60 .25
❑ 188 Alvis Whitted/Chris Howard .25 .08
❑ 189 Derrick Alexander WR .40 .15
❑ 190 Kimble Anders .40 .15
❑ 191 Donnell Bennett .25 .08
❑ 192 Dale Carter .25 .08
❑ 193 Rich Gannon .60 .25
❑ 194 Tony Gonzalez .60 .25
❑ 195 Elvis Grbac .40 .15
❑ 196 Joe Horn .40 .15
❑ 197 Kevin Lockett .25 .08
❑ 198 Byron Bam Morris .25 .08
❑ 199 Andre Rison .40 .15
❑ 200 Derrick Thomas .60 .25
❑ 201 Tamarick Vanover .25 .08
❑ 202 Gregory Favors/Rashaan Shehee .25 .08
❑ 203 Karim Abdul-Jabbar .40 .15
❑ 204 Trace Armstrong .25 .08
❑ 205 John Avery .25 .08
❑ 206 Lorenzo Bromell RC .60 .25
❑ 207 Terrell Buckley .25 .08
❑ 208 Oronde Gadsden .40 .15
❑ 209 Sam Madison .25 .08
❑ 210 Dan Marino 2.00 .75
❑ 211 O.J. McDuffie .40 .15
❑ 212 Ed Perry RC .60 .25
❑ 213 Jason Taylor .25 .08
❑ 214 Lamar Thomas .25 .08
❑ 215 Zach Thomas .60 .25
❑ 216 H.Lusk/Nate Jacquet RC 1.00 .40
❑ 217 T.Doxzon RC/D.Huard 1.50 .60
❑ 218 Gary Anderson .25 .08
❑ 219 Cris Carter .60 .25
❑ 220 Randall Cunningham .60 .25
❑ 221 Andrew Glover .25 .08
❑ 222 Matthew Hatchette .25 .08
❑ 223 Brad Johnson .60 .25
❑ 224 Ed McDaniel .25 .08
❑ 225 Randall McDaniel .25 .08
❑ 226 Randy Moss 1.50 .60
❑ 227 David Palmer .25 .08
❑ 228 John Randle .40 .15
❑ 229 Jake Reed .40 .15
❑ 230 Robert Smith .60 .25
❑ 231 Todd Steussie .25 .08
❑ 232 S.Colinet RC/K.Mays .25 .08
❑ 233 Jay Fiedler RC/T.Bouman RC 6.00 2.50
❑ 234 Drew Bledsoe .75 .30
❑ 235 Troy Brown .40 .15
❑ 236 Ben Coates .40 .15
❑ 237 Derrick Cullors .25 .08
❑ 238 Robert Edwards .25 .08
❑ 239 Terry Glenn .60 .25
❑ 240 Shawn Jefferson .25 .08
❑ 241 Ty Law .40 .15
❑ 242 Lawyer Milloy .40 .15
❑ 243 Lovett Purnell RC 1.00 .40
❑ 244 Sedrick Shaw .25 .08
❑ 245 Tony Simmons .25 .08
❑ 246 Chris Slade .25 .08
❑ 247 R.Rutledge/Anth.Ladd RC 1.00 .40
❑ 248 Chris Floyd/Harold Shaw .25 .08
❑ 249 Ink Aleaga RC 1.00 .40
❑ 250 Cameron Cleeland .25 .08
❑ 251 Kerry Collins .40 .15
❑ 252 Troy Davis .25 .08
❑ 253 Sean Dawkins .25 .08
❑ 254 Mark Fields .25 .08
❑ 255 Andre Hastings .25 .08
❑ 256 Sammy Knight .25 .08
❑ 257 Keith Poole .25 .08
❑ 258 William Roaf .25 .08
❑ 259 Lamar Smith .40 .15
❑ 260 Danny Wuerffel .25 .08
❑ 261 Josh Wilcox RC/Brett Bech RC 1.00 .40
❑ 262 Chris Bordano RC/W.Perry 1.00 .40
❑ 263 Jessie Armstead .25 .08
❑ 264 Tiki Barber .60 .25
❑ 265 Chad Bratzke .25 .08
❑ 266 Gary Brown .25 .08
❑ 267 Chris Calloway .25 .08
❑ 268 Howard Cross .25 .08
❑ 269 Kent Graham .25 .08
❑ 270 Ike Hilliard .25 .08
❑ 271 Danny Kanell .40 .15
❑ 272 Michael Strahan .40 .15
❑ 273 Amani Toomer .25 .08
❑ 274 Charles Way .25 .08
❑ 275 Greg Comella RC/M.Cherry 1.50 .60
❑ 276 Kyle Brady .25 .08
❑ 277 Keith Byars .25 .08
❑ 278 Chad Cascadden .25 .08
❑ 279 Wayne Chrebet .40 .15
❑ 280 Bryan Cox .25 .08
❑ 281 Glenn Foley .40 .15
❑ 282 Aaron Glenn .25 .08
❑ 283 Keyshawn Johnson .60 .25
❑ 284 Leon Johnson .25 .08
❑ 285 Mo Lewis .25 .08
❑ 286 Curtis Martin .60 .25
❑ 287 Otis Smith .25 .08
❑ 288 Vinny Testaverde .40 .15
❑ 289 Dedric Ward .25 .08
❑ 290 Tim Brown .60 .25
❑ 291 Rickey Dudley .25 .08
❑ 292 Jeff George .40 .15
❑ 293 Desmond Howard .40 .15
❑ 294 James Jett .40 .15
❑ 295 Lance Johnstone .25 .08
❑ 296 Randy Jordan .25 .08
❑ 297 Napoleon Kaufman .60 .25
❑ 298 Lincoln Kennedy .25 .08
❑ 299 Terry Mickens .25 .08
❑ 300 Darrell Russell .25 .08
❑ 301 Harvey Williams .25 .08
❑ 302 Ch.Woodson/Ritchie .60 .25
❑ 303 Rodney Williams/Jermaine Williams .25 .08
❑ 304 Koy Detmer .25 .08
❑ 305 Hugh Douglas .25 .08
❑ 306 Jason Dunn .25 .08
❑ 307 Irving Fryar .40 .15
❑ 308 Charlie Garner .40 .15
❑ 309 Jeff Graham .25 .08
❑ 310 Bobby Hoying .40 .15
❑ 311 Rodney Peete .25 .08
❑ 312 Allen Rossum .25 .08
❑ 313 Duce Staley .60 .25
❑ 314 William Thomas .25 .08
❑ 315 Kevin Turner .25 .08
❑ 316 K.Sinceno RC/C.Walker RC 1.00 .40
❑ 317 Jahine Arnold .25 .08
❑ 318 Jerome Bettis .60 .25
❑ 319 Will Blackwell .25 .08
❑ 320 Mark Bruener .25 .08
❑ 321 Dermontti Dawson .25 .08
❑ 322 Chris Fuamatu-Ma'afala .25 .08
❑ 323 Courtney Hawkins .25 .08
❑ 324 Richard Huntley .40 .15
❑ 325 Charles Johnson .25 .08
❑ 326 Levon Kirkland .25 .08
❑ 327 Kordell Stewart .40 .15
❑ 328 Hines Ward .60 .25
❑ 329 Dewayne Washington .25 .08
❑ 330 Tony Banks .40 .15
❑ 331 Steve Bono .25 .08
❑ 332 Isaac Bruce .60 .25
❑ 333 June Henley RC 1.25 .50
❑ 334 Robert Holcombe .25 .08
❑ 335 Mike Jones LB .25 .08
❑ 336 Eddie Kennison .40 .15
❑ 337 Amp Lee .25 .08
❑ 338 Jerald Moore .25 .08
❑ 339 Ricky Proehl .25 .08
❑ 340 J.T. Thomas .25 .08
❑ 341 Derrick Harris/Az-Zahir Hakim .40 .15
❑ 342 Roland Williams/Grant Wistrom .25 .08
❑ 343 Kurt Warner RC/T.Horne ! 12.00 5.00
❑ 344 Terrell Fletcher .25 .08
❑ 345 Greg Jackson .25 .08
❑ 346 Charlie Jones .25 .08
❑ 347 Freddie Jones .25 .08
❑ 348 Ryan Leaf .60 .25
❑ 349 Natrone Means .40 .15
❑ 350 Mikhael Ricks .25 .08

❑ 351 Junior Seau	.60	.25
❑ 352 Bryan Still	.25	.08
❑ 353 T.Stephens/R.Thelwell RC	1.25	.50
❑ 354 Greg Clark	.25	.08
❑ 355 Marc Edwards	.25	.08
❑ 356 Merton Hanks	.25	.08
❑ 357 Garrison Hearst	.40	.15
❑ 358 R.W. McQuarters	.25	.08
❑ 359 Ken Norton Jr.	.25	.08
❑ 360 Terrell Owens	.60	.25
❑ 361 Jerry Rice	1.25	.50
❑ 362 J.J. Stokes	.40	.15
❑ 363 Bryant Young	.25	.08
❑ 364 Steve Young	.75	.30
❑ 365 Chad Brown	.25	.08
❑ 366 Christian Fauria	.25	.08
❑ 367 Joey Galloway	.40	.15
❑ 368 Ahman Green	.60	.25
❑ 369 Cortez Kennedy	.25	.08
❑ 370 Jon Kitna	.60	.25
❑ 371 James McKnight	.40	.15
❑ 372 Mike Pritchard	.25	.08
❑ 373 Michael Sinclair	.25	.08
❑ 374 Shawn Springs	.25	.08
❑ 375 Ricky Watters	.40	.15
❑ 376 Darryl Williams	.25	.08
❑ 377 R.Wilson/K.Joseph RC	1.50	.60
❑ 378 Mike Alstott	.60	.25
❑ 379 Reidel Anthony	.40	.15
❑ 380 Derrick Brooks	.60	.25
❑ 381 Trent Dilfer	.60	.25
❑ 382 Warrick Dunn	.60	.25
❑ 383 Bert Emanuel	.40	.15
❑ 384 Jacquez Green	.25	.08
❑ 385 Patrick Hape	.25	.08
❑ 386 John Lynch	.40	.15
❑ 387 Dave Moore	.25	.08
❑ 388 Hardy Nickerson	.25	.08
❑ 389 Warren Sapp	.40	.15
❑ 390 Karl Williams	.25	.08
❑ 391 Blaine Bishop	.25	.08
❑ 392 Joe Bowden	.25	.08
❑ 393 Isaac Byrd RC	1.00	.40
❑ 394 Willie Davis	.25	.08
❑ 395 Al Del Greco	.25	.08
❑ 396 Kevin Dyson	.40	.15
❑ 397 Eddie George	.60	.25
❑ 398 Jackie Harris	.25	.08
❑ 399 Dave Krieg	.25	.08
❑ 400 Steve McNair	.60	.25
❑ 401 Michael Roan	.25	.08
❑ 402 Yancey Thigpen	.25	.08
❑ 403 Frank Wycheck	.25	.08
❑ 404 Derrick Mason/Steve Matthews	.40	.15
❑ 405 Stephen Alexander	.25	.08
❑ 406 Terry Allen	.40	.15
❑ 407 Jamie Asher	.25	.08
❑ 408 Stephen Davis	.60	.25
❑ 409 Darrell Green	.25	.08
❑ 410 Trent Green	.60	.25
❑ 411 Skip Hicks	.25	.08
❑ 412 Brian Mitchell	.25	.08
❑ 413 Leslie Shepherd	.25	.08
❑ 414 Michael Westbrook	.40	.15
❑ 415 T.Hardy/Rabih Abdullah RC	1.00	.40
❑ 416 C.Thomas RC/M.Quinn RC	1.00	.40
❑ 417 J.Quinn/Kelly Holcomb RC	8.00	3.00
❑ 418 Brian Alford/Blake Spence	1.00	.40
❑ 419 Andy Haase RC/Carlos King	1.00	.40
❑ 420 James Thrash RC/K.Hankton	1.50	.60
❑ 421 F.Beasley/Itula Mili RC	1.25	.50
❑ 422 Champ Bailey RC	2.00	.75
❑ 423 D'Wayne Bates RC	1.25	.50
❑ 424 Michael Bishop RC	1.50	.60
❑ 425 David Boston RC	1.50	.60
❑ 426 Shawn Bryson RC	1.50	.60
❑ 427 Tim Couch RC	1.50	.60
❑ 428 Scott Covington RC	1.50	.60
❑ 429 Daunte Culpepper RC	6.00	2.50
❑ 430 Autry Denson RC	1.25	.50
❑ 431 Troy Edwards RC	1.25	.50
❑ 432 Kevin Faulk RC	1.50	.60
❑ 433 Joe Germaine RC	1.25	.50
❑ 434 Torry Holt RC	4.00	1.50
❑ 435 Brock Huard RC	1.50	.60
❑ 436 Sedrick Irvin RC	1.00	.40
❑ 437 Edgerrin James RC	6.00	2.50
❑ 438 Andy Katzenmoyer RC	1.25	.50
❑ 439 Shaun King RC	1.25	.50
❑ 440 Rob Konrad RC	1.25	.50
❑ 441 Donovan McNabb RC	8.00	3.00
❑ 442 Cade McNown RC	1.25	.50
❑ 443 Billy Miller RC	1.00	.40
❑ 444 Dee Miller RC	1.00	.40
❑ 445 Sirr Parker RC	1.00	.40
❑ 446 Peerless Price RC	1.50	.60
❑ 447 Akili Smith RC	1.25	.50
❑ 448 Tai Streets RC	1.50	.60
❑ 449 Ricky Williams RC	3.00	1.25
❑ 450 Amos Zereoue RC	1.50	.60
❑ S1 Warrick Dunn Sample	.60	.25

2000 Pacific

❑ COMPLETE SET (450)	60.00	25.00
❑ 1 Mario Bates	.25	.08
❑ 2 David Boston	.60	.25
❑ 3 Rob Fredrickson	.25	.08
❑ 4 Terry Hardy	.25	.08
❑ 5 Rob Moore	.40	.15
❑ 6 Adrian Murrell	.40	.15
❑ 7 Michael Pittman	.25	.08
❑ 8 Jake Plummer	.40	.15
❑ 9 Simeon Rice	.40	.15
❑ 10 Frank Sanders	.40	.15
❑ 11 Aeneas Williams	.25	.08
❑ 12 M.Cody/A.McCullough	.25	.08
❑ 13 D.McKinley RC/J.Makovicka	.60	.25
❑ 14 Jamal Anderson	.60	.25
❑ 15 Chris Calloway	.25	.08
❑ 16 Chris Chandler	.40	.15
❑ 17 Bob Christian	.25	.08
❑ 18 Tim Dwight	.60	.25
❑ 19 Jammi German	.25	.08
❑ 20 Ronnie Harris	.25	.08
❑ 21 Terance Mathis	.40	.15
❑ 22 Ken Oxendine	.25	.08
❑ 23 O.J. Santiago	.25	.08
❑ 24 Bob Whitfield	.25	.08
❑ 25 E.Baker/R.Kelly	.25	.08
❑ 26 Justin Armour	.25	.08
❑ 27 Tony Banks	.40	.15
❑ 28 Peter Boulware	.25	.08
❑ 29 Stoney Case	.25	.08
❑ 30 Priest Holmes	.75	.30
❑ 31 Qadry Ismail	.40	.15
❑ 32 Patrick Johnson	.25	.08
❑ 33 Michael McCrary	.25	.08
❑ 34 Jonathan Ogden	.25	.08
❑ 35 Errict Rhett	.40	.15
❑ 36 Duane Starks	.25	.08
❑ 37 Doug Flutie	.60	.25
❑ 38 Rob Johnson	.40	.15
❑ 39 Jonathan Linton	.25	.08
❑ 40 Eric Moulds	.60	.25
❑ 41 Peerless Price	.40	.15
❑ 42 Andre Reed	.40	.15
❑ 43 Jay Riemersma	.25	.08
❑ 44 Antowain Smith	.40	.15
❑ 45 Bruce Smith	.40	.15
❑ 46 Thurman Thomas	.40	.15
❑ 47 Kevin Williams	.25	.08
❑ 48 B.Collins/S.Jackson	.25	.08
❑ 49 Michael Bates	.25	.08
❑ 50 Steve Beuerlein	.40	.15
❑ 51 Tim Biakabutuka	.40	.15
❑ 52 Antonio Edwards	.25	.08
❑ 53 Donald Hayes	.25	.08
❑ 54 Patrick Jeffers	.60	.25
❑ 55 Anthony Johnson	.25	.08
❑ 56 Jeff Lewis	.25	.08
❑ 57 Eric Metcalf	.25	.08
❑ 58 Muhsin Muhammad	.40	.15
❑ 59 Jason Peter	.25	.08
❑ 60 Wesley Walls	.25	.08
❑ 61 John Allred	.25	.08
❑ 62 Marty Booker	.40	.15
❑ 63 Curtis Conway	.40	.15
❑ 64 Bobby Engram	.25	.08
❑ 65 Curtis Enis	.25	.08
❑ 66 Shane Matthews	.40	.15
❑ 67 Cade McNown	.25	.08
❑ 68 Glyn Milburn	.25	.08
❑ 69 Jim Miller	.25	.08
❑ 70 Marcus Robinson	.60	.25
❑ 71 Ryan Wetnight	.25	.08
❑ 72 J.Allen/M.Brooks	.40	.15
❑ 73 Jeff Blake	.40	.15
❑ 74 Corey Dillon	.60	.25
❑ 75 Rodney Heath RC	.40	.15
❑ 76 Willie Jackson	.25	.08
❑ 77 Tremain Mack	.25	.08
❑ 78 Tony McGee	.25	.08
❑ 79 Carl Pickens	.40	.15
❑ 80 Darnay Scott	.40	.15
❑ 81 Akili Smith	.25	.08
❑ 82 Takeo Spikes	.25	.08
❑ 83 Craig Yeast	.25	.08
❑ 84 M.Basnight/N.Williams	.25	.08
❑ 85 Karim Abdul-Jabbar	.40	.15
❑ 86 Darrin Chiaverini	.25	.08
❑ 87 Tim Couch	.40	.15
❑ 88 Marc Edwards	.25	.08
❑ 89 Kevin Johnson	.60	.25
❑ 90 Terry Kirby	.25	.08
❑ 91 Daylon McCutcheon	.25	.08
❑ 92 Jamir Miller	.25	.08
❑ 93 Leslie Shepherd	.25	.08
❑ 94 Irv Smith	.25	.08
❑ 95 M.Campbell/J.Dearth	.25	.08
❑ 96 Z.Davis RC/D.Dunn RC	.40	.15
❑ 97 M.Hill/T.Saleh RC	.25	.08
❑ 98 Troy Aikman	1.25	.50
❑ 99 Eric Bjornson	.25	.08
❑ 100 Dexter Coakley	.25	.08
❑ 101 Greg Ellis	.25	.08
❑ 102 Rocket Ismail	.40	.15
❑ 103 David LaFleur	.25	.08
❑ 104 Ernie Mills	.25	.08
❑ 105 Jeff Ogden	.40	.15
❑ 106 R.Neufeld RC/R.Thomas	.40	.15
❑ 107 Deion Sanders	.60	.25
❑ 108 Emmitt Smith	1.25	.50
❑ 109 Chris Warren	.25	.08
❑ 110 M.Lucky/J.Tucker	.25	.08
❑ 111 Byron Chamberlain	.25	.08
❑ 112 Terrell Davis	.60	.25
❑ 113 Jason Elam	.25	.08
❑ 114 Olandis Gary	.60	.25
❑ 115 Brian Griese	.60	.25
❑ 116 Ed McCaffrey	.60	.25
❑ 117 Trevor Pryce	.25	.08
❑ 118 Bill Romanowski	.25	.08
❑ 119 Shannon Sharpe	.40	.15
❑ 120 Rod Smith	.40	.15
❑ 121 Al Wilson	.25	.08
❑ 122 A.Cooper/C.Watson	.25	.08
❑ 123 Charlie Batch	.60	.25
❑ 124 Stephen Boyd	.25	.08
❑ 125 Chris Claiborne	.25	.08
❑ 126 Germane Crowell	.25	.08
❑ 127 Terry Fair	.25	.08
❑ 128 Gus Frerotte	.25	.08
❑ 129 Jason Hanson	.25	.08
❑ 130 Greg Hill	.25	.08
❑ 131 Herman Moore	.40	.15
❑ 132 Johnnie Morton	.40	.15
❑ 133 Barry Sanders	1.50	.60
❑ 134 David Sloan	.25	.08
❑ 135 B.Olivo/C.Sauter	.25	.08
❑ 136 Corey Bradford	.40	.15
❑ 137 Tyrone Davis	.25	.08
❑ 138 Brett Favre	2.00	.75
❑ 139 Antonio Freeman	.60	.25

❑ 140 Vonnie Holliday .25 .08
❑ 141 Dorsey Levens .40 .15
❑ 142 Keith McKenzie .25 .08
❑ 143 Mike McKenzie .25 .08
❑ 144 Bill Schroeder .40 .15
❑ 145 Jeff Thomason .25 .08
❑ 146 Frank Winters .25 .08
❑ 147 Cornelius Bennett .25 .08
❑ 148 Tony Blevins RC .40 .15
❑ 149 Chad Bratzke .25 .08
❑ 150 Ken Dilger .25 .08
❑ 151 Tarik Glenn .25 .08
❑ 152 E.G. Green .25 .08
❑ 153 Marvin Harrison .60 .25
❑ 154 Edgerrin James 1.00 .40
❑ 155 Peyton Manning 1.50 .60
❑ 156 Jerome Pathon .40 .15
❑ 157 Marcus Pollard .25 .08
❑ 158 Terrence Wilkins .25 .08
❑ 159 I.Jones RC/P.Shields RC .60 .25
❑ 160 Reggie Barlow .25 .08
❑ 161 Aaron Beasley .25 .08
❑ 162 Tony Boselli .25 .08
❑ 163 Tony Brackens .25 .08
❑ 164 Kyle Brady .25 .08
❑ 165 Mark Brunell .60 .25
❑ 166 Jay Fiedler .60 .25
❑ 167 Kevin Hardy .25 .08
❑ 168 Carnell Lake .25 .08
❑ 169 Keenan McCardell .40 .15
❑ 170 Jonathan Quinn .25 .08
❑ 171 Jimmy Smith .40 .15
❑ 172 James Stewart .40 .15
❑ 173 Fred Taylor .60 .25
❑ 174 L.Jackson RC/S.Mack .60 .25
❑ 175 Derrick Alexander .40 .15
❑ 176 Donnell Bennett .25 .08
❑ 177 Donnie Edwards .25 .08
❑ 178 Tony Gonzalez .40 .15
❑ 179 Elvis Grbac .40 .15
❑ 180 James Hasty .25 .08
❑ 181 Joe Horn .40 .15
❑ 182 Lonnie Johnson .25 .08
❑ 183 Kevin Lockett .25 .08
❑ 184 Larry Parker .25 .08
❑ 185 Tony Richardson RC .40 .15
❑ 186 Rashaan Shehee .25 .08
❑ 187 Tamarick Vanover .25 .08
❑ 188 Trace Armstrong .25 .08
❑ 189 Oronde Gadsden .40 .15
❑ 190 Damon Huard .60 .25
❑ 191 Nate Jacquet .25 .08
❑ 192 James Johnson .25 .08
❑ 193 Rob Konrad .25 .08
❑ 194 Sam Madison .25 .08
❑ 195 Dan Marino 2.00 .75
❑ 196 Tony Martin .40 .15
❑ 197 O.J. McDuffie .40 .15
❑ 198 Stanley Pritchett .25 .08
❑ 199 Tim Ruddy .25 .08
❑ 200 Patrick Surtain .25 .08
❑ 201 Zach Thomas .60 .25
❑ 202 Cris Carter .60 .25
❑ 203 Duane Clemons .25 .08
❑ 204 Carlester Crumpler .25 .08
❑ 205 Daunte Culpepper .75 .30
❑ 206 Jeff George .40 .15
❑ 207 Matthew Hatchette .25 .08
❑ 208 Leroy Hoard .25 .08
❑ 209 Randy Moss 1.25 .50
❑ 210 John Randle .40 .15
❑ 211 Jake Reed .40 .15
❑ 212 Robert Smith .60 .25
❑ 213 Robert Tate .25 .08
❑ 214 Terry Allen .40 .15
❑ 215 Bruce Armstrong .25 .08
❑ 216 Drew Bledsoe .75 .30
❑ 217 Ben Coates .25 .08
❑ 218 Kevin Faulk .40 .15
❑ 219 Terry Glenn .40 .15
❑ 220 Shawn Jefferson .25 .08
❑ 221 Andy Katzenmoyer .25 .08
❑ 222 Ty Law .40 .15
❑ 223 Willie McGinest .25 .08
❑ 224 Lawyer Milloy .40 .15
❑ 225 Tony Simmons .25 .08
❑ 226 M.Bishop/S.Morey RC .40 .15
❑ 227 Cameron Cleeland .25 .08
❑ 228 Troy Davis .25 .08
❑ 229 Jake Delhomme RC 3.00 1.25
❑ 230 Andre Hastings .25 .08
❑ 231 Eddie Kennison .40 .15
❑ 232 Wilmont Perry .25 .08
❑ 233 Dino Philyaw .25 .08
❑ 234 Keith Poole .25 .08
❑ 235 William Roaf .25 .08
❑ 236 Billy Joe Tolliver .25 .08
❑ 237 Fred Weary .25 .08
❑ 238 Ricky Williams .60 .25
❑ 239 Franklin RC/M.Powell RC .60 .25
❑ 240 Jessie Armstead .25 .08
❑ 241 Tiki Barber .60 .25
❑ 242 Daniel Campbell .25 .08
❑ 243 Kerry Collins .40 .15
❑ 244 Percy Ellsworth .25 .08
❑ 245 Kent Graham .25 .08
❑ 246 Ike Hilliard .40 .15
❑ 247 Cedric Jones .25 .08
❑ 248 Bashir Levingston RC .60 .25
❑ 249 Pete Mitchell .25 .08
❑ 250 Michael Strahan .40 .15
❑ 251 Amani Toomer .25 .08
❑ 252 Charles Way .25 .08
❑ 253 Andre Weathers RC .40 .15
❑ 254 Richie Anderson .40 .15
❑ 255 Wayne Chrebet .40 .15
❑ 256 Marcus Coleman .25 .08
❑ 257 Bryan Cox .25 .08
❑ 258 Jason Fabini RC .40 .15
❑ 259 Robert Farmer RC .60 .25
❑ 260 Keyshawn Johnson .60 .25
❑ 261 Ray Lucas .40 .15
❑ 262 Curtis Martin .60 .25
❑ 263 Kevin Mawae .25 .08
❑ 264 Eric Ogbogu .25 .08
❑ 265 Bernie Parmalee .25 .08
❑ 266 Vinny Testaverde .40 .15
❑ 267 Dedric Ward .25 .08
❑ 268 Eric Barton RC .40 .15
❑ 269 Tim Brown .60 .25
❑ 270 Tony Bryant .25 .08
❑ 271 Rickey Dudley .25 .08
❑ 272 Rich Gannon .60 .25
❑ 273 Bobby Hoying .40 .15
❑ 274 James Jett .25 .08
❑ 275 Napoleon Kaufman .40 .15
❑ 276 Jon Ritchie .25 .08
❑ 277 Darrell Russell .25 .08
❑ 278 Kenny Shedd .25 .08
❑ 279 Marquis Walker RC .40 .15
❑ 280 Tyrone Wheatley .40 .15
❑ 281 Charles Woodson .40 .15
❑ 282 Luther Broughton RC .40 .15
❑ 283 Al Harris RC .25 .08
❑ 284 Greg Jefferson .25 .08
❑ 285 Dietrich Jells .25 .08
❑ 286 Charles Johnson .40 .15
❑ 287 Chad Lewis .25 .08
❑ 288 Mike Mamula .25 .08
❑ 289 Donovan McNabb 1.00 .40
❑ 290 Doug Pederson .25 .08
❑ 291 Allen Rossum .25 .08
❑ 292 Torrance Small .25 .08
❑ 293 Duce Staley .60 .25
❑ 294 Jerome Bettis .60 .25
❑ 295 Kris Brown .25 .08
❑ 296 Mark Bruener .25 .08
❑ 297 Troy Edwards .25 .08
❑ 298 Jason Gildon .25 .08
❑ 299 Richard Huntley .25 .08
❑ 300 Bobby Shaw RC .60 .25
❑ 301 Scott Shields RC .40 .15
❑ 302 Kordell Stewart .40 .15
❑ 303 Hines Ward .60 .25
❑ 304 Amos Zereoue .60 .25
❑ 305 M.Cushing RC/J.Tuman .40 .15
❑ 306 P.Gonzalez/A.Wright RC 2.00 .75
❑ 307 Isaac Bruce .60 .25
❑ 308 Kevin Carter .25 .08
❑ 309 Marshall Faulk .75 .30
❑ 310 London Fletcher RC .40 .15
❑ 311 Joe Germaine .25 .08
❑ 312 Az-Zahir Hakim .40 .15
❑ 313 Torry Holt .60 .25
❑ 314 Tony Horne .25 .08
❑ 315 Mike Jones LB .25 .08
❑ 316 Dexter McCleon RC .60 .25
❑ 317 Orlando Pace .25 .08
❑ 318 Ricky Proehl .25 .08
❑ 319 Kurt Warner 1.25 .50
❑ 320 Roland Williams .25 .08
❑ 321 Grant Wistrom .25 .08
❑ 322 J.Hodgins RC/J.Watson .25 .08
❑ 323 Jermaine Fazande .25 .08
❑ 324 Jeff Graham .25 .08
❑ 325 Jim Harbaugh .40 .15
❑ 326 Raylee Johnson .25 .08
❑ 327 Charlie Jones .25 .08
❑ 328 Freddie Jones .25 .08
❑ 329 Natrone Means .25 .08
❑ 330 Chris Penn .25 .08
❑ 331 Mikhael Ricks .25 .08
❑ 332 Junior Seau .60 .25
❑ 333 R.Davis RC/R.Reed RC .40 .15
❑ 334 Fred Beasley .25 .08
❑ 335 Brentson Buckner .25 .08
❑ 336 Greg Clark .25 .08
❑ 337 Dave Fiore RC .25 .08
❑ 338 Charlie Garner .40 .15
❑ 339 Mark Harris RC .60 .25
❑ 340 Ramos McDonald RC .40 .15
❑ 341 Terrell Owens .60 .25
❑ 342 Jerry Rice 1.25 .50
❑ 343 Lance Schulters .25 .08
❑ 344 J.J. Stokes .40 .15
❑ 345 Bryant Young .25 .08
❑ 346 Steve Young .75 .30
❑ 347 Jeff Garcia .60 .25
❑ 348 Fabien Bownes RC .25 .08
❑ 349 Chad Brown .25 .08
❑ 350 Reggie Brown .25 .08
❑ 351 Sean Dawkins .25 .08
❑ 352 Christian Fauria .25 .08
❑ 353 Ahman Green .60 .25
❑ 354 Walter Jones .25 .08
❑ 355 Cortez Kennedy .25 .08
❑ 356 Jon Kitna .60 .25
❑ 357 Derrick Mayes .40 .15
❑ 358 Charlie Rogers .25 .08
❑ 359 Shawn Springs .25 .08
❑ 360 Ricky Watters .40 .15
❑ 361 Donne Abraham .25 .08
❑ 362 Mike Alstott .60 .25
❑ 363 Reidel Anthony .25 .08
❑ 364 Ronde Barber .25 .08
❑ 365 Derrick Brooks .60 .25
❑ 366 Warrick Dunn .60 .25
❑ 367 Jacquez Green .25 .08
❑ 368 Marcus Jones .25 .08
❑ 369 Shaun King .25 .08
❑ 370 John Lynch .40 .15
❑ 371 Warren Sapp .40 .15
❑ 372 Steve White RC .25 .08
❑ 373 M.Gramatica/K.McLeod RC .40 .15
❑ 374 Blaine Bishop .25 .08
❑ 375 Al Del Greco .25 .08
❑ 376 Kevin Dyson .40 .15
❑ 377 Eddie George .60 .25
❑ 378 Jevon Kearse .60 .25
❑ 379 Derrick Mason .40 .15
❑ 380 Bruce Matthews .25 .08
❑ 381 Steve McNair .60 .25
❑ 382 Neil O'Donnell .25 .08
❑ 383 Yancey Thigpen .25 .08
❑ 384 Frank Wycheck .25 .08
❑ 385 K.Daft/L.Brown .25 .08
❑ 386 Stephen Alexander .25 .08
❑ 387 Champ Bailey .40 .15
❑ 388 Larry Centers .25 .08
❑ 389 Marco Coleman .25 .08
❑ 390 Albert Connell .25 .08
❑ 391 Stephen Davis .60 .25
❑ 392 Irving Fryar .40 .15
❑ 393 Skip Hicks .25 .08
❑ 394 Brad Johnson .60 .25
❑ 395 Michael Westbrook .40 .15
❑ 396 O.Ayanbadejo RC/L.Gordon RC .40 .15
❑ 397 D.Driver/R.Powell .60 .25
❑ 398 T.Bouman/J.Brigham RC .60 .25
❑ 399 B.Huard/S.Bonner .25 .08

❑ 400	M.Sellers/S.George RC	.40	.15
❑ 401	Shaun Alexander RC	6.00	2.50
❑ 402	LaVar Arrington RC	6.00	2.50
❑ 403	Tom Brady RC	25.00	10.00
❑ 404	Demario Brown RC	.60	.25
❑ 405	Plaxico Burress RC	2.50	1.00
❑ 406	Trung Canidate RC	1.00	.40
❑ 407	Giovanni Carmazzi RC	.60	.25
❑ 408	Kwame Cavil RC	.60	.25
❑ 409	Chrys Chukwuma RC	1.25	.50
❑ 410	Ron Dayne RC	1.25	.50
❑ 411	Reuben Droughns RC	1.50	.60
❑ 412	Ron Dugans RC	.60	.25
❑ 413	Deon Dyer RC	1.00	.40
❑ 414	Danny Farmer RC	1.00	.40
❑ 415	Chafie Fields RC	.60	.25
❑ 416	Trevor Gaylor RC	1.00	.40
❑ 417	Sherrod Gideon RC	.60	.25
❑ 418	Joey Goodspeed RC	.60	.25
❑ 419	Joe Hamilton RC	1.00	.40
❑ 420	Tony Hartley RC	.60	.25
❑ 421	Todd Husak RC	1.25	.50
❑ 422	Trevor Insley RC	.60	.25
❑ 423	Thomas Jones RC	2.00	.75
❑ 424	Marcus Knight RC	1.00	.40
❑ 425	Jamal Lewis RC	3.00	1.25
❑ 426	Anthony Lucas RC	1.50	.60
❑ 427	Tee Martin RC	1.25	.50
❑ 428	Rondell Mealey RC	.60	.25
❑ 429	Sylvester Morris RC	1.00	.40
❑ 430	Chad Morton RC	1.25	.50
❑ 431	Dennis Northcutt RC	1.25	.50
❑ 432	Chad Pennington RC	3.00	1.25
❑ 433	Rodnick Phillips RC	.60	.25
❑ 434	Mareno Philyaw RC	.60	.25
❑ 435	Jerry Porter RC	1.50	.60
❑ 436	Travis Prentice RC	1.00	.40
❑ 437	Tim Rattay RC	1.25	.50
❑ 438	Chris Redman RC	1.00	.40
❑ 439	J.R. Redmond RC	1.00	.40
❑ 440	Gari Scott RC	.60	.25
❑ 441	Keith Smith RC	.60	.25
❑ 442	Terrelle Smith RC	1.00	.40
❑ 443	R.Jay Soward RC	1.00	.40
❑ 444	Quinton Spotwood RC	.60	.25
❑ 445	Shyrone Stith RC	1.00	.40
❑ 446	Travis Taylor RC	1.25	.50
❑ 447	Troy Walters RC	1.25	.50
❑ 448	Peter Warrick RC	1.25	.50
❑ 449	Dez White RC	1.25	.50
❑ 450	Michael Wiley RC	1.00	.40

2001 Pacific

❑	COMP.SET w/o SP's (450)	50.00	25.00
❑ 1	David Boston	.60	.25
❑ 2	Mac Cody	.25	.08
❑ 3	Chris Gedney	.25	.08
❑ 4	Chris Greisen	.25	.08
❑ 5	Terry Hardy	.25	.08
❑ 6	MarTay Jenkins	.25	.08
❑ 7	Thomas Jones	.60	.25
❑ 8	Joel Makovicka	.25	.08
❑ 9	Tywan Mitchell	.25	.08
❑ 10	Rob Moore	.40	.15
❑ 11	Michael Pittman	.25	.08
❑ 12	Jake Plummer	.40	.15
❑ 13	Frank Sanders	.25	.08
❑ 14	Aeneas Williams	.25	.08
❑ 15	Jamal Anderson	.60	.25
❑ 16	Eugene Baker	.25	.08
❑ 17	Chris Chandler	.40	.15
❑ 18	Tim Dwight	.60	.25
❑ 19	Brian Finneran	.25	.08
❑ 20	Jammi German	.25	.08
❑ 21	Shawn Jefferson	.25	.08
❑ 22	Doug Johnson	.25	.08
❑ 23	Danny Kanell	.25	.08
❑ 24	Reggie Kelly	.25	.08
❑ 25	Terance Mathis	.40	.15
❑ 26	Derek Rackley	.25	.08
❑ 27	Ron Rivers	.25	.08
❑ 28	Maurice Smith	.40	.15
❑ 29	Sam Adams	.25	.08
❑ 30	Obafemi Ayanbadejo	.25	.08
❑ 31	Tony Banks	.40	.15
❑ 32	Trent Dilfer	.40	.15
❑ 33	Sam Gash	.25	.08
❑ 34	Priest Holmes	.75	.30
❑ 35	Qadry Ismail	.40	.15
❑ 36	Pat Johnson	.25	.08
❑ 37	Jamal Lewis	1.00	.40
❑ 38	Jermaine Lewis	.25	.08
❑ 39	Ray Lewis	.60	.25
❑ 40	Chris Redman	.25	.08
❑ 41	Shannon Sharpe	.40	.15
❑ 42	Brandon Stokley	.40	.15
❑ 43	Travis Taylor	.40	.15
❑ 44	Shawn Bryson	.25	.08
❑ 45	Kwame Cavil	.25	.08
❑ 46	Sam Cowart	.25	.08
❑ 47	Doug Flutie	.60	.25
❑ 48	Rob Johnson	.40	.15
❑ 49	Jonathan Linton	.25	.08
❑ 50	Jeremy McDaniel	.25	.08
❑ 51	Sammy Morris	.25	.08
❑ 52	Eric Moulds	.60	.25
❑ 53	Peerless Price	.40	.15
❑ 54	Jay Riemersma	.25	.08
❑ 55	Antowain Smith	.40	.15
❑ 56	Chris Watson	.25	.08
❑ 57	Marcellus Wiley	.25	.08
❑ 58	Michael Bates	.25	.08
❑ 59	Steve Beuerlein	.40	.15
❑ 60	Tim Biakabutuka	.40	.15
❑ 61	Isaac Byrd	.25	.08
❑ 62	Dameyune Craig	.25	.08
❑ 63	William Floyd	.25	.08
❑ 64	Karl Hankton	.25	.08
❑ 65	Donald Hayes	.25	.08
❑ 66	Chris Hetherington RC	.40	.15
❑ 67	Brad Hoover	.25	.08
❑ 68	Patrick Jeffers	.60	.25
❑ 69	Muhsin Muhammad	.40	.15
❑ 70	Iheanyi Uwaezuoke	.25	.08
❑ 71	Wesley Walls	.25	.08
❑ 72	James Allen	.40	.15
❑ 73	Marlon Barnes	.25	.08
❑ 74	D'Wayne Bates	.25	.08
❑ 75	Marty Booker	.25	.08
❑ 76	Macey Brooks	.25	.08
❑ 77	Bobby Engram	.40	.15
❑ 78	Curtis Enis	.25	.08
❑ 79	Mark Hartsell RC	.40	.15
❑ 80	Eddie Kennison	.25	.08
❑ 81	Shane Matthews	.25	.08
❑ 82	Cade McNown	.25	.08
❑ 83	Jim Miller	.25	.08
❑ 84	Marcus Robinson	.60	.25
❑ 85	Brian Urlacher	1.00	.40
❑ 86	Dez White	.25	.08
❑ 87	Brandon Bennett	.25	.08
❑ 88	Steve Bush RC	.40	.15
❑ 89	Corey Dillon	.60	.25
❑ 90	Ron Dugans	.25	.08
❑ 91	Danny Farmer	.25	.08
❑ 92	Damon Griffin	.25	.08
❑ 93	Clif Groce	.40	.15
❑ 94	Curtis Keaton	.25	.08
❑ 95	Scott Mitchell	.25	.08
❑ 96	Darnay Scott	.40	.15
❑ 97	Akili Smith	.25	.08
❑ 98	Peter Warrick	.60	.25
❑ 99	Nick Williams	.25	.08
❑ 100	Craig Yeast	.25	.08
❑ 101	Bobby Brown	.25	.08
❑ 102	Darrin Chiaverini	.25	.08
❑ 103	Tim Couch	.40	.15
❑ 104	JaJuan Dawson	.25	.08
❑ 105	Marc Edwards	.25	.08
❑ 106	Kevin Johnson	.40	.15
❑ 107	Dennis Northcutt	.40	.15
❑ 108	David Patten	.25	.08
❑ 109	Doug Pederson	.25	.08
❑ 110	Travis Prentice	.25	.08
❑ 111	Errict Rhett	.25	.08
❑ 112	Aaron Shea	.25	.08
❑ 113	Kevin Thompson	.25	.08
❑ 114	Jamel White	.25	.08
❑ 115	Spergon Wynn	.25	.08
❑ 116	Troy Aikman	1.00	.40
❑ 117	Chris Brazzell	.25	.08
❑ 118	Randall Cunningham	.60	.25
❑ 119	Jackie Harris	.25	.08
❑ 120	Damon Hodge	.25	.08
❑ 121	Rocket Ismail	.40	.15
❑ 122	David LaFleur	.25	.08
❑ 123	Wane McGarity	.25	.08
❑ 124	James McKnight	.40	.15
❑ 125	Emmitt Smith	1.25	.50
❑ 126	Clint Stoerner	.25	.08
❑ 127	Jason Tucker	.25	.08
❑ 128	Michael Wiley	.25	.08
❑ 129	Anthony Wright	.25	.08
❑ 130	Mike Anderson	.60	.25
❑ 131	Dwayne Carswell	.25	.08
❑ 132	Byron Chamberlain	.25	.08
❑ 133	Desmond Clark	.25	.08
❑ 134	Chris Cole	.25	.08
❑ 135	KaRon Coleman	.25	.08
❑ 136	Terrell Davis	.60	.25
❑ 137	Gus Frerotte	.40	.15
❑ 138	Olandis Gary	.60	.25
❑ 139	Brian Griese	.60	.25
❑ 140	Howard Griffith	.25	.08
❑ 141	Jarious Jackson	.40	.15
❑ 142	Ed McCaffrey	.60	.25
❑ 143	Scottie Montgomery RC	.40	.15
❑ 144	Rod Smith	.40	.15
❑ 145	Charlie Batch	.60	.25
❑ 146	Stoney Case	.25	.08
❑ 147	Germane Crowell	.25	.08
❑ 148	Larry Foster	.25	.08
❑ 149	Desmond Howard	.25	.08
❑ 150	Sedrick Irvin	.25	.08
❑ 151	Herman Moore	.40	.15
❑ 152	Johnnie Morton	.40	.15
❑ 153	Robert Porcher	.25	.08
❑ 154	Cory Sauter	.25	.08
❑ 155	Cory Schlesinger	.25	.08
❑ 156	David Sloan	.25	.08
❑ 157	Brian Stablein	.25	.08
❑ 158	James Stewart	.40	.15
❑ 159	Corey Bradford	.25	.08
❑ 160	Tyrone Davis	.25	.08
❑ 161	Donald Driver	.40	.15
❑ 162	Brett Favre	2.00	.75
❑ 163	Bubba Franks	.40	.15
❑ 164	Antonio Freeman	.60	.25
❑ 165	Herbert Goodman	.25	.08
❑ 166	Ahman Green	.60	.25
❑ 167	Matt Hasselbeck	.40	.15
❑ 168	William Henderson	.25	.08
❑ 169	Charles Lee	.25	.08
❑ 170	Dorsey Levens	.40	.15
❑ 171	Bill Schroeder	.40	.15
❑ 172	Darren Sharper	.25	.08
❑ 173	Matt Snider	.25	.08
❑ 174	Danny Wuerffel	.25	.08
❑ 175	Ken Dilger	.25	.08
❑ 176	Jim Finn	.25	.08
❑ 177	Lennox Gordon	.25	.08
❑ 178	E.G. Green	.25	.08
❑ 179	Marvin Harrison	.60	.25
❑ 180	Kelly Holcomb	.60	.25
❑ 181	Trevor Insley	.25	.08
❑ 182	Edgerrin James	.75	.30
❑ 183	Peyton Manning	1.50	.60
❑ 184	Kevin McDougal	.25	.08
❑ 185	Jerome Pathon	.40	.15
❑ 186	Marcus Pollard	.25	.08
❑ 187	Justin Snow	.25	.08
❑ 188	Terrence Wilkins	.25	.08
❑ 189	Reggie Barlow	.25	.08

❑	190	Kyle Brady	.25	.08
❑	191	Mark Brunell	.60	.25
❑	192	Kevin Hardy	.25	.08
❑	193	Anthony Johnson	.25	.08
❑	194	Stacey Mack	.25	.08
❑	195	Jamie Martin	.40	.15
❑	196	Keenan McCardell	.25	.08
❑	197	Daimon Shelton	.25	.08
❑	198	Jimmy Smith	.40	.15
❑	199	R.Jay Soward	.25	.08
❑	200	Shyrone Stith	.25	.08
❑	201	Fred Taylor	.60	.25
❑	202	Alvis Whitted	.25	.08
❑	203	Jermaine Williams	.25	.08
❑	204	Derrick Alexander	.40	.15
❑	205	Kimble Anders	.25	.08
❑	206	Donnell Bennett	.25	.08
❑	207	Mike Cloud	.25	.08
❑	208	Todd Collins	.25	.08
❑	209	Tony Gonzalez	.40	.15
❑	210	Elvis Grbac	.40	.15
❑	211	Dante Hall	.60	.25
❑	212	Kevin Lockett	.25	.08
❑	213	Warren Moon	.40	.15
❑	214	Frank Moreau	.25	.08
❑	215	Sylvester Morris	.25	.08
❑	216	Larry Parker	.25	.08
❑	217	Tony Richardson	.25	.08
❑	218	Trace Armstrong	.25	.08
❑	219	Autry Denson	.25	.08
❑	220	Bert Emanuel	.25	.08
❑	221	Jay Fiedler	.60	.25
❑	222	Oronde Gadsden	.40	.15
❑	223	Damon Huard	.60	.25
❑	224	James Johnson	.25	.08
❑	225	Rob Konrad	.25	.08
❑	226	Tony Martin	.25	.08
❑	227	O.J. McDuffie	.25	.08
❑	228	Mike Quinn	.25	.08
❑	229	Lamar Smith	.25	.08
❑	230	Jason Taylor	.25	.08
❑	231	Thurman Thomas	.40	.15
❑	232	Zach Thomas	.60	.25
❑	233	Todd Bouman	.40	.15
❑	234	Bubby Brister	.25	.08
❑	235	Cris Carter	.60	.25
❑	236	Daunte Culpepper	.60	.25
❑	237	John Davis RC	.40	.15
❑	238	Robert Griffith	.25	.08
❑	239	Matthew Hatchette	.25	.08
❑	240	Jim Kleinsasser	.25	.08
❑	241	Randy Moss	1.25	.50
❑	242	John Randle	.25	.08
❑	243	Robert Smith	.60	.25
❑	244	Chris Walsh RC	.25	.08
❑	245	Troy Walters	.25	.08
❑	246	Moe Williams	.40	.15
❑	247	Michael Bishop	.25	.08
❑	248	Drew Bledsoe	.75	.30
❑	249	Troy Brown	.40	.15
❑	250	Tedy Bruschi	.50	.20
❑	251	Tony Carter	.25	.08
❑	252	Shockmain Davis	.25	.08
❑	253	Kevin Faulk	.40	.15
❑	254	Terry Glenn	.40	.15
❑	255	Ty Law	.40	.15
❑	256	Lawyer Milloy	.40	.15
❑	257	J.R. Redmond	.25	.08
❑	258	Harold Shaw	.25	.08
❑	259	Tony Simmons	.25	.08
❑	260	Jermaine Wiggins	.40	.15
❑	261	Jeff Blake	.25	.08
❑	262	Aaron Brooks	.60	.25
❑	263	Cam Cleeland	.25	.08
❑	264	Andrew Glover	.25	.08
❑	265	La'Roi Glover	.25	.08
❑	266	Joe Horn	.40	.15
❑	267	Kevin Houser	.25	.08
❑	268	Willie Jackson	.25	.08
❑	269	Jerald Moore	.25	.08
❑	270	Chad Morton	.25	.08
❑	271	Keith Poole	.25	.08
❑	272	Terrelle Smith	.25	.08
❑	273	Ricky Williams	.60	.25
❑	274	Robert Wilson	.25	.08
❑	275	Jessie Armstead	.25	.08
❑	276	Tiki Barber	.60	.25
❑	277	Mike Cherry	.25	.08
❑	278	Kerry Collins	.40	.15
❑	279	Greg Comella	.25	.08
❑	280	Thabiti Davis	.25	.08
❑	281	Ron Dayne	.60	.25
❑	282	Ron Dixon	.25	.08
❑	283	Ike Hilliard	.25	.08
❑	284	Joe Jurevicius	.25	.08
❑	285	Jason Sehorn	.25	.08
❑	286	Michael Strahan	.40	.15
❑	287	Amani Toomer	.25	.08
❑	288	Craig Walendy	.25	.08
❑	289	Damon Washington RC	.40	.15
❑	290	Richie Anderson	.25	.08
❑	291	Anthony Becht	.25	.08
❑	292	Wayne Chrebet	.40	.15
❑	293	Laveranues Coles	.60	.25
❑	294	Bryan Cox	.25	.08
❑	295	Marvin Jones	.25	.08
❑	296	Mo Lewis	.25	.08
❑	297	Ray Lucas	.25	.08
❑	298	Curtis Martin	.60	.25
❑	299	Bernie Parmalee	.25	.08
❑	300	Chad Pennington	1.00	.40
❑	301	Jerald Sowell	.25	.08
❑	302	Dwight Stone	.25	.08
❑	303	Vinny Testaverde	.40	.15
❑	304	Dedric Ward	.25	.08
❑	305	Tim Brown	.60	.25
❑	306	Zack Crockett	.25	.08
❑	307	Scott Dreisbach	.25	.08
❑	308	Rickey Dudley	.25	.08
❑	309	David Dunn	.25	.08
❑	310	Mondriel Fulcher	.25	.08
❑	311	Rich Gannon	.60	.25
❑	312	James Jett	.25	.08
❑	313	Randy Jordan	.25	.08
❑	314	Napoleon Kaufman	.40	.15
❑	315	Rodney Peete	.25	.08
❑	316	Jerry Porter	.40	.15
❑	317	Andre Rison	.40	.15
❑	318	Tyrone Wheatley	.25	.08
❑	319	Charles Woodson	.25	.08
❑	320	Darnell Autry	.25	.08
❑	321	Na Brown	.25	.08
❑	322	Hugh Douglas	.25	.08
❑	323	Charles Johnson	.25	.08
❑	324	Chad Lewis	.25	.08
❑	325	Cecil Martin	.25	.08
❑	326	Donovan McNabb	.75	.30
❑	327	Brian Mitchell	.25	.08
❑	328	Todd Pinkston	.25	.08
❑	329	Ron Powlus	.25	.08
❑	330	Stanley Pritchett	.25	.08
❑	331	Torrance Small	.25	.08
❑	332	Duce Staley	.60	.25
❑	333	Troy Vincent	.25	.08
❑	334	Chris Warren	.25	.08
❑	335	Jerome Bettis	.60	.25
❑	336	Plaxico Burress	.60	.25
❑	337	Troy Edwards	.25	.08
❑	338	Chris Fuamatu-Ma'afala	.25	.08
❑	339	Cory Geason	.25	.08
❑	340	Kent Graham	.25	.08
❑	341	Courtney Hawkins	.25	.08
❑	342	Richard Huntley	.25	.08
❑	343	Tee Martin	.40	.15
❑	344	Bobby Shaw	.25	.08
❑	345	Kordell Stewart	.40	.15
❑	346	Hines Ward	.60	.25
❑	347	Destry Wright RC	.40	.15
❑	348	Amos Zereoue	.60	.25
❑	349	Isaac Bruce	.60	.25
❑	350	Trung Canidate	.40	.15
❑	351	Marshall Faulk	.75	.30
❑	352	London Fletcher	.25	.08
❑	353	Joe Germaine	.25	.08
❑	354	Trent Green	.60	.25
❑	355	Az-Zahir Hakim	.25	.08
❑	356	James Hodgins	.25	.08
❑	357	Robert Holcombe	.25	.08
❑	358	Torry Holt	.60	.25
❑	359	Tony Horne	.25	.08
❑	360	Ricky Proehl	.25	.08
❑	361	Chris Thomas RC	.40	.15
❑	362	Kurt Warner	1.25	.50
❑	363	Justin Watson	.25	.08
❑	364	Kenny Bynum	.25	.08
❑	365	Robert Chancey	.25	.08
❑	366	Curtis Conway	.40	.15
❑	367	Jermaine Fazande	.25	.08
❑	368	Terrell Fletcher	.25	.08
❑	369	Trevor Gaylor	.25	.08
❑	370	Jeff Graham	.25	.08
❑	371	Jim Harbaugh	.40	.15
❑	372	Rodney Harrison	.25	.08
❑	373	Ronney Jenkins	.25	.08
❑	374	Freddie Jones	.25	.08
❑	375	Reggie Jones	.25	.08
❑	376	Ryan Leaf	.40	.15
❑	377	Junior Seau	.60	.25
❑	378	Fred Beasley	.25	.08
❑	379	Greg Clark	.25	.08
❑	380	Jeff Garcia	.60	.25
❑	381	Charlie Garner	.40	.15
❑	382	Terry Jackson	.25	.08
❑	383	Brian Jennings	.25	.08
❑	384	Travis Jervey	.25	.08
❑	385	Jonas Lewis	.25	.08
❑	386	Terrell Owens	.60	.25
❑	387	Jerry Rice	1.25	.50
❑	388	Paul Smith	.25	.08
❑	389	J.J. Stokes	.40	.15
❑	390	Tai Streets	.25	.08
❑	391	Justin Swift	.25	.08
❑	392	Shaun Alexander	.75	.30
❑	393	Karsten Bailey	.25	.08
❑	394	Chad Brown	.25	.08
❑	395	Sean Dawkins	.25	.08
❑	396	Christian Fauria	.25	.08
❑	397	Brock Huard	.25	.08
❑	398	Darrell Jackson	.25	.08
❑	399	Jon Kitna	.60	.25
❑	400	Derrick Mayes	.25	.08
❑	401	Itula Mili	.25	.08
❑	402	Charlie Rogers	.25	.08
❑	403	Mack Strong	.40	.15
❑	404	Ricky Watters	.25	.08
❑	405	James Williams WR	.25	.08
❑	406	Rabih Abdullah	.25	.08
❑	407	Mike Alstott	.60	.25
❑	408	Reidel Anthony	.25	.08
❑	409	Derrick Brooks	.60	.25
❑	410	Warrick Dunn	.60	.25
❑	411	Jacquez Green	.25	.08
❑	412	Joe Hamilton	.25	.08
❑	413	Keyshawn Johnson	.60	.25
❑	414	Shaun King	.25	.08
❑	415	Charles Kirby RC	.60	.25
❑	416	Warren Sapp	.40	.15
❑	417	Aaron Stecker	.25	.08
❑	418	Todd Yoder	.25	.08
❑	419	Eric Zeier	.25	.08
❑	420	Chris Coleman	.25	.08
❑	421	Kevin Dyson	.40	.15
❑	422	Eddie George	.60	.25
❑	423	Jevon Kearse	.40	.15
❑	424	Erron Kinney	.25	.08
❑	425	Mike Leach	.25	.08
❑	426	Derrick Mason	.40	.15
❑	427	Steve McNair	.60	.25
❑	428	Lorenzo Neal	.25	.08
❑	429	Carl Pickens	.40	.15
❑	430	Chris Sanders	.25	.08
❑	431	Yancey Thigpen	.25	.08
❑	432	Rodney Thomas	.25	.08
❑	433	Frank Wycheck	.25	.08
❑	434	Stephen Alexander	.25	.08
❑	435	Champ Bailey	.40	.15
❑	436	Larry Centers	.25	.08
❑	437	Albert Connell	.25	.08
❑	438	Stephen Davis	.60	.25
❑	439	Zeron Flemister RC	.40	.15
❑	440	Irving Fryar	.40	.15
❑	441	Jeff George	.40	.15
❑	442	Skip Hicks	.25	.08
❑	443	Todd Husak	.25	.08
❑	444	Brad Johnson	.40	.15
❑	445	Adrian Murrell	.25	.08
❑	446	Deion Sanders	.60	.25
❑	447	Mike Sellers	.25	.08
❑	448	Derrius Thompson	.25	.08
❑	449	James Thrash	.40	.15
❑	450	Michael Westbrook	.25	.08

❑ 451 Alex Bannister AU/1750 RC 8.00 3.00
❑ 452 Kevan Barlow AU/1500 RC 15.00 6.00
❑ 453 Drew Brees AU/1000 RC 50.00 25.00
❑ 454 Travis Henry AU/1500 RC 20.00 10.00
❑ 455 Chad Johnson AU/1750 RC 30.00 12.50
❑ 456 M.McMahon AU/1000 RC 10.00 4.00
❑ 457 B.Newcombe AU/1750 RC 10.00 4.00
❑ 458 Sage Rosenfels AU/1000 RC 20.00 7.50
❑ 459 LaDain Tomlinson AU/1500 RC 150.00 75.00
❑ 460 Chris Weinke AU/1000 RC 12.00 5.00
❑ 461 Tay Cody RC 2.00 .75
❑ 462 Adam Archuleta RC 5.00 2.00
❑ 463 Will Allen RC 2.50 1.00
❑ 464 Moran Norris RC 2.00 .75
❑ 465 Tommy Polley RC 5.00 2.00
❑ 466 Ennis Davis RC 2.00 .75
❑ 467 Jamar Fletcher RC 2.50 1.00
❑ 468 Derrick Gibson RC 2.50 1.00
❑ 469 Sedrick Hodge RC 2.00 .75
❑ 470 Willie Howard RC 2.50 1.00
❑ 471 Steve Hutchinson RC 2.50 1.00
❑ 472 Michael Stone RC 2.00 .75
❑ 473 Vinny Sutherland/1750 RC 3.00 1.25
❑ 474 Joe Tafoya RC 2.00 .75
❑ 475 Maurice Williams RC 2.00 .75
❑ 476 Pork Chop Womack RC 2.00 .75
❑ 477 Chad Ward RC 2.00 .75
❑ 478 Scotty Anderson/1750 RC 3.00 1.25
❑ 479 Gary Baxter RC 2.50 1.00
❑ 480 M.Tuiasosopo/1000 RC 6.00 2.50
❑ 481 Tim Hasselbeck/1000 RC 6.00 2.50
❑ 482 Clevan Thomas RC 2.00 .75
❑ 483 Marcus Stroud RC 5.00 2.00
❑ 484 John Schlecht RC 2.00 .75
❑ 485 Brandon Spoon RC 5.00 2.00
❑ 486 Alex Lincoln RC 2.50 1.00
❑ 487 Anthony Thomas/1750 RC 4.00 1.50
❑ 488 Freddie Mitchell/1750 RC 4.00 1.50
❑ 489 Brian Allen RC 2.50 1.00
❑ 490 Zeke Moreno RC 5.00 2.00
❑ 491 Tony Driver RC 5.00 2.00
❑ 492 Kynan Forney RC 2.00 .75
❑ 493 Reggie Wayne/1750 RC 10.00 4.00
❑ 494 Larry Casher RC 2.50 1.00
❑ 495 Fred Wakefield RC 2.50 1.00
❑ 496 Jeff Backus RC 2.50 1.00
❑ 497 Jarrod Cooper RC 5.00 2.00
❑ 498 Heath Evans RC 5.00 2.00
❑ 499 James Jackson/1500 RC 3.00 1.25
❑ 500 Jabari Holloway RC 5.00 2.00
❑ 501 Quincy Morgan/1750 RC 4.00 1.50
❑ 502 Josh Booty/1000 RC 6.00 2.50
❑ 503 Ja'Mar Toombs RC 2.50 1.00
❑ 504 Jason McKinley/1000 RC 4.00 1.50
❑ 505 Reggie White/1500 RC 3.00 1.25
❑ 506 Todd Heap/1750 RC 4.00 1.50
❑ 507 Rudi Johnson/1500 RC 10.00 4.00
❑ 508 Snoop Minnis/1750 RC 3.00 1.25
❑ 509 David Terrell/1750 RC 4.00 1.50
❑ 510 Torrance Marshall RC 5.00 2.00
❑ 511 Michael Bennett/1500 RC 5.00 2.00
❑ 512 Chris Chambers/1750 RC 8.00 3.00
❑ 513 Ben Leard/1000 RC 4.00 1.50
❑ 514 Rod Gardner/1750 RC 4.00 1.50
❑ 515 Michael Vick/1000 RC 50.00 20.00
❑ 516 Josh Heupel/1000 RC 6.00 2.50
❑ 517 Jesse Palmer/1000 RC 6.00 2.50
❑ 518 Quincy Carter/1000 RC 6.00 2.50
❑ 519 A.J. Feeley/1000 RC 6.00 2.50
❑ 520 David Rivers/1000 RC 6.00 2.50
❑ 521 Deuce McAllister/1500 RC 12.00 5.00
❑ 522 LaMont Jordan/1500 RC 10.00 4.00
❑ 523 David Allen/1500 RC 8.00 3.00
❑ 524 Correll Buckhalter/1500 RC 12.00 5.00
❑ 525 Travis Minor/1500 6.00 2.50
❑ 526 Koren Robinson/1750 RC 4.00 1.50
❑ 527 Santana Moss/1750 RC 8.00 3.00
❑ 528 Robert Ferguson/1750 RC 4.00 1.50
❑ 529 T.J.Houshmndzdh/1750 RC 5.00 2.00
❑ 530 Cedrick Wilson/1750 RC 4.00 1.50

2002 Pacific

❑ COMPLETE SET (500) 100.00 50.00
❑ 1 David Boston .60 .25
❑ 2 Arnold Jackson .25 .08
❑ 3 MarTay Jenkins .25 .08
❑ 4 Thomas Jones .40 .15
❑ 5 Kwamie Lassiter .25 .08
❑ 6 Joel Makovicka .25 .08
❑ 7 Ronald McKinnon .25 .08
❑ 8 Tywan Mitchell .25 .08
❑ 9 Michael Pittman .25 .08
❑ 10 Jake Plummer .40 .15
❑ 11 Frank Sanders .25 .08
❑ 12 Kyle Vanden Bosch .25 .08
❑ 13 Jamal Anderson .40 .15
❑ 14 Keith Brooking .25 .08
❑ 15 Chris Chandler .40 .15
❑ 16 Bob Christian .25 .08
❑ 17 Alge Crumpler .40 .15
❑ 18 Brian Finneran .25 .08
❑ 19 Shawn Jefferson .25 .08
❑ 20 Patrick Kerney .25 .08
❑ 21 Terance Mathis .25 .08
❑ 22 Maurice Smith .40 .15
❑ 23 Rodney Thomas .25 .08
❑ 24 Darrick Vaughn .25 .08
❑ 25 Michael Vick 2.00 .75
❑ 26 Sam Adams .25 .08
❑ 27 Terry Allen .25 .08
❑ 28 Obafemi Ayanbadejo .25 .08
❑ 29 Peter Boulware .25 .08
❑ 30 Jason Brookins .25 .08
❑ 31 Randall Cunningham .60 .25
❑ 32 Elvis Grbac .40 .15
❑ 33 Todd Heap .25 .08
❑ 34 Qadry Ismail .40 .15
❑ 35 Jamal Lewis .60 .25
❑ 36 Ray Lewis .60 .25
❑ 37 Chris Redman .25 .08
❑ 38 Shannon Sharpe .40 .15
❑ 39 Brandon Stokley .40 .15
❑ 40 Travis Taylor .40 .15
❑ 41 Moe Williams .25 .08
❑ 42 Rod Woodson .40 .15
❑ 43 Shawn Bryson .25 .08
❑ 44 Larry Centers .25 .08
❑ 45 Nate Clements .25 .08
❑ 46 London Fletcher .25 .08
❑ 47 Reggie Germany .25 .08
❑ 48 Travis Henry .60 .25
❑ 49 Jeremy McDaniel .25 .08
❑ 50 Sammy Morris .25 .08
❑ 51 Eric Moulds .40 .15
❑ 52 Peerless Price .40 .15
❑ 53 Jay Riemersma .25 .08
❑ 54 Alex Van Pelt .25 .08
❑ 55 Tim Biakabutuka .25 .08
❑ 56 Isaac Byrd .25 .08
❑ 57 Doug Evans .25 .08
❑ 58 Donald Hayes .25 .08
❑ 59 Chris Hetherington .25 .08
❑ 60 Brad Hoover .25 .08
❑ 61 Richard Huntley .25 .08
❑ 62 Patrick Jeffers .25 .08
❑ 63 Matt Lytle .25 .08
❑ 64 Dan Morgan .25 .08
❑ 65 Muhsin Muhammad .40 .15
❑ 66 Mike Rucker RC 1.00 .40
❑ 67 Steve Smith .60 .25
❑ 68 Wesley Walls .25 .08
❑ 69 Chris Weinke .40 .15
❑ 70 James Allen .40 .15
❑ 71 Fred Baxter .25 .08
❑ 72 Marty Booker .25 .08
❑ 73 Mike Brown .60 .25
❑ 74 Rosevelt Colvin RC 1.00 .40
❑ 75 Phillip Daniels .25 .08
❑ 76 Leon Johnson .25 .08
❑ 77 Shane Matthews .25 .08
❑ 78 Jim Miller .25 .08
❑ 79 Tony Parrish .25 .08
❑ 80 Marcus Robinson .40 .15
❑ 81 David Terrell .60 .25
❑ 82 Anthony Thomas .40 .15
❑ 83 Brian Urlacher 1.00 .40
❑ 84 Ted Washington .25 .08
❑ 85 Dez White .25 .08
❑ 86 Brandon Bennett .25 .08
❑ 87 Corey Dillon .40 .15
❑ 88 Ron Dugans .25 .08
❑ 89 Danny Farmer .25 .08
❑ 90 T.J. Houshmandzadeh .40 .15
❑ 91 Chad Johnson .60 .25
❑ 92 Curtis Keaton .25 .08
❑ 93 Jon Kitna .40 .15
❑ 94 Tony McGee .25 .08
❑ 95 Lorenzo Neal .25 .08
❑ 96 Darnay Scott .25 .08
❑ 97 Akili Smith .25 .08
❑ 98 Justin Smith .25 .08
❑ 99 Takeo Spikes .25 .08
❑ 100 Peter Warrick .40 .15
❑ 101 Tim Couch .40 .15
❑ 102 JaJuan Dawson .25 .08
❑ 103 Benjamin Gay .40 .15
❑ 104 Anthony Henry .25 .08
❑ 105 James Jackson .25 .08
❑ 106 Kevin Johnson .40 .15
❑ 107 Andre King .25 .08
❑ 108 Jamir Miller .25 .08
❑ 109 Quincy Morgan .25 .08
❑ 110 Dennis Northcutt .25 .08
❑ 111 O.J. Santiago .25 .08
❑ 112 Jamel White .25 .08
❑ 113 Quincy Carter .40 .15
❑ 114 Darrin Chiaverini .60 .25
❑ 115 Dexter Coakley .25 .08
❑ 116 Joey Galloway .40 .15
❑ 117 Troy Hambrick .25 .08
❑ 118 Rocket Ismail .40 .15
❑ 119 Dat Nguyen .25 .08
❑ 120 Ken-Yon Rambo .25 .08
❑ 121 Emmitt Smith 1.50 .60
❑ 122 Reggie Swinton .25 .08
❑ 123 Robert Thomas .25 .08
❑ 124 Michael Wiley .25 .08
❑ 125 Anthony Wright .25 .08
❑ 126 Mike Anderson .60 .25
❑ 127 Dwayne Carswell .25 .08
❑ 128 Desmond Clark .25 .08
❑ 129 Chris Cole .25 .08
❑ 130 Terrell Davis .60 .25
❑ 131 Gus Frerotte .25 .08
❑ 132 Olandis Gary .40 .15
❑ 133 Brian Griese .60 .25
❑ 134 Kevin Kasper .25 .08
❑ 135 Ed McCaffrey .60 .25
❑ 136 Phil McGeoghan RC .40 .15
❑ 137 John Mobley .25 .08
❑ 138 Scottie Montgomery .25 .08
❑ 139 Deltha O'Neal .25 .08
❑ 140 Trevor Pryce .25 .08
❑ 141 Rod Smith .40 .15
❑ 142 Al Wilson .25 .08
❑ 143 Scotty Anderson .25 .08
❑ 144 Charlie Batch .40 .15
❑ 145 Aveion Cason .60 .25
❑ 146 Germane Crowell .25 .08
❑ 147 Reuben Droughns .60 .25
❑ 148 Bert Emanuel .25 .08
❑ 149 Larry Foster .25 .08
❑ 150 Az-Zahir Hakim .25 .08
❑ 151 Desmond Howard .25 .08
❑ 152 Mike McMahon .60 .25
❑ 153 Herman Moore .40 .15
❑ 154 Johnnie Morton .40 .15
❑ 155 Robert Porcher .25 .08
❑ 156 Cory Schlesinger .25 .08
❑ 157 David Sloan .25 .08
❑ 158 James Stewart .40 .15
❑ 159 Lamont Warren .25 .08
❑ 160 Donald Driver .40 .15
❑ 161 Brett Favre 1.50 .60

❑ 162 Bubba Franks .40 .15
❑ 163 Antonio Freeman .60 .25
❑ 164 Kabeer Gbaja-Biamila .40 .15
❑ 165 Terry Glenn .40 .15
❑ 166 Ahman Green .60 .25
❑ 167 William Henderson .25 .08
❑ 168 Dorsey Levens .40 .15
❑ 169 David Martin .25 .08
❑ 170 Rondell Mealey .25 .08
❑ 171 Bill Schroeder .40 .15
❑ 172 Darren Sharper .25 .08
❑ 173 Avion Black .25 .08
❑ 174 Tony Boselli .25 .08
❑ 175 Corey Bradford .25 .08
❑ 176 Marcus Coleman .25 .08
❑ 177 Leomont Evans .25 .08
❑ 178 Aaron Glenn .25 .08
❑ 179 Trevor Insley .25 .08
❑ 180 Jermaine Lewis .25 .08
❑ 181 Anthony Malbrough .25 .08
❑ 182 Frank Moreau .25 .08
❑ 183 Mike Quinn .25 .08
❑ 184 Charlie Rogers .25 .08
❑ 185 Jamie Sharper .25 .08
❑ 186 Matt Snider .25 .08
❑ 187 Gary Walker .25 .08
❑ 188 Kevin Williams RC .40 .15
❑ 189 Kailee Wong .25 .08
❑ 190 Chad Bratzke .25 .08
❑ 191 Ken Dilger .25 .08
❑ 192 Marvin Harrison .60 .25
❑ 193 Edgerrin James .75 .30
❑ 194 Kevin McDougal .25 .08
❑ 195 Rob Morris .25 .08
❑ 196 Jerome Pathon .25 .08
❑ 197 Marcus Pollard .25 .08
❑ 198 Dominic Rhodes .40 .15
❑ 199 Marcus Washington .25 .08
❑ 200 Reggie Wayne .60 .25
❑ 201 Terrence Wilkins .25 .08
❑ 202 Tony Brackens .25 .08
❑ 203 Kyle Brady .25 .08
❑ 204 Mark Brunell .60 .25
❑ 205 Donovin Darius .25 .08
❑ 206 Sean Dawkins .25 .08
❑ 207 Damon Gibson .25 .08
❑ 208 Elvis Joseph .25 .08
❑ 209 Stacey Mack .25 .08
❑ 210 Keenan McCardell .25 .08
❑ 211 Hardy Nickerson .25 .08
❑ 212 Jonathan Quinn .25 .08
❑ 213 Micah Ross RC .25 .08
❑ 214 Jimmy Smith .40 .15
❑ 215 Fred Taylor .60 .25
❑ 216 Patrick Washington .25 .08
❑ 217 Derrick Alexander .40 .15
❑ 218 Mike Cloud .25 .08
❑ 219 Donnie Edwards .25 .08
❑ 220 Tony Gonzalez .40 .15
❑ 221 Trent Green .40 .15
❑ 222 Dante Hall .60 .25
❑ 223 Priest Holmes .75 .30
❑ 224 Eddie Kennison .25 .08
❑ 225 Snoop Minnis .25 .08
❑ 226 Larry Parker .25 .08
❑ 227 Marvcus Patton .25 .08
❑ 228 Tony Richardson .25 .08
❑ 229 Mikhael Ricks .25 .08
❑ 230 Chris Chambers .60 .25
❑ 231 Jay Fiedler .40 .15
❑ 232 Oronde Gadsden .40 .15
❑ 233 Rob Konrad .25 .08
❑ 234 Sam Madison .25 .08
❑ 235 Brock Marion .25 .08
❑ 236 James McKnight .25 .08
❑ 237 Travis Minor .25 .08
❑ 238 Jeff Ogden .25 .08
❑ 239 Lamar Smith .40 .15
❑ 240 Jason Taylor .25 .08
❑ 241 Zach Thomas .60 .25
❑ 242 Dedric Ward .25 .08
❑ 243 Ricky Williams .60 .25
❑ 244 Michael Bennett .40 .15
❑ 245 Todd Bouman .25 .08
❑ 246 Cris Carter .60 .25
❑ 247 Byron Chamberlain .25 .08
❑ 248 Doug Chapman .25 .08
❑ 249 Kenny Clark RC .40 .15
❑ 250 Daunte Culpepper .60 .25
❑ 251 Nate Jacquet .25 .08
❑ 252 Jim Kleinsasser .25 .08
❑ 253 Harold Morrow .25 .08
❑ 254 Randy Moss 1.25 .50
❑ 255 Jake Reed .25 .08
❑ 256 Spergon Wynn .25 .08
❑ 257 Drew Bledsoe .75 .30
❑ 258 Tom Brady 1.50 .60
❑ 259 Troy Brown .40 .15
❑ 260 Fred Coleman .25 .08
❑ 261 Marc Edwards .25 .08
❑ 262 Kevin Faulk .40 .15
❑ 263 Bobby Hamilton .25 .08
❑ 264 Ty Law .40 .15
❑ 265 Lawyer Milloy .40 .15
❑ 266 David Patten .25 .08
❑ 267 J.R. Redmond .25 .08
❑ 268 Antowain Smith .40 .15
❑ 269 Adam Vinatieri .60 .25
❑ 270 Jermaine Wiggins .25 .08
❑ 271 Aaron Brooks .60 .25
❑ 272 Cam Cleeland .25 .08
❑ 273 Charlie Clemons RC .25 .08
❑ 274 James Fenderson RC .40 .15
❑ 275 La'Roi Glover .25 .08
❑ 276 Joe Horn .40 .15
❑ 277 Willie Jackson .25 .08
❑ 278 Sammy Knight .25 .08
❑ 279 Michael Lewis .25 .08
❑ 280 Deuce McAllister .75 .30
❑ 281 Terrelle Smith .25 .08
❑ 282 Boo Williams .25 .08
❑ 283 Robert Wilson .25 .08
❑ 284 Tiki Barber .60 .25
❑ 285 Micheal Barrow .25 .08
❑ 286 Kerry Collins .40 .15
❑ 287 Greg Comella .25 .08
❑ 288 Thabiti Davis .25 .08
❑ 289 Ron Dayne .40 .15
❑ 290 Ron Dixon .25 .08
❑ 291 Ike Hilliard .40 .15
❑ 292 Joe Jurevicius .25 .08
❑ 293 Michael Strahan .40 .15
❑ 294 Amani Toomer .40 .15
❑ 295 Damon Washington .25 .08
❑ 296 John Abraham .40 .15
❑ 297 Richie Anderson .25 .08
❑ 298 Anthony Becht .25 .08
❑ 299 Wayne Chrebet .40 .15
❑ 300 Laveranues Coles .40 .15
❑ 301 James Farrior .25 .08
❑ 302 Marvin Jones .25 .08
❑ 303 LaMont Jordan .60 .25
❑ 304 Curtis Martin .60 .25
❑ 305 Santana Moss .60 .25
❑ 306 Chad Pennington .75 .30
❑ 307 Kevin Swayne .25 .08
❑ 308 Vinny Testaverde .40 .15
❑ 309 Craig Yeast .25 .08
❑ 310 Greg Biekert .25 .08
❑ 311 Tim Brown .60 .25
❑ 312 Zack Crockett .25 .08
❑ 313 Rich Gannon .60 .25
❑ 314 Charlie Garner .40 .15
❑ 315 Sebastian Janikowski .25 .08
❑ 316 Randy Jordan .25 .08
❑ 317 Terry Kirby .25 .08
❑ 318 Jerry Porter .25 .08
❑ 319 Jerry Rice 1.25 .50
❑ 320 Jon Ritchie .25 .08
❑ 321 Tyrone Wheatley .40 .15
❑ 322 Roland Williams .25 .08
❑ 323 Charles Woodson .40 .15
❑ 324 Correll Buckhalter .40 .15
❑ 325 Brian Dawkins .40 .15
❑ 326 Hugh Douglas .25 .08
❑ 327 A.J. Feeley .60 .25
❑ 328 Chad Lewis .25 .08
❑ 329 Cecil Martin .25 .08
❑ 330 Brian Mitchell .25 .08
❑ 331 Freddie Mitchell .40 .15
❑ 332 Todd Pinkston .40 .15
❑ 333 Rod Smart RC .25 .08
❑ 334 Duce Staley .60 .25
❑ 335 James Thrash .40 .15
❑ 336 Jeremiah Trotter .25 .08
❑ 337 Troy Vincent .25 .08
❑ 338 Kendrell Bell .60 .25
❑ 339 Jerome Bettis .60 .25
❑ 340 Demetrius Brown RC .40 .15
❑ 341 Plaxico Burress .40 .15
❑ 342 Troy Edwards .25 .08
❑ 343 Chris Fuamatu-Ma'afala .25 .08
❑ 344 Jason Gildon .25 .08
❑ 345 Earl Holmes .25 .08
❑ 346 Joey Porter .60 .25
❑ 347 Chad Scott .25 .08
❑ 348 Bobby Shaw .25 .08
❑ 349 Kordell Stewart .40 .15
❑ 350 Hines Ward .60 .25
❑ 351 Amos Zereoue .60 .25
❑ 352 Adam Archuleta .25 .08
❑ 353 Dre' Bly .25 .08
❑ 354 Isaac Bruce .60 .25
❑ 355 Trung Canidate .40 .15
❑ 356 Ernie Conwell .25 .08
❑ 357 Marshall Faulk .60 .25
❑ 358 Torry Holt .60 .25
❑ 359 Leonard Little .25 .08
❑ 360 Yo Murphy .25 .08
❑ 361 Ricky Proehl .25 .08
❑ 362 Kurt Warner .60 .25
❑ 363 Aeneas Williams .25 .08
❑ 364 Drew Brees .60 .25
❑ 365 Curtis Conway .25 .08
❑ 366 Tim Dwight .40 .15
❑ 367 Terrell Fletcher .25 .08
❑ 368 Doug Flutie .60 .25
❑ 369 Jeff Graham .25 .08
❑ 370 Rodney Harrison .25 .08
❑ 371 Ronney Jenkins .25 .08
❑ 372 Raylee Johnson .25 .08
❑ 373 Freddie Jones .25 .08
❑ 374 Ryan McNeil .25 .08
❑ 375 Junior Seau .60 .25
❑ 376 LaDainian Tomlinson 1.00 .40
❑ 377 Marcellus Wiley .25 .08
❑ 378 Kevan Barlow .40 .15
❑ 379 Fred Beasley .25 .08
❑ 380 Zack Bronson RC .40 .15
❑ 381 Andre Carter .25 .08
❑ 382 Jeff Garcia .60 .25
❑ 383 Garrison Hearst .40 .15
❑ 384 Terry Jackson .25 .08
❑ 385 Eric Johnson .40 .15
❑ 386 Saladin McCullough RC .25 .08
❑ 387 Terrell Owens .60 .25
❑ 388 Ahmed Plummer .25 .08
❑ 389 J.J. Stokes .25 .08
❑ 390 Tai Streets .25 .08
❑ 391 Vinny Sutherland .25 .08
❑ 392 Bryant Young .25 .08
❑ 393 Shaun Alexander .75 .30
❑ 394 Chad Brown .25 .08
❑ 395 Kerwin Cook RC .40 .15
❑ 396 Trent Dilfer .40 .15
❑ 397 Bobby Engram .25 .08
❑ 398 Christian Fauria .25 .08
❑ 399 Matt Hasselbeck .40 .15
❑ 400 Darrell Jackson .40 .15
❑ 401 John Randle .25 .08
❑ 402 Koren Robinson .40 .15
❑ 403 Anthony Simmons .25 .08
❑ 404 Mack Strong .40 .15
❑ 405 Ricky Watters .25 .08
❑ 406 James Williams WR .25 .08
❑ 407 Mike Alstott .60 .25
❑ 408 Ronde Barber .25 .08
❑ 409 Derrick Brooks .60 .25
❑ 410 Jameel Cook .25 .08
❑ 411 Warrick Dunn .60 .25
❑ 412 Jacquez Green .25 .08
❑ 413 Brad Johnson .40 .15
❑ 414 Keyshawn Johnson .60 .25
❑ 415 Rob Johnson .40 .15
❑ 416 John Lynch .40 .15
❑ 417 Dave Moore .25 .08
❑ 418 Warren Sapp .40 .15
❑ 419 Aaron Stecker .25 .08
❑ 420 Karl Williams .25 .08
❑ 421 Drew Bennett .60 .25
❑ 422 Eddie Berlin .25 .08

❑ 423 Rafael Cooper RC .40 .15
❑ 424 Kevin Dyson .40 .15
❑ 425 Eddie George .60 .25
❑ 426 Mike Green .25 .08
❑ 427 Skip Hicks .25 .08
❑ 428 Jevon Kearse .40 .15
❑ 429 Erron Kinney .25 .08
❑ 430 Derrick Mason .40 .15
❑ 431 Justin McCareins .40 .15
❑ 432 Steve McNair .60 .25
❑ 433 Neil O'Donnell .25 .08
❑ 434 Frank Wycheck .25 .08
❑ 435 Reidel Anthony .25 .08
❑ 436 Jessie Armstead .25 .08
❑ 437 Champ Bailey .40 .15
❑ 438 Tony Banks .25 .08
❑ 439 Michael Bates .25 .08
❑ 440 Donnell Bennett .25 .08
❑ 441 Ki-Jana Carter .25 .08
❑ 442 Stephen Davis .40 .15
❑ 443 Zeron Flemister .25 .08
❑ 444 Rod Gardner .40 .15
❑ 445 Kevin Lockett .25 .08
❑ 446 Eric Metcalf .25 .08
❑ 447 Sage Rosenfels .25 .08
❑ 448 Fred Smoot .25 .08
❑ 449 Michael Westbrook .25 .08
❑ 450 Danny Wuerffel .25 .08
❑ 451 Jason McAddley RC 1.50 .60
❑ 452 Freddie Milons RC 1.50 .60
❑ 453 Bryan Thomas RC 1.50 .60
❑ 454 Levi Jones RC 1.50 .60
❑ 455 William Green RC 2.00 .75
❑ 456 Luke Staley RC 1.50 .60
❑ 457 Daniel Graham RC 2.00 .75
❑ 458 David Garrard RC 2.00 .75
❑ 459 Reche Caldwell RC 2.00 .75
❑ 460 Andra Davis RC 1.50 .60
❑ 461 Lito Sheppard RC 2.00 .75
❑ 462 Chris Hope RC 2.00 .75
❑ 463 Javon Walker RC 4.00 1.50
❑ 464 David Carr RC 5.00 2.00
❑ 465 Alan Harper RC 1.00 .40
❑ 466 Adrian Peterson RC 2.00 .75
❑ 467 Kelly Campbell RC 1.50 .60
❑ 468 Ashley Lelie RC 4.00 1.50
❑ 469 Kurt Kittner RC 1.50 .60
❑ 470 Antwaan Randle El RC 3.00 1.25
❑ 471 Ladell Betts RC 2.00 .75
❑ 472 Josh Reed RC 2.00 .75
❑ 473 Clinton Portis RC 6.00 2.50
❑ 474 Ron Johnson RC 1.50 .60
❑ 475 Eric Crouch RC 2.00 .75
❑ 476 Tracey Wistrom RC 1.50 .60
❑ 477 David Neill RC 1.50 .60
❑ 478 Ronald Curry RC 2.00 .75
❑ 479 Lamar Gordon RC 2.00 .75
❑ 480 Damien Anderson RC 1.50 .60
❑ 481 Napoleon Harris RC 2.00 .75
❑ 482 Zak Kustok RC 2.00 .75
❑ 483 Rocky Calmus RC 2.00 .75
❑ 484 Roy Williams RC 5.00 2.00
❑ 485 Joey Harrington RC 3.00 1.25
❑ 486 Maurice Morris RC 2.00 .75
❑ 487 Antonio Bryant RC 2.00 .75
❑ 488 Josh McCown RC 2.50 1.00
❑ 489 John Henderson RC 2.00 .75
❑ 490 Quentin Jammer RC 2.00 .75
❑ 491 Mike Williams RC 1.50 .60
❑ 492 Patrick Ramsey RC 2.50 1.00
❑ 493 Kenyon Coleman RC 1.00 .40
❑ 494 DeShaun Foster RC 2.00 .75
❑ 495 Brian Poli-Dixon RC 1.50 .60
❑ 496 Cliff Russell RC 1.50 .60
❑ 497 Brian Westbrook RC 3.00 1.25
❑ 498 Andre Davis RC 1.50 .60
❑ 499 Larry Tripplett RC 1.00 .40
❑ 500 Lamont Thompson RC 1.50 .60
❑ 501 T.J. Duckett RC 2.50 1.00
❑ 502 Dameon Hunter RC 1.00 .40
❑ 503 Javin Hunter RC 1.00 .40
❑ 504 Tellis Redmon RC 1.50 .60
❑ 505 Chester Taylor RC 4.00 1.50
❑ 506 Randy Fasani RC 1.50 .60
❑ 507 Julius Peppers RC 4.00 1.50
❑ 508 Jamin Elliott RC 1.00 .40
❑ 509 Chad Hutchinson RC 1.50 .60
❑ 510 Eddie Drummond RC 1.50 .60
❑ 511 Craig Nall RC 2.00 .75
❑ 512 Jabar Gaffney RC 2.00 .75
❑ 513 Jonathan Wells RC 2.00 .75
❑ 514 Shaun Hill RC 2.00 .75
❑ 515 Deion Branch RC 4.00 1.50
❑ 516 Rohan Davey RC 2.00 .75
❑ 517 J.T. O'Sullivan RC 1.50 .60
❑ 518 Tim Carter RC 1.50 .60
❑ 519 Daryl Jones RC 1.50 .60
❑ 520 Jeremy Shockey RC 6.00 2.50
❑ 521 Seth Burford RC 1.50 .60
❑ 522 Brandon Doman RC 1.50 .60
❑ 523 Jerramy Stevens RC 2.00 .75
❑ 524 Travis Stephens RC 1.50 .60
❑ 525 Marquise Walker RC 1.50 .60

2002 Pacific Adrenaline

❑ COMPLETE SET (288) 50.00 25.00
❑ 1 Damien Anderson RC 1.50 .60
❑ 2 David Boston .75 .30
❑ 3 Wendell Bryant RC 1.00 .40
❑ 4 Thomas Jones .50 .20
❑ 5 Jason McAddley RC 1.50 .60
❑ 6 Josh McCown RC 2.50 1.00
❑ 7 Jake Plummer .50 .20
❑ 8 Frank Sanders .30 .10
❑ 9 Josh Scobey RC 2.00 .75
❑ 10 Keith Brooking .30 .10
❑ 11 T.J. Duckett RC 2.50 1.00
❑ 12 Warrick Dunn .75 .30
❑ 13 Brian Finneran .30 .10
❑ 14 Kahlil Hill RC 1.50 .60
❑ 15 Shawn Jefferson .30 .10
❑ 16 Kurt Kittner RC 1.50 .60
❑ 17 Will Overstreet RC 1.00 .40
❑ 18 Michael Vick 2.50 1.00
❑ 19 Ron Johnson RC 1.50 .60
❑ 20 Jamal Lewis .75 .30
❑ 21 Ray Lewis .75 .30
❑ 22 Chris Redman .30 .10
❑ 23 Tellis Redmon RC 1.50 .60
❑ 24 Brandon Stokley .50 .20
❑ 25 Chester Taylor RC 4.00 1.50
❑ 26 Travis Taylor .50 .20
❑ 27 Anthony Weaver RC 1.50 .60
❑ 28 Drew Bledsoe 1.00 .40
❑ 29 Shawn Bryson .30 .10
❑ 30 Larry Centers .30 .10
❑ 31 Ryan Denney RC 1.50 .60
❑ 32 Travis Henry .75 .30
❑ 33 Richard Huntley .30 .10
❑ 34 Eric Moulds .50 .20
❑ 35 Peerless Price .50 .20
❑ 36 Josh Reed RC 2.00 .75
❑ 37 Isaac Byrd .30 .10
❑ 38 Randy Fasani RC 1.50 .60
❑ 39 DeShaun Foster RC 2.00 .75
❑ 40 Kyle Johnson RC 1.00 .40
❑ 41 Muhsin Muhammad .50 .20
❑ 42 Julius Peppers RC 4.00 1.50
❑ 43 Lamar Smith .50 .20
❑ 44 Steve Smith .75 .30
❑ 45 Chris Weinke .50 .20
❑ 46 Marty Booker .50 .20
❑ 47 Chris Chandler .50 .20
❑ 48 Eric McCoo RC 1.00 .40
❑ 49 Jim Miller .30 .10
❑ 50 Adrian Peterson RC 2.00 .75
❑ 51 Marcus Robinson .50 .20
❑ 52 David Terrell .75 .30
❑ 53 Anthony Thomas .50 .20
❑ 54 Brian Urlacher 1.25 .50
❑ 55 Corey Dillon .50 .20
❑ 56 Gus Frerotte .30 .10
❑ 57 Chad Johnson .75 .30
❑ 58 Jon Kitna .50 .20
❑ 59 Justin Smith .30 .10
❑ 60 Takeo Spikes .30 .10
❑ 61 Lamont Thompson RC 1.50 .60
❑ 62 Peter Warrick .50 .20
❑ 63 Michael Westbrook .30 .10
❑ 64 Tim Couch .50 .20
❑ 65 Andre Davis RC 1.50 .60
❑ 66 JaJuan Dawson .30 .10
❑ 67 William Green RC 2.00 .75
❑ 68 James Jackson .30 .10
❑ 69 Kevin Johnson .50 .20
❑ 70 Jamir Miller .30 .10
❑ 71 Quincy Morgan .30 .10
❑ 72 Jamel White .30 .10
❑ 73 Antonio Bryant RC 2.00 .75
❑ 74 Quincy Carter .50 .20
❑ 75 Woody Dantzler RC 1.50 .60
❑ 76 Joey Galloway .50 .20
❑ 77 Ennis Haywood RC 1.50 .60
❑ 78 Chad Hutchinson RC 1.50 .60
❑ 79 Rocket Ismail .50 .20
❑ 80 Emmitt Smith 2.00 .75
❑ 81 Roy Williams RC 5.00 2.00
❑ 82 Mike Anderson .75 .30
❑ 83 Terrell Davis .75 .30
❑ 84 Brian Griese .75 .30
❑ 85 Herb Haygood RC 1.00 .40
❑ 86 Ashley Lelie RC 4.00 1.50
❑ 87 Ed McCaffrey .75 .30
❑ 88 Deltha O'Neal .30 .10
❑ 89 Clinton Portis RC 6.00 2.50
❑ 90 Rod Smith .50 .20
❑ 91 Scotty Anderson .30 .10
❑ 92 Eddie Drummond RC 1.50 .60
❑ 93 Az-Zahir Hakim .30 .10
❑ 94 Joey Harrington RC 3.00 1.25
❑ 95 Mike McMahon .75 .30
❑ 96 James Mungro RC 2.00 .75
❑ 97 Bill Schroeder .30 .10
❑ 98 Luke Staley RC 1.50 .60
❑ 99 James Stewart .50 .20
❑ 100 Marques Anderson RC 2.00 .75
❑ 101 Najeh Davenport RC 2.00 .75
❑ 102 Brett Favre 2.00 .75
❑ 103 Robert Ferguson .30 .10
❑ 104 Bubba Franks .50 .20
❑ 105 Terry Glenn .50 .20
❑ 106 Ahman Green .75 .30
❑ 107 Craig Nall RC 2.00 .75
❑ 108 Javon Walker RC 4.00 1.50
❑ 109 James Allen .50 .20
❑ 110 Jarrod Baxter RC 1.50 .60
❑ 111 Corey Bradford .30 .10
❑ 112 David Carr RC 5.00 2.00
❑ 113 Delvon Flowers RC 1.50 .60
❑ 114 Jabar Gaffney RC 2.00 .75
❑ 115 Jermaine Lewis .30 .10
❑ 116 Travis Prentice .30 .10
❑ 117 Jonathan Wells RC 2.00 .75
❑ 118 Brian Allen RC 1.50 .60
❑ 119 Chad Bratzke .30 .10
❑ 120 Marvin Harrison .75 .30
❑ 121 Qadry Ismail .50 .20
❑ 122 Edgerrin James 1.00 .40
❑ 123 Peyton Manning 1.50 .60
❑ 124 Rob Morris .30 .10
❑ 125 Dominic Rhodes .50 .20
❑ 126 Reggie Wayne .75 .30
❑ 127 Tony Brackens .30 .10
❑ 128 Mark Brunell .75 .30
❑ 129 Donovin Darius .30 .10
❑ 130 David Garrard RC 2.00 .75
❑ 131 John Henderson RC 2.00 .75
❑ 132 Stacey Mack .30 .10
❑ 133 Bobby Shaw .30 .10
❑ 134 Jimmy Smith .50 .20
❑ 135 Fred Taylor .75 .30
❑ 136 Omar Easy RC 2.00 .75
❑ 137 Eddie Freeman RC 1.00 .40

❑	138	Tony Gonzalez	.50	.20
❑	139	Trent Green	.50	.20
❑	140	Priest Holmes	1.00	.40
❑	141	Eddie Kennison	.30	.10
❑	142	Snoop Minnis	.30	.10
❑	143	Johnnie Morton	.50	.20
❑	144	Ryan Sims RC	2.00	.75
❑	145	Chris Chambers	.75	.30
❑	146	Jay Fiedler	.50	.20
❑	147	Oronde Gadsden	.30	.10
❑	148	Leonard Henry RC	1.50	.60
❑	149	James McKnight	.30	.10
❑	150	Travis Minor	.30	.10
❑	151	Sam Simmons RC	1.00	.40
❑	152	Zach Thomas	.75	.30
❑	153	Ricky Williams	.75	.30
❑	154	Derrick Alexander	.50	.20
❑	155	Jeremy Allen RC	1.00	.40
❑	156	Atrews Bell RC	1.00	.40
❑	157	Michael Bennett	.50	.20
❑	158	Kelly Campbell RC	1.50	.60
❑	159	Byron Chamberlain	.30	.10
❑	160	Doug Chapman	.30	.10
❑	161	Daunte Culpepper	.75	.30
❑	162	Randy Moss	1.50	.60
❑	163	Tom Brady	2.00	.75
❑	164	Deion Branch RC	4.00	1.50
❑	165	Troy Brown	.50	.20
❑	166	Rohan Davey RC	2.00	.75
❑	167	Kevin Faulk	.50	.20
❑	168	Daniel Graham RC	2.00	.75
❑	169	David Patten	.30	.10
❑	170	Antowain Smith	.50	.20
❑	171	Antwoine Womack RC	1.50	.60
❑	172	Aaron Brooks	.75	.30
❑	173	Charlie Clemons	.30	.10
❑	174	Joe Horn	.50	.20
❑	175	Sammy Knight	.30	.10
❑	176	Deuce McAllister	1.00	.40
❑	177	J.T. O'Sullivan RC	1.50	.60
❑	178	Jerome Pathon	.50	.20
❑	179	Donte Stallworth RC	4.00	1.50
❑	180	Ricky Williams RC	1.50	.60
❑	181	Tiki Barber	.75	.30
❑	182	Tim Carter RC	1.50	.60
❑	183	Kerry Collins	.50	.20
❑	184	Ron Dayne	.50	.20
❑	185	Ike Hilliard	.50	.20
❑	186	Daryl Jones RC	1.50	.60
❑	187	Jeremy Shockey RC	6.00	2.50
❑	188	Michael Strahan	.50	.20
❑	189	Amani Toomer	.50	.20
❑	190	Wayne Chrebet	.50	.20
❑	191	Laveranues Coles	.50	.20
❑	192	Alan Harper RC	1.00	.40
❑	193	LaMont Jordan	.75	.30
❑	194	Curtis Martin	.75	.30
❑	195	Chad Morton	.30	.10
❑	196	Santana Moss	.75	.30
❑	197	Vinny Testaverde	.50	.20
❑	198	Bryan Thomas RC	1.50	.60
❑	199	Tim Brown	.75	.30
❑	200	Ronald Curry RC	2.00	.75
❑	201	Rich Gannon	.75	.30
❑	202	Charlie Garner	.50	.20
❑	203	Napoleon Harris RC	2.00	.75
❑	204	Larry Ned RC	1.50	.60
❑	205	Jerry Rice	1.50	.60
❑	206	Tyrone Wheatley	.50	.20
❑	207	Charles Woodson	.50	.20
❑	208	Michael Lewis RC	2.00	.75
❑	209	Donovan McNabb	1.00	.40
❑	210	Freddie Milons RC	1.50	.60
❑	211	Freddie Mitchell	.50	.20
❑	212	Todd Pinkston	.50	.20
❑	213	Lito Sheppard RC	2.00	.75
❑	214	Duce Staley	.75	.30
❑	215	James Thrash	.50	.20
❑	216	Brian Westbrook RC	3.00	1.25
❑	217	Kendrell Bell	.75	.30
❑	218	Jerome Bettis	.75	.30
❑	219	Plaxico Burress	.50	.20
❑	220	Verron Haynes RC	2.00	.75
❑	221	Chris Hope RC	2.00	.75
❑	222	Lee Mays RC	1.50	.60
❑	223	Antwaan Randle El RC	3.00	1.25
❑	224	Kordell Stewart	.50	.20
❑	225	Hines Ward	.75	.30
❑	226	Isaac Bruce	.75	.30
❑	227	Eric Crouch RC	2.00	.75
❑	228	Marshall Faulk	.75	.30
❑	229	Lamar Gordon RC	2.00	.75
❑	230	Torry Holt	.75	.30
❑	231	Leonard Little	.30	.10
❑	232	Robert Thomas RC	2.00	.75
❑	233	Kurt Warner	.75	.30
❑	234	Terrence Wilkins	.30	.10
❑	235	Drew Brees	.75	.30
❑	236	Seth Burford RC	1.50	.60
❑	237	Reche Caldwell RC	2.00	.75
❑	238	Curtis Conway	.30	.10
❑	239	Doug Flutie	.75	.30
❑	240	Quentin Jammer RC	2.00	.75
❑	241	Brian Poli-Dixon RC	1.50	.60
❑	242	Junior Seau	.75	.30
❑	243	LaDainian Tomlinson	1.25	.50
❑	244	Kevan Barlow	.50	.20
❑	245	Andre Carter	.30	.10
❑	246	Brandon Doman RC	1.50	.60
❑	247	Jeff Garcia	.75	.30
❑	248	Garrison Hearst	.50	.20
❑	249	Terrell Owens	.75	.30
❑	250	Derek Smith RC	1.00	.40
❑	251	J.J. Stokes	.50	.20
❑	252	Vinny Sutherland	.30	.10
❑	253	Shaun Alexander	1.00	.40
❑	254	Chad Brown	.30	.10
❑	255	Trent Dilfer	.50	.20
❑	256	Bobby Engram	.30	.10
❑	257	Darrell Jackson	.50	.20
❑	258	Nakoa McElrath RC	1.50	.60
❑	259	Maurice Morris RC	2.00	.75
❑	260	Koren Robinson	.50	.20
❑	261	Jerramy Stevens RC	2.00	.75
❑	262	Mike Alstott	.75	.30
❑	263	Derrick Brooks	.75	.30
❑	264	Brad Johnson	.50	.20
❑	265	Keyshawn Johnson	.75	.30
❑	266	Keenan McCardell	.30	.10
❑	267	Michael Pittman	.30	.10
❑	268	Warren Sapp	.50	.20
❑	269	Travis Stephens RC	1.50	.60
❑	270	Marquise Walker RC	1.50	.60
❑	271	Rocky Calmus RC	2.00	.75
❑	272	Kevin Dyson	.50	.20
❑	273	Eddie George	.75	.30
❑	274	Albert Haynesworth RC	1.50	.60
❑	275	Derrick Mason	.50	.20
❑	276	Steve McNair	.75	.30
❑	277	Dicenzo Miller RC	1.00	.40
❑	278	Jake Schifino RC	1.50	.60
❑	279	Tank Williams RC	1.50	.60
❑	280	Champ Bailey	.50	.20
❑	281	Ladell Betts RC	2.00	.75
❑	282	Stephen Davis	.50	.20
❑	283	Rod Gardner	.50	.20
❑	284	Jacquez Green	.30	.10
❑	285	Shane Matthews	.30	.10
❑	286	Patrick Ramsey RC	2.50	1.00
❑	287	Cliff Russell RC	1.50	.60
❑	288	Jeremiah Trotter	.30	.10

1996 Pacific Dynagon

❑		COMPLETE SET (144)	60.00	25.00
❑	1	Larry Centers	.75	.30
❑	2	Garrison Hearst	.75	.30
❑	3	Dave Krieg	.40	.15
❑	4	Frank Sanders	.75	.30
❑	5	Jeff George	.75	.30
❑	6	Craig Heyward	.40	.15
❑	7	Terance Mathis	.40	.15
❑	8	Eric Metcalf	.40	.15
❑	9	Todd Collins	.75	.30
❑	10	Darick Holmes	.40	.15
❑	11	Jim Kelly	1.50	.60
❑	12	Eric Moulds RC	4.00	1.50
❑	13	Bryce Paup	.40	.15
❑	14	Thurman Thomas	1.50	.60
❑	15	Tim Biakabutuka RC	1.50	.60
❑	16	Blake Brockermeyer	.40	.15
❑	17	Mark Carrier WR	.40	.15
❑	18	Kerry Collins	1.50	.60
❑	19	Derrick Moore	.40	.15
❑	20	Bobby Engram RC	1.50	.60
❑	21	Jeff Graham	.40	.15
❑	22	Erik Kramer	.40	.15
❑	23	Rashaan Salaam	.75	.30
❑	24	Steve Stenstrom	.40	.15
❑	25	Chris Zorich	.40	.15
❑	26	Jeff Blake	1.50	.60
❑	27	David Dunn	.40	.15
❑	28	Carl Pickens	.75	.30
❑	29	Darnay Scott	.75	.30
❑	30	Earnest Byner	.40	.15
❑	31	Leroy Hoard	.40	.15
❑	32	Keenan McCardell	1.50	.60
❑	33	Eric Zeier	.40	.15
❑	34	Troy Aikman	3.00	1.25
❑	35	Chris Boniol	.40	.15
❑	36	Michael Irvin	1.50	.60
❑	37	Daryl Johnston	.75	.30
❑	38	Deion Sanders	2.00	.75
❑	39	Emmitt Smith	5.00	2.00
❑	40	Stepfret Williams	.40	.15
❑	41	John Elway	6.00	2.50
❑	42	Terrell Davis	2.50	1.00
❑	43	Anthony Miller	.75	.30
❑	44	Shannon Sharpe	.75	.30
❑	45	Scott Mitchell	.75	.30
❑	46	Herman Moore	.75	.30
❑	47	Brett Perriman	.40	.15
❑	48	Barry Sanders	5.00	2.00
❑	49	Cory Schlesinger	.40	.15
❑	50	Edgar Bennett	.75	.30
❑	51	Robert Brooks	1.50	.60
❑	52	Mark Chmura	.75	.30
❑	53	Brett Favre	6.00	2.50
❑	54	Reggie White	1.50	.60
❑	55	Eddie George RC	4.00	1.50
❑	56	Steve McNair	2.50	1.00
❑	57	Chris Sanders	.75	.30
❑	58	Rodney Thomas	.40	.15
❑	59	Ben Bronson RC	.40	.15
❑	60	Zack Crockett	.40	.15
❑	61	Marshall Faulk	2.00	.75
❑	62	Jim Harbaugh	.75	.30
❑	63	Mark Brunell	2.00	.75
❑	64	Kevin Hardy RC	1.50	.60
❑	65	Willie Jackson	.75	.30
❑	66	Pete Mitchell	.75	.30
❑	67	James O.Stewart	.75	.30
❑	68	Marcus Allen	1.50	.60
❑	69	Steve Bono	.40	.15
❑	70	Lake Dawson	.40	.15
❑	71	Neil Smith	.75	.30
❑	72	Tamarick Vanover	.75	.30
❑	73	Irving Fryar	.75	.30
❑	74	Terry Kirby	.75	.30
❑	75	Dan Marino	6.00	2.50
❑	76	O.J. McDuffie	.75	.30
❑	77	Bernie Parmalee	.40	.15
❑	78	Stanley Pritchett RC	.75	.30
❑	79	Cris Carter	1.50	.60
❑	80	Qadry Ismail	.75	.30
❑	81	Chad May	.40	.15
❑	82	Warren Moon	.75	.30
❑	83	Robert Smith	.75	.30
❑	84	Drew Bledsoe	2.00	.75
❑	85	Ben Coates	.75	.30
❑	86	Terry Glenn RC	3.00	1.25
❑	87	Curtis Martin	2.50	1.00
❑	88	Willie McGinest	.40	.15
❑	89	Mario Bates	.75	.30

❑ 90 Jim Everett .40 .15
❑ 91 Wayne Martin .40 .15
❑ 92 Shane Pahukoa RC .40 .15
❑ 93 Ray Zellars .40 .15
❑ 94 Dave Brown .40 .15
❑ 95 Chris Calloway .40 .15
❑ 96 Rodney Hampton .75 .30
❑ 97 Tyrone Wheatley .75 .30
❑ 98 Wayne Chrebet 2.00 .75
❑ 99 Glenn Foley .75 .30
❑ 100 Keyshawn Johnson RC 3.00 1.25
❑ 101 Adrian Murrell .75 .30
❑ 102 Alex Van Dyke RC .75 .30
❑ 103 Tim Brown 1.50 .60
❑ 104 Billy Joe Hobert .75 .30
❑ 105 Rocket Ismail .40 .15
❑ 106 Napoleon Kaufman 1.50 .60
❑ 107 Harvey Williams .40 .15
❑ 108 Charlie Garner .75 .30
❑ 109 Rodney Peete .40 .15
❑ 110 Ricky Watters .75 .30
❑ 111 Calvin Williams .40 .15
❑ 112 Mark Bruener .40 .15
❑ 113 Kevin Greene .75 .30
❑ 114 Ernie Mills .40 .15
❑ 115 Kordell Stewart 1.50 .60
❑ 116 Yancey Thigpen .75 .30
❑ 117 Dave Barr .40 .15
❑ 118 Jerome Bettis 1.50 .60
❑ 119 Isaac Bruce 1.50 .60
❑ 120 Lawrence Phillips RC 1.50 .60
❑ 121 J.T. Thomas .40 .15
❑ 122 Ronnie Harmon .40 .15
❑ 123 Aaron Hayden RC .40 .15
❑ 124 Stan Humphries .75 .30
❑ 125 Junior Seau 1.50 .60
❑ 126 William Floyd .75 .30
❑ 127 Elvis Grbac .75 .30
❑ 128 Jerry Rice 3.00 1.25
❑ 129 J.J. Stokes 1.50 .60
❑ 130 Steve Young 2.50 1.00
❑ 131 Joey Galloway 1.50 .60
❑ 132 Cortez Kennedy .40 .15
❑ 133 Kevin Mawae .40 .15
❑ 134 Rick Mirer .75 .30
❑ 135 Chris Warren .75 .30
❑ 136 Trent Dilfer 1.50 .60
❑ 137 Jerry Ellison .40 .15
❑ 138 Alvin Harper .40 .15
❑ 139 Errict Rhett .75 .30
❑ 140 Terry Allen .75 .30
❑ 141 Brian Mitchell .40 .15
❑ 142 Gus Frerotte .75 .30
❑ 143 Michael Westbrook 1.50 .60
❑ 144 Heath Shuler .75 .30

1997 Pacific Dynagon

❑ COMPLETE SET (144) 80.00 40.00
❑ 1 Larry Centers 1.00 .40
❑ 2 Kent Graham .60 .25
❑ 3 Leeland McElroy .60 .25
❑ 4 Frank Sanders 1.00 .40
❑ 5 Jamal Anderson 1.25 .50
❑ 6 Bert Emanuel 1.00 .40
❑ 7 Bobby Hebert .60 .25
❑ 8 Terance Mathis 1.00 .40
❑ 9 Eric Metcalf 1.00 .40
❑ 10 Derrick Alexander WR 1.00 .40
❑ 11 Earnest Byner .60 .25
❑ 12 Michael Jackson 1.00 .40
❑ 13 Vinny Testaverde 1.00 .40
❑ 14 Quinn Early .60 .25
❑ 15 Jim Kelly 1.25 .50
❑ 16 Eric Moulds 1.25 .50
❑ 17 Andre Reed 1.00 .40
❑ 18 Bruce Smith 1.00 .40
❑ 19 Thurman Thomas 1.25 .50
❑ 20 Tim Biakabutuka 1.00 .40
❑ 21 Mark Carrier WR .60 .25
❑ 22 Kerry Collins 1.25 .50
❑ 23 Kevin Greene 1.00 .40
❑ 24 Anthony Johnson .60 .25
❑ 25 Wesley Walls 1.00 .40
❑ 26 Curtis Conway 1.00 .40
❑ 27 Bobby Engram 1.00 .40
❑ 28 Raymont Harris .60 .25
❑ 29 Dave Krieg .60 .25
❑ 30 Rashaan Salaam .60 .25
❑ 31 Jeff Blake 1.00 .40
❑ 32 Ki-Jana Carter .60 .25
❑ 33 Garrison Hearst 1.00 .40
❑ 34 Carl Pickens 1.00 .40
❑ 35 Darnay Scott 1.00 .40
❑ 36 Troy Aikman 2.50 1.00
❑ 37 Chris Boniol .60 .25
❑ 38 Michael Irvin 1.25 .50
❑ 39 Deion Sanders 1.25 .50
❑ 40 Emmitt Smith 4.00 1.50
❑ 41 Herschel Walker 1.00 .40
❑ 42 Terrell Davis 1.50 .60
❑ 43 John Elway 5.00 2.00
❑ 44 Ed McCaffrey 1.00 .40
❑ 45 Shannon Sharpe 1.00 .40
❑ 46 Alfred Williams .60 .25
❑ 47 Scott Mitchell 1.00 .40
❑ 48 Herman Moore 1.00 .40
❑ 49 Brett Perriman .60 .25
❑ 50 Barry Sanders 4.00 1.50
❑ 51 Edgar Bennett 1.00 .40
❑ 52 Robert Brooks 1.00 .40
❑ 53 Mark Chmura 1.00 .40
❑ 54 Brett Favre 5.00 2.00
❑ 55 Antonio Freeman 1.25 .50
❑ 56 Desmond Howard 1.00 .40
❑ 57 Reggie White 1.25 .50
❑ 58 Chris Chandler 1.00 .40
❑ 59 Eddie George 1.25 .50
❑ 60 James McKeehan .60 .25
❑ 61 Steve McNair 1.50 .60
❑ 62 Chris Sanders .60 .25
❑ 63 Sean Dawkins .60 .25
❑ 64 Ken Dilger .60 .25
❑ 65 Marshall Faulk 1.50 .60
❑ 66 Jim Harbaugh 1.00 .40
❑ 67 Marvin Harrison 1.25 .50
❑ 68 Tony Boselli .60 .25
❑ 69 Mark Brunell 1.50 .60
❑ 70 Keenan McCardell 1.00 .40
❑ 71 Natrone Means 1.00 .40
❑ 72 Jimmy Smith 1.00 .40
❑ 73 Marcus Allen 1.25 .50
❑ 74 Kimble Anders 1.00 .40
❑ 75 Dale Carter .60 .25
❑ 76 Greg Hill .60 .25
❑ 77 Derrick Thomas 1.25 .50
❑ 78 Tamarick Vanover 1.00 .40
❑ 79 Karim Abdul-Jabbar 1.25 .50
❑ 80 Dan Marino 5.00 2.00
❑ 81 O.J. McDuffie 1.00 .40
❑ 82 Jerris McPhail .60 .25
❑ 83 Zach Thomas 1.25 .50
❑ 84 Cris Carter 1.25 .50
❑ 85 Brad Johnson 1.25 .50
❑ 86 Jake Reed 1.00 .40
❑ 87 Robert Smith 1.00 .40
❑ 88 Drew Bledsoe 1.50 .60
❑ 89 Ben Coates 1.00 .40
❑ 90 Terry Glenn 1.25 .50
❑ 91 Curtis Martin 1.50 .60
❑ 92 Willie McGinest .60 .25
❑ 93 Jim Everett .60 .25
❑ 94 Michael Haynes .60 .25
❑ 95 Haywood Jeffires .60 .25
❑ 96 Ray Zellars .60 .25
❑ 97 Dave Brown .60 .25
❑ 98 Rodney Hampton 1.00 .40
❑ 99 Danny Kanell 1.00 .40
❑ 100 Thomas Lewis .60 .25
❑ 101 Wayne Chrebet 1.25 .50
❑ 102 Keyshawn Johnson 1.25 .50
❑ 103 Adrian Murrell 1.00 .40
❑ 104 Neil O'Donnell 1.00 .40
❑ 105 Tim Brown 1.25 .50
❑ 106 Rickey Dudley 1.00 .40
❑ 107 Jeff Hostetler .60 .25
❑ 108 Napoleon Kaufman 1.25 .50
❑ 109 Ty Detmer 1.00 .40
❑ 110 Jason Dunn .60 .25
❑ 111 Irving Fryar 1.00 .40
❑ 112 Chris T. Jones .60 .25
❑ 113 Ricky Watters 1.00 .40
❑ 114 Jerome Bettis 1.25 .50
❑ 115 Chad Brown .60 .25
❑ 116 Kordell Stewart 1.25 .50
❑ 117 Mike Tomczak .60 .25
❑ 118 Rod Woodson 1.00 .40
❑ 119 Tony Banks 1.00 .40
❑ 120 Isaac Bruce 1.25 .50
❑ 121 Eddie Kennison 1.00 .40
❑ 122 Lawrence Phillips .60 .25
❑ 123 Terrell Fletcher .60 .25
❑ 124 Stan Humphries 1.00 .40
❑ 125 Tony Martin 1.00 .40
❑ 126 Junior Seau 1.25 .50
❑ 127 Elvis Grbac 1.00 .40
❑ 128 Terrell Owens 1.50 .60
❑ 129 Ted Popson .60 .25
❑ 130 Jerry Rice 2.50 1.00
❑ 131 Steve Young 1.50 .60
❑ 132 John Friesz .60 .25
❑ 133 Joey Galloway 1.00 .40
❑ 134 Michael McCrary .60 .25
❑ 135 Lamar Smith 1.25 .50
❑ 136 Chris Warren 1.00 .40
❑ 137 Mike Alstott 1.25 .50
❑ 138 Trent Dilfer 1.25 .50
❑ 139 Courtney Hawkins .60 .25
❑ 140 Errict Rhett .60 .25
❑ 141 Terry Allen 1.25 .50
❑ 142 Henry Ellard .60 .25
❑ 143 Gus Frerotte .60 .25
❑ 144 Leslie Shepherd .60 .25
❑ C Mark Brunell Sample 2.00 .75

2001 Pacific Dynagon

❑ COMP.SET w/o SP's (100) 40.00 15.00
❑ 1 David Boston 1.25 .50
❑ 2 Thomas Jones .75 .30
❑ 3 Jake Plummer .75 .30
❑ 4 Jamal Anderson 1.25 .50
❑ 5 Tim Dwight 1.25 .50
❑ 6 Elvis Grbac .75 .30
❑ 7 Jamal Lewis 2.00 .75
❑ 8 Ray Lewis 1.25 .50
❑ 9 Shannon Sharpe .75 .30
❑ 10 Rob Johnson .75 .30
❑ 11 Eric Moulds .75 .30
❑ 12 Peerless Price .75 .30
❑ 13 Tim Biakabutuka .75 .30
❑ 14 Patrick Jeffers .75 .30
❑ 15 Muhsin Muhammad .75 .30
❑ 16 James Allen .75 .30
❑ 17 Cade McNown .50 .20
❑ 18 Marcus Robinson 1.25 .50
❑ 19 Brian Urlacher 2.00 .75

❑	20	Corey Dillon	1.25	.50
❑	21	Akili Smith	.50	.20
❑	22	Peter Warrick	1.25	.50
❑	23	Tim Couch	.75	.30
❑	24	Kevin Johnson	.75	.30
❑	25	Randall Cunningham	1.25	.50
❑	26	Emmitt Smith	2.50	1.00
❑	27	Mike Anderson	1.25	.50
❑	28	Terrell Davis	1.25	.50
❑	29	Brian Griese	1.25	.50
❑	30	Ed McCaffrey	1.25	.50
❑	31	Rod Smith	.75	.30
❑	32	Charlie Batch	1.25	.50
❑	33	Johnnie Morton	.75	.30
❑	34	James Stewart	.75	.30
❑	35	Brett Favre	4.00	1.50
❑	36	Antonio Freeman	1.25	.50
❑	37	Ahman Green	1.25	.50
❑	38	Marvin Harrison	1.25	.50
❑	39	Edgerrin James	1.50	.60
❑	40	Peyton Manning	3.00	1.25
❑	41	Mark Brunell	1.25	.50
❑	42	Keenan McCardell	.50	.20
❑	43	Jimmy Smith	.75	.30
❑	44	Fred Taylor	1.25	.50
❑	45	Derrick Alexander	.75	.30
❑	46	Tony Gonzalez	.75	.30
❑	47	Sylvester Morris	.50	.20
❑	48	Jay Fiedler	1.25	.50
❑	49	Oronde Gadsden	.75	.30
❑	50	Lamar Smith	.75	.30
❑	51	Cris Carter	1.25	.50
❑	52	Daunte Culpepper	1.25	.50
❑	53	Randy Moss	2.50	1.00
❑	54	Drew Bledsoe	1.50	.60
❑	55	Terry Glenn	.50	.20
❑	56	J.R. Redmond	.50	.20
❑	57	Aaron Brooks	1.25	.50
❑	58	Joe Horn	.75	.30
❑	59	Ricky Williams	1.25	.50
❑	60	Tiki Barber	1.25	.50
❑	61	Kerry Collins	.75	.30
❑	62	Ron Dayne	1.25	.50
❑	63	Amani Toomer	.50	.20
❑	64	Wayne Chrebet	.75	.30
❑	65	Curtis Martin	1.25	.50
❑	66	Vinny Testaverde	.75	.30
❑	67	Tim Brown	1.25	.50
❑	68	Rich Gannon	1.25	.50
❑	69	Tyrone Wheatley	.75	.30
❑	70	Charles Johnson	.50	.20
❑	71	Donovan McNabb	1.50	.60
❑	72	Duce Staley	1.25	.50
❑	73	Jerome Bettis	1.25	.50
❑	74	Plaxico Burress	1.25	.50
❑	75	Kordell Stewart	.75	.30
❑	76	Isaac Bruce	1.25	.50
❑	77	Marshall Faulk	1.50	.60
❑	78	Torry Holt	1.25	.50
❑	79	Kurt Warner	2.50	1.00
❑	80	Curtis Conway	.75	.30
❑	81	Doug Flutie	1.25	.50
❑	82	Jeff Garcia	1.25	.50
❑	83	Charlie Garner	.75	.30
❑	84	Terrell Owens	1.25	.50
❑	85	Jerry Rice	2.50	1.00
❑	86	Shaun Alexander	1.50	.60
❑	87	Matt Hasselbeck	.75	.30
❑	88	Darrell Jackson	1.25	.50
❑	89	Mike Alstott	1.25	.50
❑	90	Warrick Dunn	1.25	.50
❑	91	Brad Johnson	1.25	.50
❑	92	Keyshawn Johnson	1.25	.50
❑	93	Shaun King	.50	.20
❑	94	Eddie George	1.25	.50
❑	95	Jevon Kearse	.75	.30
❑	96	Derrick Mason	.75	.30
❑	97	Steve McNair	1.25	.50
❑	98	Stephen Davis	1.25	.50
❑	99	Jeff George	.75	.30
❑	100	Deion Sanders	1.25	.50
❑	101	Michael Bennett AU RC	20.00	7.50
❑	102	Drew Brees AU RC	100.00	50.00
❑	103	Chris Chambers AU RC	30.00	15.00
❑	104	LaMont Jordan AU RC	50.00	20.00
❑	105	Deuce McAllister AU RC	60.00	30.00
❑	106	Koren Robinson AU RC	20.00	7.50
❑	107	David Terrell AU RC	20.00	7.50
❑	108	LaDain Tomlinson AU RC	250.00	150.00
❑	109	Marques Tuiasosopo AU RC	20.00	7.50
❑	110	Michael Vick AU RC	150.00	75.00
❑	111	Chris Weinke AU RC	25.00	10.00
❑	112	Kevan Barlow AU RC	20.00	7.50
❑	113	Josh Booty AU RC	20.00	7.50
❑	114	Rod Gardner AU RC	20.00	8.00
❑	115	Todd Heap AU RC	20.00	7.50
❑	116	Travis Henry AU RC	40.00	20.00
❑	117	James Jackson AU RC	20.00	7.50
❑	118	Chad Johnson AU RC	80.00	40.00
❑	119	Rudi Johnson AU RC	50.00	20.00
❑	120	Ben Leard AU RC	12.00	5.00
❑	121	Quincy Morgan AU RC	20.00	7.50
❑	122	Snoop Minnis AU RC	12.00	5.00
❑	123	Freddie Mitchell AU RC	20.00	7.50
❑	124	Sage Rosenfels AU RC	20.00	7.50
❑	125	Anthony Thomas AU RC	20.00	7.50
❑	126	Reggie Wayne AU RC	40.00	20.00
❑	127	Dan Alexander AU RC	12.00	5.00
❑	128	Will Allen AU RC	10.00	4.00
❑	129	Scotty Anderson AU RC	10.00	4.00
❑	130	Adam Archuleta AU RC	12.00	5.00
❑	131	Alex Bannister AU RC	10.00	4.00
❑	133	Tay Cody AU RC	8.00	3.00
❑	134	Tony Dixon AU RC	10.00	4.00
❑	135	Heath Evans AU RC	10.00	4.00
❑	137	Derrick Gibson AU RC	10.00	4.00
❑	138	Edgerton Hartwell AU RC	8.00	3.00
❑	139	Tim Hasselbeck AU RC	12.00	5.00
❑	140	Jabari Holloway AU RC	10.00	4.00
❑	141	Torrance Marshall AU RC	12.00	5.00
❑	142	Jason McKinley AU RC	10.00	4.00
❑	143	Mike McMahon AU RC	20.00	7.50
❑	144	Bobby Newcombe AU RC	10.00	4.00
❑	145	Moran Norris AU RC	8.00	3.00
❑	146	Tommy Polley AU RC	12.00	5.00
❑	147	Vinny Sutherland AU RC	10.00	4.00
❑	149	Reggie White AU RC	10.00	4.00
❑	150	Cedrick Wilson AU RC	20.00	7.50

2002 Pacific Exclusive

❑	1	David Boston	1.50	.60
❑	2	Thomas Jones	1.00	.40
❑	3	Jake Plummer	1.00	.40
❑	4	Frank Sanders	1.00	.40
❑	5	Josh Scobey RC	2.50	1.00
❑	6	Warrick Dunn	1.50	.60
❑	7	Brian Finneran	.60	.25
❑	8	Kahlil Hill RC	2.00	.75
❑	9	Shawn Jefferson	.60	.25
❑	10	Kurt Kittner RC	2.00	.75
❑	11	Michael Vick	5.00	2.00
❑	12	Ron Johnson RC	2.00	.75
❑	13	Jamal Lewis	1.50	.60
❑	14	Ray Lewis	1.50	.60
❑	15	Chris Redman	.60	.25
❑	16	Brandon Stokley	1.00	.40
❑	17	Chester Taylor RC	5.00	2.00
❑	18	Travis Taylor	.60	.25
❑	19	Drew Bledsoe	2.00	.75
❑	20	Travis Henry	1.50	.60
❑	21	Eric Moulds	1.00	.40
❑	22	Peerless Price	1.00	.40
❑	23	Randy Fasani RC	2.00	.75
❑	24	Muhsin Muhammad	1.00	.40
❑	25	Lamar Smith	1.00	.40
❑	26	Steve Smith	1.50	.60
❑	27	Chris Weinke	1.00	.40
❑	28	Marty Booker	1.00	.40
❑	29	Jim Miller	1.00	.40
❑	30	Adrian Peterson RC	2.50	1.00
❑	31	Marcus Robinson	1.00	.40
❑	32	David Terrell	1.50	.60
❑	33	Anthony Thomas	1.00	.40
❑	34	Brian Urlacher	2.50	1.00
❑	35	Corey Dillon	1.00	.40
❑	36	Chad Johnson	1.50	.60
❑	37	Jon Kitna	1.00	.40
❑	38	Michael Westbrook	.60	.25
❑	39	Peter Warrick	1.00	.40
❑	40	Tim Couch	1.00	.40
❑	41	JaJuan Dawson	.60	.25
❑	42	James Jackson	.60	.25
❑	43	Kevin Johnson	1.00	.40
❑	44	Quincy Morgan	1.00	.40
❑	45	Quincy Carter	1.00	.40
❑	46	Joey Galloway	1.00	.40
❑	47	Troy Hambrick	.60	.25
❑	48	Chad Hutchinson RC	2.00	.75
❑	49	Rocket Ismail	1.00	.40
❑	50	Emmitt Smith	4.00	1.50
❑	51	Mike Anderson	1.50	.60
❑	52	Terrell Davis	1.50	.60
❑	53	Brian Griese	1.50	.60
❑	54	Herb Haygood RC	1.25	.50
❑	55	Ed McCaffrey	1.50	.60
❑	56	Rod Smith	1.00	.40
❑	57	Germane Crowell	.60	.25
❑	58	Az-Zahir Hakim	.60	.25
❑	59	Mike McMahon	1.50	.60
❑	60	Bill Schroeder	1.00	.40
❑	61	Luke Staley RC	2.00	.75
❑	62	James Stewart	1.00	.40
❑	63	Brett Favre	4.00	1.50
❑	64	Robert Ferguson	.60	.25
❑	65	Bubba Franks	1.00	.40
❑	66	Terry Glenn	1.00	.40
❑	67	Ahman Green	1.50	.60
❑	68	Craig Nall RC	2.50	1.00
❑	69	James Allen	1.00	.40
❑	70	Corey Bradford	.60	.25
❑	71	Jermaine Lewis	.60	.25
❑	72	Travis Prentice	.60	.25
❑	73	Brian Allen RC	2.00	.75
❑	74	Marvin Harrison	1.50	.60
❑	75	Edgerrin James	2.00	.75
❑	76	Peyton Manning	3.00	1.25
❑	77	Reggie Wayne	1.50	.60
❑	78	Mark Brunell	1.50	.60
❑	79	Patrick Johnson	.60	.25
❑	80	Jimmy Smith	1.00	.40
❑	81	Fred Taylor	1.50	.60
❑	82	Tony Gonzalez	1.00	.40
❑	83	Trent Green	1.00	.40
❑	84	Priest Holmes	2.00	.75
❑	85	Johnnie Morton	1.00	.40
❑	86	Chris Chambers	1.50	.60
❑	87	Jay Fiedler	1.00	.40
❑	88	Oronde Gadsden	1.00	.40
❑	89	Leonard Henry RC	2.00	.75
❑	90	Travis Minor	.60	.25
❑	91	Sam Simmons RC	1.25	.50
❑	92	Ricky Williams	1.50	.60
❑	93	Derrick Alexander	1.00	.40
❑	94	Michael Bennett	1.50	.60
❑	95	Daunte Culpepper	1.50	.60
❑	96	Randy Moss	3.00	1.25
❑	97	Tom Brady	4.00	1.50
❑	98	Deion Branch RC	5.00	2.00
❑	99	Troy Brown	1.00	.40
❑	100	Rohan Davey RC	2.50	1.00
❑	101	Donald Hayes	.60	.25
❑	102	David Patten	.60	.25
❑	103	Antowain Smith	1.00	.40
❑	104	Antwoine Womack RC	2.00	.75
❑	105	Aaron Brooks	1.50	.60
❑	106	Joe Horn	1.00	.40
❑	107	Deuce McAllister	1.50	.60
❑	108	J.T. O'Sullivan RC	2.00	.75
❑	109	Jerome Pathon	1.00	.40
❑	110	Tiki Barber	1.50	.60
❑	111	Tim Carter RC	2.00	.75
❑	112	Kerry Collins	1.00	.40
❑	113	Ron Dayne	1.00	.40

❑ 114 Ike Hilliard 1.00 .40
❑ 115 Amani Toomer 1.00 .40
❑ 116 Wayne Chrebet 1.00 .40
❑ 117 Laveranues Coles 1.00 .40
❑ 118 Curtis Martin 1.50 .60
❑ 119 Santana Moss 1.50 .60
❑ 120 Vinny Testaverde 1.00 .40
❑ 121 Tim Brown 1.50 .60
❑ 122 Ronald Curry RC 2.50 1.00
❑ 123 Rich Gannon 1.50 .60
❑ 124 Charlie Garner 1.00 .40
❑ 125 Larry Ned RC 2.00 .75
❑ 126 Jerry Rice 3.00 1.25
❑ 127 Tyrone Wheatley 1.00 .40
❑ 128 Donovan McNabb 2.00 .75
❑ 129 Freddie Mitchell 1.00 .40
❑ 130 Todd Pinkston 1.00 .40
❑ 131 Duce Staley 1.50 .60
❑ 132 James Thrash 1.00 .40
❑ 133 Jerome Bettis 1.50 .60
❑ 134 Plaxico Burress 1.50 .60
❑ 135 Kordell Stewart 1.00 .40
❑ 136 Hines Ward 1.50 .60
❑ 137 Amos Zereoue 1.50 .60
❑ 138 Isaac Bruce 1.50 .60
❑ 139 Trung Canidate 1.00 .40
❑ 140 Eric Crouch RC 2.50 1.00
❑ 141 Marshall Faulk 1.50 .60
❑ 142 Lamar Gordon RC 2.50 1.00
❑ 143 Torry Holt 1.50 .60
❑ 144 Kurt Warner 1.50 .60
❑ 145 Terrence Wilkins .60 .25
❑ 146 Drew Brees 1.50 .60
❑ 147 Seth Burford RC 2.00 .75
❑ 148 Reche Caldwell RC 2.50 1.00
❑ 149 Curtis Conway 1.00 .40
❑ 150 Tim Dwight 1.00 .40
❑ 151 Doug Flutie 1.50 .60
❑ 152 LaDainian Tomlinson 2.50 1.00
❑ 153 Kevan Barlow 1.00 .40
❑ 154 Brandon Doman RC 2.00 .75
❑ 155 Jeff Garcia 1.50 .60
❑ 156 Garrison Hearst 1.00 .40
❑ 157 Terrell Owens 1.50 .60
❑ 158 J.J. Stokes 1.00 .40
❑ 159 Shaun Alexander 2.00 .75
❑ 160 Trent Dilfer 1.00 .40
❑ 161 Darrell Jackson 1.00 .40
❑ 162 Koren Robinson 1.00 .40
❑ 163 Mike Alstott 1.50 .60
❑ 164 Brad Johnson 1.00 .40
❑ 165 Keyshawn Johnson 1.50 .60
❑ 166 Keenan McCardell .60 .25
❑ 167 Michael Pittman .60 .25
❑ 168 Travis Stephens RC 2.00 .75
❑ 169 Marquise Walker RC 2.00 .75
❑ 170 Kevin Dyson 1.00 .40
❑ 171 Eddie George 1.50 .60
❑ 172 Derrick Mason 1.00 .40
❑ 173 Steve McNair 1.50 .60
❑ 174 Reidel Anthony .60 .25
❑ 175 Ladell Betts RC 2.50 1.00
❑ 176 Stephen Davis 1.00 .40
❑ 177 Rod Gardner 1.00 .40
❑ 178 Jacquez Green .60 .25
❑ 179 Shane Matthews .60 .25
❑ 180 Cliff Russell RC 2.00 .75
❑ 181 Josh McCown AU/779 RC 20.00 7.50
❑ 182 T.J. Duckett RC 3.00 1.25
❑ 183 Josh Reed RC 2.50 1.00
❑ 184 DeShaun Foster AU/105 RC 50.00 25.00
❑ 185 Andre Davis AU/778 RC 20.00 7.50
❑ 186 William Green RC 2.50 1.00
❑ 187 Antonio Bryant AU/575 RC 20.00 7.50
❑ 188 Ashley Lelie AU/100 RC 80.00 30.00
❑ 189 Clinton Portis AU/524 RC 50.00 20.00
❑ 190 Joey Harrington RC 4.00 1.50
❑ 191 Javon Walker AU/519 RC 40.00 15.00
❑ 192 David Carr AU/100 RC 120.00 60.00
❑ 193 Jabar Gaffney AU/103 RC 20.00 7.50
❑ 194 Jonathan Wells AU/615 RC 20.00 7.50
❑ 195 David Garrard AU/787 RC 20.00 7.50
❑ 196 Donte Stallworth RC 5.00 2.00
❑ 197 Brian Westbrook AU/930 RC 40.00 15.00
❑ 198 Ant Randle El AU/788 RC 40.00 15.00
❑ 199 Maurice Morris AU/1045 RC 15.00 6.00
❑ 200 Patrick Ramsey RC 3.00 1.25

2002 Pacific Exclusive Retail

❑ 181 Josh McCown RC 3.00 1.25
❑ 184 DeShaun Foster RC 2.50 1.00
❑ 185 Andre Davis RC 2.50 1.00
❑ 187 Antonio Bryant RC 2.50 1.00
❑ 188 Ashley Lelie RC 5.00 2.00
❑ 189 Clinton Portis RC 8.00 3.00
❑ 191 Javon Walker RC 5.00 2.00
❑ 192 David Carr RC 6.00 2.50
❑ 193 Jabar Gaffney RC 2.50 1.00
❑ 194 Jonathan Wells RC 2.50 1.00
❑ 195 David Garrard RC 2.50 1.00
❑ 197 Brian Westbrook RC 4.00 1.50
❑ 198 Antwaan Randle El RC 4.00 1.50
❑ 199 Maurice Morris RC 2.50 1.00

1995 Pacific Gridiron

❑ COMP.BLUE SET (100) 50.00 20.00
❑ 1 Natrone Means .50 .20
❑ 2 Dave Meggett .30 .10
❑ 3 Curtis Conway .50 .20
❑ 4 Sam Adams .30 .10
❑ 5 Qadry Ismail .50 .20
❑ 6 Steve Young 2.00 .75
❑ 7 Errict Rhett .50 .20
❑ 8 Nate Lewis .30 .10
❑ 9 Barry Sanders 5.00 2.00
❑ 10 Sterling Sharpe .50 .20
❑ 11 Steve Beuerlein .50 .20
❑ 12 Irving Spikes .50 .20
❑ 13 Byron Bam Morris .30 .10
❑ 14 Eric Metcalf .50 .20
❑ 15 Michael Irvin 1.00 .40
❑ 16 Dan Marino 5.00 2.00
❑ 17 Stan Humphries .50 .20
❑ 18 Leroy Hoard .50 .20
❑ 19 Marcus Allen 1.00 .40
❑ 20 Barry Foster .50 .20
❑ 21 Ronald Moore .30 .10
❑ 22 Rodney Hampton .50 .20
❑ 23 Ben Coates .50 .20
❑ 24 Vernon Turner .30 .10
❑ 25 Shannon Sharpe .50 .20
❑ 26 Larry Centers .50 .20
❑ 27 Mack Strong RC 2.00 .75
❑ 28 Reggie White 1.00 .40
❑ 29 Harvey Williams .30 .10
❑ 30 Darnay Scott .50 .20
❑ 31 Drew Bledsoe 2.50 1.00
❑ 32 Marshall Faulk 2.00 .75
❑ 33 Troy Aikman 2.50 1.00
❑ 34 Boomer Esiason .50 .20
❑ 35 Bobby Hebert .30 .10
❑ 36 Brian Mitchell .30 .10
❑ 37 Andre Rison .50 .20
❑ 38 Brett Favre 5.00 2.00
❑ 39 Don Majkowski .30 .10
❑ 40 Johnny Johnson .30 .10
❑ 41 Mark Carrier WR .50 .20
❑ 42 James Joseph .30 .10
❑ 43 Mario Bates .50 .20
❑ 44 Craig Heyward .50 .20
❑ 45 Henry Ellard .50 .20
❑ 46 Thurman Thomas 1.00 .40
❑ 47 Jerome Bettis 1.00 .40
❑ 48 Dave Brown .50 .20
❑ 49 Lorenzo White .30 .10
❑ 50 Joe Montana 5.00 2.00
❑ 51 Vinny Testaverde .50 .20
❑ 52 Lake Dawson .50 .20
❑ 53 Michael Timpson .30 .10
❑ 54 Ricky Ervins .30 .10
❑ 55 Cris Carter 1.00 .40
❑ 56 Raymont Harris .30 .10
❑ 57 Andre Coleman .30 .10
❑ 58 Craig Erickson .30 .10
❑ 59 Jeff Hostetler .50 .20
❑ 60 Deion Sanders 1.50 .60
❑ 61 Eric Turner .30 .10
❑ 62 Daryl Johnston .50 .20
❑ 63 Bernie Parmalee .50 .20
❑ 64 Ricky Watters .50 .20
❑ 65 David Palmer .50 .20
❑ 66 Aaron Glenn .30 .10
❑ 67 Todd Kinchen .30 .10
❑ 68 Edgar Bennett .50 .20
❑ 69 Mel Gray .30 .10
❑ 70 Randall Cunningham 1.00 .40
❑ 71 Michael Haynes .50 .20
❑ 72 Chris Miller .30 .10
❑ 73 Glyn Milburn .30 .10
❑ 74 Steve McNair RC 6.00 2.50
❑ 75 Lewis Tillman .30 .10
❑ 76 Chuck Levy .30 .10
❑ 77 Carl Pickens .50 .20
❑ 78 Michael Bates .30 .10
❑ 79 Jeff Blake RC 1.50 .60
❑ 80 O.J. McDuffie 1.00 .40
❑ 81 Tim Brown 1.00 .40
❑ 82 Haywood Jeffires .30 .10
❑ 83 Jeff Burris .30 .10
❑ 84 John Elway 5.00 2.00
❑ 85 Charles Johnson .50 .20
❑ 86 Emmitt Smith 5.00 2.00
❑ 87 William Floyd .50 .20
❑ 88 Herschel Walker .50 .20
❑ 89 Rick Mirer .50 .20
❑ 90 Roosevelt Potts .30 .10
❑ 91 Rod Woodson .50 .20
❑ 92 Greg Hill .50 .20
❑ 93 Junior Seau 1.00 .40
❑ 94 Dave Krieg .30 .10
❑ 95 Jim Kelly 1.00 .40
❑ 96 Warren Moon 1.00 .40
❑ 97 Leroy Thompson .30 .10
❑ 98 Ki-Jana Carter RC 1.00 .40
❑ 99 Herman Moore 1.00 .40
❑ 100 Jerry Rice 2.50 1.00
❑ P1 Natrone Means 1.00 .40
❑ P2 Natrone Means 1.00 .40
❑ P3 Natrone Means 1.00 .40
❑ P4 Natrone Means Promo Blue 1.00 .40
❑ P5 Natrone Means Promo 1.00 .40

1996 Pacific Gridiron

❑ COMPLETE SET (125) 30.00 12.50
❑ 1 Larry Centers .40 .15
❑ 2 Garrison Hearst .40 .15
❑ 3 Dave Krieg .25 .08
❑ 4 Frank Sanders .40 .15
❑ 5 Jamal Anderson RC 1.00 .40
❑ 6 J.J. Birden .25 .08
❑ 7 Eric Metcalf .25 .08
❑ 8 Jeff George .40 .15
❑ 9 Cornelius Bennett .25 .08
❑ 10 Todd Collins .40 .15

❑ 11 Darick Holmes .25 .08
❑ 12 Jim Kelly .75 .30
❑ 13 Bryce Paup .25 .08
❑ 14 Bob Christian .25 .08
❑ 15 Kerry Collins .75 .30
❑ 16 Pete Metzelaars .25 .08
❑ 17 Derrick Moore .25 .08
❑ 18 Curtis Conway .75 .30
❑ 19 Jim Flanigan .25 .08
❑ 20 Erik Kramer .25 .08
❑ 21 Rashaan Salaam .40 .15
❑ 22 Eric Bieniemy .25 .08
❑ 23 Jeff Blake .75 .30
❑ 24 Tony McGee .25 .08
❑ 25 Darnay Scott .40 .15
❑ 26 Vashone Adams .25 .08
❑ 27 Leroy Hoard .25 .08
❑ 28 Andre Rison .40 .15
❑ 29 Tommy Vardell .25 .08
❑ 30 Troy Aikman 2.00 .75
❑ 31 Michael Irvin .75 .30
❑ 32 Daryl Johnston .40 .15
❑ 33 Deion Sanders 1.00 .40
❑ 34 Emmitt Smith 3.00 1.25
❑ 35 Terrell Davis 1.50 .60
❑ 36 John Elway 4.00 1.50
❑ 37 Ed McCaffrey .40 .15
❑ 38 Anthony Miller .40 .15
❑ 39 Scott Mitchell .40 .15
❑ 40 Brett Perriman .25 .08
❑ 41 Barry Sanders 3.00 1.25
❑ 42 Chris Spielman .25 .08
❑ 43 Edgar Bennett .40 .15
❑ 44 Robert Brooks .75 .30
❑ 45 Brett Favre 4.00 1.50
❑ 46 Antonio Freeman .75 .30
❑ 47 Reggie White .75 .30
❑ 48 Haywood Jeffires .25 .08
❑ 49 Steve McNair 1.50 .60
❑ 50 Rodney Thomas .25 .08
❑ 51 Frank Wycheck .25 .08
❑ 52 Ashley Ambrose .25 .08
❑ 53 Mark Brunell 1.25 .50
❑ 54 Ken Dilger .40 .15
❑ 55 Marshall Faulk 1.00 .40
❑ 56 Jim Harbaugh .40 .15
❑ 57 Tony Boselli .25 .08
❑ 58 Pete Mitchell .40 .15
❑ 59 James O.Stewart .40 .15
❑ 60 Marcus Allen .75 .30
❑ 61 Steve Bono .25 .08
❑ 62 Lake Dawson .25 .08
❑ 63 Tamarick Vanover .40 .15
❑ 64 Bryan Cox .25 .08
❑ 65 Dan Marino 4.00 1.50
❑ 66 O.J. McDuffie .40 .15
❑ 67 Bernie Parmalee .25 .08
❑ 68 Cris Carter .75 .30
❑ 69 Rocket Ismail .25 .08
❑ 70 Warren Moon .40 .15
❑ 71 Robert Smith .40 .15
❑ 72 Drew Bledsoe 1.25 .50
❑ 73 Vincent Brisby .25 .08
❑ 74 Ben Coates .40 .15
❑ 75 Curtis Martin 1.50 .60
❑ 76 Mario Bates .40 .15
❑ 77 Derek Brown RBK .25 .08
❑ 78 Jim Everett .25 .08
❑ 79 Dave Brown .25 .08
❑ 80 Chris Calloway .25 .08
❑ 81 Rodney Hampton .40 .15
❑ 82 Tyrone Wheatley .40 .15
❑ 83 Kyle Brady .25 .08
❑ 84 Wayne Chrebet 1.00 .40
❑ 85 Adrian Murrell .40 .15
❑ 86 Tim Brown .75 .30
❑ 87 Rob Carpenter .25 .08
❑ 88 Charlie Garner .40 .15
❑ 89 Daryl Hobbs RC .25 .08
❑ 90 Napoleon Kaufman .75 .30
❑ 91 Rodney Peete .25 .08
❑ 92 Ricky Watters .40 .15
❑ 93 Calvin Williams .25 .08
❑ 94 Kevin Greene .40 .15
❑ 95 Greg Lloyd .40 .15
❑ 96 Neil O'Donnell .40 .15
❑ 97 Erric Pegram .25 .08
❑ 98 Kordell Stewart .75 .30
❑ 99 Yancey Thigpen .40 .15
❑ 100 Rod Woodson .40 .15
❑ 101 Isaac Bruce .75 .30
❑ 102 Jerome Bettis .75 .30
❑ 103 J.T. Thomas .25 .08
❑ 104 Ronnie Harmon .25 .08
❑ 105 Aaron Hayden RC .25 .08
❑ 106 Stan Humphries .40 .15
❑ 107 Alfred Pupunu .25 .08
❑ 108 William Floyd .40 .15
❑ 109 Brent Jones .25 .08
❑ 110 Jerry Rice 2.00 .75
❑ 111 J.J. Stokes .75 .30
❑ 112 John Taylor .25 .08
❑ 113 Steve Young 1.25 .50
❑ 114 Harvey Williams .25 .08
❑ 115 John Friesz .25 .08
❑ 116 Joey Galloway .75 .30
❑ 117 Cortez Kennedy .25 .08
❑ 118 Rick Mirer .40 .15
❑ 119 Chris Warren .40 .15
❑ 120 Trent Dilfer .75 .30
❑ 121 Alvin Harper .25 .08
❑ 122 Errict Rhett .40 .15
❑ 123 Terry Allen .40 .15
❑ 124 Gus Frerotte .40 .15
❑ 125 Michael Westbrook .75 .30
❑ S1 Chris Warren Sample 1.00 .40

2001 Pacific Impressions

❑ COMP.SET w/o SP's (144) 80.00 40.00
❑ 1 David Boston 1.50 .60
❑ 2 Thomas Jones 1.00 .40
❑ 3 Rob Moore 1.00 .40
❑ 4 Michael Pittman .60 .25
❑ 5 Jake Plummer 1.00 .40
❑ 6 Jamal Anderson 1.50 .60
❑ 7 Chris Chandler 1.00 .40
❑ 8 Shawn Jefferson .60 .25
❑ 9 Terance Mathis .60 .25
❑ 10 Elvis Grbac 1.00 .40
❑ 11 Qadry Ismail 1.00 .40
❑ 12 Jamal Lewis 2.50 1.00
❑ 13 Ray Lewis 1.50 .60
❑ 14 Shannon Sharpe 1.00 .40
❑ 15 Shawn Bryson .60 .25
❑ 16 Rob Johnson 1.00 .40
❑ 17 Sammy Morris .60 .25
❑ 18 Eric Moulds 1.00 .40
❑ 19 Peerless Price 1.00 .40
❑ 20 Tim Biakabutuka 1.00 .40
❑ 21 Richard Huntley .60 .25
❑ 22 Patrick Jeffers 1.00 .40
❑ 23 Dameyune Craig .60 .25
❑ 24 Muhsin Muhammad 1.00 .40
❑ 25 James Allen 1.00 .40
❑ 26 Marcus Robinson 1.50 .60
❑ 27 Brian Urlacher 2.50 1.00
❑ 28 Corey Dillon 1.50 .60
❑ 29 Jon Kitna 1.00 .40
❑ 30 Akili Smith .60 .25
❑ 31 Peter Warrick 1.50 .60
❑ 32 Tim Couch 1.00 .40
❑ 33 Kevin Johnson 1.00 .40
❑ 34 Dennis Northcutt 1.00 .40
❑ 35 JaJuan Dawson .60 .25
❑ 36 Joey Galloway 1.00 .40
❑ 37 Rocket Ismail 1.00 .40
❑ 38 Emmitt Smith 3.00 1.25
❑ 39 Mike Anderson 1.50 .60
❑ 40 Terrell Davis 1.50 .60
❑ 41 Brian Griese 1.50 .60
❑ 42 Ed McCaffrey 1.50 .60
❑ 43 Rod Smith 1.00 .40
❑ 44 Charlie Batch 1.50 .60
❑ 45 Germane Crowell .60 .25
❑ 46 Herman Moore 1.00 .40
❑ 47 Johnnie Morton 1.00 .40
❑ 48 James Stewart 1.00 .40
❑ 49 Brett Favre 5.00 2.00
❑ 50 Antonio Freeman 1.50 .60
❑ 51 Ahman Green 1.50 .60
❑ 52 Dorsey Levens 1.00 .40
❑ 53 Bill Schroeder 1.00 .40
❑ 54 Marvin Harrison 1.50 .60
❑ 55 Edgerrin James 2.00 .75
❑ 56 Peyton Manning 4.00 1.50
❑ 57 Jerome Pathon 1.00 .40
❑ 58 Terrence Wilkins .60 .25
❑ 59 Mark Brunell 1.50 .60
❑ 60 Keenan McCardell .60 .25
❑ 61 Jimmy Smith 1.00 .40
❑ 62 Fred Taylor 1.50 .60
❑ 63 Derrick Alexander 1.00 .40
❑ 64 Tony Gonzalez 1.00 .40
❑ 65 Trent Green 1.50 .60
❑ 66 Priest Holmes 2.00 .75
❑ 67 Jay Fiedler 1.50 .60
❑ 68 Oronde Gadsden 1.00 .40
❑ 69 O.J. McDuffie .60 .25
❑ 70 Cade McNown .60 .25
❑ 71 Lamar Smith 1.00 .40
❑ 72 Zach Thomas 1.50 .60
❑ 73 Cris Carter 1.50 .60
❑ 74 Daunte Culpepper 1.50 .60
❑ 75 Randy Moss 3.00 1.25
❑ 76 Travis Prentice .60 .25
❑ 77 Drew Bledsoe 2.00 .75
❑ 78 Kevin Faulk 1.00 .40
❑ 79 Charles Johnson .60 .25
❑ 80 J.R. Redmond .60 .25
❑ 81 Jeff Blake 1.00 .40
❑ 82 Aaron Brooks 1.50 .60
❑ 83 Albert Connell .60 .25
❑ 84 Joe Horn 1.00 .40
❑ 85 Ricky Williams 1.50 .60
❑ 86 Tiki Barber 1.50 .60
❑ 87 Kerry Collins 1.00 .40
❑ 88 Ron Dayne 1.50 .60
❑ 89 Ike Hilliard 1.00 .40
❑ 90 Amani Toomer 1.00 .40
❑ 91 Richie Anderson .60 .25
❑ 92 Wayne Chrebet 1.00 .40
❑ 93 Laveranues Coles 1.50 .60
❑ 94 Curtis Martin 1.50 .60
❑ 95 Chad Pennington 2.50 1.00
❑ 96 Vinny Testaverde 1.00 .40
❑ 97 Tim Brown 1.50 .60
❑ 98 Rich Gannon 1.50 .60
❑ 99 Charlie Garner 1.00 .40
❑ 100 Jerry Rice 3.00 1.25
❑ 101 Tyrone Wheatley 1.00 .40
❑ 102 Charles Woodson 1.00 .40
❑ 103 Todd Pinkston 1.00 .40
❑ 104 Donovan McNabb 2.00 .75
❑ 105 Duce Staley 1.50 .60
❑ 106 James Thrash 1.00 .40
❑ 107 Jerome Bettis 1.50 .60
❑ 108 Plaxico Burress 1.50 .60
❑ 109 Bobby Shaw .60 .25
❑ 110 Kordell Stewart 1.00 .40
❑ 111 Hines Ward 1.50 .60
❑ 112 Isaac Bruce 1.50 .60
❑ 113 Marshall Faulk 2.00 .75
❑ 114 Az-Zahir Hakim .60 .25
❑ 115 Torry Holt 1.50 .60
❑ 116 Kurt Warner 3.00 1.25
❑ 117 Curtis Conway 1.00 .40
❑ 118 Tim Dwight 1.50 .60
❑ 119 Doug Flutie 1.50 .60
❑ 120 Jeff Graham 1.00 .40
❑ 121 Jeff Garcia 1.50 .60
❑ 122 Garrison Hearst 1.00 .40
❑ 123 Terrell Owens 1.50 .60
❑ 124 J.J. Stokes 1.00 .40

❑ 125 Tai Streets .60 .25
❑ 126 Shaun Alexander 2.00 .75
❑ 127 Matt Hasselbeck 1.00 .40
❑ 128 Darrell Jackson 1.50 .60
❑ 129 Ricky Watters 1.00 .40
❑ 130 Mike Alstott 1.50 .60
❑ 131 Warrick Dunn 1.50 .60
❑ 132 Jacquez Green .60 .25
❑ 133 Brad Johnson 1.50 .60
❑ 134 Keyshawn Johnson 1.50 .60
❑ 135 Warren Sapp 1.00 .40
❑ 136 Kevin Dyson 1.00 .40
❑ 137 Eddie George 1.50 .60
❑ 138 Jevon Kearse 1.00 .40
❑ 139 Derrick Mason 1.00 .40
❑ 140 Steve McNair 1.50 .60
❑ 141 Champ Bailey 1.50 .60
❑ 142 Stephen Davis 1.50 .60
❑ 143 Jeff George 1.00 .40
❑ 144 Michael Westbrook 1.00 .40
❑ 145 Bobby Newcombe RC 8.00 3.00
❑ 146 Corey Brown RC 8.00 3.00
❑ 147 Quentin McCord RC 8.00 3.00
❑ 148 Vinny Sutherland RC 8.00 3.00
❑ 149 Michael Vick RC 50.00 25.00
❑ 150 Chris Barnes RC 8.00 3.00
❑ 151 Tim Hasselbeck RC 12.00 5.00
❑ 152 Todd Heap RC 12.00 5.00
❑ 153 Nate Clements RC 12.00 5.00
❑ 154 Reggie Germany RC 8.00 3.00
❑ 155 Travis Henry RC 20.00 8.00
❑ 156 Dee Brown RC 12.00 5.00
❑ 157 Dan Morgan RC 12.00 5.00
❑ 158 Steve Smith RC 30.00 15.00
❑ 159 Chris Weinke RC 12.00 5.00
❑ 160 David Terrell RC 12.00 5.00
❑ 161 Anthony Thomas RC 12.00 5.00
❑ 162 T.J. Houshmandzadeh RC 15.00 6.00
❑ 163 Chad Johnson RC 30.00 15.00
❑ 164 Rudi Johnson RC 25.00 10.00
❑ 165 James Jackson RC 12.00 5.00
❑ 166 Andre King RC 8.00 3.00
❑ 167 Quincy Morgan RC 12.00 5.00
❑ 168 Quincy Carter RC 12.00 5.00
❑ 169 Kevin Kasper RC 12.00 5.00
❑ 170 Scotty Anderson RC 8.00 3.00
❑ 171 Mike McMahon RC 12.00 5.00
❑ 172 Robert Ferguson RC 12.00 5.00
❑ 173 Jamal Reynolds RC 12.00 5.00
❑ 174 Reggie Wayne RC 25.00 10.00
❑ 175 Marcus Stroud RC 12.00 5.00
❑ 176 Derrick Blaylock RC 12.00 5.00
❑ 177 Ryan Helming RC 8.00 3.00
❑ 178 Snoop Minnis RC 8.00 3.00
❑ 179 Chris Chambers RC 20.00 8.00
❑ 180 Josh Heupel RC 12.00 5.00
❑ 181 Travis Minor RC 8.00 3.00
❑ 182 Michael Bennett RC 12.00 5.00
❑ 183 Deuce McAllister RC 25.00 10.00
❑ 184 Onome Ojo RC 8.00 3.00
❑ 185 Will Allen RC 8.00 3.00
❑ 186 Jonathan Carter RC 8.00 3.00
❑ 187 Jesse Palmer RC 12.00 5.00
❑ 188 Corey Alston RC 5.00 2.00
❑ 189 LaMont Jordan RC 25.00 10.00
❑ 190 Santana Moss RC 20.00 8.00
❑ 191 Derek Combs RC 8.00 3.00
❑ 192 Derrick Gibson RC 8.00 3.00
❑ 193 Ken-Yon Rambo RC 8.00 3.00
❑ 194 Marques Tuiasosopo RC 12.00 5.00
❑ 195 Correll Buckhalter RC 15.00 6.00
❑ 196 Freddie Mitchell RC 12.00 5.00
❑ 197 Chris Taylor RC 8.00 3.00
❑ 198 Adam Archuleta RC 12.00 5.00
❑ 199 Damione Lewis RC 8.00 3.00
❑ 200 Francis St.Paul RC 8.00 3.00
❑ 201 Milton Wynn RC 8.00 3.00
❑ 202 Drew Brees RC 40.00 20.00
❑ 203 LaDainian Tomlinson RC 80.00 40.00
❑ 204 Kevan Barlow RC 12.00 5.00
❑ 205 Andre Carter RC 12.00 5.00
❑ 206 Cedrick Wilson RC 12.00 5.00
❑ 207 Alex Bannister RC 8.00 3.00
❑ 208 Josh Booty RC 12.00 5.00
❑ 209 Heath Evans RC 8.00 3.00
❑ 210 Ken Lucas RC 8.00 3.00
❑ 211 Koren Robinson RC 12.00 5.00
❑ 212 Dan Alexander RC 12.00 5.00
❑ 213 Eddie Berlin RC 8.00 3.00
❑ 214 Rod Gardner RC 12.00 5.00
❑ 215 Damerien McCants RC 8.00 3.00
❑ 216 Sage Rosenfels RC 12.00 5.00

1996 Pacific Invincible

❑ COMPLETE SET (150) 60.00 25.00
❑ 1 Larry Centers 1.00 .40
❑ 2 Garrison Hearst 1.00 .40
❑ 3 Seth Joyner .60 .25
❑ 4 Simeon Rice RC 5.00 2.00
❑ 5 Eric Swann .60 .25
❑ 6 Bert Emanuel 1.00 .40
❑ 7 Jeff George 1.00 .40
❑ 8 Craig Heyward .60 .25
❑ 9 Terance Mathis .60 .25
❑ 10 Eric Metcalf .60 .25
❑ 11 Derrick Alexander WR 1.00 .40
❑ 12 Leroy Hoard .60 .25
❑ 13 Andre Rison 1.00 .40
❑ 14 Tommy Vardell .60 .25
❑ 15 Eric Zeier .60 .25
❑ 16 Jim Kelly 2.00 .75
❑ 17 Eric Moulds RC 5.00 2.00
❑ 18 Bryce Paup .60 .25
❑ 19 Bruce Smith 1.00 .40
❑ 20 Thurman Thomas 2.00 .75
❑ 21 Tim Biakabutuka RC 2.00 .75
❑ 22 Blake Brockermeyer .60 .25
❑ 23 Kerry Collins 2.00 .75
❑ 24 Howard Griffith .60 .25
❑ 25 Lamar Lathon .60 .25
❑ 26 Mark Carrier DB .60 .25
❑ 27 Curtis Conway 2.00 .75
❑ 28 Erik Kramer .60 .25
❑ 29 Rashaan Salaam 1.00 .40
❑ 30 Alonzo Spellman .60 .25
❑ 31 Jeff Blake Braille SP 5.00 2.00
❑ 32 Harold Green .60 .25
❑ 33 Carl Pickens 1.00 .40
❑ 34 Darnay Scott 1.00 .40
❑ 35 Dan Wilkinson .60 .25
❑ 36 Troy Aikman 3.00 1.25
❑ 37 Jay Novacek .60 .25
❑ 38 Deion Sanders 2.50 1.00
❑ 39 Emmitt Smith 5.00 2.00
❑ 40 Kevin Williams .60 .25
❑ 41 Terrell Davis 2.50 1.00
❑ 42 John Elway 6.00 2.50
❑ 43 Anthony Miller 1.00 .40
❑ 44 Michael Dean Perry .60 .25
❑ 45 Shannon Sharpe 1.00 .40
❑ 46 Scott Mitchell 1.00 .40
❑ 47 Herman Moore 1.00 .40
❑ 48 Brett Perriman .60 .25
❑ 49 Barry Sanders 5.00 2.00
❑ 50 Chris Spielman .60 .25
❑ 51 Edgar Bennett 1.00 .40
❑ 52 Robert Brooks 2.00 .75
❑ 53 Brett Favre 6.00 2.50
❑ 54 Derrick Mayes RC 2.00 .75
❑ 55 Reggie White 2.00 .75
❑ 56 Eddie George RC 5.00 2.00
❑ 57 Haywood Jeffires .60 .25
❑ 58 Steve McNair 2.50 1.00
❑ 59 Chris Sanders 1.00 .40
❑ 60 Rodney Thomas .60 .25
❑ 61 Tony Bennett .60 .25
❑ 62 Quentin Coryatt .60 .25
❑ 63 Ken Dilger 1.00 .40
❑ 64 Marshall Faulk 2.50 1.00
❑ 65 Jim Harbaugh 1.00 .40
❑ 66 Tony Boselli .60 .25
❑ 67 Mark Brunell 2.00 .75
❑ 68 Kevin Hardy RC 2.00 .75
❑ 69 Desmond Howard 1.00 .40
❑ 70 James O.Stewart 1.00 .40
❑ 71 Marcus Allen 2.00 .75
❑ 72 Steve Bono .60 .25
❑ 73 Neil Smith 1.00 .40
❑ 74 Derrick Thomas 2.00 .75
❑ 75 Tamarick Vanover 1.00 .40
❑ 76 Karim Abdul-Jabbar RC 2.00 .75
❑ 77 Irving Fryar 1.00 .40
❑ 78 Eric Green .60 .25
❑ 79 Dan Marino 6.00 2.50
❑ 80 Bernie Parmalee .60 .25
❑ 81 Cris Carter 2.00 .75
❑ 82 Warren Moon 1.00 .40
❑ 83 Jake Reed 1.00 .40
❑ 84 Robert Smith 1.00 .40
❑ 85 Moe Williams RB RC 5.00 2.00
❑ 86 Drew Bledsoe 2.50 1.00
❑ 87 Ben Coates 1.00 .40
❑ 88 Terry Glenn RC 4.00 1.50
❑ 89 Curtis Martin 2.50 1.00
❑ 90 Dave Meggett .60 .25
❑ 91 Mario Bates 1.00 .40
❑ 92 Jim Everett .60 .25
❑ 93 Michael Haynes .60 .25
❑ 94 Torrance Small .60 .25
❑ 95 Ray Zellars .60 .25
❑ 96 Kyle Brady .60 .25
❑ 97 Wayne Chrebet 2.00 .75
❑ 98 Keyshawn Johnson RC 4.00 1.50
❑ 99 Adrian Murrell 1.00 .40
❑ 100 Alex Van Dyke RC 1.00 .40
❑ 101 Michael Brooks .60 .25
❑ 102 Dave Brown .60 .25
❑ 103 Chris Calloway .60 .25
❑ 104 Rodney Hampton 1.00 .40
❑ 105 Amani Toomer RC 4.00 1.50
❑ 106 Tyrone Wheatley 1.00 .40
❑ 107 Tim Brown 2.00 .75
❑ 108 Rickey Dudley RC 2.00 .75
❑ 109 Billy Joe Hobert 1.00 .40
❑ 110 Rocket Ismail 1.00 .40
❑ 111 Napoleon Kaufman 2.00 .75
❑ 112 Harvey Williams .60 .25
❑ 113 Charlie Garner 1.00 .40
❑ 114 Bobby Hoying RC 2.00 .75
❑ 115 Rodney Peete .60 .25
❑ 116 Ricky Watters 1.00 .40
❑ 117 Greg Lloyd 1.00 .40
❑ 118 Erric Pegram .60 .25
❑ 119 Kordell Stewart 2.00 .75
❑ 120 Yancey Thigpen 1.00 .40
❑ 121 Jon Witman RC 1.00 .40
❑ 122 Aaron Hayden .60 .25
❑ 123 Stan Humphries 1.00 .40
❑ 124 Tony Martin 1.00 .40
❑ 125 Leslie O'Neal .60 .25
❑ 126 Junior Seau 2.00 .75
❑ 127 Jerome Bettis 2.00 .75
❑ 128 Isaac Bruce 2.00 .75
❑ 129 Ernie Conwell RC .60 .25
❑ 130 Lawrence Phillips RC 2.00 .75
❑ 131 William Floyd 1.00 .40
❑ 132 Terrell Owens RC 10.00 4.00
❑ 133 Jerry Rice 3.00 1.25
❑ 134 J.J. Stokes 2.00 .75
❑ 135 Steve Young 2.50 1.00
❑ 136 Brian Blades .60 .25
❑ 137 Christian Fauria .60 .25
❑ 138 Joey Galloway 2.00 .75
❑ 139 Rick Mirer 1.00 .40
❑ 140 Chris Warren 1.00 .40
❑ 141 Horace Copeland .60 .25
❑ 142 Trent Dilfer 2.00 .75
❑ 143 Alvin Harper .60 .25
❑ 144 Dave Moore .60 .25
❑ 145 Errict Rhett 1.00 .40
❑ 146 Terry Allen 1.00 .40
❑ 147 Gus Frerotte 1.00 .40
❑ 148 Brian Mitchell .60 .25

- ❑ 149 Heath Shuler 1.00 .40
- ❑ 150 Michael Westbrook 2.00 .75
- ❑ PCC1 Chris Warren Promo 1.50 .60

1997 Pacific Invincible

- ❑ COMPLETE SET (150) 100.00 40.00
- ❑ 1 Larry Centers 1.00 .40
- ❑ 2 Kent Graham .60 .25
- ❑ 3 LeShon Johnson .60 .25
- ❑ 4 Leeland McElroy .60 .25
- ❑ 5 Jake Plummer RC 10.00 4.00
- ❑ 6 Frank Sanders 1.00 .40
- ❑ 7 Morten Andersen .60 .25
- ❑ 8 Jamal Anderson 1.50 .60
- ❑ 9 Bert Emanuel 1.00 .40
- ❑ 10 Bobby Hebert .60 .25
- ❑ 11 Roell Preston .60 .25
- ❑ 12 Derrick Alexander WR 1.00 .40
- ❑ 13 Michael Jackson 1.00 .40
- ❑ 14 Byron Bam Morris .60 .25
- ❑ 15 Vinny Testaverde 1.00 .40
- ❑ 16 Todd Collins .60 .25
- ❑ 17 Andre Reed 1.00 .40
- ❑ 18 Antowain Smith RC 5.00 2.00
- ❑ 19 Steve Tasker .60 .25
- ❑ 20 Thurman Thomas 1.50 .60
- ❑ 21 Tim Biakabutuka 1.00 .40
- ❑ 22 Rae Carruth RC .60 .25
- ❑ 23 Kerry Collins 1.50 .60
- ❑ 24 Kevin Greene 1.00 .40
- ❑ 25 Anthony Johnson .60 .25
- ❑ 26 Wesley Walls 1.00 .40
- ❑ 27 Darnell Autry RC 1.00 .40
- ❑ 28 Curtis Conway 1.00 .40
- ❑ 29 Raymont Harris .60 .25
- ❑ 30 Rashaan Salaam .60 .25
- ❑ 31 Jeff Blake 1.00 .40
- ❑ 32 Ki-Jana Carter .60 .25
- ❑ 33 David Dunn .60 .25
- ❑ 34 Carl Pickens 1.00 .40
- ❑ 35 Darnay Scott 1.00 .40
- ❑ 36 Troy Aikman 3.00 1.25
- ❑ 37 Michael Irvin 1.50 .60
- ❑ 38 Deion Sanders 1.50 .60
- ❑ 39 Emmitt Smith 5.00 2.00
- ❑ 40 Herschel Walker 1.00 .40
- ❑ 41 Kevin Williams .60 .25
- ❑ 42 Steve Atwater .60 .25
- ❑ 43 Terrell Davis 2.00 .75
- ❑ 44 John Elway 6.00 2.50
- ❑ 45 Ed McCaffrey 1.00 .40
- ❑ 46 Shannon Sharpe 1.00 .40
- ❑ 47 Scott Mitchell 1.00 .40
- ❑ 48 Herman Moore 1.00 .40
- ❑ 49 Brett Perriman .60 .25
- ❑ 50 Barry Sanders 5.00 2.00
- ❑ 51 Edgar Bennett 1.00 .40
- ❑ 52 Robert Brooks 1.00 .40
- ❑ 53 Brett Favre 6.00 2.50
- ❑ 54 Antonio Freeman 1.50 .60
- ❑ 55 Dorsey Levens 1.50 .60
- ❑ 56 Reggie White 1.50 .60
- ❑ 57 Eddie George 1.50 .60
- ❑ 58 Steve McNair 2.00 .75
- ❑ 59 Chris Sanders 1.00 .40
- ❑ 60 Sean Dawkins .60 .25
- ❑ 61 Marshall Faulk 2.00 .75
- ❑ 62 Jim Harbaugh 1.00 .40
- ❑ 63 Marvin Harrison 1.50 .60
- ❑ 64 Brian Stablein .60 .25
- ❑ 65 Mark Brunell 2.00 .75
- ❑ 66 Keenan McCardell 1.00 .40
- ❑ 67 Natrone Means 1.00 .40
- ❑ 68 Pete Mitchell .60 .25
- ❑ 69 Jimmy Smith 1.00 .40
- ❑ 70 Marcus Allen 1.50 .60
- ❑ 71 Kimble Anders 1.00 .40
- ❑ 72 Greg Hill .60 .25
- ❑ 73 Kevin Lockett RC 1.00 .40
- ❑ 74 Derrick Thomas 1.50 .60
- ❑ 75 Tamarick Vanover 1.00 .40
- ❑ 76 Karim Abdul-Jabbar 1.00 .40
- ❑ 77 Yatil Green RC 1.00 .40
- ❑ 78 Randal Hill .60 .25
- ❑ 79 Dan Marino 6.00 2.50
- ❑ 80 Stanley Pritchett .60 .25
- ❑ 81 Irving Spikes .60 .25
- ❑ 82 Cris Carter 1.50 .60
- ❑ 83 Brad Johnson 1.50 .60
- ❑ 84 Robert Smith 1.00 .40
- ❑ 85 Darryl Talley .60 .25
- ❑ 86 Drew Bledsoe 2.00 .75
- ❑ 87 Ben Coates 1.00 .40
- ❑ 88 Terry Glenn 1.50 .60
- ❑ 89 Curtis Martin 2.00 .75
- ❑ 90 Sedrick Shaw RC 1.00 .40
- ❑ 91 Mario Bates .60 .25
- ❑ 92 Troy Davis RC 1.00 .40
- ❑ 93 Jim Everett .60 .25
- ❑ 94 Michael Haynes .60 .25
- ❑ 95 Tiki Barber RC 12.00 5.00
- ❑ 96 Dave Brown .60 .25
- ❑ 97 Rodney Hampton 1.00 .40
- ❑ 98 Ike Hilliard RC 3.00 1.25
- ❑ 99 Danny Kanell .60 .25
- ❑ 100 Wayne Chrebet 1.50 .60
- ❑ 101 Keyshawn Johnson 1.50 .60
- ❑ 102 Adrian Murrell 1.00 .40
- ❑ 103 Neil O'Donnell 1.00 .40
- ❑ 104 Alex Van Dyke .60 .25
- ❑ 105 Joe Aska .60 .25
- ❑ 106 Tim Brown 1.50 .60
- ❑ 107 Rickey Dudley 1.00 .40
- ❑ 108 Napoleon Kaufman 1.50 .60
- ❑ 109 Carl Kidd RC .60 .25
- ❑ 110 Ty Detmer 1.00 .40
- ❑ 111 Jason Dunn .60 .25
- ❑ 112 Irving Fryar 1.00 .40
- ❑ 113 Bobby Hoying 1.00 .40
- ❑ 114 Ricky Watters 1.00 .40
- ❑ 115 Jerome Bettis 1.50 .60
- ❑ 116 Charles Johnson 1.00 .40
- ❑ 117 Greg Lloyd .60 .25
- ❑ 118 Kordell Stewart 1.50 .60
- ❑ 119 Rod Woodson 1.00 .40
- ❑ 120 Tony Banks 1.00 .40
- ❑ 121 Isaac Bruce 1.50 .60
- ❑ 122 Eddie Kennison 1.00 .40
- ❑ 123 Lawrence Phillips .60 .25
- ❑ 124 Stan Humphries 1.00 .40
- ❑ 125 Tony Martin 1.00 .40
- ❑ 126 Corey Dillon RC 12.00 5.00
- ❑ 127 Leonard Russell .60 .25
- ❑ 128 Junior Seau 1.50 .60
- ❑ 129 Jim Druckenmiller RC 1.00 .40
- ❑ 130 Marc Edwards RC 1.00 .40
- ❑ 131 Ken Norton Jr. .60 .25
- ❑ 132 Terrell Owens 2.00 .75
- ❑ 133 Jerry Rice 3.00 1.25
- ❑ 134 Iheanyi Uwaezuoke .60 .25
- ❑ 135 Steve Young 2.00 .75
- ❑ 136 John Friesz .60 .25
- ❑ 137 Joey Galloway 1.00 .40
- ❑ 138 Warren Moon 1.50 .60
- ❑ 139 Todd Peterson .60 .25
- ❑ 140 Chris Warren 1.00 .40
- ❑ 141 Mike Alstott 1.50 .60
- ❑ 142 Reidel Anthony RC 1.50 .60
- ❑ 143 Trent Dilfer 1.50 .60
- ❑ 144 Warrick Dunn RC 6.00 2.50
- ❑ 145 Errict Rhett .60 .25
- ❑ 146 Terry Allen 1.50 .60
- ❑ 147 Henry Ellard .60 .25
- ❑ 148 Gus Frerotte .60 .25
- ❑ 149 Brian Mitchell .60 .25
- ❑ 150 Leslie Shepherd .60 .25
- ❑ S1 Mark Brunell Sample 3.00 1.25

2001 Pacific Invincible

- ❑ COMP.SET w/o SP's (250) 150.00 90.00
- ❑ 1 David Boston 3.00 1.25
- ❑ 2 MarTay Jenkins 1.25 .50
- ❑ 3 Thomas Jones 2.00 .75
- ❑ 4 Rob Moore 2.00 .75
- ❑ 5 Michael Pittman 1.25 .50
- ❑ 6 Jake Plummer 2.00 .75
- ❑ 7 Frank Sanders 1.25 .50
- ❑ 8 Jamal Anderson 3.00 1.25
- ❑ 9 Chris Chandler 2.00 .75
- ❑ 10 Jammi German 1.25 .50
- ❑ 11 Shawn Jefferson 1.25 .50
- ❑ 12 Doug Johnson 1.25 .50
- ❑ 13 Terance Mathis 2.00 .75
- ❑ 14 Rodney Thomas 1.25 .50
- ❑ 15 Elvis Grbac 2.00 .75
- ❑ 16 Qadry Ismail 2.00 .75
- ❑ 17 Jamal Lewis 5.00 2.00
- ❑ 18 Jermaine Lewis 1.25 .50
- ❑ 19 Ray Lewis 3.00 1.25
- ❑ 20 Chris Redman 1.25 .50
- ❑ 21 Shannon Sharpe 2.00 .75
- ❑ 22 Travis Taylor 2.00 .75
- ❑ 23 Shawn Bryson 1.25 .50
- ❑ 24 Larry Centers 1.25 .50
- ❑ 25 Rob Johnson 2.00 .75
- ❑ 26 Jeremy McDaniel 1.25 .50
- ❑ 27 Sammy Morris 1.25 .50
- ❑ 28 Eric Moulds 2.00 .75
- ❑ 29 Peerless Price 2.00 .75
- ❑ 30 Antowain Smith 2.00 .75
- ❑ 31 Michael Bates 1.25 .50
- ❑ 32 Tim Biakabutuka 2.00 .75
- ❑ 33 Isaac Byrd 1.25 .50
- ❑ 34 Brad Hoover 1.25 .50
- ❑ 35 Patrick Jeffers 2.00 .75
- ❑ 36 Jeff Lewis 1.25 .50
- ❑ 37 Muhsin Muhammad 2.00 .75
- ❑ 38 Wesley Walls 1.25 .50
- ❑ 39 James Allen 2.00 .75
- ❑ 40 Marty Booker 1.25 .50
- ❑ 41 Macey Brooks 1.25 .50
- ❑ 42 Bobby Engram 1.25 .50
- ❑ 43 Cade McNown 1.25 .50
- ❑ 44 Marcus Robinson 3.00 1.25
- ❑ 45 Brian Urlacher 5.00 2.00
- ❑ 46 Dez White 1.25 .50
- ❑ 47 Brandon Bennett 1.25 .50
- ❑ 48 Corey Dillon 3.00 1.25
- ❑ 49 Danny Farmer 1.25 .50
- ❑ 50 Jon Kitna 3.00 1.25
- ❑ 51 Darnay Scott 2.00 .75
- ❑ 52 Akili Smith 1.25 .50
- ❑ 53 Peter Warrick 3.00 1.25
- ❑ 54 Craig Yeast 1.25 .50
- ❑ 55 Tim Couch 2.00 .75
- ❑ 56 JaJuan Dawson 1.25 .50
- ❑ 57 Curtis Enis 1.25 .50
- ❑ 58 Kevin Johnson 2.00 .75
- ❑ 59 Dennis Northcutt 2.00 .75
- ❑ 60 Travis Prentice 1.25 .50
- ❑ 61 Errict Rhett 1.25 .50
- ❑ 62 Tony Banks 2.00 .75
- ❑ 63 Randall Cunningham 3.00 1.25
- ❑ 64 Rocket Ismail 2.00 .75

❑ 65 Wane McGarity 1.25 .50
❑ 66 Carl Pickens 1.25 .50
❑ 67 Emmitt Smith 6.00 2.50
❑ 68 Jason Tucker 1.25 .50
❑ 69 Michael Wiley 1.25 .50
❑ 70 Mike Anderson 3.00 1.25
❑ 71 Terrell Davis 3.00 1.25
❑ 72 Gus Frerotte 1.25 .50
❑ 73 Olandis Gary 2.00 .75
❑ 74 Brian Griese 3.00 1.25
❑ 75 Eddie Kennison 1.25 .50
❑ 76 Ed McCaffrey 3.00 1.25
❑ 77 Rod Smith 2.00 .75
❑ 78 Charlie Batch 3.00 1.25
❑ 79 Germane Crowell 1.25 .50
❑ 80 Larry Foster 1.25 .50
❑ 81 Desmond Howard 1.25 .50
❑ 82 Herman Moore 2.00 .75
❑ 83 Johnnie Morton 2.00 .75
❑ 84 Robert Porcher 1.25 .50
❑ 85 James Stewart 2.00 .75
❑ 86 Donald Driver 2.00 .75
❑ 87 Brett Favre 10.00 4.00
❑ 88 Bubba Franks 2.00 .75
❑ 89 Antonio Freeman 3.00 1.25
❑ 90 Ahman Green 3.00 1.25
❑ 91 William Henderson 1.25 .50
❑ 92 Dorsey Levens 2.00 .75
❑ 93 Bill Schroeder 2.00 .75
❑ 94 Ken Dilger 1.25 .50
❑ 95 E.G. Green 1.25 .50
❑ 96 Marvin Harrison 3.00 1.25
❑ 97 Edgerrin James 4.00 1.50
❑ 98 Peyton Manning 8.00 3.00
❑ 99 Jerome Pathon 2.00 .75
❑ 100 Marcus Pollard 1.25 .50
❑ 101 Terrence Wilkins 1.25 .50
❑ 102 Kyle Brady 1.25 .50
❑ 103 Mark Brunell 3.00 1.25
❑ 104 Stacey Mack 1.25 .50
❑ 105 Keenan McCardell 1.25 .50
❑ 106 Jimmy Smith 2.00 .75
❑ 107 R. Jay Soward 1.25 .50
❑ 108 Shyrone Stith 1.25 .50
❑ 109 Fred Taylor 3.00 1.25
❑ 110 Derrick Alexander WR 1.25 .50
❑ 111 Kimble Anders 1.25 .50
❑ 112 Todd Collins 1.25 .50
❑ 113 Tony Gonzalez 2.00 .75
❑ 114 Trent Green 3.00 1.25
❑ 115 Priest Holmes 4.00 1.50
❑ 116 Tony Horne 1.25 .50
❑ 117 Frank Moreau 1.25 .50
❑ 118 Sylvester Morris 1.25 .50
❑ 119 Tony Richardson 1.25 .50
❑ 120 Jay Fiedler 3.00 1.25
❑ 121 Oronde Gadsden 2.00 .75
❑ 122 James Johnson 1.25 .50
❑ 123 Ray Lucas 1.25 .50
❑ 124 Tony Martin 2.00 .75
❑ 125 O.J. McDuffie 1.25 .50
❑ 126 James McKnight 2.00 .75
❑ 127 Lamar Smith 2.00 .75
❑ 128 Jason Taylor 1.25 .50
❑ 129 Zach Thomas 3.00 1.25
❑ 130 Dedric Ward 1.25 .50
❑ 131 Cris Carter 3.00 1.25
❑ 132 Daunte Culpepper 3.00 1.25
❑ 133 Randy Moss 6.00 2.50
❑ 134 Chris Walsh RC 1.25 .50
❑ 135 Troy Walters 1.25 .50
❑ 136 Moe Williams 2.00 .75
❑ 137 Drew Bledsoe 4.00 1.50
❑ 138 Troy Brown 2.00 .75
❑ 139 Kevin Faulk 2.00 .75
❑ 140 Terry Glenn 2.00 .75
❑ 141 Ty Law 2.00 .75
❑ 142 Lawyer Milloy 2.00 .75
❑ 143 David Patten 1.25 .50
❑ 144 J.R. Redmond 1.25 .50
❑ 145 Tony Simmons 1.25 .50
❑ 146 Jeff Blake 2.00 .75
❑ 147 Aaron Brooks 3.00 1.25
❑ 148 Albert Connell 1.25 .50
❑ 149 Joe Horn 2.00 .75
❑ 150 Willie Jackson 1.25 .50
❑ 151 Chad Morton 1.25 .50
❑ 152 Keith Poole 1.25 .50
❑ 153 Ricky Williams 3.00 1.25
❑ 154 Robert Wilson 1.25 .50
❑ 155 Jessie Armstead 1.25 .50
❑ 156 Tiki Barber 3.00 1.25
❑ 157 Kerry Collins 2.00 .75
❑ 158 Ron Dayne 3.00 1.25
❑ 159 Ron Dixon 1.25 .50
❑ 160 Ike Hilliard 2.00 .75
❑ 161 Jason Sehorn 1.25 .50
❑ 162 Michael Strahan 2.00 .75
❑ 163 Amani Toomer 1.25 .50
❑ 164 Richie Anderson 1.25 .50
❑ 165 Wayne Chrebet 2.00 .75
❑ 166 Laveranues Coles 3.00 1.25
❑ 167 Matthew Hatchette 1.25 .50
❑ 168 Marvin Jones 1.25 .50
❑ 169 Curtis Martin 3.00 1.25
❑ 170 Chad Pennington 5.00 2.00
❑ 171 Vinny Testaverde 2.00 .75
❑ 172 Tim Brown 3.00 1.25
❑ 173 Zack Crockett 1.25 .50
❑ 174 Rich Gannon 3.00 1.25
❑ 175 Charlie Garner 2.00 .75
❑ 176 James Jett 1.25 .50
❑ 177 Randy Jordan 1.25 .50
❑ 178 Andre Rison 2.00 .75
❑ 179 Tyrone Wheatley 2.00 .75
❑ 180 Charles Woodson 2.00 .75
❑ 181 Darnell Autry 1.25 .50
❑ 182 Charles Johnson 1.25 .50
❑ 183 Chad Lewis 1.25 .50
❑ 184 Donovan McNabb 4.00 1.50
❑ 185 Todd Pinkston 1.25 .50
❑ 186 Stanley Pritchett 1.25 .50
❑ 187 Torrance Small 1.25 .50
❑ 188 Duce Staley 3.00 1.25
❑ 189 James Thrash 2.00 .75
❑ 190 Jerome Bettis 3.00 1.25
❑ 191 Plaxico Burress 3.00 1.25
❑ 192 Troy Edwards 1.25 .50
❑ 193 Courtney Hawkins 1.25 .50
❑ 194 Richard Huntley 1.25 .50
❑ 195 Bobby Shaw 1.25 .50
❑ 196 Kordell Stewart 2.00 .75
❑ 197 Hines Ward 3.00 1.25
❑ 198 Isaac Bruce 3.00 1.25
❑ 199 Trung Canidate 2.00 .75
❑ 200 Marshall Faulk 4.00 1.50
❑ 201 Az-Zahir Hakim 1.25 .50
❑ 202 Torry Holt 3.00 1.25
❑ 203 Ricky Proehl 1.25 .50
❑ 204 Kurt Warner 6.00 2.50
❑ 205 Aeneas Williams 1.25 .50
❑ 206 Curtis Conway 2.00 .75
❑ 207 Tim Dwight 3.00 1.25
❑ 208 Jermaine Fazande 1.25 .50
❑ 209 Terrell Fletcher 1.25 .50
❑ 210 Doug Flutie 3.00 1.25
❑ 211 Jeff Graham 1.25 .50
❑ 212 Freddie Jones 1.25 .50
❑ 213 Reggie Jones 1.25 .50
❑ 214 Junior Seau 3.00 1.25
❑ 215 Fred Beasley 1.25 .50
❑ 216 Jeff Garcia 3.00 1.25
❑ 217 Terrell Owens 3.00 1.25
❑ 218 Jerry Rice 6.00 2.50
❑ 219 Paul Smith 1.25 .50
❑ 220 J.J. Stokes 2.00 .75
❑ 221 Tai Streets 1.25 .50
❑ 222 Shaun Alexander 4.00 1.50
❑ 223 Karsten Bailey 1.25 .50
❑ 224 Matt Hasselbeck 2.00 .75
❑ 225 Brock Huard 1.25 .50
❑ 226 Darrell Jackson 3.00 1.25
❑ 227 Shawn Springs 1.25 .50
❑ 228 Ricky Watters 2.00 .75
❑ 229 James Williams WR 1.25 .50
❑ 230 Mike Alstott 3.00 1.25
❑ 231 Reidel Anthony 1.25 .50
❑ 232 Warrick Dunn 3.00 1.25
❑ 233 Jacquez Green 1.25 .50
❑ 234 Brad Johnson 3.00 1.25
❑ 235 Keyshawn Johnson 3.00 1.25
❑ 236 Shaun King 1.25 .50
❑ 237 Warren Sapp 2.00 .75
❑ 238 Kevin Dyson 2.00 .75
❑ 239 Eddie George 3.00 1.25
❑ 240 Jevon Kearse 2.00 .75
❑ 241 Derrick Mason 2.00 .75
❑ 242 Steve McNair 3.00 1.25
❑ 243 Chris Sanders 1.25 .50
❑ 244 Frank Wycheck 1.25 .50
❑ 245 Stephen Alexander 1.25 .50
❑ 246 Stephen Davis 3.00 1.25
❑ 247 Irving Fryar 2.00 .75
❑ 248 Jeff George 2.00 .75
❑ 249 Kevin Lockett 1.25 .50
❑ 250 Michael Westbrook 2.00 .75
❑ 251 Bobby Newcombe RC 5.00 2.00
❑ 252 Alge Crumpler RC 12.00 5.00
❑ 253 Vinny Sutherland RC 5.00 2.00
❑ 254 Michael Vick RC 50.00 20.00
❑ 255 Travis Henry RC 12.00 5.00
❑ 256 Dan Morgan RC 8.00 3.00
❑ 257 Chris Weinke JSY RC 12.00 5.00
❑ 258 David Terrell RC 8.00 3.00
❑ 259 Anthony Thomas JSY RC 12.00 5.00
❑ 260 T.J. Houshmandzadeh RC 10.00 4.00
❑ 261 Chad Johnson RC 20.00 8.00
❑ 262 Rudi Johnson RC 15.00 6.00
❑ 263 James Jackson RC 8.00 3.00
❑ 264 Quincy Morgan RC 8.00 3.00
❑ 265 Scotty Anderson RC 5.00 2.00
❑ 266 Mike McMahon RC 8.00 3.00
❑ 267 Robert Ferguson RC 8.00 3.00
❑ 268 Reggie Wayne RC 15.00 6.00
❑ 269 Snoop Minnis RC 5.00 2.00
❑ 270 Chris Chambers RC 12.00 5.00
❑ 271 Josh Heupel RC 8.00 3.00
❑ 272 Travis Minor RC 5.00 2.00
❑ 273 Michael Bennett RC 8.00 3.00
❑ 274 Ben Leard RC 5.00 2.00
❑ 275 Deuce McAllister RC 15.00 6.00
❑ 276 Moran Norris RC 3.00 1.25
❑ 277 Jesse Palmer RC 8.00 3.00
❑ 278 LaMont Jordan RC 15.00 6.00
❑ 279 Santana Moss RC 12.00 5.00
❑ 280 Ken-Yon Rambo RC 5.00 2.00
❑ 281 M.Tuiasosopo JSY RC 20.00 8.00
❑ 282 Correll Buckhalter RC 10.00 4.00
❑ 283 A.J. Feeley RC 8.00 3.00
❑ 284 Freddie Mitchell JSY RC 10.00 4.00
❑ 285 Joey Getherall RC 5.00 2.00
❑ 286 Chris Taylor RC 5.00 2.00
❑ 287 Adam Archuleta RC 8.00 3.00
❑ 288 David Rivers RC 5.00 2.00
❑ 289 Drew Brees JSY RC 50.00 25.00
❑ 290 L.Tomlinson JSY RC 80.00 50.00
❑ 291 David Allen RC 5.00 2.00
❑ 292 Kevan Barlow RC 8.00 3.00
❑ 293 Cedrick Wilson RC 8.00 3.00
❑ 294 Alex Bannister RC 5.00 2.00
❑ 295 Josh Booty RC 8.00 3.00
❑ 296 Heath Evans RC 5.00 2.00
❑ 297 Koren Robinson RC 8.00 3.00
❑ 298 Dan Alexander RC 8.00 3.00
❑ 299 Rod Gardner RC 8.00 3.00
❑ 300 Sage Rosenfels RC 8.00 3.00

1998 Pacific Omega

❑ COMPLETE SET (250) 40.00 15.00
❑ 1 Larry Centers .25 .08
❑ 2 Rob Moore .40 .15
❑ 3 Michael Pittman RC 1.50 .75
❑ 4 Jake Plummer .60 .25

❑ 5	Simeon Rice	.40	.15
❑ 6	Frank Sanders	.40	.15
❑ 7	Eric Swann	.25	.08
❑ 8	Morten Andersen	.25	.08
❑ 9	Jamal Anderson	.60	.25
❑ 10	Chris Chandler	.40	.15
❑ 11	Harold Green	.25	.08
❑ 12	Byron Hanspard	.25	.08
❑ 13	Terance Mathis	.40	.15
❑ 14	O.J. Santiago	.25	.08
❑ 15	Peter Boulware	.25	.08
❑ 16	Jay Graham	.25	.08
❑ 17	Eric Green	.25	.08
❑ 18	Michael Jackson	.25	.08
❑ 19	Jermaine Lewis	.40	.15
❑ 20	Ray Lewis	.60	.25
❑ 21	Jonathan Ogden	.25	.08
❑ 22	Eric Zeier	.40	.15
❑ 23	Steve Christie	.25	.08
❑ 24	Todd Collins	.25	.08
❑ 25	Quinn Early	.25	.08
❑ 26	Eric Moulds	.60	.25
❑ 27	Andre Reed	.40	.15
❑ 28	Antowain Smith	.60	.25
❑ 29	Bruce Smith	.40	.15
❑ 30	Thurman Thomas	.60	.25
❑ 31	Ted Washington	.25	.08
❑ 32	Michael Bates	.25	.08
❑ 33	Tim Biakabutuka	.40	.15
❑ 34	Mark Carrier	.25	.08
❑ 35	Rae Carruth	.25	.08
❑ 36	Kerry Collins	.40	.15
❑ 37	Kevin Greene	.40	.15
❑ 38	Fred Lane	.25	.08
❑ 39	Muhsin Muhammad	.40	.15
❑ 40	Wesley Walls	.40	.15
❑ 41	Curtis Conway	.40	.15
❑ 42	Bobby Engram	.40	.15
❑ 43	Curtis Enis RC	.50	.20
❑ 44	Walt Harris	.25	.08
❑ 45	Erik Kramer	.25	.08
❑ 46	Chris Penn	.25	.08
❑ 47	Ryan Wetnight RC	.25	.08
❑ 48	Jeff Blake	.40	.15
❑ 49	Ki-Jana Carter	.25	.08
❑ 50	John Copeland	.25	.08
❑ 51	Corey Dillon	.60	.25
❑ 52	Tony McGee	.25	.08
❑ 53	Carl Pickens	.40	.15
❑ 54	Darnay Scott	.40	.15
❑ 55	Takeo Spikes RC	1.25	.50
❑ 56	Troy Aikman	1.25	.50
❑ 57	Eric Bjornson	.25	.08
❑ 58	Greg Ellis RC	.50	.20
❑ 59	Michael Irvin	.60	.25
❑ 60	Daryl Johnston	.40	.15
❑ 61	David LaFleur	.25	.08
❑ 62	Deion Sanders	.60	.25
❑ 63	Emmitt Smith	2.00	.75
❑ 64	Herschel Walker	.40	.15
❑ 65	Nicky Sualua RC	.40	.15
❑ 66	Steve Atwater	.25	.08
❑ 67	Terrell Davis	.60	.25
❑ 68	John Elway	2.50	1.00
❑ 69	Brian Griese RC	2.50	1.00
❑ 70	Ed McCaffrey	.40	.15
❑ 71	John Mobley	.25	.08
❑ 72	Marcus Nash RC	.50	.20
❑ 73	Shannon Sharpe	.40	.15
❑ 74	Neil Smith	.40	.15
❑ 75	Rod Smith	.40	.15
❑ 76	Charlie Batch RC	1.25	.50
❑ 77	Germane Crowell RC	.75	.30
❑ 78	Jason Hanson	.25	.08
❑ 79	Scott Mitchell	.40	.15
❑ 80	Herman Moore	.40	.15
❑ 81	Johnnie Morton	.40	.15
❑ 82	Barry Sanders	2.00	.75
❑ 83	Tommy Vardell	.25	.08
❑ 84	Robert Brooks	.40	.15
❑ 85	Gilbert Brown	.25	.08
❑ 86	LeRoy Butler	.25	.08
❑ 87	Mark Chmura	.40	.15
❑ 88	Brett Favre	2.50	1.00
❑ 89	Antonio Freeman	.60	.25
❑ 90	William Henderson	.40	.15
❑ 91	Vonnie Holliday RC	.75	.30
❑ 92	Dorsey Levens	.60	.25
❑ 93	Reggie White	.60	.25
❑ 94	Aaron Bailey	.25	.08
❑ 95	Quentin Coryatt	.25	.08
❑ 96	Zack Crockett	.25	.08
❑ 97	Ken Dilger	.25	.08
❑ 98	Marshall Faulk	.75	.30
❑ 99	E.G. Green RC	.75	.30
❑ 100	Marvin Harrison	.60	.25
❑ 101	Peyton Manning RC	15.00	6.00
❑ 102	Jerome Pathon RC	1.25	.50
❑ 103	Tavian Banks RC	.75	.30
❑ 104	Tony Boselli	.25	.08
❑ 105	Tony Brackens	.25	.08
❑ 106	Mark Brunell	.60	.25
❑ 107	Kevin Hardy	.25	.08
❑ 108	Keenan McCardell	.40	.15
❑ 109	Pete Mitchell	.25	.08
❑ 110	Jimmy Smith	.40	.15
❑ 111	James Stewart	.40	.15
❑ 112	Fred Taylor RC	2.00	.75
❑ 113	Kimble Anders	.40	.15
❑ 114	Dale Carter	.25	.08
❑ 115	Tony Gonzalez	.60	.25
❑ 116	Elvis Grbac	.40	.15
❑ 117	Donnell Bennett	.25	.08
❑ 118	Andre Rison	.40	.15
❑ 119	Rashaan Shehee RC	.75	.30
❑ 120	Derrick Thomas	.60	.25
❑ 121	Tamarick Vanover	.25	.08
❑ 122	Karim Abdul-Jabbar	.60	.25
❑ 123	John Avery RC	.75	.30
❑ 124	Troy Drayton	.25	.08
❑ 125	John Dutton RC	.50	.20
❑ 126	Craig Erickson	.25	.08
❑ 127	Dan Marino	2.50	1.00
❑ 128	O.J. McDuffie	.40	.15
❑ 129	Jerris McPhail	.25	.08
❑ 130	Stanley Pritchett	.25	.08
❑ 131	Larry Shannon RC	.50	.20
❑ 132	Zach Thomas	.60	.25
❑ 133	Cris Carter	.60	.25
❑ 134	Randall Cunningham	.60	.25
❑ 135	Andrew Glover	.25	.08
❑ 136	Brad Johnson	.60	.25
❑ 137	Randall McDaniel	.25	.08
❑ 138	David Palmer	.25	.08
❑ 139	John Randle	.40	.15
❑ 140	Jake Reed	.40	.15
❑ 141	Robert Smith	.60	.25
❑ 142	Drew Bledsoe	1.00	.40
❑ 143	Ben Coates	.40	.15
❑ 144	Robert Edwards RC	.75	.30
❑ 145	Terry Glenn	.60	.25
❑ 146	Shawn Jefferson	.25	.08
❑ 147	Willie McGinest	.25	.08
❑ 148	Tony Simmons RC	.75	.30
❑ 149	Chris Slade	.25	.08
❑ 150	Troy Davis	.25	.08
❑ 151	Mark Fields	.25	.08
❑ 152	Andre Hastings	.25	.08
❑ 153	Billy Joe Hobert	.25	.08
❑ 154	William Roaf	.25	.08
❑ 155	Heath Shuler	.25	.08
❑ 156	Danny Wuerffel	.40	.15
❑ 157	Ray Zellars	.25	.08
❑ 158	Jessie Armstead	.25	.08
❑ 159	Tiki Barber	.60	.25
❑ 160	Chris Calloway	.25	.08
❑ 161	Mike Cherry	.25	.08
❑ 162	Danny Kanell	.40	.15
❑ 163	Amani Toomer	.40	.15
❑ 164	Charles Way	.25	.08
❑ 165	Tyrone Wheatley	.40	.15
❑ 166	Kyle Brady	.25	.08
❑ 167	Wayne Chrebet	.60	.25
❑ 168	Glenn Foley	.40	.15
❑ 169	Scott Frost RC	.50	.20
❑ 170	Keyshawn Johnson	.60	.25
❑ 171	Leon Johnson	.25	.08
❑ 172	Alex Van Dyke	.25	.08
❑ 173	Dedric Ward	.25	.08
❑ 174	Tim Brown	.60	.25
❑ 175	Rickey Dudley	.25	.08
❑ 176	Jeff George	.40	.15
❑ 177	Desmond Howard	.40	.15
❑ 178	James Jett	.40	.15
❑ 179	Napoleon Kaufman	.60	.25
❑ 180	Darrell Russell	.25	.08
❑ 181	Charles Woodson RC	1.50	.60
❑ 182	Jason Dunn	.25	.08
❑ 183	Irving Fryar	.40	.15
❑ 184	Charlie Garner	.40	.15
❑ 185	Bobby Hoying	.40	.15
❑ 186	Chris T. Jones	.25	.08
❑ 187	Michael Timpson	.25	.08
❑ 188	Kevin Turner	.25	.08
❑ 189	Jerome Bettis	.60	.25
❑ 190	Will Blackwell	.25	.08
❑ 191	Mark Bruener	.25	.08
❑ 192	Charles Johnson	.25	.08
❑ 193	George Jones	.25	.08
❑ 194	Levon Kirkland	.25	.08
❑ 195	Kordell Stewart	.60	.25
❑ 196	Hines Ward RC	5.00	2.50
❑ 197	Tony Banks	.40	.15
❑ 198	Isaac Bruce	.60	.25
❑ 199	Ernie Conwell	.25	.08
❑ 200	Robert Holcombe RC	.75	.30
❑ 201	Eddie Kennison	.40	.15
❑ 202	Amp Lee	.25	.08
❑ 203	Orlando Pace	.25	.08
❑ 204	Charlie Jones	.25	.08
❑ 205	Freddie Jones	.25	.08
❑ 206	Ryan Leaf RC	1.25	.50
❑ 207	Natrone Means	.40	.15
❑ 208	Junior Seau	.60	.25
❑ 209	Bryan Still	.25	.08
❑ 210	Greg Clark	.25	.08
❑ 211	Jim Druckenmiller	.25	.08
❑ 212	Marc Edwards	.25	.08
❑ 213	Garrison Hearst	.60	.25
❑ 214	Terrell Owens	.60	.25
❑ 215	Jerry Rice	1.25	.50
❑ 216	J.J. Stokes	.40	.15
❑ 217	Bryant Young	.25	.08
❑ 218	Steve Young	.75	.30
❑ 219	Chad Brown	.25	.08
❑ 220	Joey Galloway	.40	.15
❑ 221	Cortez Kennedy	.25	.08
❑ 222	Jon Kitna	.60	.25
❑ 223	James McKnight	.60	.25
❑ 224	Warren Moon	.60	.25
❑ 225	Michael Sinclair	.25	.08
❑ 226	Ricky Watters	.40	.15
❑ 227	Mike Alstott	.60	.25
❑ 228	Reidel Anthony	.40	.15
❑ 229	Derrick Brooks	.60	.25
❑ 230	Trent Dilfer	.60	.25
❑ 231	Warrick Dunn	.60	.25
❑ 232	Dave Moore	.25	.08
❑ 233	Hardy Nickerson	.25	.08
❑ 234	Warren Sapp	.40	.15
❑ 235	Karl Williams	.25	.08
❑ 236	Willie Davis	.25	.08
❑ 237	Kevin Dyson RC	1.25	.50
❑ 238	Eddie George	.60	.25
❑ 239	Derrick Mason	.40	.15
❑ 240	Steve McNair	.60	.25
❑ 241	Chris Sanders	.25	.08
❑ 242	Frank Wycheck	.25	.08
❑ 243	Terry Allen	.60	.25
❑ 244	Jamie Asher	.25	.08
❑ 245	Gus Frerotte	.25	.08
❑ 246	Darrell Green	.40	.15
❑ 247	Skip Hicks RC	.75	.30
❑ 248	Brian Mitchell	.25	.08
❑ 249	Leslie Shepherd	.25	.08
❑ 250	Michael Westbrook	.40	.15

1999 Pacific Omega

❑	COMPLETE SET (250)	40.00	20.00
❑ 1	Mario Bates	.25	.08
❑ 2	David Boston RC	1.25	.50
❑ 3	Rob Moore	.40	.15
❑ 4	Adrian Murrell	.40	.15
❑ 5	Jake Plummer	.40	.15
❑ 6	Frank Sanders	.40	.15
❑ 7	Aeneas Williams	.25	.08
❑ 8	J.Makovicka/L.Shelton RC	1.25	.50
❑ 9	Jamal Anderson	.60	.25
❑ 10	Ray Buchanan	.25	.08
❑ 11	Chris Chandler	.40	.15
❑ 12	Tim Dwight	.60	.25

❑	13	Byron Hanspard	.25	.08
❑	14	Terance Mathis	.40	.15
❑	15	O.J. Santiago	.25	.08
❑	16	D.Kanell/C.Calloway	.25	.08
❑	17	Peter Boulware	.25	.08
❑	18	Priest Holmes	1.00	.40
❑	19	Patrick Johnson	.25	.08
❑	20	Jermaine Lewis	.40	.15
❑	21	Ray Lewis	.60	.25
❑	22	Michael McCrary	.25	.08
❑	23	Jonathan Ogden	.25	.08
❑	24	T.Banks/S.Mitchell	.25	.08
❑	25	Doug Flutie	.60	.25
❑	26	Rob Johnson	.40	.15
❑	27	Eric Moulds	.60	.25
❑	28	Andre Reed	.40	.15
❑	29	Antowain Smith	.60	.25
❑	30	Bruce Smith	.40	.15
❑	31	Kevin Williams	.25	.08
❑	32	S.Bryson/P.Price RC	1.25	.50
❑	33	Steve Beuerlein	.25	.08
❑	34	Tim Biakabutuka	.40	.15
❑	35	Rae Carruth	.25	.08
❑	36	Dameyune Craig RC	2.00	.75
❑	37	William Floyd	.25	.08
❑	38	Kevin Greene	.25	.08
❑	39	Muhsin Muhammad	.40	.15
❑	40	Wesley Walls	.40	.15
❑	41	Edgar Bennett	.25	.08
❑	42	Robert Chancey RC	1.50	.60
❑	43	Curtis Conway	.40	.15
❑	44	Bobby Engram	.40	.15
❑	45	Curtis Enis	.25	.08
❑	46	Cade McNown RC	1.00	.40
❑	47	Ryan Wetnight	.25	.08
❑	48	D.Bates/Mar.Booker RC	1.25	.50
❑	49	Jeff Blake	.40	.15
❑	50	Scott Covington RC	1.25	.50
❑	51	Corey Dillon	.60	.25
❑	52	James Hundon	.40	.15
❑	53	Carl Pickens	.40	.15
❑	54	Darnay Scott	.25	.08
❑	55	Akili Smith RC	1.00	.40
❑	56	Craig Yeast RC	1.00	.40
❑	57	Tim Couch RC	1.25	.50
❑	58	Ty Detmer	.40	.15
❑	59	Marc Edwards	.25	.08
❑	60	Kevin Johnson RC	1.25	.50
❑	61	Terry Kirby	.25	.08
❑	62	Sedrick Shaw	.25	.08
❑	63	Leslie Shepherd	.25	.08
❑	64	Chiaverini/McCutcheon RC	1.00	.40
❑	65	Troy Aikman	1.25	.50
❑	66	Michael Irvin	.40	.15
❑	67	David LaFleur	.25	.08
❑	68	Wane McGarity RC	.50	.20
❑	69	Ernie Mills	.25	.08
❑	70	Deion Sanders	.60	.25
❑	71	Emmitt Smith	1.25	.50
❑	72	R.Ismail/J.McKnight	.40	.15
❑	73	Bubby Brister	.25	.08
❑	74	Byron Chamberlain RC	1.00	.40
❑	75	Terrell Davis	.60	.25
❑	76	Olandis Gary RC	1.25	.50
❑	77	Brian Griese	.60	.25
❑	78	Ed McCaffrey	.40	.15
❑	79	Shannon Sharpe	.40	.15
❑	80	Rod Smith	.40	.15
❑	81	T.McGriff/A.Wilson RC	.50	.20
❑	82	Charlie Batch	.60	.25
❑	83	Chris Claiborne RC	.50	.20
❑	84	Germane Crowell	.25	.08
❑	85	Terry Fair	.25	.08
❑	86	Sedrick Irvin RC	.50	.20
❑	87	Herman Moore	.40	.15
❑	88	Johnnie Morton	.40	.15
❑	89	Barry Sanders	2.00	.75
❑	90	Mark Chmura	.25	.08
❑	91	Brett Favre	2.00	.75
❑	92	Antonio Freeman	.60	.25
❑	93	Desmond Howard	.40	.15
❑	94	Dorsey Levens	.60	.25
❑	95	Derrick Mayes	.25	.08
❑	96	Bill Schroeder	.60	.25
❑	97	A.Brooks/D.Miller RC	2.50	1.00
❑	98	E.G. Green	.25	.08
❑	99	Marvin Harrison	.60	.25
❑	100	Edgerrin James RC	5.00	2.00
❑	101	Peyton Manning	2.00	.75
❑	102	Jerome Pathon	.25	.08
❑	103	Marcus Pollard	.25	.08
❑	104	Ken Dilger	.25	.08
❑	105	Derrick Alexander WR	.40	.15
❑	106	Reggie Barlow	.25	.08
❑	107	Tony Boselli	.25	.08
❑	108	Mark Brunell	.60	.25
❑	109	George Jones	.25	.08
❑	110	Keenan McCardell	.40	.15
❑	111	Jimmy Smith	.40	.15
❑	112	James Stewart	.40	.15
❑	113	Fred Taylor	.60	.25
❑	114	Kimble Anders	.40	.15
❑	115	Mike Cloud RC	1.00	.40
❑	116	Tony Gonzalez	.60	.25
❑	117	Elvis Grbac	.40	.15
❑	118	Byron Bam Morris	.25	.08
❑	119	Andre Rison	.40	.15
❑	120	Derrick Thomas	.60	.25
❑	121	Karim Abdul-Jabbar	.40	.15
❑	122	Oronde Gadsden	.40	.15
❑	123	James Johnson RC	1.00	.40
❑	124	Rob Konrad RC	1.25	.50
❑	125	Dan Marino	2.00	.75
❑	126	O.J. McDuffie	.40	.15
❑	127	Lamar Thomas	.25	.08
❑	128	Zach Thomas	.60	.25
❑	129	Cris Carter	.60	.25
❑	130	Daunte Culpepper RC	5.00	2.00
❑	131	Randall Cunningham	.60	.25
❑	132	Matthew Hatchette	.25	.08
❑	133	Leroy Hoard	.25	.08
❑	134	David Palmer	.25	.08
❑	135	John Randle	.40	.15
❑	136	Randy Moss	1.50	.60
❑	137	Robert Smith	.60	.25
❑	138	Drew Bledsoe	.75	.30
❑	139	Ben Coates	.40	.15
❑	140	Kevin Faulk RC	1.25	.50
❑	141	Terry Glenn	.60	.25
❑	142	Shawn Jefferson	.25	.08
❑	143	Ty Law	.40	.15
❑	144	Tony Simmons	.25	.08
❑	145	Bishop RC/Katzenmoyer RC	1.25	.50
❑	146	Cameron Cleeland	.25	.08
❑	147	Andre Hastings	.25	.08
❑	148	Billy Joe Hobert	.25	.08
❑	149	Joe Johnson	.25	.08
❑	150	Keith Poole	.25	.08
❑	151	William Roaf	.25	.08
❑	152	Billy Joe Tolliver	.25	.08
❑	153	Ricky Williams RC	2.50	1.00
❑	154	Tiki Barber	.60	.25
❑	155	Gary Brown	.25	.08
❑	156	Kent Graham	.25	.08
❑	157	Ike Hilliard	.25	.08
❑	158	David Patten	.40	.15
❑	159	Jason Sehorn	.25	.08
❑	160	Amani Toomer	.25	.08
❑	161	Montgomery RC/Petit.RC	1.00	.40
❑	162	Wayne Chrebet	.40	.15
❑	163	Bryan Cox	.25	.08
❑	164	Aaron Glenn	.25	.08
❑	165	Keyshawn Johnson	.60	.25
❑	166	Leon Johnson	.25	.08
❑	167	Curtis Martin	.60	.25
❑	168	Vinny Testaverde	.40	.15
❑	169	Dedric Ward	.25	.08
❑	170	Tim Brown	.60	.25
❑	171	Rickey Dudley	.25	.08
❑	172	James Jett	.40	.15
❑	173	Napoleon Kaufman	.60	.25
❑	174	Jon Ritchie	.25	.08
❑	175	Darrell Russell	.25	.08
❑	176	Charles Woodson	.60	.25
❑	177	R.Gannon/H.Shuler	.60	.25
❑	178	Hugh Douglas	.25	.08
❑	179	Donovan McNabb RC	6.00	2.50
❑	180	Allen Rossum	.25	.08
❑	181	Duce Staley	.40	.15
❑	182	Kevin Turner	.25	.08
❑	183	C.Johnson/D.Pederson	.25	.08
❑	184	B.Gardner/C.Martin RC	1.25	.50
❑	185	Jerome Bettis	.60	.25
❑	186	Mark Bruener	.25	.08
❑	187	Troy Edwards RC	1.00	.40
❑	188	Courtney Hawkins	.25	.08
❑	189	Levon Kirkland	.25	.08
❑	190	Kordell Stewart	.40	.15
❑	191	Hines Ward	.60	.25
❑	192	M.Johnson/A.Zereoue RC	1.25	.50
❑	193	Greg Clark	.25	.08
❑	194	Terrell Fletcher	.25	.08
❑	195	Charlie Jones	.25	.08
❑	196	Cecil Collins RC	.50	.20
❑	197	Natrone Means	.40	.15
❑	198	Mikhael Ricks	.25	.08
❑	199	Junior Seau	.60	.25
❑	200	Bryan Still	.25	.08
❑	201	Ryan Thelwell RC	1.00	.40
❑	202	Garrison Hearst	.40	.15
❑	203	Terry Jackson RC	1.00	.40
❑	204	R.W. McQuarters	.25	.08
❑	205	Terrell Owens	.60	.25
❑	206	Jerry Rice	1.25	.50
❑	207	J.J. Stokes	.40	.15
❑	208	L.Phillips/T.Vardell	.25	.08
❑	209	Steve Young	.75	.30
❑	210	Karsten Bailey RC	1.00	.40
❑	211	Chad Brown	.25	.08
❑	212	Christian Fauria	.25	.08
❑	213	Joey Galloway	.40	.15
❑	214	Ahman Green	.60	.25
❑	215	Brock Huard RC	1.25	.50
❑	216	Cortez Kennedy	.25	.08
❑	217	Jon Kitna	.60	.25
❑	218	Ricky Watters	.40	.15
❑	219	Isaac Bruce	.60	.25
❑	220	Az-Zahir Hakim	.25	.08
❑	221	June Henley RC	.25	.08
❑	222	Greg Hill	.25	.08
❑	223	Torry Holt RC	3.00	1.25
❑	224	Amp Lee	.25	.08
❑	225	Ricky Proehl	.25	.08
❑	226	M.Faulk/T.Green	.75	.30
❑	227	Mike Alstott	.60	.25
❑	228	Reidel Anthony	.40	.15
❑	229	Trent Dilfer	.40	.15
❑	230	Warrick Dunn	.60	.25
❑	231	Bert Emanuel	.40	.15
❑	232	Jacquez Green	.25	.08
❑	233	Warren Sapp	.25	.08
❑	234	Shaun King RC/McFar.RC	1.25	.50
❑	235	Mike Archie RC	.50	.20
❑	236	Kevin Dyson	.40	.15
❑	237	Eddie George	.60	.25
❑	238	Derrick Mason	.40	.15
❑	239	Steve McNair	.60	.25
❑	240	Yancey Thigpen	.25	.08
❑	241	Frank Wycheck	.25	.08
❑	242	Jevon Kearse RC/Hall RC	2.00	.75
❑	243	Stephen Alexander	.25	.08
❑	244	Champ Bailey RC	1.50	.60
❑	245	Stephen Davis	.60	.25
❑	246	Skip Hicks	.25	.08
❑	247	James Thrash RC	1.25	.50
❑	248	Michael Westbrook	.40	.15
❑	249	Dan Wilkinson	.25	.08
❑	250	B.Johnson/L.Centers	.60	.25

2000 Pacific Omega

❑		COMP.SET w/o SP's (150)	20.00	7.50
❑	1	David Boston	.60	.25
❑	2	Dave Brown	.25	.08
❑	3	Rob Moore	.40	.15

❑ 4 Jake Plummer .40 .15
❑ 5 Simeon Rice .40 .15
❑ 6 Frank Sanders .40 .15
❑ 7 Jamal Anderson .60 .25
❑ 8 Chris Chandler .40 .15
❑ 9 Tim Dwight .60 .25
❑ 10 Terance Mathis .40 .15
❑ 11 Tony Banks .40 .15
❑ 12 Peter Boulware .25 .08
❑ 13 Priest Holmes .75 .30
❑ 14 Qadry Ismail .40 .15
❑ 15 Doug Flutie .60 .25
❑ 16 Rob Johnson .40 .15
❑ 17 Jonathan Linton .25 .08
❑ 18 Eric Moulds .60 .25
❑ 19 Peerless Price .40 .15
❑ 20 Antowain Smith .60 .25
❑ 21 Steve Beuerlein .25 .08
❑ 22 Tim Biakabutuka .40 .15
❑ 23 Patrick Jeffers .60 .25
❑ 24 Muhsin Muhammad .40 .15
❑ 25 Wesley Walls .40 .15
❑ 26 Bobby Engram .40 .15
❑ 27 Curtis Enis .25 .08
❑ 28 Cade McNown .25 .08
❑ 29 Marcus Robinson .60 .25
❑ 30 Willie Anderson .25 .08
❑ 31 Michael Basnight .25 .08
❑ 32 Corey Dillon .60 .25
❑ 33 Akili Smith .25 .08
❑ 34 Tim Couch .40 .15
❑ 35 Kevin Johnson .60 .25
❑ 36 Wali Rainer .25 .08
❑ 37 Troy Aikman 1.25 .50
❑ 38 Dexter Coakley .25 .08
❑ 39 Rocket Ismail .40 .15
❑ 40 Emmitt Smith 1.25 .50
❑ 41 Chris Warren .25 .08
❑ 42 Terrell Davis .60 .25
❑ 43 Olandis Gary .60 .25
❑ 44 Brian Griese .60 .25
❑ 45 Ed McCaffrey .60 .25
❑ 46 Rod Smith .40 .15
❑ 47 Charlie Batch .60 .25
❑ 48 Germane Crowell .25 .08
❑ 49 Herman Moore .40 .15
❑ 50 Johnnie Morton .40 .15
❑ 51 Barry Sanders 1.50 .60
❑ 52 Corey Bradford .40 .15
❑ 53 Brett Favre 2.00 .75
❑ 54 Antonio Freeman .60 .25
❑ 55 Dorsey Levens .40 .15
❑ 56 Bill Schroeder .40 .15
❑ 57 Ken Dilger .25 .08
❑ 58 Marvin Harrison .60 .25
❑ 59 Edgerrin James 1.00 .40
❑ 60 Peyton Manning 1.50 .60
❑ 61 Jerome Pathon .40 .15
❑ 62 Terrence Wilkins .25 .08
❑ 63 Mark Brunell .60 .25
❑ 64 Keenan McCardell .40 .15
❑ 65 Jimmy Smith .40 .15
❑ 66 Fred Taylor .60 .25
❑ 67 Derrick Alexander .40 .15
❑ 68 Donnell Bennett .25 .08
❑ 69 Tony Gonzalez .40 .15
❑ 70 Elvis Grbac .40 .15
❑ 71 Tony Richardson RC .25 .08
❑ 72 Oronde Gadsden .40 .15
❑ 73 Damon Huard .60 .25
❑ 74 James Johnson .25 .08
❑ 75 Dan Marino 2.00 .75
❑ 76 Tony Martin .40 .15
❑ 77 O.J. McDuffie .40 .15
❑ 78 Cris Carter .60 .25
❑ 79 Daunte Culpepper .75 .30
❑ 80 Randy Moss 1.25 .50
❑ 81 Robert Smith .60 .25
❑ 82 Drew Bledsoe .75 .30
❑ 83 Kevin Faulk .40 .15
❑ 84 Terry Glenn .40 .15
❑ 85 P.J. Franklin RC .40 .15
❑ 86 Keith Poole .40 .15
❑ 87 Ricky Williams .60 .25
❑ 88 Tiki Barber .60 .25
❑ 89 Kerry Collins .40 .15
❑ 90 Ike Hilliard .40 .15
❑ 91 Amani Toomer .40 .15
❑ 92 Wayne Chrebet .40 .15
❑ 93 Ray Lucas .40 .15
❑ 94 Curtis Martin .60 .25
❑ 95 Vinny Testaverde .40 .15
❑ 96 Tim Brown .60 .25
❑ 97 Rich Gannon .60 .25
❑ 98 James Jett .25 .08
❑ 99 Napoleon Kaufman .40 .15
❑ 100 Tyrone Wheatley .40 .15
❑ 101 Charles Woodson .40 .15
❑ 102 Brian Dawkins .60 .25
❑ 103 Charles Johnson .40 .15
❑ 104 Donovan McNabb 1.00 .40
❑ 105 Torrance Small .25 .08
❑ 106 Duce Staley .60 .25
❑ 107 Jerome Bettis .60 .25
❑ 108 Troy Edwards .25 .08
❑ 109 Richard Huntley .25 .08
❑ 110 Kordell Stewart .40 .15
❑ 111 Hines Ward .60 .25
❑ 112 Isaac Bruce .60 .25
❑ 113 Marshall Faulk .75 .30
❑ 114 Az-Zahir Hakim .40 .15
❑ 115 Torry Holt .60 .25
❑ 116 Tony Home .25 .08
❑ 117 Kurt Warner 1.25 .50
❑ 118 Jermaine Fazande .25 .08
❑ 119 Jeff Graham .25 .08
❑ 120 Jim Harbaugh .40 .15
❑ 121 Mikhael Ricks .25 .08
❑ 122 Junior Seau .60 .25
❑ 123 Jeff Garcia .60 .25
❑ 124 Charlie Garner .40 .15
❑ 125 Terrell Owens .60 .25
❑ 126 Jerry Rice 1.25 .50
❑ 127 J.J. Stokes .40 .15
❑ 128 Jon Kitna .60 .25
❑ 129 Derrick Mayes .40 .15
❑ 130 Charlie Rogers .25 .08
❑ 131 Shawn Springs .25 .08
❑ 132 Ricky Watters .40 .15
❑ 133 Mike Alstott .60 .25
❑ 134 Reidel Anthony .25 .08
❑ 135 Warrick Dunn .60 .25
❑ 136 Jacquez Green .25 .08
❑ 137 Shaun King .25 .08
❑ 138 Warren Sapp .40 .15
❑ 139 Kevin Dyson .40 .15
❑ 140 Eddie George .60 .25
❑ 141 Jevon Kearse .60 .25
❑ 142 Steve McNair .60 .25
❑ 143 Yancey Thigpen .25 .08
❑ 144 Frank Wycheck .25 .08
❑ 145 Champ Bailey .40 .15
❑ 146 Larry Centers .25 .08
❑ 147 Albert Connell .25 .08
❑ 148 Stephen Davis .60 .25
❑ 149 Brad Johnson .60 .25
❑ 150 Michael Westbrook .40 .15
❑ 151 Thomas Jones RC 12.00 5.00
❑ 152 Jay Tant RC 4.00 1.50
❑ 153 Doug Johnson RC 8.00 3.00
❑ 154 Mareno Philyaw RC 4.00 1.50
❑ 155 Jamal Lewis RC 20.00 7.50
❑ 156 Chris Redman RC 6.00 2.50
❑ 157 Travis Taylor RC 8.00 3.00
❑ 158 Kwame Cavil RC 4.00 1.50
❑ 159 Corey Moore RC 4.00 1.50
❑ 160 Deon Grant RC 6.00 2.50
❑ 161 Frank Murphy RC 4.00 1.50
❑ 162 Dez White RC 8.00 3.00
❑ 163 Ron Dugans RC 4.00 1.50
❑ 164 Tony Hartley RC 4.00 1.50
❑ 165 Curtis Keaton RC 6.00 2.50
❑ 166 Peter Warrick RC 8.00 3.00
❑ 167 Courtney Brown RC 8.00 3.00
❑ 168 JaJuan Dawson RC 4.00 1.50
❑ 169 Dennis Northcutt RC 8.00 3.00
❑ 170 Travis Prentice RC 6.00 2.50
❑ 171 Aaron Shea RC 6.00 2.50
❑ 172 Michael Wiley RC 6.00 2.50
❑ 173 Chris Cole RC 6.00 2.50
❑ 174 Jarious Jackson RC 6.00 2.50
❑ 175 Deltha O'Neal RC 8.00 3.00
❑ 176 Reuben Droughns RC 8.00 3.00
❑ 177 Bubba Franks RC 8.00 3.00
❑ 178 Anthony Lucas RC 4.00 1.50
❑ 179 Rondell Mealey RC 4.00 1.50
❑ 180 Ibn Green RC 4.00 1.50
❑ 181 Kevin McDougal RC 6.00 2.50
❑ 182 R.Jay Soward RC 6.00 2.50
❑ 183 Shyrone Stith RC 6.00 2.50
❑ 184 Dante Hall RC 15.00 6.00
❑ 185 Frank Moreau RC 6.00 2.50
❑ 186 Sylvester Morris RC 6.00 2.50
❑ 187 Deon Dyer RC 6.00 2.50
❑ 188 Ben Kelly RC 4.00 1.50
❑ 189 Quinton Spotwood RC 4.00 1.50
❑ 190 Troy Walters RC 8.00 3.00
❑ 191 Tom Brady RC 80.00 40.00
❑ 192 J.R. Redmond RC 6.00 2.50
❑ 193 David Stachelski RC 4.00 1.50
❑ 194 Marc Bulger RC 15.00 6.00
❑ 195 Sherrod Gideon RC 4.00 1.50
❑ 196 Chad Morton RC 8.00 3.00
❑ 197 Ron Dayne RC 8.00 3.00
❑ 198 Anthony Becht RC 8.00 3.00
❑ 199 Laveranues Coles RC 10.00 4.00
❑ 200 Chad Pennington RC 20.00 7.50
❑ 201 Sebastian Janikowski RC 8.00 3.00
❑ 202 Marcus Knight RC 6.00 2.50
❑ 203 Jerry Porter RC 10.00 4.00
❑ 204 Todd Pinkston RC 8.00 3.00
❑ 205 Gari Scott RC 4.00 1.50
❑ 206 Plaxico Burress RC 15.00 6.00
❑ 207 Danny Farmer RC 6.00 2.50
❑ 208 Tee Martin RC 8.00 3.00
❑ 209 Hank Poteat RC 6.00 2.50
❑ 210 Trung Canidate RC 6.00 2.50
❑ 211 Patrick Batteaux RC 4.00 1.50
❑ 212 Trevor Gaylor RC 6.00 2.50
❑ 213 Ronney Jenkins RC 6.00 2.50
❑ 214 Terrence McCaskey RC 4.00 1.50
❑ 215 JaJuan Seider RC 4.00 1.50
❑ 216 Giovanni Carmazzi RC 4.00 1.50
❑ 217 Chafie Fields RC 4.00 1.50
❑ 218 Jonas Lewis RC 4.00 1.50
❑ 219 Tim Rattay RC 8.00 3.00
❑ 220 Shaun Alexander RC 40.00 15.00
❑ 221 Darrell Jackson RC 15.00 6.00
❑ 222 James Williams RC 6.00 2.50
❑ 223 Joe Hamilton RC 6.00 2.50
❑ 224 Erron Kinney RC 8.00 3.00
❑ 225 Todd Husak RC 8.00 3.00
❑ 226 P.Burress/D.Farmer 8.00 3.00
❑ 227 R.Dayne/J.Hamilton 3.00 1.25
❑ 228 P.Warrick/R.Dugans 4.00 1.50
❑ 229 T.Jones/C.Keaton 6.00 2.50
❑ 230 S.Alexander/R.Droughns 20.00 7.50
❑ 231 T.Taylor/D.Jackson 8.00 3.00
❑ 232 G.Carmazzi/T.Rattay 4.00 1.50
❑ 233 T.Canidate/J.R.Redmond 3.00 1.25
❑ 234 Syl.Morris/R.Soward 3.00 1.25
❑ 235 T.Prentice/T.Gaylor 3.00 1.25
❑ 236 T.Pinkston/S.Gideon 4.00 1.50
❑ 237 F.Murphy/D.White 4.00 1.50
❑ 238 C.Redman/T.Brady 50.00 20.00
❑ 239 J.Lewis/Tee Martin 10.00 4.00
❑ 240 R.Mealey/S.Stith 3.00 1.25
❑ 241 M.Wiley/C.Morton 3.00 1.25
❑ 242 L.Coles/S.Janikowski 4.00 1.50
❑ 243 T.Walters/T.Husak 4.00 1.50
❑ 244 M.Bulger/J.Porter 10.00 4.00
❑ 245 M.Philyaw/D.Johnson 4.00 1.50
❑ 246 D.Northcutt/C.Brown 4.00 1.50
❑ 247 J.Jackson/C.Cole 3.00 1.25

- ❑ 248 J.Dawson/G.Scott 2.00 .75
- ❑ 249 Q.Spotwood/C.Fields 2.00 .75
- ❑ 250 C.Pennington/J.Williams 10.00 4.00

1997 Pacific Philadelphia

- ❑ COMPLETE SET (330) 50.00 25.00
- ❑ 1 Kevin Butler .20 .07
- ❑ 2 Larry Centers .30 .10
- ❑ 3 Kent Graham .20 .07
- ❑ 4 Leeland McElroy .20 .07
- ❑ 5 Ronald McKinnon RC .30 .10
- ❑ 6 Johnny McWilliams .20 .07
- ❑ 7 Brad Otis .20 .07
- ❑ 8 Frank Sanders .30 .10
- ❑ 9 Rob Selby .20 .07
- ❑ 10 Cedric Smith .20 .07
- ❑ 11 Joe Staysniak .20 .07
- ❑ 12 Cornelius Bennett .20 .07
- ❑ 13 David Brandon .20 .07
- ❑ 14 Tyrone Brown .20 .07
- ❑ 15 John Burrough .20 .07
- ❑ 16 Browning Nagle .20 .07
- ❑ 17 Dan Owens .20 .07
- ❑ 18 Anthony Phillips .20 .07
- ❑ 19 Roell Preston .20 .07
- ❑ 20 Darnell Walker .20 .07
- ❑ 21 Bob Whitfield .20 .07
- ❑ 22 Mike Zandofsky .20 .07
- ❑ 23 Vashone Adams .20 .07
- ❑ 24 Derrick Alexander WR .30 .10
- ❑ 25 Harold Bishop .20 .07
- ❑ 26 Jeff Blackshear .20 .07
- ❑ 27 Donald Brady RC .20 .07
- ❑ 28 Mike Frederick .20 .07
- ❑ 29 Tim Goad .20 .07
- ❑ 30 DeRon Jenkins .20 .07
- ❑ 31 Ray Lewis .75 .30
- ❑ 32 Rick Lyle .20 .07
- ❑ 33 Byron Bam Morris .20 .07
- ❑ 34 Chris Brantley .20 .07
- ❑ 35 Jeff Burris .20 .07
- ❑ 36 Todd Collins .20 .07
- ❑ 37 Rob Coons .20 .07
- ❑ 38 Corbin Lacina RC .20 .07
- ❑ 39 Emanuel Martin .20 .07
- ❑ 40 Marlo Perry .20 .07
- ❑ 41 Shawn Price .20 .07
- ❑ 42 Thomas Smith .20 .07
- ❑ 43 Matt Stevens RC .20 .07
- ❑ 44 Thurman Thomas .50 .20
- ❑ 45 Jay Barker .20 .07
- ❑ 46 Tim Biakabutuka .30 .10
- ❑ 47 Kerry Collins .50 .20
- ❑ 48 Matt Elliott .20 .07
- ❑ 49 Howard Griffith .20 .07
- ❑ 50 Anthony Johnson .20 .07
- ❑ 51 John Kasay .20 .07
- ❑ 52 Muhsin Muhammad .30 .10
- ❑ 53 Winslow Oliver .20 .07
- ❑ 54 Walter Rasby .20 .07
- ❑ 55 Gerald Williams .20 .07
- ❑ 56 Mark Butterfield .20 .07
- ❑ 57 Bryan Cox .20 .07
- ❑ 58 Mike Faulkerson .20 .07
- ❑ 59 Paul Grasmanis .20 .07
- ❑ 60 Robert Green .20 .07
- ❑ 61 Jack Jackson .20 .07
- ❑ 62 Bobby Neely .20 .07
- ❑ 63 Todd Perry .20 .07
- ❑ 64 Evan Pilgrim .20 .07
- ❑ 65 Octus Polk .20 .07
- ❑ 66 Rashaan Salaam .20 .07
- ❑ 67 Willie Anderson .20 .07
- ❑ 68 Jeff Blake .30 .10
- ❑ 69 Scott Brumfield .20 .07
- ❑ 70 Jeff Cothran .20 .07
- ❑ 71 Gerald Dixon .20 .07
- ❑ 72 Garrison Hearst .30 .10
- ❑ 73 James Hundon RC .50 .20
- ❑ 74 Brian Milne .20 .07
- ❑ 75 Troy Sadowski .20 .07
- ❑ 76 Tom Tumulty .20 .07
- ❑ 77 Kimo von Oelhoffen RC 5.00 2.00
- ❑ 78 Troy Aikman 1.00 .40
- ❑ 79 Dale Hellestrae .20 .07
- ❑ 80 Roger Harper .20 .07
- ❑ 81 Michael Irvin .50 .20
- ❑ 82 John Jett .20 .07
- ❑ 83 Kelvin Martin .20 .07
- ❑ 84 Deion Sanders .50 .20
- ❑ 85 Darrin Smith .20 .07
- ❑ 86 Emmitt Smith 1.50 .60
- ❑ 87 Herschel Walker .30 .10
- ❑ 88 Charlie Williams .20 .07
- ❑ 89 Glenn Cadrez .20 .07
- ❑ 90 Dwayne Carswell RC .50 .20
- ❑ 91 Terrell Davis .60 .25
- ❑ 92 David Diaz-infante .20 .07
- ❑ 93 John Elway 2.00 .75
- ❑ 94 Harald Hasselback .20 .07
- ❑ 95 Tory James .20 .07
- ❑ 96 Bill Musgrave .20 .07
- ❑ 97 Ralph Tamm .20 .07
- ❑ 98 Maa Tanuvasa RC .20 .07
- ❑ 99 Gary Zimmerman .20 .07
- ❑ 100 Shane Bonham .20 .07
- ❑ 101 Stephen Boyd RC .20 .07
- ❑ 102 Jeff Hartings RC 1.00 .40
- ❑ 103 Hessley Hempstead .20 .07
- ❑ 104 Scott Kowalkowski .20 .07
- ❑ 105 Herman Moore .30 .10
- ❑ 106 Barry Sanders 1.50 .60
- ❑ 107 Tony Semple .20 .07
- ❑ 108 Ryan Stewart .20 .07
- ❑ 109 Mike Wells .20 .07
- ❑ 110 Richard Woodley .20 .07
- ❑ 111 Brett Favre 2.00 .75
- ❑ 112 Bernardo Harris RC .30 .10
- ❑ 113 Keith McKenzie RC .20 .07
- ❑ 114 Terry Mickens .20 .07
- ❑ 115 Doug Pederson RC .50 .20
- ❑ 116 Jeff Thomason RC .20 .07
- ❑ 117 Adam Timmerman RC .20 .07
- ❑ 118 Reggie White .50 .20
- ❑ 119 Bruce Wilkerson .20 .07
- ❑ 120 Gabe Wilkins RC .20 .07
- ❑ 121 Tyrone Williams RC .20 .07
- ❑ 122 Al Del Greco .20 .07
- ❑ 123 Anthony Dorsett .20 .07
- ❑ 124 Josh Evans .20 .07
- ❑ 125 Eddie George .50 .20
- ❑ 126 Lemanski Hall RC .20 .07
- ❑ 127 Ronnie Harmon .20 .07
- ❑ 128 Steve McNair .60 .25
- ❑ 129 Michael Roan .20 .07
- ❑ 130 Marcus Robertson .20 .07
- ❑ 131 Jon Runyan .20 .07
- ❑ 132 Chris Sanders .20 .07
- ❑ 133 Kerwin Bell .20 .07
- ❑ 134 Marshall Faulk .60 .25
- ❑ 135 Clif Groce RC .20 .07
- ❑ 136 Jim Harbaugh .30 .10
- ❑ 137 Marvin Harrison .50 .20
- ❑ 138 Eric Mahlum .20 .07
- ❑ 139 Tony Mandarich .20 .07
- ❑ 140 Dedric Mathis .20 .07
- ❑ 141 Marcus Pollard RC .20 .07
- ❑ 142 Scott Slutzker .20 .07
- ❑ 143 Mark Stock .20 .07
- ❑ 144 Bucky Brooks .20 .07
- ❑ 145 Mark Brunell .60 .25
- ❑ 146 Kendricke Bullard .20 .07
- ❑ 147 Randy Jordan .20 .07
- ❑ 148 Jeff Kopp .20 .07
- ❑ 149 Le'Shai Maston .20 .07
- ❑ 150 Keenan McCardell .30 .10
- ❑ 151 Clyde Simmons .20 .07
- ❑ 152 Jimmy Smith .30 .10
- ❑ 153 Rich Tylski RC .20 .07
- ❑ 154 Dave Widell .20 .07
- ❑ 155 Marcus Allen .50 .20
- ❑ 156 Keith Cash .20 .07
- ❑ 157 Donnie Edwards .30 .10
- ❑ 158 Trezelle Jenkins .20 .07
- ❑ 159 Sean LaChapelle .20 .07
- ❑ 160 Greg Manusky .20 .07
- ❑ 161 Steve Matthews .20 .07
- ❑ 162 Pellom McDaniels .20 .07
- ❑ 163 Chris Penn .20 .07
- ❑ 164 Danny Villa .20 .07
- ❑ 165 Jerome Woods .20 .07
- ❑ 166 Karim Abdul-Jabbar .50 .20
- ❑ 167 John Bock .20 .07
- ❑ 168 O.J. Brigance RC .20 .07
- ❑ 169 Norman Hand RC .20 .07
- ❑ 170 Anthony Harris .20 .07
- ❑ 171 Larry Izzo RC .20 .07
- ❑ 172 Charles Jordan .20 .07
- ❑ 173 Dan Marino 2.00 .75
- ❑ 174 Everett McIver .20 .07
- ❑ 175 Joe Nedney RC .20 .07
- ❑ 176 Robert Wilson RC .20 .07
- ❑ 177 David Dixon .20 .07
- ❑ 178 Charles Evans .20 .07
- ❑ 179 Hunter Goodwin RC .20 .07
- ❑ 180 Ben Hanks .20 .07
- ❑ 181 Warren Moon .50 .20
- ❑ 182 Harold Morrow RC .50 .20
- ❑ 183 Fernando Smith .20 .07
- ❑ 184 Robert Smith .30 .10
- ❑ 185 Sean Vanhorse .20 .07
- ❑ 186 Jay Walker .20 .07
- ❑ 187 Dewayne Washington .20 .07
- ❑ 188 Moe Williams .50 .20
- ❑ 189 Mike Bartrum .20 .07
- ❑ 190 Drew Bledsoe .60 .25
- ❑ 191 Troy Brown .30 .10
- ❑ 192 Chad Eaton RC .20 .07
- ❑ 193 Sam Gash .20 .07
- ❑ 194 Mike Gisler .20 .07
- ❑ 195 Curtis Martin .60 .25
- ❑ 196 David Richards .20 .07
- ❑ 197 Todd Rucci .20 .07
- ❑ 198 Chris Sullivan .20 .07
- ❑ 199 Adam Vinatieri RC 50.00 30.00
- ❑ 200 Doug Brien .20 .07
- ❑ 201 Derek Brown RBK .20 .07
- ❑ 202 Lee DeRamus .20 .07
- ❑ 203 Jim Everett .20 .07
- ❑ 204 Mercury Hayes .20 .07
- ❑ 205 Joe Johnson .20 .07
- ❑ 206 Henry Lusk RC .20 .07
- ❑ 207 Andy McCollum .20 .07
- ❑ 208 Alex Molden .20 .07
- ❑ 209 Ray Zellars .20 .07
- ❑ 210 Marcus Buckley .20 .07
- ❑ 211 Doug Coleman RC .20 .07
- ❑ 212 Percy Ellsworth RC .20 .07
- ❑ 213 Rodney Hampton .30 .10
- ❑ 214 Brian Saxton .20 .07
- ❑ 215 Jason Sehorn .30 .10
- ❑ 216 Stan White .20 .07
- ❑ 217 Corey Widmer .20 .07
- ❑ 218 Rodney Young .20 .07
- ❑ 219 Rob Zatechka .20 .07
- ❑ 220 Henry Bailey .20 .07
- ❑ 221 Chad Cascadden RC .20 .07
- ❑ 222 Wayne Chrebet .50 .20
- ❑ 223 Tyrone Davis .20 .07
- ❑ 224 Kwame Ellis .20 .07
- ❑ 225 Glenn Foley .30 .10
- ❑ 226 Erik Howard .20 .07
- ❑ 227 Gary Jones S .20 .07
- ❑ 228 Adrian Murrell .30 .10
- ❑ 229 Marc Spindler .20 .07
- ❑ 230 Lonnie Young .20 .07
- ❑ 231 Eric Zomalt .20 .07
- ❑ 232 Tim Brown .50 .20
- ❑ 233 Aundray Bruce .20 .07
- ❑ 234 Darren Carrington .20 .07
- ❑ 235 Rick Cunningham .20 .07
- ❑ 236 Rob Holmberg .20 .07
- ❑ 237 Jeff Hostetler .20 .07

❑ 238 Lorenzo Lynch .20 .07
❑ 239 Barrett Robbins .20 .07
❑ 240 Dan Turk .20 .07
❑ 241 Harvey Williams .20 .07
❑ 242 Brian Dawkins .50 .20
❑ 243 Ty Detmer .30 .10
❑ 244 Troy Drake .20 .07
❑ 245 Rhett Hall .20 .07
❑ 246 Joe Panos .20 .07
❑ 247 Johnny Thomas .20 .07
❑ 248 Kevin Turner .20 .07
❑ 249 Ricky Watters .30 .10
❑ 250 Derrick Witherspoon RC .20 .07
❑ 251 Sylvester Wright .20 .07
❑ 252 Jerome Bettis .50 .20
❑ 253 Carlos Emmons RC .20 .07
❑ 254 Jason Gildon .20 .07
❑ 255 Jonathan Hayes .20 .07
❑ 256 Kevin Henry .20 .07
❑ 257 Jerry Olsavsky .20 .07
❑ 258 Erric Pegram .20 .07
❑ 259 Brendan Stai .20 .07
❑ 260 Justin Strzelczyk .20 .07
❑ 261 Mike Tomczak .20 .07
❑ 262 Tony Banks .30 .10
❑ 263 Hayward Clay .20 .07
❑ 264 Percell Gaskins .20 .07
❑ 265 Eddie Kennison .30 .10
❑ 266 Aaron Laing .20 .07
❑ 267 Keith Lyle .20 .07
❑ 268 Jamie Martin RC 2.50 1.00
❑ 269 Lawrence Phillips .20 .07
❑ 270 Zach Wiegert .20 .07
❑ 271 Toby Wright .20 .07
❑ 272 Darren Bennett .20 .07
❑ 273 Tony Berti .20 .07
❑ 274 Freddie Bradley .20 .07
❑ 275 Joe Cocozzo .20 .07
❑ 276 Andre Coleman .20 .07
❑ 277 Marco Coleman .20 .07
❑ 278 Rodney Harrison RC 1.00 .40
❑ 279 David Hendrix .20 .07
❑ 280 Leonard Russell .20 .07
❑ 281 Sean Salisbury .20 .07
❑ 282 Dennis Brown .20 .07
❑ 283 Chris Dalman .20 .07
❑ 284 Brent Jones .30 .10
❑ 285 Sean Manuel .20 .07
❑ 286 Marquez Pope .20 .07
❑ 287 Jerry Rice 1.00 .40
❑ 288 Kirk Scrafford .20 .07
❑ 289 Iheanyi Uwaezuoke .30 .10
❑ 290 Tommy Vardell .20 .07
❑ 291 Steve Young .60 .25
❑ 292 James Atkins .20 .07
❑ 293 T.J. Cunningham .20 .07
❑ 294 Stan Gelbaugh .20 .07
❑ 295 James Logan .20 .07
❑ 296 James McKnight RC 1.50 .60
❑ 297 Rick Mirer .20 .07
❑ 298 Todd Peterson .20 .07
❑ 299 Fred Thomas .20 .07
❑ 300 Rick Tuten .20 .07
❑ 301 Chris Warren .30 .10
❑ 302 Donnie Abraham RC .50 .20
❑ 303 Trent Dilfer .50 .20
❑ 304 Kenneth Gant .20 .07
❑ 305 Jeff Gooch .30 .10
❑ 306 Courtney Hawkins .20 .07
❑ 307 Tyoka Jackson RC .20 .07
❑ 308 Melvin Johnson S RC .20 .07
❑ 309 Lonnie Marts .20 .07
❑ 310 Hardy Nickerson .20 .07
❑ 311 Errict Rhett .20 .07
❑ 312 Terry Allen .50 .20
❑ 313 Flipper Anderson .20 .07
❑ 314 William Bell .20 .07
❑ 315 Scott Blanton .20 .07
❑ 316 Leomont Evans RC .20 .07
❑ 317 Gus Frerotte .20 .07
❑ 318 Darryl Morrison .20 .07
❑ 319 Matt Turk .20 .07
❑ 320 Jeff Uhlenhake .20 .07
❑ 321 Brian Walker RC .20 .07
❑ 322 Mark Brunell LL .50 .20
❑ 323 Barry Sanders LL .75 .30
❑ 324 Isaac Bruce LL .50 .20
❑ 325 Terry Allen LL .30 .10
❑ 326 Steve Young LL .50 .20
❑ 327 Jerry Rice LL .50 .20
❑ 328 Ricky Watters LL .30 .10
❑ 329 Kevin Greene LL .20 .07
❑ 330 Brett Favre LL 1.00 .40
❑ S1 Mark Brunell Sample 2.00 .75

1997 Pacific Philadelphia Gold

❑ COMPLETE SET (200) 30.00 15.00
❑ 1 Ryan Christopherson .15 .05
❑ 2 James Dexter .15 .05
❑ 3 Boomer Esiason .25 .08
❑ 4 Jarius Hayes .15 .05
❑ 5 Eric Hill .15 .05
❑ 6 Trey Junkin .15 .05
❑ 7 Kwamie Lassiter .40 .15
❑ 8 Patrick Bates .15 .05
❑ 9 Brad Edwards .15 .05
❑ 10 Roman Fortin .15 .05
❑ 11 Harper Le Bel .15 .05
❑ 12 Lorenzo Styles .15 .05
❑ 13 Robbie Tobeck .15 .05
❑ 14 Mike Caldwell .15 .05
❑ 15 Eric Green .15 .05
❑ 16 Brian Kinchen .15 .05
❑ 17 Eric Turner .15 .05
❑ 18 Jerrol Williams .15 .05
❑ 19 Eric Zeier .25 .08
❑ 20 Darick Holmes .15 .05
❑ 21 Ken Irvin .15 .05
❑ 22 Jerry Ostroski .15 .05
❑ 23 Andre Reed .25 .08
❑ 24 Steve Tasker .15 .05
❑ 25 Thurman Thomas .40 .15
❑ 26 Steve Beuerlein .25 .08
❑ 27 Kerry Collins .40 .15
❑ 28 Eric Davis .15 .05
❑ 29 Norberto Garrido .15 .05
❑ 30 Lamar Lathon .15 .05
❑ 31 Andre Royal .15 .05
❑ 32 Tony Carter .15 .05
❑ 33 Jerry Fontenot .15 .05
❑ 34 Raymont Harris .15 .05
❑ 35 Anthony Marshall .15 .05
❑ 36 Barry Minter .15 .05
❑ 37 Steve Stenstrom .15 .05
❑ 38 Donnell Woolford .15 .05
❑ 39 Ken Blackman .15 .05
❑ 40 Jeff Blake .25 .08
❑ 41 Carl Pickens .25 .08
❑ 42 Artie Smith .15 .05
❑ 43 Ramondo Stallings .15 .05
❑ 44 Melvin Tuten .15 .05
❑ 45 Joe Walter .15 .05
❑ 46 Troy Aikman 1.00 .40
❑ 47 Billy Davis .15 .05
❑ 48 Chad Hennings .15 .05
❑ 49 Emmitt Smith 1.50 .60
❑ 50 George Teague .15 .05
❑ 51 Kevin Williams .15 .05
❑ 52 Terrell Davis .60 .25
❑ 53 John Elway 2.00 .75
❑ 54 Tom Nalen .15 .05
❑ 55 Bill Romanowski .15 .05
❑ 56 Rod Smith WR .40 .15
❑ 57 Dan Williams .15 .05
❑ 58 Mike Compton .15 .05
❑ 59 Eric Lynch .15 .05
❑ 60 Aubrey Matthews .15 .05
❑ 61 Pete Metzelaars .15 .05
❑ 62 Herman Moore .25 .08
❑ 63 Barry Sanders 1.50 .60
❑ 64 Keith Washington .15 .05
❑ 65 Edgar Bennett .25 .08
❑ 66 Brett Favre 2.00 .75
❑ 67 Lamont Hollinquest .15 .05
❑ 68 Keith Jackson .15 .05
❑ 69 Derrick Mayes .25 .08
❑ 70 Andre Rison .25 .08
❑ 71 Eddie George .40 .15
❑ 72 Mel Gray .15 .05
❑ 73 Darryll Lewis .15 .05
❑ 74 John Henry Mills .15 .05
❑ 75 Rodney Thomas .15 .05
❑ 76 Gary Walker .15 .05
❑ 77 Troy Auzenne .15 .05
❑ 78 Sammie Burroughs .15 .05
❑ 79 Jim Harbaugh .25 .08
❑ 80 Tony McCoy .15 .05
❑ 81 Brian Stablein .15 .05
❑ 82 Kipp Vickers .15 .05
❑ 83 Aaron Beasley .15 .05
❑ 84 Mark Brunell .60 .25
❑ 85 Don Davey .15 .05
❑ 86 Chris Hudson .15 .05
❑ 87 Greg Huntington .15 .05
❑ 88 Ernie Logan .15 .05
❑ 89 Donnell Bennett .15 .05
❑ 90 Anthony Davis .15 .05
❑ 91 Tim Grunhard .15 .05
❑ 92 Danan Hughes .15 .05
❑ 93 Tony Richardson .25 .08
❑ 94 Tracy Simien .15 .05
❑ 95 Karim Abdul-Jabbar .40 .15
❑ 96 Dwight Hollier .15 .05
❑ 97 John Kidd .15 .05
❑ 98 Dan Marino 2.00 .75
❑ 99 Jerris McPhail .15 .05
❑ 100 Irving Spikes .15 .05
❑ 101 Richmond Webb .15 .05
❑ 102 Jeff Brady .15 .05
❑ 103 Richard Brown .15 .05
❑ 104 Corey Fuller .15 .05
❑ 105 John Gerak .15 .05
❑ 106 Scottie Graham .15 .05
❑ 107 Amp Lee .15 .05
❑ 108 Drew Bledsoe .60 .25
❑ 109 Tedy Bruschi .75 .30
❑ 110 Todd Collins .15 .05
❑ 111 Bob Kratch .15 .05
❑ 112 Curtis Martin .60 .25
❑ 113 Dave Meggett .15 .05
❑ 114 Tom Tupa .15 .05
❑ 115 Eric Allen .15 .05
❑ 116 Mario Bates .15 .05
❑ 117 Clarence Jones .15 .05
❑ 118 Sean Lumpkin .15 .05
❑ 119 Doug Nussmeier .15 .05
❑ 120 Irv Smith .15 .05
❑ 121 Winfred Tubbs .15 .05
❑ 122 Willie Beamon .15 .05
❑ 123 Greg Bishop .15 .05
❑ 124 Dave Brown .15 .05
❑ 125 Gary Downs .15 .05
❑ 126 Thomas Lewis .15 .05
❑ 127 Michael Strahan .25 .08
❑ 128 Tyrone Wheatley .25 .08
❑ 129 Matt Brock .15 .05
❑ 130 Mike Chalenski .15 .05
❑ 131 Roger Duffy .15 .05
❑ 132 John Hudson .15 .05
❑ 133 Frank Reich .15 .05
❑ 134 David Williams T .15 .05
❑ 135 Greg Biekert .15 .05
❑ 136 Mike Jones LB .15 .05
❑ 137 Napoleon Kaufman .40 .15
❑ 138 Carl Kidd .15 .05
❑ 139 Terry McDaniel .15 .05
❑ 140 Mike Morton .15 .05
❑ 141 Olanda Truitt .15 .05
❑ 142 Gary Anderson K .15 .05
❑ 143 Richard Cooper .15 .05
❑ 144 Jimmie Johnson TE .15 .05
❑ 145 Joe Kelly .15 .05

❑ 146	William Thomas	.15	.05
❑ 147	Ricky Watters	.25	.08
❑ 148	Ed West	.15	.05
❑ 149	Michael Zordich	.15	.05
❑ 150	Jerome Bettis	.40	.15
❑ 151	Dermontti Dawson	.15	.05
❑ 152	Lethon Flowers	.15	.05
❑ 153	Charles Johnson	.25	.08
❑ 154	Darren Perry	.15	.05
❑ 155	Kordell Stewart	.40	.15
❑ 156	Will Wolford	.15	.05
❑ 157	Isaac Bruce	.40	.15
❑ 158	Kevin Carter	.15	.05
❑ 159	Torin Dorn	.15	.05
❑ 160	Leo Goeas	.15	.05
❑ 161	Gerald McBurrows	.15	.05
❑ 162	Chuck Osborne	.15	.05
❑ 163	J.T. Thomas	.15	.05
❑ 164	Dwayne Gordon	.15	.05
❑ 165	Stan Humphries	.25	.08
❑ 166	Shawn Lee	.15	.05
❑ 167	Chris Mims	.15	.05
❑ 168	John Parrella	.15	.05
❑ 169	Junior Seau	.40	.15
❑ 170	Bryan Still	.15	.05
❑ 171	Curtis Buckley	.15	.05
❑ 172	William Floyd	.25	.08
❑ 173	Merton Hanks	.15	.05
❑ 174	Terry Kirby	.25	.08
❑ 175	Jerry Rice	1.00	.40
❑ 176	J.J. Stokes	.25	.08
❑ 177	Jeff Wilkins	.15	.05
❑ 178	Bryant Young	.15	.05
❑ 179	Sam Adams	.15	.05
❑ 180	John Friesz	.15	.05
❑ 181	Joey Galloway	.25	.08
❑ 182	Pete Kendall	.15	.05
❑ 183	Jason Kyle	.15	.05
❑ 184	Darryl Williams	.15	.05
❑ 185	Ronnie Williams	.15	.05
❑ 186	Mike Alstott	.40	.15
❑ 187	Trent Dilfer	.40	.15
❑ 188	Tyrone Legette	.15	.05
❑ 189	Martin Mayhew	.15	.05
❑ 190	Jason Odom	.15	.05
❑ 191	Warren Sapp	.25	.08
❑ 192	Karl Williams	.15	.05
❑ 193	Terry Allen	.40	.15
❑ 194	Romeo Bandison	.15	.05
❑ 195	Alcides Catanho	.15	.05
❑ 196	Gus Frerotte	.15	.05
❑ 197	William Gaines	.15	.05
❑ 198	Ken Harvey	.15	.05
❑ 199	Trevor Matich	.15	.05
❑ 200	Scott Turner	.15	.05
❑ S1	Mark Brunell Sample	1.00	.40

1993 Pacific Prisms

❑	COMPLETE SET (109)	40.00	15.00
❑ 1	Chris Miller	.75	.30
❑ 2	Mike Pritchard	.75	.30
❑ 3	Andre Rison	.75	.30
❑ 4	Deion Sanders	2.50	1.00
❑ 5	Tony Smith RB	.40	.15
❑ 6	Jim Kelly	1.50	.60
❑ 7	Andre Reed	.75	.30
❑ 8	Thurman Thomas	1.50	.60
❑ 9	Neal Anderson	.40	.15
❑ 10	Jim Harbaugh	1.50	.60
❑ 11	Donnell Woolford	.40	.15
❑ 12	David Klingler	.40	.15
❑ 13	Carl Pickens	.75	.30
❑ 14	Alfred Williams	.40	.15
❑ 15	Michael Jackson	.75	.30
❑ 16	Bernie Kosar	.75	.30
❑ 17	Tommy Vardell	.40	.15
❑ 18	Troy Aikman	4.00	1.50
❑ 19	Alvin Harper	.75	.30
❑ 20	Michael Irvin	1.50	.60
❑ 21	Russell Maryland	.40	.15
❑ 22	Emmitt Smith	8.00	3.00
❑ 23	John Elway	8.00	3.00
❑ 24	Tommy Maddox	1.50	.60
❑ 25	Shannon Sharpe	1.50	.60
❑ 26	Herman Moore	1.50	.60
❑ 27	Rodney Peete	.40	.15
❑ 28	Barry Sanders	6.00	2.50
❑ 29	Pat Swilling	.40	.15
❑ 30	Terrell Buckley	.40	.15
❑ 31	Brett Favre	10.00	4.00
❑ 32	Sterling Sharpe	1.50	.60
❑ 33	Reggie White	1.50	.60
❑ 34	Ernest Givins	.75	.30
❑ 35	Haywood Jeffires	.75	.30
❑ 36	Warren Moon	1.50	.60
❑ 37	Lorenzo White	.40	.15
❑ 38	Steve Emtman	.40	.15
❑ 39	Jeff George	1.50	.60
❑ 40	Reggie Langhorne	.40	.15
❑ 41	Dale Carter	.40	.15
❑ 42	Joe Montana	8.00	3.00
❑ 43	Derrick Thomas	1.50	.60
❑ 44	Barry Word	.40	.15
❑ 45	Nick Bell	.40	.15
❑ 46	Eric Dickerson	.75	.30
❑ 47	Jeff Jaeger	.40	.15
❑ 48	Jerome Bettis RC	12.00	5.00
❑ 49	Henry Ellard	.75	.30
❑ 50	Jim Everett	.75	.30
❑ 51	Cleveland Gary	.40	.15
❑ 52	Marco Coleman	.40	.15
❑ 53	Mark Higgs	.40	.15
❑ 54	Keith Jackson	.75	.30
❑ 55	Dan Marino	8.00	3.00
❑ 56	Troy Vincent	.40	.15
❑ 57	Terry Allen	1.50	.60
❑ 58	Jack Del Rio	.40	.15
❑ 59	Sean Salisbury	.40	.15
❑ 60	Robert Smith RC	5.00	2.00
❑ 61	Drew Bledsoe RC	10.00	4.00
❑ 62	Marv Cook	.40	.15
❑ 63	Irving Fryar	.75	.30
❑ 64	Leonard Russell	.75	.30
❑ 65	Andre Tippett	.40	.15
❑ 66	Morten Andersen	.40	.15
❑ 67	Vaughn Dunbar	.40	.15
❑ 68	Eric Martin	.40	.15
❑ 69	Dave Brown RC	1.50	.60
❑ 70	Rodney Hampton	.75	.30
❑ 71	Phil Simms	.75	.30
❑ 72	Lawrence Taylor	1.50	.60
❑ 73	Ronnie Lott	.75	.30
❑ 74	Johnny Mitchell	.40	.15
❑ 75	Rob Moore	.75	.30
❑ 76	Browning Nagle	.40	.15
❑ 77	Fred Barnett	.75	.30
❑ 78	Randall Cunningham	1.50	.60
❑ 79	Herschel Walker	.75	.30
❑ 80	Gary Clark	.75	.30
❑ 81	Ken Harvey	.40	.15
❑ 82	Garrison Hearst RC	3.00	1.25
❑ 83	Ricky Proehl	.40	.15
❑ 84	Barry Foster	.75	.30
❑ 85	Ernie Mills	.40	.15
❑ 86	Neil O'Donnell	1.50	.60
❑ 87	Stan Humphries	.75	.30
❑ 88	Leslie O'Neal	.75	.30
❑ 89	Junior Seau	1.50	.60
❑ 90	Amp Lee	.40	.15
❑ 91	Jerry Rice	5.00	2.00
❑ 92	Ricky Watters	1.50	.60
❑ 93	Steve Young	4.00	1.50
❑ 94	Cortez Kennedy	.75	.30
❑ 95	Rick Mirer RC	1.50	.60
❑ 96	Eugene Robinson	.40	.15
❑ 97	Chris Warren	.75	.30
❑ 98	John L. Williams	.40	.15
❑ 99	Reggie Cobb	.40	.15
❑ 100	Lawrence Dawsey	.40	.15
❑ 101	Santana Dotson	.75	.30
❑ 102	Courtney Hawkins	.40	.15
❑ 103	Reggie Brooks RC	.75	.30
❑ 104	Ricky Ervins	.40	.15
❑ 105	Desmond Howard	.75	.30
❑ 106	Art Monk	.75	.30
❑ 107	Mark Rypien	.40	.15
❑ 108	Ricky Sanders	.40	.15
❑ NNO	Checklist Card	.40	.15
❑ P22	Emmitt Smith Promo	10.00	4.00
❑ P61	Drew Bledsoe Promo	4.00	1.50

1994 Pacific Prisms

❑	COMPLETE SET (128)	50.00	20.00
❑ 1	Troy Aikman UER	4.00	1.50
❑ 2	Marcus Allen	1.25	.50
❑ 3	Morten Andersen	.40	.15
❑ 4	Fred Barnett	.75	.30
❑ 5	Mario Bates RC	1.25	.50
❑ 6	Edgar Bennett	1.25	.50
❑ 7	Rod Bernstine	.40	.15
❑ 8	Jerome Bettis	2.00	.75
❑ 9	Steve Beuerlein	.75	.30
❑ 10	Brian Blades	.75	.30
❑ 11	Drew Bledsoe	3.00	1.25
❑ 12	Vincent Brisby	.75	.30
❑ 13	Reggie Brooks	.75	.30
❑ 14	Derek Brown RBK	.40	.15
❑ 15	Gary Brown	.40	.15
❑ 16	Tim Brown	1.25	.50
❑ 17	Marion Butts	.40	.15
❑ 18	Keith Byars	.40	.15
❑ 19	Cody Carlson	.40	.15
❑ 20	Anthony Carter	.75	.30
❑ 21	Tom Carter	.40	.15
❑ 22	Gary Clark	.75	.30
❑ 23	Ben Coates	.75	.30
❑ 24	Reggie Cobb	.40	.15
❑ 25	Curtis Conway	.75	.30
❑ 26	John Copeland	.40	.15
❑ 27	Randall Cunningham	1.25	.50
❑ 28	Willie Davis	.75	.30
❑ 29	Sean Dawkins RC	1.25	.50
❑ 30	Lawrence Dawsey	.40	.15
❑ 31	Richard Dent	.75	.30
❑ 32	Trent Dilfer RC	3.00	1.25
❑ 33	Troy Drayton	.40	.15
❑ 34	Vaughn Dunbar	.40	.15
❑ 35	Henry Ellard	.75	.30
❑ 36	John Elway	8.00	3.00
❑ 37	Craig Erickson	.40	.15
❑ 38	Boomer Esiason	.75	.30
❑ 39	Marshall Faulk RC	10.00	5.00
❑ 40	Brett Favre	8.00	3.00
❑ 41	William Floyd RC	1.25	.50
❑ 42	Glenn Foley RC	1.25	.50
❑ 43	Barry Foster	.40	.15
❑ 44	Irving Fryar	.75	.30
❑ 45	Jeff George	1.25	.50
❑ 46	Scottie Graham RC	.75	.30
❑ 47	Rodney Hampton	.75	.30
❑ 48	Jim Harbaugh	1.25	.50
❑ 49	Alvin Harper	.75	.30
❑ 50	Courtney Hawkins	.40	.15
❑ 51	Garrison Hearst	1.25	.50
❑ 52	Vaughn Hebron	.40	.15

Card		
❑ 53 Greg Hill RC	1.25	.50
❑ 54 Jeff Hostetler	.75	.30
❑ 55 Michael Irvin	1.25	.50
❑ 56 Qadry Ismail	.75	.30
❑ 57 Rocket Ismail	.75	.30
❑ 58 Anthony Johnson	.75	.30
❑ 59 Charles Johnson RC	1.25	.50
❑ 60 Johnny Johnson	.40	.15
❑ 61 Brent Jones	.75	.30
❑ 62 Kyle Clifton	.40	.15
❑ 63 Jim Kelly	.75	.30
❑ 64 Cortez Kennedy	.75	.30
❑ 65 Terry Kirby	1.25	.50
❑ 66 David Klingler	.40	.15
❑ 67 Erik Kramer	.75	.30
❑ 68 Reggie Langhorne	.40	.15
❑ 69 Chuck Levy RC	.40	.15
❑ 70 Dan Marino	8.00	3.00
❑ 71 O.J.McDuffie	1.25	.50
❑ 72 Natrone Means	1.25	.50
❑ 73 Eric Metcalf	.75	.30
❑ 74 Glyn Milburn	.75	.30
❑ 75 Anthony Miller	.75	.30
❑ 76 Rick Mirer	1.25	.50
❑ 77 Johnny Mitchell	.40	.15
❑ 78 Scott Mitchell	.75	.30
❑ 79 Joe Montana	8.00	3.00
❑ 80 Warren Moon	.75	.30
❑ 81 Derrick Moore	.40	.15
❑ 82 Herman Moore	1.25	.50
❑ 83 Rob Moore	.75	.30
❑ 84 Ronald Moore	.40	.15
❑ 85 Johnnie Morton RC	4.00	1.50
❑ 86 Neil O'Donnell	.75	.30
❑ 87 David Palmer RC	1.25	.50
❑ 88 Erric Pegram	.40	.15
❑ 89 Carl Pickens	.75	.30
❑ 90 Anthony Pleasant	.40	.15
❑ 91 Roosevelt Potts	.40	.15
❑ 92 Mike Pritchard	.40	.15
❑ 93 Andre Reed	.75	.30
❑ 94 Errict Rhett RC	1.25	.50
❑ 95 Jerry Rice	4.00	1.50
❑ 96 Andre Rison	.75	.30
❑ 97 Greg Robinson	.40	.15
❑ 98 T.J.Rubley RC	.40	.15
❑ 99 Leonard Russell	.40	.15
❑ 100 Barry Sanders	6.00	2.50
❑ 101 Deion Sanders	2.50	1.00
❑ 102 Ricky Sanders	.40	.15
❑ 103 Junior Seau	1.25	.50
❑ 104 Shannon Sharpe	.75	.30
❑ 105 Sterling Sharpe	.75	.30
❑ 106 Heath Shuler RC	1.25	.50
❑ 107 Phil Simms	.75	.30
❑ 108 Webster Slaughter	.40	.15
❑ 109 Bruce Smith	1.25	.50
❑ 110 Emmitt Smith	8.00	3.00
❑ 111 Irv Smith	.40	.15
❑ 112 Robert Smith	1.25	.50
❑ 113 Vinny Testaverde	.75	.30
❑ 114 Derrick Thomas	1.25	.50
❑ 115 Thurman Thomas	.75	.30
❑ 116 Leroy Thompson	.40	.15
❑ 117 Lewis Tillman	.40	.15
❑ 118 Michael Timpson	.40	.15
❑ 119 Herschel Walker	.75	.30
❑ 120 Chris Warren	.75	.30
❑ 121 Ricky Watters	.75	.30
❑ 122 Lorenzo White	.40	.15
❑ 123 Reggie White	1.25	.50
❑ 124 Dan Wilkinson RC	.75	.30
❑ 125 Kevin Williams WR	.75	.30
❑ 126 Steve Young	3.00	1.25
❑ CL1 Checklist 1	.30	.10
❑ CL2 Checklist 2	.30	.10
❑ S1 Sterling Sharpe Promo	1.00	.40

1995 Pacific Prisms

Card		
❑ COMPLETE SET (216)	80.00	30.00
❑ COMP.SERIES 1 (108)	40.00	15.00
❑ COMP.SERIES 2 (108)	40.00	15.00
❑ 1 Chuck Levy	.25	.08
❑ 2 Ronald Moore	.25	.08
❑ 3 Jay Schroeder	.25	.08
❑ 4 Bert Emanuel	1.00	.40
❑ 5 Terance Mathis	.50	.20
❑ 6 Andre Rison	.50	.20
❑ 7 Bucky Brooks	.25	.08
❑ 8 Jeff Burris	.25	.08
❑ 9 Jim Kelly	1.00	.40
❑ 10 Lewis Tillman	.25	.08
❑ 11 Steve Walsh	.25	.08
❑ 12 Chris Zorich	.25	.08
❑ 13 Jeff Blake RC	2.50	1.00
❑ 14 Steve Broussard	.25	.08
❑ 15 Jeff Cothran	.25	.08
❑ 16 Earnest Byner	.25	.08
❑ 17 Leroy Hoard	.25	.08
❑ 18 Vinny Testaverde	.50	.20
❑ 19 Troy Aikman	2.50	1.00
❑ 20 Alvin Harper	.25	.08
❑ 21 Leon Lett	.25	.08
❑ 22 Jay Novacek	.50	.20
❑ 23 John Elway	5.00	2.00
❑ 24 Karl Mecklenburg	.25	.08
❑ 25 Leonard Russell	.25	.08
❑ 26 Mel Gray	.25	.08
❑ 27 Dave Krieg	.25	.08
❑ 28 Barry Sanders	4.00	1.50
❑ 29 Chris Spielman	.50	.20
❑ 30 Robert Brooks	1.00	.40
❑ 31 LeShon Johnson	.50	.20
❑ 32 Sterling Sharpe	.50	.20
❑ 33 Ernest Givins	.25	.08
❑ 34 Billy Joe Tolliver	.25	.08
❑ 35 Lorenzo White	.25	.08
❑ 36 Charles Arbuckle	.25	.08
❑ 37 Sean Dawkins	.50	.20
❑ 38 Marshall Faulk	3.00	1.25
❑ 39 Marcus Allen	1.00	.40
❑ 40 Donnell Bennett	.50	.20
❑ 41 Matt Blundin RC	.25	.08
❑ 42 Greg Hill	.50	.20
❑ 43 Tim Brown	1.00	.40
❑ 44 Billy Joe Hobert	.50	.20
❑ 45 Rocket Ismail	.50	.20
❑ 46 James Jett	.50	.20
❑ 47 Tim Bowens	.25	.08
❑ 48 Irving Fryar	.50	.20
❑ 49 O.J. McDuffie	1.00	.40
❑ 50 Irving Spikes	.50	.20
❑ 51 Terry Allen	.50	.20
❑ 52 Cris Carter	1.00	.40
❑ 53 Amp Lee	.25	.08
❑ 54 Drew Bledsoe	1.50	.60
❑ 55 Willie McGinest	.50	.20
❑ 56 Leroy Thompson	.25	.08
❑ 57 Michael Timpson	.25	.08
❑ 58 Michael Haynes	.50	.20
❑ 59 Derrell Mitchell RC	.25	.08
❑ 60 Dave Brown	.50	.20
❑ 61 Thomas Lewis	.50	.20
❑ 62 Dave Meggett	.25	.08
❑ 63 Boomer Esiason	.50	.20
❑ 64 Aaron Glenn	.25	.08
❑ 65 Ronnie Lott	.50	.20
❑ 66 Randall Cunningham	1.00	.40
❑ 67 Charlie Garner	1.00	.40
❑ 68 Herschel Walker	.50	.20
❑ 69 Barry Foster	.50	.20
❑ 70 Charles Johnson	.50	.20
❑ 71 Jim Miller RC	3.00	1.25
❑ 72 Rod Woodson	.50	.20
❑ 73 Andre Coleman	.25	.08
❑ 74 Natrone Means	.50	.20
❑ 75 Shannon Mitchell RC	.25	.08
❑ 76 Junior Seau	1.00	.40
❑ 77 Elvis Grbac	1.00	.40
❑ 78 Deion Sanders	1.50	.60
❑ 79 Adam Walker RC	.25	.08
❑ 80 Ricky Watters	.50	.20
❑ 81 Michael Bates	.25	.08
❑ 82 Brian Blades	.50	.20
❑ 83 Eugene Robinson	.25	.08
❑ 84 Chris Warren	.50	.20
❑ 85 Jerome Bettis	1.00	.40
❑ 86 Troy Drayton	.25	.08
❑ 87 Chris Miller	.25	.08
❑ 88 Trent Dilfer	1.00	.40
❑ 89 Hardy Nickerson	.25	.08
❑ 90 Errict Rhett	.50	.20
❑ 91 Henry Ellard	.50	.20
❑ 92 Gus Frerotte	.50	.20
❑ 93 Ricky Ervins	.25	.08
❑ 94 Dave Barr RC	.25	.08
❑ 95 Kyle Brady RC	1.00	.40
❑ 96 Mark Bruener RC	.50	.20
❑ 97 Ki-Jana Carter RC	1.00	.40
❑ 98 Kerry Collins RC	5.00	2.00
❑ 99 Joey Galloway RC	5.00	2.00
❑ 100 Napoleon Kaufman RC	4.00	1.50
❑ 101 Steve McNair RC	10.00	4.00
❑ 102 Craig Newsome RC	.25	.08
❑ 103 Rashaan Salaam RC	.50	.20
❑ 104 Kordell Stewart RC	5.00	2.00
❑ 105 J.J. Stokes RC	1.00	.40
❑ 106 Rodney Thomas RC	.50	.20
❑ 107 Michael Westbrook RC	1.00	.40
❑ 108 Tyrone Wheatley RC	4.00	1.50
❑ 109 Larry Centers	.50	.20
❑ 110 Garrison Hearst	1.00	.40
❑ 111 Jamir Miller	.25	.08
❑ 112 Jeff George	.50	.20
❑ 113 Craig Heyward	.50	.20
❑ 114 Cornelius Bennett	.50	.20
❑ 115 Andre Reed	.50	.20
❑ 116 Randy Baldwin	.25	.08
❑ 117 Tommy Barnhardt	.25	.08
❑ 118 Sam Mills	.50	.20
❑ 119 Brian O'Neal	.25	.08
❑ 120 Frank Reich	.25	.08
❑ 121 Tony Smith RB	.25	.08
❑ 122 Lawyer Tillman	.25	.08
❑ 123 Jack Trudeau	.25	.08
❑ 124 Vernon Turner	.25	.08
❑ 125 Curtis Conway	1.00	.40
❑ 126 Erik Kramer	.25	.08
❑ 127 Nate Lewis	.25	.08
❑ 128 Carl Pickens	.50	.20
❑ 129 Darnay Scott	.50	.20
❑ 130 Dan Wilkinson	.50	.20
❑ 131 Derrick Alexander WR	1.00	.40
❑ 132 Carl Banks	.25	.08
❑ 133 Michael Irvin	1.00	.40
❑ 134 Emmitt Smith	4.00	1.50
❑ 135 Kevin Williams WR	.50	.20
❑ 136 Glyn Milburn	.25	.08
❑ 137 Anthony Miller	.50	.20
❑ 138 Shannon Sharpe	.50	.20
❑ 139 Scott Mitchell	.50	.20
❑ 140 Herman Moore	1.00	.40
❑ 141 Edgar Bennett	.50	.20
❑ 142 Brett Favre	5.00	2.00
❑ 143 Reggie White	1.00	.40
❑ 144 Gary Brown	.25	.08
❑ 145 Haywood Jeffires	.25	.08
❑ 146 Webster Slaughter	.25	.08
❑ 147 Craig Erickson	.25	.08
❑ 148 Paul Justin	.25	.08
❑ 149 Lamont Warren	.25	.08
❑ 150 Steve Beuerlein	.50	.20
❑ 151 Derek Brown TE	.25	.08
❑ 152 Mark Brunell	1.50	.60
❑ 153 Reggie Cobb	.25	.08
❑ 154 Desmond Howard	.50	.20
❑ 155 Kelvin Pritchett	.25	.08
❑ 156 James O. Stewart RC	4.00	1.50
❑ 157 Cedric Tillman	.25	.08
❑ 158 Kimble Anders	.50	.20
❑ 159 Lake Dawson	.50	.20
❑ 160 Keith Byars	.25	.08
❑ 161 Dan Marino	5.00	2.00
❑ 162 Bernie Parmalee	.50	.20

❑ 163 Qadry Ismail .50 .20
❑ 164 Warren Moon .50 .20
❑ 165 Jake Reed .50 .20
❑ 166 Marion Butts .25 .08
❑ 167 Ben Coates .50 .20
❑ 168 Mario Bates .50 .20
❑ 169 Quinn Early .50 .20
❑ 170 Jim Everett .25 .08
❑ 171 Rodney Hampton .50 .20
❑ 172 Mike Horan .25 .08
❑ 173 Mike Sherrard .25 .08
❑ 174 Johnny Johnson .25 .08
❑ 175 Adrian Murrell .50 .20
❑ 176 Andrew Glover RC .25 .08
❑ 177 Jeff Hostetler .50 .20
❑ 178 Harvey Williams .25 .08
❑ 179 Fred Barnett .50 .20
❑ 180 Vaughn Hebron .25 .08
❑ 181 Jeff Sydner .25 .08
❑ 182 Kevin Greene .50 .20
❑ 183 Byron Bam Morris .25 .08
❑ 184 Neil O'Donnell .50 .20
❑ 185 Stan Humphries .50 .20
❑ 186 Tony Martin .50 .20
❑ 187 Mark Seay .50 .20
❑ 188 William Floyd .50 .20
❑ 189 Rickey Jackson .25 .08
❑ 190 Jerry Rice 2.50 1.00
❑ 191 Steve Young 2.00 .75
❑ 192 Cortez Kennedy .50 .20
❑ 193 Rick Mirer .50 .20
❑ 194 Jessie Hester .25 .08
❑ 195 Curtis Martin UER RC 10.00 4.00
❑ 196 Horace Copeland .25 .08
❑ 197 Charles Wilson .25 .08
❑ 198 Reggie Brooks .50 .20
❑ 199 Brian Mitchell .25 .08
❑ 200 Heath Shuler .50 .20
❑ 201 Justin Armour RC .25 .08
❑ 202 Jay Barker RC .25 .08
❑ 203 Zack Crockett RC .50 .20
❑ 204 Christian Fauria RC .50 .20
❑ 205 Antonio Freeman RC 4.00 1.50
❑ 206 Chad May RC .25 .08
❑ 207 Frank Sanders RC 1.00 .40
❑ 208 Steve Stenstrom RC .25 .08
❑ 209 Lorenzo Styles RC .25 .08
❑ 210 Sherman Williams RC .25 .08
❑ 211 Ray Zellars RC .50 .20
❑ 212 Eric Zeier RC 1.00 .40
❑ 213 Joey Galloway 2.00 .75
❑ 214 Napoleon Kaufman 1.50 .60
❑ 215 Rashaan Salaam .50 .20
❑ 216 J.J. Stokes 1.00 .40
❑ NNO Steve Beuerlein EE 1.00 .40
❑ NNO Barry Foster EE 1.00 .40
❑ P1 Natrone Means Promo 1.00 .40
❑ P2 Natrone Means Promo 1.00 .40

1999 Pacific Prisms

❑ COMPLETE SET (150) 80.00 30.00
❑ 1 David Boston RC 2.00 .75
❑ 2 Rob Moore .60 .25
❑ 3 Adrian Murrell .60 .25
❑ 4 Jake Plummer .60 .25
❑ 5 Frank Sanders .60 .25
❑ 6 Jamal Anderson 1.00 .40
❑ 7 Chris Chandler .60 .25
❑ 8 Tim Dwight .60 .25
❑ 9 Terance Mathis .60 .25
❑ 10 Peter Boulware .40 .15
❑ 11 Priest Holmes 1.50 .60
❑ 12 Pat Johnson .40 .15
❑ 13 Jermaine Lewis .60 .25
❑ 14 Doug Flutie 1.00 .40
❑ 15 Eric Moulds 1.00 .40
❑ 16 Peerless Price RC 2.00 .75
❑ 17 Antowain Smith 1.00 .40
❑ 18 Bruce Smith .60 .25
❑ 19 Steve Beuerlein .40 .15
❑ 20 Tim Biakabutuka .60 .25
❑ 21 Muhsin Muhammad .60 .25
❑ 22 Wesley Walls .60 .25
❑ 23 Edgar Bennett .40 .15
❑ 24 Curtis Conway .60 .25
❑ 25 Bobby Engram .60 .25
❑ 26 Curtis Enis .40 .15
❑ 27 Cade McNown RC 1.00 .40
❑ 28 Jeff Blake .60 .25
❑ 29 Scott Covington RC 2.00 .75
❑ 30 Corey Dillon 1.00 .40
❑ 31 Carl Pickens .60 .25
❑ 32 Akili Smith RC 1.00 .40
❑ 33 Craig Yeast RC 1.00 .40
❑ 34 Tim Couch RC 2.00 .75
❑ 35 Ty Detmer .60 .25
❑ 36 Kevin Johnson RC 2.00 .75
❑ 37 Terry Kirby .40 .15
❑ 38 Leslie Shepherd .40 .15
❑ 39 Troy Aikman 2.00 .75
❑ 40 Michael Irvin .60 .25
❑ 41 Deion Sanders 1.00 .40
❑ 42 Emmitt Smith 2.00 .75
❑ 43 Bubby Brister .40 .15
❑ 44 Terrell Davis 1.00 .40
❑ 45 Brian Griese 1.00 .40
❑ 46 Ed McCaffrey .60 .25
❑ 47 Shannon Sharpe .60 .25
❑ 48 Rod Smith .60 .25
❑ 49 Charlie Batch 1.00 .40
❑ 50 Germane Crowell .40 .15
❑ 51 Sedrick Irvin RC 1.50 .60
❑ 52 Herman Moore .60 .25
❑ 53 Johnnie Morton .60 .25
❑ 54 Barry Sanders 3.00 1.25
❑ 55 Mark Chmura .40 .15
❑ 56 Brett Favre 3.00 1.25
❑ 57 Antonio Freeman 1.00 .40
❑ 58 Dorsey Levens 1.00 .40
❑ 59 Ken Dilger .40 .15
❑ 60 Marvin Harrison 1.00 .40
❑ 61 Edgerrin James RC 6.00 2.50
❑ 62 Peyton Manning 3.00 1.25
❑ 63 Jerome Pathon .40 .15
❑ 64 Mark Brunell 1.00 .40
❑ 65 Keenan McCardell .60 .25
❑ 66 Jimmy Smith .60 .25
❑ 67 Fred Taylor 1.00 .40
❑ 68 Derrick Alexander .60 .25
❑ 69 Mike Cloud RC 1.00 .40
❑ 70 Tony Gonzalez 1.00 .40
❑ 71 Elvis Grbac .60 .25
❑ 72 Andre Rison .60 .25
❑ 73 Cecil Collins RC 1.50 .60
❑ 74 Oronde Gadsden .60 .25
❑ 75 James Johnson RC 1.00 .40
❑ 76 Dan Marino 3.00 1.25
❑ 77 O.J. McDuffie .60 .25
❑ 78 Lamar Thomas .40 .15
❑ 79 Cris Carter 1.00 .40
❑ 80 Daunte Culpepper RC 6.00 2.50
❑ 81 Randall Cunningham 1.00 .40
❑ 82 Matthew Hatchette .40 .15
❑ 83 Randy Moss 2.50 1.00
❑ 84 John Randle .60 .25
❑ 85 Robert Smith 1.00 .40
❑ 86 Drew Bledsoe 1.25 .50
❑ 87 Ben Coates .60 .25
❑ 88 Kevin Faulk RC 2.00 .75
❑ 89 Terry Glenn 1.00 .40
❑ 90 Shawn Jefferson .40 .15
❑ 91 Cam Cleeland .40 .15
❑ 92 Billy Joe Hobert .40 .15
❑ 93 Keith Poole .40 .15
❑ 94 Ricky Williams RC 3.00 1.25
❑ 95 Gary Brown .40 .15
❑ 96 Kent Graham .40 .15
❑ 97 Ike Hilliard .40 .15
❑ 98 Amani Toomer .40 .15
❑ 99 Wayne Chrebet .60 .25
❑ 100 Keyshawn Johnson 1.00 .40
❑ 101 Curtis Martin 1.00 .40
❑ 102 Vinny Testaverde .60 .25
❑ 103 Tim Brown 1.00 .40
❑ 104 James Jett .60 .25
❑ 105 Napoleon Kaufman 1.00 .40
❑ 106 Charles Woodson 1.00 .40
❑ 107 Koy Detmer .40 .15
❑ 108 Donovan McNabb RC 8.00 3.00
❑ 109 Duce Staley 1.00 .40
❑ 110 Kevin Turner .40 .15
❑ 111 Jerome Bettis 1.00 .40
❑ 112 Mark Bruener .40 .15
❑ 113 Troy Edwards RC 1.00 .40
❑ 114 Levon Kirkland .40 .15
❑ 115 Kordell Stewart .60 .25
❑ 116 Amos Zereoue RC 2.00 .75
❑ 117 Isaac Bruce 1.00 .40
❑ 118 Marshall Faulk 1.25 .50
❑ 119 Joe Germaine RC 1.00 .40
❑ 120 Trent Green 1.00 .40
❑ 121 Torry Holt RC 5.00 2.00
❑ 122 Ryan Leaf 1.00 .40
❑ 123 Natrone Means .60 .25
❑ 124 Mikhael Ricks .40 .15
❑ 125 Junior Seau 1.00 .40
❑ 126 Garrison Hearst .60 .25
❑ 127 Terrell Owens 1.00 .40
❑ 128 Jerry Rice 2.00 .75
❑ 129 J.J. Stokes .60 .25
❑ 130 Steve Young 1.25 .50
❑ 131 Chad Brown .40 .15
❑ 132 Joey Galloway .60 .25
❑ 133 Brock Huard RC 2.00 .75
❑ 134 Jon Kitna 1.00 .40
❑ 135 Ricky Watters .60 .25
❑ 136 Mike Alstott 1.00 .40
❑ 137 Reidel Anthony .60 .25
❑ 138 Trent Dilfer .60 .25
❑ 139 Warrick Dunn 1.00 .40
❑ 140 Jacquez Green .40 .15
❑ 141 Shaun King RC 1.00 .40
❑ 142 Darnell McDonald RC 1.00 .40
❑ 143 Eddie George 1.00 .40
❑ 144 Steve McNair 1.00 .40
❑ 145 Yancey Thigpen .40 .15
❑ 146 Frank Wycheck .40 .15
❑ 147 Champ Bailey RC 2.50 1.00
❑ 148 Albert Connell .40 .15
❑ 149 Skip Hicks .40 .15
❑ 150 Michael Westbrook .40 .15

2001 Pacific Prism Atomic

❑ COMP.SET w/o SP's (148) 60.00 30.00
❑ 1 David Boston 1.50 .60
❑ 2 Thomas Jones 1.00 .40
❑ 3 Rob Moore 1.00 .40
❑ 4 Michael Pittman .60 .25
❑ 5 Jake Plummer 1.00 .40
❑ 6 Jamal Anderson 1.50 .60
❑ 7 Chris Chandler 1.00 .40
❑ 8 Shawn Jefferson .60 .25
❑ 9 Terance Mathis .60 .25
❑ 10 Elvis Grbac 1.00 .40

❑ 11 Qadry Ismail 1.00 .40
❑ 12 Jamal Lewis 2.50 1.00
❑ 13 Ray Lewis 1.50 .60
❑ 14 Shannon Sharpe 1.00 .40
❑ 15 Shawn Bryson .60 .25
❑ 16 Rob Johnson 1.00 .40
❑ 17 Sammy Morris .60 .25
❑ 18 Eric Moulds 1.00 .40
❑ 19 Peerless Price 1.00 .40
❑ 20 Tim Biakabutuka 1.00 .40
❑ 21 Richard Huntley .60 .25
❑ 22 Patrick Jeffers 1.00 .40
❑ 23 Jeff Lewis .60 .25
❑ 24 Muhsin Muhammad 1.00 .40
❑ 25 James Allen 1.00 .40
❑ 26 Cade McNown .60 .25
❑ 27 Marcus Robinson 1.50 .60
❑ 28 Brian Urlacher 2.50 1.00
❑ 29 Corey Dillon 1.50 .60
❑ 30 Jon Kitna 1.00 .40
❑ 31 Akili Smith .60 .25
❑ 32 Peter Warrick 1.50 .60
❑ 33 Tim Couch 1.00 .40
❑ 34 Kevin Johnson 1.00 .40
❑ 35 Dennis Northcutt 1.00 .40
❑ 36 Travis Prentice .60 .25
❑ 37 Tony Banks 1.00 .40
❑ 38 Joey Galloway 1.00 .40
❑ 39 Rocket Ismail 1.00 .40
❑ 40 Emmitt Smith 3.00 1.25
❑ 41 Anthony Wright .60 .25
❑ 42 Mike Anderson 1.50 .60
❑ 43 Terrell Davis 1.50 .60
❑ 44 Olandis Gary 1.00 .40
❑ 45 Brian Griese 1.50 .60
❑ 46 Ed McCaffrey 1.50 .60
❑ 47 Rod Smith 1.00 .40
❑ 48 Charlie Batch 1.50 .60
❑ 49 Germane Crowell .60 .25
❑ 50 Herman Moore 1.00 .40
❑ 51 Johnnie Morton 1.00 .40
❑ 52 James Stewart 1.00 .40
❑ 53 Brett Favre 5.00 2.00
❑ 54 Antonio Freeman 1.50 .60
❑ 55 Ahman Green 1.50 .60
❑ 56 Dorsey Levens 1.00 .40
❑ 57 Bill Schroeder 1.00 .40
❑ 58 Marvin Harrison 1.50 .60
❑ 59 Edgerrin James 2.00 .75
❑ 60 Peyton Manning 4.00 1.50
❑ 61 Jerome Pathon 1.00 .40
❑ 62 Terrence Wilkins .60 .25
❑ 63 Mark Brunell 1.50 .60
❑ 64 Keenan McCardell .60 .25
❑ 65 Jimmy Smith 1.00 .40
❑ 66 Fred Taylor 1.50 .60
❑ 67 Derrick Alexander .60 .25
❑ 68 Tony Gonzalez 1.00 .40
❑ 69 Trent Green 1.50 .60
❑ 70 Priest Holmes 2.00 .75
❑ 71 Sylvester Morris .60 .25
❑ 72 Jay Fiedler 1.50 .60
❑ 73 Oronde Gadsden 1.00 .40
❑ 74 O.J. McDuffie .60 .25
❑ 75 Lamar Smith 1.00 .40
❑ 76 Zach Thomas 1.50 .60
❑ 77 Daunte Culpepper 1.50 .60
❑ 78 Cris Carter 1.50 .60
❑ 79 Randy Moss 3.00 1.25
❑ 80 Chris Walsh RC .60 .25
❑ 81 Moe Williams 1.00 .40
❑ 82 Drew Bledsoe 2.00 .75
❑ 83 Kevin Faulk 1.00 .40
❑ 84 Terry Glenn 1.00 .40
❑ 85 Charles Johnson .60 .25
❑ 86 J.R. Redmond .60 .25
❑ 87 Jeff Blake 1.00 .40
❑ 88 Aaron Brooks 1.50 .60
❑ 89 Albert Connell .60 .25
❑ 90 Joe Horn 1.00 .40
❑ 91 Ricky Williams 1.50 .60
❑ 92 Tiki Barber 1.50 .60
❑ 93 Kerry Collins 1.00 .40
❑ 94 Ron Dayne 1.50 .60
❑ 95 Ike Hilliard 1.00 .40
❑ 96 Amani Toomer 1.00 .40
❑ 97 Richie Anderson .60 .25
❑ 98 Wayne Chrebet 1.00 .40
❑ 99 Curtis Martin 1.50 .60
❑ 100 Chad Pennington 2.50 1.00
❑ 101 Vinny Testaverde 1.00 .40
❑ 102 Tim Brown 1.50 .60
❑ 103 Rich Gannon 1.50 .60
❑ 104 Charlie Garner 1.00 .40
❑ 105 Jerry Rice 3.00 1.25
❑ 106 Tyrone Wheatley 1.00 .40
❑ 107 Charles Woodson 1.00 .40
❑ 108 Darnell Autry .60 .25
❑ 109 Donovan McNabb 2.00 .75
❑ 110 Duce Staley 1.50 .60
❑ 111 James Thrash 1.00 .40
❑ 112 Jerome Bettis 1.50 .60
❑ 113 Plaxico Burress 1.50 .60
❑ 114 Bobby Shaw .60 .25
❑ 115 Kordell Stewart 1.00 .40
❑ 116 Hines Ward 1.50 .60
❑ 117 Isaac Bruce 1.50 .60
❑ 118 Marshall Faulk 2.00 .75
❑ 119 Az-Zahir Hakim 1.00 .40
❑ 120 Torry Holt 1.50 .60
❑ 121 Kurt Warner 3.00 1.25
❑ 122 Curtis Conway 1.00 .40
❑ 123 Tim Dwight 1.50 .60
❑ 124 Doug Flutie 1.50 .60
❑ 125 Dave Dickenson RC 6.00 2.50
❑ 126 Jeff Garcia 1.50 .60
❑ 127 Terrell Owens 1.50 .60
❑ 128 J.J. Stokes 1.00 .40
❑ 129 Tai Streets .60 .25
❑ 130 Shaun Alexander 2.00 .75
❑ 131 Trent Dilfer 1.00 .40
❑ 132 Matt Hasselbeck 1.00 .40
❑ 133 Darrell Jackson 1.50 .60
❑ 134 Ricky Watters 1.00 .40
❑ 135 Mike Alstott 1.50 .60
❑ 136 Warrick Dunn 1.50 .60
❑ 137 Brad Johnson 1.50 .60
❑ 138 Keyshawn Johnson 1.50 .60
❑ 139 Warren Sapp 1.00 .40
❑ 140 Kevin Dyson 1.00 .40
❑ 141 Eddie George 1.50 .60
❑ 142 Jevon Kearse 1.00 .40
❑ 143 Derrick Mason 1.00 .40
❑ 144 Steve McNair 1.50 .60
❑ 145 Champ Bailey 1.00 .40
❑ 146 Stephen Davis 1.50 .60
❑ 147 Jeff George 1.00 .40
❑ 148 Michael Westbrook 1.00 .40
❑ 149 Quentin McCord RC 6.00 2.50
❑ 150 Vinny Sutherland RC 6.00 2.50
❑ 151 Michael Vick RC 50.00 20.00
❑ 152 Chris Barnes RC 6.00 2.50
❑ 153 Reggie Germany RC 6.00 2.50
❑ 154 Travis Henry RC 15.00 6.00
❑ 155 Dee Brown RC 10.00 4.00
❑ 156 Dan Morgan RC 10.00 4.00
❑ 157 Steve Smith RC 25.00 12.50
❑ 158 Chris Weinke RC 10.00 4.00
❑ 159 David Terrell RC 10.00 4.00
❑ 160 Anthony Thomas RC 10.00 4.00
❑ 161 Chad Johnson RC 25.00 10.00
❑ 162 Rudi Johnson RC 20.00 7.50
❑ 163 James Jackson RC 10.00 4.00
❑ 164 Andre King RC 6.00 2.50
❑ 165 Quincy Morgan RC 10.00 4.00
❑ 166 Quincy Carter RC 10.00 4.00
❑ 167 Kevin Kasper RC 10.00 4.00
❑ 168 Scotty Anderson RC 6.00 2.50
❑ 169 Mike McMahon RC 10.00 4.00
❑ 170 Robert Ferguson RC 10.00 4.00
❑ 171 Reggie Wayne RC 20.00 7.50
❑ 172 Derrick Blaylock RC 10.00 4.00
❑ 173 Snoop Minnis RC 6.00 2.50
❑ 174 Chris Chambers RC 15.00 6.00
❑ 175 Josh Heupel RC 10.00 4.00
❑ 176 Travis Minor RC 6.00 2.50
❑ 177 Michael Bennett RC 10.00 4.00
❑ 178 Deuce McAllister RC 20.00 7.50
❑ 179 Jonathan Carter RC 6.00 2.50
❑ 180 Jesse Palmer RC 10.00 4.00
❑ 181 LaMont Jordan RC 20.00 7.50
❑ 182 Santana Moss RC 15.00 6.00
❑ 183 Ken-Yon Rambo RC 6.00 2.50
❑ 184 Marques Tuiasosopo RC 10.00 4.00
❑ 185 Correll Buckhalter RC 12.00 5.00
❑ 186 Freddie Mitchell RC 10.00 4.00
❑ 187 Milton Wynn RC 6.00 2.50
❑ 188 Drew Brees RC 30.00 12.50
❑ 189 LaDainian Tomlinson RC 50.00 25.00
❑ 190 Kevan Barlow RC 10.00 4.00
❑ 191 Cedrick Wilson RC 10.00 4.00
❑ 192 Alex Bannister RC 6.00 2.50
❑ 193 Josh Booty RC 10.00 4.00
❑ 194 Koren Robinson RC 10.00 4.00
❑ 195 Eddie Berlin RC 6.00 2.50
❑ 196 Rod Gardner RC 10.00 4.00
❑ 197 Damerien McCants RC 6.00 2.50
❑ 198 Sage Rosenfels RC 10.00 4.00
❑ NNO Eddie George SAMPLE 1.25 .50
❑ NNO Jamal Lewis SAMPLE 2.00 .75
❑ NNO Randy Moss SAMPLE 2.50 1.00
❑ NNO Emmitt Smith SAMPLE 2.50 1.00

2000 Pacific Prism Prospects

❑ COMP.SET w/o SP's (100) 25.00 10.00
❑ 1 David Boston .75 .30
❑ 2 Jake Plummer .50 .20
❑ 3 Jamal Anderson .75 .30
❑ 4 Chris Chandler .50 .20
❑ 5 Tim Dwight .75 .30
❑ 6 Terance Mathis .50 .20
❑ 7 Tony Banks .50 .20
❑ 8 Priest Holmes 1.00 .40
❑ 9 Doug Flutie .75 .30
❑ 10 Rob Johnson .50 .20
❑ 11 Eric Moulds .75 .30
❑ 12 Antowain Smith .50 .20
❑ 13 Steve Beuerlein .50 .20
❑ 14 Tim Biakabutuka .50 .20
❑ 15 Muhsin Muhammad .50 .20
❑ 16 Bobby Engram .50 .20
❑ 17 Curtis Enis .30 .10
❑ 18 Cade McNown .30 .10
❑ 19 Marcus Robinson .75 .30
❑ 20 Corey Dillon .75 .30
❑ 21 Akili Smith .30 .10
❑ 22 Tim Couch .50 .20
❑ 23 Kevin Johnson .75 .30
❑ 24 Troy Aikman 1.50 .60
❑ 25 Joey Galloway .50 .20
❑ 26 Rocket Ismail .50 .20
❑ 27 Emmitt Smith 1.50 .60
❑ 28 Terrell Davis .75 .30
❑ 29 Olandis Gary .75 .30
❑ 30 Brian Griese .75 .30
❑ 31 Charlie Batch .75 .30
❑ 32 Herman Moore .50 .20
❑ 33 Johnnie Morton .50 .20
❑ 34 Brett Favre 2.50 1.00
❑ 35 Antonio Freeman .75 .30
❑ 36 Dorsey Levens .50 .20
❑ 37 Marvin Harrison .75 .30
❑ 38 Edgerrin James 1.25 .50
❑ 39 Peyton Manning 2.00 .75
❑ 40 Mark Brunell .75 .30
❑ 41 Keenan McCardell .50 .20
❑ 42 Jimmy Smith .50 .20
❑ 43 Fred Taylor .75 .30
❑ 44 Donnell Bennett .30 .10
❑ 45 Tony Gonzalez .50 .20
❑ 46 Elvis Grbac .50 .20
❑ 47 Damon Huard .75 .30

❑ 48	James Johnson	.30	.10
❑ 49	Cris Carter	.75	.30
❑ 50	Daunte Culpepper	1.00	.40
❑ 51	Randy Moss	1.50	.60
❑ 52	Robert Smith	.75	.30
❑ 53	Drew Bledsoe	1.00	.40
❑ 54	Kevin Faulk	.50	.20
❑ 55	Terry Glenn	.50	.20
❑ 56	Jeff Blake	.50	.20
❑ 57	Ricky Williams	.75	.30
❑ 58	Kerry Collins	.50	.20
❑ 59	Ike Hilliard	.50	.20
❑ 60	Amani Toomer	.50	.20
❑ 61	Wayne Chrebet	.50	.20
❑ 62	Curtis Martin	.75	.30
❑ 63	Vinny Testaverde	.50	.20
❑ 64	Tim Brown	.75	.30
❑ 65	Rich Gannon	.75	.30
❑ 66	Napoleon Kaufman	.50	.20
❑ 67	Tyrone Wheatley	.50	.20
❑ 68	Donovan McNabb	1.25	.50
❑ 69	Duce Staley	.75	.30
❑ 70	Jerome Bettis	.75	.30
❑ 71	Troy Edwards	.30	.10
❑ 72	Kordell Stewart	.50	.20
❑ 73	Isaac Bruce	.75	.30
❑ 74	Torry Holt	.75	.30
❑ 75	Marshall Faulk	1.00	.40
❑ 76	Kurt Warner	1.50	.60
❑ 77	Jermaine Fazande	.30	.10
❑ 78	Jim Harbaugh	.50	.20
❑ 79	Ryan Leaf	.50	.20
❑ 80	Junior Seau	.75	.30
❑ 81	Jeff Garcia	.75	.30
❑ 82	J.J. Stokes	.50	.20
❑ 83	Terrell Owens	.75	.30
❑ 84	Jerry Rice	1.50	.60
❑ 85	Jon Kitna	.75	.30
❑ 86	Derrick Mayes	.50	.20
❑ 87	Ricky Watters	.50	.20
❑ 88	Mike Alstott	.75	.30
❑ 89	Warrick Dunn	.75	.30
❑ 90	Jacquez Green	.30	.10
❑ 91	Shaun King	.30	.10
❑ 92	Eddie George	.75	.30
❑ 93	Jevon Kearse	.75	.30
❑ 94	Steve McNair	.75	.30
❑ 95	Carl Pickens	.50	.20
❑ 96	Stephen Davis	.75	.30
❑ 97	Jeff George	.50	.20
❑ 98	Brad Johnson	.75	.30
❑ 99	Deion Sanders	.75	.30
❑ 100	Michael Westbrook	.50	.20
❑ 101	Jabari Issa RC	3.00	1.25
❑ 102	Thomas Jones RC	10.00	4.00
❑ 103	Sekou Sanyika RC	3.00	1.25
❑ 104	Jay Tant RC	3.00	1.25
❑ 105	Raynoch Thompson RC	5.00	2.00
❑ 106	Doug Johnson RC	6.00	2.50
❑ 107	Mark Simoneau RC	5.00	2.00
❑ 108	Jamal Lewis RC	15.00	6.00
❑ 109	Chris Redman RC	5.00	2.00
❑ 110	Travis Taylor RC	6.00	2.50
❑ 111	Kwame Cavil RC	3.00	1.25
❑ 112	Corey Moore RC	3.00	1.25
❑ 113	Rashard Anderson RC	5.00	2.00
❑ 114	Lester Towns RC	3.00	1.25
❑ 115	Paul Edinger RC	6.00	2.50
❑ 116	Brian Urlacher RC	25.00	10.00
❑ 117	Dez White RC	6.00	2.50
❑ 118	Ron Dugans RC	3.00	1.25
❑ 119	Danny Farmer RC	5.00	2.00
❑ 120	Curtis Keaton RC	5.00	2.00
❑ 121	Peter Warrick RC	6.00	2.50
❑ 122	Courtney Brown RC	6.00	2.50
❑ 123	Lamar Chapman RC	3.00	1.25
❑ 124	JaJuan Dawson RC	3.00	1.25
❑ 125	Dennis Northcutt RC	6.00	2.50
❑ 126	Travis Prentice RC	5.00	2.00
❑ 127	Aaron Shea RC	5.00	2.00
❑ 128	Spergon Wynn RC	5.00	2.00
❑ 129	Dwayne Goodrich RC	3.00	1.25
❑ 130	Orantes Grant RC	3.00	1.25
❑ 131	Kareem Larrimore RC	3.00	1.25
❑ 132	Michael Wiley RC	5.00	2.00
❑ 133	Mike Anderson RC	8.00	3.00
❑ 134	Chris Cole RC	5.00	2.00
❑ 135	Jarious Jackson RC	5.00	2.00
❑ 136	Jerry Johnson RC	3.00	1.25
❑ 137	Kenoy Kennedy RC	3.00	1.25
❑ 138	Deltha O'Neal RC	6.00	2.50
❑ 139	Reuben Droughns RC	8.00	3.00
❑ 140	Barrett Green RC	3.00	1.25
❑ 141	Bubba Franks RC	6.00	2.50
❑ 142	Kevin McDougal RC	5.00	2.00
❑ 143	Marcus Washington RC	5.00	2.00
❑ 144	T.J. Slaughter RC	3.00	1.25
❑ 145	R.Jay Soward RC	5.00	2.00
❑ 146	Shyrone Stith RC	5.00	2.00
❑ 147	William Bartee RC	5.00	2.00
❑ 148	Dante Hall RC	12.00	5.00
❑ 149	Frank Moreau RC	5.00	2.00
❑ 150	Sylvester Morris RC	5.00	2.00
❑ 151	Deon Dyer RC	5.00	2.00
❑ 152	Ben Kelly RC	3.00	1.25
❑ 153	Tyrone Carter RC	6.00	2.50
❑ 154	Doug Chapman RC	5.00	2.00
❑ 155	Troy Walters RC	6.00	2.50
❑ 156	Tom Brady RC	60.00	30.00
❑ 157	Patrick Pass RC	5.00	2.00
❑ 158	J.R. Redmond RC	5.00	2.00
❑ 159	Marc Bulger RC	12.00	5.00
❑ 160	Darren Howard RC	5.00	2.00
❑ 161	Chad Morton RC	6.00	2.50
❑ 162	Mareno Philyaw RC	3.00	1.25
❑ 163	Terrelle Smith RC	5.00	2.00
❑ 164	Ralph Brown RC	3.00	1.25
❑ 165	Ron Dayne RC	6.00	2.50
❑ 166	Brandon Short RC	5.00	2.00
❑ 167	John Abraham RC	6.00	2.50
❑ 168	Anthony Becht RC	6.00	2.50
❑ 169	Laveranues Coles RC	8.00	3.00
❑ 170	Shaun Ellis RC	6.00	2.50
❑ 171	Chad Pennington RC	15.00	6.00
❑ 172	Sebastian Janikowski RC	6.00	2.50
❑ 173	Jerry Porter RC	8.00	3.00
❑ 174	Todd Pinkston RC	6.00	2.50
❑ 175	Gari Scott RC	3.00	1.25
❑ 176	Corey Simon RC	6.00	2.50
❑ 177	Plaxico Burress RC	12.00	5.00
❑ 178	Tee Martin RC	6.00	2.50
❑ 179	Hank Poteat RC	5.00	2.00
❑ 180	Rogers Beckett RC	5.00	2.00
❑ 181	Trevor Gaylor RC	5.00	2.00
❑ 182	Ronney Jenkins RC	5.00	2.00
❑ 183	Giovanni Carmazzi RC	3.00	1.25
❑ 184	Chafie Fields RC	3.00	1.25
❑ 185	Ahmed Plummer RC	6.00	2.50
❑ 186	Tim Rattay RC	6.00	2.50
❑ 187	Jeff Ulbrich RC	3.00	1.25
❑ 188	Shaun Alexander RC	30.00	12.50
❑ 189	Darrell Jackson RC	12.00	5.00
❑ 190	Rodnick Phillips RC	3.00	1.25
❑ 191	James Williams RC	5.00	2.00
❑ 192	Trung Canidate RC	5.00	2.00
❑ 193	Joe Hamilton RC	5.00	2.00
❑ 194	DeMario Brown RC	3.00	1.25
❑ 195	Keith Bulluck RC	6.00	2.50
❑ 196	Chris Coleman RC	6.00	2.50
❑ 197	Erron Kinney RC	6.00	2.50
❑ 198	Billy Volek RC	10.00	4.00
❑ 199	Todd Husak RC	6.00	2.50
❑ 200	Chris Samuels RC	5.00	2.00

1998 Paramount

❑	COMPLETE SET (250)	60.00	30.00
❑ 1	Larry Centers	.20	.07
❑ 2	Chris Gedney	.20	.07
❑ 3	Rob Moore	.30	.10
❑ 4	Jake Plummer	.50	.20
❑ 5	Simeon Rice	.30	.10
❑ 6	Frank Sanders	.30	.10
❑ 7	Mark Smith DE	.20	.07
❑ 8	Eric Swann	.20	.07
❑ 9	Jamal Anderson	.50	.20
❑ 10	Chris Chandler	.30	.10
❑ 11	Bert Emanuel	.30	.10
❑ 12	Tony Graziani	.20	.07
❑ 13	Byron Hanspard	.20	.07
❑ 14	Terance Mathis	.30	.10
❑ 15	O.J. Santiago	.20	.07
❑ 16	Chuck Smith	.20	.07
❑ 17	Derrick Alexander WR	.30	.10
❑ 18	Peter Boulware	.20	.07
❑ 19	Jay Graham	.20	.07
❑ 20	Priest Holmes RC	25.00	10.00
❑ 21	Michael Jackson	.20	.07
❑ 22	Byron Bam Morris	.20	.07
❑ 23	Vinny Testaverde	.30	.10
❑ 24	Eric Zeier	.30	.10
❑ 25	Todd Collins	.20	.07
❑ 26	Quinn Early	.20	.07
❑ 27	Bryce Paup	.20	.07
❑ 28	Andre Reed	.30	.10
❑ 29	Jay Riemersma	.20	.07
❑ 30	Antowain Smith	.50	.20
❑ 31	Bruce Smith	.30	.10
❑ 32	Thurman Thomas	.50	.20
❑ 33	Michael Bates	.20	.07
❑ 34	Mark Carrier WR	.20	.07
❑ 35	Rae Carruth	.20	.07
❑ 36	Kerry Collins	.30	.10
❑ 37	Fred Lane	.20	.07
❑ 38	Lamar Lathon	.20	.07
❑ 39	Muhsin Muhammad	.30	.10
❑ 40	Wesley Walls	.30	.10
❑ 41	Darnell Autry	.20	.07
❑ 42	Curtis Conway	.30	.10
❑ 43	Raymont Harris	.20	.07
❑ 44	Tyrone Hughes	.20	.07
❑ 45	Chris Penn	.20	.07
❑ 46	Ricky Proehl	.20	.07
❑ 47	Steve Stenstrom	.20	.07
❑ 48	Ryan Wetnight RC	.20	.07
❑ 49	Jeff Blake	.30	.10
❑ 50	Ki-Jana Carter	.20	.07
❑ 51	Corey Dillon	.50	.20
❑ 52	David Dunn	.20	.07
❑ 53	Boomer Esiason	.20	.07
❑ 54	Brian Milne	.20	.07
❑ 55	Carl Pickens	.30	.10
❑ 56	Darnay Scott	.30	.10
❑ 57	Troy Aikman	1.00	.40
❑ 58	Eric Bjornson	.20	.07
❑ 59	Michael Irvin	.50	.20
❑ 60	Daryl Johnston	.30	.10
❑ 61	Anthony Miller	.20	.07
❑ 62	Deion Sanders	.50	.20
❑ 63	Emmitt Smith	1.50	.60
❑ 64	Omar Stoutmire RC	.20	.07
❑ 65	Sherman Williams	.20	.07
❑ 66	Terrell Davis	.50	.20
❑ 67	John Elway	2.00	.75
❑ 68	Darrien Gordon	.20	.07
❑ 69	Ed McCaffrey	.30	.10
❑ 70	Bill Romanowski	.20	.07
❑ 71	Shannon Sharpe	.30	.10
❑ 72	Neil Smith	.30	.10
❑ 73	Rod Smith WR	.30	.10
❑ 74	Maa Tanuvasa	.20	.07
❑ 75	Tommie Boyd	.20	.07
❑ 76	Glyn Milburn	.20	.07
❑ 77	Scott Mitchell	.30	.10
❑ 78	Herman Moore	.30	.10
❑ 79	Johnnie Morton	.30	.10
❑ 80	Robert Porcher	.20	.07
❑ 81	Barry Sanders	1.50	.60
❑ 82	Bryant Westbrook	.20	.07
❑ 83	Robert Brooks	.30	.10
❑ 84	LeRoy Butler	.20	.07
❑ 85	Mark Chmura	.30	.10
❑ 86	Brett Favre	2.00	.75

❑ 87	Antonio Freeman	.50	.20
❑ 88	Dorsey Levens	.50	.20
❑ 89	Eugene Robinson	.20	.07
❑ 90	Bill Schroeder RC	1.50	.60
❑ 91	Reggie White	.50	.20
❑ 92	Aaron Bailey	.20	.07
❑ 93	Quentin Coryatt	.20	.07
❑ 94	Zack Crockett	.20	.07
❑ 95	Sean Dawkins	.20	.07
❑ 96	Ken Dilger	.20	.07
❑ 97	Marshall Faulk	.60	.25
❑ 98	Jim Harbaugh	.30	.10
❑ 99	Marvin Harrison	.50	.20
❑ 100	Bryan Barker	.20	.07
❑ 101	Tony Boselli	.20	.07
❑ 102	Tony Brackens	.20	.07
❑ 103	Mark Brunell	.50	.20
❑ 104	Mike Hollis	.20	.07
❑ 105	Keenan McCardell	.30	.10
❑ 106	Natrone Means	.30	.10
❑ 107	Jimmy Smith	.30	.10
❑ 108	James Stewart	.30	.10
❑ 109	Marcus Allen	.50	.20
❑ 110	Kimble Anders	.30	.10
❑ 111	Dale Carter	.20	.07
❑ 112	Tony Gonzalez	.50	.20
❑ 113	Elvis Grbac	.30	.10
❑ 114	Greg Hill	.20	.07
❑ 115	Andre Rison	.30	.10
❑ 116	Will Shields	.20	.07
❑ 117	Derrick Thomas	.50	.20
❑ 118	Karim Abdul-Jabbar	.50	.20
❑ 119	Trace Armstrong	.20	.07
❑ 120	Damon Huard RC	2.50	1.00
❑ 121	Charles Jordan	.20	.07
❑ 122	Dan Marino	2.00	.75
❑ 123	O.J. McDuffie	.30	.10
❑ 124	Irving Spikes	.20	.07
❑ 125	Zach Thomas	.50	.20
❑ 126	Cris Carter	.50	.20
❑ 127	Charles Woodson RC	2.00	.75
❑ 128	Brad Johnson	.50	.20
❑ 129	Randall McDaniel	.20	.07
❑ 130	John Randle	.30	.10
❑ 131	Jake Reed	.30	.10
❑ 132	Robert Smith	.50	.20
❑ 133	Todd Steussie	.20	.07
❑ 134	Bruce Armstrong	.20	.07
❑ 135	Drew Bledsoe	.75	.30
❑ 136	Ben Coates	.30	.10
❑ 137	Derrick Cullors RC	.20	.07
❑ 138	Terry Glenn	.50	.20
❑ 139	Shawn Jefferson	.20	.07
❑ 140	Curtis Martin	.50	.20
❑ 141	Chris Slade	.20	.07
❑ 142	Larry Whigham	.20	.07
❑ 143	Troy Davis	.20	.07
❑ 144	Andre Hastings	.20	.07
❑ 145	Randal Hill	.20	.07
❑ 146	Sammy Knight RC	.50	.20
❑ 147	William Roaf	.20	.07
❑ 148	Heath Shuler	.20	.07
❑ 149	Danny Wuerffel	.30	.10
❑ 150	Ray Zellars	.20	.07
❑ 151	Jessie Armstead	.20	.07
❑ 152	Tiki Barber	.50	.20
❑ 153	Chris Calloway	.20	.07
❑ 154	Danny Kanell	.30	.10
❑ 155	David Patten RC	1.50	.60
❑ 156	Michael Strahan	.30	.10
❑ 157	Charles Way	.20	.07
❑ 158	Tyrone Wheatley	.30	.10
❑ 159	Kyle Brady	.20	.07
❑ 160	Wayne Chrebet	.50	.20
❑ 161	Glenn Foley	.30	.10
❑ 162	Aaron Glenn	.20	.07
❑ 163	Leon Johnson	.20	.07
❑ 164	Adrian Murrell	.30	.10
❑ 165	Neil O'Donnell	.30	.10
❑ 166	Dedric Ward	.20	.07
❑ 167	Tim Brown	.50	.20
❑ 168	Rickey Dudley	.20	.07
❑ 169	Jeff George	.30	.10
❑ 170	Desmond Howard	.30	.10
❑ 171	James Jett	.30	.10
❑ 172	Napoleon Kaufman	.50	.20
❑ 173	Chester McGlockton	.20	.07
❑ 174	Darrell Russell	.20	.07
❑ 175	Ty Detmer	.30	.10
❑ 176	Irving Fryar	.30	.10
❑ 177	Charlie Garner	.30	.10
❑ 178	Bobby Hoying	.30	.10
❑ 179	Chad Lewis	.30	.10
❑ 180	Duce Staley	.60	.25
❑ 181	Kevin Turner	.20	.07
❑ 182	Ricky Watters	.30	.10
❑ 183	Jerome Bettis	.50	.20
❑ 184	Will Blackwell	.20	.07
❑ 185	Charles Johnson	.20	.07
❑ 186	George Jones	.20	.07
❑ 187	Levon Kirkland	.20	.07
❑ 188	Carnell Lake	.20	.07
❑ 189	Kordell Stewart	.50	.20
❑ 190	Yancey Thigpen	.20	.07
❑ 191	Tony Banks	.30	.10
❑ 192	Isaac Bruce	.50	.20
❑ 193	Ernie Conwell	.20	.07
❑ 194	Craig Heyward	.20	.07
❑ 195	Eddie Kennison	.30	.10
❑ 196	Amp Lee	.20	.07
❑ 197	Orlando Pace	.20	.07
❑ 198	Torrance Small	.20	.07
❑ 199	Gary Brown	.20	.07
❑ 200	Kenny Bynum RC	.20	.07
❑ 201	Freddie Jones	.20	.07
❑ 202	Tony Martin	.30	.10
❑ 203	Eric Metcalf	.20	.07
❑ 204	Junior Seau	.50	.20
❑ 205	Craig Whelihan RC	.20	.07
❑ 206	William Floyd	.20	.07
❑ 207	Merton Hanks	.20	.07
❑ 208	Garrison Hearst	.50	.20
❑ 209	Brent Jones	.20	.07
❑ 210	Terrell Owens	.50	.20
❑ 211	Jerry Rice	1.00	.40
❑ 212	J.J. Stokes	.30	.10
❑ 213	Rod Woodson	.30	.10
❑ 214	Steve Young	.50	.20
❑ 215	Steve Broussard	.20	.07
❑ 216	Joey Galloway	.30	.10
❑ 217	Cortez Kennedy	.20	.07
❑ 218	Jon Kitna	.50	.20
❑ 219	James McKnight	.50	.20
❑ 220	Warren Moon	.50	.20
❑ 221	Michael Sinclair	.20	.07
❑ 222	Ryan Leaf RC	1.25	.50
❑ 223	Darryl Williams	.20	.07
❑ 224	Mike Alstott	.50	.20
❑ 225	Reidel Anthony	.30	.10
❑ 226	Derrick Brooks	.50	.20
❑ 227	Horace Copeland	.20	.07
❑ 228	Trent Dilfer	.50	.20
❑ 229	Warrick Dunn	.50	.20
❑ 230	Hardy Nickerson	.20	.07
❑ 231	Warren Sapp	.30	.10
❑ 232	Karl Williams	.20	.07
❑ 233	Blaine Bishop	.20	.07
❑ 234	Willie Davis	.20	.07
❑ 235	Eddie George	.50	.20
❑ 236	Derrick Mason	.30	.10
❑ 237	Bruce Matthews	.20	.07
❑ 238	Steve McNair	.50	.20
❑ 239	Chris Sanders	.20	.07
❑ 240	Rodney Thomas	.20	.07
❑ 241	Frank Wycheck	.20	.07
❑ 242	Terry Allen	.50	.20
❑ 243	Jamie Asher	.20	.07
❑ 244	Larry Bowie	.20	.07
❑ 245	Albert Connell	.20	.07
❑ 246	Stephen Davis	.20	.07
❑ 247	Gus Frerotte	.20	.07
❑ 248	Ken Harvey	.20	.07
❑ 249	Leslie Shepherd	.20	.07
❑ 250	Michael Westbrook	.30	.10
❑ S1	Mark Brunell Sample	1.00	.40

1999 Paramount

❑	COMPLETE SET (250)	50.00	20.00
❑ 1	David Boston RC	1.25	.50
❑ 2	Larry Centers	.20	.07
❑ 3	Joel Makovicka RC	1.25	.50
❑ 4	Eric Metcalf	.20	.07
❑ 5	Rob Moore	.30	.10
❑ 6	Adrian Murrell	.30	.10
❑ 7	Jake Plummer	.30	.10
❑ 8	Frank Sanders	.30	.10
❑ 9	Aeneas Williams	.20	.07
❑ 10	Morten Andersen	.20	.07
❑ 11	Jamal Anderson	.50	.20
❑ 12	Chris Chandler	.30	.10
❑ 13	Tim Dwight	.50	.20
❑ 14	Terance Mathis	.30	.10
❑ 15	Jeff Paulk RC	.40	.15
❑ 16	O.J. Santiago	.20	.07
❑ 17	Chuck Smith	.20	.07
❑ 18	Peter Boulware	.20	.07
❑ 19	Priest Holmes	.75	.30
❑ 20	Michael Jackson	.20	.07
❑ 21	Jermaine Lewis	.30	.10
❑ 22	Ray Lewis	.50	.20
❑ 23	Michael McCrary	.20	.07
❑ 24	Bennie Thompson	.20	.07
❑ 25	Rod Woodson	.30	.10
❑ 26	Shawn Bryson RC	1.25	.50
❑ 27	Doug Flutie	.50	.20
❑ 28	Eric Moulds	.50	.20
❑ 29	Peerless Price RC	1.25	.50
❑ 30	Andre Reed	.30	.10
❑ 31	Jay Riemersma	.20	.07
❑ 32	Antowain Smith	.50	.20
❑ 33	Bruce Smith	.30	.10
❑ 34	Michael Bates	.20	.07
❑ 35	Steve Beuerlein	.20	.07
❑ 36	Tim Biakabutuka	.30	.10
❑ 37	Kevin Greene	.20	.07
❑ 38	Anthony Johnson	.20	.07
❑ 39	Fred Lane	.20	.07
❑ 40	Muhsin Muhammad	.30	.10
❑ 41	Wesley Walls	.30	.10
❑ 42	D'Wayne Bates RC	.75	.30
❑ 43	Edgar Bennett	.20	.07
❑ 44	Marty Booker RC	1.25	.50
❑ 45	Curtis Conway	.30	.10
❑ 46	Bobby Engram	.30	.10
❑ 47	Curtis Enis	.20	.07
❑ 48	Erik Kramer	.20	.07
❑ 49	Cade McNown RC	.75	.30
❑ 50	Jeff Blake	.30	.10
❑ 51	Scott Covington RC	1.25	.50
❑ 52	Corey Dillon	.50	.20
❑ 53	Quincy Jackson RC	.40	.15
❑ 54	Carl Pickens	.30	.10
❑ 55	Darnay Scott	.20	.07
❑ 56	Akili Smith RC	.75	.30
❑ 57	Craig Yeast RC	.75	.30
❑ 58	Jerry Ball	.20	.07
❑ 59	Darrin Chiaverini RC	.75	.30
❑ 60	Tim Couch RC	1.25	.50
❑ 61	Ty Detmer	.30	.10
❑ 62	Kevin Johnson RC	1.25	.50
❑ 63	Terry Kirby	.20	.07
❑ 64	Daylon McCutcheon RC	.40	.15
❑ 65	Irv Smith	.20	.07
❑ 66	Troy Aikman	1.00	.40
❑ 67	Ebenezer Ekuban RC	.75	.30
❑ 68	Michael Irvin	.30	.10
❑ 69	Daryl Johnston	.20	.07
❑ 70	Wane McGarity RC	.40	.15
❑ 71	Dat Nguyen RC	1.25	.50
❑ 72	Deion Sanders	.50	.20
❑ 73	Emmitt Smith	1.00	.40
❑ 74	Bubby Brister	.20	.07
❑ 75	Terrell Davis	.50	.20
❑ 76	Jason Elam	.20	.07

❑ 77 Olandis Gary RC 1.25 .50
❑ 78 Brian Griese .50 .20
❑ 79 Ed McCaffrey .30 .10
❑ 80 Travis McGriff RC .40 .15
❑ 81 Shannon Sharpe .30 .10
❑ 82 Rod Smith .30 .10
❑ 83 Charlie Batch .50 .20
❑ 84 Chris Claiborne RC .40 .15
❑ 85 Germane Crowell .20 .07
❑ 86 Sedrick Irvin RC .40 .15
❑ 87 Herman Moore .30 .10
❑ 88 Johnnie Morton .30 .10
❑ 89 Barry Sanders 1.50 .60
❑ 90 Robert Brooks .30 .10
❑ 91 Aaron Brooks RC 2.50 1.00
❑ 92 Mark Chmura .20 .07
❑ 93 Brett Favre 1.50 .60
❑ 94 Antonio Freeman .50 .20
❑ 95 Vonnie Holliday .20 .07
❑ 96 Dorsey Levens .50 .20
❑ 97 De'Mond Parker RC .40 .15
❑ 98 Ken Dilger .20 .07
❑ 99 Marvin Harrison .50 .20
❑ 100 Edgerrin James RC 5.00 2.00
❑ 101 Peyton Manning 1.50 .60
❑ 102 Jerome Pathon .20 .07
❑ 103 Mike Peterson RC .75 .30
❑ 104 Marcus Pollard .20 .07
❑ 105 Tavian Banks .20 .07
❑ 106 Reggie Barlow .20 .07
❑ 107 Tony Boselli .20 .07
❑ 108 Mark Brunell .50 .20
❑ 109 Keenan McCardell .30 .10
❑ 110 Bryce Paup .20 .07
❑ 111 Jimmy Smith .30 .10
❑ 112 Fred Taylor .50 .20
❑ 113 Dave Thomas RC .20 .07
❑ 114 Kimble Anders .30 .10
❑ 115 Donnell Bennett .20 .07
❑ 116 Mike Cloud RC .75 .30
❑ 117 Tony Gonzalez .50 .20
❑ 118 Elvis Grbac .30 .10
❑ 119 Larry Parker RC 1.25 .50
❑ 120 Andre Rison .30 .10
❑ 121 Brian Shay RC .40 .15
❑ 122 Karim Abdul-Jabbar .30 .10
❑ 123 Oronde Gadsden .30 .10
❑ 124 James Johnson RC .75 .30
❑ 125 Rob Konrad RC .75 .30
❑ 126 Dan Marino 1.50 .60
❑ 127 O.J. McDuffie .30 .10
❑ 128 Zach Thomas .50 .20
❑ 129 Cris Carter .50 .20
❑ 130 Daunte Culpepper RC 5.00 2.00
❑ 131 Randall Cunningham .50 .20
❑ 132 Matthew Hatchette .20 .07
❑ 133 Leroy Hoard .20 .07
❑ 134 Randy Moss 1.25 .50
❑ 135 John Randle .30 .10
❑ 136 Jake Reed .30 .10
❑ 137 Robert Smith .50 .20
❑ 138 Michael Bishop RC 1.25 .50
❑ 139 Drew Bledsoe .60 .25
❑ 140 Ben Coates .30 .10
❑ 141 Kevin Faulk RC 1.25 .50
❑ 142 Terry Glenn .50 .20
❑ 143 Shawn Jefferson .20 .07
❑ 144 Andy Katzenmoyer RC .75 .30
❑ 145 Tony Simmons .20 .07
❑ 146 Cuncho Brown RC .40 .15
❑ 147 Cam Cleeland .20 .07
❑ 148 Mark Fields .20 .07
❑ 149 La'Roi Glover RC .50 .20
❑ 150 Andre Hastings .20 .07
❑ 151 Billy Joe Hobert .20 .07
❑ 152 William Roaf .20 .07
❑ 153 Billy Joe Tolliver .20 .07
❑ 154 Ricky Williams RC 2.50 1.00
❑ 155 Jessie Armstead .20 .07
❑ 156 Tiki Barber .50 .20
❑ 157 Gary Brown .20 .07
❑ 158 Kent Graham .20 .07
❑ 159 Ike Hilliard .20 .07
❑ 160 Joe Montgomery RC .75 .30
❑ 161 Amani Toomer .20 .07
❑ 162 Charles Way .20 .07
❑ 163 Wayne Chrebet .30 .10

❑ 164 Bryan Cox .20 .07
❑ 165 Aaron Glenn .20 .07
❑ 166 Keyshawn Johnson .50 .20
❑ 167 Leon Johnson .20 .07
❑ 168 Curtis Martin .50 .20
❑ 169 Vinny Testaverde .30 .10
❑ 170 Dedric Ward .20 .07
❑ 171 Tim Brown .50 .20
❑ 172 Dameane Douglas RC 1.25 .50
❑ 173 Rickey Dudley .20 .07
❑ 174 James Jett .30 .10
❑ 175 Napoleon Kaufman .50 .20
❑ 176 Darrell Russell .20 .07
❑ 177 Harvey Williams .20 .07
❑ 178 Charles Woodson .50 .20
❑ 179 Na Brown RC .75 .30
❑ 180 Hugh Douglas .20 .07
❑ 181 Cecil Martin RC .75 .30
❑ 182 Donovan McNabb RC 6.00 2.50
❑ 183 Duce Staley .50 .20
❑ 184 Kevin Turner .20 .07
❑ 185 Jerome Bettis .50 .20
❑ 186 Troy Edwards RC .75 .30
❑ 187 Jason Gildon .20 .07
❑ 188 Courtney Hawkins .20 .07
❑ 189 Malcolm Johnson RC .40 .15
❑ 190 Kordell Stewart .30 .10
❑ 191 Jerame Tuman RC 1.25 .50
❑ 192 Amos Zereoue RC 1.25 .50
❑ 193 Isaac Bruce .50 .20
❑ 194 Kevin Carter .20 .07
❑ 195 Jeremaine Copeland RC .40 .15
❑ 196 Joe Germaine RC .75 .30
❑ 197 Az-Zahir Hakim .20 .07
❑ 198 Torry Holt RC 3.00 1.25
❑ 199 Amp Lee .20 .07
❑ 200 Ricky Proehl .20 .07
❑ 201 Charlie Jones .20 .07
❑ 202 Freddie Jones .20 .07
❑ 203 Ryan Leaf .50 .20
❑ 204 Natrone Means .30 .10
❑ 205 Mikhael Ricks .20 .07
❑ 206 Junior Seau .50 .20
❑ 207 Bryan Still .20 .07
❑ 208 Garrison Hearst .30 .10
❑ 209 Terry Jackson RC .75 .30
❑ 210 R.W. McQuarters .20 .07
❑ 211 Ken Norton Jr. .20 .07
❑ 212 Terrell Owens .50 .20
❑ 213 Jerry Rice 1.00 .40
❑ 214 J.J. Stokes .30 .10
❑ 215 Tai Streets RC 1.25 .50
❑ 216 Steve Young .60 .25
❑ 217 Karsten Bailey RC .75 .30
❑ 218 Chad Brown .20 .07
❑ 219 Joey Galloway .30 .10
❑ 220 Ahman Green .50 .20
❑ 221 Brock Huard RC 1.25 .50
❑ 222 Cortez Kennedy .20 .07
❑ 223 Jon Kitna .50 .20
❑ 224 Shawn Springs .20 .07
❑ 225 Ricky Watters .30 .10
❑ 226 Mike Alstott .50 .20
❑ 227 Reidel Anthony .30 .10
❑ 228 Trent Dilfer .30 .10
❑ 229 Warrick Dunn .50 .20
❑ 230 Bert Emanuel .30 .10
❑ 231 Martin Gramatica RC .40 .15
❑ 232 Jacquez Green .20 .07
❑ 233 Shaun King RC .75 .30
❑ 234 Anthony McFarland RC 1.25 .50
❑ 235 Warren Sapp .30 .10
❑ 236 Willie Davis .20 .07
❑ 237 Kevin Dyson .30 .10
❑ 238 Eddie George .50 .20
❑ 239 Darran Hall RC .40 .15
❑ 240 Jackie Harris .20 .07
❑ 241 Steve McNair .50 .20
❑ 242 Yancey Thigpen .20 .07
❑ 243 Frank Wycheck .20 .07
❑ 244 Stephen Alexander .20 .07
❑ 245 Champ Bailey RC 1.50 .60
❑ 246 Stephen Davis .50 .20
❑ 247 Darrell Green .20 .07
❑ 248 Skip Hicks .20 .07
❑ 249 Brian Mitchell .20 .07
❑ 250 Michael Westbrook .30 .10

2000 Paramount

❑ COMPLETE SET (249) 40.00 15.00
❑ 1 David Boston .50 .20
❑ 2 Thomas Jones RC 1.25 .50
❑ 3 Rob Moore .30 .10
❑ 4 Jake Plummer .30 .10
❑ 5 Simeon Rice .30 .10
❑ 6 Frank Sanders .30 .10
❑ 7 Raynoch Thompson RC .30 .10
❑ 8 Jamal Anderson .50 .20
❑ 9 Chris Chandler .30 .10
❑ 10 Bob Christian .20 .08
❑ 11 Tim Dwight .50 .20
❑ 12 Byron Hanspard .20 .08
❑ 13 Terance Mathis .30 .10
❑ 14 Mareno Philyaw RC .60 .25
❑ 15 Tony Banks .30 .10
❑ 16 Priest Holmes .60 .25
❑ 17 Qadry Ismail .30 .10
❑ 18 Pat Johnson .20 .08
❑ 19 Jamal Lewis RC 2.00 .75
❑ 20 Chris Redman RC .60 .25
❑ 21 Shannon Sharpe .30 .10
❑ 22 Travis Taylor RC .75 .30
❑ 23 Erik Flowers RC 1.00 .40
❑ 24 Doug Flutie .50 .20
❑ 25 Rob Johnson .30 .10
❑ 26 Jonathan Linton .20 .08
❑ 27 Corey Moore RC .60 .25
❑ 28 Eric Moulds .50 .20
❑ 29 Peerless Price .30 .10
❑ 30 Jay Riemersma .20 .08
❑ 31 Antowain Smith .30 .10
❑ 32 Rashard Anderson RC .60 .25
❑ 33 Steve Beuerlein .30 .10
❑ 34 Tim Biakabutuka .30 .10
❑ 35 Donald Hayes .20 .08
❑ 36 Patrick Jeffers .50 .20
❑ 37 Jeff Lewis .20 .08
❑ 38 Muhsin Muhammad .30 .10
❑ 39 Wesley Walls .20 .08
❑ 40 Bobby Engram .30 .10
❑ 41 Curtis Enis .20 .08
❑ 42 Cade McNown .20 .08
❑ 43 Jim Miller .20 .08
❑ 44 Marcus Robinson .50 .20
❑ 45 Brian Urlacher RC 3.00 1.25
❑ 46 Dez White RC .75 .30
❑ 47 Michael Basnight .20 .08
❑ 48 Corey Dillon .50 .20
❑ 49 Ron Dugans RC .60 .25
❑ 50 Willie Jackson .20 .08
❑ 51 Darnay Scott .30 .10
❑ 52 Akili Smith .20 .08
❑ 53 Peter Warrick RC .75 .30
❑ 54 Courtney Brown RC .75 .30
❑ 55 Darrin Chiaverini .20 .08
❑ 56 Tim Couch .30 .10
❑ 57 Kevin Johnson .50 .20
❑ 58 Terry Kirby .20 .08
❑ 59 Dennis Northcutt RC .75 .30
❑ 60 Travis Prentice RC .60 .25
❑ 61 Leslie Shepherd .20 .08
❑ 62 Troy Aikman 1.00 .40
❑ 63 Joey Galloway .30 .10
❑ 64 Rocket Ismail .30 .10
❑ 65 David LaFleur .20 .08
❑ 66 Emmitt Smith 1.00 .40
❑ 67 Jason Tucker .20 .08

❑ 68	Chris Warren	.20	.08
❑ 69	Michael Wiley RC	.60	.25
❑ 70	Desmond Clark	.30	.10
❑ 71	Chris Cole RC	.60	.25
❑ 72	Terrell Davis	.50	.20
❑ 73	Olandis Gary	.50	.20
❑ 74	Brian Griese	.50	.20
❑ 75	Jarious Jackson RC	.60	.25
❑ 76	Ed McCaffrey	.50	.20
❑ 77	Deltha O'Neal RC	.75	.30
❑ 78	Rod Smith	.30	.10
❑ 79	Charlie Batch	.50	.20
❑ 80	Germane Crowell	.20	.08
❑ 81	Reuben Droughns RC	1.00	.50
❑ 82	Terry Fair	.20	.08
❑ 83	Herman Moore	.30	.10
❑ 84	Johnnie Morton	.30	.10
❑ 85	Barry Sanders	1.25	.50
❑ 86	James Stewart	.30	.10
❑ 87	Corey Bradford	.30	.10
❑ 88	Tyrone Davis	.20	.08
❑ 89	Brett Favre	1.50	.60
❑ 90	Bubba Franks RC	.75	.30
❑ 91	Antonio Freeman	.50	.20
❑ 92	Matt Hasselbeck	.30	.10
❑ 93	Dorsey Levens	.30	.10
❑ 94	Anthony Lucas RC	.60	.25
❑ 95	Bill Schroeder	.30	.10
❑ 96	Ken Dilger	.20	.08
❑ 97	E.G. Green	.20	.08
❑ 98	Marvin Harrison	.50	.20
❑ 99	Edgerrin James	.75	.30
❑ 100	Peyton Manning	1.25	.50
❑ 101	Jerome Pathon	.30	.10
❑ 102	Marcus Washington RC	.60	.25
❑ 103	Terrence Wilkins	.20	.08
❑ 104	Kyle Brady	.20	.08
❑ 105	Mark Brunell	.50	.20
❑ 106	Kevin Hardy	.20	.08
❑ 107	Keenan McCardell	.30	.10
❑ 108	Jimmy Smith	.30	.10
❑ 109	R.Jay Soward RC	.60	.25
❑ 110	Shyrone Stith RC	.60	.25
❑ 111	Fred Taylor	.50	.20
❑ 112	Alvis Whitted	.20	.08
❑ 113	Derrick Alexander	.30	.10
❑ 114	Kimble Anders	.20	.08
❑ 115	Donnell Bennett	.20	.08
❑ 116	Tony Gonzalez	.30	.10
❑ 117	Elvis Grbac	.30	.10
❑ 118	Kevin Lockett	.20	.08
❑ 119	Sylvester Morris RC	.60	.25
❑ 120	Tony Richardson RC	.30	.10
❑ 121	Deon Dyer RC	.60	.25
❑ 122	Oronde Gadsden	.30	.10
❑ 123	Damon Huard	.50	.20
❑ 124	James Johnson	.20	.08
❑ 125	Dan Marino	1.50	.60
❑ 126	Tony Martin	.30	.10
❑ 127	O.J. McDuffie	.30	.10
❑ 128	Zach Thomas	.50	.20
❑ 129	Cris Carter	.50	.20
❑ 130	Daunte Culpepper	.60	.25
❑ 131	Leroy Hoard	.20	.08
❑ 132	Chris Hovan RC	.60	.25
❑ 133	Randy Moss	1.00	.40
❑ 134	John Randle	.30	.10
❑ 135	Robert Smith	.50	.20
❑ 136	Troy Walters RC	.75	.30
❑ 137	Drew Bledsoe	.60	.25
❑ 138	Tom Brady RC	20.00	7.50
❑ 139	Troy Brown	.30	.10
❑ 140	Kevin Faulk	.20	.08
❑ 141	Terry Glenn	.30	.10
❑ 142	J.R. Redmond RC	.60	.25
❑ 143	Tony Simmons	.20	.08
❑ 144	David Stachelski RC	.60	.25
❑ 145	Jeff Blake	.30	.10
❑ 146	Marc Bulger RC	1.50	.60
❑ 147	Cam Cleeland	.20	.08
❑ 148	Sherrod Gideon RC	.60	.25
❑ 149	Darren Howard RC	.60	.25
❑ 150	Chad Morton RC	.75	.30
❑ 151	Keith Poole	.20	.08
❑ 152	Ricky Williams	.50	.20
❑ 153	Tiki Barber	.50	.20
❑ 154	Kerry Collins	.30	.10
❑ 155	Ron Dayne RC	.75	.30
❑ 156	Ike Hilliard	.30	.10
❑ 157	Joe Jurevicius	.20	.08
❑ 158	Pete Mitchell	.20	.08
❑ 159	Joe Montgomery	.20	.08
❑ 160	Amani Toomer	.30	.10
❑ 161	John Abraham RC	.75	.30
❑ 162	Anthony Becht RC	.75	.30
❑ 163	Wayne Chrebet	.30	.10
❑ 164	Laveranues Coles RC	1.00	.40
❑ 165	Ray Lucas	.30	.10
❑ 166	Curtis Martin	.50	.20
❑ 167	Chad Pennington RC	2.00	.75
❑ 168	Vinny Testaverde	.30	.10
❑ 169	Dedric Ward	.20	.08
❑ 170	Tim Brown	.50	.20
❑ 171	Rich Gannon	.50	.20
❑ 172	Bobby Hoying	.30	.10
❑ 173	James Jett	.20	.08
❑ 174	Napoleon Kaufman	.30	.10
❑ 175	Jerry Porter RC	1.00	.40
❑ 176	Tyrone Wheatley	.30	.10
❑ 177	Charles Woodson	.50	.20
❑ 178	Dameane Douglas	.20	.08
❑ 179	Charles Johnson	.30	.10
❑ 180	Donovan McNabb	.75	.30
❑ 181	Todd Pinkston RC	.75	.30
❑ 182	Gari Scott RC	.60	.25
❑ 183	Torrance Small	.20	.08
❑ 184	Duce Staley	.50	.20
❑ 185	Jerome Bettis	.50	.20
❑ 186	Plaxico Burress RC	1.50	.60
❑ 187	Troy Edwards	.20	.08
❑ 188	Danny Farmer RC	.60	.25
❑ 189	Richard Huntley	.20	.08
❑ 190	Tee Martin RC	.75	.30
❑ 191	Kordell Stewart	.30	.10
❑ 192	Hines Ward	.50	.20
❑ 193	Isaac Bruce	.50	.20
❑ 194	Trung Canidate RC	.60	.25
❑ 195	Marshall Faulk	.60	.25
❑ 196	Az-Zahir Hakim	.30	.10
❑ 197	Torry Holt	.50	.20
❑ 198	Tony Horne	.20	.08
❑ 199	Ricky Proehl	.20	.08
❑ 200	Kurt Warner	1.00	.40
❑ 201	Jermaine Fazande	.20	.08
❑ 202	Trevor Gaylor RC	.60	.25
❑ 203	Jeff Graham	.20	.08
❑ 204	Jim Harbaugh	.30	.10
❑ 205	Freddie Jones	.20	.08
❑ 206	Mikhael Ricks	.20	.08
❑ 207	Junior Seau	.50	.20
❑ 208	Fred Beasley	.20	.08
❑ 209	Giovanni Carmazzi RC	.60	.25
❑ 210	Jeff Garcia	.50	.20
❑ 211	Charlie Garner	.30	.10
❑ 212	Terrell Owens	.50	.20
❑ 213	Tim Rattay RC	.75	.30
❑ 214	Jerry Rice	1.00	.40
❑ 215	J.J. Stokes	.30	.10
❑ 216	Steve Young	.60	.25
❑ 217	Shaun Alexander RC	4.00	1.50
❑ 218	Sean Dawkins	.20	.08
❑ 219	Darrell Jackson RC	1.50	.60
❑ 220	Jon Kitna	.50	.20
❑ 221	Derrick Mayes	.30	.10
❑ 222	Charlie Rogers	.20	.08
❑ 223	Shawn Springs	.20	.08
❑ 224	Ricky Watters	.30	.10
❑ 225	Mike Alstott	.50	.20
❑ 226	Reidel Anthony	.20	.08
❑ 227	Warrick Dunn	.50	.20
❑ 228	Jacquez Green	.20	.08
❑ 229	Joe Hamilton RC	.60	.25
❑ 230	Keyshawn Johnson	.50	.20
❑ 231	Shaun King	.20	.08
❑ 232	Warren Sapp	.30	.10
❑ 233	Keith Bulluck RC	.75	.30
❑ 234	Kevin Dyson	.30	.10
❑ 235	Eddie George	.50	.20
❑ 236	Jevon Kearse	.50	.20
❑ 237	Erron Kinney RC	.75	.30
❑ 238	Steve McNair	.50	.20
❑ 239	Neil O'Donnell	.20	.08
❑ 240	Yancy Thigpen	.20	.08
❑ 241	Frank Wycheck	.20	.08
❑ 243	Champ Bailey	.30	.10
❑ 244	Larry Centers	.20	.08
❑ 245	Albert Connell	.20	.08
❑ 246	Stephen Davis	.50	.20
❑ 247	Todd Husak RC	.75	.30
❑ 248	Brad Johnson	.50	.20
❑ 249	Chris Samuels RC	.60	.25
❑ 250	Michael Westbrook	.30	.10

1964 Philadelphia

❑	COMPLETE SET (198)	900.00	600.00
❑	WRAPPER (1-CENT)	40.00	30.00
❑	WRAPPER (5-CENT)	20.00	10.00
❑ 1	Raymond Berry !	20.00	10.00
❑ 2	Tom Gilburg	2.50	1.25
❑ 3	John Mackey RC	30.00	18.00
❑ 4	Gino Marchetti	5.00	2.50
❑ 5	Jim Martin	2.50	1.25
❑ 6	Tom Matte RC	6.00	3.00
❑ 7	Jimmy Orr	3.00	1.50
❑ 8	Jim Parker	4.00	2.00
❑ 9	Bill Pellington	2.50	1.25
❑ 10	Alex Sandusky	2.50	1.25
❑ 11	Dick Szymanski	2.50	1.25
❑ 12	Johnny Unitas	45.00	25.00
❑ 13	Baltimore Colts	3.00	1.50
❑ 14	Colts Play/Don Shula	35.00	20.00
❑ 15	Doug Atkins	5.00	2.50
❑ 16	Ronnie Bull	2.50	1.25
❑ 17	Mike Ditka	40.00	25.00
❑ 18	Joe Fortunato	2.50	1.25
❑ 19	Willie Galimore	3.00	1.50
❑ 20	Joe Marconi	2.50	1.25
❑ 21	Bennie McRae RC	2.50	1.25
❑ 22	Johnny Morris	2.50	1.25
❑ 23	Richie Petitbon	2.50	1.25
❑ 24	Mike Pyle	2.50	1.25
❑ 25	Roosevelt Taylor RC	4.00	2.00
❑ 26	Bill Wade	3.00	1.50
❑ 27	Chicago Bears	3.00	1.50
❑ 28	Bears Play/George Halas	12.00	6.00
❑ 29	Johnny Brewer	2.50	1.25
❑ 30	Jim Brown	90.00	50.00
❑ 31	Gary Collins RC	8.00	4.00
❑ 32	Vince Costello	2.50	1.25
❑ 33	Galen Fiss	2.50	1.25
❑ 34	Bill Glass	2.50	1.25
❑ 35	Ernie Green RC	3.00	1.50
❑ 36	Rich Kreitling	2.50	1.25
❑ 37	John Morrow	2.50	1.25
❑ 38	Frank Ryan	3.00	1.50
❑ 39	Charlie Scales RC	2.50	1.25
❑ 40	Dick Schafrath RC	2.50	1.25
❑ 41	Cleveland Browns	3.00	1.50
❑ 42	Cleveland Browns Play	2.50	1.25
❑ 43	Don Bishop	2.50	1.25
❑ 44	Frank Clarke RC	3.00	1.50
❑ 45	Mike Connelly	2.50	1.25
❑ 46	Lee Folkins	2.50	1.25
❑ 47	Cornell Green RC	8.00	4.00
❑ 48	Bob Lilly	40.00	25.00
❑ 49	Amos Marsh	2.50	1.25
❑ 50	Tommy McDonald	5.00	2.50
❑ 51	Don Meredith	35.00	20.00
❑ 52	Pettis Norman RC	3.00	1.50
❑ 53	Don Perkins	4.00	2.00
❑ 54	Guy Reese	2.50	1.25
❑ 55	Dallas Cowboys	3.00	1.50
❑ 56	Cowboys Play/T.Landry	20.00	12.00

❑ 57 Terry Barr 2.50 1.25
❑ 58 Roger Brown 3.00 1.50
❑ 59 Gail Cogdill 2.50 1.25
❑ 60 John Gordy 2.50 1.25
❑ 61 Dick Lane 4.00 2.00
❑ 62 Yale Lary 4.00 2.00
❑ 63 Dan Lewis 2.50 1.25
❑ 64 Darris McCord 2.50 1.25
❑ 65 Earl Morrall 3.00 1.50
❑ 66 Joe Schmidt 5.00 2.50
❑ 67 Pat Studstill RC 3.00 1.50
❑ 68 Wayne Walker RC 3.00 1.50
❑ 69 Detroit Lions 3.00 1.50
❑ 70 Detroit Lions 2.50 1.25
❑ 71 Herb Adderley RC 35.00 20.00
❑ 72 Willie Davis DE RC 30.00 18.00
❑ 73 Forrest Gregg 5.00 2.50
❑ 74 Paul Hornung 35.00 20.00
❑ 75 Hank Jordan 5.00 2.50
❑ 76 Jerry Kramer 6.00 3.00
❑ 77 Tom Moore 3.00 1.50
❑ 78 Jim Ringo 5.00 2.50
❑ 79 Bart Starr 60.00 35.00
❑ 80 Jim Taylor 25.00 15.00
❑ 81 Jesse Whittenton RC 3.00 1.50
❑ 82 Willie Wood 8.00 4.00
❑ 83 Green Bay Packers 6.00 3.00
❑ 84 Packers Play/Lombardi 35.00 20.00
❑ 85 Jon Arnett 2.50 1.25
❑ 86 Pervis Atkins RC 2.50 1.25
❑ 87 Dick Bass 3.00 1.50
❑ 88 Carroll Dale 4.00 2.00
❑ 89 Roman Gabriel 6.00 3.00
❑ 90 Ed Meador 2.50 1.25
❑ 91 Merlin Olsen RC 50.00 30.00
❑ 92 Jack Pardee RC 4.00 2.00
❑ 93 Jim Phillips 2.50 1.25
❑ 94 Carver Shannon 2.50 1.25
❑ 95 Frank Varrichione 2.50 1.25
❑ 96 Danny Villanueva 2.50 1.25
❑ 97 Los Angeles Rams 3.00 1.50
❑ 98 Los Angeles Rams Play 2.50 1.25
❑ 99 Grady Alderman RC 3.00 1.50
❑ 100 Larry Bowie 2.50 1.25
❑ 101 Bill Brown RC 6.00 3.00
❑ 102 Paul Flatley RC 2.50 1.25
❑ 103 Rip Hawkins 2.50 1.25
❑ 104 Jim Marshall 8.00 4.00
❑ 105 Tommy Mason 3.00 1.50
❑ 106 Jim Prestel 2.50 1.25
❑ 107 Jerry Reichow 2.50 1.25
❑ 108 Ed Sharockman 2.50 1.25
❑ 109 Fran Tarkenton 35.00 20.00
❑ 110 Mick Tingelhoff RC 6.00 3.00
❑ 111 Minnesota Vikings 3.00 1.50
❑ 112 Vikings Play/Van Brock. 4.00 2.00
❑ 113 Erich Barnes 2.50 1.25
❑ 114 Roosevelt Brown 4.00 2.00
❑ 115 Don Chandler 2.50 1.25
❑ 116 Darrell Dess 2.50 1.25
❑ 117 Frank Gifford 35.00 20.00
❑ 118 Dick James 2.50 1.25
❑ 119 Jim Katcavage 2.50 1.25
❑ 120 John Lovetere 2.50 1.25
❑ 121 Dick Lynch RC 3.00 1.50
❑ 122 Jim Patton 2.50 1.25
❑ 123 Del Shofner 2.50 1.25
❑ 124 Y.A.Tittle 20.00 10.00
❑ 125 New York Giants 3.00 1.50
❑ 126 New York Giants Play 2.50 1.25
❑ 127 Sam Baker 2.50 1.25
❑ 128 Maxie Baughan 2.50 1.25
❑ 129 Timmy Brown 3.00 1.50
❑ 130 Mike Clark 2.50 1.25
❑ 131 Irv Cross RC 3.00 1.50
❑ 132 Ted Dean 2.50 1.25
❑ 133 Ron Goodwin 2.50 1.25
❑ 134 King Hill 2.50 1.25
❑ 135 Clarence Peaks 2.50 1.25
❑ 136 Pete Retzlaff 3.00 1.50
❑ 137 Jim Schrader 2.50 1.25
❑ 138 Norm Snead 3.00 1.50
❑ 139 Philadelphia Eagles 3.00 1.50
❑ 140 Philadelphia Eagles Play 2.50 1.25
❑ 141 Gary Ballman RC 2.50 1.25
❑ 142 Charley Bradshaw RC 2.50 1.25
❑ 143 Ed Brown 3.00 1.50
❑ 144 John Henry Johnson 4.00 2.00
❑ 145 Joe Krupa 2.50 1.25
❑ 146 Bill Mack 2.50 1.25
❑ 147 Lou Michaels 2.50 1.25
❑ 148 Buzz Nutter 2.50 1.25
❑ 149 Myron Pottios 2.50 1.25
❑ 150 John Reger 2.50 1.25
❑ 151 Mike Sandusky 2.50 1.25
❑ 152 Clendon Thomas 2.50 1.25
❑ 153 Pittsburgh Steelers 3.00 1.50
❑ 154 Pittsburgh Steelers Play 2.50 1.25
❑ 155 Kermit Alexander RC 3.00 1.50
❑ 156 Bernie Casey 3.00 1.50
❑ 157 Dan Colchico 2.50 1.25
❑ 158 Clyde Conner 2.50 1.25
❑ 159 Tommy Davis 2.50 1.25
❑ 160 Matt Hazeltine 2.50 1.25
❑ 161 Jim Johnson RC 20.00 10.00
❑ 162 Don Lisbon RC 2.50 1.25
❑ 163 Lamar McHan 2.50 1.25
❑ 164 Bob St.Clair 4.00 2.00
❑ 165 J.D. Smith 2.50 1.25
❑ 166 Abe Woodson 2.50 1.25
❑ 167 San Francisco 49ers 3.00 1.50
❑ 168 San Francisco 49ers Play 2.50 1.25
❑ 169 Garland Boyette UER 2.50 1.25
❑ 170 Bobby Joe Conrad 3.00 1.50
❑ 171 Bob DeMarco RC 2.50 1.25
❑ 172 Ken Gray RC 2.50 1.25
❑ 173 Jimmy Hill 2.50 1.25
❑ 174 Charlie Johnson 3.00 1.50
❑ 175 Ernie McMillan 2.50 1.25
❑ 176 Dale Meinert 2.50 1.25
❑ 177 Luke Owens 2.50 1.25
❑ 178 Sonny Randle 2.50 1.25
❑ 179 Joe Robb 2.50 1.25
❑ 180 Bill Stacy 2.50 1.25
❑ 181 St. Louis Cardinals 3.00 1.50
❑ 182 St. Louis Cardinals Play 2.50 1.25
❑ 183 Bill Barnes 2.50 1.25
❑ 184 Don Bosseler 2.50 1.25
❑ 185 Sam Huff 6.00 3.00
❑ 186 Sonny Jurgensen 20.00 10.00
❑ 187 Bob Khayat 2.50 1.25
❑ 188 Riley Mattson 2.50 1.25
❑ 189 Bobby Mitchell 6.00 3.00
❑ 190 John Nisby 2.50 1.25
❑ 191 Vince Promuto 2.50 1.25
❑ 192 Joe Rutgens 2.50 1.25
❑ 193 Lonnie Sanders 2.50 1.25
❑ 194 Jim Steffen 2.50 1.25
❑ 195 Washington Redskins 3.00 1.50
❑ 196 Washington Redskins Play 2.50 1.25
❑ 197 Checklist 1 UER ! 30.00 18.00
❑ 198 Checklist 2 UER ! 55.00 30.00

1965 Philadelphia

❑ COMPLETE SET (198) 800.00 500.00
❑ WRAPPER (5-CENT) 20.00 10.00
❑ 1 Colts Team ! 15.00 7.50
❑ 2 Raymond Berry 10.00 5.00
❑ 3 Bob Boyd DB 2.00 1.00
❑ 4 Wendell Harris 2.00 1.00
❑ 5 Jerry Logan 2.00 1.00
❑ 6 Tony Lorick 2.00 1.00
❑ 7 Lou Michaels 2.00 1.00
❑ 8 Lenny Moore 8.00 4.00
❑ 9 Jimmy Orr 3.00 1.50
❑ 10 Jim Parker 4.00 2.00
❑ 11 Dick Szymanski 2.00 1.00
❑ 12 Johnny Unitas 40.00 25.00
❑ 13 Bob Vogel RC 2.00 1.00
❑ 14 Colts Play/Don Shula 20.00 12.00
❑ 15 Chicago Bears 3.00 1.50
❑ 16 Jon Arnett 2.00 1.00
❑ 17 Doug Atkins 5.00 2.50
❑ 18 Rudy Bukich RC 3.00 1.50
❑ 19 Mike Ditka 40.00 25.00
❑ 20 Dick Evey 2.00 1.00
❑ 21 Joe Fortunato 2.00 1.00
❑ 22 Bobby Joe Green RC 2.00 1.00
❑ 23 Johnny Morris 2.00 1.00
❑ 24 Mike Pyle 2.00 1.00
❑ 25 Roosevelt Taylor 3.00 1.50
❑ 26 Bill Wade 3.00 1.50
❑ 27 Bob Wetoska 2.00 1.00
❑ 28 Bears Play/George Halas 8.00 4.00
❑ 29 Cleveland Browns 3.00 1.50
❑ 30 Walter Beach 2.00 1.00
❑ 31 Jim Brown 80.00 50.00
❑ 32 Gary Collins 3.00 1.50
❑ 33 Bill Glass 2.00 1.00
❑ 34 Ernie Green 2.00 1.00
❑ 35 Jim Houston RC 2.00 1.00
❑ 36 Dick Modzelewski 2.00 1.00
❑ 37 Bernie Parrish 2.00 1.00
❑ 38 Walter Roberts 2.00 1.00
❑ 39 Frank Ryan 3.00 1.50
❑ 40 Dick Schafrath 2.00 1.00
❑ 41 Paul Warfield RC 90.00 50.00
❑ 42 Cleveland Browns 2.00 1.00
❑ 43 Dallas Cowboys 3.00 1.50
❑ 44 Frank Clarke 3.00 1.50
❑ 45 Mike Connelly 2.00 1.00
❑ 46 Buddy Dial 2.00 1.00
❑ 47 Bob Lilly 35.00 20.00
❑ 48 Tony Liscio RC 2.00 1.00
❑ 49 Tommy McDonald 5.00 2.50
❑ 50 Don Meredith 25.00 15.00
❑ 51 Pettis Norman 2.00 1.00
❑ 52 Don Perkins 4.00 2.00
❑ 53 Mel Renfro RC 40.00 25.00
❑ 54 Jim Ridlon 2.00 1.00
❑ 55 Jerry Tubbs 2.00 1.00
❑ 56 Cowboys Play/T.Landry 15.00 7.50
❑ 57 Detroit Lions 3.00 1.50
❑ 58 Terry Barr 2.00 1.00
❑ 59 Roger Brown 2.00 1.00
❑ 60 Gail Cogdill 2.00 1.00
❑ 61 Jim Gibbons 2.00 1.00
❑ 62 John Gordy 2.00 1.00
❑ 63 Yale Lary 4.00 2.00
❑ 64 Dick LeBeau RC 3.00 1.50
❑ 65 Earl Morrall 3.00 1.50
❑ 66 Nick Pietrosante 2.00 1.00
❑ 67 Pat Studstill 2.00 1.00
❑ 68 Wayne Walker 3.00 1.50
❑ 69 Tom Watkins 2.00 1.00
❑ 70 Detroit Lions 3.00 1.50
❑ 71 Green Bay Packers 6.00 3.00
❑ 72 Herb Adderley 8.00 4.00
❑ 73 Willie Davis DE 8.00 4.00
❑ 74 Boyd Dowler 4.00 2.00
❑ 75 Forrest Gregg 5.00 2.50
❑ 76 Paul Hornung 35.00 20.00
❑ 77 Hank Jordan 5.00 2.50
❑ 78 Tom Moore 3.00 1.50
❑ 79 Ray Nitschke 20.00 12.00
❑ 80 Elijah Pitts RC 8.00 4.00
❑ 81 Bart Starr 50.00 30.00
❑ 82 Jim Taylor 20.00 12.00
❑ 83 Willie Wood 6.00 3.00
❑ 84 Packers Play/Lombardi 20.00 12.00
❑ 85 Los Angeles Rams 3.00 1.50
❑ 86 Dick Bass 3.00 1.50
❑ 87 Roman Gabriel 5.00 2.50
❑ 88 Roosevelt Grier 4.00 2.00
❑ 89 Deacon Jones 10.00 5.00
❑ 90 Lamar Lundy RC 4.00 2.00
❑ 91 Marlin McKeever 2.00 1.00
❑ 92 Ed Meador 2.00 1.00
❑ 93 Bill Munson RC 4.00 2.00
❑ 94 Merlin Olsen 15.00 7.50
❑ 95 Bobby Smith 2.00 1.00
❑ 96 Frank Varrichione 2.00 1.00
❑ 97 Ben Wilson 2.00 1.00

❑ 98 Los Angeles Rams 2.00 1.00
❑ 99 Minnesota Vikings 3.00 1.50
❑ 100 Grady Alderman 2.00 1.00
❑ 101 Hal Bedsole RC 2.00 1.00
❑ 102 Bill Brown 3.00 1.50
❑ 103 Bill Butler 2.00 1.00
❑ 104 Fred Cox RC 3.00 1.50
❑ 105 Carl Eller RC 30.00 18.00
❑ 106 Paul Flatley 2.00 1.00
❑ 107 Jim Marshall 6.00 3.00
❑ 108 Tommy Mason 2.00 1.00
❑ 109 George Rose 2.00 1.00
❑ 110 Fran Tarkenton 25.00 15.00
❑ 111 Mick Tingelhoff 3.00 1.50
❑ 112 Vikings Play/Van Brock. 4.00 2.00
❑ 113 New York Giants 3.00 1.50
❑ 114 Erich Barnes 2.00 1.00
❑ 115 Roosevelt Brown 4.00 2.00
❑ 116 Clarence Childs 2.00 1.00
❑ 117 Jerry Hillebrand 2.00 1.00
❑ 118 Greg Larson RC 2.00 1.00
❑ 119 Dick Lynch 2.00 1.00
❑ 120 Joe Morrison RC 4.00 2.00
❑ 121 Lou Slaby 2.00 1.00
❑ 122 Aaron Thomas RC 2.00 1.00
❑ 123 Steve Thurlow 2.00 1.00
❑ 124 Ernie Wheelwright RC 2.00 1.00
❑ 125 Gary Wood RC 3.00 1.50
❑ 126 New York Giants 2.00 1.00
❑ 127 Philadelphia Eagles 3.00 1.50
❑ 128 Sam Baker 2.00 1.00
❑ 129 Maxie Baughan 2.00 1.00
❑ 130 Timmy Brown 3.00 1.50
❑ 131 Jack Concannon RC 2.00 1.00
❑ 132 Irv Cross 3.00 1.50
❑ 133 Earl Gros 2.00 1.00
❑ 134 Dave Lloyd 2.00 1.00
❑ 135 Floyd Peters RC 2.00 1.00
❑ 136 Nate Ramsey 2.00 1.00
❑ 137 Pete Retzlaff 3.00 1.50
❑ 138 Jim Ringo 4.00 2.00
❑ 139 Norm Snead 4.00 2.00
❑ 140 Philadelphia Eagles 2.00 1.00
❑ 141 Pittsburgh Steelers 3.00 1.50
❑ 142 John Baker 2.00 1.00
❑ 143 Gary Ballman 2.00 1.00
❑ 144 Charley Bradshaw 2.00 1.00
❑ 145 Ed Brown 2.00 1.00
❑ 146 Dick Haley 2.00 1.00
❑ 147 John Henry Johnson 4.00 2.00
❑ 148 Brady Keys 2.00 1.00
❑ 149 Ray Lemek 2.00 1.00
❑ 150 Ben McGee 2.00 1.00
❑ 151 Clarence Peaks 2.00 1.00
❑ 152 Myron Pottios 2.00 1.00
❑ 153 Clendon Thomas 2.00 1.00
❑ 154 Pittsburgh Steelers 2.00 1.00
❑ 155 St. Louis Cardinals 3.00 1.50
❑ 156 Jim Bakken RC 3.00 1.50
❑ 157 Joe Childress 2.00 1.00
❑ 158 Bobby Joe Conrad 3.00 1.50
❑ 159 Bob DeMarco 2.00 1.00
❑ 160 Pat Fischer RC 4.00 2.00
❑ 161 Irv Goode 2.00 1.00
❑ 162 Ken Gray 2.00 1.00
❑ 163 Charlie Johnson 3.00 1.50
❑ 164 Bill Koman 2.00 1.00
❑ 165 Dale Meinert 2.00 1.00
❑ 166 Jerry Stovall RC 3.00 1.50
❑ 167 Abe Woodson 2.00 1.00
❑ 168 St. Louis Cardinals 2.00 1.00
❑ 169 San Francisco 49ers 3.00 1.50
❑ 170 Kermit Alexander 2.00 1.00
❑ 171 John Brodie 10.00 5.00
❑ 172 Bernie Casey 3.00 1.50
❑ 173 John David Crow 3.00 1.50
❑ 174 Tommy Davis 2.00 1.00
❑ 175 Matt Hazeltine 2.00 1.00
❑ 176 Jim Johnson 4.00 2.00
❑ 177 Charlie Krueger RC 2.00 1.00
❑ 178 Roland Lakes 2.00 1.00
❑ 179 George Mira RC 3.00 1.50
❑ 180 Dave Parks RC 3.00 1.50
❑ 181 John Thomas RC 2.00 1.00
❑ 182 49ers Play/Christiansen 2.00 1.00
❑ 183 Washington Redskins 3.00 1.50
❑ 184 Pervis Atkins 2.00 1.00
❑ 185 Preston Carpenter 2.00 1.00
❑ 186 Angelo Coia 2.00 1.00
❑ 187 Sam Huff 6.00 3.00
❑ 188 Sonny Jurgensen 15.00 7.50
❑ 189 Paul Krause RC 20.00 12.00
❑ 190 Jim Martin 2.00 1.00
❑ 191 Bobby Mitchell 5.00 2.50
❑ 192 John Nisby 2.00 1.00
❑ 193 John Paluck 2.00 1.00
❑ 194 Vince Promuto 2.00 1.00
❑ 195 Charley Taylor RC 50.00 30.00
❑ 196 Washington Redskins 2.00 1.00
❑ 197 Checklist 1 ! 30.00 15.00
❑ 198 Checklist 2 UER ! 50.00 25.00

1966 Philadelphia

❑ COMPLETE SET (198) 900.00 600.00
❑ WRAPPER (5-CENT) 20.00 10.00
❑ 1 Falcons Insignia ! 12.00 6.00
❑ 2 Larry Benz 2.00 1.00
❑ 3 Dennis Claridge 2.00 1.00
❑ 4 Perry Lee Dunn 2.00 1.00
❑ 5 Dan Grimm 2.00 1.00
❑ 6 Alex Hawkins 2.00 1.00
❑ 7 Ralph Heck 2.00 1.00
❑ 8 Frank Lasky 2.00 1.00
❑ 9 Guy Reese 2.00 1.00
❑ 10 Bob Richards 2.00 1.00
❑ 11 Ron Smith RC 2.00 1.00
❑ 12 Ernie Wheelwright 2.00 1.00
❑ 13 Falcons Roster 3.00 1.50
❑ 14 Baltimore Colts 3.00 1.50
❑ 15 Raymond Berry 8.00 4.00
❑ 16 Bob Boyd DB 2.00 1.00
❑ 17 Jerry Logan 2.00 1.00
❑ 18 John Mackey 6.00 3.00
❑ 19 Tom Matte 4.00 2.00
❑ 20 Lou Michaels 2.00 1.00
❑ 21 Lenny Moore 8.00 4.00
❑ 22 Jimmy Orr 3.00 1.50
❑ 23 Jim Parker 4.00 2.00
❑ 24 Johnny Unitas 40.00 25.00
❑ 25 Bob Vogel 2.00 1.00
❑ 26 Colts Play/Moore/Parker 4.00 2.00
❑ 27 Chicago Bears 3.00 1.50
❑ 28 Doug Atkins 4.00 2.00
❑ 29 Rudy Bukich 2.00 1.00
❑ 30 Ronnie Bull 2.00 1.00
❑ 31 Dick Butkus RC ! 250.00 150.00
❑ 32 Mike Ditka 35.00 20.00
❑ 33 Joe Fortunato 2.00 1.00
❑ 34 Bobby Joe Green 2.00 1.00
❑ 35 Roger LeClerc 2.00 1.00
❑ 36 Johnny Morris 2.00 1.00
❑ 37 Mike Pyle 2.00 1.00
❑ 38 Gale Sayers RC ! 225.00 125.00
❑ 39 Bears Play/Gale Sayers 35.00 20.00
❑ 40 Cleveland Browns 3.00 1.50
❑ 41 Jim Brown 80.00 50.00
❑ 42 Gary Collins 3.00 1.50
❑ 43 Ross Fichtner 2.00 1.00
❑ 44 Ernie Green 2.00 1.00
❑ 45 Gene Hickerson RC 15.00 7.50
❑ 46 Jim Houston 2.00 1.00
❑ 47 John Morrow 2.00 1.00
❑ 48 Walter Roberts 2.00 1.00
❑ 49 Frank Ryan 3.00 1.50
❑ 50 Dick Schafrath 2.00 1.00
❑ 51 Paul Wiggin RC 2.00 1.00
❑ 52 Cleveland Browns 2.00 1.00
❑ 53 Dallas Cowboys 3.00 1.50
❑ 54 George Andrie RC UER 3.00 1.50
❑ 55 Frank Clarke 3.00 1.50
❑ 56 Mike Connelly 2.00 1.00
❑ 57 Cornell Green 4.00 2.00
❑ 58 Bob Hayes RC 50.00 30.00
❑ 59 Chuck Howley RC 18.00 10.00
❑ 60 Bob Lilly 20.00 12.00
❑ 61 Don Meredith 25.00 15.00
❑ 62 Don Perkins 3.00 1.50
❑ 63 Mel Renfro 15.00 7.50
❑ 64 Danny Villanueva 2.00 1.00
❑ 65 Dallas Cowboys 2.00 1.00
❑ 66 Detroit Lions 3.00 1.50
❑ 67 Roger Brown 2.00 1.00
❑ 68 John Gordy 2.00 1.00
❑ 69 Alex Karras 10.00 5.00
❑ 70 Dick LeBeau 2.00 1.00
❑ 71 Amos Marsh 2.00 1.00
❑ 72 Milt Plum 3.00 1.50
❑ 73 Bobby Smith 2.00 1.00
❑ 74 Wayne Rasmussen 2.00 1.00
❑ 75 Pat Studstill 2.00 1.00
❑ 76 Wayne Walker 2.00 1.00
❑ 77 Tom Watkins 2.00 1.00
❑ 78 Detroit Lions 2.00 1.00
❑ 79 Green Bay Packers 6.00 3.00
❑ 80 Herb Adderley 6.00 3.00
❑ 81 Lee Roy Caffey RC 4.00 2.00
❑ 82 Don Chandler 3.00 1.50
❑ 83 Willie Davis DE 6.00 3.00
❑ 84 Boyd Dowler 4.00 2.00
❑ 85 Forrest Gregg 4.00 2.00
❑ 86 Tom Moore 3.00 1.50
❑ 87 Ray Nitschke 15.00 7.50
❑ 88 Bart Starr 50.00 30.00
❑ 89 Jim Taylor 20.00 12.00
❑ 90 Willie Wood 6.00 3.00
❑ 91 Green Bay Packers 2.00 1.00
❑ 92 Los Angeles Rams 3.00 1.50
❑ 93 Willie Brown WR 2.00 1.00
❑ 94 Roman Gabriel/D.Bass 4.00 2.00
❑ 95 Bruce Gossett RC 3.00 1.50
❑ 96 Deacon Jones 6.00 3.00
❑ 97 Tommy McDonald 5.00 2.50
❑ 98 Marlin McKeever 2.00 1.00
❑ 99 Aaron Martin 2.00 1.00
❑ 100 Ed Meador 2.00 1.00
❑ 101 Bill Munson 3.00 1.50
❑ 102 Merlin Olsen 8.00 4.00
❑ 103 Jim Stiger 2.00 1.00
❑ 104 Rams Play/W.Brown 3.00 1.50
❑ 105 Minnesota Vikings 3.00 1.50
❑ 106 Grady Alderman 2.00 1.00
❑ 107 Bill Brown 3.00 1.50
❑ 108 Fred Cox 2.00 1.00
❑ 109 Paul Flatley 2.00 1.00
❑ 110 Rip Hawkins 2.00 1.00
❑ 111 Tommy Mason 2.00 1.00
❑ 112 Ed Sharockman 2.00 1.00
❑ 113 Gordon Smith 2.00 1.00
❑ 114 Fran Tarkenton 30.00 15.00
❑ 115 Mick Tingelhoff 3.00 1.50
❑ 116 Bobby Walden RC**/C 2.00 1.00
❑ 117 Minnesota Vikings 2.00 1.00
❑ 118 New York Giants 3.00 1.50
❑ 119 Roosevelt Brown 4.00 2.00
❑ 120 Henry Carr RC 3.00 1.50
❑ 121 Clarence Childs 2.00 1.00
❑ 122 Tucker Frederickson RC 3.00 1.50
❑ 123 Jerry Hillebrand 2.00 1.00
❑ 124 Greg Larson 2.00 1.00
❑ 125 Spider Lockhart RC 3.00 1.50
❑ 126 Dick Lynch 2.00 1.00
❑ 127 Earl Morrall/Scholtz 3.00 1.50
❑ 128 Joe Morrison 2.00 1.00
❑ 129 Steve Thurlow 2.00 1.00
❑ 130 New York Giants 2.00 1.00
❑ 131 Philadelphia Eagles 3.00 1.50
❑ 132 Sam Baker 2.00 1.00
❑ 133 Maxie Baughan 2.00 1.00
❑ 134 Bob Brown OT RC 12.00 6.00
❑ 135 Timmy Brown 3.00 1.50
❑ 136 Irv Cross 3.00 1.50
❑ 137 Earl Gros 2.00 1.00
❑ 138 Ray Poage 2.00 1.00

❑ 139 Nate Ramsey	2.00	1.00
❑ 140 Pete Retzlaff	3.00	1.50
❑ 141 Jim Ringo	4.00	2.00
❑ 142 Norm Snead	4.00	2.00
❑ 143 Philadelphia Eagles	2.00	1.00
❑ 144 Pittsburgh Steelers	3.00	1.50
❑ 145 Gary Ballman	2.00	1.00
❑ 146 Charley Bradshaw	2.00	1.00
❑ 147 Jim Butler	2.00	1.00
❑ 148 Mike Clark	2.00	1.00
❑ 149 Dick Hoak RC	2.00	1.00
❑ 150 Roy Jefferson RC	3.00	1.50
❑ 151 Frank Lambert	2.00	1.00
❑ 152 Mike Lind	2.00	1.00
❑ 153 Bill Nelsen RC	4.00	2.00
❑ 154 Clarence Peaks	2.00	1.00
❑ 155 Clendon Thomas	2.00	1.00
❑ 156 Pittsburgh Steelers	2.00	1.00
❑ 157 St. Louis Cardinals	3.00	1.50
❑ 158 Jim Bakken	2.00	1.00
❑ 159 Bobby Joe Conrad	3.00	1.50
❑ 160 Willis Crenshaw RC	2.00	1.00
❑ 161 Bob DeMarco	2.00	1.00
❑ 162 Pat Fischer	3.00	1.50
❑ 163 Charlie Johnson	3.00	1.50
❑ 164 Dale Meinert	2.00	1.00
❑ 165 Sonny Randle	2.00	1.00
❑ 166 Sam Silas RC	2.00	1.00
❑ 167 Bill Triplett	2.00	1.00
❑ 168 Larry Wilson	4.00	2.00
❑ 169 St. Louis Cardinals	2.00	1.00
❑ 170 San Francisco 49ers	3.00	1.50
❑ 171 Kermit Alexander	2.00	1.00
❑ 172 Bruce Bosley	2.00	1.00
❑ 173 John Brodie	6.00	3.00
❑ 174 Bernie Casey	3.00	1.50
❑ 175 John David Crow	4.00	2.00
❑ 176 Tommy Davis	2.00	1.00
❑ 177 Jim Johnson	4.00	2.00
❑ 178 Gary Lewis RC	2.00	1.00
❑ 179 Dave Parks	2.00	1.00
❑ 180 Walter Rock RC	3.00	1.50
❑ 181 Ken Willard RC	4.00	2.00
❑ 182 San Francisco 49ers	2.00	1.00
❑ 183 Washington Redskins	3.00	1.50
❑ 184 Rickie Harris	2.00	1.00
❑ 185 Sonny Jurgensen	8.00	4.00
❑ 186 Paul Krause	6.00	3.00
❑ 187 Bobby Mitchell	6.00	3.00
❑ 188 Vince Promuto	2.00	1.00
❑ 189 Pat Richter RC	2.00	1.00
❑ 190 Joe Rutgens	2.00	1.00
❑ 191 Johnny Sample	2.00	1.00
❑ 192 Lonnie Sanders	2.00	1.00
❑ 193 Jim Steffen	2.00	1.00
❑ 194 Charley Taylor	15.00	7.50
❑ 195 Washington Redskins	2.00	1.00
❑ 196 Referee Signals	3.00	1.50
❑ 197 Checklist 1 !	25.00	12.50
❑ 198 Checklist 2 UER !	50.00	25.00

1967 Philadelphia

❑ COMPLETE SET (198)	650.00	425.00
❑ WRAPPER (5-CENT)	20.00	10.00
❑ 1 Falcons Team !	10.00	5.00
❑ 2 Junior Coffey RC	3.00	1.50
❑ 3 Alex Hawkins	2.00	1.00
❑ 4 Randy Johnson RC	3.00	1.50
❑ 5 Lou Kirouac	2.00	1.00
❑ 6 Billy Martin RC	2.00	1.00
❑ 7 Tommy Nobis RC	20.00	10.00
❑ 8 Jerry Richardson RC	4.00	2.00
❑ 9 Marion Rushing	2.00	1.00
❑ 10 Ron Smith	2.00	1.00
❑ 11 Ernie Wheelwright UER	2.00	1.00
❑ 12 Atlanta Falcons	2.00	1.00
❑ 13 Baltimore Colts	3.00	1.50
❑ 14 Raymond Berry UER	7.00	3.50
❑ 15 Bob Boyd DB	2.00	1.00
❑ 16 Ordell Braase	2.00	1.00
❑ 17 Alvin Haymond RC	2.00	1.00
❑ 18 Tony Lorick	2.00	1.00
❑ 19 Lenny Lyles	2.00	1.00
❑ 20 John Mackey	5.00	2.50
❑ 21 Tom Matte	3.00	1.50
❑ 22 Lou Michaels	2.00	1.00
❑ 23 Johnny Unitas	40.00	25.00
❑ 24 Baltimore Colts	2.00	1.00
❑ 25 Chicago Bears	3.00	1.50
❑ 26 Rudy Bukich UER	2.00	1.00
❑ 27 Ronnie Bull	2.00	1.00
❑ 28 Dick Butkus	75.00	45.00
❑ 29 Mike Ditka	30.00	18.00
❑ 30 Dick Gordon RC	3.00	1.50
❑ 31 Roger LeClerc	2.00	1.00
❑ 32 Bennie McRae	2.00	1.00
❑ 33 Richie Petitbon	2.00	1.00
❑ 34 Mike Pyle	2.00	1.00
❑ 35 Gale Sayers	75.00	45.00
❑ 36 Chicago Bears	2.00	1.00
❑ 37 Cleveland Browns	3.00	1.50
❑ 38 Johnny Brewer	2.00	1.00
❑ 39 Gary Collins	3.00	1.50
❑ 40 Ross Fichtner	2.00	1.00
❑ 41 Ernie Green	2.00	1.00
❑ 42 Gene Hickerson	5.00	2.50
❑ 43 Leroy Kelly RC	40.00	25.00
❑ 44 Frank Ryan	3.00	1.50
❑ 45 Dick Schafrath	2.00	1.00
❑ 46 Paul Warfield	18.00	10.00
❑ 47 John Wooten	2.00	1.00
❑ 48 Cleveland Browns	2.00	1.00
❑ 49 Dallas Cowboys	3.00	1.50
❑ 50 George Andrie	2.00	1.00
❑ 51 Cornell Green	3.00	1.50
❑ 52 Bob Hayes	20.00	10.00
❑ 53 Chuck Howley	4.00	2.00
❑ 54 Lee Roy Jordan RC	20.00	12.00
❑ 55 Bob Lilly	15.00	7.50
❑ 56 Dave Manders RC	2.00	1.00
❑ 57 Don Meredith	25.00	15.00
❑ 58 Dan Reeves RC	30.00	18.00
❑ 59 Mel Renfro	6.00	3.00
❑ 60 Dallas Cowboys	3.00	1.50
❑ 61 Detroit Lions	3.00	1.50
❑ 62 Roger Brown	3.00	1.50
❑ 63 Gail Cogdill	2.00	1.00
❑ 64 John Gordy	2.00	1.00
❑ 65 Ron Kramer	2.00	1.00
❑ 66 Dick LeBeau	2.00	1.00
❑ 67 Mike Lucci RC	4.00	2.00
❑ 68 Amos Marsh	2.00	1.00
❑ 69 Tom Nowatzke	2.00	1.00
❑ 70 Pat Studstill	2.00	1.00
❑ 71 Karl Sweetan	2.00	1.00
❑ 72 Detroit Lions	2.00	1.00
❑ 73 Green Bay Packers	5.00	2.50
❑ 74 Herb Adderley UER	6.00	3.00
❑ 75 Lee Roy Caffey	3.00	1.50
❑ 76 Willie Davis DE	5.00	2.50
❑ 77 Forrest Gregg	4.00	2.00
❑ 78 Hank Jordan	4.00	2.00
❑ 79 Ray Nitschke	12.00	6.00
❑ 80 Dave Robinson RC	6.00	3.00
❑ 81 Bob Skoronski	3.00	1.50
❑ 82 Bart Starr	50.00	30.00
❑ 83 Willie Wood	5.00	2.50
❑ 84 Green Bay Packers	3.00	1.50
❑ 85 Los Angeles Rams	3.00	1.50
❑ 86 Dick Bass	3.00	1.50
❑ 87 Maxie Baughan	2.00	1.00
❑ 88 Roman Gabriel	4.00	2.00
❑ 89 Bruce Gossett	2.00	1.00
❑ 90 Deacon Jones	5.00	2.50
❑ 91 Tommy McDonald	5.00	2.50
❑ 92 Marlin McKeever	2.00	1.00
❑ 93 Tom Moore	2.00	1.00
❑ 94 Merlin Olsen	6.00	3.00
❑ 95 Clancy Williams	2.00	1.00
❑ 96 Los Angeles Rams	2.00	1.00
❑ 97 Minnesota Vikings	3.00	1.50
❑ 98 Grady Alderman	2.00	1.00
❑ 99 Bill Brown	3.00	1.50
❑ 100 Fred Cox	2.00	1.00
❑ 101 Paul Flatley	2.00	1.00
❑ 102 Dale Hackbart RC	2.00	1.00
❑ 103 Jim Marshall	4.00	2.00
❑ 104 Tommy Mason	2.00	1.00
❑ 105 Milt Sunde RC	2.00	1.00
❑ 106 Fran Tarkenton	20.00	10.00
❑ 107 Mick Tingelhoff	3.00	1.50
❑ 108 Minnesota Vikings	2.00	1.00
❑ 109 New York Giants	3.00	1.50
❑ 110 Henry Carr	2.00	1.00
❑ 111 Clarence Childs	2.00	1.00
❑ 112 Allen Jacobs	2.00	1.00
❑ 113 Homer Jones RC	3.00	1.50
❑ 114 Tom Kennedy	2.00	1.00
❑ 115 Spider Lockhart	2.00	1.00
❑ 116 Joe Morrison	2.00	1.00
❑ 117 Francis Peay	2.00	1.00
❑ 118 Jeff Smith LB	2.00	1.00
❑ 119 Aaron Thomas	2.00	1.00
❑ 120 New York Giants	2.00	1.00
❑ 121 Saints Insignia	3.00	1.50
❑ 122 Charley Bradshaw	2.00	1.00
❑ 123 Paul Hornung	25.00	12.50
❑ 124 Elbert Kimbrough	2.00	1.00
❑ 125 Earl Leggett RC	2.00	1.00
❑ 126 Obert Logan	2.00	1.00
❑ 127 Riley Mattson	2.00	1.00
❑ 128 John Morrow	2.00	1.00
❑ 129 Bob Scholtz	2.00	1.00
❑ 130 Dave Whitsell RC	2.00	1.00
❑ 131 Gary Wood	2.00	1.00
❑ 132 Saints Roster UER 121	3.00	1.50
❑ 133 Philadelphia Eagles	3.00	1.50
❑ 134 Sam Baker	2.00	1.00
❑ 135 Bob Brown OT	5.00	2.00
❑ 136 Timmy Brown	3.00	1.50
❑ 137 Earl Gros	2.00	1.00
❑ 138 Dave Lloyd	2.00	1.00
❑ 139 Floyd Peters	2.00	1.00
❑ 140 Pete Retzlaff	3.00	1.50
❑ 141 Joe Scarpati	2.00	1.00
❑ 142 Norm Snead	3.00	1.50
❑ 143 Jim Skaggs	2.00	1.00
❑ 144 Philadelphia Eagles	2.00	1.00
❑ 145 Pittsburgh Steelers	3.00	1.50
❑ 146 Bill Asbury	2.00	1.00
❑ 147 John Baker	2.00	1.00
❑ 148 Gary Ballman	2.00	1.00
❑ 149 Mike Clark	2.00	1.00
❑ 150 Riley Gunnels	2.00	1.00
❑ 151 John Hilton	2.00	1.00
❑ 152 Roy Jefferson	3.00	1.50
❑ 153 Brady Keys	2.00	1.00
❑ 154 Ben McGee	2.00	1.00
❑ 155 Bill Nelsen	3.00	1.50
❑ 156 Pittsburgh Steelers	2.00	1.00
❑ 157 St. Louis Cardinals	3.00	1.50
❑ 158 Jim Bakken	2.00	1.00
❑ 159 Bobby Joe Conrad	3.00	1.50
❑ 160 Ken Gray	2.00	1.00
❑ 161 Charlie Johnson	3.00	1.50
❑ 162 Joe Robb	2.00	1.00
❑ 163 Johnny Roland RC	3.00	1.50
❑ 164 Roy Shivers	2.00	1.00
❑ 165 Jackie Smith RC	15.00	7.50
❑ 166 Jerry Stovall	2.00	1.00
❑ 167 Larry Wilson	4.00	2.00
❑ 168 St. Louis Cardinals	2.00	1.00
❑ 169 San Francisco 49ers	3.00	1.50
❑ 170 Kermit Alexander	2.00	1.00
❑ 171 Bruce Bosley	2.00	1.00
❑ 172 John Brodie	6.00	3.00
❑ 173 Bernie Casey	3.00	1.50
❑ 174 Tommy Davis	2.00	1.00
❑ 175 Howard Mudd	2.00	1.00
❑ 176 Dave Parks	2.00	1.00
❑ 177 John Thomas	2.00	1.00
❑ 178 Dave Wilcox RC	10.00	5.00
❑ 179 Ken Willard	3.00	1.50

❑ 180 San Francisco 49ers 2.00 1.00
❑ 181 Washington Redskins 3.00 1.50
❑ 182 Charlie Gogolak RC 2.00 1.00
❑ 183 Chris Hanburger RC 5.00 2.50
❑ 184 Len Hauss RC 3.00 1.50
❑ 185 Sonny Jurgensen 7.00 3.50
❑ 186 Bobby Mitchell 5.00 2.50
❑ 187 Brig Owens 2.00 1.00
❑ 188 Jim Shorter 2.00 1.00
❑ 189 Jerry Smith RC 3.00 1.50
❑ 190 Charley Taylor 8.00 4.00
❑ 191 A.D. Whitfield 2.00 1.00
❑ 192 Washington Redskins 2.00 1.00
❑ 193 Browns Play/Leroy Kelly 6.00 3.00
❑ 194 New York Giants PC 2.00 1.00
❑ 195 Atlanta Falcons PC 2.00 1.00
❑ 196 Referee Signals 3.00 1.50
❑ 197 Checklist 1 ! 20.00 12.00
❑ 198 Checklist 2 UER ! 40.00 20.00

1991 Pinnacle

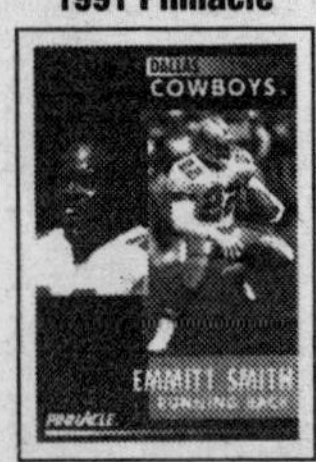

❑ COMPLETE SET (415) 20.00 7.50
❑ 1 Warren Moon .40 .15
❑ 2 Morten Andersen .10 .02
❑ 3 Rohn Stark .10 .02
❑ 4 Mark Bortz .10 .02
❑ 5 Mark Higgs RC .10 .02
❑ 6 Troy Aikman 2.00 .75
❑ 7 John Elway 3.00 1.25
❑ 8 Neal Anderson .20 .07
❑ 9 Chris Doleman .10 .02
❑ 10 Jay Schroeder .10 .02
❑ 11 Sterling Sharpe .40 .15
❑ 12 Steve DeBerg .10 .02
❑ 13 Ronnie Lott .20 .07
❑ 14 Sean Landeta .10 .02
❑ 15 Jim Everett .20 .07
❑ 16 Jim Breech .10 .02
❑ 17 Barry Foster .20 .07
❑ 18 Mike Merriweather .10 .02
❑ 19 Eric Metcalf .20 .07
❑ 20 Mark Carrier DB .20 .07
❑ 21 James Brooks .20 .07
❑ 22 Nate Odomes .10 .02
❑ 23 Rodney Hampton .40 .15
❑ 24 Chris Miller .20 .07
❑ 25 Roger Craig .20 .07
❑ 26 Louis Oliver .10 .02
❑ 27 Allen Pinkett .10 .02
❑ 28 Bubby Brister .10 .02
❑ 29 Reyna Thompson .10 .02
❑ 30 Issiac Holt .10 .02
❑ 31 Steve Broussard .10 .02
❑ 32 Christian Okoye .10 .02
❑ 33 Dave Meggett .20 .07
❑ 34 Andre Reed .20 .07
❑ 35 Shane Conlan .10 .02
❑ 36 Eric Ball .10 .02
❑ 37 Johnny Bailey .10 .02
❑ 38 Don Majkowski .10 .02
❑ 39 Gerald Williams .10 .02
❑ 40 Kevin Mack .10 .02
❑ 41 Jeff Herrod .10 .02
❑ 42 Emmitt Smith 6.00 2.50
❑ 43 Wendell Davis .10 .02
❑ 44 Lorenzo White .10 .02
❑ 45 Andre Rison .20 .07
❑ 46 Jerry Gray .10 .02
❑ 47 Dennis Smith .10 .02
❑ 48 Gaston Green .10 .02
❑ 49 Dermontti Dawson .10 .02
❑ 50 Jeff Hostetler .20 .07
❑ 51 Nick Lowery .10 .02
❑ 52 Merril Hoge .10 .02
❑ 53 Bobby Hebert .10 .02
❑ 54 Scott Case .10 .02
❑ 55 Jack Del Rio .20 .07
❑ 56 Cornelius Bennett .20 .07
❑ 57 Tony Mandarich .10 .02
❑ 58 Bill Brooks .10 .02
❑ 59 Jessie Tuggle .10 .02
❑ 60 Hugh Millen RC .10 .02
❑ 61 Tony Bennett .20 .07
❑ 62 Cris Dishman RC .10 .02
❑ 63 Darryl Henley RC .10 .02
❑ 64 Duane Bickett .10 .02
❑ 65 Jay Hilgenberg .10 .02
❑ 66 Joe Montana 3.00 1.25
❑ 67 Bill Fralic .10 .02
❑ 68 Sam Mills .10 .02
❑ 69 Bruce Armstrong .10 .02
❑ 70 Dan Marino 3.00 1.25
❑ 71 Jim Lachey .10 .02
❑ 72 Rod Woodson .40 .15
❑ 73 Simon Fletcher .10 .02
❑ 74 Bruce Matthews .20 .07
❑ 75 Howie Long .40 .15
❑ 76 John Friesz .40 .15
❑ 77 Karl Mecklenburg .10 .02
❑ 78 John L. Williams UER .10 .02
❑ 79 Rob Burnett RC .20 .07
❑ 80 Anthony Carter .20 .07
❑ 81 Henry Ellard .20 .07
❑ 82 Don Beebe .10 .02
❑ 83 Louis Lipps .10 .02
❑ 84 Greg McMurtry .10 .02
❑ 85 Will Wolford .10 .02
❑ 86 Eric Green .10 .02
❑ 87 Irving Fryar .20 .07
❑ 88 John Offerdahl .10 .02
❑ 89 John Alt .10 .02
❑ 90 Tom Tupa .10 .02
❑ 91 Don Mosebar .10 .02
❑ 92 Jeff George .50 .20
❑ 93 Vinny Testaverde .20 .07
❑ 94 Greg Townsend .10 .02
❑ 95 Derrick Fenner .10 .02
❑ 96 Brian Mitchell .20 .07
❑ 97 Herschel Walker .20 .07
❑ 98 Ricky Proehl .10 .02
❑ 99 Mark Clayton .20 .07
❑ 100 Derrick Thomas .40 .15
❑ 101 Jim Harbaugh .40 .15
❑ 102 Barry Word .10 .02
❑ 103 Jerry Rice 2.00 .75
❑ 104 Keith Byars .10 .02
❑ 105 Marion Butts .20 .07
❑ 106 Rich Moran .10 .02
❑ 107 Thurman Thomas .40 .15
❑ 108 Stephone Paige .10 .02
❑ 109 D.J. Johnson .10 .02
❑ 110 William Perry .20 .07
❑ 111 Haywood Jeffires .20 .07
❑ 112 Rodney Peete .20 .07
❑ 113 Andy Heck .10 .02
❑ 114 Kevin Ross .10 .02
❑ 115 Michael Carter .10 .02
❑ 116 Tim McKyer .10 .02
❑ 117 Kenneth Davis .10 .02
❑ 118 Richmond Webb .10 .02
❑ 119 Rich Camarillo .10 .02
❑ 120 James Francis .10 .02
❑ 121 Craig Heyward .20 .07
❑ 122 Hardy Nickerson .20 .07
❑ 123 Michael Brooks .10 .02
❑ 124 Fred Barnett .40 .15
❑ 125 Cris Carter 1.00 .40
❑ 126 Brian Jordan .20 .07
❑ 127 Pat Leahy .10 .02
❑ 128 Kevin Greene .20 .07
❑ 129 Trace Armstrong .10 .02
❑ 130 Eugene Lockhart .10 .02
❑ 131 Albert Lewis .10 .02
❑ 132 Ernie Jones .10 .02
❑ 133 Eric Martin .10 .02
❑ 134 Anthony Thompson .10 .02
❑ 135 Tim Krumrie .10 .02
❑ 136 James Lofton .20 .07
❑ 137 John Taylor .20 .07
❑ 138 Jeff Cross .10 .02
❑ 139 Tommy Kane .10 .02
❑ 140 Robb Thomas .10 .02
❑ 141 Gary Anderson K .10 .02
❑ 142 Mark Murphy .10 .02
❑ 143 Rickey Jackson .10 .02
❑ 144 Ken O'Brien .10 .02
❑ 145 Ernest Givins .20 .07
❑ 146 Jessie Hester .10 .02
❑ 147 Deion Sanders .75 .30
❑ 148 Keith Henderson RC .10 .02
❑ 149 Chris Singleton .10 .02
❑ 150 Rod Bernstine .10 .02
❑ 151 Quinn Early .20 .07
❑ 152 Boomer Esiason .20 .07
❑ 153 Mike Gann .10 .02
❑ 154 Dino Hackett .10 .02
❑ 155 Perry Kemp .10 .02
❑ 156 Mark Ingram .20 .07
❑ 157 Daryl Johnston .75 .30
❑ 158 Eugene Daniel .10 .02
❑ 159 Dalton Hilliard .10 .02
❑ 160 Rufus Porter .10 .02
❑ 161 Tunch Ilkin .10 .02
❑ 162 James Hasty .10 .02
❑ 163 Keith McKeller .10 .02
❑ 164 Heath Sherman .10 .02
❑ 165 Vai Sikahema .10 .02
❑ 166 Pat Terrell .10 .02
❑ 167 Anthony Munoz .20 .07
❑ 168 Brad Edwards RC .10 .02
❑ 169 Tom Rathman .10 .02
❑ 170 Steve McMichael .20 .07
❑ 171 Vaughan Johnson .10 .02
❑ 172 Nate Lewis RC .10 .02
❑ 173 Mark Rypien .20 .07
❑ 174 Rob Moore .50 .20
❑ 175 Tim Green .10 .02
❑ 176 Tony Casillas .10 .02
❑ 177 Jon Hand .10 .02
❑ 178 Todd McNair .10 .02
❑ 179 Toi Cook RC .10 .02
❑ 180 Eddie Brown .10 .02
❑ 181 Mark Jackson .10 .02
❑ 182 Pete Stoyanovich .10 .02
❑ 183 Bryce Paup RC .40 .15
❑ 184 Anthony Miller .20 .07
❑ 185 Dan Saleaumua .10 .02
❑ 186 Guy McIntyre .10 .02
❑ 187 Broderick Thomas .10 .02
❑ 188 Frank Warren .10 .02
❑ 189 Drew Hill .10 .02
❑ 190 Reggie White .40 .15
❑ 191 Chris Hinton .10 .02
❑ 192 David Little .10 .02
❑ 193 David Fulcher .10 .02
❑ 194 Clarence Verdin .10 .02
❑ 195 Junior Seau .60 .25
❑ 196 Blair Thomas .10 .02
❑ 197 Stan Brock .10 .02
❑ 198 Gary Clark .40 .15
❑ 199 Michael Irvin .40 .15
❑ 200 Ronnie Harmon .10 .02
❑ 201 Steve Young 2.00 .75
❑ 202 Brian Noble .10 .02
❑ 203 Dan Stryzinski .10 .02
❑ 204 Darryl Talley .10 .02
❑ 205 David Alexander .10 .02
❑ 206 Pat Swilling .20 .07
❑ 207 Gary Plummer .10 .02
❑ 208 Robert Delpino .10 .02
❑ 209 Norm Johnson .10 .02
❑ 210 Mike Singletary .20 .07
❑ 211 Anthony Johnson .40 .15
❑ 212 Eric Allen .10 .02
❑ 213 Gill Fenerty .10 .02
❑ 214 Neil Smith .40 .15
❑ 215 Joe Phillips .10 .02
❑ 216 Ottis Anderson .20 .07
❑ 217 LeRoy Butler .20 .07
❑ 218 Ray Childress .10 .02
❑ 219 Rodney Holman .10 .02
❑ 220 Kevin Fagan .10 .02
❑ 221 Bruce Smith .40 .15

Card		
❑ 222 Brad Muster	.10	.02
❑ 223 Mike Horan	.10	.02
❑ 224 Steve Atwater	.10	.02
❑ 225 Rich Gannon	.50	.20
❑ 226 Anthony Pleasant	.10	.02
❑ 227 Steve Jordan	.10	.02
❑ 228 Lomas Brown	.10	.02
❑ 229 Jackie Slater	.10	.02
❑ 230 Brad Baxter	.10	.02
❑ 231 Joe Morris	.10	.02
❑ 232 Marcus Allen	.40	.15
❑ 233 Chris Warren	.40	.15
❑ 234 Johnny Johnson	.10	.02
❑ 235 Phil Simms	.20	.07
❑ 236 Dave Krieg	.20	.07
❑ 237 Jim McMahon	.20	.07
❑ 238 Richard Dent	.20	.07
❑ 239 John Washington RC	.10	.02
❑ 240 Sammie Smith	.10	.02
❑ 241 Brian Brennan	.10	.02
❑ 242 Cortez Kennedy	.40	.15
❑ 243 Tim McDonald	.10	.02
❑ 244 Charles Haley	.20	.07
❑ 245 Joey Browner	.10	.02
❑ 246 Eddie Murray	.10	.02
❑ 247 Bob Golic	.10	.02
❑ 248 Myron Guyton	.10	.02
❑ 249 Dennis Byrd	.10	.02
❑ 250 Barry Sanders	3.00	1.25
❑ 251 Clay Matthews	.20	.07
❑ 252 Pepper Johnson	.10	.02
❑ 253 Eric Swann RC	.40	.15
❑ 254 Lamar Lathon	.10	.02
❑ 255 Andre Tippett	.10	.02
❑ 256 Tom Newberry	.10	.02
❑ 257 Kyle Clifton	.10	.02
❑ 258 Leslie O'Neal	.20	.07
❑ 259 Bubba McDowell	.10	.02
❑ 260 Scott Davis	.10	.02
❑ 261 Wilber Marshall	.10	.02
❑ 262 Marv Cook	.10	.02
❑ 263 Jeff Lageman	.10	.02
❑ 264 Michael Young	.10	.02
❑ 265 Gary Zimmerman	.10	.02
❑ 266 Mike Munchak	.20	.07
❑ 267 David Treadwell	.10	.02
❑ 268 Steve Wisniewski	.10	.02
❑ 269 Mark Duper	.20	.07
❑ 270 Chris Spielman	.20	.07
❑ 271 Brett Perriman	.40	.15
❑ 272 Lionel Washington	.10	.02
❑ 273 Lawrence Taylor	.40	.15
❑ 274 Mark Collins	.10	.02
❑ 275 Mark Carrier WR	.40	.15
❑ 276 Paul Gruber	.10	.02
❑ 277 Earnest Byner	.10	.02
❑ 278 Andre Collins	.10	.02
❑ 279 Reggie Cobb	.10	.02
❑ 280 Art Monk	.20	.07
❑ 281 Henry Jones RC	.20	.07
❑ 282 Mike Pritchard RC	.40	.15
❑ 283 Moe Gardner RC	.10	.02
❑ 284 Chris Zorich RC	.40	.15
❑ 285 Keith Traylor RC	.10	.02
❑ 286 Mike Dumas RC	.10	.02
❑ 287 Ed King RC	.10	.02
❑ 288 Russell Maryland RC	.40	.15
❑ 289 Alfred Williams RC	.10	.02
❑ 290 Derek Russell RC	.10	.02
❑ 291 Vinnie Clark RC	.10	.02
❑ 292 Mike Croel RC	.10	.02
❑ 293 Todd Marinovich RC	.10	.02
❑ 294 Phil Hansen RC	.10	.02
❑ 295 Aaron Craver RC	.10	.02
❑ 296 Nick Bell RC	.10	.02
❑ 297 Kenny Walker RC	.10	.02
❑ 298 Roman Phifer RC	.10	.02
❑ 299 Kanavis McGhee RC	.10	.02
❑ 300 Ricky Ervins RC	.20	.07
❑ 301 Jim Price RC	.10	.02
❑ 302 John Johnson RC	.10	.02
❑ 303 George Thornton RC	.10	.02
❑ 304 Huey Richardson RC	.10	.02
❑ 305 Harry Colon RC	.10	.02
❑ 306 Antone Davis RC	.10	.02
❑ 307 Todd Lyght RC	.10	.02
❑ 308 Bryan Cox RC	.40	.15
❑ 309 Brad Goebel RC	.10	.02
❑ 310 Eric Moten RC	.10	.02
❑ 311 John Kasay RC	.20	.07
❑ 312 Esera Tuaolo RC	.10	.02
❑ 313 Bobby Wilson RC	.10	.02
❑ 314 Mo Lewis RC	.20	.07
❑ 315 Harvey Williams RC	.40	.15
❑ 316 Mike Stonebreaker	.10	.02
❑ 317 Charles McRae RC	.10	.02
❑ 318 John Flannery RC	.10	.02
❑ 319 Ted Washington RC	.10	.02
❑ 320 Stanley Richard RC	.10	.02
❑ 321 Browning Nagle RC	.10	.02
❑ 322 Ed McCaffrey RC	5.00	2.00
❑ 323 Jeff Graham RC WR	.40	.15
❑ 324 Stan Thomas	.10	.02
❑ 325 Lawrence Dawsey RC	.20	.07
❑ 326 Eric Bieniemy RC	.10	.02
❑ 327 Tim Barnett RC	.10	.02
❑ 328 Erric Pegram RC	.40	.15
❑ 329 Lamar Rogers RC	.10	.02
❑ 330 Ernie Mills RC	.20	.07
❑ 331 Pat Harlow RC	.10	.02
❑ 332 Greg Lewis RC	.10	.02
❑ 333 Jarrod Bunch RC	.10	.02
❑ 334 Dan McGwire RC	.10	.02
❑ 335 Randal Hill RC	.20	.07
❑ 336 Leonard Russell RC	.40	.15
❑ 337 Carnell Lake	.10	.02
❑ 338 Brian Blades	.20	.07
❑ 339 Darrell Green	.10	.02
❑ 340 Bobby Humphrey	.10	.02
❑ 341 Mervyn Fernandez	.10	.02
❑ 342 Ricky Sanders	.10	.02
❑ 343 Keith Jackson	.20	.07
❑ 344 Carl Banks	.10	.02
❑ 345 Gill Byrd	.10	.02
❑ 346 Al Toon	.20	.07
❑ 347 Stephen Baker	.10	.02
❑ 348 Randall Cunningham	.40	.15
❑ 349 Flipper Anderson	.10	.02
❑ 350 Jay Novacek	.40	.15
❑ 351 Steve Young/B.Smith HH	.40	.15
❑ 352 Barry Sanders/Browner HH	.75	.30
❑ 353 Joe Montana/M.Carrier HH	.75	.30
❑ 354 Thurman Thomas/L.Taylor	.20	.07
❑ 355 Jerry Rice/Darr.Green HH	.50	.20
❑ 356 Warren Moon Tech	.20	.07
❑ 357 Anthony Munoz TECH	.10	.02
❑ 358 Barry Sanders Tech	1.25	.50
❑ 359 Jerry Rice Tech	1.25	.50
❑ 360 Joey Browner TECH	.10	.02
❑ 361 Morten Andersen TECH	.10	.02
❑ 362 Sean Landeta TECH	.10	.02
❑ 363 Thurman Thomas GW	.40	.15
❑ 364 Emmitt Smith GW	3.00	1.25
❑ 365 Gaston Green GW	.10	.02
❑ 366 Barry Sanders GW	1.25	.50
❑ 367 Christian Okoye GW	.10	.02
❑ 368 Earnest Byner GW	.10	.02
❑ 369 Neal Anderson GW	.10	.02
❑ 370 Herschel Walker GW	.20	.07
❑ 371 Rodney Hampton GW	.40	.15
❑ 372 Darryl Talley IDOL	.10	.02
❑ 373 Mark Carrier IDOL	.10	.02
❑ 374 Jim Breech IDOL	.10	.02
❑ 375 R.Hampton/O.Anderson ID	.10	.02
❑ 376 Kevin Mack IDOL	.10	.02
❑ 377 S.Jordan/O.Robertson ID	.10	.02
❑ 378 B.Esiason/B.Jones ID	.10	.02
❑ 379 Steve DeBerg IDOL	.20	.07
❑ 380 Al Toon IDOL	.10	.02
❑ 381 Ronnie Lott/C.Taylor ID	.20	.07
❑ 382 Henry Ellard IDOL	.10	.02
❑ 383 Troy Aikman/Staubach ID	1.25	.50
❑ 384 T.Thomas/E.Campbell ID	.40	.15
❑ 385 Dan Marino/Bradshaw ID	1.50	.60
❑ 386 Howie Long/Joe Greene ID	.20	.07
❑ 387 Franco Harris IR	.20	.07
❑ 388 Esera Tuaolo	.10	.02
❑ 389 Super Bowl XXVI	.10	.02
❑ 390 Charles Mann	.10	.02
❑ 391 Kenny Walker Succeed	.10	.02
❑ 392 Reggie Roby	.10	.02
❑ 393 Bruce Pickens RC	.10	.02
❑ 394 Ray Childress SIDE	.10	.02
❑ 395 Karl Mecklenburg SIDE	.10	.02
❑ 396 Dean Biasucci SIDE	.10	.02
❑ 397 John Alt SIDE	.10	.02
❑ 398 Marcus Allen SL	.20	.07
❑ 399 John Offerdahl SIDE	.10	.02
❑ 400 Richard Tardits RC SIDE	.10	.02
❑ 401 Al Toon SIDE	.10	.02
❑ 402 Joey Browner SIDE	.10	.02
❑ 403 Spencer Tillman RC SIDE	.10	.02
❑ 404 Jay Novacek SIDE	.20	.07
❑ 405 Stephen Braggs SIDE	.10	.02
❑ 406 Mike Tice RC SIDE	.10	.02
❑ 407 Kevin Greene SIDE	.20	.07
❑ 408 Reggie White SIDE	.20	.07
❑ 409 Brian Noble SIDE	.10	.02
❑ 410 Bart Oates SIDE	.10	.02
❑ 411 Art Monk SIDE	.20	.07
❑ 412 Ron Wolfley SIDE	.10	.02
❑ 413 Louis Lipps SIDE	.10	.02
❑ 414 Dante Jones RC SIDE	.20	.07
❑ 415 Kenneth Davis SIDE	.10	.02
❑ P1 Emmitt Smith Promo	25.00	12.50

1992 Pinnacle

Card		
❑ COMPLETE SET (360)	25.00	12.50
❑ 1 Reggie White	.50	.20
❑ 2 Eric Green	.15	.05
❑ 3 Craig Heyward	.30	.10
❑ 4 Phil Simms	.30	.10
❑ 5 Pepper Johnson	.15	.05
❑ 6 Sean Landeta	.15	.05
❑ 7 Dino Hackett	.15	.05
❑ 8 Andre Ware	.15	.05
❑ 9 Ricky Nattiel	.15	.05
❑ 10 Jim Price	.15	.05
❑ 11 Jim Ritcher	.15	.05
❑ 12 Kelly Stouffer	.15	.05
❑ 13 Ray Crockett	.15	.05
❑ 14 Steve Tasker	.30	.10
❑ 15 Barry Sanders	3.00	1.25
❑ 16 Pat Swilling	.15	.05
❑ 17 Moe Gardner	.15	.05
❑ 18 Steve Young	2.00	.75
❑ 19 Chris Spielman	.30	.10
❑ 20 Richard Dent	.30	.10
❑ 21 Anthony Munoz	.30	.10
❑ 22 Thurman Thomas	.50	.20
❑ 23 Ricky Sanders	.15	.05
❑ 24 Steve Atwater	.15	.05
❑ 25 Tony Tolbert	.15	.05
❑ 26 Haywood Jeffires	.30	.10
❑ 27 Duane Bickett	.15	.05
❑ 28 Tim McDonald	.15	.05
❑ 29 Cris Carter	.75	.30
❑ 30 Derrick Thomas	.50	.20
❑ 31 Hugh Millen	.15	.05
❑ 32 Bart Oates	.15	.05
❑ 33 Darryl Talley	.15	.05
❑ 34 Marion Butts	.15	.05
❑ 35 Pete Stoyanovich	.15	.05
❑ 36 Ronnie Lott	.30	.10
❑ 37 Simon Fletcher	.15	.05
❑ 38 Morten Andersen	.15	.05
❑ 39 Clyde Simmons	.15	.05
❑ 40 Mark Rypien	.15	.05
❑ 41 Henry Ellard	.30	.10
❑ 42 Michael Irvin	.50	.20
❑ 43 Louis Lipps	.15	.05
❑ 44 John L. Williams	.15	.05
❑ 45 Broderick Thomas	.15	.05

Card		
❑ 46 Don Majkowski	.15	.05
❑ 47 William Perry	.30	.10
❑ 48 David Fulcher	.15	.05
❑ 49 Tony Bennett	.15	.05
❑ 50 Clay Matthews	.30	.10
❑ 51 Warren Moon	.50	.20
❑ 52 Bruce Armstrong	.15	.05
❑ 53 Bill Brooks	.15	.05
❑ 54 Greg Townsend	.15	.05
❑ 55 Steve Broussard	.15	.05
❑ 56 Mel Gray	.30	.10
❑ 57 Kevin Mack	.15	.05
❑ 58 Emmitt Smith	4.00	2.00
❑ 59 Mike Croel	.15	.05
❑ 60 Brian Mitchell	.30	.10
❑ 61 Bennie Blades	.15	.05
❑ 62 Carnell Lake	.15	.05
❑ 63 Cornelius Bennett	.30	.10
❑ 64 Darrell Thompson	.15	.05
❑ 65 Jessie Hester	.15	.05
❑ 66 Marv Cook	.15	.05
❑ 67 Tim Brown	.50	.20
❑ 68 Mark Duper	.15	.05
❑ 69 Robert Delpino	.15	.05
❑ 70 Eric Martin	.15	.05
❑ 71 Wendell Davis	.15	.05
❑ 72 Vaughan Johnson	.15	.05
❑ 73 Brian Blades	.30	.10
❑ 74 Ed King	.15	.05
❑ 75 Gaston Green	.15	.05
❑ 76 Christian Okoye	.15	.05
❑ 77 Rohn Stark	.15	.05
❑ 78 Kevin Greene	.30	.10
❑ 79 Jay Novacek	.30	.10
❑ 80 Chip Lohmiller	.15	.05
❑ 81 Cris Dishman	.15	.05
❑ 82 Ethan Horton	.15	.05
❑ 83 Pat Harlow	.15	.05
❑ 84 Mark Ingram	.15	.05
❑ 85 Mark Carrier DB	.15	.05
❑ 86 Sam Mills	.15	.05
❑ 87 Mark Higgs	.15	.05
❑ 88 Keith Jackson	.30	.10
❑ 89 Gary Anderson K	.15	.05
❑ 90 Ken Harvey	.15	.05
❑ 91 Anthony Carter	.30	.10
❑ 92 Randall McDaniel	.15	.05
❑ 93 Johnny Johnson	.15	.05
❑ 94 Shane Conlan	.15	.05
❑ 95 Sterling Sharpe	.50	.20
❑ 96 Guy McIntyre	.15	.05
❑ 97 Albert Lewis	.15	.05
❑ 98 Chris Doleman	.15	.05
❑ 99 Andre Rison	.30	.10
❑ 100 Bobby Hebert	.15	.05
❑ 101 Dan Owens	.15	.05
❑ 102 Rodney Hampton	.30	.10
❑ 103 Ernie Jones	.15	.05
❑ 104 Reggie Cobb	.15	.05
❑ 105 Wilber Marshall	.15	.05
❑ 106 Mike Munchak	.30	.10
❑ 107 Cortez Kennedy	.30	.10
❑ 108 Todd Lyght	.15	.05
❑ 109 Burt Grossman	.15	.05
❑ 110 Ferrell Edmunds	.15	.05
❑ 111 Jim Everett	.30	.10
❑ 112 Hardy Nickerson	.30	.10
❑ 113 Andre Tippett	.15	.05
❑ 114 Ronnie Harmon	.15	.05
❑ 115 Andre Waters	.15	.05
❑ 116 Ernest Givins	.30	.10
❑ 117 Eric Hill	.15	.05
❑ 118 Erric Pegram	.30	.10
❑ 119 Jarrod Bunch	.15	.05
❑ 120 Marcus Allen	.50	.20
❑ 121 Barry Foster	.30	.10
❑ 122 Kent Hull	.15	.05
❑ 123 Neal Anderson	.15	.05
❑ 124 Stephen Braggs	.15	.05
❑ 125 Nick Lowery	.15	.05
❑ 126 Jeff Hostetler	.30	.10
❑ 127 Michael Carter	.15	.05
❑ 128 Don Warren	.15	.05
❑ 129 Brad Baxter	.15	.05
❑ 130 John Taylor	.30	.10
❑ 131 Harold Green	.15	.05
❑ 132 Mike Merriweather	.15	.05
❑ 133 Gary Clark	.50	.20
❑ 134 Vince Buck	.15	.05
❑ 135 Dan Saleaumua	.15	.05
❑ 136 Gary Zimmerman	.15	.05
❑ 137 Richmond Webb	.15	.05
❑ 138 Art Monk	.30	.10
❑ 139 Mervyn Fernandez	.15	.05
❑ 140 Mark Jackson	.15	.05
❑ 141 Freddie Joe Nunn	.15	.05
❑ 142 Jeff Lageman	.15	.05
❑ 143 Kenny Walker	.15	.05
❑ 144 Mark Carrier WR	.30	.10
❑ 145 Jon Vaughn	.15	.05
❑ 146 Greg Davis	.15	.05
❑ 147 Bubby Brister	.15	.05
❑ 148 Mo Lewis	.15	.05
❑ 149 Howie Long	.50	.20
❑ 150 Rod Bernstine	.15	.05
❑ 151 Nick Bell	.15	.05
❑ 152 Terry Allen	.50	.20
❑ 153 William Fuller	.15	.05
❑ 154 Dexter Carter	.15	.05
❑ 155 Gene Atkins	.15	.05
❑ 156 Don Beebe	.15	.05
❑ 157 Mark Collins	.15	.05
❑ 158 Jerry Ball	.15	.05
❑ 159 Fred Barnett	.50	.20
❑ 160 Rodney Holman	.15	.05
❑ 161 Stephen Baker	.15	.05
❑ 162 Jeff Graham	.50	.20
❑ 163 Leonard Russell	.30	.10
❑ 164 Jeff Gossett	.15	.05
❑ 165 Vinny Testaverde	.30	.10
❑ 166 Maurice Hurst	.15	.05
❑ 167 Louis Oliver	.15	.05
❑ 168 Jim Morrissey	.15	.05
❑ 169 Greg Kragen	.15	.05
❑ 170 Andre Collins	.15	.05
❑ 171 Dave Meggett	.30	.10
❑ 172 Keith Henderson	.15	.05
❑ 173 Vince Newsome	.15	.05
❑ 174 Chris Hinton	.15	.05
❑ 175 James Hasty	.15	.05
❑ 176 John Offerdahl	.15	.05
❑ 177 Lomas Brown	.15	.05
❑ 178 Neil O'Donnell	.30	.10
❑ 179 Leonard Marshall	.15	.05
❑ 180 Bubba McDowell	.15	.05
❑ 181 Herman Moore	.50	.20
❑ 182 Rob Moore	.30	.10
❑ 183 Earnest Byner	.15	.05
❑ 184 Keith McCants	.15	.05
❑ 185 Floyd Turner	.15	.05
❑ 186 Steve Jordan	.15	.05
❑ 187 Nate Odomes	.15	.05
❑ 188 Jeff Herrod	.15	.05
❑ 189 Jim Harbaugh	.50	.20
❑ 190 Jessie Tuggle	.15	.05
❑ 191 Al Smith	.15	.05
❑ 192 Lawrence Dawsey	.30	.10
❑ 193 Steve Bono RC	.50	.20
❑ 194 Greg Lloyd	.30	.10
❑ 195 Steve Wisniewski	.15	.05
❑ 196 Larry Kelm	.15	.05
❑ 197 Tommy Kane	.15	.05
❑ 198 Mark Schlereth RC	.15	.05
❑ 199 Ray Childress	.15	.05
❑ 200 Vincent Brown	.15	.05
❑ 201 Rodney Peete	.30	.10
❑ 202 Dennis Smith	.15	.05
❑ 203 Bruce Matthews	.15	.05
❑ 204 Rickey Jackson	.15	.05
❑ 205 Eric Allen	.15	.05
❑ 206 Rich Camarillo	.15	.05
❑ 207 Jim Lachey	.15	.05
❑ 208 Kevin Ross	.15	.05
❑ 209 Irving Fryar	.30	.10
❑ 210 Mark Clayton	.30	.10
❑ 211 Keith Byars	.15	.05
❑ 212 John Elway	3.00	1.25
❑ 213 Harris Barton	.15	.05
❑ 214 Aeneas Williams	.30	.10
❑ 215 Rich Gannon	.50	.20
❑ 216 Toi Cook	.15	.05
❑ 217 Rod Woodson	.50	.20
❑ 218 Gary Anderson RB	.15	.05
❑ 219 Reggie Roby	.15	.05
❑ 220 Karl Mecklenburg	.15	.05
❑ 221 Rufus Porter	.15	.05
❑ 222 Jon Hand	.15	.05
❑ 223 Tim Barnett	.15	.05
❑ 224 Eric Swann	.30	.10
❑ 225 Eugene Robinson	.15	.05
❑ 226 Michael Young	.15	.05
❑ 227 Frank Warren	.15	.05
❑ 228 Mike Kenn	.15	.05
❑ 229 Tim Green	.15	.05
❑ 230 Barry Word	.15	.05
❑ 231 Mike Pritchard	.30	.10
❑ 232 John Kasay	.15	.05
❑ 233 Derek Russell	.15	.05
❑ 234 Jim Breech	.15	.05
❑ 235 Pierce Holt	.15	.05
❑ 236 Tim Krumrie	.15	.05
❑ 237 William Roberts	.15	.05
❑ 238 Erik Kramer	.30	.10
❑ 239 Brett Perriman	.50	.20
❑ 240 Reyna Thompson	.15	.05
❑ 241 Chris Miller	.30	.10
❑ 242 Drew Hill	.15	.05
❑ 243 Curtis Duncan	.15	.05
❑ 244 Seth Joyner	.15	.05
❑ 245 Ken Norton Jr.	.30	.10
❑ 246 Calvin Williams	.30	.10
❑ 247 James Joseph	.15	.05
❑ 248 Bennie Thompson RC	.15	.05
❑ 249 Tunch Ilkin	.15	.05
❑ 250 Brad Edwards	.15	.05
❑ 251 Jeff Jaeger	.15	.05
❑ 252 Gill Byrd	.15	.05
❑ 253 Jeff Feagles	.15	.05
❑ 254 Jamie Dukes RC	.15	.05
❑ 255 Greg McMurtry	.15	.05
❑ 256 Anthony Johnson	.30	.10
❑ 257 Lamar Lathon	.15	.05
❑ 258 John Roper	.15	.05
❑ 259 Lorenzo White	.15	.05
❑ 260 Brian Noble	.15	.05
❑ 261 Chris Singleton	.15	.05
❑ 262 Todd Marinovich	.15	.05
❑ 263 Jay Hilgenberg	.15	.05
❑ 264 Kyle Clifton	.15	.05
❑ 265 Tony Casillas	.15	.05
❑ 266 James Francis	.15	.05
❑ 267 Eddie Anderson	.15	.05
❑ 268 Tim Harris	.15	.05
❑ 269 James Lofton	.30	.10
❑ 270 Jay Schroeder	.15	.05
❑ 271 Ed West	.15	.05
❑ 272 Don Mosebar	.15	.05
❑ 273 Jackie Slater	.15	.05
❑ 274 Fred McAfee RC	.15	.05
❑ 275 Steve Sewell	.15	.05
❑ 276 Charles Mann	.15	.05
❑ 277 Ron Hall	.15	.05
❑ 278 Darrell Green	.15	.05
❑ 279 Jeff Cross	.15	.05
❑ 280 Jeff Wright	.15	.05
❑ 281 Issiac Holt	.15	.05
❑ 282 Dermontti Dawson	.15	.05
❑ 283 Michael Haynes	.30	.10
❑ 284 Tony Mandarich	.15	.05
❑ 285 Leroy Hoard	.30	.10
❑ 286 Darryl Henley	.15	.05
❑ 287 Tim McGee	.15	.05
❑ 288 Willie Gault	.30	.10
❑ 289 Dalton Hilliard	.15	.05
❑ 290 Tim McKyer	.15	.05
❑ 291 Tom Waddle	.15	.05
❑ 292 Eric Thomas	.15	.05
❑ 293 Herschel Walker	.30	.10
❑ 294 Donnell Woolford	.15	.05
❑ 295 James Brooks	.30	.10
❑ 296 Brad Muster	.15	.05
❑ 297 Brent Jones	.30	.10
❑ 298 Erik Howard	.15	.05
❑ 299 Alvin Harper	.30	.10
❑ 300 Joey Browner	.15	.05
❑ 301 Jack Del Rio	.15	.05
❑ 302 Cleveland Gary	.15	.05
❑ 303 Brett Favre	6.00	3.00
❑ 304 Freeman McNeil	.15	.05
❑ 305 Willie Green	.15	.05
❑ 306 Percy Snow	.15	.05

Card		
❏ 307 Neil Smith	.50	.20
❏ 308 Eric Bieniemy	.15	.05
❏ 309 Keith Traylor	.15	.05
❏ 310 Ernie Mills	.15	.05
❏ 311 Will Wolford	.15	.05
❏ 312 Robert Young	.15	.05
❏ 313 Anthony Smith	.15	.05
❏ 314 Robert Porcher RC	.50	.20
❏ 315 Leon Searcy RC	.15	.05
❏ 316 Amp Lee RC	.15	.05
❏ 317 Siran Stacy RC	.15	.05
❏ 318 Patrick Rowe RC	.15	.05
❏ 319 Chris Mims RC	.15	.05
❏ 320 Matt Elliott RC	.15	.05
❏ 321 Ricardo McDonald RC	.15	.05
❏ 322 Keith Hamilton RC	.30	.10
❏ 323 Edgar Bennett RC	.50	.20
❏ 324 Chris Hakel RC	.15	.05
❏ 325 Dexter McNabb RC	.15	.05
❏ 326 Rod Milstead RC	.15	.05
❏ 327 Joe Bowden RC	.15	.05
❏ 328 Brian Bollinger RC	.15	.05
❏ 329 Darryl Williams RC	.15	.05
❏ 330 Tommy Vardell RC	.15	.05
❏ 331 Glenn Parker SIDE	.15	.05
❏ 332 Herschel Walker SIDE	.15	.05
❏ 333 Mike Cofer SIDE	.15	.05
❏ 334 Mark Rypien SIDE	.15	.05
❏ 335 Andre Rison GW	.30	.10
❏ 336 Henry Ellard GW	.15	.05
❏ 337 Rob Moore GW	.15	.05
❏ 338 Fred Barnett GW	.15	.05
❏ 339 Mark Clayton GW	.15	.05
❏ 340 Eric Martin GW	.15	.05
❏ 341 Irving Fryar GW	.15	.05
❏ 342 Tim Brown GW	.30	.10
❏ 343 Sterling Sharpe GW	.30	.10
❏ 344 Gary Clark GW	.15	.05
❏ 345 John Mackey HOF	.15	.05
❏ 346 Lem Barney HOF	.15	.05
❏ 347 John Riggins HOF	.30	.10
❏ 348 Marion Butts IDOL	.15	.05
❏ 349 Jeff Lageman IDOL	.15	.05
❏ 350 Eric Green IDOL	.15	.05
❏ 351 Reggie White/Bob.Jones I	.30	.10
❏ 352 Marv Cook IDOL	.15	.05
❏ 353 John Elway/Staubach ID	1.25	.50
❏ 354 Steve Tasker IDOL	.15	.05
❏ 355 Nick Lowery IDOL	.15	.05
❏ 356 Mark Clayton/Warfield ID	.15	.05
❏ 357 Warren Moon/R.Gabriel ID	.30	.10
❏ 358 Eric Metcalf	.30	.10
❏ 359 Charles Haley	.30	.10
❏ 360 Terrell Buckley RC	.15	.05
❏ P1 Promo Panel	5.00	2.00

1993 Pinnacle

Card		
❏ COMPLETE SET (360)	20.00	7.50
❏ 1 Brett Favre	3.00	1.25
❏ 2 Tommy Vardell	.10	.02
❏ 3 Jarrod Bunch	.10	.02
❏ 4 Mike Croel	.10	.02
❏ 5 Morten Andersen	.10	.02
❏ 6 Barry Foster	.20	.07
❏ 7 Chris Spielman	.20	.07
❏ 8 Jim Jeffcoat	.10	.02
❏ 9 Ken Ruettgers	.10	.02
❏ 10 Cris Dishman	.10	.02
❏ 11 Ricky Watters	.40	.15
❏ 12 Alfred Williams	.10	.02
❏ 13 Mark Kelso	.10	.02
❏ 14 Moe Gardner	.10	.02
❏ 15 Terry Allen	.40	.15
❏ 16 Willie Gault	.10	.02
❏ 17 Bubba McDowell	.10	.02
❏ 18 Brian Mitchell	.20	.07
❏ 19 Karl Mecklenburg	.10	.02
❏ 20 Jim Everett	.20	.07
❏ 21 Bobby Humphrey	.10	.02
❏ 22 Tim Krumrie	.10	.02
❏ 23 Ken Norton Jr.	.20	.07
❏ 24 Wendell Davis	.10	.02
❏ 25 Brad Baxter	.10	.02
❏ 26 Mel Gray	.20	.07
❏ 27 Jon Vaughn	.10	.02
❏ 28 James Hasty	.10	.02
❏ 29 Chris Warren	.20	.07
❏ 30 Tim Harris	.10	.02
❏ 31 Eric Metcalf	.20	.07
❏ 32 Rob Moore	.20	.07
❏ 33 Charles Haley	.20	.07
❏ 34 Leonard Marshall	.10	.02
❏ 35 Jeff Graham	.20	.07
❏ 36 Eugene Robinson	.10	.02
❏ 37 Darryl Talley	.10	.02
❏ 38 Brent Jones	.20	.07
❏ 39 Reggie Roby	.10	.02
❏ 40 Bruce Armstrong	.10	.02
❏ 41 Audray McMillian	.10	.02
❏ 42 Bern Brostek	.10	.02
❏ 43 Tony Bennett	.10	.02
❏ 44 Albert Lewis	.10	.02
❏ 45 Derrick Thomas	.40	.15
❏ 46 Cris Carter	.40	.15
❏ 47 Richmond Webb	.10	.02
❏ 48 Sean Landeta	.10	.02
❏ 49 Cleveland Gary	.10	.02
❏ 50 Mark Carrier DB	.10	.02
❏ 51 Lawrence Dawsey	.10	.02
❏ 52 Lamar Lathon	.10	.02
❏ 53 Nick Bell	.10	.02
❏ 54 Curtis Duncan	.10	.02
❏ 55 Irving Fryar	.20	.07
❏ 56 Seth Joyner	.10	.02
❏ 57 Jay Novacek	.20	.07
❏ 58 John L. Williams	.10	.02
❏ 59 Amp Lee	.10	.02
❏ 60 Marion Butts	.10	.02
❏ 61 Clyde Simmons	.10	.02
❏ 62 Rich Gannon	.40	.15
❏ 63 Anthony Johnson	.20	.07
❏ 64 Dave Meggett	.10	.02
❏ 65 James Francis	.10	.02
❏ 66 Trace Armstrong	.10	.02
❏ 67 Mo Lewis	.10	.02
❏ 68 Cornelius Bennett	.20	.07
❏ 69 Mark Duper	.10	.02
❏ 70 Frank Reich	.20	.07
❏ 71 Eric Green	.10	.02
❏ 72 Bruce Matthews	.10	.02
❏ 73 Steve Broussard	.10	.02
❏ 74 Anthony Carter	.20	.07
❏ 75 Sterling Sharpe	.40	.15
❏ 76 Mike Kenn	.10	.02
❏ 77 Andre Rison	.20	.07
❏ 78 Todd Marinovich	.10	.02
❏ 79 Vincent Brown	.10	.02
❏ 80 Harold Green	.10	.02
❏ 81 Art Monk	.20	.07
❏ 82 Reggie Cobb	.10	.02
❏ 83 Johnny Johnson	.10	.02
❏ 84 Tommy Kane	.10	.02
❏ 85 Rohn Stark	.10	.02
❏ 86 Steve Tasker	.20	.07
❏ 87 Ronnie Harmon	.10	.02
❏ 88 Pepper Johnson	.10	.02
❏ 89 Hardy Nickerson	.20	.07
❏ 90 Alvin Harper	.20	.07
❏ 91 Louis Oliver	.10	.02
❏ 92 Rod Woodson	.40	.15
❏ 93 Sam Mills	.10	.02
❏ 94 Randall McDaniel	.10	.02
❏ 95 Johnny Holland	.10	.02
❏ 96 Jackie Slater	.10	.02
❏ 97 Don Mosebar	.10	.02
❏ 98 Andre Ware	.10	.02
❏ 99 Kelvin Martin	.10	.02
❏ 100 Emmitt Smith	2.50	1.00
❏ 101 Michael Brooks	.10	.02
❏ 102 Dan Saleaumua	.10	.02
❏ 103 John Elway	2.50	1.00
❏ 104 Henry Jones	.10	.02
❏ 105 William Perry	.20	.07
❏ 106 James Lofton	.20	.07
❏ 107 Carnell Lake	.10	.02
❏ 108 Chip Lohmiller	.10	.02
❏ 109 Andre Tippett	.10	.02
❏ 110 Barry Word	.10	.02
❏ 111 Haywood Jeffires	.20	.07
❏ 112 Kenny Walker	.10	.02
❏ 113 John Randle	.20	.07
❏ 114 Donnell Woolford	.10	.02
❏ 115 Johnny Bailey	.10	.02
❏ 116 Marcus Allen	.40	.15
❏ 117 Mark Jackson	.10	.02
❏ 118 Ray Agnew	.10	.02
❏ 119 Gill Byrd	.10	.02
❏ 120 Kyle Clifton	.10	.02
❏ 121 Marv Cook	.10	.02
❏ 122 Jerry Ball	.10	.02
❏ 123 Steve Jordan	.10	.02
❏ 124 Shannon Sharpe	.40	.15
❏ 125 Brian Blades	.20	.07
❏ 126 Rodney Hampton	.20	.07
❏ 127 Bobby Hebert	.10	.02
❏ 128 Jessie Tuggle	.10	.02
❏ 129 Tom Newberry	.10	.02
❏ 130 Keith McCants	.10	.02
❏ 131 Richard Dent	.20	.07
❏ 132 Herman Moore	.40	.15
❏ 133 Michael Irvin	.40	.15
❏ 134 Ernest Givins	.20	.07
❏ 135 Mark Rypien	.10	.02
❏ 136 Leonard Russell	.20	.07
❏ 137 Reggie White	.40	.15
❏ 138 Thurman Thomas	.40	.15
❏ 139 Nick Lowery	.10	.02
❏ 140 Al Smith	.10	.02
❏ 141 Jackie Harris	.10	.02
❏ 142 Duane Bickett	.10	.02
❏ 143 Lawyer Tillman	.10	.02
❏ 144 Steve Wisniewski	.10	.02
❏ 145 Derrick Fenner	.10	.02
❏ 146 Harris Barton	.10	.02
❏ 147 Rich Camarillo	.10	.02
❏ 148 John Offerdahl	.10	.02
❏ 149 Mike Johnson	.10	.02
❏ 150 Ricky Reynolds	.10	.02
❏ 151 Fred Barnett	.20	.07
❏ 152 Nate Newton	.20	.07
❏ 153 Chris Doleman	.10	.02
❏ 154 Todd Scott	.10	.02
❏ 155 Tim McKyer	.10	.02
❏ 156 Ken Harvey	.10	.02
❏ 157 Jeff Feagles	.10	.02
❏ 158 Vince Workman	.10	.02
❏ 159 Bart Oates	.10	.02
❏ 160 Chris Miller	.20	.07
❏ 161 Pete Stoyanovich	.10	.02
❏ 162 Steve Wallace	.10	.02
❏ 163 Dermontti Dawson	.10	.02
❏ 164 Kenneth Davis	.10	.02
❏ 165 Mike Munchak	.20	.07
❏ 166 George Jamison	.10	.02
❏ 167 Christian Okoye	.10	.02
❏ 168 Chris Hinton	.10	.02
❏ 169 Vaughan Johnson	.10	.02
❏ 170 Gaston Green	.10	.02
❏ 171 Kevin Greene	.20	.07
❏ 172 Rob Burnett	.10	.02
❏ 173 Norm Johnson	.10	.02
❏ 174 Eric Hill	.10	.02
❏ 175 Lomas Brown	.10	.02
❏ 176 Chip Banks	.10	.02
❏ 177 Greg Townsend	.10	.02
❏ 178 David Fulcher	.10	.02
❏ 179 Gary Anderson RB	.10	.02
❏ 180 Brian Washington	.10	.02
❏ 181 Brett Perriman	.40	.15
❏ 182 Chris Chandler	.20	.07
❏ 183 Phil Hansen	.10	.02
❏ 184 Mark Clayton	.10	.02
❏ 185 Frank Warren	.10	.02

❑ 186 Tim Brown .40 .15
❑ 187 Mark Stepnoski .10 .02
❑ 188 Bryan Cox .10 .02
❑ 189 Gary Zimmerman .10 .02
❑ 190 Neil O'Donnell .40 .15
❑ 191 Anthony Smith .10 .02
❑ 192 Craig Heyward .20 .07
❑ 193 Keith Byars .10 .02
❑ 194 Sean Salisbury .10 .02
❑ 195 Todd Lyght .10 .02
❑ 196 Jessie Hester .10 .02
❑ 197 Rufus Porter .10 .02
❑ 198 Steve Christie .10 .02
❑ 199 Nate Lewis .10 .02
❑ 200 Barry Sanders 2.00 .75
❑ 201 Michael Haynes .20 .07
❑ 202 John Taylor .20 .07
❑ 203 John Friesz .20 .07
❑ 204 William Fuller .10 .02
❑ 205 Dennis Smith .10 .02
❑ 206 Adrian Cooper .10 .02
❑ 207 Henry Thomas .10 .02
❑ 208 Gerald Williams .10 .02
❑ 209 Chris Burkett .10 .02
❑ 210 Broderick Thomas .10 .02
❑ 211 Marvin Washington .10 .02
❑ 212 Bennie Blades .10 .02
❑ 213 Tony Casillas .10 .02
❑ 214 Bubby Brister .10 .02
❑ 215 Don Griffin .10 .02
❑ 216 Jeff Cross .10 .02
❑ 217 Derrick Walker .10 .02
❑ 218 Lorenzo White .10 .02
❑ 219 Ricky Sanders .10 .02
❑ 220 Rickey Jackson .10 .02
❑ 221 Simon Fletcher .10 .02
❑ 222 Troy Vincent .10 .02
❑ 223 Gary Clark .20 .07
❑ 224 Stanley Richard .10 .02
❑ 225 Dave Krieg .20 .07
❑ 226 Warren Moon .40 .15
❑ 227 Reggie Langhorne .10 .02
❑ 228 Kent Hull .10 .02
❑ 229 Ferrell Edmunds .10 .02
❑ 230 Cortez Kennedy .20 .07
❑ 231 Hugh Millen .10 .02
❑ 232 Eugene Chung .10 .02
❑ 233 Rodney Peete .10 .02
❑ 234 Tom Waddle .10 .02
❑ 235 David Klingler .10 .02
❑ 236 Mark Carrier WR .20 .07
❑ 237 Jay Schroeder .10 .02
❑ 238 James Jones DT .10 .02
❑ 239 Phil Simms .20 .07
❑ 240 Steve Atwater .10 .02
❑ 241 Jeff Herrod .10 .02
❑ 242 Dale Carter .10 .02
❑ 243 Glenn Cadrez RC .10 .02
❑ 244 Wayne Martin .10 .02
❑ 245 Willie Davis .40 .15
❑ 246 Lawrence Taylor .40 .15
❑ 247 Stan Humphries .20 .07
❑ 248 Byron Evans .10 .02
❑ 249 Wilber Marshall .10 .02
❑ 250 Michael Bankston RC .10 .02
❑ 251 Steve McMichael .20 .07
❑ 252 Brad Edwards .10 .02
❑ 253 Will Wolford .10 .02
❑ 254 Paul Gruber .10 .02
❑ 255 Steve Young 1.25 .50
❑ 256 Chuck Cecil .10 .02
❑ 257 Pierce Holt .10 .02
❑ 258 Anthony Miller .20 .07
❑ 259 Carl Banks .10 .02
❑ 260 Brad Muster .10 .02
❑ 261 Clay Matthews .20 .07
❑ 262 Rod Bernstine .10 .02
❑ 263 Tim Barnett .10 .02
❑ 264 Greg Lloyd .20 .07
❑ 265 Sean Jones .10 .02
❑ 266 J.J. Birden .10 .02
❑ 267 Tim McDonald .10 .02
❑ 268 Charles Mann .10 .02
❑ 269 Bruce Smith .40 .15
❑ 270 Sean Gilbert .20 .07
❑ 271 Ricardo McDonald .10 .02
❑ 272 Jeff Hostetler .20 .07
❑ 273 Russell Maryland .10 .02
❑ 274 Dave Brown RC .40 .15
❑ 275 Ronnie Lott .20 .07
❑ 276 Jim Kelly .40 .15
❑ 277 Joe Montana 2.50 1.00
❑ 278 Eric Allen .10 .02
❑ 279 Browning Nagle .10 .02
❑ 280 Neal Anderson .10 .02
❑ 281 Troy Aikman 1.25 .50
❑ 282 Ed McCaffrey .40 .15
❑ 283 Robert Jones .10 .02
❑ 284 Dalton Hilliard .10 .02
❑ 285 Johnny Mitchell .10 .02
❑ 286 Jay Hilgenberg .10 .02
❑ 287 Eric Martin .10 .02
❑ 288 Steve Emtman .10 .02
❑ 289 Vaughn Dunbar .10 .02
❑ 290 Mark Wheeler .10 .02
❑ 291 Leslie O'Neal .20 .07
❑ 292 Jerry Rice 1.50 .60
❑ 293 Neil Smith .40 .15
❑ 294 Kerry Cash .10 .02
❑ 295 Dan McGwire .10 .02
❑ 296 Carl Pickens .20 .07
❑ 297 Terrell Buckley .10 .02
❑ 298 Randall Cunningham .40 .15
❑ 299 Santana Dotson .20 .07
❑ 300 Keith Jackson .20 .07
❑ 301 Jim Lachey .10 .02
❑ 302 Dan Marino 2.50 1.00
❑ 303 Lee Williams .10 .02
❑ 304 Burt Grossman .10 .02
❑ 305 Kevin Mack .10 .02
❑ 306 Pat Swilling .10 .02
❑ 307 Arthur Marshall RC .10 .02
❑ 308 Jim Harbaugh .40 .15
❑ 309 Kurt Barber .10 .02
❑ 310 Harvey Williams .20 .07
❑ 311 Ricky Ervins .10 .02
❑ 312 Flipper Anderson .10 .02
❑ 313 Bernie Kosar .20 .07
❑ 314 Boomer Esiason .20 .07
❑ 315 Deion Sanders .75 .30
❑ 316 Ray Childress .10 .02
❑ 317 Howie Long .40 .15
❑ 318 Henry Ellard .20 .07
❑ 319 Marco Coleman .10 .02
❑ 320 Chris Mims .10 .02
❑ 321 Quentin Coryatt .20 .07
❑ 322 Jason Hanson .10 .02
❑ 323 Ricky Proehl .10 .02
❑ 324 Randal Hill .10 .02
❑ 325 Vinny Testaverde .20 .07
❑ 326 Jeff George .40 .15
❑ 327 Junior Seau .40 .15
❑ 328 Earnest Byner .10 .02
❑ 329 Andre Reed .20 .07
❑ 330 Phillippi Sparks .10 .02
❑ 331 Kevin Ross .10 .02
❑ 332 Clarence Verdin .10 .02
❑ 333 Darryl Henley .10 .02
❑ 334 Dana Hall .10 .02
❑ 335 Greg McMurtry .10 .02
❑ 336 Ron Hall .10 .02
❑ 337 Darrell Green .10 .02
❑ 338 Carlton Bailey .10 .02
❑ 339 Irv Eatman .10 .02
❑ 340 Greg Kragen .10 .02
❑ 341 Wade Wilson .10 .02
❑ 342 Klaus Wilmsmeyer .10 .02
❑ 343 Derek Brown TE .10 .02
❑ 344 Erik Williams .10 .02
❑ 345 Jim McMahon .20 .07
❑ 346 Mike Sherrard .10 .02
❑ 347 Mark Bavaro .10 .02
❑ 348 Anthony Munoz .20 .07
❑ 349 Eric Dickerson .20 .07
❑ 350 Steve Beuerlein .20 .07
❑ 351 Tim McGee .10 .02
❑ 352 Terry McDaniel .10 .02
❑ 353 Dan Fouts HOF .10 .02
❑ 354 Chuck Noll HOF .20 .07
❑ 355 Bill Walsh RC HOF .20 .07
❑ 356 Larry Little HOF .10 .02
❑ 357 Todd Marinovich HH .10 .02
❑ 358 Jeff George HH .40 .15
❑ 359 Bernie Kosar HH .20 .07
❑ 360 Rob Moore HH .20 .07
❑ NNO Franco Harris AU/3000 25.00 12.50

1994 Pinnacle

❑ COMPLETE SET (270) 20.00 8.00
❑ 1 Deion Sanders .50 .20
❑ 2 Eric Metcalf .20 .07
❑ 3 Barry Sanders 2.00 .75
❑ 4 Ernest Givins .20 .07
❑ 5 Phil Simms .20 .07
❑ 6 Rod Woodson .20 .07
❑ 7 Michael Irvin .40 .15
❑ 8 Cortez Kennedy .20 .07
❑ 9 Eric Martin .10 .02
❑ 10 Jeff Hostetler .20 .07
❑ 11 Sterling Sharpe .20 .07
❑ 12 John Elway 2.50 1.00
❑ 13 Neal Anderson .10 .02
❑ 14 Terry Kirby .40 .15
❑ 15 Jim Everett .20 .07
❑ 16 Lawrence Dawsey .10 .02
❑ 17 Kelvin Martin .10 .02
❑ 18 Tim McGee .10 .02
❑ 19 Cris Carter .50 .20
❑ 20 Ronnie Harmon .10 .02
❑ 21 Jim Kelly .40 .15
❑ 22 Steve Young 1.00 .40
❑ 23 Johnny Johnson .10 .02
❑ 24 Sean Gilbert .10 .02
❑ 25 Brian Mitchell .10 .02
❑ 26 Carl Pickens .20 .07
❑ 27 Tim Brown .40 .15
❑ 28 Reggie Langhorne .10 .02
❑ 29 Webster Slaughter .10 .02
❑ 30 Alvin Harper .20 .07
❑ 31 Andre Rison .20 .07
❑ 32 Derrick Thomas .40 .15
❑ 33 Irving Fryar .20 .07
❑ 34 Vinny Testaverde .20 .07
❑ 35 Steve Beuerlein .20 .07
❑ 36 Brett Favre 2.50 1.00
❑ 37 Barry Foster .10 .02
❑ 38 Vaughan Johnson .10 .02
❑ 39 Carlton Bailey .10 .02
❑ 40 Steve Emtman .10 .02
❑ 41 Anthony Miller .20 .07
❑ 42 Jeff Cross .10 .02
❑ 43 Trace Armstrong .10 .02
❑ 44 Derek Russell .10 .02
❑ 45 Vincent Brisby .20 .07
❑ 46 Mark Jackson .10 .02
❑ 47 Eugene Robinson .10 .02
❑ 48 John Friesz .20 .07
❑ 49 Scott Mitchell .20 .07
❑ 50 Steve Atwater .10 .02
❑ 51 Ken Norton .20 .07
❑ 52 Vincent Brown .10 .02
❑ 53 Morten Andersen .10 .02
❑ 54 Gary Anderson K .10 .02
❑ 55 Eric Curry .10 .02
❑ 56 Henry Jones .10 .02
❑ 57 Flipper Anderson .10 .02
❑ 58 Pat Swilling .10 .02
❑ 59 Erric Pegram .10 .02
❑ 60 Bruce Matthews .10 .02
❑ 61 Willie Davis .20 .07
❑ 62 O.J.McDuffie .40 .15
❑ 63 Qadry Ismail .40 .15
❑ 64 Anthony Smith .10 .02

❑ 65 Eric Allen .10 .02
❑ 66 Marion Butts .10 .02
❑ 67 Chris Miller .10 .02
❑ 68 Terrell Buckley .10 .02
❑ 69 Thurman Thomas .40 .15
❑ 70 Roosevelt Potts .10 .02
❑ 71 Tony McGee .10 .02
❑ 72 Jason Hanson .10 .02
❑ 73 Victor Bailey .10 .02
❑ 74 Albert Lewis .10 .02
❑ 75 Nate Odomes .10 .02
❑ 76 Ben Coates .20 .07
❑ 77 Warren Moon .40 .15
❑ 78 Derek Brown RBK .10 .02
❑ 79 David Klingler .10 .02
❑ 80 Cleveland Gary .10 .02
❑ 81 Emmitt Smith 2.00 .75
❑ 82 Jay Novacek .20 .07
❑ 83 Dana Stubblefield .20 .07
❑ 84 Michael Brooks .10 .02
❑ 85 James Jett .10 .02
❑ 86 J.J. Birden .10 .02
❑ 87 William Fuller .10 .02
❑ 88 Glyn Milburn .20 .07
❑ 89 Tim Worley .10 .02
❑ 90 Brett Perriman .20 .07
❑ 91 Randall Cunningham .40 .15
❑ 92 Drew Bledsoe 1.00 .40
❑ 93 Jerome Bettis .60 .25
❑ 94 Boomer Esiason .20 .07
❑ 95 Garrison Hearst .40 .15
❑ 96 Bruce Smith .40 .15
❑ 97 Jackie Harris .10 .02
❑ 98 Jeff George .40 .15
❑ 99 Tom Waddle .10 .02
❑ 100 John Copeland .10 .02
❑ 101 Bobby Hebert .10 .02
❑ 102 Joe Montana 2.50 1.00
❑ 103 Herman Moore .40 .15
❑ 104 Rick Mirer .40 .15
❑ 105 Ricky Watters .20 .07
❑ 106 Neil O'Donnell .40 .15
❑ 107 Herschel Walker .20 .07
❑ 108 Rob Moore .20 .07
❑ 109 Reggie Brooks .20 .07
❑ 110 Tommy Vardell .10 .02
❑ 111 Eric Green .10 .02
❑ 112 Stan Humphries .20 .07
❑ 113 Greg Robinson .10 .02
❑ 114 Eric Swann .20 .07
❑ 115 Courtney Hawkins .10 .02
❑ 116 Andre Reed .20 .07
❑ 117 Steve McMichael .20 .07
❑ 118 Gary Brown .10 .02
❑ 119 Terry Allen .20 .07
❑ 120 Dan Marino 2.50 1.00
❑ 121 Gary Clark .20 .07
❑ 122 Chris Warren .20 .07
❑ 123 Pierce Holt .10 .02
❑ 124 Anthony Carter .20 .07
❑ 125 Quentin Coryatt .10 .02
❑ 126 Harold Green .10 .02
❑ 127 Leonard Russell .10 .02
❑ 128 Tim McDonald .10 .02
❑ 129 Chris Spielman .20 .07
❑ 130 Cody Carlson .10 .02
❑ 131 Ronald Moore .10 .02
❑ 132 Renaldo Turnbull .10 .02
❑ 133 Ronnie Lott .20 .07
❑ 134 Natrone Means .40 .15
❑ 135 Keith Byars .10 .02
❑ 136 Henry Ellard .20 .07
❑ 137 Steve Jordan .10 .02
❑ 138 Calvin Williams .20 .07
❑ 139 Brian Blades .20 .07
❑ 140 Michael Jackson .20 .07
❑ 141 Charles Haley .20 .07
❑ 142 Curtis Conway .40 .15
❑ 143 Nick Lowery .10 .02
❑ 144 Bill Brooks .10 .02
❑ 145 Michael Haynes .20 .07
❑ 146 Willie Green .10 .02
❑ 147 Duane Bickett .10 .02
❑ 148 Shannon Sharpe .20 .07
❑ 149 Ricky Proehl .10 .02
❑ 150 Troy Aikman 1.25 .50
❑ 151 Mike Sherrard .10 .02
❑ 152 Reggie Cobb .10 .02
❑ 153 Norm Johnson .10 .02
❑ 154 Neil Smith .20 .07
❑ 155 James Francis .10 .02
❑ 156 Greg McMurtry .10 .02
❑ 157 Greg Townsend .10 .02
❑ 158 Mel Gray .10 .02
❑ 159 Rocket Ismail .20 .07
❑ 160 Leslie O'Neal .10 .02
❑ 161 Johnny Mitchell .10 .02
❑ 162 Brent Jones .20 .07
❑ 163 Chris Doleman .10 .02
❑ 164 Seth Joyner .10 .02
❑ 165 Marco Coleman .10 .02
❑ 166 Mark Higgs .10 .02
❑ 167 John L. Williams .10 .02
❑ 168 Darrell Green .10 .02
❑ 169 Mark Carrier WR .20 .07
❑ 170 Reggie White .40 .15
❑ 171 Darryl Talley .10 .02
❑ 172 Russell Maryland .10 .02
❑ 173 Mark Collins .10 .02
❑ 174 Chris Jacke .10 .02
❑ 175 Richard Dent .20 .07
❑ 176 John Taylor .20 .07
❑ 177 Rodney Hampton .20 .07
❑ 178 Dwight Stone .10 .02
❑ 179 Cornelius Bennett .20 .07
❑ 180 Cris Dishman .10 .02
❑ 181 Jerry Rice 1.25 .50
❑ 182 Rod Bernstine .10 .02
❑ 183 Keith Hamilton .10 .02
❑ 184 Keith Jackson .10 .02
❑ 185 Craig Erickson .10 .02
❑ 186 Marcus Allen .40 .15
❑ 187 Marcus Robertson .10 .02
❑ 188 Junior Seau .40 .15
❑ 189 LeShon Johnson RC .20 .07
❑ 190 Perry Klein RC .10 .02
❑ 191 Bryant Young RC .40 .15
❑ 192 Byron Bam Morris RC .20 .07
❑ 193 Jeff Cothran RC .10 .02
❑ 194 Lamar Smith RC 1.50 .60
❑ 195 Calvin Jones RC .10 .02
❑ 196 James Bostic RC .40 .15
❑ 197 Dan Wilkinson RC .20 .07
❑ 198 Marshall Faulk RC 6.00 2.50
❑ 199 Heath Shuler RC .40 .15
❑ 200 Willie McGinest RC .40 .15
❑ 201 Trev Alberts RC .20 .07
❑ 202 Trent Dilfer RC 1.50 .60
❑ 203 Sam Adams RC .20 .07
❑ 204 Charles Johnson RC .40 .15
❑ 205 Johnnie Morton RC 1.50 .60
❑ 206 Thomas Lewis RC .20 .07
❑ 207 Greg Hill RC .40 .15
❑ 208 William Floyd RC .40 .15
❑ 209 Derrick Alexander WR RC .40 .15
❑ 210 Darnay Scott RC .75 .30
❑ 211 Lake Dawson RC .20 .07
❑ 212 Errict Rhett RC .40 .15
❑ 213 Kevin Lee RC .10 .02
❑ 214 Chuck Levy RC .10 .02
❑ 215 David Palmer RC .40 .15
❑ 216 Ryan Yarborough RC .10 .02
❑ 217 Charlie Garner RC 1.50 .60
❑ 218 Mario Bates RC .40 .15
❑ 219 Jamir Miller RC .20 .07
❑ 220 Bucky Brooks RC .10 .02
❑ 221 Donnell Bennett RC .40 .15
❑ 222 Kevin Greene .20 .07
❑ 223 LeRoy Butler .10 .02
❑ 224 Anthony Pleasant .10 .02
❑ 225 Steve Christie .10 .02
❑ 226 Bill Romanowski .10 .02
❑ 227 Darren Carrington .10 .02
❑ 228 Chester McGlockton .10 .02
❑ 229 Jack Del Rio .10 .02
❑ 230 Kevin Smith .10 .02
❑ 231 Chris Zorich .10 .02
❑ 232 Donnell Woolford .10 .02
❑ 233 Tony Casillas .10 .02
❑ 234 Terry McDaniel .10 .02
❑ 235 Ray Childress .10 .02
❑ 236 John Randle .20 .07
❑ 237 Clyde Simmons .10 .02
❑ 238 Dante Jones .10 .02
❑ 239 Karl Mecklenburg .10 .02
❑ 240 Daryl Johnston .20 .07
❑ 241 Hardy Nickerson .20 .07
❑ 242 Jeff Lageman .10 .02
❑ 243 Lewis Tillman .10 .02
❑ 244 Jim McMahon .20 .07
❑ 245 Mike Pritchard .10 .02
❑ 246 Harvey Williams .20 .07
❑ 247 Sean Jones .10 .02
❑ 248 Stevon Moore .10 .02
❑ 249 Pete Metzelaars .10 .02
❑ 250 Mike Johnson .10 .02
❑ 251 Chris Slade .10 .02
❑ 252 Jessie Hester .10 .02
❑ 253 Louis Oliver .10 .02
❑ 254 Ken Harvey .10 .02
❑ 255 Bryan Cox .10 .02
❑ 256 Erik Kramer .20 .07
❑ 257 Andy Harmon .10 .02
❑ 258 Rickey Jackson .10 .02
❑ 259 Mark Carrier DB .10 .02
❑ 260 Greg Lloyd .20 .07
❑ 261 Robert Brooks .40 .15
❑ 262 Dave Brown .20 .07
❑ 263 Dennis Smith .10 .02
❑ 264 Michael Dean Perry .20 .07
❑ 265 Dan Saleaumua .10 .02
❑ 266 Mo Lewis .10 .02
❑ 267 AFC Checklist .10 .02
❑ 268 AFC Checklist .10 .02
❑ 269 NFC Checklist .10 .02
❑ 270 NFC Checklist .10 .02
❑ 271SP Jerry Rice TD King SP 8.00 4.00
❑ NNO Drew Bledsoe Pin.Passer 40.00 15.00

1995 Pinnacle

❑ COMPLETE SET (250) 20.00 8.00
❑ 1 Reggie White .40 .15
❑ 2 Troy Aikman 1.00 .40
❑ 3 Willie Davis .20 .07
❑ 4 Jerry Rice 1.00 .40
❑ 5 Bruce Smith .40 .15
❑ 6 Keith Byars .10 .02
❑ 7 Chris Warren .20 .07
❑ 8 Erik Kramer .10 .02
❑ 9 Leon Lett .10 .02
❑ 10 Greg Lloyd .20 .07
❑ 11 Jackie Harris .10 .02
❑ 12 Irving Fryar .20 .07
❑ 13 Rodney Hampton .20 .07
❑ 14 Michael Irvin .40 .15
❑ 15 Michael Haynes .20 .07
❑ 16 Irving Spikes .20 .07
❑ 17 Calvin Williams .20 .07
❑ 18 Ken Norton Jr. .20 .07
❑ 19 Herman Moore .40 .15
❑ 20 Lewis Tillman .10 .02
❑ 21 Cortez Kennedy .20 .07
❑ 22 Dan Marino 2.00 .75
❑ 23 Erric Pegram .20 .07
❑ 24 Tim Brown .40 .15
❑ 25 Jeff Blake RC .75 .30
❑ 26 Brett Favre 2.00 .75
❑ 27 Garrison Hearst .40 .15
❑ 28 Ronnie Harmon .10 .02
❑ 29 Qadry Ismail .20 .07
❑ 30 Ben Coates .20 .07
❑ 31 Deion Sanders .60 .25
❑ 32 John Elway 2.00 .75

❑ 33 Natrone Means .20 .07
❑ 34 Derrick Alexander WR .40 .15
❑ 35 Craig Heyward .20 .07
❑ 36 Jake Reed .20 .07
❑ 37 Steve Walsh .10 .02
❑ 38 John Randle .20 .07
❑ 39 Barry Sanders 1.50 .60
❑ 40 Tydus Winans .10 .02
❑ 41 Thomas Lewis .20 .07
❑ 42 Jim Kelly .40 .15
❑ 43 Gus Frerotte .20 .07
❑ 44 Cris Carter .40 .15
❑ 45 Kevin Williams WR .20 .07
❑ 46 Dave Meggett .10 .02
❑ 47 Pat Swilling .10 .02
❑ 48 Neil O'Donnell .20 .07
❑ 49 Terance Mathis .20 .07
❑ 50 Desmond Howard .20 .07
❑ 51 Bryant Young .20 .07
❑ 52 Stan Humphries .20 .07
❑ 53 Alvin Harper .10 .02
❑ 54 Henry Ellard .20 .07
❑ 55 Jessie Hester .10 .02
❑ 56 Lorenzo White .10 .02
❑ 57 John Friesz .20 .07
❑ 58 Anthony Smith .10 .02
❑ 59 Bert Emanuel .40 .15
❑ 60 Gary Clark .10 .02
❑ 61 Bill Brooks .10 .02
❑ 62 Steve Young .75 .30
❑ 63 Jerome Bettis .40 .15
❑ 64 John Taylor .10 .02
❑ 65 Ricky Proehl .10 .02
❑ 66 Junior Seau .40 .15
❑ 67 Bubby Brister .10 .02
❑ 68 Neil Smith .20 .07
❑ 69 Dan McGwire .10 .02
❑ 70 Brett Perriman .20 .07
❑ 71 Chris Spielman .20 .07
❑ 72 Jeff George .20 .07
❑ 73 Emmitt Smith 1.00 .40
❑ 74 Chris Penn .10 .02
❑ 75 Derrick Fenner .10 .02
❑ 76 Reggie Brooks .20 .07
❑ 77 Chris Chandler .20 .07
❑ 78 Rod Woodson .20 .07
❑ 79 Isaac Bruce .60 .25
❑ 80 Reggie Cobb .10 .02
❑ 81 Bryce Paup .20 .07
❑ 82 Warren Moon .20 .07
❑ 83 Bryan Reeves .10 .02
❑ 84 Lake Dawson .20 .07
❑ 85 Larry Centers .20 .07
❑ 86 Marshall Faulk 1.25 .50
❑ 87 Jim Harbaugh .20 .07
❑ 88 Ray Childress .10 .02
❑ 89 Eric Metcalf .20 .07
❑ 90 Ernie Mills .10 .02
❑ 91 Lamar Lathon .10 .02
❑ 92 Errict Rhett .20 .07
❑ 93 David Klingler .20 .07
❑ 94 Vincent Brown .10 .02
❑ 95 Andre Rison .20 .07
❑ 96 Brian Mitchell .10 .02
❑ 97 Mark Rypien .10 .02
❑ 98 Eugene Robinson .10 .02
❑ 99 Eric Green .10 .02
❑ 100 Rocket Ismail .20 .07
❑ 101 Flipper Anderson .10 .02
❑ 102 Randall Cunningham .40 .15
❑ 103 Ricky Watters .20 .07
❑ 104 Amp Lee .10 .02
❑ 105 Ernest Givins .10 .02
❑ 106 Daryl Johnston .20 .07
❑ 107 Dave Krieg .10 .02
❑ 108 Dana Stubblefield .20 .07
❑ 109 Torrance Small .10 .02
❑ 110 Yancey Thigpen RC .20 .07
❑ 111 Chester McGlockton .20 .07
❑ 112 Craig Erickson .10 .02
❑ 113 Herschel Walker .20 .07
❑ 114 Mike Sherrard .10 .02
❑ 115 Tony McGee .10 .02
❑ 116 Adrian Murrell .20 .07
❑ 117 Frank Reich .10 .02
❑ 118 Hardy Nickerson .10 .02
❑ 119 Andre Reed .20 .07
❑ 120 Leonard Russell .10 .02
❑ 121 Eric Allen .10 .02
❑ 122 Jeff Hostetler .20 .07
❑ 123 Barry Foster .20 .07
❑ 124 Anthony Miller .20 .07
❑ 125 Shawn Jefferson .10 .02
❑ 126 Richie Anderson RC .50 .20
❑ 127 Steve Bono .20 .07
❑ 128 Seth Joyner .10 .02
❑ 129 Darnay Scott .20 .07
❑ 130 Johnny Mitchell .10 .02
❑ 131 Eric Swann .20 .07
❑ 132 Drew Bledsoe .60 .25
❑ 133 Marcus Allen .40 .15
❑ 134 Carl Pickens .20 .07
❑ 135 Michael Brooks .10 .02
❑ 136 John L. Williams .10 .02
❑ 137 Steve Beuerlein .20 .07
❑ 138 Robert Smith .40 .15
❑ 139 O.J. McDuffie .40 .15
❑ 140 Haywood Jeffires .10 .02
❑ 141 Aeneas Williams .10 .02
❑ 142 Rick Mirer .20 .07
❑ 143 William Floyd .20 .07
❑ 144 Fred Barnett .20 .07
❑ 145 Leroy Hoard .10 .02
❑ 146 Terry Kirby .20 .07
❑ 147 Boomer Esiason .20 .07
❑ 148 Ken Harvey .10 .02
❑ 149 Cleveland Gary .10 .02
❑ 150 Brian Blades .20 .07
❑ 151 Eric Turner .10 .02
❑ 152 Vinny Testaverde .20 .07
❑ 153 Ronald Moore UER .10 .02
❑ 154 Curtis Conway .40 .15
❑ 155 Johnnie Morton .20 .07
❑ 156 Kenneth Davis .10 .02
❑ 157 Scott Mitchell .20 .07
❑ 158 Sean Gilbert .20 .07
❑ 159 Shannon Sharpe .20 .07
❑ 160 Mark Seay .20 .07
❑ 161 Cornelius Bennett .20 .07
❑ 162 Heath Shuler .20 .07
❑ 163 Byron Bam Morris .10 .02
❑ 164 Robert Brooks .40 .15
❑ 165 Glyn Milburn .10 .02
❑ 166 Gary Brown .10 .02
❑ 167 Jim Everett .10 .02
❑ 168 Steve Atwater .10 .02
❑ 169 Darren Woodson .20 .07
❑ 170 Mark Ingram .10 .02
❑ 171 Donnell Woolford .10 .02
❑ 172 Trent Dilfer .40 .15
❑ 173 Charlie Garner .40 .15
❑ 174 Charles Johnson .20 .07
❑ 175 Mike Pritchard .10 .02
❑ 176 Derek Brown RBK .10 .02
❑ 177 Chris Miller .10 .02
❑ 178 Charles Haley .20 .07
❑ 179 J.J. Birden .10 .02
❑ 180 Jeff Graham .10 .02
❑ 181 Bernie Parmalee .20 .07
❑ 182 Mark Brunell .60 .25
❑ 183 Greg Hill .20 .07
❑ 184 Michael Timpson .10 .02
❑ 185 Terry Allen .20 .07
❑ 186 Ricky Ervins .10 .02
❑ 187 Dave Brown .20 .07
❑ 188 Dan Wilkinson .20 .07
❑ 189 Jay Novacek .20 .07
❑ 190 Harvey Williams .10 .02
❑ 191 Mario Bates .20 .07
❑ 192 Steve Young LAW .50 .20
❑ 193 Joe Montana 2.00 .75
❑ 194 Steve Young PP .50 .20
❑ 195 Troy Aikman PP .60 .25
❑ 196 Drew Bledsoe PP .40 .15
❑ 197 Dan Marino PP 1.00 .40
❑ 198 John Elway PP 1.00 .40
❑ 199 Brett Favre PP 1.00 .40
❑ 200 Heath Shuler PP .20 .07
❑ 201 Warren Moon PP .10 .02
❑ 202 Jim Kelly PP .40 .15
❑ 203 Jeff Hostetler PP .20 .07
❑ 204 Rick Mirer PP .20 .07
❑ 205 Dave Brown PP .20 .07
❑ 206 Randall Cunningham PP .20 .07
❑ 207 Neil O'Donnell PP .20 .07
❑ 208 Jim Everett PP .10 .02
❑ 209 Ki-Jana Carter RC .40 .15
❑ 210 Steve McNair RC 3.00 1.25
❑ 211 Michael Westbrook RC .40 .15
❑ 212 Kerry Collins RC 1.50 .60
❑ 213 Joey Galloway RC 1.50 .60
❑ 214 Kyle Brady RC .40 .15
❑ 215 J.J. Stokes RC .40 .15
❑ 216 Tyrone Wheatley RC 1.25 .50
❑ 217 Rashaan Salaam RC .20 .07
❑ 218 Napoleon Kaufman RC 1.25 .50
❑ 219 Frank Sanders RC .40 .15
❑ 220 Stoney Case RC .10 .02
❑ 221 Todd Collins RC .20 .07
❑ 222 Warren Sapp RC 1.50 .60
❑ 223 Sherman Williams RC .10 .02
❑ 224 Rob Johnson RC 1.00 .40
❑ 225 Mark Bruener RC .20 .07
❑ 226 Derrick Brooks RC 1.50 .60
❑ 227 Chad May RC .10 .02
❑ 228 James A.Stewart RC .10 .02
❑ 229 Ray Zellars RC .20 .07
❑ 230 Dave Barr RC .10 .02
❑ 231 Kordell Stewart RC 1.50 .60
❑ 232 Jimmy Oliver RC .10 .02
❑ 233 Tony Boselli RC .40 .15
❑ 234 James O. Stewart RC 1.25 .50
❑ 235 Derrick Alexander DE RC .10 .02
❑ 236 Lovell Pinkney RC .10 .02
❑ 237 John Walsh RC .10 .02
❑ 238 Tyrone Davis RC .10 .02
❑ 239 Joe Aska RC .10 .02
❑ 240 Korey Stringer RC .20 .07
❑ 241 Hugh Douglas RC .40 .15
❑ 242 Christian Fauria RC .20 .07
❑ 243 Terrell Fletcher RC .10 .02
❑ 244 Dan Marino CL .60 .25
❑ 245 Drew Bledsoe CL .40 .15
❑ 246 John Elway CL .40 .15
❑ 247 Emmitt Smith CL .50 .20
❑ 248 Steve Young CL .40 .15
❑ 249 Barry Sanders CL .60 .25
❑ 250 Jerry Rice/Seau CL .40 .15
❑ 251SP Deion Sanders SP 4.00 1.50

1996 Pinnacle

❑ COMPLETE SET (200) 20.00 8.00
❑ 1 Emmitt Smith 1.50 .60
❑ 2 Robert Brooks .40 .15
❑ 3 Joey Galloway .40 .15
❑ 4 Dan Marino 2.00 .75
❑ 5 Frank Sanders .20 .07
❑ 6 Cris Carter .40 .15
❑ 7 Jeff Blake .40 .15
❑ 8 Steve McNair .75 .30
❑ 9 Tamarick Vanover .20 .07
❑ 10 Andre Reed .20 .07
❑ 11 Junior Seau .40 .15
❑ 12 Alvin Harper .10 .02
❑ 13 Trent Dilfer .40 .15
❑ 14 Kordell Stewart .40 .15
❑ 15 Kyle Brady .10 .02
❑ 16 Charles Haley .20 .07
❑ 17 Greg Lloyd .20 .07
❑ 18 Mario Bates .20 .07
❑ 19 Shannon Sharpe .20 .07
❑ 20 Scott Mitchell .20 .07
❑ 21 Craig Heyward .10 .02

❑ 22	Marcus Allen	.40	.15
❑ 23	Curtis Martin	.75	.30
❑ 24	Drew Bledsoe	.60	.25
❑ 25	Jerry Rice	1.00	.40
❑ 26	Charlie Garner	.20	.07
❑ 27	Michael Irvin	.40	.15
❑ 28	Curtis Conway	.40	.15
❑ 29	Terrell Davis	.75	.30
❑ 30	Jeff Hostetler	.10	.02
❑ 31	Neil O'Donnell	.20	.07
❑ 32	Erric Rhett	.20	.07
❑ 33	Stan Humphries	.20	.07
❑ 34	Jeff Graham	.10	.02
❑ 35	Floyd Turner	.10	.02
❑ 36	Vincent Brisby	.10	.02
❑ 37	Steve Young	.75	.30
❑ 38	Carl Pickens	.20	.07
❑ 39	Terance Mathis	.10	.02
❑ 40	Brett Favre	2.00	.75
❑ 41	Ki-Jana Carter	.20	.07
❑ 42	Jim Everett	.10	.02
❑ 43	Marshall Faulk	.50	.20
❑ 44	William Floyd	.20	.07
❑ 45	Deion Sanders	.60	.25
❑ 46	Garrison Hearst	.20	.07
❑ 47	Chris Sanders	.20	.07
❑ 48	Isaac Bruce	.40	.15
❑ 49	Natrone Means	.20	.07
❑ 50	Troy Aikman	1.00	.40
❑ 51	Ben Coates	.20	.07
❑ 52	Tony Martin	.20	.07
❑ 53	Rod Woodson	.20	.07
❑ 54	Edgar Bennett	.20	.07
❑ 55	Eric Zeier	.10	.02
❑ 56	Steve Bono	.10	.02
❑ 57	Tim Brown	.40	.15
❑ 58	Kevin Williams	.10	.02
❑ 59	Erik Kramer	.10	.02
❑ 60	Jim Kelly	.40	.15
❑ 61	Larry Centers	.20	.07
❑ 62	Terrell Fletcher	.10	.02
❑ 63	Michael Westbrook	.40	.15
❑ 64	Kerry Collins	.40	.15
❑ 65	Jay Novacek	.10	.02
❑ 66	J.J. Stokes	.40	.15
❑ 67	John Elway	2.00	.75
❑ 68	Jim Harbaugh	.20	.07
❑ 69	Aeneas Williams	.10	.02
❑ 70	Tyrone Wheatley	.20	.07
❑ 71	Chris Warren	.20	.07
❑ 72	Rodney Thomas	.10	.02
❑ 73	Jeff George	.20	.07
❑ 74	Rick Mirer	.20	.07
❑ 75	Yancey Thigpen	.20	.07
❑ 76	Herman Moore	.20	.07
❑ 77	Gus Frerotte	.20	.07
❑ 78	Anthony Miller	.20	.07
❑ 79	Ricky Watters	.20	.07
❑ 80	Sherman Williams	.10	.02
❑ 81	Hardy Nickerson	.10	.02
❑ 82	Henry Ellard	.10	.02
❑ 83	Aaron Craver	.10	.02
❑ 84	Rodney Peete	.10	.02
❑ 85	Eric Metcalf	.10	.02
❑ 86	Brian Blades	.10	.02
❑ 87	Rob Moore	.20	.07
❑ 88	Kimble Anders	.20	.07
❑ 89	Harvey Williams	.10	.02
❑ 90	Thurman Thomas	.40	.15
❑ 91	Dave Brown	.10	.02
❑ 92	Terry Allen	.20	.07
❑ 93	Ken Norton Jr.	.10	.02
❑ 94	Reggie White	.40	.15
❑ 95	Mark Chmura	.20	.07
❑ 96	Bert Emanuel	.20	.07
❑ 97	Brett Perriman	.10	.02
❑ 98	Antonio Freeman	.40	.15
❑ 99	Brian Mitchell	.10	.02
❑ 100	Orlando Thomas	.10	.02
❑ 101	Aaron Hayden	.10	.02
❑ 102	Quinn Early	.10	.02
❑ 103	Lovell Pinkney	.10	.02
❑ 104	Napoleon Kaufman	.40	.15
❑ 105	Daryl Johnston	.20	.07
❑ 106	Steve Tasker	.10	.02
❑ 107	Brent Jones	.10	.02
❑ 108	Mark Brunell	.60	.25
❑ 109	Leslie O'Neal	.10	.02
❑ 110	Irving Fryar	.20	.07
❑ 111	Jim Miller	.40	.15
❑ 112	Sean Dawkins	.10	.02
❑ 113	Boomer Esiason	.20	.07
❑ 114	Heath Shuler	.20	.07
❑ 115	Bruce Smith	.20	.07
❑ 116	Russell Maryland	.10	.02
❑ 117	Jake Reed	.20	.07
❑ 118	O.J. McDuffie	.20	.07
❑ 119	Erik Williams	.10	.02
❑ 120	Willie McGinest	.10	.02
❑ 121	Terry Kirby	.20	.07
❑ 122	Fred Barnett	.10	.02
❑ 123	Andre Hastings	.10	.02
❑ 124	Dale Hellestrae	.10	.02
❑ 125	Darren Woodson	.20	.07
❑ 126	Steve Atwater	.10	.02
❑ 127	Quentin Coryatt	.10	.02
❑ 128	Derrick Thomas	.40	.15
❑ 129	Nate Newton	.10	.02
❑ 130	Kevin Greene	.20	.07
❑ 131	Barry Sanders	1.50	.60
❑ 132	Warren Moon	.20	.07
❑ 133	Rashaan Salaam	.20	.07
❑ 134	Rodney Hampton	.20	.07
❑ 135	James O.Stewart	.20	.07
❑ 136	Erric Pegram	.10	.02
❑ 137	Bryan Cox	.10	.02
❑ 138	Adrian Murrell	.20	.07
❑ 139	Robert Smith	.20	.07
❑ 140	Bernie Parmalee	.10	.02
❑ 141	Bryce Paup	.10	.02
❑ 142	Darick Holmes	.10	.02
❑ 143	Hugh Douglas	.20	.07
❑ 144	Ken Dilger	.20	.07
❑ 145	Derek Loville	.10	.02
❑ 146	Horace Copeland	.10	.02
❑ 147	Wayne Chrebet	.60	.25
❑ 148	Andre Coleman	.10	.02
❑ 149	Greg Hill	.20	.07
❑ 150	Eric Swann	.10	.02
❑ 151	Tyrone Hughes	.10	.02
❑ 152	Ernie Mills	.10	.02
❑ 153	Terry Glenn RC	1.25	.50
❑ 154	Cedric Jones RC	.10	.02
❑ 155	Leeland McElroy RC	.20	.07
❑ 156	Bobby Engram RC	.40	.15
❑ 157	Willie Anderson RC	.10	.02
❑ 158	Mike Alstott RC	1.25	.50
❑ 159	Alex Van Dyke RC	.20	.07
❑ 160	Jeff Lewis RC	.20	.07
❑ 161	Keyshawn Johnson RC	1.25	.50
❑ 162	Regan Upshaw RC	.10	.02
❑ 163	Eric Moulds RC	1.50	.60
❑ 164	Tim Biakabutuka RC	.40	.15
❑ 165	Kevin Hardy RC	.40	.15
❑ 166	Marvin Harrison RC	3.00	1.25
❑ 167	Karim Abdul-Jabbar RC	.40	.15
❑ 168	Tony Brackens RC	.40	.15
❑ 169	Stepfret Williams RC	.20	.07
❑ 170	Eddie George RC	1.50	.60
❑ 171	Lawrence Phillips RC	.40	.15
❑ 172	Danny Kanell RC	.40	.15
❑ 173	Derrick Mayes RC	.40	.15
❑ 174	Daryl Gardener RC	.10	.02
❑ 175	Jonathan Ogden RC	.40	.15
❑ 176	Alex Molden RC	.10	.02
❑ 177	Chris Darkins RC	.10	.02
❑ 178	Stephen Davis RC	2.00	.75
❑ 179	Rickey Dudley RC	.40	.15
❑ 180	Eddie Kennison RC	.40	.15
❑ 181	Simeon Rice RC	1.00	.40
❑ 182	Bobby Hoying RC	.40	.15
❑ 183	Troy Aikman BF6	.50	.20
❑ 184	Emmitt Smith BF6	1.00	.40
❑ 185	Michael Irvin BF6	.20	.07
❑ 186	Deion Sanders BF6	.40	.15
❑ 187	Daryl Johnston BF6	.20	.07
❑ 188	Jay Novacek BF6	.10	.02
❑ 189	Steve Young BF6	.40	.15
❑ 190	Jerry Rice BF6	.50	.20
❑ 191	J.J. Stokes BF6	.40	.15
❑ 192	Ken Norton BF6	.10	.02
❑ 193	William Floyd BF6	.20	.07
❑ 194	Brent Jones BF6	.10	.02
❑ 195	Dan Marino CL	.40	.15
❑ 196	Brett Favre CL	.40	.15
❑ 197	Emmitt Smith CL	.40	.15
❑ 198	Barry Sanders CL	.40	.15
❑ 199	ESmith/Mar/Fav/BSand CL	.40	.15
❑ 200	Brett Favre PackBack	2.00	.75

1997 Pinnacle

❑	COMPLETE SET (200)	20.00	7.50
❑ 1	Brett Favre	2.00	.75
❑ 2	Dan Marino	2.00	.75
❑ 3	Emmitt Smith	1.50	.60
❑ 4	Steve Young	.60	.25
❑ 5	Drew Bledsoe	.60	.25
❑ 6	Eddie George	.50	.20
❑ 7	Barry Sanders	1.50	.60
❑ 8	Jerry Rice	1.00	.40
❑ 9	John Elway	2.00	.75
❑ 10	Troy Aikman	1.00	.40
❑ 11	Kerry Collins	.50	.20
❑ 12	Rick Mirer	.20	.07
❑ 13	Jim Harbaugh	.30	.10
❑ 14	Elvis Grbac	.30	.10
❑ 15	Gus Frerotte	.20	.07
❑ 16	Neil O'Donnell	.30	.10
❑ 17	Jeff George	.30	.10
❑ 18	Kordell Stewart	.50	.20
❑ 19	Junior Seau	.50	.20
❑ 20	Vinny Testaverde	.30	.10
❑ 21	Terry Glenn	.50	.20
❑ 22	Anthony Johnson	.20	.07
❑ 23	Boomer Esiason	.30	.10
❑ 24	Terrell Owens	.60	.25
❑ 25	Natrone Means	.30	.10
❑ 26	Marcus Allen	.50	.20
❑ 27	James Jett	.30	.10
❑ 28	Chris T. Jones	.20	.07
❑ 29	Stan Humphries	.30	.10
❑ 30	Keith Byars	.20	.07
❑ 31	John Friesz	.20	.07
❑ 32	Mike Alstott	.50	.20
❑ 33	Eddie Kennison	.30	.10
❑ 34	Eric Moulds	.50	.20
❑ 35	Frank Sanders	.30	.10
❑ 36	Daryl Johnston	.30	.10
❑ 37	Cris Carter	.50	.20
❑ 38	Erric Rhett	.20	.07
❑ 39	Ben Coates	.30	.10
❑ 40	Shannon Sharpe	.30	.10
❑ 41	Jamal Anderson	.50	.20
❑ 42	Tim Biakabutuka	.30	.10
❑ 43	Jeff Blake	.30	.10
❑ 44	Michael Irvin	.50	.20
❑ 45	Terrell Davis	.60	.25
❑ 46	Byron Bam Morris	.20	.07
❑ 47	Rashaan Salaam	.20	.07
❑ 48	Adrian Murrell	.30	.10
❑ 49	Ty Detmer	.30	.10
❑ 50	Terry Allen	.50	.20
❑ 51	Mark Brunell	.60	.25
❑ 52	O.J. McDuffie	.30	.10
❑ 53	Willie McGinest	.20	.07
❑ 54	Chris Warren	.30	.10
❑ 55	Trent Dilfer	.50	.20
❑ 56	Jerome Bettis	.50	.20
❑ 57	Tamarick Vanover	.30	.10
❑ 58	Ki-Jana Carter	.20	.07
❑ 59	Ray Zellars	.20	.07
❑ 60	J.J. Stokes	.30	.10
❑ 61	Cornelius Bennett	.20	.07

❑ 62 Scott Mitchell	.30	.10
❑ 63 Tyrone Wheatley	.30	.10
❑ 64 Steve McNair	.60	.25
❑ 65 Tony Banks	.30	.10
❑ 66 James O.Stewart	.30	.10
❑ 67 Robert Smith	.30	.10
❑ 68 Thurman Thomas	.50	.20
❑ 69 Mark Chmura	.30	.10
❑ 70 Napoleon Kaufman	.50	.20
❑ 71 Ken Norton	.20	.07
❑ 72 Herschel Walker	.30	.10
❑ 73 Joey Galloway	.30	.10
❑ 74 Neil Smith	.30	.10
❑ 75 Simeon Rice	.30	.10
❑ 76 Michael Jackson	.30	.10
❑ 77 Muhsin Muhammad	.30	.10
❑ 78 Kevin Hardy	.20	.07
❑ 79 Irving Fryar	.30	.10
❑ 80 Jeff Hostetler	.20	.07
❑ 81 Eric Swann	.20	.07
❑ 82 Jim Everett	.20	.07
❑ 83 Karim Abdul-Jabbar	.50	.20
❑ 84 Garrison Hearst	.30	.10
❑ 85 Lawrence Phillips	.20	.07
❑ 86 Bryan Cox	.20	.07
❑ 87 Larry Centers	.30	.10
❑ 88 Wesley Walls	.30	.10
❑ 89 Curtis Conway	.30	.10
❑ 90 Darnay Scott	.30	.10
❑ 91 Anthony Miller	.20	.07
❑ 92 Edgar Bennett	.30	.10
❑ 93 Willie Green	.20	.07
❑ 94 Kent Graham	.20	.07
❑ 95 Dave Brown	.20	.07
❑ 96 Wayne Chrebet	.50	.20
❑ 97 Ricky Watters	.30	.10
❑ 98 Tony Martin	.30	.10
❑ 99 Warren Moon	.50	.20
❑ 100 Curtis Martin	.60	.25
❑ 101 Dorsey Levens	.50	.20
❑ 102 Jim Pyne	.20	.07
❑ 103 Antonio Freeman	.50	.20
❑ 104 Leeland McElroy	.20	.07
❑ 105 Isaac Bruce	.50	.20
❑ 106 Chris Sanders	.20	.07
❑ 107 Tim Brown	.50	.20
❑ 108 Greg Lloyd	.20	.07
❑ 109 Terrell Buckley	.20	.07
❑ 110 Deion Sanders	.50	.20
❑ 111 Carl Pickens	.30	.10
❑ 112 Bobby Engram	.30	.10
❑ 113 Andre Reed	.30	.10
❑ 114 Terance Mathis	.30	.10
❑ 115 Herman Moore	.30	.10
❑ 116 Robert Brooks	.30	.10
❑ 117 Ken Dilger	.20	.07
❑ 118 Keenan McCardell	.30	.10
❑ 119 Andre Hastings	.20	.07
❑ 120 Willie Davis	.20	.07
❑ 121 Bruce Smith	.30	.10
❑ 122 Rob Moore	.30	.10
❑ 123 Johnnie Morton	.30	.10
❑ 124 Sean Dawkins	.20	.07
❑ 125 Mario Bates	.20	.07
❑ 126 Henry Ellard	.20	.07
❑ 127 Derrick Alexander WR	.30	.10
❑ 128 Kevin Greene	.30	.10
❑ 129 Derrick Thomas	.50	.20
❑ 130 Rod Woodson	.30	.10
❑ 131 Rodney Hampton	.30	.10
❑ 132 Marshall Faulk	.60	.25
❑ 133 Michael Westbrook	.30	.10
❑ 134 Erik Kramer	.20	.07
❑ 135 Todd Collins	.20	.07
❑ 136 Bill Romanowski	.20	.07
❑ 137 Jake Reed	.30	.10
❑ 138 Heath Shuler	.20	.07
❑ 139 Keyshawn Johnson	.50	.20
❑ 140 Marvin Harrison	.50	.20
❑ 141 Andre Rison	.30	.10
❑ 142 Zach Thomas	.50	.20
❑ 143 Eric Metcalf	.30	.10
❑ 144 Amani Toomer	.30	.10
❑ 145 Desmond Howard	.30	.10
❑ 146 Jimmy Smith	.30	.10
❑ 147 Brad Johnson	.50	.20
❑ 148 Troy Vincent	.20	.07
❑ 149 Bryce Paup	.20	.07
❑ 150 Reggie White	.50	.20
❑ 151 Jake Plummer RC	2.50	1.00
❑ 152 Darnell Autry RC	.30	.10
❑ 153 Tiki Barber RC	3.00	1.25
❑ 154 Pat Barnes RC	.50	.20
❑ 155 Orlando Pace RC	.50	.20
❑ 156 Peter Boulware RC	.50	.20
❑ 157 Shawn Springs RC	.30	.10
❑ 158 Troy Davis RC	.30	.10
❑ 159 Ike Hilliard RC	.75	.30
❑ 160 Jim Druckenmiller RC	.30	.10
❑ 161 Warrick Dunn RC	1.50	.50
❑ 162 James Farrior RC	.50	.20
❑ 163 Tony Gonzalez RC	1.50	.60
❑ 164 Darrell Russell RC	.20	.07
❑ 165 Byron Hanspard RC	.30	.10
❑ 166 Corey Dillon RC	3.00	1.25
❑ 167 Kenny Holmes RC	.50	.20
❑ 168 Walter Jones RC	.50	.20
❑ 169 Danny Wuerffel RC	.50	.20
❑ 170 Tom Knight RC	.20	.07
❑ 171 David LaFleur RC	.20	.07
❑ 172 Kevin Lockett RC	.30	.10
❑ 173 Will Blackwell RC	.30	.10
❑ 174 Reidel Anthony RC	.50	.20
❑ 175 Dwayne Rudd RC	.50	.20
❑ 176 Yatil Green RC	.30	.10
❑ 177 Antowain Smith RC	1.25	.50
❑ 178 Rae Carruth RC	.20	.07
❑ 179 Bryant Westbrook RC	.20	.07
❑ 180 Reinard Wilson RC	.30	.10
❑ 181 Joey Kent RC	.50	.20
❑ 182 Renaldo Wynn RC	.20	.07
❑ 183 Brett Favre I	1.00	.40
❑ 184 Emmitt Smith I	.75	.30
❑ 185 Dan Marino I	1.00	.40
❑ 186 Troy Aikman I	.50	.20
❑ 187 Jerry Rice I	.50	.20
❑ 188 Drew Bledsoe I	.30	.10
❑ 189 Eddie George I	.50	.20
❑ 190 Terry Glenn I	.30	.10
❑ 191 John Elway I	1.00	.40
❑ 192 Steve Young I	.30	.10
❑ 193 Mark Brunell I	.50	.20
❑ 194 Barry Sanders I	.75	.30
❑ 195 Kerry Collins I	.30	.10
❑ 196 Curtis Martin I	.50	.20
❑ 197 Terrell Davis I	.50	.20
❑ 198 Bledsoe/KCollins/Marino CL	.50	.20
❑ 199 SYoung/Brunell/JGeorge CL	.20	.07
❑ 200 Aikman/Elway/Mirer CL	.20	.07

1997 Pinnacle Certified

❑ COMPLETE SET (150)	40.00	15.00
❑ 1 Emmitt Smith	3.00	1.25
❑ 2 Dan Marino	4.00	1.50
❑ 3 Brett Favre	4.00	1.50
❑ 4 Steve Young	1.25	.50
❑ 5 Kerry Collins	1.00	.40
❑ 6 Troy Aikman	2.00	.75
❑ 7 Drew Bledsoe	1.25	.50
❑ 8 Eddie George	1.00	.40
❑ 9 Jerry Rice	2.00	.75
❑ 10 John Elway	4.00	1.50
❑ 11 Barry Sanders	3.00	1.25
❑ 12 Mark Brunell	1.25	.50
❑ 13 Elvis Grbac	.60	.25
❑ 14 Tony Banks	.60	.25
❑ 15 Vinny Testaverde	.60	.25
❑ 16 Rick Mirer	.40	.15
❑ 17 Carl Pickens	.60	.25
❑ 18 Deion Sanders	1.00	.40
❑ 19 Terry Glenn	1.00	.40
❑ 20 Heath Shuler	.40	.15
❑ 21 Dave Brown	.40	.15
❑ 22 Keyshawn Johnson	1.00	.40
❑ 23 Jeff George	.60	.25
❑ 24 Ricky Watters	.60	.25
❑ 25 Kordell Stewart	1.00	.40
❑ 26 Junior Seau	1.00	.40
❑ 27 Terrell Owens	1.25	.50
❑ 28 Warren Moon	1.00	.40
❑ 29 Isaac Bruce	1.00	.40
❑ 30 Steve McNair	1.25	.50
❑ 31 Gus Frerotte	.40	.15
❑ 32 Trent Dilfer	1.00	.40
❑ 33 Shannon Sharpe	.60	.25
❑ 34 Scott Mitchell	.60	.25
❑ 35 Antonio Freeman	1.00	.40
❑ 36 Jim Harbaugh	.60	.25
❑ 37 Natrone Means	.60	.25
❑ 38 Marcus Allen	1.00	.40
❑ 39 Karim Abdul-Jabbar	.60	.25
❑ 40 Tim Biakabutuka	.60	.25
❑ 41 Jeff Blake	.60	.25
❑ 42 Michael Irvin	1.00	.40
❑ 43 Herschel Walker	.60	.25
❑ 44 Curtis Martin	1.25	.50
❑ 45 Eddie Kennison	.60	.25
❑ 46 Napoleon Kaufman	1.00	.40
❑ 47 Larry Centers	.60	.25
❑ 48 Jamal Anderson	1.00	.40
❑ 49 Derrick Alexander WR	.60	.25
❑ 50 Bruce Smith	.60	.25
❑ 51 Wesley Walls	.60	.25
❑ 52 Rod Smith WR	1.00	.40
❑ 53 Keenan McCardell	.60	.25
❑ 54 Robert Brooks	.60	.25
❑ 55 Willie Green	.40	.15
❑ 56 Jake Reed	.60	.25
❑ 57 Joey Galloway	.60	.25
❑ 58 Eric Metcalf	.60	.25
❑ 59 Chris Sanders	.40	.15
❑ 60 Jeff Hostetler	.40	.15
❑ 61 Kevin Greene	.60	.25
❑ 62 Frank Sanders	.60	.25
❑ 63 Dorsey Levens	1.00	.40
❑ 64 Sean Dawkins	.40	.15
❑ 65 Cris Carter	1.00	.40
❑ 66 Andre Hastings	.40	.15
❑ 67 Amani Toomer	.60	.25
❑ 68 Adrian Murrell	.60	.25
❑ 69 Ty Detmer	.60	.25
❑ 70 Yancey Thigpen	.60	.25
❑ 71 Jim Everett	.40	.15
❑ 72 Todd Collins	.40	.15
❑ 73 Curtis Conway	.60	.25
❑ 74 Herman Moore	.60	.25
❑ 75 Neil O'Donnell	.60	.25
❑ 76 Rod Woodson	.60	.25
❑ 77 Tony Martin	.60	.25
❑ 78 Kent Graham	.40	.15
❑ 79 Andre Reed	.60	.25
❑ 80 Reggie White	1.00	.40
❑ 81 Thurman Thomas	1.00	.40
❑ 82 Garrison Hearst	.60	.25
❑ 83 Chris Warren	.60	.25
❑ 84 Wayne Chrebet	1.00	.40
❑ 85 Chris T. Jones	.40	.15
❑ 86 Anthony Miller	.40	.15
❑ 87 Chris Chandler	.60	.25
❑ 88 Terrell Davis	1.25	.50
❑ 89 Mike Alstott	1.00	.40
❑ 90 Terry Allen	1.00	.40
❑ 91 Jerome Bettis	1.00	.40
❑ 92 Stan Humphries	.60	.25
❑ 93 Andre Rison	.60	.25
❑ 94 Marshall Faulk	1.25	.50
❑ 95 Erik Kramer	.40	.15
❑ 96 O.J. McDuffie	.60	.25
❑ 97 Robert Smith	.60	.25
❑ 98 Keith Byars	.40	.15
❑ 99 Rodney Hampton	.60	.25
❑ 100 Desmond Howard	.60	.25
❑ 101 Lawrence Phillips	.40	.15

❑ 102 Michael Westbrook .60 .25
❑ 103 Johnnie Morton .60 .25
❑ 104 Ben Coates .60 .25
❑ 105 J.J. Stokes .60 .25
❑ 106 Terance Mathis .60 .25
❑ 107 Errict Rhett .40 .15
❑ 108 Tim Brown 1.00 .40
❑ 109 Marvin Harrison 1.00 .40
❑ 110 Muhsin Muhammad .60 .25
❑ 111 Byron Bam Morris .40 .15
❑ 112 Mario Bates .40 .15
❑ 113 Jimmy Smith .60 .25
❑ 114 Irving Fryar .60 .25
❑ 115 Tamarick Vanover .60 .25
❑ 116 Brad Johnson 1.00 .40
❑ 117 Rashaan Salaam .40 .15
❑ 118 Ki-Jana Carter .40 .15
❑ 119 Tyrone Wheatley .60 .25
❑ 120 John Friesz .40 .15
❑ 121 Orlando Pace RC 1.25 .50
❑ 122 Jim Druckenmiller RC .60 .25
❑ 123 Byron Hanspard RC .60 .25
❑ 124 David LaFleur RC .30 .10
❑ 125 Reidel Anthony RC 1.25 .50
❑ 126 Antowain Smith RC 4.00 1.50
❑ 127 Bryant Westbrook RC .30 .10
❑ 128 Fred Lane RC .60 .25
❑ 129 Tiki Barber RC 8.00 3.00
❑ 130 Shawn Springs RC .60 .25
❑ 131 Ike Hilliard RC 2.50 1.00
❑ 132 James Farrior RC 1.25 .50
❑ 133 Darrell Russell RC .30 .10
❑ 134 Walter Jones RC 1.25 .50
❑ 135 Tom Knight RC .30 .10
❑ 136 Yatil Green RC .60 .25
❑ 137 Joey Kent RC .60 .25
❑ 138 Kevin Lockett RC .60 .25
❑ 139 Troy Davis RC .60 .25
❑ 140 Darnell Autry RC .60 .25
❑ 141 Pat Barnes RC 1.25 .50
❑ 142 Rae Carruth RC .30 .10
❑ 143 Will Blackwell RC .60 .25
❑ 144 Warrick Dunn RC 4.00 1.50
❑ 145 Corey Dillon RC 8.00 3.00
❑ 146 Dwayne Rudd RC 1.25 .50
❑ 147 Reinard Wilson RC .60 .25
❑ 148 Peter Boulware RC 1.25 .50
❑ 149 Tony Gonzalez RC 4.00 1.50
❑ 150 Danny Wuerffel RC 1.00 .40

1997 Pinnacle Inscriptions

❑ COMPLETE SET (50) 20.00 7.50
❑ 1 Mark Brunell 1.25 .50
❑ 2 Steve Young 1.25 .50
❑ 3 Rick Mirer .40 .15
❑ 4 Brett Favre 4.00 1.50
❑ 5 Tony Banks .60 .25
❑ 6 Elvis Grbac .60 .25
❑ 7 John Elway 4.00 1.50
❑ 8 Troy Aikman 2.00 .75
❑ 9 Neil O'Donnell .60 .25
❑ 10 Kordell Stewart 1.00 .40
❑ 11 Drew Bledsoe 1.25 .50
❑ 12 Kerry Collins 1.00 .40
❑ 13 Dan Marino 4.00 1.50
❑ 14 Jeff George .60 .25
❑ 15 Scott Mitchell .60 .25
❑ 16 Jim Harbaugh .60 .25
❑ 17 Dave Brown .40 .15
❑ 18 Jeff Blake .60 .25
❑ 19 Trent Dilfer 1.00 .40
❑ 20 Barry Sanders 3.00 1.25
❑ 21 Jerry Rice 2.00 .75
❑ 22 Emmitt Smith 3.00 1.25
❑ 23 Vinny Testaverde .60 .25
❑ 24 Warren Moon 1.00 .40
❑ 25 Junior Seau 1.00 .40
❑ 26 Gus Frerotte .40 .15
❑ 27 Heath Shuler .40 .15
❑ 28 Erik Kramer .40 .15
❑ 29 Boomer Esiason .60 .25
❑ 30 Jim Kelly 1.00 .40
❑ 31 Mark Brunell TNL 1.00 .40
❑ 32 Steve Young TNL 1.00 .40
❑ 33 Brett Favre TNL 2.50 1.00
❑ 34 Tony Banks TNL .60 .25
❑ 35 John Elway TNL 2.50 1.00
❑ 36 Troy Aikman TNL 1.25 .50
❑ 37 Kordell Stewart TNL 1.00 .40
❑ 38 Drew Bledsoe TNL 1.00 .40
❑ 39 Kerry Collins TNL .60 .25
❑ 40 Dan Marino TNL 2.50 1.00
❑ 41 Jim Harbaugh TNL .60 .25
❑ 42 Jeff Blake TNL .60 .25
❑ 43 Barry Sanders TNL 2.00 .75
❑ 44 Jerry Rice TNL 1.25 .50
❑ 45 Emmitt Smith TNL 2.00 .75
❑ 46 Rick Mirer TNL .40 .15
❑ 47 Jeff George TNL .40 .15
❑ 48 Neil O'Donnell TNL .60 .25
❑ 49 Elvis Grbac TNL .60 .25
❑ 50 Scott Mitchell TNL .40 .15
❑ P13 Dan Marino PROMO 2.50 1.00

1997 Pinnacle Inside

❑ COMPLETE SET (150) 20.00 7.50
❑ 1 Troy Aikman 1.00 .40
❑ 2 Dan Marino 2.00 .75
❑ 3 Barry Sanders 1.50 .60
❑ 4 Drew Bledsoe .60 .25
❑ 5 Kerry Collins .50 .20
❑ 6 Emmitt Smith 1.50 .60
❑ 7 Brett Favre 2.00 .75
❑ 8 John Elway 2.00 .75
❑ 9 Jerry Rice 1.00 .40
❑ 10 Mark Brunell .60 .25
❑ 11 Elvis Grbac .30 .10
❑ 12 Junior Seau .50 .20
❑ 13 Eddie George .50 .20
❑ 14 Steve Young .60 .25
❑ 15 Terrell Davis .60 .25
❑ 16 Thurman Thomas .50 .20
❑ 17 Deion Sanders .50 .20
❑ 18 Terrell Owens .60 .25
❑ 19 Neil O'Donnell .30 .10
❑ 20 Carl Pickens .30 .10
❑ 21 Marcus Allen .50 .20
❑ 22 Ricky Watters .30 .10
❑ 23 Vinny Testaverde .30 .10
❑ 24 Kordell Stewart .50 .20
❑ 25 Tony Banks .50 .20
❑ 26 Terry Glenn .50 .20
❑ 27 Todd Collins .20 .07
❑ 28 Robert Brooks .30 .10
❑ 29 Heath Shuler .20 .07
❑ 30 Shannon Sharpe .30 .10
❑ 31 Michael Westbrook .30 .10
❑ 32 Reggie White .50 .20
❑ 33 Brad Johnson .50 .20
❑ 34 Tamarick Vanover .30 .10
❑ 35 Larry Centers .30 .10
❑ 36 Terance Mathis .30 .10
❑ 37 Hardy Nickerson .20 .07
❑ 38 Jamal Anderson .50 .20
❑ 39 Kevin Hardy .20 .07
❑ 40 Stan Humphries .30 .10
❑ 41 Chris Warren .30 .10
❑ 42 Tim Brown .50 .20
❑ 43 Joey Galloway .30 .10
❑ 44 Boomer Esiason .30 .10
❑ 45 Jake Reed .30 .10
❑ 46 Kent Graham .20 .07
❑ 47 Marshall Faulk .60 .25
❑ 48 Sean Dawkins .20 .07
❑ 49 Dave Brown .20 .07
❑ 50 Willie Green .20 .07
❑ 51 Andre Hastings .20 .07
❑ 52 Erik Kramer .20 .07
❑ 53 Michael Irvin .50 .20
❑ 54 Gus Frerotte .20 .07
❑ 55 Winslow Oliver .20 .07
❑ 56 Jimmy Smith .30 .10
❑ 57 Derrick Alexander WR .30 .10
❑ 58 Adrian Murrell .30 .10
❑ 59 Ki-Jana Carter .20 .07
❑ 60 Garrison Hearst .30 .10
❑ 61 Chris Sanders .20 .07
❑ 62 Johnnie Morton .30 .10
❑ 63 Lawrence Phillips .20 .07
❑ 64 Bobby Engram .30 .10
❑ 65 Tim Biakabutuka .30 .10
❑ 66 Anthony Johnson .20 .07
❑ 67 Keyshawn Johnson .50 .20
❑ 68 Jeff George .30 .10
❑ 69 Errict Rhett .20 .07
❑ 70 Cris Carter .50 .20
❑ 71 Chris T. Jones .20 .07
❑ 72 Eric Moulds .50 .20
❑ 73 Rick Mirer .20 .07
❑ 74 Keenan McCardell .30 .10
❑ 75 Simeon Rice .30 .10
❑ 76 Eddie Kennison .30 .10
❑ 77 Herman Moore .30 .10
❑ 78 Jim Harbaugh .30 .10
❑ 79 Robert Smith .30 .10
❑ 80 Bruce Smith .30 .10
❑ 81 John Friesz .20 .07
❑ 82 Irving Fryar .30 .10
❑ 83 Edgar Bennett .30 .10
❑ 84 Ty Detmer .30 .10
❑ 85 Curtis Conway .30 .10
❑ 86 Napoleon Kaufman .50 .20
❑ 87 Tony Martin .30 .10
❑ 88 Amani Toomer .30 .10
❑ 89 Willie McGinest .20 .07
❑ 90 Daryl Johnston .30 .10
❑ 91 Stanley Pritchett .20 .07
❑ 92 Chris Chandler .30 .10
❑ 93 Natrone Means .30 .10
❑ 94 Kimble Anders .30 .10
❑ 95 Steve McNair .60 .25
❑ 96 Curtis Martin .60 .25
❑ 97 O.J. McDuffie .30 .10
❑ 98 Ben Coates .30 .10
❑ 99 Jerome Bettis .50 .20
❑ 100 Andre Reed .30 .10
❑ 101 Jeff Blake .30 .10
❑ 102 Wesley Walls .30 .10
❑ 103 Warren Moon .50 .20
❑ 104 Isaac Bruce .50 .20
❑ 105 Terry Allen .50 .20
❑ 106 Rodney Hampton .30 .10
❑ 107 Karim Abdul-Jabbar .50 .20
❑ 108 Marvin Harrison .50 .20
❑ 109 Dorsey Levens .50 .20
❑ 110 Rashaan Salaam .20 .07
❑ 111 Scott Mitchell .30 .10
❑ 112 Darnay Scott .30 .10
❑ 113 Aeneas Williams .20 .07
❑ 114 Trent Dilfer .50 .20
❑ 115 Antonio Freeman .50 .20
❑ 116 Jim Everett .20 .07
❑ 117 Muhsin Muhammad .30 .10
❑ 118 Rickey Dudley .30 .10

❑ 119 Mike Alstott	.50	.20
❑ 120 Jim Druckenmiller RC	.30	.10
❑ 121 Tiki Barber RC	3.00	1.25
❑ 122 Ike Hilliard RC	.75	.30
❑ 123 Orlando Pace RC	.50	.20
❑ 124 Jake Plummer RC	2.50	1.00
❑ 125 Yatil Green RC	.30	.10
❑ 126 Byron Hanspard RC	.30	.10
❑ 127 James Farrior RC	.50	.20
❑ 128 Corey Dillon RC	3.00	1.25
❑ 129 Pat Barnes RC	.50	.20
❑ 130 Kenny Holmes RC	.50	.20
❑ 131 Rae Carruth RC	.20	.07
❑ 132 Danny Wuerffel RC	.50	.20
❑ 133 Darnell Autry RC	.30	.10
❑ 134 Reidel Anthony RC	.50	.20
❑ 135 Darrell Russell RC	.20	.07
❑ 136 Will Blackwell RC	.30	.10
❑ 137 Peter Boulware RC	.50	.20
❑ 138 Shawn Springs RC	.30	.10
❑ 139 Joey Kent RC	.50	.20
❑ 140 Troy Davis RC	.30	.10
❑ 141 Antowain Smith RC	1.25	.50
❑ 142 Walter Jones RC	.50	.20
❑ 143 Tony Gonzalez RC	1.50	.60
❑ 144 David LaFleur RC	.20	.07
❑ 145 Warrick Dunn RC	1.50	.60
❑ 146 Bryant Westbrook RC	.20	.07
❑ 147 Dwayne Rudd RC	.50	.20
❑ 148 Tom Knight RC	.20	.07
❑ 149 Kevin Lockett RC	.30	.10
❑ 150 Checklist	.20	.07
❑ P1 Troy Aikman Promo	1.00	.40
❑ P2 Dan Marino Promo	2.00	.75
❑ P7 Brett Favre Promo	2.00	.75

1997 Pinnacle Totally Certified Platinum Red

❑ COMPLETE SET (150)	150.00	60.00
❑ 1 Emmitt Smith	12.00	5.00
❑ 2 Dan Marino	15.00	6.00
❑ 3 Brett Favre	15.00	6.00
❑ 4 Steve Young	5.00	2.00
❑ 5 Kerry Collins	4.00	1.50
❑ 6 Troy Aikman	8.00	3.00
❑ 7 Drew Bledsoe	5.00	2.00
❑ 8 Eddie George	4.00	1.50
❑ 9 Jerry Rice	8.00	3.00
❑ 10 John Elway	15.00	6.00
❑ 11 Barry Sanders	12.00	5.00
❑ 12 Mark Brunell	5.00	2.00
❑ 13 Elvis Grbac	2.50	1.00
❑ 14 Tony Banks	2.50	1.00
❑ 15 Vinny Testaverde	2.50	1.00
❑ 16 Rick Mirer	1.50	.60
❑ 17 Carl Pickens	2.50	1.00
❑ 18 Deion Sanders	4.00	1.50
❑ 19 Terry Glenn	4.00	1.50
❑ 20 Heath Shuler	1.50	.60
❑ 21 Dave Brown	1.50	.60
❑ 22 Keyshawn Johnson	4.00	1.50
❑ 23 Jeff George	2.50	1.00
❑ 24 Ricky Watters	2.50	1.00
❑ 25 Kordell Stewart	4.00	1.50
❑ 26 Junior Seau	4.00	1.50
❑ 27 Terrell Owens	5.00	2.00
❑ 28 Warren Moon	4.00	1.50
❑ 29 Isaac Bruce	4.00	1.50
❑ 30 Steve McNair	5.00	2.00
❑ 31 Gus Frerotte	1.50	.60
❑ 32 Trent Dilfer	4.00	1.50
❑ 33 Shannon Sharpe	2.50	1.00
❑ 34 Scott Mitchell	2.50	1.00
❑ 35 Antonio Freeman	4.00	1.50
❑ 36 Jim Harbaugh	2.50	1.00
❑ 37 Natrone Means	2.50	1.00
❑ 38 Marcus Allen	4.00	1.50
❑ 39 Karim Abdul-Jabbar	4.00	1.50
❑ 40 Tim Biakabutuka	2.50	1.00
❑ 41 Jeff Blake	2.50	1.00
❑ 42 Michael Irvin	4.00	1.50
❑ 43 Herschel Walker	2.50	1.00
❑ 44 Curtis Martin	5.00	2.00
❑ 45 Eddie Kennison	2.50	1.00
❑ 46 Napoleon Kaufman	4.00	1.50
❑ 47 Larry Centers	2.50	1.00
❑ 48 Jamal Anderson	4.00	1.50
❑ 49 Derrick Alexander WR	2.50	1.00
❑ 50 Bruce Smith	2.50	1.00
❑ 51 Wesley Walls	2.50	1.00
❑ 52 Rod Smith WR	4.00	1.50
❑ 53 Keenan McCardell	2.50	1.00
❑ 54 Robert Brooks	2.50	1.00
❑ 55 Willie Green	1.50	.60
❑ 56 Jake Reed	2.50	1.00
❑ 57 Joey Galloway	2.50	1.00
❑ 58 Eric Metcalf	2.50	1.00
❑ 59 Chris Sanders	1.50	.60
❑ 60 Jeff Hostetler	1.50	.60
❑ 61 Kevin Greene	2.50	1.00
❑ 62 Frank Sanders	2.50	1.00
❑ 63 Dorsey Levens	4.00	1.50
❑ 64 Sean Dawkins	1.50	.60
❑ 65 Cris Carter	4.00	1.50
❑ 66 Andre Hastings	1.50	.60
❑ 67 Amani Toomer	2.50	1.00
❑ 68 Adrian Murrell	2.50	1.00
❑ 69 Ty Detmer	2.50	1.00
❑ 70 Yancey Thigpen	1.50	.60
❑ 71 Jim Everett	1.50	.60
❑ 72 Todd Collins	1.50	.60
❑ 73 Curtis Conway	2.50	1.00
❑ 74 Herman Moore	2.50	1.00
❑ 75 Neil O'Donnell	2.50	1.00
❑ 76 Rod Woodson	2.50	1.00
❑ 77 Tony Martin	2.50	1.00
❑ 78 Kent Graham	1.50	.60
❑ 79 Andre Reed	2.50	1.00
❑ 80 Reggie White	4.00	1.50
❑ 81 Thurman Thomas	4.00	1.50
❑ 82 Garrison Hearst	2.50	1.00
❑ 83 Chris Warren	2.50	1.00
❑ 84 Wayne Chrebet	4.00	1.50
❑ 85 Chris T. Jones	1.50	.60
❑ 86 Anthony Miller	1.50	.60
❑ 87 Chris Chandler	2.50	1.00
❑ 88 Terrell Davis	5.00	2.00
❑ 89 Mike Alstott	4.00	1.50
❑ 90 Terry Allen	4.00	1.50
❑ 91 Jerome Bettis	4.00	1.50
❑ 92 Stan Humphries	2.50	1.00
❑ 93 Andre Rison	2.50	1.00
❑ 94 Marshall Faulk	5.00	2.00
❑ 95 Erik Kramer	1.50	.60
❑ 96 O.J. McDuffie	2.50	1.00
❑ 97 Robert Smith	2.50	1.00
❑ 98 Keith Byars	1.50	.60
❑ 99 Rodney Hampton	2.50	1.00
❑ 100 Desmond Howard	2.50	1.00
❑ 101 Lawrence Phillips	1.50	.60
❑ 102 Michael Westbrook	2.50	1.00
❑ 103 Johnnie Morton	2.50	1.00
❑ 104 Ben Coates	2.50	1.00
❑ 105 J.J. Stokes	2.50	1.00
❑ 106 Terance Mathis	2.50	1.00
❑ 107 Errict Rhett	1.50	.60
❑ 108 Tim Brown	4.00	1.50
❑ 109 Marvin Harrison	4.00	1.50
❑ 110 Muhsin Muhammad	2.50	1.00
❑ 111 Byron Bam Morris	1.50	.60
❑ 112 Mario Bates	1.50	.60
❑ 113 Jimmy Smith	2.50	1.00
❑ 114 Irving Fryar	2.50	1.00
❑ 115 Tamarick Vanover	2.50	1.00
❑ 116 Brad Johnson	4.00	1.50
❑ 117 Rashaan Salaam	1.50	.60
❑ 118 Ki-Jana Carter	1.50	.60
❑ 119 Tyrone Wheatley	2.50	1.00
❑ 120 John Friesz	1.50	.60
❑ 121 Orlando Pace RC	4.00	1.50
❑ 122 Jim Druckenmiller RC	2.00	.75
❑ 123 Byron Hanspard RC	2.50	1.00
❑ 124 David LaFleur RC	1.00	.40
❑ 125 Reidel Anthony RC	4.00	1.50
❑ 126 Antowain Smith RC	10.00	4.00
❑ 127 Bryant Westbrook RC	1.00	.40
❑ 128 Fred Lane RC	2.00	.75
❑ 129 Tiki Barber RC	25.00	10.00
❑ 130 Shawn Springs RC	2.00	.75
❑ 131 Ike Hilliard RC	6.00	3.00
❑ 132 James Farrior RC	4.00	1.50
❑ 133 Darrell Russell RC	1.00	.40
❑ 134 Walter Jones RC	4.00	1.50
❑ 135 Tom Knight RC	1.00	.40
❑ 136 Yatil Green RC	2.00	.75
❑ 137 Joey Kent RC	2.00	.75
❑ 138 Kevin Lockett RC	2.00	.75
❑ 139 Troy Davis RC	2.00	.75
❑ 140 Darnell Autry RC	2.00	.75
❑ 141 Pat Barnes RC	4.00	1.50
❑ 142 Rae Carruth RC	1.00	.40
❑ 143 Will Blackwell RC	2.00	.75
❑ 144 Warrick Dunn RC	12.00	5.00
❑ 145 Corey Dillon RC	25.00	10.00
❑ 146 Dwayne Rudd RC	4.00	1.50
❑ 147 Reinard Wilson RC	2.00	.75
❑ 148 Peter Boulware RC	4.00	1.50
❑ 149 Tony Gonzalez RC	12.00	5.00
❑ 150 Danny Wuerffel RC	4.00	1.50

1997 Pinnacle X-Press

❑ COMPLETE SET (150)	20.00	7.50
❑ 1 Drew Bledsoe	.60	.25
❑ 2 Steve Young	.60	.25
❑ 3 Brett Favre	2.00	.75
❑ 4 John Elway	2.00	.75
❑ 5 Dan Marino	2.00	.75
❑ 6 Jerry Rice	1.00	.40
❑ 7 Tony Banks	.30	.10
❑ 8 Kerry Collins	.50	.20
❑ 9 Mark Brunell	.60	.25
❑ 10 Troy Aikman	1.00	.40
❑ 11 Barry Sanders	1.50	.60
❑ 12 Elvis Grbac	.30	.10
❑ 13 Eddie George	.50	.20
❑ 14 Terry Glenn	.50	.20
❑ 15 Kordell Stewart	.50	.20
❑ 16 Junior Seau	.50	.20
❑ 17 Herman Moore	.30	.10
❑ 18 Gus Frerotte	.20	.07
❑ 19 Warren Moon	.50	.20
❑ 20 Emmitt Smith	1.50	.60
❑ 21 Henry Ellard	.20	.07
❑ 22 Rashaan Salaam	.20	.07
❑ 23 Sean Dawkins	.20	.07
❑ 24 Tyrone Wheatley	.30	.10
❑ 25 Lawrence Phillips	.20	.07
❑ 26 Ty Detmer	.30	.10
❑ 27 Vinny Testaverde	.30	.10
❑ 28 Dorsey Levens	.50	.20
❑ 29 Ricky Watters	.30	.10
❑ 30 Natrone Means	.30	.10
❑ 31 Curtis Conway	.30	.10
❑ 32 Larry Centers	.30	.10
❑ 33 Johnnie Morton	.30	.10

❑ 34 Desmond Howard	.30	.10
❑ 35 Marcus Allen	.50	.20
❑ 36 Cris Carter	.50	.20
❑ 37 James O.Stewart	.30	.10
❑ 38 Frank Sanders	.30	.10
❑ 39 Bruce Smith	.30	.10
❑ 40 Carl Pickens	.30	.10
❑ 41 Neil O'Donnell	.30	.10
❑ 42 Trent Dilfer	.50	.20
❑ 43 Rodney Peete	.20	.07
❑ 44 Terance Mathis	.30	.10
❑ 45 Muhsin Muhammad	.30	.10
❑ 46 Jake Reed	.30	.10
❑ 47 Jim Harbaugh	.30	.10
❑ 48 Todd Collins	.20	.07
❑ 49 Ki-Jana Carter	.20	.07
❑ 50 Scott Mitchell	.30	.10
❑ 51 Kevin Hardy	.20	.07
❑ 52 Stanley Pritchett	.20	.07
❑ 53 Dave Brown	.20	.07
❑ 54 Jeff George	.30	.10
❑ 55 Stan Humphries	.30	.10
❑ 56 Isaac Bruce	.50	.20
❑ 57 Eric Moulds	.50	.20
❑ 58 Robert Brooks	.30	.10
❑ 59 Steve McNair	.60	.25
❑ 60 Adrian Murrell	.30	.10
❑ 61 Rodney Hampton	.30	.10
❑ 62 Michael Jackson	.30	.10
❑ 63 Tamarick Vanover	.30	.10
❑ 64 Edgar Bennett	.30	.10
❑ 65 Andre Hastings	.20	.07
❑ 66 Robert Smith	.30	.10
❑ 67 Thurman Thomas	.50	.20
❑ 68 Tim Biakabutuka	.30	.10
❑ 69 Rick Mirer	.20	.07
❑ 70 Deion Sanders	.50	.20
❑ 71 Curtis Martin	.60	.25
❑ 72 Garrison Hearst	.30	.10
❑ 73 Kent Graham	.20	.07
❑ 74 Anthony Johnson	.20	.07
❑ 75 Antonio Freeman	.50	.20
❑ 76 Marshall Faulk	.60	.25
❑ 77 O.J. McDuffie	.30	.10
❑ 78 Heath Shuler	.20	.07
❑ 79 Napoleon Kaufman	.50	.20
❑ 80 Aeneas Williams	.20	.07
❑ 81 Hardy Nickerson	.20	.07
❑ 82 Keenan McCardell	.30	.10
❑ 83 Erik Kramer	.20	.07
❑ 84 Ben Coates	.30	.10
❑ 85 Shannon Sharpe	.30	.10
❑ 86 Tony Martin	.30	.10
❑ 87 Chris Sanders	.20	.07
❑ 88 Jamal Anderson	.50	.20
❑ 89 Karim Abdul-Jabbar	.50	.20
❑ 90 Keyshawn Johnson	.50	.20
❑ 91 Terrell Owens	.60	.25
❑ 92 Michael Irvin	.50	.20
❑ 93 John Friesz	.20	.07
❑ 94 Chris Warren	.30	.10
❑ 95 Errict Rhett	.20	.07
❑ 96 Terry Allen	.50	.20
❑ 97 Michael Westbrook	.30	.10
❑ 98 Simeon Rice	.30	.10
❑ 99 Willie Green	.20	.07
❑ 100 Jerome Bettis	.50	.20
❑ 101 Reggie White	.50	.20
❑ 102 Bert Emanuel	.30	.10
❑ 103 Zach Thomas	.50	.20
❑ 104 Tim Brown	.50	.20
❑ 105 Darnay Scott	.30	.10
❑ 106 Terrell Davis	.60	.25
❑ 107 Andre Reed	.30	.10
❑ 108 Amani Toomer	.30	.10
❑ 109 Irving Fryar	.30	.10
❑ 110 Joey Galloway	.30	.10
❑ 111 Marvin Harrison	.50	.20
❑ 112 Derrick Alexander WR	.30	.10
❑ 113 Jeff Blake	.30	.10
❑ 114 Brad Johnson	.50	.20
❑ 115 Eddie Kennison	.30	.10
❑ 116 Rae Carruth RC	.20	.07
❑ 117 Tony Gonzalez RC	1.25	.50
❑ 118 Joey Kent RC	.50	.20
❑ 119 Peter Boulware RC	.50	.20
❑ 120 Orlando Pace RC	.50	.20
❑ 121 David LaFleur RC	.20	.07
❑ 122 Darnell Autry RC	.30	.10
❑ 123 Tiki Barber RC	2.50	1.00
❑ 124 Troy Davis RC	.30	.10
❑ 125 Jim Druckenmiller RC	.30	.10
❑ 126 Corey Dillon RC	2.50	1.00
❑ 127 Ike Hilliard RC	.60	.25
❑ 128 Reidel Anthony RC	.50	.20
❑ 129 Byron Hanspard RC	.30	.10
❑ 130 Antowain Smith RC	1.00	.40
❑ 131 Jake Plummer RC	2.00	.75
❑ 132 Warrick Dunn RC	1.25	.50
❑ 133 Bryant Westbrook RC	.20	.07
❑ 134 Darrell Russell RC	.20	.07
❑ 135 Yatil Green RC	.30	.10
❑ 136 Shawn Springs RC	.30	.10
❑ 137 Danny Wuerffel RC	.50	.20
❑ 138 Brett Favre PP	1.00	.40
❑ 139 Emmitt Smith PP	.75	.30
❑ 140 Barry Sanders PP	.75	.30
❑ 141 Troy Aikman PP	.50	.20
❑ 142 Drew Bledsoe PP	.50	.20
❑ 143 Jerry Rice PP	.50	.20
❑ 144 Dan Marino PP	1.00	.40
❑ 145 John Elway PP	1.00	.40
❑ 146 Kerry Collins PP	.30	.10
❑ 147 Mark Brunell PP	.50	.20
❑ 148 Brett Favre CL	.50	.20
❑ 149 Dan Marino CL	.50	.20
❑ 150 Troy Aikman CL	.50	.20

1992 Playoff

❑ COMPLETE SET (150)	25.00	10.00
❑ 1 Emmitt Smith	8.00	4.00
❑ 2 Steve Young	3.00	1.50
❑ 3 Jack Del Rio	.25	.08
❑ 4 Bobby Hebert	.25	.08
❑ 5 Shannon Sharpe	.75	.30
❑ 6 Gary Clark	.75	.30
❑ 7 Christian Okoye	.25	.08
❑ 8 Ernest Givins	.40	.15
❑ 9 Mike Horan	.25	.08
❑ 10 Dennis Gentry	.25	.08
❑ 11 Michael Irvin	.75	.30
❑ 12 Eric Floyd	.25	.08
❑ 13 Brent Jones	.40	.15
❑ 14 Anthony Carter	.40	.15
❑ 15 Tony Martin	.40	.15
❑ 16 Greg Lewis UER	.25	.08
❑ 17 Todd McNair	.25	.08
❑ 18 Earnest Byner	.25	.08
❑ 19 Steve Beuerlein	.40	.15
❑ 20 Roger Craig	.40	.15
❑ 21 Mark Higgs	.25	.08
❑ 22 Guy McIntyre	.25	.08
❑ 23 Don Warren	.25	.08
❑ 24 Alvin Harper	.40	.15
❑ 25 Mark Jackson	.25	.08
❑ 26 Chris Doleman	.25	.08
❑ 27 Jesse Sapolu	.25	.08
❑ 28 Tony Tolbert	.25	.08
❑ 29 Wendell Davis	.25	.08
❑ 30 Dan Saleaumua	.25	.08
❑ 31 Jeff Bostic	.25	.08
❑ 32 Jay Novacek	.40	.15
❑ 33 Cris Carter	1.00	.40
❑ 34 Tony Paige	.25	.08
❑ 35 Greg Kragen	.25	.08
❑ 36 Jeff Dellenbach	.25	.08
❑ 37 Keith DeLong	.25	.08
❑ 38 Todd Scott	.25	.08
❑ 39 Jeff Feagles	.25	.08
❑ 40 Mike Saxon	.25	.08
❑ 41 Martin Mayhew	.25	.08
❑ 42 Steve Bono RC	.75	.30
❑ 43 Willie Davis WR RC	.40	.15
❑ 44 Mark Stepnoski	.40	.15
❑ 45 Harry Newsome	.25	.08
❑ 46 Thane Gash	.25	.08
❑ 47 Gaston Green	.25	.08
❑ 48 James Washington	.25	.08
❑ 49 Kenny Walker	.25	.08
❑ 50 Jeff Davidson RC	.25	.08
❑ 51 Shane Conlan	.25	.08
❑ 52 Richard Dent	.40	.15
❑ 53 Haywood Jeffires	.40	.15
❑ 54 Harry Galbreath	.25	.08
❑ 55 Terry Allen	.75	.30
❑ 56 Tommy Barnhardt	.25	.08
❑ 57 Mike Golic	.25	.08
❑ 58 Dalton Hilliard	.25	.08
❑ 59 Danny Copeland	.25	.08
❑ 60 Jerry Fontenot RC	.25	.08
❑ 61 Kelvin Martin	.25	.08
❑ 62 Mark Kelso	.25	.08
❑ 63 Wymon Henderson	.25	.08
❑ 64 Mark Rypien	.25	.08
❑ 65 Bobby Humphrey	.25	.08
❑ 66 Rich Gannon UER	.75	.30
❑ 67 Darren Lewis	.25	.08
❑ 68 Barry Foster	.40	.15
❑ 69 Ken Norton Jr.	.40	.15
❑ 70 James Lofton	.40	.15
❑ 71 Trace Armstrong	.25	.08
❑ 72 Vestee Jackson	.25	.08
❑ 73 Clyde Simmons	.25	.08
❑ 74 Brad Muster	.25	.08
❑ 75 Cornelius Bennett	.40	.15
❑ 76 Mike Merriweather	.25	.08
❑ 77 John Elway	4.00	1.50
❑ 78 Herschel Walker	.40	.15
❑ 79 Hassan Jones UER	.25	.08
❑ 80 Jim Harbaugh	.75	.30
❑ 81 Issiac Holt	.25	.08
❑ 82 David Alexander	.25	.08
❑ 83 Brian Mitchell	.40	.15
❑ 84 Mark Tuinei	.25	.08
❑ 85 Tom Rathman	.25	.08
❑ 86 Reggie White	.75	.30
❑ 87 William Perry	.40	.15
❑ 88 Jeff Wright	.25	.08
❑ 89 Keith Kartz	.25	.08
❑ 90 Andre Waters	.25	.08
❑ 91 Darryl Talley	.25	.08
❑ 92 Morten Andersen	.25	.08
❑ 93 Tom Waddle	.25	.08
❑ 94 Felix Wright UER	.25	.08
❑ 95 Keith Jackson	.40	.15
❑ 96 Art Monk	.40	.15
❑ 97 Seth Joyner	.25	.08
❑ 98 Steve McMichael	.40	.15
❑ 99 Thurman Thomas	.75	.30
❑ 100 Warren Moon	.75	.30
❑ 101 Tony Casillas	.25	.08
❑ 102 Vance Johnson	.25	.08
❑ 103 Doug Dawson RC	.25	.08
❑ 104 Bill Maas	.25	.08
❑ 105 Mark Clayton	.40	.15
❑ 106 Hoby Brenner	.25	.08
❑ 107 Gary Anderson K	.25	.08
❑ 108 Marc Logan	.25	.08
❑ 109 Ricky Sanders	.25	.08
❑ 110 Vai Sikahema	.25	.08
❑ 111 Neil Smith	.75	.30
❑ 112 Cody Carlson	.25	.08
❑ 113 Jimmie Jones	.25	.08
❑ 114 Pat Swilling	.25	.08
❑ 115 Neil O'Donnell	.40	.15
❑ 116 Chip Lohmiller	.25	.08
❑ 117 Mike Croel	.25	.08
❑ 118 Pete Metzelaars	.25	.08
❑ 119 Ray Childress	.25	.08
❑ 120 Fred Banks	.25	.08
❑ 121 Derek Kennard	.25	.08
❑ 122 Daryl Johnston	.75	.30
❑ 123 Lorenzo White UER	.25	.08

Card		
❑ 124 Hardy Nickerson	.40	.15
❑ 125 Derrick Thomas	.75	.30
❑ 126 Steve Walsh	.25	.08
❑ 127 Doug Widell	.25	.08
❑ 128 Calvin Williams	.40	.15
❑ 129 Tim Harris	.25	.08
❑ 130 Rod Woodson	.75	.30
❑ 131 Craig Heyward	.40	.15
❑ 132 Barry Word	.25	.08
❑ 133 Mark Duper	.25	.08
❑ 134 Tim Johnson	.25	.08
❑ 135 John Gesek	.25	.08
❑ 136 Steve Jackson	.25	.08
❑ 137 Dave Krieg	.40	.15
❑ 138 Barry Sanders	4.00	1.50
❑ 139 Michael Haynes	.40	.15
❑ 140 Eric Metcalf	.40	.15
❑ 141 Stan Humphries	.75	.30
❑ 142 Sterling Sharpe	.75	.30
❑ 143 Todd Marinovich	.25	.08
❑ 144 Rodney Hampton	.40	.15
❑ 145 Rodney Peete	.40	.15
❑ 146 Darryl Williams RC	.25	.08
❑ 147 Darren Perry RC	.25	.08
❑ 148 Terrell Buckley RC	.25	.08
❑ 149 Amp Lee RC	.25	.08
❑ 150 Ricky Watters	.75	.30

1993 Playoff

Card		
❑ COMPLETE SET (315)	25.00	10.00
❑ 1 Troy Aikman	1.50	.60
❑ 2 Jerry Rice	2.00	.75
❑ 3 Keith Jackson	.20	.07
❑ 4 Sean Gilbert	.20	.07
❑ 5 Jim Kelly	.40	.15
❑ 6 Junior Seau	.40	.15
❑ 7 Deion Sanders	1.00	.40
❑ 8 Joe Montana	3.00	1.25
❑ 9 Terrell Buckley	.10	.02
❑ 10 Emmitt Smith	3.00	1.25
❑ 11 Pete Stoyanovich	.10	.02
❑ 12 Randall Cunningham	.40	.15
❑ 13 Boomer Esiason	.20	.07
❑ 14 Mike Saxon	.10	.02
❑ 15 Chuck Cecil	.10	.02
❑ 16 Vinny Testaverde	.20	.07
❑ 17 Jeff Hostetler	.20	.07
❑ 18 Mark Clayton	.10	.02
❑ 19 Nick Bell	.10	.02
❑ 20 Frank Reich	.20	.07
❑ 21 Henry Ellard	.20	.07
❑ 22 Andre Reed	.20	.07
❑ 23 Mark Ingram	.10	.02
❑ 24 Mike Brim	.10	.02
❑ 25A Bernie Kosar ERR Kozar	.20	.07
❑ 25B Bernie Kosar COR	.20	.07
❑ 26 Jeff George	.40	.15
❑ 27 Tommy Maddox	.40	.15
❑ 28 Kent Graham RC	.40	.15
❑ 29 David Klingler	.10	.02
❑ 30 Robert Delpino	.10	.02
❑ 31 Kevin Fagan	.10	.02
❑ 32 Mark Bavaro	.10	.02
❑ 33 Harold Green	.10	.02
❑ 34 Shawn McCarthy	.10	.02
❑ 35 Ricky Proehl	.10	.02
❑ 36 Eugene Robinson	.10	.02
❑ 37 Phil Simms	.20	.07
❑ 38 David Lang	.10	.02
❑ 39 Santana Dotson	.20	.07
❑ 40 Brett Perriman	.40	.15
❑ 41 Jim Harbaugh	.40	.15
❑ 42 Keith Byars	.10	.02
❑ 43 Quentin Coryatt	.20	.07
❑ 44 Louis Oliver	.10	.02
❑ 45 Howie Long	.40	.15
❑ 46 Mike Sherrard	.10	.02
❑ 47 Earnest Byner	.10	.02
❑ 48 Neil Smith	.40	.15
❑ 49 Audray McMillian	.10	.02
❑ 50 Vaughn Dunbar	.10	.02
❑ 51 Ronnie Lott	.20	.07
❑ 52 Clyde Simmons	.10	.02
❑ 53 Kevin Scott	.10	.02
❑ 54 Bubby Brister	.10	.02
❑ 55 Randal Hill	.10	.02
❑ 56 Pat Swilling	.10	.02
❑ 57 Steve Beuerlein	.20	.07
❑ 58 Gary Clark	.20	.07
❑ 59 Brian Noble	.10	.02
❑ 60 Leslie O'Neal	.20	.07
❑ 61 Vincent Brown	.10	.02
❑ 62 Edgar Bennett	.40	.15
❑ 63 Anthony Carter	.20	.07
❑ 64 Glenn Cadrez RC UER	.10	.02
❑ 65 Dalton Hilliard	.10	.02
❑ 66 James Lofton	.20	.07
❑ 67 Walter Stanley	.10	.02
❑ 68 Tim Harris	.10	.02
❑ 69 Carl Banks	.10	.02
❑ 70 Andre Ware	.10	.02
❑ 71 Karl Mecklenburg	.10	.02
❑ 72 Russell Maryland	.10	.02
❑ 73 Leroy Thompson	.10	.02
❑ 74 Tommy Kane	.10	.02
❑ 75 Dan Marino	3.00	1.25
❑ 76 Darrell Fullington	.10	.02
❑ 77 Jessie Tuggle	.10	.02
❑ 78 Bruce Smith	.40	.15
❑ 79 Neal Anderson	.10	.02
❑ 80 Kevin Mack	.10	.02
❑ 81 Shane Dronett	.10	.02
❑ 82 Nick Lowery	.10	.02
❑ 83 Sheldon White	.10	.02
❑ 84 Flipper Anderson	.10	.02
❑ 85 Jeff Herrod	.10	.02
❑ 86 Dwight Stone	.10	.02
❑ 87 Dave Krieg	.20	.07
❑ 88 Bryan Cox	.10	.02
❑ 89 Greg McMurtry	.10	.02
❑ 90 Rickey Jackson	.10	.02
❑ 91 Ernie Mills	.10	.02
❑ 92 Browning Nagle	.10	.02
❑ 93 John Taylor	.20	.07
❑ 94 Eric Dickerson	.20	.07
❑ 95 Johnny Holland	.10	.02
❑ 96 Anthony Miller	.20	.07
❑ 97 Fred Barnett	.20	.07
❑ 98 Ricky Ervins UER	.10	.02
❑ 99 Leonard Russell	.20	.07
❑ 100 Lawrence Taylor	.40	.15
❑ 101 Tony Casillas	.10	.02
❑ 102 John Elway	3.00	1.25
❑ 103 Bennie Blades	.10	.02
❑ 104 Harry Sydney	.10	.02
❑ 105 Bubba McDowell	.10	.02
❑ 106 Todd McNair	.10	.02
❑ 107 Steve Smith	.10	.02
❑ 108 Jim Everett	.20	.07
❑ 109 Bobby Humphrey	.10	.02
❑ 110 Rich Gannon	.40	.15
❑ 111 Marv Cook	.10	.02
❑ 112 Wayne Martin	.10	.02
❑ 113 Sean Landeta	.10	.02
❑ 114 Brad Baxter UER	.10	.02
❑ 115 Reggie White	.40	.15
❑ 116 Johnny Johnson	.10	.02
❑ 117 Jeff Graham	.20	.07
❑ 118 Darren Carrington RC	.10	.02
❑ 119 Ricky Watters	.40	.15
❑ 120 Art Monk	.20	.07
❑ 121 Cornelius Bennett	.20	.07
❑ 122 Wade Wilson	.10	.02
❑ 123 Daniel Stubbs	.10	.02
❑ 124 Brad Muster	.10	.02
❑ 125 Mike Tomczak	.10	.02
❑ 126 Jay Novacek	.20	.07
❑ 127 Shannon Sharpe	.40	.15
❑ 128 Rodney Peete	.10	.02
❑ 129 Daryl Johnston	.40	.15
❑ 130 Warren Moon	.40	.15
❑ 131 Willie Gault	.10	.02
❑ 132 Tony Martin	.40	.15
❑ 133 Terry Allen	.40	.15
❑ 134 Hugh Millen	.10	.02
❑ 135 Rob Moore	.20	.07
❑ 136 Andy Harmon RC	.20	.07
❑ 137 Kelvin Martin	.10	.02
❑ 138 Rod Woodson	.40	.15
❑ 139 Nate Lewis	.10	.02
❑ 140 Darryl Talley	.10	.02
❑ 141 Guy McIntyre	.10	.02
❑ 142 John L. Williams	.10	.02
❑ 143 Brad Edwards	.10	.02
❑ 144 Trace Armstrong	.10	.02
❑ 145 Kenneth Davis	.10	.02
❑ 146 Clay Matthews	.20	.07
❑ 147 Gaston Green	.10	.02
❑ 148 Chris Spielman	.20	.07
❑ 149 Cody Carlson	.10	.02
❑ 150 Derrick Thomas	.40	.15
❑ 151 Terry McDaniel	.10	.02
❑ 152 Kevin Greene	.20	.07
❑ 153 Roger Craig	.20	.07
❑ 154 Craig Heyward	.20	.07
❑ 155 Rodney Hampton	.20	.07
❑ 156 Heath Sherman	.10	.02
❑ 157 Mark Stepnoski	.10	.02
❑ 158 Chris Chandler	.20	.07
❑ 159 Rod Bernstine	.10	.02
❑ 160 Pierce Holt	.10	.02
❑ 161 Wilber Marshall	.10	.02
❑ 162 Reggie Cobb	.10	.02
❑ 163 Tom Rathman	.10	.02
❑ 164 Michael Haynes	.20	.07
❑ 165 Nate Odomes	.10	.02
❑ 166 Tom Waddle	.10	.02
❑ 167 Eric Ball	.10	.02
❑ 168 Brett Favre UER	4.00	1.50
❑ 169 Michael Jackson	.20	.07
❑ 170 Lorenzo White	.10	.02
❑ 171 Cleveland Gary	.10	.02
❑ 172 Jay Schroeder	.10	.02
❑ 173 Tony Paige	.10	.02
❑ 174 Jack Del Rio	.10	.02
❑ 175 Jon Vaughn	.10	.02
❑ 176 Morten Andersen UER	.10	.02
❑ 177 Chris Burkett	.10	.02
❑ 178 Vai Sikahema	.10	.02
❑ 179 Ronnie Harmon	.10	.02
❑ 180 Amp Lee	.10	.02
❑ 181 Chip Lohmiller	.10	.02
❑ 182 Steve Broussard	.10	.02
❑ 183 Don Beebe	.10	.02
❑ 184 Tommy Vardell	.10	.02
❑ 185 Keith Jennings	.10	.02
❑ 186 Simon Fletcher	.10	.02
❑ 187 Mel Gray	.20	.07
❑ 188 Vince Workman	.10	.02
❑ 189 Haywood Jeffires	.20	.07
❑ 190 Barry Word	.10	.02
❑ 191 Ethan Horton	.10	.02
❑ 192 Mark Higgs	.10	.02
❑ 193 Irving Fryar	.20	.07
❑ 194 Charles Haley	.20	.07
❑ 195 Steve Bono	.20	.07
❑ 196 Mike Golic	.10	.02
❑ 197 Gary Anderson K	.10	.02
❑ 198 Sterling Sharpe	.40	.15
❑ 199 Andre Tippett	.10	.02
❑ 200 Thurman Thomas	.40	.15
❑ 201 Chris Miller	.20	.07
❑ 202 Henry Jones	.10	.02
❑ 203 Mo Lewis	.10	.02
❑ 204 Marion Butts	.10	.02
❑ 205 Mike Johnson	.10	.02
❑ 206 Alvin Harper	.20	.07
❑ 207 Ray Childress	.10	.02
❑ 208 Anthony Johnson	.20	.07
❑ 209 Tony Bennett	.10	.02
❑ 210 Anthony Newman RC	.10	.02
❑ 211 Christian Okoye	.10	.02
❑ 212 Marcus Allen	.40	.15

Card		
❑ 213 Jackie Harris	.10	.02
❑ 214 Mark Duper	.10	.02
❑ 215 Cris Carter	.40	.15
❑ 216 John Stephens	.10	.02
❑ 217 Barry Sanders	2.50	1.00
❑ 218A H.Moore ERR Sherman	1.25	.50
❑ 218B Herman Moore COR	2.50	1.00
❑ 219 Marvin Washington	.10	.02
❑ 220 Calvin Williams	.20	.07
❑ 221 John Randle	.20	.07
❑ 222 Marco Coleman	.10	.02
❑ 223 Eric Martin	.10	.02
❑ 224 Dave Meggett	.10	.02
❑ 225 Brian Washington	.10	.02
❑ 226 Barry Foster	.20	.07
❑ 227 Michael Zordich	.10	.02
❑ 228 Stan Humphries	.20	.07
❑ 229 Mike Cofer	.10	.02
❑ 230 Chris Warren	.20	.07
❑ 231 Keith McCants	.10	.02
❑ 232 Mark Rypien	.10	.02
❑ 233 James Francis	.10	.02
❑ 234 Andre Rison	.20	.07
❑ 235 William Perry	.20	.07
❑ 236 Chip Banks	.10	.02
❑ 237 Willie Davis	.40	.15
❑ 238 Chris Doleman	.10	.02
❑ 239 Tim Brown	.40	.15
❑ 240 Darren Perry	.10	.02
❑ 241 Johnny Bailey	.10	.02
❑ 242 Ernest Givins	.20	.07
❑ 243 John Carney	.10	.02
❑ 244 Cortez Kennedy	.20	.07
❑ 245 Lawrence Dawsey	.10	.02
❑ 246 Martin Mayhew	.10	.02
❑ 247 Shane Conlan	.10	.02
❑ 248 J.J. Birden	.10	.02
❑ 249 Quinn Early	.20	.07
❑ 250 Michael Irvin	.40	.15
❑ 251 Neil O'Donnell	.40	.15
❑ 252 Stan Gelbaugh	.10	.02
❑ 253 Drew Hill	.10	.02
❑ 254 Wendell Davis	.10	.02
❑ 255 Tim Johnson	.10	.02
❑ 256 Seth Joyner	.10	.02
❑ 257 Derrick Fenner	.10	.02
❑ 258 Steve Young	1.50	.60
❑ 259 Jackie Slater	.10	.02
❑ 260 Eric Metcalf	.20	.07
❑ 261 Rufus Porter	.10	.02
❑ 262 Ken Norton Jr.	.20	.07
❑ 263 Tim McDonald	.10	.02
❑ 264 Mark Jackson	.10	.02
❑ 265 Hardy Nickerson	.20	.07
❑ 266 Anthony Munoz	.20	.07
❑ 267 Mark Carrier WR	.20	.07
❑ 268 Mike Pritchard	.20	.07
❑ 269 Steve Emtman	.10	.02
❑ 270 Ricky Sanders	.10	.02
❑ 271 Robert Massey	.10	.02
❑ 272 Pete Metzelaars	.10	.02
❑ 273 Reggie Langhorne	.10	.02
❑ 274 Tim McGee	.10	.02
❑ 275 Reggie Rivers RC	.10	.02
❑ 276 Jimmie Jones	.10	.02
❑ 277 Lorenzo White TB	.10	.02
❑ 278 Emmitt Smith TB	2.00	.75
❑ 279 Thurman Thomas TB	.40	.15
❑ 280 Barry Sanders TB	1.50	.60
❑ 281 Rodney Hampton TB	.20	.07
❑ 282 Barry Foster TB	.20	.07
❑ 283 Troy Aikman PC	1.00	.40
❑ 284 Michael Irvin PC	.20	.07
❑ 285 Brett Favre PC	2.50	1.00
❑ 286 Sterling Sharpe PC	.20	.07
❑ 287 Steve Young PC	1.00	.40
❑ 288 Jerry Rice PC	1.25	.50
❑ 289 Stan Humphries PC	.20	.07
❑ 290 Anthony Miller PC	.20	.07
❑ 291 Dan Marino PC	2.00	.75
❑ 292 Keith Jackson PC	.10	.02
❑ 293 Patrick Bates RC	.10	.02
❑ 294 Jerome Bettis RC	10.00	4.00
❑ 295 Drew Bledsoe RC	6.00	2.50
❑ 296 Tom Carter RC	.20	.07
❑ 297 Curtis Conway RC	1.00	.40
❑ 298 John Copeland RC	.20	.07
❑ 299 Eric Curry RC	.10	.02
❑ 300 Reggie Brooks RC	.20	.07
❑ 301 Steve Everitt RC	.10	.02
❑ 302 Deon Figures RC	.10	.02
❑ 303 Garrison Hearst RC	2.00	.75
❑ 304 Qadry Ismail RC UER	.40	.15
❑ 305 Marvin Jones RC	.10	.02
❑ 306 Lincoln Kennedy RC	.10	.02
❑ 307 O.J.McDuffie RC	.40	.15
❑ 308 Rick Mirer RC	.40	.15
❑ 309 Wayne Simmons RC	.10	.02
❑ 310 Irv Smith RC	.10	.02
❑ 311 Robert Smith RC	3.00	1.25
❑ 312 Dana Stubblefield RC	.40	.15
❑ 313 George Teague RC	.20	.07
❑ 314 Dan Williams RC	.10	.02
❑ 315 Kevin Williams RC WR	.40	.15
❑ NNO Santa Claus	2.00	.75

1994 Playoff

Card		
❑ COMPLETE SET (336)	30.00	12.50
❑ 1 Joe Montana	4.00	1.50
❑ 2 Derrick Thomas	.50	.20
❑ 3 Dan Marino	4.00	1.50
❑ 4 Cris Carter	.75	.30
❑ 5 Boomer Esiason	.30	.10
❑ 6 Bruce Smith	.50	.20
❑ 7 Andre Rison	.30	.10
❑ 8 Curtis Conway	.50	.20
❑ 9 Michael Irvin	.50	.20
❑ 10 Shannon Sharpe	.30	.10
❑ 11 Pat Swilling	.15	.05
❑ 12 John Parrella	.15	.05
❑ 13 Mel Gray	.15	.05
❑ 14 Ray Childress	.15	.05
❑ 15 Willie Davis	.30	.10
❑ 16 Rocket Ismail	.30	.10
❑ 17 Jim Everett	.30	.10
❑ 18 Mark Higgs	.15	.05
❑ 19 Trace Armstrong	.15	.05
❑ 20 Jim Kelly	.50	.20
❑ 21 Rob Burnett	.15	.05
❑ 22 Jay Novacek	.30	.10
❑ 23 Robert Delpino	.15	.05
❑ 24 Brett Perriman	.30	.10
❑ 25 Troy Aikman	2.00	.75
❑ 26 Reggie White	.50	.20
❑ 27 Lorenzo White	.15	.05
❑ 28 Bubba McDowell	.15	.05
❑ 29 Steve Emtman	.15	.05
❑ 30 Brett Favre	4.00	1.50
❑ 31 Derek Russell	.15	.05
❑ 32 Jeff Hostetler	.30	.10
❑ 33 Henry Ellard	.30	.10
❑ 34 Jack Del Rio	.15	.05
❑ 35 Mike Saxon	.15	.05
❑ 36 Rickey Jackson	.15	.05
❑ 37 Phil Simms	.30	.10
❑ 38 Quinn Early	.30	.10
❑ 39 Russell Copeland	.15	.05
❑ 40 Carl Pickens	.30	.10
❑ 41 Lance Gunn	.15	.05
❑ 42 Bernie Kosar	.30	.10
❑ 43 John Elway	4.00	1.50
❑ 44 George Teague	.15	.05
❑ 45 Nick Lowery	.15	.05
❑ 46 Haywood Jeffires	.30	.10
❑ 47 Will Shields	.15	.05
❑ 48 Daryl Johnston	.30	.10
❑ 49 Pete Metzelaars	.15	.05
❑ 50 Warren Moon	.50	.20
❑ 51 Cornelius Bennett	.30	.10
❑ 52 Vinny Testaverde	.30	.10
❑ 53 John Mangum RC	.15	.05
❑ 54 Tommy Vardell	.15	.05
❑ 55 Lincoln Coleman RC	.15	.05
❑ 56 Karl Mecklenburg	.15	.05
❑ 57 Jackie Harris	.15	.05
❑ 58 Curtis Duncan	.15	.05
❑ 59 Quentin Coryatt	.15	.05
❑ 60 Tim Brown	.50	.20
❑ 61 Irving Fryar	.30	.10
❑ 62 Sean Gilbert	.15	.05
❑ 63 Qadry Ismail	.50	.20
❑ 64 Irv Smith	.15	.05
❑ 65 Mark Jackson	.15	.05
❑ 66 Ronnie Lott	.30	.10
❑ 67 Henry Jones	.15	.05
❑ 68 Horace Copeland	.15	.05
❑ 69 John Copeland	.15	.05
❑ 70 Mark Carrier WR	.30	.10
❑ 71 Michael Jackson	.30	.10
❑ 72 Jason Elam	.30	.10
❑ 73 Rod Bernstine	.15	.05
❑ 74 Wayne Simmons	.15	.05
❑ 75 Cody Carlson	.15	.05
❑ 76 Alexander Wright	.15	.05
❑ 77 Shane Conlan	.15	.05
❑ 78 Keith Jackson	.15	.05
❑ 79 Sean Salisbury	.15	.05
❑ 80 Vaughan Johnson	.15	.05
❑ 81 Rob Moore	.30	.10
❑ 82 Andre Reed	.30	.10
❑ 83 David Klingler	.15	.05
❑ 84 Jim Harbaugh	.50	.20
❑ 85 John Jett RC	.15	.05
❑ 86 Sterling Sharpe	.30	.10
❑ 87 Webster Slaughter	.15	.05
❑ 88 J.J. Birden	.15	.05
❑ 89 O.J.McDuffie	.50	.20
❑ 90 Andre Tippett	.15	.05
❑ 91 Don Beebe	.15	.05
❑ 92 Mark Stepnoski	.15	.05
❑ 93 Neil Smith	.30	.10
❑ 94 Terry Kirby	.50	.20
❑ 95 Wade Wilson	.15	.05
❑ 96 Darryl Talley	.15	.05
❑ 97 Anthony Smith	.15	.05
❑ 98 Willie Roaf	.15	.05
❑ 99 Mo Lewis	.15	.05
❑ 100 James Washington	.15	.05
❑ 101 Nate Odomes	.15	.05
❑ 102 Chris Gedney	.15	.05
❑ 103 Joe Walter	.15	.05
❑ 104 Alvin Harper	.30	.10
❑ 105 Simon Fletcher	.15	.05
❑ 106 Rodney Peete	.15	.05
❑ 107 Terrell Buckley	.15	.05
❑ 108 Jeff George	.50	.20
❑ 109 James Jett	.15	.05
❑ 110 Tony Casillas	.15	.05
❑ 111 Marco Coleman	.15	.05
❑ 112 Anthony Carter	.30	.10
❑ 113 Lincoln Kennedy	.15	.05
❑ 114 Chris Calloway	.15	.05
❑ 115 Randall Cunningham	.50	.20
❑ 116 Steve Beuerlein	.30	.10
❑ 117 Neil O'Donnell	.50	.20
❑ 118 Stan Humphries	.30	.10
❑ 119 John Taylor	.30	.10
❑ 120 Cortez Kennedy	.30	.10
❑ 121 Santana Dotson	.30	.10
❑ 122 Thomas Smith	.15	.05
❑ 123 Kevin Williams WR	.30	.10
❑ 124 Andre Ware	.15	.05
❑ 125 Ethan Horton	.15	.05
❑ 126 Mike Sherrard	.15	.05
❑ 127 Fred Barnett	.30	.10
❑ 128 Ricky Proehl	.15	.05
❑ 129 Kevin Greene	.30	.10
❑ 130 John Carney	.15	.05
❑ 131 Tim McDonald	.15	.05
❑ 132 Rick Mirer	.50	.20
❑ 133 Blair Thomas	.15	.05
❑ 134 Hardy Nickerson	.30	.10
❑ 135 Heath Sherman	.15	.05

❑	136	Andre Hastings	.30	.10
❑	137	Randal Hill	.15	.05
❑	138	Mike Cofer	.15	.05
❑	139	Brian Blades	.30	.10
❑	140	Earnest Byner	.15	.05
❑	141	Bill Bates	.30	.10
❑	142	Junior Seau	.50	.20
❑	143	Johnny Bailey	.15	.05
❑	144	Dwight Stone	.15	.05
❑	145	Todd Kelly	.15	.05
❑	146	Tyrone Montgomery	.15	.05
❑	147	Herschel Walker	.30	.10
❑	148	Gary Clark	.30	.10
❑	149	Eric Green	.15	.05
❑	150	Steve Young	1.50	.60
❑	151	Anthony Miller	.30	.10
❑	152	Dana Stubblefield	.30	.10
❑	153	Dean Wells RC	.15	.05
❑	154	Vincent Brisby	.30	.10
❑	155	Chris Chandler	.30	.10
❑	156	Clyde Simmons	.15	.05
❑	157	Rod Woodson	.30	.10
❑	158	Nate Lewis	.15	.05
❑	159	Martin Harrison	.15	.05
❑	160	Kelvin Martin	.15	.05
❑	161	Craig Erickson	.15	.05
❑	162	Johnny Mitchell	.15	.05
❑	163	Calvin Williams	.30	.10
❑	164	Deon Figures	.15	.05
❑	165	Tom Rathman	.15	.05
❑	166	Rick Hamilton	.15	.05
❑	167	John L. Williams	.15	.05
❑	168	Demetrius DuBose	.15	.05
❑	169	Michael Brooks	.15	.05
❑	170	Marion Butts	.15	.05
❑	171	Brent Jones	.30	.10
❑	172	Bobby Hebert	.15	.05
❑	173	Brad Edwards	.15	.05
❑	174	David Wyman	.15	.05
❑	175	Herman Moore	.50	.20
❑	176	LeRoy Butler	.15	.05
❑	177	Reggie Langhorne	.15	.05
❑	178	Dave Krieg	.30	.10
❑	179	Patrick Bates	.15	.05
❑	180	Erik Kramer	.30	.10
❑	181	Troy Drayton	.15	.05
❑	182	Dave Meggett	.15	.05
❑	183	Eric Allen	.15	.05
❑	184	Mark Bavaro	.15	.05
❑	185	Leslie O'Neal	.15	.05
❑	186	Jerry Rice	2.00	.75
❑	187	Desmond Howard	.30	.10
❑	188	Deion Sanders	.75	.30
❑	189	Bill Maas	.15	.05
❑	190	Frank Wycheck RC	2.00	.75
❑	191	Ernest Givins	.30	.10
❑	192	Terry McDaniel	.15	.05
❑	193	Bryan Cox	.15	.05
❑	194	Guy McIntyre	.15	.05
❑	195	Pierce Holt	.15	.05
❑	196	Fred Stokes	.15	.05
❑	197	Mike Pritchard	.15	.05
❑	198	Terry Obee	.15	.05
❑	199	Mark Collins	.15	.05
❑	200	Drew Bledsoe	1.25	.50
❑	201	Barry Word	.15	.05
❑	202	Derrick Lassic	.15	.05
❑	203	Chris Spielman	.30	.10
❑	204	John Jurkovic RC	.30	.10
❑	205	Ken Norton Jr.	.30	.10
❑	206	Dale Carter	.15	.05
❑	207	Chris Doleman	.15	.05
❑	208	Keith Hamilton	.15	.05
❑	209	Andy Harmon	.15	.05
❑	210	John Friesz	.30	.10
❑	211	Steve Bono	.30	.10
❑	212	Mark Rypien	.15	.05
❑	213	Ricky Sanders	.15	.05
❑	214	Michael Haynes	.30	.10
❑	215	Todd McNair	.15	.05
❑	216	Leon Lett	.15	.05
❑	217	Scott Mitchell	.30	.10
❑	218	Mike Morris RC	.15	.05
❑	219	Darrin Smith	.15	.05
❑	220	Jim McMahon	.30	.10
❑	221	Garrison Hearst	.50	.20
❑	222	Leroy Thompson	.15	.05
❑	223	Darren Carrington	.15	.05
❑	224	Pete Stoyanovich	.15	.05
❑	225	Chris Miller	.15	.05
❑	226	Bruce Smith SP	.30	.10
❑	227	Simon Fletcher SP	.15	.05
❑	228	Reggie White SP	.50	.20
❑	229	Neil Smith SP	.30	.10
❑	230	Chris Doleman SP	.15	.05
❑	231	Keith Hamilton SP	.15	.05
❑	232	Dana Stubblefield SP	.15	.05
❑	233	Erric Pegram GA	.15	.05
❑	234	Thurman Thomas GA	.50	.20
❑	235	Lewis Tillman GA	.15	.05
❑	236	Harold Green GA	.15	.05
❑	237	Eric Metcalf GA	.30	.10
❑	238	Emmitt Smith GA	3.00	1.25
❑	239	Glyn Milburn GA	.30	.10
❑	240	Barry Sanders GA	3.00	1.25
❑	241	Edgar Bennett GA	.30	.10
❑	242	Gary Brown GA	.15	.05
❑	243	Roosevelt Potts GA	.15	.05
❑	244	Marcus Allen GA	.50	.20
❑	245	Greg Robinson GA	.15	.05
❑	246	Jerome Bettis GA	.75	.30
❑	247	Keith Byars GA	.15	.05
❑	248	Robert Smith GA	.50	.20
❑	249	Leonard Russell GA	.15	.05
❑	250	Derek Brown RBK GA	.15	.05
❑	251	Rodney Hampton GA	.30	.10
❑	252	Johnny Johnson GA	.15	.05
❑	253	Vaughn Hebron GA	.15	.05
❑	254	Ronald Moore GA	.15	.05
❑	255	Barry Foster GA	.15	.05
❑	256	Natrone Means GA	.50	.20
❑	257	Ricky Watters GA	.30	.10
❑	258	Chris Warren GA	.50	.20
❑	259	Vince Workman GA	.15	.05
❑	260	Reggie Brooks GA	.15	.05
❑	261	Carolina Panthers	.40	.15
❑	262	Jacksonville Jaguars	.40	.15
❑	263	Troy Aikman SB	1.00	.40
❑	264	Barry Sanders SB	1.50	.60
❑	265	Emmitt Smith SB	1.50	.60
❑	266	Michael Irvin SB	.50	.20
❑	267	Jerry Rice SB	1.00	.40
❑	268	Shannon Sharpe SB	.30	.10
❑	269	Bob Kratch SB	.15	.05
❑	270	Howard Ballard SB	.15	.05
❑	271	Erik Williams SB	.15	.05
❑	272	Guy McIntyre SB	.15	.05
❑	273	Kevin Williams WR SB	.30	.10
❑	274	Mel Gray SB	.15	.05
❑	275	Eddie Murray SB	.15	.05
❑	276	Mark Stepnoski SB	.15	.05
❑	277	Tommy Barnhardt SB	.15	.05
❑	278	Derrick Thomas SB	.30	.10
❑	279	Ken Norton Jr. SB	.30	.10
❑	280	Chris Spielman SB	.15	.05
❑	281	Deion Sanders SB	.50	.20
❑	282	Mark Collins SB	.15	.05
❑	283	Bruce Smith SB	.30	.10
❑	284	Reggie White SB	.50	.20
❑	285	Sean Gilbert SB	.15	.05
❑	286	Cortez Kennedy SB	.30	.10
❑	287	Steve Atwater SB	.15	.05
❑	288	Tim McDonald SB	.15	.05
❑	289	Jerome Bettis SB	.75	.30
❑	290	Dana Stubblefield SB	.30	.10
❑	291	Bert Emanuel RC	.50	.20
❑	292	Jeff Burris RC	.30	.10
❑	293	Bucky Brooks RC	.15	.05
❑	294	Dan Wilkinson RC	.30	.10
❑	295	Darnay Scott RC	1.00	.40
❑	296	Derrick Alexander WR RC	.50	.20
❑	297	Antonio Langham RC	.30	.10
❑	298	Shante Carver RC	.15	.05
❑	299	Shelby Hill RC	.15	.05
❑	300	Larry Allen RC	.50	.20
❑	301	Johnnie Morton RC	2.00	.75
❑	302	Van Malone RC	.15	.05
❑	303	Aaron Taylor RC	.15	.05
❑	304	Marshall Faulk RC	6.00	2.50
❑	305	Eric Mahlum RC	.15	.05
❑	306	Trev Alberts RC	.30	.10
❑	307	Greg Hill RC	.50	.20
❑	308	Donnell Bennett RC	.50	.20
❑	309	Rob Fredrickson RC	.30	.10
❑	310	James Folston RC	.15	.05
❑	311	Isaac Bruce RC	5.00	2.00
❑	312	Tim Ruddy RC	.15	.05
❑	313	Aubrey Beavers RC	.15	.05
❑	314	David Palmer RC	.50	.20
❑	315	Dewayne Washington RC	.30	.10
❑	316	Willie McGinest RC	.50	.20
❑	317	Mario Bates RC	.50	.20
❑	318	Kevin Lee RC	.15	.05
❑	319	Jason Sehorn RC	.75	.30
❑	320	Thomas Randolph RC	.15	.05
❑	321	Ryan Yarborough RC	.15	.05
❑	322	Bernard Williams RC	.15	.05
❑	323	Chuck Levy RC	.15	.05
❑	324	Jamir Miller RC	.30	.10
❑	325	Charles Johnson RC	.50	.20
❑	326	Bryant Young RC	.50	.20
❑	327	William Floyd RC	.50	.20
❑	328	Kevin Mitchell RC	.15	.05
❑	329	Sam Adams RC	.30	.10
❑	330	Kevin Mawae RC	.50	.20
❑	331	Errict Rhett RC	.50	.20
❑	332	Trent Dilfer RC	1.50	.60
❑	333	Heath Shuler RC	.50	.20
❑	334	Aaron Glenn RC	.50	.20
❑	335	Todd Steussie RC	.30	.10
❑	336	Toby Wright RC	.15	.05
❑	NNO	Gale Sayers Play.Club	4.00	1.50
❑	NNO	Gale Sayers AUTO	60.00	25.00

1993 Playoff Contenders

❑		COMPLETE SET (150)	20.00	7.50
❑	1	Brett Favre	3.00	1.50
❑	2	Thurman Thomas	.40	.15
❑	3	Barry Word	.10	.02
❑	4	Herman Moore	.40	.15
❑	5	Reggie Langhorne	.10	.02
❑	6	Wilber Marshall	.10	.02
❑	7	Ricky Watters	.40	.15
❑	8	Marcus Allen	.40	.15
❑	9	Jeff Hostetler	.20	.07
❑	10	Steve Young	1.00	.40
❑	11	Bobby Hebert	.10	.02
❑	12	David Klingler	.10	.02
❑	13	Craig Heyward	.20	.07
❑	14	Andre Reed	.20	.07
❑	15	Tommy Vardell	.10	.02
❑	16	Anthony Carter	.20	.07
❑	17	Mel Gray	.20	.07
❑	18	Dan Marino	2.50	1.00
❑	19	Haywood Jeffires	.20	.07
❑	20	Joe Montana	2.50	1.00
❑	21	Tim Brown	.40	.15
❑	22	Jim McMahon	.20	.07
❑	23	Scott Mitchell	.40	.15
❑	24	Rickey Jackson	.10	.02
❑	25	Troy Aikman	1.50	.60
❑	26	Rodney Hampton	.20	.07
❑	27	Fred Barnett	.20	.07
❑	28	Gary Clark	.20	.07
❑	29	Barry Foster	.20	.07
❑	30	Brian Blades	.20	.07
❑	31	Tim McDonald	.10	.02
❑	32	Kelvin Martin	.10	.02
❑	33	Henry Jones	.10	.02
❑	34	Erric Pegram	.20	.07
❑	35	Don Beebe	.10	.02
❑	36	Eric Metcalf	.20	.07
❑	37	Charles Haley	.20	.07

❑ 38 Robert Delpino .10 .02
❑ 39 Leonard Russell UER .20 .07
❑ 40 Jackie Harris .10 .02
❑ 41 Ernest Givins .20 .07
❑ 42 Willie Davis .40 .15
❑ 43 Alexander Wright .10 .02
❑ 44 Keith Byars .10 .02
❑ 45 Dave Meggett .10 .02
❑ 46 Johnny Johnson .10 .02
❑ 47 Mark Bavaro .10 .02
❑ 48 Seth Joyner .10 .02
❑ 49 Junior Seau .40 .15
❑ 50 Emmitt Smith 2.50 1.25
❑ 51 Shannon Sharpe .40 .15
❑ 52 Rodney Peete .10 .02
❑ 53 Andre Rison .20 .07
❑ 54 Cornelius Bennett .20 .07
❑ 55 Mark Carrier WR .20 .07
❑ 56 Mark Clayton .10 .02
❑ 57 Warren Moon .40 .15
❑ 58 J.J. Birden .10 .02
❑ 59 Howie Long .40 .15
❑ 60 Irving Fryar .20 .07
❑ 61 Mark Jackson .10 .02
❑ 62 Eric Martin .10 .02
❑ 63 Herschel Walker .20 .07
❑ 64 Cortez Kennedy .20 .07
❑ 65 Steve Beuerlein .20 .07
❑ 66 Jim Kelly .40 .15
❑ 67 Bernie Kosar Cowboys .20 .07
❑ 68 Pat Swilling .10 .02
❑ 69 Michael Irvin .40 .15
❑ 70 Harvey Williams .20 .07
❑ 71 Steve Smith .10 .02
❑ 72 Wade Wilson .10 .02
❑ 73 Phil Simms .20 .07
❑ 74 Vinny Testaverde .20 .07
❑ 75 Barry Sanders 2.50 1.00
❑ 76 Ken Norton Jr. .20 .07
❑ 77 Rod Woodson .40 .15
❑ 78 Webster Slaughter .10 .02
❑ 79 Derrick Thomas .40 .15
❑ 80 Mike Sherrard .10 .02
❑ 81 Calvin Williams .20 .07
❑ 82 Jay Novacek .20 .07
❑ 83 Michael Brooks .10 .02
❑ 84 Randall Cunningham .40 .15
❑ 85 Chris Warren .20 .07
❑ 86 Johnny Mitchell .10 .02
❑ 87 Jim Harbaugh .40 .15
❑ 88 Rod Bernstine .10 .02
❑ 89 John Elway 2.50 1.00
❑ 90 Jerry Rice 1.50 .60
❑ 91 Brent Jones .20 .07
❑ 92 Cris Carter .40 .15
❑ 93 Alvin Harper .20 .07
❑ 94 Horace Copeland RC .20 .07
❑ 95 Rocket Ismail .20 .07
❑ 96 Darrin Smith RC .20 .07
❑ 97 Reggie Brooks RC .20 .07
❑ 98 Demetrius DuBose RC .10 .02
❑ 99 Eric Curry RC .10 .02
❑ 100 Rick Mirer RC .40 .15
❑ 101 Carlton Gray RC UER .10 .02
❑ 102 Dana Stubblefield RC .40 .15
❑ 103 Todd Kelly RC .10 .02
❑ 104 Natrone Means RC .40 .15
❑ 105 Darrien Gordon RC .10 .02
❑ 106 Deon Figures RC .10 .02
❑ 107 Garrison Hearst RC 1.25 .50
❑ 108 Ronald Moore RC .20 .07
❑ 109 Leonard Renfro RC .10 .02
❑ 110 Lester Holmes .10 .02
❑ 111 Vaughn Hebron RC .10 .02
❑ 112 Marvin Jones RC .10 .02
❑ 113 Irv Smith RC .10 .02
❑ 114 Willie Roaf RC .20 .07
❑ 115 Derek Brown RC RBK .20 .07
❑ 116 Vincent Brisby RC .40 .15
❑ 117 Drew Bledsoe RC 4.00 1.50
❑ 118 Gino Torretta RC .20 .07
❑ 119 Robert Smith RC 2.00 .75
❑ 120 Qadry Ismail RC .40 .15
❑ 121 O.J.McDuffie RC .40 .15
❑ 122 Terry Kirby RC .40 .15
❑ 123 Troy Drayton RC .20 .07
❑ 124 Jerome Bettis RC 6.00 2.50
❑ 125 Patrick Bates RC .10 .02
❑ 126 Roosevelt Potts RC .10 .02
❑ 127 Tom Carter RC .20 .07
❑ 128 Patrick Robinson RC .10 .02
❑ 129 Brad Hopkins RC .10 .02
❑ 130 George Teague RC .20 .07
❑ 131 Wayne Simmons RC .10 .02
❑ 132 Mark Brunell RC 2.50 1.00
❑ 133 Ryan McNeil RC .40 .15
❑ 134 Dan Williams RC .10 .02
❑ 135 Glyn Milburn RC .40 .15
❑ 136 Kevin Williams RC WR .40 .15
❑ 137 Derrick Lassic RC .10 .02
❑ 138 Steve Everitt RC .10 .02
❑ 139 Lance Gunn RC .10 .02
❑ 140 John Copeland RC .20 .07
❑ 141 Curtis Conway RC 1.00 .40
❑ 142 Thomas Smith RC .20 .07
❑ 143 Russell Copeland RC .20 .07
❑ 144 Lincoln Kennedy RC .10 .02
❑ 145 Boomer Esiason CL .10 .02
❑ 146 Neil Smith CL .10 .02
❑ 147 Jack Del Rio CL .10 .02
❑ 148 Morten Andersen CL .10 .02
❑ 149 Sterling Sharpe CL .20 .07
❑ 150 Reggie White CL .20 .07

1994 Playoff Contenders

❑ COMPLETE SET (120) 20.00 7.50
❑ 1 Drew Bledsoe 1.00 .40
❑ 2 Barry Sanders 2.50 1.00
❑ 3 Jerry Rice 1.50 .60
❑ 4 Rod Woodson .20 .07
❑ 5 Irving Fryar .20 .07
❑ 6 Charles Haley .20 .07
❑ 7 Chris Warren .20 .07
❑ 8 Craig Erickson .10 .02
❑ 9 Eric Metcalf .20 .07
❑ 10 Marcus Allen .40 .15
❑ 11 Chris Miller .10 .02
❑ 12 Andre Rison .20 .07
❑ 13 Art Monk .20 .07
❑ 14 Calvin Williams .20 .07
❑ 15 Shannon Sharpe .20 .07
❑ 16 Rodney Hampton .20 .07
❑ 17 Marion Butts .10 .02
❑ 18 John Jurkovic RC .20 .07
❑ 19 Jim Kelly .40 .15
❑ 20 Emmitt Smith 2.50 1.00
❑ 21 Jeff Hostetler .20 .07
❑ 22 Barry Foster .10 .02
❑ 23 Boomer Esiason .20 .07
❑ 24 Jim Harbaugh .40 .15
❑ 25 Joe Montana 3.00 1.25
❑ 26 Jeff George .40 .15
❑ 27 Warren Moon .40 .15
❑ 28 Steve Young 1.25 .50
❑ 29 Randall Cunningham .40 .15
❑ 30 Shawn Jefferson .10 .02
❑ 31 Cortez Kennedy .20 .07
❑ 32 Reggie Brooks .20 .07
❑ 33 Alvin Harper .20 .07
❑ 34 Brent Jones .20 .07
❑ 35 O.J.McDuffie .40 .15
❑ 36 Jerome Bettis .60 .25
❑ 37 Daryl Johnston .20 .07
❑ 38 Herman Moore .40 .15
❑ 39 Dave Meggett .10 .02
❑ 40 Reggie White .40 .15
❑ 41 Junior Seau .40 .15
❑ 42 Dan Marino 3.00 1.25
❑ 43 Scott Mitchell .20 .07
❑ 44 John Elway 3.00 1.25
❑ 45 Troy Aikman 1.50 .60
❑ 46 Terry Allen .20 .07
❑ 47 David Klingler .10 .02
❑ 48 Stan Humphries .20 .07
❑ 49 Rick Mirer .40 .15
❑ 50 Neil O'Donnell .40 .15
❑ 51 Keith Jackson .10 .02
❑ 52 Ricky Watters .20 .07
❑ 53 Dave Brown .20 .07
❑ 54 Neil Smith .20 .07
❑ 55 Johnny Mitchell .10 .02
❑ 56 Jackie Harris .10 .02
❑ 57 Terry Kirby .40 .15
❑ 58 Willie Davis .20 .07
❑ 59 Rob Moore .20 .07
❑ 60 Nate Newton .10 .02
❑ 61 Deion Sanders .75 .30
❑ 62 John Taylor .20 .07
❑ 63 Sterling Sharpe .20 .07
❑ 64 Natrone Means .40 .15
❑ 65 Steve Beuerlein .20 .07
❑ 66 Erik Kramer .20 .07
❑ 67 Qadry Ismail .40 .15
❑ 68 Johnny Johnson .10 .02
❑ 69 Herschel Walker .20 .07
❑ 70 Mark Stepnoski .10 .02
❑ 71 Brett Favre 3.00 1.25
❑ 72 Dana Stubblefield .20 .07
❑ 73 Bruce Smith .40 .15
❑ 74 Leroy Hoard .10 .02
❑ 75 Steve Walsh .10 .02
❑ 76 Jay Novacek .20 .07
❑ 77 Derrick Thomas .40 .15
❑ 78 Keith Byars .10 .02
❑ 79 Ben Coates .20 .07
❑ 80 Lorenzo Neal .10 .02
❑ 81 Ronnie Lott .20 .07
❑ 82 Tim Brown .40 .15
❑ 83 Michael Irvin .40 .15
❑ 84 Ronald Moore .10 .02
❑ 85 Andre Reed .20 .07
❑ 86 James Jett .10 .02
❑ 87 Curtis Conway .40 .15
❑ 88 Bernie Parmalee RC .40 .15
❑ 89 Keith Cash .10 .02
❑ 90 Russell Copeland .10 .02
❑ 91 Kevin Williams WR .20 .07
❑ 92 Gary Brown .10 .02
❑ 93 Thurman Thomas .40 .15
❑ 94 Jamir Miller RC .20 .07
❑ 95 Bert Emanuel RC .40 .15
❑ 96 Bucky Brooks RC .10 .02
❑ 97 Jeff Burris RC .20 .07
❑ 98 Antonio Langham RC .20 .07
❑ 99 Derrick Alexander WR RC .40 .15
❑ 100 Dan Wilkinson RC .20 .07
❑ 101 Shante Carver RC .10 .02
❑ 102 Johnnie Morton RC 2.00 .75
❑ 103 LeShon Johnson RC .20 .07
❑ 104 Marshall Faulk RC 6.00 2.50
❑ 105 Greg Hill RC .40 .15
❑ 106 Lake Dawson RC .20 .07
❑ 107 Irving Spikes RC .20 .07
❑ 108 David Palmer RC .40 .15
❑ 109 Willie McGinest RC .40 .15
❑ 110 Joe Johnson RC .10 .02
❑ 111 Aaron Glenn RC .40 .15
❑ 112 Charlie Garner RC 1.50 .60
❑ 113 Charles Johnson RC .40 .15
❑ 114 Byron Bam Morris RC .20 .07
❑ 115 Bryant Young RC .40 .15
❑ 116 William Floyd RC .40 .15
❑ 117 Trent Dilfer RC 1.50 .60
❑ 118 Errict Rhett RC .40 .15
❑ 119 Heath Shuler RC .40 .15
❑ 120 Gus Frerotte RC .40 .15

1995 Playoff Contenders

❑ COMPLETE SET (150) 25.00 10.00
❑ 1 Steve Young 1.00 .40
❑ 2 Jeff Blake RC .75 .30
❑ 3 Rick Mirer .20 .07
❑ 4 Brett Favre 2.50 1.25

❑	5 Heath Shuler	.20	.07
❑	6 Steve Bono	.20	.07
❑	7 John Elway	2.50	1.00
❑	8 Troy Aikman	1.25	.50
❑	9 Rodney Peete	.10	.02
❑	10 Gus Frerotte	.20	.07
❑	11 Drew Bledsoe	.75	.30
❑	12 Jim Kelly	.40	.15
❑	13 Dan Marino	2.50	1.00
❑	14 Errict Rhett	.20	.07
❑	15 Jeff Hostetler	.20	.07
❑	16 Erik Kramer	.10	.02
❑	17 Jim Everett	.10	.02
❑	18 Elvis Grbac	.40	.15
❑	19 Scott Mitchell	.20	.07
❑	20 Barry Sanders	2.00	.75
❑	21 Deion Sanders	.75	.30
❑	22 Emmitt Smith	2.00	.75
❑	23 Garrison Hearst	.40	.15
❑	24 Mario Bates	.20	.07
❑	25 Mark Brunell	.75	.30
❑	26 Robert Smith	.40	.15
❑	27 Rodney Hampton	.20	.07
❑	28 Marshall Faulk	1.50	.60
❑	29 Greg Hill	.20	.07
❑	30 Bernie Parmalee	.20	.07
❑	31 Natrone Means	.20	.07
❑	32 Marcus Allen	.40	.15
❑	33 Byron Bam Morris	.10	.02
❑	34 Edgar Bennett	.20	.07
❑	35 Vincent Brisby	.10	.02
❑	36 Jerome Bettis	.40	.15
❑	37 Craig Heyward	.20	.07
❑	38 Anthony Miller	.20	.07
❑	39 Curtis Conway	.40	.15
❑	40 William Floyd	.20	.07
❑	41 Chris Warren	.20	.07
❑	42 Terry Kirby	.20	.07
❑	43 Herschel Walker	.20	.07
❑	44 Eric Metcalf	.20	.07
❑	45 Darnay Scott	.20	.07
❑	46 Jackie Harris	.10	.02
❑	47 Dana Stubblefield	.20	.07
❑	48 Daryl Johnston	.20	.07
❑	49 Dave Meggett	.10	.02
❑	50 Ricky Watters	.20	.07
❑	51 Ken Norton	.20	.07
❑	52 Boomer Esiason	.20	.07
❑	53 Lake Dawson	.20	.07
❑	54 Eric Green	.10	.02
❑	55 Junior Seau	.40	.15
❑	56 Yancey Thigpen RC	.40	.15
❑	57 James Jett	.20	.07
❑	58 Leonard Russell	.10	.02
❑	59 Brent Jones	.10	.02
❑	60 Trent Dilfer	.40	.15
❑	61 Terance Mathis	.20	.07
❑	62 Jeff George	.20	.07
❑	63 Alvin Harper	.10	.02
❑	64 Terry Allen	.20	.07
❑	65 Stan Humphries	.20	.07
❑	66 Robert Green	.10	.02
❑	67 Bryce Paup	.20	.07
❑	68 Tamarick Vanover RC	.40	.15
❑	69 Desmond Howard	.20	.07
❑	70 Derek Loville	.10	.02
❑	71 Dave Brown	.20	.07
❑	72 Carl Pickens	.20	.07
❑	73 Gary Clark	.10	.02
❑	74 Gary Brown	.10	.02
❑	75 Brett Perriman	.20	.07
❑	76 Charlie Garner	.40	.15
❑	77 Ben Coates	.20	.07
❑	78 Bruce Smith	.40	.15
❑	79 Erric Pegram	.20	.07
❑	80 Jerry Rice	1.25	.50
❑	81 Tim Brown	.40	.15
❑	82 John Taylor	.10	.02
❑	83 Will Moore	.10	.02
❑	84 Jay Novacek	.20	.07
❑	85 Kevin Williams	.20	.07
❑	86 Rocket Ismail	.20	.07
❑	87 Robert Brooks	.40	.15
❑	88 Michael Irvin	.40	.15
❑	89 Mark Chmura	.40	.15
❑	90 Shannon Sharpe	.20	.07
❑	91 Henry Ellard	.20	.07
❑	92 Reggie White	.40	.15
❑	93 Isaac Bruce	.75	.30
❑	94 Charles Haley	.20	.07
❑	95 Jake Reed	.20	.07
❑	96 Pete Metzelaars	.10	.02
❑	97 Dave Krieg	.10	.02
❑	98 Tony Martin	.20	.07
❑	99 Charles Jordan RC	.20	.07
❑	100 Bert Emanuel	.40	.15
❑	101 Andre Rison	.20	.07
❑	102 Jeff Graham	.10	.02
❑	103 O.J. McDuffie	.40	.15
❑	104 Randall Cunningham	.40	.15
❑	105 Harvey Williams	.10	.02
❑	106 Cris Carter	.40	.15
❑	107 Irving Fryar	.20	.07
❑	108 Jim Harbaugh	.20	.07
❑	109 Bernie Kosar	.10	.02
❑	110 Charles Johnson	.20	.07
❑	111 Warren Moon	.20	.07
❑	112 Neil O'Donnell	.20	.07
❑	113 Fred Barnett	.20	.07
❑	114 Herman Moore	.40	.15
❑	115 Chris Miller	.10	.02
❑	116 Vinny Testaverde	.20	.07
❑	117 Craig Erickson	.10	.02
❑	118 Qadry Ismail	.20	.07
❑	119 Willie Davis	.20	.07
❑	120 Michael Jackson	.20	.07
❑	121 Stoney Case RC	.40	.15
❑	122 Frank Sanders RC	.40	.15
❑	123 Todd Collins RC	.40	.15
❑	124 Kerry Collins RC	1.50	.60
❑	125 Sherman Williams RC	.10	.02
❑	126 Terrell Davis RC	2.50	1.00
❑	127 Luther Elliss RC	.10	.02
❑	128 Steve McNair RC	3.00	1.25
❑	129 Chris Sanders RC	.40	.15
❑	130 Ki-Jana Carter RC	.40	.15
❑	131 Rodney Thomas RC	.40	.15
❑	132 Tony Boselli RC	.40	.15
❑	133 Rob Johnson RC	1.00	.40
❑	134 James O. Stewart RC	1.25	.50
❑	135 Chad May RC	.10	.02
❑	136 Eric Bjornson RC	.20	.07
❑	137 Tyrone Wheatley RC	1.25	.50
❑	138 Kyle Brady RC	.40	.15
❑	139 Curtis Martin RC	3.00	1.25
❑	140 Eric Zeier RC	.40	.15
❑	141 Ray Zellars RC	.20	.07
❑	142 Napoleon Kaufman RC	1.25	.50
❑	143 Mike Mamula RC	.20	.07
❑	144 Mark Bruener RC	.20	.07
❑	145 Kordell Stewart RC	1.50	.60
❑	146 J.J. Stokes RC	.40	.15
❑	147 Joey Galloway RC	1.50	.60
❑	148 Warren Sapp RC	1.50	.60
❑	149 Michael Westbrook RC	.40	.15
❑	150 Rashaan Salaam RC	.40	.15

1996 Playoff Contenders Open Field Foil

❑	COMPLETE SET (100)	120.00	50.00
❑	1 Brett Favre P	12.00	5.00
❑	2 Steve Young R	10.00	4.00
❑	3 Herman Moore P	1.50	.60
❑	4 Jim Harbaugh G	1.25	.50
❑	5 Curtis Martin P	5.00	2.00
❑	6 Junior Seau P	3.00	1.25
❑	7 John Elway P	12.00	5.00
❑	8 Troy Aikman R	12.00	5.00
❑	9 Terry Allen G	1.25	.50
❑	10 Kordell Stewart P	3.00	1.25
❑	11 Drew Bledsoe G	3.00	1.25
❑	12 Jim Kelly G	2.00	.75
❑	13 Dan Marino R	25.00	10.00
❑	14 Andre Rison P	1.50	.60
❑	15 Jeff Hostetler G	.75	.30
❑	16 Scott Mitchell R	3.00	1.25
❑	17 Carl Pickens G	1.25	.50
❑	18 Larry Centers G	1.25	.50
❑	19 Craig Heyward R	1.50	.60
❑	20 Barry Sanders R	20.00	7.50
❑	21 Deion Sanders P	4.00	1.50
❑	22 Emmitt Smith P	10.00	4.00
❑	23 Rashaan Salaam R	3.00	1.25
❑	24 Mario Bates P	1.00	.40
❑	25 Lawrence Phillips P	1.50	.60
❑	26 Napoleon Kaufman G	2.00	.75
❑	27 Rodney Hampton G	1.25	.50
❑	28 Marshall Faulk R	5.00	2.00
❑	29 Trent Dilfer G	2.00	.75
❑	30 Leeland McElroy R	3.00	1.25
❑	31 Marcus Allen G	2.00	.75
❑	32 Ricky Watters P	1.50	.60
❑	33 Karim Abdul-Jabbar P	3.00	1.25
❑	34 Herschel Walker R	3.00	1.25
❑	35 Thurman Thomas G	2.00	.75
❑	36 Jerome Bettis G	2.00	.75
❑	37 Gus Frerotte R	3.00	1.25
❑	38 Neil O'Donnell G	1.25	.50
❑	39 Rick Mirer G	1.25	.50
❑	40 Mike Alstott G	2.50	1.00
❑	41 Vinny Testaverde G	1.25	.50
❑	42 Derek Loville G	.75	.30
❑	43 Ben Coates G	1.25	.50
❑	44 Steve McNair G	3.00	1.25
❑	45 Bobby Engram R	5.00	2.00
❑	46 Yancey Thigpen G	1.25	.50
❑	47 Lake Dawson P	1.00	.40
❑	48 Terrell Davis G	3.00	1.25
❑	49 Kerry Collins P	3.00	1.25
❑	50 Eric Metcalf G	.75	.30
❑	51 Stanley Pritchett G	.75	.30
❑	52 Robert Brooks P	1.50	.60
❑	53 Isaac Bruce P	3.00	1.25
❑	54 Tim Brown P	3.00	1.25
❑	55 Edgar Bennett G	1.25	.50
❑	56 Warren Moon P	3.00	1.25
❑	57 Jerry Rice P	6.00	2.50
❑	58 Michael Westbrook G	2.00	.75
❑	59 Keyshawn Johnson P	3.00	1.25
❑	60 Steve Bono G	.75	.30
❑	61 Derrick Mayes R	5.00	2.00
❑	62 Erik Kramer G	.75	.30
❑	63 Rodney Peete G	.75	.30
❑	64 Eddie Kennison G	2.00	.75
❑	65 Derrick Thomas G	2.00	.75
❑	66 Joey Galloway R	3.00	1.25
❑	67 Amani Toomer R	6.00	2.50
❑	68 Reggie White R	5.00	2.00
❑	69 Heath Shuler P	1.50	.60
❑	70 Dave Brown G	.75	.30
❑	71 Tony Banks R	5.00	2.00
❑	72 Chris Warren G	1.25	.50
❑	73 J.J. Stokes G	2.00	.75
❑	74 Rickey Dudley R	5.00	2.00
❑	75 Stan Humphries G	1.25	.50
❑	76 Jason Dunn R	1.50	.60

❑ 77 Tyrone Wheatley G 1.25 .50
❑ 78 Jim Everett G .75 .30
❑ 79 Cris Carter G 2.00 .75
❑ 80 Alex Van Dyke R 3.00 1.25
❑ 81 O.J. McDuffie P 3.00 1.25
❑ 82 Mark Chmura G 1.25 .50
❑ 83 Terry Glenn R 5.00 2.00
❑ 84 Boomer Esiason G 1.25 .50
❑ 85 Bruce Smith G 1.25 .50
❑ 86 Curtis Conway G 1.25 .50
❑ 87 Ki-Jana Carter R 3.00 1.25
❑ 88 Tamarick Vanover P 1.50 .60
❑ 89 Michael Jackson R 3.00 1.25
❑ 90 Mark Brunell G 3.00 1.25
❑ 91 Tim Biakabutuka G 2.00 .75
❑ 92 Anthony Miller G 1.25 .50
❑ 93 Marvin Harrison G 6.00 2.50
❑ 94 Jeff George G 1.25 .50
❑ 95 Jeff Blake G 2.00 .75
❑ 96 Eddie George P 4.00 1.50
❑ 97 Eric Moulds R 6.00 2.50
❑ 98 Mike Tomczak R 1.50 .60
❑ 99 Chris Sanders G 1.25 .50
❑ 100 Chris Chandler G 1.25 .50

1996 Playoff Contenders Pennants

❑ COMPLETE SET (100) 120.00 50.00
❑ 1 Brett Favre R 30.00 12.50
❑ 2 Steve Young R 12.00 5.00
❑ 3 Herman Moore R 4.00 1.50
❑ 4 Jim Harbaugh R 4.00 1.50
❑ 5 Curtis Martin R 12.00 5.00
❑ 6 Junior Seau G 2.50 1.00
❑ 7 John Elway R 30.00 12.50
❑ 8 Troy Aikman P 8.00 3.00
❑ 9 Terry Allen G 1.50 .60
❑ 10 Kordell Stewart R 6.00 2.50
❑ 11 Drew Bledsoe G 5.00 2.00
❑ 12 Jim Kelly P 3.00 1.25
❑ 13 Dan Marino P 15.00 6.00
❑ 14 Andre Rison G 1.50 .60
❑ 15 Jeff Hostetler G .75 .30
❑ 16 Scott Mitchell G 1.50 .60
❑ 17 Carl Pickens R 4.00 1.50
❑ 18 Larry Centers P 1.00 .40
❑ 19 Craig Heyward G .75 .30
❑ 20 Barry Sanders P 12.00 5.00
❑ 21 Deion Sanders R 10.00 4.00
❑ 22 Emmitt Smith R 25.00 10.00
❑ 23 Rashaan Salaam R 4.00 1.50
❑ 24 Mario Bates G 1.50 .60
❑ 25 Lawrence Phillips G 2.50 1.00
❑ 26 Napoleon Kaufman G 2.50 1.00
❑ 27 Rodney Hampton G 1.50 .60
❑ 28 Marshall Faulk P 4.00 1.50
❑ 29 Trent Dilfer G 2.50 1.00
❑ 30 Leeland McElroy P 2.00 .75
❑ 31 Marcus Allen P 3.00 1.25
❑ 32 Ricky Watters G 1.50 .60
❑ 33 Karim Abdul-Jabbar G 2.50 1.00
❑ 34 Herschel Walker P 2.00 .75
❑ 35 Thurman Thomas R 6.00 2.50
❑ 36 Jerome Bettis P 3.00 1.25
❑ 37 Gus Frerotte G 1.50 .60
❑ 38 Neil O'Donnell G 1.50 .60
❑ 39 Rick Mirer G 1.50 .60
❑ 40 Mike Alstott R 6.00 2.50
❑ 41 Vinny Testaverde R 4.00 1.50
❑ 42 Derek Loville G .75 .30
❑ 43 Ben Coates G 1.50 .60
❑ 44 Steve McNair R 12.00 5.00
❑ 45 Bobby Engram P 3.00 1.25
❑ 46 Yancey Thigpen G 1.50 .60
❑ 47 Lake Dawson G .75 .30
❑ 48 Terrell Davis P 8.00 3.00
❑ 49 Kerry Collins R 6.00 2.50
❑ 50 Eric Metcalf G .75 .30
❑ 51 Stanley Pritchett R 2.00 .75
❑ 52 Robert Brooks R 4.00 1.50
❑ 53 Isaac Bruce G 2.50 1.00
❑ 54 Tim Brown G 2.50 1.00
❑ 55 Edgar Bennett P 1.00 .40
❑ 56 Warren Moon G 1.50 .60
❑ 57 Jerry Rice R 15.00 6.00
❑ 58 Michael Westbrook G 2.50 1.00
❑ 59 Keyshawn Johnson G 2.50 1.00
❑ 60 Steve Bono R .75 .30
❑ 61 Derrick Mayes P 3.00 1.25
❑ 62 Erik Kramer P 1.00 .40
❑ 63 Rodney Peete G .75 .30
❑ 64 Eddie Kennison G 2.50 1.00
❑ 65 Derrick Thomas G 2.50 1.00
❑ 66 Joey Galloway R 6.00 2.50
❑ 67 Amani Toomer P 3.00 1.25
❑ 68 Reggie White G 2.50 1.00
❑ 69 Heath Shuler G 1.50 .60
❑ 70 Dave Brown G .75 .30
❑ 71 Tony Banks P 3.00 1.25
❑ 72 Chris Warren G 1.50 .60
❑ 73 J.J. Stokes G 2.50 1.00
❑ 74 Rickey Dudley P 3.00 1.25
❑ 75 Stan Humphries G 1.50 .60
❑ 76 Jason Dunn P 1.00 .40
❑ 77 Tyrone Wheatley G 1.50 .60
❑ 78 Jim Everett G .75 .30
❑ 79 Cris Carter P 3.00 1.25
❑ 80 Alex Van Dyke P 1.00 .40
❑ 81 O.J. McDuffie G 1.50 .60
❑ 82 Mark Chmura P 1.00 .40
❑ 83 Terry Glenn P 3.00 1.25
❑ 84 Boomer Esiason R 4.00 1.50
❑ 85 Bruce Smith G 1.50 .60
❑ 86 Curtis Conway G 1.50 .60
❑ 87 Ki-Jana Carter G 1.50 .60
❑ 88 Tamarick Vanover G 1.50 .60
❑ 89 Michael Jackson G 1.50 .60
❑ 90 Mark Brunell G 5.00 2.00
❑ 91 Tim Biakabutuka R 6.00 2.50
❑ 92 Anthony Miller G 1.50 .60
❑ 93 Marvin Harrison R 15.00 6.00
❑ 94 Jeff George P 2.00 .75
❑ 95 Jeff Blake R 6.00 2.50
❑ 96 Eddie George G 4.00 1.50
❑ 97 Eric Moulds P 4.00 1.50
❑ 98 Mike Tomczak G .75 .30
❑ 99 Chris Sanders G 1.50 .60
❑ 100 Chris Chandler G 1.50 .60

1997 Playoff Contenders

❑ COMPLETE SET (150) 40.00 15.00
❑ 1 Kent Graham .40 .15
❑ 2 Leeland McElroy .40 .15
❑ 3 Rob Moore .60 .25
❑ 4 Frank Sanders .60 .25
❑ 5 Jake Plummer RC 5.00 2.00
❑ 6 Chris Chandler .60 .25
❑ 7 Bert Emanuel .60 .25
❑ 8 O.J. Santiago RC .60 .25
❑ 9 Byron Hanspard RC .60 .25
❑ 10 Vinny Testaverde .60 .25
❑ 11 Michael Jackson .60 .25
❑ 12 Earnest Byner .40 .15
❑ 13 Jermaine Lewis 1.00 .40
❑ 14 Derrick Alexander WR .60 .25
❑ 15 Jay Graham RC .60 .25
❑ 16 Todd Collins .40 .15
❑ 17 Thurman Thomas 1.00 .40
❑ 18 Bruce Smith .60 .25
❑ 19 Andre Reed .60 .25
❑ 20 Quinn Early .40 .15
❑ 21 Antowain Smith RC 2.50 1.00
❑ 22 Kerry Collins 1.00 .40
❑ 23 Tim Biakabutuka .60 .25
❑ 24 Anthony Johnson .40 .15
❑ 25 Wesley Walls .60 .25
❑ 26 Fred Lane RC .60 .25
❑ 27 Rae Carruth RC .40 .15
❑ 28 Raymont Harris .40 .15
❑ 29 Rick Mirer .40 .15
❑ 30 Darnell Autry RC .60 .25
❑ 31 Jeff Blake .60 .25
❑ 32 Ki-Jana Carter .40 .15
❑ 33 Carl Pickens .60 .25
❑ 34 Darnay Scott .60 .25
❑ 35 Corey Dillon RC 6.00 2.50
❑ 36 Troy Aikman 2.00 .75
❑ 37 Emmitt Smith 3.00 1.25
❑ 38 Michael Irvin 1.00 .40
❑ 39 Deion Sanders 1.00 .40
❑ 40 Anthony Miller .40 .15
❑ 41 Eric Bjornson .40 .15
❑ 42 David LaFleur RC .40 .15
❑ 43 John Elway 4.00 1.50
❑ 44 Terrell Davis 1.25 .50
❑ 45 Shannon Sharpe .60 .25
❑ 46 Ed McCaffrey .60 .25
❑ 47 Rod Smith WR 1.00 .40
❑ 48 Scott Mitchell .60 .25
❑ 49 Barry Sanders 3.00 1.25
❑ 50 Herman Moore .60 .25
❑ 51 Brett Favre 4.00 1.50
❑ 52 Dorsey Levens 1.00 .40
❑ 53 William Henderson .60 .25
❑ 54 Derrick Mayes .60 .25
❑ 55 Antonio Freeman 1.00 .40
❑ 56 Robert Brooks .60 .25
❑ 57 Mark Chmura .60 .25
❑ 58 Reggie White 1.00 .40
❑ 59 Darren Sharper RC 1.00 .40
❑ 60 Jim Harbaugh .60 .25
❑ 61 Marshall Faulk 1.25 .50
❑ 62 Marvin Harrison 1.00 .40
❑ 63 Mark Brunell 1.25 .50
❑ 64 Natrone Means .60 .25
❑ 65 Jimmy Smith .60 .25
❑ 66 Keenan McCardell .60 .25
❑ 67 Elvis Grbac .60 .25
❑ 68 Greg Hill .40 .15
❑ 69 Marcus Allen 1.00 .40
❑ 70 Andre Rison .60 .25
❑ 71 Kimble Anders .60 .25
❑ 72 Tony Gonzalez RC 3.00 1.25
❑ 73 Pat Barnes RC 1.00 .40
❑ 74 Dan Marino 4.00 1.50
❑ 75 Karim Abdul-Jabbar .60 .25
❑ 76 Zach Thomas 1.00 .40
❑ 77 O.J. McDuffie .60 .25
❑ 78 Brian Manning RC .40 .15
❑ 79 Brad Johnson 1.00 .40
❑ 80 Cris Carter 1.00 .40
❑ 81 Jake Reed .60 .25
❑ 82 Robert Smith .60 .25
❑ 83 Drew Bledsoe 1.25 .50
❑ 84 Curtis Martin 1.25 .50
❑ 85 Ben Coates .60 .25
❑ 86 Terry Glenn 1.00 .40
❑ 87 Shawn Jefferson .40 .15
❑ 88 Heath Shuler .40 .15
❑ 89 Mario Bates .40 .15
❑ 90 Andre Hastings .40 .15
❑ 91 Troy Davis RC .60 .25
❑ 92 Danny Wuerffel RC 1.00 .40
❑ 93 Dave Brown .40 .15
❑ 94 Chris Calloway .40 .15

Card		
❑ 95 Tiki Barber RC	6.00	2.50
❑ 96 Mike Cherry RC	.40	.15
❑ 97 Neil O'Donnell	.60	.25
❑ 98 Keyshawn Johnson	1.00	.40
❑ 99 Adrian Murrell	.60	.25
❑ 100 Wayne Chrebet	1.00	.40
❑ 101 Dedric Ward RC	.60	.25
❑ 102 Leon Johnson RC	.60	.25
❑ 103 Jeff George	.60	.25
❑ 104 Napoleon Kaufman	1.00	.40
❑ 105 Tim Brown	1.00	.40
❑ 106 James Jett	.60	.25
❑ 107 Ty Detmer	.60	.25
❑ 108 Ricky Watters	.60	.25
❑ 109 Irving Fryar	.60	.25
❑ 110 Michael Timpson	.40	.15
❑ 111 Chad Lewis RC	2.00	.75
❑ 112 Kordell Stewart	1.00	.40
❑ 113 Jerome Bettis	1.00	.40
❑ 114 Charles Johnson	.60	.25
❑ 115 George Jones RC	.60	.25
❑ 116 Will Blackwell RC	.60	.25
❑ 117 Stan Humphries	.60	.25
❑ 118 Junior Seau	1.00	.40
❑ 119 Freddie Jones RC	.60	.25
❑ 120 Steve Young	1.25	.50
❑ 121 Jerry Rice	2.00	.75
❑ 122 Garrison Hearst	.60	.25
❑ 123 William Floyd	.60	.25
❑ 124 Terrell Owens	1.25	.50
❑ 125 J.J. Stokes	.60	.25
❑ 126 Marc Edwards RC	.40	.15
❑ 127 Jim Druckenmiller RC	.60	.25
❑ 128 Warren Moon	1.00	.40
❑ 129 Chris Warren	.60	.25
❑ 130 Joey Galloway	.60	.25
❑ 131 Shawn Springs RC	.60	.25
❑ 132 Tony Banks	.60	.25
❑ 133 Lawrence Phillips	.40	.15
❑ 134 Isaac Bruce	1.00	.40
❑ 135 Eddie Kennison	.60	.25
❑ 136 Orlando Pace RC	1.00	.40
❑ 137 Trent Dilfer	1.00	.40
❑ 138 Mike Alstott	1.00	.40
❑ 139 Horace Copeland	.40	.15
❑ 140 Jackie Harris	.40	.15
❑ 141 Warrick Dunn RC	3.00	1.25
❑ 142 Reidel Anthony RC	1.00	.40
❑ 143 Steve McNair	1.25	.50
❑ 144 Eddie George	1.00	.40
❑ 145 Chris Sanders	.40	.15
❑ 146 Gus Frerotte	.40	.15
❑ 147 Terry Allen	1.00	.40
❑ 148 Henry Ellard	.40	.15
❑ 149 Leslie Shepherd	.40	.15
❑ 150 Michael Westbrook	.60	.25
❑ S1 Terrell Davis Sample	2.00	.75

1998 Playoff Contenders Leather

Card		
❑ COMPLETE SET (100)	200.00	100.00
❑ 1 Adrian Murrell	1.50	.60
❑ 2 Michael Pittman	2.50	1.00
❑ 3 Jake Plummer	2.50	1.00
❑ 4 Andre Wadsworth	1.50	.60
❑ 5 Jamal Anderson	2.50	1.00
❑ 6 Chris Chandler	1.50	.60
❑ 7 Tim Dwight	2.50	1.00
❑ 8 Pat Johnson	1.50	.60
❑ 9 Jermaine Lewis	1.50	.60
❑ 10 Doug Flutie	2.50	1.00
❑ 11 Antowain Smith	2.50	1.00
❑ 12 Muhsin Muhammad	1.50	.60
❑ 13 Bobby Engram	1.50	.60
❑ 14 Curtis Enis	.75	.30
❑ 15 Alonzo Mayes	.75	.30
❑ 16 Corey Dillon	2.50	1.00
❑ 17 Carl Pickens	1.50	.60
❑ 18 Troy Aikman	5.00	2.00
❑ 19 Michael Irvin	2.50	1.00
❑ 20 Deion Sanders	2.50	1.00
❑ 21 Emmitt Smith	8.00	3.00
❑ 22 Terrell Davis	2.50	1.00
❑ 23 John Elway	10.00	4.00
❑ 24 Brian Griese	5.00	2.00
❑ 25 Rod Smith WR	1.50	.60
❑ 26 Charlie Batch	2.50	1.00
❑ 27 Germane Crowell	.75	.30
❑ 28 Terry Fair	.75	.30
❑ 29 Herman Moore	1.50	.60
❑ 30 Barry Sanders	8.00	3.00
❑ 31 Brett Favre	10.00	4.00
❑ 32 Antonio Freeman	2.50	1.00
❑ 33 Vonnie Holliday	1.50	.60
❑ 34 Reggie White	2.50	1.00
❑ 35 Marshall Faulk	3.00	1.25
❑ 36 Marvin Harrison	2.50	1.00
❑ 37 Peyton Manning	25.00	10.00
❑ 38 Jerome Pathon	2.50	1.00
❑ 39 Tavian Banks	1.50	.60
❑ 40 Mark Brunell	2.50	1.00
❑ 41 Keenan McCardell	1.50	.60
❑ 42 Fred Taylor	4.00	1.50
❑ 43 Elvis Grbac	1.50	.60
❑ 44 Andre Rison	1.50	.60
❑ 45 Rashaan Shehee	.75	.30
❑ 46 Karim Abdul-Jabbar	2.50	1.00
❑ 47 John Avery	.75	.30
❑ 48 Dan Marino	10.00	4.00
❑ 49 O.J. McDuffie	1.50	.60
❑ 50 Cris Carter	2.50	1.00
❑ 51 Brad Johnson	2.50	1.00
❑ 52 Randy Moss	15.00	6.00
❑ 53 Robert Smith	2.50	1.00
❑ 54 Drew Bledsoe	4.00	1.50
❑ 55 Ben Coates	1.50	.60
❑ 56 Robert Edwards	1.50	.60
❑ 57 Chris Floyd	.75	.30
❑ 58 Terry Glenn	2.50	1.00
❑ 59 Cameron Cleeland	.75	.30
❑ 60 Kerry Collins	1.50	.60
❑ 61 Danny Kanell	1.50	.60
❑ 62 Charles Way	1.00	.40
❑ 63 Glenn Foley	1.00	.40
❑ 64 Keyshawn Johnson	2.50	1.00
❑ 65 Curtis Martin	2.50	1.00
❑ 66 Tim Brown	2.50	1.00
❑ 67 Jeff George	1.50	.60
❑ 68 Napoleon Kaufman	2.50	1.00
❑ 69 Charles Woodson	3.00	1.25
❑ 70 Irving Fryar	1.50	.60
❑ 71 Bobby Hoying	1.50	.60
❑ 72 Jerome Bettis	2.50	1.00
❑ 73 Kordell Stewart	2.50	1.00
❑ 74 Hines Ward	10.00	5.00
❑ 75 Ryan Leaf	2.50	1.00
❑ 76 Natrone Means	1.50	.60
❑ 77 Mikhael Ricks	.75	.30
❑ 78 Junior Seau	2.50	1.00
❑ 79 Garrison Hearst	2.50	1.00
❑ 80 Terrell Owens	2.50	1.00
❑ 81 Jerry Rice	5.00	2.00
❑ 82 Steve Young	3.00	1.25
❑ 83 Joey Galloway	1.50	.60
❑ 84 Ahman Green	12.00	5.00
❑ 85 Warren Moon	2.50	1.00
❑ 86 Ricky Watters	1.50	.60
❑ 87 Tony Banks	1.50	.60
❑ 88 Isaac Bruce	2.50	1.00
❑ 89 Robert Holcombe	1.50	.60
❑ 90 Mike Alstott	2.50	1.00
❑ 91 Trent Dilfer	2.50	1.00
❑ 92 Warrick Dunn	2.50	1.00
❑ 93 Jacquez Green	1.50	.60
❑ 94 Kevin Dyson	2.50	1.00
❑ 95 Eddie George	2.50	1.00
❑ 96 Steve McNair	2.50	1.00
❑ 97 Yancey Thigpen	1.00	.40
❑ 98 Terry Allen	2.50	1.00
❑ 99 Skip Hicks	1.50	.60
❑ 100 Michael Westbrook	1.50	.60

1998 Playoff Contenders Ticket

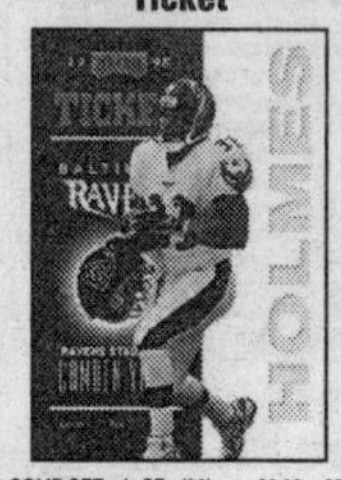

Card		
❑ COMP.SET w/o SPs (80)	60.00	25.00
❑ 1 Rob Moore	1.25	.50
❑ 2 Jake Plummer	2.00	.75
❑ 3 Jamal Anderson	2.00	.75
❑ 4 Terance Mathis	1.25	.50
❑ 5 Priest Holmes RC	60.00	30.00
❑ 6 Michael Jackson	.75	.30
❑ 7 Eric Zeier	1.25	.50
❑ 8 Andre Reed	1.25	.50
❑ 9 Antowain Smith	2.00	.75
❑ 10 Bruce Smith	1.25	.50
❑ 11 Thurman Thomas	2.00	.75
❑ 12 Rocket Ismail	.75	.30
❑ 13 Wesley Walls	1.25	.50
❑ 14 Curtis Conway	1.25	.50
❑ 15 Jeff Blake	1.25	.50
❑ 16 Corey Dillon	2.00	.75
❑ 17 Carl Pickens	1.25	.50
❑ 18 Troy Aikman	4.00	1.50
❑ 19 Michael Irvin	2.00	.75
❑ 20 Ernie Mills	.75	.30
❑ 21 Deion Sanders	2.00	.75
❑ 22 Emmitt Smith	6.00	2.50
❑ 23 Terrell Davis	2.00	.75
❑ 24 John Elway	8.00	3.00
❑ 25 Neil Smith	1.25	.50
❑ 26 Rod Smith WR	1.25	.50
❑ 27 Herman Moore	1.25	.50
❑ 28 Johnnie Morton	1.25	.50
❑ 29 Barry Sanders	6.00	2.50
❑ 30 Robert Brooks	1.25	.50
❑ 31 Brett Favre	8.00	3.00
❑ 32 Antonio Freeman	2.00	.75
❑ 33 Dorsey Levens	2.00	.75
❑ 34 Reggie White	2.00	.75
❑ 35 Marshall Faulk	2.50	1.00
❑ 36 Mark Brunell	2.00	.75
❑ 37 Jimmy Smith	1.25	.50
❑ 38 James Stewart	1.25	.50
❑ 39 Donnell Bennett	.75	.30
❑ 40 Andre Rison	1.25	.50
❑ 41 Derrick Thomas	2.00	.75
❑ 42 Karim Abdul-Jabbar	2.00	.75
❑ 43 Dan Marino	8.00	3.00
❑ 44 Cris Carter	2.00	.75
❑ 45 Brad Johnson	2.00	.75
❑ 46 Robert Smith	2.00	.75
❑ 47 Drew Bledsoe	3.00	1.25
❑ 48 Terry Glenn	2.00	.75
❑ 49 Lamar Smith	1.25	.50
❑ 50 Ike Hilliard	1.25	.50
❑ 51 Danny Kanell	1.25	.50
❑ 52 Wayne Chrebet	2.00	.75
❑ 53 Keyshawn Johnson	2.00	.75
❑ 54 Curtis Martin	2.00	.75
❑ 55 Tim Brown	2.00	.75
❑ 56 Rickey Dudley	.75	.30
❑ 57 Jeff George	1.25	.50
❑ 58 Napoleon Kaufman	2.00	.75
❑ 59 Irving Fryar	1.25	.50
❑ 60 Jerome Bettis	2.00	.75

❑ 61 Charles Johnson .75 .30
❑ 62 Kordell Stewart 2.00 .75
❑ 63 Natrone Means 1.25 .50
❑ 64 Bryan Still .75 .30
❑ 65 Garrison Hearst 2.00 .75
❑ 66 Jerry Rice 4.00 1.50
❑ 67 Steve Young 2.50 1.00
❑ 68 Joey Galloway 1.25 .50
❑ 69 Warren Moon 2.00 .75
❑ 70 Ricky Watters 1.25 .50
❑ 71 Isaac Bruce 2.00 .75
❑ 72 Mike Alstott 2.00 .75
❑ 73 Reidel Anthony 1.25 .50
❑ 74 Trent Dilfer 2.00 .75
❑ 75 Warrick Dunn 2.00 .75
❑ 76 Warren Sapp 1.25 .50
❑ 77 Eddie George 2.00 .75
❑ 78 Steve McNair 2.00 .75
❑ 79 Terry Allen 2.00 .75
❑ 80 Gus Frerotte .75 .30
❑ 81 Andre Wadsworth AUTO 25.00 10.00
❑ 82 Tim Dwight AUTO 40.00 15.00
❑ 83 Curtis Enis AUTO/400 40.00 15.00
❑ 85 Charlie Batch AUTO 40.00 15.00
❑ 86 Germane Crowell AUTO 25.00 10.00
❑ 87 Pey.Manning AUTO/200 2500.00 1800.00
❑ 88 Jerome Pathon AUTO 40.00 15.00
❑ 89 Fred Taylor AUTO 80.00 40.00
❑ 90 Tavian Banks AUTO 25.00 10.00
❑ 92 Randy Moss AUTO/300 400.00 250.00
❑ 93 Robert Edwards AUTO 25.00 10.00
❑ 94 Hines Ward AUTO 250.00 125.00
❑ 95 Ryan Leaf AUTO/200 60.00 25.00
❑ 96 Mikhael Ricks AUTO 25.00 10.00
❑ 97 Ahman Green AUTO 100.00 50.00
❑ 98 Jacquez Green AUTO 25.00 10.00
❑ 99 Kevin Dyson AUTO 40.00 15.00
❑ 100 Skip Hicks AUTO 25.00 10.00
❑ 103 C.Fuamatu-Ma'afala AU 25.00 10.00

1999 Playoff Contenders SSD

❑ COMPLETE SET (200) 2000.00 1000.00
❑ COMP.SET w/o RC/PT's (141) 60.00 25.00
❑ 1 Randy Moss 5.00 2.00
❑ 2 Randall Cunningham 2.00 .75
❑ 3 Cris Carter 2.00 .75
❑ 4 Robert Smith 2.00 .75
❑ 5 Jake Reed 1.25 .50
❑ 6 Albert Connell .75 .30
❑ 7 Jeff George 1.25 .50
❑ 8 Brett Favre 6.00 2.50
❑ 9 Antonio Freeman 2.00 .75
❑ 10 Dorsey Levens 2.00 .75
❑ 11 Mark Chmura 1.25 .50
❑ 12 Mike Alstott 2.00 .75
❑ 13 Warrick Dunn 2.00 .75
❑ 14 Trent Dilfer 1.25 .50
❑ 15 Jacquez Green .75 .30
❑ 16 Reidel Anthony .75 .30
❑ 17 Warren Sapp 1.25 .50
❑ 18 Amani Toomer .75 .30
❑ 19 Curtis Enis .75 .30
❑ 20 Curtis Conway 1.25 .50
❑ 21 Bobby Engram 1.25 .50
❑ 22 Barry Sanders 6.00 2.50
❑ 23 Charlie Batch 2.00 .75
❑ 24 Herman Moore 1.25 .50
❑ 25 Johnnie Morton 1.25 .50
❑ 26 Greg Hill .75 .30
❑ 27 Germane Crowell .75 .30
❑ 28 Kerry Collins 1.25 .50
❑ 29 Ike Hilliard .75 .30
❑ 30 Joe Jurevicius 1.25 .50
❑ 31 Stephen Davis 2.00 .75
❑ 32 Brad Johnson 2.00 .75
❑ 33 Skip Hicks .75 .30
❑ 34 Michael Westbrook 1.25 .50
❑ 35 Jake Plummer 1.25 .50
❑ 36 Adrian Murrell .75 .30
❑ 37 Frank Sanders 1.25 .50
❑ 38 Rob Moore 1.25 .50
❑ 39 Gary Brown .75 .30
❑ 40 Duce Staley 2.00 .75
❑ 41 Charles Johnson 1.25 .50
❑ 42 Emmitt Smith 4.00 1.50
❑ 43 Troy Aikman 4.00 1.50
❑ 44 Michael Irvin 1.25 .50
❑ 45 Deion Sanders 2.00 .75
❑ 46 Rocket Ismail 1.25 .50
❑ 47 Jerry Rice 4.00 1.50
❑ 48 Terrell Owens 2.00 .75
❑ 49 Steve Young 2.50 1.00
❑ 50 Garrison Hearst 1.25 .50
❑ 51 J.J. Stokes 1.25 .50
❑ 52 Lawrence Phillips 1.25 .50
❑ 53 Jamal Anderson 2.00 .75
❑ 54 Chris Chandler 1.25 .50
❑ 55 Terance Mathis 1.25 .50
❑ 56 Tim Dwight 2.00 .75
❑ 57 Charlie Garner 1.25 .50
❑ 58 Chris Calloway 1.25 .50
❑ 59 Eddie Kennison 1.25 .50
❑ 60 Billy Joe Hobert .75 .30
❑ 61 Tim Biakabutuka 1.25 .50
❑ 62 Muhsin Muhammad 1.25 .50
❑ 63 Olandis Gary/1825 RC 25.00 10.00
❑ 64 Wesley Walls 1.25 .50
❑ 65 Isaac Bruce 2.00 .75
❑ 66 Marshall Faulk 2.50 1.00
❑ 67 Kordell Stewart 1.25 .50
❑ 68 Jerome Bettis 2.00 .75
❑ 69 Hines Ward 2.00 .75
❑ 70 Corey Dillon 2.00 .75
❑ 71 Carl Pickens 1.25 .50
❑ 72 Darnay Scott 1.25 .50
❑ 73 Steve McNair 2.00 .75
❑ 74 Eddie George 2.00 .75
❑ 75 Yancey Thigpen .75 .30
❑ 76 Kevin Dyson 1.25 .50
❑ 77 Fred Taylor 2.00 .75
❑ 78 Mark Brunell 2.00 .75
❑ 79 Jimmy Smith 1.25 .50
❑ 80 Keenan McCardell 1.25 .50
❑ 81 James Stewart 1.25 .50
❑ 82 Jermaine Lewis 1.25 .50
❑ 83 Priest Holmes 3.00 1.25
❑ 84 Stoney Case .75 .30
❑ 85 Errict Rhett 1.25 .50
❑ 86 Bill Schroeder 2.00 .75
❑ 87 Terry Kirby .75 .30
❑ 88 Leslie Shepherd .75 .30
❑ 89 Terrence Wilkins/825 RC 20.00 7.50
❑ 90 Dan Marino 6.00 2.50
❑ 91 O.J. McDuffie 1.25 .50
❑ 92 Karim Abdul-Jabbar 1.25 .50
❑ 93 Zach Thomas 2.00 .75
❑ 94 Terry Allen 1.25 .50
❑ 95 Tony Martin 1.25 .50
❑ 96 Drew Bledsoe 2.50 1.00
❑ 97 Terry Glenn 2.00 .75
❑ 98 Ben Coates 1.25 .50
❑ 99 Tony Simmons .75 .30
❑ 100 Curtis Martin 2.00 .75
❑ 101 Keyshawn Johnson 2.00 .75
❑ 102 Vinny Testaverde 1.25 .50
❑ 103 Wayne Chrebet 2.00 .75
❑ 104 Peyton Manning 6.00 2.50
❑ 105 Marvin Harrison 2.00 .75
❑ 106 E.G. Green .75 .30
❑ 107 Doug Flutie 2.00 .75
❑ 108 Thurman Thomas 1.25 .50
❑ 109 Andre Reed 1.25 .50
❑ 110 Eric Moulds 2.00 .75
❑ 111 Antowain Smith 2.00 .75
❑ 112 Bruce Smith 1.25 .50
❑ 113 Terrell Davis 2.00 .75
❑ 114 John Elway 6.00 2.50
❑ 115 Ed McCaffrey 1.25 .50
❑ 116 Rod Smith 1.25 .50
❑ 117 Shannon Sharpe 1.25 .50
❑ 118 Jeff Garcia AU/325 RC 100.00 50.00
❑ 119 Brian Griese 2.00 .75
❑ 120 Justin Watson/325 RC 25.00 10.00
❑ 121 Bubby Brister 1.25 .50
❑ 122 Ryan Leaf 2.00 .75
❑ 123 Natrone Means 1.25 .50
❑ 124 Mikhael Ricks .75 .30
❑ 125 Junior Seau 2.00 .75
❑ 126 Jim Harbaugh 1.25 .50
❑ 127 Andre Rison 1.25 .50
❑ 128 Elvis Grbac 1.25 .50
❑ 129 Bam Morris .75 .30
❑ 130 Rashaan Shehee .75 .30
❑ 131 Warren Moon 2.00 .75
❑ 132 Tony Gonzalez 2.00 .75
❑ 133 Derrick Alexander 1.25 .50
❑ 134 Jon Kitna 2.00 .75
❑ 135 Ricky Watters 1.25 .50
❑ 136 Joey Galloway 1.25 .50
❑ 137 Ahman Green 2.00 .75
❑ 138 Derrick Mayes 1.25 .50
❑ 139 Tyrone Wheatley 1.25 .50
❑ 140 Napoleon Kaufman 2.00 .75
❑ 141 Tim Brown 2.00 .75
❑ 142 Charles Woodson 2.00 .75
❑ 143 Rich Gannon 2.00 .75
❑ 144 Rickey Dudley .75 .30
❑ 145 Az-Zahir Hakim .75 .30
❑ 146 Kurt Warner AU/1825 RC 50.00 25.00
❑ 147 Sean Bennett AU/1325 RC 15.00 6.00
❑ 148 Bran.Stokley AU/1325 RC 30.00 12.50
❑ 149 Amos Zereoue AU/1325 RC 25.00 10.00
❑ 150 Brock Huard AU/1325 RC 25.00 10.00
❑ 151 Tim Couch AU/1025 RC 30.00 12.50
❑ 152 Ricky Williams AU/725 RC 60.00 30.00
❑ 153 Donov McNabb AU/525 RC 200.00 100.00
❑ 154 Edgerrin James AU/525 RC 120.00 60.00
❑ 155 Torry Holt AU/1025 RC 80.00 40.00
❑ 156 D.Culpepper AU/1025 RC 120.00 50.00
❑ 157 Akili Smith AU/1025 RC 20.00 7.50
❑ 158 Champ Bailey AU/1725 RC 30.00 12.50
❑ 159 Chris Claiborne AU/1825 RC 20.00 7.50
❑ 160A C McAlister No AU/1825 RC 15.00 6.00
❑ 160B Jason Tucker AU/1825 15.00 6.00
❑ 161 Troy Edwards AU/1225 RC 20.00 7.50
❑ 162 Jevon Kearse AU/325 RC 80.00 40.00
❑ 163 Darnell McDonald AU/1825 RC 20.00 7.50
❑ 164 David Boston AU/1025 RC 25.00 10.00
❑ 165 Peerless Price AU/1325 RC 25.00 10.00
❑ 166 C.Collins AU/1025 RC 15.00 6.00
❑ 167 Rob Konrad AU/1325 RC 20.00 7.50
❑ 168 Cade McNown AU/1025 RC 20.00 7.50
❑ 169 Shawn Bryson AU/1825 RC 20.00 7.50
❑ 170 Kevin Faulk AU/1325 RC 25.00 10.00
❑ 171 Corby Jones AU/1825 RC 15.00 6.00
❑ 172A Jam Johnson No AU/1325 RC 15.00 6.00
❑ 172B Patrick Jeffers AU/1325 25.00 10.00
❑ 173 Autry Denson AU/1825 RC 20.00 7.50
❑ 174 Sedrick Irvin AU/1825 RC 15.00 6.00
❑ 175 Michael Bishop AU/1825 RC 25.00 10.00
❑ 176 Joe Germaine AU/825 RC 25.00 10.00
❑ 177 De'Mond Parker AU/1325 RC 15.00 6.00
❑ 178A Shaun King No AU/1825 RC 15.00 6.00
❑ 178B Ray Lucas AU/1825 25.00 10.00
❑ 179 D'Wayne Bates AU/1825 RC 20.00 7.50
❑ 180 Tai Streets AU/1825 RC 25.00 10.00
❑ 181 Na Brown AU/1825 RC 20.00 7.50
❑ 182 Desmond Clark AU/1825 RC 20.00 7.50
❑ 183 Jim Kleinsasser AU/1825 RC 20.00 7.50
❑ 184 Kevin Johnson AU/1325 RC 25.00 10.00
❑ 185 Joe Montgomery AU/1325 RC 20.00 7.50
❑ 186 John Elway PT 10.00 4.00
❑ 187 Dan Marino PT 10.00 4.00
❑ 188 Jerry Rice PT 6.00 2.50
❑ 189 Barry Sanders PT 10.00 4.00
❑ 190 Steve Young PT 4.00 1.50
❑ 191 Doug Flutie PT 2.50 1.00
❑ 192 Troy Aikman PT 6.00 2.50
❑ 193 Drew Bledsoe PT 4.00 1.50
❑ 194 Brett Favre PT 10.00 4.00
❑ 195 Randall Cunningham PT 2.50 1.00
❑ 196 Terrell Davis PT 2.50 1.00

❑ 197 Kordell Stewart PT 2.50 1.00
❑ 198 Keyshawn Johnson PT 2.50 1.00
❑ 199 Jake Plummer PT 2.50 1.00
❑ 200 Peyton Manning PT 10.00 4.00
❑ 201 Jay Fiedler/1825 AU 25.00 10.00
❑ 202 Kevin Daft/325 AU 40.00 20.00

2000 Playoff Contenders

❑ COMP.SET w/o SP's (100) 20.00 7.50
❑ 1 David Boston .75 .30
❑ 2 Jake Plummer .50 .20
❑ 3 Chris Chandler .50 .20
❑ 4 Jamal Anderson .75 .30
❑ 5 Tim Dwight .75 .30
❑ 6 Qadry Ismail .50 .20
❑ 7 Tony Banks .50 .20
❑ 8 Lamar Smith .50 .20
❑ 9 Doug Flutie .75 .30
❑ 10 Eric Moulds .75 .30
❑ 11 Peerless Price .50 .20
❑ 12 Rob Johnson .50 .20
❑ 13 Muhsin Muhammad .50 .20
❑ 14 Reggie White .75 .30
❑ 15 Steve Beuerlein .50 .20
❑ 16 Cade McNown .30 .10
❑ 17 Derrick Alexander .50 .20
❑ 18 Marcus Robinson .50 .20
❑ 19 Akili Smith .30 .10
❑ 20 Corey Dillon .75 .30
❑ 21 Kevin Johnson .75 .30
❑ 22 Tim Couch .50 .20
❑ 23 Emmitt Smith 1.50 .60
❑ 24 Joey Galloway .50 .20
❑ 25 Rocket Ismail .50 .20
❑ 26 Troy Aikman 1.50 .60
❑ 27 Brian Griese .75 .30
❑ 28 Ed McCaffrey .75 .30
❑ 29 John Elway 2.50 1.00
❑ 30 Olandis Gary .75 .30
❑ 31 Rod Smith .50 .20
❑ 32 Terrell Davis .75 .30
❑ 33 Charlie Batch .75 .30
❑ 34 Germane Crowell .30 .10
❑ 35 James Stewart .50 .20
❑ 36 Barry Sanders 2.00 .75
❑ 37 Antonio Freeman .75 .30
❑ 38 Brett Favre 2.50 1.00
❑ 39 Dorsey Levens .50 .20
❑ 40 Edgerrin James 1.25 .50
❑ 41 Marvin Harrison .75 .30
❑ 42 Peyton Manning 2.00 .75
❑ 43 Fred Taylor .75 .30
❑ 44 Jimmy Smith .50 .20
❑ 45 Mark Brunell .75 .30
❑ 46 Elvis Grbac .50 .20
❑ 47 Tony Gonzalez .50 .20
❑ 48 Dan Marino 2.50 1.00
❑ 49 Joe Horn .50 .20
❑ 50 Jay Fiedler .75 .30
❑ 51 Thurman Thomas .50 .20
❑ 52 Cris Carter .75 .30
❑ 53 Daunte Culpepper 1.00 .40
❑ 54 Randy Moss 1.50 .60
❑ 55 Robert Smith .75 .30
❑ 56 Drew Bledsoe 1.00 .40
❑ 57 Terry Glenn .50 .20
❑ 58 Ricky Williams .75 .30
❑ 59 Amani Toomer .30 .10
❑ 60 Kerry Collins .50 .20
❑ 61 Curtis Martin .75 .30
❑ 62 Vinny Testaverde .50 .20
❑ 63 Wayne Chrebet .50 .20
❑ 64 Rich Gannon .75 .30
❑ 65 Tim Brown .75 .30
❑ 66 Tyrone Wheatley .50 .20
❑ 67 Donovan McNabb 1.25 .50
❑ 68 Duce Staley .75 .30
❑ 69 Jerome Bettis .75 .30
❑ 70 Jermaine Fazande .30 .10
❑ 71 Junior Seau .75 .30
❑ 72 Donald Hayes .30 .10
❑ 73 Charlie Garner .50 .20
❑ 74 Jeff Garcia .75 .30
❑ 75 Jerry Rice 1.50 .60
❑ 76 Steve Young 1.00 .40
❑ 77 Terrell Owens .75 .30
❑ 78 Tiki Barber .75 .30
❑ 79 Tim Biakabutuka .50 .20
❑ 80 Ricky Watters .50 .20
❑ 81 Isaac Bruce .75 .30
❑ 82 Kurt Warner 1.50 .60
❑ 83 Marshall Faulk 1.00 .40
❑ 84 Torry Holt .75 .30
❑ 85 Keyshawn Johnson .75 .30
❑ 86 Mike Alstott .75 .30
❑ 87 Shaun King .30 .10
❑ 88 Warren Sapp .50 .20
❑ 89 Warrick Dunn .75 .30
❑ 90 Eddie George .75 .30
❑ 91 Jevon Kearse .75 .30
❑ 92 Steve McNair .75 .30
❑ 93 Carl Pickens .50 .20
❑ 94 Albert Connell .30 .10
❑ 95 Brad Johnson .75 .30
❑ 96 Bruce Smith .50 .20
❑ 97 Deion Sanders .75 .30
❑ 98 Jeff George .50 .20
❑ 99 Michael Westbrook .50 .20
❑ 100 Stephen Davis .75 .30
❑ 101 Courtney Brown AU RC 60.00 30.00
❑ 102 Corey Simon AU RC 20.00 7.50
❑ 103 Brian Urlacher AU RC 80.00 40.00
❑ 104 Deon Grant AU RC 15.00 6.00
❑ 105 Peter Warrick AU RC 20.00 7.50
❑ 106 Jamal Lewis AU RC 50.00 25.00
❑ 107 Thomas Jones EXCH
❑ 108 Plaxico Burress AU RC 50.00 20.00
❑ 109 Travis Taylor AU RC 25.00 10.00
❑ 110 Ron Dayne AU RC 40.00 20.00
❑ 111 Bubba Franks AU RC 20.00 7.50
❑ 112 Chad Pennington AU RC 80.00 40.00
❑ 113 Shaun Alexander AU RC 120.00 60.00
❑ 114 Sylvester Morris AU RC 15.00 6.00
❑ 115 Mike Anderson AU RC 30.00 12.50
❑ 116 R.Jay Soward AU RC 15.00 6.00
❑ 117 Trung Canidate AU RC 15.00 6.00
❑ 118 Dennis Northcutt AU RC 20.00 7.50
❑ 119 Todd Pinkston AU RC 20.00 7.50
❑ 120 Jerry Porter AU RC 40.00 15.00
❑ 121 Travis Prentice AU RC 15.00 6.00
❑ 122 Giovanni Carmazzi AU RC 10.00 4.00
❑ 123 Ron Dugans AU RC 10.00 4.00
❑ 124 Dez White AU RC 20.00 7.50
❑ 125 Chris Cole AU RC 15.00 6.00
❑ 126 Ron Dixon AU RC 15.00 6.00
❑ 127 Chris Redman AU RC 15.00 6.00
❑ 128 J.R. Redmond AU RC 20.00 7.50
❑ 129 Laveranues Coles AU RC 30.00 15.00
❑ 130 JaJuan Dawson AU RC 10.00 4.00
❑ 131 Darrell Jackson AU RC 30.00 12.50
❑ 132 Reuben Droughns AU RC 30.00 12.50
❑ 133 Doug Chapman AU RC 15.00 6.00
❑ 134 Curtis Keaton AU RC 15.00 6.00
❑ 135 Gari Scott AU RC 10.00 4.00
❑ 136 Danny Farmer AU RC 15.00 6.00
❑ 137 Trevor Gaylor AU RC 15.00 6.00
❑ 138 Avion Black AU RC 15.00 6.00
❑ 139 Michael Wiley AU RC 15.00 6.00
❑ 140 Sammy Morris AU RC 20.00 10.00
❑ 141 Tee Martin AU RC 20.00 7.50
❑ 142 Troy Walters AU RC 20.00 7.50
❑ 143 Marc Bulger AU RC 50.00 20.00
❑ 144 Tom Brady AU RC 350.00 250.00
❑ 145 Todd Husak AU RC 20.00 7.50
❑ 146 Tim Rattay AU RC 20.00 7.50
❑ 147 Jarious Jackson AU RC 15.00 6.00
❑ 148 Joe Hamilton AU RC 15.00 6.00
❑ 149 Shyrone Stith AU RC 15.00 6.00
❑ 150 Kwame Cavil AU RC 10.00 4.00
❑ 151 Antonio Banks ET AU RC 6.00 2.50
❑ 152 Jonathan Brown ET AU RC 6.00 2.50
❑ 153 Ontiwaun Carter ET AU RC 6.00 2.50
❑ 154 Jeremaine Copeland ET 6.00 2.50
❑ 155 Ralph Dawkins ET AU RC 8.00 3.00
❑ 156 Marques Douglas ET AU RC 6.00 2.50
❑ 157 Kevin Drake ET AU RC 6.00 2.50
❑ 158 Damon Dunn ET AU RC 8.00 3.00
❑ 159 Todd Floyd ET AU RC 6.00 2.50
❑ 160 Tony Graziani ET AU 8.00 3.00
❑ 161 Derrick Ham ET EXCH
❑ 162 Duane Hawthorne ET AU RC 8.00 3.00
❑ 163 Alonzo Johnson ET AU RC 6.00 2.50
❑ 164 Mark Kacmarynski ET AU RC 6.00 2.50
❑ 165 Eric Kresser ET AU 6.00 2.50
❑ 166 Jim Kubiak ET AU RC 8.00 3.00
❑ 167 Blaine McElmurry ET AU RC 6.00 2.50
❑ 168 Scott Milanovich ET AU 10.00 4.00
❑ 169 Norman Miller ET AU RC 6.00 2.50
❑ 170 Sean Morey ET AU RC 8.00 3.00
❑ 171 Jeff Ogden ET AU 8.00 3.00
❑ 172 Pepe Pearson ET AU RC 8.00 3.00
❑ 173 Ron Powlus ET AU RC 10.00 4.00
❑ 174 Jason Shelley ET AU RC 8.00 3.00
❑ 175 Ben Snell ET AU RC 8.00 3.00
❑ 176 Aaron Stecker ET AU RC 8.00 3.00
❑ 177 L.C. Stevens ET AU 6.00 2.50
❑ 178 Mike Sutton ET AU RC 6.00 2.50
❑ 179 Damian Vaughn ET AU RC 6.00 2.50
❑ 180 Ted White ET AU 6.00 2.50
❑ 181 Marcus Crandell ET AU RC 8.00 3.00
❑ 182 Darryl Daniel ET AU RC 8.00 3.00
❑ 183 Jesse Haynes ET AU 6.00 2.50
❑ 184 Matt Lytle ET AU RC 8.00 3.00
❑ 185 Deon Mitchell ET AU RC 8.00 3.00
❑ 186 Kendrick Nord ET AU RC 6.00 2.50
❑ 187 Ronnie Powell EXCH
❑ 188 Selucio Sanford ET AU RC 8.00 3.00
❑ 189 Corey Thomas ET AU 6.00 2.50
❑ 190 Vershan Jackson ET AU RC 6.00 2.50
❑ 191 Jake Plummer PT 20.00 7.50
❑ 192 Jim Kelly PT AU 40.00 15.00
❑ 193 Bernie Kosar PT AU 40.00 15.00
❑ 194 Marvin Harrison PT AU 40.00 15.00
❑ 195 Fred Taylor PT EXCH
❑ 196 Kerry Collins PT AU 30.00 12.50
❑ 197 Kurt Warner PT AU 60.00 25.00
❑ 198 Jevon Kearse PT AU 30.00 12.50
❑ 199 Brad Johnson PT AU 30.00 12.50
❑ 200 Jeff George PT AU 30.00 12.50

2001 Playoff Contenders

❑ COMP.SET w/o SP's (100) 25.00 10.00
❑ 1 David Boston 1.00 .40
❑ 2 Jake Plummer .60 .25
❑ 3 Jamal Anderson 1.00 .40
❑ 4 Chris Chandler .60 .25
❑ 5 Elvis Grbac .60 .25
❑ 6 Brandon Stokley .60 .25
❑ 7 Travis Taylor .60 .25
❑ 8 Ray Lewis 1.00 .40
❑ 9 Rob Johnson .60 .25
❑ 10 Eric Moulds .60 .25
❑ 11 Tim Biakabutuka .60 .25
❑ 12 Muhsin Muhammad .60 .25
❑ 13 James Allen .60 .25

❑ 14 Brian Urlacher	1.50	.60
❑ 15 Peter Warrick	1.00	.40
❑ 16 Corey Dillon	1.00	.40
❑ 17 Tim Couch	.60	.25
❑ 18 Kevin Johnson	.60	.25
❑ 19 Rickey Dudley	.40	.10
❑ 20 Emmitt Smith	2.00	.75
❑ 21 Joey Galloway	.60	.25
❑ 22 Brian Griese	1.00	.40
❑ 23 Terrell Davis	1.00	.40
❑ 24 Mike Anderson	1.00	.40
❑ 25 Ed McCaffrey	1.00	.40
❑ 26 Rod Smith	.60	.25
❑ 27 Charlie Batch	1.00	.40
❑ 28 James Stewart	.60	.25
❑ 29 Germane Crowell	.40	.10
❑ 30 Johnnie Morton	.60	.25
❑ 31 Brett Favre	3.00	1.25
❑ 32 Ahman Green	1.00	.40
❑ 33 Antonio Freeman	1.00	.40
❑ 34 Peyton Manning	2.50	1.00
❑ 35 Edgerrin James	1.25	.50
❑ 36 Marvin Harrison	1.00	.40
❑ 37 Jerome Pathon	.60	.25
❑ 38 Mark Brunell	1.00	.40
❑ 39 Fred Taylor	1.00	.40
❑ 40 Keenan McCardell	.40	.10
❑ 41 Jimmy Smith	.60	.25
❑ 42 Trent Green	1.00	.40
❑ 43 Priest Holmes	1.25	.50
❑ 44 Tony Gonzalez	.60	.25
❑ 45 Derrick Alexander	.60	.25
❑ 46 Jay Fiedler	1.00	.40
❑ 47 Lamar Smith	.60	.25
❑ 48 Zach Thomas	1.00	.40
❑ 49 Oronde Gadsden	.60	.25
❑ 50 Daunte Culpepper	1.00	.40
❑ 51 Randy Moss	2.00	.75
❑ 52 Cris Carter	1.00	.40
❑ 53 Drew Bledsoe	1.25	.50
❑ 54 J.R. Redmond	.40	.10
❑ 55 Troy Brown	.60	.25
❑ 56 Aaron Brooks	1.00	.40
❑ 57 Ricky Williams	1.00	.40
❑ 58 Joe Horn	.60	.25
❑ 59 Kerry Collins	.60	.25
❑ 60 Tiki Barber	1.00	.40
❑ 61 Ron Dayne	1.00	.40
❑ 62 Ike Hilliard	.60	.25
❑ 63 Vinny Testaverde	.60	.25
❑ 64 Curtis Martin	1.00	.40
❑ 65 Wayne Chrebet	.60	.25
❑ 66 Laveranues Coles	1.00	.40
❑ 67 Rich Gannon	1.00	.40
❑ 68 Tyrone Wheatley	.60	.25
❑ 69 Tim Brown	1.00	.40
❑ 70 Jerry Rice	2.00	.75
❑ 71 Donovan McNabb	1.25	.50
❑ 72 Duce Staley	1.00	.40
❑ 73 Todd Pinkston	.60	.25
❑ 74 Kordell Stewart	.60	.25
❑ 75 Jerome Bettis	1.00	.40
❑ 76 Plaxico Burress	1.00	.40
❑ 77 Doug Flutie	1.00	.40
❑ 78 Junior Seau	1.00	.40
❑ 79 Jeff Garcia	1.00	.40
❑ 80 Garrison Hearst	.60	.25
❑ 81 Terrell Owens	1.00	.40
❑ 82 Matt Hasselbeck	.60	.25
❑ 83 Ricky Watters	.60	.25
❑ 84 Shaun Alexander	1.25	.50
❑ 85 Darrell Jackson	1.00	.40
❑ 86 Kurt Warner	2.00	.75
❑ 87 Marshall Faulk	1.25	.50
❑ 88 Isaac Bruce	1.00	.40
❑ 89 Torry Holt	1.00	.40
❑ 90 Brad Johnson	1.00	.40
❑ 91 Keyshawn Johnson	1.00	.40
❑ 92 Warrick Dunn	1.00	.40
❑ 93 Warren Sapp	.60	.25
❑ 94 Steve McNair	1.00	.40
❑ 95 Eddie George	1.00	.40
❑ 96 Derrick Mason	.60	.25
❑ 97 Jevon Kearse	.60	.25
❑ 98 Stephen Davis	1.00	.40
❑ 99 Bruce Smith	.60	.25
❑ 100 Michael Westbrook	.60	.25

❑ 101 Adam Archuleta/50 RC	80.00	40.00
❑ 102 Alex Bannister AU RC	15.00	6.00
❑ 103 Alge Crumpler AU RC	30.00	15.00
❑ 104 Andre Carter AU/100 RC	50.00	25.00
❑ 105 Anthony Thomas AU/600 RC	25.00	10.00
❑ 106 Ben Leard AU RC	10.00	4.00
❑ 107 Bobby Newcombe AU RC	15.00	6.00
❑ 108 Brian Allen AU RC	10.00	4.00
❑ 109 Carlos Polk AU RC	10.00	4.00
❑ 110 Casey Hampton No Auto RC	25.00	10.00
❑ 111 Cedric Scott AU RC	10.00	4.00
❑ 112 Cedrick Wilson AU RC	30.00	12.50
❑ 113 Chad Johnson AU RC	125.00	75.00
❑ 114 Chris Chambers AU/170 RC	150.00	75.00
❑ 115 Chris Weinke AU/350 RC	30.00	15.00
❑ 116 Correll Buckhalter AU/590 RC	30.00	12.50
❑ 117 Damione Lewis AU RC	25.00	10.00
❑ 118 Dan Morgan AU RC	40.00	15.00
❑ 119 Daniel Guy AU RC	10.00	4.00
❑ 120 David Allen AU RC	10.00	4.00
❑ 121 David Terrell AU/500 RC	25.00	10.00
❑ 122 Ken Lucas AU/276 RC	10.00	4.00
❑ 123 Deu McAllister AU/500 RC	80.00	40.00
❑ 124 Drew Brees AU/500 RC	200.00	125.00
❑ 125 Eddie Berlin AU RC	10.00	4.00
❑ 126 Boo Williams AU/50 RC	60.00	30.00
❑ 127 Ennis Davis AU RC	10.00	4.00
❑ 128 Freddie Mitchell AU RC	25.00	10.00
❑ 129 Gary Baxter AU RC	15.00	6.00
❑ 130 Gerard Warren AU/200 RC	40.00	15.00
❑ 131 Hakim Akbar AU RC	10.00	4.00
❑ 132 Heath Evans AU RC	10.00	4.00
❑ 133 Jabari Holloway AU RC	15.00	6.00
❑ 134 Jamal Reynolds AU/500 RC	15.00	6.00
❑ 135 James Jackson AU RC	15.00	6.00
❑ 136 Jamie Winborn AU RC	10.00	4.00
❑ 137 Javon Green AU RC	10.00	4.00
❑ 138 Jesse Palmer AU RC	25.00	10.00
❑ 139 Dominic Rhodes AU/300 RC	60.00	30.00
❑ 140 Josh Heupel AU/150 RC	50.00	20.00
❑ 141 Justin Smith AU RC	15.00	6.00
❑ 142 Karon Riley AU RC	10.00	4.00
❑ 143 Keith Adams/50 RC	80.00	40.00
❑ 144 Kendrell Bell AU RC	30.00	15.00
❑ 145 Kenny Smith AU RC	15.00	6.00
❑ 146 Ken. Walker AU/50 RC	80.00	40.00
❑ 147 Ken-Yon Rambo AU RC	10.00	4.00
❑ 148 Kevan Barlow AU RC	30.00	15.00
❑ 149 Koren Robinson AU/400 RC	30.00	12.50
❑ 150 L.Tomlinson AU/600 RC	750.00	450.00
❑ 151 LaMont Jordan AU/50 RC	500.00	350.00
❑ 152 Leonard Davis/50 RC	80.00	40.00
❑ 153 Marcus Stroud AU RC	25.00	10.00
❑ 154 Marques Tuiasosopo AU RC	25.00	10.00
❑ 155 Snoop Minnis AU/295 RC	15.00	6.00
❑ 156 Michael Bennett AU/600 RC	30.00	15.00
❑ 157 Michael Vick AU/327 RC	300.00	150.00
❑ 158 Mike McMahon AU/529 RC	30.00	15.00
❑ 159 Moran Norris AU RC	10.00	4.00
❑ 160 Morlon Greenwood AU RC	10.00	4.00
❑ 161 Nate Clements/50 RC	80.00	40.00
❑ 162 Quincy Carter AU SP RC	80.00	40.00
❑ 163 Quincy Morgan AU RC	25.00	10.00
❑ 164 Jamar Fletcher/50 RC	80.00	40.00
❑ 165 Reggie Germany AU RC	10.00	4.00
❑ 166 Reggie Wayne AU/400 RC	100.00	60.00
❑ 167 Reggie White AU RC	10.00	4.00
❑ 168 Richard Seymour/50 RC	100.00	50.00
❑ 169 Robert Carswell/50 RC	60.00	30.00
❑ 170 Robert Ferguson AU RC	25.00	10.00
❑ 171 Rod Gardner AU/75 RC	120.00	60.00
❑ 172 Ronney Daniels AU RC	10.00	4.00
❑ 173 Rudi Johnson AU RC	80.00	40.00
❑ 174 Sage Rosenfels AU/400 RC	25.00	10.00
❑ 175 Santana Moss AU/500 RC	60.00	30.00
❑ 176 Shaun Rogers AU RC	25.00	10.00
❑ 177 Houshmandzadeh AU RC	50.00	25.00
❑ 178 Tim Hasselbeck AU RC	25.00	10.00
❑ 179 Todd Heap AU/169 RC	100.00	50.00
❑ 180 Tony Stewart AU RC	15.00	6.00
❑ 181 Torrance Marshall AU RC	15.00	6.00
❑ 182 Travis Henry AU/369 RC	60.00	30.00
❑ 183 Travis Minor AU RC	25.00	10.00
❑ 184 Vinny Sutherland AU RC	15.00	6.00
❑ 185 Will Allen AU RC	15.00	6.00
❑ 186 Willie Howard AU RC	10.00	4.00
❑ 187 W Middlebrooks/50 RC	60.00	30.00

❑ 188 Derrick Blaylock AU/200 RC	60.00	30.00
❑ 189 A.J. Feeley AU/200 RC	80.00	30.00
❑ 190 Steve Smith AU/300 RC	200.00	100.00
❑ 191 Onome Ojo AU/200 RC	15.00	6.00
❑ 192 Dee Brown AU/300 RC	25.00	10.00
❑ 193 Kevin Kasper AU/200 RC	25.00	10.00
❑ 194 Dave Dickenson AU/300 RC	25.00	10.00
❑ 195 Chris Barnes AU/200 RC	25.00	10.00
❑ 196 Scotty Anderson AU/300 RC	25.00	10.00
❑ 197 Chris Taylor AU/300 RC	15.00	6.00
❑ 198 Cedric James AU/300 SP RC	25.00	10.00
❑ 199 Justin McCareins AU/200 RC	50.00	20.00
❑ 200 Tommy Polley AU/200 RC	25.00	10.00

2002 Playoff Contenders

❑ COMP.SET w/o SP's (100)	25.00	10.00
❑ 1 Drew Bledsoe	1.25	.50
❑ 2 Travis Henry	1.00	.40
❑ 3 Eric Moulds	.60	.25
❑ 4 Chris Chambers	1.00	.40
❑ 5 Ricky Williams	1.00	.40
❑ 6 Zach Thomas	1.00	.40
❑ 7 Tom Brady	2.50	1.00
❑ 8 Antowain Smith	.60	.25
❑ 9 Troy Brown	.60	.25
❑ 10 Curtis Martin	1.00	.40
❑ 11 Vinny Testaverde	.60	.25
❑ 12 Chad Pennington	1.25	.50
❑ 13 Jeff Blake	.40	.15
❑ 14 Jamal Lewis	1.00	.40
❑ 15 Ray Lewis	1.00	.40
❑ 16 Michael Westbrook	.40	.15
❑ 17 Corey Dillon	.60	.25
❑ 18 Peter Warrick	.60	.25
❑ 19 Tim Couch	.60	.25
❑ 20 Quincy Morgan	.60	.25
❑ 21 Kevin Johnson	.60	.25
❑ 22 Kordell Stewart	.60	.25
❑ 23 Plaxico Burress	.60	.25
❑ 24 Jerome Bettis	1.00	.40
❑ 25 James Allen	.60	.25
❑ 26 Corey Bradford	.40	.15
❑ 27 Mark Brunell	1.00	.40
❑ 28 Fred Taylor	1.00	.40
❑ 29 Jimmy Smith	.60	.25
❑ 30 Peyton Manning	2.00	.75
❑ 31 Reggie Wayne	1.00	.40
❑ 32 Marvin Harrison	1.00	.40
❑ 33 Edgerrin James	1.25	.50
❑ 34 Steve McNair	1.00	.40
❑ 35 Eddie George	1.00	.40
❑ 36 Jevon Kearse	.60	.25
❑ 37 Derrick Mason	.60	.25
❑ 38 Brian Griese	1.00	.40
❑ 39 Terrell Davis	1.00	.40
❑ 40 Ed McCaffrey	1.00	.40
❑ 41 Rod Smith	.60	.25
❑ 42 Trent Green	.60	.25
❑ 43 Priest Holmes	1.25	.50
❑ 44 Johnnie Morton	.60	.25
❑ 45 Tony Gonzalez	.60	.25
❑ 46 Rich Gannon	1.00	.40
❑ 47 Tim Brown	1.00	.40
❑ 48 Jerry Rice	2.00	.75
❑ 49 Charlie Garner	.60	.25
❑ 50 Drew Brees	1.00	.40
❑ 51 LaDainian Tomlinson	1.50	.60
❑ 52 Junior Seau	1.00	.40
❑ 53 Quincy Carter	.60	.25

❑ 54 Emmitt Smith 2.50 1.00
❑ 55 Joey Galloway .60 .25
❑ 56 Kerry Collins .60 .25
❑ 57 Tiki Barber 1.00 .40
❑ 58 Michael Strahan .60 .25
❑ 59 Donovan McNabb 1.25 .50
❑ 60 Duce Staley 1.00 .40
❑ 61 Antonio Freeman 1.00 .40
❑ 62 Derrius Thompson .40 .15
❑ 63 Stephen Davis .60 .25
❑ 64 Rod Gardner .60 .25
❑ 65 Anthony Thomas .60 .25
❑ 66 Marty Booker .60 .25
❑ 67 Brian Urlacher 1.50 .60
❑ 68 James Stewart .60 .25
❑ 69 Az-Zahir Hakim .40 .15
❑ 70 Brett Favre 2.50 1.00
❑ 71 Ahman Green 1.00 .40
❑ 72 Donald Driver .60 .25
❑ 73 Daunte Culpepper 1.00 .40
❑ 74 Michael Bennett .60 .25
❑ 75 Randy Moss 2.00 .75
❑ 76 Michael Vick 3.00 1.25
❑ 77 Warrick Dunn 1.00 .40
❑ 78 Chris Weinke .60 .25
❑ 79 Lamar Smith .60 .25
❑ 80 Steve Smith 1.00 .40
❑ 81 Aaron Brooks 1.00 .40
❑ 82 Deuce McAllister 1.25 .50
❑ 83 Joe Horn .60 .25
❑ 84 Brad Johnson .60 .25
❑ 85 Keyshawn Johnson 1.00 .40
❑ 86 Mike Alstott 1.00 .40
❑ 87 Warren Sapp .60 .25
❑ 88 Jake Plummer .60 .25
❑ 89 Thomas Jones .60 .25
❑ 90 David Boston 1.00 .40
❑ 91 Kurt Warner 1.00 .40
❑ 92 Marshall Faulk 1.00 .40
❑ 93 Isaac Bruce 1.00 .40
❑ 94 Torry Holt 1.00 .40
❑ 95 Jeff Garcia 1.00 .40
❑ 96 Garrison Hearst .60 .25
❑ 97 Kevan Barlow .60 .25
❑ 98 Terrell Owens 1.00 .40
❑ 99 Trent Dilfer .60 .25
❑ 100 Shaun Alexander 1.25 .50
❑ 101 Adrian Peterson AU/360 RC 40.00 20.00
❑ 102 A.Haynesworth No Auto RC 30.00 12.50
❑ 103 Alex Brown AU/410 RC 40.00 20.00
❑ 104 Andra Davis AU/510 RC 15.00 6.00
❑ 105 Andre Davis AU/360 RC 30.00 12.50
❑ 106 Andre Lott AU/750 RC 15.00 6.00
❑ 107 Anthony Weaver AU/450 RC 15.00 6.00
❑ 108 Antonio Bryant AU/165 RC 80.00 40.00
❑ 109 Antw Randle El AU/135 RC 120.00 60.00
❑ 110 Ashley Lelie AU/360 RC 50.00 20.00
❑ 111 Brian Poli-Dixon AU/460 RC 20.007.50
❑ 112 Brian Westbrook AU/600 RC 60.00 35.00
❑ 113 Bryant McKinnie AU/600 RC 30.00 12.50
❑ 114 C Hutchinson AU/450 RC 20.00 7.50
❑ 115 Charles Grant AU/450 RC 20.00 7.50
❑ 116 Chester Taylor AU/315 RC 50.0025.00
❑ 117 Cliff Russell AU/545 RC 20.00 7.50
❑ 118 Clinton Portis AU/360 RC 150.0075.00
❑ 119 R.McMichael AU/400 RC 30.00 12.50
❑ 120 Damien Anderson AU/460 RC 15.00 6.00
❑ 121 Daniel Graham AU/185 RC 50.0020.00
❑ 122 David Carr AU/250 RC 100.00 50.00
❑ 123 David Garrard AU/310 RC 60.0030.00
❑ 124 Deion Branch AU/650 RC 50.00 20.00
❑ 125 John Simon AU/400 RC 20.00 7.50
❑ 126 DeShaun Foster AU/310 RC 60.00 30.00
❑ 127 Donte Stallworth AU/302 RC 60.00 30.00
❑ 128 Dwight Freeney AU/410 RC 60.0035.00
❑ 129 Ed Reed AU/550 RC 50.00 25.00
❑ 130 Eric Crouch AU/280 RC 30.00 12.50
❑ 131 Freddie Milons AU/380 RC 20.00 7.50
❑ 132 Jabar Gaffney AU/315 RC 30.0012.50
❑ 133 Javon Walker AU/435 RC 80.00 40.00
❑ 134 Jeremy Shockey AU/160 RC 200.00 125.00
❑ 135 Jeramy Stevens AU/250 RC 30.00 12.50
❑ 136 Joey Harrington AU/250 RC 60.0025.00
❑ 137 John Henderson AU/560 RC 30.00 12.50
❑ 138 Jonathan Wells AU/485 RC 40.00 15.00
❑ 139 Josh McCown AU/595 RC 40.00 25.00
❑ 140 Josh Reed AU/290 RC 40.00 15.00
❑ 141 Josh Scobey AU/615 RC 15.00 6.00
❑ 142 Julius Peppers AU/40 RC 350.00 250.00
❑ 143 Kalimba Edwards AU/510 RC 20.00 7.50
❑ 144 Kelly Campbell AU/360 RC 30.0012.50
❑ 145 Ken Simonton AU/650 RC 15.00 6.00
❑ 146 Keyuo Craver AU/850 RC 15.00 6.00
❑ 147 Kahlil Hill AU/850 RC 20.00 7.50
❑ 148 Kurt Kittner AU/235 RC 20.00 7.50
❑ 149 Ladell Betts AU/600 RC 40.00 20.00
❑ 150 Lamar Gordon AU/600 RC 30.00 12.50
❑ 151 Levar Fisher AU/760 RC 15.00 6.00
❑ 152 Lito Sheppard AU/410 RC 30.00 12.50
❑ 153 Luke Staley AU/360 RC 20.00 7.50
❑ 154 Marquise Walker AU/330 RC 30.00 12.50
❑ 155 Maurice Morris AU/153 RC 60.0030.00
❑ 156 Mike Rumph AU/510 RC 30.00 12.50
❑ 157 Mike Williams AU/500 RC 20.00 7.50
❑ 158 Najeh Davenport AU/460 RC 30.00 12.50
❑ 159 Napoleon Harris AU/900 RC 20.007.50
❑ 160 Patrick Ramsey AU/575 RC 50.00 20.00
❑ 161 Buchanon No AU/310 RC 50.00 20.00
❑ 162 Quentin Jammer AU/300 RC 30.00 12.50
❑ 163 Randy Fasani AU/500 RC 20.00 7.50
❑ 164 Reche Caldwell AU/340 RC 30.00 12.50
❑ 165 Robert Thomas AU/460 RC 30.00 12.50
❑ 166 Rocky Calmus AU/385 RC 30.0012.50
❑ 167 Rohan Davey AU/295 RC 50.00 25.00
❑ 168 Ron Johnson AU/385 RC 20.00 7.50
❑ 169 Roy Williams AU/250 RC 100.0050.00
❑ 170 Ryan Sims No AU/360 RC 30.00 12.50
❑ 171 Tavon Mason AU/690 RC 15.00 6.00
❑ 172 Terry Charles AU/750 RC 15.00 6.00
❑ 173 T.J. Duckett AU/335 RC 40.00 15.00
❑ 174 Tim Carter AU/600 RC 20.00 7.50
❑ 175 Travis Stephens AU/170 RC 50.00 25.00
❑ 176 Trev Faulk AU/600 RC 15.00 6.00
❑ 177 Wendell Bryant AU/560 RC 15.006.00
❑ 178 William Green AU/317 RC 30.0012.50
❑ 179 Woody Dantzler AU/185 RC 30.0012.50
❑ 180 Tony Fisher AU/340 RC 30.00 12.50
❑ 181 Javin Hunter AU/400 RC 15.00 6.00
❑ 182 Daryl Jones AU/400 RC 20.00 7.50
❑ 183 Jesse Chatman AU/400 RC 30.00 12.50
❑ 184 J.T. O'Sullivan AU/340 RC 20.00 7.50
❑ 185 Josh Norman AU/340 RC 30.00 12.50
❑ 186 James Mungro AU/100 RC 80.0040.00

2003 Playoff Contenders

❑ COMP.SET w/o SP's (100) 20.00 7.50
❑ UNPRICED CHAMPION.TICKET #'d TO 1
❑ 1 Roy Williams .75 .30
❑ 2 Antonio Bryant .50 .20
❑ 3 Jeremy Shockey 1.25 .50
❑ 4 Kerry Collins .50 .20
❑ 5 Tiki Barber .75 .30
❑ 6 Michael Strahan .50 .20
❑ 7 Donovan McNabb 1.00 .40
❑ 8 Duce Staley .50 .20
❑ 9 Todd Pinkston .50 .20
❑ 10 Patrick Ramsey .75 .30
❑ 11 Laveranues Coles .50 .20
❑ 12 Rod Gardner .50 .20
❑ 13 Drew Bledsoe .75 .30
❑ 14 Travis Henry .50 .20
❑ 15 Eric Moulds .50 .20
❑ 16 Josh Reed .50 .20
❑ 17 Ricky Williams .75 .30
❑ 18 Jay Fiedler .50 .20
❑ 19 Chris Chambers .75 .30
❑ 20 Zach Thomas .75 .30
❑ 21 Junior Seau .75 .30
❑ 22 Tom Brady 2.00 .75
❑ 23 Troy Brown .50 .20
❑ 24 Chad Pennington 1.00 .40
❑ 25 Curtis Martin .75 .30
❑ 26 Santana Moss .50 .20
❑ 27 Emmitt Smith 2.00 .75
❑ 28 Jeff Garcia .75 .30
❑ 29 Terrell Owens .75 .30
❑ 30 Kevan Barlow .50 .20
❑ 31 Shaun Alexander .75 .30
❑ 32 Matt Hasselbeck .50 .20
❑ 33 Koren Robinson .50 .20
❑ 34 Kurt Warner .75 .30
❑ 35 Marshall Faulk .75 .30
❑ 36 Torry Holt .75 .30
❑ 37 Isaac Bruce .75 .30
❑ 38 Clinton Portis 1.25 .50
❑ 39 Jake Plummer .50 .20
❑ 40 Rod Smith .50 .20
❑ 41 Ed McCaffrey .75 .30
❑ 42 Ashley Lelie .75 .30
❑ 43 Priest Holmes 1.00 .40
❑ 44 Trent Green .50 .20
❑ 45 Tony Gonzalez .50 .20
❑ 46 Jerry Rice 1.50 .60
❑ 47 Rich Gannon .50 .20
❑ 48 Tim Brown .75 .30
❑ 49 Jerry Porter .50 .20
❑ 50 Charles Woodson .50 .20
❑ 51 LaDainian Tomlinson .75 .30
❑ 52 Drew Brees .75 .30
❑ 53 David Boston .50 .20
❑ 54 Brian Urlacher 1.25 .50
❑ 55 Kordell Stewart .50 .20
❑ 56 Marty Booker .50 .20
❑ 57 Joey Harrington 1.25 .50
❑ 58 Brett Favre 2.00 .75
❑ 59 Ahman Green .75 .30
❑ 60 Donald Driver .50 .20
❑ 61 Javon Walker .50 .20
❑ 62 Randy Moss 1.25 .50
❑ 63 Daunte Culpepper .75 .30
❑ 64 Michael Bennett .50 .20
❑ 65 Jamal Lewis .75 .30
❑ 66 Ray Lewis .75 .30
❑ 67 Corey Dillon .50 .20
❑ 68 Chad Johnson .75 .30
❑ 69 William Green .50 .20
❑ 70 Tim Couch .30 .10
❑ 71 Quincy Morgan .50 .20
❑ 72 Plaxico Burress .50 .20
❑ 73 Tommy Maddox .75 .30
❑ 74 Hines Ward .75 .30
❑ 75 Antwaan Randle El .75 .30
❑ 76 Michael Vick 2.00 .75
❑ 77 Peerless Price .50 .20
❑ 78 Warrick Dunn .50 .20
❑ 79 T.J. Duckett .50 .20
❑ 80 Julius Peppers .75 .30
❑ 81 Stephen Davis .50 .20
❑ 82 Deuce McAllister .75 .30
❑ 83 Aaron Brooks .75 .30
❑ 84 Joe Horn .50 .20
❑ 85 Donte Stallworth .75 .30
❑ 86 Mike Alstott .75 .30
❑ 87 Brad Johnson .50 .20
❑ 88 Keyshawn Johnson .75 .30
❑ 89 Warren Sapp .50 .20
❑ 90 David Carr 1.25 .50
❑ 91 Jabar Gaffney .50 .20
❑ 92 Peyton Manning 1.25 .50
❑ 93 Edgerrin James .75 .30
❑ 94 Marvin Harrison .75 .30
❑ 95 Mark Brunell .50 .20
❑ 96 Fred Taylor .75 .30
❑ 97 Jimmy Smith .50 .20
❑ 98 Steve McNair .75 .30
❑ 99 Eddie George .50 .20
❑ 100 Jevon Kearse .50 .20
❑ 101 Lee Suggs AU/499 RC 30.00 15.00
❑ 102 Charles Rogers AU/204 RC 50.00 25.00
❑ 103 Brandon Lloyd AU/589 RC 40.00 20.00
❑ 104 Terrence Edwards AU/399 RC 15.00 6.00
❑ 105 Mike Pinkard AU/849 RC 12.00 5.00
❑ 106 DeWayne White AU/524 RC 12.00 5.00

❑ 107 Jero McDougle AU/339 RC 20.00 7.50
❑ 108 Jimmy Kennedy AU/514 RC 20.00 7.50
❑ 109 William Joseph AU/764 RC 15.00 6.00
❑ 110 E.J. Henderson AU/774 RC 20.00 7.50
❑ 111 Mike Doss AU/574 RC 20.00 7.50
❑ 112A C.Simms Blu AU/310 RC 120.00 60.00
❑ 112B C.Simms Blk AU/79 RC 200.00 125.00
❑ 113 Cecil Sapp AU/474 RC 15.00 6.00
❑ 114 Justin Gage AU/579 RC 20.00 7.50
❑ 115 Sam Aiken AU/664 RC 15.00 6.00
❑ 116 Doug Gabriel AU/389 RC 40.00 20.00
❑ 117 Jason Witten AU/599 RC 50.00 25.00
❑ 118 Bennie Joppru AU/449 RC 20.00 7.50
❑ 119 Chris Kelsay AU/864 RC 15.00 6.00
❑ 120 John.Sullivan/924 RC 10.00 4.00
❑ 121 Kevin Williams AU/764 RC 20.00 7.50
❑ 122 Rien Long AU/849 RC 12.00 5.00
❑ 123 Kenny Peterson/674 RC 15.00 6.00
❑ 124 Boss Bailey AU/564 RC 20.00 7.50
❑ 125 Denn Weathersby AU/774 RC 12.00 5.00
❑ 126A Car.Palmer Blk AU/36 RC 600.00 400.00
❑ 126B Car.Palmer Blu AU/158 RC 450.00 250.00
❑ 127 Byron Leftwich AU/169 RC 350.00 175.00
❑ 128 Kyle Boller AU/439 RC 30.00 12.50
❑ 129 Rex Grossman AU/494 RC 120.00 60.00
❑ 130 Dave Ragone AU/344 RC 20.00 7.50
❑ 131 Brian St.Pierre AU/554 RC 15.00 6.00
❑ 132 Kliff Kingsbury AU/879 RC 20.00 7.50
❑ 133 Seneca Wallace AU/864 RC 30.00 15.00
❑ 134 Larry Johnson AU/344 RC 400.00 200.00
❑ 135 Willis McGahee AU/369 RC 120.00 60.00
❑ 136 Justin Fargas AU/354 RC 20.00 7.50
❑ 137 Onterrio Smith AU/414 RC 20.00 7.50
❑ 138 Chris Brown AU/279 RC 50.00 25.00
❑ 139 Musa Smith AU/379 RC 30.00 15.00
❑ 140 Artose Pinner AU/364 RC 20.00 7.50
❑ 141 Andre Johnson AU/199 RC 150.00 75.00
❑ 142 Kell Washington AU/472 RC 30.00 12.50
❑ 143 Taylor Jacobs AU/349 RC 15.00 6.00
❑ 144 Bryant Johnson AU/389 RC 20.00 7.50
❑ 145 Tyrone Calico AU/499 RC 20.00 7.50
❑ 146 Anquan Boldin AU/524 RC 80.00 40.00
❑ 147 Bethel Johnson AU/484 RC 30.00 12.50
❑ 148 Nate Burleson AU/549 RC 30.00 15.00
❑ 149 Kevin Curtis AU/455 RC 30.00 15.00
❑ 150 Dallas Clark AU/539 RC 40.00 20.00
❑ 151 Teyo Johnson AU/389 RC 20.00 7.50
❑ 152 Terrell Suggs AU/564 RC 30.00 15.00
❑ 153 DeWayne Robertson/689 RC 12.00 5.00
❑ 154 Terence Newman AU/364 RC 40.00 15.00
❑ 155 Marcus Trufant AU/739 RC 20.00 7.50
❑ 156 Tony Romo AU/999 RC 300.00 150.00
❑ 157 Brooks Bollinger AU/974 RC 20.00 7.50
❑ 158 Ken Dorsey AU/774 RC 20.00 7.50
❑ 159 Kirk Farmer AU/999 RC 15.00 6.00
❑ 160 Jason Gesser AU/999 RC 15.00 6.00
❑ 161 Brock Forsey AU/999 RC 15.00 6.00
❑ 162 Quentin Griffin AU/999 RC 20.00 7.50
❑ 163 Avon Cobourne AU/974 RC 12.00 5.00
❑ 164 Domanick Davis AU/999 RC 30.00 12.50
❑ 165 Tony Hollings AU/974 RC 20.00 7.50
❑ 166 LaBran.Toefield AU/799 RC 20.00 7.50
❑ 167 Arlen Harris AU/974 RC 20.00 7.50
❑ 168 Sult McCullough AU/989 RC 15.00 6.00
❑ 169 Visant Shiancoe AU/999 RC 12.00 5.00
❑ 170 L.J. Smith AU/974 RC 20.00 7.50
❑ 171 LaTaren Dunbar AU/999 RC 12.00 5.00
❑ 172 Walter Young AU/889 RC 12.00 5.00
❑ 173 Bobby Wade AU/989 RC 15.00 6.00
❑ 174 Zuriel Smith AU/989 RC 12.00 5.00
❑ 175 Adrian Madise AU/999 RC 15.00 6.00
❑ 176 Ken Hamlin AU/989 RC 20.00 7.50
❑ 177 Carl Ford AU/999 RC 12.00 5.00
❑ 178 Cortez Hankton AU/989 RC 15.00 6.00
❑ 179 J.R. Tolver AU/889 RC 15.00 6.00
❑ 180 Keenan Howry AU/999 RC 15.00 6.00
❑ 181 Billy McMullen AU/899 RC 15.00 6.00
❑ 182 Amaz Battle AU/989 RC 25.00 10.00
❑ 183 Shaun McDonald AU/899 RC 15.00 6.00
❑ 184 Andre Woolfolk AU/989 RC 15.00 6.00
❑ 185 Sammy Davis AU/999 RC 12.00 5.00
❑ 186 Calvin Pace AU/999 RC 12.00 5.00
❑ 187 Michael Haynes AU/999 RC 15.00 6.00
❑ 188 Ty Warren AU/999 RC 15.00 6.00
❑ 189 Nick Barnett AU/999 RC 20.00 7.50
❑ 190 Troy Polamalu AU/989 RC 135.00 75.00
❑ 191 Eric Parker AU/589 RC 25.00 10.00
❑ 192 Justin Griffith AU/589 RC 15.00 6.00
❑ 193 David Tyree AU/599 RC 15.00 6.00
❑ 194 Pisa Tinoisamoa/599 RC 20.00 7.50
❑ 195 Rashean Mathis AU/589 RC 12.00 5.00
❑ 196 Mike Sherman AU/574 RC 30.00 12.50
❑ 197 Dave Wannstedt AU/574 RC 20.00 7.50
❑ 198 Dick Vermeil AU/574 RC 30.00 12.50
❑ 199 Tony Dungy AU/574 RC 60.00 35.00
❑ 200 Mike Martz AU/574 RC 20.00 7.50

2004 Playoff Contenders

❑ COMP.SET w/o SP's (100) 20.00 7.50
❑ AU PRINT RUNS ANNOUNCED BY PLAYOFF
❑ 1 Anquan Boldin .75 .30
❑ 2 Emmitt Smith 1.50 .60
❑ 3 Josh McCown .50 .20
❑ 4 Michael Vick 1.50 .60
❑ 5 Peerless Price .50 .20
❑ 6 T.J. Duckett .50 .20
❑ 7 Warrick Dunn .50 .20
❑ 8 Jamal Lewis .75 .30
❑ 9 Kyle Boller .75 .30
❑ 10 Ray Lewis .75 .30
❑ 11 Drew Bledsoe .75 .30
❑ 12 Eric Moulds .50 .20
❑ 13 Travis Henry .50 .20
❑ 14 Willis McGahee .75 .30
❑ 15 DeShaun Foster .50 .20
❑ 16 Jake Delhomme .75 .30
❑ 17 Stephen Davis .50 .20
❑ 18 Steve Smith .75 .30
❑ 19 Brian Urlacher 1.00 .40
❑ 20 Rex Grossman .75 .30
❑ 21 Thomas Jones .50 .20
❑ 22 Carson Palmer 1.00 .40
❑ 23 Chad Johnson .75 .30
❑ 24 Rudi Johnson .50 .20
❑ 25 Jeff Garcia .75 .30
❑ 26 Lee Suggs .75 .30
❑ 27 William Green .50 .20
❑ 28 Keyshawn Johnson .50 .20
❑ 29 Roy Williams S .50 .20
❑ 30 Eddie George .50 .20
❑ 31 Ashley Lelie .50 .20
❑ 32 Jake Plummer .50 .20
❑ 33 Quentin Griffin .75 .30
❑ 34 Rod Smith .50 .20
❑ 35 Charles Rogers .50 .20
❑ 36 Joey Harrington .75 .30
❑ 37 Ahman Green .75 .30
❑ 38 Brett Favre 2.00 .75
❑ 39 Javon Walker .50 .20
❑ 40 Andre Johnson .75 .30
❑ 41 David Carr .75 .30
❑ 42 Domanick Davis .75 .30
❑ 43 Edgerrin James .75 .30
❑ 44 Marvin Harrison .75 .30
❑ 45 Peyton Manning 1.25 .50
❑ 46 Byron Leftwich 1.00 .40
❑ 47 Fred Taylor .50 .20
❑ 48 Jimmy Smith .50 .20
❑ 49 Priest Holmes 1.00 .40
❑ 50 Tony Gonzalez .50 .20
❑ 51 Trent Green .50 .20
❑ 52 A.J. Feeley .75 .30
❑ 53 Chris Chambers .50 .20
❑ 54 Deion Sanders .75 .30
❑ 55 Daunte Culpepper .75 .30
❑ 56 Michael Bennett .50 .20
❑ 57 Randy Moss 1.00 .40
❑ 58 Corey Dillon .50 .20
❑ 59 Deion Branch .75 .30
❑ 60 Tom Brady 2.00 .75
❑ 61 Aaron Brooks .50 .20
❑ 62 Deuce McAllister .75 .30
❑ 63 Donte Stallworth .50 .20
❑ 64 Joe Horn .50 .20
❑ 65 Amani Toomer .50 .20
❑ 66 Jeremy Shockey .75 .30
❑ 67 Michael Strahan .50 .20
❑ 68 Tiki Barber .75 .30
❑ 69 Chad Pennington .75 .30
❑ 70 Curtis Martin .75 .30
❑ 71 Santana Moss .50 .20
❑ 72 Jerry Porter .50 .20
❑ 73 Jerry Rice 1.50 .60
❑ 74 Warren Sapp .50 .20
❑ 75 Brian Westbrook .50 .20
❑ 76 Donovan McNabb 1.00 .40
❑ 77 Jevon Kearse .50 .20
❑ 78 Terrell Owens .75 .30
❑ 79 Antwaan Randle El .75 .30
❑ 80 Hines Ward .75 .30
❑ 81 Jerome Bettis .75 .30
❑ 82 LaDainian Tomlinson 1.00 .40
❑ 83 Kevan Barlow .50 .20
❑ 84 Tim Rattay .50 .20
❑ 85 Koren Robinson .50 .20
❑ 86 Matt Hasselbeck .50 .20
❑ 87 Shaun Alexander .75 .30
❑ 88 Isaac Bruce .50 .20
❑ 89 Marc Bulger .75 .30
❑ 90 Marshall Faulk .75 .30
❑ 91 Torry Holt .75 .30
❑ 92 Brad Johnson .50 .20
❑ 93 Mike Alstott .50 .20
❑ 94 Chris Brown .75 .30
❑ 95 Derrick Mason .50 .20
❑ 96 Steve McNair .75 .30
❑ 97 Clinton Portis .75 .30
❑ 98 LaVar Arrington 1.50 .60
❑ 99 Laveranues Coles .50 .20
❑ 100 Mark Brunell .50 .20
❑ 101 Adimchinobe Echemandu AU RC 12.00 5.00
❑ 102 Ahmad Carroll AU/574* RC 20.00 8.00
❑ 103 Andy Hall AU RC 15.00 6.00
❑ 104 B.J. Johnson AU RC 12.00 5.00
❑ 105 B.J. Symons AU RC 15.00 6.00
❑ 106 Roethlisberger AU/541* RC 350.00 175.00
❑ 107 Ben Troupe AU/540* RC 20.00 8.00
❑ 108 Ben Watson AU/660* RC 30.00 15.00
❑ 109 Bernard Berrian AU/653* RC 40.00 20.00
❑ 110 Brandon Miree AU RC 12.00 5.00
❑ 111 Bruce Perry AU RC 15.00 6.00
❑ 112 Carlos Francis AU RC 15.00 6.00
❑ 113 Casey Bramlet AU RC 12.00 5.00
❑ 114 Cedric Cobbs AU/630* RC 20.00 8.00
❑ 115 Chris Gamble AU/490* RC 20.00 8.00
❑ 116 Chris Perry AU/478* RC 50.00 25.00
❑ 117 Clarence Moore AU RC 15.00 6.00
❑ 118 Cody Pickett AU RC 15.00 6.00
❑ 119 Craig Krenzel AU RC 20.00 8.00
❑ 120 D.J. Hackett AU/325* RC 30.00 15.00
❑ 121 D.J. Williams AU/490* RC 25.00 12.50
❑ 122 Darius Watts AU RC 15.00 6.00
❑ 123 DeAngelo Hall AU RC 30.00 12.50
❑ 124 Derrick Hamilton AU/373* RC 15.00 6.00
❑ 125 Derrick Ward AU RC 12.00 5.00
❑ 126 Devard Darling AU/325* RC 20.00 8.00
❑ 127 D.Henderson AU/475* RC 30.00 12.50
❑ 128 Drew Carter AU RC 15.00 6.00
❑ 129 Drew Henson AU/415* RC 30.00 12.50
❑ 130 D.Robinson AU/660* RC 25.00 10.00
❑ 131 Eli Manning AU/372* RC 300.00 150.00
❑ 132 Ernest Wilford AU/365* RC 35.00 20.00
❑ 133 Greg Jones AU/553* RC 40.00 15.00
❑ 134 J.P. Losman AU/358* RC 80.00 40.00
❑ 135 Jamaar Taylor AU RC 15.00 6.00
❑ 136 Jared Lorenzen AU RC 15.00 6.00
❑ 137 Jarrett Payton AU RC 15.00 6.00
❑ 138 Jason Babin AU RC 20.00 8.00
❑ 139 Jeff Smoker AU RC 20.00 8.00
❑ 140 J.Cotchery AU/325* RC 30.00 15.00
❑ 141 Jim Sorgi AU RC 20.00 8.00
❑ 142 John Navarre AU RC 20.00 8.00
❑ 143 Johnnie Morant AU/325* RC 30.00 15.00

❑ 144 Jonathan Vilma AU SP RC 30.00 12.50
❑ 145 Josh Harris AU/555* RC 15.00 6.00
❑ 146 Julius Jones AU/252* RC 120.00 60.00
❑ 147 Keary Colbert AU/495* RC 40.00 20.00
❑ 148 Kel.Winslow AU/135* RC 200.00 125.00
❑ 149 Kenechi Udeze AU/475* RC 25.00 12.50
❑ 150 Kevin Jones AU/327* RC 80.00 40.00
❑ 151 L.Fitzgerald AU/50* RC 750.00 400.00
❑ 152 Lee Evans AU/375* RC 50.00 25.00
❑ 153 Luke McCown AU/543* RC 20.00 8.00
❑ 154 Matt Mauck AU RC 15.00 6.00
❑ 155 Matt Schaub AU/367* RC 150.00 90.00
❑ 156 Maurice Mann AU RC 12.00 5.00
❑ 157 Mewelde Moore AU/435* RC 30.00 12.50
❑ 158 Michael Clayton AU/325* RC 80.00 40.00
❑ 159 Michael Jenkins AU/412* RC 40.00 20.00
❑ 160 M.Turner AU/535* RC 100.00 60.00
❑ 161 P.K. Sam AU/300* RC 20.00 8.00
❑ 162 Philip Rivers AU/556* RC 200.00 125.00
❑ 163 Quincy Wilson AU/350* RC 20.00 8.00
❑ 164 Ran Carthon AU RC 12.00 5.00
❑ 165 Rashaun Woods AU RC 15.00 6.00
❑ 166 Re.Williams AU/336* RC 60.00 25.00
❑ 167 R.Colclough AU/640* RC 25.00 10.00
❑ 168 Robert Gallery AU/310* RC 40.00 15.00
❑ 169 Roy Williams AU/564* RC 100.00 50.00
❑ 170 Samie Parker AU/356* RC 30.00 15.00
❑ 171 Sean Jones AU RC 15.00 6.00
❑ 172 S.Taylor/575* RC No Auto 30.00 12.50
❑ 173 Sloan Thomas AU RC 12.00 5.00
❑ 174 Steven Jackson AU/333* RC 150.00 90.00
❑ 175 Tatum Bell AU/539* RC 80.00 40.00
❑ 176 Tommie Harris AU/365* RC 30.00 15.00
❑ 177 Triandos Luke AU RC 15.00 6.00
❑ 178 Troy Fleming AU RC 12.00 5.00
❑ 179 Vince Wilfork AU/315* RC 25.00 10.00
❑ 180 Will Smith AU/565* RC 20.00 8.00
❑ 181 Marcus Tubbs AU RC 15.00 6.00
❑ 182 Michael Boulware AU RC 20.00 8.00
❑ 183 Kris Wilson AU RC 15.00 6.00
❑ 184 Richard Smith AU RC 12.00 5.00
❑ 185 Teddy Lehman AU RC 20.00 8.00
❑ 186 Chris Cooley AU RC 30.00 15.00
❑ 187 Thomas Tapeh AU RC 12.00 5.00
❑ 188A Willie Parker Blk AU RC 120.00 60.00
❑ 188B Willie Parker Blu AU RC 250.00 150.00
❑ 189 Patrick Crayton AU RC 30.00 15.00
❑ 190 Kendrick Starling AU RC 12.00 5.00
❑ 191 B.J. Sams AU RC 15.00 6.00
❑ 192 Derick Armstrong AU EXCH 12.00 5.00
❑ 193 Wes Welker AU RC 40.00 20.00
❑ 194 Erik Coleman AU RC 15.00 6.00
❑ 195 Gibril Wilson AU RC 20.00 8.00
❑ 196 Andy Reid AU/335* RC 30.00 12.50
❑ 197 Brian Billick AU/585* RC 30.00 12.50
❑ 198 Jeff Fisher AU/585* RC 25.00 12.50
❑ 199 Jon Gruden AU/585* RC 20.00 8.00
❑ 200 Marvin Lewis AU/585* RC 25.00 12.50

2005 Playoff Contenders

❑ COMP.SET w/o RC's (100) 20.00 7.50
❑ AU PRINT RUNS ANNOUNCED BY PLAYOFF
❑ EXCH EXPIRATION: 8/1/2007
❑ UNPRICED CHAMPION.PRINT RUN 1 SET
❑ 1 Anquan Boldin .50 .20
❑ 2 Kurt Warner .50 .20
❑ 3 Larry Fitzgerald .75 .30
❑ 4 Michael Vick 1.25 .50
❑ 5 T.J. Duckett .50 .20
❑ 6 Warrick Dunn .50 .20
❑ 7 Derrick Mason .50 .20
❑ 8 Jamal Lewis .75 .30
❑ 9 Kyle Boller .50 .20
❑ 10 Ray Lewis .75 .30
❑ 11 J.P. Losman .75 .30
❑ 12 Lee Evans .50 .20
❑ 13 Willis McGahee .75 .30
❑ 14 DeShaun Foster .50 .20
❑ 15 Jake Delhomme .75 .30
❑ 16 Steve Smith .50 .20
❑ 17 Brian Urlacher .75 .30
❑ 18 Muhsin Muhammad .50 .20
❑ 19 Rex Grossman .50 .20
❑ 20 Carson Palmer .75 .30
❑ 21 Chad Johnson .75 .30
❑ 22 Rudi Johnson .50 .20
❑ 23 Lee Suggs .50 .20
❑ 24 Trent Dilfer .50 .20
❑ 25 Drew Bledsoe .75 .30
❑ 26 Jason Witten .50 .20
❑ 27 Julius Jones 1.00 .40
❑ 28 Keyshawn Johnson .50 .20
❑ 29 Ashley Lelie .50 .20
❑ 30 Jake Plummer .50 .20
❑ 31 Rod Smith .50 .20
❑ 32 Tatum Bell .50 .20
❑ 33 Joey Harrington .75 .30
❑ 34 Kevin Jones .75 .30
❑ 35 Roy Williams WR .75 .30
❑ 36 Ahman Green .75 .30
❑ 37 Brett Favre 2.00 .75
❑ 38 Javon Walker .50 .20
❑ 39 Andre Johnson .50 .20
❑ 40 David Carr .75 .30
❑ 41 Domanick Davis .50 .20
❑ 42 Edgerrin James .75 .30
❑ 43 Marvin Harrison .75 .30
❑ 44 Peyton Manning 1.25 .50
❑ 45 Reggie Wayne .50 .20
❑ 46 Byron Leftwich .75 .30
❑ 47 Fred Taylor .50 .20
❑ 48 Jimmy Smith .50 .20
❑ 49 Priest Holmes .75 .30
❑ 50 Tony Gonzalez .50 .20
❑ 51 Trent Green .50 .20
❑ 52 Chris Chambers .50 .20
❑ 53 Ricky Williams .50 .20
❑ 54 Daunte Culpepper .75 .30
❑ 55 Michael Bennett .50 .20
❑ 56 Nate Burleson .50 .20
❑ 57 Corey Dillon .50 .20
❑ 58 Deion Branch .50 .20
❑ 59 Tom Brady 2.00 .75
❑ 60 Aaron Brooks .50 .20
❑ 61 Deuce McAllister .75 .30
❑ 62 Joe Horn .50 .20
❑ 63 Eli Manning 1.50 .60
❑ 64 Jeremy Shockey .75 .30
❑ 65 Plaxico Burress .50 .20
❑ 66 Tiki Barber .75 .30
❑ 67 Chad Pennington .75 .30
❑ 68 Curtis Martin .75 .30
❑ 69 Laveranues Coles .50 .20
❑ 70 Kerry Collins .50 .20
❑ 71 LaMont Jordan .75 .30
❑ 72 Randy Moss .75 .30
❑ 73 Brian Westbrook .50 .20
❑ 74 Donovan McNabb 1.00 .40
❑ 75 Terrell Owens .75 .30
❑ 76 Ben Roethlisberger 2.00 .75
❑ 77 Duce Staley .50 .20
❑ 78 Hines Ward .75 .30
❑ 79 Jerome Bettis .75 .30
❑ 80 Antonio Gates .75 .30
❑ 81 Drew Brees .75 .30
❑ 82 LaDainian Tomlinson 1.00 .40
❑ 83 Brandon Lloyd .40 .15
❑ 84 Kevan Barlow .50 .20
❑ 85 Darrell Jackson .50 .20
❑ 86 Matt Hasselbeck .50 .20
❑ 87 Shaun Alexander 1.00 .40
❑ 88 Isaac Bruce .50 .20
❑ 89 Marc Bulger .75 .30
❑ 90 Steven Jackson 1.00 .40
❑ 91 Torry Holt .75 .30
❑ 92 Brian Griese .50 .20
❑ 93 Derrick Brooks .50 .20
❑ 94 Chris Brown .50 .20
❑ 95 Drew Bennett .50 .20
❑ 96 Steve McNair .75 .30
❑ 97 Travis Henry .50 .20
❑ 98 Clinton Portis .75 .30
❑ 99 LaVar Arrington .75 .30
❑ 100 Santana Moss .50 .20
❑ 101 Aaron Rodgers AU/530* RC 120.00 60.00
❑ 102 Adam Jones AU RC 20.00 7.50
❑ 103 A.McPherson AU/365* RC 40.00 20.00
❑ 104 Alvin Pearman AU RC 20.00 7.50
❑ 105 Airese Currie AU RC 20.00 7.50
❑ 106 Alex Smith QB AU/401* RC 150.00 75.00
❑ 107 Andrew Walter AU/99* RC 250.00 125.00
❑ 108 Anthony Davis AU/366* RC 30.00 15.00
❑ 109 Antrel Rolle AU RC 20.00 7.50
❑ 110 Brandon Jacobs AU RC 60.00 35.00
❑ 111 Brandon Jones AU RC 20.00 7.50
❑ 112 Braylon Edwards AU RC 80.00 40.00
❑ 113 Bryant McFadden AU/315* RC 40.00 20.00
❑ 114 Carlos Rogers AU RC 30.00 15.00
❑ 115 Cad.Williams AU/380* RC 150.00 75.00
❑ 116 Cedric Benson AU/289* RC 150.00 90.00
❑ 117 Houston AU/116* RC EX 250.00 125.00
❑ 118 Chad Owens AU RC 20.00 7.50
❑ 119 Charlie Frye AU RC 60.00 30.00
❑ 120 Chris Henry AU RC 50.00 25.00
❑ 121 Ciatrick Fason AU RC 20.00 7.50
❑ 122 Courtney Roby AU RC 20.00 7.50
❑ 123 Craig Bragg AU/425* RC 40.00 20.00
❑ 124 C.Thorpe AU/416* RC 40.00 20.00
❑ 125 Damien Nash AU RC 15.00 6.00
❑ 126 Dan Cody AU/315* RC 40.00 20.00
❑ 127 Dan Orlovsky AU RC 25.00 10.00
❑ 128 Dante Ridgeway AU/373* RC 30.00 15.00
❑ 129 Darren Sproles AU/454* RC 30.00 15.00
❑ 130 David Greene AU RC 25.00 10.00
❑ 131 David Pollack AU RC 20.00 7.50
❑ 132 Deandra Cobb AU/440* RC 30.00 15.00
❑ 133 DeMarcus Ware AU RC 30.00 15.00
❑ 134 Derek Anderson AU/450* RC 60.00 35.00
❑ 135 Derrick Johnson AU RC 40.00 15.00
❑ 136 Erasmus James AU RC 20.00 7.50
❑ 137 Eric Shelton AU RC 20.00 7.50
❑ 138 Fabian Washington AU RC 20.00 7.50
❑ 139 Frank Gore AU RC 100.00 50.00
❑ 140 F.Gibson AU/476* RC EXCH 50.00 20.00
❑ 141 Heath Miller AU/510* RC 80.00 40.00
❑ 142 J.J. Arrington AU/465* RC 50.00 25.00
❑ 143 J.R. Russell AU/489* RC 30.00 15.00
❑ 144 Jason Campbell AU RC 75.00 40.00
❑ 145 Jason White AU RC 15.00 6.00
❑ 146 Jerome Mathis AU/416* RC 30.00 15.00
❑ 147 Josh Davis AU RC 12.00 5.00
❑ 148 Kay-Jay Harris AU RC 12.00 5.00
❑ 149 Kyle Orton AU RC 40.00 15.00
❑ 150 Larry Brackins AU RC 12.00 5.00
❑ 151 Lionel Gates AU/241* RC 40.00 20.00
❑ 152 Marion Barber AU RC 60.00 35.00
❑ 153 Mark Bradley AU RC 25.00 10.00
❑ 154 Mark Clayton AU/494* RC 50.00 20.00
❑ 155 Marlin Jackson AU RC 20.00 7.50
❑ 156 Matt Jones AU/165* RC 150.00 75.00
❑ 157 Matt Roth AU RC 20.00 7.50
❑ 158 Maurice Clarett AU/89* 135.00 75.00
❑ 159 Mike Williams AU/73* 300.00 150.00
❑ 160 Paris Warren AU/241* RC 50.00 25.00
❑ 161 Rasheed Marshall AU RC 15.00 6.00
❑ 162 Reggie Brown AU/528* RC 50.00 25.00
❑ 163 Roddy White AU RC 20.00 7.50
❑ 164 Ronnie Brown AU/550* RC 120.00 60.00
❑ 165 Roscoe Parrish AU RC 20.00 7.50
❑ 166 Royd.Williams AU/491* RC 30.00 15.00
❑ 167 R.Fitzpatrick AU/284* RC 50.00 25.00
❑ 168 Ryan Moats AU RC 30.00 15.00
❑ 169 Shaun Cody AU RC 15.00 6.00
❑ 170 Shawne Merriman AU RC 50.00 30.00
❑ 171 Stefan LeFors AU RC 20.00 7.50
❑ 172 Steve Savoy AU RC 12.00 5.00
❑ 173 T.A. McLendon AU RC 12.00 5.00
❑ 174 Tab Perry AU RC 20.00 7.50
❑ 175 Taylor Stubblefield AU RC 12.00 5.00
❑ 176 Terrence Murphy AU RC 20.00 7.50
❑ 177 Thomas Davis AU RC 15.00 6.00
❑ 178 Travis Johnson AU RC 15.00 6.00
❑ 179 T.Williamson AU/402* RC 50.00 30.00

- ❑ 180 Vernand Morency AU RC 15.00 6.00
- ❑ 181 Vincent Jackson AU RC 20.00 7.50
- ❑ 182 Alex Smith TE AU RC 20.00 7.50
- ❑ 183 Channing Crowder AU RC 15.00 6.00
- ❑ 184 Darrent Williams AU RC 40.00 15.00
- ❑ 185 Derrick Wimbush AU RC 15.00 6.00
- ❑ 186 James Kilian AU RC 15.00 6.00
- ❑ 187 Josh Cribbs AU RC 15.00 6.00
- ❑ 188 LeRon McCoy AU RC 12.00 5.00
- ❑ 189 Luis Castillo AU RC 20.00 7.50
- ❑ 190 Matt Cassel AU RC 30.00 15.00
- ❑ 191 Mike Patterson AU RC 15.00 6.00
- ❑ 192 Nate Washington AU RC 20.00 7.50
- ❑ 193 Noah Herron AU RC 20.00 7.50
- ❑ 194 Fred Amey AU RC 15.00 6.00
- ❑ 195 Tyson Thompson AU RC 25.00 10.00
- ❑ 196 Mike Nugent AU RC 15.00 6.00
- ❑ 197 Odell Thurman AU RC 25.00 10.00
- ❑ 198 Chris Carr AU RC 20.00 7.50
- ❑ 199 Bo Scaife AU RC 15.00 6.00
- ❑ 200 Billy Bajema AU RC 12.00 5.00

2006 Playoff Contenders

- ❑ COMP.SET w/o RC's (100) 20.00 8.00
- ❑ 1 Anquan Boldin .50 .20
- ❑ 2 Edgerrin James .75 .30
- ❑ 3 Larry Fitzgerald .75 .30
- ❑ 4 Alge Crumpler .50 .20
- ❑ 5 Michael Vick 1.00 .40
- ❑ 6 Warrick Dunn .50 .20
- ❑ 7 Steve McNair .50 .20
- ❑ 8 Mark Clayton .50 .20
- ❑ 9 Derrick Mason .40 .15
- ❑ 10 Lee Evans .50 .20
- ❑ 11 Willis McGahee .75 .30
- ❑ 12 Jake Delhomme .50 .20
- ❑ 13 Keyshawn Johnson .50 .20
- ❑ 14 Steve Smith .75 .30
- ❑ 15 Cedric Benson .75 .30
- ❑ 16 Brian Urlacher .75 .30
- ❑ 17 Thomas Jones .50 .20
- ❑ 18 Carson Palmer .75 .30
- ❑ 19 Chad Johnson .50 .20
- ❑ 20 Rudi Johnson .50 .20
- ❑ 21 T.J. Houshmandzadeh .50 .20
- ❑ 22 Charlie Frye .50 .20
- ❑ 23 Braylon Edwards .75 .30
- ❑ 24 Reuben Droughns .50 .20
- ❑ 25 Tony Romo 5.00 2.00
- ❑ 26 Julius Jones .75 .30
- ❑ 27 Roy Williams S .50 .20
- ❑ 28 Terrell Owens .75 .30
- ❑ 29 Javon Walker .50 .20
- ❑ 30 Rod Smith .50 .20
- ❑ 31 Tatum Bell .50 .20
- ❑ 32 Roy Williams WR .75 .30
- ❑ 33 Kevin Jones .75 .30
- ❑ 34 Brett Favre 1.50 .60
- ❑ 35 Robert Ferguson .40 .15
- ❑ 36 Samkon Gado .75 .30
- ❑ 37 Andre Johnson .50 .20
- ❑ 38 David Carr .50 .20
- ❑ 39 Domanick Davis .50 .20
- ❑ 40 Eric Moulds .50 .20
- ❑ 41 Dallas Clark .40 .15
- ❑ 42 Marvin Harrison .75 .30
- ❑ 43 Peyton Manning 1.25 .50
- ❑ 44 Reggie Wayne .50 .20
- ❑ 45 Matt Jones .75 .30
- ❑ 46 Byron Leftwich .50 .20
- ❑ 47 Fred Taylor .50 .20
- ❑ 48 Larry Johnson 1.00 .40
- ❑ 49 Priest Holmes .50 .20
- ❑ 50 Tony Gonzalez .50 .20
- ❑ 51 Trent Green .50 .20
- ❑ 52 Chris Chambers .50 .20
- ❑ 53 Daunte Culpepper .75 .30
- ❑ 54 Ronnie Brown .75 .30
- ❑ 55 Chester Taylor .50 .20
- ❑ 56 Brad Johnson .50 .20
- ❑ 57 Corey Dillon .50 .20
- ❑ 58 Deion Branch .50 .20
- ❑ 59 Tom Brady 1.25 .50
- ❑ 60 Tedy Bruschi .75 .30
- ❑ 61 Deuce McAllister .50 .20
- ❑ 62 Donte Stallworth .50 .20
- ❑ 63 Drew Brees .75 .30
- ❑ 64 Eli Manning 1.00 .40
- ❑ 65 Jeremy Shockey .75 .30
- ❑ 66 Tiki Barber .75 .30
- ❑ 67 Chad Pennington .50 .20
- ❑ 68 Curtis Martin .75 .30
- ❑ 69 Laveranues Coles .50 .20
- ❑ 70 Randy Moss .75 .30
- ❑ 71 LaMont Jordan .50 .20
- ❑ 72 Jerry Porter .50 .20
- ❑ 73 Donovan McNabb .75 .30
- ❑ 74 Reggie Brown .50 .20
- ❑ 75 Ben Roethlisberger 1.25 .50
- ❑ 76 Hines Ward .75 .30
- ❑ 77 Willie Parker 1.00 .40
- ❑ 78 Antonio Gates .75 .30
- ❑ 79 Philip Rivers .75 .30
- ❑ 80 LaDainian Tomlinson 1.00 .40
- ❑ 81 Alex Smith QB 1.00 .40
- ❑ 82 Antonio Bryant .50 .20
- ❑ 83 Kevan Barlow .50 .20
- ❑ 84 Darrell Jackson .50 .20
- ❑ 85 Matt Hasselbeck .50 .20
- ❑ 86 Nate Burleson .50 .20
- ❑ 87 Shaun Alexander .75 .30
- ❑ 88 Marc Bulger .50 .20
- ❑ 89 Steven Jackson .75 .30
- ❑ 90 Isaac Bruce .50 .20
- ❑ 91 Torry Holt .50 .20
- ❑ 92 Cadillac Williams .75 .30
- ❑ 93 Chris Simms .50 .20
- ❑ 94 Joey Galloway .50 .20
- ❑ 95 Chris Brown .50 .20
- ❑ 96 David Givens .50 .20
- ❑ 97 Drew Bennett .40 .15
- ❑ 98 Clinton Portis .75 .30
- ❑ 99 Santana Moss .50 .20
- ❑ 100 Mark Brunell .50 .20
- ❑ 101 Malcolm Floyd AU RC 20.00 8.00
- ❑ 102 Bart Scott AU RC 60.00 35.00
- ❑ 103 Reggie McNeal AU/457* RC 25.00 10.00
- ❑ 104 Domenik Hixon AU/586* RC 25.00 10.00
- ❑ 105 Vince Young AU/487* RC 350.00 200.00
- ❑ 106 Marcedes Lewis AU RC 20.00 8.00
- ❑ 107 Wali Lundy AU/400* RC EXCH 50.00 25.00
- ❑ 108 Tarvaris Jackson AU RC 60.00 30.00
- ❑ 109 Ko Simpson AU RC 15.00 6.00
- ❑ 110 Jason Allen AU RC 20.00 8.00
- ❑ 111 Anthony Fasano AU RC 20.00 8.00
- ❑ 112 Joe Klopfenstein AU RC 15.00 6.00
- ❑ 113 Marques Hagans AU RC 12.00 5.00
- ❑ 114 Jason Avant AU RC 20.00 8.00
- ❑ 115 Santonio Holmes AU RC 80.00 40.00
- ❑ 116 Marcus Vick AU/149* RC 150.00 75.00
- ❑ 117 Antonio Cromartie AU/322* RC 30.00 15.00
- ❑ 118 DeAngelo Williams AU RC 100.00 50.00
- ❑ 119 Laurence Maroney AU RC 150.00 75.00
- ❑ 120 Daniel Bullocks AU RC 20.00 8.00
- ❑ 121 Jonathan Orr AU RC 15.00 6.00
- ❑ 122 Mike Bell AU RC 40.00 15.00
- ❑ 123 Kellen Clemens AU RC 50.00 25.00
- ❑ 124 Tim Jennings AU RC 15.00 6.00
- ❑ 125 Cory Rodgers AU RC 20.00 8.00
- ❑ 126 Jerome Harrison AU RC 20.00 8.00
- ❑ 127 Brad Smith AU/570* RC 25.00 10.00
- ❑ 128 Jeff Webb AU/250* RC EXCH 40.00 20.00
- ❑ 129 Will Blackmon AU RC 15.00 6.00
- ❑ 130 Quinton Ganther AU RC 15.00 6.00
- ❑ 131 Drew Olson AU RC 15.00 6.00
- ❑ 132 Omar Jacobs AU RC 15.00 6.00
- ❑ 133 Adam Jennings AU RC 15.00 6.00
- ❑ 134 Cedric Humes AU RC 20.00 8.00
- ❑ 135 Derrick Ross AU/250* RC EXCH 50.00 25.00
- ❑ 136 Charlie Whitehurst AU RC 40.00 20.00
- ❑ 137 Bobby Carpenter AU RC 25.00 10.00
- ❑ 138 Darryl Tapp AU RC 15.00 6.00
- ❑ 139 A.J. Hawk AU/399* RC 100.00 50.00
- ❑ 140 Bruce Gradkowski AU RC 30.00 12.00
- ❑ 141 Chad Greenway AU RC 20.00 8.00
- ❑ 142 John David Washington AU RC 15.00 6.00
- ❑ 143 Kamerion Wimbley AU RC 25.00 10.00
- ❑ 144 LenDale White AU/549* RC 60.00 30.00
- ❑ 145 Johnathan Joseph AU/549* RC 25.00 10.00
- ❑ 146 Maurice Drew AU RC 120.00 60.00
- ❑ 147 Brandon Marshall AU/608* RC 80.00 40.00
- ❑ 148 Vernon Davis AU/537* RC 80.00 40.00
- ❑ 149 Joseph Addai AU RC 200.00 100.00
- ❑ 150 Bennie Brazell AU RC 12.00 5.00
- ❑ 151 D.J. Shockley AU RC 20.00 8.00
- ❑ 152 Jay Cutler AU/501* RC 350.00 200.00
- ❑ 153 Wendell Mathis AU RC 15.00 6.00
- ❑ 154 Demetrius Williams AU RC 30.00 15.00
- ❑ 155 Dusty Dvoracek AU RC 25.00 10.00
- ❑ 156 DeMario Minter AU RC 15.00 6.00
- ❑ 157 Marcus Maxey AU RC 15.00 6.00
- ❑ 158 Brodie Croyle AU RC 50.00 30.00
- ❑ 159 Jeremy Bloom AU/473* RC 40.00 20.00
- ❑ 160 Todd Watkins AU RC 12.00 5.00
- ❑ 161 Cory Ross AU RC 20.00 8.00
- ❑ 162 Tamba Hali AU/500* RC 25.00 10.00
- ❑ 163 P.J. Daniels AU/555* RC 20.00 8.00
- ❑ 164 Brandon Williams AU RC 20.00 8.00
- ❑ 165 Devin Hester AU RC 60.00 30.00
- ❑ 166 Kelly Jennings AU/393* RC 25.00 10.00
- ❑ 167 Dawan Landry AU RC 20.00 8.00
- ❑ 168 Greg Jennings AU RC 40.00 20.00
- ❑ 169 Mathias Kiwanuka AU RC 25.00 10.00
- ❑ 170 Leon Washington AU RC 50.00 25.00
- ❑ 171 Richard Marshall AU RC 15.00 6.00
- ❑ 172 Haloti Ngata AU RC 20.00 8.00
- ❑ 173 Sinorice Moss AU RC 30.00 15.00
- ❑ 174 Greg Blue AU RC 15.00 6.00
- ❑ 175 Chris Barclay AU RC 15.00 6.00
- ❑ 176 D'Qwell Jackson AU RC 15.00 6.00
- ❑ 177 Eric Smith AU RC 12.00 5.00
- ❑ 178 Ethan Kilmer AU RC 20.00 8.00
- ❑ 179 Mike Hass AU RC 20.00 8.00
- ❑ 180 Derek Hagan AU RC 25.00 10.00
- ❑ 181 Travis Wilson AU RC 20.00 8.00
- ❑ 182 Reggie Bush AU/645* RC 500.00 300.00
- ❑ 183 Maurice Stovall AU/579* RC 40.00 20.00
- ❑ 184 Skyler Green AU RC 15.00 6.00
- ❑ 185 Calvin Lowry AU RC 15.00 6.00
- ❑ 186 Jerious Norwood AU RC 60.00 35.00
- ❑ 187 Brodrick Bunkley AU/518* RC 20.00 8.00
- ❑ 188 Ernie Sims AU/611* RC 25.00 10.00
- ❑ 189 Ingle Martin AU RC 20.00 8.00
- ❑ 190 Anthony Mix AU RC 15.00 6.00
- ❑ 191 Patrick Cobbs AU RC 15.00 6.00
- ❑ 192 Delanie Walker AU/212* RC 120.00 60.00
- ❑ 193 Gabe Watson AU RC 15.00 6.00
- ❑ 194 Willie Reid AU/515* RC 25.00 10.00
- ❑ 195 Michael Huff AU RC 30.00 15.00
- ❑ 196 Mario Williams AU/395* RC 40.00 20.00
- ❑ 197 Chad Jackson AU RC 40.00 20.00
- ❑ 198 David Kirtman AU RC 15.00 6.00
- ❑ 199 B.Calhoun AU/407* RC EXCH 40.00 15.00
- ❑ 200 M.Robinson AU/512* RC EXCH 50.00 30.00
- ❑ 201 D.Ferguson AU/386* RC 30.00 12.00
- ❑ 202 Donte Whitner AU/518* RC 20.00 8.00
- ❑ 203 Roman Harper AU RC 15.00 6.00
- ❑ 204 Manny Lawson AU RC 15.00 6.00
- ❑ 205 DeMeco Ryans AU RC 30.00 15.00
- ❑ 206 Anthony Smith AU RC 30.00 15.00
- ❑ 207 Thomas Howard AU RC 20.00 8.00
- ❑ 208 John McCargo AU RC 12.00 5.00
- ❑ 209 David Pittman AU RC 15.00 6.00
- ❑ 210 Danieal Manning AU RC 20.00 8.00
- ❑ 211 Nate Salley AU RC 12.00 5.00
- ❑ 212 Jimmy Williams AU/524* RC 20.00 8.00
- ❑ 213 Rocky McIntosh AU RC 20.00 8.00
- ❑ 214 Montell Owens AU RC 12.00 5.00
- ❑ 215 Devin Aromashodu AU RC 12.00 5.00
- ❑ 216 Ben Obomanu AU RC 12.00 5.00
- ❑ 217 David Anderson AU RC 15.00 6.00
- ❑ 218 Marques Colston AU RC 120.00 60.00
- ❑ 219 Miles Austin AU RC 20.00 8.00

Card		
❑ 220 Tony Scheffler AU/526* RC	40.00	20.00
❑ 221 Leonard Pope AU/495* RC	20.00	8.00
❑ 222 David Thomas AU RC	20.00	8.00
❑ 223 Dominique Byrd AU RC	15.00	6.00
❑ 224 Owen Daniels AU RC	20.00	8.00
❑ 225 Garrett Mills AU RC	15.00	6.00
❑ 226 Hank Baskett AU RC	25.00	12.50
❑ 227 Jason Carter AU RC	15.00	6.00
❑ 228 Sam Hurd AU RC	20.00	8.00
❑ 229 C.Sharon AU/250* RC EXCH	120.00	60.00
❑ 230 Chris Hannon AU RC	12.00	5.00
❑ 231 John Madsen AU RC	20.00	8.00
❑ 232 Shaun Bodiford AU RC	12.00	5.00
❑ 233 Mike Espy AU RC	20.00	8.00
❑ 234 Abdul Hodge AU RC	20.00	8.00
❑ 235 Anthony Montgomery AU RC	15.00	6.00
❑ 236 Matt Leinart AU/567* RC	300.00	150.00
❑ 237 Bernard Pollard AU/307* RC	30.00	15.00
❑ 238 Pat Watkins AU/343* RC	60.00	30.00
❑ 239 Cedric Griffin AU/357* RC	30.00	15.00
❑ 240 A.J. Nicholson AU RC	12.00	5.00
❑ 241 Claude Wroten AU/306* RC	60.00	30.00
❑ 242 Tye Hill AU/368* RC	30.00	15.00

2003 Playoff Hogg Heaven

Card		
❑ COMP.SET w/o SP's (150)	30.00	12.50
❑ 1 Emmitt Smith	2.50	1.00
❑ 2 Marcel Shipp	.60	.25
❑ 3 Michael Vick	2.50	1.00
❑ 4 Warrick Dunn	.60	.25
❑ 5 T.J. Duckett	.60	.25
❑ 6 Peerless Price	.60	.25
❑ 7 Brian Finneran	.40	.15
❑ 8 Chris Redman	.40	.15
❑ 9 Jamal Lewis	1.00	.40
❑ 10 Todd Heap	.60	.25
❑ 11 Travis Taylor	.60	.25
❑ 12 Ray Lewis	1.00	.40
❑ 13 Peter Boulware	.40	.15
❑ 14 Ed Reed	.60	.25
❑ 15 Drew Bledsoe	1.00	.40
❑ 16 Travis Henry	.60	.25
❑ 17 Eric Moulds	.60	.25
❑ 18 Josh Reed	.60	.25
❑ 19 Takeo Spikes	.40	.15
❑ 20 Julius Peppers	1.00	.40
❑ 21 Stephen Davis	.60	.25
❑ 22 Muhsin Muhammad	.60	.25
❑ 23 Wesley Walls	.40	.15
❑ 24 Anthony Thomas	.60	.25
❑ 25 Brian Urlacher	1.50	.60
❑ 26 Marty Booker	.60	.25
❑ 27 Mike Brown	.60	.25
❑ 28 Kordell Stewart	.60	.25
❑ 29 Dez White	.40	.15
❑ 30 Corey Dillon	.60	.25
❑ 31 Chad Johnson	1.00	.40
❑ 32 Peter Warrick	.60	.25
❑ 33 Tim Couch	.40	.15
❑ 34 William Green	.60	.25
❑ 35 Andre Davis	.40	.15
❑ 36 Quincy Morgan	.60	.25
❑ 37 Kevin Johnson	.60	.25
❑ 38 Dennis Northcutt	.40	.15
❑ 39 Antonio Bryant	.60	.25
❑ 40 Terry Glenn	.40	.15
❑ 41 Joey Galloway	.60	.25
❑ 42 Roy Williams	1.00	.40
❑ 43 Darren Woodson	.40	.15
❑ 44 Jake Plummer	.60	.25
❑ 45 Clinton Portis	1.50	.60
❑ 46 Mike Anderson	.60	.25
❑ 47 Rod Smith	.60	.25
❑ 48 Ed McCaffrey	.60	.25
❑ 49 Ashley Lelie	1.00	.40
❑ 50 Shannon Sharpe	.60	.25
❑ 51 Al Wilson	.40	.15
❑ 52 Joey Harrington	1.50	.60
❑ 53 James Stewart	.60	.25
❑ 54 Brett Favre	2.50	1.00
❑ 55 Ahman Green	1.00	.40
❑ 56 Darren Sharper	.40	.15
❑ 57 Donald Driver	.60	.25
❑ 58 Javon Walker	.60	.25
❑ 59 Robert Ferguson	.40	.15
❑ 60 David Carr	1.50	.60
❑ 61 Jabar Gaffney	.60	.25
❑ 62 Stacey Mack	.40	.15
❑ 63 Marvin Harrison	1.00	.40
❑ 64 Peyton Manning	1.50	.60
❑ 65 Edgerrin James	1.00	.40
❑ 66 Reggie Wayne	.60	.25
❑ 67 Fred Taylor	1.00	.40
❑ 68 Mark Brunell	.60	.25
❑ 69 Jimmy Smith	.60	.25
❑ 70 Hugh Douglas	.40	.15
❑ 71 Priest Holmes	1.25	.50
❑ 72 Trent Green	.60	.25
❑ 73 Tony Gonzalez	.60	.25
❑ 74 Marc Boerigter	.60	.25
❑ 75 Ricky Williams	1.00	.40
❑ 76 Jay Fiedler	.60	.25
❑ 77 Chris Chambers	1.00	.40
❑ 78 Zach Thomas	1.00	.40
❑ 79 Jason Taylor	.40	.15
❑ 80 Junior Seau	1.00	.40
❑ 81 Randy McMichael	.60	.25
❑ 82 Patrick Surtain	.40	.15
❑ 83 Randy Moss	1.50	.60
❑ 84 Michael Bennett	.60	.25
❑ 85 Daunte Culpepper	1.00	.40
❑ 86 Tom Brady	2.50	1.00
❑ 87 Troy Brown	.60	.25
❑ 88 Ty Law	.60	.25
❑ 89 Aaron Brooks	1.00	.40
❑ 90 Deuce McAllister	1.00	.40
❑ 91 Donte Stallworth	1.00	.40
❑ 92 Joe Horn	.60	.25
❑ 93 Michael Strahan	.60	.25
❑ 94 Kerry Collins	.60	.25
❑ 95 Tiki Barber	1.00	.40
❑ 96 Amani Toomer	.60	.25
❑ 97 Jeremy Shockey	1.50	.60
❑ 98 Chad Pennington	1.25	.50
❑ 99 Curtis Martin	1.00	.40
❑ 100 Santana Moss	.60	.25
❑ 101 Rich Gannon	.60	.25
❑ 102 Jerry Rice	2.00	.75
❑ 103 Tim Brown	1.00	.40
❑ 104 Jerry Porter	.60	.25
❑ 105 Charlie Garner	.60	.25
❑ 106 Charles Woodson	.60	.25
❑ 107 Donovan McNabb	1.25	.50
❑ 108 Duce Staley	.60	.25
❑ 109 James Thrash	.40	.15
❑ 110 Chad Lewis	.40	.15
❑ 111 Troy Vincent	.40	.15
❑ 112 Tommy Maddox	1.00	.40
❑ 113 Plaxico Burress	.60	.25
❑ 114 Hines Ward	1.00	.40
❑ 115 Antwaan Randle El	1.00	.40
❑ 116 Jerome Bettis	1.00	.40
❑ 117 Kendrell Bell	.60	.25
❑ 118 LaDainian Tomlinson	1.00	.40
❑ 119 Drew Brees	1.00	.40
❑ 120 David Boston	.60	.25
❑ 121 Jeff Garcia	1.00	.40
❑ 122 Terrell Owens	1.00	.40
❑ 123 Tai Streets	.60	.25
❑ 124 Kevan Barlow	.60	.25
❑ 125 Matt Hasselbeck	.60	.25
❑ 126 Koren Robinson	.60	.25
❑ 127 Shaun Alexander	1.00	.40
❑ 128 Kurt Warner	1.00	.40
❑ 129 Marc Bulger	1.00	.40
❑ 130 Marshall Faulk	1.00	.40
❑ 131 Torry Holt	1.00	.40
❑ 132 Isaac Bruce	1.00	.40
❑ 133 Brad Johnson	.60	.25
❑ 134 Keyshawn Johnson	1.00	.40
❑ 135 Warren Sapp	.60	.25
❑ 136 Derrick Brooks	.60	.25
❑ 137 John Lynch	.60	.25
❑ 138 Michael Pittman	.40	.15
❑ 139 Mike Alstott	1.00	.40
❑ 140 Steve McNair	1.00	.40
❑ 141 Eddie George	.60	.25
❑ 142 Jevon Kearse	.60	.25
❑ 143 Keith Bulluck	.40	.15
❑ 144 Derrick Mason	.60	.25
❑ 145 Patrick Ramsey	1.00	.40
❑ 146 Ladell Betts	.60	.25
❑ 147 Laveranues Coles	.60	.25
❑ 148 Rod Gardner	.60	.25
❑ 149 Champ Bailey	.60	.25
❑ 150 Bruce Smith	.40	.15
❑ 151 Ken Dorsey RC	6.00	2.50
❑ 152 Lee Suggs RC	6.00	2.50
❑ 153 Domanick Davis RC	6.00	2.50
❑ 154 Quentin Griffin RC	6.00	2.50
❑ 155 LaBrandon Toefield RC	6.00	2.50
❑ 156 B.J. Askew RC	6.00	2.50
❑ 157 Jason Witten RC	10.00	4.00
❑ 158 Bennie Joppru RC	6.00	2.50
❑ 159 L.J. Smith RC	6.00	2.50
❑ 160 Billy McMullen RC	5.00	2.00
❑ 161 Shaun McDonald RC	6.00	2.50
❑ 162 Brandon Lloyd RC	6.00	2.50
❑ 163 Sam Aiken RC	5.00	2.00
❑ 164 Bobby Wade RC	6.00	2.50
❑ 165 Justin Gage RC	6.00	2.50
❑ 166 Doug Gabriel RC	6.00	2.50
❑ 167 David Kircus RC	6.00	2.50
❑ 168 Arnaz Battle RC	6.00	2.50
❑ 169 Kareem Kelly RC	5.00	2.00
❑ 170 Talman Gardner RC	6.00	2.50
❑ 171 Ryan Hoag RC	3.00	1.25
❑ 172 LaTarence Dunbar RC	5.00	2.00
❑ 173 Johnathan Sullivan RC	5.00	2.00
❑ 174 Kevin Williams RC	6.00	2.50
❑ 175 Jimmy Kennedy RC	8.00	3.00
❑ 176 Ty Warren RC	6.00	2.50
❑ 177 William Joseph RC	6.00	2.50
❑ 178 Michael Haynes RC	6.00	2.50
❑ 179 Jerome McDougle RC	6.00	2.50
❑ 180 Calvin Pace RC	3.00	1.25
❑ 181 Tyler Brayton RC	6.00	2.50
❑ 182 Chris Kelsay RC	6.00	2.50
❑ 183 DeWayne White RC	5.00	2.00
❑ 184 E.J. Henderson RC	6.00	2.50
❑ 185 Charles Rogers RC	6.00	2.50
❑ 186 Terry Pierce RC	5.00	2.00
❑ 187 Nick Barnett RC	6.00	2.50
❑ 188 Boss Bailey RC	6.00	2.50
❑ 189 Pisa Tinoisamoa RC	6.00	2.50
❑ 190 Chaun Thompson RC	3.00	1.25
❑ 191 Andre Woolfolk RC	6.00	2.50
❑ 192 Sammy Davis RC	6.00	2.50
❑ 193 Eugene Wilson RC	6.00	2.50
❑ 194 Drayton Florence RC	3.00	1.25
❑ 195 Ricky Manning RC	6.00	2.50
❑ 196 Donald Strickland RC	3.00	1.25
❑ 197 Dennis Weathersby RC	3.00	1.25
❑ 198 Troy Polamalu RC	25.00	12.50
❑ 199 Ken Hamlin RC	6.00	2.50
❑ 200 Mike Doss RC	6.00	2.50
❑ 201 Carson Palmer JSY RC	30.00	12.50
❑ 202 Byron Leftwich JSY RC	25.00	10.00
❑ 203 Kyle Boller JSY RC	8.00	3.00
❑ 204 Rex Grossman JSY RC	25.00	10.00
❑ 205 Andre Johnson JSY RC	15.00	6.00
❑ 206 Bryant Johnson JSY RC	8.00	3.00
❑ 207 Larry Johnson JSY RC	30.00	15.00
❑ 208 Taylor Jacobs JSY RC	6.00	2.50
❑ 209 Bethel Johnson JSY RC	8.00	3.00
❑ 210 Anquan Boldin JSY RC	20.00	7.50
❑ 211 Tyrone Calico JSY RC	8.00	3.00
❑ 212 Teyo Johnson JSY RC	8.00	3.00
❑ 213 Kelley Washington JSY RC	8.00	3.00
❑ 214 Musa Smith JSY RC	8.00	3.00
❑ 215 Chris Brown JSY RC	8.00	3.00
❑ 216 Justin Fargas JSY RC	8.00	3.00

❑ 217 Artose Pinner JSY RC 8.00 3.00
❑ 218 Onterrio Smith JSY RC 8.00 3.00
❑ 219 Brian St.Pierre JSY RC 8.00 3.00
❑ 220 Dave Ragone JSY RC 8.00 3.00
❑ 221 Dallas Clark JSY RC 8.00 3.00
❑ 222 Seneca Wallace JSY RC 8.00 3.00
❑ 223 Terrell Suggs JSY RC 12.00 5.00
❑ 224 Terence Newman JSY RC 15.00 6.00
❑ 225 DeWayne Robertson JSY RC 8.003.00
❑ 226 Marcus Trufant JSY RC 8.00 3.00
❑ 227 Kliff Kingsbury JSY RC 6.00 2.50
❑ 228 Kevin Curtis JSY RC 8.00 3.00
❑ 229 Willis McGahee JSY RC 20.00 7.50
❑ 230 Nate Burleson JSY RC 8.00 3.00

2004 Playoff Hogg Heaven

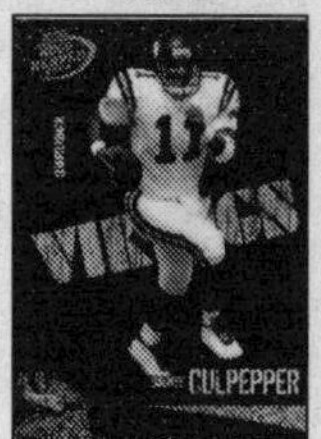

❑ COMP.SET w/o SP's (100) 30.00 12.50
❑ 151-180 RPH RC PRINT RUN 750 SER.#'d SETS
❑ 1 Anquan Boldin 1.00 .40
❑ 2 Emmitt Smith 2.00 .75
❑ 3 Josh McCown .60 .25
❑ 4 Michael Vick 2.00 .75
❑ 5 Peerless Price .60 .25
❑ 6 T.J. Duckett .60 .25
❑ 7 Jamal Lewis 1.00 .40
❑ 8 Kyle Boller 1.00 .40
❑ 9 Ray Lewis 1.00 .40
❑ 10 Terrell Owens 1.00 .40
❑ 11 Drew Bledsoe 1.00 .40
❑ 12 Eric Moulds .60 .25
❑ 13 Travis Henry .60 .25
❑ 14 Jake Delhomme 1.00 .40
❑ 15 Stephen Davis .60 .25
❑ 16 Steve Smith 1.00 .40
❑ 17 Anthony Thomas .60 .25
❑ 18 Brian Urlacher 1.25 .50
❑ 19 Rex Grossman 1.00 .40
❑ 20 Carson Palmer 1.25 .50
❑ 21 Chad Johnson 1.00 .40
❑ 22 Peter Warrick .60 .25
❑ 23 Rudi Johnson .60 .25
❑ 24 Andre Davis .40 .15
❑ 25 Lee Suggs 1.00 .40
❑ 26 Keyshawn Johnson .60 .25
❑ 27 Quincy Carter .60 .25
❑ 28 Roy Williams S .60 .25
❑ 29 Ashley Lelie .60 .25
❑ 30 Jake Plummer .60 .25
❑ 31 Rod Smith .60 .25
❑ 32 Charles Rogers .60 .25
❑ 33 Joey Harrington 1.00 .40
❑ 34 Ahman Green 1.00 .40
❑ 35 Brett Favre 2.50 1.00
❑ 36 Javon Walker .60 .25
❑ 37 Andre Johnson 1.00 .40
❑ 38 David Carr 1.00 .40
❑ 39 Domanick Davis 1.00 .40
❑ 40 Edgerrin James 1.00 .40
❑ 41 Marvin Harrison 1.00 .40
❑ 42 Peyton Manning 1.50 .60
❑ 43 Reggie Wayne .60 .25
❑ 44 Byron Leftwich 1.25 .50
❑ 45 Fred Taylor .60 .25
❑ 46 Jimmy Smith .60 .25
❑ 47 Priest Holmes 1.25 .50
❑ 48 Tony Gonzalez .60 .25
❑ 49 Trent Green .60 .25
❑ 50 A.J. Feeley 1.00 .40
❑ 51 Chris Chambers .60 .25
❑ 52 Ricky Williams 1.00 .40
❑ 53 Zach Thomas 1.00 .40
❑ 54 Daunte Culpepper 1.00 .40
❑ 55 Michael Bennett .60 .25
❑ 56 Randy Moss 1.25 .50
❑ 57 Deion Branch 1.00 .40
❑ 58 Tom Brady 2.50 1.00
❑ 59 Ty Law .60 .25
❑ 60 Aaron Brooks .60 .25
❑ 61 Deuce McAllister 1.00 .40
❑ 62 Joe Horn .60 .25
❑ 63 Jeremy Shockey 1.00 .40
❑ 64 Kerry Collins .60 .25
❑ 65 Michael Strahan .60 .25
❑ 66 Tiki Barber 1.00 .40
❑ 67 Chad Pennington 1.00 .40
❑ 68 Curtis Martin 1.00 .40
❑ 69 Santana Moss .60 .25
❑ 70 Jerry Rice 2.00 .75
❑ 71 Rich Gannon .60 .25
❑ 72 Tim Brown 1.00 .40
❑ 73 Brian Westbrook .60 .25
❑ 74 Donovan McNabb 1.25 .50
❑ 75 Jevon Kearse .60 .25
❑ 76 Hines Ward 1.00 .40
❑ 77 Jerome Bettis 1.00 .40
❑ 78 Kendrell Bell .60 .25
❑ 79 David Boston .60 .25
❑ 80 Drew Brees 1.00 .40
❑ 81 LaDainian Tomlinson 1.25 .50
❑ 82 Jeff Garcia 1.00 .40
❑ 83 Kevan Barlow .60 .25
❑ 84 Tim Rattay .40 .15
❑ 85 Koren Robinson .60 .25
❑ 86 Matt Hasselbeck .60 .25
❑ 87 Shaun Alexander 1.00 .40
❑ 88 Isaac Bruce .60 .25
❑ 89 Marc Bulger 1.00 .40
❑ 90 Marshall Faulk 1.00 .40
❑ 91 Torry Holt 1.00 .40
❑ 92 Brad Johnson .60 .25
❑ 93 Keenan McCardell .40 .15
❑ 94 Warren Sapp .60 .25
❑ 95 Derrick Mason .60 .25
❑ 96 Steve McNair 1.00 .40
❑ 97 Eddie George .60 .25
❑ 98 Clinton Portis 1.00 .40
❑ 99 Laveranues Coles .60 .25
❑ 100 Mark Brunell .60 .25
❑ 101 Adimchinobe Echemandu RC 5.002.00
❑ 102 Ahmad Carroll RC 6.00 2.50
❑ 103 Andy Hall RC 5.00 2.00
❑ 104 B.J. Symons RC 6.00 2.50
❑ 105 Bradlee Van Pelt RC 6.00 2.50
❑ 106 Brandon Miree RC 5.00 2.00
❑ 107 Bruce Perry RC 6.00 2.50
❑ 108 Carlos Francis RC 5.00 2.00
❑ 109 Casey Bramlet RC 5.00 2.00
❑ 110 Chris Gamble RC 6.00 2.50
❑ 111 Clarence Moore RC 6.00 2.50
❑ 112 Cody Pickett RC 6.00 2.50
❑ 113 Craig Krenzel RC 6.00 2.50
❑ 114 D.J. Hackett RC 5.00 2.00
❑ 115 D.J. Williams RC 6.00 2.50
❑ 116 Derrick Ward RC 3.00 1.25
❑ 117 Drew Carter RC 6.00 2.50
❑ 118 Ernest Wilford RC 6.00 2.50
❑ 119 Drew Henson RC 6.00 2.50
❑ 120 Jamaar Taylor RC 6.00 2.50
❑ 121 Jared Lorenzen RC 5.00 2.00
❑ 122 Jarrett Payton RC 6.00 2.50
❑ 123 Jason Babin RC 6.00 2.50
❑ 124 Jeff Smoker RC 6.00 2.50
❑ 125 Jeris McIntyre RC 5.00 2.00
❑ 126 Jerricho Cotchery RC 6.00 2.50
❑ 127 Jim Sorgi RC 6.00 2.50
❑ 128 John Navarre RC 6.00 2.50
❑ 129 Johnnie Morant RC 6.00 2.50
❑ 130 Sean Taylor RC 6.00 2.50
❑ 131 Jonathan Vilma RC 6.00 2.50
❑ 132 Josh Harris RC 6.00 2.50
❑ 133 Kenechi Udeze RC 6.00 2.50
❑ 134 Marcus Tubbs RC 6.00 2.50
❑ 135 Mark Jones RC 5.00 2.00
❑ 136 Matt Mauck RC 6.00 2.50
❑ 137 Maurice Mann RC 5.00 2.00
❑ 138 Michael Turner RC 8.00 3.00
❑ 139 P.K. Sam RC 5.00 2.00
❑ 140 Patrick Crayton RC 6.00 2.50
❑ 141 Quincy Wilson RC 5.00 2.00
❑ 142 Ran Carthon RC 5.00 2.00
❑ 143 Ryan Krause RC 5.00 2.00
❑ 144 Samie Parker RC 6.00 2.50
❑ 145 Sloan Thomas RC 5.00 2.00
❑ 146 Tommie Harris RC 6.00 2.50
❑ 147 Triandos Luke RC 6.00 2.50
❑ 148 Troy Fleming RC 5.00 2.00
❑ 149 Vince Wilfork RC 6.00 2.50
❑ 150 Will Smith RC 6.00 2.50
❑ 151 Larry Fitzgerald RPH RC 20.00 7.50
❑ 152 DeAngelo Hall RPH RC 8.00 3.00
❑ 153 Matt Schaub RPH RC 20.00 7.50
❑ 154 Michael Jenkins RPH RC 6.00 2.50
❑ 155 Devard Darling RPH RC 6.00 2.50
❑ 156 J.P. Losman RPH RC 12.00 5.00
❑ 157 Lee Evans RPH RC 8.00 3.00
❑ 158 Keary Colbert RPH RC 8.00 3.00
❑ 159 Bernard Berrian RPH RC 10.00 4.00
❑ 160 Chris Perry RPH RC 10.00 4.00
❑ 161 Kellen Winslow RPH RC 12.00 5.00
❑ 162 Luke McCown RPH RC 6.00 2.50
❑ 163 Julius Jones RPH RC 20.00 7.50
❑ 164 Darius Watts RPH RC 6.00 2.50
❑ 165 Tatum Bell RPH RC 12.00 5.00
❑ 166 Kevin Jones RPH RC 15.00 6.00
❑ 167 Roy Williams RPH RC 15.00 6.00
❑ 168 Greg Jones RPH RC 6.00 2.50
❑ 169 Reggie Williams RPH RC 8.00 3.00
❑ 170 Ben Watson RPH RC 6.00 2.50
❑ 171 Cedric Cobbs RPH RC 6.00 2.50
❑ 172 D.Henderson RPH RC 5.00 2.00
❑ 173 Eli Manning RPH RC 30.00 15.00
❑ 174 Roethlisberger RPH RC 50.00 25.00
❑ 175 Philip Rivers RPH RC 20.00 10.00
❑ 176 Derrick Hamilton RPH RC 5.00 2.00
❑ 177 Rashaun Woods RPH RC 6.00 2.50
❑ 178 Steven Jackson RPH RC 20.00 7.50
❑ 179 Michael Clayton RPH RC 12.00 5.00
❑ 180 Ben Troupe RPH RC 6.00 2.50

2001 Playoff Honors

❑ COMP.SET w/o SP's (100) 25.00 10.00
❑ 1 Rob Johnson .60 .25
❑ 2 Eric Moulds .60 .25
❑ 3 Marvin Harrison 1.00 .40
❑ 4 Edgerrin James 1.25 .50
❑ 5 Peyton Manning 2.50 1.00
❑ 6 Jay Fiedler 1.00 .40
❑ 7 Lamar Smith .60 .25
❑ 8 Zach Thomas 1.00 .40
❑ 9 Dan Marino 3.00 1.25
❑ 10 Drew Bledsoe 1.25 .50
❑ 11 Terry Glenn .60 .25
❑ 12 Wayne Chrebet .60 .25
❑ 13 Curtis Martin 1.00 .40
❑ 14 Chad Pennington 1.50 .60
❑ 15 Vinny Testaverde .60 .25
❑ 16 Corey Dillon 1.00 .40
❑ 17 Jon Kitna 1.00 .40
❑ 18 Akili Smith .40 .15
❑ 19 Peter Warrick 1.00 .40
❑ 20 Kevin Johnson .60 .25
❑ 21 Tim Couch .60 .25
❑ 22 Eddie George 1.00 .40

❑ 23 Steve McNair 1.00 .40
❑ 24 Jevon Kearse .60 .25
❑ 25 Jerome Bettis 1.00 .40
❑ 26 Kordell Stewart .60 .25
❑ 27 Plaxico Burress 1.00 .40
❑ 28 Mark Brunell 1.00 .40
❑ 29 Keenan McCardell .40 .15
❑ 30 Jimmy Smith .60 .25
❑ 31 Fred Taylor 1.00 .40
❑ 32 Elvis Grbac .60 .25
❑ 33 Jamal Lewis 1.50 .60
❑ 34 Ray Lewis 1.00 .40
❑ 35 Mike Anderson 1.00 .40
❑ 36 Terrell Davis 1.00 .40
❑ 37 John Elway 3.00 1.25
❑ 38 Brian Griese 1.00 .40
❑ 39 Ed McCaffrey 1.00 .40
❑ 40 Tony Gonzalez .60 .25
❑ 41 Trent Green 1.00 .40
❑ 42 Sylvester Morris .40 .15
❑ 43 Tim Brown 1.00 .40
❑ 44 Rich Gannon 1.00 .40
❑ 45 Charlie Garner .60 .25
❑ 46 Tyrone Wheatley .60 .25
❑ 47 Charles Woodson .60 .25
❑ 48 Tim Dwight 1.00 .40
❑ 49 Doug Flutie 1.00 .40
❑ 50 Junior Seau 1.00 .40
❑ 51 Shaun Alexander 1.25 .50
❑ 52 Matt Hasselbeck .60 .25
❑ 53 Ricky Watters .60 .25
❑ 54 Tony Banks .60 .25
❑ 55 Joey Galloway .60 .25
❑ 56 Emmitt Smith 2.00 .75
❑ 57 Troy Aikman 1.50 .60
❑ 58 Kerry Collins .60 .25
❑ 59 Ron Dayne 1.00 .40
❑ 60 Donovan McNabb 1.25 .50
❑ 61 Duce Staley 1.00 .40
❑ 62 David Boston 1.00 .40
❑ 63 Thomas Jones .60 .25
❑ 64 Jake Plummer .60 .25
❑ 65 Stephen Davis 1.00 .40
❑ 66 Jeff George .60 .25
❑ 67 Michael Westbrook .60 .25
❑ 68 Deion Sanders 1.00 .40
❑ 69 James Allen .60 .25
❑ 70 Cade McNown .40 .15
❑ 71 Marcus Robinson 1.00 .40
❑ 72 Brian Urlacher 1.50 .60
❑ 73 Germane Crowell .40 .15
❑ 74 Charlie Batch 1.00 .40
❑ 75 James Stewart .60 .25
❑ 76 Brett Favre 3.00 1.25
❑ 77 Antonio Freeman 1.00 .40
❑ 78 Ahman Green 1.00 .40
❑ 79 Cris Carter 1.00 .40
❑ 80 Daunte Culpepper 1.00 .40
❑ 81 Randy Moss 2.00 .75
❑ 82 Mike Alstott 1.00 .40
❑ 83 Warrick Dunn 1.00 .40
❑ 84 Brad Johnson 1.00 .40
❑ 85 Keyshawn Johnson 1.00 .40
❑ 86 Warren Sapp .60 .25
❑ 87 Jamal Anderson 1.00 .40
❑ 88 Chris Chandler .60 .25
❑ 89 Isaac Bruce 1.00 .40
❑ 90 Marshall Faulk 1.25 .50
❑ 91 Torry Holt 1.00 .40
❑ 92 Kurt Warner 2.00 .75
❑ 93 Aaron Brooks 1.00 .40
❑ 94 Albert Connell .40 .15
❑ 95 Ricky Williams 1.00 .40
❑ 96 Jeff Garcia 1.00 .40
❑ 97 Terrell Owens 1.00 .40
❑ 98 Steve Young 1.00 .40
❑ 99 Jerry Rice 2.00 .75
❑ 100 Jeff Lewis .40 .15
❑ 101 Rashard Casey RC 6.00 2.50
❑ 102 A.J. Feeley RC 10.00 4.00
❑ 103 Josh Booty RC 10.00 4.00
❑ 104 LaMont Jordan RC 20.00 7.50
❑ 105 Ben Leard RC 6.00 2.50
❑ 106 David Rivers RC 6.00 2.50
❑ 107 Tim Hasselbeck RC 10.00 4.00
❑ 108 Jason McKinley RC 6.00 2.50
❑ 109 Correll Buckhalter RC 12.00 5.00
❑ 110 Dan Alexander RC 10.00 4.00
❑ 111 Derrick Blaylock RC 10.00 4.00
❑ 112 Chris Barnes RC 6.00 2.50
❑ 113 Dee Brown RC 10.00 4.00
❑ 114 Derek Combs RC 6.00 2.50
❑ 115 David Allen RC 6.00 2.50
❑ 116 DeAngelo Evans RC 6.00 2.50
❑ 117 Reggie White RC 6.00 2.50
❑ 118 Heath Evans RC 6.00 2.50
❑ 119 George Layne RC 6.00 2.50
❑ 120 Moran Norris RC 4.00 1.50
❑ 121 Bhawoh Jue RC 10.00 4.00
❑ 122 Dustin McClintock RC 6.00 2.50
❑ 123 Ja'Mar Toombs RC 6.00 2.50
❑ 124 Steve Smith RC 25.00 12.50
❑ 125 Milton Wynn RC 6.00 2.50
❑ 126 Justin McCareins RC 10.00 4.00
❑ 127 Jarrod Cooper RC 10.00 4.00
❑ 128 Vinny Sutherland RC 6.00 2.50
❑ 129 Alex Bannister RC 6.00 2.50
❑ 130 Scotty Anderson RC 6.00 2.50
❑ 131 Onome Ojo RC 6.00 2.50
❑ 132 Damerien McCants RC 6.00 2.50
❑ 133 Eddie Berlin RC 6.00 2.50
❑ 134 Jonathan Carter RC 6.00 2.50
❑ 135 Bobby Newcombe RC 10.00 4.00
❑ 136 Cedrick Wilson RC 10.00 4.00
❑ 137 Kevin Kasper RC 10.00 4.00
❑ 138 Francis St. Paul RC 6.00 2.50
❑ 139 David Martin RC 6.00 2.50
❑ 140 T.J. Houshmandzadeh RC 12.00 5.00
❑ 141 John Capel RC 6.00 2.50
❑ 142 Reggie Germany RC 6.00 2.50
❑ 143 Chris Taylor RC 6.00 2.50
❑ 144 Ken-Yon Rambo RC 6.00 2.50
❑ 145 Richmond Flowers RC 6.00 2.50
❑ 146 Quentin McCord RC 6.00 2.50
❑ 147 Andre King RC 6.00 2.50
❑ 148 Boo Williams RC 6.00 2.50
❑ 149 Daniel Guy RC 4.00 1.50
❑ 150 Javon Green RC 6.00 2.50
❑ 151 Ronney Daniels RC 4.00 1.50
❑ 152 Alge Crumpler RC 12.00 6.00
❑ 153 Tony Driver RC 6.00 2.50
❑ 154 Shad Meier RC 6.00 2.50
❑ 155 Jabari Holloway RC 6.00 2.50
❑ 156 Ryan Pickett RC 4.00 1.50
❑ 157 Cedric James RC 6.00 2.50
❑ 158 Tony Stewart RC 10.00 4.00
❑ 159 Sean Brewer RC 4.00 1.50
❑ 160 Orlando Huff RC 4.00 1.50
❑ 161 Nate Clements RC 10.00 4.00
❑ 162 Will Allen RC 6.00 2.50
❑ 163 Willie Middlebrooks RC 6.00 2.50
❑ 164 Jamar Fletcher RC 6.00 2.50
❑ 165 Ken Lucas RC 6.00 2.50
❑ 166 Fred Smoot RC 10.00 4.00
❑ 167 Michael Stone RC 4.00 1.50
❑ 168 Tony Dixon RC 6.00 2.50
❑ 169 Andre Dyson RC 4.00 1.50
❑ 170 Gary Baxter RC 6.00 2.50
❑ 171 Adam Archuleta RC 10.00 4.00
❑ 172 Derrick Gibson RC 6.00 2.50
❑ 173 Edgerton Hartwell RC 4.00 1.50
❑ 174 Jamal Reynolds RC 10.00 4.00
❑ 175 Richard Seymour RC 10.00 4.00
❑ 176 Brandon Manumaleuna RC 6.00 2.50
❑ 177 Idrees Bashir RC 4.00 1.50
❑ 178 DeLawrence Grant RC 4.00 1.50
❑ 179 Karon Riley RC 4.00 1.50
❑ 180 Cedric Scott RC 6.00 2.50
❑ 181 Damione Lewis RC 6.00 2.50
❑ 182 Marcus Stroud RC 10.00 4.00
❑ 183 Casey Hampton RC 10.00 4.00
❑ 184 Willie Howard RC 6.00 2.50
❑ 185 Shaun Rogers RC 10.00 4.00
❑ 186 Kenny Smith RC 6.00 2.50
❑ 187 Marcus Bell DT RC 6.00 2.50
❑ 188 Mario Fatafehi RC 6.00 2.50
❑ 189 Kendrell Bell RC 12.00 5.00
❑ 190 Tommy Polley RC 10.00 4.00
❑ 191 Jamie Winborn RC 6.00 2.50
❑ 192 Sedrick Hodge RC 4.00 1.50
❑ 193 Torrance Marshall RC 10.00 4.00
❑ 194 Eric Westmoreland RC 6.00 2.50
❑ 195 Brian Allen RC 4.00 1.50
❑ 196 Morlon Greenwood RC 6.00 2.50
❑ 197 Brandon Spoon RC 10.00 4.00
❑ 198 Carlos Polk RC 4.00 1.50
❑ 199 Alex Lincoln RC 6.00 2.50
❑ 200 Keith Adams RC 4.00 1.50
❑ 201 Kevan Barlow JSY RC 10.00 4.00
❑ 202 Michael Bennett JSY RC 10.00 4.00
❑ 203 Drew Brees JSY RC 30.00 12.00
❑ 204 Quincy Carter JSY RC 10.00 4.00
❑ 205 Andre Carter JSY RC 10.00 4.00
❑ 206 Chris Chambers JSY RC 15.00 6.00
❑ 207 Robert Ferguson JSY RC 10.00 4.00
❑ 208 Rod Gardner JSY RC 10.00 4.00
❑ 210 Travis Henry JSY RC 15.00 6.00
❑ 212 Chad Johnson JSY RC 25.00 10.00
❑ 213 Rudi Johnson JSY RC 20.00 7.50
❑ 214 Sage Rosenfels JSY RC 10.00 4.00
❑ 215 Deuce McAllister JSY RC 20.00 7.50
❑ 216 Mike McMahon JSY RC 10.00 4.00
❑ 217 Snoop Minnis JSY RC 6.00 2.50
❑ 218 Travis Minor JSY RC 6.00 2.50
❑ 219 Freddie Mitchell JSY RC 10.00 4.00
❑ 220 Quincy Morgan JSY RC 10.00 4.00
❑ 222 Santana Moss JSY RC 15.00 6.00
❑ 223 Jesse Palmer JSY RC 10.00 4.00
❑ 224 Koren Robinson JSY RC 10.00 4.00
❑ 225 Josh Heupel JSY RC 10.00 4.00
❑ 226 Justin Smith JSY RC 10.00 4.00
❑ 227 David Terrell JSY RC 10.00 4.00
❑ 228 Anthony Thomas JSY RC 10.00 4.00
❑ 229 LaDainian Tomlinson JSY RC 60.00 35.00
❑ 230 Marques Tuiasosopo JSY RC 10.00 4.00
❑ 231 Michael Vick JSY RC 40.00 15.00
❑ 232 Gerard Warren JSY RC 10.00 4.00
❑ 233 Reggie Wayne JSY RC 20.00 7.50
❑ 234 Chris Weinke JSY RC 10.00 4.00
❑ 235 Leonard Davis JSY RC 6.00 2.50

2002 Playoff Honors

❑ COMP.SET w/o SP's (100) 25.00 10.00
❑ 1 David Boston 1.00 .40
❑ 2 Jake Plummer .60 .25
❑ 3 Warrick Dunn 1.00 .40
❑ 4 Michael Vick 3.00 1.25
❑ 5 Jamal Lewis 1.00 .40
❑ 6 Chris Redman .40 .15
❑ 7 Ray Lewis 1.00 .40
❑ 8 Drew Bledsoe 1.25 .50
❑ 9 Travis Henry 1.00 .40
❑ 10 Eric Moulds .60 .25
❑ 11 Lamar Smith .60 .25
❑ 12 Steve Smith 1.00 .40
❑ 13 Chris Weinke .60 .25
❑ 14 Chris Chandler .60 .25
❑ 15 David Terrell 1.00 .40
❑ 16 Anthony Thomas .60 .25
❑ 17 Brian Urlacher 1.50 .60
❑ 18 Corey Dillon .60 .25
❑ 19 Peter Warrick .60 .25
❑ 20 Tim Couch .60 .25
❑ 21 James Jackson .40 .15
❑ 22 Kevin Johnson .60 .25
❑ 23 Quincy Carter .60 .25
❑ 24 Joey Galloway .60 .25
❑ 25 Emmitt Smith 2.50 1.00
❑ 26 Terrell Davis 1.00 .40
❑ 27 Brian Griese 1.00 .40
❑ 28 Rod Smith .60 .25
❑ 29 Germane Crowell .40 .15
❑ 30 Az-Zahir Hakim .40 .15

#	Card	Hi	Lo
31	Mike McMahon	1.00	.40
32	Brett Favre	2.50	1.00
33	Terry Glenn	.60	.25
34	Ahman Green	1.00	.40
35	James Allen	.60	.25
36	Corey Bradford	.40	.15
37	Marvin Harrison	1.00	.40
38	Peyton Manning	2.00	.75
39	Edgerrin James	1.25	.50
40	Reggie Wayne	1.00	.40
41	Mark Brunell	1.00	.40
42	Fred Taylor	1.00	.40
43	Jimmy Smith	.60	.25
44	Tony Gonzalez	.60	.25
45	Trent Green	.60	.25
46	Priest Holmes	1.25	.50
47	Snoop Minnis	.40	.15
48	Chris Chambers	1.00	.40
49	Jay Fiedler	.60	.25
50	Ricky Williams	1.00	.40
51	Zach Thomas	1.00	.40
52	Randy Moss	2.00	.75
53	Daunte Culpepper	1.00	.40
54	Michael Bennett	.60	.25
55	Tom Brady	2.50	1.00
56	Troy Brown	.60	.25
57	Antowain Smith	.60	.25
58	Aaron Brooks	1.00	.40
59	Deuce McAllister	1.00	.40
60	Tiki Barber	1.00	.40
61	Kerry Collins	.60	.25
62	Amani Toomer	.60	.25
63	Michael Strahan	.60	.25
64	Curtis Martin	1.00	.40
65	Vinny Testaverde	.60	.25
66	Chad Pennington	1.25	.50
67	Laveranues Coles	.60	.25
68	Tim Brown	1.00	.40
69	Rich Gannon	1.00	.40
70	Jerry Rice	2.00	.75
71	Donovan McNabb	1.25	.50
72	Freddie Mitchell	.60	.25
73	Duce Staley	1.00	.40
74	Jerome Bettis	1.00	.40
75	Plaxico Burress	.60	.25
76	Kordell Stewart	.60	.25
77	Drew Brees	1.00	.40
78	Doug Flutie	1.00	.40
79	LaDainian Tomlinson	1.50	.60
80	Jeff Garcia	1.00	.40
81	Garrison Hearst	.60	.25
82	Terrell Owens	1.00	.40
83	Shaun Alexander	1.25	.50
84	Trent Dilfer	.60	.25
85	Koren Robinson	.60	.25
86	Isaac Bruce	1.00	.40
87	Marshall Faulk	1.00	.40
88	Torry Holt	1.00	.40
89	Kurt Warner	1.00	.40
90	Mike Alstott	1.00	.40
91	Brad Johnson	.60	.25
92	Keyshawn Johnson	1.00	.40
93	Keenan McCardell	.40	.15
94	Steve McNair	1.00	.40
95	Eddie George	1.00	.40
96	Jevon Kearse	.60	.25
97	Derrick Mason	.60	.25
98	Stephen Davis	.60	.25
99	Sage Rosenfels	.40	.15
100	Rod Gardner	.60	.25
101	Randy Fasani RC	5.00	2.00
102	Kurt Kittner RC	5.00	2.00
103	Brandon Doman RC	5.00	2.00
104	Craig Nall RC	6.00	2.50
105	J.T. O'Sullivan RC	5.00	2.00
106	Seth Burford RC	5.00	2.00
107	Jeff Kelly RC	5.00	2.00
108	Ronald Curry RC	6.00	2.50
109	Wes Pate RC	3.00	1.25
110	Chad Hutchinson RC	5.00	2.00
111	Major Applewhite RC	6.00	2.50
112	Preston Parsons RC	3.00	1.25
113	David Priestley RC	5.00	2.00
114	Lamar Gordon RC	6.00	2.50
115	Brian Westbrook RC	10.00	4.00
116	Jonathan Wells RC	6.00	2.50
117	Omar Easy RC	6.00	2.50
118	Verron Haynes RC	6.00	2.50
119	Josh Scobey RC	6.00	2.50
120	Larry Ned RC	5.00	2.00
121	Adrian Peterson RC	6.00	2.50
122	Brian Allen RC	5.00	2.00
123	Chester Taylor RC	12.00	5.00
124	Luke Staley RC	5.00	2.00
125	Antwoine Womack RC	5.00	2.00
126	Leonard Henry RC	5.00	2.00
127	Jesse Chatman RC	6.00	2.50
128	Damien Anderson RC	5.00	2.00
129	Eric McCoo RC	3.00	1.25
130	Tellis Redmon RC	5.00	2.00
131	Joe Burns RC	5.00	2.00
132	Delvon Flowers RC	5.00	2.00
133	Ken Simonton RC	3.00	1.25
134	Ricky Williams RC	5.00	2.00
135	Dicenzo Miller RC	3.00	1.25
136	James Mungro RC	6.00	2.50
137	Randy McMichael RC	10.00	4.00
138	Deion Branch RC	12.00	5.00
139	Terry Charles RC	5.00	2.00
140	Herb Haygood RC	3.00	1.25
141	Jason McAddley RC	5.00	2.00
142	Jake Schifino RC	5.00	2.00
143	Freddie Milons RC	5.00	2.00
144	Kahlil Hill RC	5.00	2.00
145	Lamont Brightful RC	3.00	1.25
146	Chris Luzar RC	5.00	2.00
147	Daryl Jones RC	5.00	2.00
148	Woody Dantzler RC	5.00	2.00
149	Kelly Campbell RC	5.00	2.00
150	Brian Poli-Dixon RC	5.00	2.00
151	Atrews Bell RC	3.00	1.25
152	Jarrod Baxter RC	5.00	2.00
153	Eddie Drummond RC	5.00	2.00
154	Jerramy Stevens RC	6.00	2.50
155	Doug Jolley RC	6.00	2.50
156	Jamar Martin RC	5.00	2.00
157	Najeh Davenport RC	6.00	2.50
158	Dwight Freeney RC	10.00	4.00
159	Bryan Thomas RC	5.00	2.00
160	Charles Grant RC	6.00	2.50
161	Kalimba Edwards RC	6.00	2.50
162	Ryan Denney RC	5.00	2.00
163	Will Overstreet RC	3.00	1.25
164	Dennis Johnson RC	3.00	1.25
165	Alex Brown RC	6.00	2.50
166	Kenyon Coleman RC	3.00	1.25
167	Ryan Sims RC	6.00	2.50
168	John Henderson RC	6.00	2.50
169	Wendell Bryant RC	3.00	1.25
170	Albert Haynesworth RC	5.00	2.00
171	Larry Tripplett RC	3.00	1.25
172	Eddie Freeman RC	3.00	1.25
173	Anthony Weaver RC	5.00	2.00
174	Quentin Jammer RC	6.00	2.50
175	Phillip Buchanon RC	6.00	2.50
176	Lito Sheppard RC	6.00	2.50
177	Mike Rumph RC	5.00	2.00
178	Roosevelt Williams RC	3.00	1.25
179	Derek Ross RC	5.00	2.00
180	Mike Echols RC	3.00	1.25
181	Keyou Craver RC	5.00	2.00
182	Ed Reed RC	10.00	4.00
183	Lamont Thompson RC	5.00	2.00
184	Tank Williams RC	5.00	2.00
185	Michael Lewis RC	6.00	2.50
186	Napoleon Harris RC	6.00	2.50
187	Robert Thomas RC	6.00	2.50
188	Raonall Smith RC	5.00	2.00
189	Levar Fisher RC	3.00	1.25
190	Rocky Calmus RC	6.00	2.50
191	Andra Davis RC	5.00	2.00
192	Nick Rolovich RC	5.00	2.00
193	Zak Kustok RC	6.00	2.50
194	Dusty Bonner RC	3.00	1.25
195	Tony Fisher RC	6.00	2.50
196	Sam Simmons RC	3.00	1.25
197	Lee Mays RC	5.00	2.00
198	Jamin Elliott RC	3.00	1.25
199	Javin Hunter RC	3.00	1.25
200	Kendall Newson RC	3.00	1.25
201	Ladell Betts JSY RC	10.00	4.00
202	Antonio Bryant JSY RC	10.00	4.00
203	Reche Caldwell JSY RC	10.00	4.00
204	David Carr JSY RC	25.00	10.00
205	Tim Carter JSY RC	8.00	3.00
206	Eric Crouch JSY RC	10.00	4.00
207	Rohan Davey JSY RC	10.00	4.00
208	Andre Davis JSY RC	8.00	3.00
209	T.J. Duckett JSY RC	12.00	5.00
210	DeShaun Foster JSY RC	10.00	4.00
211	Jabar Gaffney JSY RC	10.00	4.00
212	David Garrard JSY RC	12.00	5.00
213	Daniel Graham JSY RC	10.00	4.00
214	William Green JSY RC	10.00	4.00
215	Joey Harrington JSY RC	15.00	6.00
216	Ron Johnson JSY RC	8.00	3.00
217	Ashley Lelie JSY RC	20.00	7.50
218	Josh McCown JSY RC	12.00	5.00
219	Maurice Morris JSY RC	10.00	4.00
220	Julius Peppers JSY RC	20.00	7.50
221	Clinton Portis JSY RC	30.00	12.50
222	Patrick Ramsey JSY RC	12.00	5.00
223	Antwaan Randle El JSY RC	15.00	6.00
224	Josh Reed JSY RC	10.00	4.00
225	Cliff Russell JSY RC	8.00	3.00
226	Jeremy Shockey JSY RC	30.00	12.50
227	Donte Stallworth JSY RC	20.00	7.50
228	Travis Stephens JSY RC	8.00	3.00
229	Javon Walker JSY RC	20.00	10.00
230	Marquise Walker JSY RC	8.00	3.00
231	Roy Williams JSY RC	25.00	12.50
232	Mike Williams JSY RC	8.00	3.00
RWH1	Payton/Smith JSY/250	120.00	50.00
RWH1A	Payton/Smith AUTO/22	400.00	200.00

2003 Playoff Honors

#	Card	Hi	Lo
	COMP.SET w/o SP's (100)	20.00	7.50
1	Aaron Brooks	1.00	.40
2	Ahman Green	1.00	.40
3	Amani Toomer	.60	.25
4	Anthony Thomas	.60	.25
5	Antonio Bryant	.60	.25
6	Antwaan Randle El	1.00	.40
7	Ashley Lelie	1.00	.40
8	Brad Johnson	.60	.25
9	Brett Favre	2.50	1.00
10	Brian Urlacher	1.50	.60
11	Bruce Smith	.60	.25
12	Chad Johnson	1.00	.40
13	Chad Pennington	1.25	.50
14	Charlie Garner	.60	.25
15	Chris Chambers	1.00	.40
16	Clinton Portis	1.50	.60
17	Corey Dillon	.60	.25
18	Curtis Martin	1.00	.40
19	Daunte Culpepper	1.00	.40
20	David Boston	.60	.25
21	David Carr	1.50	.60
22	Deuce McAllister	1.00	.40
23	Donald Driver	.60	.25
24	Donovan McNabb	1.25	.50
25	Donte Stallworth	1.00	.40
26	Drew Bledsoe	1.00	.40
27	Drew Brees	1.00	.40
28	Duce Staley	.60	.25
29	Ed McCaffrey	1.00	.40
30	Eddie George	.60	.25
31	Edgerrin James	1.00	.40
32	Emmitt Smith	2.50	1.00
33	Eric Moulds	.60	.25
34	Fred Taylor	1.00	.40
35	Garrison Hearst	.60	.25

❑ 36 Hines Ward 1.00 .40
❑ 37 Isaac Bruce 1.00 .40
❑ 38 Jabar Gaffney .60 .25
❑ 39 Jake Plummer .60 .25
❑ 40 Jamal Lewis 1.00 .40
❑ 41 Jay Fiedler .60 .25
❑ 42 Jeff Garcia 1.00 .40
❑ 43 Jeremy Shockey 1.50 .60
❑ 44 Jerome Bettis 1.00 .40
❑ 45 Jerry Porter .60 .25
❑ 46 Jerry Rice 2.00 .75
❑ 47 Jevon Kearse .60 .25
❑ 48 Jimmy Smith .60 .25
❑ 49 Joe Horn .60 .25
❑ 50 Joey Harrington 1.50 .60
❑ 51 Josh Reed .60 .25
❑ 52 Julius Peppers 1.00 .40
❑ 53 Kendrell Bell .60 .25
❑ 54 Kerry Collins .60 .25
❑ 55 Keyshawn Johnson 1.00 .40
❑ 56 Kordell Stewart .60 .25
❑ 57 Koren Robinson .60 .25
❑ 58 Kurt Warner 1.00 .40
❑ 59 LaDainian Tomlinson 1.00 .40
❑ 60 Laveranues Coles .60 .25
❑ 61 Mark Brunell .60 .25
❑ 62 Marshall Faulk 1.00 .40
❑ 63 Marvin Harrison 1.00 .40
❑ 64 Matt Hasselbeck .60 .25
❑ 65 Michael Bennett .60 .25
❑ 66 Michael Strahan .60 .25
❑ 67 Michael Vick 2.50 1.00
❑ 68 Mike Alstott 1.00 .40
❑ 69 Patrick Ramsey 1.00 .40
❑ 70 Peerless Price .60 .25
❑ 71 Peyton Manning 1.50 .60
❑ 72 Plaxico Burress .60 .25
❑ 73 Priest Holmes 1.25 .50
❑ 74 Randy Moss 1.50 .60
❑ 75 Ray Lewis 1.00 .40
❑ 76 Rich Gannon .60 .25
❑ 77 Ricky Williams 1.00 .40
❑ 78 Rod Gardner .60 .25
❑ 79 Rod Smith .60 .25
❑ 80 Roy Williams 1.00 .40
❑ 81 Shaun Alexander 1.00 .40
❑ 82 Stephen Davis .60 .25
❑ 83 Steve McNair 1.00 .40
❑ 84 T.J. Duckett .60 .25
❑ 85 Terrell Owens 1.00 .40
❑ 86 Tiki Barber 1.00 .40
❑ 87 Tim Brown 1.00 .40
❑ 88 Tim Couch .40 .15
❑ 89 Todd Heap .60 .25
❑ 90 Tom Brady 2.50 1.00
❑ 91 Tommy Maddox 1.00 .40
❑ 92 Tony Gonzalez .60 .25
❑ 93 Torry Holt 1.00 .40
❑ 94 Travis Henry .60 .25
❑ 95 Trent Green .60 .25
❑ 96 Troy Brown .60 .25
❑ 97 Warren Sapp .60 .25
❑ 98 Warrick Dunn .60 .25
❑ 99 William Green .60 .25
❑ 100 Zach Thomas 1.00 .40
❑ 101 Chris Simms RC 8.00 3.00
❑ 102 Brooks Bollinger RC 5.00 2.00
❑ 103 Gibran Hamdan RC 2.50 1.00
❑ 104 Ken Dorsey RC 5.00 2.00
❑ 105 Jason Gesser RC 5.00 2.00
❑ 106 Brad Banks RC 4.00 1.50
❑ 107 Tony Romo RC 50.00 25.00
❑ 108 B.J. Askew RC 5.00 2.00
❑ 109 Domanick Davis RC 5.00 2.00
❑ 110 Lee Suggs RC 5.00 2.00
❑ 111 LaBrandon Toefield RC 5.00 2.00
❑ 112 Brock Forsey RC 5.00 2.00
❑ 113 Malaefou MacKenzie RC 2.50 1.00
❑ 114 Andrew Pinnock RC 4.00 1.50
❑ 115 Ahmaad Galloway RC 4.00 1.50
❑ 116 Tony Hollings RC 5.00 2.00
❑ 117 Charles Rogers RC 5.00 2.00
❑ 118 Billy McMullen RC 4.00 1.50
❑ 119 Shaun McDonald RC 5.00 2.00
❑ 120 Brandon Lloyd RC 5.00 2.00
❑ 121 Sam Aiken RC 4.00 1.50
❑ 122 Bobby Wade RC 5.00 2.00
❑ 123 Justin Gage RC 5.00 2.00
❑ 124 Adrian Madise RC 4.00 1.50
❑ 125 Jon Olinger RC 2.50 1.00
❑ 126 Doug Gabriel RC 5.00 2.00
❑ 127 J.R. Tolver RC 4.00 1.50
❑ 128 David Kircus RC 5.00 2.00
❑ 129 Zuriel Smith RC 2.50 1.00
❑ 130 LaTarence Dunbar RC 4.00 1.50
❑ 131 Amaz Battle RC 5.00 2.00
❑ 132 Willie Ponder RC 2.50 1.00
❑ 133 Kareem Kelly RC 4.00 1.50
❑ 134 David Tyree RC 4.00 1.50
❑ 135 Keenan Howry RC 5.00 2.00
❑ 136 Taco Wallace RC 4.00 1.50
❑ 137 Walter Young RC 2.50 1.00
❑ 138 Talman Gardner RC 5.00 2.00
❑ 139 DeAndrew Rubin RC 2.50 1.00
❑ 140 Kevin Walter RC 4.00 1.50
❑ 141 Carl Ford RC 2.50 1.00
❑ 142 Travis Anglin RC 2.50 1.00
❑ 143 Ryan Hoag RC 2.50 1.00
❑ 144 Terrence Edwards RC 4.00 1.50
❑ 145 Bennie Joppru RC 5.00 2.00
❑ 146 L.J. Smith RC 5.00 2.00
❑ 147 Jason Witten RC 8.00 3.00
❑ 148 Andre Woolfolk RC 5.00 2.00
❑ 149 Nnamdi Asomugha RC 4.00 1.50
❑ 150 Troy Polamalu RC 25.00 12.50
❑ 151 Nate Hybl RC 10.00 4.00
❑ 152 Curt Anes RC 5.00 2.00
❑ 153 Avon Cobourne RC 5.00 2.00
❑ 154 Cecil Sapp RC 8.00 3.00
❑ 155 Casey Urlacher RC 10.00 4.00
❑ 156 Dwone Hicks RC 5.00 2.00
❑ 157 Jeremi Johnson RC 8.00 3.00
❑ 158 Kirk Farmer RC 8.00 3.00
❑ 159 James MacPherson RC 10.00 4.00
❑ 160 Chris Davis RC 8.00 3.00
❑ 161 Brandon Drumm RC 5.00 2.00
❑ 162 J.T. Wall RC 5.00 2.00
❑ 163 Casey Moore RC 8.00 3.00
❑ 164 Mike Seidman RC 5.00 2.00
❑ 165 Visanthe Shiancoe RC 8.00 3.00
❑ 166 George Wrighster RC 8.00 3.00
❑ 167 Dan Curley RC 5.00 2.00
❑ 168 Donald Lee RC 8.00 3.00
❑ 169 Aaron Walker RC 8.00 3.00
❑ 170 Trent Smith RC 5.00 2.00
❑ 171 Spencer Nead RC 8.00 3.00
❑ 172 Richard Angulo RC 8.00 3.00
❑ 173 Mike Pinkard RC 5.00 2.00
❑ 174 Johnathan Sullivan RC 8.00 3.00
❑ 175 Kevin Williams RC 10.00 4.00
❑ 176 Jimmy Kennedy RC 10.00 4.00
❑ 177 Ty Warren RC 10.00 4.00
❑ 178 William Joseph RC 10.00 4.00
❑ 179 Michael Haynes RC 10.00 4.00
❑ 180 Jerome McDougle RC 10.00 4.00
❑ 181 Calvin Pace RC 8.00 3.00
❑ 182 Tyler Brayton RC 10.00 4.00
❑ 183 Chris Kelsay RC 10.00 4.00
❑ 184 Osi Umenyiora RC 15.00 6.00
❑ 185 Alonzo Jackson RC 8.00 3.00
❑ 186 DeWayne White RC 8.00 3.00
❑ 187 Kenny Peterson RC 8.00 3.00
❑ 188 Nick Barnett RC 10.00 4.00
❑ 189 Boss Bailey RC 10.00 4.00
❑ 190 E.J. Henderson RC 10.00 4.00
❑ 191 Pisa Tinoisamoa RC 10.00 4.00
❑ 192 Sammy Davis RC 10.00 4.00
❑ 193 Charles Tillman RC 12.00 5.00
❑ 194 Eugene Wilson RC 10.00 4.00
❑ 195 Drayton Florence RC 5.00 2.00
❑ 196 Ricky Manning RC 10.00 4.00
❑ 197 Rashean Mathis RC 8.00 3.00
❑ 198 Ken Hamlin RC 10.00 4.00
❑ 199 Mike Doss RC 10.00 4.00
❑ 200 Julian Battle RC 8.00 3.00
❑ 201 Andre Johnson JSY RC 15.00 6.00
❑ 202 Anquan Boldin JSY RC 20.00 10.00
❑ 203 Artose Pinner JSY RC 8.00 3.00
❑ 204 Bethel Johnson JSY RC 8.00 3.00
❑ 205 Brian St.Pierre JSY RC 8.00 3.00
❑ 206 Bryant Johnson JSY RC 8.00 3.00
❑ 207 Byron Leftwich JSY RC 25.00 10.00
❑ 208 Carson Palmer JSY RC 30.00 12.50
❑ 209 Chris Brown JSY RC 8.00 3.00
❑ 210 Dallas Clark JSY RC 8.00 3.00
❑ 211 Dave Ragone JSY RC 8.00 3.00
❑ 212 DeWayne Robertson JSY RC 8.00 3.00
❑ 213 Justin Fargas JSY RC 8.00 3.00
❑ 214 Kelley Washington JSY RC 8.00 3.00
❑ 215 Kevin Curtis JSY RC 8.00 3.00
❑ 216 Kliff Kingsbury JSY RC 6.00 2.50
❑ 217 Kyle Boller JSY RC 8.00 3.00
❑ 218 Larry Johnson JSY RC 30.00 15.00
❑ 219 Marcus Trufant JSY RC 8.00 3.00
❑ 220 Musa Smith JSY RC 8.00 3.00
❑ 221 Nate Burleson JSY RC 8.00 3.00
❑ 222 Onterrio Smith JSY RC 8.00 3.00
❑ 223 Rex Grossman JSY RC 25.00 10.00
❑ 224 Seneca Wallace JSY RC 8.00 3.00
❑ 225 Taylor Jacobs JSY RC 6.00 2.50
❑ 226 Terrell Suggs JSY RC 12.00 5.00
❑ 227 Terence Newman JSY RC 15.00 6.00
❑ 228 Teyo Johnson JSY RC 8.00 3.00
❑ 229 Tyrone Calico JSY RC 8.00 3.00
❑ 230 Willis McGahee JSY RC 20.00 7.50

2004 Playoff Honors

❑ COMP.SET w/o SP's (100) 20.00 7.50
❑ 201-233 JSY RC PRINT RUN 750 #'d SETS
❑ 1 Anquan Boldin 1.00 .40
❑ 2 Emmitt Smith 2.00 .75
❑ 3 Josh McCown .60 .25
❑ 4 Michael Vick 2.00 .75
❑ 5 Peerless Price .60 .25
❑ 6 T.J. Duckett .60 .25
❑ 7 Warrick Dunn .60 .25
❑ 8 Jamal Lewis 1.00 .40
❑ 9 Kyle Boller 1.00 .40
❑ 10 Ray Lewis 1.00 .40
❑ 11 Drew Bledsoe 1.00 .40
❑ 12 Eric Moulds .60 .25
❑ 13 Travis Henry .60 .25
❑ 14 DeShaun Foster .60 .25
❑ 15 Jake Delhomme 1.00 .40
❑ 16 Steve Smith 1.00 .40
❑ 17 Stephen Davis .60 .25
❑ 18 Brian Urlacher 1.25 .50
❑ 19 Rex Grossman 1.00 .40
❑ 20 Thomas Jones .60 .25
❑ 21 Carson Palmer 1.25 .50
❑ 22 Chad Johnson 1.00 .40
❑ 23 Rudi Johnson .60 .25
❑ 24 Jeff Garcia 1.00 .40
❑ 25 Lee Suggs 1.00 .40
❑ 26 Keyshawn Johnson .60 .25
❑ 27 Quincy Carter .60 .25
❑ 28 Roy Williams S .60 .25
❑ 29 Jake Plummer .60 .25
❑ 30 Quentin Griffin 1.00 .40
❑ 31 Rod Smith .60 .25
❑ 32 Charles Rogers .60 .25
❑ 33 Joey Harrington 1.00 .40
❑ 34 Ahman Green 1.00 .40
❑ 35 Brett Favre 2.50 1.00
❑ 36 Javon Walker .60 .25
❑ 37 Andre Johnson 1.00 .40
❑ 38 David Carr 1.00 .40
❑ 39 Domanick Davis 1.00 .40
❑ 40 Edgerrin James 1.00 .40
❑ 41 Marvin Harrison 1.00 .40
❑ 42 Peyton Manning 1.50 .60
❑ 43 Byron Leftwich 1.25 .50
❑ 44 Fred Taylor .60 .25

❑ 45 Jimmy Smith .60 .25
❑ 46 Priest Holmes 1.25 .50
❑ 47 Tony Gonzalez .60 .25
❑ 48 Trent Green .60 .25
❑ 49 A.J. Feeley 1.00 .40
❑ 50 Chris Chambers .60 .25
❑ 51 Ricky Williams 1.00 .40
❑ 52 Daunte Culpepper 1.00 .40
❑ 53 Michael Bennett .60 .25
❑ 54 Randy Moss 1.25 .50
❑ 55 Corey Dillon .60 .25
❑ 56 Deion Branch 1.00 .40
❑ 57 Tom Brady 2.50 1.00
❑ 58 Aaron Brooks .60 .25
❑ 59 Deuce McAllister 1.00 .40
❑ 60 Joe Horn .60 .25
❑ 61 Jeremy Shockey 1.00 .40
❑ 62 Michael Strahan .60 .25
❑ 63 Tiki Barber 1.00 .40
❑ 64 Chad Pennington 1.00 .40
❑ 65 Curtis Martin 1.00 .40
❑ 66 Santana Moss .60 .25
❑ 67 Jerry Rice 2.00 .75
❑ 68 Justin Fargas .60 .25
❑ 69 Kerry Collins .60 .25
❑ 70 Tim Brown 1.00 .40
❑ 71 Brian Westbrook .60 .25
❑ 72 Donovan McNabb 1.25 .50
❑ 73 Jevon Kearse .60 .25
❑ 74 Terrell Owens 1.00 .40
❑ 75 Duce Staley .60 .25
❑ 76 Hines Ward 1.00 .40
❑ 77 Jerome Bettis 1.00 .40
❑ 78 Tommy Maddox .60 .25
❑ 79 Drew Brees 1.00 .40
❑ 80 LaDainian Tomlinson 1.25 .50
❑ 81 Kevan Barlow .60 .25
❑ 82 Tim Rattay .40 .15
❑ 83 Koren Robinson .60 .25
❑ 84 Matt Hasselbeck .60 .25
❑ 85 Shaun Alexander 1.00 .40
❑ 86 Isaac Bruce .60 .25
❑ 87 Marc Bulger 1.00 .40
❑ 88 Marshall Faulk 1.00 .40
❑ 89 Torry Holt 1.00 .40
❑ 90 Brad Johnson .60 .25
❑ 91 Charlie Garner .60 .25
❑ 92 Keenan McCardell .40 .15
❑ 93 Chris Brown 1.00 .40
❑ 94 Derrick Mason .60 .25
❑ 95 Eddie George .60 .25
❑ 96 Steve McNair 1.00 .40
❑ 97 Clinton Portis 1.00 .40
❑ 98 LaVar Arrington 2.00 .75
❑ 99 Laveranues Coles .60 .25
❑ 100 Mark Brunell .60 .25
❑ 101 Drew Henson RC 5.00 2.00
❑ 102 Craig Krenzel RC 5.00 2.00
❑ 103 Andy Hall RC 4.00 1.50
❑ 104 Josh Harris RC 5.00 2.00
❑ 105 Jim Sorgi RC 5.00 2.00
❑ 106 Jeff Smoker RC 5.00 2.00
❑ 107 John Navarre RC 5.00 2.00
❑ 108 Cody Pickett RC 5.00 2.00
❑ 109 Casey Bramlet RC 4.00 1.50
❑ 110 Matt Mauck RC 5.00 2.00
❑ 111 B.J. Symons RC 5.00 2.00
❑ 112 Bradlee Van Pelt RC 5.00 2.00
❑ 113 Michael Turner RC 6.00 2.50
❑ 114 Troy Fleming RC 4.00 1.50
❑ 115 Adimchinobe Echemandu RC 4.001.50
❑ 116 Quincy Wilson RC 4.00 1.50
❑ 117 Derrick Ward RC 2.50 1.00
❑ 118 Bruce Perry RC 5.00 2.00
❑ 119 Brandon Miree RC 4.00 1.50
❑ 120 Carlos Francis RC 4.00 1.50
❑ 121 Samie Parker RC 5.00 2.00
❑ 122 Jerricho Cotchery RC 5.00 2.00
❑ 123 Ernest Wilford RC 5.00 2.00
❑ 124 Johnnie Morant RC 5.00 2.00
❑ 125 Maurice Mann RC 4.00 1.50
❑ 126 D.J. Hackett RC 4.00 1.50
❑ 127 Drew Carter RC 5.00 2.00
❑ 128 P.K. Sam RC 4.00 1.50
❑ 129 Jamaar Taylor RC 5.00 2.00
❑ 130 Ryan Krause RC 4.00 1.50
❑ 131 Triandos Luke RC 5.00 2.00
❑ 132 Jeris McIntyre RC 4.00 1.50
❑ 133 Clarence Moore RC 5.00 2.00
❑ 134 Mark Jones RC 4.00 1.50
❑ 135 Sloan Thomas RC 4.00 1.50
❑ 136 Jonathan Smith RC 4.00 1.50
❑ 137 Patrick Crayton RC 5.00 2.00
❑ 138 Derek Abney RC 5.00 2.00
❑ 139 Kris Wilson RC 5.00 2.00
❑ 140 Sean Taylor RC 5.00 2.00
❑ 141 Jonathan Vilma RC 5.00 2.00
❑ 142 Tommie Harris RC 5.00 2.00
❑ 143 D.J. Williams RC 5.00 2.00
❑ 144 Will Smith RC 5.00 2.00
❑ 145 Kenechi Udeze RC 5.00 2.00
❑ 146 Vince Wilfork RC 5.00 2.00
❑ 147 Marcus Tubbs RC 5.00 2.00
❑ 148 Ahmad Carroll RC 5.00 2.00
❑ 149 Jason Babin RC 5.00 2.00
❑ 150 Chris Gamble RC 5.00 2.00
❑ 151 Willie Parker RC 30.00 15.00
❑ 152 Darnell Dockett RC 6.00 2.50
❑ 153 Nate Poole RC 4.00 1.50
❑ 154 Matt Kegel RC 8.00 3.00
❑ 155 Kendrick Starling RC 4.00 1.50
❑ 156 Tramon Douglas RC 4.00 1.50
❑ 157 Ryan Dinwiddie RC 6.00 2.50
❑ 158 Brian Gaither RC 4.00 1.50
❑ 159 Ran Carthon RC 6.00 2.50
❑ 160 Derick Armstrong 4.00 1.50
❑ 161 Chris Cooley RC 8.00 3.00
❑ 162 Casey Clausen RC 8.00 3.00
❑ 163 Omar Jenkins RC 4.00 1.50
❑ 164 Justin Jenkins RC 6.00 2.50
❑ 165 Wes Welker RC 10.00 4.00
❑ 166 Terrance Copper RC 6.00 2.50
❑ 167 Jarrett Payton RC 5.00 2.00
❑ 168 Zamir Cobb RC 8.00 3.00
❑ 169 Derrick Knight RC 6.00 2.50
❑ 170 Romby Bryant RC 4.00 1.50
❑ 171 Larry Croom RC 6.00 2.50
❑ 172 Thomas Tapeh RC 6.00 2.50
❑ 173 Brock Lesnar RC 8.00 3.00
❑ 174 Richard Smith RC 6.00 2.50
❑ 175 Ricky Ray RC 6.00 2.50
❑ 176 John Booth RC 4.00 1.50
❑ 177 Huey Whittaker RC 8.00 3.00
❑ 178 Fred Russell RC 8.00 3.00
❑ 179 Ben Hartsock RC 8.00 3.00
❑ 180 Tim Euhus RC 8.00 3.00
❑ 181 Ricardo Colclough RC 8.00 3.00
❑ 182 Keiwan Ratliff RC 6.00 2.50
❑ 183 Shawntae Spencer RC 8.00 3.00
❑ 184 Joey Thomas RC 8.00 3.00
❑ 185 Keith Smith RC 6.00 2.50
❑ 186 Derrick Strait RC 8.00 3.00
❑ 187 Jeremy LeSueur RC 6.00 2.50
❑ 188 Matt Ware RC 8.00 3.00
❑ 189 Rich Gardner RC 6.00 2.50
❑ 190 Daryl Smith RC 8.00 3.00
❑ 191 Dontarrious Thomas RC 8.00 3.00
❑ 192 Courtney Watson RC 8.00 3.00
❑ 193 Karlos Dansby RC 8.00 3.00
❑ 194 Teddy Lehman RC 8.00 3.00
❑ 195 Michael Boulware RC 8.00 3.00
❑ 196 Bob Sanders RC 20.00 8.00
❑ 197 Travis LaBoy RC 8.00 3.00
❑ 198 Antwan Odom RC 8.00 3.00
❑ 199 Marquise Hill RC 6.00 2.50
❑ 200 Terry Johnson RC 6.00 2.50
❑ 201 Larry Fitzgerald JSY RC 15.00 6.00
❑ 202 DeAngelo Hall JSY RC 8.00 3.00
❑ 203 Matt Schaub JSY RC 15.00 6.00
❑ 204 Michael Jenkins JSY RC 6.00 2.50
❑ 205 Devard Darling JSY RC 6.00 2.50
❑ 206 J.P. Losman JSY RC 10.00 4.00
❑ 207 Lee Evans JSY RC 8.00 3.00
❑ 208 Keary Colbert JSY RC 8.00 3.00
❑ 209 Bernard Berrian JSY RC 8.00 3.00
❑ 210 Chris Perry JSY RC 8.00 3.00
❑ 211 Kellen Winslow JSY RC 10.00 4.00
❑ 212 Luke McCown JSY RC 6.00 2.50
❑ 213 Julius Jones JSY RC 15.00 6.00
❑ 214 Darius Watts JSY RC 6.00 2.50
❑ 215 Tatum Bell JSY RC 10.00 4.00
❑ 216 Kevin Jones JSY RC 12.00 5.00
❑ 217 Roy Williams JSY RC 12.00 5.00
❑ 218 Dunta Robinson JSY RC 6.00 2.50
❑ 219 Greg Jones JSY RC 6.00 2.50
❑ 220 Reggie Williams JSY RC 8.00 3.00
❑ 221 Mewelde Moore JSY RC 6.00 2.50
❑ 222 Ben Watson JSY RC 6.00 2.50
❑ 223 Cedric Cobbs JSY RC 6.00 2.50
❑ 224 Devery Henderson JSY RC 5.00 2.00
❑ 225 Eli Manning JSY RC 25.00 10.00
❑ 226 Robert Gallery JSY RC 6.00 2.50
❑ 227 Philip Rivers JSY RC 15.00 7.50
❑ 229 Derrick Hamilton JSY RC 5.00 2.00
❑ 230 Rashaun Woods JSY RC 6.00 2.50
❑ 231 Steven Jackson JSY RC 15.00 6.00
❑ 232 Michael Clayton JSY RC 10.00 4.00
❑ 233 Ben Troupe JSY RC 6.00 2.50
❑ 227 B.Roethlisberger JSY RC 40.00 20.00

2005 Playoff Honors

❑ COMP.SET w/o SP's (100) 20.00 7.50
❑ 101-150 INSERTED IN HOBBY PACKS
❑ 101-150 PRINT RUN 699 SER.#'d SETS
❑ COMMON ROOKIE (151-200) 3.00 1.25
❑ ROOKIE SEMISTARS 151-200 5.00 2.00
❑ ROOKIE UNL.STARS 151-200 6.00 2.50
❑ 151-200 INSERTED IN RETAIL PACKS
❑ 151-200 PRINT RUN 399 SER.#'d SETS
❑ ROOKIE JSY PRINT RUN 750 SER.#'d SETS
❑ 1 Anquan Boldin .60 .25
❑ 2 Larry Fitzgerald 1.00 .40
❑ 3 Kurt Warner .60 .25
❑ 4 Michael Vick 1.50 .60
❑ 5 Alge Crumpler .60 .25
❑ 6 Warrick Dunn .60 .25
❑ 7 Jamal Lewis 1.00 .40
❑ 8 Kyle Boller .60 .25
❑ 9 Ray Lewis 1.00 .40
❑ 10 Derrick Mason .60 .25
❑ 11 Eric Moulds .60 .25
❑ 12 J.P. Losman 1.00 .40
❑ 13 Willis McGahee 1.00 .40
❑ 14 Jake Delhomme 1.00 .40
❑ 15 Steve Smith .60 .25
❑ 16 DeShaun Foster .60 .25
❑ 17 Rex Grossman .60 .25
❑ 18 Brian Urlacher 1.00 .40
❑ 19 Muhsin Muhammad .60 .25
❑ 20 Carson Palmer 1.00 .40
❑ 21 Chad Johnson 1.00 .40
❑ 22 Rudi Johnson .60 .25
❑ 23 Lee Suggs .60 .25
❑ 24 Trent Dilfer .60 .25
❑ 25 Reuben Droughns .60 .25
❑ 26 Drew Bledsoe 1.00 .40
❑ 27 Julius Jones 1.25 .50
❑ 28 Keyshawn Johnson .60 .25
❑ 29 Roy Williams S .60 .25
❑ 30 Ashley Lelie .60 .25
❑ 31 Jake Plummer .60 .25
❑ 32 Rod Smith .60 .25
❑ 33 Tatum Bell .60 .25
❑ 34 Joey Harrington 1.00 .40
❑ 35 Kevin Jones 1.00 .40
❑ 36 Roy Williams WR 1.00 .40
❑ 37 Ahman Green 1.00 .40
❑ 38 Brett Favre 2.50 1.00
❑ 39 Javon Walker .60 .25
❑ 40 Andre Johnson .60 .25
❑ 41 David Carr 1.00 .40
❑ 42 Domanick Davis .60 .25

❑ 43 Marvin Harrison 1.00 .40
❑ 44 Edgerrin James 1.00 .40
❑ 45 Peyton Manning 1.50 .60
❑ 46 Reggie Wayne .60 .25
❑ 47 Fred Taylor .60 .25
❑ 48 Byron Leftwich 1.00 .40
❑ 49 Jimmy Smith .60 .25
❑ 50 Priest Holmes 1.00 .40
❑ 51 Tony Gonzalez .60 .25
❑ 52 Trent Green .60 .25
❑ 53 A.J. Feeley .60 .25
❑ 54 Chris Chambers .60 .25
❑ 55 Daunte Culpepper 1.00 .40
❑ 56 Nate Burleson .60 .25
❑ 57 Michael Bennett .60 .25
❑ 58 Corey Dillon .60 .25
❑ 59 Deion Branch .60 .25
❑ 60 Tedy Bruschi .60 .25
❑ 61 Tom Brady 2.50 1.00
❑ 62 Aaron Brooks .60 .25
❑ 63 Deuce McAllister 1.00 .40
❑ 64 Joe Horn .60 .25
❑ 65 Eli Manning 2.00 .75
❑ 66 Tiki Barber 1.00 .40
❑ 67 Plaxico Burress .60 .25
❑ 68 Jeremy Shockey 1.00 .40
❑ 69 Chad Pennington 1.00 .40
❑ 70 Curtis Martin 1.00 .40
❑ 71 Laveranues Coles .60 .25
❑ 72 Kerry Collins .60 .25
❑ 73 Randy Moss 1.00 .40
❑ 74 LaMont Jordan 1.00 .40
❑ 75 Brian Westbrook .60 .25
❑ 76 Donovan McNabb 1.25 .50
❑ 77 Terrell Owens 1.00 .40
❑ 78 Ben Roethlisberger 2.50 1.00
❑ 79 Hines Ward 1.00 .40
❑ 80 Duce Staley .60 .25
❑ 81 Jerome Bettis 1.00 .40
❑ 82 Drew Brees 1.00 .40
❑ 83 LaDainian Tomlinson 1.25 .50
❑ 84 Antonio Gates 1.00 .40
❑ 85 Kevan Barlow .60 .25
❑ 86 Brandon Lloyd .50 .20
❑ 87 Darrell Jackson .60 .25
❑ 88 Matt Hasselbeck .60 .25
❑ 89 Shaun Alexander 1.25 .50
❑ 90 Marc Bulger 1.00 .40
❑ 91 Torry Holt 1.00 .40
❑ 92 Steven Jackson 1.25 .50
❑ 93 Brian Griese .60 .25
❑ 94 Michael Clayton 1.00 .40
❑ 95 Drew Bennett .60 .25
❑ 96 Steve McNair 1.00 .40
❑ 97 Chris Brown .60 .25
❑ 98 Clinton Portis 1.00 .40
❑ 99 LaVar Arrington 1.00 .40
❑ 100 Santana Moss .60 .25
❑ 101 Cedric Benson RC 10.00 4.00
❑ 102 Mike Williams 10.00 4.00
❑ 103 DeMarcus Ware RC 8.00 3.00
❑ 104 Shawne Merriman RC 8.00 3.00
❑ 105 Thomas Davis RC 5.00 2.00
❑ 106 Derrick Johnson RC 8.00 3.00
❑ 107 David Pollack RC 5.00 2.00
❑ 108 Erasmus James RC 5.00 2.00
❑ 109 Marcus Spears RC 5.00 2.00
❑ 110 Fabian Washington RC 5.00 2.00
❑ 111 Aaron Rodgers RC 15.00 6.00
❑ 112 Marlin Jackson RC 5.00 2.00
❑ 113 Heath Miller RC 12.00 5.00
❑ 114 Alex Smith TE RC 5.00 2.00
❑ 115 Chris Henry RC 5.00 2.00
❑ 116 David Greene RC 5.00 2.00
❑ 117 Brandon Jones RC 5.00 2.00
❑ 118 Marion Barber RC 8.00 3.00
❑ 119 Brandon Jacobs RC 6.00 2.50
❑ 120 Jerome Mathis RC 5.00 2.00
❑ 121 Craphonso Thorpe RC 4.00 1.50
❑ 122 Manuel White RC 4.00 1.50
❑ 123 Alvin Pearman RC 5.00 2.00
❑ 124 Darren Sproles RC 5.00 2.00
❑ 125 Fred Gibson RC 4.00 1.50
❑ 126 Roydell Williams RC 5.00 2.00
❑ 127 Airese Currie RC 5.00 2.00
❑ 128 Damien Nash RC 4.00 1.50
❑ 129 Dan Orlovsky RC 6.00 2.50
❑ 130 Adrian McPherson RC 5.00 2.00
❑ 131 Larry Brackins RC 4.00 1.50
❑ 132 Rasheed Marshall RC 5.00 2.00
❑ 133 Cedric Houston RC 5.00 2.00
❑ 134 Chad Owens RC 5.00 2.00
❑ 135 Tab Perry RC 5.00 2.00
❑ 136 Dante Ridgeway RC UER 4.00 1.50
❑ 137 Craig Bragg RC 4.00 1.50
❑ 138 Deandra Cobb RC 4.00 1.50
❑ 139 Derek Anderson RC 5.00 2.00
❑ 140 Travis Johnson RC 4.00 1.50
❑ 141 Paris Warren RC 4.00 1.50
❑ 142 LeRon McCoy RC 4.00 1.50
❑ 143 James Kilian RC 5.00 2.00
❑ 144 Matt Cassel RC 8.00 3.00
❑ 145 Lionel Gates RC 4.00 1.50
❑ 146 Harry Williams RC 4.00 1.50
❑ 147 Anthony Davis RC 4.00 1.50
❑ 148 Noah Herron RC 5.00 2.00
❑ 149 Ryan Fitzpatrick RC 8.00 3.00
❑ 150 J.R. Russell RC 4.00 1.50
❑ 151 Cole Magner RC 3.00 1.25
❑ 152 Luis Castillo RC 6.00 2.50
❑ 153 Mike Patterson RC 6.00 2.50
❑ 154 Brodney Pool RC 6.00 2.50
❑ 155 Barrett Ruud RC 6.00 2.50
❑ 156 Shaun Cody RC 6.00 2.50
❑ 157 Stanford Routt RC 5.00 2.00
❑ 158 Josh Bullocks RC 6.00 2.50
❑ 159 Kevin Burnett RC 6.00 2.50
❑ 160 Corey Webster RC 6.00 2.50
❑ 161 Lofa Tatupu RC 8.00 3.00
❑ 162 Matt Roth RC 6.00 2.50
❑ 163 Mike Nugent RC 6.00 2.50
❑ 164 Odell Thurman RC 6.00 2.50
❑ 165 Ronald Bartell RC 5.00 2.00
❑ 166 Nick Collins RC 6.00 2.50
❑ 167 Dan Cody RC 6.00 2.50
❑ 168 Darrent Williams RC 6.00 2.50
❑ 169 Justin Miller RC 5.00 2.00
❑ 170 Jerome Collins RC 5.00 2.00
❑ 171 Justin Green RC 6.00 2.50
❑ 172 Eric Green RC 3.00 1.25
❑ 173 Joel Dreessen RC 5.00 2.00
❑ 174 Bo Scaife RC 5.00 2.00
❑ 175 Antonio Perkins RC 5.00 2.00
❑ 176 Nehemiah Broughton RC 5.00 2.00
❑ 177 Patrick Estes RC 5.00 2.00
❑ 178 Billy Bajema RC 5.00 2.00
❑ 179 Madison Hedgecock RC 6.00 2.50
❑ 180 Roscoe Crosby RC 5.00 2.00
❑ 181 Kendrick Mosley RC 3.00 1.25
❑ 182 Tyson Thompson RC 10.00 4.00
❑ 183 Fred Amey RC 5.00 2.00
❑ 184 Brock Berlin RC 5.00 2.00
❑ 185 Gino Guidugli RC 3.00 1.25
❑ 186 Walter Reyes RC 5.00 2.00
❑ 187 Lydell Ross RC 5.00 2.00
❑ 188 Carlyle Holiday RC 5.00 2.00
❑ 189 Bryan Randall RC 5.00 2.00
❑ 190 Derrick Tinsley RC 5.00 2.00
❑ 191 Ryan Grant RC 6.00 2.50
❑ 192 Bobby Purify RC 5.00 2.00
❑ 193 Leonard Weaver RC 5.00 2.00
❑ 194 Vincent Fuller RC 5.00 2.00
❑ 195 Tony Brown RC 5.00 2.00
❑ 196 Zach Tuiasosopo RC 3.00 1.25
❑ 197 Craig Ochs RC 5.00 2.00
❑ 198 Ruvell Martin RC 12.00 5.00
❑ 199 Manuel Wright RC 6.00 2.50
❑ 200 Travis Daniels RC 5.00 2.00
❑ 201 Adam Jones JSY RC 8.00 3.00
❑ 202 Alex Smith QB JSY RC 20.00 7.50
❑ 203 Andrew Walter JSY RC 10.00 4.00
❑ 204 Antrel Rolle JSY RC 8.00 3.00
❑ 205 Braylon Edwards JSY RC 20.00 7.50
❑ 206 Cadillac Williams JSY RC 25.00 10.00
❑ 207 Carlos Rogers JSY RC 10.00 4.00
❑ 208 Charlie Frye JSY RC 12.00 5.00
❑ 209 Ciatrick Fason JSY RC 8.00 3.00
❑ 210 Courtney Roby JSY RC 8.00 3.00
❑ 211 Eric Shelton JSY RC 8.00 3.00
❑ 212 Frank Gore JSY RC 12.00 5.00
❑ 213 J.J. Arrington JSY RC 10.00 4.00
❑ 214 Jason Campbell JSY RC 10.00 4.00
❑ 215 Kyle Orton JSY RC 10.00 4.00
❑ 216 Mark Bradley JSY RC 8.00 3.00
❑ 217 Mark Clayton JSY RC 10.00 4.00
❑ 218 Matt Jones JSY RC 15.00 6.00
❑ 219 Maurice Clarett JSY 8.00 3.00
❑ 220 Reggie Brown JSY RC 8.00 3.00
❑ 221 Ronnie Brown JSY RC 20.00 7.50
❑ 222 Roddy White JSY RC 8.00 3.00
❑ 223 Ryan Moats JSY RC 8.00 3.00
❑ 224 Roscoe Parrish JSY RC 8.00 3.00
❑ 225 Stefan LeFors JSY RC 8.00 3.00
❑ 226 Terrence Murphy JSY RC 8.00 3.00
❑ 227 Troy Williamson JSY RC 12.00 5.00
❑ 228 Vernand Morency JSY RC 8.00 3.00
❑ 229 Vincent Jackson JSY RC 8.00 3.00

1996 Playoff Illusions

❑ COMPLETE SET (120) 50.00 20.00
❑ COMP.SERIES 1 (63) 10.00 4.00
❑ COMP.SERIES 2 (57) 40.00 15.00
❑ 1 Troy Aikman 1.50 .60
❑ 2 Larry Centers .30 .10
❑ 3 Terance Mathis .15 .05
❑ 4 Michael Irvin .60 .25
❑ 5 Jim Kelly .60 .25
❑ 6 Tim Biakabutuka RC .60 .25
❑ 7 Rashaan Salaam .30 .10
❑ 8 Ki-Jana Carter .30 .10
❑ 9 Anthony Miller .30 .10
❑ 10 Deion Sanders .75 .30
❑ 11 Scott Mitchell .30 .10
❑ 12 Robert Brooks .60 .25
❑ 13 Willie Davis .15 .05
❑ 14 Zack Crockett .15 .05
❑ 15 James O.Stewart .30 .10
❑ 16 Tamarick Vanover .30 .10
❑ 17 Stanley Pritchett .15 .05
❑ 18 Warren Moon .30 .10
❑ 19 Shawn Jefferson .15 .05
❑ 20 Shannon Sharpe .30 .10
❑ 21 Jim Everett .15 .05
❑ 22 Dave Brown .15 .05
❑ 23 Adrian Murrell .30 .10
❑ 24 Rickey Dudley RC .60 .25
❑ 25 Chris T. Jones .30 .10
❑ 26 Andre Hastings .15 .05
❑ 27 Stan Humphries .30 .10
❑ 28 Steve Young 1.25 .50
❑ 29 Joey Galloway .60 .25
❑ 30 Jim Harbaugh .30 .10
❑ 31 Eddie Kennison RC .60 .25
❑ 32 Mike Alstott RC 2.00 .75
❑ 33 Michael Westbrook .60 .25
❑ 34 Leeland McElroy RC .30 .10
❑ 35 Erik Kramer .15 .05
❑ 36 Mark Chmura .30 .10
❑ 37 Cris Carter .60 .25
❑ 38 Ben Coates .30 .10
❑ 39 Wayne Chrebet 1.00 .40
❑ 40 Jerome Bettis .60 .25
❑ 41 Tim Brown .60 .25
❑ 42 Jason Dunn RC .30 .10
❑ 43 William Henderson .60 .25
❑ 44 Rick Mirer .30 .10
❑ 45 J.J. Stokes .60 .25
❑ 46 Rodney Peete .15 .05
❑ 47 Neil O'Donnell .30 .10
❑ 48 Tyrone Wheatley .30 .10
❑ 49 Terry Glenn RC 2.00 .75
❑ 50 Junior Seau .60 .25
❑ 51 Jake Reed .30 .10

❑	52 O.J. McDuffie	.30	.10
❑	53 Steve Bono	.15	.05
❑	54 Steve McNair	1.25	.50
❑	55 Antonio Freeman	.60	.25
❑	56 Johnnie Morton	.30	.10
❑	57 Eric Metcalf	.15	.05
❑	58 Andre Reed	.30	.10
❑	59 Bobby Engram RC	.60	.25
❑	60 Gus Frerotte	.30	.10
❑	61 Jeff Blake	.60	.25
❑	62 Erric Pegram	.15	.05
❑	63 Jeff Hostetler	.15	.05
❑	64 Edgar Bennett	.60	.25
❑	65 Eddie George RC	4.00	1.50
❑	66 Marvin Harrison RC	8.00	3.00
❑	67 LeShon Johnson	.30	.10
❑	68 Jamal Anderson RC	1.50	.60
❑	69 Thurman Thomas	1.25	.50
❑	70 Barry Sanders	5.00	2.00
❑	71 Muhsin Muhammad RC	3.00	1.25
❑	72 Robert Green	.30	.10
❑	73 Garrison Hearst	.60	.25
❑	74 John Elway	6.00	2.50
❑	75 Herman Moore	.60	.25
❑	76 Chris Chandler	.30	.10
❑	77 Marshall Faulk	1.50	.60
❑	78 Mark Brunell	2.00	.75
❑	79 Tony Banks RC	1.25	.50
❑	80 Terrell Davis	2.50	1.00
❑	81 Marcus Allen	1.25	.50
❑	82 Dan Marino	6.00	2.50
❑	83 Robert Smith	.60	.25
❑	84 Curtis Martin	2.50	1.00
❑	85 Amani Toomer RC	4.00	1.50
❑	86 Napoleon Kaufman	.60	.25
❑	87 Ricky Watters	.60	.25
❑	88 Kordell Stewart	1.25	.50
❑	89 Keyshawn Johnson RC	3.00	1.25
❑	90 Emmitt Smith	5.00	2.00
❑	91 Chris Warren	.60	.25
❑	92 Isaac Bruce	1.25	.50
❑	93 Terry Allen	.60	.25
❑	94 Trent Dilfer	.60	.25
❑	95 Vinny Testaverde	.60	.25
❑	96 Bruce Smith	1.25	.50
❑	97 Kerry Collins	1.25	.50
❑	98 Curtis Conway	1.25	.50
❑	99 Karim Abdul-Jabbar RC	1.25	.50
❑	100 Brett Favre	6.00	2.50
❑	101 Carl Pickens	.60	.25
❑	102 Brett Perriman	.30	.10
❑	103 Keith Jackson	.30	.10
❑	104 Drew Bledsoe	2.00	.75
❑	105 Rodney Hampton	.30	.10
❑	106 Ray Zellars	.30	.10
❑	107 Jeff Graham	.30	.10
❑	108 Irving Fryar	.60	.25
❑	109 Lawrence Phillips RC	1.25	.50
❑	110 Jerry Rice	3.00	1.25
❑	111 Mike Tomczak	.30	.10
❑	112 Tony Martin	.60	.25
❑	113 Brian Blades	.60	.25
❑	114 Bill Brooks	.30	.10
❑	115 Rob Moore	.60	.25
❑	116 Quinn Early	.30	.10
❑	117 Darnay Scott	.60	.25
❑	118 Ken Dilger	.30	.10
❑	119 Derek Loville	.30	.10
❑	120 Reggie White	1.25	.50
❑	P1 Robert Brooks Promo	.75	.30

1998 Playoff Momentum Hobby

❑	COMPLETE SET (250)	250.00	100.00
❑	1 Jake Plummer	2.50	1.00
❑	2 Eric Metcalf	1.00	.40
❑	3 Adrian Murrell	1.50	.60
❑	4 Larry Centers	1.00	.40
❑	5 Frank Sanders	1.50	.60
❑	6 Rob Moore	1.50	.60
❑	7 Andre Wadsworth RC	4.00	1.50
❑	8 Chris Chandler	1.50	.60
❑	9 Jamal Anderson	2.50	1.00
❑	10 Tony Martin	1.50	.60
❑	11 Terance Mathis	1.50	.60
❑	12 Tim Dwight RC	5.00	2.00

❑	13 Jammi German RC	2.50	1.00
❑	14 O.J. Santiago	1.00	.40
❑	15 Jim Harbaugh	1.50	.60
❑	16 Eric Zeier	1.50	.60
❑	17 Duane Starks RC	2.50	1.00
❑	18 Rod Woodson	1.50	.60
❑	19 Errict Rhett	1.50	.60
❑	20 Jay Graham	1.00	.40
❑	21 Ray Lewis	2.50	1.00
❑	22 Michael Jackson	1.00	.40
❑	23 Jermaine Lewis	1.50	.60
❑	24 Patrick Johnson RC	4.00	1.50
❑	25 Eric Green	1.00	.40
❑	26 Doug Flutie	2.50	1.00
❑	27 Rob Johnson	1.50	.60
❑	28 Antowain Smith	2.50	1.00
❑	29 Thurman Thomas	2.50	1.00
❑	30 Jonathan Linton RC	4.00	1.50
❑	31 Bruce Smith	1.50	.60
❑	32 Eric Moulds	2.50	1.00
❑	33 Kevin Williams	1.00	.40
❑	34 Andre Reed	1.50	.60
❑	35 Steve Beuerlein	1.50	.60
❑	36 Kerry Collins	1.50	.60
❑	37 Anthony Johnson	1.00	.40
❑	38 Fred Lane	1.00	.40
❑	39 William Floyd	1.00	.40
❑	40 Rocket Ismail	1.00	.40
❑	41 Wesley Walls	1.50	.60
❑	42 Muhsin Muhammad	1.50	.60
❑	43 Rae Carruth	1.00	.40
❑	44 Kevin Greene	1.50	.60
❑	45 Greg Lloyd	1.00	.40
❑	46 Moses Moreno RC	2.50	1.00
❑	47 Erik Kramer	1.00	.40
❑	48 Edgar Bennett	1.00	.40
❑	49 Curtis Enis RC	2.50	1.00
❑	50 Curtis Conway	1.50	.60
❑	51 Bobby Engram	1.50	.60
❑	52 Alonzo Mayes RC	2.50	1.00
❑	53 Jeff Blake	1.50	.60
❑	54 Neil O'Donnell	1.50	.60
❑	55 Corey Dillon	2.50	1.00
❑	56 Takeo Spikes RC	5.00	2.00
❑	57 Carl Pickens	1.50	.60
❑	58 Tony McGee	1.00	.40
❑	59 Darnay Scott	1.50	.60
❑	60 Troy Aikman	5.00	2.00
❑	61 Deion Sanders	2.50	1.00
❑	62 Emmitt Smith	8.00	3.00
❑	63 Darren Woodson	1.00	.40
❑	64 Chris Warren	1.50	.60
❑	65 Daryl Johnston	1.50	.60
❑	66 Ernie Mills	1.00	.40
❑	67 Billy Davis	1.00	.40
❑	68 Michael Irvin	2.50	1.00
❑	69 David LaFleur	1.00	.40
❑	70 John Elway	10.00	4.00
❑	71 Brian Griese RC	10.00	4.00
❑	72 Steve Atwater	1.00	.40
❑	73 Terrell Davis	2.50	1.00
❑	74 Rod Smith	1.50	.60
❑	75 Marcus Nash RC	2.50	1.00
❑	76 Shannon Sharpe	1.50	.60
❑	77 Ed McCaffrey	1.50	.60
❑	78 Neil Smith	1.50	.60
❑	79 Charlie Batch RC	5.00	2.00
❑	80 Germane Crowell RC	4.00	1.50
❑	81 Scott Mitchell	1.50	.60
❑	82 Barry Sanders	8.00	3.00
❑	83 Terry Fair RC	4.00	1.50
❑	84 Herman Moore	1.50	.60
❑	85 Johnnie Morton	1.50	.60
❑	86 Brett Favre	10.00	4.00
❑	87 Rick Mirer	1.00	.40
❑	88 Dorsey Levens	2.50	1.00
❑	89 William Henderson	1.50	.60
❑	90 Derrick Mayes	1.50	.60
❑	91 Antonio Freeman	2.50	1.00
❑	92 Robert Brooks	1.50	.60
❑	93 Mark Chmura	1.50	.60
❑	94 Vonnie Holliday RC	4.00	1.50
❑	95 Reggie White	2.50	1.00
❑	96 E.G. Green RC	4.00	1.50
❑	97 Jerome Pathon RC	5.00	2.00
❑	98 Peyton Manning RC	50.00	25.00
❑	99 Marshall Faulk	3.00	1.25
❑	100 Zack Crockett	1.00	.40
❑	101 Ken Dilger	1.00	.40
❑	102 Marvin Harrison	2.50	1.00
❑	103 Mark Brunell	2.50	1.00
❑	104 Jonathan Quinn RC	5.00	2.00
❑	105 Tavian Banks RC	4.00	1.50
❑	106 Fred Taylor RC	8.00	3.00
❑	107 James Stewart	1.50	.60
❑	108 Jimmy Smith	1.50	.60
❑	109 Keenan McCardell	1.50	.60
❑	110 Elvis Grbac	1.50	.60
❑	111 Rich Gannon	2.50	1.00
❑	112 Rashaan Shehee RC	4.00	1.50
❑	113 Donnell Bennett	1.00	.40
❑	114 Kimble Anders	1.50	.60
❑	115 Derrick Thomas	2.50	1.00
❑	116 Kevin Lockett	1.00	.40
❑	117 Derrick Alexander WR	1.50	.60
❑	118 Tony Gonzalez	2.50	1.00
❑	119 Andre Rison	1.50	.60
❑	120 Craig Erickson	1.00	.40
❑	121 Dan Marino	10.00	4.00
❑	122 John Avery RC	4.00	1.50
❑	123 Karim Abdul-Jabbar	2.50	1.00
❑	124 Zach Thomas	2.50	1.00
❑	125 O.J. McDuffie	1.50	.60
❑	126 Troy Drayton	1.00	.40
❑	127 Randall Cunningham	2.50	1.00
❑	128 Brad Johnson	2.50	1.00
❑	129 Robert Smith	2.50	1.00
❑	130 Cris Carter	2.50	1.00
❑	131 Randy Moss RC	30.00	12.50
❑	132 Jake Reed	1.50	.60
❑	133 John Randle	1.50	.60
❑	134 Drew Bledsoe	4.00	1.50
❑	135 Tony Simmons RC	4.00	1.50
❑	136 Sedrick Shaw	1.00	.40
❑	137 Chris Floyd RC	2.50	1.00
❑	138 Robert Edwards RC	4.00	1.50
❑	139 Rod Rutledge RC	2.50	1.00
❑	140 Shawn Jefferson	1.00	.40
❑	141 Ben Coates	1.50	.60
❑	142 Terry Glenn	2.50	1.00
❑	143 Heath Shuler	1.00	.40
❑	144 Danny Wuerffel	1.50	.60
❑	145 Troy Davis	1.00	.40
❑	146 Qadry Ismail	1.50	.60
❑	147 Ray Zellars	1.00	.40
❑	148 Lamar Smith	1.50	.60
❑	149 Cameron Cleeland RC	2.50	1.00
❑	150 Sean Dawkins	1.00	.40
❑	151 Andre Hastings	1.00	.40
❑	152 Danny Kanell	1.50	.60
❑	153 Tiki Barber	2.50	1.00
❑	154 Tyrone Wheatley	1.50	.60
❑	155 Charles Way	1.00	.40
❑	156 Gary Brown	1.00	.40
❑	157 Shaun Williams RC	4.00	1.50
❑	158 Chris Calloway	1.00	.40
❑	159 Amani Toomer	1.50	.60
❑	160 Brian Alford RC	2.50	1.00
❑	161 Joe Jurevicius RC	5.00	2.00
❑	162 Ike Hilliard	1.50	.60
❑	163 Michael Strahan	1.50	.60
❑	164 Glenn Foley	1.50	.60
❑	165 Vinny Testaverde	1.50	.60
❑	166 Keyshawn Johnson	2.50	1.00
❑	167 Curtis Martin	2.50	1.00
❑	168 Leon Johnson	1.00	.40
❑	169 Keith Byars	1.00	.40

❑	170 Wayne Chrebet	2.50	1.00
❑	171 Kyle Brady	1.00	.40
❑	172 Dedric Ward	1.00	.40
❑	173 Jeff George	1.50	.60
❑	174 Charles Woodson RC	10.00	4.00
❑	175 Napoleon Kaufman	2.50	1.00
❑	176 Jon Ritchie RC	4.00	1.50
❑	177 Tim Brown	2.50	1.00
❑	178 James Jett	1.50	.60
❑	179 Rickey Dudley	1.00	.40
❑	180 Bobby Hoying	1.50	.60
❑	181 Duce Staley	3.00	1.25
❑	182 Charlie Garner	1.50	.60
❑	183 Irving Fryar	1.50	.60
❑	184 Jeff Graham	1.00	.40
❑	185 Jason Dunn	1.00	.40
❑	186 Kordell Stewart	2.50	1.00
❑	187 Jerome Bettis	2.50	1.00
❑	188 Andre Coleman	1.00	.40
❑	189 Chris Fuamatu-Ma'afala RC	4.00	1.50
❑	190 Charles Johnson	1.00	.40
❑	191 Hines Ward RC	20.00	10.00
❑	192 Mark Bruener	1.00	.40
❑	193 Courtney Hawkins	1.00	.40
❑	194 Will Blackwell	1.00	.40
❑	195 Levon Kirkland	1.00	.40
❑	196 Mikhael Ricks RC	4.00	1.50
❑	197 Ryan Leaf RC	5.00	2.00
❑	198 Natrone Means	1.50	.60
❑	199 Junior Seau	2.50	1.00
❑	200 Bryan Still	1.00	.40
❑	201 Freddie Jones	1.00	.40
❑	202 Steve Young	3.00	1.25
❑	203 Jim Druckenmiller	1.00	.40
❑	204 Garrison Hearst	2.50	1.00
❑	205 R.W. McQuarters RC	4.00	1.50
❑	206 Merton Hanks	1.00	.40
❑	207 Marc Edwards	1.00	.40
❑	208 Jerry Rice	5.00	2.00
❑	209 Terrell Owens	2.50	1.00
❑	210 J.J. Stokes	1.50	.60
❑	211 Tony Banks	1.50	.60
❑	212 Robert Holcombe RC	4.00	1.50
❑	213 Greg Hill	1.00	.40
❑	214 Amp Lee	1.00	.40
❑	215 Jerald Moore	1.00	.40
❑	216 Isaac Bruce	2.50	1.00
❑	217 Az-Zahir Hakim RC	5.00	2.00
❑	218 Eddie Kennison	1.50	.60
❑	219 Grant Wistrom RC	4.00	1.50
❑	220 Warren Moon	2.50	1.00
❑	221 Ahman Green RC	25.00	10.00
❑	222 Steve Broussard	1.00	.40
❑	223 Ricky Watters	1.50	.60
❑	224 James McKnight	2.50	1.00
❑	225 Joey Galloway	1.50	.60
❑	226 Mike Pritchard	1.00	.40
❑	227 Trent Dilfer	2.50	1.00
❑	228 Warrick Dunn	2.50	1.00
❑	229 Mike Alstott	2.50	1.00
❑	230 John Lynch	1.50	.60
❑	231 Jacquez Green RC	4.00	1.50
❑	232 Reidel Anthony	1.50	.60
❑	233 Bert Emanuel	1.50	.60
❑	234 Warren Sapp	1.50	.60
❑	235 Steve McNair	2.50	1.00
❑	236 Eddie George	2.50	1.00
❑	237 Chris Sanders	1.00	.40
❑	238 Yancey Thigpen	1.00	.40
❑	239 Willie Davis	1.00	.40
❑	240 Kevin Dyson RC	5.00	2.00
❑	241 Frank Wycheck	1.00	.40
❑	242 Trent Green	2.50	1.00
❑	243 Gus Frerotte	1.00	.40
❑	244 Skip Hicks RC	4.00	1.50
❑	245 Terry Allen	2.50	1.00
❑	246 Stephen Davis	1.00	.40
❑	247 Stephen Alexander RC	4.00	1.50
❑	248 Michael Westbrook	1.50	.60
❑	249 Dana Stubblefield SP	2.50	1.00
❑	250 Dan Wilkinson SP	2.50	1.00

1999 Playoff Momentum SSD

❑	COMPLETE SET (200)	300.00	150.00
❑	COMP.SHORT SET (150)	100.00	50.00
❑	1 Rob Moore	.50	.20
❑	2 Adrian Murrell	.50	.20
❑	3 Frank Sanders	.50	.20
❑	4 Andre Wadsworth	.30	.10
❑	5 Tim Dwight	.75	.30
❑	6 Terance Mathis	.50	.20
❑	7 Priest Holmes	1.25	.50
❑	8 Jermaine Lewis	.50	.20
❑	9 Scott Mitchell	.30	.10
❑	10 Patrick Johnson	.30	.10
❑	11 Tony Banks	.50	.20
❑	12 Thurman Thomas	.50	.20
❑	13 Andre Reed	.50	.20
❑	14 Bruce Smith	.50	.20
❑	15 Tim Biakabutuka	.50	.20
❑	16 Muhsin Muhammad	.50	.20
❑	17 Wesley Walls	.50	.20
❑	18 Rae Carruth	.30	.10
❑	19 Curtis Conway	.50	.20
❑	20 Bobby Engram	.50	.20
❑	21 Jeff Blake	.50	.20
❑	22 Darnay Scott	.30	.10
❑	23 Ty Detmer	.50	.20
❑	24 Leslie Shepherd	.30	.10
❑	25 Sedrick Shaw	.30	.10
❑	26 Michael Irvin	.50	.20
❑	27 Rocket Ismail	.50	.20
❑	28 Ed McCaffrey	.50	.20
❑	29 Marcus Nash	.30	.10
❑	30 Shannon Sharpe	.50	.20
❑	31 Neil Smith	.50	.20
❑	32 Rod Smith	.50	.20
❑	33 Bubby Brister	.30	.10
❑	34 Germane Crowell	.30	.10
❑	35 Johnnie Morton	.50	.20
❑	36 Bill Schroeder	.75	.30
❑	37 Mark Chmura	.30	.10
❑	38 Marvin Harrison	.75	.30
❑	39 E.G. Green	.30	.10
❑	40 Jerome Pathon	.30	.10
❑	41 Keenan McCardell	.50	.20
❑	42 Jimmy Smith	.50	.20
❑	43 Kyle Brady	.30	.10
❑	44 Tavian Banks	.30	.10
❑	45 Warren Moon	.75	.30
❑	46 Derrick Alexander WR	.50	.20
❑	47 Elvis Grbac	.50	.20
❑	48 Andre Rison	.50	.20
❑	49 Byron Bam Morris	.30	.10
❑	50 Rashaan Shehee	.30	.10
❑	51 Karim Abdul-Jabbar	.50	.20
❑	52 John Avery	.30	.10
❑	53 Tony Martin	.50	.20
❑	54 O.J. McDuffie	.50	.20
❑	55 Oronde Gadsden	.50	.20
❑	56 Robert Smith	.75	.30
❑	57 Jeff George	.50	.20
❑	58 Jake Reed	.50	.20
❑	59 Leroy Hoard	.30	.10
❑	60 Terry Allen	.50	.20
❑	61 Terry Glenn	.75	.30
❑	62 Ben Coates	.50	.20
❑	63 Tony Simmons	.30	.10
❑	64 Cameron Cleeland	.30	.10
❑	65 Eddie Kennison	.50	.20
❑	66 Billy Joe Hobert	.30	.10
❑	67 Amani Toomer	.30	.10
❑	68 Kerry Collins	.50	.20
❑	69 Ike Hilliard	.30	.10
❑	70 Gary Brown	.30	.10
❑	71 Joe Jurevicius	.50	.20
❑	72 Wayne Chrebet	.50	.20
❑	73 Vinny Testaverde	.50	.20
❑	74 Charles Woodson	.75	.30
❑	75 James Jett	.50	.20
❑	76 Charles Johnson	.30	.10
❑	77 Duce Staley	.75	.30
❑	78 Hines Ward	.75	.30
❑	79 Jim Harbaugh	.50	.20
❑	80 Ryan Leaf	.75	.30
❑	81 Junior Seau	.75	.30
❑	82 Mikhael Ricks	.30	.10
❑	83 Garrison Hearst	.50	.20
❑	84 J.J. Stokes	.50	.20
❑	85 Lawrence Phillips	.50	.20
❑	86 Derrick Mayes	.30	.10
❑	87 Mike Pritchard	.30	.10
❑	88 Ahman Green	.75	.30
❑	89 Ricky Watters	.50	.20
❑	90 Robert Holcombe	.30	.10
❑	91 Isaac Bruce	.75	.30
❑	92 Trent Dilfer	.50	.20
❑	93 Reidel Anthony	.30	.10
❑	94 Jacquez Green	.30	.10
❑	95 Warren Sapp	.30	.10
❑	96 Kevin Dyson	.50	.20
❑	97 Yancey Thigpen	.30	.10
❑	98 Stephen Davis	.75	.30
❑	99 Irving Fryar	.50	.20
❑	100 Michael Westbrook	.50	.20
❑	101 Jake Plummer	.75	.30
❑	102 Jamal Anderson	1.25	.50
❑	103 Chris Chandler	.75	.30
❑	104 Doug Flutie	.75	.30
❑	105 Eric Moulds	1.25	.50
❑	106 Antowain Smith	1.25	.50
❑	107 Jonathan Linton	.50	.20
❑	108 Curtis Enis	.50	.20
❑	109 Corey Dillon	1.25	.50
❑	110 Carl Pickens	.75	.30
❑	111 Emmitt Smith	2.50	1.00
❑	112 Troy Aikman	2.50	1.00
❑	113 Deion Sanders	1.25	.50
❑	114 John Elway	4.00	1.50
❑	115 Terrell Davis	1.25	.50
❑	116 Brian Griese	1.25	.50
❑	117 Barry Sanders	4.00	1.50
❑	118 Charlie Batch	.75	.30
❑	119 Herman Moore	.75	.30
❑	120 Brett Favre	4.00	1.50
❑	121 Antonio Freeman	1.25	.50
❑	122 Dorsey Levens	1.25	.50
❑	123 Peyton Manning	4.00	1.50
❑	124 Fred Taylor	1.25	.50
❑	125 Mark Brunell	.75	.30
❑	126 Dan Marino	4.00	1.50
❑	127 Randy Moss	3.00	1.25
❑	128 Cris Carter	1.25	.50
❑	129 Randall Cunningham	1.25	.50
❑	130 Drew Bledsoe	1.50	.60
❑	131 Keyshawn Johnson	1.25	.50
❑	132 Curtis Martin	1.25	.50
❑	133 Tim Brown	1.25	.50
❑	134 Napoleon Kaufman	1.25	.50
❑	135 Kordell Stewart	.75	.30
❑	136 Jerome Bettis	1.25	.50
❑	137 Natrone Means	.75	.30
❑	138 Jerry Rice	2.50	1.00
❑	139 Steve Young	1.50	.60
❑	140 Terrell Owens	1.25	.50
❑	141 Joey Galloway	.75	.30
❑	142 Jon Kitna	.75	.30
❑	143 Marshall Faulk	1.50	.60
❑	144 Kurt Warner RC	12.00	5.00
❑	145 Warrick Dunn	1.25	.50
❑	146 Mike Alstott	1.25	.50
❑	147 Eddie George	.75	.30
❑	148 Steve McNair	1.25	.50
❑	149 Brad Johnson	1.25	.50
❑	150 Skip Hicks	.50	.20
❑	151 Tim Couch RC	5.00	2.00
❑	152 Donovan McNabb RC	20.00	7.50
❑	153 Akili Smith RC	.75	.30
❑	154 Edgerrin James RC	15.00	6.00
❑	155 Ricky Williams RC	8.00	3.00
❑	156 Torry Holt RC	10.00	4.00
❑	157 Champ Bailey RC	6.00	2.50

❑ 158 David Boston RC	5.00	2.00
❑ 159 Chris Claiborne RC	2.50	1.00
❑ 160 Chris McAlister RC	4.00	1.50
❑ 161 Daunte Culpepper RC	15.00	6.00
❑ 162 Cade McNown RC	4.00	1.50
❑ 163 Troy Edwards RC	4.00	1.50
❑ 164 Jevon Kearse RC	8.00	3.00
❑ 165 Kevin Johnson RC	5.00	2.00
❑ 166 James Johnson RC	4.00	1.50
❑ 167 Reginald Kelly RC	2.50	1.00
❑ 168 Rob Konrad RC	5.00	2.00
❑ 169 Jim Kleinsasser RC	5.00	2.00
❑ 170 Kevin Faulk RC	5.00	2.00
❑ 171 Joe Montgomery RC	4.00	1.50
❑ 172 Shaun King RC	4.00	1.50
❑ 173 Peerless Price RC	5.00	2.00
❑ 174 Mike Cloud RC	4.00	1.50
❑ 175 Jermaine Fazande RC	4.00	1.50
❑ 176 D'Wayne Bates RC	4.00	1.50
❑ 177 Brock Huard RC	5.00	2.00
❑ 178 Marty Booker RC	5.00	2.00
❑ 179 Karsten Bailey RC	4.00	1.50
❑ 180 Shawn Bryson RC	5.00	2.00
❑ 181 Jeff Paulk RC	2.50	1.00
❑ 182 Travis McGriff RC	2.50	1.00
❑ 183 Amos Zereoue RC	5.00	2.00
❑ 184 Craig Yeast RC	4.00	1.50
❑ 185 Joe Germaine RC	4.00	1.50
❑ 186 Dameane Douglas RC	4.00	1.50
❑ 187 Sedrick Irvin RC	2.50	1.00
❑ 188 Brandon Stokley RC	6.00	2.50
❑ 189 Larry Parker RC	5.00	2.00
❑ 190 Sean Bennett RC	2.50	1.00
❑ 191 Wane McGarity RC	2.50	1.00
❑ 192 Olandis Gary RC	5.00	2.00
❑ 193 Na Brown RC	4.00	1.50
❑ 194 Aaron Brooks RC	8.00	3.00
❑ 195 Cecil Collins RC	2.50	1.00
❑ 196 Darrin Chiaverini RC	4.00	1.50
❑ 197 Kevin Daft RC	4.00	1.50
❑ 198 Darnell McDonald RC	4.00	1.50
❑ 199 Joel Makovicka RC	5.00	2.00
❑ 200 Michael Bishop RC	5.00	2.00

2000 Playoff Momentum

❑ COMP.SET w/o SP's (100)	15.00	6.00
❑ 1 David Boston	.60	.25
❑ 2 Jake Plummer	.40	.15
❑ 3 Chris Chandler	.40	.15
❑ 4 Jamal Anderson	.60	.25
❑ 5 Tim Dwight	.60	.25
❑ 6 Qadry Ismail	.40	.15
❑ 7 Peerless Price	.40	.15
❑ 8 Antowain Smith	.40	.15
❑ 9 Eric Moulds	.60	.25
❑ 10 Rob Johnson	.40	.15
❑ 11 Natrone Means	.25	.08
❑ 12 Muhsin Muhammad	.40	.15
❑ 13 Steve Beuerlein	.40	.15
❑ 14 Patrick Jeffers	.60	.25
❑ 15 Curtis Enis	.25	.08
❑ 16 Cade McNown	.25	.08
❑ 17 Marcus Robinson	.60	.25
❑ 18 Corey Dillon	.60	.25
❑ 19 Akili Smith	.25	.08
❑ 20 Carl Pickens	.40	.15
❑ 21 Tim Couch	.40	.15
❑ 22 Kevin Johnson	.60	.25
❑ 23 Troy Aikman	1.25	.50
❑ 24 Emmitt Smith	1.25	.50
❑ 25 Joey Galloway	.40	.15
❑ 26 Rocket Ismail	.40	.15
❑ 27 Olandis Gary	.60	.25
❑ 28 John Elway	2.00	.75
❑ 29 Brian Griese	.60	.25
❑ 30 Ed McCaffrey	.60	.25
❑ 31 Terrell Davis	.60	.25
❑ 32 Charlie Batch	.60	.25
❑ 33 James Stewart	.40	.15
❑ 34 Germane Crowell	.25	.08
❑ 35 Barry Sanders	1.50	.60
❑ 36 Herman Moore	.40	.15
❑ 37 Antonio Freeman	.60	.25
❑ 38 Dorsey Levens	.40	.15
❑ 39 Brett Favre	2.00	.75
❑ 40 Edgerrin James	1.00	.40
❑ 41 Marvin Harrison	.60	.25
❑ 42 Peyton Manning	1.50	.60
❑ 43 Fred Taylor	.60	.25
❑ 44 Keenan McCardell	.40	.15
❑ 45 Mark Brunell	.60	.25
❑ 46 Jimmy Smith	.40	.15
❑ 47 Elvis Grbac	.40	.15
❑ 48 Tony Gonzalez	.40	.15
❑ 49 James Johnson	.25	.08
❑ 50 Dan Marino	2.00	.75
❑ 51 Thurman Thomas	.40	.15
❑ 52 Cris Carter	.60	.25
❑ 53 Robert Smith	.60	.25
❑ 54 Randy Moss	1.25	.50
❑ 55 Daunte Culpepper	.75	.30
❑ 56 Terry Glenn	.40	.15
❑ 57 Kevin Faulk	.40	.15
❑ 58 Drew Bledsoe	.75	.30
❑ 59 Ricky Williams	.60	.25
❑ 60 Amani Toomer	.40	.15
❑ 61 Kerry Collins	.40	.15
❑ 62 Vinny Testaverde	.40	.15
❑ 63 Curtis Martin	.60	.25
❑ 64 Rich Gannon	.60	.25
❑ 65 Tyrone Wheatley	.40	.15
❑ 66 Napoleon Kaufman	.40	.15
❑ 67 Tim Brown	.60	.25
❑ 68 Duce Staley	.60	.25
❑ 69 Donovan McNabb	1.00	.40
❑ 70 Kordell Stewart	.40	.15
❑ 71 Troy Edwards	.25	.08
❑ 72 Jerome Bettis	.60	.25
❑ 73 Jim Harbaugh	.40	.15
❑ 74 Jermaine Fazande	.25	.08
❑ 75 Steve Young	.75	.30
❑ 76 Charlie Garner	.40	.15
❑ 77 Terrell Owens	.60	.25
❑ 78 Jerry Rice	1.25	.50
❑ 79 Jeff Garcia	.60	.25
❑ 80 Ricky Watters	.40	.15
❑ 81 Jon Kitna	.60	.25
❑ 82 Marshall Faulk	.75	.30
❑ 83 Isaac Bruce	.60	.25
❑ 84 Torry Holt	.60	.25
❑ 85 Kurt Warner	1.25	.50
❑ 86 Keyshawn Johnson	.60	.25
❑ 87 Warrick Dunn	.60	.25
❑ 88 Mike Alstott	.60	.25
❑ 89 Warren Sapp	.40	.15
❑ 90 Shaun King	.25	.08
❑ 91 Eddie George	.60	.25
❑ 92 Steve McNair	.60	.25
❑ 93 Jevon Kearse	.60	.25
❑ 94 Bruce Smith	.40	.15
❑ 95 Deion Sanders	.60	.25
❑ 96 Albert Connell	.25	.08
❑ 97 Michael Westbrook	.40	.15
❑ 98 Brad Johnson	.60	.25
❑ 99 Jeff George	.40	.15
❑ 100 Stephen Davis	.60	.25
❑ 101 Peter Warrick RC	8.00	3.00
❑ 102 Jamal Lewis RC	20.00	7.50
❑ 103 Thomas Jones RC	12.00	5.00
❑ 104 Plaxico Burress RC	15.00	6.00
❑ 105 Travis Taylor RC	8.00	3.00
❑ 106 Ron Dayne RC	8.00	3.00
❑ 107 Bubba Franks RC	8.00	3.00
❑ 108 Sebastian Janikowski RC	8.00	3.00
❑ 109 Chad Pennington RC	20.00	7.50
❑ 110 Shaun Alexander RC	40.00	15.00
❑ 111 Sylvester Morris RC	6.00	2.50
❑ 112 Anthony Becht RC	8.00	3.00
❑ 113 R.Jay Soward RC	6.00	2.50
❑ 114 Trung Canidate RC	6.00	2.50
❑ 115 Dennis Northcutt RC	8.00	3.00
❑ 116 Todd Pinkston RC	8.00	3.00
❑ 117 Jerry Porter RC	10.00	4.00
❑ 118 Travis Prentice RC	6.00	2.50
❑ 119 Giovanni Carmazzi RC	4.00	1.50
❑ 120 Ron Dugans RC	4.00	1.50
❑ 121 Erron Kinney RC	8.00	3.00
❑ 122 Dez White RC	8.00	3.00
❑ 123 Chris Cole RC	6.00	2.50
❑ 124 Ron Dixon RC	6.00	2.50
❑ 125 Chris Redman RC	6.00	2.50
❑ 126 J.R. Redmond RC	6.00	2.50
❑ 127 Laveranues Coles RC	10.00	4.00
❑ 128 JaJuan Dawson RC	4.00	1.50
❑ 129 Darrell Jackson RC	15.00	6.00
❑ 130 Reuben Droughns RC	10.00	4.00
❑ 131 Doug Chapman RC	6.00	2.50
❑ 132 Terrelle Smith RC	6.00	2.50
❑ 133 Curtis Keaton RC	6.00	2.50
❑ 134 Gari Scott RC	4.00	1.50
❑ 135 Courtney Brown RC	8.00	3.00
❑ 136 Corey Simon RC	8.00	3.00
❑ 137 Brian Urlacher RC	30.00	12.50
❑ 138 Shaun Ellis RC	8.00	3.00
❑ 139 John Abraham RC	8.00	3.00
❑ 140 Deltha O'Neal RC	8.00	3.00
❑ 141 Rashard Anderson RC	6.00	2.50
❑ 142 Ahmed Plummer RC	8.00	3.00
❑ 143 Chris Hovan RC	6.00	2.50
❑ 144 Erik Flowers RC	6.00	2.50
❑ 145 Rob Morris RC	6.00	2.50
❑ 146 Keith Bulluck RC	8.00	3.00
❑ 147 Darren Howard RC	6.00	2.50
❑ 148 John Engelberger RC	6.00	2.50
❑ 149 Ian Gold RC	6.00	2.50
❑ 150 Raynoch Thompson RC	6.00	2.50
❑ 151 Cornelius Griffin RC	6.00	2.50
❑ 152 Rogers Beckett RC	6.00	2.50
❑ 153 Dwayne Goodrich RC	4.00	1.50
❑ 154 Barrett Green RC	4.00	1.50
❑ 155 Kevin Thompson RC	4.00	1.50
❑ 156 Ben Kelly RC	4.00	1.50
❑ 157 Danny Farmer RC	6.00	2.50
❑ 158 Aaron Shea RC	6.00	2.50
❑ 159 Trevor Gaylor RC	6.00	2.50
❑ 160 Mike Brown RC	12.00	5.00
❑ 161 Frank Moreau RC	6.00	2.50
❑ 162 Deon Dyer RC	6.00	2.50
❑ 163 Avion Black RC	6.00	2.50
❑ 164 Spergon Wynn RC	6.00	2.50
❑ 165 Billy Volek RC	12.00	5.00
❑ 166 Michael Wiley RC	6.00	2.50
❑ 167 Dante Hall RC	15.00	6.00
❑ 168 Ronney Jenkins RC	6.00	2.50
❑ 169 Sammy Morris RC	6.00	2.50
❑ 170 Kevin McDougal RC	6.00	2.50
❑ 171 Tee Martin RC	8.00	3.00
❑ 172 Troy Walters RC	8.00	3.00
❑ 173 Chad Morton RC	8.00	3.00
❑ 174 Jamel White RC	6.00	2.50
❑ 175 Shockmain Davis RC	4.00	1.50
❑ 176 Mario Edwards RC	6.00	2.50
❑ 177 Brandon Short RC	6.00	2.50
❑ 178 James Williams RC	6.00	2.50
❑ 179 Mike Anderson RC	10.00	4.00
❑ 180 Tom Brady RC	80.00	50.00
❑ 181 Na'il Diggs RC	6.00	2.50
❑ 182 Todd Husak RC	8.00	3.00
❑ 183 JaJuan Seider RC	4.00	1.50
❑ 184 Tim Rattay RC	8.00	3.00
❑ 185 Jarious Jackson RC	6.00	2.50
❑ 186 Joe Hamilton RC	6.00	2.50
❑ 187 Shyrone Stith RC	6.00	2.50
❑ 188 Mondriel Fulcher RC	4.00	1.50
❑ 189 Bashir Yamini RC	4.00	1.50
❑ 190 Herbert Goodman RC	6.00	2.50
❑ 191 Mike Green RC	6.00	2.50
❑ 192 Demario Brown RC	4.00	1.50
❑ 193 Charles Lee RC	4.00	1.50
❑ 194 Doug Johnson RC	8.00	3.00
❑ 195 Windrell Hayes RC	6.00	2.50
❑ 196 Julian Peterson RC	8.00	3.00
❑ 197 Kwame Cavil RC	4.00	1.50
❑ 198 Hank Poteat RC	6.00	2.50
❑ 199 Clint Stoerner RC	6.00	2.50
❑ 200 Mark Simoneau RC	6.00	2.50

2002 Playoff Piece of the Game

❑ COMP.SET w/o SP's (75)	50.00	30.00
❑ 1 Daunte Culpepper	1.50	.60
❑ 2 Tim Couch	1.00	.40
❑ 3 Michael Vick	5.00	2.00
❑ 4 Brett Favre	4.00	1.50
❑ 5 Drew Bledsoe	2.00	.75
❑ 6 Mark Brunell	1.50	.60
❑ 7 Jake Plummer	1.00	.40
❑ 8 Mike McMahon	1.50	.60
❑ 9 Brian Griese	1.50	.60
❑ 10 Aaron Brooks	1.50	.60

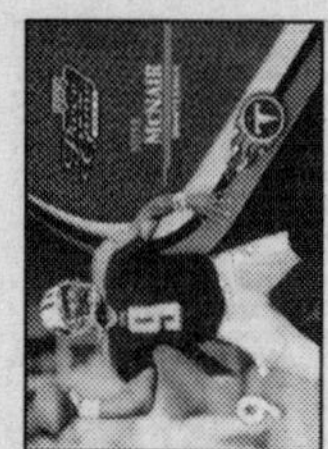

❑ 11 Chris Weinke 1.00 .40
❑ 12 Peyton Manning 3.00 1.25
❑ 13 Trent Green 1.00 .40
❑ 14 Quincy Carter 1.00 .40
❑ 15 Tom Brady 4.00 1.50
❑ 16 Vinny Testaverde 1.00 .40
❑ 17 Drew Brees 1.50 .60
❑ 18 Kordell Stewart 1.00 .40
❑ 19 Kerry Collins 1.00 .40
❑ 20 Kurt Warner 1.50 .60
❑ 21 Rich Gannon 1.50 .60
❑ 22 Jeff Garcia 1.50 .60
❑ 23 Shaun Alexander 2.00 .75
❑ 24 Doug Flutie 1.50 .60
❑ 25 Donovan McNabb 2.00 .75
❑ 26 Steve McNair 1.50 .60
❑ 27 Michael Bennett 1.50 .60
❑ 28 Jamal Lewis 1.50 .60
❑ 29 Marshall Faulk 1.50 .60
❑ 30 Curtis Martin 1.50 .60
❑ 31 James Jackson .60 .25
❑ 32 Terrell Davis 1.50 .60
❑ 33 Travis Henry 1.50 .60
❑ 34 Corey Dillon 1.00 .40
❑ 35 Deuce McAllister 2.00 .75
❑ 36 Priest Holmes 2.00 .75
❑ 37 Antowain Smith 1.00 .40
❑ 38 Anthony Thomas 1.00 .40
❑ 39 Ricky Williams 1.50 .60
❑ 40 Charlie Garner 1.00 .40
❑ 41 Jerome Bettis 1.50 .60
❑ 42 Ahman Green 1.50 .60
❑ 43 Emmitt Smith 4.00 1.50
❑ 44 Edgerrin James 2.00 .75
❑ 45 Warrick Dunn 1.50 .60
❑ 46 LaDainian Tomlinson 2.50 1.00
❑ 47 Fred Taylor 1.50 .60
❑ 48 Eddie George 1.50 .60
❑ 49 Garrison Hearst 1.00 .40
❑ 50 Stephen Davis 1.00 .40
❑ 51 Snoop Minnis .60 .25
❑ 52 Troy Brown 1.00 .40
❑ 53 Cris Carter 1.50 .60
❑ 54 Jerry Rice 3.00 1.25
❑ 55 Terry Glenn 1.00 .40
❑ 56 Plaxico Burress 1.50 .60
❑ 57 David Boston 1.50 .60
❑ 58 Marvin Harrison 1.50 .60
❑ 59 Randy Moss 3.00 1.25
❑ 60 Eric Moulds 1.00 .40
❑ 61 Rod Smith 1.00 .40
❑ 62 Freddie Mitchell 1.00 .40
❑ 63 Chris Chambers 1.50 .60
❑ 64 Keyshawn Johnson 1.50 .60
❑ 65 Terrell Owens 1.50 .60
❑ 66 Isaac Bruce 1.50 .60
❑ 67 Tim Brown 1.50 .60
❑ 68 Tony Gonzalez 1.00 .40
❑ 69 Jevon Kearse 1.50 .60
❑ 70 Warren Sapp 1.00 .40
❑ 71 Junior Seau 1.50 .60
❑ 72 Michael Strahan 1.00 .40
❑ 73 Ray Lewis 1.50 .60
❑ 74 Zach Thomas 1.50 .60
❑ 75 Brian Urlacher 2.50 1.00
❑ 76 Quentin Jammer RC 6.00 2.50
❑ 77 Kurt Kittner RC 5.00 2.00
❑ 78 Chad Hutchinson RC 5.00 2.00
❑ 79 Randy Fasani RC 5.00 2.00
❑ 80 Lamar Gordon RC 6.00 2.50
❑ 81 Brian Westbrook RC 10.00 4.00
❑ 82 Josh Scobey RC 6.00 2.50
❑ 83 Chester Taylor RC 12.00 5.00
❑ 84 Luke Staley RC 5.00 2.00
❑ 85 Deion Branch RC 12.00 5.00
❑ 86 Terry Charles RC 5.00 2.00
❑ 87 Kahlil Hill RC 5.00 2.00
❑ 88 Freddie Milons RC 5.00 2.00
❑ 89 Woody Dantzler RC 5.00 2.00
❑ 90 Kelly Campbell RC 5.00 2.00
❑ 91 Dwight Freeney RC 10.00 4.00
❑ 92 Bryan Thomas RC 5.00 2.00
❑ 93 Ryan Sims RC 6.00 2.50
❑ 94 John Henderson RC 6.00 2.50
❑ 95 Wendell Bryant RC 3.00 1.25
❑ 96 Albert Haynesworth RC 5.00 2.00
❑ 97 Phillip Buchanon RC 6.00 2.50
❑ 98 Lito Sheppard RC 6.00 2.50
❑ 99 Ed Reed RC 10.00 4.00
❑ 100 Napoleon Harris RC 6.00 2.50
❑ 101 David Carr JSY RC 30.00 12.50
❑ 102 Rohan Davey JSY RC 10.00 4.00
❑ 103 Joey Harrington JSY RC 15.00 6.00
❑ 104 Josh McCown JSY RC 12.00 5.00
❑ 105 Patrick Ramsey JSY RC 12.00 5.00
❑ 106 Ladell Betts JSY RC 10.00 4.00
❑ 107 T.J. Duckett JSY RC 12.00 5.00
❑ 108 DeShaun Foster JSY RC 10.00 4.00
❑ 109 William Green JSY RC 10.00 4.00
❑ 110 Maurice Morris JSY RC 10.00 4.00
❑ 111 Clinton Portis JSY RC 40.00 15.00
❑ 112 Travis Stephens JSY RC 8.00 3.00
❑ 113 Antonio Bryant JSY RC 10.00 4.00
❑ 114 Reche Caldwell JSY RC 10.00 4.00
❑ 115 Tim Carter JSY RC 8.00 3.00
❑ 116 Eric Crouch JSY RC 10.00 4.00
❑ 117 Andre Davis JSY RC 8.00 3.00
❑ 118 Jabar Gaffney JSY RC 10.00 4.00
❑ 119 Ron Johnson JSY RC 8.00 3.00
❑ 120 Ashley Lelie JSY RC 20.00 7.50
❑ 121 Antwaan Randle El JSY RC 15.00 6.00
❑ 122 Josh Reed JSY RC 10.00 4.00
❑ 123 Cliff Russell JSY RC 8.00 3.00
❑ 124 Donte Stallworth JSY RC 20.00 7.50
❑ 125 Javon Walker JSY RC 20.00 7.50
❑ 126 Marquise Walker JSY RC 8.00 3.00
❑ 127 Jeremy Shockey JSY RC 40.00 15.00
❑ 128 Daniel Graham JSY RC 10.00 4.00
❑ 129 David Garrard JSY RC 12.00 5.00
❑ 130 Roy Williams JSY RC 30.00 12.50
❑ 131 Julius Peppers JSY RC 20.00 7.50
❑ 132 Mike Williams JSY RC 8.00 3.00

2001 Playoff Preferred

❑ COMP.SET w/o SP's (100) 60.00 30.00
❑ 1 Elvis Grbac .75 .30
❑ 2 Ray Lewis 1.25 .50
❑ 3 Travis Taylor .75 .30
❑ 4 Rob Johnson .75 .30
❑ 5 Eric Moulds .75 .30
❑ 6 Corey Dillon 1.25 .50
❑ 7 Peter Warrick 1.25 .50
❑ 8 Tim Couch .75 .30
❑ 9 Kevin Johnson .75 .30
❑ 10 Brian Griese 1.25 .50
❑ 11 Mike Anderson 1.25 .50
❑ 12 Rod Smith .75 .30
❑ 13 Terrell Davis 1.25 .50
❑ 14 Olandis Gary .75 .30
❑ 15 Peyton Manning 3.00 1.25
❑ 16 Edgerrin James 1.50 .60
❑ 17 Marvin Harrison 1.25 .50
❑ 18 Terrence Wilkins .50 .20
❑ 19 Mark Brunell 1.25 .50
❑ 20 Fred Taylor 1.25 .50
❑ 21 Keenan McCardell .50 .20
❑ 22 Jimmy Smith .75 .30
❑ 23 Stacey Mack .50 .20
❑ 24 Trent Green 1.25 .50
❑ 25 Priest Holmes 1.50 .60
❑ 26 Tony Gonzalez .75 .30
❑ 27 Jay Fiedler 1.25 .50
❑ 28 Lamar Smith .75 .30
❑ 29 Zach Thomas 1.25 .50
❑ 30 Drew Bledsoe 1.50 .60
❑ 31 Antowain Smith .75 .30
❑ 32 Troy Brown .75 .30
❑ 33 Tom Brady 12.00 6.00
❑ 34 Vinny Testaverde .75 .30
❑ 35 Wayne Chrebet .75 .30
❑ 36 Curtis Martin 1.25 .50
❑ 37 Rich Gannon 1.25 .50
❑ 38 Tyrone Wheatley .75 .30
❑ 39 Jerry Rice 2.50 1.00
❑ 40 Tim Brown 1.25 .50
❑ 41 Charles Woodson .75 .30
❑ 42 Charlie Garner .75 .30
❑ 43 Kordell Stewart .75 .30
❑ 44 Jerome Bettis 1.25 .50
❑ 45 Doug Flutie 1.25 .50
❑ 46 Junior Seau 1.25 .50
❑ 47 Matt Hasselbeck .75 .30
❑ 48 Trent Dilfer .75 .30
❑ 49 Shaun Alexander 1.50 .60
❑ 50 Ricky Watters .75 .30
❑ 51 Eddie George 1.25 .50
❑ 52 Steve McNair 1.25 .50
❑ 53 Jevon Kearse .75 .30
❑ 54 David Boston 1.25 .50
❑ 55 Jake Plummer .75 .30
❑ 56 Chris Chandler .75 .30
❑ 57 Maurice Smith .50 .20
❑ 58 Muhsin Muhammad .75 .30
❑ 59 Wesley Walls .50 .20
❑ 60 James Allen .75 .30
❑ 61 Marcus Robinson 1.25 .50
❑ 62 Brian Urlacher 2.00 .75
❑ 63 Clint Stoerner .50 .20
❑ 64 Ryan Leaf .75 .30
❑ 65 Emmitt Smith 2.50 1.00
❑ 66 Joey Galloway .75 .30
❑ 67 Charlie Batch 1.25 .50
❑ 68 James Stewart .75 .30
❑ 69 Brett Favre 4.00 1.50
❑ 70 Ahman Green 1.25 .50
❑ 71 Bill Schroeder .75 .30
❑ 72 Bubba Franks .75 .30
❑ 73 Daunte Culpepper 1.25 .50
❑ 74 Randy Moss 2.50 1.00
❑ 75 Cris Carter 1.25 .50
❑ 76 Aaron Brooks 1.25 .50
❑ 77 Ricky Williams 1.25 .50
❑ 78 Albert Connell .50 .20
❑ 79 Kerry Collins .75 .30
❑ 80 Ron Dayne 1.25 .50
❑ 81 Jason Sehorn .50 .20
❑ 82 Amani Toomer .75 .30
❑ 83 Donovan McNabb 1.50 .60
❑ 84 James Thrash .75 .30
❑ 85 Duce Staley 1.25 .50
❑ 86 Jeff Garcia 1.25 .50
❑ 87 Garrison Hearst .75 .30
❑ 88 Terrell Owens 1.25 .50
❑ 89 Kurt Warner 2.50 1.00
❑ 90 Marshall Faulk 1.50 .60
❑ 91 Torry Holt 1.25 .50
❑ 92 Isaac Bruce 1.25 .50
❑ 93 Brad Johnson 1.25 .50
❑ 94 Warrick Dunn 1.25 .50
❑ 95 Mike Alstott 1.25 .50
❑ 96 Keyshawn Johnson 1.25 .50
❑ 97 Warren Sapp .75 .30
❑ 98 Tony Banks .75 .30
❑ 99 Stephen Davis 1.25 .50
❑ 100 Champ Bailey .75 .30
❑ 101 Michael Vick RC 30.00 12.50

❑ 102 Drew Brees RC 25.00 10.00
❑ 103 Marques Tuiasosopo RC 6.00 2.50
❑ 104 Sage Rosenfels RC 6.00 2.50
❑ 105 Jesse Palmer RC 6.00 2.50
❑ 106 Mike McMahon RC 6.00 2.50
❑ 107 A.J. Feeley RC 6.00 2.50
❑ 108 Josh Booty RC 6.00 2.50
❑ 109 Josh Heupel RC 6.00 2.50
❑ 110 Henry Burris RC 4.00 1.50
❑ 111 Roderick Robinson RC 4.00 1.50
❑ 112 Tory Woodbury RC 4.00 1.50
❑ 113 Dave Dickenson RC 4.00 1.50
❑ 114 Deuce McAllister RC 12.00 5.00
❑ 115 Michael Bennett RC 6.00 2.50
❑ 116 Rudi Johnson RC 12.00 5.00
❑ 117 Derrick Blaylock RC 6.00 2.50
❑ 118 Dee Brown RC 6.00 2.50
❑ 119 Eric Kelly RC 2.50 1.00
❑ 120 Dominic Rhodes RC 10.00 4.00
❑ 121 Jason Brookins RC 6.00 2.50
❑ 122 Nick Goings RC 6.00 2.50
❑ 123 Markus Steele RC 4.00 1.50
❑ 124 Benjamin Gay RC 6.00 2.50
❑ 125 Tony Taylor RC 4.00 1.50
❑ 126 Elvis Joseph RC 4.00 1.50
❑ 127 Tay Cody RC 2.50 1.00
❑ 128 Heath Evans RC 4.00 1.50
❑ 129 George Layne RC 4.00 1.50
❑ 130 Moran Norris RC 2.50 1.00
❑ 131 Jameel Cook RC 4.00 1.50
❑ 132 Patrick Washington RC 4.00 1.50
❑ 133 Chad Johnson RC 15.00 6.00
❑ 134 Santana Moss RC 10.00 4.00
❑ 135 Reggie Wayne RC 12.00 5.00
❑ 136 Robert Ferguson RC 6.00 2.50
❑ 137 Steve Smith RC 15.00 7.50
❑ 138 Justin McCareins RC 6.00 2.50
❑ 139 Vinny Sutherland RC 4.00 1.50
❑ 140 Alex Bannister RC 4.00 1.50
❑ 141 Scotty Anderson RC 4.00 1.50
❑ 142 Onome Ojo RC 4.00 1.50
❑ 143 Damerien McCants RC 4.00 1.50
❑ 144 Eddie Berlin RC 4.00 1.50
❑ 145 Cedrick Wilson RC 6.00 2.50
❑ 146 Kevin Kasper RC 6.00 2.50
❑ 147 T.J. Houshmandzadeh RC 8.00 3.00
❑ 148 Reggie Germany RC 4.00 1.50
❑ 149 Chris Taylor RC 4.00 1.50
❑ 150 Ken-Yon Rambo RC 4.00 1.50
❑ 151 Quentin McCord RC 4.00 1.50
❑ 152 Andre King RC 4.00 1.50
❑ 153 Arnold Jackson RC 4.00 1.50
❑ 154 Tim Baker RC 2.50 1.00
❑ 155 Drew Bennett RC 12.00 5.00
❑ 156 Cedric James RC 4.00 1.50
❑ 157 Todd Heap RC 6.00 2.50
❑ 158 Alge Crumpler RC 8.00 4.00
❑ 159 Sean Brewer RC 2.50 1.00
❑ 160 Shad Meier RC 4.00 1.50
❑ 161 Brandon Manumaleuna RC 4.00 1.50
❑ 162 Tony Stewart RC 6.00 2.50
❑ 163 David Martin RC 4.00 1.50
❑ 164 Matt Dominguez RC 4.00 1.50
❑ 165 Boo Williams RC 4.00 1.50
❑ 166 Justin Smith RC 6.00 2.50
❑ 167 Andre Carter RC 6.00 2.50
❑ 168 Jamal Reynolds RC 6.00 2.50
❑ 169 Ryan Pickett RC 2.50 1.00
❑ 170 Aaron Schobel RC 6.00 2.50
❑ 171 Derrick Burgess RC 6.00 2.50
❑ 172 DeLawrence Grant RC 2.50 1.00
❑ 173 Karon Riley RC 2.50 1.00
❑ 174 Richard Seymour RC 6.00 2.50
❑ 175 Marcus Stroud RC 6.00 2.50
❑ 176 Casey Hampton RC 6.00 2.50
❑ 177 Shaun Rogers RC 6.00 2.50
❑ 178 Kris Jenkins RC 6.00 2.50
❑ 179 Eric Downing RC 2.50 1.00
❑ 180 Kenny Smith RC 4.00 1.50
❑ 181 Marcus Bell RC 4.00 1.50
❑ 182 Dan Morgan RC 6.00 2.50
❑ 183 Kendrell Bell RC 8.00 3.00
❑ 184 Tommy Polley RC 6.00 2.50
❑ 185 Jamie Winborn RC 4.00 1.50
❑ 186 Quinton Caver RC 4.00 1.50
❑ 187 Sedrick Hodge RC 2.50 1.00
❑ 188 Brian Allen RC 2.50 1.00
❑ 189 Torrance Marshall RC 6.00 2.50
❑ 190 Willie Middlebrooks RC 4.00 1.50
❑ 191 Jamar Fletcher RC 4.00 1.50
❑ 192 Ken Lucas RC 4.00 1.50
❑ 193 Fred Smoot RC 6.00 2.50
❑ 194 Andre Dyson RC 2.50 1.00
❑ 195 Anthony Henry RC 6.00 2.50
❑ 196 Adam Archuleta RC 6.00 2.50
❑ 197 Idrees Bashir RC 2.50 1.00
❑ 198 Adrian Wilson RC 4.00 1.50
❑ 199 Cory Bird RC 6.00 2.50
❑ 200 Jarrod Cooper RC 6.00 2.50
❑ 201 L Tomlinson JSY/400 RC 60.00 35.00
❑ 202 Chris Weinke JSY/400 RC 10.00 4.00
❑ 203 Anthony Thomas FB/400 RC 12.00 5.00
❑ 204 Koren Robinson JSY/400 RC 12.00 5.00
❑ 205 James Jackson JSY/400 RC 10.00 4.00
❑ 206 Kevan Barlow FB/400 RC 10.00 4.00
❑ 207 Quincy Morgan JSY/400 RC 12.00 5.00
❑ 208 Nate Clements JSY/400 RC 8.00 3.00
❑ 209 Travis Henry JSY/400 RC 15.00 6.00
❑ 210 Damione Lewis FB/400 RC 8.00 3.00
❑ 211 Snoop Minnis FB/400 RC 10.00 4.00
❑ 212 David Terrell FB/600 RC 8.00 3.00
❑ 213 Gerard Warren JSY/600 RC 8.00 3.00
❑ 214 Chris Chambers JSY/600 RC 15.00 6.00
❑ 215 Will Allen FB/750 RC 6.00 2.50
❑ 216 Leonard Davis JSY/750 RC 6.00 2.50
❑ 217 Travis Minor JSY/750 RC 8.00 3.00
❑ 218 Will Peterson FB/750 RC 6.00 2.50
❑ 219 Rod Gardner FB/750 RC 6.00 2.50
❑ 220 Freddie Mitchell FB/750 RC 8.00 3.00
❑ 221 Derrick Gibson FB/750 RC 6.00 2.50
❑ 222 K Vanden Bosch JSY/750 RC 10.00 4.00
❑ 223 LaMont Jordan FB/750 RC 15.00 6.00
❑ 224 Quincy Carter FB/750 RC 8.00 3.00
❑ 225 C Buckhalter FB/750 RC 12.00 5.00

1998 Playoff Prestige Hobby

❑ COMP.HOBBY SET (200) 100.00 40.00
❑ 1 John Elway 8.00 3.00
❑ 2 Steve Atwater .75 .30
❑ 3 Terrell Davis 2.00 .75
❑ 4 Bill Romanowski .75 .30
❑ 5 Rod Smith 1.25 .50
❑ 6 Shannon Sharpe 1.25 .50
❑ 7 Ed McCaffrey 1.25 .50
❑ 8 Neil Smith 1.25 .50
❑ 9 Brett Favre 8.00 3.00
❑ 10 Dorsey Levens 2.00 .75
❑ 11 LeRoy Butler .75 .30
❑ 12 Antonio Freeman 2.00 .75
❑ 13 Robert Brooks 1.25 .50
❑ 14 Mark Chmura 1.25 .50
❑ 15 Gilbert Brown .75 .30
❑ 16 Kordell Stewart 2.00 .75
❑ 17 Jerome Bettis 2.00 .75
❑ 18 Carnell Lake .75 .30
❑ 19 Dermontti Dawson .75 .30
❑ 20 Charles Johnson .75 .30
❑ 21 Greg Lloyd .75 .30
❑ 22 Levon Kirkland .75 .30
❑ 23 Steve Young 2.50 1.00
❑ 24 Jim Druckenmiller .75 .30
❑ 25 Garrison Hearst 2.00 .75
❑ 26 Merton Hanks .75 .30
❑ 27 Ken Norton .75 .30
❑ 28 Jerry Rice 4.00 1.50
❑ 29 Terrell Owens 2.00 .75
❑ 30 J.J. Stokes 1.25 .50
❑ 31 Trent Dilfer 2.00 .75
❑ 32 Warrick Dunn 2.00 .75
❑ 33 Mike Alstott 2.00 .75
❑ 34 Reidel Anthony 1.25 .50
❑ 35 Warren Sapp 1.25 .50
❑ 36 Elvis Grbac 1.25 .50
❑ 37 Kimble Anders 1.25 .50
❑ 38 Ted Popson .75 .30
❑ 39 Derrick Thomas 2.00 .75
❑ 40 Tony Gonzalez 2.00 .75
❑ 41 Andre Rison 1.25 .50
❑ 42 Derrick Alexander 1.25 .50
❑ 43 Brad Johnson 2.00 .75
❑ 44 Robert Smith 2.00 .75
❑ 45 Randall McDaniel .75 .30
❑ 46 Cris Carter 2.00 .75
❑ 47 Jake Reed 1.25 .50
❑ 48 John Randle 1.25 .50
❑ 49 Drew Bledsoe 3.00 1.25
❑ 50 Willie Clay .75 .30
❑ 51 Chris Slade .75 .30
❑ 52 Willie McGinest .75 .30
❑ 53 Shawn Jefferson .75 .30
❑ 54 Ben Coates 1.25 .50
❑ 55 Terry Glenn 2.00 .75
❑ 56 Jason Hanson .75 .30
❑ 57 Scott Mitchell 1.25 .50
❑ 58 Barry Sanders 6.00 2.50
❑ 59 Herman Moore 1.25 .50
❑ 60 Johnnie Morton 1.25 .50
❑ 61 Mark Brunell 2.00 .75
❑ 62 James Stewart 1.25 .50
❑ 63 Tony Boselli .75 .30
❑ 64 Jimmy Smith 1.25 .50
❑ 65 Keenan McCardell 1.25 .50
❑ 66 Dan Marino 8.00 3.00
❑ 67 Troy Drayton .75 .30
❑ 68 Bernie Parmalee .75 .30
❑ 69 Karim Abdul-Jabbar 2.00 .75
❑ 70 Zach Thomas 2.00 .75
❑ 71 O.J. McDuffie 1.25 .50
❑ 72 Tim Bowens .75 .30
❑ 73 Danny Kanell 1.25 .50
❑ 74 Tiki Barber 2.00 .75
❑ 75 Tyrone Wheatley 1.25 .50
❑ 76 Charles Way .75 .30
❑ 77 Jason Sehorn 1.25 .50
❑ 78 Ike Hilliard 1.25 .50
❑ 79 Michael Strahan 1.25 .50
❑ 80 Troy Aikman 4.00 1.50
❑ 81 Deion Sanders 2.00 .75
❑ 82 Emmitt Smith 6.00 2.50
❑ 83 Darren Woodson .75 .30
❑ 84 Daryl Johnston 1.25 .50
❑ 85 Michael Irvin 2.00 .75
❑ 86 David LaFleur .75 .30
❑ 87 Glenn Foley 1.25 .50
❑ 88 Neil O'Donnell 1.25 .50
❑ 89 Keyshawn Johnson 2.00 .75
❑ 90 Aaron Glenn .75 .30
❑ 91 Wayne Chrebet 2.00 .75
❑ 92 Curtis Martin 2.00 .75
❑ 93 Steve McNair 2.00 .75
❑ 94 Eddie George 2.00 .75
❑ 95 Bruce Matthews .75 .30
❑ 96 Frank Wycheck .75 .30
❑ 97 Yancey Thigpen .75 .30
❑ 98 Gus Frerotte .75 .30
❑ 99 Terry Allen 2.00 .75
❑ 100 Michael Westbrook 1.25 .50
❑ 101 Jamie Asher .75 .30
❑ 102 Marshall Faulk 2.50 1.00
❑ 103 Zack Crockett .75 .30
❑ 104 Ken Dilger .75 .30
❑ 105 Marvin Harrison 2.00 .75
❑ 106 Chris Chandler 1.25 .50
❑ 107 Byron Hanspard .75 .30
❑ 108 Jamal Anderson 2.00 .75
❑ 109 Terance Mathis 1.25 .50
❑ 110 Peter Boulware .75 .30
❑ 111 Michael Jackson .75 .30
❑ 112 Jim Harbaugh 1.25 .50
❑ 113 Errict Rhett 1.25 .50
❑ 114 Antowain Smith 2.00 .75
❑ 115 Thurman Thomas 2.00 .75

❑ 116 Bruce Smith 1.25 .50
❑ 117 Doug Flutie 2.00 .75
❑ 118 Rob Johnson 1.25 .50
❑ 119 Kerry Collins 1.25 .50
❑ 120 Fred Lane .75 .30
❑ 121 Wesley Walls 1.25 .50
❑ 122 William Floyd .75 .30
❑ 123 Kevin Greene 1.25 .50
❑ 124 Erik Kramer .75 .30
❑ 125 Darnell Autry .75 .30
❑ 126 Curtis Conway 1.25 .50
❑ 127 Edgar Bennett .75 .30
❑ 128 Jeff Blake 1.25 .50
❑ 129 Corey Dillon 2.00 .75
❑ 130 Carl Pickens 1.25 .50
❑ 131 Darnay Scott 1.25 .50
❑ 132 Jake Plummer 2.00 .75
❑ 133 Larry Centers .75 .30
❑ 134 Frank Sanders 1.25 .50
❑ 135 Rob Moore 1.25 .50
❑ 136 Adrian Murrell 1.25 .50
❑ 137 Troy Davis .75 .30
❑ 138 Ray Zellars .75 .30
❑ 139 Willie Roaf .75 .30
❑ 140 Andre Hastings .75 .30
❑ 141 Jeff George 1.25 .50
❑ 142 Napoleon Kaufman 2.00 .75
❑ 143 Desmond Howard 1.25 .50
❑ 144 Tim Brown 2.00 .75
❑ 145 James Jett 1.25 .50
❑ 146 Rickey Dudley .75 .30
❑ 147 Bobby Hoying 1.25 .50
❑ 148 Duce Staley 2.50 1.00
❑ 149 Charlie Garner 1.25 .50
❑ 150 Irving Fryar 1.25 .50
❑ 151 Chris T. Jones .75 .30
❑ 152 Tony Banks 1.25 .50
❑ 153 Craig Heyward .75 .30
❑ 154 Isaac Bruce 2.00 .75
❑ 155 Eddie Kennison 1.25 .50
❑ 156 Junior Seau 2.00 .75
❑ 157 Tony Martin 1.25 .50
❑ 158 Freddie Jones .75 .30
❑ 159 Natrone Means 1.25 .50
❑ 160 Warren Moon 2.00 .75
❑ 161 Steve Broussard .75 .30
❑ 162 Joey Galloway 1.25 .50
❑ 163 Brian Blades .75 .30
❑ 164 Ricky Watters 1.25 .50
❑ 165 Peyton Manning RC 25.00 12.50
❑ 166 Ryan Leaf RC 3.00 1.25
❑ 167 Andre Wadsworth RC 2.50 1.00
❑ 168 Charles Woodson RC 4.00 1.50
❑ 169 Curtis Enis RC 1.50 .60
❑ 170 Fred Taylor RC 5.00 2.00
❑ 171 Kevin Dyson RC 3.00 1.25
❑ 172 Robert Edwards RC 2.50 1.00
❑ 173 Randy Moss RC 12.00 6.00
❑ 174 R.W. McQuarters RC 2.50 1.00
❑ 175 John Avery RC 2.50 1.00
❑ 176 Marcus Nash RC 1.50 .60
❑ 177 Jerome Pathon RC 3.00 1.25
❑ 178 Jacquez Green RC 2.50 1.00
❑ 179 Robert Holcombe RC 2.50 1.00
❑ 180 Pat Johnson RC 2.50 1.00
❑ 181 Germane Crowell RC 2.50 1.00
❑ 182 Tony Simmons RC 2.50 1.00
❑ 183 Joe Jurevicius RC 3.00 1.25
❑ 184 Mikhael Ricks RC 2.50 1.00
❑ 185 Charlie Batch RC 3.00 1.25
❑ 186 Jon Ritchie RC 2.50 1.00
❑ 187 Scott Frost RC 1.50 .60
❑ 188 Skip Hicks RC 2.50 1.00
❑ 189 Brian Alford RC 1.50 .60
❑ 190 E.G. Green RC 2.50 1.00
❑ 191 Jammi German RC 1.50 .60
❑ 192 Ahman Green RC 12.00 5.00
❑ 193 Chris Floyd RC 1.50 .60
❑ 194 Larry Shannon RC 1.50 .60
❑ 195 Jonathan Quinn RC 3.00 1.25
❑ 196 Rashaan Shehee RC 2.50 1.00
❑ 197 Brian Griese RC 6.00 2.50
❑ 198 Hines Ward RC 10.00 5.00
❑ 199 Michael Pittman RC 4.00 2.00
❑ 200 Az-Zahir Hakim RC 3.00 1.25

1999 Playoff Prestige EXP

❑ COMPLETE SET (200) 50.00 25.00
❑ 1 Anthony McFarland RC 1.50 .60
❑ 2 Al Wilson RC 1.00 .40
❑ 3 Jevon Kearse RC 2.50 1.00
❑ 4 Aaron Brooks RC 3.00 1.25
❑ 5 Travis McGriff RC .75 .30
❑ 6 Jeff Paulk RC .75 .30
❑ 7 Shawn Bryson RC 1.50 .60
❑ 8 Karsten Bailey RC 1.00 .40
❑ 9 Mike Cloud RC 1.00 .40
❑ 10 James Johnson RC 1.00 .40
❑ 11 Tai Streets RC 1.50 .60
❑ 12 Jermaine Fazande RC 1.00 .40
❑ 13 Ebenezer Ekuban RC 1.00 .40
❑ 14 Joe Montgomery RC 1.00 .40
❑ 15 Craig Yeast RC 1.00 .40
❑ 16 Joe Germaine RC 1.00 .40
❑ 17 Andy Katzenmoyer RC 1.00 .40
❑ 18 Kevin Faulk RC 1.50 .60
❑ 19 Chris McAlister RC 1.00 .40
❑ 20 Sedrick Irvin RC .75 .30
❑ 21 Brock Huard RC 1.50 .60
❑ 22 Cade McNown RC 1.00 .40
❑ 23 Shaun King RC 1.00 .40
❑ 24 Amos Zereoue RC 1.50 .60
❑ 25 Dameane Douglas RC 1.00 .40
❑ 26 D'Wayne Bates RC 1.00 .40
❑ 27 Kevin Johnson RC 1.50 .60
❑ 28 Rob Konrad RC 1.50 .60
❑ 29 Troy Edwards RC 1.00 .40
❑ 30 Peerless Price RC 1.50 .60
❑ 31 Daunte Culpepper RC 6.00 2.50
❑ 32 Akili Smith RC 1.00 .40
❑ 33 David Boston RC 1.50 .60
❑ 34 Chris Claiborne RC .75 .30
❑ 35 Torry Holt RC 4.00 1.50
❑ 36 Champ Bailey RC 2.00 .75
❑ 37 Edgerrin James RC 6.00 2.50
❑ 38 Donovan McNabb RC 8.00 3.00
❑ 39 Ricky Williams RC 3.00 1.25
❑ 40 Tim Couch RC 1.50 .60
❑ 41 Charles Woodson RP 1.00 .40
❑ 42 Skip Hicks RP .40 .15
❑ 43 Brian Griese RP 1.00 .40
❑ 44 Tim Dwight RP 1.00 .40
❑ 45 Ryan Leaf RP .60 .25
❑ 46 Curtis Enis RP .40 .15
❑ 47 Charlie Batch RP 1.00 .40
❑ 48 Fred Taylor RP 1.00 .40
❑ 49 Peyton Manning RP 1.50 .60
❑ 50 Randy Moss RP 1.25 .50
❑ 51 Jim Harbaugh .60 .25
❑ 52 Warren Moon 1.00 .40
❑ 53 Jeff George .60 .25
❑ 54 Rich Gannon 1.00 .40
❑ 55 Scott Mitchell .40 .15
❑ 56 Kerry Collins .60 .25
❑ 57 Brad Johnson 1.00 .40
❑ 58 Charles Johnson .40 .15
❑ 59 Chris Calloway .40 .15
❑ 60 Tyrone Wheatley .60 .25
❑ 61 Michael Westbrook .60 .25
❑ 62 Skip Hicks .40 .15
❑ 63 Terry Allen .60 .25
❑ 64 Albert Connell .40 .15
❑ 65 Kevin Dyson .60 .25
❑ 66 Frank Wycheck .40 .15
❑ 67 Yancey Thigpen .40 .15
❑ 68 Steve McNair 1.00 .40
❑ 69 Eddie George 1.00 .40
❑ 70 Eric Zeier .40 .15
❑ 71 Jacquez Green .40 .15
❑ 72 Reidel Anthony .60 .25
❑ 73 Warren Sapp .60 .25
❑ 74 Mike Alstott 1.00 .40
❑ 75 Warrick Dunn 1.00 .40
❑ 76 Trent Dilfer .60 .25
❑ 77 Ahman Green 1.00 .40
❑ 78 Joey Galloway .60 .25
❑ 79 Ricky Watters .60 .25
❑ 80 Jon Kitna 1.00 .40
❑ 81 Amp Lee .40 .15
❑ 82 Isaac Bruce 1.00 .40
❑ 83 Robert Holcombe .40 .15
❑ 84 Greg Hill .40 .15
❑ 85 Marshall Faulk 1.25 .50
❑ 86 Trent Green 1.00 .40
❑ 87 J.J. Stokes .60 .25
❑ 88 Terrell Owens 1.00 .40
❑ 89 Jerry Rice 2.00 .75
❑ 90 Garrison Hearst .60 .25
❑ 91 Steve Young 1.25 .50
❑ 92 Junior Seau 1.00 .40
❑ 93 Mikhael Ricks .40 .15
❑ 94 Natrone Means .60 .25
❑ 95 Ryan Leaf 1.00 .40
❑ 96 Courtney Hawkins .40 .15
❑ 97 Chris Fuamatu-Ma'afala UER .40 .15
❑ 98 Jerome Bettis 1.00 .40
❑ 99 Kordell Stewart .60 .25
❑ 100 Bobby Hoying .60 .25
❑ 101 Charlie Garner .60 .25
❑ 102 Duce Staley 1.00 .40
❑ 103 Charles Woodson 1.00 .40
❑ 104 James Jett .60 .25
❑ 105 Rickey Dudley .40 .15
❑ 106 Tim Brown 1.00 .40
❑ 107 Napoleon Kaufman 1.00 .40
❑ 108 Wayne Chrebet .60 .25
❑ 109 Keyshawn Johnson 1.00 .40
❑ 110 Vinny Testaverde .60 .25
❑ 111 Curtis Martin 1.00 .40
❑ 112 Joe Jurevicius .60 .25
❑ 113 Tiki Barber 1.00 .40
❑ 114 Ike Hilliard .40 .15
❑ 115 Kent Graham .40 .15
❑ 116 Gary Brown .40 .15
❑ 117 Lamar Smith .60 .25
❑ 118 Eddie Kennison .60 .25
❑ 119 Cam Cleeland .40 .15
❑ 120 Tony Simmons .40 .15
❑ 121 Ben Coates .60 .25
❑ 122 Darick Holmes .40 .15
❑ 123 Terry Glenn 1.00 .40
❑ 124 Drew Bledsoe 1.25 .50
❑ 125 Leroy Hoard .40 .15
❑ 126 Jake Reed .60 .25
❑ 127 Randy Moss 2.50 1.00
❑ 128 Cris Carter 1.00 .40
❑ 129 Robert Smith 1.00 .40
❑ 130 Randall Cunningham 1.00 .40
❑ 131 Lamar Thomas .40 .15
❑ 132 John Avery .40 .15
❑ 133 O.J. McDuffie .60 .25
❑ 134 Dan Marino 3.00 1.25
❑ 135 Karim Abdul-Jabbar .60 .25
❑ 136 Rashaan Shehee .40 .15
❑ 137 Derrick Alexander WR .60 .25
❑ 138 Byron Bam Morris .40 .15
❑ 139 Andre Rison .60 .25
❑ 140 Elvis Grbac .60 .25
❑ 141 Tavian Banks .40 .15
❑ 142 Keenan McCardell .60 .25
❑ 143 Jimmy Smith .60 .25
❑ 144 Fred Taylor 1.00 .40
❑ 145 Mark Brunell 1.00 .40
❑ 146 Jerome Pathon .40 .15
❑ 147 Marvin Harrison 1.00 .40
❑ 148 Peyton Manning 3.00 1.25
❑ 149 Robert Brooks .60 .25
❑ 150 Mark Chmura .40 .15
❑ 151 Antonio Freeman 1.00 .40
❑ 152 Dorsey Levens 1.00 .40

☐ 153	Brett Favre	3.00	1.25
☐ 154	Johnnie Morton	.60	.25
☐ 155	Germane Crowell	.40	.15
☐ 156	Barry Sanders	3.00	1.25
☐ 157	Herman Moore	.60	.25
☐ 158	Charlie Batch	1.00	.40
☐ 159	Marcus Nash	.40	.15
☐ 160	Shannon Sharpe	.60	.25
☐ 161	Rod Smith	.60	.25
☐ 162	Ed McCaffrey	.60	.25
☐ 163	Terrell Davis	1.00	.40
☐ 164	John Elway	3.00	1.25
☐ 165	Ernie Mills	.40	.15
☐ 166	Michael Irvin	.60	.25
☐ 167	Deion Sanders	1.00	.40
☐ 168	Emmitt Smith	2.00	.75
☐ 169	Troy Aikman	2.00	.75
☐ 170	Chris Spielman	.40	.15
☐ 171	Terry Kirby	.40	.15
☐ 172	Ty Detmer	.60	.25
☐ 173	Leslie Shepherd	.40	.15
☐ 174	Darnay Scott	.40	.15
☐ 175	Jeff Blake	.60	.25
☐ 176	Carl Pickens	.60	.25
☐ 177	Corey Dillon	1.00	.40
☐ 178	Bobby Engram	.60	.25
☐ 179	Curtis Conway	.60	.25
☐ 180	Curtis Enis	.40	.15
☐ 181	Muhsin Muhammad	.60	.25
☐ 182	Steve Beuerlein	.40	.15
☐ 183	Tim Biakabutuka	.60	.25
☐ 184	Bruce Smith	.60	.25
☐ 185	Andre Reed	.60	.25
☐ 186	Thurman Thomas	.60	.25
☐ 187	Eric Moulds	1.00	.40
☐ 188	Antowain Smith	1.00	.40
☐ 189	Doug Flutie	1.00	.40
☐ 190	Jermaine Lewis	.60	.25
☐ 191	Priest Holmes	1.50	.60
☐ 192	O.J. Santiago	.40	.15
☐ 193	Tim Dwight	1.00	.40
☐ 194	Terance Mathis	.60	.25
☐ 195	Chris Chandler	.60	.25
☐ 196	Jamal Anderson	1.00	.40
☐ 197	Rob Moore	.60	.25
☐ 198	Frank Sanders	.60	.25
☐ 199	Adrian Murrell	.60	.25
☐ 200	Jake Plummer	.60	.25
☐ RR1	Barry Sanders RFR	20.00	7.50

1999 Playoff Prestige SSD

☐	COMPLETE SET (200)	150.00	75.00
☐	COMP.SET w/o SP's (150)	50.00	25.00
☐ 1	Jake Plummer	.75	.30
☐ 2	Adrian Murrell	.75	.30
☐ 3	Frank Sanders	.75	.30
☐ 4	Rob Moore	.75	.30
☐ 5	Jamal Anderson	1.25	.50
☐ 6	Chris Chandler	.75	.30
☐ 7	Terance Mathis	.75	.30
☐ 8	Tim Dwight	1.25	.50
☐ 9	O.J. Santiago	.50	.20
☐ 10	Priest Holmes	2.00	.75
☐ 11	Jermaine Lewis	.75	.30
☐ 12	Doug Flutie	1.25	.50
☐ 13	Antowain Smith	1.25	.50
☐ 14	Eric Moulds	1.25	.50
☐ 15	Thurman Thomas	.75	.30
☐ 16	Andre Reed	.75	.30
☐ 17	Bruce Smith	.75	.30
☐ 18	Tim Biakabutuka	.75	.30
☐ 19	Steve Beuerlein	.50	.20
☐ 20	Muhsin Muhammad	.75	.30
☐ 21	Curtis Enis	.50	.20
☐ 22	Curtis Conway	.75	.30
☐ 23	Bobby Engram	.75	.30
☐ 24	Corey Dillon	1.25	.50
☐ 25	Carl Pickens	.75	.30
☐ 26	Jeff Blake	.75	.30
☐ 27	Darnay Scott	.50	.20
☐ 28	Leslie Shepherd	.50	.20
☐ 29	Ty Detmer	.75	.30
☐ 30	Terry Kirby	.50	.20
☐ 31	Chris Spielman	.50	.20
☐ 32	Troy Aikman	3.00	1.25
☐ 33	Emmitt Smith	3.00	1.25
☐ 34	Deion Sanders	1.25	.50
☐ 35	Michael Irvin	.75	.30
☐ 36	Ernie Mills	.50	.20
☐ 37	John Elway	5.00	2.00
☐ 38	Terrell Davis	1.25	.50
☐ 39	Ed McCaffrey	.75	.30
☐ 40	Rod Smith	.75	.30
☐ 41	Shannon Sharpe	.75	.30
☐ 42	Marcus Nash	.50	.20
☐ 43	Charlie Batch	1.25	.50
☐ 44	Herman Moore	.75	.30
☐ 45	Barry Sanders	5.00	2.00
☐ 46	Germane Crowell	.50	.20
☐ 47	Johnnie Morton	.75	.30
☐ 48	Brett Favre	5.00	2.00
☐ 49	Dorsey Levens	1.25	.50
☐ 50	Antonio Freeman	1.25	.50
☐ 51	Mark Chmura	.50	.20
☐ 52	Robert Brooks	.75	.30
☐ 53	Peyton Manning	5.00	2.00
☐ 54	Marvin Harrison	1.25	.50
☐ 55	Jerome Pathon	.50	.20
☐ 56	Mark Brunell	1.25	.50
☐ 57	Fred Taylor	1.25	.50
☐ 58	Jimmy Smith	.75	.30
☐ 59	Keenan McCardell	.75	.30
☐ 60	Tavian Banks	.50	.20
☐ 61	Elvis Grbac	.75	.30
☐ 62	Andre Rison	.75	.30
☐ 63	Byron Bam Morris	.50	.20
☐ 64	Derrick Alexander WR	.75	.30
☐ 65	Rashaan Shehee	.50	.20
☐ 66	Karim Abdul-Jabbar	.75	.30
☐ 67	Dan Marino	5.00	2.00
☐ 68	O.J. McDuffie	.75	.30
☐ 69	John Avery	.50	.20
☐ 70	Lamar Thomas	.50	.20
☐ 71	Randall Cunningham	1.25	.50
☐ 72	Robert Smith	1.25	.50
☐ 73	Cris Carter	1.25	.50
☐ 74	Randy Moss	4.00	1.50
☐ 75	Jake Reed	.75	.30
☐ 76	Leroy Hoard	.50	.20
☐ 77	Drew Bledsoe	2.00	.75
☐ 78	Terry Glenn	1.25	.50
☐ 79	Darick Holmes	.50	.20
☐ 80	Ben Coates	.75	.30
☐ 81	Tony Simmons	.50	.20
☐ 82	Cam Cleeland	.50	.20
☐ 83	Eddie Kennison	.75	.30
☐ 84	Lamar Smith	.75	.30
☐ 85	Gary Brown	.50	.20
☐ 86	Kent Graham	.50	.20
☐ 87	Ike Hilliard	.50	.20
☐ 88	Tiki Barber	1.25	.50
☐ 89	Joe Jurevicius	.75	.30
☐ 90	Curtis Martin	1.25	.50
☐ 91	Vinny Testaverde	.75	.30
☐ 92	Keyshawn Johnson	1.25	.50
☐ 93	Wayne Chrebet	.75	.30
☐ 94	Napoleon Kaufman	1.25	.50
☐ 95	Tim Brown	1.25	.50
☐ 96	Rickey Dudley	.50	.20
☐ 97	James Jett	.75	.30
☐ 98	Charles Woodson	1.25	.50
☐ 99	Duce Staley	1.25	.50
☐ 100	Charlie Garner	.75	.30
☐ 101	Bobby Hoying	.75	.30
☐ 102	Kordell Stewart	.75	.30
☐ 103	Jerome Bettis	1.25	.50
☐ 104	Chris Fuamatu-Ma'afala	.50	.20
☐ 105	Courtney Hawkins	.50	.20
☐ 106	Ryan Leaf	1.25	.50
☐ 107	Natrone Means	.75	.30
☐ 108	Mikhael Ricks	.50	.20
☐ 109	Junior Seau	1.25	.50
☐ 110	Steve Young	2.00	.75
☐ 111	Garrison Hearst	.75	.30
☐ 112	Jerry Rice	3.00	1.25
☐ 113	Terrell Owens	1.25	.50
☐ 114	J.J. Stokes	.75	.30
☐ 115	Trent Green	1.25	.50
☐ 116	Marshall Faulk	1.50	.60
☐ 117	Greg Hill	.50	.20
☐ 118	Robert Holcombe	.50	.20
☐ 119	Isaac Bruce	1.25	.50
☐ 120	Amp Lee	.50	.20
☐ 121	Jon Kitna	1.25	.50
☐ 122	Ricky Watters	.75	.30
☐ 123	Joey Galloway	.75	.30
☐ 124	Ahman Green	1.25	.50
☐ 125	Trent Dilfer	.75	.30
☐ 126	Warrick Dunn	1.25	.50
☐ 127	Mike Alstott	1.25	.50
☐ 128	Warren Sapp	.75	.30
☐ 129	Reidel Anthony	.75	.30
☐ 130	Jacquez Green	.50	.20
☐ 131	Eric Zeier	.50	.20
☐ 132	Eddie George	1.25	.50
☐ 133	Steve McNair	1.25	.50
☐ 134	Yancey Thigpen	.50	.20
☐ 135	Frank Wycheck	.50	.20
☐ 136	Kevin Dyson	.75	.30
☐ 137	Albert Connell	.50	.20
☐ 138	Terry Allen	.75	.30
☐ 139	Skip Hicks	.50	.20
☐ 140	Michael Westbrook	.75	.30
☐ 141	Tyrone Wheatley	.75	.30
☐ 142	Chris Calloway	.50	.20
☐ 143	Charles Johnson	.50	.20
☐ 144	Brad Johnson	1.25	.50
☐ 145	Kerry Collins	.75	.30
☐ 146	Scott Mitchell	.50	.20
☐ 147	Rich Gannon	1.25	.50
☐ 148	Jeff George	.75	.30
☐ 149	Warren Moon	1.25	.50
☐ 150	Jim Harbaugh	.75	.30
☐ 151	Randy Moss RP	6.00	2.50
☐ 152	Peyton Manning RP	8.00	3.00
☐ 153	Fred Taylor RP	2.50	1.00
☐ 154	Charlie Batch RP	2.50	1.00
☐ 155	Curtis Enis RP	1.50	.60
☐ 156	Ryan Leaf RP	1.50	.60
☐ 157	Tim Dwight RP	1.50	.60
☐ 158	Brian Griese RP	2.50	1.00
☐ 159	Skip Hicks RP	1.50	.60
☐ 160	Charles Woodson RP	2.50	1.00
☐ 161	Tim Couch RC	4.00	1.50
☐ 162	Ricky Williams RC	6.00	2.50
☐ 163	Donovan McNabb RC	15.00	6.00
☐ 164	Edgerrin James RC	12.00	5.00
☐ 165	Champ Bailey RC	5.00	2.00
☐ 166	Torry Holt RC	8.00	3.00
☐ 167	Chris Claiborne RC	2.00	.75
☐ 168	David Boston RC	4.00	1.50
☐ 169	Akili Smith RC	1.50	.60
☐ 170	Daunte Culpepper RC	12.00	5.00
☐ 171	Peerless Price RC	4.00	1.50
☐ 172	Troy Edwards RC	3.00	1.25
☐ 173	Rob Konrad RC	4.00	1.50
☐ 174	Kevin Johnson RC	4.00	1.50
☐ 175	D'Wayne Bates RC	3.00	1.25
☐ 176	Dameane Douglas RC	3.00	1.25
☐ 177	Amos Zereoue RC	4.00	1.50
☐ 178	Shaun King RC	3.00	1.25
☐ 179	Cade McNown RC	3.00	1.25
☐ 180	Brock Huard RC	4.00	1.50
☐ 181	Sedrick Irvin RC	2.00	.75
☐ 182	Chris McAlister RC	3.00	1.25
☐ 183	Kevin Faulk RC	4.00	1.50
☐ 184	Andy Katzenmoyer RC	3.00	1.25
☐ 185	Joe Germaine RC	3.00	1.25
☐ 186	Craig Yeast RC	3.00	1.25
☐ 187	Joe Montgomery RC	3.00	1.25
☐ 188	Ebenezer Ekuban RC	3.00	1.25
☐ 189	Jermaine Fazande RC	3.00	1.25

❑ 190 Tai Streets RC	4.00	1.50
❑ 191 James Johnson RC	3.00	1.25
❑ 192 Mike Cloud RC	3.00	1.25
❑ 193 Karsten Bailey RC	3.00	1.25
❑ 194 Shawn Bryson RC	4.00	1.50
❑ 195 Jeff Paulk RC	2.00	.75
❑ 196 Travis McGriff RC	2.00	.75
❑ 197 Aaron Brooks RC	6.00	2.50
❑ 198 Jevon Kearse RC	6.00	2.50
❑ 199 Al Wilson RC	3.00	1.25
❑ 200 Anthony McFarland RC	4.00	1.50

2000 Playoff Prestige

❑ COMPLETE SET (300)	350.00	175.00
❑ COMP.SET w/o SP's (200)	25.00	10.00
❑ 1 Frank Sanders	.40	.15
❑ 2 Rob Moore	.40	.15
❑ 3 Michael Pittman	.25	.08
❑ 4 Jake Plummer	.40	.15
❑ 5 David Boston	.60	.25
❑ 6 Chris Chandler	.40	.15
❑ 7 Tim Dwight	.60	.25
❑ 8 Shawn Jefferson	.25	.08
❑ 9 Terance Mathis	.40	.15
❑ 10 Jamal Anderson	.60	.25
❑ 11 Byron Hanspard	.25	.08
❑ 12 Ken Oxendine	.25	.08
❑ 13 Priest Holmes	.75	.30
❑ 14 Tony Banks	.40	.15
❑ 15 Shannon Sharpe	.40	.15
❑ 16 Rod Woodson	.40	.15
❑ 17 Jermaine Lewis	.40	.15
❑ 18 Qadry Ismail	.40	.15
❑ 19 Eric Moulds	.60	.25
❑ 20 Doug Flutie	.60	.25
❑ 21 Jay Riemersma	.25	.08
❑ 22 Antowain Smith	.40	.15
❑ 23 Jonathan Linton	.25	.08
❑ 24 Peerless Price	.40	.15
❑ 25 Rob Johnson	.40	.15
❑ 26 Muhsin Muhammad	.40	.15
❑ 27 Wesley Walls	.25	.08
❑ 28 Tim Biakabutuka	.40	.15
❑ 29 Steve Beuerlein	.40	.15
❑ 30 Patrick Jeffers	.60	.25
❑ 31 Natrone Means	.25	.08
❑ 32 Curtis Enis	.25	.08
❑ 33 Bobby Engram	.40	.15
❑ 34 Marcus Robinson	.60	.25
❑ 35 Marty Booker	.40	.15
❑ 36 Cade McNown	.25	.08
❑ 37 Darnay Scott	.40	.15
❑ 38 Carl Pickens	.40	.15
❑ 39 Corey Dillon	.60	.25
❑ 40 Akili Smith	.25	.08
❑ 41 Michael Basnight	.25	.08
❑ 42 Karim Abdul-Jabbar	.40	.15
❑ 43 Tim Couch	.40	.15
❑ 44 Kevin Johnson	.60	.25
❑ 45 Darrin Chiaverini	.25	.08
❑ 46 Errict Rhett	.40	.15
❑ 47 Emmitt Smith	1.25	.50
❑ 48 Deion Sanders	.60	.25
❑ 49 Michael Irvin	.40	.15
❑ 50 Rocket Ismail	.40	.15
❑ 51 Troy Aikman	1.25	.50
❑ 52 Jason Tucker	.25	.08
❑ 53 Joey Galloway	.40	.15
❑ 54 David LaFleur	.25	.08

❑ 55 Wane McGarity	.25	.08
❑ 56 Ed McCaffrey	.60	.25
❑ 57 Rod Smith	.40	.15
❑ 58 Brian Griese	.60	.25
❑ 59 John Elway	2.00	.75
❑ 60 Gus Frerotte	.25	.08
❑ 61 Neil Smith	.25	.08
❑ 62 Terrell Davis	.60	.25
❑ 63 Olandis Gary	.60	.25
❑ 64 Johnnie Morton	.40	.15
❑ 65 Charlie Batch	.60	.25
❑ 66 Barry Sanders	1.50	.60
❑ 67 James Stewart	.40	.15
❑ 68 Germane Crowell	.25	.08
❑ 69 Sedrick Irvin	.25	.08
❑ 70 Herman Moore	.40	.15
❑ 71 Corey Bradford	.40	.15
❑ 72 Dorsey Levens	.40	.15
❑ 73 Antonio Freeman	.60	.25
❑ 74 Brett Favre	2.00	.75
❑ 75 De'Mond Parker	.25	.08
❑ 76 Bill Schroeder	.40	.15
❑ 77 Donald Driver	.60	.25
❑ 78 E.G. Green	.25	.08
❑ 79 Marvin Harrison	.60	.25
❑ 80 Peyton Manning	1.50	.60
❑ 81 Terrence Wilkins	.25	.08
❑ 82 Edgerrin James	1.00	.40
❑ 83 Keenan McCardell	.40	.15
❑ 84 Mark Brunell	.60	.25
❑ 85 Fred Taylor	.60	.25
❑ 86 Jimmy Smith	.40	.15
❑ 87 Derrick Alexander	.40	.15
❑ 88 Andre Rison	.40	.15
❑ 89 Elvis Grbac	.40	.15
❑ 90 Tony Gonzalez	.40	.15
❑ 91 Donnell Bennett	.25	.08
❑ 92 Warren Moon	.60	.25
❑ 93 Kimble Anders	.25	.08
❑ 94 Tony Richardson RC	.40	.15
❑ 95 Jay Fiedler	.60	.25
❑ 96 Zach Thomas	.60	.25
❑ 97 Oronde Gadsden	.40	.15
❑ 98 Dan Marino	2.00	.75
❑ 99 O.J. McDuffie	.40	.15
❑ 100 Tony Martin	.40	.15
❑ 101 James Johnson	.25	.08
❑ 102 Rob Konrad	.25	.08
❑ 103 Damon Huard	.60	.25
❑ 104 Thurman Thomas	.40	.15
❑ 105 Randy Moss	1.25	.50
❑ 106 Cris Carter	.60	.25
❑ 107 Robert Smith	.60	.25
❑ 108 Randall Cunningham	.60	.25
❑ 109 John Randle	.40	.15
❑ 110 Leroy Hoard	.25	.08
❑ 111 Daunte Culpepper	.75	.30
❑ 112 Matthew Hatchette	.25	.08
❑ 113 Troy Brown	.40	.15
❑ 114 Tony Simmons	.25	.08
❑ 115 Terry Glenn	.40	.15
❑ 116 Ben Coates	.25	.08
❑ 117 Drew Bledsoe	.75	.30
❑ 118 Terry Allen	.40	.15
❑ 119 Kevin Faulk	.25	.08
❑ 120 Ricky Williams	.60	.25
❑ 121 Jake Delhomme RC	3.00	1.25
❑ 122 Jake Reed	.40	.15
❑ 123 Jeff Blake	.40	.15
❑ 124 Amani Toomer	.40	.15
❑ 125 Kerry Collins	.40	.15
❑ 126 Tiki Barber	.60	.25
❑ 127 Ike Hilliard	.40	.15
❑ 128 Joe Montgomery	.25	.08
❑ 129 Sean Bennett	.25	.08
❑ 130 Curtis Martin	.60	.25
❑ 131 Vinny Testaverde	.40	.15
❑ 132 Wayne Chrebet	.40	.15
❑ 133 Ray Lucas	.40	.15
❑ 134 Tyrone Wheatley	.40	.15
❑ 135 Napoleon Kaufman	.40	.15
❑ 136 Tim Brown	.60	.25
❑ 137 Rickey Dudley	.25	.08
❑ 138 James Jett	.25	.08
❑ 139 Rich Gannon	.60	.25
❑ 140 Charles Woodson	.40	.15
❑ 141 Duce Staley	.60	.25

❑ 142 Donovan McNabb	1.00	.40
❑ 143 Na Brown	.25	.08
❑ 144 Kordell Stewart	.40	.15
❑ 145 Jerome Bettis	.60	.25
❑ 146 Hines Ward	.60	.25
❑ 147 Troy Edwards	.25	.08
❑ 148 Curtis Conway	.40	.15
❑ 149 Junior Seau	.60	.25
❑ 150 Jim Harbaugh	.40	.15
❑ 151 Jermaine Fazande	.25	.08
❑ 152 Terrell Owens	.60	.25
❑ 153 J.J. Stokes	.40	.15
❑ 154 Charlie Garner	.40	.15
❑ 155 Jerry Rice	1.25	.50
❑ 156 Garrison Hearst	.40	.15
❑ 157 Steve Young	.75	.30
❑ 158 Jeff Garcia	.60	.25
❑ 159 Derrick Mayes	.40	.15
❑ 160 Ahman Green	.60	.25
❑ 161 Ricky Watters	.40	.15
❑ 162 Jon Kitna	.60	.25
❑ 163 Karsten Bailey	.25	.08
❑ 164 Sean Dawkins	.25	.08
❑ 165 Az-Zahir Hakim	.40	.15
❑ 166 Isaac Bruce	.60	.25
❑ 167 Marshall Faulk	.75	.30
❑ 168 Trent Green	.60	.25
❑ 169 Kurt Warner	1.25	.50
❑ 170 Torry Holt	.60	.25
❑ 171 Robert Holcombe	.25	.08
❑ 172 Kevin Carter	.25	.08
❑ 173 Keyshawn Johnson	.60	.25
❑ 174 Jacquez Green	.25	.08
❑ 175 Reidel Anthony	.25	.08
❑ 176 Warren Sapp	.40	.15
❑ 177 Mike Alstott	.60	.25
❑ 178 Warrick Dunn	.60	.25
❑ 179 Trent Dilfer	.40	.15
❑ 180 Shaun King	.25	.08
❑ 181 Neil O'Donnell	.25	.08
❑ 182 Eddie George	.60	.25
❑ 183 Yancey Thigpen	.25	.08
❑ 184 Steve McNair	.60	.25
❑ 185 Kevin Dyson	.40	.15
❑ 186 Frank Wycheck	.25	.08
❑ 187 Jevon Kearse	.60	.25
❑ 188 Adrian Murrell	.25	.08
❑ 189 Jeff George	.40	.15
❑ 190 Stephen Davis	.60	.25
❑ 191 Stephen Alexander	.25	.08
❑ 192 Darrell Green	.25	.08
❑ 193 Skip Hicks	.25	.08
❑ 194 Brad Johnson	.60	.25
❑ 195 Michael Westbrook	.40	.15
❑ 196 Albert Connell	.25	.08
❑ 197 Irving Fryar	.40	.15
❑ 198 Bruce Smith	.40	.15
❑ 199 Champ Bailey	.40	.15
❑ 200 Larry Centers	.25	.08
❑ 201 Jake Plummer PP	1.25	.50
❑ 202 Doug Flutie PP	1.25	.50
❑ 203 Eric Moulds PP	1.25	.50
❑ 204 Muhsin Muhammad PP	1.25	.50
❑ 205 Marcus Robinson PP	1.25	.50
❑ 206 Cade McNown PP	1.25	.50
❑ 207 Corey Dillon PP	1.25	.50
❑ 208 Tim Couch PP	1.25	.50
❑ 209 Kevin Johnson PP	1.25	.50
❑ 210 Emmitt Smith PP	3.00	1.25
❑ 211 Troy Aikman PP	3.00	1.25
❑ 212 Brian Griese PP	1.25	.50
❑ 213 Olandis Gary PP	1.25	.50
❑ 214 Germane Crowell PP	1.25	.50
❑ 215 Brett Favre PP	5.00	2.00
❑ 216 Charlie Batch PP	1.25	.50
❑ 217 Antonio Freeman PP	1.25	.50
❑ 218 Dorsey Levens PP	1.25	.50
❑ 219 Peyton Manning PP	4.00	1.50
❑ 220 Edgerrin James PP	2.50	1.00
❑ 221 Marvin Harrison PP	1.25	.50
❑ 222 Fred Taylor PP	1.25	.50
❑ 223 Mark Brunell PP	1.25	.50
❑ 224 Jimmy Smith PP	1.25	.50
❑ 225 Dan Marino PP	5.00	2.00
❑ 226 Randy Moss PP	3.00	1.25
❑ 227 Cris Carter PP	1.25	.50
❑ 228 Robert Smith PP	1.25	.50

❑ 229 Drew Bledsoe PP	2.00	.75
❑ 230 Terry Glenn PP	1.25	.50
❑ 231 Ricky Williams PP	1.25	.50
❑ 232 Amani Toomer PP	1.25	.50
❑ 233 Keyshawn Johnson PP	1.25	.50
❑ 234 Curtis Martin PP	1.25	.50
❑ 235 Ray Lucas PP	1.25	.50
❑ 236 Tim Brown PP	1.25	.50
❑ 237 Duce Staley PP	1.25	.50
❑ 238 Donovan McNabb PP	2.50	1.00
❑ 239 Jerry Rice PP	3.00	1.25
❑ 240 Jon Kitna PP	1.25	.50
❑ 241 Isaac Bruce PP	1.25	.50
❑ 242 Kurt Warner PP	3.00	1.25
❑ 243 Torry Holt PP	1.25	.50
❑ 244 Mike Alstott PP	1.25	.50
❑ 245 Marshall Faulk PP	2.00	.75
❑ 246 Shaun King PP	.25	.08
❑ 247 Eddie George PP	1.25	.50
❑ 248 Steve McNair PP	1.25	.50
❑ 249 Stephen Davis PP	1.25	.50
❑ 250 Brad Johnson PP	1.25	.50
❑ 251 Rondell Mealey RC	2.50	1.00
❑ 252 Peter Warrick RC	4.00	1.50
❑ 253 Courtney Brown RC	1.25	.50
❑ 254 Plaxico Burress RC	8.00	3.00
❑ 255 Corey Simon RC	1.25	.50
❑ 256 Thomas Jones RC	6.00	2.50
❑ 257 Travis Taylor RC	1.25	.50
❑ 258 Shaun Alexander RC	20.00	7.50
❑ 259 Chris Redman RC	1.25	.50
❑ 260 Chad Pennington RC	10.00	4.00
❑ 261 Jamal Lewis RC	10.00	4.00
❑ 262 Bubba Franks RC	4.00	1.50
❑ 263 Dez White RC	4.00	1.50
❑ 264 Ron Dayne RC	4.00	1.50
❑ 265 Sylvester Morris RC	3.00	1.25
❑ 266 R.Jay Soward RC	3.00	1.25
❑ 267 Sherrod Gideon RC	2.50	1.00
❑ 268 Travis Prentice RC	3.00	1.25
❑ 269 Darrell Jackson RC	8.00	3.00
❑ 270 Giovanni Carmazzi RC	2.50	1.00
❑ 271 Anthony Lucas RC	2.50	1.00
❑ 272 Danny Farmer RC	3.00	1.25
❑ 273 Dennis Northcutt RC	4.00	1.50
❑ 274 Troy Walters RC	4.00	1.50
❑ 275 Laveranues Coles RC	5.00	2.00
❑ 276 Tee Martin RC	4.00	1.50
❑ 277 J.R. Redmond RC	3.00	1.25
❑ 278 Jerry Porter RC	5.00	2.00
❑ 279 Sebastian Janikowski RC	4.00	1.50
❑ 280 Michael Wiley RC	3.00	1.25
❑ 281 Reuben Droughns RC	5.00	2.00
❑ 282 Trung Canidate RC	3.00	1.25
❑ 283 Shyrone Stith RC	3.00	1.25
❑ 284 Trevor Gaylor RC	3.00	1.25
❑ 285 Marc Bulger RC	8.00	3.00
❑ 286 Tom Brady RC	40.00	20.00
❑ 287 Todd Husak RC	4.00	1.50
❑ 288 Jarious Jackson RC	3.00	1.25
❑ 289 Terrelle Smith RC	3.00	1.25
❑ 290 Chad Morton RC	4.00	1.50
❑ 291 Chris Cole RC	4.00	1.50
❑ 292 Kwame Cavil RC	2.50	1.00
❑ 293 JaJuan Dawson RC	2.50	1.00
❑ 294 Curtis Keaton RC	3.00	1.25
❑ 295 Tim Rattay RC	4.00	1.50
❑ 296 Joe Hamilton RC	3.00	1.25
❑ 297 Gari Scott RC	2.50	1.00
❑ 298 Mike Anderson RC	5.00	2.00
❑ 299 Ron Dugans RC	2.50	1.00
❑ 300 Todd Pinkston RC	4.00	1.50

2002 Playoff Prestige

❑ COMP.SET w/o SP's (150)	40.00	15.00
❑ 1 David Boston	1.25	.50
❑ 2 MarTay Jenkins	.50	.20
❑ 3 Jake Plummer	.75	.30
❑ 4 Chris Chandler	.75	.30
❑ 5 Jamal Anderson	.75	.30
❑ 6 Michael Vick	4.00	1.50
❑ 7 Maurice Smith	.75	.30
❑ 8 Elvis Grbac	.75	.30
❑ 9 Jamal Lewis	1.25	.50
❑ 10 Todd Heap	.50	.20
❑ 11 Qadry Ismail	.75	.30
❑ 12 Shannon Sharpe	.75	.30
❑ 13 Ray Lewis	1.25	.50
❑ 14 Rod Woodson	.75	.30
❑ 15 Travis Henry	1.25	.50
❑ 16 Rob Johnson	.75	.30
❑ 17 Eric Moulds	.75	.30
❑ 18 Nate Clements	.50	.20
❑ 19 Donald Hayes	.50	.20
❑ 20 Muhsin Muhammad	.75	.30
❑ 21 Steve Smith	1.25	.50
❑ 22 Wesley Walls	.50	.20
❑ 23 Chris Weinke	.75	.30
❑ 24 James Allen	.75	.30
❑ 25 David Terrell	1.25	.50
❑ 26 Anthony Thomas	.75	.30
❑ 27 Dez White	.50	.20
❑ 28 Brian Urlacher	2.00	.75
❑ 29 Mike Brown	1.25	.50
❑ 30 Corey Dillon	.75	.30
❑ 31 Chad Johnson	1.25	.50
❑ 32 Peter Warrick	.75	.30
❑ 33 Justin Smith	.50	.20
❑ 34 Tim Couch	.75	.30
❑ 35 James Jackson	.50	.20
❑ 36 Quincy Morgan	.50	.20
❑ 37 Kevin Johnson	.75	.30
❑ 38 Gerard Warren	.50	.20
❑ 39 Anthony Henry	.50	.20
❑ 40 Quincy Carter	.75	.30
❑ 41 Joey Galloway	.75	.30
❑ 42 Rocket Ismail	.75	.30
❑ 43 Ryan Leaf	.75	.30
❑ 44 Emmitt Smith	3.00	1.25
❑ 45 Troy Hambrick	.50	.20
❑ 46 Mike Anderson	1.25	.50
❑ 47 Terrell Davis	1.25	.50
❑ 48 Brian Griese	1.25	.50
❑ 49 Rod Smith	.75	.30
❑ 50 Ed McCaffrey	1.25	.50
❑ 51 Charlie Batch	.75	.30
❑ 52 Johnnie Morton	.75	.30
❑ 53 Germane Crowell	.50	.20
❑ 54 James Stewart	.75	.30
❑ 55 Shaun Rogers	.50	.20
❑ 56 Brett Favre	3.00	1.25
❑ 57 Antonio Freeman	1.25	.50
❑ 58 Ahman Green	1.25	.50
❑ 59 Bill Schroeder	.75	.30
❑ 60 Kabeer Gbaja-Biamila	.75	.30
❑ 61 Marvin Harrison	1.25	.50
❑ 62 Terrence Wilkins	.50	.20
❑ 63 Dominic Rhodes	.75	.30
❑ 64 Reggie Wayne	1.25	.50
❑ 65 Edgerrin James	1.50	.60
❑ 66 Mark Brunell	1.25	.50
❑ 67 Keenan McCardell	.50	.20
❑ 68 Jimmy Smith	.75	.30
❑ 69 Fred Taylor	1.25	.50
❑ 70 Derrick Alexander	.75	.30
❑ 71 Tony Gonzalez	.75	.30
❑ 72 Trent Green	.75	.30
❑ 73 Priest Holmes	1.50	.60
❑ 74 Snoop Minnis	.50	.20
❑ 75 Chris Chambers	1.25	.50
❑ 76 Jay Fiedler	.75	.30
❑ 77 Travis Minor	.50	.20
❑ 78 Lamar Smith	.75	.30
❑ 79 Zach Thomas	1.25	.50
❑ 80 Michael Bennett	.75	.30
❑ 81 Cris Carter	1.25	.50
❑ 82 Daunte Culpepper	1.25	.50
❑ 83 Randy Moss	2.50	1.00
❑ 84 Drew Bledsoe	1.50	.60
❑ 85 Tom Brady	3.00	1.25
❑ 86 Troy Brown	.75	.30
❑ 87 Antowain Smith	.75	.30
❑ 88 Aaron Brooks	1.25	.50
❑ 89 Joe Horn	.75	.30
❑ 90 Deuce McAllister	1.50	.60
❑ 91 Ricky Williams	1.25	.50
❑ 92 Kerry Collins	.75	.30
❑ 93 Ron Dayne	.75	.30
❑ 94 Michael Strahan	.75	.30
❑ 95 Jason Sehorn	.50	.20
❑ 96 Wayne Chrebet	.75	.30
❑ 97 Laveranues Coles	.75	.30
❑ 98 LaMont Jordan	1.25	.50
❑ 99 Curtis Martin	1.25	.50
❑ 100 Santana Moss	1.25	.50
❑ 101 Vinny Testaverde	.75	.30
❑ 102 Tim Brown	1.25	.50
❑ 103 Jerry Porter	.50	.20
❑ 104 Jerry Rice	2.50	1.00
❑ 105 Charlie Garner	.75	.30
❑ 106 Tyrone Wheatley	.75	.30
❑ 107 Charles Woodson	.75	.30
❑ 108 Correll Buckhalter	.75	.30
❑ 109 Todd Pinkston	.75	.30
❑ 110 Freddie Mitchell	.75	.30
❑ 111 James Thrash	.75	.30
❑ 112 Duce Staley	1.25	.50
❑ 113 Jerome Bettis	1.25	.50
❑ 114 Plaxico Burress	.75	.30
❑ 115 Kordell Stewart	.75	.30
❑ 116 Hines Ward	1.25	.50
❑ 117 Kendrell Bell	1.25	.50
❑ 118 Drew Brees	1.25	.50
❑ 119 Curtis Conway	.50	.20
❑ 120 Doug Flutie	1.25	.50
❑ 121 LaDainian Tomlinson	2.00	.75
❑ 122 Junior Seau	1.25	.50
❑ 123 Kevan Barlow	.75	.30
❑ 124 Jeff Garcia	1.25	.50
❑ 125 Garrison Hearst	.75	.30
❑ 126 Terrell Owens	1.25	.50
❑ 127 Andre Carter	.50	.20
❑ 128 Shaun Alexander	1.50	.60
❑ 129 Matt Hasselbeck	.75	.30
❑ 130 Koren Robinson	.75	.30
❑ 131 Ricky Watters	.75	.30
❑ 132 Isaac Bruce	1.25	.50
❑ 133 Trung Canidate	.75	.30
❑ 134 Marshall Faulk	1.25	.50
❑ 135 Torry Holt	1.25	.50
❑ 136 Kurt Warner	1.25	.50
❑ 137 Mike Alstott	1.25	.50
❑ 138 Warrick Dunn	1.25	.50
❑ 139 Brad Johnson	.75	.30
❑ 140 Keyshawn Johnson	1.25	.50
❑ 141 Warren Sapp	.75	.30
❑ 142 Eddie George	1.25	.50
❑ 143 Derrick Mason	.75	.30
❑ 144 Steve McNair	1.25	.50
❑ 145 Jevon Kearse	.75	.30
❑ 146 Stephen Davis	.75	.30
❑ 147 Rod Gardner	.75	.30
❑ 148 Champ Bailey	.75	.30
❑ 149 Bruce Smith	.50	.20
❑ 150 Houston Texans	1.50	.60
❑ 151 David Carr RC	10.00	4.00
❑ 152 Julius Peppers RC	8.00	3.00
❑ 153 Joey Harrington RC	6.00	2.50
❑ 154 Quentin Jammer RC	4.00	1.50
❑ 155 Ryan Sims RC	4.00	1.50
❑ 156 Bryant McKinnie RC	3.00	1.25
❑ 157 Roy Williams RC	10.00	4.00
❑ 158 John Henderson RC	4.00	1.50
❑ 159 Dwight Freeney RC	6.00	2.50
❑ 160 Wendell Bryant RC	2.00	.75
❑ 161 Donte Stallworth RC	8.00	3.00
❑ 162 Jeremy Shockey RC	12.00	5.00
❑ 163 Albert Haynesworth RC	3.00	1.25
❑ 164 William Green RC	4.00	1.50
❑ 165 Phillip Buchanon RC	4.00	1.50
❑ 166 T.J. Duckett RC	5.00	2.00
❑ 167 Ashley Lelie RC	8.00	3.00
❑ 168 Javon Walker RC	8.00	3.00
❑ 169 Daniel Graham RC	4.00	1.50

❑ 170 Napoleon Harris RC 4.00 1.50
❑ 171 Lito Sheppard RC 4.00 1.50
❑ 172 Robert Thomas RC 4.00 1.50
❑ 173 Patrick Ramsey RC 5.00 2.00
❑ 174 Jabar Gaffney RC 4.00 1.50
❑ 175 DeShaun Foster RC 4.00 1.50
❑ 176 Kalimba Edwards RC 4.00 1.50
❑ 177 Josh Reed RC 4.00 1.50
❑ 178 Larry Tripplett RC 2.00 .75
❑ 179 Andre Davis RC 3.00 1.25
❑ 180 Reche Caldwell RC 4.00 1.50
❑ 181 Levar Fisher RC 2.00 .75
❑ 182 Clinton Portis RC 12.00 5.00
❑ 183 Anthony Weaver RC 3.00 1.25
❑ 184 Maurice Morris RC 4.00 1.50
❑ 185 Ladell Betts RC 4.00 1.50
❑ 186 Antwaan Randle El RC 6.00 2.50
❑ 187 Antonio Bryant RC 4.00 1.50
❑ 188 Rocky Calmus RC 4.00 1.50
❑ 189 Josh McCown RC 5.00 2.00
❑ 190 Lamar Gordon RC 4.00 1.50
❑ 191 Marquise Walker RC 3.00 1.25
❑ 192 Cliff Russell RC 3.00 1.25
❑ 193 Eric Crouch RC 4.00 1.50
❑ 194 Dennis Johnson RC 2.00 .75
❑ 195 Alex Brown RC 4.00 1.50
❑ 196 David Garrard RC 4.00 1.50
❑ 197 Rohan Davey RC 4.00 1.50
❑ 198 Alan Harper RC 2.00 .75
❑ 199 Ron Johnson RC 3.00 1.25
❑ 200 Andra Davis RC 3.00 1.25
❑ 201 Kurt Kittner RC 3.00 1.25
❑ 202 Freddie Milons RC 3.00 1.25
❑ 203 Adrian Peterson RC 4.00 1.50
❑ 204 Luke Staley RC 3.00 1.25
❑ 205 Tracey Wistrom RC 3.00 1.25
❑ 206 Woody Dantzler RC 3.00 1.25
❑ 207 Chad Hutchinson RC 3.00 1.25
❑ 208 Zak Kustok RC 4.00 1.50
❑ 209 Damien Anderson RC 3.00 1.25
❑ 210 James Mungro RC 4.00 1.50
❑ 211 Cortlen Johnson RC 2.00 .75
❑ 212 Demontray Carter RC 2.00 .75
❑ 213 Kelly Campbell RC 3.00 1.25
❑ 214 Brian Poli-Dixon RC 3.00 1.25
❑ 215 Mike Rumph RC 4.00 1.50
❑ 216 Najeh Davenport RC 4.00 1.50

2003 Playoff Prestige

❑ COMP.SET w/o SP's (150) 30.00 12.50
❑ 1 David Boston .75 .30
❑ 2 Thomas Jones .75 .30
❑ 3 Jake Plummer .75 .30
❑ 4 Marcel Shipp .75 .30
❑ 5 T.J. Duckett .75 .30
❑ 6 Warrick Dunn .75 .30
❑ 7 Michael Vick 3.00 1.25
❑ 8 Jeff Blake .50 .20
❑ 9 Todd Heap .75 .30
❑ 10 Jamal Lewis 1.25 .50
❑ 11 Ray Lewis 1.25 .50
❑ 12 Drew Bledsoe 1.25 .50
❑ 13 Travis Henry .75 .30
❑ 14 Eric Moulds .75 .30
❑ 15 Peerless Price .75 .30
❑ 16 Josh Reed .75 .30
❑ 17 DeShaun Foster .50 .20
❑ 18 Muhsin Muhammad .75 .30
❑ 19 Steve Smith 1.25 .50
❑ 20 Julius Peppers 1.25 .50
❑ 21 Marty Booker .75 .30
❑ 22 David Terrell .75 .30
❑ 23 Anthony Thomas .75 .30
❑ 24 Brian Urlacher 2.00 .75
❑ 25 Corey Dillon .75 .30
❑ 26 Chad Johnson 1.25 .50
❑ 27 Jon Kitna .75 .30
❑ 28 Peter Warrick .75 .30
❑ 29 Tim Couch .50 .20
❑ 30 Andre Davis .50 .20
❑ 31 William Green .75 .30
❑ 32 Quincy Morgan .75 .30
❑ 33 Dennis Northcutt .75 .30
❑ 34 Antonio Bryant .75 .30
❑ 35 Quincy Carter .75 .30
❑ 36 Troy Hambrick .50 .20
❑ 37 Chad Hutchinson .50 .20
❑ 38 Emmitt Smith 3.00 1.25
❑ 39 Roy Williams 1.25 .50
❑ 40 Brian Griese 1.25 .50
❑ 41 Ashley Lelie 1.25 .50
❑ 42 Ed McCaffrey .75 .30
❑ 43 Clinton Portis 2.00 .75
❑ 44 Rod Smith .75 .30
❑ 45 Germane Crowell .50 .20
❑ 46 Az-Zahir Hakim .50 .20
❑ 47 Joey Harrington 2.00 .75
❑ 48 James Stewart .75 .30
❑ 49 Donald Driver .75 .30
❑ 50 Brett Favre 3.00 1.25
❑ 51 Terry Glenn .50 .20
❑ 52 Ahman Green 1.25 .50
❑ 53 Javon Walker .75 .30
❑ 54 Corey Bradford .50 .20
❑ 55 David Carr 2.00 .75
❑ 56 Jabar Gaffney .75 .30
❑ 57 Jonathan Wells .50 .20
❑ 58 Marvin Harrison 1.25 .50
❑ 59 Edgerrin James 1.25 .50
❑ 60 Peyton Manning 2.00 .75
❑ 61 James Mungro .50 .20
❑ 62 Reggie Wayne .75 .30
❑ 63 Mark Brunell .75 .30
❑ 64 David Garrard .50 .20
❑ 65 Stacey Mack .50 .20
❑ 66 Jimmy Smith .75 .30
❑ 67 Fred Taylor 1.25 .50
❑ 68 Marc Boerigter .75 .30
❑ 69 Tony Gonzalez .75 .30
❑ 70 Trent Green .75 .30
❑ 71 Priest Holmes 1.50 .60
❑ 72 Eddie Kennison .50 .20
❑ 73 Cris Carter 1.25 .50
❑ 74 Chris Chambers 1.25 .50
❑ 75 Jay Fiedler .75 .30
❑ 76 Randy McMichael .75 .30
❑ 77 Zach Thomas .75 .30
❑ 78 Ricky Williams 1.25 .50
❑ 79 Michael Bennett .75 .30
❑ 80 Todd Bouman .50 .20
❑ 81 Daunte Culpepper 1.25 .50
❑ 82 Randy Moss 2.00 .75
❑ 83 Tom Brady 3.00 1.25
❑ 84 Deion Branch 1.25 .50
❑ 85 Troy Brown .75 .30
❑ 86 Kevin Faulk .50 .20
❑ 87 Antowain Smith .75 .30
❑ 88 Aaron Brooks 1.25 .50
❑ 89 Joe Horn .75 .30
❑ 90 Deuce McAllister 1.25 .50
❑ 91 Donte Stallworth 1.25 .50
❑ 92 Tiki Barber 1.25 .50
❑ 93 Kerry Collins .75 .30
❑ 94 Jeremy Shockey 2.00 .75
❑ 95 Michael Strahan .75 .30
❑ 96 Amani Toomer .75 .30
❑ 97 Laveranues Coles .75 .30
❑ 98 LaMont Jordan 1.25 .50
❑ 99 Curtis Martin 1.25 .50
❑ 100 Santana Moss .75 .30
❑ 101 Chad Pennington 1.50 .60
❑ 102 Tim Brown 1.25 .50
❑ 103 Rich Gannon .75 .30
❑ 104 Charlie Garner .75 .30
❑ 105 Jerry Rice 2.50 1.00
❑ 106 Charles Woodson .75 .30
❑ 107 Antonio Freeman .75 .30
❑ 108 Dorsey Levens .50 .20
❑ 109 Donovan McNabb 1.50 .60
❑ 110 Duce Staley .75 .30
❑ 111 James Thrash .50 .20
❑ 112 Jerome Bettis 1.25 .50
❑ 113 Plaxico Burress .75 .30
❑ 114 Tommy Maddox 1.25 .50
❑ 115 Antwaan Randle El 1.25 .50
❑ 116 Kordell Stewart .75 .30
❑ 117 Hines Ward 1.25 .50
❑ 118 Drew Brees 1.25 .50
❑ 119 Curtis Conway .50 .20
❑ 120 Junior Seau 1.25 .50
❑ 121 LaDainian Tomlinson 1.25 .50
❑ 122 Kevan Barlow .75 .30
❑ 123 Jeff Garcia 1.25 .50
❑ 124 Garrison Hearst .75 .30
❑ 125 Terrell Owens 1.25 .50
❑ 126 Shaun Alexander 1.25 .50
❑ 127 Trent Dilfer .75 .30
❑ 128 Darrell Jackson .75 .30
❑ 129 Maurice Morris .50 .20
❑ 130 Koren Robinson .50 .20
❑ 131 Isaac Bruce 1.25 .50
❑ 132 Marc Bulger 1.25 .50
❑ 133 Marshall Faulk 1.25 .50
❑ 134 Torry Holt 1.25 .50
❑ 135 Kurt Warner 1.25 .50
❑ 136 Mike Alstott 1.25 .50
❑ 137 Brad Johnson .75 .30
❑ 138 Keyshawn Johnson 1.25 .50
❑ 139 Dexter Jackson RC 1.25 .50
❑ 140 Warren Sapp .75 .30
❑ 141 Kevin Dyson .75 .30
❑ 142 Eddie George .75 .30
❑ 143 Jevon Kearse .75 .30
❑ 144 Derrick Mason .75 .30
❑ 145 Steve McNair 1.25 .50
❑ 146 Stephen Davis .75 .30
❑ 147 Rod Gardner .75 .30
❑ 148 Shane Matthews .50 .20
❑ 149 Patrick Ramsey 1.25 .50
❑ 150 Derrius Thompson .50 .20
❑ 151 Byron Leftwich RC 10.00 4.00
❑ 152 Carson Palmer RC 12.00 5.00
❑ 153 Chris Simms RC 5.00 2.00
❑ 154 Kliff Kingsbury RC 2.50 1.00
❑ 155 Dave Ragone RC 3.00 1.25
❑ 156 Jason Gesser RC 3.00 1.25
❑ 157 Ken Dorsey RC 3.00 1.25
❑ 158 Kyle Boller RC 3.00 1.25
❑ 159 Brad Banks RC 2.50 1.00
❑ 160 Rex Grossman RC 10.00 4.00
❑ 161 Seneca Wallace RC 3.00 1.25
❑ 162 Brian St.Pierre RC 3.00 1.25
❑ 163 Larry Johnson RC 12.00 6.00
❑ 164 Earnest Graham RC 2.50 1.00
❑ 165 Musa Smith RC 3.00 1.25
❑ 166 Lee Suggs RC 3.00 1.25
❑ 167 Willis McGahee RC 8.00 3.00
❑ 168 Onterrio Smith RC 3.00 1.25
❑ 170 Sultan McCullough RC 2.50 1.00
❑ 171 Chris Brown RC 3.00 1.25
❑ 172 Justin Fargas RC 3.00 1.25
❑ 173 Avon Cobourne RC 1.50 .60
❑ 174 Dahrran Diedrick RC 3.00 1.25
❑ 175 LaBrandon Toefield RC 3.00 1.25
❑ 176 Artose Pinner RC 3.00 1.25
❑ 177 Quentin Griffin RC 3.00 1.25
❑ 178 ReShard Lee RC 3.00 1.25
❑ 179 Andrew Pinnock RC 2.50 1.00
❑ 180 B.J. Askew RC 3.00 1.25
❑ 181 Andre Johnson RC 6.00 2.50
❑ 182 Brandon Lloyd RC 3.00 1.25
❑ 183 Bryant Johnson RC 3.00 1.25
❑ 184 Charles Rogers RC 3.00 1.25
❑ 185 Doug Gabriel RC 3.00 1.25
❑ 186 Justin Gage RC 3.00 1.25
❑ 187 Kareem Kelly RC 2.50 1.00
❑ 188 Kelley Washington RC 3.00 1.25
❑ 189 Taylor Jacobs RC 2.50 1.00
❑ 190 Terrence Edwards RC 2.50 1.00
❑ 191 Anquan Boldin RC 8.00 3.00
❑ 192 Billy McMullen RC 2.50 1.00
❑ 193 Talman Gardner RC 3.00 1.25
❑ 194 Arnaz Battle RC 3.00 1.25

- ❑ 195 Sam Aiken RC 2.50 1.00
- ❑ 196 Bobby Wade RC 3.00 1.25
- ❑ 197 Mike Bush RC 1.50 .60
- ❑ 198 Keenan Howry RC 3.00 1.25
- ❑ 199 Jerel Myers RC 1.50 .60
- ❑ 200 Dallas Clark RC 3.00 1.25
- ❑ 201 Mike Pinkard RC 1.50 .60
- ❑ 202 Teyo Johnson RC 3.00 1.25
- ❑ 203 Trent Smith RC 2.50 1.00
- ❑ 204 George Wrighster RC 2.50 1.00
- ❑ 205 Jason Witten RC 5.00 2.00
- ❑ 206 Cory Redding RC 2.50 1.00
- ❑ 207 DeWayne White RC 2.50 1.00
- ❑ 208 Jerome McDougle RC 3.00 1.25
- ❑ 209 Michael Haynes RC 3.00 1.25
- ❑ 210 Chris Kelsay RC 3.00 1.25
- ❑ 211 Calvin Pace RC 2.50 1.00
- ❑ 212 Kenny King RC 2.50 1.00
- ❑ 213 Jimmy Kennedy RC 3.00 1.25
- ❑ 214 William Joseph RC 3.00 1.25
- ❑ 215 DeWayne Robertson RC 3.00 1.25
- ❑ 216 Jarret Johnson RC 2.50 1.00
- ❑ 217 Rien Long RC 1.50 .60
- ❑ 218 Boss Bailey RC 3.00 1.25
- ❑ 219 Terrell Suggs RC 5.00 2.00
- ❑ 220 Terry Pierce RC 2.50 1.00
- ❑ 221 Bradie James RC 3.00 1.25
- ❑ 222 Angelo Crowell RC 2.50 1.00
- ❑ 223 Andre Woolfolk RC 3.00 1.25
- ❑ 224 Dennis Weathersby RC 1.50 .60
- ❑ 225 Marcus Trufant RC 3.00 1.25
- ❑ 226 Terence Newman RC 6.00 2.50
- ❑ 227 Ricky Manning RC 3.00 1.25
- ❑ 228 Mike Doss RC 3.00 1.25
- ❑ 229 Julian Battle RC 2.50 1.00
- ❑ 230 Rashean Mathis RC 2.50 1.00

2004 Playoff Prestige

- ❑ COMP.SET w/o RC's (150) 25.00 10.00
- ❑ 1 Anquan Boldin 1.00 .40
- ❑ 2 Emmitt Smith 2.00 .75
- ❑ 3 Jeff Blake .40 .15
- ❑ 4 Marcel Shipp .60 .25
- ❑ 5 Michael Vick 2.00 .75
- ❑ 6 Peerless Price .60 .25
- ❑ 7 T.J. Duckett .60 .25
- ❑ 8 Warrick Dunn .60 .25
- ❑ 9 Ed Reed .60 .25
- ❑ 10 Jamal Lewis 1.00 .40
- ❑ 11 Kyle Boller 1.00 .40
- ❑ 12 Ray Lewis 1.00 .40
- ❑ 13 Todd Heap .60 .25
- ❑ 14 Drew Bledsoe 1.00 .40
- ❑ 15 Eric Moulds .60 .25
- ❑ 16 Josh Reed .40 .15
- ❑ 17 Travis Henry .60 .25
- ❑ 18 DeShaun Foster .60 .25
- ❑ 19 Stephen Davis .60 .25
- ❑ 20 Jake Delhomme 1.00 .40
- ❑ 21 Julius Peppers 1.00 .40
- ❑ 22 Steve Smith 1.00 .40
- ❑ 23 Anthony Thomas .60 .25
- ❑ 24 Brian Urlacher 1.25 .50
- ❑ 25 Marty Booker .60 .25
- ❑ 26 Rex Grossman 1.00 .40
- ❑ 27 Chad Johnson 1.00 .40
- ❑ 28 Corey Dillon .60 .25
- ❑ 29 Carson Palmer 1.25 .50
- ❑ 30 Peter Warrick .60 .25
- ❑ 31 Rudi Johnson .60 .25
- ❑ 32 Andre Davis .40 .15
- ❑ 33 Quincy Morgan .60 .25
- ❑ 34 William Green .60 .25
- ❑ 35 Kelly Holcomb .60 .25
- ❑ 36 Antonio Bryant .60 .25
- ❑ 37 Quincy Carter .60 .25
- ❑ 38 Roy Williams S .60 .25
- ❑ 39 Terence Newman .60 .25
- ❑ 40 Terry Glenn .40 .15
- ❑ 41 Troy Hambrick .40 .15
- ❑ 42 Ashley Lelie .60 .25
- ❑ 43 Clinton Portis 1.00 .40
- ❑ 44 Rod Smith .60 .25
- ❑ 45 Shannon Sharpe .60 .25
- ❑ 46 Mike Anderson .60 .25
- ❑ 47 Jake Plummer .60 .25
- ❑ 48 Charles Rogers .60 .25
- ❑ 49 Joey Harrington 1.00 .40
- ❑ 50 Ahman Green 1.00 .40
- ❑ 51 Brett Favre 2.50 1.00
- ❑ 52 Donald Driver .60 .25
- ❑ 53 Javon Walker .60 .25
- ❑ 54 Robert Ferguson .40 .15
- ❑ 55 Andre Johnson 1.00 .40
- ❑ 56 David Carr 1.00 .40
- ❑ 57 Domanick Davis 1.00 .40
- ❑ 58 Jabar Gaffney .60 .25
- ❑ 59 Dwight Freeney .60 .25
- ❑ 60 Dallas Clark .60 .25
- ❑ 61 Edgerrin James 1.00 .40
- ❑ 62 Marvin Harrison 1.00 .40
- ❑ 63 Peyton Manning 1.50 .60
- ❑ 64 Reggie Wayne .60 .25
- ❑ 65 Byron Leftwich 1.25 .50
- ❑ 66 Fred Taylor .60 .25
- ❑ 67 Jimmy Smith .60 .25
- ❑ 68 Johnnie Morton .60 .25
- ❑ 69 Priest Holmes 1.25 .50
- ❑ 70 Tony Gonzalez .60 .25
- ❑ 71 Trent Green .60 .25
- ❑ 72 Chris Chambers .60 .25
- ❑ 73 Jay Fiedler .40 .15
- ❑ 74 Randy McMichael .40 .15
- ❑ 75 Ricky Williams 1.00 .40
- ❑ 76 Zach Thomas 1.00 .40
- ❑ 77 Daunte Culpepper 1.00 .40
- ❑ 78 Kelly Campbell .40 .15
- ❑ 79 Michael Bennett .60 .25
- ❑ 80 Moe Williams .40 .15
- ❑ 81 Nate Burleson 1.00 .40
- ❑ 82 Randy Moss 1.25 .50
- ❑ 83 Deion Branch 1.00 .40
- ❑ 84 Kevin Faulk .40 .15
- ❑ 85 Tom Brady 2.50 1.00
- ❑ 86 Troy Brown .60 .25
- ❑ 87 Tedy Bruschi .60 .25
- ❑ 88 Aaron Brooks .60 .25
- ❑ 89 Deuce McAllister 1.00 .40
- ❑ 90 Donte Stallworth .60 .25
- ❑ 91 Joe Horn .60 .25
- ❑ 92 Amani Toomer .60 .25
- ❑ 93 Ike Hilliard .40 .15
- ❑ 94 Jeremy Shockey 1.00 .40
- ❑ 95 Kerry Collins .60 .25
- ❑ 96 Michael Strahan .60 .25
- ❑ 97 Tiki Barber 1.00 .40
- ❑ 98 Chad Pennington 1.00 .40
- ❑ 99 Curtis Martin 1.00 .40
- ❑ 100 LaMont Jordan 1.00 .40
- ❑ 101 Santana Moss .60 .25
- ❑ 102 Charlie Garner .60 .25
- ❑ 103 Jerry Porter .60 .25
- ❑ 104 Jerry Rice 2.00 .75
- ❑ 105 Justin Fargas .60 .25
- ❑ 106 Rich Gannon .60 .25
- ❑ 107 Rod Woodson .60 .25
- ❑ 108 Tim Brown 1.00 .40
- ❑ 109 Brian Westbrook .60 .25
- ❑ 110 Correll Buckhalter .60 .25
- ❑ 111 Donovan McNabb 1.25 .50
- ❑ 112 Freddie Mitchell .60 .25
- ❑ 113 James Thrash .40 .15
- ❑ 114 Amos Zereoue .40 .15
- ❑ 115 Antwaan Randle El 1.00 .40
- ❑ 116 Hines Ward 1.00 .40
- ❑ 117 Joey Porter .60 .25
- ❑ 118 Kendrell Bell .60 .25
- ❑ 119 Plaxico Burress .60 .25
- ❑ 120 David Boston .60 .25
- ❑ 121 Drew Brees 1.00 .40
- ❑ 122 LaDainian Tomlinson 1.25 .50
- ❑ 123 Jeff Garcia 1.00 .40
- ❑ 124 Kevan Barlow .60 .25
- ❑ 125 Tai Streets .40 .15
- ❑ 126 Terrell Owens 1.00 .40
- ❑ 127 Tim Rattay .40 .15
- ❑ 128 Darrell Jackson .60 .25
- ❑ 129 Koren Robinson .60 .25
- ❑ 130 Matt Hasselbeck .60 .25
- ❑ 131 Shaun Alexander 1.00 .40
- ❑ 132 Isaac Bruce .60 .25
- ❑ 133 Marc Bulger 1.00 .40
- ❑ 134 Marshall Faulk 1.00 .40
- ❑ 135 Torry Holt 1.00 .40
- ❑ 136 Brad Johnson .60 .25
- ❑ 137 Derrick Brooks .60 .25
- ❑ 138 Keenan McCardell .40 .15
- ❑ 139 Keyshawn Johnson .60 .25
- ❑ 140 Mike Alstott .60 .25
- ❑ 141 Derrick Mason .60 .25
- ❑ 142 Drew Bennett .60 .25
- ❑ 143 Jevon Kearse .60 .25
- ❑ 144 Justin McCareins .40 .15
- ❑ 145 Steve McNair 1.00 .40
- ❑ 146 Tyrone Calico .60 .25
- ❑ 147 Bruce Smith .60 .25
- ❑ 148 Laveranues Coles .60 .25
- ❑ 149 Patrick Ramsey .60 .25
- ❑ 150 LaVar Arrington 2.00 .75
- ❑ 151 Eli Manning RC 12.00 6.00
- ❑ 152 Larry Fitzgerald RC 8.00 3.00
- ❑ 153 Philip Rivers RC 8.00 3.00
- ❑ 154 Sean Taylor RC 2.50 1.00
- ❑ 155 Kellen Winslow RC 5.00 2.00
- ❑ 156 Roy Williams RC 6.00 2.50
- ❑ 157 DeAngelo Hall RC 3.00 1.25
- ❑ 158 Reggie Williams RC 3.00 1.25
- ❑ 159 Ben Roethlisberger RC 15.00 7.50
- ❑ 160 Jonathan Vilma RC 2.50 1.00
- ❑ 161 Lee Evans RC 3.00 1.25
- ❑ 162 Tommie Harris RC 2.50 1.00
- ❑ 163 Michael Clayton RC 5.00 2.00
- ❑ 164 D.J. Williams SP RC 25.00 10.00
- ❑ 165 Will Smith RC 2.50 1.00
- ❑ 166 Kenechi Udeze RC 2.50 1.00
- ❑ 167 Vince Wilfork SP RC 25.00 10.00
- ❑ 168 J.P. Losman RC 5.00 2.00
- ❑ 169 Steven Jackson SP RC 50.00 25.00
- ❑ 170 Ahmad Carroll RC 2.50 1.00
- ❑ 171 Chris Perry RC 5.00 2.00
- ❑ 172 Jason Babin SP RC 30.00 15.00
- ❑ 173 Chris Gamble RC 2.50 1.00
- ❑ 174 Michael Jenkins RC 2.50 1.00
- ❑ 175 Kevin Jones RC 6.00 2.50
- ❑ 176 Rashaun Woods RC 2.50 1.00
- ❑ 177 Ben Watson RC 2.50 1.00
- ❑ 178 Karlos Dansby RC 2.50 1.00
- ❑ 179 Teddy Lehman RC 2.50 1.00
- ❑ 180 Ricardo Colclough SP RC 30.00 15.00
- ❑ 181 Daryl Smith RC 2.50 1.00
- ❑ 182 Ben Troupe RC 2.50 1.00
- ❑ 183 Tatum Bell RC 5.00 2.00
- ❑ 184 Julius Jones RC 8.00 3.00
- ❑ 185 Bob Sanders RC 6.00 2.50
- ❑ 186 Devery Henderson RC 2.00 .75
- ❑ 187 Dwan Edwards RC 1.25 .50
- ❑ 188 Michael Boulware RC 2.50 1.00
- ❑ 189 Darius Watts RC 2.50 1.00
- ❑ 190 Greg Jones RC 2.50 1.00
- ❑ 191 Antwan Odom RC 2.50 1.00
- ❑ 192 Sean Jones SP RC 25.00 10.00
- ❑ 193 Courtney Watson RC 2.50 1.00
- ❑ 194 Keary Colbert RC 3.00 1.25
- ❑ 195 Keith Smith RC 2.00 .75
- ❑ 196 Derrick Strait RC 2.50 1.00
- ❑ 197 Bernard Berrian RC 3.00 1.25
- ❑ 198 Devard Darling RC 2.50 1.00
- ❑ 199 Matt Schaub RC 8.00 3.00
- ❑ 200 Will Poole RC 2.50 1.00
- ❑ 201 Samie Parker RC 2.50 1.00
- ❑ 202 Luke McCown SP RC 30.00 15.00
- ❑ 203 Jerricho Cotchery RC 2.50 1.00
- ❑ 204 Mewelde Moore RC 2.50 1.00

❑ 205 Ernest Wilford RC 2.50 1.00
❑ 206 Cedric Cobbs SP RC 30.00 15.00
❑ 207 Johnnie Morant RC 2.50 1.00
❑ 208 Craig Krenzel RC 2.50 1.00
❑ 209 Michael Turner RC 3.00 1.25
❑ 210 D.J. Hackett RC 2.00 .75
❑ 211 P.K. Sam RC 2.00 .75
❑ 212 Josh Harris RC 2.50 1.00
❑ 213 Drew Henson RC 2.50 1.00
❑ 214 Jeff Smoker RC 2.50 1.00
❑ 215 John Navarre RC 2.50 1.00
❑ 216 Cody Pickett RC 2.50 1.00
❑ 217 Quincy Wilson RC 2.00 .75
❑ 218 Derek Abney RC 2.50 1.00
❑ 219 Maurice Clarett SP RC 25.00 10.00
❑ 220 Mike Williams SP RC 25.00 10.00
❑ 221 B.J. Johnson RC 2.00 .75
❑ 222 Brandon Everage RC 2.00 .75
❑ 223 Derek McCoy RC 2.00 .75
❑ 224 Jared Lorenzen RC 2.00 .75
❑ 225 Jarrett Payton RC 2.50 1.00
❑ 226 Jason Fife RC 2.00 .75
❑ 227 Robert Kent RC 1.25 .50

2005 Playoff Prestige

❑ COMP.SET w/o SP's (234) 100.00 50.00
❑ COMP.SET w/o RC's (150) 25.00 10.00
❑ ONE 151-244 DRAFT PICK PER PACK
❑ 1 Anquan Boldin .60 .25
❑ 2 Emmitt Smith 2.00 .75
❑ 3 Josh McCown .60 .25
❑ 4 Larry Fitzgerald 1.00 .40
❑ 5 Michael Vick 1.50 .60
❑ 6 Peerless Price .50 .20
❑ 7 Alge Crumpler .60 .25
❑ 8 T.J. Duckett .60 .25
❑ 9 Warrick Dunn .60 .25
❑ 10 Ed Reed .60 .25
❑ 11 Jamal Lewis 1.00 .40
❑ 12 Kyle Boller .60 .25
❑ 13 Ray Lewis 1.00 .40
❑ 14 Todd Heap .60 .25
❑ 15 Drew Bledsoe 1.00 .40
❑ 16 Eric Moulds .60 .25
❑ 17 Lee Evans .60 .25
❑ 18 Travis Henry .60 .25
❑ 19 Willis McGahee 1.00 .40
❑ 20 Anthony Thomas .60 .25
❑ 21 Brian Urlacher 1.00 .40
❑ 22 Rex Grossman .60 .25
❑ 23 David Terrell .60 .25
❑ 24 Thomas Jones .60 .25
❑ 25 Carson Palmer 1.00 .40
❑ 26 Chad Johnson 1.00 .40
❑ 27 Peter Warrick .50 .20
❑ 28 Rudi Johnson .60 .25
❑ 29 Antonio Bryant .50 .20
❑ 30 William Green .50 .20
❑ 31 Jeff Garcia .60 .25
❑ 32 Kellen Winslow 1.00 .40
❑ 33 Lee Suggs .60 .25
❑ 34 Drew Henson .60 .25
❑ 35 Julius Jones 1.25 .50
❑ 36 Jason Witten .60 .25
❑ 37 Keyshawn Johnson .60 .25
❑ 38 Roy Williams S .60 .25
❑ 39 Ashley Lelie .60 .25
❑ 40 Champ Bailey .60 .25
❑ 41 Jake Plummer .60 .25
❑ 42 Reuben Droughns .60 .25
❑ 43 Rod Smith .60 .25
❑ 44 Charles Rogers .60 .25
❑ 45 Joey Harrington 1.00 .40
❑ 46 Kevin Jones 1.00 .40
❑ 47 Roy Williams WR 1.00 .40
❑ 48 Ahman Green 1.00 .40
❑ 49 Donald Driver .60 .25
❑ 50 Javon Walker .60 .25
❑ 51 Brett Favre 2.50 1.00
❑ 52 Andre Johnson .60 .25
❑ 53 David Carr 1.00 .40
❑ 54 Domanick Davis .60 .25
❑ 55 Jabar Gaffney .50 .20
❑ 56 Edgerrin James 1.00 .40
❑ 57 Marvin Harrison 1.00 .40
❑ 58 Brandon Stokley .60 .25
❑ 59 Peyton Manning 1.50 .60
❑ 60 Reggie Wayne .60 .25
❑ 61 Byron Leftwich 1.00 .40
❑ 62 Fred Taylor .60 .25
❑ 63 Jimmy Smith .60 .25
❑ 64 Priest Holmes 1.00 .40
❑ 65 Tony Gonzalez .60 .25
❑ 66 Johnnie Morton .60 .25
❑ 67 Trent Green .60 .25
❑ 68 Chris Chambers .60 .25
❑ 69 Randy McMichael .50 .20
❑ 70 A.J. Feeley .60 .25
❑ 71 Zach Thomas 1.00 .40
❑ 72 Daunte Culpepper 1.00 .40
❑ 73 Marcus Robinson .60 .25
❑ 74 Mewelde Moore .60 .25
❑ 75 Nate Burleson .60 .25
❑ 76 Onterrio Smith .60 .25
❑ 77 Randy Moss 1.00 .40
❑ 78 Corey Dillon .60 .25
❑ 79 Tom Brady 2.50 1.00
❑ 80 Deion Branch .60 .25
❑ 81 Tedy Bruschi .60 .25
❑ 82 David Givens .60 .25
❑ 83 David Patten .50 .20
❑ 84 Aaron Brooks .60 .25
❑ 85 Deuce McAllister 1.00 .40
❑ 86 Donte Stallworth .60 .25
❑ 87 Joe Horn .60 .25
❑ 88 Eli Manning 2.00 .75
❑ 89 Jeremy Shockey 1.00 .40
❑ 90 Kurt Warner .60 .25
❑ 91 Michael Strahan .60 .25
❑ 92 Tiki Barber 1.00 .40
❑ 93 Amani Toomer .60 .25
❑ 94 Chad Pennington 1.00 .40
❑ 95 Curtis Martin 1.00 .40
❑ 96 Santana Moss .60 .25
❑ 97 Justin McCareins .50 .20
❑ 98 Charles Woodson .60 .25
❑ 99 Kerry Collins .60 .25
❑ 100 Warren Sapp .60 .25
❑ 101 Jerry Porter .60 .25
❑ 102 Donovan McNabb 1.25 .50
❑ 103 Jevon Kearse .60 .25
❑ 104 Terrell Owens 1.00 .40
❑ 105 Brian Westbrook .60 .25
❑ 106 Todd Pinkston .50 .20
❑ 107 Duce Staley .60 .25
❑ 108 Hines Ward 1.00 .40
❑ 109 Jerome Bettis 1.00 .40
❑ 110 Joey Porter .60 .25
❑ 111 Plaxico Burress .60 .25
❑ 112 Ben Roethlisberger 2.50 1.00
❑ 113 Drew Brees 1.00 .40
❑ 114 LaDainian Tomlinson 1.25 .50
❑ 115 Keenan McCardell .50 .20
❑ 116 Philip Rivers 1.00 .40
❑ 117 Antonio Gates 1.00 .40
❑ 118 Eric Johnson .60 .25
❑ 119 Kevan Barlow .60 .25
❑ 120 Brandon Lloyd .50 .20
❑ 121 Tim Rattay .50 .20
❑ 122 Darrell Jackson .60 .25
❑ 123 Koren Robinson .60 .25
❑ 124 Jerry Rice 2.00 .75
❑ 125 Matt Hasselbeck .60 .25
❑ 126 Shaun Alexander 1.25 .50
❑ 127 Isaac Bruce .60 .25
❑ 128 Marc Bulger 1.00 .40
❑ 129 Marshall Faulk 1.00 .40
❑ 130 Steven Jackson 1.25 .50
❑ 131 Torry Holt 1.00 .40
❑ 132 Derrick Brooks .60 .25
❑ 133 Michael Clayton 1.00 .40
❑ 134 Michael Pittman .50 .20
❑ 135 Chris Simms .60 .25
❑ 136 Chris Brown .60 .25
❑ 137 Derrick Mason .60 .25
❑ 138 Drew Bennett .60 .25
❑ 139 Steve McNair 1.00 .40
❑ 140 Clinton Portis 1.00 .40
❑ 141 LaVar Arrington 1.00 .40
❑ 142 Laveranues Coles .60 .25
❑ 143 Patrick Ramsey .60 .25
❑ 144 Rod Gardner .60 .25
❑ 145 DeShaun Foster .60 .25
❑ 146 Stephen Davis .60 .25
❑ 147 Jake Delhomme 1.00 .40
❑ 148 Muhsin Muhammad .60 .25
❑ 149 Steve Smith .60 .25
❑ 150 Keary Colbert .60 .25
❑ 151 Aaron Rodgers SP RC 50.00 20.00
❑ 152 Adrian McPherson SP RC 30.00 12.50
❑ 153 Alex Smith QB RC 10.00 4.00
❑ 154 Andrew Walter RC 4.00 1.50
❑ 155 Brock Berlin RC 2.00 .75
❑ 156 Charlie Frye SP RC 40.00 20.00
❑ 157 Chris Rix RC 2.00 .75
❑ 158 Dan Orlovsky RC 3.00 1.25
❑ 159 Darian Durant RC 2.50 1.00
❑ 160 David Greene RC 2.50 1.00
❑ 161 Derek Anderson RC 2.50 1.00
❑ 162 Gino Guidugli RC 1.25 .50
❑ 163 Jason Campbell RC 4.00 1.50
❑ 164 Jason White RC 2.50 1.00
❑ 165 Kyle Orton RC 4.00 1.50
❑ 166 Matt Jones SP RC 40.00 15.00
❑ 167 Ryan Fitzpatrick RC 4.00 1.50
❑ 168 Stefan LeFors RC 2.50 1.00
❑ 169 Timmy Chang RC 2.00 .75
❑ 170 Alvin Pearman RC 2.50 1.00
❑ 171 Anthony Davis RC 2.00 .75
❑ 172 Brandon Jacobs RC 3.00 1.25
❑ 173 Cadillac Williams RC 12.00 5.00
❑ 174 Cedric Benson RC 5.00 2.00
❑ 175 Cedric Houston RC 2.50 1.00
❑ 176 Ciatrick Fason RC 2.50 1.00
❑ 177 Damien Nash RC 2.00 .75
❑ 178 Darren Sproles RC 2.50 1.00
❑ 179 Eric Shelton SP RC 25.00 10.00
❑ 180 Frank Gore SP RC 40.00 15.00
❑ 181 J.J. Arrington SP RC 30.00 12.50
❑ 182 Kay-Jay Harris RC 2.00 .75
❑ 183 Marion Barber RC 4.00 1.50
❑ 184 Ronnie Brown RC 10.00 4.00
❑ 185 Ryan Moats RC 2.50 1.00
❑ 186 T.A. McLendon RC 1.25 .50
❑ 187 Vernand Morency RC 2.50 1.00
❑ 188 Walter Reyes RC 2.00 .75
❑ 189 Braylon Edwards RC 8.00 3.00
❑ 190 Charles Frederick RC 2.00 .75
❑ 191 Chris Henry RC 2.50 1.00
❑ 192 Courtney Roby RC 2.50 1.00
❑ 193 Craig Bragg RC 2.00 .75
❑ 194 Craphonso Thorpe SP RC 20.00 7.50
❑ 195 Dante Ridgeway RC 2.00 .75
❑ 196 Fred Amey RC 2.00 .75
❑ 197 Fred Gibson RC 2.00 .75
❑ 198 J.R. Russell RC 2.00 .75
❑ 199 Jerome Mathis SP RC 25.00 10.00
❑ 200 Josh Davis RC 2.00 .75
❑ 201 Larry Brackins RC 1.25 .50
❑ 202 Mark Bradley RC 2.50 1.00
❑ 203 Mark Clayton SP RC 30.00 12.50
❑ 204 Mike Williams 6.00 2.50
❑ 205 Reggie Brown RC 2.50 1.00
❑ 206 Roddy White RC 2.50 1.00
❑ 207 Roscoe Parrish RC 2.50 1.00
❑ 208 Roydell Williams RC 2.50 1.00
❑ 209 Steve Savoy RC 1.25 .50
❑ 210 Tab Perry RC 2.50 1.00
❑ 211 Taylor Stubblefield RC 1.25 .50
❑ 212 Terrence Murphy RC 2.50 1.00
❑ 213 Troy Williamson RC 5.00 2.00
❑ 214 Vincent Jackson RC 2.50 1.00
❑ 215 Alex Smith TE RC 2.50 1.00

Card	Hi	Lo
❑ 216 Heath Miller RC	6.00	2.50
❑ 217 Dan Cody RC	2.50	1.00
❑ 218 David Pollack RC	2.50	1.00
❑ 219 Erasmus James RC	2.50	1.00
❑ 220 Justin Tuck RC	2.50	1.00
❑ 221 Marcus Spears RC	2.50	1.00
❑ 222 Matt Roth RC	2.50	1.00
❑ 223 Anttaj Hawthorne RC	2.00	.75
❑ 224 Mike Patterson RC	2.50	1.00
❑ 225 Shaun Cody RC	2.50	1.00
❑ 226 Travis Johnson RC	2.00	.75
❑ 227 Channing Crowder RC	2.50	1.00
❑ 228 Darryl Blackstock RC	2.00	.75
❑ 229 DeMarcus Ware RC	4.00	1.50
❑ 230 Derrick Johnson RC	4.00	1.50
❑ 231 Kevin Burnett RC	2.50	1.00
❑ 232 Shawne Merriman RC	4.00	1.50
❑ 233 Adam Jones RC	2.50	1.00
❑ 234 Antrel Rolle RC	2.50	1.00
❑ 235 Brandon Browner RC	2.00	.75
❑ 236 Bryant McFadden RC	2.50	1.00
❑ 237 Carlos Rogers RC	3.00	1.25
❑ 238 Corey Webster RC	2.50	1.00
❑ 239 Fabian Washington RC	2.50	1.00
❑ 240 Justin Miller RC	2.00	.75
❑ 241 Marlin Jackson RC	2.50	1.00
❑ 242 Ernest Shazor RC	2.50	1.00
❑ 243 Josh Bullocks RC	2.50	1.00
❑ 244 Thomas Davis RC	2.50	1.00

2006 Playoff Prestige

Card	Hi	Lo
❑ COMP.SET w/o SP's (239)	100.00	50.00
❑ COMP.SET w/o RC's (150)	25.00	10.00
❑ ONE ROOKIE PER HOBBY PACK		
❑ 1 Anquan Boldin	.60	.25
❑ 2 J.J. Arrington	.60	.25
❑ 3 Josh McCown	.60	.25
❑ 4 Larry Fitzgerald	1.00	.40
❑ 5 Marcel Shipp	.50	.20
❑ 6 Alge Crumpler	.60	.25
❑ 7 Michael Vick	1.25	.50
❑ 8 T.J. Duckett	.60	.25
❑ 9 Warrick Dunn	.60	.25
❑ 10 Michael Jenkins	.60	.25
❑ 11 Derrick Mason	.50	.20
❑ 12 Jamal Lewis	.60	.25
❑ 13 Kyle Boller	.60	.25
❑ 14 Mark Clayton	.60	.25
❑ 15 Ray Lewis	1.00	.40
❑ 16 Eric Moulds	.60	.25
❑ 17 J.P. Losman	.60	.25
❑ 18 Lee Evans	.60	.25
❑ 19 Willis McGahee	1.00	.40
❑ 20 Jake Delhomme	.60	.25
❑ 21 Julius Peppers	.60	.25
❑ 22 Keary Colbert	.50	.20
❑ 23 Stephen Davis	.60	.25
❑ 24 Steve Smith	1.00	.40
❑ 25 Brian Urlacher	1.00	.40
❑ 26 Cedric Benson	1.00	.40
❑ 27 Kyle Orton	.60	.25
❑ 28 Mark Bradley	.60	.25
❑ 29 Muhsin Muhammad	.60	.25
❑ 30 Thomas Jones	.60	.25
❑ 31 Carson Palmer	1.00	.40
❑ 32 Chad Johnson	.60	.25
❑ 33 Rudi Johnson	.60	.25
❑ 34 T.J. Houshmandzadeh	.60	.25
❑ 35 Braylon Edwards	1.00	.40
❑ 36 Dennis Northcutt	.50	.20
❑ 37 Antonio Bryant	.60	.25
❑ 38 Reuben Droughns	.60	.25
❑ 39 Trent Dilfer	.60	.25
❑ 40 Drew Bledsoe	1.00	.40
❑ 41 Jason Witten	.60	.25
❑ 42 Julius Jones	1.00	.40
❑ 43 Keyshawn Johnson	.60	.25
❑ 44 Roy Williams S	.60	.25
❑ 45 Terry Glenn	.60	.25
❑ 46 Ashley Lelie	.60	.25
❑ 47 Jake Plummer	.60	.25
❑ 48 Mike Anderson	.60	.25
❑ 49 Rod Smith	.60	.25
❑ 50 Tatum Bell	.60	.25
❑ 51 Joey Harrington	.60	.25
❑ 52 Kevin Jones	1.00	.40
❑ 53 Mike Williams	1.00	.40
❑ 54 Roy Williams WR	1.00	.40
❑ 55 Aaron Rodgers	1.00	.40
❑ 56 Brett Favre	2.00	.75
❑ 57 Donald Driver	.60	.25
❑ 58 Javon Walker	.60	.25
❑ 59 Ahman Green	.60	.25
❑ 60 Andre Johnson	.60	.25
❑ 61 Corey Bradford	.50	.20
❑ 62 David Carr	.60	.25
❑ 63 Domanick Davis	.60	.25
❑ 64 Jabar Gaffney	.50	.20
❑ 65 Brandon Stokley	.60	.25
❑ 66 Dallas Clark	.50	.20
❑ 67 Edgerrin James	1.00	.40
❑ 68 Marvin Harrison	1.00	.40
❑ 69 Peyton Manning	1.50	.60
❑ 70 Reggie Wayne	.60	.25
❑ 71 Byron Leftwich	.60	.25
❑ 72 Fred Taylor	.60	.25
❑ 73 Jimmy Smith	.60	.25
❑ 74 Matt Jones	1.00	.40
❑ 75 Reggie Williams	.60	.25
❑ 76 Eddie Kennison	.50	.20
❑ 77 Larry Johnson	1.25	.50
❑ 78 Priest Holmes	.60	.25
❑ 79 Tony Gonzalez	.60	.25
❑ 80 Trent Green	.60	.25
❑ 81 Chris Chambers	.60	.25
❑ 82 Marty Booker	.50	.20
❑ 83 Randy McMichael	.50	.20
❑ 84 Ricky Williams	.60	.25
❑ 85 Ronnie Brown	1.00	.40
❑ 86 Zach Thomas	1.00	.40
❑ 87 Daunte Culpepper	1.00	.40
❑ 88 Mewelde Moore	.50	.20
❑ 89 Nate Burleson	.60	.25
❑ 90 Jim Kleinsasser	.50	.20
❑ 91 Corey Dillon	.60	.25
❑ 92 David Givens	.60	.25
❑ 93 Deion Branch	.60	.25
❑ 94 Tedy Bruschi	1.00	.40
❑ 95 Tom Brady	1.50	.60
❑ 96 Aaron Brooks	.60	.25
❑ 97 Deuce McAllister	.60	.25
❑ 98 Donte Stallworth	.60	.25
❑ 99 Joe Horn	.60	.25
❑ 100 Amani Toomer	.60	.25
❑ 101 Eli Manning	1.25	.50
❑ 102 Jeremy Shockey	1.00	.40
❑ 103 Plaxico Burress	.60	.25
❑ 104 Tiki Barber	1.00	.40
❑ 105 Chad Pennington	.60	.25
❑ 106 Curtis Martin	1.00	.40
❑ 107 Justin McCareins	.50	.20
❑ 108 Laveranues Coles	.60	.25
❑ 109 Jerry Porter	.60	.25
❑ 110 Kerry Collins	.60	.25
❑ 111 LaMont Jordan	.60	.25
❑ 112 Randy Moss	1.00	.40
❑ 113 Brian Westbrook	.60	.25
❑ 114 Donovan McNabb	1.00	.40
❑ 115 Terrell Owens	1.00	.40
❑ 116 L.J. Smith	.50	.20
❑ 117 Ben Roethlisberger	1.50	.60
❑ 118 Hines Ward	1.00	.40
❑ 119 Heath Miller	1.00	.40
❑ 120 Willie Parker	1.25	.50
❑ 121 Jerome Bettis	1.00	.40
❑ 122 Antonio Gates	1.00	.40
❑ 123 Drew Brees	1.00	.40
❑ 124 Keenan McCardell	.50	.20
❑ 125 LaDainian Tomlinson	1.25	.50
❑ 126 Alex Smith QB	1.25	.50
❑ 127 Brandon Lloyd	.60	.25
❑ 128 Frank Gore	1.00	.40
❑ 129 Kevan Barlow	.60	.25
❑ 130 Darrell Jackson	.60	.25
❑ 131 Joe Jurevicius	.60	.25
❑ 132 Matt Hasselbeck	.60	.25
❑ 133 Shaun Alexander	1.00	.40
❑ 134 Isaac Bruce	.60	.25
❑ 135 Marc Bulger	.60	.25
❑ 136 Marshall Faulk	.60	.25
❑ 137 Steven Jackson	1.00	.40
❑ 138 Torry Holt	.60	.25
❑ 139 Cadillac Williams	1.00	.40
❑ 140 Derrick Brooks	.60	.25
❑ 141 Joey Galloway	.60	.25
❑ 142 Michael Clayton	.60	.25
❑ 143 Brandon Jones	.50	.20
❑ 144 Chris Brown	.60	.25
❑ 145 Steve McNair	.60	.25
❑ 146 Tyrone Calico	.50	.20
❑ 147 Clinton Portis	1.00	.40
❑ 148 Mark Brunell	.60	.25
❑ 149 Santana Moss	.60	.25
❑ 150 David Patten	.50	.20
❑ 151 A.J. Hawk SP RC	60.00	30.00
❑ 152 Abdul Hodge RC	3.00	1.25
❑ 153 Alan Zemaitis RC	3.00	1.25
❑ 154 Andre Hall RC	2.50	1.00
❑ 155 Anthony Fasano RC	3.00	1.25
❑ 156 Ashton Youboty RC	3.00	1.25
❑ 157 Erik Meyer RC	2.50	1.00
❑ 158 Bobby Carpenter RC	3.00	1.25
❑ 159 Brad Smith RC	3.00	1.25
❑ 160 Brandon Kirsch RC	3.00	1.25
❑ 161 Brandon Marshall SP RC	25.00	12.50
❑ 162 Brandon Williams RC	3.00	1.25
❑ 163 Brian Calhoun SP RC	25.00	12.50
❑ 164 Brodie Croyle SP RC	30.00	15.00
❑ 165 Brodrick Bunkley RC	3.00	1.25
❑ 166 Bruce Gradkowski RC	5.00	2.00
❑ 167 Cedric Griffin RC	2.50	1.00
❑ 168 Cedric Humes RC	3.00	1.25
❑ 169 Chad Greenway RC	3.00	1.25
❑ 170 Chad Jackson RC	5.00	2.00
❑ 171 Charlie Whitehurst RC	4.00	1.50
❑ 172 Cory Rodgers RC	3.00	1.25
❑ 173 D.J. Shockley RC	3.00	1.25
❑ 174 Darnell Bing RC	3.00	1.25
❑ 175 Darrell Hackney RC	2.50	1.00
❑ 176 David Thomas SP RC	25.00	12.50
❑ 177 D'Brickashaw Ferguson RC	3.00	1.25
❑ 178 DeAngelo Williams RC	8.00	3.00
❑ 179 Dee Webb RC	2.50	1.00
❑ 180 Delanie Walker RC	2.50	1.00
❑ 181 DeMeco Ryans RC	4.00	1.50
❑ 182 Demetrius Williams RC	4.00	1.50
❑ 183 Derek Hagan RC	3.00	1.25
❑ 184 Devin Aromashodu RC	2.50	1.00
❑ 185 Dominique Byrd RC	2.50	1.00
❑ 186 DonTrell Moore RC	2.50	1.00
❑ 187 D'Qwell Jackson RC	2.50	1.00
❑ 188 Drew Olson RC	2.50	1.00
❑ 189 Eric Winston RC	1.50	.60
❑ 190 Ernie Sims RC	4.00	1.50
❑ 191 Gerald Riggs RC	3.00	1.25
❑ 192 Greg Jennings RC	5.00	2.00
❑ 193 Greg Lee RC	2.50	1.00
❑ 194 Haloti Ngata RC	3.00	1.25
❑ 195 Hank Baskett RC	3.00	1.25
❑ 196 Jason Avant RC	3.00	1.25
❑ 197 Jason Carter RC	2.50	1.00
❑ 198 Jay Cutler RC	12.00	5.00
❑ 199 Jeff Webb RC	2.50	1.00
❑ 200 Jeremy Bloom RC	2.50	1.00
❑ 201 Jerious Norwood RC	5.00	2.00
❑ 202 Jerome Harrison RC	3.00	1.25
❑ 203 Jimmy Williams RC	3.00	1.25
❑ 204 Joe Klopfenstein RC	2.50	1.00
❑ 205 Johnathan Joseph RC	2.50	1.00
❑ 206 Jonathan Orr RC	2.50	1.00
❑ 207 Joseph Addai RC	10.00	4.00
❑ 208 Kai Parham RC	3.00	1.25
❑ 209 Kamerion Wimbley RC	3.00	1.25

❑ 210	Kellen Clemens RC	4.00	1.50
❑ 211	Kelly Jennings RC	3.00	1.25
❑ 212	Ko Simpson RC	2.50	1.00
❑ 213	Laurence Maroney RC	8.00	3.00
❑ 214	Lawrence Vickers RC	2.50	1.00
❑ 215	LenDale White RC	6.00	2.50
❑ 216	Leon Washington RC	5.00	2.00
❑ 217	Leonard Pope RC	3.00	1.25
❑ 218	Marcedes Lewis RC	3.00	1.25
❑ 219	Marcus Vick SP RC	30.00	15.00
❑ 220	Mario Williams RC	5.00	2.00
❑ 221	Martin Nance RC	2.50	1.00
❑ 222	Mathias Kiwanuka RC	4.00	1.50
❑ 223	Matt Leinart RC	12.00	5.00
❑ 224	Maurice Drew SP RC	30.00	15.00
❑ 225	Maurice Stovall SP RC	25.00	12.50
❑ 226	Michael Huff RC	4.00	1.50
❑ 227	Michael Robinson SP RC	30.00	15.00
❑ 228	Mike Hass RC	3.00	1.25
❑ 229	Omar Jacobs RC	2.50	1.00
❑ 230	Paul Pinegar RC	2.50	1.00
❑ 231	Reggie Bush RC	20.00	8.00
❑ 232	Reggie McNeal RC	2.50	1.00
❑ 233	Rodrique Wright RC	1.50	.60
❑ 234	Santonio Holmes RC	6.00	2.50
❑ 235	Sinorice Moss RC	4.00	1.50
❑ 236	Skyler Green RC	3.00	1.25
❑ 237	Tamba Hali RC	3.00	1.25
❑ 238	Tarvaris Jackson RC	5.00	2.00
❑ 239	Taurean Henderson RC	3.00	1.25
❑ 240	Terrence Whitehead RC	2.50	1.00
❑ 241	Tim Day SP RC	20.00	10.00
❑ 242	Todd Watkins RC	2.50	1.00
❑ 243	Travis Wilson RC	3.00	1.25
❑ 244	Tye Hill RC	3.00	1.25
❑ 245	Vernon Davis RC	6.00	2.50
❑ 246	Vince Young RC	12.00	5.00
❑ 247	Wali Lundy RC	2.50	1.00
❑ 248	Wendell Mathis RC	2.50	1.00
❑ 249	Willie Reid SP RC	25.00	12.50
❑ 250	Winston Justice RC	3.00	1.25

1996 Playoff Prime

❑	COMPLETE SET (200)	100.00	40.00
❑	COMP. BRONZE SET (100)	15.00	6.00
❑ 1	Brett Favre	3.00	1.25
❑ 2	Jerry Rice	1.50	.60
❑ 3	Troy Aikman	1.50	.60
❑ 4	Bruce Smith	.25	.08
❑ 5	Marshall Faulk	.60	.25
❑ 6	Erik Kramer	.10	.02
❑ 7	Carl Pickens	.25	.08
❑ 8	Anthony Miller	.25	.08
❑ 9	Cris Carter	.50	.20
❑ 10	Todd Kinchen	.10	.02
❑ 11	Stoney Case	.10	.02
❑ 12	Chris Calloway	.10	.02
❑ 13	Andre Rison	.25	.08
❑ 14	Bill Brooks	.10	.02
❑ 15	Shawn Jefferson	.10	.02
❑ 16	Eric Zeier	.10	.02
❑ 17	Yancey Thigpen	.25	.08
❑ 18	Edgar Bennett	.25	.08
❑ 19	Garrison Hearst	.25	.08
❑ 20	Daryl Johnston	.25	.08
❑ 21	Tyrone Wheatley	.25	.08
❑ 22	Darick Holmes	.10	.02
❑ 23	Dave Brown	.10	.02
❑ 24	Leeland McElroy RC	.25	.08
❑ 25	Craig Heyward	.10	.02
❑ 26	Kevin Hardy RC	.50	.20
❑ 27	Scott Mitchell	.25	.08
❑ 28	Willie Green	.10	.02
❑ 29	Vincent Brisby	.10	.02
❑ 30	Mike Tomczak	.10	.02
❑ 31	Luther Elliss	.10	.02
❑ 32	Mike Pritchard	.10	.02
❑ 33	Robert Green	.10	.02
❑ 34	Jeff Graham	.10	.02
❑ 35	Tamarick Vanover	.25	.08
❑ 36	William Floyd	.25	.08
❑ 37	Alvin Harper	.10	.02
❑ 38	Stan Humphries	.25	.08
❑ 39	Herman Moore	.25	.08
❑ 40	Tony Martin	.25	.08
❑ 41	Jonathan Ogden RC	.50	.20
❑ 42	Randall Cunningham	.50	.20
❑ 43	Chris Warren	.25	.08
❑ 44	Bobby Hebert	.10	.02
❑ 45	Jerome Bettis	.50	.20
❑ 46	Joey Galloway	.50	.20
❑ 47	Ernie Mills	.10	.02
❑ 48	Steve McNair	1.00	.40
❑ 49	Karim Abdul-Jabbar RC	.50	.20
❑ 50	Chad May	.10	.02
❑ 51	Jim Everett	.10	.02
❑ 52	Robert Smith	.25	.08
❑ 53	Tony Boselli	.10	.02
❑ 54	William Henderson	.50	.20
❑ 55	Terry Glenn RC UER	1.50	.60
❑ 56	Neil O'Donnell	.25	.08
❑ 57	Chris Chandler	.25	.08
❑ 58	Michael Jackson	.25	.08
❑ 59	Jason Dunn RC	.25	.08
❑ 60	James O. Stewart	.25	.08
❑ 61	Greg Hill	.25	.08
❑ 62	Mark Carrier WR	.10	.02
❑ 63	Bernie Parmalee	.10	.02
❑ 64	Chris Sanders	.25	.08
❑ 65	Jeff Hostetler	.10	.02
❑ 66	Eric Moulds RC	2.00	.75
❑ 67	James Jett	.25	.08
❑ 68	Henry Ellard	.10	.02
❑ 69	Mario Bates	.25	.08
❑ 70	Natrone Means	.25	.08
❑ 71	Bobby Engram RC	.50	.20
❑ 72	Christian Fauria	.10	.02
❑ 73	Gus Frerotte	.25	.08
❑ 74	Aaron Hayden	.10	.02
❑ 75	Reggie White	.50	.20
❑ 76	Dave Meggett	.10	.02
❑ 77	Harvey Williams	.10	.02
❑ 78	Terance Mathis	.10	.02
❑ 79	Byron Bam Morris	.10	.02
❑ 80	Trent Dilfer	.50	.20
❑ 81	Irving Fryar	.25	.08
❑ 82	Quinn Early	.10	.02
❑ 83	Lake Dawson	.10	.02
❑ 84	Todd Collins	.25	.08
❑ 85	Eric Metcalf	.10	.02
❑ 86	Tim Biakabutuka RC	.50	.20
❑ 87	Rob Johnson	.50	.20
❑ 88	Charlie Garner	.25	.08
❑ 89	Mike Mamula	.10	.02
❑ 90	Steve Walsh	.10	.02
❑ 91	Charles Haley	.25	.08
❑ 92	Mike Alstott RC	1.50	.60
❑ 93	Wayne Chrebet	.75	.30
❑ 94	Vinny Testaverde	.25	.08
❑ 95	Fred Barnett	.10	.02
❑ 96	Boomer Esiason	.25	.08
❑ 97	Zack Crockett	.10	.02
❑ 98	Kevin Williams	.10	.02
❑ 99	Eric Bieniemy	.10	.02
❑ 100	Bryan Cox	.10	.02
❑ 101	Larry Centers	1.00	.40
❑ 102	Jeff George	1.00	.40
❑ 103	Bryce Paup	1.00	.40
❑ 104	Kerry Collins	2.00	.75
❑ 105	Derrick Moore	.50	.20
❑ 106	Adrian Murrell	1.00	.40
❑ 107	Harold Green	.50	.20
❑ 108	Ki-Jana Carter	1.00	.40
❑ 109	Sherman Williams	.50	.20
❑ 110	Deion Sanders	4.00	2.00
❑ 111	Emmitt Smith	8.00	3.00
❑ 112	Shannon Sharpe	1.00	.40
❑ 113	Johnnie Morton	1.00	.40
❑ 114	Eddie Kennison RC	2.00	.75
❑ 115	Marvin Harrison RC	10.00	4.00
❑ 116	Amani Toomer RC	2.00	.75
❑ 117	Rickey Dudley RC	2.00	.75
❑ 118	Alex Van Dyke RC	1.00	.40
❑ 119	Dorsey Levens	2.00	.75
❑ 120	Antonio Freeman	2.00	.75
❑ 121	Willie Davis WR	1.00	.40
❑ 122	Lamont Warren	.50	.20
❑ 123	Sean Dawkins	.50	.20
❑ 124	Willie Jackson	1.00	.40
❑ 125	Kimble Anders	.50	.20
❑ 126	Dan Marino	10.00	4.00
❑ 127	Terry Kirby	1.00	.40
❑ 128	Amp Lee	.50	.20
❑ 129	Jake Reed	1.00	.40
❑ 130	Curtis Martin	4.00	1.50
❑ 131	Ray Zellars	.50	.20
❑ 132	Herschel Walker	1.00	.40
❑ 133	Mike Sherrard	.50	.20
❑ 134	Kyle Brady	1.00	.40
❑ 135	Rocket Ismail	1.00	.40
❑ 136	Ricky Watters	1.00	.40
❑ 137	Kordell Stewart	2.00	.75
❑ 138	Andre Hastings	.10	.02
❑ 139	Ronnie Harmon	.50	.20
❑ 140	Terrell Fletcher	.50	.20
❑ 141	J.J. Stokes	2.00	.75
❑ 142	Brent Jones	.50	.20
❑ 143	Tony McGee	.50	.20
❑ 144	Brian Blades	1.00	.40
❑ 145	Isaac Bruce	2.00	.75
❑ 146	Errict Rhett	1.00	.40
❑ 147	Warren Sapp	.50	.20
❑ 148	Horace Copeland	.50	.20
❑ 149	Heath Shuler	1.00	.40
❑ 150	Michael Westbrook	2.00	.75
❑ 151	Frank Sanders	1.50	.60
❑ 152	Rob Moore	1.50	.60
❑ 153	Bert Emanuel	1.50	.60
❑ 154	J.J. Birden	.75	.30
❑ 155	Thurman Thomas	2.50	1.00
❑ 156	Jim Kelly	2.50	1.00
❑ 157	Curtis Conway	1.50	.60
❑ 158	Darnay Scott	1.50	.60
❑ 159	Jeff Blake	2.50	1.00
❑ 160	Jay Novacek	1.50	.60
❑ 161	Michael Irvin	2.50	1.00
❑ 162	John Elway	12.00	5.00
❑ 163	Terrell Davis	6.00	2.50
❑ 164	Barry Sanders	8.00	3.00
❑ 165	Brett Perriman	1.50	.60
❑ 166	Keyshawn Johnson RC	5.00	2.00
❑ 167	Eddie George RC	6.00	2.50
❑ 168	Derrick Mayes RC	2.50	1.00
❑ 169	Simeon Rice RC	6.00	2.50
❑ 170	Lawrence Phillips RC	1.50	.60
❑ 171	Robert Brooks	1.50	.60
❑ 172	Mark Chmura	1.50	.60
❑ 173	Rodney Thomas	.75	.30
❑ 174	Jim Harbaugh	1.50	.60
❑ 175	Ken Dilger	1.50	.60
❑ 176	Mark Brunell	5.00	2.00
❑ 177	Steve Bono	1.50	.60
❑ 178	Marcus Allen	2.50	1.00
❑ 179	O.J. McDuffie	1.50	.60
❑ 180	Eric Green	.75	.30
❑ 181	Warren Moon	2.50	1.00
❑ 182	Drew Bledsoe	5.00	2.00
❑ 183	Ben Coates	1.50	.60
❑ 184	Michael Haynes	1.50	.60
❑ 185	Rodney Hampton	1.50	.60
❑ 186	Rashaan Salaam	1.50	.60
❑ 187	Napoleon Kaufman	2.50	1.00
❑ 188	Tim Brown	2.50	1.00
❑ 189	Rodney Peete	.75	.30
❑ 190	Calvin Williams	.75	.30
❑ 191	Erric Pegram	1.50	.60
❑ 192	Mark Bruener	.75	.30
❑ 193	Junior Seau	2.50	1.00
❑ 194	Steve Young	6.00	2.50
❑ 195	Derek Loville	.75	.30
❑ 196	Rick Mirer	1.50	.60
❑ 197	Mark Rypien	.75	.30
❑ 198	Jackie Harris	.75	.30

❑ 199	Terry Allen	1.50	.60
❑ 200	Brian Mitchell	.75	.30

2002 Playoff Prime Signatures

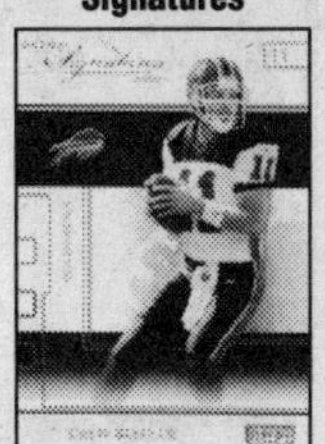

❑ 1	Aaron Brooks	5.00	2.00
❑ 2	Brett Favre	12.00	5.00
❑ 3	Drew Bledsoe	6.00	2.50
❑ 4	Jake Plummer	3.00	1.25
❑ 5	Jeff Blake	2.00	.75
❑ 6	Jevon Kearse	3.00	1.25
❑ 7	Ricky Williams	5.00	2.00
❑ 8	Terrell Davis	6.00	2.50
❑ 9	Chris Chambers	5.00	2.00
❑ 10	Cris Carter	5.00	2.00
❑ 11	Emmitt Smith	12.00	5.00
❑ 12	Randall Cunningham	3.00	1.25
❑ 13	Corey Dillon	3.00	1.25
❑ 14	Brian Griese	5.00	2.00
❑ 15	Isaac Bruce	5.00	2.00
❑ 16	Koren Robinson	3.00	1.25
❑ 17	David Terrell	5.00	2.00
❑ 18	Mark Brunell	5.00	2.00
❑ 19	Eric Moulds	3.00	1.25
❑ 20	Kevan Barlow	3.00	1.25
❑ 21	David Boston	5.00	2.00
❑ 22	LaMont Jordan	5.00	2.00
❑ 23	Jimmy Smith	3.00	1.25
❑ 24	Marvin Harrison	5.00	2.00
❑ 25	Marcus Robinson	3.00	1.25
❑ 26	Ray Lewis	5.00	2.00
❑ 27	Mike Anderson	5.00	2.00
❑ 28	Randy Moss	10.00	4.00
❑ 29	Michael Bennett	3.00	1.25
❑ 30	Quincy Carter	3.00	1.25
❑ 31	Tim Brown	5.00	2.00
❑ 32	Michael Strahan	3.00	1.25
❑ 33	Tony Gonzalez	3.00	1.25
❑ 34	Santana Moss	5.00	2.00
❑ 35	Torry Holt	5.00	2.00
❑ 36	Anthony Thomas	3.00	1.25
❑ 37	Chris Weinke	3.00	1.25
❑ 38	Deuce McAllister	6.00	2.50
❑ 39	Drew Brees	5.00	2.00
❑ 40	Edgerrin James	6.00	2.50
❑ 41	Freddie Mitchell	3.00	1.25
❑ 42	James Jackson	2.00	.75
❑ 43	Kendrell Bell	5.00	2.00
❑ 44	LaDainian Tomlinson	8.00	3.00
❑ 45	Mike McMahon	5.00	2.00
❑ 46	Quincy Morgan	3.00	1.25
❑ 47	Robert Ferguson	2.00	.75
❑ 48	Steve Smith	5.00	2.00
❑ 49	Terrell Owens	5.00	2.00
❑ 50	Eddie George	5.00	2.00
❑ 51	Kurt Warner	5.00	2.00
❑ 52	Chad Johnson	5.00	2.00
❑ 53	Dan Marino	15.00	6.00
❑ 54	Jim Kelly	8.00	3.00
❑ 55	John Elway	15.00	6.00
❑ 56	Michael Irvin	5.00	2.00
❑ 57	Phil Simms	3.00	1.25
❑ 58	Steve Young	8.00	3.00
❑ 59	Troy Aikman	8.00	3.00
❑ 60	Warren Moon	5.00	2.00
❑ 61	Barry Sanders	8.00	3.00
❑ 62	Joe Montana	20.00	7.50
❑ 63	Joe Namath	6.00	2.50
❑ 64	Thurman Thomas	3.00	1.25
❑ 65	T.J. Duckett RC	15.00	6.00
❑ 66	William Green RC	12.00	5.00
❑ 67	Travis Stephens RC	10.00	4.00
❑ 68	Tim Carter RC	10.00	4.00
❑ 69	Terry Charles RC	10.00	4.00
❑ 70	Roy Williams RC	30.00	12.50
❑ 71	Marquise Walker RC	10.00	4.00
❑ 72	Rohan Davey RC	12.00	5.00
❑ 73	Quentin Jammer RC	12.00	5.00
❑ 74	Reche Caldwell RC	12.00	5.00
❑ 75	Maurice Morris RC	12.00	5.00
❑ 76	Woody Dantzler RC	10.00	4.00
❑ 77	Patrick Ramsey RC	15.00	6.00
❑ 78	Tavon Mason RC	6.00	2.50
❑ 79	Ladell Betts RC	12.00	5.00
❑ 80	Kahlil Hill RC	10.00	4.00
❑ 81	Josh Scobey RC	12.00	5.00
❑ 82	Brian Westbrook RC	20.00	7.50
❑ 83	Javon Walker RC	25.00	10.00
❑ 84	DeShaun Foster RC	12.00	5.00
❑ 85	Kelly Campbell RC	10.00	4.00
❑ 86	Ashley Lelie RC	25.00	10.00
❑ 87	Donte Stallworth RC	25.00	10.00
❑ 88	David Carr RC	40.00	15.00
❑ 89	Kurt Kittner RC	10.00	4.00
❑ 90	Clinton Portis RC	50.00	20.00
❑ 91	Josh Reed RC	12.00	5.00
❑ 92	Joey Harrington RC	20.00	7.50
❑ 93	Antwaan Randle El RC	20.00	7.50
❑ 94	Randy Fasani RC	10.00	4.00
❑ 95	Cliff Russell RC	10.00	4.00
❑ 96	John Henderson RC	12.00	5.00
❑ 97	Luke Staley RC	10.00	4.00
❑ 98	Antonio Bryant RC	12.00	5.00
❑ 99	Jonathan Wells RC	12.00	5.00
❑ 100	Chester Taylor RC	25.00	10.00
❑ 101	Lamar Gordon RC	12.00	5.00
❑ 102	Deion Branch RC	25.00	10.00
❑ 103	Josh McCown RC	15.00	6.00
❑ 104	Andre Davis RC	10.00	4.00
❑ 105	Freddie Milons RC	10.00	4.00
❑ 106	David Garrard RC	12.00	5.00
❑ 107	Chad Hutchinson RC	10.00	4.00
❑ 108	Jabar Gaffney RC	12.00	5.00
❑ 109	Eric Crouch RC	12.00	5.00
❑ 110	Albert Haynesworth RC	10.00	4.00
❑ NNO	Jeff Garcia TIN	5.00	2.00

2004 Playoff Prime Signatures

❑ 1	Anquan Boldin	4.00	1.50
❑ 2	Josh McCown	3.00	1.25
❑ 3	Alge Crumpler	3.00	1.25
❑ 4	Michael Vick	8.00	3.00
❑ 5	Jamal Lewis	4.00	1.50
❑ 6	Todd Heap	3.00	1.25
❑ 7	Jim Kelly	6.00	2.50
❑ 8	Thurman Thomas	4.00	1.50
❑ 9	Travis Henry	3.00	1.25
❑ 10	Jake Delhomme	4.00	1.50
❑ 11	Stephen Davis	3.00	1.25
❑ 12	Steve Smith	4.00	1.50
❑ 13	Brian Urlacher	5.00	2.00
❑ 14	Dick Butkus	6.00	2.50
❑ 15	Gale Sayers	6.00	2.50
❑ 16	Mike Ditka	5.00	2.00
❑ 17	Mike Singletary	5.00	2.00
❑ 18	Rex Grossman	4.00	1.50
❑ 19	Richard Dent	3.00	1.25
❑ 20	Chad Johnson	4.00	1.50
❑ 21	Rudi Johnson	3.00	1.25
❑ 22	Jim Brown	8.00	3.00
❑ 23	Lee Suggs	4.00	1.50
❑ 24	Ozzie Newsome	4.00	1.50
❑ 25	Paul Warfield	4.00	1.50
❑ 26	Quincy Morgan	3.00	1.25
❑ 27	William Green	3.00	1.25
❑ 28	Antonio Bryant	3.00	1.25
❑ 29	Herschel Walker	4.00	1.50
❑ 30	Jimmy Johnson	4.00	1.50
❑ 31	Keyshawn Johnson	3.00	1.25
❑ 32	Roger Staubach	8.00	3.00
❑ 33	Terence Newman	3.00	1.25
❑ 34	Tony Dorsett	5.00	2.00
❑ 35	Terrell Davis	4.00	1.50
❑ 36	Joey Harrington	4.00	1.50
❑ 37	Ahman Green	4.00	1.50
❑ 38	Javon Walker	3.00	1.25
❑ 39	Paul Hornung	5.00	2.00
❑ 40	Reggie White	5.00	2.00
❑ 41	Robert Ferguson	2.50	1.00
❑ 42	Sterling Sharpe	4.00	1.50
❑ 43	David Carr	4.00	1.50
❑ 44	Domanick Davis	4.00	1.50
❑ 45	Earl Campbell	5.00	2.00
❑ 46	Peyton Manning	6.00	2.50
❑ 47	Reggie Wayne	3.00	1.25
❑ 48	Dante Hall	4.00	1.50
❑ 49	Priest Holmes	5.00	2.00
❑ 50	Trent Green	3.00	1.25
❑ 51	A.J. Feeley	4.00	1.50
❑ 52	Don Shula	5.00	2.00
❑ 53	Chris Chambers	3.00	1.25
❑ 54	Travis Minor	2.50	1.00
❑ 55	Fran Tarkenton	6.00	2.50
❑ 56	Bill Belichick	5.00	2.00
❑ 57	Tom Brady	8.00	3.00
❑ 58	Aaron Brooks	3.00	1.25
❑ 59	Deuce McAllister	4.00	1.50
❑ 60	Boo Williams	2.50	1.00
❑ 61	Joe Horn	3.00	1.25
❑ 62	Lawrence Taylor	5.00	2.00
❑ 63	Mark Bavaro	2.50	1.00
❑ 64	Michael Strahan	3.00	1.25
❑ 65	Tiki Barber	4.00	1.50
❑ 66	Herman Edwards	4.00	1.50
❑ 67	Joe Namath	8.00	3.00
❑ 68	Justin McCareins	2.50	1.00
❑ 69	LaMont Jordan	4.00	1.50
❑ 70	Santana Moss	3.00	1.25
❑ 71	Bo Jackson	8.00	3.00
❑ 72	Fred Biletnikoff	5.00	2.00
❑ 73	George Blanda	5.00	2.00
❑ 74	Jim Plunkett	4.00	1.50
❑ 75	Marcus Allen	5.00	2.00
❑ 76	Barry Switzer	10.00	4.00
❑ 77	Correll Buckhalter	3.00	1.25
❑ 78	Donovan McNabb	5.00	2.00
❑ 79	Antwaan Randle El	4.00	1.50
❑ 80	Bill Cowher	5.00	2.00
❑ 81	Franco Harris	6.00	2.50
❑ 82	Jack Lambert	6.00	2.50
❑ 83	Joe Greene	5.00	2.00
❑ 84	Kendrell Bell	3.00	1.25
❑ 85	L.C. Greenwood	4.00	1.50
❑ 86	Mel Blount	4.00	1.50
❑ 87	Terry Bradshaw	8.00	3.00
❑ 88	LaDainian Tomlinson	5.00	2.00
❑ 89	Andre Carter	2.50	1.00
❑ 90	Bill Walsh	5.00	2.00
❑ 91	Shaun Alexander	4.00	1.50
❑ 92	Steve Largent	5.00	2.00
❑ 93	Matt Hasselbeck	3.00	1.25
❑ 94	Torry Holt	4.00	1.50
❑ 95	Clinton Portis	4.00	1.50
❑ 96	Laveranues Coles	3.00	1.25
❑ 97	Mark Brunell	3.00	1.25
❑ 98	Patrick Ramsey	3.00	1.25
❑ 99	Reuben Droughns	3.00	1.25
❑ 100	Sonny Jurgensen	4.00	1.50
❑ 101	Mauck AU RC/Luke AU RC	25.00	10.00
❑ 102	D.Wll AU RC/Miree AU RC	20.00	7.50
❑ 103	Fmcs AU RC/Mmt AU RC	25.00	10.00
❑ 104	Vilma AU RC/Ward AU RC	25.00	10.00
❑ 105	Wlfrk AU RC/Sam AU RC	20.00	7.50
❑ 106	Srgi AU RC/Crthn AU RC	25.00	10.00

❑ 107 Flmng AU RC/Pytn AU RC 25.00 10.00
❑ 108 Bbin AU RC/Symns AU RC 25.00 10.00
❑ 109 J.Hrrs AU RC/Mre AU RC 25.00 10.00
❑ 110 M.Mnn AU RC/Brmlt AU RC 20.00 7.50
❑ 111 S.Jns AU RC/Eche.AU RC 20.00 7.50
❑ 112 A.Hll AU RC/B.Pry AU RC 25.00 10.00
❑ 113 J.Tylr AU RC/Lmzn AU RC 25.00 10.00
❑ 114 Gmble AU RC/Crtr AU RC 25.00 10.00
❑ 115 Hnsn AU RC/Krnzl AU RC 25.00 10.00
❑ 116 T.Hrrs AU RC/Crrll AU RC 25.00 10.00
❑ 117 Smkr AU RC/Hcktt AU RC 25.00 10.00
❑ 118 Wlfrd AU RC/Ctchry AU RC 25.00 10.00
❑ 119 W.Smth AU RC/Ude.AU RC 25.00 10.00
❑ 120 Prkr AU RC/Turner AU RC 40.00 20.00
❑ 121 Thom.AU RC/B.Jhn.AU RC 20.00 7.50
❑ 122 Nava.AU RC/Pick.AU RC 25.00 10.00
❑ 123 Colcl.AU RC/Q.Wil.AU RC 25.00 10.00
❑ 124 S.Taylor RC/Cooley AU RC 30.00 12.50
❑ 125 M.Boul.AU RC/Lehman RC 20.00 7.50
❑ 126 J.P. Losman AU RC 80.00 40.00
❑ 127 Lee Evans AU RC 60.00 30.00
❑ 128 Ben Watson AU RC 40.00 20.00
❑ 129 Cedric Cobbs AU RC 40.00 20.00
❑ 130 Devard Darling AU RC 40.00 20.00
❑ 131 Chris Perry AU RC 60.00 30.00
❑ 132 Kellen Winslow AU RC 80.00 30.00
❑ 133 Luke McCown AU RC 40.00 20.00
❑ 134 B.Roethlisberger AU RC 350.00 200.00
❑ 135 Dunta Robinson AU RC 50.00 25.00
❑ 136 Greg Jones AU RC 50.00 30.00
❑ 137 Reggie Williams AU RC 50.00 25.00
❑ 138 Ben Troupe AU RC 40.00 20.00
❑ 139 Tatum Bell AU RC 80.00 40.00
❑ 140 Darius Watts AU RC 40.00 20.00
❑ 141 Robert Gallery AU RC 40.00 20.00
❑ 142 Philip Rivers AU RC 200.00 100.00
❑ 143 Julius Jones AU RC 150.00 75.00
❑ 144 Eli Manning AU RC 300.00 150.00
❑ 145 Bernard Berrian AU RC 50.00 25.00
❑ 146 Roy Williams AU RC 120.00 60.00
❑ 147 Kevin Jones AU RC 100.00 50.00
❑ 148 Mewelde Moore AU RC 40.00 20.00
❑ 149 DeAngelo Hall AU RC 50.00 25.00
❑ 150 Michael Jenkins AU RC 40.00 20.00
❑ 151 Matt Schaub AU RC 125.00 75.00
❑ 152 Keary Colbert AU RC 60.00 25.00
❑ 153 Devery Henderson AU RC 30.00 15.00
❑ 154 Michael Clayton AU RC 80.00 30.00
❑ 155 Larry Fitzgerald AU RC 120.00 60.00
❑ 156 Rashaun Woods AU RC 40.00 20.00
❑ 157 Derrick Hamilton AU RC 40.00 20.00
❑ 158 Steven Jackson AU RC 150.00 75.00

1996 Playoff Trophy Contenders

❑ COMPLETE SET (120) 20.00 7.50
❑ 1 Brett Favre 2.00 .75
❑ 2 Troy Aikman 1.00 .40
❑ 3 Dan Marino 2.00 .75
❑ 4 Emmitt Smith 1.50 .60
❑ 5 Marshall Faulk .50 .20
❑ 6 Jeff Blake .40 .15
❑ 7 John Elway 2.00 .75
❑ 8 Steve Young .75 .30
❑ 9 Curtis Martin .75 .30
❑ 10 Kordell Stewart .40 .15
❑ 11 Drew Bledsoe .60 .25
❑ 12 Jim Kelly .40 .15
❑ 13 Steve Bono .10 .02
❑ 14 Neil O'Donnell .20 .07
❑ 15 Jeff Hostetler .10 .02
❑ 16 Jim Harbaugh .20 .07
❑ 17 Jim Everett .10 .02
❑ 18 Erric Pegram .10 .02
❑ 19 Tyrone Wheatley .20 .07
❑ 20 Barry Sanders 1.50 .60
❑ 21 Deion Sanders .60 .25
❑ 22 Harvey Williams .10 .02
❑ 23 Garrison Hearst .20 .07
❑ 24 Aaron Hayden RC .10 .02
❑ 25 Dorsey Levens .40 .15
❑ 26 Napoleon Kaufman .40 .15
❑ 27 Rodney Hampton .20 .07
❑ 28 Scott Mitchell .20 .07
❑ 29 Greg Hill .20 .07
❑ 30 Charlie Garner .20 .07
❑ 31 Rashaan Salaam .20 .07
❑ 32 Errict Rhett .20 .07
❑ 33 Byron Bam Morris .10 .02
❑ 34 Edgar Bennett .20 .07
❑ 35 Jeff George .20 .07
❑ 36 Rodney Peete .10 .02
❑ 37 Stan Humphries .20 .07
❑ 38 Kimble Anders .20 .07
❑ 39 Natrone Means .20 .07
❑ 40 Sherman Williams .10 .02
❑ 41 Eric Metcalf .10 .02
❑ 42 Chris Warren .20 .07
❑ 43 Marcus Allen .40 .15
❑ 44 Bill Brooks .10 .02
❑ 45 Wayne Chrebet .60 .25
❑ 46 Irving Fryar .20 .07
❑ 47 Tony Martin .20 .07
❑ 48 Daryl Johnston .20 .07
❑ 49 O.J. McDuffie .20 .07
❑ 50 Frank Sanders .20 .07
❑ 51 Ken Norton .10 .02
❑ 52 Jake Reed .20 .07
❑ 53 Bert Emanuel .20 .07
❑ 54 Floyd Turner .10 .02
❑ 55 Junior Seau .40 .15
❑ 56 Ernie Mills .10 .02
❑ 57 Mark Pike .10 .02
❑ 58 Warren Moon .20 .07
❑ 59 Mike Mamula .10 .02
❑ 60 Kerry Collins .40 .15
❑ 61 Nate Newton .10 .02
❑ 62 Terry Allen .20 .07
❑ 63 Bernie Parmalee .10 .02
❑ 64 James O.Stewart .20 .07
❑ 65 Isaac Bruce .40 .15
❑ 66 Lake Dawson .10 .02
❑ 67 Terance Mathis .10 .02
❑ 68 Chris Sanders .20 .07
❑ 69 Anthony Miller .20 .07
❑ 70 Jay Novacek .10 .02
❑ 71 Sean Dawkins .10 .02
❑ 72 J.J. Birden .10 .02
❑ 73 Calvin Williams .10 .02
❑ 74 Rick Mirer .20 .07
❑ 75 Steve McNair .75 .30
❑ 76 Lamont Warren .10 .02
❑ 77 Rod Woodson .20 .07
❑ 78 Larry Brown .10 .02
❑ 79 Zack Crockett .10 .02
❑ 80 Jerry Rice 1.00 .40
❑ 81 Tim Brown .40 .15
❑ 82 Yancey Thigpen .20 .07
❑ 83 J.J. Stokes .40 .15
❑ 84 Herman Moore .20 .07
❑ 85 Kevin Williams .10 .02
❑ 86 Gus Frerotte .20 .07
❑ 87 Robert Brooks .40 .15
❑ 88 Michael Irvin .40 .15
❑ 89 Steve Tasker .10 .02
❑ 90 Joey Galloway .40 .15
❑ 91 Kevin Greene .20 .07
❑ 92 Reggie White .40 .15
❑ 93 Cris Carter .40 .15
❑ 94 Charles Haley .20 .07
❑ 95 Bryce Paup .10 .02
❑ 96 Heath Shuler .20 .07
❑ 97 Eric Zeier .10 .02
❑ 98 Antonio Freeman .40 .15
❑ 99 Erik Kramer .10 .02
❑ 100 Derek Loville .10 .02
❑ 101 Rodney Thomas .10 .02
❑ 102 Terrell Davis .75 .30
❑ 103 Ricky Watters .20 .07
❑ 104 Craig Heyward .10 .02
❑ 105 Terry Kirby .20 .07
❑ 106 Bruce Smith .20 .07
❑ 107 Curtis Conway .40 .15
❑ 108 Charles Johnson .10 .02
❑ 109 Brett Perriman .10 .02
❑ 110 Carl Pickens .20 .07
❑ 111 Michael Westbrook .40 .15
❑ 112 Brent Jones .10 .02
❑ 113 Ken Dilger .20 .07
❑ 114 Fred Barnett .10 .02
❑ 115 Mark Bruener .10 .02
❑ 116 Tamarick Vanover .20 .07
❑ 117 Quinn Early .10 .02
❑ 118 Mark Chmura .20 .07
❑ 119 Andre Hastings .10 .02
❑ 120 Craig Newsome .10 .02

1997 Playoff Zone

❑ COMPLETE SET (150) 25.00 10.00
❑ 1 Brett Favre 2.00 .75
❑ 2 Dorsey Levens .50 .20
❑ 3 William Henderson .30 .10
❑ 4 Derrick Mayes .30 .10
❑ 5 Antonio Freeman .50 .20
❑ 6 Robert Brooks .30 .10
❑ 7 Mark Chmura .30 .10
❑ 8 Reggie White .50 .20
❑ 9 Randall Cunningham .50 .20
❑ 10 Brad Johnson .50 .20
❑ 11 Robert Smith .30 .10
❑ 12 Cris Carter .50 .20
❑ 13 Jake Reed .30 .10
❑ 14 Trent Dilfer .50 .20
❑ 15 Errict Rhett .20 .07
❑ 16 Mike Alstott .50 .20
❑ 17 Scott Mitchell .30 .10
❑ 18 Barry Sanders 1.50 .60
❑ 19 Herman Moore .30 .10
❑ 20 Erik Kramer .20 .07
❑ 21 Rick Mirer .20 .07
❑ 22 Rashaan Salaam .20 .07
❑ 23 Troy Aikman 1.00 .40
❑ 24 Deion Sanders .50 .20
❑ 25 Emmitt Smith 1.50 .60
❑ 26 Daryl Johnston .30 .10
❑ 27 Anthony Miller .20 .07
❑ 28 Eric Bjornson .20 .07
❑ 29 Michael Irvin .50 .20
❑ 30 Chris T. Jones .20 .07
❑ 31 Ty Detmer .30 .10
❑ 32 Ricky Watters .30 .10
❑ 33 Irving Fryar .30 .10
❑ 34 Rodney Peete .20 .07
❑ 35 Jeff Hostetler .20 .07
❑ 36 Terry Allen .50 .20
❑ 37 Michael Westbrook .30 .10
❑ 38 Gus Frerotte .20 .07
❑ 39 Frank Sanders .30 .10
❑ 40 Larry Centers .30 .10
❑ 41 Kent Graham .20 .07
❑ 42 Dave Brown .20 .07
❑ 43 Rodney Hampton .30 .10
❑ 44 Tyrone Wheatley .30 .10
❑ 45 Chris Calloway .20 .07
❑ 46 Ernie Mills .20 .07

❑ 47	Tim Biakabutuka	.30	.10
❑ 48	Anthony Johnson	.20	.07
❑ 49	Wesley Walls	.30	.10
❑ 50	Muhsin Muhammad	.30	.10
❑ 51	Kerry Collins	.50	.20
❑ 52	Terrell Owens	.60	.25
❑ 53	Garrison Hearst	.30	.10
❑ 54	Jerry Rice	1.00	.40
❑ 55	Steve Young	.60	.25
❑ 56	Lawrence Phillips	.20	.07
❑ 57	Isaac Bruce	.50	.20
❑ 58	Eddie Kennison	.30	.10
❑ 59	Tony Banks	.30	.10
❑ 60	Heath Shuler	.20	.07
❑ 61	Andre Hastings	.20	.07
❑ 62	Mario Bates	.20	.07
❑ 63	Chris Chandler	.30	.10
❑ 64	Jamal Anderson	.50	.20
❑ 65	Bert Emanuel	.30	.10
❑ 66	Drew Bledsoe	.60	.25
❑ 67	Curtis Martin	.60	.25
❑ 68	Ben Coates	.30	.10
❑ 69	Terry Glenn	.50	.20
❑ 70	Dan Marino	2.00	.75
❑ 71	Karim Abdul-Jabbar	.50	.20
❑ 72	Fred Barnett	.20	.07
❑ 73	O.J. McDuffie	.30	.10
❑ 74	Jim Harbaugh	.30	.10
❑ 75	Marshall Faulk	.60	.25
❑ 76	Zack Crockett	.20	.07
❑ 77	Ken Dilger	.20	.07
❑ 78	Marvin Harrison	.50	.20
❑ 79	Keyshawn Johnson	.50	.20
❑ 80	Neil O'Donnell	.30	.10
❑ 81	Adrian Murrell	.30	.10
❑ 82	Wayne Chrebet	.50	.20
❑ 83	Todd Collins	.20	.07
❑ 84	Thurman Thomas	.50	.20
❑ 85	Bruce Smith	.30	.10
❑ 86	Eric Moulds	.50	.20
❑ 87	Rob Johnson	.50	.20
❑ 88	Mark Brunell	.60	.25
❑ 89	Natrone Means	.30	.10
❑ 90	Jimmy Smith	.30	.10
❑ 91	Keenan McCardell	.30	.10
❑ 92	Kordell Stewart	.50	.20
❑ 93	Jerome Bettis	.50	.20
❑ 94	Charles Johnson	.30	.10
❑ 95	Courtney Hawkins	.20	.07
❑ 96	Greg Lloyd	.20	.07
❑ 97	Ki-Jana Carter	.20	.07
❑ 98	Carl Pickens	.30	.10
❑ 99	Jeff Blake	.30	.10
❑ 100	Steve McNair	.60	.25
❑ 101	Chris Sanders	.20	.07
❑ 102	Eddie George	.50	.20
❑ 103	Vinny Testaverde	.30	.10
❑ 104	Michael Jackson	.30	.10
❑ 105	Derrick Alexander WR	.30	.10
❑ 106	Willie Green	.20	.07
❑ 107	Shannon Sharpe	.30	.10
❑ 108	Rod Smith WR	.50	.20
❑ 109	Terrell Davis	.60	.25
❑ 110	John Elway	2.00	.75
❑ 111	Elvis Grbac	.30	.10
❑ 112	Greg Hill	.20	.07
❑ 113	Marcus Allen	.50	.20
❑ 114	Derrick Thomas	.50	.20
❑ 115	Brett Perriman	.20	.07
❑ 116	Andre Rison	.30	.10
❑ 117	Rickey Dudley	.30	.10
❑ 118	Tim Brown	.50	.20
❑ 119	Desmond Howard	.30	.10
❑ 120	Napoleon Kaufman	.50	.20
❑ 121	Jeff George	.30	.10
❑ 122	Warren Moon	.50	.20
❑ 123	John Friesz	.20	.07
❑ 124	Chris Warren	.30	.10
❑ 125	Joey Galloway	.30	.10
❑ 126	Stan Humphries	.30	.10
❑ 127	Tony Martin	.30	.10
❑ 128	Eric Metcalf	.30	.10
❑ 129	Jim Everett	.20	.07
❑ 130	Warrick Dunn RC	1.50	.60
❑ 131	Reidel Anthony RC	.50	.20
❑ 132	Derrick Mason RC	1.00	.40
❑ 133	Joey Kent RC	.50	.20
❑ 134	Will Blackwell RC	.30	.10
❑ 135	Jim Druckenmiller RC	.30	.10
❑ 136	Byron Hanspard RC	.30	.10
❑ 137	John Allred RC	.20	.07
❑ 138	David LaFleur RC	.20	.07
❑ 139	Danny Wuerffel RC	.50	.20
❑ 140	Tiki Barber RC	3.00	1.25
❑ 141	Ike Hilliard RC	.75	.30
❑ 142	Troy Davis RC	.30	.10
❑ 143	Leon Johnson RC	.30	.10
❑ 144	Tony Gonzalez RC	1.50	.60
❑ 145	Jake Plummer RC	2.50	1.00
❑ 146	Antowain Smith RC	1.25	.50
❑ 147	Rae Carruth RC	.20	.07
❑ 148	Darnell Autry RC	.30	.10
❑ 149	Corey Dillon RC	3.00	1.25
❑ 150	Orlando Pace RC	.50	.20

2000 Private Stock

❑	COMP.SET w/o SP's (100)	25.00	10.00
❑ 1	Rob Moore	.60	.25
❑ 2	Jake Plummer	.60	.25
❑ 3	Frank Sanders	.60	.25
❑ 4	Jamal Anderson	1.00	.40
❑ 5	Chris Chandler	.60	.25
❑ 6	Tim Dwight	1.00	.40
❑ 7	Tony Banks	.60	.25
❑ 8	Priest Holmes	1.25	.50
❑ 9	Doug Flutie	1.00	.40
❑ 10	Rob Johnson	.60	.25
❑ 11	Eric Moulds	1.00	.40
❑ 12	Antowain Smith	.60	.25
❑ 13	Steve Beuerlein	.40	.15
❑ 14	Tim Biakabutuka	.60	.25
❑ 15	Patrick Jeffers	1.00	.40
❑ 16	Muhsin Muhammad	.60	.25
❑ 17	Curtis Enis	.40	.15
❑ 18	Cade McNown	.40	.15
❑ 19	Marcus Robinson	1.00	.40
❑ 20	Corey Dillon	1.00	.40
❑ 21	Akili Smith	.40	.15
❑ 22	Tim Couch	.60	.25
❑ 23	Kevin Johnson	1.00	.40
❑ 24	Troy Aikman	2.00	.75
❑ 25	Rocket Ismail	.60	.25
❑ 26	Emmitt Smith	2.00	.75
❑ 27	Terrell Davis	1.00	.40
❑ 28	Olandis Gary	1.00	.40
❑ 29	Brian Griese	1.00	.40
❑ 30	Ed McCaffrey	.60	.25
❑ 31	Charlie Batch	1.00	.40
❑ 32	Germane Crowell	.40	.15
❑ 33	Herman Moore	.60	.25
❑ 34	Barry Sanders	2.50	1.00
❑ 35	Brett Favre	3.00	1.25
❑ 36	Antonio Freeman	1.00	.40
❑ 37	Dorsey Levens	.60	.25
❑ 38	Marvin Harrison	1.00	.40
❑ 39	Edgerrin James	1.50	.60
❑ 40	Peyton Manning	2.50	1.00
❑ 41	Terrence Wilkins	.40	.15
❑ 42	Mark Brunell	1.00	.40
❑ 43	Keenan McCardell	.60	.25
❑ 44	Jimmy Smith	.60	.25
❑ 45	Fred Taylor	1.00	.40
❑ 46	Derrick Alexander	.60	.25
❑ 47	Donnell Bennett	.40	.15
❑ 48	Tony Gonzalez	.60	.25
❑ 49	Elvis Grbac	.60	.25
❑ 50	Damon Huard	1.00	.40
❑ 51	James Johnson	.40	.15
❑ 52	Dan Marino	3.00	1.25
❑ 53	O.J. McDuffie	.60	.25
❑ 54	Cris Carter	1.00	.40
❑ 55	Daunte Culpepper	1.25	.50
❑ 56	Randy Moss	2.00	.75
❑ 57	Robert Smith	1.00	.40
❑ 58	Drew Bledsoe	1.25	.50
❑ 59	Kevin Faulk	.60	.25
❑ 60	Terry Glenn	.60	.25
❑ 61	Keith Poole	.60	.25
❑ 62	Ricky Williams	1.00	.40
❑ 63	Kerry Collins	.60	.25
❑ 64	Ike Hilliard	.60	.25
❑ 65	Amani Toomer	.60	.25
❑ 66	Wayne Chrebet	.60	.25
❑ 67	Ray Lucas	.60	.25
❑ 68	Curtis Martin	1.00	.40
❑ 69	Tim Brown	1.00	.40
❑ 70	Rich Gannon	1.00	.40
❑ 71	Napoleon Kaufman	.60	.25
❑ 72	Donovan McNabb	1.50	.60
❑ 73	Duce Staley	1.00	.40
❑ 74	Jerome Bettis	1.00	.40
❑ 75	Troy Edwards	.40	.15
❑ 76	Kordell Stewart	.60	.25
❑ 77	Isaac Bruce	1.00	.40
❑ 78	Marshall Faulk	1.25	.50
❑ 79	Torry Holt	1.00	.40
❑ 80	Kurt Warner	2.00	.75
❑ 81	Jermaine Fazande	.40	.15
❑ 82	Jim Harbaugh	.60	.25
❑ 83	Junior Seau	1.00	.40
❑ 84	Charlie Garner	.60	.25
❑ 85	Terrell Owens	1.00	.40
❑ 86	Jerry Rice	2.00	.75
❑ 87	Jon Kitna	1.00	.40
❑ 88	Derrick Mayes	.60	.25
❑ 89	Ricky Watters	.60	.25
❑ 90	Mike Alstott	1.00	.40
❑ 91	Warrick Dunn	1.00	.40
❑ 92	Jacquez Green	.40	.15
❑ 93	Shaun King	.40	.15
❑ 94	Eddie George	1.00	.40
❑ 95	Jevon Kearse	1.00	.40
❑ 96	Steve McNair	1.00	.40
❑ 97	Yancey Thigpen	.40	.15
❑ 98	Stephen Davis	1.00	.40
❑ 99	Brad Johnson	1.00	.40
❑ 100	Michael Westbrook	.60	.25
❑ 101	Thomas Jones RC	25.00	10.00
❑ 102	Doug Johnson RC	15.00	6.00
❑ 103	Mareno Philyaw RC	10.00	4.00
❑ 104	Jamal Lewis RC	40.00	15.00
❑ 105	Chris Redman RC	12.00	5.00
❑ 106	Travis Taylor RC	15.00	6.00
❑ 107	Frank Murphy RC	10.00	4.00
❑ 108	Dez White RC	15.00	6.00
❑ 109	Ron Dugans RC	10.00	4.00
❑ 110	Curtis Keaton RC	12.00	5.00
❑ 111	Peter Warrick RC	15.00	6.00
❑ 112	Courtney Brown RC	15.00	6.00
❑ 113	JaJuan Dawson RC	10.00	4.00
❑ 114	Dennis Northcutt RC	15.00	6.00
❑ 115	Travis Prentice RC	12.00	5.00
❑ 116	Michael Wiley RC	12.00	5.00
❑ 117	Chris Cole RC	12.00	5.00
❑ 118	Jarious Jackson RC	12.00	5.00
❑ 119	Reuben Droughns RC	20.00	7.50
❑ 120	Bubba Franks RC	15.00	6.00
❑ 121	Anthony Lucas RC	10.00	4.00
❑ 122	Rondell Mealey RC	10.00	4.00
❑ 123	R.Jay Soward RC	12.00	5.00
❑ 124	Shyrone Stith RC	12.00	5.00
❑ 125	Sylvester Morris RC	12.00	5.00
❑ 126	Quinton Spotwood RC	10.00	4.00
❑ 127	Troy Walters RC	15.00	6.00
❑ 128	Tom Brady RC	120.00	60.00
❑ 129	J.R. Redmond RC	12.00	5.00
❑ 130	Marc Bulger RC	30.00	12.50
❑ 131	Sherrod Gideon RC	10.00	4.00
❑ 132	Ron Dayne RC	15.00	6.00
❑ 133	Anthony Becht RC	15.00	6.00
❑ 134	Laveranues Coles RC	20.00	7.50
❑ 135	Chad Pennington RC	40.00	15.00
❑ 136	Sebastian Janikowski RC	15.00	6.00

❑ 137	Jerry Porter RC	20.00	7.50
❑ 138	Todd Pinkston RC	15.00	6.00
❑ 139	Gari Scott RC	10.00	4.00
❑ 140	Plaxico Burress RC	30.00	12.50
❑ 141	Danny Farmer RC	12.00	5.00
❑ 142	Tee Martin RC	15.00	6.00
❑ 143	Trung Canidate RC	12.00	5.00
❑ 144	Trevor Gaylor RC	12.00	5.00
❑ 145	Giovanni Carmazzi RC	10.00	4.00
❑ 146	Tim Rattay RC	15.00	6.00
❑ 147	Shaun Alexander RC	60.00	30.00
❑ 148	Darrell Jackson RC	25.00	10.00
❑ 149	Joe Hamilton RC	12.00	5.00
❑ 150	Todd Husak RC	15.00	6.00
❑ S1	Jon Kitna Sample	1.00	.40

2001 Private Stock

❑	COMP.SET w/o SP's (100)	60.00	30.00
❑ 1	David Boston	1.25	.50
❑ 2	Thomas Jones	.75	.30
❑ 3	Jake Plummer	.75	.30
❑ 4	Jamal Anderson	1.25	.50
❑ 5	Chris Chandler	.75	.30
❑ 6	Eric Zeier	.50	.20
❑ 7	Elvis Grbac	.75	.30
❑ 8	Jamal Lewis	2.00	.75
❑ 9	Shannon Sharpe	.75	.30
❑ 10	Rob Johnson	.75	.30
❑ 11	Eric Moulds	1.25	.50
❑ 12	Peerless Price	.75	.30
❑ 13	Tim Biakabutuka	.75	.30
❑ 14	Jeff Lewis	.50	.20
❑ 15	Muhsin Muhammad	.75	.30
❑ 16	James Allen	.75	.30
❑ 17	Cade McNown	.50	.20
❑ 18	Marcus Robinson	1.25	.50
❑ 19	Brian Urlacher	2.00	.75
❑ 20	Corey Dillon	1.25	.50
❑ 21	Jon Kitna	1.25	.50
❑ 22	Akili Smith	.50	.20
❑ 23	Peter Warrick	1.25	.50
❑ 24	Tim Couch	.75	.30
❑ 25	Kevin Johnson	.75	.30
❑ 26	Travis Prentice	.50	.20
❑ 27	Rocket Ismail	.75	.30
❑ 28	Emmitt Smith	2.50	1.00
❑ 29	Mike Anderson	1.25	.50
❑ 30	Terrell Davis	1.25	.50
❑ 31	Brian Griese	1.25	.50
❑ 32	Ed McCaffrey	1.25	.50
❑ 33	Charlie Batch	1.25	.50
❑ 34	Germane Crowell	.50	.20
❑ 35	James Stewart	.75	.30
❑ 36	Brett Favre	4.00	1.50
❑ 37	Antonio Freeman	1.25	.50
❑ 38	Ahman Green	1.25	.50
❑ 39	Marvin Harrison	1.25	.50
❑ 40	Edgerrin James	1.50	.60
❑ 41	Peyton Manning	3.00	1.25
❑ 42	Mark Brunell	1.25	.50
❑ 43	Jimmy Smith	.75	.30
❑ 44	Fred Taylor	1.25	.50
❑ 45	Derrick Alexander	.75	.30
❑ 46	Tony Gonzalez	.75	.30
❑ 47	Trent Green	1.25	.50
❑ 48	Priest Holmes	1.50	.60
❑ 49	Jay Fiedler	1.25	.50
❑ 50	Oronde Gadsden	.75	.30
❑ 51	Lamar Smith	.75	.30
❑ 52	Cris Carter	1.25	.50
❑ 53	Daunte Culpepper	1.25	.50
❑ 54	Randy Moss	2.50	1.00
❑ 55	Drew Bledsoe	1.50	.60
❑ 56	Kevin Faulk	.75	.30
❑ 57	Terry Glenn	.75	.30
❑ 58	Jeff Blake	.75	.30
❑ 59	Aaron Brooks	1.25	.50
❑ 60	Joe Horn	.75	.30
❑ 61	Ricky Williams	1.25	.50
❑ 62	Tiki Barber	1.25	.50
❑ 63	Kerry Collins	.75	.30
❑ 64	Ron Dayne	1.25	.50
❑ 65	Amani Toomer	.75	.30
❑ 66	Wayne Chrebet	.75	.30
❑ 67	Curtis Martin	1.25	.50
❑ 68	Vinny Testaverde	.75	.30
❑ 69	Tim Brown	1.25	.50
❑ 70	Rich Gannon	1.25	.50
❑ 71	Charlie Garner	.75	.30
❑ 72	Jerry Rice	2.50	1.00
❑ 73	Tyrone Wheatley	.75	.30
❑ 74	Donovan McNabb	1.50	.60
❑ 75	Duce Staley	1.25	.50
❑ 76	Jerome Bettis	1.25	.50
❑ 77	Kordell Stewart	.75	.30
❑ 78	Hines Ward	1.25	.50
❑ 79	Isaac Bruce	1.25	.50
❑ 80	Marshall Faulk	1.50	.60
❑ 81	Torry Holt	1.25	.50
❑ 82	Kurt Warner	2.50	1.00
❑ 83	Curtis Conway	.75	.30
❑ 84	Doug Flutie	1.25	.50
❑ 85	Jeff Garcia	1.25	.50
❑ 86	Terrell Owens	1.25	.50
❑ 87	Shaun Alexander	1.50	.60
❑ 88	Matt Hasselbeck	.75	.30
❑ 89	Darrell Jackson	1.25	.50
❑ 90	Ricky Watters	.75	.30
❑ 91	Mike Alstott	1.25	.50
❑ 92	Warrick Dunn	1.25	.50
❑ 93	Keyshawn Johnson	1.25	.50
❑ 94	Brad Johnson	1.25	.50
❑ 95	Eddie George	1.25	.50
❑ 96	Derrick Mason	.75	.30
❑ 97	Steve McNair	1.25	.50
❑ 98	Stephen Davis	1.25	.50
❑ 99	Jeff George	.75	.30
❑ 100	Michael Westbrook	.75	.30
❑ 101	Bobby Newcombe RC	12.00	5.00
❑ 102	Corey Brown RC	12.00	5.00
❑ 103	Alge Crumpler RC	25.00	10.00
❑ 104	Vinny Sutherland RC	12.00	5.00
❑ 105	Michael Vick RC	60.00	30.00
❑ 106	Chris Barnes RC	12.00	5.00
❑ 107	Todd Heap RC	15.00	6.00
❑ 108	Nate Clements RC	15.00	6.00
❑ 109	Tim Hasselbeck RC	15.00	6.00
❑ 110	Travis Henry RC	25.00	10.00
❑ 111	Dee Brown RC	15.00	6.00
❑ 112	Dan Morgan RC	15.00	6.00
❑ 113	Steve Smith RC	40.00	15.00
❑ 114	Chris Weinke RC	15.00	6.00
❑ 115	John Capel RC	12.00	5.00
❑ 116	David Terrell RC	15.00	6.00
❑ 117	Anthony Thomas RC	15.00	6.00
❑ 118	T.J. Houshmandzadeh RC	20.00	8.00
❑ 119	Chad Johnson RC	40.00	15.00
❑ 120	Rudi Johnson RC	30.00	12.00
❑ 121	James Jackson RC	15.00	6.00
❑ 122	Quincy Morgan RC	15.00	6.00
❑ 123	Quincy Carter RC	15.00	6.00
❑ 124	Kevin Kasper RC	15.00	6.00
❑ 125	Scotty Anderson RC	12.00	5.00
❑ 126	Mike McMahon RC	15.00	6.00
❑ 127	Robert Ferguson RC	15.00	6.00
❑ 128	David Martin RC	12.00	5.00
❑ 129	Jamal Reynolds RC	15.00	6.00
❑ 130	Reggie Wayne RC	30.00	12.00
❑ 131	Richmond Flowers RC	12.00	5.00
❑ 132	Marcus Stroud RC	15.00	6.00
❑ 133	Derrick Blaylock RC	15.00	6.00
❑ 134	Snoop Minnis RC	12.00	5.00
❑ 135	Chris Chambers RC	25.00	10.00
❑ 136	Jamar Fletcher RC	12.00	5.00
❑ 137	Josh Heupel RC	15.00	6.00
❑ 138	Travis Minor RC	12.00	5.00
❑ 139	Michael Bennett RC	15.00	6.00
❑ 140	Deuce McAllister RC	30.00	12.00
❑ 141	Moran Norris RC	8.00	3.00
❑ 142	Onomo Ojo RC	12.00	5.00
❑ 143	Will Allen RC	12.00	5.00
❑ 144	Jonathan Carter RC	12.00	5.00
❑ 145	Jesse Palmer RC	15.00	6.00
❑ 146	LaMont Jordan RC	30.00	12.00
❑ 147	Santana Moss RC	25.00	10.00
❑ 148	Derek Combs RC	12.00	5.00
❑ 149	Derrick Gibson RC	12.00	5.00
❑ 150	Javon Green RC	12.00	5.00
❑ 151	Ken-Yon Rambo RC	12.00	5.00
❑ 152	Marques Tuiasosopo RC	15.00	6.00
❑ 153	Correll Buckhalter RC	20.00	8.00
❑ 154	Freddie Mitchell RC	15.00	6.00
❑ 155	Joey Getherall RC	12.00	5.00
❑ 156	Chris Taylor RC	12.00	5.00
❑ 157	Adam Archuleta RC	15.00	6.00
❑ 158	David Rivers RC	12.00	5.00
❑ 159	Francis St. Paul RC	12.00	5.00
❑ 160	Drew Brees RC	50.00	25.00
❑ 161	LaDainian Tomlinson RC	100.00	50.00
❑ 162	David Allen RC	12.00	5.00
❑ 163	Kevan Barlow RC	15.00	6.00
❑ 164	Andre Carter RC	15.00	6.00
❑ 165	Cedrick Wilson RC	15.00	6.00
❑ 166	Alex Bannister RC	12.00	5.00
❑ 167	Josh Booty RC	15.00	6.00
❑ 168	Heath Evans RC	12.00	5.00
❑ 169	Koren Robinson RC	15.00	6.00
❑ 170	Margin Hooks RC	8.00	3.00
❑ 171	Dan Alexander RC	15.00	6.00
❑ 172	Eddie Berlin RC	12.00	5.00
❑ 173	Rod Gardner RC	15.00	6.00
❑ 174	Damerien McCants RC	12.00	5.00
❑ 175	Sage Rosenfels RC	15.00	6.00

2002 Private Stock

❑	COMP.SET w/o SP's (100)	40.00	15.00
❑ 1	David Boston	1.50	.60
❑ 2	Thomas Jones	1.00	.40
❑ 3	Jake Plummer	1.00	.40
❑ 4	Jamal Anderson	1.00	.40
❑ 5	Warrick Dunn	1.50	.60
❑ 6	Shawn Jefferson	.60	.25
❑ 7	Michael Vick	5.00	2.00
❑ 8	Jamal Lewis	1.50	.60
❑ 9	Chris Redman	.60	.25
❑ 10	Travis Taylor	1.00	.40
❑ 11	Travis Henry	1.50	.60
❑ 12	Eric Moulds	1.00	.40
❑ 13	Peerless Price	1.00	.40
❑ 14	Muhsin Muhammad	1.00	.40
❑ 15	Lamar Smith	1.00	.40
❑ 16	Chris Weinke	1.00	.40
❑ 17	Marty Booker	.60	.25
❑ 18	Jim Miller	.60	.25
❑ 19	Anthony Thomas	1.00	.40
❑ 20	Corey Dillon	1.00	.40
❑ 21	Darnay Scott	.60	.25
❑ 22	Peter Warrick	1.00	.40
❑ 23	Tim Couch	1.00	.40
❑ 24	James Jackson	.60	.25
❑ 25	Kevin Johnson	1.00	.40
❑ 26	Quincy Carter	1.00	.40
❑ 27	Rocket Ismail	1.00	.40
❑ 28	Emmitt Smith	4.00	1.50
❑ 29	Mike Anderson	1.50	.60

❑ 30 Terrell Davis 1.50 .60
❑ 31 Brian Griese 1.50 .60
❑ 32 Rod Smith 1.00 .40
❑ 33 Mike McMahon 1.50 .60
❑ 34 Johnnie Morton 1.00 .40
❑ 35 Brett Favre 4.00 1.50
❑ 36 Antonio Freeman 1.50 .60
❑ 37 Ahman Green 1.50 .60
❑ 38 Corey Bradford .60 .25
❑ 39 Jermaine Lewis .60 .25
❑ 40 Jamie Sharper .60 .25
❑ 41 Marvin Harrison 1.50 .60
❑ 42 Edgerrin James 2.00 .75
❑ 43 Mark Brunell 1.50 .60
❑ 44 Jimmy Smith 1.00 .40
❑ 45 Fred Taylor 1.50 .60
❑ 46 Tony Gonzalez 1.00 .40
❑ 47 Trent Green 1.00 .40
❑ 48 Priest Holmes 2.00 .75
❑ 49 Chris Chambers 1.50 .60
❑ 50 Jay Fiedler 1.00 .40
❑ 51 James McKnight .60 .25
❑ 52 Ricky Williams 1.50 .60
❑ 53 Michael Bennett 1.00 .40
❑ 54 Cris Carter 1.50 .60
❑ 55 Daunte Culpepper 1.50 .60
❑ 56 Randy Moss 3.00 1.25
❑ 57 Drew Bledsoe 1.50 .60
❑ 58 Tom Brady 4.00 1.50
❑ 59 Troy Brown 1.00 .40
❑ 60 Antowain Smith 1.00 .40
❑ 61 Aaron Brooks 1.50 .60
❑ 62 Joe Horn 1.00 .40
❑ 63 Deuce McAllister 2.00 .75
❑ 64 Tiki Barber 1.50 .60
❑ 65 Kerry Collins 1.00 .40
❑ 66 Ron Dayne 1.00 .40
❑ 67 Laveranues Coles 1.00 .40
❑ 68 Curtis Martin 1.50 .60
❑ 69 Vinny Testaverde 1.00 .40
❑ 70 Tim Brown 1.50 .60
❑ 71 Rich Gannon 1.50 .60
❑ 72 Jerry Rice 3.00 1.25
❑ 73 Correll Buckhalter 1.00 .40
❑ 74 Duce Staley 1.50 .60
❑ 75 James Thrash 1.00 .40
❑ 76 Jerome Bettis 1.50 .60
❑ 77 Plaxico Burress 1.00 .40
❑ 78 Kordell Stewart 1.00 .40
❑ 79 Hines Ward 1.50 .60
❑ 80 Isaac Bruce 1.50 .60
❑ 81 Marshall Faulk 1.50 .60
❑ 82 Torry Holt 1.50 .60
❑ 83 Kurt Warner 1.50 .60
❑ 84 Drew Brees 1.50 .60
❑ 85 Doug Flutie 1.50 .60
❑ 86 LaDainian Tomlinson 2.50 1.00
❑ 87 Jeff Garcia 1.50 .60
❑ 88 Garrison Hearst 1.00 .40
❑ 89 Terrell Owens 1.50 .60
❑ 90 Shaun Alexander 2.00 .75
❑ 91 Trent Dilfer 1.00 .40
❑ 92 Darrell Jackson 1.00 .40
❑ 93 Ricky Watters 1.00 .40
❑ 94 Brad Johnson 1.00 .40
❑ 95 Keyshawn Johnson 1.50 .60
❑ 96 Eddie George 1.50 .60
❑ 97 Derrick Mason 1.00 .40
❑ 98 Steve McNair 1.50 .60
❑ 99 Stephen Davis 1.00 .40
❑ 100 Rod Gardner 1.00 .40
❑ 101 Damien Anderson FB/20
❑ 102 Ladell Betts FB/46 40.00 15.00
❑ 103 Antonio Bryant FB/80 40.00 15.00
❑ 104 Wendell Bryant FB/77 30.00 12.50
❑ 105 Reche Caldwell FB/17
❑ 106 Kelly Campbell FB/6
❑ 107 David Carr FB/8
❑ 108 Eric Crouch FB/7
❑ 109 Ronald Curry FB/1
❑ 110 Rohan Davey FB/6
❑ 111 Andre Davis FB/88 40.00 15.00
❑ 112 T.J. Duckett FB/8
❑ 113 DeShaun Foster FB/26 80.00 40.00
❑ 114 Jabar Gaffney FB/10
❑ 115 David Garrard FB/9
❑ 116 Lamar Gordon FB/28 60.00 25.00
❑ 117 Daniel Graham FB/89 40.00 15.00
❑ 118 William Green FB/1
❑ 119 Joey Harrington FB/3
❑ 120 Napoleon Harris FB/8
❑ 121 Verron Haynes FB/35 40.00 15.00
❑ 122 John Henderson FB/98 30.00 12.50
❑ 123 Kahlil Hill FB/3
❑ 124 Quentin Jammer FB/6
❑ 125 Ron Johnson FB/3
❑ 126 Kurt Kittner FB/15
❑ 127 Zak Kustok FB/10
❑ 128 Ashley Lelie FB/8
❑ 129 Josh McCown FB/12
❑ 130 Freddie Milons FB/15
❑ 131 Maurice Morris FB/9
❑ 132 James Mungro FB/23 40.00 15.00
❑ 133 David Neill FB/11
❑ 134 Adrian Peterson FB/3
❑ 135 Brian Poli-Dixon FB/82 30.00 12.50
❑ 136 Clinton Portis FB/28 150.00 60.00
❑ 137 Patrick Ramsey FB/7
❑ 138 Antwaan Randle El FB/11
❑ 139 Josh Reed FB/25 40.00 15.00
❑ 140 Cliff Russell FB/1
❑ 141 Josh Scobey FB/1
❑ 142 Lito Sheppard FB/3
❑ 143 Jeremy Shockey FB/88 50.00 20.00
❑ 144 Luke Staley FB/6
❑ 145 Donte Stallworth FB/4
❑ 146 Lamont Thompson FB/19
❑ 147 Javon Walker FB/80 50.00 20.00
❑ 148 Marquise Walker FB/4
❑ 149 Brian Westbrook FB/20
❑ 150 Roy Williams FB/38 80.00 40.00

1991 Pro Line Portraits

❑ COMPLETE SET (300) 6.00 3.00
❑ 1 Jim Kelly .20 .07
❑ 2 Carl Banks .05 .01
❑ 3 Neal Anderson .10 .02
❑ 4 James Brooks .05 .01
❑ 5 Reggie Langhorne .05 .01
❑ 6 Robert Awalt .05 .01
❑ 7 Greg Kragen .05 .01
❑ 8 Steve Young .60 .25
❑ 9 Nick Bell RC .05 .01
❑ 10 Ray Childress .10 .02
❑ 11 Albert Bentley .05 .01
❑ 12 Albert Lewis .05 .01
❑ 13 Howie Long .10 .02
❑ 14 Flipper Anderson .05 .01
❑ 15 Mark Clayton .10 .02
❑ 16 Jarrod Bunch RC .05 .01
❑ 17 Bruce Armstrong .05 .01
❑ 18 Vinnie Clark RC .05 .01
❑ 19 Rob Moore .10 .02
❑ 20 Eric Allen .05 .01
❑ 21 Timm Rosenbach .05 .01
❑ 22 Gary Anderson K .05 .01
❑ 23 Martin Bayless .05 .01
❑ 24 Kevin Fagan .05 .01
❑ 25 Brian Blades .10 .02
❑ 26 Gary Anderson RB .05 .01
❑ 27 Earnest Byner .10 .02
❑ 28 O.J.Simpson RET .20 .07
❑ 29 Dan Henning CO .05 .01
❑ 30 Sean Landeta .05 .01
❑ 31 James Lofton .10 .02
❑ 32 Mike Singletary .10 .02
❑ 33 David Fulcher .05 .01
❑ 34 Mark Murphy .05 .01
❑ 35 Issiac Holt .05 .01
❑ 36 Dennis Smith .05 .01
❑ 37 Lomas Brown .05 .01
❑ 38 Ernest Givins .10 .02
❑ 39 Duane Bickett .05 .01
❑ 40 Barry Word .05 .01
❑ 41 Tony Mandarich .05 .01
❑ 42 Cleveland Gary .05 .01
❑ 43 Ferrell Edmunds .05 .01
❑ 44 Randal Hill RC .10 .02
❑ 45 Irving Fryar .10 .02
❑ 46 Henry Jones RC .10 .02
❑ 47 Blair Thomas .05 .01
❑ 48 Andre Waters .05 .01
❑ 49 J.T. Smith .05 .01
❑ 50 Thomas Everett .05 .01
❑ 51 Marion Butts .10 .02
❑ 52 Tom Rathman .05 .01
❑ 53 Vann McElroy .05 .01
❑ 54 Mark Carrier WR .10 .02
❑ 55 Jim Lachey .05 .01
❑ 56 Joe Theismann RET .10 .02
❑ 57 Jerry Glanville CO .05 .01
❑ 58 Doug Riesenberg .05 .01
❑ 59 Cornelius Bennett .10 .02
❑ 60 Mark Carrier DB .10 .02
❑ 61 Rodney Holman .05 .01
❑ 62 Leroy Hoard .10 .02
❑ 63 Michael Irvin .20 .07
❑ 64 Bobby Humphrey .05 .01
❑ 65 Mel Gray .10 .02
❑ 66 Brian Noble .05 .01
❑ 67 Al Smith .05 .01
❑ 68 Eric Dickerson .10 .02
❑ 69 Steve DeBerg .10 .02
❑ 70 Jay Schroeder .05 .01
❑ 71 Irv Pankey .05 .01
❑ 72 Reggie Roby .05 .01
❑ 73 Wade Wilson .05 .01
❑ 74 Johnny Rembert .05 .01
❑ 75 Russell Maryland RC .10 .02
❑ 76 Al Toon .10 .02
❑ 77 Randall Cunningham .20 .07
❑ 78 Lonnie Young .05 .01
❑ 79 Carnell Lake .05 .01
❑ 80 Burt Grossman .05 .01
❑ 81 Jim Mora CO .05 .01
❑ 82 Dave Krieg .05 .01
❑ 83 Bruce Hill .05 .01
❑ 84 Ricky Sanders .05 .01
❑ 85 Roger Staubach RET .20 .07
❑ 86 Richard Williamson CO .05 .01
❑ 87 Everson Walls .05 .01
❑ 88 Shane Conlan .05 .01
❑ 89 Mike Ditka CO .20 .07
❑ 90 Mark Bortz .05 .01
❑ 91 Tim McGee .05 .01
❑ 92 Michael Dean Perry .10 .02
❑ 93 Danny Noonan .05 .01
❑ 94 Mark Jackson .05 .01
❑ 95 Chris Miller .10 .02
❑ 96 Ed McCaffrey RC .75 .30
❑ 97 Lorenzo White .10 .02
❑ 98 Ray Donaldson .05 .01
❑ 99 Nick Lowery .05 .01
❑ 100 Steve Smith .05 .01
❑ 101 Jackie Slater .05 .01
❑ 102 Louis Oliver .05 .01
❑ 103 Kanavis McGhee RC .05 .01
❑ 104 Ray Agnew .05 .01
❑ 105 Sam Mills .10 .02
❑ 106 Bill Pickel .05 .01
❑ 107 Keith Byars .10 .02
❑ 108 Ricky Proehl .05 .01
❑ 109 Merril Hoge .05 .01
❑ 110 Rod Bernstine .05 .01
❑ 111 Andy Heck .05 .01
❑ 112 Broderick Thomas .05 .01
❑ 113 Andre Collins .05 .01
❑ 114 Paul Warfield RET .10 .02
❑ 115 Bill Belichick CO RC 1.50 .60
❑ 116 Ottis Anderson .10 .02
❑ 117 Andre Reed .10 .02
❑ 118 Andre Rison .10 .02
❑ 119 Dexter Carter .05 .01

❑ 120 Anthony Munoz .10 .02
❑ 121 Bernie Kosar .10 .02
❑ 122 Alonzo Highsmith .05 .01
❑ 123 David Treadwell .05 .01
❑ 124 Rodney Peete .10 .02
❑ 125 Haywood Jeffires .10 .02
❑ 126 Clarence Verdin .05 .01
❑ 127 Christian Okoye .05 .01
❑ 128 Greg Townsend .05 .01
❑ 129 Tom Newberry .05 .01
❑ 130 Keith Sims .05 .01
❑ 131 Myron Guyton .05 .01
❑ 132 Andre Tippett .05 .01
❑ 133 Steve Walsh .05 .01
❑ 134 Erik McMillan .05 .01
❑ 135 Jim McMahon .10 .02
❑ 136 Derek Hill .05 .01
❑ 137 D.J. Johnson .05 .01
❑ 138 Leslie O'Neal .10 .02
❑ 139 Pierce Holt .05 .01
❑ 140 Cortez Kennedy .10 .02
❑ 141 Danny Peebles .05 .01
❑ 142 Alvin Walton .05 .01
❑ 143 Drew Pearson RET .05 .01
❑ 144 Dick MacPherson CO .05 .01
❑ 145 Erik Howard .05 .01
❑ 146 Steve Tasker .10 .02
❑ 147 Bill Fralic .05 .01
❑ 148 Don Warren .05 .01
❑ 149 Eric Thomas .05 .01
❑ 150 Jack Pardee CO .05 .01
❑ 151 Gary Zimmerman .05 .01
❑ 152 Leonard Marshall .05 .01
❑ 153 Chris Spielman .10 .02
❑ 154 Sam Wyche CO .05 .01
❑ 155 Rohn Stark .05 .01
❑ 156 Stephone Paige .05 .01
❑ 157 Lionel Washington .05 .01
❑ 158 Henry Ellard .10 .02
❑ 159 Dan Marino 1.50 .60
❑ 160 Lindy Infante CO .05 .01
❑ 161 Dan McGwire RC .05 .01
❑ 162 Ken O'Brien .05 .01
❑ 163 Tim McDonald .05 .01
❑ 164 Louis Lipps .05 .01
❑ 165 Billy Joe Tolliver .05 .01
❑ 166 Harris Barton .05 .01
❑ 167 Tony Woods .05 .01
❑ 168 Matt Millen .10 .02
❑ 169 Gale Sayers RET .20 .07
❑ 170 Ron Meyer CO .05 .01
❑ 171 William Roberts .05 .01
❑ 172 Thurman Thomas .20 .07
❑ 173 Steve McMichael .05 .01
❑ 174 Ickey Woods .05 .01
❑ 175 Eugene Lockhart .05 .01
❑ 176 George Seifert CO .10 .02
❑ 177 Keith Jones .05 .01
❑ 178 Jack Trudeau .05 .01
❑ 179 Kevin Porter .05 .01
❑ 180 Ronnie Lott .10 .02
❑ 181 M. Schottenheimer CO .05 .01
❑ 182 Morten Andersen .05 .01
❑ 183 Anthony Thompson .05 .01
❑ 184 Tim Worley .05 .01
❑ 185 Billy Ray Smith .05 .01
❑ 186 David Whitmore RC .05 .01
❑ 187 Jacob Green .05 .01
❑ 188 Browning Nagle RC .05 .01
❑ 189 Franco Harris RET .10 .02
❑ 190 Art Shell CO .10 .02
❑ 191 Bart Oates .05 .01
❑ 192 William Perry .10 .02
❑ 193 Chuck Noll CO .10 .02
❑ 194 Troy Aikman .75 .30
❑ 195 Jeff George .10 .02
❑ 196 Derrick Thomas .20 .07
❑ 197 Roger Craig .10 .02
❑ 198 John Fourcade .05 .01
❑ 199 Rod Woodson .20 .07
❑ 200 Anthony Miller .10 .02
❑ 201 Jerry Rice .75 .30
❑ 202 Eugene Robinson .05 .01
❑ 203 Charles Mann .05 .01
❑ 204 Mel Blount RET .10 .02
❑ 205 Don Shula CO .10 .02
❑ 206 Jumbo Elliott .05 .01
❑ 207 Jay Hilgenberg .05 .01
❑ 208 Deron Cherry .05 .01
❑ 209 Dan Reeves CO .10 .02
❑ 210 Roman Phifer RC .05 .01
❑ 211 David Little .05 .01
❑ 212 Lee Williams .05 .01
❑ 213 John Taylor .10 .02
❑ 214 Monte Coleman .05 .01
❑ 215 Walter Payton RET .50 .20
❑ 216 John Robinson CO .05 .01
❑ 217 Pepper Johnson .05 .01
❑ 218 Tom Thayer .05 .01
❑ 219 Dan Saleaumua .05 .01
❑ 220 Ernest Spears RC .05 .01
❑ 221 Bubby Brister .05 .01
❑ 222 Junior Seau .20 .07
❑ 223 Brent Jones .10 .02
❑ 224 Rufus Porter .05 .01
❑ 225 Jack Kemp RET .20 .07
❑ 226 Wayne Fontes CO .05 .01
❑ 227 Phil Simms .10 .02
❑ 228 Shaun Gayle .05 .01
❑ 229 Bill Maas .05 .01
❑ 230 Renaldo Turnbull .05 .01
❑ 231 Bryan Hinkle .05 .01
❑ 232 Gary Plummer .05 .01
❑ 233 Jerry Burns CO .05 .01
❑ 234 Lawrence Taylor .10 .02
❑ 235 Joe Gibbs CO .10 .02
❑ 236 Neil Smith .20 .07
❑ 237 Rich Kotite CO .05 .01
❑ 238 Jim Covert .05 .01
❑ 239 Tim Grunhard .05 .01
❑ 240 Joe Bugel CO .05 .01
❑ 241 David Wyman .05 .01
❑ 242 Maury Buford .05 .01
❑ 243 Kevin Ross .05 .01
❑ 244 Jimmy Johnson CO .10 .02
❑ 245 Jim Morrissey RC .05 .01
❑ 246 Jeff Hostetler .10 .02
❑ 247 Andre Ware .10 .02
❑ 248 Steve Largent RET .20 .07
❑ 249 Chuck Knox CO .05 .01
❑ 250 Boomer Esiason .10 .02
❑ 251 Kevin Butler .05 .01
❑ 252 Bruce Smith .20 .07
❑ 253 Webster Slaughter .10 .02
❑ 254 Mike Sherrard .05 .01
❑ 255 Steve Broussard .05 .01
❑ 256 Warren Moon .20 .07
❑ 257 John Elway 1.50 .60
❑ 258 Bob Golic .05 .01
❑ 259 Jim Everett .10 .02
❑ 260 Bruce Coslet CO .05 .01
❑ 261 James Francis .05 .01
❑ 262 Eric Dorsey .05 .01
❑ 263 Marcus Dupree .05 .01
❑ 264 Hart Lee Dykes .05 .01
❑ 265 Vinny Testaverde .10 .02
❑ 266 Chip Lohmiller .05 .01
❑ 267 John Riggins RET .10 .02
❑ 268 Mike Schad .05 .01
❑ 269 Kevin Greene .10 .02
❑ 270 Dean Biasucci .05 .01
❑ 271 Mike Pritchard RC .10 .02
❑ 272 Ted Washington RC .05 .01
❑ 273 Alfred Williams RC .05 .01
❑ 274 Chris Zorich RC .10 .02
❑ 275 Reggie Barrett .05 .01
❑ 276 Chris Hinton .05 .01
❑ 277 Tracy Johnson RC .05 .01
❑ 278 Jim Harbaugh .10 .02
❑ 279 John Roper .05 .01
❑ 280 Mike Dumas RC .05 .01
❑ 281 Herman Moore RC .20 .07
❑ 282 Eric Turner RC .10 .02
❑ 283 Steve Atwater .05 .01
❑ 284 Michael Cofer .05 .01
❑ 285 Darion Conner .05 .01
❑ 286 Darryl Talley .05 .01
❑ 287 Donnell Woolford .05 .01
❑ 288 Keith McCants .05 .01
❑ 289 Ray Handley CO .05 .01
❑ 290 Ahmad Rashad RET .10 .02
❑ 291 Eric Swann RC .10 .02
❑ 292 Dalton Hilliard .05 .01
❑ 293 Rickey Jackson .10 .02
❑ 294 Vaughan Johnson .05 .01
❑ 295 Eric Martin .05 .01
❑ 296 Pat Swilling .10 .02
❑ 297 Anthony Carter .10 .02
❑ 298 Guy McIntyre .05 .01
❑ 299 Bennie Blades .05 .01
❑ 300 Paul Farren .05 .01
❑ P1 Derrick Thomas Promo .50 .20
❑ PLC1 Ahmad Rashad Family .75 .30
❑ PLC2 Payne Stewart .75 .30
❑ NNO Emmitt Smith 15.00 6.00
❑ NNO Santa '91 Sendaway SP .75 .30

1992 Pro Line Portraits

❑ COMPLETE SET (167) 6.00 2.50
❑ 301 Steve Emtman RC .05 .01
❑ 302 Al Edwards .05 .01
❑ 303 Wendell Davis .05 .01
❑ 304 Lewis Billups .05 .01
❑ 305 Brian Brennan .05 .01
❑ 306 John Gesek .05 .01
❑ 307 Terrell Buckley RC .05 .01
❑ 308 Johnny Mitchell RC .05 .01
❑ 309 LeRoy Butler .05 .01
❑ 310 William Fuller .05 .01
❑ 311 Bill Brooks .10 .02
❑ 312 Dino Hackett .05 .01
❑ 313 Willie Gault .10 .02
❑ 314 Aaron Cox .05 .01
❑ 315 Jeff Cross .05 .01
❑ 316 Emmitt Smith 2.00 .75
❑ 317 Marv Cook .05 .01
❑ 318 Gill Fenerty .05 .01
❑ 319 Jeff Carlson RC .05 .01
❑ 320 Brad Baxter .05 .01
❑ 321 Fred Barnett .10 .02
❑ 322 Kurt Barber RC .05 .01
❑ 323 Eric Green .10 .02
❑ 324 Greg Clark RC .05 .01
❑ 325 Keith DeLong .05 .01
❑ 326 Patrick Hunter .05 .01
❑ 327 Troy Vincent RC .05 .01
❑ 328 Gary Clark .10 .02
❑ 329 Joe Montana 2.50 1.00
❑ 330 Michael Haynes .10 .02
❑ 331 Edgar Bennett RC .20 .07
❑ 332 Darren Lewis .05 .01
❑ 333 Derrick Fenner .05 .01
❑ 334 Rob Burnett .05 .01
❑ 335 Alvin Harper .10 .02
❑ 336 Vance Johnson .05 .01
❑ 337 William White .05 .01
❑ 338 Sterling Sharpe .20 .07
❑ 339 Sean Jones .05 .01
❑ 340 Jeff Herrod .05 .01
❑ 341 Chris Martin .05 .01
❑ 342 Ethan Horton .05 .01
❑ 343 Robert Delpino .05 .01
❑ 344 Mark Higgs .05 .01
❑ 345 Chris Doleman .10 .02
❑ 346 Tommy Hodson .05 .01
❑ 347 Craig Heyward .10 .02
❑ 348 Cary Conklin .05 .01
❑ 349 James Hasty .05 .01
❑ 350 Antone Davis .05 .01
❑ 351 Ernie Jones .05 .01
❑ 352 Greg Lloyd .10 .02
❑ 353 John Friesz .10 .02
❑ 354 Charles Haley .10 .02

❑ 355 Tracy Scroggins RC .05 .01
❑ 356 Paul Gruber .05 .01
❑ 357 Ricky Ervins .05 .01
❑ 358 Brad Muster .05 .01
❑ 359 Deion Sanders .50 .20
❑ 360 Mitch Frerotte RC .05 .01
❑ 361 Stan Thomas .05 .01
❑ 362 Harold Green .10 .02
❑ 363 Eric Metcalf .20 .07
❑ 364 Ken Norton Jr. .10 .02
❑ 365 Dave Widell .05 .01
❑ 366 Mike Tomczak .05 .01
❑ 367 Bubba McDowell .05 .01
❑ 368 Jessie Hester .05 .01
❑ 369 Ervin Randle .05 .01
❑ 370 Anthony Smith DT .05 .01
❑ 371 Pat Terrell .05 .01
❑ 372 Jim C. Jensen .05 .01
❑ 373 Mike Merriweather .05 .01
❑ 374 Chris Singleton .05 .01
❑ 375 Floyd Turner .05 .01
❑ 376 Jim Sweeney .05 .01
❑ 377 Keith Jackson .10 .02
❑ 378 Walter Reeves .05 .01
❑ 379 Neil O'Donnell .10 .02
❑ 380 Nate Lewis .05 .01
❑ 381 Keith Henderson .05 .01
❑ 382 Kelly Stouffer .05 .01
❑ 383 Ricky Reynolds .05 .01
❑ 384 Joe Jacoby .05 .01
❑ 385 Fred Biletnikoff RET .10 .02
❑ 386 Jessie Tuggle .05 .01
❑ 387 Tom Waddle .05 .01
❑ 388 David Shula RC CO .05 .01
❑ 389 Van Waiters RC .05 .01
❑ 390 Jay Novacek .10 .02
❑ 391 Michael Young .05 .01
❑ 392 Mike Holmgren RC CO .20 .07
❑ 393 Doug Smith .05 .01
❑ 394 Mike Prior .05 .01
❑ 395 Harvey Williams .10 .02
❑ 396 Aaron Wallace .05 .01
❑ 397 Tony Zendejas .05 .01
❑ 398 Sammie Smith .05 .01
❑ 399 Henry Thomas .05 .01
❑ 400 Jon Vaughn .05 .01
❑ 401 Brian Washington .05 .01
❑ 402 Leon Searcy RC .05 .01
❑ 403 Lance Smith .05 .01
❑ 404 Warren Williams .05 .01
❑ 405 Bobby Ross CO RC .05 .01
❑ 406 Harry Sydney .05 .01
❑ 407 John L. Williams .05 .01
❑ 408 Ken Willis .05 .01
❑ 409 Brian Mitchell .10 .02
❑ 410 Dick Butkus RET .10 .02
❑ 411 Chuck Knox CO .05 .01
❑ 412 Robert Porcher RC .20 .07
❑ 413 Calvin Williams .10 .02
❑ 414 Bill Cowher CO RC .75 .30
❑ 415 Eric Moore .05 .01
❑ 416 Derek Brown RC TE .05 .01
❑ 417 Dennis Green CO RC .10 .02
❑ 418 Tom Flores CO .05 .01
❑ 419 Dale Carter RC .10 .02
❑ 420 Tony Dorsett RET .10 .02
❑ 421 Marco Coleman RC .05 .01
❑ 422 Sam Wyche CO .05 .01
❑ 423 Ray Crockett .05 .01
❑ 424 Dan Fouts RET .10 .02
❑ 425 Hugh Millen .05 .01
❑ 426 Quentin Coryatt RC .05 .01
❑ 427 Brian Jordan .10 .02
❑ 428 Frank Gifford RET .10 .02
❑ 429 Toby Caston RC .05 .01
❑ 430 Ted Marchibroda CO .05 .01
❑ 431 Cris Carter .20 .07
❑ 432 Tim Krumrie .05 .01
❑ 433 Otto Graham RET .10 .02
❑ 434 Vaughn Dunbar RC .05 .01
❑ 435 John Fina RC .05 .01
❑ 436 Sonny Jurgensen RET .10 .02
❑ 437 Robert Jones RC .05 .01
❑ 438 Steve DeOssie .05 .01
❑ 439 Eddie LeBaron RET .05 .01
❑ 440 Chester McGlockton RC .10 .02
❑ 441 Ken Stabler RET .10 .02
❑ 442 Joe DeLamielleure RET .10 .02
❑ 443 Charley Taylor RET .05 .01
❑ 444 Greg Skrepenak RC .05 .01
❑ 445 Y.A.Tittle RET .10 .02
❑ 446 Chuck Smith RC .05 .01
❑ 447 Kellen Winslow RET .05 .01
❑ 448 Kevin Smith RC DB .05 .01
❑ 449 Phillippi Sparks RC .05 .01
❑ 450 Alonzo Spellman RC .10 .02
❑ 451 Mark Rypien .05 .01
❑ 452 Darryl Williams RC .05 .01
❑ 453 Tommy Vardell RC .05 .01
❑ 454 Tommy Maddox RC 1.50 .60
❑ 455 Steve Israel RC .05 .01
❑ 456 Marquez Pope RC .05 .01
❑ 457 Eugene Chung RC .05 .01
❑ 458 Lynn Swann RET .10 .02
❑ 459 Sean Gilbert RC .10 .02
❑ 460 Chris Mims RC .05 .01
❑ 461 Al Davis OWN .10 .02
❑ 462 Richard Todd RET .05 .01
❑ 463 Mike Fox .05 .01
❑ 464 David Klingler RC .05 .01
❑ 465 Darren Woodson RC .20 .07
❑ 466 Jason Hanson RC .10 .02
❑ 467 Lem Barney RET .05 .01
❑ NNO Santa Sendaway 1.00 .40
❑ NNO Mrs.Claus Sendaway 1.00 .40

1993 Pro Line Live

❑ COMPLETE SET (285) 15.00 7.00
❑ 1 Michael Haynes .10 .02
❑ 2 Chris Hinton .05 .01
❑ 3 Pierce Holt .05 .01
❑ 4 Chris Miller .10 .02
❑ 5 Mike Pritchard .10 .02
❑ 6 Andre Rison .10 .02
❑ 7 Deion Sanders .50 .20
❑ 8 Jessie Tuggle .05 .01
❑ 9 Lincoln Kennedy RC .05 .01
❑ 10 Roger Harper RC .05 .01
❑ 11 Cornelius Bennett .10 .02
❑ 12 Henry Jones .05 .01
❑ 13 Jim Kelly .25 .08
❑ 14 Bill Brooks .05 .01
❑ 15 Nate Odomes .05 .01
❑ 16 Andre Reed .10 .02
❑ 17 Frank Reich .10 .02
❑ 18 Bruce Smith .25 .08
❑ 19 Steve Tasker .10 .02
❑ 20 Thurman Thomas .25 .08
❑ 21 Thomas Smith RC .10 .02
❑ 22 John Parrella RC .05 .01
❑ 23 Neal Anderson .05 .01
❑ 24 Mark Carrier DB .05 .01
❑ 25 Jim Harbaugh .25 .08
❑ 26 Darren Lewis .05 .01
❑ 27 Steve McMichael .10 .02
❑ 28 Alonzo Spellman .05 .01
❑ 29 Tom Waddle .05 .01
❑ 30 Curtis Conway RC .40 .15
❑ 31 Carl Simpson RC .05 .01
❑ 32 David Fulcher .05 .01
❑ 33 Harold Green .05 .01
❑ 34 David Klingler .05 .01
❑ 35 Tim Krumrie .05 .01
❑ 36 Carl Pickens .10 .02
❑ 37 Alfred Williams .05 .01
❑ 38 Darryl Williams .05 .01
❑ 39 John Copeland RC .10 .02
❑ 40 Tony McGee RC .10 .02
❑ 41 Bernie Kosar .10 .02
❑ 42 Kevin Mack .05 .01
❑ 43 Clay Matthews .10 .02
❑ 44 Eric Metcalf .10 .02
❑ 45 Michael Dean Perry .10 .02
❑ 46 Vinny Testaverde .10 .02
❑ 47 Jerry Ball .05 .01
❑ 48 Tommy Vardell .05 .01
❑ 49 Steve Everitt RC .05 .01
❑ 50 Dan Footman RC .05 .01
❑ 51 Troy Aikman .75 .30
❑ 52 Daryl Johnston .25 .08
❑ 53 Tony Casillas .05 .01
❑ 54 Charles Haley .10 .02
❑ 55 Alvin Harper .10 .02
❑ 56 Michael Irvin .25 .08
❑ 57 Robert Jones .05 .01
❑ 58 Russell Maryland .05 .01
❑ 59 Nate Newton .10 .02
❑ 60 Ken Norton Jr. .10 .02
❑ 61 Jay Novacek .10 .02
❑ 62 Emmitt Smith 1.50 .60
❑ 63 Kevin Smith .10 .02
❑ 64 Kevin Williams RC WR .05 .01
❑ 65 Darrin Smith RC .10 .02
❑ 66 Steve Atwater .05 .01
❑ 67 Rod Bernstine .05 .01
❑ 68 Mike Croel .05 .01
❑ 69 John Elway 1.50 .60
❑ 70 Tommy Maddox .25 .08
❑ 71 Karl Mecklenburg .05 .01
❑ 72 Shannon Sharpe .25 .08
❑ 73 Dennis Smith .05 .01
❑ 74 Dan Williams RC .05 .01
❑ 75 Glyn Milburn RC .25 .08
❑ 76 Pat Swilling .05 .01
❑ 77 Bennie Blades .05 .01
❑ 78 Herman Moore .25 .08
❑ 79 Rodney Peete .05 .01
❑ 80 Brett Perriman .25 .08
❑ 81 Barry Sanders 1.25 .50
❑ 82 Chris Spielman .10 .02
❑ 83 Andre Ware .05 .01
❑ 84 Ryan McNeil RC .25 .08
❑ 85 Antonio London RC .05 .01
❑ 86 Tony Bennett .05 .01
❑ 87 Terrell Buckley .05 .01
❑ 88 Brett Favre 2.00 .75
❑ 89 Brian Noble .05 .01
❑ 90 Ken O'Brien .05 .01
❑ 91 Sterling Sharpe .25 .08
❑ 92 Reggie White .25 .08
❑ 93 John Stephens .05 .01
❑ 94 Wayne Simmons RC .05 .01
❑ 95 George Teague RC .10 .02
❑ 96 Ray Childress .05 .01
❑ 97 Curtis Duncan .05 .01
❑ 98 Ernest Givins .10 .02
❑ 99 Haywood Jeffires .10 .02
❑ 100 Bubba McDowell .05 .01
❑ 101 Warren Moon .25 .08
❑ 102 Al Smith .05 .01
❑ 103 Lorenzo White .05 .01
❑ 104 Brad Hopkins RC .05 .01
❑ 105 Micheal Barrow RC .25 .08
❑ 106 Duane Bickett .05 .01
❑ 107 Quentin Coryatt .10 .02
❑ 108 Steve Emtman .05 .01
❑ 109 Jeff George .25 .08
❑ 110 Anthony Johnson .10 .02
❑ 111 Reggie Langhorne .05 .01
❑ 112 Jack Trudeau .05 .01
❑ 113 Clarence Verdin .05 .01
❑ 114 Jessie Hester .05 .01
❑ 115 Roosevelt Potts RC .05 .01
❑ 116 Dale Carter .05 .01
❑ 117 Dave Krieg .10 .02
❑ 118 Nick Lowery .05 .01
❑ 119 Christian Okoye .05 .01
❑ 120 Neil Smith .25 .08
❑ 121 Derrick Thomas .25 .08
❑ 122 Harvey Williams .10 .02
❑ 123 Barry Word .05 .01
❑ 124 Joe Montana 1.50 .60
❑ 125 Marcus Allen .25 .08

❑ 126 James Lofton .10 .02
❑ 127 Nick Bell .05 .01
❑ 128 Tim Brown .25 .08
❑ 129 Eric Dickerson .10 .02
❑ 130 Jeff Hostetler .10 .02
❑ 131 Howie Long .25 .08
❑ 132 Todd Marinovich .05 .01
❑ 133 Greg Townsend .05 .01
❑ 134 Patrick Bates RC .05 .01
❑ 135 Billy Joe Hobert RC .25 .08
❑ 136 Flipper Anderson .05 .01
❑ 137 Shane Conlan .05 .01
❑ 138 Henry Ellard .10 .02
❑ 139 Jim Everett .10 .02
❑ 140 Cleveland Gary .05 .01
❑ 141 Sean Gilbert .10 .02
❑ 142 Todd Lyght .05 .01
❑ 143 Jerome Bettis RC 4.00 1.50
❑ 144 Troy Drayton RC .10 .02
❑ 145 Louis Oliver .05 .01
❑ 146 Marco Coleman .05 .01
❑ 147 Bryan Cox .05 .01
❑ 148 Mark Duper .05 .01
❑ 149 Irving Fryar .10 .02
❑ 150 Mark Higgs .05 .01
❑ 151 Keith Jackson .10 .02
❑ 152 Dan Marino 1.50 .60
❑ 153 Troy Vincent .05 .01
❑ 154 Richmond Webb .05 .01
❑ 155 O.J.McDuffie RC .25 .08
❑ 156 Terry Kirby RC .25 .08
❑ 157 Terry Allen .25 .08
❑ 158 Anthony Carter .10 .02
❑ 159 Cris Carter .25 .08
❑ 160 Chris Doleman .05 .01
❑ 161 Randall McDaniel .05 .01
❑ 162 Audray McMillian .05 .01
❑ 163 Henry Thomas .05 .01
❑ 164 Gary Zimmerman .05 .01
❑ 165 Robert Smith RC 1.25 .50
❑ 166 Qadry Ismail RC .25 .08
❑ 167 Vincent Brown .05 .01
❑ 168 Marv Cook .05 .01
❑ 169 Greg McMurtry .05 .01
❑ 170 Jon Vaughn .05 .01
❑ 171 Leonard Russell .10 .02
❑ 172 Andre Tippett .05 .01
❑ 173 Scott Zolak .05 .01
❑ 174 Drew Bledsoe RC 2.50 1.00
❑ 175 Chris Slade RC .10 .02
❑ 176 Morten Andersen .05 .01
❑ 177 Vaughn Dunbar .05 .01
❑ 178 Rickey Jackson .05 .01
❑ 179 Vaughan Johnson .05 .01
❑ 180 Eric Martin .05 .01
❑ 181 Sam Mills .05 .01
❑ 182 Brad Muster .05 .01
❑ 183 Willie Roaf RC .10 .02
❑ 184 Irv Smith RC .05 .01
❑ 185 Reggie Freeman RC .05 .01
❑ 186 Michael Brooks .05 .01
❑ 187 Dave Brown RC .25 .08
❑ 188 Rodney Hampton .10 .02
❑ 189 Pepper Johnson .05 .01
❑ 190 Ed McCaffrey .25 .08
❑ 191 Dave Meggett .05 .01
❑ 192 Bart Oates .05 .01
❑ 193 Phil Simms .10 .02
❑ 194 Lawrence Taylor .25 .08
❑ 195 Michael Strahan RC 1.00 .40
❑ 196 Brad Baxter .05 .01
❑ 197 Johnny Johnson .05 .01
❑ 198 Boomer Esiason .10 .02
❑ 199 Ronnie Lott .10 .02
❑ 200 Johnny Mitchell .05 .01
❑ 201 Rob Moore .10 .02
❑ 202 Browning Nagle .05 .01
❑ 203 Blair Thomas .05 .01
❑ 204 Marvin Jones RC .05 .01
❑ 205 Coleman Rudolph RC .05 .01
❑ 206 Eric Allen .05 .01
❑ 207 Fred Barnett .10 .02
❑ 208 Tim Harris .05 .01
❑ 209 Randall Cunningham .25 .08
❑ 210 Seth Joyner .05 .01
❑ 211 Clyde Simmons .05 .01
❑ 212 Herschel Walker .10 .02
❑ 213 Calvin Williams .10 .02
❑ 214 Lester Holmes RC .05 .01
❑ 215 Leonard Renfro RC .05 .01
❑ 216 Chris Chandler .10 .02
❑ 217 Gary Clark .10 .02
❑ 218 Ken Harvey .05 .01
❑ 219 Randal Hill .05 .01
❑ 220 Steve Beuerlein .10 .02
❑ 221 Ricky Proehl .05 .01
❑ 222 Timm Rosenbach .05 .01
❑ 223 Garrison Hearst RC .75 .30
❑ 224 Ernest Dye RC .05 .01
❑ 225 Bubby Brister .05 .01
❑ 226 Dermontti Dawson .05 .01
❑ 227 Barry Foster .10 .02
❑ 228 Kevin Greene .10 .02
❑ 229 Merril Hoge .05 .01
❑ 230 Greg Lloyd .10 .02
❑ 231 Neil O'Donnell .25 .08
❑ 232 Rod Woodson .25 .08
❑ 233 Deon Figures RC .05 .01
❑ 234 Chad Brown RC LB .10 .02
❑ 235 Marion Butts .05 .01
❑ 236 Gill Byrd .05 .01
❑ 237 Ronnie Harmon .05 .01
❑ 238 Stan Humphries .10 .02
❑ 239 Anthony Miller .10 .02
❑ 240 Leslie O'Neal .10 .02
❑ 241 Stanley Richard .05 .01
❑ 242 Junior Seau .25 .08
❑ 243 Darrien Gordon RC .05 .01
❑ 244 Natrone Means RC .25 .08
❑ 245 Dana Hall .05 .01
❑ 246 Brent Jones .10 .02
❑ 247 Tim McDonald .05 .01
❑ 248 Steve Bono .10 .02
❑ 249 Jerry Rice 1.00 .40
❑ 250 John Taylor .10 .02
❑ 251 Ricky Watters .25 .08
❑ 252 Steve Young .75 .30
❑ 253 Dana Stubblefield RC .25 .08
❑ 254 Todd Kelly RC .05 .01
❑ 255 Brian Blades .10 .02
❑ 256 Ferrell Edmunds .05 .01
❑ 257 Stan Gelbaugh .05 .01
❑ 258 Cortez Kennedy .10 .02
❑ 259 Dan McGwire .05 .01
❑ 260 Chris Warren .10 .02
❑ 261 John L. Williams .05 .01
❑ 262 David Wyman .05 .01
❑ 263 Rick Mirer RC .25 .08
❑ 264 Carlton Gray RC .05 .01
❑ 265 Marty Carter .05 .01
❑ 266 Reggie Cobb .05 .01
❑ 267 Lawrence Dawsey .05 .01
❑ 268 Santana Dotson .10 .02
❑ 269 Craig Erickson .10 .02
❑ 270 Paul Gruber .05 .01
❑ 271 Keith McCants .05 .01
❑ 272 Broderick Thomas .05 .01
❑ 273 Eric Curry RC .05 .01
❑ 274 Demetrius DuBose RC .05 .01
❑ 275 Earnest Byner UER .05 .01
❑ 276 Ricky Ervins .05 .01
❑ 277 Brad Edwards .05 .01
❑ 278 Jim Lachey .05 .01
❑ 279 Charles Mann .05 .01
❑ 280 Carl Banks .05 .01
❑ 281 Art Monk .10 .02
❑ 282 Mark Rypien .05 .01
❑ 283 Ricky Sanders .05 .01
❑ 284 Tom Carter RC .10 .02
❑ 285 Reggie Brooks RC .10 .02
❑ P1 Troy Aikman Promo 1.25 .50
❑ P2 Troy Aikman Promo 1.00 .40

1993 Pro Line Portraits

❑ COMPLETE SET (44) 6.00 2.50
❑ 468 Willie Roaf RC .10 .02
❑ 469 Terry Allen .20 .07
❑ 470 Jerry Ball .05 .01
❑ 471 Patrick Bates RC .05 .01
❑ 472 Ray Bentley .05 .01
❑ 473 Jerome Bettis RC 4.00 1.50
❑ 474 Steve Beuerlein .10 .02
❑ 475 Drew Bledsoe RC 2.50 1.00
❑ 476 Dave Brown RC .20 .07

❑ 477 Gill Byrd .05 .01
❑ 478 Tony Casillas .05 .01
❑ 479 Chuck Cecil .05 .01
❑ 480 Reggie Cobb .05 .01
❑ 481 Pat Harlow .05 .01
❑ 482 John Copeland RC .10 .02
❑ 483 Bryan Cox .05 .01
❑ 484 Eric Curry RC .05 .01
❑ 485 Jeff Lageman .05 .01
❑ 486 Brett Favre UER 2.00 .75
❑ 487 Barry Foster .10 .02
❑ 488 Gaston Green .05 .01
❑ 489 Rodney Hampton .10 .02
❑ 490 Tim Harris .05 .01
❑ 491 Garrison Hearst RC .75 .30
❑ 492 Tony Smith RB .05 .01
❑ 493 Marvin Jones RC .05 .01
❑ 494 Lincoln Kennedy RC .05 .01
❑ 495 Wilber Marshall .05 .01
❑ 496 Terry McDaniel .05 .01
❑ 497 Rick Mirer RC .20 .07
❑ 498 Art Monk .10 .02
❑ 499 Mike Munchak .10 .02
❑ 500 Frank Reich .10 .02
❑ 501 Barry Sanders 1.50 .60
❑ 502 Shannon Sharpe .20 .07
❑ 503 Gino Torretta RC .05 .01
❑ 504 Ricky Watters .20 .07
❑ 505 Richmond Webb .05 .01
❑ 506 Reggie White .20 .07
❑ 507 Bert Jones TB .05 .01
❑ 508 Billy Kilmer TB .05 .01
❑ 509 John Mackey TB .05 .01
❑ 510 Archie Manning TB .10 .02
❑ 511 Harvey Martin TB .05 .01

1993 Pro Line Profiles

❑ COMPLETE SET (117) 6.00 2.50
❑ COMMON RAY CHILDRESS .04 .01
❑ COMMON JEFF GEORGE .04 .01
❑ COMMON FRANCO HARRIS .08 .02
❑ COMMON KEITH JACKSON .04 .01
❑ COMMON JIMMY JOHNSON .15 .03
❑ COMMON JAMES LOFTON .08 .02
❑ COMMON DAN MARINO .60 .25
❑ COMMON JOE MONTANA .75 .30
❑ COMMON JAY NOVACEK .04 .01
❑ COMMON GALE SAYERS .08 .02
❑ COMMON EMMITT SMITH .60 .25
❑ COMMON HERSCHEL WALKER .08 .02
❑ COMMON STEVE YOUNG .30 .10

1994 Pro Line Live

Card		
❑ COMPLETE SET (405)	20.00	7.50
❑ 1 Emmitt Smith	1.25	.50
❑ 2 Andre Rison	.10	.02
❑ 3 Deion Sanders	.40	.15
❑ 4 Jeff George	.25	.08
❑ 5 Cornelius Bennett	.10	.02
❑ 6 Jim Kelly	.25	.08
❑ 7 Andre Reed	.10	.02
❑ 8 Bruce Smith	.25	.08
❑ 9 Thurman Thomas	.25	.08
❑ 10 Mark Carrier DB	.05	.01
❑ 11 Curtis Conway	.25	.08
❑ 12 Donnell Woolford	.05	.01
❑ 13 Chris Zorich	.05	.01
❑ 14 Erik Kramer	.10	.02
❑ 15 John Copeland	.05	.01
❑ 16 Harold Green	.05	.01
❑ 17 David Klingler	.05	.01
❑ 18 Tony McGee	.05	.01
❑ 19 Carl Pickens	.10	.02
❑ 20 Michael Jackson	.10	.02
❑ 21 Eric Metcalf	.10	.02
❑ 22 Michael Dean Perry	.10	.02
❑ 23 Vinny Testaverde	.10	.02
❑ 24 Eric Turner	.05	.01
❑ 25 Tommy Vardell	.05	.01
❑ 26 Troy Aikman	.75	.30
❑ 27 Charles Haley	.10	.02
❑ 28 Michael Irvin	.25	.08
❑ 29 Pierce Holt	.05	.01
❑ 30 Russell Maryland	.05	.01
❑ 31 Erik Williams	.05	.01
❑ 32 Thomas Everett	.05	.01
❑ 33 Steve Atwater	.05	.01
❑ 34 John Elway	1.50	.60
❑ 35 Glyn Milburn	.10	.02
❑ 36 Shannon Sharpe	.10	.02
❑ 37 Anthony Miller	.10	.02
❑ 38 Barry Sanders	1.25	.50
❑ 39 Chris Spielman	.10	.02
❑ 40 Pat Swilling	.05	.01
❑ 41 Brett Perriman	.10	.02
❑ 42 Herman Moore	.25	.08
❑ 43 Scott Mitchell	.10	.02
❑ 44 Edgar Bennett	.25	.08
❑ 45 Terrell Buckley	.05	.01
❑ 46 LeRoy Butler	.05	.01
❑ 47 Brett Favre	1.50	.60
❑ 48 Jackie Harris	.05	.01
❑ 49 Sterling Sharpe	.10	.02
❑ 50 Reggie White	.25	.08
❑ 51 Gary Brown	.05	.01
❑ 52 Cody Carlson	.05	.01
❑ 53 Ray Childress	.05	.01
❑ 54 Ernest Givins	.10	.02
❑ 55 Bruce Matthews	.05	.01
❑ 56 Quentin Coryatt	.05	.01
❑ 57 Steve Emtman	.05	.01
❑ 58 Roosevelt Potts	.05	.01
❑ 59 Tony Bennett	.05	.01
❑ 60 Marcus Allen	.25	.08
❑ 61 Joe Montana	1.50	.60
❑ 62 Neil Smith	.10	.02
❑ 63 Derrick Thomas	.25	.08
❑ 64 Dale Carter	.05	.01
❑ 65 Tim Brown	.25	.08
❑ 66 Jeff Hostetler	.10	.02
❑ 67 Terry McDaniel	.05	.01
❑ 68 Chester McGlockton	.05	.01
❑ 69 Anthony Smith	.05	.01
❑ 70 Albert Lewis	.05	.01
❑ 71 Jerome Bettis	.50	.20
❑ 72 Shane Conlan	.05	.01
❑ 73 Troy Drayton	.05	.01
❑ 74 Sean Gilbert	.05	.01
❑ 75 Chris Miller	.05	.01
❑ 76 Bryan Cox	.05	.01
❑ 77 Irving Fryar	.10	.02
❑ 78 Keith Jackson	.05	.01
❑ 79 Terry Kirby	.25	.08
❑ 80 Dan Marino	1.50	.60
❑ 81 O.J.McDuffie	.25	.08
❑ 82 Terry Allen	.10	.02
❑ 83 Cris Carter	.40	.15
❑ 84 Chris Doleman	.05	.01
❑ 85 Randall McDaniel	.05	.01
❑ 86 John Randle	.10	.02
❑ 87 Robert Smith	.25	.08
❑ 88 Jason Belser	.05	.01
❑ 89 Jack Del Rio	.05	.01
❑ 90 Vincent Brown	.05	.01
❑ 91 Ben Coates	.10	.02
❑ 92 Chris Slade	.05	.01
❑ 93 Derek Brown RBK	.05	.01
❑ 94 Morten Andersen	.05	.01
❑ 95 Willie Roaf	.05	.01
❑ 96 Irv Smith	.05	.01
❑ 97 Tyrone Hughes	.10	.02
❑ 98 Michael Haynes	.10	.02
❑ 99 Jim Everett	.10	.02
❑ 100 Michael Brooks	.05	.01
❑ 101 Leroy Thompson	.05	.01
❑ 102 Rodney Hampton	.10	.02
❑ 103 Dave Meggett	.05	.01
❑ 104 Phil Simms	.10	.02
❑ 105 Boomer Esiason	.10	.02
❑ 106 Johnny Johnson	.05	.01
❑ 107 Gary Anderson K	.05	.01
❑ 108 Mo Lewis	.05	.01
❑ 109 Ronnie Lott	.10	.02
❑ 110 Johnny Mitchell	.05	.01
❑ 111 Howard Cross	.05	.01
❑ 112 Victor Bailey	.05	.01
❑ 113 Fred Barnett	.10	.02
❑ 114 Randall Cunningham	.25	.08
❑ 115 Calvin Williams	.10	.02
❑ 116 Steve Beuerlein	.10	.02
❑ 117 Gary Clark	.10	.02
❑ 118 Ronald Moore	.05	.01
❑ 119 Ricky Proehl	.05	.01
❑ 120 Eric Swann	.10	.02
❑ 121 Barry Foster	.05	.01
❑ 122 Kevin Greene	.10	.02
❑ 123 Greg Lloyd	.10	.02
❑ 124 Neil O'Donnell	.25	.08
❑ 125 Rod Woodson	.10	.02
❑ 126 Ronnie Harmon	.05	.01
❑ 127 Mark Higgs	.05	.01
❑ 128 Stan Humphries	.10	.02
❑ 129 Leslie O'Neal	.05	.01
❑ 130 Chris Mims	.05	.01
❑ 131 Stanley Richard	.05	.01
❑ 132 Junior Seau	.25	.08
❑ 133 Brent Jones	.10	.02
❑ 134 Tim McDonald	.05	.01
❑ 135 Jerry Rice	.75	.30
❑ 136 Dana Stubblefield	.10	.02
❑ 137 Ricky Watters	.10	.02
❑ 138 Steve Young	.60	.25
❑ 139 Cortez Kennedy	.10	.02
❑ 140 Rick Mirer	.25	.08
❑ 141 Eugene Robinson	.05	.01
❑ 142 Chris Warren	.10	.02
❑ 143 Nate Odomes	.05	.01
❑ 144 Howard Ballard	.05	.01
❑ 145 Flipper Anderson	.05	.01
❑ 146 Chris Jacke	.05	.01
❑ 147 Santana Dotson	.10	.02
❑ 148 Craig Erickson	.05	.01
❑ 149 Hardy Nickerson	.10	.02
❑ 150 Lawrence Dawsey	.05	.01
❑ 151 Terry Wooden	.05	.01
❑ 152 Ethan Horton	.05	.01
❑ 153 John Kasay	.05	.01
❑ 154 Desmond Howard	.10	.02
❑ 155 Ken Harvey	.05	.01
❑ 156 William Fuller	.05	.01
❑ 157 Clyde Simmons	.05	.01
❑ 158 Randal Hill	.05	.01
❑ 159 Garrison Hearst	.25	.08
❑ 160 Mike Pritchard	.05	.01
❑ 161 Jessie Tuggle	.05	.01
❑ 162 Erric Pegram	.05	.01
❑ 163 Kevin Ross	.05	.01
❑ 164 Bill Brooks	.05	.01
❑ 165 Darryl Talley	.05	.01
❑ 166 Steve Tasker	.10	.02
❑ 167 Pete Stoyanovich	.05	.01
❑ 168 Dante Jones	.05	.01
❑ 169 Vencie Glenn	.05	.01
❑ 170 Tom Waddle	.05	.01
❑ 171 Harlon Barnett	.05	.01
❑ 172 Trace Armstrong	.05	.01
❑ 173 Tim Worley	.05	.01
❑ 174 Alfred Williams	.05	.01
❑ 175 Louis Oliver	.05	.01
❑ 176 Darryl Williams	.05	.01
❑ 177 Clay Matthews	.05	.01
❑ 178 Kyle Clifton	.05	.01
❑ 179 Alvin Harper	.10	.02
❑ 180 Jay Novacek	.10	.02
❑ 181 Ken Norton Jr.	.10	.02
❑ 182 Kevin Williams WR	.10	.02
❑ 183 Daryl Johnston	.10	.02
❑ 184 Rod Bernstine	.05	.01
❑ 185 Karl Mecklenburg	.05	.01
❑ 186 Dennis Smith	.05	.01
❑ 187 Robert Delpino	.05	.01
❑ 188 Bennie Blades	.05	.01
❑ 189 Jason Hanson	.05	.01
❑ 190 Derrick Moore	.05	.01
❑ 191 Mark Clayton	.05	.01
❑ 192 Webster Slaughter	.05	.01
❑ 193 Haywood Jeffires	.10	.02
❑ 194 Bubba McDowell	.05	.01
❑ 195 Warren Moon	.25	.08
❑ 196 Al Smith	.05	.01
❑ 197 Bill Romanowski	.05	.01
❑ 198 John Carney	.05	.01
❑ 199 Kerry Cash	.05	.01
❑ 200 Darren Carrington	.05	.01
❑ 201 Jeff Lageman	.05	.01
❑ 202 Tracy Simien	.05	.01
❑ 203 Willie Davis	.10	.02
❑ 204 Dan Saleaumua	.05	.01
❑ 205 Rocket Ismail	.10	.02
❑ 206 James Jett	.05	.01
❑ 207 Todd Lyght	.05	.01
❑ 208 Roman Phifer	.05	.01
❑ 209 Jimmie Jones	.05	.01
❑ 210 Jeff Cross	.05	.01
❑ 211 Eric Davis	.05	.01
❑ 212 Keith Byars	.05	.01
❑ 213 Richmond Webb	.05	.01
❑ 214 Anthony Carter	.10	.02
❑ 215 Henry Thomas	.05	.01
❑ 216 Andre Tippett	.05	.01
❑ 217 Rickey Jackson	.05	.01
❑ 218 Vaughan Johnson	.05	.01
❑ 219 Eric Martin	.05	.01
❑ 220 Sam Mills	.05	.01
❑ 221 Renaldo Turnbull	.05	.01
❑ 222 Mark Collins	.05	.01
❑ 223 Mike Johnson	.05	.01
❑ 224 Rob Moore	.10	.02
❑ 225 Seth Joyner	.05	.01
❑ 226 Herschel Walker	.10	.02
❑ 227 Eric Green	.05	.01
❑ 228 Marion Butts	.05	.01
❑ 229 John Friesz	.10	.02
❑ 230 John Taylor	.10	.02
❑ 231 Dexter Carter	.05	.01
❑ 232 Brian Blades	.10	.02
❑ 233 Reggie Cobb	.05	.01
❑ 234 Paul Gruber	.05	.01
❑ 235 Ricky Reynolds	.05	.01
❑ 236 Vince Workman	.05	.01
❑ 237 Darrell Green	.05	.01
❑ 238 Jim Lachey	.05	.01
❑ 239 James Hasty	.05	.01
❑ 240 Howie Long	.25	.08
❑ 241 Aeneas Williams	.05	.01

❑ 242 Mike Kenn .05 .01
❑ 243 Henry Jones .05 .01
❑ 244 Kenneth Davis .05 .01
❑ 245 Tim Krumrie .05 .01
❑ 246 Derrick Fenner .05 .01
❑ 247 Mark Carrier WR .10 .02
❑ 248 Robert Porcher .05 .01
❑ 249 Darren Woodson .10 .02
❑ 250 Kevin Smith .05 .01
❑ 251 Mark Stepnoski .05 .01
❑ 252 Simon Fletcher .05 .01
❑ 253 Derek Russell .05 .01
❑ 254 Mike Croel .05 .01
❑ 255 Johnny Holland .05 .01
❑ 256 Bryce Paup .10 .02
❑ 257 Cris Dishman .05 .01
❑ 258 Sean Jones .05 .01
❑ 259 Marcus Robertson .05 .01
❑ 260 Steve Jackson .05 .01
❑ 261 Jeff Herrod .05 .01
❑ 262 John Alt .05 .01
❑ 263 Nick Lowery .05 .01
❑ 264 Greg Robinson .05 .01
❑ 265 Alexander Wright .05 .01
❑ 266 Steve Wisniewski .05 .01
❑ 267 Henry Ellard .10 .02
❑ 268 Tracy Scroggins .05 .01
❑ 269 Jackie Slater .05 .01
❑ 270 Troy Vincent .05 .01
❑ 271 Qadry Ismail .25 .08
❑ 272 Steve Jordan .05 .01
❑ 273 Leonard Russell .05 .01
❑ 274 Maurice Hurst .05 .01
❑ 275 Scottie Graham RC .10 .02
❑ 276 Carlton Bailey .05 .01
❑ 277 John Elliott .05 .01
❑ 278 Corey Miller .05 .01
❑ 279 Brad Baxter .05 .01
❑ 280 Brian Washington .05 .01
❑ 281 Tim Harris .05 .01
❑ 282 Byron Evans .05 .01
❑ 283 Dermontti Dawson .05 .01
❑ 284 Carnell Lake .05 .01
❑ 285 Jeff Graham .05 .01
❑ 286 Merton Hanks .10 .02
❑ 287 Harris Barton .05 .01
❑ 288 Guy McIntyre .05 .01
❑ 289 Kelvin Martin .05 .01
❑ 290 John L. Williams .05 .01
❑ 291 Courtney Hawkins .05 .01
❑ 292 Vaughn Hebron .05 .01
❑ 293 Brian Mitchell .05 .01
❑ 294 Andre Collins .05 .01
❑ 295 Art Monk .10 .02
❑ 296 Mark Rypien .05 .01
❑ 297 Ricky Sanders .05 .01
❑ 298 Eric Hill .05 .01
❑ 299 Larry Centers .25 .08
❑ 300 Norm Johnson .05 .01
❑ 301 Pete Metzelaars .05 .01
❑ 302 Ricardo McDonald .05 .01
❑ 303 Stevon Moore .05 .01
❑ 304 Mike Sherrard .05 .01
❑ 305 Andy Harmon .05 .01
❑ 306 Anthony Johnson .10 .02
❑ 307 J.J. Birden .05 .01
❑ 308 Neal Anderson .05 .01
❑ 309 Lewis Tillman .05 .01
❑ 310 Richard Dent .10 .02
❑ 311 Nate Newton .05 .01
❑ 312 Sean Dawkins RC .25 .08
❑ 313 Lawrence Taylor .25 .08
❑ 314 Wilber Marshall .05 .01
❑ 315 Tom Carter .05 .01
❑ 316 Reggie Brooks .10 .02
❑ 317 Eric Curry .05 .01
❑ 318 Horace Copeland .05 .01
❑ 319 Natrone Means .25 .08
❑ 320 Eric Allen .05 .01
❑ 321 Marvin Jones .05 .01
❑ 322 Keith Hamilton .05 .01
❑ 323 Vincent Brisby .10 .02
❑ 324 Drew Bledsoe .75 .30
❑ 325 Tom Rathman .05 .01
❑ 326 Ed McCaffrey .25 .08
❑ 327 Steve Israel .05 .01
❑ 328 Dan Wilkinson RC .10 .02
❑ 329 Marshall Faulk RC 5.00 2.00
❑ 330 Heath Shuler RC .25 .08
❑ 331 Willie McGinest RC .25 .08
❑ 332 Trev Alberts RC .10 .02
❑ 333 Trent Dilfer RC 1.25 .50
❑ 334 Bryant Young RC .25 .08
❑ 335 Sam Adams RC .10 .02
❑ 336 Antonio Langham RC .10 .02
❑ 337 Jamir Miller RC .10 .02
❑ 338 John Thierry RC .05 .01
❑ 339 Aaron Glenn RC .25 .08
❑ 340 Joe Johnson RC .05 .01
❑ 341 Bernard Williams RC .05 .01
❑ 342 Wayne Gandy RC .05 .01
❑ 343 Aaron Taylor RC .05 .01
❑ 344 Charles Johnson RC .25 .08
❑ 345 Dewayne Washington RC .10 .02
❑ 346 Todd Steussie RC .10 .02
❑ 347 Tim Bowens RC .10 .02
❑ 348 Johnnie Morton RC .50 .20
❑ 349 Rob Fredrickson RC .10 .02
❑ 350 Shante Carver RC .05 .01
❑ 351 Thomas Lewis RC .10 .02
❑ 352 Greg Hill RC .25 .08
❑ 353 Henry Ford RC .05 .01
❑ 354 Jeff Burris RC .10 .02
❑ 355 William Floyd RC .25 .08
❑ 356 Derrick Alexander WR RC .25 .08
❑ 357 Darnay Scott RC .50 .20
❑ 358 Isaac Bruce RC 4.00 2.00
❑ 359 Errict Rhett RC .25 .08
❑ 360 Kevin Lee RC .05 .01
❑ 361 Chuck Levy RC .05 .01
❑ 362 David Palmer RC .25 .08
❑ 363 Ryan Yarborough RC .05 .01
❑ 364 Charlie Garner RC 1.25 .50
❑ 365 Isaac Davis RC .05 .01
❑ 366 Mario Bates RC .25 .08
❑ 367 Bert Emanuel RC .25 .08
❑ 368 Thomas Randolph RC .05 .01
❑ 369 Bucky Brooks RC .05 .01
❑ 370 Allen Aldridge RC .05 .01
❑ 371 Charlie Ward RC .25 .08
❑ 372 Aubrey Beavers RC .05 .01
❑ 373 Donnell Bennett RC .25 .08
❑ 374 Jason Sehorn RC .40 .15
❑ 375 Lonnie Johnson RC .05 .01
❑ 376 Tyronne Drakeford RC .05 .01
❑ 377 Andre Coleman RC .05 .01
❑ 378 Lamar Smith RC 1.25 .50
❑ 379 Calvin Jones RC .05 .01
❑ 380 LeShon Johnson RC .10 .02
❑ 381 Byron Bam Morris RC .10 .02
❑ 382 Lake Dawson RC .10 .02
❑ 383 Corey Sawyer RC .10 .02
❑ 384 Willie Jackson RC .25 .08
❑ 385 Perry Klein RC .05 .01
❑ 386 Ronnie Woolfork RC .05 .01
❑ 387 Doug Nussmeier RC .05 .01
❑ 388 Rob Waldrop RC .05 .01
❑ 389 Glenn Foley RC .25 .08
❑ 390 Troy Aikman/Irvin CC .40 .15
❑ 391 Jerry Rice/S.Young CC .40 .15
❑ 392 Brett Favre/St.Sharpe CC .75 .30
❑ 393 Jim Kelly/A.Reed CC .25 .08
❑ 394 John Elway/Sh.Sharpe CC .75 .30
❑ 395 Carolina Panthers .15 .05
❑ 396 Jacksonville Jaguars .15 .05
❑ 397 Checklist 1 .05 .01
❑ 398 Checklist 2 .05 .01
❑ 399 Checklist 3 .05 .01
❑ 400 Checklist 4 .05 .01
❑ 401 Sterling Sharpe ILL .10 .02
❑ 402 Derrick Thomas ILL .10 .02
❑ 403 Joe Montana ILL .60 .25
❑ 404 Emmitt Smith ILL .50 .20
❑ 405 Barry Sanders ILL .60 .25
❑ ES1 E.Smith MVP/15000 15.00 6.00
❑ JB1 Jerome Bettis ROY 12.00 5.00
❑ P1 Troy Aikman Promo 1.25 .50
❑ PR1 Emmitt Smith Promo 2.00 .75

1995 Pro Line

❑ COMPLETE SET (400) 20.00 8.00
❑ 1 Garrison Hearst .25 .08
❑ 2 Anthony Miller .10 .02
❑ 3 Brett Favre 1.50 .60
❑ 4 Jessie Hester .05 .01
❑ 5 Mike Fox .05 .01
❑ 6 Jeff Blake RC .60 .25
❑ 7 J.J. Birden .05 .01
❑ 8 Greg Jackson .05 .01
❑ 9 Leon Lett .05 .01
❑ 10 Bruce Matthews .05 .01
❑ 11 Andre Reed .10 .02
❑ 12 Joe Montana 1.50 .60
❑ 13 Craig Heyward .10 .02
❑ 14 Henry Ellard UER .10 .02
❑ 15 Chris Spielman .10 .02
❑ 16 Tony Woods .05 .01
❑ 17 Carl Banks .05 .01
❑ 18 Eric Zeier RC .25 .08
❑ 19 Michael Brooks .05 .01
❑ 20 Kevin Ross .05 .01
❑ 21 Qadry Ismail .10 .02
❑ 22 Mel Gray .05 .01
❑ 23 Ty Law RC 1.25 .50
❑ 24 Mark Collins .05 .01
❑ 25 Neil O'Donnell .10 .02
❑ 26 Ellis Johnson RC .05 .01
❑ 27 Rick Mirer .10 .02
❑ 28 Fred Barnett .10 .02
❑ 29 Mike Mamula RC .05 .01
❑ 30 Jim Jeffcoat .05 .01
❑ 31 Reggie Cobb .05 .01
❑ 32 Mark Carrier WR UER .10 .02
❑ 33 Darnay Scott .10 .02
❑ 34 Michael Jackson .10 .02
❑ 35 Terrell Buckley .05 .01
❑ 36 Nolan Harrison .05 .01
❑ 37 Thurman Thomas .25 .08
❑ 38 Anthony Smith .05 .01
❑ 39 Phillippi Sparks .05 .01
❑ 40 Cornelius Bennett .10 .02
❑ 41 Robert Young .05 .01
❑ 42 Pierce Holt .05 .01
❑ 43 Greg Lloyd .10 .02
❑ 44 Chad May RC .05 .01
❑ 45 Darrien Gordon .05 .01
❑ 46 Bryan Cox .05 .01
❑ 47 Junior Seau .25 .08
❑ 48 Al Smith .05 .01
❑ 49 Chris Slade .05 .01
❑ 50 Hardy Nickerson .05 .01
❑ 51 Brad Baxter .05 .01
❑ 52 Darryll Lewis .05 .01
❑ 53 Bryant Young .10 .02
❑ 54 Chris Warren .10 .02
❑ 55 Darion Conner .05 .01
❑ 56 Thomas Everett .05 .01
❑ 57 Charles Haley .10 .02
❑ 58 Chris Mims .05 .01
❑ 59 Sean Jones .05 .01
❑ 60 Tamarick Vanover RC .25 .08
❑ 61 Daryl Johnston .10 .02
❑ 62 Rashaan Salaam RC .10 .02
❑ 63 James Hasty .05 .01
❑ 64 Dante Jones .05 .01
❑ 65 Darren Perry UER .05 .01
❑ 66 Troy Drayton .05 .01
❑ 67 Mark Fields RC .25 .08
❑ 68 Brian Williams LB RC .05 .01
❑ 69 Steve Bono UER .10 .02
❑ 70 Eric Allen .05 .01
❑ 71 Chris Zorich .05 .01
❑ 72 Dave Brown .10 .02
❑ 73 Ken Norton Jr. .10 .02

- ❑ 74 Wayne Martin .05 .01
- ❑ 75 Mo Lewis .05 .01
- ❑ 76 Johnny Mitchell .05 .01
- ❑ 77 Todd Lyght .05 .01
- ❑ 78 Erric Pegram .10 .02
- ❑ 79 Kevin Greene .10 .02
- ❑ 80 Randal Hill .05 .01
- ❑ 81 Brett Perriman .10 .02
- ❑ 82 Mike Sherrard .05 .01
- ❑ 83 Curtis Conway .25 .08
- ❑ 84 Mark Tuinei .05 .01
- ❑ 85 Mark Seay .10 .02
- ❑ 86 Randy Baldwin .05 .01
- ❑ 87 Ricky Ervins .05 .01
- ❑ 88 Chester McGlockton .10 .02
- ❑ 89 Tyrone Wheatley RC 1.00 .40
- ❑ 90 Micheal Barrow UER .05 .01
- ❑ 91 Kenneth Davis .05 .01
- ❑ 92 Napoleon Kaufman RC 1.00 .40
- ❑ 93 Webster Slaughter .05 .01
- ❑ 94 Darren Woodson .10 .02
- ❑ 95 Pete Stoyanovich .05 .01
- ❑ 96 Jimmie Jones .05 .01
- ❑ 97 Craig Erickson .05 .01
- ❑ 98 Michael Westbrook RC .25 .08
- ❑ 99 Steve McNair RC 2.50 1.00
- ❑ 100 Errict Rhett .10 .02
- ❑ 101 Devin Bush RC .05 .01
- ❑ 102 Dewayne Washington .10 .02
- ❑ 103 Bart Oates .05 .01
- ❑ 104 Aaron Pierce .05 .01
- ❑ 105 Warren Sapp RC 1.25 .50
- ❑ 106 Eric Green .05 .01
- ❑ 107 Glyn Milburn .05 .01
- ❑ 108 Johnny Johnson .05 .01
- ❑ 109 Marshall Faulk 1.00 .40
- ❑ 110 William Thomas .05 .01
- ❑ 111 George Koonce .05 .01
- ❑ 112 Dana Stubblefield .10 .02
- ❑ 113 Steve Tovar .05 .01
- ❑ 114 Steve Israel .05 .01
- ❑ 115 Brent Williams .05 .01
- ❑ 116 Shane Conlan .05 .01
- ❑ 117 Winston Moss .05 .01
- ❑ 118 Nate Newton .10 .02
- ❑ 119 Michael Irvin .25 .08
- ❑ 120 Jeff Lageman .05 .01
- ❑ 121 Ki-Jana Carter RC .25 .08
- ❑ 122 Dan Marino 1.50 .60
- ❑ 123 Tony Casillas .05 .01
- ❑ 124 Kevin Carter RC .25 .08
- ❑ 125 Warren Moon .10 .02
- ❑ 126 Byron Bam Morris .05 .01
- ❑ 127 Ben Coates .10 .02
- ❑ 128 Michael Bankston .05 .01
- ❑ 129 Anthony Parker .05 .01
- ❑ 130 LeRoy Butler .05 .01
- ❑ 131 Tony Bennett .05 .01
- ❑ 132 Alvin Harper .05 .01
- ❑ 133 Tim Brown .25 .08
- ❑ 134 Tom Carter .05 .01
- ❑ 135 Lorenzo White .05 .01
- ❑ 136 Shane Dronett .05 .01
- ❑ 137 John Elliott UER .05 .01
- ❑ 138 Korey Stringer RC .10 .02
- ❑ 139 Jerry Rice .75 .30
- ❑ 140 Sherman Williams RC .05 .01
- ❑ 141 Kevin Turner .05 .01
- ❑ 142 Randall Cunningham .25 .08
- ❑ 143 Vinny Testaverde .10 .02
- ❑ 144 Tim Bowens .05 .01
- ❑ 145 Russell Maryland .05 .01
- ❑ 146 Chris Miller .05 .01
- ❑ 147 Vince Buck .05 .01
- ❑ 148 Willie Clay .05 .01
- ❑ 149 Jeff Graham .05 .01
- ❑ 150 Shannon Sharpe .10 .02
- ❑ 151 Carnell Lake .05 .01
- ❑ 152 Mark Bruener RC .10 .02
- ❑ 153 James Washington .05 .01
- ❑ 154 Pepper Johnson .05 .01
- ❑ 155 Bert Emanuel .25 .08
- ❑ 156 Mark Stepnoski .05 .01
- ❑ 157 Robert Jones .05 .01
- ❑ 158 Cris Dishman .05 .01
- ❑ 159 Henry Jones .05 .01
- ❑ 160 Henry Thomas .05 .01
- ❑ 161 John L. Williams .05 .01
- ❑ 162 Joe Cain .05 .01
- ❑ 163 Mike Johnson .05 .01
- ❑ 164 Merton Hanks .05 .01
- ❑ 165 Deion Sanders .40 .15
- ❑ 166 William Floyd .10 .02
- ❑ 167 Leroy Thompson .05 .01
- ❑ 168 Ray Childress .05 .01
- ❑ 169 Donnell Woolford .05 .01
- ❑ 170 Tony Siragusa .05 .01
- ❑ 171 Chad Brown .10 .02
- ❑ 172 Stanley Richard .05 .01
- ❑ 173 Rob Johnson RC .75 .30
- ❑ 174 Derrick Brooks RC 1.25 .50
- ❑ 175 Drew Bledsoe .50 .20
- ❑ 176 Maurice Hurst .05 .01
- ❑ 177 Ricky Watters .10 .02
- ❑ 178 Myron Guyton .05 .01
- ❑ 179 Ricky Proehl .05 .01
- ❑ 180 Haywood Jeffires .05 .01
- ❑ 181 Michael Strahan .25 .08
- ❑ 182 Charles Wilson .05 .01
- ❑ 183 Mark Carrier DB .05 .01
- ❑ 184 James O. Stewart RC 1.00 .40
- ❑ 185 Andy Harmon .05 .01
- ❑ 186 Ronnie Lott .10 .02
- ❑ 187 Clay Matthews .10 .02
- ❑ 188 John Carney .05 .01
- ❑ 189 Andre Rison .10 .02
- ❑ 190 Aeneas Williams .05 .01
- ❑ 191 Alexander Wright .05 .01
- ❑ 192 Desmond Howard .10 .02
- ❑ 193 Herman Moore .25 .08
- ❑ 194 Alfred Williams .05 .01
- ❑ 195 Tyrone Poole RC .25 .08
- ❑ 196 Darren Mickell .05 .01
- ❑ 197 Steve Young .60 .25
- ❑ 198 Roman Phifer .05 .01
- ❑ 199 Darrell Green .05 .01
- ❑ 200 Terry Wooden .05 .01
- ❑ 201 Chris Calloway .05 .01
- ❑ 202 Lewis Tillman .05 .01
- ❑ 203 Cris Carter .25 .08
- ❑ 204 Jim Everett .05 .01
- ❑ 205 Adrian Murrell .10 .02
- ❑ 206 Barry Sanders 1.25 .50
- ❑ 207 Mario Bates .10 .02
- ❑ 208 Shawn Lee .05 .01
- ❑ 209 Charles Mincy .05 .01
- ❑ 210 Kerry Collins RC 1.25 .50
- ❑ 211 Steve Walsh .05 .01
- ❑ 212 Chris Chandler .10 .02
- ❑ 213 Bennie Blades .05 .01
- ❑ 214 Kevin Williams WR .10 .02
- ❑ 215 Jim Kelly .25 .08
- ❑ 216 Marion Butts .05 .01
- ❑ 217 Jay Novacek .10 .02
- ❑ 218 Shawn Jefferson .05 .01
- ❑ 219 O.J. McDuffie .25 .08
- ❑ 220 Ray Seals .05 .01
- ❑ 221 Arthur Marshall .05 .01
- ❑ 222 Karl Mecklenburg .05 .01
- ❑ 223 Terance Mathis .10 .02
- ❑ 224 David Klingler .10 .02
- ❑ 225 Rod Woodson .10 .02
- ❑ 226 Quentin Coryatt .10 .02
- ❑ 227 Leroy Hoard .05 .01
- ❑ 228 Brian Blades .10 .02
- ❑ 229 Rob Moore .10 .02
- ❑ 230 Boomer Esiason .10 .02
- ❑ 231 Dave Krieg .05 .01
- ❑ 232 Sterling Sharpe .10 .02
- ❑ 233 Marcus Allen .25 .08
- ❑ 234 John Randle .10 .02
- ❑ 235 Craig Powell RC .05 .01
- ❑ 236 John Elway 1.50 .60
- ❑ 237 Mark Ingram .05 .01
- ❑ 238 Cortez Kennedy .10 .02
- ❑ 239 Brent Jones .05 .01
- ❑ 240 Ken Harvey .05 .01
- ❑ 241 Keenan McCardell .25 .08
- ❑ 242 Dan Wilkinson .10 .02
- ❑ 243 Don Beebe .05 .01
- ❑ 244 Jack Del Rio .05 .01
- ❑ 245 Byron Evans .05 .01
- ❑ 246 Ronald Moore .05 .01
- ❑ 247 Edgar Bennett .10 .02
- ❑ 248 William Fuller .05 .01
- ❑ 249 James Williams LB .05 .01
- ❑ 250 Neil Smith .10 .02
- ❑ 251 Sam Mills .10 .02
- ❑ 252 Willie McGinest .10 .02
- ❑ 253 Howard Cross .05 .01
- ❑ 254 Troy Aikman .75 .30
- ❑ 255 Herschel Walker .10 .02
- ❑ 256 Dale Carter .10 .02
- ❑ 257 Sean Dawkins .10 .02
- ❑ 258 Greg Hill .10 .02
- ❑ 259 Stan Humphries .10 .02
- ❑ 260 Erik Kramer .05 .01
- ❑ 261 Leslie O'Neal .10 .02
- ❑ 262 Trezelle Jenkins RC .05 .01
- ❑ 263 Antonio Langham .05 .01
- ❑ 264 Bryce Paup .10 .02
- ❑ 265 Jake Reed .10 .02
- ❑ 266 Richmond Webb .05 .01
- ❑ 267 Eric Davis .05 .01
- ❑ 268 Mark McMillian .05 .01
- ❑ 269 John Walsh RC .05 .01
- ❑ 270 Irving Fryar .10 .02
- ❑ 271 Rocket Ismail .10 .02
- ❑ 272 Phil Hansen .05 .01
- ❑ 273 J.J. Stokes RC .25 .08
- ❑ 274 Craig Newsome RC .05 .01
- ❑ 275 Leonard Russell .05 .01
- ❑ 276 Derrick Deese .05 .01
- ❑ 277 Broderick Thomas .05 .01
- ❑ 278 Bobby Houston .05 .01
- ❑ 279 Lamar Lathon .05 .01
- ❑ 280 Eugene Robinson .05 .01
- ❑ 281 Dan Saleaumua .05 .01
- ❑ 282 Kyle Brady RC .25 .08
- ❑ 283 John Taylor .05 .01
- ❑ 284 Tony Boselli RC .25 .08
- ❑ 285 Seth Joyner .05 .01
- ❑ 286 Steve Beuerlein .10 .02
- ❑ 287 Sam Adams .05 .01
- ❑ 288 Frank Reich .05 .01
- ❑ 289 Patrick Hunter .05 .01
- ❑ 290 Sean Gilbert .10 .02
- ❑ 291 Dermontti Dawson UER .10 .02
- ❑ 292 Shaun Gayle .05 .01
- ❑ 293 Vincent Brown .05 .01
- ❑ 294 Terry Kirby .10 .02
- ❑ 295 Courtney Hawkins .05 .01
- ❑ 296 Carl Pickens .10 .02
- ❑ 297 Luther Elliss RC .05 .01
- ❑ 298 Steve Atwater .05 .01
- ❑ 299 James Francis .05 .01
- ❑ 300 Rob Burnett .05 .01
- ❑ 301 Keith Hamilton .05 .01
- ❑ 302 Rob Fredrickson .05 .01
- ❑ 303 Jerome Bettis .25 .08
- ❑ 304 Emmitt Smith 1.25 .50
- ❑ 305 Clyde Simmons .05 .01
- ❑ 306 Reggie White .25 .08
- ❑ 307 Rodney Hampton .10 .02
- ❑ 308 Steve Emtman .05 .01
- ❑ 309 Hugh Douglas RC .25 .08
- ❑ 310 Bernie Parmalee .10 .02
- ❑ 311 Trent Dilfer .25 .08
- ❑ 312 Flipper Anderson .05 .01
- ❑ 313 Heath Shuler .10 .02
- ❑ 314 Rod Smith DB .10 .02
- ❑ 315 Ray Zellars RC .10 .02
- ❑ 316 Robert Brooks .25 .08
- ❑ 317 Lee Woodall .05 .01
- ❑ 318 Robert Porcher .05 .01
- ❑ 319 Todd Collins RC .10 .02
- ❑ 320 Willie Roaf .05 .01
- ❑ 321 Erik Williams .05 .01
- ❑ 322 Steve Wisniewski .05 .01
- ❑ 323 Derrick Alexander DE RC .05 .01
- ❑ 324 Frank Warren .05 .01
- ❑ 325 Kelvin Pritchett .05 .01
- ❑ 326 Dennis Gibson .05 .01
- ❑ 327 Jason Belser .05 .01
- ❑ 328 Vincent Brisby .05 .01
- ❑ 329 Calvin Williams .10 .02
- ❑ 330 Derek Brown RBK .05 .01
- ❑ 331 Blake Brockermeyer .05 .01
- ❑ 332 Jeff Herrod .05 .01
- ❑ 333 Darryl Williams .05 .01
- ❑ 334 Aaron Glenn .05 .01

	Card	Price 1	Price 2
❑	335 Eric Metcalf	.10	.02
❑	336 Billy Milner RC	.05	.01
❑	337 Terry McDaniel	.05	.01
❑	338 Trace Armstrong	.05	.01
❑	339 Yancey Thigpen RC	.10	.02
❑	340 Jackie Harris	.05	.01
❑	341 Jeff George	.10	.02
❑	342 Darryl Talley	.05	.01
❑	343 Marcus Robertson	.05	.01
❑	344 Robert Massey	.05	.01
❑	345 Jessie Tuggle	.05	.01
❑	346 Scott Mitchell	.10	.02
❑	347 Harvey Williams	.05	.01
❑	348 Jack Jackson RC	.05	.01
❑	349 Brian Mitchell	.05	.01
❑	350 Lawrence Dawsey	.05	.01
❑	351 Erik Howard	.05	.01
❑	352 Quinn Early	.10	.02
❑	353 Terry Allen	.10	.02
❑	354 Simon Fletcher	.05	.01
❑	355 Eric Turner	.05	.01
❑	356 Natrone Means	.10	.02
❑	357 Frank Sanders RC	.25	.08
❑	358 Michael Timpson	.05	.01
❑	359 Michael Haynes	.10	.02
❑	360 Ruben Brown RC	.25	.08
❑	361 Troy Vincent UER	.05	.01
❑	362 Floyd Turner	.05	.01
❑	363 Larry Centers	.10	.02
❑	364 Eric Swann	.10	.02
❑	365 Albert Lewis	.05	.01
❑	366 Barry Foster	.10	.02
❑	367 Michael Dean Perry	.05	.01
❑	368 Jumpy Geathers UER	.05	.01
❑	369 Kordell Stewart RC	1.25	.50
❑	370 Chuck Smith	.05	.01
❑	371 Lake Dawson	.10	.02
❑	372 Terry Hoage	.05	.01
❑	373 Jeff Cross	.05	.01
❑	374 Tony McGee	.05	.01
❑	375 Eric Curry	.05	.01
❑	376 Harold Green	.05	.01
❑	377 Eric Hill	.05	.01
❑	378 Ray Buchanan	.05	.01
❑	379 Willie Davis	.10	.02
❑	380 Chris T.Jones RC	.05	.01
❑	381 Martin Mayhew	.05	.01
❑	382 Anthony Pleasant	.05	.01
❑	383 Joey Galloway RC	1.25	.50
❑	384 Anthony Morgan	.05	.01
❑	385 Harlon Barnett	.05	.01
❑	386 Bruce Smith	.25	.08
❑	387 Jeff Hostetler	.10	.02
❑	388 Randall McDaniel	.05	.01
❑	389 Dave Meggett	.05	.01
❑	390 Bill Romanowski	.05	.01
❑	391 Gary Brown	.05	.01
❑	392 Charles Johnson	.10	.02
❑	393 Chris Doleman	.05	.01
❑	394 Tony Martin	.10	.02
❑	395 Raymont Harris	.05	.01
❑	396 John Copeland	.05	.01
❑	397 Emmitt Smith CL	.25	.08
❑	398 Steve Young CL	.10	.02
❑	399 Marshall Faulk CL	.50	.20
❑	400 Ki-Jana Carter CL	.10	.02
❑	HP1 Marshall Faulk Sample	1.50	.60
❑	P1 Marshall Faulk Promo	1.50	.60
❑	P2 Jerome Bettis Natl. Promo	1.50	.60

1995 Pro Line Series 2

	Card	Price 1	Price 2
❑	COMPLETE SET (75)	15.00	6.00
❑	1 Jim Kelly	.25	.08
❑	2 Steve Walsh	.05	.01
❑	3 Jeff Blake	.25	.08
❑	4 Vinny Testaverde	.10	.02
❑	5 Jeff Hostetler	.10	.02
❑	6 Dan Marino	1.50	.60
❑	7 Cris Carter	.25	.08
❑	8 Drew Bledsoe	.50	.20
❑	9 Jim Everett	.05	.01
❑	10 Neil O'Donnell	.10	.02
❑	11 Rodney Hampton	.10	.02
❑	12 Troy Aikman	.75	.30
❑	13 John Elway	1.50	.60
❑	14 Barry Sanders	1.25	.50
❑	15 Reggie White	.25	.08
❑	16 Marshall Faulk	1.00	.40
❑	17 Marcus Allen	.25	.08
❑	18 James O. Stewart	.25	.08
❑	19 Randall Cunningham	.25	.08
❑	20 Natrone Means	.10	.02
❑	21 Rick Mirer	.10	.02
❑	22 Jerry Rice	.75	.30
❑	23 Errict Rhett	.10	.02
❑	24 Heath Shuler	.10	.02
❑	25 Jerome Bettis	.25	.08
❑	26 Garrison Hearst	.25	.08
❑	27 Jeff George	.10	.02
❑	28 Andre Reed	.10	.02
❑	29 Warren Moon	.10	.02
❑	30 Ben Coates	.10	.02
❑	31 Mario Bates	.10	.02
❑	32 Byron Bam Morris	.05	.01
❑	33 Dave Brown	.10	.02
❑	34 Emmitt Smith	1.25	.50
❑	35 Anthony Miller	.10	.02
❑	36 Herman Moore	.25	.08
❑	37 Brett Favre	1.50	.60
❑	38 Steve Bono	.10	.02
❑	39 Stan Humphries	.10	.02
❑	40 Steve Young	.60	.25
❑	41 Trent Dilfer	.25	.08
❑	42 Chris Miller	.05	.01
❑	43 Herschel Walker	.10	.02
❑	44 Michael Irvin	.25	.08
❑	45 Junior Seau	.25	.08
❑	46 Deion Sanders	.40	.15
❑	47 William Floyd	.10	.02
❑	48 Ki-Jana Carter	.10	.02
❑	49 Kerry Collins	.40	.15
❑	50 Steve McNair	.75	.30
❑	51 Tony Boselli	.10	.02
❑	52 Kyle Brady	.25	.08
❑	53 Mike Mamula	.05	.01
❑	54 Warren Sapp	.25	.08
❑	55 J.J. Stokes	.10	.02
❑	56 Joey Galloway	.40	.15
❑	57 Hugh Douglas	.10	.02
❑	58 Michael Westbrook	.25	.08
❑	59 Napoleon Kaufman	.25	.08
❑	60 Rashaan Salaam	.10	.02
❑	61 Tyrone Wheatley	.25	.08
❑	62 Terrell Fletcher RC	.05	.01
❑	63 Eric Metcalf	.10	.02
❑	64 Kevin Carter	.25	.08
❑	65 Andre Rison	.10	.02
❑	66 Eric Green	.05	.01
❑	67 Dave Meggett	.05	.01
❑	68 Ricky Watters	.10	.02
❑	69 Steve Beuerlein	.10	.02
❑	70 Craig Erickson	.05	.01
❑	71 Michael Dean Perry	.05	.01
❑	72 Alvin Harper	.05	.01
❑	73 Rob Moore	.10	.02
❑	74 Frank Reich	.05	.01
❑	75 Checklist	.05	.01

1996 Pro Line

	Card	Price 1	Price 2
❑	COMPLETE SET (350)	25.00	10.00
❑	1 Troy Aikman	1.00	.40
❑	2 Steve Young	.75	.30
❑	3 John Elway	2.00	.75
❑	4 Jim Kelly	.40	.15
❑	5 Dan Marino	2.00	.75
❑	6 Brett Favre	2.00	.75
❑	7 Kerry Collins	.40	.15
❑	8 Jeff Blake	.40	.15
❑	9 Stan Humphries	.20	.07
❑	10 Steve Bono	.10	.02
❑	11 Jeff George	.20	.07
❑	12 Mark Brunell	.60	.25
❑	13 Scott Mitchell	.20	.07
❑	14 Steve McNair	.75	.30
❑	15 Jeff Hostetler	.10	.02
❑	16 Jim Everett	.10	.02
❑	17 Rick Mirer	.20	.07
❑	18 Boomer Esiason	.20	.07
❑	19 Neil O'Donnell	.20	.07
❑	20 Dave Brown	.10	.02
❑	21 Erik Kramer	.10	.02
❑	22 Trent Dilfer	.40	.15
❑	23 Jim Harbaugh	.20	.07
❑	24 Vinny Testaverde	.20	.07
❑	25 Thurman Thomas	.40	.15
❑	26 Rodney Peete	.10	.02
❑	27 Gus Frerotte	.20	.07
❑	28 Warren Moon	.20	.07
❑	29 Eric Zeier	.10	.02
❑	30 Randall Cunningham	.40	.15
❑	31 Heath Shuler	.20	.07
❑	32 John Friesz	.10	.02
❑	33 Tommy Maddox	.40	.15
❑	34 Glenn Foley	.20	.07
❑	35 Drew Bledsoe	.60	.25
❑	36 Kordell Stewart	.40	.15
❑	37 Natrone Means	.20	.07
❑	38 Errict Rhett	.20	.07
❑	39 Rashaan Salaam	.20	.07
❑	40 Emmitt Smith	1.50	.60
❑	41 Larry Centers	.20	.07
❑	42 Terrell Davis	.75	.30
❑	43 Marshall Faulk	.50	.20
❑	44 Rodney Hampton	.20	.07
❑	45 Byron Bam Morris	.10	.02
❑	46 Chris Warren	.20	.07
❑	47 Curtis Martin	.75	.30
❑	48 Ricky Watters	.20	.07
❑	49 Marcus Allen	.40	.15
❑	50 Barry Sanders	1.50	.60
❑	51 Edgar Bennett	.20	.07
❑	52 Adrian Murrell	.20	.07
❑	53 James O. Stewart	.20	.07
❑	54 Leroy Hoard	.10	.02
❑	55 Jerome Bettis	.40	.15
❑	56 Craig Heyward	.10	.02
❑	57 Harvey Williams	.10	.02
❑	58 Bernie Parmalee	.10	.02
❑	59 Garrison Hearst	.20	.07
❑	60 Terry Allen	.20	.07
❑	61 Charlie Garner	.20	.07
❑	62 Dorsey Levens	.40	.15
❑	63 Derek Loville	.10	.02
❑	64 Greg Hill	.20	.07
❑	65 Derrick Moore	.10	.02
❑	66 Rodney Thomas	.10	.02
❑	67 Daryl Johnston	.20	.07
❑	68 Mario Bates	.20	.07
❑	69 Aaron Hayden RC	.10	.02
❑	70 Napoleon Kaufman	.40	.15
❑	71 Terry Kirby	.20	.07
❑	72 Glyn Milburn	.10	.02
❑	73 Robert Smith	.20	.07
❑	74 Ki-Jana Carter	.20	.07
❑	75 Tyrone Wheatley	.20	.07
❑	76 Erric Pegram	.10	.02

❑	77	Brian Mitchell	.10	.02
❑	78	Vaughn Dunbar	.10	.02
❑	79	Dave Meggett	.10	.02
❑	80	Scottie Graham	.10	.02
❑	81	Darick Holmes	.10	.02
❑	82	Marion Butts	.10	.02
❑	83	Harold Green	.10	.02
❑	84	Zack Crockett	.10	.02
❑	85	Amp Lee	.10	.02
❑	86	Lamont Warren	.10	.02
❑	87	Mark Chmura	.20	.07
❑	88	Irving Fryar	.20	.07
❑	89	Tim Brown	.40	.15
❑	90	Michael Irvin	.40	.15
❑	91	Tony Martin	.20	.07
❑	92	Alvin Harper	.10	.02
❑	93	Darnay Scott	.20	.07
❑	94	Eric Metcalf	.10	.02
❑	95	Michael Timpson	.10	.02
❑	96	Sean Dawkins	.10	.02
❑	97	Qadry Ismail	.20	.07
❑	98	Yancey Thigpen	.20	.07
❑	99	Joey Galloway	.40	.15
❑	100	Herman Moore	.20	.07
❑	101	J.J. Stokes	.40	.15
❑	102	Wayne Chrebet	.60	.25
❑	103	Ernest Givins	.10	.02
❑	104	Michael Jackson	.20	.07
❑	105	Henry Ellard	.10	.02
❑	106	Thomas Lewis	.10	.02
❑	107	Anthony Miller	.20	.07
❑	108	Terance Mathis	.10	.02
❑	109	Horace Copeland	.10	.02
❑	110	Rocket Ismail	.10	.02
❑	111	Quinn Early	.10	.02
❑	112	Haywood Jeffires	.10	.02
❑	113	Mark Carrier WR	.10	.02
❑	114	Brent Jones	.10	.02
❑	115	Ben Coates	.20	.07
❑	116	Ken Dilger	.20	.07
❑	117	Irv Smith	.10	.02
❑	118	Jay Novacek	.10	.02
❑	119	Tony McGee	.10	.02
❑	120	Troy Drayton	.10	.02
❑	121	Johnny Mitchell	.10	.02
❑	122	Rob Moore	.20	.07
❑	123	Kevin Williams WR	.10	.02
❑	124	O.J. McDuffie	.20	.07
❑	125	Carl Pickens	.20	.07
❑	126	Curtis Conway	.40	.15
❑	127	Ed McCaffrey	.20	.07
❑	128	Arthur Marshall	.10	.02
❑	129	Ernie Mills	.10	.02
❑	130	Cris Carter	.40	.15
❑	131	Isaac Bruce	.40	.15
❑	132	Brian Blades	.10	.02
❑	133	Michael Westbrook	.40	.15
❑	134	Andre Reed	.20	.07
❑	135	Andre Rison	.20	.07
❑	136	Brett Perriman	.10	.02
❑	137	Willie Jackson	.20	.07
❑	138	Ryan Yarborough	.10	.02
❑	139	Chris T. Jones	.20	.07
❑	140	Jerry Rice	1.00	.40
❑	141	Lake Dawson	.10	.02
❑	142	Robert Brooks	.40	.15
❑	143	Vincent Brisby	.10	.02
❑	144	Desmond Howard	.20	.07
❑	145	Johnnie Morton	.20	.07
❑	146	Steve Tasker	.10	.02
❑	147	Ty Detmer	.20	.07
❑	148	Todd Kinchen	.10	.02
❑	149	Mike Sherrard	.10	.02
❑	150	Eric Green	.10	.02
❑	151	Mark Bruener	.10	.02
❑	152	Kyle Brady	.10	.02
❑	153	Frank Sanders	.20	.07
❑	154	Willie Green	.10	.02
❑	155	Jeff Graham	.10	.02
❑	156	Bert Emanuel	.20	.07
❑	157	Courtney Hawkins	.10	.02
❑	158	Mark Seay	.10	.02
❑	159	Chris Calloway	.10	.02
❑	160	John Taylor	.10	.02
❑	161	Fred Barnett	.10	.02
❑	162	Tamarick Vanover	.20	.07
❑	163	Keenan McCardell	.40	.15
❑	164	Bill Brooks	.10	.02
❑	165	Alexander Wright	.10	.02
❑	166	Jake Reed	.20	.07
❑	167	Floyd Turner	.10	.02
❑	168	Mike Pritchard	.10	.02
❑	169	Lawrence Dawsey	.10	.02
❑	170	Shawn Jefferson	.10	.02
❑	171	Michael Haynes	.10	.02
❑	172	Shannon Sharpe	.20	.07
❑	173	Jackie Harris	.10	.02
❑	174	Daryl Hobbs RC	.10	.02
❑	175	Chris Sanders	.20	.07
❑	176	Willie Davis	.10	.02
❑	177	Marco Coleman	.10	.02
❑	178	Pat Swilling	.10	.02
❑	179	Alonzo Spellman	.10	.02
❑	180	Simon Fletcher	.10	.02
❑	181	Sean Gilbert	.10	.02
❑	182	Tracy Scroggins	.10	.02
❑	183	Hugh Douglas	.20	.07
❑	184	Eric Swann	.10	.02
❑	185	Russell Maryland	.10	.02
❑	186	Warren Sapp	.10	.02
❑	187	Jim Flanigan	.10	.02
❑	188	Cortez Kennedy	.10	.02
❑	189	Andy Harmon	.10	.02
❑	190	Dan Saleaumua	.10	.02
❑	191	Kelvin Pritchett	.10	.02
❑	192	John Randle	.20	.07
❑	193	Dan Wilkinson	.10	.02
❑	194	Chester McGlockton	.10	.02
❑	195	Leon Lett	.10	.02
❑	196	Neil Smith	.20	.07
❑	197	Mike Mamula	.10	.02
❑	198	Mike Jones	.10	.02
❑	199	Reggie White	.40	.15
❑	200	Anthony Pleasant	.10	.02
❑	201	Phil Hansen	.10	.02
❑	202	Ray Seals	.10	.02
❑	203	Tony Bennett	.10	.02
❑	204	Leslie O'Neal	.10	.02
❑	205	Jeff Cross	.10	.02
❑	206	Anthony Cook	.10	.02
❑	207	Clyde Simmons	.10	.02
❑	208	Renaldo Turnbull	.10	.02
❑	209	Charles Haley	.20	.07
❑	210	John Copeland	.10	.02
❑	211	John Thierry	.10	.02
❑	212	Michael Strahan	.20	.07
❑	213	Jeff Lageman	.10	.02
❑	214	William Fuller	.10	.02
❑	215	Rickey Jackson	.10	.02
❑	216	Wayne Martin	.10	.02
❑	217	Steve Emtman	.10	.02
❑	218	Shawn Lee	.10	.02
❑	219	Chris Zorich	.10	.02
❑	220	Henry Thomas	.10	.02
❑	221	Dana Stubblefield	.20	.07
❑	222	D'Marco Farr	.10	.02
❑	223	Pierce Holt	.10	.02
❑	224	Sean Jones	.10	.02
❑	225	Robert Porcher	.10	.02
❑	226	Kevin Carter	.10	.02
❑	227	Chris Doleman	.10	.02
❑	228	Tony Tolbert	.10	.02
❑	229	Bruce Smith	.20	.07
❑	230	Marvin Washington	.10	.02
❑	231	Blaine Bishop	.10	.02
❑	232	Bryant Young	.20	.07
❑	233	Rob Burnett	.10	.02
❑	234	Lawrence Phillips RC	.40	.15
❑	235	Trev Alberts	.10	.02
❑	236	Eric Curry	.10	.02
❑	237	Anthony Smith	.10	.02
❑	238	Sam Mills	.10	.02
❑	239	Seth Joyner	.10	.02
❑	240	Quentin Coryatt	.10	.02
❑	241	Levon Kirkland	.10	.02
❑	242	Cornelius Bennett	.10	.02
❑	243	Chris Spielman	.10	.02
❑	244	Mo Lewis	.10	.02
❑	245	Lee Woodall	.10	.02
❑	246	Derrick Thomas	.40	.15
❑	247	Willie McGinest	.10	.02
❑	248	Terry Wooden	.10	.02
❑	249	Greg Lloyd	.20	.07
❑	250	Jack Del Rio	.10	.02
❑	251	Hardy Nickerson	.10	.02
❑	252	Micheal Barrow	.10	.02
❑	253	Lamar Lathon	.10	.02
❑	254	Bryan Cox	.10	.02
❑	255	Randy Kirk	.10	.02
❑	256	Jessie Tuggle	.10	.02
❑	257	Roman Phifer	.10	.02
❑	258	Ken Harvey	.10	.02
❑	259	Junior Seau	.40	.15
❑	260	Pepper Johnson	.10	.02
❑	261	Chris Slade	.10	.02
❑	262	Gary Plummer	.10	.02
❑	263	Wayne Simmons	.10	.02
❑	264	Bryce Paup	.10	.02
❑	265	William Thomas	.10	.02
❑	266	Kevin Greene	.20	.07
❑	267	Bobby Engram RC	.40	.15
❑	268	Ken Norton	.10	.02
❑	269	Eric Hill	.10	.02
❑	270	Darion Conner	.10	.02
❑	271	Tyrone Poole	.10	.02
❑	272	Cris Dishman	.10	.02
❑	273	Marcus Jones RC	.10	.02
❑	274	Rod Woodson	.20	.07
❑	275	Mark McMillian	.10	.02
❑	276	Dale Carter	.10	.02
❑	277	Darrell Green	.10	.02
❑	278	Donnell Woolford	.10	.02
❑	279	Troy Vincent	.10	.02
❑	280	Larry Brown	.10	.02
❑	281	Aeneas Williams	.10	.02
❑	282	Eric Allen	.10	.02
❑	283	Ray Buchanan	.10	.02
❑	284	Ty Law	.40	.15
❑	285	Eric Davis	.10	.02
❑	286	Todd Lyght	.10	.02
❑	287	Terry McDaniel	.10	.02
❑	288	Darryll Lewis	.10	.02
❑	289	Deion Sanders	.60	.25
❑	290	Phillippi Sparks	.10	.02
❑	291	Bobby Taylor	.10	.02
❑	292	Mark Collins	.10	.02
❑	293	Steve Atwater	.10	.02
❑	294	Stanley Richard	.20	.07
❑	295	Stevon Moore	.10	.02
❑	296	Bennie Blades	.10	.02
❑	297	Tim McDonald	.10	.02
❑	298	Shaun Gayle	.10	.02
❑	299	Darren Woodson	.20	.07
❑	300	Mark Carrier DB	.10	.02
❑	301	Carnell Lake	.10	.02
❑	302	James Washington	.10	.02
❑	303	LeRoy Butler	.10	.02
❑	304	Henry Jones	.10	.02
❑	305	Darryl Williams	.10	.02
❑	306	Darren Perry	.10	.02
❑	307	Merton Hanks	.10	.02
❑	308	Orlando Thomas	.10	.02
❑	309	Eric Turner	.10	.02
❑	310	Nate Newton	.10	.02
❑	311	Steve Wisniewski	.10	.02
❑	312	Derrick Deese	.10	.02
❑	313	Larry Allen	.10	.02
❑	314	Aaron Taylor	.10	.02
❑	315	Blake Brockermeyer	.10	.02
❑	316	William Roaf	.10	.02
❑	317	Jumbo Elliott	.10	.02
❑	318	Keyshawn Johnson RC	1.00	.40
❑	319	Karim Abdul-Jabbar RC	.40	.15
❑	320	Kevin Hardy RC	.40	.15
❑	321	Duane Clemons RC	.10	.02
❑	322	Jevon Langford RC	.10	.02
❑	323	Mike Alstott RC	1.00	.40
❑	324	Scott Greene RC	.10	.02
❑	325	Derrick Mayes RC	.40	.15
❑	326	Chris Doering RC	.10	.02
❑	327	Amani Toomer RC	1.00	.40
❑	328	Eric Moulds RC	1.25	.50
❑	329	Alex Molden RC	.10	.02
❑	330	Lawyer Milloy RC	.50	.20
❑	331	Daryl Gardener RC	.10	.02
❑	332	Randall Godfrey RC	.10	.02
❑	333	Willie Anderson RC	.10	.02
❑	334	Tony Banks RC	.40	.15
❑	335	Jeff Lewis RC	.20	.07
❑	336	Roman Oben RC	.10	.02
❑	337	Andre Johnson RC	.10	.02

❑	338	Brian Roche RC	.10	.02
❑	339	Johnny McWilliams RC	.20	.07
❑	340	Alex Van Dyke RC	.20	.07
❑	341	Ray Mickens RC	.10	.02
❑	342	Marvin Harrison RC	2.50	1.00
❑	343	Terry Glenn RC	1.00	.40
❑	344	Tim Biakabutuka RC	.40	.15
❑	345	Simeon Rice RC	1.00	.40
❑	346	Cedric Jones RC	.10	.02
❑	347	Eddie George RC	1.25	.50
❑	348	Drew Bledsoe CL	.40	.15
❑	349	Emmitt Smith CL	.50	.20
❑	350	Keyshawn Johnson CL	.40	.15

1997 Pro Line

❑		COMPLETE SET (300)	25.00	10.00
❑	1	Larry Centers	.30	.10
❑	2	Kent Graham	.20	.07
❑	3	LeShon Johnson	.20	.07
❑	4	Leeland McElroy	.20	.07
❑	5	Rob Moore	.30	.10
❑	6	Simeon Rice	.30	.10
❑	7	Frank Sanders	.30	.10
❑	8	Eric Swann	.20	.07
❑	9	Aeneas Williams	.20	.07
❑	10	Jamal Anderson	.50	.20
❑	11	Cornelius Bennett	.20	.07
❑	12	Ray Buchanan	.20	.07
❑	13	Bert Emanuel	.30	.10
❑	14	Terance Mathis	.30	.10
❑	15	Eric Metcalf	.30	.10
❑	16	Jessie Tuggle	.20	.07
❑	17	Derrick Alexander WR	.30	.10
❑	18	Earnest Byner	.20	.07
❑	19	Michael Jackson	.30	.10
❑	20	Antonio Langham	.20	.07
❑	21	Ray Lewis	.75	.30
❑	22	Byron Bam Morris	.20	.07
❑	23	Jonathan Ogden	.20	.07
❑	24	Vinny Testaverde	.30	.10
❑	25	Eric Moulds	.50	.20
❑	26	Todd Collins	.20	.07
❑	27	Quinn Early	.20	.07
❑	28	Phil Hansen	.20	.07
❑	29	Darick Holmes	.20	.07
❑	30	Bryce Paup	.20	.07
❑	31	Andre Reed	.30	.10
❑	32	Bruce Smith	.30	.10
❑	33	Chris Spielman	.20	.07
❑	34	Matt Stevens	.20	.07
❑	35	Steve Tasker	.20	.07
❑	36	Thurman Thomas	.50	.20
❑	37	Mark Carrier WR	.20	.07
❑	38	Kerry Collins	.50	.20
❑	39	Tim Biakabutuka	.30	.10
❑	40	Eric Davis	.20	.07
❑	41	Kevin Greene	.30	.10
❑	42	Anthony Johnson	.20	.07
❑	43	Lamar Lathon	.20	.07
❑	44	Sam Mills	.20	.07
❑	45	Wesley Walls	.30	.10
❑	46	Muhsin Muhammad	.30	.10
❑	47	Mark Carrier DB	.20	.07
❑	48	Curtis Conway	.30	.10
❑	49	Bryan Cox	.20	.07
❑	50	Bobby Engram	.30	.10
❑	51	Raymont Harris	.20	.07
❑	52	Walt Harris	.20	.07
❑	53	Rick Mirer	.20	.07
❑	54	Rashaan Salaam	.30	.10
❑	55	Alonzo Spellman	.20	.07
❑	56	Ashley Ambrose	.20	.07
❑	57	Jeff Blake	.30	.10
❑	58	Ki-Jana Carter	.20	.07
❑	59	John Copeland	.20	.07
❑	60	James Francis	.20	.07
❑	61	Tony McGee	.20	.07
❑	62	Carl Pickens	.30	.10
❑	63	Darnay Scott	.30	.10
❑	64	Steve Tovar	.20	.07
❑	65	Dan Wilkinson	.20	.07
❑	66	Troy Aikman	1.00	.40
❑	67	Eric Bjornson	.20	.07
❑	68	Michael Irvin	.50	.20
❑	69	Daryl Johnston	.30	.10
❑	70	Nate Newton	.20	.07
❑	71	Deion Sanders	.50	.20
❑	72	Emmitt Smith	1.50	.60
❑	73	Kevin Smith	.20	.07
❑	74	Kevin Williams	.20	.07
❑	75	Darren Woodson	.20	.07
❑	76	Mark Tuinei	.20	.07
❑	77	Steve Atwater	.20	.07
❑	78	Terrell Davis	.60	.25
❑	79	John Elway	2.00	.75
❑	80	Ed McCaffrey	.30	.10
❑	81	Anthony Miller	.20	.07
❑	82	John Mobley	.20	.07
❑	83	Michael Dean Perry	.20	.07
❑	84	Shannon Sharpe	.30	.10
❑	85	Alfred Williams	.20	.07
❑	86	Reggie Brown LB	.30	.10
❑	87	Luther Elliss	.20	.07
❑	88	Scott Mitchell	.30	.10
❑	89	Herman Moore	.30	.10
❑	90	Johnnie Morton	.30	.10
❑	91	Brett Perriman	.20	.07
❑	92	Robert Porcher	.20	.07
❑	93	Barry Sanders	1.50	.60
❑	94	Henry Thomas	.20	.07
❑	95	Edgar Bennett	.30	.10
❑	96	Robert Brooks	.30	.10
❑	97	Gilbert Brown	.30	.10
❑	98	LeRoy Butler	.20	.07
❑	99	Mark Chmura	.30	.10
❑	100	Brett Favre	2.00	.75
❑	101	Santana Dotson	.20	.07
❑	102	Antonio Freeman	.50	.20
❑	103	Dorsey Levens	.50	.20
❑	104	Wayne Simmons	.20	.07
❑	105	Reggie White	.50	.20
❑	106	Willie Davis	.20	.07
❑	107	Eddie George	.50	.20
❑	108	Darryll Lewis	.20	.07
❑	109	Steve McNair	.60	.25
❑	110	Marcus Robertson	.20	.07
❑	111	Chris Sanders	.20	.07
❑	112	Al Smith	.20	.07
❑	113	Tony Bennett	.20	.07
❑	114	Quentin Coryatt	.20	.07
❑	115	Ken Dilger	.20	.07
❑	116	Sean Dawkins	.20	.07
❑	117	Marshall Faulk	.60	.25
❑	118	Jim Harbaugh	.30	.10
❑	119	Marvin Harrison	.50	.20
❑	120	Jeff Herrod	.20	.07
❑	121	Tony Boselli	.20	.07
❑	122	Tony Brackens	.20	.07
❑	123	Mark Brunell	.60	.25
❑	124	Kevin Hardy	.20	.07
❑	125	Jeff Lageman	.20	.07
❑	126	Keenan McCardell	.30	.10
❑	127	Natrone Means	.30	.10
❑	128	Eddie Robinson	.20	.07
❑	129	Jimmy Smith	.30	.10
❑	130	James O.Stewart	.30	.10
❑	131	Marcus Allen	.50	.20
❑	132	Dale Carter	.20	.07
❑	133	Mark Collins	.20	.07
❑	134	Lake Dawson	.20	.07
❑	135	Greg Hill	.20	.07
❑	136	Sean LaChapelle	.20	.07
❑	137	Chris Penn	.20	.07
❑	138	Derrick Thomas	.50	.20
❑	139	Tamarick Vanover	.30	.10
❑	140	Elvis Grbac	.30	.10
❑	141	Karim Abdul-Jabbar	.50	.20
❑	142	Fred Barnett	.20	.07
❑	143	Terrell Buckley	.20	.07
❑	144	Daryl Gardener	.20	.07
❑	145	Randal Hill	.20	.07
❑	146	Dan Marino	2.00	.75
❑	147	O.J. McDuffie	.30	.10
❑	148	Jerris McPhail	.20	.07
❑	149	Zach Thomas	.50	.20
❑	150	Cris Carter	.50	.20
❑	151	Dixon Edwards	.20	.07
❑	152	Leroy Hoard	.20	.07
❑	153	Qadry Ismail	.30	.10
❑	154	Brad Johnson	.50	.20
❑	155	John Randle	.30	.10
❑	156	Jake Reed	.30	.10
❑	157	Robert Smith	.30	.10
❑	158	Orlando Thomas	.20	.07
❑	159	Dewayne Washington	.20	.07
❑	160	Drew Bledsoe	.60	.25
❑	161	Tedy Bruschi	1.00	.40
❑	162	Willie Clay	.20	.07
❑	163	Ben Coates	.30	.10
❑	164	Terry Glenn	.50	.20
❑	165	Shawn Jefferson	.20	.07
❑	166	Ty Law	.30	.10
❑	167	Curtis Martin	.60	.25
❑	168	Willie McGinest	.20	.07
❑	169	Chris Slade	.20	.07
❑	170	Eric Allen	.20	.07
❑	171	Mario Bates	.20	.07
❑	172	Heath Shuler	.20	.07
❑	173	Michael Haynes	.20	.07
❑	174	Wayne Martin	.20	.07
❑	175	Torrance Small	.20	.07
❑	176	Dave Brown	.20	.07
❑	177	Chris Calloway	.20	.07
❑	178	Rodney Hampton	.30	.10
❑	179	Danny Kanell	.30	.10
❑	180	Thomas Lewis	.20	.07
❑	181	Jason Sehorn	.30	.10
❑	182	Amani Toomer	.30	.10
❑	183	Charles Way	.30	.10
❑	184	Tyrone Wheatley	.30	.10
❑	185	Wayne Chrebet	.50	.20
❑	186	Hugh Douglas	.20	.07
❑	187	Aaron Glenn	.20	.07
❑	188	Jeff Graham	.20	.07
❑	189	Keyshawn Johnson	.50	.20
❑	190	Mo Lewis	.20	.07
❑	191	Adrian Murrell	.30	.10
❑	192	Neil O'Donnell	.30	.10
❑	193	Tim Brown	.50	.20
❑	194	Rickey Dudley	.30	.10
❑	195	Jeff George	.30	.10
❑	196	Napoleon Kaufman	.50	.20
❑	197	Russell Maryland	.20	.07
❑	198	Terry McDaniel	.20	.07
❑	199	Chester McGlockton	.20	.07
❑	200	Desmond Howard	.30	.10
❑	201	Pat Swilling	.20	.07
❑	202	Ty Detmer	.30	.10
❑	203	Jason Dunn	.20	.07
❑	204	Ray Farmer	.20	.07
❑	205	Irving Fryar	.30	.10
❑	206	Chris T. Jones	.20	.07
❑	207	Bobby Taylor	.20	.07
❑	208	William Thomas	.20	.07
❑	209	Hollis Thomas RC	.20	.07
❑	210	Kevin Turner	.20	.07
❑	211	Ricky Watters	.30	.10
❑	212	Jerome Bettis	.50	.20
❑	213	Andre Hastings	.20	.07
❑	214	Charles Johnson	.30	.10
❑	215	Levon Kirkland	.20	.07
❑	216	Carnell Lake	.20	.07
❑	217	Greg Lloyd	.20	.07
❑	218	Darren Perry	.20	.07
❑	219	Kordell Stewart	.50	.20
❑	220	Rod Woodson	.30	.10
❑	221	Andre Coleman	.20	.07
❑	222	Marco Coleman	.20	.07
❑	223	Leonard Russell	.20	.07
❑	224	Stan Humphries	.30	.10
❑	225	Shawn Lee	.20	.07
❑	226	Tony Martin	.30	.10
❑	227	Chris Mims	.20	.07

❑ 228 Junior Seau .50 .20
❑ 229 Chris Doleman .20 .07
❑ 230 William Floyd .30 .10
❑ 231 Merton Hanks .20 .07
❑ 232 Brent Jones .30 .10
❑ 233 Terry Kirby .30 .10
❑ 234 Ken Norton .20 .07
❑ 235 Terrell Owens .60 .25
❑ 236 Jerry Rice 1.00 .40
❑ 237 Bryant Young .20 .07
❑ 238 Steve Young .60 .25
❑ 239 Garrison Hearst .30 .10
❑ 240 Brian Blades .20 .07
❑ 241 Chad Brown .20 .07
❑ 242 John Friesz .20 .07
❑ 243 Joey Galloway .30 .10
❑ 244 Cortez Kennedy .20 .07
❑ 245 Chris Warren .30 .10
❑ 246 Darryl Williams .20 .07
❑ 247 Tony Banks .30 .10
❑ 248 Isaac Bruce .50 .20
❑ 249 Kevin Carter .20 .07
❑ 250 Eddie Kennison .30 .10
❑ 251 Todd Lyght .20 .07
❑ 252 Leslie O'Neal .20 .07
❑ 253 Anthony Parker .20 .07
❑ 254 Roman Phifer .20 .07
❑ 255 Lawrence Phillips .20 .07
❑ 256 Mike Alstott .50 .20
❑ 257 Derrick Brooks .50 .20
❑ 258 Trent Dilfer .50 .20
❑ 259 Jackie Harris .20 .07
❑ 260 Hardy Nickerson .20 .07
❑ 261 Errict Rhett .20 .07
❑ 262 Warren Sapp .30 .10
❑ 263 Terry Allen .50 .20
❑ 264 Jamie Asher .20 .07
❑ 265 Henry Ellard .20 .07
❑ 266 Gus Frerotte .20 .07
❑ 267 Sean Gilbert .20 .07
❑ 268 Darrell Green .30 .10
❑ 269 Ken Harvey .20 .07
❑ 270 Brian Mitchell .20 .07
❑ 271 Michael Westbrook .30 .10
❑ 272 Koy Detmer RC 1.00 .40
❑ 273 Yatil Green RC .30 .10
❑ 274 Troy Davis RC .30 .10
❑ 275 Darrell Russell RC .20 .07
❑ 276 Warrick Dunn RC 1.50 .60
❑ 277 David LaFleur RC .20 .07
❑ 278 Tony Gonzalez RC 1.50 .60
❑ 279 Jake Plummer RC 2.50 1.00
❑ 280 Antowain Smith RC 1.25 .50
❑ 281 Peter Boulware RC .50 .20
❑ 282 Shawn Springs RC .30 .10
❑ 283 Bryant Westbrook RC .20 .07
❑ 284 Rae Carruth RC .20 .07
❑ 285 Corey Dillon RC 3.00 1.25
❑ 286 Byron Hanspard RC .30 .10
❑ 287 Greg Jones RC .20 .07
❑ 288 Trevor Pryce RC .50 .20
❑ 289 Michael Booker RC .20 .07
❑ 290 Orlando Pace RC .50 .20
❑ 291 James Farrior RC .50 .20
❑ 292 Walter Jones RC .50 .20
❑ 293 Reinard Wilson RC .30 .10
❑ 294 Ike Hilliard RC .75 .30
❑ 295 Kenard Lang RC .30 .10
❑ 296 Reidel Anthony RC .50 .20
❑ 297 Brett Favre CL .50 .20
❑ 298 Kerry Collins CL .30 .10
❑ 299 Drew Bledsoe CL .30 .10
❑ 300 Terrell Davis CL .50 .20

1996 Pro Line DC3

❑ COMPLETE SET (100) 20.00 7.50
❑ 1 Emmitt Smith 1.50 .60
❑ 2 Larry Centers .20 .07
❑ 3 Jeff George .20 .07
❑ 4 Jim Kelly .40 .15
❑ 5 Kerry Collins .40 .15
❑ 6 Erik Kramer .10 .02
❑ 7 Jeff Blake .40 .15
❑ 8 Andre Rison .20 .07
❑ 9 John Elway 2.00 .75
❑ 10 Herman Moore .20 .07
❑ 11 Robert Brooks .40 .15

❑ 12 Steve McNair .75 .30
❑ 13 Jim Harbaugh .20 .07
❑ 14 Mark Brunell .60 .25
❑ 15 Steve Bono .10 .02
❑ 16 Dan Marino 2.00 .75
❑ 17 Warren Moon .20 .07
❑ 18 Drew Bledsoe .60 .25
❑ 19 Jim Everett .10 .02
❑ 20 Rodney Hampton .20 .07
❑ 21 Kyle Brady .10 .02
❑ 22 Jeff Hostetler .10 .02
❑ 23 Neil O'Donnell .20 .07
❑ 24 Ricky Watters .20 .07
❑ 25 Isaac Bruce .40 .15
❑ 26 Steve Young .75 .30
❑ 27 Stan Humphries .20 .07
❑ 28 Joey Galloway .40 .15
❑ 29 Errict Rhett .20 .07
❑ 30 Terry Allen .20 .07
❑ 31 Eric Swann .10 .02
❑ 32 Craig Heyward .10 .02
❑ 33 Bryce Paup .10 .02
❑ 34 Sam Mills .10 .02
❑ 35 Jim Flanigan .10 .02
❑ 36 Carl Pickens .20 .07
❑ 37 Pepper Johnson .10 .02
❑ 38 Troy Aikman 1.00 .40
❑ 39 Terrell Davis .75 .30
❑ 40 Scott Mitchell .20 .07
❑ 41 Brett Favre 2.00 .75
❑ 42 Chris Sanders .20 .07
❑ 43 Marshall Faulk .50 .20
❑ 44 James O. Stewart .20 .07
❑ 45 Marcus Allen .40 .15
❑ 46 Bernie Parmalee .10 .02
❑ 47 Cris Carter .40 .15
❑ 48 Ben Coates .20 .07
❑ 49 Quinn Early .10 .02
❑ 50 Tyrone Wheatley .20 .07
❑ 51 Adrian Murrell .20 .07
❑ 52 Tim Brown .40 .15
❑ 53 Yancey Thigpen .20 .07
❑ 54 Andy Harmon .10 .02
❑ 55 Jerome Bettis .40 .15
❑ 56 Jerry Rice 1.00 .40
❑ 57 Natrone Means .20 .07
❑ 58 Chris Warren .20 .07
❑ 59 Warren Sapp .10 .02
❑ 60 Michael Westbrook .40 .15
❑ 61 Aeneas Williams .10 .02
❑ 62 Eric Metcalf .10 .02
❑ 63 Bruce Smith .20 .07
❑ 64 Rashaan Salaam .20 .07
❑ 65 Michael Irvin .40 .15
❑ 66 Anthony Miller .20 .07
❑ 67 Barry Sanders 1.50 .60
❑ 68 Reggie White .40 .15
❑ 69 Rodney Thomas .10 .02
❑ 70 Zack Crockett .10 .02
❑ 71 Neil Smith .20 .07
❑ 72 Bryan Cox .10 .02
❑ 73 Curtis Martin .75 .30
❑ 74 Eric Allen .10 .02
❑ 75 Hugh Douglas .20 .07
❑ 76 Napoleon Kaufman .40 .15
❑ 77 Greg Lloyd .20 .07
❑ 78 Charlie Garner .20 .07
❑ 79 Lee Woodall .10 .02
❑ 80 Tony Martin .20 .07
❑ 81 Cortez Kennedy .10 .02
❑ 82 Gus Frerotte .20 .07
❑ 83 Darick Holmes .10 .02
❑ 84 Jay Novacek .10 .02
❑ 85 Brett Perriman .10 .02
❑ 86 Mark Chmura .20 .07
❑ 87 Chester McGlockton .10 .02
❑ 88 Dave Brown .10 .02
❑ 89 William Thomas .10 .02
❑ 90 Ken Norton .10 .02
❑ 91 Junior Seau .40 .15
❑ 92 Deion Sanders .60 .25
❑ 93 J.J. Stokes .40 .15
❑ 94 Kordell Stewart .40 .15
❑ 95 Tamarick Vanover .20 .07
❑ 96 Ken Harvey .10 .02
❑ 97 John Randle .20 .07
❑ 98 Lamont Warren .10 .02
❑ 99 Dorsey Levens .40 .15
❑ 100 Frank Sanders .20 .07
❑ S1 Emmitt Smith Sample 2.00 .80

1997 Pro Line DC3

❑ COMPLETE SET (100) 15.00 6.00
❑ 1 Emmitt Smith 1.50 .60
❑ 2 Rod Woodson .30 .10
❑ 3 Eddie George .50 .20
❑ 4 Ty Detmer .30 .10
❑ 5 Zach Thomas .50 .20
❑ 6 Kevin Greene .30 .10
❑ 7 Michael Jackson .30 .10
❑ 8 Isaac Bruce .50 .20
❑ 9 Joey Galloway .30 .10
❑ 10 Bryant Young .20 .07
❑ 11 Terrell Davis .60 .25
❑ 12 Mark Brunell .60 .25
❑ 13 Marvin Harrison .50 .20
❑ 14 Jake Reed .30 .10
❑ 15 Terry Allen .50 .20
❑ 16 Kordell Stewart .50 .20
❑ 17 Reggie White .50 .20
❑ 18 Michael Irvin .50 .20
❑ 19 Tony Martin .30 .10
❑ 20 Barry Sanders 1.50 .60
❑ 21 Tony Boselli .20 .07
❑ 22 Carl Pickens .30 .10
❑ 23 Simeon Rice .30 .10
❑ 24 Adrian Murrell .30 .10
❑ 25 Lamar Lathon .20 .07
❑ 26 Thurman Thomas .50 .20
❑ 27 Tim Brown .50 .20
❑ 28 Karim Abdul-Jabbar .50 .20
❑ 29 Brad Johnson .50 .20
❑ 30 Keenan McCardell .30 .10
❑ 31 Keyshawn Johnson .50 .20
❑ 32 Ricky Watters .30 .10
❑ 33 Michael McCrary .20 .07
❑ 34 Brett Favre 2.00 .75
❑ 35 Steve McNair .60 .25
❑ 36 Herman Moore .30 .10
❑ 37 Tony Banks .30 .10
❑ 38 Deion Sanders .50 .20
❑ 39 Kerry Collins .50 .20
❑ 40 Shannon Sharpe .30 .10
❑ 41 Drew Bledsoe .60 .25
❑ 42 Jim Everett .20 .07
❑ 43 Jamal Anderson .50 .20
❑ 44 Irving Fryar .30 .10
❑ 45 Terry Glenn .50 .20
❑ 46 Jerry Rice 1.00 .40

❑ 47 Curtis Martin .60 .25
❑ 48 Curtis Conway .30 .10
❑ 49 Jerome Bettis .50 .20
❑ 50 Vinny Testaverde .30 .10
❑ 51 Mike Alstott .50 .20
❑ 52 Anthony Johnson .20 .07
❑ 53 Dan Marino 2.00 .75
❑ 54 Junior Seau .50 .20
❑ 55 Steve Young .60 .25
❑ 56 Troy Aikman 1.00 .40
❑ 57 Jimmy Smith .30 .10
❑ 58 Cris Carter .50 .20
❑ 59 Gus Frerotte .20 .07
❑ 60 Marcus Allen .50 .20
❑ 61 Rodney Hampton .30 .10
❑ 62 Bruce Smith .30 .10
❑ 63 LeRoy Butler .20 .07
❑ 64 Jeff Blake .30 .10
❑ 65 Antonio Freeman .50 .20
❑ 66 John Elway 2.00 .75
❑ 67 B.Favre/Rison CL .50 .20
❑ 68 Barry Sanders REW .75 .30
❑ 69 Troy Aikman REW .50 .20
❑ 70 Jerome Bettis REW .30 .10
❑ 71 Mark Brunell REW .50 .20
❑ 72 Junior Seau REW .30 .10
❑ 73 John Elway REW 1.00 .40
❑ 74 Chad Brown REW .20 .07
❑ 75 Irving Fryar REW .20 .07
❑ 76 Drew Bledsoe REW .50 .20
❑ 77 Jerry Rice REW .50 .20
❑ 78 Larry Centers REW .20 .07
❑ 79 Terrell Davis REW .50 .20
❑ 80 Carl Pickens REW .20 .07
❑ 81 Emmitt Smith REW .75 .30
❑ 82 Kerry Collins REW .30 .10
❑ 83 Eddie Kennison REW .30 .10
❑ 84 Kordell Stewart REW .30 .10
❑ 85 Natrone Means REW .30 .10
❑ 86 Curtis Martin REW UER .50 .20
❑ 87 Dorsey Levens REW .50 .20
❑ 88 Desmond Howard REW .30 .10
❑ 89 Brett Favre REW CL .50 .20
❑ 90 Brett Favre T10 1.00 .40
❑ 91 Terrell Davis T10 .50 .20
❑ 92 Kevin Greene T10 .20 .07
❑ 93 Terry Allen T10 .20 .07
❑ 94 Barry Sanders T10 .75 .30
❑ 95 John Elway T10 1.00 .40
❑ 96 Ricky Watters T10 .20 .07
❑ 97 Reggie White T10 .30 .10
❑ 98 Jerome Bettis T10 .30 .10
❑ 99 Jerry Rice T10 .50 .20
❑ 100 Brett Favre T10 CL .50 .20

1998 Pro Line DC3

❑ COMPLETE SET (100) 25.00 10.00
❑ 1 Drew Bledsoe 1.25 .50
❑ 2 Emmitt Smith 2.50 1.00
❑ 3 Dana Stubblefield .30 .10
❑ 4 Brett Favre 3.00 1.25
❑ 5 Derrick Alexander WR .50 .20
❑ 6 Bert Emanuel .50 .20
❑ 7 Joey Galloway .50 .20
❑ 8 Terrell Davis .75 .30
❑ 9 Mark Brunell .75 .30
❑ 10 Marshall Faulk 1.00 .40
❑ 11 Jake Reed .50 .20
❑ 12 Terry Allen .75 .30
❑ 13 Kordell Stewart .75 .30
❑ 14 Reggie White .75 .30
❑ 15 Michael Irvin .75 .30
❑ 16 Tony Martin .50 .20
❑ 17 Barry Sanders 2.50 1.00
❑ 18 Carl Pickens .50 .20
❑ 19 Bobby Hoying .50 .20
❑ 20 Adrian Murrell .50 .20
❑ 21 Jeff George .50 .20
❑ 22 Tim Brown .75 .30
❑ 23 Karim Abdul-Jabbar .75 .30
❑ 24 Robert Smith .75 .30
❑ 25 Eddie George .75 .30
❑ 26 Corey Dillon .75 .30
❑ 27 Keyshawn Johnson .75 .30
❑ 28 Ricky Watters .50 .20
❑ 29 Robert Brooks .50 .20
❑ 30 Antonio Freeman .75 .30
❑ 31 Danny Kanell .50 .20
❑ 32 Steve McNair .75 .30
❑ 33 Antowain Smith .75 .30
❑ 34 Warrick Dunn .75 .30
❑ 35 Napoleon Kaufman .75 .30
❑ 36 Trent Dilfer .75 .30
❑ 37 Herman Moore .50 .20
❑ 38 Brad Johnson .75 .30
❑ 39 Deion Sanders .75 .30
❑ 40 Kerry Collins .50 .20
❑ 41 Shannon Sharpe .50 .20
❑ 42 Irving Fryar .50 .20
❑ 43 Dorsey Levens .75 .30
❑ 44 Jerry Rice 1.50 .60
❑ 45 Curtis Martin .75 .30
❑ 46 Jerome Bettis .75 .30
❑ 47 Raymont Harris .30 .10
❑ 48 Vinny Testaverde .50 .20
❑ 49 Dan Marino 3.00 1.25
❑ 50 Junior Seau .75 .30
❑ 51 Steve Young .75 .30
❑ 52 Troy Aikman 1.50 .60
❑ 53 Jimmy Smith .50 .20
❑ 54 Ben Coates .50 .20
❑ 55 Gus Frerotte .30 .10
❑ 56 Marcus Allen .75 .30
❑ 57 Bruce Smith .50 .20
❑ 58 Jeff Blake .50 .20
❑ 59 John Elway 3.00 1.25
❑ 60 Rod Smith WR .50 .20
❑ 61 Andre Rison .50 .20
❑ 62 Isaac Bruce .75 .30
❑ 63 Cris Carter .75 .30
❑ 64 Danny Wuerffel .50 .20
❑ 65 Rob Moore .50 .20
❑ 66 Garrison Hearst .75 .30
❑ 67 Warren Moon .75 .30
❑ 68 Jerome Bettis CL .30 .10
❑ 69 Marcus Allen DCR .50 .20
❑ 70 James O.Stewart DCR .50 .20
❑ 71 Karim Abdul-Jabbar DCR .50 .20
❑ 72 Joey Galloway DCR .50 .20
❑ 73 Corey Dillon DCR .50 .20
❑ 74 Andre Rison DCR .30 .10
❑ 75 Napoleon Kaufman DCR .50 .20
❑ 76 Dorsey Levens DCR .50 .20
❑ 77 Irving Fryar DCR .30 .10
❑ 78 Eric Metcalf DCR .30 .10
❑ 79 Darrien Gordon DCR .30 .10
❑ 80 Neil O'Donnell DCR .50 .20
❑ 81 Rod Woodson DCR .50 .20
❑ 82 Rob Johnson DCR .50 .20
❑ 83 Michael Westbrook DCR .50 .20
❑ 84 Jake Plummer DCR .50 .20
❑ 85 Bobby Hoying DCR .30 .10
❑ 86 Adrian Murrell DCR .30 .10
❑ 87 Jim Druckenmiller DCR .30 .10
❑ 88 Warren Moon DCR .50 .20
❑ 89 Dorsey Levens DCR CL .30 .10
❑ 90 Tony Gonzalez RU .75 .30
❑ 91 Jim Druckenmiller RU .30 .10
❑ 92 Corey Dillon RU .50 .20
❑ 93 Darrell Russell RU .30 .10
❑ 94 Byron Hanspard RU .30 .10
❑ 95 Rae Carruth RU .30 .10
❑ 96 Peter Boulware RU .30 .10
❑ 97 Troy Davis RU .30 .10
❑ 98 Reidel Anthony RU .50 .20
❑ 99 Tiki Barber RU .75 .30
❑ 100 Jake Plummer RU CL .50 .20

1997 Pro Line Gems

❑ COMPLETE SET (100) 20.00 10.00
❑ 1 Brett Favre 2.00 .75
❑ 2 Robert Brooks .30 .10
❑ 3 Reggie White .50 .20
❑ 4 Drew Bledsoe .60 .25
❑ 5 Curtis Martin .60 .25
❑ 6 Terry Glenn .50 .20
❑ 7 Kerry Collins .50 .20
❑ 8 Kevin Greene .30 .10
❑ 9 Troy Aikman 1.00 .40
❑ 10 Emmitt Smith 1.50 .60
❑ 11 Deion Sanders .50 .20
❑ 12 John Elway 2.00 .75
❑ 13 Terrell Davis .60 .25
❑ 14 Kordell Stewart .50 .20
❑ 15 Jerome Bettis .50 .20
❑ 16 Steve Young .60 .25
❑ 17 Jerry Rice 1.00 .40
❑ 18 Bruce Smith .30 .10
❑ 19 Thurman Thomas .50 .20
❑ 20 Jim Harbaugh .30 .10
❑ 21 Marshall Faulk .60 .25
❑ 22 Marvin Harrison .50 .20
❑ 23 Ricky Watters .30 .10
❑ 24 Seth Joyner .20 .07
❑ 25 Mark Brunell .60 .25
❑ 26 Natrone Means .30 .10
❑ 27 Dan Marino 2.00 .75
❑ 28 Zach Thomas .50 .20
❑ 29 Karim Abdul-Jabbar .50 .20
❑ 30 Isaac Bruce .50 .20
❑ 31 Eddie Kennison .30 .10
❑ 32 Tony Banks .30 .10
❑ 33 Tony Martin .30 .10
❑ 34 Junior Seau .50 .20
❑ 35 Barry Sanders 1.50 .60
❑ 36 Herman Moore .30 .10
❑ 37 Leeland McElroy .20 .07
❑ 38 Jamal Anderson .50 .20
❑ 39 Rick Mirer .20 .07
❑ 40 Rashaan Salaam .20 .07
❑ 41 Vinny Testaverde .30 .10
❑ 42 Elvis Grbac .30 .10
❑ 43 Cris Carter .50 .20
❑ 44 Brad Johnson .50 .20
❑ 45 Keyshawn Johnson .50 .20
❑ 46 Adrian Murrell .30 .10
❑ 47 Joey Galloway .30 .10
❑ 48 Trent Dilfer .50 .20
❑ 49 Gus Frerotte .20 .07
❑ 50 Terry Allen .50 .20
❑ 51 Tim Brown .50 .20
❑ 52 Desmond Howard .30 .10
❑ 53 Jeff George .30 .10
❑ 54 Heath Shuler .20 .07
❑ 55 Steve McNair .60 .25
❑ 56 Eddie George .50 .20
❑ 57 Jeff Blake .30 .10
❑ 58 Carl Pickens .30 .10
❑ 59 Dave Brown .20 .07
❑ 60 Brett Favre CL .50 .20
❑ 61 Antowain Smith PL .50 .20
❑ 62 Emmitt Smith PL .75 .30
❑ 63 Terry Glenn PL .30 .10
❑ 64 Herman Moore PL .30 .10

❑ 65 Barry Sanders PL	.75	.30
❑ 66 Derrick Thomas PL	.50	.20
❑ 67 Brett Favre PL	1.00	.40
❑ 68 Warrick Dunn PL	.60	.25
❑ 69 Emmitt Smith PL	.75	.30
❑ 70 Brett Favre CL	.50	.20
❑ 71 Orlando Pace RC	.50	.20
❑ 72 Darrell Russell RC	.20	.07
❑ 73 Shawn Springs RC	.30	.10
❑ 74 Warrick Dunn RC	1.50	.60
❑ 75 Tiki Barber RC	3.00	1.25
❑ 76 Tom Knight RC	.20	.07
❑ 77 Peter Boulware RC	.50	.20
❑ 78 David LaFleur RC	.20	.07
❑ 79 Tony Gonzalez RC	1.50	.60
❑ 80 Yatil Green RC	.30	.10
❑ 81 Ike Hilliard RC	.75	.30
❑ 82 James Farrior RC	.50	.20
❑ 83 Jim Druckenmiller RC	.30	.10
❑ 84 Jon Harris RC	.20	.07
❑ 85 Walter Jones RC	.50	.20
❑ 86 Reidel Anthony RC	.50	.20
❑ 87 Jake Plummer RC	2.50	1.00
❑ 88 Reinard Wilson RC	.30	.10
❑ 89 Kevin Lockett RC	.30	.10
❑ 90 Rae Carruth RC	.20	.07
❑ 91 Byron Hanspard RC	.30	.10
❑ 92 Renaldo Wynn RC	.20	.07
❑ 93 Troy Davis RC	.30	.10
❑ 94 Duce Staley RC	4.00	1.50
❑ 95 Kenard Lang RC	.30	.10
❑ 96 Freddie Jones RC	.30	.10
❑ 97 Corey Dillon RC	3.00	1.25
❑ 98 Antowain Smith RC	1.25	.50
❑ 99 Dwayne Rudd RC	.50	.20
❑ 100 Warrick Dunn CL	.60	.25
❑ CR1 Brett Favre Ring/1997	40.00	15.00

1996 Pro Line Intense

❑ COMPLETE SET (100)	15.00	6.00
❑ 1 Kerry Collins	.25	.10
❑ 2 Jeff George	.10	.07
❑ 3 Mark Brunell	.50	.20
❑ 4 Steve McNair	.60	.25
❑ 5 Rick Mirer	.10	.07
❑ 6 Dave Brown	.05	.02
❑ 7 Rashaan Salaam	.05	.02
❑ 8 Marshall Faulk	.30	.10
❑ 9 Errict Pegram	.05	.02
❑ 10 Cris Carter	.25	.10
❑ 11 Eric Allen	.05	.02
❑ 12 Jim Kelly	.25	.10
❑ 13 Jeff Blake	.25	.10
❑ 14 Stan Humphries	.10	.07
❑ 15 Scott Mitchell	.10	.07
❑ 16 Jeff Hostetler	.05	.02
❑ 17 Rodney Peete	.05	.02
❑ 18 Warren Moon	.10	.07
❑ 19 Errict Rhett	.10	.07
❑ 20 Terrell Davis	.60	.25
❑ 21 J.J. Stokes	.25	.10
❑ 22 Marco Coleman	.05	.02
❑ 23 Heath Shuler	.10	.07
❑ 24 Duane Clemons RC	.05	.02
❑ 25 Amani Toomer RC	.75	.30
❑ 26 Leslie O'Neal	.05	.02
❑ 27 Tamarick Vanover	.10	.07
❑ 28 Steve Bono	.05	.02
❑ 29 Jim Everett	.05	.02
❑ 30 Erik Kramer	.05	.02
❑ 31 Trent Dilfer	.25	.10
❑ 32 Jim Harbaugh	.10	.07
❑ 33 Vinny Testaverde	.10	.07
❑ 34 Rodney Hampton	.10	.07
❑ 35 Chris Warren	.10	.07
❑ 36 Curtis Martin	.60	.25
❑ 37 Eddie Kennison RC	.25	.10
❑ 38 Herman Moore	.10	.07
❑ 39 Terance Mathis	.05	.02
❑ 40 Carl Pickens	.10	.07
❑ 41 Isaac Bruce	.25	.10
❑ 42 Reggie White	.25	.10
❑ 43 Junior Seau	.25	.10
❑ 44 Bryce Paup	.05	.02
❑ 45 Deion Sanders	.30	.10
❑ 46 Thurman Thomas	.25	.10
❑ 47 Gus Frerotte	.10	.07
❑ 48 Tony Mandarich	.05	.02
❑ 49 Michael Irvin	.25	.10
❑ 50 Wayne Chrebet	.30	.10
❑ 51 Bobby Engram RC	.25	.10
❑ 52 Marcus Jones RC	.05	.02
❑ 53 Daryl Gardener RC	.05	.02
❑ 54 Alex Van Dyke RC	.10	.07
❑ 55 Andre Rison	.10	.07
❑ 56 Regan Upshaw RC	.05	.02
❑ 57 Jason Dunn RC	.10	.07
❑ 58 Mark Chmura	.10	.07
❑ 59 Ray Lewis RC	2.00	.75
❑ 60 Rickey Dudley RC	.25	.10
❑ 61 Leeland McElroy RC	.10	.07
❑ 62 Derrick Thomas	.25	.10
❑ 63 Bobby Hoying RC	.25	.10
❑ 64 Robert Brooks	.10	.07
❑ 65 Tim Brown	.25	.10
❑ 66 Michael Westbrook	.25	.10
❑ 67 Jim Miller	.25	.10
❑ 68 Aaron Hayden	.05	.02
❑ 69 Marcus Allen	.25	.10
❑ 70 Troy Aikman	.75	.30
❑ 71 Steve Young	.50	.20
❑ 72 Neil O'Donnell	.10	.07
❑ 73 Drew Bledsoe	.50	.20
❑ 74 Emmitt Smith	1.25	.50
❑ 75 Ki-Jana Carter	.10	.07
❑ 76 Irving Fryar	.10	.07
❑ 77 Joey Galloway	.25	.10
❑ 78 Russell Maryland	.05	.02
❑ 79 Kordell Stewart	.25	.10
❑ 80 Barry Sanders	1.25	.50
❑ 81 Bryan Cox	.05	.02
❑ 82 Keyshawn Johnson RC	.75	.30
❑ 83 Karim Abdul-Jabbar RC	.25	.10
❑ 84 Kevin Hardy RC	.25	.10
❑ 85 Rodney Thomas	.05	.02
❑ 86 John Elway	1.50	.40
❑ 87 Dan Marino	1.50	.60
❑ 88 Brett Favre	1.50	.60
❑ 89 Eric Metcalf	.05	.02
❑ 90 Jonathan Ogden RC	.25	.10
❑ 91 Eddie George RC	1.00	.40
❑ 92 Simeon Rice RC	.60	.25
❑ 93 Tim Biakabutuka RC	.25	.10
❑ 94 Terry Glenn RC	.75	.30
❑ 95 Marvin Harrison RC	2.00	.75
❑ 96 Lawrence Phillips RC	.25	.10
❑ 97 Natrone Means	.10	.07
❑ 98 Jerry Rice	.75	.30
❑ 99 Ricky Watters	.10	.07
❑ 100 Emmitt Smith CL	.25	.10

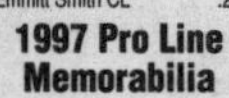

1997 Pro Line Memorabilia

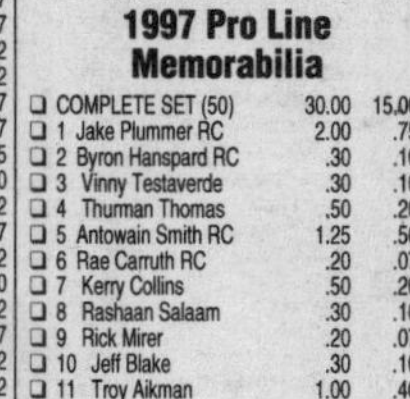

❑ COMPLETE SET (50)	30.00	15.00
❑ 1 Jake Plummer RC	2.00	.75
❑ 2 Byron Hanspard RC	.30	.10
❑ 3 Vinny Testaverde	.30	.10
❑ 4 Thurman Thomas	.50	.20
❑ 5 Antowain Smith RC	1.25	.50
❑ 6 Rae Carruth RC	.20	.07
❑ 7 Kerry Collins	.50	.20
❑ 8 Rashaan Salaam	.30	.10
❑ 9 Rick Mirer	.20	.07
❑ 10 Jeff Blake	.30	.10
❑ 11 Troy Aikman	1.00	.40

❑ 12 Emmitt Smith	1.50	.60
❑ 13 John Elway	2.00	.75
❑ 14 Terrell Davis	.60	.25
❑ 15 Barry Sanders	1.50	.60
❑ 16 Herman Moore	.30	.10
❑ 17 Brett Favre	2.00	.75
❑ 18 Reggie White	.50	.20
❑ 19 Dorsey Levens	.50	.20
❑ 20 Eddie George	.50	.20
❑ 21 Jim Harbaugh	.30	.10
❑ 22 Mark Brunell	.60	.25
❑ 23 Tony Gonzalez RC	1.25	.50
❑ 24 Elvis Grbac	.30	.10
❑ 25 Dan Marino	2.00	.75
❑ 26 Karim Abdul-Jabbar	.50	.20
❑ 27 Brad Johnson	.50	.20
❑ 28 Drew Bledsoe	.60	.25
❑ 29 Curtis Martin	.60	.25
❑ 30 Terry Glenn	.50	.20
❑ 31 Heath Shuler	.20	.07
❑ 32 Danny Wuerffel RC	.50	.20
❑ 33 Ike Hilliard RC	.75	.30
❑ 34 Keyshawn Johnson	.50	.20
❑ 35 Darrell Russell RC	.20	.07
❑ 36 Jeff George	.30	.10
❑ 37 Ricky Watters	.30	.10
❑ 38 Bobby Hoying	.30	.10
❑ 39 Jerome Bettis	.50	.20
❑ 40 Kordell Stewart	.50	.20
❑ 41 Junior Seau	.50	.20
❑ 42 Shawn Springs RC	.30	.10
❑ 43 Jim Druckenmiller RC	.30	.10
❑ 44 Steve Young	.60	.25
❑ 45 Jerry Rice	1.00	.40
❑ 46 Orlando Pace RC	.50	.20
❑ 47 Isaac Bruce	.50	.20
❑ 48 Warrick Dunn RC	1.25	.50
❑ 49 Gus Frerotte	.20	.07
❑ 50 Brett Favre CL	.50	.20

1989 Pro Set

❑ COMPLETE SET (561)	25.00	10.00
❑ COMP.SERIES 1 (440)	6.00	3.00
❑ COMP.SERIES 2 (100)	20.00	10.00
❑ COMP.FINAL FACT.SET (21)	2.00	.75
❑ 1 Stacey Bailey	.04	.01
❑ 2 Aundray Bruce RC	.04	.01
❑ 3 Rick Bryan	.04	.01
❑ 4 Bobby Butler	.04	.01
❑ 5 Scott Case RC	.04	.01
❑ 6 Tony Casillas	.04	.01
❑ 7 Floyd Dixon	.04	.01

Card		
❑ 8 Rick Donnelly	.04	.01
❑ 9 Bill Fralic	.04	.01
❑ 10 Mike Gann	.04	.01
❑ 11 Mike Kenn	.04	.01
❑ 12 Chris Miller RC	.25	.08
❑ 13 John Rade	.04	.01
❑ 14 Gerald Riggs UER	.10	.02
❑ 15 John Settle RC	.04	.01
❑ 16 Marion Campbell CO	.04	.01
❑ 17 Cornelius Bennett	.10	.02
❑ 18 Derrick Burroughs	.04	.01
❑ 19 Shane Conlan	.04	.01
❑ 20 Ronnie Harmon	.10	.02
❑ 21 Kent Hull RC	.04	.01
❑ 22 Jim Kelly	.50	.20
❑ 23 Mark Kelso	.04	.01
❑ 24 Pete Metzelaars	.04	.01
❑ 25 Scott Norwood RC**	.04	.01
❑ 26 Andre Reed	.25	.08
❑ 27 Fred Smerlas	.04	.01
❑ 28 Bruce Smith	.25	.08
❑ 29 Leonard Smith	.04	.01
❑ 30 Art Still	.04	.01
❑ 31 Darryl Talley	.10	.02
❑ 32 Thurman Thomas RC	1.25	.50
❑ 33 Will Wolford RC	.04	.01
❑ 34 Marv Levy CO	.04	.01
❑ 35 Neal Anderson	.10	.02
❑ 36 Kevin Butler	.04	.01
❑ 37 Jim Covert	.04	.01
❑ 38 Richard Dent	.10	.02
❑ 39 Dave Duerson	.04	.01
❑ 40 Dennis Gentry	.04	.01
❑ 41 Dan Hampton	.10	.02
❑ 42 Jay Hilgenberg	.04	.01
❑ 43 Dennis McKinnon UER	.04	.01
❑ 44 Jim McMahon	.10	.02
❑ 45 Steve McMichael	.10	.02
❑ 46 Brad Muster RC	.04	.01
❑ 47A William Perry ERR SP	6.00	2.50
❑ 47B Ron Morris RC	.04	.01
❑ 48 Ron Rivera	.04	.01
❑ 49 Vestee Jackson RC	.04	.01
❑ 50 Mike Singletary	.10	.02
❑ 51 Mike Tomczak	.10	.02
❑ 52 Keith Van Horne RC	.04	.01
❑ 53A Mike Ditka CO	.25	.08
❑ 53B Mike Ditka CO HOF	.25	.08
❑ 54 Lewis Billups	.04	.01
❑ 55 James Brooks	.10	.02
❑ 56 Eddie Brown	.04	.01
❑ 57 Jason Buck RC	.04	.01
❑ 58 Boomer Esiason	.10	.02
❑ 59 David Fulcher	.10	.02
❑ 60A Rodney Holman RC ERR	.10	.02
❑ 60B Rodney Holman RC COR	.25	.08
❑ 61 Reggie Williams	.04	.01
❑ 62 Joe Kelly RC	.04	.01
❑ 63 Tim Krumrie	.04	.01
❑ 64 Tim McGee	.04	.01
❑ 65 Max Montoya	.04	.01
❑ 66 Anthony Munoz	.10	.02
❑ 67 Jim Skow	.04	.01
❑ 68 Eric Thomas RC	.04	.01
❑ 69 Leon White	.04	.01
❑ 70 Ickey Woods RC	.10	.02
❑ 71 Carl Zander	.04	.01
❑ 72 Sam Wyche CO	.04	.01
❑ 73 Brian Brennan	.04	.01
❑ 74 Earnest Byner	.04	.01
❑ 75 Hanford Dixon	.04	.01
❑ 76 Mike Pagel	.04	.01
❑ 77 Bernie Kosar	.10	.02
❑ 78 Reggie Langhorne RC	.04	.01
❑ 79 Kevin Mack	.04	.01
❑ 80 Clay Matthews	.10	.02
❑ 81 Gerald McNeil	.04	.01
❑ 82 Frank Minnifield	.04	.01
❑ 83 Cody Risien	.04	.01
❑ 84 Webster Slaughter	.10	.02
❑ 85 Felix Wright	.04	.01
❑ 86 Bud Carson CO UER	.04	.01
❑ 87 Bill Bates	.10	.02
❑ 88 Kevin Brooks	.04	.01
❑ 89 Michael Irvin RC	1.50	.60
❑ 90 Jim Jeffcoat	.04	.01
❑ 91 Ed Too Tall Jones	.10	.02
❑ 92 Eugene Lockhart RC	.04	.01
❑ 93 Nate Newton RC	.10	.02
❑ 94 Danny Noonan	.04	.01
❑ 95 Steve Pelluer	.04	.01
❑ 96 Herschel Walker	.10	.02
❑ 97 Everson Walls	.04	.01
❑ 98 Jimmy Johnson RC CO	.10	.02
❑ 99 Keith Bishop	.04	.01
❑ 100A John Elway DRAFT	6.00	2.50
❑ 100B John Elway TRADE	2.00	.75
❑ 101 Simon Fletcher RC	.04	.01
❑ 102 Mike Harden	.04	.01
❑ 103 Mike Horan	.04	.01
❑ 104 Mark Jackson	.04	.01
❑ 105 Vance Johnson	.10	.02
❑ 106 Rulon Jones	.04	.01
❑ 107 Clarence Kay	.04	.01
❑ 108 Karl Mecklenburg	.04	.01
❑ 109 Ricky Nattiel	.04	.01
❑ 110 Steve Sewell RC	.04	.01
❑ 111 Dennis Smith	.10	.02
❑ 112 Gerald Willhite	.04	.01
❑ 113 Sammy Winder	.04	.01
❑ 114 Dan Reeves CO	.04	.01
❑ 115 Jim Arnold	.04	.01
❑ 116 Jerry Ball RC	.04	.01
❑ 117 Bennie Blades RC	.04	.01
❑ 118 Lomas Brown	.04	.01
❑ 119 Mike Cofer	.04	.01
❑ 120 Garry James	.04	.01
❑ 121 James Jones FB	.04	.01
❑ 122 Chuck Long	.04	.01
❑ 123 Pete Mandley	.04	.01
❑ 124 Eddie Murray	.04	.01
❑ 125 Chris Spielman RC	.25	.08
❑ 126 Dennis Gibson	.04	.01
❑ 127 Wayne Fontes CO	.04	.01
❑ 128 John Anderson	.04	.01
❑ 129 Brent Fullwood RC	.04	.01
❑ 130 Mark Cannon	.04	.01
❑ 131 Tim Harris	.04	.01
❑ 132 Mark Lee	.04	.01
❑ 133 Don Majkowski RC	.10	.02
❑ 134 Mark Murphy	.04	.01
❑ 135 Brian Noble	.04	.01
❑ 136 Ken Ruettgers RC	.04	.01
❑ 137 Johnny Holland	.04	.01
❑ 138 Randy Wright	.04	.01
❑ 139 Lindy Infante CO	.04	.01
❑ 140 Steve Brown	.04	.01
❑ 141 Ray Childress	.04	.01
❑ 142 Jeff Donaldson	.04	.01
❑ 143 Ernest Givins	.10	.02
❑ 144 John Grimsley	.04	.01
❑ 145 Alonzo Highsmith	.04	.01
❑ 146 Drew Hill	.04	.01
❑ 147 Robert Lyles	.04	.01
❑ 148 Bruce Matthews RC	.75	.30
❑ 149 Warren Moon	.25	.08
❑ 150 Mike Munchak	.10	.02
❑ 151 Allen Pinkett RC	.04	.01
❑ 152 Mike Rozier	.04	.01
❑ 153 Tony Zendejas	.04	.01
❑ 154 Jerry Glanville CO	.04	.01
❑ 155 Albert Bentley	.04	.01
❑ 156 Dean Biasucci	.04	.01
❑ 157 Duane Bickett	.04	.01
❑ 158 Bill Brooks	.10	.02
❑ 159 Chris Chandler RC	1.00	.40
❑ 160 Pat Beach	.04	.01
❑ 161 Ray Donaldson	.04	.01
❑ 162 Jon Hand	.04	.01
❑ 163 Chris Hinton	.04	.01
❑ 164 Rohn Stark	.04	.01
❑ 165 Fredd Young	.04	.01
❑ 166 Ron Meyer CO	.04	.01
❑ 167 Lloyd Burruss	.04	.01
❑ 168 Carlos Carson	.04	.01
❑ 169 Deron Cherry	.10	.02
❑ 170 Irv Eatman	.04	.01
❑ 171 Dino Hackett	.04	.01
❑ 172 Steve DeBerg	.04	.01
❑ 173 Albert Lewis	.04	.01
❑ 174 Nick Lowery	.04	.01
❑ 175 Bill Maas	.04	.01
❑ 176 Christian Okoye	.04	.01
❑ 177 Stephone Paige	.04	.01
❑ 178 Mark Adickes	.04	.01
❑ 179 Kevin Ross RC	.10	.02
❑ 180 Neil Smith RC	.50	.20
❑ 181 M. Schottenheimer CO	.04	.01
❑ 182 Marcus Allen	.25	.08
❑ 183 Tim Brown RC	1.50	.60
❑ 184 Willie Gault	.10	.02
❑ 185 Bo Jackson	.30	.10
❑ 186 Howie Long	.25	.08
❑ 187 Vann McElroy	.04	.01
❑ 188 Matt Millen	.10	.02
❑ 189 Don Mosebar RC	.04	.01
❑ 190 Bill Pickel	.04	.01
❑ 191 Jerry Robinson UER	.04	.01
❑ 192 Jay Schroeder	.04	.01
❑ 193A Stacey Toran	.04	.01
❑ 193B Stacey Toran	.50	.20
❑ 194 Mike Shanahan CO RC	.10	.02
❑ 195 Greg Bell	.04	.01
❑ 196 Ron Brown	.04	.01
❑ 197 Aaron Cox RC	.04	.01
❑ 198 Henry Ellard	.25	.08
❑ 199 Jim Everett	.10	.02
❑ 200 Jerry Gray	.04	.01
❑ 201 Kevin Greene	.25	.08
❑ 202 Pete Holohan	.04	.01
❑ 203 LeRoy Irvin	.04	.01
❑ 204 Mike Lansford	.04	.01
❑ 205 Tom Newberry RC	.04	.01
❑ 206 Mel Owens	.04	.01
❑ 207 Jackie Slater	.04	.01
❑ 208 Doug Smith	.04	.01
❑ 209 Mike Wilcher	.04	.01
❑ 210 John Robinson CO	.04	.01
❑ 211 John Bosa	.04	.01
❑ 212 Mark Brown	.04	.01
❑ 213 Mark Clayton	.10	.02
❑ 214A Ferrell Edmonds RC ERR	.50	.20
❑ 214B Ferrell Edmunds RC COR	.04	.01
❑ 215 Roy Foster	.04	.01
❑ 216 Lorenzo Hampton	.04	.01
❑ 217 Jim C.Jensen RC UER	.04	.01
❑ 218 William Judson	.04	.01
❑ 219 Eric Kumerow RC	.04	.01
❑ 220 Dan Marino	2.00	.75
❑ 221 John Offerdahl	.04	.01
❑ 222 Fuad Reveiz	.04	.01
❑ 223 Reggie Roby	.04	.01
❑ 224 Brian Sochia	.04	.01
❑ 225 Don Shula CO RC	.25	.08
❑ 226 Alfred Anderson	.04	.01
❑ 227 Joey Browner	.04	.01
❑ 228 Anthony Carter	.10	.02
❑ 229 Chris Doleman	.10	.02
❑ 230 Hassan Jones RC	.04	.01
❑ 231 Steve Jordan	.04	.01
❑ 232 Tommy Kramer	.04	.01
❑ 233 Carl Lee RC	.04	.01
❑ 234 Kirk Lowdermilk RC	.04	.01
❑ 235 Randall McDaniel RC	.25	.08
❑ 236 Doug Martin	.04	.01
❑ 237 Keith Millard	.04	.01
❑ 238 Darrin Nelson	.04	.01
❑ 239 Jesse Solomon	.04	.01
❑ 240 Scott Studwell	.04	.01
❑ 241 Wade Wilson	.10	.02
❑ 242 Gary Zimmerman	.04	.01
❑ 243 Jerry Burns CO	.04	.01
❑ 244 Bruce Armstrong RC	.04	.01
❑ 245 Raymond Clayborn	.04	.01
❑ 246 Reggie Dupard	.04	.01
❑ 247 Tony Eason	.04	.01
❑ 248 Sean Farrell	.04	.01
❑ 249 Doug Flutie	.75	.25
❑ 250 Brent Williams RC	.04	.01
❑ 251 Roland James	.04	.01
❑ 252 Ronnie Lippett	.04	.01
❑ 253 Fred Marion	.04	.01
❑ 254 Larry McGrew	.04	.01
❑ 255 Stanley Morgan	.04	.01
❑ 256 Johnny Rembert RC	.04	.01
❑ 257 John Stephens RC	.04	.01
❑ 258 Andre Tippett	.04	.01
❑ 259 Garin Veris	.04	.01
❑ 260A Raymond Berry CO	.04	.01
❑ 260B Raymond Berry CO HOF	.04	.01
❑ 261 Morten Andersen	.04	.01

No.	Player	Mint	Ex
262	Hoby Brenner	.04	.01
263	Stan Brock	.04	.01
264	Brad Edelman	.04	.01
265	Jumpy Geathers	.04	.01
266A	Bobby Hebert Passers	.50	.20
266B	Bobby Hebert Passes	.04	.01
267	Craig Heyward RC	.25	.08
268	Lonzell Hill	.04	.01
269	Dalton Hilliard	.04	.01
270	Rickey Jackson	.10	.02
271	Steve Korte	.04	.01
272	Eric Martin	.04	.01
273	Rueben Mayes	.04	.01
274	Sam Mills	.10	.02
275	Brett Perriman RC	.25	.08
276	Pat Swilling	.10	.02
277	John Tice	.04	.01
278	Jim Mora CO	.04	.01
279	Eric Moore RC	.04	.01
280	Carl Banks	.04	.01
281	Mark Bavaro	.10	.02
282	Maurice Carthon	.04	.01
283	Mark Collins RC	.04	.01
284	Erik Howard	.04	.01
285	Terry Kinard	.04	.01
286	Sean Landeta	.04	.01
287	Lionel Manuel	.04	.01
288	Leonard Marshall	.04	.01
289	Joe Morris	.04	.01
290	Bart Oates	.04	.01
291	Phil Simms	.10	.02
292	Lawrence Taylor	.25	.08
293	Bill Parcells RC CO	.10	.02
294	Dave Cadigan	.04	.01
295	Kyle Clifton RC	.04	.01
296	Alex Gordon	.04	.01
297	James Hasty RC	.04	.01
298	Johnny Hector	.04	.01
299	Bobby Humphery	.04	.01
300	Pat Leahy	.04	.01
301	Marty Lyons	.04	.01
302	Reggie McElroy RC	.04	.01
303	Erik McMillan RC	.04	.01
304	Freeman McNeil	.04	.01
305	Ken O'Brien	.04	.01
306	Pat Ryan	.04	.01
307	Mickey Shuler	.04	.01
308	Al Toon	.10	.02
309	Jo Jo Townsell	.04	.01
310	Roger Vick	.04	.01
311	Joe Walton CO	.04	.01
312	Jerome Brown	.10	.02
313	Keith Byars	.10	.02
314	Cris Carter RC	1.50	.60
315	Randall Cunningham	.40	.15
316	Terry Hoage	.04	.01
317	Wes Hopkins	.04	.01
318	Keith Jackson RC	.25	.08
319	Mike Quick	.04	.01
320	Mike Reichenbach	.04	.01
321	Dave Rimington	.04	.01
322	John Teltschik	.04	.01
323	Anthony Toney	.04	.01
324	Andre Waters	.04	.01
325	Reggie White	.25	.08
326	Luis Zendejas	.04	.01
327	Buddy Ryan CO	.04	.01
328	Robert Awalt	.04	.01
329	Tim McDonald RC	.10	.02
330	Roy Green	.10	.02
331	Neil Lomax	.04	.01
332	Cedric Mack	.04	.01
333	Stump Mitchell	.04	.01
334	Niko Noga RC	.04	.01
335	Jay Novacek RC	.25	.08
336	Freddie Joe Nunn	.04	.01
337	Luis Sharpe	.04	.01
338	Vai Sikahema	.04	.01
339	J.T. Smith	.04	.01
340	Ron Wolfley	.04	.01
341	Gene Stallings RC CO	.10	.02
342	Gary Anderson K	.04	.01
343	Bubby Brister RC	.25	.08
344	Dermontti Dawson RC	.10	.02
345	Thomas Everett RC	.04	.01
346	Delton Hall RC	.04	.01
347	Bryan Hinkle RC	.04	.01
348	Merril Hoge RC	.04	.01
349	Tunch Ilkin RC	.04	.01
350	Aaron Jones RC	.04	.01
351	Louis Lipps	.10	.02
352	David Little	.04	.01
353	Hardy Nickerson RC	.25	.08
354	Rod Woodson RC	.50	.20
355A	Chuck Noll RC CO 1/3	.10	.02
355B	Chuck Noll RC CO 1/2	.10	.02
356	Gary Anderson RB	.04	.01
357	Rod Bernstine RC	.04	.01
358	Gill Byrd	.04	.01
359	Vencie Glenn	.04	.01
360	Dennis McKnight	.04	.01
361	Lionel James	.04	.01
362	Mark Malone	.04	.01
363A	Anthony Miller RC 14.8	.25	.08
363B	Anthony Miller RC 3	.25	.08
364	Ralf Mojsiejenko	.04	.01
365	Leslie O'Neal	.10	.02
366	Jamie Holland RC	.04	.01
367	Lee Williams	.04	.01
368	Dan Henning CO	.04	.01
369	Harris Barton RC	.04	.01
370	Michael Carter	.04	.01
371	Mike Cofer RC K	.04	.01
372	Roger Craig	.25	.08
373	Riki Ellison RC	.04	.01
374	Jim Fahnhorst	.04	.01
375	John Frank	.04	.01
376	Jeff Fuller	.04	.01
377	Don Griffin	.04	.01
378	Charles Haley	.25	.08
379	Ronnie Lott	.10	.02
380	Tim McKyer	.04	.01
381	Joe Montana	2.00	.75
382	Tom Rathman	.04	.01
383	Jerry Rice	1.50	.60
384	John Taylor RC	.25	.08
385	Keena Turner	.04	.01
386	Michael Walter	.04	.01
387	Bubba Paris	.04	.01
388	Steve Young	1.00	.40
389	George Seifert RC CO	.10	.02
390	Brian Blades RC	.25	.08
391A	B.Bosworth Seattle	.30	.10
391B	B.Bosworth Seahawks	.10	.02
392	Jeff Bryant	.04	.01
393	Jacob Green	.04	.01
394	Norm Johnson	.04	.01
395	Dave Krieg	.10	.02
396	Steve Largent	.25	.08
397	Bryan Millard RC	.04	.01
398	Paul Moyer	.04	.01
399	Joe Nash	.04	.01
400	Rufus Porter RC	.04	.01
401	Eugene Robinson RC	.04	.01
402	Bruce Scholtz	.04	.01
403	Kelly Stouffer RC	.04	.01
404A	Curt Warner 1455	1.25	.50
404B	Curt Warner 6074	.10	.02
405	John L.Williams	.04	.01
406	Tony Woods RC	.04	.01
407	David Wyman	.04	.01
408	Chuck Knox CO	.04	.01
409	Mark Carrier RC WR	.25	.08
410	Randy Grimes	.04	.01
411	Paul Gruber RC	.04	.01
412	Harry Hamilton	.04	.01
413	Ron Holmes	.04	.01
414	Donald Igwebuike	.04	.01
415	Dan Turk	.04	.01
416	Ricky Reynolds	.04	.01
417	Bruce Hill RC	.04	.01
418	Lars Tate	.04	.01
419	Vinny Testaverde	.30	.10
420	James Wilder	.04	.01
421	Ray Perkins CO	.04	.01
422	Jeff Bostic	.04	.01
423	Kelvin Bryant	.04	.01
424	Gary Clark	.25	.08
425	Monte Coleman	.04	.01
426	Darrell Green	.10	.02
427	Joe Jacoby	.04	.01
428	Jim Lachey	.04	.01
429	Charles Mann	.04	.01
430	Dexter Manley	.04	.01
431	Darryl Grant	.04	.01
432	Mark May RC	.04	.01
433	Art Monk	.10	.02
434	Mark Rypien RC	.25	.08
435	Ricky Sanders	.04	.01
436	Alvin Walton RC	.04	.01
437	Don Warren	.04	.01
438	Jamie Morris	.04	.01
439	Doug Williams	.10	.02
440	Joe Gibbs RC CO	.10	.02
441	Marcus Cotton	.04	.01
442	Joel Williams	.04	.01
443	Joe Devlin	.04	.01
444	Robb Riddick	.04	.01
445	William Perry	.10	.02
446	Thomas Sanders RC	.04	.01
447	Brian Blados	.04	.01
448	Cris Collinsworth	.10	.02
449	Stanford Jennings	.04	.01
450	Barry Krauss UER	.04	.01
451	Ozzie Newsome	.10	.02
452	Mike Oliphant RC	.04	.01
453	Tony Dorsett	.25	.08
454	Bruce McNorton	.04	.01
455	Eric Dickerson	.10	.02
456	Keith Bostic	.04	.01
457	Sam Clancy RC	.04	.01
458	Jack Del Rio RC	.25	.08
459	Mike Webster	.10	.02
460	Bob Golic	.04	.01
461	Otis Wilson	.04	.01
462	Mike Haynes	.10	.02
463	Greg Townsend	.04	.01
464	Mark Duper	.10	.02
465	E.J. Junior	.04	.01
466	Troy Stradford	.04	.01
467	Mike Merriweather	.04	.01
468	Irving Fryar	.25	.08
469	Vaughan Johnson RC**	.04	.01
470	Pepper Johnson	.04	.01
471	Gary Reasons RC	.04	.01
472	Perry Williams RC	.04	.01
473	Wesley Walker	.04	.01
474	Anthony Bell RC	.04	.01
475	Earl Ferrell	.04	.01
476	Craig Wolfley	.04	.01
477	Billy Ray Smith	.04	.01
478A	Jim McMahon NOTR	.10	.02
478B	Jim McMahon TR	.10	.02
478C	Jim McMahon	40.00	15.00
479	Eric Wright	.04	.01
480A	Earnest Byner NOTR	.04	.01
480B	Earnest Byner TR	.30	.10
480C	Earnest Byner	40.00	15.00
481	Russ Grimm	.04	.01
482	Wilber Marshall	.04	.01
483A	Gerald Riggs	.10	.02
483B	Gerald Riggs	.30	.10
483C	Gerald Riggs	40.00	15.00
484	Brian Davis RC	.04	.01
485	Shawn Collins RC	.04	.01
486	Deion Sanders RC	2.00	.75
487	Trace Armstrong RC	.04	.01
488	Donnell Woolford RC	.10	.02
489	Eric Metcalf RC	.25	.08
490	Troy Aikman RC	6.00	2.50
491	Steve Walsh RC	.10	.02
492	Steve Atwater RC	.25	.08
493	Bobby Humphrey RC	.04	.01
494	Barry Sanders RC	8.00	3.00
495	Tony Mandarich RC	.04	.01
496	David Williams RC	.04	.01
497	Andre Rison RC UER	1.00	.40
498	Derrick Thomas RC	1.50	.60
499	Cleveland Gary RC	.04	.01
500	Bill Hawkins RC	.04	.01
501	Louis Oliver RC	.10	.02
502	Sammie Smith RC	.04	.01
503	Hart Lee Dykes RC	.04	.01
504	Wayne Martin RC	.04	.01
505	Brian Williams OL RC	.04	.01
506	Jeff Lageman RC	.10	.02
507	Eric Hill RC	.04	.01
508	Joe Wolf RC	.04	.01
509	Timm Rosenbach RC	.04	.01
510	Tom Ricketts	.04	.01
511	Tim Worley RC	.04	.01

❑ 512 Burt Grossman RC .04 .01
❑ 513 Keith DeLong RC .04 .01
❑ 514 Andy Heck RC .04 .01
❑ 515 Broderick Thomas RC .25 .08
❑ 516 Don Beebe RC .25 .08
❑ 517 James Thornton RC .04 .01
❑ 518 Eric Kattus .04 .01
❑ 519 Bruce Kozerski RC .04 .01
❑ 520 Brian Washington RC .04 .01
❑ 521 Rodney Peete RC .50 .20
❑ 522 Erik Affholter RC .04 .01
❑ 523 Anthony Dilweg RC .04 .01
❑ 524 O'Brien Alston .04 .01
❑ 525 Mike Elkins .04 .01
❑ 526 Jonathan Hayes RC .04 .01
❑ 527 Terry McDaniel RC .04 .01
❑ 528 Frank Stams RC .04 .01
❑ 529 Darryl Ingram RC .04 .01
❑ 530 Henry Thomas .04 .01
❑ 531 Eric Coleman DB .04 .01
❑ 532 Sheldon White RC .04 .01
❑ 533 Eric Allen RC .25 .08
❑ 534 Robert Drummond .04 .01
❑ 535A G.Williams RC bal 10.00 5.00
❑ 535B G.Williams RC w/o scout .25 .08
❑ 535C G.Williams RC w/scout .04 .01
❑ 536 Billy Joe Tolliver RC .04 .01
❑ 537 Daniel Stubbs RC .04 .01
❑ 538 Wesley Walls RC .40 .15
❑ 539A James Jefferson RC*ERR .30 .10
❑ 539B James Jefferson RC*COR .04 .01
❑ 540 Tracy Rocker .04 .01
❑ 541 Art Shell CO .10 .02
❑ 542 Lemuel Stinson RC .04 .01
❑ 543 Tyrone Braxton RC UER .04 .01
❑ 544 David Treadwell RC .04 .01
❑ 545 Flipper Anderson RC .25 .08
❑ 546 Dave Meggett RC .25 .08
❑ 547 Lewis Tillman RC .04 .01
❑ 548 Carnell Lake RC .25 .08
❑ 549 Marion Butts RC .10 .02
❑ 550 Sterling Sharpe RC 1.00 .40
❑ 551 Ezra Johnson .04 .01
❑ 552 Clarence Verdin RC** .04 .01
❑ 553 Mervyn Fernandez RC**/C .04 .01
❑ 554 Ottis Anderson .10 .02
❑ 555 Gary Hogeboom .04 .01
❑ 556 Paul Palmer TR .04 .01
❑ 557 Jesse Solomon TR .04 .01
❑ 558 Chip Banks TR .04 .01
❑ 559 Steve Pelluer TR .04 .01
❑ 560 Darrin Nelson TR .04 .01
❑ 561 Herschel Walker TR .10 .02
❑ CC1 Pete Rozelle .50 .20

1990 Pro Set

❑ COMPLETE SET (801) 25.00 10.00
❑ COMP.SERIES 1 (377) 10.00 4.00
❑ COMP.SERIES 2 (392) 10.00 4.00
❑ COMP.FINAL SERIES (32) 4.00 1.50
❑ COMP.FINAL FACT. (32) 5.00 2.00
❑ 1A Ba.Sanders ROY Hawaii 80.00 30.00
❑ 1B Barry Sanders ROY .60 .25
❑ 2A Joe Montana POY 3521 ERR .50 .20
❑ 2B Joe Montana POY 3130 COR .50 .20
❑ 3 Lindy Infante UER .04 .01
❑ 4 Warren Moon MOY UER .25 .08
❑ 5 Keith Millard .04 .01
❑ 6 Derrick Thomas D.ROY .25 .08
❑ 7 Ottis Anderson .10 .02
❑ 8 Joe Montana LL UER .50 .20
❑ 9 Christian Okoye .04 .01
❑ 10 Thurman Thomas LL .25 .08
❑ 11 Mike Cofer .04 .01
❑ 12 Dalton Hilliard UER .04 .01
❑ 13 Sterling Sharpe LL .25 .08
❑ 14 Rich Camarillo .04 .01
❑ 15A Walter Stanley LL 87/8 .50 .20
❑ 15B Walter Stanley COR .04 .01
❑ 16 Rod Woodson .25 .08
❑ 17 Felix Wright .04 .01
❑ 18A Chris Doleman ERR .50 .20
❑ 18B Chris Doleman COR .50 .20
❑ 19A Andre Ware RC w/o strip .10 .02
❑ 19B Andre Ware RC w/stripe .10 .02
❑ 20A Mo Elewonibi RC .04 .01
❑ 20B Mo Elewonibi RC .04 .01
❑ 21A Percy Snow .50 .20
❑ 21B Percy Snow .04 .01
❑ 22A Anthony Thompson RC w/o .04 .01
❑ 22B Anthony Thompson RC w/ .04 .01
❑ 23 Buck Buchanan .04 .01
❑ 24 Bob Griese .10 .02
❑ 25A Franco Harris ERR .50 .20
❑ 25B Franco Harris COR .10 .02
❑ 26 Ted Hendricks .04 .01
❑ 27A Jack Lambert ERR .50 .20
❑ 27B Jack Lambert COR .50 .20
❑ 28 Tom Landry HOF .10 .02
❑ 29 Bob St.Clair .04 .01
❑ 30 Aundray Bruce UER .04 .01
❑ 31 Tony Casillas UER .04 .01
❑ 32 Shawn Collins .04 .01
❑ 33 Marcus Cotton .04 .01
❑ 34 Bill Fralic .04 .01
❑ 35 Chris Miller .10 .02
❑ 36 Deion Sanders UER .50 .20
❑ 37 John Settle .04 .01
❑ 38 Jerry Glanville CO .04 .01
❑ 39 Cornelius Bennett .10 .02
❑ 40 Jim Kelly .25 .08
❑ 41 Mark Kelso UER .04 .01
❑ 42 Scott Norwood .04 .01
❑ 43 Nate Odomes RC .10 .02
❑ 44 Scott Radecic .04 .01
❑ 45 Jim Ritcher RC .04 .01
❑ 46 Leonard Smith .04 .01
❑ 47 Darryl Talley .04 .01
❑ 48 Marv Levy CO .04 .01
❑ 49 Neal Anderson .10 .02
❑ 50 Kevin Butler .04 .01
❑ 51 Jim Covert .04 .01
❑ 52 Richard Dent .10 .02
❑ 53 Jay Hilgenberg .04 .01
❑ 54 Steve McMichael .10 .02
❑ 55 Ron Morris .04 .01
❑ 56 John Roper .04 .01
❑ 57 Mike Singletary .10 .02
❑ 58 Keith Van Horne .04 .01
❑ 59 Mike Ditka CO .25 .08
❑ 60 Lewis Billups .04 .01
❑ 61 Eddie Brown .04 .01
❑ 62 Jason Buck .04 .01
❑ 63A Rickey Dixon RC ERR .50 .20
❑ 63B Rickey Dixon RC COR .50 .20
❑ 64 Tim McGee .04 .01
❑ 65 Eric Thomas .04 .01
❑ 66 Ickey Woods .04 .01
❑ 67 Carl Zander .04 .01
❑ 68A Sam Wyche CO ERR .50 .20
❑ 68B Sam Wyche CO COR .50 .20
❑ 69 Paul Farren .04 .01
❑ 70 Thane Gash RC .04 .01
❑ 71 David Grayson .04 .01
❑ 72 Bernie Kosar .10 .02
❑ 73 Reggie Langhorne .04 .01
❑ 74 Eric Metcalf .25 .08
❑ 75A Ozzie Newsome ERR .50 .20
❑ 75B Ozzie Newsome COR .50 .20
❑ 75C Cody Risien SP .50 .20
❑ 76 Felix Wright .04 .01
❑ 77 Bud Carson CO .04 .01
❑ 78 Troy Aikman .75 .30
❑ 79 Michael Irvin .25 .08
❑ 80 Jim Jeffcoat .04 .01
❑ 81 Crawford Ker .04 .01
❑ 82 Eugene Lockhart .04 .01
❑ 83 Kelvin Martin RC .04 .01
❑ 84 Ken Norton Jr. RC .25 .08
❑ 85 Jimmy Johnson CO .10 .02
❑ 86 Steve Atwater .04 .01
❑ 87 Tyrone Braxton .04 .01
❑ 88 John Elway 1.25 .50
❑ 89 Simon Fletcher .04 .01
❑ 90 Ron Holmes .04 .01
❑ 91 Bobby Humphrey .04 .01
❑ 92 Vance Johnson .04 .01
❑ 93 Ricky Nattiel .04 .01
❑ 94 Dan Reeves CO .04 .01
❑ 95 Jim Arnold .04 .01
❑ 96 Jerry Ball .04 .01
❑ 97 Bennie Blades .04 .01
❑ 98 Lomas Brown .04 .01
❑ 99 Michael Cofer .04 .01
❑ 100 Richard Johnson .04 .01
❑ 101 Eddie Murray .04 .01
❑ 102 Barry Sanders 1.25 .50
❑ 103 Chris Spielman .25 .08
❑ 104 William White RC .04 .01
❑ 105 Eric Williams RC .04 .01
❑ 106 Wayne Fontes CO UER .04 .01
❑ 107 Brent Fullwood .04 .01
❑ 108 Ron Hallstrom RC .04 .01
❑ 109 Tim Harris .04 .01
❑ 110A Johnny Holland ERR .50 .20
❑ 110B Johnny Holland COR .50 .20
❑ 111A Perry Kemp ERR .50 .20
❑ 111B Perry Kemp COR .50 .20
❑ 112 Don Majkowski .04 .01
❑ 113 Mark Murphy .04 .01
❑ 114A Sterling Sharpe ERR Gle .25 .08
❑ 114B Sterling Sharpe COR Chi .50 .20
❑ 115 Ed West RC .04 .01
❑ 116 Lindy Infante CO .04 .01
❑ 117 Steve Brown .04 .01
❑ 118 Ray Childress .04 .01
❑ 119 Ernest Givins .10 .02
❑ 120 John Grimsley .04 .01
❑ 121 Alonzo Highsmith .04 .01
❑ 122 Drew Hill .04 .01
❑ 123 Bubba McDowell .04 .01
❑ 124 Dean Steinkuhler .04 .01
❑ 125 Lorenzo White FPSC .10 .02
❑ 126 Tony Zendejas .04 .01
❑ 127 Jack Pardee CO .04 .01
❑ 128 Albert Bentley .04 .01
❑ 129 Dean Biasucci .04 .01
❑ 130 Duane Bickett .04 .01
❑ 131 Bill Brooks .04 .01
❑ 132 Jon Hand .04 .01
❑ 133 Mike Prior .04 .01
❑ 134A Andre Rison NOTR .25 .08
❑ 134B Andre Rison TR .25 .08
❑ 134C Andre Rison TR Lud/back .25 .08
❑ 135 Rohn Stark .04 .01
❑ 136 Donnell Thompson .04 .01
❑ 137 Clarence Verdin .04 .01
❑ 138 Fredd Young .04 .01
❑ 139 Ron Meyer CO .04 .01
❑ 140 John Alt RC .04 .01
❑ 141 Steve DeBerg .04 .01
❑ 142 Irv Eatman .04 .01
❑ 143 Dino Hackett .04 .01
❑ 144 Nick Lowery .04 .01
❑ 145 Bill Maas .04 .01
❑ 146 Stephone Paige .04 .01
❑ 147 Neil Smith .25 .08
❑ 148 M. Schottenheimer CO .04 .01
❑ 149 Steve Beuerlein FPSC .10 .02
❑ 150 Tim Brown .25 .08
❑ 151 Mike Dyal .04 .01
❑ 152A Mervyn Fernandez ERR .75 .30
❑ 152B Mervyn Fernandez COR .75 .30
❑ 153 Willie Gault .10 .02
❑ 154 Bob Golic .04 .01
❑ 155 Bo Jackson .30 .10
❑ 156 Don Mosebar .04 .01
❑ 157 Steve Smith .04 .01
❑ 158 Greg Townsend .04 .01
❑ 159 Bruce Wilkerson RC .04 .01
❑ 160 Steve Wisniewski .10 .02
❑ 161A Art Shell CO ERR .50 .20
❑ 161B Art Shell CO COR 8.00 3.00

No.	Card	Price	Price
161C	Art Shell CO COR	.50	.20
162	Flipper Anderson	.04	.01
163	Greg Bell UER	.04	.01
164	Henry Ellard	.10	.02
165	Jim Everett	.10	.02
166	Jerry Gray	.04	.01
167	Kevin Greene	.10	.02
168	Pete Holohan	.04	.01
169	Larry Kelm RC	.04	.01
170	Tom Newberry	.04	.01
171	Vince Newsome RC	.04	.01
172	Irv Pankey	.04	.01
173	Jackie Slater	.04	.01
174	Fred Strickland RC	.04	.01
175	Mike Wilcher UER	.04	.01
176	John Robinson CO UER	.04	.01
177	Mark Clayton	.10	.02
178	Roy Foster	.04	.01
179	Harry Galbreath RC	.04	.01
180	Jim C. Jensen	.04	.01
181	Dan Marino	1.25	.50
182	Louis Oliver	.04	.01
183	Sammie Smith	.04	.01
184	Brian Sochia	.04	.01
185	Don Shula CO	.10	.02
186	Joey Browner	.04	.01
187	Anthony Carter	.10	.02
188	Chris Doleman	.04	.01
189	Steve Jordan	.04	.01
190	Carl Lee	.04	.01
191	Randall McDaniel	.10	.02
192	Mike Merriweather	.04	.01
193	Keith Millard	.04	.01
194	Al Noga	.04	.01
195	Scott Studwell	.04	.01
196	Henry Thomas	.04	.01
197	Herschel Walker	.10	.02
198	Wade Wilson	.10	.02
199	Gary Zimmerman	.04	.01
200	Jerry Burns CO	.04	.01
201	Vincent Brown RC	.04	.01
202	Hart Lee Dykes	.04	.01
203	Sean Farrell	.04	.01
204A	Fred Marion belt	250.00	100.00
204B	Fred Marion no belt	.04	.01
205	Stanley Morgan UER	.04	.01
206	Eric Sievers RC	.04	.01
207	John Stephens	.04	.01
208	Andre Tippett	.04	.01
209	Rod Rust CO	.04	.01
210A	Morten Andersen ERR	.50	.20
210B	Morten Andersen COR	.50	.20
211	Brad Edelman	.04	.01
212	John Fourcade	.04	.01
213	Dalton Hilliard	.04	.01
214	Rickey Jackson	.10	.02
215	Vaughan Johnson	.04	.01
216A	Eric Martin ERR	.50	.20
216B	Eric Martin COR	.50	.20
217	Sam Mills	.10	.02
218	Pat Swilling UER	.10	.02
219	Frank Warren RC	.04	.01
220	Jim Wilks	.04	.01
221A	Jim Mora CO ERR	.50	.20
221B	Jim Mora CO COR	.50	.20
222	Raul Allegre	.04	.01
223	Carl Banks	.04	.01
224	John Elliott	.04	.01
225	Erik Howard	.04	.01
226	Pepper Johnson	.04	.01
227	Leonard Marshall UER	.04	.01
228	Dave Meggett	.10	.02
229	Bart Oates	.04	.01
230	Phil Simms	.10	.02
231	Lawrence Taylor	.25	.08
232	Bill Parcells CO	.10	.02
233	Troy Benson	.04	.01
234	Kyle Clifton UER	.04	.01
235	Johnny Hector	.04	.01
236	Jeff Lageman	.04	.01
237	Pat Leahy	.04	.01
238	Freeman McNeil	.04	.01
239	Ken O'Brien	.04	.01
240	Al Toon	.10	.02
241	Jo Jo Townsell	.04	.01
242	Bruce Coslet CO	.04	.01
243	Eric Allen	.04	.01
244	Jerome Brown	.04	.01
245	Keith Byars	.04	.01
246	Cris Carter	.50	.20
247	Randall Cunningham	.25	.08
248	Keith Jackson	.10	.02
249	Mike Quick	.04	.01
250	Clyde Simmons	.04	.01
251	Andre Waters	.04	.01
252	Reggie White	.25	.08
253	Buddy Ryan CO	.04	.01
254	Rich Camarillo	.04	.01
255	Earl Ferrell	.04	.01
256	Roy Green	.10	.02
257	Ken Harvey RC	.25	.08
258	Ernie Jones RC	.04	.01
259	Tim McDonald	.04	.01
260	Timm Rosenbach UER	.04	.01
261	Luis Sharpe	.04	.01
262	Vai Sikahema	.04	.01
263	J.T. Smith	.04	.01
264	Ron Wolfley UER	.04	.01
265	Joe Bugel CO	.04	.01
266	Gary Anderson K	.04	.01
267	Bubby Brister	.04	.01
268	Merril Hoge	.04	.01
269	Carnell Lake	.04	.01
270	Louis Lipps	.10	.02
271	David Little	.04	.01
272	Greg Lloyd	.25	.08
273	Keith Willis	.04	.01
274	Tim Worley	.04	.01
275	Chuck Noll CO	.10	.02
276	Marion Butts	.10	.02
277	Gill Byrd	.04	.01
278	Vencie Glenn UER	.04	.01
279	Burt Grossman	.04	.01
280	Gary Plummer	.04	.01
281	Billy Ray Smith	.04	.01
282	Billy Joe Tolliver	.04	.01
283	Dan Henning CO	.04	.01
284	Harris Barton	.04	.01
285	Michael Carter	.04	.01
286	Mike Cofer	.04	.01
287	Roger Craig	.10	.02
288	Don Griffin	.04	.01
289A	Charles Haley ERR	10.00	4.00
289B	Charles Haley COR 5 fum	.75	.30
290	Pierce Holt RC	.04	.01
291	Ronnie Lott	.10	.02
292	Guy McIntyre	.04	.01
293	Joe Montana	1.25	.50
294	Tom Rathman	.04	.01
295	Jerry Rice	.75	.30
296	Jesse Sapolu RC	.04	.01
297	John Taylor	.10	.02
298	Michael Walter	.04	.01
299	George Seifert CO	.10	.02
300	Jeff Bryant	.04	.01
301	Jacob Green	.04	.01
302	Norm Johnson UER	.04	.01
303	Bryan Millard	.04	.01
304	Joe Nash	.04	.01
305	Eugene Robinson	.04	.01
306	John L. Williams	.04	.01
307	David Wyman	.04	.01
308	Chuck Knox CO	.04	.01
309	Mark Carrier WR	.25	.08
310	Paul Gruber	.04	.01
311	Harry Hamilton	.04	.01
312	Bruce Hill	.04	.01
313	Donald Igwebuike	.04	.01
314	Kevin Murphy	.04	.01
315	Ervin Randle	.04	.01
316	Mark Robinson	.04	.01
317	Lars Tate	.04	.01
318	Vinny Testaverde	.10	.02
319A	Ray Perkins CO ERR	.75	.30
319B	Ray Perkins CO COR	.04	.01
320	Earnest Byner	.04	.01
321	Gary Clark	.25	.08
322	Darryl Grant	.04	.01
323	Darrell Green	.10	.02
324	Jim Lachey	.04	.01
325	Charles Mann	.04	.01
326	Wilber Marshall	.04	.01
327	Ralf Mojsiejenko	.04	.01
328	Art Monk	.10	.02
329	Gerald Riggs	.10	.02
330	Mark Rypien	.10	.02
331	Ricky Sanders	.04	.01
332	Alvin Walton	.04	.01
333	Joe Gibbs CO	.10	.02
334	Aloha Stadium	.04	.01
335	Brian Blades PB	.04	.01
336	James Brooks PB	.04	.01
337	Shane Conlan PB	.04	.01
338A	Eric Dickerson PB SP	3.00	1.25
338B	Lud Denny Promo	200.00	75.00
339	Ray Donaldson PB	.04	.01
340	Ferrell Edmunds PB	.04	.01
341	Boomer Esiason PB	.04	.01
342	David Fulcher PB	.04	.01
343A	Chris Hinton PB	8.00	3.00
343B	Chris Hinton PB	.04	.01
344	Rodney Holman PB	.04	.01
345	Kent Hull PB	.04	.01
346	Tunch Ilkin PB	.04	.01
347	Mike Johnson PB	.04	.01
348	Greg Kragen PB	.04	.01
349	Dave Krieg PB	.10	.02
350	Albert Lewis PB	.04	.01
351	Howie Long PB	.10	.02
352	Bruce Matthews PB	.04	.01
353	Clay Matthews PB	.04	.01
354	Erik McMillan PB	.04	.01
355	Karl Mecklenburg PB	.04	.01
356	Anthony Miller PB	.04	.01
357	Frank Minnifield PB	.04	.01
358	Max Montoya PB	.04	.01
359	Warren Moon PB	.25	.08
360	Mike Munchak PB	.04	.01
361	Anthony Munoz PB	.04	.01
362	John Offerdahl PB	.04	.01
363	Christian Okoye PB	.04	.01
364	Leslie O'Neal PB	.04	.01
365	Rufus Porter PB UER	.04	.01
366	Andre Reed PB	.10	.02
367	Johnny Rembert PB	.04	.01
368	Reggie Roby PB	.04	.01
369	Kevin Ross PB	.04	.01
370	Webster Slaughter PB	.04	.01
371	Bruce Smith PB	.10	.02
372	Dennis Smith PB	.04	.01
373	Derrick Thomas PB	.10	.02
374	Thurman Thomas PB	.25	.08
375	David Treadwell PB	.04	.01
376	Lee Williams PB	.04	.01
377	Rod Woodson PB	.10	.02
378	Bud Carson CO PB	.04	.01
379	Eric Allen PB	.04	.01
380	Neal Anderson PB	.10	.02
381	Jerry Ball PB	.04	.01
382	Joey Browner PB	.04	.01
383	Rich Camarillo PB	.04	.01
384	Mark Carrier WR PB	.04	.01
385	Roger Craig PB	.10	.02
386A	Randall Cunningham PB	.50	.20
386B	Randall Cunningham PB	.50	.20
387	Chris Doleman PB	.04	.01
388	Henry Ellard PB	.04	.01
389	Bill Fralic PB	.04	.01
390	Brent Fullwood PB	.04	.01
391	Jerry Gray PB	.04	.01
392	Kevin Greene PB	.10	.02
393	Tim Harris PB	.04	.01
394	Jay Hilgenberg PB	.04	.01
395	Dalton Hilliard PB	.04	.01
396	Keith Jackson PB	.10	.02
397	Vaughan Johnson PB	.04	.01
398	Steve Jordan PB	.04	.01
399	Carl Lee PB	.04	.01
400	Ronnie Lott PB	.10	.02
401	Don Majkowski PB	.04	.01
402	Charles Mann PB	.04	.01
403	Randall McDaniel PB	.04	.01
404	Tim McDonald PB	.04	.01
405	Guy McIntyre PB	.04	.01
406	Dave Meggett PB	.04	.01
407	Keith Millard PB	.04	.01
408	Joe Montana PB	.50	.20
409	Eddie Murray PB	.04	.01
410	Tom Newberry PB	.04	.01
411	Jerry Rice PB	.50	.20
412	Mark Rypien PB	.04	.01

Card		
413 Barry Sanders PB	.60	.25
414 Luis Sharpe PB	.04	.01
415 Sterling Sharpe PB	.04	.01
416 Mike Singletary PB	.10	.02
417 Jackie Slater PB	.04	.01
418 Doug Smith PB	.04	.01
419 Chris Spielman PB	.04	.01
420 Pat Swilling PB	.04	.01
421 John Taylor PB	.04	.01
422 Lawrence Taylor PB	.10	.02
423 Reggie White PB	.10	.02
424 Ron Wolfley PB	.04	.01
425 Gary Zimmerman PB	.04	.01
426 John Robinson CO PB	.04	.01
427 Scott Case UER	.04	.01
428 Mike Kenn	.04	.01
429 Mike Gann	.04	.01
430 Tim Green RC	.04	.01
431 Michael Haynes RC	.25	.08
432 Jessie Tuggle RC UER	.04	.01
433 John Rade	.04	.01
434 Andre Rison	.25	.08
435 Don Beebe	.10	.02
436 Ray Bentley	.04	.01
437 Shane Conlan	.04	.01
438 Kent Hull	.04	.01
439 Pete Metzelaars	.04	.01
440 Andre Reed UER	.25	.08
441 Frank Reich FPSC	.25	.08
442 Leon Seals RC	.04	.01
443 Bruce Smith	.25	.08
444 Thurman Thomas	.25	.08
445 Will Wolford	.04	.01
446 Trace Armstrong	.04	.01
447 Mark Bortz RC	.04	.01
448 Tom Thayer RC	.04	.01
449A Dan Hampton ERR	.50	.20
449B Dan Hampton COR	10.00	4.00
450 Shaun Gayle RC	.04	.01
451 Dennis Gentry	.04	.01
452 Jim Harbaugh	.25	.08
453 Vestee Jackson	.04	.01
454 Brad Muster	.04	.01
455 William Perry	.10	.02
456 Ron Rivera	.04	.01
457 James Thornton	.04	.01
458 Mike Tomczak	.10	.02
459 Donnell Woolford	.04	.01
460 Eric Ball	.04	.01
461 James Brooks	.10	.02
462 David Fulcher	.04	.01
463 Boomer Esiason	.10	.02
464 Rodney Holman	.04	.01
465 Bruce Kozerski	.04	.01
466 Tim Krumrie	.04	.01
467 Anthony Munoz	.10	.02
468 Brian Blados	.04	.01
469 Mike Baab	.04	.01
470 Brian Brennan	.04	.01
471 Raymond Clayborn	.04	.01
472 Mike Johnson	.04	.01
473 Kevin Mack	.04	.01
474 Clay Matthews	.10	.02
475 Frank Minnifield	.04	.01
476 Gregg Rakoczy RC	.04	.01
477 Webster Slaughter	.10	.02
478 James Dixon	.04	.01
479 Robert Awalt UER	.04	.01
480 Dennis McKinnon UER	.04	.01
481 Danny Noonan	.04	.01
482 Jesse Solomon	.04	.01
483 Daniel Stubbs UER	.04	.01
484 Steve Walsh	.10	.02
485 Michael Brooks RC	.04	.01
486 Mark Jackson	.04	.01
487 Greg Kragen	.04	.01
488 Ken Lanier RC	.04	.01
489 Karl Mecklenburg	.04	.01
490 Steve Sewell	.04	.01
491 Dennis Smith	.04	.01
492 David Treadwell	.04	.01
493 Michael Young RC	.04	.01
494 Robert Clark RC	.04	.01
495 Dennis Gibson	.04	.01
496A Kevin Glover RC C/G	.50	.20
496B Kevin Glover RC C	.04	.01
497 Mel Gray	.10	.02
498 Rodney Peete	.10	.02
499 Dave Brown DB	.04	.01
500 Jerry Holmes	.04	.01
501 Chris Jacke	.04	.01
502 Alan Veingrad	.04	.01
503 Mark Lee	.04	.01
504 Tony Mandarich	.04	.01
505 Brian Noble	.04	.01
506 Jeff Query	.04	.01
507 Ken Ruettgers	.04	.01
508 Patrick Allen	.04	.01
509 Curtis Duncan	.04	.01
510 William Fuller	.10	.02
511 Haywood Jeffires RC	.25	.08
512 Sean Jones	.10	.02
513 Terry Kinard	.04	.01
514 Bruce Matthews	.10	.02
515 Gerald McNeil	.04	.01
516 Greg Montgomery RC	.04	.01
517 Warren Moon	.25	.08
518 Mike Munchak	.10	.02
519 Allen Pinkett	.04	.01
520 Pat Beach	.04	.01
521 Eugene Daniel	.04	.01
522 Kevin Call	.04	.01
523 Ray Donaldson	.04	.01
524 Jeff Herrod RC	.04	.01
525 Keith Taylor	.04	.01
526 Jack Trudeau	.04	.01
527 Deron Cherry	.04	.01
528 Jeff Donaldson	.04	.01
529 Albert Lewis	.04	.01
530 Pete Mandley	.04	.01
531 Chris Martin RC	.04	.01
532 Christian Okoye	.04	.01
533 Steve Pelluer	.04	.01
534 Kevin Ross	.04	.01
535 Dan Saleaumua	.04	.01
536 Derrick Thomas	.25	.08
537 Mike Webster	.10	.02
538 Marcus Allen	.25	.08
539 Greg Bell	.04	.01
540 Thomas Benson	.04	.01
541 Ron Brown	.04	.01
542 Scott Davis	.04	.01
543 Riki Ellison	.04	.01
544 Jamie Holland	.04	.01
545 Howie Long	.25	.08
546 Terry McDaniel	.04	.01
547 Max Montoya	.04	.01
548 Jay Schroeder	.04	.01
549 Lionel Washington	.04	.01
550 Robert Delpino FPSC	.04	.01
551 Bobby Humphery	.04	.01
552 Mike Lansford	.04	.01
553 Michael Stewart RC	.04	.01
554 Doug Smith	.04	.01
555 Curt Warner	.04	.01
556 Alvin Wright RC	.04	.01
557 Jeff Cross	.04	.01
558 Jeff Dellenbach RC	.04	.01
559 Mark Duper	.10	.02
560 Ferrell Edmunds	.04	.01
561 Tim McKyer	.04	.01
562 John Offerdahl	.04	.01
563 Reggie Roby	.04	.01
564 Pete Stoyanovich	.04	.01
565 Alfred Anderson	.04	.01
566 Ray Berry	.04	.01
567 Rick Fenney	.04	.01
568 Rich Gannon RC	1.50	.60
569 Tim Irwin	.04	.01
570 Hassan Jones	.04	.01
571 Cris Carter	.50	.20
572 Kirk Lowdermilk	.04	.01
573 Reggie Rutland RC	.04	.01
574 Ken Stills	.04	.01
575 Bruce Armstrong	.04	.01
576 Irving Fryar	.10	.02
577 Roland James	.04	.01
578 Robert Perryman	.04	.01
579 Cedric Jones	.04	.01
580 Steve Grogan	.10	.02
581 Johnny Rembert	.04	.01
582 Ed Reynolds	.04	.01
583 Brent Williams	.04	.01
584 Marc Wilson	.04	.01
585 Hoby Brenner	.04	.01
586 Stan Brock	.04	.01
587 Jim Dombrowski RC	.04	.01
588 Joel Hilgenberg RC	.04	.01
589 Robert Massey	.04	.01
590 Floyd Turner FPSC	.04	.01
591 Ottis Anderson	.10	.02
592 Mark Bavaro	.04	.01
593 Maurice Carthon	.04	.01
594 Eric Dorsey RC	.04	.01
595 Myron Guyton	.04	.01
596 Jeff Hostetler RC	.25	.08
597 Sean Landeta	.04	.01
598 Lionel Manuel	.04	.01
599 Odessa Turner RC	.04	.01
600 Perry Williams	.04	.01
601 James Hasty	.04	.01
602 Erik McMillan	.04	.01
603 Alex Gordon UER	.04	.01
604 Ron Stallworth	.04	.01
605 Byron Evans RC	.04	.01
606 Ron Heller RC OT	.04	.01
607 Wes Hopkins	.04	.01
608 Mickey Shuler UER	.04	.01
609 Seth Joyner	.10	.02
610 Jim McMahon	.10	.02
611 Mike Pitts	.04	.01
612 Izel Jenkins RC	.04	.01
613 Anthony Bell	.04	.01
614 David Galloway	.04	.01
615 Eric Hill	.04	.01
616 Cedric Mack	.04	.01
617 Freddie Joe Nunn	.04	.01
618 Tootie Robbins	.04	.01
619 Tom Tupa RC	.04	.01
620 Joe Wolf	.04	.01
621 Dermontti Dawson	.10	.02
622 Thomas Everett	.04	.01
623 Tunch Ilkin	.04	.01
624 Hardy Nickerson	.10	.02
625 Gerald Williams RC	.04	.01
626 Rod Woodson	.25	.08
627A Rod Bernstine TE	.50	.20
627B Rod Bernstine RB	.04	.01
628 Courtney Hall	.04	.01
629 Ronnie Harmon	.10	.02
630A Anthony Miller WR	.25	.08
630B Anthony Miller WR-KR	.10	.02
631 Joe Phillips	.04	.01
632A Leslie O'Neal LB-DE	8.00	3.00
632B Leslie O'Neal LB	.15	.05
632C Leslie O'Neal COR	.10	.02
633A David Richards RC G-T	.15	.05
633B David Richards RC G	.15	.05
634 Mark Vlasic FPSC	.04	.01
635 Lee Williams	.04	.01
636 Chet Brooks	.04	.01
637 Keena Turner	.04	.01
638 Kevin Fagan RC	.04	.01
639 Brent Jones RC	.25	.08
640 Matt Millen	.10	.02
641 Bubba Paris	.04	.01
642 Bill Romanowski RC	1.00	.40
643 Fred Smerlas UER	.04	.01
644 Dave Waymer	.04	.01
645 Steve Young	.50	.20
646 Brian Blades	.10	.02
647 Andy Heck	.04	.01
648 Dave Krieg	.10	.02
649 Rufus Porter	.04	.01
650 Kelly Stouffer	.04	.01
651 Tony Woods	.04	.01
652 Gary Anderson RB	.04	.01
653 Reuben Davis	.04	.01
654 Randy Grimes	.04	.01
655 Ron Hall	.04	.01
656 Eugene Marve	.04	.01
657A Curt Jarvis ERR	.50	.20
657B Curt Jarvis COR	10.00	4.00
658 Ricky Reynolds	.04	.01
659 Broderick Thomas	.04	.01
660 Jeff Bostic	.04	.01
661 Todd Bowles RC	.04	.01
662 Ravin Caldwell	.04	.01
663 Russ Grimm UER	.04	.01
664 Joe Jacoby	.04	.01
665 Mark May	.04	.01

❑ 666 Walter Stanley .04 .01
❑ 667 Don Warren .04 .01
❑ 668 Stan Humphries RC .25 .08
❑ 669A Jeff George Illinois SP 1.00 .40
❑ 669B Jeff George RC .50 .20
❑ 670 Blair Thomas RC .10 .02
❑ 671 Cortez Kennedy RC UER .25 .08
❑ 672 Keith McCants RC .04 .01
❑ 673 Junior Seau RC 1.25 .50
❑ 674 Mark Carrier RC DB .25 .08
❑ 675 Andre Ware .10 .02
❑ 676 Chris Singleton RC UER .04 .01
❑ 677 Richmond Webb RC .04 .01
❑ 678 Ray Agnew RC .04 .01
❑ 679 Anthony Smith RC .04 .01
❑ 680 James Francis RC .04 .01
❑ 681 Percy Snow .04 .01
❑ 682 Renaldo Turnbull RC .04 .01
❑ 683 Lamar Lathon RC .10 .02
❑ 684 James Williams DB RC .04 .01
❑ 685 Emmitt Smith RC 5.00 2.00
❑ 686 Tony Bennett RC .25 .08
❑ 687 Darrell Thompson RC .04 .01
❑ 688 Steve Broussard RC .04 .01
❑ 689 Eric Green RC .10 .02
❑ 690 Ben Smith RC .04 .01
❑ 691 Bern Brostek RC UER .04 .01
❑ 692 Rodney Hampton RC .25 .08
❑ 693 Dexter Carter RC .04 .01
❑ 694 Rob Moore RC .50 .20
❑ 695 Alexander Wright RC .04 .01
❑ 696 Darion Conner RC .10 .02
❑ 697 Reggie Rembert RC UER .04 .01
❑ 698A Terry Wooden RC 90 .50 .20
❑ 698B Terry Wooden RC 51 .04 .01
❑ 699 Reggie Cobb RC .04 .01
❑ 700 Anthony Thompson .04 .01
❑ 701 Fred Washington RC .04 .01
❑ 702 Ron Cox RC .04 .01
❑ 703 Robert Blackmon RC .04 .01
❑ 704 Dan Owens RC .04 .01
❑ 705 Anthony Johnson RC .25 .08
❑ 706 Aaron Wallace RC .04 .01
❑ 707 Harold Green RC .25 .08
❑ 708 Keith Sims RC .04 .01
❑ 709 Tim Grunhard RC .04 .01
❑ 710 Jeff Alm RC .04 .01
❑ 711 Carwell Gardner RC .04 .01
❑ 712 Kenny Davidson RC .04 .01
❑ 713 Vince Buck RC .04 .01
❑ 714 Leroy Hoard RC .25 .08
❑ 715 Andre Collins RC .04 .01
❑ 716 Dennis Brown RC .04 .01
❑ 717 LeRoy Butler RC .25 .08
❑ 718A Pat Terrell RC 41 .50 .20
❑ 718B Pat Terrell RC 37 .04 .01
❑ 719 Mike Bellamy RC .04 .01
❑ 720 Mike Fox RC .04 .01
❑ 721 Alton Montgomery RC .04 .01
❑ 722 Eric Davis RC .10 .02
❑ 723A Oliver Barnett RC DT .50 .20
❑ 723B Oliver Barnett RC NT .04 .01
❑ 724 Houston Hoover RC .04 .01
❑ 725 Howard Ballard RC .04 .01
❑ 726 Keith McKeller RC .04 .01
❑ 727 Wendell Davis RC .04 .01
❑ 728 Peter Tom Willis RC .04 .01
❑ 729 Bernard Clark .04 .01
❑ 730 Doug Widell RC .04 .01
❑ 731 Eric Andolsek .04 .01
❑ 732 Jeff Campbell RC .04 .01
❑ 733 Marc Spindler RC .04 .01
❑ 734 Keith Woodside .04 .01
❑ 735 Willis Peguese RC .04 .01
❑ 736 Frank Stams .04 .01
❑ 737 Jeff Uhlenhake .04 .01
❑ 738 Todd Kalis .04 .01
❑ 739 Tommy Hodson RC UER .04 .01
❑ 740 Greg McMurtry RC .04 .01
❑ 741 Mike Buck RC .04 .01
❑ 742 Kevin Haverdink UER .04 .01
❑ 743A Johnny Bailey RC 46 .10 .02
❑ 743B Johnny Bailey RC 22 .10 .02
❑ 744A Eric Moore .15 .05
❑ 744B Eric Moore 10.00 4.00
❑ 745 Tony Stargell RC .04 .01
❑ 746 Fred Barnett RC .25 .08
❑ 747 Walter Reeves .04 .01
❑ 748 Derek Hill .04 .01
❑ 749 Quinn Early .25 .08
❑ 750 Ronald Lewis .04 .01
❑ 751 Ken Clark RC .04 .01
❑ 752 Garry Lewis RC .04 .01
❑ 753 James Lofton .10 .02
❑ 754 Steve Tasker UER .25 .08
❑ 755 Jim Shofner CO .04 .01
❑ 756 Jimmie Jones RC .04 .01
❑ 757 Jay Novacek .25 .08
❑ 758 Jessie Hester RC .04 .01
❑ 759 Barry Word RC .04 .01
❑ 760 Eddie Anderson RC .04 .01
❑ 761 Cleveland Gary .04 .01
❑ 762 Marcus Dupree RC .04 .01
❑ 763 David Griggs RC .04 .01
❑ 764 Rueben Mayes .04 .01
❑ 765 Stephen Baker FPSC .04 .01
❑ 766 Reyna Thompson RC UER .04 .01
❑ 767 Everson Walls .04 .01
❑ 768 Brad Baxter RC .04 .01
❑ 769 Steve Walsh .10 .02
❑ 770 Heath Sherman RC .04 .01
❑ 771 Johnny Johnson RC .10 .02
❑ 772A Dexter Manley ERR 30.00 15.00
❑ 772B Dexter Manley .04 .01
❑ 773 Ricky Proehl RC .25 .08
❑ 774 Frank Cornish .04 .01
❑ 775 Tommy Kane RC .04 .01
❑ 776 Derrick Fenner RC .04 .01
❑ 777 Steve Christie RC .04 .01
❑ 778 Wayne Haddix RC .04 .01
❑ 779 Richard Williamson UER .04 .01
❑ 780 Brian Mitchell RC .25 .08
❑ 781 American Bowl/London .04 .01
❑ 782 American Bowl/Berlin .04 .01
❑ 783 American Bowl/Tokyo .04 .01
❑ 784 American Bowl/Montreal .04 .01
❑ 785A Berlin Wall .75 .30
❑ 785B Berlin Wall .75 .30
❑ 786 Al Davis NEWS .04 .01
❑ 787 Falcons Back in Black .04 .01
❑ 788 NFL Goes International .04 .01
❑ 789 Overseas Appeal .04 .01
❑ 790 Photo Contest .04 .01
❑ 791 Photo Contest .04 .01
❑ 792 Photo Contest .04 .01
❑ 793 Photo Contest .04 .01
❑ 794 Barry Sanders PHOTO .50 .20
❑ 795 Photo Contest .04 .01
❑ 796 Photo Contest .04 .01
❑ 797 Photo Contest .04 .01
❑ 798 Cris Carter PC .04 .01
❑ 799 Ronnie Lott School .10 .02
❑ 800D Mark Carrier DB D-ROY .10 .02
❑ 800O Emmitt Smith O-ROY 1.50 .60
❑ 1990 Santa Claus SP .50 .20
❑ CC2 Paul Tagliabue SP .40 .15
❑ CC3 Joe Robbie Mem SP .50 .20
❑ SC Super Pro SP .50 .20
❑ SC4 Fred Washington UER .04 .01
❑ SP1 Payne Stewart SP 1.00 .40
❑ NNO Lombardi HOLO/10000* 60.00 25.00
❑ NNO Super Bowl XXIV Logo .04 .01

1991 Pro Set

❑ COMPLETE SET (850) 20.00 8.00
❑ COMP.SERIES 1 (405) 8.00 3.00
❑ COMP.SERIES 2 (407) 8.00 3.00
❑ COMP.FINAL FACT. (38) 4.00 2.00
❑ 1D Mark Carrier DB D-ROY .10 .02
❑ 1O Emmitt Smith O-ROY 1.25 .50
❑ 3 Joe Montana POY .50 .20
❑ 4 Art Shell .10 .02
❑ 5 Mike Singletary .10 .02
❑ 6 Bruce Smith .10 .02
❑ 7 Barry Word Comeback .05 .01
❑ 8A Jim Kelly LL w/LOGO .25 .08
❑ 8B Jim Kelly LL NO LOGO .25 .08
❑ 8C Jim Kelly LL Reg NO LOGO 6.00 3.00
❑ 9 Warren Moon LL .10 .02
❑ 10 Barry Sanders LL .50 .20
❑ 11 Jerry Rice LL .40 .15
❑ 12 Jay Novacek .10 .02
❑ 13 Thurman Thomas LL .10 .02
❑ 14 Nick Lowery .05 .01
❑ 15 Mike Horan .05 .01
❑ 16 Clarence Verdin .05 .01
❑ 17 Kevin Clark LL RC .05 .01
❑ 18 Mark Carrier DB LL .10 .02
❑ 19A Derrick Thomas LL Bills 20.00 7.50
❑ 19B Derrick Thomas LL COR .10 .02
❑ 20 Ottis Anderson ML .10 .02
❑ 21 Roger Craig ML .10 .02
❑ 22 Art Monk ML .10 .02
❑ 23 Chuck Noll ML .10 .02
❑ 24 Randall Cunningham ML .10 .02
❑ 25 Dan Marino ML .50 .20
❑ 26 49ers Road Record ML .05 .01
❑ 27 Earl Campbell HOF .05 .01
❑ 28 John Hannah HOF .05 .01
❑ 29 Stan Jones HOF .05 .01
❑ 30 Tex Schramm HOF .05 .01
❑ 31 Jan Stenerud HOF .05 .01
❑ 32 Russell Maryland RC TW .10 .02
❑ 33 Chris Zorich RC TW .10 .02
❑ 34 Darryll Lewis RC Thorpe .10 .02
❑ 35 Alfred Williams RC TW .05 .01
❑ 36 Rocket Ismail RC TW 1.00 .40
❑ 37 Ty Detmer RC HH .40 .15
❑ 38 Andre Ware Heisman .10 .02
❑ 39 Barry Sanders HH .50 .20
❑ 40 Tim Brown HH .10 .02
❑ 41 Vinny Testaverde HH .10 .02
❑ 42 Bo Jackson HH .30 .10
❑ 43 Mike Rozier HH .05 .01
❑ 44 Herschel Walker HH .10 .02
❑ 45 Marcus Allen HH .10 .02
❑ 46A James Lofton SB .10 .02
❑ 46B James Lofton SB .10 .02
❑ 47A Bruce Smith SB black ink .10 .02
❑ 47B Bruce Smith SB white ink .10 .02
❑ 48 Myron Guyton SB .05 .01
❑ 49 Stephen Baker SB .05 .01
❑ 50 Mark Ingram SB UER .05 .01
❑ 51 Ottis Anderson SB .10 .02
❑ 52 Thurman Thomas SB .25 .08
❑ 53 Matt Bahr SB .05 .01
❑ 54 Scott Norwood SB .05 .01
❑ 55 Stephen Baker .05 .01
❑ 56 Carl Banks .05 .01
❑ 57 Mark Collins .05 .01
❑ 58 Steve DeOssie .05 .01
❑ 59 Eric Dorsey .05 .01
❑ 60 John Elliott .05 .01
❑ 61 Myron Guyton .05 .01
❑ 62 Rodney Hampton .25 .08
❑ 63 Jeff Hostetler .10 .02
❑ 64 Erik Howard .05 .01
❑ 65 Mark Ingram .10 .02
❑ 66 Greg Jackson RC .05 .01
❑ 67 Leonard Marshall .05 .01
❑ 68 Dave Meggett .10 .02
❑ 69 Eric Moore .05 .01
❑ 70 Bart Oates .05 .01
❑ 71 Gary Reasons .05 .01
❑ 72 Bill Parcells CO .10 .02
❑ 73 Howard Ballard .05 .01
❑ 74A Corn.Bennett w/LOGO .25 .08
❑ 74B Corn.Bennett NO LOGO .05 .01
❑ 75 Shane Conlan .05 .01
❑ 76 Kent Hull .05 .01
❑ 77 Kirby Jackson RC .05 .01
❑ 78A Jim Kelly w/LOGO .60 .25
❑ 78B Jim Kelly NO LOGO .25 .08

❑ 79 Mark Kelso	.05	.01
❑ 80 Nate Odomes	.05	.01
❑ 81 Andre Reed	.10	.02
❑ 82 Jim Ritcher	.05	.01
❑ 83 Bruce Smith	.25	.08
❑ 84 Darryl Talley	.05	.01
❑ 85 Steve Tasker	.10	.02
❑ 86 Thurman Thomas	.25	.08
❑ 87 James Williams	.05	.01
❑ 88 Will Wolford	.05	.01
❑ 89 Jeff Wright RC UER	.05	.01
❑ 90 Marv Levy CO	.05	.01
❑ 91 Steve Broussard	.05	.01
❑ 92A Darion Conner ERR '99	10.00	4.00
❑ 92B Darion Conner COR	.25	.08
❑ 93 Bill Fralic	.05	.01
❑ 94 Tim Green	.05	.01
❑ 95 Michael Haynes	.25	.08
❑ 96 Chris Hinton	.05	.01
❑ 97 Chris Miller UER	.10	.02
❑ 98 Deion Sanders UER	.40	.15
❑ 99 Jerry Glanville CO	.05	.01
❑ 100 Kevin Butler	.05	.01
❑ 101 Mark Carrier DB	.10	.02
❑ 102 Jim Covert	.05	.01
❑ 103 Richard Dent	.10	.02
❑ 104 Jim Harbaugh	.25	.08
❑ 105 Brad Muster	.05	.01
❑ 106 Lemuel Stinson	.05	.01
❑ 107 Keith Van Horne	.05	.01
❑ 108 Mike Ditka CO UER	.25	.08
❑ 109 Lewis Billups	.05	.01
❑ 110 James Brooks	.10	.02
❑ 111 Boomer Esiason	.10	.02
❑ 112 James Francis	.05	.01
❑ 113 David Fulcher	.05	.01
❑ 114 Rodney Holman	.05	.01
❑ 115 Tim McGee	.05	.01
❑ 116 Anthony Munoz	.10	.02
❑ 117 Sam Wyche CO	.05	.01
❑ 118 Paul Farren	.05	.01
❑ 119 Thane Gash	.05	.01
❑ 120 Mike Johnson	.05	.01
❑ 121A Bernie Kosar w/LOGO	.10	.02
❑ 121B Bernie Kosar NO LOGO	.10	.02
❑ 122 Clay Matthews	.10	.02
❑ 123 Eric Metcalf	.10	.02
❑ 124 Frank Minnifield	.05	.01
❑ 125A Webster Slaughter	.10	.02
❑ 125B Webster Slaughter	.10	.02
❑ 126 Bill Belichick CO RC	1.50	.60
❑ 127 Tommie Agee	.05	.01
❑ 128 Troy Aikman	.75	.30
❑ 129 Jack Del Rio	.10	.02
❑ 130 John Gesek RC	.05	.01
❑ 131 Issiac Holt	.05	.01
❑ 132 Michael Irvin	.25	.08
❑ 133 Ken Norton	.10	.02
❑ 134 Daniel Stubbs	.05	.01
❑ 135 Jimmy Johnson CO	.10	.02
❑ 136 Steve Atwater	.05	.01
❑ 137 Michael Brooks	.05	.01
❑ 138 John Elway	1.25	.50
❑ 139 Wymon Henderson	.05	.01
❑ 140 Bobby Humphrey	.05	.01
❑ 141 Mark Jackson	.05	.01
❑ 142 Karl Mecklenburg	.05	.01
❑ 143 Doug Widell	.05	.01
❑ 144 Dan Reeves CO	.05	.01
❑ 145 Eric Andolsek	.05	.01
❑ 146 Jerry Ball	.05	.01
❑ 147 Bennie Blades	.05	.01
❑ 148 Lomas Brown	.05	.01
❑ 149 Robert Clark	.05	.01
❑ 150 Michael Cofer	.05	.01
❑ 151 Dan Owens	.05	.01
❑ 152 Rodney Peete	.10	.02
❑ 153 Wayne Fontes CO	.05	.01
❑ 154 Tim Harris	.05	.01
❑ 155 Johnny Holland	.05	.01
❑ 156 Don Majkowski	.05	.01
❑ 157 Tony Mandarich	.05	.01
❑ 158 Mark Murphy	.05	.01
❑ 159 Brian Noble	.05	.01
❑ 160 Jeff Query	.05	.01
❑ 161 Sterling Sharpe	.25	.08
❑ 162 Lindy Infante CO	.05	.01
❑ 163 Ray Childress	.05	.01
❑ 164 Ernest Givins	.10	.02
❑ 165 Richard Johnson CB	.05	.01
❑ 166 Bruce Matthews	.10	.02
❑ 167 Warren Moon	.25	.08
❑ 168 Mike Munchak	.10	.02
❑ 169 Al Smith	.05	.01
❑ 170 Lorenzo White	.05	.01
❑ 171 Jack Pardee CO	.05	.01
❑ 172 Albert Bentley	.05	.01
❑ 173 Duane Bickett	.05	.01
❑ 174 Bill Brooks	.05	.01
❑ 175A E.Dickerson w/LOGO	.40	.15
❑ 175B E.Dickerson NO LOGO 667	1.25	.50
❑ 175C E.Dickerson NO LOGO 677	.25	.08
❑ 176 Ray Donaldson	.05	.01
❑ 177 Jeff George	.25	.08
❑ 178 Jeff Herrod	.05	.01
❑ 179 Clarence Verdin	.05	.01
❑ 180 Ron Meyer CO	.05	.01
❑ 181 John Alt	.05	.01
❑ 182 Steve DeBerg	.05	.01
❑ 183 Albert Lewis	.05	.01
❑ 184 Nick Lowery UER	.05	.01
❑ 185 Christian Okoye	.05	.01
❑ 186 Stephone Paige	.05	.01
❑ 187 Kevin Porter	.05	.01
❑ 188 Derrick Thomas	.25	.08
❑ 189 Marty Schottenheimer CO	.05	.01
❑ 190 Willie Gault	.10	.02
❑ 191 Howie Long	.25	.08
❑ 192 Terry McDaniel	.05	.01
❑ 193 Jay Schroeder UER	.05	.01
❑ 194 Steve Smith	.05	.01
❑ 195 Greg Townsend	.05	.01
❑ 196 Lionel Washington	.05	.01
❑ 197 Steve Wisniewski UER	.05	.01
❑ 198 Art Shell CO	.10	.02
❑ 199 Henry Ellard	.10	.02
❑ 200 Jim Everett	.10	.02
❑ 201 Jerry Gray	.05	.01
❑ 202 Kevin Greene	.10	.02
❑ 203 Buford McGee	.05	.01
❑ 204 Tom Newberry	.05	.01
❑ 205 Frank Stams	.05	.01
❑ 206 Alvin Wright	.05	.01
❑ 207 John Robinson CO	.05	.01
❑ 208 Jeff Cross	.05	.01
❑ 209 Mark Duper	.10	.02
❑ 210 Dan Marino	1.25	.50
❑ 211A Tim McKyer	.10	.02
❑ 211B Tim McKyer TR	.25	.08
❑ 212 John Offerdahl	.05	.01
❑ 213 Sammie Smith	.05	.01
❑ 214 Richmond Webb	.05	.01
❑ 215 Jarvis Williams	.05	.01
❑ 216 Don Shula CO	.10	.02
❑ 217A D.Fullington ERR	.10	.02
❑ 217B D.Fullington COR	.10	.02
❑ 218 Tim Irwin	.05	.01
❑ 219 Mike Merriweather	.05	.01
❑ 220 Keith Millard	.05	.01
❑ 221 Al Noga	.05	.01
❑ 222 Henry Thomas	.05	.01
❑ 223 Wade Wilson	.10	.02
❑ 224 Gary Zimmerman	.05	.01
❑ 225 Jerry Burns CO	.05	.01
❑ 226 Bruce Armstrong	.05	.01
❑ 227 Marv Cook FPSC	.05	.01
❑ 228 Hart Lee Dykes	.05	.01
❑ 229 Tommy Hodson	.05	.01
❑ 230 Ronnie Lippett	.05	.01
❑ 231 Ed Reynolds	.05	.01
❑ 232 Chris Singleton	.05	.01
❑ 233 John Stephens	.05	.01
❑ 234 Dick MacPherson CO	.05	.01
❑ 235 Stan Brock	.05	.01
❑ 236 Craig Heyward	.10	.02
❑ 237 Vaughan Johnson	.05	.01
❑ 238 Robert Massey	.05	.01
❑ 239 Brett Maxie	.05	.01
❑ 240 Rueben Mayes	.05	.01
❑ 241 Pat Swilling	.10	.02
❑ 242 Renaldo Turnbull	.05	.01
❑ 243 Jim Mora CO	.05	.01
❑ 244 Kyle Clifton	.05	.01
❑ 245 Jeff Criswell	.05	.01
❑ 246 James Hasty	.05	.01
❑ 247 Erik McMillan	.05	.01
❑ 248 Scott Mersereau RC	.05	.01
❑ 249 Ken O'Brien	.05	.01
❑ 250A Blair Thomas w/LOGO	.25	.08
❑ 250B Blair Thomas NO LOGO	.10	.02
❑ 251 Al Toon	.10	.02
❑ 252 Bruce Coslet CO	.05	.01
❑ 253 Eric Allen	.05	.01
❑ 254 Fred Barnett	.25	.08
❑ 255 Keith Byars	.05	.01
❑ 256 Randall Cunningham	.25	.08
❑ 257 Seth Joyner	.10	.02
❑ 258 Clyde Simmons	.05	.01
❑ 259 Jessie Small	.05	.01
❑ 260 Andre Waters	.05	.01
❑ 261 Rich Kotite CO	.05	.01
❑ 262 Roy Green	.05	.01
❑ 263 Ernie Jones	.05	.01
❑ 264 Tim McDonald	.05	.01
❑ 265 Timm Rosenbach	.05	.01
❑ 266 Rod Saddler	.05	.01
❑ 267 Luis Sharpe	.05	.01
❑ 268 Anthony Thompson UER	.05	.01
❑ 269 Marcus Turner RC	.05	.01
❑ 270 Joe Bugel CO	.05	.01
❑ 271 Gary Anderson K	.05	.01
❑ 272 Dermontti Dawson	.05	.01
❑ 273 Eric Green	.05	.01
❑ 274 Merril Hoge	.05	.01
❑ 275 Tunch Ilkin	.05	.01
❑ 276 D.J. Johnson	.05	.01
❑ 277 Louis Lipps	.05	.01
❑ 278 Rod Woodson	.25	.08
❑ 279 Chuck Noll CO	.10	.02
❑ 280 Martin Bayless	.05	.01
❑ 281 Marion Butts UER	.10	.02
❑ 282 Gill Byrd	.05	.01
❑ 283 Burt Grossman	.05	.01
❑ 284 Courtney Hall	.05	.01
❑ 285 Anthony Miller	.10	.02
❑ 286 Leslie O'Neal	.10	.02
❑ 287 Billy Joe Tolliver	.05	.01
❑ 288 Dan Henning CO	.05	.01
❑ 289 Dexter Carter	.05	.01
❑ 290 Michael Carter	.05	.01
❑ 291 Kevin Fagan	.05	.01
❑ 292 Pierce Holt	.05	.01
❑ 293 Guy McIntyre	.05	.01
❑ 294 Tom Rathman	.05	.01
❑ 295 John Taylor	.10	.02
❑ 296 Steve Young	.75	.30
❑ 297 George Seifert CO	.10	.02
❑ 298 Brian Blades	.10	.02
❑ 299 Jeff Bryant	.05	.01
❑ 300 Norm Johnson	.05	.01
❑ 301 Tommy Kane	.05	.01
❑ 302 Cortez Kennedy UER	.25	.08
❑ 303 Bryan Millard	.05	.01
❑ 304 John L. Williams	.05	.01
❑ 305 David Wyman	.05	.01
❑ 306A Chuck Knox CO w/LOGO	.05	.01
❑ 306B Chuck Knox CO NO LOGO	.50	.20
❑ 307 Gary Anderson RB	.05	.01
❑ 308 Reggie Cobb	.05	.01
❑ 309 Randy Grimes	.05	.01
❑ 310 Harry Hamilton	.05	.01
❑ 311 Bruce Hill	.05	.01
❑ 312 Eugene Marve	.05	.01
❑ 313 Ervin Randle	.05	.01
❑ 314 Vinny Testaverde	.10	.02
❑ 315 Richard Williamson CO	.05	.01
❑ 316 Earnest Byner	.05	.01
❑ 317 Gary Clark	.25	.08
❑ 318A Andre Collins	.10	.02
❑ 318B Andre Collins	.10	.02
❑ 319 Darryl Grant	.05	.01
❑ 320 Chip Lohmiller	.05	.01
❑ 321 Martin Mayhew	.05	.01
❑ 322 Mark Rypien	.10	.02
❑ 323 Alvin Walton	.05	.01
❑ 324 Joe Gibbs CO UER	.10	.02
❑ 325 Jerry Glanville REP	.05	.01
❑ 326A J.Elway REP LOGO	4.00	2.00
❑ 326B J.Elway REP NO LOGO	2.00	.75
❑ 327 Boomer Esiason REP	.05	.01
❑ 328A Steve Tasker REP	4.00	2.00

❑ 328B Steve Tasker REP 2.00 .75
❑ 329 Jerry Rice REP .40 .15
❑ 330 Jeff Rutledge REP .05 .01
❑ 331 K.C. Defense REP .05 .01
❑ 332 49ers Streak REP .05 .01
❑ 333 Monday Meeting REP .05 .01
❑ 334A R.Cunningham w/LOGO .05 .01
❑ 334B R.Cunningham NO LOGO .05 .01
❑ 335A Bo/Barry REP w/LOGO .50 .20
❑ 335B Bo/Barry REP NO LOGO .50 .20
❑ 336 Lawrence Taylor REP .25 .08
❑ 337 Warren Moon REP .25 .08
❑ 338 Alan Grant REP .05 .01
❑ 339 Todd McNair REP .05 .01
❑ 340A Miami Dolphins REP .05 .01
❑ 340B Miami Dolphins REP .05 .01
❑ 341A Highest Scoring REP 4.00 2.00
❑ 341B Highest Scoring REP 2.00 .75
❑ 342 Matt Bahr REP .05 .01
❑ 343 Robert Tisch NEW .05 .01
❑ 344 Sam Jankovich NEW .05 .01
❑ 345 In-the-Grasp NEW .05 .01
❑ 346 Bo Jackson NEW .10 .02
❑ 347 NFL Teacher of the .05 .01
❑ 348 Ronnie Lott NEW .10 .02
❑ 349 Super Bowl XXV .10 .02
❑ 350 Whitney Houston RC NEW .05 .01
❑ 351 U.S. Troops in .05 .01
❑ 352 Art McNally OFF .05 .01
❑ 353 Dick Jorgensen OFF .05 .01
❑ 354 Jerry Seeman OFF .05 .01
❑ 355 Jim Tunney OFF .05 .01
❑ 356 Gerry Austin OFF .05 .01
❑ 357 Gene Barth OFF .05 .01
❑ 358 Red Cashion OFF .05 .01
❑ 359 Tom Dooley OFF .05 .01
❑ 360 Johnny Grier OFF .05 .01
❑ 361 Pat Haggerty OFF .05 .01
❑ 362 Dale Hamer OFF .05 .01
❑ 363 Dick Hantak OFF .05 .01
❑ 364 Jerry Markbreit OFF .05 .01
❑ 365 Gordon McCarter OFF .05 .01
❑ 366 Bob McElwee OFF .05 .01
❑ 367 Howard Roe OFF .05 .01
❑ 368 Tom White OFF .05 .01
❑ 369 Norm Schachter OFF .05 .01
❑ 370A Warren Moon Crack .25 .08
❑ 370B Warren Moon Crack .25 .08
❑ 371A Boomer Esiason .50 .20
❑ 371B Boomer Esiason .10 .02
❑ 372A Troy Aikman Str.ST .40 .15
❑ 372B Troy Aikman Str.LT .40 .15
❑ 373A Carl Banks .50 .20
❑ 373B Carl Banks .05 .01
❑ 374A Jim Everett .50 .20
❑ 374B Jim Everett .10 .02
❑ 375A Anth.Munoz dificul .10 .02
❑ 375B Anth.Munoz dificil .10 .02
❑ 375C Anth.Munoz large type .10 .02
❑ 375D Anth.Munoz Quedate .10 .02
❑ 376A Ray Childress 1.25 .50
❑ 376B Ray Childress .05 .01
❑ 377A Charles Mann 1.25 .50
❑ 377B Charles Mann .05 .01
❑ 378A Jackie Slater 1.25 .50
❑ 378B Jackie Slater .05 .01
❑ 379 Jerry Rice PB .40 .15
❑ 380 Andre Rison PB .10 .02
❑ 381 Jim Lachey NFC .05 .01
❑ 382 Jackie Slater NFC .05 .01
❑ 383 Randall McDaniel NFC .05 .01
❑ 384 Mark Bortz NFC .05 .01
❑ 385 Jay Hilgenberg NFC .05 .01
❑ 386 Keith Jackson NFC .05 .01
❑ 387 Joe Montana PB .50 .20
❑ 388 Barry Sanders PB .50 .20
❑ 389 Neal Anderson NFC .05 .01
❑ 390 Reggie White NFC .25 .08
❑ 391 Chris Doleman NFC .05 .01
❑ 392 Jerome Brown NFC .05 .01
❑ 393 Charles Haley NFC .05 .01
❑ 394 Lawrence Taylor PB .25 .08
❑ 395 Pepper Johnson NFC .05 .01
❑ 396 Mike Singletary NFC .10 .02
❑ 397 Darrell Green NFC .05 .01
❑ 398 Carl Lee NFC .05 .01
❑ 399 Joey Browner NFC .05 .01
❑ 400 Ronnie Lott NFC .10 .02
❑ 401 Sean Landeta NFC .05 .01
❑ 402 Morten Andersen NFC .05 .01
❑ 403 Mel Gray NFC .05 .01
❑ 404 Reyna Thompson NFC .05 .01
❑ 405 Jimmy Johnson CO NFC .10 .02
❑ 406 Andre Reed AFC .10 .02
❑ 407 Anthony Miller AFC .10 .02
❑ 408 Anthony Munoz AFC .10 .02
❑ 409 Bruce Armstrong AFC .05 .01
❑ 410 Bruce Matthews AFC .05 .01
❑ 411 Mike Munchak AFC .05 .01
❑ 412 Kent Hull AFC .05 .01
❑ 413 Rodney Holman AFC .05 .01
❑ 414 Warren Moon PB .25 .08
❑ 415 Thurman Thomas PB .25 .08
❑ 416 Marion Butts AFC .10 .02
❑ 417 Bruce Smith AFC .10 .02
❑ 418 Greg Townsend AFC .05 .01
❑ 419 Ray Childress AFC .05 .01
❑ 420 Derrick Thomas PB .25 .08
❑ 421 Leslie O'Neal AFC .10 .02
❑ 422 John Offerdahl AFC .05 .01
❑ 423 Shane Conlan AFC .05 .01
❑ 424 Rod Woodson PB .25 .08
❑ 425 Albert Lewis AFC .05 .01
❑ 426 Steve Atwater AFC .05 .01
❑ 427 David Fulcher AFC .05 .01
❑ 428 Rohn Stark AFC .05 .01
❑ 429 Nick Lowery AFC .05 .01
❑ 430 Clarence Verdin AFC .05 .01
❑ 431 Steve Tasker AFC .05 .01
❑ 432 Art Shell CO AFC .10 .02
❑ 433 Scott Case .05 .01
❑ 434 Tory Epps UER .05 .01
❑ 435 Mike Gann UER .05 .01
❑ 436 Brian Jordan FPSC UER .10 .02
❑ 437 Mike Kenn .05 .01
❑ 438 John Rade .05 .01
❑ 439 Andre Rison .10 .02
❑ 440 Mike Rozier .05 .01
❑ 441 Jessie Tuggle .05 .01
❑ 442 Don Beebe .05 .01
❑ 443 John Davis RC .05 .01
❑ 444 James Lofton .10 .02
❑ 445 Keith McKeller .05 .01
❑ 446 Jamie Mueller .05 .01
❑ 447 Scott Norwood .05 .01
❑ 448 Frank Reich .10 .02
❑ 449 Leon Seals .05 .01
❑ 450 Leonard Smith .05 .01
❑ 451 Neal Anderson .10 .02
❑ 452 Trace Armstrong .05 .01
❑ 453 Mark Bortz .05 .01
❑ 454 Wendell Davis .05 .01
❑ 455 Shaun Gayle .05 .01
❑ 456 Jay Hilgenberg .05 .01
❑ 457 Steve McMichael .10 .02
❑ 458 Mike Singletary .10 .02
❑ 459 Donnell Woolford .05 .01
❑ 460 Jim Breech .05 .01
❑ 461 Eddie Brown .05 .01
❑ 462 Barney Bussey RC .05 .01
❑ 463 Bruce Kozerski .05 .01
❑ 464 Tim Krumrie .05 .01
❑ 465 Bruce Reimers .05 .01
❑ 466 Kevin Walker RC .05 .01
❑ 467 Ickey Woods .05 .01
❑ 468 Carl Zander UER .05 .01
❑ 469 Mike Baab .05 .01
❑ 470 Brian Brennan .05 .01
❑ 471 Rob Burnett RC .10 .02
❑ 472 Raymond Clayborn .05 .01
❑ 473 Reggie Langhorne .05 .01
❑ 474 Kevin Mack .05 .01
❑ 475 Anthony Pleasant .05 .01
❑ 476 Joe Morris .05 .01
❑ 477 Dan Fike .05 .01
❑ 478 Ray Horton .05 .01
❑ 479 Jim Jeffcoat .05 .01
❑ 480 Jimmie Jones .05 .01
❑ 481 Kelvin Martin .05 .01
❑ 482 Nate Newton .10 .02
❑ 483 Danny Noonan .05 .01
❑ 484 Jay Novacek .25 .08
❑ 485 Emmitt Smith 2.50 1.00
❑ 486 James Washington RC .05 .01
❑ 487 Simon Fletcher .05 .01
❑ 488 Ron Holmes .05 .01
❑ 489 Mike Horan .05 .01
❑ 490 Vance Johnson .05 .01
❑ 491 Keith Kartz .05 .01
❑ 492 Greg Kragen .05 .01
❑ 493 Ken Lanier .05 .01
❑ 494 Warren Powers .05 .01
❑ 495 Dennis Smith .05 .01
❑ 496 Jeff Campbell .05 .01
❑ 497 Ken Dallafior .05 .01
❑ 498 Dennis Gibson .05 .01
❑ 499 Kevin Glover .05 .01
❑ 500 Mel Gray .10 .02
❑ 501 Eddie Murray .05 .01
❑ 502 Barry Sanders 1.25 .50
❑ 503 Chris Spielman .10 .02
❑ 504 William White .05 .01
❑ 505 Matt Brock RC .05 .01
❑ 506 Robert Brown .05 .01
❑ 507 LeRoy Butler .10 .02
❑ 508 James Campen RC .05 .01
❑ 509 Jerry Holmes .05 .01
❑ 510 Perry Kemp .05 .01
❑ 511 Ken Ruettgers .05 .01
❑ 512 Scott Stephen RC .05 .01
❑ 513 Ed West .05 .01
❑ 514 Cris Dishman RC .05 .01
❑ 515 Curtis Duncan .05 .01
❑ 516 Drew Hill UER .05 .01
❑ 517 Haywood Jeffires .10 .02
❑ 518 Sean Jones .10 .02
❑ 519 Lamar Lathon .05 .01
❑ 520 Don Maggs .05 .01
❑ 521 Bubba McDowell .05 .01
❑ 522 Johnny Meads .05 .01
❑ 523A Chip Banks ERR No Text .50 .20
❑ 523B Chip Banks COR .05 .01
❑ 524 Pat Beach .05 .01
❑ 525 Sam Clancy .05 .01
❑ 526 Eugene Daniel .05 .01
❑ 527 Jon Hand .05 .01
❑ 528 Jessie Hester .05 .01
❑ 529A Mike Prior ERR No Text .50 .20
❑ 529B Mike Prior COR .05 .01
❑ 530 Keith Taylor .05 .01
❑ 531 Donnell Thompson .05 .01
❑ 532 Dino Hackett .05 .01
❑ 533 David Lutz RC .05 .01
❑ 534 Chris Martin .05 .01
❑ 535 Kevin Ross .05 .01
❑ 536 Dan Saleaumua .05 .01
❑ 537 Neil Smith .25 .08
❑ 538 Percy Snow .05 .01
❑ 539 Robb Thomas .05 .01
❑ 540 Barry Word .05 .01
❑ 541 Marcus Allen .25 .08
❑ 542 Eddie Anderson .05 .01
❑ 543 Scott Davis .05 .01
❑ 544 Mervyn Fernandez .05 .01
❑ 545 Ethan Horton .05 .01
❑ 546 Ronnie Lott .10 .02
❑ 547 Don Mosebar .05 .01
❑ 548 Jerry Robinson .05 .01
❑ 549 Aaron Wallace .05 .01
❑ 550 Flipper Anderson .05 .01
❑ 551 Cleveland Gary .05 .01
❑ 552 Damone Johnson RC .05 .01
❑ 553 Duval Love RC .05 .01
❑ 554 Irv Pankey .05 .01
❑ 555 Mike Piel .05 .01
❑ 556 Jackie Slater .05 .01
❑ 557 Michael Stewart .05 .01
❑ 558 Pat Terrell .05 .01
❑ 559 J.B. Brown .05 .01
❑ 560 Mark Clayton .10 .02
❑ 561 Ferrell Edmunds .05 .01
❑ 562 Harry Galbreath .05 .01
❑ 563 David Griggs .05 .01
❑ 564 Jim C. Jensen .05 .01
❑ 565 Louis Oliver .05 .01
❑ 566 Tony Paige .05 .01
❑ 567 Keith Sims .05 .01
❑ 568 Joey Browner .05 .01
❑ 569 Anthony Carter .10 .02
❑ 570 Chris Doleman .05 .01
❑ 571 Rich Gannon UER .25 .08

❑ 572 Hassan Jones .05 .01
❑ 573 Steve Jordan .05 .01
❑ 574 Carl Lee .05 .01
❑ 575 Randall McDaniel .05 .01
❑ 576 Herschel Walker .10 .02
❑ 577 Ray Agnew .05 .01
❑ 578 Vincent Brown .05 .01
❑ 579 Irving Fryar .10 .02
❑ 580 Tim Goad .05 .01
❑ 581 Maurice Hurst .05 .01
❑ 582 Fred Marion .05 .01
❑ 583 Johnny Rembert .05 .01
❑ 584 Andre Tippett .05 .01
❑ 585 Brent Williams .05 .01
❑ 586 Morten Andersen .05 .01
❑ 587 Toi Cook RC .05 .01
❑ 588 Jim Dombrowski .05 .01
❑ 589 Dalton Hilliard .05 .01
❑ 590 Rickey Jackson .05 .01
❑ 591 Eric Martin .05 .01
❑ 592 Sam Mills .05 .01
❑ 593 Bobby Hebert .05 .01
❑ 594 Steve Walsh .05 .01
❑ 595 Ottis Anderson .10 .02
❑ 596 Pepper Johnson .05 .01
❑ 597 Bob Kratch RC .05 .01
❑ 598 Sean Landeta .05 .01
❑ 599 Doug Riesenberg .05 .01
❑ 600 William Roberts .05 .01
❑ 601 Phil Simms .10 .02
❑ 602 Lawrence Taylor .25 .08
❑ 603 Everson Walls .05 .01
❑ 604 Brad Baxter .05 .01
❑ 605 Dennis Byrd .05 .01
❑ 606 Jeff Lageman .05 .01
❑ 607 Pat Leahy .05 .01
❑ 608 Rob Moore .25 .08
❑ 609 Joe Mott .05 .01
❑ 610 Tony Stargell .05 .01
❑ 611 Brian Washington .05 .01
❑ 612 Marvin Washington RC .05 .01
❑ 613 David Alexander .05 .01
❑ 614 Jerome Brown .05 .01
❑ 615 Byron Evans .05 .01
❑ 616 Ron Heller .05 .01
❑ 617 Wes Hopkins .05 .01
❑ 618 Keith Jackson .10 .02
❑ 619 Heath Sherman .05 .01
❑ 620 Reggie White .25 .08
❑ 621 Calvin Williams .10 .02
❑ 622 Ken Harvey .10 .02
❑ 623 Eric Hill .05 .01
❑ 624 Johnny Johnson .05 .01
❑ 625 Freddie Joe Nunn .05 .01
❑ 626 Ricky Proehl .05 .01
❑ 627 Tootie Robbins .05 .01
❑ 628 Jay Taylor .05 .01
❑ 629 Tom Tupa .05 .01
❑ 630 Jim Wahler RC .05 .01
❑ 631 Bubby Brister .05 .01
❑ 632 Thomas Everett .05 .01
❑ 633 Bryan Hinkle .05 .01
❑ 634 Carnell Lake .05 .01
❑ 635 David Little .05 .01
❑ 636 Hardy Nickerson .10 .02
❑ 637 Gerald Williams .05 .01
❑ 638 Keith Willis .05 .01
❑ 639 Tim Worley .05 .01
❑ 640 Rod Bernstine .05 .01
❑ 641 Frank Cornish .05 .01
❑ 642 Gary Plummer .05 .01
❑ 643 Henry Rolling RC .05 .01
❑ 644 Sam Seale .05 .01
❑ 645 Junior Seau .25 .08
❑ 646 Billy Ray Smith .05 .01
❑ 647 Broderick Thompson .05 .01
❑ 648 Derrick Walker RC .05 .01
❑ 649 Todd Bowles .05 .01
❑ 650 Don Griffin .05 .01
❑ 651 Charles Haley .10 .02
❑ 652 Brent Jones UER .10 .02
❑ 653 Joe Montana 1.25 .50
❑ 654 Jerry Rice .75 .30
❑ 655 Bill Romanowski .05 .01
❑ 656 Michael Walter .05 .01
❑ 657 Dave Waymer .05 .01
❑ 658 Jeff Chadwick .05 .01
❑ 659 Derrick Fenner .05 .01
❑ 660 Nesby Glasgow .05 .01
❑ 661 Jacob Green .05 .01
❑ 662 Dwayne Harper RC .05 .01
❑ 663 Andy Heck .05 .01
❑ 664 Dave Krieg .10 .02
❑ 665 Rufus Porter .05 .01
❑ 666 Eugene Robinson .05 .01
❑ 667 Mark Carrier WR .25 .08
❑ 668 Steve Christie .05 .01
❑ 669 Reuben Davis .05 .01
❑ 670 Paul Gruber .05 .01
❑ 671 Wayne Haddix .05 .01
❑ 672 Ron Hall .05 .01
❑ 673 Keith McCants UER .05 .01
❑ 674 Ricky Reynolds .05 .01
❑ 675 Mark Robinson .05 .01
❑ 676 Jeff Bostic .05 .01
❑ 677 Darrell Green .05 .01
❑ 678 Markus Koch .05 .01
❑ 679 Jim Lachey .05 .01
❑ 680 Charles Mann .05 .01
❑ 681 Wilber Marshall .05 .01
❑ 682 Art Monk .10 .02
❑ 683 Gerald Riggs .05 .01
❑ 684 Ricky Sanders .05 .01
❑ 685 Ray Handley NEW .05 .01
❑ 686 NFL announces NEW .05 .01
❑ 687 Miami gets NEW .05 .01
❑ 688 Giants' George Young NEW .05 .01
❑ 689 Five-millionth fan NEW .05 .01
❑ 690 Sports Illustrated NEW .05 .01
❑ 691 American Bowl NEW .05 .01
❑ 692 American Bowl NEW .05 .01
❑ 693 American Bowl NEW .05 .01
❑ 694A Russell Maryland .25 .08
❑ 694B Joe Ferguson LEG .05 .01
❑ 695 Carl Hairston LEG .10 .02
❑ 696 Dan Hampton LEG .10 .02
❑ 697 Mike Haynes LEG .05 .01
❑ 698 Marty Lyons LEG .05 .01
❑ 699 Ozzie Newsome LEGEND .10 .02
❑ 700 Scott Studwell LEG .05 .01
❑ 701 Mike Webster LEG .05 .01
❑ 702 Dwayne Woodruff LEG .05 .01
❑ 703 Larry Kennan CO .05 .01
❑ 704 Stan Gelbaugh RC LL .10 .02
❑ 705 John Brantley LL .05 .01
❑ 706 Danny Lockett LL .05 .01
❑ 707 Anthony Parker RC LL .10 .02
❑ 708 Dan Crossman LL .05 .01
❑ 709 Eric Wilkerson LL .05 .01
❑ 710 Judd Garrett RC LL .05 .01
❑ 711 Tony Baker LL .05 .01
❑ 712 Ran.Cunningham PHOTO .05 .01
❑ 713 2nd Place BW PHOTO .05 .01
❑ 714 3rd Place BW PHOTO .05 .01
❑ 715 1st Place Color PHOTO .05 .01
❑ 716 2nd Place Color PHOTO .05 .01
❑ 717 3rd Place Color PHOTO .05 .01
❑ 718 1st Place Color PHOTO .05 .01
❑ 719 2nd Place Color PHOTO .05 .01
❑ 720 3rd Place Color PHOTO .05 .01
❑ 721 Ray Bentley .05 .01
❑ 722 Earnest Byner .05 .01
❑ 723 Bill Fralic .05 .01
❑ 724 Joe Jacoby .05 .01
❑ 725 Howie Long .25 .08
❑ 726 Dan Marino THINK .50 .20
❑ 727 Ron Rivera .05 .01
❑ 728 Mike Singletary .10 .02
❑ 729 Cornelius Bennett .10 .02
❑ 730 Russell Maryland .25 .08
❑ 731 Eric Turner RC .10 .02
❑ 732 Bruce Pickens RC UER .05 .01
❑ 733 Mike Croel RC .05 .01
❑ 734 Todd Lyght RC .05 .01
❑ 735 Eric Swann RC .25 .08
❑ 736 Charles McRae RC .05 .01
❑ 737 Antone Davis RC .05 .01
❑ 738 Stanley Richard RC .05 .01
❑ 739 Herman Moore RC .25 .08
❑ 740 Pat Harlow RC .05 .01
❑ 741 Alvin Harper RC .25 .08
❑ 742 Mike Pritchard RC .25 .08
❑ 743 Leonard Russell RC .25 .08
❑ 744 Huey Richardson RC .05 .01
❑ 745 Dan McGwire RC .05 .01
❑ 746 Bobby Wilson RC .05 .01
❑ 747 Alfred Williams .05 .01
❑ 748 Vinnie Clark RC .05 .01
❑ 749 Kelvin Pritchett RC .10 .02
❑ 750 Harvey Williams RC .25 .08
❑ 751 Stan Thomas .05 .01
❑ 752 Randal Hill RC .10 .02
❑ 753 Todd Marinovich RC .05 .01
❑ 754 Ted Washington RC .05 .01
❑ 755 Henry Jones RC .10 .02
❑ 756 Jarrod Bunch RC .05 .01
❑ 757 Mike Dumas RC .05 .01
❑ 758 Ed King RC .05 .01
❑ 759 Reggie Johnson RC .05 .01
❑ 760 Roman Phifer RC .05 .01
❑ 761 Mike Jones DE RC .05 .01
❑ 762 Brett Favre RC 8.00 3.00
❑ 763 Browning Nagle RC .05 .01
❑ 764 Esera Tuaolo RC .05 .01
❑ 765 George Thornton RC .05 .01
❑ 766 Dixon Edwards RC .05 .01
❑ 767 Darryll Lewis .10 .02
❑ 768 Eric Bieniemy RC .05 .01
❑ 769 Shane Curry .05 .01
❑ 770 Jerome Henderson RC .05 .01
❑ 771 Wesley Carroll RC .05 .01
❑ 772 Nick Bell RC .05 .01
❑ 773 John Flannery RC .05 .01
❑ 774 Ricky Watters RC 1.50 .60
❑ 775 Jeff Graham RC WR .25 .08
❑ 776 Eric Moten RC .05 .01
❑ 777 Jesse Campbell RC .05 .01
❑ 778 Chris Zorich .10 .02
❑ 779 Joe Valerio .05 .01
❑ 780 Doug Thomas RC .05 .01
❑ 781 Lamar Rogers RC UER .05 .01
❑ 782 John Johnson RC .05 .01
❑ 783 Phil Hansen RC .05 .01
❑ 784 Kanavis McGhee RC .05 .01
❑ 785 Calvin Stephens RC UER .05 .01
❑ 786 James Jones RC DT .05 .01
❑ 787 Reggie Barrett .05 .01
❑ 788 Aeneas Williams RC .25 .08
❑ 789 Aaron Craver RC .05 .01
❑ 790 Keith Traylor RC .05 .01
❑ 791 Godfrey Myles RC .05 .01
❑ 792 Mo Lewis RC .10 .02
❑ 793 James Richard RC .05 .01
❑ 794 Carlos Jenkins RC .05 .01
❑ 795 Lawrence Dawsey RC .10 .02
❑ 796 Don Davey .05 .01
❑ 797 Jake Reed RC .50 .20
❑ 798 Dave McCloughan .05 .01
❑ 799 Erik Williams RC .10 .02
❑ 800 Steve Jackson RC .05 .01
❑ 801 Bob Dahl .05 .01
❑ 802 Ernie Mills RC .10 .02
❑ 803 David Daniels RC .05 .01
❑ 804 Rob Selby RC .05 .01
❑ 805 Ricky Ervins RC .10 .02
❑ 806 Tim Barnett RC .05 .01
❑ 807 Chris Gardocki RC .25 .08
❑ 808 Kevin Donnalley RC .05 .01
❑ 809 Robert Wilson RC .05 .01
❑ 810 Chuck Webb RC .05 .01
❑ 811 Darryl Wren RC .05 .01
❑ 812 Ed McCaffrey RC 2.00 .75
❑ 813 Shula's 300th Victory .05 .01
❑ 814 Raiders-49ers sell .05 .01
❑ 815 NFL International NEWS .05 .01
❑ 816 Moe Gardner RC .05 .01
❑ 817 Tim McKyer .05 .01
❑ 818 Tom Waddle RC .05 .01
❑ 819 Michael Jackson RC WR .25 .08
❑ 820 Tony Casillas .05 .01
❑ 821 Gaston Green .05 .01
❑ 822 Kenny Walker RC .05 .01
❑ 823 Willie Green RC .05 .01
❑ 824 Erik Kramer RC .25 .08
❑ 825 William Fuller .10 .02
❑ 826 Allen Pinkett .05 .01
❑ 827 Rick Venturi CO .05 .01
❑ 828 Bill Maas .05 .01
❑ 829 Jeff Jaeger .05 .01
❑ 830 Robert Delpino .05 .01
❑ 831 Mark Higgs RC .05 .01

❑ 832 Reggie Roby	.05	.01
❑ 833 Terry Allen RC	1.50	.60
❑ 834 Cris Carter	.50	.20
❑ 835 John Randle RC	.60	.25
❑ 836 Hugh Millen RC	.05	.01
❑ 837 Jon Vaughn RC	.05	.01
❑ 838 Gill Fenerty	.05	.01
❑ 839 Floyd Turner	.05	.01
❑ 840 Irv Eatman	.05	.01
❑ 841 Lonnie Young	.05	.01
❑ 842 Jim McMahon	.10	.02
❑ 843 Randal Hill	.05	.01
❑ 844 Barry Foster FPSC	.10	.02
❑ 845 Neil O'Donnell RC	.25	.08
❑ 846 John Friesz FPSC	.25	.08
❑ 847 Broderick Thomas	.05	.01
❑ 848 Brian Mitchell	.10	.02
❑ 849 Mike Utley RC	.10	.02
❑ 850 Mike Croel ROY	.05	.01
❑ SC1 SB XXVI Theme Art	.25	.08
❑ SC3 Jim Thorpe Pioneer	.75	.30
❑ SC4 Otto Graham Pioneer	.75	.30
❑ SC5 Paul Brown Pioneer	.75	.30
❑ PSS1 Walter Payton	.50	.20
❑ PSS2 Red Grange	.50	.20
❑ MVPC25 Ottis Anderson	.25	.08
❑ AU336 L.Taylor REP AU/500	175.00	100.00
❑ AU394 L.Taylor PB AU/500	175.00	100.00
❑ AU699 O.Newsome AU/500	50.00	25.00
❑ AU824 Erik Kramer AU	50.00	25.00
❑ NNO Mini Pro Set Gazette	.25	.08
❑ NNO Pro Set Gazette	.25	.08
❑ NNO Santa Claus	.50	.20
❑ NNO Super Bowl XXV Art	.25	.08
❑ NNO Super Bowl XXV Logo	.25	.08

1991 Pro Set Platinum

❑ COMPLETE SET (315)	10.00	5.00
❑ COMP.SERIES 1 (150)	4.00	2.00
❑ COMP.SERIES 2 (165)	6.00	3.00
❑ 1 Chris Miller	.10	.02
❑ 2 Andre Rison	.25	.08
❑ 3 Tim Green	.05	.01
❑ 4 Jessie Tuggle	.05	.01
❑ 5 Thurman Thomas	.25	.08
❑ 6 Darryl Talley	.05	.01
❑ 7 Kent Hull	.05	.01
❑ 8 Bruce Smith	.25	.08
❑ 9 Shane Conlan	.05	.01
❑ 10 Jim Harbaugh	.25	.08
❑ 11 Neal Anderson	.10	.02
❑ 12 Mark Bortz	.05	.01
❑ 13 Richard Dent	.10	.02
❑ 14 Steve McMichael	.05	.01
❑ 15 James Brooks	.05	.01
❑ 16 Boomer Esiason	.10	.02
❑ 17 Tim Krumrie	.05	.01
❑ 18 James Francis	.05	.01
❑ 19 Lewis Billups	.05	.01
❑ 20 Eric Metcalf	.25	.08
❑ 21 Kevin Mack	.05	.01
❑ 22 Clay Matthews	.10	.02
❑ 23 Mike Johnson	.05	.01
❑ 24 Troy Aikman	.75	.30
❑ 25 Emmitt Smith	2.50	1.00
❑ 26 Daniel Stubbs	.05	.01
❑ 27 Ken Norton	.10	.02
❑ 28 John Elway	1.25	.50
❑ 29 Bobby Humphrey	.05	.01
❑ 30 Simon Fletcher	.05	.01
❑ 31 Karl Mecklenburg	.05	.01
❑ 32 Rodney Peete	.10	.02
❑ 33 Barry Sanders	1.25	.50
❑ 34 Michael Cofer	.05	.01
❑ 35 Jerry Ball	.05	.01
❑ 36 Sterling Sharpe	.25	.08
❑ 37 Tony Mandarich	.05	.01
❑ 38 Brian Noble	.05	.01
❑ 39 Tim Harris	.05	.01
❑ 40 Warren Moon	.10	.02
❑ 41 Ernest Givins UER	.10	.02
❑ 42 Mike Munchak	.10	.02
❑ 43 Sean Jones	.10	.02
❑ 44 Ray Childress	.10	.02
❑ 45 Jeff George	.25	.08
❑ 46 Albert Bentley	.05	.01
❑ 47 Duane Bickett	.05	.01
❑ 48 Steve DeBerg	.10	.02
❑ 49 Christian Okoye	.10	.02
❑ 50 Neil Smith	.25	.08
❑ 51 Derrick Thomas	.25	.08
❑ 52 Willie Gault	.10	.02
❑ 53 Don Mosebar	.05	.01
❑ 54 Howie Long	.25	.08
❑ 55 Greg Townsend	.05	.01
❑ 56 Terry McDaniel	.10	.02
❑ 57 Jackie Slater	.05	.01
❑ 58 Jim Everett	.10	.02
❑ 59 Cleveland Gary	.05	.01
❑ 60 Mike Piel	.05	.01
❑ 61 Jerry Gray	.05	.01
❑ 62 Dan Marino	1.25	.50
❑ 63 Sammie Smith	.05	.01
❑ 64 Richmond Webb	.05	.01
❑ 65 Louis Oliver	.05	.01
❑ 66 Ferrell Edmunds	.05	.01
❑ 67 Jeff Cross	.05	.01
❑ 68 Wade Wilson	.05	.01
❑ 69 Chris Doleman	.10	.02
❑ 70 Joey Browner	.05	.01
❑ 71 Keith Millard	.05	.01
❑ 72 John Stephens	.05	.01
❑ 73 Andre Tippett	.05	.01
❑ 74 Brent Williams	.05	.01
❑ 75 Craig Heyward	.10	.02
❑ 76 Eric Martin	.05	.01
❑ 77 Pat Swilling	.10	.02
❑ 78 Sam Mills	.10	.02
❑ 79 Jeff Hostetler	.10	.02
❑ 80 Ottis Anderson	.10	.02
❑ 81 Lawrence Taylor	.25	.08
❑ 82 Pepper Johnson	.05	.01
❑ 83 Blair Thomas	.05	.01
❑ 84 Al Toon	.10	.02
❑ 85 Ken O'Brien	.05	.01
❑ 86 Erik McMillan	.05	.01
❑ 87 Dennis Byrd	.10	.02
❑ 88 Randall Cunningham	.25	.08
❑ 89 Fred Barnett	.25	.08
❑ 90 Seth Joyner	.10	.02
❑ 91 Reggie White	.25	.08
❑ 92 Timm Rosenbach	.05	.01
❑ 93 Johnny Johnson	.05	.01
❑ 94 Tim McDonald	.05	.01
❑ 95 Freddie Joe Nunn	.05	.01
❑ 96 Bubby Brister	.10	.02
❑ 97 Gary Anderson K UER	.05	.01
❑ 98 Merril Hoge	.05	.01
❑ 99 Keith Willis	.05	.01
❑ 100 Rod Woodson	.25	.08
❑ 101 Billy Joe Tolliver	.05	.01
❑ 102 Marion Butts	.10	.02
❑ 103 Rod Bernstine	.05	.01
❑ 104 Lee Williams	.05	.01
❑ 105 Burt Grossman UER	.05	.01
❑ 106 Tom Rathman	.05	.01
❑ 107 John Taylor	.10	.02
❑ 108 Michael Carter	.05	.01
❑ 109 Guy McIntyre	.05	.01
❑ 110 Pierce Holt	.05	.01
❑ 111 John L. Williams	.05	.01
❑ 112 Dave Krieg	.10	.02
❑ 113 Bryan Millard	.05	.01
❑ 114 Cortez Kennedy	.25	.08
❑ 115 Derrick Fenner	.05	.01
❑ 116 Vinny Testaverde	.10	.02
❑ 117 Reggie Cobb	.05	.01
❑ 118 Gary Anderson RB	.05	.01
❑ 119 Bruce Hill	.05	.01
❑ 120 Wayne Haddix	.05	.01
❑ 121 Broderick Thomas	.05	.01
❑ 122 Keith McCants	.05	.01
❑ 123 Andre Collins	.10	.02
❑ 124 Earnest Byner	.05	.01
❑ 125 Jim Lachey	.05	.01
❑ 126 Mark Rypien	.10	.02
❑ 127 Charles Mann	.05	.01
❑ 128 Nick Lowery	.05	.01
❑ 129 Chip Lohmiller	.05	.01
❑ 130 Mike Horan	.05	.01
❑ 131 Rohn Stark	.05	.01
❑ 132 Sean Landeta	.05	.01
❑ 133 Clarence Verdin	.05	.01
❑ 134 Johnny Bailey	.05	.01
❑ 135 Herschel Walker	.10	.02
❑ 136 Bo Jackson PP	.30	.10
❑ 137 Dexter Carter PP	.05	.01
❑ 138 Warren Moon PP	.10	.02
❑ 139 Joe Montana PP	1.25	.50
❑ 140 Jerry Rice PP	.75	.30
❑ 141 Deion Sanders PP	.40	.15
❑ 142 Ronnie Lippett PP	.05	.01
❑ 143 Terance Mathis	.25	.08
❑ 144 Gaston Green PP	.05	.01
❑ 145 Dean Biasucci PP	.05	.01
❑ 146 Charles Haley PP	.10	.02
❑ 147 Derrick Thomas PP	.25	.08
❑ 148 Lawrence Taylor PP	.10	.02
❑ 149 Art Shell CO PP	.10	.02
❑ 150 Bill Parcells CO PP	.10	.02
❑ 151 Steve Broussard	.05	.01
❑ 152 Darion Conner	.05	.01
❑ 153 Bill Fralic	.05	.01
❑ 154 Mike Gann	.05	.01
❑ 155 Tim McKyer	.05	.01
❑ 156 Don Beebe UER	.05	.01
❑ 157 Cornelius Bennett	.10	.02
❑ 158 Andre Reed	.25	.08
❑ 159 Leonard Smith	.05	.01
❑ 160 Will Wolford	.05	.01
❑ 161 Mark Carrier DB	.10	.02
❑ 162 Wendell Davis	.05	.01
❑ 163 Jay Hilgenberg	.05	.01
❑ 164 Brad Muster	.05	.01
❑ 165 Mike Singletary	.10	.02
❑ 166 Eddie Brown	.05	.01
❑ 167 David Fulcher	.05	.01
❑ 168 Rodney Holman	.05	.01
❑ 169 Anthony Munoz	.10	.02
❑ 170 Craig Taylor RC	.05	.01
❑ 171 Mike Baab	.05	.01
❑ 172 David Grayson	.05	.01
❑ 173 Reggie Langhorne	.05	.01
❑ 174 Joe Morris	.05	.01
❑ 175 Kevin Gogan RC	.05	.01
❑ 176 Jack Del Rio	.10	.02
❑ 177 Issiac Holt	.05	.01
❑ 178 Michael Irvin	.25	.08
❑ 179 Jay Novacek	.25	.08
❑ 180 Steve Atwater	.05	.01
❑ 181 Mark Jackson	.05	.01
❑ 182 Ricky Nattiel	.05	.01
❑ 183 Warren Powers	.05	.01
❑ 184 Dennis Smith	.05	.01
❑ 185 Bennie Blades	.05	.01
❑ 186 Lomas Brown UER	.05	.01
❑ 187 Robert Clark UER	.05	.01
❑ 188 Mel Gray	.10	.02
❑ 189 Chris Spielman	.10	.02
❑ 190 Johnny Holland	.05	.01
❑ 191 Don Majkowski	.05	.01
❑ 192 Bryce Paup RC	.25	.08
❑ 193 Darrell Thompson	.05	.01
❑ 194 Ed West UER	.05	.01
❑ 195 Cris Dishman RC	.10	.02
❑ 196 Drew Hill	.10	.02
❑ 197 Bruce Matthews	.10	.02
❑ 198 Bubba McDowell	.05	.01
❑ 199 Allen Pinkett	.05	.01
❑ 200 Bill Brooks	.10	.02
❑ 201 Jeff Herrod	.05	.01
❑ 202 Anthony Johnson	.10	.02
❑ 203 Mike Prior	.05	.01

Card		
❑ 204 John Alt	.05	.01
❑ 205 Stephone Paige	.05	.01
❑ 206 Kevin Ross	.05	.01
❑ 207 Dan Saleaumua	.05	.01
❑ 208 Barry Word	.05	.01
❑ 209 Marcus Allen	.25	.08
❑ 210 Roger Craig	.10	.02
❑ 211 Ronnie Lott	.10	.02
❑ 212 Winston Moss	.05	.01
❑ 213 Jay Schroeder	.05	.01
❑ 214 Robert Delpino	.05	.01
❑ 215 Henry Ellard	.10	.02
❑ 216 Kevin Greene	.10	.02
❑ 217 Tom Newberry	.05	.01
❑ 218 Michael Stewart	.05	.01
❑ 219 Mark Duper	.10	.02
❑ 220 Mark Higgs RC	.05	.01
❑ 221 John Offerdahl UER	.05	.01
❑ 222 Keith Sims	.05	.01
❑ 223 Anthony Carter	.10	.02
❑ 224 Cris Carter	.50	.20
❑ 225 Steve Jordan	.05	.01
❑ 226 Randall McDaniel	.05	.01
❑ 227 Al Noga	.05	.01
❑ 228 Ray Agnew	.05	.01
❑ 229 Bruce Armstrong	.05	.01
❑ 230 Irving Fryar	.10	.02
❑ 231 Greg McMurtry	.05	.01
❑ 232 Chris Singleton	.05	.01
❑ 233 Morten Andersen	.05	.01
❑ 234 Vince Buck	.05	.01
❑ 235 Gill Fenerty	.05	.01
❑ 236 Rickey Jackson	.10	.02
❑ 237 Vaughan Johnson	.05	.01
❑ 238 Carl Banks	.05	.01
❑ 239 Mark Collins	.05	.01
❑ 240 Rodney Hampton	.25	.08
❑ 241 Dave Meggett	.10	.02
❑ 242 Bart Oates	.05	.01
❑ 243 Kyle Clifton	.05	.01
❑ 244 Jeff Lageman	.10	.02
❑ 245 Freeman McNeil UER	.10	.02
❑ 246 Rob Moore	.25	.08
❑ 247 Eric Allen	.05	.01
❑ 248 Keith Byars	.10	.02
❑ 249 Keith Jackson	.10	.02
❑ 250 Jim McMahon	.10	.02
❑ 251 Andre Waters	.05	.01
❑ 252 Ken Harvey	.10	.02
❑ 253 Ernie Jones	.05	.01
❑ 254 Luis Sharpe	.05	.01
❑ 255 Anthony Thompson	.05	.01
❑ 256 Tom Tupa	.05	.01
❑ 257 Eric Green	.10	.02
❑ 258 Barry Foster	.10	.02
❑ 259 Bryan Hinkle	.05	.01
❑ 260 Tunch Ilkin	.05	.01
❑ 261 Louis Lipps	.05	.01
❑ 262 Gill Byrd	.05	.01
❑ 263 John Friesz	.10	.02
❑ 264 Anthony Miller	.10	.02
❑ 265 Junior Seau	.25	.08
❑ 266 Ronnie Harmon	.10	.02
❑ 267 Harris Barton	.05	.01
❑ 268 Todd Bowles	.05	.01
❑ 269 Don Griffin	.05	.01
❑ 270 Bill Romanowski	.05	.01
❑ 271 Steve Young	.75	.30
❑ 272 Brian Blades	.10	.02
❑ 273 Jacob Green	.05	.01
❑ 274 Rufus Porter	.05	.01
❑ 275 Eugene Robinson	.05	.01
❑ 276 Mark Carrier WR	.10	.02
❑ 277 Reuben Davis	.05	.01
❑ 278 Paul Gruber	.05	.01
❑ 279 Gary Clark	.25	.08
❑ 280 Darrell Green	.10	.02
❑ 281 Wilber Marshall	.05	.01
❑ 282 Matt Millen	.10	.02
❑ 283 Alvin Walton	.05	.01
❑ 284 Joe Gibbs CO UER	.10	.02
❑ 285 Don Shula CO UER	.10	.02
❑ 286 Larry Brown RC DB	.10	.02
❑ 287 Mike Croel RC	.05	.01
❑ 288 Antone Davis RC	.05	.01
❑ 289 Ricky Ervins RC UER	.10	.02
❑ 290 Brett Favre RC	8.00	3.00
❑ 291 Pat Harlow RC	.05	.01
❑ 292 Michael Jackson RC WR	.25	.08
❑ 293 Henry Jones RC	.10	.02
❑ 294 Aaron Craver RC	.05	.01
❑ 295 Nick Bell RC	.05	.01
❑ 296 Todd Lyght RC	.10	.02
❑ 297 Todd Marinovich RC	.05	.01
❑ 298 Russell Maryland RC	.10	.02
❑ 299 Kanavis McGhee RC	.05	.01
❑ 300 Dan McGwire RC	.10	.02
❑ 301 Charles McRae RC	.05	.01
❑ 302 Eric Moten RC	.05	.01
❑ 303 Jerome Henderson RC	.05	.01
❑ 304 Browning Nagle RC	.05	.01
❑ 305 Mike Pritchard RC	.25	.08
❑ 306 Stanley Richard RC	.10	.02
❑ 307 Randal Hill RC	.10	.02
❑ 308 Leonard Russell RC	.10	.02
❑ 309 Eric Swann RC	.10	.02
❑ 310 Phil Hansen RC	.05	.01
❑ 311 Moe Gardner RC	.05	.01
❑ 312 Jon Vaughn RC	.05	.01
❑ 313 Aeneas Williams RC	.25	.08
❑ 314 Alfred Williams RC	.05	.01
❑ 315 Harvey Williams RC	.25	.08
❑ PM1 Emmitt Smith Plat.	250.00	125.00
❑ PM2 Paul Brown Plat.	60.00	25.00

1992 Pro Set

Card		
❑ COMPLETE SET (700)	15.00	6.00
❑ COMP.SERIES 1 (400)	8.00	3.00
❑ COMP.SERIES 2 (300)	8.00	3.00
❑ 1 Mike Croel LL	.05	.01
❑ 2 Thurman Thomas LL	.25	.08
❑ 3 Wayne Fontes CO LL	.05	.01
❑ 4 Anthony Munoz LL	.10	.02
❑ 5 Steve Young LL	.30	.10
❑ 6 Warren Moon LL	.10	.02
❑ 7 Emmitt Smith LL	.60	.25
❑ 8 Haywood Jeffires LL	.05	.01
❑ 9 Marv Cook LL	.05	.01
❑ 10 Michael Irvin LL	.25	.08
❑ 11 Thurman Thomas LL	.25	.08
❑ 12 Chip Lohmiller LL UER	.05	.01
❑ 13 Barry Sanders LL	.50	.20
❑ 14 Reggie Roby LL	.05	.01
❑ 15 Mel Gray LL	.05	.01
❑ 16 Ronnie Lott LL	.10	.02
❑ 17 Pat Swilling LL	.05	.01
❑ 18 Reggie White LL	.10	.02
❑ 19 Haywood Jeffires ML	.05	.01
❑ 20 Pat Leahy MILE	.05	.01
❑ 21 James Lofton MILE	.10	.02
❑ 22 Art Monk MILE	.10	.02
❑ 23 Don Shula MILE	.10	.02
❑ 24A Nick Lowery MILE ERR	.05	.01
❑ 24B Nick Lowery MILE COR	.05	.01
❑ 25 John Elway ML	.50	.20
❑ 26 Chicago Bears MILE	.05	.01
❑ 27 Marcus Allen MILE	.10	.02
❑ 28 Terrell Buckley RC	.05	.01
❑ 29 Amp Lee RC	.05	.01
❑ 30 Chris Mims RC	.05	.01
❑ 31 Leon Searcy RC	.05	.01
❑ 32 Jimmy Smith RC	3.00	1.25
❑ 33 Siran Stacy RC	.05	.01
❑ 34 Pete Gogolak INN	.05	.01
❑ 35 Cheerleaders INN	.05	.01
❑ 36 Houston Astrodome INN	.05	.01
❑ 37 Week 1 REPLAY	.05	.01
❑ 38 Week 2 REPLAY	.05	.01
❑ 39 Week 3 REPLAY	.05	.01
❑ 40 Week 4 REPLAY	.05	.01
❑ 41 Week 5 REPLAY	.05	.01
❑ 42 Week 6 REPLAY	.05	.01
❑ 43 Thurman Thomas REP	.10	.02
❑ 44 Week 8 REPLAY	.05	.01
❑ 45 Week 9 REPLAY UER	.05	.01
❑ 46 Week 10 REPLAY	.05	.01
❑ 47 Week 11 REPLAY	.05	.01
❑ 48 Week 12 REPLAY	.05	.01
❑ 49 M.Irvin/S.Beuerlein REP	.10	.02
❑ 50 Week 14 REPLAY	.05	.01
❑ 51 Week 15 REPLAY	.05	.01
❑ 52 Week 16 REPLAY	.05	.01
❑ 53 Week 17 REPLAY	.05	.01
❑ 54 AFC Wild Card REPLAY	.05	.01
❑ 55 AFC Wild Card REPLAY	.05	.01
❑ 56 NFC Wild Card REPLAY	.05	.01
❑ 57 NFC Wild Card REPLAY	.05	.01
❑ 58 AFC Divis. Playoff REPLAY	.05	.01
❑ 59 Thurman Thomas REP	.10	.02
❑ 60 Erik Kramer REP	.05	.01
❑ 61 NFC Divis. Playoff REPLAY	.05	.01
❑ 62 AFC Championship REPLAY	.05	.01
❑ 63 NFC Championship REPLAY	.05	.01
❑ 64 Super Bowl XXVI REPLAY	.05	.01
❑ 65 Super Bowl XXVI REPLAY	.05	.01
❑ 66 Super Bowl XXVI REPLAY	.05	.01
❑ 67 Super Bowl XXVI REPLAY	.05	.01
❑ 68 Super Bowl XXVI REPLAY	.05	.01
❑ 69 Thurman Thomas REP	.10	.02
❑ 70 Super Bowl XXVI REPLAY	.05	.01
❑ 71 Super Bowl XXVI REPLAY	.05	.01
❑ 72 Super Bowl XXVI REPLAY	.05	.01
❑ 73 Jeff Bostic	.05	.01
❑ 74 Earnest Byner	.05	.01
❑ 75 Gary Clark	.25	.08
❑ 76 Andre Collins	.05	.01
❑ 77 Darrell Green	.05	.01
❑ 78 Joe Jacoby	.05	.01
❑ 79 Jim Lachey	.05	.01
❑ 80 Chip Lohmiller	.05	.01
❑ 81 Charles Mann	.05	.01
❑ 82 Martin Mayhew	.05	.01
❑ 83 Matt Millen	.10	.02
❑ 84 Brian Mitchell	.10	.02
❑ 85 Art Monk	.10	.02
❑ 86 Gerald Riggs	.05	.01
❑ 87 Mark Rypien	.05	.01
❑ 88 Fred Stokes	.05	.01
❑ 89 Bobby Wilson	.05	.01
❑ 90 Joe Gibbs CO	.10	.02
❑ 91 Howard Ballard	.05	.01
❑ 92 Cornelius Bennett UER	.10	.02
❑ 93 Kenneth Davis	.05	.01
❑ 94 Al Edwards	.05	.01
❑ 95 Kent Hull	.05	.01
❑ 96 Kirby Jackson	.05	.01
❑ 97 Mark Kelso	.05	.01
❑ 98 James Lofton	.10	.02
❑ 99 Keith McKeller	.05	.01
❑ 100 Nate Odomes	.05	.01
❑ 101 Jim Ritcher	.05	.01
❑ 102 Leon Seals	.05	.01
❑ 103 Steve Tasker	.10	.02
❑ 104 Darryl Talley	.05	.01
❑ 105 Thurman Thomas	.25	.08
❑ 106 Will Wolford	.05	.01
❑ 107 Jeff Wright	.05	.01
❑ 108 Marv Levy CO	.05	.01
❑ 109 Darion Conner	.05	.01
❑ 110 Bill Fralic	.05	.01
❑ 111 Moe Gardner	.05	.01
❑ 112 Michael Haynes	.10	.02
❑ 113 Chris Miller	.10	.02
❑ 114 Erric Pegram	.10	.02
❑ 115 Bruce Pickens	.05	.01
❑ 116 Andre Rison	.10	.02
❑ 117 Jerry Glanville CO	.05	.01
❑ 118 Neal Anderson	.05	.01
❑ 119 Trace Armstrong	.05	.01
❑ 120 Wendell Davis	.05	.01
❑ 121 Richard Dent	.10	.02
❑ 122 Jay Hilgenberg	.05	.01
❑ 123 Lemuel Stinson	.05	.01

❑ 124 Stan Thomas .05 .01
❑ 125 Tom Waddle .05 .01
❑ 126 Mike Ditka CO .25 .08
❑ 127 James Brooks .10 .02
❑ 128 Eddie Brown .05 .01
❑ 129 David Fulcher .05 .01
❑ 130 Harold Green .05 .01
❑ 131 Tim Krumrie UER .05 .01
❑ 132 Anthony Munoz .10 .02
❑ 133 Craig Taylor .05 .01
❑ 134 Eric Thomas .05 .01
❑ 135 David Shula RC CO .05 .01
❑ 136 Mike Baab .05 .01
❑ 137 Brian Brennan .05 .01
❑ 138 Michael Jackson .10 .02
❑ 139 James Jones DT UER .05 .01
❑ 140 Ed King .05 .01
❑ 141 Clay Matthews .10 .02
❑ 142 Eric Metcalf .10 .02
❑ 143 Joe Morris .05 .01
❑ 144A Bill Belichick CO NPO .25 .08
❑ 144B Bill Belichick CO .25 .08
❑ 145 Steve Beuerlein .10 .02
❑ 146 Larry Brown DB .05 .01
❑ 147 Ray Horton .05 .01
❑ 148 Ken Norton .10 .02
❑ 149 Mike Saxon .05 .01
❑ 150 Emmitt Smith 1.50 .60
❑ 151 Mark Stepnoski .10 .02
❑ 152 Alexander Wright .05 .01
❑ 153 Jimmy Johnson CO .10 .02
❑ 154 Mike Croel .05 .01
❑ 155 John Elway 1.25 .50
❑ 156 Gaston Green .05 .01
❑ 157 Wymon Henderson .05 .01
❑ 158 Karl Mecklenburg UER .05 .01
❑ 159 Warren Powers .05 .01
❑ 160 Steve Sewell UER .05 .01
❑ 161 Doug Widell .05 .01
❑ 162 Dan Reeves CO .05 .01
❑ 163 Eric Andolsek .05 .01
❑ 164 Jerry Ball .05 .01
❑ 165 Bennie Blades .05 .01
❑ 166 Ray Crockett .05 .01
❑ 167 Willie Green .05 .01
❑ 168 Erik Kramer .10 .02
❑ 169 Barry Sanders 1.25 .50
❑ 170 Chris Spielman UER .05 .01
❑ 171 Wayne Fontes CO .05 .01
❑ 172 Vinnie Clark .05 .01
❑ 173 Tony Mandarich .05 .01
❑ 174 Brian Noble .05 .01
❑ 175 Bryce Paup .25 .08
❑ 176 Sterling Sharpe .25 .08
❑ 177 Darrell Thompson .05 .01
❑ 178 Esera Tuaolo UER .05 .01
❑ 179 Ed West .05 .01
❑ 180 Mike Holmgren RC CO .25 .08
❑ 181 Ray Childress .05 .01
❑ 182 Cris Dishman .05 .01
❑ 183 Curtis Duncan .05 .01
❑ 184 William Fuller .05 .01
❑ 185 Lamar Lathon .05 .01
❑ 186 Warren Moon .25 .08
❑ 187 Bo Orlando RC .05 .01
❑ 188 Lorenzo White .05 .01
❑ 189 Jack Pardee CO .05 .01
❑ 190 Chip Banks .05 .01
❑ 191 Dean Biasucci UER .05 .01
❑ 192 Bill Brooks .05 .01
❑ 193 Ray Donaldson .05 .01
❑ 194 Jeff Herrod .05 .01
❑ 195 Mike Prior .05 .01
❑ 196 Mark Vander Poel .05 .01
❑ 197 Clarence Verdin .05 .01
❑ 198 Ted Marchibroda CO .05 .01
❑ 199 John Alt .05 .01
❑ 200 Deron Cherry .05 .01
❑ 201 Steve DeBerg .05 .01
❑ 202 Nick Lowery .05 .01
❑ 203 Neil Smith .25 .08
❑ 204 Derrick Thomas .25 .08
❑ 205 Joe Valerio .05 .01
❑ 206 Barry Word .05 .01
❑ 207 M. Schottenheimer CO .05 .01
❑ 208 Marcus Allen .25 .08
❑ 209 Nick Bell .05 .01
❑ 210 Tim Brown .25 .08
❑ 211 Howie Long .25 .08
❑ 212 Ronnie Lott .10 .02
❑ 213 Todd Marinovich .05 .01
❑ 214 Greg Townsend .05 .01
❑ 215 Steve Wright .05 .01
❑ 216 Art Shell CO .10 .02
❑ 217 Flipper Anderson .05 .01
❑ 218 Robert Delpino .05 .01
❑ 219 Henry Ellard .10 .02
❑ 220 Kevin Greene .10 .02
❑ 221 Todd Lyght .05 .01
❑ 222 Tom Newberry .05 .01
❑ 223 Roman Phifer .05 .01
❑ 224 Michael Stewart .05 .01
❑ 225 Chuck Knox CO .05 .01
❑ 226 Aaron Craver .05 .01
❑ 227 Jeff Cross .05 .01
❑ 228 Mark Duper .05 .01
❑ 229 Ferrell Edmunds .05 .01
❑ 230 Jim C. Jensen .05 .01
❑ 231 Louis Oliver UER .05 .01
❑ 232 Reggie Roby .05 .01
❑ 233 Sammie Smith .05 .01
❑ 234 Don Shula CO .10 .02
❑ 235 Joey Browner .05 .01
❑ 236 Anthony Carter .10 .02
❑ 237 Chris Doleman .05 .01
❑ 238 Steve Jordan .05 .01
❑ 239 Kirk Lowdermilk .05 .01
❑ 240 Henry Thomas .05 .01
❑ 241 Herschel Walker .10 .02
❑ 242 Felix Wright .05 .01
❑ 243 Dennis Green CO RC .10 .02
❑ 244 Ray Agnew .05 .01
❑ 245 Marv Cook .05 .01
❑ 246 Irving Fryar UER .10 .02
❑ 247 Pat Harlow .05 .01
❑ 248 Hugh Millen .05 .01
❑ 249 Leonard Russell .10 .02
❑ 250 Andre Tippett .05 .01
❑ 251 Jon Vaughn .05 .01
❑ 252 Dick MacPherson CO .05 .01
❑ 253 Morten Andersen .05 .01
❑ 254 Bobby Hebert .05 .01
❑ 255 Joel Hilgenberg .05 .01
❑ 256 Vaughan Johnson .05 .01
❑ 257 Sam Mills .05 .01
❑ 258 Pat Swilling .05 .01
❑ 259 Floyd Turner .05 .01
❑ 260 Steve Walsh .05 .01
❑ 261 Jim Mora CO UER .05 .01
❑ 262 Stephen Baker .05 .01
❑ 263 Mark Collins .05 .01
❑ 264 Rodney Hampton .10 .02
❑ 265 Jeff Hostetler .10 .02
❑ 266 Erik Howard .05 .01
❑ 267 Sean Landeta .05 .01
❑ 268 Gary Reasons UER .05 .01
❑ 269 Everson Walls .05 .01
❑ 270 Ray Handley CO .05 .01
❑ 271 Louie Aguiar RC .05 .01
❑ 272 Brad Baxter .05 .01
❑ 273 Chris Burkett .05 .01
❑ 274 Irv Eatman .05 .01
❑ 275 Jeff Lageman .05 .01
❑ 276 Freeman McNeil .05 .01
❑ 277 Rob Moore .10 .02
❑ 278 Lonnie Young .05 .01
❑ 279 Bruce Coslet CO .05 .01
❑ 280 Jerome Brown .05 .01
❑ 281 Keith Byars .05 .01
❑ 282 Bruce Collie UER .05 .01
❑ 283 Keith Jackson .10 .02
❑ 284 James Joseph .05 .01
❑ 285 Seth Joyner .05 .01
❑ 286 Andre Waters .05 .01
❑ 287 Reggie White .25 .08
❑ 288 Rich Kotite CO .05 .01
❑ 289 Rich Camarillo .05 .01
❑ 290 Garth Jax .05 .01
❑ 291 Ernie Jones .05 .01
❑ 292 Tim McDonald .05 .01
❑ 293 Rod Saddler .05 .01
❑ 294 Anthony Thompson UER .05 .01
❑ 295 Tom Tupa UER .05 .01
❑ 296 Ron Wolfley .05 .01
❑ 297 Joe Bugel CO .05 .01
❑ 298 Gary Anderson K .05 .01
❑ 299 Jeff Graham .25 .08
❑ 300 Eric Green .05 .01
❑ 301 Bryan Hinkle .05 .01
❑ 302 Tunch Ilkin .05 .01
❑ 303 Louis Lipps .05 .01
❑ 304 Neil O'Donnell .10 .02
❑ 305 Rod Woodson .25 .08
❑ 306 Bill Cowher CO RC .75 .30
❑ 307 Eric Bieniemy .05 .01
❑ 308 Marion Butts .05 .01
❑ 309 John Friesz .10 .02
❑ 310 Courtney Hall .05 .01
❑ 311 Ronnie Harmon .05 .01
❑ 312 Henry Rolling .05 .01
❑ 313 Billy Ray Smith .05 .01
❑ 314 George Thornton .05 .01
❑ 315 Bobby Ross CO RC .05 .01
❑ 316 Todd Bowles .05 .01
❑ 317 Michael Carter .05 .01
❑ 318 Don Griffin .05 .01
❑ 319 Charles Haley .10 .02
❑ 320 Brent Jones .10 .02
❑ 321 John Taylor .10 .02
❑ 322 Ted Washington .05 .01
❑ 323 Steve Young .60 .25
❑ 324 George Seifert CO .10 .02
❑ 325 Brian Blades .10 .02
❑ 326 Jacob Green .05 .01
❑ 327 Patrick Hunter .05 .01
❑ 328 Tommy Kane .05 .01
❑ 329 Cortez Kennedy .10 .02
❑ 330 Dave Krieg .10 .02
❑ 331 Rufus Porter .05 .01
❑ 332 John L. Williams .05 .01
❑ 333 Tom Flores CO .05 .01
❑ 334 Gary Anderson RB .05 .01
❑ 335 Mark Carrier WR .10 .02
❑ 336 Reuben Davis .05 .01
❑ 337 Lawrence Dawsey .10 .02
❑ 338 Keith McCants UER .05 .01
❑ 339 Vinny Testaverde .10 .02
❑ 340 Broderick Thomas .05 .01
❑ 341 Robert Wilson .05 .01
❑ 342 Sam Wyche CO .05 .01
❑ 343 1991 Teacher of .05 .01
❑ 344 Owners Reject Instant .05 .01
❑ 345 NFL Experience .05 .01
❑ 346 Chuck Noll Retires .10 .02
❑ 347 Isaac Curtis .05 .01
❑ 348 Michael Irvin/D.Pearson .10 .02
❑ 349 Barry Sanders/B.Sims .50 .20
❑ 350 Todd Marinovich/K.Stable .05 .01
❑ 351 Leonard Russell/C.James .10 .02
❑ 352 Bob Golic .05 .01
❑ 353 Pat Harlow .05 .01
❑ 354 Esera Tuaolo .05 .01
❑ 355 Mark Schlereth RC Envir. .05 .01
❑ 356 Trace Armstrong .05 .01
❑ 357 Eric Bieniemy .05 .01
❑ 358 Bill Romanowski .05 .01
❑ 359 Irv Eatman .05 .01
❑ 360 Jonathan Hayes .05 .01
❑ 361 Atlanta Falcons .05 .01
❑ 362 Chicago Bears .05 .01
❑ 363 Dallas Cowboys .05 .01
❑ 364 Detroit Lions .05 .01
❑ 365 Green Bay Packers .05 .01
❑ 366 Los Angeles Rams .05 .01
❑ 367 Minnesota Vikings .05 .01
❑ 368 New Orleans Saints UER .05 .01
❑ 369 New York Giants .05 .01
❑ 370 Philadelphia Eagles .05 .01
❑ 371 Phoenix Cardinals .05 .01
❑ 372 San Francisco 49ers .05 .01
❑ 373 Tampa Bay Buccaneers .05 .01
❑ 374 Washington Redskins .05 .01
❑ 375 Steve Atwater PB UER .05 .01
❑ 376 Cornelius Bennett PB .10 .02
❑ 377 Tim Brown PB .10 .02
❑ 378 Marion Butts PB .05 .01
❑ 379 Ray Childress PB .05 .01
❑ 380 Mark Clayton PB .05 .01
❑ 381 Marv Cook PB .05 .01
❑ 382 Cris Dishman PB .05 .01
❑ 383 William Fuller PB .05 .01

❑ 384 Gaston Green PB .05 .01
❑ 385 Jeff Jaeger PB .05 .01
❑ 386 Haywood Jeffires PB .10 .02
❑ 387 James Lofton PB .10 .02
❑ 388 Ronnie Lott PB .10 .02
❑ 389 Karl Mecklenburg PB UER .05 .01
❑ 390 Warren Moon PB .10 .02
❑ 391 Anthony Munoz PB .05 .01
❑ 392 Dennis Smith PB .05 .01
❑ 393 Neil Smith PB .10 .02
❑ 394 Darryl Talley PB .05 .01
❑ 395 Derrick Thomas PB .10 .02
❑ 396 Thurman Thomas PB .10 .02
❑ 397 Greg Townsend PB .05 .01
❑ 398 Richmond Webb PB .05 .01
❑ 399 Rod Woodson PB .10 .02
❑ 400 Dan Reeves CO PB .05 .01
❑ 401 Troy Aikman PB .40 .15
❑ 402 Eric Allen PB .05 .01
❑ 403 Bennie Blades PB .05 .01
❑ 404 Lomas Brown PB .05 .01
❑ 405 Mark Carrier DB PB .05 .01
❑ 406 Gary Clark PB .10 .02
❑ 407 Mel Gray PB .05 .01
❑ 408 Darrell Green PB .05 .01
❑ 409 Michael Irvin PB .25 .08
❑ 410 Vaughan Johnson PB .05 .01
❑ 411 Seth Joyner PB .05 .01
❑ 412 Jim Lachey PB .05 .01
❑ 413 Chip Lohmiller PB .05 .01
❑ 414 Charles Mann PB .05 .01
❑ 415 Chris Miller PB .10 .02
❑ 416 Sam Mills PB .05 .01
❑ 417 Bart Oates PB .05 .01
❑ 418 Jerry Rice PB .40 .15
❑ 419 Andre Rison PB .10 .02
❑ 420 Mark Rypien PB .05 .01
❑ 421 Barry Sanders PB .50 .20
❑ 422 Deion Sanders PB .25 .08
❑ 423 Mark Schlereth PB .05 .01
❑ 424 Mike Singletary PB .05 .01
❑ 425 Emmitt Smith PB .60 .25
❑ 426 Pat Swilling PB .05 .01
❑ 427 Reggie White PB .10 .02
❑ 428 Rick Bryan .05 .01
❑ 429 Tim Green .05 .01
❑ 430 Drew Hill .05 .01
❑ 431 Norm Johnson .05 .01
❑ 432 Keith Jones .05 .01
❑ 433 Mike Pritchard .10 .02
❑ 434 Deion Sanders .50 .20
❑ 435 Tony Smith RC RB .05 .01
❑ 436 Jessie Tuggle .05 .01
❑ 437 Steve Christie .05 .01
❑ 438 Shane Conlan .05 .01
❑ 439 Matt Darby RC .05 .01
❑ 440 John Fina RC .05 .01
❑ 441 Henry Jones .05 .01
❑ 442 Jim Kelly .25 .08
❑ 443 Pete Metzelaars .05 .01
❑ 444 Andre Reed .10 .02
❑ 445 Bruce Smith .25 .08
❑ 446 Troy Auzenne RC .05 .01
❑ 447 Mark Carrier DB .05 .01
❑ 448 Will Furrer RC .05 .01
❑ 449 Jim Harbaugh .25 .08
❑ 450 Brad Muster .05 .01
❑ 451 Darren Lewis .05 .01
❑ 452 Mike Singletary .10 .02
❑ 453 Alonzo Spellman RC .10 .02
❑ 454 Chris Zorich .10 .02
❑ 455 Jim Breech .05 .01
❑ 456 Boomer Esiason .10 .02
❑ 457 Derrick Fenner .05 .01
❑ 458 James Francis .05 .01
❑ 459 David Klingler RC .05 .01
❑ 460 Tim McGee .05 .01
❑ 461 Carl Pickens RC .25 .08
❑ 462 Alfred Williams .05 .01
❑ 463 Darryl Williams RC .05 .01
❑ 464 Mark Bavaro .05 .01
❑ 465 Jay Hilgenberg .05 .01
❑ 466 Leroy Hoard .10 .02
❑ 467 Bernie Kosar .10 .02
❑ 468 Michael Dean Perry .10 .02
❑ 469 Todd Philcox RC .05 .01
❑ 470 Patrick Rowe RC .05 .01
❑ 471 Tommy Vardell RC .05 .01
❑ 472 Everson Walls .05 .01
❑ 473 Troy Aikman .75 .30
❑ 474 Kenneth Gant RC .05 .01
❑ 475 Charles Haley .10 .02
❑ 476 Michael Irvin .25 .08
❑ 477 Robert Jones RC .05 .01
❑ 478 Russell Maryland .05 .01
❑ 479 Jay Novacek .10 .02
❑ 480 Kevin Smith RC DB .05 .01
❑ 481 Tony Tolbert .05 .01
❑ 482 Steve Atwater .05 .01
❑ 483 Shane Dronett RC .05 .01
❑ 484 Simon Fletcher .05 .01
❑ 485 Greg Lewis .05 .01
❑ 486 Tommy Maddox RC 2.00 .75
❑ 487 Shannon Sharpe .25 .08
❑ 488 Dennis Smith .05 .01
❑ 489 Sammie Smith .05 .01
❑ 490 Kenny Walker .05 .01
❑ 491 Lomas Brown .05 .01
❑ 492 Mike Farr .05 .01
❑ 493 Mel Gray .10 .02
❑ 494 Jason Hanson RC .10 .02
❑ 495 Herman Moore .25 .08
❑ 496 Rodney Peete .10 .02
❑ 497 Robert Porcher RC .25 .08
❑ 498 Kelvin Pritchett .05 .01
❑ 499 Andre Ware .05 .01
❑ 500 Sanjay Beach RC .05 .01
❑ 501 Edgar Bennett RC .25 .08
❑ 502 Lewis Billups .05 .01
❑ 503 Terrell Buckley .05 .01
❑ 504 Ty Detmer .25 .08
❑ 505 Brett Favre 2.50 1.25
❑ 506 Johnny Holland .05 .01
❑ 507 Dexter McNabb RC .05 .01
❑ 508 Vince Workman .05 .01
❑ 509 Cody Carlson .05 .01
❑ 510 Ernest Givins .10 .02
❑ 511 Jerry Gray .05 .01
❑ 512 Haywood Jeffires .10 .02
❑ 513 Bruce Matthews .05 .01
❑ 514 Bubba McDowell .05 .01
❑ 515 Bucky Richardson RC .05 .01
❑ 516 Webster Slaughter .05 .01
❑ 517 Al Smith .05 .01
❑ 518 Mel Agee .05 .01
❑ 519 Ashley Ambrose RC .25 .08
❑ 520 Kevin Call .05 .01
❑ 521 Ken Clark .05 .01
❑ 522 Quentin Coryatt RC .05 .01
❑ 523 Steve Emtman RC .05 .01
❑ 524 Jeff George .25 .08
❑ 525 Jessie Hester .05 .01
❑ 526 Anthony Johnson .10 .02
❑ 527 Tim Barnett .05 .01
❑ 528 Martin Bayless .05 .01
❑ 529 J.J. Birden .05 .01
❑ 530 Dale Carter RC .10 .02
❑ 531 Dave Krieg .10 .02
❑ 532 Albert Lewis .05 .01
❑ 533 Nick Lowery .05 .01
❑ 534 Christian Okoye .05 .01
❑ 535 Harvey Williams .25 .08
❑ 536 Aundray Bruce .05 .01
❑ 537 Eric Dickerson .10 .02
❑ 538 Willie Gault .10 .02
❑ 539 Ethan Horton .05 .01
❑ 540 Jeff Jaeger .05 .01
❑ 541 Napoleon McCallum .05 .01
❑ 542 Chester McGlockton RC .10 .02
❑ 543 Steve Smith .05 .01
❑ 544 Steve Wisniewski .05 .01
❑ 545 Marc Boutte RC .05 .01
❑ 546 Pat Carter .05 .01
❑ 547 Jim Everett .10 .02
❑ 548 Cleveland Gary .05 .01
❑ 549 Sean Gilbert RC .10 .02
❑ 550 Steve Israel RC .05 .01
❑ 551 Todd Kinchen RC .05 .01
❑ 552 Jackie Slater .05 .01
❑ 553 Tony Zendejas .05 .01
❑ 554 Robert Clark .05 .01
❑ 555 Mark Clayton .10 .02
❑ 556 Marco Coleman RC .05 .01
❑ 557 Bryan Cox .10 .02
❑ 558 Keith Jackson .10 .02
❑ 559 Dan Marino 1.25 .50
❑ 560 John Offerdahl .05 .01
❑ 561 Troy Vincent RC .05 .01
❑ 562 Richmond Webb .05 .01
❑ 563 Terry Allen .25 .08
❑ 564 Cris Carter .50 .20
❑ 565 Roger Craig .10 .02
❑ 566 Rich Gannon .25 .08
❑ 567 Hassan Jones .05 .01
❑ 568 Randall McDaniel .05 .01
❑ 569 Al Noga .05 .01
❑ 570 Todd Scott .05 .01
❑ 571 Van Waiters RC .05 .01
❑ 572 Bruce Armstrong .05 .01
❑ 573 Gene Chilton RC .05 .01
❑ 574 Eugene Chung RC .05 .01
❑ 575 Todd Collins RC .05 .01
❑ 576 Hart Lee Dykes .05 .01
❑ 577 David Howard RC .05 .01
❑ 578 Eugene Lockhart .05 .01
❑ 579 Greg McMurtry .05 .01
❑ 580 Rod Smith DB RC .05 .01
❑ 581 Gene Atkins .05 .01
❑ 582 Vince Buck .05 .01
❑ 583 Wesley Carroll .05 .01
❑ 584 Jim Dombrowski .05 .01
❑ 585 Vaughn Dunbar RC .05 .01
❑ 586 Craig Heyward .10 .02
❑ 587 Dalton Hilliard .05 .01
❑ 588 Wayne Martin .05 .01
❑ 589 Renaldo Turnbull .05 .01
❑ 590 Carl Banks .05 .01
❑ 591 Derek Brown RC TE .05 .01
❑ 592 Jarrod Bunch .05 .01
❑ 593 Mark Ingram .05 .01
❑ 594 Ed McCaffrey .30 .10
❑ 595 Phil Simms .10 .02
❑ 596 Phillippi Sparks RC .05 .01
❑ 597 Lawrence Taylor .25 .08
❑ 598 Lewis Tillman .05 .01
❑ 599 Kyle Clifton .05 .01
❑ 600 Mo Lewis .05 .01
❑ 601 Terance Mathis .10 .02
❑ 602 Scott Mersereau .05 .01
❑ 603 Johnny Mitchell RC .05 .01
❑ 604 Browning Nagle .05 .01
❑ 605 Ken O'Brien .05 .01
❑ 606 Al Toon .10 .02
❑ 607 Marvin Washington .05 .01
❑ 608 Eric Allen .05 .01
❑ 609 Fred Barnett .25 .08
❑ 610 John Booty .05 .01
❑ 611 Randall Cunningham .25 .08
❑ 612 Rich Miano .05 .01
❑ 613 Clyde Simmons .05 .01
❑ 614 Siran Stacy .05 .01
❑ 615 Herschel Walker .10 .02
❑ 616 Calvin Williams .10 .02
❑ 617 Chris Chandler .25 .08
❑ 618 Randal Hill .05 .01
❑ 619 Johnny Johnson .05 .01
❑ 620 Lorenzo Lynch .05 .01
❑ 621 Robert Massey .05 .01
❑ 622 Ricky Proehl .05 .01
❑ 623 Timm Rosenbach .05 .01
❑ 624 Tony Sacca RC .05 .01
❑ 625 Aeneas Williams UER .10 .02
❑ 626 Bubby Brister .05 .01
❑ 627 Barry Foster .10 .02
❑ 628 Merril Hoge .05 .01
❑ 629 D.J. Johnson .05 .01
❑ 630 David Little .05 .01
❑ 631 Greg Lloyd .10 .02
❑ 632 Ernie Mills .05 .01
❑ 633 Leon Searcy RC .05 .01
❑ 634 Dwight Stone .05 .01
❑ 635 Sam Anno RC .05 .01
❑ 636 Burt Grossman .05 .01
❑ 637 Stan Humphries .25 .08
❑ 638 Nate Lewis .05 .01
❑ 639 Anthony Miller .10 .02
❑ 640 Chris Mims .25 .08
❑ 641 Marquez Pope RC .05 .01
❑ 642 Stanley Richard .05 .01
❑ 643 Junior Seau .25 .08
❑ 644 Brian Bollinger RC .05 .01

❑ 645 Steve Bono RC .25 .08
❑ 646 Dexter Carter .05 .01
❑ 647 Dana Hall RC .05 .01
❑ 648 Amp Lee .05 .01
❑ 649 Joe Montana 1.25 .50
❑ 650 Tom Rathman .05 .01
❑ 651 Jerry Rice .75 .30
❑ 652 Ricky Watters .25 .08
❑ 653 Robert Blackmon .05 .01
❑ 654 John Kasay .05 .01
❑ 655 Ronnie Lee RC .05 .01
❑ 656 Dan McGwire .05 .01
❑ 657 Ray Roberts RC .05 .01
❑ 658 Kelly Stouffer .05 .01
❑ 659 Chris Warren .25 .08
❑ 660 Tony Woods .05 .01
❑ 661 David Wyman .05 .01
❑ 662 Reggie Cobb .05 .01
❑ 663A Steve DeBerg ERR .10 .02
❑ 663B Steve DeBerg COR .10 .02
❑ 664 Santana Dotson RC .10 .02
❑ 665 Willie Drewery .05 .01
❑ 666 Paul Gruber .05 .01
❑ 667 Ron Hall .05 .01
❑ 668 Courtney Hawkins RC .10 .02
❑ 669 Charles McRae .05 .01
❑ 670 Ricky Reynolds .05 .01
❑ 671 Monte Coleman .05 .01
❑ 672 Brad Edwards .05 .01
❑ 673 Jumpy Geathers UER .05 .01
❑ 674 Kelly Goodburn .05 .01
❑ 675 Kurt Gouveia .05 .01
❑ 676 Chris Hakel RC .05 .01
❑ 677 Wilber Marshall .05 .01
❑ 678 Ricky Sanders .05 .01
❑ 679 Mark Schlereth .05 .01
❑ 680 Buffalo Bills .05 .01
❑ 681 Cincinnati Bengals .05 .01
❑ 682 Cleveland Browns .05 .01
❑ 683 Denver Broncos .05 .01
❑ 684 Houston Oilers .05 .01
❑ 685 Indianapolis Colts .05 .01
❑ 686 Tracy Simien SG .05 .01
❑ 687 Los Angeles Raiders .05 .01
❑ 688 Miami Dolphins .05 .01
❑ 689 New England Patriots .05 .01
❑ 690 New York Jets .05 .01
❑ 691 Pittsburgh Steelers .05 .01
❑ 692 San Diego Chargers .05 .01
❑ 693 Seattle Seahawks .05 .01
❑ 694 Play Smart .05 .01
❑ 695 Hank Williams Jr. NEW .05 .01
❑ 696 3 Brothers in NFL NEWS .05 .01
❑ 697 Japan Bowl NEWS .05 .01
❑ 698 Georgia Dome NEWS .05 .01
❑ 699 Theme Art NEWS .05 .01
❑ 700 Mark Rypien SB MVP NEW .05 .01
❑ AU150 Emmitt Smith AU/1000 120.00 60.00
❑ AU168 Erik Kramer AU/1000 30.00 12.50
❑ NNO E.Smith Power Preview .75 .30
❑ NNO Santa Claus .50 .20
❑ SC5 Super Bowl XXVI Logo .30 .10
❑ P1 Cover Card Promo 1.00 .40

1993 Pro Set

❑ COMPLETE SET (449) 15.00 6.00
❑ 1 Marco Coleman .05 .01
❑ 2 Steve Young LL .30 .10
❑ 3 Mike Holmgren .10 .02
❑ 4 John Elway LL .75 .30
❑ 5 Steve Young LL .30 .10
❑ 6 Dan Marino LL .75 .30
❑ 7 Emmitt Smith LL .75 .30
❑ 8 Sterling Sharpe LL .10 .02
❑ 9 Jay Novacek .10 .02
❑ 10 Sterling Sharpe LL .10 .02
❑ 11 Thurman Thomas LL .10 .02
❑ 12 Pete Stoyanovich .05 .01
❑ 13 Greg Montgomery .05 .01
❑ 14 Johnny Bailey .05 .01
❑ 15 Jon Vaughn .05 .01
❑ 16 Audray McMillian .05 .01
❑ 17 Clyde Simmons .05 .01
❑ 18 Cortez Kennedy .05 .01
❑ 19 AFC Wildcard .05 .01
❑ 20 AFC Wildcard .05 .01
❑ 21 NFC Wildcard .05 .01
❑ 22 NFC Wildcard .05 .01
❑ 23 AFC Divisional .05 .01
❑ 24 Dan Marino REP .75 .30
❑ 25 Troy Aikman REP .50 .20
❑ 26 Ricky Watters REP .10 .02
❑ 27 AFC Championship .05 .01
❑ 28 NFC Championship .05 .01
❑ 29 Super Bowl XXVIII Logo .05 .01
❑ 30 Troy Aikman .75 .30
❑ 31 Thomas Everett .05 .01
❑ 32 Charles Haley .10 .02
❑ 33 Alvin Harper .10 .02
❑ 34 Michael Irvin .25 .08
❑ 35 Robert Jones .05 .01
❑ 36 Russell Maryland .05 .01
❑ 37 Ken Norton .10 .02
❑ 38 Jay Novacek .10 .02
❑ 39 Emmitt Smith 1.50 .50
❑ 40 Darrin Smith RC .10 .02
❑ 41 Mark Stepnoski .05 .01
❑ 42 Kevin Williams RC WR .25 .08
❑ 43 Daryl Johnston .25 .08
❑ 44 Derrick Lassic RC .05 .01
❑ 45 Don Beebe .05 .01
❑ 46 Cornelius Bennett .10 .02
❑ 47 Bill Brooks .05 .01
❑ 48 Kenneth Davis .05 .01
❑ 49 Jim Kelly .25 .08
❑ 50 Andre Reed .10 .02
❑ 51 Bruce Smith .25 .08
❑ 52 Thomas Smith RC .10 .02
❑ 53 Darryl Talley .05 .01
❑ 54 Thurman Thomas .25 .08
❑ 55 Russell Copeland RC .10 .02
❑ 56 Steve Christie .05 .01
❑ 57 Pete Metzelaars .05 .01
❑ 58 Frank Reich .10 .02
❑ 59 Henry Jones .05 .01
❑ 60 Vinnie Clark .05 .01
❑ 61 Eric Dickerson .10 .02
❑ 62 Jumpy Geathers .05 .01
❑ 63 Roger Harper RC .05 .01
❑ 64 Michael Haynes .10 .02
❑ 65 Bobby Hebert .05 .01
❑ 66 Lincoln Kennedy RC .05 .01
❑ 67 Chris Miller .10 .02
❑ 68 Andre Rison .10 .02
❑ 69 Deion Sanders .50 .20
❑ 70 Jessie Tuggle .05 .01
❑ 71 Ron George .05 .01
❑ 72 Erric Pegram .10 .02
❑ 73 Melvin Jenkins .05 .01
❑ 74 Pierce Holt .05 .01
❑ 75 Neal Anderson .05 .01
❑ 76 Mark Carrier DB .05 .01
❑ 77 Curtis Conway RC .40 .15
❑ 78 Richard Dent .10 .02
❑ 79 Jim Harbaugh .25 .08
❑ 80 Craig Heyward .10 .02
❑ 81 Darren Lewis .05 .01
❑ 82 Alonzo Spellman .05 .01
❑ 83 Tom Waddle .05 .01
❑ 84 Wendell Davis .05 .01
❑ 85 Chris Zorich .05 .01
❑ 86 Carl Simpson RC .05 .01
❑ 87 Chris Gedney RC .05 .01
❑ 88 Trace Armstrong .05 .01
❑ 89 Peter Tom Willis .05 .01
❑ 90 John Copeland RC .10 .02
❑ 91 Derrick Fenner .05 .01
❑ 92 James Francis .05 .01
❑ 93 Harold Green .05 .01
❑ 94 David Klingler .05 .01
❑ 95 Tim Krumrie .05 .01
❑ 96 Tony McGee RC .10 .02
❑ 97 Carl Pickens .10 .02
❑ 98 Alfred Williams .05 .01
❑ 99 Doug Pelfrey RC .05 .01
❑ 100 Lance Gunn RC .05 .01
❑ 101 Jay Schroeder .05 .01
❑ 102 Steve Tovar RC .05 .01
❑ 103 Jeff Query .05 .01
❑ 104 Ty Parten RC .05 .01
❑ 105 Jerry Ball .05 .01
❑ 106 Mark Carrier WR .10 .02
❑ 107 Rob Burnett .05 .01
❑ 108 Michael Jackson .10 .02
❑ 109 Mike Johnson .05 .01
❑ 110 Bernie Kosar .10 .02
❑ 111 Clay Matthews .10 .02
❑ 112 Eric Metcalf .10 .02
❑ 113 Michael Dean Perry .10 .02
❑ 114 Vinny Testaverde .10 .02
❑ 115 Eric Turner .05 .01
❑ 116 Tommy Vardell .05 .01
❑ 117 Leroy Hoard .10 .02
❑ 118 Steve Everitt RC .05 .01
❑ 119 Everson Walls .05 .01
❑ 120 Steve Atwater .05 .01
❑ 121 Rod Bernstine .05 .01
❑ 122 Mike Croel .05 .01
❑ 123 John Elway 1.50 .60
❑ 124 Simon Fletcher .05 .01
❑ 125 Glyn Milburn RC .25 .08
❑ 126 Reggie Rivers RC .05 .01
❑ 127 Shannon Sharpe .25 .08
❑ 128 Dennis Smith .05 .01
❑ 129 Dan Williams RC .05 .01
❑ 130 Rondell Jones RC .05 .01
❑ 131 Jason Elam RC .25 .08
❑ 132 Arthur Marshall RC .05 .01
❑ 133 Gary Zimmerman .05 .01
❑ 134 Karl Mecklenburg .05 .01
❑ 135 Bennie Blades .05 .01
❑ 136 Lomas Brown .05 .01
❑ 137 Bill Fralic .05 .01
❑ 138 Mel Gray .10 .02
❑ 139 Willie Green .05 .01
❑ 140 Ryan McNeil RC .25 .08
❑ 141 Rodney Peete .05 .01
❑ 142 Barry Sanders 1.25 .50
❑ 143 Chris Spielman .10 .02
❑ 144 Pat Swilling .05 .01
❑ 145 Andre Ware .05 .01
❑ 146 Herman Moore .25 .08
❑ 147 Tim McKyer .05 .01
❑ 148 Brett Perriman .25 .08
❑ 149 Antonio London RC .05 .01
❑ 150 Edgar Bennett .25 .08
❑ 151 Terrell Buckley .05 .01
❑ 152 Brett Favre 2.00 .75
❑ 153 Jackie Harris .05 .01
❑ 154 Johnny Holland .05 .01
❑ 155 Sterling Sharpe .25 .08
❑ 156 Tim Hauck .05 .01
❑ 157 George Teague RC .10 .02
❑ 158 Reggie White .25 .08
❑ 159 Mark Clayton .05 .01
❑ 160 Ty Detmer .25 .08
❑ 161 Wayne Simmons RC .05 .01
❑ 162 Mark Brunell RC 1.50 .60
❑ 163 Tony Bennett .05 .01
❑ 164 Brian Noble .05 .01
❑ 165 Cody Carlson .05 .01
❑ 166 Ray Childress .05 .01
❑ 167 Cris Dishman .05 .01
❑ 168 Curtis Duncan .05 .01
❑ 169 Brad Hopkins RC .05 .01
❑ 170 Haywood Jeffires .10 .02
❑ 171 Wilber Marshall .05 .01
❑ 172 Micheal Barrow RC UER .25 .08
❑ 173 Bubba McDowell .05 .01
❑ 174 Warren Moon .25 .08
❑ 175 Webster Slaughter .05 .01
❑ 176 Travis Hannah RC .05 .01
❑ 177 Lorenzo White .05 .01

❑ 178 Ernest Givins UER .10 .02
❑ 179 Keith McCants .05 .01
❑ 180 Kerry Cash .05 .01
❑ 181 Quentin Coryatt .10 .02
❑ 182 Kirk Lowdermilk .05 .01
❑ 183 Rodney Culver .05 .01
❑ 184 Rohn Stark .05 .01
❑ 185 Steve Emtman .05 .01
❑ 186 Jeff George .25 .08
❑ 187 Jeff Herrod .05 .01
❑ 188 Reggie Langhorne .05 .01
❑ 189 Roosevelt Potts RC .05 .01
❑ 190 Jack Trudeau .05 .01
❑ 191 Will Wolford .05 .01
❑ 192 Jessie Hester .05 .01
❑ 193 Anthony Johnson .10 .02
❑ 194 Ray Buchanan RC .25 .08
❑ 195 Dale Carter .05 .01
❑ 196 Willie Davis .25 .08
❑ 197 John Alt .05 .01
❑ 198 Joe Montana 1.50 .60
❑ 199 Will Shields RC .25 .08
❑ 200 Neil Smith .25 .08
❑ 201 Derrick Thomas .25 .08
❑ 202 Harvey Williams .10 .02
❑ 203 Marcus Allen .25 .08
❑ 204 J.J. Birden .05 .01
❑ 205 Tim Barnett .05 .01
❑ 206 Albert Lewis .05 .01
❑ 207 Nick Lowery .05 .01
❑ 208 Dave Krieg .10 .02
❑ 209 Keith Cash .05 .01
❑ 210 Patrick Bates RC .05 .01
❑ 211 Nick Bell .05 .01
❑ 212 Tim Brown .25 .08
❑ 213 Willie Gault .05 .01
❑ 214 Ethan Horton .05 .01
❑ 215 Jeff Hostetler .10 .02
❑ 216 Howie Long .25 .08
❑ 217 Greg Townsend .05 .01
❑ 218 Rocket Ismail .10 .02
❑ 219 Alexander Wright .05 .01
❑ 220 Greg Robinson RC .05 .01
❑ 221 Billy Joe Hobert RC .25 .08
❑ 222 Steve Wisniewski .05 .01
❑ 223 Steve Smith .05 .01
❑ 224 Vince Evans .05 .01
❑ 225 Flipper Anderson .05 .01
❑ 226 Jerome Bettis RC 4.00 1.50
❑ 227 Troy Drayton RC .10 .02
❑ 228 Henry Ellard .10 .02
❑ 229 Jim Everett .10 .02
❑ 230 Tony Zendejas .05 .01
❑ 231 Todd Lyght .05 .01
❑ 232 Todd Kinchen .05 .01
❑ 233 Jackie Slater .05 .01
❑ 234 Fred Stokes .05 .01
❑ 235 Russell White RC .10 .02
❑ 236 Cleveland Gary .05 .01
❑ 237 Sean LaChapelle RC .05 .01
❑ 238 Steve Israel .05 .01
❑ 239 Shane Conlan .05 .01
❑ 240 Keith Byars .05 .01
❑ 241 Marco Coleman .05 .01
❑ 242 Bryan Cox .05 .01
❑ 243 Irving Fryar .10 .02
❑ 244 Richmond Webb .05 .01
❑ 245 Mark Higgs .05 .01
❑ 246 Terry Kirby RC .25 .08
❑ 247 Mark Ingram .05 .01
❑ 248 John Offerdahl .05 .01
❑ 249 Keith Jackson .10 .02
❑ 250 Dan Marino 1.50 .60
❑ 251 O.J.McDuffie RC .25 .08
❑ 252 Louis Oliver .05 .01
❑ 253 Pete Stoyanovich .05 .01
❑ 254 Troy Vincent .05 .01
❑ 255 Anthony Carter .10 .02
❑ 256 Cris Carter .25 .08
❑ 257 Roger Craig .10 .02
❑ 258 Jack Del Rio .05 .01
❑ 259 Chris Doleman .05 .01
❑ 260 Barry Word .05 .01
❑ 261 Qadry Ismail RC .25 .08
❑ 262 Jim McMahon .10 .02
❑ 263 Robert Smith RC 1.25 .50
❑ 264 Fred Strickland .05 .01
❑ 265 Randall McDaniel .05 .01
❑ 266 Carl Lee .05 .01
❑ 267 Olanda Truitt RC UER .05 .01
❑ 268 Terry Allen .25 .08
❑ 269 Audray McMillian .05 .01
❑ 270 Drew Bledsoe RC 2.50 1.00
❑ 271 Eugene Chung .05 .01
❑ 272 Marv Cook .05 .01
❑ 273 Pat Harlow .05 .01
❑ 274 Greg McMurtry .05 .01
❑ 275 Leonard Russell .10 .02
❑ 276 Chris Slade RC .10 .02
❑ 277 Andre Tippett .05 .01
❑ 278 Vincent Brisby RC .25 .08
❑ 279 Ben Coates .50 .20
❑ 280 Sam Gash RC .25 .08
❑ 281 Bruce Armstrong .05 .01
❑ 282 Rod Smith DB .05 .01
❑ 283 Michael Timpson .05 .01
❑ 284 Scott Sisson RC .05 .01
❑ 285 Morten Andersen .05 .01
❑ 286 Reggie Freeman RC .05 .01
❑ 287 Dalton Hilliard .05 .01
❑ 288 Rickey Jackson .05 .01
❑ 289 Vaughan Johnson .05 .01
❑ 290 Eric Martin .05 .01
❑ 291 Sam Mills .05 .01
❑ 292 Brad Muster .05 .01
❑ 293 Willie Roaf RC .10 .02
❑ 294 Irv Smith RC .05 .01
❑ 295 Wade Wilson .05 .01
❑ 296 Derek Brown RC RBK .10 .02
❑ 297 Quinn Early .10 .02
❑ 298 Steve Walsh .05 .01
❑ 299 Renaldo Turnbull .05 .01
❑ 300 Jessie Armstead RC .10 .02
❑ 301 Carlton Bailey .05 .01
❑ 302 Michael Brooks .05 .01
❑ 303 Rodney Hampton .10 .02
❑ 304 Ed McCaffrey .25 .08
❑ 305 Dave Meggett .05 .01
❑ 306 Bart Oates .05 .01
❑ 307 Mike Sherrard .05 .01
❑ 308 Phil Simms .10 .02
❑ 309 Lawrence Taylor .25 .08
❑ 310 Mark Jackson .05 .01
❑ 311 Jarrod Bunch .05 .01
❑ 312 Howard Cross .05 .01
❑ 313 Michael Strahan RC 1.00 .40
❑ 314 Marcus Buckley RC .05 .01
❑ 315 Brad Baxter .05 .01
❑ 316 Adrian Murrell RC .25 .08
❑ 317 Boomer Esiason .10 .02
❑ 318 Johnny Johnson .05 .01
❑ 319 Marvin Jones RC .05 .01
❑ 320 Jeff Lageman .05 .01
❑ 321 Ronnie Lott .10 .02
❑ 322 Leonard Marshall .05 .01
❑ 323 Johnny Mitchell .05 .01
❑ 324 Rob Moore .10 .02
❑ 325 Browning Nagle .05 .01
❑ 326 Blair Thomas .05 .01
❑ 327 Brian Washington .05 .01
❑ 328 Terance Mathis .10 .02
❑ 329 Kyle Clifton .05 .01
❑ 330 Eric Allen .05 .01
❑ 331 Victor Bailey RC .05 .01
❑ 332 Fred Barnett .10 .02
❑ 333 Mark Bavaro .05 .01
❑ 334 Randall Cunningham .25 .08
❑ 335 Ken O'Brien .05 .01
❑ 336 Seth Joyner .05 .01
❑ 337 Leonard Renfro RC .05 .01
❑ 338 Heath Sherman .05 .01
❑ 339 Clyde Simmons .05 .01
❑ 340 Herschel Walker .10 .02
❑ 341 Calvin Williams .10 .02
❑ 342 Bubby Brister .05 .01
❑ 343 Vaughn Hebron RC .05 .01
❑ 344 Keith Millard .05 .01
❑ 345 Johnny Bailey .05 .01
❑ 346 Steve Beuerlein .10 .02
❑ 347 Chuck Cecil .05 .01
❑ 348 Larry Centers RC .25 .08
❑ 349 Chris Chandler .10 .02
❑ 350 Ernest Dye RC .05 .01
❑ 351 Garrison Hearst RC .75 .30
❑ 352 Randal Hill .05 .01
❑ 353 John Booty .05 .01
❑ 354 Gary Clark .10 .02
❑ 355 Ronald Moore RC .10 .02
❑ 356 Ricky Proehl .05 .01
❑ 357 Eric Swann .10 .02
❑ 358 Ken Harvey .05 .01
❑ 359 Ben Coleman RC .05 .01
❑ 360 Deon Figures RC .05 .01
❑ 361 Barry Foster .10 .02
❑ 362 Jeff Graham .10 .02
❑ 363 Eric Green .05 .01
❑ 364 Kevin Greene .10 .02
❑ 365 Andre Hastings RC .10 .02
❑ 366 Greg Lloyd .10 .02
❑ 367 Neil O'Donnell .25 .08
❑ 368 Dwight Stone .05 .01
❑ 369 Mike Tomczak .05 .01
❑ 370 Rod Woodson .25 .08
❑ 371 Chad Brown RC LB .10 .02
❑ 372 Ernie Mills .05 .01
❑ 373 Darren Perry .05 .01
❑ 374 Leon Searcy .05 .01
❑ 375 Marion Butts .05 .01
❑ 376 John Carney .05 .01
❑ 377 Ronnie Harmon .05 .01
❑ 378 Stan Humphries .10 .02
❑ 379 Nate Lewis .05 .01
❑ 380 Natrone Means RC .25 .08
❑ 381 Anthony Miller .10 .02
❑ 382 Chris Mims .05 .01
❑ 383 Leslie O'Neal .10 .02
❑ 384 Joe Cocozzo RC .05 .01
❑ 385 Junior Seau .25 .08
❑ 386 Jerrol Williams .05 .01
❑ 387 John Friesz .10 .02
❑ 388 Darrien Gordon RC .05 .01
❑ 389 Derrick Walker .05 .01
❑ 390 Dana Hall .05 .01
❑ 391 Brent Jones .10 .02
❑ 392 Todd Kelly RC .05 .01
❑ 393 Amp Lee .05 .01
❑ 394 Tim McDonald .05 .01
❑ 395 Jerry Rice 1.00 .40
❑ 396 Dana Stubblefield RC .25 .08
❑ 397 John Taylor .10 .02
❑ 398 Ricky Watters .25 .08
❑ 399 Steve Young .75 .30
❑ 400 Steve Bono .10 .02
❑ 401 Adrian Hardy .05 .01
❑ 402 Tom Rathman .05 .01
❑ 403 Elvis Grbac RC UER 1.50 .60
❑ 404 Bill Romanowski .05 .01
❑ 405 Brian Blades .10 .02
❑ 406 Ferrell Edmunds .05 .01
❑ 407 Carlton Gray RC .05 .01
❑ 408 Cortez Kennedy .10 .02
❑ 409 Kelvin Martin .05 .01
❑ 410 Dan McGwire .05 .01
❑ 411 Rick Mirer RC .25 .08
❑ 412 Rufus Porter .05 .01
❑ 413 Chris Warren .10 .02
❑ 414 Jon Vaughn .05 .01
❑ 415 John L. Williams .05 .01
❑ 416 Eugene Robinson .05 .01
❑ 417 Michael McCrary RC .10 .02
❑ 418 Michael Bates RC .05 .01
❑ 419 Stan Gelbaugh .05 .01
❑ 420 Reggie Cobb .05 .01
❑ 421 Eric Curry RC .05 .01
❑ 422 Lawrence Dawsey .05 .01
❑ 423 Santana Dotson .10 .02
❑ 424 Craig Erickson .10 .02
❑ 425 Ron Hall .05 .01
❑ 426 Courtney Hawkins .05 .01
❑ 427 Broderick Thomas .05 .01
❑ 428 Vince Workman .05 .01
❑ 429 Demetrius DuBose RC .05 .01
❑ 430 Lamar Thomas RC .05 .01
❑ 431 John Lynch RC .60 .25
❑ 432 Hardy Nickerson .10 .02
❑ 433 Horace Copeland RC .10 .02
❑ 434 Steve DeBerg .05 .01
❑ 435 Joe Jacoby .05 .01
❑ 436 Tom Carter RC .10 .02
❑ 437 Andre Collins .05 .01
❑ 438 Darrell Green .05 .01

❑ 439	Desmond Howard	.10	.02
❑ 440	Chip Lohmiller	.05	.01
❑ 441	Charles Mann	.05	.01
❑ 442	Tim McGee	.05	.01
❑ 443	Art Monk	.10	.02
❑ 444	Mark Rypien	.05	.01
❑ 445	Ricky Sanders	.05	.01
❑ 446	Brian Mitchell	.10	.02
❑ 447	Reggie Brooks RC	.10	.02
❑ 448	Carl Banks	.05	.01
❑ 449	Cary Conklin	.05	.01
❑ NNO	Santa Claus	1.50	.60

2000 Quantum Leaf

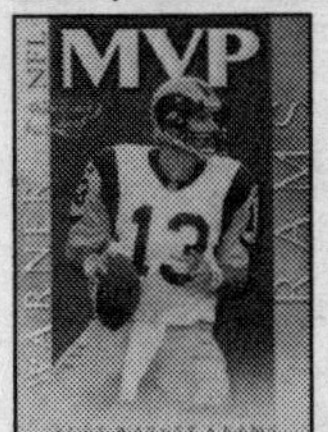

❑	COMPLETE SET (350)	150.00	60.00
❑	COMP.SET w/o SP's (300)	25.00	10.00
❑	COMP.ROOKIE UPDATE (31)	20.00	10.00
❑ 1	Frank Sanders	.75	.30
❑ 2	Adrian Murrell	.75	.30
❑ 3	Rob Moore	.75	.30
❑ 4	Simeon Rice	.75	.30
❑ 5	Michael Pittman	.50	.20
❑ 6	Jake Plummer	.75	.30
❑ 7	David Boston	1.25	.50
❑ 8	Mario Bates	.50	.20
❑ 9	Chris Chandler	.75	.30
❑ 10	Tim Dwight	1.25	.50
❑ 11	Chris Calloway	.50	.20
❑ 12	Terance Mathis	.75	.30
❑ 13	Jamal Anderson	1.25	.50
❑ 14	Byron Hanspard	.50	.20
❑ 15	Ken Oxendine	.50	.20
❑ 16	Tony Graziani	.50	.20
❑ 17	Bob Christian	.50	.20
❑ 18	Priest Holmes	1.50	.60
❑ 19	Tony Banks	.75	.30
❑ 20	Patrick Johnson	.50	.20
❑ 21	Rod Woodson	.75	.30
❑ 22	Jermaine Lewis	.50	.20
❑ 23	Errict Rhett	.75	.30
❑ 24	Stoney Case	.50	.20
❑ 25	Peter Boulware	.50	.20
❑ 26	Qadry Ismail	.75	.30
❑ 27	Brandon Stokley	.75	.30
❑ 28	Andre Reed	.75	.30
❑ 29	Eric Moulds	1.25	.50
❑ 30	Doug Flutie	1.25	.50
❑ 31	Bruce Smith	.75	.30
❑ 32	Jay Riemersma	.50	.20
❑ 33	Antowain Smith	.75	.30
❑ 34	Thurman Thomas	.75	.30
❑ 35	Jonathan Linton	.50	.20
❑ 36	Peerless Price	.75	.30
❑ 37	Rob Johnson	.75	.30
❑ 38	Sam Gash	.50	.20
❑ 39	Muhsin Muhammad	.75	.30
❑ 40	Wesley Walls	.50	.20
❑ 41	Fred Lane	.50	.20
❑ 42	Kevin Greene	.50	.20
❑ 43	Tim Biakabutuka	.75	.30
❑ 44	Steve Beuerlein	.75	.30
❑ 45	Donald Hayes	.50	.20
❑ 46	Patrick Jeffers	1.25	.50
❑ 47	Curtis Enis	.50	.20
❑ 48	Bobby Engram	.50	.20
❑ 49	Curtis Conway	.75	.30
❑ 50	Marcus Robinson	1.25	.50
❑ 51	Marty Booker	.75	.30
❑ 52	Cade McNown	.50	.20
❑ 53	Shane Matthews	.75	.30
❑ 54	Jim Miller	.50	.20
❑ 55	Darnay Scott	.75	.30
❑ 56	Carl Pickens	.75	.30
❑ 57	Corey Dillon	1.25	.50
❑ 58	Jeff Blake	.75	.30
❑ 59	Akili Smith	.50	.20
❑ 60	Michael Basnight	.50	.20
❑ 61	Karim Abdul-Jabbar	.75	.30
❑ 62	Tim Couch	.75	.30
❑ 63	Kevin Johnson	1.25	.50
❑ 64	Terry Kirby	.50	.20
❑ 65	Ty Detmer	.75	.30
❑ 66	Leslie Shepherd	.50	.20
❑ 67	Darrin Chiaverini	.50	.20
❑ 68	Emmitt Smith	2.50	1.00
❑ 69	Deion Sanders	1.25	.50
❑ 70	Michael Irvin	.75	.30
❑ 71	Rocket Ismail	.75	.30
❑ 72	Troy Aikman	2.50	1.00
❑ 73	Daryl Johnston	.75	.30
❑ 74	Chris Warren	.50	.20
❑ 75	Jason Garrett	.75	.30
❑ 76	Jason Tucker	.50	.20
❑ 77	Lawyer Milloy	.75	.30
❑ 78	Dexter Coakley	.50	.20
❑ 79	Greg Ellis	.50	.20
❑ 80	David LaFleur	.50	.20
❑ 81	Todd Lyght	.50	.20
❑ 82	Ernie Mills	.50	.20
❑ 83	Wane McGarity	.50	.20
❑ 84	Chris Brazzell RC	.75	.30
❑ 85	Ed McCaffrey	1.25	.50
❑ 86	Rod Smith	.75	.30
❑ 87	Shannon Sharpe	.75	.30
❑ 88	Brian Griese	1.25	.50
❑ 89	John Elway	4.00	1.50
❑ 90	Neil Smith	.75	.30
❑ 91	Terrell Davis	1.25	.50
❑ 92	Olandis Gary	1.25	.50
❑ 93	Derek Loville	.50	.20
❑ 94	John Avery	.50	.20
❑ 95	Bubby Brister	.50	.20
❑ 96	Byron Chamberlain	.50	.20
❑ 97	Dale Carter	.50	.20
❑ 98	Johnnie Morton	.75	.30
❑ 99	Charlie Batch	1.25	.50
❑ 100	Barry Sanders	3.00	1.25
❑ 101	Germane Crowell	.50	.20
❑ 102	Gus Frerotte	.50	.20
❑ 103	Desmond Howard	.50	.20
❑ 104	Terry Fair	.50	.20
❑ 105	Ron Rivers	.50	.20
❑ 106	Greg Hill	.50	.20
❑ 107	Sedrick Irvin	.50	.20
❑ 108	David Sloan	.50	.20
❑ 109	Herman Moore	.75	.30
❑ 110	Robert Porcher	.50	.20
❑ 111	Corey Bradford	.75	.30
❑ 112	Dorsey Levens	.75	.30
❑ 113	Antonio Freeman	1.25	.50
❑ 114	Brett Favre	4.00	1.50
❑ 115	De'Mond Parker	.50	.20
❑ 116	Bill Schroeder	.75	.30
❑ 117	Matt Hasselbeck	.75	.30
❑ 118	Donald Driver	1.25	.50
❑ 119	Basil Mitchell	.50	.20
❑ 120	E.G. Green	.50	.20
❑ 121	Ken Dilger	.50	.20
❑ 122	Marvin Harrison	1.25	.50
❑ 123	Peyton Manning	3.00	1.25
❑ 124	Terrence Wilkins	.50	.20
❑ 125	Edgerrin James	2.00	.75
❑ 126	Jerome Pathon	.75	.30
❑ 127	Marcus Pollard	.50	.20
❑ 128	Keenan McCardell	.75	.30
❑ 129	Mark Brunell	1.25	.50
❑ 130	Fred Taylor	1.25	.50
❑ 131	Jimmy Smith	.75	.30
❑ 132	James Stewart	.75	.30
❑ 133	Kyle Brady	.50	.20
❑ 134	Tony Brackens	.50	.20
❑ 135	Derrick Thomas	1.25	.50
❑ 136	Rashaan Shehee	.50	.20
❑ 137	Derrick Alexander	.75	.30
❑ 138	Bam Morris	.50	.20
❑ 139	Andre Rison	.75	.30
❑ 140	Elvis Grbac	.75	.30
❑ 141	Tony Gonzalez	.75	.30
❑ 142	Donnell Bennett	.50	.20
❑ 143	Warren Moon	1.25	.50
❑ 144	Tamarick Vanover	.50	.20
❑ 145	Kimble Anders	.50	.20
❑ 146	Tony Richardson RC	.75	.30
❑ 147	Zach Thomas	1.25	.50
❑ 148	Oronde Gadsden	.75	.30
❑ 149	Dan Marino	4.00	1.50
❑ 150	O.J. McDuffie	.75	.30
❑ 151	Tony Martin	.75	.30
❑ 152	Cecil Collins	.50	.20
❑ 153	James Johnson	.50	.20
❑ 154	Rob Konrad	.50	.20
❑ 155	Yatil Green	.50	.20
❑ 156	Damon Huard	1.25	.50
❑ 157	Nate Jacquet	.50	.20
❑ 158	Stanley Pritchett	.50	.20
❑ 159	Sam Madison	.50	.20
❑ 160	Randy Moss	2.50	1.00
❑ 161	Cris Carter	1.25	.50
❑ 162	Robert Smith	1.25	.50
❑ 163	Randall Cunningham	1.25	.50
❑ 164	Jake Reed	.75	.30
❑ 165	John Randle	.75	.30
❑ 166	Leroy Hoard	.50	.20
❑ 167	Jeff George	.75	.30
❑ 168	Daunte Culpepper	1.50	.60
❑ 169	Matthew Hatchette	.50	.20
❑ 170	Robert Tate	.50	.20
❑ 171	Ty Law	.75	.30
❑ 172	Troy Brown	.75	.30
❑ 173	Tony Simmons	.50	.20
❑ 174	Terry Glenn	.75	.30
❑ 175	Ben Coates	.50	.20
❑ 176	Drew Bledsoe	1.50	.60
❑ 177	Terry Allen	.75	.30
❑ 178	Kevin Faulk	.75	.30
❑ 179	Shawn Jefferson	.50	.20
❑ 180	Andy Katzenmoyer	.50	.20
❑ 181	Willie McGinest	.50	.20
❑ 182	Cameron Cleeland	.50	.20
❑ 183	Eddie Kennison	.75	.30
❑ 184	Ricky Williams	1.25	.50
❑ 185	Danny Wuerffel	.50	.20
❑ 186	Brett Bech	.50	.20
❑ 187	Billy Joe Hobert	.50	.20
❑ 188	Jake Delhomme RC	5.00	2.00
❑ 189	Wilmont Perry	.50	.20
❑ 190	Keith Poole	.50	.20
❑ 191	Ashley Ambrose	.50	.20
❑ 192	Amani Toomer	.50	.20
❑ 193	Kerry Collins	.75	.30
❑ 194	Tiki Barber	1.25	.50
❑ 195	Ike Hilliard	.75	.30
❑ 196	Jason Sehorn	.50	.20
❑ 197	Joe Montgomery	.50	.20
❑ 198	Joe Jurevicius	.50	.20
❑ 199	Michael Strahan	.75	.30
❑ 200	Sean Bennett	.50	.20
❑ 201	Jessie Armstead	.50	.20
❑ 202	Pete Mitchell	.50	.20
❑ 203	Curtis Martin	1.25	.50
❑ 204	Vinny Testaverde	.75	.30
❑ 205	Keyshawn Johnson	1.25	.50
❑ 206	Wayne Chrebet	.75	.30
❑ 207	Ray Lucas	.75	.30
❑ 208	Tyrone Wheatley	.75	.30
❑ 209	Napoleon Kaufman	.75	.30
❑ 210	Tim Brown	1.25	.50
❑ 211	Rickey Dudley	.50	.20
❑ 212	James Jett	.50	.20
❑ 213	Rich Gannon	1.25	.50
❑ 214	Charles Woodson	.75	.30
❑ 215	Zack Crockett	.50	.20
❑ 216	Darrell Russell	.50	.20
❑ 217	Duce Staley	1.25	.50
❑ 218	Donovan McNabb	2.00	.75
❑ 219	Charles Johnson	.75	.30
❑ 220	Dameane Douglas	.50	.20
❑ 221	Doug Pederson	.50	.20
❑ 222	Torrance Small	.50	.20
❑ 223	Troy Vincent	.50	.20
❑ 224	Na Brown	.50	.20
❑ 225	Kordell Stewart	.75	.30
❑ 226	Jerome Bettis	1.25	.50

❑ 227	Hines Ward	1.25	.50
❑ 228	Troy Edwards	.50	.20
❑ 229	Richard Huntley	.50	.20
❑ 230	Mark Bruener	.50	.20
❑ 231	Pete Gonzalez	.50	.20
❑ 232	Levon Kirkland	.50	.20
❑ 233	Bobby Shaw RC	1.25	.50
❑ 234	Amos Zereoue	1.25	.50
❑ 235	Natrone Means	.50	.20
❑ 236	Junior Seau	1.25	.50
❑ 237	Jim Harbaugh	.75	.30
❑ 238	Ryan Leaf	.75	.30
❑ 239	Mikhael Ricks	.50	.20
❑ 240	Jermaine Fazande	.50	.20
❑ 241	Jeff Graham	.50	.20
❑ 242	Tremayne Stephens	.50	.20
❑ 243	Terrell Owens	1.25	.50
❑ 244	J.J. Stokes	.75	.30
❑ 245	Charlie Garner	.75	.30
❑ 246	Jerry Rice	2.50	1.00
❑ 247	Garrison Hearst	.75	.30
❑ 248	Steve Young	1.50	.60
❑ 249	Jeff Garcia	1.25	.50
❑ 250	Fred Beasley	.50	.20
❑ 251	Bryant Young	.50	.20
❑ 252	Derrick Mayes	.75	.30
❑ 253	Ahman Green	1.25	.50
❑ 254	Joey Galloway	.75	.30
❑ 255	Ricky Watters	.75	.30
❑ 256	Jon Kitna	1.25	.50
❑ 257	Sean Dawkins	.50	.20
❑ 258	Sam Adams	.50	.20
❑ 259	Christian Fauria	.50	.20
❑ 260	Shawn Springs	.50	.20
❑ 261	Az-Zahir Hakim	.75	.30
❑ 262	Isaac Bruce	1.25	.50
❑ 263	Marshall Faulk	1.50	.60
❑ 264	Trent Green	1.25	.50
❑ 265	Kurt Warner	2.50	1.00
❑ 266	Torry Holt	1.25	.50
❑ 267	Robert Holcombe	.50	.20
❑ 268	Kevin Carter	.50	.20
❑ 269	Amp Lee	.50	.20
❑ 270	Roland Williams	.50	.20
❑ 271	Jacquez Green	.50	.20
❑ 272	Reidel Anthony	.50	.20
❑ 273	Warren Sapp	.75	.30
❑ 274	Mike Alstott	1.25	.50
❑ 275	Warrick Dunn	1.25	.50
❑ 276	Trent Dilfer	.75	.30
❑ 277	Shaun King	.50	.20
❑ 278	Bert Emanuel	.50	.20
❑ 279	Eric Zeier	.50	.20
❑ 280	Neil O'Donnell	.50	.20
❑ 281	Eddie George	1.25	.50
❑ 282	Yancey Thigpen	.50	.20
❑ 283	Steve McNair	1.25	.50
❑ 284	Kevin Dyson	.75	.30
❑ 285	Frank Wycheck	.50	.20
❑ 286	Jevon Kearse	1.25	.50
❑ 287	Bruce Matthews	.50	.20
❑ 288	Lorenzo Neal	.50	.20
❑ 289	Stephen Davis	1.25	.50
❑ 290	Stephen Alexander	.50	.20
❑ 291	Darrell Green	.50	.20
❑ 292	Skip Hicks	.50	.20
❑ 293	Brad Johnson	1.25	.50
❑ 294	Michael Westbrook	.75	.30
❑ 295	Albert Connell	.50	.20
❑ 296	Irving Fryar	.75	.30
❑ 297	Champ Bailey	.75	.30
❑ 298	Larry Centers	.50	.20
❑ 299	Brian Mitchell	.50	.20
❑ 300	James Thrash	1.25	.50
❑ 301	LaVar Arrington RC	10.00	5.00
❑ 302	Peter Warrick RC	2.50	1.00
❑ 303	Courtney Brown RC	2.50	1.00
❑ 304	Plaxico Burress RC	5.00	2.00
❑ 305	Corey Simon RC	2.50	1.00
❑ 306	Thomas Jones RC	4.00	1.50
❑ 307	Travis Taylor RC	2.50	1.00
❑ 308	Shaun Alexander RC	12.00	5.00
❑ 309	Chris Redman RC	2.00	.75
❑ 310	Chad Pennington RC	6.00	2.50
❑ 311	Jamal Lewis RC	6.00	2.50
❑ 312	Brian Urlacher RC	10.00	4.00
❑ 313	Keith Bulluck RC	2.50	1.00
❑ 314	Bubba Franks RC	2.50	1.00
❑ 315	Dez White RC	2.50	1.00
❑ 316	Ahmed Plummer RC	2.50	1.00
❑ 317	Ron Dayne RC	2.50	1.00
❑ 318	Shaun Ellis RC	2.50	1.00
❑ 319	Sylvester Morris RC	2.00	.75
❑ 320	Deltha O'Neal RC	2.50	1.00
❑ 321	R.Jay Soward RC	2.00	.75
❑ 322	Sherrod Gideon RC	1.50	.60
❑ 323	John Abraham RC	2.50	1.00
❑ 324	Travis Prentice RC	2.00	.75
❑ 325	Darrell Jackson RC	5.00	2.00
❑ 326	Giovanni Carmazzi RC	1.50	.60
❑ 327	Anthony Lucas RC	1.50	.60
❑ 328	Danny Farmer RC	2.00	.75
❑ 329	Dennis Northcutt RC	2.50	1.00
❑ 330	Troy Walters RC	2.50	1.00
❑ 331	Laveranues Coles RC	3.00	1.25
❑ 332	Tee Martin RC	2.50	1.00
❑ 333	J.R. Redmond RC	2.00	.75
❑ 334	Jerry Porter RC	3.00	1.25
❑ 335	Sebastian Janikowski RC	2.00	.75
❑ 336	Michael Wiley RC	2.00	.75
❑ 337	Reuben Droughns RC	2.00	.75
❑ 338	Trung Canidate RC	2.00	.75
❑ 339	Shyrone Stith RC	1.50	.60
❑ 340	Trevor Gaylor RC	1.50	.60
❑ 341	Rob Morris RC	2.50	1.00
❑ 342	Marc Bulger RC	5.00	2.00
❑ 343	Tom Brady RC	25.00	12.50
❑ 344	Todd Husak RC	2.50	1.00
❑ 345	Gari Scott RC	1.50	.60
❑ 346	Erron Kinney RC	2.50	1.00
❑ 347	Julian Peterson RC	2.50	1.00
❑ 348	Doug Chapman RC	2.00	.75
❑ 349	Ron Dugans RC	1.50	.60
❑ 350	Todd Pinkston RC	2.50	1.00
❑ 351	Deon Grant RC	1.25	.50
❑ 352	Na'il Diggs RC	1.25	.50
❑ 353	Raynoch Thompson RC	1.25	.50
❑ 354	Mario Edwards RC	1.25	.50
❑ 355	John Engelberger RC	1.25	.50
❑ 356	Dwayne Goodrich RC	.75	.30
❑ 357	Ben Kelly RC	.75	.30
❑ 358	Sekou Sanyika RC	.75	.30
❑ 359	Brandon Short RC	1.25	.50
❑ 360	Jabari Issa RC	.75	.30
❑ 361	Darwin Walker RC	.75	.30
❑ 362	Jerry Johnson RC	.75	.30
❑ 363	Robaire Smith RC	.75	.30
❑ 364	Mark Roman RC	1.25	.50
❑ 365	Leonardo Carson RC	.75	.30
❑ 366	Mark Simoneau RC	1.25	.50
❑ 367	Hank Poteat RC	1.25	.50
❑ 368	Darren Howard RC	1.25	.50
❑ 369	David Macklin RC	.75	.30
❑ 370	Adalius Thomas RC	3.00	1.25
❑ 371	Ralph Brown RC	.75	.30
❑ 372	Mondriel Fulcher RC	.75	.30
❑ 373	Sammy Morris RC	1.25	.50
❑ 374	Rondell Mealey RC	.75	.30
❑ 375	Deon Dyer RC	1.25	.50
❑ 376	Mareno Philyaw RC	.75	.30
❑ 377	Thomas Hamner RC	.75	.30
❑ 378	Jarious Jackson RC	1.25	.50
❑ 379	Joe Hamilton RC	1.25	.50
❑ 380	Tim Rattay RC	2.00	.75
❑ 381	Chris Hovan RC	1.25	.50
❑ SB1	Kurt Warner MVP/1000	8.00	3.00
❑ SB1A	Kurt Warner MVP AU/100	80.00	30.00
❑ NFL1	Kurt Warner MVP/1000	8.00	3.00
❑ NFL1A	Kurt Warner MVP AU/100	80.00	30.00
❑ QLP10	Dan Marino Promo	3.00	1.50

2001 Quantum Leaf

❑	COMP.SET w/o SP's (200)	25.00	10.00
❑	COMP.ROOKIE UPDATE (36)	20.00	7.50
❑ 1	David Boston	1.00	.40
❑ 2	Frank Sanders	.40	.15
❑ 3	Jake Plummer	.60	.25
❑ 4	Michael Pittman	.40	.15
❑ 5	Rob Moore	.60	.25
❑ 6	Thomas Jones	.60	.25
❑ 7	Chris Chandler	.60	.25
❑ 8	Doug Johnson	.40	.15
❑ 9	Jamal Anderson	1.00	.40
❑ 10	Tim Dwight	1.00	.40
❑ 11	Chris Redman	.40	.15
❑ 12	Jamal Lewis	1.50	.60
❑ 13	Qadry Ismail	.60	.25
❑ 14	Ray Lewis	1.00	.40
❑ 15	Rod Woodson	.60	.25
❑ 16	Shannon Sharpe	.60	.25
❑ 17	Travis Taylor	.60	.25
❑ 18	Trent Dilfer	.60	.25
❑ 19	Doug Flutie	1.00	.40
❑ 20	Eric Moulds	.60	.25
❑ 21	Jay Riemersma	.40	.15
❑ 22	Peerless Price	.60	.25
❑ 23	Rob Johnson	.60	.25
❑ 24	Sammy Morris	.40	.15
❑ 25	Shawn Bryson	.40	.15
❑ 26	Donald Hayes	.40	.15
❑ 27	Muhsin Muhammad	.60	.25
❑ 28	Patrick Jeffers	.60	.25
❑ 29	Reggie White DE	.60	.25
❑ 30	Steve Beuerlein	.60	.25
❑ 31	Tim Biakabutuka	.60	.25
❑ 32	Wesley Walls	.40	.15
❑ 33	Brian Urlacher	1.50	.60
❑ 34	Cade McNown	.40	.15
❑ 35	Dez White	.40	.15
❑ 36	James Allen	.60	.25
❑ 37	Marcus Robinson	1.00	.40
❑ 38	Marty Booker	.40	.15
❑ 39	Akili Smith	.40	.15
❑ 40	Corey Dillon	1.00	.40
❑ 41	Danny Farmer	.40	.15
❑ 42	Peter Warrick	1.00	.40
❑ 43	Ron Dugans	.40	.15
❑ 44	Courtney Brown	.60	.25
❑ 45	Dennis Northcutt	.60	.25
❑ 46	JaJuan Dawson	.40	.15
❑ 47	Kevin Johnson	.60	.25
❑ 48	Tim Couch	.60	.25
❑ 49	Travis Prentice	.40	.15
❑ 50	Anthony Wright	.40	.15
❑ 51	Emmitt Smith	2.00	.75
❑ 52	James McKnight	.60	.25
❑ 53	Joey Galloway	.60	.25
❑ 54	Rocket Ismail	.60	.25
❑ 55	Randall Cunningham	1.00	.40
❑ 56	Troy Aikman	1.50	.60
❑ 57	Brian Griese	1.00	.40
❑ 58	Ed McCaffrey	1.00	.40
❑ 59	Gus Frerotte	.40	.15
❑ 60	John Elway	3.00	1.25
❑ 61	Mike Anderson	1.00	.40
❑ 62	Olandis Gary	.60	.25
❑ 63	Rod Smith	.60	.25
❑ 64	Terrell Davis	1.00	.40
❑ 65	Barry Sanders	2.00	.75
❑ 66	Charlie Batch	1.00	.40
❑ 67	Germane Crowell	.40	.15
❑ 68	Herman Moore	.60	.25
❑ 69	James Stewart	.60	.25
❑ 70	Johnnie Morton	.60	.25
❑ 71	Ahman Green	1.00	.40
❑ 72	Antonio Freeman	1.00	.40
❑ 73	Bill Schroeder	.60	.25
❑ 74	Brett Favre	3.00	1.25
❑ 75	Dorsey Levens	.60	.25
❑ 76	Matt Hasselbeck	.60	.25
❑ 77	Edgerrin James	1.25	.50
❑ 78	Jerome Pathon	.60	.25
❑ 79	Ken Dilger	.40	.15
❑ 80	Marvin Harrison	1.00	.40

❑ 81 Peyton Manning 2.50 1.00
❑ 82 Fred Taylor 1.00 .40
❑ 83 Hardy Nickerson .40 .15
❑ 84 Jimmy Smith .60 .25
❑ 85 Keenan McCardell .40 .15
❑ 86 Mark Brunell 1.00 .40
❑ 87 Tony Brackens .40 .15
❑ 88 Derrick Alexander .60 .25
❑ 89 Elvis Grbac .60 .25
❑ 90 Sylvester Morris .40 .15
❑ 91 Tony Gonzalez .60 .25
❑ 92 Tony Richardson .40 .15
❑ 93 Warren Moon .60 .25
❑ 94 Dan Marino 3.00 1.25
❑ 95 Jay Fiedler 1.00 .40
❑ 96 Lamar Smith .60 .25
❑ 97 Oronde Gadsden .60 .25
❑ 98 Sam Madison .40 .15
❑ 99 Thurman Thomas .40 .15
❑ 100 Tony Martin .60 .25
❑ 101 Zach Thomas 1.00 .40
❑ 102 Cris Carter 1.00 .40
❑ 103 Daunte Culpepper 1.00 .40
❑ 104 John Randle .60 .25
❑ 105 Randy Moss 2.00 .75
❑ 106 Robert Smith .60 .25
❑ 107 Drew Bledsoe 1.25 .50
❑ 108 J.R. Redmond .40 .15
❑ 109 Kevin Faulk .60 .25
❑ 110 Michael Bishop .40 .15
❑ 111 Terry Glenn .60 .25
❑ 112 Troy Brown .60 .25
❑ 113 Aaron Brooks 1.00 .40
❑ 114 Jake Reed .60 .25
❑ 115 Jeff Blake .60 .25
❑ 116 Joe Horn .60 .25
❑ 117 La'Roi Glover .40 .15
❑ 118 Ricky Williams 1.00 .40
❑ 119 Willie Jackson .40 .15
❑ 120 Amani Toomer .40 .15
❑ 121 Ike Hilliard .60 .25
❑ 122 Jason Sehorn .40 .15
❑ 123 Kerry Collins .60 .25
❑ 124 Michael Strahan .60 .25
❑ 125 Ron Dayne 1.00 .40
❑ 126 Ron Dixon .40 .15
❑ 127 Tiki Barber 1.00 .40
❑ 128 Chad Pennington 1.50 .60
❑ 129 Curtis Martin 1.00 .40
❑ 130 Dedric Ward .40 .15
❑ 131 Laveranues Coles 1.00 .40
❑ 132 Vinny Testaverde .60 .25
❑ 133 Wayne Chrebet .60 .25
❑ 134 Charles Woodson .60 .25
❑ 135 Napoleon Kaufman .60 .25
❑ 136 Rich Gannon 1.00 .40
❑ 137 Tim Brown 1.00 .40
❑ 138 Tyrone Wheatley .60 .25
❑ 139 Charles Johnson .40 .15
❑ 140 Donovan McNabb 1.25 .50
❑ 141 Duce Staley 1.00 .40
❑ 142 Hugh Douglas .40 .15
❑ 143 Na Brown .40 .15
❑ 144 Todd Pinkston .40 .15
❑ 145 Bobby Shaw .40 .15
❑ 146 Hines Ward 1.00 .40
❑ 147 Jerome Bettis 1.00 .40
❑ 148 Kordell Stewart .60 .25
❑ 149 Levon Kirkland .40 .15
❑ 150 Plaxico Burress 1.00 .40
❑ 151 Richard Huntley .40 .15
❑ 152 Troy Edwards .40 .15
❑ 153 Jim Harbaugh .60 .25
❑ 154 Junior Seau 1.00 .40
❑ 155 Ryan Leaf .60 .25
❑ 156 Charlie Garner .60 .25
❑ 157 Jeff Garcia 1.00 .40
❑ 158 Jerry Rice 2.00 .75
❑ 159 Steve Young 1.25 .50
❑ 160 Terrell Owens 1.00 .40
❑ 161 Brock Huard .40 .15
❑ 162 Darrell Jackson 1.00 .40
❑ 163 Derrick Mayes .40 .15
❑ 164 Ricky Watters .60 .25
❑ 165 Shaun Alexander 1.25 .50
❑ 166 Az-Zahir Hakim .40 .15
❑ 167 Isaac Bruce 1.00 .40
❑ 168 Kurt Warner 2.00 .75
❑ 169 Marshall Faulk 1.25 .50
❑ 170 Torry Holt 1.00 .40
❑ 171 Trent Green 1.00 .40
❑ 172 Derrick Brooks 1.00 .40
❑ 173 Jacquez Green .40 .15
❑ 174 John Lynch .60 .25
❑ 175 Keyshawn Johnson 1.00 .40
❑ 176 Mike Alstott 1.00 .40
❑ 177 Reidel Anthony .40 .15
❑ 178 Shaun King .40 .15
❑ 179 Warren Sapp .60 .25
❑ 180 Warrick Dunn 1.00 .40
❑ 181 Carl Pickens .40 .15
❑ 182 Derrick Mason .60 .25
❑ 183 Eddie George 1.00 .40
❑ 184 Frank Wycheck .40 .15
❑ 185 Jevon Kearse .60 .25
❑ 186 Neil O'Donnell .40 .15
❑ 187 Steve McNair 1.00 .40
❑ 188 Yancey Thigpen .40 .15
❑ 189 Albert Connell .40 .15
❑ 190 Andre Reed .40 .15
❑ 191 Brad Johnson 1.00 .40
❑ 192 Bruce Smith .40 .15
❑ 193 Champ Bailey .60 .25
❑ 194 Darrell Green .40 .15
❑ 195 Deion Sanders 1.00 .40
❑ 196 Irving Fryar .60 .25
❑ 197 James Thrash .60 .25
❑ 198 Jeff George .60 .25
❑ 199 Michael Westbrook .60 .25
❑ 200 Stephen Davis 1.00 .40
❑ 201 Michael Vick RC 12.00 5.00
❑ 202 Drew Brees RC 8.00 3.00
❑ 203 Chris Weinke RC 2.00 .75
❑ 204 Sage Rosenfels RC 2.00 .75
❑ 205 Josh Heupel RC 2.00 .75
❑ 206 Marques Tuiasosopo RC 2.00 .75
❑ 207 Mike McMahon SP RC 40.00 15.00
❑ 208 Deuce McAllister SP RC 80.00 30.00
❑ 209 LaMont Jordan RC 4.00 1.50
❑ 210 LaDainian Tomlinson RC 20.00 10.00
❑ 211 James Jackson RC 2.00 .75
❑ 212 Anthony Thomas RC 2.00 .75
❑ 213 Travis Henry RC 3.00 1.25
❑ 214 Travis Minor RC 1.25 .50
❑ 215 Rudi Johnson RC 4.00 1.50
❑ 216 Michael Bennett RC 2.00 .75
❑ 217 Kevan Barlow RC 2.00 .75
❑ 218 Dan Alexander RC 1.25 .50
❑ 219 Correll Buckhalter SP RC 50.00 20.00
❑ 220 Moran Norris RC .75 .30
❑ 221 Jesse Palmer RC 2.00 .75
❑ 222 Heath Evans RC 1.25 .50
❑ 223 David Terrell SP RC 40.00 15.00
❑ 224 Santana Moss RC 3.00 1.25
❑ 225 Rod Gardner RC 2.00 .75
❑ 226 Quincy Morgan SP RC 50.00 20.00
❑ 227 Freddie Mitchell RC 2.00 .75
❑ 228 Reggie Wayne RC 4.00 1.50
❑ 229 Bobby Newcombe RC 1.25 .50
❑ 230 Casey Hampton RC 2.00 .75
❑ 231 Robert Ferguson RC 2.00 .75
❑ 232 Ken-Yon Rambo RC 1.25 .50
❑ 233 Alex Bannister RC 1.25 .50
❑ 234 Koren Robinson RC 2.00 .75
❑ 235 Chad Johnson RC 5.00 2.00
❑ 236 Chris Chambers RC 3.00 1.25
❑ 237 Snoop Minnis RC 1.25 .50
❑ 238 Vinny Sutherland RC 1.25 .50
❑ 239 Cedrick Wilson RC 2.00 .75
❑ 240 T.J. Houshmandzadeh RC 2.50 1.00
❑ 241 Todd Heap RC 2.00 .75
❑ 242 Alge Crumpler RC 2.50 1.00
❑ 243 Jabari Holloway RC 1.25 .50
❑ 244 Tony Stewart RC 2.00 .75
❑ 245 Jamal Reynolds RC 2.00 .75
❑ 246 Andre Carter SP RC 40.00 15.00
❑ 247 Justin Smith SP RC 40.00 15.00
❑ 248 Richard Seymour RC 2.00 .75
❑ 249 Marcus Stroud RC 2.00 .75
❑ 250 Damione Lewis RC 1.25 .50
❑ 251 Gerard Warren SP RC 50.00 20.00
❑ 252 Tommy Polley SP RC 40.00 15.00
❑ 253 Dan Morgan RC 2.00 .75
❑ 254 Jamar Fletcher RC 1.25 .50
❑ 255 Ken Lucas RC 2.00 .75
❑ 256 Fred Smoot SP RC 40.00 15.00
❑ 257 Nate Clements RC 2.00 .75
❑ 258 Will Allen RC 1.25 .50
❑ 259 Derrick Gibson RC 1.25 .50
❑ 260 Adam Archuleta RC 2.00 .75
❑ 261 Karon Riley RC .75 .30
❑ 262 Cedric Scott RC 1.25 .50
❑ 263 Kenny Smith RC 1.25 .50
❑ 264 Willie Howard RC 1.25 .50
❑ 265 Shaun Rogers RC 2.00 .75
❑ 266 Ennis Davis RC .75 .30
❑ 267 Morlon Greenwood RC 1.25 .50
❑ 268 Gary Baxter RC 1.25 .50
❑ 269 Keith Adams RC .75 .30
❑ 270 Brian Allen RC .75 .30
❑ 271 Carlos Polk RC .75 .30
❑ 272 Torrance Marshall RC 2.00 .75
❑ 273 Jamie Winborn RC 1.25 .50
❑ 274 Hakim Akbar RC .75 .30
❑ 275 David Rivers RC 1.25 .50
❑ 276 Ben Leard RC 1.25 .50
❑ 277 Tim Hasselbeck RC 2.00 .75
❑ 278 DeAngelo Evans RC 1.25 .50
❑ 279 David Allen RC 1.25 .50
❑ 280 Reggie White RC 1.25 .50
❑ 281 Ja'Mar Toombs RC 1.25 .50
❑ 282 Dustin McClintock RC 1.25 .50
❑ 283 Boo Williams RC 1.25 .50
❑ 284 Ronney Daniels RC .75 .30
❑ 285 Daniel Guy RC .75 .30
❑ 286 Javon Green RC 1.25 .50
❑ 287 Marcellus Rivers RC 1.25 .50
❑ 288 Rashon Burns RC .75 .30
❑ 289 Jevaris Johnson RC .75 .30
❑ 290 David Warren RC .75 .30
❑ 291 John Capel RC 1.25 .50
❑ 292 Kendrell Bell RC 4.00 1.50
❑ 294 Willie Middlebrooks RC 1.25 .50
❑ 295 Reggie Germany RC 1.25 .50
❑ 296 Quincy Carter RC 2.00 .75

2004 Reflections

❑ COMP.SET w/o SP's (100) 40.00 15.00
❑ 1 Emmitt Smith 3.00 1.25
❑ 2 Anquan Boldin 1.50 .60
❑ 3 Josh McCown 1.00 .40
❑ 4 Michael Vick 3.00 1.25
❑ 5 Peerless Price 1.00 .40
❑ 6 T.J. Duckett 1.00 .40
❑ 7 Todd Heap 1.00 .40
❑ 8 Jamal Lewis 1.50 .60
❑ 9 Kyle Boller 1.50 .60
❑ 10 Drew Bledsoe 1.50 .60
❑ 11 Travis Henry 1.00 .40
❑ 12 Eric Moulds 1.00 .40
❑ 13 Jake Delhomme 1.50 .60
❑ 14 Steve Smith 1.50 .60
❑ 15 Stephen Davis 1.00 .40
❑ 16 Rex Grossman 1.50 .60
❑ 17 Brian Urlacher 2.00 .75
❑ 18 Anthony Thomas 1.00 .40
❑ 19 Rudi Johnson 1.00 .40
❑ 20 Carson Palmer 2.00 .75
❑ 21 Chad Johnson 1.50 .60
❑ 22 Jeff Garcia 1.50 .60
❑ 23 Andre Davis .60 .25
❑ 24 Quincy Morgan 1.00 .40
❑ 25 Keyshawn Johnson 1.00 .40

❑ 26	Roy Williams S	1.00	.40
❑ 27	Quincy Carter	1.00	.40
❑ 28	Ashley Lelie	1.00	.40
❑ 29	Champ Bailey	1.00	.40
❑ 30	Jake Plummer	1.00	.40
❑ 31	Az-Zahir Hakim	.60	.25
❑ 32	Joey Harrington	1.50	.60
❑ 33	Charles Rogers	1.00	.40
❑ 34	Javon Walker	1.00	.40
❑ 35	Ahman Green	1.50	.60
❑ 36	Brett Favre	4.00	1.50
❑ 37	Domanick Davis	1.50	.60
❑ 38	David Carr	1.50	.60
❑ 39	Andre Johnson	1.50	.60
❑ 40	Edgerrin James	1.50	.60
❑ 41	Marvin Harrison	1.50	.60
❑ 42	Dwight Freeney	1.00	.40
❑ 43	Peyton Manning	2.50	1.00
❑ 44	Fred Taylor	1.00	.40
❑ 45	Jimmy Smith	1.00	.40
❑ 46	Byron Leftwich	2.00	.75
❑ 47	Dante Hall	1.50	.60
❑ 48	Tony Gonzalez	1.00	.40
❑ 49	Trent Green	1.00	.40
❑ 50	Priest Holmes	2.00	.75
❑ 51	Zach Thomas	1.50	.60
❑ 52	A.J. Feeley	1.50	.60
❑ 53	Chris Chambers	1.00	.40
❑ 54	Ricky Williams	1.50	.60
❑ 55	Randy Moss	2.00	.75
❑ 56	Onterrio Smith	1.00	.40
❑ 57	Daunte Culpepper	1.50	.60
❑ 58	Tom Brady	4.00	1.50
❑ 59	Troy Brown	1.00	.40
❑ 60	Corey Dillon	1.00	.40
❑ 61	Donte Stallworth	1.00	.40
❑ 62	Deuce McAllister	1.50	.60
❑ 63	Aaron Brooks	1.00	.40
❑ 64	Amani Toomer	1.00	.40
❑ 65	Jeremy Shockey	1.50	.60
❑ 66	Michael Strahan	1.00	.40
❑ 67	Curtis Martin	1.50	.60
❑ 68	Chad Pennington	1.50	.60
❑ 69	Santana Moss	1.00	.40
❑ 70	Jerry Porter	1.00	.40
❑ 71	Jerry Rice	3.00	1.25
❑ 72	Rich Gannon	1.00	.40
❑ 73	Tim Brown	1.50	.60
❑ 74	Terrell Owens	1.50	.60
❑ 75	Brian Westbrook	1.00	.40
❑ 76	Donovan McNabb	2.00	.75
❑ 77	Tommy Maddox	1.00	.40
❑ 78	Hines Ward	1.50	.60
❑ 79	Duce Staley	1.00	.40
❑ 80	Donnie Edwards	.60	.25
❑ 81	LaDainian Tomlinson	2.00	.75
❑ 82	Drew Brees	1.50	.60
❑ 83	Brandon Lloyd	1.00	.40
❑ 84	Tim Rattay	.60	.25
❑ 85	Kevan Barlow	1.00	.40
❑ 86	Koren Robinson	1.00	.40
❑ 87	Shaun Alexander	1.50	.60
❑ 88	Matt Hasselbeck	1.00	.40
❑ 89	Torry Holt	1.50	.60
❑ 90	Marc Bulger	1.50	.60
❑ 91	Marshall Faulk	1.50	.60
❑ 92	Brad Johnson	1.00	.40
❑ 93	Keenan McCardell	.60	.25
❑ 94	Charlie Garner	1.00	.40
❑ 95	Steve McNair	1.50	.60
❑ 96	Chris Brown	1.50	.60
❑ 97	Eddie George	1.00	.40
❑ 98	Mark Brunell	1.00	.40
❑ 99	Laveranues Coles	1.00	.40
❑ 100	Clinton Portis	1.50	.60
❑ 101	Kris Wilson/750 RC	6.00	2.50
❑ 102	Carlos Francis/750 RC	5.00	2.00
❑ 103	D.J. Williams/750 RC	6.00	2.50
❑ 104	Devery Henderson/450 RC	6.00	2.50
❑ 105	Craig Krenzel/750 RC	6.00	2.50
❑ 106	Jonathan Vilma/750 RC	6.00	2.50
❑ 107	Luke McCown/750 RC	6.00	2.50
❑ 108	Michael Turner/750 RC	8.00	3.00
❑ 109	Richard Seigler/750 RC	5.00	2.00
❑ 110	Stuart Schweigert/750 RC	6.00	2.50
❑ 111	Ben Watson/750 RC	6.00	2.50
❑ 112	Chris Perry/450 RC	12.00	5.00
❑ 113	Jason Fife/750 RC	5.00	2.00
❑ 114	Eli Manning/450 RC	40.00	20.00
❑ 115	Matt Kegel/750 RC	6.00	2.50
❑ 116	Kellen Winslow/450 RC	15.00	6.00
❑ 117	Chris Cooley/750 RC	6.00	2.50
❑ 118	Quincy Wilson/750 RC	5.00	2.00
❑ 119	Samie Parker/750 RC	6.00	2.50
❑ 120	Vince Wilfork/750 RC	6.00	2.50
❑ 121	Bernard Berrian/750 RC	8.00	3.00
❑ 122	Ahmad Carroll/750 RC	6.00	2.50
❑ 123	Derrick Hamilton/750 RC	5.00	2.00
❑ 124	Rich Gardner/750 RC	5.00	2.00
❑ 125	Jeff Smoker/750 RC	6.00	2.50
❑ 126	Kenechi Udeze/750 RC	6.00	2.50
❑ 127	Mewelde Moore/750 RC	6.00	2.50
❑ 128	Keyaron Fox/750 RC	5.00	2.00
❑ 129	Sean Jones/750 RC	5.00	2.00
❑ 130	Will Poole/750 RC	6.00	2.50
❑ 131	Travelle Wharton/750 RC	3.00	1.25
❑ 132	Demorrio Williams/750 RC	6.00	2.50
❑ 133	Jason Babin/750 RC	6.00	2.50
❑ 134	Ernest Wilford/750 RC	6.00	2.50
❑ 135	Jerricho Cotchery/750 RC	6.00	2.50
❑ 136	Kevin Jones/450 RC	20.00	7.50
❑ 137	Michael Boulware/750 RC	6.00	2.50
❑ 138	D.J. Hackett/750 RC	5.00	2.00
❑ 139	Sean Taylor/450 RC	8.00	3.00
❑ 140	Will Smith/750 RC	6.00	2.50
❑ 141	John Standeford/750 RC	5.00	2.00
❑ 142	Max Starks/750 RC	5.00	2.00
❑ 143	Cody Pickett/750 RC	6.00	2.50
❑ 144	Derrick Strait/750 RC	6.00	2.50
❑ 145	Greg Jones/450 RC	8.00	3.00
❑ 146	John Navarre/750 RC	6.00	2.50
❑ 147	Larry Fitzgerald/450 RC	25.00	10.00
❑ 148	Michael Clayton/450 RC	15.00	6.00
❑ 149	Rashaun Woods/450 RC	8.00	3.00
❑ 150	Shawn Andrews/750 RC	6.00	2.50
❑ 151	B.J. Symons/750 RC	6.00	2.50
❑ 152	Cedric Cobbs/450 RC	8.00	3.00
❑ 153	Darius Watts/750 RC	6.00	2.50
❑ 154	B.J. Johnson/750 RC	5.00	2.00
❑ 155	Ricardo Colclough/750 RC	6.00	2.50
❑ 156	Josh Harris/750 RC	6.00	2.50
❑ 157	Derek Abney/750 RC	6.00	2.50
❑ 158	Kendrick Starling/750 RC	3.00	1.25
❑ 159	Robert Gallery/450 RC	8.00	3.00
❑ 160	Tatum Bell/450 RC	15.00	6.00
❑ 161	Ben Hartsock/750 RC	6.00	2.50
❑ 162	Dwan Edwards/750 RC	3.00	1.25
❑ 163	Darnell Dockett/750 RC	5.00	2.00
❑ 164	Igor Olshansky/750 RC	6.00	2.50
❑ 165	Justin Smiley/750 RC	6.00	2.50
❑ 166	Julius Jones/450 RC	25.00	10.00
❑ 167	Matt Mauck/750 RC	6.00	2.50
❑ 168	Derek McCoy/750 RC	5.00	2.00
❑ 169	Chris Pittman/750 RC	6.00	2.50
❑ 170	Teddy Lehman/750 RC	6.00	2.50
❑ 171	Ben Troupe/450 RC	8.00	3.00
❑ 172	Chris Gamble/750 RC	6.00	2.50
❑ 173	DeAngelo Hall/750 RC	8.00	3.00
❑ 174	Dunta Robinson/750 RC	6.00	2.50
❑ 175	Jason Shivers/750 RC	5.00	2.00
❑ 176	Keary Colbert/450 RC	10.00	4.00
❑ 177	Jared Lorenzen/750 RC	5.00	2.00
❑ 178	Philip Rivers/450 RC	25.00	12.50
❑ 179	Roy Williams/450 RC	20.00	7.50
❑ 180	Bob Sanders/750 RC	15.00	6.00
❑ 181	Antwan Odom/750 RC	6.00	2.50
❑ 182	Josh Davis/750 RC	5.00	2.00
❑ 183	Courtney Watson/750 RC	6.00	2.50
❑ 184	Devard Darling/750 RC	6.00	2.50
❑ 185	J.P. Losman/450 RC	15.00	6.00
❑ 186	Johnnie Morant/750 RC	6.00	2.50
❑ 187	Lee Evans/450 RC	10.00	4.00
❑ 188	Michael Jenkins/450 RC	8.00	3.00
❑ 189	Reggie Williams/450 RC	10.00	4.00
❑ 190	Steven Jackson/450 RC	25.00	10.00
❑ 191	Roethlisberger/450 RC	60.00	30.00
❑ 192	P.K. Sam/750 RC	5.00	2.00
❑ 193	Derrick Knight/750 RC	5.00	2.00
❑ 194	Drew Henson/450 RC	8.00	3.00
❑ 195	Marquise Hill/750 RC	5.00	2.00
❑ 196	Karlos Dansby/750 RC	6.00	2.50
❑ 197	Matt Schaub/750 RC	20.00	7.50
❑ 198	Ben Utecht/750 RC	3.00	1.25
❑ 199	Darrion Scott/750 RC	6.00	2.50
❑ 200	Tommie Harris/750 RC	6.00	2.50
❑ 201	Andrae Thurman RC	3.00	1.25
❑ 202	Matt Kranchick RC	6.00	2.50
❑ 203	Shaun Phillips RC	5.00	2.00
❑ 204	Landon Johnson RC	5.00	2.00
❑ 205	Jeff Dugan RC	3.00	1.25
❑ 206	Wes Welker RC	6.00	2.50
❑ 207	Michael Gaines RC	5.00	2.00
❑ 208	Jamaar Taylor RC	6.00	2.50
❑ 209	Brandon Chillar RC	5.00	2.00
❑ 210	Jermaine Green RC	5.00	2.00
❑ 211	Triandos Luke RC	6.00	2.50
❑ 212	Brandon Miree RC	5.00	2.00
❑ 213	Dexter Reid RC	3.00	1.25
❑ 214	Isaac Hilton RC	5.00	2.00
❑ 215	Adrian Jones RC	5.00	2.00
❑ 216	Grant Wiley RC	5.00	2.00
❑ 217	Matt Cherry RC	3.00	1.25
❑ 218	Courtney Anderson RC	5.00	2.00
❑ 219	Antonio Smith RC	5.00	2.00
❑ 220	Sean Tufts RC	5.00	2.00
❑ 221	Johnny Lamar RC	6.00	2.50
❑ 222	Shawn Johnson RC	5.00	2.00
❑ 223	Jason Peters RC	6.00	2.50
❑ 224	Rodney Leisle RC	3.00	1.25
❑ 225	Lane Danielsen RC	6.00	2.50
❑ 226	Zack Abron RC	5.00	2.00
❑ 227	Romar Crenshaw RC	3.00	1.25
❑ 228	Keiwan Ratliff RC	5.00	2.00
❑ 229	Chad Lavalais RC	5.00	2.00
❑ 230	Jason Wright RC	5.00	2.00
❑ 231	Rayshun Reed RC	3.00	1.25
❑ 232	Patrick Crayton RC	6.00	2.50
❑ 233	Casey Bramlet RC	5.00	2.00
❑ 234	Nathaniel Adibi RC	6.00	2.50
❑ 235	Dontarrious Thomas RC	6.00	2.50
❑ 236	B.J. Sander RC	5.00	2.00
❑ 237	Ryan McGuffey RC	3.00	1.25
❑ 238	Shawntae Spencer RC	6.00	2.50
❑ 239	Amon Gordon RC	3.00	1.25
❑ 240	Vernon Carey RC	5.00	2.00
❑ 241	Stanford Samuels RC	5.00	2.00
❑ 242	Thomas Tapeh RC	5.00	2.00
❑ 243	Keith Smith RC	5.00	2.00
❑ 244	Casey Clausen RC	6.00	2.50
❑ 245	Jake Grove RC	3.00	1.25
❑ 246	Omar Nazel RC	5.00	2.00
❑ 247	Jammal Lord RC	6.00	2.50
❑ 248	Jeremy LeSueur RC	5.00	2.00
❑ 249	Daryl Smith RC	6.00	2.50
❑ 250	Nat Dorsey RC	3.00	1.25
❑ 251	Tim Anderson RC	6.00	2.50
❑ 252	Chris Snee RC	5.00	2.00
❑ 253	Sean Ryan RC	5.00	2.00
❑ 254	Tank Johnson RC	5.00	2.00
❑ 255	Marquis Cooper RC	5.00	2.00
❑ 256	Josh Scobee RC	3.00	1.25
❑ 257	Justin Jenkins RC	5.00	2.00
❑ 258	Nate Lawrie RC	5.00	2.00
❑ 259	Randy Starks RC	5.00	2.00
❑ 260	Caleb Miller RC	5.00	2.00
❑ 261	A.J. Ricker RC	3.00	1.25
❑ 262	Andy Hall RC	5.00	2.00
❑ 263	Troy Fleming RC	5.00	2.00
❑ 264	Matt Ware RC	6.00	2.50
❑ 265	Christian Ferrara RC	5.00	2.00
❑ 266	Stacy Andrews RC	5.00	2.00
❑ 267	Reggie Torbor RC	5.00	2.00
❑ 268	Jeris McIntyre RC	5.00	2.00
❑ 269	Jarrett Payton RC	5.00	2.00
❑ 270	Ronald Jones RC	3.00	1.25
❑ 271	Kelly Butler RC	5.00	2.00
❑ 272	Bryan Hickman RC	6.00	2.50
❑ 273	Chris Collins RC	5.00	2.00
❑ 274	Ryan Dinwiddie RC	5.00	2.00
❑ 275	Robert Geathers RC	5.00	2.00
❑ 276	Niko Koutouvides RC	5.00	2.00
❑ 277	Clarence Farmer RC	5.00	2.00
❑ 278	Jim Sorgi RC	6.00	2.50
❑ 279	Ran Carthon RC	5.00	2.00
❑ 280	Michael Waddell RC	3.00	1.25
❑ 281	Andrew Strojny RC	3.00	1.25
❑ 282	Sloan Thomas RC	5.00	2.00
❑ 283	Tim Euhus RC	6.00	2.50
❑ 284	Lawrence Richardson RC	6.00	2.50
❑ 285	Nate Kaeding RC	6.00	2.50
❑ 286	Ryan Krause RC	5.00	2.00

❑ 287 Derrick Ward RC 3.00 1.25
❑ 288 Nathan Vasher RC 8.00 3.00
❑ 289 Bobby McCray RC 5.00 2.00
❑ 290 Scott Rislov RC 6.00 2.50
❑ 291 Ryan Boschetti RC 3.00 1.25
❑ 292 Fred Russell RC 6.00 2.50
❑ 293 Von Hutchins RC 5.00 2.00
❑ 294 Derrick Crawford RC 3.00 1.25

2005 Reflections

❑ COMP.SET w/o SP's (100) 30.00 12.50
❑ 101-175 PRINT RUN 899 SER.#'d SETS
❑ 176-225 PRINT RUN 699 SER.#'d SETS
❑ 226-275 PRINT RUN 499 SER.#'d SETS
❑ 276-300 PRINT RUN 299 SER.#'d SETS
❑ OVERALL DRAFT PICK ODDS 1:3
❑ UNPRICED RAINBOW PRINT RUN 1 SET
❑ 1 Larry Fitzgerald 1.25 .50
❑ 2 Anquan Boldin .75 .30
❑ 3 Josh McCown .75 .30
❑ 4 Michael Vick 2.00 .75
❑ 5 Warrick Dunn .75 .30
❑ 6 Peerless Price .60 .25
❑ 7 Ray Lewis 1.25 .50
❑ 8 Jamal Lewis 1.25 .50
❑ 9 Kyle Boller .75 .30
❑ 10 Derrick Mason .75 .30
❑ 11 J.P. Losman 1.25 .50
❑ 12 Willis McGahee 1.25 .50
❑ 13 Lee Evans .75 .30
❑ 14 Eric Moulds .75 .30
❑ 15 Jake Delhomme 1.25 .50
❑ 16 Keary Colbert .75 .30
❑ 17 DeShaun Foster .75 .30
❑ 18 Brian Urlacher 1.25 .50
❑ 19 Rex Grossman .75 .30
❑ 20 Muhsin Muhammad .75 .30
❑ 21 Carson Palmer 1.25 .50
❑ 22 Rudi Johnson .75 .30
❑ 23 Chad Johnson 1.25 .50
❑ 24 Julius Jones 1.50 .60
❑ 25 Keyshawn Johnson .75 .30
❑ 26 Drew Bledsoe 1.25 .50
❑ 27 Tatum Bell .75 .30
❑ 28 Jake Plummer .75 .30
❑ 29 Ashley Lelie .75 .30
❑ 30 Roy Williams WR 1.25 .50
❑ 31 Kevin Jones 1.25 .50
❑ 32 Jeff Garcia .75 .30
❑ 33 Brett Favre 3.00 1.25
❑ 34 Ahman Green 1.25 .50
❑ 35 Javon Walker .75 .30
❑ 36 David Carr 1.25 .50
❑ 37 Andre Johnson .75 .30
❑ 38 Domanick Davis .75 .30
❑ 39 Peyton Manning 2.00 .75
❑ 40 Reggie Wayne .75 .30
❑ 41 Edgerrin James 1.25 .50
❑ 42 Marvin Harrison 1.25 .50
❑ 43 Byron Leftwich 1.25 .50
❑ 44 Fred Taylor .75 .30
❑ 45 Jimmy Smith .75 .30
❑ 46 Priest Holmes 1.25 .50
❑ 47 Larry Johnson 1.25 .50
❑ 48 Trent Green .75 .30
❑ 49 A.J. Feeley .75 .30
❑ 50 Chris Chambers .75 .30
❑ 51 Randy McMichael .60 .25
❑ 52 Daunte Culpepper 1.25 .50
❑ 53 Onterrio Smith .75 .30
❑ 54 Nate Burleson .75 .30
❑ 55 Tom Brady 3.00 1.25
❑ 56 Corey Dillon .75 .30
❑ 57 Deion Branch .75 .30
❑ 58 David Givens .75 .30
❑ 59 Aaron Brooks .75 .30
❑ 60 Deuce McAllister 1.25 .50
❑ 61 Joe Horn .75 .30
❑ 62 Eli Manning 2.50 1.00
❑ 63 Jeremy Shockey 1.25 .50
❑ 64 Tiki Barber 1.25 .50
❑ 65 Chad Pennington 1.25 .50
❑ 66 Curtis Martin 1.25 .50
❑ 67 Laveranues Coles .75 .30
❑ 68 Kerry Collins .75 .30
❑ 69 Jerry Porter .75 .30
❑ 70 Randy Moss 1.25 .50
❑ 71 Donovan McNabb 1.50 .60
❑ 72 Terrell Owens 1.25 .50
❑ 73 Brian Dawkins .75 .30
❑ 74 Brian Westbrook .75 .30
❑ 75 Ben Roethlisberger 3.00 1.25
❑ 76 Jerome Bettis 1.25 .50
❑ 77 Hines Ward 1.25 .50
❑ 78 Duce Staley .75 .30
❑ 79 Drew Brees 1.25 .50
❑ 80 LaDainian Tomlinson 1.50 .60
❑ 81 Antonio Gates 1.25 .50
❑ 82 Tim Rattay .60 .25
❑ 83 Kevan Barlow .75 .30
❑ 84 Eric Johnson .75 .30
❑ 85 Shaun Alexander 1.50 .60
❑ 86 Darrell Jackson .75 .30
❑ 87 Matt Hasselbeck .75 .30
❑ 88 Marc Bulger 1.25 .50
❑ 89 Steven Jackson 1.50 .60
❑ 90 Marshall Faulk 1.25 .50
❑ 91 Torry Holt 1.25 .50
❑ 92 Michael Pittman .60 .25
❑ 93 Brian Griese .75 .30
❑ 94 Michael Clayton 1.25 .50
❑ 95 Steve McNair 1.25 .50
❑ 96 Billy Volek .75 .30
❑ 97 Chris Brown .75 .30
❑ 98 Clinton Portis 1.25 .50
❑ 99 Patrick Ramsey .75 .30
❑ 100 Santana Moss .75 .30
❑ 101 James Kilian RC 6.00 2.50
❑ 102 Matt Cassel RC 10.00 4.00
❑ 103 Keron Henry RC 3.00 1.25
❑ 104 Adrian McPherson RC 6.00 2.50
❑ 105 Marcus Randall RC 5.00 2.00
❑ 106 Roydel Williams RC 6.00 2.50
❑ 107 Dante Ridgeway RC 5.00 2.00
❑ 108 Marcus Maxwell RC 5.00 2.00
❑ 109 Paris Warren RC 5.00 2.00
❑ 110 Courtney Roby RC 6.00 2.50
❑ 111 Mark Bradley RC 6.00 2.50
❑ 112 Brandon Jones RC 6.00 2.50
❑ 113 Chase Lyman RC 5.00 2.00
❑ 114 LeRon McCoy RC 5.00 2.00
❑ 115 Adam Bergen RC 6.00 2.50
❑ 116 Harry Williams RC 5.00 2.00
❑ 117 Lance Moore RC 3.00 1.25
❑ 118 Jason Anderson RC 5.00 2.00
❑ 119 Lionel Gates RC 5.00 2.00
❑ 120 Darrell Shropshire RC 5.00 2.00
❑ 121 Will Matthews RC 5.00 2.00
❑ 122 Noah Herron RC 6.00 2.50
❑ 123 Jerome Collins RC 5.00 2.00
❑ 124 Stanford Routt RC 5.00 2.00
❑ 125 Nick Collins RC 6.00 2.50
❑ 126 Maurice Clarett 6.00 2.50
❑ 127 Kelvin Hayden RC 5.00 2.00
❑ 128 Bo Scaife RC 5.00 2.00
❑ 129 Eric King RC 5.00 2.00
❑ 130 Kerry Rhodes RC 6.00 2.50
❑ 131 Darrent Williams RC 6.00 2.50
❑ 132 Stanley Wilson RC 5.00 2.00
❑ 133 Nick Speegle RC 5.00 2.00
❑ 134 Brodney Pool RC 6.00 2.50
❑ 135 Ellis Hobbs RC 6.00 2.50
❑ 136 Sean Considine RC 6.00 2.50
❑ 137 Josh Bullocks RC 6.00 2.50
❑ 138 Jovan Haye RC 5.00 2.00
❑ 139 Jimmy Verdon RC 3.00 1.25
❑ 140 Ryan Riddle RC 3.00 1.25
❑ 141 Luis Castillo RC 6.00 2.50
❑ 142 Jesse Lumsden RC 3.00 1.25
❑ 143 David Baas RC 5.00 2.00
❑ 144 Chris Spencer RC 6.00 2.50
❑ 145 Jamaal Brown RC 6.00 2.50
❑ 146 Marcus Lawrence RC 5.00 2.00
❑ 147 Todd Mortensen RC 5.00 2.00
❑ 148 Shane Boyd RC 3.00 1.25
❑ 149 Darian Durant RC 6.00 2.50
❑ 150 Chance Mock RC 3.00 1.25
❑ 151 Damien Nash RC 5.00 2.00
❑ 152 Deandra Cobb RC 5.00 2.00
❑ 153 Jamaica Rector RC 3.00 1.25
❑ 154 Carlyle Holiday RC 5.00 2.00
❑ 155 Nehemiah Broughton RC 5.00 2.00
❑ 156 Efrem Hill RC 5.00 2.00
❑ 157 Dominic Robinson RC 3.00 1.25
❑ 158 Rick Razzano RC 6.00 2.50
❑ 159 Rasheed Marshall RC 6.00 2.50
❑ 160 Lofa Tatupu RC 8.00 3.00
❑ 161 Robert McCune RC 5.00 2.00
❑ 162 Channing Crowder RC 6.00 2.50
❑ 163 Ryan Claridge RC 5.00 2.00
❑ 164 Fred Amey RC 5.00 2.00
❑ 165 Jordan Beck RC 5.00 2.00
❑ 166 Leroy Hill RC 6.00 2.50
❑ 167 Travis Daniels RC 5.00 2.00
❑ 168 Jerome Carter RC 5.00 2.00
❑ 169 Chad Friehauf RC 5.00 2.00
❑ 170 Scott Starks RC 5.00 2.00
❑ 171 Marviel Underwood RC 5.00 2.00
❑ 172 Domonique Foxworth RC 6.00 2.50
❑ 173 Jon Goldsberry RC 6.00 2.50
❑ 174 Jonathan Babineaux RC 5.00 2.00
❑ 175 Sione Pouha RC 6.00 2.50
❑ 176 Kerry Wright RC 5.00 2.00
❑ 177 Jason White RC 6.00 2.50
❑ 178 Matt Jones RC 15.00 6.00
❑ 179 Gino Guidugli RC 3.00 1.25
❑ 180 Timmy Chang RC 5.00 2.00
❑ 181 Chris Rix RC 5.00 2.00
❑ 182 Ryan Fitzpatrick RC 10.00 4.00
❑ 183 Brock Berlin RC 5.00 2.00
❑ 184 Bryan Randall RC 5.00 2.00
❑ 185 Stefan LeFors RC 6.00 2.50
❑ 186 Larry Brackins RC 5.00 2.00
❑ 187 Charles Frederick RC 5.00 2.00
❑ 188 J.R. Russell RC 5.00 2.00
❑ 189 Vincent Jackson RC 6.00 2.50
❑ 190 Josh Davis RC 5.00 2.00
❑ 191 Chad Owens RC 6.00 2.50
❑ 192 Airese Currie RC 6.00 2.50
❑ 193 Chauncey Stovall RC 3.00 1.25
❑ 194 Jovan Witherspoon RC 3.00 1.25
❑ 195 Trent Cole RC 6.00 2.50
❑ 196 Tab Perry RC 6.00 2.50
❑ 197 Cedric Houston RC 6.00 2.50
❑ 198 Brandon Jacobs RC 8.00 3.00
❑ 199 Bobby Purify RC 5.00 2.00
❑ 200 Marion Barber RC 10.00 4.00
❑ 201 Alvin Pearman RC 6.00 2.50
❑ 202 Madison Hedgecock RC 6.00 2.50
❑ 203 Justin Green RC 6.00 2.50
❑ 204 Manuel White RC 5.00 2.00
❑ 205 Kevin Everett RC 6.00 2.50
❑ 206 Matthew Tant RC 3.00 1.25
❑ 207 Bryant McFadden RC 6.00 2.50
❑ 208 Ryan Moats RC 6.00 2.50
❑ 209 Fabian Washington RC 6.00 2.50
❑ 210 Oshiomogho Atogwe RC 5.00 2.00
❑ 211 Dustin Fox RC 6.00 2.50
❑ 212 Shaun Cody RC 6.00 2.50
❑ 213 Matt Roth RC 6.00 2.50
❑ 214 Vincent Burns RC 5.00 2.00
❑ 215 Bill Swancutt RC 5.00 2.00
❑ 216 Brady Poppinga RC 6.00 2.50
❑ 217 Logan Mankins RC 8.00 3.00
❑ 218 Michael Roos RC 3.00 1.25
❑ 219 Alfred Fincher RC 5.00 2.00
❑ 220 Darryl Blackstock RC 5.00 2.00
❑ 221 Jared Newberry RC 5.00 2.00
❑ 222 Khalif Barnes RC 5.00 2.00
❑ 223 Alex Barron RC 3.00 1.25
❑ 224 Patrick Estes RC 5.00 2.00
❑ 225 Elton Brown RC 3.00 1.25
❑ 226 David Greene RC 8.00 3.00

❑ 227 Dan Orlovsky RC	10.00	4.00
❑ 228 Derek Anderson RC	8.00	3.00
❑ 229 Kyle Orton RC	12.00	5.00
❑ 230 Chris Henry RC	8.00	3.00
❑ 231 Fred Gibson RC	6.00	2.50
❑ 232 Craphonso Thorpe RC	6.00	2.50
❑ 233 Terrence Murphy RC	8.00	3.00
❑ 234 Steve Savoy RC	4.00	1.50
❑ 235 Roscoe Parrish RC	8.00	3.00
❑ 236 Reggie Brown RC	8.00	3.00
❑ 237 Craig Bragg RC	6.00	2.50
❑ 238 Eric Shelton RC	8.00	3.00
❑ 239 T.A. McLendon RC	4.00	1.50
❑ 240 Walter Reyes RC	6.00	2.50
❑ 241 Anthony Davis RC	6.00	2.50
❑ 242 J.J. Arrington RC	10.00	4.00
❑ 243 Frank Gore RC	15.00	6.00
❑ 244 Alex Smith TE RC	8.00	3.00
❑ 245 Jeb Huckeba RC	8.00	3.00
❑ 246 Adam Jones RC	8.00	3.00
❑ 247 Brandon Browner RC	6.00	2.50
❑ 248 Carlos Rogers RC	10.00	4.00
❑ 249 Corey Webster RC	8.00	3.00
❑ 250 Justin Miller RC	6.00	2.50
❑ 251 Eric Green RC	4.00	1.50
❑ 252 Kurt Campbell RC	6.00	2.50
❑ 253 Ronald Bartell RC	6.00	2.50
❑ 254 Billy Bajema RC	6.00	2.50
❑ 255 Vincent Fuller RC	6.00	2.50
❑ 256 Donte Nicholson RC	8.00	3.00
❑ 257 Derrick Johnson RC	12.00	5.00
❑ 258 Mike Patterson RC	8.00	3.00
❑ 259 Anttaj Hawthorne RC	6.00	2.50
❑ 260 Erasmus James RC	8.00	3.00
❑ 261 David Pollack RC	8.00	3.00
❑ 262 Garrett Cross RC	4.00	1.50
❑ 263 Justin Tuck RC	8.00	3.00
❑ 264 DeMarcus Ware RC	12.00	5.00
❑ 265 Odell Thurman RC	8.00	3.00
❑ 266 Barrett Ruud RC	8.00	3.00
❑ 267 Lance Mitchell RC	6.00	2.50
❑ 268 Kevin Burnett RC	8.00	3.00
❑ 269 Daven Holly RC	6.00	2.50
❑ 270 James Butler RC	6.00	2.50
❑ 271 Kirk Morrison RC	8.00	3.00
❑ 272 Mike Nugent RC	8.00	3.00
❑ 273 Zach Tuiasosopo RC	4.00	1.50
❑ 274 Kay-Jay Harris RC	6.00	2.50
❑ 275 Darren Sproles RC	8.00	3.00
❑ 276 Ciatrick Fason RC	8.00	3.00
❑ 277 Charlie Frye RC	15.00	6.00
❑ 278 Vernand Morency RC	8.00	3.00
❑ 279 Jason Campbell RC	12.00	5.00
❑ 280 Antrel Rolle RC	8.00	3.00
❑ 281 Derrick Johnson RC	12.00	5.00
❑ 282 Shawne Merriman RC	12.00	5.00
❑ 283 Marlin Jackson RC	8.00	3.00
❑ 284 Jerome Mathis RC	8.00	3.00
❑ 285 Mike Williams	15.00	6.00
❑ 286 Dan Cody RC	8.00	3.00
❑ 287 Travis Johnson RC	8.00	3.00
❑ 288 Thomas Davis RC	8.00	3.00
❑ 289 Marcus Spears RC	8.00	3.00
❑ 290 Andrew Walter RC	12.00	5.00
❑ 291 Heath Miller RC	20.00	7.50
❑ 292 Mark Clayton RC	10.00	4.00
❑ 293 Troy Williamson RC	15.00	6.00
❑ 294 Roddy White RC	8.00	3.00
❑ 295 Braylon Edwards RC	25.00	10.00
❑ 296 Cedric Benson RC	15.00	6.00
❑ 297 Cadillac Williams RC	40.00	20.00
❑ 298 Ronnie Brown RC	30.00	12.50
❑ 299 Alex Smith QB RC	30.00	12.50
❑ 300 Aaron Rodgers RC	25.00	10.00

1997 Revolution

❑ COMPLETE SET (150)	80.00	40.00
❑ 1 Larry Centers	.75	.30
❑ 2 Kent Graham	.50	.20
❑ 3 Leeland McElroy	.50	.20
❑ 4 Rob Moore	.75	.30
❑ 5 Jake Plummer RC	8.00	3.00
❑ 6 Jamal Anderson	1.25	.50
❑ 7 Bert Emanuel	.75	.30
❑ 8 Byron Hanspard RC	.75	.30
❑ 9 Terance Mathis	.75	.30
❑ 10 O.J. Santiago RC	.75	.30
❑ 11 Derrick Alexander WR	.75	.30
❑ 12 Peter Boulware RC	1.25	.50
❑ 13 Jay Graham RC	.75	.30
❑ 14 Michael Jackson	.75	.30
❑ 15 Vinny Testaverde	.75	.30
❑ 16 Todd Collins	.50	.20
❑ 17 Andre Reed	.75	.30
❑ 18 Jay Riemersma	.50	.20
❑ 19 Antowain Smith RC	4.00	1.50
❑ 20 Bruce Smith	.75	.30
❑ 21 Thurman Thomas	1.25	.50
❑ 22 Rae Carruth RC	.50	.20
❑ 23 Kerry Collins	1.25	.50
❑ 24 Anthony Johnson	.50	.20
❑ 25 Muhsin Muhammad	.75	.30
❑ 26 Wesley Walls	.75	.30
❑ 27 Curtis Conway	.75	.30
❑ 28 Bobby Engram	.75	.30
❑ 29 Raymont Harris	.50	.20
❑ 30 Rick Mirer	.50	.20
❑ 31 Rashaan Salaam	.50	.20
❑ 32 Jeff Blake	.75	.30
❑ 33 Corey Dillon RC	10.00	4.00
❑ 34 Carl Pickens	.75	.30
❑ 35 Darnay Scott	.75	.30
❑ 36 Troy Aikman	2.50	1.00
❑ 37 Michael Irvin	1.25	.50
❑ 38 Daryl Johnston	.75	.30
❑ 39 Deion Sanders	1.25	.50
❑ 40 Emmitt Smith	4.00	1.50
❑ 41 Terrell Davis	1.50	.60
❑ 42 John Elway	5.00	2.00
❑ 43 Ed McCaffrey	.75	.30
❑ 44 Shannon Sharpe	.75	.30
❑ 45 Neil Smith	.75	.30
❑ 46 Scott Mitchell	.75	.30
❑ 47 Herman Moore	.75	.30
❑ 48 Johnnie Morton	.75	.30
❑ 49 Barry Sanders	4.00	1.50
❑ 50 Robert Brooks	.75	.30
❑ 51 LeRoy Butler	.50	.20
❑ 52 Brett Favre	5.00	2.00
❑ 53 Antonio Freeman	1.25	.50
❑ 54 Dorsey Levens	1.25	.50
❑ 55 Reggie White	1.25	.50
❑ 56 Sean Dawkins	.50	.20
❑ 57 Ken Dilger	.50	.20
❑ 58 Marshall Faulk	1.50	.60
❑ 59 Jim Harbaugh	.75	.30
❑ 60 Marvin Harrison	1.25	.50
❑ 61 Mark Brunell	1.50	.60
❑ 62 Keenan McCardell	.75	.30
❑ 63 Natrone Means	.75	.30
❑ 64 Jimmy Smith	.75	.30
❑ 65 James O.Stewart	.75	.30
❑ 66 Marcus Allen	1.25	.50
❑ 67 Tony Gonzalez RC	5.00	2.00
❑ 68 Elvis Grbac	.75	.30
❑ 69 Greg Hill	.50	.20
❑ 70 Andre Rison	.75	.30
❑ 71 Karim Abdul-Jabbar	1.25	.50
❑ 72 Fred Barnett	.50	.20
❑ 73 Dan Marino	5.00	2.00
❑ 74 O.J. McDuffie	.75	.30
❑ 75 Irving Spikes	.50	.20
❑ 76 Cris Carter	1.25	.50
❑ 77 Matthew Hatchette RC	.75	.30
❑ 78 Brad Johnson	1.25	.50
❑ 79 Jake Reed	.75	.30
❑ 80 Robert Smith	.75	.30
❑ 81 Drew Bledsoe	1.50	.60
❑ 82 Ben Coates	.75	.30
❑ 83 Terry Glenn	1.25	.50
❑ 84 Curtis Martin	1.50	.60
❑ 85 Dave Meggett	.50	.20
❑ 86 Troy Davis RC	.75	.30
❑ 87 Andre Hastings	.50	.20
❑ 88 Heath Shuler	.50	.20
❑ 89 Irv Smith	.50	.20
❑ 90 Danny Wuerffel RC	1.25	.50
❑ 91 Ray Zellars	.50	.20
❑ 92 Tiki Barber RC	10.00	4.00
❑ 93 Dave Brown	.50	.20
❑ 94 Chris Calloway	.50	.20
❑ 95 Rodney Hampton	.75	.30
❑ 96 Amani Toomer	.75	.30
❑ 97 Wayne Chrebet	1.25	.50
❑ 98 Keyshawn Johnson	1.25	.50
❑ 99 Adrian Murrell	.75	.30
❑ 100 Neil O'Donnell	.75	.30
❑ 101 Dedric Ward RC	.75	.30
❑ 102 Tim Brown	1.25	.50
❑ 103 Rickey Dudley	.75	.30
❑ 104 Jeff George	.75	.30
❑ 105 Desmond Howard	.75	.30
❑ 106 Napoleon Kaufman	1.25	.50
❑ 107 Ty Detmer	.75	.30
❑ 108 Jason Dunn	.50	.20
❑ 109 Irving Fryar	.75	.30
❑ 110 Rodney Peete	.50	.20
❑ 111 Ricky Watters	.75	.30
❑ 112 Jerome Bettis	1.25	.50
❑ 113 Will Blackwell RC	.75	.30
❑ 114 Charles Johnson	.75	.30
❑ 115 Kordell Stewart	1.25	.50
❑ 116 Tony Banks	.75	.30
❑ 117 Isaac Bruce	1.25	.50
❑ 118 Ernie Conwell	.50	.20
❑ 119 Eddie Kennison	.75	.30
❑ 120 Lawrence Phillips	.50	.20
❑ 121 Stan Humphries	.75	.30
❑ 122 Tony Martin	.75	.30
❑ 123 Eric Metcalf	.75	.30
❑ 124 Junior Seau	1.25	.50
❑ 125 Jim Druckenmiller RC	.75	.30
❑ 126 Kevin Greene	.75	.30
❑ 127 Garrison Hearst	.75	.30
❑ 128 Terrell Owens	1.50	.60
❑ 129 Jerry Rice	2.50	1.00
❑ 130 J.J. Stokes	.75	.30
❑ 131 Rod Woodson	.75	.30
❑ 132 Steve Young	1.50	.60
❑ 133 Joey Galloway	.75	.30
❑ 134 Cortez Kennedy	.50	.20
❑ 135 Jon Kitna RC	6.00	2.50
❑ 136 Warren Moon	1.25	.50
❑ 137 Chris Warren	.75	.30
❑ 138 Mike Alstott	1.25	.50
❑ 139 Reidel Anthony RC	1.25	.50
❑ 140 Trent Dilfer	1.25	.50
❑ 141 Warrick Dunn RC	5.00	2.00
❑ 142 Willie Davis	.50	.20
❑ 143 Eddie George	1.25	.50
❑ 144 Steve McNair	1.50	.60
❑ 145 Chris Sanders	.50	.20
❑ 146 Terry Allen	1.25	.50
❑ 147 Jamie Asher	.50	.20
❑ 148 Henry Ellard	.50	.20
❑ 149 Gus Frerotte	.50	.20
❑ 150 Leslie Shepherd	.50	.20
❑ S1 Mark Brunell Sample	1.00	.40

1998 Revolution

❑ COMPLETE SET (150)	100.00	40.00
❑ 1 Larry Centers	.75	.30
❑ 2 Leeland McElroy	.75	.30
❑ 3 Rob Moore	1.25	.50
❑ 4 Jake Plummer	2.00	.75
❑ 5 Frank Sanders	1.25	.50
❑ 6 Jamal Anderson	2.00	.75
❑ 7 Chris Chandler	1.25	.50
❑ 8 Byron Hanspard	.75	.30
❑ 9 Jay Graham	.75	.30
❑ 10 Michael Jackson	.75	.30
❑ 11 Vinny Testaverde	1.25	.50
❑ 12 Eric Zeier	1.25	.50
❑ 13 Todd Collins	.75	.30

❑ 14 Quinn Early	.75	.30
❑ 15 Andre Reed	1.25	.50
❑ 16 Antowain Smith	2.00	.75
❑ 17 Bruce Smith	1.25	.50
❑ 18 Thurman Thomas	2.00	.75
❑ 19 Rae Carruth	.75	.30
❑ 20 Kerry Collins	1.25	.50
❑ 21 Wesley Walls	1.25	.50
❑ 22 Darnell Autry	.75	.30
❑ 23 Curtis Conway	1.25	.50
❑ 24 Bobby Engram	1.25	.50
❑ 25 Curtis Enis RC	1.25	.50
❑ 26 Raymont Harris	.75	.30
❑ 27 Jeff Blake	1.25	.50
❑ 28 Corey Dillon	2.00	.75
❑ 29 Carl Pickens	1.25	.50
❑ 30 Darnay Scott	1.25	.50
❑ 31 Troy Aikman	4.00	1.50
❑ 32 Michael Irvin	2.00	.75
❑ 33 Deion Sanders	2.00	.75
❑ 34 Emmitt Smith	6.00	2.50
❑ 35 Steve Atwater	.75	.30
❑ 36 Terrell Davis	2.00	.75
❑ 37 John Elway	8.00	3.00
❑ 38 Brian Griese RC	5.00	2.00
❑ 39 Ed McCaffrey	1.25	.50
❑ 40 Marcus Nash RC	1.25	.50
❑ 41 Shannon Sharpe	1.25	.50
❑ 42 Neil Smith	1.25	.50
❑ 43 Rod Smith	1.25	.50
❑ 44 Charlie Batch RC	2.50	1.00
❑ 45 Germane Crowell RC	2.00	.75
❑ 46 Scott Mitchell	1.25	.50
❑ 47 Herman Moore	1.25	.50
❑ 48 Barry Sanders	6.00	2.50
❑ 49 Robert Brooks	1.25	.50
❑ 50 Mark Chmura	1.25	.50
❑ 51 Brett Favre	8.00	3.00
❑ 52 Antonio Freeman	2.00	.75
❑ 53 Dorsey Levens	2.00	.75
❑ 54 Aaron Bailey	.75	.30
❑ 55 Ken Dilger	.75	.30
❑ 56 Marshall Faulk	2.50	1.00
❑ 57 Marvin Harrison	2.00	.75
❑ 58 Peyton Manning RC	25.00	10.00
❑ 59 Tavian Banks RC	2.00	.75
❑ 60 Tony Brackens	.75	.30
❑ 61 Mark Brunell	2.00	.75
❑ 62 Keenan McCardell	1.25	.50
❑ 63 Natrone Means	1.25	.50
❑ 64 Jimmy Smith	1.25	.50
❑ 65 James Stewart	1.25	.50
❑ 66 Fred Taylor RC	4.00	1.50
❑ 67 Tony Gonzalez	2.00	.75
❑ 68 Elvis Grbac	1.25	.50
❑ 69 Greg Hill	.75	.30
❑ 70 Andre Rison	1.25	.50
❑ 71 Derrick Thomas	2.00	.75
❑ 72 Karim Abdul-Jabbar	2.00	.75
❑ 73 John Avery RC	2.00	.75
❑ 74 Troy Drayton	.75	.30
❑ 75 Dan Marino	8.00	3.00
❑ 76 O.J. McDuffie	1.25	.50
❑ 77 Cris Carter	2.00	.75
❑ 78 Brad Johnson	2.00	.75
❑ 79 John Randle	1.25	.50
❑ 80 Jake Reed	1.25	.50
❑ 81 Robert Smith	2.00	.75
❑ 82 Drew Bledsoe	3.00	1.25
❑ 83 Ben Coates	1.25	.50
❑ 84 Robert Edwards RC	2.00	.75
❑ 85 Terry Glenn	2.00	.75
❑ 86 Tony Simmons RC	2.00	.75
❑ 87 Troy Davis	.75	.30
❑ 88 Heath Shuler	.75	.30
❑ 89 Danny Wuerffel	1.25	.50
❑ 90 Ray Zellars	.75	.30
❑ 91 Tiki Barber	2.00	.75
❑ 92 Joe Jurevicius RC	2.50	1.00
❑ 93 Danny Kanell	1.25	.50
❑ 94 Charles Way	.75	.30
❑ 95 Tyrone Wheatley	1.25	.50
❑ 96 Wayne Chrebet	2.00	.75
❑ 97 Glenn Foley	1.25	.50
❑ 98 Keyshawn Johnson	2.00	.75
❑ 99 Curtis Martin	2.00	.75
❑ 100 Tim Brown	2.00	.75
❑ 101 Rickey Dudley	.75	.30
❑ 102 Jeff George	1.25	.50
❑ 103 Desmond Howard	1.25	.50
❑ 104 Napoleon Kaufman	2.00	.75
❑ 105 Charles Woodson RC	3.00	1.25
❑ 106 Jason Dunn	.75	.30
❑ 107 Irving Fryar	1.25	.50
❑ 108 Charlie Garner	1.25	.50
❑ 109 Bobby Hoying	1.25	.50
❑ 110 Jerome Bettis	2.00	.75
❑ 111 Mark Bruener	.75	.30
❑ 112 Charles Johnson	.75	.30
❑ 113 Levon Kirkland	.75	.30
❑ 114 Kordell Stewart	2.00	.75
❑ 115 Hines Ward RC	10.00	5.00
❑ 116 Tony Banks	1.25	.50
❑ 117 Isaac Bruce	2.00	.75
❑ 118 Robert Holcombe RC	2.00	.75
❑ 119 Eddie Kennison	1.25	.50
❑ 120 Freddie Jones	.75	.30
❑ 121 Ryan Leaf RC	2.50	1.00
❑ 122 Tony Martin	1.25	.50
❑ 123 Junior Seau	2.00	.75
❑ 124 Jim Druckenmiller	.75	.30
❑ 125 Garrison Hearst	2.00	.75
❑ 126 Terrell Owens	2.00	.75
❑ 127 Jerry Rice	4.00	1.50
❑ 128 J.J. Stokes	1.25	.50
❑ 129 Steve Young	2.50	1.00
❑ 130 Joey Galloway	1.25	.50
❑ 131 Ahman Green RC	12.00	5.00
❑ 132 Cortez Kennedy	.75	.30
❑ 133 Jon Kitna	2.00	.75
❑ 134 James McKnight	2.00	.75
❑ 135 Warren Moon	2.00	.75
❑ 136 Mike Alstott	2.00	.75
❑ 137 Reidel Anthony	1.25	.50
❑ 138 Trent Dilfer	2.00	.75
❑ 139 Warrick Dunn	2.00	.75
❑ 140 Warren Sapp	1.25	.50
❑ 141 Kevin Dyson RC	2.50	1.00
❑ 142 Eddie George	2.00	.75
❑ 143 Steve McNair	2.00	.75
❑ 144 Chris Sanders	.75	.30
❑ 145 Frank Wycheck	.75	.30
❑ 146 Stephen Alexander RC	2.00	.75
❑ 147 Terry Allen	2.00	.75
❑ 148 Gus Frerotte	.75	.30
❑ 149 Skip Hicks RC	2.00	.75
❑ 150 Michael Westbrook	1.25	.50
❑ S1 Warrick Dunn Sample	1.00	.40

1999 Revolution

❑ COMPLETE SET (175)	100.00	50.00
❑ 1 David Boston RC	2.50	1.00
❑ 2 Joel Makovicka RC SP	3.00	1.25
❑ 3 Rob Moore	.75	.30
❑ 4 Adrian Murrell	.75	.30
❑ 5 Jake Plummer	.75	.30
❑ 6 Frank Sanders	.75	.30
❑ 7 Jamal Anderson	1.25	.50
❑ 8 Chris Chandler	.75	.30
❑ 9 Tim Dwight	1.25	.50
❑ 10 Terance Mathis	.75	.30
❑ 11 Jeff Paulk RC SP	1.50	.60
❑ 12 O.J. Santiago	.50	.20
❑ 13 Peter Boulware	.50	.20
❑ 14 Priest Holmes	2.00	.75
❑ 15 Michael Jackson	.50	.20
❑ 16 Jermaine Lewis	.75	.30
❑ 17 Doug Flutie	1.25	.50
❑ 18 Eric Moulds	1.25	.50
❑ 19 Peerless Price RC SP	3.00	1.25
❑ 20 Andre Reed	.75	.30
❑ 21 Antowain Smith	1.25	.50
❑ 22 Bruce Smith	.75	.30
❑ 23 Steve Beuerlein	.50	.20
❑ 24 Kevin Greene	.75	.30
❑ 25 Fred Lane	.50	.20
❑ 26 Muhsin Muhammad	.75	.30
❑ 27 Wesley Walls	.75	.30
❑ 28 Marty Booker RC SP	3.00	1.25
❑ 29 Curtis Conway	.75	.30
❑ 30 Bobby Engram	.75	.30
❑ 31 Curtis Enis	.50	.20
❑ 32 Erik Kramer	.50	.20
❑ 33 Cade McNown RC	2.00	.75
❑ 34 Scott Covington RC	2.50	1.00
❑ 35 Corey Dillon	1.25	.50
❑ 36 Carl Pickens	.75	.30
❑ 37 Darnay Scott	.50	.20
❑ 38 Akili Smith RC	2.00	.75
❑ 39 Craig Yeast RC SP	2.50	1.00
❑ 40 Darrin Chiaverini RC SP	2.50	1.00
❑ 41 Tim Couch RC	2.50	1.00
❑ 42 Ty Detmer	.75	.30
❑ 43 Kevin Johnson RC	2.50	1.00
❑ 44 Terry Kirby	.50	.20
❑ 45 Daylon McCutcheon RC SP	1.50	.60
❑ 46 Irv Smith	.50	.20
❑ 47 Troy Aikman	2.50	1.00
❑ 48 Michael Irvin	.75	.30
❑ 49 Wane McGarity RC SP	1.50	.60
❑ 50 Dat Nguyen RC SP	3.00	1.25
❑ 51 Deion Sanders	1.25	.50
❑ 52 Emmitt Smith	2.50	1.00
❑ 53 Terrell Davis	1.25	.50
❑ 54 John Elway	4.00	1.50
❑ 55 Brian Griese	1.25	.50
❑ 56 Ed McCaffrey	.75	.30
❑ 57 Travis McGriff RC SP	1.50	.60
❑ 58 Shannon Sharpe	.75	.30
❑ 59 Rod Smith WR	.75	.30
❑ 60 Charlie Batch	1.25	.50
❑ 61 Chris Claiborne RC	1.25	.50
❑ 62 Sedrick Irvin RC	1.25	.50
❑ 63 Herman Moore	.75	.30
❑ 64 Johnnie Morton	.75	.30
❑ 65 Barry Sanders	4.00	1.50
❑ 66 Aaron Brooks RC SP	6.00	2.50
❑ 67 Mark Chmura	.50	.20
❑ 68 Brett Favre	4.00	1.50
❑ 69 Antonio Freeman	1.25	.50
❑ 70 Dorsey Levens	1.25	.50
❑ 71 De'Mond Parker RC SP	1.50	.60
❑ 72 Marvin Harrison	1.25	.50
❑ 73 Edgerrin James RC	8.00	3.00
❑ 74 Peyton Manning	4.00	1.50
❑ 75 Jerome Pathon	.50	.20
❑ 76 Mike Peterson RC SP	2.50	1.00
❑ 77 Reggie Barlow	.50	.20
❑ 78 Mark Brunell	1.25	.50
❑ 79 Keenan McCardell	.75	.30
❑ 80 Jimmy Smith	.75	.30
❑ 81 Fred Taylor	1.25	.50
❑ 82 Mike Cloud RC	2.00	.75
❑ 83 Tony Gonzalez	1.25	.50
❑ 84 Elvis Grbac	.75	.30
❑ 85 Larry Parker RC SP	3.00	1.25
❑ 86 Andre Rison	.75	.30

❑ 87 Brian Shay RC SP 1.50 .60
❑ 88 Karim Abdul-Jabbar .75 .30
❑ 89 Oronde Gadsden .75 .30
❑ 90 James Johnson RC 2.00 .75
❑ 91 Rob Konrad RC 2.00 .75
❑ 92 Dan Marino 4.00 1.50
❑ 93 O.J. McDuffie .75 .30
❑ 94 Cris Carter 1.25 .50
❑ 95 Daunte Culpepper RC 8.00 3.00
❑ 96 Randall Cunningham 1.25 .50
❑ 97 Jim Kleinsasser RC SP 2.50 1.00
❑ 98 Randy Moss 3.00 1.25
❑ 99 Jake Reed .75 .30
❑ 100 Robert Smith 1.25 .50
❑ 101 Drew Bledsoe 1.50 .60
❑ 102 Ben Coates .75 .30
❑ 103 Kevin Faulk RC 2.50 1.00
❑ 104 Terry Glenn 1.25 .50
❑ 105 Shawn Jefferson .50 .20
❑ 106 Andy Katzenmoyer RC SP 2.50 1.00
❑ 107 Cameron Cleeland .50 .20
❑ 108 Andre Hastings .50 .20
❑ 109 Billy Joe Tolliver .50 .20
❑ 110 Ricky Williams RC 4.00 1.50
❑ 111 Gary Brown .50 .20
❑ 112 Kent Graham .50 .20
❑ 113 Ike Hilliard .50 .20
❑ 114 Joe Montgomery RC SP 2.50 1.00
❑ 115 Amani Toomer .50 .20
❑ 116 Wayne Chrebet .75 .30
❑ 117 Keyshawn Johnson 1.25 .50
❑ 118 Leon Johnson .50 .20
❑ 119 Curtis Martin 1.25 .50
❑ 120 Vinny Testaverde .75 .30
❑ 121 Dedric Ward .50 .20
❑ 122 Tim Brown 1.25 .50
❑ 123 Dameane Douglas RC SP 3.00 1.25
❑ 124 Rickey Dudley .50 .20
❑ 125 James Jett .75 .30
❑ 126 Napoleon Kaufman 1.25 .50
❑ 127 Charles Woodson 1.25 .50
❑ 128 Na Brown RC SP 2.50 1.00
❑ 129 Cecil Martin RC SP 2.50 1.00
❑ 130 Donovan McNabb RC 10.00 4.00
❑ 131 Duce Staley 1.25 .50
❑ 132 Kevin Turner .50 .20
❑ 133 Jerome Bettis 1.25 .50
❑ 134 Troy Edwards RC 2.00 .75
❑ 135 Courtney Hawkins .50 .20
❑ 136 Malcolm Johnson RC SP 1.50 .60
❑ 137 Kordell Stewart .75 .30
❑ 138 Jerame Tuman RC SP 3.00 1.25
❑ 139 Amos Zereoue RC 2.50 1.00
❑ 140 Isaac Bruce 1.25 .50
❑ 141 Joe Germaine RC 2.00 .75
❑ 142 Torry Holt RC SP 6.00 2.50
❑ 143 Amp Lee .50 .20
❑ 144 Ricky Proehl .50 .20
❑ 145 Freddie Jones .50 .20
❑ 146 Ryan Leaf 1.25 .50
❑ 147 Natrone Means .75 .30
❑ 148 Mikhael Ricks .50 .20
❑ 149 Garrison Hearst .75 .30
❑ 150 Terry Jackson RC SP 2.50 1.00
❑ 151 Terrell Owens 1.25 .50
❑ 152 Jerry Rice 2.50 1.00
❑ 153 J.J. Stokes .75 .30
❑ 154 Steve Young 1.50 .60
❑ 155 Karsten Bailey RC 2.00 .75
❑ 156 Joey Galloway .75 .30
❑ 157 Ahman Green 1.25 .50
❑ 158 Brock Huard RC 2.50 1.00
❑ 159 Jon Kitna 1.25 .50
❑ 160 Ricky Watters .75 .30
❑ 161 Mike Alstott 1.25 .50
❑ 162 Reidel Anthony .75 .30
❑ 163 Trent Dilfer .75 .30
❑ 164 Warrick Dunn 1.25 .50
❑ 165 Shaun King RC 2.00 .75
❑ 166 Anthony McFarland RC 2.50 1.00
❑ 167 Kevin Dyson .75 .30
❑ 168 Eddie George 1.25 .50
❑ 169 Darran Hall RC 1.25 .50
❑ 170 Steve McNair 1.25 .50
❑ 171 Frank Wycheck .50 .20
❑ 172 Stephen Alexander .50 .20
❑ 173 Champ Bailey RC 3.00 1.25
❑ 174 Skip Hicks .50 .20
❑ 175 Michael Westbrook .75 .30

2000 Revolution

❑ COMP.SET w/o SP's (100) 40.00 20.00
❑ 1 David Boston 1.25 .50
❑ 2 Jake Plummer .75 .30
❑ 3 Frank Sanders .75 .30
❑ 4 Jamal Anderson 1.25 .50
❑ 5 Chris Chandler .75 .30
❑ 6 Tim Dwight 1.25 .50
❑ 7 Terance Mathis .75 .30
❑ 8 Tony Banks .75 .30
❑ 9 Qadry Ismail .75 .30
❑ 10 Shannon Sharpe .50 .20
❑ 11 Rob Johnson .75 .30
❑ 12 Eric Moulds 1.25 .50
❑ 13 Peerless Price .75 .30
❑ 14 Antowain Smith .75 .30
❑ 15 Steve Beuerlein .75 .30
❑ 16 Tim Biakabutuka .75 .30
❑ 17 Muhsin Muhammad .75 .30
❑ 18 Curtis Enis .50 .20
❑ 19 Cade McNown .50 .20
❑ 20 Marcus Robinson 1.25 .50
❑ 21 Corey Dillon 1.25 .50
❑ 22 Akili Smith .50 .20
❑ 23 Tim Couch .75 .30
❑ 24 Kevin Johnson 1.25 .50
❑ 25 Troy Aikman 2.50 1.00
❑ 26 Rocket Ismail .75 .30
❑ 27 Emmitt Smith 2.50 1.00
❑ 28 Terrell Davis 1.25 .50
❑ 29 Brian Griese 1.25 .50
❑ 30 Ed McCaffrey 1.25 .50
❑ 31 Charlie Batch 1.25 .50
❑ 32 Herman Moore .75 .30
❑ 33 James Stewart .75 .30
❑ 34 Brett Favre 4.00 1.50
❑ 35 Antonio Freeman 1.25 .50
❑ 36 Dorsey Levens .75 .30
❑ 37 Marvin Harrison 1.25 .50
❑ 38 Edgerrin James 2.00 .75
❑ 39 Peyton Manning 3.00 1.25
❑ 40 Terrence Wilkins .50 .20
❑ 41 Mark Brunell 1.25 .50
❑ 42 Keenan McCardell .75 .30
❑ 43 Jimmy Smith .75 .30
❑ 44 Fred Taylor 1.25 .50
❑ 45 Derrick Alexander .75 .30
❑ 46 Tony Gonzalez .75 .30
❑ 47 Elvis Grbac .75 .30
❑ 48 Damon Huard 1.25 .50
❑ 49 James Johnson .50 .20
❑ 50 O.J. McDuffie .75 .30
❑ 51 Cris Carter 1.25 .50
❑ 52 Daunte Culpepper 1.50 .60
❑ 53 Randy Moss 2.50 1.00
❑ 54 Robert Smith 1.25 .50
❑ 55 Drew Bledsoe 1.50 .60
❑ 56 Terry Glenn .75 .30
❑ 57 Jeff Blake .75 .30
❑ 58 Ricky Williams 1.25 .50
❑ 59 Tiki Barber 1.25 .50
❑ 60 Kerry Collins .75 .30
❑ 61 Ike Hilliard .75 .30
❑ 62 Amani Toomer .50 .20
❑ 63 Wayne Chrebet .75 .30
❑ 64 Curtis Martin 1.25 .50
❑ 65 Vinny Testaverde .75 .30
❑ 66 Dedric Ward .50 .20
❑ 67 Tim Brown 1.25 .50
❑ 68 Napoleon Kaufman .75 .30
❑ 69 Tyrone Wheatley .75 .30
❑ 70 Charles Johnson .75 .30
❑ 71 Donovan McNabb 2.00 .75
❑ 72 Duce Staley 1.25 .50
❑ 73 Jerome Bettis 1.25 .50
❑ 74 Troy Edwards .50 .20
❑ 75 Kordell Stewart .75 .30
❑ 76 Isaac Bruce 1.25 .50
❑ 77 Marshall Faulk 1.50 .60
❑ 78 Az-Zahir Hakim .50 .20
❑ 79 Torry Holt 1.25 .50
❑ 80 Kurt Warner 2.50 1.00
❑ 81 Curtis Conway .75 .30
❑ 82 Jermaine Fazande .50 .20
❑ 83 Ryan Leaf .75 .30
❑ 84 Junior Seau 1.25 .50
❑ 85 Jeff Garcia 1.25 .50
❑ 86 Charlie Garner .75 .30
❑ 87 Terrell Owens 1.25 .50
❑ 88 Jerry Rice 2.50 1.00
❑ 89 Jon Kitna 1.25 .50
❑ 90 Derrick Mayes .75 .30
❑ 91 Ricky Watters .75 .30
❑ 92 Mike Alstott 1.25 .50
❑ 93 Warrick Dunn 1.25 .50
❑ 94 Keyshawn Johnson 1.25 .50
❑ 95 Shaun King .50 .20
❑ 96 Eddie George 1.25 .50
❑ 97 Jevon Kearse 1.25 .50
❑ 98 Steve McNair 1.25 .50
❑ 99 Stephen Davis 1.25 .50
❑ 100 Brad Johnson 1.25 .50
❑ 101 Thomas Jones RC 20.00 7.50
❑ 102 Doug Johnson RC 10.00 4.00
❑ 103 Jamal Lewis RC 25.00 10.00
❑ 104 Chris Redman RC 8.00 3.00
❑ 105 Travis Taylor RC 10.00 4.00
❑ 106 Troy Walters RC 10.00 4.00
❑ 107 Kwame Cavil RC 5.00 2.00
❑ 108 Sammy Morris RC 8.00 3.00
❑ 109 Dez White RC 10.00 4.00
❑ 110 Ron Dugans RC 5.00 2.00
❑ 111 Danny Farmer RC 8.00 3.00
❑ 112 Curtis Keaton RC 8.00 3.00
❑ 113 Peter Warrick RC 10.00 4.00
❑ 114 Dennis Northcutt RC 10.00 4.00
❑ 115 Travis Prentice RC 8.00 3.00
❑ 116 Kevin Thompson RC 5.00 2.00
❑ 117 Spergon Wynn RC 8.00 3.00
❑ 118 Michael Wiley RC 8.00 3.00
❑ 119 Mike Anderson RC 12.00 5.00
❑ 120 Chris Cole RC 8.00 3.00
❑ 121 Jarious Jackson RC 8.00 3.00
❑ 122 Charles Lee RC 5.00 2.00
❑ 123 Anthony Lucas RC 5.00 2.00
❑ 124 R.Jay Soward RC 8.00 3.00
❑ 125 Shyrone Stith RC 8.00 3.00
❑ 126 Sylvester Morris RC 8.00 3.00
❑ 127 Doug Chapman RC 8.00 3.00
❑ 128 Tom Brady RC 135.00 75.00
❑ 129 Gari Scott RC 5.00 2.00
❑ 130 J.R. Redmond RC 8.00 3.00
❑ 131 Ron Dayne RC 10.00 4.00
❑ 132 Ron Dixon RC 8.00 3.00
❑ 133 Laveranues Coles RC 12.00 5.00
❑ 134 Ronney Jenkins RC 8.00 3.00
❑ 135 Chad Pennington RC 25.00 10.00
❑ 136 Jerry Porter RC 12.00 5.00
❑ 137 Todd Pinkston RC 10.00 4.00
❑ 138 Plaxico Burress RC 20.00 7.50
❑ 139 Trung Canidate RC 8.00 3.00
❑ 140 Troy Walters RC 10.00 4.00
❑ 141 Giovanni Carmazzi RC 5.00 2.00
❑ 142 Tim Rattay RC 10.00 4.00
❑ 143 Shaun Alexander RC 40.00 20.00
❑ 144 Darrell Jackson RC 20.00 7.50
❑ 145 James Williams RC 8.00 3.00
❑ 146 Joe Hamilton RC 8.00 3.00
❑ 147 Aaron Stecker RC 10.00 4.00
❑ 148 Erron Kinney RC 10.00 4.00
❑ 149 Billy Volek RC 15.00 6.00
❑ 150 Todd Husak RC 10.00 4.00

1989 Score

Card		
❑ COMPLETE SET (330)	100.00	50.00
❑ COMP.FACT.SET (330)	100.00	50.00
❑ 1 Joe Montana	4.00	1.50
❑ 2 Bo Jackson	.60	.25
❑ 3 Boomer Esiason	.20	.07
❑ 4 Roger Craig	.50	.20
❑ 5 Ed Too Tall Jones	.20	.07
❑ 6 Phil Simms	.20	.07
❑ 7 Dan Hampton	.20	.07
❑ 8 John Settle RC	.10	.02
❑ 9 Bernie Kosar	.20	.07
❑ 10 Al Toon	.20	.07
❑ 11 Bubby Brister RC	1.00	.40
❑ 12 Mark Clayton	.20	.07
❑ 13 Dan Marino	4.00	1.50
❑ 14 Joe Morris	.10	.02
❑ 15 Warren Moon	.50	.20
❑ 16 Chuck Long	.10	.02
❑ 17 Mark Jackson	.10	.02
❑ 18 Michael Irvin RC	10.00	4.00
❑ 19 Bruce Smith	.50	.20
❑ 20 Anthony Carter	.20	.07
❑ 21 Charles Haley	.50	.20
❑ 22 Dave Duerson	.10	.02
❑ 23 Troy Stradford	.10	.02
❑ 24 Freeman McNeil	.10	.02
❑ 25 Jerry Gray	.10	.02
❑ 26 Bill Maas	.10	.02
❑ 27 Chris Chandler RC	5.00	2.00
❑ 28 Tom Newberry RC	.10	.02
❑ 29 Albert Lewis	.10	.02
❑ 30 Jay Schroeder	.10	.02
❑ 31 Dalton Hilliard	.10	.02
❑ 32 Tony Eason	.10	.02
❑ 33 Rick Donnelly UER	.10	.02
❑ 34 Herschel Walker	.20	.07
❑ 35 Wesley Walker	.10	.02
❑ 36 Chris Doleman	.20	.07
❑ 37 Pat Swilling	.20	.07
❑ 38 Joey Browner	.10	.02
❑ 39 Shane Conlan	.10	.02
❑ 40 Mike Tomczak	.20	.07
❑ 41 Webster Slaughter	.20	.07
❑ 42 Ray Donaldson	.10	.02
❑ 43 Christian Okoye	.10	.02
❑ 44 John Bosa	.10	.02
❑ 45 Aaron Cox RC	.10	.02
❑ 46 Bobby Hebert	.20	.07
❑ 47 Carl Banks	.10	.02
❑ 48 Jeff Fuller	.10	.02
❑ 49 Gerald Willhite	.10	.02
❑ 50 Mike Singletary	.20	.07
❑ 51 Stanley Morgan	.10	.02
❑ 52 Mark Bavaro	.20	.07
❑ 53 Mickey Shuler	.10	.02
❑ 54 Keith Millard	.10	.02
❑ 55 Andre Tippett	.10	.02
❑ 56 Vance Johnson	.20	.07
❑ 57 Bennie Blades RC	.20	.07
❑ 58 Tim Harris	.10	.02
❑ 59 Hanford Dixon	.10	.02
❑ 60 Chris Miller RC	1.00	.40
❑ 61 Cornelius Bennett	.50	.20
❑ 62 Neal Anderson	.20	.07
❑ 63 Ickey Woods RC UER	.50	.20
❑ 64 Gary Anderson RB	.10	.02
❑ 65 Vaughan Johnson RC	.10	.02
❑ 66 Ronnie Lippett	.10	.02
❑ 67 Mike Quick	.10	.02
❑ 68 Roy Green	.20	.07
❑ 69 Tim Krumrie	.10	.02
❑ 70 Mark Malone	.10	.02
❑ 71 James Jones FB	.10	.02
❑ 72 Cris Carter RC	12.00	5.00
❑ 73 Ricky Nattiel	.10	.02
❑ 74 Jim Arnold UER	.10	.02
❑ 75 Randall Cunningham	1.00	.40
❑ 76 John L.Williams	.10	.02
❑ 77 Paul Gruber RC	.10	.02
❑ 78 Rod Woodson RC	3.00	1.25
❑ 79 Ray Childress	.10	.02
❑ 80 Doug Williams	.20	.07
❑ 81 Deron Cherry	.20	.07
❑ 82 John Offerdahl	.10	.02
❑ 83 Louis Lipps	.20	.07
❑ 84 Neil Lomax	.10	.02
❑ 85 Wade Wilson	.20	.07
❑ 86 Tim Brown RC	12.00	5.00
❑ 87 Chris Hinton	.10	.02
❑ 88 Stump Mitchell	.10	.02
❑ 89 Tunch Ilkin RC	.10	.02
❑ 90 Steve Pelluer	.10	.02
❑ 91 Brian Noble	.10	.02
❑ 92 Reggie White	.50	.20
❑ 93 Aundray Bruce RC	.10	.02
❑ 94 Garry James	.10	.02
❑ 95 Drew Hill	.10	.02
❑ 96 Anthony Munoz	.20	.07
❑ 97 James Wilder	.10	.02
❑ 98 Dexter Manley	.10	.02
❑ 99 Lee Williams	.10	.02
❑ 100 Dave Krieg	.20	.07
❑ 101A Keith Jackson RC 84	.50	.20
❑ 101B Keith Jackson RC 88	.50	.20
❑ 102 Luis Sharpe	.10	.02
❑ 103 Kevin Greene	.50	.20
❑ 104 Duane Bickett	.10	.02
❑ 105 Mark Rypien RC	.50	.20
❑ 106 Curt Warner	.10	.02
❑ 107 Jacob Green	.10	.02
❑ 108 Gary Clark	.50	.20
❑ 109 Bruce Matthews RC	2.50	1.00
❑ 110 Bill Fralic	.10	.02
❑ 111 Bill Bates	.20	.07
❑ 112 Jeff Bryant	.10	.02
❑ 113 Charles Mann	.10	.02
❑ 114 Richard Dent	.20	.07
❑ 115 Bruce Hill RC	.10	.02
❑ 116 Mark May RC	.10	.02
❑ 117 Mark Collins RC	.10	.02
❑ 118 Ron Holmes	.10	.02
❑ 119 Scott Case RC	.10	.02
❑ 120 Tom Rathman	.10	.02
❑ 121 Dennis McKinnon	.10	.02
❑ 122A Ricky Sanders ERR 46	.25	.08
❑ 122B Ricky Sanders COR 83	.50	.20
❑ 123 Michael Carter	.10	.02
❑ 124 Ozzie Newsome	.20	.07
❑ 125 Irving Fryar UER	.20	.07
❑ 126A Ron Hall RC ERR	.25	.08
❑ 126B Ron Hall RC COR	.50	.20
❑ 127 Clay Matthews	.20	.07
❑ 128 Leonard Marshall	.10	.02
❑ 129 Kevin Mack	.10	.02
❑ 130 Art Monk	.20	.07
❑ 131 Garin Veris	.10	.02
❑ 132 Steve Jordan	.10	.02
❑ 133 Frank Minnifield	.10	.02
❑ 134 Eddie Brown	.10	.02
❑ 135 Stacey Bailey	.10	.02
❑ 136 Rickey Jackson	.20	.07
❑ 137 Henry Ellard	.20	.07
❑ 138 Jim Burt	.10	.02
❑ 139 Jerome Brown	.20	.07
❑ 140 Rodney Holman RC	.10	.02
❑ 141 Sammy Winder	.10	.02
❑ 142 Marcus Cotton	.10	.02
❑ 143 Jim Jeffcoat	.10	.02
❑ 144 Rueben Mayes	.10	.02
❑ 145 Jim McMahon	.20	.07
❑ 146 Reggie Williams	.10	.02
❑ 147 John Anderson	.10	.02
❑ 148 Harris Barton RC	.10	.02
❑ 149 Phillip Epps	.10	.02
❑ 150 Jay Hilgenberg	.10	.02
❑ 151 Earl Ferrell	.10	.02
❑ 152 Andre Reed	.50	.20
❑ 153 Dennis Gentry	.10	.02
❑ 154 Max Montoya	.10	.02
❑ 155 Darrin Nelson	.10	.02
❑ 156 Jeff Chadwick	.10	.02
❑ 157 James Brooks	.20	.07
❑ 158 Keith Bishop	.10	.02
❑ 159 Robert Awalt	.10	.02
❑ 160 Marty Lyons	.10	.02
❑ 161 Johnny Hector	.10	.02
❑ 162 Tony Casillas	.10	.02
❑ 163 Kyle Clifton RC	.10	.02
❑ 164 Cody Risien	.10	.02
❑ 165 Jamie Holland RC	.10	.02
❑ 166 Merril Hoge RC	.10	.02
❑ 167 Chris Spielman RC	1.00	.40
❑ 168 Carlos Carson	.10	.02
❑ 169 Jerry Ball RC	.10	.02
❑ 170 Don Majkowski RC	.50	.20
❑ 171 Everson Walls	.10	.02
❑ 172 Mike Rozier	.10	.02
❑ 173 Matt Millen	.20	.07
❑ 174 Karl Mecklenburg	.10	.02
❑ 175 Paul Palmer	.10	.02
❑ 176 Brian Blades RC UER	.50	.20
❑ 177 Brent Fullwood RC	.10	.02
❑ 178 Anthony Miller RC	.50	.20
❑ 179 Brian Sochia	.10	.02
❑ 180 Stephen Baker RC	.10	.02
❑ 181 Jesse Solomon	.10	.02
❑ 182 John Grimsley	.10	.02
❑ 183 Timmy Newsome	.10	.02
❑ 184 Steve Sewell RC	.10	.02
❑ 185 Dean Biasucci	.10	.02
❑ 186 Alonzo Highsmith	.10	.02
❑ 187 Randy Grimes	.10	.02
❑ 188A Mark Carrier RC WR ERR	1.00	.40
❑ 188B Mark Carrier RC WR COR	1.00	.40
❑ 189 Vann McElroy	.10	.02
❑ 190 Greg Bell	.10	.02
❑ 191 Quinn Early RC	1.00	.40
❑ 192 Lawrence Taylor	.50	.20
❑ 193 Albert Bentley	.10	.02
❑ 194 Ernest Givins	.20	.07
❑ 195 Jackie Slater	.10	.02
❑ 196 Jim Sweeney	.10	.02
❑ 197 Freddie Joe Nunn	.10	.02
❑ 198 Keith Byars	.20	.07
❑ 199 Hardy Nickerson RC	.50	.20
❑ 200 Steve Beuerlein RC	4.00	1.50
❑ 201 Bruce Armstrong RC	.50	.20
❑ 202 Lionel Manuel	.10	.02
❑ 203 J.T. Smith	.10	.02
❑ 204 Mark Ingram RC	.50	.20
❑ 205 Fred Smerlas	.10	.02
❑ 206 Bryan Hinkle RC	.10	.02
❑ 207 Steve McMichael	.20	.07
❑ 208 Nick Lowery	.10	.02
❑ 209 Jack Trudeau	.10	.02
❑ 210 Lorenzo Hampton	.10	.02
❑ 211 Thurman Thomas RC	8.00	3.00
❑ 212 Steve Young	1.50	.60
❑ 213 James Lofton	.50	.20
❑ 214 Jim Covert	.10	.02
❑ 215 Ronnie Lott	.20	.07
❑ 216 Stephone Paige	.10	.02
❑ 217 Mark Duper	.20	.07
❑ 218A Willie Gault ERR 93	.25	.08
❑ 218B Willie Gault COR 83	.50	.20
❑ 219 Ken Ruettgers RC	.10	.02
❑ 220 Kevin Ross RC	.10	.02
❑ 221 Jerry Rice	3.00	1.50
❑ 222 Billy Ray Smith	.10	.02
❑ 223 Jim Kelly	1.00	.40
❑ 224 Vinny Testaverde	1.00	.40
❑ 225 Steve Largent	.50	.20
❑ 226 Warren Williams RC	.10	.02
❑ 227 Morten Andersen	.10	.02
❑ 228 Bill Brooks	.20	.07
❑ 229 Reggie Langhorne RC	.10	.02
❑ 230 Pepper Johnson	.10	.02
❑ 231 Pat Leahy	.10	.02
❑ 232 Fred Marion	.10	.02
❑ 233 Gary Zimmerman	.10	.02
❑ 234 Marcus Allen	.50	.20
❑ 235 Gaston Green RC	.10	.02

- ❑ 236 John Stephens RC .10 .02
- ❑ 237 Terry Kinard .10 .02
- ❑ 238 John Taylor RC .50 .20
- ❑ 239 Brian Bosworth .20 .07
- ❑ 240 Anthony Toney .10 .02
- ❑ 241 Ken O'Brien .10 .02
- ❑ 242 Howie Long .50 .20
- ❑ 243 Doug Flutie 2.50 1.00
- ❑ 244 Jim Everett .50 .20
- ❑ 245 Broderick Thomas RC .10 .02
- ❑ 246 Deion Sanders RC 12.00 5.00
- ❑ 247 Donnell Woolford RC .10 .02
- ❑ 248 Wayne Martin RC .10 .02
- ❑ 249 David Williams RC .10 .02
- ❑ 250 Bill Hawkins RC .10 .02
- ❑ 251 Eric Hill RC .10 .02
- ❑ 252 Burt Grossman RC .10 .02
- ❑ 253 Tracy Rocker .10 .02
- ❑ 254 Steve Wisniewski RC .50 .20
- ❑ 255 Jessie Small RC .10 .02
- ❑ 256 David Braxton .10 .02
- ❑ 257 Barry Sanders RC 40.00 15.00
- ❑ 258 Derrick Thomas RC 6.00 3.00
- ❑ 259 Eric Metcalf RC 1.00 .40
- ❑ 260 Keith DeLong RC .10 .02
- ❑ 261 Hart Lee Dykes RC .10 .02
- ❑ 262 Sammie Smith RC .10 .02
- ❑ 263 Steve Atwater RC .50 .20
- ❑ 264 Eric Ball RC .10 .02
- ❑ 265 Don Beebe RC .50 .20
- ❑ 266 Brian Williams OL RC .10 .02
- ❑ 267 Jeff Lageman RC .10 .02
- ❑ 268 Tim Worley RC .10 .02
- ❑ 269 Tony Mandarich RC .10 .02
- ❑ 270 Troy Aikman RC 30.00 12.50
- ❑ 271 Andy Heck RC .10 .02
- ❑ 272 Andre Rison RC 5.00 2.50
- ❑ 273 AFC Champ/Woods/Esiason .10 .02
- ❑ 274 NFC Champ/Joe Montana 1.00 .40
- ❑ 275 Joe Montana/Jerry Rice 2.00 .75
- ❑ 276 Rodney Carter .10 .02
- ❑ 277 Mark Jackson/V.Johnson/Nattiel .10 .02
- ❑ 278 John L. Williams .10 .02
- ❑ 279 Joe Montana/Jerry Rice 2.00 .75
- ❑ 280 Roy Green/Lomax .10 .02
- ❑ 281 Ran.Cunningham/K.Jackson .10 .02
- ❑ 282 Chris Doleman and .10 .02
- ❑ 283 Mark Duper and .10 .02
- ❑ 284 Bo Jackson/Marcus Allen .60 .25
- ❑ 285 Frank Minnifield AP .10 .02
- ❑ 286 Bruce Matthews AP .40 .15
- ❑ 287 Joey Browner AP .10 .02
- ❑ 288 Jay Hilgenberg AP .10 .02
- ❑ 289 Carl Lee RC AP .10 .02
- ❑ 290 Scott Norwood AP RC .10 .02
- ❑ 291 John Taylor AP .50 .20
- ❑ 292 Jerry Rice AP 1.50 .60
- ❑ 293A Keith Jackson AP 84 .50 .20
- ❑ 293B Keith Jackson AP 88 .50 .20
- ❑ 294 Gary Zimmerman AP .10 .02
- ❑ 295 Lawrence Taylor AP .50 .20
- ❑ 296 Reggie White AP .50 .20
- ❑ 297 Roger Craig AP .20 .07
- ❑ 298 Boomer Esiason AP .20 .07
- ❑ 299 Cornelius Bennett AP .20 .07
- ❑ 300 Mike Horan AP .10 .02
- ❑ 301 Deron Cherry AP .10 .02
- ❑ 302 Tom Newberry AP .10 .02
- ❑ 303 Mike Singletary AP .20 .07
- ❑ 304 Shane Conlan AP .10 .02
- ❑ 305A Tim Brown AP ERR 80 2.00 .75
- ❑ 305B Tim Brown AP COR 81 2.00 .75
- ❑ 306 Henry Ellard AP .20 .07
- ❑ 307 Bruce Smith AP .20 .07
- ❑ 308 Tim Krumrie AP .10 .02
- ❑ 309 Anthony Munoz AP .20 .07
- ❑ 310 Darrell Green SPD .10 .02
- ❑ 311 Anthony Miller SPD .50 .20
- ❑ 312 Wesley Walker SPEED .10 .02
- ❑ 313 Ron Brown SPEED .10 .02
- ❑ 314 Bo Jackson SPD .60 .25
- ❑ 315 Phillip Epps SPEED .10 .02
- ❑ 316A Eric Thomas RC SPD 31 .25 .08
- ❑ 316B Eric Thomas RC SPD 22 .50 .20
- ❑ 317 Herschel Walker SPD .20 .07
- ❑ 318 Jacob Green PRED .10 .02
- ❑ 319 Andre Tippett PRED .10 .02
- ❑ 320 Freddie Joe Nunn PRED .10 .02
- ❑ 321 Reggie White PRED .50 .20
- ❑ 322 Lawrence Taylor PRED .50 .20
- ❑ 323 Greg Townsend PRED .10 .02
- ❑ 324 Tim Harris PRED .10 .02
- ❑ 325 Bruce Smith PRED .20 .07
- ❑ 326 Tony Dorsett RB .50 .20
- ❑ 327 Steve Largent RB .50 .20
- ❑ 328 Tim Brown RB 2.00 .75
- ❑ 329 Joe Montana RB 1.50 .60
- ❑ 330 Tom Landry Tribute 1.00 .40

1989 Score Supplemental

- ❑ COMP.FACT.SET (110) 8.00 3.00
- ❑ 331S Herschel Walker .40 .15
- ❑ 332S Allen Pinkett RC .10 .02
- ❑ 333S Sterling Sharpe RC 3.00 1.25
- ❑ 334S Alvin Walton RC .10 .02
- ❑ 335S Frank Reich RC .40 .15
- ❑ 336S James Thornton RC .10 .02
- ❑ 337S David Fulcher .20 .07
- ❑ 338S Raul Allegre .10 .02
- ❑ 339S John Elway 4.00 2.00
- ❑ 340S Michael Cofer .10 .02
- ❑ 341S Jim Skow .10 .02
- ❑ 342S Steve DeBerg .10 .02
- ❑ 343S Mervyn Fernandez RC .10 .02
- ❑ 344S Mike Lansford .10 .02
- ❑ 345S Reggie Roby .10 .02
- ❑ 346S Raymond Clayborn .10 .02
- ❑ 347S Lonzell Hill .10 .02
- ❑ 348S Ottis Anderson .20 .07
- ❑ 349S Erik McMillan RC .10 .02
- ❑ 350S Al Harris RC .10 .02
- ❑ 351S Jack Del Rio RC .40 .15
- ❑ 352S Gary Anderson K .10 .02
- ❑ 353S Jim McMahon .20 .07
- ❑ 354S Keena Turner .10 .02
- ❑ 355S Tony Woods RC .10 .02
- ❑ 356S Donald Igwebuike .10 .02
- ❑ 357S Gerald Riggs .20 .07
- ❑ 358S Eddie Murray .10 .02
- ❑ 359S Dino Hackett .10 .02
- ❑ 360S Brad Muster RC .10 .02
- ❑ 361S Paul Palmer .10 .02
- ❑ 362S Jerry Robinson .10 .02
- ❑ 363S Simon Fletcher RC .20 .07
- ❑ 364S Tommy Kramer .10 .02
- ❑ 365S Jim C.Jensen RC .10 .02
- ❑ 366S Lorenzo White RC .40 .15
- ❑ 367S Fredd Young .10 .02
- ❑ 368S Ron Jaworski .10 .02
- ❑ 369S Mel Owens .10 .02
- ❑ 370S Dave Waymer .10 .02
- ❑ 371S Sean Landeta .10 .02
- ❑ 372S Sam Mills .20 .07
- ❑ 373S Todd Blackledge .10 .02
- ❑ 374S Jo Jo Townsell .10 .02
- ❑ 375S Ron Wolfley .10 .02
- ❑ 376S Ralf Mojsiejenko .10 .02
- ❑ 377S Eric Wright .10 .02
- ❑ 378S Nesby Glasgow .10 .02
- ❑ 379S Darryl Talley .20 .07
- ❑ 380S Eric Allen RC UER .40 .15
- ❑ 381S Dennis Smith .20 .07
- ❑ 382S John Tice .10 .02
- ❑ 383S Jesse Solomon .10 .02
- ❑ 384S Bo Jackson FB/BB 1.00 .40
- ❑ 385S Mike Merriweather .10 .02
- ❑ 386S Maurice Carthon .10 .02
- ❑ 387S David Grayson .10 .02
- ❑ 388S Wilber Marshall .10 .02
- ❑ 389S David Wyman .10 .02
- ❑ 390S Thomas Everett RC .10 .02
- ❑ 391S Alex Gordon .10 .02
- ❑ 392S D.J. Dozier .10 .02
- ❑ 393S Scott Radecic RC .10 .02
- ❑ 394S Eric Thomas .10 .02
- ❑ 395S Mike Gann .10 .02
- ❑ 396S William Perry .20 .07
- ❑ 397S Carl Hairston .10 .02
- ❑ 398S Billy Ard .10 .02
- ❑ 399S Donnell Thompson .10 .02
- ❑ 400S Mike Webster .20 .07
- ❑ 401S Scott Davis RC .10 .02
- ❑ 402S Sean Farrell .10 .02
- ❑ 403S Mike Golic RC .10 .02
- ❑ 404S Mike Kenn .10 .02
- ❑ 405S Keith Van Horne RC .10 .02
- ❑ 406S Bob Golic .10 .02
- ❑ 407S Neil Smith RC 2.00 .75
- ❑ 408S Dermontti Dawson RC .20 .07
- ❑ 409S Leslie O'Neal .20 .07
- ❑ 410S Matt Bahr .10 .02
- ❑ 411S Guy McIntyre RC .10 .02
- ❑ 412S Bryan Millard .10 .02
- ❑ 413S Joe Jacoby .10 .02
- ❑ 414S Rob Taylor RC .10 .02
- ❑ 415S Tony Zendejas .10 .02
- ❑ 416S Vai Sikahema .10 .02
- ❑ 417S Gary Reasons RC .10 .02
- ❑ 418S Shawn Collins RC .10 .02
- ❑ 419S Mark Green RC .10 .02
- ❑ 420S Courtney Hall RC .10 .02
- ❑ 421S Bobby Humphrey RC .10 .02
- ❑ 422S Myron Guyton RC .10 .02
- ❑ 423S Darryl Ingram RC .10 .02
- ❑ 424S Chris Jacke RC .10 .02
- ❑ 425S Keith Jones RC .10 .02
- ❑ 426S Robert Massey RC .10 .02
- ❑ 427S Bubba McDowell RC .40 .15
- ❑ 428S Dave Meggett RC .40 .15
- ❑ 429S Louis Oliver RC .20 .07
- ❑ 430S Danny Peebles .10 .02
- ❑ 431S Rodney Peete RC .75 .30
- ❑ 432S Jeff Query RC .10 .02
- ❑ 433S Timm Rosenbach RC UER .10 .02
- ❑ 434S Frank Stams RC .10 .02
- ❑ 435S Lawyer Tillman RC .10 .02
- ❑ 436S Billy Joe Tolliver RC .10 .02
- ❑ 437S Floyd Turner RC .20 .07
- ❑ 438S Steve Walsh RC .20 .07
- ❑ 439S Joe Wolf RC .10 .02
- ❑ 440S Trace Armstrong RC .10 .02

1990 Score

- ❑ COMPLETE SET (660) 15.00 6.00
- ❑ COMP.FACT.SET (665) 20.00 7.50
- ❑ 1 Joe Montana 1.25 .50
- ❑ 2 Christian Okoye .04 .01
- ❑ 3 Mike Singletary UER .10 .02
- ❑ 4 Jim Everett UER .10 .02
- ❑ 5 Phil Simms .10 .02
- ❑ 6 Brent Fullwood .04 .01
- ❑ 7 Bill Fralic .04 .01
- ❑ 8 Leslie O'Neal .10 .02
- ❑ 9 John Taylor .25 .08

Card		
❑ 10 Bo Jackson	.30	.10
❑ 11 John Stephens	.04	.01
❑ 12 Art Monk	.10	.02
❑ 13 Dan Marino	1.25	.50
❑ 14 John Settle	.04	.01
❑ 15 Don Majkowski	.04	.01
❑ 16 Bruce Smith	.25	.08
❑ 17 Brad Muster	.04	.01
❑ 18 Jason Buck	.04	.01
❑ 19 James Brooks	.10	.02
❑ 20 Barry Sanders	1.25	.50
❑ 21 Troy Aikman	.75	.30
❑ 22 Allen Pinkett	.04	.01
❑ 23 Duane Bickett	.04	.01
❑ 24 Kevin Ross	.04	.01
❑ 25 John Elway	1.25	.50
❑ 26 Jeff Query	.04	.01
❑ 27 Eddie Murray	.04	.01
❑ 28 Richard Dent	.10	.02
❑ 29 Lorenzo White	.04	.01
❑ 30 Eric Metcalf	.25	.08
❑ 31 Jeff Dellenbach RC	.04	.01
❑ 32 Leon White	.04	.01
❑ 33 Jim Jeffcoat	.04	.01
❑ 34 Herschel Walker	.10	.02
❑ 35 Mike Johnson UER	.04	.01
❑ 36 Joe Phillips	.04	.01
❑ 37 Willie Gault	.10	.02
❑ 38 Keith Millard	.04	.01
❑ 39 Fred Marion	.04	.01
❑ 40 Boomer Esiason	.10	.02
❑ 41 Dermontti Dawson	.10	.02
❑ 42 Dino Hackett	.04	.01
❑ 43 Reggie Roby	.04	.01
❑ 44 Roger Vick	.04	.01
❑ 45 Bobby Hebert	.04	.01
❑ 46 Don Beebe	.10	.02
❑ 47 Neal Anderson	.10	.02
❑ 48 Johnny Holland	.04	.01
❑ 49 Bobby Humphery	.04	.01
❑ 50 Lawrence Taylor	.25	.08
❑ 51 Billy Ray Smith	.04	.01
❑ 52 Robert Perryman	.04	.01
❑ 53 Gary Anderson K	.04	.01
❑ 54 Raul Allegre	.04	.01
❑ 55 Pat Swilling	.10	.02
❑ 56 Chris Doleman	.04	.01
❑ 57 Andre Reed	.25	.08
❑ 58 Seth Joyner	.10	.02
❑ 59 Bart Oates	.04	.01
❑ 60 Bernie Kosar	.10	.02
❑ 61 Dave Krieg	.10	.02
❑ 62 Lars Tate	.04	.01
❑ 63 Scott Norwood	.04	.01
❑ 64 Kyle Clifton	.04	.01
❑ 65 Alan Veingrad	.04	.01
❑ 66 Gerald Riggs UER	.10	.02
❑ 67 Tim Worley	.04	.01
❑ 68 Rodney Holman	.04	.01
❑ 69 Tony Zendejas	.04	.01
❑ 70 Chris Miller	.25	.08
❑ 71 Wilber Marshall	.04	.01
❑ 72 Skip McClendon RC	.04	.01
❑ 73 Jim Covert	.04	.01
❑ 74 Sam Mills	.10	.02
❑ 75 Chris Hinton	.04	.01
❑ 76 Irv Eatman	.04	.01
❑ 77 Bubba Paris UER	.04	.01
❑ 78 John Elliott UER	.04	.01
❑ 79 Thomas Everett	.04	.01
❑ 80 Steve Smith	.04	.01
❑ 81 Jackie Slater	.04	.01
❑ 82 Kelvin Martin RC	.04	.01
❑ 83 Jo Jo Townsell	.04	.01
❑ 84 Jim C. Jensen	.04	.01
❑ 85 Bobby Humphrey	.04	.01
❑ 86 Mike Dyal	.04	.01
❑ 87 Andre Rison UER	.25	.08
❑ 88 Brian Sochia	.04	.01
❑ 89 Greg Bell	.04	.01
❑ 90 Dalton Hilliard	.04	.01
❑ 91 Carl Banks	.04	.01
❑ 92 Dennis Smith	.04	.01
❑ 93 Bruce Matthews	.10	.02
❑ 94 Charles Haley	.10	.02
❑ 95 Deion Sanders	.50	.20
❑ 96 Stephone Paige	.04	.01
❑ 97 Marion Butts FSC	.10	.02
❑ 98 Howie Long	.25	.08
❑ 99 Donald Igwebuike	.04	.01
❑ 100 Roger Craig UER	.10	.02
❑ 101 Charles Mann	.04	.01
❑ 102 Fredd Young	.04	.01
❑ 103 Chris Jacke	.04	.01
❑ 104 Scott Case	.04	.01
❑ 105 Warren Moon	.25	.08
❑ 106 Clyde Simmons	.04	.01
❑ 107 Steve Atwater	.04	.01
❑ 108 Morten Andersen	.04	.01
❑ 109 Eugene Marve	.04	.01
❑ 110 Thurman Thomas	.25	.08
❑ 111 Carnell Lake	.04	.01
❑ 112 Jim Kelly	.25	.08
❑ 113 Stanford Jennings	.04	.01
❑ 114 Jacob Green	.04	.01
❑ 115 Karl Mecklenburg	.04	.01
❑ 116 Ray Childress	.04	.01
❑ 117 Erik McMillan	.04	.01
❑ 118 Harry Newsome	.04	.01
❑ 119 James Dixon	.04	.01
❑ 120 Hassan Jones	.04	.01
❑ 121 Eric Allen	.04	.01
❑ 122 Felix Wright	.04	.01
❑ 123 Merril Hoge	.04	.01
❑ 124 Eric Ball	.04	.01
❑ 125 Flipper Anderson FSC	.04	.01
❑ 126 James Jefferson	.04	.01
❑ 127 Tim McDonald	.04	.01
❑ 128 Larry Kinnebrew	.04	.01
❑ 129 Mark Collins	.04	.01
❑ 130 Ickey Woods	.04	.01
❑ 131 Jeff Donaldson UER	.04	.01
❑ 132 Rich Camarillo	.04	.01
❑ 133 Melvin Bratton RC	.04	.01
❑ 134A Kevin Butler	.35	.12
❑ 134B Kevin Butler	.50	.20
❑ 135 Albert Bentley	.04	.01
❑ 136A Vai Sikahema	.35	.12
❑ 136B Vai Sikahema	.50	.20
❑ 137 Todd McNair RC	.04	.01
❑ 138 Alonzo Highsmith	.04	.01
❑ 139 Brian Blades	.10	.02
❑ 140 Jeff Lageman	.04	.01
❑ 141 Eric Thomas	.04	.01
❑ 142 Derek Hill	.04	.01
❑ 143 Rick Fenney	.04	.01
❑ 144 Herman Heard	.04	.01
❑ 145 Steve Young	.50	.20
❑ 146 Kent Hull	.04	.01
❑ 147A Joey Browner face left	.35	.12
❑ 147B Joey Browner straight	.50	.20
❑ 148 Frank Minnifield	.04	.01
❑ 149 Robert Massey	.04	.01
❑ 150 Dave Meggett	.10	.02
❑ 151 Bubba McDowell	.04	.01
❑ 152 Rickey Dixon RC	.04	.01
❑ 153 Ray Donaldson	.04	.01
❑ 154 Alvin Walton	.04	.01
❑ 155 Mike Cofer	.04	.01
❑ 156 Darryl Talley	.04	.01
❑ 157 A.J. Johnson	.04	.01
❑ 158 Jerry Gray	.04	.01
❑ 159 Keith Byars	.04	.01
❑ 160 Andy Heck	.04	.01
❑ 161 Mike Munchak	.10	.02
❑ 162 Dennis Gentry	.04	.01
❑ 163 Timm Rosenbach UER	.04	.01
❑ 164 Randall McDaniel	.10	.02
❑ 165 Pat Leahy	.04	.01
❑ 166 Bubby Brister	.04	.01
❑ 167 Aundray Bruce	.04	.01
❑ 168 Bill Brooks	.04	.01
❑ 169 Eddie Anderson RC	.04	.01
❑ 170 Ronnie Lott	.10	.02
❑ 171 Jay Hilgenberg	.04	.01
❑ 172 Joe Nash	.04	.01
❑ 173 Simon Fletcher	.04	.01
❑ 174 Shane Conlan	.04	.01
❑ 175 Sean Landeta	.04	.01
❑ 176 John Alt RC	.04	.01
❑ 177 Clay Matthews	.10	.02
❑ 178 Anthony Munoz	.10	.02
❑ 179 Pete Holohan	.04	.01
❑ 180 Robert Awalt	.04	.01
❑ 181 Rohn Stark	.04	.01
❑ 182 Vance Johnson	.04	.01
❑ 183 David Fulcher	.04	.01
❑ 184 Robert Delpino FSC	.04	.01
❑ 185 Drew Hill	.04	.01
❑ 186 Reggie Langhorne UER	.04	.01
❑ 187 Lonzell Hill	.04	.01
❑ 188 Tom Rathman UER	.04	.01
❑ 189 Greg Montgomery RC	.04	.01
❑ 190 Leonard Smith	.04	.01
❑ 191 Chris Spielman	.25	.08
❑ 192 Tom Newberry	.04	.01
❑ 193 Cris Carter	.50	.20
❑ 194 Kevin Porter RC	.04	.01
❑ 195 Donnell Thompson	.04	.01
❑ 196 Vaughan Johnson	.04	.01
❑ 197 Steve McMichael	.10	.02
❑ 198 Jim Sweeney	.04	.01
❑ 199 Rich Karlis UER	.04	.01
❑ 200 Jerry Rice	.75	.30
❑ 201 Dan Hampton UER	.10	.02
❑ 202 Jim Lachey	.04	.01
❑ 203 Reggie White	.25	.08
❑ 204 Jerry Ball	.04	.01
❑ 205 Russ Grimm	.04	.01
❑ 206 Tim Green RC	.04	.01
❑ 207 Shawn Collins	.04	.01
❑ 208A R.Mojsiejenko Chargers	.15	.05
❑ 208B R.Mojsiejenko Redskins	.50	.20
❑ 209 Trace Armstrong	.04	.01
❑ 210 Keith Jackson	.10	.02
❑ 211 Jamie Holland	.04	.01
❑ 212 Mark Clayton	.10	.02
❑ 213 Jeff Cross	.04	.01
❑ 214 Bob Gagliano	.04	.01
❑ 215 Louis Oliver UER	.04	.01
❑ 216 Jim Arnold	.04	.01
❑ 217 Robert Clark RC	.04	.01
❑ 218 Gill Byrd	.04	.01
❑ 219 Rodney Peete	.10	.02
❑ 220 Anthony Miller	.25	.08
❑ 221 Steve Grogan	.10	.02
❑ 222 Vince Newsome RC	.04	.01
❑ 223 Thomas Benson	.04	.01
❑ 224 Kevin Murphy	.04	.01
❑ 225 Henry Ellard	.10	.02
❑ 226 Richard Johnson	.04	.01
❑ 227 Jim Skow	.04	.01
❑ 228 Keith Jones	.04	.01
❑ 229 Dave Brown DB	.04	.01
❑ 230 Marcus Allen	.25	.08
❑ 231 Steve Walsh	.10	.02
❑ 232 Jim Harbaugh	.25	.08
❑ 233 Mel Gray	.10	.02
❑ 234 David Treadwell	.04	.01
❑ 235 John Offerdahl	.04	.01
❑ 236 Gary Reasons	.04	.01
❑ 237 Tim Krumrie	.04	.01
❑ 238 Dave Duerson	.04	.01
❑ 239 Gary Clark UER	.25	.08
❑ 240 Mark Jackson	.04	.01
❑ 241 Mark Murphy	.04	.01
❑ 242 Jerry Holmes	.04	.01
❑ 243 Tim McGee	.04	.01
❑ 244 Mike Tomczak	.10	.02
❑ 245 Sterling Sharpe UER	.25	.08
❑ 246 Bennie Blades	.04	.01
❑ 247 Ken Harvey RC UER	.25	.08
❑ 248 Ron Heller	.04	.01
❑ 249 Louis Lipps	.10	.02
❑ 250 Wade Wilson	.10	.02
❑ 251 Freddie Joe Nunn	.04	.01
❑ 252 Jerome Brown UER	.04	.01
❑ 253 Myron Guyton	.04	.01
❑ 254 Nate Odomes RC	.10	.02
❑ 255 Rod Woodson	.25	.08
❑ 256 Cornelius Bennett	.10	.02
❑ 257 Keith Woodside	.04	.01
❑ 258 Jeff Uhlenhake UER	.04	.01
❑ 259 Harry Hamilton	.04	.01
❑ 260 Mark Bavaro	.04	.01
❑ 261 Vinny Testaverde	.10	.02
❑ 262 Steve DeBerg	.04	.01
❑ 263 Steve Wisniewski UER	.10	.02
❑ 264 Pete Mandley	.04	.01
❑ 265 Tim Harris	.04	.01
❑ 266 Jack Trudeau	.04	.01

❑ 267	Mark Kelso	.04	.01
❑ 268	Brian Noble	.04	.01
❑ 269	Jessie Tuggle RC	.04	.01
❑ 270	Ken O'Brien	.04	.01
❑ 271	David Little	.04	.01
❑ 272	Pete Stoyanovich	.04	.01
❑ 273	Odessa Turner RC	.04	.01
❑ 274	Anthony Toney	.04	.01
❑ 275	Tunch Ilkin	.04	.01
❑ 276	Carl Lee	.04	.01
❑ 277	Hart Lee Dykes	.04	.01
❑ 278	Al Noga	.04	.01
❑ 279	Greg Lloyd	.25	.08
❑ 280	Billy Joe Tolliver	.04	.01
❑ 281	Kirk Lowdermilk	.04	.01
❑ 282	Earl Ferrell	.04	.01
❑ 283	Eric Sievers RC	.04	.01
❑ 284	Steve Jordan	.04	.01
❑ 285	Burt Grossman	.04	.01
❑ 286	Johnny Rembert	.04	.01
❑ 287	Jeff Jaeger RC	.04	.01
❑ 288	James Hasty	.04	.01
❑ 289	Tony Mandarich DP	.04	.01
❑ 290	Chris Singleton RC	.04	.01
❑ 291	Lynn James RC	.04	.01
❑ 292	Andre Ware RC	.25	.08
❑ 293	Ray Agnew RC	.04	.01
❑ 294	Joel Smeenge RC	.04	.01
❑ 295	Marc Spindler RC	.04	.01
❑ 296	Renaldo Turnbull RC	.04	.01
❑ 297	Reggie Rembert RC	.04	.01
❑ 298	Jeff Alm RC	.04	.01
❑ 299	Cortez Kennedy RC	.25	.08
❑ 300	Blair Thomas RC	.10	.02
❑ 301	Pat Terrell RC	.04	.01
❑ 302	Junior Seau RC	1.25	.50
❑ 303	Mo Elewonibi RC	.04	.01
❑ 304	Tony Bennett RC	.25	.08
❑ 305	Percy Snow RC	.04	.01
❑ 306	Richmond Webb RC	.04	.01
❑ 307	Rodney Hampton RC	.25	.08
❑ 308	Barry Foster RC	.25	.08
❑ 309	John Friesz RC	.25	.08
❑ 310	Ben Smith RC	.04	.01
❑ 311	Joe Montana HG	.50	.20
❑ 312	Jim Everett HG	.10	.02
❑ 313	Mark Rypien HG	.10	.02
❑ 314	Phil Simms HG UER	.10	.02
❑ 315	Don Majkowski HG	.04	.01
❑ 316	Boomer Esiason HG	.04	.01
❑ 317	Warren Moon HG Moon	.25	.08
❑ 318	Jim Kelly HG	.25	.08
❑ 319	Bernie Kosar HG UER	.10	.02
❑ 320	Dan Marino HG UER	.50	.20
❑ 321	Christian Okoye GF	.04	.01
❑ 322	Thurman Thomas GF	.25	.08
❑ 323	James Brooks GF	.10	.02
❑ 324	Bobby Humphrey GF	.04	.01
❑ 325	Barry Sanders GF	.60	.25
❑ 326	Neal Anderson GF	.04	.01
❑ 327	Dalton Hilliard GF	.04	.01
❑ 328	Greg Bell GF	.04	.01
❑ 329	Roger Craig GF UER	.10	.02
❑ 330	Bo Jackson GF	.30	.10
❑ 331	Don Warren	.04	.01
❑ 332	Rufus Porter	.04	.01
❑ 333	Sammie Smith	.04	.01
❑ 334	Lewis Tillman	.04	.01
❑ 335	Michael Walter	.04	.01
❑ 336	Marc Logan	.04	.01
❑ 337	Ron Hallstrom RC	.04	.01
❑ 338	Stanley Morgan	.04	.01
❑ 339	Mark Robinson	.04	.01
❑ 340	Frank Reich	.25	.08
❑ 341	Chip Lohmiller FSC	.04	.01
❑ 342	Steve Beuerlein	.10	.02
❑ 343	John L. Williams	.04	.01
❑ 344	Irving Fryar	.25	.08
❑ 345	Anthony Carter	.10	.02
❑ 346	Al Toon	.10	.02
❑ 347	J.T. Smith	.04	.01
❑ 348	Pierce Holt RC	.04	.01
❑ 349	Ferrell Edmunds	.04	.01
❑ 350	Mark Rypien	.10	.02
❑ 351	Paul Gruber	.04	.01
❑ 352	Ernest Givins	.10	.02
❑ 353	Ervin Randle	.04	.01
❑ 354	Guy McIntyre	.04	.01
❑ 355	Webster Slaughter	.10	.02
❑ 356	Reuben Davis	.04	.01
❑ 357	Rickey Jackson	.10	.02
❑ 358	Earnest Byner	.04	.01
❑ 359	Eddie Brown	.04	.01
❑ 360	Troy Stradford	.04	.01
❑ 361	Pepper Johnson	.04	.01
❑ 362	Ravin Caldwell	.04	.01
❑ 363	Chris Mohr RC	.04	.01
❑ 364	Jeff Bryant	.04	.01
❑ 365	Bruce Collie	.04	.01
❑ 366	Courtney Hall	.04	.01
❑ 367	Jerry Olsavsky	.04	.01
❑ 368	David Galloway	.04	.01
❑ 369	Wes Hopkins	.04	.01
❑ 370	Johnny Hector	.04	.01
❑ 371	Clarence Verdin	.04	.01
❑ 372	Nick Lowery	.04	.01
❑ 373	Tim Brown	.25	.08
❑ 374	Kevin Greene	.10	.02
❑ 375	Leonard Marshall	.04	.01
❑ 376	Roland James	.04	.01
❑ 377	Scott Studwell	.04	.01
❑ 378	Jarvis Williams	.04	.01
❑ 379	Mike Saxon	.04	.01
❑ 380	Kevin Mack	.04	.01
❑ 381	Joe Kelly	.04	.01
❑ 382	Tom Thayer RC	.04	.01
❑ 383	Roy Green	.10	.02
❑ 384	Michael Brooks RC	.04	.01
❑ 385	Michael Cofer	.04	.01
❑ 386	Ken Ruettgers	.04	.01
❑ 387	Dean Steinkuhler	.04	.01
❑ 388	Maurice Carthon	.04	.01
❑ 389	Ricky Sanders	.04	.01
❑ 390	Winston Moss RC	.04	.01
❑ 391	Tony Woods	.04	.01
❑ 392	Keith DeLong	.04	.01
❑ 393	David Wyman	.04	.01
❑ 394	Vencie Glenn	.04	.01
❑ 395	Harris Barton	.04	.01
❑ 396	Bryan Hinkle	.04	.01
❑ 397	Derek Kennard	.04	.01
❑ 398	Heath Sherman RC	.04	.01
❑ 399	Troy Benson	.04	.01
❑ 400	Gary Zimmerman	.04	.01
❑ 401	Mark Duper	.10	.02
❑ 402	Eugene Lockhart	.04	.01
❑ 403	Tim Manoa	.04	.01
❑ 404	Reggie Williams	.04	.01
❑ 405	Mark Bortz RC	.04	.01
❑ 406	Mike Kenn	.04	.01
❑ 407	John Grimsley	.04	.01
❑ 408	Bill Romanowski RC	1.00	.40
❑ 409	Perry Kemp	.04	.01
❑ 410	Norm Johnson	.04	.01
❑ 411	Broderick Thomas	.04	.01
❑ 412	Joe Wolf	.04	.01
❑ 413	Andre Waters	.04	.01
❑ 414	Jason Staurovsky	.04	.01
❑ 415	Eric Martin	.04	.01
❑ 416	Joe Prokop	.04	.01
❑ 417	Steve Sewell	.04	.01
❑ 418	Cedric Jones	.04	.01
❑ 419	Alphonso Carreker	.04	.01
❑ 420	Keith Willis	.04	.01
❑ 421	Bobby Butler	.04	.01
❑ 422	John Roper	.04	.01
❑ 423	Tim Spencer	.04	.01
❑ 424	Jesse Sapolu RC	.04	.01
❑ 425	Ron Wolfley	.04	.01
❑ 426	Doug Smith	.04	.01
❑ 427	William Howard	.04	.01
❑ 428	Keith Van Horne	.04	.01
❑ 429	Tony Jordan	.04	.01
❑ 430	Mervyn Fernandez	.04	.01
❑ 431	Shaun Gayle RC	.04	.01
❑ 432	Ricky Nattiel	.04	.01
❑ 433	Albert Lewis	.04	.01
❑ 434	Fred Banks RC	.04	.01
❑ 435	Henry Thomas	.04	.01
❑ 436	Chet Brooks	.04	.01
❑ 437	Mark Ingram	.10	.02
❑ 438	Jeff Gossett	.04	.01
❑ 439	Mike Wilcher	.04	.01
❑ 440	Deron Cherry UER	.04	.01
❑ 441	Mike Rozier	.04	.01
❑ 442	Jon Hand	.04	.01
❑ 443	Ozzie Newsome	.10	.02
❑ 444	Sammy Martin	.04	.01
❑ 445	Luis Sharpe	.04	.01
❑ 446	Lee Williams	.04	.01
❑ 447	Chris Martin RC	.04	.01
❑ 448	Kevin Fagan RC	.04	.01
❑ 449	Gene Lang	.04	.01
❑ 450	Greg Townsend	.04	.01
❑ 451	Robert Lyles	.04	.01
❑ 452	Eric Hill	.04	.01
❑ 453	John Teltschik	.04	.01
❑ 454	Vestee Jackson	.04	.01
❑ 455	Bruce Reimers	.04	.01
❑ 456	Butch Rolle RC	.04	.01
❑ 457	Lawyer Tillman	.04	.01
❑ 458	Andre Tippett	.04	.01
❑ 459	James Thornton	.04	.01
❑ 460	Randy Grimes	.04	.01
❑ 461	Larry Roberts	.04	.01
❑ 462	Ron Holmes	.04	.01
❑ 463	Mike Wise DE	.04	.01
❑ 464	Danny Copeland RC	.04	.01
❑ 465	Bruce Wilkerson RC	.04	.01
❑ 466	Mike Quick	.04	.01
❑ 467	Mickey Shuler	.04	.01
❑ 468	Mike Prior	.04	.01
❑ 469	Ron Rivera	.04	.01
❑ 470	Dean Biasucci	.04	.01
❑ 471	Perry Williams	.04	.01
❑ 472	Darren Comeaux UER	.04	.01
❑ 473	Freeman McNeil	.04	.01
❑ 474	Tyrone Braxton	.04	.01
❑ 475	Jay Schroeder	.04	.01
❑ 476	Naz Worthen	.04	.01
❑ 477	Lionel Washington	.04	.01
❑ 478	Carl Zander	.04	.01
❑ 479	Al(Bubba) Baker	.10	.02
❑ 480	Mike Merriweather	.04	.01
❑ 481	Mike Gann	.04	.01
❑ 482	Brent Williams	.04	.01
❑ 483	Eugene Robinson	.04	.01
❑ 484	Ray Horton	.04	.01
❑ 485	Bruce Armstrong	.04	.01
❑ 486	John Fourcade	.04	.01
❑ 487	Lewis Billups	.04	.01
❑ 488	Scott Davis	.04	.01
❑ 489	Kenneth Sims	.04	.01
❑ 490	Chris Chandler	.25	.08
❑ 491	Mark Lee	.04	.01
❑ 492	Johnny Meads	.04	.01
❑ 493	Tim Irwin	.04	.01
❑ 494	E.J. Junior	.04	.01
❑ 495	Hardy Nickerson	.10	.02
❑ 496	Rob McGovern	.04	.01
❑ 497	Fred Strickland RC	.04	.01
❑ 498	Reggie Rutland RC	.04	.01
❑ 499	Mel Owens	.04	.01
❑ 500	Derrick Thomas	.25	.08
❑ 501	Jerrol Williams	.04	.01
❑ 502	Maurice Hurst RC	.04	.01
❑ 503	Larry Kelm RC	.04	.01
❑ 504	Herman Fontenot	.04	.01
❑ 505	Pat Beach	.04	.01
❑ 506	Haywood Jeffires RC	.25	.08
❑ 507	Neil Smith	.25	.08
❑ 508	Cleveland Gary FSC	.04	.01
❑ 509	William Perry	.10	.02
❑ 510	Michael Carter	.04	.01
❑ 511	Walker Lee Ashley	.04	.01
❑ 512	Bob Golic	.04	.01
❑ 513	Danny Villa RC	.04	.01
❑ 514	Matt Millen	.10	.02
❑ 515	Don Griffin	.04	.01
❑ 516	Jonathan Hayes	.04	.01
❑ 517	Gerald Williams RC	.04	.01
❑ 518	Scott Fulhage	.04	.01
❑ 519	Irv Pankey	.04	.01
❑ 520	Randy Dixon RC	.04	.01
❑ 521	Terry McDaniel	.04	.01
❑ 522	Dan Saleaumua	.04	.01
❑ 523	Darrin Nelson	.04	.01
❑ 524	Leonard Griffin	.04	.01
❑ 525	Michael Ball RC	.04	.01
❑ 526	Ernie Jones RC	.04	.01
❑ 527	Tony Eason UER	.04	.01

❑ 528 Ed Reynolds .04 .01
❑ 529 Gary Hogeboom .04 .01
❑ 530 Don Mosebar .04 .01
❑ 531 Ottis Anderson .10 .02
❑ 532 Bucky Scribner .04 .01
❑ 533 Aaron Cox .04 .01
❑ 534 Sean Jones .10 .02
❑ 535 Doug Flutie .50 .20
❑ 536 Leo Lewis .04 .01
❑ 537 Art Still .04 .01
❑ 538 Matt Bahr .04 .01
❑ 539 Keena Turner .04 .01
❑ 540 Sammy Winder .04 .01
❑ 541 Mike Webster .10 .02
❑ 542 Doug Riesenberg RC .04 .01
❑ 543 Dan Fike .04 .01
❑ 544 Clarence Kay .04 .01
❑ 545 Jim Burt .04 .01
❑ 546 Mike Horan .04 .01
❑ 547 Al Harris .04 .01
❑ 548 Maury Buford .04 .01
❑ 549 Jerry Robinson .04 .01
❑ 550 Tracy Rocker .04 .01
❑ 551 Karl Mecklenburg CC .04 .01
❑ 552 Lawrence Taylor CC .25 .08
❑ 553 Derrick Thomas CC .25 .08
❑ 554 Mike Singletary CC .10 .02
❑ 555 Tim Harris CC .04 .01
❑ 556 Jerry Rice RM .50 .20
❑ 557 Art Monk RM .10 .02
❑ 558 Mark Carrier WR RM .10 .02
❑ 559 Andre Reed RM .10 .02
❑ 560 Sterling Sharpe RM .25 .08
❑ 561 Herschel Walker GF .10 .02
❑ 562 Ottis Anderson GF .10 .02
❑ 563 Randall Cunningham HG .10 .02
❑ 564 John Elway HG .50 .20
❑ 565 David Fulcher AP .04 .01
❑ 566 Ronnie Lott AP .10 .02
❑ 567 Jerry Gray AP .04 .01
❑ 568 Albert Lewis AP .04 .01
❑ 569 Karl Mecklenburg AP .04 .01
❑ 570 Mike Singletary AP .10 .02
❑ 571 Lawrence Taylor AP .25 .08
❑ 572 Tim Harris AP .04 .01
❑ 573 Keith Millard AP .04 .01
❑ 574 Reggie White AP .25 .08
❑ 575 Chris Doleman AP .04 .01
❑ 576 Dave Meggett AP .10 .02
❑ 577 Rod Woodson AP .25 .08
❑ 578 Sean Landeta AP .04 .01
❑ 579 Eddie Murray AP .04 .01
❑ 580 Barry Sanders AP .60 .25
❑ 581 Christian Okoye AP .04 .01
❑ 582 Joe Montana AP .50 .20
❑ 583 Jay Hilgenberg AP .04 .01
❑ 584 Bruce Matthews AP .10 .02
❑ 585 Tom Newberry AP .04 .01
❑ 586 Gary Zimmerman AP .04 .01
❑ 587 Anthony Munoz AP .10 .02
❑ 588 Keith Jackson AP .10 .02
❑ 589 Sterling Sharpe AP .25 .08
❑ 590 Jerry Rice AP .50 .20
❑ 591 Bo Jackson RB .30 .10
❑ 592 Steve Largent RB .25 .08
❑ 593 Flipper Anderson RB .04 .01
❑ 594 Joe Montana RB .50 .20
❑ 595 Franco Harris HOF .10 .02
❑ 596 Bob St. Clair HOF .04 .01
❑ 597 Tom Landry HOF .10 .02
❑ 598 Jack Lambert HOF .10 .02
❑ 599 Ted Hendricks HOF .04 .01
❑ 600A Buck Buchanan HOF ERR 83 .10 .02
❑ 600B Buck Buchanan HOF COR 63 .10
.02
❑ 601 Bob Griese HOF .10 .02
❑ 602 Super Bowl Wrap .04 .01
❑ 603A Vince Lombardi w/o logo .20 .07
❑ 603B Vince Lombardi Curt.logo .20 .07
❑ 604 Mark Carrier WR UER .10 .02
❑ 605 Randall Cunningham .25 .08
❑ 606 Percy Snow C90 .04 .01
❑ 607 Andre Ware C90 .25 .08
❑ 608 Blair Thomas C90 .10 .02
❑ 609 Eric Green C90 .04 .01
❑ 610 Reggie Rembert C90 .04 .01
❑ 611 Richmond Webb C90 .04 .01
❑ 612 Bern Brostek C90 .04 .01
❑ 613 James Williams C90 .04 .01
❑ 614 Mark Carrier DB C90 .10 .02
❑ 615 Renaldo Turnbull C90 .04 .01
❑ 616 Cortez Kennedy C90 .10 .02
❑ 617 Keith McCants C90 .04 .01
❑ 618 Anthony Thompson RC .04 .01
❑ 619 LeRoy Butler RC .25 .08
❑ 620 Aaron Wallace RC .04 .01
❑ 621 Alexander Wright RC .04 .01
❑ 622 Keith McCants RC .04 .01
❑ 623 Jimmie Jones RC .04 .01
❑ 624 Anthony Johnson RC .25 .08
❑ 625 Fred Washington RC .04 .01
❑ 626 Mike Bellamy RC .04 .01
❑ 627 Mark Carrier DB RC .25 .08
❑ 628 Harold Green RC .25 .08
❑ 629 Eric Green RC .10 .02
❑ 630 Andre Collins RC .04 .01
❑ 631 Lamar Lathon RC .10 .02
❑ 632 Terry Wooden RC .04 .01
❑ 633 Jesse Anderson RC .04 .01
❑ 634 Jeff George RC .50 .20
❑ 635 Carwell Gardner RC .04 .01
❑ 636 Darrell Thompson RC .04 .01
❑ 637 Vince Buck RC .04 .01
❑ 638 Mike Jones TE RC .04 .01
❑ 639 Charles Arbuckle RC .04 .01
❑ 640 Dennis Brown RC .04 .01
❑ 641 James Williams DB RC .04 .01
❑ 642 Bern Brostek RC .04 .01
❑ 643 Darion Conner RC .10 .02
❑ 644 Mike Fox RC .04 .01
❑ 645 Cary Conklin RC .04 .01
❑ 646 Tim Grunhard RC .04 .01
❑ 647 Ron Cox RC .04 .01
❑ 648 Keith Sims RC .04 .01
❑ 649 Alton Montgomery RC .04 .01
❑ 650 Greg McMurtry RC .04 .01
❑ 651 Scott Mitchell RC .25 .08
❑ 652 Tim Ryan DE RC .04 .01
❑ 653 Jeff Mills RC .04 .01
❑ 654 Ricky Proehl RC .25 .08
❑ 655 Steve Broussard RC .04 .01
❑ 656 Peter Tom Willis RC .04 .01
❑ 657 Dexter Carter RC .04 .01
❑ 658 Tony Casillas .04 .01
❑ 659 Joe Morris .04 .01
❑ 660 Greg Kragen .04 .01
❑ B1 Matt Stover FF .25 .08
❑ B2 Demetrius Davis .04 .01
❑ B3 Ken McMichel .04 .01
❑ B4 Judd Garrett FF .04 .01
❑ B5 Elliott Searcy .04 .01

1990 Score Supplemental

❑ COMP.FACT.SET (110) 80.00 40.00
❑ 1T Marcus Dupree RC** .15 .05
❑ 2T Jerry Kauric .15 .05
❑ 3T Everson Walls .15 .05
❑ 4T Elliott Smith .15 .05
❑ 5T Donald Evans RC UER .30 .10
❑ 6T Jerry Holmes .15 .05
❑ 7T Dan Stryzinski RC .15 .05
❑ 8T Gerald McNeil .15 .05
❑ 9T Rick Tuten RC .15 .05
❑ 10T Mickey Shuler .15 .05
❑ 11T Jay Novacek .60 .25
❑ 12T Eric Williams RC .15 .05
❑ 13T Stanley Morgan .15 .05
❑ 14T Wayne Haddix RC .15 .05
❑ 15T Gary Anderson RB .15 .05
❑ 16T Stan Humphries RC .60 .25
❑ 17T Raymond Clayborn .15 .05
❑ 18T Mark Boyer RC .15 .05
❑ 19T Dave Waymer .15 .05
❑ 20T Andre Rison .60 .25
❑ 21T Daniel Stubbs .15 .05
❑ 22T Mike Rozier .15 .05
❑ 23T Damian Johnson .15 .05
❑ 24T Don Smith RBK RC .15 .05
❑ 25T Max Montoya .15 .05
❑ 26T Terry Kinard .15 .05
❑ 27T Herb Welch .15 .05
❑ 28T Cliff Odom .15 .05
❑ 29T John Kidd .15 .05
❑ 30T Barry Word RC .15 .05
❑ 31T Rich Karlis .15 .05
❑ 32T Mike Baab .15 .05
❑ 33T Ronnie Harmon .30 .10
❑ 34T Jeff Donaldson .15 .05
❑ 35T Riki Ellison .15 .05
❑ 36T Steve Walsh .30 .10
❑ 37T Bill Lewis RC .15 .05
❑ 38T Tim McKyer .15 .05
❑ 39T James Wilder .15 .05
❑ 40T Tony Paige .15 .05
❑ 41T Derrick Fenner RC .15 .05
❑ 42T Thane Gash RC .15 .05
❑ 43T Dave Duerson .15 .05
❑ 44T Clarence Weathers .15 .05
❑ 45T Matt Bahr .15 .05
❑ 46T Alonzo Highsmith .15 .05
❑ 47T Joe Kelly .15 .05
❑ 48T Chris Hinton .15 .05
❑ 49T Bobby Humphery .15 .05
❑ 50T Greg Bell .15 .05
❑ 51T Fred Smerlas .15 .05
❑ 52T Walter Stanley .15 .05
❑ 53T Jim Skow .15 .05
❑ 54T Renaldo Turnbull .15 .05
❑ 55T Bern Brostek .15 .05
❑ 56T Charles Wilson RC .15 .05
❑ 57T Keith McCants .15 .05
❑ 58T Alexander Wright .30 .10
❑ 59T Ian Beckles RC .15 .05
❑ 60T Eric Davis RC .30 .10
❑ 61T Chris Singleton .15 .05
❑ 62T Rob Moore RC 2.50 1.00
❑ 63T Darion Conner .30 .10
❑ 64T Tim Grunhard .15 .05
❑ 65T Junior Seau 6.00 2.50
❑ 66T Tony Stargell RC .15 .05
❑ 67T Anthony Thompson .15 .05
❑ 68T Cortez Kennedy .60 .25
❑ 69T Darrell Thompson .15 .05
❑ 70T Calvin Williams RC .60 .25
❑ 71T Rodney Hampton .60 .25
❑ 72T Terry Wooden .15 .05
❑ 73T Leo Goeas RC .15 .05
❑ 74T Ken Willis .15 .05
❑ 75T Ricky Proehl .60 .25
❑ 76T Steve Christie RC .15 .05
❑ 77T Andre Ware .60 .25
❑ 78T Jeff George 2.50 1.00
❑ 79T Walter Wilson .15 .05
❑ 80T Johnny Bailey RC .15 .05
❑ 81T Harold Green .30 .10
❑ 82T Mark Carrier DB .60 .25
❑ 83T Frank Cornish .15 .05
❑ 84T James Williams .15 .05
❑ 85T James Francis RC .15 .05
❑ 86T Percy Snow .15 .05
❑ 87T Anthony Johnson .60 .25
❑ 88T Tim Ryan DE .15 .05
❑ 89T Dan Owens RC .15 .05
❑ 90T Aaron Wallace RC .15 .05
❑ 91T Steve Broussard .15 .05
❑ 92T Eric Green .15 .05
❑ 93T Blair Thomas .30 .10
❑ 94T Robert Blackmon RC .15 .05
❑ 95T Alan Grant RC .15 .05
❑ 96T Andre Collins .15 .05
❑ 97T Dexter Carter .15 .05
❑ 98T Reggie Cobb RC .15 .05
❑ 99T Dennis Brown .15 .05

❑ 100T	Kenny Davidson RC	.15	.05
❑ 101T	Emmitt Smith RC	60.00	30.00
❑ 102T	Jeff Alm	.15	.05
❑ 103T	Alton Montgomery	.15	.05
❑ 104T	Tony Bennett	.60	.25
❑ 105T	Johnny Johnson RC	.30	.10
❑ 106T	Leroy Hoard RC	.60	.25
❑ 107T	Ray Agnew	.15	.05
❑ 108T	Richmond Webb	.15	.05
❑ 109T	Keith Sims	.15	.05
❑ 110T	Barry Foster	.60	.25

1991 Score

❑	COMPLETE SET (686)	20.00	7.50
❑	COMP.FACT.SET (690)	25.00	12.50
❑ 1	Joe Montana	1.25	.50
❑ 2	Eric Allen	.05	.01
❑ 3	Rohn Stark	.05	.01
❑ 4	Frank Reich	.10	.02
❑ 5	Derrick Thomas	.25	.08
❑ 6	Mike Singletary	.10	.02
❑ 7	Boomer Esiason	.10	.02
❑ 8	Matt Millen	.10	.02
❑ 9	Chris Spielman	.10	.02
❑ 10	Gerald McNeil	.05	.01
❑ 11	Nick Lowery	.05	.01
❑ 12	Randall Cunningham	.25	.08
❑ 13	Marion Butts	.10	.02
❑ 14	Tim Brown	.25	.08
❑ 15	Emmitt Smith	2.50	1.00
❑ 16	Rich Camarillo	.05	.01
❑ 17	Mike Merriweather	.05	.01
❑ 18	Derrick Fenner	.05	.01
❑ 19	Clay Matthews	.10	.02
❑ 20	Barry Sanders	1.25	.50
❑ 21	James Brooks	.10	.02
❑ 22	Alton Montgomery	.05	.01
❑ 23	Steve Atwater	.05	.01
❑ 24	Ron Morris	.05	.01
❑ 25	Brad Muster	.05	.01
❑ 26	Andre Rison	.10	.02
❑ 27	Brian Brennan	.05	.01
❑ 28	Leonard Smith	.05	.01
❑ 29	Kevin Butler	.05	.01
❑ 30	Tim Harris	.05	.01
❑ 31	Jay Novacek	.25	.08
❑ 32	Eddie Murray	.05	.01
❑ 33	Keith Woodside	.05	.01
❑ 34	Ray Crockett RC	.05	.01
❑ 35	Eugene Lockhart	.05	.01
❑ 36	Bill Romanowski	.05	.01
❑ 37	Eddie Brown	.05	.01
❑ 38	Eugene Daniel	.05	.01
❑ 39	Scott Fulhage	.05	.01
❑ 40	Harold Green	.10	.02
❑ 41	Mark Jackson	.05	.01
❑ 42	Sterling Sharpe	.25	.08
❑ 43	Mel Gray	.10	.02
❑ 44	Jerry Holmes	.05	.01
❑ 45	Allen Pinkett	.05	.01
❑ 46	Warren Powers	.05	.01
❑ 47	Rodney Peete	.10	.02
❑ 48	Lorenzo White	.05	.01
❑ 49	Dan Owens	.05	.01
❑ 50	James Francis	.05	.01
❑ 51	Ken Norton	.10	.02
❑ 52	Ed West	.05	.01
❑ 53	Andre Reed	.10	.02
❑ 54	John Grimsley	.05	.01
❑ 55	Michael Cofer	.05	.01
❑ 56	Chris Doleman	.05	.01
❑ 57	Pat Swilling	.10	.02
❑ 58	Jessie Tuggle	.05	.01
❑ 59	Mike Johnson	.05	.01
❑ 60	Steve Walsh	.05	.01
❑ 61	Sam Mills	.05	.01
❑ 62	Don Mosebar	.05	.01
❑ 63	Jay Hilgenberg	.05	.01
❑ 64	Cleveland Gary	.05	.01
❑ 65	Andre Tippett	.05	.01
❑ 66	Tom Newberry	.05	.01
❑ 67	Maurice Hurst	.05	.01
❑ 68	Louis Oliver	.05	.01
❑ 69	Fred Marion	.05	.01
❑ 70	Christian Okoye	.05	.01
❑ 71	Marv Cook FSC	.05	.01
❑ 72	Darryl Talley	.05	.01
❑ 73	Rick Fenney	.05	.01
❑ 74	Kelvin Martin	.05	.01
❑ 75	Howie Long	.25	.08
❑ 76	Steve Wisniewski	.05	.01
❑ 77	Karl Mecklenburg	.05	.01
❑ 78	Dan Saleaumua	.05	.01
❑ 79	Ray Childress	.05	.01
❑ 80	Henry Ellard	.10	.02
❑ 81	Ernest Givins UER	.10	.02
❑ 82	Ferrell Edmunds	.05	.01
❑ 83	Steve Jordan	.05	.01
❑ 84	Tony Mandarich	.05	.01
❑ 85	Eric Martin	.05	.01
❑ 86	Rich Gannon FSC	.25	.08
❑ 87	Irving Fryar	.10	.02
❑ 88	Tom Rathman	.05	.01
❑ 89	Dan Hampton	.10	.02
❑ 90	Barry Word	.05	.01
❑ 91	Kevin Greene	.10	.02
❑ 92	Sean Landeta	.05	.01
❑ 93	Trace Armstrong	.05	.01
❑ 94	Dennis Byrd	.05	.01
❑ 95	Timm Rosenbach	.05	.01
❑ 96	Anthony Toney	.05	.01
❑ 97	Tim Krumrie	.05	.01
❑ 98	Jerry Ball	.05	.01
❑ 99	Tim Green	.05	.01
❑ 100	Bo Jackson	.30	.10
❑ 101	Myron Guyton	.05	.01
❑ 102	Mike Mularkey	.05	.01
❑ 103	Jerry Gray	.05	.01
❑ 104	Scott Stephen RC	.05	.01
❑ 105	Anthony Bell	.05	.01
❑ 106	Lomas Brown	.05	.01
❑ 107	David Little	.05	.01
❑ 108	Brad Baxter FSC	.05	.01
❑ 109	Freddie Joe Nunn	.05	.01
❑ 110	Dave Meggett	.10	.02
❑ 111	Mark Rypien	.10	.02
❑ 112	Warren Williams	.05	.01
❑ 113	Ron Rivera	.05	.01
❑ 114	Terance Mathis	.10	.02
❑ 115	Anthony Munoz	.10	.02
❑ 116	Jeff Bryant	.05	.01
❑ 117	Issiac Holt	.05	.01
❑ 118	Steve Sewell	.05	.01
❑ 119	Tim Newton	.05	.01
❑ 120	Emile Harry	.05	.01
❑ 121	Gary Anderson K	.05	.01
❑ 122	Mark Lee	.05	.01
❑ 123	Alfred Anderson	.05	.01
❑ 124	Anthony Blaylock	.05	.01
❑ 125	Earnest Byner	.05	.01
❑ 126	Bill Maas	.05	.01
❑ 127	Keith Taylor	.05	.01
❑ 128	Cliff Odom	.05	.01
❑ 129	Bob Golic	.05	.01
❑ 130	Bart Oates	.05	.01
❑ 131	Jim Arnold	.05	.01
❑ 132	Jeff Herrod	.05	.01
❑ 133	Bruce Armstrong	.05	.01
❑ 134	Craig Heyward	.10	.02
❑ 135	Joey Browner	.05	.01
❑ 136	Darren Comeaux	.05	.01
❑ 137	Pat Beach	.05	.01
❑ 138	Dalton Hilliard	.05	.01
❑ 139	David Treadwell	.05	.01
❑ 140	Gary Anderson RB	.05	.01
❑ 141	Eugene Robinson	.05	.01
❑ 142	Scott Case	.05	.01
❑ 143	Paul Farren	.05	.01
❑ 144	Gill Fenerty	.05	.01
❑ 145	Tim Irwin	.05	.01
❑ 146	Norm Johnson	.05	.01
❑ 147	Willie Gault	.10	.02
❑ 148	Clarence Verdin	.05	.01
❑ 149	Jeff Uhlenhake	.05	.01
❑ 150	Erik McMillan	.05	.01
❑ 151	Kevin Ross	.05	.01
❑ 152	Pepper Johnson	.05	.01
❑ 153	Bryan Hinkle	.05	.01
❑ 154	Gary Clark	.25	.08
❑ 155	Robert Delpino	.05	.01
❑ 156	Doug Smith	.05	.01
❑ 157	Chris Martin	.05	.01
❑ 158	Ray Berry	.05	.01
❑ 159	Steve Christie	.05	.01
❑ 160	Don Smith RB	.05	.01
❑ 161	Greg McMurtry	.05	.01
❑ 162	Jack Del Rio	.10	.02
❑ 163	Floyd Dixon	.05	.01
❑ 164	Buford McGee	.05	.01
❑ 165	Brett Maxie	.05	.01
❑ 166	Morten Andersen	.05	.01
❑ 167	Kent Hull	.05	.01
❑ 168	Skip McClendon	.05	.01
❑ 169	Keith Sims	.05	.01
❑ 170	Leonard Marshall	.05	.01
❑ 171	Tony Woods	.05	.01
❑ 172	Byron Evans	.05	.01
❑ 173	Rob Burnett RC	.10	.02
❑ 174	Tory Epps	.05	.01
❑ 175	Toi Cook RC	.05	.01
❑ 176	John Elliott	.05	.01
❑ 177	Tommie Agee	.05	.01
❑ 178	Keith Van Horne	.05	.01
❑ 179	Dennis Smith	.05	.01
❑ 180	James Lofton	.10	.02
❑ 181	Art Monk	.10	.02
❑ 182	Anthony Carter	.10	.02
❑ 183	Louis Lipps	.05	.01
❑ 184	Bruce Hill	.05	.01
❑ 185	Michael Young	.05	.01
❑ 186	Eric Green	.05	.01
❑ 187	Barney Bussey RC	.05	.01
❑ 188	Curtis Duncan	.05	.01
❑ 189	Robert Awalt	.05	.01
❑ 190	Johnny Johnson	.05	.01
❑ 191	Jeff Cross	.05	.01
❑ 192	Keith McKeller	.05	.01
❑ 193	Robert Brown	.05	.01
❑ 194	Vincent Brown	.05	.01
❑ 195	Calvin Williams	.10	.02
❑ 196	Sean Jones	.10	.02
❑ 197	Willie Drewrey	.05	.01
❑ 198	Bubba McDowell	.05	.01
❑ 199	Al Noga	.05	.01
❑ 200	Ronnie Lott	.10	.02
❑ 201	Warren Moon	.25	.08
❑ 202	Chris Hinton	.05	.01
❑ 203	Jim Sweeney	.05	.01
❑ 204	Wayne Haddix	.05	.01
❑ 205	Tim Jorden RC	.05	.01
❑ 206	Marvin Allen	.05	.01
❑ 207	Jim Morrissey RC	.05	.01
❑ 208	Ben Smith	.05	.01
❑ 209	William White	.05	.01
❑ 210	Jim C. Jensen	.05	.01
❑ 211	Doug Reed	.05	.01
❑ 212	Ethan Horton	.05	.01
❑ 213	Chris Jacke	.05	.01
❑ 214	Johnny Hector	.05	.01
❑ 215	Drew Hill UER	.05	.01
❑ 216	Roy Green	.05	.01
❑ 217	Dean Steinkuhler	.05	.01
❑ 218	Cedric Mack	.05	.01
❑ 219	Chris Miller	.10	.02
❑ 220	Keith Byars	.05	.01
❑ 221	Lewis Billups	.05	.01
❑ 222	Roger Craig	.10	.02
❑ 223	Shaun Gayle	.05	.01
❑ 224	Mike Rozier	.05	.01
❑ 225	Troy Aikman	.75	.30
❑ 226	Bobby Humphrey	.05	.01
❑ 227	Eugene Marve	.05	.01
❑ 228	Michael Carter	.05	.01

❑ 229 Richard Johnson CB RC .05 .01
❑ 230 Billy Joe Tolliver .05 .01
❑ 231 Mark Murphy .05 .01
❑ 232 John L. Williams .05 .01
❑ 233 Ronnie Harmon .05 .01
❑ 234 Thurman Thomas .25 .08
❑ 235 Martin Mayhew .05 .01
❑ 236 Richmond Webb .05 .01
❑ 237 Gerald Riggs UER .10 .02
❑ 238 Mike Prior .05 .01
❑ 239 Mike Gann .05 .01
❑ 240 Alvin Walton .05 .01
❑ 241 Tim McGee .05 .01
❑ 242 Bruce Matthews .10 .02
❑ 243 Johnny Holland .05 .01
❑ 244 Martin Bayless .05 .01
❑ 245 Eric Metcalf .10 .02
❑ 246 John Alt .05 .01
❑ 247 Max Montoya .05 .01
❑ 248 Rod Bernstine .05 .01
❑ 249 Paul Gruber .05 .01
❑ 250 Charles Haley .10 .02
❑ 251 Scott Norwood .05 .01
❑ 252 Michael Haddix .05 .01
❑ 253 Ricky Sanders .05 .01
❑ 254 Ervin Randle .05 .01
❑ 255 Duane Bickett .05 .01
❑ 256 Mike Munchak .10 .02
❑ 257 Keith Jones .05 .01
❑ 258 Riki Ellison .05 .01
❑ 259 Vince Newsome .05 .01
❑ 260 Lee Williams .05 .01
❑ 261 Steve Smith .05 .01
❑ 262 Sam Clancy .05 .01
❑ 263 Pierce Holt .05 .01
❑ 264 Jim Harbaugh .25 .08
❑ 265 Dino Hackett .05 .01
❑ 266 Andy Heck .05 .01
❑ 267 Leo Goeas .05 .01
❑ 268 Russ Grimm .05 .01
❑ 269 Gill Byrd .05 .01
❑ 270 Neal Anderson .10 .02
❑ 271 Jackie Slater .05 .01
❑ 272 Joe Nash .05 .01
❑ 273 Todd Bowles .05 .01
❑ 274 D.J. Dozier .05 .01
❑ 275 Kevin Fagan .05 .01
❑ 276 Don Warren .05 .01
❑ 277 Jim Jeffcoat .05 .01
❑ 278 Bruce Smith .25 .08
❑ 279 Cortez Kennedy .25 .08
❑ 280 Thane Gash .05 .01
❑ 281 Perry Kemp .05 .01
❑ 282 John Taylor .10 .02
❑ 283 Stephone Paige .05 .01
❑ 284 Paul Skansi .05 .01
❑ 285 Shawn Collins .05 .01
❑ 286 Mervyn Fernandez .05 .01
❑ 287 Daniel Stubbs .05 .01
❑ 288 Chip Lohmiller .05 .01
❑ 289 Brian Blades .10 .02
❑ 290 Mark Carrier WR .25 .08
❑ 291 Carl Zander .05 .01
❑ 292 David Wyman .05 .01
❑ 293 Jeff Bostic .05 .01
❑ 294 Irv Pankey .05 .01
❑ 295 Keith Millard .05 .01
❑ 296 Jamie Mueller .05 .01
❑ 297 Bill Fralic .05 .01
❑ 298 Wendell Davis FSC .05 .01
❑ 299 Ken Clarke .05 .01
❑ 300 Wymon Henderson .05 .01
❑ 301 Jeff Campbell .05 .01
❑ 302 Cody Carlson RC .05 .01
❑ 303 Matt Brock RC .05 .01
❑ 304 Maurice Carthon .05 .01
❑ 305 Scott Mersereau RC .05 .01
❑ 306 Steve Wright RC .05 .01
❑ 307 J.B. Brown .05 .01
❑ 308 Ricky Reynolds .05 .01
❑ 309 Darryl Pollard .05 .01
❑ 310 Donald Evans .05 .01
❑ 311 Nick Bell RC .05 .01
❑ 312 Pat Harlow RC .05 .01
❑ 313 Dan McGwire RC .05 .01
❑ 314 Mike Dumas RC .05 .01
❑ 315 Mike Croel RC .05 .01
❑ 316 Chris Smith RC .05 .01
❑ 317 Kenny Walker RC .05 .01
❑ 318 Todd Lyght RC .05 .01
❑ 319 Mike Stonebreaker .05 .01
❑ 320 Randall Cunningham 90 .10 .02
❑ 321 Terance Mathis 90 .25 .08
❑ 322 Gaston Green 90 .05 .01
❑ 323 Johnny Bailey 90 .05 .01
❑ 324 Donnie Elder 90 .05 .01
❑ 325 Dwight Stone 90 UER .05 .01
❑ 326 J.J.Birden RC 90 .10 .02
❑ 327 Alexander Wright 90 .05 .01
❑ 328 Eric Metcalf 90 .10 .02
❑ 329 Andre Rison TL .10 .02
❑ 330 Warren Moon TL UER .10 .02
❑ 331 Steve Tasker DT .05 .01
❑ 332 Mel Gray DT .10 .02
❑ 333 Nick Lowery DT .05 .01
❑ 334 Sean Landeta DT .05 .01
❑ 335 David Fulcher DT .05 .01
❑ 336 Joey Browner DT .05 .01
❑ 337 Albert Lewis DT .05 .01
❑ 338 Rod Woodson DT .10 .02
❑ 339 Shane Conlan DT .05 .01
❑ 340 Pepper Johnson DT .05 .01
❑ 341 Chris Spielman DT .05 .01
❑ 342 Derrick Thomas DT .10 .02
❑ 343 Ray Childress DT .05 .01
❑ 344 Reggie White DT .10 .02
❑ 345 Bruce Smith DT .10 .02
❑ 346 Darrell Green .05 .01
❑ 347 Ray Bentley .05 .01
❑ 348 Herschel Walker .10 .02
❑ 349 Rodney Holman .05 .01
❑ 350 Al Toon .10 .02
❑ 351 Harry Hamilton .05 .01
❑ 352 Albert Lewis .05 .01
❑ 353 Renaldo Turnbull .05 .01
❑ 354 Junior Seau .25 .08
❑ 355 Merril Hoge .05 .01
❑ 356 Shane Conlan .05 .01
❑ 357 Jay Schroeder .05 .01
❑ 358 Steve Broussard .05 .01
❑ 359 Mark Bavaro .05 .01
❑ 360 Jim Lachey .05 .01
❑ 361 Greg Townsend .05 .01
❑ 362 Dave Krieg .10 .02
❑ 363 Jessie Hester .05 .01
❑ 364 Steve Tasker .10 .02
❑ 365 Ron Hall .05 .01
❑ 366 Pat Leahy .05 .01
❑ 367 Jim Everett .10 .02
❑ 368 Felix Wright .05 .01
❑ 369 Ricky Proehl .05 .01
❑ 370 Anthony Miller .10 .02
❑ 371 Keith Jackson .10 .02
❑ 372 Pete Stoyanovich .05 .01
❑ 373 Tommy Kane .05 .01
❑ 374 Richard Johnson .05 .01
❑ 375 Randall McDaniel .05 .01
❑ 376 John Stephens .05 .01
❑ 377 Haywood Jeffires .10 .02
❑ 378 Rodney Hampton .25 .08
❑ 379 Tim Grunhard .05 .01
❑ 380 Jerry Rice .75 .30
❑ 381 Ken Harvey .10 .02
❑ 382 Vaughan Johnson .05 .01
❑ 383 J.T. Smith .05 .01
❑ 384 Carnell Lake .05 .01
❑ 385 Dan Marino 1.25 .50
❑ 386 Kyle Clifton .05 .01
❑ 387 Wilber Marshall .05 .01
❑ 388 Pete Holohan .05 .01
❑ 389 Gary Plummer .05 .01
❑ 390 William Perry .10 .02
❑ 391 Mark Robinson .05 .01
❑ 392 Nate Odomes .05 .01
❑ 393 Ickey Woods .05 .01
❑ 394 Reyna Thompson .05 .01
❑ 395 Deion Sanders .40 .15
❑ 396 Harris Barton .05 .01
❑ 397 Sammie Smith .05 .01
❑ 398 Vinny Testaverde .10 .02
❑ 399 Ray Donaldson .05 .01
❑ 400 Tim McKyer .05 .01
❑ 401 Nesby Glasgow .05 .01
❑ 402 Brent Williams .05 .01
❑ 403 Rob Moore .25 .08
❑ 404 Bubby Brister .05 .01
❑ 405 David Fulcher .05 .01
❑ 406 Reggie Cobb .05 .01
❑ 407 Jerome Brown .05 .01
❑ 408 Erik Howard .05 .01
❑ 409 Tony Paige .05 .01
❑ 410 John Elway 1.25 .50
❑ 411 Charles Mann .05 .01
❑ 412 Luis Sharpe .05 .01
❑ 413 Hassan Jones .05 .01
❑ 414 Frank Minnifield .05 .01
❑ 415 Steve DeBerg .05 .01
❑ 416 Mark Carrier DB .10 .02
❑ 417 Brian Jordan FSC .10 .02
❑ 418 Reggie Langhorne .05 .01
❑ 419 Don Majkowski .05 .01
❑ 420 Marcus Allen .25 .08
❑ 421 Michael Brooks .05 .01
❑ 422 Vai Sikahema .05 .01
❑ 423 Dermontti Dawson .05 .01
❑ 424 Jacob Green .05 .01
❑ 425 Flipper Anderson .05 .01
❑ 426 Bill Brooks .05 .01
❑ 427 Keith McCants .05 .01
❑ 428 Ken O'Brien .05 .01
❑ 429 Fred Barnett FSC .25 .08
❑ 430 Mark Duper .10 .02
❑ 431 Mark Kelso .05 .01
❑ 432 Leslie O'Neal .10 .02
❑ 433 Ottis Anderson .10 .02
❑ 434 Jesse Sapolu .05 .01
❑ 435 Gary Zimmerman .05 .01
❑ 436 Kevin Porter .05 .01
❑ 437 Anthony Thompson .05 .01
❑ 438 Robert Clark .05 .01
❑ 439 Chris Warren .25 .08
❑ 440 Gerald Williams .05 .01
❑ 441 Jim Skow .05 .01
❑ 442 Rick Donnelly .05 .01
❑ 443 Guy McIntyre .05 .01
❑ 444 Jeff Lageman .05 .01
❑ 445 John Offerdahl .05 .01
❑ 446 Clyde Simmons .05 .01
❑ 447 John Kidd .05 .01
❑ 448 Chip Banks .05 .01
❑ 449 Johnny Meads .05 .01
❑ 450 Rickey Jackson .05 .01
❑ 451 Lee Johnson .05 .01
❑ 452 Michael Irvin .25 .08
❑ 453 Leon Seals .05 .01
❑ 454 Darrell Thompson .05 .01
❑ 455 Everson Walls .05 .01
❑ 456 LeRoy Butler .10 .02
❑ 457 Marcus Dupree .05 .01
❑ 458 Kirk Lowdermilk .05 .01
❑ 459 Chris Singleton .05 .01
❑ 460 Seth Joyner .10 .02
❑ 461 Rueben Mayes UER .05 .01
❑ 462 Ernie Jones .05 .01
❑ 463 Greg Kragen .05 .01
❑ 464 Bennie Blades .05 .01
❑ 465 Mark Bortz .05 .01
❑ 466 Tony Stargell .05 .01
❑ 467 Mike Cofer .05 .01
❑ 468 Randy Grimes .05 .01
❑ 469 Tim Worley .05 .01
❑ 470 Kevin Mack .05 .01
❑ 471 Wes Hopkins .05 .01
❑ 472 Will Wolford .05 .01
❑ 473 Sam Seale .05 .01
❑ 474 Jim Ritcher .05 .01
❑ 475 Jeff Hostetler FSC .25 .08
❑ 476 Mitchell Price RC .05 .01
❑ 477 Ken Lanier .05 .01
❑ 478 Naz Worthen .05 .01
❑ 479 Ed Reynolds .05 .01
❑ 480 Mark Clayton .10 .02
❑ 481 Matt Bahr .05 .01
❑ 482 Gary Reasons .05 .01
❑ 483 David Szott .05 .01
❑ 484 Barry Foster .10 .02
❑ 485 Bruce Reimers .05 .01
❑ 486 Dean Biasucci .05 .01
❑ 487 Cris Carter .50 .20
❑ 488 Albert Bentley .05 .01
❑ 489 Robert Massey .05 .01

❑ 490 Al Smith .05 .01
❑ 491 Greg Lloyd .25 .08
❑ 492 Steve McMichael UER .10 .02
❑ 493 Jeff Wright RC .05 .01
❑ 494 Scott Davis .05 .01
❑ 495 Freeman McNeil .05 .01
❑ 496 Simon Fletcher .05 .01
❑ 497 Terry McDaniel .05 .01
❑ 498 Heath Sherman .05 .01
❑ 499 Jeff Jaeger .05 .01
❑ 500 Mark Collins .05 .01
❑ 501 Tim Goad .05 .01
❑ 502 Jeff George .25 .08
❑ 503 Jimmie Jones .05 .01
❑ 504 Henry Thomas .05 .01
❑ 505 Steve Young .75 .30
❑ 506 William Roberts .05 .01
❑ 507 Neil Smith .25 .08
❑ 508 Mike Saxon .05 .01
❑ 509 Johnny Bailey .05 .01
❑ 510 Broderick Thomas .05 .01
❑ 511 Wade Wilson .10 .02
❑ 512 Hart Lee Dykes .05 .01
❑ 513 Hardy Nickerson .10 .02
❑ 514 Tim McDonald .05 .01
❑ 515 Frank Cornish .05 .01
❑ 516 Jarvis Williams .05 .01
❑ 517 Carl Lee .05 .01
❑ 518 Carl Banks .05 .01
❑ 519 Mike Golic .05 .01
❑ 520 Brian Noble .05 .01
❑ 521 James Hasty .05 .01
❑ 522 Bubba Paris .05 .01
❑ 523 Kevin Walker RC .05 .01
❑ 524 William Fuller .10 .02
❑ 525 Eddie Anderson .05 .01
❑ 526 Roger Ruzek .05 .01
❑ 527 Robert Blackmon .05 .01
❑ 528 Vince Buck .05 .01
❑ 529 Lawrence Taylor .25 .08
❑ 530 Reggie Roby .05 .01
❑ 531 Doug Riesenberg .05 .01
❑ 532 Joe Jacoby .05 .01
❑ 533 Kirby Jackson RC .05 .01
❑ 534 Robb Thomas .05 .01
❑ 535 Don Griffin .05 .01
❑ 536 Andre Waters .05 .01
❑ 537 Marc Logan .05 .01
❑ 538 James Thornton .05 .01
❑ 539 Ray Agnew .05 .01
❑ 540 Frank Stams .05 .01
❑ 541 Brett Perriman .25 .08
❑ 542 Andre Ware .10 .02
❑ 543 Kevin Haverdink .05 .01
❑ 544 Greg Jackson RC .05 .01
❑ 545 Tunch Ilkin .05 .01
❑ 546 Dexter Carter .05 .01
❑ 547 Rod Woodson .25 .08
❑ 548 Donnell Woolford .05 .01
❑ 549 Mark Boyer .05 .01
❑ 550 Jeff Query .05 .01
❑ 551 Burt Grossman .05 .01
❑ 552 Mike Kenn .05 .01
❑ 553 Richard Dent .10 .02
❑ 554 Gaston Green .05 .01
❑ 555 Phil Simms .10 .02
❑ 556 Brent Jones .25 .08
❑ 557 Ronnie Lippett .05 .01
❑ 558 Mike Horan .05 .01
❑ 559 Danny Noonan .05 .01
❑ 560 Reggie White .25 .08
❑ 561 Rufus Porter .05 .01
❑ 562 Aaron Wallace .05 .01
❑ 563 Vance Johnson .05 .01
❑ 564A Aaron Craver RC ERR .05 .01
❑ 564B Aaron Craver RC COR .05 .01
❑ 565A Russell Maryland RC ERR .25 .08
❑ 565B Russell Maryland RC COR .25 .08
❑ 566 Paul Justin RC .05 .01
❑ 567 Walter Dean .05 .01
❑ 568 Herman Moore RC .25 .08
❑ 569 Bill Musgrave RC .05 .01
❑ 570 Rob Carpenter RC WR .05 .01
❑ 571 Greg Lewis RC .05 .01
❑ 572 Ed King RC .05 .01
❑ 573 Ernie Mills RC .10 .02
❑ 574 Jake Reed RC .50 .20
❑ 575 Ricky Watters RC 1.50 .60
❑ 576 Derek Russell RC .05 .01
❑ 577 Shawn Moore RC .05 .01
❑ 578 Eric Bieniemy RC .05 .01
❑ 579 Chris Zorich RC .25 .08
❑ 580 Scott Miller .05 .01
❑ 581 Jarrod Bunch RC .05 .01
❑ 582 Ricky Ervins RC .10 .02
❑ 583 Browning Nagle RC .05 .01
❑ 584 Eric Turner RC .10 .02
❑ 585 William Thomas RC .05 .01
❑ 586 Stanley Richard RC .05 .01
❑ 587 Adrian Cooper RC .05 .01
❑ 588 Harvey Williams RC .25 .08
❑ 589 Alvin Harper RC .25 .08
❑ 590 John Carney .05 .01
❑ 591 Mark Vander Poel RC .05 .01
❑ 592 Mike Pritchard RC .25 .08
❑ 593 Eric Moten RC .05 .01
❑ 594 Moe Gardner RC .05 .01
❑ 595 Wesley Carroll RC .05 .01
❑ 596 Eric Swann RC .25 .08
❑ 597 Joe Kelly .05 .01
❑ 598 Steve Jackson RC .05 .01
❑ 599 Kelvin Pritchett RC .10 .02
❑ 600 Jesse Campbell RC .05 .01
❑ 601 Darryll Lewis RC UER .10 .02
❑ 602 Howard Griffith .05 .01
❑ 603 Blaise Bryant .05 .01
❑ 604 Vinnie Clark RC .05 .01
❑ 605 Mel Agee RC .05 .01
❑ 606 Bobby Wilson RC .05 .01
❑ 607 Kevin Donnalley RC .05 .01
❑ 608 Randal Hill RC .10 .02
❑ 609 Stan Thomas .05 .01
❑ 610 Mike Heldt .05 .01
❑ 611 Brett Favre RC 8.00 3.00
❑ 612 Lawrence Dawsey RC UER .10 .02
❑ 613 Dennis Gibson .05 .01
❑ 614 Dean Dingman .05 .01
❑ 615 Bruce Pickens RC .05 .01
❑ 616 Todd Marinovich RC .05 .01
❑ 617 Gene Atkins .05 .01
❑ 618 Marcus Dupree .05 .01
❑ 619 Warren Moon Man of Year .10 .02
❑ 620 Joe Montana TM .50 .20
❑ 621 Neal Anderson MVP .05 .01
❑ 622 James Brooks MVP .10 .02
❑ 623 Thurman Thomas TM .10 .02
❑ 624 Bobby Humphrey MVP .05 .01
❑ 625 Kevin Mack MVP .05 .01
❑ 626 Mark Carrier WR MVP .05 .01
❑ 627 Johnny Johnson TM .05 .01
❑ 628 Marion Butts MVP .10 .02
❑ 629 Steve DeBerg MVP .05 .01
❑ 630 Jeff George TM .10 .02
❑ 631 Troy Aikman TM .40 .15
❑ 632 Dan Marino TM .50 .20
❑ 633 Randall Cunningham TM .10 .02
❑ 634 Andre Rison TM .10 .02
❑ 635 Pepper Johnson MVP .05 .01
❑ 636 Pat Leahy MVP .05 .01
❑ 637 Barry Sanders TM .50 .20
❑ 638 Warren Moon TM .10 .02
❑ 639 Sterling Sharpe TM .05 .01
❑ 640 Bruce Armstrong MVP .05 .01
❑ 641 Bo Jackson TM .10 .02
❑ 642 Henry Ellard MVP .10 .02
❑ 643 Earnest Byner MVP .05 .01
❑ 644 Pat Swilling MVP .05 .01
❑ 645 John L. Williams MVP .05 .01
❑ 646 Rod Woodson TM .10 .02
❑ 647 Chris Doleman MVP .05 .01
❑ 648 Joey Browner CC .05 .01
❑ 649 Erik McMillan CC .05 .01
❑ 650 David Fulcher CC .05 .01
❑ 651A Ronnie Lott CC ERR .10 .02
❑ 651B Ronnie Lott CC COR .10 .02
❑ 652 Louis Oliver CC .05 .01
❑ 653 Mark Robinson CC .05 .01
❑ 654 Dennis Smith CC .05 .01
❑ 655 Reggie White SA ERR .10 .02
❑ 656 Charles Haley SA .05 .01
❑ 657 Leslie O'Neal SA .10 .02
❑ 658 Kevin Greene SA .10 .02
❑ 659 Dennis Byrd SA .05 .01
❑ 660 Bruce Smith SA .10 .02
❑ 661 Derrick Thomas SACK .10 .02
❑ 662 Steve DeBerg TL .05 .01
❑ 663 Barry Sanders TL .50 .20
❑ 664 Thurman Thomas TL .10 .02
❑ 665 Jerry Rice TL .40 .15
❑ 666 Derrick Thomas TL .10 .02
❑ 667 Bruce Smith TL .10 .02
❑ 668 Mark Carrier DB TL .05 .01
❑ 669 Richard Johnson CB TL .05 .01
❑ 670 Jan Stenerud HOF .05 .01
❑ 671 Stan Jones HOF .05 .01
❑ 672 John Hannah HOF .05 .01
❑ 673 Tex Schramm HOF .05 .01
❑ 674 Earl Campbell HOF .25 .08
❑ 675 Emmitt Smith/Carrier ROY .75 .30
❑ 676 Warren Moon DT .10 .02
❑ 677 Barry Sanders DT .50 .20
❑ 678 Thurman Thomas DT .25 .08
❑ 679 Andre Reed DT .10 .02
❑ 680 Andre Rison DT .10 .02
❑ 681 Keith Jackson DT .05 .01
❑ 682 Bruce Armstrong DT .05 .01
❑ 683 Jim Lachey DT .05 .01
❑ 684 Bruce Matthews DT .05 .01
❑ 685 Mike Munchak DT .05 .01
❑ 686 Don Mosebar DT .05 .01
❑ B1 Jeff Hostetler BONUS SB .25 .08
❑ B2 Matt Bahr SB .05 .01
❑ B3 Ottis Anderson SB .10 .02
❑ B4 Ottis Anderson SB .10 .02

1991 Score Supplemental

❑ COMPLETE FACT.SET (110) 4.00 1.50
❑ 1T Ronnie Lott .10 .02
❑ 2T Matt Millen .10 .02
❑ 3T Tim McKyer .05 .01
❑ 4T Vince Newsome .05 .01
❑ 5T Gaston Green .05 .01
❑ 6T Brett Perriman .25 .08
❑ 7T Roger Craig .10 .02
❑ 8T Pete Holohan .05 .01
❑ 9T Tony Zendejas .05 .01
❑ 10T Lee Williams .05 .01
❑ 11T Mike Stonebreaker .05 .01
❑ 12T Felix Wright .05 .01
❑ 13T Lonnie Young .05 .01
❑ 14T Hugh Millen RC .05 .01
❑ 15T Roy Green .05 .01
❑ 16T Greg Davis RC .05 .01
❑ 17T Dexter Manley .05 .01
❑ 18T Ted Washington RC .05 .01
❑ 19T Norm Johnson .05 .01
❑ 20T Joe Morris .05 .01
❑ 21T Robert Perryman .05 .01
❑ 22T Mike Iaquaniello RC UER .05 .01
❑ 23T Gerald Perry RC UER .05 .01
❑ 24T Zeke Mowatt .05 .01
❑ 25T Rich Miano RC .05 .01
❑ 26T Nick Bell .05 .01
❑ 27T Terry Orr RC .05 .01
❑ 28T Matt Stover RC .25 .08
❑ 29T Bubba Paris .05 .01
❑ 30T Ron Brown .05 .01
❑ 31T Don Davey .05 .01
❑ 32T Lee Rouson .05 .01
❑ 33T Terry Hoage UER .05 .01
❑ 34T Tony Covington .05 .01
❑ 35T John Rienstra .05 .01
❑ 36T Charles Dimry RC .05 .01

❑ 37T Todd Marinovich	.05	.01
❑ 38T Winston Moss	.05	.01
❑ 39T Vestee Jackson	.05	.01
❑ 40T Brian Hansen	.05	.01
❑ 41T Irv Eatman	.05	.01
❑ 42T Jarrod Bunch	.05	.01
❑ 43T Kanavis McGhee RC	.05	.01
❑ 44T Vai Sikahema	.05	.01
❑ 45T Charles McRae RC	.05	.01
❑ 46T Quinn Early	.10	.02
❑ 47T Jeff Faulkner RC	.05	.01
❑ 48T William Frizzell RC	.05	.01
❑ 49T John Booty	.05	.01
❑ 50T Tim Harris	.05	.01
❑ 51T Derek Russell	.05	.01
❑ 52T John Flannery RC	.05	.01
❑ 53T Tim Barnett RC	.05	.01
❑ 54T Alfred Williams RC	.05	.01
❑ 55T Dan McGwire	.05	.01
❑ 56T Ernie Mills	.05	.01
❑ 57T Stanley Richard	.05	.01
❑ 58T Huey Richardson RC	.05	.01
❑ 59T Jerome Henderson RC	.05	.01
❑ 60T Bryan Cox RC	.25	.08
❑ 61T Russell Maryland	.10	.02
❑ 62T Reginald Jones RC	.05	.01
❑ 63T Mo Lewis RC	.10	.02
❑ 64T Moe Gardner	.05	.01
❑ 65T Wesley Carroll	.05	.01
❑ 66T Michael Jackson RC WR	.25	.08
❑ 67T Shawn Jefferson RC	.10	.02
❑ 68T Chris Zorich	.10	.02
❑ 69T Kenny Walker	.05	.01
❑ 70T Erric Pegram RC	.25	.08
❑ 71T Alvin Harper	.25	.08
❑ 72T Harry Colon RC	.05	.01
❑ 73T Scott Miller	.05	.01
❑ 74T Lawrence Dawsey	.10	.02
❑ 75T Phil Hansen RC	.05	.01
❑ 76T Roman Phifer RC	.05	.01
❑ 77T Greg Lewis	.05	.01
❑ 78T Merton Hanks RC	.25	.08
❑ 79T James Jones RC DT	.05	.01
❑ 80T Vinnie Clark	.05	.01
❑ 81T R.J. Kors	.05	.01
❑ 82T Mike Pritchard	.25	.08
❑ 83T Stan Thomas	.05	.01
❑ 84T Lamar Rogers RC	.05	.01
❑ 85T Erik Williams RC	.10	.02
❑ 86T Keith Traylor RC	.05	.01
❑ 87T Mike Dumas	.05	.01
❑ 88T Mel Agee	.05	.01
❑ 89T Harvey Williams	.25	.08
❑ 90T Todd Lyght	.05	.01
❑ 91T Jake Reed	.40	.15
❑ 92T Pat Harlow	.05	.01
❑ 93T Antone Davis RC	.05	.01
❑ 94T Aeneas Williams RC	.25	.08
❑ 95T Eric Bieniemy	.05	.01
❑ 96T John Kasay RC	.10	.02
❑ 97T Robert Wilson RC	.05	.01
❑ 98T Ricky Ervins	.10	.02
❑ 99T Mike Croel	.05	.01
❑ 100T David Lang RC	.05	.01
❑ 101T Esera Tuaolo RC	.05	.01
❑ 102T Randal Hill	.10	.02
❑ 103T Jon Vaughn RC	.05	.01
❑ 104T Dave McCloughan	.05	.01
❑ 105T David Daniels RC	.05	.01
❑ 106T Eric Moten	.05	.01
❑ 107T Anthony Morgan RC	.05	.01
❑ 108T Ed King	.05	.01
❑ 109T Leonard Russell RC	.10	.02
❑ 110T Aaron Craver	.05	.01

1992 Score

❑ COMPLETE SET (550)	25.00	12.50
❑ 1 Barry Sanders	2.00	.75
❑ 2 Pat Swilling	.05	.01
❑ 3 Moe Gardner	.05	.01
❑ 4 Steve Young	1.00	.40
❑ 5 Chris Spielman	.10	.02
❑ 6 Richard Dent	.10	.02
❑ 7 Anthony Munoz	.10	.02
❑ 8 Martin Mayhew	.05	.01
❑ 9 Terry McDaniel	.05	.01
❑ 10 Thurman Thomas	.25	.08
❑ 11 Ricky Sanders	.05	.01
❑ 12 Steve Atwater	.05	.01
❑ 13 Tony Tolbert	.05	.01
❑ 14 Vince Workman	.05	.01
❑ 15 Haywood Jeffires	.10	.02
❑ 16 Duane Bickett	.05	.01
❑ 17 Jeff Uhlenhake	.05	.01
❑ 18 Tim McDonald	.05	.01
❑ 19 Cris Carter	.50	.20
❑ 20 Derrick Thomas	.25	.08
❑ 21 Hugh Millen	.05	.01
❑ 22 Bart Oates	.05	.01
❑ 23 Eugene Robinson	.05	.01
❑ 24 Jerrol Williams	.05	.01
❑ 25 Reggie White	.25	.08
❑ 26 Marion Butts	.05	.01
❑ 27 Jim Sweeney	.05	.01
❑ 28 Tom Newberry	.05	.01
❑ 29 Pete Stoyanovich	.05	.01
❑ 30 Ronnie Lott	.10	.02
❑ 31 Simon Fletcher	.05	.01
❑ 32 Dino Hackett	.05	.01
❑ 33 Morten Andersen	.05	.01
❑ 34 Clyde Simmons	.05	.01
❑ 35 Mark Rypien	.05	.01
❑ 36 Greg Montgomery	.05	.01
❑ 37 Nate Lewis	.05	.01
❑ 38 Henry Ellard	.10	.02
❑ 39 Luis Sharpe	.05	.01
❑ 40 Michael Irvin	.25	.08
❑ 41 Louis Lipps	.05	.01
❑ 42 John L. Williams	.05	.01
❑ 43 Broderick Thomas	.05	.01
❑ 44 Michael Haynes	.10	.02
❑ 45 Don Majkowski	.05	.01
❑ 46 William Perry	.10	.02
❑ 47 David Fulcher	.05	.01
❑ 48 Tony Bennett	.05	.01
❑ 49 Clay Matthews	.10	.02
❑ 50 Warren Moon	.25	.08
❑ 51 Bruce Armstrong	.05	.01
❑ 52 Harry Newsome	.05	.01
❑ 53 Bill Brooks	.05	.01
❑ 54 Greg Townsend	.05	.01
❑ 55 Tom Rathman	.05	.01
❑ 56 Sean Landeta	.05	.01
❑ 57 Kyle Clifton	.05	.01
❑ 58 Steve Broussard	.05	.01
❑ 59 Mark Carrier WR	.10	.02
❑ 60 Mel Gray	.10	.02
❑ 61 Tim Krumrie	.05	.01
❑ 62 Rufus Porter	.05	.01
❑ 63 Kevin Mack	.05	.01
❑ 64 Todd Bowles	.05	.01
❑ 65 Emmitt Smith	2.50	1.25
❑ 66 Mike Croel	.05	.01
❑ 67 Brian Mitchell	.10	.02
❑ 68 Bennie Blades	.05	.01
❑ 69 Carnell Lake	.05	.01
❑ 70 Cornelius Bennett	.10	.02
❑ 71 Darrell Thompson	.05	.01
❑ 72 Wes Hopkins	.05	.01
❑ 73 Jessie Hester	.05	.01
❑ 74 Irv Eatman	.05	.01
❑ 75 Marv Cook	.05	.01
❑ 76 Tim Brown	.25	.08
❑ 77 Pepper Johnson	.05	.01
❑ 78 Mark Duper	.05	.01
❑ 79 Robert Delpino	.05	.01
❑ 80 Charles Mann	.05	.01
❑ 81 Brian Jordan	.10	.02
❑ 82 Wendell Davis	.05	.01
❑ 83 Lee Johnson	.05	.01
❑ 84 Ricky Reynolds	.05	.01
❑ 85 Vaughan Johnson	.05	.01
❑ 86 Brian Blades	.10	.02
❑ 87 Sam Seale	.05	.01
❑ 88 Ed King	.05	.01
❑ 89 Gaston Green	.05	.01
❑ 90 Christian Okoye	.05	.01
❑ 91 Chris Jacke	.05	.01
❑ 92 Rohn Stark	.05	.01
❑ 93 Kevin Greene	.10	.02
❑ 94 Jay Novacek	.10	.02
❑ 95 Chip Lohmiller	.05	.01
❑ 96 Cris Dishman	.05	.01
❑ 97 Ethan Horton	.05	.01
❑ 98 Pat Harlow	.05	.01
❑ 99 Mark Ingram	.05	.01
❑ 100 Mark Carrier DB	.05	.01
❑ 101 Deron Cherry	.05	.01
❑ 102 Sam Mills	.05	.01
❑ 103 Mark Higgs	.05	.01
❑ 104 Keith Jackson	.10	.02
❑ 105 Steve Tasker	.10	.02
❑ 106 Ken Harvey	.05	.01
❑ 107 Bryan Hinkle	.05	.01
❑ 108 Anthony Carter	.10	.02
❑ 109 Johnny Hector	.05	.01
❑ 110 Randall McDaniel	.05	.01
❑ 111 Johnny Johnson	.05	.01
❑ 112 Shane Conlan	.05	.01
❑ 113 Ray Horton	.05	.01
❑ 114 Sterling Sharpe	.25	.08
❑ 115 Guy McIntyre	.05	.01
❑ 116 Tom Waddle	.05	.01
❑ 117 Albert Lewis	.05	.01
❑ 118 Riki Ellison	.05	.01
❑ 119 Chris Doleman	.05	.01
❑ 120 Andre Rison	.10	.02
❑ 121 Bobby Hebert	.05	.01
❑ 122 Dan Owens	.05	.01
❑ 123 Rodney Hampton	.10	.02
❑ 124 Ron Holmes	.05	.01
❑ 125 Ernie Jones	.05	.01
❑ 126 Michael Carter	.05	.01
❑ 127 Reggie Cobb	.05	.01
❑ 128 Esera Tuaolo	.05	.01
❑ 129 Wilber Marshall	.05	.01
❑ 130 Mike Munchak	.10	.02
❑ 131 Cortez Kennedy	.10	.02
❑ 132 Lamar Lathon	.05	.01
❑ 133 Todd Lyght	.05	.01
❑ 134 Jeff Feagles	.05	.01
❑ 135 Burt Grossman	.05	.01
❑ 136 Mike Cofer	.05	.01
❑ 137 Frank Warren	.05	.01
❑ 138 Jarvis Williams	.05	.01
❑ 139 Eddie Brown	.05	.01
❑ 140 John Elliott	.05	.01
❑ 141 Jim Everett	.10	.02
❑ 142 Hardy Nickerson	.10	.02
❑ 143 Eddie Murray	.05	.01
❑ 144 Andre Tippett	.05	.01
❑ 145 Heath Sherman	.05	.01
❑ 146 Ronnie Harmon	.05	.01
❑ 147 Eric Metcalf	.10	.02
❑ 148 Tony Martin	.10	.02
❑ 149 Chris Burkett	.05	.01
❑ 150 Andre Waters	.05	.01
❑ 151 Ray Donaldson	.05	.01
❑ 152 Paul Gruber	.05	.01
❑ 153 Chris Singleton	.05	.01
❑ 154 Clarence Kay	.05	.01
❑ 155 Ernest Givins	.10	.02
❑ 156 Eric Hill	.05	.01
❑ 157 Jesse Sapolu	.05	.01
❑ 158 Jack Del Rio	.05	.01
❑ 159 Erric Pegram	.10	.02
❑ 160 Joey Browner	.05	.01
❑ 161 Marcus Allen	.25	.08
❑ 162 Eric Moten	.05	.01
❑ 163 Donnell Thompson	.05	.01
❑ 164 Chuck Cecil	.05	.01
❑ 165 Matt Millen	.10	.02
❑ 166 Barry Foster	.10	.02
❑ 167 Kent Hull	.05	.01

❑ 168 Tony Jones WR .05 .01
❑ 169 Mike Prior .05 .01
❑ 170 Neal Anderson .05 .01
❑ 171 Roger Craig .10 .02
❑ 172 Felix Wright .05 .01
❑ 173 James Francis .05 .01
❑ 174 Eugene Lockhart .05 .01
❑ 175 Dalton Hilliard .05 .01
❑ 176 Nick Lowery .05 .01
❑ 177 Tim McKyer .05 .01
❑ 178 Lorenzo White .05 .01
❑ 179 Jeff Hostetler .10 .02
❑ 180 Jackie Harris RC .25 .08
❑ 181 Ken Norton .10 .02
❑ 182 Flipper Anderson .05 .01
❑ 183 Don Warren .05 .01
❑ 184 Brad Baxter .05 .01
❑ 185 John Taylor .10 .02
❑ 186 Harold Green .05 .01
❑ 187 James Washington .05 .01
❑ 188 Aaron Craver .05 .01
❑ 189 Mike Merriweather .05 .01
❑ 190 Gary Clark .25 .08
❑ 191 Vince Buck .05 .01
❑ 192 Cleveland Gary .05 .01
❑ 193 Dan Saleaumua .05 .01
❑ 194 Gary Zimmerman .05 .01
❑ 195 Richmond Webb .05 .01
❑ 196 Gary Plummer .05 .01
❑ 197 Willie Green .05 .01
❑ 198 Chris Warren .25 .08
❑ 199 Mike Pritchard .10 .02
❑ 200 Art Monk .10 .02
❑ 201 Matt Stover .05 .01
❑ 202 Tim Grunhard .05 .01
❑ 203 Mervyn Fernandez .05 .01
❑ 204 Mark Jackson .05 .01
❑ 205 Freddie Joe Nunn .05 .01
❑ 206 Stan Thomas .05 .01
❑ 207 Keith McKeller .05 .01
❑ 208 Jeff Lageman .05 .01
❑ 209 Kenny Walker .05 .01
❑ 210 Dave Krieg .10 .02
❑ 211 Dean Biasucci .05 .01
❑ 212 Herman Moore .25 .08
❑ 213 Jon Vaughn .05 .01
❑ 214 Howard Cross .05 .01
❑ 215 Greg Davis .05 .01
❑ 216 Bubby Brister .05 .01
❑ 217 John Kasay .05 .01
❑ 218 Ron Hall .05 .01
❑ 219 Mo Lewis .05 .01
❑ 220 Eric Green .05 .01
❑ 221 Scott Case .05 .01
❑ 222 Sean Jones .05 .01
❑ 223 Winston Moss .05 .01
❑ 224 Reggie Langhorne .05 .01
❑ 225 Greg Lewis .05 .01
❑ 226 Todd McNair .05 .01
❑ 227 Rod Bernstine .05 .01
❑ 228 Joe Jacoby .05 .01
❑ 229 Brad Muster .05 .01
❑ 230 Nick Bell .05 .01
❑ 231 Terry Allen .25 .08
❑ 232 Cliff Odom .05 .01
❑ 233 Brian Hansen .05 .01
❑ 234 William Fuller .05 .01
❑ 235 Issiac Holt .05 .01
❑ 236 Dexter Carter .05 .01
❑ 237 Gene Atkins .05 .01
❑ 238 Pat Beach .05 .01
❑ 239 Tim McGee .05 .01
❑ 240 Dermontti Dawson .05 .01
❑ 241 Dan Fike .05 .01
❑ 242 Don Beebe .05 .01
❑ 243 Jeff Bostic .05 .01
❑ 244 Mark Collins .05 .01
❑ 245 Steve Sewell .05 .01
❑ 246 Steve Walsh .05 .01
❑ 247 Erik Kramer .10 .02
❑ 248 Scott Norwood .05 .01
❑ 249 Jesse Solomon .05 .01
❑ 250 Jerry Ball .05 .01
❑ 251 Eugene Daniel .05 .01
❑ 252 Michael Stewart .05 .01
❑ 253 Fred Barnett .25 .08
❑ 254 Rodney Holman .05 .01
❑ 255 Stephen Baker .05 .01
❑ 256 Don Griffin .05 .01
❑ 257 Will Wolford .05 .01
❑ 258 Perry Kemp .05 .01
❑ 259 Leonard Russell .10 .02
❑ 260 Jeff Gossett .05 .01
❑ 261 Dwayne Harper .05 .01
❑ 262 Vinny Testaverde .10 .02
❑ 263 Maurice Hurst .05 .01
❑ 264 Tony Casillas .05 .01
❑ 265 Louis Oliver .05 .01
❑ 266 Jim Morrissey .05 .01
❑ 267 Kenneth Davis .05 .01
❑ 268 John Alt .05 .01
❑ 269 Michael Zordich RC .05 .01
❑ 270 Brian Brennan .05 .01
❑ 271 Greg Kragen .05 .01
❑ 272 Andre Collins .05 .01
❑ 273 Dave Meggett .10 .02
❑ 274 Scott Fulhage .05 .01
❑ 275 Tony Zendejas .05 .01
❑ 276 Herschel Walker .10 .02
❑ 277 Keith Henderson .05 .01
❑ 278 Johnny Bailey .05 .01
❑ 279 Vince Newsome .05 .01
❑ 280 Chris Hinton .05 .01
❑ 281 Robert Blackmon .05 .01
❑ 282 James Hasty .05 .01
❑ 283 John Offerdahl .05 .01
❑ 284 Wesley Carroll .05 .01
❑ 285 Lomas Brown .05 .01
❑ 286 Neil O'Donnell .10 .02
❑ 287 Kevin Porter .05 .01
❑ 288 Lionel Washington .05 .01
❑ 289 Carlton Bailey RC .05 .01
❑ 290 Leonard Marshall .05 .01
❑ 291 John Carney .05 .01
❑ 292 Bubba McDowell .05 .01
❑ 293 Nate Newton .05 .01
❑ 294 Dave Waymer .05 .01
❑ 295 Rob Moore .10 .02
❑ 296 Earnest Byner .05 .01
❑ 297 Jason Staurovsky .05 .01
❑ 298 Keith McCants .05 .01
❑ 299 Floyd Turner .05 .01
❑ 300 Steve Jordan .05 .01
❑ 301 Nate Odomes .05 .01
❑ 302 Gerald Riggs .05 .01
❑ 303 Marvin Washington .05 .01
❑ 304 Anthony Thompson .05 .01
❑ 305 Steve DeBerg .05 .01
❑ 306 Jim Harbaugh .25 .08
❑ 307 Larry Brown DB .05 .01
❑ 308 Roger Ruzek .05 .01
❑ 309 Jessie Tuggle .05 .01
❑ 310 Al Smith .05 .01
❑ 311 Mark Kelso .05 .01
❑ 312 Lawrence Dawsey .10 .02
❑ 313 Steve Bono RC .25 .08
❑ 314 Greg Lloyd .10 .02
❑ 315 Steve Wisniewski .05 .01
❑ 316 Gill Fenerty .05 .01
❑ 317 Mark Stepnoski .10 .02
❑ 318 Derek Russell .05 .01
❑ 319 Chris Martin .05 .01
❑ 320 Shaun Gayle .05 .01
❑ 321 Bob Golic .05 .01
❑ 322 Larry Kelm .05 .01
❑ 323 Mike Brim RC .05 .01
❑ 324 Tommy Kane .05 .01
❑ 325 Mark Schlereth RC .05 .01
❑ 326 Ray Childress .05 .01
❑ 327 Richard Brown RC .05 .01
❑ 328 Vincent Brown .05 .01
❑ 329 Mike Farr UER .05 .01
❑ 330 Eric Swann .10 .02
❑ 331 Bill Fralic .05 .01
❑ 332 Rodney Peete .10 .02
❑ 333 Jerry Gray .05 .01
❑ 334 Ray Berry .05 .01
❑ 335 Dennis Smith .05 .01
❑ 336 Jeff Herrod .05 .01
❑ 337 Tony Mandarich .05 .01
❑ 338 Matt Bahr .05 .01
❑ 339 Mike Saxon .05 .01
❑ 340 Bruce Matthews .05 .01
❑ 341 Rickey Jackson .05 .01
❑ 342 Eric Allen .05 .01
❑ 343 Lonnie Young .05 .01
❑ 344 Steve McMichael .10 .02
❑ 345 Willie Gault .10 .02
❑ 346 Barry Word .05 .01
❑ 347 Rich Camarillo .05 .01
❑ 348 Bill Romanowski .05 .01
❑ 349 Jim Lachey .05 .01
❑ 350 Jim Ritcher .05 .01
❑ 351 Irving Fryar .10 .02
❑ 352 Gary Anderson K .05 .01
❑ 353 Henry Rolling .05 .01
❑ 354 Mark Bortz .05 .01
❑ 355 Mark Clayton .10 .02
❑ 356 Keith Woodside .05 .01
❑ 357 Jonathan Hayes .05 .01
❑ 358 Derrick Fenner .05 .01
❑ 359 Keith Byars .05 .01
❑ 360 Drew Hill .05 .01
❑ 361 Harris Barton .05 .01
❑ 362 John Kidd .05 .01
❑ 363 Aeneas Williams .10 .02
❑ 364 Brian Washington .05 .01
❑ 365 John Stephens .05 .01
❑ 366 Norm Johnson .05 .01
❑ 367 Darryl Henley .05 .01
❑ 368 William White .05 .01
❑ 369 Mark Murphy .05 .01
❑ 370 Myron Guyton .05 .01
❑ 371 Leon Seals .05 .01
❑ 372 Rich Gannon .25 .08
❑ 373 Toi Cook .05 .01
❑ 374 Anthony Johnson .10 .02
❑ 375 Rod Woodson .25 .08
❑ 376 Alexander Wright .05 .01
❑ 377 Kevin Butler .05 .01
❑ 378 Neil Smith .25 .08
❑ 379 Gary Anderson RB .05 .01
❑ 380 Reggie Roby .05 .01
❑ 381 Jeff Bryant .05 .01
❑ 382 Ray Crockett .05 .01
❑ 383 Richard Johnson CB .05 .01
❑ 384 Hassan Jones .05 .01
❑ 385 Karl Mecklenburg .05 .01
❑ 386 Jeff Jaeger .05 .01
❑ 387 Keith Willis .05 .01
❑ 388 Phil Simms .10 .02
❑ 389 Kevin Ross .05 .01
❑ 390 Chris Miller .10 .02
❑ 391 Brian Noble .05 .01
❑ 392 Jamie Dukes RC .05 .01
❑ 393 George Jamison .05 .01
❑ 394 Rickey Dixon .05 .01
❑ 395 Carl Lee .05 .01
❑ 396 Jon Hand .05 .01
❑ 397 Kirby Jackson .05 .01
❑ 398 Pat Terrell .05 .01
❑ 399 Howie Long .25 .08
❑ 400 Michael Young .05 .01
❑ 401 Keith Sims .05 .01
❑ 402 Tommy Barnhardt .05 .01
❑ 403 Greg McMurtry .05 .01
❑ 404 Keith Van Horne .05 .01
❑ 405 Seth Joyner .05 .01
❑ 406 Jim Jeffcoat .05 .01
❑ 407 Courtney Hall .05 .01
❑ 408 Tony Covington .05 .01
❑ 409 Jacob Green .05 .01
❑ 410 Charles Haley .10 .02
❑ 411 Darryl Talley .05 .01
❑ 412 Jeff Cross .05 .01
❑ 413 John Elway 2.00 .75
❑ 414 Donald Evans .05 .01
❑ 415 Jackie Slater .05 .01
❑ 416 John Friesz .10 .02
❑ 417 Anthony Smith .05 .01
❑ 418 Gill Byrd .05 .01
❑ 419 Willie Drewrey .05 .01
❑ 420 Jay Hilgenberg .05 .01
❑ 421 David Treadwell .05 .01
❑ 422 Curtis Duncan .05 .01
❑ 423 Sammie Smith .05 .01
❑ 424 Henry Thomas .05 .01
❑ 425 James Lofton .10 .02
❑ 426 Fred Marion .05 .01
❑ 427 Bryce Paup .25 .08
❑ 428 Michael Timpson RC .05 .01

❑ 429	Reyna Thompson	.05	.01
❑ 430	Mike Kenn	.05	.01
❑ 431	Bill Maas	.05	.01
❑ 432	Quinn Early	.10	.02
❑ 433	Everson Walls	.05	.01
❑ 434	Jimmie Jones	.05	.01
❑ 435	Dwight Stone	.05	.01
❑ 436	Harry Colon	.05	.01
❑ 437	Don Mosebar	.05	.01
❑ 438	Calvin Williams	.10	.02
❑ 439	Tom Tupa	.05	.01
❑ 440	Darrell Green	.05	.01
❑ 441	Eric Thomas	.05	.01
❑ 442	Terry Wooden	.05	.01
❑ 443	Brett Perriman	.25	.08
❑ 444	Todd Marinovich	.05	.01
❑ 445	Jim Breech	.05	.01
❑ 446	Eddie Anderson	.05	.01
❑ 447	Jay Schroeder	.05	.01
❑ 448	William Roberts	.05	.01
❑ 449	Brad Edwards	.05	.01
❑ 450	Tunch Ilkin	.05	.01
❑ 451	Ivy Joe Hunter RC	.05	.01
❑ 452	Robert Clark	.05	.01
❑ 453	Tim Barnett	.05	.01
❑ 454	Jarrod Bunch	.05	.01
❑ 455	Tim Harris	.05	.01
❑ 456	James Brooks	.10	.02
❑ 457	Trace Armstrong	.05	.01
❑ 458	Michael Brooks	.05	.01
❑ 459	Andy Heck	.05	.01
❑ 460	Greg Jackson	.05	.01
❑ 461	Vance Johnson	.05	.01
❑ 462	Kirk Lowdermilk	.05	.01
❑ 463	Erik McMillan	.05	.01
❑ 464	Scott Mersereau	.05	.01
❑ 465	Jeff Wright	.05	.01
❑ 466	Mike Tomczak	.05	.01
❑ 467	David Alexander	.05	.01
❑ 468	Bryan Millard	.05	.01
❑ 469	John Randle	.10	.02
❑ 470	Joel Hilgenberg	.05	.01
❑ 471	Bennie Thompson RC	.05	.01
❑ 472	Freeman McNeil	.05	.01
❑ 473	Terry Orr RC	.05	.01
❑ 474	Mike Horan	.05	.01
❑ 475	Leroy Hoard	.10	.02
❑ 476	Patrick Rowe RC	.05	.01
❑ 477	Siran Stacy RC	.05	.01
❑ 478	Amp Lee RC	.05	.01
❑ 479	Eddie Blake RC	.05	.01
❑ 480	Joe Bowden RC	.05	.01
❑ 481	Rod Milstead RC	.05	.01
❑ 482	Keith Hamilton RC	.10	.02
❑ 483	Darryl Williams RC	.05	.01
❑ 484	Robert Porcher RC	.25	.08
❑ 485	Ed Cunningham RC	.05	.01
❑ 486	Chris Mims RC	.05	.01
❑ 487	Chris Hakel RC	.05	.01
❑ 488	Jimmy Smith RC	4.00	1.50
❑ 489	Todd Harrison RC	.05	.01
❑ 490	Edgar Bennett RC	.25	.08
❑ 491	Dexter McNabb RC	.05	.01
❑ 492	Leon Searcy RC	.05	.01
❑ 493	Tommy Vardell RC	.05	.01
❑ 494	Terrell Buckley RC	.05	.01
❑ 495	Kevin Turner RC	.05	.01
❑ 496	Russ Campbell RC	.05	.01
❑ 497	Torrance Small RC	.10	.02
❑ 498	Nate Turner RC	.05	.01
❑ 499	Cornelius Benton RC	.05	.01
❑ 500	Matt Elliott RC	.05	.01
❑ 501	Robert Stewart RC	.05	.01
❑ 502	Muhammad Shamsid-Deen RC	.05	.01
❑ 503	George Williams RC	.05	.01
❑ 504	Pumpy Tudors RC	.05	.01
❑ 505	Matt LaBounty RC	.05	.01
❑ 506	Darryl Hardy RC	.05	.01
❑ 507	Derrick Moore RC	.10	.02
❑ 508	Willie Clay RC	.05	.01
❑ 509	Bob Whitfield RC	.05	.01
❑ 510	Ricardo McDonald RC	.05	.01
❑ 511	Carlos Huerta RC	.05	.01
❑ 512	Selwyn Jones RC	.05	.01
❑ 513	Steve Gordon RC	.05	.01
❑ 514	Bob Meeks RC	.05	.01
❑ 515	Bennie Blades CC	.05	.01
❑ 516	Andre Waters CC	.05	.01
❑ 517	Bubba McDowell CC	.05	.01
❑ 518	Kevin Porter CC	.05	.01
❑ 519	Carnell Lake CC	.05	.01
❑ 520	Leonard Russell ROY	.10	.02
❑ 521	Mike Croel ROY	.05	.01
❑ 522	Lawrence Dawsey ROY	.05	.01
❑ 523	Moe Gardner ROY	.05	.01
❑ 524	Steve Broussard LBM	.05	.01
❑ 525	Dave Meggett LBM	.05	.01
❑ 526	Darrell Green LBM	.05	.01
❑ 527	Tony Jones WR LBM	.05	.01
❑ 528	Barry Sanders LBM	1.00	.40
❑ 529	Pat Swilling SA	.05	.01
❑ 530	Reggie White SA	.10	.02
❑ 531	William Fuller SA	.05	.01
❑ 532	Simon Fletcher SA	.05	.01
❑ 533	Derrick Thomas SA	.10	.02
❑ 534	Mark Rypien MOY	.05	.01
❑ 535	John Mackey HOF	.05	.01
❑ 536	John Riggins HOF	.10	.02
❑ 537	Lem Barney HOF	.05	.01
❑ 538	Shawn McCarthy RC 90	.05	.01
❑ 539	Al Edwards 90	.05	.01
❑ 540	Alexander Wright 90	.05	.01
❑ 541	Ray Crockett 90	.05	.01
❑ 542	Steve Young/J.Taylor 90	.25	.08
❑ 543	Nate Lewis 90	.05	.01
❑ 544	Dexter Carter 90	.05	.01
❑ 545	Reggie Rutland 90	.05	.01
❑ 546	Jon Vaughn 90	.05	.01
❑ 547	Chris Martin 90	.05	.01
❑ 548	Warren Moon HL	.10	.02
❑ 549	Super Bowl Highlights	.05	.01
❑ 550	Robb Thomas	.05	.01
❑ NNO	Dick Butkus Promo	8.00	4.00

1993 Score

❑	COMPLETE SET (440)	15.00	6.00
❑ 1	Barry Sanders	1.25	.50
❑ 2	Moe Gardner	.05	.01
❑ 3	Ricky Watters	.25	.08
❑ 4	Todd Lyght	.05	.01
❑ 5	Rodney Hampton	.10	.02
❑ 6	Curtis Duncan	.05	.01
❑ 7	Barry Word	.05	.01
❑ 8	Reggie Cobb	.05	.01
❑ 9	Mike Kenn	.05	.01
❑ 10	Michael Irvin	.25	.08
❑ 11	Bryan Cox	.05	.01
❑ 12	Chris Doleman	.05	.01
❑ 13	Rod Woodson	.25	.08
❑ 14	Emmitt Smith	1.50	.60
❑ 15	Pete Stoyanovich	.05	.01
❑ 16	Steve Young	.75	.30
❑ 17	Randall McDaniel	.05	.01
❑ 18	Cortez Kennedy	.10	.02
❑ 19	Mel Gray	.10	.02
❑ 20	Barry Foster	.10	.02
❑ 21	Tim Brown	.25	.08
❑ 22	Todd McNair	.05	.01
❑ 23	Anthony Johnson	.10	.02
❑ 24	Nate Odomes	.05	.01
❑ 25	Brett Favre	2.00	.75
❑ 26	Jack Del Rio	.05	.01
❑ 27	Terry McDaniel	.05	.01
❑ 28	Haywood Jeffires	.10	.02
❑ 29	Jay Novacek	.10	.02
❑ 30	Wilber Marshall	.05	.01
❑ 31	Richmond Webb	.05	.01
❑ 32	Steve Atwater	.05	.01
❑ 33	James Lofton	.10	.02
❑ 34	Harold Green	.05	.01
❑ 35	Eric Metcalf	.10	.02
❑ 36	Bruce Matthews	.05	.01
❑ 37	Albert Lewis	.05	.01
❑ 38	Jeff Herrod	.05	.01
❑ 39	Vince Workman	.05	.01
❑ 40	John Elway	1.50	.60
❑ 41	Brett Perriman	.25	.08
❑ 42	Jon Vaughn	.05	.01
❑ 43	Terry Allen	.25	.08
❑ 44	Clyde Simmons	.05	.01
❑ 45	Bennie Thompson	.05	.01
❑ 46	Wendell Davis	.05	.01
❑ 47	Bobby Hebert	.05	.01
❑ 48	John Offerdahl	.05	.01
❑ 49	Jeff Graham	.10	.02
❑ 50	Steve Wisniewski	.05	.01
❑ 51	Louis Oliver	.05	.01
❑ 52	Rohn Stark	.05	.01
❑ 53	Cleveland Gary	.05	.01
❑ 54	John Randle	.10	.02
❑ 55	Jim Everett	.10	.02
❑ 56	Donnell Woolford	.05	.01
❑ 57	Pepper Johnson	.05	.01
❑ 58	Irving Fryar	.10	.02
❑ 59	Greg Townsend	.05	.01
❑ 60	Chris Burkett	.05	.01
❑ 61	Johnny Johnson	.05	.01
❑ 62	Ronnie Harmon	.05	.01
❑ 63	Don Griffin	.05	.01
❑ 64	Wayne Martin	.05	.01
❑ 65	John L. Williams	.05	.01
❑ 66	Brad Edwards	.05	.01
❑ 67	Toi Cook	.05	.01
❑ 68	Lawrence Dawsey	.05	.01
❑ 69	Johnny Bailey	.05	.01
❑ 70	Mike Brim	.05	.01
❑ 71	Andre Rison	.10	.02
❑ 72	Cornelius Bennett	.10	.02
❑ 73	Brad Muster	.05	.01
❑ 74	Broderick Thomas	.05	.01
❑ 75	Tom Waddle	.05	.01
❑ 76	Paul Gruber	.05	.01
❑ 77	Jackie Harris	.05	.01
❑ 78	Kenneth Davis	.05	.01
❑ 79	Norm Johnson	.05	.01
❑ 80	Jim Jeffcoat	.05	.01
❑ 81	Chris Warren	.10	.02
❑ 82	Greg Kragen	.05	.01
❑ 83	Ricky Reynolds	.05	.01
❑ 84	Hardy Nickerson	.10	.02
❑ 85	Brian Mitchell	.10	.02
❑ 86	Rufus Porter	.05	.01
❑ 87	Greg Jackson	.05	.01
❑ 88	Seth Joyner	.05	.01
❑ 89	Tim Grunhard	.05	.01
❑ 90	Tim Harris	.05	.01
❑ 91	Sterling Sharpe	.25	.08
❑ 92	Daniel Stubbs	.05	.01
❑ 93	Rob Burnett	.05	.01
❑ 94	Rich Camarillo	.05	.01
❑ 95	Al Smith	.05	.01
❑ 96	Thurman Thomas	.25	.08
❑ 97	Morten Andersen	.05	.01
❑ 98	Reggie White	.25	.08
❑ 99	Gill Byrd	.05	.01
❑ 100	Pierce Holt	.05	.01
❑ 101	Tim McGee	.05	.01
❑ 102	Rickey Jackson	.05	.01
❑ 103	Vince Newsome	.05	.01
❑ 104	Chris Spielman	.10	.02
❑ 105	Tim McDonald	.05	.01
❑ 106	James Francis	.05	.01
❑ 107	Andre Tippett	.05	.01
❑ 108	Sam Mills	.05	.01
❑ 109	Hugh Millen	.05	.01
❑ 110	Brad Baxter	.05	.01
❑ 111	Ricky Sanders	.05	.01
❑ 112	Marion Butts	.05	.01
❑ 113	Fred Barnett	.10	.02
❑ 114	Wade Wilson	.05	.01
❑ 115	Dave Meggett	.05	.01
❑ 116	Kevin Greene	.10	.02
❑ 117	Reggie Langhorne	.05	.01

❑ 118 Simon Fletcher .05 .01
❑ 119 Tommy Vardell .05 .01
❑ 120 Darion Conner .05 .01
❑ 121 Darren Lewis .05 .01
❑ 122 Charles Mann .05 .01
❑ 123 David Fulcher .05 .01
❑ 124 Tommy Kane .05 .01
❑ 125 Richard Brown .05 .01
❑ 126 Nate Lewis .05 .01
❑ 127 Tony Tolbert .05 .01
❑ 128 Greg Lloyd .10 .02
❑ 129 Herman Moore .25 .08
❑ 130 Robert Massey .05 .01
❑ 131 Chris Jacke .05 .01
❑ 132 Keith Byars .05 .01
❑ 133 William Fuller .05 .01
❑ 134 Rob Moore .10 .02
❑ 135 Duane Bickett .05 .01
❑ 136 Jarrod Bunch .05 .01
❑ 137 Ethan Horton .05 .01
❑ 138 Leonard Russell .10 .02
❑ 139 Darryl Henley .05 .01
❑ 140 Tony Bennett .05 .01
❑ 141 Harry Newsome .05 .01
❑ 142 Kelvin Martin .05 .01
❑ 143 Audray McMillian .05 .01
❑ 144 Chip Lohmiller .05 .01
❑ 145 Henry Jones .05 .01
❑ 146 Rod Bernstine .05 .01
❑ 147 Darryl Talley .05 .01
❑ 148 Clarence Verdin .05 .01
❑ 149 Derrick Thomas .25 .08
❑ 150 Raleigh McKenzie .05 .01
❑ 151 Phil Hansen .05 .01
❑ 152 Lin Elliott RC .05 .01
❑ 153 Chip Banks .05 .01
❑ 154 Shannon Sharpe .25 .08
❑ 155 David Williams .05 .01
❑ 156 Gaston Green .05 .01
❑ 157 Trace Armstrong .05 .01
❑ 158 Todd Scott .05 .01
❑ 159 Stan Humphries .10 .02
❑ 160 Christian Okoye .05 .01
❑ 161 Dennis Smith .05 .01
❑ 162 Derek Kennard .05 .01
❑ 163 Melvin Jenkins .05 .01
❑ 164 Tommy Barnhardt .05 .01
❑ 165 Eugene Robinson .05 .01
❑ 166 Tom Rathman .05 .01
❑ 167 Chris Chandler .10 .02
❑ 168 Steve Broussard .05 .01
❑ 169 Wymon Henderson .05 .01
❑ 170 Bryce Paup .10 .02
❑ 171 Kent Hull .05 .01
❑ 172 Willie Davis .25 .08
❑ 173 Richard Dent .10 .02
❑ 174 Rodney Peete .05 .01
❑ 175 Clay Matthews .10 .02
❑ 176 Erik Williams .05 .01
❑ 177 Mike Cofer .05 .01
❑ 178 Mark Kelso .05 .01
❑ 179 Kurt Gouveia .05 .01
❑ 180 Keith McCants .05 .01
❑ 181 Jim Arnold .05 .01
❑ 182 Sean Jones .05 .01
❑ 183 Chuck Cecil .05 .01
❑ 184 Mark Rypien .05 .01
❑ 185 William Perry .10 .02
❑ 186 Mark Jackson .05 .01
❑ 187 Jim Dombrowski .05 .01
❑ 188 Heath Sherman .05 .01
❑ 189 Bubba McDowell .05 .01
❑ 190 Fuad Reveiz .05 .01
❑ 191 Darren Perry .05 .01
❑ 192 Karl Mecklenburg .05 .01
❑ 193 Frank Reich .10 .02
❑ 194 Tony Casillas .05 .01
❑ 195 Jerry Ball .05 .01
❑ 196 Jessie Hester .05 .01
❑ 197 David Lang .05 .01
❑ 198 Sean Landeta .05 .01
❑ 199 Jerry Gray .05 .01
❑ 200 Mark Higgs .05 .01
❑ 201 Bruce Armstrong .05 .01
❑ 202 Vaughan Johnson .05 .01
❑ 203 Calvin Williams .10 .02
❑ 204 Leonard Marshall .05 .01
❑ 205 Mike Munchak .10 .02
❑ 206 Kevin Ross .05 .01
❑ 207 Daryl Johnston .25 .08
❑ 208 Jay Schroeder .05 .01
❑ 209 Mo Lewis .05 .01
❑ 210 Carlton Haselrig .05 .01
❑ 211 Cris Carter .25 .08
❑ 212 Marv Cook .05 .01
❑ 213 Mark Duper .05 .01
❑ 214 Jackie Slater .05 .01
❑ 215 Mike Prior .05 .01
❑ 216 Warren Moon .25 .08
❑ 217 Mike Saxon .05 .01
❑ 218 Derrick Fenner .05 .01
❑ 219 Brian Washington .05 .01
❑ 220 Jessie Tuggle .05 .01
❑ 221 Jeff Hostetler .10 .02
❑ 222 Deion Sanders .50 .20
❑ 223 Neal Anderson .05 .01
❑ 224 Kevin Mack .05 .01
❑ 225 Tommy Maddox .25 .08
❑ 226 Neil Smith .25 .08
❑ 227 Ronnie Lott .10 .02
❑ 228 Flipper Anderson .05 .01
❑ 229 Keith Jackson .10 .02
❑ 230 Pat Swilling .05 .01
❑ 231 Carl Banks .05 .01
❑ 232 Eric Allen .05 .01
❑ 233 Randal Hill .05 .01
❑ 234 Burt Grossman .05 .01
❑ 235 Jerry Rice 1.00 .40
❑ 236 Santana Dotson .10 .02
❑ 237 Andre Reed .10 .02
❑ 238 Troy Aikman .75 .30
❑ 239 Ray Childress .05 .01
❑ 240 Phil Simms .10 .02
❑ 241 Steve McMichael .10 .02
❑ 242 Browning Nagle .05 .01
❑ 243 Anthony Miller .10 .02
❑ 244 Earnest Byner .05 .01
❑ 245 Jay Hilgenberg .05 .01
❑ 246 Jeff George .25 .08
❑ 247 Marco Coleman .05 .01
❑ 248 Mark Carrier DB .05 .01
❑ 249 Howie Long .25 .08
❑ 250 Ed McCaffrey .25 .08
❑ 251 Jim Kelly .25 .08
❑ 252 Henry Ellard .10 .02
❑ 253 Joe Montana 1.50 .60
❑ 254 Dale Carter .05 .01
❑ 255 Boomer Esiason .10 .02
❑ 256 Gary Clark .10 .02
❑ 257 Carl Pickens .10 .02
❑ 258 Dave Krieg .10 .02
❑ 259 Russell Maryland .05 .01
❑ 260 Randall Cunningham .25 .08
❑ 261 Leslie O'Neal .10 .02
❑ 262 Vinny Testaverde .10 .02
❑ 263 Ricky Ervins .05 .01
❑ 264 Chris Mims .05 .01
❑ 265 Dan Marino 1.50 .60
❑ 266 Eric Martin .05 .01
❑ 267 Bruce Smith .25 .08
❑ 268 Jim Harbaugh .25 .08
❑ 269 Steve Emtman .05 .01
❑ 270 Ricky Proehl .05 .01
❑ 271 Vaughn Dunbar .05 .01
❑ 272 Junior Seau .25 .08
❑ 273 Sean Gilbert .10 .02
❑ 274 Jim Lachey .05 .01
❑ 275 Dalton Hilliard .05 .01
❑ 276 David Klingler .05 .01
❑ 277 Robert Jones .05 .01
❑ 278 David Treadwell .05 .01
❑ 279 Tracy Scroggins .05 .01
❑ 280 Terrell Buckley .05 .01
❑ 281 Quentin Coryatt .10 .02
❑ 282 Jason Hanson .05 .01
❑ 283 Shane Conlan .05 .01
❑ 284 Guy McIntyre .05 .01
❑ 285 Gary Zimmerman .05 .01
❑ 286 Marty Carter .05 .01
❑ 287 Jim Sweeney .05 .01
❑ 288 Arthur Marshall RC .05 .01
❑ 289 Eugene Chung .05 .01
❑ 290 Mike Pritchard .10 .02
❑ 291 Jim Ritcher .05 .01
❑ 292 Todd Marinovich .05 .01
❑ 293 Courtney Hall .05 .01
❑ 294 Mark Collins .05 .01
❑ 295 Troy Auzenne .05 .01
❑ 296 Aeneas Williams .05 .01
❑ 297 Andy Heck .05 .01
❑ 298 Shaun Gayle .05 .01
❑ 299 Kevin Fagan .05 .01
❑ 300 Carnell Lake .05 .01
❑ 301 Bernie Kosar .10 .02
❑ 302 Maurice Hurst .05 .01
❑ 303 Mike Merriweather .05 .01
❑ 304 Reggie Roby .05 .01
❑ 305 Darryl Williams .05 .01
❑ 306 Jerome Bettis RC 5.00 2.50
❑ 307 Curtis Conway RC .40 .15
❑ 308 Drew Bledsoe RC 2.50 1.00
❑ 309 John Copeland RC .10 .02
❑ 310 Eric Curry RC .05 .01
❑ 311 Lincoln Kennedy RC .05 .01
❑ 312 Dan Williams RC .05 .01
❑ 313 Patrick Bates RC .05 .01
❑ 314 Tom Carter RC .10 .02
❑ 315 Garrison Hearst RC .75 .30
❑ 316 Joel Hilgenberg .05 .01
❑ 317 Harris Barton .05 .01
❑ 318 Jeff Lageman .05 .01
❑ 319 Charles Mincy RC .05 .01
❑ 320 Ricardo McDonald .05 .01
❑ 321 Lorenzo White .05 .01
❑ 322 Troy Vincent .05 .01
❑ 323 Bennie Blades .05 .01
❑ 324 Dana Hall .05 .01
❑ 325 Ken Norton Jr. .10 .02
❑ 326 Will Wolford .05 .01
❑ 327 Neil O'Donnell .25 .08
❑ 328 Tracy Simien .05 .01
❑ 329 Darrell Green .05 .01
❑ 330 Kyle Clifton .05 .01
❑ 331 Elbert Shelley RC .05 .01
❑ 332 Jeff Wright .05 .01
❑ 333 Mike Johnson .05 .01
❑ 334 John Gesek .05 .01
❑ 335 Michael Brooks .05 .01
❑ 336 George Jamison .05 .01
❑ 337 Johnny Holland .05 .01
❑ 338 Lamar Lathon .05 .01
❑ 339 Bern Brostek .05 .01
❑ 340 Steve Jordan .05 .01
❑ 341 Gene Atkins .05 .01
❑ 342 Aaron Wallace .05 .01
❑ 343 Adrian Cooper .05 .01
❑ 344 Amp Lee .05 .01
❑ 345 Vincent Brown .05 .01
❑ 346 James Hasty .05 .01
❑ 347 Ron Hall .05 .01
❑ 348 Matt Elliott .05 .01
❑ 349 Tim Krumrie .05 .01
❑ 350 Mark Stepnoski .05 .01
❑ 351 Matt Stover .05 .01
❑ 352 James Washington .05 .01
❑ 353 Marc Spindler .05 .01
❑ 354 Frank Warren .05 .01
❑ 355 Vai Sikahema .05 .01
❑ 356 Dan Saleaumua .05 .01
❑ 357 Mark Clayton .05 .01
❑ 358 Brent Jones .10 .02
❑ 359 Andy Harmon RC .10 .02
❑ 360 Anthony Parker .05 .01
❑ 361 Chris Hinton .05 .01
❑ 362 Greg Montgomery .05 .01
❑ 363 Greg McMurtry .05 .01
❑ 364 Craig Heyward .10 .02
❑ 365 D.J. Johnson .05 .01
❑ 366 Bill Romanowski .05 .01
❑ 367 Steve Christie .05 .01
❑ 368 Art Monk .10 .02
❑ 369 Howard Ballard .05 .01
❑ 370 Andre Collins .05 .01
❑ 371 Alvin Harper .10 .02
❑ 372 Blaise Winter RC .05 .01
❑ 373 Al Del Greco .05 .01
❑ 374 Eric Green .05 .01
❑ 375 Chris Mohr .05 .01
❑ 376 Tom Newberry .05 .01
❑ 377 Cris Dishman .05 .01
❑ 378 Jumpy Geathers .05 .01

❑ 379 Don Mosebar	.05	.01
❑ 380 Andre Ware	.05	.01
❑ 381 Marvin Washington	.05	.01
❑ 382 Bobby Humphrey	.05	.01
❑ 383 Marc Logan	.05	.01
❑ 384 Lomas Brown	.05	.01
❑ 385 Steve Tasker	.10	.02
❑ 386 Chris Miller	.10	.02
❑ 387 Tony Paige	.05	.01
❑ 388 Charles Haley	.10	.02
❑ 389 Rich Moran	.05	.01
❑ 390 Mike Sherrard	.05	.01
❑ 391 Nick Lowery	.05	.01
❑ 392 Henry Thomas	.05	.01
❑ 393 Keith Sims	.05	.01
❑ 394 Thomas Everett	.05	.01
❑ 395 Steve Wallace	.05	.01
❑ 396 John Carney	.05	.01
❑ 397 Tim Johnson	.05	.01
❑ 398 Jeff Gossett	.05	.01
❑ 399 Anthony Smith	.05	.01
❑ 400 Kelvin Pritchett	.05	.01
❑ 401 Dermontti Dawson	.05	.01
❑ 402 Alfred Williams	.05	.01
❑ 403 Michael Haynes	.10	.02
❑ 404 Bart Oates	.05	.01
❑ 405 Ken Lanier	.05	.01
❑ 406 Vencie Glenn	.05	.01
❑ 407 John Taylor	.10	.02
❑ 408 Nate Newton	.10	.02
❑ 409 Mark Carrier WR	.10	.02
❑ 410 Ken Harvey	.05	.01
❑ 411 Troy Aikman SB	.40	.15
❑ 412 Charles Haley SB	.05	.01
❑ 413 Warren Moon/Jeffires DT	.10	.02
❑ 414 Henry Jones DT	.05	.01
❑ 415 Rickey Jackson DT	.05	.01
❑ 416 Clyde Simmons DT	.05	.01
❑ 417 Dale Carter ROY	.05	.01
❑ 418 Carl Pickens ROY	.10	.02
❑ 419 Vaughn Dunbar ROY	.05	.01
❑ 420 Santana Dotson ROY	.05	.01
❑ 421 Steve Emtman 90	.05	.01
❑ 422 Louis Oliver 90	.05	.01
❑ 423 Carl Pickens 90	.10	.02
❑ 424 Eddie Anderson 90	.05	.01
❑ 425 Deion Sanders 90	.25	.08
❑ 426 Jon Vaughn 90	.05	.01
❑ 427 Darren Lewis 90	.05	.01
❑ 428 Kevin Ross 90	.05	.01
❑ 429 David Brandon 90	.05	.01
❑ 430 Dave Meggett 90	.05	.01
❑ 431 Jerry Rice HL	.50	.20
❑ 432 Sterling Sharpe HL	.10	.02
❑ 433 Art Monk HL	.05	.01
❑ 434 James Lofton HL	.05	.01
❑ 435 Lawrence Taylor	.10	.02
❑ 436 Bill Walsh RC HOF	.10	.02
❑ 437 Chuck Noll HOF	.10	.02
❑ 438 Dan Fouts HOF	.05	.01
❑ 439 Larry Little HOF	.05	.01
❑ 440 Steve Young MOY	.40	.15
❑ NNO Dick Butkus AU/3000	40.00	25.00

1994 Score

❑ COMPLETE SET (330)	12.00	5.00
❑ 1 Barry Sanders	1.25	.50
❑ 2 Troy Aikman	.75	.30
❑ 3 Sterling Sharpe	.10	.02
❑ 4 Deion Sanders	.50	.20
❑ 5 Bruce Smith	.25	.08
❑ 6 Eric Metcalf	.10	.02
❑ 7 John Elway	1.50	.60
❑ 8 Bruce Matthews	.05	.01
❑ 9 Rickey Jackson	.05	.01
❑ 10 Cortez Kennedy	.10	.02
❑ 11 Jerry Rice	.75	.30
❑ 12 Stanley Richard	.05	.01
❑ 13 Rod Woodson	.10	.02
❑ 14 Eric Swann	.10	.02
❑ 15 Eric Allen	.05	.01
❑ 16 Richard Dent	.10	.02
❑ 17 Carl Pickens	.10	.02
❑ 18 Rohn Stark	.05	.01
❑ 19 Marcus Allen	.25	.08
❑ 20 Steve Wisniewski	.05	.01
❑ 21 Jerome Bettis	.50	.20
❑ 22 Darrell Green	.05	.01
❑ 23 Lawrence Dawsey	.05	.01
❑ 24 Larry Centers	.25	.08
❑ 25 Steve Jordan	.05	.01
❑ 26 Johnny Johnson	.05	.01
❑ 27 Phil Simms	.10	.02
❑ 28 Bruce Armstrong	.05	.01
❑ 29 Willie Roaf	.05	.01
❑ 30 Andre Rison	.10	.02
❑ 31 Henry Jones	.05	.01
❑ 32 Warren Moon	.25	.08
❑ 33 Sean Gilbert	.05	.01
❑ 34 Ben Coates	.10	.02
❑ 35 Seth Joyner	.05	.01
❑ 36 Ronnie Harmon	.05	.01
❑ 37 Quentin Coryatt	.05	.01
❑ 38 Ricky Sanders	.05	.01
❑ 39 Gerald Williams	.05	.01
❑ 40 Emmitt Smith	1.00	.40
❑ 41 Jason Hanson	.05	.01
❑ 42 Kevin Smith	.05	.01
❑ 43 Irving Fryar	.10	.02
❑ 44 Boomer Esiason	.10	.02
❑ 45 Darryl Talley	.05	.01
❑ 46 Paul Gruber	.05	.01
❑ 47 Anthony Smith	.05	.01
❑ 48 John Copeland	.05	.01
❑ 49 Michael Jackson	.10	.02
❑ 50 Shannon Sharpe	.10	.02
❑ 51 Reggie White	.25	.08
❑ 52 Andre Collins	.05	.01
❑ 53 Jack Del Rio	.05	.01
❑ 54 John Elliott	.05	.01
❑ 55 Kevin Greene	.10	.02
❑ 56 Steve Young	.60	.25
❑ 57 Erric Pegram	.05	.01
❑ 58 Donnell Woolford	.05	.01
❑ 59 Darryl Williams	.05	.01
❑ 60 Michael Irvin	.25	.08
❑ 61 Mel Gray	.05	.01
❑ 62 Greg Montgomery	.05	.01
❑ 63 Neil Smith	.10	.02
❑ 64 Andy Harmon	.05	.01
❑ 65 Dan Marino	1.50	.60
❑ 66 Leonard Russell	.05	.01
❑ 67 Joe Montana	1.50	.60
❑ 68 John Taylor	.10	.02
❑ 69 Cris Dishman	.05	.01
❑ 70 Cornelius Bennett	.10	.02
❑ 71 Harold Green	.05	.01
❑ 72 Anthony Pleasant	.05	.01
❑ 73 Dennis Smith	.05	.01
❑ 74 Bryce Paup	.10	.02
❑ 75 Jeff George	.25	.08
❑ 76 Henry Ellard	.10	.02
❑ 77 Randall McDaniel	.05	.01
❑ 78 Derek Brown RBK	.05	.01
❑ 79 Johnny Mitchell	.05	.01
❑ 80 Leroy Thompson	.05	.01
❑ 81 Junior Seau	.25	.08
❑ 82 Kelvin Martin	.05	.01
❑ 83 Guy McIntyre	.05	.01
❑ 84 Elbert Shelley	.05	.01
❑ 85 Louis Oliver	.05	.01
❑ 86 Tommy Vardell	.05	.01
❑ 87 Jeff Herrod	.05	.01
❑ 88 Edgar Bennett	.25	.08
❑ 89 Reggie Langhorne	.05	.01
❑ 90 Terry Kirby	.25	.08
❑ 91 Marcus Robertson	.05	.01
❑ 92 Mark Collins	.05	.01
❑ 93 Calvin Williams	.10	.02
❑ 94 Barry Foster	.05	.01
❑ 95 Brent Jones	.10	.02
❑ 96 Reggie Cobb	.05	.01
❑ 97 Ray Childress	.05	.01
❑ 98 Chris Miller	.05	.01
❑ 99 John Carney	.05	.01
❑ 100 Ricky Proehl	.05	.01
❑ 101 Renaldo Turnbull	.05	.01
❑ 102 John Randle	.10	.02
❑ 103 Flipper Anderson	.05	.01
❑ 104 Scottie Graham RC	.10	.02
❑ 105 Webster Slaughter	.05	.01
❑ 106 Tyrone Hughes	.10	.02
❑ 107 Ken Norton Jr.	.10	.02
❑ 108 Jim Kelly	.25	.08
❑ 109 Michael Haynes	.10	.02
❑ 110 Mark Carrier DB	.05	.01
❑ 111 Eddie Murray	.05	.01
❑ 112 Glyn Milburn	.10	.02
❑ 113 Jackie Harris	.05	.01
❑ 114 Dean Biasucci	.05	.01
❑ 115 Tim Brown	.25	.08
❑ 116 Mark Higgs	.05	.01
❑ 117 Steve Emtman	.05	.01
❑ 118 Clay Matthews	.05	.01
❑ 119 Clyde Simmons	.05	.01
❑ 120 Howard Ballard	.05	.01
❑ 121 Ricky Watters	.10	.02
❑ 122 William Fuller	.05	.01
❑ 123 Robert Brooks	.25	.08
❑ 124 Brian Blades	.10	.02
❑ 125 Leslie O'Neal	.05	.01
❑ 126 Gary Clark	.10	.02
❑ 127 Jim Sweeney	.05	.01
❑ 128 Vaughan Johnson	.05	.01
❑ 129 Gary Brown	.05	.01
❑ 130 Todd Lyght	.05	.01
❑ 131 Nick Lowery	.05	.01
❑ 132 Ernest Givins	.10	.02
❑ 133 Lomas Brown	.05	.01
❑ 134 Craig Erickson	.05	.01
❑ 135 James Francis	.05	.01
❑ 136 Andre Reed	.10	.02
❑ 137 Jim Everett	.10	.02
❑ 138 Nate Odomes	.05	.01
❑ 139 Tom Waddle	.05	.01
❑ 140 Stevon Moore	.05	.01
❑ 141 Rod Bernstine	.05	.01
❑ 142 Brett Favre	1.50	.60
❑ 143 Roosevelt Potts	.05	.01
❑ 144 Chester McGlockton	.05	.01
❑ 145 LeRoy Butler	.05	.01
❑ 146 Charles Haley	.10	.02
❑ 147 Rodney Hampton	.10	.02
❑ 148 George Teague	.05	.01
❑ 149 Gary Anderson K	.05	.01
❑ 150 Mark Stepnoski	.05	.01
❑ 151 Courtney Hawkins	.05	.01
❑ 152 Tim Grunhard	.05	.01
❑ 153 David Klingler	.05	.01
❑ 154 Erik Williams	.05	.01
❑ 155 Herman Moore	.25	.08
❑ 156 Daryl Johnston	.10	.02
❑ 157 Chris Zorich	.05	.01
❑ 158 Shane Conlan	.05	.01
❑ 159 Santana Dotson	.10	.02
❑ 160 Sam Mills	.05	.01
❑ 161 Ronnie Lott	.10	.02
❑ 162 Jesse Sapolu	.05	.01
❑ 163 Marion Butts	.05	.01
❑ 164 Eugene Robinson	.05	.01
❑ 165 Mark Schlereth	.05	.01
❑ 166 John L. Williams	.05	.01
❑ 167 Anthony Miller	.10	.02
❑ 168 Rich Camarillo	.05	.01
❑ 169 Jeff Lageman	.05	.01
❑ 170 Michael Brooks	.05	.01
❑ 171 Scott Mitchell	.10	.02
❑ 172 Duane Bickett	.05	.01
❑ 173 Willie Davis	.10	.02
❑ 174 Maurice Hurst	.05	.01
❑ 175 Brett Perriman	.10	.02
❑ 176 Jay Novacek	.10	.02
❑ 177 Terry Allen	.10	.02

❑ 178 Pete Metzelaars .05 .01
❑ 179 Erik Kramer .10 .02
❑ 180 Neal Anderson .05 .01
❑ 181 Ethan Horton .05 .01
❑ 182 Tony Bennett .05 .01
❑ 183 Gary Zimmerman .05 .01
❑ 184 Jeff Hostetler .10 .02
❑ 185 Jeff Cross .05 .01
❑ 186 Vincent Brown .05 .01
❑ 187 Herschel Walker .10 .02
❑ 188 Courtney Hall .05 .01
❑ 189 Norm Johnson .05 .01
❑ 190 Hardy Nickerson .10 .02
❑ 191 Greg Townsend .05 .01
❑ 192 Mike Munchak .10 .02
❑ 193 Dante Jones .05 .01
❑ 194 Vinny Testaverde .10 .02
❑ 195 Vance Johnson .05 .01
❑ 196 Chris Jacke .05 .01
❑ 197 Will Wolford .05 .01
❑ 198 Terry McDaniel .05 .01
❑ 199 Bryan Cox .05 .01
❑ 200 Nate Newton .05 .01
❑ 201 Keith Byars .05 .01
❑ 202 Neil O'Donnell .25 .08
❑ 203 Harris Barton .05 .01
❑ 204 Thurman Thomas .25 .08
❑ 205 Jeff Query .05 .01
❑ 206 Russell Maryland .05 .01
❑ 207 Pat Swilling .05 .01
❑ 208 Haywood Jeffires .10 .02
❑ 209 John Alt .05 .01
❑ 210 O.J.McDuffie .25 .08
❑ 211 Keith Sims .05 .01
❑ 212 Eric Martin .05 .01
❑ 213 Kyle Clifton .05 .01
❑ 214 Luis Sharpe .05 .01
❑ 215 Thomas Everett .05 .01
❑ 216 Chris Warren .10 .02
❑ 217 Chris Doleman .05 .01
❑ 218 Tony Jones T .05 .01
❑ 219 Karl Mecklenburg .05 .01
❑ 220 Rob Moore .10 .02
❑ 221 Jessie Hester .05 .01
❑ 222 Jeff Jaeger .05 .01
❑ 223 Keith Jackson .05 .01
❑ 224 Mo Lewis .05 .01
❑ 225 Mike Horan .05 .01
❑ 226 Eric Green .05 .01
❑ 227 Jim Ritcher .05 .01
❑ 228 Eric Curry .05 .01
❑ 229 Stan Humphries .10 .02
❑ 230 Mike Johnson .05 .01
❑ 231 Alvin Harper .10 .02
❑ 232 Bennie Blades .05 .01
❑ 233 Cris Carter .50 .20
❑ 234 Morten Andersen .05 .01
❑ 235 Brian Washington .05 .01
❑ 236 Eric Hill .05 .01
❑ 237 Natrone Means .25 .08
❑ 238 Carlton Bailey .05 .01
❑ 239 Anthony Carter .10 .02
❑ 240 Jessie Tuggle .05 .01
❑ 241 Tim Irwin .05 .01
❑ 242 Mark Carrier WR .10 .02
❑ 243 Steve Atwater .05 .01
❑ 244 Sean Jones .05 .01
❑ 245 Bernie Kosar .10 .02
❑ 246 Richmond Webb .05 .01
❑ 247 Dave Meggett .05 .01
❑ 248 Vincent Brisby .10 .02
❑ 249 Fred Barnett .10 .02
❑ 250 Greg Lloyd .10 .02
❑ 251 Tim McDonald .05 .01
❑ 252 Mike Pritchard .05 .01
❑ 253 Greg Robinson .05 .01
❑ 254 Tony McGee .05 .01
❑ 255 Chris Spielman .10 .02
❑ 256 Keith Loneker RC .05 .01
❑ 257 Derrick Thomas .25 .08
❑ 258 Wayne Martin .05 .01
❑ 259 Art Monk .10 .02
❑ 260 Andy Heck .05 .01
❑ 261 Chip Lohmiller .05 .01
❑ 262 Simon Fletcher .05 .01
❑ 263 Ricky Reynolds .05 .01
❑ 264 Chris Hinton .05 .01
❑ 265 Ronald Moore .05 .01
❑ 266 Rocket Ismail .10 .02
❑ 267 Pete Stoyanovich .05 .01
❑ 268 Mark Jackson .05 .01
❑ 269 Randall Cunningham .25 .08
❑ 270 Dermontti Dawson .05 .01
❑ 271 Bill Romanowski .05 .01
❑ 272 Tim Johnson .05 .01
❑ 273 Steve Tasker .10 .02
❑ 274 Keith Hamilton .05 .01
❑ 275 Pierce Holt .05 .01
❑ 276 Heath Shuler RC .25 .08
❑ 277 Marshall Faulk RC 5.00 2.00
❑ 278 Charles Johnson RC .25 .08
❑ 279 Sam Adams RC .10 .02
❑ 280 Trev Alberts RC .10 .02
❑ 281 Derrick Alexander WR RC .25 .08
❑ 282 Bryant Young RC .25 .08
❑ 283 Greg Hill RC .25 .08
❑ 284 Darnay Scott RC .50 .20
❑ 285 Willie McGinest RC .25 .08
❑ 286 Thomas Randolph RC .05 .01
❑ 287 Errict Rhett RC .25 .08
❑ 288 Lamar Smith RC 1.25 .50
❑ 289 William Floyd RC .25 .08
❑ 290 Johnnie Morton RC .50 .20
❑ 291 Jamir Miller RC .10 .02
❑ 292 David Palmer RC .25 .08
❑ 293 Dan Wilkinson RC .10 .02
❑ 294 Trent Dilfer RC 1.25 .50
❑ 295 Antonio Langham RC .10 .02
❑ 296 Chuck Levy RC .05 .01
❑ 297 John Thierry RC .05 .01
❑ 298 Kevin Lee RC .05 .01
❑ 299 Aaron Glenn RC .25 .08
❑ 300 Charlie Garner RC 1.25 .50
❑ 301 Lonnie Johnson RC .05 .01
❑ 302 LeShon Johnson RC .10 .02
❑ 303 Thomas Lewis RC .10 .02
❑ 304 Ryan Yarborough RC .05 .01
❑ 305 Mario Bates RC .25 .08
❑ 306 Buffalo Bills TC .05 .01
❑ 307 Cincinnati Bengals TC .05 .01
❑ 308 Cleveland Browns TC .05 .01
❑ 309 Denver Broncos TC .05 .01
❑ 310 Houston Oilers TC .05 .01
❑ 311 Indianapolis Colts TC .05 .01
❑ 312 Kansas City Chiefs TC .05 .01
❑ 313 Los Angeles Raiders TC .05 .01
❑ 314 Miami Dolphins TC .05 .01
❑ 315 New England Patriots TC .05 .01
❑ 316 New York Jets TC .05 .01
❑ 317 Pittsburgh Steelers TC .05 .01
❑ 318 San Diego Charges TC .05 .01
❑ 319 Seattle Seahawks TC .05 .01
❑ 320 Garrison Hearst FF .25 .08
❑ 321 Drew Bledsoe FF .75 .30
❑ 322 Tyrone Hughes FF .10 .02
❑ 323 James Jett FF .05 .01
❑ 324 Tom Carter FF .05 .01
❑ 325 Reggie Brooks FF .05 .01
❑ 326 Dana Stubblefield FF .10 .02
❑ 327 Jerome Bettis FF .25 .08
❑ 328 Chris Slade FF .05 .01
❑ 329 Rick Mirer FF .25 .08
❑ 330 Emmitt Smith MVP .50 .20

1995 Score

❑ COMPLETE SET (275) 15.00 6.00
❑ 1 Steve Young .60 .25
❑ 2 Barry Sanders 1.25 .50
❑ 3 Jerry Rice .75 .30
❑ 4 Marshall Faulk 1.00 .40
❑ 5 Terance Mathis .10 .02
❑ 6 Rod Woodson .10 .02
❑ 7 Seth Joyner .05 .01
❑ 8 Michael Timpson .05 .01
❑ 9 Deion Sanders .50 .20
❑ 10 Emmitt Smith 1.25 .50
❑ 11 Cris Carter .25 .08
❑ 12 Jake Reed .10 .02
❑ 13 Reggie White .25 .08
❑ 14 Shannon Sharpe .10 .02
❑ 15 Troy Aikman .75 .30
❑ 16 Andre Reed .10 .02
❑ 17 Tyrone Hughes .10 .02
❑ 18 Sterling Sharpe .10 .02
❑ 19 Jerome Bettis .25 .08
❑ 20 Irving Fryar .10 .02
❑ 21 Warren Moon .10 .02
❑ 22 Ben Coates .10 .02
❑ 23 Frank Reich .05 .01
❑ 24 Henry Ellard .10 .02
❑ 25 Steve Atwater .05 .01
❑ 26 Willie Davis .10 .02
❑ 27 Michael Irvin .25 .08
❑ 28 Harvey Williams .05 .01
❑ 29 Aeneas Williams .05 .01
❑ 30 Errict Rhett .10 .02
❑ 31 Lorenzo White .05 .01
❑ 32 John Elway 1.50 .60
❑ 33 Rodney Hampton .10 .02
❑ 34 Webster Slaughter .05 .01
❑ 35 Eric Turner .05 .01
❑ 36 Dan Marino 1.50 .60
❑ 37 Daryl Johnston .10 .02
❑ 38 Bruce Smith .25 .08
❑ 39 Ronald Moore .05 .01
❑ 40 Larry Centers .10 .02
❑ 41 Curtis Conway .25 .08
❑ 42 Drew Bledsoe .50 .20
❑ 43 Quinn Early .10 .02
❑ 44 Marcus Allen .25 .08
❑ 45 Andre Rison .10 .02
❑ 46 Jeff Blake RC .50 .20
❑ 47 Barry Foster .10 .02
❑ 48 Antonio Langham .05 .01
❑ 49 Herman Moore .25 .08
❑ 50 Flipper Anderson .05 .01
❑ 51 Rick Mirer .10 .02
❑ 52 Jay Novacek .10 .02
❑ 53 Tim Bowens .05 .01
❑ 54 Carl Pickens .10 .02
❑ 55 Lewis Tillman .05 .01
❑ 56 Lawrence Dawsey .05 .01
❑ 57 Leroy Hoard .05 .01
❑ 58 Steve Broussard .05 .01
❑ 59 Dave Krieg .05 .01
❑ 60 John Taylor .05 .01
❑ 61 Johnny Mitchell .05 .01
❑ 62 Jessie Hester .05 .01
❑ 63 Johnny Bailey .05 .01
❑ 64 Brett Favre 1.50 .60
❑ 65 Bryce Paup .10 .02
❑ 66 J.J. Birden .05 .01
❑ 67 Steve Tasker .10 .02
❑ 68 Edgar Bennett .10 .02
❑ 69 Ray Buchanan .05 .01
❑ 70 Brent Jones .05 .01
❑ 71 Dave Meggett .05 .01
❑ 72 Jeff Graham .05 .01
❑ 73 Michael Brooks .05 .01
❑ 74 Ricky Ervins .05 .01
❑ 75 Chris Warren .10 .02
❑ 76 Natrone Means .10 .02
❑ 77 Tim Brown .25 .08
❑ 78 Jim Everett .05 .01
❑ 79 Chris Calloway .05 .01
❑ 80 John L. Williams .05 .01
❑ 81 Chris Chandler .10 .02
❑ 82 Tim McDonald .05 .01
❑ 83 Calvin Williams .10 .02
❑ 84 Tony McGee .05 .01
❑ 85 Erik Kramer .05 .01
❑ 86 Eric Green .05 .01
❑ 87 Nate Newton .10 .02
❑ 88 Leonard Russell .05 .01

❑ 89 Jeff George	.10	.02
❑ 90 Raymont Harris	.05	.01
❑ 91 Darnay Scott	.10	.02
❑ 92 Brian Mitchell	.05	.01
❑ 93 Craig Erickson	.05	.01
❑ 94 Cortez Kennedy	.10	.02
❑ 95 Derrick Alexander WR	.25	.08
❑ 96 Charles Haley	.10	.02
❑ 97 Randall Cunningham	.25	.08
❑ 98 Haywood Jeffires	.05	.01
❑ 99 Ronnie Harmon	.05	.01
❑ 100 Dale Carter	.10	.02
❑ 101 Dave Brown	.10	.02
❑ 102 Michael Haynes	.10	.02
❑ 103 Johnny Johnson	.05	.01
❑ 104 William Floyd	.10	.02
❑ 105 Jeff Hostetler	.10	.02
❑ 106 Bernie Parmalee	.10	.02
❑ 107 Mo Lewis	.05	.01
❑ 108 Byron Bam Morris	.05	.01
❑ 109 Vincent Brisby	.05	.01
❑ 110 John Randle	.10	.02
❑ 111 Steve Walsh	.05	.01
❑ 112 Terry Allen	.10	.02
❑ 113 Greg Lloyd	.10	.02
❑ 114 Merton Hanks	.05	.01
❑ 115 Mel Gray	.05	.01
❑ 116 Jim Kelly	.25	.08
❑ 117 Don Beebe	.05	.01
❑ 118 Floyd Turner	.05	.01
❑ 119 Neil Smith	.10	.02
❑ 120 Keith Byars	.05	.01
❑ 121 Rocket Ismail	.10	.02
❑ 122 Leslie O'Neal	.10	.02
❑ 123 Mike Sherrard	.05	.01
❑ 124 Marion Butts	.05	.01
❑ 125 Andre Coleman	.05	.01
❑ 126 Charles Johnson	.10	.02
❑ 127 Derrick Fenner	.05	.01
❑ 128 Vinny Testaverde	.10	.02
❑ 129 Chris Spielman	.10	.02
❑ 130 Bert Emanuel	.25	.08
❑ 131 Craig Heyward	.10	.02
❑ 132 Anthony Miller	.10	.02
❑ 133 Rob Moore	.10	.02
❑ 134 Gary Brown	.05	.01
❑ 135 David Klingler	.10	.02
❑ 136 Sean Dawkins	.10	.02
❑ 137 Terry McDaniel	.05	.01
❑ 138 Fred Barnett	.10	.02
❑ 139 Bryan Cox	.05	.01
❑ 140 Andrew Jordan	.05	.01
❑ 141 Leroy Thompson	.05	.01
❑ 142 Richmond Webb	.05	.01
❑ 143 Kimble Anders	.10	.02
❑ 144 Mario Bates	.10	.02
❑ 145 Irv Smith	.05	.01
❑ 146 Carnell Lake	.05	.01
❑ 147 Mark Seay	.10	.02
❑ 148 Dana Stubblefield	.10	.02
❑ 149 Kelvin Martin	.05	.01
❑ 150 Pete Metzelaars	.05	.01
❑ 151 Roosevelt Potts	.05	.01
❑ 152 Bubby Brister	.05	.01
❑ 153 Trent Dilfer	.25	.08
❑ 154 Ricky Proehl	.05	.01
❑ 155 Aaron Glenn	.05	.01
❑ 156 Eric Metcalf	.10	.02
❑ 157 Kevin Williams WR	.10	.02
❑ 158 Charlie Garner	.25	.08
❑ 159 Glyn Milburn	.05	.01
❑ 160 Fuad Reveiz	.05	.01
❑ 161 Brett Perriman	.10	.02
❑ 162 Neil O'Donnell	.10	.02
❑ 163 Tony Martin	.10	.02
❑ 164 Sam Adams	.05	.01
❑ 165 John Friesz	.10	.02
❑ 166 Bryant Young	.10	.02
❑ 167 Junior Seau	.25	.08
❑ 168 Ken Harvey	.05	.01
❑ 169 Bill Brooks	.05	.01
❑ 170 Eugene Robinson	.05	.01
❑ 171 Ricky Sanders	.10	.02
❑ 172 Rodney Peete	.05	.01
❑ 173 Boomer Esiason	.10	.02
❑ 174 Reggie Roby	.05	.01
❑ 175 Michael Jackson	.10	.02
❑ 176 Gus Frerotte	.10	.02
❑ 177 Terry Kirby	.10	.02
❑ 178 Jessie Tuggle	.05	.01
❑ 179 Courtney Hawkins	.05	.01
❑ 180 Heath Shuler	.10	.02
❑ 181 Jack Del Rio	.05	.01
❑ 182 O.J. McDuffie	.25	.08
❑ 183 Ricky Watters	.10	.02
❑ 184 Willie Roaf	.05	.01
❑ 185 Glenn Foley	.05	.01
❑ 186 Blair Thomas	.05	.01
❑ 187 Darren Woodson	.10	.02
❑ 188 Kevin Greene	.10	.02
❑ 189 Jeff Burris	.05	.01
❑ 190 Jay Schroeder	.05	.01
❑ 191 Stan Humphries	.10	.02
❑ 192 Irving Spikes	.10	.02
❑ 193 Jim Harbaugh	.10	.02
❑ 194 Robert Brooks	.25	.08
❑ 195 Greg Hill	.10	.02
❑ 196 Herschel Walker	.10	.02
❑ 197 Brian Blades	.10	.02
❑ 198 Mark Ingram	.05	.01
❑ 199 Kevin Turner	.05	.01
❑ 200 Lake Dawson	.10	.02
❑ 201 Alvin Harper	.05	.01
❑ 202 Derek Brown RBK	.05	.01
❑ 203 Qadry Ismail	.10	.02
❑ 204 Reggie Brooks	.10	.02
❑ 205 Steve Young SS	.30	.10
❑ 206 Emmitt Smith SS	.60	.25
❑ 207 Stan Humphries SS	.05	.01
❑ 208 Barry Sanders SS	.60	.25
❑ 209 Marshall Faulk SS	.40	.15
❑ 210 Drew Bledsoe SS	.25	.08
❑ 211 Jerry Rice SS	.40	.15
❑ 212 Tim Brown SS	.10	.02
❑ 213 Cris Carter SS	.25	.08
❑ 214 Dan Marino SS	.75	.30
❑ 215 Troy Aikman SS	.40	.15
❑ 216 Jerome Bettis SS	.10	.02
❑ 217 Deion Sanders SS	.25	.08
❑ 218 Junior Seau SS	.10	.02
❑ 219 John Elway SS	.75	.30
❑ 220 Warren Moon SS	.05	.01
❑ 221 Sterling Sharpe SS	.10	.02
❑ 222 Marcus Allen SS	.25	.08
❑ 223 Michael Irvin SS	.10	.02
❑ 224 Brett Favre SS	.75	.30
❑ 225 Rodney Hampton SS	.05	.01
❑ 226 Dave Brown SS	.10	.02
❑ 227 Ben Coates SS	.10	.02
❑ 228 Jim Kelly SS	.25	.08
❑ 229 Heath Shuler SS	.10	.02
❑ 230 Herman Moore SS	.25	.08
❑ 231 Jeff Hostetler SS	.10	.02
❑ 232 Rick Mirer SS	.10	.02
❑ 233 Byron Bam Morris SS	.05	.01
❑ 234 Terance Mathis SS	.05	.01
❑ 235 John Elway/B.Sanders CL	.40	.15
❑ 236 Troy Aikman CL	.25	.08
❑ 237 Jerry Rice CL	.25	.08
❑ 238 Emmitt Smith CL	.50	.20
❑ 239 Steve Young CL	.25	.08
❑ 240 Drew Bledsoe CL	.25	.08
❑ 241 Marshall Faulk CL	.25	.08
❑ 242 Dan Marino CL	.40	.15
❑ 243 Junior Seau CL	.10	.02
❑ 244 Ray Zellars RC	.10	.02
❑ 245 Rob Johnson RC	.75	.30
❑ 246 Tony Boselli RC	.25	.08
❑ 247 Kevin Carter RC	.25	.08
❑ 248 Steve McNair RC	2.50	1.00
❑ 249 Tyrone Wheatley RC	.75	.30
❑ 250 Steve Stenstrom RC	.05	.01
❑ 251 Stoney Case RC	.05	.01
❑ 252 Rodney Thomas RC	.10	.02
❑ 253 Michael Westbrook RC	.25	.08
❑ 254 Derrick Alexander DE RC	.05	.01
❑ 255 Kyle Brady RC	.25	.08
❑ 256 Kerry Collins RC	1.25	.50
❑ 257 Rashaan Salaam RC	.10	.02
❑ 258 Frank Sanders RC	.25	.08
❑ 259 John Walsh RC	.05	.01
❑ 260 Sherman Williams RC	.05	.01
❑ 261 Ki-Jana Carter RC	.25	.08
❑ 262 Jack Jackson RC	.05	.01
❑ 263 J.J. Stokes RC	.25	.08
❑ 264 Kordell Stewart RC	1.25	.50
❑ 265 Dave Barr RC	.05	.01
❑ 266 Eddie Goines RC	.05	.01
❑ 267 Warren Sapp RC	1.25	.50
❑ 268 James O. Stewart RC	.75	.30
❑ 269 Joey Galloway RC	1.25	.50
❑ 270 Tyrone Davis RC	.05	.01
❑ 271 Napoleon Kaufman RC	1.00	.40
❑ 272 Mark Bruener RC	.10	.02
❑ 273 Todd Collins RC	.10	.02
❑ 274 Billy Williams RC	.05	.01
❑ 275 James A.Stewart RC	.05	.01
❑ P264 Kordell Stewart PROMO	2.50	1.00
❑ AD3 Steve Young	3.00	1.25

1996 Score

❑ COMPLETE SET (275)	20.00	7.50
❑ 1 Emmitt Smith	1.25	.50
❑ 2 Flipper Anderson	.10	.02
❑ 3 Kordell Stewart	.40	.15
❑ 4 Bruce Smith	.20	.07
❑ 5 Marshall Faulk	.50	.20
❑ 6 William Floyd	.20	.07
❑ 7 Darren Woodson	.20	.07
❑ 8 Lake Dawson	.10	.02
❑ 9 Terry Allen	.20	.07
❑ 10 Ki-Jana Carter	.20	.07
❑ 11 Tony Boselli	.10	.02
❑ 12 Christian Fauria	.10	.02
❑ 13 Jeff George	.20	.07
❑ 14 Dan Marino	1.50	.60
❑ 15 Rodney Thomas	.10	.02
❑ 16 Anthony Miller	.20	.07
❑ 17 Chris Sanders	.20	.07
❑ 18 Natrone Means	.20	.07
❑ 19 Curtis Conway	.40	.15
❑ 20 Ben Coates	.20	.07
❑ 21 Alvin Harper	.10	.02
❑ 22 Frank Sanders	.20	.07
❑ 23 Boomer Esiason	.20	.07
❑ 24 Lovell Pinkney	.10	.02
❑ 25 Troy Aikman	.75	.30
❑ 26 Quinn Early	.10	.02
❑ 27 Adrian Murrell	.20	.07
❑ 28 Chris Spielman	.10	.02
❑ 29 Tyrone Wheatley	.20	.07
❑ 30 Tim Brown	.40	.15
❑ 31 Erik Kramer	.10	.02
❑ 32 Warren Moon	.20	.07
❑ 33 Jimmy Oliver	.10	.02
❑ 34 Herman Moore	.20	.07
❑ 35 Quentin Coryatt	.10	.02
❑ 36 Heath Shuler	.20	.07
❑ 37 Jim Kelly	.40	.15
❑ 38 Mike Morris	.10	.02
❑ 39 Harvey Williams	.10	.02
❑ 40 Vinny Testaverde	.20	.07
❑ 41 Steve McNair	.60	.25
❑ 42 Jerry Rice	.75	.30
❑ 43 Darick Holmes	.10	.02
❑ 44 Kyle Brady	.10	.02
❑ 45 Greg Lloyd	.20	.07
❑ 46 Kerry Collins	.40	.15
❑ 47 Willie McGinest	.10	.02
❑ 48 Isaac Bruce	.40	.15
❑ 49 Carnell Lake	.10	.02
❑ 50 Charles Haley	.20	.07
❑ 51 Troy Vincent	.10	.02

52	Randall Cunningham	.40	.15
53	Rashaan Salaam	.20	.07
54	Willie Jackson	.20	.07
55	Chris Warren	.20	.07
56	Michael Irvin	.40	.15
57	Mario Bates	.20	.07
58	Warren Sapp	.10	.02
59	John Elway	1.50	.60
60	Shannon Sharpe	.20	.07
61	Cornelius Bennett	.10	.02
62	Robert Brooks	.40	.15
63	Rodney Hampton	.20	.07
64	Ken Norton Jr.	.10	.02
65	Bryce Paup	.10	.02
66	Eric Swann	.10	.02
67	Rodney Peete	.10	.02
68	Larry Centers	.20	.07
69	Lamont Warren	.10	.02
70	Jay Novacek	.10	.02
71	Cris Carter	.40	.15
72	Terrell Fletcher	.10	.02
73	Andre Rison	.20	.07
74	Ricky Watters	.20	.07
75	Napoleon Kaufman	.40	.15
76	Reggie White	.40	.15
77	Yancey Thigpen	.20	.07
78	Terry Kirby	.20	.07
79	Deion Sanders	.40	.15
80	Irving Fryar	.20	.07
81	Marcus Allen	.40	.15
82	Carl Pickens	.20	.07
83	Drew Bledsoe	.50	.20
84	Eric Metcalf	.10	.02
85	Robert Smith	.20	.07
86	Tamarick Vanover	.20	.07
87	Henry Ellard	.10	.02
88	Kevin Greene	.20	.07
89	Mark Brunell	.50	.20
90	Terrell Davis	.60	.25
91	Brian Mitchell	.10	.02
92	Aaron Bailey	.10	.02
93	Rocket Ismail	.10	.02
94	Dave Brown	.10	.02
95	Rod Woodson	.20	.07
96	Sean Gilbert	.10	.02
97	Mark Seay	.10	.02
98	Zack Crockett	.10	.02
99	Scott Mitchell	.20	.07
100	Erric Pegram	.10	.02
101	David Palmer	.10	.02
102	Vincent Brisby	.10	.02
103	Brett Perriman	.10	.02
104	Jim Everett	.10	.02
105	Tony Martin	.20	.07
106	Desmond Howard	.20	.07
107	Stan Humphries	.20	.07
108	Bill Brooks	.10	.02
109	Neil Smith	.20	.07
110	Michael Westbrook	.40	.15
111	Herschel Walker	.20	.07
112	Andre Coleman	.10	.02
113	Derrick Alexander WR	.20	.07
114	Jeff Blake	.40	.15
115	Sherman Williams	.10	.02
116	James O.Stewart	.20	.07
117	Hardy Nickerson	.10	.02
118	Elvis Grbac	.20	.07
119	Brett Favre	1.50	.60
120	Mike Sherrard	.10	.02
121	Edgar Bennett	.20	.07
122	Calvin Williams	.10	.02
123	Brian Blades	.10	.02
124	Jeff Graham	.10	.02
125	Gary Brown	.10	.02
126	Bernie Parmalee	.10	.02
127	Kimble Anders	.20	.07
128	Hugh Douglas	.20	.07
129	James A.Stewart	.10	.02
130	Eric Bjornson	.10	.02
131	Ken Dilger	.20	.07
132	Jerome Bettis	.40	.15
133	Cortez Kennedy	.10	.02
134	Bryan Cox	.10	.02
135	Darnay Scott	.20	.07
136	Bert Emanuel	.20	.07
137	Steve Bono	.10	.02
138	Charles Johnson	.10	.02
139	Glyn Milburn	.10	.02
140	Derrick Alexander DE	.10	.02
141	Dave Meggett	.10	.02
142	Trent Dilfer	.40	.15
143	Eric Zeier	.10	.02
144	Jim Harbaugh	.20	.07
145	Antonio Freeman	.40	.15
146	Orlando Thomas	.10	.02
147	Russell Maryland	.10	.02
148	Chad May	.10	.02
149	Craig Heyward	.10	.02
150	Aeneas Williams	.10	.02
151	Kevin Williams WR	.10	.02
152	Charlie Garner	.20	.07
153	J.J. Stokes	.40	.15
154	Stoney Case	.10	.02
155	Mark Chmura	.20	.07
156	Mark Bruener	.10	.02
157	Derek Loville	.10	.02
158	Justin Armour	.10	.02
159	Brent Jones	.10	.02
160	Aaron Craver	.10	.02
161	Terance Mathis	.10	.02
162	Chris Zorich	.10	.02
163	Glenn Foley	.20	.07
164	Johnny Mitchell	.10	.02
165	Junior Seau	.40	.15
166	Willie Davis	.10	.02
167	Rick Mirer	.20	.07
168	Mike Jones LB	.10	.02
169	Greg Hill	.20	.07
170	Steve Tasker	.10	.02
171	Tony Bennett	.10	.02
172	Jeff Hostetler	.10	.02
173	Dave Krieg	.10	.02
174	Mark Carrier WR	.10	.02
175	Michael Haynes	.10	.02
176	Chris Chandler	.20	.07
177	Ernie Mills	.10	.02
178	Jake Reed	.20	.07
179	Errict Rhett	.20	.07
180	Garrison Hearst	.20	.07
181	Derrick Thomas	.40	.15
182	Aaron Hayden RC	.10	.02
183	Jackie Harris	.10	.02
184	Curtis Martin	.60	.25
185	Neil O'Donnell	.20	.07
186	Derrick Moore	.10	.02
187	Steve Young	.60	.25
188	Pat Swilling	.10	.02
189	Amp Lee	.10	.02
190	Rob Johnson	.40	.15
191	Todd Collins	.20	.07
192	J.J. Birden	.10	.02
193	O.J. McDuffie	.20	.07
194	Shawn Jefferson	.10	.02
195	Sean Dawkins	.10	.02
196	Fred Barnett	.10	.02
197	Roosevelt Potts	.10	.02
198	Rob Moore	.20	.07
199	Kevin Miniefield	.10	.02
200	Barry Sanders	1.25	.50
201	Floyd Turner	.10	.02
202	Wayne Chrebet	.60	.25
203	Andre Reed	.20	.07
204	Tyrone Hughes	.10	.02
205	Keenan McCardell	.40	.15
206	Gus Frerotte	.20	.07
207	Daryl Johnston	.20	.07
208	Steve Broussard	.10	.02
209	Steve Atwater	.10	.02
210	Thurman Thomas	.40	.15
211	Andre Hastings	.10	.02
212	Joey Galloway	.40	.15
213	Kevin Carter	.10	.02
214	Keyshawn Johnson RC	1.00	.40
215	Tony Brackens RC	.40	.15
216	Stepfret Williams RC	.20	.07
217	Mike Alstott RC	1.00	.40
218	Terry Glenn RC	1.00	.40
219	Tim Biakabutuka RC	.40	.15
220	Eric Moulds RC	1.25	.50
221	Jeff Lewis RC	.20	.07
222	Bobby Engram RC	.40	.15
223	Cedric Jones RC	.10	.02
224	Stanley Pritchett RC	.20	.07
225	Kevin Hardy RC	.40	.15
226	Alex Van Dyke RC	.20	.07
227	Willie Anderson RC	.10	.02
228	Regan Upshaw RC	.10	.02
229	Leeland McElroy RC	.20	.07
230	Marvin Harrison RC	2.50	1.00
231	Eddie George RC	1.25	.50
232	Lawrence Phillips RC	.40	.15
233	Daryl Gardener RC	.10	.02
234	Alex Molden RC	.10	.02
235	Derrick Mayes RC	.40	.15
236	John Mobley RC	.10	.02
237	Israel Ifeanyi RC	.10	.02
238	Pete Kendall RC	.10	.02
239	Danny Kanell RC	.40	.15
240	Jonathan Ogden RC	.40	.15
241	Reggie Brown LB RC	.10	.02
242	Marcus Jones RC	.10	.02
243	Jon Stark RC	.10	.02
244	Barry Sanders SE	.60	.25
245	Brett Favre SE	.75	.30
246	John Elway SE	.75	.30
247	Dan Marino SE	.75	.30
248	Drew Bledsoe SE	.40	.15
249	Michael Irvin SE	.20	.07
250	Troy Aikman SE	.40	.15
251	Emmitt Smith SE	.50	.20
252	Steve Young SE	.40	.15
253	Jerry Rice SE	.40	.15
254	Jeff Blake SE	.20	.07
255	Tim Brown SE	.20	.07
256	Eric Metcalf SE	.10	.02
257	Rodney Hampton SE	.10	.02
258	Scott Mitchell SE	.10	.02
259	Garrison Hearst SE	.20	.07
260	Larry Centers SE	.20	.07
261	Neil O'Donnell SE	.20	.07
262	Orlando Thomas SE	.10	.02
263	Hugh Douglas SE	.10	.02
264	Bill Brooks SE	.10	.02
265	Harvey Williams SE	.10	.02
266	Charles Haley SE	.20	.07
267	Greg Lloyd SE	.20	.07
268	Daryl Johnston SE	.20	.07
269	Dan Marino CL	.40	.15
270	Jeff Blake CL	.20	.07
271	John Elway CL	.40	.15
272	Emmitt Smith CL	.40	.15
273	Brett Favre CL	.40	.15
274	Jerry Rice CL	.40	.15
275	Five Star Players CL	.40	.15
P1	Barry Sanders Promo	2.00	.75

1997 Score

	COMPLETE SET (330)	25.00	10.00
1	John Elway	2.00	.75
2	Drew Bledsoe	.60	.25
3	Brett Favre	2.00	.75
4	Emmitt Smith	1.50	.60
5	Kerry Collins	.50	.20
6	Jerry Rice	1.00	.40
7	Kordell Stewart	.50	.20
8	Barry Sanders	1.50	.60
9	Dan Marino	2.00	.75
10	Steve Young	.60	.25
11	Erik Kramer	.20	.07
12	Warren Moon	.50	.20
13	Chris Calloway	.20	.07
14	Doug Evans	.20	.07
15	Darren Woodson	.20	.07

❑	16	Alonzo Spellman	.20	.07
❑	17	Greg Hill	.20	.07
❑	18	Aaron Craver	.20	.07
❑	19	Jeff Hostetler	.20	.07
❑	20	William Thomas	.20	.07
❑	21	Marco Coleman	.20	.07
❑	22	Wayne Simmons	.20	.07
❑	23	Donnell Woolford	.20	.07
❑	24	Vinny Testaverde	.30	.10
❑	25	Ed McCaffrey	.30	.10
❑	26	Jim Everett	.20	.07
❑	27	Gilbert Brown	.30	.10
❑	28	Jason Dunn	.20	.07
❑	29	Stanley Pritchett	.20	.07
❑	30	Joey Galloway	.30	.10
❑	31	Amani Toomer	.30	.10
❑	32	Chris Penn	.20	.07
❑	33	Aeneas Williams	.20	.07
❑	34	Bobby Taylor	.20	.07
❑	35	Bryan Still	.20	.07
❑	36	Ty Law	.30	.10
❑	37	Shannon Sharpe	.30	.10
❑	38	Marty Carter	.20	.07
❑	39	Sam Mills	.20	.07
❑	40	William Floyd	.30	.10
❑	41	Brad Johnson	.50	.20
❑	42	Sean Dawkins	.20	.07
❑	43	Michael Irvin	.50	.20
❑	44	Jeff George	.30	.10
❑	45	Brent Jones	.30	.10
❑	46	Mark Brunell	.60	.25
❑	47	Rob Moore	.30	.10
❑	48	Hardy Nickerson	.20	.07
❑	49	Chris Chandler	.30	.10
❑	50	Willie Anderson	.20	.07
❑	51	Isaac Bruce	.50	.20
❑	52	Natrone Means	.30	.10
❑	53	Tony Banks	.30	.10
❑	54	Marshall Faulk	.60	.25
❑	55	Michael Westbrook	.30	.10
❑	56	Bruce Smith	.30	.10
❑	57	Jamal Anderson	.50	.20
❑	58	Jackie Harris	.20	.07
❑	59	Sean Gilbert	.20	.07
❑	60	Ki-Jana Carter	.20	.07
❑	61	Eric Moulds	.50	.20
❑	62	James O.Stewart	.30	.10
❑	63	Jeff Blake	.30	.10
❑	64	O.J. McDuffie	.30	.10
❑	65	Neil Smith	.30	.10
❑	66	Kevin Smith	.20	.07
❑	67	Terry Allen	.50	.20
❑	68	Sean LaChapelle	.20	.07
❑	69	Rashaan Salaam	.20	.07
❑	70	Jeff Graham	.20	.07
❑	71	Mark Carrier WR	.20	.07
❑	72	Allen Aldridge	.20	.07
❑	73	Keenan McCardell	.30	.10
❑	74	Willie McGinest	.20	.07
❑	75	Napoleon Kaufman	.50	.20
❑	76	Jerris McPhail	.20	.07
❑	77	Eric Swann	.20	.07
❑	78	Kimble Anders	.30	.10
❑	79	Charles Johnson	.30	.10
❑	80	Bryan Cox	.20	.07
❑	81	Johnnie Morton	.30	.10
❑	82	Andre Rison	.30	.10
❑	83	Corey Miller	.20	.07
❑	84	Troy Drayton	.20	.07
❑	85	Jim Harbaugh	.30	.10
❑	86	Wesley Walls	.30	.10
❑	87	Bryce Paup	.20	.07
❑	88	Curtis Martin	.60	.25
❑	89	Michael Sinclair	.20	.07
❑	90	Chris T. Jones	.20	.07
❑	91	Jake Reed	.30	.10
❑	92	LeRoy Butler	.20	.07
❑	93	Reggie Tongue	.20	.07
❑	94	Bert Emanuel	.30	.10
❑	95	Stan Humphries	.30	.10
❑	96	Neil O'Donnell	.30	.10
❑	97	Troy Vincent	.20	.07
❑	98	Mike Alstott	.50	.20
❑	99	Chad Cota	.20	.07
❑	100	Marvin Harrison	.50	.20
❑	101	Terrell Owens	.60	.25
❑	102	Dave Brown	.20	.07
❑	103	Harvey Williams	.20	.07
❑	104	Desmond Howard	.30	.10
❑	105	Carl Pickens	.30	.10
❑	106	Kent Graham	.20	.07
❑	107	Michael Bates	.20	.07
❑	108	Terrell Davis	.60	.25
❑	109	Marcus Allen	.50	.20
❑	110	Ray Zellars	.20	.07
❑	111	Chris Warren	.30	.10
❑	112	Phillippi Sparks	.20	.07
❑	113	Craig Erickson	.20	.07
❑	114	Eddie George	.50	.20
❑	115	Daryl Johnston	.30	.10
❑	116	Ricky Watters	.30	.10
❑	117	Tedy Bruschi	1.00	.40
❑	118	Mike Mamula	.20	.07
❑	119	Ken Harvey	.20	.07
❑	120	John Randle	.30	.10
❑	121	Mark Chmura	.30	.10
❑	122	Sam Gash	.20	.07
❑	123	John Kasay	.20	.07
❑	124	Barry Minter	.20	.07
❑	125	Raymont Harris	.20	.07
❑	126	Derrick Thomas	.50	.20
❑	127	Trent Dilfer	.50	.20
❑	128	Carnell Lake	.20	.07
❑	129	Brian Dawkins	.50	.20
❑	130	Tyronne Drakeford	.20	.07
❑	131	Daryl Gardener	.20	.07
❑	132	Fred Strickland	.20	.07
❑	133	Kevin Hardy	.20	.07
❑	134	Winslow Oliver	.20	.07
❑	135	Herman Moore	.30	.10
❑	136	Keith Byars	.20	.07
❑	137	Harold Green	.20	.07
❑	138	Ty Detmer	.30	.10
❑	139	Lamar Thomas	.20	.07
❑	140	Elvis Grbac	.30	.10
❑	141	Edgar Bennett	.30	.10
❑	142	Cornelius Bennett	.20	.07
❑	143	Tony Tolbert	.20	.07
❑	144	James Hasty	.20	.07
❑	145	Ben Coates	.30	.10
❑	146	Errict Rhett	.20	.07
❑	147	Jason Sehorn	.30	.10
❑	148	Michael Jackson	.30	.10
❑	149	John Mobley	.20	.07
❑	150	Walt Harris	.20	.07
❑	151	Terry Kirby	.30	.10
❑	152	Devin Wyman	.20	.07
❑	153	Ray Crockett	.20	.07
❑	154	Quinn Early	.20	.07
❑	155	Rodney Thomas	.20	.07
❑	156	Mark Seay	.20	.07
❑	157	Derrick Alexander WR	.30	.10
❑	158	Lamar Lathon	.20	.07
❑	159	Anthony Miller	.20	.07
❑	160	Shawn Wooden RC	.20	.07
❑	161	Antonio Freeman	.50	.20
❑	162	Cortez Kennedy	.20	.07
❑	163	Rickey Dudley	.30	.10
❑	164	Tony Carter	.20	.07
❑	165	Kevin Williams	.20	.07
❑	166	Reggie White	.50	.20
❑	167	Tim Bowens	.20	.07
❑	168	Roy Barker	.20	.07
❑	169	Adrian Murrell	.30	.10
❑	170	Anthony Johnson	.20	.07
❑	171	Terry Glenn	.50	.20
❑	172	Jeff Lewis	.20	.07
❑	173	Dorsey Levens	.50	.20
❑	174	Willie Jackson	.20	.07
❑	175	Willie Clay	.20	.07
❑	176	Richmond Webb	.20	.07
❑	177	Shawn Lee	.20	.07
❑	178	Joe Aska	.20	.07
❑	179	Rod Woodson	.30	.10
❑	180	Jim Schwantz RC	.20	.07
❑	181	Alfred Williams	.20	.07
❑	182	Ferric Collons	.20	.07
❑	183	Ken Norton Jr.	.20	.07
❑	184	Rick Mirer	.20	.07
❑	185	Leeland McElroy	.20	.07
❑	186	Rodney Hampton	.30	.10
❑	187	Ted Popson	.20	.07
❑	188	Fred Barnett	.20	.07
❑	189	Junior Seau	.50	.20
❑	190	Micheal Barrow	.20	.07
❑	191	Corey Widmer	.20	.07
❑	192	Rodney Peete	.20	.07
❑	193	Rod Smith WR	.50	.20
❑	194	Muhsin Muhammad	.30	.10
❑	195	Keith Jackson	.20	.07
❑	196	Jimmy Smith	.30	.10
❑	197	Dave Meggett	.20	.07
❑	198	Lawrence Phillips	.20	.07
❑	199	Chad Brown	.20	.07
❑	200	Darrin Smith	.20	.07
❑	201	Larry Centers	.30	.10
❑	202	Kevin Greene	.30	.10
❑	203	Sherman Williams	.20	.07
❑	204	Chris Sanders	.20	.07
❑	205	Shawn Jefferson	.20	.07
❑	206	Thurman Thomas	.50	.20
❑	207	Keyshawn Johnson	.50	.20
❑	208	Bryant Young	.20	.07
❑	209	Tim Biakabutuka	.30	.10
❑	210	Troy Aikman	1.00	.40
❑	211	Quentin Coryatt	.20	.07
❑	212	Karim Abdul-Jabbar	.50	.20
❑	213	Brian Blades	.20	.07
❑	214	Ray Farmer	.20	.07
❑	215	Simeon Rice	.30	.10
❑	216	Tyrone Braxton	.20	.07
❑	217	Jerome Woods	.20	.07
❑	218	Charles Way	.30	.10
❑	219	Garrison Hearst	.30	.10
❑	220	Bobby Engram	.30	.10
❑	221	Billy Davis RC	.20	.07
❑	222	Ken Dilger	.20	.07
❑	223	Robert Smith	.30	.10
❑	224	John Friesz	.20	.07
❑	225	Charlie Garner	.30	.10
❑	226	Jerome Bettis	.50	.20
❑	227	Darnay Scott	.30	.10
❑	228	Terance Mathis	.30	.10
❑	229	Brian Williams LB	.20	.07
❑	230	Cris Carter	.50	.20
❑	231	Michael Haynes	.20	.07
❑	232	Cedric Jones	.20	.07
❑	233	Danny Kanell	.30	.10
❑	234	Deion Sanders	.50	.20
❑	235	Steve Atwater	.20	.07
❑	236	Jonathan Ogden	.20	.07
❑	237	Lake Dawson	.20	.07
❑	238	Eric Allen	.20	.07
❑	239	Eddie Kennison	.30	.10
❑	240	Irving Fryar	.30	.10
❑	241	Michael Strahan	.30	.10
❑	242	Steve McNair	.60	.25
❑	243	Terrell Buckley	.20	.07
❑	244	Merton Hanks	.20	.07
❑	245	Jessie Armstead	.20	.07
❑	246	Dana Stubblefield	.20	.07
❑	247	Brett Perriman	.20	.07
❑	248	Mark Collins	.20	.07
❑	249	Willie Roaf	.20	.07
❑	250	Gus Frerotte	.20	.07
❑	251	William Fuller	.20	.07
❑	252	Tamarick Vanover	.30	.10
❑	253	Scott Mitchell	.30	.10
❑	254	Eric Metcalf	.30	.10
❑	255	Herschel Walker	.30	.10
❑	256	Robert Brooks	.30	.10
❑	257	Zach Thomas	.50	.20
❑	258	Alvin Harper	.20	.07
❑	259	Wayne Chrebet	.50	.20
❑	260	Bill Romanowski	.20	.07
❑	261	Willie Green	.20	.07
❑	262	Dale Carter	.20	.07
❑	263	Chris Slade	.20	.07
❑	264	J.J. Stokes	.30	.10
❑	265	Tim Brown	.50	.20
❑	266	Eric Davis	.20	.07
❑	267	Mark Carrier DB	.20	.07
❑	268	Tony Martin	.30	.10
❑	269	Tyrone Wheatley	.30	.10
❑	270	Eugene Robinson	.20	.07
❑	271	Curtis Conway	.30	.10
❑	272	Michael Timpson	.20	.07
❑	273	Orlando Pace RC	.50	.20
❑	274	Tiki Barber RC	3.00	1.25
❑	275	Byron Hanspard RC	.30	.10
❑	276	Warrick Dunn RC	1.50	.60

❑ 277 Rae Carruth RC	.20	.07
❑ 278 Bryant Westbrook RC	.20	.07
❑ 279 Antowain Smith RC	1.25	.50
❑ 280 Peter Boulware RC	.50	.20
❑ 281 Reidel Anthony RC	.50	.20
❑ 282 Troy Davis RC	.30	.10
❑ 283 Jake Plummer RC	2.50	1.00
❑ 284 Chris Canty RC	.20	.07
❑ 285 Dwayne Rudd RC	.50	.20
❑ 286 Ike Hilliard RC	.75	.30
❑ 287 Reinard Wilson RC	.30	.10
❑ 288 Corey Dillon RC	3.00	1.25
❑ 289 Tony Gonzalez RC	1.50	.60
❑ 290 Darnell Autry RC	.30	.10
❑ 291 Kevin Lockett RC	.30	.10
❑ 292 Darrell Russell RC	.20	.07
❑ 293 Jim Druckenmiller RC	.30	.10
❑ 294 Shon Mitchell RC	.20	.07
❑ 295 Joey Kent RC	.50	.20
❑ 296 Shawn Springs RC	.30	.10
❑ 297 James Farrior RC	.50	.20
❑ 298 Sedrick Shaw RC	.30	.10
❑ 299 Marcus Harris RC	.20	.07
❑ 300 Danny Wuerffel RC	.50	.20
❑ 301 Marc Edwards RC	.20	.07
❑ 302 Michael Booker RC	.20	.07
❑ 303 David LaFleur RC	.20	.07
❑ 304 Mike Adams WR RC	.20	.07
❑ 305 Pat Barnes RC	.50	.20
❑ 306 George Jones RC	.30	.10
❑ 307 Yatil Green RC	.30	.10
❑ 308 Drew Bledsoe TBP	.50	.20
❑ 309 Troy Aikman TBP	.50	.20
❑ 310 Terrell Davis TBP	.30	.10
❑ 311 Jim Everett TBP	.20	.07
❑ 312 John Elway TBP	1.00	.40
❑ 313 Barry Sanders TBP	.75	.30
❑ 314 Jim Harbaugh TBP	.30	.10
❑ 315 Steve Young TBP	.50	.20
❑ 316 Dan Marino TBP	1.00	.40
❑ 317 Michael Irvin TBP	.50	.20
❑ 318 Emmitt Smith TBP	.75	.30
❑ 319 Jeff Hostetler TBP	.20	.07
❑ 320 Mark Brunell TBP	.50	.20
❑ 321 Jeff Blake TBP	.50	.20
❑ 322 Scott Mitchell TBP	.20	.07
❑ 323 Boomer Esiason TBP	.30	.10
❑ 324 Jerome Bettis TBP	.50	.20
❑ 325 Warren Moon TBP	.30	.10
❑ 326 Neil O'Donnell TBP	.30	.10
❑ 327 Jim Kelly TBP	.50	.20
❑ 328 Dan Marino CL	.50	.20
❑ 329 John Elway CL	.50	.20
❑ 330 Drew Bledsoe CL	.30	.10
❑ P1 Troy Aikman Promo	1.00	.40
❑ P2 Brett Favre Promo	2.00	.75
❑ P3 Dan Marino Promo	2.00	.75
❑ P4 Barry Sanders Promo	1.50	.60

1998 Score

❑ COMPLETE SET (270)	40.00	15.00
❑ 1 John Elway	2.00	.75
❑ 2 Kordell Stewart	.50	.20
❑ 3 Warrick Dunn	.50	.20
❑ 4 Brad Johnson	.50	.20
❑ 5 Kerry Collins	.30	.10
❑ 6 Danny Kanell	.30	.10
❑ 7 Emmitt Smith	1.50	.60
❑ 8 Jamal Anderson	.50	.20
❑ 9 Jim Harbaugh	.30	.10
❑ 10 Tony Martin	.30	.10
❑ 11 Rod Smith	.30	.10
❑ 12 Dorsey Levens	.50	.20
❑ 13 Steve McNair	.50	.20
❑ 14 Derrick Thomas	.50	.20
❑ 15 Rob Moore	.30	.10
❑ 16 Peter Boulware	.20	.07
❑ 17 Terry Allen	.50	.20
❑ 18 Joey Galloway	.30	.10
❑ 19 Jerome Bettis	.50	.20
❑ 20 Carl Pickens	.30	.10
❑ 21 Napoleon Kaufman	.50	.20
❑ 22 Troy Aikman	1.00	.40
❑ 23 Curtis Conway	.30	.10
❑ 24 Adrian Murrell	.30	.10
❑ 25 Elvis Grbac	.30	.10
❑ 26 Garrison Hearst	.50	.20
❑ 27 Chris Sanders	.20	.07
❑ 28 Scott Mitchell	.30	.10
❑ 29 Junior Seau	.50	.20
❑ 30 Chris Chandler	.30	.10
❑ 31 Kevin Hardy	.20	.07
❑ 32 Terrell Davis	.50	.20
❑ 33 Keyshawn Johnson	.50	.20
❑ 34 Natrone Means	.30	.10
❑ 35 Antowain Smith	.50	.20
❑ 36 Jake Plummer	.50	.20
❑ 37 Isaac Bruce	.50	.20
❑ 38 Tony Banks	.30	.10
❑ 39 Reidel Anthony	.30	.10
❑ 40 Darren Woodson	.20	.07
❑ 41 Corey Dillon	.50	.20
❑ 42 Antonio Freeman	.50	.20
❑ 43 Eddie George	.50	.20
❑ 44 Yancey Thigpen	.20	.07
❑ 45 Tim Brown	.50	.20
❑ 46 Wayne Chrebet	.50	.20
❑ 47 Andre Rison	.30	.10
❑ 48 Michael Strahan	.30	.10
❑ 49 Deion Sanders	.50	.20
❑ 50 Eric Moulds	.50	.20
❑ 51 Mark Brunell	.50	.20
❑ 52 Rae Carruth	.20	.07
❑ 53 Warren Sapp	.30	.10
❑ 54 Mark Chmura	.30	.10
❑ 55 Darrell Green	.30	.10
❑ 56 Quinn Early	.20	.07
❑ 57 Barry Sanders	1.50	.60
❑ 58 Neil O'Donnell	.30	.10
❑ 59 Tony Brackens	.20	.07
❑ 60 Willie Davis	.20	.07
❑ 61 Shannon Sharpe	.30	.10
❑ 62 Shawn Springs	.20	.07
❑ 63 Tony Gonzalez	.50	.20
❑ 64 Rodney Thomas	.20	.07
❑ 65 Terance Mathis	.30	.10
❑ 66 Brett Favre	2.00	.75
❑ 67 Eric Swann	.20	.07
❑ 68 Kevin Turner	.20	.07
❑ 69 Tyrone Wheatley	.30	.10
❑ 70 Trent Dilfer	.50	.20
❑ 71 Bryan Cox	.20	.07
❑ 72 Lake Dawson	.20	.07
❑ 73 Will Blackwell	.20	.07
❑ 74 Fred Lane	.20	.07
❑ 75 Ty Detmer	.30	.10
❑ 76 Eddie Kennison	.30	.10
❑ 77 Jimmy Smith	.30	.10
❑ 78 Chris Calloway	.20	.07
❑ 79 Shawn Jefferson	.20	.07
❑ 80 Dan Marino	2.00	.75
❑ 81 LeRoy Butler	.20	.07
❑ 82 William Roaf	.20	.07
❑ 83 Rick Mirer	.20	.07
❑ 84 Dermontti Dawson	.20	.07
❑ 85 Errict Rhett	.30	.10
❑ 86 Lamar Thomas	.20	.07
❑ 87 Lamar Lathon	.20	.07
❑ 88 John Randle	.30	.10
❑ 89 Darryl Williams	.20	.07
❑ 90 Keenan McCardell	.30	.10
❑ 91 Erik Kramer	.20	.07
❑ 92 Ken Dilger	.20	.07
❑ 93 Dave Meggett	.20	.07
❑ 94 Jeff Blake	.30	.10
❑ 95 Ed McCaffrey	.30	.10
❑ 96 Charles Johnson	.20	.07
❑ 97 Irving Spikes	.20	.07
❑ 98 Mike Alstott	.50	.20
❑ 99 Vincent Brisby	.20	.07
❑ 100 Michael Westbrook	.30	.10
❑ 101 Rickey Dudley	.20	.07
❑ 102 Bert Emanuel	.30	.10
❑ 103 Daryl Johnston	.30	.10
❑ 104 Lawrence Phillips	.20	.07
❑ 105 Eric Bieniemy	.20	.07
❑ 106 Bryant Westbrook	.20	.07
❑ 107 Rob Johnson	.30	.10
❑ 108 Ray Zellars	.20	.07
❑ 109 Anthony Johnson	.20	.07
❑ 110 Reggie White	.50	.20
❑ 111 Wesley Walls	.30	.10
❑ 112 Amani Toomer	.30	.10
❑ 113 Gary Brown	.20	.07
❑ 114 Brian Blades	.20	.07
❑ 115 Alex Van Dyke	.20	.07
❑ 116 Michael Haynes	.20	.07
❑ 117 Jessie Armstead	.20	.07
❑ 118 James Jett	.30	.10
❑ 119 Troy Drayton	.20	.07
❑ 120 Craig Heyward	.20	.07
❑ 121 Steve Atwater	.20	.07
❑ 122 Tiki Barber	.50	.20
❑ 123 Karim Abdul-Jabbar	.50	.20
❑ 124 Kimble Anders	.30	.10
❑ 125 Frank Sanders	.30	.10
❑ 126 David Sloan	.20	.07
❑ 127 Andre Hastings	.20	.07
❑ 128 Vinny Testaverde	.30	.10
❑ 129 Robert Smith	.50	.20
❑ 130 Horace Copeland	.20	.07
❑ 131 Larry Centers	.20	.07
❑ 132 J.J. Stokes	.30	.10
❑ 133 Ike Hilliard	.30	.10
❑ 134 Muhsin Muhammad	.30	.10
❑ 135 Sean Dawkins	.20	.07
❑ 136 Raymont Harris	.20	.07
❑ 137 Lamar Smith	.30	.10
❑ 138 David Palmer	.20	.07
❑ 139 Steve Young	.60	.25
❑ 140 Bryan Still	.20	.07
❑ 141 Keith Byars	.20	.07
❑ 142 Cris Carter	.50	.20
❑ 143 Charlie Garner	.30	.10
❑ 144 Drew Bledsoe	.75	.30
❑ 145 Simeon Rice	.30	.10
❑ 146 Merton Hanks	.20	.07
❑ 147 Aeneas Williams	.20	.07
❑ 148 Rodney Hampton	.30	.10
❑ 149 Zach Thomas	.50	.20
❑ 150 Mark Bruener	.20	.07
❑ 151 Jason Dunn	.20	.07
❑ 152 Danny Wuerffel	.30	.10
❑ 153 Jim Druckenmiller	.20	.07
❑ 154 Greg Hill	.20	.07
❑ 155 Earnest Byner	.20	.07
❑ 156 Greg Lloyd	.20	.07
❑ 157 John Mobley	.20	.07
❑ 158 Tim Biakabutuka	.30	.10
❑ 159 Terrell Owens	.50	.20
❑ 160 O.J. McDuffie	.30	.10
❑ 161 Glenn Foley	.30	.10
❑ 162 Derrick Brooks	.50	.20
❑ 163 Dave Brown	.20	.07
❑ 164 Ki-Jana Carter	.20	.07
❑ 165 Bobby Hoying	.30	.10
❑ 166 Randal Hill	.20	.07
❑ 167 Michael Irvin	.50	.20
❑ 168 Bruce Smith	.30	.10
❑ 169 Troy Davis	.20	.07
❑ 170 Derrick Mayes	.30	.10
❑ 171 Henry Ellard	.30	.10
❑ 172 Dana Stubblefield	.20	.07
❑ 173 Willie McGinest	.20	.07
❑ 174 Leeland McElroy	.20	.07
❑ 175 Edgar Bennett	.20	.07
❑ 176 Robert Porcher	.20	.07
❑ 177 Randall Cunningham	.50	.20
❑ 178 Jim Everett	.20	.07
❑ 179 Jake Reed	.30	.10
❑ 180 Quentin Coryatt	.20	.07
❑ 181 William Floyd	.20	.07
❑ 182 Jason Sehorn	.30	.10

❑ 183	Carnell Lake	.20	.07
❑ 184	Dexter Coakley	.20	.07
❑ 185	Derrick Alexander WR	.30	.10
❑ 186	Johnnie Morton	.30	.10
❑ 187	Irving Fryar	.30	.10
❑ 188	Warren Moon	.50	.20
❑ 189	Todd Collins	.20	.07
❑ 190	Ken Norton Jr.	.20	.07
❑ 191	Terry Glenn	.50	.20
❑ 192	Rashaan Salaam	.20	.07
❑ 193	Jerry Rice	1.00	.40
❑ 194	James O.Stewart	.30	.10
❑ 195	David LaFleur	.20	.07
❑ 196	Eric Green	.20	.07
❑ 197	Gus Frerotte	.20	.07
❑ 198	Willie Green	.20	.07
❑ 199	Marshall Faulk	.60	.25
❑ 200	Brett Perriman	.20	.07
❑ 201	Darnay Scott	.30	.10
❑ 202	Marvin Harrison	.50	.20
❑ 203	Joe Aska	.20	.07
❑ 204	Darrien Gordon	.20	.07
❑ 205	Herman Moore	.30	.10
❑ 206	Curtis Martin	.50	.20
❑ 207	Derek Loville	.20	.07
❑ 208	Dale Carter	.20	.07
❑ 209	Heath Shuler	.20	.07
❑ 210	Jonathan Ogden	.20	.07
❑ 211	Leslie Shepherd	.20	.07
❑ 212	Tony Boselli	.20	.07
❑ 213	Eric Metcalf	.20	.07
❑ 214	Neil Smith	.30	.10
❑ 215	Anthony Miller	.20	.07
❑ 216	Jeff George	.30	.10
❑ 217	Charles Way	.20	.07
❑ 218	Mario Bates	.30	.10
❑ 219	Ben Coates	.30	.10
❑ 220	Michael Jackson	.20	.07
❑ 221	Thurman Thomas	.50	.20
❑ 222	Kyle Brady	.20	.07
❑ 223	Marcus Allen	.50	.20
❑ 224	Robert Brooks	.30	.10
❑ 225	Yatil Green	.20	.07
❑ 226	Byron Hanspard	.20	.07
❑ 227	Andre Reed	.30	.10
❑ 228	Chris Warren	.30	.10
❑ 229	Jackie Harris	.20	.07
❑ 230	Ricky Watters	.30	.10
❑ 231	Bobby Engram	.30	.10
❑ 232	Tamarick Vanover	.20	.07
❑ 233	Peyton Manning RC	15.00	6.00
❑ 234	Curtis Enis RC	.75	.30
❑ 235	Randy Moss RC	8.00	3.00
❑ 236	Charles Woodson RC	1.50	.60
❑ 237	Robert Edwards RC	1.00	.40
❑ 238	Jacquez Green RC	1.00	.40
❑ 239	Keith Brooking RC	1.50	.60
❑ 240	Jerome Pathon RC	1.50	.60
❑ 241	Kevin Dyson RC	1.50	.60
❑ 242	Fred Taylor RC	2.00	.75
❑ 243	Tavian Banks RC	1.00	.40
❑ 244	Marcus Nash RC	.75	.30
❑ 245	Brian Griese RC	2.50	1.00
❑ 246	Andre Wadsworth RC	1.00	.40
❑ 247	Ahman Green RC	6.00	2.50
❑ 248	Joe Jurevicius RC	1.50	.60
❑ 249	Germane Crowell RC	1.00	.40
❑ 250	Skip Hicks RC	1.00	.40
❑ 251	Ryan Leaf RC	1.50	.60
❑ 252	Hines Ward RC	6.00	2.50
❑ 253	John Elway OS	1.00	.40
❑ 254	Mark Brunell OS	.50	.20
❑ 255	Brett Favre OS	1.00	.40
❑ 256	Troy Aikman OS	.50	.20
❑ 257	Warrick Dunn OS	.30	.10
❑ 258	Barry Sanders OS	.75	.30
❑ 259	Eddie George OS	.50	.20
❑ 260	Kordell Stewart OS	.50	.20
❑ 261	Emmitt Smith OS	.75	.30
❑ 262	Steve Young OS	.50	.20
❑ 263	Terrell Davis OS	.50	.20
❑ 264	Dorsey Levens OS	.30	.10
❑ 265	Dan Marino OS	1.00	.40
❑ 266	Jerry Rice OS	.50	.20
❑ 267	Drew Bledsoe OS	.50	.20
❑ 268	Brett Favre CL	.60	.25
❑ 269	Barry Sanders CL	.50	.20
❑ 270	Terrell Davis CL	.50	.20
❑ 251AU	Ryan Leaf AUTO	40.00	15.00

1999 Score

❑	COMPLETE SET (275)	60.00	25.00
❑	COMP.SET w/o SP's (220)	15.00	6.00
❑ 1	Randy Moss	1.50	.60
❑ 2	Randall Cunningham	.60	.25
❑ 3	Cris Carter	.60	.25
❑ 4	Robert Smith	.60	.25
❑ 5	Jake Reed	.40	.15
❑ 6	Leroy Hoard	.25	.08
❑ 7	John Randle	.40	.15
❑ 8	Brett Favre	2.00	.75
❑ 9	Antonio Freeman	.60	.25
❑ 10	Dorsey Levens	.60	.25
❑ 11	Robert Brooks	.40	.15
❑ 12	Derrick Mayes	.40	.15
❑ 13	Mark Chmura	.40	.15
❑ 14	Darick Holmes	.25	.08
❑ 15	Vonnie Holliday	.25	.08
❑ 16	Mike Alstott	.60	.25
❑ 17	Warrick Dunn	.60	.25
❑ 18	Trent Dilfer	.40	.15
❑ 19	Jacquez Green	.25	.08
❑ 20	Reidel Anthony	.40	.15
❑ 21	Warren Sapp	.40	.15
❑ 22	Bert Emanuel	.40	.15
❑ 23	Curtis Enis	.25	.08
❑ 24	Curtis Conway	.40	.15
❑ 25	Bobby Engram	.40	.15
❑ 26	Erik Kramer	.40	.15
❑ 27	Moses Moreno	.25	.08
❑ 28	Edgar Bennett	.25	.08
❑ 29	Barry Sanders	2.00	.75
❑ 30	Charlie Batch	.60	.25
❑ 31	Herman Moore	.40	.15
❑ 32	Johnnie Morton	.40	.15
❑ 33	Germane Crowell	.25	.08
❑ 34	Terry Fair	.25	.08
❑ 35	Gary Brown	.25	.08
❑ 36	Kent Graham	.25	.08
❑ 37	Kerry Collins	.40	.15
❑ 38	Charles Way	.25	.08
❑ 39	Tiki Barber	.60	.25
❑ 40	Ike Hilliard	.25	.08
❑ 41	Joe Jurevicius	.40	.15
❑ 42	Michael Strahan	.40	.15
❑ 43	Jason Sehorn	.25	.08
❑ 44	Brad Johnson	.60	.25
❑ 45	Terry Allen	.40	.15
❑ 46	Skip Hicks	.25	.08
❑ 47	Michael Westbrook	.40	.15
❑ 48	Leslie Shepherd	.25	.08
❑ 49	Stephen Alexander	.25	.08
❑ 50	Albert Connell	.25	.08
❑ 51	Darrell Green	.40	.15
❑ 52	Jake Plummer	.40	.15
❑ 53	Adrian Murrell	.40	.15
❑ 54	Frank Sanders	.40	.15
❑ 55	Rob Moore	.40	.15
❑ 56	Larry Centers	.25	.08
❑ 57	Simeon Rice	.40	.15
❑ 58	Andre Wadsworth	.25	.08
❑ 59	Duce Staley	.60	.25
❑ 60	Charles Johnson	.25	.08
❑ 61	Charlie Garner	.40	.15
❑ 62	Bobby Hoying	.40	.15
❑ 63	Daryl Johnston	.40	.15
❑ 64	Emmitt Smith	1.25	.50
❑ 65	Troy Aikman	1.25	.50
❑ 66	Michael Irvin	.40	.15
❑ 67	Deion Sanders	.60	.25
❑ 68	Chris Warren	.25	.08
❑ 69	Darren Woodson	.25	.08
❑ 70	Rod Woodson	.40	.15
❑ 71	Travis Jervey	.25	.08
❑ 72	Jerry Rice	1.25	.50
❑ 73	Terrell Owens	.60	.25
❑ 74	Steve Young	.75	.30
❑ 75	Garrison Hearst	.40	.15
❑ 76	J.J. Stokes	.40	.15
❑ 77	Ken Norton	.25	.08
❑ 78	R.W. McQuarters	.25	.08
❑ 79	Bryant Young	.25	.08
❑ 80	Jamal Anderson	.60	.25
❑ 81	Chris Chandler	.40	.15
❑ 82	Terance Mathis	.40	.15
❑ 83	Tim Dwight	.60	.25
❑ 84	O.J. Santiago	.25	.08
❑ 85	Chris Calloway	.25	.08
❑ 86	Keith Brooking	.25	.08
❑ 87	Eddie Kennison	.40	.15
❑ 88	Willie Roaf	.25	.08
❑ 89	Cam Cleeland	.25	.08
❑ 90	Lamar Smith	.40	.15
❑ 91	Sean Dawkins	.25	.08
❑ 92	Tim Biakabutuka	.40	.15
❑ 93	Muhsin Muhammad	.40	.15
❑ 94	Steve Beuerlein	.25	.08
❑ 95	Rae Carruth	.25	.08
❑ 96	Wesley Walls	.40	.15
❑ 97	Kevin Greene	.40	.15
❑ 98	Trent Green	.60	.25
❑ 99	Tony Banks	.40	.15
❑ 100	Greg Hill	.25	.08
❑ 101	Robert Holcombe	.25	.08
❑ 102	Isaac Bruce	.60	.25
❑ 103	Amp Lee	.25	.08
❑ 104	Az-Zahir Hakim	.25	.08
❑ 105	Warren Moon	.60	.25
❑ 106	Jeff George	.40	.15
❑ 107	Rocket Ismail	.40	.15
❑ 108	Kordell Stewart	.40	.15
❑ 109	Jerome Bettis	.60	.25
❑ 110	Courtney Hawkins	.25	.08
❑ 111	Chris Fuamatu-Ma'afala	.25	.08
❑ 112	Levon Kirkland	.25	.08
❑ 113	Hines Ward	.60	.25
❑ 114	Will Blackwell	.25	.08
❑ 115	Corey Dillon	.60	.25
❑ 116	Carl Pickens	.40	.15
❑ 117	Neil O'Donnell	.40	.15
❑ 118	Jeff Blake	.40	.15
❑ 119	Darnay Scott	.25	.08
❑ 120	Takeo Spikes	.25	.08
❑ 121	Steve McNair	.60	.25
❑ 122	Frank Wycheck	.25	.08
❑ 123	Eddie George	.60	.25
❑ 124	Chris Sanders	.25	.08
❑ 125	Yancey Thigpen	.25	.08
❑ 126	Kevin Dyson	.40	.15
❑ 127	Blaine Bishop	.25	.08
❑ 128	Fred Taylor	.60	.25
❑ 129	Mark Brunell	.60	.25
❑ 130	Jimmy Smith	.40	.15
❑ 131	Keenan McCardell	.40	.15
❑ 132	Kyle Brady	.25	.08
❑ 133	Tavian Banks	.25	.08
❑ 134	James Stewart	.40	.15
❑ 135	Kevin Hardy	.25	.08
❑ 136	Jonathan Quinn	.25	.08
❑ 137	Jermaine Lewis	.40	.15
❑ 138	Priest Holmes	1.00	.40
❑ 139	Scott Mitchell	.40	.15
❑ 140	Eric Zeier	.40	.15
❑ 141	Patrick Johnson	.25	.08
❑ 142	Ray Lewis	.60	.25
❑ 143	Terry Kirby	.25	.08
❑ 144	Ty Detmer	.25	.08
❑ 145	Irv Smith	.25	.08
❑ 146	Chris Spielman	.25	.08
❑ 147	Antonio Langham	.25	.08
❑ 148	Dan Marino	2.00	.75
❑ 149	O.J. McDuffie	.40	.15
❑ 150	Oronde Gadsden	.40	.15

❑ 151	Karim Abdul-Jabbar	.40	.15
❑ 152	Yatil Green	.25	.08
❑ 153	Zach Thomas	.60	.25
❑ 154	John Avery	.25	.08
❑ 155	Lamar Thomas	.25	.08
❑ 156	Drew Bledsoe	.75	.30
❑ 157	Terry Glenn	.60	.25
❑ 158	Ben Coates	.40	.15
❑ 159	Shawn Jefferson	.25	.08
❑ 160	Sedrick Shaw	.25	.08
❑ 161	Tony Simmons	.25	.08
❑ 162	Ty Law	.40	.15
❑ 163	Robert Edwards	.25	.08
❑ 164	Curtis Martin	.60	.25
❑ 165	Keyshawn Johnson	.60	.25
❑ 166	Vinny Testaverde	.40	.15
❑ 167	Aaron Glenn	.25	.08
❑ 168	Wayne Chrebet	.40	.15
❑ 169	Dedric Ward	.25	.08
❑ 170	Peyton Manning	2.00	.75
❑ 171	Marshall Faulk	.75	.30
❑ 172	Marvin Harrison	.60	.25
❑ 173	Jerome Pathon	.25	.08
❑ 174	Ken Dilger	.25	.08
❑ 175	E.G. Green	.25	.08
❑ 176	Doug Flutie	.60	.25
❑ 177	Thurman Thomas	.40	.15
❑ 178	Andre Reed	.40	.15
❑ 179	Eric Moulds	.60	.25
❑ 180	Antowain Smith	.60	.25
❑ 181	Bruce Smith	.40	.15
❑ 182	Rob Johnson	.40	.15
❑ 183	Terrell Davis	.60	.25
❑ 184	John Elway	2.00	.75
❑ 185	Ed McCaffrey	.40	.15
❑ 186	Rod Smith	.40	.15
❑ 187	Shannon Sharpe	.40	.15
❑ 188	Marcus Nash	.25	.08
❑ 189	Brian Griese	.60	.25
❑ 190	Neil Smith	.40	.15
❑ 191	Bubby Brister	.25	.08
❑ 192	Ryan Leaf	.60	.25
❑ 193	Natrone Means	.40	.15
❑ 194	Mikhael Ricks	.25	.08
❑ 195	Junior Seau	.60	.25
❑ 196	Jim Harbaugh	.40	.15
❑ 197	Bryan Still	.25	.08
❑ 198	Freddie Jones	.25	.08
❑ 199	Andre Rison	.40	.15
❑ 200	Elvis Grbac	.40	.15
❑ 201	Byron Bam Morris	.25	.08
❑ 202	Rashaan Shehee	.25	.08
❑ 203	Kimble Anders	.40	.15
❑ 204	Donnell Bennett	.25	.08
❑ 205	Tony Gonzalez	.60	.25
❑ 206	Derrick Alexander WR	.40	.15
❑ 207	Jon Kitna	.60	.25
❑ 208	Ricky Watters	.40	.15
❑ 209	Joey Galloway	.40	.15
❑ 210	Ahman Green	.60	.25
❑ 211	Shawn Springs	.25	.08
❑ 212	Michael Sinclair	.25	.08
❑ 213	Napoleon Kaufman	.60	.25
❑ 214	Tim Brown	.60	.25
❑ 215	Charles Woodson	.60	.25
❑ 216	Harvey Williams	.25	.08
❑ 217	Jon Ritchie	.25	.08
❑ 218	Rich Gannon	.60	.25
❑ 219	Rickey Dudley	.25	.08
❑ 220	James Jett	.40	.15
❑ 221	Tim Couch RC	3.00	1.25
❑ 222	Ricky Williams RC	4.00	1.50
❑ 223	Donovan McNabb RC	10.00	4.00
❑ 224	Edgerrin James RC	8.00	3.00
❑ 225	Torry Holt RC	6.00	2.50
❑ 226	Daunte Culpepper RC	8.00	3.00
❑ 227	Akili Smith RC	2.00	.75
❑ 228	Champ Bailey RC	4.00	1.50
❑ 229	Chris Claiborne RC	1.25	.50
❑ 230	Chris McAlister RC	2.00	.75
❑ 231	Troy Edwards RC	2.00	.75
❑ 232	Jevon Kearse RC	5.00	2.00
❑ 233	Shaun King RC	2.00	.75
❑ 234	David Boston RC	3.00	1.25
❑ 235	Peerless Price RC	3.00	1.25
❑ 236	Cecil Collins RC	1.25	.50
❑ 237	Rob Konrad RC	2.00	.75
❑ 238	Cade McNown UER RC	2.00	.75
❑ 239	Shawn Bryson RC	3.00	1.25
❑ 240	Kevin Faulk RC	3.00	1.25
❑ 241	Scott Covington RC	3.00	1.25
❑ 242	James Johnson RC	2.00	.75
❑ 243	Mike Cloud RC	2.00	.75
❑ 244	Aaron Brooks RC	4.00	1.50
❑ 245	Sedrick Irvin RC	1.25	.50
❑ 246	Amos Zereoue RC	3.00	1.25
❑ 247	Jermaine Fazande RC	2.00	.75
❑ 248	Joe Germaine RC	2.00	.75
❑ 249	Brock Huard RC	3.00	1.25
❑ 250	Craig Yeast RC	2.00	.75
❑ 251	Travis McGriff RC	1.25	.50
❑ 252	D'Wayne Bates RC	2.00	.75
❑ 253	Na Brown RC	2.00	.75
❑ 254	Tai Streets RC	3.00	1.25
❑ 255	Andy Katzenmoyer RC	2.00	.75
❑ 256	Kevin Johnson RC	3.00	1.25
❑ 257	Joe Montgomery RC	2.00	.75
❑ 258	Karsten Bailey RC	2.00	.75
❑ 259	De'Mond Parker RC	1.25	.50
❑ 260	Reginald Kelly RC	1.25	.50
❑ 261	Eddie George AP	1.50	.60
❑ 262	Jamal Anderson AP	1.50	.60
❑ 263	Barry Sanders AP	6.00	2.50
❑ 264	Fred Taylor AP	1.50	.60
❑ 265	Keyshawn Johnson AP	1.50	.60
❑ 266	Jerry Rice AP	4.00	1.50
❑ 267	Doug Flutie AP	1.50	.60
❑ 268	Deion Sanders AP	1.50	.60
❑ 269	Randall Cunningham AP	1.50	.60
❑ 270	Steve Young AP	2.50	1.00
❑ 271	J.Elway/T.Davis GC	5.00	2.00
❑ 272	P.Manning/M.Faulk GC	5.00	2.00
❑ 273	B.Favre/A.Freeman GC	6.00	2.50
❑ 274	T.Aikman/E.Smith GC	4.00	1.50
❑ 275	C.Carter/R.Moss GC	4.00	1.50

1999 Score Supplemental

❑	COMPLETE SET (110)	25.00	10.00
❑	COMP.FACT.SET (110)	30.00	12.50
❑ S1	Chris Greisen RC	1.00	.40
❑ S2	Sherdrick Bonner RC	.60	.25
❑ S3	Joel Makovicka RC	1.50	.60
❑ S4	Andy McCullough RC	.60	.25
❑ S5	Jeff Paulk RC	.60	.25
❑ S6	Brandon Stokley RC	2.00	.75
❑ S7	Sheldon Jackson RC	1.00	.40
❑ S8	Bobby Collins RC	.60	.25
❑ S9	Kamil Loud RC	.60	.25
❑ S10	Antoine Winfield RC	1.00	.40
❑ S11	Jerry Azumah RC	1.00	.40
❑ S12	James Allen RC	1.50	.60
❑ S13	Nick Williams RC	1.00	.40
❑ S14	Michael Basnight RC	.60	.25
❑ S15	Damon Griffin RC	1.00	.40
❑ S16	Ronnie Powell RC	.60	.25
❑ S17	Darrin Chiaverini RC	1.00	.40
❑ S18	Mark Campbell RC	1.00	.40
❑ S19	Mike Lucky RC	1.00	.40
❑ S20	Wane McGarity RC	.60	.25
❑ S21	Jason Tucker RC	1.00	.40
❑ S22	Ebenezer Ekuban RC	1.00	.40
❑ S23	Robert Thomas RC	1.00	.40
❑ S24	Dat Nguyen RC	1.00	.40
❑ S25	Olandis Gary RC	1.50	.60
❑ S26	Desmond Clark RC	1.50	.60
❑ S27	Andre Cooper RC	.60	.25
❑ S28	Chris Watson RC	.60	.25
❑ S29	Al Wilson RC	1.50	.60
❑ S30	Cory Sauter RC	.60	.25
❑ S31	Brock Olivo RC	.60	.25
❑ S32	Basil Mitchell RC	.60	.25
❑ S33	Matt Snider RC	.60	.25
❑ S34	Antuan Edwards RC	1.00	.40
❑ S35	Mike McKenzie RC	1.00	.40
❑ S36	Terrence Wilkins RC	1.00	.40
❑ S37	Fernando Bryant RC	1.00	.40
❑ S38	Larry Parker RC	1.50	.60
❑ S39	Autry Denson RC	1.00	.40
❑ S40	Jim Kleinsasser RC	1.50	.60
❑ S41	Michael Bishop RC	1.50	.60
❑ S42	Andy Katzenmoyer	.25	.08
❑ S43	Brett Bech RC	.60	.25
❑ S44	Sean Bennett RC	.60	.25
❑ S45	Dan Campbell RC	.60	.25
❑ S46	Ray Lucas RC	1.50	.60
❑ S47	Scott Dreisbach RC	1.00	.40
❑ S48	Cecil Martin RC	1.00	.40
❑ S49	Dameane Douglas RC	1.00	.40
❑ S50	Jed Weaver RC	1.00	.40
❑ S51	Jerame Tuman RC	1.50	.60
❑ S52	Steve Heiden RC	1.50	.60
❑ S53	Jeff Garcia RC	4.00	1.50
❑ S54	Terry Jackson RC	1.00	.40
❑ S55	Charlie Rogers RC	1.00	.40
❑ S56	Lamar King RC	1.00	.40
❑ S57	Kurt Warner RC	8.00	3.00
❑ S58	Dre' Bly RC	1.50	.60
❑ S59	Justin Watson RC	.60	.25
❑ S60	Rabih Abdullah RC	1.00	.40
❑ S61	Martin Gramatica RC	.60	.25
❑ S62	Darnell McDonald RC	1.00	.40
❑ S63	Anthony McFarland RC	1.00	.40
❑ S64	Larry Brown TE RC	.60	.25
❑ S65	Kevin Daft RC	1.00	.40
❑ S66	Mike Sellers	.15	.05
❑ S67	Ken Oxendine	.15	.05
❑ S68	Errict Rhett	.25	.08
❑ S69	Stoney Case	.15	.05
❑ S70	Jonathan Linton	.15	.05
❑ S71	Marcus Robinson	1.00	.40
❑ S72	Shane Matthews	.25	.08
❑ S73	Cade McNown	1.00	.40
❑ S74	Akili Smith	.15	.05
❑ S75	Karim Abdul-Jabbar	.25	.08
❑ S76	Tim Couch	1.50	.60
❑ S77	Kevin Johnson	.40	.15
❑ S78	Ron Rivers	.15	.05
❑ S79	Bill Schroeder	.40	.15
❑ S80	Edgerrin James	2.50	1.00
❑ S81	Cecil Collins	.75	.30
❑ S82	Matthew Hatchette	.15	.05
❑ S83	Daunte Culpepper	2.50	1.00
❑ S84	Ricky Williams	1.25	.50
❑ S85	Tyrone Wheatley	.40	.15
❑ S86	Donovan McNabb	3.00	1.25
❑ S87	Marshall Faulk	.50	.20
❑ S88	Torry Holt	2.00	.75
❑ S89	Stephen Davis	.40	.15
❑ S90	Brad Johnson	.40	.15
❑ S91	Jake Plummer SS	.25	.08
❑ S92	Emmitt Smith SS	.75	.30
❑ S93	Troy Aikman SS	.75	.30
❑ S94	John Elway SS	1.25	.50
❑ S95	Terrell Davis SS	.40	.15
❑ S96	Barry Sanders SS	1.25	.50
❑ S97	Brett Favre SS	1.25	.50
❑ S98	Antonio Freeman SS	.40	.15
❑ S99	Peyton Manning SS	1.25	.50
❑ S100	Fred Taylor SS	.40	.15
❑ S101	Mark Brunell SS	.40	.15
❑ S102	Dan Marino SS	1.25	.50
❑ S103	Randy Moss SS	1.00	.40
❑ S104	Cris Carter SS	.40	.15
❑ S105	Drew Bledsoe SS	.50	.20
❑ S106	Terry Glenn SS	.40	.15
❑ S107	Keyshawn Johnson SS	.40	.15
❑ S108	Jerry Rice SS	.75	.30
❑ S109	Steve Young SS	.50	.20
❑ S110	Eddie George SS	.40	.15

2000 Score

❑ COMP.SET w/o SP's (220)	20.00	7.50
❑ 1 Michael Pittman	.25	.08
❑ 2 Jake Plummer	.40	.15
❑ 3 Rob Moore	.40	.15
❑ 4 David Boston	.60	.25
❑ 5 Frank Sanders	.40	.15
❑ 6 Jamal Anderson	.60	.25
❑ 7 Chris Chandler	.40	.15
❑ 8 Tim Dwight	.60	.25
❑ 9 Terance Mathis	.40	.15
❑ 10 Shawn Jefferson	.25	.08
❑ 11 Ashley Ambrose	.25	.08
❑ 12 Peter Boulware	.25	.08
❑ 13 Priest Holmes	.75	.30
❑ 14 Tony Banks	.40	.15
❑ 15 Qadry Ismail	.40	.15
❑ 16 Shannon Sharpe	.40	.15
❑ 17 Rod Woodson	.40	.15
❑ 18 Matt Stover	.25	.08
❑ 19 Michael McCrary	.25	.08
❑ 20 Doug Flutie	.60	.25
❑ 21 Rob Johnson	.40	.15
❑ 22 Eric Moulds	.60	.25
❑ 23 Peerless Price	.40	.15
❑ 24 Jonathan Linton	.25	.08
❑ 25 Antowain Smith	.40	.15
❑ 26 Jay Riemersma	.25	.08
❑ 27 Muhsin Muhammad	.40	.15
❑ 28 Tim Biakabutuka	.40	.15
❑ 29 Patrick Jeffers	.60	.25
❑ 30 Wesley Walls	.25	.08
❑ 31 Steve Beuerlein	.40	.15
❑ 32 John Kasay	.25	.08
❑ 33 Curtis Enis	.25	.08
❑ 34 Cade McNown	.25	.08
❑ 35 Marcus Robinson	.60	.25
❑ 36 Bobby Engram	.25	.08
❑ 37 Eddie Kennison	.25	.08
❑ 38 Akili Smith	.25	.08
❑ 39 Carl Pickens	.40	.15
❑ 40 Corey Dillon	.60	.25
❑ 41 Darnay Scott	.40	.15
❑ 42 Errict Rhett	.40	.15
❑ 43 Karim Abdul-Jabbar	.40	.15
❑ 44 Tim Couch	.40	.15
❑ 45 Kevin Johnson	.60	.25
❑ 46 Darrin Chiaverini	.25	.08
❑ 47 Terry Kirby	.25	.08
❑ 48 Jason Tucker	.25	.08
❑ 49 Rocket Ismail	.40	.15
❑ 50 Joey Galloway	.40	.15
❑ 51 Michael Irvin	.40	.15
❑ 52 Troy Aikman	1.25	.50
❑ 53 Emmitt Smith	1.25	.50
❑ 54 David LaFleur	.25	.08
❑ 55 Trevor Pryce	.25	.08
❑ 56 Brian Griese	.60	.25
❑ 57 Olandis Gary	.60	.25
❑ 58 Terrell Davis	.60	.25
❑ 59 Rod Smith	.40	.15
❑ 60 Ed McCaffrey	.60	.25
❑ 61 Gus Frerotte	.25	.08
❑ 62 Jason Elam	.25	.08
❑ 63 Kavika Pittman	.25	.08
❑ 64 James Stewart	.40	.15
❑ 65 Charlie Batch	.60	.25
❑ 66 Johnnie Morton	.40	.15
❑ 67 Herman Moore	.40	.15
❑ 68 Germane Crowell	.25	.08
❑ 69 Barry Sanders	1.50	.60
❑ 70 Chris Claiborne	.25	.08
❑ 71 Brett Favre	2.00	.75
❑ 72 Antonio Freeman	.60	.25
❑ 73 Dorsey Levens	.40	.15
❑ 74 De'Mond Parker	.25	.08
❑ 75 Corey Bradford	.40	.15
❑ 76 Basil Mitchell	.25	.08
❑ 77 Bill Schroeder	.40	.15
❑ 78 Peyton Manning	1.50	.60
❑ 79 Marvin Harrison	.60	.25
❑ 80 Terrence Wilkins	.25	.08
❑ 81 Edgerrin James	1.00	.40
❑ 82 E.G. Green	.25	.08
❑ 83 Chad Bratzke	.25	.08
❑ 84 Mark Brunell	.60	.25
❑ 85 Fred Taylor	.60	.25
❑ 86 Jimmy Smith	.40	.15
❑ 87 Keenan McCardell	.40	.15
❑ 88 Kevin Hardy	.25	.08
❑ 89 Aaron Beasley	.25	.08
❑ 90 Elvis Grbac	.40	.15
❑ 91 Derrick Alexander	.40	.15
❑ 92 Tony Gonzalez	.40	.15
❑ 93 Donnell Bennett	.25	.08
❑ 94 Warren Moon	.60	.25
❑ 95 Andre Rison	.40	.15
❑ 96 James Hasty	.25	.08
❑ 97 Dan Marino	2.00	.75
❑ 98 Thurman Thomas	.40	.15
❑ 99 James Johnson	.25	.08
❑ 100 O.J. McDuffie	.40	.15
❑ 101 Tony Martin	.40	.15
❑ 102 Oronde Gadsden	.40	.15
❑ 103 Zach Thomas	.60	.25
❑ 104 Sam Madison	.25	.08
❑ 105 Jay Fiedler	.60	.25
❑ 106 Damon Huard	.60	.25
❑ 107 Robert Smith	.60	.25
❑ 108 Leroy Hoard	.25	.08
❑ 109 Randy Moss	1.25	.50
❑ 110 Cris Carter	.60	.25
❑ 111 Daunte Culpepper	.75	.30
❑ 112 John Randle	.40	.15
❑ 113 Randall Cunningham	.60	.25
❑ 114 Gary Anderson	.25	.08
❑ 115 Drew Bledsoe DP	.75	.30
❑ 116 Terry Glenn	.40	.15
❑ 117 Kevin Faulk	.40	.15
❑ 118 Terry Allen SP	15.00	7.50
❑ 119 Adam Vinatieri	.60	.25
❑ 120 Ty Law	.40	.15
❑ 121 Lawyer Milloy	.40	.15
❑ 122 Troy Brown	.40	.15
❑ 123 Ben Coates	.25	.08
❑ 124 Cam Cleeland	.25	.08
❑ 125 Jeff Blake	.40	.15
❑ 126 Ricky Williams	.60	.25
❑ 127 Jake Reed	.40	.15
❑ 128 Jake Delhomme RC	2.50	1.00
❑ 129 Andrew Glover	.25	.08
❑ 130 Keith Poole	.25	.08
❑ 131 Joe Horn	.40	.15
❑ 132 Kerry Collins	.40	.15
❑ 133 Joe Montgomery	.25	.08
❑ 134 Sean Bennett	.25	.08
❑ 135 Amani Toomer	.25	.08
❑ 136 Ike Hilliard	.40	.15
❑ 137 Joe Jurevicius	.25	.08
❑ 138 Tiki Barber	.60	.25
❑ 139 Victor Green	.25	.08
❑ 140 Ray Lucas	.40	.15
❑ 141 Vinny Testaverde	.40	.15
❑ 142 Curtis Martin	.60	.25
❑ 143 Wayne Chrebet	.40	.15
❑ 144 Tyrone Wheatley	.40	.15
❑ 145 Rich Gannon	.60	.25
❑ 146 Napoleon Kaufman	.40	.15
❑ 147 Tim Brown	.25	.08
❑ 148 Rickey Dudley	.25	.08
❑ 149 Charles Woodson	.60	.25
❑ 150 James Jett	.25	.08
❑ 151 Duce Staley	.60	.25
❑ 152 Charles Johnson	.40	.15
❑ 153 Donovan McNabb	1.00	.40
❑ 154 Troy Vincent	.25	.08
❑ 155 Troy Edwards	.25	.08
❑ 156 Jerome Bettis	.60	.25
❑ 157 Kordell Stewart	.40	.15
❑ 158 Richard Huntley	.25	.08
❑ 159 Hines Ward	.60	.25
❑ 160 Levon Kirkland	.25	.08
❑ 161 Ryan Leaf	.40	.15
❑ 162 Jim Harbaugh	.40	.15
❑ 163 Jermaine Fazande	.25	.08
❑ 164 Natrone Means	.25	.08
❑ 165 Junior Seau	.60	.25
❑ 166 Curtis Conway	.40	.15
❑ 167 Freddie Jones	.25	.08
❑ 168 Jeff Graham	.25	.08
❑ 169 Terrell Owens	.60	.25
❑ 170 Jeff Garcia	.60	.25
❑ 171 Jerry Rice	1.25	.50
❑ 172 Steve Young	.75	.30
❑ 173 Garrison Hearst	.40	.15
❑ 174 Charlie Garner	.40	.15
❑ 175 Fred Beasley	.25	.08
❑ 176 Bryant Young	.25	.08
❑ 177 Derrick Mayes	.40	.15
❑ 178 Sean Dawkins	.25	.08
❑ 179 Jon Kitna	.60	.25
❑ 180 Ricky Watters	.40	.15
❑ 181 Charlie Rogers	.25	.08
❑ 182 Kurt Warner	1.25	.50
❑ 183 Marshall Faulk	.75	.30
❑ 184 Isaac Bruce	.60	.25
❑ 185 Az-Zahir Hakim	.40	.15
❑ 186 Trent Green	.60	.25
❑ 187 Jeff Wilkins	.25	.08
❑ 188 Torry Holt	.60	.25
❑ 189 London Fletcher RC	.40	.15
❑ 190 Robert Holcombe	.25	.08
❑ 191 Todd Lyght	.25	.08
❑ 192 Keyshawn Johnson	.60	.25
❑ 193 Derrick Brooks	.60	.25
❑ 194 Warren Sapp	.40	.15
❑ 195 Shaun King	.25	.08
❑ 196 Warrick Dunn	.60	.25
❑ 197 Mike Alstott	.60	.25
❑ 198 Jacquez Green	.25	.08
❑ 199 Reidel Anthony	.25	.08
❑ 200 Martin Gramatica	.25	.08
❑ 201 Donnie Abraham	.25	.08
❑ 202 Steve McNair	.60	.25
❑ 203 Eddie George	.60	.25
❑ 204 Jevon Kearse	.60	.25
❑ 205 Frank Wycheck	.25	.08
❑ 206 Kevin Dyson	.40	.15
❑ 207 Yancey Thigpen	.25	.08
❑ 208 Al Del Greco	.25	.08
❑ 209 Jeff George	.40	.15
❑ 210 Adrian Murrell	.40	.15
❑ 211 Brad Johnson	.60	.25
❑ 212 Stephen Davis	.60	.25
❑ 213 Stephen Alexander	.25	.08
❑ 214 Michael Westbrook	.40	.15
❑ 215 Darrell Green	.25	.08
❑ 216 Champ Bailey	.60	.25
❑ 217 Albert Connell	.25	.08
❑ 218 Larry Centers	.25	.08
❑ 219 Bruce Smith	.40	.15
❑ 220 Deion Sanders	.60	.25
❑ 221 Ricky Williams SS	.60	.25
❑ 222 Edgerrin James SS	1.00	.40
❑ 223 Tim Couch SS	.40	.15
❑ 224 Cade McNown SS	.30	.10
❑ 225 Olandis Gary SS	.75	.30
❑ 226 Torry Holt SS	.75	.30
❑ 227 Donovan McNabb SS	1.00	.40
❑ 228 Shaun King SS	.25	.08
❑ 229 Kevin Johnson SS	.75	.30
❑ 230 Kurt Warner SS	1.50	.60
❑ 231 Tony Gonzalez AP	.50	.20
❑ 232 Frank Wycheck AP	.30	.10
❑ 233 Eddie George AP	.75	.30
❑ 234 Mark Brunell AP	.75	.30
❑ 235 Corey Dillon AP	.75	.30
❑ 236 Peyton Manning AP	2.00	.75
❑ 237 Keyshawn Johnson AP	.75	.30
❑ 238 Rich Gannon AP	.75	.30
❑ 239 Terry Glenn AP	.50	.20
❑ 240 Tony Brackens AP	.30	.10
❑ 241 Edgerrin James AP	1.00	.40

❑ 242 Tim Brown AP .75 .30
❑ 243 Michael Strahan AP .50 .20
❑ 244 Kurt Warner AP 1.50 .60
❑ 245 Brad Johnson AP .75 .30
❑ 246 Aeneas Williams AP .30 .10
❑ 247 Marshall Faulk AP 1.00 .40
❑ 248 Dexter Coakley AP .30 .10
❑ 249 Warren Sapp AP .50 .20
❑ 250 Mike Alstott AP .75 .30
❑ 251 David Sloan AP .30 .10
❑ 252 Cris Carter AP .75 .30
❑ 253 Muhsin Muhammad AP .30 .10
❑ 254 Isaac Bruce AP .75 .30
❑ 255 Wesley Walls AP .30 .10
❑ 256 Steve Beuerlein LL .50 .20
❑ 257 Kurt Warner LL 1.50 .60
❑ 258 Peyton Manning LL 2.00 .75
❑ 259 Brad Johnson LL .75 .30
❑ 260 Edgerrin James LL 1.00 .40
❑ 261 Curtis Martin LL .75 .30
❑ 262 Stephen Davis LL .75 .30
❑ 263 Emmitt Smith LL 1.50 .60
❑ 264 Marvin Harrison LL .75 .30
❑ 265 Jimmy Smith LL .50 .20
❑ 266 Randy Moss LL 1.50 .60
❑ 267 Marcus Robinson LL .75 .30
❑ 268 Kevin Carter LL .30 .10
❑ 269 Simeon Rice LL .50 .20
❑ 270 Robert Porcher LL .30 .10
❑ 271 Jevon Kearse LL .75 .30
❑ 272 Mike Vanderjagt LL .30 .10
❑ 273 Olindo Mare LL .30 .10
❑ 274 Todd Peterson LL .30 .10
❑ 275 Mike Hollis LL .30 .10
❑ 276 Mike Anderson RC/500 30.00 12.50
❑ 277 Peter Warrick RC 2.00 .75
❑ 278 Courtney Brown RC .75 .30
❑ 279 Plaxico Burress RC 4.00 1.50
❑ 280 Corey Simon RC .75 .30
❑ 281 Thomas Jones RC 3.00 1.25
❑ 282 Travis Taylor RC .75 .30
❑ 283 Shaun Alexander RC 10.00 4.00
❑ 284 Patrick Pass RC/500 20.00 7.50
❑ 285 Chris Redman RC .50 .20
❑ 286 Chad Pennington RC 5.00 2.00
❑ 287 Jamal Lewis RC 5.00 2.00
❑ 288 Brian Urlacher RC 8.00 3.00
❑ 289 Bubba Franks RC 2.00 .75
❑ 290 Dez White RC 2.00 .75
❑ 291 Frank Moreau RC/500 20.00 7.50
❑ 292 Ron Dayne RC 2.00 .75
❑ 293 Sylvester Morris RC .50 .20
❑ 294 R.Jay Soward RC 1.50 .60
❑ 295 Curtis Keaton RC 1.50 .60
❑ 296 Spergon Wynn RC/500 20.00 7.50
❑ 297 Rondell Mealey RC 1.50 .60
❑ 298 Travis Prentice RC 1.50 .60
❑ 299 Darrell Jackson RC 4.00 1.50
❑ 300 Giovanni Carmazzi RC 1.50 .60
❑ 301 Anthony Lucas RC 1.50 .60
❑ 302 Danny Farmer RC 1.50 .60
❑ 303 Dennis Northcutt RC 2.00 .75
❑ 304 Troy Walters RC 2.00 .75
❑ 305 Laveranues Coles RC 2.50 1.00
❑ 306 Kwame Cavil RC 1.50 .60
❑ 307 Tee Martin RC 2.00 .75
❑ 308 J.R. Redmond RC 1.50 .60
❑ 309 Tim Rattay RC 2.00 .75
❑ 310 Jerry Porter RC 2.50 1.00
❑ 311 Michael Wiley RC 1.50 .60
❑ 312 Reuben Droughns RC 2.50 1.00
❑ 313 Trung Canidate RC 1.50 .60
❑ 314 Shyrone Stith RC 1.50 .60
❑ 315 Marc Bulger RC 4.00 1.50
❑ 316 Tom Brady RC 25.00 10.00
❑ 317 Doug Johnson RC 2.00 .75
❑ 318 Todd Husak RC 2.00 .75
❑ 319 Gari Scott RC 1.50 .60
❑ 320 Windrell Hayes RC/500 20.00 7.50
❑ 321 Chris Cole RC 1.50 .60
❑ 322 Sammy Morris RC 1.50 .60
❑ 323 Trevor Gaylor RC 1.50 .60
❑ 324 Jarious Jackson RC 1.50 .60
❑ 325 Doug Chapman RC/500 20.00 7.50
❑ 326 Ron Dugans RC 1.50 .60
❑ 327 Ron Dixon RC/500 20.00 7.50
❑ 328 Joe Hamilton RC 1.50 .60
❑ 329 Todd Pinkston RC 2.00 .75
❑ 330 Chad Morton RC 2.00 .75

2001 Score

❑ COMP.SET w/o SP's (220) 25.00 10.00
❑ 1 David Boston .50 .20
❑ 2 Frank Sanders .20 .07
❑ 3 Jake Plummer .30 .10
❑ 4 Michael Pittman .20 .07
❑ 5 Rob Moore .30 .10
❑ 6 Thomas Jones .30 .10
❑ 7 Chris Chandler .30 .10
❑ 8 Doug Johnson .20 .07
❑ 9 Jamal Anderson .50 .20
❑ 10 Tim Dwight .50 .20
❑ 11 Brandon Stokley .30 .10
❑ 12 Chris Redman .20 .07
❑ 13 Jamal Lewis .75 .30
❑ 14 Qadry Ismail .30 .10
❑ 15 Ray Lewis .50 .20
❑ 16 Rod Woodson .30 .10
❑ 17 Shannon Sharpe .30 .10
❑ 18 Travis Taylor .30 .10
❑ 19 Trent Dilfer .30 .10
❑ 20 Elvis Grbac .30 .10
❑ 21 Eric Moulds .30 .10
❑ 22 Jay Riemersma .20 .07
❑ 23 Peerless Price .30 .10
❑ 24 Rob Johnson .30 .10
❑ 25 Sam Cowart .20 .07
❑ 26 Sammy Morris .20 .07
❑ 27 Shawn Bryson .20 .07
❑ 28 Donald Hayes .20 .07
❑ 29 Muhsin Muhammad .30 .10
❑ 30 Patrick Jeffers .30 .10
❑ 31 Reggie White DE .50 .20
❑ 32 Steve Beuerlein .30 .10
❑ 33 Tim Biakabutuka .30 .10
❑ 34 Wesley Walls .20 .07
❑ 35 Brian Urlacher .75 .30
❑ 36 Cade McNown .20 .07
❑ 37 Dez White .20 .07
❑ 38 James Allen .30 .10
❑ 39 Marcus Robinson .50 .20
❑ 40 Marty Booker .20 .07
❑ 41 Akili Smith .20 .07
❑ 42 Corey Dillon .50 .20
❑ 43 Danny Farmer .20 .07
❑ 44 Peter Warrick .50 .20
❑ 45 Ron Dugans .20 .07
❑ 46 Takeo Spikes .20 .07
❑ 47 Courtney Brown .30 .10
❑ 48 Dennis Northcutt .30 .10
❑ 49 JaJuan Dawson .20 .07
❑ 50 Kevin Johnson .30 .10
❑ 51 Tim Couch .30 .10
❑ 52 Travis Prentice .20 .07
❑ 53 Anthony Wright .20 .07
❑ 54 Emmitt Smith 1.00 .40
❑ 55 James McKnight .30 .10
❑ 56 Joey Galloway .30 .10
❑ 57 Rocket Ismail .30 .10
❑ 58 Randall Cunningham .50 .20
❑ 59 Troy Aikman .75 .30
❑ 60 Brian Griese .50 .20
❑ 61 Ed McCaffrey .50 .20
❑ 62 Gus Frerotte .20 .07
❑ 63 John Elway 1.50 .60
❑ 64 Mike Anderson .50 .20
❑ 65 Olandis Gary .30 .10
❑ 66 Rod Smith .30 .10
❑ 67 Terrell Davis .50 .20
❑ 68 Barry Sanders 1.00 .40
❑ 69 Charlie Batch .50 .20
❑ 70 Germane Crowell .20 .07
❑ 71 Herman Moore .30 .10
❑ 72 James Stewart .30 .10
❑ 73 Johnnie Morton .30 .10
❑ 74 Robert Porcher .20 .07
❑ 75 Jim Harbaugh .30 .10
❑ 76 Ahman Green .50 .20
❑ 77 Antonio Freeman .50 .20
❑ 78 Bill Schroeder .30 .10
❑ 79 Brett Favre 1.50 .60
❑ 80 Bubba Franks .30 .10
❑ 81 Dorsey Levens .30 .10
❑ 82 E.G. Green .20 .07
❑ 83 Edgerrin James .60 .25
❑ 84 Jerome Pathon .30 .10
❑ 85 Ken Dilger .20 .07
❑ 86 Marcus Pollard .20 .07
❑ 87 Marvin Harrison .50 .20
❑ 88 Peyton Manning 1.25 .50
❑ 89 Terrence Wilkins .20 .07
❑ 90 Fred Taylor .50 .20
❑ 91 Hardy Nickerson .20 .07
❑ 92 Jimmy Smith .30 .10
❑ 93 Keenan McCardell .20 .07
❑ 94 Kyle Brady .20 .07
❑ 95 Mark Brunell .50 .20
❑ 96 Tony Brackens .20 .07
❑ 97 Derrick Alexander .30 .10
❑ 98 Sylvester Morris .20 .07
❑ 99 Tony Gonzalez .30 .10
❑ 100 Tony Richardson .20 .07
❑ 101 Kimble Anders .20 .07
❑ 102 Warren Moon .50 .20
❑ 103 Dan Marino 1.50 .60
❑ 104 Jay Fiedler .50 .20
❑ 105 Lamar Smith .30 .10
❑ 106 O.J. McDuffie .20 .07
❑ 107 Oronde Gadsden .30 .10
❑ 108 Sam Madison .20 .07
❑ 109 Thurman Thomas .20 .07
❑ 110 Tony Martin .20 .07
❑ 111 Zach Thomas .50 .20
❑ 112 Cris Carter .50 .20
❑ 113 Daunte Culpepper .50 .20
❑ 114 Matthew Hatchette .20 .07
❑ 115 Randy Moss 1.00 .40
❑ 116 Robert Smith .50 .20
❑ 117 Drew Bledsoe .60 .25
❑ 118 J.R. Redmond .20 .07
❑ 119 Kevin Faulk .30 .10
❑ 120 Michael Bishop .20 .07
❑ 121 Terry Glenn .30 .10
❑ 122 Troy Brown .30 .10
❑ 123 Ty Law .30 .10
❑ 124 Aaron Brooks .50 .20
❑ 125 Darren Howard .20 .07
❑ 126 Jake Reed .30 .10
❑ 127 Jeff Blake .30 .10
❑ 128 Joe Horn .30 .10
❑ 129 La'Roi Glover .20 .07
❑ 130 Ricky Williams .50 .20
❑ 131 Willie Jackson .20 .07
❑ 132 Albert Connell .20 .07
❑ 133 Amani Toomer .20 .07
❑ 134 Ike Hilliard .30 .10
❑ 135 Jason Sehorn .20 .07
❑ 136 Jessie Armstead .20 .07
❑ 137 Kerry Collins .30 .10
❑ 138 Michael Strahan .30 .10
❑ 139 Ron Dayne .50 .20
❑ 140 Ron Dixon .20 .07
❑ 141 Tiki Barber .50 .20
❑ 142 Anthony Becht .20 .07
❑ 143 Chad Pennington .75 .30
❑ 144 Curtis Martin .50 .20
❑ 145 Dedric Ward .20 .07
❑ 146 Laveranues Coles .50 .20
❑ 147 Vinny Testaverde .30 .10
❑ 148 Wayne Chrebet .30 .10
❑ 149 Andre Rison .30 .10
❑ 150 Charles Woodson .30 .10
❑ 151 Darrell Russell .20 .07

❑ 152	Napoleon Kaufman	.30	.10
❑ 153	Rich Gannon	.50	.20
❑ 154	Tim Brown	.50	.20
❑ 155	Tyrone Wheatley	.30	.10
❑ 156	Chad Lewis	.20	.07
❑ 157	Charles Johnson	.20	.07
❑ 158	Donovan McNabb	.60	.25
❑ 159	Duce Staley	.50	.20
❑ 160	Hugh Douglas	.20	.07
❑ 161	Na Brown	.20	.07
❑ 162	Todd Pinkston	.20	.07
❑ 163	James Thrash	.30	.10
❑ 164	Bobby Shaw	.20	.07
❑ 165	Hines Ward	.50	.20
❑ 166	Jerome Bettis	.50	.20
❑ 167	Kordell Stewart	.30	.10
❑ 168	Levon Kirkland	.20	.07
❑ 169	Plaxico Burress	.50	.20
❑ 170	Richard Huntley	.20	.07
❑ 171	Troy Edwards	.20	.07
❑ 172	Jeff Graham	.20	.07
❑ 173	Junior Seau	.50	.20
❑ 174	Doug Flutie	.50	.20
❑ 175	Charlie Garner	.30	.10
❑ 176	Jeff Garcia	.50	.20
❑ 177	Jerry Rice	1.00	.40
❑ 178	Steve Young	.50	.20
❑ 179	Terrell Owens	.50	.20
❑ 180	Brock Huard	.20	.07
❑ 181	Darrell Jackson	.50	.20
❑ 182	Derrick Mayes	.30	.10
❑ 183	Ricky Watters	.30	.10
❑ 184	Shaun Alexander	.60	.25
❑ 185	Matt Hasselbeck	.30	.10
❑ 186	John Randle	.30	.10
❑ 187	Az-Zahir Hakim	.20	.07
❑ 188	Isaac Bruce	.50	.20
❑ 189	Kurt Warner	1.00	.40
❑ 190	Marshall Faulk	.60	.25
❑ 191	Torry Holt	.50	.20
❑ 192	Trent Green	.50	.20
❑ 193	Derrick Brooks	.50	.20
❑ 194	Jacquez Green	.20	.07
❑ 195	John Lynch	.30	.10
❑ 196	Keyshawn Johnson	.50	.20
❑ 197	Mike Alstott	.50	.20
❑ 198	Reidel Anthony	.20	.07
❑ 199	Shaun King	.20	.07
❑ 200	Warren Sapp	.30	.10
❑ 201	Warrick Dunn	.50	.20
❑ 202	Ryan Leaf	.30	.10
❑ 203	Carl Pickens	.20	.07
❑ 204	Derrick Mason	.30	.10
❑ 205	Eddie George	.50	.20
❑ 206	Frank Wycheck	.20	.07
❑ 207	Jevon Kearse	.30	.10
❑ 208	Neil O'Donnell	.20	.07
❑ 209	Steve McNair	.50	.20
❑ 210	Yancey Thigpen	.20	.07
❑ 211	Andre Reed	.30	.10
❑ 212	Brad Johnson	.50	.20
❑ 213	Bruce Smith	.30	.10
❑ 214	Champ Bailey	.50	.20
❑ 215	Darrell Green	.20	.07
❑ 216	Deion Sanders	.50	.20
❑ 217	Irving Fryar	.30	.10
❑ 218	Jeff George	.30	.10
❑ 219	Michael Westbrook	.30	.10
❑ 220	Stephen Davis	.50	.20
❑ 221	Terrell Owens AP	1.00	.40
❑ 222	Peyton Manning AP	2.50	1.00
❑ 223	Stephen Davis AP	1.00	.40
❑ 224	Marvin Harrison AP	1.00	.40
❑ 225	Donovan McNabb AP	1.25	.50
❑ 226	Edgerrin James AP	1.25	.50
❑ 227	Eric Moulds AP	.60	.25
❑ 228	Daunte Culpepper AP	1.00	.40
❑ 229	Eddie George AP	1.00	.40
❑ 230	Cris Carter AP	1.00	.40
❑ 231	Rich Gannon AP	1.00	.40
❑ 232	Jeff Garcia AP	1.00	.40
❑ 233	Jimmy Smith AP	.60	.25
❑ 234	Tony Gonzalez AP	.60	.25
❑ 235	Torry Holt AP	1.00	.40
❑ 236	Jevon Kearse AP	.60	.25
❑ 237	Ray Lewis AP	1.00	.40
❑ 238	Warren Sapp AP	.60	.25
❑ 239	Brian Urlacher AP	1.50	.60
❑ 240	Champ Bailey AP	.60	.25
❑ 241	Peyton Manning LL	2.50	1.00
❑ 242	Jeff Garcia LL	1.00	.40
❑ 243	Elvis Grbac LL	.60	.25
❑ 244	Daunte Culpepper LL	1.00	.40
❑ 245	Brett Favre LL	3.00	1.25
❑ 246	Edgerrin James LL	1.25	.50
❑ 247	Robert Smith LL	.60	.25
❑ 248	Eddie George LL	1.00	.40
❑ 249	Mike Anderson LL	1.00	.40
❑ 250	Corey Dillon LL	1.00	.40
❑ 251	Torry Holt LL	1.00	.40
❑ 252	Rod Smith LL	.60	.25
❑ 253	Isaac Bruce LL	1.00	.40
❑ 254	Terrell Owens LL	1.00	.40
❑ 255	Randy Moss LL	2.00	.75
❑ 256	La'Roi Glover LL	.40	.15
❑ 257	Trace Armstrong LL	.40	.15
❑ 258	Warren Sapp LL	.60	.25
❑ 259	Hugh Douglas LL	.40	.15
❑ 260	Jason Taylor LL	.40	.15
❑ 261	Mike Anderson SS	1.00	.40
❑ 262	Jamal Lewis SS	1.25	.50
❑ 263	Sylvester Morris SS	.40	.15
❑ 264	Darrell Jackson SS	1.00	.40
❑ 265	Peter Warrick SS	1.00	.40
❑ 266	Ron Dayne SS	1.00	.40
❑ 267	Shaun Alexander SS	1.25	.50
❑ 268	Plaxico Burress SS	1.00	.40
❑ 269	Brian Urlacher SS	1.50	.60
❑ 270	Courtney Brown SS	.60	.25
❑ 271	Michael Vick RC	12.00	5.00
❑ 272	Drew Brees RC	8.00	3.00
❑ 273	Chris Weinke RC	1.00	.40
❑ 274	Quincy Carter RC	2.00	.75
❑ 275	Sage Rosenfels RC	1.00	.40
❑ 276	Josh Heupel RC	2.00	.75
❑ 277	David Rivers RC	1.25	.50
❑ 278	Ben Leard RC	1.25	.50
❑ 279	Marques Tuiasosopo RC	2.00	.75
❑ 280	Mike McMahon RC	2.00	.75
❑ 281	Deuce McAllister RC	4.00	1.50
❑ 282	LaMont Jordan RC	4.00	1.50
❑ 283	LaDainian Tomlinson RC	20.00	8.00
❑ 284	James Jackson RC	2.00	.75
❑ 285	Anthony Thomas RC	2.00	.75
❑ 286	Travis Henry RC	3.00	1.25
❑ 287	Travis Minor RC	1.25	.50
❑ 288	Rudi Johnson RC	4.00	1.50
❑ 289	Michael Bennett RC	2.00	.75
❑ 290	Kevan Barlow RC	2.00	.75
❑ 291	Reggie White RC	1.25	.50
❑ 292	Moran Norris RC	.75	.30
❑ 293	Ja'Mar Toombs RC	1.25	.50
❑ 294	Heath Evans RC	1.25	.50
❑ 295	David Terrell RC	2.00	.75
❑ 296	Santana Moss RC	3.00	1.25
❑ 297	Rod Gardner RC	2.00	.75
❑ 298	Quincy Morgan RC	2.00	.75
❑ 299	Freddie Mitchell RC	2.00	.75
❑ 300	Boo Williams RC	1.25	.50
❑ 301	Reggie Wayne RC	4.00	1.50
❑ 302	Ronney Daniels RC	.75	.30
❑ 303	Bobby Newcombe RC	1.25	.50
❑ 304	Vinny Sutherland RC	1.25	.50
❑ 305	Cedrick Wilson RC	2.00	.75
❑ 306	Robert Ferguson RC	2.00	.75
❑ 307	Ken-Yon Rambo RC	1.25	.50
❑ 308	Alex Bannister RC	1.25	.50
❑ 309	Koren Robinson RC	2.00	.75
❑ 310	Chad Johnson RC	5.00	2.00
❑ 311	Chris Chambers RC	3.00	1.25
❑ 312	Javon Green RC	1.25	.50
❑ 313	Snoop Minnis RC	1.25	.50
❑ 314	Scotty Anderson RC	1.25	.50
❑ 315	Todd Heap RC	2.00	.75
❑ 316	Alge Crumpler RC	2.50	1.00
❑ 317	Marcellus Rivers RC	1.25	.50
❑ 318	Rashon Burns RC	.75	.30
❑ 319	Jamal Reynolds RC	2.00	.75
❑ 320	Andre Carter RC	2.00	.75
❑ 321	Justin Smith RC	2.00	.75
❑ 322	Gerard Warren RC	2.00	.75
❑ 323	Tommy Polley RC	2.00	.75
❑ 324	Dan Morgan RC	1.00	.40
❑ 325	Torrance Marshall RC	2.00	.75
❑ 326	Correll Buckhalter RC	2.50	1.00
❑ 327	Derrick Gibson RC	1.25	.50
❑ 328	Adam Archuleta RC	2.00	.75
❑ 329	Jamar Fletcher RC	1.25	.50
❑ 330	Nate Clements RC	2.00	.75

2002 Score

❑	COMPLETE SET (330)	50.00	20.00
❑ 1	David Boston	.50	.20
❑ 2	Arnold Jackson	.20	.07
❑ 3	MarTay Jenkins	.20	.07
❑ 4	Thomas Jones	.30	.10
❑ 5	Kwamie Lassiter	.20	.07
❑ 6	Michael Pittman	.20	.07
❑ 7	Jake Plummer	.30	.10
❑ 8	Chris Chandler	.30	.10
❑ 9	Alge Crumpler	.30	.10
❑ 10	Terance Mathis	.20	.07
❑ 11	Maurice Smith	.30	.10
❑ 12	Ray Buchanan	.20	.07
❑ 13	Jamal Anderson	.30	.10
❑ 14	Keith Brooking	.20	.07
❑ 15	Michael Vick	1.50	.60
❑ 16	Obafemi Ayanbadejo	.20	.07
❑ 17	Jason Brookins	.20	.07
❑ 18	Randall Cunningham	.20	.07
❑ 19	Elvis Grbac	.30	.10
❑ 20	Todd Heap	.20	.07
❑ 21	Qadry Ismail	.30	.10
❑ 22	Shannon Sharpe	.30	.10
❑ 23	Travis Taylor	.30	.10
❑ 24	Ray Lewis	.50	.20
❑ 25	Jamal Lewis	.50	.20
❑ 26	Larry Centers	.20	.07
❑ 27	Rob Johnson	.30	.10
❑ 28	Shawn Bryson	.20	.07
❑ 29	Eric Moulds	.30	.10
❑ 30	Peerless Price	.30	.10
❑ 31	Nate Clements	.20	.07
❑ 32	Travis Henry	.50	.20
❑ 33	Isaac Byrd	.20	.07
❑ 34	Nick Goings	.20	.07
❑ 35	Donald Hayes	.20	.07
❑ 36	Richard Huntley	.20	.07
❑ 37	Muhsin Muhammad	.30	.10
❑ 38	Steve Smith	.50	.20
❑ 39	Wesley Walls	.20	.07
❑ 40	Chris Weinke	.30	.10
❑ 41	James Allen	.30	.10
❑ 42	Marty Booker	.20	.07
❑ 43	Jim Miller	.20	.07
❑ 44	David Terrell	.50	.20
❑ 45	Dez White	.20	.07
❑ 46	Brian Urlacher	.75	.30
❑ 47	Mike Brown	.50	.20
❑ 48	Anthony Thomas	.30	.10
❑ 49	T.J. Houshmandzadeh	.30	.10
❑ 50	Chad Johnson	.50	.20
❑ 51	Darnay Scott	.20	.07
❑ 52	Peter Warrick	.30	.10
❑ 53	Akili Smith	.20	.07
❑ 54	Jon Kitna	.30	.10
❑ 55	Justin Smith	.20	.07
❑ 56	Corey Dillon	.30	.10
❑ 57	Benjamin Gay	.30	.10
❑ 58	Kevin Johnson	.30	.10
❑ 59	Quincy Morgan	.20	.07
❑ 60	James Jackson	.20	.07
❑ 61	Anthony Henry	.20	.07

❑	62	Gerard Warren	.20	.07
❑	63	Jamir Miller	.20	.07
❑	64	Tim Couch	.30	.10
❑	65	Quincy Carter	.30	.10
❑	66	Joey Galloway	.30	.10
❑	67	Troy Hambrick	.20	.07
❑	68	Rocket Ismail	.30	.10
❑	69	Dexter Coakley	.20	.07
❑	70	Darren Woodson	.20	.07
❑	71	Emmitt Smith	1.25	.50
❑	72	Mike Anderson	.50	.20
❑	73	Terrell Davis	.50	.20
❑	74	Kevin Kasper	.20	.07
❑	75	Rod Smith	.30	.10
❑	76	Ed McCaffrey	.50	.20
❑	77	Olandis Gary	.30	.10
❑	78	Dwayne Carswell	.20	.07
❑	79	Deltha O'Neal	.20	.07
❑	80	Brian Griese	.50	.20
❑	81	Scotty Anderson	.20	.07
❑	82	Johnnie Morton	.30	.10
❑	83	Cory Schlesinger	.20	.07
❑	84	James Stewart	.30	.10
❑	85	Shaun Rogers	.20	.07
❑	86	Mike McMahon	.50	.20
❑	87	Charlie Batch	.30	.10
❑	88	Robert Porcher	.20	.07
❑	89	Bubba Franks	.30	.10
❑	90	Robert Ferguson	.20	.07
❑	91	Antonio Freeman	.50	.20
❑	92	Ahman Green	.50	.20
❑	93	Bill Schroeder	.30	.10
❑	94	Kabeer Gbaja-Biamila	.30	.10
❑	95	Jamal Reynolds	.20	.07
❑	96	Darren Sharper	.20	.07
❑	97	Brett Favre	1.25	.50
❑	98	Marvin Harrison	.50	.20
❑	99	Dominic Rhodes	.30	.10
❑	100	Edgerrin James	.60	.25
❑	101	Reggie Wayne	.50	.20
❑	102	Terrence Wilkins	.20	.07
❑	103	Ken Dilger	.20	.07
❑	104	Peyton Manning	1.00	.40
❑	105	Elvis Joseph	.20	.07
❑	106	Stacey Mack	.20	.07
❑	107	Fred Taylor	.50	.20
❑	108	Keenan McCardell	.20	.07
❑	109	Jimmy Smith	.30	.10
❑	110	Mark Brunell	.50	.20
❑	111	Derrick Alexander	.30	.10
❑	112	Tony Gonzalez	.30	.10
❑	113	Trent Green	.30	.10
❑	114	Snoop Minnis	.20	.07
❑	115	Priest Holmes	.60	.25
❑	116	Chris Chambers	.50	.20
❑	117	Jay Fiedler	.30	.10
❑	118	Oronde Gadsden	.30	.10
❑	119	Travis Minor	.20	.07
❑	120	Lamar Smith	.30	.10
❑	121	Zach Thomas	.50	.20
❑	122	Michael Bennett	.30	.10
❑	123	Todd Bouman	.20	.07
❑	124	Cris Carter	.50	.20
❑	125	Byron Chamberlain	.20	.07
❑	126	Randy Moss	1.00	.40
❑	127	Jake Reed	.30	.10
❑	128	Daunte Culpepper	.50	.20
❑	129	Drew Bledsoe	.50	.20
❑	130	Troy Brown	.30	.10
❑	131	David Patten	.20	.07
❑	132	J.R. Redmond	.20	.07
❑	133	Antowain Smith	.30	.10
❑	134	Ty Law	.30	.10
❑	135	Richard Seymour	.20	.07
❑	136	Adam Vinatieri	.50	.20
❑	137	Tom Brady	1.25	.50
❑	138	Joe Horn	.30	.10
❑	139	Willie Jackson	.20	.07
❑	140	Deuce McAllister	.60	.25
❑	141	Boo Williams	.20	.07
❑	142	Ricky Williams	.50	.20
❑	143	La'Roi Glover	.20	.07
❑	144	Sammy Knight	.20	.07
❑	145	Aaron Brooks	.50	.20
❑	146	Tiki Barber	.50	.20
❑	147	Ron Dayne	.30	.10
❑	148	Ike Hilliard	.30	.10
❑	149	Amani Toomer	.30	.10
❑	150	Will Allen	.20	.07
❑	151	Michael Strahan	.30	.10
❑	152	Jason Sehorn	.20	.07
❑	153	Kerry Collins	.30	.10
❑	154	Anthony Becht	.20	.07
❑	155	Wayne Chrebet	.30	.10
❑	156	Laveranues Coles	.30	.10
❑	157	LaMont Jordan	.50	.20
❑	158	Santana Moss	.50	.20
❑	159	Chad Pennington	.60	.25
❑	160	John Abraham	.30	.10
❑	161	Vinny Testaverde	.30	.10
❑	162	Curtis Martin	.50	.20
❑	163	Tim Brown	.50	.20
❑	164	Rich Gannon	.50	.20
❑	165	Charlie Garner	.30	.10
❑	166	Jerry Porter	.20	.07
❑	167	Marques Tuiasosopo	.30	.10
❑	168	Tyrone Wheatley	.30	.10
❑	169	Charles Woodson	.30	.10
❑	170	Jerry Rice	1.00	.40
❑	171	Correll Buckhalter	.30	.10
❑	172	Chad Lewis	.20	.07
❑	173	Brian Mitchell	.20	.07
❑	174	Freddie Mitchell	.30	.10
❑	175	Todd Pinkston	.30	.10
❑	176	Duce Staley	.50	.20
❑	177	Tony Stewart	.20	.07
❑	178	James Thrash	.30	.10
❑	179	Hugh Douglas	.20	.07
❑	180	Donovan McNabb	.60	.25
❑	181	Plaxico Burress	.30	.10
❑	182	Chris Fuamatu-Ma'afala	.20	.07
❑	183	Kordell Stewart	.30	.10
❑	184	Hines Ward	.50	.20
❑	185	Amos Zereoue	.50	.20
❑	186	Kendrell Bell	.50	.20
❑	187	Casey Hampton	.20	.07
❑	188	Jerome Bettis	.50	.20
❑	189	Drew Brees	.50	.20
❑	190	Curtis Conway	.20	.07
❑	191	Tim Dwight	.30	.10
❑	192	Doug Flutie	.50	.20
❑	193	Junior Seau	.50	.20
❑	194	Marcellus Wiley	.20	.07
❑	195	Ryan McNeil	.20	.07
❑	196	Jeff Graham	.20	.07
❑	197	LaDainian Tomlinson	.75	.30
❑	198	Kevan Barlow	.30	.10
❑	199	Garrison Hearst	.30	.10
❑	200	Eric Johnson	.30	.10
❑	201	Terrell Owens	.50	.20
❑	202	J.J. Stokes	.30	.10
❑	203	Andre Carter	.20	.07
❑	204	Jeff Garcia	.50	.20
❑	205	Trent Dilfer	.30	.10
❑	206	Matt Hasselbeck	.30	.10
❑	207	Darrell Jackson	.30	.10
❑	208	Koren Robinson	.30	.10
❑	209	Ricky Watters	.30	.10
❑	210	John Randle	.20	.07
❑	211	Shaun Alexander	.60	.25
❑	212	Isaac Bruce	.50	.20
❑	213	Trung Canidate	.30	.10
❑	214	Marshall Faulk	.50	.20
❑	215	Az-Zahir Hakim	.20	.07
❑	216	Torry Holt	.50	.20
❑	217	Yo Murphy	.20	.07
❑	218	Ricky Proehl	.20	.07
❑	219	Adam Archuleta	.20	.07
❑	220	Dre Bly	.20	.07
❑	221	London Fletcher	.20	.07
❑	222	Tommy Polley	.20	.07
❑	223	Aeneas Williams	.20	.07
❑	224	Kurt Warner	.50	.20
❑	225	Mike Alstott	.50	.20
❑	226	Warrick Dunn	.50	.20
❑	227	Jacquez Green	.20	.07
❑	228	Derrick Brooks	.50	.20
❑	229	John Lynch	.30	.10
❑	230	Warren Sapp	.30	.10
❑	231	Ronde Barber	.20	.07
❑	232	Brad Johnson	.30	.10
❑	233	Keyshawn Johnson	.50	.20
❑	234	Drew Bennett	.50	.20
❑	235	Kevin Dyson	.30	.10
❑	236	Eddie George	.50	.20
❑	237	Derrick Mason	.30	.10
❑	238	Justin McCareins	.30	.10
❑	239	Frank Wycheck	.20	.07
❑	240	Jevon Kearse	.30	.10
❑	241	Samari Rolle	.20	.07
❑	242	Steve McNair	.50	.20
❑	243	Tony Banks	.20	.07
❑	244	Stephen Davis	.30	.10
❑	245	Michael Westbrook	.20	.07
❑	246	Champ Bailey	.30	.10
❑	247	Darrell Green	.20	.07
❑	248	Bruce Smith	.20	.07
❑	249	Fred Smoot	.20	.07
❑	250	Rod Gardner	.30	.10
❑	251	David Carr RC	3.00	1.25
❑	252	Joey Harrington RC	2.00	.75
❑	253	Patrick Ramsey RC	1.50	.60
❑	254	Kurt Kittner RC	.60	.25
❑	255	Eric Crouch RC	1.25	.50
❑	256	Josh McCown RC	1.50	.60
❑	257	David Garrard RC	1.25	.50
❑	258	Rohan Davey RC	1.25	.50
❑	259	Ronald Curry RC	1.25	.50
❑	260	Chad Hutchinson RC	.60	.25
❑	261	William Green RC	1.25	.50
❑	262	T.J. Duckett RC	1.50	.60
❑	263	Clinton Portis RC	4.00	1.50
❑	264	DeShaun Foster RC	1.25	.50
❑	265	Luke Staley RC	.60	.25
❑	266	Wes Pate RC	.50	.20
❑	267	Travis Stephens RC	.60	.25
❑	268	Adrian Peterson RC	1.25	.50
❑	269	Zak Kustok RC	1.25	.50
❑	270	Maurice Morris RC	1.25	.50
❑	271	Lamar Gordon RC	1.25	.50
❑	272	Chester Taylor RC	2.50	1.00
❑	273	Najeh Davenport RC	1.25	.50
❑	274	Ladell Betts RC	1.25	.50
❑	275	Ashley Lelie RC	2.50	1.00
❑	276	Josh Reed RC	1.25	.50
❑	277	Cliff Russell RC	.60	.25
❑	278	Javon Walker RC	2.50	1.00
❑	279	Ron Johnson RC	.60	.25
❑	280	Antwaan Randle El RC	2.00	.75
❑	281	Andre Davis RC	.60	.25
❑	282	Marquise Walker RC	.60	.25
❑	283	Kelly Campbell RC	.60	.25
❑	284	Tavon Mason RC	.50	.20
❑	285	Antonio Bryant RC	1.25	.50
❑	286	Jabar Gaffney RC	1.25	.50
❑	287	Donte Stallworth RC	2.50	1.00
❑	288	Tim Carter RC	.60	.25
❑	289	Reche Caldwell RC	1.25	.50
❑	290	Freddie Milons RC	.60	.25
❑	291	Brian Poli-Dixon RC	.60	.25
❑	292	Brian Westbrook RC	2.00	.75
❑	293	Josh Scobey RC	1.25	.50
❑	294	Jeremy Shockey RC	4.00	1.50
❑	295	Daniel Graham RC	1.25	.50
❑	296	Deion Branch RC	2.50	1.00
❑	297	Julius Peppers RC	2.50	1.00
❑	298	Kalimba Edwards RC	1.25	.50
❑	299	Dwight Freeney RC	2.00	.75
❑	300	Terry Charles RC	.60	.25
❑	301	Alex Brown RC	1.25	.50
❑	302	Jason McAddley RC	.60	.25
❑	303	Michael Lewis RC	1.25	.50
❑	304	Dennis Johnson RC	.50	.20
❑	305	Albert Haynesworth RC	.60	.25
❑	306	Ryan Sims RC	1.25	.50
❑	307	Larry Tripplett RC	.50	.20
❑	308	Anthony Weaver RC	.60	.25
❑	309	Wendell Bryant RC	.50	.20
❑	310	John Henderson RC	1.25	.50
❑	311	Alan Harper RC	.50	.20
❑	312	Napoleon Harris RC	1.25	.50
❑	313	Bryan Thomas RC	.60	.25
❑	314	Andra Davis RC	.60	.25
❑	315	Levar Fisher RC	.50	.20
❑	316	Woody Dantzler RC	.60	.25
❑	317	Robert Thomas RC	1.25	.50
❑	318	Quentin Jammer RC	1.25	.50
❑	319	Lito Sheppard RC	1.25	.50
❑	320	Travis Fisher RC	1.25	.50
❑	321	Roy Williams RC	3.00	1.25
❑	322	Phillip Buchanon RC	1.25	.50

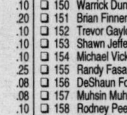

❑ 323	Joseph Jefferson RC	.60	.25
❑ 324	Ed Reed RC	2.00	.75
❑ 325	Lamont Thompson RC	.60	.25
❑ 326	Raonall Smith RC	.60	.25
❑ 327	Mike Rumph RC	1.25	.50
❑ 328	Rocky Calmus RC	1.25	.50
❑ 329	Bryant McKinnie RC	.60	.25
❑ 330	Mike Williams RC	.60	.25

2003 Score

❑	COMPLETE SET (327)	50.00	20.00
❑ 1	Jeff Blake	.20	.08
❑ 2	Todd Heap	.30	.10
❑ 3	Ron Johnson	.20	.08
❑ 4	Jamal Lewis	.50	.20
❑ 5	Ray Lewis	.50	.20
❑ 6	Chris Redman	.20	.08
❑ 7	Ed Reed	.30	.10
❑ 8	Travis Taylor	.20	.08
❑ 9	Anthony Weaver	.20	.08
❑ 10	Drew Bledsoe	.50	.20
❑ 11	Larry Centers	.20	.08
❑ 12	Nate Clements	.20	.08
❑ 13	Travis Henry	.30	.10
❑ 14	Eric Moulds	.30	.10
❑ 15	Peerless Price	.30	.10
❑ 16	Josh Reed	.30	.10
❑ 17	Coy Wire	.20	.08
❑ 18	Corey Dillon	.30	.10
❑ 19	T.J. Houshmandzadeh	.20	.08
❑ 20	Chad Johnson	.50	.20
❑ 21	Jon Kitna	.30	.10
❑ 22	Lorenzo Neal	.20	.08
❑ 23	Peter Warrick	.30	.10
❑ 24	Nicolas Luchey RC	.20	.08
❑ 25	Tim Couch	.20	.08
❑ 26	Andre Davis	.20	.08
❑ 27	William Green	.30	.10
❑ 28	Kevin Johnson	.30	.10
❑ 29	Quincy Morgan	.30	.10
❑ 30	Dennis Northcutt	.30	.10
❑ 31	Jamel White	.20	.08
❑ 32	Mike Anderson	.30	.10
❑ 33	Steve Beuerlein	.20	.08
❑ 34	Jason Elam	.20	.08
❑ 35	Olandis Gary	.30	.10
❑ 36	Brian Griese	.50	.20
❑ 37	Ashley Lelie	.50	.20
❑ 38	Ed McCaffrey	.30	.10
❑ 39	Clinton Portis	.75	.30
❑ 40	Shannon Sharpe	.30	.10
❑ 41	Rod Smith	.30	.10
❑ 42	James Allen	.30	.10
❑ 43	Corey Bradford	.20	.08
❑ 44	David Carr	.75	.30
❑ 45	JaJuan Dawson	.20	.08
❑ 46	Jabar Gaffney	.30	.10
❑ 47	Aaron Glenn	.20	.08
❑ 48	Billy Miller	.20	.08
❑ 49	Jonathan Wells	.20	.08
❑ 50	Dwight Freeney	.30	.10
❑ 51	Marvin Harrison	.50	.20
❑ 52	Qadry Ismail	.30	.10
❑ 53	Edgerrin James	.50	.20
❑ 54	Peyton Manning	.75	.30
❑ 55	James Mungro	.20	.08
❑ 56	Marcus Pollard	.20	.08
❑ 57	Reggie Wayne	.30	.10
❑ 58	Kyle Brady	.20	.08
❑ 59	Mark Brunell	.30	.10
❑ 60	David Garrard	.20	.08
❑ 61	John Henderson	.20	.08
❑ 62	Stacey Mack	.20	.08
❑ 63	Jimmy Smith	.30	.10
❑ 64	Fred Taylor	.50	.20
❑ 65	Marc Boerigter	.30	.10
❑ 66	Tony Gonzalez	.30	.10
❑ 67	Trent Green	.30	.10
❑ 68	Priest Holmes	.60	.25
❑ 69	Eddie Kennison	.20	.08
❑ 70	Snoop Minnis	.20	.08
❑ 71	Johnnie Morton	.30	.10
❑ 72	Cris Carter	.50	.20
❑ 73	Chris Chambers	.50	.20
❑ 74	Robert Edwards	.20	.08
❑ 75	Jay Fiedler	.30	.10
❑ 76	Ray Lucas	.20	.08
❑ 77	Randy McMichael	.30	.10
❑ 78	Travis Minor	.20	.08
❑ 79	Zach Thomas	.30	.10
❑ 80	Ricky Williams	.50	.20
❑ 81	Tom Brady	1.25	.50
❑ 82	Deion Branch	.50	.20
❑ 83	Troy Brown	.30	.10
❑ 84	Tedy Bruschi	.50	.20
❑ 85	Kevin Faulk	.20	.08
❑ 86	Daniel Graham	.20	.08
❑ 87	David Patten	.20	.08
❑ 88	Antowain Smith	.30	.10
❑ 89	Adam Vinatieri	.50	.20
❑ 90	Donnie Abraham	.20	.08
❑ 91	Anthony Becht	.20	.08
❑ 92	Wayne Chrebet	.30	.10
❑ 93	Laveranues Coles	.30	.10
❑ 94	LaMont Jordan	.50	.20
❑ 95	Curtis Martin	.50	.20
❑ 96	Chad Morton	.20	.08
❑ 97	Santana Moss	.30	.10
❑ 98	Chad Pennington	.60	.25
❑ 99	Vinny Testaverde	.30	.10
❑ 100	Tim Brown	.50	.20
❑ 101	Phillip Buchanon	.20	.08
❑ 102	Rich Gannon	.30	.10
❑ 103	Charlie Garner	.30	.10
❑ 104	Doug Jolley	.20	.08
❑ 105	Jerry Porter	.30	.10
❑ 106	Jerry Rice	1.00	.40
❑ 107	Marques Tuiasosopo	.30	.10
❑ 108	Charles Woodson	.30	.10
❑ 109	Rod Woodson	.30	.10
❑ 110	Kendrell Bell	.30	.10
❑ 111	Jerome Bettis	.50	.20
❑ 112	Plaxico Burress	.30	.10
❑ 113	Tommy Maddox	.50	.20
❑ 114	Joey Porter	.50	.20
❑ 115	Antwaan Randle El	.50	.20
❑ 116	Kordell Stewart	.30	.10
❑ 117	Hines Ward	.50	.20
❑ 118	Amos Zereoue	.30	.10
❑ 119	Drew Brees	.50	.20
❑ 120	Reche Caldwell	.20	.08
❑ 121	Curtis Conway	.20	.08
❑ 122	Tim Dwight	.30	.10
❑ 123	Doug Flutie	.50	.20
❑ 124	Quentin Jammer	.20	.08
❑ 125	Ben Leber	.20	.08
❑ 126	Josh Norman	.20	.08
❑ 127	Junior Seau	.50	.20
❑ 128	LaDainian Tomlinson	.50	.20
❑ 129	Keith Bulluck	.20	.08
❑ 130	Rocky Calmus	.20	.08
❑ 131	Kevin Carter	.20	.08
❑ 132	Kevin Dyson	.30	.10
❑ 133	Eddie George	.30	.10
❑ 134	Albert Haynesworth	.20	.08
❑ 135	Jevon Kearse	.30	.10
❑ 136	Derrick Mason	.30	.10
❑ 137	Justin McCareins	.20	.08
❑ 138	Steve McNair	.50	.20
❑ 139	Frank Wycheck	.20	.08
❑ 140	David Boston	.30	.10
❑ 141	MarTay Jenkins	.20	.08
❑ 142	Freddie Jones	.20	.08
❑ 143	Thomas Jones	.30	.10
❑ 144	Jason McAddley	.20	.08
❑ 145	Josh McCown	.30	.10
❑ 146	Jake Plummer	.30	.10
❑ 147	Marcel Shipp	.30	.10
❑ 148	Alge Crumpler	.30	.10
❑ 149	T.J. Duckett	.30	.10
❑ 150	Warrick Dunn	.30	.10
❑ 151	Brian Finneran	.20	.08
❑ 152	Trevor Gaylor	.20	.08
❑ 153	Shawn Jefferson	.20	.08
❑ 154	Michael Vick	1.25	.50
❑ 155	Randy Fasani	.20	.08
❑ 156	DeShaun Foster	.20	.08
❑ 157	Muhsin Muhammad	.30	.10
❑ 158	Rodney Peete	.20	.08
❑ 159	Julius Peppers	.50	.20
❑ 160	Lamar Smith	.20	.08
❑ 161	Steve Smith	.50	.20
❑ 162	Chris Weinke	.30	.10
❑ 163	Wesley Walls	.20	.08
❑ 164	Marty Booker	.30	.10
❑ 165	Mike Brown	.30	.10
❑ 166	Chris Chandler	.20	.08
❑ 167	Jim Miller	.20	.08
❑ 168	Marcus Robinson	.30	.10
❑ 169	David Terrell	.30	.10
❑ 170	Anthony Thomas	.30	.10
❑ 171	Brian Urlacher	.75	.30
❑ 172	Dez White	.20	.08
❑ 173	Antonio Bryant	.30	.10
❑ 174	Quincy Carter	.30	.10
❑ 175	Dexter Coakley	.20	.08
❑ 176	Joey Galloway	.30	.10
❑ 177	La'Roi Glover	.20	.08
❑ 178	Troy Hambrick	.20	.08
❑ 179	Chad Hutchinson	.20	.08
❑ 180	Rocket Ismail	.30	.10
❑ 181	Emmitt Smith	1.25	.50
❑ 182	Roy Williams	.50	.20
❑ 183	Scotty Anderson	.20	.08
❑ 184	Germane Crowell	.20	.08
❑ 185	Az-Zahir Hakim	.20	.08
❑ 186	Joey Harrington	.75	.30
❑ 187	Cory Schlesinger	.20	.08
❑ 188	Bill Schroeder	.30	.10
❑ 189	James Stewart	.30	.10
❑ 190	Marques Anderson	.20	.08
❑ 191	Najeh Davenport	.20	.08
❑ 192	Donald Driver	.30	.10
❑ 193	Brett Favre	1.25	.50
❑ 194	Bubba Franks	.30	.10
❑ 195	Terry Glenn	.20	.08
❑ 196	Ahman Green	.50	.20
❑ 197	Darren Sharper	.20	.08
❑ 198	Javon Walker	.30	.10
❑ 199	D'Wayne Bates	.20	.08
❑ 200	Michael Bennett	.30	.10
❑ 201	Todd Bouman	.20	.08
❑ 202	Byron Chamberlain	.20	.08
❑ 203	Daunte Culpepper	.50	.20
❑ 204	Randy Moss	.75	.30
❑ 205	Kelly Campbell	.30	.10
❑ 206	Aaron Brooks	.50	.20
❑ 207	Charles Grant	.20	.08
❑ 208	Joe Horn	.30	.10
❑ 209	Michael Lewis	.20	.08
❑ 210	Deuce McAllister	.50	.20
❑ 211	Jerome Pathon	.30	.10
❑ 212	Donte Stallworth	.50	.20
❑ 213	Boo Williams	.20	.08
❑ 214	Tiki Barber	.50	.20
❑ 215	Tim Carter	.30	.10
❑ 216	Kerry Collins	.30	.10
❑ 217	Ron Dayne	.20	.08
❑ 218	Jesse Palmer	.20	.08
❑ 219	Will Peterson	.20	.08
❑ 220	Jason Sehorn	.20	.08
❑ 221	Jeremy Shockey	.75	.30
❑ 222	Michael Strahan	.30	.10
❑ 223	Amani Toomer	.30	.10
❑ 224	Koy Detmer	.20	.08
❑ 225	Antonio Freeman	.30	.10
❑ 226	Dorsey Levens	.20	.08
❑ 227	Chad Lewis	.20	.08
❑ 228	Donovan McNabb	.60	.25
❑ 229	Freddie Mitchell	.30	.10
❑ 230	Duce Staley	.30	.10
❑ 231	James Thrash	.20	.08
❑ 232	Brian Westbrook	.30	.10

❑ 233 Kevan Barlow .30 .10
❑ 234 Andre Carter .20 .08
❑ 235 Jeff Garcia .50 .20
❑ 236 Garrison Hearst .30 .10
❑ 237 Eric Johnson .30 .10
❑ 238 Terrell Owens .50 .20
❑ 239 Jamal Robertson .30 .10
❑ 240 Tai Streets .20 .08
❑ 241 Shaun Alexander .50 .20
❑ 242 Trent Dilfer .30 .10
❑ 243 Bobby Engram .20 .08
❑ 244 Matt Hasselbeck .30 .10
❑ 245 Darrell Jackson .30 .10
❑ 246 Maurice Morris .20 .08
❑ 247 Koren Robinson .20 .08
❑ 248 Jerramy Stevens .20 .08
❑ 249 Isaac Bruce .50 .20
❑ 250 Marc Bulger .50 .20
❑ 251 Marshall Faulk .50 .20
❑ 252 Lamar Gordon .20 .08
❑ 253 Torry Holt .50 .20
❑ 254 Ricky Proehl .20 .08
❑ 255 Kurt Warner .50 .20
❑ 256 Aeneas Williams .20 .08
❑ 257 Mike Alstott .50 .20
❑ 258 Ken Dilger .20 .08
❑ 259 Brad Johnson .30 .10
❑ 260 Keyshawn Johnson .50 .20
❑ 261 Rob Johnson .30 .10
❑ 262 John Lynch .30 .10
❑ 263 Keenan McCardell .20 .08
❑ 264 Michael Pittman .20 .08
❑ 265 Warren Sapp .30 .10
❑ 266 Marquise Walker .20 .08
❑ 267 Champ Bailey .30 .10
❑ 268 Stephen Davis .30 .10
❑ 269 Rod Gardner .30 .10
❑ 270 Darrell Green .20 .08
❑ 271 Shane Matthews .20 .08
❑ 272 Damerien McCants .20 .08
❑ 273 Patrick Ramsey .50 .20
❑ 274 Bruce Smith .30 .10
❑ 275 Kenny Watson .20 .08
❑ 276 Carson Palmer RC 5.00 2.00
❑ 277 Byron Leftwich RC 4.00 1.50
❑ 278 Kyle Boller RC 1.25 .50
❑ 279 Chris Simms RC 2.00 .75
❑ 280 Dave Ragone RC 1.25 .50
❑ 281 Rex Grossman RC 4.00 1.50
❑ 282 Brian St.Pierre RC 1.25 .50
❑ 283 Larry Johnson RC 5.00 2.50
❑ 284 Lee Suggs RC 1.25 .50
❑ 285 Justin Fargas RC 1.25 .50
❑ 286 Onterrio Smith RC 1.25 .50
❑ 287 Willis McGahee RC 3.00 1.25
❑ 288 Chris Brown RC 1.25 .50
❑ 289 Musa Smith RC 1.25 .50
❑ 290 Artose Pinner RC 1.25 .50
❑ 291 Cecil Sapp RC 1.00 .40
❑ 292 Derek Watson SP RC
❑ 293 LaBrandon Toefield RC 1.25 .50
❑ 294 Charles Rogers RC 1.25 .50
❑ 295 Andre Johnson RC 2.50 1.00
❑ 296 Taylor Jacobs RC 1.00 .40
❑ 297 Bryant Johnson RC 1.25 .50
❑ 298 Kelley Washington RC 1.25 .50
❑ 299 Brandon Lloyd RC 1.25 .50
❑ 300 Justin Gage RC 1.25 .50
❑ 301 Tyrone Calico RC 1.25 .50
❑ 302 Kevin Curtis RC 1.25 .50
❑ 303 Sam Aiken RC 1.00 .40
❑ 304 Doug Gabriel RC 1.25 .50
❑ 305 Talman Gardner RC 1.25 .50
❑ 306 Jason Witten RC 2.00 .75
❑ 307 Mike Pinkard RC .60 .25
❑ 308 Teyo Johnson RC 1.25 .50
❑ 309 Bennie Joppru RC 1.25 .50
❑ 310 Dallas Clark RC 1.25 .50
❑ 311 Terrell Suggs RC 2.00 .75
❑ 312 Chris Kelsay RC 1.25 .50
❑ 313 Jerome McDougle RC 1.25 .50
❑ 314 Andrew Williams RC 1.00 .40
❑ 315 Michael Haynes RC 1.25 .50
❑ 316 Jimmy Kennedy RC 1.25 .50
❑ 317 Kevin Williams RC 1.25 .50
❑ 318 Ken Dorsey RC 1.25 .50
❑ 319 William Joseph RC 1.25 .50
❑ 320 Kenny Peterson RC 1.00 .40
❑ 321 Rien Long RC .60 .25
❑ 322 Boss Bailey RC 1.25 .50
❑ 323 E.J. Henderson SP RC
❑ 324 Terence Newman RC 2.50 1.00
❑ 325 Marcus Trufant RC 1.25 .50
❑ 326 Andre Woolfolk RC 1.25 .50
❑ 327 Dennis Weathersby RC .60 .25
❑ 328 Eugene Wilson SP RC
❑ 329 Mike Doss RC 1.25 .50
❑ 330 Rashean Mathis RC 1.00 .40

2004 Score

❑ COMPLETE SET (440) 80.00 40.00
❑ 1 Emmitt Smith 1.00 .40
❑ 2 Anquan Boldin .50 .20
❑ 3 Bryant Johnson .20 .07
❑ 4 Marcel Shipp .30 .10
❑ 5 Josh McCown .30 .10
❑ 6 Dexter Jackson .20 .07
❑ 7 Bertrand Berry .20 .07
❑ 8 Freddie Jones .20 .07
❑ 9 Duane Starks .20 .07
❑ 10 Michael Vick 1.00 .40
❑ 11 T.J. Duckett .30 .10
❑ 12 Warrick Dunn .30 .10
❑ 13 Peerless Price .30 .10
❑ 14 Alge Crumpler .30 .10
❑ 15 Brian Finneran .20 .07
❑ 16 Jason Webster .20 .07
❑ 17 Dez White .30 .10
❑ 18 Keith Brooking .20 .07
❑ 19 Rod Coleman .20 .07
❑ 20 Jamal Lewis .50 .20
❑ 21 Kyle Boller .50 .20
❑ 22 Todd Heap .30 .10
❑ 23 Jonathan Ogden .20 .07
❑ 24 Travis Taylor .20 .07
❑ 25 Ray Lewis .50 .20
❑ 26 Peter Boulware .30 .10
❑ 27 Terrell Suggs .30 .10
❑ 28 Chris McAlister .20 .07
❑ 29 Ed Reed .30 .10
❑ 30 Drew Bledsoe .50 .20
❑ 31 Travis Henry .30 .10
❑ 32 Eric Moulds .30 .10
❑ 33 Josh Reed .20 .07
❑ 34 Willis McGahee .50 .20
❑ 35 Takeo Spikes .20 .07
❑ 36 Lawyer Milloy .30 .10
❑ 37 Troy Vincent .20 .07
❑ 38 Sam Adams .20 .07
❑ 39 Nate Clements .20 .07
❑ 40 Jake Delhomme .50 .20
❑ 41 Stephen Davis .30 .10
❑ 42 DeShaun Foster .30 .10
❑ 43 Muhsin Muhammad .30 .10
❑ 44 Steve Smith .50 .20
❑ 45 Ricky Proehl .20 .07
❑ 46 Julius Peppers .50 .20
❑ 47 Kris Jenkins .20 .07
❑ 48 Dan Morgan .20 .07
❑ 49 Ricky Manning .20 .07
❑ 50 Brad Hoover .20 .07
❑ 51 Carson Palmer .60 .25
❑ 52 Rudi Johnson .30 .10
❑ 53 Corey Dillon .30 .10
❑ 54 Chad Johnson .50 .20
❑ 55 Peter Warrick .30 .10
❑ 56 Kelley Washington .20 .07
❑ 57 Kevin Hardy .20 .07
❑ 58 Tory James .20 .07
❑ 59 Ickey Woods .50 .20
❑ 60 Anthony Thomas .30 .10
❑ 61 Thomas Jones .30 .10
❑ 62 Rex Grossman .50 .20
❑ 63 Marty Booker .30 .10
❑ 64 Justin Gage .30 .10
❑ 65 David Terrell .30 .10
❑ 66 Brian Urlacher .60 .25
❑ 67 Mike Brown .20 .07
❑ 68 Charles Tillman .30 .10
❑ 69 Jeff Garcia .50 .20
❑ 70 Lee Suggs .50 .20
❑ 71 William Green .30 .10
❑ 72 Kelly Holcomb .30 .10
❑ 73 Quincy Morgan .30 .10
❑ 74 Andre Davis .20 .07
❑ 75 Dennis Northcutt .20 .07
❑ 76 Gerard Warren .20 .07
❑ 77 Courtney Brown .30 .10
❑ 78 Joey Harrington .50 .20
❑ 79 Shawn Bryson .20 .07
❑ 80 Charles Rogers .30 .10
❑ 81 Mikhael Ricks .20 .07
❑ 82 Artose Pinner .20 .07
❑ 83 Az-Zahir Hakim .20 .07
❑ 84 Dre Bly .20 .07
❑ 85 Fernando Bryant .20 .07
❑ 86 Boss Bailey .30 .10
❑ 87 Tai Streets .20 .07
❑ 88 Jake Plummer .30 .10
❑ 89 Quentin Griffin .50 .20
❑ 90 Mike Anderson .30 .10
❑ 91 Garrison Hearst .30 .10
❑ 92 Rod Smith .30 .10
❑ 93 Ashley Lelie .30 .10
❑ 94 Shannon Sharpe .30 .10
❑ 95 Al Wilson .20 .07
❑ 96 Champ Bailey .30 .10
❑ 97 Jason Elam .20 .07
❑ 98 John Lynch .30 .10
❑ 99 Quincy Carter .30 .10
❑ 100 Antonio Bryant .30 .10
❑ 101 Terry Glenn .20 .07
❑ 102 Keyshawn Johnson .30 .10
❑ 103 Jason Witten .30 .10
❑ 104 La'Roi Glover .20 .07
❑ 105 Dat Nguyen .20 .07
❑ 106 Dexter Coakley .20 .07
❑ 107 Terence Newman .30 .10
❑ 108 Darren Woodson .20 .07
❑ 109 Roy Williams S .30 .10
❑ 110 Brett Favre 1.25 .50
❑ 111 Ahman Green .50 .20
❑ 112 Najeh Davenport .20 .07
❑ 113 Donald Driver .30 .10
❑ 114 Robert Ferguson .20 .07
❑ 115 Javon Walker .30 .10
❑ 116 Bubba Franks .30 .10
❑ 117 Kabeer Gbaja-Biamila .30 .10
❑ 118 Darren Sharper .20 .07
❑ 119 Mike McKenzie .20 .07
❑ 120 Nick Barnett .30 .10
❑ 121 David Carr .50 .20
❑ 122 Domanick Davis .50 .20
❑ 123 Andre Johnson .50 .20
❑ 124 Corey Bradford .20 .07
❑ 125 Jabar Gaffney .30 .10
❑ 126 Billy Miller .20 .07
❑ 127 Gary Walker .20 .07
❑ 128 Jamie Sharper .20 .07
❑ 129 Aaron Glenn .20 .07
❑ 130 Robaire Smith .20 .07
❑ 131 Peyton Manning .75 .30
❑ 132 Edgerrin James .50 .20
❑ 133 Dominic Rhodes .30 .10
❑ 134 Marvin Harrison .50 .20
❑ 135 Reggie Wayne .30 .10
❑ 136 Brandon Stokley .30 .10
❑ 137 Marcus Pollard .20 .07
❑ 138 Dallas Clark .30 .10
❑ 139 Mike Vanderjagt .20 .07
❑ 140 Dwight Freeney .30 .10
❑ 141 Mike Doss .20 .07
❑ 142 Byron Leftwich .60 .25

❑ 143 Fred Taylor .30 .10
❑ 144 LaBrandon Toefield .20 .07
❑ 145 Jimmy Smith .30 .10
❑ 146 Kevin Johnson .20 .07
❑ 147 Marcus Stroud .20 .07
❑ 148 John Henderson .20 .07
❑ 149 Donovin Darius .20 .07
❑ 150 Deon Grant .20 .07
❑ 151 Rashean Mathis .20 .07
❑ 152 Trent Green .30 .10
❑ 153 Priest Holmes .60 .25
❑ 154 Johnnie Morton .30 .10
❑ 155 Eddie Kennison .20 .07
❑ 156 Marc Boerigter .30 .10
❑ 157 Tony Gonzalez .30 .10
❑ 158 Dante Hall .50 .20
❑ 159 Tony Richardson .20 .07
❑ 160 Gary Stills .20 .07
❑ 161 Daunte Culpepper .50 .20
❑ 162 Michael Bennett .30 .10
❑ 163 Moe Williams .20 .07
❑ 164 Onterrio Smith .30 .10
❑ 165 Jim Kleinsasser .20 .07
❑ 166 Antoine Winfield .20 .07
❑ 167 Nate Burleson .50 .20
❑ 168 Randy Moss .60 .25
❑ 169 Marcus Robinson .30 .10
❑ 170 Chris Hovan .20 .07
❑ 171 Brian Russell RC .50 .20
❑ 172 A.J. Feeley .50 .20
❑ 173 Jay Fiedler .20 .07
❑ 174 Ricky Williams .50 .20
❑ 175 Chris Chambers .30 .10
❑ 176 David Boston .30 .10
❑ 177 Randy McMichael .20 .07
❑ 178 Jason Taylor .20 .07
❑ 179 Adewale Ogunleye .30 .10
❑ 180 Zach Thomas .50 .20
❑ 181 Junior Seau .50 .20
❑ 182 Patrick Surtain .20 .07
❑ 183 Tom Brady 1.25 .50
❑ 184 Kevin Faulk .20 .07
❑ 185 Troy Brown .30 .10
❑ 186 Deion Branch .50 .20
❑ 187 David Givens .30 .10
❑ 188 Bethel Johnson .30 .10
❑ 189 Richard Seymour .20 .07
❑ 190 Tedy Bruschi .30 .10
❑ 191 Ty Law .30 .10
❑ 192 Rodney Harrison .20 .07
❑ 193 Willie McGinest .20 .07
❑ 194 Adam Vinatieri .50 .20
❑ 195 Aaron Brooks .30 .10
❑ 196 Deuce McAllister .50 .20
❑ 197 Joe Horn .30 .10
❑ 198 Donte Stallworth .30 .10
❑ 199 Jerome Pathon .20 .07
❑ 200 Boo Williams .20 .07
❑ 201 Charles Grant .20 .07
❑ 202 Darren Howard .20 .07
❑ 203 Michael Lewis .20 .07
❑ 204 Johnathan Sullivan .20 .07
❑ 205 LeCharles Bentley RC .20 .07
❑ 206 Kerry Collins .30 .10
❑ 207 Tiki Barber .50 .20
❑ 208 Amani Toomer .30 .10
❑ 209 Ike Hilliard .20 .07
❑ 210 Tim Carter .20 .07
❑ 211 Jeremy Shockey .50 .20
❑ 212 Michael Strahan .30 .10
❑ 213 Will Allen .20 .07
❑ 214 Will Peterson .20 .07
❑ 215 William Joseph .20 .07
❑ 216 Chad Pennington .50 .20
❑ 217 Curtis Martin .50 .20
❑ 218 LaMont Jordan .50 .20
❑ 219 Santana Moss .30 .10
❑ 220 Justin McCareins .20 .07
❑ 221 Wayne Chrebet .30 .10
❑ 222 Anthony Becht .20 .07
❑ 223 Shaun Ellis .20 .07
❑ 224 John Abraham .20 .07
❑ 225 DeWayne Robertson .20 .07
❑ 226 Rich Gannon .30 .10
❑ 227 Justin Fargas .30 .10
❑ 228 Tyrone Wheatley .20 .07
❑ 229 Jerry Rice 1.00 .40
❑ 230 Tim Brown .50 .20
❑ 231 Jerry Porter .30 .10
❑ 232 Teyo Johnson .20 .07
❑ 233 Charles Woodson .30 .10
❑ 234 Phillip Buchanon .20 .07
❑ 235 Rod Woodson .30 .10
❑ 236 Warren Sapp .30 .10
❑ 237 Donovan McNabb .60 .25
❑ 238 Brian Westbrook .30 .10
❑ 239 Correll Buckhalter .30 .10
❑ 240 Chad Lewis .20 .07
❑ 241 L.J. Smith .30 .10
❑ 242 Terrell Owens .50 .20
❑ 243 Todd Pinkston .20 .07
❑ 244 Freddie Mitchell .30 .10
❑ 245 Jevon Kearse .30 .10
❑ 246 Brian Dawkins .30 .10
❑ 247 Corey Simon .30 .10
❑ 248 Tommy Maddox .30 .10
❑ 249 Duce Staley .30 .10
❑ 250 Jerome Bettis .50 .20
❑ 251 Hines Ward .50 .20
❑ 252 Plaxico Burress .30 .10
❑ 253 Antwaan Randle El .50 .20
❑ 254 Kendrell Bell .30 .10
❑ 255 Joey Porter .30 .10
❑ 256 Alan Faneca .50 .20
❑ 257 Casey Hampton .20 .07
❑ 258 Drew Brees .50 .20
❑ 259 Doug Flutie .50 .20
❑ 260 LaDainian Tomlinson .60 .25
❑ 261 Reche Caldwell .20 .07
❑ 262 Tim Dwight .30 .10
❑ 263 Eric Parker .20 .07
❑ 264 Kevin Dyson .20 .07
❑ 265 Antonio Gates .50 .20
❑ 266 Quentin Jammer. .20 .07
❑ 267 Zeke Moreno .20 .07
❑ 268 Tim Rattay .20 .07
❑ 269 Kevan Barlow .30 .10
❑ 270 Cedrick Wilson .20 .07
❑ 271 Brandon Lloyd .30 .10
❑ 272 Fred Beasley .20 .07
❑ 273 Andre Carter .20 .07
❑ 274 Julian Peterson .20 .07
❑ 275 Ahmed Plummer .20 .07
❑ 276 Tony Parrish .20 .07
❑ 277 Bryant Young .20 .07
❑ 278 Matt Hasselbeck .30 .10
❑ 279 Shaun Alexander .50 .20
❑ 280 Maurice Morris .20 .07
❑ 281 Koren Robinson .30 .10
❑ 282 Darrell Jackson .30 .10
❑ 283 Bobby Engram .20 .07
❑ 284 Grant Wistrom .20 .07
❑ 285 Chad Brown .20 .07
❑ 286 Marcus Trufant .20 .07
❑ 287 Bobby Taylor .20 .07
❑ 288 Marc Bulger .50 .20
❑ 289 Kurt Warner .50 .20
❑ 290 Marshall Faulk .50 .20
❑ 291 Lamar Gordon .20 .07
❑ 292 Torry Holt .50 .20
❑ 293 Isaac Bruce .30 .10
❑ 294 Leonard Little .20 .07
❑ 295 Aeneas Williams .20 .07
❑ 296 Orlando Pace .20 .07
❑ 297 Tommy Polley .20 .07
❑ 298 Pisa Tinoisamoa .20 .07
❑ 299 Brad Johnson .30 .10
❑ 300 Michael Pittman .20 .07
❑ 301 Charlie Garner .30 .10
❑ 302 Mike Alstott .30 .10
❑ 303 Keenan McCardell .20 .07
❑ 304 Joey Galloway .30 .10
❑ 305 Joe Jurevicius .20 .07
❑ 306 Anthony McFarland .20 .07
❑ 307 Derrick Brooks .30 .10
❑ 308 Ronde Barber .20 .07
❑ 309 Shelton Quarles .20 .07
❑ 310 Steve McNair .50 .20
❑ 311 Eddie George .30 .10
❑ 312 Chris Brown .50 .20
❑ 313 Derrick Mason .30 .10
❑ 314 Tyrone Calico .30 .10
❑ 315 Drew Bennett .30 .10
❑ 316 Kevin Carter .20 .07
❑ 317 Keith Bulluck .20 .07
❑ 318 Samari Rolle .20 .07
❑ 319 Albert Haynesworth .20 .07
❑ 320 Erron Kinney .20 .07
❑ 321 Mark Brunell .30 .10
❑ 322 Patrick Ramsey .30 .10
❑ 323 Laveranues Coles .30 .10
❑ 324 Rod Gardner .30 .10
❑ 325 Damerien McCants .20 .07
❑ 326 Clinton Portis .50 .20
❑ 327 LaVar Arrington 1.00 .40
❑ 328 Shawn Springs .20 .07
❑ 329 Fred Smoot .20 .07
❑ 330 James Thrash .20 .07
❑ 331 Marvin Harrison PB .30 .10
❑ 332 Steve McNair PB .30 .10
❑ 333 Ray Lewis PB .30 .10
❑ 334 Trent Green PB .20 .07
❑ 335 Peyton Manning PB .50 .20
❑ 336 Priest Holmes PB .50 .20
❑ 337 Clinton Portis PB .50 .20
❑ 338 Torry Holt PB .30 .10
❑ 339 Anquan Boldin PB .20 .07
❑ 340 Daunte Culpepper PB .30 .10
❑ 341 Ahman Green PB .30 .10
❑ 342 Brian Urlacher PB .50 .20
❑ 343 Donovan McNabb PB .50 .20
❑ 344 Marc Bulger PB .30 .10
❑ 345 Shaun Alexander PB .30 .10
❑ 346 Peyton Manning LL .50 .20
❑ 347 Daunte Culpepper LL .30 .10
❑ 348 Brett Favre LL .50 .20
❑ 349 Steve McNair LL .30 .10
❑ 350 Tom Brady LL .50 .20
❑ 351 Jamal Lewis LL .30 .10
❑ 352 Deuce McAllister LL .30 .10
❑ 353 Clinton Portis LL .50 .20
❑ 354 Ahman Green LL .30 .10
❑ 355 LaDainian Tomlinson LL .40 .15
❑ 356 Torry Holt LL .30 .10
❑ 357 Anquan Boldin LL .20 .07
❑ 358 Randy Moss LL .50 .20
❑ 359 Chad Johnson LL .30 .10
❑ 360 Marvin Harrison LL .30 .10
❑ 361 Peyton Manning HL .50 .20
❑ 362 Jamal Lewis HL .30 .10
❑ 363 Ray Lewis HL .30 .10
❑ 364 Anquan Boldin HL .20 .07
❑ 365 Terrell Suggs HL .20 .07
❑ 366 Jamal Lewis HL .30 .10
❑ 367 Priest Holmes HL .50 .20
❑ 368 Tom Brady HL .50 .20
❑ 369 Marc Bulger HL .30 .10
❑ 370 Steve McNair HL .30 .10
❑ 371 Eli Manning RC 8.00 3.00
❑ 372 Robert Gallery RC 1.25 .50
❑ 373 Larry Fitzgerald RC 4.00 1.50
❑ 374 Philip Rivers RC 4.00 1.50
❑ 375 Sean Taylor RC 1.25 .50
❑ 376 Kellen Winslow RC 2.50 1.00
❑ 377 Roy Williams RC 3.00 1.25
❑ 378 DeAngelo Hall RC 1.50 .60
❑ 379 Reggie Williams RC 1.50 .60
❑ 380 Dunta Robinson RC 1.25 .50
❑ 381 Ben Roethlisberger RC 10.00 4.00
❑ 382 Jonathan Vilma RC 1.25 .50
❑ 383 Lee Evans RC 1.50 .60
❑ 384 Tommie Harris RC 1.25 .50
❑ 385 Michael Clayton RC 2.50 1.00
❑ 386 D.J. Williams RC 1.25 .50
❑ 387 Will Smith RC 1.25 .50
❑ 388 Kenechi Udeze RC 1.25 .50
❑ 389 Vince Wilfork RC 1.25 .50
❑ 390 J.P. Losman RC 2.50 1.00
❑ 391 Marcus Tubbs RC 1.25 .50
❑ 392 Steven Jackson RC 4.00 1.50
❑ 393 Ahmad Carroll RC 1.25 .50
❑ 394 Chris Perry RC 2.00 .75
❑ 395 Jason Babin RC 1.25 .50
❑ 396 Chris Gamble RC 1.25 .50
❑ 397 Michael Jenkins RC 1.25 .50
❑ 398 Kevin Jones RC 3.00 1.25
❑ 399 Rashaun Woods RC 1.25 .50
❑ 400 Ben Watson RC 1.25 .50
❑ 401 Karlos Dansby RC 1.25 .50
❑ 402 Igor Olshansky RC 1.25 .50
❑ 403 Junior Siavii RC 1.25 .50

❑ 404	Teddy Lehman RC	1.25	.50
❑ 405	Ricardo Colclough RC	1.25	.50
❑ 406	Daryl Smith RC	1.25	.50
❑ 407	Ben Troupe RC	1.25	.50
❑ 408	Tatum Bell RC	2.50	1.00
❑ 409	Travis LaBoy RC	1.25	.50
❑ 410	Julius Jones RC	4.00	1.50
❑ 411	Mewelde Moore RC	1.25	.50
❑ 412	Drew Henson RC	1.25	.50
❑ 413	Dontarrious Thomas RC	1.25	.50
❑ 414	Keiwan Ratliff RC	1.00	.40
❑ 415	Devery Henderson RC	1.00	.40
❑ 416	Dwan Edwards RC	.60	.25
❑ 417	Michael Boulware RC	1.25	.50
❑ 418	Darius Watts RC	1.25	.50
❑ 419	Greg Jones RC	1.25	.50
❑ 420	Madieu Williams RC	1.00	.40
❑ 421	Antwan Odom RC	1.25	.50
❑ 422	Shawntae Spencer RC	1.25	.50
❑ 423	Sean Jones RC	1.00	.40
❑ 424	Courtney Watson RC	1.25	.50
❑ 425	Kris Wilson RC	1.25	.50
❑ 426	Keary Colbert RC	1.50	.60
❑ 427	Marquise Hill RC	1.00	.40
❑ 428	Darnell Dockett RC	1.00	.40
❑ 429	Stuart Schweigert RC	1.25	.50
❑ 430	Ben Hartsock RC	1.25	.50
❑ 431	Joey Thomas RC	1.25	.50
❑ 432	Randy Starks RC	1.00	.40
❑ 433	Keith Smith RC	1.00	.40
❑ 434	Derrick Hamilton RC	1.00	.40
❑ 435	Bernard Berrian RC	1.50	.60
❑ 436	Chris Cooley RC	1.25	.50
❑ 437	Devard Darling RC	1.25	.50
❑ 438	Matt Schaub RC	4.00	1.50
❑ 439	Luke McCown RC	1.25	.50
❑ 440	Cedric Cobbs RC	1.25 -	.50

2005 Score

❑	COMPLETE SET (385)	80.00	40.00
❑	ONE ROOKIE PER PACK		
❑ 1	Anquan Boldin	.30	.10
❑ 2	Bertrand Berry	.25	.08
❑ 3	Bryant Johnson	.25	.08
❑ 4	Darnell Dockett	.25	.08
❑ 5	Freddie Jones	.25	.08
❑ 6	Josh McCown	.30	.10
❑ 7	Karlos Dansby	.25	.08
❑ 8	Larry Fitzgerald	.50	.20
❑ 9	Alge Crumpler	.30	.10
❑ 10	DeAngelo Hall	.30	.10
❑ 11	Keith Brooking	.25	.08
❑ 12	Michael Jenkins	.30	.10
❑ 13	Michael Vick	.75	.30
❑ 14	Peerless Price	.25	.08
❑ 15	Rod Coleman	.25	.08
❑ 16	T.J. Duckett	.30	.10
❑ 17	Warrick Dunn	.30	.10
❑ 18	Chris McAlister	.25	.08
❑ 19	Clarence Moore	.25	.08
❑ 20	Ed Reed	.30	.10
❑ 21	Jamal Lewis	.50	.20
❑ 22	Jonathan Ogden	.25	.08
❑ 23	Kyle Boller	.30	.10
❑ 24	Peter Boulware	.25	.08
❑ 25	Ray Lewis	.50	.20
❑ 26	Terrell Suggs	.30	.10
❑ 27	Todd Heap	.30	.10
❑ 28	Drew Bledsoe	.50	.20
❑ 29	Eric Moulds	.30	.10
❑ 30	Josh Reed	.25	.08
❑ 31	Lee Evans	.30	.10
❑ 32	Nate Clements	.25	.08
❑ 33	Takeo Spikes	.25	.08
❑ 34	Travis Henry	.30	.10
❑ 35	Willis McGahee	.50	.20
❑ 36	Dan Morgan	.25	.08
❑ 37	DeShaun Foster	.30	.10
❑ 38	Jake Delhomme	.50	.20
❑ 39	Julius Peppers	.30	.10
❑ 40	Keary Colbert	.30	.10
❑ 41	Kris Jenkins	.25	.08
❑ 42	Muhsin Muhammad	.30	.10
❑ 43	Nick Goings	.25	.08
❑ 44	Stephen Davis	.30	.10
❑ 45	Steve Smith	.30	.10
❑ 46	Anthony Thomas	.30	.10
❑ 47	Adewale Ogunleye	.25	.08
❑ 48	Bernard Berrian	.25	.08
❑ 49	Brian Urlacher	.50	.20
❑ 50	David Terrell	.30	.10
❑ 51	Mike Brown	.25	.08
❑ 52	Rex Grossman	.30	.10
❑ 53	Thomas Jones	.30	.10
❑ 54	Tommie Harris	.25	.08
❑ 55	Carson Palmer	.50	.20
❑ 56	Chad Johnson	.50	.20
❑ 57	Chris Perry	.30	.10
❑ 58	Kelley Washington	.25	.08
❑ 59	Madieu Williams	.25	.08
❑ 60	Peter Warrick	.25	.08
❑ 61	Rudi Johnson	.30	.10
❑ 62	T.J. Houshmandzadeh	.25	.08
❑ 63	Tory James	.25	.08
❑ 64	Andre Davis	.25	.08
❑ 65	Antonio Bryant	.25	.08
❑ 66	Dennis Northcutt	.25	.08
❑ 67	Gerard Warren	.25	.08
❑ 68	Jeff Garcia	.30	.10
❑ 69	Kellen Winslow Jr.	.50	.20
❑ 70	Lee Suggs	.30	.10
❑ 71	William Green	.25	.08
❑ 72	Drew Henson	.30	.10
❑ 73	Jason Witten	.30	.10
❑ 74	Julius Jones	.60	.25
❑ 75	Keyshawn Johnson	.30	.10
❑ 76	La'Roi Glover	.25	.08
❑ 77	J.P. Losman	.50	.20
❑ 78	Roy Williams S	.30	.10
❑ 79	Terence Newman	.25	.08
❑ 80	Terry Glenn	.25	.08
❑ 81	Al Wilson	.25	.08
❑ 82	Ashley Lelie	.30	.10
❑ 83	Champ Bailey	.30	.10
❑ 84	D.J. Williams	.25	.08
❑ 85	Jake Plummer	.30	.10
❑ 86	Jason Elam	.25	.08
❑ 87	John Lynch	.30	.10
❑ 88	Reuben Droughns	.30	.10
❑ 89	Rod Smith	.30	.10
❑ 90	Tatum Bell	.30	.10
❑ 91	Trent Dilfer	.30	.10
❑ 92	Charles Rogers	.30	.10
❑ 93	Dre' Bly	.25	.08
❑ 94	Joey Harrington	.50	.20
❑ 95	Kevin Jones	.50	.20
❑ 96	Roy Williams WR	.50	.20
❑ 97	Shawn Bryson	.25	.08
❑ 98	Tai Streets	.25	.08
❑ 99	Teddy Lehman	.25	.08
❑ 100	Ahman Green	.50	.20
❑ 101	Brett Favre	1.25	.50
❑ 102	Bubba Franks	.30	.10
❑ 103	Darren Sharper	.25	.08
❑ 104	Donald Driver	.30	.10
❑ 105	Javon Walker	.30	.10
❑ 106	Najeh Davenport	.25	.08
❑ 107	Nick Barnett	.25	.08
❑ 108	Robert Ferguson	.25	.08
❑ 109	Aaron Glenn	.25	.08
❑ 110	Andre Johnson	.30	.10
❑ 111	Corey Bradford	.25	.08
❑ 112	David Carr	.50	.20
❑ 113	Domanick Davis	.30	.10
❑ 114	Dunta Robinson	.30	.10
❑ 115	Jabar Gaffney	.25	.08
❑ 116	Jamie Sharper	.25	.08
❑ 117	Jason Babin	.25	.08
❑ 118	Brandon Stokley	.30	.10
❑ 119	Dallas Clark	.25	.08
❑ 120	Dwight Freeney	.30	.10
❑ 121	Edgerrin James	.50	.20
❑ 122	Marcus Pollard	.25	.08
❑ 123	Marvin Harrison	.50	.20
❑ 124	Peyton Manning	.75	.30
❑ 125	Reggie Wayne	.30	.10
❑ 126	Robert Mathis RC	1.25	.50
❑ 127	Byron Leftwich	.50	.20
❑ 128	Daryl Smith	.25	.08
❑ 129	Donovan Darius	.25	.08
❑ 130	Ernest Wilford	.25	.08
❑ 131	Fred Taylor	.30	.10
❑ 132	Jimmy Smith	.30	.10
❑ 133	John Henderson	.25	.08
❑ 134	Marcus Stroud	.25	.08
❑ 135	Reggie Williams	.30	.10
❑ 136	Dante Hall	.30	.10
❑ 137	Eddie Kennison	.25	.08
❑ 138	Jared Allen	.30	.10
❑ 139	Johnnie Morton	.30	.10
❑ 140	Larry Johnson	.50	.20
❑ 141	Priest Holmes	.50	.20
❑ 142	Samie Parker	.25	.08
❑ 143	Tony Gonzalez	.30	.10
❑ 144	Trent Green	.30	.10
❑ 145	A.J. Feeley	.30	.10
❑ 146	Chris Chambers	.30	.10
❑ 147	Jason Taylor	.25	.08
❑ 148	Junior Seau	.30	.10
❑ 149	Marty Booker	.30	.10
❑ 150	Patrick Surtain	.25	.08
❑ 151	Randy McMichael	.25	.08
❑ 152	Sammy Morris	.25	.08
❑ 153	Zach Thomas	.50	.20
❑ 154	Daunte Culpepper	.50	.20
❑ 155	Jim Kleinsasser	.25	.08
❑ 156	Kelly Campbell	.25	.08
❑ 157	Kevin Williams	.25	.08
❑ 158	Marcus Robinson	.30	.10
❑ 159	Mewelde Moore	.30	.10
❑ 160	Michael Bennett	.30	.10
❑ 161	Nate Burleson	.30	.10
❑ 162	Onterrio Smith	.30	.10
❑ 163	Randy Moss	.50	.20
❑ 164	Adam Vinatieri	.50	.20
❑ 165	Corey Dillon	.30	.10
❑ 166	David Givens	.30	.10
❑ 167	David Patten	.25	.08
❑ 168	Deion Branch	.30	.10
❑ 169	Mike Vrabel	.30	.10
❑ 170	Richard Seymour	.30	.10
❑ 171	Tedy Bruschi	.30	.10
❑ 172	Tom Brady	1.25	.50
❑ 173	Troy Brown	.30	.10
❑ 174	Ty Law	.30	.10
❑ 175	Aaron Brooks	.30	.10
❑ 176	Charles Grant	.25	.08
❑ 177	Deuce McAllister	.50	.20
❑ 178	Devery Henderson	.25	.08
❑ 179	Donte Stallworth	.30	.10
❑ 180	Jerome Pathon	.25	.08
❑ 181	Joe Horn	.30	.10
❑ 182	Will Smith	.25	.08
❑ 183	Amani Toomer	.30	.10
❑ 184	Eli Manning	1.00	.40
❑ 185	Gibril Wilson	.25	.08
❑ 186	Ike Hilliard	.30	.10
❑ 187	Jeremy Shockey	.50	.20
❑ 188	Michael Strahan	.30	.10
❑ 189	Tiki Barber	.50	.20
❑ 190	Jamaar Taylor	.25	.08
❑ 191	Tim Carter	.25	.08
❑ 192	Chad Pennington	.50	.20
❑ 193	DeWayne Robertson	.25	.08
❑ 194	Curtis Martin	.50	.20
❑ 195	John Abraham	.25	.08
❑ 196	Jonathan Vilma	.30	.10
❑ 197	Justin McCareins	.25	.08
❑ 198	LaMont Jordan	.50	.20
❑ 199	Santana Moss	.30	.10
❑ 200	Shaun Ellis	.25	.08
❑ 201	Wayne Chrebet	.30	.10
❑ 202	Charles Woodson	.30	.10

❑ 203 Doug Jolley .25 .08
❑ 204 Jerry Porter .30 .10
❑ 205 Justin Fargas .25 .08
❑ 206 Kerry Collins .30 .10
❑ 207 Robert Gallery .30 .10
❑ 208 Ronald Curry .30 .10
❑ 209 Sebastian Janikowski .25 .08
❑ 210 Tyrone Wheatley .25 .08
❑ 211 Warren Sapp .30 .10
❑ 212 Brian Dawkins .30 .10
❑ 213 Brian Westbrook .30 .10
❑ 214 Chad Lewis .25 .08
❑ 215 Corey Simon .25 .08
❑ 216 Donovan McNabb .60 .25
❑ 217 Freddie Mitchell .25 .08
❑ 218 Jevon Kearse .30 .10
❑ 219 L.J. Smith .25 .08
❑ 220 Lito Sheppard .25 .08
❑ 221 Terrell Owens .50 .20
❑ 222 Todd Pinkston .25 .08
❑ 223 Alan Faneca .50 .20
❑ 224 Antwaan Randle El .30 .10
❑ 225 Ben Roethlisberger 1.25 .50
❑ 226 Duce Staley .30 .10
❑ 227 Hines Ward .50 .20
❑ 228 James Farrior .25 .08
❑ 229 Jerome Bettis .50 .20
❑ 230 Joey Porter .30 .10
❑ 231 Kendrell Bell .30 .10
❑ 232 Plaxico Burress .30 .10
❑ 233 Troy Polamalu .75 .30
❑ 234 Antonio Gates .50 .20
❑ 235 Reche Caldwell .25 .08
❑ 236 Doug Flutie .50 .20
❑ 237 Drew Brees .50 .20
❑ 238 Eric Parker .25 .08
❑ 239 Keenan McCardell .25 .08
❑ 240 LaDainian Tomlinson .60 .25
❑ 241 Philip Rivers .50 .20
❑ 242 Quentin Jammer .25 .08
❑ 243 Tim Dwight .25 .08
❑ 244 Brandon Lloyd .25 .08
❑ 245 Bryant Young .25 .08
❑ 246 Cedrick Wilson .25 .08
❑ 247 Eric Johnson .30 .10
❑ 248 Julian Peterson .25 .08
❑ 249 Kevan Barlow .30 .10
❑ 250 Rashaun Woods .30 .10
❑ 251 Maurice Hicks RC .50 .20
❑ 252 Tim Rattay .25 .08
❑ 253 Bobby Engram .25 .08
❑ 254 Chad Brown .25 .08
❑ 255 Darrell Jackson .30 .10
❑ 256 Grant Wistrom .25 .08
❑ 257 Jerramy Stevens .25 .08
❑ 258 Koren Robinson .30 .10
❑ 259 Marcus Trufant .25 .08
❑ 260 Matt Hasselbeck .30 .10
❑ 261 Michael Boulware .25 .08
❑ 262 Shaun Alexander .60 .25
❑ 263 Isaac Bruce .30 .10
❑ 264 Leonard Little .25 .08
❑ 265 Marc Bulger .50 .20
❑ 266 Marshall Faulk .50 .20
❑ 267 Orlando Pace .25 .08
❑ 268 Pisa Tinoisamoa .25 .08
❑ 269 Shaun McDonald .25 .08
❑ 270 Steven Jackson .60 .25
❑ 271 Torry Holt .50 .20
❑ 272 Anthony McFarland .25 .08
❑ 273 Brian Griese .30 .10
❑ 274 Charlie Garner .30 .10
❑ 275 Derrick Brooks .30 .10
❑ 276 Joe Jurevicius .25 .08
❑ 277 Joey Galloway .30 .10
❑ 278 Michael Clayton .50 .20
❑ 279 Michael Pittman .25 .08
❑ 280 Mike Alstott .30 .10
❑ 281 Ronde Barber .25 .08
❑ 282 Albert Haynesworth .25 .08
❑ 283 Ben Troupe .25 .08
❑ 284 Billy Volek .30 .10
❑ 285 Chris Brown .30 .10
❑ 286 Derrick Mason .30 .10
❑ 287 Drew Bennett .30 .10
❑ 288 Keith Bulluck .25 .08
❑ 289 Kevin Carter .25 .08
❑ 290 Samari Rolle .25 .08
❑ 291 Steve McNair .50 .20
❑ 292 Tyrone Calico .30 .10
❑ 293 Chris Cooley .30 .10
❑ 294 Clinton Portis .50 .20
❑ 295 Fred Smoot .25 .08
❑ 296 LaVar Arrington .50 .20
❑ 297 Laveranues Coles .30 .10
❑ 298 Patrick Ramsey .30 .10
❑ 299 Rod Gardner .30 .10
❑ 300 Sean Taylor .30 .10
❑ 301 Michael Vick PB .50 .20
❑ 302 Daunte Culpepper PB .30 .10
❑ 303 Donovan McNabb PB .50 .20
❑ 304 Brian Westbrook PB .25 .08
❑ 305 Tiki Barber PB .30 .10
❑ 306 Ahman Green PB .30 .10
❑ 307 Joe Horn PB .25 .08
❑ 308 Javon Walker PB .25 .08
❑ 309 Torry Holt PB .30 .10
❑ 310 Muhsin Muhammad PB .25 .08
❑ 311 Jason Witten PB .25 .08
❑ 312 Alge Crumpler PB .25 .08
❑ 313 Peyton Manning PB .50 .20
❑ 314 Tom Brady PB .50 .20
❑ 315 Drew Brees PB .30 .10
❑ 316 LaDainian Tomlinson PB .50 .20
❑ 317 Rudi Johnson PB .25 .08
❑ 318 Jerome Bettis PB .30 .10
❑ 319 Marvin Harrison PB .30 .10
❑ 320 Hines Ward PB .30 .10
❑ 321 Andre Johnson PB .25 .08
❑ 322 Chad Johnson PB .30 .10
❑ 323 Tony Gonzalez PB .25 .08
❑ 324 Adam Vinatieri PB .30 .10
❑ 325 David Akers PB .25 .08
❑ 326 Takeo Spikes PB .25 .08
❑ 327 Joey Porter PB .25 .08
❑ 328 Tedy Bruschi PB .30 .10
❑ 329 Ed Reed PB .30 .10
❑ 330 Terrell Owens PB .30 .10
❑ 331 Alex Smith QB RC 4.00 1.50
❑ 332 Ronnie Brown RC 4.00 1.50
❑ 333 Braylon Edwards RC 3.00 1.25
❑ 334 Cedric Benson RC 2.00 .75
❑ 335 Cadillac Williams RC 5.00 2.00
❑ 336 Adam Jones RC 1.00 .40
❑ 337 Troy Williamson RC 2.00 .75
❑ 338 Antrel Rolle RC 1.00 .40
❑ 339 Carlos Rogers RC 1.25 .50
❑ 340 Mike Williams 2.00 .75
❑ 341 DeMarcus Ware RC 1.50 .60
❑ 342 Shawne Merriman RC 1.50 .60
❑ 343 Thomas Davis RC 1.00 .40
❑ 344 Derrick Johnson RC 1.50 .60
❑ 345 Travis Johnson RC 1.00 .40
❑ 346 David Pollack RC 1.00 .40
❑ 347 Erasmus James RC 1.00 .40
❑ 348 Marcus Spears RC 1.00 .40
❑ 349 Matt Jones RC 2.50 1.00
❑ 350 Mark Clayton RC 1.25 .50
❑ 351 Fabian Washington RC 1.00 .40
❑ 352 Aaron Rodgers RC 3.00 1.25
❑ 353 Jason Campbell RC 1.50 .60
❑ 354 Roddy White RC 1.00 .40
❑ 355 Marlin Jackson RC 1.00 .40
❑ 356 Heath Miller RC 2.50 1.00
❑ 357 Mike Patterson RC 1.00 .40
❑ 358 Reggie Brown RC 1.00 .40
❑ 359 Shaun Cody RC 1.00 .40
❑ 360 Mark Bradley RC 1.00 .40
❑ 361 J.J. Arrington RC 1.25 .50
❑ 362 Dan Cody RC 1.00 .40
❑ 363 Eric Shelton RC 1.00 .40
❑ 364 Roscoe Parrish RC 1.00 .40
❑ 365 Terrence Murphy RC 1.00 .40
❑ 366 Vincent Jackson RC 1.00 .40
❑ 367 Frank Gore RC 2.00 .75
❑ 368 Charlie Frye RC 2.00 .75
❑ 369 Courtney Roby RC 1.00 .40
❑ 370 Andrew Walter RC 1.50 .60
❑ 371 Vernand Morency RC 1.00 .40
❑ 372 Ryan Moats RC 1.00 .40
❑ 373 Chris Henry RC 1.00 .40
❑ 374 David Greene RC 1.00 .40
❑ 375 Brandon Jones RC 1.00 .40
❑ 376 Maurice Clarett 1.00 .40
❑ 377 Kyle Orton RC 1.50 .60
❑ 378 Marion Barber RC 1.50 .60
❑ 379 Brandon Jacobs RC 1.25 .50
❑ 380 Ciatrick Fason RC 1.00 .40
❑ 381 Jerome Mathis RC 1.00 .40
❑ 382 Craphonso Thorpe RC 1.00 .40
❑ 383 Stefan LeFors RC 1.00 .40
❑ 384 Darren Sproles RC 1.00 .40
❑ 385 Fred Gibson RC 1.00 .40

2002 Score QBC Materials

❑ AUTOGRAPH CARDS TOO SCARCE TO PRICE
❑ 1 Donovan McNabb JSY 25.00 10.00
❑ 2 Jake Plummer JSY 10.00 4.00
❑ 3 Jeff Garcia JSY 12.00 5.00
❑ 4 Peyton Manning JSY 30.00 12.50
❑ 5 Rob Johnson JSY 10.00 4.00
❑ 6 Trent Dilfer JSY 10.00 4.00
❑ 7 Bernie Kosar JSY 10.00 4.00
❑ 8 Boomer Esiason JSY 12.00 5.00
❑ 9 Jim Everett JSY 10.00 4.00
❑ 10 Jim Kelly JSY 12.00 5.00
❑ 11 Steve Young JSY 20.00 7.50
❑ 12 Warren Moon JSY 12.00 5.00
❑ 13 Donovan McNabb FB 25.00 10.00
❑ 14 Jeff Garcia FB 12.00 5.00
❑ 15 Peyton Manning FB 30.00 12.50
❑ 16 Boomer Esiason FB 12.00 5.00
❑ 17 Jim Kelly FB 12.00 5.00
❑ 18 Steve Young FB 20.00 7.50
❑ 19 Warren Moon FB 12.00 5.00
❑ 20 Peyton Manning JSY 30.00 12.50
❑ 21 Doug Flutie JSY 15.00 6.00
❑ 22 Jeff Garcia JSY 12.00 5.00
❑ 23 Jake Plummer JSY 10.00 4.00
❑ 24 Aaron Brooks JSY 12.00 5.00
❑ 25 John Elway JSY 40.00 25.00
❑ 26 Boomer Esiason JSY 10.00 4.00
❑ 27 Warren Moon JSY 12.00 5.00
❑ 28 Jim Everett JSY 10.00 4.00
❑ 29 John Elway FB 40.00 25.00
❑ 30 Warren Moon FB 12.00 5.00
❑ 31 Jake Plummer FB 10.00 4.00
❑ 32 Peyton Manning FB 30.00 12.50
❑ 33 Jeff Garcia FB 12.00 5.00
❑ 34 Aaron Brooks FB 12.00 5.00
❑ 35 Doug Flutie FB 15.00 6.00
❑ 36 Boomer Esiason FB 12.00 5.00
❑ 37 Ken O'Brien JSY 8.00 3.00

1997 Score Board NFL Experience

❑ COMPLETE SET (100) 12.00 5.00
❑ 1 Emmitt Smith 1.25 .50
❑ 2 Kordell Stewart .40 .15
❑ 3 Antonio Freeman .40 .15
❑ 4 William Thomas .15 .05
❑ 5 Simeon Rice .25 .08
❑ 6 Drew Bledsoe .50 .20
❑ 7 Elvis Grbac .25 .08
❑ 8 Ken Dilger .15 .05
❑ 9 John Elway 1.50 .60
❑ 10 Curtis Conway .25 .08
❑ 11 Adrian Murrell .25 .08
❑ 12 Karim Abdul-Jabbar .40 .15
❑ 13 Terry Allen .40 .15
❑ 14 Lawrence Phillips .15 .05

❑	15 Barry Sanders	1.25	.50
❑	16 Shannon Sharpe	.25	.08
❑	17 Troy Aikman	.75	.30
❑	18 Kevin Greene	.25	.08
❑	19 Cris Carter	.40	.15
❑	20 Jim Kelly	.40	.15
❑	21 Eric Metcalf	.25	.08
❑	22 Joey Galloway	.25	.08
❑	23 Eddie George	.40	.15
❑	24 Scott Mitchell	.25	.08
❑	25 Neil O'Donnell	.25	.08
❑	26 Ben Coates	.25	.08
❑	27 Andre Reed	.25	.08
❑	28 Michael Jackson	.25	.08
❑	29 Keith Jackson	.15	.05
❑	30 J.J. Stokes	.25	.08
❑	31 Rickey Dudley	.25	.08
❑	32 Ricky Watters	.25	.08
❑	33 Marcus Allen	.40	.15
❑	34 Brett Favre	1.50	.60
❑	35 Kevin Hardy	.15	.05
❑	36 Jim Everett	.15	.05
❑	37 Zach Thomas	.40	.15
❑	38 Lamar Lathon	.15	.05
❑	39 LeShon Johnson	.15	.05
❑	40 Bruce Smith	.25	.08
❑	41 Junior Seau	.40	.15
❑	42 Tony Banks	.25	.08
❑	43 Brian Mitchell	.15	.05
❑	44 Chris T. Jones	.15	.05
❑	45 Ty Detmer	.25	.08
❑	46 Robert Brooks	.25	.08
❑	47 Derrick Thomas	.40	.15
❑	48 Dan Wilkinson	.15	.05
❑	49 Michael Sinclair	.15	.05
❑	50 Dave Brown	.15	.05
❑	51 Carl Pickens	.25	.08
❑	52 Jim Harbaugh	.25	.08
❑	53 Wayne Chrebet	.40	.15
❑	54 Warren Moon	.40	.15
❑	55 Steve Young	.50	.20
❑	56 Sean Gilbert	.15	.05
❑	57 Jerome Bettis	.40	.15
❑	58 Dan Marino	1.50	.60
❑	59 Terrell Davis	.60	.25
❑	60 Mark Brunell	.50	.20
❑	61 Kent Graham	.15	.05
❑	62 Rashaan Salaam	.25	.08
❑	63 Tony Martin	.25	.08
❑	64 Robert Smith	.25	.08
❑	65 Thurman Thomas	.40	.15
❑	66 Marshall Faulk	.50	.20
❑	67 Dale Carter	.15	.05
❑	68 Stan Humphries	.25	.08
❑	69 Isaac Bruce	.40	.15
❑	70 Warren Sapp	.25	.08
❑	71 Kerry Collins	.40	.15
❑	72 Jamal Anderson	.40	.15
❑	73 Chris Chandler	.25	.08
❑	74 Herman Moore	.25	.08
❑	75 Rodney Hampton	.25	.08
❑	76 Tim Brown	.40	.15
❑	77 Keenan McCardell	.25	.08
❑	78 Anthony Miller	.15	.05
❑	79 Jake Reed	.25	.08
❑	80 Earnest Byner	.15	.05
❑	81 Chris Warren	.25	.08
❑	82 Deion Sanders	.40	.15
❑	83 Mike Tomczak	.15	.05
❑	84 Curtis Martin	.50	.20
❑	85 John Friesz	.15	.05
❑	86 Gus Frerotte	.15	.05
❑	87 Vinny Testaverde	.25	.08
❑	88 Jason Dunn	.15	.05
❑	89 James O.Stewart	.25	.08
❑	90 Steve Bono	.25	.08
❑	91 Levon Kirkland	.15	.05
❑	92 Merton Hanks	.15	.05
❑	93 Marvin Harrison	.40	.15
❑	94 Reggie Brooks	.15	.05
❑	95 Reggie White	.40	.15
❑	96 Jeff Blake	.25	.08
❑	97 Terry Glenn	.40	.15
❑	98 Jerry Rice	.75	.30
❑	99 Keyshawn Johnson	.40	.15
❑	100 Edgar Bennett CL	.15	.05
❑	P1 Promo Sheet	3.00	1.20

1997 Score Board Playbook

❑	COMPLETE SET (100)	15.00	6.00
❑	1 Warren Moon	.40	.15
❑	2 Troy Aikman	.75	.30
❑	3 Jeff George	.25	.08
❑	4 Brett Favre	1.50	.60
❑	5 Jim Harbaugh	.25	.08
❑	6 Jeff Blake	.25	.08
❑	7 John Elway	1.50	.60
❑	8 Mark Brunell	.50	.20
❑	9 Steve McNair	.50	.20
❑	10 Kordell Stewart	.40	.15
❑	11 Drew Bledsoe	.50	.20
❑	12 Kerry Collins	.40	.15
❑	13 Dan Marino	1.50	.60
❑	14 Jim Druckenmiller RC	.25	.08
❑	15 Todd Collins	.15	.05
❑	16 Jake Plummer RC	2.00	.75
❑	17 Pat Barnes RC	.15	.05
❑	18 Vinny Testaverde	.25	.08
❑	19 Scott Mitchell	.25	.08
❑	20 Rob Johnson	.40	.15
❑	21 Elvis Grbac	.25	.08
❑	22 Danny Wuerffel RC	.40	.15
❑	23 Neil O'Donnell	.25	.08
❑	24 Tony Banks	.25	.08
❑	25 Stan Humphries	.25	.08
❑	26 Brad Johnson	.40	.15
❑	27 Trent Dilfer	.40	.15
❑	28 Ty Detmer	.25	.08
❑	29 Steve Young	.50	.20
❑	30 Gus Frerotte	.15	.05
❑	31 Leeland McElroy	.15	.05
❑	32 Byron Hanspard RC	.25	.08
❑	33 Jamal Anderson	.40	.15
❑	34 Thurman Thomas	.40	.15
❑	35 Antowain Smith RC	1.00	.40
❑	36 Tim Biakabutuka	.25	.08
❑	37 Raymont Harris	.15	.05
❑	38 Corey Dillon RC	2.50	1.00
❑	39 Emmitt Smith	1.25	.50
❑	40 Terrell Davis	.50	.20
❑	41 Barry Sanders	1.25	.50
❑	42 Dorsey Levens	.40	.15
❑	43 Marshall Faulk	.50	.20
❑	44 Natrone Means	.25	.08
❑	45 Marcus Allen	.40	.15
❑	46 Karim Abdul-Jabbar	.40	.15
❑	47 Robert Smith	.25	.08
❑	48 Curtis Martin	.50	.20
❑	49 Troy Davis RC	.25	.08
❑	50 Tiki Barber RC	2.50	1.00
❑	51 Adrian Murrell	.25	.08
❑	52 Napoleon Kaufman	.40	.15
❑	53 Ricky Watters	.25	.08
❑	54 Jerome Bettis	.40	.15
❑	55 Lawrence Phillips	.15	.05
❑	56 Garrison Hearst	.25	.08
❑	57 Warrick Dunn RC	1.25	.50
❑	58 Eddie George	.40	.15
❑	59 Terry Allen	.40	.15
❑	60 Michael Jackson	.25	.08
❑	61 Rae Carruth RC	.15	.05
❑	62 Carl Pickens	.25	.08
❑	63 Michael Irvin	.40	.15
❑	64 Shannon Sharpe	.25	.08
❑	65 Herman Moore	.25	.08
❑	66 Robert Brooks	.25	.08
❑	67 Antonio Freeman	.40	.15
❑	68 Marvin Harrison	.40	.15
❑	69 Keenan McCardell	.25	.08
❑	70 Jimmy Smith	.25	.08
❑	71 Cris Carter	.40	.15
❑	72 Ben Coates	.25	.08
❑	73 Terry Glenn	.40	.15
❑	74 Ike Hilliard RC	.60	.25
❑	75 Keyshawn Johnson	.40	.15
❑	76 Eddie Kennison	.25	.08
❑	77 Tim Brown	.40	.15
❑	78 Irving Fryar	.25	.08
❑	79 Jake Reed	.25	.08
❑	80 Isaac Bruce	.40	.15
❑	81 Tony Martin	.25	.08
❑	82 Jerry Rice	.75	.30
❑	83 Joey Galloway	.25	.08
❑	84 Reidel Anthony RC	.40	.15
❑	85 Yatil Green RC	.25	.08
❑	86 Tony Gonzalez RC	1.25	.50
❑	87 Simeon Rice	.25	.08
❑	88 Peter Boulware RC	.40	.15
❑	89 Bruce Smith	.25	.08
❑	90 Reinard Wilson RC	.25	.08
❑	91 Deion Sanders	.40	.15
❑	92 Bryant Westbrook RC	.15	.05
❑	93 Reggie White	.40	.15
❑	94 Dwayne Rudd RC	.15	.05
❑	95 Darrell Russell RC	.15	.05
❑	96 Greg Lloyd	.15	.05
❑	97 Junior Seau	.40	.15
❑	98 Shawn Springs RC	.25	.08
❑	99 Cortez Kennedy	.15	.05
❑	100 Kordell Stewart CL	.25	.08

1993 Select

❑	COMPLETE SET (200)	20.00	7.50
❑	1 Steve Young	2.00	.75
❑	2 Andre Reed	.40	.15
❑	3 Deion Sanders	1.25	.50
❑	4 Harold Green	.20	.07
❑	5 Wendell Davis	.20	.07
❑	6 Mike Johnson	.20	.07
❑	7 Troy Aikman	2.00	.75
❑	8 Johnny Mitchell	.20	.07
❑	9 Dale Carter	.20	.07
❑	10 Bruce Matthews	.20	.07
❑	11 Terrell Buckley	.20	.07
❑	12 Steve Emtman	.20	.07
❑	13 Neil Smith	.75	.30
❑	14 Tim Brown	.75	.30

❑ 15 Chris Doleman .20 .07
❑ 16 Dan Marino 4.00 1.50
❑ 17 Terry McDaniel .20 .07
❑ 18 Neal Anderson .20 .07
❑ 19 Phil Simms .40 .15
❑ 20 Jeff Lageman .20 .07
❑ 21 Jerry Rice 2.50 1.00
❑ 22 Dermontti Dawson .20 .07
❑ 23 Reggie Cobb .20 .07
❑ 24 Junior Seau .75 .30
❑ 25 Darrell Green .20 .07
❑ 26 Chris Warren .40 .15
❑ 27 Randall Cunningham .75 .30
❑ 28 Bruce Smith .75 .30
❑ 29 Bryan Cox .20 .07
❑ 30 David Klingler .20 .07
❑ 31 Chip Lohmiller .20 .07
❑ 32 Eric Metcalf .40 .15
❑ 33 Ken Norton Jr. .40 .15
❑ 34 John Elway 4.00 1.50
❑ 35 Harris Barton .20 .07
❑ 36 Tim Barnett .20 .07
❑ 37 Rodney Hampton .40 .15
❑ 38 Desmond Howard .40 .15
❑ 39 Tom Rathman .20 .07
❑ 40 Derrick Thomas .75 .30
❑ 41 Randal Hill .20 .07
❑ 42 Steve Wisniewski .20 .07
❑ 43 Brett Favre 5.00 2.00
❑ 44 Darryl Talley .20 .07
❑ 45 Shane Conlan .20 .07
❑ 46 Anthony Miller .40 .15
❑ 47 Randall McDaniel .20 .07
❑ 48 Rod Woodson .75 .30
❑ 49 Eric Martin .20 .07
❑ 50 Ronnie Lott .40 .15
❑ 51 Chris Spielman .40 .15
❑ 52 Vincent Brown .20 .07
❑ 53 Donnell Woolford .20 .07
❑ 54 Richmond Webb .20 .07
❑ 55 Emmitt Smith 3.00 1.25
❑ 56 Haywood Jeffires .40 .15
❑ 57 Jim Kelly .75 .30
❑ 58 James Francis .20 .07
❑ 59 Steve Wallace .20 .07
❑ 60 Jarrod Bunch .20 .07
❑ 61 Lawrence Dawsey .20 .07
❑ 62 Steve Atwater .20 .07
❑ 63 Art Monk .40 .15
❑ 64 Eric Green .20 .07
❑ 65 Lawrence Taylor .75 .30
❑ 66 Ronnie Harmon .20 .07
❑ 67 Fred Barnett .40 .15
❑ 68 Cortez Kennedy .40 .15
❑ 69 Mark Collins .20 .07
❑ 70 Howie Long .75 .30
❑ 71 Jackie Harris .20 .07
❑ 72 Irving Fryar .40 .15
❑ 73 Jim Everett .40 .15
❑ 74 Troy Vincent .20 .07
❑ 75 Cris Carter .75 .30
❑ 76 Boomer Esiason .40 .15
❑ 77 Sam Mills .20 .07
❑ 78 Lorenzo White .20 .07
❑ 79 Andre Rison .40 .15
❑ 80 Quentin Coryatt .40 .15
❑ 81 Steve McMichael .40 .15
❑ 82 Nick Lowery .20 .07
❑ 83 Michael Irvin .75 .30
❑ 84 Thurman Thomas .75 .30
❑ 85 Bill Romanowski .20 .07
❑ 86 Carl Pickens .40 .15
❑ 87 Tim McDonald .20 .07
❑ 88 Bernie Kosar .40 .15
❑ 89 Greg Lloyd .40 .15
❑ 90 Barry Sanders 3.00 1.25
❑ 91 Shannon Sharpe .75 .30
❑ 92 Henry Thomas .20 .07
❑ 93 Barry Foster .40 .15
❑ 94 Antone Davis .20 .07
❑ 95 Stan Humphries .40 .15
❑ 96 Eric Swann .40 .15
❑ 97 Mike Pritchard .40 .15
❑ 98 Reggie White .75 .30
❑ 99 Jeff Hostetler .40 .15
❑ 100 Flipper Anderson .20 .07
❑ 101 Gary Clark .40 .15
❑ 102 Morten Andersen .20 .07
❑ 103 Leonard Russell .40 .15
❑ 104 Chris Hinton .20 .07
❑ 105 John Stephens .20 .07
❑ 106 Byron Evans .20 .07
❑ 107 Warren Moon .75 .30
❑ 108 Marv Cook .20 .07
❑ 109 Carlton Gray RC .20 .07
❑ 110 Jay Novacek .40 .15
❑ 111 Gary Anderson K .20 .07
❑ 112 Andre Tippett .20 .07
❑ 113 Cornelius Bennett .40 .15
❑ 114 Clyde Simmons .20 .07
❑ 115 Jeff George .75 .30
❑ 116 Audray McMillian .20 .07
❑ 117 Mark Carrier WR .40 .15
❑ 118 Vaughan Johnson .20 .07
❑ 119 Kevin Greene .40 .15
❑ 120 John Taylor .40 .15
❑ 121 Jerry Ball .20 .07
❑ 122 Pat Swilling .20 .07
❑ 123 George Teague RC .40 .15
❑ 124 Ricky Reynolds .20 .07
❑ 125 Marcus Allen .75 .30
❑ 126 Henry Jones .20 .07
❑ 127 Ricky Watters .75 .30
❑ 128 Leon Searcy .20 .07
❑ 129 Chris Miller .40 .15
❑ 130 Jim Harbaugh .75 .30
❑ 131 Luis Sharpe .20 .07
❑ 132 Simon Fletcher .20 .07
❑ 133 Eric Allen .20 .07
❑ 134 Carlton Haselrig .20 .07
❑ 135 Harvey Williams .40 .15
❑ 136 Leslie O'Neal .40 .15
❑ 137 Sterling Sharpe .75 .30
❑ 138 Tim Harris .20 .07
❑ 139 Mark Rypien .20 .07
❑ 140 Harry Galbreath .20 .07
❑ 141 Sean Gilbert .40 .15
❑ 142 Keith Jackson .40 .15
❑ 143 Mark Clayton .20 .07
❑ 144 Guy McIntyre .20 .07
❑ 145 Jessie Tuggle .20 .07
❑ 146 Leonard Marshall .20 .07
❑ 147 Willie Davis .75 .30
❑ 148 Herman Moore .75 .30
❑ 149 Charles Haley .40 .15
❑ 150 Amp Lee .20 .07
❑ 151 Gary Zimmerman .20 .07
❑ 152 Bennie Blades .20 .07
❑ 153 Pierce Holt .20 .07
❑ 154 Edgar Bennett .75 .30
❑ 155 Joe Montana 4.00 1.50
❑ 156 Ted Washington .20 .07
❑ 157 Hardy Nickerson .40 .15
❑ 158 Rohn Stark .20 .07
❑ 159 Brent Jones .40 .15
❑ 160 Eugene Robinson .20 .07
❑ 161 Pepper Johnson .20 .07
❑ 162 Dan Saleaumua .20 .07
❑ 163 Seth Joyner .20 .07
❑ 164 Bruce Armstrong .20 .07
❑ 165 Mike Munchak .40 .15
❑ 166 Drew Bledsoe RC 5.00 2.00
❑ 167 Curtis Conway RC 1.25 .50
❑ 168 Lincoln Kennedy RC .20 .07
❑ 169 Dana Stubblefield RC .75 .30
❑ 170 Wayne Simmons RC .20 .07
❑ 171 Garrison Hearst RC 2.00 .75
❑ 172 Jerome Bettis RC 8.00 3.00
❑ 173 Eric Curry RC .20 .07
❑ 174 Natrone Means RC .75 .30
❑ 175 Glyn Milburn RC .75 .30
❑ 176 Marvin Jones RC .20 .07
❑ 177 O.J.McDuffie RC .75 .30
❑ 178 Dan Williams RC .20 .07
❑ 179 Rick Mirer RC .75 .30
❑ 180 John Copeland RC .40 .15
❑ 181 Willie Roaf RC .40 .15
❑ 182 Patrick Bates RC .20 .07
❑ 183 Troy Drayton RC .40 .15
❑ 184 Vincent Brisby RC .75 .30
❑ 185 Irv Smith RC .20 .07
❑ 186 Marion Butts .20 .07
❑ 187 Wayne Martin .20 .07
❑ 188 Brian Blades .40 .15
❑ 189 Mel Gray .40 .15
❑ 190 Mark Stepnoski .20 .07
❑ 191 Ernest Givins .40 .15
❑ 192 Steve Tasker .40 .15
❑ 193 Tim Grunhard .20 .07
❑ 194 Stanley Richard .20 .07
❑ 195 Jeff Wright .20 .07
❑ 196 Rodney Peete .20 .07
❑ 197 Tunch Ilkin .20 .07
❑ 198 Rich Camarillo .20 .07
❑ 199 Erik Williams .20 .07
❑ 200 Pete Stoyanovich .20 .07
❑ S21 Jerry Rice SAMPLE 2.50 1.00

1994 Select

❑ COMPLETE SET (225) 15.00 6.00
❑ 1 Emmitt Smith 2.50 1.00
❑ 2 Bruce Smith .40 .15
❑ 3 Randall McDaniel .10 .02
❑ 4 Drew Bledsoe 1.25 .50
❑ 5 Rod Woodson .20 .07
❑ 6 Richard Dent .20 .07
❑ 7 Norm Johnson .10 .02
❑ 8 Jim Everett .20 .07
❑ 9 Harold Green .10 .02
❑ 10 John Elway 3.00 1.25
❑ 11 Barry Sanders 2.50 1.00
❑ 12 Sterling Sharpe .20 .07
❑ 13 Marcus Robertson .10 .02
❑ 14 Steve Wisniewski .10 .02
❑ 15 Irving Fryar .20 .07
❑ 16 Tyrone Hughes .20 .07
❑ 17 Garrison Hearst .40 .15
❑ 18 Randall Cunningham .40 .15
❑ 19 Junior Seau .40 .15
❑ 20 Rick Mirer .40 .15
❑ 21 Jerry Rice 1.50 .60
❑ 22 Eric Metcalf .20 .07
❑ 23 Roosevelt Potts .10 .02
❑ 24 Neil Smith .20 .07
❑ 25 Jerome Bettis .75 .30
❑ 26 Keith Hamilton .10 .02
❑ 27 Hardy Nickerson .20 .07
❑ 28 Steve Tasker .20 .07
❑ 29 Johnny Johnson .10 .02
❑ 30 Tom Carter .10 .02
❑ 31 Andre Rison .20 .07
❑ 32 Cortez Kennedy .20 .07
❑ 33 Mark Carrier DB .10 .02
❑ 34 Shannon Sharpe .20 .07
❑ 35 Eric Swann .20 .07
❑ 36 Steve Young 1.25 .50
❑ 37 Johnny Mitchell .10 .02
❑ 38 Dermontti Dawson .10 .02
❑ 39 Mike Johnson .10 .02
❑ 40 Troy Aikman 1.50 .60
❑ 41 Pierce Holt .10 .02
❑ 42 Derrick Thomas .40 .15
❑ 43 Reggie Cobb .10 .02
❑ 44 Michael Jackson .20 .07
❑ 45 Lomas Brown .10 .02
❑ 46 Jeff Hostetler .20 .07
❑ 47 Pete Stoyanovich .10 .02
❑ 48 Reggie White .40 .15
❑ 49 Quentin Coryatt .10 .02
❑ 50 Cris Carter .75 .30
❑ 51 Sean Gilbert .10 .02
❑ 52 Chris Slade .10 .02
❑ 53 Ronnie Harmon .10 .02

Card		
❑ 54 Renaldo Turnbull	.10	.02
❑ 55 Fred Barnett	.20	.07
❑ 56 John Elliott	.10	.02
❑ 57 Deion Sanders	.75	.30
❑ 58 John Carney	.10	.02
❑ 59 Louis Oliver	.10	.02
❑ 60 Greg Lloyd	.20	.07
❑ 61 Chris Hinton	.10	.02
❑ 62 Ronald Moore	.10	.02
❑ 63 Vincent Brown	.10	.02
❑ 64 Tony McGee	.10	.02
❑ 65 Erik Williams	.10	.02
❑ 66 Thurman Thomas	.40	.15
❑ 67 Neil O'Donnell	.40	.15
❑ 68 Scott Mitchell	.20	.07
❑ 69 Keith Byars	.10	.02
❑ 70 Henry Ellard	.20	.07
❑ 71 Chris Spielman	.20	.07
❑ 72 LeRoy Butler	.10	.02
❑ 73 Tim Brown	.40	.15
❑ 74 Darrell Green	.10	.02
❑ 75 Bruce Matthews	.10	.02
❑ 76 Stan Humphries	.20	.07
❑ 77 Will Wolford	.10	.02
❑ 78 John Taylor	.20	.07
❑ 79 Joe Montana	3.00	1.25
❑ 80 Chris Warren	.20	.07
❑ 81 Michael Brooks	.10	.02
❑ 82 Vance Johnson	.10	.02
❑ 83 Rob Moore	.20	.07
❑ 84 Herschel Walker	.20	.07
❑ 85 Alvin Harper	.20	.07
❑ 86 Wayne Martin	.10	.02
❑ 87 Leslie O'Neal	.10	.02
❑ 88 Flipper Anderson	.10	.02
❑ 89 Tommy Vardell	.10	.02
❑ 90 Mike Sherrard	.10	.02
❑ 91 Chris Jacke	.10	.02
❑ 92 Jim Kelly	.40	.15
❑ 93 Jeff Graham	.10	.02
❑ 94 Bryan Cox	.10	.02
❑ 95 Michael Irvin	.40	.15
❑ 96 Jeff Lageman	.10	.02
❑ 97 Webster Slaughter	.10	.02
❑ 98 Eugene Robinson	.10	.02
❑ 99 Vencie Glenn	.10	.02
❑ 100 Sean Jones	.10	.02
❑ 101 Calvin Williams	.20	.07
❑ 102 Jim Harbaugh	.40	.15
❑ 103 Eric Curry	.10	.02
❑ 104 Terry Allen	.20	.07
❑ 105 Darryl Williams	.10	.02
❑ 106 Gary Clark	.20	.07
❑ 107 Marcus Allen	.40	.15
❑ 108 Chip Lohmiller	.10	.02
❑ 109 Vaughan Johnson	.10	.02
❑ 110 Herman Moore	.40	.15
❑ 111 Barry Foster	.10	.02
❑ 112 Rocket Ismail	.20	.07
❑ 113 Erric Pegram	.10	.02
❑ 114 Anthony Miller	.20	.07
❑ 115 Shane Conlan	.10	.02
❑ 116 David Klingler	.10	.02
❑ 117 Mark Collins	.10	.02
❑ 118 Tony Bennett	.10	.02
❑ 119 Donnell Woolford	.10	.02
❑ 120 Reggie Brooks	.20	.07
❑ 121 Sam Mills	.10	.02
❑ 122 Greg Montgomery	.10	.02
❑ 123 Kevin Greene	.20	.07
❑ 124 Terry McDaniel	.10	.02
❑ 125 Henry Jones	.10	.02
❑ 126 Ricky Watters	.20	.07
❑ 127 Dan Marino	3.00	1.25
❑ 128 Steve Atwater	.10	.02
❑ 129 Ricky Proehl	.10	.02
❑ 130 Ernest Givins	.20	.07
❑ 131 John L. Williams	.10	.02
❑ 132 John Randle	.20	.07
❑ 133 Jay Novacek	.20	.07
❑ 134 Boomer Esiason	.20	.07
❑ 135 Jessie Hester	.10	.02
❑ 136 Courtney Hawkins	.10	.02
❑ 137 Ben Coates	.20	.07
❑ 138 Stevon Moore	.10	.02
❑ 139 Eric Allen	.10	.02
❑ 140 Jessie Tuggle	.10	.02

Card		
❑ 141 Marion Butts	.10	.02
❑ 142 Brett Favre	3.00	1.25
❑ 143 Andre Reed	.20	.07
❑ 144 Rodney Hampton	.20	.07
❑ 145 Keith Sims	.10	.02
❑ 146 Derek Brown RBK	.10	.02
❑ 147 Eric Green	.10	.02
❑ 148 Greg Robinson	.10	.02
❑ 149 Nate Newton	.10	.02
❑ 150 Mark Higgs	.10	.02
❑ 151 Nick Lowery	.10	.02
❑ 152 Craig Erickson	.10	.02
❑ 153 Anthony Carter	.20	.07
❑ 154 Simon Fletcher	.10	.02
❑ 155 Ronnie Lott	.20	.07
❑ 156 Gary Brown	.10	.02
❑ 157 Brent Jones	.20	.07
❑ 158 Jim Sweeney	.10	.02
❑ 159 Robert Brooks	.40	.15
❑ 160 Keith Jackson	.10	.02
❑ 161 Daryl Johnston	.20	.07
❑ 162 Tom Waddle	.10	.02
❑ 163 Eric Martin	.10	.02
❑ 164 Cornelius Bennett	.20	.07
❑ 165 Tim McDonald	.10	.02
❑ 166 Chris Doleman	.10	.02
❑ 167 Gary Zimmerman	.10	.02
❑ 168 Al Smith	.10	.02
❑ 169 Mark Carrier WR	.20	.07
❑ 170 Harris Barton	.10	.02
❑ 171 Ray Childress	.10	.02
❑ 172 Darryl Talley	.10	.02
❑ 173 James Jett	.10	.02
❑ 174 Mark Stepnoski	.10	.02
❑ 175 Jeff Query	.10	.02
❑ 176 Charles Haley	.20	.07
❑ 177 Rod Bernstine	.10	.02
❑ 178 Richmond Webb	.10	.02
❑ 179 Rich Camarillo	.10	.02
❑ 180 Pat Swilling	.10	.02
❑ 181 Chris Miller	.10	.02
❑ 182 Mike Pritchard	.10	.02
❑ 183 Checklist NFC	.10	.02
❑ 184 Natrone Means	.40	.15
❑ 185 Erik Kramer	.20	.07
❑ 186 Clyde Simmons	.10	.02
❑ 187 Checklist AFC/NFC	.10	.02
❑ 188 Warren Moon	.40	.15
❑ 189 Michael Haynes	.20	.07
❑ 190 Terry Kirby	.40	.15
❑ 191 Brian Blades	.20	.07
❑ 192 Haywood Jeffires	.20	.07
❑ 193 Thomas Everett	.10	.02
❑ 194 Morten Andersen	.10	.02
❑ 195 Dana Stubblefield	.20	.07
❑ 196 Ken Norton	.20	.07
❑ 197 Art Monk	.20	.07
❑ 198 Seth Joyner	.10	.02
❑ 199 Heath Shuler RC	.40	.15
❑ 200 Marshall Faulk RC	6.00	2.50
❑ 201 Charles Johnson RC	.40	.15
❑ 202 Derrick Alexander WR RC	.40	.15
❑ 203 Greg Hill RC	.40	.15
❑ 204 Darnay Scott RC	1.00	.40
❑ 205 Willie McGinest RC	.40	.15
❑ 206 Thomas Randolph RC	.10	.02
❑ 207 Errict Rhett RC	.40	.15
❑ 208 William Floyd RC	.40	.15
❑ 209 Johnnie Morton RC	2.00	.75
❑ 210 David Palmer RC	.40	.15
❑ 211 Dan Wilkinson RC	.20	.07
❑ 212 Trent Dilfer RC	1.25	.50
❑ 213 Antonio Langham RC	.20	.07
❑ 214 Chuck Levy RC	.10	.02
❑ 215 John Thierry RC	.10	.02
❑ 216 Kevin Lee RC	.10	.02
❑ 217 Aaron Glenn RC	.40	.15
❑ 218 Charlie Garner RC	1.50	.60
❑ 219 Jeff Burris RC	.20	.07
❑ 220 LeShon Johnson RC	.20	.07
❑ 221 Thomas Lewis RC	.20	.07
❑ 222 Ryan Yarborough RC	.10	.02
❑ 223 Mario Bates RC	.40	.15
❑ 224 Checklist NFC/AFC	.10	.02
❑ 225 Checklist AFC	.10	.02
❑ SR1 Marshall Faulk SR	40.00	15.00
❑ SR2 Dan Wilkinson SR	8.00	3.00

1996 Select

Card		
❑ COMPLETE SET (200)	20.00	8.00
❑ 1 Troy Aikman	1.00	.40
❑ 2 Marshall Faulk	.50	.20
❑ 3 Kordell Stewart	.40	.15
❑ 4 Larry Centers	.20	.07
❑ 5 Tamarick Vanover	.20	.07
❑ 6 Ken Norton Jr.	.10	.02
❑ 7 Steve Tasker	.10	.02
❑ 8 Dan Marino	2.00	.75
❑ 9 Heath Shuler	.20	.07
❑ 10 Anthony Miller	.20	.07
❑ 11 Mario Bates	.20	.07
❑ 12 Natrone Means	.20	.07
❑ 13 Darren Woodson	.20	.07
❑ 14 Chris Sanders	.20	.07
❑ 15 Chris Warren	.20	.07
❑ 16 Eric Metcalf	.10	.02
❑ 17 Quentin Coryatt	.10	.02
❑ 18 Jeff Hostetler	.10	.02
❑ 19 Brett Favre	2.00	.75
❑ 20 Curtis Martin	.75	.30
❑ 21 Floyd Turner	.10	.02
❑ 22 Curtis Conway	.40	.15
❑ 23 Orlando Thomas	.10	.02
❑ 24 Lee Woodall	.10	.02
❑ 25 Darick Holmes	.10	.02
❑ 26 Marcus Allen	.40	.15
❑ 27 Ricky Watters	.20	.07
❑ 28 Herman Moore	.20	.07
❑ 29 Rodney Hampton	.20	.07
❑ 30 Alvin Harper	.10	.02
❑ 31 Jeff Blake	.40	.15
❑ 32 Wayne Chrebet	.60	.25
❑ 33 Jerry Rice	1.00	.40
❑ 34 Dave Krieg	.10	.02
❑ 35 Mark Brunell	.60	.25
❑ 36 Terry Allen	.20	.07
❑ 37 Emmitt Smith	1.50	.60
❑ 38 Bryan Cox	.10	.02
❑ 39 Tony Martin	.20	.07
❑ 40 John Elway	2.00	.75
❑ 41 Warren Moon	.20	.07
❑ 42 Yancey Thigpen	.20	.07
❑ 43 Jeff George	.20	.07
❑ 44 Rodney Thomas	.10	.02
❑ 45 Joey Galloway	.40	.15
❑ 46 Jim Kelly	.40	.15
❑ 47 Drew Bledsoe	.60	.25
❑ 48 Greg Lloyd	.20	.07
❑ 49 Michael Irvin	.40	.15
❑ 50 Quinn Early	.10	.02
❑ 51 Brent Jones	.10	.02
❑ 52 Rashaan Salaam	.20	.07
❑ 53 James O.Stewart	.20	.07
❑ 54 Gus Frerotte	.20	.07
❑ 55 Edgar Bennett	.20	.07
❑ 56 Lamont Warren	.10	.02
❑ 57 Napoleon Kaufman	.40	.15
❑ 58 Kevin Williams	.10	.02
❑ 59 Irving Fryar	.20	.07
❑ 60 Trent Dilfer	.40	.15
❑ 61 Eric Zeier	.10	.02
❑ 62 Tyrone Wheatley	.20	.07
❑ 63 Isaac Bruce	.40	.15
❑ 64 Terrell Davis	.75	.30
❑ 65 Lake Dawson	.10	.02
❑ 66 Carnell Lake	.10	.02
❑ 67 Kerry Collins	.40	.15

❑ 68	Kyle Brady	.10	.02
❑ 69	Rodney Peete	.10	.02
❑ 70	Carl Pickens	.20	.07
❑ 71	Robert Smith	.20	.07
❑ 72	Rod Woodson	.20	.07
❑ 73	Deion Sanders	.60	.25
❑ 74	Sean Dawkins	.10	.02
❑ 75	William Floyd	.20	.07
❑ 76	Barry Sanders	1.50	.60
❑ 77	Ben Coates	.20	.07
❑ 78	Neil O'Donnell	.20	.07
❑ 79	Bill Brooks	.10	.02
❑ 80	Steve Bono	.10	.02
❑ 81	Jay Novacek	.10	.02
❑ 82	Bernie Parmalee	.10	.02
❑ 83	Derek Loville	.10	.02
❑ 84	Frank Sanders	.20	.07
❑ 85	Robert Brooks	.40	.15
❑ 86	Jim Harbaugh	.20	.07
❑ 87	Rick Mirer	.20	.07
❑ 88	Craig Heyward	.10	.02
❑ 89	Greg Hill	.20	.07
❑ 90	Andre Coleman	.10	.02
❑ 91	Shannon Sharpe	.20	.07
❑ 92	Hugh Douglas	.20	.07
❑ 93	Andre Hastings	.10	.02
❑ 94	Bryce Paup	.10	.02
❑ 95	Jim Everett	.10	.02
❑ 96	Brian Mitchell	.10	.02
❑ 97	Jeff Graham	.10	.02
❑ 98	Steve McNair	.75	.30
❑ 99	Charlie Garner	.20	.07
❑ 100	Willie McGinest	.10	.02
❑ 101	Harvey Williams	.10	.02
❑ 102	Daryl Johnston	.20	.07
❑ 103	Cris Carter	.40	.15
❑ 104	J.J. Stokes	.40	.15
❑ 105	Garrison Hearst	.20	.07
❑ 106	Mark Chmura	.20	.07
❑ 107	Derrick Thomas	.40	.15
❑ 108	Errict Rhett	.20	.07
❑ 109	Terance Mathis	.10	.02
❑ 110	Dave Brown	.10	.02
❑ 111	Erric Pegram	.10	.02
❑ 112	Scott Mitchell	.20	.07
❑ 113	Aaron Bailey	.10	.02
❑ 114	Stan Humphries	.20	.07
❑ 115	Bruce Smith	.20	.07
❑ 116	Rob Johnson	.40	.15
❑ 117	O.J. McDuffie	.20	.07
❑ 118	Brian Blades	.10	.02
❑ 119	Steve Atwater	.10	.02
❑ 120	Tyrone Hughes	.10	.02
❑ 121	Michael Westbrook	.40	.15
❑ 122	Ki-Jana Carter	.20	.07
❑ 123	Adrian Murrell	.20	.07
❑ 124	Steve Young	.75	.30
❑ 125	Charles Haley	.20	.07
❑ 126	Vincent Brisby	.10	.02
❑ 127	Jerome Bettis	.40	.15
❑ 128	Erik Kramer	.10	.02
❑ 129	Roosevelt Potts	.10	.02
❑ 130	Tim Brown	.40	.15
❑ 131	Reggie White	.40	.15
❑ 132	Jake Reed	.20	.07
❑ 133	Junior Seau	.40	.15
❑ 134	Stoney Case	.10	.02
❑ 135	Kimble Anders	.20	.07
❑ 136	Brett Perriman	.10	.02
❑ 137	Todd Collins	.20	.07
❑ 138	Sherman Williams	.10	.02
❑ 139	Hardy Nickerson	.10	.02
❑ 140	Ernie Mills	.10	.02
❑ 141	Glyn Milburn	.10	.02
❑ 142	Terry Kirby	.20	.07
❑ 143	Bert Emanuel	.20	.07
❑ 144	Aeneas Williams	.10	.02
❑ 145	Aaron Craver	.10	.02
❑ 146	Jackie Harris	.10	.02
❑ 147	Thurman Thomas	.40	.15
❑ 148	Aaron Hayden RC	.10	.02
❑ 149	Antonio Freeman	.40	.15
❑ 150	Kevin Greene	.20	.07
❑ 151	Kevin Hardy RC	.40	.15
❑ 152	Eric Moulds RC	1.50	.60
❑ 153	Tim Biakabutuka RC	.40	.15
❑ 154	Keyshawn Johnson RC	1.25	.50
❑ 155	Jeff Lewis RC	.20	.07
❑ 156	Stepfret Williams RC	.20	.07
❑ 157	Tony Brackens RC	.40	.15
❑ 158	Mike Alstott RC	1.25	.50
❑ 159	Willie Anderson RC	.10	.02
❑ 160	Marvin Harrison RC	3.00	1.25
❑ 161	Regan Upshaw RC	.10	.02
❑ 162	Bobby Engram RC	.40	.15
❑ 163	Leeland McElroy RC	.20	.07
❑ 164	Alex Van Dyke RC	.20	.07
❑ 165	Stanley Pritchett RC	.20	.07
❑ 166	Cedric Jones RC	.10	.02
❑ 167	Terry Glenn RC	1.25	.50
❑ 168	Eddie George RC	1.50	.60
❑ 169	Lawrence Phillips RC	.40	.15
❑ 170	Jonathan Ogden RC	.40	.15
❑ 171	Danny Kanell RC	.40	.15
❑ 172	Alex Molden RC	.10	.02
❑ 173	Daryl Gardener RC	.10	.02
❑ 174	Derrick Mayes RC	.40	.15
❑ 175	Marco Battaglia RC	.10	.02
❑ 176	Jon Stark RC	.10	.02
❑ 177	Karim Abdul-Jabbar RC	.40	.15
❑ 178	Stephen Davis RC	2.00	.75
❑ 179	Rickey Dudley RC	.40	.15
❑ 180	Eddie Kennison RC	.40	.15
❑ 181	Barry Sanders FF	.75	.30
❑ 182	Brett Favre FF	1.00	.40
❑ 183	John Elway FF	1.00	.40
❑ 184	Steve Young FF	.40	.15
❑ 185	Michael Irvin FF	.20	.07
❑ 186	Jerry Rice FF	.50	.20
❑ 187	Emmitt Smith FF	.75	.30
❑ 188	Isaac Bruce FF	.40	.15
❑ 189	Chris Warren FF	.20	.07
❑ 190	Errict Rhett FF	.20	.07
❑ 191	Herman Moore FF	.20	.07
❑ 192	Carl Pickens FF	.20	.07
❑ 193	Cris Carter FF	.40	.15
❑ 194	Terrell Davis FF	.40	.15
❑ 195	Rodney Thomas FF	.10	.02
❑ 196	Dan Marino CL	.40	.15
❑ 197	Drew Bledsoe CL	.20	.07
❑ 198	Emmitt Smith CL	.40	.15
❑ 199	Jerry Rice CL	.40	.15
❑ 200	Barry Sanders/Elway CL	.40	.15

2001 Select

❑	COMP.SET w/o SPs (220)	30.00	12.50
❑ 1	David Boston	.75	.30
❑ 2	Frank Sanders	.30	.10
❑ 3	Jake Plummer	.50	.20
❑ 4	Michael Pittman	.30	.10
❑ 5	Rob Moore	.50	.20
❑ 6	Thomas Jones	.50	.20
❑ 7	Chris Chandler	.50	.20
❑ 8	Doug Johnson	.30	.10
❑ 9	Jamal Anderson	.75	.30
❑ 10	Tim Dwight	.75	.30
❑ 11	Brandon Stokley	.50	.20
❑ 12	Chris Redman	.30	.10
❑ 13	Jamal Lewis	1.25	.50
❑ 14	Qadry Ismail	.50	.20
❑ 15	Ray Lewis	.75	.30
❑ 16	Rod Woodson	.50	.20
❑ 17	Shannon Sharpe	.50	.20
❑ 18	Travis Taylor	.50	.20
❑ 19	Trent Dilfer	.50	.20
❑ 20	Elvis Grbac	.50	.20
❑ 21	Eric Moulds	.50	.20
❑ 22	Jay Riemersma	.30	.10
❑ 23	Peerless Price	.50	.20
❑ 24	Rob Johnson	.50	.20
❑ 25	Sam Cowart	.30	.10
❑ 26	Sammy Morris	.30	.10
❑ 27	Shawn Bryson	.30	.10
❑ 28	Donald Hayes	.30	.10
❑ 29	Muhsin Muhammad	.50	.20
❑ 30	Patrick Jeffers	.50	.20
❑ 31	Reggie White DE	.75	.30
❑ 32	Steve Beuerlein	.50	.20
❑ 33	Tim Biakabutuka	.50	.20
❑ 34	Wesley Walls	.30	.10
❑ 35	Brian Urlacher	1.25	.50
❑ 36	Cade McNown	.30	.10
❑ 37	Dez White	.30	.10
❑ 38	James Allen	.50	.20
❑ 39	Marcus Robinson	.75	.30
❑ 40	Marty Booker	.30	.10
❑ 41	Akili Smith	.30	.10
❑ 42	Corey Dillon	.75	.30
❑ 43	Danny Farmer	.30	.10
❑ 44	Peter Warrick	.75	.30
❑ 45	Ron Dugans	.30	.10
❑ 46	Takeo Spikes	.30	.10
❑ 47	Courtney Brown	.50	.20
❑ 48	Dennis Northcutt	.50	.20
❑ 49	JaJuan Dawson	.30	.10
❑ 50	Kevin Johnson	.50	.20
❑ 51	Tim Couch	.50	.20
❑ 52	Travis Prentice	.30	.10
❑ 53	Anthony Wright	.30	.10
❑ 54	Emmitt Smith	1.50	.60
❑ 55	James McKnight	.50	.20
❑ 56	Joey Galloway	.50	.20
❑ 57	Rocket Ismail	.50	.20
❑ 58	Randall Cunningham	.75	.30
❑ 59	Troy Aikman	1.25	.50
❑ 60	Brian Griese	.75	.30
❑ 61	Ed McCaffrey	.75	.30
❑ 62	Gus Frerotte	.30	.10
❑ 63	John Elway	2.50	1.00
❑ 64	Mike Anderson	.75	.30
❑ 65	Olandis Gary	.50	.20
❑ 66	Rod Smith	.50	.20
❑ 67	Terrell Davis	.75	.30
❑ 68	Barry Sanders	1.50	.60
❑ 69	Charlie Batch	.75	.30
❑ 70	Germane Crowell	.30	.10
❑ 71	Herman Moore	.50	.20
❑ 72	James Stewart	.50	.20
❑ 73	Johnnie Morton	.50	.20
❑ 74	Robert Porcher	.30	.10
❑ 75	Jim Harbaugh	.50	.20
❑ 76	Ahman Green	.75	.30
❑ 77	Antonio Freeman	.75	.30
❑ 78	Bill Schroeder	.50	.20
❑ 79	Brett Favre	2.50	1.00
❑ 80	Bubba Franks	.50	.20
❑ 81	Dorsey Levens	.50	.20
❑ 82	E.G. Green	.30	.10
❑ 83	Edgerrin James	1.00	.40
❑ 84	Jerome Pathon	.50	.20
❑ 85	Ken Dilger	.30	.10
❑ 86	Marcus Pollard	.30	.10
❑ 87	Marvin Harrison	.75	.30
❑ 88	Peyton Manning	2.00	.75
❑ 89	Terrence Wilkins	.30	.10
❑ 90	Fred Taylor	.75	.30
❑ 91	Hardy Nickerson	.30	.10
❑ 92	Jimmy Smith	.50	.20
❑ 93	Keenan McCardell	.30	.10
❑ 94	Kyle Brady	.30	.10
❑ 95	Mark Brunell	.75	.30
❑ 96	Tony Brackens	.30	.10
❑ 97	Derrick Alexander WR	.50	.20
❑ 98	Sylvester Morris	.30	.10
❑ 99	Tony Gonzalez	.50	.20
❑ 100	Tony Richardson	.30	.10
❑ 101	Kimble Anders	.30	.10
❑ 102	Warren Moon	.75	.30
❑ 103	Dan Marino	2.50	1.00
❑ 104	Jay Fiedler	.75	.30
❑ 105	Lamar Smith	.50	.20
❑ 106	O.J. McDuffie	.30	.10
❑ 107	Oronde Gadsden	.50	.20

❑ 108 Sam Madison .30 .10
❑ 109 Thurman Thomas .50 .20
❑ 110 Tony Martin .30 .10
❑ 111 Zach Thomas .75 .30
❑ 112 Cris Carter .75 .30
❑ 113 Daunte Culpepper .75 .30
❑ 114 Matthew Hatchette .30 .10
❑ 115 Randy Moss 1.50 .60
❑ 116 Robert Smith .75 .30
❑ 117 Drew Bledsoe 1.00 .40
❑ 118 J.R. Redmond .30 .10
❑ 119 Kevin Faulk .50 .20
❑ 120 Michael Bishop .30 .10
❑ 121 Terry Glenn .50 .20
❑ 122 Troy Brown .50 .20
❑ 123 Ty Law .50 .20
❑ 124 Aaron Brooks .75 .30
❑ 125 Darren Howard .30 .10
❑ 126 Jake Reed .50 .20
❑ 127 Jeff Blake .50 .20
❑ 128 Joe Horn .50 .20
❑ 129 La'Roi Glover .30 .10
❑ 130 Ricky Williams .75 .30
❑ 131 Willie Jackson .30 .10
❑ 132 Albert Connell .30 .10
❑ 133 Amani Toomer .50 .20
❑ 134 Ike Hilliard .50 .20
❑ 135 Jason Sehorn .30 .10
❑ 136 Jessie Armstead .30 .10
❑ 137 Kerry Collins .50 .20
❑ 138 Michael Strahan .50 .20
❑ 139 Ron Dayne .75 .30
❑ 140 Ron Dixon .30 .10
❑ 141 Tiki Barber .75 .30
❑ 142 Anthony Becht .30 .10
❑ 143 Chad Pennington 1.25 .50
❑ 144 Curtis Martin .75 .30
❑ 145 Dedric Ward .30 .10
❑ 146 Laveranues Coles .75 .30
❑ 147 Vinny Testaverde .50 .20
❑ 148 Wayne Chrebet .50 .20
❑ 149 Andre Rison .50 .20
❑ 150 Charles Woodson .50 .20
❑ 151 Darrell Russell .30 .10
❑ 152 Napoleon Kaufman .50 .20
❑ 153 Rich Gannon .75 .30
❑ 154 Tim Brown .75 .30
❑ 155 Tyrone Wheatley .50 .20
❑ 156 Chad Lewis .30 .10
❑ 157 Charles Johnson .30 .10
❑ 158 Donovan McNabb 1.00 .40
❑ 159 Duce Staley .75 .30
❑ 160 Hugh Douglas .30 .10
❑ 161 Na Brown .30 .10
❑ 162 Todd Pinkston .30 .10
❑ 163 James Thrash .50 .20
❑ 164 Bobby Shaw .30 .10
❑ 165 Hines Ward .75 .30
❑ 166 Jerome Bettis .75 .30
❑ 167 Kordell Stewart .50 .20
❑ 168 Levon Kirkland .30 .10
❑ 169 Plaxico Burress .75 .30
❑ 170 Richard Huntley .30 .10
❑ 171 Troy Edwards .30 .10
❑ 172 Jeff Graham .30 .10
❑ 173 Junior Seau .75 .30
❑ 174 Doug Flutie .75 .30
❑ 175 Charlie Garner .50 .20
❑ 176 Jeff Garcia .75 .30
❑ 177 Jerry Rice 1.50 .60
❑ 178 Steve Young 1.00 .40
❑ 179 Terrell Owens .75 .30
❑ 180 Brock Huard .30 .10
❑ 181 Darrell Jackson .75 .30
❑ 182 Derrick Mayes .30 .10
❑ 183 Ricky Watters .50 .20
❑ 184 Shaun Alexander 1.00 .40
❑ 185 Matt Hasselbeck .50 .20
❑ 186 John Randle .50 .20
❑ 187 Az-Zahir Hakim .30 .10
❑ 188 Isaac Bruce .75 .30
❑ 189 Kurt Warner 1.50 .60
❑ 190 Marshall Faulk 1.00 .40
❑ 191 Torry Holt .75 .30
❑ 192 Trent Green .75 .30
❑ 193 Derrick Brooks .75 .30
❑ 194 Jacquez Green .30 .10
❑ 195 John Lynch .50 .20
❑ 196 Keyshawn Johnson .75 .30
❑ 197 Mike Alstott .75 .30
❑ 198 Reidel Anthony .30 .10
❑ 199 Shaun King .30 .10
❑ 200 Warren Sapp .50 .20
❑ 201 Warrick Dunn .75 .30
❑ 202 Ryan Leaf .50 .20
❑ 203 Carl Pickens .30 .10
❑ 204 Derrick Mason .50 .20
❑ 205 Eddie George .75 .30
❑ 206 Frank Wycheck .30 .10
❑ 207 Jevon Kearse .50 .20
❑ 208 Neil O'Donnell .30 .10
❑ 209 Steve McNair .75 .30
❑ 210 Yancey Thigpen .30 .10
❑ 211 Andre Reed .50 .20
❑ 212 Brad Johnson .75 .30
❑ 213 Bruce Smith .50 .20
❑ 214 Champ Bailey .75 .30
❑ 215 Darrell Green .30 .10
❑ 216 Deion Sanders .75 .30
❑ 217 Irving Fryar .50 .20
❑ 218 Jeff George .50 .20
❑ 219 Michael Westbrook .50 .20
❑ 220 Stephen Davis .75 .30
❑ 221 Terrell Owens AP 2.00 .75
❑ 222 Peyton Manning AP 6.00 2.50
❑ 223 Stephen Davis AP 2.00 .75
❑ 224 Marvin Harrison AP 2.00 .75
❑ 225 Donovan McNabb AP 3.00 1.25
❑ 226 Edgerrin James AP 3.00 1.25
❑ 227 Eric Moulds AP 1.25 .50
❑ 228 Daunte Culpepper AP 2.00 .75
❑ 229 Eddie George AP 2.00 .75
❑ 230 Cris Carter AP 2.00 .75
❑ 231 Rich Gannon AP 2.00 .75
❑ 232 Jeff Garcia AP 2.00 .75
❑ 233 Jimmy Smith AP 1.25 .50
❑ 234 Tony Gonzalez AP 1.25 .50
❑ 235 Torry Holt AP 2.00 .75
❑ 236 Jevon Kearse AP 1.25 .50
❑ 237 Ray Lewis AP 2.00 .75
❑ 238 Warren Sapp AP 1.25 .50
❑ 239 Brian Urlacher AP 4.00 1.50
❑ 240 Champ Bailey AP 1.25 .50
❑ 241 Peyton Manning LL 6.00 2.50
❑ 242 Jeff Garcia LL 2.00 .75
❑ 243 Elvis Grbac LL 1.25 .50
❑ 244 Daunte Culpepper LL 2.00 .75
❑ 245 Brett Favre LL 8.00 3.00
❑ 246 Edgerrin James LL 3.00 1.25
❑ 247 Robert Smith LL 1.25 .50
❑ 248 Eddie George LL 2.00 .75
❑ 249 Mike Anderson LL 2.00 .75
❑ 250 Corey Dillon LL 2.00 .75
❑ 251 Torry Holt LL 2.00 .75
❑ 252 Rod Smith LL 1.25 .50
❑ 253 Isaac Bruce LL 2.00 .75
❑ 254 Terrell Owens LL 2.00 .75
❑ 255 Randy Moss LL 5.00 2.00
❑ 256 La'Roi Glover LL .75 .30
❑ 257 Trace Armstrong LL .75 .30
❑ 258 Warren Sapp LL 1.25 .50
❑ 259 Hugh Douglas LL .75 .30
❑ 260 Jason Taylor LL .75 .30
❑ 261 Mike Anderson SS 2.00 .75
❑ 262 Jamal Lewis SS 3.00 1.25
❑ 263 Sylvester Morris SS .75 .30
❑ 264 Darrell Jackson SS 2.00 .75
❑ 265 Peter Warrick SS 2.00 .75
❑ 266 Ron Dayne SS 2.00 .75
❑ 267 Shaun Alexander SS 3.00 1.25
❑ 268 Plaxico Burress SS 2.00 .75
❑ 269 Brian Urlacher SS 4.00 1.50
❑ 270 Courtney Brown SS 1.25 .50
❑ 271 Michael Vick RC 50.00 20.00
❑ 272 Drew Brees RC 40.00 20.00
❑ 273 Chris Weinke RC 12.00 5.00
❑ 274 Quincy Carter RC 12.00 5.00
❑ 275 Sage Rosenfels RC 12.00 5.00
❑ 276 Josh Heupel RC 12.00 5.00
❑ 277 David Rivers RC 8.00 3.00
❑ 278 Ben Leard RC 8.00 3.00
❑ 279 Marques Tuiasosopo RC 12.00 5.00
❑ 280 Mike McMahon RC 12.00 5.00
❑ 281 Deuce McAllister RC 25.00 10.00
❑ 282 LaMont Jordan RC 25.00 10.00
❑ 283 LaDainian Tomlinson RC 80.00 40.00
❑ 284 James Jackson RC 12.00 5.00
❑ 285 Anthony Thomas RC 12.00 5.00
❑ 286 Travis Henry RC 20.00 7.50
❑ 287 Travis Minor RC 8.00 3.00
❑ 288 Rudi Johnson RC 25.00 10.00
❑ 289 Michael Bennett RC 12.00 5.00
❑ 290 Kevan Barlow RC 12.00 5.00
❑ 291 Reggie White RC 8.00 3.00
❑ 292 Moran Norris RC 5.00 2.00
❑ 293 Ja'Mar Toombs RC 8.00 3.00
❑ 294 Heath Evans RC 8.00 3.00
❑ 295 David Terrell RC 12.00 5.00
❑ 296 Santana Moss RC 20.00 7.50
❑ 297 Rod Gardner RC 12.00 5.00
❑ 298 Quincy Morgan RC 12.00 5.00
❑ 299 Freddie Mitchell RC 12.00 5.00
❑ 300 Boo Williams RC 8.00 3.00
❑ 301 Reggie Wayne RC 25.00 10.00
❑ 302 Ronney Daniels RC 5.00 2.00
❑ 303 Bobby Newcombe RC 8.00 3.00
❑ 304 Vinny Sutherland RC 8.00 3.00
❑ 305 Cedrick Wilson RC 12.00 5.00
❑ 306 Robert Ferguson RC 12.00 5.00
❑ 307 Ken-Yon Rambo RC 8.00 3.00
❑ 308 Alex Bannister RC 8.00 3.00
❑ 309 Koren Robinson RC 12.00 5.00
❑ 310 Chad Johnson RC 30.00 12.50
❑ 311 Chris Chambers RC 20.00 7.50
❑ 312 Javon Green RC 8.00 3.00
❑ 313 Snoop Minnis RC 8.00 3.00
❑ 314 Scotty Anderson RC 8.00 3.00
❑ 315 Todd Heap RC 12.00 5.00
❑ 316 Alge Crumpler RC 15.00 6.00
❑ 317 Marcellus Rivers RC 8.00 3.00
❑ 318 Rashon Burns RC 5.00 2.00
❑ 319 Jamal Reynolds RC 12.00 5.00
❑ 320 Andre Carter RC 12.00 5.00
❑ 321 Justin Smith RC 12.00 5.00
❑ 322 Gerard Warren RC 12.00 5.00
❑ 323 Tommy Polley RC 12.00 5.00
❑ 324 Dan Morgan RC 12.00 5.00
❑ 325 Torrance Marshall RC 12.00 5.00
❑ 326 Correll Buckhalter RC 15.00 6.00
❑ 327 Derrick Gibson RC 8.00 3.00
❑ 328 Adam Archuleta RC 12.00 5.00
❑ 329 Jamar Fletcher RC 8.00 3.00
❑ 330 Nate Clements RC 12.00 5.00

2006 Select

❑ COMP.SET w/o RC's (330) 50.00 25.00
❑ 331-430 RC PRINT RUN 599 SETS
❑ 1 Kurt Warner .50 .20
❑ 2 J.J. Arrington .50 .20
❑ 3 Anquan Boldin .50 .20
❑ 4 Larry Fitzgerald .75 .30
❑ 5 Marcel Shipp .40 .15
❑ 6 Bryant Johnson .40 .15
❑ 7 Bertrand Berry .40 .15
❑ 8 John Navarre .40 .15
❑ 9 Michael Vick 1.00 .40
❑ 10 Warrick Dunn .50 .20
❑ 11 Roddy White .50 .20
❑ 12 Alge Crumpler .50 .20
❑ 13 T.J. Duckett .50 .20
❑ 14 Michael Jenkins .50 .20
❑ 15 DeAngelo Hall .50 .20
❑ 16 Brian Finneran .40 .15

❑ 17 Kyle Boller .40 .15
❑ 18 Jamal Lewis .50 .20
❑ 19 Chester Taylor .50 .20
❑ 20 Derrick Mason .40 .15
❑ 21 Mark Clayton .50 .20
❑ 22 Todd Heap .50 .20
❑ 23 Ray Lewis .75 .30
❑ 24 Devard Darling .40 .15
❑ 25 J.P. Losman .50 .20
❑ 26 Willis McGahee .75 .30
❑ 27 Lee Evans .50 .20
❑ 28 Eric Moulds .50 .20
❑ 29 Lawyer Milloy .40 .15
❑ 30 Josh Reed .40 .15
❑ 31 Kelly Holcomb .40 .15
❑ 32 Jake Delhomme .50 .20
❑ 33 DeShaun Foster .50 .20
❑ 34 Steve Smith .75 .30
❑ 35 Julius Peppers .50 .20
❑ 36 Drew Carter .40 .15
❑ 37 Chris Gamble .40 .15
❑ 38 Stephen Davis .50 .20
❑ 39 Keary Colbert .40 .15
❑ 40 Nick Goings .40 .15
❑ 41 Eric Shelton .40 .15
❑ 42 Rex Grossman .75 .30
❑ 43 Thomas Jones .50 .20
❑ 44 Cedric Benson .75 .30
❑ 45 Muhsin Muhammad .50 .20
❑ 46 Brian Urlacher .75 .30
❑ 47 Mark Bradley .50 .20
❑ 48 Kyle Orton .50 .20
❑ 49 Tommie Harris .40 .15
❑ 50 Adrian Peterson .40 .15
❑ 51 Bernard Berrian .40 .15
❑ 52 Justin Gage .40 .15
❑ 53 Carson Palmer .75 .30
❑ 54 Rudi Johnson .50 .20
❑ 55 Chad Johnson .50 .20
❑ 56 T.J. Houshmandzadeh .50 .20
❑ 57 Chris Henry .40 .15
❑ 58 Chris Perry .50 .20
❑ 59 Jon Kitna .40 .15
❑ 60 Deltha O'Neal .40 .15
❑ 61 Charlie Frye .50 .20
❑ 62 Reuben Droughns .50 .20
❑ 63 Braylon Edwards .75 .30
❑ 64 Kellen Winslow .75 .30
❑ 65 Antonio Bryant .50 .20
❑ 66 Trent Dilfer .50 .20
❑ 67 Dennis Northcutt .40 .15
❑ 68 Drew Bledsoe .75 .30
❑ 69 Julius Jones .75 .30
❑ 70 Marion Barber .50 .20
❑ 71 Terry Glenn .50 .20
❑ 72 Keyshawn Johnson .50 .20
❑ 73 Roy Williams S .50 .20
❑ 74 Jason Witten .50 .20
❑ 75 Terence Newman .40 .15
❑ 76 Drew Henson .40 .15
❑ 77 Patrick Crayton .40 .15
❑ 78 Jake Plummer .50 .20
❑ 79 Mike Anderson .50 .20
❑ 80 Tatum Bell .50 .20
❑ 81 Ashley Lelie .50 .20
❑ 82 Rod Smith .50 .20
❑ 83 D.J. Williams .40 .15
❑ 84 Darius Watts .40 .15
❑ 85 Ron Dayne .50 .20
❑ 86 Jeb Putzier .40 .15
❑ 87 Joey Harrington .50 .20
❑ 88 Kevin Jones .75 .30
❑ 89 Roy Williams WR .75 .30
❑ 90 Mike Williams .75 .30
❑ 91 Charles Rogers .50 .20
❑ 92 Teddy Lehman .40 .15
❑ 93 Marcus Pollard .40 .15
❑ 94 Artose Pinner .40 .15
❑ 95 Brett Favre 1.50 .60
❑ 96 Ahman Green .50 .20
❑ 97 Najeh Davenport .40 .15
❑ 98 Samkon Gado .75 .30
❑ 99 Javon Walker .50 .20
❑ 100 Donald Driver .50 .20
❑ 101 Aaron Rodgers .75 .30
❑ 102 Robert Ferguson .40 .15
❑ 103 David Carr .50 .20
❑ 104 Domanick Davis .50 .20
❑ 105 Andre Johnson .50 .20
❑ 106 Jabar Gaffney .40 .15
❑ 107 Jonathan Wells .40 .15
❑ 108 Vernand Morency .40 .15
❑ 109 Corey Bradford .40 .15
❑ 110 Jerome Mathis .40 .15
❑ 111 Peyton Manning 1.25 .50
❑ 112 Edgerrin James .75 .30
❑ 113 Marvin Harrison .75 .30
❑ 114 Reggie Wayne .50 .20
❑ 115 Dwight Freeney .50 .20
❑ 116 Dallas Clark .40 .15
❑ 117 Dominic Rhodes .50 .20
❑ 118 Jim Sorgi .40 .15
❑ 119 Brandon Stokley .50 .20
❑ 120 Bob Sanders .50 .20
❑ 121 Mike Doss .40 .15
❑ 122 Marlin Jackson .40 .15
❑ 123 Byron Leftwich .50 .20
❑ 124 Fred Taylor .50 .20
❑ 125 Jimmy Smith .50 .20
❑ 126 Matt Jones .75 .30
❑ 127 Ernest Wilford .40 .15
❑ 128 Greg Jones .40 .15
❑ 129 Mike Peterson .40 .15
❑ 130 Reggie Williams .50 .20
❑ 131 Rashean Mathis .40 .15
❑ 132 Trent Green .50 .20
❑ 133 Larry Johnson 1.00 .40
❑ 134 Priest Holmes .50 .20
❑ 135 Eddie Kennison .40 .15
❑ 136 Tony Gonzalez .50 .20
❑ 137 Kendrell Bell .40 .15
❑ 138 Samie Parker .40 .15
❑ 139 Dante Hall .50 .20
❑ 140 Tony Richardson .40 .15
❑ 141 Gus Frerotte .40 .15
❑ 142 Ronnie Brown .75 .30
❑ 143 Neil Rackers .40 .15
❑ 144 Chris Chambers .50 .20
❑ 145 Zach Thomas .75 .30
❑ 146 Cliff Russell .40 .15
❑ 147 David Boston .40 .15
❑ 148 Wes Welker .40 .15
❑ 149 Marty Booker .40 .15
❑ 150 Randy McMichael .40 .15
❑ 151 Daunte Culpepper .75 .30
❑ 152 Mewelde Moore .40 .15
❑ 153 Nate Burleson .50 .20
❑ 154 Troy Williamson .50 .20
❑ 155 Koren Robinson .50 .20
❑ 156 Erasmus James .40 .15
❑ 157 Marcus Robinson .50 .20
❑ 158 E.J. Henderson .40 .15
❑ 159 Brad Johnson .50 .20
❑ 160 Michael Bennett .40 .15
❑ 161 Travis Taylor .40 .15
❑ 162 Tom Brady 1.25 .50
❑ 163 Corey Dillon .50 .20
❑ 164 Deion Branch .50 .20
❑ 165 Tedy Bruschi .75 .30
❑ 166 Ben Watson .40 .15
❑ 167 Daniel Graham .40 .15
❑ 168 Bethel Johnson .40 .15
❑ 169 Kevin Faulk .40 .15
❑ 170 David Givens .50 .20
❑ 171 Troy Brown .50 .20
❑ 172 Aaron Brooks .50 .20
❑ 173 Deuce McAllister .50 .20
❑ 174 Joe Horn .50 .20
❑ 175 Donte Stallworth .50 .20
❑ 176 Antowain Smith .40 .15
❑ 177 Devery Henderson .40 .15
❑ 178 Eli Manning 1.00 .40
❑ 179 Tiki Barber .75 .30
❑ 180 Plaxico Burress .50 .20
❑ 181 Jeremy Shockey .75 .30
❑ 182 Osi Umenyiora .40 .15
❑ 183 Gibril Wilson .40 .15
❑ 184 Brandon Jacobs .40 .15
❑ 185 Michael Strahan .50 .20
❑ 186 Will Allen .40 .15
❑ 187 Amani Toomer .50 .20
❑ 188 Chad Pennington .50 .20
❑ 189 Curtis Martin .75 .30
❑ 190 Laveranues Coles .50 .20
❑ 191 Jonathan Vilma .50 .20
❑ 192 Ty Law .50 .20
❑ 193 Cedric Houston .40 .15
❑ 194 Justin McCareins .40 .15
❑ 195 Jerald Sowell .40 .15
❑ 196 Josh Brown .40 .15
❑ 197 LaMont Jordan .50 .20
❑ 198 Randy Moss .75 .30
❑ 199 Jerry Porter .50 .20
❑ 200 Doug Gabriel .40 .15
❑ 201 Johnnie Morant .40 .15
❑ 202 Zack Crockett .40 .15
❑ 203 Derrick Burgess .40 .15
❑ 204 Donovan McNabb .75 .30
❑ 205 Brian Westbrook .50 .20
❑ 206 Reggie Brown .50 .20
❑ 207 Terrell Owens .75 .30
❑ 208 Ryan Moats .40 .15
❑ 209 Correll Buckhalter .50 .20
❑ 210 Jevon Kearse .50 .20
❑ 211 L.J. Smith .40 .15
❑ 212 Lamar Gordon .40 .15
❑ 213 Greg Lewis .40 .15
❑ 214 Ben Roethlisberger 1.25 .50
❑ 215 Willie Parker 1.00 .40
❑ 216 Jerome Bettis .75 .30
❑ 217 Hines Ward .75 .30
❑ 218 Troy Polamalu 1.00 .40
❑ 219 Heath Miller .75 .30
❑ 220 Antwaan Randle El .50 .20
❑ 221 Duce Staley .50 .20
❑ 222 Cedrick Wilson .40 .15
❑ 223 James Farrior .40 .15
❑ 224 Drew Brees .75 .30
❑ 225 LaDainian Tomlinson 1.00 .40
❑ 226 Keenan McCardell .40 .15
❑ 227 Antonio Gates .75 .30
❑ 228 Shawne Merriman .50 .20
❑ 229 Philip Rivers .75 .30
❑ 230 Vincent Jackson .40 .15
❑ 231 Donnie Edwards .40 .15
❑ 232 Eric Parker .40 .15
❑ 233 Reche Caldwell .40 .15
❑ 234 Alex Smith QB 1.00 .40
❑ 235 Frank Gore .75 .30
❑ 236 Brandon Lloyd .50 .20
❑ 237 Kevan Barlow .50 .20
❑ 238 Rashaun Woods .40 .15
❑ 239 Arnaz Battle .40 .15
❑ 240 Matt Hasselbeck .50 .20
❑ 241 Shaun Alexander .75 .30
❑ 242 Darrell Jackson .50 .20
❑ 243 Jerramy Stevens .50 .20
❑ 244 Lofa Tatupu .50 .20
❑ 245 D.J. Hackett .40 .15
❑ 246 Bobby Engram .40 .15
❑ 247 Joe Jurevicius .50 .20
❑ 248 Maurice Morris .40 .15
❑ 249 Marc Bulger .50 .20
❑ 250 Steven Jackson .75 .30
❑ 251 Torry Holt .50 .20
❑ 252 Isaac Bruce .50 .20
❑ 253 Kevin Curtis .40 .15
❑ 254 Marshall Faulk .50 .20
❑ 255 Shaun McDonald .40 .15
❑ 256 Chris Simms .50 .20
❑ 257 Cadillac Williams .75 .30
❑ 258 Joey Galloway .50 .20
❑ 259 Michael Clayton .50 .20
❑ 260 Derrick Brooks .50 .20
❑ 261 Ronde Barber .40 .15
❑ 262 Michael Pittman .40 .15
❑ 263 Alex Smith TE .40 .15
❑ 264 Simeon Rice .40 .15
❑ 265 Steve McNair .50 .20
❑ 266 Chris Brown .50 .20
❑ 267 Drew Bennett .40 .15
❑ 268 Brandon Jones .40 .15
❑ 269 Adam Jones .40 .15
❑ 270 Keith Bulluck .40 .15
❑ 271 Ben Troupe .40 .15
❑ 272 Jarrett Payton .40 .15
❑ 273 Tyrone Calico .40 .15
❑ 274 Bobby Wade .40 .15
❑ 275 Troy Fleming .40 .15
❑ 276 Mark Brunell .50 .20
❑ 277 Clinton Portis .75 .30

❑ 278 Santana Moss .50 .20
❑ 279 Jason Campbell .50 .20
❑ 280 Chris Cooley .40 .15
❑ 281 Carlos Rogers .40 .15
❑ 282 Ladell Betts .40 .15
❑ 283 Patrick Ramsey .50 .20
❑ 284 Taylor Jacobs .40 .15
❑ 285 James Thrash .40 .15
❑ 286 Adrian Wilson .40 .15
❑ 287 London Fletcher .40 .15
❑ 288 Lance Briggs .50 .20
❑ 289 Robert Mathis .40 .15
❑ 290 Rod Coleman .40 .15
❑ 291 Bart Scott RC 2.50 1.00
❑ 292 Brian Moorman RC .60 .25
❑ 293 Shayne Graham RC .60 .25
❑ 294 Kevin Kaesviharn RC .60 .25
❑ 295 Leigh Bodden RC .60 .25
❑ 296 Lousaka Polite RC .60 .25
❑ 297 Todd Devoe RC 1.25 .50
❑ 298 Scottie Vines .60 .25
❑ 299 Cullen Jenkins RC .60 .25
❑ 300 Donovan Morgan RC .60 .25
❑ 301 C.C. Brown .60 .25
❑ 302 Demarcus Faggins RC .60 .25
❑ 303 Shantee Orr RC .60 .25
❑ 304 Vashon Pearson RC .60 .25
❑ 305 Reggie Hayward RC .60 .25
❑ 306 Paul Spicer RC .60 .25
❑ 307 Kenny Wright RC .60 .25
❑ 308 Rich Alexis RC .60 .25
❑ 309 Terrence Melton RC .60 .25
❑ 310 Willie Whitehead RC .60 .25
❑ 311 Kendrick Clancy RC .60 .25
❑ 312 Mark Brown RC .60 .25
❑ 313 Tommy Kelly .60 .25
❑ 314 Josh Parry RC .60 .25
❑ 315 Malcolm Floyd RC 1.25 .50
❑ 316 Mike Adams RC .60 .25
❑ 317 Ben Emanuel RC .60 .25
❑ 318 Brandon Moore RC .60 .25
❑ 319 Chartric Darby RC .60 .25
❑ 320 Bryce Fisher RC .60 .25
❑ 321 D.D. Lewis RC .60 .25
❑ 322 Jimmy Williams DB RC .60 .25
❑ 323 Robert Pollard RC .60 .25
❑ 324 Chris Johnson RC .60 .25
❑ 325 Edell Shepherd RC .60 .25
❑ 326 O.J. Small RC .60 .25
❑ 327 Brad Kassell RC .60 .25
❑ 328 M.Leinart/R.Bush 8.00 3.00
❑ 329 M.Leinart/V.Young 5.00 2.00
❑ 330 White/Leinart/Bush 8.00 3.00
❑ 331 Matt Leinart RC 25.00 10.00
❑ 332 Chad Greenway RC 6.00 2.50
❑ 333 Devin Aromashodu RC 5.00 2.00
❑ 334 DeAngelo Williams RC 15.00 6.00
❑ 335 Travis Wilson RC 6.00 2.50
❑ 336 Leon Washington RC 10.00 4.00
❑ 337 Maurice Stovall RC 6.00 2.50
❑ 338 Michael Huff RC 8.00 3.00
❑ 339 Charlie Whitehurst RC 8.00 3.00
❑ 340 Vince Young RC 25.00 10.00
❑ 341 Jerious Norwood RC 10.00 4.00
❑ 342 D'Brickashaw Ferguson RC 6.00 2.50
❑ 343 Taurean Henderson RC 6.00 2.50
❑ 344 Dominique Byrd RC 5.00 2.00
❑ 345 Sinorice Moss RC 8.00 3.00
❑ 346 Martin Nance RC 5.00 2.00
❑ 347 Vernon Davis RC 12.00 5.00
❑ 348 Ko Simpson RC 5.00 2.00
❑ 349 Jerome Harrison RC 6.00 2.50
❑ 350 Jay Cutler RC 25.00 10.00
❑ 351 Alan Zemaitis RC 6.00 2.50
❑ 352 Haloti Ngata RC 6.00 2.50
❑ 353 Greg Lee RC 5.00 2.00
❑ 354 Laurence Maroney RC 20.00 8.00
❑ 355 Bobby Carpenter RC 6.00 2.50
❑ 356 Jonathan Orr RC 5.00 2.00
❑ 357 Marcedes Lewis RC 6.00 2.50
❑ 358 Brodrick Bunkley RC 6.00 2.50
❑ 359 Todd Watkins RC 5.00 2.00
❑ 360 Reggie Bush RC 60.00 25.00
❑ 361 Jimmy Williams RC 6.00 2.50
❑ 362 Maurice Drew RC 15.00 6.00
❑ 363 Mario Williams RC 10.00 4.00
❑ 364 Derek Hagan RC 6.00 2.50
❑ 365 Santonio Holmes RC 12.00 5.00
❑ 366 Tye Hill RC 6.00 2.50
❑ 367 Jason Avant RC 6.00 2.50
❑ 368 Tamba Hali RC 6.00 2.50
❑ 369 Joe Klopfenstein RC 5.00 2.00
❑ 370 LenDale White RC 12.00 5.00
❑ 371 DeMeco Ryans RC 8.00 3.00
❑ 372 Bruce Gradkowski RC 10.00 4.00
❑ 373 A.J. Hawk RC 12.00 5.00
❑ 374 Gabe Watson RC 5.00 2.00
❑ 375 Devin Hester RC 12.00 5.00
❑ 376 Demetrius Williams RC 8.00 3.00
❑ 377 Joseph Addai RC 20.00 8.00
❑ 378 Leonard Pope RC 6.00 2.50
❑ 379 Omar Jacobs RC 5.00 2.00
❑ 380 Brad Smith RC 6.00 2.50
❑ 381 Michael Robinson RC 10.00 4.00
❑ 382 Brodie Croyle RC 10.00 4.00
❑ 383 Anthony Fasano RC 6.00 2.50
❑ 384 Brian Calhoun RC 6.00 2.50
❑ 385 Chad Jackson RC 10.00 4.00
❑ 386 Drew Olson RC 5.00 2.00
❑ 387 Greg Jennings RC 12.00 5.00
❑ 388 Andre Hall RC 5.00 2.00
❑ 389 Ryan Gilbert RC 5.00 2.00
❑ 390 Tim Day RC 5.00 2.00
❑ 391 Brandon Williams RC 6.00 2.50
❑ 392 Mark Anderson RC 15.00 6.00
❑ 393 DonTrell Moore RC 5.00 2.00
❑ 394 Kellen Clemens RC 8.00 3.00
❑ 395 Ernie Sims RC 8.00 3.00
❑ 396 Cedric Humes RC 6.00 2.50
❑ 397 Brandon Kirsch RC 6.00 2.50
❑ 398 Tony Scheffler RC 6.00 2.50
❑ 399 Kelly Jennings RC 6.00 2.50
❑ 400 Manny Lawson RC 6.00 2.50
❑ 401 Terrence Whitehead RC 5.00 2.00
❑ 402 Marcus Vick RC 5.00 2.00
❑ 403 De'Arrius Howard RC 6.00 2.50
❑ 404 Wendell Mathis RC 5.00 2.00
❑ 405 Abdul Hodge RC 6.00 2.50
❑ 406 Owen Daniels RC 6.00 2.50
❑ 407 Mike Hass RC 6.00 2.50
❑ 408 Brett Elliott RC 6.00 2.50
❑ 409 Kamerion Wimbley RC 6.00 2.50
❑ 410 Jeremy Bloom RC 5.00 2.00
❑ 411 D.J. Shockley RC 6.00 2.50
❑ 412 Darnell Bing RC 6.00 2.50
❑ 413 Miles Austin RC 5.00 2.00
❑ 414 D'Qwell Jackson RC 5.00 2.00
❑ 415 Tarvaris Jackson RC 10.00 4.00
❑ 416 Mathias Kiwanuka RC 8.00 3.00
❑ 417 Mike Bell RC 10.00 4.00
❑ 418 Paul Pinegar RC 5.00 2.00
❑ 419 David Thomas RC 6.00 2.50
❑ 420 Hank Baskett RC 6.00 2.50
❑ 421 P.J. Daniels RC 5.00 2.00
❑ 422 Jon Alston RC 6.00 2.50
❑ 423 Reggie McNeal RC 5.00 2.00
❑ 424 Brandon Marshall RC 6.00 2.50
❑ 425 Gerald Riggs RC 6.00 2.50
❑ 426 Delanie Walker RC 5.00 2.00
❑ 427 Erik Meyer RC 5.00 2.00
❑ 428 Jeff Webb RC 5.00 2.00
❑ 429 Skyler Green RC 6.00 2.50
❑ 430 Thomas Howard RC 6.00 2.50

1995 Select Certified

❑ COMPLETE SET (135) 40.00 15.00
❑ 1 Marshall Faulk 4.00 1.50
❑ 2 Heath Shuler .50 .20
❑ 3 Garrison Hearst 1.00 .40
❑ 4 Errict Rhett .50 .20
❑ 5 Jeff George .50 .20
❑ 6 Jerome Bettis 1.00 .40
❑ 7 Jim Kelly 1.00 .40
❑ 8 Rick Mirer .50 .20
❑ 9 Willie Davis .50 .20
❑ 10 Steve Young 2.50 1.00
❑ 11 Erik Kramer .25 .08
❑ 12 Natrone Means .50 .20
❑ 13 Jeff Blake RC 3.00 1.25
❑ 14 Neil O'Donnell .50 .20
❑ 15 Andre Rison .50 .20
❑ 16 Randall Cunningham 1.00 .40
❑ 17 Emmitt Smith 5.00 2.00
❑ 18 Tim Brown 1.00 .40
❑ 19 Shannon Sharpe .50 .20
❑ 20 Boomer Esiason .50 .20
❑ 21 Barry Sanders 5.00 2.00
❑ 22 Rodney Hampton .50 .20
❑ 23 Robert Brooks 1.00 .40
❑ 24 Jim Everett .25 .08
❑ 25 Gary Brown .25 .08
❑ 26 Drew Bledsoe 1.25 .50
❑ 27 Desmond Howard .50 .20
❑ 28 Cris Carter 1.00 .40
❑ 29 Marcus Allen 1.00 .40
❑ 30 Dan Marino 6.00 2.50
❑ 31 Warren Moon .50 .20
❑ 32 Dave Krieg .25 .08
❑ 33 Ben Coates .50 .20
❑ 34 Terance Mathis .50 .20
❑ 35 Mario Bates .50 .20
❑ 36 Andre Reed .50 .20
❑ 37 Dave Brown .50 .20
❑ 38 Jeff Graham .25 .08
❑ 39 Johnny Mitchell .25 .08
❑ 40 Carl Pickens .50 .20
❑ 41 Jeff Hostetler .50 .20
❑ 42 Vinny Testaverde .50 .20
❑ 43 Ricky Watters .50 .20
❑ 44 Troy Aikman 3.00 1.25
❑ 45 Byron Bam Morris .25 .08
❑ 46 John Elway 6.00 2.50
❑ 47 Junior Seau 1.00 .40
❑ 48 Scott Mitchell .50 .20
❑ 49 Jerry Rice 3.00 1.25
❑ 50 Brett Favre 6.00 2.50
❑ 51 Chris Warren .50 .20
❑ 52 Chris Chandler .50 .20
❑ 53 Lorenzo White .25 .08
❑ 54 Craig Erickson .25 .08
❑ 55 Alvin Harper .25 .08
❑ 56 Steve Beuerlein .50 .20
❑ 57 Edgar Bennett .50 .20
❑ 58 Steve Bono .50 .20
❑ 59 Eric Green .25 .08
❑ 60 Jake Reed .50 .20
❑ 61 Terry Kirby .50 .20
❑ 62 Vincent Brisby .25 .08
❑ 63 Lake Dawson .50 .20
❑ 64 Torrance Small .25 .08
❑ 65 Mark Brunell 1.25 .50
❑ 66 Haywood Jeffires .25 .08
❑ 67 Flipper Anderson .25 .08
❑ 68 Ronald Moore .25 .08
❑ 69 LeShon Johnson .50 .20
❑ 70 Rocket Ismail .50 .20
❑ 71 Herman Moore 1.00 .40
❑ 72 Charlie Garner 1.00 .40
❑ 73 Anthony Miller .50 .20
❑ 74 Greg Lloyd .50 .20
❑ 75 Michael Irvin 1.00 .40
❑ 76 Stan Humphries .50 .20
❑ 77 Leroy Hoard .25 .08
❑ 78 Deion Sanders Mail Out 3.00 1.25
❑ 79 Darnay Scott .50 .20
❑ 80 Chris Miller .25 .08
❑ 81 Curtis Conway 1.00 .40
❑ 82 Trent Dilfer 1.00 .40
❑ 83 Bruce Smith 1.00 .40
❑ 84 Reggie Brooks .50 .20
❑ 85 Frank Reich .25 .08
❑ 86 Henry Ellard .50 .20
❑ 87 Eric Metcalf .50 .20
❑ 88 Sean Gilbert .50 .20

❑ 89 Larry Centers	.50	.20
❑ 90 Ricky Ervins	.25	.08
❑ 91 Craig Heyward	.50	.20
❑ 92 Rod Woodson	.50	.20
❑ 93 Steve Walsh	.25	.08
❑ 94 Fred Barnett	.50	.20
❑ 95 William Floyd	.50	.20
❑ 96 Harvey Williams	.25	.08
❑ 97 Greg Hill	.50	.20
❑ 98 Irving Fryar	.50	.20
❑ 99 Kevin Williams WR	.50	.20
❑ 100 Herschel Walker	.50	.20
❑ 101 Sean Dawkins	.50	.20
❑ 102 Michael Haynes	.50	.20
❑ 103 Reggie White	1.00	.40
❑ 104 Robert Smith	1.00	.40
❑ 105 Todd Collins RC	1.00	.40
❑ 106 Michael Westbrook RC	2.00	.75
❑ 107 Frank Sanders RC	2.00	.75
❑ 108 Christian Fauria RC	1.00	.40
❑ 109 Stoney Case RC	.50	.20
❑ 110 Jimmy Oliver RC	.50	.20
❑ 111 Mark Bruener RC	1.00	.40
❑ 112 Rodney Thomas RC	1.00	.40
❑ 113 Chris T.Jones RC	.50	.20
❑ 114 James A.Stewart RC	.50	.20
❑ 115 Kevin Carter RC	2.00	.75
❑ 116 Eric Zeier RC	2.00	.75
❑ 117 Curtis Martin RC	15.00	6.00
❑ 118 James O. Stewart RC	5.00	2.00
❑ 119 Joe Aska RC	.50	.20
❑ 120 Ken Dilger RC	2.00	.75
❑ 121 Tyrone Wheatley RC	5.00	2.00
❑ 122 Ray Zellars RC	1.00	.40
❑ 123 Kyle Brady RC	2.00	.75
❑ 124 Chad May RC	.50	.20
❑ 125 Napoleon Kaufman RC	5.00	2.00
❑ 126 Terrell Davis RC	12.00	5.00
❑ 127 Warren Sapp RC	6.00	2.50
❑ 128 Sherman Williams RC	.50	.20
❑ 129 Kordell Stewart RC	8.00	3.00
❑ 130 Ki-Jana Carter RC	2.00	.75
❑ 131 Terrell Fletcher RC	.50	.20
❑ 132 Rashaan Salaam RC	1.00	.40
❑ 133 J.J. Stokes RC	2.00	.75
❑ 134 Kerry Collins RC	8.00	3.00
❑ 135 Joey Galloway RC	8.00	3.00
❑ P7 Dan Marino Promo	5.00	2.00
❑ P10 Steve Young Promo	2.00	.75
❑ P44 Troy Aikman Promo	2.50	1.00

1996 Select Certified

❑ COMPLETE SET (125)	50.00	20.00
❑ 1 Isaac Bruce	.75	.30
❑ 2 Rick Mirer	.40	.15
❑ 3 Jake Reed	.40	.15
❑ 4 Reggie White	.75	.30
❑ 5 Harvey Williams	.20	.07
❑ 6 Jim Everett	.20	.07
❑ 7 Tony Martin	.40	.15
❑ 8 Craig Heyward	.20	.07
❑ 9 Tamarick Vanover	.40	.15
❑ 10 Hugh Douglas	.40	.15
❑ 11 Erik Kramer	.20	.07
❑ 12 Charlie Garner	.40	.15
❑ 13 Erric Pegram	.20	.07
❑ 14 Scott Mitchell	.40	.15
❑ 15 Michael Westbrook	.75	.30
❑ 16 Robert Smith	.40	.15
❑ 17 Kerry Collins	.75	.30
❑ 18 Derek Loville	.20	.07
❑ 19 Jeff Blake	.75	.30
❑ 20 Terry Kirby	.40	.15
❑ 21 Bruce Smith	.40	.15
❑ 22 Stan Humphries	.40	.15
❑ 23 Rodney Thomas	.20	.07
❑ 24 Wayne Chrebet	1.00	.40
❑ 25 Napoleon Kaufman	.75	.30
❑ 26 Marshall Faulk	1.00	.40
❑ 27 Emmitt Smith	3.00	1.25
❑ 28 Natrone Means	.40	.15
❑ 29 Neil O'Donnell	.40	.15
❑ 30 Warren Moon	.40	.15
❑ 31 Junior Seau	.75	.30
❑ 32 Chris Sanders	.40	.15
❑ 33 Barry Sanders	3.00	1.25
❑ 34 Jeff Graham	.20	.07
❑ 35 Kordell Stewart	.75	.30
❑ 36 Jim Harbaugh	.40	.15
❑ 37 Chris Warren	.40	.15
❑ 38 Cris Carter	.75	.30
❑ 39 J.J. Stokes	.75	.30
❑ 40 Tyrone Wheatley	.40	.15
❑ 41 Terrell Davis	1.50	.60
❑ 42 Mark Brunell	1.25	.50
❑ 43 Steve Young	1.50	.60
❑ 44 Rodney Hampton	.40	.15
❑ 45 Drew Bledsoe	1.25	.50
❑ 46 Larry Centers	.40	.15
❑ 47 Ken Norton Jr.	.20	.07
❑ 48 Deion Sanders	1.25	.50
❑ 49 Alvin Harper	.20	.07
❑ 50 Trent Dilfer	.75	.30
❑ 51 Steve McNair	1.50	.60
❑ 52 Robert Brooks	.75	.30
❑ 53 Edgar Bennett	.40	.15
❑ 54 Troy Aikman	2.00	.75
❑ 55 Dan Marino	4.00	1.50
❑ 56 Steve Bono	.20	.07
❑ 57 Marcus Allen	.75	.30
❑ 58 Rodney Peete	.20	.07
❑ 59 Ben Coates	.40	.15
❑ 60 Yancey Thigpen	.40	.15
❑ 61 Tim Brown	.75	.30
❑ 62 Jerry Rice	2.00	.75
❑ 63 Quinn Early	.20	.07
❑ 64 Ricky Watters	.40	.15
❑ 65 Thurman Thomas	.75	.30
❑ 66 Greg Lloyd	.40	.15
❑ 67 Eric Metcalf	.20	.07
❑ 68 Jeff George	.40	.15
❑ 69 John Elway	4.00	1.50
❑ 70 Frank Sanders	.40	.15
❑ 71 Curtis Conway	.75	.30
❑ 72 Greg Hill	.40	.15
❑ 73 Darick Holmes	.20	.07
❑ 74 Herman Moore	.40	.15
❑ 75 Carl Pickens	.40	.15
❑ 76 Eric Zeier	.20	.07
❑ 77 Curtis Martin	1.50	.60
❑ 78 Rashaan Salaam	.40	.15
❑ 79 Joey Galloway	.75	.30
❑ 80 Jeff Hostetler	.20	.07
❑ 81 Jim Kelly	.75	.30
❑ 82 Dave Brown	.20	.07
❑ 83 Sean Dawkins	.20	.07
❑ 84 Michael Irvin	.75	.30
❑ 85 Brett Favre	4.00	1.50
❑ 86 Cedric Jones RC	.25	.08
❑ 87 Jeff Lewis RC	.50	.20
❑ 88 Alex Van Dyke RC	.50	.20
❑ 89 Regan Upshaw RC	.25	.08
❑ 90 Karim Abdul-Jabbar RC	1.00	.40
❑ 91 Marvin Harrison RC	12.00	5.00
❑ 92 Stephen Davis RC	8.00	3.00
❑ 93 Terry Glenn RC	4.00	1.50
❑ 94 Kevin Hardy RC	1.00	.40
❑ 95 Stanley Pritchett RC	.25	.08
❑ 96 Willie Anderson RC	.25	.08
❑ 97 Lawrence Phillips RC	.50	.20
❑ 98 Bobby Hoying RC	1.00	.40
❑ 99 Amani Toomer RC	4.00	1.50
❑ 100 Eddie George RC	6.00	2.50
❑ 101 Stepfret Williams RC	.25	.08
❑ 102 Eric Moulds RC	5.00	2.00
❑ 103 Simeon Rice RC	2.50	1.00
❑ 104 John Mobley RC	.25	.08
❑ 105 Keyshawn Johnson RC	4.00	1.50
❑ 106 Daryl Gardener RC	.25	.08
❑ 107 Tony Banks RC	1.00	.40
❑ 108 Bobby Engram RC	1.00	.40
❑ 109 Jonathan Ogden RC	1.00	.40
❑ 110 Eddie Kennison RC	1.00	.40
❑ 111 Danny Kanell RC	1.00	.40
❑ 112 Tony Brackens RC	1.00	.40
❑ 113 Tim Biakabutuka RC	1.00	.40
❑ 114 Leeland McElroy RC	.50	.20
❑ 115 Rickey Dudley RC	1.00	.40
❑ 116 Troy Aikman SS	1.00	.40
❑ 117 Brett Favre SS	2.00	.75
❑ 118 Drew Bledsoe SS	.75	.30
❑ 119 Steve Young SS	.75	.30
❑ 120 Kerry Collins SS	.75	.30
❑ 121 John Elway SS	2.00	.75
❑ 122 Dan Marino SS	2.00	.75
❑ 123 Kordell Stewart SS	.75	.30
❑ 124 Jeff Blake SS	.40	.15
❑ 125 Jim Harbaugh SS	.40	.15

1993 SP

❑ COMPLETE SET (270)	60.00	25.00
❑ 1 Curtis Conway FOIL RC	4.00	1.50
❑ 2 John Copeland FOIL RC	.75	.30
❑ 3 Kevin Williams RC WR FOIL	1.50	.60
❑ 4 Dan Williams FOIL RC	.75	.30
❑ 5 Patrick Bates FOIL RC	.75	.30
❑ 6 Jerome Bettis FOIL RC	25.00	15.00
❑ 7 O.J.McDuffie FOIL RC	3.00	1.25
❑ 8 Robert Smith FOIL RC	8.00	3.00
❑ 9 Drew Bledsoe FOIL RC	30.00	12.50
❑ 10 Irv Smith FOIL RC	.75	.30
❑ 11 Marvin Jones FOIL RC	.75	.30
❑ 12 Victor Bailey FOIL RC	.75	.30
❑ 13 Garrison Hearst FOIL RC	8.00	3.00
❑ 14 Natrone Means FOIL RC	3.00	1.25
❑ 15 Todd Kelly FOIL RC	.75	.30
❑ 16 Rick Mirer FOIL RC	3.00	1.25
❑ 17 Eric Curry FOIL RC	.75	.30
❑ 18 Reggie Brooks FOIL RC	1.50	.60
❑ 19 Eric Dickerson	.50	.20
❑ 20 Roger Harper RC	.30	.10
❑ 21 Michael Haynes	.50	.20
❑ 22 Bobby Hebert	.30	.10
❑ 23 Lincoln Kennedy RC	.30	.10
❑ 24 Chris Miller	.50	.20
❑ 25 Mike Pritchard	.50	.20
❑ 26 Andre Rison	.50	.20
❑ 27 Deion Sanders	1.50	.60
❑ 28 Cornelius Bennett	.50	.20
❑ 29 Kenneth Davis	.30	.10
❑ 30 Henry Jones	.30	.10
❑ 31 Jim Kelly	1.00	.40
❑ 32 John Parrella RC	.30	.10
❑ 33 Andre Reed	.50	.20
❑ 34 Bruce Smith	1.00	.40
❑ 35 Thomas Smith RC	.50	.20
❑ 36 Thurman Thomas	1.00	.40
❑ 37 Neal Anderson	.30	.10
❑ 38 Myron Baker RC	.30	.10
❑ 39 Mark Carrier DB	.30	.10
❑ 40 Richard Dent	.50	.20
❑ 41 Chris Gedney RC	.30	.10
❑ 42 Jim Harbaugh	1.00	.40
❑ 43 Craig Heyward	.50	.20
❑ 44 Carl Simpson RC	.30	.10

❑ 45 Alonzo Spellman .30 .10
❑ 46 Derrick Fenner .30 .10
❑ 47 Harold Green .30 .10
❑ 48 David Klingler .30 .10
❑ 49 Ricardo McDonald .30 .10
❑ 50 Tony McGee RC .50 .20
❑ 51 Carl Pickens .50 .20
❑ 52 Steve Tovar RC .30 .10
❑ 53 Alfred Williams .30 .10
❑ 54 Darryl Williams .30 .10
❑ 55 Jerry Ball .30 .10
❑ 56 Mike Caldwell RC .30 .10
❑ 57 Mark Carrier WR .50 .20
❑ 58 Steve Everitt RC .30 .10
❑ 59 Dan Footman RC .30 .10
❑ 60 Pepper Johnson .30 .10
❑ 61 Bernie Kosar .50 .20
❑ 62 Eric Metcalf .50 .20
❑ 63 Michael Dean Perry .50 .20
❑ 64 Troy Aikman 2.50 1.25
❑ 65 Charles Haley .50 .20
❑ 66 Michael Irvin 1.00 .40
❑ 67 Robert Jones .30 .10
❑ 68 Derrick Lassic RC .30 .10
❑ 69 Russell Maryland .30 .10
❑ 70 Ken Norton Jr. .50 .20
❑ 71 Darrin Smith RC .50 .20
❑ 72 Emmitt Smith 5.00 2.50
❑ 73 Steve Atwater .30 .10
❑ 74 Rod Bernstine .30 .10
❑ 75 Jason Elam RC 1.00 .40
❑ 76 John Elway 5.00 2.00
❑ 77 Simon Fletcher .30 .10
❑ 78 Tommy Maddox 1.00 .40
❑ 79 Glyn Milburn RC 1.00 .40
❑ 80 Derek Russell .30 .10
❑ 81 Shannon Sharpe 1.00 .40
❑ 82 Bennie Blades .30 .10
❑ 83 Willie Green .30 .10
❑ 84 Antonio London RC .30 .10
❑ 85 Ryan McNeil RC 1.00 .40
❑ 86 Herman Moore 1.00 .40
❑ 87 Rodney Peete .30 .10
❑ 88 Barry Sanders 4.00 1.50
❑ 89 Chris Spielman .50 .20
❑ 90 Pat Swilling .30 .10
❑ 91 Mark Brunell RC 15.00 6.00
❑ 92 Terrell Buckley .30 .10
❑ 93 Brett Favre 6.00 3.00
❑ 94 Jackie Harris .30 .10
❑ 95 Sterling Sharpe 1.00 .40
❑ 96 John Stephens .30 .10
❑ 97 Wayne Simmons RC .30 .10
❑ 98 George Teague RC .50 .20
❑ 99 Reggie White 1.00 .40
❑ 100 Micheal Barrow RC 1.00 .40
❑ 101 Cody Carlson .30 .10
❑ 102 Ray Childress .30 .10
❑ 103 Brad Hopkins RC .30 .10
❑ 104 Haywood Jeffires .50 .20
❑ 105 Wilber Marshall .30 .10
❑ 106 Warren Moon 1.00 .40
❑ 107 Webster Slaughter .30 .10
❑ 108 Lorenzo White .30 .10
❑ 109 John Baylor .30 .10
❑ 110 Duane Bickett .30 .10
❑ 111 Quentin Coryatt .50 .20
❑ 112 Steve Emtman .30 .10
❑ 113 Jeff George 1.00 .40
❑ 114 Jessie Hester .30 .10
❑ 115 Anthony Johnson .50 .20
❑ 116 Reggie Langhorne .30 .10
❑ 117 Roosevelt Potts RC .30 .10
❑ 118 Marcus Allen 1.00 .40
❑ 119 J.J. Birden .30 .10
❑ 120 Willie Davis 1.00 .40
❑ 121 Jaime Fields RC .30 .10
❑ 122 Joe Montana 5.00 2.00
❑ 123 Will Shields RC 1.00 .40
❑ 124 Neil Smith 1.00 .40
❑ 125 Derrick Thomas 1.00 .40
❑ 126 Harvey Williams .50 .20
❑ 127 Tim Brown 1.00 .40
❑ 128 Billy Joe Hobert RC 1.00 .40
❑ 129 Jeff Hostetler .50 .20
❑ 130 Ethan Horton .30 .10
❑ 131 Rocket Ismail .50 .20
❑ 132 Howie Long 1.00 .40
❑ 133 Terry McDaniel .30 .10
❑ 134 Greg Robinson RC .30 .10
❑ 135 Anthony Smith .30 .10
❑ 136 Flipper Anderson .30 .10
❑ 137 Marc Boutte .30 .10
❑ 138 Shane Conlan .30 .10
❑ 139 Troy Drayton RC .50 .20
❑ 140 Henry Ellard .50 .20
❑ 141 Jim Everett .50 .20
❑ 142 Cleveland Gary .30 .10
❑ 143 Sean Gilbert .50 .20
❑ 144 Robert Young .30 .10
❑ 145 Marco Coleman .30 .10
❑ 146 Bryan Cox .30 .10
❑ 147 Irving Fryar .50 .20
❑ 148 Keith Jackson .50 .20
❑ 149 Terry Kirby RC 1.00 .40
❑ 150 Dan Marino 5.00 2.00
❑ 151 Scott Mitchell 1.00 .40
❑ 152 Louis Oliver .30 .10
❑ 153 Troy Vincent .30 .10
❑ 154 Anthony Carter .50 .20
❑ 155 Cris Carter 1.00 .40
❑ 156 Roger Craig .50 .20
❑ 157 Chris Doleman .30 .10
❑ 158 Qadry Ismail RC 2.00 .75
❑ 159 Steve Jordan .30 .10
❑ 160 Randall McDaniel .30 .10
❑ 161 Audray McMillian .30 .10
❑ 162 Barry Word .30 .10
❑ 163 Vincent Brown .30 .10
❑ 164 Marv Cook .30 .10
❑ 165 Sam Gash RC 1.00 .40
❑ 166 Pat Harlow .30 .10
❑ 167 Greg McMurtry .30 .10
❑ 168 Todd Rucci RC .30 .10
❑ 169 Leonard Russell .50 .20
❑ 170 Scott Sisson RC .30 .10
❑ 171 Chris Slade RC .50 .20
❑ 172 Morten Andersen .30 .10
❑ 173 Derek Brown RC RBK .50 .20
❑ 174 Reggie Freeman RC .30 .10
❑ 175 Rickey Jackson .30 .10
❑ 176 Eric Martin .30 .10
❑ 177 Wayne Martin .30 .10
❑ 178 Brad Muster .30 .10
❑ 179 Willie Roaf RC .50 .20
❑ 180 Renaldo Turnbull .30 .10
❑ 181 Derek Brown TE .30 .10
❑ 182 Marcus Buckley RC .30 .10
❑ 183 Jarrod Bunch .30 .10
❑ 184 Rodney Hampton .50 .20
❑ 185 Ed McCaffrey 1.00 .40
❑ 186 Kanavis McGhee .30 .10
❑ 187 Mike Sherrard .30 .10
❑ 188 Phil Simms .50 .20
❑ 189 Lawrence Taylor 1.00 .40
❑ 190 Kurt Barber .30 .10
❑ 191 Boomer Esiason .50 .20
❑ 192 Johnny Johnson .30 .10
❑ 193 Ronnie Lott .50 .20
❑ 194 Johnny Mitchell .30 .10
❑ 195 Rob Moore .50 .20
❑ 196 Adrian Murrell RC 1.00 .40
❑ 197 Browning Nagle .30 .10
❑ 198 Marvin Washington .30 .10
❑ 199 Eric Allen .30 .10
❑ 200 Fred Barnett .50 .20
❑ 201 Randall Cunningham 1.00 .40
❑ 202 Byron Evans .30 .10
❑ 203 Tim Harris .30 .10
❑ 204 Seth Joyner .30 .10
❑ 205 Leonard Renfro RC .30 .10
❑ 206 Heath Sherman .30 .10
❑ 207 Clyde Simmons .30 .10
❑ 208 Johnny Bailey .30 .10
❑ 209 Steve Beuerlein .50 .20
❑ 210 Chuck Cecil .30 .10
❑ 211 Larry Centers RC 1.00 .40
❑ 212 Gary Clark .50 .20
❑ 213 Ernest Dye RC .30 .10
❑ 214 Ken Harvey .30 .10
❑ 215 Randal Hill .30 .10
❑ 216 Ricky Proehl .30 .10
❑ 217 Deon Figures RC .30 .10
❑ 218 Barry Foster .50 .20
❑ 219 Eric Green .30 .10
❑ 220 Kevin Greene .50 .20
❑ 221 Carlton Haselrig .30 .10
❑ 222 Andre Hastings RC .50 .20
❑ 223 Greg Lloyd .50 .20
❑ 224 Neil O'Donnell 1.00 .40
❑ 225 Rod Woodson 1.00 .40
❑ 226 Marion Butts .30 .10
❑ 227 Darren Carrington RC .30 .10
❑ 228 Darrien Gordon RC .30 .10
❑ 229 Ronnie Harmon .30 .10
❑ 230 Stan Humphries .50 .20
❑ 231 Anthony Miller .50 .20
❑ 232 Chris Mims .30 .10
❑ 233 Leslie O'Neal .50 .20
❑ 234 Junior Seau 1.00 .40
❑ 235 Dana Hall .30 .10
❑ 236 Adrian Hardy .30 .10
❑ 237 Brent Jones .50 .20
❑ 238 Tim McDonald .30 .10
❑ 239 Tom Rathman .30 .10
❑ 240 Jerry Rice 3.00 1.50
❑ 241 Dana Stubblefield RC 1.00 .40
❑ 242 Ricky Watters 1.00 .40
❑ 243 Steve Young 2.50 1.25
❑ 244 Brian Blades .50 .20
❑ 245 Ferrell Edmunds .30 .10
❑ 246 Carlton Gray RC .30 .10
❑ 247 Cortez Kennedy .50 .20
❑ 248 Kelvin Martin .30 .10
❑ 249 Dan McGwire .30 .10
❑ 250 Jon Vaughn .30 .10
❑ 251 Chris Warren .50 .20
❑ 252 John L. Williams .30 .10
❑ 253 Reggie Cobb .30 .10
❑ 254 Horace Copeland RC .50 .20
❑ 255 Lawrence Dawsey .30 .10
❑ 256 Demetrius DuBose RC .30 .10
❑ 257 Craig Erickson .50 .20
❑ 258 Courtney Hawkins .30 .10
❑ 259 John Lynch RC 8.00 3.00
❑ 260 Hardy Nickerson .50 .20
❑ 261 Lamar Thomas RC .30 .10
❑ 262 Carl Banks .30 .10
❑ 263 Tom Carter RC .50 .20
❑ 264 Brad Edwards .30 .10
❑ 265 Kurt Gouveia .30 .10
❑ 266 Desmond Howard .50 .20
❑ 267 Charles Mann .30 .10
❑ 268 Art Monk .50 .20
❑ 269 Mark Rypien .30 .10
❑ 270 Ricky Sanders .30 .10
❑ P1 Joe Montana Promo 5.00 2.00

1994 SP

❑ COMPLETE SET (200) 50.00 25.00
❑ 1 Dan Wilkinson FOIL RC 1.25 .50
❑ 2 Heath Shuler FOIL RC .75 .30
❑ 3 Marshall Faulk FOIL RC 20.00 7.50
❑ 4 Willie McGinest FOIL RC 2.00 .75
❑ 5 Trent Dilfer FOIL RC 5.00 2.00
❑ 6 Bryant Young FOIL RC 1.25 .50
❑ 7 Antonio Langham FOIL RC .40 .15
❑ 8 John Thierry FOIL RC .40 .15
❑ 9 Aaron Glenn FOIL RC 1.25 .50
❑ 10 Charles Johnson FOIL RC 1.25 .50
❑ 11 Dewayne Washington FOIL RC .40 .15
❑ 12 Johnnie Morton FOIL RC 3.00 1.25
❑ 13 Greg Hill FOIL RC .75 .30

❑ 14 William Floyd FOIL RC .75 .30
❑ 15 Derrick Alexander WR FOIL RC 1.25 .50
❑ 16 Darnay Scott FOIL RC 1.25 .50
❑ 17 Errict Rhett FOIL RC 1.25 .50
❑ 18 Charlie Garner FOIL RC 3.00 1.25
❑ 19 Thomas Lewis FOIL RC .40 .15
❑ 20 David Palmer FOIL RC 1.25 .50
❑ 21 Andre Reed .30 .10
❑ 22 Thurman Thomas .50 .20
❑ 23 Bruce Smith .50 .20
❑ 24 Jim Kelly .50 .20
❑ 25 Cornelius Bennett .30 .10
❑ 26 Bucky Brooks RC .15 .05
❑ 27 Jeff Burris RC .30 .10
❑ 28 Jim Harbaugh .50 .20
❑ 29 Tony Bennett .15 .05
❑ 30 Quentin Coryatt .15 .05
❑ 31 Floyd Turner .15 .05
❑ 32 Roosevelt Potts .15 .05
❑ 33 Jeff Herrod .15 .05
❑ 34 Irving Fryar .30 .10
❑ 35 Bryan Cox .15 .05
❑ 36 Dan Marino 4.00 1.50
❑ 37 Terry Kirby .50 .20
❑ 38 Michael Stewart .15 .05
❑ 39 Bernie Kosar .30 .10
❑ 40 Aubrey Beavers RC .15 .05
❑ 41 Vincent Brisby .30 .10
❑ 42 Ben Coates .30 .10
❑ 43 Drew Bledsoe 2.00 .75
❑ 44 Marion Butts .15 .05
❑ 45 Chris Slade .15 .05
❑ 46 Michael Timpson .15 .05
❑ 47 Ray Crittenden RC .15 .05
❑ 48 Rob Moore .30 .10
❑ 49 Johnny Mitchell .15 .05
❑ 50 Art Monk .30 .10
❑ 51 Boomer Esiason .30 .10
❑ 52 Ronnie Lott .30 .10
❑ 53 Ryan Yarborough RC .15 .05
❑ 54 Carl Pickens .30 .10
❑ 55 David Klingler .15 .05
❑ 56 Harold Green .15 .05
❑ 57 John Copeland .15 .05
❑ 58 Louis Oliver .15 .05
❑ 59 Corey Sawyer .30 .10
❑ 60 Michael Jackson .30 .10
❑ 61 Mark Rypien .15 .05
❑ 62 Vinny Testaverde .30 .10
❑ 63 Eric Metcalf .30 .10
❑ 64 Eric Turner .15 .05
❑ 65 Haywood Jeffires .30 .10
❑ 66 Micheal Barrow .15 .05
❑ 67 Cody Carlson .15 .05
❑ 68 Gary Brown .15 .05
❑ 69 Bucky Richardson .15 .05
❑ 70 Al Smith .15 .05
❑ 71 Eric Green .15 .05
❑ 72 Neil O'Donnell .50 .20
❑ 73 Barry Foster .15 .05
❑ 74 Greg Lloyd .30 .10
❑ 75 Rod Woodson .30 .10
❑ 76 Byron Bam Morris RC .30 .10
❑ 77 John L. Williams .15 .05
❑ 78 Anthony Miller .30 .10
❑ 79 Mike Pritchard .15 .05
❑ 80 John Elway 4.00 1.50
❑ 81 Shannon Sharpe .30 .10
❑ 82 Steve Atwater .15 .05
❑ 83 Simon Fletcher .15 .05
❑ 84 Glyn Milburn .30 .10
❑ 85 Mark Collins .15 .05
❑ 86 Keith Cash .15 .05
❑ 87 Willie Davis .30 .10
❑ 88 Joe Montana 4.00 1.50
❑ 89 Marcus Allen .50 .20
❑ 90 Neil Smith .30 .10
❑ 91 Derrick Thomas .50 .20
❑ 92 Tim Brown .50 .20
❑ 93 Jeff Hostetler .30 .10
❑ 94 Terry McDaniel .15 .05
❑ 95 Rocket Ismail .30 .10
❑ 96 Rob Fredrickson RC .30 .10
❑ 97 Harvey Williams .30 .10
❑ 98 Steve Wisniewski .15 .05
❑ 99 Stan Humphries .30 .10
❑ 100 Natrone Means .50 .20
❑ 101 Leslie O'Neal .15 .05
❑ 102 Junior Seau .50 .20
❑ 103 Ronnie Harmon .15 .05
❑ 104 Shawn Jefferson .15 .05
❑ 105 Howard Ballard .15 .05
❑ 106 Rick Mirer .50 .20
❑ 107 Cortez Kennedy .30 .10
❑ 108 Chris Warren .30 .10
❑ 109 Brian Blades .30 .10
❑ 110 Sam Adams RC .30 .10
❑ 111 Gary Clark .30 .10
❑ 112 Steve Beuerlein .30 .10
❑ 113 Ronald Moore .15 .05
❑ 114 Eric Swann .30 .10
❑ 115 Clyde Simmons .15 .05
❑ 116 Seth Joyner .15 .05
❑ 117 Troy Aikman 2.00 .75
❑ 118 Charles Haley .30 .10
❑ 119 Alvin Harper .30 .10
❑ 120 Michael Irvin .50 .20
❑ 121 Daryl Johnston .30 .10
❑ 122 Emmitt Smith 3.00 1.25
❑ 123 Shante Carver RC .15 .05
❑ 124 Dave Brown .30 .10
❑ 125 Rodney Hampton .30 .10
❑ 126 Dave Meggett .15 .05
❑ 127 Chris Calloway .15 .05
❑ 128 Mike Sherrard .15 .05
❑ 129 Carlton Bailey .15 .05
❑ 130 Randall Cunningham .50 .20
❑ 131 William Fuller .15 .05
❑ 132 Eric Allen .15 .05
❑ 133 Calvin Williams .30 .10
❑ 134 Herschel Walker .30 .10
❑ 135 Bernard Williams RC .15 .05
❑ 136 Henry Ellard .30 .10
❑ 137 Ethan Horton .15 .05
❑ 138 Desmond Howard .30 .10
❑ 139 Reggie Brooks .30 .10
❑ 140 John Friesz .30 .10
❑ 141 Tom Carter .15 .05
❑ 142 Terry Allen .30 .10
❑ 143 Adrian Cooper .15 .05
❑ 144 Qadry Ismail .50 .20
❑ 145 Warren Moon .50 .20
❑ 146 Henry Thomas .15 .05
❑ 147 Todd Steussie RC .30 .10
❑ 148 Cris Carter .75 .30
❑ 149 Andy Heck .15 .05
❑ 150 Curtis Conway .50 .20
❑ 151 Erik Kramer .30 .10
❑ 152 Lewis Tillman .15 .05
❑ 153 Dante Jones .15 .05
❑ 154 Alonzo Spellman .15 .05
❑ 155 Herman Moore .50 .20
❑ 156 Broderick Thomas .15 .05
❑ 157 Scott Mitchell .30 .10
❑ 158 Barry Sanders 3.00 1.25
❑ 159 Chris Spielman .30 .10
❑ 160 Pat Swilling .15 .05
❑ 161 Bennie Blades .15 .05
❑ 162 Sterling Sharpe .30 .10
❑ 163 Brett Favre 4.00 1.50
❑ 164 Reggie Cobb .15 .05
❑ 165 Reggie White .50 .20
❑ 166 Sean Jones .15 .05
❑ 167 George Teague .15 .05
❑ 168 LeShon Johnson RC .30 .10
❑ 169 Courtney Hawkins .15 .05
❑ 170 Jackie Harris .15 .05
❑ 171 Craig Erickson .15 .05
❑ 172 Santana Dotson .30 .10
❑ 173 Eric Curry .15 .05
❑ 174 Hardy Nickerson .30 .10
❑ 175 Derek Brown RBK .15 .05
❑ 176 Jim Everett .30 .10
❑ 177 Michael Haynes .30 .10
❑ 178 Tyrone Hughes .30 .10
❑ 179 Wayne Martin .15 .05
❑ 180 Willie Roaf .15 .05
❑ 181 Irv Smith .15 .05
❑ 182 Jeff George .50 .20
❑ 183 Andre Rison .30 .10
❑ 184 Erric Pegram .15 .05
❑ 185 Bert Emanuel RC 1.00 .40
❑ 186 Chris Doleman .15 .05
❑ 187 Ron George .15 .05
❑ 188 Chris Miller .15 .05
❑ 189 Troy Drayton .15 .05
❑ 190 Chris Chandler .30 .10
❑ 191 Jerome Bettis 1.00 .40
❑ 192 Jimmie Jones .15 .05
❑ 193 Sean Gilbert .15 .05
❑ 194 Jerry Rice 2.00 .75
❑ 195 Brent Jones .30 .10
❑ 196 Deion Sanders 1.00 .40
❑ 197 Steve Young 1.50 .60
❑ 198 Ricky Watters .30 .10
❑ 199 Dana Stubblefield .30 .10
❑ 200 Ken Norton Jr. .30 .10
❑ RB1 Dan Marino RB 25.00 10.00
❑ RB2 Jerry Rice RB 25.00 12.50
❑ P16 Joe Montana Promo 4.00 1.50

1995 SP

❑ COMPLETE SET (200) 50.00 20.00
❑ 1 Ki-Jana Carter FOIL RC 2.00 .75
❑ 2 Eric Zeier FOIL RC 2.00 .75
❑ 3 Steve McNair FOIL RC 12.00 5.00
❑ 4 Michael Westbrook FOIL RC 2.00 .75
❑ 5 Kerry Collins FOIL RC 6.00 2.50
❑ 6 Joey Galloway FOIL RC 5.00 2.00
❑ 7 Kevin Carter FOIL RC 2.00 .75
❑ 8 Mike Mamula RC .50 .20
❑ 9 Kyle Brady FOIL RC 2.00 .75
❑ 10 J.J. Stokes FOIL RC 2.00 .75
❑ 11 Tyrone Poole RC 2.00 .75
❑ 12 Rashaan Salaam FOIL RC 1.00 .40
❑ 13 Sherman Williams FOIL RC .50 .20
❑ 14 Luther Elliss RC .50 .20
❑ 15 James O. Stewart FOIL RC 4.00 1.50
❑ 16 Tamarick Vanover FOIL RC 2.00 .75
❑ 17 Napoleon Kaufman FOIL RC 4.00 1.50
❑ 18 Curtis Martin FOIL RC 12.00 6.00
❑ 19 Tyrone Wheatley FOIL RC 4.00 1.50
❑ 20 Frank Sanders FOIL RC 2.00 .75
❑ 21 Devin Bush .20 .07
❑ 22 Terance Mathis .40 .15
❑ 23 Bert Emanuel .75 .30
❑ 24 Eric Metcalf .40 .15
❑ 25 Craig Heyward .40 .15
❑ 26 Jeff George .40 .15
❑ 27 Mark Carrier WR .40 .15
❑ 28 Pete Metzelaars .20 .07
❑ 29 Frank Reich .20 .07
❑ 30 Sam Mills .40 .15
❑ 31 John Kasay .20 .07
❑ 32 Willie Green .40 .15
❑ 33 Jeff Graham .20 .07
❑ 34 Curtis Conway .75 .30
❑ 35 Steve Walsh .20 .07
❑ 36 Erik Kramer .20 .07
❑ 37 Michael Timpson .20 .07
❑ 38 Mark Carrier DB .20 .07
❑ 39 Troy Aikman 2.00 .75
❑ 40 Michael Irvin .75 .30
❑ 41 Charles Haley .40 .15
❑ 42 Deion Sanders 1.25 .50
❑ 43 Jay Novacek .40 .15
❑ 44 Emmitt Smith 3.00 1.25
❑ 45 Herman Moore .75 .30
❑ 46 Scott Mitchell UER .40 .15

Card		
❑ 47 Bennie Blades	.20	.07
❑ 48 Johnnie Morton	.40	.15
❑ 49 Chris Spielman	.40	.15
❑ 50 Barry Sanders	3.00	1.25
❑ 51 Edgar Bennett	.40	.15
❑ 52 Reggie White	.75	.30
❑ 53 Sean Jones	.20	.07
❑ 54 Mark Ingram	.20	.07
❑ 55 Robert Brooks	.75	.30
❑ 56 Brett Favre	4.00	1.50
❑ 57 Lovell Pinkney RC	.50	.20
❑ 58 Chris Miller	.20	.07
❑ 59 Isaac Bruce	1.25	.50
❑ 60 Roman Phifer	.20	.07
❑ 61 Sean Gilbert	.40	.15
❑ 62 Jerome Bettis	.75	.30
❑ 63 Derrick Alexander DE RC	.50	.20
❑ 64 Cris Carter	.75	.30
❑ 65 Jake Reed	.40	.15
❑ 66 Robert Smith	.75	.30
❑ 67 David Palmer	.40	.15
❑ 68 Warren Moon	.40	.15
❑ 69 Ray Zellars RC	1.00	.40
❑ 70 Jim Everett	.20	.07
❑ 71 Michael Haynes	.40	.15
❑ 72 Quinn Early	.40	.15
❑ 73 Willie Roaf	.20	.07
❑ 74 Mario Bates	.40	.15
❑ 75 Mike Sherrard	.20	.07
❑ 76 Chris Calloway	.20	.07
❑ 77 Dave Brown	.40	.15
❑ 78 Thomas Lewis	.40	.15
❑ 79 Herschel Walker	.40	.15
❑ 80 Rodney Hampton	.40	.15
❑ 81 Fred Barnett	.40	.15
❑ 82 Calvin Williams	.40	.15
❑ 83 Randall Cunningham	.75	.30
❑ 84 Charlie Garner	.75	.30
❑ 85 Bobby Taylor RC	3.00	1.25
❑ 86 Ricky Watters	.40	.15
❑ 87 Dave Krieg	.20	.07
❑ 88 Rob Moore	.40	.15
❑ 89 Eric Swann	.40	.15
❑ 90 Clyde Simmons	.20	.07
❑ 91 Seth Joyner	.20	.07
❑ 92 Garrison Hearst	.75	.30
❑ 93 Jerry Rice	2.00	.75
❑ 94 Bryant Young	.40	.15
❑ 95 Brent Jones	.20	.07
❑ 96 Ken Norton	.40	.15
❑ 97 William Floyd	.40	.15
❑ 98 Steve Young	1.50	.60
❑ 99 Warren Sapp RC	5.00	2.00
❑ 100 Trent Dilfer	.75	.30
❑ 101 Alvin Harper	.20	.07
❑ 102 Hardy Nickerson	.20	.07
❑ 103 Derrick Brooks RC	5.00	2.00
❑ 104 Errict Rhett	.40	.15
❑ 105 Henry Ellard	.40	.15
❑ 106 Ken Harvey	.20	.07
❑ 107 Gus Frerotte	.40	.15
❑ 108 Brian Mitchell	.20	.07
❑ 109 Terry Allen	.40	.15
❑ 110 Heath Shuler	.40	.15
❑ 111 Jim Kelly	.75	.30
❑ 112 Andre Reed	.40	.15
❑ 113 Bruce Smith	.75	.30
❑ 114 Darick Holmes RC	1.00	.40
❑ 115 Bryce Paup	.40	.15
❑ 116 Cornelius Bennett	.40	.15
❑ 117 Carl Pickens	.40	.15
❑ 118 Darnay Scott	.40	.15
❑ 119 Jeff Blake RC	2.00	.75
❑ 120 Steve Tovar	.20	.07
❑ 121 Tony McGee	.20	.07
❑ 122 Dan Wilkinson	.40	.15
❑ 123 Craig Powell RC	.20	.07
❑ 124 Vinny Testaverde	.40	.15
❑ 125 Eric Turner	.20	.07
❑ 126 Leroy Hoard	.20	.07
❑ 127 Lorenzo White	.20	.07
❑ 128 Andre Rison	.40	.15
❑ 129 Shannon Sharpe	.40	.15
❑ 130 Terrell Davis RC	10.00	4.00
❑ 131 Anthony Miller	.40	.15
❑ 132 Mike Pritchard	.20	.07
❑ 133 Steve Atwater	.20	.07
❑ 134 John Elway	4.00	1.50
❑ 135 Haywood Jeffires	.20	.07
❑ 136 Gary Brown	.20	.07
❑ 137 Al Smith	.20	.07
❑ 138 Rodney Thomas RC	1.00	.40
❑ 139 Chris Chandler	.40	.15
❑ 140 Mel Gray	.20	.07
❑ 141 Craig Erickson	.20	.07
❑ 142 Sean Dawkins	.40	.15
❑ 143 Ken Dilger RC	2.00	.75
❑ 144 Ellis Johnson RC	.50	.20
❑ 145 Quentin Coryatt	.40	.15
❑ 146 Marshall Faulk	2.50	1.00
❑ 147 Tony Boselli RC	2.00	.75
❑ 148 Rob Johnson RC	3.00	1.25
❑ 149 Desmond Howard	.40	.15
❑ 150 Steve Beuerlein	.40	.15
❑ 151 Reggie Cobb	.20	.07
❑ 152 Jeff Lageman	.20	.07
❑ 153 Willie Davis	.40	.15
❑ 154 Marcus Allen	.75	.30
❑ 155 Neil Smith	.40	.15
❑ 156 Greg Hill	.40	.15
❑ 157 Steve Bono	.40	.15
❑ 158 Derrick Thomas	.75	.30
❑ 159 Jeff Hostetler	.40	.15
❑ 160 Harvey Williams	.20	.07
❑ 161 Rocket Ismail	.40	.15
❑ 162 Chester McGlockton	.40	.15
❑ 163 Terry McDaniel	.20	.07
❑ 164 Tim Brown	.75	.30
❑ 165 Terry Kirby	.40	.15
❑ 166 Irving Fryar	.40	.15
❑ 167 O.J. McDuffie	.75	.30
❑ 168 Bryan Cox	.20	.07
❑ 169 Eric Green	.20	.07
❑ 170 Dan Marino	4.00	1.50
❑ 171 Ben Coates	.40	.15
❑ 172 Vincent Brisby	.20	.07
❑ 173 Chris Slade	.20	.07
❑ 174 Ty Law RC	4.00	1.50
❑ 175 Vincent Brown	.20	.07
❑ 176 Drew Bledsoe	1.25	.50
❑ 177 Johnny Mitchell	.20	.07
❑ 178 Boomer Esiason	.40	.15
❑ 179 Wayne Chrebet RC	6.00	3.00
❑ 180 Mo Lewis	.20	.07
❑ 181 Ronald Moore	.20	.07
❑ 182 Aaron Glenn	.20	.07
❑ 183 Mark Bruener RC	1.00	.40
❑ 184 Neil O'Donnell	.40	.15
❑ 185 Charles Johnson	.40	.15
❑ 186 Greg Lloyd	.40	.15
❑ 187 Rod Woodson	.40	.15
❑ 188 Byron Bam Morris	.20	.07
❑ 189 Terrell Fletcher RC	.50	.20
❑ 190 Terrance Shaw RC UER	.50	.20
❑ 191 Stan Humphries	.40	.15
❑ 192 Junior Seau	.75	.30
❑ 193 Leslie O'Neal	.40	.15
❑ 194 Natrone Means	.40	.15
❑ 195 Christian Fauria RC	1.00	.40
❑ 196 Rick Mirer	.40	.15
❑ 197 Sam Adams	.20	.07
❑ 198 Cortez Kennedy	.40	.15
❑ 199 Eugene Robinson	.20	.07
❑ 200 Chris Warren	.40	.15
❑ DM1 Dan Marino Tribute	20.00	7.50
❑ JM1 Joe Montana Salute	20.00	7.50
❑ JMAP Joe Montana Promo	4.00	1.50
❑ NNO Dan Marino TRI Jumbo	25.00	10.00
❑ NNO Joe Montana SAL Jumbo	25.00	10.00
❑ P113 Dan Marino Promo	3.00	1.25

1996 SP

Card		
❑ COMPLETE SET (188)	100.00	40.00
❑ 1 Keyshawn Johnson RC	8.00	4.00
❑ 2 Kevin Hardy RC	.75	.30
❑ 3 Simeon Rice RC	3.00	1.25
❑ 4 Jonathan Ogden RC	1.25	.50
❑ 5 Eddie George RC	10.00	4.00
❑ 6 Terry Glenn RC	6.00	2.50
❑ 7 Terrell Owens RC	20.00	12.00
❑ 8 Tim Biakabutuka RC	2.00	.75
❑ 9 Lawrence Phillips RC	.75	.30
❑ 10 Alex Molden RC	.40	.15
❑ 11 Regan Upshaw RC	.40	.15
❑ 12 Rickey Dudley RC	1.25	.50
❑ 13 Duane Clemons RC	.40	.15
❑ 14 John Mobley RC	.75	.30
❑ 15 Eddie Kennison RC	2.00	.75
❑ 16 Karim Abdul-Jabbar RC	1.25	.50
❑ 17 Eric Moulds RC	8.00	3.00
❑ 18 Marvin Harrison RC	20.00	10.00
❑ 19 Stepfret Williams RC	.40	.15
❑ 20 Stephen Davis RC	12.00	5.00
❑ 21 Deion Sanders	1.25	.50
❑ 22 Emmitt Smith	3.00	1.25
❑ 23 Troy Aikman	2.00	.75
❑ 24 Michael Irvin	.75	.30
❑ 25 Herschel Walker	.40	.15
❑ 26 Kavika Pittman RC	.20	.07
❑ 27 Andre Hastings	.20	.07
❑ 28 Jerome Bettis	.75	.30
❑ 29 Mike Tomczak	.20	.07
❑ 30 Kordell Stewart	.75	.30
❑ 31 Charles Johnson	.20	.07
❑ 32 Greg Lloyd	.40	.15
❑ 33 Brett Favre	4.00	1.50
❑ 34 Mark Chmura	.40	.15
❑ 35 Edgar Bennett	.40	.15
❑ 36 Robert Brooks	.40	.15
❑ 37 Craig Newsome	.20	.07
❑ 38 Reggie White	.75	.30
❑ 39 Jim Harbaugh	.40	.15
❑ 40 Marshall Faulk	1.00	.40
❑ 41 Sean Dawkins	.20	.07
❑ 42 Quentin Coryatt	.20	.07
❑ 43 Ray Buchanan	.20	.07
❑ 44 Ken Dilger	.40	.15
❑ 45 Jerry Rice	2.00	.75
❑ 46 J.J. Stokes	.75	.30
❑ 47 Steve Young	1.50	.60
❑ 48 Derek Loville	.20	.07
❑ 49 Terry Kirby	.40	.15
❑ 50 Ken Norton	.20	.07
❑ 51 Tamarick Vanover	.40	.15
❑ 52 Marcus Allen	.75	.30
❑ 53 Steve Bono	.20	.07
❑ 54 Neil Smith	.40	.15
❑ 55 Derrick Thomas	.75	.30
❑ 56 Dale Carter	.20	.07
❑ 57 Terance Mathis	.20	.07
❑ 58 Eric Metcalf	.20	.07
❑ 59 Jamal Anderson RC	1.50	.60
❑ 60 Bert Emanuel	.40	.15
❑ 61 Craig Heyward	.20	.07
❑ 62 Cornelius Bennett	.20	.07
❑ 63 Tony Martin	.40	.15
❑ 64 Stan Humphries	.40	.15

❑ 65 Andre Coleman	.20	.07
❑ 66 Junior Seau	.75	.30
❑ 67 Terrell Fletcher	.20	.07
❑ 68 John Carney	.20	.07
❑ 69 Charlie Jones RC	.40	.15
❑ 70 Ricky Watters	.40	.15
❑ 71 Charlie Garner	.40	.15
❑ 72 Bobby Hoying RC	.75	.30
❑ 73 Jason Dunn RC	.40	.15
❑ 74 Bobby Taylor	.20	.07
❑ 75 Irving Fryar	.40	.15
❑ 76 Jim Kelly	.75	.30
❑ 77 Thurman Thomas	.75	.30
❑ 78 Bruce Smith	.40	.15
❑ 79 Bryce Paup	.20	.07
❑ 80 Darick Holmes	.20	.07
❑ 81 Andre Reed	.40	.15
❑ 82 Glyn Milburn	.20	.07
❑ 83 Brett Perriman	.20	.07
❑ 84 Herman Moore	.40	.15
❑ 85 Scott Mitchell	.40	.15
❑ 86 Barry Sanders	3.00	1.25
❑ 87 Johnnie Morton	.40	.15
❑ 88 Dan Marino	4.00	1.50
❑ 89 O.J. McDuffie	.40	.15
❑ 90 Stanley Pritchett RC	.20	.07
❑ 91 Zach Thomas RC	4.00	1.50
❑ 92 Daryl Gardener RC	.20	.07
❑ 93 Rashaan Salaam	.40	.15
❑ 94 Erik Kramer	.20	.07
❑ 95 Curtis Conway	.75	.30
❑ 96 Bobby Engram RC	.75	.30
❑ 97 Walt Harris RC	.20	.07
❑ 98 Bryan Cox	.20	.07
❑ 99 John Elway	4.00	1.50
❑ 100 Terrell Davis	1.50	.60
❑ 101 Anthony Miller	.40	.15
❑ 102 Shannon Sharpe	.40	.15
❑ 103 Tory James RC	.75	.30
❑ 104 Jeff Lewis RC	.40	.15
❑ 105 Joey Galloway	.75	.30
❑ 106 Chris Warren	.40	.15
❑ 107 Rick Mirer	.40	.15
❑ 108 Cortez Kennedy	.20	.07
❑ 109 Michael Sinclair	.20	.07
❑ 110 John Friesz	.20	.07
❑ 111 Warren Moon	.40	.15
❑ 112 Cris Carter	.75	.30
❑ 113 Jake Reed	.40	.15
❑ 114 Robert Smith	.40	.15
❑ 115 John Randle	.40	.15
❑ 116 Orlando Thomas	.20	.07
❑ 117 Jeff Hostetler	.20	.07
❑ 118 Tim Brown	.75	.30
❑ 119 Joe Aska	.20	.07
❑ 120 Napoleon Kaufman	.75	.30
❑ 121 Terry McDaniel	.20	.07
❑ 122 Harvey Williams	.20	.07
❑ 123 Trent Dilfer	.75	.30
❑ 124 Reggie Brooks	.20	.07
❑ 125 Alvin Harper	.20	.07
❑ 126 Mike Alstott RC	5.00	2.00
❑ 127 Hardy Nickerson	.20	.07
❑ 128 Mario Bates	.40	.15
❑ 129 Jim Everett	.20	.07
❑ 130 Tyrone Hughes	.20	.07
❑ 131 Michael Haynes	.20	.07
❑ 132 Eric Allen	.20	.07
❑ 133 Isaac Bruce	.75	.30
❑ 134 Kevin Carter	.20	.07
❑ 135 Leslie O'Neal	.20	.07
❑ 136 Tony Banks RC	.75	.30
❑ 137 Chris Chandler	.40	.15
❑ 138 Steve McNair	1.50	.60
❑ 139 Chris Sanders	.40	.15
❑ 140 Ronnie Harmon	.20	.07
❑ 141 Willie Davis	.20	.07
❑ 142 Michael Westbrook	.75	.30
❑ 143 Terry Allen	.40	.15
❑ 144 Brian Mitchell	.20	.07
❑ 145 Henry Ellard	.20	.07
❑ 146 Gus Frerotte	.40	.15
❑ 147 Kerry Collins	.75	.30
❑ 148 Sam Mills	.20	.07
❑ 149 Wesley Walls	.40	.15
❑ 150 Kevin Greene	.40	.15
❑ 151 Muhsin Muhammad RC	4.00	1.50
❑ 152 Winslow Oliver	.20	.07
❑ 153 Jeff Blake	.75	.30
❑ 154 Carl Pickens	.40	.15
❑ 155 Darnay Scott	.40	.15
❑ 156 Garrison Hearst	.40	.15
❑ 157 Marco Battaglia RC	.20	.07
❑ 158 Drew Bledsoe	1.25	.50
❑ 159 Curtis Martin	1.50	.60
❑ 160 Shawn Jefferson	.20	.07
❑ 161 Ben Coates	.40	.15
❑ 162 Lawyer Milloy RC	2.50	1.00
❑ 163 Tyrone Wheatley	.40	.15
❑ 164 Rodney Hampton	.40	.15
❑ 165 Chris Calloway	.20	.07
❑ 166 Dave Brown	.20	.07
❑ 167 Amani Toomer RC	5.00	2.00
❑ 168 Vinny Testaverde	.40	.15
❑ 169 Michael Jackson	.40	.15
❑ 170 Eric Turner	.20	.07
❑ 171 DeRon Jenkins	.20	.07
❑ 172 Jermaine Lewis RC	.75	.30
❑ 173 Frank Sanders	.40	.15
❑ 174 Rob Moore	.40	.15
❑ 175 Kent Graham	.20	.07
❑ 176 Leeland McElroy RC	.40	.15
❑ 177 Larry Centers	.40	.15
❑ 178 Eric Swann	.20	.07
❑ 179 Mark Brunell	1.25	.50
❑ 180 Willie Jackson	.40	.15
❑ 181 James O. Stewart	.40	.15
❑ 182 Natrone Means	.40	.15
❑ 183 Tony Brackens RC	.75	.30
❑ 184 Adrian Murrell	.40	.15
❑ 185 Neil O'Donnell	.40	.15
❑ 186 Hugh Douglas	.40	.15
❑ 187 Wayne Chrebet	1.00	.40
❑ 188 Alex Van Dyke RC	.40	.15
❑ SP13 Dan Marino Promo	3.00	1.25

1997 SP Authentic

❑ COMPLETE SET (198)	100.00	50.00
❑ 1 Orlando Pace RC	2.00	.75
❑ 2 Darrell Russell RC	.50	.20
❑ 3 Shawn Springs RC	1.00	.40
❑ 4 Peter Boulware RC	4.00	1.50
❑ 5 Bryant Westbrook RC	1.00	.40
❑ 6 Walter Jones RC	2.00	.75
❑ 7 Ike Hilliard RC	4.00	1.50
❑ 8 James Farrior RC	3.00	1.25
❑ 9 Tom Knight RC	.50	.20
❑ 10 Warrick Dunn RC	15.00	6.00
❑ 11 Tony Gonzalez RC	15.00	6.00
❑ 12 Reinard Wilson RC	1.00	.40
❑ 13 Yatil Green RC	1.00	.40
❑ 14 Reidel Anthony RC	2.00	.75
❑ 15 Kenny Holmes RC	.50	.20
❑ 16 Dwayne Rudd RC	.50	.20
❑ 17 Renaldo Wynn RC	.50	.20
❑ 18 David LaFleur RC	.50	.20
❑ 19 Antowain Smith RC	8.00	3.00
❑ 20 Jim Druckenmiller RC	1.00	.40
❑ 21 Rae Carruth RC	.50	.20
❑ 22 Byron Hanspard RC	1.00	.40
❑ 23 Jake Plummer RC	12.00	5.00
❑ 24 Joey Kent RC	1.00	.40
❑ 25 Corey Dillon RC	20.00	7.50
❑ 26 Danny Wuerffel RC	5.00	2.00
❑ 27 Will Blackwell RC	.50	.20
❑ 28 Troy Davis RC	1.00	.40
❑ 29 Darnell Autry RC	1.00	.40
❑ 30 Pat Barnes RC	1.00	.40
❑ 31 Kent Graham	.50	.20
❑ 32 Simeon Rice	.75	.30
❑ 33 Frank Sanders	.75	.30
❑ 34 Rob Moore	.75	.30
❑ 35 Eric Swann	.50	.20
❑ 36 Chris Chandler	.75	.30
❑ 37 Jamal Anderson	1.25	.50
❑ 38 Terance Mathis	.75	.30
❑ 39 Bert Emanuel	.75	.30
❑ 40 Michael Booker	.50	.20
❑ 41 Vinny Testaverde	.75	.30
❑ 42 Byron Bam Morris	.50	.20
❑ 43 Michael Jackson	.75	.30
❑ 44 Derrick Alexander WR	.75	.30
❑ 45 Jamie Sharper RC	2.00	.75
❑ 46 Kim Herring RC	.50	.20
❑ 47 Todd Collins	.50	.20
❑ 48 Thurman Thomas	1.25	.50
❑ 49 Andre Reed	.75	.30
❑ 50 Quinn Early	.50	.20
❑ 51 Bryce Paup	.50	.20
❑ 52 Lonnie Johnson	.50	.20
❑ 53 Kerry Collins	1.25	.50
❑ 54 Anthony Johnson	.50	.20
❑ 55 Tim Biakabutuka	.75	.30
❑ 56 Muhsin Muhammad	.75	.30
❑ 57 Sam Mills	.50	.20
❑ 58 Wesley Walls	.75	.30
❑ 59 Rick Mirer	.50	.20
❑ 60 Raymont Harris	.50	.20
❑ 61 Curtis Conway	.75	.30
❑ 62 Bobby Engram	.75	.30
❑ 63 Bryan Cox	.50	.20
❑ 64 John Allred RC	.50	.20
❑ 65 Jeff Blake	.75	.30
❑ 66 Ki-Jana Carter	.50	.20
❑ 67 Darnay Scott	.75	.30
❑ 68 Carl Pickens	.75	.30
❑ 69 Dan Wilkinson	.50	.20
❑ 70 Troy Aikman	2.50	1.25
❑ 71 Emmitt Smith	4.00	2.00
❑ 72 Michael Irvin	1.25	.50
❑ 73 Deion Sanders	1.25	.50
❑ 74 Anthony Miller	.50	.20
❑ 75 Antonio Anderson RC	.50	.20
❑ 76 John Elway	5.00	2.00
❑ 77 Terrell Davis	1.50	.60
❑ 78 Rod Smith WR	1.25	.50
❑ 79 Shannon Sharpe	.75	.30
❑ 80 Neil Smith	.75	.30
❑ 81 Trevor Pryce RC	2.00	.75
❑ 82 Scott Mitchell	.75	.30
❑ 83 Barry Sanders	4.00	1.50
❑ 84 Herman Moore	.75	.30
❑ 85 Johnnie Morton	.75	.30
❑ 86 Matt Russell RC	.50	.20
❑ 87 Brett Favre	5.00	2.50
❑ 88 Edgar Bennett	.75	.30
❑ 89 Robert Brooks	.75	.30
❑ 90 Antonio Freeman	1.25	.50
❑ 91 Reggie White	1.25	.50
❑ 92 Craig Newsome	.50	.20
❑ 93 Jim Harbaugh	.75	.30
❑ 94 Marshall Faulk	1.50	.60
❑ 95 Sean Dawkins	.50	.20
❑ 96 Marvin Harrison	1.25	.50
❑ 97 Quentin Coryatt	.50	.20
❑ 98 Tarik Glenn RC	1.00	.40
❑ 99 Mark Brunell	1.50	.60
❑ 100 Natrone Means	.75	.30
❑ 101 Keenan McCardell	.75	.30
❑ 102 Jimmy Smith	.75	.30
❑ 103 Tony Brackens	.50	.20
❑ 104 Kevin Hardy	.50	.20
❑ 105 Elvis Grbac	.75	.30
❑ 106 Marcus Allen	1.25	.50
❑ 107 Greg Hill	.50	.20
❑ 108 Derrick Thomas	1.25	.50
❑ 109 Dale Carter	.50	.20
❑ 110 Dan Marino	5.00	2.00
❑ 111 Karim Abdul-Jabbar	.75	.30
❑ 112 Brian Manning RC	.50	.20
❑ 113 Daryl Gardener	.50	.20
❑ 114 Troy Drayton	.50	.20
❑ 115 Zach Thomas	1.25	.50

❑ 116	Jason Taylor RC	12.00	5.00
❑ 117	Brad Johnson	1.25	.50
❑ 118	Robert Smith	.75	.30
❑ 119	John Randle	.75	.30
❑ 120	Cris Carter	1.25	.50
❑ 121	Jake Reed	.75	.30
❑ 122	Randall Cunningham	1.25	.50
❑ 123	Drew Bledsoe	1.50	.60
❑ 124	Curtis Martin	1.50	.60
❑ 125	Terry Glenn	1.25	.50
❑ 126	Willie McGinest	.50	.20
❑ 127	Chris Canty RC	.50	.20
❑ 128	Sedrick Shaw RC	1.00	.40
❑ 129	Heath Shuler	.50	.20
❑ 130	Mario Bates	.50	.20
❑ 131	Ray Zellars	.50	.20
❑ 132	Andre Hastings	.50	.20
❑ 133	Dave Brown	.50	.20
❑ 134	Tyrone Wheatley	.75	.30
❑ 135	Rodney Hampton	.75	.30
❑ 136	Chris Calloway	.50	.20
❑ 137	Tiki Barber RC	30.00	15.00
❑ 138	Neil O'Donnell	.75	.30
❑ 139	Adrian Murrell	.75	.30
❑ 140	Wayne Chrebet	1.25	.50
❑ 141	Keyshawn Johnson	1.25	.50
❑ 142	Hugh Douglas	.50	.20
❑ 143	Jeff George	.75	.30
❑ 144	Napoleon Kaufman	1.25	.50
❑ 145	Tim Brown	1.25	.50
❑ 146	Desmond Howard	.75	.30
❑ 147	Rickey Dudley	.75	.30
❑ 148	Terry McDaniel	.50	.20
❑ 149	Ty Detmer	.75	.30
❑ 150	Ricky Watters	.75	.30
❑ 151	Chris T. Jones	.50	.20
❑ 152	Irving Fryar	.75	.30
❑ 153	Mike Mamula	.50	.20
❑ 154	Jon Harris RC	.50	.20
❑ 155	Kordell Stewart	1.25	.50
❑ 156	Jerome Bettis	1.25	.50
❑ 157	Charles Johnson	.75	.30
❑ 158	Greg Lloyd	.50	.20
❑ 159	George Jones RC	.50	.20
❑ 160	Terrell Fletcher	.50	.20
❑ 161	Stan Humphries	.75	.30
❑ 162	Tony Martin	.75	.30
❑ 163	Eric Metcalf	.75	.30
❑ 164	Junior Seau	1.25	.50
❑ 165	Rod Woodson	.75	.30
❑ 166	Steve Young	1.50	.60
❑ 167	Terry Kirby	.75	.30
❑ 168	Garrison Hearst	.75	.30
❑ 169	Jerry Rice	2.50	1.25
❑ 170	Ken Norton	.50	.20
❑ 171	Kevin Greene	.75	.30
❑ 172	Lamar Smith	1.25	.50
❑ 173	Warren Moon	1.25	.50
❑ 174	Chris Warren	.75	.30
❑ 175	Cortez Kennedy	.50	.20
❑ 176	Joey Galloway	.75	.30
❑ 177	Tony Banks	.75	.30
❑ 178	Isaac Bruce	1.25	.50
❑ 179	Eddie Kennison	.75	.30
❑ 180	Kevin Carter	.50	.20
❑ 181	Craig Heyward	.50	.20
❑ 182	Trent Dilfer	1.25	.50
❑ 183	Errict Rhett	.50	.20
❑ 184	Mike Alstott	1.25	.50
❑ 185	Hardy Nickerson	.50	.20
❑ 186	Ronde Barber RC	12.00	5.00
❑ 187	Steve McNair	1.50	.60
❑ 188	Eddie George	1.25	.50
❑ 189	Chris Sanders	.50	.20
❑ 190	Blaine Bishop	.50	.20
❑ 191	Derrick Mason RC	12.00	5.00
❑ 192	Gus Frerotte	.50	.20
❑ 193	Terry Allen	1.25	.50
❑ 194	Brian Mitchell	.50	.20
❑ 195	Alvin Harper	.50	.20
❑ 196	Jeff Hostetler	.50	.20
❑ 197	Leslie Shepherd	.50	.20
❑ 198	Stephen Davis	1.25	.50
❑ A1	Aikman Audio Blue	4.00	1.50
❑ A2	Aikman Audio Pro Bowl	10.00	4.00
❑ A3	Aikman Audio White/500	30.00	15.00

1998 SP Authentic

❑	COMP.SET w/o SP's (84)	40.00	20.00
❑	*HAND NUMBERED RCs: .5X TO .8X		
❑ 1	Andre Wadsworth RC	25.00	10.00
❑ 2	Corey Chavous RC	40.00	15.00
❑ 3	Keith Brooking RC	40.00	15.00
❑ 4	Duane Starks RC	15.00	7.50
❑ 5	Pat Johnson RC	25.00	10.00
❑ 6	Jason Peter RC	15.00	7.50
❑ 7	Curtis Enis RC	15.00	7.50
❑ 8	Takeo Spikes RC	40.00	15.00
❑ 9	Greg Ellis RC	15.00	7.50
❑ 10	Marcus Nash RC	15.00	7.50
❑ 11	Brian Griese RC	50.00	20.00
❑ 12	Germane Crowell RC	25.00	10.00
❑ 13	Vonnie Holliday RC	25.00	10.00
❑ 14	Peyton Manning RC	800.00	400.00
❑ 15	Jerome Pathon RC	25.00	10.00
❑ 16	Fred Taylor RC	50.00	20.00
❑ 17	John Avery RC	25.00	10.00
❑ 18	Randy Moss RC	120.00	60.00
❑ 19	Robert Edwards RC	15.00	7.50
❑ 20	Tony Simmons RC	25.00	10.00
❑ 21	Shaun Williams RC	25.00	10.00
❑ 22	Joe Jurevicius RC	40.00	15.00
❑ 23	Charles Woodson RC	50.00	20.00
❑ 24	Tra Thomas RC	15.00	7.50
❑ 25	Grant Wistrom RC	25.00	10.00
❑ 26	Ryan Leaf RC	40.00	15.00
❑ 27	Ahman Green RC	80.00	30.00
❑ 28	Jacquez Green RC	25.00	10.00
❑ 29	Kevin Dyson RC	40.00	15.00
❑ 30	Stephen Alexander RC	25.00	10.00
❑ 31	John Elway TW	20.00	7.50
❑ 32	Jerry Rice TW	12.00	5.00
❑ 33	Emmitt Smith TW	20.00	7.50
❑ 34	Steve Young TW	8.00	3.00
❑ 35	Jerome Bettis TW	6.00	2.50
❑ 36	Deion Sanders TW	6.00	2.50
❑ 37	Andre Rison TW	4.00	1.50
❑ 38	Warren Moon TW	6.00	2.50
❑ 39	Mark Brunell TW	6.00	2.50
❑ 40	Ricky Watters TW	4.00	1.50
❑ 41	Dan Marino TW	25.00	10.00
❑ 42	Brett Favre TW	25.00	10.00
❑ 43	Jake Plummer	1.00	.40
❑ 44	Adrian Murrell	.60	.25
❑ 45	Eric Swann	.40	.15
❑ 46	Jamal Anderson	1.00	.40
❑ 47	Chris Chandler	.60	.25
❑ 48	Jim Harbaugh	.60	.25
❑ 49	Michael Jackson	.40	.15
❑ 50	Jermaine Lewis	.60	.25
❑ 51	Rob Johnson	.60	.25
❑ 52	Antowain Smith	1.00	.40
❑ 53	Thurman Thomas	1.00	.40
❑ 54	Kerry Collins	.60	.25
❑ 55	Fred Lane	.40	.15
❑ 56	Rae Carruth	.40	.15
❑ 57	Erik Kramer	.40	.15
❑ 58	Curtis Conway	.60	.25
❑ 59	Corey Dillon	1.00	.40
❑ 60	Neil O'Donnell	.60	.25
❑ 61	Carl Pickens	.60	.25
❑ 62	Troy Aikman	2.00	.75
❑ 63	Emmitt Smith	3.00	1.25
❑ 64	Deion Sanders	1.00	.40
❑ 65	Terrell Davis	1.00	.40
❑ 66	John Elway	4.00	1.50
❑ 67	Rod Smith	.60	.25
❑ 68	Scott Mitchell	.60	.25
❑ 69	Barry Sanders	3.00	1.25
❑ 70	Herman Moore	.60	.25
❑ 71	Brett Favre	4.00	1.50
❑ 72	Dorsey Levens	1.00	.40
❑ 73	Antonio Freeman	1.00	.40
❑ 74	Marshall Faulk	1.25	.50
❑ 75	Marvin Harrison	1.00	.40
❑ 76	Mark Brunell	1.00	.40
❑ 77	Keenan McCardell	.60	.25
❑ 78	Jimmy Smith	.60	.25
❑ 79	Andre Rison	.60	.25
❑ 80	Elvis Grbac	.60	.25
❑ 81	Derrick Alexander	.60	.25
❑ 82	Dan Marino	4.00	1.50
❑ 83	Karim Abdul-Jabbar	1.00	.40
❑ 84	O.J. McDuffie	.60	.25
❑ 85	Brad Johnson	1.00	.40
❑ 86	Cris Carter	1.00	.40
❑ 87	Robert Smith	1.00	.40
❑ 88	Drew Bledsoe	1.50	.60
❑ 89	Terry Glenn	1.00	.40
❑ 90	Ben Coates	.60	.25
❑ 91	Lamar Smith	.60	.25
❑ 92	Danny Wuerffel	.60	.25
❑ 93	Tiki Barber	1.00	.40
❑ 94	Danny Kanell	.60	.25
❑ 95	Ike Hilliard	.60	.25
❑ 96	Curtis Martin	1.00	.40
❑ 97	Keyshawn Johnson	1.00	.40
❑ 98	Glenn Foley	.60	.25
❑ 99	Jeff George	.60	.25
❑ 100	Tim Brown	1.00	.40
❑ 101	Napoleon Kaufman	1.00	.40
❑ 102	Bobby Hoying	.60	.25
❑ 103	Charlie Garner	.60	.25
❑ 104	Irving Fryar	.60	.25
❑ 105	Kordell Stewart	1.00	.40
❑ 106	Jerome Bettis	1.00	.40
❑ 107	Charles Johnson	.40	.15
❑ 108	Tony Banks	.60	.25
❑ 109	Isaac Bruce	1.00	.40
❑ 110	Natrone Means	.60	.25
❑ 111	Junior Seau	1.00	.40
❑ 112	Steve Young	1.25	.50
❑ 113	Jerry Rice	2.00	.75
❑ 114	Garrison Hearst	1.00	.40
❑ 115	Ricky Watters	.60	.25
❑ 116	Warren Moon	1.00	.40
❑ 117	Joey Galloway	.60	.25
❑ 118	Trent Dilfer	1.00	.40
❑ 119	Warrick Dunn	1.25	.50
❑ 120	Mike Alstott	1.00	.40
❑ 121	Steve McNair	1.00	.40
❑ 122	Eddie George	1.00	.40
❑ 123	Yancey Thigpen	.40	.15
❑ 124	Gus Frerotte	.40	.15
❑ 125	Terry Allen	1.00	.40
❑ 126	Michael Westbrook	.60	.25
❑ AE13	Dan Marino SAMPLE	2.00	.75

1999 SP Authentic

❑	COMP.SET w/o SPs (90)	35.00	15.00
❑	*HAND NUMBERED RCs: .5X TO .8X		
❑ 1	Jake Plummer	.60	.25
❑ 2	Adrian Murrell	.60	.25
❑ 3	Frank Sanders	.60	.25
❑ 4	Jamal Anderson	1.00	.40

- ❑ 5 Chris Chandler .60 .25
- ❑ 6 Terance Mathis .60 .25
- ❑ 7 Priest Holmes 1.50 .60
- ❑ 8 Jermaine Lewis .60 .25
- ❑ 9 Antowain Smith 1.00 .40
- ❑ 10 Doug Flutie 1.00 .40
- ❑ 11 Eric Moulds 1.00 .40
- ❑ 12 Muhsin Muhammad .60 .25
- ❑ 13 Tim Biakabutuka .60 .25
- ❑ 14 Wesley Walls .60 .25
- ❑ 15 Curtis Enis .40 .15
- ❑ 16 Bobby Engram .60 .25
- ❑ 17 Corey Dillon 1.00 .40
- ❑ 18 Darnay Scott .60 .25
- ❑ 19 Terry Kirby .40 .15
- ❑ 20 Ty Detmer .60 .25
- ❑ 21 Troy Aikman 2.00 .75
- ❑ 22 Michael Irvin .60 .25
- ❑ 23 Emmitt Smith 2.00 .75
- ❑ 24 Terrell Davis 1.00 .40
- ❑ 25 Brian Griese 1.00 .40
- ❑ 26 Rod Smith .60 .25
- ❑ 27 Shannon Sharpe .60 .25
- ❑ 28 Barry Sanders 3.00 1.25
- ❑ 29 Charlie Batch 1.00 .40
- ❑ 30 Herman Moore .60 .25
- ❑ 31 Johnnie Morton .60 .25
- ❑ 32 Brett Favre 3.00 1.25
- ❑ 33 Antonio Freeman 1.00 .40
- ❑ 34 Dorsey Levens 1.00 .40
- ❑ 35 Mark Chmura .60 .25
- ❑ 36 Peyton Manning 3.00 1.25
- ❑ 37 Marvin Harrison 1.00 .40
- ❑ 38 Mark Brunell 1.00 .40
- ❑ 39 Fred Taylor 1.00 .40
- ❑ 40 Jimmy Smith .60 .25
- ❑ 41 Elvis Grbac .60 .25
- ❑ 42 Andre Rison .60 .25
- ❑ 43 Dan Marino 3.00 1.25
- ❑ 44 O.J. McDuffie .60 .25
- ❑ 45 Yatil Green .40 .15
- ❑ 46 Randall Cunningham 1.00 .40
- ❑ 47 Randy Moss 3.00 1.25
- ❑ 48 Robert Smith 1.00 .40
- ❑ 49 Cris Carter 1.00 .40
- ❑ 50 Drew Bledsoe 1.25 .50
- ❑ 51 Ben Coates .40 .15
- ❑ 52 Terry Glenn 1.00 .40
- ❑ 53 Eddie Kennison .60 .25
- ❑ 54 Cam Cleeland .40 .15
- ❑ 55 Ike Hilliard .60 .25
- ❑ 56 Gary Brown .40 .15
- ❑ 57 Kerry Collins .60 .25
- ❑ 58 Vinny Testaverde .60 .25
- ❑ 59 Keyshawn Johnson 1.00 .40
- ❑ 60 Wayne Chrebet 1.00 .40
- ❑ 61 Curtis Martin 1.00 .40
- ❑ 62 Tim Brown 1.00 .40
- ❑ 63 Napoleon Kaufman 1.00 .40
- ❑ 64 Charles Woodson 1.00 .40
- ❑ 65 Duce Staley 1.00 .40
- ❑ 66 Charles Johnson .60 .25
- ❑ 67 Kordell Stewart .60 .25
- ❑ 68 Jerome Bettis 1.00 .40
- ❑ 69 Marshall Faulk 1.25 .50
- ❑ 70 Isaac Bruce 1.00 .40
- ❑ 71 Trent Green 1.00 .40
- ❑ 72 Jim Harbaugh .60 .25
- ❑ 73 Junior Seau 1.00 .40
- ❑ 74 Natrone Means .60 .25
- ❑ 75 Steve Young 1.25 .50
- ❑ 76 Jerry Rice 2.00 .75
- ❑ 77 Terrell Owens 1.00 .40
- ❑ 78 Lawrence Phillips .60 .25
- ❑ 79 Joey Galloway .60 .25
- ❑ 80 Ricky Watters .60 .25
- ❑ 81 Jon Kitna 1.00 .40
- ❑ 82 Warrick Dunn 1.00 .40
- ❑ 83 Trent Dilfer .60 .25
- ❑ 84 Mike Alstott 1.00 .40
- ❑ 85 Eddie George 1.00 .40
- ❑ 86 Steve McNair 1.00 .40
- ❑ 87 Yancey Thigpen .40 .15
- ❑ 88 Brad Johnson 1.00 .40
- ❑ 89 Skip Hicks .40 .15
- ❑ 90 Michael Westbrook .60 .25
- ❑ 91 Ricky Williams RC 40.00 15.00
- ❑ 92 Tim Couch RC 25.00 10.00
- ❑ 93 Akili Smith RC 20.00 7.50
- ❑ 94 Edgerrin James RC 80.00 30.00
- ❑ 95 Donovan McNabb RC 100.00 40.00
- ❑ 96 Torry Holt RC 60.00 30.00
- ❑ 97 Cade McNown RC 20.00 7.50
- ❑ 98 Shaun King RC 20.00 7.50
- ❑ 99 Daunte Culpepper RC 80.00 30.00
- ❑ 100 Brock Huard RC 25.00 10.00
- ❑ 101 Chris Claiborne RC 12.00 5.00
- ❑ 102 James Johnson RC 20.00 7.50
- ❑ 103 Rob Konrad RC 25.00 10.00
- ❑ 104 Peerless Price RC 25.00 10.00
- ❑ 105 Kevin Faulk RC 25.00 10.00
- ❑ 106 Andy Katzenmoyer RC 20.00 7.50
- ❑ 107 Troy Edwards RC 20.00 7.50
- ❑ 108 Kevin Johnson RC 25.00 10.00
- ❑ 109 Mike Cloud RC 20.00 7.50
- ❑ 110 David Boston RC 25.00 10.00
- ❑ 111 Champ Bailey RC 30.00 12.50
- ❑ 112 D'Wayne Bates RC 20.00 7.50
- ❑ 113 Joe Germaine RC 20.00 7.50
- ❑ 114 Antoine Winfield RC 20.00 7.50
- ❑ 115 Fernando Bryant RC 20.00 7.50
- ❑ 116 Jevon Kearse RC 40.00 15.00
- ❑ 117 Chris McAlister RC 20.00 7.50
- ❑ 118 Brandon Stokley RC 25.00 10.00
- ❑ 119 Karsten Bailey RC 20.00 7.50
- ❑ 120 Daylon McCutcheon RC 20.00 7.50
- ❑ 121 Jermaine Fazande RC 20.00 7.50
- ❑ 122 Joel Makovicka RC 25.00 10.00
- ❑ 123 Ebenezer Ekuban RC 20.00 7.50
- ❑ 124 Joe Montgomery RC 20.00 7.50
- ❑ 125 Sean Bennett RC 12.00 5.00
- ❑ 126 Na Brown RC 20.00 7.50
- ❑ 127 De'Mond Parker RC 12.00 5.00
- ❑ 128 Sedrick Irvin RC 12.00 5.00
- ❑ 129 Terry Jackson RC 20.00 7.50
- ❑ 130 Jeff Paulk RC 12.00 5.00
- ❑ 131 Cecil Collins RC 12.00 5.00
- ❑ 132 Bobby Collins RC 12.00 5.00
- ❑ 133 Amos Zereoue RC 25.00 10.00
- ❑ 134 Travis McGriff RC 12.00 5.00
- ❑ 135 Larry Parker RC 25.00 10.00
- ❑ 136 Wane McGarity RC 12.00 5.00
- ❑ 137 Cecil Martin RC 20.00 7.50
- ❑ 138 Al Wilson RC 20.00 7.50
- ❑ 139 Jim Kleinsasser RC 20.00 7.50
- ❑ 140 Dat Nguyen RC 20.00 7.50
- ❑ 141 Marty Booker RC 25.00 10.00
- ❑ 142 Reginald Kelly RC 12.00 5.00
- ❑ 143 Scott Covington RC 25.00 10.00
- ❑ 144 Antuan Edwards RC 20.00 7.50
- ❑ 145 Craig Yeast RC 20.00 7.50
- ❑ WPA W.Payton AU/100 500.00 350.00
- ❑ WPSP W.Payton Jsy AU/34 1000.00700.00

2000 SP Authentic

- ❑ COMP.SET w/o SP's (90) 15.00 6.00
- ❑ 1 Jake Plummer .60 .25
- ❑ 2 David Boston 1.00 .40
- ❑ 3 Frank Sanders .60 .25
- ❑ 4 Chris Chandler .60 .25
- ❑ 5 Jamal Anderson 1.00 .40
- ❑ 6 Shawn Jefferson .40 .15
- ❑ 7 Tony Banks .60 .25
- ❑ 8 Shannon Sharpe .60 .25
- ❑ 9 Rob Johnson .60 .25
- ❑ 10 Antowain Smith .60 .25
- ❑ 11 Muhsin Muhammad .60 .25
- ❑ 12 Steve Beuerlein .60 .25
- ❑ 13 Cade McNown .40 .15
- ❑ 14 Curtis Enis .40 .15
- ❑ 15 Marcus Robinson 1.00 .40
- ❑ 16 Akili Smith .40 .15
- ❑ 17 Corey Dillon 1.00 .40
- ❑ 18 Tim Couch .60 .25
- ❑ 19 Kevin Johnson 1.00 .40
- ❑ 20 Errict Rhett .40 .15
- ❑ 21 Troy Aikman 2.00 .75
- ❑ 22 Emmitt Smith 2.50 1.00
- ❑ 23 Rocket Ismail .60 .25
- ❑ 24 Joey Galloway .60 .25
- ❑ 25 Terrell Davis 1.00 .40
- ❑ 26 Olandis Gary 1.00 .40
- ❑ 27 Ed McCaffrey 1.00 .40
- ❑ 28 Brian Griese 1.00 .40
- ❑ 29 Charlie Batch 1.00 .40
- ❑ 30 Germane Crowell .40 .15
- ❑ 31 James O. Stewart .60 .25
- ❑ 32 Brett Favre 3.00 1.25
- ❑ 33 Antonio Freeman 1.00 .40
- ❑ 34 Dorsey Levens .60 .25
- ❑ 35 Peyton Manning 2.50 1.00
- ❑ 36 Edgerrin James 1.50 .60
- ❑ 37 Marvin Harrison 1.00 .40
- ❑ 38 Mark Brunell 1.00 .40
- ❑ 39 Fred Taylor 1.00 .40
- ❑ 40 Jimmy Smith .60 .25
- ❑ 41 Elvis Grbac .60 .25
- ❑ 42 Tony Gonzalez .60 .25
- ❑ 43 James Johnson .40 .15
- ❑ 44 Oronde Gadsden .60 .25
- ❑ 45 Damon Huard 1.00 .40
- ❑ 46 Randy Moss 2.00 .75
- ❑ 47 Cris Carter 1.00 .40
- ❑ 48 Daunte Culpepper 1.25 .50
- ❑ 49 Drew Bledsoe 1.25 .50
- ❑ 50 Terry Glenn .60 .25
- ❑ 51 Ricky Williams 1.00 .40
- ❑ 52 Jeff Blake .60 .25
- ❑ 53 Keith Poole .40 .15
- ❑ 54 Kerry Collins .60 .25
- ❑ 55 Amani Toomer .60 .25
- ❑ 56 Ike Hilliard .60 .25
- ❑ 57 Wayne Chrebet .60 .25
- ❑ 58 Curtis Martin 1.00 .40
- ❑ 59 Vinny Testaverde .60 .25
- ❑ 60 Tim Brown 1.00 .40
- ❑ 61 Rich Gannon 1.00 .40
- ❑ 62 Tyrone Wheatley .60 .25
- ❑ 63 Duce Staley 1.00 .40
- ❑ 64 Donovan McNabb 1.50 .60
- ❑ 65 Troy Edwards .40 .15
- ❑ 66 Jerome Bettis 1.00 .40
- ❑ 67 Kordell Stewart .60 .25
- ❑ 68 Marshall Faulk 1.25 .50
- ❑ 69 Kurt Warner 1.50 .60
- ❑ 70 Isaac Bruce 1.00 .40
- ❑ 71 Torry Holt 1.00 .40
- ❑ 72 Ryan Leaf .60 .25
- ❑ 73 Jim Harbaugh .60 .25
- ❑ 74 Jermaine Fazande .40 .15
- ❑ 75 Jerry Rice 2.00 .75
- ❑ 76 Terrell Owens 1.00 .40
- ❑ 77 Jeff Garcia 1.00 .40
- ❑ 78 Ricky Watters .60 .25
- ❑ 79 Jon Kitna 1.00 .40
- ❑ 80 Derrick Mayes .60 .25
- ❑ 81 Shaun King .40 .15
- ❑ 82 Mike Alstott 1.00 .40
- ❑ 83 Keyshawn Johnson 1.00 .40
- ❑ 84 Warrick Dunn 1.00 .40
- ❑ 85 Eddie George 1.00 .40
- ❑ 86 Steve McNair 1.00 .40
- ❑ 87 Jevon Kearse 1.00 .40
- ❑ 88 Brad Johnson 1.00 .40
- ❑ 89 Stephen Davis 1.00 .40
- ❑ 90 Michael Westbrook .60 .25
- ❑ 91 Anthony Lucas RC 10.00 4.00

❑ 92 Avion Black RC 15.00 6.00
❑ 93 Dante Hall RC 40.00 15.00
❑ 94 Darrell Jackson RC 30.00 12.50
❑ 95 Deltha O'Neal RC 20.00 7.50
❑ 96 Erron Kinney RC 20.00 7.50
❑ 97 Doug Chapman RC 15.00 6.00
❑ 98 Frank Murphy RC 10.00 4.00
❑ 99 Gari Scott RC 10.00 4.00
❑ 100 Giovanni Carmazzi RC 10.00 4.00
❑ 101 JaJuan Dawson RC 10.00 4.00
❑ 102 Jarious Jackson RC 15.00 6.00
❑ 103 Rashard Anderson RC 15.00 6.00
❑ 104 Michael Wiley RC 15.00 6.00
❑ 105 Spergon Wynn RC 15.00 6.00
❑ 106 Muneer Moore RC 10.00 4.00
❑ 107 Ahmed Plummer RC 20.00 7.50
❑ 108 Chad Morton RC 20.00 7.50
❑ 109 Rob Morris RC 15.00 6.00
❑ 110 Ron Dixon RC 15.00 6.00
❑ 111 Rondell Mealey RC 10.00 4.00
❑ 112 Sebastian Janikowski RC 20.00 7.50
❑ 113 Shaun Ellis RC 20.00 7.50
❑ 114 Rogers Beckett RC 15.00 6.00
❑ 115 Shyrone Stith RC 15.00 6.00
❑ 116 Tim Rattay RC 20.00 7.50
❑ 117 Todd Husak RC 20.00 7.50
❑ 118 Tom Brady RC 800.00 500.00
❑ 119 Trevor Gaylor RC 15.00 6.00
❑ 120 Windrell Hayes RC 15.00 6.00
❑ 121 Anthony Becht RC 20.00 7.50
❑ 122 Brian Urlacher RC 80.00 40.00
❑ 123 Bubba Franks RC 20.00 7.50
❑ 124 Chad Pennington RC 80.00 30.00
❑ 125 Chris Redman RC 15.00 6.00
❑ 126 Corey Simon RC 20.00 7.50
❑ 127 Curtis Keaton RC 15.00 6.00
❑ 128 Danny Farmer RC 15.00 6.00
❑ 129 Dennis Northcutt RC 20.00 7.50
❑ 130 Dez White RC 20.00 7.50
❑ 131 J.R. Redmond RC 15.00 6.00
❑ 132 Jamal Lewis RC 80.00 30.00
❑ 133 Jerry Porter RC 50.00 20.00
❑ 134 Joe Hamilton RC 15.00 6.00
❑ 135 Laveranues Coles RC 40.00 15.00
❑ 136 R.Jay Soward RC 15.00 6.00
❑ 137 Reuben Droughns RC 40.00 15.00
❑ 138 Ron Dayne RC 30.00 12.50
❑ 139 Ron Dugans RC 10.00 4.00
❑ 140 Shaun Alexander RC 150.00 75.00
❑ 141 Sylvester Morris RC 15.00 6.00
❑ 142 Tee Martin RC 20.00 7.50
❑ 143 Thomas Jones RC 40.00 15.00
❑ 144 Todd Pinkston RC 20.00 7.50
❑ 145 Travis Prentice RC 15.00 6.00
❑ 146 Travis Taylor RC 20.00 7.50
❑ 147 Trung Canidate RC 15.00 6.00
❑ 148 Courtney Brown RC 20.00 7.50
❑ 149 Plaxico Burress RC 50.00 20.00
❑ 150 Peter Warrick RC 20.00 7.50
❑ 151 Billy Volek RC 50.00 20.00
❑ 152 Bobby Shaw RC 10.00 4.00
❑ 153 Brad Hoover RC 15.00 6.00
❑ 154 Brian Finneran RC 20.00 7.50
❑ 155 Charles Lee RC 10.00 4.00
❑ 156 Chris Cole RC 10.00 4.00
❑ 157 Clint Stoerner RC 15.00 6.00
❑ 158 Doug Johnson RC 20.00 7.50
❑ 159 Frank Moreau RC 15.00 6.00
❑ 160 Jake Delhomme RC 80.00 40.00
❑ 161 KaRon Coleman RC 10.00 4.00
❑ 162 Kevin McDougal RC 10.00 4.00
❑ 163 Larry Foster RC 10.00 4.00
❑ 164 Mike Anderson RC 25.00 10.00
❑ 165 Patrick Pass RC 10.00 4.00
❑ 166 Reggie Jones RC 10.00 4.00
❑ 167 Sammy Morris RC 15.00 6.00
❑ 168 Shockmain Davis RC 10.00 4.00
❑ 169 Terrelle Smith RC 10.00 4.00
❑ 170 Ronney Jenkins RC 10.00 4.00
❑ 171 Troy Walters RC 15.00 6.00

2001 SP Authentic

❑ COMP.SET w/o SP's (90) 20.00 7.50
❑ *SINGLE COLOR SWATCH: .3X TO .8X
❑ 1 Jake Plummer .60 .25
❑ 2 Thomas Jones .60 .25
❑ 3 Frank Sanders .40 .15
❑ 4 Jamal Anderson 1.00 .40
❑ 5 Chris Chandler .60 .25
❑ 6 Tony Martin .60 .25
❑ 7 Jamal Lewis 1.25 .50
❑ 8 Elvis Grbac .60 .25
❑ 9 Travis Taylor .60 .25
❑ 10 Peerless Price .60 .25
❑ 11 Rob Johnson .60 .25
❑ 12 Eric Moulds .60 .25
❑ 13 Muhsin Muhammad .60 .25
❑ 14 Isaac Byrd .40 .15
❑ 15 Wesley Walls .40 .15
❑ 16 James Allen .60 .25
❑ 17 Marcus Robinson 1.00 .40
❑ 18 Brian Urlacher 1.25 .50
❑ 19 Jon Kitna .60 .25
❑ 20 Peter Warrick 1.00 .40
❑ 21 Corey Dillon 1.00 .40
❑ 22 Kevin Johnson .60 .25
❑ 23 JaJuan Dawson .40 .15
❑ 24 Tim Couch .60 .25
❑ 25 Rocket Ismail .60 .25
❑ 26 Emmitt Smith 2.00 .75
❑ 27 Joey Galloway .60 .25
❑ 28 Terrell Davis 1.00 .40
❑ 29 Mike Anderson 1.00 .40
❑ 30 Brian Griese 1.00 .40
❑ 31 Ed McCaffrey 1.00 .40
❑ 32 Charlie Batch 1.00 .40
❑ 33 James O. Stewart .60 .25
❑ 34 Johnnie Morton .60 .25
❑ 35 Brett Favre 3.00 1.25
❑ 36 Antonio Freeman 1.00 .40
❑ 37 Bill Schroeder .40 .15
❑ 38 Ahman Green 1.00 .40
❑ 39 Peyton Manning 2.50 1.00
❑ 40 Edgerrin James 1.25 .50
❑ 41 Marvin Harrison 1.00 .40
❑ 42 Mark Brunell 1.00 .40
❑ 43 Fred Taylor 1.00 .40
❑ 44 Jimmy Smith .60 .25
❑ 45 Tony Gonzalez .60 .25
❑ 46 Trent Green 1.00 .40
❑ 47 Oronde Gadsden .60 .25
❑ 48 Jay Fiedler 1.00 .40
❑ 49 Lamar Smith .60 .25
❑ 50 Randy Moss 2.00 .75
❑ 51 Cris Carter 1.00 .40
❑ 52 Daunte Culpepper 1.00 .40
❑ 53 Drew Bledsoe 1.25 .50
❑ 54 Terry Glenn .60 .25
❑ 55 Antowain Smith .60 .25
❑ 56 Ricky Williams 1.00 .40
❑ 57 Joe Horn .60 .25
❑ 58 Aaron Brooks 1.00 .40
❑ 59 Kerry Collins .60 .25
❑ 60 Tiki Barber 1.00 .40
❑ 61 Ron Dayne 1.00 .40
❑ 62 Vinny Testaverde .60 .25
❑ 63 Wayne Chrebet .60 .25
❑ 64 Curtis Martin 1.00 .40
❑ 65 Tim Brown 1.00 .40
❑ 66 Rich Gannon 1.00 .40
❑ 67 Jerry Rice 2.00 .75
❑ 68 Duce Staley 1.00 .40
❑ 69 Donovan McNabb 1.25 .50
❑ 70 Kordell Stewart .60 .25
❑ 71 Jerome Bettis 1.00 .40
❑ 72 Marshall Faulk 1.25 .50
❑ 73 Kurt Warner 1.50 .60
❑ 74 Isaac Bruce 1.00 .40
❑ 75 Doug Flutie 1.00 .40
❑ 76 Junior Seau 1.00 .40
❑ 77 Jeff Garcia 1.00 .40
❑ 78 Garrison Hearst .60 .25
❑ 79 Terrell Owens 1.00 .40
❑ 80 Ricky Watters .60 .25
❑ 81 Matt Hasselbeck .60 .25
❑ 82 Brad Johnson 1.00 .40
❑ 83 Warrick Dunn 1.00 .40
❑ 84 Mike Alstott 1.00 .40
❑ 85 Kevin Dyson .60 .25
❑ 86 Eddie George 1.00 .40
❑ 87 Steve McNair 1.00 .40
❑ 88 Champ Bailey .60 .25
❑ 89 Michael Westbrook .60 .25
❑ 90 Stephen Davis 1.00 .40
❑ 91 Michael Vick JSY AU RC 1000.00 500.00
❑ 92 Rod Gardner JSY AU RC 80.00 30.00
❑ 93 Freddie Mitchell JSY AU RC 60.00 25.00
❑ 94 Koren Robinson JSY/500 RC 50.00 20.00
❑ 95 David Terrell JSY/500 RC 25.00 10.00
❑ 96 Michael Bennett JSY RC 40.00 15.00
❑ 97 Robert Ferguson JSY RC 40.00 15.00
❑ 98 Deuce McAllister JSY RC 100.00 50.00
❑ 99 Travis Henry JSY RC 50.00 30.00
❑ 100 Andre Carter JSY RC 25.00 10.00
❑ 101 Drew Brees JSY RC 150.00 75.00
❑ 102 Santana Moss JSY/500 RC 80.00 50.00
❑ 103 Chris Weinke JSY/390 RC 40.00 15.00
❑ 104 Chad Johnson JSY/160 RC 400.00 250.00
❑ 105 Reggie Wayne JSY RC 100.00 60.00
❑ 106 Kevan Barlow JSY/500 RC 40.00 15.00
❑ 107 Chr Chambers JSY/500 RC 80.00 40.00
❑ 108 Todd Heap JSY/500 RC 80.00 40.00
❑ 109 A Thomas JSY/500 RC 30.00 12.50
❑ 110 James Jackson JSY/500 RC 25.00 10.00
❑ 111 Rudi Johnson JSY/500 RC 120.00 60.00
❑ 112 Mike McMahon JSY RC 25.00 10.00
❑ 113 Josh Heupel JSY RC 30.00 12.00
❑ 114 Travis Minor JSY/500 RC 30.00 12.50
❑ 115 Quincy Morgan JSY/500 RC 30.00 12.50
❑ 116 Dan Morgan JSY/500 RC 30.00 12.50
❑ 117 Jesse Palmer JSY/500 RC 50.00 20.00
❑ 118 Sage Rosenfels JSY/300 RC 50.00 20.00
❑ 119 Marq Tuiasosopo JSY RC 25.00 10.00
❑ 120 L.Tomlinson JSY/500 RC 800.00 450.00
❑ 123 Alge Crumpler AU RC 30.00 15.00
❑ 124 Arnold Jackson AU RC 20.00 7.50
❑ 125 Bobby Newcombe AU RC 20.00 7.50
❑ 126 Brand Manumaleuna AU RC 20.00 7.50
❑ 127 Cedrick Wilson AU RC 35.00 20.00
❑ 128 Brian Allen AU RC 15.00 6.00
❑ 129 Dee Brown AU RC 25.00 10.00
❑ 130 Damerien McCants AU RC 20.00 7.50
❑ 131 Dave Dickenson AU RC 20.00 7.50
❑ 132 Derrick Blaylock AU RC 40.00 20.00
❑ 133 Eddie Berlin AU RC 20.00 7.50
❑ 134 Francis St.Paul AU RC 20.00 7.50
❑ 135 Jamar Fletcher AU RC 20.00 7.50
❑ 136 Josh Booty AU RC 25.00 10.00
❑ 137 Scotty Anderson AU RC 20.00 7.50
❑ 138 Ken-Yon Rambo AU RC 20.00 7.50
❑ 139 Kenyatta Walker AU RC 15.00 6.00
❑ 140 Kevin Kasper AU RC 25.00 10.00
❑ 141 Snoop Minnis AU RC 20.00 7.50
❑ 142 Houshmandzadeh AU RC 50.00 25.00
❑ 143 Quincy Carter AU RC 25.00 10.00
❑ 144 Ronney Daniels AU RC 15.00 6.00
❑ 145 Sedrick Hodge AU RC 15.00 6.00
❑ 146 Steve Smith AU RC 135.00 75.00
❑ 147 Tim Hasselbeck AU RC 25.00 10.00
❑ 148 Vinny Sutherland AU RC 20.00 7.50
❑ 149 Richard Seymour AU RC 60.00 30.00
❑ 150 Jamie Winborn AU 20.00 7.50
❑ 151 Gerard Warren RC 12.00 5.00
❑ 152 Justin Smith RC 12.00 5.00
❑ 153 David Martin RC 10.00 4.00
❑ 154 Jamal Reynolds RC 12.00 5.00
❑ 155 Dominic Rhodes RC 20.00 10.00

❑ 156 Nate Clements RC 12.00 5.00
❑ 157 Michael Lewis RC 12.00 5.00
❑ 158 Andre King RC 10.00 4.00
❑ 159 Benjamin Gay RC 12.00 5.00
❑ 160 Correll Buckhalter RC 30.00 15.00
❑ 161 Roderick Robinson RC 10.00 4.00
❑ 162 Moran Norris RC 8.00 3.00
❑ 163 Onome Ojo RC 10.00 4.00
❑ 164 Will Allen RC 10.00 4.00
❑ 165 Jonathan Carter RC 10.00 4.00
❑ 166 LaMont Jordan RC 40.00 15.00
❑ 167 DeLawrence Grant RC 8.00 3.00
❑ 168 Derrick Gibson RC 10.00 4.00
❑ 169 A.J. Feeley RC 20.00 7.50
❑ 170 Tim Baker RC 8.00 3.00
❑ 171 Kendrell Bell RC 25.00 10.00
❑ 172 Zeke Moreno RC 12.00 5.00
❑ 173 Carlos Polk RC 8.00 3.00
❑ 174 Ken Lucas RC 10.00 4.00
❑ 175 Heath Evans RC 10.00 4.00
❑ 176 Elvis Joseph RC 10.00 4.00
❑ 177 Damione Lewis RC 10.00 4.00
❑ 178 Tommy Polley RC 12.00 5.00
❑ 179 Fred Smoot RC 12.00 5.00
❑ 180 Jason Brookins RC 12.00 5.00
❑ 181 Nick Goings RC 12.00 5.00
❑ 182 Drew Bennett RC 25.00 10.00
❑ 183 Justin McCareins RC 15.00 6.00
❑ 184 Kabeer Gbaja-Biamila RC 25.00 10.00
❑ 185 Edgerton Hartwell RC 8.00 3.00
❑ 186 Robert Carswell RC 8.00 3.00
❑ 187 Aaron Schobel RC 12.00 5.00
❑ 188 Dan Alexander RC 12.00 5.00
❑ 189 Jamie Winborn RC 10.00 4.00
❑ 190 Karon Riley RC 8.00 3.00
❑ EG Eddie George SAMPLE 3.00 1.50

2002 SP Authentic

❑ COMP.SET w/o SP's (90) 25.00 10.00
❑ 1 Tom Brady 2.00 .75
❑ 2 Antowain Smith .60 .25
❑ 3 Troy Brown .60 .25
❑ 4 Kurt Warner 1.00 .40
❑ 5 Marshall Faulk 1.00 .40
❑ 6 Isaac Bruce 1.00 .40
❑ 7 Kordell Stewart .60 .25
❑ 8 Jerome Bettis 1.00 .40
❑ 9 Plaxico Burress .60 .25
❑ 10 Hines Ward 1.00 .40
❑ 11 Donovan McNabb 1.25 .50
❑ 12 Duce Staley 1.00 .40
❑ 13 Dorsey Levens .60 .25
❑ 14 Antonio Freeman 1.00 .40
❑ 15 Jerry Rice 2.00 .75
❑ 16 Rich Gannon 1.00 .40
❑ 17 Tim Brown 1.00 .40
❑ 18 Jim Miller .60 .25
❑ 19 Marty Booker .60 .25
❑ 20 Brian Urlacher 1.25 .50
❑ 21 Jamal Lewis 1.00 .40
❑ 22 Chris Redman .40 .15
❑ 23 Ray Lewis 1.00 .40
❑ 24 Brett Favre 2.50 1.00
❑ 25 Ahman Green 1.00 .40
❑ 26 Terry Glenn .60 .25
❑ 27 Keyshawn Johnson 1.00 .40
❑ 28 Keenan McCardell .40 .15
❑ 29 Michael Pittman .40 .15
❑ 30 Curtis Martin 1.00 .40
❑ 31 Vinny Testaverde .60 .25
❑ 32 Chad Pennington 1.25 .50
❑ 33 Wayne Chrebet .60 .25
❑ 34 Terrell Owens 1.00 .40
❑ 35 Garrison Hearst .60 .25
❑ 36 Jay Fiedler .60 .25
❑ 37 Ricky Williams 1.00 .40
❑ 38 Chris Chambers 1.00 .40
❑ 39 Shaun Alexander 1.25 .50
❑ 40 Darrell Jackson .60 .25
❑ 41 Drew Bledsoe 1.25 .50
❑ 42 Travis Henry 1.00 .40
❑ 43 Eric Moulds .60 .25
❑ 44 Stephen Davis .60 .25
❑ 45 Rod Gardner .60 .25
❑ 46 Brian Griese 1.00 .40
❑ 47 Olandis Gary .60 .25
❑ 48 Shannon Sharpe .60 .25
❑ 49 Tim Couch .60 .25
❑ 50 Kevin Johnson .60 .25
❑ 51 Steve McNair 1.00 .40
❑ 52 Eddie George 1.00 .40
❑ 53 Aaron Brooks 1.00 .40
❑ 54 Deuce McAllister 1.25 .50
❑ 55 Joe Horn .60 .25
❑ 56 Michael Vick 2.50 1.00
❑ 57 Warrick Dunn 1.00 .40
❑ 58 Kerry Collins .60 .25
❑ 59 Tiki Barber 1.00 .40
❑ 60 Amani Toomer .60 .25
❑ 61 Jake Plummer .60 .25
❑ 62 David Boston 1.00 .40
❑ 63 Thomas Jones .60 .25
❑ 64 Edgerrin James 1.25 .50
❑ 65 Marvin Harrison 1.00 .40
❑ 66 Mark Brunell 1.00 .40
❑ 67 Jimmy Smith .60 .25
❑ 68 Fred Taylor 1.00 .40
❑ 69 Corey Dillon .60 .25
❑ 70 Jon Kitna .60 .25
❑ 71 Michael Westbrook .40 .15
❑ 72 Trent Green .60 .25
❑ 73 Priest Holmes 1.25 .50
❑ 74 Tony Gonzalez .60 .25
❑ 75 Daunte Culpepper 1.00 .40
❑ 76 Michael Bennett .60 .25
❑ 77 Randy Moss 1.50 .60
❑ 78 Drew Brees 1.00 .40
❑ 79 Curtis Conway .40 .15
❑ 80 Junior Seau 1.00 .40
❑ 81 Quincy Carter .60 .25
❑ 82 Emmitt Smith 2.50 1.00
❑ 83 Joey Galloway .60 .25
❑ 84 Cory Schlesinger .40 .15
❑ 85 James Stewart .60 .25
❑ 86 Az-Zahir Hakim .40 .15
❑ 87 Rodney Peete .60 .25
❑ 88 Lamar Smith .60 .25
❑ 89 Corey Bradford .40 .15
❑ 90 Jermaine Lewis .40 .15
❑ 91 Peyton Manning AU 120.00 60.00
❑ 92 Anthony Thomas AU 25.00 12.50
❑ 93 LaDainian Tomlinson AU 80.00 40.00
❑ 94 Jeff Garcia AU 25.00 10.00
❑ 95 Kurt Warner SC 3.00 1.25
❑ 96 Brett Favre SC 8.00 3.00
❑ 97 Michael Vick SC 10.00 4.00
❑ 98 Donovan McNabb SC 4.00 1.50
❑ 99 Daunte Culpepper SC 3.00 1.25
❑ 100 Tom Brady SC 8.00 3.00
❑ 101 Drew Brees SC 3.00 1.25
❑ 102 Kordell Stewart SC 2.00 .75
❑ 103 Steve McNair SC 3.00 1.25
❑ 104 Peyton Manning SC 6.00 2.50
❑ 105 Mark Brunell SC 3.00 1.25
❑ 106 Jeff Garcia SC 3.00 1.25
❑ 107 Aaron Brooks SC 3.00 1.25
❑ 108 Rich Gannon SC 3.00 1.25
❑ 109 Tim Couch SC 2.00 .75
❑ 110 Jake Plummer SC 3.00 1.25
❑ 111 Drew Bledsoe SC 4.00 1.50
❑ 112 Brian Griese SC 3.00 1.25
❑ 113 Quincy Carter SC 2.00 .75
❑ 114 Vinny Testaverde SC 2.00 .75
❑ 115 Chad Pennington SC 4.00 1.50
❑ 116 Brad Johnson SC 2.00 .75
❑ 117 Trent Dilfer SC 2.00 .75
❑ 118 Jim Miller SC 2.00 .75
❑ 119 Tommy Maddox SC 8.00 3.00
❑ 120 Trent Green SC 2.00 .75
❑ 121 Rodney Peete SC 2.00 .75
❑ 122 Jay Fiedler SC 2.00 .75
❑ 123 Kerry Collins SC 2.00 .75
❑ 124 Chris Redman SC 2.00 .75
❑ 125 Marshall Faulk SS 4.00 1.50
❑ 126 Donovan McNabb SS 5.00 2.00
❑ 127 Michael Vick SS 12.00 5.00
❑ 128 Brett Favre SS 10.00 4.00
❑ 129 Peyton Manning SS 8.00 3.00
❑ 130 Kurt Warner SS 4.00 1.50
❑ 131 Curtis Martin SS 4.00 1.50
❑ 132 Randy Moss SS 8.00 3.00
❑ 133 Edgerrin James SS 5.00 2.00
❑ 134 Jerome Bettis SS 4.00 1.50
❑ 135 Emmitt Smith SS 10.00 4.00
❑ 136 LaDainian Tomlinson SS 6.00 2.50
❑ 137 Jeff Garcia SS 4.00 1.50
❑ 138 Kordell Stewart SS 2.50 1.00
❑ 139 Anthony Thomas SS 2.50 1.00
❑ 140 Tom Brady SS 10.00 4.00
❑ 141 Daunte Culpepper SS 4.00 1.50
❑ 142 Drew Bledsoe SS 5.00 2.00
❑ 143 Ricky Williams SS 4.00 1.50
❑ 144 Warrick Dunn SS 4.00 1.50
❑ 145 Steve McNair SS 4.00 1.50
❑ 146 Rich Gannon SS 4.00 1.50
❑ 147 Jake Plummer SS 2.50 1.00
❑ 148 Jerry Rice SS 8.00 3.00
❑ 149 Mark Brunell SS 4.00 1.50
❑ 150 Brian Griese SS 4.00 1.50
❑ 151 Eddie George SS 4.00 1.50
❑ 152 Tim Couch SS 2.50 1.00
❑ 153 Keyshawn Johnson SS 4.00 1.50
❑ 154 Shannon Sharpe SS 2.50 1.00
❑ 155 Phillip Buchanon RC 12.00 5.00
❑ 156 Brian Allen RC 10.00 4.00
❑ 157 Brian Westbrook RC 40.00 20.00
❑ 158 Lito Sheppard RC 12.00 5.00
❑ 159 Daryl Jones RC 10.00 4.00
❑ 160 Javin Hunter RC 6.00 2.50
❑ 161 Derrick Lewis RC 6.00 2.50
❑ 162 Javon Walker RC 30.00 15.00
❑ 163 Tank Williams RC 10.00 4.00
❑ 164 Shaun Hill RC 12.00 5.00
❑ 165 Napoleon Harris RC 12.00 5.00
❑ 166 Herb Haygood RC 6.00 2.50
❑ 167 Jake Schifino RC 10.00 4.00
❑ 168 Quentin Jammer RC 12.00 5.00
❑ 169 Jason McAddley RC 10.00 4.00
❑ 170 Jerramy Stevens RC 12.00 5.00
❑ 171 Jesse Chatman RC 12.00 5.00
❑ 172 Larry Ned RC 10.00 4.00
❑ 173 Najeh Davenport RC 12.00 5.00
❑ 174 Lamont Thompson RC 10.00 4.00
❑ 175 Darrell Hill RC 10.00 4.00
❑ 176 Ryan Sims RC 12.00 5.00
❑ 177 Ryan Denney RC 10.00 4.00
❑ 178 Jamin Elliott RC 6.00 2.50
❑ 179 Sam Simmons RC 6.00 2.50
❑ 180 Seth Burford RC 10.00 4.00
❑ 181 Tellis Redmon RC 10.00 4.00
❑ 182 Ben Leber RC 12.00 5.00
❑ 183 Kendall Newson RC 6.00 2.50
❑ 184 Marques Anderson RC 12.00 5.00
❑ 185 Adrian Peterson AU RC 20.00 7.50
❑ 186 Haynesworth AU RC EXCH
❑ 187 Antwoine Womack AU RC 20.00 7.50
❑ 188 Brandon Doman AU RC 20.00 7.50
❑ 189 Craig Nall AU RC 30.00 12.50
❑ 190 Chad Hutchinson AU RC 20.00 7.50
❑ 191 Chester Taylor AU RC 40.00 20.00
❑ 192 Damien Anderson AU RC 20.00 7.50
❑ 193 Deion Branch AU RC 50.00 25.00
❑ 194 Dusty Bonner AU RC 15.00 6.00
❑ 195 Ed Reed AU RC 50.00 20.00
❑ 196 Eric McCoo AU RC 15.00 6.00
❑ 197 J.T. O'Sullivan AU RC 20.00 7.50
❑ 198 Kalimba Edwards AU RC 25.00 10.00
❑ 199 Jonathan Wells AU RC 25.00 10.00
❑ 200 Josh Scobey AU RC 20.00 7.50
❑ 201 Kelly Campbell AU RC 30.00 15.00
❑ 202 Kurt Kittner AU RC 20.00 7.50
❑ 203 Lamar Gordon AU RC 25.00 10.00
❑ 204 Lee Mays AU RC 20.00 7.50

❑ 205	Leonard Henry AU RC	20.00	7.50
❑ 206	Luke Staley AU RC	20.00	7.50
❑ 207	Justin Peelle AU RC	15.00	6.00
❑ 208	Randy Fasani AU RC	20.00	7.50
❑ 209	Ricky Williams AU RC	25.00	10.00
❑ 210	Ronald Curry AU RC	30.00	15.00
❑ 211	Travis Stephens AU RC	20.00	7.50
❑ 212	Wendell Bryant AU RC	15.00	6.00
❑ 213	Woody Dantzler AU RC	20.00	7.50
❑ 214	Kahlil Hill AU RC	20.00	7.50
❑ 215	Donte Stallworth JSY RC	50.00	25.00
❑ 216	Joe Harrington AU/280 RC	80.00	30.00
❑ 217	Cliff Russell JSY RC	30.00	12.50
❑ 218	Clinton Portis JSY RC	100.00	50.00
❑ 219	Daniel Graham JSY RC	30.00	15.00
❑ 220	David Garrard JSY RC	60.00	25.00
❑ 221	DeShaun Foster JSY RC	50.00	25.00
❑ 222	Julius Peppers JSY RC	50.00	25.00
❑ 223	Jeremy Shockey JSY RC	60.00	30.00
❑ 224	Patrick Ramsey JSY RC	50.00	20.00
❑ 225	Josh Reed JSY RC	30.00	12.50
❑ 226	LaDell Betts JSY RC	30.00	12.50
❑ 227	Mike Williams JSY/350 RC	30.00	12.50
❑ 228	Reche Caldwell JSY RC	30.00	12.50
❑ 229	Rohan Davey JSY RC	30.00	12.50
❑ 230	Ron Johnson JSY RC	30.00	12.50
❑ 231	Roy Williams JSY/350 RC	80.00	40.00
❑ 232	T.J. Duckett JSY RC	30.00	12.50
❑ 233	Tim Carter JSY RC	30.00	12.50
❑ 234	William Green JSY RC	30.00	12.50
❑ 235	Randle El JSY AU RC	100.00	50.00
❑ 237	David Carr JSY AU RC	250.00	125.00
❑ 238	Andre Davis JSY AU RC	50.00	25.00
❑ 239	Eric Crouch JSY AU RC	50.00	20.00
❑ 240	Antonio Bryant JSY AU RC	60.00	30.00
❑ 241	Jabar Gaffney JSY AU RC	50.00	25.00
❑ 242	Marquise Walker JSY AU RC	50.00	25.00
❑ 243	Maurice Morris JSY AU RC	50.00	25.00
❑ 244	Josh McCown JSY AU RC	80.00	30.00
❑ AP1	Walter Payton AU/34	500.00	350.00
❑ SW1	Walter Payton JSY/150	120.00	50.00
❑ SW1	W.Payton Gold JSY/34	200.00	100.00
❑ SCPS	Payt/Smith JSY/250	120.00	60.00
❑ SCPSG	Payt/Smith Gld JSY/34	300.00	175.00

2003 SP Authentic

❑	COMP.SET w/o SP's (90)	20.00	7.50
❑ 1	Donovan McNabb	1.25	.50
❑ 2	Tim Couch	.40	.15
❑ 3	Joey Harrington	1.25	.50
❑ 4	Brett Favre	2.50	1.00
❑ 5	Jeff Garcia	1.00	.40
❑ 6	Kerry Collins	.60	.25
❑ 7	Michael Vick	2.00	.75
❑ 8	David Carr	1.25	.50
❑ 9	Steve McNair	1.00	.40
❑ 10	Chad Pennington	1.25	.50
❑ 11	Patrick Ramsey	1.00	.40
❑ 12	Rich Gannon	.60	.25
❑ 13	Kurt Warner	1.00	.40
❑ 14	Brad Johnson	.60	.25
❑ 15	Jay Fiedler	.60	.25
❑ 16	Jake Plummer	.60	.25
❑ 17	Mark Brunell	.60	.25
❑ 18	Peyton Manning	1.50	.60
❑ 19	Brian Griese	1.00	.40
❑ 20	Kordell Stewart	.60	.25
❑ 21	Kelly Holcomb	.60	.25
❑ 22	Josh McCown	.60	.25
❑ 23	Matt Hasselbeck	.60	.25
❑ 24	Marc Bulger	1.00	.40
❑ 25	Chris Redman	.40	.15
❑ 26	Rodney Peete	.60	.25
❑ 27	Jake Delhomme	1.00	.40
❑ 28	Jon Kitna	.60	.25
❑ 29	Trent Green	.60	.25
❑ 30	Quincy Carter	.60	.25
❑ 31	Chad Hutchinson	.40	.15
❑ 32	Edgerrin James	1.00	.40
❑ 33	Deuce McAllister	1.00	.40
❑ 34	Ricky Williams	1.00	.40
❑ 35	Priest Holmes	1.25	.50
❑ 36	Curtis Martin	1.00	.40
❑ 37	Shaun Alexander	1.00	.40
❑ 38	Eddie George	.60	.25
❑ 39	Marshall Faulk	1.00	.40
❑ 40	Garrison Hearst	.60	.25
❑ 41	Ahman Green	1.00	.40
❑ 42	Corey Dillon	.60	.25
❑ 43	Jamal Lewis	1.00	.40
❑ 44	William Green	.60	.25
❑ 45	Travis Henry	.60	.25
❑ 46	Mike Alstott	1.00	.40
❑ 47	Amos Zereoue	.60	.25
❑ 48	Stephen Davis	.60	.25
❑ 49	Duce Staley	.60	.25
❑ 50	Fred Taylor	1.00	.40
❑ 51	Anthony Thomas	.60	.25
❑ 52	Charlie Garner	.60	.25
❑ 53	Kevan Barlow	.60	.25
❑ 54	Brian Urlacher	1.25	.50
❑ 55	Junior Seau	1.00	.40
❑ 56	Zach Thomas	1.00	.40
❑ 57	Ray Lewis	1.00	.40
❑ 58	Jerry Porter	.60	.25
❑ 59	Marty Booker	.60	.25
❑ 60	Javon Walker	.60	.25
❑ 61	Donald Driver	.60	.25
❑ 62	Amani Toomer	.60	.25
❑ 63	Peerless Price	.60	.25
❑ 64	Santana Moss	.60	.25
❑ 65	Laveranues Coles	.60	.25
❑ 66	Troy Brown	.60	.25
❑ 67	Chris Chambers	1.00	.40
❑ 68	Rod Smith	.60	.25
❑ 69	Ashley Lelie	1.00	.40
❑ 70	Plaxico Burress	.60	.25
❑ 71	Keyshawn Johnson	1.00	.40
❑ 72	Isaac Bruce	1.00	.40
❑ 73	Torry Holt	1.00	.40
❑ 74	Koren Robinson	.60	.25
❑ 75	Derrick Mason	.60	.25
❑ 76	Kevin Johnson	.60	.25
❑ 77	Andre' Davis	.40	.15
❑ 78	Antonio Bryant	.60	.25
❑ 79	Eric Moulds	.60	.25
❑ 80	Jerry Rice	2.00	.75
❑ 81	Tim Brown	1.00	.40
❑ 82	Antwaan Randle El	1.00	.40
❑ 83	Donte Stallworth	1.00	.40
❑ 84	Randy Moss	1.50	.60
❑ 85	Chad Johnson	1.00	.40
❑ 86	Hines Ward	1.00	.40
❑ 87	Rod Gardner	.60	.25
❑ 88	Marvin Harrison	1.00	.40
❑ 89	David Boston	.60	.25
❑ 90	Julius Peppers	1.00	.40
❑ 91	Dewayne White RC	5.00	2.00
❑ 92	Casey Fitzsimmons RC	6.00	2.50
❑ 93	Aaron Moorehead RC	6.00	2.50
❑ 94	Jimmy Farris RC	5.00	2.00
❑ 95	Eric Parker RC	6.00	2.50
❑ 96	Michael Haynes RC	6.00	2.50
❑ 97	J.J. Moses RC	5.00	2.00
❑ 98	Ken Hamlin RC	6.00	2.50
❑ 99	William Joseph RC	6.00	2.50
❑ 100	Alonzo Jackson RC	5.00	2.00
❑ 101	Tyler Brayton RC	6.00	2.50
❑ 102	Eddie Moore RC	5.00	2.00
❑ 103	Cleo Lemon RC	15.00	6.00
❑ 104	Arlen Harris RC	6.00	2.50
❑ 105	Cortez Hankton RC	5.00	2.00
❑ 106	Angelo Crowell RC	5.00	2.00
❑ 107	Johnathan Sullivan RC	5.00	2.00
❑ 108	Pisa Tinoisamoa RC	6.00	2.50
❑ 109	Boss Bailey RC	6.00	2.50
❑ 110	Tommy Jones RC	3.00	1.25
❑ 111	E.J. Henderson RC	6.00	2.50
❑ 112	Jimmy Kennedy RC	6.00	2.50
❑ 113	Nnamdi Asomugha RC	5.00	2.00
❑ 114	Hanik Milligan RC	5.00	2.00
❑ 115	Sammy Davis RC	6.00	2.50
❑ 116	Drayton Florence RC	3.00	1.25
❑ 117	Andre Woolfolk RC	6.00	2.50
❑ 118	Dennis Weathersby RC	3.00	1.25
❑ 119	Mike Doss RC	6.00	2.50
❑ 120	Troy Polamalu RC	30.00	18.00
❑ 121	Clinton Portis SS	6.00	2.50
❑ 122	Daunte Culpepper SS	5.00	2.00
❑ 123	Jeremy Shockey SS	6.00	2.50
❑ 124	Drew Brees SS	5.00	2.00
❑ 125	Marshall Faulk SS	5.00	2.00
❑ 126	Emmitt Smith SS	10.00	4.00
❑ 127	Terrell Owens SS	5.00	2.00
❑ 128	Ricky Williams SS	5.00	2.00
❑ 129	Deuce McAllister SS	5.00	2.00
❑ 130	Ahman Green SS	5.00	2.00
❑ 131	Chad Pennington SS	5.00	2.00
❑ 132	Plaxico Burress SS	5.00	2.00
❑ 133	Steve McNair SS	5.00	2.00
❑ 134	Keyshawn Johnson SS	5.00	2.00
❑ 135	Jeff Garcia SS	5.00	2.00
❑ 136	Drew Bledsoe SS	5.00	2.00
❑ 137	Jerry Rice SS	8.00	3.00
❑ 138	Randy Moss SS	6.00	2.50
❑ 139	David Carr SS	6.00	2.50
❑ 140	Joey Harrington SS	6.00	2.50
❑ 141	Michael Vick SS	10.00	4.00
❑ 142	Tom Brady SS	10.00	4.00
❑ 143	Brian Urlacher SS	6.00	2.50
❑ 144	Brett Favre SS	10.00	4.00
❑ 145	Kurt Warner SS	5.00	2.00
❑ 146	LaDainian Tomlinson SS	5.00	2.00
❑ 147	Aaron Brooks SS	5.00	2.00
❑ 148	Edgerrin James SS	5.00	2.00
❑ 149	Peyton Manning SS	6.00	2.50
❑ 150	Donovan McNabb SS	5.00	2.00
❑ 151	Jason Gesser RC	12.00	5.00
❑ 152	Ken Dorsey RC	12.00	5.00
❑ 153	Jason Johnson RC	6.00	2.50
❑ 154	Avon Cobourne RC	6.00	2.50
❑ 155	Andrew Pinnock RC	10.00	4.00
❑ 156	Kirk Farmer RC	6.00	2.50
❑ 157	Reno Mahe RC	12.00	5.00
❑ 158	Lon Sheriff RC	6.00	2.50
❑ 159	Marquel Blackwell RC	6.00	2.50
❑ 160	Quentin Griffin RC	12.00	5.00
❑ 161	Rashean Mathis RC	10.00	4.00
❑ 162	Lee Suggs RC	15.00	6.00
❑ 163	Jeremi Johnson RC	10.00	4.00
❑ 164	Ovie Mughelli RC	6.00	2.50
❑ 165	Nick Barnett RC	15.00	6.00
❑ 166	Brock Forsey RC	12.00	5.00
❑ 167	Malaefou MacKenzie RC	6.00	2.50
❑ 168	Ahmaad Galloway RC	10.00	4.00
❑ 169	Cecil Sapp RC	10.00	4.00
❑ 170	Kerry Carter RC	10.00	4.00
❑ 171	Dahrran Diedrick RC	12.00	5.00
❑ 171A	Terrence Edwards RC	10.00	4.00
❑ 172	Joffrey Reynolds RC	6.00	2.50
❑ 173	Sultan McCullough RC	10.00	4.00
❑ 174	Brandon Drumm RC	6.00	2.50
❑ 175	Casey Moore RC	10.00	4.00
❑ 176	Gerald Hayes RC	6.00	2.50
❑ 178	Jamal Burke RC	6.00	2.50
❑ 179	Antonio Chatman RC	12.00	5.00
❑ 180	Reggie Newhouse RC	10.00	4.00
❑ 181	Chris Horn RC	6.00	2.50
❑ 182	Denero Marriott RC	6.00	2.50
❑ 183	DeAndrew Rubin RC	6.00	2.50
❑ 184	Taco Wallace RC	10.00	4.00
❑ 185	Doug Gabriel RC	12.00	5.00
❑ 186	Willie Ponder RC	6.00	2.50
❑ 187	David Tyree RC	10.00	4.00
❑ 188	Kevin Walter RC	10.00	4.00

❑ 189 Zuriel Smith RC 6.00 2.50
❑ 190 Keenan Howry RC 12.00 5.00
❑ 191 C.J. Jones RC 6.00 2.50
❑ 192 Amaz Battle RC 12.00 5.00
❑ 193 Walter Young RC 6.00 2.50
❑ 194 Anthony Adams RC 10.00 4.00
❑ 195 Jerome McDougle RC 12.00 5.00
❑ 196 Will Heller RC 10.00 4.00
❑ 197 Cecil Moore RC 6.00 2.50
❑ 198 Mike Seidman RC 6.00 2.50
❑ 199 Jason Witten RC 20.00 10.00
❑ 200 L.J. Smith RC 12.00 5.00
❑ 201 Bennie Joppru RC 12.00 5.00
❑ 202 Donald Lee RC 10.00 4.00
❑ 203 Aaron Walker RC 10.00 4.00
❑ 204 Antonio Brown RC 6.00 2.50
❑ 205 George Wrighster RC 10.00 4.00
❑ 206 Danny Curley RC 6.00 2.50
❑ 207 Mike Banks RC 6.00 2.50
❑ 208 Mike Pinkard RC 6.00 2.50
❑ 209 Ryan Hoag RC 6.00 2.50
❑ 210 Brad Pyatt RC 10.00 4.00
❑ 211 Charles Rogers RC 12.00 5.00
❑ 212 Chris Simms AU/250 RC 200.00 100.00
❑ 213 Nate Hybl AU RC 20.00 7.50
❑ 214 Brandon Lloyd AU RC 50.00 20.00
❑ 215 ReShard Lee AU RC 20.00 7.50
❑ 216 Dwone Hicks AU RC 12.00 5.00
❑ 217 Tony Romo AU RC 300.00 150.00
❑ 218 Brett Engemann AU RC 12.00 5.00
❑ 219 Nick Maddox AU RC 12.00 5.00
❑ 220 James MacPherson AU RC 12.00 5.00
❑ 221 Juston Wood AU RC 12.00 5.00
❑ 222 Adrian Madise AU RC 15.00 6.00
❑ 223 Shaun McDonald AU RC 20.00 7.50
❑ 224 Carl Ford AU RC 12.00 5.00
❑ 225 Vishante Shiancoe AU RC 15.00 6.00
❑ 226 Gibran Hamdan AU RC 12.00 5.00
❑ 227 Brooks Bollinger AU RC 20.00 7.50
❑ 228 B.J. Askew AU RC 20.00 7.50
❑ 229 Domanick Davis AU RC 30.00 12.50
❑ 230 LaBrandon Toefield AU RC 20.00 7.50
❑ 231 Bobby Wade AU RC 20.00 7.50
❑ 232 Justin Gage AU RC 20.00 7.50
❑ 233 Billy McMullen AU RC 15.00 6.00
❑ 234 David Kircus AU RC 25.00 10.00
❑ 235 J.R. Tolver AU RC 15.00 6.00
❑ 236 Sam Aiken AU RC 15.00 6.00
❑ 237 LaTarence Dunbar AU RC 15.00 6.00
❑ 238 Kassim Osgood AU RC 20.00 7.50
❑ 239 Tony Hollings AU RC 20.00 7.50
❑ 240 Justin Griffith AU RC 15.00 6.00
❑ 241 Brian St.Pierre JSY RC 30.00 12.50
❑ 242 Kevin Curtis JSY RC 40.00 20.00
❑ 243 Dallas Clark JSY RC 40.00 15.00
❑ 244 Willis McGahee JSY RC 100.00 50.00
❑ 245 Terence Newman JSY RC 30.00 15.00
❑ 246 Justin Fargas JSY AU RC 40.00 20.00
❑ 247 Artose Pinner JSY RC 30.00 12.50
❑ 248 Kelley Washington JSY RC 40.00 15.00
❑ 249 DeWayne Robertson JSY RC 25.00 10.00
❑ 250 Nate Burleson JSY RC 30.00 12.50
❑ 251 Kliff Kingsbury JSY RC 25.00 10.00
❑ 252 Bethel Johnson JSY RC 30.00 12.50
❑ 253 Anquan Boldin JSY RC 60.00 30.00
❑ 254 Bryant Johnson JSY AU RC 40.00 20.00
❑ 255 Terrell Suggs JSY AU RC 60.00 30.00
❑ 256 Musa Smith JSY RC 30.00 12.50
❑ 257 Chris Brown JSY RC 30.00 12.50
❑ 258 Marcus Trufant JSY RC 30.00 12.50
❑ 259 Teyo Johnson JSY RC 30.00 12.50
❑ 260 Tyrone Calico JSY RC 40.00 15.00
❑ 261 Dave Ragone JSY AU RC 40.00 20.00
❑ 262 Kyle Boller JSY AU RC 50.00 25.00
❑ 263 Onterrio Smith JSY AU RC 40.00 20.00
❑ 264 Rex Grossman JSY RC 100.00 40.00
❑ 265 Larry Johnson JSY RC 200.00 100.00
❑ 266 Seneca Wallace JSY AU RC 80.00 40.00
❑ 268 Taylor Jacobs JSY AU RC 40.00 20.00
❑ 269 Byron Leftwich JSY AU RC 300.00 150.00
❑ 270 Carson Palmer JSY AU RC 700.00 400.00

2004 SP Authentic

❑ COMP.SET w/o SP's (90) 25.00 10.00
❑ 151-185 AU RC PRINT RUN 990 SER.#'d SETS
❑ 186-200 JSY AU RC PRINT RUN 799
❑ 201-206 JSY AU RC PRINT RUN 499
❑ 207-216 JSY AU RC PRINT RUN 299
❑ 1 Josh McCown .60 .25
❑ 2 Anquan Boldin 1.00 .40
❑ 3 Michael Vick 2.00 .75
❑ 4 Peerless Price .60 .25
❑ 5 Todd Heap .60 .25
❑ 6 Kyle Boller 1.00 .40
❑ 7 Jamal Lewis 1.00 .40
❑ 8 Drew Bledsoe 1.00 .40
❑ 9 Travis Henry .60 .25
❑ 10 Eric Moulds .60 .25
❑ 11 Steve Smith 1.00 .40
❑ 12 Stephen Davis .60 .25
❑ 13 Jake Delhomme 1.00 .40
❑ 14 Rex Grossman 1.00 .40
❑ 15 Brian Urlacher 1.25 .50
❑ 16 Thomas Jones .60 .25
❑ 17 Chad Johnson 1.00 .40
❑ 18 Rudi Johnson .60 .25
❑ 19 Carson Palmer 1.25 .50
❑ 20 William Green .60 .25
❑ 21 Andre Davis .40 .15
❑ 22 Jeff Garcia 1.00 .40
❑ 23 Roy Williams S .60 .25
❑ 24 Eddie George .60 .25
❑ 25 Keyshawn Johnson .60 .25
❑ 26 Ashley Lelie .60 .25
❑ 27 Jake Plummer .60 .25
❑ 28 Champ Bailey .60 .25
❑ 29 Charles Rogers .60 .25
❑ 30 Joey Harrington 1.00 .40
❑ 31 Ahman Green 1.00 .40
❑ 32 Brett Favre 2.50 1.00
❑ 33 Javon Walker .60 .25
❑ 34 David Carr 1.00 .40
❑ 35 Domanick Davis 1.00 .40
❑ 36 Andre Johnson 1.00 .40
❑ 37 Marvin Harrison 1.00 .40
❑ 38 Edgerrin James 1.00 .40
❑ 39 Peyton Manning 1.50 .60
❑ 40 Byron Leftwich 1.25 .50
❑ 41 Fred Taylor .60 .25
❑ 42 Trent Green .60 .25
❑ 43 Tony Gonzalez .60 .25
❑ 44 Priest Holmes 1.25 .50
❑ 45 Ricky Williams 1.00 .40
❑ 46 Chris Chambers .60 .25
❑ 47 Jay Fiedler .40 .15
❑ 48 Daunte Culpepper 1.00 .40
❑ 49 Randy Moss 1.25 .50
❑ 50 Onterrio Smith .60 .25
❑ 51 Tom Brady 2.50 1.00
❑ 52 Troy Brown .60 .25
❑ 53 Corey Dillon .60 .25
❑ 54 Deuce McAllister 1.00 .40
❑ 55 Aaron Brooks .60 .25
❑ 56 Joe Horn .60 .25
❑ 57 Amani Toomer .60 .25
❑ 58 Kurt Warner 1.00 .40
❑ 59 Jeremy Shockey 1.00 .40
❑ 60 Chad Pennington 1.00 .40
❑ 61 Santana Moss .60 .25
❑ 62 Curtis Martin 1.00 .40
❑ 63 Rich Gannon .60 .25
❑ 64 Jerry Rice 2.00 .75
❑ 65 Jerry Porter .60 .25
❑ 66 Terrell Owens 1.00 .40
❑ 67 Jevon Kearse .60 .25
❑ 68 Donovan McNabb 1.25 .50
❑ 69 Hines Ward 1.00 .40
❑ 70 Plaxico Burress .60 .25
❑ 71 Tommy Maddox .60 .25
❑ 72 Drew Brees 1.00 .40
❑ 73 LaDainian Tomlinson 1.25 .50
❑ 74 Tim Rattay .40 .15
❑ 75 Brandon Lloyd .60 .25
❑ 76 Kevan Barlow .60 .25
❑ 77 Shaun Alexander 1.00 .40
❑ 78 Koren Robinson .60 .25
❑ 79 Matt Hasselbeck .60 .25
❑ 80 Marshall Faulk 1.00 .40
❑ 81 Torry Holt 1.00 .40
❑ 82 Marc Bulger 1.00 .40
❑ 83 Brad Johnson .60 .25
❑ 84 Joey Galloway .60 .25
❑ 85 Steve McNair 1.00 .40
❑ 86 Derrick Mason .60 .25
❑ 87 Chris Brown 1.00 .40
❑ 88 Mark Brunell .60 .25
❑ 89 Laveranues Coles .60 .25
❑ 90 Clinton Portis 1.00 .40
❑ 91 Triandos Luke RC 8.00 3.00
❑ 92 Keith Smith RC 6.00 2.50
❑ 93 Shaun Phillips RC 6.00 2.50
❑ 94 D.J. Williams RC 8.00 3.00
❑ 95 Keiwan Ratliff RC 6.00 2.50
❑ 96 Madieu Williams RC 6.00 2.50
❑ 97 Chris Cooley RC 8.00 3.00
❑ 98 Stuart Schweigert RC 8.00 3.00
❑ 99 Sloan Thomas RC 6.00 2.50
❑ 100 Chad Lavalais RC 6.00 2.50
❑ 101 Jared Allen RC 15.00 6.00
❑ 102 Brian Jones RC 6.00 2.50
❑ 103 Matt Ware RC 8.00 3.00
❑ 104 Daryl Smith RC 8.00 3.00
❑ 105 J.R. Reed RC 6.00 2.50
❑ 106 D.J. Hackett RC 6.00 2.50
❑ 107 Jeris McIntyre RC 6.00 2.50
❑ 108 Dexter Reid RC 4.00 1.50
❑ 109 Courtney Anderson RC 6.00 2.50
❑ 110 Courtney Watson RC 8.00 3.00
❑ 111 Larry Croom RC 6.00 2.50
❑ 112 Jonathan Smith RC 6.00 2.50
❑ 113 Vernon Carey RC 6.00 2.50
❑ 114 Michael Gaines RC 6.00 2.50
❑ 115 Chris Snee RC 6.00 2.50
❑ 116 Nathan Vasher RC 10.00 4.00
❑ 117 Teddy Lehman RC 8.00 3.00
❑ 118 Marcus Tubbs RC 8.00 3.00
❑ 119 Ben Utecht RC 4.00 1.50
❑ 120 Maurice Mann RC 6.00 2.50
❑ 121 Thomas Tapeh RC 6.00 2.50
❑ 122 Will Allen RC 8.00 3.00
❑ 123 Demorrio Williams RC 8.00 3.00
❑ 124 Ran Carthon RC 6.00 2.50
❑ 125 Tim Euhus RC 8.00 3.00
❑ 126 Bradlee Van Pelt RC 8.00 3.00
❑ 127 Patrick Crayton RC 8.00 3.00
❑ 128 Ryan Krause RC 6.00 2.50
❑ 129 Joey Thomas RC 8.00 3.00
❑ 130 Antwan Odom RC 8.00 3.00
❑ 131 Karlos Dansby RC 8.00 3.00
❑ 132 Junior Siavii RC 8.00 3.00
❑ 133 Jamaar Taylor RC 8.00 3.00
❑ 134 Kendrick Starling RC 4.00 1.50
❑ 135 Wes Welker RC 10.00 4.00
❑ 136 Igor Olshansky RC 8.00 3.00
❑ 137 Mark Jones RC 6.00 2.50
❑ 138 Bruce Thornton RC 4.00 1.50
❑ 139 Michael Boulware RC 8.00 3.00
❑ 140 Matt Mauck RC 8.00 3.00
❑ 141 Clarence Moore RC 8.00 3.00
❑ 142 Derrick Strait RC 8.00 3.00
❑ 143 Jarrett Payton RC 8.00 3.00
❑ 144 Dontarrious Thomas RC 8.00 3.00
❑ 145 Shawntae Spencer RC 8.00 3.00
❑ 146 Bob Sanders RC 20.00 10.00
❑ 147 Darrell Dockett RC 6.00 2.50
❑ 148 Sean Taylor RC 8.00 3.00
❑ 149 Jason Babin RC 8.00 3.00
❑ 150 Ricardo Colclough RC 8.00 3.00

❑ 151 Brandon Chillar AU RC 15.00 6.00
❑ 152 Clarence Farmer AU RC 15.00 6.00
❑ 153 B.J. Symons AU RC 20.00 7.50
❑ 154 John Navarre AU RC 20.00 7.50
❑ 155 P.K. Sam AU RC EXCH 20.00 7.50
❑ 156 Casey Clausen AU RC 20.00 7.50
❑ 157 Drew Henson AU RC 20.00 7.50
❑ 158 Kris Wilson AU RC 20.00 7.50
❑ 159 Vince Wilfork AU RC 25.00 10.00
❑ 160 Michael Turner AU RC 80.00 40.00
❑ 161 Jonathan Vilma AU RC 30.00 12.50
❑ 162 Samie Parker AU RC 20.00 7.50
❑ 163 B.J. Sams AU RC 20.00 7.50
❑ 164 A.Echemandu AU RC 15.00 6.00
❑ 165 Ernest Wilford AU RC 20.00 7.50
❑ 166 Troy Fleming AU RC 20.00 7.50
❑ 167 Tommie Harris AU RC 25.00 12.50
❑ 168 Jammal Lord AU RC 20.00 7.50
❑ 169 Kenechi Udeze AU RC 20.00 7.50
❑ 170 Chris Gamble AU RC 25.00 10.00
❑ 171 Carlos Francis AU RC 15.00 6.00
❑ 172 Mewelde Moore AU RC 20.00 7.50
❑ 173 Jared Lorenzen AU RC 15.00 6.00
❑ 174 Jeff Smoker AU RC 20.00 7.50
❑ 175 Ben Hartsock AU RC 20.00 7.50
❑ 176 Jerricho Cotchery AU RC 20.00 7.50
❑ 177 Josh Harris AU RC 20.00 7.50
❑ 178 Cody Pickett AU RC 20.00 7.50
❑ 179 Quincy Wilson AU RC 15.00 6.00
❑ 180 Will Smith AU RC EXCH 20.00 7.50
❑ 181 Ahmad Carroll AU RC 25.00 10.00
❑ 182 B.J. Johnson AU RC 15.00 6.00
❑ 183 Dunta Robinson AU RC 25.00 10.00
❑ 184 Craig Krenzel AU RC 20.00 7.50
❑ 185 Johnnie Morant AU RC 20.00 7.50
❑ 186 Cedric Cobbs JSY AU RC 50.00 20.00
❑ 187 Matt Schaub JSY AU RC 250.00 125.00
❑ 188 Bernard Berrian JSY AU RC 100.00 60.00
❑ 189 Devard Darling JSY AU RC 50.00 20.00
❑ 190 Ben Watson JSY AU RC 80.00 30.00
❑ 191 Darius Watts JSY AU RC 50.00 20.00
❑ 192 DeAngelo Hall JSY AU RC 60.00 30.00
❑ 193 Ben Troupe JSY AU RC 50.00 20.00
❑ 194 Mich Jenkins JSY AU RC 50.00 20.00
❑ 195 Keary Colbert JSY AU RC 60.00 25.00
❑ 196 Robert Gallery JSY AU RC 50.00 20.00
❑ 197 Greg Jones JSY AU RC 60.00 30.00
❑ 198 Mich.Clayton JSY AU RC 100.00 40.00
❑ 199 Luke McCown JSY AU RC 50.00 20.00
❑ 200 Derrick Hamilton JSY AU RC 50.00 20.00
❑ 201 Ras.Woods JSY AU RC 50.00 20.00
❑ 202 Chris Perry JSY AU RC 80.00 30.00
❑ 203 D.Henderson JSY AU RC 60.00 30.00
❑ 204 Tatum Bell JSY AU RC 120.00 60.00
❑ 205 Lee Evans JSY AU RC 100.00 50.00
❑ 206 J.P. Losman JSY AU RC 120.00 60.00
❑ 207 Kel.Winslow JSY AU RC 120.00 60.00
❑ 208 Reg.Williams JSY AU RC 100.00 60.00
❑ 209 Julius Jones JSY AU RC 300.00 150.00
❑ 210 S.Jackson JSY AU RC 350.00 200.00
❑ 211 Kevin Jones JSY AU RC 200.00 100.00
❑ 212 Roy Williams JSY AU RC 250.00 125.00
❑ 213 Roethlisberger JSY AU RC 600.00 300.00
❑ 214 Philip Rivers JSY AU RC 500.00 250.00
❑ 215 L.Fitzgerald JSY AU RC 300.00 150.00
❑ 216 Eli Manning JSY AU RC 600.00 300.00

2005 SP Authentic

❑ COMP.SET w/o RC's (90) 25.00 10.00
❑ 91-180 PRINT RUN 750 SER.#'d SETS
❑ 181-220/254-257 PRINT RUN 850 SETS
❑ 221-253 PRINT RUN 99-899 SER.#'d SETS
❑ UNPRICED NFL LOGO PATCHES #'d TO 1
❑ EXCH EXPIRATION:12/20/2008
❑ 1 Kurt Warner .60 .25
❑ 2 Larry Fitzgerald 1.00 .40
❑ 3 Anquan Boldin .60 .25
❑ 4 Michael Vick 1.50 .60
❑ 5 Alge Crumpler .60 .25
❑ 6 Warrick Dunn .60 .25
❑ 7 Kyle Boller .60 .25
❑ 8 Jamal Lewis 1.00 .40
❑ 9 J.P. Losman 1.00 .40
❑ 10 Willis McGahee 1.00 .40
❑ 11 Lee Evans .60 .25
❑ 12 Jake Delhomme 1.00 .40
❑ 13 DeShaun Foster .60 .25
❑ 14 Muhsin Muhammad .60 .25
❑ 15 Walter Payton 4.00 1.50
❑ 16 Brian Urlacher 1.00 .40
❑ 17 Carson Palmer 1.00 .40
❑ 18 Rudi Johnson .60 .25
❑ 19 Chad Johnson 1.00 .40
❑ 20 Lee Suggs .60 .25
❑ 21 Antonio Bryant .50 .20
❑ 22 Julius Jones 1.25 .50
❑ 23 Drew Bledsoe 1.00 .40
❑ 24 Keyshawn Johnson .60 .25
❑ 25 Tatum Bell .60 .25
❑ 26 Jake Plummer .60 .25
❑ 27 Roy Williams WR 1.00 .40
❑ 28 Kevin Jones 1.00 .40
❑ 29 Jeff Garcia .60 .25
❑ 30 Brett Favre 2.50 1.00
❑ 31 Ahman Green 1.00 .40
❑ 32 Javon Walker .60 .25
❑ 33 David Carr 1.00 .40
❑ 34 Andre Johnson .60 .25
❑ 35 Domanick Davis .60 .25
❑ 36 Peyton Manning 1.50 .60
❑ 37 Edgerrin James 1.00 .40
❑ 38 Reggie Wayne .60 .25
❑ 39 Byron Leftwich 1.00 .40
❑ 40 Fred Taylor .60 .25
❑ 41 Jimmy Smith .60 .25
❑ 42 Priest Holmes 1.00 .40
❑ 43 Larry Johnson 1.00 .40
❑ 44 Trent Green .60 .25
❑ 45 Randy McMichael .50 .20
❑ 46 Chris Chambers .60 .25
❑ 47 Ricky Williams .60 .25
❑ 48 Daunte Culpepper 1.00 .40
❑ 49 Nate Burleson .60 .25
❑ 50 Tom Brady 2.50 1.00
❑ 51 Corey Dillon .60 .25
❑ 52 David Givens .60 .25
❑ 53 Aaron Brooks .60 .25
❑ 54 Deuce McAllister 1.00 .40
❑ 55 Joe Horn .60 .25
❑ 56 Eli Manning 2.00 .75
❑ 57 Jeremy Shockey 1.00 .40
❑ 58 Tiki Barber 1.00 .40
❑ 59 Chad Pennington 1.00 .40
❑ 60 Santana Moss .60 .25
❑ 61 Curtis Martin 1.00 .40
❑ 62 Randy Moss 1.00 .40
❑ 63 LaMont Jordan 1.00 .40
❑ 64 Kerry Collins .60 .25
❑ 65 Donovan McNabb 1.25 .50
❑ 66 Brian Westbrook .60 .25
❑ 67 Terrell Owens 1.00 .40
❑ 68 Ben Roethlisberger 2.50 1.00
❑ 69 Hines Ward 1.00 .40
❑ 70 Jerome Bettis 1.00 .40
❑ 71 Drew Brees 1.00 .40
❑ 72 Antonio Gates 1.00 .40
❑ 73 LaDainian Tomlinson 1.25 .50
❑ 74 Kevan Barlow .60 .25
❑ 75 Brandon Lloyd .50 .20
❑ 76 Matt Hasselbeck .60 .25
❑ 77 Shaun Alexander 1.25 .50
❑ 78 Darrell Jackson .60 .25
❑ 79 Marc Bulger 1.00 .40
❑ 80 Steven Jackson 1.25 .50
❑ 81 Torry Holt 1.00 .40
❑ 82 Brian Griese .60 .25
❑ 83 Michael Clayton 1.00 .40
❑ 84 Michael Pittman .50 .20
❑ 85 Steve McNair 1.00 .40
❑ 86 Drew Bennett .60 .25
❑ 87 Chris Brown .60 .25
❑ 88 Clinton Portis 1.00 .40
❑ 89 Patrick Ramsey .60 .25
❑ 90 Laveranues Coles .60 .25
❑ 91 Nehemiah Broughton RC 6.00 2.50
❑ 92 Madison Hedgecock RC 8.00 3.00
❑ 93 Damien Nash RC 6.00 2.50
❑ 94 Michael Boley RC 6.00 2.50
❑ 95 Lionel Gates RC 6.00 2.50
❑ 96 Noah Herron RC 8.00 3.00
❑ 97 Bo Scaife RC 6.00 2.50
❑ 98 Joel Dreessen RC 6.00 2.50
❑ 99 Rasheed Marshall RC 8.00 3.00
❑ 100 Andre Maddox RC 6.00 2.50
❑ 101 Tab Perry RC 8.00 3.00
❑ 102 Dante Ridgeway RC 6.00 2.50
❑ 103 Patrick Estes RC 6.00 2.50
❑ 104 Billy Bajema RC 6.00 2.50
❑ 105 Paris Warren RC 6.00 2.50
❑ 106 LeRon McCoy RC 6.00 2.50
❑ 107 Adam Bergen RC 8.00 3.00
❑ 108 Manuel White RC 6.00 2.50
❑ 109 Stephen Spach RC 6.00 2.50
❑ 110 Donte Nicholson RC 8.00 3.00
❑ 111 Brodney Pool RC 8.00 3.00
❑ 112 Stanford Routt RC 6.00 2.50
❑ 113 Josh Bullocks RC 8.00 3.00
❑ 114 Ronald Bartell RC 6.00 2.50
❑ 115 Nick Collins RC 8.00 3.00
❑ 116 Darrent Williams RC 8.00 3.00
❑ 117 Justin Miller RC 6.00 2.50
❑ 118 Kelvin Hayden RC 6.00 2.50
❑ 119 Bryant McFadden RC 8.00 3.00
❑ 120 Oshiomogho Atogwe RC 6.00 2.50
❑ 121 Stanley Wilson RC 6.00 2.50
❑ 122 Eric Green RC 4.00 1.50
❑ 123 Michael Hawkins RC 6.00 2.50
❑ 124 Marcus Spears RC 8.00 3.00
❑ 125 Ellis Hobbs RC 8.00 3.00
❑ 126 Scott Starks RC 6.00 2.50
❑ 127 Domonique Foxworth RC 8.00 3.00
❑ 128 Sean Considine RC 8.00 3.00
❑ 129 James Sanders RC 8.00 3.00
❑ 130 Travis Daniels RC 6.00 2.50
❑ 131 Vincent Fuller RC 6.00 2.50
❑ 132 Marviel Underwood RC 6.00 2.50
❑ 133 Jerome Carter RC 6.00 2.50
❑ 134 Kerry Rhodes RC 8.00 3.00
❑ 135 Fred Amey RC 6.00 2.50
❑ 136 Eric King RC 6.00 2.50
❑ 137 Derrick Johnson CB RC 8.00 3.00
❑ 138 Luis Castillo RC 8.00 3.00
❑ 139 Shaun Cody RC 8.00 3.00
❑ 140 Matt Roth RC 8.00 3.00
❑ 141 Jonathan Babineaux RC 6.00 2.50
❑ 142 Justin Tuck RC 8.00 3.00
❑ 143 Sione Pouha RC 8.00 3.00
❑ 144 Daven Holly RC 8.00 3.00
❑ 145 Vincent Burns RC 6.00 2.50
❑ 146 Derrick Johnson RC 12.00 5.00
❑ 147 Lofa Tatupu RC 12.00 5.00
❑ 148 Odell Thurman RC 8.00 3.00
❑ 149 Rick Razzano RC 8.00 3.00
❑ 150 Channing Crowder RC 8.00 3.00
❑ 151 Kirk Morrison RC 8.00 3.00
❑ 152 Alfred Fincher RC 6.00 2.50
❑ 153 Jordan Beck RC 6.00 2.50
❑ 154 Darryl Blackstock RC 6.00 2.50
❑ 155 Leroy Hill RC 8.00 3.00
❑ 156 Jammal Brown RC 8.00 3.00
❑ 157 Alex Barron RC 4.00 1.50
❑ 158 Chris Spencer RC 8.00 3.00
❑ 159 Logan Mankins RC 10.00 4.00
❑ 160 David Baas RC 6.00 2.50
❑ 161 Michael Roos RC 4.00 1.50
❑ 162 Kurt Campbell RC 6.00 2.50
❑ 163 Khalif Barnes RC 6.00 2.50
❑ 164 Antonio Perkins RC 6.00 2.50
❑ 165 Vonta Leach RC 8.00 3.00
❑ 166 Brady Poppinga RC 8.00 3.00
❑ 167 Trent Cole RC 8.00 3.00
❑ 168 Dave Rayner RC 6.00 2.50

❑ 169	Bill Swancutt RC	6.00	2.50
❑ 170	Eric Moore RC	6.00	2.50
❑ 171	Justin Green RC	8.00	3.00
❑ 172	Shaun Suisham RC	6.00	2.50
❑ 173	C.J. Mosley RC	6.00	2.50
❑ 174	Ryan Riddle RC	4.00	1.50
❑ 175	Darrell Shropshire RC	6.00	2.50
❑ 176	Boomer Grigsby RC	10.00	4.00
❑ 177	Rian Wallace RC	6.00	2.50
❑ 178	Lance Mitchell RC	6.00	2.50
❑ 179	Nick Speegle RC	6.00	2.50
❑ 180	Tyson Thompson RC	10.00	4.00
❑ 181	Dan Orlovsky AU RC	20.00	7.50
❑ 182	Anthony Davis AU RC	12.00	5.00
❑ 183	Kay-Jay Harris AU RC	12.00	5.00
❑ 184	Walter Reyes AU RC	12.00	5.00
❑ 185	Darren Sproles AU RC	15.00	6.00
❑ 186	Marlin Jackson AU RC	15.00	6.00
❑ 187	Corey Webster AU RC	15.00	6.00
❑ 188	Marion Barber AU RC	60.00	35.00
❑ 189	Chris Henry AU RC EXCH	20.00	7.50
❑ 190	Derek Anderson AU RC	35.00	20.00
❑ 191	David Pollack AU RC EXCH	20.00	7.50
❑ 192	Anttaj Hawthorne AU RC	12.00	5.00
❑ 193	David Greene AU RC	20.00	7.50
❑ 194	Erasmus James AU RC	15.00	6.00
❑ 195	Ryan Fitzpatrick AU RC	25.00	10.00
❑ 196	Derrick Johnson AU	25.00	10.00
❑ 197	Barrett Ruud AU RC	15.00	6.00
❑ 198	Kevin Burnett AU RC	15.00	6.00
❑ 199	C.Houston AU RC EXCH	20.00	10.00
❑ 200	J.R. Russell AU RC	12.00	5.00
❑ 201	Larry Brackins AU RC	12.00	5.00
❑ 202	Thomas Davis AU RC	15.00	6.00
❑ 203	Fred Gibson AU RC	12.00	5.00
❑ 204	Craphonso Thorpe AU RC	12.00	5.00
❑ 205	Brandon Jacobs AU RC	60.00	35.00
❑ 206	Taylor Stubblefield AU RC	10.00	4.00
❑ 207	Shawne Merriman AU RC	50.00	25.00
❑ 208	Travis Johnson AU RC	12.00	5.00
❑ 209	Adrian McPherson AU RC	15.00	6.00
❑ 210	Brandon Jones AU RC	15.00	6.00
❑ 211	Jerome Mathis AU RC	15.00	6.00
❑ 212	Alex Smith TE AU RC	15.00	6.00
❑ 213	Fabian Washington AU RC	15.00	6.00
❑ 214	Mike Nugent AU RC	15.00	6.00
❑ 215	Chase Lyman AU RC	12.00	5.00
❑ 216	Roydell Williams AU RC	15.00	6.00
❑ 217	Matt Cassel AU RC	30.00	15.00
❑ 218	Alvin Pearman AU RC	15.00	6.00
❑ 219	DeMarcus Ware AU RC	25.00	12.50
❑ 220	Mike Patterson AU RC	15.00	6.00
❑ 221	C.Roby JSY/899 AU RC	50.00	20.00
❑ 222	E.Shelton JSY/899 AU RC	50.00	20.00
❑ 223	S.LeFors JSY/899 AU RC	50.00	20.00
❑ 224	Frank Gore JSY/899 AU RC	200.00	100.00
❑ 225	Ryan Moats JSY/899 AU RC	80.00	50.00
❑ 226	A.Walter JSY/899 AU RC	80.00	30.00
❑ 227	A.Jones JSY/899 AU RC	50.00	20.00
❑ 228	C.Rogers JSY/699 AU RC	50.00	20.00
❑ 229	T.Murphy JSY/899 AU RC	50.00	20.00
❑ 230	Kyle Orton JSY/699 AU RC	60.00	30.00
❑ 231	C.Fason JSY/699 AU RC	60.00	25.00
❑ 232	V.Morency JSY/699 AU RC	50.00	20.00
❑ 233	R.Parrish JSY/699 AU RC	60.00	30.00
❑ 234	V.Jackson JSY/699 AU RC	60.00	30.00
❑ 235	M.Bradley JSY/699 AU RC	60.00	30.00
❑ 236	Re.Brown JSY/599 AU RC	80.00	40.00
❑ 237	Ro.White JSY/499 AU RC	60.00	30.00
❑ 238	M.Clayton JSY/499 AU RC	100.00	50.00
❑ 239	Antrel Rolle JSY/499 AU RC	50.00	20.00
❑ 240	Maurice Clarett JSY/499 AU	50.00	20.00
❑ 241	J.Arrington JSY/699 AU RC	60.00	25.00
❑ 242	Matt Jones JSY/399 AU RC	100.00	50.00
❑ 243	Ro.Brown JSY/299 AU RC	250.00	125.00
❑ 244	C.Frye JSY/499 AU RC	100.00	40.00
❑ 245	J.Campbell JSY/299 AU RC	150.00	75.00
❑ 246	T.Willmsn JSY/299 AU RC	100.00	40.00
❑ 247	B.Edwrd JSY/299 AU RC	150.00	75.00
❑ 248	A.Smith QB JSY/299 AU RC	300.00	150.00
❑ 249	C.Wllms JSY/299 AU RC	250.00	125.00
❑ 250	H.Miller JSY/299 AU RC	100.00	40.00
❑ 251	C.Benson JSY/99 AU RC	400.00	250.00
❑ 252	A.Rodgers JSY/99 AU RC	400.00	250.00
❑ 253	M.Williams JSY/99 AU	250.00	125.00
❑ 254	Chris Carr AU RC	20.00	7.50
❑ 255	Deandra Cobb AU RC	12.00	5.00
❑ 256	James Kilian AU RC	15.00	6.00
❑ 257	Airese Currie AU RC	15.00	6.00

2006 SP Authentic

❑ 1	Edgerrin James	1.00	.40
❑ 2	Larry Fitzgerald	1.00	.40
❑ 3	Anquan Boldin	.60	.25
❑ 4	Michael Vick	1.25	.50
❑ 5	Warrick Dunn	.60	.25
❑ 6	Alge Crumpler	.60	.25
❑ 7	Steve McNair	.60	.25
❑ 8	Jamal Lewis	.60	.25
❑ 9	Derrick Mason	.50	.20
❑ 10	Willis McGahee	1.00	.40
❑ 11	Lee Evans	.60	.25
❑ 12	Jake Delhomme	.60	.25
❑ 13	Steve Smith	1.00	.40
❑ 14	DeShaun Foster	.60	.25
❑ 15	Rex Grossman	1.00	.40
❑ 16	Thomas Jones	.60	.25
❑ 17	Brian Urlacher	1.00	.40
❑ 18	Carson Palmer	1.00	.40
❑ 19	Chad Johnson	.60	.25
❑ 20	Rudi Johnson	.60	.25
❑ 21	Charlie Frye	.60	.25
❑ 22	Braylon Edwards	1.00	.40
❑ 23	Reuben Droughns	.60	.25
❑ 24	Drew Bledsoe	1.00	.40
❑ 25	Terrell Owens	1.00	.40
❑ 26	Julius Jones	1.00	.40
❑ 27	Jake Plummer	.60	.25
❑ 28	Tatum Bell	.60	.25
❑ 29	Javon Walker	.60	.25
❑ 30	Kevin Jones	1.00	.40
❑ 31	Roy Williams WR	1.00	.40
❑ 32	Brett Favre	2.00	.75
❑ 33	Donald Driver	.60	.25
❑ 34	David Carr	.60	.25
❑ 35	Ron Dayne	.60	.25
❑ 36	Andre Johnson	.60	.25
❑ 37	Peyton Manning	1.50	.60
❑ 38	Marvin Harrison	1.00	.40
❑ 39	Reggie Wayne	.60	.25
❑ 40	Byron Leftwich	.60	.25
❑ 41	Fred Taylor	.60	.25
❑ 42	Matt Jones	1.00	.40
❑ 43	Trent Green	.60	.25
❑ 44	Larry Johnson	1.25	.50
❑ 45	Tony Gonzalez	.60	.25
❑ 46	Daunte Culpepper	1.00	.40
❑ 47	Ronnie Brown	1.00	.40
❑ 48	Chris Chambers	.60	.25
❑ 49	Chester Taylor	.60	.25
❑ 50	Troy Williamson	.60	.25
❑ 51	Tom Brady	1.50	.60
❑ 52	Corey Dillon	.60	.25
❑ 53	Troy Brown	.60	.25
❑ 54	Drew Brees	1.00	.40
❑ 55	Deuce McAllister	.60	.25
❑ 56	Joe Horn	.60	.25
❑ 57	Eli Manning	1.25	.50
❑ 58	Tiki Barber	1.00	.40
❑ 59	Plaxico Burress	.60	.25
❑ 60	Laveranues Coles	.60	.25
❑ 61	Chad Pennington	.60	.25
❑ 62	Aaron Brooks	.60	.25
❑ 63	Randy Moss	1.00	.40
❑ 64	LaMont Jordan	.60	.25
❑ 65	Donovan McNabb	1.00	.40
❑ 66	Brian Westbrook	.60	.25
❑ 67	Ben Roethlisberger	1.50	.60
❑ 68	Willie Parker	1.25	.50
❑ 69	Hines Ward	1.00	.40
❑ 70	Philip Rivers	1.00	.40
❑ 71	LaDainian Tomlinson	1.25	.50
❑ 72	Antonio Gates	1.00	.40
❑ 73	Alex Smith QB	1.25	.50
❑ 74	Frank Gore	1.00	.40
❑ 75	Antonio Bryant	.60	.25
❑ 76	Matt Hasselbeck	.60	.25
❑ 77	Shaun Alexander	1.00	.40
❑ 78	Darrell Jackson	.60	.25
❑ 79	Marc Bulger	.60	.25
❑ 80	Steven Jackson	1.00	.40
❑ 81	Torry Holt	.60	.25
❑ 82	Chris Simms	.60	.25
❑ 83	Cadillac Williams	1.00	.40
❑ 84	Joey Galloway	.60	.25
❑ 85	Travis Henry	.50	.20
❑ 86	Drew Bennett	.50	.20
❑ 87	David Givens	.60	.25
❑ 88	Mark Brunell	.60	.25
❑ 89	Clinton Portis	1.00	.40
❑ 90	Santana Moss	.60	.25
❑ 91	Bernard Pollard RC	10.00	4.00
❑ 92	Brodie Croyle RC	20.00	8.00
❑ 93	Cedric Griffin RC	10.00	4.00
❑ 94	Marques Colston RC	50.00	20.00
❑ 95	Daniel Bullocks RC	12.00	5.00
❑ 96	Darryl Tapp RC	10.00	4.00
❑ 97	David Thomas RC	12.00	5.00
❑ 98	Montell Owens RC	10.00	4.00
❑ 99	DeMeco Ryans RC	15.00	6.00
❑ 100	Devin Hester RC	25.00	10.00
❑ 101	Donte Whitner RC	12.00	5.00
❑ 102	D'Qwell Jackson RC	10.00	4.00
❑ 103	Patrick Cobbs RC	10.00	4.00
❑ 104	Haloti Ngata RC	12.00	5.00
❑ 105	Lawrence Vickers RC	10.00	4.00
❑ 106	Jeff King RC	10.00	4.00
❑ 107	Jeremy Bloom RC	10.00	4.00
❑ 108	Johnathan Joseph RC	10.00	4.00
❑ 109	DeDe Dorsey RC	10.00	4.00
❑ 110	Marcus Vick RC	10.00	4.00
❑ 111	Bobby Carpenter RC	12.00	5.00
❑ 112	Manny Lawson RC	12.00	5.00
❑ 113	Nick Mangold RC	10.00	4.00
❑ 114	Quinn Sypniewski RC	10.00	4.00
❑ 115	Richard Marshall RC	10.00	4.00
❑ 116	Rocky McIntosh RC	12.00	5.00
❑ 117	Roman Harper RC	10.00	4.00
❑ 118	Tamba Hali RC	12.00	5.00
❑ 119	Tony Scheffler RC	12.00	5.00
❑ 120	Wali Lundy RC	12.00	5.00
❑ 121	A.J. Nicholson RC	5.00	2.00
❑ 122	Abdul Hodge RC	10.00	4.00
❑ 123	Adam Jennings RC	8.00	3.00
❑ 124	Alan Zemaitis RC	10.00	4.00
❑ 125	Andrew Whitworth RC	5.00	2.00
❑ 126	Anthony Schlegel RC	8.00	3.00
❑ 127	Anthony Smith RC	12.00	5.00
❑ 128	Antoine Bethea RC	12.00	5.00
❑ 129	Barry Cofield RC	10.00	4.00
❑ 130	Brandon Johnson RC	8.00	3.00
❑ 131	Calvin Lowry RC	10.00	4.00
❑ 132	Shaun Bodiford RC	8.00	3.00
❑ 133	Charlie Peprah RC	8.00	3.00
❑ 134	Claude Wroten RC	5.00	2.00
❑ 135	Clint Ingram RC	10.00	4.00
❑ 136	Cortland Finnegan RC	10.00	4.00
❑ 137	Daryn Colledge RC	10.00	4.00
❑ 138	David Anderson RC	8.00	3.00
❑ 139	David Kirtman RC	8.00	3.00
❑ 140	Boone Stutz RC	8.00	3.00
❑ 141	Delanie Walker RC	8.00	3.00
❑ 142	Sam Hurd RC	15.00	6.00
❑ 143	Derrick Martin RC	8.00	3.00
❑ 144	Willie Andrews RC	8.00	3.00
❑ 145	Dusty Dvoracek RC	10.00	4.00
❑ 146	Elvis Dumervil RC	5.00	2.00
❑ 147	Eric Smith RC	8.00	3.00
❑ 148	Freddie Keiaho RC	8.00	3.00
❑ 149	Gabe Watson RC	8.00	3.00
❑ 150	Gerris Wilkinson RC	5.00	2.00
❑ 151	Greg Blue RC	8.00	3.00
❑ 152	Guy Whimper RC	5.00	2.00

❑ 153 Jamar Williams RC 8.00 3.00
❑ 154 James Anderson RC 5.00 2.00
❑ 155 Jason Spitz RC 10.00 4.00
❑ 156 Jeff Webb RC 8.00 3.00
❑ 157 Jeremy Mincey RC 8.00 3.00
❑ 158 Jeremy Trueblood RC 8.00 3.00
❑ 159 Omar Gaither RC 8.00 3.00
❑ 160 Jon Alston RC 10.00 4.00
❑ 161 Julian Jenkins RC 8.00 3.00
❑ 162 Keith Ellison RC 8.00 3.00
❑ 163 Kevin McMahan RC 8.00 3.00
❑ 164 Kyle Williams RC 10.00 4.00
❑ 165 Leon Williams RC 8.00 3.00
❑ 166 Mark Anderson RC 15.00 6.00
❑ 167 LaJuan Ramsey RC 10.00 4.00
❑ 168 Nate Salley RC 8.00 3.00
❑ 169 Rob Ninkovich RC 8.00 3.00
❑ 170 Parys Haralson RC 8.00 3.00
❑ 171 Pat Watkins RC 10.00 4.00
❑ 172 Paul McQuistan RC 5.00 2.00
❑ 173 Rashad Butler RC 5.00 2.00
❑ 174 Ray Edwards RC 8.00 3.00
❑ 175 Reed Doughty RC 8.00 3.00
❑ 176 Ronnie Prude RC 8.00 3.00
❑ 177 Stephen Tulloch RC 8.00 3.00
❑ 178 Tim Jennings RC 8.00 3.00
❑ 179 Jarrad Page RC 10.00 4.00
❑ 180 Victor Adeyanju RC 8.00 3.00
❑ 181 Andre Hall AU RC 12.00 5.00
❑ 182 Anthony Fasano AU RC 15.00 6.00
❑ 183 Antonio Cromartie AU RC 15.00 6.00
❑ 184 Ashton Youboty AU RC 12.00 5.00
❑ 185 Kamerion Wimbley AU RC 15.00 6.00
❑ 186 Brad Smith AU RC 15.00 6.00
❑ 187 Brodrick Bunkley AU RC 12.00 5.00
❑ 188 Bruce Gradkowski AU RC 25.00 10.00
❑ 189 Chad Greenway AU RC 15.00 6.00
❑ 190 Cory Rodgers AU RC 12.00 5.00
❑ 191 D.J. Shockley AU RC 15.00 6.00
❑ 192 Danieal Manning AU RC 15.00 6.00
❑ 193 Darnell Bing AU RC 12.00 5.00
❑ 194 Darrell Hackney AU RC 12.00 5.00
❑ 195 D.Ferguson AU RC EXCH 15.00 6.00
❑ 196 Dominique Byrd AU RC 12.00 5.00
❑ 197 Drew Olson AU RC 12.00 5.00
❑ 198 Ernie Sims AU RC 15.00 6.00
❑ 199 Garrett Mills AU/99 RC 150.00 75.00
❑ 200 Gerald Riggs AU RC 12.00 5.00
❑ 201 Greg Jennings AU RC 30.00 15.00
❑ 202 Greg Lee AU RC 12.00 5.00
❑ 203 Hank Baskett AU RC 20.00 10.00
❑ 204 Ingle Martin AU RC 15.00 6.00
❑ 205 Jason Allen AU RC 12.00 5.00
❑ 206 Jerome Harrison AU RC 15.00 6.00
❑ 207 Jimmy Williams AU RC 15.00 6.00
❑ 208 John McCargo AU RC 10.00 4.00
❑ 209 Josh Betts AU RC 12.00 5.00
❑ 210 Leonard Pope AU RC 15.00 6.00
❑ 211 Marques Hagans AU RC 12.00 5.00
❑ 212 Martin Nance AU RC 12.00 5.00
❑ 213 Mathias Kiwanuka AU RC 20.00 8.00
❑ 214 Mike Bell AU RC 30.00 12.00
❑ 215 Mike Hass AU RC 15.00 6.00
❑ 216 Owen Daniels AU RC 15.00 6.00
❑ 217 P.J. Daniels AU RC 12.00 5.00
❑ 218 Reggie McNeal AU RC 12.00 5.00
❑ 219 Skyler Green AU RC 12.00 5.00
❑ 220 Terrence Whitehead AU RC 12.00 5.00
❑ 221 Thomas Howard AU RC 12.00 5.00
❑ 222 Tye Hill AU RC 12.00 5.00
❑ 223 Will Blackmon AU RC 12.00 5.00
❑ 224 Willie Reid AU RC 15.00 6.00
❑ 225 Winston Justice AU RC 15.00 6.00
❑ 226 Jay Cutler AU/99 RC 600.00 450.00
❑ 227 Joseph Addai AU/99 RC 500.00 300.00
❑ 228 Br.Williams JSY/999 AU RC 40.00 15.00
❑ 229 B.Calhoun JSY/999 AU RC 40.00 15.00
❑ 230 Ch.Jackson JSY/699 AU RC 80.00 30.00
❑ 231 C.Whitehurst JSY/999 AU RC 50.00 25.00
❑ 232 DeA.Williams JSY/175 AU RC 400.00 250.00
❑ 233 Dem.Williams JSY/999 AU RC 50.00 25.00
❑ 234 Derek Hagan JSY/999 AU RC 40.00 15.00
❑ 235 Jason Avant JSY/999 AU RC 40.00 15.00
❑ 236 J.Norwood JSY/999 AU RC 100.00 50.00
❑ 237 J.Klopfenstein JSY/999 AU RC 30.00 12.00
❑ 238 K.Clemens JSY/999 AU RC 60.00 30.00
❑ 239 K.Jennings JSY/199 AU RC 80.00 40.00
❑ 240 L.Maroney JSY/999 AU RC 250.00 125.00
❑ 241 L.White JSY/999 AU RC 250.00 125.00
❑ 242 L.Washington JSY/999 AU RC 60.00 30.00
❑ 243 M.Lewis JSY/999 AU RC 40.00 15.00
❑ 244 M.McNeill JSY/260 AU RC 80.00 30.00
❑ 245 Ma.Williams JSY/699 AU RC 60.00 30.00
❑ 246 Matt Leinart JSY/299 AU RC 550.00 350.00
❑ 247 M.Drew JSY/999 AU RC 200.00 100.00
❑ 248 M.Stovall JSY/999 AU RC 40.00 15.00
❑ 249 Michael Huff JSY/999 AU RC 50.00 20.00
❑ 250 M.Robinson JSY/999 AU RC 50.00 20.00
❑ 251 Omar Jacobs/750 RC 10.00 4.00
❑ 252 Reggie Bush JSY/299 AU RC 1000.00 600.00
❑ 253 S.Holmes JSY/399 AU RC 150.00 75.00
❑ 254 Sinorice Moss JSY/99 AU RC 250.00 150.00
❑ 255 T.Jackson JSY/999 AU RC 80.00 40.00
❑ 256 Travis Wilson JSY/999 AU RC 40.00 15.00
❑ 257 V.Davis JSY/699 AU RC 100.00 50.00
❑ 258 Vince Young JSY/270 AU RC 750.00 400.00
❑ 259 A.J. Hawk JSY/399 AU RC 100.00 50.00
❑ 260 B.Marshall JSY/999 AU RC 60.00 30.00

2001 SP Game Used Edition

❑ COMP.SET w/o SP's (90) 100.00 50.00
❑ 1 Jake Plummer 1.50 .60
❑ 2 David Boston 2.50 1.00
❑ 3 Frank Sanders 1.00 .40
❑ 4 Jamal Anderson 2.50 1.00
❑ 5 Doug Johnson 1.00 .40
❑ 6 Shawn Jefferson 1.00 .40
❑ 7 Jamal Lewis 4.00 1.50
❑ 8 Shannon Sharpe 1.50 .60
❑ 9 Qadry Ismail 1.50 .60
❑ 10 Shawn Bryson 1.00 .40
❑ 11 Rob Johnson 1.50 .60
❑ 12 Eric Moulds 1.50 .60
❑ 13 Muhsin Muhammad 1.50 .60
❑ 14 Brad Hoover 1.00 .40
❑ 15 Tim Biakabutuka 1.50 .60
❑ 16 Cade McNown 1.00 .40
❑ 17 Marcus Robinson 2.50 1.00
❑ 18 Brian Urlacher 4.00 1.50
❑ 19 Akili Smith 1.00 .40
❑ 20 Peter Warrick 2.50 1.00
❑ 21 Corey Dillon 2.50 1.00
❑ 22 Kevin Johnson 1.50 .60
❑ 23 Rickey Dudley 1.00 .40
❑ 24 Tim Couch 1.50 .60
❑ 25 Tony Banks 1.00 .40
❑ 26 Emmitt Smith 5.00 2.00
❑ 27 Carl Pickens 1.00 .40
❑ 28 Terrell Davis 2.50 1.00
❑ 29 Mike Anderson 2.50 1.00
❑ 30 Brian Griese 2.50 1.00
❑ 31 Ed McCaffrey 2.50 1.00
❑ 32 Charlie Batch 2.50 1.00
❑ 33 Germane Crowell 1.00 .40
❑ 34 James O. Stewart 1.50 .60
❑ 35 Brett Favre 8.00 3.00
❑ 36 Antonio Freeman 2.50 1.00
❑ 37 Ahman Green 2.50 1.00
❑ 38 Peyton Manning 6.00 2.50
❑ 39 Edgerrin James 3.00 1.25
❑ 40 Marvin Harrison 2.50 1.00
❑ 41 Mark Brunell 2.50 1.00
❑ 42 Fred Taylor 2.50 1.00
❑ 43 Jimmy Smith 1.50 .60
❑ 44 Tony Gonzalez 1.50 .60
❑ 45 Derrick Alexander 1.50 .60
❑ 46 Oronde Gadsden 1.50 .60
❑ 47 Ray Lucas 1.00 .40
❑ 48 Lamar Smith 1.50 .60
❑ 49 Randy Moss 5.00 2.00
❑ 50 Cris Carter 2.50 1.00
❑ 51 Daunte Culpepper 2.50 1.00
❑ 52 Drew Bledsoe 3.00 1.25
❑ 53 Terry Glenn 1.50 .60
❑ 54 Ricky Williams 2.50 1.00
❑ 55 Jeff Blake 1.50 .60
❑ 56 Joe Horn 1.50 .60
❑ 57 Aaron Brooks 2.50 1.00
❑ 58 Kerry Collins 1.50 .60
❑ 59 Tiki Barber 2.50 1.00
❑ 60 Ron Dayne 2.50 1.00
❑ 61 Vinny Testaverde 1.50 .60
❑ 62 Wayne Chrebet 1.50 .60
❑ 63 Curtis Martin 2.50 1.00
❑ 64 Tim Brown 2.50 1.00
❑ 65 Rich Gannon 2.50 1.00
❑ 66 Tyrone Wheatley 1.50 .60
❑ 67 Duce Staley 2.50 1.00
❑ 68 Donovan McNabb 3.00 1.25
❑ 69 Kordell Stewart 1.50 .60
❑ 70 Jerome Bettis 2.50 1.00
❑ 71 Marshall Faulk 3.00 1.25
❑ 72 Kurt Warner 5.00 2.00
❑ 73 Isaac Bruce 2.50 1.00
❑ 74 Doug Flutie 2.50 1.00
❑ 75 Curtis Conway 1.50 .60
❑ 76 Jeff Garcia 2.50 1.00
❑ 77 Jerry Rice 5.00 2.00
❑ 78 Charlie Garner 1.50 .60
❑ 79 Terrell Owens 2.50 1.00
❑ 80 Ricky Watters 1.00 .40
❑ 81 Matt Hasselbeck 1.50 .60
❑ 82 Levon Kirkland 1.00 .40
❑ 83 Keyshawn Johnson 2.50 1.00
❑ 84 Brad Johnson 2.50 1.00
❑ 85 Mike Alstott 2.50 1.00
❑ 86 Eddie George 2.50 1.00
❑ 87 Steve McNair 2.50 1.00
❑ 88 Jeff George 1.50 .60
❑ 89 Michael Westbrook 2.50 1.00
❑ 90 Stephen Davis 2.50 1.00
❑ 91 Michael Vick JSY RC 60.00 25.00
❑ 92 Chris Weinke JSY RC 15.00 6.00
❑ 93 Drew Brees JSY RC 50.00 25.00
❑ 94 Deuce McAllister JSY RC 30.00 12.50
❑ 95 Michael Bennett JSY RC 15.00 6.00
❑ 96 LaDain Tomlinson JSY RC 100.00 50.00
❑ 97 Kevan Barlow JSY RC 15.00 6.00
❑ 98 Travis Minor JSY RC 12.00 5.00
❑ 99 Rudi Johnson JSY RC 30.00 12.50
❑ 100 Todd Heap JSY RC 15.00 6.00
❑ 101 Freddie Mitchell JSY RC 15.00 6.00
❑ 102 Santana Moss JSY RC 25.00 10.00
❑ 103 Reggie Wayne JSY RC 30.00 12.50
❑ 104 Koren Robinson JSY RC 15.00 6.00
❑ 105 Josh Heupel JSY RC 15.00 6.00
❑ 106 Rod Gardner JSY RC 15.00 6.00
❑ 107 Quincy Morgan JSY RC 15.00 6.00
❑ 108 Chad Johnson JSY RC 40.00 15.00
❑ 109 Dan Morgan JSY RC 15.00 6.00
❑ 110 Gerard Warren JSY RC 15.00 6.00
❑ 111 Chris Chambers JSY RC 25.00 10.00
❑ 112 James Jackson JSY RC 15.00 6.00
❑ 113 Jesse Palmer JSY RC 15.00 6.00
❑ 114 Sage Rosenfels JSY RC 15.00 6.00
❑ 115 Mike McMahon JSY RC 15.00 6.00
❑ 116 Marques Tuiasosopo JSY RC 15.00 6.00
❑ 117 Robert Ferguson JSY RC 15.00 6.00
❑ 118 Travis Henry JSY RC 25.00 10.00
❑ 119 Richard Seymour JSY RC 15.00 6.00
❑ 120 Andre Carter JSY RC 15.00 6.00
❑ 121 LaMont Jordan RC 15.00 6.00
❑ 122 Vinny Sutherland RC 5.00 2.00
❑ 123 Nate Clements RC 8.00 3.00
❑ 124 David Terrell RC 8.00 3.00
❑ 125 A.J. Feeley RC 8.00 3.00
❑ 126 David Rivers RC 5.00 2.00
❑ 127 Snoop Minnis RC 5.00 2.00
❑ 128 Josh Booty RC 8.00 3.00
❑ 129 Correll Buckhalter RC 10.00 4.00
❑ 130 Will Allen RC 5.00 2.00
❑ 131 Dan Alexander RC 8.00 3.00

❑ 132	Leonard Davis RC	5.00	2.00
❑ 133	Anthony Thomas RC	8.00	3.00
❑ 134	Alge Crumpler RC	10.00	5.00
❑ 135	Jamal Reynolds RC	8.00	3.00
❑ 136	Ken-Yon Rambo RC	5.00	2.00
❑ 137	Bobby Newcombe RC	5.00	2.00
❑ 138	Alex Bannister RC	5.00	2.00
❑ 139	Jabari Holloway RC	5.00	2.00
❑ 140	Jamar Fletcher RC	5.00	2.00
❑ 141	Adam Archuleta RC	8.00	3.00
❑ 142	Heath Evans RC	5.00	2.00
❑ 143	Scotty Anderson RC	5.00	2.00
❑ 144	Moran Norris RC	3.00	1.25
❑ 145	Justin Smith RC	8.00	3.00
❑ 146	Quincy Carter RC	8.00	3.00
❑ 147	Ronney Daniels RC	3.00	1.25
❑ 148	Ben Leard RC	5.00	2.00
❑ 149	Fred Smoot RC	8.00	3.00
❑ 150	Milton Wynn RC	5.00	2.00

2003 SP Game Used Edition

❑	COMP.SET w/o SP's (90)	60.00	30.00
❑ 1	Chad Hutchinson	1.25	.50
❑ 2	Quincy Carter	2.00	.75
❑ 3	Joey Galloway	2.00	.75
❑ 4	Kerry Collins	2.00	.75
❑ 5	Jeremy Shockey	5.00	2.00
❑ 6	Amani Toomer	2.00	.75
❑ 7	A.J. Feeley	2.00	.75
❑ 8	Duce Staley	2.00	.75
❑ 9	Dorsey Levens	1.25	.50
❑ 10	Ladell Betts	2.00	.75
❑ 11	Patrick Ramsey	3.00	1.25
❑ 12	Anthony Thomas	2.00	.75
❑ 13	Marty Booker	2.00	.75
❑ 14	Brian Urlacher	5.00	2.00
❑ 15	Joey Harrington	5.00	2.00
❑ 16	James Stewart	2.00	.75
❑ 17	Az-Zahir Hakim	1.25	.50
❑ 18	Donald Driver	2.00	.75
❑ 19	Javon Walker	2.00	.75
❑ 20	Kordell Stewart	2.00	.75
❑ 21	Randy Moss	5.00	2.00
❑ 22	Shaun Hill	1.25	.50
❑ 23	Brian Finneran	1.25	.50
❑ 24	T.J. Duckett	2.00	.75
❑ 25	Warrick Dunn	2.00	.75
❑ 26	Rodney Peete	1.25	.50
❑ 27	Stephen Davis	2.00	.75
❑ 28	Muhsin Muhammad	2.00	.75
❑ 29	Aaron Brooks	3.00	1.25
❑ 30	Deuce McAllister	3.00	1.25
❑ 31	Joe Horn	2.00	.75
❑ 32	Keyshawn Johnson	3.00	1.25
❑ 33	Brad Johnson	2.00	.75
❑ 34	Keenan McCardell	1.25	.50
❑ 35	Jake Plummer	2.00	.75
❑ 36	Josh McCown	2.00	.75
❑ 37	Thomas Jones	2.00	.75
❑ 38	Tai Streets	1.25	.50
❑ 39	Kevan Barlow	2.00	.75
❑ 40	Garrison Hearst	2.00	.75
❑ 41	Maurice Morris	1.25	.50
❑ 42	Matt Hasselbeck	2.00	.75
❑ 43	Koren Robinson	2.00	.75
❑ 44	Marc Bulger	3.00	1.25
❑ 45	Trung Canidate	2.00	.75
❑ 46	Emmitt Smith	8.00	3.00
❑ 47	Alex Van Pelt	1.25	.50
❑ 48	Travis Henry	2.00	.75
❑ 49	Eric Moulds	2.00	.75
❑ 50	Jason Taylor	1.25	.50
❑ 51	Jay Fiedler	2.00	.75
❑ 52	Randy McMichael	2.00	.75
❑ 53	Tom Brady	8.00	3.00
❑ 54	Antowain Smith	2.00	.75
❑ 55	Troy Brown	2.00	.75
❑ 56	Curtis Martin	3.00	1.25
❑ 57	Vinny Testaverde	2.00	.75
❑ 58	Santana Moss	2.00	.75
❑ 59	Jamal Lewis	3.00	1.25
❑ 60	Chris Redman	1.25	.50
❑ 61	Ray Lewis	3.00	1.25
❑ 62	Jon Kitna	2.00	.75
❑ 63	Peter Warrick	2.00	.75
❑ 64	Kelly Holcomb	2.00	.75
❑ 65	William Green	2.00	.75
❑ 66	Kevin Johnson	2.00	.75
❑ 67	Amos Zereoue	2.00	.75
❑ 68	Tommy Maddox	3.00	1.25
❑ 69	Hines Ward	3.00	1.25
❑ 70	Corey Bradford	1.25	.50
❑ 71	Jonathan Wells	1.25	.50
❑ 72	Jabar Gaffney	2.00	.75
❑ 73	Edgerrin James	3.00	1.25
❑ 74	David Garrard	1.25	.50
❑ 75	Mark Brunell	2.00	.75
❑ 76	Jimmy Smith	2.00	.75
❑ 77	Steve McNair	3.00	1.25
❑ 78	Kevin Dyson	2.00	.75
❑ 79	Terrell Davis	3.00	1.25
❑ 80	Shannon Sharpe	2.00	.75
❑ 81	Rod Smith	2.00	.75
❑ 82	Trent Green	2.00	.75
❑ 83	Priest Holmes	4.00	1.50
❑ 84	Tony Gonzalez	2.00	.75
❑ 85	Jerry Rice	6.00	2.50
❑ 86	Charlie Garner	2.00	.75
❑ 87	Jerry Porter	2.00	.75
❑ 88	Reche Caldwell	1.25	.50
❑ 89	Tim Dwight	2.00	.75
❑ 90	Junior Seau	3.00	1.25
❑ 91	Carson Palmer RC	50.00	20.00
❑ 92	Byron Leftwich RC	40.00	15.00
❑ 93	Dave Ragone RC	12.00	5.00
❑ 94	Kyle Boller RC	12.00	5.00
❑ 95	Rex Grossman RC	40.00	15.00
❑ 96	Chris Simms RC	20.00	7.50
❑ 97	Kliff Kingsbury RC	10.00	4.00
❑ 98	Jason Gesser RC	12.00	5.00
❑ 99	Brad Banks RC	10.00	4.00
❑ 100	Ken Dorsey RC	12.00	5.00
❑ 101	Juston Wood RC	6.00	2.50
❑ 102	Brian St.Pierre RC	12.00	5.00
❑ 103	Domanick Davis RC	12.00	5.00
❑ 104	Quentin Griffin RC	12.00	5.00
❑ 105	B.J. Askew RC	12.00	5.00
❑ 106	Onterrio Smith RC	12.00	5.00
❑ 107	Seneca Wallace RC	12.00	5.00
❑ 108	Artose Pinner RC	12.00	5.00
❑ 109	Justin Fargas RC	12.00	5.00
❑ 110	Chris Brown RC	12.00	5.00
❑ 111	Willis McGahee RC	30.00	12.50
❑ 112	Larry Johnson RC	50.00	25.00
❑ 113	Lee Suggs RC	12.00	5.00
❑ 114	Billy McMullen RC	10.00	4.00
❑ 115	Sultan McCullough RC	10.00	4.00
❑ 116	Musa Smith RC	12.00	5.00
❑ 117	Earnest Graham RC	10.00	4.00
❑ 118	Antwone Savage RC	6.00	2.50
❑ 119	Kirk Farmer RC	6.00	2.50
❑ 120	Kareem Kelly RC	10.00	4.00
❑ 121	J.R. Tolver RC	10.00	4.00
❑ 122	Tyrone Calico RC	15.00	6.00
❑ 123	Kevin Curtis RC	12.00	5.00
❑ 124	Bobby Wade RC	12.00	5.00
❑ 125	Justin Gage RC	12.00	5.00
❑ 126	Bryant Johnson RC	12.00	5.00
❑ 127	Doug Gabriel RC	12.00	5.00
❑ 128	Teyo Johnson RC	12.00	5.00
❑ 129	Brandon Lloyd RC	12.00	5.00
❑ 130	Kelley Washington RC	12.00	5.00
❑ 131	Talman Gardner RC	12.00	5.00
❑ 132	Anquan Boldin RC	30.00	12.50
❑ 133	Taylor Jacobs RC	10.00	4.00
❑ 134	Andre Johnson RC	25.00	10.00
❑ 135	Charles Rogers RC	12.00	5.00
❑ 136	Antonio Bryant JSY	12.00	5.00
❑ 137	Donovan McNabb JSY/99	30.00	15.00
❑ 138	Rod Gardner JSY	8.00	3.00
❑ 139	Ahman Green JSY	12.00	5.00
❑ 140	Brett Favre JSY/99	40.00	15.00
❑ 141	Daunte Culpepper JSY	12.00	5.00
❑ 142	Michael Bennett JSY	12.00	5.00
❑ 143	Michael Vick JSY/99	50.00	20.00
❑ 144	Jeff Garcia JSY	15.00	6.00
❑ 145	Terrell Owens JSY	12.00	5.00
❑ 146	Shaun Alexander JSY	12.00	5.00
❑ 147	Torry Holt JSY	12.00	5.00
❑ 148	Isaac Bruce JSY	10.00	4.00
❑ 149	Marshall Faulk JSY/99	20.00	7.50
❑ 150	Kurt Warner JSY/99	25.00	10.00
❑ 151	Drew Bledsoe JSY	12.00	5.00
❑ 152	Josh Reed JSY	10.00	4.00
❑ 153	Peerless Price JSY	10.00	4.00
❑ 154	David Boston JSY	10.00	4.00
❑ 155	Ricky Williams JSY/99	25.00	10.00
❑ 156	Chris Chambers JSY	12.00	5.00
❑ 157	Wayne Chrebet JSY	10.00	4.00
❑ 158	Chad Pennington JSY/99	25.00	12.50
❑ 159	Laveranues Coles JSY	10.00	4.00
❑ 160	Corey Dillon JSY	10.00	4.00
❑ 161	Tim Couch JSY	8.00	3.00
❑ 162	Jerome Bettis JSY	12.00	5.00
❑ 163	Plaxico Burress JSY	12.00	5.00
❑ 164	Antwaan Randle El JSY	12.00	5.00
❑ 165	David Carr JSY/99	30.00	15.00
❑ 166	Marvin Harrison JSY	10.00	4.00
❑ 167	Peyton Manning JSY	15.00	6.00
❑ 168	Fred Taylor JSY	10.00	4.00
❑ 169	Eddie George JSY	10.00	4.00
❑ 170	Clinton Portis JSY/99	30.00	15.00
❑ 171	Ashley Lelie JSY	10.00	4.00
❑ 172	Rich Gannon JSY	12.00	5.00
❑ 173	Phillip Buchanon JSY	10.00	4.00
❑ 174	Tim Brown JSY	12.00	5.00
❑ 175	LaDainian Tomlinson JSY	12.00	5.00
❑ 176	Drew Brees JSY/99	30.00	15.00
❑ 177	Jason Johnson RC	6.00	2.50
❑ 178	Sam Aiken RC	10.00	4.00
❑ 179	Nate Burleson RC	12.00	5.00
❑ 180	Tony Romo RC	60.00	30.00
❑ 181	Arnaz Battle RC	12.00	5.00

2004 SP Game Used Edition

❑ 1	Anquan Boldin	3.00	1.25
❑ 2	Marcel Shipp	2.00	.75
❑ 3	Josh McCown	2.00	.75
❑ 4	Michael Vick	6.00	2.50
❑ 5	T.J. Duckett	2.00	.75
❑ 6	Peerless Price	2.00	.75
❑ 7	Jamal Lewis	3.00	1.25
❑ 8	Todd Heap	2.00	.75
❑ 9	Kyle Boller	3.00	1.25
❑ 10	Drew Bledsoe	3.00	1.25
❑ 11	Travis Henry	2.00	.75
❑ 12	Eric Moulds	2.00	.75
❑ 13	Jake Delhomme	3.00	1.25
❑ 14	Stephen Davis	2.00	.75
❑ 15	Julius Peppers	3.00	1.25
❑ 16	Anthony Thomas	2.00	.75
❑ 17	Rex Grossman	3.00	1.25
❑ 18	Brian Urlacher	4.00	1.50

❑ 19 Carson Palmer 4.00 1.50
❑ 20 Chad Johnson 3.00 1.25
❑ 21 Rudi Johnson 2.00 .75
❑ 22 Jeff Garcia 3.00 1.25
❑ 23 Dennis Northcutt 1.25 .50
❑ 24 Andre Davis 1.25 .50
❑ 25 Quincy Carter 2.00 .75
❑ 26 Roy Williams S 2.00 .75
❑ 27 Keyshawn Johnson 2.00 .75
❑ 28 Quentin Griffin 3.00 1.25
❑ 29 Jake Plummer 2.00 .75
❑ 30 Ashley Lelie 2.00 .75
❑ 31 Shannon Sharpe 2.00 .75
❑ 32 Joey Harrington 3.00 1.25
❑ 33 Charles Rogers 2.00 .75
❑ 34 Az-Zahir Hakim 1.25 .50
❑ 35 Brett Favre 8.00 3.00
❑ 36 Javon Walker 2.00 .75
❑ 37 Ahman Green 3.00 1.25
❑ 38 Andre Johnson 3.00 1.25
❑ 39 David Carr 3.00 1.25
❑ 40 Domanick Davis 3.00 1.25
❑ 41 Peyton Manning 5.00 2.00
❑ 42 Edgerrin James 3.00 1.25
❑ 43 Marvin Harrison 3.00 1.25
❑ 44 Byron Leftwich 4.00 1.50
❑ 45 Fred Taylor 2.00 .75
❑ 46 Jimmy Smith 2.00 .75
❑ 47 Priest Holmes 4.00 1.50
❑ 48 Trent Green 2.00 .75
❑ 49 Dante Hall 3.00 1.25
❑ 50 Tony Gonzalez 2.00 .75
❑ 51 Ricky Williams 3.00 1.25
❑ 52 Jay Fiedler 1.25 .50
❑ 53 Chris Chambers 2.00 .75
❑ 54 Randy Moss 4.00 1.50
❑ 55 Daunte Culpepper 3.00 1.25
❑ 56 Moe Williams 1.25 .50
❑ 57 Tom Brady 8.00 3.00
❑ 58 Deion Branch 3.00 1.25
❑ 59 Corey Dillon 2.00 .75
❑ 60 Deuce McAllister 3.00 1.25
❑ 61 Aaron Brooks 2.00 .75
❑ 62 Joe Horn 2.00 .75
❑ 63 Jeremy Shockey 3.00 1.25
❑ 64 Amani Toomer 2.00 .75
❑ 65 Michael Strahan 2.00 .75
❑ 66 Curtis Martin 3.00 1.25
❑ 67 Chad Pennington 3.00 1.25
❑ 68 Santana Moss 2.00 .75
❑ 69 Jerry Rice 6.00 2.50
❑ 70 Tim Brown 3.00 1.25
❑ 71 Jerry Porter 2.00 .75
❑ 72 Donovan McNabb 4.00 1.50
❑ 73 Brian Westbrook 2.00 .75
❑ 74 Terrell Owens 3.00 1.25
❑ 75 Hines Ward 3.00 1.25
❑ 76 Plaxico Burress 2.00 .75
❑ 77 Duce Staley 2.00 .75
❑ 78 LaDainian Tomlinson 4.00 1.50
❑ 79 Quentin Jammer 1.25 .50
❑ 80 Drew Brees 3.00 1.25
❑ 81 Brandon Lloyd 2.00 .75
❑ 82 Kevan Barlow 2.00 .75
❑ 83 Tim Rattay 1.25 .50
❑ 84 Matt Hasselbeck 2.00 .75
❑ 85 Shaun Alexander 3.00 1.25
❑ 86 Darrell Jackson 2.00 .75
❑ 87 Marc Bulger 3.00 1.25
❑ 88 Torry Holt 3.00 1.25
❑ 89 Marshall Faulk 3.00 1.25
❑ 90 Isaac Bruce 2.00 .75
❑ 91 Brad Johnson 2.00 .75
❑ 92 Derrick Brooks 2.00 .75
❑ 93 Warren Sapp 2.00 .75
❑ 94 Steve McNair 3.00 1.25
❑ 95 Derrick Mason 2.00 .75
❑ 96 Eddie George 2.00 .75
❑ 97 Clinton Portis 3.00 1.25
❑ 98 Mark Brunell 2.00 .75
❑ 99 Laveranues Coles 2.00 .75
❑ 100 LaVar Arrington 6.00 2.50
❑ 101 Ben Troupe RC 12.00 5.00
❑ 102 Chris Gamble RC 12.00 5.00
❑ 103 DeAngelo Hall RC 15.00 6.00
❑ 104 Dunta Robinson RC 12.00 5.00
❑ 105 Jason Shivers RC 6.00 2.50
❑ 106 Keary Colbert RC 15.00 6.00
❑ 107 Craig Krenzel RC 12.00 5.00
❑ 108 Philip Rivers RC 40.00 15.00
❑ 109 Roy Williams RC 30.00 12.50
❑ 110 Will Allen RC 12.00 5.00
❑ 111 Bob Sanders RC 25.00 10.00
❑ 112 Kris Wilson RC 12.00 5.00
❑ 113 D.J. Williams RC 12.00 5.00
❑ 114 Devery Henderson RC 10.00 4.00
❑ 115 Carlos Francis RC 10.00 4.00
❑ 116 Jonathan Vilma RC 12.00 5.00
❑ 117 Luke McCown RC 12.00 5.00
❑ 118 Michael Turner RC 15.00 6.00
❑ 119 Richard Seigler RC 10.00 4.00
❑ 120 Jared Lorenzen RC 10.00 4.00
❑ 121 P.K. Sam RC 10.00 4.00
❑ 122 Justin Smiley RC 12.00 5.00
❑ 123 Marquise Hill RC 10.00 4.00
❑ 124 Ernest Wilford RC 12.00 5.00
❑ 125 Jerricho Cotchery RC 12.00 5.00
❑ 126 Kevin Jones RC 30.00 12.50
❑ 127 Michael Boulware RC 12.00 5.00
❑ 128 Jarrett Payton RC 12.00 5.00
❑ 129 Sean Taylor RC 12.00 5.00
❑ 130 Will Smith RC 12.00 5.00
❑ 131 Bernard Berrian RC 15.00 6.00
❑ 132 Ahmad Carroll RC 12.00 5.00
❑ 133 Derrick Hamilton RC 10.00 4.00
❑ 134 Dwan Edwards RC 6.00 2.50
❑ 135 Jeff Smoker RC 12.00 5.00
❑ 136 Kenechi Udeze RC 15.00 6.00
❑ 137 Mewelde Moore RC 12.00 5.00
❑ 138 Joey Thomas RC 12.00 5.00
❑ 139 Sean Jones RC 10.00 4.00
❑ 140 Will Poole RC 12.00 5.00
❑ 141 Casey Clausen RC 12.00 5.00
❑ 142 Stuart Schweigert RC 12.00 5.00
❑ 143 Cody Pickett RC 12.00 5.00
❑ 144 Derrick Strait RC 12.00 5.00
❑ 145 Greg Jones RC 12.00 5.00
❑ 146 John Navarre RC 12.00 5.00
❑ 147 Larry Fitzgerald RC 30.00 12.50
❑ 148 Michael Clayton RC 25.00 10.00
❑ 149 Rashaun Woods RC 12.00 5.00
❑ 150 Shawn Andrews RC 12.00 5.00
❑ 151 B.J. Symons RC 12.00 5.00
❑ 152 Cedric Cobbs RC 12.00 5.00
❑ 153 Darius Watts RC 12.00 5.00
❑ 154 B.J. Johnson RC 10.00 4.00
❑ 155 Max Starks RC 10.00 4.00
❑ 156 Josh Harris RC 12.00 5.00
❑ 157 Kendrick Starling RC 6.00 2.50
❑ 158 Brandon Miree RC 10.00 4.00
❑ 159 Robert Gallery RC 12.00 5.00
❑ 160 Tatum Bell RC 25.00 10.00
❑ 161 Ben Hartsock RC 12.00 5.00
❑ 162 Derek Abney RC 12.00 5.00
❑ 163 Ricardo Colclough RC 12.00 5.00
❑ 164 Justin Jenkins RC 10.00 4.00
❑ 165 Chris Cooley RC 12.00 5.00
❑ 166 Julius Jones RC 40.00 15.00
❑ 167 Matt Mauck RC 12.00 5.00
❑ 168 Vernon Carey RC 10.00 4.00
❑ 169 John Standeford RC 10.00 4.00
❑ 170 Teddy Lehman RC 12.00 5.00
❑ 171 Ben Roethlisberger RC 120.00 60.00
❑ 172 Ben Utecht RC 6.00 2.50
❑ 173 D.J. Hackett RC 10.00 4.00
❑ 174 Drew Henson RC 12.00 5.00
❑ 175 Rich Gardner RC 10.00 4.00
❑ 176 Karlos Dansby RC 12.00 5.00
❑ 177 Matt Schaub RC 40.00 15.00
❑ 178 Darrion Scott RC 12.00 5.00
❑ 179 Keyaron Fox RC 10.00 4.00
❑ 180 Tommie Harris RC 12.00 5.00
❑ 181 Ben Watson RC 12.00 5.00
❑ 182 Chris Perry RC 20.00 7.50
❑ 183 Travelle Wharton RC 6.00 2.50
❑ 184 Eli Manning RC 100.00 50.00
❑ 185 Demorrio Williams RC 12.00 5.00
❑ 186 Kellen Winslow RC 25.00 10.00
❑ 187 Jason Babin RC 12.00 5.00
❑ 188 Quincy Wilson RC 10.00 4.00
❑ 189 Samie Parker RC 12.00 5.00
❑ 190 Vince Wilfork RC 12.00 5.00
❑ 191 Antwan Odom RC 12.00 5.00
❑ 192 Josh Davis RC 10.00 4.00
❑ 193 Courtney Watson RC 12.00 5.00
❑ 194 Devard Darling RC 12.00 5.00
❑ 195 J.P. Losman RC 25.00 10.00
❑ 196 Johnnie Morant RC 12.00 5.00
❑ 197 Lee Evans RC 15.00 6.00
❑ 198 Michael Jenkins RC 12.00 5.00
❑ 199 Reggie Williams RC 15.00 6.00
❑ 200 Steven Jackson RC 40.00 15.00

1998 SPx Finite

❑ COMP.SERIES 1 (190) 750.00 400.00
❑ COMP.SERIES 2 (180) 750.00 400.00
❑ 1 Jake Plummer 2.50 1.00
❑ 2 Eric Swann 1.00 .40
❑ 3 Rob Moore 1.50 .60
❑ 4 Jamal Anderson 2.50 1.00
❑ 5 Byron Hanspard 1.00 .40
❑ 6 Cornelius Bennett 1.00 .40
❑ 7 Michael Jackson 1.00 .40
❑ 8 Peter Boulware 1.00 .40
❑ 9 Jermaine Lewis 1.50 .60
❑ 10 Antowain Smith 2.50 1.00
❑ 11 Bruce Smith 1.50 .60
❑ 12 Bryce Paup 1.00 .40
❑ 13 Rae Carruth 1.00 .40
❑ 14 Michael Bates 1.00 .40
❑ 15 Fred Lane 1.00 .40
❑ 16 Darnell Autry 1.50 .60
❑ 17 Curtis Conway 1.50 .60
❑ 18 Erik Kramer 1.00 .40
❑ 19 Corey Dillon 2.50 1.00
❑ 20 Darnay Scott 1.50 .60
❑ 21 Reinard Wilson 1.00 .40
❑ 22 Troy Aikman 5.00 2.00
❑ 23 David LaFleur 1.00 .40
❑ 24 Emmitt Smith 8.00 3.00
❑ 25 John Elway 10.00 4.00
❑ 26 John Mobley 1.00 .40
❑ 27 Terrell Davis 2.50 1.00
❑ 28 Rod Smith 1.50 .60
❑ 29 Bryant Westbrook 1.00 .40
❑ 30 Scott Mitchell 1.50 .60
❑ 31 Barry Sanders 8.00 3.00
❑ 32 Dorsey Levens 2.50 1.00
❑ 33 Antonio Freeman 2.50 1.00
❑ 34 Reggie White 2.50 1.00
❑ 35 Marshall Faulk 3.00 1.25
❑ 36 Marvin Harrison 2.50 1.00
❑ 37 Ken Dilger 1.00 .40
❑ 38 Mark Brunell 2.50 1.00
❑ 39 Keenan McCardell 1.50 .60
❑ 40 Renaldo Wynn 1.00 .40
❑ 41 Marcus Allen 2.50 1.00
❑ 42 Elvis Grbac 1.50 .60
❑ 43 Andre Rison 1.50 .60
❑ 44 Yatil Green 1.00 .40
❑ 45 Zach Thomas 2.50 1.00
❑ 46 Karim Abdul-Jabbar 2.50 1.00
❑ 47 John Randle 1.50 .60
❑ 48 Brad Johnson 2.50 1.00
❑ 49 Jake Reed 1.50 .60
❑ 50 Danny Wuerffel 1.50 .60
❑ 51 Andre Hastings 1.00 .40
❑ 52 Drew Bledsoe 4.00 1.50
❑ 53 Terry Glenn 2.50 1.00
❑ 54 Ty Law 1.50 .60
❑ 55 Danny Kanell 1.50 .60
❑ 56 Tiki Barber 2.50 1.00
❑ 57 Jessie Armstead 1.00 .40

❑ 58 Glenn Foley 1.50 .60
❑ 59 James Farrior 1.00 .40
❑ 60 Wayne Chrebet 2.50 1.00
❑ 61 Tim Brown 2.50 1.00
❑ 62 Napoleon Kaufman 2.50 1.00
❑ 63 Darrell Russell 1.00 .40
❑ 64 Bobby Hoying 1.50 .60
❑ 65 Irving Fryar 1.50 .60
❑ 66 Charlie Garner 1.50 .60
❑ 67 Will Blackwell 1.00 .40
❑ 68 Kordell Stewart 2.50 1.00
❑ 69 Levon Kirkland 1.00 .40
❑ 70 Tony Banks 1.50 .60
❑ 71 Ryan McNeil 1.00 .40
❑ 72 Isaac Bruce 2.50 1.00
❑ 73 Tony Martin 1.50 .60
❑ 74 Junior Seau 2.50 1.00
❑ 75 Natrone Means 1.50 .60
❑ 76 Jerry Rice 5.00 2.00
❑ 77 Garrison Hearst 2.50 1.00
❑ 78 Terrell Owens 2.50 1.00
❑ 79 Warren Moon 2.50 1.00
❑ 80 Joey Galloway 1.50 .60
❑ 81 Chad Brown 1.00 .40
❑ 82 Warrick Dunn 2.50 1.00
❑ 83 Mike Alstott 2.50 1.00
❑ 84 Hardy Nickerson 1.00 .40
❑ 85 Steve McNair 2.50 1.00
❑ 86 Chris Sanders 1.00 .40
❑ 87 Darryll Lewis 1.00 .40
❑ 88 Gus Frerotte 1.00 .40
❑ 89 Terry Allen 2.50 1.00
❑ 90 Chris Dishman 1.00 .40
❑ 91 Kordell Stewart PM 3.00 1.25
❑ 92 Jerry Rice PM 6.00 2.50
❑ 93 Michael Irvin PM 3.00 1.25
❑ 94 Brett Favre PM 12.00 5.00
❑ 95 Jeff George PM 2.00 .75
❑ 96 Joey Galloway PM 2.00 .75
❑ 97 John Elway PM 12.00 5.00
❑ 98 Troy Aikman PM 6.00 2.50
❑ 99 Steve Young PM 4.00 1.50
❑ 100 Andre Rison PM 2.00 .75
❑ 101 Ben Coates PM 2.00 .75
❑ 102 Robert Brooks PM 2.00 .75
❑ 103 Dan Marino PM 12.00 5.00
❑ 104 Isaac Bruce PM 3.00 1.25
❑ 105 Junior Seau PM 3.00 1.25
❑ 106 Jake Plummer PM 3.00 1.25
❑ 107 Curtis Conway PM 2.00 .75
❑ 108 Jeff Blake PM 2.00 .75
❑ 109 Rod Smith PM 2.00 .75
❑ 110 Barry Sanders PM 10.00 4.00
❑ 111 Deion Sanders PM 3.00 1.25
❑ 112 Drew Bledsoe PM 5.00 2.00
❑ 113 Emmitt Smith PM 10.00 4.00
❑ 114 Herman Moore PM 2.00 .75
❑ 115 Dorsey Levens PM 3.00 1.25
❑ 116 Jimmy Smith PM 2.00 .75
❑ 117 Tony Martin PM 1.25 .50
❑ 118 Carl Pickens PM 2.00 .75
❑ 119 Keyshawn Johnson PM 3.00 1.25
❑ 120 Cris Carter PM 3.00 1.25
❑ 121 Warrick Dunn YM 5.00 2.00
❑ 122 Marshall Faulk YM 6.00 2.50
❑ 123 Trent Dilfer YM 5.00 2.00
❑ 124 Napoleon Kaufman YM 5.00 2.00
❑ 125 Corey Dillon YM 5.00 2.00
❑ 126 Darrell Russell YM 2.00 .75
❑ 127 Danny Kanell YM 3.00 1.25
❑ 128 Reidel Anthony YM 3.00 1.25
❑ 129 Steve McNair YM 5.00 2.00
❑ 130 Ike Hilliard YM 3.00 1.25
❑ 131 Tony Banks YM 3.00 1.25
❑ 132 Yatil Green YM 2.00 .75
❑ 133 J.J. Stokes YM 3.00 1.25
❑ 134 Fred Lane YM 2.00 .75
❑ 135 Bryant Westbrook YM 2.00 .75
❑ 136 Jake Plummer YM 5.00 2.00
❑ 137 Byron Hanspard YM 2.00 .75
❑ 138 Rae Carruth YM 2.00 .75
❑ 139 Keyshawn Johnson YM 5.00 2.00
❑ 140 Jim Druckenmiller YM 2.00 .75
❑ 141 Amani Toomer YM 3.00 1.25
❑ 142 Troy Davis YM 2.00 .75
❑ 143 Antowain Smith YM 5.00 2.00
❑ 144 Shawn Springs YM 2.00 .75
❑ 145 Rickey Dudley YM 2.00 .75
❑ 146 Terry Glenn YM 5.00 2.00
❑ 147 Johnnie Morton YM 3.00 1.25
❑ 148 David LaFleur YM 2.00 .75
❑ 149 Eddie Kennison YM 3.00 1.25
❑ 150 Bobby Hoying YM 3.00 1.25
❑ 151 Junior Seau PE 6.00 2.50
❑ 152 Shannon Sharpe PE 4.00 1.50
❑ 153 Bruce Smith PE 4.00 1.50
❑ 154 Brett Favre PE 20.00 7.50
❑ 155 Emmitt Smith PE 15.00 6.00
❑ 156 Keenan McCardell PE 2.50 1.00
❑ 157 Kordell Stewart PE 6.00 2.50
❑ 158 Troy Aikman PE 10.00 4.00
❑ 159 Steve Young PE 6.00 2.50
❑ 160 Tim Brown PE 6.00 2.50
❑ 161 Eddie George PE 6.00 2.50
❑ 162 Herman Moore PE 4.00 1.50
❑ 163 Dan Marino PE 20.00 7.50
❑ 164 Dorsey Levens PE 6.00 2.50
❑ 165 Jerry Rice PE 10.00 4.00
❑ 166 Warren Sapp PE 4.00 1.50
❑ 167 Robert Smith PE 6.00 2.50
❑ 168 Mark Brunell PE 6.00 2.50
❑ 169 Terrell Davis PE 6.00 2.50
❑ 170 Jerome Bettis PE 6.00 2.50
❑ 171 Dan Marino HG 30.00 12.50
❑ 172 Barry Sanders HG 25.00 10.00
❑ 173 Marcus Allen HG 8.00 3.00
❑ 174 Brett Favre HG 30.00 12.50
❑ 175 Warrick Dunn HG 8.00 3.00
❑ 176 Eddie George HG 8.00 3.00
❑ 177 John Elway HG 30.00 12.50
❑ 178 Troy Aikman HG 15.00 6.00
❑ 179 Cris Carter HG 8.00 3.00
❑ 180 Terrell Davis HG 8.00 3.00
❑ 181 Peyton Manning RC 250.00 125.00
❑ 182 Ryan Leaf RC 25.00 12.50
❑ 183 Andre Wadsworth RC 20.00 10.00
❑ 184 Charles Woodson RC 30.00 15.00
❑ 185 Curtis Enis RC 15.00 7.50
❑ 186 Grant Wistrom RC 20.00 10.00
❑ 187 Fred Taylor RC 40.00 15.00
❑ 188 Takeo Spikes RC 25.00 12.50
❑ 189 Kevin Dyson RC 25.00 12.50
❑ 190 Robert Edwards RC 20.00 10.00
❑ 191 Adrian Murrell 1.00 .40
❑ 192 Simeon Rice 1.00 .40
❑ 193 Frank Sanders 1.00 .40
❑ 194 Chris Chandler 1.00 .40
❑ 195 Terance Mathis 1.00 .40
❑ 196 Keith Brooking RC 1.50 .60
❑ 197 Jim Harbaugh 1.00 .40
❑ 198 Errict Rhett 1.00 .40
❑ 199 Pat Johnson RC 2.50 1.00
❑ 200 Rob Johnson 1.00 .40
❑ 201 Andre Reed 1.00 .40
❑ 202 Thurman Thomas 1.50 .60
❑ 203 Kerry Collins 1.00 .40
❑ 204 William Floyd .60 .25
❑ 205 Sean Gilbert .60 .25
❑ 206 Bobby Engram 1.00 .40
❑ 207 Edgar Bennett 1.00 .40
❑ 208 Walt Harris 1.00 .40
❑ 209 Carl Pickens 1.00 .40
❑ 210 Neil O'Donnell 1.00 .40
❑ 211 Tony McGee .60 .25
❑ 212 Deion Sanders 1.50 .60
❑ 213 Michael Irvin 1.50 .60
❑ 214 Greg Ellis RC 1.25 .50
❑ 215 Shannon Sharpe 1.00 .40
❑ 216 Neil Smith 1.00 .40
❑ 217 Marcus Nash RC 1.25 .50
❑ 218 Brian Griese RC 30.00 12.50
❑ 219 Johnnie Morton 1.00 .40
❑ 220 Herman Moore 1.50 .60
❑ 221 Charlie Batch RC 20.00 7.50
❑ 222 Robert Brooks 1.00 .40
❑ 223 Mark Chmura 1.00 .40
❑ 224 Brett Favre 6.00 2.50
❑ 225 Jerome Pathon RC 5.00 2.00
❑ 226 Zack Crockett .60 .25
❑ 227 Dan Footman .60 .25
❑ 228 Jimmy Smith 1.00 .40
❑ 229 Bryce Paup .60 .25
❑ 230 James Stewart 1.00 .40
❑ 231 Derrick Thomas 1.50 .60
❑ 232 Derrick Alexander 1.00 .40
❑ 233 Tony Gonzalez 1.50 .60
❑ 234 Dan Marino 6.00 2.50
❑ 235 O.J. McDuffie 1.00 .40
❑ 236 Troy Drayton .60 .25
❑ 237 Cris Carter 1.50 .60
❑ 238 Robert Smith 1.50 .60
❑ 239 Randy Moss RC 80.00 30.00
❑ 240 Lamar Smith 1.00 .40
❑ 241 Sean Dawkins .60 .25
❑ 242 Alex Molden .60 .25
❑ 243 Ben Coates 1.00 .40
❑ 244 Ted Johnson .60 .25
❑ 245 Sedrick Shaw .60 .25
❑ 246 Ike Hilliard 1.00 .40
❑ 247 Jason Sehorn 1.00 .40
❑ 248 Michael Strahan 1.00 .40
❑ 249 Keyshawn Johnson 1.50 .60
❑ 250 Curtis Martin 1.50 .60
❑ 251 Jeff George 1.00 .40
❑ 252 Rickey Dudley .60 .25
❑ 253 James Jett 1.00 .40
❑ 254 Bobby Taylor 1.00 .40
❑ 255 Rodney Peete 1.00 .40
❑ 256 William Thomas 1.00 .40
❑ 257 Jerome Bettis 1.50 .60
❑ 258 Charles Johnson .60 .25
❑ 259 Chris Fuamatu-Ma'afala RC 2.50 1.00
❑ 260 Eddie Kennison 1.00 .40
❑ 261 Az-Zahir Hakim RC 5.00 2.00
❑ 262 Robert Holcombe RC 2.50 1.00
❑ 263 Bryan Still .60 .25
❑ 264 Mikhael Ricks RC 2.50 1.00
❑ 265 Charlie Jones .60 .25
❑ 266 J.J. Stokes 1.00 .40
❑ 267 Marc Edwards .60 .25
❑ 268 Steve Young 2.00 .75
❑ 269 Ricky Watters 1.00 .40
❑ 270 Cortez Kennedy .60 .25
❑ 271 Shawn Springs .60 .25
❑ 272 Trent Dilfer 1.50 .60
❑ 273 Warren Sapp 1.00 .40
❑ 274 Reidel Anthony 1.00 .40
❑ 275 Yancey Thigpen .60 .25
❑ 276 Chris Sanders .60 .25
❑ 277 Eddie George 1.50 .60
❑ 278 Leslie Shepherd .60 .25
❑ 279 Skip Hicks RC 2.50 1.00
❑ 280 Dana Stubblefield .60 .25
❑ 281 John Elway ET 8.00 3.00
❑ 282 Brett Favre ET 8.00 3.00
❑ 283 Junior Seau ET 2.00 .75
❑ 284 Barry Sanders ET 6.00 2.50
❑ 285 Jerry Rice ET 4.00 1.50
❑ 286 Antonio Freeman ET 2.00 .75
❑ 287 Peyton Manning ET 30.00 12.50
❑ 288 Warrick Dunn ET 2.00 .75
❑ 289 Steve Young ET 2.50 1.00
❑ 290 Dan Marino ET 8.00 3.00
❑ 291 Jerome Bettis ET 2.00 .75
❑ 292 Ryan Leaf ET 2.00 .75
❑ 293 Deion Sanders ET 2.00 .75
❑ 294 Eddie George ET 2.00 .75
❑ 295 Joey Galloway ET 1.25 .50
❑ 296 Troy Aikman ET 4.00 1.50
❑ 297 Andre Wadsworth ET 1.25 .50
❑ 298 Terrell Davis ET 2.00 .75
❑ 299 Steve McNair ET 2.00 .75
❑ 300 Jake Plummer ET 2.00 .75
❑ 301 Emmitt Smith ET 6.00 2.50
❑ 302 Isaac Bruce ET 2.00 .75
❑ 303 Kordell Stewart ET 2.00 .75
❑ 304 Dorsey Levens ET 2.00 .75
❑ 305 Antowain Smith ET 2.00 .75
❑ 306 Drew Bledsoe ET 3.00 1.25
❑ 307 Marshall Faulk ET 2.50 1.00
❑ 308 Herman Moore ET 1.25 .50
❑ 309 Mark Brunell ET 2.00 .75
❑ 310 Charles Woodson ET 5.00 2.00
❑ 311 Peyton Manning NS 30.00 12.50
❑ 312 Curtis Enis NS 1.50 .60
❑ 313 Terry Fair NS RC 2.50 1.00
❑ 314 Andre Wadsworth NS 2.50 1.00
❑ 315 Anthony Simmons NS RC 2.50 1.00
❑ 316 Jacquez Green NS RC 8.00 3.00
❑ 317 Takeo Spikes NS 5.00 2.00
❑ 318 Vonnie Holliday NS RC 8.00 3.00

❑ 319	Kyle Turley NS RC	5.00	2.00
❑ 320	Keith Brooking NS	5.00	2.00
❑ 321	Randy Moss NS	20.00	7.50
❑ 322	Shaun Williams NS RC	2.50	1.00
❑ 323	Greg Ellis NS	1.50	.60
❑ 324	Mikhael Ricks NS	2.50	1.00
❑ 325	Charles Woodson NS	8.00	3.00
❑ 326	Corey Chavous NS RC	5.00	2.00
❑ 327	Stephen Alexander NS RC	8.00	3.00
❑ 328	Marcus Nash NS	1.50	.60
❑ 329	Tra Thomas NS RC	2.50	1.00
❑ 330	Duane Starks NS RC	5.00	2.00
❑ 331	John Avery NS RC	2.50	1.00
❑ 332	Kevin Dyson NS	5.00	2.00
❑ 333	Fred Taylor NS	10.00	4.00
❑ 334	Grant Wistrom NS	2.50	1.00
❑ 335	Ryan Leaf NS	5.00	2.00
❑ 336	Robert Edwards NS	2.50	1.00
❑ 337	Jason Peter NS RC	2.50	1.00
❑ 338	Brian Griese NS	12.00	5.00
❑ 339	Charlie Batch NS	5.00	2.00
❑ 340	Pat Johnson NS	2.50	1.00
❑ 341	John Elway SS	15.00	6.00
❑ 342	Curtis Enis SS	1.50	.60
❑ 343	Antonio Freeman SS	4.00	1.50
❑ 344	Mark Brunell SS	4.00	1.50
❑ 345	Robert Edwards SS	2.50	1.00
❑ 346	Ryan Leaf SS	4.00	1.50
❑ 347	Steve Young SS	5.00	2.00
❑ 348	Jerome Bettis SS	4.00	1.50
❑ 349	Antowain Smith SS	4.00	1.50
❑ 350	Tim Brown SS	4.00	1.50
❑ 351	Peyton Manning SS	30.00	12.50
❑ 352	Troy Aikman SS	8.00	3.00
❑ 353	Natrone Means SS	2.50	1.00
❑ 354	Dan Marino SS	15.00	6.00
❑ 355	Junior Seau SS	1.50	.60
❑ 356	Brad Johnson SS	4.00	1.50
❑ 357	Jerry Rice SS	8.00	3.00
❑ 358	Drew Bledsoe SS	6.00	2.50
❑ 359	Fred Taylor SS	8.00	3.00
❑ 360	Emmitt Smith SS	12.00	5.00
❑ 361	Terrell Davis UV	8.00	3.00
❑ 362	Kordell Stewart UV	6.00	2.50
❑ 363	Barry Sanders UV	20.00	7.50
❑ 364	Jake Plummer UV	6.00	2.50
❑ 365	Brett Favre UV	25.00	10.00
❑ 366	Curtis Enis UV	6.00	2.50
❑ 367	Eddie George UV	6.00	2.50
❑ 368	Napoleon Kaufman UV	6.00	2.50
❑ 369	Randy Moss UV	40.00	15.00
❑ 370	Warrick Dunn UV	6.00	2.50
❑ S8	Troy Aikman Sample	1.00	.40
❑ S234	Dan Marino Sample	2.00	.75

1999 SPx

❑	COMPLETE SET (135)	2000.00	1000.00
❑	COMP.SET w/o SP's (90)	25.00	12.50
❑	*HAND NUMBERED RCs: .5X TO .8X		
❑ 1	Jake Plummer	1.00	.40
❑ 2	Adrian Murrell	1.00	.40
❑ 3	Frank Sanders	1.00	.40
❑ 4	Jamal Anderson	1.50	.60
❑ 5	Chris Chandler	1.00	.40
❑ 6	Terance Mathis	1.00	.40
❑ 7	Tony Banks	1.00	.40
❑ 8	Priest Holmes	2.50	1.00
❑ 9	Jermaine Lewis	1.00	.40
❑ 10	Antowain Smith	1.50	.60
❑ 11	Doug Flutie	1.50	.60
❑ 12	Eric Moulds	1.50	.60
❑ 13	Tim Biakabutuka	1.00	.40
❑ 14	Steve Beuerlein	1.00	.40
❑ 15	Muhsin Muhammad	1.00	.40
❑ 16	Bobby Engram	1.00	.40
❑ 17	Curtis Conway	1.00	.40
❑ 18	Curtis Enis	.60	.25
❑ 19	Corey Dillon	1.50	.60
❑ 20	Jeff Blake	1.00	.40
❑ 21	Carl Pickens	1.00	.40
❑ 22	Ty Detmer	1.00	.40
❑ 23	Terry Kirby	.60	.25
❑ 24	Leslie Shepherd	.60	.25
❑ 25	Troy Aikman	3.00	1.25
❑ 26	Emmitt Smith	3.00	1.25
❑ 27	Deion Sanders	1.50	.60
❑ 28	Terrell Davis	1.50	.60
❑ 29	Rod Smith	1.00	.40
❑ 30	Bubby Brister	1.00	.40
❑ 31	Barry Sanders	5.00	2.00
❑ 32	Herman Moore	1.00	.40
❑ 33	Charlie Batch	1.50	.60
❑ 34	Brett Favre	5.00	2.00
❑ 35	Antonio Freeman	1.50	.60
❑ 36	Dorsey Levens	1.50	.60
❑ 37	Peyton Manning	5.00	2.00
❑ 38	Marvin Harrison	1.50	.60
❑ 39	Jerome Pathon	.60	.25
❑ 40	Mark Brunell	1.50	.60
❑ 41	Jimmy Smith	1.00	.40
❑ 42	Fred Taylor	1.50	.60
❑ 43	Elvis Grbac	1.00	.40
❑ 44	Andre Rison	1.00	.40
❑ 45	Warren Moon	1.50	.60
❑ 46	Dan Marino	5.00	2.00
❑ 47	Karim Abdul-Jabbar	1.00	.40
❑ 48	O.J. McDuffie	1.00	.40
❑ 49	Randall Cunningham	1.50	.60
❑ 50	Robert Smith	1.50	.60
❑ 51	Randy Moss	4.00	1.50
❑ 52	Drew Bledsoe	2.00	.75
❑ 53	Terry Glenn	1.50	.60
❑ 54	Tony Simmons	.60	.25
❑ 55	Danny Wuerffel	.60	.25
❑ 56	Cam Cleeland	.60	.25
❑ 57	Kerry Collins	1.00	.40
❑ 58	Gary Brown	.60	.25
❑ 59	Ike Hilliard	.60	.25
❑ 60	Vinny Testaverde	1.00	.40
❑ 61	Curtis Martin	1.50	.60
❑ 62	Keyshawn Johnson	1.50	.60
❑ 63	Rich Gannon	1.50	.60
❑ 64	Napoleon Kaufman	1.50	.60
❑ 65	Tim Brown	1.50	.60
❑ 66	Duce Staley	1.50	.60
❑ 67	Doug Pederson	.60	.25
❑ 68	Charles Johnson	.60	.25
❑ 69	Kordell Stewart	1.00	.40
❑ 70	Jerome Bettis	1.50	.60
❑ 71	Trent Green	1.50	.60
❑ 72	Marshall Faulk	2.00	.75
❑ 73	Ryan Leaf	1.50	.60
❑ 74	Natrone Means	1.00	.40
❑ 75	Jim Harbaugh	1.00	.40
❑ 76	Steve Young	2.00	.75
❑ 77	Garrison Hearst	1.00	.40
❑ 78	Jerry Rice	3.00	1.25
❑ 79	Terrell Owens	1.50	.60
❑ 80	Ricky Watters	1.00	.40
❑ 81	Joey Galloway	1.00	.40
❑ 82	Jon Kitna	1.50	.60
❑ 83	Warrick Dunn	1.50	.60
❑ 84	Trent Dilfer	1.00	.40
❑ 85	Mike Alstott	1.50	.60
❑ 86	Steve McNair	1.50	.60
❑ 87	Eddie George	1.50	.60
❑ 88	Yancey Thigpen	.60	.25
❑ 89	Skip Hicks	.60	.25
❑ 90	Michael Westbrook	1.00	.40
❑ 91	Amos Zereoue RC	15.00	6.00
❑ 92	Chris Claiborne AU RC	25.00	10.00
❑ 93	Scott Covington RC	15.00	6.00
❑ 94	Jeff Paulk RC	10.00	4.00
❑ 95	Brandon Stokley AU RC	40.00	15.00
❑ 96	Antoine Winfield RC	12.00	5.00
❑ 97	Reginald Kelly RC	10.00	4.00
❑ 98	Jermaine Fazande AU RC	15.00	6.00
❑ 99	Andy Katzenmoyer RC	12.00	5.00
❑ 100	Craig Yeast RC	12.00	5.00
❑ 101	Joe Montgomery RC	12.00	5.00
❑ 102	Darrin Chiaverini RC	12.00	5.00
❑ 103	Travis McGriff RC	10.00	4.00
❑ 104	Jevon Kearse RC	30.00	12.50
❑ 105	Joel Makovicka AU RC	15.00	6.00
❑ 106	Aaron Brooks RC	20.00	8.00
❑ 107	Chris McAlister RC	12.00	5.00
❑ 108	Jim Kleinsasser RC	15.00	6.00
❑ 109	Ebenezer Ekuban RC	12.00	5.00
❑ 110	Karsten Bailey RC	12.00	5.00
❑ 111	Sedrick Irvin AU RC	12.00	5.00
❑ 112	D'Wayne Bates AU RC	12.00	5.00
❑ 113	Joe Germaine AU RC	15.00	6.00
❑ 114	Cecil Collins AU RC	15.00	6.00
❑ 115	Mike Cloud RC	12.00	5.00
❑ 116	James Johnson RC	12.00	5.00
❑ 117	Champ Bailey AU RC	40.00	15.00
❑ 118	Rob Konrad RC	15.00	6.00
❑ 119	Peerless Price AU RC	30.00	12.50
❑ 120	Kevin Faulk AU RC	25.00	10.00
❑ 121	Dameane Douglas RC	10.00	4.00
❑ 122	Kevin Johnson AU RC	15.00	6.00
❑ 123	Troy Edwards AU RC	25.00	10.00
❑ 124	Edgerrin James AU RC	100.00	50.00
❑ 125	David Boston AU RC	25.00	10.00
❑ 126	Michael Bishop AU RC	25.00	10.00
❑ 127	Shaun King AU RC SP	50.00	25.00
❑ 127X	Shaun King EXCH	10.00	4.00
❑ 128	Brock Huard AU RC	15.00	6.00
❑ 129	Torry Holt AU RC	60.00	30.00
❑ 130	Cade McNown AU/500 RC	40.00	15.00
❑ 131	Tim Couch AU/500 RC	40.00	15.00
❑ 132	Donovan McNabb AU RC	120.00	60.00
❑ 132X	Donovan McNabb EXCH	5.00	2.00
❑ 133	Akili Smith AU/500 RC	40.00	15.00
❑ 134	D.Culpepper AU/500 RC	200.00	100.00
❑ 135	Ricky Williams AU/500 RC	80.00	30.00
❑ S8	Troy Aikman Sample	2.00	.75

2000 SPx

❑	COMP.SET w/o SP's (90)	20.00	7.50
❑ 1	Jake Plummer	.60	.25
❑ 2	David Boston	1.00	.40
❑ 3	Frank Sanders	.60	.25
❑ 4	Chris Chandler	.60	.25
❑ 5	Jamal Anderson	1.00	.40
❑ 6	Shawn Jefferson	.40	.15
❑ 7	Qadry Ismail	.60	.25
❑ 8	Tony Banks	.60	.25
❑ 9	Shannon Sharpe	.60	.25
❑ 10	Rob Johnson	.60	.25
❑ 11	Eric Moulds	1.00	.40
❑ 12	Muhsin Muhammad	.60	.25
❑ 13	Steve Beuerlein	.40	.15
❑ 14	Cade McNown	.40	.15
❑ 15	Marcus Robinson	1.00	.40
❑ 16	Akili Smith	.40	.15
❑ 17	Corey Dillon	1.00	.40
❑ 18	Darnay Scott	.60	.25
❑ 19	Tim Couch	.60	.25
❑ 20	Kevin Johnson	1.00	.40
❑ 21	Errict Rhett	.40	.15
❑ 22	Troy Aikman	2.00	.75
❑ 23	Emmitt Smith	2.00	.75
❑ 24	Joey Galloway	.60	.25
❑ 25	Terrell Davis	1.00	.40

❑ 26 Olandis Gary 1.00 .40
❑ 27 Brian Griese 1.00 .40
❑ 28 Charlie Batch 1.00 .40
❑ 29 Germane Crowell .40 .15
❑ 30 James Stewart .60 .25
❑ 31 Brett Favre 3.00 1.25
❑ 32 Antonio Freeman 1.00 .40
❑ 33 Dorsey Levens .60 .25
❑ 34 Peyton Manning 2.50 1.00
❑ 35 Edgerrin James 1.50 .60
❑ 36 Marvin Harrison 1.00 .40
❑ 37 Mark Brunell 1.00 .40
❑ 38 Fred Taylor 1.00 .40
❑ 39 Jimmy Smith .60 .25
❑ 40 Keenan McCardell .60 .25
❑ 41 Elvis Grbac .60 .25
❑ 42 Tony Gonzalez .60 .25
❑ 43 Tony Martin .60 .25
❑ 44 Jay Fiedler 1.00 .40
❑ 45 Damon Huard 1.00 .40
❑ 46 Randy Moss 2.00 .75
❑ 47 Robert Smith 1.00 .40
❑ 48 Cris Carter 1.00 .40
❑ 49 Daunte Culpepper 1.25 .50
❑ 50 Drew Bledsoe 1.25 .50
❑ 51 Terry Glenn .60 .25
❑ 52 Ricky Williams 1.00 .40
❑ 53 Jeff Blake .60 .25
❑ 54 Keith Poole .40 .15
❑ 55 Kerry Collins .60 .25
❑ 56 Amani Toomer .60 .25
❑ 57 Ike Hilliard .60 .25
❑ 58 Ray Lucas .60 .25
❑ 59 Curtis Martin 1.00 .40
❑ 60 Vinny Testaverde .60 .25
❑ 61 Tim Brown 1.00 .40
❑ 62 Rich Gannon 1.00 .40
❑ 63 Tyrone Wheatley .60 .25
❑ 64 Napoleon Kaufman .60 .25
❑ 65 Duce Staley 1.00 .40
❑ 66 Donovan McNabb 1.50 .60
❑ 67 Troy Edwards .40 .15
❑ 68 Jerome Bettis 1.00 .40
❑ 69 Kordell Stewart .60 .25
❑ 70 Marshall Faulk 1.25 .50
❑ 71 Kurt Warner 1.50 .60
❑ 72 Isaac Bruce 1.00 .40
❑ 73 Torry Holt 1.00 .40
❑ 74 Ryan Leaf .60 .25
❑ 75 Jim Harbaugh .60 .25
❑ 76 Jerry Rice 2.00 .75
❑ 77 Terrell Owens 1.00 .40
❑ 78 Jeff Garcia 1.00 .40
❑ 79 Ricky Watters .60 .25
❑ 80 Jon Kitna 1.00 .40
❑ 81 Derrick Mayes .60 .25
❑ 82 Shaun King .40 .15
❑ 83 Mike Alstott 1.00 .40
❑ 84 Keyshawn Johnson 1.00 .40
❑ 85 Eddie George 1.00 .40
❑ 86 Steve McNair 1.00 .40
❑ 87 Jevon Kearse 1.00 .40
❑ 88 Brad Johnson 1.00 .40
❑ 89 Stephen Davis 1.00 .40
❑ 90 Michael Westbrook .60 .25
❑ 91 Anthony Lucas RC 8.00 3.00
❑ 92 Avion Black RC 12.00 5.00
❑ 93 Corey Moore RC 8.00 3.00
❑ 94 Chris Cole RC 12.00 5.00
❑ 95 Chris Hovan RC 12.00 5.00
❑ 96 Dante Hall RC 30.00 12.50
❑ 97 Darrell Jackson RC 30.00 12.50
❑ 98 Deltha O'Neal RC 15.00 6.00
❑ 99 Doug Chapman RC 12.00 5.00
❑ 100 Doug Johnson RC 15.00 6.00
❑ 101 Erron Kinney RC 15.00 6.00
❑ 102 Frank Moreau RC 12.00 5.00
❑ 103 Patrick Pass RC 12.00 5.00
❑ 104 Gari Scott RC 8.00 3.00
❑ 105 Giovanni Carmazzi RC 8.00 3.00
❑ 106 JaJuan Dawson RC 8.00 3.00
❑ 107 James Williams RC 12.00 5.00
❑ 108 Jarious Jackson RC 12.00 5.00
❑ 109 John Abraham RC 20.00 7.50
❑ 110 Keith Bulluck RC 15.00 6.00
❑ 111 Jonas Lewis RC 8.00 3.00
❑ 112 Mike Green RC 12.00 5.00
❑ 113 Ronney Jenkins RC 12.00 5.00
❑ 114 Michael Wiley RC 12.00 5.00
❑ 115 Mike Anderson RC 20.00 10.00
❑ 116 Mareno Philyaw RC 8.00 3.00
❑ 117 Muneer Moore RC 8.00 3.00
❑ 118 Paul Smith RC 12.00 5.00
❑ 119 Raynoch Thompson RC 12.00 5.00
❑ 120 Rob Morris RC 12.00 5.00
❑ 121 Ron Dixon RC 12.00 5.00
❑ 122 Rondell Mealey RC 8.00 3.00
❑ 123 Sebastian Janikowski RC 15.00 6.00
❑ 124 Shaun Ellis RC 15.00 6.00
❑ 125 Charles Lee RC 12.00 5.00
❑ 126 Shyrone Stith RC 12.00 5.00
❑ 127 Thomas Hamner RC 8.00 3.00
❑ 128 Tim Rattay RC 15.00 6.00
❑ 129 Todd Husak RC 15.00 6.00
❑ 130 Tom Brady RC 300.00 150.00
❑ 131 Trevor Gaylor RC 12.00 5.00
❑ 132 Windrell Hayes RC 12.00 5.00
❑ 133 Anthony Becht JSY AU RC 25.00 10.00
❑ 134 Brian Urlacher JSY AU RC 135.00 75.00
❑ 135 Bubba Franks JSY AU RC 30.00 12.50
❑ 136 C Pennington JSY AU RC 60.00 35.00
❑ 137 Chr Redman JSY AU RC 25.00 10.00
❑ 138 Corey Simon JSY AU RC 30.00 12.50
❑ 139 Curtis Keaton JSY AU RC 25.00 10.00
❑ 140 Danny Farmer JSY AU RC 25.00 10.00
❑ 141 Den Northcutt JSY AU RC 30.00 12.50
❑ 142 Dez White JSY AU RC 30.00 12.50
❑ 143 J.R. Redmond JSY AU SP RC 25.00 10.00
❑ 144 Jamal Lewis JSY AU RC 50.00 25.00
❑ 145 Jerry Porter JSY AU RC 50.00 20.00
❑ 146 Joe Hamilton EXCH 3.00 1.25
❑ 147 Laver Coles JSY AU RC 40.00 20.00
❑ 148 R.Jay Soward JSY AU RC 25.00 10.00
❑ 149 Reu Droughns JSY AU RC 40.00 15.00
❑ 150 Ron Dayne JSY AU RC 40.00 15.00
❑ 151 Ron Dugans JSY AU RC 20.00 7.50
❑ 152 Sha Alexander JSY AU RC 150.00 75.00
❑ 153 Sylvester Morris JSY AU RC 25.00 10.00
❑ 154 Tee Martin JSY AU RC 30.00 12.50
❑ 155 Th.Jones JSY AU RC SP 200.00 125.00
❑ 156 Todd Pinkston JSY AU RC 30.00 12.50
❑ 157 Travis Prentice JSY AU RC 25.00 10.00
❑ 158 Travis Taylor JSY AU SP RC 40.00 15.00
❑ 159 Trung Canidate JSY AU RC 25.00 10.00
❑ 160 Courtney Brown JSY AU RC 30.00 12.50
❑ 161 Peter Warrick JSY AU RC 30.00 12.50
❑ 162 Plaxico Burress JSY AU RC 100.00 40.00
❑ S1 Peyton Manning Sample 4.00 1.50

2001 SPx

❑ COMP.SET w/o SP's (90) 20.00 7.50
❑ 1 Jake Plummer .60 .25
❑ 2 David Boston 1.00 .40
❑ 3 Jamal Anderson 1.00 .40
❑ 4 Chris Chandler .60 .25
❑ 5 Tony Martin .60 .25
❑ 6 Elvis Grbac .60 .25
❑ 7 Qadry Ismail .60 .25
❑ 8 Ray Lewis 1.00 .40
❑ 9 Rob Johnson .60 .25
❑ 10 Shawn Bryson .40 .15
❑ 11 Eric Moulds .60 .25
❑ 12 Tim Biakabutuka .60 .25
❑ 13 Jeff Lewis .40 .15
❑ 14 Muhsin Muhammad .60 .25
❑ 15 Shane Matthews .40 .15
❑ 16 Marcus Robinson 1.00 .40
❑ 17 Brian Urlacher 1.50 .60
❑ 18 Jon Kitna .40 .15
❑ 19 Peter Warrick 1.00 .40
❑ 20 Corey Dillon 1.00 .40
❑ 21 Tim Couch .60 .25
❑ 22 Travis Prentice .40 .15
❑ 23 Kevin Johnson .60 .25
❑ 24 Rocket Ismail .60 .25
❑ 25 Emmitt Smith 2.00 .75
❑ 26 Joey Galloway .60 .25
❑ 27 Terrell Davis 1.00 .40
❑ 28 Brian Griese 1.00 .40
❑ 29 Rod Smith .60 .25
❑ 30 Ed McCaffrey 1.00 .40
❑ 31 Charlie Batch 1.00 .40
❑ 32 Germane Crowell .40 .15
❑ 33 James O. Stewart .60 .25
❑ 34 Brett Favre 3.00 1.25
❑ 35 Antonio Freeman 1.00 .40
❑ 36 Ahman Green 1.00 .40
❑ 37 Peyton Manning 2.50 1.00
❑ 38 Edgerrin James 1.25 .50
❑ 39 Marvin Harrison 1.00 .40
❑ 40 Mark Brunell 1.00 .40
❑ 41 Fred Taylor 1.00 .40
❑ 42 Jimmy Smith .60 .25
❑ 43 Tony Gonzalez .60 .25
❑ 44 Trent Green 1.00 .40
❑ 45 Priest Holmes 1.25 .50
❑ 46 Lamar Smith .60 .25
❑ 47 Jay Fiedler 1.00 .40
❑ 48 Oronde Gadsden .60 .25
❑ 49 Daunte Culpepper 1.00 .40
❑ 50 Randy Moss 2.00 .75
❑ 51 Cris Carter 1.00 .40
❑ 52 Drew Bledsoe 1.25 .50
❑ 53 Troy Brown .60 .25
❑ 54 Ricky Williams 1.00 .40
❑ 55 Joe Horn .60 .25
❑ 56 Aaron Brooks 1.00 .40
❑ 57 Albert Connell .40 .15
❑ 58 Kerry Collins .60 .25
❑ 59 Tiki Barber 1.00 .40
❑ 60 Ron Dayne 1.00 .40
❑ 61 Vinny Testaverde .60 .25
❑ 62 Wayne Chrebet .60 .25
❑ 63 Curtis Martin 1.00 .40
❑ 64 Tim Brown 1.00 .40
❑ 65 Jerry Rice 2.00 .75
❑ 66 Rich Gannon 1.00 .40
❑ 67 Duce Staley 1.00 .40
❑ 68 Donovan McNabb 1.25 .50
❑ 69 Kordell Stewart .60 .25
❑ 70 Jerome Bettis 1.00 .40
❑ 71 Marshall Faulk 1.25 .50
❑ 72 Kurt Warner 2.00 .75
❑ 73 Isaac Bruce 1.00 .40
❑ 74 Torry Holt 1.00 .40
❑ 75 Doug Flutie 1.00 .40
❑ 76 Junior Seau 1.00 .40
❑ 77 Jeff Garcia 1.00 .40
❑ 78 Garrison Hearst .60 .25
❑ 79 Terrell Owens 1.00 .40
❑ 80 Ricky Watters .60 .25
❑ 81 Matt Hasselbeck .60 .25
❑ 82 Brad Johnson 1.00 .40
❑ 83 Keyshawn Johnson 1.00 .40
❑ 84 Warrick Dunn 1.00 .40
❑ 85 Mike Alstott 1.00 .40
❑ 86 Kevin Dyson .60 .25
❑ 87 Eddie George 1.00 .40
❑ 88 Steve McNair 1.00 .40
❑ 89 Michael Westbrook .60 .25
❑ 90 Stephen Davis 1.00 .40
❑ 91B D McAllister JSY AU/250 RC 100.00 50.00
❑ 91G D McAllister JSY AU/250 RC 100.00 50.00
❑ 92B Fr Mitchell JSY AU/250 RC 30.00 12.50
❑ 92G Fr Mitchell JSY AU/250 RC 30.00 12.50
❑ 93B Koren Robinson/999 RC 10.00 4.00
❑ 93G Koren Robinson/999 RC 10.00 4.00
❑ 94B David Terrell/999 RC 10.00 4.00
❑ 94G David Terrell/999 RC 10.00 4.00
❑ 95B M Vick JSY AU/250 RC 300.00 150.00
❑ 95G M Vick JSY AU/250 RC 300.00 150.00
❑ 96B M Bennett JSY AU/550 RC 30.00 12.50
❑ 96G M Bennett JSY AU/550 RC 30.00 12.50

	No.	Player	Price 1	Price 2
❑	97B	Robert Ferguson/999 RC	10.00	4.00
❑	97G	Robert Ferguson/999 RC	10.00	4.00
❑	98B	Rod Gardner/999 RC	10.00	4.00
❑	98G	Rod Gardner/999 RC	10.00	4.00
❑	99B	Travis Henry JSY AU/550 RC	50.00	30.00
❑	99G	Travis Henry JSY AU/550 RC	50.00	30.00
❑	100B	C Johnson JSY AU/550 RC	100.00	60.00
❑	100G	C Johnson JSY AU/550 RC	100.00	60.00
❑	101B	Drew Brees JSY AU/250 RC	175.00	100.00
❑	101G	Drew Brees JSY AU/250 RC	175.00	100.00
❑	102B	S Moss JSY AU/550 RC	50.00	30.00
❑	102G	S Moss JSY AU/550 RC	50.00	30.00
❑	103B	C Weinke JSY AU/550 RC	25.00	10.00
❑	103G	C Weinke JSY AU/550 RC	25.00	10.00
❑	104B	R Seymour JSY AU/900 RC	40.00	20.00
❑	104G	R Seymour JSY AU/900 RC	40.00	20.00
❑	105B	Reggie Wayne/999 RC	25.00	10.00
❑	105G	Reggie Wayne/999 RC	25.00	10.00
❑	106B	K Barlow JSY AU/550 RC	30.00	12.50
❑	106G	K Barlow JSY AU/550 RC	30.00	12.50
❑	107B	Chambers JSY AU/900 RC	50.00	25.00
❑	107G	Chambers JSY AU/900 RC	50.00	25.00
❑	108B	Todd Heap JSY AU/900 RC	30.00	12.50
❑	108G	Todd Heap JSY AU/900 RC	30.00	12.50
❑	109B	A Thomas JSY AU/550 RC	30.00	12.50
❑	109G	A Thomas JSY AU/550 RC	30.00	12.50
❑	110B	J Jackson JSY AU/550 RC	25.00	10.00
❑	110G	J Jackson JSY AU/550 RC	25.00	10.00
❑	111B	R Johnson JSY AU/900 RC	80.00	40.00
❑	111G	R Johnson JSY AU/900 RC	80.00	40.00
❑	112B	McMahon JSY AU/900 RC	25.00	10.00
❑	112G	McMahon JSY AU/900 RC	25.00	10.00
❑	113G	Josh Heupel JSY AU/900 RC	100.00	50.00
❑	114B	T Minor JSY AU/900 RC	25.00	10.00
❑	114G	T Minor JSY AU/900 RC	25.00	10.00
❑	115B	Quincy Morgan/999 RC	10.00	4.00
❑	115G	Quincy Morgan/999 RC	10.00	4.00
❑	116B	D Morgan JSY AU/900 RC	20.00	10.00
❑	116G	D Morgan JSY AU/900 RC	20.00	10.00
❑	117B	J Palmer JSY AU/900 RC	25.00	10.00
❑	117G	J Palmer JSY AU/900 RC	25.00	10.00
❑	118B	S Rosenfels JSY AU/900 RC	25.00	10.00
❑	118G	S Rosenfels JSY AU/900 RC	25.00	10.00
❑	119B	Tuiasosopo JSY AU/900 RC	30.00	12.50
❑	119G	Tuiasosopo JSY AU/900 RC	30.00	12.50
❑	120B	Damerien McCants/999 RC	6.00	2.50
❑	120G	Damerien McCants/999 RC	6.00	2.50
❑	121B	Snoop Minnis/999 RC	6.00	2.50
❑	121G	Snoop Minnis/999 RC	6.00	2.50
❑	122B	L Tomlinson JSY/250 RC	300.00	150.00
❑	122G	L Tomlinson JSY/250 RC	300.00	150.00
❑	123B	Quincy Carter/999 RC	10.00	4.00
❑	123G	Quincy Carter/999 RC	10.00	4.00
❑	124B	Arnold Jackson/999 RC	6.00	2.50
❑	124G	Arnold Jackson/999 RC	6.00	2.50
❑	125B	Justin McCareins/999 RC	10.00	4.00
❑	125G	Justin McCareins/999 RC	10.00	4.00
❑	126B	Eddie Berlin/999 RC	6.00	2.50
❑	126G	Eddie Berlin/999 RC	6.00	2.50
❑	127B	Quentin McCord/999 RC	6.00	2.50
❑	127G	Quentin McCord/999 RC	6.00	2.50
❑	128B	Vinny Sutherland/999 RC	6.00	2.50
❑	128G	Vinny Sutherland/999 RC	6.00	2.50
❑	129B	Willie Middlebrooks/999 RC	6.00	2.50
❑	129G	Willie Middlebrooks/999 RC	6.00	2.50
❑	130B	Dan Alexander/999 RC	10.00	4.00
❑	130G	Dan Alexander/999 RC	10.00	4.00
❑	131B	Dee Brown/999 RC	10.00	4.00
❑	131G	Dee Brown/999 RC	10.00	4.00
❑	132B	Andre Carter/999 RC	10.00	4.00
❑	132G	Andre Carter/999 RC	10.00	4.00
❑	133B	Justin Smith/999 RC	10.00	4.00
❑	133G	Justin Smith/999 RC	10.00	4.00
❑	134B	Houshmandzadeh/999 RC	12.00	5.00
❑	134G	Houshmandzadeh/999 RC	12.00	5.00
❑	135B	Andre King/999 RC	6.00	2.50
❑	135G	Andre King/999 RC	6.00	2.50
❑	136B	Nick Goings/999 RC	10.00	4.00
❑	136G	Nick Goings/999 RC	10.00	4.00
❑	137B	Scotty Anderson/999 RC	6.00	2.50
❑	137G	Scotty Anderson/999 RC	6.00	2.50
❑	138B	David Martin/999 RC	6.00	2.50
❑	138G	David Martin/999 RC	6.00	2.50
❑	139B	Derrick Blaylock/999 RC	12.00	5.00
❑	139G	Derrick Blaylock/999 RC	12.00	5.00
❑	140B	Onome Ojo/999 RC	6.00	2.50
❑	140G	Onome Ojo/999 RC	6.00	2.50
❑	141B	Jonathan Carter/999 RC	6.00	2.50
❑	141G	Jonathan Carter/999 RC	6.00	2.50
❑	142B	LaMont Jordan/999 RC	20.00	7.50
❑	142G	LaMont Jordan/999 RC	20.00	7.50
❑	143B	Dominic Rhodes/999 RC	15.00	6.00
❑	143G	Dominic Rhodes/999 RC	15.00	6.00
❑	145B	A.J. Feeley/999 RC	10.00	4.00
❑	145G	A.J. Feeley/999 RC	10.00	4.00
❑	146B	Correll Buckhalter/999 RC	12.00	5.00
❑	146G	Correll Buckhalter/999 RC	12.00	5.00
❑	147B	Steve Smith/999 RC	25.00	12.50
❑	147G	Steve Smith/999 RC	25.00	12.50
❑	148B	Dave Dickenson/999 RC	6.00	2.50
❑	148G	Dave Dickenson/999 RC	6.00	2.50
❑	149B	Cedrick Wilson/999 RC	10.00	4.00
❑	149G	Cedrick Wilson/999 RC	10.00	4.00
❑	150B	Jamie Winborn/999 RC	6.00	2.50
❑	150G	Jamie Winborn/999 RC	6.00	2.50
❑	151B	Alex Bannister/999 RC	6.00	2.50
❑	151G	Alex Bannister/999 RC	6.00	2.50
❑	152B	Heath Evans/999 RC	6.00	2.50
❑	152G	Heath Evans/999 RC	6.00	2.50
❑	153B	Josh Booty/999 RC	10.00	4.00
❑	153G	Josh Booty/999 RC	10.00	4.00
❑	154B	Adam Archuleta/999 RC	10.00	4.00
❑	154G	Adam Archuleta/999 RC	10.00	4.00
❑	155B	Francis St.Paul/999 RC	6.00	2.50
❑	155G	Francis St.Paul/999 RC	6.00	2.50
❑	156B	Andre Dyson/999 RC	4.00	1.50
❑	156G	Andre Dyson/999 RC	4.00	1.50
❑	RM	Randy Moss SAMPLE	2.00	.75

2002 SPx

	No.	Player	Price 1	Price 2
❑		COMP.SET w/o SP's (90)	20.00	7.50
❑	1	Drew Bledsoe	1.25	.50
❑	2	Peerless Price	.60	.25
❑	3	Travis Henry	1.00	.40
❑	4	Ricky Williams	1.00	.40
❑	5	Jay Fiedler	.60	.25
❑	6	Tom Brady	2.50	1.00
❑	7	Troy Brown	.60	.25
❑	8	Antowain Smith	.60	.25
❑	9	Santana Moss	1.00	.40
❑	10	Curtis Martin	1.00	.40
❑	11	Vinny Testaverde	.60	.25
❑	12	Jamal Lewis	1.00	.40
❑	13	Chris Redman	.40	.15
❑	14	Travis Taylor	.60	.25
❑	15	Corey Dillon	.60	.25
❑	16	T.J. Houshmandzadeh	.60	.25
❑	17	Peter Warrick	.60	.25
❑	18	Courtney Brown	.60	.25
❑	19	Kevin Johnson	.60	.25
❑	20	Tim Couch	.60	.25
❑	21	Hines Ward	1.00	.40
❑	22	Jerome Bettis	1.00	.40
❑	23	Kordell Stewart	.60	.25
❑	24	Corey Bradford	.40	.15
❑	25	Jermaine Lewis	.40	.15
❑	26	Edgerrin James	1.25	.50
❑	27	Marvin Harrison	1.00	.40
❑	28	Peyton Manning	2.00	.75
❑	29	Jimmy Smith	.60	.25
❑	30	Mark Brunell	1.00	.40
❑	31	Fred Taylor	1.00	.40
❑	32	Eddie George	1.00	.40
❑	33	Steve McNair	1.00	.40
❑	34	Brian Griese	1.00	.40
❑	35	Shannon Sharpe	.60	.25
❑	36	Rod Smith	.60	.25
❑	37	Trent Green	.60	.25
❑	38	Johnnie Morton	.60	.25
❑	39	Priest Holmes	1.25	.50
❑	40	Jerry Rice	2.00	.75
❑	41	Rich Gannon	1.00	.40
❑	42	Tim Brown	1.00	.40
❑	43	Drew Brees	1.00	.40
❑	44	Junior Seau	1.00	.40
❑	45	LaDainian Tomlinson	1.50	.60
❑	46	Emmitt Smith	2.50	1.00
❑	47	Quincy Carter	.60	.25
❑	48	Rocket Ismail	.60	.25
❑	49	Amani Toomer	.60	.25
❑	50	Kerry Collins	.60	.25
❑	51	Ron Dayne	.60	.25
❑	52	Donovan McNabb	1.25	.50
❑	53	Duce Staley	1.00	.40
❑	54	Antonio Freeman	1.00	.40
❑	55	Rod Gardner	.60	.25
❑	56	Stephen Davis	.60	.25
❑	57	Brian Urlacher	1.50	.60
❑	58	Anthony Thomas	.60	.25
❑	59	Jim Miller	.60	.25
❑	60	Marty Booker	.60	.25
❑	61	Az-Zahir Hakim	.40	.15
❑	62	James Stewart	.60	.25
❑	63	Ahman Green	1.00	.40
❑	64	Brett Favre	2.50	1.00
❑	65	Robert Ferguson	.40	.15
❑	66	Terry Glenn	.60	.25
❑	67	Randy Moss	2.00	.75
❑	68	Daunte Culpepper	1.00	.40
❑	69	Michael Bennett	.60	.25
❑	70	Michael Vick	3.00	1.25
❑	71	Warrick Dunn	1.00	.40
❑	72	Rodney Peete	.60	.25
❑	73	Muhsin Muhammad	.60	.25
❑	74	Aaron Brooks	1.00	.40
❑	75	Deuce McAllister	1.25	.50
❑	76	Keyshawn Johnson	1.00	.40
❑	77	Michael Pittman	.40	.15
❑	78	Brad Johnson	.60	.25
❑	79	Thomas Jones	.60	.25
❑	80	David Boston	1.00	.40
❑	81	Jake Plummer	.60	.25
❑	82	Terrell Owens	1.00	.40
❑	83	Garrison Hearst	.60	.25
❑	84	Jeff Garcia	1.00	.40
❑	85	Darrell Jackson	.60	.25
❑	86	Shaun Alexander	1.25	.50
❑	87	Trent Dilfer	.60	.25
❑	88	Isaac Bruce	1.00	.40
❑	89	Kurt Warner	1.00	.40
❑	90	Marshall Faulk	1.00	.40
❑	91	Saleem Rasheed RC	10.00	4.00
❑	92	Jason McAddley RC	8.00	3.00
❑	93	Brandon Doman RC	8.00	3.00
❑	94	Mike Rumph RC	10.00	4.00
❑	95	Wendell Bryant RC	5.00	2.00
❑	96	Bryan Thomas RC	8.00	3.00
❑	97	Anthony Weaver RC	8.00	3.00
❑	98	Chester Taylor RC	20.00	7.50
❑	99	Ed Reed RC	15.00	6.00
❑	100	Lamar Gordon RC	10.00	4.00
❑	101	Tellis Redmon RC	8.00	3.00
❑	102	Ben Leber RC	10.00	4.00
❑	103	Javin Hunter RC	5.00	2.00
❑	104	Javon Walker RC	20.00	7.50
❑	105	Shaun Hill RC	10.00	4.00
❑	106	Raonall Smith RC	8.00	3.00
❑	107	Darrell Hill RC	8.00	3.00
❑	108	Kalimba Edwards RC	10.00	4.00
❑	109	Robert Thomas RC	10.00	4.00
❑	110	Craig Nall RC	10.00	4.00
❑	111	Marques Anderson RC	10.00	4.00
❑	112	Najeh Davenport RC	10.00	4.00
❑	113	Jonathan Wells RC	10.00	4.00
❑	114	Dwight Freeney RC	15.00	6.00
❑	115	Larry Tripplett RC	5.00	2.00
❑	116	T.J. Duckett RC	12.00	5.00
❑	117	John Henderson RC	10.00	4.00
❑	118	Albert Haynesworth RC	8.00	3.00
❑	119	Tank Williams RC	8.00	3.00
❑	120	Ryan Sims RC	10.00	4.00
❑	121	Leonard Henry RC	8.00	3.00
❑	122	Clinton Portis RC	50.00	20.00

❑ 123 Josh Reed RC 10.00 4.00
❑ 124 Chad Hutchinson RC 8.00 3.00
❑ 125 Deion Branch RC 20.00 10.00
❑ 126 Rocky Calmus RC 10.00 4.00
❑ 127 Donte Stallworth RC 20.00 7.50
❑ 128 Daryl Jones RC 8.00 3.00
❑ 129 Joey Harrington RC 25.00 10.00
❑ 130 Napoleon Harris RC 10.00 4.00
❑ 131 Phillip Buchanon RC 10.00 4.00
❑ 132 Patrick Ramsey RC 12.00 5.00
❑ 133 Brian Westbrook RC 20.00 10.00
❑ 134 Freddie Milons RC 8.00 3.00
❑ 135 Lito Sheppard RC 10.00 4.00
❑ 136 Michael Lewis RC 10.00 4.00
❑ 137 Jamin Elliott RC 5.00 2.00
❑ 138 Lee Mays RC 10.00 4.00
❑ 139 Verron Haynes RC 10.00 4.00
❑ 140 Jesse Chatman RC 10.00 4.00
❑ 141 Quentin Jammer RC 10.00 4.00
❑ 142 Seth Burford RC 8.00 3.00
❑ 143 Julius Peppers RC 20.00 7.50
❑ 144 William Green RC 10.00 4.00
❑ 145 DeShaun Foster RC 10.00 4.00
❑ 146 Daniel Graham RC 10.00 4.00
❑ 147 David Garrard RC 10.00 4.00
❑ 148 Reche Caldwell RC 10.00 4.00
❑ 149 Randy Fasani RC 8.00 3.00
❑ 150 J.T. O'Sullivan RC 8.00 3.00
❑ 151 Josh McCown JSY AU RC 40.0015.00
❑ 152 Kurt Kittner JSY AU RC 20.00 7.50
❑ 153 Kahlil Hill JSY AU RC 15.00 6.00
❑ 154 Ladell Betts JSY AU RC 40.00 20.00
❑ 155 Ron Johnson JSY AU RC 15.00 6.00
❑ 156 Maurice Morris JSY AU RC 25.0010.00
❑ 157 Andre Davis JSY AU RC 25.00 10.00
❑ 158 Antonio Bryant JSY AU RC 25.0010.00
❑ 159 Roy Williams JSY AU RC 60.00 25.00
❑ 160 Lam Thompson JSY AU RC 15.006.00
❑ 161 Cliff Russell JSY AU RC 15.00 6.00
❑ 162 Woody Dantzler JSY AU RC 15.006.00
❑ 163 Travis Stephens JSY AU RC 15.006.00
❑ 164 Tony Fisher JSY AU RC 20.00 7.50
❑ 165 Eric McCoo JSY AU RC 15.00 6.00
❑ 166 Eric Crouch JSY AU RC 25.00 10.00
❑ 167 Rohan Davey JSY AU RC 20.00 7.50
❑ 168 Marquise Walker JSY AU RC 15.006.00
❑ 169 Jeremy Shockey JSY RC 50.00 20.00
❑ 170 Tim Carter JSY AU RC 20.00 7.50
❑ 171 Atrews Bell JSY AU RC 15.00 6.00
❑ 172 Ant Randle El JSY AU RC 60.00 30.00
❑ 173 Ricky Williams JSY AU RC 25.0010.00
❑ 174 Mike Williams JSY AU 15.00 6.00
❑ 175 Adrian Peterson JSY AU RC 25.00 10.00
❑ 176 Jab Gaffney JSY AU/650 RC 25.00 10.00
❑ 177 Ashley Lelie JSY AU/250 RC 60.00 30.00
❑ 178 David Carr JSY AU/250 RC 100.00 50.00

2003 SPx

❑ COMP.SET w/o SP's (110) 25.00 10.00
❑ 1 Peyton Manning 1.50 .60
❑ 2 Aaron Brooks 1.00 .40
❑ 3 Joey Harrington 1.50 .60
❑ 4 Tim Couch .40 .15
❑ 5 Jeff Garcia 1.00 .40
❑ 6 Jay Fiedler .60 .25
❑ 7 Chad Hutchinson .40 .15
❑ 8 Tommy Maddox 1.00 .40
❑ 9 Drew Brees 1.00 .40
❑ 10 Trent Green .60 .25
❑ 11 Patrick Ramsey 1.00 .40
❑ 12 Daunte Culpepper 1.00 .40
❑ 13 Kurt Warner 1.00 .40
❑ 14 Brad Johnson .60 .25
❑ 15 Rich Gannon .60 .25
❑ 16 Jake Plummer .60 .25
❑ 17 Steve McNair 1.00 .40
❑ 18 Mark Brunell .60 .25
❑ 19 Drew Bledsoe 1.00 .40
❑ 20 Kordell Stewart .60 .25
❑ 21 Kelly Holcomb .60 .25
❑ 22 Josh McCown .60 .25
❑ 23 Matt Hasselbeck .60 .25
❑ 24 Marc Bulger 1.00 .40
❑ 25 Chris Redman .40 .15
❑ 26 Rodney Peete .60 .25
❑ 27 Jake Delhomme 1.00 .40
❑ 28 Jon Kitna .60 .25
❑ 29 Kerry Collins .60 .25
❑ 30 Quincy Carter .60 .25
❑ 31 Ricky Williams 1.00 .40
❑ 32 Clinton Portis 1.50 .60
❑ 33 Deuce McAllister 1.00 .40
❑ 34 Ahman Green 1.00 .40
❑ 35 Priest Holmes 1.25 .50
❑ 36 Curtis Martin 1.00 .40
❑ 37 Michael Bennett .60 .25
❑ 38 Eddie George .60 .25
❑ 39 Marshall Faulk 1.00 .40
❑ 40 Garrison Hearst .60 .25
❑ 41 Shaun Alexander 1.00 .40
❑ 42 Corey Dillon .60 .25
❑ 43 Jamal Lewis 1.00 .40
❑ 44 William Green .60 .25
❑ 45 Travis Henry .60 .25
❑ 46 Randy Moss 1.50 .60
❑ 47 Terrell Owens 1.00 .40
❑ 48 Peerless Price .60 .25
❑ 49 David Boston .60 .25
❑ 50 Eric Moulds .60 .25
❑ 51 Marvin Harrison 1.00 .40
❑ 52 Laveranues Coles .60 .25
❑ 53 Santana Moss .60 .25
❑ 54 Troy Brown .60 .25
❑ 55 Chris Chambers 1.00 .40
❑ 56 Tim Brown 1.00 .40
❑ 57 Rod Smith .60 .25
❑ 58 Hines Ward 1.00 .40
❑ 59 Keyshawn Johnson 1.00 .40
❑ 60 Isaac Bruce 1.00 .40
❑ 61 Torry Holt 1.00 .40
❑ 62 Koren Robinson .60 .25
❑ 63 Chad Johnson 1.00 .40
❑ 64 Derrick Mason .60 .25
❑ 65 Antonio Bryant .60 .25
❑ 66 Kevin Johnson .60 .25
❑ 67 Todd Heap .60 .25
❑ 68 Tony Gonzalez .60 .25
❑ 69 Jeremy Shockey 1.50 .60
❑ 70 Brian Urlacher 1.50 .60
❑ 71 Emmitt Smith/500 20.00 7.50
❑ 72 Edgerrin James/500 10.00 4.00
❑ 73 LaDainian Tomlinson/500 8.00 3.00
❑ 74 Brett Favre/500 20.00 7.50
❑ 75 Donovan McNabb/500 10.00 4.00
❑ 76 Tom Brady/500 20.00 7.50
❑ 77 Michael Vick/500 20.00 7.50
❑ 78 David Carr/500 12.00 5.00
❑ 79 Jerry Rice/500 15.00 6.00
❑ 80 Chad Pennington/500 10.00 4.00
❑ 81 Joey Harrington XCT 1.50 .60
❑ 82 Clinton Portis XCT 1.50 .60
❑ 83 Jeremy Shockey XCT 1.50 .60
❑ 84 David Boston XCT .60 .25
❑ 85 Marshall Faulk XCT 1.00 .40
❑ 86 Emmitt Smith XCT 2.50 1.00
❑ 87 Terrell Owens XCT 1.00 .40
❑ 88 Randy Moss XCT 1.50 .60
❑ 89 Deuce McAllister XCT 1.00 .40
❑ 90 Ahman Green XCT 1.00 .40
❑ 91 Peerless Price XCT .60 .25
❑ 92 Plaxico Burress XCT .60 .25
❑ 93 Marvin Harrison XCT 1.00 .40
❑ 94 Keyshawn Johnson XCT 1.00 .40
❑ 95 Laveranues Coles XCT .60 .25
❑ 96 Drew Bledsoe XCT 1.00 .40
❑ 97 Eric Moulds XCT .60 .25
❑ 98 Chad Pennington XCT 1.25 .50
❑ 99 Jerry Rice XCT 2.00 .75
❑ 100 David Carr XCT 1.50 .60
❑ 101 Michael Vick XCT 2.50 1.00
❑ 102 Tom Brady XCT 2.50 1.00
❑ 103 Donovan McNabb XCT 1.25 .50
❑ 104 Brett Favre XCT 2.50 1.00
❑ 105 Kurt Warner XCT 1.00 .40
❑ 106 LaDainian Tomlinson XCT 1.00 .40
❑ 107 Drew Brees XCT 1.00 .40
❑ 108 Edgerrin James XCT 1.00 .40
❑ 109 Peyton Manning XCT 1.50 .60
❑ 110 Ricky Williams XCT 1.00 .40
❑ 111 Brooks Bollinger RC 10.00 4.00
❑ 112 Gibran Hamden RC 5.00 2.00
❑ 113 Jason Johnson RC 5.00 2.00
❑ 114 Tony Romo RC 50.00 25.00
❑ 115 Juston Wood RC 5.00 2.00
❑ 116 Kirk Farmer RC 5.00 2.00
❑ 117 Kliff Kingsbury RC 8.00 3.00
❑ 118 Jason Gesser RC 10.00 4.00
❑ 119 Brad Banks RC 8.00 3.00
❑ 120 Rob Adamson RC 5.00 2.00
❑ 121 Ken Dorsey RC 10.00 4.00
❑ 122 Curt Anes RC 5.00 2.00
❑ 123 George Wrighster RC 8.00 3.00
❑ 124 Brett Engemann RC 5.00 2.00
❑ 125 Aaron Walker RC 8.00 3.00
❑ 126 Nate Hybl RC 10.00 4.00
❑ 127 Chris Simms RC 15.00 6.00
❑ 128 Marquel Blackwell RC 5.00 2.00
❑ 129 Domanick Davis RC 10.00 4.00
❑ 130 Quentin Griffin RC 10.00 4.00
❑ 131 B.J. Askew RC 10.00 4.00
❑ 132 Earnest Graham RC 8.00 3.00
❑ 133 Sultan McCullough RC 8.00 3.00
❑ 134 Dahrran Diedrick RC 10.00 4.00
❑ 135 Cecil Sapp RC 8.00 3.00
❑ 136 LaBrandon Toefield RC 10.00 4.00
❑ 137 ReShard Lee RC 10.00 4.00
❑ 138 Dwone Hicks RC 5.00 2.00
❑ 139 Brock Forsey RC 10.00 4.00
❑ 140 Bethel Johnson RC 10.00 4.00
❑ 141 Andrew Pinnock RC 8.00 3.00
❑ 142 Ahmaad Galloway RC 8.00 3.00
❑ 143 J.T. Wall RC 5.00 2.00
❑ 144 Tom Lopienski RC 8.00 3.00
❑ 145 Justin Griffith RC 8.00 3.00
❑ 146 Lee Suggs RC 10.00 4.00
❑ 147 Nick Maddox RC 5.00 2.00
❑ 148 Jeremi Johnson RC 8.00 3.00
❑ 149 Doug Gabriel RC 10.00 4.00
❑ 150 Bobby Wade RC 10.00 4.00
❑ 151 Justin Gage RC 10.00 4.00
❑ 152 Arnaz Battle RC 10.00 4.00
❑ 153 Brandon Lloyd RC 10.00 4.00
❑ 154 Talman Gardner RC 10.00 4.00
❑ 155 Kareem Kelly RC 8.00 3.00
❑ 156 Billy McMullen RC 8.00 3.00
❑ 157 Antwone Savage RC 5.00 2.00
❑ 158 J.R. Tolver RC 8.00 3.00
❑ 159 Kassim Osgood RC 10.00 4.00
❑ 160 Shaun McDonald RC 10.00 4.00
❑ 161 Sam Aiken RC 8.00 3.00
❑ 162 Adrian Madise RC 8.00 3.00
❑ 163 Charles Rogers RC 10.00 4.00
❑ 164 David Kircus RC 10.00 4.00
❑ 165 Zuriel Smith RC 5.00 2.00
❑ 166 LaTarence Dunbar RC 8.00 3.00
❑ 167 Willie Ponder RC 8.00 3.00
❑ 168 David Tyree RC 5.00 2.00
❑ 169 Kevin Walter RC 8.00 3.00
❑ 170 Keenan Howry RC 10.00 4.00
❑ 171 Walter Young RC 5.00 2.00
❑ 172 DeAndrew Rubin RC 5.00 2.00
❑ 173 Carl Ford RC 5.00 2.00
❑ 174 Taco Wallace RC 8.00 3.00
❑ 175 Travis Anglin RC 5.00 2.00
❑ 176 Ryan Hoag RC 5.00 2.00
❑ 177 Ronald Bellamy RC 8.00 3.00
❑ 178 Terrence Edwards RC 8.00 3.00
❑ 179 Jerel Myers RC 5.00 2.00
❑ 180 Mike Bush RC 8.00 3.00
❑ 181 Dan Curley RC 5.00 2.00
❑ 182 Carl Morris RC 5.00 2.00
❑ 183 Reggie Newhouse RC 8.00 3.00
❑ 184 Troy Polamalu RC 40.00 20.00

❑ 185 Cecil Moore RC 5.00 2.00
❑ 186 Bennie Joppru RC 10.00 4.00
❑ 187 Donald Lee RC 8.00 3.00
❑ 188 Jason Witten RC 15.00 6.00
❑ 189 Mike Seidman RC 5.00 2.00
❑ 190 Vishante Shiancoe RC 8.00 3.00
❑ 191 Anquan Boldin JSY AU RC 50.0020.00
❑ 192 Kyle Boller JSY AU/450 RC 40.00 15.00
❑ 193 Chris Brown JSY AU RC 30.00 12.50
❑ 194 Nate Burleson JSY AU RC 30.0012.50
❑ 195 Tyro Calico JSY AU/450 RC 40.00 15.00
❑ 196 Dallas Clark JSY AU RC 40.00 20.00
❑ 197 Kevin Curtis JSY AU RC 40.00 15.00
❑ 198 Kliff Kingsbury JSY AU RC 25.0010.00
❑ 199 Justin Fargas JSY AU RC 30.00 12.50
❑ 200 Grossman JSY AU/450 RC 120.00 60.00
❑ 201 Taylor Jacobs JSY AU RC 25.00 10.00
❑ 202 An Johnson JSY AU/250 RC 150.00 75.00
❑ 203 Malae MacKenzie JSY AU RC 15.00 6.00
❑ 204 Bryant Johnson JSY AU RC 30.00 12.50
❑ 205 Larry Johnson JSY AU RC 200.00 100.00
❑ 206 T Johnson JSY AU/450 RC 50.0025.00
❑ 207 Leftwich JSY AU/250 RC 200.00 100.00
❑ 208 McGahee JSY AU/450 RC 150.0075.00
❑ 210 C.Palmer JSY AU/250 RC 300.00 150.00
❑ 211 Artose Pinner JSY AU RC 30.0012.50
❑ 212 Dave Ragone JSY AU RC 30.0012.50
❑ 213 Terrell Suggs JSY AU RC 40.00 15.00
❑ 215 Onterio Smith JSY AU RC 30.0012.50
❑ 216 Musa Smith JSY AU RC 30.00 12.50
❑ 217 Brian St.Pierre JSY AU RC 30.0012.50
❑ 218 Marcus Trufant JSY AU RC 30.00 12.50
❑ 219 Seneca Wallace JSY AU RC 30.00 12.50
❑ 220 Kell Washington JSY AU RC 40.00 15.00

2004 SPx

❑ COMP.SET w/o SP's (100) 30.00 15.00
❑ 191-221 JSY AU RC #'d TO 1499 UNLESS NOTED
❑ 1 Anquan Boldin 1.00 .40
❑ 2 Marcel Shipp .60 .25
❑ 3 Josh McCown .60 .25
❑ 4 Peerless Price .60 .25
❑ 5 Michael Vick 2.00 .75
❑ 6 T.J. Duckett .60 .25
❑ 7 Kyle Boller 1.00 .40
❑ 8 Todd Heap .60 .25
❑ 9 Jamal Lewis 1.00 .40
❑ 10 Travis Henry .60 .25
❑ 11 Drew Bledsoe 1.00 .40
❑ 12 Eric Moulds .60 .25
❑ 13 Jake Delhomme 1.00 .40
❑ 14 Steve Smith 1.00 .40
❑ 15 Stephen Davis .60 .25
❑ 16 Brian Urlacher 1.25 .50
❑ 17 Rex Grossman 1.00 .40
❑ 18 Thomas Jones .60 .25
❑ 19 Chad Johnson 1.00 .40
❑ 20 Carson Palmer 1.25 .50
❑ 21 Rudi Johnson .60 .25
❑ 22 William Green .60 .25
❑ 23 Jeff Garcia 1.00 .40
❑ 24 Andre Davis .40 .15
❑ 25 Roy Williams S .60 .25
❑ 26 Eddie George .60 .25
❑ 27 Keyshawn Johnson .60 .25
❑ 28 Jake Plummer .60 .25
❑ 29 Ashley Lelie .60 .25
❑ 30 Quentin Griffin 1.00 .40
❑ 31 Charles Rogers .60 .25
❑ 32 Olandis Gary .40 .15
❑ 33 Joey Harrington 1.00 .40
❑ 34 Brett Favre 2.50 1.00
❑ 35 Javon Walker .60 .25
❑ 36 Ahman Green 1.00 .40
❑ 37 Andre Johnson 1.00 .40
❑ 38 Domanick Davis 1.00 .40
❑ 39 David Carr 1.00 .40
❑ 40 Peyton Manning 1.50 .60
❑ 41 Edgerrin James 1.00 .40
❑ 42 Marvin Harrison 1.00 .40
❑ 43 Byron Leftwich 1.25 .50
❑ 44 Jimmy Smith .60 .25
❑ 45 Fred Taylor .60 .25
❑ 46 Trent Green .60 .25
❑ 47 Priest Holmes 1.25 .50
❑ 48 Dante Hall 1.00 .40
❑ 49 Tony Gonzalez .60 .25
❑ 50 A.J. Feeley 1.00 .40
❑ 51 Marty Booker .60 .25
❑ 52 Chris Chambers .60 .25
❑ 53 Zach Thomas 1.00 .40
❑ 54 Randy Moss 1.25 .50
❑ 55 Daunte Culpepper 1.00 .40
❑ 56 Onterrio Smith .60 .25
❑ 57 Troy Brown .60 .25
❑ 58 Corey Dillon .60 .25
❑ 59 Tom Brady 2.50 1.00
❑ 60 Deuce McAllister 1.00 .40
❑ 61 Joe Horn .60 .25
❑ 62 Aaron Brooks .60 .25
❑ 63 Jeremy Shockey 1.00 .40
❑ 64 Kurt Warner 1.00 .40
❑ 65 Tiki Barber 1.00 .40
❑ 66 Chad Pennington 1.00 .40
❑ 67 Curtis Martin 1.00 .40
❑ 68 Santana Moss .60 .25
❑ 69 Rich Gannon .60 .25
❑ 70 Jerry Rice 2.00 .75
❑ 71 Warren Sapp .60 .25
❑ 72 Donovan McNabb 1.25 .50
❑ 73 Terrell Owens 1.00 .40
❑ 74 Jevon Kearse .60 .25
❑ 75 Brian Westbrook .60 .25
❑ 76 Hines Ward 1.00 .40
❑ 77 Duce Staley .60 .25
❑ 78 Tommy Maddox .60 .25
❑ 79 LaDainian Tomlinson 1.25 .50
❑ 80 Drew Brees 1.00 .40
❑ 81 Tim Rattay .40 .15
❑ 82 Kevan Barlow .60 .25
❑ 83 Brandon Lloyd .60 .25
❑ 84 Shaun Alexander 1.00 .40
❑ 85 Matt Hasselbeck .60 .25
❑ 86 Koren Robinson .60 .25
❑ 87 Marc Bulger 1.00 .40
❑ 88 Marshall Faulk 1.00 .40
❑ 89 Torry Holt 1.00 .40
❑ 90 Isaac Bruce .60 .25
❑ 91 Brad Johnson .60 .25
❑ 92 Keenan McCardell .40 .15
❑ 93 Derrick Brooks .60 .25
❑ 94 Steve McNair 1.00 .40
❑ 95 Chris Brown 1.00 .40
❑ 96 Derrick Mason .60 .25
❑ 97 Clinton Portis 1.00 .40
❑ 98 Mark Brunell .60 .25
❑ 99 Laveranues Coles .60 .25
❑ 100 LaVar Arrington 2.00 .75
❑ 101 B.J. Johnson RC 8.00 3.00
❑ 102 Craig Krenzel RC 10.00 4.00
❑ 103 Will Smith RC 10.00 4.00
❑ 104 Jamaar Taylor RC 10.00 4.00
❑ 105 Tommie Harris RC 10.00 4.00
❑ 106 Shawn Andrews RC 10.00 4.00
❑ 107 Kendrick Starling RC 5.00 2.00
❑ 108 Jeris McIntyre RC 8.00 3.00
❑ 109 Jason Babin RC 10.00 4.00
❑ 110 Marcus Tubbs RC 10.00 4.00
❑ 111 Triandos Luke RC 10.00 4.00
❑ 112 Karlos Dansby RC 10.00 4.00
❑ 113 Vernon Carey RC 8.00 3.00
❑ 114 Ryan Krause RC 8.00 3.00
❑ 115 Daryl Smith RC 10.00 4.00
❑ 116 Ricardo Colclough RC 10.00 4.00
❑ 117 Michael Boulware RC 10.00 4.00
❑ 118 Chris Cooley RC 10.00 4.00
❑ 119 Tank Johnson RC 8.00 3.00
❑ 120 Marquise Hill RC 8.00 3.00
❑ 121 Teddy Lehman RC 10.00 4.00
❑ 122 Antwan Odom RC 10.00 4.00
❑ 123 Sean Jones RC 8.00 3.00
❑ 124 Junior Siavii RC 10.00 4.00
❑ 125 Joey Thomas RC 10.00 4.00
❑ 126 Shawntae Spencer RC 10.00 4.00
❑ 127 Dontarrious Thomas RC 10.00 4.00
❑ 128 Travis LaBoy RC 10.00 4.00
❑ 129 Justin Jenkins RC 8.00 3.00
❑ 130 Dwan Edwards RC 5.00 2.00
❑ 131 Derrick Strait RC 10.00 4.00
❑ 132 Matt Ware RC 10.00 4.00
❑ 133 Jared Lorenzen RC 8.00 3.00
❑ 134 Demorrio Williams RC 10.00 4.00
❑ 135 Bob Sanders RC 20.00 10.00
❑ 136 Justin Smiley RC 10.00 4.00
❑ 137 Casey Bramlet RC 8.00 3.00
❑ 138 Jake Grove RC 5.00 2.00
❑ 139 Thomas Tapeh RC 8.00 3.00
❑ 140 Igor Olshansky RC 10.00 4.00
❑ 141 Stuart Schweigert RC 10.00 4.00
❑ 142 Cody Pickett RC 10.00 4.00
❑ 143 Derrick Ward RC 5.00 2.00
❑ 144 Gilbert Gardner RC 8.00 3.00
❑ 145 D.J. Hackett RC 8.00 3.00
❑ 146 Marquis Cooper RC 8.00 3.00
❑ 147 Courtney Watson RC 10.00 4.00
❑ 148 Jim Sorgi RC 10.00 4.00
❑ 149 Caleb Miller RC 8.00 3.00
❑ 150 Casey Clausen RC 10.00 4.00
❑ 151 Jammal Lord RC 10.00 4.00
❑ 152 Sloan Thomas RC 8.00 3.00
❑ 153 Keyaron Fox RC 8.00 3.00
❑ 154 Adimchinobe Echemandu RC 8.003.00
❑ 155 Ryan Dinwiddie RC 8.00 3.00
❑ 156 Kris Wilson RC 10.00 4.00
❑ 157 D.J. Williams RC 12.00 5.00
❑ 158 Tim Euhus RC 10.00 4.00
❑ 159 Bradlee Van Pelt RC 12.00 5.00
❑ 160 Keiwan Ratliff RC 8.00 3.00
❑ 161 Darnell Dockett RC 8.00 3.00
❑ 162 Troy Fleming RC 8.00 3.00
❑ 163 Tramon Douglas RC 5.00 2.00
❑ 164 Jeremy LeSueur RC 8.00 3.00
❑ 165 Matt Mauck RC 10.00 4.00
❑ 166 Sean Taylor RC 12.00 5.00
❑ 167 B.J. Symons RC 12.00 5.00
❑ 168 Quincy Wilson RC 10.00 4.00
❑ 169 Ernest Wilford RC 12.00 5.00
❑ 170 Jerricho Cotchery RC 12.00 5.00
❑ 171 Michael Turner RC 15.00 6.00
❑ 172 Samie Parker RC 12.00 5.00
❑ 173 Andy Hall RC 10.00 4.00
❑ 174 Keith Smith RC 10.00 4.00
❑ 175 Josh Harris RC 12.00 5.00
❑ 176 Maurice Mann RC 10.00 4.00
❑ 177 Jonathan Vilma RC 12.00 5.00
❑ 178 Jeff Smoker RC 12.00 5.00
❑ 179 Ben Hartsock RC 12.00 5.00
❑ 180 Chris Gamble RC 12.00 5.00
❑ 181 Derrick Hamilton RC 10.00 4.00
❑ 182 John Navarre RC 12.00 5.00
❑ 183 P.K. Sam RC 10.00 4.00
❑ 184 Kenechi Udeze RC 12.00 5.00
❑ 185 Mewelde Moore RC 12.00 5.00
❑ 186 Carlos Francis RC 10.00 4.00
❑ 187 Dunta Robinson RC 12.00 5.00
❑ 188 Johnnie Morant RC 12.00 5.00
❑ 189 Ahmad Carroll RC 12.00 5.00
❑ 190 Vince Wilfork RC 12.00 5.00
❑ 191 Tatum Bell JSY AU RC 40.00 20.00
❑ 192 Cedric Cobbs JSY AU RC 20.00 7.50
❑ 193 Darius Watts JSY AU RC 20.00 7.50
❑ 194 Jul.Jones JSY AU/375 RC 120.0050.00
❑ 195 Robert Gallery JSY AU RC 20.00 7.50
❑ 196 DeAngelo Hall JSY AU RC 30.0012.50
❑ 197 Ben Watson JSY AU RC 25.00 10.00
❑ 198 Ben Troupe JSY AU RC 20.00 7.50
❑ 199 Matt Schaub JSY AU RC 60.00 30.00
❑ 200 Michael Jenkins JSY AU RC 25.00 10.00
❑ 201 Luke McCown JSY AU RC 20.00 7.50
❑ 202 Devery Henderson JSY AU RC 15.00 6.00
❑ 203 Bernard Berrian JSY AU RC 30.00 15.00
❑ 204 Keary Colbert JSY AU RC 25.0010.00

❑ 205 Devard Darling JSY AU RC 20.00 7.50
❑ 206 Lee Evans JSY AU RC 30.00 15.00
❑ 207 Greg Jones JSY AU RC 25.00 12.50
❑ 208 Mich.Clayton JSY AU RC 40.00 15.00
❑ 209 Re.Williams JSY AU RC 25.00 10.00
❑ 210 C.Perry JSY AU/799 RC 30.00 12.50
❑ 211 Rash.Woods JSY AU RC 20.00 7.50
❑ 212 J.P. Losman JSY AU RC 40.00 20.00
❑ 213 Kevin Jones JSY AU RC 40.00 15.00
❑ 214 K.Winslow JSY AU/375 RC 50.00 25.00
❑ 215 S.Jackson JSY AU/375 RC 135.00 75.00
❑ 216 Hamilton JSY AU RC EXCH 15.00 6.00
❑ 217 Ro.Will.JSY AU/375 RC 100.00 50.00
❑ 218 P.Rivers JSY AU/375 RC 150.00 75.00
❑ 219 Fitzgerald JSY AU/100 RC 250.00 125.00
❑ 220 Roethlis.JSY AU/375 RC 300.00 150.00
❑ 221 Manning JSY AU/375 RC 250.00 125.00

2005 SPx

❑ COMP.SET w/o SP's (100) 30.00 15.00
❑ 101-170 RC PRINT RUN 1199 SER.#'d SETS
❑ 171-200 RC PRINT RUN 499 SER.#'d SETS
❑ EXCH EXPIRATION: 10/25/2008
❑ JSY AU RC PRINT RUN 1275 UNLESS NOTED
❑ UNPRICED NFL LOGO AUTOS #'d OF 1
❑ 1 Larry Fitzgerald 1.00 .40
❑ 2 Anquan Boldin .60 .25
❑ 3 Josh McCown .60 .25
❑ 4 Michael Vick 1.50 .60
❑ 5 Alge Crumpler .60 .25
❑ 6 Peerless Price .50 .20
❑ 7 Ray Lewis 1.00 .40
❑ 8 Jamal Lewis 1.00 .40
❑ 9 Kyle Boller .60 .25
❑ 10 J.P. Losman 1.00 .40
❑ 11 Willis McGahee 1.00 .40
❑ 12 Eric Moulds .60 .25
❑ 13 Jake Delhomme 1.00 .40
❑ 14 DeShaun Foster .60 .25
❑ 15 Steve Smith .60 .25
❑ 16 Brian Urlacher 1.00 .40
❑ 17 Rex Grossman .60 .25
❑ 18 Muhsin Muhammad .60 .25
❑ 19 Carson Palmer 1.00 .40
❑ 20 Rudi Johnson .60 .25
❑ 21 Chad Johnson 1.00 .40
❑ 22 Julius Jones 1.25 .50
❑ 23 Keyshawn Johnson .60 .25
❑ 24 Roy Williams S .60 .25
❑ 25 Tatum Bell .60 .25
❑ 26 Jake Plummer .60 .25
❑ 27 Ashley Lelie .60 .25
❑ 28 Roy Williams WR 1.00 .40
❑ 29 Kevin Jones 1.00 .40
❑ 30 Joey Harrington 1.00 .40
❑ 31 Brett Favre 2.50 1.00
❑ 32 Ahman Green 1.00 .40
❑ 33 Javon Walker .60 .25
❑ 34 David Carr 1.00 .40
❑ 35 Andre Johnson .60 .25
❑ 36 Domanick Davis .60 .25
❑ 37 Peyton Manning 1.50 .60
❑ 38 Reggie Wayne .60 .25
❑ 39 Edgerrin James 1.00 .40
❑ 40 Marvin Harrison 1.00 .40
❑ 41 Byron Leftwich 1.00 .40
❑ 42 Fred Taylor .60 .25
❑ 43 Jimmy Smith .60 .25
❑ 44 Priest Holmes 1.00 .40
❑ 45 Larry Johnson 1.00 .40
❑ 46 Trent Green .60 .25
❑ 47 A.J. Feeley .60 .25
❑ 48 Chris Chambers .60 .25
❑ 49 Randy McMichael .50 .20
❑ 50 Daunte Culpepper 1.00 .40
❑ 51 Nate Burleson .60 .25
❑ 52 Michael Bennett .60 .25
❑ 53 Tom Brady 2.50 1.00
❑ 54 Corey Dillon .60 .25
❑ 55 Deion Branch .60 .25
❑ 56 David Givens .60 .25
❑ 57 Aaron Brooks .60 .25
❑ 58 Deuce McAllister 1.00 .40
❑ 59 Joe Horn .60 .25
❑ 60 Eli Manning 2.00 .75
❑ 61 Jeremy Shockey 1.00 .40
❑ 62 Tiki Barber 1.00 .40
❑ 63 Chad Pennington 1.00 .40
❑ 64 Curtis Martin 1.00 .40
❑ 65 Laveranues Coles .60 .25
❑ 66 Kerry Collins .60 .25
❑ 67 Jerry Porter .60 .25
❑ 68 Randy Moss 1.00 .40
❑ 69 Donovan McNabb 1.25 .50
❑ 70 Terrell Owens 1.00 .40
❑ 71 Brian Dawkins .60 .25
❑ 72 Brian Westbrook .60 .25
❑ 73 Ben Roethlisberger 2.50 1.00
❑ 74 Jerome Bettis 1.00 .40
❑ 75 Hines Ward 1.00 .40
❑ 76 Duce Staley .60 .25
❑ 77 Drew Brees 1.00 .40
❑ 78 LaDainian Tomlinson 1.25 .50
❑ 79 Antonio Gates 1.00 .40
❑ 80 Eric Parker .50 .20
❑ 81 Tim Rattay .50 .20
❑ 82 Kevan Barlow .60 .25
❑ 83 Eric Johnson .60 .25
❑ 84 Shaun Alexander 1.25 .50
❑ 85 Darrell Jackson .60 .25
❑ 86 Matt Hasselbeck .60 .25
❑ 87 Marc Bulger 1.00 .40
❑ 88 Steven Jackson 1.25 .50
❑ 89 Marshall Faulk 1.00 .40
❑ 90 Torry Holt 1.00 .40
❑ 91 Michael Pittman .50 .20
❑ 92 Brian Griese .60 .25
❑ 93 Michael Clayton 1.00 .40
❑ 94 Steve McNair 1.00 .40
❑ 95 Drew Bennett .60 .25
❑ 96 Billy Volek .60 .25
❑ 97 Chris Brown .60 .25
❑ 98 Clinton Portis 1.00 .40
❑ 99 Patrick Ramsey .60 .25
❑ 100 Santana Moss .60 .25
❑ 101 Matt Jones RC 20.00 7.50
❑ 102 Jonathan Babineaux RC 6.00 2.50
❑ 103 Darrent Williams RC 8.00 3.00
❑ 104 Timmy Chang RC 6.00 2.50
❑ 105 Kelvin Hayden RC 6.00 2.50
❑ 106 Paris Warren RC 6.00 2.50
❑ 107 Stanley Wilson RC 6.00 2.50
❑ 108 Walter Reyes RC 6.00 2.50
❑ 109 Roydell Williams RC 8.00 3.00
❑ 110 Chase Lyman RC 6.00 2.50
❑ 111 Anthony Davis RC 6.00 2.50
❑ 112 Rasheed Marshall RC 8.00 3.00
❑ 113 Jerome Carter RC 6.00 2.50
❑ 114 Mike Nugent RC 8.00 3.00
❑ 115 Brodney Pool RC 8.00 3.00
❑ 116 Sean Considine RC 8.00 3.00
❑ 117 Chris Rix RC 6.00 2.50
❑ 118 Donte Nicholson RC 8.00 3.00
❑ 119 Dustin Fox RC 8.00 3.00
❑ 120 Oshiomogho Atogwe RC 6.00 2.50
❑ 121 Vincent Fuller RC 6.00 2.50
❑ 122 Josh Bullocks RC 8.00 3.00
❑ 123 Ronald Bartell RC 6.00 2.50
❑ 124 Brock Berlin RC 6.00 2.50
❑ 125 Fabian Washington RC 8.00 3.00
❑ 126 Domonique Foxworth RC 8.00 3.00
❑ 127 Bryant McFadden RC 8.00 3.00
❑ 128 Marlin Jackson RC 8.00 3.00
❑ 129 Eric Green RC 4.00 1.50
❑ 130 Justin Miller RC 6.00 2.50
❑ 131 Lofa Tatupu RC 10.00 4.00
❑ 132 Justin Tuck RC 8.00 3.00
❑ 133 Kurt Campbell RC 6.00 2.50
❑ 134 Darryl Blackstock RC 6.00 2.50
❑ 135 Kevin Burnett RC 8.00 3.00
❑ 136 Marviel Underwood RC 6.00 2.50
❑ 137 Kirk Morrison RC 8.00 3.00
❑ 138 Alfred Fincher RC 6.00 2.50
❑ 139 Lance Mitchell RC 6.00 2.50
❑ 140 Barrett Ruud RC 8.00 3.00
❑ 141 David Pollack RC 8.00 3.00
❑ 142 Bill Swancutt RC 6.00 2.50
❑ 143 DeMarcus Ware RC 12.00 5.00
❑ 144 Steve Savoy RC 4.00 1.50
❑ 145 Matt Roth RC 8.00 3.00
❑ 146 Shaun Cody RC 8.00 3.00
❑ 147 Dan Cody RC 8.00 3.00
❑ 148 Jordan Beck RC 6.00 2.50
❑ 149 Kevin Everett RC 8.00 3.00
❑ 150 Anttaj Hawthorne RC 6.00 2.50
❑ 151 Mike Patterson RC 8.00 3.00
❑ 152 Jerome Collins RC 6.00 2.50
❑ 153 Dante Ridgeway RC 6.00 2.50
❑ 154 Bryan Randall RC 6.00 2.50
❑ 155 Marcus Maxwell RC 6.00 2.50
❑ 156 Airese Currie RC 8.00 3.00
❑ 157 Chad Owens RC 8.00 3.00
❑ 158 Brandon Jacobs RC 10.00 4.00
❑ 159 Manuel White RC 6.00 2.50
❑ 160 Ellis Hobbs RC 8.00 3.00
❑ 161 Lionel Gates RC 6.00 2.50
❑ 162 Ryan Fitzpatrick RC 12.00 5.00
❑ 163 Noah Herron RC 8.00 3.00
❑ 164 Kay-Jay Harris RC 6.00 2.50
❑ 165 T.A. McLendon RC 4.00 1.50
❑ 166 Kerry Rhodes RC 8.00 3.00
❑ 167 Nick Collins RC 8.00 3.00
❑ 168 Eric Moore RC 6.00 2.50
❑ 169 Harry Williams RC 6.00 2.50
❑ 170 Luis Castillo RC 8.00 3.00
❑ 171 James Kilian RC 10.00 4.00
❑ 172 Matt Cassel RC 15.00 6.00
❑ 173 Alvin Pearman RC 10.00 4.00
❑ 174 Dan Orlovsky RC 12.00 5.00
❑ 175 Damien Nash RC 8.00 3.00
❑ 176 Jason White RC 10.00 4.00
❑ 177 Craig Bragg RC 8.00 3.00
❑ 178 Craphonso Thorpe RC 8.00 3.00
❑ 179 Derrick Johnson RC 15.00 6.00
❑ 180 Derek Anderson RC 10.00 4.00
❑ 181 Darren Sproles RC 10.00 4.00
❑ 182 Cedric Houston RC 10.00 4.00
❑ 183 Jerome Mathis RC 10.00 4.00
❑ 184 Larry Brackins RC 8.00 3.00
❑ 185 Fred Gibson RC 8.00 3.00
❑ 186 J.R. Russell RC 8.00 3.00
❑ 187 Alex Smith TE RC 10.00 4.00
❑ 188 Deandra Cobb RC 8.00 3.00
❑ 189 Tab Perry RC 10.00 4.00
❑ 190 Travis Johnson RC 8.00 3.00
❑ 191A Marion Barber RC 15.00 6.00
❑ 191B Andrew Walter JSY AU RC 40.00 20.00
❑ 192A Erasmus James RC 10.00 4.00
❑ 192B V.Morency JSY AU RC 25.00 10.00
❑ 193A Marcus Spears RC 8.00 3.00
❑ 193B Antrel Rolle JSY AU RC 25.00 10.00
❑ 194A Channing Crowder RC 10.00 4.00
❑ 194B Adam Jones JSY AU RC 25.00 10.00
❑ 195A Odell Thurman RC 8.00 3.00
❑ 195B M.Clarett JSY AU/250 50.00 25.00
❑ 196A Shawne Merriman RC 15.00 6.00
❑ 196B Mark Bradley JSY AU RC 25.00 10.00
❑ 197A Adrian McPherson RC 10.00 4.00
❑ 197B Eric Shelton JSY AU RC 25.00 10.00
❑ 198A Chris Henry RC 10.00 4.00
❑ 198B Kyle Orton JSY AU RC 40.00 20.00
❑ 199A Thomas Davis RC 10.00 4.00
❑ 199B Ryan Moats JSY AU RC 25.00 12.50
❑ 200A Corey Webster RC 10.00 4.00
❑ 200B Frank Gore JSY AU RC 80.00 40.00
❑ 201 J.J. Arrington JSY AU RC 40.00 15.00
❑ 202 M.Williams JSY AU/250 100.00 40.00
❑ 203 V.Jackson JSY AU RC 25.00 10.00
❑ 204 Stefan LeFors JSY AU RC 25.00 10.00
❑ 205 D.Greene JSY AU RC EXCH 25.00 10.00
❑ 206 T.Murphy JSY AU RC 25.00 10.00
❑ 207 Courtney Roby JSY AU RC 25.00 10.00
❑ 208 Carlos Rogers JSY AU RC 30.00 12.50

- ❑ 209 Charlie Frye JSY AU RC 50.00 30.00
- ❑ 210 Mark Clayton JSY AU RC 30.00 12.50
- ❑ 211 Roddy White JSY AU RC 25.00 10.00
- ❑ 212 Jason Campbell JSY AU RC 40.00 25.00
- ❑ 213 Roscoe Parrish JSY AU RC 25.00 10.00
- ❑ 214 Reggie Brown JSY AU RC 30.0015.00
- ❑ 215 H.Miller JSY AU RC EXCH 60.0035.00
- ❑ 216 Williamson JSY AU/250 RC 100.00 50.00
- ❑ 217 Ciatrick Fason JSY AU RC 25.0010.00
- ❑ 218 C.Benson JSY AU/150 RC 300.00 150.00
- ❑ 219 B.Edwards JSY AU/250 RC 120.00 60.00
- ❑ 220 Ro.Brown JSY AU/250 RC 200.00 100.00
- ❑ 221 C.Williams JSY AU/250 RC 200.00 100.00
- ❑ 222 A.Smith QB JSY AU/250 RC 200.00 100.00
- ❑ 223 A.Rodgers JSY AU/250 RC 150.00 75.00

2006 SPx

- ❑ COMP.SET w/o RC's (90) 30.00 12.50
- ❑ ROOKIE PRINT RUN 1299 SER.#'d SETS
- ❑ ROOKIE PRINT RUN 399 SER.#'d SETS
- ❑ ROOKIE PRINT RUN 1650 SER.#'d SETS
- ❑ 1 Edgerrin James 1.00 .40
- ❑ 2 Kurt Warner .60 .25
- ❑ 3 Larry Fitzgerald 1.00 .40
- ❑ 4 Michael Vick 1.25 .50
- ❑ 5 Warrick Dunn .60 .25
- ❑ 6 Michael Jenkins .60 .25
- ❑ 7 Jamal Lewis .60 .25
- ❑ 8 Kyle Boller .50 .20
- ❑ 9 Derrick Mason .50 .20
- ❑ 10 Willis McGahee 1.00 .40
- ❑ 11 Lee Evans .60 .25
- ❑ 12 Jake Delhomme .60 .25
- ❑ 13 Steve Smith 1.00 .40
- ❑ 14 DeShaun Foster .60 .25
- ❑ 15 Rex Grossman 1.00 .40
- ❑ 16 Muhsin Muhammad .60 .25
- ❑ 17 Thomas Jones .60 .25
- ❑ 18 Carson Palmer 1.00 .40
- ❑ 19 Chad Johnson .60 .25
- ❑ 20 Rudi Johnson .60 .25
- ❑ 21 Charlie Frye .60 .25
- ❑ 22 Reuben Droughns .60 .25
- ❑ 23 Braylon Edwards 1.00 .40
- ❑ 24 Drew Bledsoe 1.00 .40
- ❑ 25 Terrell Owens 1.00 .40
- ❑ 26 Julius Jones 1.00 .40
- ❑ 27 Jake Plummer .60 .25
- ❑ 28 Tatum Bell .60 .25
- ❑ 29 Rod Smith .60 .25
- ❑ 30 Kevin Jones 1.00 .40
- ❑ 31 Roy Williams WR 1.00 .40
- ❑ 32 Brett Favre 2.00 .75
- ❑ 33 Ahman Green .60 .25
- ❑ 34 Donald Driver .60 .25
- ❑ 35 David Carr .60 .25
- ❑ 36 Andre Johnson .60 .25
- ❑ 37 Peyton Manning 1.50 .60
- ❑ 38 Marvin Harrison 1.00 .40
- ❑ 39 Reggie Wayne .60 .25
- ❑ 40 Byron Leftwich .60 .25
- ❑ 41 Fred Taylor .60 .25
- ❑ 42 Ernest Wilford .50 .20
- ❑ 43 Larry Johnson 1.25 .50
- ❑ 44 Trent Green .60 .25
- ❑ 45 Tony Gonzalez .60 .25
- ❑ 46 Daunte Culpepper 1.00 .40
- ❑ 47 Ronnie Brown 1.00 .40
- ❑ 48 Chris Chambers .60 .25
- ❑ 49 Troy Williamson .60 .25
- ❑ 50 Chester Taylor .60 .25
- ❑ 51 Brad Johnson .60 .25
- ❑ 52 Tom Brady 1.50 .60
- ❑ 53 Deion Branch .60 .25
- ❑ 54 Corey Dillon .60 .25
- ❑ 55 Drew Brees 1.00 .40
- ❑ 56 Deuce McAllister .60 .25
- ❑ 57 Donte Stallworth .60 .25
- ❑ 58 Eli Manning 1.25 .50
- ❑ 59 Tiki Barber 1.00 .40
- ❑ 60 Plaxico Burress .60 .25
- ❑ 61 Chad Pennington .60 .25
- ❑ 62 Curtis Martin 1.00 .40
- ❑ 63 Randy Moss 1.00 .40
- ❑ 64 LaMont Jordan .60 .25
- ❑ 65 Aaron Brooks .60 .25
- ❑ 66 Donovan McNabb 1.00 .40
- ❑ 67 Brian Westbrook .60 .25
- ❑ 68 Ben Roethlisberger 1.50 .60
- ❑ 69 Hines Ward 1.00 .40
- ❑ 70 Willie Parker 1.25 .50
- ❑ 71 LaDainian Tomlinson 1.25 .50
- ❑ 72 Philip Rivers 1.00 .40
- ❑ 73 Antonio Gates 1.00 .40
- ❑ 74 Alex Smith QB 1.25 .50
- ❑ 75 Antonio Bryant .60 .25
- ❑ 76 Frank Gore 1.00 .40
- ❑ 77 Shaun Alexander 1.00 .40
- ❑ 78 Matt Hasselbeck .60 .25
- ❑ 79 Nate Burleson .60 .25
- ❑ 80 Marc Bulger .60 .25
- ❑ 81 Steven Jackson 1.00 .40
- ❑ 82 Torry Holt .60 .25
- ❑ 83 Cadillac Williams 1.00 .40
- ❑ 84 Joey Galloway .60 .25
- ❑ 85 Chris Simms .60 .25
- ❑ 86 Billy Volek .60 .25
- ❑ 87 Drew Bennett .50 .20
- ❑ 88 Clinton Portis 1.00 .40
- ❑ 89 Santana Moss .60 .25
- ❑ 90 Mark Brunell .60 .25
- ❑ 91 Haloti Ngata RC 10.00 4.00
- ❑ 92 Willie Reid RC 10.00 4.00
- ❑ 93 Kamerion Wimbley RC 10.00 4.00
- ❑ 94 Donte Whitner RC 10.00 4.00
- ❑ 95 Ethan Kilmer RC 10.00 4.00
- ❑ 96 Johnathan Joseph RC 8.00 3.00
- ❑ 97 Brodie Croyle RC 15.00 6.00
- ❑ 98 Bobby Carpenter RC 10.00 4.00
- ❑ 99 Antonio Cromartie RC 10.00 4.00
- ❑ 100 Eric Winston RC 5.00 2.00
- ❑ 101 Nick Mangold RC 5.00 2.00
- ❑ 102 Manny Lawson RC 10.00 4.00
- ❑ 103 Claude Wroten RC 5.00 2.00
- ❑ 104 D'Qwell Jackson RC 8.00 3.00
- ❑ 105 Richard Marshall RC 8.00 3.00
- ❑ 106 Tamba Hali RC 10.00 4.00
- ❑ 107 Ko Simpson RC 8.00 3.00
- ❑ 108 Danieal Manning RC 10.00 4.00
- ❑ 109 Gabe Watson RC 8.00 3.00
- ❑ 110 Kevin McMahan RC 8.00 3.00
- ❑ 111 Jai Lewis RC 8.00 3.00
- ❑ 112 Darryl Tapp RC 8.00 3.00
- ❑ 113 John McCargo RC 8.00 3.00
- ❑ 114 Jeff King RC 8.00 3.00
- ❑ 115 Charles Davis RC 8.00 3.00
- ❑ 116 Calvin Lowry RC 10.00 4.00
- ❑ 117 Delanie Walker RC 8.00 3.00
- ❑ 118 Roman Harper RC 8.00 3.00
- ❑ 119 Nate Salley RC 8.00 3.00
- ❑ 120 Cooper Wallace RC 8.00 3.00
- ❑ 121 Bernard Pollard RC 8.00 3.00
- ❑ 122 Derrick Ross RC 8.00 3.00
- ❑ 123 Ingle Martin RC 10.00 4.00
- ❑ 124 Wali Lundy RC 10.00 4.00
- ❑ 125 Marcus Vick RC 8.00 3.00
- ❑ 126 Cedric Humes RC 10.00 4.00
- ❑ 127 Marques Hagans RC 8.00 3.00
- ❑ 128 Taurean Henderson RC 10.00 4.00
- ❑ 129 Marques Colston RC 40.00 15.00
- ❑ 130 Devin Aromashodu RC 8.00 3.00
- ❑ 131 Jonathan Orr RC 8.00 3.00
- ❑ 132 Skyler Green RC 10.00 4.00
- ❑ 133 Jeff Webb RC 8.00 3.00
- ❑ 134 Jon Alston RC 10.00 4.00
- ❑ 135 Daniel Bullocks RC 10.00 4.00
- ❑ 136 Anthony Schlegel RC 8.00 3.00
- ❑ 137 Adam Jennings RC 8.00 3.00
- ❑ 138 Gerris Wilkinson RC 5.00 2.00
- ❑ 139 James Anderson RC 5.00 2.00
- ❑ 140 Owen Daniels RC 10.00 4.00
- ❑ 141 Ray Edwards RC 8.00 3.00
- ❑ 142 Chris Gocong RC 8.00 3.00
- ❑ 143 Babatunde Oshinowo RC 8.00 3.00
- ❑ 144 Marvin Philip RC 10.00 4.00
- ❑ 145 Stanley McClover RC 8.00 3.00
- ❑ 146 DeMeco Ryans RC 12.00 5.00
- ❑ 147 Tony Scheffler RC 10.00 4.00
- ❑ 148 T.J. Williams RC 10.00 4.00
- ❑ 149 P.J. Daniels RC 8.00 3.00
- ❑ 150 Bennie Brazell RC 8.00 3.00
- ❑ 151 Will Blackmon RC 8.00 3.00
- ❑ 152 Bruce Gradkowski RC 15.00 6.00
- ❑ 153 Drew Olson RC 8.00 3.00
- ❑ 154 Darnell Bing RC 10.00 4.00
- ❑ 155 Darrell Hackney RC 8.00 3.00
- ❑ 156 Cory Rodgers RC 10.00 4.00
- ❑ 157 DonTrell Moore RC 8.00 3.00
- ❑ 158 Ernie Sims RC 12.00 5.00
- ❑ 159 Jay Cutler RC 40.00 15.00
- ❑ 160 D.J. Shockley RC 10.00 4.00
- ❑ 161 Martin Nance RC 8.00 3.00
- ❑ 162 Joseph Addai RC 25.00 10.00
- ❑ 163 Leonard Pope RC 10.00 4.00
- ❑ 164 Anthony Fasano RC 10.00 4.00
- ❑ 165 Mathias Kiwanuka RC 12.00 5.00
- ❑ 166 Greg Jennings RC 20.00 8.00
- ❑ 167 Greg Lee RC 8.00 3.00
- ❑ 168 Jerome Harrison RC 10.00 4.00
- ❑ 169 Jimmy Williams RC 10.00 4.00
- ❑ 170 Josh Betts RC 8.00 3.00
- ❑ 171 Ashton Youboty RC 10.00 4.00
- ❑ 172 Terrence Whitehead RC 8.00 3.00
- ❑ 173 Brad Smith RC 10.00 4.00
- ❑ 174 D'Brickashaw Ferguson RC 10.00 4.00
- ❑ 175 Mike Hass RC 10.00 4.00
- ❑ 176 Reggie McNeal RC 8.00 3.00
- ❑ 177 Dominique Byrd RC 8.00 3.00
- ❑ 178 Winston Justice RC 10.00 4.00
- ❑ 179 Chad Greenway RC 10.00 4.00
- ❑ 180 Tye Hill RC 10.00 4.00
- ❑ 181 Chad Jackson JSY AU RC 100.0050.00
- ❑ 182 DeA.Williams JSY AU RC 120.0060.00
- ❑ 183 Vince Young JSY AU RC 400.00200.00
- ❑ 184 S.Holmes JSY AU RC 100.00 40.00
- ❑ 185 Sinorice Moss JSY AU RC 60.00 30.00
- ❑ 186 Matt Leinart JSY AU RC 350.00175.00
- ❑ 187 Reggie Bush JSY AU RC 600.00300.00
- ❑ 188 LenDale White JSY AU RC 50.0020.00
- ❑ 189 Vernon Davis JSY AU RC 40.00 20.00
- ❑ 190 L.Maroney JSY AU RC 120.00 60.00
- ❑ 191 A.J. Hawk JSY AU RC 80.00 30.00
- ❑ 192 Marcus McNeill JSY AU RC 15.00 6.00
- ❑ 193 Kelly Jennings JSY AU RC 20.00 8.00
- ❑ 194 B.Williams JSY AU RC 20.00 8.00
- ❑ 195 Brian Calhoun JSY AU RC 20.00 8.00
- ❑ 196 Travis Wilson JSY AU RC 20.00 8.00
- ❑ 197 C.Whitehurst JSY AU RC 25.00 10.00
- ❑ 198 Omar Jacobs JSY AU RC 15.00 6.00
- ❑ 199 J.Klopfenstein JSY AU RC 15.00 6.00
- ❑ 200 Derek Hagan JSY AU RC 20.00 8.00
- ❑ 201 Michael Huff JSY AU RC 25.00 10.00
- ❑ 202 Maurice Stovall JSY AU RC 20.00 8.00
- ❑ 203 Maurice Drew JSY AU RC 60.00 35.00
- ❑ 204 Jason Avant JSY AU RC 20.00 8.00
- ❑ 205 K.Clemens JSY AU RC 25.00 10.00
- ❑ 206 J.Norwood JSY AU RC 50.00 25.00
- ❑ 207 T.Jackson JSY AU RC 40.00 20.00
- ❑ 208 B.Marshall JSY AU RC 30.00 15.00
- ❑ 209 Dem.Williams JSY AU RC 25.00 10.00
- ❑ 210 L.Washington JSY AU RC 40.00 20.00
- ❑ 211 M.Robinson JSY AU RC 30.00 12.00

❑ 212 Marcedes Lewis JSY AU RC	20.00	8.00
❑ 213 Mario Williams JSY AU RC	30.00	12.00

1991 Stadium Club

❑ COMPLETE SET (500)	60.00	30.00
❑ 1 Pepper Johnson	.20	.07
❑ 2 Emmitt Smith	5.00	2.00
❑ 3 Deion Sanders	1.50	.60
❑ 4 Andre Collins	.20	.07
❑ 5 Eric Metcalf	.40	.15
❑ 6 Richard Dent	.40	.15
❑ 7 Eric Martin	.20	.07
❑ 8 Marcus Allen	.75	.30
❑ 9 Gary Anderson K	.20	.07
❑ 10 Joey Browner	.20	.07
❑ 11 Lorenzo White	.20	.07
❑ 12 Bruce Smith	.75	.30
❑ 13 Mark Boyer	.20	.07
❑ 14 Mike Piel	.20	.07
❑ 15 Albert Bentley	.20	.07
❑ 16 Bennie Blades	.20	.07
❑ 17 Jason Staurovsky	.20	.07
❑ 18 Anthony Toney	.20	.07
❑ 19 Dave Krieg	.40	.15
❑ 20 Harvey Williams RC	.75	.30
❑ 21 Bubba Paris	.20	.07
❑ 22 Tim McGee	.20	.07
❑ 23 Brian Noble	.20	.07
❑ 24 Vinny Testaverde	.40	.15
❑ 25 Doug Widell	.20	.07
❑ 26 John Jackson WR RC	.20	.07
❑ 27 Marion Butts	.40	.15
❑ 28 Deron Cherry	.20	.07
❑ 29 Don Warren	.20	.07
❑ 30 Rod Woodson	.75	.30
❑ 31 Mike Baab	.20	.07
❑ 32 Greg Jackson RC	.20	.07
❑ 33 Jerry Robinson	.20	.07
❑ 34 Dalton Hilliard	.20	.07
❑ 35 Brian Jordan	.40	.15
❑ 36 James Thornton UER	.20	.07
❑ 37 Michael Irvin	.75	.30
❑ 38 Billy Joe Tolliver	.20	.07
❑ 39 Jeff Herrod	.20	.07
❑ 40 Scott Norwood	.20	.07
❑ 41 Ferrell Edmunds	.20	.07
❑ 42 Andre Waters	.20	.07
❑ 43 Kevin Glover	.20	.07
❑ 44 Ray Berry	.20	.07
❑ 45 Timm Rosenbach	.20	.07
❑ 46 Reuben Davis	.20	.07
❑ 47 Charles Wilson	.20	.07
❑ 48 Todd Marinovich RC	.20	.07
❑ 49 Harris Barton	.20	.07
❑ 50 Jim Breech	.20	.07
❑ 51 Ron Holmes	.20	.07
❑ 52 Chris Singleton	.20	.07
❑ 53 Pat Leahy	.20	.07
❑ 54 Tom Newberry	.20	.07
❑ 55 Greg Montgomery	.20	.07
❑ 56 Robert Blackmon	.20	.07
❑ 57 Jay Hilgenberg	.20	.07
❑ 58 Rodney Hampton	.75	.30
❑ 59 Brett Perriman	.75	.30
❑ 60 Ricky Watters RC	6.00	2.50
❑ 61 Howie Long	.75	.30
❑ 62 Frank Cornish	.20	.07
❑ 63 Chris Miller	.40	.15
❑ 64 Keith Taylor	.20	.07
❑ 65 Tony Paige	.20	.07
❑ 66 Gary Zimmerman	.20	.07
❑ 67 Mark Royals RC	.20	.07
❑ 68 Ernie Jones	.20	.07
❑ 69 David Grant	.20	.07
❑ 70 Shane Conlan	.20	.07
❑ 71 Jerry Rice	2.50	1.00
❑ 72 Christian Okoye	.20	.07
❑ 73 Eddie Murray	.20	.07
❑ 74 Reggie White	.75	.30
❑ 75 Jeff Graham RC WR	1.00	.40
❑ 76 Mark Jackson	.20	.07
❑ 77 David Grayson	.20	.07
❑ 78 Dan Stryzinski	.20	.07
❑ 79 Sterling Sharpe	.75	.30
❑ 80 Cleveland Gary	.20	.07
❑ 81 Johnny Meads	.20	.07
❑ 82 Howard Cross	.20	.07
❑ 83 Ken O'Brien	.20	.07
❑ 84 Brian Blades	.40	.15
❑ 85 Ethan Horton	.20	.07
❑ 86 Bruce Armstrong	.20	.07
❑ 87 James Washington RC	.20	.07
❑ 88 Eugene Daniel	.20	.07
❑ 89 James Lofton	.40	.15
❑ 90 Louis Oliver	.20	.07
❑ 91 Boomer Esiason	.40	.15
❑ 92 Seth Joyner	.40	.15
❑ 93 Mark Carrier WR	.75	.30
❑ 94 Brett Favre RC UER	50.00	25.00
❑ 95 Lee Williams	.20	.07
❑ 96 Neal Anderson	.40	.15
❑ 97 Brent Jones	.75	.30
❑ 98 John Alt	.20	.07
❑ 99 Rodney Peete	.40	.15
❑ 100 Steve Broussard	.20	.07
❑ 101 Cedric Mack	.20	.07
❑ 102 Pat Swilling	.40	.15
❑ 103 Stan Humphries	.75	.30
❑ 104 Darrell Thompson	.20	.07
❑ 105 Reggie Langhorne	.20	.07
❑ 106 Kenny Davidson	.20	.07
❑ 107 Jim Everett	.40	.15
❑ 108 Keith Millard	.20	.07
❑ 109 Garry Lewis	.20	.07
❑ 110 Jeff Hostetler	.40	.15
❑ 111 Lamar Lathon	.20	.07
❑ 112 Johnny Bailey	.20	.07
❑ 113 Cornelius Bennett	.40	.15
❑ 114 Travis McNeal	.20	.07
❑ 115 Jeff Lageman	.20	.07
❑ 116 Nick Bell RC	.20	.07
❑ 117 Calvin Williams	.40	.15
❑ 118 Shawn Lee RC	.20	.07
❑ 119 Anthony Munoz	.40	.15
❑ 120 Jay Novacek	.75	.30
❑ 121 Kevin Fagan	.20	.07
❑ 122 Leo Goeas	.20	.07
❑ 123 Vance Johnson	.20	.07
❑ 124 Brent Williams	.20	.07
❑ 125 Clarence Verdin	.20	.07
❑ 126 Luis Sharpe	.20	.07
❑ 127 Darrell Green	.20	.07
❑ 128 Barry Word	.20	.07
❑ 129 Steve Walsh	.20	.07
❑ 130 Bryan Hinkle	.20	.07
❑ 131 Ed West	.20	.07
❑ 132 Jeff Campbell	.20	.07
❑ 133 Dennis Byrd	.20	.07
❑ 134 Nate Odomes	.20	.07
❑ 135 Trace Armstrong	.20	.07
❑ 136 Jarvis Williams	.20	.07
❑ 137 Warren Moon	.75	.30
❑ 138 Eric Moten RC	.20	.07
❑ 139 Tony Woods	.20	.07
❑ 140 Phil Simms	.40	.15
❑ 141 Ricky Reynolds	.20	.07
❑ 142 Frank Stams	.20	.07
❑ 143 Kevin Mack	.20	.07
❑ 144 Wade Wilson	.40	.15
❑ 145 Shawn Collins	.20	.07
❑ 146 Roger Craig	.40	.15
❑ 147 Jeff Feagles RC	.20	.07
❑ 148 Norm Johnson	.20	.07
❑ 149 Terance Mathis	.40	.15
❑ 150 Reggie Cobb	.20	.07
❑ 151 Chip Banks	.20	.07
❑ 152 Darryl Pollard	.20	.07
❑ 153 Karl Mecklenburg	.20	.07
❑ 154 Ricky Proehl	.20	.07
❑ 155 Pete Stoyanovich	.20	.07
❑ 156 John Stephens	.20	.07
❑ 157 Ron Morris	.20	.07
❑ 158 Steve DeBerg	.20	.07
❑ 159 Mike Munchak	.40	.15
❑ 160 Brett Maxie	.20	.07
❑ 161 Don Beebe	.20	.07
❑ 162 Martin Mayhew	.20	.07
❑ 163 Merril Hoge	.20	.07
❑ 164 Kelvin Pritchett RC	.40	.15
❑ 165 Jim Jeffcoat	.20	.07
❑ 166 Myron Guyton	.20	.07
❑ 167 Ickey Woods	.20	.07
❑ 168 Andre Ware	.40	.15
❑ 169 Gary Plummer	.20	.07
❑ 170 Henry Ellard	.40	.15
❑ 171 Scott Davis	.20	.07
❑ 172 Randall McDaniel	.20	.07
❑ 173 Randal Hill RC	.40	.15
❑ 174 Anthony Bell	.20	.07
❑ 175 Gary Anderson RB	.20	.07
❑ 176 Byron Evans	.20	.07
❑ 177 Tony Mandarich	.20	.07
❑ 178 Jeff George	1.00	.40
❑ 179 Art Monk	.40	.15
❑ 180 Mike Kenn	.20	.07
❑ 181 Sean Landeta	.20	.07
❑ 182 Shaun Gayle	.20	.07
❑ 183 Michael Carter	.20	.07
❑ 184 Robb Thomas	.20	.07
❑ 185 Richmond Webb	.20	.07
❑ 186 Carnell Lake	.20	.07
❑ 187 Rueben Mayes	.20	.07
❑ 188 Issiac Holt	.20	.07
❑ 189 Leon Seals	.20	.07
❑ 190 Al Smith	.20	.07
❑ 191 Steve Atwater	.20	.07
❑ 192 Greg McMurtry	.20	.07
❑ 193 Al Toon	.40	.15
❑ 194 Cortez Kennedy	.75	.30
❑ 195 Gill Byrd	.20	.07
❑ 196 Carl Zander	.20	.07
❑ 197 Robert Brown	.20	.07
❑ 198 Buford McGee	.20	.07
❑ 199 Mervyn Fernandez	.20	.07
❑ 200 Mike Dumas RC	.20	.07
❑ 201 Rob Burnett RC	.40	.15
❑ 202 Brian Mitchell	.40	.15
❑ 203 Randall Cunningham	.75	.30
❑ 204 Sammie Smith	.20	.07
❑ 205 Ken Clarke	.20	.07
❑ 206 Floyd Dixon	.20	.07
❑ 207 Ken Norton	.40	.15
❑ 208 Tony Siragusa RC	.40	.15
❑ 209 Louis Lipps	.20	.07
❑ 210 Chris Martin	.20	.07
❑ 211 Jamie Mueller	.20	.07
❑ 212 Dave Waymer	.20	.07
❑ 213 Donnell Woolford	.20	.07
❑ 214 Paul Gruber	.20	.07
❑ 215 Ken Harvey	.40	.15
❑ 216 Henry Jones RC	.40	.15
❑ 217 Tommy Barnhardt RC	.20	.07
❑ 218 Arthur Cox	.20	.07
❑ 219 Pat Terrell	.20	.07
❑ 220 Curtis Duncan	.20	.07
❑ 221 Jeff Jaeger	.20	.07
❑ 222 Scott Stephen RC	.20	.07
❑ 223 Rob Moore	1.00	.40
❑ 224 Chris Hinton	.20	.07
❑ 225 Marv Cook	.20	.07
❑ 226 Patrick Hunter RC	.20	.07
❑ 227 Earnest Byner	.20	.07
❑ 228 Troy Aikman	3.00	1.25
❑ 229 Kevin Walker RC	.20	.07
❑ 230 Keith Jackson	.40	.15
❑ 231 Russell Maryland RC	.75	.30
❑ 232 Charles Haley	.40	.15
❑ 233 Nick Lowery	.20	.07
❑ 234 Erik Howard	.20	.07
❑ 235 Leonard Smith	.20	.07
❑ 236 Tim Irwin	.20	.07
❑ 237 Simon Fletcher	.20	.07
❑ 238 Thomas Everett	.20	.07

Card		
❑ 239 Reggie Roby	.20	.07
❑ 240 Leroy Hoard	.40	.15
❑ 241 Wayne Haddix	.20	.07
❑ 242 Gary Clark	.75	.30
❑ 243 Eric Andolsek	.20	.07
❑ 244 Jim Wahler RC	.20	.07
❑ 245 Vaughan Johnson	.20	.07
❑ 246 Kevin Butler	.20	.07
❑ 247 Steve Tasker	.40	.15
❑ 248 LeRoy Butler	.40	.15
❑ 249 Darion Conner	.20	.07
❑ 250 Eric Turner RC	.40	.15
❑ 251 Kevin Ross	.20	.07
❑ 252 Stephen Baker	.20	.07
❑ 253 Harold Green	.40	.15
❑ 254 Rohn Stark	.20	.07
❑ 255 Joe Nash	.20	.07
❑ 256 Jesse Sapolu	.20	.07
❑ 257 Willie Gault	.40	.15
❑ 258 Jerome Brown	.20	.07
❑ 259 Ken Willis	.20	.07
❑ 260 Courtney Hall	.20	.07
❑ 261 Hart Lee Dykes	.20	.07
❑ 262 William Fuller	.40	.15
❑ 263 Stan Thomas	.20	.07
❑ 264 Dan Marino	4.00	1.50
❑ 265 Ron Cox	.20	.07
❑ 266 Eric Green	.20	.07
❑ 267 Anthony Carter	.40	.15
❑ 268 Jerry Ball	.20	.07
❑ 269 Ron Hall	.20	.07
❑ 270 Dennis Smith	.20	.07
❑ 271 Eric Hill	.20	.07
❑ 272 Dan McGwire RC	.20	.07
❑ 273 Lewis Billups UER	.20	.07
❑ 274 Rickey Jackson	.20	.07
❑ 275 Jim Sweeney	.20	.07
❑ 276 Pat Beach	.20	.07
❑ 277 Kevin Porter	.20	.07
❑ 278 Mike Sherrard	.20	.07
❑ 279 Andy Heck	.20	.07
❑ 280 Ron Brown	.20	.07
❑ 281 Lawrence Taylor	.75	.30
❑ 282 Anthony Pleasant	.20	.07
❑ 283 Wes Hopkins	.20	.07
❑ 284 Jim Lachey	.20	.07
❑ 285 Tim Harris	.20	.07
❑ 286 Tory Epps	.20	.07
❑ 287 Wendell Davis	.20	.07
❑ 288 Bubba McDowell	.20	.07
❑ 289 Bubby Brister	.20	.07
❑ 290 Chris Zorich RC	.75	.30
❑ 291 Mike Merriweather	.20	.07
❑ 292 Burt Grossman	.20	.07
❑ 293 Erik McMillan	.20	.07
❑ 294 John Elway	4.00	1.50
❑ 295 Toi Cook RC	.20	.07
❑ 296 Tom Rathman	.20	.07
❑ 297 Matt Bahr	.20	.07
❑ 298 Chris Spielman	.40	.15
❑ 299 F.J.Nunn w/Aikman/Emmitt	.40	.15
❑ 300 Jim C. Jensen	.20	.07
❑ 301 David Fulcher UER	.20	.07
❑ 302 Tommy Hodson	.20	.07
❑ 303 Stephone Paige	.20	.07
❑ 304 Greg Townsend	.20	.07
❑ 305 Dean Biasucci	.20	.07
❑ 306 Jimmie Jones	.20	.07
❑ 307 Eugene Marve	.20	.07
❑ 308 Flipper Anderson	.20	.07
❑ 309 Darryl Talley	.20	.07
❑ 310 Mike Croel RC	.20	.07
❑ 311 Thane Gash	.20	.07
❑ 312 Perry Kemp	.20	.07
❑ 313 Heath Sherman	.20	.07
❑ 314 Mike Singletary	.40	.15
❑ 315 Chip Lohmiller	.20	.07
❑ 316 Tunch Ilkin	.20	.07
❑ 317 Junior Seau	1.25	.50
❑ 318 Mike Gann	.20	.07
❑ 319 Tim McDonald	.20	.07
❑ 320 Kyle Clifton	.20	.07
❑ 321 Dan Owens	.20	.07
❑ 322 Tim Grunhard	.20	.07
❑ 323 Stan Brock	.20	.07
❑ 324 Rodney Holman	.20	.07
❑ 325 Mark Ingram	.40	.15
❑ 326 Browning Nagle RC	.20	.07
❑ 327 Joe Montana	5.00	2.00
❑ 328 Carl Lee	.20	.07
❑ 329 John L. Williams	.20	.07
❑ 330 David Griggs	.20	.07
❑ 331 Clarence Kay	.20	.07
❑ 332 Irving Fryar	.40	.15
❑ 333 Doug Smith DT RC**	.40	.15
❑ 334 Kent Hull	.20	.07
❑ 335 Mike Wilcher	.20	.07
❑ 336 Ray Donaldson	.20	.07
❑ 337 Mark Carrier DB UER	.20	.07
❑ 338 Kelvin Martin	.20	.07
❑ 339 Keith Byars	.20	.07
❑ 340 Wilber Marshall	.20	.07
❑ 341 Ronnie Lott	.40	.15
❑ 342 Blair Thomas	.20	.07
❑ 343 Ronnie Harmon	.20	.07
❑ 344 Brian Brennan	.20	.07
❑ 345 Charles McRae RC	.20	.07
❑ 346 Michael Cofer	.20	.07
❑ 347 Keith Willis	.20	.07
❑ 348 Bruce Kozerski	.20	.07
❑ 349 Dave Meggett	.40	.15
❑ 350 John Taylor	.40	.15
❑ 351 Johnny Holland	.20	.07
❑ 352 Steve Christie	.20	.07
❑ 353 Ricky Ervins RC	.40	.15
❑ 354 Robert Massey	.20	.07
❑ 355 Derrick Thomas	.75	.30
❑ 356 Tommy Kane	.20	.07
❑ 357 Melvin Bratton	.20	.07
❑ 358 Bruce Matthews	.40	.15
❑ 359 Mark Duper	.40	.15
❑ 360 Jeff Wright RC	.20	.07
❑ 361 Barry Sanders	4.00	1.50
❑ 362 Chuck Webb RC	.20	.07
❑ 363 Darryl Grant	.20	.07
❑ 364 William Roberts	.20	.07
❑ 365 Reggie Rutland	.20	.07
❑ 366 Clay Matthews	.40	.15
❑ 367 Anthony Miller	.40	.15
❑ 368 Mike Prior	.20	.07
❑ 369 Jessie Tuggle	.20	.07
❑ 370 Brad Muster	.20	.07
❑ 371 Jay Schroeder	.20	.07
❑ 372 Greg Lloyd	.75	.30
❑ 373 Mike Cofer	.20	.07
❑ 374 James Brooks	.40	.15
❑ 375 Danny Noonan UER	.20	.07
❑ 376 Latin Berry RC	.20	.07
❑ 377 Brad Baxter	.20	.07
❑ 378 Godfrey Myles RC	.20	.07
❑ 379 Morten Andersen	.20	.07
❑ 380 Keith Woodside	.20	.07
❑ 381 Bobby Humphrey	.20	.07
❑ 382 Mike Golic	.20	.07
❑ 383 Keith McCants	.20	.07
❑ 384 Anthony Thompson	.20	.07
❑ 385 Mark Clayton	.40	.15
❑ 386 Neil Smith	.75	.30
❑ 387 Bryan Millard	.20	.07
❑ 388 Mel Gray UER	.40	.15
❑ 389 Ernest Givins	.40	.15
❑ 390 Reyna Thompson	.20	.07
❑ 391 Eric Bieniemy RC	.20	.07
❑ 392 Jon Hand	.20	.07
❑ 393 Mark Rypien	.40	.15
❑ 394 Bill Romanowski	.20	.07
❑ 395 Thurman Thomas	.75	.30
❑ 396 Jim Harbaugh	.75	.30
❑ 397 Don Mosebar	.20	.07
❑ 398 Andre Rison	.40	.15
❑ 399 Mike Johnson	.20	.07
❑ 400 Dermontti Dawson	.20	.07
❑ 401 Herschel Walker	.40	.15
❑ 402 Joe Prokop	.20	.07
❑ 403 Eddie Brown	.20	.07
❑ 404 Nate Newton	.40	.15
❑ 405 Damone Johnson RC	.20	.07
❑ 406 Jessie Hester	.20	.07
❑ 407 Jim Arnold	.20	.07
❑ 408 Ray Agnew	.20	.07
❑ 409 Michael Brooks	.20	.07
❑ 410 Keith Sims	.20	.07
❑ 411 Carl Banks	.20	.07
❑ 412 Jonathan Hayes	.20	.07
❑ 413 Richard Johnson CB RC	.20	.07
❑ 414 Darryll Lewis RC	.40	.15
❑ 415 Jeff Bryant	.20	.07
❑ 416 Leslie O'Neal	.40	.15
❑ 417 Andre Reed	.40	.15
❑ 418 Charles Mann	.20	.07
❑ 419 Keith DeLong	.20	.07
❑ 420 Bruce Hill	.20	.07
❑ 421 Matt Brock RC	.20	.07
❑ 422 Johnny Johnson	.20	.07
❑ 423 Mark Bortz	.20	.07
❑ 424 Ben Smith	.20	.07
❑ 425 Jeff Cross	.20	.07
❑ 426 Irv Pankey	.20	.07
❑ 427 Hassan Jones	.20	.07
❑ 428 Andre Tippett	.20	.07
❑ 429 Tim Worley	.20	.07
❑ 430 Daniel Stubbs	.20	.07
❑ 431 Max Montoya	.20	.07
❑ 432 Jumbo Elliott	.20	.07
❑ 433 Duane Bickett	.20	.07
❑ 434 Nate Lewis RC	.20	.07
❑ 435 Leonard Russell RC	.75	.30
❑ 436 Hoby Brenner	.20	.07
❑ 437 Ricky Sanders	.20	.07
❑ 438 Pierce Holt	.20	.07
❑ 439 Derrick Fenner	.20	.07
❑ 440 Drew Hill	.20	.07
❑ 441 Will Wolford	.20	.07
❑ 442 Albert Lewis	.20	.07
❑ 443 James Francis	.20	.07
❑ 444 Chris Jacke	.20	.07
❑ 445 Mike Farr	.20	.07
❑ 446 Stephen Braggs	.20	.07
❑ 447 Michael Haynes	.75	.30
❑ 448 Freeman McNeil UER	.20	.07
❑ 449 Kevin Donnalley RC	.20	.07
❑ 450 John Offerdahl	.20	.07
❑ 451 Eric Allen	.20	.07
❑ 452 Keith McKeller	.20	.07
❑ 453 Kevin Greene	.40	.15
❑ 454 Ronnie Lippett	.20	.07
❑ 455 Ray Childress	.20	.07
❑ 456 Mike Saxon	.20	.07
❑ 457 Mark Robinson	.20	.07
❑ 458 Greg Kragen	.20	.07
❑ 459 Steve Jordan	.20	.07
❑ 460 John Johnson RC	.20	.07
❑ 461 Sam Mills	.20	.07
❑ 462 Bo Jackson	1.00	.40
❑ 463 Mark Collins	.20	.07
❑ 464 Percy Snow	.20	.07
❑ 465 Jeff Bostic	.20	.07
❑ 466 Jacob Green	.20	.07
❑ 467 Dexter Carter	.20	.07
❑ 468 Rich Camarillo	.20	.07
❑ 469 Bill Brooks	.20	.07
❑ 470 John Carney	.20	.07
❑ 471 Don Majkowski	.20	.07
❑ 472 Ralph Tamm RC	.20	.07
❑ 473 Fred Barnett	.75	.30
❑ 474 Jim Covert	.20	.07
❑ 475 Kenneth Davis	.20	.07
❑ 476 Jerry Gray	.20	.07
❑ 477 Broderick Thomas	.20	.07
❑ 478 Chris Doleman	.20	.07
❑ 479 Haywood Jeffires	.40	.15
❑ 480 Craig Heyward	.40	.15
❑ 481 Markus Koch	.20	.07
❑ 482 Tim Krumrie	.20	.07
❑ 483 Robert Clark	.20	.07
❑ 484 Mike Rozier	.20	.07
❑ 485 Danny Villa	.20	.07
❑ 486 Gerald Williams	.20	.07
❑ 487 Steve Wisniewski	.20	.07
❑ 488 J.B. Brown	.20	.07
❑ 489 Eugene Robinson	.20	.07
❑ 490 Ottis Anderson	.40	.15
❑ 491 Tony Stargell	.20	.07
❑ 492 Jack Del Rio	.40	.15
❑ 493 Lamar Rogers RC	.20	.07
❑ 494 Ricky Nattiel	.20	.07
❑ 495 Dan Saleaumua	.20	.07
❑ 496 Checklist 1-100	.20	.07
❑ 497 Checklist 101-200	.20	.07
❑ 498 Checklist 201-300	.20	.07

❑ 499 Checklist 301-400 .20 .07
❑ 500 Checklist 401-500 .20 .07

1992 Stadium Club

❑ COMPLETE SET (700) 150.00 75.00
❑ COMP.SERIES 1 (300) 15.00 6.00
❑ COMP.SERIES 2 (300) 15.00 6.00
❑ COMP.HIGH SER.(100) 120.00 60.00
❑ 1 Mark Rypien .10 .02
❑ 2 Carlton Bailey RC .10 .02
❑ 3 Kevin Glover .10 .02
❑ 4 Vance Johnson .10 .02
❑ 5 Jim Jeffcoat .10 .02
❑ 6 Dan Saleaumua .10 .02
❑ 7 Darion Conner .10 .02
❑ 8 Don Maggs .10 .02
❑ 9 Richard Dent .15 .05
❑ 10 Mark Murphy .10 .02
❑ 11 Wesley Carroll .10 .02
❑ 12 Chris Burkett .10 .02
❑ 13 Steve Wallace .10 .02
❑ 14 Jacob Green .10 .02
❑ 15 Roger Ruzek .10 .02
❑ 16 J.B. Brown .10 .02
❑ 17 Dave Meggett .15 .05
❑ 18 D.J. Johnson .10 .02
❑ 19 Rich Gannon .30 .10
❑ 20 Kevin Mack .10 .02
❑ 21A Reggie Cobb ERR .10 .02
❑ 21B Reggie Cobb COR .10 .02
❑ 22 Nate Lewis .10 .02
❑ 23 Doug Smith .10 .02
❑ 24 Irving Fryar .15 .05
❑ 25 Anthony Thompson .10 .02
❑ 26 Duane Bickett .10 .02
❑ 27 Don Majkowski .10 .02
❑ 28 Mark Schlereth RC .10 .02
❑ 29 Melvin Jenkins .10 .02
❑ 30 Michael Haynes .15 .05
❑ 31 Greg Lewis .10 .02
❑ 32 Kenneth Davis .10 .02
❑ 33 Derrick Thomas .30 .10
❑ 34 David Williams .10 .02
❑ 35 Neal Anderson .10 .02
❑ 36 Andre Collins .10 .02
❑ 37 Jesse Solomon .10 .02
❑ 38 Barry Sanders 2.50 1.00
❑ 39 Jeff Gossett .10 .02
❑ 40 Rickey Jackson .10 .02
❑ 41 Ray Berry .10 .02
❑ 42 Leroy Hoard .15 .05
❑ 43 Eric Thomas .10 .02
❑ 44 Brian Washington .10 .02
❑ 45 Pat Terrell .10 .02
❑ 46 Eugene Robinson .10 .02
❑ 47 Luis Sharpe .10 .02
❑ 48 Jerome Brown .10 .02
❑ 49 Mark Collins .10 .02
❑ 50 Johnny Holland .10 .02
❑ 51 Tony Paige .10 .02
❑ 52 Willie Green .10 .02
❑ 53 Steve Atwater .10 .02
❑ 54 Brad Muster .10 .02
❑ 55 Cris Dishman .10 .02
❑ 56 Eddie Anderson .10 .02
❑ 57 Sam Mills .10 .02
❑ 58 Donald Evans .10 .02
❑ 59 Jon Vaughn .10 .02
❑ 60 Marion Butts .10 .02
❑ 61 Rodney Holman .10 .02
❑ 62 Dwayne White RC .10 .02
❑ 63 Martin Mayhew .10 .02
❑ 64 Jonathan Hayes .10 .02
❑ 65 Andre Rison .15 .05
❑ 66 Calvin Williams .15 .05
❑ 67 James Washington .10 .02
❑ 68 Tim Harris .10 .02
❑ 69 Jim Ritcher .10 .02
❑ 70 Johnny Johnson .10 .02
❑ 71 John Offerdahl .10 .02
❑ 72 Herschel Walker .15 .05
❑ 73 Perry Kemp .10 .02
❑ 74 Erik Howard .10 .02
❑ 75 Lamar Lathon .10 .02
❑ 76 Greg Kragen .10 .02
❑ 77 Jay Schroeder .10 .02
❑ 78 Jim Arnold .10 .02
❑ 79 Chris Miller .15 .05
❑ 80 Deron Cherry .10 .02
❑ 81 Jim Harbaugh .30 .10
❑ 82 Gill Fenerty .10 .02
❑ 83 Fred Stokes .10 .02
❑ 84 Roman Phifer .10 .02
❑ 85 Clyde Simmons .10 .02
❑ 86 Vince Newsome .10 .02
❑ 87 Lawrence Dawsey .15 .05
❑ 88 Eddie Brown .10 .02
❑ 89 Greg Montgomery .10 .02
❑ 90 Jeff Lageman .10 .02
❑ 91 Terry Wooden .10 .02
❑ 92 Nate Newton .10 .02
❑ 93 David Richards .10 .02
❑ 94 Derek Russell .10 .02
❑ 95 Steve Jordan .10 .02
❑ 96 Hugh Millen .10 .02
❑ 97 Mark Duper .10 .02
❑ 98 Sean Landeta .10 .02
❑ 99 James Thornton .10 .02
❑ 100 Darrell Green .10 .02
❑ 101 Harris Barton .10 .02
❑ 102 John Alt .10 .02
❑ 103 Mike Farr .10 .02
❑ 104 Bob Golic .10 .02
❑ 105 Gene Atkins .10 .02
❑ 106 Gary Anderson K .10 .02
❑ 107 Norm Johnson .10 .02
❑ 108 Eugene Daniel .10 .02
❑ 109 Kent Hull .10 .02
❑ 110 John Elway 2.50 1.00
❑ 111 Rich Camarillo .10 .02
❑ 112 Charles Wilson .10 .02
❑ 113 Matt Bahr .10 .02
❑ 114 Mark Carrier WR .15 .05
❑ 115 Richmond Webb .10 .02
❑ 116 Charles Mann .10 .02
❑ 117 Tim McGee .10 .02
❑ 118 Wes Hopkins .10 .02
❑ 119 Mo Lewis .10 .02
❑ 120 Warren Moon .30 .10
❑ 121 Damone Johnson .10 .02
❑ 122 Kevin Gogan .10 .02
❑ 123 Joey Browner .10 .02
❑ 124 Tommy Kane .10 .02
❑ 125 Vincent Brown .10 .02
❑ 126 Barry Word .10 .02
❑ 127 Michael Brooks .10 .02
❑ 128 Jumbo Elliott .10 .02
❑ 129 Marcus Allen .30 .10
❑ 130 Tom Waddle .10 .02
❑ 131 Jim Dombrowski .10 .02
❑ 132 Aeneas Williams .15 .05
❑ 133 Clay Matthews .15 .05
❑ 134 Thurman Thomas .30 .10
❑ 135 Dean Biasucci .10 .02
❑ 136 Moe Gardner .10 .02
❑ 137 James Campen .10 .02
❑ 138 Tim Johnson .10 .02
❑ 139 Erik Kramer .15 .05
❑ 140 Keith McCants .10 .02
❑ 141 John Carney .10 .02
❑ 142 Tunch Ilkin .10 .02
❑ 143 Louis Oliver .10 .02
❑ 144 Bill Maas .10 .02
❑ 145 Wendell Davis .10 .02
❑ 146 Pepper Johnson .10 .02
❑ 147 Howie Long .30 .10
❑ 148 Brett Maxie .10 .02
❑ 149 Tony Casillas .10 .02
❑ 150 Michael Carter .10 .02
❑ 151 Byron Evans .10 .02
❑ 152 Lorenzo White .10 .02
❑ 153 Larry Kelm .10 .02
❑ 154 Andy Heck .10 .02
❑ 155 Harry Newsome .10 .02
❑ 156 Chris Singleton .10 .02
❑ 157 Mike Kenn .10 .02
❑ 158 Jeff Faulkner .10 .02
❑ 159 Ken Lanier .10 .02
❑ 160 Darryl Talley .10 .02
❑ 161 Louie Aguiar RC .10 .02
❑ 162 Danny Copeland .10 .02
❑ 163 Kevin Porter .10 .02
❑ 164 Trace Armstrong .10 .02
❑ 165 Dermontti Dawson .10 .02
❑ 166 Fred McAfee RC .10 .02
❑ 167 Ronnie Lott .15 .05
❑ 168 Tony Mandarich .10 .02
❑ 169 Howard Cross .10 .02
❑ 170 Vestee Jackson .10 .02
❑ 171 Jeff Herrod .10 .02
❑ 172 Randy Hilliard RC .10 .02
❑ 173 Robert Wilson .10 .02
❑ 174 Joe Walter RC .10 .02
❑ 175 Chris Spielman .15 .05
❑ 176 Darryl Henley .10 .02
❑ 177 Jay Hilgenberg .10 .02
❑ 178 John Kidd .10 .02
❑ 179 Doug Widell .10 .02
❑ 180 Seth Joyner .10 .02
❑ 181 Nick Bell .10 .02
❑ 182 Don Griffin .10 .02
❑ 183 Johnny Meads .10 .02
❑ 184 Jeff Bostic .10 .02
❑ 185 Johnny Hector .10 .02
❑ 186 Jessie Tuggle .10 .02
❑ 187 Robb Thomas .10 .02
❑ 188 Shane Conlan .10 .02
❑ 189 Michael Zordich RC .10 .02
❑ 190 Emmitt Smith 3.00 1.50
❑ 191 Robert Blackmon .10 .02
❑ 192 Carl Lee .10 .02
❑ 193 Harry Galbreath .10 .02
❑ 194 Ed King .10 .02
❑ 195 Stan Thomas .10 .02
❑ 196 Andre Waters .10 .02
❑ 197 Pat Harlow .10 .02
❑ 198 Zefross Moss .10 .02
❑ 199 Bobby Hebert .10 .02
❑ 200 Doug Riesenberg .10 .02
❑ 201 Mike Croel .10 .02
❑ 202 Jeff Jaeger .10 .02
❑ 203 Gary Plummer .10 .02
❑ 204 Chris Jacke .10 .02
❑ 205 Neil O'Donnell .15 .05
❑ 206 Mark Bortz .10 .02
❑ 207 Tim Barnett .10 .02
❑ 208 Jerry Ball .10 .02
❑ 209 Chip Lohmiller .10 .02
❑ 210 Jim Everett .15 .05
❑ 211 Tim McKyer .10 .02
❑ 212 Aaron Craver .10 .02
❑ 213 John L. Williams .10 .02
❑ 214 Simon Fletcher .10 .02
❑ 215 Walter Reeves .10 .02
❑ 216 Terance Mathis .15 .05
❑ 217 Mike Pitts .10 .02
❑ 218 Bruce Matthews .10 .02
❑ 219 Howard Ballard .10 .02
❑ 220 Leonard Russell .15 .05
❑ 221 Michael Stewart .10 .02
❑ 222 Mike Merriweather .10 .02
❑ 223 Ricky Sanders .10 .02
❑ 224 Ray Horton .10 .02
❑ 225 Michael Jackson .15 .05
❑ 226 Bill Romanowski .10 .02
❑ 227 Steve McMichael UER .15 .05
❑ 228 Chris Martin .10 .02
❑ 229 Tim Green .10 .02
❑ 230 Karl Mecklenburg .10 .02
❑ 231 Felix Wright .10 .02
❑ 232 Charles McRae .10 .02
❑ 233 Pete Stoyanovich .10 .02
❑ 234 Stephen Baker .10 .02

❑	235	Herman Moore	.30	.10
❑	236	Terry McDaniel	.10	.02
❑	237	Dalton Hilliard	.10	.02
❑	238	Gill Byrd	.10	.02
❑	239	Leon Seals	.10	.02
❑	240	Rod Woodson	.30	.10
❑	241	Curtis Duncan	.10	.02
❑	242	Keith Jackson	.15	.05
❑	243	Mark Stepnoski	.15	.05
❑	244	Art Monk	.15	.05
❑	245	Matt Stover	.10	.02
❑	246	John Roper	.10	.02
❑	247	Rodney Hampton	.15	.05
❑	248	Steve Wisniewski	.10	.02
❑	249	Bryan Millard	.10	.02
❑	250	Todd Lyght	.10	.02
❑	251	Marvin Washington	.10	.02
❑	252	Eric Swann	.15	.05
❑	253	Bruce Kozerski	.10	.02
❑	254	Jon Hand	.10	.02
❑	255	Scott Fulhage	.10	.02
❑	256	Chuck Cecil	.10	.02
❑	257	Eric Martin	.10	.02
❑	258	Eric Metcalf	.15	.05
❑	259	T.J. Turner	.10	.02
❑	260	Kirk Lowdermilk	.10	.02
❑	261	Keith McKeller	.10	.02
❑	262	Wymon Henderson	.10	.02
❑	263	David Alexander	.10	.02
❑	264	George Jamison	.10	.02
❑	265	Ken Norton Jr.	.15	.05
❑	266	Jim Lachey	.10	.02
❑	267	Bo Orlando RC	.10	.02
❑	268	Nick Lowery	.10	.02
❑	269	Keith Van Horne	.10	.02
❑	270	Dwight Stone	.10	.02
❑	271	Keith DeLong	.10	.02
❑	272	James Francis	.10	.02
❑	273	Greg McMurtry	.10	.02
❑	274	Ethan Horton	.10	.02
❑	275	Stan Brock	.10	.02
❑	276	Ken Harvey	.10	.02
❑	277	Ronnie Harmon	.10	.02
❑	278	Mike Pritchard	.15	.05
❑	279	Kyle Clifton	.10	.02
❑	280	Anthony Johnson	.15	.05
❑	281	Esera Tuaolo	.10	.02
❑	282	Vernon Turner	.10	.02
❑	283	David Griggs	.10	.02
❑	284	Dino Hackett	.10	.02
❑	285	Carwell Gardner	.10	.02
❑	286	Ron Hall	.10	.02
❑	287	Reggie White	.30	.10
❑	288	Checklist 1-100	.10	.02
❑	289	Checklist 101-200	.10	.02
❑	290	Checklist 201-300	.10	.02
❑	291	Mark Clayton MC	.10	.02
❑	292	Pat Swilling MC	.10	.02
❑	293	Ernest Givins MC	.10	.02
❑	294	Broderick Thomas MC	.10	.02
❑	295	John Friesz MC	.10	.02
❑	296	Cornelius Bennett MC	.10	.02
❑	297	Anthony Carter MC	.15	.05
❑	298	Earnest Byner MC	.10	.02
❑	299	Michael Irvin MC	.30	.10
❑	300	Cortez Kennedy MC	.10	.02
❑	301	Barry Sanders MC	1.50	.60
❑	302	Mike Croel MC	.10	.02
❑	303	Emmitt Smith MC	2.00	.75
❑	304	Leonard Russell MC	.10	.02
❑	305	Neal Anderson MC	.10	.02
❑	306	Derrick Thomas MC	.15	.05
❑	307	Mark Rypien MC	.10	.02
❑	308	Reggie White MC	.15	.05
❑	309	Rod Woodson MC	.15	.05
❑	310	Rodney Hampton MC	.15	.05
❑	311	Carnell Lake	.10	.02
❑	312	Robert Delpino	.10	.02
❑	313	Brian Blades	.15	.05
❑	314	Marc Spindler	.10	.02
❑	315	Scott Norwood	.10	.02
❑	316	Frank Warren	.10	.02
❑	317	David Treadwell	.10	.02
❑	318	Steve Broussard	.10	.02
❑	319	Lorenzo Lynch	.10	.02
❑	320	Ray Agnew	.10	.02
❑	321	Derrick Walker	.10	.02
❑	322	Vinson Smith RC	.10	.02
❑	323	Gary Clark	.30	.10
❑	324	Charles Haley	.15	.05
❑	325	Keith Byars	.10	.02
❑	326	Winston Moss	.10	.02
❑	327	Paul McJulien RC UER	.10	.02
❑	328	Tony Covington	.10	.02
❑	329	Mark Carrier DB	.10	.02
❑	330	Mark Tuinei	.10	.02
❑	331	Tracy Simien RC	.10	.02
❑	332	Jeff Wright	.10	.02
❑	333	Bryan Cox	.15	.05
❑	334	Lonnie Young	.10	.02
❑	335	Clarence Verdin	.10	.02
❑	336	Dan Fike	.10	.02
❑	337	Steve Sewell	.10	.02
❑	338	Gary Zimmerman	.10	.02
❑	339	Barney Bussey	.10	.02
❑	340	William Perry	.15	.05
❑	341	Jeff Hostetler	.15	.05
❑	342	Doug Smith	.10	.02
❑	343	Cleveland Gary	.10	.02
❑	344	Todd Marinovich	.10	.02
❑	345	Rich Moran	.10	.02
❑	346	Tony Woods	.10	.02
❑	347	Vaughan Johnson	.10	.02
❑	348	Marv Cook	.10	.02
❑	349	Pierce Holt	.10	.02
❑	350	Gerald Williams	.10	.02
❑	351	Kevin Butler	.10	.02
❑	352	William White	.10	.02
❑	353	Henry Rolling	.10	.02
❑	354	James Joseph	.10	.02
❑	355	Vinny Testaverde	.15	.05
❑	356	Scott Radecic	.10	.02
❑	357	Lee Johnson	.10	.02
❑	358	Steve Tasker	.15	.05
❑	359	David Lutz	.10	.02
❑	360	Audray McMillian UER	.10	.02
❑	361	Brad Baxter	.10	.02
❑	362	Mark Dennis	.10	.02
❑	363	Erric Pegram	.15	.05
❑	364	Sean Jones	.10	.02
❑	365	William Roberts	.10	.02
❑	366	Steve Young	1.00	.40
❑	367	Joe Jacoby	.10	.02
❑	368	Richard Brown RC	.10	.02
❑	369	Keith Kartz	.10	.02
❑	370	Freddie Joe Nunn	.10	.02
❑	371	Darren Comeaux	.10	.02
❑	372	Larry Brown DB	.10	.02
❑	373	Haywood Jeffires	.15	.05
❑	374	Tom Newberry	.10	.02
❑	375	Steve Bono RC	.30	.10
❑	376	Kevin Ross	.10	.02
❑	377	Kelvin Pritchett	.10	.02
❑	378	Jessie Hester	.10	.02
❑	379	Mitchell Price	.10	.02
❑	380	Barry Foster	.15	.05
❑	381	Reyna Thompson	.10	.02
❑	382	Cris Carter	.75	.30
❑	383	Lemuel Stinson	.10	.02
❑	384	Rod Bernstine	.10	.02
❑	385	James Lofton	.15	.05
❑	386	Kevin Murphy	.10	.02
❑	387	Greg Townsend	.10	.02
❑	388	Edgar Bennett RC	.30	.10
❑	389	Rob Moore	.15	.05
❑	390	Eugene Lockhart	.10	.02
❑	391	Bern Brostek	.10	.02
❑	392	Craig Heyward	.15	.05
❑	393	Ferrell Edmunds	.10	.02
❑	394	John Kasay	.10	.02
❑	395	Jesse Sapolu	.10	.02
❑	396	Jim Breech	.10	.02
❑	397	Neil Smith	.30	.10
❑	398	Bryce Paup	.30	.10
❑	399	Tony Tolbert	.10	.02
❑	400	Bubby Brister	.10	.02
❑	401	Dennis Smith	.10	.02
❑	402	Dan Owens	.10	.02
❑	403	Steve Beuerlein	.15	.05
❑	404	Rick Tuten	.10	.02
❑	405	Eric Allen	.10	.02
❑	406	Eric Hill	.10	.02
❑	407	Don Warren	.10	.02
❑	408	Greg Jackson	.10	.02
❑	409	Chris Doleman	.10	.02
❑	410	Anthony Munoz	.15	.05
❑	411	Michael Young	.10	.02
❑	412	Cornelius Bennett	.15	.05
❑	413	Ray Childress	.10	.02
❑	414	Kevin Call	.10	.02
❑	415	Burt Grossman	.10	.02
❑	416	Scott Miller	.10	.02
❑	417	Tim Newton	.10	.02
❑	418	Robert Young	.10	.02
❑	419	Tommy Vardell RC	.10	.02
❑	420	Michael Walter	.10	.02
❑	421	Chris Port RC	.10	.02
❑	422	Carlton Haselrig RC	.10	.02
❑	423	Rodney Peete	.15	.05
❑	424	Scott Stephen	.10	.02
❑	425	Chris Warren	.30	.10
❑	426	Scott Galbraith RC	.10	.02
❑	427	Fuad Reveiz UER	.10	.02
❑	428	Irv Eatman	.10	.02
❑	429	David Szott	.10	.02
❑	430	Brent Williams	.10	.02
❑	431	Mike Horan	.10	.02
❑	432	Brent Jones	.15	.05
❑	433	Paul Gruber	.10	.02
❑	434	Carlos Huerta	.10	.02
❑	435	Scott Case	.10	.02
❑	436	Greg Davis	.10	.02
❑	437	Ken Clarke	.10	.02
❑	438	Alfred Williams	.10	.02
❑	439	Jim C. Jensen	.10	.02
❑	440	Louis Lipps	.10	.02
❑	441	Larry Roberts	.10	.02
❑	442	James Jones DT	.10	.02
❑	443	Don Mosebar	.10	.02
❑	444	Quinn Early	.15	.05
❑	445	Robert Brown	.10	.02
❑	446	Tom Thayer	.10	.02
❑	447	Michael Irvin	.30	.10
❑	448	Jarrod Bunch	.10	.02
❑	449	Riki Ellison	.10	.02
❑	450	Joe Phillips	.10	.02
❑	451	Ernest Givins	.15	.05
❑	452	Glenn Parker	.10	.02
❑	453	Brett Perriman UER	.30	.10
❑	454	Jayice Pearson RC	.10	.02
❑	455	Mark Jackson	.10	.02
❑	456	Siran Stacy RC	.10	.02
❑	457	Rufus Porter	.10	.02
❑	458	Michael Ball	.10	.02
❑	459	Craig Taylor	.10	.02
❑	460	George Thomas RC	.10	.02
❑	461	Alvin Wright	.10	.02
❑	462	Ron Hallstrom	.10	.02
❑	463	Mike Mooney RC	.10	.02
❑	464	Dexter Carter	.10	.02
❑	465	Marty Carter RC	.10	.02
❑	466	Pat Swilling	.10	.02
❑	467	Mike Golic	.10	.02
❑	468	Reggie Roby	.10	.02
❑	469	Randall McDaniel	.10	.02
❑	470	John Stephens	.10	.02
❑	471	Ricardo McDonald RC	.10	.02
❑	472	Wilber Marshall	.10	.02
❑	473	Jim Sweeney	.10	.02
❑	474	Ernie Jones	.10	.02
❑	475	Bennie Blades	.10	.02
❑	476	Don Beebe	.10	.02
❑	477	Grant Feasel	.10	.02
❑	478	Ernie Mills	.10	.02
❑	479	Tony Jones T	.10	.02
❑	480	Jeff Uhlenhake	.10	.02
❑	481	Gaston Green	.10	.02
❑	482	John Taylor	.15	.05
❑	483	Anthony Smith	.10	.02
❑	484	Tony Bennett	.10	.02
❑	485	David Brandon RC	.10	.02
❑	486	Shawn Jefferson	.10	.02
❑	487	Christian Okoye	.10	.02
❑	488	Leonard Marshall	.10	.02
❑	489	Jay Novacek	.15	.05
❑	490	Harold Green	.10	.02
❑	491	Bubba McDowell	.10	.02
❑	492	Gary Anderson RB	.10	.02
❑	493	Terrell Buckley RC	.10	.02
❑	494	Jamie Dukes RC	.10	.02
❑	495	Morten Andersen	.10	.02

❏ 496	Henry Thomas	.10	.02
❏ 497	Bill Lewis	.10	.02
❏ 498	Jeff Cross	.10	.02
❏ 499	Hardy Nickerson	.15	.05
❏ 500	Henry Ellard	.15	.05
❏ 501	Joe Bowden RC	.10	.02
❏ 502	Brian Noble	.10	.02
❏ 503	Mike Cofer	.10	.02
❏ 504	Jeff Bryant	.10	.02
❏ 505	Lomas Brown	.10	.02
❏ 506	Chip Banks	.10	.02
❏ 507	Keith Traylor	.10	.02
❏ 508	Mark Kelso	.10	.02
❏ 509	Dexter McNabb RC	.10	.02
❏ 510	Gene Chilton RC	.10	.02
❏ 511	George Thornton	.10	.02
❏ 512	Jeff Criswell	.10	.02
❏ 513	Brad Edwards	.10	.02
❏ 514	Ron Heller	.10	.02
❏ 515	Tim Brown	.30	.10
❏ 516	Keith Hamilton RC	.15	.05
❏ 517	Mark Higgs	.10	.02
❏ 518	Tommy Barnhardt	.10	.02
❏ 519	Brian Jordan	.15	.05
❏ 520	Ray Crockett	.10	.02
❏ 521	Karl Wilson	.10	.02
❏ 522	Ricky Reynolds	.10	.02
❏ 523	Max Montoya	.10	.02
❏ 524	David Little	.10	.02
❏ 525	Alonzo Mitz RC	.10	.02
❏ 526	Darryll Lewis	.10	.02
❏ 527	Keith Henderson	.10	.02
❏ 528	LeRoy Butler	.10	.02
❏ 529	Rob Burnett	.10	.02
❏ 530	Chris Chandler	.30	.10
❏ 531	Maury Buford	.10	.02
❏ 532	Mark Ingram	.10	.02
❏ 533	Mike Saxon	.10	.02
❏ 534	Bill Fralic	.10	.02
❏ 535	Craig Patterson RC	.10	.02
❏ 536	John Randle	.15	.05
❏ 537	Dwayne Harper	.10	.02
❏ 538	Chris Hakel RC	.10	.02
❏ 539	Maurice Hurst	.10	.02
❏ 540	Warren Powers UER	.10	.02
❏ 541	Will Wolford	.10	.02
❏ 542	Dennis Gibson	.10	.02
❏ 543	Jackie Slater	.10	.02
❏ 544	Floyd Turner	.10	.02
❏ 545	Guy McIntyre	.10	.02
❏ 546	Eric Green	.10	.02
❏ 547	Rohn Stark	.10	.02
❏ 548	William Fuller	.10	.02
❏ 549	Alvin Harper	.15	.05
❏ 550	Mark Clayton	.15	.05
❏ 551	Natu Tuatagaloa RC	.10	.02
❏ 552	Fred Barnett	.30	.10
❏ 553	Bob Whitfield RC	.10	.02
❏ 554	Courtney Hall	.10	.02
❏ 555	Brian Mitchell	.15	.05
❏ 556	Patrick Hunter	.10	.02
❏ 557	Rick Bryan	.10	.02
❏ 558	Anthony Carter	.15	.05
❏ 559	Jim Wahler	.10	.02
❏ 560	Joe Morris	.10	.02
❏ 561	Tony Zendejas	.10	.02
❏ 562	Mervyn Fernandez	.10	.02
❏ 563	Jamie Williams	.10	.02
❏ 564	Darrell Thompson	.10	.02
❏ 565	Adrian Cooper	.10	.02
❏ 566	Chris Goode	.10	.02
❏ 567	Jeff Davidson RC	.10	.02
❏ 568	James Hasty	.10	.02
❏ 569	Chris Mims RC	.10	.02
❏ 570	Ray Seals RC	.10	.02
❏ 571	Myron Guyton	.10	.02
❏ 572	Todd McNair	.10	.02
❏ 573	Andre Tippett	.10	.02
❏ 574	Kirby Jackson	.10	.02
❏ 575	Mel Gray	.15	.05
❏ 576	Stephone Paige	.10	.02
❏ 577	Scott Davis	.10	.02
❏ 578	John Gesek	.10	.02
❏ 579	Earnest Byner	.10	.02
❏ 580	John Friesz	.15	.05
❏ 581	Al Smith	.10	.02
❏ 582	Flipper Anderson	.10	.02
❏ 583	Amp Lee RC	.10	.02
❏ 584	Greg Lloyd	.15	.05
❏ 585	Cortez Kennedy	.15	.05
❏ 586	Keith Sims	.10	.02
❏ 587	Terry Allen	.30	.10
❏ 588	David Fulcher	.10	.02
❏ 589	Chris Hinton	.10	.02
❏ 590	Tim McDonald	.10	.02
❏ 591	Bruce Armstrong	.10	.02
❏ 592	Sterling Sharpe	.30	.10
❏ 593	Tom Rathman	.10	.02
❏ 594	Bill Brooks	.10	.02
❏ 595	Broderick Thomas	.10	.02
❏ 596	Jim Wilks	.10	.02
❏ 597	Tyrone Braxton UER	.10	.02
❏ 598	Checklist 301-400 UER	.10	.02
❏ 599	Checklist 401-500	.10	.02
❏ 600	Checklist 501-600	.10	.02
❏ 601	Andre Reed MC	.75	.30
❏ 602	Troy Aikman MC	4.00	2.00
❏ 603	Dan Marino MC	6.00	2.50
❏ 604	Randall Cunningham MC	.75	.30
❏ 605	Jim Kelly MC	1.50	.60
❏ 606	Deion Sanders MC	2.00	.75
❏ 607	Junior Seau MC	1.50	.60
❏ 608	Jerry Rice MC	4.00	2.00
❏ 609	Bruce Smith MC	.75	.30
❏ 610	Lawrence Taylor MC	1.50	.60
❏ 611	Todd Collins RC	.50	.20
❏ 612	Ty Detmer	1.50	.60
❏ 613	Browning Nagle	.50	.20
❏ 614	Tony Sacca RC UER	.50	.20
❏ 615	Boomer Esiason	.75	.30
❏ 616	Billy Joe Tolliver	.50	.20
❏ 617	Leslie O'Neal	.75	.30
❏ 618	Mark Wheeler RC	.50	.20
❏ 619	Eric Dickerson	.75	.30
❏ 620	Phil Simms	.75	.30
❏ 621	Troy Vincent RC	.50	.20
❏ 622	Jason Hanson RC	.75	.30
❏ 623	Andre Reed	.75	.30
❏ 624	Russell Maryland	.50	.20
❏ 625	Steve Emtman RC	.50	.20
❏ 626	Sean Gilbert RC	.75	.30
❏ 627	Dana Hall RC	.50	.20
❏ 628	Dan McGwire	.50	.20
❏ 629	Lewis Billups	.50	.20
❏ 630	Darryl Williams RC	.50	.20
❏ 631	Dwayne Sabb RC	.50	.20
❏ 632	Mark Royals	.50	.20
❏ 633	Cary Conklin	.50	.20
❏ 634	Al Toon	.75	.30
❏ 635	Junior Seau	1.50	.60
❏ 636	Greg Skrepenak RC UER 68	.50	.20
❏ 637	Deion Sanders	3.00	1.50
❏ 638	Steve DeOssie	.50	.20
❏ 639	Randall Cunningham	1.50	.60
❏ 640	Jim Kelly	1.50	.60
❏ 641	Michael Brandon RC	.50	.20
❏ 642	Clayton Holmes RC	.50	.20
❏ 643	Webster Slaughter	.50	.20
❏ 644	Ricky Proehl	.50	.20
❏ 645	Jerry Rice	5.00	2.50
❏ 646	Carl Banks	.50	.20
❏ 647	J.J.Birden	.50	.20
❏ 648	Tracy Scroggins RC	.50	.20
❏ 649	Alonzo Spellman RC	.75	.30
❏ 650	Joe Montana	8.00	3.00
❏ 651	Courtney Hawkins RC	.75	.30
❏ 652	Corey Widmer RC	.50	.20
❏ 653	Robert Brooks RC	4.00	1.50
❏ 654	Darren Woodson RC	1.50	.60
❏ 655	Derrick Fenner	.50	.20
❏ 656	Steve Christie	.50	.20
❏ 657	Chester McGlockton RC	.75	.30
❏ 658	Steve Israel RC	.50	.20
❏ 659	Robert Harris RC	.50	.20
❏ 660	Dan Marino	8.00	3.00
❏ 661	Ed McCaffrey	5.00	2.00
❏ 662	Johnny Mitchell RC	.50	.20
❏ 663	Timm Rosenbach	.50	.20
❏ 664	Anthony Miller	.75	.30
❏ 665	Merril Hoge	.50	.20
❏ 666	Eugene Chung RC	.50	.20
❏ 667	Rueben Mayes	.50	.20
❏ 668	Martin Bayless	.50	.20
❏ 669	Ashley Ambrose RC	1.50	.60
❏ 670	Michael Cofer UER	.50	.20
❏ 671	Shane Dronett RC	.50	.20
❏ 672	Bernie Kosar	.75	.30
❏ 673	Mike Singletary	.75	.30
❏ 674	Mike Lodish RC	.50	.20
❏ 675	Phillippi Sparks RC	.50	.20
❏ 676	Joel Steed RC	.50	.20
❏ 677	Kevin Fagan	.50	.20
❏ 678	Randal Hill	.50	.20
❏ 679	Ken O'Brien	.50	.20
❏ 680	Lawrence Taylor	1.50	.60
❏ 681	Harvey Williams	1.50	.60
❏ 682	Quentin Coryatt RC	.50	.20
❏ 683	Brett Favre	100.00	60.00
❏ 684	Robert Jones RC	.50	.20
❏ 685	Michael Dean Perry	.75	.30
❏ 686	Bruce Smith	1.50	.60
❏ 687	Troy Auzenne RC	.50	.20
❏ 688	Thomas McLemore RC	.50	.20
❏ 689	Dale Carter RC	.75	.30
❏ 690	Marc Boutte RC	.50	.20
❏ 691	Jeff George	1.50	.60
❏ 692	Dion Lambert RC	.50	.20
❏ 693	Vaughn Dunbar RC	.50	.20
❏ 694	Derek Brown TE RC	.50	.20
❏ 695	Troy Aikman	5.00	2.50
❏ 696	John Fina RC	.50	.20
❏ 697	Kevin Smith RC DB	.50	.20
❏ 698	Corey Miller RC	.50	.20
❏ 699	Lance Olberding RC	.50	.20
❏ 700	Checklist 601-700 UER	.50	.20
❏ P1	Promo Sheet Natl.	10.00	4.00
❏ P2	Promo Sheet Diam.Day	12.00	5.00

1993 Stadium Club

❏	COMPLETE SET (550)	40.00	15.00
❏	COMP.SERIES 1 (250)	25.00	10.00
❏	COMP.SERIES 2 (250)	15.00	6.00
❏	COMP.HIGH SERIES (50)	8.00	4.00
❏	COMP.HIGH FACT.SET (51)	12.00	5.00
❏ 1	Sterling Sharpe	.20	.07
❏ 2	Chris Burkett	.10	.02
❏ 3	Santana Dotson	.20	.07
❏ 4	Michael Jackson	.20	.07
❏ 5	Neal Anderson	.10	.02
❏ 6	Bryan Cox	.10	.02
❏ 7	Dennis Gibson	.10	.02
❏ 8	Jeff Graham	.20	.07
❏ 9	Roger Ruzek	.10	.02
❏ 10	Duane Bickett	.10	.02
❏ 11	Charles Mann	.10	.02
❏ 12	Tommy Maddox	.40	.15
❏ 13	Vaughn Dunbar	.10	.02
❏ 14	Gary Plummer	.10	.02
❏ 15	Chris Miller	.20	.07
❏ 16	Chris Warren	.20	.07
❏ 17	Alvin Harper	.20	.07
❏ 18	Eric Dickerson	.20	.07
❏ 19	Mike Jones	.10	.02
❏ 20	Ernest Givins	.20	.07
❏ 21	Natrone Means RC	.40	.15
❏ 22	Doug Riesenberg	.10	.02
❏ 23	Barry Word	.10	.02
❏ 24	Sean Salisbury	.10	.02
❏ 25	Derrick Fenner	.10	.02
❏ 26	David Howard	.10	.02
❏ 27	Mark Kelso	.10	.02
❏ 28	Todd Lyght	.10	.02
❏ 29	Dana Hall	.10	.02

Card	Player	Price	Low
❑ 30	Eric Metcalf	.20	.07
❑ 31	Jason Hanson	.10	.02
❑ 32	Dwight Stone	.10	.02
❑ 33	Johnny Mitchell	.10	.02
❑ 34	Reggie Roby	.10	.02
❑ 35	Terrell Buckley	.10	.02
❑ 36	Steve McMichael	.20	.07
❑ 37	Marty Carter	.10	.02
❑ 38	Seth Joyner	.10	.02
❑ 39	Rohn Stark	.10	.02
❑ 40	Eric Curry RC	.10	.02
❑ 41	Tommy Barnhardt	.10	.02
❑ 42	Karl Mecklenburg	.10	.02
❑ 43	Darion Conner	.10	.02
❑ 44	Ronnie Harmon	.10	.02
❑ 45	Cortez Kennedy	.20	.07
❑ 46	Tim Brown	.40	.15
❑ 47	Bill Lewis	.10	.02
❑ 48	Randall McDaniel	.10	.02
❑ 49	Curtis Duncan	.10	.02
❑ 50	Troy Aikman	1.50	.60
❑ 51	David Klingler	.10	.02
❑ 52	Brent Jones	.20	.07
❑ 53	Dave Krieg	.20	.07
❑ 54	Bruce Smith	.40	.15
❑ 55	Vincent Brown	.10	.02
❑ 56	O.J.McDuffie RC	.40	.15
❑ 57	Cleveland Gary	.10	.02
❑ 58	Larry Centers RC	.40	.15
❑ 59	Pepper Johnson	.10	.02
❑ 60	Dan Marino	3.00	1.25
❑ 61	Robert Porcher	.10	.02
❑ 62	Jim Harbaugh	.40	.15
❑ 63	Sam Mills	.10	.02
❑ 64	Gary Anderson RB	.10	.02
❑ 65	Neil O'Donnell	.20	.07
❑ 66	Keith Byars	.10	.02
❑ 67	Jeff Herrod	.10	.02
❑ 68	Marion Butts	.10	.02
❑ 69	Terry McDaniel	.10	.02
❑ 70	John Elway	3.00	1.25
❑ 71	Steve Broussard	.10	.02
❑ 72	Kelvin Martin	.10	.02
❑ 73	Tom Carter RC	.20	.07
❑ 74	Bryce Paup	.20	.07
❑ 75	Jim Kelly UER	.20	.07
❑ 76	Bill Romanowski	.10	.02
❑ 77	Andre Collins	.10	.02
❑ 78	Mike Farr	.10	.02
❑ 79	Henry Ellard	.20	.07
❑ 80	Dale Carter	.10	.02
❑ 81	Johnny Bailey	.10	.02
❑ 82	Garrison Hearst RC	1.50	.60
❑ 83	Brent Williams	.10	.02
❑ 84	Ricardo McDonald	.10	.02
❑ 85	Emmitt Smith	3.00	1.50
❑ 86	Vai Sikahema	.10	.02
❑ 87	Jackie Harris	.10	.02
❑ 88	Alonzo Spellman	.10	.02
❑ 89	Mark Wheeler	.10	.02
❑ 90	Dalton Hilliard	.10	.02
❑ 91	Mark Higgs	.10	.02
❑ 92	Aaron Wallace	.10	.02
❑ 93	Earnest Byner	.10	.02
❑ 94	Stanley Richard	.10	.02
❑ 95	Cris Carter	.40	.15
❑ 96	Bobby Houston RC	.10	.02
❑ 97	Craig Heyward	.20	.07
❑ 98	Bernie Kosar	.20	.07
❑ 99	Mike Croel	.10	.02
❑ 100	Deion Sanders	1.00	.40
❑ 101	Warren Moon	.20	.07
❑ 102	Christian Okoye	.10	.02
❑ 103	Ricky Watters	.40	.15
❑ 104	Eric Swann	.20	.07
❑ 105	Rodney Hampton	.20	.07
❑ 106	Daryl Johnston	.20	.07
❑ 107	Andre Reed	.20	.07
❑ 108	Jerome Bettis RC	8.00	4.00
❑ 109	Eugene Daniel	.10	.02
❑ 110	Leonard Russell	.20	.07
❑ 111	Darryl Williams	.10	.02
❑ 112	Rod Woodson	.40	.15
❑ 113	Boomer Esiason	.20	.07
❑ 114	James Hasty	.10	.02
❑ 115	Marc Boutte	.10	.02
❑ 116	Tom Waddle	.10	.02
❑ 117	Lawrence Dawsey	.10	.02
❑ 118	Mark Collins	.10	.02
❑ 119	Willie Gault	.10	.02
❑ 120	Barry Sanders	2.50	1.00
❑ 121	Leroy Hoard	.20	.07
❑ 122	Anthony Munoz	.20	.07
❑ 123	Jesse Sapolu	.10	.02
❑ 124	Art Monk	.20	.07
❑ 125	Randal Hill	.10	.02
❑ 126	John Offerdahl	.10	.02
❑ 127	Carlos Jenkins	.10	.02
❑ 128	Al Smith	.10	.02
❑ 129	Michael Irvin	.40	.15
❑ 130	Kenneth Davis	.10	.02
❑ 131	Curtis Conway RC	.75	.30
❑ 132	Steve Atwater	.10	.02
❑ 133	Neil Smith	.40	.15
❑ 134	Steve Everitt RC	.10	.02
❑ 135	Chris Mims	.10	.02
❑ 136	Rickey Jackson	.10	.02
❑ 137	Edgar Bennett	.40	.15
❑ 138	Mike Pritchard	.20	.07
❑ 139	Richard Dent	.20	.07
❑ 140	Barry Foster	.20	.07
❑ 141	Eugene Robinson	.10	.02
❑ 142	Jackie Slater	.10	.02
❑ 143	Paul Gruber	.10	.02
❑ 144	Rob Moore	.20	.07
❑ 145	Robert Smith RC	2.50	1.00
❑ 146	Lorenzo White	.10	.02
❑ 147	Tommy Vardell	.10	.02
❑ 148	Dave Meggett	.10	.02
❑ 149	Vince Workman	.10	.02
❑ 150	Terry Allen	.40	.15
❑ 151	Howie Long	.40	.15
❑ 152	Charles Haley	.20	.07
❑ 153	Pete Metzelaars	.10	.02
❑ 154	John Copeland RC	.20	.07
❑ 155	Aeneas Williams	.10	.02
❑ 156	Ricky Sanders	.10	.02
❑ 157	Andre Ware	.10	.02
❑ 158	Tony Paige	.10	.02
❑ 159	Jerome Henderson	.10	.02
❑ 160	Harold Green	.10	.02
❑ 161	Wymon Henderson	.10	.02
❑ 162	Andre Rison	.20	.07
❑ 163	Donald Evans	.10	.02
❑ 164	Todd Scott	.10	.02
❑ 165	Steve Emtman	.10	.02
❑ 166	William Fuller	.10	.02
❑ 167	Michael Dean Perry	.20	.07
❑ 168	Randall Cunningham	.40	.15
❑ 169	Toi Cook	.10	.02
❑ 170	Browning Nagle	.10	.02
❑ 171	Darryl Henley	.10	.02
❑ 172	George Teague RC	.20	.07
❑ 173	Derrick Thomas	.40	.15
❑ 174	Jay Novacek	.20	.07
❑ 175	Mark Carrier DB	.10	.02
❑ 176	Kevin Fagan	.10	.02
❑ 177	Nate Lewis	.10	.02
❑ 178	Courtney Hawkins	.10	.02
❑ 179	Robert Blackmon	.10	.02
❑ 180	Rick Mirer RC	.40	.15
❑ 181	Mike Lodish	.10	.02
❑ 182	Jarrod Bunch	.10	.02
❑ 183	Anthony Smith	.10	.02
❑ 184	Brian Noble	.10	.02
❑ 185	Eric Bieniemy	.10	.02
❑ 186	Keith Jackson	.20	.07
❑ 187	Eric Martin	.10	.02
❑ 188	Vance Johnson	.10	.02
❑ 189	Kevin Mack	.10	.02
❑ 190	Rich Camarillo	.10	.02
❑ 191	Ashley Ambrose	.10	.02
❑ 192	Ray Childress	.10	.02
❑ 193	Jim Arnold	.10	.02
❑ 194	Ricky Ervins	.10	.02
❑ 195	Gary Anderson K	.10	.02
❑ 196	Eric Allen	.10	.02
❑ 197	Roger Craig	.20	.07
❑ 198	Jon Vaughn	.10	.02
❑ 199	Tim McDonald	.10	.02
❑ 200	Broderick Thomas	.10	.02
❑ 201	Jessie Tuggle	.10	.02
❑ 202	Alonzo Mitz	.10	.02
❑ 203	Harvey Williams	.20	.07
❑ 204	Russell Maryland	.10	.02
❑ 205	Marvin Washington	.10	.02
❑ 206	Jim Everett	.20	.07
❑ 207	Trace Armstrong	.10	.02
❑ 208	Steve Young	1.50	.60
❑ 209	Tony Woods	.10	.02
❑ 210	Brett Favre	4.00	2.00
❑ 211	Nate Odomes	.10	.02
❑ 212	Ricky Proehl	.10	.02
❑ 213	Jim Dombrowski	.10	.02
❑ 214	Anthony Carter	.20	.07
❑ 215	Tracy Simien	.10	.02
❑ 216	Clay Matthews	.20	.07
❑ 217	Patrick Bates RC	.10	.02
❑ 218	Jeff George	.40	.15
❑ 219	David Fulcher	.10	.02
❑ 220	Phil Simms	.20	.07
❑ 221	Eugene Chung	.10	.02
❑ 222	Reggie Cobb	.10	.02
❑ 223	Jim Sweeney	.10	.02
❑ 224	Greg Lloyd	.20	.07
❑ 225	Sean Jones	.10	.02
❑ 226	Marvin Jones RC	.10	.02
❑ 227	Bill Brooks	.10	.02
❑ 228	Moe Gardner	.10	.02
❑ 229	Louis Oliver	.10	.02
❑ 230	Flipper Anderson	.10	.02
❑ 231	Marc Spindler	.10	.02
❑ 232	Jerry Rice	2.00	.75
❑ 233	Chip Lohmiller	.10	.02
❑ 234	Nolan Harrison	.10	.02
❑ 235	Heath Sherman	.10	.02
❑ 236	Reyna Thompson	.10	.02
❑ 237	Derrick Walker	.10	.02
❑ 238	Rufus Porter	.10	.02
❑ 239	Checklist 1-125	.10	.02
❑ 240	Checklist 126-250	.10	.02
❑ 241	John Elway MC	1.50	.60
❑ 242	Troy Aikman MC	.75	.30
❑ 243	Steve Emtman MC	.10	.02
❑ 244	Ricky Watters MC	.20	.07
❑ 245	Barry Foster MC	.10	.02
❑ 246	Dan Marino MC	1.50	.60
❑ 247	Reggie White MC	.20	.07
❑ 248	Thurman Thomas MC	.20	.07
❑ 249	Broderick Thomas MC	.10	.02
❑ 250	Joe Montana MC	1.50	.60
❑ 251	Tim Goad	.10	.02
❑ 252	Joe Nash	.10	.02
❑ 253	Anthony Johnson	.20	.07
❑ 254	Carl Pickens	.20	.07
❑ 255	Steve Beuerlein	.20	.07
❑ 256	Anthony Newman	.10	.02
❑ 257	Corey Miller	.10	.02
❑ 258	Steve DeBerg	.10	.02
❑ 259	Johnny Holland	.10	.02
❑ 260	Jerry Ball	.10	.02
❑ 261	Siupeli Malamala RC	.10	.02
❑ 262	Steve Wisniewski	.10	.02
❑ 263	Kelvin Pritchett	.10	.02
❑ 264	Chris Gardocki	.10	.02
❑ 265	Henry Thomas	.10	.02
❑ 266	Arthur Marshall RC	.10	.02
❑ 267	Quinn Early	.20	.07
❑ 268	Jonathan Hayes	.10	.02
❑ 269	Erric Pegram	.20	.07
❑ 270	Clyde Simmons	.10	.02
❑ 271	Eric Moten	.10	.02
❑ 272	Brian Mitchell	.20	.07
❑ 273	Adrian Cooper	.10	.02
❑ 274	Gaston Green	.10	.02
❑ 275	John Taylor	.20	.07
❑ 276	Jeff Uhlenhake	.10	.02
❑ 277	Phil Hansen	.10	.02
❑ 278A	Kev.Williams RC WR ERR	.40	.15
❑ 278B	Kev.Williams RC WR COR	.40	.15
❑ 279	Robert Massey	.10	.02
❑ 280A	Drew Bledsoe RC ERR	10.00	4.00
❑ 280B	Drew Bledsoe RC COR	5.00	2.00
❑ 281	Walter Reeves	.10	.02
❑ 282A	Carlton Gray RC ERR	.25	.08
❑ 282B	Carlton Gray RC COR	.15	.05
❑ 283	Derek Brown TE	.10	.02
❑ 284	Martin Mayhew	.10	.02
❑ 285	Sean Gilbert	.20	.07
❑ 286	Jessie Hester	.10	.02
❑ 287	Mark Clayton	.10	.02

❑ 288 Blair Thomas .10 .02
❑ 289 J.J. Birden .10 .02
❑ 290 Shannon Sharpe .40 .15
❑ 291 Richard Fain RC .10 .02
❑ 292 Gene Atkins .10 .02
❑ 293 Burt Grossman .10 .02
❑ 294 Chris Doleman .10 .02
❑ 295 Pat Swilling .10 .02
❑ 296 Mike Kenn .10 .02
❑ 297 Merril Hoge .10 .02
❑ 298 Don Mosebar .10 .02
❑ 299 Kevin Smith .20 .07
❑ 300 Darrell Green .10 .02
❑ 301A Dan Footman RC ERR .25 .08
❑ 301B Dan Footman RC COR .15 .05
❑ 302 Vestee Jackson .10 .02
❑ 303 Carwell Gardner .10 .02
❑ 304 Amp Lee .10 .02
❑ 305 Bruce Matthews .10 .02
❑ 306 Antone Davis .10 .02
❑ 307 Dean Biasucci .10 .02
❑ 308 Maurice Hurst .10 .02
❑ 309 John Kasay .10 .02
❑ 310 Lawrence Taylor .20 .07
❑ 311 Ken Harvey .10 .02
❑ 312 Willie Davis .20 .07
❑ 313 Tony Bennett .10 .02
❑ 314 Jay Schroeder .10 .02
❑ 315 Darren Perry .10 .02
❑ 316A Troy Drayton RC ERR .25 .08
❑ 316B Troy Drayton RC COR .15 .05
❑ 317A Dan Williams RC ERR .25 .08
❑ 317B Dan Williams RC COR .15 .05
❑ 318 Michael Haynes .20 .07
❑ 319 Renaldo Turnbull .10 .02
❑ 320 Junior Seau .40 .15
❑ 321 Ray Crockett .10 .02
❑ 322 Will Furrer .10 .02
❑ 323 Byron Evans .10 .02
❑ 324 Jim McMahon .20 .07
❑ 325 Robert Jones .10 .02
❑ 326 Eric Davis .10 .02
❑ 327 Jeff Cross .10 .02
❑ 328 Kyle Clifton .10 .02
❑ 329 Haywood Jeffires .20 .07
❑ 330 Jeff Hostetler .20 .07
❑ 331 Darryl Talley .10 .02
❑ 332 Keith McCants .10 .02
❑ 333 Mo Lewis .10 .02
❑ 334 Matt Stover .10 .02
❑ 335 Ferrell Edmunds .10 .02
❑ 336 Matt Brock .10 .02
❑ 337 Ernie Mills .10 .02
❑ 338 Shane Dronett .10 .02
❑ 339 Brad Muster .10 .02
❑ 340 Jesse Solomon .10 .02
❑ 341 John Randle .20 .07
❑ 342 Chris Spielman .20 .07
❑ 343 David Whitmore .10 .02
❑ 344 Glenn Parker .10 .02
❑ 345 Marco Coleman .10 .02
❑ 346 Kenneth Gant .10 .02
❑ 347 Cris Dishman .10 .02
❑ 348 Kenny Walker .10 .02
❑ 349A Roosevelt Potts RC ERR .25 .08
❑ 349B Roosevelt Potts RC COR .15 .05
❑ 350 Reggie White .40 .15
❑ 351 Gerald Robinson .10 .02
❑ 352 Mark Rypien .10 .02
❑ 353 Stan Humphries .20 .07
❑ 354 Chris Singleton .10 .02
❑ 355 Herschel Walker .20 .07
❑ 356 Ron Hall .10 .02
❑ 357 Ethan Horton .10 .02
❑ 358 Anthony Pleasant .10 .02
❑ 359A Thomas Smith RC ERR .25 .08
❑ 359B Thomas Smith RC COR .15 .05
❑ 360 Audray McMillian .10 .02
❑ 361 D.J. Johnson .10 .02
❑ 362 Ron Heller .10 .02
❑ 363 Bern Brostek .10 .02
❑ 364 Ronnie Lott .20 .07
❑ 365 Reggie Johnson .10 .02
❑ 366 Lin Elliott .10 .02
❑ 367 Lemuel Stinson .10 .02
❑ 368 William White .10 .02
❑ 369 Ernie Jones .10 .02
❑ 370 Tom Rathman .10 .02
❑ 371 Tommy Kane .10 .02
❑ 372 David Brandon .10 .02
❑ 373 Lee Johnson .10 .02
❑ 374 Wade Wilson .10 .02
❑ 375 Nick Lowery .10 .02
❑ 376 Bubba McDowell .10 .02
❑ 377A Wayne Simmons RC ERR .25 .08
❑ 377B Wayne Simmons RC COR .15 .05
❑ 378 Calvin Williams .20 .07
❑ 379 Courtney Hall .10 .02
❑ 380 Troy Vincent .10 .02
❑ 381 Tim McGee .10 .02
❑ 382 Russell Freeman RC .10 .02
❑ 383 Steve Tasker .20 .07
❑ 384A Michael Strahan RC ERR 2.00 .75
❑ 384B Michael Strahan RC COR 2.00 .75
❑ 385 Greg Skrepenak .10 .02
❑ 386 Jake Reed .20 .07
❑ 387 Pete Stoyanovich .10 .02
❑ 388 Levon Kirkland .10 .02
❑ 389 Mel Gray .20 .07
❑ 390 Brian Washington .10 .02
❑ 391 Don Griffin .10 .02
❑ 392 Desmond Howard .20 .07
❑ 393 Luis Sharpe .10 .02
❑ 394 Mike Johnson .10 .02
❑ 395 Andre Tippett .10 .02
❑ 396 Donnell Woolford .10 .02
❑ 397A Demetrius DuBose RC ERR .25 .08
❑ 397B Demetrius DuBose RC COR .15 .05
❑ 398 Pat Terrell .10 .02
❑ 399 Todd McNair .10 .02
❑ 400 Ken Norton .20 .07
❑ 401 Keith Hamilton .10 .02
❑ 402 Andy Heck .10 .02
❑ 403 Jeff Gossett .10 .02
❑ 404 Dexter McNabb .10 .02
❑ 405 Richmond Webb .10 .02
❑ 406 Irving Fryar .20 .07
❑ 407 Brian Hansen .10 .02
❑ 408 David Little .10 .02
❑ 409A Glyn Milburn RC ERR .40 .15
❑ 409B Glyn Milburn RC COR .20 .07
❑ 410 Doug Dawson .10 .02
❑ 411 Scott Mersereau .10 .02
❑ 412 Don Beebe .10 .02
❑ 413 Vaughan Johnson .10 .02
❑ 414 Jack Del Rio .10 .02
❑ 415A Darrien Gordon RC ERR .25 .08
❑ 415B Darrien Gordon RC COR .15 .05
❑ 416 Mark Schlereth .10 .02
❑ 417 Lomas Brown .10 .02
❑ 418 William Thomas .10 .02
❑ 419 James Francis .10 .02
❑ 420 Quentin Coryatt .20 .07
❑ 421 Tyji Armstrong .10 .02
❑ 422 Hugh Millen .10 .02
❑ 423 Adrian White RC .10 .02
❑ 424 Eddie Anderson .10 .02
❑ 425 Mark Ingram .10 .02
❑ 426 Ken O'Brien .10 .02
❑ 427 Simon Fletcher .10 .02
❑ 428 Tim McKyer .10 .02
❑ 429 Leonard Marshall .10 .02
❑ 430 Eric Green .10 .02
❑ 431 Leonard Harris .10 .02
❑ 432 Darin Jordan RC .10 .02
❑ 433 Erik Howard .10 .02
❑ 434 David Lang .10 .02
❑ 435 Eric Turner .10 .02
❑ 436 Michael Cofer .10 .02
❑ 437 Jeff Bryant .10 .02
❑ 438 Charles McRae .10 .02
❑ 439 Henry Jones .10 .02
❑ 440 Joe Montana 3.00 1.25
❑ 441 Morten Andersen .10 .02
❑ 442 Jeff Jaeger .10 .02
❑ 443 Leslie O'Neal .20 .07
❑ 444 LeRoy Butler .10 .02
❑ 445 Steve Jordan .10 .02
❑ 446 Brad Edwards .10 .02
❑ 447 J.B. Brown .10 .02
❑ 448 Kerry Cash .10 .02
❑ 449 Mark Tuinei .10 .02
❑ 450 Rodney Peete .10 .02
❑ 451 Sheldon White .10 .02
❑ 452 Wesley Carroll .10 .02
❑ 453 Brad Baxter .10 .02
❑ 454 Mike Pitts .10 .02
❑ 455 Greg Montgomery .10 .02
❑ 456 Kenny Davidson .10 .02
❑ 457 Scott Fulhage .10 .02
❑ 458 Greg Townsend .10 .02
❑ 459 Rod Bernstine .10 .02
❑ 460 Gary Clark .20 .07
❑ 461 Hardy Nickerson .20 .07
❑ 462 Sean Landeta .10 .02
❑ 463 Rob Burnett .10 .02
❑ 464 Fred Barnett .20 .07
❑ 465 John L. Williams .10 .02
❑ 466 Anthony Miller .20 .07
❑ 467 Roman Phifer .10 .02
❑ 468 Rich Moran .10 .02
❑ 469A Willie Roaf RC ERR .25 .08
❑ 469B Willie Roaf RC COR .15 .05
❑ 470 William Perry .20 .07
❑ 471 Marcus Allen .40 .15
❑ 472 Carl Lee .10 .02
❑ 473 Kurt Gouveia .10 .02
❑ 474 Jarvis Williams .10 .02
❑ 475 Alfred Williams .10 .02
❑ 476 Mark Stepnoski .10 .02
❑ 477 Steve Wallace .10 .02
❑ 478 Pat Harlow .10 .02
❑ 479 Chip Banks .10 .02
❑ 480 Cornelius Bennett .20 .07
❑ 481A Ryan McNeil RC ERR .15 .05
❑ 481B Ryan McNeil RC COR .40 .15
❑ 482 Norm Johnson .10 .02
❑ 483 Dermontti Dawson .10 .02
❑ 484 Dwayne White .10 .02
❑ 485 Derek Russell .10 .02
❑ 486 Lionel Washington .10 .02
❑ 487 Eric Hill .10 .02
❑ 488 Micheal Barrow RC .40 .15
❑ 489 Checklist 251-375 UER .10 .02
❑ 490 Checklist 376-500 UER .10 .02
❑ 491 Emmitt Smith MC 1.50 .60
❑ 492 Derrick Thomas MC .20 .07
❑ 493 Deion Sanders MC .40 .15
❑ 494 Randall Cunningham MC .20 .07
❑ 495 Sterling Sharpe MC .20 .07
❑ 496 Barry Sanders MC 1.25 .50
❑ 497 Thurman Thomas MC .20 .07
❑ 498 Brett Favre MC 2.00 .75
❑ 499 Vaughan Johnson MC .10 .02
❑ 500 Steve Young MC .75 .30
❑ 501 Marvin Jones MC .10 .02
❑ 502 Reggie Brooks RC MC .20 .07
❑ 503 Eric Curry MC .10 .02
❑ 504 Drew Bledsoe MC 2.00 .75
❑ 505 Glyn Milburn MC .20 .07
❑ 506 Jerome Bettis MC 4.00 1.50
❑ 507 Robert Smith MC 1.00 .40
❑ 508 Dana Stubblefield RC MC .40 .15
❑ 509 Tom Carter MC .20 .07
❑ 510 Rick Mirer MC .40 .15
❑ 511 Russell Copeland RC .20 .07
❑ 512 Deon Figures RC .10 .02
❑ 513 Tony McGee RC .20 .07
❑ 514 Derrick Lassic RC .10 .02
❑ 515 Everett Lindsay RC .10 .02
❑ 516 Derek Brown RC RBK .10 .02
❑ 517 Harold Alexander RC .10 .02
❑ 518 Tom Scott OL RC .10 .02
❑ 519 Elvis Grbac RC 3.00 1.25
❑ 520 Terry Kirby RC .40 .15
❑ 521 Doug Pelfrey RC .10 .02
❑ 522 Horace Copeland RC .20 .07
❑ 523 Irv Smith RC .10 .02
❑ 524 Lincoln Kennedy RC .10 .02
❑ 525 Jason Elam RC .40 .15
❑ 526 Qadry Ismail RC .40 .15
❑ 527 Artie Smith RC .10 .02
❑ 528 Tyrone Hughes RC .20 .07
❑ 529 Lance Gunn RC .10 .02
❑ 530 Vincent Brisby RC .40 .15
❑ 531 Patrick Robinson RC .10 .02
❑ 532 Rocket Ismail .20 .07
❑ 533 Willie Beamon RC .10 .02
❑ 534 Vaughn Hebron RC .10 .02
❑ 535 Darren Drozdov RC .40 .15
❑ 536 James Jett RC .40 .15

❑ 537 Michael Bates RC	.10	.02
❑ 538 Tom Rouen RC	.10	.02
❑ 539 Michael Husted RC	.10	.02
❑ 540 Greg Robinson RC	.10	.02
❑ 541 Carl Banks	.10	.02
❑ 542 Kevin Greene	.20	.07
❑ 543 Scott Mitchell	.40	.15
❑ 544 Michael Brooks	.10	.02
❑ 545 Shane Conlan	.10	.02
❑ 546 Vinny Testaverde	.20	.07
❑ 547 Robert Delpino	.10	.02
❑ 548 Bill Fralic	.10	.02
❑ 549 Carlton Bailey	.10	.02
❑ 550 Johnny Johnson	.10	.02
❑ NNO Jerry Rice RB	10.00	4.00
❑ P1 Promo Sheet	5.00	2.00

1994 Stadium Club

❑ COMPLETE SET (630)	60.00	25.00
❑ COMP.SERIES 1 (270)	25.00	10.00
❑ COMP.SERIES 2 (270)	25.00	10.00
❑ COMP.HIGH SERIES (90)	10.00	5.00
❑ 1 Dan Wilkinson RC	.20	.07
❑ 2 Chip Lohmiller	.10	.02
❑ 3 Roosevelt Potts	.10	.02
❑ 4 Martin Mayhew	.10	.02
❑ 5 Shane Conlan	.10	.02
❑ 6 Sam Adams RC	.20	.07
❑ 7 Mike Kenn	.10	.02
❑ 8 Tim Goad	.10	.02
❑ 9 Tony Jones T	.10	.02
❑ 10 Ronald Moore	.10	.02
❑ 11 Mark Bortz	.10	.02
❑ 12 Darren Carrington	.10	.02
❑ 13 Eric Martin	.10	.02
❑ 14 Eric Allen	.10	.02
❑ 15 Aaron Glenn RC	.40	.15
❑ 16 Bryan Cox	.10	.02
❑ 17 Levon Kirkland	.10	.02
❑ 18 Qadry Ismail	.40	.15
❑ 19 Shane Dronett	.10	.02
❑ 20 Chris Spielman	.20	.07
❑ 21 Rob Fredrickson RC	.20	.07
❑ 22 Wayne Simmons	.10	.02
❑ 23 Glenn Montgomery	.10	.02
❑ 24 Jason Sehorn RC	.60	.25
❑ 25 Nick Lowery	.10	.02
❑ 26 Dennis Brown	.10	.02
❑ 27 Kenneth Davis	.10	.02
❑ 28 Shante Carver RC	.10	.02
❑ 29 Ryan Yarborough RC	.10	.02
❑ 30 Cortez Kennedy	.20	.07
❑ 31 Anthony Pleasant	.10	.02
❑ 32 Jessie Tuggle	.10	.02
❑ 33 Herschel Walker	.20	.07
❑ 34 Andre Collins	.10	.02
❑ 35 William Floyd RC	.40	.15
❑ 36 Harold Green	.10	.02
❑ 37 Courtney Hawkins	.10	.02
❑ 38 Curtis Conway	.40	.15
❑ 39 Ben Coates	.20	.07
❑ 40 Natrone Means	.40	.15
❑ 41 Eric Hill	.10	.02
❑ 42 Keith Kartz	.10	.02
❑ 43 Alexander Wright	.10	.02
❑ 44 Willie Roaf	.10	.02
❑ 45 Vencie Glenn	.10	.02
❑ 46 Ronnie Lott	.20	.07
❑ 47 George Koonce	.10	.02
❑ 48 Rod Woodson	.20	.07
❑ 49 Tim Grunhard	.10	.02
❑ 50 Cody Carlson	.10	.02
❑ 51 Bryant Young RC	.40	.15
❑ 52 Jay Novacek	.20	.07
❑ 53 Darryl Talley	.10	.02
❑ 54 Harry Colon	.10	.02
❑ 55 Dave Meggett	.10	.02
❑ 56 Aubrey Beavers RC	.10	.02
❑ 57 James Folston	.10	.02
❑ 58 Willie Davis	.20	.07
❑ 59 Jason Elam	.20	.07
❑ 60 Eric Metcalf	.20	.07
❑ 61 Bruce Armstrong	.10	.02
❑ 62 Ron Heller	.10	.02
❑ 63 LeRoy Butler	.10	.02
❑ 64 Terry Obee	.10	.02
❑ 65 Kurt Gouveia	.10	.02
❑ 66 Pierce Holt	.10	.02
❑ 67 David Alexander	.10	.02
❑ 68 Deral Boykin	.10	.02
❑ 69 Carl Pickens	.20	.07
❑ 70 Broderick Thomas	.10	.02
❑ 71 Barry Sanders CT	1.25	.50
❑ 72 Qadry Ismail CT	.40	.15
❑ 73 Thurman Thomas CT	.40	.15
❑ 74 Junior Seau	.40	.15
❑ 75 Vinny Testaverde	.20	.07
❑ 76 Tyrone Hughes	.20	.07
❑ 77 Nate Newton	.10	.02
❑ 78 Eric Swann	.20	.07
❑ 79 Brad Baxter	.10	.02
❑ 80 Dana Stubblefield	.20	.07
❑ 81 Jumbo Elliott	.10	.02
❑ 82 Steve Wisniewski	.10	.02
❑ 83 Eddie Robinson	.10	.02
❑ 84 Isaac Davis	.10	.02
❑ 85 Cris Carter	.60	.25
❑ 86 Mel Gray	.10	.02
❑ 87 Cornelius Bennett	.20	.07
❑ 88 Neil O'Donnell	.40	.15
❑ 89 Jon Hand	.10	.02
❑ 90 John Elway	3.00	1.25
❑ 91 Bill Hitchcock	.10	.02
❑ 92 Neil Smith	.20	.07
❑ 93 Joe Johnson RC	.10	.02
❑ 94 Edgar Bennett	.40	.15
❑ 95 Vincent Brown	.10	.02
❑ 96 Tommy Vardell	.10	.02
❑ 97 Donnell Woolford	.10	.02
❑ 98 Lincoln Kennedy	.10	.02
❑ 99 O.J.McDuffie	.40	.15
❑ 100 Heath Shuler RC	.40	.15
❑ 101 Jerry Rice BO	.75	.30
❑ 102 Erik Williams BO	.10	.02
❑ 103 Randall McDaniel BO	.10	.02
❑ 104 Dermontti Dawson BO	.10	.02
❑ 105 Nate Newton BO	.10	.02
❑ 106 Harris Barton BO	.10	.02
❑ 107 Shannon Sharpe BO	.20	.07
❑ 108 Sterling Sharpe BO	.20	.07
❑ 109 Steve Young BO	.60	.25
❑ 110 Emmitt Smith BO	1.25	.50
❑ 111 Thurman Thomas BO	.40	.15
❑ 112 Kyle Clifton	.10	.02
❑ 113 Desmond Howard	.20	.07
❑ 114 Quinn Early	.20	.07
❑ 115 David Klingler	.10	.02
❑ 116 Bern Brostek	.10	.02
❑ 117 Gary Clark	.20	.07
❑ 118 Courtney Hall	.10	.02
❑ 119 Joe King	.10	.02
❑ 120 Quentin Coryatt	.10	.02
❑ 121 Johnnie Morton RC	2.00	.75
❑ 122 Andre Reed	.20	.07
❑ 123 Eric Davis	.10	.02
❑ 124 Jack Del Rio	.10	.02
❑ 125 Greg Lloyd	.20	.07
❑ 126 Bubba McDowell	.10	.02
❑ 127 Mark Jackson	.10	.02
❑ 128 Jeff Jaeger	.10	.02
❑ 129 Chris Warren	.20	.07
❑ 130 Tom Waddle	.10	.02
❑ 131 Tony Smith RB	.10	.02
❑ 132 Todd Collins	.10	.02
❑ 133 Mark Bavaro	.10	.02
❑ 134 Joe Phillips	.10	.02
❑ 135 Chris Jacke	.10	.02
❑ 136 Glyn Milburn	.20	.07
❑ 137 Keith Jackson	.10	.02
❑ 138 Steve Tovar	.10	.02
❑ 139 Tim Johnson	.10	.02
❑ 140 Brian Washington	.10	.02
❑ 141 Troy Drayton	.10	.02
❑ 142 Dewayne Washington RC	.20	.07
❑ 143 Erik Williams	.10	.02
❑ 144 Eric Turner	.10	.02
❑ 145 John Taylor	.20	.07
❑ 146 Richard Cooper	.10	.02
❑ 147 Van Malone	.10	.02
❑ 148 Tim Ruddy RC	.10	.02
❑ 149 Henry Jones	.10	.02
❑ 150 Tim Brown	.40	.15
❑ 151 Stan Humphries	.20	.07
❑ 152 Harry Newsome	.10	.02
❑ 153 Craig Erickson	.10	.02
❑ 154 Gary Anderson K	.10	.02
❑ 155 Ray Childress	.10	.02
❑ 156 Howard Cross	.10	.02
❑ 157 Heath Sherman	.10	.02
❑ 158 Terrell Buckley	.10	.02
❑ 159 J.B. Brown	.10	.02
❑ 160 Joe Montana	3.00	1.25
❑ 161 David Wyman	.10	.02
❑ 162 Norm Johnson	.10	.02
❑ 163 Rod Stephens	.10	.02
❑ 164 Willie McGinest RC	.40	.15
❑ 165 Barry Sanders	2.50	1.00
❑ 166 Marc Logan	.10	.02
❑ 167 Anthony Newman	.10	.02
❑ 168 Russell Maryland	.10	.02
❑ 169 Luis Sharpe	.10	.02
❑ 170 Jim Kelly	.40	.15
❑ 171 Tre Johnson RC	.10	.02
❑ 172 Johnny Mitchell	.10	.02
❑ 173 David Palmer RC	.40	.15
❑ 174 Bob Dahl	.10	.02
❑ 175 Aaron Wallace	.10	.02
❑ 176 Chris Gardocki	.10	.02
❑ 177 Hardy Nickerson	.20	.07
❑ 178 Jeff Query	.10	.02
❑ 179 Leslie O'Neal	.10	.02
❑ 180 Kevin Greene	.20	.07
❑ 181 Alonzo Spellman	.10	.02
❑ 182 Reggie Brooks	.20	.07
❑ 183 Dana Stubblefield	.20	.07
❑ 184 Tyrone Hughes	.20	.07
❑ 185 Drew Bledsoe GE	.40	.15
❑ 186 Ronald Moore GE	.10	.02
❑ 187 Jason Elam GE	.10	.02
❑ 188 Rick Mirer GE	.40	.15
❑ 189 Willie Roaf GE	.10	.02
❑ 190 Jerome Bettis GE	.40	.15
❑ 191 Brad Hopkins	.10	.02
❑ 192 Derek Brown RBK	.10	.02
❑ 193 Nolan Harrison	.10	.02
❑ 194 John Randle	.20	.07
❑ 195 Carlton Bailey	.10	.02
❑ 196 Kevin Williams WR	.20	.07
❑ 197 Greg Hill RC	.40	.15
❑ 198 Mark McMillian	.10	.02
❑ 199 Brad Edwards	.10	.02
❑ 200 Dan Marino	3.00	1.25
❑ 201 Ricky Watters	.20	.07
❑ 202 George Teague	.10	.02
❑ 203 Steve Beuerlein	.20	.07
❑ 204 Jeff Burris RC	.20	.07
❑ 205 Steve Atwater	.10	.02
❑ 206 John Thierry RC	.10	.02
❑ 207 Patrick Hunter	.10	.02
❑ 208 Wayne Gandy	.10	.02
❑ 209 Derrick Moore	.10	.02
❑ 210 Phil Simms	.20	.07
❑ 211 Kirk Lowdermilk	.10	.02
❑ 212 Patrick Robinson	.10	.02
❑ 213 Kevin Mitchell	.10	.02
❑ 214 Jonathan Hayes	.10	.02
❑ 215 Michael Dean Perry	.20	.07
❑ 216 John Fina	.10	.02
❑ 217 Anthony Smith	.10	.02
❑ 218 Paul Gruber	.10	.02
❑ 219 Carnell Lake	.10	.02
❑ 220 Carl Lee	.10	.02
❑ 221 Steve Christie	.10	.02

	Card	Player	Price	Price
❑	222	Greg Montgomery	.10	.02
❑	223	Reggie Brooks	.20	.07
❑	224	Derrick Thomas	.40	.15
❑	225	Eric Metcalf	.20	.07
❑	226	Michael Haynes	.20	.07
❑	227	Bobby Hebert	.10	.02
❑	228	Tyrone Hughes	.20	.07
❑	229	Donald Frank	.10	.02
❑	230	Vaughan Johnson	.10	.02
❑	231	Eric Thomas	.10	.02
❑	232	Ernest Givins	.20	.07
❑	233	Charles Haley	.20	.07
❑	234	Darrell Green	.10	.02
❑	235	Harold Alexander	.10	.02
❑	236	Dwayne Sabb	.10	.02
❑	237	Harris Barton	.10	.02
❑	238	Randall Cunningham	.40	.15
❑	239	Ray Buchanan	.10	.02
❑	240	Sterling Sharpe	.20	.07
❑	241	Chris Mims	.10	.02
❑	242	Mark Carrier DB	.10	.02
❑	243	Ricky Proehl	.10	.02
❑	244	Michael Brooks	.10	.02
❑	245	Sean Gilbert	.10	.02
❑	246	David Lutz	.10	.02
❑	247	Kelvin Martin	.10	.02
❑	248	Scottie Graham RC	.20	.07
❑	249	Irving Fryar	.20	.07
❑	250	Ricardo McDonald	.10	.02
❑	251	Marvcus Patton	.10	.02
❑	252	Errict Rhett RC	.40	.15
❑	253	Winston Moss	.10	.02
❑	254	Rod Bernstine	.10	.02
❑	255	Terry Wooden	.10	.02
❑	256	Antonio Langham RC	.20	.07
❑	257	Tommy Barnhardt	.10	.02
❑	258	Marvin Washington	.10	.02
❑	259	Bo Orlando	.10	.02
❑	260	Marcus Allen	.40	.15
❑	261	Mario Bates RC	.40	.15
❑	262	Marco Coleman	.10	.02
❑	263	Doug Riesenberg	.10	.02
❑	264	Jesse Sapolu	.10	.02
❑	265	Dermontti Dawson	.10	.02
❑	266	Fernando Smith RC	.10	.02
❑	267	David Szott	.10	.02
❑	268	Steve Christie	.10	.02
❑	269	Bruce Matthews	.10	.02
❑	270	Michael Irvin	.40	.15
❑	271	Seth Joyner	.10	.02
❑	272	Santana Dotson	.20	.07
❑	273	Vincent Brisby	.20	.07
❑	274	Rohn Stark	.10	.02
❑	275	John Copeland	.10	.02
❑	276	Toby Wright	.10	.02
❑	277	David Griggs	.10	.02
❑	278	Aaron Taylor	.10	.02
❑	279	Chris Doleman	.10	.02
❑	280	Reggie Brooks	.20	.07
❑	281	Flipper Anderson	.10	.02
❑	282	Alvin Harper	.20	.07
❑	283	Chris Hinton	.10	.02
❑	284	Kelvin Pritchett	.10	.02
❑	285	Russell Copeland	.10	.02
❑	286	Dwight Stone	.10	.02
❑	287	Jeff Gossett	.10	.02
❑	288	Larry Allen RC	.40	.15
❑	289	Kevin Mawae RC	.40	.15
❑	290	Mark Collins	.10	.02
❑	291	Chris Zorich	.10	.02
❑	292	Vince Buck	.10	.02
❑	293	Gene Atkins	.10	.02
❑	294	Webster Slaughter	.10	.02
❑	295	Steve Young	1.25	.50
❑	296	Dan Williams	.10	.02
❑	297	Jessie Armstead	.10	.02
❑	298	Victor Bailey	.10	.02
❑	299	John Carney	.10	.02
❑	300	Emmitt Smith	2.50	1.00
❑	301	Bucky Brooks RC	.10	.02
❑	302	Mo Lewis	.10	.02
❑	303	Eugene Daniel	.10	.02
❑	304	Tyji Armstrong	.10	.02
❑	305	Eugene Chung	.10	.02
❑	306	Rocket Ismail	.20	.07
❑	307	Sean Jones	.10	.02
❑	308	Rick Cunningham	.10	.02
❑	309	Ken Harvey	.10	.02
❑	310	Jeff George	.40	.15
❑	311	Jon Vaughn	.10	.02
❑	312	Roy Barker RC	.10	.02
❑	313	Micheal Barrow	.10	.02
❑	314	Ryan McNeil	.10	.02
❑	315	Pete Stoyanovich	.10	.02
❑	316	Darryl Williams	.10	.02
❑	317	Renaldo Turnbull	.10	.02
❑	318	Eric Green	.10	.02
❑	319	Nate Lewis	.10	.02
❑	320	Mike Flores	.10	.02
❑	321	Derek Russell	.10	.02
❑	322	Marcus Spears RC	.10	.02
❑	323	Corey Miller	.10	.02
❑	324	Derrick Thomas	.40	.15
❑	325	Steve Everitt	.10	.02
❑	326	Brent Jones	.20	.07
❑	327	Marshall Faulk RC	6.00	2.50
❑	328	Don Beebe	.10	.02
❑	329	Harry Swayne	.10	.02
❑	330	Boomer Esiason	.20	.07
❑	331	Don Mosebar	.10	.02
❑	332	Isaac Bruce RC	5.00	2.00
❑	333	Rickey Jackson	.10	.02
❑	334	Daryl Johnston	.20	.07
❑	335	Lorenzo Lynch	.10	.02
❑	336	Brian Blades	.20	.07
❑	337	Michael Timpson	.10	.02
❑	338	Reggie Cobb	.10	.02
❑	339	Joe Walter	.10	.02
❑	340	Barry Foster	.10	.02
❑	341	Richmond Webb	.10	.02
❑	342	Pat Swilling	.10	.02
❑	343	Shaun Gayle	.10	.02
❑	344	Reggie Roby	.10	.02
❑	345	Chris Calloway	.10	.02
❑	346	Doug Dawson	.10	.02
❑	347	Rob Burnett	.10	.02
❑	348	Dana Hall	.10	.02
❑	349	Horace Copeland	.10	.02
❑	350	Shannon Sharpe	.20	.07
❑	351	Rich Miano	.10	.02
❑	352	Henry Thomas	.10	.02
❑	353	Dan Saleaumua	.10	.02
❑	354	Kevin Ross	.10	.02
❑	355	Morten Andersen	.10	.02
❑	356	Anthony Blaylock	.10	.02
❑	357	Stanley Richard	.10	.02
❑	358	Albert Lewis	.10	.02
❑	359	Darren Woodson	.20	.07
❑	360	Drew Bledsoe	1.00	.40
❑	361	Eric Mahlum	.10	.02
❑	362	Trent Dilfer RC	1.50	.60
❑	363	William Roberts	.10	.02
❑	364	Robert Brooks	.40	.15
❑	365	Jason Hanson	.10	.02
❑	366	Troy Vincent	.10	.02
❑	367	William Thomas	.10	.02
❑	368	Lonnie Johnson RC	.10	.02
❑	369	Jamir Miller RC	.20	.07
❑	370	Michael Jackson	.20	.07
❑	371	Charlie Ward CT RC	.40	.15
❑	372	Shannon Sharpe CT	.20	.07
❑	373	Jackie Slater CT	.10	.02
❑	374	Steve Young CT	.60	.25
❑	375	Bobby Wilson	.10	.02
❑	376	Paul Frase	.10	.02
❑	377	Dale Carter	.10	.02
❑	378	Robert Delpino	.10	.02
❑	379	Bert Emanuel RC	.40	.15
❑	380	Rick Mirer	.40	.15
❑	381	Carlos Jenkins	.10	.02
❑	382	Gary Brown	.10	.02
❑	383	Doug Pelfrey	.10	.02
❑	384	Dexter Carter	.10	.02
❑	385	Chris Miller	.10	.02
❑	386	Charles Johnson RC	.40	.15
❑	387	James Joseph	.10	.02
❑	388	Darrin Smith	.10	.02
❑	389	James Jett	.10	.02
❑	390	Junior Seau	.40	.15
❑	391	Chris Slade	.10	.02
❑	392	Jim Harbaugh	.40	.15
❑	393	Herman Moore	.40	.15
❑	394	Thomas Randolph RC	.10	.02
❑	395	Lamar Thomas	.10	.02
❑	396	Reggie Rivers	.10	.02
❑	397	Larry Centers	.40	.15
❑	398	Chad Brown	.10	.02
❑	399	Terry Kirby	.40	.15
❑	400	Bruce Smith	.40	.15
❑	401	Keenan McCardell RC	2.00	.75
❑	402	Tim McDonald	.10	.02
❑	403	Robert Smith	.40	.15
❑	404	Matt Brock	.10	.02
❑	405	Tony McGee	.10	.02
❑	406	Ethan Horton	.10	.02
❑	407	Michael Haynes	.20	.07
❑	408	Steve Jackson	.10	.02
❑	409	Erik Kramer	.20	.07
❑	410	Jerome Bettis	.60	.25
❑	411	D.J. Johnson	.10	.02
❑	412	John Alt	.10	.02
❑	413	Jeff Lageman	.10	.02
❑	414	Rick Tuten	.10	.02
❑	415	Jeff Robinson	.10	.02
❑	416	Kevin Lee RC	.10	.02
❑	417	Thomas Lewis RC	.20	.07
❑	418	Kerry Cash	.10	.02
❑	419	Chuck Levy RC	.10	.02
❑	420	Mark Ingram	.10	.02
❑	421	Dennis Gibson	.10	.02
❑	422	Tyronne Drakeford	.10	.02
❑	423	James Washington	.10	.02
❑	424	Dante Jones	.10	.02
❑	425	Eugene Robinson	.10	.02
❑	426	Johnny Johnson	.10	.02
❑	427	Brian Mitchell	.10	.02
❑	428	Charles Mincy	.10	.02
❑	429	Mark Carrier WR	.20	.07
❑	430	Vince Workman	.10	.02
❑	431	James Francis	.10	.02
❑	432	Clay Matthews	.10	.02
❑	433	Randall McDaniel	.10	.02
❑	434	Brad Ottis	.10	.02
❑	435	Bruce Smith	.40	.15
❑	436	Cortez Kennedy BD	.10	.02
❑	437	John Randle BD	.20	.07
❑	438	Neil Smith BD	.20	.07
❑	439	Cornelius Bennett BD	.20	.07
❑	440	Junior Seau BD	.20	.07
❑	441	Derrick Thomas BD	.20	.07
❑	442	Rod Woodson BD	.20	.07
❑	443	Terry McDaniel BD	.10	.02
❑	444	Tim McDonald BD	.10	.02
❑	445	Mark Carrier DB BD	.10	.02
❑	446	Irv Smith	.10	.02
❑	447	Steve Wallace	.10	.02
❑	448	Cris Dishman	.10	.02
❑	449	Bill Brooks	.10	.02
❑	450	Jeff Hostetler	.20	.07
❑	451	Brentson Buckner RC	.10	.02
❑	452	Ken Ruettgers	.10	.02
❑	453	Marc Boutte	.10	.02
❑	454	John Offerdahl	.10	.02
❑	455	Allen Aldridge	.10	.02
❑	456	Steve Emtman	.10	.02
❑	457	Andre Rison	.20	.07
❑	458	Shawn Jefferson	.10	.02
❑	459	Todd Steussie RC	.20	.07
❑	460	Scott Mitchell	.20	.07
❑	461	Tom Carter	.10	.02
❑	462	Donnell Bennett RC	.40	.15
❑	463	James Jones DT	.10	.02
❑	464	Antone Davis	.10	.02
❑	465	Jim Everett	.20	.07
❑	466	Tony Tolbert	.10	.02
❑	467	Merril Hoge	.10	.02
❑	468	Michael Bates	.10	.02
❑	469	Phil Hansen	.10	.02
❑	470	Rodney Hampton	.20	.07
❑	471	Aeneas Williams	.10	.02
❑	472	Al Del Greco	.10	.02
❑	473	Todd Lyght	.10	.02
❑	474	Joel Steed	.10	.02
❑	475	Merton Hanks	.20	.07
❑	476	Tony Stargell	.10	.02
❑	477	Greg Robinson	.10	.02
❑	478	Roger Duffy	.10	.02
❑	479	Simon Fletcher	.10	.02
❑	480	Reggie White	.40	.15
❑	481	Lee Johnson	.10	.02
❑	482	Wayne Martin	.10	.02

Card	Mint	Ex
❑ 483 Thurman Thomas	.40	.15
❑ 484 Warren Moon	.40	.15
❑ 485 Sam Rogers RC	.10	.02
❑ 486 Erric Pegram	.10	.02
❑ 487 Will Wolford	.10	.02
❑ 488 Duane Young	.10	.02
❑ 489 Keith Hamilton	.10	.02
❑ 490 Haywood Jeffires	.20	.07
❑ 491 Trace Armstrong	.10	.02
❑ 492 J.J. Birden	.10	.02
❑ 493 Ricky Ervins	.10	.02
❑ 494 Robert Blackmon	.10	.02
❑ 495 William Perry	.20	.07
❑ 496 Robert Massey	.10	.02
❑ 497 Jim Jeffcoat	.10	.02
❑ 498 Pat Harlow	.10	.02
❑ 499 Jeff Cross	.10	.02
❑ 500 Jerry Rice	1.50	.60
❑ 501 Darnay Scott RC	1.00	.40
❑ 502 Clyde Simmons	.10	.02
❑ 503 Henry Rolling	.10	.02
❑ 504 James Hasty	.10	.02
❑ 505 Leroy Thompson	.10	.02
❑ 506 Darrell Thompson	.10	.02
❑ 507 Tim Bowens RC	.20	.07
❑ 508 Gerald Perry	.10	.02
❑ 509 Mike Croel	.10	.02
❑ 510 Sam Mills	.10	.02
❑ 511 Steve Young RZ	.60	.25
❑ 512 Hardy Nickerson RZ	.20	.07
❑ 513 Cris Carter RZ	.20	.07
❑ 514 Boomer Esiason RZ	.10	.02
❑ 515 Bruce Smith RZ	.20	.07
❑ 516 Emmitt Smith RZ	1.25	.50
❑ 517 Eugene Robinson RZ	.10	.02
❑ 518 Gary Brown RZ	.10	.02
❑ 519 Jerry Rice RZ	.75	.30
❑ 520 Troy Aikman RZ	.75	.30
❑ 521 Marcus Allen RZ	.20	.07
❑ 522 Junior Seau RZ	.20	.07
❑ 523 Sterling Sharpe RZ	.20	.07
❑ 524 Dana Stubblefield RZ	.20	.07
❑ 525 Tom Carter RZ	.10	.02
❑ 526 Pete Metzelaars	.10	.02
❑ 527 Russell Freeman	.10	.02
❑ 528 Keith Cash	.10	.02
❑ 529 Willie Drewrey	.10	.02
❑ 530 Randal Hill	.10	.02
❑ 531 Pepper Johnson	.10	.02
❑ 532 Rob Moore	.20	.07
❑ 533 Todd Kelly	.10	.02
❑ 534 Keith Byars	.10	.02
❑ 535 Mike Fox	.10	.02
❑ 536 Brett Favre	3.00	1.25
❑ 537 Terry McDaniel	.10	.02
❑ 538 Darren Perry	.10	.02
❑ 539 Maurice Hurst	.10	.02
❑ 540 Troy Aikman	1.50	.60
❑ 541 Junior Seau	.40	.15
❑ 542 Steve Broussard	.10	.02
❑ 543 Lorenzo White	.10	.02
❑ 544 Terry McDaniel	.10	.02
❑ 545 Henry Thomas	.10	.02
❑ 546 Tyrone Hughes	.20	.07
❑ 547 Mark Collins	.10	.02
❑ 548 Gary Anderson K	.10	.02
❑ 549 Darrell Green	.10	.02
❑ 550 Jerry Rice	1.25	.50
❑ 551 Cornelius Bennett	.20	.07
❑ 552 Aeneas Williams	.10	.02
❑ 553 Eric Metcalf	.20	.07
❑ 554 Jumbo Elliott	.10	.02
❑ 555 Mo Lewis	.10	.02
❑ 556 Darren Carrington	.10	.02
❑ 557 Kevin Greene	.20	.07
❑ 558 John Elway	2.50	1.00
❑ 559 Eugene Robinson	.10	.02
❑ 560 Drew Bledsoe	.75	.30
❑ 561 Fred Barnett	.20	.07
❑ 562 Bernie Parmalee RC	.40	.15
❑ 563 Bryce Paup	.20	.07
❑ 564 Donnell Woolford	.10	.02
❑ 565 Terance Mathis	.20	.07
❑ 566 Santana Dotson	.20	.07
❑ 567 Randall McDaniel	.10	.02
❑ 568 Stanley Richard	.10	.02
❑ 569 Brian Blades	.20	.07
❑ 570 Jerome Bettis	.50	.20
❑ 571 Neil Smith	.20	.07
❑ 572 Andre Reed	.20	.07
❑ 573 Michael Bankston	.10	.02
❑ 574 Dana Stubblefield	.20	.07
❑ 575 Rod Woodson	.20	.07
❑ 576 Ken Harvey	.10	.02
❑ 577 Andre Rison	.20	.07
❑ 578 Darion Conner	.10	.02
❑ 579 Michael Strahan	.40	.15
❑ 580 Barry Sanders	2.00	.75
❑ 581 Pepper Johnson	.10	.02
❑ 582 Lewis Tillman	.10	.02
❑ 583 Jeff George	.40	.15
❑ 584 Michael Haynes	.20	.07
❑ 585 Herschel Walker	.20	.07
❑ 586 Tim Brown	.40	.15
❑ 587 Jim Kelly	.40	.15
❑ 588 Ricky Watters	.20	.07
❑ 589 Randall Cunningham	.40	.15
❑ 590 Troy Aikman	1.25	.50
❑ 591 Ken Norton Jr.	.20	.07
❑ 592 Cortez Kennedy	.20	.07
❑ 593 Ricky Ervins	.10	.02
❑ 594 Cris Carter	.50	.20
❑ 595 Sterling Sharpe	.20	.07
❑ 596 John Randle	.20	.07
❑ 597 Shannon Sharpe	.20	.07
❑ 598 Ray Crittenden RC	.10	.02
❑ 599 Barry Foster	.10	.02
❑ 600 Deion Sanders	.60	.25
❑ 601 Seth Joyner	.10	.02
❑ 602 Chris Warren	.20	.07
❑ 603 Tom Rathman	.10	.02
❑ 604 Brett Favre	2.50	1.00
❑ 605 Marshall Faulk	2.00	.75
❑ 606 Terry Allen	.20	.07
❑ 607 Ben Coates	.20	.07
❑ 608 Brian Washington	.10	.02
❑ 609 Henry Ellard	.20	.07
❑ 610 Dave Meggett	.10	.02
❑ 611 Stan Humphries	.20	.07
❑ 612 Warren Moon	.40	.15
❑ 613 Marcus Allen	.40	.15
❑ 614 Ed McDaniel	.10	.02
❑ 615 Joe Montana	2.50	1.00
❑ 616 Jeff Hostetler	.20	.07
❑ 617 Johnny Johnson	.10	.02
❑ 618 Andre Coleman RC	.10	.02
❑ 619 Willie Davis	.20	.07
❑ 620 Rick Mirer	.40	.15
❑ 621 Dan Marino	2.50	1.00
❑ 622 Rob Moore	.20	.07
❑ 623 Byron Bam Morris RC	.20	.07
❑ 624 Natrone Means	.40	.15
❑ 625 Steve Young	.75	.30
❑ 626 Jim Everett	.20	.07
❑ 627 Michael Brooks	.10	.02
❑ 628 Dermontti Dawson	.10	.02
❑ 629 Reggie White	.40	.15
❑ 630 Emmitt Smith	1.50	.60
❑ 0 Micheal Barrow TSC	4.00	2.00
❑ NNO Checklist Card 1	.10	.02
❑ NNO Checklist Card 2	.10	.02
❑ NNO Checklist Card 3	.10	.02

1995 Stadium Club

Card	Mint	Ex
❑ COMPLETE SET (450)	60.00	25.00
❑ COMP.SERIES 1 (225)	30.00	12.50
❑ COMP.SERIES 2 (225)	30.00	12.50
❑ 1 Steve Young	1.25	.50
❑ 2 Stan Humphries	.20	.07
❑ 3 Chris Boniol RC	.10	.02
❑ 4 Darren Perry	.10	.02
❑ 5 Vinny Testaverde	.20	.07
❑ 6 Aubrey Beavers	.10	.02
❑ 7 Dewayne Washington	.20	.07
❑ 8 Marion Butts	.10	.02
❑ 9 George Koonce	.10	.02
❑ 10 Joe Cain	.10	.02
❑ 11 Mike Johnson	.10	.02
❑ 12 Dale Carter	.20	.07
❑ 13 Greg Biekert	.10	.02
❑ 14 Aaron Pierce	.10	.02
❑ 15 Aeneas Williams	.10	.02
❑ 16 Stephen Grant RC	.10	.02
❑ 17 Henry Jones	.10	.02
❑ 18 James Williams LB	.10	.02
❑ 19 Andy Harmon	.10	.02
❑ 20 Anthony Miller	.20	.07
❑ 21 Kevin Ross	.10	.02
❑ 22 Erik Howard	.10	.02
❑ 23 Brian Blades	.20	.07
❑ 24 Trent Dilfer	.40	.15
❑ 25 Roman Phifer	.10	.02
❑ 26 Bruce Kozerski	.10	.02
❑ 27 Henry Ellard	.20	.07
❑ 28 Rich Camarillo	.10	.02
❑ 29 Richmond Webb	.10	.02
❑ 30 George Teague	.10	.02
❑ 31 Antonio Langham	.10	.02
❑ 32 Barry Foster	.20	.07
❑ 33 Bruce Armstrong	.10	.02
❑ 34 Tim McDonald	.10	.02
❑ 35 James Harris DE	.10	.02
❑ 36 Lomas Brown	.10	.02
❑ 37 Jay Novacek	.20	.07
❑ 38 John Thierry	.10	.02
❑ 39 John Elliott	.10	.02
❑ 40 Terry McDaniel	.10	.02
❑ 41 Shawn Lee	.10	.02
❑ 42 Shane Dronett	.10	.02
❑ 43 Cornelius Bennett	.20	.07
❑ 44 Steve Bono	.20	.07
❑ 45 Byron Evans	.10	.02
❑ 46 Eugene Robinson	.10	.02
❑ 47 Tony Bennett	.10	.02
❑ 48 Michael Bankston	.10	.02
❑ 49 Willie Roaf	.10	.02
❑ 50 Bobby Houston	.10	.02
❑ 51 Ken Harvey	.10	.02
❑ 52 Bruce Matthews	.10	.02
❑ 53 Lincoln Kennedy	.10	.02
❑ 54 Todd Lyght	.10	.02
❑ 55 Paul Gruber	.10	.02
❑ 56 Corey Sawyer	.10	.02
❑ 57 Myron Guyton	.10	.02
❑ 58 John Jackson T	.10	.02
❑ 59 Sean Jones	.10	.02
❑ 60 Pepper Johnson	.10	.02
❑ 61 Steve Walsh	.10	.02
❑ 62 Corey Miller	.10	.02
❑ 63 Fuad Reveiz	.10	.02
❑ 64 Rickey Jackson	.10	.02
❑ 65 Scott Mitchell	.20	.07
❑ 66 Michael Irvin	.40	.15
❑ 67 Andre Reed	.20	.07
❑ 68 Mark Seay	.20	.07
❑ 69 Keith Byars	.10	.02
❑ 70 Marcus Allen	.40	.15
❑ 71 Shannon Sharpe	.20	.07
❑ 72 Eric Hill	.10	.02
❑ 73 James Washington	.10	.02
❑ 74 Greg Jackson	.10	.02
❑ 75 Chris Warren	.20	.07
❑ 76 Will Wolford	.10	.02
❑ 77 Anthony Smith	.10	.02
❑ 78 Cris Dishman	.10	.02
❑ 79 Carl Pickens	.20	.07
❑ 80 Tyrone Hughes	.20	.07
❑ 81 Chris Miller	.10	.02
❑ 82 Clay Matthews	.20	.07
❑ 83 Lonnie Marts	.10	.02
❑ 84 Jerome Henderson	.10	.02
❑ 85 Ben Coates	.20	.07
❑ 86 Deon Figures	.10	.02

❑ 87 Anthony Pleasant .10 .02
❑ 88 Guy McIntyre .10 .02
❑ 89 Jake Reed .20 .07
❑ 90 Rodney Hampton .20 .07
❑ 91 Santana Dotson .10 .02
❑ 92 Jeff Blackshear .10 .02
❑ 93 Willie Clay .10 .02
❑ 94 Nate Newton .20 .07
❑ 95 Bucky Brooks .10 .02
❑ 96 Lamar Lathon .10 .02
❑ 97 Tim Grunhard .10 .02
❑ 98 Harris Barton .10 .02
❑ 99 Brian Mitchell .10 .02
❑ 100 Natrone Means .20 .07
❑ 101 Sean Dawkins .20 .07
❑ 102 Chris Slade .10 .02
❑ 103 Tom Rathman .10 .02
❑ 104 Fred Barnett .20 .07
❑ 105 Gary Brown .10 .02
❑ 106 Leonard Russell .10 .02
❑ 107 Alfred Williams .10 .02
❑ 108 Kelvin Martin .10 .02
❑ 109 Alexander Wright .10 .02
❑ 110 O.J. McDuffie .40 .15
❑ 111 Mario Bates .20 .07
❑ 112 Tony Casillas .10 .02
❑ 113 Michael Timpson .10 .02
❑ 114 Robert Brooks .40 .15
❑ 115 Rob Burnett .10 .02
❑ 116 Mark Collins .10 .02
❑ 117 Chris Calloway .10 .02
❑ 118 Courtney Hawkins .10 .02
❑ 119 Marvcus Patton .10 .02
❑ 120 Greg Lloyd .20 .07
❑ 121 Ryan McNeil .10 .02
❑ 122 Gary Plummer .10 .02
❑ 123 Dwayne Sabb .10 .02
❑ 124 Jessie Hester .10 .02
❑ 125 Terance Mathis .20 .07
❑ 126 Steve Atwater .10 .02
❑ 127 Lorenzo Lynch .10 .02
❑ 128 James Francis .10 .02
❑ 129 John Fina .10 .02
❑ 130 Emmitt Smith 2.50 1.25
❑ 131 Bryan Cox .10 .02
❑ 132 Robert Blackmon .10 .02
❑ 133 Kenny Davidson .10 .02
❑ 134 Eugene Daniel .10 .02
❑ 135 Vince Buck .10 .02
❑ 136 Leslie O'Neal .20 .07
❑ 137 James Jett .20 .07
❑ 138 Johnny Johnson .10 .02
❑ 139 Michael Zordich .10 .02
❑ 140 Warren Moon .20 .07
❑ 141 William White .10 .02
❑ 142 Carl Banks .10 .02
❑ 143 Marty Carter .10 .02
❑ 144 Keith Hamilton .10 .02
❑ 145 Alvin Harper .10 .02
❑ 146 Corey Harris .10 .02
❑ 147 Elijah Alexander RC .10 .02
❑ 148 Darrell Green .10 .02
❑ 149 Yancey Thigpen RC .20 .07
❑ 150 Deion Sanders 1.00 .40
❑ 151 Burt Grossman .10 .02
❑ 152 J.B. Brown .10 .02
❑ 153 Johnny Bailey .10 .02
❑ 154 Harvey Williams .10 .02
❑ 155 Jeff Blake RC 1.00 .40
❑ 156 Al Smith .10 .02
❑ 157 Chris Doleman .10 .02
❑ 158 Garrison Hearst .40 .15
❑ 159 Bryce Paup .20 .07
❑ 160 Herman Moore .40 .15
❑ 161 Cortez Kennedy .20 .07
❑ 162 Marquez Pope .10 .02
❑ 163 Quinn Early .20 .07
❑ 164 Broderick Thomas .10 .02
❑ 165 Jeff Herrod .10 .02
❑ 166 Robert Jones .10 .02
❑ 167 Mo Lewis .10 .02
❑ 168 Ray Crittenden .10 .02
❑ 169 Raymont Harris .10 .02
❑ 170 Bruce Smith .40 .15
❑ 171 Dana Stubblefield .20 .07
❑ 172 Charles Haley .20 .07
❑ 173 Charles Johnson .20 .07
❑ 174 Shawn Jefferson .10 .02
❑ 175 Leroy Hoard .10 .02
❑ 176 Bernie Parmalee .20 .07
❑ 177 Scottie Graham .20 .07
❑ 178 Edgar Bennett .20 .07
❑ 179 Aubrey Matthews .10 .02
❑ 180 Don Beebe .10 .02
❑ 181 Eric Swann EC SP .30 .10
❑ 182 Jeff George EC SP .30 .10
❑ 183 Jim Kelly EC SP .60 .25
❑ 184 Sam Mills EC SP .30 .10
❑ 185 Mark Carrier DB EC SP .20 .07
❑ 186 Dan Wilkinson EC SP .30 .10
❑ 187 Eric Turner EC SP .20 .07
❑ 188 Troy Aikman EC SP 2.00 .75
❑ 189 John Elway EC SP 4.00 1.50
❑ 190 Barry Sanders EC SP 3.00 1.25
❑ 191 Brett Favre EC SP 4.00 2.00
❑ 192 Micheal Barrow EC SP .20 .07
❑ 193 Marshall Faulk EC SP 2.50 1.00
❑ 194 Steve Beuerlein EC SP .30 .10
❑ 195 Neil Smith EC SP .30 .10
❑ 196 Jeff Hostetler EC SP .30 .10
❑ 197 Jerome Bettis EC SP .60 .25
❑ 198 Dan Marino EC SP 4.00 1.50
❑ 199 Cris Carter EC SP .60 .25
❑ 200 Drew Bledsoe EC SP 1.00 .40
❑ 201 Jim Everett EC SP .20 .07
❑ 202 Dave Brown EC SP .30 .10
❑ 203 Boomer Esiason EC SP .30 .10
❑ 204 Randall Cunningham EC SP .30 .10
❑ 205 Rod Woodson EC SP .30 .10
❑ 206 Junior Seau EC SP .60 .25
❑ 207 Jerry Rice EC SP 2.00 .75
❑ 208 Rick Mirer EC SP .30 .10
❑ 209 Errict Rhett EC SP .30 .10
❑ 210 Heath Shuler EC SP .30 .10
❑ 211 Bobby Taylor SP RC .60 .25
❑ 212 Jesse James SP RC .20 .07
❑ 213 Devin Bush SP RC .20 .07
❑ 214 Luther Elliss SP RC .20 .07
❑ 215 Kerry Collins RC SP 2.00 .75
❑ 216 Derr.Alexander DE SP RC .20 .07
❑ 217 Rashaan Salaam RC SP .30 .10
❑ 218 J.J. Stokes RC SP .60 .25
❑ 219 Todd Collins RC SP .30 .10
❑ 220 Ki-Jana Carter RC SP .60 .25
❑ 221 Kyle Brady RC SP .60 .25
❑ 222 Kevin Carter RC SP .60 .25
❑ 223 Tony Boselli RC SP .60 .25
❑ 224 Scott Gragg SP RC .20 .07
❑ 225 Warren Sapp RC SP 2.00 .75
❑ 226 Ricky Reynolds .10 .02
❑ 227 Roosevelt Potts .10 .02
❑ 228 Jessie Tuggle .10 .02
❑ 229 Anthony Newman .10 .02
❑ 230 Randall Cunningham .40 .15
❑ 231 Jason Elam .20 .07
❑ 232 Darnay Scott .20 .07
❑ 233 Tom Carter .10 .02
❑ 234 Micheal Barrow .10 .02
❑ 235 Steve Tasker .20 .07
❑ 236 Howard Cross .10 .02
❑ 237 Charles Wilson .10 .02
❑ 238 Rob Fredrickson .10 .02
❑ 239 Russell Maryland .10 .02
❑ 240 Dan Marino 3.00 1.25
❑ 241 Rafael Robinson .10 .02
❑ 242 Ed McDaniel .10 .02
❑ 243 Brett Perriman .20 .07
❑ 244 Chuck Levy .10 .02
❑ 245 Errict Rhett .20 .07
❑ 246 Tracy Simien .10 .02
❑ 247 Steve Everitt .10 .02
❑ 248 John Jurkovic .10 .02
❑ 249 Johnny Mitchell .10 .02
❑ 250 Mark Carrier DB .10 .02
❑ 251 Merton Hanks .10 .02
❑ 252 Joe Johnson .10 .02
❑ 253 Andre Coleman .10 .02
❑ 254 Ray Buchanan .10 .02
❑ 255 Jeff George .20 .07
❑ 256 Shane Conlan .10 .02
❑ 257 Gus Frerotte .20 .07
❑ 258 Doug Pelfrey .10 .02
❑ 259 Glenn Montgomery .10 .02
❑ 260 John Elway 3.00 1.25
❑ 261 Larry Centers .20 .07
❑ 262 Calvin Williams .20 .07
❑ 263 Gene Atkins .10 .02
❑ 264 Tim Brown .40 .15
❑ 265 Leon Lett .10 .02
❑ 266 Martin Mayhew .10 .02
❑ 267 Arthur Marshall .10 .02
❑ 268 Maurice Hurst .10 .02
❑ 269 Greg Hill .20 .07
❑ 270 Junior Seau .40 .15
❑ 271 Rick Mirer .20 .07
❑ 272 Jack Del Rio .10 .02
❑ 273 Lewis Tillman .10 .02
❑ 274 Renaldo Turnbull .10 .02
❑ 275 Dan Footman .10 .02
❑ 276 John Taylor .10 .02
❑ 277 Russell Copeland .10 .02
❑ 278 Tracy Scroggins .10 .02
❑ 279 Lou Benfatti .10 .02
❑ 280 Rod Woodson .20 .07
❑ 281 Troy Drayton .10 .02
❑ 282 Quentin Coryatt .20 .07
❑ 283 Craig Heyward .20 .07
❑ 284 Jeff Cross .10 .02
❑ 285 Hardy Nickerson .10 .02
❑ 286 Dorsey Levens .75 .30
❑ 287 Derek Russell .10 .02
❑ 288 Seth Joyner .10 .02
❑ 289 Kimble Anders .20 .07
❑ 290 Drew Bledsoe .75 .30
❑ 291 Bryant Young .20 .07
❑ 292 Chris Zorich .10 .02
❑ 293 Michael Strahan .40 .15
❑ 294 Kevin Greene .20 .07
❑ 295 Aaron Glenn .10 .02
❑ 296 Jimmy Spencer RC .10 .02
❑ 297 Eric Turner .10 .02
❑ 298 William Thomas .10 .02
❑ 299 Dan Wilkinson .20 .07
❑ 300 Troy Aikman 1.50 .60
❑ 301 Terry Wooden .10 .02
❑ 302 Heath Shuler .20 .07
❑ 303 Jeff Burris .10 .02
❑ 304 Mark Stepnoski .10 .02
❑ 305 Chris Mims .10 .02
❑ 306 Todd Steussie .10 .02
❑ 307 Johnnie Morton .20 .07
❑ 308 Darryl Talley .10 .02
❑ 309 Nolan Harrison .10 .02
❑ 310 Dave Brown .20 .07
❑ 311 Brent Jones .10 .02
❑ 312 Curtis Conway .40 .15
❑ 313 Ronald Humphrey .10 .02
❑ 314 Richie Anderson RC .50 .20
❑ 315 Jim Everett .10 .02
❑ 316 Willie Davis .20 .07
❑ 317 Ed Cunningham .10 .02
❑ 318 Willie McGinest .20 .07
❑ 319 Sean Gilbert .20 .07
❑ 320 Brett Favre 3.00 1.50
❑ 321 Bennie Thompson .10 .02
❑ 322 Neil O'Donnell .20 .07
❑ 323 Vince Workman .10 .02
❑ 324 Terry Kirby .20 .07
❑ 325 Simon Fletcher .10 .02
❑ 326 Ricardo McDonald .10 .02
❑ 327 Duane Young .10 .02
❑ 328 Jim Harbaugh .20 .07
❑ 329 D.J. Johnson .10 .02
❑ 330 Boomer Esiason .20 .07
❑ 331 Donnell Woolford .10 .02
❑ 332 Mike Sherrard .10 .02
❑ 333 Tyrone Legette .10 .02
❑ 334 Larry Brown DB .10 .02
❑ 335 William Floyd .20 .07
❑ 336 Reggie Brooks .20 .07
❑ 337 Patrick Bates .10 .02
❑ 338 Jim Jeffcoat .10 .02
❑ 339 Ray Childress .10 .02
❑ 340 Cris Carter .40 .15
❑ 341 Charlie Garner .40 .15
❑ 342 Bill Hitchcock .10 .02
❑ 343 Levon Kirkland .10 .02
❑ 344 Robert Porcher .10 .02
❑ 345 Darryl Williams .10 .02
❑ 346 Vincent Brisby .10 .02
❑ 347 Kenyon Rasheed .10 .02

❑ 348	Floyd Turner	.10	.02
❑ 349	Bob Whitfield	.10	.02
❑ 350	Jerome Bettis	.40	.15
❑ 351	Brad Baxter	.10	.02
❑ 352	Darrin Smith	.10	.02
❑ 353	Lamar Thomas	.10	.02
❑ 354	Lorenzo Neal	.10	.02
❑ 355	Erik Kramer	.10	.02
❑ 356	Dwayne Harper	.10	.02
❑ 357	Doug Evans RC	.40	.15
❑ 358	Jeff Feagles	.10	.02
❑ 359	Ray Crockett	.10	.02
❑ 360	Neil Smith	.20	.07
❑ 361	Troy Vincent	.10	.02
❑ 362	Don Griffin	.10	.02
❑ 363	Michael Brooks	.10	.02
❑ 364	Carlton Gray	.10	.02
❑ 365	Thomas Smith	.10	.02
❑ 366	Ken Norton	.20	.07
❑ 367	Tony McGee	.10	.02
❑ 368	Eric Metcalf	.20	.07
❑ 369	Mel Gray	.10	.02
❑ 370	Barry Sanders	2.50	1.00
❑ 371	Rocket Ismail	.20	.07
❑ 372	Chad Brown	.20	.07
❑ 373	Qadry Ismail	.20	.07
❑ 374	Anthony Prior	.10	.02
❑ 375	Kevin Lee	.10	.02
❑ 376	Robert Young	.10	.02
❑ 377	Kevin Williams WR	.20	.07
❑ 378	Tydus Winans	.10	.02
❑ 379	Ricky Watters	.20	.07
❑ 380	Jim Kelly	.40	.15
❑ 381	Eric Swann	.20	.07
❑ 382	Mike Pritchard	.10	.02
❑ 383	Derek Brown RBK	.10	.02
❑ 384	Dennis Gibson	.10	.02
❑ 385	Byron Bam Morris	.10	.02
❑ 386	Reggie White	.40	.15
❑ 387	Jeff Graham	.10	.02
❑ 388	Marshall Faulk	2.00	.75
❑ 389	Joe Phillips	.10	.02
❑ 390	Jeff Hostetler	.20	.07
❑ 391	Irving Fryar	.20	.07
❑ 392	Stevon Moore	.10	.02
❑ 393	Bert Emanuel	.40	.15
❑ 394	Leon Searcy	.10	.02
❑ 395	Robert Smith	.40	.15
❑ 396	Michael Bates	.10	.02
❑ 397	Thomas Lewis	.20	.07
❑ 398	Joe Bowden	.10	.02
❑ 399	Steve Tovar	.10	.02
❑ 400	Jerry Rice	1.50	.60
❑ 401	Toby Wright	.10	.02
❑ 402	Daryl Johnston	.20	.07
❑ 403	Vincent Brown	.10	.02
❑ 404	Marvin Washington	.10	.02
❑ 405	Chris Spielman	.20	.07
❑ 406	Willie Jackson ET SP	.30	.10
❑ 407	Harry Boatswain ET SP	.20	.07
❑ 408	Kelvin Pritchett ET SP	.20	.07
❑ 409	Dave Widell ET SP	.20	.07
❑ 410	Frank Reich ET SP	.20	.07
❑ 411	Corey Mayfield ET SP RC	.20	.07
❑ 412	Pete Metzelaars ET SP	.20	.07
❑ 413	Keith Goganious ET SP	.20	.07
❑ 414	John Kasay ET SP	.20	.07
❑ 415	Ernest Givins ET SP	.20	.07
❑ 416	Randy Baldwin ET SP	.20	.07
❑ 417	Shawn Bouwens ET SP	.20	.07
❑ 418	Mike Fox ET SP	.20	.07
❑ 419	Mark Carrier WR ET SP	.30	.10
❑ 420	Steve Beuerlein ET SP	.30	.10
❑ 421	Steve Lofton ET SP	.20	.07
❑ 422	Jeff Lageman ET SP	.20	.07
❑ 423	Paul Butcher ET SP	.20	.07
❑ 424	Mark Brunell ET SP	1.00	.40
❑ 425	Vernon Turner ET SP	.20	.07
❑ 426	Tim McKyer ET SP	.20	.07
❑ 427	James Williams ET SP	.20	.07
❑ 428	Tommy Barnhardt ET SP	.20	.07
❑ 429	Rogerick Green ET SP	.20	.07
❑ 430	Desmond Howard ET SP	.30	.10
❑ 431	Darion Conner ET SP	.20	.07
❑ 432	Reggie Clark ET SP	.20	.07
❑ 433	Eric Guliford ET SP	.20	.07
❑ 434	Rob Johnson ET RC SP	1.25	.50
❑ 435	Sam Mills ET SP	.30	.10
❑ 436	Kordell Stewart RC SP	2.00	.75
❑ 437	James O. Stewart RC SP	1.50	.60
❑ 438	Zach Wiegert SP	.20	.07
❑ 439	Ellis Johnson RC SP	.20	.07
❑ 440	Matt O'Dwyer RC SP	.20	.07
❑ 441	Anthony Cook RC SP	.20	.07
❑ 442	Ron Davis RC SP	.20	.07
❑ 443	Chris Hudson RC SP	.20	.07
❑ 444	Hugh Douglas RC SP	.60	.25
❑ 445	Tyrone Poole RC SP	.60	.25
❑ 446	Korey Stringer RC SP	.30	.10
❑ 447	Ruben Brown RC SP	.60	.25
❑ 448	Brian DeMarco RC SP	.20	.07
❑ 449	Michael Westbrook RC SP	.60	.25
❑ 450	Steve McNair RC SP	4.00	1.50

1996 Stadium Club

❑	COMPLETE SET (360)	60.00	30.00
❑	COMP.SERIES 1 (180)	30.00	15.00
❑	COMP.SERIES 2 (180)	30.00	15.00
❑ 1	Kyle Brady	.10	.02
❑ 2	Mickey Washington	.10	.02
❑ 3	Seth Joyner	.10	.02
❑ 4	Vinny Testaverde	.25	.08
❑ 5	Thomas Randolph	.10	.02
❑ 6	Heath Shuler	.25	.08
❑ 7	Ty Law	.50	.20
❑ 8	Blake Brockermeyer	.10	.02
❑ 9	Darryll Lewis	.10	.02
❑ 10	Jeff Blake	.50	.20
❑ 11	Tyrone Hughes	.10	.02
❑ 12	Horace Copeland	.10	.02
❑ 13	Roman Phifer	.10	.02
❑ 14	Eugene Robinson	.10	.02
❑ 15	Anthony Miller	.25	.08
❑ 16	Robert Smith	.25	.08
❑ 17	Chester McGlockton	.10	.02
❑ 18	Marty Carter	.10	.02
❑ 19	Scott Mitchell	.25	.08
❑ 20	O.J. McDuffie	.25	.08
❑ 21	Stan Humphries	.25	.08
❑ 22	Eugene Daniel	.10	.02
❑ 23	Devin Bush	.10	.02
❑ 24	Darick Holmes	.10	.02
❑ 25	Ricky Watters	.25	.08
❑ 26	J.J. Stokes	.50	.20
❑ 27	George Koonce	.10	.02
❑ 28	Tamarick Vanover	.25	.08
❑ 29	Yancey Thigpen	.25	.08
❑ 30	Troy Aikman	1.25	.50
❑ 31	Rashaan Salaam	.25	.08
❑ 32	Anthony Cook	.10	.02
❑ 33	Tim McKyer	.10	.02
❑ 34	Dale Carter	.10	.02
❑ 35	Marvin Washington	.10	.02
❑ 36	Terry Allen	.25	.08
❑ 37	Keith Goganious	.10	.02
❑ 38	Pepper Johnson	.10	.02
❑ 39	Dave Brown	.10	.02
❑ 40	Levon Kirkland	.10	.02
❑ 41	Ken Dilger	.25	.08
❑ 42	Harvey Williams	.10	.02
❑ 43	Robert Blackmon	.10	.02
❑ 44	Kevin Carter	.10	.02
❑ 45	Warren Moon	.25	.08
❑ 46	Allen Aldridge	.10	.02
❑ 47	Terance Mathis	.10	.02
❑ 48	Junior Seau	.50	.20
❑ 49	William Fuller	.10	.02
❑ 50	Lee Woodall	.10	.02
❑ 51	Aeneas Williams	.10	.02
❑ 52	Thomas Smith	.10	.02
❑ 53	Chris Slade	.10	.02
❑ 54	Eric Allen	.10	.02
❑ 55	David Sloan	.10	.02
❑ 56	Hardy Nickerson	.10	.02
❑ 57	Michael Irvin	.50	.20
❑ 58	Corey Sawyer	.10	.02
❑ 59	Eric Green	.10	.02
❑ 60	Reggie White	.50	.20
❑ 61	Isaac Bruce	.50	.20
❑ 62	Darrell Green	.10	.02
❑ 63	Aaron Glenn	.10	.02
❑ 64	Mark Brunell	.75	.30
❑ 65	Mark Carrier WR	.10	.02
❑ 66	Mel Gray	.10	.02
❑ 67	Phillippi Sparks	.10	.02
❑ 68	Ernie Mills	.10	.02
❑ 69	Rick Mirer	.25	.08
❑ 70	Neil Smith	.25	.08
❑ 71	Terry McDaniel	.10	.02
❑ 72	Terrell Davis	1.00	.40
❑ 73	Alonzo Spellman	.10	.02
❑ 74	Jessie Tuggle	.10	.02
❑ 75	Terry Kirby	.25	.08
❑ 76	David Palmer	.10	.02
❑ 77	Calvin Williams	.10	.02
❑ 78	Shaun Gayle	.10	.02
❑ 79	Bryant Young	.25	.08
❑ 80	Jim Harbaugh	.25	.08
❑ 81	Michael Jackson	.25	.08
❑ 82	Dave Meggett	.10	.02
❑ 83	Henry Thomas	.10	.02
❑ 84	Jim Kelly	.50	.20
❑ 85	Frank Sanders	.25	.08
❑ 86	Daryl Johnston	.25	.08
❑ 87	Alvin Harper	.10	.02
❑ 88	John Copeland	.10	.02
❑ 89	Mark Chmura	.25	.08
❑ 90	Jim Everett	.10	.02
❑ 91	Bobby Houston	.10	.02
❑ 92	Willie Jackson	.25	.08
❑ 93	Carlton Bailey	.10	.02
❑ 94	Todd Lyght	.10	.02
❑ 95	Ken Harvey	.10	.02
❑ 96	Erric Pegram	.10	.02
❑ 97	Anthony Smith	.10	.02
❑ 98	Kimble Anders	.25	.08
❑ 99	Steve McNair	1.00	.40
❑ 100	Jeff George	.25	.08
❑ 101	Michael Timpson	.10	.02
❑ 102	Brent Jones	.10	.02
❑ 103	Mike Mamula	.10	.02
❑ 104	Jeff Cross	.10	.02
❑ 105	Craig Newsome	.10	.02
❑ 106	Howard Cross	.10	.02
❑ 107	Terry Wooden	.10	.02
❑ 108	Randall McDaniel	.10	.02
❑ 109	Andre Reed	.25	.08
❑ 110	Steve Atwater	.10	.02
❑ 111	Larry Centers	.25	.08
❑ 112	Tony Bennett	.10	.02
❑ 113	Drew Bledsoe	.75	.30
❑ 114	Terrell Fletcher	.10	.02
❑ 115	Warren Sapp	.10	.02
❑ 116	Deion Sanders	.75	.30
❑ 117	Bryce Paup	.10	.02
❑ 118	Mario Bates	.25	.08
❑ 119	Steve Tovar	.10	.02
❑ 120	Barry Sanders	2.00	.75
❑ 121	Tony Boselli	.10	.02
❑ 122	Micheal Barrow	.10	.02
❑ 123	Sam Mills	.10	.02
❑ 124	Tim Brown	.50	.20
❑ 125	Darren Perry	.10	.02
❑ 126	Brian Blades	.10	.02
❑ 127	Tyrone Wheatley	.25	.08
❑ 128	Derrick Thomas	.50	.20
❑ 129	Edgar Bennett	.25	.08
❑ 130	Cris Carter	.50	.20
❑ 131	Stephen Grant	.10	.02
❑ 132	Kevin Williams	.10	.02
❑ 133	Darnay Scott	.25	.08
❑ 134	Rod Stephens	.10	.02
❑ 135	Ken Norton	.10	.02

No.	Card		
136	Tim Biakabutuka SP RC	.50	.20
137	Willie Anderson SP RC	.10	.02
138	Lawrence Phillips SP RC	.50	.20
139	Jonathan Ogden SP RC	.50	.20
140	Simeon Rice SP RC	1.25	.50
141	Alex Van Dyke SP RC	.25	.08
142	Jerome Woods SP RC	.10	.02
143	Eric Moulds SP RC	2.00	.75
144	Mike Alstott SP RC	1.50	.60
145	Marvin Harrison SP RC	4.00	1.50
146	Duane Clemons SP RC	.10	.02
147	Regan Upshaw SP RC	.10	.02
148	Eddie Kennison SP RC	.50	.20
149	John Mobley SP RC	.10	.02
150	Keyshawn Johnson SP RC	1.50	.60
151	Marco Battaglia SP RC	.10	.02
152	Rickey Dudley SP RC	.50	.20
153	Kevin Hardy SP RC	.50	.20
154	Curtis Martin SM SP	1.00	.40
155	Dan Marino SM SP	2.50	1.00
156	Rashaan Salaam SM SP	.25	.08
157	Joey Galloway SM SP	.50	.20
158	John Elway SM SP	2.50	1.00
159	Marshall Faulk SM SP	.60	.25
160	Jerry Rice SM SP	1.25	.50
161	Darren Bennett SM SP	.10	.02
162	Tamarick Vanover SM SP	.25	.08
163	Orlando Thomas SM SP	.10	.02
164	Jim Kelly SM SP	.50	.20
165	Larry Brown SM SP	.10	.02
166	Errict Rhett SM SP	.25	.08
167	Warren Moon SM SP	.10	.02
168	Hugh Douglas SM SP	.10	.02
169	Jim Everett SM SP	.10	.02
170	AFC Championship Game SP	.10	.02
171	Larry Centers SM SP	.25	.08
172	Marcus Allen GM SP	.50	.20
173	Morten Andersen GM SP	.10	.02
174	Brett Favre GM SP	2.50	1.00
175	Jerry Rice GM SP	1.25	.50
176	Glyn Milburn GM SP	.10	.02
177	Thurman Thomas GM SP	.25	.08
178	Michael Irvin GM SP	.25	.08
179	Barry Sanders GM SP	2.00	.75
180	Dan Marino GM SP	2.50	1.00
181	Joey Galloway	.50	.20
182	Dwayne Harper	.10	.02
183	Antonio Langham	.10	.02
184	Chris Zorich	.10	.02
185	Willie McGinest	.10	.02
186	Wayne Chrebet	.75	.30
187	Dermontti Dawson	.10	.02
188	Charlie Garner	.25	.08
189	Quentin Coryatt	.10	.02
190	Rodney Hampton	.25	.08
191	Kelvin Pritchett	.10	.02
192	Willie Green	.10	.02
193	Garrison Hearst	.25	.08
194	Tracy Scroggins	.10	.02
195	Rocket Ismail	.10	.02
196	Michael Westbrook	.50	.20
197	Troy Drayton	.10	.02
198	Rob Fredrickson	.10	.02
199	Sean Lumpkin	.10	.02
200	John Elway	2.50	1.00
201	Bernie Parmalee	.10	.02
202	Chris Chandler	.25	.08
203	Lake Dawson	.10	.02
204	Orlando Thomas	.10	.02
205	Carl Pickens	.25	.08
206	Kurt Schulz	.10	.02
207	Clay Matthews	.10	.02
208	Winston Moss	.10	.02
209	Sean Dawkins	.10	.02
210	Emmitt Smith	2.00	.75
211	Mark Carrier DB	.10	.02
212	Clyde Simmons	.10	.02
213	Derrick Brooks	.50	.20
214	William Floyd	.25	.08
215	Aaron Hayden	.10	.02
216	Brian DeMarco	.10	.02
217	Ben Coates	.25	.08
218	Renaldo Turnbull	.10	.02
219	Adrian Murrell	.25	.08
220	Marcus Allen	.50	.20
221	Brett Maxie	.10	.02
222	Trev Alberts	.10	.02

No.	Card		
223	Darren Woodson	.25	.08
224	Brian Mitchell	.10	.02
225	Michael Haynes	.10	.02
226	Sean Jones	.10	.02
227	Eric Zeier	.10	.02
228	Herman Moore	.25	.08
229	Shane Conlan	.10	.02
230	Chris Warren	.25	.08
231	Dana Stubblefield	.25	.08
232	Andre Coleman	.10	.02
233	Kordell Stewart UER	.50	.20
234	Ray Crockett	.10	.02
235	Craig Heyward	.10	.02
236	Mike Fox	.10	.02
237	Derek Brown RBK	.10	.02
238	Thomas Lewis	.10	.02
239	Hugh Douglas	.25	.08
240	Tom Carter	.10	.02
241	Toby Wright	.10	.02
242	Jason Belser	.10	.02
243	Rodney Peete	.10	.02
244	Napoleon Kaufman	.50	.20
245	Merton Hanks	.10	.02
246	Harry Colon	.10	.02
247	Greg Hill	.25	.08
248	Vincent Brisby	.10	.02
249	Eric Hill	.10	.02
250	Brett Favre	2.50	1.00
251	Leroy Hoard	.10	.02
252	Eric Guliford	.10	.02
253	Stanley Richard	.25	.08
254	Carlos Jenkins	.10	.02
255	D'Marco Farr	.10	.02
256	Carlton Gray	.10	.02
257	Derek Loville	.10	.02
258	Ray Buchanan	.10	.02
259	Jake Reed	.25	.08
260	Dan Marino	2.50	1.00
261	Brad Baxter	.10	.02
262	Pat Swilling	.10	.02
263	Andy Harmon	.10	.02
264	Harold Green	.10	.02
265	Shannon Sharpe	.25	.08
266	Erik Kramer	.10	.02
267	Lamar Lathon	.10	.02
268	Stevon Moore	.10	.02
269	Tony Martin	.25	.08
270	Bruce Smith	.25	.08
271	James Washington	.10	.02
272	Tyrone Poole	.10	.02
273	Eric Swann	.10	.02
274	Dexter Carter	.10	.02
275	Greg Lloyd	.25	.08
276	Michael Zordich	.10	.02
277	Steve Wisniewski	.10	.02
278	Chris Calloway	.10	.02
279	Irv Smith	.10	.02
280	Steve Young	1.00	.40
281	James O.Stewart	.25	.08
282	Blaine Bishop	.10	.02
283	Rob Moore	.25	.08
284	Eric Metcalf	.10	.02
285	Kerry Collins	.50	.20
286	Dan Wilkinson	.10	.02
287	Curtis Conway	.50	.20
288	Jay Novacek	.10	.02
289	Henry Ellard	.10	.02
290	Curtis Martin	1.00	.40
291	Brett Perriman	.10	.02
292	Jeff Lageman	.10	.02
293	Trent Dilfer	.50	.20
294	Cortez Kennedy	.10	.02
295	Jeff Hostetler	.10	.02
296	Mark Fields	.10	.02
297	Qadry Ismail	.25	.08
298	Steve Bono	.10	.02
299	Tony Tolbert	.10	.02
300	Jerry Rice	1.25	.50
301	Marvcus Patton	.10	.02
302	Robert Brooks	.50	.20
303	Terry Ray RC	.10	.02
304	John Thierry	.10	.02
305	Errict Rhett	.25	.08
306	Ricardo McDonald	.10	.02
307	Antonio London	.10	.02
308	Lonnie Johnson	.10	.02
309	Mark Collins	.10	.02

No.	Card		
310	Marshall Faulk	.60	.25
311	Anthony Pleasant	.10	.02
312	Howard Griffith	.10	.02
313	Roosevelt Potts	.10	.02
314	Jim Flanigan	.10	.02
315	Omar Ellison RC	.10	.02
316	Boomer Esiason SP	.25	.08
317	Leslie O'Neal SP	.10	.02
318	Jerome Bettis SP	.50	.20
319	Larry Brown SP	.10	.02
320	Neil O'Donnell SP	.25	.08
321	Andre Rison SP	.25	.08
322	Cornelius Bennett SP	.10	.02
323	Quinn Early SP	.10	.02
324	Bryan Cox SP	.10	.02
325	Irving Fryar SP	.25	.08
326	Eddie Robinson SP	.10	.02
327	Chris Doleman SP	.10	.02
328	Sean Gilbert SP	.10	.02
329	Steve Walsh SP	.10	.02
330	Kevin Greene SP	.25	.08
331	Chris Spielman SP	.10	.02
332	Jeff Graham SP	.10	.02
333	Anthony Dorsett SP RC	.10	.02
334	Amani Toomer SP RC	1.50	.60
335	Walt Harris SP RC	.10	.02
336	Ray Mickens SP RC	.10	.02
337	Danny Kanell SP RC	.50	.20
338	Daryl Gardener SP RC	.10	.02
339	Jonathan Ogden SP	.25	.08
340	Eddie George SP RC	2.00	.75
341	Jeff Lewis SP RC	.25	.08
342	Terrell Owens SP RC	4.00	1.50
343	Brian Dawkins SP RC	2.00	.75
344	Tim Biakabutuka SP	.50	.20
345	Marvin Harrison SP	1.50	.60
346	Lawyer Milloy SP RC	.60	.25
347	Eric Moulds SP	.75	.30
348	Alex Van Dyke SP	.25	.08
349	John Mobley SP	.10	.02
350	Kevin Hardy SP	.50	.20
351	Ray Lewis SP RC	5.00	2.00
352	Lawrence Phillips SP	.50	.20
353	Stepfret Williams SP RC	.25	.08
354	Bobby Engram SP RC	.50	.20
355	Leeland McElroy SP RC	.25	.08
356	Marco Battaglia SP	.10	.02
357	Rickey Dudley SP	.50	.20
358	Bobby Hoying SP RC	.50	.20
359	Cedric Jones SP RC	.10	.02
360	Keyshawn Johnson SP	.50	.20
P19	Scott Mitchell Prototype	.50	.20
P31	Rashaan Salaam Prototype	.75	.30
P56	Hardy Nickerson Prototype	.50	.20
NNO	Checklist Card	.10	.02

1997 Stadium Club

No.	Card		
	COMPLETE SET (340)	60.00	25.00
	COMP.SERIES 1 (170)	30.00	15.00
	COMP.SERIES 2 (170)	30.00	15.00
1	Junior Seau	.75	.30
2	Michael Irvin	.75	.30
3	Marcus Allen	.75	.30
4	Dale Carter	.30	.10
5	Darnell Autry RC	.50	.20
6	Isaac Bruce	.75	.30
7	Darrell Green	.50	.20
8	Joey Galloway	.50	.20
9	Steve Atwater	.30	.10

❑ 10 Kordell Stewart .75 .30
❑ 11 Tony Brackens .30 .10
❑ 12 Gus Frerotte .30 .10
❑ 13 Henry Ellard .30 .10
❑ 14 Charles Way .50 .20
❑ 15 Jim Druckenmiller RC .50 .20
❑ 16 Orlando Thomas .30 .10
❑ 17 Terrell Davis 1.00 .40
❑ 18 Jim Schwantz .30 .10
❑ 19 Derrick Thomas .75 .30
❑ 20 Curtis Martin 1.00 .40
❑ 21 Deion Sanders .75 .30
❑ 22 Bruce Smith .50 .20
❑ 23 Jake Reed .50 .20
❑ 24 Leeland McElroy .30 .10
❑ 25 Jerome Bettis .75 .30
❑ 26 Neil Smith .50 .20
❑ 27 Terry Allen .75 .30
❑ 28 Gilbert Brown .50 .20
❑ 29 Steve McNair 1.00 .40
❑ 30 Kerry Collins .75 .30
❑ 31 Thurman Thomas .75 .30
❑ 32 Kenny Holmes RC .75 .30
❑ 33 Karim Abdul-Jabbar .75 .30
❑ 34 Steve Young 1.00 .40
❑ 35 Jerry Rice 1.50 .60
❑ 36 Jeff George .50 .20
❑ 37 Errict Rhett .30 .10
❑ 38 Mike Alstott .75 .30
❑ 39 Tim Brown .75 .30
❑ 40 Keyshawn Johnson .75 .30
❑ 41 Jim Harbaugh .50 .20
❑ 42 Kevin Hardy .30 .10
❑ 43 Kevin Greene .50 .20
❑ 44 Eric Metcalf .50 .20
❑ 45 Troy Aikman 1.50 .60
❑ 46 Marshall Faulk 1.00 .40
❑ 47 Shannon Sharpe .50 .20
❑ 48 Warren Moon .75 .30
❑ 49 Mark Brunell 1.00 .40
❑ 50 Dan Marino 3.00 1.25
❑ 51 Byron Hanspard RC .50 .20
❑ 52 Chris Chandler .50 .20
❑ 53 Wayne Chrebet .75 .30
❑ 54 Antonio Langham .30 .10
❑ 55 Barry Sanders 2.50 1.00
❑ 56 Curtis Conway .50 .20
❑ 57 Ricky Watters .50 .20
❑ 58 William Thomas .30 .10
❑ 59 Chris Warren .50 .20
❑ 60 Terry Glenn .75 .30
❑ 61 Peter Boulware RC .75 .30
❑ 62 Chad Cota .30 .10
❑ 63 Eddie Kennison .50 .20
❑ 64 Lamar Smith .75 .30
❑ 65 Brett Favre 3.00 1.50
❑ 66 Michael Westbrook .50 .20
❑ 67 Larry Centers .50 .20
❑ 68 Trent Dilfer .75 .30
❑ 69 Stevon Moore .30 .10
❑ 70 John Elway 3.00 1.25
❑ 71 Bryce Paup .30 .10
❑ 72 Quentin Coryatt .30 .10
❑ 73 Rashaan Salaam .30 .10
❑ 74 Thomas Lewis .30 .10
❑ 75 Drew Bledsoe 1.00 .40
❑ 76 Cris Carter .75 .30
❑ 77 Joe Bowden .30 .10
❑ 78 Allen Aldridge .30 .10
❑ 79 Zach Thomas .75 .30
❑ 80 Emmitt Smith 2.50 1.00
❑ 81 Daryl Johnston .50 .20
❑ 82 Vinny Testaverde .50 .20
❑ 83 James O.Stewart .50 .20
❑ 84 Edgar Bennett .50 .20
❑ 85 Shawn Springs RC .50 .20
❑ 86 Elvis Grbac .50 .20
❑ 87 Levon Kirkland .30 .10
❑ 88 Jeff Graham .30 .10
❑ 89 Terrell Fletcher .30 .10
❑ 90 Eddie George .75 .30
❑ 91 Jessie Tuggle .30 .10
❑ 92 Terrell Owens 1.00 .40
❑ 93 Wayne Martin .30 .10
❑ 94 Dwayne Harper .30 .10
❑ 95 Mark Collins .30 .10
❑ 96 Marvcus Patton .30 .10
❑ 97 Napoleon Kaufman .75 .30
❑ 98 Keenan McCardell .50 .20
❑ 99 Ty Detmer .50 .20
❑ 100 Reggie White .75 .30
❑ 101 William Floyd .50 .20
❑ 102 Scott Mitchell .50 .20
❑ 103 Robert Blackmon .30 .10
❑ 104 Dan Wilkinson .30 .10
❑ 105 Warren Sapp .50 .20
❑ 106 Dave Meggett .30 .10
❑ 107 Brian Mitchell .30 .10
❑ 108 Tyrone Poole .30 .10
❑ 109 Derrick Alexander WR .50 .20
❑ 110 David Palmer .30 .10
❑ 111 James Farrior RC .75 .30
❑ 112 Chad Brown .30 .10
❑ 113 Marty Carter .30 .10
❑ 114 Lawrence Phillips .30 .10
❑ 115 Wesley Walls .50 .20
❑ 116 John Friesz .30 .10
❑ 117 Roman Phifer .30 .10
❑ 118 Jason Sehorn .50 .20
❑ 119 Henry Thomas .30 .10
❑ 120 Natrone Means .50 .20
❑ 121 Ty Law .50 .20
❑ 122 Tony Gonzalez RC 3.00 1.25
❑ 123 Kevin Williams .30 .10
❑ 124 Regan Upshaw .30 .10
❑ 125 Antonio Freeman .75 .30
❑ 126 Jessie Armstead .30 .10
❑ 127 Pat Barnes RC .75 .30
❑ 128 Charlie Garner .50 .20
❑ 129 Irving Fryar .50 .20
❑ 130 Rickey Dudley .50 .20
❑ 131 Rodney Harrison RC 1.50 .60
❑ 132 Brent Jones .50 .20
❑ 133 Neil O'Donnell .50 .20
❑ 134 Darryll Lewis .30 .10
❑ 135 Jason Belser .30 .10
❑ 136 Mark Chmura .50 .20
❑ 137 Seth Joyner .30 .10
❑ 138 Herschel Walker .50 .20
❑ 139 Santana Dotson .30 .10
❑ 140 Carl Pickens .50 .20
❑ 141 Terance Mathis .50 .20
❑ 142 Walt Harris .30 .10
❑ 143 John Mobley .30 .10
❑ 144 Gabe Northern .30 .10
❑ 145 Herman Moore .50 .20
❑ 146 Michael Jackson .50 .20
❑ 147 Chris Sanders .30 .10
❑ 148 LeShon Johnson .30 .10
❑ 149 Darrell Russell RC .30 .10
❑ 150 Winslow Oliver .30 .10
❑ 151 Tamarick Vanover .50 .20
❑ 152 Tony Martin .50 .20
❑ 153 Lamar Lathon .30 .10
❑ 154 Ray Mickens .30 .10
❑ 155 Derrick Brooks .75 .30
❑ 156 Warrick Dunn RC 3.00 1.25
❑ 157 Tim McDonald .30 .10
❑ 158 Keith Lyle .30 .10
❑ 159 Terry McDaniel .30 .10
❑ 160 Andre Hastings .30 .10
❑ 161 Phillippi Sparks .30 .10
❑ 162 Tedy Bruschi 1.50 .60
❑ 163 Bryant Westbrook RC .30 .10
❑ 164 Victor Green .30 .10
❑ 165 Jimmy Smith .50 .20
❑ 166 Greg Biekert .30 .10
❑ 167 Frank Sanders .50 .20
❑ 168 Chris Doleman .30 .10
❑ 169 Phil Hansen .30 .10
❑ 170 Walter Jones RC .75 .30
❑ 171 Mark Carrier WR .30 .10
❑ 172 Greg Hill .30 .10
❑ 173 Erik Kramer .30 .10
❑ 174 Chris Spielman .30 .10
❑ 175 Tom Knight RC .30 .10
❑ 176 Sam Mills .30 .10
❑ 177 Robert Smith .50 .20
❑ 178 Dorsey Levens .75 .30
❑ 179 Chris Slade .30 .10
❑ 180 Troy Vincent .30 .10
❑ 181 Mario Bates .30 .10
❑ 182 Ed McCaffrey .50 .20
❑ 183 Mike Mamula .30 .10
❑ 184 Chad Hennings .30 .10
❑ 185 Stan Humphries .50 .20
❑ 186 Reinard Wilson RC .50 .20
❑ 187 Kevin Carter .30 .10
❑ 188 Qadry Ismail .50 .20
❑ 189 Cortez Kennedy .30 .10
❑ 190 Eric Swann .30 .10
❑ 191 Corey Dillon RC 6.00 2.50
❑ 192 Renaldo Wynn .30 .10
❑ 193 Bobby Hebert .30 .10
❑ 194 Fred Barnett .30 .10
❑ 195 Ray Lewis 1.25 .50
❑ 196 Robert Jones .30 .10
❑ 197 Brian Williams .30 .10
❑ 198 Willie McGinest .30 .10
❑ 199 Jake Plummer RC 5.00 2.00
❑ 200 Aeneas Williams .30 .10
❑ 201 Ashley Ambrose .30 .10
❑ 202 Cornelius Bennett .30 .10
❑ 203 Mo Lewis .30 .10
❑ 204 James Hasty .30 .10
❑ 205 Carnell Lake .30 .10
❑ 206 Heath Shuler .30 .10
❑ 207 Dana Stubblefield .30 .10
❑ 208 Corey Miller .30 .10
❑ 209 Ike Hilliard RC 1.25 .50
❑ 210 Bryant Young .30 .10
❑ 211 Hardy Nickerson .30 .10
❑ 212 Blaine Bishop .30 .10
❑ 213 Marcus Robertson .30 .10
❑ 214 Tony Bennett .30 .10
❑ 215 Kent Graham .30 .10
❑ 216 Steve Bono .50 .20
❑ 217 Will Blackwell RC .50 .20
❑ 218 Tyrone Braxton .30 .10
❑ 219 Eric Moulds .75 .30
❑ 220 Rod Woodson .50 .20
❑ 221 Anthony Johnson .30 .10
❑ 222 Willie Davis .30 .10
❑ 223 Darrin Smith .30 .10
❑ 224 Rick Mirer .30 .10
❑ 225 Marvin Harrison .75 .30
❑ 226 Terrell Buckley .30 .10
❑ 227 Joe Aska .30 .10
❑ 228 Yatil Green RC .50 .20
❑ 229 William Fuller .30 .10
❑ 230 Eddie Robinson .30 .10
❑ 231 Brian Blades .30 .10
❑ 232 Michael Sinclair .30 .10
❑ 233 Ken Harvey .30 .10
❑ 234 Harvey Williams .30 .10
❑ 235 Simeon Rice .50 .20
❑ 236 Chris T. Jones .30 .10
❑ 237 Bert Emanuel .50 .20
❑ 238 Corey Sawyer .30 .10
❑ 239 Chris Calloway .30 .10
❑ 240 Jeff Blake .50 .20
❑ 241 Alonzo Spellman .30 .10
❑ 242 Bryan Cox .30 .10
❑ 243 Antowain Smith RC 2.50 1.00
❑ 244 Tim Biakabutuka .50 .20
❑ 245 Ray Crockett .30 .10
❑ 246 Dwayne Rudd .30 .10
❑ 247 Glyn Milburn .30 .10
❑ 248 Gary Plummer .30 .10
❑ 249 O.J. McDuffie .50 .20
❑ 250 Willie Clay .30 .10
❑ 251 Jim Everett .30 .10
❑ 252 Eugene Daniel .30 .10
❑ 253 Corey Widmer .30 .10
❑ 254 Mel Gray .30 .10
❑ 255 Ken Norton .30 .10
❑ 256 Johnnie Morton .50 .20
❑ 257 Courtney Hawkins .30 .10
❑ 258 Ricardo McDonald .30 .10
❑ 259 Todd Lyght .30 .10
❑ 260 Micheal Barrow .30 .10
❑ 261 Aaron Glenn .30 .10
❑ 262 Jeff Herrod .30 .10
❑ 263 Troy Davis RC .50 .20
❑ 264 Eric Hill .30 .10

265	Darrien Gordon	.30	.10
266	Lake Dawson	.30	.10
267	John Randle	.50	.20
268	Henry Jones	.30	.10
269	Mickey Washington	.30	.10
270	Amani Toomer	.50	.20
271	Steve Grant	.30	.10
272	Adrian Murrell	.50	.20
273	Derrick Witherspoon	.30	.10
274	Albert Lewis	.30	.10
275	Ben Coates	.50	.20
276	Reidel Anthony RC	.75	.30
277	Jim Schwantz	.30	.10
278	Aaron Hayden	.30	.10
279	Ryan McNeil	.30	.10
280	LeRoy Butler	.30	.10
281	Craig Newsome	.30	.10
282	Bill Romanowski	.30	.10
283	Michael Bankston	.30	.10
284	Kevin Smith	.30	.10
285	Byron Bam Morris	.30	.10
286	Darnay Scott	.50	.20
287	David LaFleur RC	.30	.10
288	Randall Cunningham	.75	.30
289	Eric Davis	.30	.10
290	Todd Collins	.30	.10
291	Steve Tovar	.30	.10
292	Jermaine Lewis	.75	.30
293	Alfred Williams	.30	.10
294	Brad Johnson	.75	.30
295	Charles Johnson	.50	.20
296	Ted Johnson	.30	.10
297	Merton Hanks	.30	.10
298	Andre Coleman	.30	.10
299	Keith Jackson	.30	.10
300	Terry Kirby	.50	.20
301	Tony Banks	.50	.20
302	Terrance Shaw	.30	.10
303	Bobby Engram	.50	.20
304	Hugh Douglas	.30	.10
305	Lawyer Milloy	.50	.20
306	James Jett	.50	.20
307	Joey Kent RC	.75	.30
308	Rodney Hampton	.50	.20
309	Dewayne Washington	.30	.10
310	Kevin Lockett RC	.50	.20
311	Ki-Jana Carter	.30	.10
312	Jeff Lageman	.30	.10
313	Don Beebe	.30	.10
314	Willie Williams	.30	.10
315	Tyrone Wheatley	.50	.20
316	Leslie O'Neal	.30	.10
317	Quinn Early	.30	.10
318	Sean Gilbert	.30	.10
319	Tim Bowens	.30	.10
320	Sean Dawkins	.30	.10
321	Ken Dilger	.30	.10
322	George Koonce	.30	.10
323	Jevon Langford	.30	.10
324	Mike Caldwell	.30	.10
325	Orlando Pace RC	.75	.30
326	Garrison Hearst	.50	.20
327	Mike Tomczak	.30	.10
328	Rob Moore	.50	.20
329	Andre Reed	.50	.20
330	Kimble Anders	.50	.20
331	Qadry Ismail	.50	.20
332	Eric Allen	.30	.10
333	Dave Brown	.30	.10
334	Bennie Blades	.30	.10
335	Jamal Anderson	.75	.30
336	John Lynch	.50	.20
337	Tyrone Hughes	.30	.10
338	Ronnie Harmon	.30	.10
339	Rae Carruth RC	.30	.10
340	Robert Brooks	.50	.20
P1	Junior Seau Prototype	.50	.20
P20	Curtis Martin Prototype	1.00	.40
P21	Deion Sanders Prototype	.50	.20
P30	Kerry Collins Prototype	.75	.30
P47	Shannon Sharpe Prototype	.50	.20
P84	Edgar Bennett Prototype	.50	.20

1998 Stadium Club

	COMPLETE SET (195)	60.00	25.00
1	Barry Sanders	2.50	1.00
2	Tony Martin	.50	.20
3	Fred Lane	.30	.10
4	Darren Woodson	.30	.10
5	Andre Reed	.50	.20
6	Blaine Bishop	.30	.10
7	Robert Brooks	.50	.20
8	Tony Banks	.50	.20
9	Charles Way	.30	.10
10	Mark Brunell	.75	.30
11	Darrell Green	.50	.20
12	Aeneas Williams	.30	.10
13	Rob Johnson	.50	.20
14	Deion Sanders	.75	.30
15	Marshall Faulk	1.00	.40
16	Stephen Boyd	.30	.10
17	Adrian Murrell	.50	.20
18	Wayne Chrebet	.75	.30
19	Michael Sinclair	.30	.10
20	Dan Marino	3.00	1.25
21	Willie Davis	.30	.10
22	Chris Warren	.50	.20
23	John Mobley	.30	.10
24	Shannon Sharpe	.50	.20
25	Thurman Thomas	.75	.30
26	Corey Dillon	.75	.30
27	Zach Thomas	.75	.30
28	James Jett	.50	.20
29	Eric Metcalf	.30	.10
30	Drew Bledsoe	1.25	.50
31	Scott Greene	.30	.10
32	Simeon Rice	.50	.20
33	Robert Smith	.75	.30
34	Keenan McCardell	.50	.20
35	Jessie Armstead	.30	.10
36	Jerry Rice	1.50	.60
37	Eric Green	.30	.10
38	Terrell Owens	.75	.30
39	Tim Brown	.75	.30
40	Vinny Testaverde	.50	.20
41	Brian Stablein	.30	.10
42	Bert Emanuel	.50	.20
43	Terry Glenn	.75	.30
44	Chad Cota	.30	.10
45	Jermaine Lewis	.50	.20
46	Derrick Thomas	.75	.30
47	O.J. McDuffie	.50	.20
48	Frank Wycheck	.30	.10
49	Steve Broussard	.30	.10
50	Terrell Davis	.75	.30
51	Eric Allen	.30	.10
52	Napoleon Kaufman	.75	.30
53	Dan Wilkinson	.30	.10
54	Kerry Collins	.50	.20
55	Frank Sanders	.50	.20
56	Jeff Burris	.30	.10
57	Michael Westbrook	.50	.20
58	Michael McCrary	.30	.10
59	Bobby Hoying	.50	.20
60	Jerome Bettis	.75	.30
61	Amp Lee	.30	.10
62	Levon Kirkland	.30	.10
63	Dana Stubblefield	.30	.10
64	Terance Mathis	.50	.20
65	Mark Chmura	.50	.20
66	Bryant Westbrook	.30	.10
67	Rod Smith	.50	.20
68	Derrick Alexander	.50	.20
69	Jason Taylor	.50	.20
70	Eddie George	.75	.30
71	Elvis Grbac	.50	.20
72	Junior Seau	.75	.30
73	Marvin Harrison	.75	.30
74	Neil O'Donnell	.50	.20
75	Johnnie Morton	.50	.20
76	John Randle	.50	.20
77	Danny Kanell	.50	.20
78	Charlie Garner	.50	.20
79	J.J. Stokes	.50	.20
80	Troy Aikman	1.50	.60
81	Gus Frerotte	.30	.10
82	Jake Plummer	.75	.30
83	Andre Hastings	.30	.10
84	Steve Atwater	.30	.10
85	Larry Centers	.30	.10
86	Kevin Hardy	.30	.10
87	Willie McGinest	.30	.10
88	Joey Galloway	.50	.20
89	Charles Johnson	.30	.10
90	Warrick Dunn	.75	.30
91	Derrick Rodgers	.30	.10
92	Aaron Glenn	.30	.10
93	Shawn Jefferson	.30	.10
94	Antonio Freeman	.75	.30
95	Jake Reed	.50	.20
96	Reidel Anthony	.50	.20
97	Cris Dishman	.30	.10
98	Jason Sehorn	.50	.20
99	Herman Moore	.50	.20
100	John Elway	3.00	1.25
101	Brad Johnson	.75	.30
102	Jeff George	.50	.20
103	Emmitt Smith	2.50	1.00
104	Steve McNair	.75	.30
105	Ed McCaffrey	.50	.20
106	Errict Rhett	.50	.20
107	Dorsey Levens	.75	.30
108	Michael Jackson	.30	.10
109	Carl Pickens	.50	.20
110	James Stewart	.50	.20
111	Karim Abdul-Jabbar	.75	.30
112	Jim Harbaugh	.50	.20
113	Yancey Thigpen	.30	.10
114	Chad Brown	.30	.10
115	Chris Sanders	.30	.10
116	Cris Carter	.75	.30
117	Glenn Foley	.50	.20
118	Ben Coates	.50	.20
119	Jamal Anderson	.75	.30
120	Steve Young	1.00	.40
121	Scott Mitchell	.50	.20
122	Rob Moore	.50	.20
123	Bobby Engram	.50	.20
124	Rod Woodson	.50	.20
125	Terry Allen	.75	.30
126	Warren Sapp	.50	.20
127	Irving Fryar	.50	.20
128	Isaac Bruce	.75	.30
129	Rae Carruth	.30	.10
130	Sean Dawkins	.30	.10
131	Andre Rison	.50	.20
132	Kevin Greene	.50	.20
133	Warren Moon	.75	.30
134	Keyshawn Johnson	.75	.30
135	Jay Graham	.30	.10
136	Mike Alstott	.75	.30
137	Peter Boulware	.30	.10
138	Doug Evans	.30	.10
139	Jimmy Smith	.50	.20
140	Kordell Stewart	.75	.30
141	Tamarick Vanover	.30	.10
142	Chris Slade	.30	.10
143	Freddie Jones	.30	.10
144	Erik Kramer	.30	.10
145	Ricky Watters	.50	.20
146	Chris Chandler	.50	.20
147	Garrison Hearst	.75	.30
148	Trent Dilfer	.75	.30
149	Bruce Smith	.50	.20
150	Brett Favre	3.00	1.25
151	Will Blackwell	.30	.10

❑ 152	Rickey Dudley	.30	.10
❑ 153	Natrone Means	.50	.20
❑ 154	Curtis Conway	.50	.20
❑ 155	Tony Gonzalez	.75	.30
❑ 156	Jeff Blake	.50	.20
❑ 157	Michael Irvin	.75	.30
❑ 158	Curtis Martin	.75	.30
❑ 159	Tim McDonald	.30	.10
❑ 160	Wesley Walls	.50	.20
❑ 161	Michael Strahan	.50	.20
❑ 162	Reggie White	.75	.30
❑ 163	Jeff Graham	.30	.10
❑ 164	Ray Lewis	.75	.30
❑ 165	Antowain Smith	.75	.30
❑ 166	Ryan Leaf RC	2.50	1.00
❑ 167	Jerome Pathon RC	2.50	1.00
❑ 168	Duane Starks RC	1.25	.50
❑ 169	Brian Simmons RC	2.00	.75
❑ 170	Pat Johnson RC	2.00	.75
❑ 171	Keith Brooking RC	2.50	1.00
❑ 172	Kevin Dyson RC	2.50	1.00
❑ 173	Robert Edwards RC	2.00	.75
❑ 174	Grant Wistrom RC	2.00	.75
❑ 175	Curtis Enis RC	1.25	.50
❑ 176	John Avery RC	2.00	.75
❑ 177	Jason Peter RC	1.25	.50
❑ 178	Brian Griese RC	5.00	2.00
❑ 179	Tavian Banks RC	2.00	.75
❑ 180	Andre Wadsworth RC	2.00	.75
❑ 181	Skip Hicks RC	2.00	.75
❑ 182	Hines Ward RC	10.00	5.00
❑ 183	Greg Ellis RC	1.25	.50
❑ 184	Robert Holcombe RC	2.00	.75
❑ 185	Joe Jurevicius RC	2.50	1.00
❑ 186	Takeo Spikes RC	2.50	1.00
❑ 187	Ahman Green RC	12.00	5.00
❑ 188	Jacquez Green RC	2.00	.75
❑ 189	Randy Moss RC	12.00	6.00
❑ 190	Charles Woodson RC	3.00	1.25
❑ 191	Fred Taylor RC	4.00	1.50
❑ 192	Marcus Nash RC	1.25	.50
❑ 193	Germane Crowell RC	2.00	.75
❑ 194	Tim Dwight RC	2.50	1.00
❑ 195	Peyton Manning RC	25.00	12.50

1999 Stadium Club

❑	COMPLETE SET (200)	60.00	25.00
❑	COMP.SET w/o SP's (175)	20.00	7.50
❑	UNPRICED 1/1 PRESS PLATES EXIST		
❑	FOUR DIFF.PP's PRODUCED PER CARD		
❑ 1	Dan Marino	2.50	1.00
❑ 2	Andre Reed	.50	.20
❑ 3	Michael Westbrook	.50	.20
❑ 4	Isaac Bruce	.75	.30
❑ 5	Curtis Martin	.75	.30
❑ 6	Courtney Hawkins	.30	.10
❑ 7	Charles Way	.30	.10
❑ 8	Terrell Owens	.75	.30
❑ 9	Warrick Dunn	.75	.30
❑ 10	Jake Plummer	.50	.20
❑ 11	Chad Brown	.30	.10
❑ 12	Yancey Thigpen	.30	.10
❑ 13	Lamar Thomas	.30	.10
❑ 14	Keenan McCardell	.50	.20
❑ 15	Shannon Sharpe	.50	.20
❑ 16	Robert Brooks	.50	.20
❑ 17	Cameron Cleeland	.30	.10
❑ 18	Derrick Thomas	.75	.30
❑ 19	Mark Brunell	.75	.30
❑ 20	Jamal Anderson	.75	.30
❑ 21	Germane Crowell	.30	.10
❑ 22	Rod Smith	.50	.20
❑ 23	Ty Law	.50	.20
❑ 24	Cris Carter	.75	.30
❑ 25	Terrell Davis	.75	.30
❑ 26	Takeo Spikes	.30	.10
❑ 27	Tim Biakabutuka	.50	.20
❑ 28	Jermaine Lewis	.50	.20
❑ 29	Adrian Murrell	.50	.20
❑ 30	Doug Flutie	.75	.30
❑ 31	Curtis Enis	.30	.10
❑ 32	Skip Hicks	.30	.10
❑ 33	Steve McNair	.75	.30
❑ 34	Charles Woodson	.75	.30
❑ 35	Jessie Armstead	.30	.10
❑ 36	Shawn Springs	.30	.10
❑ 37	Levon Kirkland	.30	.10
❑ 38	Freddie Jones	.30	.10
❑ 39	Warren Sapp	.30	.10
❑ 40	Emmitt Smith	1.50	.60
❑ 41	Reidel Anthony	.50	.20
❑ 42	Tony Simmons	.30	.10
❑ 43	Andre Hastings	.30	.10
❑ 44	Byron Bam Morris	.30	.10
❑ 45	Jimmy Smith	.50	.20
❑ 46	Antonio Freeman	.75	.30
❑ 47	Herman Moore	.50	.20
❑ 48	Muhsin Muhammad	.50	.20
❑ 49	Chris Chandler	.50	.20
❑ 50	John Elway	2.50	1.00
❑ 51	Aeneas Williams	.30	.10
❑ 52	Bobby Engram	.50	.20
❑ 53	Keith Poole	.30	.10
❑ 54	Zach Thomas	.75	.30
❑ 55	Mike Alstott	.75	.30
❑ 56	Junior Seau	.75	.30
❑ 57	Aaron Glenn	.30	.10
❑ 58	Darrell Green	.30	.10
❑ 59	Thurman Thomas	.50	.20
❑ 60	Troy Aikman	1.50	.60
❑ 61	Bill Romanowski	.30	.10
❑ 62	Wesley Walls	.50	.20
❑ 63	Andre Wadsworth	.30	.10
❑ 64	Robert Smith	.75	.30
❑ 65	Elvis Grbac	.50	.20
❑ 66	Terry Fair	.30	.10
❑ 67	Ben Coates	.50	.20
❑ 68	Bert Emanuel	.50	.20
❑ 69	Jacquez Green	.30	.10
❑ 70	Barry Sanders	2.50	1.00
❑ 71	James Jett	.50	.20
❑ 72	Gary Brown	.30	.10
❑ 73	Stephen Alexander	.30	.10
❑ 74	Wayne Chrebet	.50	.20
❑ 75	Drew Bledsoe	1.00	.40
❑ 76	John Lynch	.50	.20
❑ 77	Jake Reed	.50	.20
❑ 78	Marvin Harrison	.75	.30
❑ 79	Johnnie Morton	.50	.20
❑ 80	Brett Favre	2.50	1.00
❑ 81	Charlie Batch	.75	.30
❑ 82	Antowain Smith	.75	.30
❑ 83	Mikhael Ricks	.30	.10
❑ 84	Derrick Mayes	.30	.10
❑ 85	John Mobley	.30	.10
❑ 86	Ernie Mills	.30	.10
❑ 87	Jeff Blake	.50	.20
❑ 88	Curtis Conway	.50	.20
❑ 89	Bruce Smith	.50	.20
❑ 90	Peyton Manning	2.50	1.00
❑ 91	Tyrone Davis	.30	.10
❑ 92	Ray Buchanan	.30	.10
❑ 93	Tim Dwight	.75	.30
❑ 94	O.J. McDuffie	.50	.20
❑ 95	Vonnie Holliday	.30	.10
❑ 96	Jon Kitna	.75	.30
❑ 97	Trent Dilfer	.50	.20
❑ 98	Jerome Bettis	.75	.30
❑ 99	Dedric Ward	.30	.10
❑ 100	Fred Taylor	.75	.30
❑ 101	Ike Hilliard	.30	.10
❑ 102	Frank Wycheck	.30	.10
❑ 103	Eric Moulds	.75	.30
❑ 104	Rob Moore	.50	.20
❑ 105	Ed McCaffrey	.50	.20
❑ 106	Carl Pickens	.50	.20
❑ 107	Priest Holmes	1.25	.50
❑ 108	Kevin Hardy	.30	.10
❑ 109	Terry Glenn	.75	.30
❑ 110	Keyshawn Johnson	.75	.30
❑ 111	Karim Abdul-Jabbar	.50	.20
❑ 112	Stephen Boyd	.30	.10
❑ 113	Ahman Green	.75	.30
❑ 114	Duce Staley	.75	.30
❑ 115	Vinny Testaverde	.50	.20
❑ 116	Napoleon Kaufman	.75	.30
❑ 117	Frank Sanders	.50	.20
❑ 118	Peter Boulware	.30	.10
❑ 119	Kevin Greene	.30	.10
❑ 120	Steve Young	1.00	.40
❑ 121	Darnay Scott	.30	.10
❑ 122	Deion Sanders	.75	.30
❑ 123	Corey Dillon	.75	.30
❑ 124	Randall Cunningham	.75	.30
❑ 125	Eddie George	.75	.30
❑ 126	Derrick Alexander	.30	.10
❑ 127	Mark Chmura	.30	.10
❑ 128	Michael Sinclair	.30	.10
❑ 129	Rickey Dudley	.30	.10
❑ 130	Joey Galloway	.50	.20
❑ 131	Michael Strahan	.50	.20
❑ 132	Ricky Proehl	.30	.10
❑ 133	Natrone Means	.50	.20
❑ 134	Dorsey Levens	.75	.30
❑ 135	Andre Rison	.50	.20
❑ 136	Alonzo Mayes	.30	.10
❑ 137	John Randle	.50	.20
❑ 138	Terance Mathis	.50	.20
❑ 139	Rae Carruth	.30	.10
❑ 140	Jerry Rice	1.50	.60
❑ 141	Michael Irvin	.50	.20
❑ 142	Oronde Gadsden	.50	.20
❑ 143	Jerome Pathon	.30	.10
❑ 144	Ricky Watters	.50	.20
❑ 145	J.J. Stokes	.50	.20
❑ 146	Kordell Stewart	.50	.20
❑ 147	Tim Brown	.75	.30
❑ 148	Garrison Hearst	.50	.20
❑ 149	Tony Gonzalez	.75	.30
❑ 150	Randy Moss	2.00	.75
❑ 151	Daunte Culpepper RC	6.00	2.50
❑ 152	Amos Zereoue RC	2.00	.75
❑ 153	Champ Bailey RC	2.50	1.00
❑ 154	Peerless Price RC	2.00	.75
❑ 155	Edgerrin James RC	6.00	2.50
❑ 156	Joe Germaine RC	1.50	.60
❑ 157	David Boston RC	2.00	.75
❑ 158	Kevin Faulk RC	2.00	.75
❑ 159	Troy Edwards RC	1.50	.60
❑ 160	Akili Smith RC	1.50	.60
❑ 161	Kevin Johnson RC	2.00	.75
❑ 162	Rob Konrad RC	1.50	.60
❑ 163	Shaun King RC	1.50	.60
❑ 164	James Johnson RC	1.50	.60
❑ 165	Donovan McNabb RC	8.00	3.00
❑ 166	Torry Holt RC	4.00	1.50
❑ 167	Mike Cloud RC	1.50	.60
❑ 168	Sedrick Irvin RC	1.00	.40
❑ 169	Cade McNown RC	1.50	.60
❑ 170	Ricky Williams RC	3.00	1.25
❑ 171	Karsten Bailey RC	1.50	.60
❑ 172	Cecil Collins RC	1.00	.40
❑ 173	Brock Huard RC	2.00	.75
❑ 174	D'Wayne Bates RC	1.50	.60
❑ 175	Tim Couch RC	2.00	.75
❑ 176	Torrance Small	.30	.10
❑ 177	Warren Moon	.75	.30
❑ 178	Rocket Ismail	.50	.20
❑ 179	Marshall Faulk	1.00	.40
❑ 180	Trent Green	.75	.30
❑ 181	Sean Dawkins	.30	.10
❑ 182	Pete Mitchell	.30	.10
❑ 183	Jeff Graham	.30	.10
❑ 184	Eddie Kennison	.50	.20
❑ 185	Kerry Collins	.50	.20
❑ 186	Eric Green	.30	.10
❑ 187	Kyle Brady	.30	.10
❑ 188	Tony Martin	.50	.20

❑	189 Jim Harbaugh	.50	.20
❑	190 Erik Kramer	.30	.10
❑	191 Steve Atwater	.30	.10
❑	192 Chad Bratzke	.30	.10
❑	193 Charles Johnson	.30	.10
❑	194 Damon Gibson	.30	.10
❑	195 Jeff George	.50	.20
❑	196 Scott Mitchell	.30	.10
❑	197 Terry Kirby	.30	.10
❑	198 Rich Gannon	.75	.30
❑	199 Chris Spielman	.30	.10
❑	200 Brad Johnson	.75	.30
❑	PP4 Emmitt Smith PROMO	3.00	1.25

2000 Stadium Club

❑	COMPLETE SET (175)	50.00	20.00
❑	COMP.SET w/o SP's (150)	20.00	7.50
❑	1 Peyton Manning	1.50	.60
❑	2 Pete Mitchell	.25	.08
❑	3 Napoleon Kaufman	.40	.15
❑	4 Mikhael Ricks	.25	.08
❑	5 Mike Alstott	.60	.25
❑	6 Brad Johnson	.60	.25
❑	7 Tony Gonzalez	.40	.15
❑	8 Germane Crowell	.25	.08
❑	9 Marcus Robinson	.60	.25
❑	10 Stephen Davis	.60	.25
❑	11 Terance Mathis	.40	.15
❑	12 Jake Plummer	.40	.15
❑	13 Qadry Ismail	.40	.15
❑	14 Cade McNown	.25	.08
❑	15 Zach Thomas	.60	.25
❑	16 Curtis Martin	.60	.25
❑	17 Torrance Small	.25	.08
❑	18 Steve McNair	.60	.25
❑	19 Jim Harbaugh	.40	.15
❑	20 Keyshawn Johnson	.60	.25
❑	21 Antonio Freeman	.60	.25
❑	22 Ed McCaffrey	.60	.25
❑	23 Elvis Grbac	.40	.15
❑	24 Peerless Price	.40	.15
❑	25 Jerome Bettis	.60	.25
❑	26 Yancey Thigpen	.25	.08
❑	27 Jake Delhomme RC	3.00	1.25
❑	28 Keith Poole	.25	.08
❑	29 Carl Pickens	.40	.15
❑	30 Jerry Rice	1.25	.50
❑	31 Rob Moore	.40	.15
❑	32 Reidel Anthony	.25	.08
❑	33 Jimmy Smith	.40	.15
❑	34 Ray Lucas	.40	.15
❑	35 Troy Aikman	1.25	.50
❑	36 Steve Beuerlein	.40	.15
❑	37 Charlie Batch	.60	.25
❑	38 Derrick Mayes	.40	.15
❑	39 Tim Brown	.60	.25
❑	40 Eddie George	.60	.25
❑	41 O.J. McDuffie	.40	.15
❑	42 Ike Hilliard	.40	.15
❑	43 Bill Schroeder	.40	.15
❑	44 Jim Miller	.25	.08
❑	45 Chris Chandler	.40	.15
❑	46 Fred Taylor	.60	.25
❑	47 Ricky Watters	.40	.15
❑	48 Tyrone Wheatley	.40	.15
❑	49 Bruce Smith	.40	.15
❑	50 Marshall Faulk	.75	.30
❑	51 Kevin Carter	.25	.08
❑	52 Champ Bailey	.40	.15
❑	53 Troy Edwards	.25	.08
❑	54 Doug Flutie	.60	.25
❑	55 Charles Johnson	.40	.15
❑	56 Michael Westbrook	.40	.15
❑	57 Frank Wycheck	.25	.08
❑	58 Drew Bledsoe	.75	.30
❑	59 Terrence Wilkins	.25	.08
❑	60 Ricky Williams	.60	.25
❑	61 Rod Smith	.40	.15
❑	62 Errict Rhett	.40	.15
❑	63 Vinny Testaverde	.40	.15
❑	64 Jacquez Green	.25	.08
❑	65 Curtis Conway	.40	.15
❑	66 Wayne Chrebet	.40	.15
❑	67 Albert Connell	.25	.08
❑	68 Kordell Stewart	.40	.15
❑	69 Bert Emanuel	.25	.08
❑	70 Randy Moss	1.25	.50
❑	71 Akili Smith	.25	.08
❑	72 Brian Griese	.60	.25
❑	73 Frank Sanders	.40	.15
❑	74 Wesley Walls	.25	.08
❑	75 Michael Pittman	.25	.08
❑	76 Steve Young	.75	.30
❑	77 Jevon Kearse	.60	.25
❑	78 Az-Zahir Hakim	.40	.15
❑	79 James Stewart	.40	.15
❑	80 Brett Favre	2.00	.75
❑	81 Dan Marino	2.00	.75
❑	82 Joe Horn	.40	.15
❑	83 Mark Brunell	.60	.25
❑	84 Eddie Kennison	.40	.15
❑	85 Deion Sanders	.60	.25
❑	86 Priest Holmes	.75	.30
❑	87 Terry Glenn	.40	.15
❑	88 Olandis Gary	.60	.25
❑	89 Patrick Jeffers	.60	.25
❑	90 Emmitt Smith	1.25	.50
❑	91 J.J. Stokes	.40	.15
❑	92 Warrick Dunn	.60	.25
❑	93 Damon Huard	.60	.25
❑	94 Herman Moore	.40	.15
❑	95 Corey Dillon	.60	.25
❑	96 Joey Galloway	.40	.15
❑	97 Jamal Anderson	.60	.25
❑	98 Junior Seau	.60	.25
❑	99 Robert Smith	.60	.25
❑	100 Edgerrin James	1.00	.40
❑	101 Derrick Alexander	.40	.15
❑	102 Johnnie Morton	.40	.15
❑	103 Sean Dawkins	.25	.08
❑	104 Derrick Brooks	.60	.25
❑	105 Rickey Dudley	.25	.08
❑	106 Keenan McCardell	.40	.15
❑	107 Kerry Collins	.40	.15
❑	108 Kevin Johnson	.60	.25
❑	109 Eric Moulds	.60	.25
❑	110 Terrell Davis	.60	.25
❑	111 Shawn Jefferson	.25	.08
❑	112 Donovan McNabb	1.00	.40
❑	113 Torry Holt	.60	.25
❑	114 Marvin Harrison	.60	.25
❑	115 Amani Toomer	.40	.15
❑	116 Tony Martin	.40	.15
❑	117 Curtis Enis	.25	.08
❑	118 Tiki Barber	.60	.25
❑	119 Freddie Jones	.25	.08
❑	120 Muhsin Muhammad	.40	.15
❑	121 Shaun King	.25	.08
❑	122 Isaac Bruce	.60	.25
❑	123 Duce Staley	.60	.25
❑	124 Hardy Nickerson	.25	.08
❑	125 Corey Bradford	.40	.15
❑	126 Kevin Hardy	.25	.08
❑	127 Hines Ward	.60	.25
❑	128 Charlie Garner	.40	.15
❑	129 Warren Sapp	.40	.15
❑	130 Tim Couch	.40	.15
❑	131 Kevin Dyson	.40	.15
❑	132 Rocket Ismail	.40	.15
❑	133 Tim Dwight	.60	.25
❑	134 Darnay Scott	.40	.15
❑	135 Jeff George	.40	.15
❑	136 Dorsey Levens	.40	.15
❑	137 Jeff Blake	.40	.15
❑	138 Jon Kitna	.60	.25
❑	139 Rich Gannon	.60	.25
❑	140 Cris Carter	.60	.25
❑	141 Jeff Graham	.25	.08
❑	142 James Johnson	.25	.08
❑	143 Tim Biakabutuka	.40	.15
❑	144 Bobby Engram	.40	.15
❑	145 Tony Banks	.40	.15
❑	146 Shannon Sharpe	.40	.15
❑	147 Antowain Smith	.40	.15
❑	148 Terrell Owens	.60	.25
❑	149 Rob Johnson	.40	.15
❑	150 Kurt Warner	1.25	.50
❑	151 Thomas Jones RC	4.00	1.50
❑	152 Chad Pennington RC	6.00	2.50
❑	153 Ron Dayne RC	2.50	1.00
❑	154 Tee Martin RC	2.50	1.00
❑	155 Reuben Droughns RC	3.00	1.25
❑	156 Jerry Porter RC	3.00	1.25
❑	157 R.Jay Soward RC	2.00	.75
❑	158 Sylvester Morris RC	2.00	.75
❑	159 Todd Pinkston RC	2.50	1.00
❑	160 Courtney Brown RC	2.50	1.00
❑	161 Travis Taylor RC	2.50	1.00
❑	162 Ron Dugans RC	2.00	.75
❑	163 Laveranues Coles RC	3.00	1.25
❑	164 Joe Hamilton RC	2.00	.75
❑	165 Curtis Keaton RC	2.00	.75
❑	166 Bubba Franks RC	2.50	1.00
❑	167 Dennis Northcutt RC	2.50	1.00
❑	168 Chris Redman RC	2.00	.75
❑	169 Travis Prentice RC	2.00	.75
❑	170 Shaun Alexander RC	12.00	5.00
❑	171 Jamal Lewis RC	6.00	2.50
❑	172 Peter Warrick RC	2.50	1.00
❑	173 J.R. Redmond RC	2.00	.75
❑	174 Trung Canidate RC	2.00	.75
❑	175 Plaxico Burress RC	5.00	2.00

2001 Stadium Club

❑	COMPLETE SET (175)	120.00	60.00
❑	COMP.SET w/o SPs (125)	20.00	7.50
❑	1 Peyton Manning	1.50	.60
❑	2 Akili Smith	.25	.08
❑	3 Brian Griese	.60	.25
❑	4 Wayne Chrebet	.40	.15
❑	5 Oronde Gadsden	.40	.15
❑	6 Marvin Harrison	.60	.25
❑	7 Charles Johnson	.25	.08
❑	8 Jay Fiedler	.60	.25
❑	9 Kerry Collins	.40	.15
❑	10 Troy Aikman	1.00	.40
❑	11 Donovan McNabb	.75	.30
❑	12 Ike Hilliard	.40	.15
❑	13 Warrick Dunn	.60	.25
❑	14 Derrick Alexander	.40	.15
❑	15 Jake Plummer	.40	.15
❑	16 Corey Dillon	.60	.25
❑	17 Ahman Green	.60	.25
❑	18 Keenan McCardell	.25	.08
❑	19 Derrick Mason	.40	.15
❑	20 Jerry Rice	1.25	.50
❑	21 Emmitt Smith	1.25	.50
❑	22 Dedric Ward	.25	.08
❑	23 Jamal Anderson	.60	.25
❑	24 Charlie Garner	.40	.15
❑	25 Vinny Testaverde	.40	.15
❑	26 Shaun Alexander	.75	.30
❑	27 Terry Glenn	.40	.15
❑	28 Cade McNown	.25	.08
❑	29 Germane Crowell	.25	.08

- ❑ 30 Jeff Graham .25 .08
- ❑ 31 Rich Gannon .60 .25
- ❑ 32 Jevon Kearse .40 .15
- ❑ 33 Shannon Sharpe .40 .15
- ❑ 34 Marcus Robinson .60 .25
- ❑ 35 Rod Smith .40 .15
- ❑ 36 Curtis Martin .60 .25
- ❑ 37 Robert Smith .60 .25
- ❑ 38 Marshall Faulk .75 .30
- ❑ 39 Tony Richardson .25 .08
- ❑ 40 Travis Prentice .25 .08
- ❑ 41 Edgerrin James .75 .30
- ❑ 42 Duce Staley .60 .25
- ❑ 43 Keyshawn Johnson .60 .25
- ❑ 44 Joe Horn .40 .15
- ❑ 45 Shawn Bryson .25 .08
- ❑ 46 Ray Lewis .60 .25
- ❑ 47 Fred Taylor .60 .25
- ❑ 48 Jeff George .40 .15
- ❑ 49 Sean Dawkins .25 .08
- ❑ 50 Daunte Culpepper .60 .25
- ❑ 51 Chris Chandler .40 .15
- ❑ 52 Tim Couch .40 .15
- ❑ 53 Trent Dilfer .40 .15
- ❑ 54 Steve McNair .60 .25
- ❑ 55 Kordell Stewart .40 .15
- ❑ 56 Aaron Brooks .60 .25
- ❑ 57 Michael Pittman .25 .08
- ❑ 58 Bill Schroeder .40 .15
- ❑ 59 Junior Seau .60 .25
- ❑ 60 Kurt Warner 1.25 .50
- ❑ 61 Drew Bledsoe .75 .30
- ❑ 62 Steve Beuerlein .40 .15
- ❑ 63 Mike Anderson .60 .25
- ❑ 64 Brad Johnson .60 .25
- ❑ 65 Tim Brown .60 .25
- ❑ 66 Qadry Ismail .40 .15
- ❑ 67 Doug Flutie .60 .25
- ❑ 68 Terrell Owens .60 .25
- ❑ 69 Rocket Ismail .40 .15
- ❑ 70 Charlie Batch .60 .25
- ❑ 71 Jerome Pathon .40 .15
- ❑ 72 Peter Warrick .60 .25
- ❑ 73 Hines Ward .60 .25
- ❑ 74 Ron Dayne .60 .25
- ❑ 75 Lamar Smith .40 .15
- ❑ 76 Amani Toomer .40 .15
- ❑ 77 Joey Galloway .40 .15
- ❑ 78 James Allen .40 .15
- ❑ 79 Isaac Bruce .60 .25
- ❑ 80 David Boston .60 .25
- ❑ 81 James Thrash .40 .15
- ❑ 82 Tony Gonzalez .40 .15
- ❑ 83 Jason Taylor .25 .08
- ❑ 84 Ricky Watters .40 .15
- ❑ 85 Terance Mathis .40 .15
- ❑ 86 Troy Brown .40 .15
- ❑ 87 Mark Brunell .60 .25
- ❑ 88 Rob Johnson .40 .15
- ❑ 89 Freddie Jones .25 .08
- ❑ 90 Eddie George .60 .25
- ❑ 91 Tiki Barber .60 .25
- ❑ 92 Donald Hayes .25 .08
- ❑ 93 Muhsin Muhammad .40 .15
- ❑ 94 Johnnie Morton .40 .15
- ❑ 95 Warren Sapp .40 .15
- ❑ 96 Bobby Shaw .25 .08
- ❑ 97 Randy Moss 1.25 .50
- ❑ 98 Jerome Bettis .60 .25
- ❑ 99 Antonio Freeman .60 .25
- ❑ 100 Jamal Lewis 1.00 .40
- ❑ 101 Andre Rison .40 .15
- ❑ 102 Kevin Faulk .40 .15
- ❑ 103 Jon Kitna .60 .25
- ❑ 104 Shawn Jefferson .25 .08
- ❑ 105 Kevin Johnson .40 .15
- ❑ 106 Torry Holt .60 .25
- ❑ 107 Cris Carter .60 .25
- ❑ 108 Chad Lewis .25 .08
- ❑ 109 Stephen Davis .60 .25
- ❑ 110 Jeff Blake .40 .15
- ❑ 111 Elvis Grbac .40 .15
- ❑ 112 Ed McCaffrey .60 .25
- ❑ 113 Tim Biakabutuka .40 .15
- ❑ 114 Trent Green .60 .25
- ❑ 115 Jeff Garcia .60 .25
- ❑ 116 Jacquez Green .25 .08
- ❑ 117 Shaun King .25 .08
- ❑ 118 Jimmy Smith .40 .15
- ❑ 119 James Stewart .40 .15
- ❑ 120 Brian Urlacher 1.00 .40
- ❑ 121 Tyrone Wheatley .40 .15
- ❑ 122 J.R. Redmond .25 .08
- ❑ 123 Eric Moulds .40 .15
- ❑ 124 Ricky Williams .60 .25
- ❑ 125 Brett Favre 2.00 .75
- ❑ 126 Koren Robinson RC 2.50 1.00
- ❑ 127 Richard Seymour RC 2.50 1.00
- ❑ 128 Jamal Reynolds RC 2.50 1.00
- ❑ 129 Kevin Kasper RC 2.50 1.00
- ❑ 130 LaMont Jordan RC 5.00 2.00
- ❑ 131 Reggie Wayne RC 5.00 2.00
- ❑ 132 Travis Henry RC 4.00 1.50
- ❑ 133 Alge Crumpler RC 3.00 1.25
- ❑ 134 Quincy Carter RC 2.50 1.00
- ❑ 135 Michael Bennett RC 2.50 1.00
- ❑ 136 Jamie Winborn RC 1.50 .60
- ❑ 137 Josh Heupel RC 2.50 1.00
- ❑ 138 Will Allen RC 1.50 .60
- ❑ 139 Scotty Anderson RC 1.50 .60
- ❑ 140 LaDainian Tomlinson RC 25.00 12.50
- ❑ 141 Freddie Mitchell RC 2.50 1.00
- ❑ 142 Gerard Warren RC 2.50 1.00
- ❑ 143 Chad Johnson RC 6.00 2.50
- ❑ 144 Todd Heap RC 2.50 1.00
- ❑ 145 Leonard Davis RC 1.50 .60
- ❑ 146 Kevan Barlow RC 2.50 1.00
- ❑ 147 Correll Buckhalter RC 3.00 1.25
- ❑ 148 Fred Smoot RC 2.50 1.00
- ❑ 149 Steve Smith RC 6.00 3.00
- ❑ 150 David Terrell RC 2.50 1.00
- ❑ 151 Chris Chambers RC 4.00 1.50
- ❑ 152 Mike McMahon RC 2.50 1.00
- ❑ 153 Rudi Johnson RC 5.00 2.00
- ❑ 154 Marques Tuiasosopo RC 2.50 1.00
- ❑ 155 Deuce McAllister RC 5.00 2.00
- ❑ 156 Marcus Stroud RC 2.50 1.00
- ❑ 157 Bobby Newcombe RC 1.50 .60
- ❑ 158 Rod Gardner RC 2.50 1.00
- ❑ 159 Drew Brees RC 8.00 3.00
- ❑ 160 Jesse Palmer RC 2.50 1.00
- ❑ 161 Derrick Gibson RC 1.50 .60
- ❑ 162 James Jackson RC 2.50 1.00
- ❑ 163 Dan Morgan RC 2.50 1.00
- ❑ 164 Michael Vick RC 12.00 5.00
- ❑ 165 Snoop Minnis RC 1.50 .60
- ❑ 166 Anthony Thomas RC 2.50 1.00
- ❑ 167 Andre Carter RC 2.50 1.00
- ❑ 168 Travis Minor RC 1.50 .60
- ❑ 169 Quincy Morgan RC 2.50 1.00
- ❑ 170 Justin Smith RC 2.50 1.00
- ❑ 171 Tay Cody RC 1.00 .40
- ❑ 172 Santana Moss RC 4.00 1.50
- ❑ 173 Sage Rosenfels RC 2.50 1.00
- ❑ 174 Robert Ferguson RC 2.50 1.00
- ❑ 175 Chris Weinke RC 2.50 1.00

2002 Stadium Club

- ❑ COMP.SET w/o SP's (125) 25.00 10.00
- ❑ 1 Randy Moss 1.25 .50
- ❑ 2 Kordell Stewart .40 .15
- ❑ 3 Marvin Harrison .60 .25
- ❑ 4 Chris Weinke .40 .15
- ❑ 5 James Allen .40 .15
- ❑ 6 Michael Pittman .25 .08
- ❑ 7 Quincy Carter .40 .15
- ❑ 8 Mike Anderson .60 .25
- ❑ 9 Mike McMahon .60 .25
- ❑ 10 Chris Chambers .60 .25
- ❑ 11 Laveranues Coles .40 .15
- ❑ 12 Curtis Conway .25 .08
- ❑ 13 Brad Johnson .40 .15
- ❑ 14 Shaun Alexander .75 .30
- ❑ 15 Jerry Rice 1.25 .50
- ❑ 16 Rod Gardner .40 .15
- ❑ 17 Derrick Mason .40 .15
- ❑ 18 Tom Brady 1.50 .60
- ❑ 19 Jimmy Smith .40 .15
- ❑ 20 Tim Couch .40 .15
- ❑ 21 Jim Miller .25 .08
- ❑ 22 Eric Moulds .40 .15
- ❑ 23 Michael Vick 2.00 .75
- ❑ 24 Jon Kitna .40 .15
- ❑ 25 Johnnie Morton .40 .15
- ❑ 26 Priest Holmes .75 .30
- ❑ 27 Aaron Brooks .60 .25
- ❑ 28 Duce Staley .60 .25
- ❑ 29 LaDainian Tomlinson 1.00 .40
- ❑ 30 Lamar Smith .40 .15
- ❑ 31 Rod Smith .40 .15
- ❑ 32 Richard Huntley .25 .08
- ❑ 33 Antonio Freeman .60 .25
- ❑ 34 Amani Toomer .40 .15
- ❑ 35 Hines Ward .60 .25
- ❑ 36 Marshall Faulk .60 .25
- ❑ 37 Steve McNair .60 .25
- ❑ 38 Tim Brown .60 .25
- ❑ 39 Curtis Martin .60 .25
- ❑ 40 Kevin Johnson .40 .15
- ❑ 41 Rob Johnson .40 .15
- ❑ 42 Qadry Ismail .40 .15
- ❑ 43 Daunte Culpepper .60 .25
- ❑ 44 Willie Jackson .25 .08
- ❑ 45 Jeff Garcia .60 .25
- ❑ 46 Matt Hasselbeck .40 .15
- ❑ 47 Corey Bradford .25 .08
- ❑ 48 Snoop Minnis .25 .08
- ❑ 49 Ron Dayne .40 .15
- ❑ 50 Peyton Manning 1.25 .50
- ❑ 51 Drew Bledsoe .75 .30
- ❑ 52 Terry Glenn .40 .15
- ❑ 53 Warrick Dunn .60 .25
- ❑ 54 Mark Brunell .60 .25
- ❑ 55 James Stewart .40 .15
- ❑ 56 Muhsin Muhammad .40 .15
- ❑ 57 Jake Plummer .40 .15
- ❑ 58 Terance Mathis .25 .08
- ❑ 59 Rocket Ismail .40 .15
- ❑ 60 Joe Horn .40 .15
- ❑ 61 Wayne Chrebet .40 .15
- ❑ 62 James Thrash .40 .15
- ❑ 63 Stephen Davis .40 .15
- ❑ 64 Isaac Bruce .60 .25
- ❑ 65 Peter Warrick .40 .15
- ❑ 66 Anthony Thomas .40 .15
- ❑ 67 Maurice Smith .40 .15
- ❑ 68 Tony Gonzalez .40 .15
- ❑ 69 Michael Bennett .40 .15
- ❑ 70 Ike Hilliard .40 .15
- ❑ 71 Plaxico Burress .40 .15
- ❑ 72 Darrell Jackson .40 .15
- ❑ 73 Kevan Barlow .40 .15
- ❑ 74 Ray Lewis .60 .25
- ❑ 75 Emmitt Smith 1.50 .60
- ❑ 76 Bill Schroeder .40 .15
- ❑ 77 Az-Zahir Hakim .25 .08
- ❑ 78 Troy Brown .40 .15
- ❑ 79 Keyshawn Johnson .60 .25
- ❑ 80 Tim Dwight .40 .15
- ❑ 81 Peerless Price .40 .15
- ❑ 82 Marty Booker .25 .08
- ❑ 83 Terrell Davis .60 .25
- ❑ 84 Dominic Rhodes .40 .15
- ❑ 85 Jay Fiedler .40 .15
- ❑ 86 Rich Gannon .60 .25
- ❑ 87 Terrell Owens .60 .25
- ❑ 88 Donald Hayes .25 .08
- ❑ 89 Thomas Jones .40 .15

❑ 90	Ricky Williams	.60	.25
❑ 91	Donovan McNabb	.75	.30
❑ 92	Eddie George	.60	.25
❑ 93	Germane Crowell	.25	.08
❑ 94	David Terrell	.60	.25
❑ 95	Alex Van Pelt	.25	.08
❑ 96	Antowain Smith	.40	.15
❑ 97	Jerome Bettis	.60	.25
❑ 98	Mike Alstott	.60	.25
❑ 99	Doug Flutie	.60	.25
❑ 100	Kurt Warner	.60	.25
❑ 101	Cris Carter	.60	.25
❑ 102	Oronde Gadsden	.40	.15
❑ 103	Ahman Green	.60	.25
❑ 104	Corey Dillon	.40	.15
❑ 105	Marcus Robinson	.40	.15
❑ 106	Shannon Sharpe	.40	.15
❑ 107	Kerry Collins	.40	.15
❑ 108	Garrison Hearst	.40	.15
❑ 109	David Boston	.60	.25
❑ 110	Travis Henry	.60	.25
❑ 111	James Jackson	.25	.08
❑ 112	Fred Taylor	.60	.25
❑ 113	Edgerrin James	.75	.30
❑ 114	Vinny Testaverde	.40	.15
❑ 115	Todd Pinkston	.40	.15
❑ 116	Koren Robinson	.40	.15
❑ 117	Torry Holt	.60	.25
❑ 118	Brian Griese	.60	.25
❑ 119	Trent Green	.40	.15
❑ 120	James McKnight	.25	.08
❑ 121	Charlie Garner	.40	.15
❑ 122	Tiki Barber	.60	.25
❑ 123	Joey Galloway	.40	.15
❑ 124	Quincy Morgan	.25	.08
❑ 125	Brett Favre	1.50	.60
❑ 126	Joey Harrington RC	5.00	2.00
❑ 127	Ashley Lelie RC	6.00	2.50
❑ 128	Terry Charles RC	2.50	1.00
❑ 129	Charles Grant RC	3.00	1.25
❑ 130	Levar Fisher RC	1.50	.60
❑ 131	Larry Tripplett RC	1.50	.60
❑ 132	Quentin Jammer RC	3.00	1.25
❑ 133	Ron Johnson RC	2.50	1.00
❑ 134	Maurice Morris RC	3.00	1.25
❑ 135	Roy Williams RC	8.00	3.00
❑ 136	Kurt Kittner RC	2.50	1.00
❑ 137	Dennis Johnson RC	1.50	.60
❑ 138	Seth Burford RC	2.50	1.00
❑ 139	Michael Lewis RC	3.00	1.25
❑ 140	William Green RC	3.00	1.25
❑ 141	Rohan Davey RC	3.00	1.25
❑ 142	Rocky Calmus RC	3.00	1.25
❑ 143	Robert Thomas RC	3.00	1.25
❑ 144	Travis Stephens RC	2.50	1.00
❑ 145	Ladell Betts RC	3.00	1.25
❑ 146	Daniel Graham RC	3.00	1.25
❑ 147	Chester Taylor RC	6.00	2.50
❑ 148	Tim Carter RC	2.50	1.00
❑ 149	Lito Sheppard RC	3.00	1.25
❑ 150	David Carr RC	8.00	3.00
❑ 151	Alex Brown RC	3.00	1.25
❑ 152	John Henderson RC	3.00	1.25
❑ 153	Jamar Martin RC	2.50	1.00
❑ 154	Raonall Smith RC	2.50	1.00
❑ 155	Leonard Henry RC	2.50	1.00
❑ 156	T.J. Duckett RC	4.00	1.50
❑ 157	Patrick Ramsey RC	4.00	1.50
❑ 158	Antwaan Randle El RC	5.00	2.00
❑ 159	Luke Staley RC	2.50	1.00
❑ 160	Jon McGraw RC	1.50	.60
❑ 161	Phillip Buchanon RC	3.00	1.25
❑ 162	Dwight Freeney RC	5.00	2.00
❑ 163	Mike Rumph RC	3.00	1.25
❑ 164	Albert Haynesworth RC	2.50	1.00
❑ 165	Antonio Bryant RC	3.00	1.25
❑ 166	Josh Reed RC	3.00	1.25
❑ 167	Eric Crouch RC	3.00	1.25
❑ 168	Reche Caldwell RC	3.00	1.25
❑ 169	Adrian Peterson RC	3.00	1.25
❑ 170	Jonathan Wells RC	3.00	1.25
❑ 171	Wendell Bryant RC	1.50	.60
❑ 172	Tellis Redmon RC	2.50	1.00
❑ 173	Josh McCown RC	4.00	1.50
❑ 174	DeShaun Foster RC	3.00	1.25
❑ 175	Cliff Russell RC	2.50	1.00
❑ 176	David Garrard RC	3.00	1.25
❑ 177	Brian Westbrook RC	5.00	2.00
❑ 178	Anthony Weaver RC	2.50	1.00
❑ 179	Bryan Thomas RC	2.50	1.00
❑ 180	Kalimba Edwards RC	3.00	1.25
❑ 181	Javon Walker RC	6.00	2.50
❑ 182	Marquise Walker RC	2.50	1.00
❑ 183	Deion Branch RC	6.00	2.50
❑ 184	Lamar Gordon RC	3.00	1.25
❑ 185	Jeremy Shockey RC	10.00	4.00
❑ 186	Clinton Portis RC	10.00	4.00
❑ 187	Napoleon Harris RC	3.00	1.25
❑ 188	Freddie Milons RC	2.50	1.00
❑ 189	Julius Peppers RC	6.00	2.50
❑ 190	Andre Davis RC	2.50	1.00
❑ 191	Travis Fisher RC	3.00	1.25
❑ 192	Chad Hutchinson RC	2.50	1.00
❑ 193	Najeh Davenport RC	3.00	1.25
❑ 194	Ed Reed RC	5.00	2.00
❑ 195	Donte Stallworth RC	6.00	2.50
❑ 196	Brandon Doman RC	2.50	1.00
❑ 197	Zak Kustok RC	3.00	1.25
❑ 198	Randy Fasani RC	2.50	1.00
❑ 199	J.T. O'Sullivan RC	2.50	1.00
❑ 200	Jabar Gaffney RC	3.00	1.25

2002 Sweet Spot

❑	COMP.SET w/o SP's (90)	30.00	12.50
❑ 1	Aaron Brooks	1.25	.50
❑ 2	Tim Couch	.75	.30
❑ 3	Jon Kitna	.75	.30
❑ 4	Brett Favre	3.00	1.25
❑ 5	Donovan McNabb	1.50	.60
❑ 6	Jeff Garcia	1.25	.50
❑ 7	Michael Vick	4.00	1.50
❑ 8	Mark Brunell	1.25	.50
❑ 9	Steve McNair	1.25	.50
❑ 10	Kordell Stewart	.75	.30
❑ 11	Drew Bledsoe	1.50	.60
❑ 12	Tom Brady	3.00	1.25
❑ 13	Kurt Warner	1.25	.50
❑ 14	Brian Griese	1.25	.50
❑ 15	Jim Miller	.75	.30
❑ 16	Jake Plummer	.75	.30
❑ 17	Quincy Carter	.75	.30
❑ 18	Peyton Manning	2.50	1.00
❑ 19	Keyshawn Johnson	1.25	.50
❑ 20	Travis Henry	1.25	.50
❑ 21	LaDainian Tomlinson	2.00	.75
❑ 22	Emmitt Smith	3.00	1.25
❑ 23	Michael Bennett	.75	.30
❑ 24	Duce Staley	1.25	.50
❑ 25	Thomas Jones	.75	.30
❑ 26	Deuce McAllister	1.50	.60
❑ 27	Eddie George	1.25	.50
❑ 28	Marshall Faulk	1.25	.50
❑ 29	Curtis Martin	1.25	.50
❑ 30	Ahman Green	1.25	.50
❑ 31	Priest Holmes	1.50	.60
❑ 32	Edgerrin James	1.50	.60
❑ 33	Antowain Smith	.75	.30
❑ 34	Ricky Williams	1.25	.50
❑ 35	Anthony Thomas	.75	.30
❑ 36	Jerome Bettis	1.25	.50
❑ 37	Shaun Alexander	1.50	.60
❑ 38	Kerry Collins	.75	.30
❑ 39	Drew Brees	1.25	.50
❑ 40	Chris Redman	.50	.20
❑ 41	Marc Bulger	1.25	.50
❑ 42	Jay Fiedler	.75	.30
❑ 43	Trent Green	.75	.30
❑ 44	Daunte Culpepper	1.25	.50
❑ 45	Rich Gannon	1.25	.50
❑ 46	Rodney Peete	.75	.30
❑ 47	Vinny Testaverde	.75	.30
❑ 48	Stephen Davis	.75	.30
❑ 49	James Allen	.75	.30
❑ 50	Tiki Barber	1.25	.50
❑ 51	Ron Dayne	.75	.30
❑ 52	Ray Lewis	1.25	.50
❑ 53	Corey Dillon	.75	.30
❑ 54	Brian Urlacher	2.00	.75
❑ 55	Junior Seau	1.25	.50
❑ 56	Warrick Dunn	1.25	.50
❑ 57	Fred Taylor	1.25	.50
❑ 58	Jamal Lewis	1.25	.50
❑ 59	Trent Dilfer	.75	.30
❑ 60	James Stewart	.75	.30
❑ 61	David Patten	.50	.20
❑ 62	Eric Moulds	.75	.30
❑ 63	Isaac Bruce	1.25	.50
❑ 64	Troy Brown	.75	.30
❑ 65	Terrell Owens	1.25	.50
❑ 66	Moe Williams	.50	.20
❑ 67	Joe Horn	.75	.30
❑ 68	Az-Zahir Hakim	.50	.20
❑ 69	Jimmy Smith	.75	.30
❑ 70	Michael Westbrook	.50	.20
❑ 71	Olandis Gary	.75	.30
❑ 72	Chris Chambers	1.25	.50
❑ 73	Kevin Johnson	.75	.30
❑ 74	Joey Galloway	.75	.30
❑ 75	Hines Ward	1.25	.50
❑ 76	Garrison Hearst	.75	.30
❑ 77	Wayne Chrebet	.75	.30
❑ 78	Muhsin Muhammad	.75	.30
❑ 79	Rod Gardner	.75	.30
❑ 80	Jerry Rice	2.50	1.00
❑ 81	Tim Brown	1.25	.50
❑ 82	Shannon Sharpe	.75	.30
❑ 83	Terry Glenn	.75	.30
❑ 84	Randy Moss	2.50	1.00
❑ 85	Corey Bradford	.50	.20
❑ 86	Marty Booker	.75	.30
❑ 87	Keenan McCardell	.50	.20
❑ 88	Marvin Harrison	1.25	.50
❑ 89	David Boston	1.25	.50
❑ 90	Eddie Kennison	.50	.20
❑ 91	Tim Carter RC	5.00	2.00
❑ 92	Joey Harrington RC	10.00	4.00
❑ 93	Patrick Ramsey RC	8.00	3.00
❑ 94	David Garrard RC	6.00	2.50
❑ 95	Donte Stallworth RC	12.00	5.00
❑ 96	Reche Caldwell RC	6.00	2.50
❑ 97	William Green RC	6.00	2.50
❑ 98	Josh Reed RC	6.00	2.50
❑ 99	DeShaun Foster RC	6.00	2.50
❑ 100	Jeremy Shockey RC	20.00	7.50
❑ 101	Mike Williams RC	5.00	2.00
❑ 102	Daniel Graham RC	6.00	2.50
❑ 103	Josh McCown RC	8.00	3.00
❑ 104	Javon Walker RC	12.00	5.00
❑ 105	Travis Stephens RC	5.00	2.00
❑ 106	Marquise Walker RC	5.00	2.00
❑ 107	T.J. Duckett RC	8.00	3.00
❑ 108	Damien Anderson RC	5.00	2.00
❑ 109	Quentin Jammer RC	6.00	2.50
❑ 110	Bryan Thomas RC	5.00	2.00
❑ 111	Chad Hutchinson RC	5.00	2.00
❑ 112	Brian Westbrook RC	10.00	4.00
❑ 113	Lamar Gordon RC	6.00	2.50
❑ 114	Deion Branch RC	12.00	5.00
❑ 115	Ed Reed RC	10.00	4.00
❑ 116	Jonathan Wells RC	6.00	2.50
❑ 117	Phillip Buchanon RC	6.00	2.50
❑ 118	Wendell Bryant RC	3.00	1.25
❑ 119	Kurt Kittner RC	5.00	2.00
❑ 120	Randy McMichael RC	10.00	4.00
❑ 121	Brandon Doman RC	5.00	2.00
❑ 122	Adrian Peterson RC	6.00	2.50
❑ 123	Ricky Williams RC	5.00	2.00
❑ 124	Seth Burford RC	5.00	2.00
❑ 125	Shaun Hill RC	6.00	2.50
❑ 126	Anthony Weaver RC	5.00	2.00
❑ 127	Freddie Milons RC	5.00	2.00
❑ 128	Darrell Hill RC	5.00	2.00
❑ 129	Daryl Jones RC	5.00	2.00

❑ 130	Chester Taylor RC	12.00	5.00
❑ 131	Najeh Davenport RC	6.00	2.50
❑ 132	Jason McAddley RC	5.00	2.00
❑ 133	Preston Parsons RC	3.00	1.25
❑ 134	Michael Lewis RC	6.00	2.50
❑ 135	Mike Rumph RC	6.00	2.50
❑ 136	Lamont Thompson RC	5.00	2.00
❑ 137	Dwight Freeney RC	10.00	4.00
❑ 138	Napoleon Harris RC	6.00	2.50
❑ 139	Tank Williams RC	5.00	2.00
❑ 140	Lee Mays RC	6.00	2.50
❑ 141	Robert Thomas RC	6.00	2.50
❑ 142	Tellis Redmon RC	5.00	2.00
❑ 143	Alex Brown RC	6.00	2.50
❑ 144	Ryan Sims RC	6.00	2.50
❑ 145	Larry Tripplett RC	3.00	1.25
❑ 146	Quinn Gray RC	3.00	1.25
❑ 147	Jesse Chatman RC	6.00	2.50
❑ 148	Jamin Elliott RC	3.00	1.25
❑ 149	Ben Leber RC	6.00	2.50
❑ 150	Lito Sheppard RC	6.00	2.50
❑ 151	Antonio Bryant AU/550 RC	25.00	12.50
❑ 152	Rohan Davey AU/550 RC	25.00	10.00
❑ 153	Randy Fasani AU/550 RC	15.00	6.00
❑ 154	J.T. O'Sullivan AU/550 RC	20.00	7.50
❑ 155	Ron Johnson AU/550 RC	15.00	6.00
❑ 156	Maurice Morris AU/550 RC	25.00	10.00
❑ 157	Kahlil Hill AU/550 RC	15.00	6.00
❑ 158	Ant Randle El AU/550 RC	30.00	15.00
❑ 159	Cliff Russell AU/550 RC	15.00	6.00
❑ 160	Ladell Betts AU/550 RC	20.00	7.50
❑ 161	David Carr AU/125 RC	100.00	50.00
❑ 162	Andre Davis AU/125 RC	25.00	12.50
❑ 163	Julius Peppers AU/125	125.00	75.00
❑ 164	Ashley Lelie AU/125 RC	50.00	20.00
❑ 165	Jabar Gaffney AU/125 RC	25.00	12.50
❑ 166	Clinton Portis AU/125 RC	120.00	60.00

2003 Sweet Spot

❑	COMP.SET w/o SP's (90)	30.00	12.50
❑ 1	Chad Pennington	1.50	.60
❑ 2	Aaron Brooks	1.25	.50
❑ 3	Joey Harrington	2.00	.75
❑ 4	Brett Favre	3.00	1.25
❑ 5	Donovan McNabb	1.50	.60
❑ 6	Jeff Garcia	1.25	.50
❑ 7	Michael Vick	3.00	1.25
❑ 8	David Carr	2.00	.75
❑ 9	Drew Brees	1.25	.50
❑ 10	Trent Green	.75	.30
❑ 11	Patrick Ramsey	1.25	.50
❑ 12	Tom Brady	3.00	1.25
❑ 13	Kurt Warner	1.25	.50
❑ 14	Brad Johnson	.75	.30
❑ 15	Brian Griese	1.25	.50
❑ 16	Jake Plummer	.75	.30
❑ 17	Drew Bledsoe	1.25	.50
❑ 18	Peyton Manning	2.00	.75
❑ 19	Tim Couch	.50	.20
❑ 20	Kordell Stewart	.75	.30
❑ 21	Jay Fiedler	.75	.30
❑ 22	Rich Gannon	.75	.30
❑ 23	Josh McCown	.75	.30
❑ 24	Matt Hasselbeck	.75	.30
❑ 25	Tommy Maddox	1.25	.50
❑ 26	Rodney Peete	.50	.20
❑ 27	Jake Delhomme	1.25	.50
❑ 28	Chris Redman	.50	.20
❑ 29	Mark Brunell	.75	.30
❑ 30	Marc Bulger	1.25	.50
❑ 31	Kelly Holcomb	.75	.30
❑ 32	Chad Hutchinson	.50	.20
❑ 33	Quincy Carter	.75	.30
❑ 34	Steve McNair	1.25	.50
❑ 35	Marshall Faulk	1.25	.50
❑ 36	Deuce McAllister	1.25	.50
❑ 37	Emmitt Smith	3.00	1.25
❑ 38	LaDainian Tomlinson	1.25	.50
❑ 39	Kevan Barlow	.75	.30
❑ 40	Michael Bennett	.75	.30
❑ 41	Shaun Alexander	1.25	.50
❑ 42	Edgerrin James	1.25	.50
❑ 43	Ricky Williams	1.25	.50
❑ 44	Priest Holmes	1.50	.60
❑ 45	Ahman Green	1.25	.50
❑ 46	Curtis Martin	1.25	.50
❑ 47	Anthony Thomas	.75	.30
❑ 48	Travis Henry	.75	.30
❑ 49	Jerome Bettis	1.25	.50
❑ 50	Fred Taylor	1.25	.50
❑ 51	Corey Dillon	.75	.30
❑ 52	Jamal Lewis	1.25	.50
❑ 53	William Green	.75	.30
❑ 54	Brian Urlacher	2.00	.75
❑ 55	Junior Seau	1.25	.50
❑ 56	Ray Lewis	1.25	.50
❑ 57	Julius Peppers	1.25	.50
❑ 58	Terrell Owens	1.25	.50
❑ 59	David Boston	.75	.30
❑ 60	Isaac Bruce	1.25	.50
❑ 61	Marvin Harrison	1.25	.50
❑ 62	Chris Chambers	1.25	.50
❑ 63	Chad Johnson	1.25	.50
❑ 64	Peter Warrick	.75	.30
❑ 65	Peerless Price	.75	.30
❑ 66	Antonio Bryant	.75	.30
❑ 67	Laveranues Coles	.75	.30
❑ 68	Rod Gardner	.75	.30
❑ 69	Hines Ward	1.25	.50
❑ 70	Plaxico Burress	.75	.30
❑ 71	Keyshawn Johnson	1.25	.50
❑ 72	Jabar Gaffney	.75	.30
❑ 73	Eric Moulds	.75	.30
❑ 74	Santana Moss	.75	.30
❑ 75	Koren Robinson	.75	.30
❑ 76	Jimmy Smith	.75	.30
❑ 77	Donte Stallworth	1.25	.50
❑ 78	Kevin Johnson	.75	.30
❑ 79	Quincy Morgan	.75	.30
❑ 80	Jerry Rice	2.50	1.00
❑ 81	Tim Brown	1.25	.50
❑ 82	Rod Smith	.75	.30
❑ 83	Ashley Lelie	1.25	.50
❑ 84	Randy Moss	2.00	.75
❑ 85	Torry Holt	1.25	.50
❑ 86	Troy Brown	.75	.30
❑ 87	Donald Driver	.75	.30
❑ 88	Todd Heap	.75	.30
❑ 89	Tony Gonzalez	.75	.30
❑ 90	Jeremy Shockey	2.00	.75
❑ 91	Casey Moore RC	5.00	2.00
❑ 92	Chris Crocker RC	4.00	1.50
❑ 93	Pisa Tinoisamoa RC	6.00	2.50
❑ 94	Nnamdi Asomugha RC	5.00	2.00
❑ 95	Tyler Brayton RC	6.00	2.50
❑ 96	Eddie Moore RC	5.00	2.00
❑ 97	Terrence Kiel RC	6.00	2.50
❑ 98	Casey Fitzsimmons RC	6.00	2.50
❑ 99	George Foster RC	4.00	1.50
❑ 100	J.J. Moses RC	5.00	2.00
❑ 101	Dan Klecko RC	6.00	2.50
❑ 102	Terry Pierce RC	5.00	2.00
❑ 103	Brad Pyatt RC	5.00	2.00
❑ 104	Boss Bailey RC	6.00	2.50
❑ 105	Michael Haynes RC	6.00	2.50
❑ 106	Jimmy Kennedy RC	6.00	2.50
❑ 107	Jerome McDougle RC	6.00	2.50
❑ 108	William Joseph RC	6.00	2.50
❑ 109	Visanthe Shiancoe RC	5.00	2.00
❑ 110	L.J. Smith RC	6.00	2.50
❑ 111	Avon Cobourne RC	4.00	1.50
❑ 112	Bennie Joppru RC	6.00	2.50
❑ 113	Ken Hamlin RC	6.00	2.50
❑ 114	Jeremi Johnson RC	5.00	2.00
❑ 115	Justin Griffith RC	5.00	2.00
❑ 116	Joffrey Reynolds RC	4.00	1.50
❑ 117	Kassim Osgood RC	6.00	2.50
❑ 118	Donald Lee RC	5.00	2.00
❑ 119	Denero Marriott RC	4.00	1.50
❑ 120	Jamal Burke RC	4.00	1.50
❑ 121	Michael Vick SS	25.00	10.00
❑ 122	Donovan McNabb SS	12.00	5.00
❑ 123	Jerry Rice SS	20.00	7.50
❑ 124	Brett Favre SS	25.00	10.00
❑ 125	Kurt Warner SS	10.00	4.00
❑ 126	Marshall Faulk SS	10.00	4.00
❑ 127	Ricky Williams SS	10.00	4.00
❑ 128	Emmitt Smith SS	25.00	10.00
❑ 129	Tom Brady SS	25.00	10.00
❑ 130	Randy Moss SS	15.00	6.00
❑ 131	LaDainian Tomlinson SS	10.00	4.00
❑ 132	Jeff Garcia SS	10.00	4.00
❑ 133	Brian Urlacher SS	15.00	6.00
❑ 134	Drew Bledsoe SS	10.00	4.00
❑ 135	Peyton Manning SS	15.00	6.00
❑ 136	Dave Ragone RC	8.00	3.00
❑ 137	Brian St.Pierre RC	8.00	3.00
❑ 138	Kliff Kingsbury RC	6.00	2.50
❑ 139	Marquel Blackwell RC	4.00	1.50
❑ 140	Brett Engemann RC	4.00	1.50
❑ 141	Kirk Farmer RC	4.00	1.50
❑ 142	Andrew Pinnock RC	6.00	2.50
❑ 143	Tony Romo RC	50.00	25.00
❑ 144	Nate Hybl RC	8.00	3.00
❑ 145	Ken Dorsey RC	8.00	3.00
❑ 146	Brock Forsey RC	8.00	3.00
❑ 147	Musa Smith RC	8.00	3.00
❑ 148	Domanick Davis RC	8.00	3.00
❑ 149	LaBrandon Toefield RC	8.00	3.00
❑ 150	B.J. Askew RC	8.00	3.00
❑ 151	Quentin Griffin RC	8.00	3.00
❑ 152	Ahmaad Galloway RC	6.00	2.50
❑ 153	Cecil Sapp RC	6.00	2.50
❑ 154	Justin Fargas RC	8.00	3.00
❑ 155	Sultan McCullough RC	6.00	2.50
❑ 156	Malaefou MacKenzie RC	4.00	1.50
❑ 157	Tom Lopienski RC	6.00	2.50
❑ 158	Lee Suggs RC	8.00	3.00
❑ 159	Richard Angulo RC	6.00	2.50
❑ 160	Dwone Hicks RC	4.00	1.50
❑ 161	Nate Burleson RC	8.00	3.00
❑ 162	Billy McMullen RC	6.00	2.50
❑ 163	David Tyree RC	6.00	2.50
❑ 164	Gerald Hayes RC	4.00	1.50
❑ 165	Anthony Adams RC	6.00	2.50
❑ 166	George Wrighster RC	6.00	2.50
❑ 167	Tyrone Calico RC	8.00	3.00
❑ 168	Shaun McDonald RC	8.00	3.00
❑ 169	Bobby Wade RC	8.00	3.00
❑ 170	Larry Johnson RC	30.00	15.00
❑ 171	Ryan Hoag RC	4.00	1.50
❑ 172	Doug Gabriel RC	8.00	3.00
❑ 173	Antonio Gates RC	50.00	30.00
❑ 174	Brandon Lloyd RC	8.00	3.00
❑ 175	Arnaz Battle RC	8.00	3.00
❑ 176	Kelley Washington RC	8.00	3.00
❑ 177	Antwone Savage RC	4.00	1.50
❑ 178	Keenan Howry RC	8.00	3.00
❑ 179	Adrian Madise RC	6.00	2.50
❑ 180	LaTarence Dunbar RC	6.00	2.50
❑ 181	Walter Young RC	4.00	1.50
❑ 182	Travaris Robinson RC	4.00	1.50
❑ 183	DeAndrew Rubin RC	4.00	1.50
❑ 184	Carl Ford RC	4.00	1.50
❑ 185	Zuriel Smith RC	4.00	1.50
❑ 186	Willie Ponder RC	5.00	2.00
❑ 187	Gibran Hamdan RC	5.00	2.00
❑ 188	Aaron Moorehead RC	10.00	4.00
❑ 189	Nick Barnett RC	8.00	3.00
❑ 190	Chris Brown RC	8.00	3.00
❑ 191	ReShard Lee RC	10.00	4.00
❑ 192	Anquan Boldin RC	25.00	10.00
❑ 193	Kevin Curtis RC	10.00	4.00
❑ 194	Taylor Jacobs RC	8.00	3.00
❑ 195	Sam Aiken RC	8.00	3.00
❑ 196	Aaron Walker RC	8.00	3.00
❑ 197	Mike Seidman RC	5.00	2.00
❑ 198	Jason Witten RC	15.00	6.00
❑ 199	Dallas Clark RC	10.00	4.00

❑ 200 Rashean Mathis RC 8.00 3.00
❑ 201 DeWayne Robertson RC 10.00 4.00
❑ 202 Johnathan Sullivan RC 8.00 3.00
❑ 203 Drayton Florence RC 5.00 2.00
❑ 204 Sammy Davis RC 10.00 4.00
❑ 205 Andre Woolfolk RC 10.00 4.00
❑ 206 Terence Newman RC 20.00 7.50
❑ 207 Mike Doss RC 10.00 4.00
❑ 208 Troy Polamalu RC 30.00 15.00
❑ 209 Terrell Suggs RC 15.00 6.00
❑ 210 Marcus Trufant RC 10.00 4.00
❑ 211 Seneca Wallace RC 15.00 6.00
❑ 212 Brooks Bollinger RC 15.00 6.00
❑ 213 Jason Gesser RC 15.00 6.00
❑ 214 Onterrio Smith RC 15.00 6.00
❑ 215 Artose Pinner RC 15.00 6.00
❑ 216 J.R. Tolver RC 12.00 5.00
❑ 217 Kerry Carter RC 12.00 5.00
❑ 218 Tony Hollings RC 15.00 6.00
❑ 219 Teyo Johnson RC 15.00 6.00
❑ 220 Bethel Johnson RC 15.00 6.00
❑ 221 Rex Grossman RC 50.00 25.00
❑ 222 Andre Johnson RC 40.00 15.00
❑ 223 Terrence Edwards RC 12.00 5.00
❑ 224 Willis McGahee RC 40.00 15.00
❑ 225 Charles Rogers RC 15.00 6.00
❑ 226 Chris Simms AU RC 50.00 30.00
❑ 227 Bryant Johnson AU RC 25.00 10.00
❑ 228 Byron Leftwich AU RC 80.00 30.00
❑ 229 Carson Palmer AU RC 150.00 75.00
❑ 230 Justin Gage AU RC 25.00 10.00
❑ 231 Kyle Boller AU RC 30.00 12.50

2004 Sweet Spot

❑ COMP.SET w/o SP's (100) 30.00 15.00
❑ 1 Anquan Boldin 1.25 .50
❑ 2 Emmitt Smith 2.50 1.00
❑ 3 Josh McCown .75 .30
❑ 4 Michael Vick 2.50 1.00
❑ 5 Warrick Dunn .75 .30
❑ 6 Peerless Price .75 .30
❑ 7 Jamal Lewis 1.25 .50
❑ 8 Deion Sanders 1.25 .50
❑ 9 Kyle Boller 1.25 .50
❑ 10 Drew Bledsoe 1.25 .50
❑ 11 Travis Henry .75 .30
❑ 12 Eric Moulds .75 .30
❑ 13 Jake Delhomme 1.25 .50
❑ 14 Stephen Davis .75 .30
❑ 15 Julius Peppers 1.25 .50
❑ 16 Thomas Jones .75 .30
❑ 17 Rex Grossman 1.25 .50
❑ 18 Brian Urlacher 1.50 .60
❑ 19 Carson Palmer 1.50 .60
❑ 20 Chad Johnson 1.25 .50
❑ 21 Rudi Johnson .75 .30
❑ 22 Jeff Garcia 1.25 .50
❑ 23 William Green .75 .30
❑ 24 Andre Davis .50 .20
❑ 25 Vinny Testaverde .75 .30
❑ 26 Eddie George .75 .30
❑ 27 Keyshawn Johnson .75 .30
❑ 28 Reuben Droughns .75 .30
❑ 29 Jake Plummer .75 .30
❑ 30 Ashley Lelie .75 .30
❑ 31 Rod Smith .75 .30
❑ 32 Joey Harrington 1.25 .50
❑ 33 Artose Pinner .50 .20
❑ 34 Az-Zahir Hakim .50 .20
❑ 35 Brett Favre 3.00 1.25
❑ 36 Javon Walker .75 .30
❑ 37 Ahman Green 1.25 .50
❑ 38 Andre Johnson 1.25 .50
❑ 39 David Carr 1.25 .50
❑ 40 Domanick Davis 1.25 .50
❑ 41 Peyton Manning 2.00 .75
❑ 42 Edgerrin James 1.25 .50
❑ 43 Marvin Harrison 1.25 .50
❑ 44 Byron Leftwich 1.50 .60
❑ 45 Fred Taylor .75 .30
❑ 46 Jimmy Smith .75 .30
❑ 47 Priest Holmes 1.50 .60
❑ 48 Trent Green .75 .30
❑ 49 Dante Hall 1.25 .50
❑ 50 Tony Gonzalez .75 .30
❑ 51 Randy McMichael .50 .20
❑ 52 Jay Fiedler .50 .20
❑ 53 Chris Chambers .75 .30
❑ 54 Randy Moss 1.50 .60
❑ 55 Daunte Culpepper 1.25 .50
❑ 56 Onterrio Smith .75 .30
❑ 57 Tom Brady 3.00 1.25
❑ 58 Deion Branch 1.25 .50
❑ 59 Corey Dillon .75 .30
❑ 60 Deuce McAllister 1.25 .50
❑ 61 Aaron Brooks .75 .30
❑ 62 Joe Horn .75 .30
❑ 63 Jeremy Shockey 1.25 .50
❑ 64 Tiki Barber 1.25 .50
❑ 65 Michael Strahan .75 .30
❑ 66 Curtis Martin 1.25 .50
❑ 67 Chad Pennington 1.25 .50
❑ 68 Santana Moss .75 .30
❑ 69 Charles Woodson .75 .30
❑ 70 Kerry Collins .75 .30
❑ 71 Warren Sapp .75 .30
❑ 72 Donovan McNabb 1.50 .60
❑ 73 Brian Westbrook .75 .30
❑ 74 Terrell Owens 1.25 .50
❑ 75 Hines Ward 1.25 .50
❑ 76 Plaxico Burress .75 .30
❑ 77 Duce Staley .75 .30
❑ 78 LaDainian Tomlinson 1.50 .60
❑ 79 Antonio Gates 1.25 .50
❑ 80 Drew Brees 1.25 .50
❑ 81 Eric Johnson .75 .30
❑ 82 Kevan Barlow .75 .30
❑ 83 Tim Rattay .50 .20
❑ 84 Matt Hasselbeck .75 .30
❑ 85 Shaun Alexander 1.25 .50
❑ 86 Jerry Rice 2.50 1.00
❑ 87 Marc Bulger 1.25 .50
❑ 88 Torry Holt 1.25 .50
❑ 89 Marshall Faulk 1.25 .50
❑ 90 Isaac Bruce .75 .30
❑ 91 Brad Johnson .75 .30
❑ 92 Derrick Brooks .75 .30
❑ 93 Joey Galloway .75 .30
❑ 94 Steve McNair 1.25 .50
❑ 95 Derrick Mason .75 .30
❑ 96 Chris Brown 1.25 .50
❑ 97 Clinton Portis 1.25 .50
❑ 98 Mark Brunell .75 .30
❑ 99 Laveranues Coles .75 .30
❑ 100 LaVar Arrington 2.50 1.00
❑ 101 Roger Staubach 8.00 3.00
❑ 102 Troy Aikman 6.00 2.50
❑ 103 John Elway 10.00 4.00
❑ 104 Barry Sanders 10.00 4.00
❑ 105 Fran Tarkenton 6.00 2.50
❑ 106 Archie Manning 6.00 2.50
❑ 107 Joe Namath 8.00 3.00
❑ 108 Ken Stabler 6.00 2.50
❑ 109 Howie Long 6.00 2.50
❑ 110 Kellen Winslow Sr. 5.00 2.00
❑ 111 Joe Montana 15.00 6.00
❑ 112 Joe Theismann 5.00 2.00
❑ 113 Darnell Dockett RC 6.00 2.50
❑ 114 Randy Starks RC 6.00 2.50
❑ 115 Rashad Baker RC 8.00 3.00
❑ 116 Tim Anderson RC 8.00 3.00
❑ 117 Darrion Scott RC 8.00 3.00
❑ 118 Courtney Watson RC 8.00 3.00
❑ 119 Gilbert Gardner RC 6.00 2.50
❑ 120 Marquis Cooper RC 6.00 2.50
❑ 121 Caleb Miller RC 6.00 2.50
❑ 122 Jeff Shoate RC 4.00 1.50
❑ 123 Keyaron Fox RC 6.00 2.50
❑ 124 Landon Johnson RC 6.00 2.50
❑ 125 Reggie Torbor RC 6.00 2.50
❑ 126 Demorrio Williams RC 8.00 3.00
❑ 127 Niko Koutouvides RC 6.00 2.50
❑ 128 Richard Seigler RC 6.00 2.50
❑ 129 Brandon Chillar RC 6.00 2.50
❑ 130 Nate Kaeding RC 8.00 3.00
❑ 131 Dave Ball RC 4.00 1.50
❑ 132 Josh Thomas RC 8.00 3.00
❑ 133 Josh Scobee RC 4.00 1.50
❑ 134 Wes Welker RC 10.00 4.00
❑ 135 Darrell McClover RC 6.00 2.50
❑ 136 Ben Utecht RC 4.00 1.50
❑ 137 Chris Snee RC 6.00 2.50
❑ 138 Jake Grove RC 4.00 1.50
❑ 139 Justin Smiley RC 8.00 3.00
❑ 140 Max Starks RC 6.00 2.50
❑ 141 Randall Gay RC 12.00 6.00
❑ 142 Charlie Anderson RC 4.00 1.50
❑ 143 Alain Kashama RC 8.00 3.00
❑ 144 Eric Edwards RC 10.00 4.00
❑ 145 Jacques Reeves RC 6.00 2.50
❑ 146 Jarrett Payton RC 8.00 3.00
❑ 147 Curtis Deloatch RC 6.00 2.50
❑ 148 Michael Gaines RC 6.00 2.50
❑ 149 Erik Jensen RC 6.00 2.50
❑ 150 Courtney Anderson RC 6.00 2.50
❑ 151 Bruce Thornton RC 4.00 1.50
❑ 152 Glenn Earl RC 6.00 2.50
❑ 153 Michael Waddell RC 4.00 1.50
❑ 154 J.R. Reed RC 6.00 2.50
❑ 155 Dwight Anderson RC 8.00 3.00
❑ 156 Von Hutchins RC 6.00 2.50
❑ 157 Travis LaBoy RC 8.00 3.00
❑ 158 Terry Johnson RC 6.00 2.50
❑ 159 Dwan Edwards RC 4.00 1.50
❑ 160 Colby Bockwoldt RC 8.00 3.00
❑ 161 Madieu Williams RC 6.00 2.50
❑ 162 Will Poole RC 8.00 3.00
❑ 163 Igor Olshansky RC 8.00 3.00
❑ 164 Michael Boulware RC 8.00 3.00
❑ 165 Shaun Phillips RC 6.00 2.50
❑ 166 Keith Smith RC 6.00 2.50
❑ 167 Will Smith RC 8.00 3.00
❑ 168 D.J. Williams RC 8.00 3.00
❑ 169 Derrick Strait RC 8.00 3.00
❑ 170 Karlos Dansby RC 8.00 3.00
❑ 171 Ricardo Colclough RC 8.00 3.00
❑ 172 Chad Lavalais RC 6.00 2.50
❑ 173 Teddy Lehman RC 8.00 3.00
❑ 174 Jim Sorgi RC 8.00 3.00
❑ 175 Bob Sanders RC 20.00 10.00
❑ 176 Sean Taylor RC 8.00 3.00
❑ 177 Marcus Tubbs RC 10.00 4.00
❑ 178 Daryl Smith RC 10.00 4.00
❑ 179 Bradlee Van Pelt RC 8.00 3.00
❑ 180 Shawntae Spencer RC 10.00 4.00
❑ 181 Nathan Vasher RC 12.00 5.00
❑ 182 Jared Allen RC 12.00 5.00
❑ 183 Rod Davis RC 5.00 2.00
❑ 184 Brian Jones RC 8.00 3.00
❑ 185 Will Allen RC 10.00 4.00
❑ 186 Antwan Odom RC 10.00 4.00
❑ 187 Vernon Carey RC 8.00 3.00
❑ 188 Mike Karney RC 8.00 3.00
❑ 189 Joey Thomas RC 10.00 4.00
❑ 190 Casey Bramlet RC 8.00 3.00
❑ 191 Keiwan Ratliff RC 8.00 3.00
❑ 192 Rich Gardner RC 8.00 3.00
❑ 193 Jason Babin RC 10.00 4.00
❑ 194 Dontarrious Thomas RC 10.00 4.00
❑ 195 Dexter Reid RC 5.00 2.00
❑ 196 Marquise Hill RC 8.00 3.00
❑ 197 Jonathan Smith RC 8.00 3.00
❑ 198 Larry Croom RC 8.00 3.00
❑ 199 Gibril Wilson RC 10.00 4.00
❑ 200 Erik Coleman RC 10.00 4.00
❑ 201 B.J. Sams RC 10.00 4.00
❑ 202 Bruce Perry RC 10.00 4.00
❑ 203 Brock Lesnar RC 15.00 6.00
❑ 204 Brandon Miree RC 8.00 3.00

❑ 205 Clarence Moore RC 10.00 4.00
❑ 206 Mark Jones RC 8.00 3.00
❑ 207 Patrick Crayton RC 10.00 4.00
❑ 208 Jeff Dugan RC 5.00 2.00
❑ 209 Sean Ryan RC 8.00 3.00
❑ 210 Sloan Thomas RC 8.00 3.00
❑ 211 Triandos Luke RC 12.00 5.00
❑ 212 Dexter Wynn RC 10.00 4.00
❑ 213 Matt Kranchick RC 12.00 5.00
❑ 214 Tim Euhus RC 12.00 5.00
❑ 215 Ryan Krause RC 10.00 4.00
❑ 216 Junior Siavii RC 12.00 5.00
❑ 217 Ran Carthon RC 10.00 4.00
❑ 218 Derrick Pope RC 10.00 4.00
❑ 219 Alex Lewis RC 12.00 5.00
❑ 220 Chris Cooley RC 12.00 5.00
❑ 221 Jamaar Taylor RC 12.00 5.00
❑ 222 Stuart Schweigert RC 12.00 5.00
❑ 223 Jason David RC 12.00 5.00
❑ 224 Maurice Mann RC 10.00 4.00
❑ 225 Robert Geathers RC 10.00 4.00
❑ 226 Matt Mauck RC 12.00 5.00
❑ 227 Jammal Lord RC 12.00 5.00
❑ 228 Travelle Wharton RC 6.00 2.50
❑ 229 D.J. Hackett RC 10.00 4.00
❑ 230 Thomas Tapeh RC 10.00 4.00
❑ 231 D.Robinson AU/699 RC EXCH 25.00 10.00
❑ 232 Ahmad Carroll AU/699 RC 20.00 7.50
❑ 233 Kenechi Udeze AU/699 RC 20.00 7.50
❑ 234 Tommie Harris AU/699 RC 20.00 7.50
❑ 235 Jonathan Vilma AU/699 RC 30.00 12.50
❑ 236 Vince Wilfork AU/699 RC 20.00 8.00
❑ 237 B.J. Symons AU/699 RC 20.00 7.50
❑ 238 B.J. Johnson AU/699 RC 15.00 6.00
❑ 239 Kris Wilson AU/699 RC 20.00 7.50
❑ 240 Josh Harris AU/699 RC 20.00 7.50
❑ 241 Troy Fleming AU/699 RC 15.00 6.00
❑ 242 J.Morant AU/699 RC 20.00 7.50
❑ 243 Craig Krenzel AU/699 RC 20.00 7.50
❑ 244 Q.Wilson AU/699 RC EXCH 15.00 6.00
❑ 245 P.K. Sam AU/699 RC 15.00 6.00
❑ 246 Michael Turner AU/699 RC 50.00 25.00
❑ 247 Carlos Francis AU/699 RC 20.00 7.50
❑ 248 Jared Lorenzen AU/699 RC 15.00 6.00
❑ 249 John Navarre AU/675 RC 20.00 7.50
❑ 250 Jeff Smoker AU/699 RC 20.00 7.50
❑ 251 Ernest Wilford AU/559 RC 20.00 7.50
❑ 252 Mew.Moore AU/699 RC 20.00 7.50
❑ 253 Chris Gamble AU/699 RC 20.00 8.00
❑ 254 Jerricho Cotchery AU/699 RC 20.00 7.50
❑ 255 Derrick Hamilton AU/699 RC 20.00 7.50
❑ 256 Samie Parker AU/699 RC 20.00 7.50
❑ 257 Cody Pickett AU/699 RC 25.00 10.00
❑ 259 Ben Hartsock AU/699 RC 20.00 7.50
❑ 260 Cedric Cobbs AU/699 RC 20.00 7.50
❑ 261 Matt Schaub AU/699 RC 60.00 30.00
❑ 262 Bernard Berrian AU/699 RC 25.00 12.50
❑ 263 Devard Darling AU/699 RC 20.00 7.50
❑ 264 Ben Watson AU/699 RC 20.00 7.50
❑ 265 Darius Watts AU/699 RC 20.00 7.50
❑ 266 DeAngelo Hall AU/399 RC 25.00 10.00
❑ 267 Ben Troupe AU/699 RC 20.00 7.50
❑ 268 Michael Jenkins AU/399 RC 25.00 10.00
❑ 269 Keary Colbert AU/699 RC 25.00 10.00
❑ 270 Robert Gallery AU/699 RC 20.00 8.00
❑ 271 Greg Jones AU/650 RC 25.00 12.50
❑ 272 Mic.Clayton AU/699 RC 50.00 20.00
❑ 273 Luke McCown AU/699 RC 20.00 7.50
❑ 274 Ras.Woods AU/699 RC 20.00 7.50
❑ 275 Reg.Williams AU/699 RC 25.00 10.00
❑ 276 Dev.Henderson AU/699 RC 15.00 6.00
❑ 277 Tatum Bell AU/699 RC 40.00 15.00
❑ 278 Lee Evans AU/350 RC 40.00 20.00
❑ 279 J.P. Losman AU/199 RC 60.00 30.00
❑ 280 Drew Henson AU/199 RC 40.00 15.00
❑ 281 Kel.Winslow AU/125 RC 60.00 30.00
❑ 282 Chris Perry AU/199 RC 50.00 20.00
❑ 283 Julius Jones AU/199 RC 100.00 50.00
❑ 284 Stev.Jackson AU/199 RC 100.00 50.00
❑ 285 Kevin Jones AU/199 RC 80.00 40.00
❑ 286 Roy Williams AU/149 RC 100.00 40.00
❑ 287 Roethlis AU/199 RC 200.00 100.00
❑ 288 Philip Rivers AU/199 RC 120.00 60.00
❑ 289 L.Fitzgerald AU/150 RC 100.00 50.00
❑ 290 Eli Manning AU/150 RC 150.00 75.00

2005 Sweet Spot

❑ COMP.SET w/o RCs (100) 30.00 15.00
❑ 101-142 PRINT RUN 899 SER.#'d SETS
❑ 143-182 PRINT RUN 699 SER.#'d SETS
❑ 183-222 PRINT RUN 499 SER.#'d SETS
❑ 223-242 PRINT RUN 299 SER.#'d SETS
❑ 285-302 PRINT RUN 899 SER.#'d SETS
❑ EXCH EXPIRATION: 12/9/2008
❑ 1 Larry Fitzgerald 1.25 .50
❑ 2 Anquan Boldin .75 .30
❑ 3 Kurt Warner .75 .30
❑ 4 Michael Vick 2.00 .75
❑ 5 T.J. Duckett .75 .30
❑ 6 Peerless Price .60 .25
❑ 7 Todd Heap .75 .30
❑ 8 Jamal Lewis 1.25 .50
❑ 9 Kyle Boller .75 .30
❑ 10 Derrick Mason .75 .30
❑ 11 J.P. Losman 1.25 .50
❑ 12 Willis McGahee 1.25 .50
❑ 13 Lee Evans .75 .30
❑ 14 Eric Moulds .75 .30
❑ 15 Jake Delhomme 1.25 .50
❑ 16 Keary Colbert .75 .30
❑ 17 DeShaun Foster .75 .30
❑ 18 Brian Urlacher 1.25 .50
❑ 19 Rex Grossman .75 .30
❑ 20 Muhsin Muhammad .75 .30
❑ 21 Carson Palmer 1.25 .50
❑ 22 Rudi Johnson .75 .30
❑ 23 Chad Johnson 1.25 .50
❑ 24 Julius Jones 1.50 .60
❑ 25 Keyshawn Johnson .75 .30
❑ 26 Drew Bledsoe 1.25 .50
❑ 27 Tatum Bell .75 .30
❑ 28 Jake Plummer .75 .30
❑ 29 Ashley Lelie .75 .30
❑ 30 Roy Williams WR 1.25 .50
❑ 31 Kevin Jones 1.25 .50
❑ 32 Joey Harrington 1.25 .50
❑ 33 Brett Favre 3.00 1.25
❑ 34 Ahman Green 1.25 .50
❑ 35 Javon Walker .75 .30
❑ 36 David Carr 1.25 .50
❑ 37 Andre Johnson .75 .30
❑ 38 Domanick Davis .75 .30
❑ 39 Peyton Manning 2.00 .75
❑ 40 Reggie Wayne .75 .30
❑ 41 Edgerrin James 1.25 .50
❑ 42 Marvin Harrison 1.25 .50
❑ 43 Byron Leftwich 1.25 .50
❑ 44 Fred Taylor .75 .30
❑ 45 Jimmy Smith .75 .30
❑ 46 Priest Holmes 1.25 .50
❑ 47 Tony Gonzalez .75 .30
❑ 48 Trent Green .75 .30
❑ 49 A.J. Feeley .75 .30
❑ 50 Chris Chambers .75 .30
❑ 51 Randy McMichael .60 .25
❑ 52 Daunte Culpepper 1.25 .50
❑ 53 Michael Bennett .75 .30
❑ 54 Nate Burleson .75 .30
❑ 55 Tom Brady 3.00 1.25
❑ 56 Corey Dillon .75 .30
❑ 57 Deion Branch .75 .30
❑ 58 Richard Seymour .60 .25
❑ 59 Aaron Brooks .75 .30
❑ 60 Deuce McAllister 1.25 .50
❑ 61 Joe Horn .75 .30
❑ 62 Eli Manning 2.50 1.00
❑ 63 Jeremy Shockey 1.25 .50
❑ 64 Tiki Barber 1.25 .50
❑ 65 Chad Pennington 1.25 .50
❑ 66 Curtis Martin 1.25 .50
❑ 67 Laveranues Coles .75 .30
❑ 68 Kerry Collins .75 .30
❑ 69 LaMont Jordan 1.25 .50
❑ 70 Randy Moss 1.25 .50
❑ 71 Donovan McNabb 1.50 .60
❑ 72 Terrell Owens 1.25 .50
❑ 73 Jeremiah Trotter .60 .25
❑ 74 Brian Westbrook .75 .30
❑ 75 Ben Roethlisberger 3.00 1.25
❑ 76 Willie Parker 10.00 4.00
❑ 77 Hines Ward 1.25 .50
❑ 78 Antwaan Randle El .75 .30
❑ 79 Drew Brees 1.25 .50
❑ 80 LaDainian Tomlinson 1.50 .60
❑ 81 Antonio Gates 1.25 .50
❑ 82 Tim Rattay .60 .25
❑ 83 Brandon Lloyd .60 .25
❑ 84 Eric Johnson .75 .30
❑ 85 Shaun Alexander 1.50 .60
❑ 86 Darrell Jackson .75 .30
❑ 87 Matt Hasselbeck .75 .30
❑ 88 Marc Bulger 1.25 .50
❑ 89 Steven Jackson 1.50 .60
❑ 90 Marshall Faulk 1.25 .50
❑ 91 Torry Holt 1.25 .50
❑ 92 Joey Galloway .75 .30
❑ 93 Brian Griese .75 .30
❑ 94 Michael Clayton 1.25 .50
❑ 95 Steve McNair 1.25 .50
❑ 96 Drew Bennett .75 .30
❑ 97 Chris Brown .75 .30
❑ 98 Clinton Portis 1.25 .50
❑ 99 Patrick Ramsey .75 .30
❑ 100 Santana Moss .75 .30
❑ 101 Antonio Perkins RC 5.00 2.00
❑ 102 James Sanders RC 6.00 2.50
❑ 103 Justin Green RC 6.00 2.50
❑ 104 Andre Maddox RC 5.00 2.00
❑ 105 C.C. Brown RC 5.00 2.00
❑ 106 Michael Hawkins RC 5.00 2.00
❑ 107 Deandra Cobb RC 5.00 2.00
❑ 108 Nehemiah Broughton RC 5.00 2.00
❑ 109 Madison Hedgecock RC 6.00 2.50
❑ 110 Paris Warren RC 5.00 2.00
❑ 111 Chris Harris RC 12.00 5.00
❑ 112 Matt Cassel RC 10.00 4.00
❑ 113 Justin Beriault RC 5.00 2.00
❑ 114 Roydell Williams RC 6.00 2.50
❑ 115 Alex Barron RC 3.00 1.25
❑ 116 Jammal Brown RC 6.00 2.50
❑ 117 Bo Scaife RC 5.00 2.00
❑ 118 Patrick Estes RC 5.00 2.00
❑ 119 Elton Brown RC 3.00 1.25
❑ 120 Rasheed Marshall RC 6.00 2.50
❑ 121 Jovan Haye RC 5.00 2.00
❑ 122 Nick Collins RC 6.00 2.50
❑ 123 Travis Daniels RC 5.00 2.00
❑ 124 Reynaldo Hill RC 8.00 3.00
❑ 125 Billy Bajema RC 5.00 2.00
❑ 126 Jim Leonhard RC 10.00 4.00
❑ 127 Boomer Grigsby RC 8.00 3.00
❑ 128 Chauncey Davis RC 6.00 2.50
❑ 129 David McMillan RC 10.00 4.00
❑ 130 Alfred Fincher RC 5.00 2.00
❑ 131 Kelvin Hayden RC 5.00 2.00
❑ 132 Kevin Burnett RC 6.00 2.50
❑ 133 Jonathan Welsh RC 5.00 2.00
❑ 134 Stanley Wilson RC 5.00 2.00
❑ 135 Stanford Routt RC 5.00 2.00
❑ 136 Kerry Rhodes RC 6.00 2.50
❑ 137 Ellis Hobbs RC 6.00 2.50
❑ 138 Darrent Williams RC 6.00 2.50
❑ 139 Eric King RC 5.00 2.00
❑ 140 Domonique Foxworth RC 6.00 2.50
❑ 141 Anthony Bryant RC 6.00 2.50
❑ 142 Scott Starks RC 5.00 2.00
❑ 143 Marviel Underwood RC 5.00 2.00
❑ 144 Mike Montgomery RC 8.00 3.00
❑ 145 Kevin Vickerson RC 10.00 4.00
❑ 146 Jerome Carter RC 5.00 2.00
❑ 147 Jay Ratliff RC 6.00 2.50
❑ 148 Damien Nash RC 5.00 2.00

❑ 149 Noah Herron RC 6.00 2.50
❑ 150 Jonathan Fanene RC 5.00 2.00
❑ 151 Chase Lyman RC 5.00 2.00
❑ 152 Adam Seward RC 10.00 4.00
❑ 153 Michael Boley RC 5.00 2.00
❑ 154 Pat Thomas RC 5.00 2.00
❑ 155 Evan Mathis RC 6.00 2.50
❑ 156 Derrick Johnson CB RC 6.00 2.50
❑ 157 Tab Perry RC 6.00 2.50
❑ 158 Joel Dreessen RC 5.00 2.00
❑ 159 Daven Holly RC 6.00 2.50
❑ 160 Brandon Jones RC 6.00 2.50
❑ 161 Dan Buenning RC 8.00 3.00
❑ 162 Kurt Campbell RC 5.00 2.00
❑ 163 Kerry Wright RC 5.00 2.00
❑ 164 Matt McCoy RC 5.00 2.00
❑ 165 Dave Rayner RC 5.00 2.00
❑ 166 Kirk Morrison RC 6.00 2.50
❑ 167 Lofa Tatupu RC 8.00 3.00
❑ 168 Bryant McFadden RC 6.00 2.50
❑ 169 Corey Webster RC 6.00 2.50
❑ 170 Eric Green RC 5.00 2.00
❑ 171 Fabian Washington RC 6.00 2.50
❑ 172 Donte Nicholson RC 6.00 2.50
❑ 173 Vonta Leach RC 6.00 2.50
❑ 174 Ronald Bartell RC 5.00 2.00
❑ 175 Sean Considine RC 6.00 2.50
❑ 176 Oshiomogho Atogwe RC 5.00 2.00
❑ 177 Ryan Grant RC 6.00 2.50
❑ 178 James Butler RC 5.00 2.00
❑ 179 Paul Ernster RC 5.00 2.00
❑ 180 Duke Preston RC 8.00 3.00
❑ 181 Mike Nugent RC 6.00 2.50
❑ 182 Sione Pouha RC 6.00 2.50
❑ 183 Geoff Hangartner RC 20.00 7.50
❑ 184 Justin Geisinger RC 20.00 7.50
❑ 185 Chris Kemoeatu RC 20.00 10.00
❑ 186 Ryan Fitzpatrick RC 12.00 5.00
❑ 187 Lionel Gates RC 6.00 2.50
❑ 188 Brandon Jacobs RC 10.00 4.00
❑ 189 Alvin Pearman RC 8.00 3.00
❑ 190 J.R. Russell RC 6.00 2.50
❑ 191 Manuel White RC 6.00 2.50
❑ 192 Tyson Thompson RC 10.00 4.00
❑ 193 Chad Owens RC 8.00 3.00
❑ 194 Dante Ridgeway RC 6.00 2.50
❑ 195 Stephen Spach RC 6.00 2.50
❑ 196 Scott Mruczkowski RC 15.00 6.00
❑ 197 Chris Carr RC 10.00 4.00
❑ 198 Jonathan Babineaux RC 6.00 2.50
❑ 199 Will Whitticker RC 15.00 6.00
❑ 200 Luis Castillo RC 8.00 3.00
❑ 201 Matt Roth RC 8.00 3.00
❑ 202 Shaun Cody RC 8.00 3.00
❑ 203 Justin Tuck RC 8.00 3.00
❑ 204 Vincent Burns RC 6.00 2.50
❑ 205 DeMarcus Ware RC 12.00 5.00
❑ 206 Bill Swancutt RC 6.00 2.50
❑ 207 Darryl Blackstock RC 6.00 2.50
❑ 208 Brady Poppinga RC 8.00 3.00
❑ 209 Leroy Hill RC 8.00 3.00
❑ 210 Ryan Claridge RC 6.00 2.50
❑ 211 Odell Thurman RC 8.00 3.00
❑ 212 Barrett Ruud RC 8.00 3.00
❑ 213 Lance Mitchell RC 6.00 2.50
❑ 214 Trent Cole RC 8.00 3.00
❑ 215 Jerome Mathis RC 8.00 3.00
❑ 216 Brandon Browner RC 6.00 2.50
❑ 217 Justin Miller RC 6.00 2.50
❑ 218 Thomas Davis RC 8.00 3.00
❑ 219 Brodney Pool RC 8.00 3.00
❑ 220 Dylan Gandy RC 6.00 2.50
❑ 221 Josh Bullocks RC 8.00 3.00
❑ 222 Vincent Fuller RC 6.00 2.50
❑ 223 Jordan Beck RC 6.00 2.50
❑ 224 Claude Terrell RC 20.00 7.50
❑ 225 Adrian McPherson RC 8.00 3.00
❑ 226 Jerome Collins RC 6.00 2.50
❑ 227 Cedric Houston RC 8.00 3.00
❑ 228 Daniel Loper RC 20.00 7.50
❑ 229 Adam Bergen RC 8.00 3.00
❑ 230 Jeb Huckeba RC 8.00 3.00
❑ 231 Eric Moore RC 6.00 2.50
❑ 232 Dan Cody RC 8.00 3.00
❑ 233 Alex Smith TE RC 8.00 3.00
❑ 234 Travis Johnson RC 6.00 2.50
❑ 235 Ryan Riddle RC 4.00 1.50
❑ 236 Mike Patterson RC 8.00 3.00
❑ 237 Darrell Shropshire RC 6.00 2.50
❑ 238 David Pollack RC 8.00 3.00
❑ 239 Marcus Spears RC 8.00 3.00
❑ 240 Shawne Merriman RC 12.00 5.00
❑ 241 Channing Crowder RC 8.00 3.00
❑ 242 Derrick Johnson RC 12.00 5.00
❑ 243 Kyle Orton AU/199 RC 40.00 15.00
❑ 244 David Greene AU/650 RC 20.00 7.50
❑ 245 Derek Anderson AU/650 RC 25.00 12.50
❑ 246 Dan Orlovsky AU/650 RC 25.00 10.00
❑ 247 Eric Shelton AU/650 RC 20.00 7.50
❑ 248 Stefan LeFors AU/650 RC 20.00 7.50
❑ 249 Reggie Brown AU/650 RC 25.00 10.00
❑ 250 Andrew Walter AU/650 RC 30.00 15.00
❑ 251 Mark Bradley AU/650 RC 20.00 7.50
❑ 252 Courtney Roby AU/650 RC 20.00 7.50
❑ 253 Vincent Jackson AU/650 RC 20.00 7.50
❑ 254 Terrence Murphy AU/650 RC 20.00 7.50
❑ 255 Marion Barber AU/650 RC 40.00 20.00
❑ 256 Frank Gore AU/650 RC 60.00 35.00
❑ 257 Chris Henry AU/650 RC 30.00 15.00
❑ 258 Heath Miller AU/650 RC 60.00 25.00
❑ 259 Arrington AU/650 RC EXCH 25.00 10.00
❑ 260 A.Rolle AU/650 RC EXCH 20.00 7.50
❑ 261 Fred Gibson AU/650 RC 15.00 6.00
❑ 262 Charlie Frye AU/650 RC 40.00 15.00
❑ 263 Adam Jones AU/650 RC 20.00 7.50
❑ 264 Ciatrick Fason AU/650 RC 20.00 7.50
❑ 265 Roscoe Parrish AU/650 RC 20.00 7.50
❑ 266 Erasmus James AU/650 RC 20.00 7.50
❑ 267 Carlos Rogers AU/650 RC 25.00 10.00
❑ 268 Ryan Moats AU/650 RC 25.00 10.00
❑ 269 Marlin Jackson AU/650 RC 20.00 7.50
❑ 270 Darren Sproles AU/650 RC 20.00 7.50
❑ 271 Maurice Clarett AU/199 25.00 10.00
❑ 272 Jason Campbell AU/199 RC 40.00 25.00
❑ 273 Vernand Morency AU/199 RC 20.00 7.50
❑ 274 M.Clayton AU/199 RC EX 40.00 20.00
❑ 275 Roddy White AU/650 RC 20.00 7.50
❑ 276 Williamson AU/199 RC 40.00 20.00
❑ 277 M.Williams AU/199 EXCH 40.00 20.00
❑ 278 B.Edwards AU/199 RC 80.00 40.00
❑ 279 Cedric Benson AU/199 RC 80.00 40.00
❑ 280 Cadillac Williams AU/199 RC 100.00 50.00
❑ 281 Ronnie Brown AU/199 RC 100.00 50.00
❑ 282 Matt Jones AU/199 RC 60.00 30.00
❑ 283 Alex Smith QB AU/175 RC 100.00 50.00
❑ 284 Aaron Rodgers AU/199 RC 80.00 40.00
❑ 285 Rian Wallace RC 5.00 2.00
❑ 286 Nick Speegle RC 5.00 2.00
❑ 287 Chris Spencer RC 6.00 2.50
❑ 288 Logan Mankins RC 8.00 3.00
❑ 289 David Baas RC 5.00 2.00
❑ 290 Michael Roos RC 5.00 2.00
❑ 291 Khalif Barnes RC 5.00 2.00
❑ 292 Matt Giordano RC 6.00 2.50
❑ 293 Rick Razzano RC 6.00 2.50
❑ 294 Trai Essex RC 20.00 7.50
❑ 295 Roy Manning RC 20.00 10.00
❑ 296 Gerald Sensabaugh RC 8.00 3.00
❑ 297 Nick Kaczur RC 12.00 5.00
❑ 298 Ray Willis RC 6.00 2.50
❑ 299 Jason Brown RC 6.00 2.50
❑ 300 Frank Omiyale RC 5.00 2.00
❑ 301 Fred Amey RC 5.00 2.00
❑ 302 Reggie Hodges RC 5.00 2.00

1955 Topps All American

❑ COMPLETE SET (100) 3800.00 2800.00
❑ WRAPPER (1-CENT) 300.00 250.00
❑ WRAPPER (5-CENT) 250.00 200.00
❑ 1 Herman Hickman RC ! 125.00 65.00
❑ 2 John Kimbrough 18.00 10.00
❑ 3 Ed Weir 18.00 10.00
❑ 4 Emy Pinckert 18.00 10.00
❑ 5 Bobby Grayson 18.00 10.00
❑ 6 Nile Kinnick RC UER 135.00 75.00
❑ 7 Andy Bershak 18.00 10.00
❑ 8 George Cafego RC 18.00 10.00
❑ 9 Tom Hamilton SP 30.00 20.00
❑ 10 Bill Dudley 40.00 25.00
❑ 11 Bobby Dodd SP 30.00 20.00
❑ 12 Otto Graham 175.00 100.00
❑ 13 Aaron Rosenberg 18.00 10.00
❑ 14A Gay.Tinsley RC ERR 100.00 50.00
❑ 14B Gay.Tinsley RC COR 25.00 15.00
❑ 15 Ed Kaw SP 30.00 20.00
❑ 16 Knute Rockne 275.00 175.00
❑ 17 Bob Reynolds HB 18.00 10.00
❑ 18 Pudg.Heffelfinger RC SP 40.00 25.00
❑ 19 Bruce Smith 35.00 20.00
❑ 20 Sammy Baugh 200.00 125.00
❑ 21A W.White RC SP ERR 250.00 150.00
❑ 21B W.White RC SP COR 100.00 60.00
❑ 22 Brick Muller 18.00 10.00
❑ 23 Dick Kazmaier RC 25.00 15.00
❑ 24 Ken Strong 50.00 30.00
❑ 25 Casimir Myslinski SP 30.00 20.00
❑ 26 Larry Kelley RC SP 40.00 25.00
❑ 27 Red Grange UER 300.00 200.00
❑ 28 Mel Hein RC SP 75.00 40.00
❑ 29 Leo Nomellini SP 100.00 60.00
❑ 30 Wes Fesler 18.00 10.00
❑ 31 George Sauer Sr. RC 25.00 15.00
❑ 32 Hank Foldberg 18.00 10.00
❑ 33 Bob Higgins 18.00 10.00
❑ 34 Davey O'Brien RC 50.00 30.00
❑ 35 Tom Harmon RC SP 100.00 60.00
❑ 36 Turk Edwards SP 60.00 35.00
❑ 37 Jim Thorpe ! 400.00 275.00
❑ 38 Amos A. Stagg RC 75.00 40.00
❑ 39 Jerome Holland RC 25.00 15.00
❑ 40 Donn Moomaw 18.00 10.00
❑ 41 Joseph Alexander SP 30.00 20.00
❑ 42 Eddie Tryon RC SP 40.00 25.00
❑ 43 George Savitsky 18.00 10.00
❑ 44 Ed Garbisch 18.00 10.00
❑ 45 Elmer Oliphant 18.00 10.00
❑ 46 Arnold Lassman 18.00 10.00
❑ 47 Bo McMillin RC 25.00 15.00
❑ 48 Ed Widseth 18.00 10.00
❑ 49 Don Gordon Zimmerman 18.00 10.00
❑ 50 Ken Kavanaugh 25.00 15.00
❑ 51 Duane Purvis SP 30.00 20.00
❑ 52 Johnny Lujack 90.00 50.00
❑ 53 John F. Green 18.00 10.00
❑ 54 Edwin Dooley SP 30.00 20.00
❑ 55 Frank Merritt SP 30.00 20.00
❑ 56 Ernie Nevers RC 125.00 75.00
❑ 57 Vic Hanson SP 30.00 20.00
❑ 58 Ed Franco 18.00 10.00
❑ 59 Doc Blanchard RC 50.00 30.00
❑ 60 Dan Hill 18.00 10.00
❑ 61 Charles Brickley SP 30.00 20.00
❑ 62 Harry Newman 18.00 10.00
❑ 63 Charlie Justice 35.00 20.00
❑ 64 Benny Friedman RC 30.00 18.00
❑ 65 Joe Donchess SP 30.00 20.00
❑ 66 Bruiser Kinard RC 35.00 20.00
❑ 67 Frankie Albert 25.00 15.00
❑ 68 Four Horsemen RC SP 500.00 325.00
❑ 69 Frank Sinkwich RC 25.00 15.00
❑ 70 Bill Daddio 18.00 10.00
❑ 71 Bobby Wilson 18.00 10.00
❑ 72 Chub Peabody 18.00 10.00
❑ 73 Paul Governali 25.00 15.00
❑ 74 Gene McEver 18.00 10.00
❑ 75 Hugh Gallarneau 18.00 10.00
❑ 76 Angelo Bertelli RC 25.00 15.00
❑ 77 Bowden Wyatt SP 30.00 20.00
❑ 78 Jay Berwanger RC 35.00 20.00
❑ 79 Pug Lund 18.00 10.00
❑ 80 Bennie Oosterbaan 18.00 10.00
❑ 81 Cotton Warburton 18.00 10.00
❑ 82 Alex Wojciechowicz 35.00 20.00

❑ 83 Ted Coy SP	30.00	20.00
❑ 84 Ace Parker RC SP	50.00	30.00
❑ 85 Sid Luckman	150.00	90.00
❑ 86 Albie Booth SP	30.00	20.00
❑ 87 Adolph Schultz SP	30.00	20.00
❑ 88 Ralph Kercheval	18.00	10.00
❑ 89 Marshall Goldberg	25.00	15.00
❑ 90 Charlie O'Rourke	18.00	10.00
❑ 91 Bob Odell UER	18.00	10.00
❑ 92 Biggie Munn	18.00	10.00
❑ 93 Willie Heston SP	40.00	25.00
❑ 94 Joe Bernard SP	40.00	25.00
❑ 95 Chris Cagle SP	40.00	25.00
❑ 96 Bill Hollenback SP	40.00	25.00
❑ 97 Don Hutson RC SP	225.00	150.00
❑ 98 Beattie Feathers SP	100.00	60.00
❑ 99 Don Whitmire SP	40.00	25.00
❑ 100 Fats Henry RC SP !	200.00	100.00

1956 Topps

❑ COMPLETE SET (120)	1800.00	1200.00
❑ WRAPPER (1-CENT)	250.00	200.00
❑ WRAPPER (5-CENT)	50.00	40.00
❑ 1 Johnny Carson SP !	80.00	40.00
❑ 2 Gordy Soltau	6.00	3.50
❑ 3 Frank Varrichione	6.00	3.50
❑ 4 Eddie Bell	6.00	3.50
❑ 5 Alex Webster RC	12.00	6.00
❑ 6 Norm Van Brocklin	30.00	18.00
❑ 7 Green Bay Packers	25.00	15.00
❑ 8 Lou Creekmur	15.00	7.50
❑ 9 Lou Groza	25.00	15.00
❑ 10 Tom Bienemann SP	25.00	15.00
❑ 11 George Blanda	50.00	30.00
❑ 12 Alan Ameche	12.00	6.00
❑ 13 Vic Janowicz SP	45.00	25.00
❑ 14 Dick Moegle	8.00	4.00
❑ 15 Fran Rogel	6.00	3.50
❑ 16 Harold Giancanelli	6.00	3.50
❑ 17 Emlen Tunnell	15.00	7.50
❑ 18 Tank Younger	12.00	6.00
❑ 19 Billy Howton	8.00	4.00
❑ 20 Jack Christiansen	15.00	7.50
❑ 21 Darrel Brewster	6.00	3.50
❑ 22 Chicago Cardinals SP	100.00	60.00
❑ 23 Ed Brown	8.00	4.00
❑ 24 Joe Campanella	6.00	3.50
❑ 25 Leon Heath SP	22.00	12.00
❑ 26 San Francisco 49ers	18.00	10.00
❑ 27 Dick Flanagan	6.00	3.50
❑ 28 Chuck Bednarik	25.00	15.00
❑ 29 Kyle Rote	12.00	6.00
❑ 30 Les Richter	8.00	4.00
❑ 31 Howard Ferguson	6.00	3.50
❑ 32 Dorne Dibble	6.00	3.50
❑ 33 Kenny Konz	6.00	3.50
❑ 34 Dave Mann SP	25.00	15.00
❑ 35 Rick Casares	12.00	6.00
❑ 36 Art Donovan	30.00	18.00
❑ 37 Chuck Drazenovich SP	22.00	12.00
❑ 38 Joe Arenas	6.00	3.50
❑ 39 Lynn Chandnois	6.00	3.50
❑ 40 Philadelphia Eagles	18.00	10.00
❑ 41 Roosevelt Brown RC	35.00	20.00
❑ 42 Tom Fears	25.00	15.00
❑ 43 Gary Knafelc	6.00	3.50
❑ 44 Joe Schmidt RC	50.00	30.00
❑ 45 Cleveland Browns	18.00	10.00
❑ 46 Len Teeuws RC SP	25.00	15.00
❑ 47 Bill George RC	30.00	18.00
❑ 48 Baltimore Colts	18.00	10.00
❑ 49 Eddie LeBaron SP	45.00	25.00
❑ 50 Hugh McElhenny	30.00	18.00
❑ 51 Ted Marchibroda	12.00	6.00
❑ 52 Adrian Burk	6.00	3.50
❑ 53 Frank Gifford	60.00	35.00
❑ 54 Charley Toogood	6.00	3.50
❑ 55 Tobin Rote	8.00	4.00
❑ 56 Bill Stits	6.00	3.50
❑ 57 Don Colo	6.00	3.50
❑ 58 Ollie Matson SP	75.00	40.00
❑ 59 Harlon Hill	8.00	4.00
❑ 60 Lenny Moore RC !	90.00	50.00
❑ 61 Wash.Redskins SP	90.00	50.00
❑ 62 Billy Wilson	6.00	3.50
❑ 63 Pittsburgh Steelers	18.00	10.00
❑ 64 Bob Pellegrini	6.00	3.50
❑ 65 Ken MacAfee E	6.00	3.50
❑ 66 Willard Sherman	6.00	3.50
❑ 67 Roger Zatkoff	6.00	3.50
❑ 68 Dave Middleton	6.00	3.50
❑ 69 Ray Renfro	8.00	4.00
❑ 70 Don Stonesifer SP	25.00	15.00
❑ 71 Stan Jones RC	30.00	18.00
❑ 72 Jim Mutscheller	6.00	3.50
❑ 73 Volney Peters SP	22.00	12.00
❑ 74 Leo Nomellini	20.00	12.00
❑ 75 Ray Mathews	6.00	3.50
❑ 76 Dick Bielski	6.00	3.50
❑ 77 Charley Conerly	25.00	15.00
❑ 78 Elroy Hirsch	30.00	18.00
❑ 79 Bill Forester RC	8.00	4.00
❑ 80 Jim Doran	6.00	3.50
❑ 81 Fred Morrison	6.00	3.50
❑ 82 Jack Simmons SP	25.00	15.00
❑ 83 Bill McColl	6.00	3.50
❑ 84 Bert Rechichar	6.00	3.50
❑ 85 Joe Scudero SP	22.00	12.00
❑ 86 Y.A.Tittle	50.00	30.00
❑ 87 Ernie Stautner	20.00	12.00
❑ 88 Norm Willey	6.00	3.50
❑ 89 Bob Schnelker	6.00	3.50
❑ 90 Dan Towler	12.00	6.00
❑ 91 John Martinkovic	6.00	3.50
❑ 92 Detroit Lions	18.00	10.00
❑ 93 George Ratterman	8.00	4.00
❑ 94 Chuck Ulrich SP	25.00	15.00
❑ 95 Bobby Watkins	6.00	3.50
❑ 96 Buddy Young	12.00	6.00
❑ 97 Billy Wells SP	22.00	12.00
❑ 98 Bob Toneff	6.00	3.50
❑ 99 Bill McPeak	6.00	3.50
❑ 100 Bobby Thomason	6.00	3.50
❑ 101 Roosevelt Grier RC	40.00	25.00
❑ 102 Ron Waller	6.00	3.50
❑ 103 Bobby Dillon	6.00	3.50
❑ 104 Leon Hart	12.00	6.00
❑ 105 Mike McCormack	15.00	7.50
❑ 106 John Olszewski SP	25.00	15.00
❑ 107 Bill Wightkin	6.00	3.50
❑ 108 George Shaw RC	8.00	4.00
❑ 109 Dale Atkeson SP	22.00	12.00
❑ 110 Joe Perry	25.00	15.00
❑ 111 Dale Dodrill	6.00	3.50
❑ 112 Tom Scott	6.00	3.50
❑ 113 New York Giants	18.00	10.00
❑ 114 Los Angeles Rams	18.00	10.00
❑ 115 Al Carmichael	6.00	3.50
❑ 116 Bobby Layne	50.00	30.00
❑ 117 Ed Modzelewski	6.00	3.50
❑ 118 Lamar McHan RC SP	25.00	15.00
❑ 119 Chicago Bears	18.00	10.00
❑ 120 Billy Vessels RC !	40.00	20.00
❑ AD1 Lou Groza/Don Colo Darrel Brewster	250.00	125.00
❑ NNO Checklist SP NNO!	400.00	250.00
❑ C1 Contest Card 1 !	80.00	45.00
❑ C2 Contest Card 2 !	80.00	45.00
❑ C3 Contest Card 3 !	80.00	45.00
❑ CA Contest Card A !	90.00	50.00
❑ CB Contest Card B !	110.00	70.00

1957 Topps

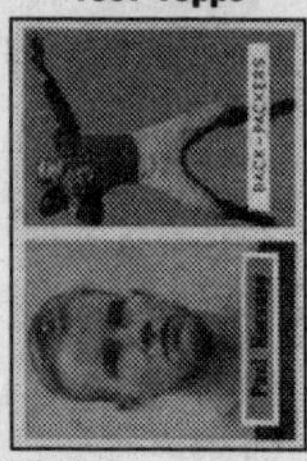

❑ COMPLETE SET (154)	2200.00	1600.00
❑ COMMON CARD (1-88)	4.00	2.50
❑ COMMON CARD (89-154)	10.00	5.00
❑ WRAPPER (1-CENT)	50.00	30.00
❑ WRAPPER (5-CENT)	75.00	50.00
❑ 1 Eddie LeBaron !	50.00	30.00
❑ 2 Pete Retzlaff RC	15.00	7.50
❑ 3 Mike McCormack	12.00	6.00
❑ 4 Lou Baldacci	4.00	2.50
❑ 5 Gino Marchetti	20.00	10.00
❑ 6 Leo Nomellini	20.00	10.00
❑ 7 Bobby Watkins	4.00	2.50
❑ 8 Dave Middleton	4.00	2.50
❑ 9 Bobby Dillon	4.00	2.50
❑ 10 Les Richter	6.00	3.50
❑ 11 Roosevelt Brown	20.00	10.00
❑ 12 Lavern Torgeson RC	4.00	2.50
❑ 13 Dick Bielski	4.00	2.50
❑ 14 Pat Summerall	20.00	10.00
❑ 15 Jack Butler RC	10.00	5.00
❑ 16 John Henry Johnson	15.00	7.50
❑ 17 Art Spinney	4.00	2.50
❑ 18 Bob St. Clair	12.00	6.00
❑ 19 Perry Jeter	4.00	2.50
❑ 20 Lou Creekmur	12.00	6.00
❑ 21 Dave Hanner	6.00	3.50
❑ 22 Norm Van Brocklin	30.00	18.00
❑ 23 Don Chandler RC	10.00	5.00
❑ 24 Al Dorow	4.00	2.50
❑ 25 Tom Scott	4.00	2.50
❑ 26 Ollie Matson	20.00	12.00
❑ 27 Fran Rogel	4.00	2.50
❑ 28 Lou Groza	25.00	15.00
❑ 29 Billy Vessels	6.00	3.50
❑ 30 Y.A.Tittle	40.00	25.00
❑ 31 George Blanda	40.00	25.00
❑ 32 Bobby Layne	40.00	25.00
❑ 33 Billy Howton	6.00	3.50
❑ 34 Bill Wade	10.00	5.00
❑ 35 Emlen Tunnell	15.00	7.50
❑ 36 Leo Elter	4.00	2.50
❑ 37 Clarence Peaks RC	6.00	3.50
❑ 38 Don Stonesifer	4.00	2.50
❑ 39 George Tarasovic	4.00	2.50
❑ 40 Darrel Brewster	4.00	2.50
❑ 41 Bert Rechichar	4.00	2.50
❑ 42 Billy Wilson	4.00	2.50
❑ 43 Ed Brown	6.00	3.50
❑ 44 Gene Gedman	4.00	2.50
❑ 45 Gary Knafelc	4.00	2.50
❑ 46 Elroy Hirsch	30.00	18.00
❑ 47 Don Heinrich	6.00	3.50
❑ 48 Gene Brito	4.00	2.50
❑ 49 Chuck Bednarik	25.00	15.00
❑ 50 Dave Mann	4.00	2.50
❑ 51 Bill McPeak	4.00	2.50
❑ 52 Kenny Konz	4.00	2.50
❑ 53 Alan Ameche	10.00	5.00
❑ 54 Gordy Soltau	4.00	2.50
❑ 55 Rick Casares	6.00	3.50
❑ 56 Charlie Ane	4.00	2.50
❑ 57 Al Carmichael	4.00	2.50
❑ 58A Willard Sherman ERR	300.00	175.00
❑ 58B Willard Sherman COR	4.00	2.50
❑ 59 Kyle Rote	10.00	5.00
❑ 60 Chuck Drazenovich	4.00	2.50
❑ 61 Bobby Walston	4.00	2.50
❑ 62 John Olszewski	4.00	2.50

❑ 63 Ray Mathews 4.00 2.50
❑ 64 Maurice Bassett 4.00 2.50
❑ 65 Art Donovan 25.00 15.00
❑ 66 Joe Arenas 4.00 2.50
❑ 67 Harlon Hill 6.00 3.50
❑ 68 Yale Lary 12.00 6.00
❑ 69 Bill Forester 6.00 3.50
❑ 70 Bob Boyd 4.00 2.50
❑ 71 Andy Robustelli 20.00 12.00
❑ 72 Sam Baker RC 6.00 3.50
❑ 73 Bob Pellegrini 4.00 2.50
❑ 74 Leo Sanford 4.00 2.50
❑ 75 Sid Watson 4.00 2.50
❑ 76 Ray Renfro 6.00 3.50
❑ 77 Carl Taseff 4.00 2.50
❑ 78 Clyde Conner 4.00 2.50
❑ 79 J.C. Caroline 4.00 2.50
❑ 80 Howard Cassady RC 15.00 7.50
❑ 81 Tobin Rote 6.00 3.50
❑ 82 Ron Waller 4.00 2.50
❑ 83 Jim Patton RC 6.00 3.50
❑ 84 Volney Peters 4.00 2.50
❑ 85 Dick Lane RC 50.00 30.00
❑ 86 Royce Womble 4.00 2.50
❑ 87 Duane Putnam RC 6.00 3.50
❑ 88 Frank Gifford ! 60.00 30.00
❑ 89 Steve Meilinger 10.00 5.00
❑ 90 Buck Lansford 10.00 5.00
❑ 91 Lindon Crow DP 8.00 4.00
❑ 92 Ernie Stautner DP 25.00 12.50
❑ 93 Preston Carpenter RC DP 8.00 4.00
❑ 94 Raymond Berry RC 135.00 75.00
❑ 95 Hugh McElhenny 30.00 18.00
❑ 96 Stan Jones 25.00 15.00
❑ 97 Dorne Dibble 10.00 5.00
❑ 98 Joe Scudero DP 8.00 4.00
❑ 99 Eddie Bell 10.00 5.00
❑ 100 Joe Childress DP 8.00 4.00
❑ 101 Elbert Nickel 12.00 6.00
❑ 102 Walt Michaels 12.00 6.00
❑ 103 Jim Mutscheller DP 8.00 4.00
❑ 104 Earl Morrall RC 50.00 30.00
❑ 105 Larry Strickland 10.00 5.00
❑ 106 Jack Christiansen 15.00 7.50
❑ 107 Fred Cone DP 8.00 4.00
❑ 108 Bud McFadin RC 12.00 6.00
❑ 109 Charley Conerly 30.00 18.00
❑ 110 Tom Runnels DP 8.00 4.00
❑ 111 Ken Keller DP 8.00 4.00
❑ 112 James Root 10.00 5.00
❑ 113 Ted Marchibroda DP 10.00 5.00
❑ 114 Don Paul DB 10.00 5.00
❑ 115 George Shaw 12.00 6.00
❑ 116 Dick Moegle 12.00 6.00
❑ 117 Don Bingham 10.00 5.00
❑ 118 Leon Hart 14.00 7.00
❑ 119 Bart Starr RC 450.00 300.00
❑ 120 Paul Miller DP 8.00 4.00
❑ 121 Alex Webster 12.00 6.00
❑ 122 Ray Wietecha DP 8.00 4.00
❑ 123 Johnny Carson 10.00 5.00
❑ 124 Tom. McDonald RC DP 30.00 18.00
❑ 125 Jerry Tubbs RC 12.00 6.00
❑ 126 Jack Scarbath 10.00 5.00
❑ 127 Ed Modzelewski DP 8.00 4.00
❑ 128 Lenny Moore 50.00 30.00
❑ 129 Joe Perry DP 25.00 15.00
❑ 130 Bill Wightkin 10.00 5.00
❑ 131 Jim Doran 10.00 5.00
❑ 132 Howard Ferguson UER 10.00 5.00
❑ 133 Tom Wilson 10.00 5.00
❑ 134 Dick James 10.00 5.00
❑ 135 Jimmy Harris 10.00 5.00
❑ 136 Chuck Ulrich 10.00 5.00
❑ 137 Lynn Chandnois 10.00 5.00
❑ 138 Johnny Unitas RC DP 450.00 300.00
❑ 139 Jim Ridlon DP 8.00 4.00
❑ 140 Zeke Bratkowski DP 10.00 5.00
❑ 141 Ray Krouse 10.00 5.00
❑ 142 John Martinkovic 10.00 5.00
❑ 143 Jim Cason DP 8.00 4.00
❑ 144 Ken MacAfee E 10.00 5.00
❑ 145 Sid Youngelman RC 12.00 6.00
❑ 146 Paul Larson 10.00 5.00
❑ 147 Len Ford 30.00 18.00
❑ 148 Bob Toneff DP 8.00 4.00
❑ 149 Ronnie Knox DP 8.00 4.00
❑ 150 Jim David RC 12.00 6.00
❑ 151 Paul Hornung RC 400.00 250.00
❑ 152 Tank Younger 14.00 7.00
❑ 153 Bill Svoboda DP 8.00 4.00
❑ 154 Fred Morrison ! 70.00 35.00
❑ AD1 Al Dorow/Harlon Hill Bert Rechich 600.00 350.00
❑ AD2 B.Watkins/G.Marchetti C.Peaks 600.00 350.00
❑ NNO1 Checklist Bazooka SP ! 750.00 500.00
❑ NNO2 Checklist Blony SP ! 750.00 500.00

1958 Topps

❑ COMPLETE SET (132) 1250.00 850.00
❑ WRAPPER (1-CENT) 60.00 35.00
❑ WRAPPER (5-CENT) 125.00 75.00
❑ 1 Gene Filipski RC ! 15.00 7.50
❑ 2 Bobby Layne 35.00 20.00
❑ 3 Joe Schmidt 12.00 6.00
❑ 4 Bill Barnes 4.00 2.00
❑ 5 Milt Plum RC 8.00 4.00
❑ 6 Billy Howton UER 5.00 2.50
❑ 7 Howard Cassady 5.00 2.50
❑ 8 Jim Dooley 4.00 2.00
❑ 9 Cleveland Browns 6.00 3.00
❑ 10 Lenny Moore 25.00 12.50
❑ 11 Darrel Brewster 4.00 2.00
❑ 12 Alan Ameche 8.00 4.00
❑ 13 Jim David 4.00 2.00
❑ 14 Jim Mutscheller 4.00 2.00
❑ 15 Andy Robustelli 10.00 5.00
❑ 16 Gino Marchetti 12.00 6.00
❑ 17 Ray Renfro 5.00 2.50
❑ 18 Yale Lary 8.00 4.00
❑ 19 Gary Glick 4.00 2.00
❑ 20 Jon Arnett RC 8.00 4.00
❑ 21 Bob Boyd 4.00 2.00
❑ 22 Johnny Unitas UER 135.00 75.00
❑ 23 Zeke Bratkowski 5.00 2.50
❑ 24 Sid Youngelman UER 4.00 2.00
❑ 25 Leo Elter 4.00 2.00
❑ 26 Kenny Konz 4.00 2.00
❑ 27 Washington Redskins 6.00 3.00
❑ 28 Carl Brettschneider 4.00 2.00
❑ 29 Chicago Bears 6.00 3.00
❑ 30 Alex Webster 5.00 2.50
❑ 31 Al Carmichael 4.00 2.00
❑ 32 Bobby Dillon 4.00 2.00
❑ 33 Steve Meilinger 4.00 2.00
❑ 34 Sam Baker 4.00 2.00
❑ 35 Chuck Bednarik 15.00 7.50
❑ 36 Bert Vic Zucco 4.00 2.00
❑ 37 George Tarasovic 4.00 2.00
❑ 38 Bill Wade 8.00 4.00
❑ 39 Dick Stanfel 5.00 2.50
❑ 40 Jerry Norton 4.00 2.00
❑ 41 San Francisco 49ers 6.00 3.00
❑ 42 Emlen Tunnell 10.00 5.00
❑ 43 Jim Doran 4.00 2.00
❑ 44 Ted Marchibroda 8.00 4.00
❑ 45 Chet Hanulak 4.00 2.00
❑ 46 Dale Dodrill 4.00 2.00
❑ 47 Johnny Carson 4.00 2.00
❑ 48 Dick Deschaine 4.00 2.00
❑ 49 Billy Wells UER 4.00 2.00
❑ 50 Larry Morris 4.00 2.00
❑ 51 Jack McClairen 4.00 2.00
❑ 52 Lou Groza 15.00 7.50
❑ 53 Rick Casares 5.00 2.50
❑ 54 Don Chandler 5.00 2.50
❑ 55 Duane Putnam 4.00 2.00
❑ 56 Gary Knafelc 4.00 2.00
❑ 57 Earl Morrall 10.00 5.00
❑ 58 Ron Kramer RC 5.00 2.50
❑ 59 Mike McCormack 8.00 4.00
❑ 60 Gern Nagler 4.00 2.00
❑ 61 New York Giants 6.00 3.00
❑ 62 Jim Brown RC ! 450.00 300.00
❑ 63 Joe Marconi RC 4.00 2.00
❑ 64 R.C. Owens RC UER 5.00 2.50
❑ 65 Jimmy Carr RC 5.00 2.50
❑ 66 Bart Starr UER 135.00 75.00
❑ 67 Tom Wilson 4.00 2.00
❑ 68 Lamar McHan 4.00 2.00
❑ 69 Chicago Cardinals 6.00 3.00
❑ 70 Jack Christiansen 8.00 4.00
❑ 71 Don McIlhenny RC 4.00 2.00
❑ 72 Ron Waller 4.00 2.00
❑ 73 Frank Gifford 50.00 25.00
❑ 74 Bert Rechichar 4.00 2.00
❑ 75 John Henry Johnson 10.00 5.00
❑ 76 Jack Butler 5.00 2.50
❑ 77 Frank Varrichione 4.00 2.00
❑ 78 Ray Mathews 4.00 2.00
❑ 79 Marv Matuszak UER 4.00 2.00
❑ 80 Harlon Hill UER 4.00 2.00
❑ 81 Lou Creekmur 8.00 4.00
❑ 82 Woodley Lewis UER 4.00 2.00
❑ 83 Don Heinrich 4.00 2.00
❑ 84 Charley Conerly 15.00 7.50
❑ 85 Los Angeles Rams 6.00 3.00
❑ 86 Y.A.Tittle 30.00 18.00
❑ 87 Bobby Walston 4.00 2.00
❑ 88 Earl Putman 4.00 2.00
❑ 89 Leo Nomellini 15.00 7.50
❑ 90 Sonny Jurgensen RC 100.00 60.00
❑ 91 Don Paul DB 4.00 2.00
❑ 92 Paige Cothren 4.00 2.00
❑ 93 Joe Perry 15.00 7.50
❑ 94 Tobin Rote 5.00 2.50
❑ 95 Billy Wilson 4.00 2.00
❑ 96 Green Bay Packers 6.00 3.00
❑ 97 Lavern Torgeson 4.00 2.00
❑ 98 Milt Davis 4.00 2.00
❑ 99 Larry Strickland 4.00 2.00
❑ 100 Matt Hazeltine RC 5.00 2.50
❑ 101 Walt Yowarsky 4.00 2.00
❑ 102 Roosevelt Brown 8.00 4.00
❑ 103 Jim Ringo 10.00 5.00
❑ 104 Joe Krupa 4.00 2.00
❑ 105 Les Richter 5.00 2.50
❑ 106 Art Donovan 20.00 12.00
❑ 107 John Olszewski 4.00 2.00
❑ 108 Ken Keller 4.00 2.00
❑ 109 Philadelphia Eagles 6.00 3.00
❑ 110 Baltimore Colts 6.00 3.00
❑ 111 Dick Bielski 4.00 2.00
❑ 112 Eddie LeBaron 8.00 4.00
❑ 113 Gene Brito 4.00 2.00
❑ 114 Willie Galimore RC 8.00 4.00
❑ 115 Detroit Lions 6.00 3.00
❑ 116 Pittsburgh Steelers 6.00 3.00
❑ 117 L.G. Dupre 5.00 2.50
❑ 118 Babe Parilli 5.00 2.50
❑ 119 Bill George 10.00 5.00
❑ 120 Raymond Berry 40.00 25.00
❑ 121 Jim Podoley UER 4.00 2.00
❑ 122 Hugh McElhenny 15.00 7.50
❑ 123 Ed Brown 5.00 2.50
❑ 124 Dick Moegle 5.00 2.50
❑ 125 Tom Scott 4.00 2.00
❑ 126 Tommy McDonald 12.00 6.00
❑ 127 Ollie Matson 20.00 10.00
❑ 128 Preston Carpenter 4.00 2.00
❑ 129 George Blanda 30.00 18.00
❑ 130 Gordy Soltau 4.00 2.00
❑ 131 Dick Nolan RC 5.00 2.50
❑ 132 Don Bosseler RC ! 20.00 10.00
❑ NNO Free Felt Initial Card 25.00 15.00

1959 Topps

Card		
❑ COMPLETE SET (176)	900.00	600.00
❑ COMMON CARD (1-88)	3.00	1.50
❑ COMMON CARD (89-176)	2.00	1.00
❑ WRAPPER (1-CENT)	90.00	50.00
❑ WRAPPER (1-CENT, REP)	80.00	50.00
❑ WRAPPER (5-CENT)	80.00	50.00
❑ 1 Johnny Unitas !	150.00	90.00
❑ 2 Gene Brito	3.00	1.50
❑ 3 Detroit Lions	6.00	3.00
❑ 4 Max McGee RC	15.00	7.50
❑ 5 Hugh McElhenny	15.00	7.50
❑ 6 Joe Schmidt	8.00	4.00
❑ 7 Kyle Rote	6.00	3.00
❑ 8 Clarence Peaks	3.00	1.50
❑ 9 Pittsburgh Steelers	3.50	1.75
❑ 10 Jim Brown	150.00	90.00
❑ 11 Ray Mathews	3.00	1.50
❑ 12 Bobby Dillon	3.00	1.50
❑ 13 Joe Childress	3.00	1.50
❑ 14 Terry Barr RC	3.00	1.50
❑ 15 Del Shofner RC	4.00	2.00
❑ 16 Bob Pellegrini UER	3.00	1.50
❑ 17 Baltimore Colts	6.00	3.00
❑ 18 Preston Carpenter	3.00	1.50
❑ 19 Leo Nomellini	10.00	5.00
❑ 20 Frank Gifford	40.00	25.00
❑ 21 Charlie Ane	3.00	1.50
❑ 22 Jack Butler	3.00	1.50
❑ 23 Bart Starr	60.00	35.00
❑ 24 Chicago Cardinals	3.50	1.75
❑ 25 Bill Barnes	3.00	1.50
❑ 26 Walt Michaels	4.00	2.00
❑ 27 Clyde Conner UER	3.00	1.50
❑ 28 Paige Cothren	3.00	1.50
❑ 29 Roosevelt Grier	6.00	3.00
❑ 30 Alan Ameche	6.00	3.00
❑ 31 Philadelphia Eagles	6.00	3.00
❑ 32 Dick Nolan	4.00	2.00
❑ 33 R.C. Owens	4.00	2.00
❑ 34 Dale Dodrill	3.00	1.50
❑ 35 Gene Gedman	3.00	1.50
❑ 36 Gene Lipscomb RC	10.00	5.00
❑ 37 Ray Renfro	4.00	2.00
❑ 38 Cleveland Browns	3.50	1.75
❑ 39 Bill Forester	4.00	2.00
❑ 40 Bobby Layne	25.00	15.00
❑ 41 Pat Summerall	10.00	5.00
❑ 42 Jerry Mertens	3.00	1.50
❑ 43 Steve Myhra	3.00	1.50
❑ 44 John Henry Johnson	8.00	4.00
❑ 45 Woodley Lewis UER	3.00	1.50
❑ 46 Green Bay Packers	8.00	4.00
❑ 47 Don Owens UER	3.00	1.50
❑ 48 Ed Beatty	3.00	1.50
❑ 49 Don Chandler	3.00	1.50
❑ 50 Ollie Matson	12.00	6.00
❑ 51 Sam Huff RC	50.00	30.00
❑ 52 Tom Miner	3.00	1.50
❑ 53 New York Giants	3.50	1.75
❑ 54 Kenny Konz	3.00	1.50
❑ 55 Raymond Berry	20.00	10.00
❑ 56 Howard Ferguson UER	3.00	1.50
❑ 57 Chuck Ulrich	3.00	1.50
❑ 58 Bob St.Clair	6.00	3.00
❑ 59 Don Burroughs RC	3.00	1.50
❑ 60 Lou Groza	15.00	7.50
❑ 61 San Francisco 49ers	6.00	3.00
❑ 62 Andy Nelson	3.00	1.50
❑ 63 Harold Bradley	3.00	1.50
❑ 64 Dave Hanner	4.00	2.00
❑ 65 Charley Conerly	10.00	5.00
❑ 66 Gene Cronin RC	3.00	1.50
❑ 67 Duane Putnam	3.00	1.50
❑ 68 Baltimore Colts	3.50	1.75
❑ 69 Ernie Stautner	8.00	4.00
❑ 70 Jon Arnett	4.00	2.00
❑ 71 Ken Panfil	3.00	1.50
❑ 72 Matt Hazeltine	3.00	1.50
❑ 73 Harley Sewell	3.00	1.50
❑ 74 Mike McCormack	6.00	3.00
❑ 75 Jim Ringo	8.00	4.00
❑ 76 Los Angeles Rams	6.00	3.00
❑ 77 Bob Gain RC	3.00	1.50
❑ 78 Buzz Nutter	3.00	1.50
❑ 79 Jerry Norton	3.00	1.50
❑ 80 Joe Perry	12.00	6.00
❑ 81 Carl Brettschneider	3.00	1.50
❑ 82 Paul Hornung	60.00	30.00
❑ 83 Philadelphia Eagles	3.50	1.75
❑ 84 Les Richter	4.00	2.00
❑ 85 Howard Cassady	4.00	2.00
❑ 86 Art Donovan	15.00	7.50
❑ 87 Jim Patton	4.00	2.00
❑ 88 Pete Retzlaff	4.00	2.00
❑ 89 Jim Mutscheller	2.00	1.00
❑ 90 Zeke Bratkowski	3.00	1.50
❑ 91 Washington Redskins	4.00	2.00
❑ 92 Art Hunter	2.00	1.00
❑ 93 Gern Nagler	2.00	1.00
❑ 94 Chuck Weber	2.00	1.00
❑ 95 Lew Carpenter RC	3.00	1.50
❑ 96 Stan Jones	5.00	2.50
❑ 97 Ralph Guglielmi UER	3.00	1.50
❑ 98 Green Bay Packers	4.00	2.00
❑ 99 Ray Wietecha	2.00	1.00
❑ 100 Lenny Moore	12.00	6.00
❑ 101 Jim Ray Smith RC UER	3.00	1.50
❑ 102 Abe Woodson RC	3.00	1.50
❑ 103 Alex Karras RC	40.00	25.00
❑ 104 Chicago Bears	4.00	2.00
❑ 105 John David Crow RC	12.00	6.00
❑ 106 Joe Fortunato RC	2.00	1.00
❑ 107 Babe Parilli	3.00	1.50
❑ 108 Proverb Jacobs	2.00	1.00
❑ 109 Gino Marchetti	8.00	4.00
❑ 110 Bill Wade	3.00	1.50
❑ 111 San Francisco 49ers	3.00	1.50
❑ 112 Karl Rubke	2.00	1.00
❑ 113 Dave Middleton UER	2.00	1.00
❑ 114 Roosevelt Brown	5.00	2.50
❑ 115 John Olszewski	2.00	1.00
❑ 116 Jerry Kramer RC	30.00	18.00
❑ 117 King Hill RC	3.00	1.50
❑ 118 Chicago Cardinals	4.00	2.00
❑ 119 Frank Varrichione	2.00	1.00
❑ 120 Rick Casares	3.00	1.50
❑ 121 George Strugar	2.00	1.00
❑ 122 Bill Glass RC	3.00	1.50
❑ 123 Don Bosseler	2.00	1.00
❑ 124 John Reger	2.00	1.00
❑ 125 Jim Ninowski RC	2.00	1.00
❑ 126 Los Angeles Rams	3.00	1.50
❑ 127 Willard Sherman	2.00	1.00
❑ 128 Bob Schnelker	2.00	1.00
❑ 129 Ollie Spencer	2.00	1.00
❑ 130 Y.A.Tittle	25.00	15.00
❑ 131 Yale Lary	5.00	2.50
❑ 132 Jim Parker RC	25.00	12.50
❑ 133 New York Giants	4.00	2.00
❑ 134 Jim Schrader	2.00	1.00
❑ 135 M.C. Reynolds	2.00	1.00
❑ 136 Mike Sandusky	2.00	1.00
❑ 137 Ed Brown	3.00	1.50
❑ 138 Al Barry	2.00	1.00
❑ 139 Detroit Lions	3.00	1.50
❑ 140 Bobby Mitchell RC	35.00	20.00
❑ 141 Larry Morris	2.00	1.00
❑ 142 Jim Phillips RC	3.00	1.50
❑ 143 Jim David	2.00	1.00
❑ 144 Joe Krupa	2.00	1.00
❑ 145 Willie Galimore	3.00	1.50
❑ 146 Pittsburgh Steelers	4.00	2.00
❑ 147 Andy Robustelli	8.00	4.00
❑ 148 Billy Wilson	2.00	1.00
❑ 149 Leo Sanford	2.00	1.00
❑ 150 Eddie LeBaron	5.00	2.50
❑ 151 Bill McColl	2.00	1.00
❑ 152 Buck Lansford UER	2.00	1.00
❑ 153 Chicago Bears	3.00	1.50
❑ 154 Leo Sugar	2.00	1.00
❑ 155 Jim Taylor RC UER	35.00	20.00
❑ 156 Lindon Crow	2.00	1.00
❑ 157 Jack McClairen	2.00	1.00
❑ 158 Vince Costello RC UER	2.00	1.00
❑ 159 Stan Wallace	2.00	1.00
❑ 160 Mel Triplett RC	2.00	1.00
❑ 161 Cleveland Browns	4.00	2.00
❑ 162 Dan Currie RC	3.00	1.50
❑ 163 L.G. Dupre UER	3.00	1.50
❑ 164 John Morrow UER	2.00	1.00
❑ 165 Jim Podoley	2.00	1.00
❑ 166 Bruce Bosley RC	2.00	1.00
❑ 167 Harlon Hill	2.00	1.00
❑ 168 Washington Redskins	3.00	1.50
❑ 169 Junior Wren	2.00	1.00
❑ 170 Tobin Rote	3.00	1.50
❑ 171 Art Spinney	2.00	1.00
❑ 172 Chuck Drazenovich UER	2.00	1.00
❑ 173 Bobby Joe Conrad RC	3.00	1.50
❑ 174 Jesse Richardson	2.00	1.00
❑ 175 Sam Baker	2.00	1.00
❑ 176 Tom Tracy RC !	8.00	4.00

1960 Topps

Card		
❑ COMPLETE SET (132)	600.00	400.00
❑ WRAPPER (1-CENT)	80.00	50.00
❑ WRAPPER (1-CENT, REP)	300.00	150.00
❑ WRAPPER (5-CENT)	80.00	50.00
❑ 1 Johnny Unitas !	80.00	40.00
❑ 2 Alan Ameche	4.00	2.00
❑ 3 Lenny Moore	10.00	5.00
❑ 4 Raymond Berry	12.00	6.00
❑ 5 Jim Parker	8.00	4.00
❑ 6 George Preas	2.50	1.25
❑ 7 Art Spinney	2.50	1.25
❑ 8 Bill Pellington RC	3.00	1.50
❑ 9 Johnny Sample RC	3.00	1.50
❑ 10 Gene Lipscomb	3.00	1.50
❑ 11 Baltimore Colts	3.00	1.50
❑ 12 Ed Brown	3.00	1.50
❑ 13 Rick Casares	3.00	1.50
❑ 14 Willie Galimore	3.00	1.50
❑ 15 Jim Dooley	2.50	1.25
❑ 16 Harlon Hill UER	2.50	1.25
❑ 17 Stan Jones	4.00	2.00
❑ 18 Bill George	4.00	2.00
❑ 19 Erich Barnes RC	3.00	1.50
❑ 20 Doug Atkins	6.00	3.00
❑ 21 Chicago Bears	3.00	1.50
❑ 22 Milt Plum	3.00	1.50
❑ 23 Jim Brown	100.00	60.00
❑ 24 Sam Baker	2.50	1.25
❑ 25 Bobby Mitchell	10.00	5.00
❑ 26 Ray Renfro	3.00	1.50
❑ 27 Billy Howton	3.00	1.50
❑ 28 Jim Ray Smith	2.50	1.25
❑ 29 Jim Shofner RC	3.00	1.50
❑ 30 Bob Gain	2.50	1.25
❑ 31 Cleveland Browns	3.00	1.50
❑ 32 Don Heinrich	2.50	1.25
❑ 33 Ed Modzelewski UER	2.50	1.25
❑ 34 Fred Cone	2.50	1.25
❑ 35 L.G. Dupre	3.00	1.50
❑ 36 Dick Bielski	2.50	1.25

- ❑ 37 Charlie Ane UER 2.50 1.25
- ❑ 38 Jerry Tubbs 3.00 1.50
- ❑ 39 Doyle Nix 2.50 1.25
- ❑ 40 Ray Krouse 2.50 1.25
- ❑ 41 Earl Morrall 4.00 2.00
- ❑ 42 Howard Cassady 3.00 1.50
- ❑ 43 Dave Middleton 2.50 1.25
- ❑ 44 Jim Gibbons RC 3.00 1.50
- ❑ 45 Darris McCord 2.50 1.25
- ❑ 46 Joe Schmidt 6.00 3.00
- ❑ 47 Terry Barr 2.50 1.25
- ❑ 48 Yale Lary 4.00 2.00
- ❑ 49 Gil Mains 2.50 1.25
- ❑ 50 Detroit Lions 3.00 1.50
- ❑ 51 Bart Starr 45.00 30.00
- ❑ 52 Jim Taylor UER 8.00 4.00
- ❑ 53 Lew Carpenter 3.00 1.50
- ❑ 54 Paul Hornung 45.00 30.00
- ❑ 55 Max McGee 4.00 2.00
- ❑ 56 Forrest Gregg RC 40.00 25.00
- ❑ 57 Jim Ringo 5.00 2.50
- ❑ 58 Bill Forester 3.00 1.50
- ❑ 59 Dave Hanner 3.00 1.50
- ❑ 60 Green Bay Packers 8.00 4.00
- ❑ 61 Bill Wade 3.00 1.50
- ❑ 62 Frank Ryan RC 4.00 2.00
- ❑ 63 Ollie Matson 10.00 5.00
- ❑ 64 Jon Arnett 3.00 1.50
- ❑ 65 Del Shofner 3.00 1.50
- ❑ 66 Jim Phillips 2.50 1.25
- ❑ 67 Art Hunter 2.50 1.25
- ❑ 68 Les Richter 3.00 1.50
- ❑ 69 Lou Michaels RC 3.00 1.50
- ❑ 70 John Baker 2.50 1.25
- ❑ 71 Los Angeles Rams 3.00 1.50
- ❑ 72 Charley Conerly 8.00 4.00
- ❑ 73 Mel Triplett 2.50 1.25
- ❑ 74 Frank Gifford 35.00 20.00
- ❑ 75 Alex Webster 3.00 1.50
- ❑ 76 Bob Schnelker 2.50 1.25
- ❑ 77 Pat Summerall 8.00 4.00
- ❑ 78 Roosevelt Brown 4.00 2.00
- ❑ 79 Jim Patton 2.50 1.25
- ❑ 80 Sam Huff 20.00 10.00
- ❑ 81 Andy Robustelli 6.00 3.00
- ❑ 82 New York Giants 3.00 1.50
- ❑ 83 Clarence Peaks 2.50 1.25
- ❑ 84 Bill Barnes 2.50 1.25
- ❑ 85 Pete Retzlaff 3.00 1.50
- ❑ 86 Bobby Walston 2.50 1.25
- ❑ 87 Chuck Bednarik UER 8.00 4.00
- ❑ 88 Bob Pellegrini 2.50 1.25
- ❑ 89 Tom Brookshier RC 3.00 1.50
- ❑ 90 Marion Campbell 3.00 1.50
- ❑ 91 Jesse Richardson 2.50 1.25
- ❑ 92 Philadelphia Eagles 3.00 1.50
- ❑ 93 Bobby Layne 30.00 18.00
- ❑ 94 John Henry Johnson 6.00 3.00
- ❑ 95 Tom Tracy UER 3.00 1.50
- ❑ 96 Preston Carpenter 2.50 1.25
- ❑ 97 Frank Varrichione UER 2.50 1.25
- ❑ 98 John Nisby 2.50 1.25
- ❑ 99 Dean Derby 2.50 1.25
- ❑ 100 George Tarasovic 2.50 1.25
- ❑ 101 Ernie Stautner 5.00 2.50
- ❑ 102 Pittsburgh Steelers 3.00 1.50
- ❑ 103 King Hill 2.50 1.25
- ❑ 104 Mal Hammack 2.50 1.25
- ❑ 105 John David Crow 3.00 1.50
- ❑ 106 Bobby Joe Conrad 3.00 1.50
- ❑ 107 Woodley Lewis 2.50 1.25
- ❑ 108 Don Gillis 2.50 1.25
- ❑ 109 Carl Brettschneider 2.50 1.25
- ❑ 110 Leo Sugar 2.50 1.25
- ❑ 111 Frank Fuller 2.50 1.25
- ❑ 112 St. Louis Cardinals 3.00 1.50
- ❑ 113 Y.A.Tittle 30.00 18.00
- ❑ 114 Joe Perry 8.00 4.00
- ❑ 115 J.D.Smith RC 3.00 1.50
- ❑ 116 Hugh McElhenny 8.00 4.00
- ❑ 117 Billy Wilson 2.50 1.25
- ❑ 118 Bob St.Clair 4.00 2.00
- ❑ 119 Matt Hazeltine 2.50 1.25
- ❑ 120 Abe Woodson 2.50 1.25
- ❑ 121 Leo Nomellini 5.00 2.50
- ❑ 122 San Francisco 49ers 3.00 1.50
- ❑ 123 Ralph Guglielmi UER 2.50 1.25
- ❑ 124 Don Bosseler 2.50 1.25
- ❑ 125 John Olszewski 2.50 1.25
- ❑ 126 Bill Anderson UER 2.50 1.25
- ❑ 127 Joe Walton RC 3.00 1.50
- ❑ 128 Jim Schrader 2.50 1.25
- ❑ 129 Ralph Felton 2.50 1.25
- ❑ 130 Gary Glick 2.50 1.25
- ❑ 131 Bob Toneff 2.50 1.25
- ❑ 132 Redskins Team ! 30.00 18.00
- ❑ AD1 Alan Ameche/Paul Hornung Tom Tracy 350.00 200.00
- ❑ AD2 Del Shofner/Milt Plum Jim Patton 200.00 125.00
- ❑ AD3 Bob St.Clair/Jim Shofner Gil Mains 200.00 125.00
- ❑ AD4 Tom Brookshier/Packers Team George Preas 200.00 125.00

1961 Topps

- ❑ COMPLETE SET (198) 1000.00 650.00
- ❑ COMMON CARD (1-132) 2.50 1.25
- ❑ COMMON CARD (133-198) 3.00 1.50
- ❑ WRAPPER (1-CENT) 275.00 200.00
- ❑ WRAPPER (1-CENT, REP) 200.00 100.00
- ❑ WRAPPER (5-CENT) 100.00 60.00
- ❑ 1 Johnny Unitas ! 100.00 50.00
- ❑ 2 Lenny Moore 12.00 6.00
- ❑ 3 Alan Ameche 4.00 2.00
- ❑ 4 Raymond Berry 12.00 6.00
- ❑ 5 Jim Mutscheller 2.50 1.25
- ❑ 6 Jim Parker 5.00 2.50
- ❑ 7 Gino Marchetti 6.00 3.00
- ❑ 8 Gene Lipscomb 4.00 2.00
- ❑ 9 Baltimore Colts 3.00 1.50
- ❑ 10 Bill Wade 3.00 1.50
- ❑ 11 Johnny Morris RC 6.00 3.00
- ❑ 12 Rick Casares 3.00 1.50
- ❑ 13 Harlon Hill 2.50 1.25
- ❑ 14 Stan Jones 4.00 2.00
- ❑ 15 Doug Atkins 5.00 2.50
- ❑ 16 Bill George 4.00 2.00
- ❑ 17 J.C. Caroline 2.50 1.25
- ❑ 18 Chicago Bears 3.00 1.50
- ❑ 19 Eddie LeBaron IA 3.00 1.50
- ❑ 20 Eddie LeBaron 3.00 1.50
- ❑ 21 Don McIlhenny 2.50 1.25
- ❑ 22 L.G. Dupre 3.00 1.50
- ❑ 23 Jim Doran 2.50 1.25
- ❑ 24 Billy Howton 3.00 1.50
- ❑ 25 Buzz Guy 2.50 1.25
- ❑ 26 Jack Patera RC 2.50 1.25
- ❑ 27 Tom Franckhauser RC 2.50 1.25
- ❑ 28 Cowboys Team 15.00 7.50
- ❑ 29 Jim Ninowski 2.50 1.25
- ❑ 30 Dan Lewis RC 2.50 1.25
- ❑ 31 Nick Pietrosante RC 3.00 1.50
- ❑ 32 Gail Cogdill RC 3.00 1.50
- ❑ 33 Jim Gibbons 2.50 1.25
- ❑ 34 Jim Martin 2.50 1.25
- ❑ 35 Alex Karras 15.00 7.50
- ❑ 36 Joe Schmidt 5.00 2.50
- ❑ 37 Detroit Lions 3.00 1.50
- ❑ 38 Paul Hornung IA 18.00 9.00
- ❑ 39 Bart Starr 40.00 25.00
- ❑ 40 Paul Hornung 40.00 25.00
- ❑ 41 Jim Taylor 35.00 20.00
- ❑ 42 Max McGee 4.00 2.00
- ❑ 43 Boyd Dowler RC 8.00 4.00
- ❑ 44 Jim Ringo 5.00 2.50
- ❑ 45 Hank Jordan RC 30.00 18.00
- ❑ 46 Bill Forester 3.00 1.50
- ❑ 47 Green Bay Packers 15.00 7.50
- ❑ 48 Frank Ryan 3.00 1.50
- ❑ 49 Jon Arnett 3.00 1.50
- ❑ 50 Ollie Matson 8.00 4.00
- ❑ 51 Jim Phillips 2.50 1.25
- ❑ 52 Del Shofner 3.00 1.50
- ❑ 53 Art Hunter 2.50 1.25
- ❑ 54 Gene Brito 2.50 1.25
- ❑ 55 Lindon Crow 2.50 1.25
- ❑ 56 Los Angeles Rams 3.00 1.50
- ❑ 57 Johnny Unitas IA 25.00 15.00
- ❑ 58 Y.A.Tittle 30.00 18.00
- ❑ 59 John Brodie RC 40.00 25.00
- ❑ 60 J.D. Smith 2.50 1.25
- ❑ 61 R.C. Owens 3.00 1.50
- ❑ 62 Clyde Conner 2.50 1.25
- ❑ 63 Bob St.Clair 4.00 2.00
- ❑ 64 Leo Nomellini 6.00 3.00
- ❑ 65 Abe Woodson 2.50 1.25
- ❑ 66 San Francisco 49ers 3.00 1.50
- ❑ 67 Checklist Card 40.00 25.00
- ❑ 68 Milt Plum 3.00 1.50
- ❑ 69 Ray Renfro 3.00 1.50
- ❑ 70 Bobby Mitchell 8.00 4.00
- ❑ 71 Jim Brown 125.00 75.00
- ❑ 72 Mike McCormack 4.00 2.00
- ❑ 73 Jim Ray Smith 2.50 1.25
- ❑ 74 Sam Baker 2.50 1.25
- ❑ 75 Walt Michaels 3.00 1.50
- ❑ 76 Cleveland Browns 3.00 1.50
- ❑ 77 Jim Brown IA 35.00 20.00
- ❑ 78 George Shaw 2.50 1.25
- ❑ 79 Hugh McElhenny 8.00 4.00
- ❑ 80 Clancy Osborne 2.50 1.25
- ❑ 81 Dave Middleton 2.50 1.25
- ❑ 82 Frank Youso 2.50 1.25
- ❑ 83 Don Joyce 2.50 1.25
- ❑ 84 Ed Culpepper 2.50 1.25
- ❑ 85 Charley Conerly 8.00 4.00
- ❑ 86 Mel Triplett 2.50 1.25
- ❑ 87 Kyle Rote 3.00 1.50
- ❑ 88 Roosevelt Brown 4.00 2.00
- ❑ 89 Ray Wietecha 2.50 1.25
- ❑ 90 Andy Robustelli 5.00 2.50
- ❑ 91 Sam Huff 8.00 4.00
- ❑ 92 Jim Patton 2.50 1.25
- ❑ 93 New York Giants 3.00 1.50
- ❑ 94 Charley Conerly IA 6.00 3.00
- ❑ 95 Sonny Jurgensen 25.00 15.00
- ❑ 96 Tommy McDonald 5.00 2.50
- ❑ 97 Bill Barnes 2.50 1.25
- ❑ 98 Bobby Walston 2.50 1.25
- ❑ 99 Pete Retzlaff 3.00 1.50
- ❑ 100 Jim McCusker 2.50 1.25
- ❑ 101 Chuck Bednarik 8.00 4.00
- ❑ 102 Tom Brookshier 3.00 1.50
- ❑ 103 Philadelphia Eagles 3.00 1.50
- ❑ 104 Bobby Layne 30.00 18.00
- ❑ 105 John Henry Johnson 4.00 2.00
- ❑ 106 Tom Tracy 3.00 1.50
- ❑ 107 Buddy Dial RC 2.50 1.25
- ❑ 108 Jimmy Orr RC 4.00 2.00
- ❑ 109 Mike Sandusky 2.50 1.25
- ❑ 110 John Reger 2.50 1.25
- ❑ 111 Junior Wren 2.50 1.25
- ❑ 112 Pittsburgh Steelers 3.00 1.50
- ❑ 113 Bobby Layne IA 10.00 5.00
- ❑ 114 John Roach 2.50 1.25
- ❑ 115 Sam Etcheverry RC 3.00 1.50
- ❑ 116 John David Crow 3.00 1.50
- ❑ 117 Mal Hammack 2.50 1.25
- ❑ 118 Sonny Randle RC 3.00 1.50
- ❑ 119 Leo Sugar 2.50 1.25
- ❑ 120 Jerry Norton 2.50 1.25
- ❑ 121 St. Louis Cardinals 3.00 1.50
- ❑ 122 Checklist Card 50.00 30.00
- ❑ 123 Ralph Guglielmi 2.50 1.25

Card		
❑ 124 Dick James	2.50	1.25
❑ 125 Don Bosseler	2.50	1.25
❑ 126 Joe Walton	2.50	1.25
❑ 127 Bill Anderson	2.50	1.25
❑ 128 Vince Promuto RC	2.50	1.25
❑ 129 Bob Toneff	2.50	1.25
❑ 130 John Paluck	2.50	1.25
❑ 131 Washington Redskins	3.00	1.50
❑ 132 Milt Plum IA !	2.50	1.25
❑ 133 Abner Haynes !	8.00	4.00
❑ 134 Mel Branch UER	4.00	2.00
❑ 135 Jerry Cornelison UER	3.00	1.50
❑ 136 Bill Krisher	3.00	1.50
❑ 137 Paul Miller	3.00	1.50
❑ 138 Jack Spikes	4.00	2.00
❑ 139 Johnny Robinson RC	8.00	4.00
❑ 140 Cotton Davidson RC	4.00	2.00
❑ 141 Dave Smith RB	3.00	1.50
❑ 142 Bill Groman	3.00	1.50
❑ 143 Rich Michael	3.00	1.50
❑ 144 Mike Dukes	3.00	1.50
❑ 145 George Blanda	25.00	15.00
❑ 146 Billy Cannon	6.00	3.00
❑ 147 Dennit Morris	3.00	1.50
❑ 148 Jacky Lee UER	4.00	2.00
❑ 149 Al Dorow	3.00	1.50
❑ 150 Don Maynard RC	50.00	25.00
❑ 151 Art Powell RC	8.00	4.00
❑ 152 Sid Youngelman	3.00	1.50
❑ 153 Bob Mischak	3.00	1.50
❑ 154 Larry Grantham	3.00	1.50
❑ 155 Tom Saidock	3.00	1.50
❑ 156 Roger Donnahoo	3.00	1.50
❑ 157 Laverne Torczon	3.00	1.50
❑ 158 Archie Matsos RC	4.00	2.00
❑ 159 Elbert Dubenion	4.00	2.00
❑ 160 Wray Carlton RC	4.00	2.00
❑ 161 Rich McCabe	3.00	1.50
❑ 162 Ken Rice	3.00	1.50
❑ 163 Art Baker RC	3.00	1.50
❑ 164 Tom Rychlec	3.00	1.50
❑ 165 Mack Yoho	3.00	1.50
❑ 166 Jack Kemp	100.00	50.00
❑ 167 Paul Lowe	6.00	3.00
❑ 168 Ron Mix	10.00	5.00
❑ 169 Paul Maguire UER	6.00	3.00
❑ 170 Volney Peters	3.00	1.50
❑ 171 Ernie Wright RC	4.00	2.00
❑ 172 Ron Nery RC	3.00	1.50
❑ 173 Dave Kocourek RC	4.00	2.00
❑ 174 Jim Colclough	3.00	1.50
❑ 175 Babe Parilli	4.00	2.00
❑ 176 Billy Lott	3.00	1.50
❑ 177 Fred Bruney	3.00	1.50
❑ 178 Ross O'Hanley	3.00	1.50
❑ 179 Walt Cudzik	3.00	1.50
❑ 180 Charley Leo	3.00	1.50
❑ 181 Bob Dee	3.00	1.50
❑ 182 Jim Otto RC	40.00	25.00
❑ 183 Eddie Macon	3.00	1.50
❑ 184 Dick Christy	3.00	1.50
❑ 185 Alan Miller	3.00	1.50
❑ 186 Tom Flores RC	20.00	10.00
❑ 187 Joe Cannavino	3.00	1.50
❑ 188 Don Manoukian	3.00	1.50
❑ 189 Bob Coolbaugh	3.00	1.50
❑ 190 Lionel Taylor RC	8.00	4.00
❑ 191 Bud McFadin	3.00	1.50
❑ 192 Goose Gonsoulin RC	6.00	3.00
❑ 193 Frank Tripucka	4.00	2.00
❑ 194 Gene Mingo RC	4.00	2.00
❑ 195 Eldon Danenhauer	3.00	1.50
❑ 196 Bob McNamara	3.00	1.50
❑ 197 Dave Rolle UER	3.00	1.50
❑ 198 Checklist UER !	100.00	60.00
❑ AD1 Jim Martin/George Shaw Jim Ray Smith	200.00	125.00

1962 Topps

Card		
❑ COMPLETE SET (176)	2000.00	1200.00
❑ WRAPPER (1-CENT)	250.00	175.00
❑ WRAPPER (5-CENT,STARS)	50.00	25.00
❑ WRAPPER (5-CENT,BUCKS)	40.00	25.00
❑ 1 Johnny Unitas !	200.00	125.00
❑ 2 Lenny Moore	12.00	6.00
❑ 3 Alex Hawkins RC SP	10.00	5.00
❑ 4 Joe Perry	8.00	4.00
❑ 5 Raymond Berry SP	40.00	25.00
❑ 6 Steve Myhra	4.00	2.00
❑ 7 Tom Gilburg SP	8.00	4.00
❑ 8 Gino Marchetti	8.00	4.00
❑ 9 Bill Pellington	4.00	2.00
❑ 10 Andy Nelson	4.00	2.00
❑ 11 Wendell Harris SP	8.00	4.00
❑ 12 Baltimore Colts	6.00	3.00
❑ 13 Bill Wade SP	10.00	5.00
❑ 14 Willie Galimore	5.00	2.50
❑ 15 Johnny Morris SP	8.00	4.00
❑ 16 Rick Casares	5.00	2.50
❑ 17 Mike Ditka RC	225.00	125.00
❑ 18 Stan Jones	6.00	3.00
❑ 19 Roger LeClerc	4.00	2.00
❑ 20 Angelo Coia	4.00	2.00
❑ 21 Doug Atkins	7.00	3.50
❑ 22 Bill George	6.00	3.00
❑ 23 Richie Petitbon RC	5.00	2.50
❑ 24 Ronnie Bull RC SP	8.00	4.00
❑ 25 Chicago Bears	6.00	3.00
❑ 26 Howard Cassady	5.00	2.50
❑ 27 Ray Renfro SP	10.00	5.00
❑ 28 Jim Brown	175.00	100.00
❑ 29 Rich Kreitling	4.00	2.00
❑ 30 Jim Ray Smith	4.00	2.00
❑ 31 John Morrow	4.00	2.00
❑ 32 Lou Groza	15.00	7.50
❑ 33 Bob Gain	4.00	2.00
❑ 34 Bernie Parrish	4.00	2.00
❑ 35 Jim Shofner	4.00	2.00
❑ 36 Ernie Davis RC SP	150.00	90.00
❑ 37 Cleveland Browns	6.00	3.00
❑ 38 Eddie LeBaron	5.00	2.50
❑ 39 Don Meredith SP	100.00	60.00
❑ 40 J.W. Lockett SP	8.00	4.00
❑ 41 Don Perkins RC	10.00	5.00
❑ 42 Billy Howton	5.00	2.50
❑ 43 Dick Bielski	4.00	2.00
❑ 44 Mike Connelly RC	4.00	2.00
❑ 45 Jerry Tubbs SP	8.00	4.00
❑ 46 Don Bishop SP	8.00	4.00
❑ 47 Dick Moegle	4.00	2.00
❑ 48 Bobby Plummer SP	8.00	4.00
❑ 49 Cowboys Team	20.00	12.00
❑ 50 Milt Plum	5.00	2.50
❑ 51 Dan Lewis	4.00	2.00
❑ 52 Nick Pietrosante SP	8.00	4.00
❑ 53 Gail Cogdill	4.00	2.00
❑ 54 Jim Gibbons	4.00	2.00
❑ 55 Jim Martin	4.00	2.00
❑ 56 Yale Lary	6.00	3.00
❑ 57 Darris McCord	4.00	2.00
❑ 58 Alex Karras	25.00	15.00
❑ 59 Joe Schmidt	7.00	3.50
❑ 60 Dick Lane	6.00	3.00
❑ 61 John Lomakoski SP	8.00	4.00
❑ 62 Detroit Lions SP	18.00	10.00
❑ 63 Bart Starr SP	125.00	75.00
❑ 64 Paul Hornung SP	100.00	60.00
❑ 65 Tom Moore SP	12.00	6.00
❑ 66 Jim Taylor SP	50.00	30.00
❑ 67 Max McGee SP	12.00	6.00
❑ 68 Jim Ringo SP	15.00	7.50
❑ 69 Fuzzy Thurston RC SP	20.00	12.00
❑ 70 Forrest Gregg	7.00	3.50
❑ 71 Boyd Dowler	6.00	3.00
❑ 72 Hank Jordan SP	15.00	7.50
❑ 73 Bill Forester SP	10.00	5.00
❑ 74 Earl Gros SP	8.00	4.00
❑ 75 Packers Team SP	35.00	20.00
❑ 76 Checklist SP	80.00	45.00
❑ 77 Zeke Bratkowski SP	10.00	5.00
❑ 78 Jon Arnett SP	10.00	5.00
❑ 79 Ollie Matson SP	35.00	20.00
❑ 80 Dick Bass SP	10.00	5.00
❑ 81 Jim Phillips	4.00	2.00
❑ 82 Carroll Dale RC	5.00	2.50
❑ 83 Frank Varrichione	4.00	2.00
❑ 84 Art Hunter	4.00	2.00
❑ 85 Danny Villanueva RC	4.00	2.00
❑ 86 Les Richter SP	8.00	4.00
❑ 87 Lindon Crow	4.00	2.00
❑ 88 Roman Gabriel RC SP	60.00	35.00
❑ 89 Los Angeles Rams SP	18.00	10.00
❑ 90 Fran Tarkenton RC SP	225.00	125.00
❑ 91 Jerry Reichow SP	8.00	4.00
❑ 92 Hugh McElhenny SP	30.00	18.00
❑ 93 Mel Triplett SP	8.00	4.00
❑ 94 Tommy Mason RC SP	12.00	6.00
❑ 95 Dave Middleton SP	8.00	4.00
❑ 96 Frank Youso SP	8.00	4.00
❑ 97 Mike Mercer SP	8.00	4.00
❑ 98 Rip Hawkins SP	8.00	4.00
❑ 99 Cliff Livingston SP	8.00	4.00
❑ 100 Roy Winston RC SP	8.00	4.00
❑ 101 Vikings Team SP	25.00	15.00
❑ 102 Y.A.Tittle	40.00	25.00
❑ 103 Joe Walton	4.00	2.00
❑ 104 Frank Gifford	50.00	30.00
❑ 105 Alex Webster	5.00	2.50
❑ 106 Del Shofner	5.00	2.50
❑ 107 Don Chandler	4.00	2.00
❑ 108 Andy Robustelli	7.00	3.50
❑ 109 Jim Katcavage RC	5.00	2.50
❑ 110 Sam Huff SP	40.00	25.00
❑ 111 Erich Barnes	4.00	2.00
❑ 112 Jim Patton	4.00	2.00
❑ 113 Jerry Hillebrand SP	8.00	4.00
❑ 114 New York Giants	6.00	3.00
❑ 115 Sonny Jurgensen	40.00	25.00
❑ 116 Tommy McDonald	8.00	4.00
❑ 117 Ted Dean SP	8.00	4.00
❑ 118 Clarence Peaks	4.00	2.00
❑ 119 Bobby Walston	4.00	2.00
❑ 120 Pete Retzlaff SP	10.00	5.00
❑ 121 Jim Schrader SP	8.00	4.00
❑ 122 J.D. Smith T	4.00	2.00
❑ 123 King Hill	4.00	2.00
❑ 124 Maxie Baughan	5.00	2.50
❑ 125 Pete Case SP	8.00	4.00
❑ 126 Philadelphia Eagles	6.00	3.00
❑ 127 Bobby Layne	40.00	25.00
❑ 128 Tom Tracy	5.00	2.50
❑ 129 John Henry Johnson	6.00	3.00
❑ 130 Buddy Dial SP	10.00	5.00
❑ 131 Preston Carpenter	4.00	2.00
❑ 132 Lou Michaels SP	8.00	4.00
❑ 133 Gene Lipscomb SP	10.00	5.00
❑ 134 Ernie Stautner SP	20.00	12.00
❑ 135 John Reger SP	8.00	4.00
❑ 136 Myron Pottios RC	4.00	2.00
❑ 137 Bob Ferguson SP	8.00	4.00
❑ 138 Pittsburgh Steelers SP	18.00	10.00
❑ 139 Sam Etcheverry	5.00	2.50
❑ 140 John David Crow SP	10.00	5.00
❑ 141 Bobby Joe Conrad SP	10.00	5.00
❑ 142 Prentice Gautt RC SP	8.00	4.00
❑ 143 Frank Mestnik	4.00	2.00
❑ 144 Sonny Randle	5.00	2.50
❑ 145 Gerry Perry UER	4.00	2.00

❑ 146 Jerry Norton 4.00 2.00
❑ 147 Jimmy Hill 4.00 2.00
❑ 148 Bill Stacy 4.00 2.00
❑ 149 Fate Echols SP 8.00 4.00
❑ 150 St. Louis Cardinals 6.00 3.00
❑ 151 Billy Kilmer RC 35.00 20.00
❑ 152 John Brodie 18.00 10.00
❑ 153 J.D. Smith RB 5.00 2.50
❑ 154 C.R. Roberts SP 8.00 4.00
❑ 155 Monty Stickles 4.00 2.00
❑ 156 Clyde Conner UER 4.00 2.00
❑ 157 Bob St.Clair 6.00 3.00
❑ 158 Tommy Davis RC 4.00 2.00
❑ 159 Leo Nomellini 8.00 4.00
❑ 160 Matt Hazeltine 4.00 2.00
❑ 161 Abe Woodson 4.00 2.00
❑ 162 Dave Baker 4.00 2.00
❑ 163 San Francisco 49ers 6.00 3.00
❑ 164 Norm Snead RC SP 30.00 18.00
❑ 165 Dick James 5.00 2.50
❑ 166 Bobby Mitchell 8.00 4.00
❑ 167 Sam Horner 4.00 2.00
❑ 168 Bill Barnes 4.00 2.00
❑ 169 Bill Anderson 4.00 2.00
❑ 170 Fred Dugan 4.00 2.00
❑ 171 John Aveni SP 8.00 4.00
❑ 172 Bob Toneff 4.00 2.00
❑ 173 Jim Kerr 4.00 2.00
❑ 174 Leroy Jackson SP 8.00 4.00
❑ 175 Washington Redskins 6.00 3.00
❑ 176 Checklist ! 100.00 60.00

1963 Topps

❑ COMPLETE SET (170) 1350.00 850.00
❑ WRAPPER (1-CENT) 450.00 300.00
❑ WRAPPER (5-CENT) 80.00 50.00
❑ 1 Johnny Unitas ! 135.00 75.00
❑ 2 Lenny Moore 8.00 4.00
❑ 3 Jimmy Orr 3.00 1.50
❑ 4 Raymond Berry 8.00 4.00
❑ 5 Jim Parker 5.00 2.50
❑ 6 Alex Sandusky 2.50 1.25
❑ 7 Dick Szymanski RC 2.50 1.25
❑ 8 Gino Marchetti 6.00 3.00
❑ 9 Billy Ray Smith RC 3.00 1.50
❑ 10 Bill Pellington 2.50 1.25
❑ 11 Bob Boyd RC DB 2.50 1.25
❑ 12 Baltimore Colts SP 10.00 5.00
❑ 13 Frank Ryan SP 8.00 4.00
❑ 14 Jim Brown SP 200.00 100.00
❑ 15 Ray Renfro SP 8.00 4.00
❑ 16 Rich Kreitling SP 6.00 3.50
❑ 17 Mike McCormack SP 10.00 5.00
❑ 18 Jim Ray Smith SP 6.00 3.50
❑ 19 Lou Groza SP 25.00 15.00
❑ 20 Bill Glass SP 6.00 3.50
❑ 21 Galen Fiss SP 6.00 3.50
❑ 22 Don Fleming RC SP 8.00 4.00
❑ 23 Bob Gain SP 6.00 3.50
❑ 24 Cleveland Browns SP 10.00 5.00
❑ 25 Milt Plum 3.00 1.50
❑ 26 Dan Lewis 2.50 1.25
❑ 27 Nick Pietrosante 2.50 1.25
❑ 28 Gail Cogdill 2.50 1.25
❑ 29 Harley Sewell 2.50 1.25
❑ 30 Jim Gibbons 2.50 1.25
❑ 31 Carl Brettschneider 2.50 1.25
❑ 32 Dick Lane 5.00 2.50
❑ 33 Yale Lary 5.00 2.50
❑ 34 Roger Brown RC 3.00 1.50
❑ 35 Joe Schmidt 6.00 3.00
❑ 36 Detroit Lions SP 10.00 5.00
❑ 37 Roman Gabriel 8.00 4.00
❑ 38 Zeke Bratkowski 3.00 1.50
❑ 39 Dick Bass 3.00 1.50
❑ 40 Jon Arnett 3.00 1.50
❑ 41 Jim Phillips 2.50 1.25
❑ 42 Frank Varrichione 2.50 1.25
❑ 43 Danny Villanueva 2.50 1.25
❑ 44 Deacon Jones RC 50.00 30.00
❑ 45 Lindon Crow 2.50 1.25
❑ 46 Marlin McKeever 2.50 1.25
❑ 47 Ed Meador RC 2.50 1.25
❑ 48 Los Angeles Rams 4.00 2.00
❑ 49 Y.A.Tittle SP 50.00 30.00
❑ 50 Del Shofner SP 6.00 3.50
❑ 51 Alex Webster SP 8.00 4.00
❑ 52 Phil King SP 6.00 3.50
❑ 53 Jack Stroud SP 6.00 3.50
❑ 54 Darrell Dess SP 6.00 3.50
❑ 55 Jim Katcavage SP 6.00 3.50
❑ 56 Roosevelt Grier SP 10.00 5.00
❑ 57 Erich Barnes SP 6.00 3.50
❑ 58 Jim Patton SP 6.00 3.50
❑ 59 Sam Huff SP 20.00 12.00
❑ 60 New York Giants 4.00 2.00
❑ 61 Bill Wade 3.00 1.50
❑ 62 Mike Ditka 60.00 35.00
❑ 63 Johnny Morris 2.50 1.25
❑ 64 Roger LeClerc 2.50 1.25
❑ 65 Roger Davis RC 2.50 1.25
❑ 66 Joe Marconi 2.50 1.25
❑ 67 Herman Lee 2.50 1.25
❑ 68 Doug Atkins 6.00 3.00
❑ 69 Joe Fortunato 2.50 1.25
❑ 70 Bill George 5.00 2.50
❑ 71 Richie Petitbon 3.00 1.50
❑ 72 Bears Team SP 10.00 5.00
❑ 73 Eddie LeBaron SP 10.00 5.00
❑ 74 Don Meredith SP 60.00 35.00
❑ 75 Don Perkins SP 10.00 5.00
❑ 76 Amos Marsh SP 6.00 3.50
❑ 77 Billy Howton SP 8.00 4.00
❑ 78 Andy Cvercko SP 6.00 3.50
❑ 79 Sam Baker SP 6.00 3.50
❑ 80 Jerry Tubbs SP 6.00 3.50
❑ 81 Don Bishop SP 6.00 3.50
❑ 82 Bob Lilly RC SP 175.00 100.00
❑ 83 Jerry Norton SP 6.00 3.50
❑ 84 Cowboys Team SP 20.00 12.00
❑ 85 Checklist 25.00 15.00
❑ 86 Bart Starr 75.00 40.00
❑ 87 Jim Taylor 30.00 18.00
❑ 88 Boyd Dowler 5.00 2.50
❑ 89 Forrest Gregg 6.00 3.00
❑ 90 Fuzzy Thurston 6.00 3.00
❑ 91 Jim Ringo 6.00 3.00
❑ 92 Ron Kramer 3.00 1.50
❑ 93 Hank Jordan 6.00 3.00
❑ 94 Bill Forester 3.00 1.50
❑ 95 Willie Wood RC 40.00 25.00
❑ 96 Ray Nitschke RC 125.00 75.00
❑ 97 Green Bay Packers 15.00 7.50
❑ 98 Fran Tarkenton 60.00 35.00
❑ 99 Tommy Mason 3.00 1.50
❑ 100 Mel Triplett 2.50 1.25
❑ 101 Jerry Reichow 2.50 1.25
❑ 102 Frank Youso 2.50 1.25
❑ 103 Hugh McElhenny 8.00 4.00
❑ 104 Gerald Huth 2.50 1.25
❑ 105 Ed Sharockman 2.50 1.25
❑ 106 Rip Hawkins 2.50 1.25
❑ 107 Jim Marshall RC 35.00 20.00
❑ 108 Jim Prestel 2.50 1.25
❑ 109 Minnesota Vikings 4.00 2.00
❑ 110 Sonny Jurgensen SP 25.00 15.00
❑ 111 Timmy Brown RC SP 10.00 5.00
❑ 112 Tommy McDonald SP 15.00 7.50
❑ 113 Clarence Peaks SP 6.00 3.50
❑ 114 Pete Retzlaff SP 8.00 4.00
❑ 115 Jim Schrader SP 6.00 3.50
❑ 116 Jim McCusker SP 6.00 3.50
❑ 117 Don Burroughs SP 6.00 3.50
❑ 118 Maxie Baughan SP 6.00 3.50
❑ 119 Riley Gunnels SP 6.00 3.50
❑ 120 Jimmy Carr SP 6.00 3.50
❑ 121 Philadelphia Eagles SP 10.00 5.00
❑ 122 Ed Brown SP 8.00 4.00
❑ 123 John H.Johnson SP 15.00 7.50
❑ 124 Buddy Dial SP 6.00 3.50
❑ 125 Bill Red Mack SP 6.00 3.50
❑ 126 Preston Carpenter SP 6.00 3.50
❑ 127 Ray Lemek SP 6.00 3.50
❑ 128 Buzz Nutter SP 6.00 3.50
❑ 129 Ernie Stautner SP 15.00 7.50
❑ 130 Lou Michaels SP 6.00 3.50
❑ 131 Clendon Thomas RC SP 6.00 3.50
❑ 132 Tom Bettis SP 6.00 3.50
❑ 133 Pittsburgh Steelers SP 10.00 5.00
❑ 134 John Brodie 8.00 4.00
❑ 135 J.D. Smith 2.50 1.25
❑ 136 Billy Kilmer 5.00 2.50
❑ 137 Bernie Casey RC 3.00 1.50
❑ 138 Tommy Davis 2.50 1.25
❑ 139 Ted Connolly 2.50 1.25
❑ 140 Bob St.Clair 5.00 2.50
❑ 141 Abe Woodson 2.50 1.25
❑ 142 Matt Hazeltine 2.50 1.25
❑ 143 Leo Nomellini 6.00 3.00
❑ 144 Dan Colchico 2.50 1.25
❑ 145 San Francisco 49ers SP 10.00 5.00
❑ 146 Charlie Johnson RC 8.00 4.00
❑ 147 John David Crow 3.00 1.50
❑ 148 Bobby Joe Conrad 3.00 1.50
❑ 149 Sonny Randle 2.50 1.25
❑ 150 Prentice Gautt 2.50 1.25
❑ 151 Taz Anderson 2.50 1.25
❑ 152 Ernie McMillan RC 3.00 1.50
❑ 153 Jimmy Hill 2.50 1.25
❑ 154 Bill Koman 2.50 1.25
❑ 155 Larry Wilson RC 20.00 12.00
❑ 156 Don Owens 2.50 1.25
❑ 157 St. Louis Cardinals SP 10.00 5.00
❑ 158 Norm Snead SP 10.00 5.00
❑ 159 Bobby Mitchell SP 15.00 7.50
❑ 160 Bill Barnes SP 6.00 3.50
❑ 161 Fred Dugan SP 6.00 3.50
❑ 162 Don Bosseler SP 6.00 3.50
❑ 163 John Nisby SP 6.00 3.50
❑ 164 Riley Mattson SP 6.00 3.50
❑ 165 Bob Toneff SP 6.00 3.50
❑ 166 Rod Breedlove SP 6.00 3.50
❑ 167 Dick James SP 6.00 3.50
❑ 168 Claude Crabb SP 6.00 3.50
❑ 169 Washington Redskins SP 10.00 5.00
❑ 170 Checklist UER ! 50.00 30.00
❑ AD1 C.Johnson/Crow/Conrad 200.00125.00

1964 Topps

❑ COMPLETE SET (176) 1500.001000.00
❑ WRAPPER (1-CENT) 40.00 30.00
❑ WRAPPER (5-CENT, PENN) 90.00 60.00
❑ WRAP. (5-CENT, 8-CARD) 150.00 90.00
❑ 1 Tommy Addison SP ! 30.00 15.00
❑ 2 Houston Antwine RC 4.00 2.00
❑ 3 Nick Buoniconti 25.00 15.00
❑ 4 Ron Burton SP 10.00 5.00
❑ 5 Gino Cappelletti 5.00 2.50

❑ 6 Jim Colclough SP 6.00 3.00
❑ 7 Bob Dee SP 6.00 3.00
❑ 8 Larry Eisenhauer 4.00 2.00
❑ 9 Dick Felt SP 6.00 3.00
❑ 10 Larry Garron 4.00 2.00
❑ 11 Art Graham 4.00 2.00
❑ 12 Ron Hall DB 4.00 2.00
❑ 13 Charles Long 4.00 2.00
❑ 14 Don McKinnon 4.00 2.00
❑ 15 Don Oakes SP 6.00 3.00
❑ 16 Ross O'Hanley SP 6.00 3.00
❑ 17 Babe Parilli SP 10.00 5.00
❑ 18 Jesse Richardson SP 6.00 3.00
❑ 19 Jack Rudolph SP 6.00 3.00
❑ 20 Don Webb RC 4.00 2.00
❑ 21 Boston Patriots 6.00 3.00
❑ 22 Ray Abruzzese 4.00 2.00
❑ 23 Stew Barber RC 4.00 2.00
❑ 24 Dave Behrman 4.00 2.00
❑ 25 Al Bemiller 4.00 2.00
❑ 26 Elbert Dubenion SP 10.00 5.00
❑ 27 Jim Dunaway RC SP 6.00 3.00
❑ 28 Booker Edgerson SP 6.00 3.00
❑ 29 Cookie Gilchrist SP 25.00 15.00
❑ 30 Jack Kemp SP 120.00 60.00
❑ 31 Daryle Lamonica RC 75.00 40.00
❑ 32 Bill Miller 4.00 2.00
❑ 33 Herb Paterra RC 4.00 2.00
❑ 34 Ken Rice SP 6.00 3.00
❑ 35 Ed Rutkowski 4.00 2.00
❑ 36 George Saimes RC 4.00 2.00
❑ 37 Tom Sestak 4.00 2.00
❑ 38 Billy Shaw SP 15.00 7.50
❑ 39 Mike Stratton 5.00 2.50
❑ 40 Gene Sykes 4.00 2.00
❑ 41 John Tracey SP 6.00 3.00
❑ 42 Sid Youngelman SP 6.00 3.00
❑ 43 Buffalo Bills 6.00 3.00
❑ 44 Eldon Danenhauer SP 6.00 3.00
❑ 45 Jim Fraser SP 6.00 3.00
❑ 46 Chuck Gavin SP 6.00 3.00
❑ 47 Goose Gonsoulin SP 10.00 5.00
❑ 48 Ernie Barnes RC 4.00 2.00
❑ 49 Tom Janik 4.00 2.00
❑ 50 Billy Joe RC 5.00 2.50
❑ 51 Ike Lassiter RC 4.00 2.00
❑ 52 John McCormick QB SP 6.00 3.00
❑ 53 Bud McFadin SP 6.00 3.00
❑ 54 Gene Mingo SP 6.00 3.00
❑ 55 Charlie Mitchell 4.00 2.00
❑ 56 John Nocera SP 6.00 3.00
❑ 57 Tom Nomina 4.00 2.00
❑ 58 Harold Olson SP 6.00 3.00
❑ 59 Bob Scarpitto 4.00 2.00
❑ 60 John Sklopan 4.00 2.00
❑ 61 Mickey Slaughter 4.00 2.00
❑ 62 Don Stone 4.00 2.00
❑ 63 Jerry Sturm 4.00 2.00
❑ 64 Lionel Taylor SP 12.00 6.00
❑ 65 Broncos Team SP 20.00 10.00
❑ 66 Scott Appleton RC 4.00 2.00
❑ 67 Tony Banfield SP 6.00 3.00
❑ 68 George Blanda SP 75.00 40.00
❑ 69 Billy Cannon 6.00 3.00
❑ 70 Doug Cline SP 6.00 3.00
❑ 71 Gary Cutsinger SP 6.00 3.00
❑ 72 Willard Dewveall SP 6.00 3.00
❑ 73 Don Floyd SP 6.00 3.00
❑ 74 Freddy Glick SP 6.00 3.00
❑ 75 Charlie Hennigan SP 10.00 5.00
❑ 76 Ed Husmann SP 6.00 3.00
❑ 77 Bobby Jancik SP 6.00 3.00
❑ 78 Jacky Lee SP 10.00 5.00
❑ 79 Bob McLeod SP 6.00 3.00
❑ 80 Rich Michael SP 6.00 3.00
❑ 81 Larry Onesti RC 4.00 2.00
❑ 82 Checklist Card UER 60.00 30.00
❑ 83 Bob Schmidt SP 6.00 3.00
❑ 84 Walt Suggs SP 6.00 3.00
❑ 85 Bob Talamini SP 6.00 3.00
❑ 86 Charley Tolar SP 6.00 3.00
❑ 87 Don Trull RC 4.00 2.00
❑ 88 Houston Oilers 6.00 3.00
❑ 89 Fred Arbanas 4.00 2.00
❑ 90 Bobby Bell RC 40.00 25.00
❑ 91 Mel Branch SP 10.00 5.00
❑ 92 Buck Buchanan RC 40.00 25.00
❑ 93 Ed Budde RC 4.00 2.00
❑ 94 Chris Burford SP 10.00 5.00
❑ 95 Walt Corey RC 5.00 2.50
❑ 96 Len Dawson SP 75.00 40.00
❑ 97 Dave Grayson RC 4.00 2.00
❑ 98 Abner Haynes 6.00 3.00
❑ 99 Sherrill Headrick SP 10.00 5.00
❑ 100 E.J. Holub 4.00 2.00
❑ 101 Bobby Hunt RC 4.00 2.00
❑ 102 Frank Jackson SP 6.00 3.00
❑ 103 Curtis McClinton 5.00 2.50
❑ 104 Jerry Mays SP 10.00 5.00
❑ 105 Johnny Robinson SP 12.00 6.00
❑ 106 Jack Spikes SP 6.00 3.00
❑ 107 Smokey Stover SP 6.00 3.00
❑ 108 Jim Tyrer RC 8.00 4.00
❑ 109 Duane Wood SP 6.00 3.00
❑ 110 Kansas City Chiefs 6.00 3.00
❑ 111 Dick Christy SP 6.00 3.00
❑ 112 Dan Ficca SP 6.00 3.00
❑ 113 Larry Grantham 4.00 2.00
❑ 114 Curley Johnson SP 6.00 3.00
❑ 115 Gene Heeter 4.00 2.00
❑ 116 Jack Klotz 4.00 2.00
❑ 117 Pete Liske RC 5.00 2.50
❑ 118 Bob McAdam 4.00 2.00
❑ 119 Dee Mackey SP 6.00 3.00
❑ 120 Bill Mathis SP 10.00 5.00
❑ 121 Don Maynard 35.00 20.00
❑ 122 Dainard Paulson SP 6.00 3.00
❑ 123 Gerry Philbin RC 5.00 2.50
❑ 124 Mark Smolinski SP 6.00 3.00
❑ 125 Matt Snell RC 20.00 10.00
❑ 126 Mike Taliaferro 4.00 2.00
❑ 127 Bake Turner RC SP 10.00 5.00
❑ 128 Jeff Ware 4.00 2.00
❑ 129 Clyde Washington 4.00 2.00
❑ 130 Dick Wood RC 4.00 2.00
❑ 131 New York Jets 6.00 3.00
❑ 132 Dalva Allen SP 6.00 3.00
❑ 133 Dan Birdwell 4.00 2.00
❑ 134 Dave Costa RC 4.00 2.00
❑ 135 Dobie Craig 4.00 2.00
❑ 136 Clem Daniels 5.00 2.50
❑ 137 Cotton Davidson SP 10.00 5.00
❑ 138 Claude Gibson 4.00 2.00
❑ 139 Tom Flores SP 15.00 7.50
❑ 140 Wayne Hawkins SP 6.00 3.00
❑ 141 Ken Herock 4.00 2.00
❑ 142 Jon Jelacic SP 6.00 3.00
❑ 143 Joe Krakoski 4.00 2.00
❑ 144 Archie Matsos SP 6.00 3.00
❑ 145 Mike Mercer 4.00 2.00
❑ 146 Alan Miller SP 6.00 3.00
❑ 147 Bob Mischak SP 6.00 3.00
❑ 148 Jim Otto SP 30.00 18.00
❑ 149 Clancy Osborne SP 6.00 3.00
❑ 150 Art Powell SP 12.00 6.00
❑ 151 Bo Roberson 4.00 2.00
❑ 152 Fred Williamson SP 30.00 18.00
❑ 153 Oakland Raiders 6.00 3.00
❑ 154 Chuck Allen RC SP 10.00 5.00
❑ 155 Lance Alworth 50.00 30.00
❑ 156 George Blair 4.00 2.00
❑ 157 Earl Faison 4.00 2.00
❑ 158 Sam Gruneisen 4.00 2.00
❑ 159 John Hadl RC 40.00 25.00
❑ 160 Dick Harris SP 6.00 3.00
❑ 161 Emil Karas SP 6.00 3.00
❑ 162 Dave Kocourek SP 6.00 3.00
❑ 163 Ernie Ladd 8.00 4.00
❑ 164 Keith Lincoln 6.00 3.00
❑ 165 Paul Lowe SP 12.00 6.00
❑ 166 Charley McNeil 4.00 2.00
❑ 167 Jacque MacKinnon SP RC 6.00 3.00
❑ 168 Ron Mix SP 20.00 10.00
❑ 169 Don Norton SP 6.00 3.00
❑ 170 Don Rogers SP 6.00 3.00
❑ 171 Tobin Rote SP 10.00 5.00
❑ 172 Henry Schmidt SP RC 6.00 3.00
❑ 173 Bud Whitehead 4.00 2.00
❑ 174 Ernie Wright SP 10.00 5.00
❑ 175 San Diego Chargers 6.00 3.00
❑ 176 Checklist SP UER ! 160.00 80.00

1965 Topps

❑ COMPLETE SET (176) 4000.00 2500.00
❑ WRAPPER (5-CENT) 150.00 90.00
❑ 1 Tommy Addison SP ! 35.00 20.00
❑ 2 Houston Antwine SP 12.00 7.00
❑ 3 Nick Buoniconti SP 30.00 18.00
❑ 4 Ron Burton SP 20.00 10.00
❑ 5 Gino Cappelletti SP 20.00 10.00
❑ 6 Jim Colclough 7.00 3.50
❑ 7 Bob Dee SP 12.00 7.00
❑ 8 Larry Eisenhauer 7.00 3.50
❑ 9 J.D. Garrett 7.00 3.50
❑ 10 Larry Garron 7.00 3.50
❑ 11 Art Graham SP 12.00 7.00
❑ 12 Ron Hall DB 7.00 3.50
❑ 13 Charles Long 7.00 3.50
❑ 14 Jon Morris RC 10.00 5.00
❑ 15 Billy Neighbors SP 12.00 7.00
❑ 16 Ross O'Hanley 7.00 3.50
❑ 17 Babe Parilli SP 20.00 10.00
❑ 18 Tony Romeo SP 12.00 7.00
❑ 19 Jack Rudolph SP 12.00 7.00
❑ 20 Bob Schmidt 7.00 3.50
❑ 21 Don Webb SP 12.00 7.00
❑ 22 Jim Whalen SP 12.00 7.00
❑ 23 Stew Barber 7.00 3.50
❑ 24 Glenn Bass SP 12.00 7.00
❑ 25 Al Bemiller SP 12.00 7.00
❑ 26 Wray Carlton SP 12.00 7.00
❑ 27 Tom Day 7.00 3.50
❑ 28 Elbert Dubenion SP 15.00 7.50
❑ 29 Jim Dunaway 7.00 3.50
❑ 30 Pete Gogolak RC SP 20.00 10.00
❑ 31 Dick Hudson SP 12.00 7.00
❑ 32 Harry Jacobs SP 12.00 7.00
❑ 33 Billy Joe SP 15.00 7.50
❑ 34 Tom Keating RC SP 12.00 7.00
❑ 35 Jack Kemp SP ! 150.00 75.00
❑ 36 Daryle Lamonica SP 50.00 30.00
❑ 37 Paul Maguire SP 20.00 10.00
❑ 38 Ron McDole RC SP 12.00 7.00
❑ 39 George Saimes SP 12.00 7.00
❑ 40 Tom Sestak SP 12.00 7.00
❑ 41 Billy Shaw SP 20.00 10.00
❑ 42 Mike Stratton SP 12.00 7.00
❑ 43 John Tracey SP 12.00 7.00
❑ 44 Ernie Warlick 7.00 3.50
❑ 45 Odell Barry 7.00 3.50
❑ 46 Willie Brown RC SP 100.00 60.00
❑ 47 Gerry Bussell SP 12.00 7.00
❑ 48 Eldon Danenhauer SP 12.00 7.00
❑ 49 Al Denson SP 12.00 7.00
❑ 50 Hewritt Dixon RC SP 15.00 7.50
❑ 51 Cookie Gilchrist SP 30.00 18.00
❑ 52 Goose Gonsoulin SP 15.00 7.50
❑ 53 Abner Haynes SP 20.00 10.00
❑ 54 Jerry Hopkins 7.00 3.50
❑ 55 Ray Jacobs SP 12.00 7.00
❑ 56 Jacky Lee SP 15.00 7.50
❑ 57 John McCormick QB 7.00 3.50

❑ 58 Bob McCullough SP 12.00 7.00
❑ 59 John McGeever 7.00 3.50
❑ 60 Charlie Mitchell SP 12.00 7.00
❑ 61 Jim Perkins SP 12.00 7.00
❑ 62 Bob Scarpitto SP 12.00 7.00
❑ 63 Mickey Slaughter SP 12.00 7.00
❑ 64 Jerry Sturm SP 12.00 7.00
❑ 65 Lionel Taylor SP 20.00 10.00
❑ 66 Scott Appleton SP 12.00 7.00
❑ 67 Johnny Baker SP 12.00 7.00
❑ 68 Sonny Bishop SP 12.00 7.00
❑ 69 George Blanda SP 125.00 75.00
❑ 70 Sid Blanks SP 12.00 7.00
❑ 71 Ode Burrell SP 12.00 7.00
❑ 72 Doug Cline SP 12.00 7.00
❑ 73 Willard Dewveall 7.00 3.50
❑ 74 Larry Elkins RC 7.00 3.50
❑ 75 Don Floyd SP 12.00 7.00
❑ 76 Freddy Glick 7.00 3.50
❑ 77 Tom Goode SP 12.00 7.00
❑ 78 Charlie Hennigan SP 20.00 10.00
❑ 79 Ed Husmann 7.00 3.50
❑ 80 Bobby Jancik SP 12.00 7.00
❑ 81 Bud McFadin SP 12.00 7.00
❑ 82 Bob McLeod SP 12.00 7.00
❑ 83 Jim Norton SP 12.00 7.00
❑ 84 Walt Suggs 7.00 3.50
❑ 85 Bob Talamini 7.00 3.50
❑ 86 Charley Tolar SP 12.00 7.00
❑ 87 Checklist SP ! 175.00 100.00
❑ 88 Don Trull SP 12.00 7.00
❑ 89 Fred Arbanas SP 12.00 7.00
❑ 90 Pete Beathard RC SP 12.00 7.00
❑ 91 Bobby Bell SP 40.00 25.00
❑ 92 Mel Branch SP 12.00 7.00
❑ 93 Tommy Brooker SP 12.00 7.00
❑ 94 Buck Buchanan SP 35.00 20.00
❑ 95 Ed Budde SP 12.00 7.00
❑ 96 Chris Burford SP 12.00 7.00
❑ 97 Walt Corey 7.00 3.50
❑ 98 Jerry Cornelison 7.00 3.50
❑ 99 Len Dawson SP 100.00 60.00
❑ 100 Jon Gilliam SP 12.00 7.00
❑ 101 Sherrill Headrick SP UER 12.00 7.00
❑ 102 Dave Hill SP 12.00 7.00
❑ 103 E.J. Holub SP 12.00 7.00
❑ 104 Bobby Hunt SP 12.00 7.00
❑ 105 Frank Jackson SP 12.00 7.00
❑ 106 Jerry Mays 10.00 5.00
❑ 107 Curtis McClinton SP 15.00 7.50
❑ 108 Bobby Ply SP 12.00 7.00
❑ 109 Johnny Robinson SP 15.00 7.50
❑ 110 Jim Tyrer SP 12.00 7.00
❑ 111 Bill Baird SP 12.00 7.00
❑ 112 Ralph Baker RC SP 12.00 7.00
❑ 113 Sam DeLuca SP 12.00 7.00
❑ 114 Larry Grantham SP 15.00 7.50
❑ 115 Gene Heeter SP 12.00 7.00
❑ 116 Winston Hill RC SP 20.00 10.00
❑ 117 John Huarte RC SP 30.00 18.00
❑ 118 Cosmo Iacavazzi SP 12.00 7.00
❑ 119 Curley Johnson SP 12.00 7.00
❑ 120 Dee Mackey UER 7.00 3.50
❑ 121 Don Maynard 50.00 30.00
❑ 122 Joe Namath RC SP ! 1800.00 1200.00
❑ 123 Dainard Paulson 7.00 3.50
❑ 124 Gerry Philbin SP 12.00 7.00
❑ 125 Sherman Plunkett RC SP 15.00 7.50
❑ 126 Mark Smolinski 7.00 3.50
❑ 127 Matt Snell SP 30.00 18.00
❑ 128 Mike Taliaferro SP 12.00 7.00
❑ 129 Bake Turner SP 12.00 7.00
❑ 130 Clyde Washington SP 12.00 7.00
❑ 131 Verlon Biggs RC SP 12.00 7.00
❑ 132 Dalva Allen 7.00 3.50
❑ 133 Fred Biletnikoff RC SP 225.00 150.00
❑ 134 Billy Cannon SP 20.00 10.00
❑ 135 Dave Costa SP 12.00 7.00
❑ 136 Clem Daniels SP 15.00 7.50
❑ 137 Ben Davidson RC SP 60.00 35.00
❑ 138 Cotton Davidson SP 15.00 7.50
❑ 139 Tom Flores SP 20.00 10.00
❑ 140 Claude Gibson 7.00 3.50
❑ 141 Wayne Hawkins 7.00 3.50
❑ 142 Archie Matsos SP 12.00 7.00
❑ 143 Mike Mercer SP 12.00 7.00
❑ 144 Bob Mischak SP 12.00 7.00
❑ 145 Jim Otto 30.00 18.00
❑ 146 Art Powell UER 10.00 5.00
❑ 147 Warren Powers DB SP 12.00 7.00
❑ 148 Ken Rice SP 12.00 7.00
❑ 149 Bo Roberson SP 12.00 7.00
❑ 150 Harry Schuh RC 7.00 3.50
❑ 151 Larry Todd SP 12.00 7.00
❑ 152 Fred Williamson SP 30.00 15.00
❑ 153 J.R. Williamson 7.00 3.50
❑ 154 Chuck Allen 10.00 5.00
❑ 155 Lance Alworth 75.00 50.00
❑ 156 Frank Buncom 7.00 3.50
❑ 157 Steve DeLong RC SP 12.00 7.00
❑ 158 Earl Faison SP 15.00 7.50
❑ 159 Kenny Graham SP 12.00 7.00
❑ 160 George Gross SP 12.00 7.00
❑ 161 John Hadl SP 35.00 20.00
❑ 162 Emil Karas SP 12.00 7.00
❑ 163 Dave Kocourek SP 12.00 7.00
❑ 164 Ernie Ladd SP 20.00 10.00
❑ 165 Keith Lincoln SP 20.00 10.00
❑ 166 Paul Lowe SP 20.00 10.00
❑ 167 Jacque MacKinnon 7.00 3.50
❑ 168 Ron Mix 20.00 12.00
❑ 169 Don Norton SP 12.00 7.00
❑ 170 Bob Petrich 7.00 3.50
❑ 171 Rick Redman SP 12.00 7.00
❑ 172 Pat Shea 7.00 3.50
❑ 173 Walt Sweeney RC SP 15.00 7.50
❑ 174 Dick Westmoreland RC 7.00 3.50
❑ 175 Ernie Wright SP 20.00 10.00
❑ 176 Checklist SP ! 225.00 125.00

1966 Topps

❑ COMPLETE SET (132) 1500.00 950.00
❑ WRAPPER (5-CENT) 60.00 30.00
❑ 1 Tommy Addison ! 20.00 10.00
❑ 2 Houston Antwine 5.00 3.00
❑ 3 Nick Buoniconti 10.00 5.00
❑ 4 Gino Cappelletti 7.00 3.50
❑ 5 Bob Dee 5.00 3.00
❑ 6 Larry Garron 5.00 3.00
❑ 7 Art Graham 5.00 3.00
❑ 8 Ron Hall DB 5.00 3.00
❑ 9 Charles Long 5.00 3.00
❑ 10 Jon Morris 5.00 3.00
❑ 11 Don Oakes 5.00 3.00
❑ 12 Babe Parilli 7.00 3.50
❑ 13 Don Webb 5.00 3.00
❑ 14 Jim Whalen 5.00 3.00
❑ 15 Funny Ring Checklist ! 300.00 200.00
❑ 16 Stew Barber 5.00 3.00
❑ 17 Glenn Bass 5.00 3.00
❑ 18 Dave Behrman 5.00 3.00
❑ 19 Al Bemiller 5.00 3.00
❑ 20 Butch Byrd RC 7.00 3.50
❑ 21 Wray Carlton 5.00 3.00
❑ 22 Tom Day 5.00 3.00
❑ 23 Elbert Dubenion 7.00 3.50
❑ 24 Jim Dunaway 5.00 3.00
❑ 25 Dick Hudson 5.00 3.00
❑ 26 Jack Kemp 150.00 75.00
❑ 27 Daryle Lamonica 20.00 12.00
❑ 28 Tom Sestak 5.00 3.00
❑ 29 Billy Shaw 10.00 5.00
❑ 30 Mike Stratton 5.00 3.00
❑ 31 Eldon Danenhauer 5.00 3.00
❑ 32 Cookie Gilchrist 10.00 5.00
❑ 33 Goose Gonsoulin 7.00 3.50
❑ 34 Wendell Hayes RC 10.00 5.00
❑ 35 Abner Haynes 10.00 5.00
❑ 36 Jerry Hopkins 5.00 3.00
❑ 37 Ray Jacobs 5.00 3.00
❑ 38 Charlie Janerette 5.00 3.00
❑ 39 Ray Kubala 5.00 3.00
❑ 40 John McCormick QB 5.00 3.00
❑ 41 Leroy Moore 5.00 3.00
❑ 42 Bob Scarpitto 5.00 3.00
❑ 43 Mickey Slaughter 5.00 3.00
❑ 44 Jerry Sturm 5.00 3.00
❑ 45 Lionel Taylor 10.00 5.00
❑ 46 Scott Appleton 5.00 3.00
❑ 47 Johnny Baker 5.00 3.00
❑ 48 George Blanda 35.00 20.00
❑ 49 Sid Blanks 5.00 3.00
❑ 50 Danny Brabham 5.00 3.00
❑ 51 Ode Burrell 5.00 3.00
❑ 52 Gary Cutsinger 5.00 3.00
❑ 53 Larry Elkins 5.00 3.00
❑ 54 Don Floyd 5.00 3.00
❑ 55 Willie Frazier RC 7.00 3.50
❑ 56 Freddy Glick 5.00 3.00
❑ 57 Charlie Hennigan 7.00 3.50
❑ 58 Bobby Jancik 5.00 3.00
❑ 59 Rich Michael 5.00 3.00
❑ 60 Don Trull 5.00 3.00
❑ 61 Checklist 55.00 30.00
❑ 62 Fred Arbanas 5.00 3.00
❑ 63 Pete Beathard 5.00 3.00
❑ 64 Bobby Bell 10.00 5.00
❑ 65 Ed Budde 5.00 3.00
❑ 66 Chris Burford 5.00 3.00
❑ 67 Len Dawson 40.00 25.00
❑ 68 Jon Gilliam 5.00 3.00
❑ 69 Sherrill Headrick 5.00 3.00
❑ 70 E.J. Holub UER 5.00 3.00
❑ 71 Bobby Hunt 5.00 3.00
❑ 72 Curtis McClinton 7.00 3.50
❑ 73 Jerry Mays 5.00 3.00
❑ 74 Johnny Robinson 7.00 3.50
❑ 75 Otis Taylor RC 25.00 15.00
❑ 76 Tom Erlandson 7.00 3.50
❑ 77 Norm Evans RC 10.00 5.00
❑ 78 Tom Goode 7.00 3.50
❑ 79 Mike Hudock 7.00 3.50
❑ 80 Frank Jackson 7.00 3.50
❑ 81 Billy Joe 7.00 3.50
❑ 82 Dave Kocourek 7.00 3.50
❑ 83 Bo Roberson 7.00 3.50
❑ 84 Jack Spikes 7.00 3.50
❑ 85 Jim Warren RC 7.00 3.50
❑ 86 Willie West RC 7.00 3.50
❑ 87 Dick Westmoreland 7.00 3.50
❑ 88 Eddie Wilson 7.00 3.50
❑ 89 Dick Wood 7.00 3.50
❑ 90 Verlon Biggs 7.00 3.50
❑ 91 Sam DeLuca 5.00 3.00
❑ 92 Winston Hill 5.00 3.00
❑ 93 Dee Mackey 5.00 3.00
❑ 94 Bill Mathis 5.00 3.00
❑ 95 Don Maynard 30.00 18.00
❑ 96 Joe Namath 250.00 150.00
❑ 97 Dainard Paulson 5.00 3.00
❑ 98 Gerry Philbin 7.00 3.50
❑ 99 Sherman Plunkett 5.00 3.00
❑ 100 Paul Rochester 5.00 3.00
❑ 101 George Sauer Jr. RC 15.00 7.50
❑ 102 Matt Snell 10.00 5.00
❑ 103 Jim Turner RC 7.00 3.50
❑ 104 Fred Biletnikoff UER 50.00 30.00
❑ 105 Bill Budness 5.00 3.00
❑ 106 Billy Cannon 10.00 5.00
❑ 107 Clem Daniels 7.00 3.50
❑ 108 Ben Davidson 15.00 7.50
❑ 109 Cotton Davidson 7.00 3.50
❑ 110 Claude Gibson 5.00 3.00
❑ 111 Wayne Hawkins 5.00 3.00
❑ 112 Ken Herock 5.00 3.00

❑ 113 Bob Mischak	5.00	3.00
❑ 114 Gus Otto	5.00	3.00
❑ 115 Jim Otto	20.00	12.00
❑ 116 Art Powell	10.00	5.00
❑ 117 Harry Schuh	5.00	3.00
❑ 118 Chuck Allen	5.00	3.00
❑ 119 Lance Alworth	40.00	25.00
❑ 120 Frank Buncom	5.00	3.00
❑ 121 Steve DeLong	5.00	3.00
❑ 122 John Farris	5.00	3.00
❑ 123 Kenny Graham	5.00	3.00
❑ 124 Sam Gruneisen	5.00	3.00
❑ 125 John Hadl	10.00	5.00
❑ 126 Walt Sweeney	5.00	3.00
❑ 127 Keith Lincoln	10.00	5.00
❑ 128 Ron Mix	10.00	5.00
❑ 129 Don Norton	5.00	3.00
❑ 130 Pat Shea	5.00	3.00
❑ 131 Ernie Wright	10.00	5.00
❑ 132 Checklist !	100.00	50.00

1967 Topps

❑ COMPLETE SET (132)	700.00	400.00
❑ WRAPPER (5-CENT)	60.00	30.00
❑ 1 John Huarte !	18.00	10.00
❑ 2 Babe Parilli	4.00	2.00
❑ 3 Gino Cappelletti	4.00	2.00
❑ 4 Larry Garron	3.00	1.50
❑ 5 Tommy Addison	3.00	1.50
❑ 6 Jon Morris	3.00	1.50
❑ 7 Houston Antwine	3.00	1.50
❑ 8 Don Oakes	3.00	1.50
❑ 9 Larry Eisenhauer	3.00	1.50
❑ 10 Jim Hunt	3.00	1.50
❑ 11 Jim Whalen	3.00	1.50
❑ 12 Art Graham	3.00	1.50
❑ 13 Nick Buoniconti	6.00	3.00
❑ 14 Bob Dee	3.00	1.50
❑ 15 Keith Lincoln	6.00	3.00
❑ 16 Tom Flores	4.00	2.00
❑ 17 Art Powell	4.00	2.00
❑ 18 Stew Barber	3.00	1.50
❑ 19 Wray Carlton	3.00	1.50
❑ 20 Elbert Dubenion	4.00	2.00
❑ 21 Jim Dunaway	3.00	1.50
❑ 22 Dick Hudson	3.00	1.50
❑ 23 Harry Jacobs	3.00	1.50
❑ 24 Jack Kemp	80.00	40.00
❑ 25 Ron McDole	3.00	1.50
❑ 26 George Saimes	3.00	1.50
❑ 27 Tom Sestak	3.00	1.50
❑ 28 Billy Shaw	6.00	3.00
❑ 29 Mike Stratton	3.00	1.50
❑ 30 Nemiah Wilson RC	3.00	1.50
❑ 31 John McCormick QB	3.00	1.50
❑ 32 Rex Mirich	3.00	1.50
❑ 33 Dave Costa	3.00	1.50
❑ 34 Goose Gonsoulin	4.00	2.00
❑ 35 Abner Haynes	6.00	3.00
❑ 36 Wendell Hayes	4.00	2.00
❑ 37 Archie Matsos	3.00	1.50
❑ 38 John Bramlett	3.00	1.50
❑ 39 Jerry Sturm	3.00	1.50
❑ 40 Max Leetzow	3.00	1.50
❑ 41 Bob Scarpitto	3.00	1.50
❑ 42 Lionel Taylor	6.00	3.00
❑ 43 Al Denson	3.00	1.50
❑ 44 Miller Farr RC	3.00	1.50
❑ 45 Don Trull	3.00	1.50
❑ 46 Jacky Lee	4.00	2.00
❑ 47 Bobby Jancik	3.00	1.50
❑ 48 Ode Burrell	3.00	1.50
❑ 49 Larry Elkins	3.00	1.50
❑ 50 W.K. Hicks	3.00	1.50
❑ 51 Sid Blanks	3.00	1.50
❑ 52 Jim Norton	3.00	1.50
❑ 53 Bobby Maples RC	3.00	1.50
❑ 54 Bob Talamini	3.00	1.50
❑ 55 Walt Suggs	3.00	1.50
❑ 56 Gary Cutsinger	3.00	1.50
❑ 57 Danny Brabham	3.00	1.50
❑ 58 Ernie Ladd	6.00	3.00
❑ 59 Checklist	50.00	25.00
❑ 60 Pete Beathard	3.00	1.50
❑ 61 Len Dawson	30.00	18.00
❑ 62 Bobby Hunt	3.00	1.50
❑ 63 Bert Coan	3.00	1.50
❑ 64 Curtis McClinton	4.00	2.00
❑ 65 Johnny Robinson	4.00	2.00
❑ 66 E.J. Holub	3.00	1.50
❑ 67 Jerry Mays	3.00	1.50
❑ 68 Jim Tyrer	4.00	2.00
❑ 69 Bobby Bell	6.00	3.00
❑ 70 Fred Arbanas	3.00	1.50
❑ 71 Buck Buchanan	6.00	3.00
❑ 72 Chris Burford	3.00	1.50
❑ 73 Otis Taylor	6.00	3.00
❑ 74 Cookie Gilchrist	8.00	4.00
❑ 75 Earl Faison	3.00	1.50
❑ 76 George Wilson Jr.	4.00	2.00
❑ 77 Rick Norton	3.00	1.50
❑ 78 Frank Jackson	4.00	2.00
❑ 79 Joe Auer	3.00	1.50
❑ 80 Willie West	3.00	1.50
❑ 81 Jim Warren	3.00	1.50
❑ 82 Wahoo McDaniel RC	50.00	30.00
❑ 83 Ernie Park	3.00	1.50
❑ 84 Billy Neighbors	3.00	1.50
❑ 85 Norm Evans	4.00	2.00
❑ 86 Tom Nomina	3.00	1.50
❑ 87 Rich Zecher	3.00	1.50
❑ 88 Dave Kocourek	3.00	1.50
❑ 89 Bill Baird	3.00	1.50
❑ 90 Ralph Baker	3.00	1.50
❑ 91 Verlon Biggs	3.00	1.50
❑ 92 Sam DeLuca	3.00	1.50
❑ 93 Larry Grantham	4.00	2.00
❑ 94 Jim Harris	3.00	1.50
❑ 95 Winston Hill	3.00	1.50
❑ 96 Bill Mathis	3.00	1.50
❑ 97 Don Maynard	20.00	12.00
❑ 98 Joe Namath	150.00	75.00
❑ 99 Gerry Philbin	4.00	2.00
❑ 100 Paul Rochester	3.00	1.50
❑ 101 George Sauer Jr.	4.00	2.00
❑ 102 Matt Snell	6.00	3.00
❑ 103 Daryle Lamonica	10.00	5.00
❑ 104 Glenn Bass	3.00	1.50
❑ 105 Jim Otto	6.00	3.00
❑ 106 Fred Biletnikoff	30.00	18.00
❑ 107 Cotton Davidson	4.00	2.00
❑ 108 Larry Todd	3.00	1.50
❑ 109 Billy Cannon	6.00	3.00
❑ 110 Clem Daniels	4.00	2.00
❑ 111 Dave Grayson	3.00	1.50
❑ 112 Kent McCloughan RC	3.00	1.50
❑ 113 Bob Svihus	3.00	1.50
❑ 114 Ike Lassiter	3.00	1.50
❑ 115 Harry Schuh	3.00	1.50
❑ 116 Ben Davidson	8.00	4.00
❑ 117 Tom Day	3.00	1.50
❑ 118 Scott Appleton	3.00	1.50
❑ 119 Steve Tensi RC	3.00	1.50
❑ 120 John Hadl	6.00	3.00
❑ 121 Paul Lowe	4.00	2.00
❑ 122 Jim Allison	3.00	1.50
❑ 123 Lance Alworth	35.00	20.00
❑ 124 Jacque MacKinnon	3.00	1.50
❑ 125 Ron Mix	6.00	3.00
❑ 126 Bob Petrich	3.00	1.50
❑ 127 Howard Kindig	3.00	1.50
❑ 128 Steve DeLong	3.00	1.50
❑ 129 Chuck Allen	3.00	1.50
❑ 130 Frank Buncom	3.00	1.50
❑ 131 Speedy Duncan RC	4.00	2.00
❑ 132 Checklist !	70.00	35.00

1968 Topps

❑ COMPLETE SET (219)	550.00	350.00
❑ COMMON CARD (1-131)	1.50	.75
❑ COMMON CARD (132-219)	2.00	1.00
❑ WRAPPER (5-CENT, SER.1)	20.00	10.00
❑ WRAPPER (5-CENT, SER.2)	30.00	20.00
❑ 1 Bart Starr !	40.00	25.00
❑ 2 Dick Bass	2.00	1.00
❑ 3 Grady Alderman	1.50	.75
❑ 4 Obert Logan	1.50	.75
❑ 5 Ernie Koy RC	2.00	1.00
❑ 6 Don Hultz	1.50	.75
❑ 7 Earl Gros	1.50	.75
❑ 8 Jim Bakken	1.50	.75
❑ 9 George Mira	2.00	1.00
❑ 10 Carl Kammerer	1.50	.75
❑ 11 Willie Frazier	1.50	.75
❑ 12 Kent McCloughan UER	1.50	.75
❑ 13 George Sauer Jr.	2.00	1.00
❑ 14 Jack Clancy	1.50	.75
❑ 15 Jim Tyrer	2.00	1.00
❑ 16 Bobby Maples	1.50	.75
❑ 17 Bo Hickey	1.50	.75
❑ 18 Frank Buncom	1.50	.75
❑ 19 Keith Lincoln	2.00	1.00
❑ 20 Jim Whalen	1.50	.75
❑ 21 Junior Coffey	1.50	.75
❑ 22 Billy Ray Smith	1.50	.75
❑ 23 Johnny Morris	1.50	.75
❑ 24 Ernie Green	1.50	.75
❑ 25 Don Meredith	25.00	15.00
❑ 26 Wayne Walker	1.50	.75
❑ 27 Carroll Dale	2.00	1.00
❑ 28 Bernie Casey	2.00	1.00
❑ 29 Dave Osborn RC	2.00	1.00
❑ 30 Ray Poage	1.50	.75
❑ 31 Homer Jones	1.50	.75
❑ 32 Sam Baker	1.50	.75
❑ 33 Bill Saul	1.50	.75
❑ 34 Ken Willard	2.00	1.00
❑ 35 Bobby Mitchell	4.00	2.00
❑ 36 Gary Garrison RC	2.00	1.00
❑ 37 Billy Cannon	2.00	1.00
❑ 38 Ralph Baker	1.50	.75
❑ 39 Howard Twilley RC	4.00	2.00
❑ 40 Wendell Hayes	2.00	1.00
❑ 41 Jim Norton	1.50	.75
❑ 42 Tom Beer	1.50	.75
❑ 43 Chris Burford	1.50	.75
❑ 44 Stew Barber	1.50	.75
❑ 45 Leroy Mitchell UER	1.50	.75
❑ 46 Dan Grimm	1.50	.75
❑ 47 Jerry Logan	1.50	.75
❑ 48 Andy Livingston	1.50	.75
❑ 49 Paul Warfield	15.00	7.50
❑ 50 Don Perkins	3.00	1.50
❑ 51 Ron Kramer	1.50	.75
❑ 52 Bob Jeter RC	2.00	1.00
❑ 53 Les Josephson RC	2.00	1.00
❑ 54 Bobby Walden	1.50	.75
❑ 55 Checklist	15.00	7.50

❑ 56 Walter Roberts 1.50 .75
❑ 57 Henry Carr 1.50 .75
❑ 58 Gary Ballman 1.50 .75
❑ 59 J.R. Wilburn 1.50 .75
❑ 60 Jim Hart RC 10.00 5.00
❑ 61 Jim Johnson 3.00 1.50
❑ 62 Chris Hanburger 2.00 1.00
❑ 63 John Hadl 3.00 1.50
❑ 64 Hewritt Dixon 2.00 1.00
❑ 65 Joe Namath 80.00 50.00
❑ 66 Jim Warren 1.50 .75
❑ 67 Curtis McClinton 2.00 1.00
❑ 68 Bob Talamini 1.50 .75
❑ 69 Steve Tensi 1.50 .75
❑ 70 Dick Van Raaphorst UER 1.50 .75
❑ 71 Art Powell 2.00 1.00
❑ 72 Jim Nance RC 4.00 2.00
❑ 73 Bob Riggle 1.50 .75
❑ 74 John Mackey 5.00 2.50
❑ 75 Gale Sayers 40.00 25.00
❑ 76 Gene Hickerson 2.50 1.25
❑ 77 Dan Reeves 10.00 5.00
❑ 78 Tom Nowatzke 1.50 .75
❑ 79 Elijah Pitts 3.00 1.50
❑ 80 Lamar Lundy 2.00 1.00
❑ 81 Paul Flatley 1.50 .75
❑ 82 Dave Whitsell 1.50 .75
❑ 83 Spider Lockhart 2.00 1.00
❑ 84 Dave Lloyd 1.50 .75
❑ 85 Roy Jefferson 2.00 1.00
❑ 86 Jackie Smith 6.00 3.00
❑ 87 John David Crow 2.00 1.00
❑ 88 Sonny Jurgensen 6.00 3.00
❑ 89 Ron Mix 3.00 1.50
❑ 90 Clem Daniels 2.00 1.00
❑ 91 Cornell Gordon 1.50 .75
❑ 92 Tom Goode 1.50 .75
❑ 93 Bobby Bell 3.00 1.50
❑ 94 Walt Suggs 1.50 .75
❑ 95 Eric Crabtree 1.50 .75
❑ 96 Sherrill Headrick 1.50 .75
❑ 97 Wray Carlton 1.50 .75
❑ 98 Gino Cappelletti 2.00 1.00
❑ 99 Tommy McDonald 4.00 2.00
❑ 100 Johnny Unitas 35.00 20.00
❑ 101 Richie Petitbon 1.50 .75
❑ 102 Erich Barnes 1.50 .75
❑ 103 Bob Hayes 8.00 4.00
❑ 104 Milt Plum 2.00 1.00
❑ 105 Boyd Dowler 2.00 1.00
❑ 106 Ed Meador 1.50 .75
❑ 107 Fred Cox 1.50 .75
❑ 108 Steve Stonebreaker RC 1.50 .75
❑ 109 Aaron Thomas 1.50 .75
❑ 110 Norm Snead 2.00 1.00
❑ 111 Paul Martha RC 1.50 .75
❑ 112 Jerry Stovall 1.50 .75
❑ 113 Kay McFarland 1.50 .75
❑ 114 Pat Richter 1.50 .75
❑ 115 Rick Redman 1.50 .75
❑ 116 Tom Keating 1.50 .75
❑ 117 Matt Snell 2.00 1.00
❑ 118 Dick Westmoreland 1.50 .75
❑ 119 Jerry Mays 1.50 .75
❑ 120 Sid Blanks 1.50 .75
❑ 121 Al Denson 1.50 .75
❑ 122 Bobby Hunt 1.50 .75
❑ 123 Mike Mercer 1.50 .75
❑ 124 Nick Buoniconti 3.00 1.50
❑ 125 Ron Vanderkelen RC 1.50 .75
❑ 126 Ordell Braase 1.50 .75
❑ 127 Dick Butkus 45.00 30.00
❑ 128 Gary Collins 2.00 1.00
❑ 129 Mel Renfro 6.00 3.00
❑ 130 Alex Karras 5.00 2.50
❑ 131 Herb Adderley ! 5.00 2.50
❑ 132 Roman Gabriel ! 4.00 2.00
❑ 133 Bill Brown 2.50 1.25
❑ 134 Kent Kramer 2.00 1.00
❑ 135 Tucker Frederickson 2.50 1.25
❑ 136 Nate Ramsey 2.00 1.00
❑ 137 Marv Woodson 2.00 1.00
❑ 138 Ken Gray 2.00 1.00
❑ 139 John Brodie 5.00 2.50
❑ 140 Jerry Smith 2.00 1.00
❑ 141 Brad Hubbert 2.00 1.00
❑ 142 George Blanda 20.00 10.00
❑ 143 Pete Lammons RC 2.00 1.00
❑ 144 Doug Moreau 2.00 1.00
❑ 145 E.J. Holub 2.00 1.00
❑ 146 Ode Burrell 2.00 1.00
❑ 147 Bob Scarpitto 2.00 1.00
❑ 148 Andre White 2.00 1.00
❑ 149 Jack Kemp 50.00 30.00
❑ 150 Art Graham 2.00 1.00
❑ 151 Tommy Nobis 6.00 3.00
❑ 152 Willie Richardson RC 2.50 1.25
❑ 153 Jack Concannon 2.00 1.00
❑ 154 Bill Glass 2.00 1.00
❑ 155 Craig Morton RC 10.00 5.00
❑ 156 Pat Studstill 2.00 1.00
❑ 157 Ray Nitschke 10.00 5.00
❑ 158 Roger Brown 2.00 1.00
❑ 159 Joe Kapp RC 5.00 2.50
❑ 160 Jim Taylor 15.00 7.50
❑ 161 Fran Tarkenton 20.00 10.00
❑ 162 Mike Ditka 30.00 18.00
❑ 163 Andy Russell RC 6.00 3.00
❑ 164 Larry Wilson 4.00 2.00
❑ 165 Tommy Davis 2.00 1.00
❑ 166 Paul Krause 4.00 2.00
❑ 167 Speedy Duncan 2.00 1.00
❑ 168 Fred Biletnikoff 15.00 7.50
❑ 169 Don Maynard 10.00 5.00
❑ 170 Frank Emanuel 2.00 1.00
❑ 171 Len Dawson 15.00 7.50
❑ 172 Miller Farr 2.00 1.00
❑ 173 Floyd Little RC 20.00 10.00
❑ 174 Lonnie Wright 2.00 1.00
❑ 175 Paul Costa 2.00 1.00
❑ 176 Don Trull 2.00 1.00
❑ 177 Jerry Simmons 2.00 1.00
❑ 178 Tom Matte 2.50 1.25
❑ 179 Bennie McRae 2.00 1.00
❑ 180 Jim Kanicki 2.00 1.00
❑ 181 Bob Lilly 15.00 7.50
❑ 182 Tom Watkins 2.00 1.00
❑ 183 Jim Grabowski RC 4.00 2.00
❑ 184 Jack Snow RC 4.00 2.00
❑ 185 Gary Cuozzo RC 2.50 1.25
❑ 186 Billy Kilmer 4.00 2.00
❑ 187 Jim Katcavage 2.00 1.00
❑ 188 Floyd Peters 2.00 1.00
❑ 189 Bill Nelsen 2.50 1.25
❑ 190 Bobby Joe Conrad 2.50 1.25
❑ 191 Kermit Alexander 2.00 1.00
❑ 192 Charley Taylor UER 6.00 3.00
❑ 193 Lance Alworth 20.00 10.00
❑ 194 Daryle Lamonica 5.00 2.50
❑ 195 Al Atkinson 2.00 1.00
❑ 196 Bob Griese RC 90.00 50.00
❑ 197 Buck Buchanan 4.00 2.00
❑ 198 Pete Beathard 2.00 1.00
❑ 199 Nemiah Wilson 2.00 1.00
❑ 200 Ernie Wright 2.00 1.00
❑ 201 George Saimes 2.00 1.00
❑ 202 John Charles 2.00 1.00
❑ 203 Randy Johnson 2.00 1.00
❑ 204 Tony Lorick 2.00 1.00
❑ 205 Dick Evey 2.00 1.00
❑ 206 Leroy Kelly 10.00 5.00
❑ 207 Lee Roy Jordan 6.00 3.00
❑ 208 Jim Gibbons 2.00 1.00
❑ 209 Donny Anderson RC 4.00 2.00
❑ 210 Maxie Baughan 2.00 1.00
❑ 211 Joe Morrison 2.00 1.00
❑ 212 Jim Snowden 2.00 1.00
❑ 213 Lenny Lyles 2.00 1.00
❑ 214 Bobby Joe Green 2.00 1.00
❑ 215 Frank Ryan 2.50 1.25
❑ 216 Cornell Green 2.50 1.25
❑ 217 Karl Sweetan 2.00 1.00
❑ 218 Dave Williams 2.00 1.00
❑ 219A Checklist Green ! 18.00 10.00
❑ 219B Checklist Blue ! 20.00 12.00

1969 Topps

❑ COMPLETE SET (263) 550.00 350.00
❑ COMMON CARD (1-132) 1.50 .75
❑ COMMON CARD (133-263) 2.00 1.00
❑ WRAPPER (5-CENT) 30.00 15.00
❑ 1 Leroy Kelly ! 20.00 10.00
❑ 2 Paul Flatley 1.50 .75
❑ 3 Jim Cadile 1.50 .75
❑ 4 Erich Barnes 1.50 .75
❑ 5 Willie Richardson 1.50 .75
❑ 6 Bob Hayes 5.00 2.50
❑ 7 Bob Jeter 1.50 .75
❑ 8 Jim Colclough 1.50 .75
❑ 9 Sherrill Headrick 1.50 .75
❑ 10 Jim Dunaway 1.50 .75
❑ 11 Bill Munson 2.00 1.00
❑ 12 Jack Pardee 2.00 1.00
❑ 13 Jim Lindsey 1.50 .75
❑ 14 Dave Whitsell 1.50 .75
❑ 15 Tucker Frederickson 1.50 .75
❑ 16 Alvin Haymond 2.00 1.00
❑ 17 Andy Russell 2.00 1.00
❑ 18 Tom Beer 1.50 .75
❑ 19 Bobby Maples 1.50 .75
❑ 20 Len Dawson 8.00 4.00
❑ 21 Willis Crenshaw 1.50 .75
❑ 22 Tommy Davis 1.50 .75
❑ 23 Rickie Harris 1.50 .75
❑ 24 Jerry Simmons 1.50 .75
❑ 25 Johnny Unitas 40.00 25.00
❑ 26 Brian Piccolo RC UER 80.00 50.00
❑ 27 Bob Matheson 1.50 .75
❑ 28 Howard Twilley 2.00 1.00
❑ 29 Jim Turner 2.00 1.00
❑ 30 Pete Banaszak RC 2.00 1.00
❑ 31 Lance Rentzel RC 2.00 1.00
❑ 32 Bill Triplett 1.50 .75
❑ 33 Boyd Dowler 2.00 1.00
❑ 34 Merlin Olsen 5.00 2.50
❑ 35 Joe Kapp 3.00 1.50
❑ 36 Dan Abramowicz RC 4.00 2.00
❑ 37 Spider Lockhart 2.00 1.00
❑ 38 Tom Day 1.50 .75
❑ 39 Art Graham 1.50 .75
❑ 40 Bob Cappadona 1.50 .75
❑ 41 Gary Ballman 1.50 .75
❑ 42 Clendon Thomas 1.50 .75
❑ 43 Jackie Smith 4.00 2.00
❑ 44 Dave Wilcox 3.00 1.50
❑ 45 Jerry Smith 1.50 .75
❑ 46 Dan Grimm 1.50 .75
❑ 47 Tom Matte 2.00 1.00
❑ 48 John Stofa 1.50 .75
❑ 49 Rex Mirich 1.50 .75
❑ 50 Miller Farr 1.50 .75
❑ 51 Gale Sayers 40.00 25.00
❑ 52 Bill Nelsen 2.00 1.00
❑ 53 Bob Lilly 6.00 3.00
❑ 54 Wayne Walker 1.50 .75
❑ 55 Ray Nitschke 5.00 2.50
❑ 56 Ed Meador 1.50 .75
❑ 57 Lonnie Warwick 1.50 .75
❑ 58 Wendell Hayes 1.50 .75

❑ 59 Dick Anderson RC 5.00 2.50
❑ 60 Don Maynard 6.00 3.00
❑ 61 Tony Lorick 1.50 .75
❑ 62 Pete Gogolak 1.50 .75
❑ 63 Nate Ramsey 1.50 .75
❑ 64 Dick Shiner 1.50 .75
❑ 65 Larry Wilson UER 3.00 1.50
❑ 66 Ken Willard 2.00 1.00
❑ 67 Charley Taylor 5.00 2.50
❑ 68 Billy Cannon 2.00 1.00
❑ 69 Lance Alworth 8.00 4.00
❑ 70 Jim Nance 2.00 1.00
❑ 71 Nick Rassas 1.50 .75
❑ 72 Lenny Lyles 1.50 .75
❑ 73 Bennie McRae 1.50 .75
❑ 74 Bill Glass 1.50 .75
❑ 75 Don Meredith 25.00 15.00
❑ 76 Dick LeBeau 1.50 .75
❑ 77 Carroll Dale 2.00 1.00
❑ 78 Ron McDole 1.50 .75
❑ 79 Charley King 1.50 .75
❑ 80 Checklist UER 15.00 7.50
❑ 81 Dick Bass 2.00 1.00
❑ 82 Roy Winston 1.50 .75
❑ 83 Don McCall 1.50 .75
❑ 84 Jim Katcavage 2.00 1.00
❑ 85 Norm Snead 2.00 1.00
❑ 86 Earl Gros 1.50 .75
❑ 87 Don Brumm 1.50 .75
❑ 88 Sonny Bishop 1.50 .75
❑ 89 Fred Arbanas 1.50 .75
❑ 90 Karl Noonan 1.50 .75
❑ 91 Dick Witcher 1.50 .75
❑ 92 Vince Promuto 1.50 .75
❑ 93 Tommy Nobis 4.00 2.00
❑ 94 Jerry Hill 1.50 .75
❑ 95 Ed O'Bradovich RC 1.50 .75
❑ 96 Ernie Kellerman 1.50 .75
❑ 97 Chuck Howley 2.00 1.00
❑ 98 Hewritt Dixon 1.50 .75
❑ 99 Ron Mix 3.00 1.50
❑ 100 Joe Namath 75.00 40.00
❑ 101 Billy Gambrell 1.50 .75
❑ 102 Elijah Pitts 2.00 1.00
❑ 103 Billy Truax RC 2.00 1.00
❑ 104 Ed Sharockman 1.50 .75
❑ 105 Doug Atkins 3.00 1.50
❑ 106 Greg Larson 1.50 .75
❑ 107 Israel Lang 1.50 .75
❑ 108 Houston Antwine 1.50 .75
❑ 109 Paul Guidry 1.50 .75
❑ 110 Al Denson 1.50 .75
❑ 111 Roy Jefferson 2.00 1.00
❑ 112 Chuck Latourette 1.50 .75
❑ 113 Jim Johnson 3.00 1.50
❑ 114 Bobby Mitchell 4.00 2.00
❑ 115 Randy Johnson 1.50 .75
❑ 116 Lou Michaels 1.50 .75
❑ 117 Rudy Kuechenberg 1.50 .75
❑ 118 Walt Suggs 1.50 .75
❑ 119 Goldie Sellers 1.50 .75
❑ 120 Larry Csonka RC ! 75.00 40.00
❑ 121 Jim Houston 1.50 .75
❑ 122 Craig Baynham 1.50 .75
❑ 123 Alex Karras 5.00 2.50
❑ 124 Jim Grabowski 2.00 1.00
❑ 125 Roman Gabriel 3.00 1.50
❑ 126 Larry Bowie 1.50 .75
❑ 127 Dave Parks 2.00 1.00
❑ 128 Ben Davidson 3.00 1.50
❑ 129 Steve DeLong 1.50 .75
❑ 130 Fred Hill 1.50 .75
❑ 131 Ernie Koy 2.00 1.00
❑ 132A Checklist no border ! 15.00 7.50
❑ 132B Checklist bordered ! 20.00 10.00
❑ 133 Dick Hoak 2.00 1.00
❑ 134 Larry Stallings RC 2.00 1.00
❑ 135 Clifton McNeil RC 2.00 1.00
❑ 136 Walter Rock 2.00 1.00
❑ 137 Billy Lothridge 2.00 1.00
❑ 138 Bob Vogel 2.00 1.00
❑ 139 Dick Butkus 40.00 25.00
❑ 140 Frank Ryan 2.50 1.25
❑ 141 Larry Garron 2.00 1.00
❑ 142 George Saimes 2.00 1.00
❑ 143 Frank Buncom 2.00 1.00
❑ 144 Don Perkins 2.50 1.25
❑ 145 Johnnie Robinson UER 2.00 1.00
❑ 146 Lee Roy Caffey 2.50 1.25
❑ 147 Bernie Casey 2.50 1.25
❑ 148 Billy Martin E 2.00 1.00
❑ 149 Gene Howard 2.00 1.00
❑ 150 Fran Tarkenton 20.00 10.00
❑ 151 Eric Crabtree 2.00 1.00
❑ 152 W.K. Hicks 2.00 1.00
❑ 153 Bobby Bell 4.00 2.00
❑ 154 Sam Baker 2.00 1.00
❑ 155 Marv Woodson 2.00 1.00
❑ 156 Dave Williams 2.00 1.00
❑ 157 Bruce Bosley UER 2.00 1.00
❑ 158 Carl Kammerer 2.00 1.00
❑ 159 Jim Burson 2.00 1.00
❑ 160 Roy Hilton 2.00 1.00
❑ 161 Bob Griese 25.00 15.00
❑ 162 Bob Talamini 2.00 1.00
❑ 163 Jim Otto 4.00 2.00
❑ 164 Ronnie Bull 2.00 1.00
❑ 165 Walter Johnson RC 2.00 1.00
❑ 166 Lee Roy Jordan 4.00 2.00
❑ 167 Mike Lucci 2.50 1.25
❑ 168 Willie Wood 4.00 2.00
❑ 169 Maxie Baughan 2.00 1.00
❑ 170 Bill Brown 2.50 1.25
❑ 171 John Hadl 4.00 2.00
❑ 172 Gino Cappelletti 2.50 1.25
❑ 173 George Butch Byrd 2.50 1.25
❑ 174 Steve Stonebreaker 2.00 1.00
❑ 175 Joe Morrison 2.00 1.00
❑ 176 Joe Scarpati 2.00 1.00
❑ 177 Bobby Walden 2.00 1.00
❑ 178 Roy Shivers 2.00 1.00
❑ 179 Kermit Alexander 2.00 1.00
❑ 180 Pat Richter 2.00 1.00
❑ 181 Pete Perreault 2.00 1.00
❑ 182 Pete Duranko 2.00 1.00
❑ 183 Leroy Mitchell 2.00 1.00
❑ 184 Jim Simon 2.00 1.00
❑ 185 Billy Ray Smith 2.00 1.00
❑ 186 Jack Concannon 2.00 1.00
❑ 187 Ben Davis 2.00 1.00
❑ 188 Mike Clark 2.00 1.00
❑ 189 Jim Gibbons 2.00 1.00
❑ 190 Dave Robinson 2.50 1.25
❑ 191 Otis Taylor 2.50 1.25
❑ 192 Nick Buoniconti 4.00 2.00
❑ 193 Matt Snell 2.50 1.25
❑ 194 Bruce Gossett 2.00 1.00
❑ 195 Mick Tingelhoff 2.50 1.25
❑ 196 Earl Leggett 2.00 1.00
❑ 197 Pete Case 2.00 1.00
❑ 198 Tom Woodeshick RC 2.00 1.00
❑ 199 Ken Kortas 2.00 1.00
❑ 200 Jim Hart 4.00 2.00
❑ 201 Fred Biletnikoff 10.00 5.00
❑ 202 Jacque MacKinnon 2.00 1.00
❑ 203 Jim Whalen 2.00 1.00
❑ 204 Matt Hazeltine 2.00 1.00
❑ 205 Charlie Gogolak 2.00 1.00
❑ 206 Ray Ogden 2.00 1.00
❑ 207 John Mackey 4.00 2.00
❑ 208 Roosevelt Taylor 2.00 1.00
❑ 209 Gene Hickerson 2.50 1.25
❑ 210 Dave Edwards RC 2.50 1.25
❑ 211 Tom Sestak 2.00 1.00
❑ 212 Ernie Wright 2.00 1.00
❑ 213 Dave Costa 2.00 1.00
❑ 214 Tom Vaughn 2.00 1.00
❑ 215 Bart Starr 35.00 20.00
❑ 216 Les Josephson 2.00 1.00
❑ 217 Fred Cox 2.00 1.00
❑ 218 Mike Tilleman 2.00 1.00
❑ 219 Darrell Dess 2.00 1.00
❑ 220 Dave Lloyd 2.00 1.00
❑ 221 Pete Beathard 2.00 1.00
❑ 222 Buck Buchanan 4.00 2.00
❑ 223 Frank Emanuel 2.00 1.00
❑ 224 Paul Martha 2.00 1.00
❑ 225 Johnny Roland 2.00 1.00
❑ 226 Gary Lewis 2.00 1.00
❑ 227 Sonny Jurgensen UER 6.00 3.00
❑ 228 Jim Butler 2.00 1.00
❑ 229 Mike Curtis RC 6.00 3.00
❑ 230 Richie Petitbon 2.00 1.00
❑ 231 George Sauer Jr. 2.50 1.25
❑ 232 George Blanda 20.00 10.00
❑ 233 Gary Garrison 2.00 1.00
❑ 234 Gary Collins 2.50 1.25
❑ 235 Craig Morton 4.00 2.00
❑ 236 Tom Nowatzke 2.00 1.00
❑ 237 Donny Anderson 2.50 1.25
❑ 238 Deacon Jones 4.00 2.00
❑ 239 Grady Alderman 2.00 1.00
❑ 240 Billy Kilmer 4.00 2.00
❑ 241 Mike Taliaferro 2.00 1.00
❑ 242 Stew Barber 2.00 1.00
❑ 243 Bobby Hunt 2.00 1.00
❑ 244 Homer Jones 2.00 1.00
❑ 245 Bob Brown OT 4.00 2.00
❑ 246 Bill Asbury 2.00 1.00
❑ 247 Charlie Johnson 2.50 1.25
❑ 248 Chris Hanburger 2.50 1.25
❑ 249 John Brodie 6.00 3.00
❑ 250 Earl Morrall 2.50 1.25
❑ 251 Floyd Little 5.00 2.50
❑ 252 Jerrel Wilson RC 2.00 1.00
❑ 253 Jim Keyes 2.00 1.00
❑ 254 Mel Renfro 4.00 2.00
❑ 255 Herb Adderley 4.00 2.00
❑ 256 Jack Snow 2.50 1.25
❑ 257 Charlie Durkee 2.00 1.00
❑ 258 Charlie Harper 2.00 1.00
❑ 259 J.R. Wilburn 2.00 1.00
❑ 260 Charlie Krueger 2.00 1.00
❑ 261 Pete Jacques 2.00 1.00
❑ 262 Gerry Philbin 2.00 1.00
❑ 263 Daryle Lamonica ! 10.00 5.00

1970 Topps

❑ COMPLETE SET (263) 475.00 300.00
❑ COMMON CARD (1-132) 1.00 .40
❑ COMMON CARD (133-263) 1.25 .50
❑ WRAPPER (10-CENT) 12.00 8.00
❑ 1 Len Dawson UER ! 20.00 12.00
❑ 2 Doug Hart 1.00 .40
❑ 3 Verlon Biggs 1.00 .40
❑ 4 Ralph Neely RC 1.50 .60
❑ 5 Harmon Wages 1.00 .40
❑ 6 Dan Conners 1.00 .40
❑ 7 Gino Cappelletti 1.50 .60
❑ 8 Erich Barnes 1.00 .40
❑ 9 Checklist 10.00 5.00
❑ 10 Bob Griese 15.00 7.50
❑ 11 Ed Flanagan 1.00 .40
❑ 12 George Seals 1.00 .40
❑ 13 Harry Jacobs 1.00 .40
❑ 14 Mike Haffner 1.00 .40

❑ 15 Bob Vogel 1.00 .40
❑ 16 Bill Peterson 1.00 .40
❑ 17 Spider Lockhart 1.00 .40
❑ 18 Billy Truax 1.00 .40
❑ 19 Jim Beirne 1.00 .40
❑ 20 Leroy Kelly 6.00 3.00
❑ 21 Dave Lloyd 1.00 .40
❑ 22 Mike Tilleman 1.00 .40
❑ 23 Gary Garrison 1.00 .40
❑ 24 Larry Brown RC 8.00 4.00
❑ 25 Jan Stenerud RC 12.00 6.00
❑ 26 Rolf Krueger 1.00 .40
❑ 27 Roland Lakes 1.00 .40
❑ 28 Dick Hoak 1.00 .40
❑ 29 Gene Washington Vik RC 2.50 1.25
❑ 30 Bart Starr 20.00 10.00
❑ 31 Dave Grayson 1.00 .40
❑ 32 Jerry Rush 1.00 .40
❑ 33 Len St. Jean 1.00 .40
❑ 34 Randy Edmunds 1.00 .40
❑ 35 Matt Snell 1.50 .60
❑ 36 Paul Costa 1.00 .40
❑ 37 Mike Pyle 1.00 .40
❑ 38 Roy Hilton 1.00 .40
❑ 39 Steve Tensi 1.00 .40
❑ 40 Tommy Nobis 2.50 1.25
❑ 41 Pete Case 1.00 .40
❑ 42 Andy Rice 1.00 .40
❑ 43 Elvin Bethea RC 8.00 4.00
❑ 44 Jack Snow 1.50 .60
❑ 45 Mel Renfro 2.50 1.25
❑ 46 Andy Livingston 1.00 .40
❑ 47 Gary Ballman 1.00 .40
❑ 48 Bob DeMarco 1.00 .40
❑ 49 Steve DeLong 1.00 .40
❑ 50 Daryle Lamonica 4.00 2.00
❑ 51 Jim Lynch RC 1.00 .40
❑ 52 Mel Farr RC 1.00 .40
❑ 53 Bob Long RC 1.00 .40
❑ 54 John Elliott 1.00 .40
❑ 55 Ray Nitschke 5.00 2.50
❑ 56 Jim Shorter 1.00 .40
❑ 57 Dave Wilcox 2.50 1.25
❑ 58 Eric Crabtree 1.00 .40
❑ 59 Alan Page RC 30.00 15.00
❑ 60 Jim Nance 1.50 .60
❑ 61 Glen Ray Hines 1.00 .40
❑ 62 John Mackey 2.50 1.25
❑ 63 Ron McDole 1.00 .40
❑ 64 Tom Beier 1.00 .40
❑ 65 Bill Nelsen 1.50 .60
❑ 66 Paul Flatley 1.00 .40
❑ 67 Sam Brunelli 1.00 .40
❑ 68 Jack Pardee 1.50 .60
❑ 69 Brig Owens 1.00 .40
❑ 70 Gale Sayers 25.00 12.50
❑ 71 Lee Roy Jordan 2.50 1.25
❑ 72 Harold Jackson RC 5.00 2.50
❑ 73 John Hadl 2.50 1.25
❑ 74 Dave Parks 1.00 .40
❑ 75 Lem Barney RC 14.00 7.00
❑ 76 Johnny Roland 1.00 .40
❑ 77 Ed Budde 1.00 .40
❑ 78 Ben McGee 1.00 .40
❑ 79 Ken Bowman 1.00 .40
❑ 80 Fran Tarkenton 15.00 7.50
❑ 81 G.Washington 49er RC 5.00 2.50
❑ 82 Larry Grantham 1.00 .40
❑ 83 Bill Brown 1.50 .60
❑ 84 John Charles 1.00 .40
❑ 85 Fred Biletnikoff 7.00 3.50
❑ 86 Royce Berry 1.00 .40
❑ 87 Bob Lilly 5.00 2.50
❑ 88 Earl Morrall 1.50 .60
❑ 89 Jerry LeVias RC 1.50 .60
❑ 90 O.J. Simpson RC 80.00 40.00
❑ 91 Mike Howell 1.00 .40
❑ 92 Ken Gray 1.00 .40
❑ 93 Chris Hanburger 1.00 .40
❑ 94 Larry Seiple RC 1.00 .40
❑ 95 Rich Jackson RC 1.00 .40
❑ 96 Rockne Freitas 1.00 .40
❑ 97 Dick Post RC 1.50 .60
❑ 98 Ben Hawkins RC 1.00 .40
❑ 99 Ken Reaves 1.00 .40
❑ 100 Roman Gabriel 2.50 1.25
❑ 101 Dave Rowe 1.00 .40
❑ 102 Dave Robinson 1.00 .40
❑ 103 Otis Taylor 1.50 .60
❑ 104 Jim Turner 1.00 .40
❑ 105 Joe Morrison 1.00 .40
❑ 106 Dick Evey 1.00 .40
❑ 107 Ray Mansfield 1.00 .40
❑ 108 Grady Alderman 1.00 .40
❑ 109 Bruce Gossett 1.00 .40
❑ 110 Bob Trumpy RC 4.00 2.00
❑ 111 Jim Hunt 1.00 .40
❑ 112 Larry Stallings 1.00 .40
❑ 113A Lance Rentzel Red 1.50 .60
❑ 113B Lance Rentzel Black 1.50 .60
❑ 114 Bubba Smith RC 25.00 12.50
❑ 115 Norm Snead 1.50 .60
❑ 116 Jim Otto 2.50 1.25
❑ 117 Bo Scott RC 1.00 .40
❑ 118 Rick Redman 1.00 .40
❑ 119 George Butch Byrd 1.00 .40
❑ 120 George Webster RC 1.50 .60
❑ 121 Chuck Walton RC 1.00 .40
❑ 122 Dave Costa 1.00 .40
❑ 123 Al Dodd 1.00 .40
❑ 124 Len Hauss 1.00 .40
❑ 125 Deacon Jones 2.50 1.25
❑ 126 Randy Johnson 1.00 .40
❑ 127 Ralph Heck 1.00 .40
❑ 128 Emerson Boozer RC 1.50 .60
❑ 129 Johnny Robinson 1.50 .60
❑ 130 John Brodie 5.00 2.50
❑ 131 Gale Gillingham RC 1.00 .40
❑ 132 Checklist DP 6.00 3.00
❑ 133 Chuck Walker 1.25 .50
❑ 134 Bennie McRae 1.25 .50
❑ 135 Paul Warfield 7.00 3.50
❑ 136 Dan Darragh 1.25 .50
❑ 137 Paul Robinson RC 1.25 .50
❑ 138 Ed Philpott 1.25 .50
❑ 139 Craig Morton 3.00 1.50
❑ 140 Tom Dempsey RC 2.00 .75
❑ 141 Al Nelson 1.25 .50
❑ 142 Tom Matte 2.00 .75
❑ 143 Dick Schafrath 1.25 .50
❑ 144 Willie Brown 4.00 2.00
❑ 145 Charley Taylor UER 5.00 2.50
❑ 146 John Huard 1.25 .50
❑ 147 Dave Osborn 1.25 .50
❑ 148 Gene Mingo 1.25 .50
❑ 149 Larry Hand 1.25 .50
❑ 150 Joe Namath 50.00 25.00
❑ 151 Tom Mack RC 10.00 5.00
❑ 152 Kenny Graham 1.25 .50
❑ 153 Don Herrmann 1.25 .50
❑ 154 Bobby Bell 3.00 1.50
❑ 155 Hoyle Granger 1.25 .50
❑ 156 Claude Humphrey RC 2.00 .75
❑ 157 Clifton McNeil 1.25 .50
❑ 158 Mick Tingelhoff 2.00 .75
❑ 159 Don Horn RC 1.25 .50
❑ 160 Larry Wilson 3.00 1.50
❑ 161 Tom Neville 1.25 .50
❑ 162 Larry Csonka 20.00 10.00
❑ 163 Doug Buffone RC 1.25 .50
❑ 164 Cornell Green 2.00 .75
❑ 165 Haven Moses RC 2.00 .75
❑ 166 Billy Kilmer 3.00 1.50
❑ 167 Tim Rossovich RC 1.25 .50
❑ 168 Bill Bergey RC 4.00 2.00
❑ 169 Gary Collins 2.00 .75
❑ 170 Floyd Little 3.00 1.50
❑ 171 Tom Keating 1.25 .50
❑ 172 Pat Fischer 1.25 .50
❑ 173 Walt Sweeney 1.25 .50
❑ 174 Greg Larson 1.25 .50
❑ 175 Carl Eller 3.00 1.50
❑ 176 George Sauer Jr. 2.00 .75
❑ 177 Jim Hart 3.00 1.50
❑ 178 Bob Brown OT 3.00 1.50
❑ 179 Mike Garrett RC 2.00 .75
❑ 180 Johnny Unitas 25.00 15.00
❑ 181 Tom Regner 1.25 .50
❑ 182 Bob Jeter 1.25 .50
❑ 183 Gail Cogdill 1.25 .50
❑ 184 Earl Gros 1.25 .50
❑ 185 Dennis Partee 1.25 .50
❑ 186 Charlie Krueger 1.25 .50
❑ 187 Martin Baccaglio 1.25 .50
❑ 188 Charles Long 1.25 .50
❑ 189 Bob Hayes 4.00 2.00
❑ 190 Dick Butkus 25.00 12.50
❑ 191 Al Bemiller 1.25 .50
❑ 192 Dick Westmoreland 1.25 .50
❑ 193 Joe Scarpati 1.25 .50
❑ 194 Ron Snidow 1.25 .50
❑ 195 Earl McCullouch RC 1.25 .50
❑ 196 Jake Kupp 1.25 .50
❑ 197 Bob Lurtsema 1.25 .50
❑ 198 Mike Current 1.25 .50
❑ 199 Charlie Smith RB 1.25 .50
❑ 200 Sonny Jurgensen 6.00 3.00
❑ 201 Mike Curtis 2.00 .75
❑ 202 Aaron Brown RC 1.25 .50
❑ 203 Richie Petitbon 1.25 .50
❑ 204 Walt Suggs 1.25 .50
❑ 205 Roy Jefferson 1.25 .50
❑ 206 Russ Washington RC 1.25 .50
❑ 207 Woody Peoples RC 1.25 .50
❑ 208 Dave Williams 1.25 .50
❑ 209 John Zook RC 1.25 .50
❑ 210 Tom Woodeshick 1.25 .50
❑ 211 Howard Fest 1.25 .50
❑ 212 Jack Concannon 1.25 .50
❑ 213 Jim Marshall 3.00 1.50
❑ 214 Jon Morris 1.25 .50
❑ 215 Dan Abramowicz 2.00 .75
❑ 216 Paul Martha 1.25 .50
❑ 217 Ken Willard 1.25 .50
❑ 218 Walter Rock 1.25 .50
❑ 219 Garland Boyette 1.25 .50
❑ 220 Buck Buchanan 3.00 1.50
❑ 221 Bill Munson 2.00 .75
❑ 222 David Lee RC 1.25 .50
❑ 223 Karl Noonan 1.25 .50
❑ 224 Harry Schuh 1.25 .50
❑ 225 Jackie Smith 3.00 1.50
❑ 226 Gerry Philbin 1.25 .50
❑ 227 Ernie Koy 1.25 .50
❑ 228 Chuck Howley 2.00 .75
❑ 229 Billy Shaw 3.00 1.50
❑ 230 Jerry Hillebrand 1.25 .50
❑ 231 Bill Thompson RC 2.00 .75
❑ 232 Carroll Dale 2.00 .75
❑ 233 Gene Hickerson 2.50 1.00
❑ 234 Jim Butler 1.25 .50
❑ 235 Greg Cook RC 1.25 .50
❑ 236 Lee Roy Caffey 1.25 .50
❑ 237 Merlin Olsen 4.00 2.00
❑ 238 Fred Cox 1.25 .50
❑ 239 Nate Ramsey 1.25 .50
❑ 240 Lance Alworth 7.00 3.50
❑ 241 Chuck Hinton 1.25 .50
❑ 242 Jerry Smith 1.25 .50
❑ 243 Tony Baker FB 1.25 .50
❑ 244 Nick Buoniconti 3.00 1.50
❑ 245 Jim Johnson 3.00 1.50
❑ 246 Willie Richardson 1.25 .50
❑ 247 Fred Dryer RC 10.00 5.00
❑ 248 Bobby Maples 1.25 .50
❑ 249 Alex Karras 4.00 2.00
❑ 250 Joe Kapp 2.00 .75
❑ 251 Ben Davidson 3.00 1.50
❑ 252 Mike Stratton 1.25 .50
❑ 253 Les Josephson 1.25 .50
❑ 254 Don Maynard 6.00 3.00
❑ 255 Houston Antwine 1.25 .50
❑ 256 Mac Percival RC 1.25 .50

❑ 257 George Goeddeke	1.25	.50
❑ 258 Homer Jones	1.25	.50
❑ 259 Bob Berry	1.25	.50
❑ 260A Calvin Hill RC Red	15.00	7.50
❑ 260B Calvin Hill RC Black	20.00	10.00
❑ 261 Willie Wood	3.00	1.50
❑ 262 Ed Weisacosky	1.25	.50
❑ 263 Jim Tyrer !	3.00	1.50

1971 Topps

❑ COMPLETE SET (263)	500.00	300.00
❑ COMMON CARD (1-132)	.75	.30
❑ COMMON CARD (133-263)	1.00	.40
❑ 1 Johnny Unitas !	30.00	15.00
❑ 2 Jim Butler	.75	.30
❑ 3 Marty Schottenheimer RC	12.00	6.00
❑ 4 Joe O'Donnell	.75	.30
❑ 5 Tom Dempsey	1.25	.50
❑ 6 Chuck Allen	.75	.30
❑ 7 Ernie Kellerman	.75	.30
❑ 8 Walt Garrison RC	2.00	.75
❑ 9 Bill Van Heusen	.75	.30
❑ 10 Lance Alworth	8.00	4.00
❑ 11 Greg Landry RC	2.00	.75
❑ 12 Larry Krause	.75	.30
❑ 13 Buck Buchanan	2.00	.75
❑ 14 Roy Gerela RC	1.25	.50
❑ 15 Clifton McNeil	.75	.30
❑ 16 Bob Brown OT	2.00	.75
❑ 17 Lloyd Mumphord	.75	.30
❑ 18 Gary Cuozzo	.75	.30
❑ 19 Don Maynard	5.00	2.50
❑ 20 Larry Wilson	2.00	.75
❑ 21 Charlie Smith RB	.75	.30
❑ 22 Ken Avery	.75	.30
❑ 23 Billy Walik	.75	.30
❑ 24 Jim Johnson	2.00	.75
❑ 25 Dick Butkus	25.00	12.50
❑ 26 Charley Taylor UER	4.00	2.00
❑ 27 Checklist UER	8.00	4.00
❑ 28 Lionel Aldridge RC	.75	.30
❑ 29 Billy Lothridge	.75	.30
❑ 30 Terry Hanratty RC	1.25	.50
❑ 31 Lee Roy Jordan	2.00	.75
❑ 32 Rick Volk RC	.75	.30
❑ 33 Howard Kindig	.75	.30
❑ 34 Carl Garrett RC	.75	.30
❑ 35 Bobby Bell	2.00	.75
❑ 36 Gene Hickerson	1.50	.60
❑ 37 Dave Parks	.75	.30
❑ 38 Paul Martha	.75	.30
❑ 39 George Blanda	15.00	7.50
❑ 40 Tom Woodeshick	.75	.30
❑ 41 Alex Karras	3.00	1.50
❑ 42 Rick Redman	.75	.30
❑ 43 Zeke Moore	.75	.30
❑ 44 Jack Snow	1.25	.50
❑ 45 Larry Csonka	15.00	7.50
❑ 46 Karl Kassulke	.75	.30
❑ 47 Jim Hart	2.00	.75
❑ 48 Al Atkinson	.75	.30
❑ 49 Horst Muhlmann RC	.75	.30
❑ 50 Sonny Jurgensen	5.00	2.50
❑ 51 Ron Johnson RC	1.25	.50
❑ 52 Cas Banaszek	.75	.30
❑ 53 Bubba Smith	8.00	4.00
❑ 54 Bobby Douglass RC	1.25	.50
❑ 55 Willie Wood	2.00	.75
❑ 56 Bake Turner	.75	.30
❑ 57 Mike Morgan LB	.75	.30
❑ 58 George Butch Byrd	1.25	.50
❑ 59 Don Horn	.75	.30
❑ 60 Tommy Nobis	2.00	.75
❑ 61 Jan Stenerud	4.00	2.00
❑ 62 Altie Taylor RC	.75	.30
❑ 63 Gary Pettigrew	.75	.30
❑ 64 Spike Jones RC	.75	.30
❑ 65 Duane Thomas RC	2.00	.75
❑ 66 Marty Domres RC	.75	.30
❑ 67 Dick Anderson	1.25	.50
❑ 68 Ken Iman	.75	.30
❑ 69 Miller Farr	.75	.30
❑ 70 Daryle Lamonica	3.00	1.50
❑ 71 Alan Page	12.00	6.00
❑ 72 Pat Matson	.75	.30
❑ 73 Emerson Boozer	.75	.30
❑ 74 Pat Fischer	.75	.30
❑ 75 Gary Collins	1.25	.50
❑ 76 John Fuqua RC	1.25	.50
❑ 77 Bruce Gossett	.75	.30
❑ 78 Ed O'Bradovich	.75	.30
❑ 79 Bob Tucker RC	1.25	.50
❑ 80 Mike Curtis	1.25	.50
❑ 81 Rich Jackson	.75	.30
❑ 82 Tom Janik	.75	.30
❑ 83 Gale Gillingham	.75	.30
❑ 84 Jim Mitchell TE	.75	.30
❑ 85 Charlie Johnson	1.25	.50
❑ 86 Edgar Chandler	.75	.30
❑ 87 Cyril Pinder	.75	.30
❑ 88 Johnny Robinson	1.25	.50
❑ 89 Ralph Neely	.75	.30
❑ 90 Dan Abramowicz	.75	.30
❑ 91 Mercury Morris RC	5.00	2.50
❑ 92 Steve DeLong	.75	.30
❑ 93 Larry Stallings	.75	.30
❑ 94 Tom Mack	2.00	.75
❑ 95 Hewritt Dixon	.75	.30
❑ 96 Fred Cox	.75	.30
❑ 97 Chris Hanburger	.75	.30
❑ 98 Gerry Philbin	.75	.30
❑ 99 Ernie Wright	.75	.30
❑ 100 John Brodie	4.00	2.00
❑ 101 Tucker Frederickson	.75	.30
❑ 102 Bobby Walden	.75	.30
❑ 103 Dick Gordon	.75	.30
❑ 104 Walter Johnson	.75	.30
❑ 105 Mike Lucci	1.25	.50
❑ 106 Checklist DP	6.00	3.00
❑ 107 Ron Berger	.75	.30
❑ 108 Dan Sullivan	.75	.30
❑ 109 George Kunz RC	.75	.30
❑ 110 Floyd Little	2.00	.75
❑ 111 Zeke Bratkowski	1.25	.50
❑ 112 Haven Moses	1.25	.50
❑ 113 Ken Houston RC	15.00	7.50
❑ 114 Willie Lanier RC	15.00	7.50
❑ 115 Larry Brown	2.00	.75
❑ 116 Tim Rossovich	.75	.30
❑ 117 Errol Linden	.75	.30
❑ 118 Mel Renfro	2.00	.75
❑ 119 Mike Garrett	.75	.30
❑ 120 Fran Tarkenton	15.00	7.50
❑ 121 Garo Yepremian RC	2.00	.75
❑ 122 Glen Condren	.75	.30
❑ 123 Johnny Roland	.75	.30
❑ 124 Dave Herman	.75	.30
❑ 125 Merlin Olsen	3.00	1.50
❑ 126 Doug Buffone	.75	.30
❑ 127 Earl McCullouch	.75	.30
❑ 128 Spider Lockhart	.75	.30
❑ 129 Ken Willard	.75	.30
❑ 130 Gene Washington Vik	.75	.30
❑ 131 Mike Phipps RC	1.25	.50
❑ 132 Andy Russell	1.25	.50
❑ 133 Ray Nitschke !	4.00	2.00
❑ 134 Jerry Logan	1.00	.40
❑ 135 MacArthur Lane RC	1.50	.60
❑ 136 Jim Turner	1.00	.40
❑ 137 Kent McCloughan	1.00	.40
❑ 138 Paul Guidry	1.00	.40
❑ 139 Otis Taylor	1.50	.60
❑ 140 Virgil Carter RC	1.00	.40
❑ 141 Joe Dawkins	1.00	.40
❑ 142 Steve Preece	1.00	.40
❑ 143 Mike Bragg RC	1.00	.40
❑ 144 Bob Lilly	5.00	2.50
❑ 145 Joe Kapp	1.50	.60
❑ 146 Al Dodd	1.00	.40
❑ 147 Nick Buoniconti	2.50	1.25
❑ 148 Speedy Duncan	1.00	.40
❑ 149 Cedrick Hardman RC	1.00	.40
❑ 150 Gale Sayers	25.00	12.50
❑ 151 Jim Otto	2.50	1.25
❑ 152 Billy Truax	1.00	.40
❑ 153 John Elliott	1.00	.40
❑ 154 Dick LeBeau	1.00	.40
❑ 155 Bill Bergey	1.50	.60
❑ 156 Terry Bradshaw RC !	200.00	125.00
❑ 157 Leroy Kelly	6.00	3.00
❑ 158 Paul Krause	2.50	1.25
❑ 159 Ted Vactor	1.00	.40
❑ 160 Bob Griese	15.00	7.50
❑ 161 Ernie McMillan	1.00	.40
❑ 162 Donny Anderson	1.50	.60
❑ 163 John Pitts	1.00	.40
❑ 164 Dave Costa	1.00	.40
❑ 165 Gene Washington 49er	1.50	.60
❑ 166 John Zook	1.00	.40
❑ 167 Pete Gogolak	1.00	.40
❑ 168 Erich Barnes	1.00	.40
❑ 169 Alvin Reed	1.00	.40
❑ 170 Jim Nance	1.50	.60
❑ 171 Craig Morton	2.50	1.25
❑ 172 Gary Garrison	1.00	.40
❑ 173 Joe Scarpati	1.00	.40
❑ 174 Adrian Young UER	1.00	.40
❑ 175 John Mackey	2.50	1.25
❑ 176 Mac Percival	1.00	.40
❑ 177 Preston Pearson RC	4.00	2.00
❑ 178 Fred Biletnikoff	8.00	4.00
❑ 179 Mike Battle RC	1.00	.40
❑ 180 Len Dawson	8.00	4.00
❑ 181 Les Josephson	1.00	.40
❑ 182 Royce Berry	1.00	.40
❑ 183 Herman Weaver	1.00	.40
❑ 184 Norm Snead	1.50	.60
❑ 185 Sam Brunelli	1.00	.40
❑ 186 Jim Kiick RC	5.00	2.50
❑ 187 Austin Denney	1.00	.40
❑ 188 Roger Wehrli RC	6.00	3.00
❑ 189 Dave Wilcox	2.50	1.25
❑ 190 Bob Hayes	2.50	1.25
❑ 191 Joe Morrison	1.00	.40
❑ 192 Manny Sistrunk	1.00	.40
❑ 193 Don Cockroft RC	1.00	.40
❑ 194 Lee Bouggess	1.00	.40
❑ 195 Bob Berry	1.00	.40
❑ 196 Ron Sellers	1.00	.40
❑ 197 George Webster	1.00	.40
❑ 198 Hoyle Granger	1.00	.40
❑ 199 Bob Vogel	1.00	.40
❑ 200 Bart Starr	20.00	10.00
❑ 201 Mike Mercer	1.00	.40
❑ 202 Dave Smith WR	1.00	.40
❑ 203 Lee Roy Caffey	1.00	.40
❑ 204 Mick Tingelhoff	1.50	.60
❑ 205 Matt Snell	1.50	.60
❑ 206 Jim Tyrer	1.00	.40
❑ 207 Willie Brown	2.50	1.25
❑ 208 Bob Johnson RC	1.00	.40
❑ 209 Deacon Jones	2.50	1.25
❑ 210 Charlie Sanders RC	5.00	2.00
❑ 211 Jake Scott RC	6.00	3.00
❑ 212 Bob Anderson RC	1.00	.40
❑ 213 Charlie Krueger	1.00	.40
❑ 214 Jim Bakken	1.00	.40
❑ 215 Harold Jackson	1.50	.60
❑ 216 Bill Brundige	1.00	.40
❑ 217 Calvin Hill	5.00	2.50
❑ 218 Claude Humphrey	1.00	.40

❑	219 Glen Ray Hines	1.00	.40
❑	220 Bill Nelsen	1.50	.60
❑	221 Roy Hilton	1.00	.40
❑	222 Don Herrmann	1.00	.40
❑	223 John Bramlett	1.00	.40
❑	224 Ken Ellis	1.00	.40
❑	225 Dave Osborn	1.50	.60
❑	226 Edd Hargett RC	1.00	.40
❑	227 Gene Mingo	1.00	.40
❑	228 Larry Grantham	1.00	.40
❑	229 Dick Post	1.00	.40
❑	230 Roman Gabriel	2.50	1.25
❑	231 Mike Eischeid	1.00	.40
❑	232 Jim Lynch	1.00	.40
❑	233 Lemar Parrish RC	1.50	.60
❑	234 Cecil Turner	1.00	.40
❑	235 Dennis Shaw RC	1.00	.40
❑	236 Mel Farr	1.00	.40
❑	237 Curt Knight	1.00	.40
❑	238 Chuck Howley	1.50	.60
❑	239 Bruce Taylor RC	1.00	.40
❑	240 Jerry LeVias	1.00	.40
❑	241 Bob Lurtsema	1.00	.40
❑	242 Earl Morrall	1.50	.60
❑	243 Kermit Alexander	1.00	.40
❑	244 Jackie Smith	2.50	1.25
❑	245 Joe Greene RC	50.00	30.00
❑	246 Harmon Wages	1.00	.40
❑	247 Errol Mann	1.00	.40
❑	248 Mike McCoy DT RC	1.00	.40
❑	249 Milt Morin RC	1.00	.40
❑	250 Joe Namath	60.00	35.00
❑	251 Jackie Burkett	1.00	.40
❑	252 Steve Chomyszak	1.00	.40
❑	253 Ed Sharockman	1.00	.40
❑	254 Robert Holmes RC	1.00	.40
❑	255 John Hadl	2.50	1.25
❑	256 Cornell Gordon	1.00	.40
❑	257 Mark Moseley RC	1.50	.60
❑	258 Gus Otto	1.00	.40
❑	259 Mike Taliaferro	1.00	.40
❑	260 O.J.Simpson	25.00	12.50
❑	261 Paul Warfield	8.00	4.00
❑	262 Jack Concannon	1.00	.40
❑	263 Tom Matte !	2.50	1.25

1972 Topps

❑	COMPLETE SET (351)	2500.00	1500.00
❑	COMMON CARD (1-132)	.50	.25
❑	COMMON CARD (133-263)	.60	.30
❑	COMMON CARD (264-351)	18.00	10.00
❑	WRAPPER (10-CENT)	10.00	6.00
❑	WRAPPER SER.3 (10-CENT)	20.00	15.00
❑	1 L.Csonka/Litt/Hubb LL	4.00	2.00
❑	2 NFC Rushing Leaders	.50	.25
❑	3 B.Griese/Dawson/Cart LL	2.00	.75
❑	4 R.Staubach/Lan/Kil LL	5.00	2.50
❑	5 AFC Receiving Leaders	1.00	.40
❑	6 NFC Receiving Leaders	.50	.25
❑	7 Yepre/Stener/O'Brien LL	.50	.25
❑	8 NFC Scoring Leaders	.50	.25
❑	9 Jim Kiick	2.00	.75
❑	10 Otis Taylor	1.00	.40
❑	11 Bobby Joe Green	.50	.25
❑	12 Ken Ellis	.50	.25
❑	13 John Riggins RC	20.00	10.00
❑	14 Dave Parks	.50	.25
❑	15 John Hadl	2.00	.75
❑	16 Ron Hornsby	.50	.25
❑	17 Chip Myers RC	.50	.25
❑	18 Billy Kilmer	2.00	.75
❑	19 Fred Hoaglin	.50	.25
❑	20 Carl Eller	2.00	.75
❑	21 Steve Zabel	.50	.25
❑	22 Vic Washington RC	.50	.25
❑	23 Len St. Jean	.50	.25
❑	24 Bill Thompson	.50	.25
❑	25 Steve Owens RC	2.00	.75
❑	26 Ken Burrough RC	1.00	.40
❑	27 Mike Clark	.50	.25
❑	28 Willie Brown	2.00	.75
❑	29 Checklist	6.00	3.00
❑	30 Marlin Briscoe RC	.50	.25
❑	31 Jerry Logan	.50	.25
❑	32 Donny Anderson	1.00	.40
❑	33 Rich McGeorge	.50	.25
❑	34 Charlie Durkee	.50	.25
❑	35 Willie Lanier	4.00	2.00
❑	36 Chris Farasopoulos	.50	.25
❑	37 Ron Shanklin RC	.50	.25
❑	38 Forrest Blue RC	.50	.25
❑	39 Ken Reaves	.50	.25
❑	40 Roman Gabriel	2.00	.75
❑	41 Mac Percival	.50	.25
❑	42 Lem Barney	3.00	1.50
❑	43 Nick Buoniconti	2.00	.75
❑	44 Charlie Gogolak	.50	.25
❑	45 Bill Bradley RC	1.00	.40
❑	46 Joe Jones DE	.50	.25
❑	47 Dave Williams	.50	.25
❑	48 Pete Athas	.50	.25
❑	49 Virgil Carter	.50	.25
❑	50 Floyd Little	2.00	.75
❑	51 Curt Knight	.50	.25
❑	52 Bobby Maples	.50	.25
❑	53 Charlie West	.50	.25
❑	54 Marv Hubbard RC	1.00	.40
❑	55 Archie Manning RC	20.00	10.00
❑	56 Jim O'Brien RC	1.00	.40
❑	57 Wayne Patrick	.50	.25
❑	58 Ken Bowman	.50	.25
❑	59 Roger Wehrli	1.25	.50
❑	60 Charlie Sanders	1.25	.50
❑	61 Jan Stenerud	2.00	.75
❑	62 Willie Ellison	.50	.25
❑	63 Walt Sweeney	.50	.25
❑	64 Ron Smith	.50	.25
❑	65 Jim Plunkett RC	20.00	10.00
❑	66 Herb Adderley UER	2.00	.75
❑	67 Mike Reid RC	2.00	.75
❑	68 Richard Caster RC	1.00	.40
❑	69 Dave Wilcox	2.00	.75
❑	70 Leroy Kelly	3.00	1.50
❑	71 Bob Lee RC	.50	.25
❑	72 Verlon Biggs	.50	.25
❑	73 Henry Allison	.50	.25
❑	74 Steve Ramsey	.50	.25
❑	75 Claude Humphrey	1.00	.40
❑	76 Bob Grim RC	.50	.25
❑	77 John Fuqua	1.00	.40
❑	78 Ken Houston	4.00	2.00
❑	79 Checklist DP	5.00	2.50
❑	80 Bob Griese	8.00	4.00
❑	81 Lance Rentzel	1.00	.40
❑	82 Ed Podolak RC	1.00	.40
❑	83 Ike Hill	.50	.25
❑	84 George Farmer	.50	.25
❑	85 John Brockington RC	2.00	.75
❑	86 Jim Otto	2.00	.75
❑	87 Richard Neal	.50	.25
❑	88 Jim Hart	2.00	.75
❑	89 Bob Babich	.50	.25
❑	90 Gene Washington 49er	1.00	.40
❑	91 John Zook	.50	.25
❑	92 Bobby Duhon	.50	.25
❑	93 Ted Hendricks RC	15.00	7.50
❑	94 Rockne Freitas	.50	.25
❑	95 Larry Brown	2.00	.75
❑	96 Mike Phipps	1.00	.40
❑	97 Julius Adams	.50	.25
❑	98 Dick Anderson	1.00	.40
❑	99 Fred Willis	.50	.25
❑	100 Joe Namath	35.00	20.00
❑	101 L.C.Greenwood RC	15.00	7.50
❑	102 Mark Nordquist	.50	.25
❑	103 Robert Holmes	.50	.25
❑	104 Ron Yary RC	5.00	2.00
❑	105 Bob Hayes	2.00	.75
❑	106 Lyle Alzado RC	15.00	7.50
❑	107 Bob Berry	.50	.25
❑	108 Phil Villapiano RC	1.00	.40
❑	109 Dave Elmendorf	.50	.25
❑	110 Gale Sayers	20.00	10.00
❑	111 Jim Tyrer	.50	.25
❑	112 Mel Gray RC	2.00	.75
❑	113 Gerry Philbin	.50	.25
❑	114 Bob James	.50	.25
❑	115 Garo Yepremian	1.00	.40
❑	116 Dave Robinson	1.00	.40
❑	117 Jeff Queen	.50	.25
❑	118 Norm Snead	1.00	.40
❑	119 Jim Nance IA	1.00	.40
❑	120 Terry Bradshaw IA	15.00	7.50
❑	121 Jim Kiick IA	1.00	.40
❑	122 Roger Staubach IA	20.00	12.00
❑	123 Bo Scott IA	.50	.25
❑	124 John Brodie IA	2.00	.75
❑	125 Rick Volk IA	.50	.25
❑	126 John Riggins IA	6.00	3.00
❑	127 Bubba Smith IA	2.00	.75
❑	128 Roman Gabriel IA	1.00	.40
❑	129 Calvin Hill IA	1.00	.40
❑	130 Bill Nelsen IA	.50	.25
❑	131 Tom Matte IA	1.00	.40
❑	132 Bob Griese IA	4.00	2.00
❑	133 AFC Semi-Final	1.00	.40
❑	134 NFC Semi-Final	1.00	.40
❑	135 AFC Semi-Final	1.00	.40
❑	136 NFC Semi-Final	1.00	.40
❑	137 AFC Title Game/Unitas	3.00	1.50
❑	138 NFC Title Game/Bob Lilly	2.00	.75
❑	139 Super Bowl VI/Staubach	5.00	2.50
❑	140 Larry Csonka	8.00	4.00
❑	141 Rick Volk	.60	.30
❑	142 Roy Jefferson	1.00	.40
❑	143 Raymond Chester RC	1.00	.40
❑	144 Bobby Douglass	.60	.30
❑	145 Bob Lilly	5.00	2.50
❑	146 Harold Jackson	1.00	.40
❑	147 Pete Gogolak	.60	.30
❑	148 Art Malone	.60	.30
❑	149 Ed Flanagan	.60	.30
❑	150 Terry Bradshaw	40.00	25.00
❑	151 MacArthur Lane	1.00	.40
❑	152 Jack Snow	1.00	.40
❑	153 Al Beauchamp	.60	.30
❑	154 Bob Anderson	.60	.30
❑	155 Ted Kwalick RC	.60	.30
❑	156 Dan Pastorini RC	2.00	.75
❑	157 Emmitt Thomas RC	2.00	.75
❑	158 Randy Vataha RC	.60	.30
❑	159 Al Atkinson	.60	.30
❑	160 O.J.Simpson	15.00	7.50
❑	161 Jackie Smith	2.00	.75
❑	162 Ernie Kellerman	.60	.30
❑	163 Dennis Partee	.60	.30
❑	164 Jake Kupp	.60	.30
❑	165 Johnny Unitas	20.00	10.00
❑	166 Clint Jones RC	.60	.30
❑	167 Paul Warfield	6.00	3.00
❑	168 Roland McDole	.60	.30
❑	169 Daryle Lamonica	2.00	.75
❑	170 Dick Butkus	15.00	7.50
❑	171 Jim Butler	.60	.30
❑	172 Mike McCoy DT	.60	.30
❑	173 Dave Smith WR	.60	.30
❑	174 Greg Landry	1.00	.40
❑	175 Tom Dempsey	1.00	.40
❑	176 John Charles	.60	.30
❑	177 Bobby Bell	2.00	.75
❑	178 Don Horn	.60	.30
❑	179 Bob Trumpy	2.00	.75
❑	180 Duane Thomas	1.00	.40
❑	181 Merlin Olsen	3.00	1.50
❑	182 Dave Herman	.60	.30
❑	183 Jim Nance	1.00	.40
❑	184 Pete Beathard	.60	.30
❑	185 Bob Tucker	.60	.30
❑	186 Gene Upshaw RC	15.00	7.50
❑	187 Bo Scott	.60	.30
❑	188 J.D.Hill RC	.60	.30
❑	189 Bruce Gossett	.60	.30
❑	190 Bubba Smith	4.00	2.00

❑ 191 Edd Hargett .60 .30
❑ 192 Gary Garrison .60 .30
❑ 193 Jake Scott 1.00 .40
❑ 194 Fred Cox .60 .30
❑ 195 Sonny Jurgensen 4.00 2.00
❑ 196 Greg Brezina RC .60 .30
❑ 197 Ed O'Bradovich .60 .30
❑ 198 John Rowser .60 .30
❑ 199 Altie Taylor UER .60 .30
❑ 200 Roger Staubach RC ! 175.00 100.00
❑ 201 Leroy Keyes RC .60 .30
❑ 202 Garland Boyette .60 .30
❑ 203 Tom Beer .60 .30
❑ 204 Buck Buchanan 2.00 .75
❑ 205 Larry Wilson 2.00 .75
❑ 206 Scott Hunter RC .60 .30
❑ 207 Ron Johnson .60 .30
❑ 208 Sam Brunelli .60 .30
❑ 209 Deacon Jones 2.00 .75
❑ 210 Fred Biletnikoff 6.00 3.00
❑ 211 Bill Nelsen 1.00 .40
❑ 212 George Nock .60 .30
❑ 213 Dan Abramowicz 1.00 .40
❑ 214 Irv Goode .60 .30
❑ 215 Isiah Robertson RC 1.00 .40
❑ 216 Tom Matte 1.00 .40
❑ 217 Pat Fischer .60 .30
❑ 218 Gene Washington Vik .60 .30
❑ 219 Paul Robinson .60 .30
❑ 220 John Brodie 4.00 2.00
❑ 221 Manny Fernandez RC 1.00 .40
❑ 222 Errol Mann .60 .30
❑ 223 Dick Gordon .60 .30
❑ 224 Calvin Hill 2.00 .75
❑ 225 Fran Tarkenton 12.00 6.00
❑ 226 Jim Turner .60 .30
❑ 227 Jim Mitchell TE .60 .30
❑ 228 Pete Liske .60 .30
❑ 229 Carl Garrett .60 .30
❑ 230 Joe Greene 20.00 10.00
❑ 231 Gale Gillingham .60 .30
❑ 232 Norm Bulaich RC 1.00 .40
❑ 233 Spider Lockhart .60 .30
❑ 234 Ken Willard .60 .30
❑ 235 George Blanda 12.00 6.00
❑ 236 Wayne Mulligan .60 .30
❑ 237 Dave Lewis .60 .30
❑ 238 Dennis Shaw .60 .30
❑ 239 Fair Hooker .60 .30
❑ 240 Larry Little RC 15.00 7.50
❑ 241 Mike Garrett .60 .30
❑ 242 Glen Ray Hines .60 .30
❑ 243 Myron Pottios .60 .30
❑ 244 Charlie Joiner RC 20.00 10.00
❑ 245 Len Dawson 6.00 3.00
❑ 246 W.K. Hicks .60 .30
❑ 247 Les Josephson .60 .30
❑ 248 Lance Alworth UER 6.00 3.00
❑ 249 Frank Nunley .60 .30
❑ 250 Mel Farr IA .60 .30
❑ 251 Johnny Unitas IA 8.00 4.00
❑ 252 George Farmer IA .60 .30
❑ 253 Duane Thomas IA 1.00 .40
❑ 254 John Hadl IA 2.00 .75
❑ 255 Vic Washington IA .60 .30
❑ 256 Don Horn IA .60 .30
❑ 257 L.C.Greenwood IA 2.00 .75
❑ 258 Bob Lee IA .60 .30
❑ 259 Larry Csonka IA 4.00 2.00
❑ 260 Mike McCoy DT IA .60 .30
❑ 261 Greg Landry IA 1.00 .40
❑ 262 Ray May IA .60 .30
❑ 263 Bobby Douglass IA .60 .30
❑ 264 Charlie Sanders AP ! 30.00 15.00
❑ 265 Ron Yary AP 30.00 15.00
❑ 266 Rayfield Wright AP 30.00 15.00
❑ 267 Larry Little AP 35.00 20.00
❑ 268 John Niland AP 30.00 15.00
❑ 269 Forrest Blue AP 30.00 15.00
❑ 270 Otis Taylor AP 30.00 15.00
❑ 271 Paul Warfield AP 50.00 30.00
❑ 272 Bob Griese AP 70.00 40.00
❑ 273 John Brockington AP 30.00 15.00
❑ 274 Floyd Little AP 30.00 15.00
❑ 275 Garo Yepremian AP 30.00 15.00
❑ 276 Jerrel Wilson AP 18.00 10.00
❑ 277 Carl Eller AP 30.00 15.00
❑ 278 Bubba Smith AP 40.00 25.00
❑ 279 Alan Page AP 40.00 25.00
❑ 280 Bob Lilly AP 60.00 30.00
❑ 281 Ted Hendricks AP 50.00 30.00
❑ 282 Dave Wilcox AP 30.00 15.00
❑ 283 Willie Lanier AP 35.00 20.00
❑ 284 Jim Johnson AP 30.00 15.00
❑ 285 Willie Brown AP 35.00 20.00
❑ 286 Bill Bradley AP 30.00 15.00
❑ 287 Ken Houston AP 35.00 20.00
❑ 288 Mel Farr 18.00 10.00
❑ 289 Kermit Alexander 18.00 10.00
❑ 290 John Gilliam RC 25.00 12.50
❑ 291 Steve Spurrier RC 100.00 50.00
❑ 292 Walter Johnson 18.00 10.00
❑ 293 Jack Pardee 25.00 12.50
❑ 294 Checklist UER 80.00 50.00
❑ 295 Winston Hill 18.00 10.00
❑ 296 Hugo Hollas 18.00 10.00
❑ 297 Ray May RC 18.00 10.00
❑ 298 Jim Bakken 18.00 10.00
❑ 299 Larry Carwell 18.00 10.00
❑ 300 Alan Page 50.00 30.00
❑ 301 Walt Garrison 25.00 12.50
❑ 302 Mike Lucci 25.00 12.50
❑ 303 Nemiah Wilson 18.00 10.00
❑ 304 Carroll Dale 25.00 12.50
❑ 305 Jim Kanicki 18.00 10.00
❑ 306 Preston Pearson 30.00 15.00
❑ 307 Lemar Parrish 25.00 12.50
❑ 308 Earl Morrall 25.00 12.50
❑ 309 Tommy Nobis 25.00 12.50
❑ 310 Rich Jackson 18.00 10.00
❑ 311 Doug Cunningham 18.00 10.00
❑ 312 Jim Marsalis 18.00 10.00
❑ 313 Jim Beirne 18.00 10.00
❑ 314 Tom McNeill 18.00 10.00
❑ 315 Milt Morin 18.00 10.00
❑ 316 Rayfield Wright RC 25.00 12.50
❑ 317 Jerry LeVias 25.00 12.50
❑ 318 Travis Williams RC 25.00 12.50
❑ 319 Edgar Chandler 18.00 10.00
❑ 320 Bob Wallace 18.00 10.00
❑ 321 Delles Howell 18.00 10.00
❑ 322 Emerson Boozer 25.00 12.50
❑ 323 George Atkinson RC 25.00 12.50
❑ 324 Mike Montler 18.00 10.00
❑ 325 Randy Johnson 18.00 10.00
❑ 326 Mike Curtis UER 25.00 12.50
❑ 327 Miller Farr 18.00 10.00
❑ 328 Horst Muhlmann 18.00 10.00
❑ 329 John Niland RC 25.00 12.50
❑ 330 Andy Russell 30.00 15.00
❑ 331 Mercury Morris 40.00 25.00
❑ 332 Jim Johnson 30.00 15.00
❑ 333 Jerrel Wilson 18.00 10.00
❑ 334 Charley Taylor 40.00 25.00
❑ 335 Dick LeBeau 18.00 10.00
❑ 336 Jim Marshall 30.00 15.00
❑ 337 Tom Mack 30.00 15.00
❑ 338 Steve Spurrier IA 60.00 30.00
❑ 339 Floyd Little IA 25.00 12.50
❑ 340 Len Dawson IA 40.00 25.00
❑ 341 Dick Butkus IA 70.00 40.00
❑ 342 Larry Brown IA 25.00 12.50
❑ 343 Joe Namath IA 175.00 100.00
❑ 344 Jim Turner IA 18.00 10.00
❑ 345 Doug Cunningham IA 18.00 10.00
❑ 346 Edd Hargett IA 18.00 10.00
❑ 347 Steve Owens IA 18.00 10.00
❑ 348 George Blanda IA 50.00 30.00
❑ 349 Ed Podolak IA 18.00 10.00
❑ 350 Rich Jackson IA 18.00 10.00
❑ 351 Ken Willard IA ! 40.00 25.00

1973 Topps

❑ COMPLETE SET (528) 400.00 200.00
❑ 1 Simpson/L.Brown LL 8.00 3.00
❑ 2 Passing Leaders 1.00 .40
❑ 3 Jackson/Biletnikoff LL 1.50 .60
❑ 4 Scoring Leaders .50 .25
❑ 5 Interception Leaders .50 .25
❑ 6 Punting Leaders .50 .25
❑ 7 Bob Trumpy 1.50 .60
❑ 8 Mel Tom .50 .25
❑ 9 Clarence Ellis .50 .25
❑ 10 John Niland .50 .25
❑ 11 Randy Jackson .50 .25
❑ 12 Greg Landry 1.50 .60
❑ 13 Cid Edwards .50 .25
❑ 14 Phil Olsen .50 .25
❑ 15 Terry Bradshaw 25.00 15.00
❑ 16 Al Cowlings RC 1.50 .60
❑ 17 Walker Gillette .50 .25
❑ 18 Bob Atkins .50 .25
❑ 19 Diron Talbert RC .50 .25
❑ 20 Jim Johnson 1.50 .60
❑ 21 Howard Twilley 1.00 .40
❑ 22 Dick Enderle .50 .25
❑ 23 Wayne Colman .50 .25
❑ 24 John Schmitt .50 .25
❑ 25 George Blanda 10.00 5.00
❑ 26 Milt Morin .50 .25
❑ 27 Mike Current .50 .25
❑ 28 Rex Kern RC .50 .25
❑ 29 MacArthur Lane 1.00 .40
❑ 30 Alan Page 3.00 1.50
❑ 31 Randy Vataha .50 .25
❑ 32 Jim Kearney .50 .25
❑ 33 Steve Smith T .50 .25
❑ 34 Ken Anderson RC 15.00 7.50
❑ 35 Calvin Hill 1.50 .60
❑ 36 Andy Maurer .50 .25
❑ 37 Joe Taylor .50 .25
❑ 38 Deacon Jones 1.50 .60
❑ 39 Mike Weger .50 .25
❑ 40 Roy Gerela 1.00 .40
❑ 41 Les Josephson .50 .25
❑ 42 Dave Washington .50 .25
❑ 43 Bill Curry RC 1.00 .40
❑ 44 Fred Heron .50 .25
❑ 45 John Brodie 3.00 1.50
❑ 46 Roy Winston .50 .25
❑ 47 Mike Bragg .50 .25
❑ 48 Mercury Morris 1.50 .60
❑ 49 Jim Files .50 .25
❑ 50 Gene Upshaw 3.00 1.50
❑ 51 Hugo Hollas .50 .25
❑ 52 Rod Sherman .50 .25
❑ 53 Ron Snidow .50 .25
❑ 54 Steve Tannen RC .50 .25
❑ 55 Jim Carter RC .50 .25
❑ 56 Lydell Mitchell RC 1.50 .60
❑ 57 Jack Rudnay RC .50 .25
❑ 58 Halvor Hagen .50 .25
❑ 59 Tom Dempsey 1.00 .40
❑ 60 Fran Tarkenton 10.00 5.00
❑ 61 Lance Alworth 5.00 2.50
❑ 62 Vern Holland .50 .25
❑ 63 Steve DeLong .50 .25
❑ 64 Art Malone .50 .25
❑ 65 Isiah Robertson 1.00 .40
❑ 66 Jerry Rush .50 .25
❑ 67 Bryant Salter .50 .25
❑ 68 Checklist 1-132 5.00 2.50
❑ 69 J.D. Hill .50 .25
❑ 70 Forrest Blue .50 .25
❑ 71 Myron Pottios .50 .25
❑ 72 Norm Thompson RC .50 .25
❑ 73 Paul Robinson .50 .25
❑ 74 Larry Grantham .50 .25
❑ 75 Manny Fernandez 1.00 .40
❑ 76 Kent Nix .50 .25
❑ 77 Art Shell RC 15.00 7.50
❑ 78 George Saimes .50 .25
❑ 79 Don Cockroft .50 .25
❑ 80 Bob Tucker 1.00 .40
❑ 81 Don McCauley RC .50 .25
❑ 82 Bob Brown DT .50 .25
❑ 83 Larry Carwell .50 .25
❑ 84 Mo Moorman .50 .25
❑ 85 John Gilliam 1.00 .40
❑ 86 Wade Key .50 .25
❑ 87 Ross Brupbacher .50 .25
❑ 88 Dave Lewis .50 .25
❑ 89 Franco Harris RC 50.00 25.00
❑ 90 Tom Mack 1.50 .60
❑ 91 Mike Tilleman .50 .25
❑ 92 Carl Mauck .50 .25
❑ 93 Larry Hand .50 .25
❑ 94 Dave Foley RC .50 .25
❑ 95 Frank Nunley .50 .25
❑ 96 John Charles .50 .25
❑ 97 Jim Bakken .50 .25

Card		
❑ 98 Pat Fischer	1.00	.40
❑ 99 Randy Rasmussen	.50	.25
❑ 100 Larry Csonka	6.00	3.00
❑ 101 Mike Siani RC	.50	.25
❑ 102 Tom Roussel	.50	.25
❑ 103 Clarence Scott RC	1.00	.40
❑ 104 Charlie Johnson	1.00	.40
❑ 105 Rick Volk	.50	.25
❑ 106 Willie Young	.50	.25
❑ 107 Emmitt Thomas	1.00	.40
❑ 108 Jon Morris	.50	.25
❑ 109 Clarence Williams	.50	.25
❑ 110 Rayfield Wright	1.00	.40
❑ 111 Norm Bulaich	.50	.25
❑ 112 Mike Eischeid	.50	.25
❑ 113 Speedy Thomas	.50	.25
❑ 114 Glen Holloway	.50	.25
❑ 115 Jack Ham RC	30.00	15.00
❑ 116 Jim Nettles	.50	.25
❑ 117 Errol Mann	.50	.25
❑ 118 John Mackey	1.50	.60
❑ 119 George Kunz	.50	.25
❑ 120 Bob James	.50	.25
❑ 121 Garland Boyette	.50	.25
❑ 122 Mel Phillips	.50	.25
❑ 123 Johnny Roland	.50	.25
❑ 124 Doug Swift	.50	.25
❑ 125 Archie Manning	4.00	2.00
❑ 126 Dave Herman	.50	.25
❑ 127 Carleton Oats	.50	.25
❑ 128 Bill Van Heusen	.50	.25
❑ 129 Rich Jackson	.50	.25
❑ 130 Len Hauss	1.00	.40
❑ 131 Billy Parks RC	.50	.25
❑ 132 Ray May	.50	.25
❑ 133 NFC Semi/Staubach	5.00	2.00
❑ 134 AFC Semi/Immac.Rec.	2.50	1.00
❑ 135 NFC Semi-Final	1.00	.40
❑ 136 AFC Semi/L.Csonka	2.00	.75
❑ 137 NFC Title Game/Kilmer	1.50	.60
❑ 138 AFC Title Game	1.00	.40
❑ 139 Super Bowl VII	1.50	.60
❑ 140 Dwight White RC	3.00	1.25
❑ 141 Jim Marsalis	.50	.25
❑ 142 Doug Van Horn	.50	.25
❑ 143 Al Matthews	.50	.25
❑ 144 Bob Windsor	.50	.25
❑ 145 Dave Hampton RC	.50	.25
❑ 146 Horst Muhlmann	.50	.25
❑ 147 Wally Hilgenberg RC	.50	.25
❑ 148 Ron Smith	.50	.25
❑ 149 Coy Bacon RC	1.00	.40
❑ 150 Winston Hill	.50	.25
❑ 151 Ron Jessie RC	1.00	.40
❑ 152 Ken Iman	.50	.25
❑ 153 Ron Saul	.50	.25
❑ 154 Jim Braxton RC	1.00	.40
❑ 155 Bubba Smith	2.50	1.25
❑ 156 Gary Cuozzo	1.00	.40
❑ 157 Charlie Krueger	1.00	.40
❑ 158 Tim Foley RC	1.00	.40
❑ 159 Lee Roy Jordan	1.50	.60
❑ 160 Bob Brown OT	1.50	.60
❑ 161 Margene Adkins	.50	.25
❑ 162 Ron Widby	.50	.25
❑ 163 Jim Houston	.50	.25
❑ 164 Joe Dawkins	.50	.25
❑ 165 L.C.Greenwood	4.00	2.00
❑ 166 Richmond Flowers RC	.50	.25
❑ 167 Curley Culp RC	1.50	.60
❑ 168 Len St. Jean	.50	.25
❑ 169 Walter Rock	.50	.25
❑ 170 Bill Bradley	1.00	.40
❑ 171 Ken Riley RC	1.50	.60
❑ 172 Rich Coady	.50	.25
❑ 173 Don Hansen	.50	.25
❑ 174 Lionel Aldridge	.50	.25
❑ 175 Don Maynard	4.00	2.00
❑ 176 Dave Osborn	1.00	.40
❑ 177 Jim Bailey	.50	.25
❑ 178 John Pitts	.50	.25
❑ 179 Dave Parks	.50	.25
❑ 180 Chester Marcol RC	.50	.25
❑ 181 Len Rohde	.50	.25
❑ 182 Jeff Staggs	.50	.25
❑ 183 Gene Hickerson	1.25	.50
❑ 184 Charlie Evans	.50	.25
❑ 185 Mel Renfro	1.50	.60
❑ 186 Marvin Upshaw	.50	.25
❑ 187 George Atkinson	1.00	.40
❑ 188 Norm Evans	1.00	.40
❑ 189 Steve Ramsey	.50	.25
❑ 190 Dave Chapple	.50	.25
❑ 191 Gerry Mullins	.50	.25
❑ 192 John Didion	.50	.25
❑ 193 Bob Gladieux	.50	.25
❑ 194 Don Hultz	.50	.25
❑ 195 Mike Lucci	.50	.25
❑ 196 John Wilbur	.50	.25
❑ 197 George Farmer	.50	.25
❑ 198 Tommy Casanova RC	1.00	.40
❑ 199 Russ Washington	.50	.25
❑ 200 Claude Humphrey	1.50	.60
❑ 201 Pat Hughes	.50	.25
❑ 202 Zeke Moore	.50	.25
❑ 203 Chip Glass	.50	.25
❑ 204 Glenn Ressler	.50	.25
❑ 205 Willie Ellison	1.00	.40
❑ 206 John Leypoldt	.50	.25
❑ 207 Johnny Fuller	.50	.25
❑ 208 Bill Hayhoe	.50	.25
❑ 209 Ed Bell	.50	.25
❑ 210 Willie Brown	1.50	.60
❑ 211 Carl Eller	1.50	.60
❑ 212 Mark Nordquist	.50	.25
❑ 213 Larry Willingham	.50	.25
❑ 214 Nick Buoniconti	1.50	.60
❑ 215 John Hadl	1.50	.60
❑ 216 Jethro Pugh RC	1.50	.60
❑ 217 Leroy Mitchell	.50	.25
❑ 218 Billy Newsome	.50	.25
❑ 219 John McMakin	.50	.25
❑ 220 Larry Brown	1.50	.60
❑ 221 Clarence Scott RC	.50	.25
❑ 222 Paul Naumoff	.50	.25
❑ 223 Ted Fritsch Jr.	.50	.25
❑ 224 Checklist 133-264	5.00	2.50
❑ 225 Dan Pastorini	1.50	.60
❑ 226 Joe Beauchamp UER	.50	.25
❑ 227 Pat Matson	.50	.25
❑ 228 Tony McGee DT	.50	.25
❑ 229 Mike Phipps	1.00	.40
❑ 230 Harold Jackson	1.50	.60
❑ 231 Willie Williams	.50	.25
❑ 232 Spike Jones	.50	.25
❑ 233 Jim Tyrer	.50	.25
❑ 234 Roy Hilton	.50	.25
❑ 235 Phil Villapiano	1.00	.40
❑ 236 Charley Taylor UER	3.00	1.50
❑ 237 Malcolm Snider	.50	.25
❑ 238 Vic Washington	.50	.25
❑ 239 Grady Alderman	.50	.25
❑ 240 Dick Anderson	1.00	.40
❑ 241 Ron Yankowski	.50	.25
❑ 242 Billy Masters	.50	.25
❑ 243 Herb Adderley	1.50	.60
❑ 244 David Ray	.50	.25
❑ 245 John Riggins	8.00	4.00
❑ 246 Mike Wagner RC	1.50	.60
❑ 247 Don Morrison	.50	.25
❑ 248 Earl McCullouch	.50	.25
❑ 249 Dennis Wirgowski	.50	.25
❑ 250 Chris Hanburger	1.00	.40
❑ 251 Pat Sullivan RC	1.50	.60
❑ 252 Walt Sweeney	.50	.25
❑ 253 Willie Alexander	.50	.25
❑ 254 Doug Dressler	.50	.25
❑ 255 Walter Johnson	.50	.25
❑ 256 Ron Hornsby	.50	.25
❑ 257 Ben Hawkins	.50	.25
❑ 258 Donnie Green RC	.50	.25
❑ 259 Fred Hoaglin	.50	.25
❑ 260 Jerrel Wilson	.50	.25
❑ 261 Horace Jones	.50	.25
❑ 262 Woody Peoples	.50	.25
❑ 263 Jim Hill RC	.50	.25
❑ 264 John Fuqua	.50	.25
❑ 265 Donny Anderson KP	1.00	.40
❑ 266 Roman Gabriel KP	1.50	.60
❑ 267 Mike Garrett KP	1.00	.40
❑ 268 Rufus Mayes RC	.50	.25
❑ 269 Chip Myrtle	.50	.25
❑ 270 Bill Stanfill RC	1.00	.40
❑ 271 Clint Jones	.50	.25
❑ 272 Miller Farr	.50	.25
❑ 273 Harry Schuh	.50	.25
❑ 274 Bob Hayes	1.50	.60
❑ 275 Bobby Douglass	1.00	.40
❑ 276 Gus Hollomon	.50	.25
❑ 277 Del Williams	.50	.25
❑ 278 Julius Adams	.50	.25
❑ 279 Herman Weaver	.50	.25
❑ 280 Joe Greene	8.00	4.00
❑ 281 Wes Chesson	.50	.25
❑ 282 Charlie Harraway	.50	.25
❑ 283 Paul Guidry	.50	.25
❑ 284 Terry Owens	.50	.25
❑ 285 Jan Stenerud	1.50	.60
❑ 286 Pete Athas	.50	.25
❑ 287 Dale Lindsey	.50	.25
❑ 288 Jack Tatum RC	15.00	6.00
❑ 289 Floyd Little	1.50	.60
❑ 290 Bob Johnson	.50	.25
❑ 291 Tommy Hart RC	.50	.25
❑ 292 Tom Mitchell	.50	.25
❑ 293 Walt Patulski RC	.50	.25
❑ 294 Jim Skaggs	.50	.25
❑ 295 Bob Griese	6.00	3.00
❑ 296 Mike McCoy DT	.50	.25
❑ 297 Mel Gray	1.00	.40
❑ 298 Bobby Bryant	.50	.25
❑ 299 Blaine Nye RC	.50	.25
❑ 300 Dick Butkus	12.00	6.00
❑ 301 Charlie Cowan RC	.50	.25
❑ 302 Mark Lomas	.50	.25
❑ 303 Josh Ashton	.50	.25
❑ 304 Happy Feller	.50	.25
❑ 305 Ron Shanklin	.50	.25
❑ 306 Wayne Rasmussen	.50	.25
❑ 307 Jerry Smith	.50	.25
❑ 308 Ken Reaves	.50	.25
❑ 309 Ron East	.50	.25
❑ 310 Otis Taylor	1.50	.60
❑ 311 John Garlington	.50	.25
❑ 312 Lyle Alzado	4.00	2.00
❑ 313 Remi Prudhomme	.50	.25
❑ 314 Cornelius Johnson	.50	.25
❑ 315 Lemar Parrish	1.00	.40
❑ 316 Jim Kiick	1.50	.60
❑ 317 Steve Zabel	.50	.25
❑ 318 Alden Roche	.50	.25
❑ 319 Tom Blanchard	.50	.25
❑ 320 Fred Biletnikoff	4.00	2.00
❑ 321 Ralph Neely	1.00	.40
❑ 322 Dan Dierdorf RC	20.00	7.50
❑ 323 Richard Caster	1.00	.40
❑ 324 Gene Howard	.50	.25
❑ 325 Elvin Bethea	1.50	.60
❑ 326 Carl Garrett	1.00	.40
❑ 327 Ron Billingsley	.50	.25
❑ 328 Charlie West	.50	.25
❑ 329 Tom Neville	.50	.25
❑ 330 Ted Kwalick	1.00	.40
❑ 331 Rudy Redmond	.50	.25
❑ 332 Henry Davis	.50	.25
❑ 333 John Zook	.50	.25
❑ 334 Jim Turner	.50	.25
❑ 335 Len Dawson	5.00	2.50
❑ 336 Bob Chandler RC	1.00	.40
❑ 337 Al Beauchamp	.50	.25
❑ 338 Tom Matte	1.00	.40
❑ 339 Paul Laaveg	.50	.25
❑ 340 Ken Ellis	.50	.25
❑ 341 Jim Langer RC	10.00	5.00
❑ 342 Ron Porter	.50	.25
❑ 343 Jack Youngblood RC	15.00	7.50
❑ 344 Cornell Green	1.50	.60
❑ 345 Marv Hubbard	1.00	.40
❑ 346 Bruce Taylor	.50	.25
❑ 347 Sam Havrilak	.50	.25
❑ 348 Walt Sumner	.50	.25
❑ 349 Steve O'Neal	.50	.25
❑ 350 Ron Johnson	1.00	.40
❑ 351 Rockne Freitas	.50	.25
❑ 352 Larry Stallings	.50	.25
❑ 353 Jim Cadile	.50	.25
❑ 354 Ken Burrough	1.00	.40
❑ 355 Jim Plunkett	4.00	2.00
❑ 356 Dave Long	.50	.25
❑ 357 Ralph Anderson	.50	.25
❑ 358 Checklist 265-396	5.00	2.50

❑ 359 Gene Washington Vik 1.00 .40
❑ 360 Dave Wilcox 1.50 .60
❑ 361 Paul Smith .50 .25
❑ 362 Alvin Wyatt .50 .25
❑ 363 Charlie Smith RB .50 .25
❑ 364 Royce Berry .50 .25
❑ 365 Dave Elmendorf .50 .25
❑ 366 Scott Hunter 1.00 .40
❑ 367 Bob Kuechenberg RC 3.00 1.25
❑ 368 Pete Gogolak .50 .25
❑ 369 Dave Edwards .50 .25
❑ 370 Lem Barney 2.50 1.25
❑ 371 Verlon Biggs .50 .25
❑ 372 John Reaves RC .50 .25
❑ 373 Ed Podolak 1.00 .40
❑ 374 Chris Farasopoulos .50 .25
❑ 375 Gary Garrison .50 .25
❑ 376 Tom Funchess .50 .25
❑ 377 Bobby Joe Green .50 .25
❑ 378 Don Brumm .50 .25
❑ 379 Jim O'Brien .50 .25
❑ 380 Paul Krause 1.50 .60
❑ 381 Leroy Kelly 2.50 1.25
❑ 382 Ray Mansfield .50 .25
❑ 383 Dan Abramowicz 1.00 .40
❑ 384 John Outlaw RC .50 .25
❑ 385 Tommy Nobis 1.50 .60
❑ 386 Tom Domres .50 .25
❑ 387 Ken Willard .50 .25
❑ 388 Mike Stratton .50 .25
❑ 389 Fred Dryer 2.50 1.25
❑ 390 Jake Scott 1.50 .60
❑ 391 Rich Houston .50 .25
❑ 392 Virgil Carter .50 .25
❑ 393 Tody Smith .50 .25
❑ 394 Ernie Calloway .50 .25
❑ 395 Charlie Sanders 1.25 .50
❑ 396 Fred Willis .50 .25
❑ 397 Curt Knight .50 .25
❑ 398 Nemiah Wilson .50 .25
❑ 399 Carroll Dale 1.00 .40
❑ 400 Joe Namath 30.00 15.00
❑ 401 Wayne Mulligan .50 .25
❑ 402 Jim Harrison .50 .25
❑ 403 Tim Rossovich .50 .25
❑ 404 David Lee .50 .25
❑ 405 Frank Pitts .50 .25
❑ 406 Jim Marshall 1.50 .60
❑ 407 Bob Brown TE .50 .25
❑ 408 John Rowser .50 .25
❑ 409 Mike Montler .50 .25
❑ 410 Willie Lanier 1.50 .60
❑ 411 Bill Bell K .50 .25
❑ 412 Cedrick Hardman .50 .25
❑ 413 Bob Anderson .50 .25
❑ 414 Earl Morrall 1.50 .60
❑ 415 Ken Houston 1.50 .60
❑ 416 Jack Snow 1.00 .40
❑ 417 Dick Cunningham .50 .25
❑ 418 Greg Larson .50 .25
❑ 419 Mike Bass 1.00 .40
❑ 420 Mike Reid 1.50 .60
❑ 421 Walt Garrison 1.50 .60
❑ 422 Pete Liske .50 .25
❑ 423 Jim Yarbrough .50 .25
❑ 424 Rich McGeorge .50 .25
❑ 425 Bobby Howfield .50 .25
❑ 426 Pete Banaszak .50 .25
❑ 427 Willie Holman .50 .25
❑ 428 Dale Hackbart .50 .25
❑ 429 Fair Hooker .50 .25
❑ 430 Ted Hendricks 5.00 2.50
❑ 431 Mike Garrett 1.00 .40
❑ 432 Glen Ray Hines .50 .25
❑ 433 Fred Cox .50 .25
❑ 434 Bobby Walden .50 .25
❑ 435 Bobby Bell 1.50 .60
❑ 436 Dave Rowe .50 .25
❑ 437 Bob Berry .50 .25
❑ 438 Bill Thompson .50 .25
❑ 439 Jim Beirne .50 .25
❑ 440 Larry Little 3.00 1.50
❑ 441 Rocky Thompson .50 .25
❑ 442 Brig Owens .50 .25
❑ 443 Richard Neal .50 .25
❑ 444 Al Nelson .50 .25
❑ 445 Chip Myers .50 .25
❑ 446 Ken Bowman .50 .25
❑ 447 Jim Purnell .50 .25
❑ 448 Altie Taylor .50 .25
❑ 449 Linzy Cole .50 .25
❑ 450 Bob Lilly 5.00 2.50
❑ 451 Charlie Ford .50 .25
❑ 452 Milt Sunde .50 .25
❑ 453 Doug Wyatt .50 .25
❑ 454 Don Nottingham RC 1.00 .40
❑ 455 Johnny Unitas 15.00 7.50
❑ 456 Frank Lewis RC 1.00 .40
❑ 457 Roger Wehrli 1.00 .40
❑ 458 Jim Cheyunski .50 .25
❑ 459 Jerry Sherk RC 1.00 .40
❑ 460 Gene Washington 49er 1.00 .40
❑ 461 Jim Otto 1.50 .60
❑ 462 Ed Budde .50 .25
❑ 463 Jim Mitchell TE 1.00 .40
❑ 464 Emerson Boozer 1.00 .40
❑ 465 Garo Yepremian 1.50 .60
❑ 466 Pete Duranko .50 .25
❑ 467 Charlie Joiner 8.00 4.00
❑ 468 Spider Lockhart 1.00 .40
❑ 469 Marty Domres .50 .25
❑ 470 John Brockington 1.50 .60
❑ 471 Ed Flanagan .50 .25
❑ 472 Roy Jefferson 1.00 .40
❑ 473 Julian Fagan .50 .25
❑ 474 Bill Brown 1.00 .40
❑ 475 Roger Staubach 30.00 15.00
❑ 476 Jan White RC .50 .25
❑ 477 Pat Holmes .50 .25
❑ 478 Bob DeMarco .50 .25
❑ 479 Merlin Olsen 2.50 1.25
❑ 480 Andy Russell 1.50 .60
❑ 481 Steve Spurrier 20.00 10.00
❑ 482 Nate Ramsey .50 .25
❑ 483 Dennis Partee .50 .25
❑ 484 Jerry Simmons .50 .25
❑ 485 Donny Anderson 1.50 .60
❑ 486 Ralph Baker .50 .25
❑ 487 Ken Stabler RC ! 60.00 35.00
❑ 488 Ernie McMillan .50 .25
❑ 489 Ken Burrow .50 .25
❑ 490 Jack Gregory RC .50 .25
❑ 491 Larry Seiple 1.00 .40
❑ 492 Mick Tingelhoff 1.00 .40
❑ 493 Craig Morton 1.50 .60
❑ 494 Cecil Turner .50 .25
❑ 495 Steve Owens 1.50 .60
❑ 496 Rickie Harris .50 .25
❑ 497 Buck Buchanan 1.50 .60
❑ 498 Checklist 397-528 5.00 2.50
❑ 499 Billy Kilmer 1.50 .60
❑ 500 O.J.Simpson 15.00 7.50
❑ 501 Bruce Gossett .50 .25
❑ 502 Art Thoms RC .50 .25
❑ 503 Larry Kaminski .50 .25
❑ 504 Larry Smith RB .50 .25
❑ 505 Bruce Van Dyke .50 .25
❑ 506 Alvin Reed .50 .25
❑ 507 Delles Howell .50 .25
❑ 508 Leroy Keyes .50 .25
❑ 509 Bo Scott 1.00 .40
❑ 510 Ron Yary 1.50 .60
❑ 511 Paul Warfield 5.00 2.50
❑ 512 Mac Percival .50 .25
❑ 513 Essex Johnson .50 .25
❑ 514 Jackie Smith 1.50 .60
❑ 515 Norm Snead 1.50 .60
❑ 516 Charlie Stukes .50 .25
❑ 517 Reggie Rucker RC 1.00 .40
❑ 518 Bill Sandeman UER .50 .25
❑ 519 Mel Farr 1.00 .40
❑ 520 Raymond Chester 1.00 .40
❑ 521 Fred Carr RC 1.00 .40
❑ 522 Jerry LeVias 1.00 .40
❑ 523 Jim Strong .50 .25
❑ 524 Roland McDole .50 .25
❑ 525 Dennis Shaw .50 .25
❑ 526 Dave Manders .50 .25
❑ 527 Skip Vanderbundt .50 .25
❑ 528 Mike Sensibaugh RC ! 1.50 .60

1974 Topps

❑ COMPLETE SET (528) 300.00 175.00
❑ 1 O.J.Simpson RB UER 20.00 10.00

❑ 2 Blaine Nye .40 .20
❑ 3 Don Hansen .40 .20
❑ 4 Ken Bowman .40 .20
❑ 5 Carl Eller 1.50 .60
❑ 6 Jerry Smith .40 .20
❑ 7 Ed Podolak .40 .20
❑ 8 Mel Gray 1.50 .60
❑ 9 Pat Matson .40 .20
❑ 10 Floyd Little 1.50 .60
❑ 11 Frank Pitts .40 .20
❑ 12 Vern Den Herder RC .75 .30
❑ 13 John Fuqua .75 .30
❑ 14 Jack Tatum 2.00 .75
❑ 15 Winston Hill .40 .20
❑ 16 John Beasley .40 .20
❑ 17 David Lee .40 .20
❑ 18 Rich Coady .40 .20
❑ 19 Ken Willard .40 .20
❑ 20 Coy Bacon .75 .30
❑ 21 Ben Hawkins .40 .20
❑ 22 Paul Guidry .40 .20
❑ 23 Norm Snead HOR .75 .30
❑ 24 Jim Yarbrough .40 .20
❑ 25 Jack Reynolds RC 3.00 1.25
❑ 26 Josh Ashton .40 .20
❑ 27 Donnie Green .40 .20
❑ 28 Bob Hayes 1.50 .60
❑ 29 John Zook .40 .20
❑ 30 Bobby Bryant .40 .20
❑ 31 Scott Hunter .75 .30
❑ 32 Dan Dierdorf 6.00 3.00
❑ 33 Curt Knight .40 .20
❑ 34 Elmo Wright RC .40 .20
❑ 35 Essex Johnson .40 .20
❑ 36 Walt Sumner .40 .20
❑ 37 Marv Montgomery .40 .20
❑ 38 Tim Foley .75 .30
❑ 39 Mike Siani .40 .20
❑ 40 Joe Greene 6.00 3.00
❑ 41 Bobby Howfield .40 .20
❑ 42 Del Williams .40 .20
❑ 43 Don McCauley .40 .20
❑ 44 Randy Jackson .40 .20
❑ 45 Ron Smith .40 .20
❑ 46 Gene Washington 49er .75 .30
❑ 47 Po James .40 .20
❑ 48 Solomon Freelon .40 .20
❑ 49 Bob Windsor HOR .40 .20
❑ 50 John Hadl 1.50 .60
❑ 51 Greg Larson .40 .20
❑ 52 Steve Owens .75 .30
❑ 53 Jim Cheyunski .40 .20
❑ 54 Rayfield Wright .75 .30
❑ 55 Dave Hampton .40 .20
❑ 56 Ron Widby .40 .20
❑ 57 Milt Sunde .40 .20
❑ 58 Billy Kilmer 1.50 .60
❑ 59 Bobby Bell 1.50 .60
❑ 60 Jim Bakken .40 .20
❑ 61 Rufus Mayes .40 .20
❑ 62 Vic Washington .40 .20
❑ 63 Gene Washington Vik .75 .30
❑ 64 Clarence Scott .40 .20
❑ 65 Gene Upshaw 2.00 .75
❑ 66 Larry Seiple .75 .30
❑ 67 John McMakin .40 .20
❑ 68 Ralph Baker .40 .20
❑ 69 Lydell Mitchell .75 .30
❑ 70 Archie Manning 2.50 1.25
❑ 71 George Farmer .40 .20

❑ 72 Ron East .40 .20
❑ 73 Al Nelson .40 .20
❑ 74 Pat Hughes .40 .20
❑ 75 Fred Willis .40 .20
❑ 76 Larry Walton .40 .20
❑ 77 Tom Neville .40 .20
❑ 78 Ted Kwalick .40 .20
❑ 79 Walt Patulski .40 .20
❑ 80 John Niland .40 .20
❑ 81 Ted Fritsch Jr. .40 .20
❑ 82 Paul Krause 1.50 .60
❑ 83 Jack Snow .75 .30
❑ 84 Mike Bass .40 .20
❑ 85 Jim Tyrer .40 .20
❑ 86 Ron Yankowski .40 .20
❑ 87 Mike Phipps .75 .30
❑ 88 Al Beauchamp .40 .20
❑ 89 Riley Odoms RC 1.50 .60
❑ 90 MacArthur Lane .40 .20
❑ 91 Art Thoms .40 .20
❑ 92 Marlin Briscoe .40 .20
❑ 93 Bruce Van Dyke .40 .20
❑ 94 Tom Myers RC .40 .20
❑ 95 Calvin Hill 1.50 .60
❑ 96 Bruce Laird .40 .20
❑ 97 Tony McGee DT .40 .20
❑ 98 Len Rohde .40 .20
❑ 99 Tom McNeill .40 .20
❑ 100 Delles Howell .40 .20
❑ 101 Gary Garrison .40 .20
❑ 102 Dan Goich .40 .20
❑ 103 Len St. Jean .40 .20
❑ 104 Zeke Moore .40 .20
❑ 105 Ahmad Rashad RC 20.00 10.00
❑ 106 Mel Renfro 1.50 .60
❑ 107 Jim Mitchell TE .40 .20
❑ 108 Ed Budde .40 .20
❑ 109 Harry Schuh .40 .20
❑ 110 Greg Pruitt RC 4.00 2.00
❑ 111 Ed Flanagan .40 .20
❑ 112 Larry Stallings .40 .20
❑ 113 Chuck Foreman RC 4.00 2.00
❑ 114 Royce Berry .40 .20
❑ 115 Gale Gillingham .40 .20
❑ 116 Charlie Johnson HOR 1.50 .60
❑ 117 Checklist 1-132 UER 4.00 2.00
❑ 118 Bill Butler .40 .20
❑ 119 Roy Jefferson .75 .30
❑ 120 Bobby Douglass .75 .30
❑ 121 Harold Carmichael RC 12.00 6.00
❑ 122 George Kunz AP .40 .20
❑ 123 Larry Little 2.00 .75
❑ 124 Forrest Blue AP .40 .20
❑ 125 Ron Yary 1.50 .60
❑ 126 Tom Mack AP 1.50 .60
❑ 127 Bob Tucker AP .75 .30
❑ 128 Paul Warfield 4.00 2.00
❑ 129 Fran Tarkenton 10.00 5.00
❑ 130 O.J.Simpson 12.00 6.00
❑ 131 Larry Csonka 6.00 3.00
❑ 132 Bruce Gossett AP .40 .20
❑ 133 Bill Stanfill AP .75 .30
❑ 134 Alan Page 2.50 1.25
❑ 135 Paul Smith AP .40 .20
❑ 136 Claude Humphrey AP .75 .30
❑ 137 Jack Ham 10.00 5.00
❑ 138 Lee Roy Jordan 1.50 .60
❑ 139 Phil Villapiano AP .75 .30
❑ 140 Ken Ellis AP .40 .20
❑ 141 Willie Brown 1.50 .60
❑ 142 Dick Anderson AP .75 .30
❑ 143 Bill Bradley AP .75 .30
❑ 144 Jerrel Wilson AP .40 .20
❑ 145 Reggie Rucker .75 .30
❑ 146 Marty Domres .40 .20
❑ 147 Bob Kowalkowski .40 .20
❑ 148 John Matuszak RC 6.00 2.50
❑ 149 Mike Adamle RC .75 .30
❑ 150 Johnny Unitas 15.00 7.50
❑ 151 Charlie Ford .40 .20
❑ 152 Bob Klein RC .40 .20
❑ 153 Jim Merlo .40 .20
❑ 154 Willie Young .40 .20
❑ 155 Donny Anderson .75 .30
❑ 156 Brig Owens .40 .20
❑ 157 Bruce Jarvis .40 .20
❑ 158 Ron Carpenter RC .40 .20
❑ 159 Don Cockroft .40 .20
❑ 160 Tommy Nobis 1.50 .60
❑ 161 Craig Morton 1.50 .60
❑ 162 Jon Staggers .40 .20
❑ 163 Mike Eischeid .40 .20
❑ 164 Jerry Sisemore RC .40 .20
❑ 165 Cedrick Hardman .40 .20
❑ 166 Bill Thompson .75 .30
❑ 167 Jim Lynch .75 .30
❑ 168 Bob Moore .40 .20
❑ 169 Glen Edwards .40 .20
❑ 170 Mercury Morris 1.50 .60
❑ 171 Julius Adams .40 .20
❑ 172 Cotton Speyrer .40 .20
❑ 173 Bill Munson .75 .30
❑ 174 Benny Johnson .40 .20
❑ 175 Burgess Owens RC .40 .20
❑ 176 Cid Edwards .40 .20
❑ 177 Doug Buffone .40 .20
❑ 178 Charlie Cowan .40 .20
❑ 179 Bob Newland .40 .20
❑ 180 Ron Johnson .75 .30
❑ 181 Bob Rowe .40 .20
❑ 182 Len Hauss .40 .20
❑ 183 Joe DeLamielleure RC 8.00 3.00
❑ 184 Sherman White RC .40 .20
❑ 185 Fair Hooker .40 .20
❑ 186 Nick Mike-Mayer .40 .20
❑ 187 Ralph Neely .40 .20
❑ 188 Rich McGeorge .40 .20
❑ 189 Ed Marinaro RC 4.00 1.50
❑ 190 Dave Wilcox 1.50 .60
❑ 191 Joe Owens RC .40 .20
❑ 192 Bill Van Heusen .40 .20
❑ 193 Jim Kearney .40 .20
❑ 194 Otis Sistrunk RC 1.50 .60
❑ 195 Ron Shanklin .40 .20
❑ 196 Bill Lenkaitis .40 .20
❑ 197 Tom Drougas .40 .20
❑ 198 Larry Hand .40 .20
❑ 199 Mack Alston .40 .20
❑ 200 Bob Griese 6.00 3.00
❑ 201 Earlie Thomas .40 .20
❑ 202 Carl Gersbach .40 .20
❑ 203 Jim Harrison .40 .20
❑ 204 Jake Kupp .40 .20
❑ 205 Merlin Olsen 2.00 .75
❑ 206 Spider Lockhart .75 .30
❑ 207 Walker Gillette .40 .20
❑ 208 Verlon Biggs .40 .20
❑ 209 Bob James .40 .20
❑ 210 Bob Trumpy 1.50 .60
❑ 211 Jerry Sherk .40 .20
❑ 212 Andy Maurer .40 .20
❑ 213 Fred Carr .40 .20
❑ 214 Mick Tingelhoff .75 .30
❑ 215 Steve Spurrier 15.00 7.50
❑ 216 Richard Harris .40 .20
❑ 217 Charlie Greer .40 .20
❑ 218 Buck Buchanan 1.50 .60
❑ 219 Ray Guy RC 10.00 5.00
❑ 220 Franco Harris 12.00 6.00
❑ 221 Darryl Stingley RC 1.50 .60
❑ 222 Rex Kern .40 .20
❑ 223 Toni Fritsch .75 .30
❑ 224 Levi Johnson .40 .20
❑ 225 Bob Kuechenberg .75 .30
❑ 226 Elvin Bethea 1.50 .60
❑ 227 Al Woodall RC .75 .30
❑ 228 Terry Owens .40 .20
❑ 229 Bivian Lee .40 .20
❑ 230 Dick Butkus 10.00 5.00
❑ 231 Jim Bertelsen RC .75 .30
❑ 232 John Mendenhall RC .40 .20
❑ 233 Conrad Dobler RC 1.50 .60
❑ 234 J.D. Hill .75 .30
❑ 235 Ken Houston 1.50 .60
❑ 236 Dave Lewis .40 .20
❑ 237 John Garlington .40 .20
❑ 238 Bill Sandeman .40 .20
❑ 239 Alden Roche .40 .20
❑ 240 John Gilliam .75 .30
❑ 241 Bruce Taylor .40 .20
❑ 242 Vern Winfield .40 .20
❑ 243 Bobby Maples .40 .20
❑ 244 Wendell Hayes .40 .20
❑ 245 George Blanda 8.00 4.00
❑ 246 Dwight White .75 .30
❑ 247 Sandy Durko .40 .20
❑ 248 Tom Mitchell .40 .20
❑ 249 Chuck Walton .40 .20
❑ 250 Bob Lilly 4.00 2.00
❑ 251 Doug Swift .40 .20
❑ 252 Lynn Dickey RC 1.50 .60
❑ 253 Jerome Barkum RC .40 .20
❑ 254 Clint Jones .40 .20
❑ 255 Billy Newsome .40 .20
❑ 256 Bob Asher .40 .20
❑ 257 Joe Scibelli .40 .20
❑ 258 Tom Blanchard .40 .20
❑ 259 Norm Thompson .40 .20
❑ 260 Larry Brown 1.50 .60
❑ 261 Paul Seymour .40 .20
❑ 262 Checklist 133-264 4.00 2.00
❑ 263 Doug Dieken RC .40 .20
❑ 264 Lemar Parrish .75 .30
❑ 265 Bob Lee UER .40 .20
❑ 266 Bob Brown DT .40 .20
❑ 267 Roy Winston .40 .20
❑ 268 Randy Beisler .40 .20
❑ 269 Joe Dawkins .40 .20
❑ 270 Tom Dempsey .75 .30
❑ 271 Jack Rudnay .40 .20
❑ 272 Art Shell 5.00 2.50
❑ 273 Mike Wagner .75 .30
❑ 274 Rick Cash .40 .20
❑ 275 Greg Landry 1.50 .60
❑ 276 Glenn Ressler .40 .20
❑ 277 Billy Joe DuPree RC 3.00 1.25
❑ 278 Norm Evans .40 .20
❑ 279 Billy Parks .40 .20
❑ 280 John Riggins 6.00 3.00
❑ 281 Lionel Aldridge .40 .20
❑ 282 Steve O'Neal .40 .20
❑ 283 Craig Clemons .40 .20
❑ 284 Willie Williams .40 .20
❑ 285 Isiah Robertson .75 .30
❑ 286 Dennis Shaw .40 .20
❑ 287 Bill Brundige .40 .20
❑ 288 John Leypoldt .40 .20
❑ 289 John DeMarie .40 .20
❑ 290 Mike Reid 1.50 .60
❑ 291 Greg Brezina .40 .20
❑ 292 Willie Buchanon RC .40 .20
❑ 293 Dave Osborn .75 .30
❑ 294 Mel Phillips .40 .20
❑ 295 Haven Moses .75 .30
❑ 296 Wade Key .40 .20
❑ 297 Marvin Upshaw .40 .20
❑ 298 Ray Mansfield .40 .20
❑ 299 Edgar Chandler .40 .20
❑ 300 Marv Hubbard .75 .30
❑ 301 Herman Weaver .40 .20
❑ 302 Jim Bailey .40 .20
❑ 303 D.D.Lewis RC 1.50 .60
❑ 304 Ken Burrough .75 .30
❑ 305 Jake Scott 1.50 .60
❑ 306 Randy Rasmussen .40 .20
❑ 307 Pettis Norman .40 .20
❑ 308 Carl Johnson .40 .20
❑ 309 Joe Taylor .40 .20
❑ 310 Pete Gogolak .40 .20
❑ 311 Tony Baker FB .40 .20
❑ 312 John Richardson .40 .20
❑ 313 Dave Robinson .75 .30
❑ 314 Reggie McKenzie RC 1.50 .60
❑ 315 Isaac Curtis RC 1.50 .60
❑ 316 Thom Darden .40 .20
❑ 317 Ken Reaves .40 .20
❑ 318 Malcolm Snider .40 .20
❑ 319 Jeff Siemon RC .75 .30
❑ 320 Dan Abramowicz .75 .30
❑ 321 Lyle Alzado 2.00 .75
❑ 322 John Reaves .40 .20
❑ 323 Morris Stroud .40 .20
❑ 324 Bobby Walden .40 .20
❑ 325 Randy Vataha .40 .20
❑ 326 Nemiah Wilson .40 .20
❑ 327 Paul Naumoff .40 .20
❑ 328 O.J.Simpson/Brock. LL 3.00 1.50
❑ 329 R.Staubach/Stabler LL 5.00 2.50
❑ 330 Harold Carmichael/Wil LL 1.50 .60
❑ 331 Scoring Leaders .75 .30
❑ 332 Interception Leaders .75 .30

❑ 333 Punting Leaders .75 .30
❑ 334 Dennis Nelson .40 .20
❑ 335 Walt Garrison .75 .30
❑ 336 Tody Smith .40 .20
❑ 337 Ed Bell .40 .20
❑ 338 Bryant Salter .40 .20
❑ 339 Wayne Colman .40 .20
❑ 340 Garo Yepremian .75 .30
❑ 341 Bob Newton .40 .20
❑ 342 Vince Clements RC .40 .20
❑ 343 Ken Iman .40 .20
❑ 344 Jim Tolbert .40 .20
❑ 345 Chris Hanburger .75 .30
❑ 346 Dave Foley .40 .20
❑ 347 Tommy Casanova .75 .30
❑ 348 John James .40 .20
❑ 349 Clarence Williams .40 .20
❑ 350 Leroy Kelly 1.50 .60
❑ 351 Stu Voigt RC .75 .30
❑ 352 Skip Vanderbundt .40 .20
❑ 353 Pete Duranko .40 .20
❑ 354 John Outlaw .40 .20
❑ 355 Jan Stenerud 1.50 .60
❑ 356 Barry Pearson .40 .20
❑ 357 Brian Dowling RC .40 .20
❑ 358 Dan Conners .40 .20
❑ 359 Bob Bell .40 .20
❑ 360 Rick Volk .40 .20
❑ 361 Pat Toomay .75 .30
❑ 362 Bob Gresham .40 .20
❑ 363 John Schmitt .40 .20
❑ 364 Mel Rogers .40 .20
❑ 365 Manny Fernandez .75 .30
❑ 366 Ernie Jackson .40 .20
❑ 367 Gary Huff RC .75 .30
❑ 368 Bob Grim .40 .20
❑ 369 Ernie McMillan .40 .20
❑ 370 Dave Elmendorf .40 .20
❑ 371 Mike Bragg .40 .20
❑ 372 John Skorupan .40 .20
❑ 373 Howard Fest .40 .20
❑ 374 Jerry Tagge RC .75 .30
❑ 375 Art Malone .40 .20
❑ 376 Bob Babich .40 .20
❑ 377 Jim Marshall 1.50 .60
❑ 378 Bob Hoskins .40 .20
❑ 379 Don Zimmerman .40 .20
❑ 380 Ray May .40 .20
❑ 381 Emmitt Thomas .75 .30
❑ 382 Terry Hanratty .75 .30
❑ 383 John Hannah RC 15.00 7.50
❑ 384 George Atkinson .40 .20
❑ 385 Ted Hendricks 3.00 1.50
❑ 386 Jim O'Brien .40 .20
❑ 387 Jethro Pugh .75 .30
❑ 388 Elbert Drungo .40 .20
❑ 389 Richard Caster .75 .30
❑ 390 Deacon Jones 1.50 .60
❑ 391 Checklist 265-396 4.00 2.00
❑ 392 Jess Phillips .40 .20
❑ 393 Garry Lyle UER .40 .20
❑ 394 Jim Files .40 .20
❑ 395 Jim Hart 1.50 .60
❑ 396 Dave Chapple .40 .20
❑ 397 Jim Langer 2.00 .75
❑ 398 John Wilbur .40 .20
❑ 399 Dwight Harrison .40 .20
❑ 400 John Brockington .75 .30
❑ 401 Ken Anderson 6.00 3.00
❑ 402 Mike Tilleman .40 .20
❑ 403 Charlie Hall .40 .20
❑ 404 Tommy Hart .40 .20
❑ 405 Norm Bulaich .75 .30
❑ 406 Jim Turner .40 .20
❑ 407 Mo Moorman .40 .20
❑ 408 Ralph Anderson .40 .20
❑ 409 Jim Otto 1.50 .60
❑ 410 Andy Russell 1.50 .60
❑ 411 Glenn Doughty .40 .20
❑ 412 Altie Taylor .40 .20
❑ 413 Marv Bateman .40 .20
❑ 414 Willie Alexander .40 .20
❑ 415 Bill Zapalac RC .40 .20
❑ 416 Russ Washington .40 .20
❑ 417 Joe Federspiel .40 .20
❑ 418 Craig Cotton .40 .20
❑ 419 Randy Johnson .40 .20
❑ 420 Harold Jackson 1.50 .60
❑ 421 Roger Wehrli 1.00 .40
❑ 422 Charlie Harraway .40 .20
❑ 423 Spike Jones .40 .20
❑ 424 Bob Johnson .40 .20
❑ 425 Mike McCoy DT .40 .20
❑ 426 Dennis Havig .40 .20
❑ 427 Bob McKay RC .40 .20
❑ 428 Steve Zabel .40 .20
❑ 429 Horace Jones .40 .20
❑ 430 Jim Johnson 1.50 .60
❑ 431 Roy Gerela .75 .30
❑ 432 Tom Graham RC .40 .20
❑ 433 Curley Culp .75 .30
❑ 434 Ken Mendenhall .40 .20
❑ 435 Jim Plunkett 2.50 1.25
❑ 436 Julian Fagan .40 .20
❑ 437 Mike Garrett .75 .30
❑ 438 Bobby Joe Green .40 .20
❑ 439 Jack Gregory .40 .20
❑ 440 Charlie Sanders 1.00 .40
❑ 441 Bill Curry .75 .30
❑ 442 Bob Pollard .40 .20
❑ 443 David Ray .40 .20
❑ 444 Terry Metcalf RC 3.00 1.50
❑ 445 Pat Fischer .75 .30
❑ 446 Bob Chandler .75 .30
❑ 447 Bill Bergey .75 .30
❑ 448 Walter Johnson .40 .20
❑ 449 Charle Young RC 1.50 .60
❑ 450 Chester Marcol .40 .20
❑ 451 Ken Stabler 20.00 10.00
❑ 452 Preston Pearson 1.50 .60
❑ 453 Mike Current .40 .20
❑ 454 Ron Bolton .40 .20
❑ 455 Mark Lomas .40 .20
❑ 456 Raymond Chester .75 .30
❑ 457 Jerry LeVias .75 .30
❑ 458 Skip Butler .40 .20
❑ 459 Mike Livingston RC .40 .20
❑ 460 AFC Semi-Final .75 .30
❑ 461 NFC Semi/Staubach 4.00 2.00
❑ 462 Playoff Champs/Stabler 3.00 1.50
❑ 463 SB VIII/Tarkenton 2.00 .75
❑ 464 Wayne Mulligan .40 .20
❑ 465 Horst Muhlmann .40 .20
❑ 466 Milt Morin .40 .20
❑ 467 Don Parish .40 .20
❑ 468 Richard Neal .40 .20
❑ 469 Ron Jessie .75 .30
❑ 470 Terry Bradshaw 25.00 12.50
❑ 471 Fred Dryer 1.50 .60
❑ 472 Jim Carter .40 .20
❑ 473 Ken Burrow .40 .20
❑ 474 Wally Chambers RC .75 .30
❑ 475 Dan Pastorini 1.50 .60
❑ 476 Don Morrison .40 .20
❑ 477 Carl Mauck .40 .20
❑ 478 Larry Cole RC .75 .30
❑ 479 Jim Kiick 1.50 .60
❑ 480 Willie Lanier 1.50 .60
❑ 481 Don Herrmann .75 .30
❑ 482 George Hunt .40 .20
❑ 483 Bob Howard RC .40 .20
❑ 484 Myron Pottios .40 .20
❑ 485 Jackie Smith 1.50 .60
❑ 486 Vern Holland .40 .20
❑ 487 Jim Braxton .40 .20
❑ 488 Joe Reed .40 .20
❑ 489 Wally Hilgenberg .40 .20
❑ 490 Fred Biletnikoff 4.00 2.00
❑ 491 Bob DeMarco .40 .20
❑ 492 Mark Nordquist .40 .20
❑ 493 Larry Brooks .40 .20
❑ 494 Pete Athas .40 .20
❑ 495 Emerson Boozer .75 .30
❑ 496 L.C.Greenwood 2.00 .75
❑ 497 Rockne Freitas .40 .20
❑ 498 Checklist 397-528 UER 4.00 2.00
❑ 499 Joe Schmiesing .40 .20
❑ 500 Roger Staubach 25.00 12.50
❑ 501 Al Cowlings UER .75 .30
❑ 502 Sam Cunningham RC 1.50 .60
❑ 503 Dennis Partee .40 .20
❑ 504 John Didion .40 .20
❑ 505 Nick Buoniconti 1.50 .60
❑ 506 Carl Garrett .75 .30
❑ 507 Doug Van Horn .40 .20
❑ 508 Jamie Rivers .40 .20
❑ 509 Jack Youngblood 4.00 2.00
❑ 510 Charley Taylor UER 2.50 1.25
❑ 511 Ken Riley 1.50 .60
❑ 512 Joe Ferguson RC 3.00 1.25
❑ 513 Bill Lueck .40 .20
❑ 514 Ray Brown DB RC .40 .20
❑ 515 Fred Cox .40 .20
❑ 516 Joe Jones DE .40 .20
❑ 517 Larry Schreiber .40 .20
❑ 518 Dennis Wirgowski .40 .20
❑ 519 Leroy Mitchell .40 .20
❑ 520 Otis Taylor 1.50 .60
❑ 521 Henry Davis .40 .20
❑ 522 Bruce Barnes .40 .20
❑ 523 Charlie Smith RB .40 .20
❑ 524 Bert Jones RC 5.00 2.00
❑ 525 Lem Barney 2.00 .75
❑ 526 John Fitzgerald RC .40 .20
❑ 527 Tom Funchess .40 .20
❑ 528 Steve Tannen 1.50 .60

1975 Topps

❑ COMPLETE SET (528) 300.00 175.00
❑ 1 McCutcheon/Armstrong LL 1.50 .60
❑ 2 Jurgensen/K.Anderson LL 1.50 .60
❑ 3 Receiving Leaders 1.50 .60
❑ 4 Scoring Leaders .75 .30
❑ 5 Interception Leaders .75 .30
❑ 6 Punting Leaders 1.50 .60
❑ 7 George Blanda HL 5.00 2.50
❑ 8 George Blanda 5.00 2.50
❑ 9 Ralph Baker .30 .15
❑ 10 Don Woods .30 .15
❑ 11 Bob Asher .30 .15
❑ 12 Mel Blount RC 20.00 10.00
❑ 13 Sam Cunningham .75 .30
❑ 14 Jackie Smith 1.50 .60
❑ 15 Greg Landry .75 .30
❑ 16 Buck Buchanan 1.50 .60
❑ 17 Haven Moses .75 .30
❑ 18 Clarence Ellis .30 .15
❑ 19 Jim Carter .30 .15
❑ 20 Charley Taylor UER 2.00 .75
❑ 21 Jess Phillips .30 .15
❑ 22 Larry Seiple .30 .15
❑ 23 Doug Dieken .30 .15
❑ 24 Ron Saul .30 .15
❑ 25 Isaac Curtis 1.50 .60
❑ 26 Gary Larsen RC .30 .15
❑ 27 Bruce Jarvis .30 .15
❑ 28 Steve Zabel .30 .15
❑ 29 John Mendenhall .30 .15
❑ 30 Rick Volk .30 .15
❑ 31 Checklist 1-132 4.00 2.00
❑ 32 Dan Abramowicz .75 .30
❑ 33 Bubba Smith 1.50 .60
❑ 34 David Ray .30 .15
❑ 35 Dan Dierdorf 4.00 2.00
❑ 36 Randy Rasmussen .30 .15
❑ 37 Bob Howard .30 .15
❑ 38 Gary Huff .75 .30
❑ 39 Rocky Bleier RC 20.00 10.00
❑ 40 Mel Gray .75 .30
❑ 41 Tony McGee DT .30 .15
❑ 42 Larry Hand .30 .15
❑ 43 Wendell Hayes .30 .15
❑ 44 Doug Wilkerson RC .30 .15

❑ 45 Paul Smith .30 .15
❑ 46 Dave Robinson .75 .30
❑ 47 Bivian Lee .30 .15
❑ 48 Jim Mandich RC .75 .30
❑ 49 Greg Pruitt 1.50 .60
❑ 50 Dan Pastorini 1.50 .60
❑ 51 Ron Pritchard .30 .15
❑ 52 Dan Conners .30 .15
❑ 53 Fred Cox .30 .15
❑ 54 Tony Greene .30 .15
❑ 55 Craig Morton 1.50 .60
❑ 56 Jerry Sisemore .30 .15
❑ 57 Glenn Doughty .30 .15
❑ 58 Larry Schreiber .30 .15
❑ 59 Charlie Waters RC 4.00 2.00
❑ 60 Jack Youngblood 1.50 .60
❑ 61 Bill Lenkaitis .30 .15
❑ 62 Greg Brezina .30 .15
❑ 63 Bob Pollard .30 .15
❑ 64 Mack Alston .30 .15
❑ 65 Drew Pearson RC 20.00 10.00
❑ 66 Charlie Stukes .30 .15
❑ 67 Emerson Boozer .75 .30
❑ 68 Dennis Partee .30 .15
❑ 69 Bob Newton .30 .15
❑ 70 Jack Tatum 1.50 .60
❑ 71 Frank Lewis .30 .15
❑ 72 Bob Young .30 .15
❑ 73 Julius Adams .30 .15
❑ 74 Paul Naumoff .30 .15
❑ 75 Otis Taylor 1.50 .60
❑ 76 Dave Hampton .30 .15
❑ 77 Mike Current .30 .15
❑ 78 Brig Owens .30 .15
❑ 79 Bobby Scott .30 .15
❑ 80 Harold Carmichael 3.00 1.50
❑ 81 Bill Stanfill .30 .15
❑ 82 Bob Babich .30 .15
❑ 83 Vic Washington .30 .15
❑ 84 Mick Tingelhoff .75 .30
❑ 85 Bob Trumpy 1.50 .60
❑ 86 Earl Edwards .30 .15
❑ 87 Ron Hornsby .30 .15
❑ 88 Don McCauley .30 .15
❑ 89 Jim Johnson 1.50 .60
❑ 90 Andy Russell .75 .30
❑ 91 Cornell Green 1.50 .60
❑ 92 Charlie Cowan .30 .15
❑ 93 Jon Staggers .30 .15
❑ 94 Billy Newsome .30 .15
❑ 95 Willie Brown 1.50 .60
❑ 96 Carl Mauck .30 .15
❑ 97 Doug Buffone .30 .15
❑ 98 Preston Pearson .75 .30
❑ 99 Jim Bakken .30 .15
❑ 100 Bob Griese 5.00 2.50
❑ 101 Bob Windsor .30 .15
❑ 102 Rockne Freitas .30 .15
❑ 103 Jim Marsalis .30 .15
❑ 104 Bill Thompson .75 .30
❑ 105 Ken Burrow .30 .15
❑ 106 Diron Talbert .30 .15
❑ 107 Joe Federspiel .30 .15
❑ 108 Norm Bulaich .75 .30
❑ 109 Bob DeMarco .30 .15
❑ 110 Tom Wittum .30 .15
❑ 111 Larry Hefner .30 .15
❑ 112 Tody Smith .30 .15
❑ 113 Stu Voigt .30 .15
❑ 114 Horst Muhlmann .30 .15
❑ 115 Ahmad Rashad 6.00 3.00
❑ 116 Joe Dawkins .30 .15
❑ 117 George Kunz .30 .15
❑ 118 D.D.Lewis .75 .30
❑ 119 Levi Johnson .30 .15
❑ 120 Len Dawson 4.00 2.00
❑ 121 Jim Bertelsen .30 .15
❑ 122 Ed Bell .30 .15
❑ 123 Art Thoms .30 .15
❑ 124 Joe Beauchamp .30 .15
❑ 125 Jack Ham 6.00 3.00
❑ 126 Carl Garrett .30 .15
❑ 127 Roger Finnie .30 .15
❑ 128 Howard Twilley .75 .30
❑ 129 Bruce Barnes .30 .15
❑ 130 Nate Wright .30 .15
❑ 131 Jerry Tagge .30 .15
❑ 132 Floyd Little 1.50 .60
❑ 133 John Zook .30 .15
❑ 134 Len Hauss .30 .15
❑ 135 Archie Manning 1.50 .60
❑ 136 Po James .30 .15
❑ 137 Walt Sumner .30 .15
❑ 138 Randy Beisler .30 .15
❑ 139 Willie Alexander .30 .15
❑ 140 Garo Yepremian .75 .30
❑ 141 Chip Myers .30 .15
❑ 142 Jim Braxton .30 .15
❑ 143 Doug Van Horn .30 .15
❑ 144 Stan White .30 .15
❑ 145 Roger Staubach 20.00 10.00
❑ 146 Herman Weaver .30 .15
❑ 147 Marvin Upshaw .30 .15
❑ 148 Bob Klein .30 .15
❑ 149 Earlie Thomas .30 .15
❑ 150 John Brockington .75 .30
❑ 151 Mike Siani .30 .15
❑ 152 Sam Davis RC .30 .15
❑ 153 Mike Wagner .75 .30
❑ 154 Larry Stallings .30 .15
❑ 155 Wally Chambers .30 .15
❑ 156 Randy Vataha .30 .15
❑ 157 Jim Marshall 1.50 .60
❑ 158 Jim Turner .30 .15
❑ 159 Walt Sweeney .30 .15
❑ 160 Ken Anderson 4.00 2.00
❑ 161 Ray Brown DB .30 .15
❑ 162 John Didion .30 .15
❑ 163 Tom Dempsey .30 .15
❑ 164 Clarence Scott .30 .15
❑ 165 Gene Washington 49er .75 .30
❑ 166 Willie Rodgers RC .30 .15
❑ 167 Doug Swift .30 .15
❑ 168 Rufus Mayes .30 .15
❑ 169 Marv Bateman .30 .15
❑ 170 Lydell Mitchell .75 .30
❑ 171 Ron Smith .30 .15
❑ 172 Bill Munson .75 .30
❑ 173 Bob Grim .30 .15
❑ 174 Ed Budde .30 .15
❑ 175 Bob Lilly UER 4.00 2.00
❑ 176 Jim Youngblood RC 1.50 .60
❑ 177 Steve Tannen .30 .15
❑ 178 Rich McGeorge .30 .15
❑ 179 Jim Tyrer .30 .15
❑ 180 Forrest Blue .30 .15
❑ 181 Jerry LeVias .75 .30
❑ 182 Joe Gilliam RC 1.50 .60
❑ 183 Jim Otis RC .75 .30
❑ 184 Mel Tom .30 .15
❑ 185 Paul Seymour .30 .15
❑ 186 George Webster .30 .15
❑ 187 Pete Duranko .30 .15
❑ 188 Essex Johnson .30 .15
❑ 189 Bob Lee .75 .30
❑ 190 Gene Upshaw 1.50 .60
❑ 191 Tom Myers .30 .15
❑ 192 Don Zimmerman .30 .15
❑ 193 John Garlington .30 .15
❑ 194 Skip Butler .30 .15
❑ 195 Tom Mitchell .30 .15
❑ 196 Jim Langer 1.50 .60
❑ 197 Ron Carpenter .30 .15
❑ 198 Dave Foley .30 .15
❑ 199 Bert Jones 1.50 .60
❑ 200 Larry Brown .75 .30
❑ 201 Biletnikoff/C.Taylor AP 2.00 .75
❑ 202 All Pro Tackles .30 .15
❑ 203 L.Little/T.Mack AP 1.50 .60
❑ 204 All Pro Centers .30 .15
❑ 205 Hannah/Gillingham AP 1.50 .60
❑ 206 Dan Dierdorf/W.Hill AP 1.50 .60
❑ 207 All Pro Tight Ends .75 .30
❑ 208 F.Tarkenton/Stabler AP 4.00 2.00
❑ 209 Simpson/McCutch. AP 3.00 1.50
❑ 210 All Pro Backs .75 .30
❑ 211 All Pro Receivers .75 .30
❑ 212 All Pro Kickers .30 .15
❑ 213 Youngblood/Bethea AP 1.50 .60
❑ 214 All Pro Tackles .75 .30
❑ 215 M.Olsen/M.Reid AP 1.50 .60
❑ 216 Carl Eller/L.Alzado AP 1.50 .60
❑ 217 Hendricks/Villapiano AP 1.50 .60
❑ 218 Willie Lanier/Jordan AP 1.50 .60
❑ 219 All Pro Linebackers .75 .30
❑ 220 All Pro Cornerbacks .30 .15
❑ 221 All Pro Cornerbacks .30 .15
❑ 222 K.Houston/D.Anderson AP .75 .30
❑ 223 Cliff Harris/J.Tatum AP 1.50 .60
❑ 224 All Pro Punters .75 .30
❑ 225 All Pro Returners .75 .30
❑ 226 Ted Kwalick .30 .15
❑ 227 Spider Lockhart .75 .30
❑ 228 Mike Livingston .30 .15
❑ 229 Larry Cole .30 .15
❑ 230 Gary Garrison .30 .15
❑ 231 Larry Brooks .30 .15
❑ 232 Bobby Howfield .30 .15
❑ 233 Fred Carr .30 .15
❑ 234 Norm Evans .30 .15
❑ 235 Dwight White .75 .30
❑ 236 Conrad Dobler .75 .30
❑ 237 Garry Lyle .30 .15
❑ 238 Darryl Stingley 1.50 .60
❑ 239 Tom Graham .30 .15
❑ 240 Chuck Foreman 1.50 .60
❑ 241 Ken Riley .75 .30
❑ 242 Don Morrison .30 .15
❑ 243 Lynn Dickey .75 .30
❑ 244 Don Cockroft .30 .15
❑ 245 Claude Humphrey .75 .30
❑ 246 John Skorupan .30 .15
❑ 247 Raymond Chester .75 .30
❑ 248 Cas Banaszek .30 .15
❑ 249 Art Malone .30 .15
❑ 250 Ed Flanagan .30 .15
❑ 251 Checklist 133-264 4.00 2.00
❑ 252 Nemiah Wilson .30 .15
❑ 253 Ron Jessie .30 .15
❑ 254 Jim Lynch .30 .15
❑ 255 Bob Tucker .75 .30
❑ 256 Terry Owens .30 .15
❑ 257 John Fitzgerald .30 .15
❑ 258 Jack Snow .75 .30
❑ 259 Garry Puetz .30 .15
❑ 260 Mike Phipps .75 .30
❑ 261 Al Matthews .30 .15
❑ 262 Bob Kuechenberg .30 .15
❑ 263 Ron Yankowski .30 .15
❑ 264 Ron Shanklin .30 .15
❑ 265 Bobby Douglass .75 .30
❑ 266 Josh Ashton .30 .15
❑ 267 Bill Van Heusen .30 .15
❑ 268 Jeff Siemon .30 .15
❑ 269 Bob Newland .30 .15
❑ 270 Gale Gillingham .30 .15
❑ 271 Zeke Moore .30 .15
❑ 272 Mike Tilleman .30 .15
❑ 273 John Leypoldt .30 .15
❑ 274 Ken Mendenhall .30 .15
❑ 275 Norm Snead .75 .30
❑ 276 Bill Bradley .75 .30
❑ 277 Jerry Smith .30 .15
❑ 278 Clarence Davis .30 .15
❑ 279 Jim Yarbrough .30 .15
❑ 280 Lemar Parrish .30 .15
❑ 281 Bobby Bell 1.50 .60
❑ 282 Lynn Swann RC UER ! 60.00 30.00
❑ 283 John Hicks .30 .15
❑ 284 Coy Bacon .75 .30
❑ 285 Lee Roy Jordan 1.50 .60
❑ 286 Willie Buchanon .30 .15
❑ 287 Al Woodall .30 .15
❑ 288 Reggie Rucker .75 .30
❑ 289 John Schmitt .30 .15
❑ 290 Carl Eller 1.50 .60
❑ 291 Jake Scott .75 .30
❑ 292 Donny Anderson .75 .30
❑ 293 Charley Wade .30 .15
❑ 294 John Tanner .30 .15
❑ 295 Charlie Johnson .75 .30
❑ 296 Tom Blanchard .30 .15
❑ 297 Curley Culp .75 .30
❑ 298 Jeff Van Note RC .75 .30
❑ 299 Bob James .30 .15
❑ 300 Franco Harris 8.00 4.00
❑ 301 Tim Berra .75 .30
❑ 302 Bruce Gossett .30 .15
❑ 303 Verlon Biggs .30 .15
❑ 304 Bob Kowalkowski .30 .15
❑ 305 Marv Hubbard .30 .15

❑ 306 Ken Avery .30 .15
❑ 307 Mike Adamle .30 .15
❑ 308 Don Herrmann .30 .15
❑ 309 Chris Fletcher .30 .15
❑ 310 Roman Gabriel 1.50 .60
❑ 311 Billy Joe DuPree 1.50 .60
❑ 312 Fred Dryer 1.50 .60
❑ 313 John Riggins 5.00 2.50
❑ 314 Bob McKay .30 .15
❑ 315 Ted Hendricks 1.50 .60
❑ 316 Bobby Bryant .30 .15
❑ 317 Don Nottingham .30 .15
❑ 318 John Hannah 4.00 2.00
❑ 319 Rich Coady .30 .15
❑ 320 Phil Villapiano .75 .30
❑ 321 Jim Plunkett 1.50 .60
❑ 322 Lyle Alzado 1.50 .60
❑ 323 Ernie Jackson .30 .15
❑ 324 Billy Parks .30 .15
❑ 325 Willie Lanier 1.50 .60
❑ 326 John James .30 .15
❑ 327 Joe Ferguson .75 .30
❑ 328 Ernie Holmes RC 1.50 .60
❑ 329 Bruce Laird .30 .15
❑ 330 Chester Marcol .30 .15
❑ 331 Dave Wilcox 1.50 .60
❑ 332 Pat Fischer .75 .30
❑ 333 Steve Owens .75 .30
❑ 334 Royce Berry .30 .15
❑ 335 Russ Washington .30 .15
❑ 336 Walker Gillette .30 .15
❑ 337 Mark Nordquist .30 .15
❑ 338 James Harris RC 1.50 .60
❑ 339 Warren Koegel .30 .15
❑ 340 Emmitt Thomas .75 .30
❑ 341 Walt Garrison .75 .30
❑ 342 Thom Darden .30 .15
❑ 343 Mike Eischeid .30 .15
❑ 344 Ernie McMillan .30 .15
❑ 345 Nick Buoniconti 1.50 .60
❑ 346 George Farmer .30 .15
❑ 347 Sam Adams OL .30 .15
❑ 348 Larry Cipa .30 .15
❑ 349 Bob Moore .30 .15
❑ 350 Otis Armstrong RC 1.50 .60
❑ 351 George Blanda RB 3.00 1.50
❑ 352 Fred Cox RB .75 .30
❑ 353 Tom Dempsey RB .75 .30
❑ 354 Ken Houston RB 1.50 .60
❑ 355 O.J.Simpson RB 5.00 2.50
❑ 356 Ron Smith RB .75 .30
❑ 357 Bob Atkins .30 .15
❑ 358 Pat Sullivan .75 .30
❑ 359 Joe DeLamielleure 2.50 1.00
❑ 360 Lawr. McCutcheon RC 1.50 .60
❑ 361 David Lee .30 .15
❑ 362 Mike McCoy DT .30 .15
❑ 363 Skip Vanderbundt .30 .15
❑ 364 Mark Moseley .75 .30
❑ 365 Lem Barney 1.50 .60
❑ 366 Doug Dressler .30 .15
❑ 367 Dan Fouts RC 40.00 20.00
❑ 368 Bob Hyland .30 .15
❑ 369 John Outlaw .30 .15
❑ 370 Roy Gerela .30 .15
❑ 371 Isiah Robertson .75 .30
❑ 372 Jerome Barkum .30 .15
❑ 373 Ed Podolak .30 .15
❑ 374 Milt Morin .30 .15
❑ 375 John Niland .30 .15
❑ 376 Checklist 265-396 UER 4.00 2.00
❑ 377 Ken Iman .30 .15
❑ 378 Manny Fernandez .75 .30
❑ 379 Dave Gallagher .30 .15
❑ 380 Ken Stabler 15.00 7.50
❑ 381 Mack Herron .30 .15
❑ 382 Bill McClard .30 .15
❑ 383 Ray May .30 .15
❑ 384 Don Hansen .30 .15
❑ 385 Elvin Bethea 1.50 .60
❑ 386 Joe Scibelli .30 .15
❑ 387 Neal Craig .30 .15
❑ 388 Marty Domres .30 .15
❑ 389 Ken Ellis .30 .15
❑ 390 Charle Young .75 .30
❑ 391 Tommy Hart .30 .15
❑ 392 Moses Denson .30 .15
❑ 393 Larry Walton .30 .15
❑ 394 Dave Green .30 .15
❑ 395 Ron Johnson .75 .30
❑ 396 Ed Bradley RC .30 .15
❑ 397 J.T. Thomas .30 .15
❑ 398 Jim Bailey .30 .15
❑ 399 Barry Pearson .30 .15
❑ 400 Fran Tarkenton 8.00 4.00
❑ 401 Jack Rudnay .30 .15
❑ 402 Rayfield Wright .75 .30
❑ 403 Roger Wehrli 1.00 .40
❑ 404 Vern Den Herder .30 .15
❑ 405 Fred Biletnikoff 3.00 1.50
❑ 406 Ken Grandberry .30 .15
❑ 407 Bob Adams .30 .15
❑ 408 Jim Merlo .30 .15
❑ 409 John Pitts .30 .15
❑ 410 Dave Osborn .75 .30
❑ 411 Dennis Havig .30 .15
❑ 412 Bob Johnson .30 .15
❑ 413 Ken Burrough UER .75 .30
❑ 414 Jim Cheyunski .30 .15
❑ 415 MacArthur Lane .30 .15
❑ 416 Joe Theismann RC 25.00 12.50
❑ 417 Mike Boryla RC .30 .15
❑ 418 Bruce Taylor .30 .15
❑ 419 Chris Hanburger .75 .30
❑ 420 Tom Mack 1.50 .60
❑ 421 Errol Mann .30 .15
❑ 422 Jack Gregory .30 .15
❑ 423 Harrison Davis .30 .15
❑ 424 Burgess Owens .30 .15
❑ 425 Joe Greene 5.00 2.50
❑ 426 Morris Stroud .30 .15
❑ 427 John DeMarie .30 .15
❑ 428 Mel Renfro 1.50 .60
❑ 429 Cid Edwards .30 .15
❑ 430 Mike Reid 1.50 .60
❑ 431 Jack Mildren RC .30 .15
❑ 432 Jerry Simmons .30 .15
❑ 433 Ron Yary 1.50 .60
❑ 434 Howard Stevens .30 .15
❑ 435 Ray Guy 2.00 .75
❑ 436 Tommy Nobis 1.50 .60
❑ 437 Solomon Freelon .30 .15
❑ 438 J.D. Hill .75 .30
❑ 439 Toni Linhart .30 .15
❑ 440 Dick Anderson .75 .30
❑ 441 Guy Morriss .30 .15
❑ 442 Bob Hoskins .30 .15
❑ 443 John Hadl 1.50 .60
❑ 444 Roy Jefferson .30 .15
❑ 445 Charlie Sanders 1.00 .40
❑ 446 Pat Curran .30 .15
❑ 447 David Knight .30 .15
❑ 448 Bob Brown DT .30 .15
❑ 449 Pete Gogolak .30 .15
❑ 450 Terry Metcalf 1.50 .60
❑ 451 Bill Bergey 1.50 .60
❑ 452 Dan Abramowicz HL .75 .30
❑ 453 Otis Armstrong HL .75 .30
❑ 454 Cliff Branch HL 1.50 .60
❑ 455 John James HL .30 .15
❑ 456 Lydell Mitchell HL .75 .30
❑ 457 Lemar Parrish HL .75 .30
❑ 458 Ken Stabler HL 5.00 2.50
❑ 459 Lynn Swann HL 8.00 4.00
❑ 460 Emmitt Thomas HL .30 .15
❑ 461 Terry Bradshaw 20.00 10.00
❑ 462 Jerrel Wilson .30 .15
❑ 463 Walter Johnson .30 .15
❑ 464 Golden Richards .75 .30
❑ 465 Tommy Casanova .75 .30
❑ 466 Randy Jackson .30 .15
❑ 467 Ron Bolton .30 .15
❑ 468 Joe Owens .30 .15
❑ 469 Wally Hilgenberg .30 .15
❑ 470 Riley Odoms .75 .30
❑ 471 Otis Sistrunk .75 .30
❑ 472 Eddie Ray .30 .15
❑ 473 Reggie McKenzie .75 .30
❑ 474 Elbert Drungo .30 .15
❑ 475 Mercury Morris 1.50 .60
❑ 476 Dan Dickel .30 .15
❑ 477 Merritt Kersey .30 .15
❑ 478 Mike Holmes .30 .15
❑ 479 Clarence Williams .30 .15
❑ 480 Billy Kilmer 1.50 .60
❑ 481 Altie Taylor .30 .15
❑ 482 Dave Elmendorf .30 .15
❑ 483 Bob Rowe .30 .15
❑ 484 Pete Athas .30 .15
❑ 485 Winston Hill .30 .15
❑ 486 Bo Matthews .30 .15
❑ 487 Earl Thomas .30 .15
❑ 488 Jan Stenerud 1.50 .60
❑ 489 Steve Holden .30 .15
❑ 490 Cliff Harris RC 4.00 2.00
❑ 491 Boobie Clark RC .75 .30
❑ 492 Joe Taylor .30 .15
❑ 493 Tom Neville .30 .15
❑ 494 Wayne Colman .30 .15
❑ 495 Jim Mitchell TE .30 .15
❑ 496 Paul Krause 1.50 .60
❑ 497 Jim Otto 1.50 .60
❑ 498 John Rowser .30 .15
❑ 499 Larry Little 1.50 .60
❑ 500 O.J.Simpson 10.00 5.00
❑ 501 John Dutton RC 1.50 .60
❑ 502 Pat Hughes .30 .15
❑ 503 Malcolm Snider .30 .15
❑ 504 Fred Willis .30 .15
❑ 505 Harold Jackson 1.50 .60
❑ 506 Mike Bragg .30 .15
❑ 507 Jerry Sherk .75 .30
❑ 508 Mirro Roder .30 .15
❑ 509 Tom Sullivan .30 .15
❑ 510 Jim Hart 1.50 .60
❑ 511 Cedrick Hardman .30 .15
❑ 512 Blaine Nye .30 .15
❑ 513 Elmo Wright .30 .15
❑ 514 Herb Orvis .30 .15
❑ 515 Richard Caster .75 .30
❑ 516 Doug Kotar RC .30 .15
❑ 517 Checklist 397-528 4.00 2.00
❑ 518 Jesse Freitas .30 .15
❑ 519 Ken Houston 1.50 .60
❑ 520 Alan Page 1.50 .60
❑ 521 Tim Foley .75 .30
❑ 522 Bill Olds .30 .15
❑ 523 Bobby Maples .30 .15
❑ 524 Cliff Branch RC 15.00 7.50
❑ 525 Merlin Olsen 1.50 .60
❑ 526 AFC Champs/Brad./Harris 4.00 2.00
❑ 527 NFC Champs/Foreman 1.50 .60
❑ 528 Super Bowl IX/Bradshaw 5.00 2.50

1976 Topps

❑ COMPLETE SET (528) 350.00 200.00
❑ 1 George Blanda RB ! 5.00 2.50
❑ 2 Neal Colzie RB .75 .30
❑ 3 Chuck Foreman RB .75 .30
❑ 4 Jim Marshall RB .75 .30
❑ 5 Terry Metcalf RB .75 .30
❑ 6 O.J.Simpson RB 3.00 1.50
❑ 7 Fran Tarkenton RB 3.00 1.50
❑ 8 Charley Taylor RB 1.50 .60
❑ 9 Ernie Holmes .75 .30
❑ 10 Ken Anderson 1.50 .60
❑ 11 Bobby Bryant .30 .15
❑ 12 Jerry Smith .75 .30
❑ 13 David Lee .30 .15
❑ 14 Robert Newhouse RC 1.50 .60
❑ 15 Vern Den Herder .30 .15
❑ 16 John Hannah 1.50 .60
❑ 17 J.D. Hill .75 .30

❑ 18 James Harris .75 .30
❑ 19 Willie Buchanon .30 .15
❑ 20 Charle Young .75 .30
❑ 21 Jim Yarbrough .30 .15
❑ 22 Ronnie Coleman .30 .15
❑ 23 Don Cockroft .30 .15
❑ 24 Willie Lanier 1.50 .60
❑ 25 Fred Biletnikoff 3.00 1.50
❑ 26 Ron Yankowski .30 .15
❑ 27 Spider Lockhart .30 .15
❑ 28 Bob Johnson .30 .15
❑ 29 J.T. Thomas .30 .15
❑ 30 Ron Yary 1.50 .60
❑ 31 Brad Dusek RC .30 .15
❑ 32 Raymond Chester .75 .30
❑ 33 Larry Little 1.50 .60
❑ 34 Pat Leahy RC 1.50 .60
❑ 35 Steve Bartkowski RC 4.00 2.00
❑ 36 Tom Myers .30 .15
❑ 37 Bill Van Heusen .30 .15
❑ 38 Russ Washington .30 .15
❑ 39 Tom Sullivan .30 .15
❑ 40 Curley Culp .75 .30
❑ 41 Johnnie Gray .30 .15
❑ 42 Bob Klein .30 .15
❑ 43 Lem Barney 1.50 .60
❑ 44 Harvey Martin RC 6.00 3.00
❑ 45 Reggie Rucker .75 .30
❑ 46 Neil Clabo .30 .15
❑ 47 Ray Hamilton .30 .15
❑ 48 Joe Ferguson .75 .30
❑ 49 Ed Podolak .30 .15
❑ 50 Ray Guy 1.50 .60
❑ 51 Glen Edwards .30 .15
❑ 52 Jim LeClair .30 .15
❑ 53 Mike Barnes .30 .15
❑ 54 Nat Moore RC 1.50 .60
❑ 55 Billy Kilmer 1.50 .60
❑ 56 Larry Stallings .30 .15
❑ 57 Jack Gregory .30 .15
❑ 58 Steve Mike-Mayer .30 .15
❑ 59 Virgil Livers .30 .15
❑ 60 Jerry Sherk .75 .30
❑ 61 Guy Morriss .30 .15
❑ 62 Barty Smith .30 .15
❑ 63 Jerome Barkum .30 .15
❑ 64 Ira Gordon .30 .15
❑ 65 Paul Krause 1.50 .60
❑ 66 John McMakin .30 .15
❑ 67 Checklist 1-132 3.00 1.50
❑ 68 Charlie Johnson UER .75 .30
❑ 69 Tommy Nobis 1.50 .60
❑ 70 Lydell Mitchell .75 .30
❑ 71 Vern Holland .30 .15
❑ 72 Tim Foley .75 .30
❑ 73 Golden Richards .75 .30
❑ 74 Bryant Salter .30 .15
❑ 75 Terry Bradshaw 20.00 10.00
❑ 76 Ted Hendricks 1.50 .60
❑ 77 Rich Saul RC .30 .15
❑ 78 John Smith RC .30 .15
❑ 79 Altie Taylor .30 .15
❑ 80 Cedrick Hardman .30 .15
❑ 81 Ken Payne .30 .15
❑ 82 Zeke Moore .30 .15
❑ 83 Alvin Maxson .30 .15
❑ 84 Wally Hilgenberg .30 .15
❑ 85 John Niland .30 .15
❑ 86 Mike Sensibaugh .30 .15
❑ 87 Ron Johnson .75 .30
❑ 88 Winston Hill .30 .15
❑ 89 Charlie Joiner 4.00 2.00
❑ 90 Roger Wehrli .75 .30
❑ 91 Mike Bragg .30 .15
❑ 92 Dan Dickel .30 .15
❑ 93 Earl Morrall .75 .30
❑ 94 Pat Toomay .30 .15
❑ 95 Gary Garrison .30 .15
❑ 96 Ken Geddes .30 .15
❑ 97 Mike Current .30 .15
❑ 98 Bob Avellini RC .75 .30
❑ 99 Dave Pureifory .30 .15
❑ 100 Franco Harris 8.00 4.00
❑ 101 Randy Logan .30 .15
❑ 102 John Fitzgerald .30 .15
❑ 103 Gregg Bingham RC .75 .30
❑ 104 Jim Plunkett 1.50 .60
❑ 105 Carl Eller 1.50 .60
❑ 106 Larry Walton .30 .15
❑ 107 Clarence Scott .30 .15
❑ 108 Skip Vanderbundt .30 .15
❑ 109 Boobie Clark .75 .30
❑ 110 Tom Mack 1.50 .60
❑ 111 Bruce Laird .30 .15
❑ 112 Dave Dalby RC .30 .15
❑ 113 John Leypoldt .30 .15
❑ 114 Barry Pearson .30 .15
❑ 115 Larry Brown .75 .30
❑ 116 Jackie Smith 1.50 .60
❑ 117 Pat Hughes .30 .15
❑ 118 Al Woodall .30 .15
❑ 119 John Zook .30 .15
❑ 120 Jake Scott .75 .30
❑ 121 Rich Glover .30 .15
❑ 122 Ernie Jackson .30 .15
❑ 123 Otis Armstrong 1.50 .60
❑ 124 Bob Grim .30 .15
❑ 125 Jeff Siemon .75 .30
❑ 126 Harold Hart .30 .15
❑ 127 John DeMarie .30 .15
❑ 128 Dan Fouts 12.00 6.00
❑ 129 Jim Kearney .30 .15
❑ 130 John Dutton .75 .30
❑ 131 Calvin Hill 1.50 .60
❑ 132 Toni Fritsch .30 .15
❑ 133 Ron Jessie .30 .15
❑ 134 Don Nottingham .30 .15
❑ 135 Lemar Parrish .30 .15
❑ 136 Russ Francis RC 1.50 .60
❑ 137 Joe Reed .30 .15
❑ 138 C.L. Whittington .30 .15
❑ 139 Otis Sistrunk .75 .30
❑ 140 Lynn Swann 20.00 10.00
❑ 141 Jim Carter .30 .15
❑ 142 Mike Montler .30 .15
❑ 143 Walter Johnson .30 .15
❑ 144 Doug Kotar .30 .15
❑ 145 Roman Gabriel 1.50 .60
❑ 146 Billy Newsome .30 .15
❑ 147 Ed Bradley .30 .15
❑ 148 Walter Payton RC 250.00 125.00
❑ 149 Johnny Fuller .30 .15
❑ 150 Alan Page 1.50 .60
❑ 151 Frank Grant .30 .15
❑ 152 Dave Green .30 .15
❑ 153 Nelson Munsey .30 .15
❑ 154 Jim Mandich .30 .15
❑ 155 Lawrence McCutcheon 1.50 .60
❑ 156 Steve Ramsey .30 .15
❑ 157 Ed Flanagan .30 .15
❑ 158 Randy White RC 20.00 10.00
❑ 159 Gerry Mullins .30 .15
❑ 160 Jan Stenerud 1.50 .60
❑ 161 Steve Odom .30 .15
❑ 162 Roger Finnie .30 .15
❑ 163 Norm Snead .75 .30
❑ 164 Jeff Van Note .75 .30
❑ 165 Bill Bergey 1.50 .60
❑ 166 Allen Carter .30 .15
❑ 167 Steve Holden .30 .15
❑ 168 Sherman White .30 .15
❑ 169 Bob Berry .30 .15
❑ 170 Ken Houston 1.50 .60
❑ 171 Bill Olds .30 .15
❑ 172 Larry Seiple .30 .15
❑ 173 Cliff Branch 4.00 2.00
❑ 174 Reggie McKenzie .75 .30
❑ 175 Dan Pastorini 1.50 .60
❑ 176 Paul Naumoff .30 .15
❑ 177 Checklist 133-264 3.00 1.50
❑ 178 Durwood Keeton .30 .15
❑ 179 Earl Thomas .30 .15
❑ 180 L.C.Greenwood 1.50 .60
❑ 181 John Outlaw .30 .15
❑ 182 Frank Nunley .30 .15
❑ 183 Dave Jennings RC .75 .30
❑ 184 MacArthur Lane .30 .15
❑ 185 Chester Marcol .30 .15
❑ 186 J.J. Jones .30 .15
❑ 187 Tom DeLeone .30 .15
❑ 188 Steve Zabel .30 .15
❑ 189 Ken Johnson DT .30 .15
❑ 190 Rayfield Wright .75 .30
❑ 191 Brent McClanahan .30 .15
❑ 192 Pat Fischer .75 .30
❑ 193 Roger Carr RC .75 .30
❑ 194 Manny Fernandez .75 .30
❑ 195 Roy Gerela .30 .15
❑ 196 Dave Elmendorf .30 .15
❑ 197 Bob Kowalkowski .30 .15
❑ 198 Phil Villapiano .75 .30
❑ 199 Will Wynn .30 .15
❑ 200 Terry Metcalf 1.50 .60
❑ 201 Tarkenton/Anderson LL 2.00 .75
❑ 202 Receiving Leaders .75 .30
❑ 203 O.J.Simpson/J.Otis LL 2.50 1.25
❑ 204 Simpson/Foreman LL 2.50 1.25
❑ 205 M.Blount/P.Krause LL 1.50 .60
❑ 206 Punting Leaders .75 .30
❑ 207 Ken Ellis .30 .15
❑ 208 Ron Saul .30 .15
❑ 209 Toni Linhart .30 .15
❑ 210 Jim Langer 1.50 .60
❑ 211 Jeff Wright S .30 .15
❑ 212 Moses Denson .30 .15
❑ 213 Earl Edwards .30 .15
❑ 214 Walker Gillette .30 .15
❑ 215 Bob Trumpy .75 .30
❑ 216 Emmitt Thomas .75 .30
❑ 217 Lyle Alzado 1.50 .60
❑ 218 Carl Garrett .75 .30
❑ 219 Van Green .30 .15
❑ 220 Jack Lambert RC 35.00 20.00
❑ 221 Spike Jones .30 .15
❑ 222 John Hadl 1.50 .60
❑ 223 Billy Johnson RC 1.50 .60
❑ 224 Tony McGee DT .30 .15
❑ 225 Preston Pearson .75 .30
❑ 226 Isiah Robertson .75 .30
❑ 227 Errol Mann .30 .15
❑ 228 Paul Seal .30 .15
❑ 229 Roland Harper RC .30 .15
❑ 230 Ed White RC .75 .30
❑ 231 Joe Theismann 6.00 3.00
❑ 232 Jim Cheyunski .30 .15
❑ 233 Bill Stanfill .75 .30
❑ 234 Marv Hubbard .30 .15
❑ 235 Tommy Casanova .75 .30
❑ 236 Bob Hyland .30 .15
❑ 237 Jesse Freitas .30 .15
❑ 238 Norm Thompson .30 .15
❑ 239 Charlie Smith WR .30 .15
❑ 240 John James .30 .15
❑ 241 Alden Roche .30 .15
❑ 242 Gordon Jolley .30 .15
❑ 243 Larry Ely .30 .15
❑ 244 Richard Caster .30 .15
❑ 245 Joe Greene 5.00 2.00
❑ 246 Larry Schreiber .30 .15
❑ 247 Terry Schmidt .30 .15
❑ 248 Jerrel Wilson .30 .15
❑ 249 Marty Domres .30 .15
❑ 250 Isaac Curtis .75 .30
❑ 251 Harold McLinton .30 .15
❑ 252 Fred Dryer 1.50 .60
❑ 253 Bill Lenkaitis .30 .15
❑ 254 Don Hardeman .30 .15
❑ 255 Bob Griese 4.00 2.00
❑ 256 Oscar Roan RC .30 .15
❑ 257 Randy Gradishar RC 2.50 1.25
❑ 258 Bob Thomas RC .30 .15
❑ 259 Joe Owens .30 .15
❑ 260 Cliff Harris 1.50 .60
❑ 261 Frank Lewis .30 .15
❑ 262 Mike McCoy DT .30 .15
❑ 263 Rickey Young RC .30 .15
❑ 264 Brian Kelley RC .30 .15
❑ 265 Charlie Sanders .75 .30
❑ 266 Jim Hart 1.50 .60
❑ 267 Greg Gantt .30 .15
❑ 268 John Ward .30 .15
❑ 269 Al Beauchamp .30 .15
❑ 270 Jack Tatum 1.50 .60
❑ 271 Jim Lash .30 .15
❑ 272 Diron Talbert .30 .15
❑ 273 Checklist 265-396 3.00 1.50
❑ 274 Steve Spurrier 8.00 3.00
❑ 275 Greg Pruitt 1.50 .60
❑ 276 Jim Mitchell TE .30 .15
❑ 277 Jack Rudnay .30 .15
❑ 278 Freddie Solomon RC .75 .30

279	Frank LeMaster	.30	.15
280	Wally Chambers	.30	.15
281	Mike Collier	.30	.15
282	Clarence Williams	.30	.15
283	Mitch Hoopes	.30	.15
284	Ron Bolton	.30	.15
285	Harold Jackson	1.50	.60
286	Greg Landry	.75	.30
287	Tony Greene	.30	.15
288	Howard Stevens	.30	.15
289	Roy Jefferson	.30	.15
290	Jim Bakken	.30	.15
291	Doug Sutherland	.30	.15
292	Marvin Cobb RC	.30	.15
293	Mack Alston	.30	.15
294	Rod McNeill	.30	.15
295	Gene Upshaw	1.50	.60
296	Dave Gallagher	.30	.15
297	Larry Ball	.30	.15
298	Ron Howard	.30	.15
299	Don Strock RC	1.50	.60
300	O.J.Simpson	8.00	4.00
301	Ray Mansfield	.30	.15
302	Larry Marshall	.30	.15
303	Dick Himes	.30	.15
304	Ray Wersching RC	.30	.15
305	John Riggins	4.00	2.00
306	Bob Parsons	.30	.15
307	Ray Brown DB	.30	.15
308	Len Dawson	3.00	1.50
309	Andy Maurer	.30	.15
310	Jack Youngblood	1.50	.60
311	Essex Johnson	.30	.15
312	Stan White	.30	.15
313	Drew Pearson	5.00	2.00
314	Rockne Freitas	.30	.15
315	Mercury Morris	1.50	.60
316	Willie Alexander	.30	.15
317	Paul Warfield	3.00	1.50
318	Bob Chandler	.75	.30
319	Bobby Walden	.30	.15
320	Riley Odoms	.75	.30
321	Mike Boryla	.30	.15
322	Bruce Van Dyke	.30	.15
323	Pete Banaszak	.30	.15
324	Darryl Stingley	1.50	.60
325	John Mendenhall	.30	.15
326	Dan Dierdorf	2.00	.75
327	Bruce Taylor	.30	.15
328	Don McCauley	.30	.15
329	John Reaves UER	.30	.15
330	Chris Hanburger	.75	.30
331	NFC Champs/Staubach	3.00	1.50
332	AFC Champs/F.Harris	2.00	.75
333	Super Bowl X/Bradshaw	2.50	1.25
334	Godwin Turk	.30	.15
335	Dick Anderson	.75	.30
336	Woody Green	.30	.15
337	Pat Curran	.30	.15
338	Council Rudolph	.30	.15
339	Joe Lavender	.30	.15
340	John Gilliam	.75	.30
341	Steve Furness RC	.75	.30
342	D.D. Lewis	.75	.30
343	Duane Carrell	.30	.15
344	Jon Morris	.30	.15
345	John Brockington	.75	.30
346	Mike Phipps	.75	.30
347	Lyle Blackwood RC	.30	.15
348	Julius Adams	.30	.15
349	Terry Hermeling	.30	.15
350	Rolland Lawrence RC	.30	.15
351	Glenn Doughty	.30	.15
352	Doug Swift	.30	.15
353	Mike Strachan	.30	.15
354	Craig Morton	1.50	.60
355	George Blanda	5.00	2.50
356	Garry Puetz	.30	.15
357	Carl Mauck	.30	.15
358	Walt Patulski	.30	.15
359	Stu Voigt	.30	.15
360	Fred Carr	.30	.15
361	Po James	.30	.15
362	Otis Taylor	1.50	.60
363	Jeff West	.30	.15
364	Gary Huff	.75	.30
365	Dwight White	.75	.30
366	Dan Ryczek	.30	.15
367	Jon Keyworth RC	.30	.15
368	Mel Renfro	1.50	.60
369	Bruce Coslet RC	1.50	.60
370	Len Hauss	.30	.15
371	Rick Volk	.30	.15
372	Howard Twilley	.75	.30
373	Cullen Bryant RC	.75	.30
374	Bob Babich	.30	.15
375	Herman Weaver	.30	.15
376	Steve Grogan RC	3.00	1.25
377	Bubba Smith	1.50	.60
378	Burgess Owens	.30	.15
379	Al Matthews	.30	.15
380	Art Shell	1.50	.60
381	Larry Brown	.30	.15
382	Horst Muhlmann	.30	.15
383	Ahmad Rashad	2.50	1.25
384	Bobby Maples	.30	.15
385	Jim Marshall	1.50	.60
386	Joe Dawkins	.30	.15
387	Dennis Partee	.30	.15
388	Eddie McMillan RC	.30	.15
389	Randy Johnson	.30	.15
390	Bob Kuechenberg	.30	.15
391	Rufus Mayes	.30	.15
392	Lloyd Mumphord	.30	.15
393	Ike Harris	.30	.15
394	Dave Hampton	.30	.15
395	Roger Staubach	20.00	10.00
396	Doug Buffone	.30	.15
397	Howard Fest	.30	.15
398	Wayne Mulligan	.30	.15
399	Bill Bradley	.75	.30
400	Chuck Foreman	1.50	.60
401	Jack Snow	.75	.30
402	Bob Howard	.30	.15
403	John Matuszak	1.50	.60
404	Bill Munson	.75	.30
405	Andy Russell	.75	.30
406	Skip Butler	.30	.15
407	Hugh McKinnis	.30	.15
408	Bob Penchion	.30	.15
409	Mike Bass	.30	.15
410	George Kunz	.30	.15
411	Ron Pritchard	.30	.15
412	Barry Smith	.30	.15
413	Norm Bulaich	.30	.15
414	Marv Bateman	.30	.15
415	Ken Stabler	12.00	6.00
416	Conrad Dobler	.75	.30
417	Bob Tucker	.75	.30
418	Gene Washington 49er	.75	.30
419	Ed Marinaro	1.50	.60
420	Jack Ham	4.00	2.00
421	Jim Turner	.30	.15
422	Chris Fletcher	.30	.15
423	Carl Barzilauskas	.30	.15
424	Robert Brazile RC	1.50	.60
425	Harold Carmichael	2.00	.75
426	Ron Jaworski RC	5.00	2.00
427	Ed Too Tall Jones RC	20.00	10.00
428	Larry McCarren	.30	.15
429	Mike Thomas RC	.30	.15
430	Joe DeLamielleure	1.50	.60
431	Tom Blanchard	.30	.15
432	Ron Carpenter	.30	.15
433	Levi Johnson	.30	.15
434	Sam Cunningham	.75	.30
435	Garo Yepremian	.75	.30
436	Mike Livingston	.30	.15
437	Larry Csonka	4.00	2.00
438	Doug Dieken	.75	.30
439	Bill Lueck	.30	.15
440	Tom MacLeod	.30	.15
441	Mick Tingelhoff	.75	.30
442	Terry Hanratty	.75	.30
443	Mike Siani	.30	.15
444	Dwight Harrison	.30	.15
445	Jim Otis	.75	.30
446	Jack Reynolds	.75	.30
447	Jean Fugett RC	.75	.30
448	Dave Beverly	.30	.15
449	Bernard Jackson RC	.30	.15
450	Charley Taylor	2.00	.75
451	Atlanta Falcons CL	2.00	.75
452	Baltimore Colts CL	2.00	.75
453	Buffalo Bills CL	2.00	.75
454	Chicago Bears CL	2.00	.75
455	Cincinnati Bengals CL	2.00	.75
456	Cleveland Browns CL	2.00	.75
457	Dallas Cowboys CL	2.00	.75
458	Denver Broncos CL UER	2.00	.75
459	Detroit Lions CL	2.00	.75
460	Green Bay Packers CL	2.00	.75
461	Houston Oilers CL	2.00	.75
462	Kansas City Chiefs CL	2.00	.75
463	Los Angeles Rams CL	2.00	.75
464	Miami Dolphins CL	2.00	.75
465	Minnesota Vikings CL	2.00	.75
466	New England Patriots CL	2.00	.75
467	New Orleans Saints CL	2.00	.75
468	New York Giants CL	2.00	.75
469	New York Jets CL	2.00	.75
470	Oakland Raiders CL	2.00	.75
471	Philadelphia Eagles CL	2.00	.75
472	Pittsburgh Steelers CL	2.00	.75
473	St. Louis Cardinals CL	2.00	.75
474	San Diego Chargers CL	2.00	.75
475	San Francisco 49ers CL	2.00	.75
476	Seattle Seahawks CL	2.00	.75
477	Tampa Bay Buccaneers CL	2.00	.75
478	Washington Redskins CL	2.00	.75
479	Fred Cox	.30	.15
480	Mel Blount	6.00	3.00
481	John Bunting RC	.75	.30
482	Ken Mendenhall	.30	.15
483	Will Harrell	.30	.15
484	Marlin Briscoe	.30	.15
485	Archie Manning	1.50	.60
486	Tody Smith	.30	.15
487	George Hunt	.30	.15
488	Roscoe Word	.30	.15
489	Paul Seymour	.30	.15
490	Lee Roy Jordan	1.50	.60
491	Chip Myers	.30	.15
492	Norm Evans	.30	.15
493	Jim Bertelsen	.30	.15
494	Mark Moseley	.75	.30
495	George Buehler	.30	.15
496	Charlie Hall	.30	.15
497	Marvin Upshaw	.30	.15
498	Tom Banks RC	.30	.15
499	Randy Vataha	.30	.15
500	Fran Tarkenton	6.00	3.00
501	Mike Wagner	.75	.30
502	Art Malone	.30	.15
503	Fred Cook	.30	.15
504	Rich McGeorge	.30	.15
505	Ken Burrough	.75	.30
506	Nick Mike-Mayer	.30	.15
507	Checklist 397-528	3.00	1.50
508	Steve Owens	.75	.30
509	Brad Van Pelt RC	.30	.15
510	Ken Riley	.75	.30
511	Art Thoms	.30	.15
512	Ed Bell	.30	.15
513	Tom Wittum	.30	.15
514	Jim Braxton	.30	.15
515	Nick Buoniconti	1.50	.60
516	Brian Sipe RC	6.00	2.50
517	Jim Lynch	.30	.15
518	Prentice McCray	.30	.15
519	Tom Dempsey	.30	.15
520	Mel Gray	.75	.30
521	Nate Wright	.30	.15
522	Rocky Bleier	6.00	3.00
523	Dennis Johnson RC	.30	.15
524	Jerry Sisemore	.30	.15
525	Bert Jones	.30	.15
526	Perry Smith	.30	.15
527	Blaine Nye	.30	.15
528	Bob Moore !	1.50	.60

1977 Topps

	COMPLETE SET (528)	250.00	125.00
1	K.Stabler/J.Harris LL !	2.50	1.25
2	Drew Pearson/M.Lane LL	1.00	.40
3	W.Payton/Simpson LL	10.00	5.00
4	Scoring Leaders	.50	.20
5	Interception Leaders	.50	.20
6	Punting Leaders	.25	.10
7	Mike Phipps	.50	.20
8	Rick Volk	.25	.10

❑	9	Steve Furness	.50	.20
❑	10	Isaac Curtis	.50	.20
❑	11	Nate Wright	.50	.20
❑	12	Jean Fugett	.25	.10
❑	13	Ken Mendenhall	.25	.10
❑	14	Sam Adams OL	.25	.10
❑	15	Charlie Waters	1.00	.40
❑	16	Bill Stanfill	.25	.10
❑	17	John Holland	.25	.10
❑	18	Pat Haden RC	2.00	.75
❑	19	Bob Young	.25	.10
❑	20	Wally Chambers	.25	.10
❑	21	Lawrence Gaines	.25	.10
❑	22	Larry McCarren	.25	.10
❑	23	Horst Muhlmann	.25	.10
❑	24	Phil Villapiano	.50	.20
❑	25	Greg Pruitt	.50	.20
❑	26	Ron Howard	.25	.10
❑	27	Craig Morton	1.00	.40
❑	28	Rufus Mayes	.25	.10
❑	29	Lee Roy Selmon RC UER	12.00	6.00
❑	30	Ed White	.50	.20
❑	31	Harold McLinton	.25	.10
❑	32	Glenn Doughty	.25	.10
❑	33	Bob Kuechenberg	1.00	.40
❑	34	Duane Carrell	.25	.10
❑	35	Riley Odoms	.25	.10
❑	36	Bobby Scott	.25	.10
❑	37	Nick Mike-Mayer	.25	.10
❑	38	Bill Lenkaitis	.25	.10
❑	39	Roland Harper	.50	.20
❑	40	Tommy Hart	.25	.10
❑	41	Mike Sensibaugh	.25	.10
❑	42	Rusty Jackson	.25	.10
❑	43	Levi Johnson	.25	.10
❑	44	Mike McCoy DT	.25	.10
❑	45	Roger Staubach	20.00	10.00
❑	46	Fred Cox	.25	.10
❑	47	Bob Babich	.25	.10
❑	48	Reggie McKenzie	.50	.20
❑	49	Dave Jennings	.25	.10
❑	50	Mike Haynes RC	10.00	4.00
❑	51	Larry Brown	.50	.20
❑	52	Marvin Cobb	.25	.10
❑	53	Fred Cook	.25	.10
❑	54	Freddie Solomon	.50	.20
❑	55	John Riggins	2.50	1.25
❑	56	John Bunting	.50	.20
❑	57	Ray Wersching	.50	.20
❑	58	Mike Livingston	.25	.10
❑	59	Billy Johnson	.50	.20
❑	60	Mike Wagner	.25	.10
❑	61	Waymond Bryant	.25	.10
❑	62	Jim Otis	.50	.20
❑	63	Ed Galigher	.25	.10
❑	64	Randy Vataha	.25	.10
❑	65	Jim Zorn RC	4.00	1.50
❑	66	Jon Keyworth	.25	.10
❑	67	Checklist 1-132	2.00	.75
❑	68	Henry Childs	.25	.10
❑	69	Thom Darden	.25	.10
❑	70	George Kunz	.25	.10
❑	71	Lenvil Elliott	.25	.10
❑	72	Curtis Johnson	.25	.10
❑	73	Doug Van Horn	.25	.10
❑	74	Joe Theismann	4.00	2.00
❑	75	Dwight White	.50	.20
❑	76	Scott Laidlaw	.25	.10
❑	77	Monte Johnson	.25	.10
❑	78	Dave Beverly	.25	.10
❑	79	Jim Mitchell TE	.25	.10
❑	80	Jack Youngblood	1.00	.40
❑	81	Mel Gray	.50	.20
❑	82	Dwight Harrison	.25	.10
❑	83	John Hadl	.50	.20
❑	84	Matt Blair RC	1.00	.40
❑	85	Charlie Sanders	.60	.25
❑	86	Noah Jackson	.25	.10
❑	87	Ed Marinaro	.50	.20
❑	88	Bob Howard	.25	.10
❑	89	John McDaniel	.25	.10
❑	90	Dan Dierdorf	1.50	.60
❑	91	Mark Moseley	.50	.20
❑	92	Cleo Miller	.25	.10
❑	93	Andre Tillman	.25	.10
❑	94	Bruce Taylor	.25	.10
❑	95	Bert Jones	1.00	.40
❑	96	Anthony Davis RC	1.00	.40
❑	97	Don Goode	.25	.10
❑	98	Ray Rhodes RC	6.00	3.00
❑	99	Mike Webster RC	12.00	6.00
❑	100	O.J.Simpson	6.00	3.00
❑	101	Doug Plank RC	.25	.10
❑	102	Efren Herrera	.50	.20
❑	103	Charlie Smith WR	.25	.10
❑	104	Carlos Brown RC	1.00	.40
❑	105	Jim Marshall	1.00	.40
❑	106	Paul Naumoff	.25	.10
❑	107	Walter White	.25	.10
❑	108	John Cappelletti RC	3.00	1.25
❑	109	Chip Myers	.25	.10
❑	110	Ken Stabler	10.00	5.00
❑	111	Joe Ehrmann	.25	.10
❑	112	Rick Engles	.25	.10
❑	113	Jack Dolbin RC	.25	.10
❑	114	Ron Bolton	.25	.10
❑	115	Mike Thomas	.25	.10
❑	116	Mike Fuller	.25	.10
❑	117	John Hill	.25	.10
❑	118	Richard Todd RC	1.00	.40
❑	119	Duriel Harris RC	.50	.20
❑	120	John James	.25	.10
❑	121	Lionel Antoine	.25	.10
❑	122	John Skorupan	.25	.10
❑	123	Skip Butler	.25	.10
❑	124	Bob Tucker	.25	.10
❑	125	Paul Krause	1.00	.40
❑	126	Dave Hampton	.25	.10
❑	127	Tom Wittum	.25	.10
❑	128	Gary Huff	.50	.20
❑	129	Emmitt Thomas	.25	.10
❑	130	Drew Pearson	2.00	.75
❑	131	Ron Saul	.25	.10
❑	132	Steve Niehaus	.25	.10
❑	133	Fred Carr	1.00	.40
❑	134	Norm Bulaich	.25	.10
❑	135	Bob Trumpy	.50	.20
❑	136	Greg Landry	.50	.20
❑	137	George Buehler	.25	.10
❑	138	Reggie Rucker	.50	.20
❑	139	Julius Adams	.25	.10
❑	140	Jack Ham	2.50	1.25
❑	141	Wayne Morris RC	.25	.10
❑	142	Marv Bateman	.25	.10
❑	143	Bobby Maples	.25	.10
❑	144	Harold Carmichael	1.00	.40
❑	145	Bob Avellini	.50	.20
❑	146	Harry Carson RC	3.00	1.50
❑	147	Lawrence Pillers	.25	.10
❑	148	Ed Williams RC	.25	.10
❑	149	Dan Pastorini	.50	.20
❑	150	Ron Yary	1.00	.40
❑	151	Joe Lavender	.25	.10
❑	152	Pat McInally RC	.50	.20
❑	153	Lloyd Mumphord	.25	.10
❑	154	Cullen Bryant	.50	.20
❑	155	Willie Lanier	1.00	.40
❑	156	Gene Washington 49er	.50	.20
❑	157	Scott Hunter	.25	.10
❑	158	Jim Merlo	.25	.10
❑	159	Randy Grossman	.50	.20
❑	160	Blaine Nye	.25	.10
❑	161	Ike Harris	.25	.10
❑	162	Doug Dieken	.25	.10
❑	163	Guy Morriss	.25	.10
❑	164	Bob Parsons	.25	.10
❑	165	Steve Grogan	1.00	.40
❑	166	John Brockington	.50	.20
❑	167	Charlie Joiner	2.50	1.25
❑	168	Ron Carpenter	.25	.10
❑	169	Jeff Wright S	.25	.10
❑	170	Chris Hanburger	.25	.10
❑	171	Roosevelt Leaks RC	.50	.20
❑	172	Larry Little	1.00	.40
❑	173	John Matuszak	.50	.20
❑	174	Joe Ferguson	.50	.20
❑	175	Brad Van Pelt	.50	.20
❑	176	Dexter Bussey RC	.50	.20
❑	177	Steve Largent RC	40.00	20.00
❑	178	Dewey Selmon	.50	.20
❑	179	Randy Gradishar	1.00	.40
❑	180	Mel Blount	3.00	1.50
❑	181	Dan Neal	.25	.10
❑	182	Rich Szaro	.25	.10
❑	183	Mike Boryla	.25	.10
❑	184	Steve Jones	.25	.10
❑	185	Paul Warfield	2.50	1.25
❑	186	Greg Buttle RC	.25	.10
❑	187	Rich McGeorge	.25	.10
❑	188	Leon Gray RC	.50	.20
❑	189	John Shinners	.25	.10
❑	190	Toni Linhart	.25	.10
❑	191	Robert Miller	.25	.10
❑	192	Jake Scott	.25	.10
❑	193	Jon Morris	.25	.10
❑	194	Randy Crowder	.25	.10
❑	195	Lynn Swann UER	18.00	10.00
❑	196	Marsh White	.25	.10
❑	197	Rod Perry RC	1.00	.40
❑	198	Willie Hall	.25	.10
❑	199	Mike Hartenstine	.25	.10
❑	200	Jim Bakken	.25	.10
❑	201	Atlanta Falcons CL UER	1.25	.50
❑	202	Baltimore Colts CL	1.25	.50
❑	203	Buffalo Bills CL	1.25	.50
❑	204	Chicago Bears CL	1.25	.50
❑	205	Cincinnati Bengals CL	1.25	.50
❑	206	Cleveland Browns CL	1.25	.50
❑	207	Dallas Cowboys CL	1.25	.50
❑	208	Denver Broncos CL	1.25	.50
❑	209	Detroit Lions CL	1.25	.50
❑	210	Green Bay Packers CL	1.25	.50
❑	211	Houston Oilers CL	1.25	.50
❑	212	Kansas City Chiefs CL	1.25	.50
❑	213	Los Angeles Rams CL	1.25	.50
❑	214	Miami Dolphins CL	1.25	.50
❑	215	Minnesota Vikings CL	1.25	.50
❑	216	New England Patriots CL	1.25	.50
❑	217	New Orleans Saints CL	1.25	.50
❑	218	New York Giants CL	1.25	.50
❑	219	New York Jets CL	1.25	.50
❑	220	Oakland Raiders CL	1.25	.50
❑	221	Philadelphia Eagles CL	1.25	.50
❑	222	Pittsburgh Steelers CL	1.25	.50
❑	223	St. Louis Cardinals CL	1.25	.50
❑	224	San Diego Chargers CL	1.25	.50
❑	225	San Francisco 49ers CL	1.25	.50
❑	226	Seattle Seahawks CL	1.25	.50
❑	227	Tampa Bay Buccaneers CL	1.25	.50
❑	228	Washington Redskins CL	1.25	.50
❑	229	Sam Cunningham	.50	.20
❑	230	Alan Page	1.00	.40
❑	231	Eddie Brown S	.25	.10
❑	232	Stan White	.25	.10
❑	233	Vern Den Herder	.25	.10
❑	234	Clarence Davis	.25	.10
❑	235	Ken Anderson	1.00	.40
❑	236	Karl Chandler	.25	.10
❑	237	Will Harrell	.25	.10
❑	238	Clarence Scott	.25	.10
❑	239	Bo Rather	.25	.10
❑	240	Robert Brazile	.50	.20
❑	241	Bob Bell	.25	.10
❑	242	Rolland Lawrence	.25	.10
❑	243	Tom Sullivan	.25	.10
❑	244	Larry Brunson	.25	.10
❑	245	Terry Bradshaw	20.00	10.00
❑	246	Rich Saul	.25	.10
❑	247	Cleveland Elam	.25	.10
❑	248	Don Woods	.25	.10
❑	249	Bruce Laird	.25	.10
❑	250	Coy Bacon	.50	.20
❑	251	Russ Francis	1.00	.40
❑	252	Jim Braxton	.25	.10

❑ 253	Perry Smith	.25	.10
❑ 254	Jerome Barkum	.25	.10
❑ 255	Garo Yepremian	.50	.20
❑ 256	Checklist 133-264	2.00	.75
❑ 257	Tony Galbreath RC	.50	.20
❑ 258	Troy Archer	.25	.10
❑ 259	Brian Sipe	1.00	.40
❑ 260	Billy Joe DuPree	.50	.20
❑ 261	Bobby Walden	.25	.10
❑ 262	Larry Marshall	.25	.10
❑ 263	Ted Fritsch Jr.	.25	.10
❑ 264	Larry Hand	.25	.10
❑ 265	Tom Mack	1.00	.40
❑ 266	Ed Bradley	.25	.10
❑ 267	Pat Leahy	.50	.20
❑ 268	Louis Carter	.25	.10
❑ 269	Archie Griffin RC	6.00	3.00
❑ 270	Art Shell	1.00	.40
❑ 271	Stu Voigt	.25	.10
❑ 272	Prentice McCray	.25	.10
❑ 273	MacArthur Lane	.25	.10
❑ 274	Dan Fouts	6.00	3.00
❑ 275	Charlie Young	.50	.20
❑ 276	Wilbur Jackson RC	.25	.10
❑ 277	John Hicks	.25	.10
❑ 278	Nat Moore	1.00	.40
❑ 279	Virgil Livers	.25	.10
❑ 280	Curley Culp	.50	.20
❑ 281	Rocky Bleier	2.50	1.25
❑ 282	John Zook	.25	.10
❑ 283	Tom DeLeone	.25	.10
❑ 284	Danny White RC	10.00	5.00
❑ 285	Otis Armstrong	.50	.20
❑ 286	Larry Walton	.25	.10
❑ 287	Jim Carter	.25	.10
❑ 288	Don McCauley	.25	.10
❑ 289	Frank Grant	.25	.10
❑ 290	Roger Wehrli	.60	.25
❑ 291	Mick Tingelhoff	.50	.20
❑ 292	Bernard Jackson	.25	.10
❑ 293	Tom Owen RC	.25	.10
❑ 294	Mike Esposito	.25	.10
❑ 295	Fred Biletnikoff	2.50	1.25
❑ 296	Revie Sorey RC	.25	.10
❑ 297	John McMakin	.25	.10
❑ 298	Dan Ryczek	.25	.10
❑ 299	Wayne Moore	.25	.10
❑ 300	Franco Harris	4.00	2.00
❑ 301	Rick Upchurch RC	1.00	.40
❑ 302	Jim Stienke	.25	.10
❑ 303	Charlie Davis	.25	.10
❑ 304	Don Cockroft	.25	.10
❑ 305	Ken Burrough	.50	.20
❑ 306	Clark Gaines	.25	.10
❑ 307	Bobby Douglass	.25	.10
❑ 308	Ralph Perretta	.25	.10
❑ 309	Wally Hilgenberg	.25	.10
❑ 310	Monte Jackson RC	.50	.20
❑ 311	Chris Bahr RC	.50	.20
❑ 312	Jim Cheyunski	.25	.10
❑ 313	Mike Patrick	.25	.10
❑ 314	Ed Too Tall Jones	5.00	2.50
❑ 315	Bill Bradley	.25	.10
❑ 316	Benny Malone	.25	.10
❑ 317	Paul Seymour	.25	.10
❑ 318	Jim Laslavic	.25	.10
❑ 319	Frank Lewis	.50	.20
❑ 320	Ray Guy	1.00	.40
❑ 321	Allan Ellis	.25	.10
❑ 322	Conrad Dobler	.50	.20
❑ 323	Chester Marcol	.25	.10
❑ 324	Doug Kotar	.25	.10
❑ 325	Lemar Parrish	.50	.20
❑ 326	Steve Holden	.25	.10
❑ 327	Jeff Van Note	.50	.20
❑ 328	Howard Stevens	.25	.10
❑ 329	Brad Dusek	.50	.20
❑ 330	Joe DeLamielleure	1.00	.40
❑ 331	Jim Plunkett	1.00	.40
❑ 332	Checklist 265-396	2.00	.75
❑ 333	Lou Piccone	.25	.10
❑ 334	Ray Hamilton	.25	.10
❑ 335	Jan Stenerud	1.00	.40
❑ 336	Jeris White	.25	.10
❑ 337	Sherman Smith RC	.25	.10
❑ 338	Dave Green	.25	.10
❑ 339	Terry Schmidt	.25	.10
❑ 340	Sammie White RC	1.00	.40
❑ 341	Jon Kolb RC	.25	.10
❑ 342	Randy White	8.00	4.00
❑ 343	Bob Klein	.25	.10
❑ 344	Bob Kowalkowski	.25	.10
❑ 345	Terry Metcalf	.50	.20
❑ 346	Joe Danelo	.25	.10
❑ 347	Ken Payne	.25	.10
❑ 348	Neal Craig	.25	.10
❑ 349	Dennis Johnson	.25	.10
❑ 350	Bill Bergey	.50	.20
❑ 351	Raymond Chester	.25	.10
❑ 352	Bob Matheson	.25	.10
❑ 353	Mike Kadish	.25	.10
❑ 354	Mark Van Eeghen RC	1.00	.40
❑ 355	L.C.Greenwood	1.00	.40
❑ 356	Sam Hunt	.25	.10
❑ 357	Darrell Austin	.25	.10
❑ 358	Jim Turner	.25	.10
❑ 359	Ahmad Rashad	2.00	.75
❑ 360	Walter Payton	40.00	15.00
❑ 361	Mark Arneson	.25	.10
❑ 362	Jerrel Wilson	.25	.10
❑ 363	Steve Bartkowski	1.00	.40
❑ 364	John Watson	.25	.10
❑ 365	Ken Riley	.50	.20
❑ 366	Gregg Bingham	.25	.10
❑ 367	Golden Richards	.50	.20
❑ 368	Clyde Powers	.25	.10
❑ 369	Diron Talbert	.25	.10
❑ 370	Lydell Mitchell	.50	.20
❑ 371	Bob Jackson	.25	.10
❑ 372	Jim Mandich	.25	.10
❑ 373	Frank LeMaster	.25	.10
❑ 374	Benny Ricardo	.25	.10
❑ 375	Lawrence McCutcheon	.50	.20
❑ 376	Lynn Dickey	.50	.20
❑ 377	Phil Wise	.25	.10
❑ 378	Tony McGee DT	.25	.10
❑ 379	Norm Thompson	.25	.10
❑ 380	Dave Casper RC	4.00	1.50
❑ 381	Glen Edwards	.25	.10
❑ 382	Bob Thomas	.25	.10
❑ 383	Bob Chandler	.50	.20
❑ 384	Rickey Young	.50	.20
❑ 385	Carl Eller	1.00	.40
❑ 386	Lyle Alzado	1.00	.40
❑ 387	John Leypoldt	.25	.10
❑ 388	Gordon Bell	.25	.10
❑ 389	Mike Bragg	.25	.10
❑ 390	Jim Langer	1.00	.40
❑ 391	Vern Holland	.25	.10
❑ 392	Nelson Munsey	.25	.10
❑ 393	Mack Mitchell	.25	.10
❑ 394	Tony Adams RC	.25	.10
❑ 395	Preston Pearson	.50	.20
❑ 396	Emanuel Zanders	.25	.10
❑ 397	Vince Papale RC	20.00	8.00
❑ 398	Joe Fields RC	.50	.20
❑ 399	Craig Clemons	.25	.10
❑ 400	Fran Tarkenton	5.00	2.50
❑ 401	Andy Johnson	.25	.10
❑ 402	Willie Buchanon	.25	.10
❑ 403	Pat Curran	.25	.10
❑ 404	Ray Jarvis	.25	.10
❑ 405	Joe Greene	2.50	1.25
❑ 406	Bill Simpson	.25	.10
❑ 407	Ronnie Coleman	.25	.10
❑ 408	J.K. McKay RC	.50	.20
❑ 409	Pat Fischer	.50	.20
❑ 410	John Dutton	.50	.20
❑ 411	Boobie Clark	.25	.10
❑ 412	Pat Tilley RC	1.00	.40
❑ 413	Don Strock	.50	.20
❑ 414	Brian Kelley	.25	.10
❑ 415	Gene Upshaw	1.00	.40
❑ 416	Mike Montler	.25	.10
❑ 417	Checklist 397-528	2.00	.75
❑ 418	John Gilliam	.25	.10
❑ 419	Brent McClanahan	.25	.10
❑ 420	Jerry Sherk	.25	.10
❑ 421	Roy Gerela	.25	.10
❑ 422	Tim Fox	.50	.20
❑ 423	John Ebersole	.25	.10
❑ 424	James Scott RC	.25	.10
❑ 425	Delvin Williams RC	.50	.20
❑ 426	Spike Jones	.25	.10
❑ 427	Harvey Martin	1.00	.40
❑ 428	Don Herrmann	.25	.10
❑ 429	Calvin Hill	.50	.20
❑ 430	Isiah Robertson	.25	.10
❑ 431	Tony Greene	.25	.10
❑ 432	Bob Johnson	.25	.10
❑ 433	Lem Barney	1.00	.40
❑ 434	Eric Torkelson	.25	.10
❑ 435	John Mendenhall	.25	.10
❑ 436	Larry Seiple	.50	.20
❑ 437	Art Kuehn	.25	.10
❑ 438	John Vella	.25	.10
❑ 439	Greg Latta	.25	.10
❑ 440	Roger Carr	.50	.20
❑ 441	Doug Sutherland	.25	.10
❑ 442	Mike Kruczek RC	.25	.10
❑ 443	Steve Zabel	.25	.10
❑ 444	Mike Pruitt RC	1.00	.40
❑ 445	Harold Jackson	.50	.20
❑ 446	George Jakowenko	.25	.10
❑ 447	John Fitzgerald	.25	.10
❑ 448	Carey Joyce	.25	.10
❑ 449	Jim LeClair	.25	.10
❑ 450	Ken Houston	1.00	.40
❑ 451	Steve Grogan RB	.50	.20
❑ 452	Jim Marshall RB	.50	.20
❑ 453	O.J.Simpson RB	2.50	1.25
❑ 454	Fran Tarkenton RB	3.00	1.50
❑ 455	Jim Zorn RB	.50	.20
❑ 456	Robert Pratt	.25	.10
❑ 457	Walker Gillette	.25	.10
❑ 458	Charlie Hall	.25	.10
❑ 459	Robert Newhouse	.50	.20
❑ 460	John Hannah	1.00	.40
❑ 461	Ken Reaves	.25	.10
❑ 462	Herman Weaver	.25	.10
❑ 463	James Harris	.50	.20
❑ 464	Howard Twilley	.50	.20
❑ 465	Jeff Siemon	.50	.20
❑ 466	John Outlaw	.25	.10
❑ 467	Chuck Muncie RC	1.00	.40
❑ 468	Bob Moore	.25	.10
❑ 469	Robert Woods	.25	.10
❑ 470	Cliff Branch	2.00	.75
❑ 471	Johnnie Gray	.25	.10
❑ 472	Don Hardeman	.25	.10
❑ 473	Steve Ramsey	.25	.10
❑ 474	Steve Mike-Mayer	.25	.10
❑ 475	Gary Garrison	.25	.10
❑ 476	Walter Johnson	.25	.10
❑ 477	Neil Clabo	.25	.10
❑ 478	Len Hauss	.25	.10
❑ 479	Darryl Stingley	.50	.20
❑ 480	Jack Lambert	8.00	4.00
❑ 481	Mike Adamle	.50	.20
❑ 482	David Lee	.25	.10
❑ 483	Tom Mullen	.25	.10
❑ 484	Claude Humphrey	.25	.10
❑ 485	Jim Hart	1.00	.40
❑ 486	Bobby Thompson RB	.25	.10
❑ 487	Jack Rudnay	.25	.10
❑ 488	Rich Sowells	.25	.10
❑ 489	Reuben Gant	.25	.10
❑ 490	Cliff Harris	1.00	.40
❑ 491	Bob Brown DT	.25	.10
❑ 492	Don Nottingham	.25	.10
❑ 493	Ron Jessie	.25	.10
❑ 494	Otis Sistrunk	.50	.20
❑ 495	Billy Kilmer	.50	.20
❑ 496	Oscar Roan	.25	.10
❑ 497	Bill Van Heusen	.25	.10
❑ 498	Randy Logan	.25	.10
❑ 499	John Smith	.25	.10
❑ 500	Chuck Foreman	.50	.20
❑ 501	J.T. Thomas	.25	.10
❑ 502	Steve Schubert	.25	.10
❑ 503	Mike Barnes	.25	.10
❑ 504	J.V. Cain	.25	.10
❑ 505	Larry Csonka	3.00	1.50
❑ 506	Elvin Bethea	1.00	.40
❑ 507	Ray Easterling	.25	.10
❑ 508	Joe Reed	.25	.10
❑ 509	Steve Odom	.25	.10
❑ 510	Tommy Casanova	.25	.10
❑ 511	Dave Dalby	.25	.10
❑ 512	Richard Caster	.25	.10
❑ 513	Fred Dryer	1.00	.40

❑ 514	Jeff Kinney	.25	.10
❑ 515	Bob Griese	3.00	1.50
❑ 516	Butch Johnson RC	1.00	.40
❑ 517	Gerald Irons	.25	.10
❑ 518	Don Calhoun	.25	.10
❑ 519	Jack Gregory	.25	.10
❑ 520	Tom Banks	.25	.10
❑ 521	Bobby Bryant	.25	.10
❑ 522	Reggie Harrison	.25	.10
❑ 523	Terry Hermeling	.25	.10
❑ 524	David Taylor	.25	.10
❑ 525	Brian Baschnagel RC	.50	.20
❑ 526	AFC Champ/Stabler	1.00	.40
❑ 527	NFC Championship	.50	.20
❑ 528	Super Bowl XI	1.00	.40

1978 Topps

❑	COMPLETE SET (528)	150.00	80.00
❑ 1	Gary Huff HL !	1.00	.40
❑ 2	Craig Morton HL	1.00	.40
❑ 3	Walter Payton HL	8.00	3.00
❑ 4	O.J.Simpson HL	2.00	.75
❑ 5	Fran Tarkenton HL	2.00	.75
❑ 6	Bob Thomas HL	.20	.07
❑ 7	Joe Pisarcik	.50	.20
❑ 8	Skip Thomas	.20	.07
❑ 9	Roosevelt Leaks	.20	.07
❑ 10	Ken Houston	1.00	.40
❑ 11	Tom Blanchard	.20	.07
❑ 12	Jim Turner	.20	.07
❑ 13	Tom DeLeone	.20	.07
❑ 14	Jim LeClair	.20	.07
❑ 15	Bob Avellini	.50	.20
❑ 16	Tony McGee DT	.20	.07
❑ 17	James Harris	.50	.20
❑ 18	Terry Nelson	.20	.07
❑ 19	Rocky Bleier	2.00	.75
❑ 20	Joe DeLamielleure	1.00	.40
❑ 21	Richard Caster	.20	.07
❑ 22	A.J.Duhe RC	1.00	.40
❑ 23	John Outlaw	.20	.07
❑ 24	Danny White	1.25	.50
❑ 25	Larry Csonka	2.50	1.00
❑ 26	David Hill RC	.50	.20
❑ 27	Mark Arneson	.20	.07
❑ 28	Jack Tatum	.50	.20
❑ 29	Norm Thompson	.20	.07
❑ 30	Sammie White	.50	.20
❑ 31	Dennis Johnson	.20	.07
❑ 32	Robin Earl	.20	.07
❑ 33	Don Cockroft	.20	.07
❑ 34	Bob Johnson	.20	.07
❑ 35	John Hannah	1.00	.40
❑ 36	Scott Hunter	.20	.07
❑ 37	Ken Burrough	.50	.20
❑ 38	Wilbur Jackson	.50	.20
❑ 39	Rich McGeorge	.20	.07
❑ 40	Lyle Alzado	1.00	.40
❑ 41	John Ebersole	.20	.07
❑ 42	Gary Green RC	.20	.07
❑ 43	Art Kuehn	.20	.07
❑ 44	Glen Edwards	.50	.20
❑ 45	Lawrence McCutcheon	.50	.20
❑ 46	Duriel Harris	.20	.07
❑ 47	Rich Szaro	.20	.07
❑ 48	Mike Washington	.20	.07
❑ 49	Stan White	.20	.07
❑ 50	Dave Casper	1.00	.40
❑ 51	Len Hauss	.20	.07
❑ 52	James Scott	.20	.07
❑ 53	Brian Sipe	1.00	.40
❑ 54	Gary Shirk	.20	.07
❑ 55	Archie Griffin	1.00	.40
❑ 56	Mike Patrick	.20	.07
❑ 57	Mario Clark	.20	.07
❑ 58	Jeff Siemon	.20	.07
❑ 59	Steve Mike-Mayer	.20	.07
❑ 60	Randy White	4.00	2.00
❑ 61	Darrell Austin	.20	.07
❑ 62	Tom Sullivan	.20	.07
❑ 63	Johnny Rodgers RC	1.00	.40
❑ 64	Ken Reaves	.20	.07
❑ 65	Terry Bradshaw	12.00	6.00
❑ 66	Fred Steinfort	.20	.07
❑ 67	Curley Culp	.50	.20
❑ 68	Ted Hendricks	1.00	.40
❑ 69	Raymond Chester	.20	.07
❑ 70	Jim Langer	1.00	.40
❑ 71	Calvin Hill	.50	.20
❑ 72	Mike Hartenstine	.20	.07
❑ 73	Gerald Irons	.20	.07
❑ 74	Billy Brooks	.50	.20
❑ 75	John Mendenhall	.20	.07
❑ 76	Andy Johnson	.20	.07
❑ 77	Tom Wittum	.20	.07
❑ 78	Lynn Dickey	.50	.20
❑ 79	Carl Eller	1.00	.40
❑ 80	Tom Mack	1.00	.40
❑ 81	Clark Gaines	.20	.07
❑ 82	Lem Barney	1.00	.40
❑ 83	Mike Montler	.20	.07
❑ 84	Jon Kolb	.20	.07
❑ 85	Bob Chandler	.50	.20
❑ 86	Robert Newhouse	.50	.20
❑ 87	Frank LeMaster	.20	.07
❑ 88	Jeff West	.20	.07
❑ 89	Lyle Blackwood	.50	.20
❑ 90	Gene Upshaw	1.00	.40
❑ 91	Frank Grant	.20	.07
❑ 92	Tom Hicks	.20	.07
❑ 93	Mike Pruitt	.50	.20
❑ 94	Chris Bahr	.20	.07
❑ 95	Russ Francis	.50	.20
❑ 96	Norris Thomas	.20	.07
❑ 97	Gary Barbaro RC	.50	.20
❑ 98	Jim Merlo	.20	.07
❑ 99	Karl Chandler	.20	.07
❑ 100	Fran Tarkenton	4.00	1.50
❑ 101	Abdul Salaam	.20	.07
❑ 102	Marv Kellum	.20	.07
❑ 103	Herman Weaver	.20	.07
❑ 104	Roy Gerela	.20	.07
❑ 105	Harold Jackson	.50	.20
❑ 106	Dewey Selmon	.50	.20
❑ 107	Checklist 1-132	1.00	.40
❑ 108	Clarence Davis	.20	.07
❑ 109	Robert Pratt	.20	.07
❑ 110	Harvey Martin	1.00	.40
❑ 111	Brad Dusek	.20	.07
❑ 112	Greg Latta	.20	.07
❑ 113	Tony Peters	.20	.07
❑ 114	Jim Braxton	.20	.07
❑ 115	Ken Riley	.50	.20
❑ 116	Steve Nelson	.20	.07
❑ 117	Rick Upchurch	.50	.20
❑ 118	Spike Jones	.20	.07
❑ 119	Doug Kotar	.20	.07
❑ 120	Bob Griese	2.50	1.00
❑ 121	Burgess Owens	.20	.07
❑ 122	Rolf Benirschke RC	.50	.20
❑ 123	Haskel Stanback RC	.20	.07
❑ 124	J.T. Thomas	.20	.07
❑ 125	Ahmad Rashad	1.50	.60
❑ 126	Rick Kane	.20	.07
❑ 127	Elvin Bethea	1.00	.40
❑ 128	Dave Dalby	.20	.07
❑ 129	Mike Barnes	.20	.07
❑ 130	Isiah Robertson	.20	.07
❑ 131	Jim Plunkett	1.00	.40
❑ 132	Allan Ellis	.20	.07
❑ 133	Mike Bragg	.20	.07
❑ 134	Bob Jackson	.20	.07
❑ 135	Coy Bacon	.20	.07
❑ 136	John Smith	.20	.07
❑ 137	Chuck Muncie	.50	.20
❑ 138	Johnnie Gray	.20	.07
❑ 139	Jimmy Robinson	.20	.07
❑ 140	Tom Banks	.20	.07
❑ 141	Marvin Powell RC	.20	.07
❑ 142	Jerrel Wilson	.20	.07
❑ 143	Ron Howard	.20	.07
❑ 144	Rob Lytle RC	.50	.20
❑ 145	L.C.Greenwood	1.00	.40
❑ 146	Morris Owens	.20	.07
❑ 147	Joe Reed	.20	.07
❑ 148	Mike Kadish	.20	.07
❑ 149	Phil Villapiano	.50	.20
❑ 150	Lydell Mitchell	.50	.20
❑ 151	Randy Logan	.20	.07
❑ 152	Mike Williams RC	.20	.07
❑ 153	Jeff Van Note	.50	.20
❑ 154	Steve Schubert	.20	.07
❑ 155	Billy Kilmer	.50	.20
❑ 156	Boobie Clark	.20	.07
❑ 157	Charlie Hall	.20	.07
❑ 158	Raymond Clayborn RC	1.00	.40
❑ 159	Jack Gregory	.20	.07
❑ 160	Cliff Harris	1.00	.40
❑ 161	Joe Fields	.20	.07
❑ 162	Don Nottingham	.20	.07
❑ 163	Ed White	.50	.20
❑ 164	Toni Fritsch	.20	.07
❑ 165	Jack Lambert	4.00	2.00
❑ 166	NFC Champs/Staubach	1.50	.60
❑ 167	AFC Champs/Lytle	.50	.20
❑ 168	Super Bowl XII/Dorsett	3.00	1.50
❑ 169	Neal Colzie RC	.20	.07
❑ 170	Cleveland Elam	.20	.07
❑ 171	David Lee	.20	.07
❑ 172	Jim Otis	.20	.07
❑ 173	Archie Manning	1.00	.40
❑ 174	Jim Carter	.20	.07
❑ 175	Jean Fugett	.20	.07
❑ 176	Willie Parker C	.20	.07
❑ 177	Haven Moses	.50	.20
❑ 178	Horace King RC	.20	.07
❑ 179	Bob Thomas	.20	.07
❑ 180	Monte Jackson	.20	.07
❑ 181	Steve Zabel	.20	.07
❑ 182	John Fitzgerald	.20	.07
❑ 183	Mike Livingston	.20	.07
❑ 184	Larry Poole	.20	.07
❑ 185	Isaac Curtis	.50	.20
❑ 186	Chuck Ramsey	.20	.07
❑ 187	Bob Klein	.20	.07
❑ 188	Ray Rhodes	1.00	.40
❑ 189	Otis Sistrunk	.50	.20
❑ 190	Bill Bergey	.50	.20
❑ 191	Sherman Smith	.50	.20
❑ 192	Dave Green	.20	.07
❑ 193	Carl Mauck	.20	.07
❑ 194	Reggie Harrison	.20	.07
❑ 195	Roger Carr	.50	.20
❑ 196	Steve Bartkowski	1.00	.40
❑ 197	Ray Wersching	.20	.07
❑ 198	Willie Buchanon	.20	.07
❑ 199	Neil Clabo	.20	.07
❑ 200	Walter Payton UER	25.00	12.50
❑ 201	Sam Adams OL	.20	.07
❑ 202	Larry Gordon	.20	.07
❑ 203	Pat Tilley	.50	.20
❑ 204	Mack Mitchell	.20	.07
❑ 205	Ken Anderson	1.00	.40
❑ 206	Scott Dierking	.20	.07
❑ 207	Jack Rudnay	.20	.07
❑ 208	Jim Stienke	.20	.07
❑ 209	Bill Simpson	.20	.07
❑ 210	Errol Mann	.20	.07
❑ 211	Bucky Dilts	.20	.07
❑ 212	Reuben Gant	.20	.07
❑ 213	Thomas Henderson RC	1.50	.60
❑ 214	Steve Furness	.50	.20
❑ 215	John Riggins	2.00	.75
❑ 216	Keith Krepfle RC	.20	.07
❑ 217	Fred Dean RC	.50	.20
❑ 218	Emanuel Zanders	.20	.07
❑ 219	Don Testerman	.20	.07
❑ 220	George Kunz	.20	.07
❑ 221	Darryl Stingley	.50	.20
❑ 222	Ken Sanders	.20	.07
❑ 223	Gary Huff	.20	.07
❑ 224	Gregg Bingham	.20	.07
❑ 225	Jerry Sherk	.20	.07

	No.	Card		
❑	226	Doug Plank	.20	.07
❑	227	Ed Taylor	.20	.07
❑	228	Emery Moorehead	.20	.07
❑	229	Reggie Williams RC	1.00	.40
❑	230	Claude Humphrey	.20	.07
❑	231	Randy Cross RC	2.00	.75
❑	232	Jim Hart	1.00	.40
❑	233	Bobby Bryant	.20	.07
❑	234	Larry Brown	.20	.07
❑	235	Mark Van Eeghen	.50	.20
❑	236	Terry Hermeling	.20	.07
❑	237	Steve Odom	.20	.07
❑	238	Jan Stenerud	1.00	.40
❑	239	Andre Tillman	.20	.07
❑	240	Tom Jackson RC	5.00	2.00
❑	241	Ken Mendenhall	.20	.07
❑	242	Tim Fox	.20	.07
❑	243	Don Herrmann	.20	.07
❑	244	Eddie McMillan	.20	.07
❑	245	Greg Pruitt	.50	.20
❑	246	J.K. McKay	.20	.07
❑	247	Larry Keller	.20	.07
❑	248	Dave Jennings	.50	.20
❑	249	Bo Harris	.20	.07
❑	250	Revie Sorey	.20	.07
❑	251	Tony Greene	.20	.07
❑	252	Butch Johnson	.50	.20
❑	253	Paul Naumoff	.20	.07
❑	254	Rickey Young	.50	.20
❑	255	Dwight White	.50	.20
❑	256	Joe Lavender	.20	.07
❑	257	Checklist 133-264	1.00	.40
❑	258	Ronnie Coleman	.20	.07
❑	259	Charlie Smith WR	.20	.07
❑	260	Ray Guy	1.00	.40
❑	261	David Taylor	.20	.07
❑	262	Bill Lenkaitis	.20	.07
❑	263	Jim Mitchell TE	.20	.07
❑	264	Delvin Williams	.20	.07
❑	265	Jack Youngblood	1.00	.40
❑	266	Chuck Crist	.20	.07
❑	267	Richard Todd	.50	.20
❑	268	Dave Logan RC	1.00	.40
❑	269	Rufus Mayes	.20	.07
❑	270	Brad Van Pelt	.20	.07
❑	271	Chester Marcol	.20	.07
❑	272	J.V. Cain	.20	.07
❑	273	Larry Seiple	.20	.07
❑	274	Brent McClanahan	.20	.07
❑	275	Mike Wagner	.20	.07
❑	276	Diron Talbert	.20	.07
❑	277	Brian Baschnagel	.20	.07
❑	278	Ed Podolak	.20	.07
❑	279	Don Goode	.20	.07
❑	280	John Dutton	.50	.20
❑	281	Don Calhoun	.20	.07
❑	282	Monte Johnson	.20	.07
❑	283	Ron Jessie	.20	.07
❑	284	Jon Morris	.20	.07
❑	285	Riley Odoms	.20	.07
❑	286	Marv Bateman	.20	.07
❑	287	Joe Klecko RC	1.00	.40
❑	288	Oliver Davis	.20	.07
❑	289	John McDaniel	.20	.07
❑	290	Roger Staubach	12.00	6.00
❑	291	Brian Kelley	.20	.07
❑	292	Mike Hogan	.20	.07
❑	293	John Leypoldt	.20	.07
❑	294	Jack Novak	.20	.07
❑	295	Joe Greene	2.00	.75
❑	296	John Hill	.20	.07
❑	297	Danny Buggs	.20	.07
❑	298	Ted Albrecht	.20	.07
❑	299	Nelson Munsey	.20	.07
❑	300	Chuck Foreman	.50	.20
❑	301	Dan Pastorini	.50	.20
❑	302	Tommy Hart	.20	.07
❑	303	Dave Beverly	.20	.07
❑	304	Tony Reed RC	.50	.20
❑	305	Cliff Branch	1.50	.60
❑	306	Clarence Duren	.20	.07
❑	307	Randy Rasmussen	.20	.07
❑	308	Oscar Roan	.20	.07
❑	309	Lenvil Elliott	.20	.07
❑	310	Dan Dierdorf	1.00	.40
❑	311	Johnny Perkins	.20	.07
❑	312	Rafael Septien RC	.50	.20
❑	313	Terry Beeson	.20	.07
❑	314	Lee Roy Selmon	2.00	.75
❑	315	Tony Dorsett RC	40.00	25.00
❑	316	Greg Landry	.50	.20
❑	317	Jake Scott	.20	.07
❑	318	Dan Peiffer	.20	.07
❑	319	John Bunting	.50	.20
❑	320	John Stallworth RC	20.00	10.00
❑	321	Bob Howard	.20	.07
❑	322	Larry Little	1.00	.40
❑	323	Reggie McKenzie	.50	.20
❑	324	Duane Carrell	.20	.07
❑	325	Ed Simonini	.20	.07
❑	326	John Vella	.20	.07
❑	327	Wesley Walker RC	3.00	1.50
❑	328	Jon Keyworth	.20	.07
❑	329	Ron Bolton	.20	.07
❑	330	Tommy Casanova	.20	.07
❑	331	R.Staubach/B.Griese LL	4.00	2.00
❑	332	A.Rashad/Mitchell LL	1.00	.40
❑	333	W.Payton/VanEeghenLL	3.00	1.25
❑	334	W.Payton/E.Mann LL	3.00	1.25
❑	335	Interception Leaders	.20	.07
❑	336	Punting Leaders	.50	.20
❑	337	Robert Brazile	.50	.20
❑	338	Charlie Joiner	1.50	.60
❑	339	Joe Ferguson	.50	.20
❑	340	Bill Thompson	.20	.07
❑	341	Sam Cunningham	.50	.20
❑	342	Curtis Johnson	.20	.07
❑	343	Jim Marshall	1.00	.40
❑	344	Charlie Sanders	.50	.20
❑	345	Willie Hall	.20	.07
❑	346	Pat Haden	1.00	.40
❑	347	Jim Bakken	.20	.07
❑	348	Bruce Taylor	.20	.07
❑	349	Barty Smith	.20	.07
❑	350	Drew Pearson	1.50	.60
❑	351	Mike Webster	2.50	1.00
❑	352	Bobby Hammond	.20	.07
❑	353	Dave Mays	.20	.07
❑	354	Pat McInally	.20	.07
❑	355	Toni Linhart	.20	.07
❑	356	Larry Hand	.20	.07
❑	357	Ted Fritsch Jr.	.20	.07
❑	358	Larry Marshall	.20	.07
❑	359	Waymond Bryant	.20	.07
❑	360	Louie Kelcher RC	.50	.20
❑	361	Stanley Morgan RC	2.00	.75
❑	362	Bruce Harper RC	.50	.20
❑	363	Bernard Jackson	.20	.07
❑	364	Walter White	.20	.07
❑	365	Ken Stabler	8.00	4.00
❑	366	Fred Dryer	1.00	.40
❑	367	Ike Harris	.20	.07
❑	368	Norm Bulaich	.20	.07
❑	369	Merv Krakau	.20	.07
❑	370	John James	.20	.07
❑	371	Bennie Cunningham RC	.20	.07
❑	372	Doug Van Horn	.20	.07
❑	373	Thom Darden	.20	.07
❑	374	Eddie Edwards RC	.20	.07
❑	375	Mike Thomas	.20	.07
❑	376	Fred Cook	.20	.07
❑	377	Mike Phipps	.50	.20
❑	378	Paul Krause	1.00	.40
❑	379	Harold Carmichael	1.00	.40
❑	380	Mike Haynes	1.00	.40
❑	381	Wayne Morris	.20	.07
❑	382	Greg Buttle	.20	.07
❑	383	Jim Zorn	1.00	.40
❑	384	Jack Dolbin	.20	.07
❑	385	Charlie Waters	.50	.20
❑	386	Dan Ryczek	.20	.07
❑	387	Joe Washington RC	1.00	.40
❑	388	Checklist 265-396	1.00	.40
❑	389	James Hunter	.20	.07
❑	390	Billy Johnson	.50	.20
❑	391	Jim Allen RC	.20	.07
❑	392	George Buehler	.20	.07
❑	393	Harry Carson	1.00	.40
❑	394	Cleo Miller	.20	.07
❑	395	Gary Burley	.20	.07
❑	396	Mark Moseley	.50	.20
❑	397	Virgil Livers	.20	.07
❑	398	Joe Ehrmann	.20	.07
❑	399	Freddie Solomon	.20	.07
❑	400	O.J.Simpson	4.00	2.00
❑	401	Julius Adams	.20	.07
❑	402	Artimus Parker	.20	.07
❑	403	Gene Washington 49er	.50	.20
❑	404	Herman Edwards	.50	.20
❑	405	Craig Morton	1.00	.40
❑	406	Alan Page	1.00	.40
❑	407	Larry McCarren	.20	.07
❑	408	Tony Galbreath	.50	.20
❑	409	Roman Gabriel	1.00	.40
❑	410	Efren Herrera	.20	.07
❑	411	Jim Smith RC	1.00	.40
❑	412	Bill Bryant	.20	.07
❑	413	Doug Dieken	.20	.07
❑	414	Marvin Cobb	.20	.07
❑	415	Fred Biletnikoff	2.00	.75
❑	416	Joe Theismann	2.50	1.00
❑	417	Roland Harper	.20	.07
❑	418	Derrel Luce	.20	.07
❑	419	Ralph Perretta	.20	.07
❑	420	Louis Wright RC	1.00	.40
❑	421	Prentice McCray	.20	.07
❑	422	Garry Puetz	.20	.07
❑	423	Alfred Jenkins RC	1.00	.40
❑	424	Paul Seymour	.20	.07
❑	425	Garo Yepremian	.50	.20
❑	426	Emmitt Thomas	.20	.07
❑	427	Dexter Bussey	.20	.07
❑	428	John Sanders	.20	.07
❑	429	Ed Too Tall Jones	2.00	.75
❑	430	Ron Yary	1.00	.40
❑	431	Frank Lewis	.50	.20
❑	432	Jerry Golsteyn	.20	.07
❑	433	Clarence Scott	.20	.07
❑	434	Pete Johnson RC	1.00	.40
❑	435	Charle Young	.50	.20
❑	436	Harold McLinton	.20	.07
❑	437	Noah Jackson	.20	.07
❑	438	Bruce Laird	.20	.07
❑	439	John Matuszak	.50	.20
❑	440	Nat Moore	.50	.20
❑	441	Leon Gray	.20	.07
❑	442	Jerome Barkum	.20	.07
❑	443	Steve Largent	12.00	6.00
❑	444	John Zook	.20	.07
❑	445	Preston Pearson	.50	.20
❑	446	Conrad Dobler	.50	.20
❑	447	Wilbur Summers	.20	.07
❑	448	Lou Piccone	.20	.07
❑	449	Ron Jaworski	1.00	.40
❑	450	Jack Ham	1.50	.60
❑	451	Mick Tingelhoff	.50	.20
❑	452	Clyde Powers	.20	.07
❑	453	John Cappelletti	1.00	.40
❑	454	Dick Ambrose	.20	.07
❑	455	Lemar Parrish	.20	.07
❑	456	Ron Saul	.20	.07
❑	457	Bob Parsons	.20	.07
❑	458	Glenn Doughty	.20	.07
❑	459	Don Woods	.20	.07
❑	460	Art Shell	1.00	.40
❑	461	Sam Hunt	.20	.07
❑	462	Lawrence Pillers	.20	.07
❑	463	Henry Childs	.20	.07
❑	464	Roger Wehrli	.50	.20
❑	465	Otis Armstrong	.50	.20
❑	466	Bob Baumhower RC	2.00	.75
❑	467	Ray Jarvis	.20	.07
❑	468	Guy Morriss	.20	.07
❑	469	Matt Blair	.50	.20
❑	470	Billy Joe DuPree	.50	.20
❑	471	Roland Hooks	.20	.07
❑	472	Joe Danelo	.20	.07
❑	473	Reggie Rucker	.50	.20
❑	474	Vern Holland	.20	.07
❑	475	Mel Blount	1.50	.60
❑	476	Eddie Brown S	.20	.07
❑	477	Bo Rather	.20	.07
❑	478	Don McCauley	.20	.07
❑	479	Glen Walker	.20	.07
❑	480	Randy Gradishar	1.00	.40
❑	481	Dave Rowe	.20	.07
❑	482	Pat Leahy	.50	.20
❑	483	Mike Fuller	.20	.07
❑	484	David Lewis RC	.20	.07
❑	485	Steve Grogan	1.00	.40
❑	486	Mel Gray	.50	.20

	Card		
❑	487 Eddie Payton RC	.50	.20
❑	488 Checklist 397-528	1.00	.40
❑	489 Stu Voigt	.20	.07
❑	490 Rolland Lawrence	.20	.07
❑	491 Nick Mike-Mayer	.20	.07
❑	492 Troy Archer	.20	.07
❑	493 Benny Malone	.20	.07
❑	494 Golden Richards	.50	.20
❑	495 Chris Hanburger	.20	.07
❑	496 Dwight Harrison	.20	.07
❑	497 Gary Fencik RC	1.00	.40
❑	498 Rich Saul	.20	.07
❑	499 Dan Fouts	4.00	2.00
❑	500 Franco Harris	4.00	2.00
❑	501 Atlanta Falcons TL	.75	.30
❑	502 Baltimore Colts TL	.75	.30
❑	503 Bills TL/O.J.Simpson	1.50	.60
❑	504 Bears TL/Walter Payton	2.00	.75
❑	505 Bengals TL/Reg.Williams	.75	.30
❑	506 Cleveland Browns TL	.75	.30
❑	507 Cowboys TL/T.Dorsett	2.50	1.00
❑	508 Denver Broncos TL	1.00	.40
❑	509 Detroit Lions TL	.75	.30
❑	510 Green Bay Packers TL	1.00	.40
❑	511 Houston Oilers TL	.75	.30
❑	512 Kansas City Chiefs TL	.75	.30
❑	513 Los Angeles Rams TL	.75	.30
❑	514 Miami Dolphins TL	1.00	.40
❑	515 Minnesota Vikings TL	.75	.30
❑	516 New England Patriots TL	.75	.30
❑	517 New Orleans Saints TL	.75	.30
❑	518 New York Giants TL	.75	.30
❑	519 Jets TL/Wesley Walker	.75	.30
❑	520 Oakland Raiders TL	1.00	.40
❑	521 Philadelphia Eagles TL	.75	.30
❑	522 Steelers TL/Harris/Blount	1.00	.40
❑	523 St.Louis Cardinals TL	.75	.30
❑	524 San Diego Chargers TL	1.00	.40
❑	525 San Francisco 49ers TL	.75	.30
❑	526 Seahawks TL/S.Largent	1.50	.60
❑	527 Tampa Bay Bucs TL	.75	.30
❑	528 Redskins TL/Ken Houston	1.00	.40

1979 Topps

	Card		
❑	COMPLETE SET (528)	150.00	75.00
❑	1 Staubach/Bradshaw LL	8.00	4.00
❑	2 S.Largent/R.Young LL	1.00	.40
❑	3 E.Campbell/W.Payton LL	8.00	4.00
❑	4 Scoring Leaders	.20	.07
❑	5 Interception Leaders	.20	.07
❑	6 Punting Leaders	.20	.07
❑	7 Johnny Perkins	.20	.07
❑	8 Charles Phillips	.20	.07
❑	9 Derrel Luce	.20	.07
❑	10 John Riggins	1.25	.50
❑	11 Chester Marcol	.20	.07
❑	12 Bernard Jackson	.20	.07
❑	13 Dave Logan	.20	.07
❑	14 Bo Harris	.20	.07
❑	15 Alan Page	1.00	.40
❑	16 John Smith	.20	.07
❑	17 Dwight McDonald	.20	.07
❑	18 John Cappelletti	.50	.20
❑	19 Steelers TL/Harris/Dungy	12.00	5.00
❑	20 Bill Bergey	.50	.20
❑	21 Jerome Barkum	.20	.07
❑	22 Larry Csonka	2.50	1.00
❑	23 Joe Ferguson	.50	.20
❑	24 Ed Too Tall Jones	1.25	.50
❑	25 Dave Jennings	.50	.20
❑	26 Horace King	.20	.07
❑	27 Steve Little	.50	.20
❑	28 Morris Bradshaw	.20	.07
❑	29 Joe Ehrmann	.20	.07
❑	30 Ahmad Rashad	1.00	.40
❑	31 Joe Lavender	.20	.07
❑	32 Dan Neal	.20	.07
❑	33 Johnny Evans	.20	.07
❑	34 Pete Johnson	.50	.20
❑	35 Mike Haynes	1.00	.40
❑	36 Tim Mazzetti	.20	.07
❑	37 Mike Barber RC	.20	.07
❑	38 49ers TL/O.J.Simpson	1.50	.60
❑	39 Bill Gregory	.20	.07
❑	40 Randy Gradishar	1.00	.40
❑	41 Richard Todd	.50	.20
❑	42 Henry Marshall	.20	.07
❑	43 John Hill	.20	.07
❑	44 Sidney Thornton	.20	.07
❑	45 Ron Jessie	.20	.07
❑	46 Bob Baumhower	.50	.20
❑	47 Johnnie Gray	.20	.07
❑	48 Doug Williams RC	6.00	3.00
❑	49 Don McCauley	.20	.07
❑	50 Ray Guy	.50	.20
❑	51 Bob Klein	.20	.07
❑	52 Golden Richards	.20	.07
❑	53 Mark Miller QB	.20	.07
❑	54 John Sanders	.20	.07
❑	55 Gary Burley	.20	.07
❑	56 Steve Nelson	.20	.07
❑	57 Buffalo Bills TL	.75	.30
❑	58 Bobby Bryant	.20	.07
❑	59 Rick Kane	.20	.07
❑	60 Larry Little	1.00	.40
❑	61 Ted Fritsch Jr.	.20	.07
❑	62 Larry Mallory	.20	.07
❑	63 Marvin Powell	.20	.07
❑	64 Jim Hart	1.00	.40
❑	65 Joe Greene	1.50	.60
❑	66 Walter White	.20	.07
❑	67 Gregg Bingham	.20	.07
❑	68 Errol Mann	.20	.07
❑	69 Bruce Laird	.20	.07
❑	70 Drew Pearson	1.00	.40
❑	71 Steve Bartkowski	1.00	.40
❑	72 Ted Albrecht	.20	.07
❑	73 Charlie Hall	.20	.07
❑	74 Pat McInally	.20	.07
❑	75 Bubba Baker RC	1.00	.40
❑	76 New England Pats TL	.75	.30
❑	77 Steve DeBerg RC	2.00	.75
❑	78 John Yarno	.20	.07
❑	79 Stu Voigt	.20	.07
❑	80 Frank Corral AP	.20	.07
❑	81 Troy Archer	.20	.07
❑	82 Bruce Harper	.20	.07
❑	83 Tom Jackson	1.50	.60
❑	84 Larry Brown	.50	.20
❑	85 Wilbert Montgomery RC	1.00	.40
❑	86 Butch Johnson	.50	.20
❑	87 Mike Kadish	.20	.07
❑	88 Ralph Perretta	.20	.07
❑	89 David Lee	.20	.07
❑	90 Mark Van Eeghen	.50	.20
❑	91 John McDaniel	.20	.07
❑	92 Gary Fencik	.50	.20
❑	93 Mack Mitchell	.20	.07
❑	94 Cincinnati Bengals TL/Jauron	1.00	.40
❑	95 Steve Grogan	1.00	.40
❑	96 Garo Yepremian	.50	.20
❑	97 Barty Smith	.20	.07
❑	98 Frank Reed	.20	.07
❑	99 Jim Clack	.20	.07
❑	100 Chuck Foreman	.50	.20
❑	101 Joe Klecko	1.00	.40
❑	102 Pat Tilley	.50	.20
❑	103 Conrad Dobler	.50	.20
❑	104 Craig Colquitt	.20	.07
❑	105 Dan Pastorini	.50	.20
❑	106 Rod Perry AP	.20	.07
❑	107 Nick Mike-Mayer	.20	.07
❑	108 John Matuszak	.50	.20
❑	109 David Taylor	.20	.07
❑	110 Billy Joe DuPree	.50	.20
❑	111 Harold McLinton	.20	.07
❑	112 Virgil Livers	.20	.07
❑	113 Cleveland Browns TL	.75	.30
❑	114 Checklist 1-132	1.00	.40
❑	115 Ken Anderson	1.00	.40
❑	116 Bill Lenkaitis	.20	.07
❑	117 Bucky Dilts	.20	.07
❑	118 Tony Greene	.20	.07
❑	119 Bobby Hammond	.20	.07
❑	120 Nat Moore	.50	.20
❑	121 Pat Leahy	.50	.20
❑	122 James Harris	.50	.20
❑	123 Lee Roy Selmon	1.25	.50
❑	124 Bennie Cunningham	.50	.20
❑	125 Matt Blair AP	.50	.20
❑	126 Jim Allen	.20	.07
❑	127 Alfred Jenkins	.50	.20
❑	128 Arthur Whittington	.20	.07
❑	129 Norm Thompson	.20	.07
❑	130 Pat Haden	1.00	.40
❑	131 Freddie Solomon	.20	.07
❑	132 Bears TL/W.Payton	2.00	.75
❑	133 Mark Moseley	.20	.07
❑	134 Cleo Miller	.20	.07
❑	135 Ross Browner RC	.50	.20
❑	136 Don Calhoun	.20	.07
❑	137 David Whitehurst	.20	.07
❑	138 Terry Beeson	.20	.07
❑	139 Ken Stone	.20	.07
❑	140 Brad Van Pelt AP	.20	.07
❑	141 Wesley Walker	1.00	.40
❑	142 Jan Stenerud	1.00	.40
❑	143 Henry Childs	.20	.07
❑	144 Otis Armstrong	1.00	.40
❑	145 Dwight White	.50	.20
❑	146 Steve Wilson	.20	.07
❑	147 Tom Skladany RC	.20	.07
❑	148 Lou Piccone	.20	.07
❑	149 Monte Johnson	.20	.07
❑	150 Joe Washington	.50	.20
❑	151 Eagles TL/W.Montgomery	.75	.30
❑	152 Fred Dean	.20	.07
❑	153 Rolland Lawrence	.20	.07
❑	154 Brian Baschnagel	.20	.07
❑	155 Joe Theismann	2.00	.75
❑	156 Marvin Cobb	.20	.07
❑	157 Dick Ambrose	.20	.07
❑	158 Mike Patrick	.20	.07
❑	159 Gary Shirk	.20	.07
❑	160 Tony Dorsett	12.00	6.00
❑	161 Greg Buttle	.20	.07
❑	162 A.J. Duhe	.50	.20
❑	163 Mick Tingelhoff	.50	.20
❑	164 Ken Burrough	.50	.20
❑	165 Mike Wagner	.20	.07
❑	166 AFC Champs/F.Harris	1.00	.40
❑	167 NFC Championship	.50	.20
❑	168 Super Bowl XIII/Harris	1.25	.50
❑	169 Raiders TL/Ted Hendricks	1.00	.40
❑	170 O.J.Simpson	4.00	1.50
❑	171 Doug Nettles	.20	.07
❑	172 Dan Dierdorf	1.00	.40
❑	173 Dave Beverly	.20	.07
❑	174 Jim Zorn	1.00	.40
❑	175 Mike Thomas	.20	.07
❑	176 John Outlaw	.20	.07
❑	177 Jim Turner	.20	.07
❑	178 Freddie Scott	.20	.07
❑	179 Mike Phipps	.50	.20
❑	180 Jack Youngblood	1.00	.40
❑	181 Sam Hunt	.20	.07
❑	182 Tony Hill RC	1.00	.40
❑	183 Gary Barbaro	.20	.07
❑	184 Archie Griffin	.50	.20
❑	185 Jerry Sherk	.20	.07
❑	186 Bobby Jackson	.20	.07
❑	187 Don Woods	.20	.07
❑	188 New York Giants TL	.75	.30
❑	189 Raymond Chester	.20	.07
❑	190 Joe DeLamielleure AP	1.00	.40
❑	191 Tony Galbreath	.50	.20
❑	192 Robert Brazile AP	.50	.20
❑	193 Neil O'Donoghue	.20	.07
❑	194 Mike Webster	1.00	.40
❑	195 Ed Simonini	.20	.07
❑	196 Benny Malone	.20	.07
❑	197 Tom Wittum	.20	.07
❑	198 Steve Largent	8.00	4.00

❑ 199	Tommy Hart	.20	.07
❑ 200	Fran Tarkenton	3.00	1.50
❑ 201	Leon Gray AP	.20	.07
❑ 202	Leroy Harris	.20	.07
❑ 203	Eric Williams LB	.20	.07
❑ 204	Thom Darden AP	.20	.07
❑ 205	Ken Riley	.50	.20
❑ 206	Clark Gaines	.20	.07
❑ 207	Kansas City Chiefs TL	.75	.30
❑ 208	Joe Danelo	.20	.07
❑ 209	Glen Walker	.20	.07
❑ 210	Art Shell	1.00	.40
❑ 211	Jon Keyworth	.20	.07
❑ 212	Herman Edwards	.20	.07
❑ 213	John Fitzgerald	.20	.07
❑ 214	Jim Smith	.50	.20
❑ 215	Coy Bacon	.50	.20
❑ 216	Dennis Johnson RBK RC	.20	.07
❑ 217	John Jefferson RC	3.00	1.50
❑ 218	Gary Weaver	.20	.07
❑ 219	Tom Blanchard	.20	.07
❑ 220	Bert Jones	1.00	.40
❑ 221	Stanley Morgan	1.00	.40
❑ 222	James Hunter	.20	.07
❑ 223	Jim O'Bradovich	.20	.07
❑ 224	Carl Mauck	.20	.07
❑ 225	Chris Bahr	.20	.07
❑ 226	Jets TL/Wesley Walker	.75	.30
❑ 227	Roland Harper	.20	.07
❑ 228	Randy Dean	.20	.07
❑ 229	Bob Jackson	.20	.07
❑ 230	Sammie White	.50	.20
❑ 231	Mike Dawson	.20	.07
❑ 232	Checklist 133-264	1.00	.40
❑ 233	Ken MacAfee RC	.20	.07
❑ 234	Jon Kolb AP	.20	.07
❑ 235	Willie Hall	.20	.07
❑ 236	Ron Saul AP	.20	.07
❑ 237	Haskel Stanback	.20	.07
❑ 238	Zenon Andrusyshyn	.20	.07
❑ 239	Norris Thomas	.20	.07
❑ 240	Rick Upchurch	.50	.20
❑ 241	Robert Pratt	.20	.07
❑ 242	Julius Adams	.20	.07
❑ 243	Rich McGeorge	.20	.07
❑ 244	Seahawks TL/S.Largent	1.25	.50
❑ 245	Blair Bush RC	.20	.07
❑ 246	Billy Johnson	.50	.20
❑ 247	Randy Rasmussen	.20	.07
❑ 248	Brian Kelley	.20	.07
❑ 249	Mike Pruitt	.50	.20
❑ 250	Harold Carmichael	1.00	.40
❑ 251	Mike Hartenstine	.20	.07
❑ 252	Robert Newhouse	.50	.20
❑ 253	Gary Danielson RC	1.00	.40
❑ 254	Mike Fuller	.20	.07
❑ 255	L.C.Greenwood	1.00	.40
❑ 256	Lemar Parrish	.20	.07
❑ 257	Ike Harris	.20	.07
❑ 258	Ricky Bell RC	1.00	.40
❑ 259	Willie Parker C	.20	.07
❑ 260	Gene Upshaw	1.00	.40
❑ 261	Glenn Doughty	.20	.07
❑ 262	Steve Zabel	.20	.07
❑ 263	Atlanta Falcons TL	.75	.30
❑ 264	Ray Wersching	.20	.07
❑ 265	Lawrence McCutcheon	.50	.20
❑ 266	Willie Buchanon AP	.20	.07
❑ 267	Matt Robinson	.20	.07
❑ 268	Reggie Rucker	.50	.20
❑ 269	Doug Van Horn	.20	.07
❑ 270	Lydell Mitchell	.50	.20
❑ 271	Vern Holland	.20	.07
❑ 272	Eason Ramson	.20	.07
❑ 273	Steve Towle	.20	.07
❑ 274	Jim Marshall	1.00	.40
❑ 275	Mel Blount	1.25	.50
❑ 276	Bob Kuziel	.20	.07
❑ 277	James Scott	.20	.07
❑ 278	Tony Reed	.20	.07
❑ 279	Dave Green	.20	.07
❑ 280	Toni Linhart	.20	.07
❑ 281	Andy Johnson	.20	.07
❑ 282	Los Angeles Rams TL	.75	.30
❑ 283	Phil Villapiano	.50	.20
❑ 284	Dexter Bussey	.20	.07
❑ 285	Craig Morton	1.00	.40
❑ 286	Guy Morriss	.20	.07
❑ 287	Lawrence Pillers	.20	.07
❑ 288	Gerald Irons	.20	.07
❑ 289	Scott Perry	.20	.07
❑ 290	Randy White	2.00	.75
❑ 291	Jack Gregory	.20	.07
❑ 292	Bob Chandler	.20	.07
❑ 293	Rich Szaro	.20	.07
❑ 294	Sherman Smith	.20	.07
❑ 295	Tom Banks AP	.20	.07
❑ 296	Revie Sorey AP	.20	.07
❑ 297	Ricky Thompson	.20	.07
❑ 298	Ron Yary	1.00	.40
❑ 299	Lyle Blackwood	.20	.07
❑ 300	Franco Harris	2.50	1.25
❑ 301	Oilers TL/E.Campbell	3.00	1.50
❑ 302	Scott Bull	.20	.07
❑ 303	Dewey Selmon	.50	.20
❑ 304	Jack Rudnay	.20	.07
❑ 305	Fred Biletnikoff	2.00	.75
❑ 306	Jeff West	.20	.07
❑ 307	Shafer Suggs	.20	.07
❑ 308	Ozzie Newsome RC	12.00	6.00
❑ 309	Boobie Clark	.20	.07
❑ 310	James Lofton RC	12.00	6.00
❑ 311	Joe Pisarcik	.20	.07
❑ 312	Bill Simpson AP	.20	.07
❑ 313	Haven Moses	.50	.20
❑ 314	Jim Merlo	.20	.07
❑ 315	Preston Pearson	.50	.20
❑ 316	Larry Tearry	.20	.07
❑ 317	Tom Dempsey	.20	.07
❑ 318	Greg Latta	.20	.07
❑ 319	Redskins TL/John Riggins	1.50	.60
❑ 320	Jack Ham	1.25	.50
❑ 321	Harold Jackson	.50	.20
❑ 322	George Roberts	.20	.07
❑ 323	Ron Jaworski	1.00	.40
❑ 324	Jim Otis	.20	.07
❑ 325	Roger Carr	.50	.20
❑ 326	Jack Tatum	.50	.20
❑ 327	Derrick Gaffney	.20	.07
❑ 328	Reggie Williams	1.00	.40
❑ 329	Doug Dieken	.20	.07
❑ 330	Efren Herrera	.20	.07
❑ 331	Earl Campbell RB	6.00	3.00
❑ 332	Tony Galbreath RB	.20	.07
❑ 333	Bruce Harper RB	.20	.07
❑ 334	John James RB	.20	.07
❑ 335	Walter Payton RB	4.00	1.50
❑ 336	Rickey Young RB	.20	.07
❑ 337	Jeff Van Note	.50	.20
❑ 338	Chargers TL/J.Jefferson	1.00	.40
❑ 339	Stan Walters RC	.20	.07
❑ 340	Louis Wright	.50	.20
❑ 341	Horace Ivory	.20	.07
❑ 342	Andre Tillman	.20	.07
❑ 343	Greg Coleman RC	.20	.07
❑ 344	Doug English RC	1.00	.40
❑ 345	Ted Hendricks	1.00	.40
❑ 346	Rich Saul	.20	.07
❑ 347	Mel Gray	.50	.20
❑ 348	Toni Fritsch	.20	.07
❑ 349	Cornell Webster	.20	.07
❑ 350	Ken Houston	1.00	.40
❑ 351	Ron Johnson DB RC	.50	.20
❑ 352	Doug Kotar	.20	.07
❑ 353	Brian Sipe	1.00	.40
❑ 354	Billy Brooks	.20	.07
❑ 355	John Dutton	.50	.20
❑ 356	Don Goode	.20	.07
❑ 357	Detroit Lions TL	.75	.30
❑ 358	Reuben Gant	.20	.07
❑ 359	Bob Parsons	.20	.07
❑ 360	Cliff Harris	1.00	.40
❑ 361	Raymond Clayborn	.50	.20
❑ 362	Scott Dierking	.20	.07
❑ 363	Bill Bryan	.20	.07
❑ 364	Mike Livingston	.20	.07
❑ 365	Otis Sistrunk	.50	.20
❑ 366	Charle Young	.50	.20
❑ 367	Keith Wortman	.20	.07
❑ 368	Checklist 265-396	1.00	.40
❑ 369	Mike Michel	.20	.07
❑ 370	Delvin Williams AP	.20	.07
❑ 371	Steve Furness	.50	.20
❑ 372	Emery Moorehead	.20	.07
❑ 373	Clarence Scott	.20	.07
❑ 374	Rufus Mayes	.20	.07
❑ 375	Chris Hanburger	.20	.07
❑ 376	Baltimore Colts TL	.75	.30
❑ 377	Bob Avellini	.50	.20
❑ 378	Jeff Siemon	.20	.07
❑ 379	Roland Hooks	.20	.07
❑ 380	Russ Francis	.50	.20
❑ 381	Roger Wehrli	.50	.20
❑ 382	Joe Fields	.20	.07
❑ 383	Archie Manning	1.00	.40
❑ 384	Rob Lytle	.20	.07
❑ 385	Thomas Henderson	.50	.20
❑ 386	Morris Owens	.20	.07
❑ 387	Dan Fouts	3.00	1.50
❑ 388	Chuck Crist	.20	.07
❑ 389	Ed O'Neil	.20	.07
❑ 390	Earl Campbell RC	30.00	15.00
❑ 391	Randy Grossman	.20	.07
❑ 392	Monte Jackson	.20	.07
❑ 393	John Mendenhall	.20	.07
❑ 394	Miami Dolphins TL	1.00	.40
❑ 395	Isaac Curtis	.50	.20
❑ 396	Mike Bragg	.20	.07
❑ 397	Doug Plank	.20	.07
❑ 398	Mike Barnes	.20	.07
❑ 399	Calvin Hill	.50	.20
❑ 400	Roger Staubach	10.00	5.00
❑ 401	Doug Beaudoin	.20	.07
❑ 402	Chuck Ramsey	.20	.07
❑ 403	Mike Hogan	.20	.07
❑ 404	Mario Clark	.20	.07
❑ 405	Riley Odoms	.20	.07
❑ 406	Carl Eller	1.00	.40
❑ 407	Packers TL/J.Lofton	1.50	.60
❑ 408	Mark Arneson	.20	.07
❑ 409	Vince Ferragamo RC	1.00	.40
❑ 410	Cleveland Elam	.20	.07
❑ 411	Donnie Shell RC	4.00	1.50
❑ 412	Ray Rhodes	1.00	.40
❑ 413	Don Cockroft	.20	.07
❑ 414	Don Bass	.50	.20
❑ 415	Cliff Branch	1.00	.40
❑ 416	Diron Talbert	.20	.07
❑ 417	Tom Hicks	.20	.07
❑ 418	Roosevelt Leaks	.20	.07
❑ 419	Charlie Joiner	1.00	.40
❑ 420	Lyle Alzado	1.00	.40
❑ 421	Sam Cunningham	.50	.20
❑ 422	Larry Keller	.20	.07
❑ 423	Jim Mitchell TE	.20	.07
❑ 424	Randy Logan	.20	.07
❑ 425	Jim Langer	1.00	.40
❑ 426	Gary Green	.20	.07
❑ 427	Luther Blue	.20	.07
❑ 428	Dennis Johnson	.20	.07
❑ 429	Danny White	1.00	.40
❑ 430	Roy Gerela	.20	.07
❑ 431	Jimmy Robinson	.20	.07
❑ 432	Minnesota Vikings TL	.75	.30
❑ 433	Oliver Davis	.20	.07
❑ 434	Lenvil Elliott	.20	.07
❑ 435	Willie Miller RC	.20	.07
❑ 436	Brad Dusek	.20	.07
❑ 437	Bob Thomas	.20	.07
❑ 438	Ken Mendenhall	.20	.07
❑ 439	Clarence Davis	.20	.07
❑ 440	Bob Griese	2.50	1.00
❑ 441	Tony McGee DT	.20	.07
❑ 442	Ed Taylor	.20	.07
❑ 443	Ron Howard	.20	.07
❑ 444	Wayne Morris	.20	.07
❑ 445	Charlie Waters	.50	.20
❑ 446	Rick Danmeier	.20	.07
❑ 447	Paul Naumoff	.20	.07
❑ 448	Keith Krepfle	.20	.07
❑ 449	Rusty Jackson	.20	.07
❑ 450	John Stallworth	4.00	2.00
❑ 451	New Orleans Saints TL	.75	.30
❑ 452	Ron Mikolajczyk	.20	.07
❑ 453	Fred Dryer	1.00	.40
❑ 454	Jim LeClair	.20	.07
❑ 455	Greg Pruitt	.50	.20
❑ 456	Jake Scott	.20	.07
❑ 457	Steve Schubert	.20	.07
❑ 458	George Kunz	.20	.07
❑ 459	Mike Williams	.20	.07

❑ 460 Dave Casper AP 1.00 .40
❑ 461 Sam Adams OL .20 .07
❑ 462 Abdul Salaam .20 .07
❑ 463 Terdell Middleton .50 .20
❑ 464 Mike Wood .20 .07
❑ 465 Bill Thompson AP .20 .07
❑ 466 Larry Gordon .20 .07
❑ 467 Benny Ricardo .20 .07
❑ 468 Reggie McKenzie .50 .20
❑ 469 Cowboys TL/T.Dorsett 1.50 .60
❑ 470 Rickey Young .50 .20
❑ 471 Charlie Smith WR .20 .07
❑ 472 Al Dixon .20 .07
❑ 473 Tom DeLeone .20 .07
❑ 474 Louis Breeden .50 .20
❑ 475 Jack Lambert 2.00 .75
❑ 476 Terry Hermeling .20 .07
❑ 477 J.K. McKay .20 .07
❑ 478 Stan White .20 .07
❑ 479 Terry Nelson .20 .07
❑ 480 Walter Payton 20.00 10.00
❑ 481 Dave Dalby .20 .07
❑ 482 Burgess Owens .20 .07
❑ 483 Rolf Benirschke .20 .07
❑ 484 Jack Dolbin .20 .07
❑ 485 John Hannah 1.00 .40
❑ 486 Checklist 397-528 1.00 .40
❑ 487 Greg Landry .50 .20
❑ 488 St. Louis Cardinals TL .75 .30
❑ 489 Paul Krause 1.00 .40
❑ 490 John James .20 .07
❑ 491 Merv Krakau .20 .07
❑ 492 Dan Doornink .20 .07
❑ 493 Curtis Johnson .20 .07
❑ 494 Rafael Septien .20 .07
❑ 495 Jean Fugett .20 .07
❑ 496 Frank LeMaster .20 .07
❑ 497 Allan Ellis .20 .07
❑ 498 Billy Waddy RC .50 .20
❑ 499 Hank Bauer .20 .07
❑ 500 Terry Bradshaw UER 10.00 5.00
❑ 501 Larry McCarren .20 .07
❑ 502 Fred Cook .20 .07
❑ 503 Chuck Muncie .50 .20
❑ 504 Herman Weaver .20 .07
❑ 505 Eddie Edwards .20 .07
❑ 506 Tony Peters .20 .07
❑ 507 Denver Broncos TL .75 .30
❑ 508 Jimbo Elrod .20 .07
❑ 509 David Hill .20 .07
❑ 510 Harvey Martin .50 .20
❑ 511 Terry Miller .50 .20
❑ 512 June Jones RC .50 .20
❑ 513 Randy Cross 1.00 .40
❑ 514 Duriel Harris .20 .07
❑ 515 Harry Carson 1.00 .40
❑ 516 Tim Fox .20 .07
❑ 517 John Zook .20 .07
❑ 518 Bob Tucker .20 .07
❑ 519 Kevin Long RC .20 .07
❑ 520 Ken Stabler 6.00 3.00
❑ 521 John Bunting .50 .20
❑ 522 Rocky Bleier 1.25 .50
❑ 523 Noah Jackson .20 .07
❑ 524 Cliff Parsley .20 .07
❑ 525 Louie Kelcher AP .50 .20
❑ 526 Bucs TL/Ricky Bell .75 .30
❑ 527 Bob Brudzinski RC .20 .07
❑ 528 Danny Buggs .20 .07

1980 Topps

❑ COMPLETE SET (528) 75.00 40.00
❑ 1 Ottis Anderson RB 1.00 .40
❑ 2 Harold Carmichael RB 1.00 .40
❑ 3 Dan Fouts RB 1.00 .40
❑ 4 Paul Krause RB .50 .20
❑ 5 Rick Upchurch RB .50 .20
❑ 6 Garo Yepremian RB .20 .07
❑ 7 Harold Jackson .50 .20
❑ 8 Mike Williams .20 .07
❑ 9 Calvin Hill .50 .20
❑ 10 Jack Ham 1.00 .40
❑ 11 Dan Melville .20 .07
❑ 12 Matt Robinson .20 .07
❑ 13 Billy Campfield .20 .07
❑ 14 Phil Tabor .20 .07
❑ 15 Randy Hughes UER .20 .07

❑ 16 Andre Tillman .20 .07
❑ 17 Isaac Curtis .50 .20
❑ 18 Charley Hannah .20 .07
❑ 19 Redskins TL/J.Riggins 1.00 .40
❑ 20 Jim Zorn .50 .20
❑ 21 Brian Baschnagel .20 .07
❑ 22 Jon Keyworth .20 .07
❑ 23 Phil Villapiano .20 .07
❑ 24 Richard Osborne .20 .07
❑ 25 Rich Saul AP .20 .07
❑ 26 Doug Beaudoin .20 .07
❑ 27 Cleveland Elam .20 .07
❑ 28 Charlie Joiner 1.00 .40
❑ 29 Dick Ambrose .20 .07
❑ 30 Mike Reinfeldt RC .20 .07
❑ 31 Matt Bahr RC 1.00 .40
❑ 32 Keith Krepfle .20 .07
❑ 33 Herb Scott .20 .07
❑ 34 Doug Kotar .20 .07
❑ 35 Bob Griese 1.50 .60
❑ 36 Jerry Butler RC 1.00 .40
❑ 37 Rolland Lawrence .20 .07
❑ 38 Gary Weaver .20 .07
❑ 39 Chiefs TL/J.T.Smith .50 .20
❑ 40 Chuck Muncie .50 .20
❑ 41 Mike Hartenstine .20 .07
❑ 42 Sammie White .50 .20
❑ 43 Ken Clark .20 .07
❑ 44 Clarence Harmon .20 .07
❑ 45 Bert Jones 1.00 .40
❑ 46 Mike Washington .20 .07
❑ 47 Joe Fields .20 .07
❑ 48 Mike Wood .20 .07
❑ 49 Oliver Davis .20 .07
❑ 50 Stan Walters AP .20 .07
❑ 51 Riley Odoms .20 .07
❑ 52 Steve Pisarkiewicz .20 .07
❑ 53 Tony Hill 1.00 .40
❑ 54 Scott Perry .20 .07
❑ 55 George Martin RC .20 .07
❑ 56 George Roberts .20 .07
❑ 57 Seahawks TL/S. Largent 1.00 .40
❑ 58 Billy Johnson .50 .20
❑ 59 Reuben Gant .20 .07
❑ 60 Dennis Harrah RC .20 .07
❑ 61 Rocky Bleier 1.00 .40
❑ 62 Sam Hunt .20 .07
❑ 63 Allan Ellis .20 .07
❑ 64 Ricky Thompson .20 .07
❑ 65 Ken Stabler 4.00 2.00
❑ 66 Dexter Bussey .20 .07
❑ 67 Ken Mendenhall .20 .07
❑ 68 Woodrow Lowe .20 .07
❑ 69 Thom Darden .20 .07
❑ 70 Randy White 1.50 .60
❑ 71 Ken MacAfee .20 .07
❑ 72 Ron Jaworski 1.00 .40
❑ 73 William Andrews RC 1.00 .40
❑ 74 Jimmy Robinson .20 .07
❑ 75 Roger Wehrli AP .40 .15
❑ 76 Dolphins TL/L.Csonka 1.00 .40
❑ 77 Jack Rudnay .20 .07
❑ 78 James Lofton 2.00 .75
❑ 79 Robert Brazile .50 .20
❑ 80 Russ Francis .50 .20
❑ 81 Ricky Bell 1.00 .40
❑ 82 Bob Avellini .50 .20
❑ 83 Bobby Jackson .20 .07
❑ 84 Mike Bragg .20 .07
❑ 85 Cliff Branch 1.00 .40
❑ 86 Blair Bush .20 .07
❑ 87 Sherman Smith .20 .07
❑ 88 Glen Edwards .20 .07
❑ 89 Don Cockroft .20 .07
❑ 90 Louis Wright .50 .20
❑ 91 Randy Grossman .20 .07
❑ 92 Carl Hairston RC 1.00 .40
❑ 93 Archie Manning 1.00 .40
❑ 94 New York Giants TL .50 .20
❑ 95 Preston Pearson .50 .20
❑ 96 Rusty Chambers .20 .07
❑ 97 Greg Coleman .20 .07
❑ 98 Charle Young .20 .07
❑ 99 Matt Cavanaugh RC .50 .20
❑ 100 Jesse Baker .20 .07
❑ 101 Doug Plank .20 .07
❑ 102 Checklist 1-132 .75 .30
❑ 103 Luther Bradley RC .20 .07
❑ 104 Bob Kuziel .20 .07
❑ 105 Craig Morton .50 .20
❑ 106 Sherman White .20 .07
❑ 107 Jim Breech RC .50 .20
❑ 108 Hank Bauer .20 .07
❑ 109 Tom Blanchard .20 .07
❑ 110 Ozzie Newsome 2.00 .75
❑ 111 Steve Furness .20 .07
❑ 112 Frank LeMaster .20 .07
❑ 113 Cowboys TL/T.Dorsett 1.00 .40
❑ 114 Doug Van Horn .20 .07
❑ 115 Delvin Williams .20 .07
❑ 116 Lyle Blackwood .20 .07
❑ 117 Derrick Gaffney .20 .07
❑ 118 Cornell Webster .20 .07
❑ 119 Sam Cunningham .50 .20
❑ 120 Jim Youngblood AP .50 .20
❑ 121 Bob Thomas .20 .07
❑ 122 Jack Thompson RC .50 .20
❑ 123 Randy Cross 1.00 .40
❑ 124 Karl Lorch RC .20 .07
❑ 125 Mel Gray .20 .07
❑ 126 John James .20 .07
❑ 127 Terdell Middleton .20 .07
❑ 128 Leroy Jones .20 .07
❑ 129 Tom DeLeone .20 .07
❑ 130 John Stallworth 1.50 .60
❑ 131 Jimmie Giles RC .50 .20
❑ 132 Philadelphia Eagles TL 1.00 .40
❑ 133 Gary Green .20 .07
❑ 134 John Dutton .50 .20
❑ 135 Harry Carson 1.00 .40
❑ 136 Bob Kuechenberg .50 .20
❑ 137 Ike Harris .20 .07
❑ 138 Tommy Kramer RC 1.00 .40
❑ 139 Sam Adams OL .20 .07
❑ 140 Doug English .50 .20
❑ 141 Steve Schubert .20 .07
❑ 142 Rusty Jackson .20 .07
❑ 143 Reese McCall .20 .07
❑ 144 Scott Dierking .20 .07
❑ 145 Ken Houston 1.00 .40
❑ 146 Bob Martin .20 .07
❑ 147 Sam McCullum .20 .07
❑ 148 Tom Banks .20 .07
❑ 149 Willie Buchanon .20 .07
❑ 150 Greg Pruitt .50 .20
❑ 151 Denver Broncos TL 1.00 .40
❑ 152 Don Smith RC .20 .07
❑ 153 Pete Johnson .50 .20
❑ 154 Charlie Smith WR .20 .07
❑ 155 Mel Blount 1.00 .40
❑ 156 John Mendenhall .20 .07
❑ 157 Danny White 1.00 .40
❑ 158 Jimmy Cefalo RC .50 .20
❑ 159 Richard Bishop AP .20 .07
❑ 160 Walter Payton 12.00 6.00
❑ 161 Dave Dalby .20 .07
❑ 162 Preston Dennard .20 .07
❑ 163 Johnnie Gray .20 .07
❑ 164 Russell Erxleben .20 .07
❑ 165 Toni Fritsch AP .20 .07
❑ 166 Terry Hermeling .20 .07
❑ 167 Roland Hooks .20 .07
❑ 168 Roger Carr .20 .07
❑ 169 San Diego Chargers TL 1.00 .40
❑ 170 Ottis Anderson RC 4.00 1.50
❑ 171 Brian Sipe 1.00 .40
❑ 172 Leonard Thompson .20 .07

	No.	Player	Mint	Exc
❑	173	Tony Reed	.20	.07
❑	174	Bob Tucker	.20	.07
❑	175	Joe Greene	1.00	.40
❑	176	Jack Dolbin	.20	.07
❑	177	Chuck Ramsey	.20	.07
❑	178	Paul Hofer	.20	.07
❑	179	Randy Logan	.20	.07
❑	180	David Lewis AP	.20	.07
❑	181	Duriel Harris	.20	.07
❑	182	June Jones	.50	.20
❑	183	Larry McCarren	.20	.07
❑	184	Ken Johnson RB	.20	.07
❑	185	Charlie Waters	.50	.20
❑	186	Noah Jackson	.20	.07
❑	187	Reggie Williams	.50	.20
❑	188	New England Patriots TL	.50	.20
❑	189	Carl Eller	1.00	.40
❑	190	Ed White AP	.20	.07
❑	191	Mario Clark	.20	.07
❑	192	Roosevelt Leaks	.20	.07
❑	193	Ted McKnight	.20	.07
❑	194	Danny Buggs	.20	.07
❑	195	Lester Hayes RC	2.00	.75
❑	196	Clarence Scott	.20	.07
❑	197	Saints TL/Wes Chandler	.50	.20
❑	198	Richard Caster	.20	.07
❑	199	Louie Giammona	.20	.07
❑	200	Terry Bradshaw	8.00	3.00
❑	201	Ed Newman	.20	.07
❑	202	Fred Dryer	1.00	.40
❑	203	Dennis Franks	.20	.07
❑	204	Bob Breunig RC	.50	.20
❑	205	Alan Page	1.00	.40
❑	206	Earnest Gray RC	.20	.07
❑	207	Vikings TL/A.Rashad	1.00	.40
❑	208	Horace Ivory	.20	.07
❑	209	Isaac Hagins	.20	.07
❑	210	Gary Johnson AP	.20	.07
❑	211	Kevin Long	.20	.07
❑	212	Bill Thompson	.20	.07
❑	213	Don Bass	.20	.07
❑	214	George Starke RC	.20	.07
❑	215	Efren Herrera	.20	.07
❑	216	Theo Bell	.20	.07
❑	217	Monte Jackson	.20	.07
❑	218	Reggie McKenzie	.20	.07
❑	219	Bucky Dilts	.20	.07
❑	220	Lyle Alzado	1.00	.40
❑	221	Tim Foley	.20	.07
❑	222	Mark Arneson	.20	.07
❑	223	Fred Quillan	.20	.07
❑	224	Benny Ricardo	.20	.07
❑	225	Phil Simms RC	12.00	6.00
❑	226	Bears TL/Walter Payton	1.25	.50
❑	227	Max Runager	.20	.07
❑	228	Barty Smith	.20	.07
❑	229	Jay Saldi	.50	.20
❑	230	John Hannah	1.00	.40
❑	231	Tim Wilson	.20	.07
❑	232	Jeff Van Note	.20	.07
❑	233	Henry Marshall	.20	.07
❑	234	Diron Talbert	.20	.07
❑	235	Garo Yepremian	.50	.20
❑	236	Larry Brown	.20	.07
❑	237	Clarence Williams RB	.20	.07
❑	238	Burgess Owens	.20	.07
❑	239	Vince Ferragamo	.50	.20
❑	240	Rickey Young	.20	.07
❑	241	Dave Logan	.20	.07
❑	242	Larry Gordon	.20	.07
❑	243	Terry Miller	.20	.07
❑	244	Baltimore Colts TL	1.00	.40
❑	245	Steve DeBerg	1.00	.40
❑	246	Checklist 133-264	.75	.30
❑	247	Greg Latta	.20	.07
❑	248	Raymond Clayborn	.50	.20
❑	249	Jim Clack	.20	.07
❑	250	Drew Pearson	1.00	.40
❑	251	John Bunting	.50	.20
❑	252	Rob Lytle	.20	.07
❑	253	Jim Hart	1.00	.40
❑	254	John McDaniel	.20	.07
❑	255	Dave Pear AP	.20	.07
❑	256	Donnie Shell	1.00	.40
❑	257	Dan Doornink	.20	.07
❑	258	Wallace Francis RC	1.00	.40
❑	259	Dave Beverly	.20	.07
❑	260	Lee Roy Selmon	1.00	.40
❑	261	Doug Dieken	.20	.07
❑	262	Gary Davis	.20	.07
❑	263	Bob Rush	.20	.07
❑	264	Buffalo Bills TL	.50	.20
❑	265	Greg Landry	.50	.20
❑	266	Jan Stenerud	1.00	.40
❑	267	Tom Hicks	.20	.07
❑	268	Pat McInally	.20	.07
❑	269	Tim Fox	.20	.07
❑	270	Harvey Martin	.50	.20
❑	271	Dan Lloyd	.20	.07
❑	272	Mike Barber	.20	.07
❑	273	Wendell Tyler RC	1.00	.40
❑	274	Jeff Komlo	.20	.07
❑	275	Wes Chandler RC	1.00	.40
❑	276	Brad Dusek	.20	.07
❑	277	Charlie Johnson NT	.20	.07
❑	278	Dennis Swilley	.20	.07
❑	279	Johnny Evans	.20	.07
❑	280	Jack Lambert	1.50	.60
❑	281	Vern Den Herder	.20	.07
❑	282	Tampa Bay Bucs TL	1.00	.40
❑	283	Bob Klein	.20	.07
❑	284	Jim Turner	.20	.07
❑	285	Marvin Powell AP	.50	.20
❑	286	Aaron Kyle	.20	.07
❑	287	Dan Neal	.20	.07
❑	288	Wayne Morris	.20	.07
❑	289	Steve Bartkowski	.50	.20
❑	290	Dave Jennings AP	.50	.20
❑	291	John Smith	.20	.07
❑	292	Bill Gregory	.20	.07
❑	293	Frank Lewis	.20	.07
❑	294	Fred Cook	.20	.07
❑	295	David Hill AP	.20	.07
❑	296	Wade Key	.20	.07
❑	297	Sidney Thornton	.20	.07
❑	298	Charlie Hall	.20	.07
❑	299	Joe Lavender	.20	.07
❑	300	Tom Rafferty RC	.20	.07
❑	301	Mike Renfro RC	.50	.20
❑	302	Wilbur Jackson	.50	.20
❑	303	Packers TL/J.Lofton	1.00	.40
❑	304	Henry Childs	.20	.07
❑	305	Russ Washington AP	.20	.07
❑	306	Jim LeClair	.20	.07
❑	307	Tommy Hart	.20	.07
❑	308	Gary Barbaro	.20	.07
❑	309	Billy Taylor	.20	.07
❑	310	Ray Guy	.50	.20
❑	311	Don Hasselbeck RC	.50	.20
❑	312	Doug Williams	1.00	.40
❑	313	Nick Mike-Mayer	.20	.07
❑	314	Don McCauley	.20	.07
❑	315	Wesley Walker	1.00	.40
❑	316	Dan Dierdorf	1.00	.40
❑	317	Dave Brown DB RC	.50	.20
❑	318	Leroy Harris	.20	.07
❑	319	Steelers TL/Harris/Lambrt	1.00	.40
❑	320	Mark Moseley AP UER	.20	.07
❑	321	Mark Dennard	.20	.07
❑	322	Terry Nelson	.20	.07
❑	323	Tom Jackson	1.00	.40
❑	324	Rick Kane	.20	.07
❑	325	Jerry Sherk	.20	.07
❑	326	Ray Preston	.20	.07
❑	327	Golden Richards	.20	.07
❑	328	Randy Dean	.20	.07
❑	329	Rick Danmeier	.20	.07
❑	330	Tony Dorsett	6.00	3.00
❑	331	R.Staubach/Fouts LL	3.00	1.50
❑	332	Receiving Leaders	.50	.20
❑	333	Sacks Leaders	1.00	.40
❑	334	Scoring Leaders	1.00	.40
❑	335	Interception Leaders	1.00	.40
❑	336	Punting Leaders	1.00	.40
❑	337	Freddie Solomon	.20	.07
❑	338	Cincinnati Bengals TL/Jauron	1.00	.40
❑	339	Ken Stone	.20	.07
❑	340	Greg Buttle AP	.20	.07
❑	341	Bob Baumhower	.50	.20
❑	342	Billy Waddy	.20	.07
❑	343	Cliff Parsley	.20	.07
❑	344	Walter White	.20	.07
❑	345	Mike Thomas	.20	.07
❑	346	Neil O'Donoghue	.20	.07
❑	347	Freddie Scott	.20	.07
❑	348	Joe Ferguson	.50	.20
❑	349	Doug Nettles	.20	.07
❑	350	Mike Webster	1.00	.40
❑	351	Ron Saul	.20	.07
❑	352	Julius Adams	.20	.07
❑	353	Rafael Septien	.20	.07
❑	354	Cleo Miller	.20	.07
❑	355	Keith Simpson AP	.20	.07
❑	356	Johnny Perkins	.20	.07
❑	357	Jerry Sisemore	.20	.07
❑	358	Arthur Whittington	.20	.07
❑	359	Cardinals TL/Anderson	1.00	.40
❑	360	Rick Upchurch	.50	.20
❑	361	Kim Bokamper RC	.20	.07
❑	362	Roland Harper	.20	.07
❑	363	Pat Leahy	.20	.07
❑	364	Louis Breeden	.20	.07
❑	365	John Jefferson	1.00	.40
❑	366	Jerry Eckwood	.20	.07
❑	367	David Whitehurst	.20	.07
❑	368	Willie Parker C	.20	.07
❑	369	Ed Simonini	.20	.07
❑	370	Jack Youngblood	1.00	.40
❑	371	Don Warren RC	1.00	.40
❑	372	Andy Johnson	.20	.07
❑	373	D.D. Lewis	.50	.20
❑	374A	B.Reece RC ERR	1.00	.40
❑	374B	Beasley Reece RC COR	.50	.20
❑	375	L.C.Greenwood	1.00	.40
❑	376	Cleveland Browns TL	.50	.20
❑	377	Herman Edwards	.20	.07
❑	378	Rob Carpenter RC RB	.20	.07
❑	379	Herman Weaver	.20	.07
❑	380	Gary Fencik	.20	.07
❑	381	Don Strock	.50	.20
❑	382	Art Shell	1.00	.40
❑	383	Tim Mazzetti	.20	.07
❑	384	Bruce Harper	.20	.07
❑	385	Al (Bubba) Baker	.50	.20
❑	386	Conrad Dobler	.20	.07
❑	387	Stu Voigt	.20	.07
❑	388	Ken Anderson	1.00	.40
❑	389	Pat Tilley	.20	.07
❑	390	John Riggins	1.00	.40
❑	391	Checklist 265-396	.75	.30
❑	392	Fred Dean	.20	.07
❑	393	Benny Barnes RC	.20	.07
❑	394	Los Angeles Rams TL	.50	.20
❑	395	Brad Van Pelt	.20	.07
❑	396	Eddie Hare	.20	.07
❑	397	John Sciarra RC	.20	.07
❑	398	Bob Jackson	.20	.07
❑	399	John Yarno	.20	.07
❑	400	Franco Harris	2.00	.75
❑	401	Ray Wersching	.20	.07
❑	402	Virgil Livers	.20	.07
❑	403	Raymond Chester	.20	.07
❑	404	Leon Gray	.20	.07
❑	405	Richard Todd	.50	.20
❑	406	Larry Little	1.00	.40
❑	407	Ted Fritsch Jr.	.20	.07
❑	408	Larry Mucker	.20	.07
❑	409	Jim Allen	.20	.07
❑	410	Randy Gradishar	1.00	.40
❑	411	Atlanta Falcons TL	1.00	.40
❑	412	Louie Kelcher	.50	.20
❑	413	Robert Newhouse	.50	.20
❑	414	Gary Shirk	.20	.07
❑	415	Mike Haynes	1.00	.40
❑	416	Craig Colquitt	.20	.07
❑	417	Lou Piccone	.20	.07
❑	418	Clay Matthews RC	2.50	1.00
❑	419	Marvin Cobb	.20	.07
❑	420	Harold Carmichael	1.00	.40
❑	421	Uwe Von Schamann	.50	.20
❑	422	Mike Phipps	.50	.20
❑	423	Nolan Cromwell RC	1.00	.40
❑	424	Glenn Doughty	.20	.07
❑	425	Bob Young AP	.20	.07
❑	426	Tony Galbreath	.20	.07
❑	427	Luke Prestridge RC	.20	.07
❑	428	Terry Beeson	.20	.07
❑	429	Jack Tatum	.50	.20
❑	430	Lemar Parrish AP	.20	.07
❑	431	Chester Marcol	.20	.07
❑	432	Houston Oilers TL	1.00	.40

No.	Player	Nrmt	Exc
❑ 433	John Fitzgerald	.20	.07
❑ 434	Gary Jeter RC	.50	.20
❑ 435	Steve Grogan	1.00	.40
❑ 436	Jon Kolb UER	.20	.07
❑ 437	Jim O'Bradovich UER	.20	.07
❑ 438	Gerald Irons	.20	.07
❑ 439	Jeff West	.20	.07
❑ 440	Wilbert Montgomery	.50	.20
❑ 441	Norris Thomas	.20	.07
❑ 442	James Scott	.20	.07
❑ 443	Curtis Brown	.20	.07
❑ 444	Ken Fantetti	.20	.07
❑ 445	Pat Haden	1.00	.40
❑ 446	Carl Mauck	.20	.07
❑ 447	Bruce Laird	.20	.07
❑ 448	Otis Armstrong	.20	.07
❑ 449	Gene Upshaw	1.00	.40
❑ 450	Steve Largent	6.00	3.00
❑ 451	Benny Malone	.20	.07
❑ 452	Steve Nelson	.20	.07
❑ 453	Mark Cotney	.20	.07
❑ 454	Joe Danelo	.20	.07
❑ 455	Billy Joe DuPree	.50	.20
❑ 456	Ron Johnson DB	.20	.07
❑ 457	Archie Griffin	.50	.20
❑ 458	Reggie Rucker	.20	.07
❑ 459	Claude Humphrey	.20	.07
❑ 460	Lydell Mitchell	.50	.20
❑ 461	Steve Towle	.20	.07
❑ 462	Revie Sorey	.20	.07
❑ 463	Tom Skladany	.20	.07
❑ 464	Clark Gaines	.20	.07
❑ 465	Frank Corral	.20	.07
❑ 466	Steve Fuller RC	.50	.20
❑ 467	Ahmad Rashad	1.00	.40
❑ 468	Oakland Raiders TL	1.00	.40
❑ 469	Brian Peets	.20	.07
❑ 470	Pat Donovan RC	.50	.20
❑ 471	Ken Burrough	.20	.07
❑ 472	Don Calhoun	.20	.07
❑ 473	Bill Bryan	.20	.07
❑ 474	Terry Jackson	.20	.07
❑ 475	Joe Theismann	1.25	.50
❑ 476	Jim Smith	.50	.20
❑ 477	Joe DeLamielleure	1.00	.40
❑ 478	Mike Pruitt AP	.50	.20
❑ 479	Steve Mike-Mayer	.20	.07
❑ 480	Bill Bergey	.50	.20
❑ 481	Mike Fuller	.20	.07
❑ 482	Bob Parsons	.20	.07
❑ 483	Billy Brooks	.20	.07
❑ 484	Jerome Barkum	.20	.07
❑ 485	Larry Csonka	1.50	.60
❑ 486	John Hill	.20	.07
❑ 487	Mike Dawson	.20	.07
❑ 488	Detroit Lions TL	.50	.20
❑ 489	Ted Hendricks	1.00	.40
❑ 490	Dan Pastorini	.50	.20
❑ 491	Stanley Morgan	1.00	.40
❑ 492	AFC Champs/Bleier	1.00	.40
❑ 493	NFC Champs/Ferragamo	.50	.20
❑ 494	Super Bowl XIV	1.00	.40
❑ 495	Dwight White	.50	.20
❑ 496	Haven Moses	.20	.07
❑ 497	Guy Morriss	.20	.07
❑ 498	Dewey Selmon	.50	.20
❑ 499	Dave Butz RC	1.00	.40
❑ 500	Chuck Foreman	.50	.20
❑ 501	Chris Bahr	.20	.07
❑ 502	Mark Miller QB	.20	.07
❑ 503	Tony Greene	.20	.07
❑ 504	Brian Kelley	.20	.07
❑ 505	Joe Washington	.50	.20
❑ 506	Butch Johnson	.50	.20
❑ 507	New York Jets TL	.50	.20
❑ 508	Steve Little	.20	.07
❑ 509	Checklist 397-528	.75	.30
❑ 510	Mark Van Eeghen	.20	.07
❑ 511	Gary Danielson	.50	.20
❑ 512	Manu Tuiasosopo	.20	.07
❑ 513	Paul Coffman RC	.50	.20
❑ 514	Cullen Bryant	.20	.07
❑ 515	Nat Moore	.50	.20
❑ 516	Bill Lenkaitis	.20	.07
❑ 517	Lynn Cain RC	.20	.07
❑ 518	Gregg Bingham	.20	.07
❑ 519	Ted Albrecht	.20	.07
❑ 520	Dan Fouts	2.00	.75
❑ 521	Bernard Jackson	.20	.07
❑ 522	Coy Bacon	.20	.07
❑ 523	Tony Franklin RC	.50	.20
❑ 524	Bo Harris	.20	.07
❑ 525	Bob Grupp AP	.20	.07
❑ 526	San Francisco 49ers TL	1.00	.40
❑ 527	Steve Wilson	.20	.07
❑ 528	Bennie Cunningham	.50	.20

1981 Topps

No.	Player	Nrmt	Exc
❑	COMPLETE SET (528)	200.00	100.00
❑ 1	Ron Jaworski/B.Sipe LL	.75	.30
❑ 2	K.Winslow/Cooper LL	.75	.30
❑ 3	Sack Leaders	.40	.15
❑ 4	Scoring Leaders	.15	.05
❑ 5	Interception Leaders	.40	.15
❑ 6	Punting Leaders	.15	.05
❑ 7	Don Calhoun	.15	.05
❑ 8	Jack Tatum	.40	.15
❑ 9	Reggie Rucker	.15	.05
❑ 10	Mike Webster	.75	.30
❑ 11	Vince Evans RC	.75	.30
❑ 12	Ottis Anderson SA	.75	.30
❑ 13	Leroy Harris	.15	.05
❑ 14	Gordon King	.15	.05
❑ 15	Harvey Martin	.40	.15
❑ 16	Johnny Lam Jones RC	.40	.15
❑ 17	Ken Greene	.15	.05
❑ 18	Frank Lewis	.15	.05
❑ 19	Seahawks TL/Largent	.75	.30
❑ 20	Lester Hayes	.75	.30
❑ 21	Uwe Von Schamann	.15	.05
❑ 22	Joe Washington	.15	.05
❑ 23	Louie Kelcher	.15	.05
❑ 24	Willie Miller	.15	.05
❑ 25	Steve Grogan	.75	.30
❑ 26	John Hill	.15	.05
❑ 27	Stan White	.15	.05
❑ 28	William Andrews SA	.40	.15
❑ 29	Clarence Scott	.15	.05
❑ 30	Leon Gray AP	.15	.05
❑ 31	Craig Colquitt	.15	.05
❑ 32	Doug Williams	.75	.30
❑ 33	Bob Breunig	.40	.15
❑ 34	Billy Taylor	.15	.05
❑ 35	Harold Carmichael	.75	.30
❑ 36	Ray Wersching	.15	.05
❑ 37	Dennis Johnson LB RC	.15	.05
❑ 38	Archie Griffin	.40	.15
❑ 39	Los Angeles Rams TL	.40	.15
❑ 40	Gary Fencik	.40	.15
❑ 41	Lynn Dickey	.15	.05
❑ 42	Steve Bartkowski SA	.40	.15
❑ 43	Art Shell	.75	.30
❑ 44	Wilbur Jackson	.15	.05
❑ 45	Frank Corral	.15	.05
❑ 46	Ted McKnight	.15	.05
❑ 47	Joe Klecko	.40	.15
❑ 48	Dan Doornink	.15	.05
❑ 49	Doug Dieken	.15	.05
❑ 50	Jerry Robinson RC	.40	.15
❑ 51	Wallace Francis	.15	.05
❑ 52	Dave Preston RC	.15	.05
❑ 53	Jay Saldi	.15	.05
❑ 54	Rush Brown	.15	.05
❑ 55	Phil Simms	3.00	1.50
❑ 56	Nick Mike-Mayer	.15	.05
❑ 57	Redskins TL/A.Monk	2.00	.75
❑ 58	Mike Renfro	.15	.05
❑ 59	Ted Brown SA	.15	.05
❑ 60	Steve Nelson	.15	.05
❑ 61	Sidney Thornton	.15	.05
❑ 62	Kent Hill	.15	.05
❑ 63	Don Bessillieu	.15	.05
❑ 64	Fred Cook	.15	.05
❑ 65	Raymond Chester	.15	.05
❑ 66	Rick Kane	.15	.05
❑ 67	Mike Fuller	.15	.05
❑ 68	Dewey Selmon	.40	.15
❑ 69	Charles White RC	.75	.30
❑ 70	Jeff Van Note	.15	.05
❑ 71	Robert Newhouse	.40	.15
❑ 72	Roynell Young RC	.15	.05
❑ 73	Lynn Cain SA	.15	.05
❑ 74	Mike Friede	.15	.05
❑ 75	Earl Cooper RC	.15	.05
❑ 76	New Orleans Saints TL	.40	.15
❑ 77	Rick Danmeier	.15	.05
❑ 78	Darrol Ray	.15	.05
❑ 79	Gregg Bingham	.15	.05
❑ 80	John Hannah	.75	.30
❑ 81	Jack Thompson	.40	.15
❑ 82	Rick Upchurch	.40	.15
❑ 83	Mike Butler	.15	.05
❑ 84	Don Warren	.15	.05
❑ 85	Mark Van Eeghen	.15	.05
❑ 86	J.T.Smith RC	.75	.30
❑ 87	Herman Weaver	.15	.05
❑ 88	Terry Bradshaw SA	2.00	.75
❑ 89	Charlie Hall	.15	.05
❑ 90	Donnie Shell	.75	.30
❑ 91	Ike Harris	.15	.05
❑ 92	Charlie Johnson NT	.15	.05
❑ 93	Rickey Watts	.15	.05
❑ 94	New England Patriots TL	.75	.30
❑ 95	Drew Pearson	.75	.30
❑ 96	Neil O'Donoghue	.15	.05
❑ 97	Conrad Dobler	.15	.05
❑ 98	Jewerl Thomas RC	.15	.05
❑ 99	Mike Barber	.15	.05
❑ 100	Billy Sims RC	3.00	1.25
❑ 101	Vern Den Herder	.15	.05
❑ 102	Greg Landry	.40	.15
❑ 103	Joe Cribbs SA	.40	.15
❑ 104	Mark Murphy S RC	.15	.05
❑ 105	Chuck Muncie	.40	.15
❑ 106	Alfred Jackson	.40	.15
❑ 107	Chris Bahr	.15	.05
❑ 108	Gordon Jones	.15	.05
❑ 109	Willie Harper RC	.15	.05
❑ 110	Dave Jennings	.15	.05
❑ 111	Bennie Cunningham	.15	.05
❑ 112	Jerry Sisemore	.15	.05
❑ 113	Cleveland Browns TL	.75	.30
❑ 114	Rickey Young	.15	.05
❑ 115	Ken Anderson	.75	.30
❑ 116	Randy Gradishar	.75	.30
❑ 117	Eddie Lee Ivery RC	.15	.05
❑ 118	Wesley Walker	.75	.30
❑ 119	Chuck Foreman	.40	.15
❑ 120	Nolan Cromwell UER	.40	.15
❑ 121	Curtis Dickey SA	.15	.05
❑ 122	Wayne Morris	.15	.05
❑ 123	Greg Stemrick	.15	.05
❑ 124	Coy Bacon	.15	.05
❑ 125	Jim Zorn	.40	.15
❑ 126	Henry Childs	.15	.05
❑ 127	Checklist 1-132	.75	.30
❑ 128	Len Walterscheid	.15	.05
❑ 129	Johnny Evans	.15	.05
❑ 130	Gary Barbaro	.15	.05
❑ 131	Jim Smith	.15	.05
❑ 132	New York Jets TL	.40	.15
❑ 133	Curtis Brown	.15	.05
❑ 134	D.D. Lewis	.15	.05
❑ 135	Jim Plunkett	.75	.30
❑ 136	Nat Moore	.40	.15
❑ 137	Don McCauley	.15	.05
❑ 138	Tony Dorsett SA	.75	.30
❑ 139	Julius Adams	.15	.05
❑ 140	Ahmad Rashad	.75	.30
❑ 141	Rich Saul	.15	.05
❑ 142	Ken Fantetti	.15	.05
❑ 143	Kenny Johnson	.15	.05
❑ 144	Clark Gaines	.15	.05

❑ 145 Mark Moseley .15 .05
❑ 146 Vernon Perry RC .15 .05
❑ 147 Jerry Eckwood .15 .05
❑ 148 Freddie Solomon .15 .05
❑ 149 Jerry Sherk .15 .05
❑ 150 Kellen Winslow RC 8.00 4.00
❑ 151 Packers TL/Lofton .75 .30
❑ 152 Ross Browner .15 .05
❑ 153 Dan Fouts SA .75 .30
❑ 154 Woody Peoples .15 .05
❑ 155 Jack Lambert 1.00 .40
❑ 156 Mike Dennis .15 .05
❑ 157 Rafael Septien .15 .05
❑ 158 Archie Manning .75 .30
❑ 159 Don Hasselbeck .15 .05
❑ 160 Alan Page .75 .30
❑ 161 Arthur Whittington .15 .05
❑ 162 Billy Waddy .15 .05
❑ 163 Horace Belton .15 .05
❑ 164 Luke Prestridge .15 .05
❑ 165 Joe Theismann .75 .30
❑ 166 Morris Towns .15 .05
❑ 167 Dave Brown DB .15 .05
❑ 168 Ezra Johnson .15 .05
❑ 169 Tampa Bay Bucs TL .15 .05
❑ 170 Joe DeLamielleure .75 .30
❑ 171 Earnest Gray SA .15 .05
❑ 172 Mike Thomas .15 .05
❑ 173 Jim Haslett RC 2.00 .75
❑ 174 David Woodley RC .40 .15
❑ 175 Al(Bubba) Baker .40 .15
❑ 176 Nesby Glasgow RC .15 .05
❑ 177 Pat Leahy .15 .05
❑ 178 Tom Brahaney .15 .05
❑ 179 Herman Edwards .15 .05
❑ 180 Junior Miller RC .15 .05
❑ 181 Richard Wood RC .15 .05
❑ 182 Lenvil Elliott .15 .05
❑ 183 Sammie White .40 .15
❑ 184 Russell Erxleben .15 .05
❑ 185 Ed Too Tall Jones .75 .30
❑ 186 Ray Guy SA .40 .15
❑ 187 Haven Moses .15 .05
❑ 188 New York Giants TL .40 .15
❑ 189 David Whitehurst .15 .05
❑ 190 John Jefferson .75 .30
❑ 191 Terry Beeson .15 .05
❑ 192 Dan Ross RC .40 .15
❑ 193 Dave Williams RB RC .15 .05
❑ 194 Art Monk RC 15.00 6.00
❑ 195 Roger Wehrli .40 .15
❑ 196 Ricky Feacher .15 .05
❑ 197 Miami Dolphins TL .75 .30
❑ 198 Carl Roaches RC .15 .05
❑ 199 Billy Campfield .15 .05
❑ 200 Ted Hendricks .75 .30
❑ 201 Fred Smerlas RC .75 .30
❑ 202 Walter Payton SA 3.00 1.25
❑ 203 Luther Bradley .15 .05
❑ 204 Herb Scott .15 .05
❑ 205 Jack Youngblood .75 .30
❑ 206 Danny Pittman .15 .05
❑ 207 Houston Oilers TL .40 .15
❑ 208 Vagas Ferguson RC .40 .15
❑ 209 Mark Dennard .15 .05
❑ 210 Lemar Parrish .15 .05
❑ 211 Bruce Harper .15 .05
❑ 212 Ed Simonini .15 .05
❑ 213 Nick Lowery RC .75 .30
❑ 214 Kevin House RC .40 .15
❑ 215 Mike Kenn RC .75 .30
❑ 216 Joe Montana RC 150.00 75.00
❑ 217 Joe Senser .15 .05
❑ 218 Lester Hayes SA .40 .15
❑ 219 Gene Upshaw .75 .30
❑ 220 Franco Harris 1.25 .50
❑ 221 Ron Bolton .15 .05
❑ 222 Charles Alexander RC .40 .15
❑ 223 Matt Robinson .15 .05
❑ 224 Ray Oldham .15 .05
❑ 225 George Martin .15 .05
❑ 226 Buffalo Bills TL .75 .30
❑ 227 Tony Franklin .15 .05
❑ 228 George Cumby .15 .05
❑ 229 Butch Johnson .40 .15
❑ 230 Mike Haynes .75 .30
❑ 231 Rob Carpenter .40 .15
❑ 232 Steve Fuller .40 .15
❑ 233 John Sawyer .15 .05
❑ 234 Kenny King SA .15 .05
❑ 235 Jack Ham .75 .30
❑ 236 Jimmy Rogers .15 .05
❑ 237 Bob Parsons .15 .05
❑ 238 Marty Lyons RC .75 .30
❑ 239 Pat Tilley .15 .05
❑ 240 Dennis Harrah .15 .05
❑ 241 Thom Darden .15 .05
❑ 242 Rolf Benirschke .15 .05
❑ 243 Gerald Small .15 .05
❑ 244 Atlanta Falcons TL .75 .30
❑ 245 Roger Carr .15 .05
❑ 246 Sherman White .15 .05
❑ 247 Ted Brown .15 .05
❑ 248 Matt Cavanaugh .40 .15
❑ 249 John Dutton .15 .05
❑ 250 Bill Bergey .40 .15
❑ 251 Jim Allen .15 .05
❑ 252 Mike Nelms SA .15 .05
❑ 253 Tom Blanchard .15 .05
❑ 254 Ricky Thompson .15 .05
❑ 255 John Matuszak .40 .15
❑ 256 Randy Grossman .15 .05
❑ 257 Ray Griffin RC .15 .05
❑ 258 Lynn Cain .15 .05
❑ 259 Checklist 133-264 .75 .30
❑ 260 Mike Pruitt .40 .15
❑ 261 Chris Ward RC .15 .05
❑ 262 Fred Steinfort .15 .05
❑ 263 James Owens .15 .05
❑ 264 Bears TL/Payton/Hampton 1.50 .60
❑ 265 Dan Fouts 1.50 .60
❑ 266 Arnold Morgado .15 .05
❑ 267 John Jefferson SA .75 .30
❑ 268 Bill Lenkaitis .15 .05
❑ 269 James Jones COW .15 .05
❑ 270 Brad Van Pelt .15 .05
❑ 271 Steve Largent 2.50 1.25
❑ 272 Elvin Bethea .75 .30
❑ 273 Cullen Bryant .15 .05
❑ 274 Gary Danielson .40 .15
❑ 275 Tony Galbreath .15 .05
❑ 276 Dave Butz .15 .05
❑ 277 Steve Mike-Mayer .15 .05
❑ 278 Ron Johnson DB .15 .05
❑ 279 Tom DeLeone .15 .05
❑ 280 Ron Jaworski .75 .30
❑ 281 Mel Gray .15 .05
❑ 282 San Diego Chargers TL .75 .30
❑ 283 Mark Brammer RC .15 .05
❑ 284 Alfred Jenkins SA .40 .15
❑ 285 Greg Buttle .15 .05
❑ 286 Randy Hughes .15 .05
❑ 287 Delvin Williams .15 .05
❑ 288 Brian Baschnagel .15 .05
❑ 289 Gary Jeter .15 .05
❑ 290 Stanley Morgan .75 .30
❑ 291 Gerry Ellis .15 .05
❑ 292 Al Richardson .15 .05
❑ 293 Jimmie Giles .40 .15
❑ 294 Dave Jennings SA .15 .05
❑ 295 Wilbert Montgomery .40 .15
❑ 296 Dave Pureifory .15 .05
❑ 297 Greg Hawthorne .15 .05
❑ 298 Dick Ambrose .15 .05
❑ 299 Terry Hermeling .15 .05
❑ 300 Danny White .75 .30
❑ 301 Ken Burrough .15 .05
❑ 302 Paul Hofer .15 .05
❑ 303 Denver Broncos TL .75 .30
❑ 304 Eddie Payton .40 .15
❑ 305 Isaac Curtis .40 .15
❑ 306 Benny Ricardo .15 .05
❑ 307 Riley Odoms .15 .05
❑ 308 Bob Chandler .15 .05
❑ 309 Larry Heater .15 .05
❑ 310 Art Still RC .75 .30
❑ 311 Harold Jackson .40 .15
❑ 312 Charlie Joiner SA .75 .30
❑ 313 Jeff Nixon .15 .05
❑ 314 Aundra Thompson .15 .05
❑ 315 Richard Todd .40 .15
❑ 316 Dan Hampton RC 3.00 1.25
❑ 317 Doug Marsh .15 .05
❑ 318 Louie Giammona .15 .05
❑ 319 49ers TL/Dwight Clark .75 .30
❑ 320 Manu Tuiasosopo .15 .05
❑ 321 Rich Milot .15 .05
❑ 322 Mike Guman RC .15 .05
❑ 323 Bob Kuechenberg .40 .15
❑ 324 Tom Skladany .15 .05
❑ 325 Dave Logan .15 .05
❑ 326 Bruce Laird .15 .05
❑ 327 James Jones COW SA .15 .05
❑ 328 Joe Danelo .15 .05
❑ 329 Kenny King RC .40 .15
❑ 330 Pat Donovan .15 .05
❑ 331 Earl Cooper RB .40 .15
❑ 332 John Jefferson RB .75 .30
❑ 333 Kenny King RB .40 .15
❑ 334 Rod Martin RB .40 .15
❑ 335 Jim Plunkett RB .75 .30
❑ 336 Bill Thompson RB .40 .15
❑ 337 John Cappelletti .40 .15
❑ 338 Lions TL/Billy Sims .75 .30
❑ 339 Don Smith .15 .05
❑ 340 Rod Perry .15 .05
❑ 341 David Lewis .15 .05
❑ 342 Mark Gastineau RC 1.00 .40
❑ 343 Steve Largent SA .75 .30
❑ 344 Charle Young .15 .05
❑ 345 Toni Fritsch .15 .05
❑ 346 Matt Blair .40 .15
❑ 347 Don Bass .15 .05
❑ 348 Jim Jensen RC .40 .15
❑ 349 Karl Lorch .15 .05
❑ 350 Brian Sipe .40 .15
❑ 351 Theo Bell .15 .05
❑ 352 Sam Adams OL .15 .05
❑ 353 Paul Coffman .15 .05
❑ 354 Eric Harris .15 .05
❑ 355 Tony Hill .40 .15
❑ 356 J.T. Turner .15 .05
❑ 357 Frank LeMaster .15 .05
❑ 358 Jim Jodat .15 .05
❑ 359 Raiders TL/Hendricks .75 .30
❑ 360 Joe Cribbs RC .75 .30
❑ 361 James Lofton SA .75 .30
❑ 362 Dexter Bussey .15 .05
❑ 363 Bobby Jackson .15 .05
❑ 364 Steve DeBerg .75 .30
❑ 365 Ottis Anderson 1.00 .40
❑ 366 Tom Myers .15 .05
❑ 367 John James .15 .05
❑ 368 Reese McCall .15 .05
❑ 369 Jack Reynolds .40 .15
❑ 370 Gary Johnson .15 .05
❑ 371 Jimmy Cefalo .15 .05
❑ 372 Horace Ivory .15 .05
❑ 373 Garo Yepremian .15 .05
❑ 374 Brian Kelley .15 .05
❑ 375 Terry Bradshaw 6.00 2.50
❑ 376 Cowboys TL/Tony Dorsett .75 .30
❑ 377 Randy Logan .15 .05
❑ 378 Tim Wilson .15 .05
❑ 379 Archie Manning SA .75 .30
❑ 380 Revie Sorey .15 .05
❑ 381 Randy Holloway .15 .05
❑ 382 Henry Lawrence .15 .05
❑ 383 Pat McInally .15 .05
❑ 384 Kevin Long .15 .05
❑ 385 Louis Wright .40 .15
❑ 386 Leonard Thompson .15 .05
❑ 387 Jan Stenerud .40 .15
❑ 388 Raymond Butler RC .15 .05
❑ 389 Checklist 265-396 .75 .30
❑ 390 Steve Bartkowski .40 .15
❑ 391 Clarence Harmon .15 .05
❑ 392 Wilbert Montgomery SA .40 .15
❑ 393 Billy Joe DuPree .40 .15
❑ 394 Kansas City Chiefs TL .40 .15
❑ 395 Earnest Gray .15 .05
❑ 396 Ray Hamilton .15 .05
❑ 397 Brenard Wilson .15 .05
❑ 398 Calvin Hill .75 .30
❑ 399 Robin Cole .15 .05
❑ 400 Walter Payton 12.00 6.00
❑ 401 Jim Hart .75 .30
❑ 402 Ron Yary .75 .30
❑ 403 Cliff Branch .75 .30
❑ 404 Roland Hooks .15 .05
❑ 405 Ken Stabler 3.00 1.50

Card	Player	Price 1	Price 2
❑ 406	Chuck Ramsey	.15	.05
❑ 407	Mike Nelms RC	.15	.05
❑ 408	Ron Jaworski SA	.40	.15
❑ 409	James Hunter	.15	.05
❑ 410	Lee Roy Selmon	.75	.30
❑ 411	Baltimore Colts TL	.40	.15
❑ 412	Henry Marshall	.15	.05
❑ 413	Preston Pearson	.40	.15
❑ 414	Richard Bishop	.15	.05
❑ 415	Greg Pruitt	.40	.15
❑ 416	Matt Bahr	.40	.15
❑ 417	Tom Mullady	.15	.05
❑ 418	Glen Edwards	.15	.05
❑ 419	Sam McCullum	.15	.05
❑ 420	Stan Walters	.15	.05
❑ 421	George Roberts	.15	.05
❑ 422	Dwight Clark RC	5.00	2.00
❑ 423	Pat Thomas RC	.15	.05
❑ 424	Bruce Harper SA	.15	.05
❑ 425	Craig Morton	.40	.15
❑ 426	Derrick Gaffney	.15	.05
❑ 427	Pete Johnson	.15	.05
❑ 428	Wes Chandler	.75	.30
❑ 429	Burgess Owens	.15	.05
❑ 430	James Lofton	2.00	.75
❑ 431	Tony Reed	.15	.05
❑ 432	Vikings TL/A.Rashad	.75	.30
❑ 433	Ron Springs RC	.40	.15
❑ 434	Tim Fox	.15	.05
❑ 435	Ozzie Newsome	2.00	.75
❑ 436	Steve Furness	.15	.05
❑ 437	Will Lewis	.15	.05
❑ 438	Mike Hartenstine	.15	.05
❑ 439	John Bunting	.15	.05
❑ 440	Eddie Murray RC	.75	.30
❑ 441	Mike Pruitt SA	.40	.15
❑ 442	Larry Swider	.15	.05
❑ 443	Steve Freeman	.15	.05
❑ 444	Bruce Hardy RC	.15	.05
❑ 445	Pat Haden	.40	.15
❑ 446	Curtis Dickey RC	.15	.05
❑ 447	Doug Wilkerson	.15	.05
❑ 448	Alfred Jenkins	.40	.15
❑ 449	Dave Dalby	.15	.05
❑ 450	Robert Brazile	.15	.05
❑ 451	Bobby Hammond	.15	.05
❑ 452	Raymond Clayborn	.15	.05
❑ 453	Jim Miller P RC	.15	.05
❑ 454	Roy Simmons	.15	.05
❑ 455	Charlie Waters	.40	.15
❑ 456	Ricky Bell	.75	.30
❑ 457	Ahmad Rashad SA	.75	.30
❑ 458	Don Cockroft	.15	.05
❑ 459	Keith Krepfle	.15	.05
❑ 460	Marvin Powell	.15	.05
❑ 461	Tommy Kramer	.75	.30
❑ 462	Jim LeClair	.15	.05
❑ 463	Freddie Scott	.15	.05
❑ 464	Rob Lytle	.15	.05
❑ 465	Johnnie Gray	.15	.05
❑ 466	Doug France RC	.15	.05
❑ 467	Carlos Carson RC	.40	.15
❑ 468	Cardinals TL/O.Anderson	.75	.30
❑ 469	Efren Herrera	.15	.05
❑ 470	Randy White	1.00	.40
❑ 471	Richard Caster	.15	.05
❑ 472	Andy Johnson	.15	.05
❑ 473	Billy Sims SA	.75	.30
❑ 474	Joe Lavender	.15	.05
❑ 475	Harry Carson	.40	.15
❑ 476	John Stallworth	1.00	.40
❑ 477	Bob Thomas	.15	.05
❑ 478	Keith Wright RC	.15	.05
❑ 479	Ken Stone	.15	.05
❑ 480	Carl Hairston	.40	.15
❑ 481	Reggie McKenzie	.15	.05
❑ 482	Bob Griese	1.50	.60
❑ 483	Mike Bragg	.15	.05
❑ 484	Scott Dierking	.15	.05
❑ 485	David Hill	.15	.05
❑ 486	Brian Sipe SA	.40	.15
❑ 487	Rod Martin RC	.40	.15
❑ 488	Cincinnati Bengals TL	.40	.15
❑ 489	Preston Dennard	.15	.05
❑ 490	John Smith	.15	.05
❑ 491	Mike Reinfeldt	.15	.05
❑ 492	NFC Champs/Jaworski	.75	.30
❑ 493	AFC Champs/Plunkett	.75	.30
❑ 494	Super Bowl XV/J.Plunkett	.75	.30
❑ 495	Joe Greene	.75	.30
❑ 496	Charlie Joiner	.75	.30
❑ 497	Rolland Lawrence	.15	.05
❑ 498	Al(Bubba) Baker SA	.40	.15
❑ 499	Brad Dusek	.15	.05
❑ 500	Tony Dorsett	4.00	2.00
❑ 501	Robin Earl	.15	.05
❑ 502	Theotis Brown RC	.15	.05
❑ 503	Joe Ferguson	.40	.15
❑ 504	Beasley Reece	.15	.05
❑ 505	Lyle Alzado	.75	.30
❑ 506	Tony Nathan RC	.75	.30
❑ 507	Philadelphia Eagles TL	.40	.15
❑ 508	Herb Orvis	.15	.05
❑ 509	Clarence Williams RB	.15	.05
❑ 510	Ray Guy	.40	.15
❑ 511	Jeff Komlo	.15	.05
❑ 512	Freddie Solomon SA	.15	.05
❑ 513	Tim Mazzetti	.15	.05
❑ 514	Elvis Peacock RC	.15	.05
❑ 515	Russ Francis	.40	.15
❑ 516	Roland Harper	.15	.05
❑ 517	Checklist 397-528	.75	.30
❑ 518	Billy Johnson	.40	.15
❑ 519	Dan Dierdorf	.75	.30
❑ 520	Fred Dean	.15	.05
❑ 521	Jerry Butler	.15	.05
❑ 522	Ron Saul	.15	.05
❑ 523	Charlie Smith WR	.15	.05
❑ 524	Kellen Winslow SA	3.00	1.50
❑ 525	Bert Jones	.75	.30
❑ 526	Steelers TL/Fr.Harris	.75	.30
❑ 527	Duriel Harris	.15	.05
❑ 528	William Andrews	.75	.30

1982 Topps

Card	Player	Price 1	Price 2
❑	COMPLETE SET (528)	80.00	40.00
❑ 1	Ken Anderson RB	.75	.30
❑ 2	Dan Fouts RB	.75	.30
❑ 3	LeRoy Irvin RB	.15	.05
❑ 4	Stump Mitchell RB	.15	.05
❑ 5	George Rogers RB	.75	.30
❑ 6	Dan Ross RB	.15	.05
❑ 7	AFC Champs/K.Anderson	.75	.30
❑ 8	NFC Champs/E.Cooper	.75	.30
❑ 9	Super Bowl XVI/A.Munoz	.75	.30
❑ 10	Baltimore Colts TL	.15	.05
❑ 11	Raymond Butler	.15	.05
❑ 12	Roger Carr	.15	.05
❑ 13	Curtis Dickey	.40	.15
❑ 14	Zachary Dixon	.15	.05
❑ 15	Nesby Glasgow	.15	.05
❑ 16	Bert Jones	.75	.30
❑ 17	Bruce Laird	.15	.05
❑ 18	Reese McCall	.15	.05
❑ 19	Randy McMillan	.15	.05
❑ 20	Ed Simonini	.15	.05
❑ 21	Buffalo Bills TL	.40	.15
❑ 22	Mark Brammer	.15	.05
❑ 23	Curtis Brown	.15	.05
❑ 24	Jerry Butler	.15	.05
❑ 25	Mario Clark	.15	.05
❑ 26	Joe Cribbs	.40	.15
❑ 27	Joe Cribbs IA	.40	.15
❑ 28	Joe Ferguson	.40	.15
❑ 29	Jim Haslett	.75	.30
❑ 30	Frank Lewis	.15	.05
❑ 31	Frank Lewis IA	.15	.05
❑ 32	Shane Nelson	.15	.05
❑ 33	Charles Romes	.15	.05
❑ 34	Bill Simpson	.15	.05
❑ 35	Fred Smerlas	.15	.05
❑ 36	Bengals TL/C.Collinswort	.40	.15
❑ 37	Charles Alexander	.15	.05
❑ 38	Ken Anderson	.75	.30
❑ 39	Ken Anderson IA	.75	.30
❑ 40	Jim Breech	.15	.05
❑ 41	Jim Breech IA	.15	.05
❑ 42	Louis Breeden	.15	.05
❑ 43	Ross Browner	.15	.05
❑ 44	Cris Collinsworth RC	2.00	.75
❑ 45	Cris Collinsworth IA	.75	.30
❑ 46	Isaac Curtis	.15	.05
❑ 47	Pete Johnson	.15	.05
❑ 48	Pete Johnson IA	.15	.05
❑ 49	Steve Kreider	.15	.05
❑ 50	Pat McInally	.15	.05
❑ 51	Anthony Munoz RC	8.00	4.00
❑ 52	Dan Ross	.15	.05
❑ 53	David Verser RC	.15	.05
❑ 54	Reggie Williams	.40	.15
❑ 55	Browns TL/O.Newsome	.40	.15
❑ 56	Lyle Alzado	.75	.30
❑ 57	Dick Ambrose	.15	.05
❑ 58	Ron Bolton	.15	.05
❑ 59	Steve Cox	.15	.05
❑ 60	Joe DeLamielleure	.75	.30
❑ 61	Tom DeLeone	.15	.05
❑ 62	Doug Dieken	.15	.05
❑ 63	Ricky Feacher	.15	.05
❑ 64	Don Goode	.15	.05
❑ 65	Robert L.Jackson RC	.15	.05
❑ 66	Dave Logan	.15	.05
❑ 67	Ozzie Newsome	1.00	.40
❑ 68	Ozzie Newsome IA	.75	.30
❑ 69	Greg Pruitt	.40	.15
❑ 70	Mike Pruitt	.40	.15
❑ 71	Mike Pruitt IA	.40	.15
❑ 72	Reggie Rucker	.15	.05
❑ 73	Clarence Scott	.15	.05
❑ 74	Brian Sipe	.40	.15
❑ 75	Charles White	.40	.15
❑ 76	Denver Broncos TL	.40	.15
❑ 77	Rubin Carter	.15	.05
❑ 78	Steve Foley	.15	.05
❑ 79	Randy Gradishar	.40	.15
❑ 80	Tom Jackson	.75	.30
❑ 81	Craig Morton	.40	.15
❑ 82	Craig Morton IA	.40	.15
❑ 83	Riley Odoms	.15	.05
❑ 84	Rick Parros	.15	.05
❑ 85	Dave Preston	.15	.05
❑ 86	Tony Reed	.15	.05
❑ 87	Bob Swenson RC	.15	.05
❑ 88	Bill Thompson	.15	.05
❑ 89	Rick Upchurch	.40	.15
❑ 90	Steve Watson RC	.40	.15
❑ 91	Steve Watson IA	.15	.05
❑ 92	Houston Oilers TL	.15	.05
❑ 93	Mike Barber	.15	.05
❑ 94	Elvin Bethea	.75	.30
❑ 95	Gregg Bingham	.15	.05
❑ 96	Robert Brazile	.15	.05
❑ 97	Ken Burrough	.15	.05
❑ 98	Toni Fritsch	.15	.05
❑ 99	Leon Gray	.15	.05
❑ 100	Gifford Nielsen RC	.40	.15
❑ 101	Vernon Perry	.15	.05
❑ 102	Mike Reinfeldt	.15	.05
❑ 103	Mike Renfro	.15	.05
❑ 104	Carl Roaches	.15	.05
❑ 105	Ken Stabler	2.00	.75
❑ 106	Greg Stemrick	.15	.05
❑ 107	J.C. Wilson	.15	.05
❑ 108	Tim Wilson	.15	.05
❑ 109	Kansas City Chiefs TL	.15	.05
❑ 110	Gary Barbaro	.15	.05
❑ 111	Brad Budde RC	.15	.05
❑ 112	Joe Delaney RC	.75	.30
❑ 113	Joe Delaney IA	.40	.15
❑ 114	Steve Fuller	.15	.05
❑ 115	Gary Green	.15	.05
❑ 116	James Hadnot	.15	.05
❑ 117	Eric Harris	.15	.05

Card		
❑ 118 Billy Jackson	.15	.05
❑ 119 Bill Kenney RC	.15	.05
❑ 120 Nick Lowery	.75	.30
❑ 121 Nick Lowery IA	.40	.15
❑ 122 Henry Marshall	.15	.05
❑ 123 J.T.Smith	.40	.15
❑ 124 Art Still	.15	.05
❑ 125 Miami Dolphins TL	.40	.15
❑ 126 Bob Baumhower	.40	.15
❑ 127 Glenn Blackwood RC	.15	.05
❑ 128 Jimmy Cefalo	.15	.05
❑ 129 A.J. Duhe	.40	.15
❑ 130 Andra Franklin RC	.15	.05
❑ 131 Duriel Harris	.15	.05
❑ 132 Nat Moore	.40	.15
❑ 133 Tony Nathan	.40	.15
❑ 134 Ed Newman	.15	.05
❑ 135 Earnie Rhone	.15	.05
❑ 136 Don Strock	.15	.05
❑ 137 Tommy Vigorito	.15	.05
❑ 138 Uwe Von Schamann	.15	.05
❑ 139 Uwe Von Schamann IA	.15	.05
❑ 140 David Woodley	.40	.15
❑ 141 New England Pats TL	.40	.15
❑ 142 Julius Adams	.15	.05
❑ 143 Richard Bishop	.15	.05
❑ 144 Matt Cavanaugh	.15	.05
❑ 145 Raymond Clayborn	.15	.05
❑ 146 Tony Collins RC	.15	.05
❑ 147 Vagas Ferguson	.15	.05
❑ 148 Tim Fox	.15	.05
❑ 149 Steve Grogan	.40	.15
❑ 150 John Hannah	.75	.30
❑ 151 John Hannah IA	.40	.15
❑ 152 Don Hasselbeck	.15	.05
❑ 153 Mike Haynes	.40	.15
❑ 154 Harold Jackson	.40	.15
❑ 155 Andy Johnson	.15	.05
❑ 156 Stanley Morgan	.40	.15
❑ 157 Stanley Morgan IA	.40	.15
❑ 158 Steve Nelson	.15	.05
❑ 159 Rod Shoate	.15	.05
❑ 160 Jets TL/F.McNeil	.40	.15
❑ 161 Dan Alexander RC	.15	.05
❑ 162 Mike Augustyniak	.15	.05
❑ 163 Jerome Barkum	.15	.05
❑ 164 Greg Buttle	.15	.05
❑ 165 Scott Dierking	.15	.05
❑ 166 Joe Fields	.15	.05
❑ 167 Mark Gastineau	.40	.15
❑ 168 Mark Gastineau IA	.40	.15
❑ 169 Bruce Harper	.15	.05
❑ 170 Johnny Lam Jones	.15	.05
❑ 171 Joe Klecko	.40	.15
❑ 172 Joe Klecko IA	.40	.15
❑ 173 Pat Leahy	.40	.15
❑ 174 Pat Leahy IA	.15	.05
❑ 175 Marty Lyons	.40	.15
❑ 176 Freeman McNeil RC	.75	.30
❑ 177 Marvin Powell	.15	.05
❑ 178 Chuck Ramsey	.15	.05
❑ 179 Darrol Ray	.15	.05
❑ 180 Abdul Salaam	.15	.05
❑ 181 Richard Todd	.40	.15
❑ 182 Richard Todd IA	.40	.15
❑ 183 Wesley Walker	.40	.15
❑ 184 Chris Ward	.15	.05
❑ 185 Oakland Raiders TL	.40	.15
❑ 186 Cliff Branch	.75	.30
❑ 187 Bob Chandler	.15	.05
❑ 188 Ray Guy	.40	.15
❑ 189 Lester Hayes	.40	.15
❑ 190 Ted Hendricks	.75	.30
❑ 191 Monte Jackson	.15	.05
❑ 192 Derrick Jensen	.15	.05
❑ 193 Kenny King	.15	.05
❑ 194 Rod Martin	.15	.05
❑ 195 John Matuszak	.40	.15
❑ 196 Matt Millen RC	1.50	.60
❑ 197 Derrick Ramsey	.15	.05
❑ 198 Art Shell	.75	.30
❑ 199 Mark Van Eeghen	.15	.05
❑ 200 Arthur Whittington	.15	.05
❑ 201 Marc Wilson RC	.40	.15
❑ 202 Steelers TL/Fr.Harris	.75	.30
❑ 203 Mel Blount	.75	.30
❑ 204 Terry Bradshaw	5.00	2.00
❑ 205 Terry Bradshaw IA	1.25	.50
❑ 206 Craig Colquitt	.15	.05
❑ 207 Bennie Cunningham	.15	.05
❑ 208 Russell Davis RC	.15	.05
❑ 209 Gary Dunn	.15	.05
❑ 210 Jack Ham	.75	.30
❑ 211 Franco Harris	1.00	.40
❑ 212 Franco Harris IA	.75	.30
❑ 213 Jack Lambert	.75	.30
❑ 214 Jack Lambert IA	.75	.30
❑ 215 Mark Malone RC	.75	.30
❑ 216 Frank Pollard RC	.15	.05
❑ 217 Donnie Shell	.75	.30
❑ 218 Jim Smith	.15	.05
❑ 219 John Stallworth	.75	.30
❑ 220 John Stallworth IA	.75	.30
❑ 221 David Trout	.15	.05
❑ 222 Mike Webster	.75	.30
❑ 223 San Diego Chargers TL	.75	.30
❑ 224 Rolf Benirschke	.15	.05
❑ 225 Rolf Benirschke IA	.15	.05
❑ 226 James Brooks RC	.75	.30
❑ 227 Willie Buchanon	.15	.05
❑ 228 Wes Chandler	.75	.30
❑ 229 Wes Chandler IA	.40	.15
❑ 230 Dan Fouts	1.00	.40
❑ 231 Dan Fouts IA	.75	.30
❑ 232 Gary Johnson	.15	.05
❑ 233 Charlie Joiner	.75	.30
❑ 234 Charlie Joiner IA	.75	.30
❑ 235 Louie Kelcher	.15	.05
❑ 236 Chuck Muncie	.40	.15
❑ 237 Chuck Muncie IA	.15	.05
❑ 238 George Roberts	.15	.05
❑ 239 Ed White	.15	.05
❑ 240 Doug Wilkerson	.15	.05
❑ 241 Kellen Winslow	2.00	.75
❑ 242 Kellen Winslow IA	.75	.30
❑ 243 Seahawks TL/S.Largent	.75	.30
❑ 244 Theotis Brown	.15	.05
❑ 245 Dan Doornink	.15	.05
❑ 246 John Harris	.15	.05
❑ 247 Efren Herrera	.15	.05
❑ 248 David Hughes	.15	.05
❑ 249 Steve Largent	2.00	.75
❑ 250 Steve Largent IA	.75	.30
❑ 251 Sam McCullum	.15	.05
❑ 252 Sherman Smith	.15	.05
❑ 253 Manu Tuiasosopo	.15	.05
❑ 254 John Yarno	.15	.05
❑ 255 Jim Zorn	.40	.15
❑ 256 Jim Zorn IA	.40	.15
❑ 257 J.Montana/Anderson LL	4.00	2.00
❑ 258 Kellen Winslow/Clark LL	.75	.30
❑ 259 QB Sack Leaders	.15	.05
❑ 260 Scoring Leaders	.40	.15
❑ 261 Interception Leaders	.40	.15
❑ 262 Punting Leaders	.15	.05
❑ 263 Brothers: Bahr	.15	.05
❑ 264 Brothers: Blackwood	.40	.15
❑ 265 Brothers: Brock	.15	.05
❑ 266 Brothers: Griffin	.40	.15
❑ 267 Brothers: Hannah	.75	.30
❑ 268 Brothers: Jackson	.15	.05
❑ 269 Walter/Eddie Payton	1.00	.40
❑ 270 Brothers: Selmon	.75	.30
❑ 271 Atlanta Falcons TL	.40	.15
❑ 272 William Andrews	.40	.15
❑ 273 William Andrews IA	.40	.15
❑ 274 Steve Bartkowski	.40	.15
❑ 275 Steve Bartkowski IA	.40	.15
❑ 276 Bobby Butler RC	.15	.05
❑ 277 Lynn Cain	.15	.05
❑ 278 Wallace Francis	.15	.05
❑ 279 Alfred Jackson	.15	.05
❑ 280 John James	.15	.05
❑ 281 Alfred Jenkins	.15	.05
❑ 282 Alfred Jenkins IA	.15	.05
❑ 283 Kenny Johnson	.15	.05
❑ 284 Mike Kenn	.75	.30
❑ 285 Fulton Kuykendall	.15	.05
❑ 286 Mick Luckhurst RC	.15	.05
❑ 287 Mick Luckhurst IA	.15	.05
❑ 288 Junior Miller	.15	.05
❑ 289 Al Richardson	.15	.05
❑ 290 R.C.Thielemann RC	.15	.05
❑ 291 Jeff Van Note	.15	.05
❑ 292 Bears TL/Walter Payton	.75	.30
❑ 293 Brian Baschnagel	.15	.05
❑ 294 Robin Earl	.15	.05
❑ 295 Vince Evans	.40	.15
❑ 296 Gary Fencik	.15	.05
❑ 297 Dan Hampton	.75	.30
❑ 298 Noah Jackson	.15	.05
❑ 299 Ken Margerum	.15	.05
❑ 300 Jim Osborne	.15	.05
❑ 301 Bob Parsons	.15	.05
❑ 302 Walter Payton	10.00	4.00
❑ 303 Walter Payton IA	3.00	1.25
❑ 304 Revie Sorey	.15	.05
❑ 305 Matt Suhey RC	.75	.30
❑ 306 Rickey Watts	.15	.05
❑ 307 Cowboys TL/Dorsett	.75	.30
❑ 308 Bob Breunig	.15	.05
❑ 309 Doug Cosbie RC	.15	.05
❑ 310 Pat Donovan	.15	.05
❑ 311 Tony Dorsett	1.50	.60
❑ 312 Tony Dorsett IA	.75	.30
❑ 313 Michael Downs RC	.15	.05
❑ 314 Billy Joe DuPree	.40	.15
❑ 315 John Dutton	.15	.05
❑ 316 Tony Hill	.40	.15
❑ 317 Butch Johnson	.40	.15
❑ 318 Ed Too Tall Jones	.75	.30
❑ 319 James Jones COW	.15	.05
❑ 320 Harvey Martin	.40	.15
❑ 321 Drew Pearson	.75	.30
❑ 322 Herb Scott	.15	.05
❑ 323 Rafael Septien	.15	.05
❑ 324 Rafael Septien IA	.15	.05
❑ 325 Ron Springs	.40	.15
❑ 326 Dennis Thurman RC	.15	.05
❑ 327 Everson Walls RC	.75	.30
❑ 328 Everson Walls IA	.75	.30
❑ 329 Danny White	.75	.30
❑ 330 Danny White IA	.40	.15
❑ 331 Randy White	.75	.30
❑ 332 Randy White IA	.75	.30
❑ 333 Detroit Lions TL	.40	.15
❑ 334 Jim Allen	.15	.05
❑ 335 Al(Bubba) Baker	.40	.15
❑ 336 Dexter Bussey	.15	.05
❑ 337 Doug English	.40	.15
❑ 338 Ken Fantetti	.15	.05
❑ 339 William Gay	.15	.05
❑ 340 David Hill	.15	.05
❑ 341 Eric Hipple RC	.15	.05
❑ 342 Rick Kane	.15	.05
❑ 343 Eddie Murray	.75	.30
❑ 344 Eddie Murray IA	.40	.15
❑ 345 Ray Oldham	.15	.05
❑ 346 Dave Pureifory	.15	.05
❑ 347 Freddie Scott	.15	.05
❑ 348 Freddie Scott IA	.15	.05
❑ 349 Billy Sims	.75	.30
❑ 350 Billy Sims IA	.75	.30
❑ 351 Tom Skladany	.15	.05
❑ 352 Leonard Thompson	.15	.05
❑ 353 Stan White	.15	.05
❑ 354 Packers TL/Lofton	.75	.30
❑ 355 Paul Coffman	.15	.05
❑ 356 George Cumby	.15	.05
❑ 357 Lynn Dickey	.15	.05
❑ 358 Lynn Dickey IA	.15	.05
❑ 359 Gerry Ellis	.15	.05
❑ 360 Maurice Harvey	.15	.05
❑ 361 Harlan Huckleby	.15	.05
❑ 362 John Jefferson	.75	.30
❑ 363 Mark Lee RC	.15	.05
❑ 364 James Lofton	1.00	.40
❑ 365 James Lofton IA	.75	.30
❑ 366 Jan Stenerud	.40	.15
❑ 367 Jan Stenerud IA	.40	.15
❑ 368 Rich Wingo	.15	.05
❑ 369 Los Angeles Rams TL	.40	.15
❑ 370 Frank Corral	.15	.05
❑ 371 Nolan Cromwell	.40	.15
❑ 372 Nolan Cromwell IA	.40	.15
❑ 373 Preston Dennard	.15	.05
❑ 374 Mike Fanning	.15	.05
❑ 375 Doug France	.15	.05
❑ 376 Mike Guman	.15	.05
❑ 377 Pat Haden	.40	.15
❑ 378 Dennis Harrah	.15	.05

	Card	Price 1	Price 2
❑	379 Drew Hill RC	.75	.30
❑	380 LeRoy Irvin RC	.15	.05
❑	381 Cody Jones	.15	.05
❑	382 Rod Perry	.15	.05
❑	383 Rich Saul	.15	.05
❑	384 Pat Thomas	.15	.05
❑	385 Wendell Tyler	.40	.15
❑	386 Wendell Tyler IA	.40	.15
❑	387 Billy Waddy	.15	.05
❑	388 Jack Youngblood	.75	.30
❑	389 Minnesota Vikings TL	.15	.05
❑	390 Matt Blair	.15	.05
❑	391 Ted Brown	.15	.05
❑	392 Ted Brown IA	.15	.05
❑	393 Rick Danmeier	.15	.05
❑	394 Tommy Kramer	.40	.15
❑	395 Mark Mullaney	.15	.05
❑	396 Eddie Payton	.15	.05
❑	397 Ahmad Rashad	.75	.30
❑	398 Joe Senser	.15	.05
❑	399 Joe Senser IA	.15	.05
❑	400 Sammie White	.40	.15
❑	401 Sammie White IA	.15	.05
❑	402 Ron Yary	.75	.30
❑	403 Rickey Young	.15	.05
❑	404 Saints TL/Ric.Jackson	.40	.15
❑	405 Russell Erxleben	.15	.05
❑	406 Elois Grooms	.15	.05
❑	407 Jack Holmes	.15	.05
❑	408 Archie Manning	.75	.30
❑	409 Derland Moore	.15	.05
❑	410 George Rogers RC	.75	.30
❑	411 George Rogers IA	.75	.30
❑	412 Toussaint Tyler	.15	.05
❑	413 Dave Waymer RC	.15	.05
❑	414 Wayne Wilson	.15	.05
❑	415 New York Giants TL	.15	.05
❑	416 Scott Brunner RC	.15	.05
❑	417 Rob Carpenter	.15	.05
❑	418 Harry Carson	.40	.15
❑	419 Bill Currier	.15	.05
❑	420 Joe Danelo	.15	.05
❑	421 Joe Danelo IA	.15	.05
❑	422 Mark Haynes RC	.15	.05
❑	423 Terry Jackson	.15	.05
❑	424 Dave Jennings	.15	.05
❑	425 Gary Jeter	.15	.05
❑	426 Brian Kelley	.15	.05
❑	427 George Martin	.15	.05
❑	428 Curtis McGriff	.15	.05
❑	429 Bill Neill	.15	.05
❑	430 Johnny Perkins	.15	.05
❑	431 Beasley Reece	.15	.05
❑	432 Gary Shirk	.15	.05
❑	433 Phil Simms	2.00	.75
❑	434 Lawrence Taylor RC	20.00	7.50
❑	435 Lawrence Taylor IA	10.00	4.00
❑	436 Brad Van Pelt	.15	.05
❑	437 Philadelphia Eagles TL	.40	.15
❑	438 John Bunting	.15	.05
❑	439 Billy Campfield	.15	.05
❑	440 Harold Carmichael	.75	.30
❑	441 Harold Carmichael IA	.75	.30
❑	442 Herman Edwards	.15	.05
❑	443 Tony Franklin	.15	.05
❑	444 Tony Franklin IA	.15	.05
❑	445 Carl Hairston	.15	.05
❑	446 Dennis Harrison	.15	.05
❑	447 Ron Jaworski	.75	.30
❑	448 Charlie Johnson NT	.15	.05
❑	449 Keith Krepfle	.15	.05
❑	450 Frank LeMaster	.15	.05
❑	451 Randy Logan	.15	.05
❑	452 Wilbert Montgomery	.40	.15
❑	453 Wilbert Montgomery IA	.40	.15
❑	454 Hubie Oliver	.15	.05
❑	455 Jerry Robinson	.15	.05
❑	456 Jerry Robinson IA	.15	.05
❑	457 Jerry Sisemore	.15	.05
❑	458 Charlie Smith WR	.15	.05
❑	459 Stan Walters	.15	.05
❑	460 Brenard Wilson	.15	.05
❑	461 Roynell Young	.15	.05
❑	462 Cardinals TL/O.Anderson	.40	.15
❑	463 Ottis Anderson	.75	.30
❑	464 Ottis Anderson IA	.75	.30
❑	465 Carl Birdsong	.15	.05
❑	466 Rush Brown	.15	.05
❑	467 Mel Gray	.40	.15
❑	468 Ken Greene	.15	.05
❑	469 Jim Hart	.75	.30
❑	470 E.J.Junior RC	.40	.15
❑	471 Neil Lomax RC	.75	.30
❑	472 Stump Mitchell RC	.75	.30
❑	473 Wayne Morris	.15	.05
❑	474 Neil O'Donoghue	.15	.05
❑	475 Pat Tilley	.15	.05
❑	476 Pat Tilley IA	.15	.05
❑	477 49ers TL/Dwight Clark	.40	.15
❑	478 Dwight Clark	.75	.30
❑	479 Dwight Clark IA	.75	.30
❑	480 Earl Cooper	.15	.05
❑	481 Randy Cross	.40	.15
❑	482 Johnny Davis RC	.15	.05
❑	483 Fred Dean	.15	.05
❑	484 Fred Dean IA	.15	.05
❑	485 Dwight Hicks RC	.75	.30
❑	486 Ronnie Lott RC	20.00	7.50
❑	487 Ronnie Lott IA	6.00	3.00
❑	488 Joe Montana	20.00	7.50
❑	489 Joe Montana IA	12.00	5.00
❑	490 Ricky Patton	.15	.05
❑	491 Jack Reynolds	.40	.15
❑	492 Freddie Solomon	.15	.05
❑	493 Ray Wersching	.15	.05
❑	494 Charle Young	.15	.05
❑	495 Tampa Bay Bucs TL	.40	.15
❑	496 Cedric Brown	.15	.05
❑	497 Neal Colzie	.15	.05
❑	498 Jerry Eckwood	.15	.05
❑	499 Jimmie Giles	.40	.15
❑	500 Hugh Green RC	.75	.30
❑	501 Kevin House	.15	.05
❑	502 Kevin House IA	.15	.05
❑	503 Cecil Johnson	.15	.05
❑	504 James Owens	.15	.05
❑	505 Lee Roy Selmon	.75	.30
❑	506 Mike Washington	.15	.05
❑	507 James Wilder RC	.40	.15
❑	508 Doug Williams	.40	.15
❑	509 Redskins TL/Monk	.75	.30
❑	510 Perry Brooks	.15	.05
❑	511 Dave Butz	.40	.15
❑	512 Wilbur Jackson	.15	.05
❑	513 Joe Lavender	.15	.05
❑	514 Terry Metcalf	.40	.15
❑	515 Art Monk	3.00	1.25
❑	516 Mark Moseley	.15	.05
❑	517 Mark Murphy	.15	.05
❑	518 Mike Nelms	.15	.05
❑	519 Lemar Parrish	.15	.05
❑	520 John Riggins	.75	.30
❑	521 Joe Theismann	.75	.30
❑	522 Ricky Thompson	.15	.05
❑	523 Don Warren UER	.15	.05
❑	524 Joe Washington	.40	.15
❑	525 Checklist 1-132	.50	.20
❑	526 Checklist 133-264	.50	.20
❑	527 Checklist 265-396	.50	.20
❑	528 Checklist 397-528	.50	.20

1983 Topps

	Card	Price 1	Price 2
❑	COMPLETE SET (396)	60.00	30.00
❑	1 Ken Anderson RB	.60	.25
❑	2 Tony Dorsett RB	.60	.25
❑	3 Dan Fouts RB	.60	.25
❑	4 Joe Montana RB	3.00	1.50
❑	5 Mark Moseley RB	.30	.10
❑	6 Mike Nelms RB	.10	.02
❑	7 Darrol Ray RB	.10	.02
❑	8 John Riggins RB	.60	.25
❑	9 Fulton Walker RB	.10	.02
❑	10 NFC Champs/Riggins	.60	.25
❑	11 AFC Championship	.30	.10
❑	12 Super Bowl XVII/J.Riggins	.10	.02
❑	13 Atlanta Falcons TL	.30	.10
❑	14 William Andrews DP	.30	.10
❑	15 Steve Bartkowski	.30	.10
❑	16 Bobby Butler	.10	.02
❑	17 Buddy Curry	.10	.02
❑	18 Alfred Jackson DP	.10	.02
❑	19 Alfred Jenkins	.10	.02
❑	20 Kenny Johnson	.10	.02
❑	21 Mike Kenn	.10	.02
❑	22 Mick Luckhurst	.10	.02
❑	23 Junior Miller	.10	.02
❑	24 Al Richardson	.10	.02
❑	25 Gerald Riggs RC DP	.30	.10
❑	26 R.C. Thielemann	.10	.02
❑	27 Jeff Van Note	.10	.02
❑	28 Bears TL/W.Payton	1.00	.40
❑	29 Brian Baschnagel	.10	.02
❑	30 Dan Hampton	.60	.25
❑	31 Mike Hartenstine	.10	.02
❑	32 Noah Jackson	.10	.02
❑	33 Jim McMahon RC	8.00	4.00
❑	34 Emery Moorehead DP	.10	.02
❑	35 Bob Parsons	.10	.02
❑	36 Walter Payton	6.00	3.00
❑	37 Terry Schmidt	.10	.02
❑	38 Mike Singletary RC	8.00	4.00
❑	39 Matt Suhey DP	.30	.10
❑	40 Rickey Watts DP	.10	.02
❑	41 Otis Wilson RC DP	.30	.10
❑	42 Cowboys TL/Tony Dorsett	.60	.25
❑	43 Bob Breunig	.30	.10
❑	44 Doug Cosbie	.10	.02
❑	45 Pat Donovan	.10	.02
❑	46 Tony Dorsett DP	1.00	.40
❑	47 Tony Hill	.30	.10
❑	48 Butch Johnson DP	.30	.10
❑	49 Ed Too Tall Jones DP	.60	.25
❑	50 Harvey Martin DP	.30	.10
❑	51 Drew Pearson	.60	.25
❑	52 Rafael Septien	.10	.02
❑	53 Ron Springs DP	.10	.02
❑	54 Dennis Thurman	.10	.02
❑	55 Everson Walls	.30	.10
❑	56 Danny White DP	.60	.25
❑	57 Randy White	.60	.25
❑	58 Detroit Lions TL	.30	.10
❑	59 Al(Bubba) Baker DP	.30	.10
❑	60 Dexter Bussey DP	.10	.02
❑	61 Gary Danielson DP	.10	.02
❑	62 Keith Dorney DP	.10	.02
❑	63 Doug English	.10	.02
❑	64 Ken Fantetti DP	.10	.02
❑	65 Alvin Hall DP	.10	.02
❑	66 David Hill DP	.10	.02
❑	67 Eric Hipple	.10	.02
❑	68 Eddie Murray DP	.30	.10
❑	69 Freddie Scott	.10	.02
❑	70 Billy Sims DP	.30	.10
❑	71 Tom Skladany DP	.10	.02
❑	72 Leonard Thompson DP	.10	.02
❑	73 Bobby Watkins	.10	.02
❑	74 Green Bay Packers TL	.10	.02
❑	75 John Anderson	.10	.02
❑	76 Paul Coffman	.10	.02
❑	77 Lynn Dickey	.10	.02
❑	78 Mike Douglass DP	.10	.02
❑	79 Eddie Lee Ivery	.10	.02
❑	80 John Jefferson DP	.60	.25
❑	81 Ezra Johnson	.10	.02
❑	82 Mark Lee	.10	.02
❑	83 James Lofton	.60	.25
❑	84 Larry McCarren	.10	.02
❑	85 Jan Stenerud DP	.30	.10
❑	86 Los Angeles Rams TL	.10	.02
❑	87 Bill Bain DP	.10	.02
❑	88 Nolan Cromwell	.30	.10
❑	89 Preston Dennard	.10	.02
❑	90 Vince Ferragamo DP	.30	.10

❑ 91 Mike Guman .10 .02
❑ 92 Kent Hill .10 .02
❑ 93 Mike Lansford RC DP .10 .02
❑ 94 Rod Perry .10 .02
❑ 95 Pat Thomas DP .10 .02
❑ 96 Jack Youngblood .60 .25
❑ 97 Minnesota Vikings TL .10 .02
❑ 98 Matt Blair .10 .02
❑ 99 Ted Brown .10 .02
❑ 100 Greg Coleman .10 .02
❑ 101 Randy Holloway .10 .02
❑ 102 Tommy Kramer .30 .10
❑ 103 Doug Martin DP .10 .02
❑ 104 Mark Mullaney .10 .02
❑ 105 Joe Senser .10 .02
❑ 106 Willie Teal DP .10 .02
❑ 107 Sammie White .30 .10
❑ 108 Rickey Young .10 .02
❑ 109 New Orleans Saints TL .30 .10
❑ 110 Stan Brock RC .10 .02
❑ 111 Bruce Clark RC .10 .02
❑ 112 Russell Erxleben DP .10 .02
❑ 113 Russell Gary .10 .02
❑ 114 Jeff Groth DP .10 .02
❑ 115 John Hill DP .10 .02
❑ 116 Derland Moore .10 .02
❑ 117 George Rogers .30 .10
❑ 118 Ken Stabler 1.50 .60
❑ 119 Wayne Wilson .10 .02
❑ 120 New York Giants TL .10 .02
❑ 121 Scott Brunner .10 .02
❑ 122 Rob Carpenter .10 .02
❑ 123 Harry Carson .30 .10
❑ 124 Joe Danelo DP .10 .02
❑ 125 Earnest Gray .10 .02
❑ 126 Mark Haynes DP .30 .10
❑ 127 Terry Jackson .10 .02
❑ 128 Dave Jennings .10 .02
❑ 129 Brian Kelley .10 .02
❑ 130 George Martin .10 .02
❑ 131 Tom Mullady .10 .02
❑ 132 Johnny Perkins .10 .02
❑ 133 Lawrence Taylor 5.00 2.00
❑ 134 Brad Van Pelt .10 .02
❑ 135 Butch Woolfolk DP RC .10 .02
❑ 136 Philadelphia Eagles TL .30 .10
❑ 137 Harold Carmichael .60 .25
❑ 138 Herman Edwards .10 .02
❑ 139 Tony Franklin DP .10 .02
❑ 140 Carl Hairston DP .10 .02
❑ 141 Dennis Harrison DP .10 .02
❑ 142 Ron Jaworski DP .30 .10
❑ 143 Frank LeMaster .10 .02
❑ 144 Wilbert Montgomery DP .30 .10
❑ 145 Guy Morriss .10 .02
❑ 146 Jerry Robinson .10 .02
❑ 147 Max Runager .10 .02
❑ 148 Ron Smith DP RC .10 .02
❑ 149 John Spagnola .10 .02
❑ 150 Stan Walters DP .10 .02
❑ 151 Roynell Young DP .10 .02
❑ 152 Cardinals TL/O.Anderson .30 .10
❑ 153 Ottis Anderson .60 .25
❑ 154 Carl Birdsong .10 .02
❑ 155 Dan Dierdorf DP .60 .25
❑ 156 Roy Green RC .60 .25
❑ 157 Elois Grooms .10 .02
❑ 158 Neil Lomax DP .30 .10
❑ 159 Wayne Morris .10 .02
❑ 160 Tootie Robbins RC .10 .02
❑ 161 Luis Sharpe RC .10 .02
❑ 162 Pat Tilley .10 .02
❑ 163 San Francisco 49ers TL .10 .02
❑ 164 Dwight Clark .60 .25
❑ 165 Randy Cross .30 .10
❑ 166 Russ Francis .30 .10
❑ 167 Dwight Hicks .10 .02
❑ 168 Ronnie Lott 2.50 1.25
❑ 169 Joe Montana DP 10.00 4.00
❑ 170 Jeff Moore .10 .02
❑ 171 Renaldo Nehemiah RC DP .60 .25
❑ 172 Freddie Solomon .10 .02
❑ 173 Ray Wersching DP .10 .02
❑ 174 Tampa Bay Bucs TL .10 .02
❑ 175 Cedric Brown .10 .02
❑ 176 Bill Capece .10 .02
❑ 177 Neal Colzie .10 .02
❑ 178 Jimmie Giles .10 .02
❑ 179 Hugh Green .30 .10
❑ 180 Kevin House DP .10 .02
❑ 181 James Owens .10 .02
❑ 182 Lee Roy Selmon .60 .25
❑ 183 Mike Washington .10 .02
❑ 184 James Wilder .10 .02
❑ 185 Doug Williams DP .30 .10
❑ 186 Redskins TL/John Riggins .60 .25
❑ 187 Jeff Bostic RC DP 1.00 .40
❑ 188 Charlie Brown RC .30 .10
❑ 189 Vernon Dean DP RC .10 .02
❑ 190 Joe Jacoby RC 1.00 .40
❑ 191 Dexter Manley RC .30 .10
❑ 192 Rich Milot .10 .02
❑ 193 Art Monk DP 1.00 .40
❑ 194 Mark Moseley DP .10 .02
❑ 195 Mike Nelms .10 .02
❑ 196 Neal Olkewicz DP .10 .02
❑ 197 Tony Peters .10 .02
❑ 198 John Riggins DP .60 .25
❑ 199 Joe Theismann .60 .25
❑ 200 Don Warren .10 .02
❑ 201 Jeris White DP .10 .02
❑ 202 J.Theismann/K.Anderson LL .60 .25
❑ 203 Receiving Leaders .30 .10
❑ 204 Tony Dorsett/F.McNeil LL .60 .25
❑ 205 M.Allen/W.Tyler LL 1.25 .50
❑ 206 Interception Leaders .30 .10
❑ 207 Punting Leaders .10 .02
❑ 208 Baltimore Colts TL .10 .02
❑ 209 Matt Bouza .10 .02
❑ 210 Johnie Cooks RC DP .10 .02
❑ 211 Curtis Dickey .10 .02
❑ 212 Nesby Glasgow DP .10 .02
❑ 213 Derrick Hatchett .10 .02
❑ 214 Randy McMillan .10 .02
❑ 215 Mike Pagel RC .30 .10
❑ 216 Rohn Stark RC DP .30 .10
❑ 217 Donnell Thompson RC DP .10 .02
❑ 218 Leo Wisniewski DP .10 .02
❑ 219 Buffalo Bills TL .30 .10
❑ 220 Curtis Brown .10 .02
❑ 221 Jerry Butler .10 .02
❑ 222 Greg Cater DP .10 .02
❑ 223 Joe Cribbs .30 .10
❑ 224 Joe Ferguson .30 .10
❑ 225 Roosevelt Leaks .10 .02
❑ 226 Frank Lewis .10 .02
❑ 227 Eugene Marve RC .10 .02
❑ 228 Fred Smerlas DP .10 .02
❑ 229 Ben Williams DP .10 .02
❑ 230 Cincinnati Bengals TL .10 .02
❑ 231 Charles Alexander .10 .02
❑ 232 Ken Anderson DP .60 .25
❑ 233 Jim Breech DP .10 .02
❑ 234 Ross Browner .10 .02
❑ 235 Cris Collinsworth DP .60 .25
❑ 236 Isaac Curtis .10 .02
❑ 237 Pete Johnson .10 .02
❑ 238 Steve Kreider DP .10 .02
❑ 239 Max Montoya RC DP .10 .02
❑ 240 Anthony Munoz 1.00 .40
❑ 241 Ken Riley .10 .02
❑ 242 Dan Ross .10 .02
❑ 243 Reggie Williams .30 .10
❑ 244 Cleveland Browns TL .30 .10
❑ 245 Chip Banks RC DP .30 .10
❑ 246 Tom Cousineau RC DP .30 .10
❑ 247 Joe DeLamielleure DP .30 .10
❑ 248 Doug Dieken DP .10 .02
❑ 249 Hanford Dixon RC .10 .02
❑ 250 Ricky Feacher DP .10 .02
❑ 251 Lawrence Johnson DP .10 .02
❑ 252 Dave Logan DP .10 .02
❑ 253 Paul McDonald DP .10 .02
❑ 254 Ozzie Newsome DP .60 .25
❑ 255 Mike Pruitt .30 .10
❑ 256 Clarence Scott DP .10 .02
❑ 257 Brian Sipe DP .30 .10
❑ 258 Dwight Walker DP .10 .02
❑ 259 Charles White .30 .10
❑ 260 Denver Broncos TL .10 .02
❑ 261 Steve DeBerg DP .30 .10
❑ 262 Randy Gradishar DP .30 .10
❑ 263 Rulon Jones RC DP .10 .02
❑ 264 Rich Karlis DP .10 .02
❑ 265 Don Latimer .10 .02
❑ 266 Rick Parros DP .10 .02
❑ 267 Luke Prestridge .10 .02
❑ 268 Rick Upchurch .30 .10
❑ 269 Steve Watson DP .10 .02
❑ 270 Gerald Willhite DP .10 .02
❑ 271 Houston Oilers TL .10 .02
❑ 272 Harold Bailey .10 .02
❑ 273 Jesse Baker DP .10 .02
❑ 274 Gregg Bingham DP .10 .02
❑ 275 Robert Brazile DP .10 .02
❑ 276 Donnie Craft .10 .02
❑ 277 Daryl Hunt .10 .02
❑ 278 Archie Manning DP .30 .10
❑ 279 Gifford Nielsen .10 .02
❑ 280 Mike Renfro .10 .02
❑ 281 Carl Roaches DP .10 .02
❑ 282 Kansas City Chiefs TL .30 .10
❑ 283 Gary Barbaro .10 .02
❑ 284 Joe Delaney .10 .02
❑ 285 Jeff Gossett RC .60 .25
❑ 286 Gary Green DP .10 .02
❑ 287 Eric Harris DP .10 .02
❑ 288 Billy Jackson DP .10 .02
❑ 289 Bill Kenney DP .10 .02
❑ 290 Nick Lowery .60 .25
❑ 291 Henry Marshall .10 .02
❑ 292 Art Still DP .10 .02
❑ 293 Raiders TL/M.Allen 2.00 .75
❑ 294 Marcus Allen RC DP 15.00 6.00
❑ 295 Lyle Alzado .60 .25
❑ 296 Chris Bahr DP .10 .02
❑ 297 Cliff Branch .60 .25
❑ 298 Todd Christensen RC .75 .30
❑ 299 Ray Guy .30 .10
❑ 300 Frank Hawkins DP .10 .02
❑ 301 Lester Hayes DP .10 .02
❑ 302 Ted Hendricks DP .60 .25
❑ 303 Kenny King DP .10 .02
❑ 304 Rod Martin .10 .02
❑ 305 Matt Millen DP .60 .25
❑ 306 Burgess Owens .10 .02
❑ 307 Jim Plunkett .60 .25
❑ 308 Miami Dolphins TL .30 .10
❑ 309 Bob Baumhower .10 .02
❑ 310 Glenn Blackwood .10 .02
❑ 311 Lyle Blackwood DP .10 .02
❑ 312 A.J. Duhe .10 .02
❑ 313 Andra Franklin .10 .02
❑ 314 Duriel Harris .10 .02
❑ 315 Bob Kuechenberg DP .30 .10
❑ 316 Don McNeal .10 .02
❑ 317 Tony Nathan .30 .10
❑ 318 Ed Newman .10 .02
❑ 319 Earnie Rhone DP .10 .02
❑ 320 Joe Rose DP .10 .02
❑ 321 Don Strock DP .10 .02
❑ 322 Uwe Von Schamann .10 .02
❑ 323 David Woodley DP .30 .10
❑ 324 New England Pats TL .10 .02
❑ 325 Julius Adams .10 .02
❑ 326 Pete Brock .10 .02
❑ 327 Rich Camarillo RC DP .10 .02
❑ 328 Tony Collins DP .10 .02
❑ 329 Steve Grogan .30 .10
❑ 330 John Hannah .60 .25
❑ 331 Don Hasselbeck .10 .02
❑ 332 Mike Haynes .30 .10
❑ 333 Roland James RC .10 .02
❑ 334A Stanley Morgan ERR IL .60 .25
❑ 334B Stanley Morgan COR .30 .10
❑ 335 Steve Nelson .10 .02
❑ 336 Kenneth Sims DP .10 .02
❑ 337 Mark Van Eeghen .30 .10
❑ 338 New York Jets TL .30 .10
❑ 339 Greg Buttle .10 .02
❑ 340 Joe Fields .10 .02
❑ 341 Mark Gastineau DP .30 .10
❑ 342 Bruce Harper .10 .02
❑ 343 Bobby Jackson .10 .02
❑ 344 Bobby Jones .10 .02
❑ 345 Johnny Lam Jones DP .10 .02
❑ 346 Joe Klecko .30 .10
❑ 347 Marty Lyons .10 .02
❑ 348 Freeman McNeil .60 .25
❑ 349 Lance Mehl RC .10 .02
❑ 350 Marvin Powell DP .10 .02

Card		
❑ 351 Darrol Ray DP	.10	.02
❑ 352 Abdul Salaam	.10	.02
❑ 353 Richard Todd	.30	.10
❑ 354 Wesley Walker	.30	.10
❑ 355 Steelers TL/Franco Harris	.60	.25
❑ 356 Gary Anderson K RC DP	6.00	3.00
❑ 357 Mel Blount DP	.60	.25
❑ 358 Terry Bradshaw DP	1.50	.60
❑ 359 Larry Brown	.10	.02
❑ 360 Bennie Cunningham	.10	.02
❑ 361 Gary Dunn	.10	.02
❑ 362 Franco Harris	.75	.30
❑ 363 Jack Lambert	.60	.25
❑ 364 Frank Pollard	.10	.02
❑ 365 Donnie Shell	.30	.10
❑ 366 John Stallworth	.60	.25
❑ 367 Loren Toews	.10	.02
❑ 368 Mike Webster DP	.60	.25
❑ 369 Dwayne Woodruff RC	.10	.02
❑ 370 San Diego Chargers TL	.30	.10
❑ 371 Rolf Benirschke DP	.10	.02
❑ 372 James Brooks	.60	.25
❑ 373 Wes Chandler	.30	.10
❑ 374 Dan Fouts DP	.60	.25
❑ 375 Tim Fox	.10	.02
❑ 376 Gary Johnson	.10	.02
❑ 377 Charlie Joiner DP	.60	.25
❑ 378 Louie Kelcher	.10	.02
❑ 379 Chuck Muncie	.10	.02
❑ 380 Cliff Thrift	.10	.02
❑ 381 Doug Wilkerson	.10	.02
❑ 382 Kellen Winslow	.75	.30
❑ 383 Seattle Seahawks TL	.10	.02
❑ 384 Kenny Easley RC	.60	.25
❑ 385 Jacob Green RC	.30	.10
❑ 386 John Harris	.10	.02
❑ 387 Michael Jackson	.10	.02
❑ 388 Norm Johnson RC	.10	.02
❑ 389 Steve Largent	1.25	.50
❑ 390 Keith Simpson	.10	.02
❑ 391 Sherman Smith	.10	.02
❑ 392 Jeff West DP	.10	.02
❑ 393 Jim Zorn DP	.30	.10
❑ 394 Checklist 1-132	.50	.20
❑ 395 Checklist 133-264	.50	.20
❑ 396 Checklist 265-396	.50	.20

1984 Topps

Card		
❑ COMPLETE SET (396)	200.00	100.00
❑ COMP.FACT.SET (396)	350.00	200.00
❑ 1 Eric Dickerson RB	.50	.20
❑ 2 Ali Haji-Sheikh RB	.25	.08
❑ 3 Franco Harris RB	.50	.20
❑ 4 Mark Moseley RB	.25	.08
❑ 5 John Riggins RB	.50	.20
❑ 6 Jan Stenerud RB	.25	.08
❑ 7 AFC Champs/M.Allen	.50	.20
❑ 8 NFC Champs/Riggins	.25	.08
❑ 9 Super Bowl XVIII/Allen UER	.50	.20
❑ 10 Indianapolis Colts TL	.10	.02
❑ 11 Raul Allegre RC	.10	.02
❑ 12 Curtis Dickey	.25	.08
❑ 13 Ray Donaldson RC	.25	.08
❑ 14 Nesby Glasgow	.10	.02
❑ 15 Chris Hinton RC	.50	.20
❑ 16 Vernon Maxwell RC	.10	.02
❑ 17 Randy McMillan	.10	.02
❑ 18 Mike Pagel	.25	.08
❑ 19 Rohn Stark	.25	.08
❑ 20 Leo Wisniewski	.10	.02
❑ 21 Buffalo Bills TL	.25	.08
❑ 22 Jerry Butler	.10	.02
❑ 23 Joe Danelo	.10	.02
❑ 24 Joe Ferguson	.25	.08
❑ 25 Steve Freeman	.10	.02
❑ 26 Roosevelt Leaks	.25	.08
❑ 27 Frank Lewis	.10	.02
❑ 28 Eugene Marve	.10	.02
❑ 29 Booker Moore	.10	.02
❑ 30 Fred Smerlas	.10	.02
❑ 31 Ben Williams	.25	.08
❑ 32 Cincinnati Bengals TL	.25	.08
❑ 33 Charles Alexander	.10	.02
❑ 34 Ken Anderson	.50	.20
❑ 35 Ken Anderson IR	.50	.20
❑ 36 Jim Breech	.10	.02
❑ 37 Cris Collinsworth	.50	.20
❑ 38 Cris Collinsworth IR	.50	.20
❑ 39 Isaac Curtis	.25	.08
❑ 40 Eddie Edwards	.10	.02
❑ 41 Ray Horton RC	.10	.02
❑ 42 Pete Johnson	.25	.08
❑ 43 Steve Kreider	.10	.02
❑ 44 Max Montoya	.10	.02
❑ 45 Anthony Munoz	.50	.20
❑ 46 Reggie Williams	.25	.08
❑ 47 Cleveland Browns TL	.25	.08
❑ 48 Matt Bahr	.25	.08
❑ 49 Chip Banks	.10	.02
❑ 50 Tom Cousineau	.10	.02
❑ 51 Joe DeLamielleure	.50	.20
❑ 52 Doug Dieken	.10	.02
❑ 53 Bob Golic RC	.50	.20
❑ 54 Bobby Jones	.10	.02
❑ 55 Dave Logan	.10	.02
❑ 56 Clay Matthews	.50	.20
❑ 57 Paul McDonald	.10	.02
❑ 58 Ozzie Newsome	.50	.20
❑ 59 Ozzie Newsome IR	.50	.20
❑ 60 Mike Pruitt	.25	.08
❑ 61 Denver Broncos TL	.25	.08
❑ 62 Barney Chavous RC	.10	.02
❑ 63 John Elway RC !	80.00	30.00
❑ 64 Steve Foley	.10	.02
❑ 65 Tom Jackson	.50	.20
❑ 66 Rich Karlis	.10	.02
❑ 67 Luke Prestridge	.10	.02
❑ 68 Zach Thomas WR	.10	.02
❑ 69 Rick Upchurch	.25	.08
❑ 70 Steve Watson	.25	.08
❑ 71 Sammy Winder RC	.25	.08
❑ 72 Louis Wright	.25	.08
❑ 73 Houston Oilers TL	.10	.02
❑ 74 Jesse Baker	.10	.02
❑ 75 Gregg Bingham	.10	.02
❑ 76 Robert Brazile	.25	.08
❑ 77 Steve Brown RC	.10	.02
❑ 78 Chris Dressel	.10	.02
❑ 79 Doug France	.10	.02
❑ 80 Florian Kempf	.10	.02
❑ 81 Carl Roaches	.25	.08
❑ 82 Tim Smith WR RC	.25	.08
❑ 83 Willie Tullis	.10	.02
❑ 84 Kansas City Chiefs TL	.10	.02
❑ 85 Mike Bell RC	.10	.02
❑ 86 Theotis Brown	.10	.02
❑ 87 Carlos Carson	.50	.20
❑ 88 Carlos Carson IR	.25	.08
❑ 89 Deron Cherry RC	.25	.08
❑ 90 Gary Green	.10	.02
❑ 91 Billy Jackson	.10	.02
❑ 92 Bill Kenney	.25	.08
❑ 93 Bill Kenney IR	.25	.08
❑ 94 Nick Lowery	.50	.20
❑ 95 Henry Marshall	.10	.02
❑ 96 Art Still	.10	.02
❑ 97 Los Angeles Raiders TL	.25	.08
❑ 98 Marcus Allen	5.00	2.50
❑ 99 Marcus Allen IR	2.50	1.00
❑ 100 Lyle Alzado	.25	.08
❑ 101 Lyle Alzado IR	.25	.08
❑ 102 Chris Bahr	.10	.02
❑ 103 Malcolm Barnwell RC	.10	.02
❑ 104 Cliff Branch	.50	.20
❑ 105 Todd Christensen	.50	.20
❑ 106 Todd Christensen IR	.50	.20
❑ 107 Ray Guy	.50	.20
❑ 108 Frank Hawkins	.10	.02
❑ 109 Lester Hayes	.25	.08
❑ 110 Ted Hendricks	.50	.20
❑ 111 Howie Long RC	15.00	6.00
❑ 112 Rod Martin	.25	.08
❑ 113 Vann McElroy RC	.10	.02
❑ 114 Jim Plunkett	.50	.20
❑ 115 Greg Pruitt	.25	.08
❑ 116 Dolphins TL/M.Duper	.50	.20
❑ 117 Bob Baumhower	.10	.02
❑ 118 Doug Betters RC	.10	.02
❑ 119 A.J. Duhe	.10	.02
❑ 120 Mark Duper RC	.50	.20
❑ 121 Andra Franklin	.10	.02
❑ 122 William Judson	.10	.02
❑ 123 Dan Marino RC !	80.00	30.00
❑ 124 Dan Marino IR	12.00	5.00
❑ 125 Nat Moore	.25	.08
❑ 126 Ed Newman	.10	.02
❑ 127 Reggie Roby RC	.25	.08
❑ 128 Gerald Small	.10	.02
❑ 129 Dwight Stephenson RC	3.00	1.25
❑ 130 Uwe Von Schamann	.10	.02
❑ 131 New England Pats TL	.10	.02
❑ 132 Rich Camarillo	.25	.08
❑ 133 Tony Collins	.25	.08
❑ 134 Tony Collins IR	.10	.02
❑ 135 Bob Cryder	.10	.02
❑ 136 Steve Grogan	.25	.08
❑ 137 John Hannah	.50	.20
❑ 138 Brian Holloway RC	.10	.02
❑ 139 Roland James	.10	.02
❑ 140 Stanley Morgan	.25	.08
❑ 141 Rick Sanford	.10	.02
❑ 142 Mosi Tatupu RC	.10	.02
❑ 143 Andre Tippett RC	.50	.20
❑ 144 New York Jets TL	.25	.08
❑ 145 Jerome Barkum	.10	.02
❑ 146 Mark Gastineau	.25	.08
❑ 147 Mark Gastineau IR	.25	.08
❑ 148 Bruce Harper	.10	.02
❑ 149 Johnny Lam Jones	.10	.02
❑ 150 Joe Klecko	.25	.08
❑ 151 Pat Leahy	.10	.02
❑ 152 Freeman McNeil	.25	.08
❑ 153 Lance Mehl	.10	.02
❑ 154 Marvin Powell	.25	.08
❑ 155 Darrol Ray	.10	.02
❑ 156 Pat Ryan RC	.10	.02
❑ 157 Kirk Springs	.10	.02
❑ 158 Wesley Walker	.25	.08
❑ 159 Steelers TL/F.Harris	.50	.20
❑ 160 Walter Abercrombie RC	.25	.08
❑ 161 Gary Anderson K	.50	.20
❑ 162 Terry Bradshaw	2.00	.75
❑ 163 Craig Colquitt	.10	.02
❑ 164 Bennie Cunningham	.10	.02
❑ 165 Franco Harris	.50	.20
❑ 166 Franco Harris IR	.50	.20
❑ 167 Jack Lambert	.50	.20
❑ 168 Jack Lambert IR	.50	.20
❑ 169 Frank Pollard	.10	.02
❑ 170 Donnie Shell	.25	.08
❑ 171 Mike Webster	.25	.08
❑ 172 Keith Willis RC	.10	.02
❑ 173 Rick Woods	.10	.02
❑ 174 Chargers TL/K.Winslow	.50	.20
❑ 175 Rolf Benirschke	.10	.02
❑ 176 James Brooks	.25	.08
❑ 177 Maury Buford	.10	.02
❑ 178 Wes Chandler	.25	.08
❑ 179 Dan Fouts	.60	.25
❑ 180 Dan Fouts IR	.50	.20
❑ 181 Charlie Joiner	.50	.20
❑ 182 Linden King	.10	.02
❑ 183 Chuck Muncie	.25	.08
❑ 184 Billy Ray Smith RC	.50	.20
❑ 185 Danny Walters RC	.10	.02
❑ 186 Kellen Winslow	.60	.25
❑ 187 Kellen Winslow IR	.50	.20
❑ 188 Seahawks TL/C.Warner	.50	.20
❑ 189 Steve August	.10	.02
❑ 190 Dave Brown DB	.10	.02
❑ 191 Zachary Dixon	.10	.02
❑ 192 Kenny Easley	.25	.08
❑ 193 Jacob Green	.10	.02

- ❑ 194 Norm Johnson .25 .08
- ❑ 195 Dave Krieg RC 1.50 .60
- ❑ 196 Steve Largent 1.00 .40
- ❑ 197 Steve Largent IR .50 .20
- ❑ 198 Curt Warner RC .50 .20
- ❑ 199 Curt Warner IR .50 .20
- ❑ 200 Jeff West .10 .02
- ❑ 201 Charle Young .10 .02
- ❑ 202 D.Marino/Bartkow. LL 6.00 2.50
- ❑ 203 Receiving Leaders .25 .08
- ❑ 204 Eric Dickerson/Warner LL .50 .20
- ❑ 205 Scoring Leaders .10 .02
- ❑ 206 Interception Leaders .10 .02
- ❑ 207 Punting Leaders .10 .02
- ❑ 208 Atlanta Falcons TL .25 .08
- ❑ 209 William Andrews .25 .08
- ❑ 210 William Andrews IR .25 .08
- ❑ 211 Stacey Bailey RC .10 .02
- ❑ 212 Steve Bartkowski .50 .20
- ❑ 213 Steve Bartkowski IR .25 .08
- ❑ 214 Ralph Giacomarro .10 .02
- ❑ 215 Billy Johnson .25 .08
- ❑ 216 Mike Kenn .25 .08
- ❑ 217 Mick Luckhurst .10 .02
- ❑ 218 Gerald Riggs .50 .20
- ❑ 219 R.C. Thielemann .10 .02
- ❑ 220 Jeff Van Note .25 .08
- ❑ 221 Bears TL/W.Payton .75 .30
- ❑ 222 Jim Covert RC .50 .20
- ❑ 223 Leslie Frazier .10 .02
- ❑ 224 Willie Gault RC .50 .20
- ❑ 225 Mike Hartenstine .10 .02
- ❑ 226 Noah Jackson UER .10 .02
- ❑ 227 Jim McMahon 1.25 .50
- ❑ 228 Walter Payton 4.00 2.00
- ❑ 229 Walter Payton IR 1.25 .50
- ❑ 230 Mike Richardson RC .10 .02
- ❑ 231 Terry Schmidt .10 .02
- ❑ 232 Mike Singletary 1.25 .50
- ❑ 233 Matt Suhey .25 .08
- ❑ 234 Bob Thomas .10 .02
- ❑ 235 Cowboys TL/T.Dorsett .50 .20
- ❑ 236 Bob Breunig .10 .02
- ❑ 237 Doug Cosbie .25 .08
- ❑ 238 Tony Dorsett 1.00 .40
- ❑ 239 Tony Dorsett IR .50 .20
- ❑ 240 John Dutton .10 .02
- ❑ 241 Tony Hill .25 .08
- ❑ 242 Ed Too Tall Jones .50 .20
- ❑ 243 Drew Pearson .50 .20
- ❑ 244 Rafael Septien .10 .02
- ❑ 245 Ron Springs .25 .08
- ❑ 246 Dennis Thurman .10 .02
- ❑ 247 Everson Walls .10 .02
- ❑ 248 Danny White .50 .20
- ❑ 249 Randy White .50 .20
- ❑ 250 Detroit Lions TL .25 .08
- ❑ 251 Jeff Chadwick RC .25 .08
- ❑ 252 Garry Cobb .10 .02
- ❑ 253 Doug English .25 .08
- ❑ 254 William Gay .10 .02
- ❑ 255 Eric Hipple .25 .08
- ❑ 256 James Jones FB RC .25 .08
- ❑ 257 Bruce McNorton .10 .02
- ❑ 258 Eddie Murray .25 .08
- ❑ 259 Ulysses Norris .10 .02
- ❑ 260 Billy Sims .50 .20
- ❑ 261 Billy Sims IR .25 .08
- ❑ 262 Leonard Thompson .10 .02
- ❑ 263 Packers TL/J.Lofton .50 .20
- ❑ 264 John Anderson .10 .02
- ❑ 265 Paul Coffman .25 .08
- ❑ 266 Lynn Dickey .25 .08
- ❑ 267 Gerry Ellis .10 .02
- ❑ 268 John Jefferson .50 .20
- ❑ 269 John Jefferson IR .50 .20
- ❑ 270 Ezra Johnson .10 .02
- ❑ 271 Tim Lewis RC .10 .02
- ❑ 272 James Lofton .50 .20
- ❑ 273 James Lofton IR .50 .20
- ❑ 274 Larry McCarren .10 .02
- ❑ 275 Jan Stenerud .25 .08
- ❑ 276 Rams TL/E.Dickerson .50 .20
- ❑ 277 Mike Barber .10 .02
- ❑ 278 Jim Collins .10 .02
- ❑ 279 Nolan Cromwell .25 .08
- ❑ 280 Eric Dickerson RC 10.00 4.00
- ❑ 281 Eric Dickerson IR 2.00 .75
- ❑ 282 George Farmer South. .10 .02
- ❑ 283 Vince Ferragamo .25 .08
- ❑ 284 Kent Hill .10 .02
- ❑ 285 John Misko .10 .02
- ❑ 286 Jackie Slater RC 4.00 1.50
- ❑ 287 Jack Youngblood .25 .08
- ❑ 288 Minnesota Vikings TL .10 .02
- ❑ 289 Ted Brown .25 .08
- ❑ 290 Greg Coleman .10 .02
- ❑ 291 Steve Dils .10 .02
- ❑ 292 Tony Galbreath .10 .02
- ❑ 293 Tommy Kramer .25 .08
- ❑ 294 Doug Martin .10 .02
- ❑ 295 Darrin Nelson RC .25 .08
- ❑ 296 Benny Ricardo .10 .02
- ❑ 297 John Swain .10 .02
- ❑ 298 John Turner .10 .02
- ❑ 299 New Orleans Saints TL .25 .08
- ❑ 300 Morten Andersen RC 1.50 .60
- ❑ 301 Russell Erxleben .10 .02
- ❑ 302 Jeff Groth .10 .02
- ❑ 303 Rickey Jackson RC .50 .20
- ❑ 304 Johnnie Poe RC .10 .02
- ❑ 305 George Rogers .25 .08
- ❑ 306 Richard Todd .25 .08
- ❑ 307 Jim Wilks RC .10 .02
- ❑ 308 Dave Wilson RC .10 .02
- ❑ 309 Wayne Wilson .10 .02
- ❑ 310 New York Giants TL .10 .02
- ❑ 311 Leon Bright .10 .02
- ❑ 312 Scott Brunner .10 .02
- ❑ 313 Rob Carpenter .10 .02
- ❑ 314 Harry Carson .25 .08
- ❑ 315 Earnest Gray .10 .02
- ❑ 316 Ali Haji-Sheikh RC .10 .02
- ❑ 317 Mark Haynes .25 .08
- ❑ 318 Dave Jennings .10 .02
- ❑ 319 Brian Kelley .10 .02
- ❑ 320 Phil Simms .75 .30
- ❑ 321 Lawrence Taylor 3.00 1.50
- ❑ 322 Lawrence Taylor IR 1.50 .60
- ❑ 323 Brad Van Pelt .10 .02
- ❑ 324 Butch Woolfolk .10 .02
- ❑ 325 Eagles TL/M.Quick .25 .08
- ❑ 326 Harold Carmichael .25 .08
- ❑ 327 Herman Edwards .10 .02
- ❑ 328 Michael Haddix RC .10 .02
- ❑ 329 Dennis Harrison .10 .02
- ❑ 330 Ron Jaworski .25 .08
- ❑ 331 Wilbert Montgomery .25 .08
- ❑ 332 Hubie Oliver .10 .02
- ❑ 333 Mike Quick RC .50 .20
- ❑ 334 Jerry Robinson .10 .02
- ❑ 335 Max Runager .10 .02
- ❑ 336 Michael Williams .10 .02
- ❑ 337 Cardinals TL/O.Anderson .25 .08
- ❑ 338 Ottis Anderson .50 .20
- ❑ 339 Al(Bubba) Baker .25 .08
- ❑ 340 Carl Birdsong .10 .02
- ❑ 341 David Galloway .10 .02
- ❑ 342 Roy Green .25 .08
- ❑ 343 Roy Green IR .25 .08
- ❑ 344 Curtis Greer RC .10 .02
- ❑ 345 Neil Lomax .25 .08
- ❑ 346 Doug Marsh .10 .02
- ❑ 347 Stump Mitchell .25 .08
- ❑ 348 Lionel Washington RC .25 .08
- ❑ 349 49ers TL/D.Clark .25 .08
- ❑ 350 Dwaine Board .10 .02
- ❑ 351 Dwight Clark .50 .20
- ❑ 352 Dwight Clark IR .25 .08
- ❑ 353 Roger Craig RC ! 3.00 1.25
- ❑ 354 Fred Dean .25 .08
- ❑ 355 Fred Dean IR w/Marino .50 .20
- ❑ 356 Dwight Hicks .25 .08
- ❑ 357 Ronnie Lott 1.50 .60
- ❑ 358 Joe Montana 10.00 4.00
- ❑ 359 Joe Montana IR 3.00 1.50
- ❑ 360 Freddie Solomon .10 .02
- ❑ 361 Wendell Tyler .10 .02
- ❑ 362 Ray Wersching .10 .02
- ❑ 363 Eric Wright RC .25 .08
- ❑ 364 Tampa Bay Bucs TL .10 .02
- ❑ 365 Gerald Carter .10 .02
- ❑ 366 Hugh Green .25 .08
- ❑ 367 Kevin House .25 .08
- ❑ 368 Michael Morton RC .10 .02
- ❑ 369 James Owens .10 .02
- ❑ 370 Booker Reese .10 .02
- ❑ 371 Lee Roy Selmon .50 .20
- ❑ 372 Jack Thompson .25 .08
- ❑ 373 James Wilder .25 .08
- ❑ 374 Steve Wilson .10 .02
- ❑ 375 Redskins TL/J.Riggins .50 .20
- ❑ 376 Jeff Bostic .10 .02
- ❑ 377 Charlie Brown .50 .20
- ❑ 378 Charlie Brown IR .25 .08
- ❑ 379 Dave Butz .25 .08
- ❑ 380 Darrell Green RC 10.00 5.00
- ❑ 381 Russ Grimm RC 1.00 .40
- ❑ 382 Joe Jacoby .25 .08
- ❑ 383 Dexter Manley .25 .08
- ❑ 384 Art Monk 1.00 .40
- ❑ 385 Mark Moseley .25 .08
- ❑ 386 Mark Murphy .10 .02
- ❑ 387 Mike Nelms .10 .02
- ❑ 388 John Riggins .50 .20
- ❑ 389 John Riggins IR .50 .20
- ❑ 390 Joe Theismann .50 .20
- ❑ 391 Joe Theismann IR .50 .20
- ❑ 392 Don Warren .25 .08
- ❑ 393 Joe Washington .25 .08
- ❑ 394 Checklist 1-132 .30 .10
- ❑ 395 Checklist 133-264 .30 .10
- ❑ 396 Checklist 265-396 .30 .10

1984 Topps USFL

- ❑ COMP.FACT.SET (132) 300.00 150.00
- ❑ COMPLETE SET (132) 300.00 150.00
- ❑ 1 Luther Bradley 2.00 .75
- ❑ 2 Frank Corral 2.00 .75
- ❑ 3 Trumaine Johnson 2.00 .75
- ❑ 4 Greg Landry 2.50 1.25
- ❑ 5 Kit Lathrop 2.00 .75
- ❑ 6 Kevin Long 2.00 .75
- ❑ 7 Tim Spencer 2.00 .75
- ❑ 8 Stan White 2.00 .75
- ❑ 9 Buddy Aydelette 2.00 .75
- ❑ 10 Tom Banks 2.00 .75
- ❑ 11 Fred Bohannon 2.00 .75
- ❑ 12 Joe Cribbs 4.00 2.00
- ❑ 13 Joey Jones 2.00 .75
- ❑ 14 Scott Norwood XRC 2.50 1.25
- ❑ 15 Jim Smith 2.50 1.25
- ❑ 16 Cliff Stoudt 4.00 2.00
- ❑ 17 Vince Evans 4.00 2.00
- ❑ 18 Vagas Ferguson 2.00 .75
- ❑ 19 John Gillen 2.00 .75
- ❑ 20 Kris Haines 2.00 .75
- ❑ 21 Glenn Hyde 2.00 .75
- ❑ 22 Mark Keel 2.00 .75
- ❑ 23 Gary Lewis XRC 2.00 .75
- ❑ 24 Doug Plank 2.00 .75
- ❑ 25 Neil Balholm 2.00 .75
- ❑ 26 David Dumars 2.00 .75
- ❑ 27 David Martin XRC 2.00 .75
- ❑ 28 Craig Penrose 2.00 .75
- ❑ 29 Dave Stalls 2.00 .75
- ❑ 30 Harry Sydney XRC 2.00 .75
- ❑ 31 Vincent White 2.00 .75
- ❑ 32 George Yarno 2.00 .75
- ❑ 33 Kiki DeAyala 2.00 .75
- ❑ 34 Sam Harrell 2.00 .75
- ❑ 35 Mike Hawkins 2.00 .75
- ❑ 36 Jim Kelly XRC 80.00 40.00

Card		
❑ 37 Mark Rush	2.00	.75
❑ 38 Ricky Sanders XRC	6.00	3.00
❑ 39 Paul Bergmann	2.00	.75
❑ 40 Tom Dinkel	2.00	.75
❑ 41 Wyatt Henderson	2.00	.75
❑ 42 Vaughan Johnson XRC	2.50	1.25
❑ 43 Willie McClendon Geor.	2.00	.75
❑ 44 Matt Robinson	2.00	.75
❑ 45 George Achica	2.00	.75
❑ 46 Mark Adickes	2.00	.75
❑ 47 Howard Carson	2.00	.75
❑ 48 Kevin Nelson	2.00	.75
❑ 49 Jeff Partridge	2.00	.75
❑ 50 Jo Jo Townsell	2.50	1.25
❑ 51 Eddie Weaver	2.00	.75
❑ 52 Steve Young XRC	120.00	60.00
❑ 53 Derrick Crawford	2.00	.75
❑ 54 Walter Lewis	2.00	.75
❑ 55 Phil McKinnely	2.00	.75
❑ 56 Vic Minore	2.00	.75
❑ 57 Gary Shirk	2.00	.75
❑ 58 Reggie White XRC	60.00	30.00
❑ 59 Anthony Carter XRC	12.00	5.00
❑ 60 John Corker	2.00	.75
❑ 61 David Greenwood	2.00	.75
❑ 62 Bobby Hebert XRC	4.00	2.00
❑ 63 Derek Holloway	2.00	.75
❑ 64 Ken Lacy	2.00	.75
❑ 65 Tyrone McGriff	2.00	.75
❑ 66 Ray Pinney	2.00	.75
❑ 67 Gary Barbaro	2.00	.75
❑ 68 Sam Bowers	2.00	.75
❑ 69 Clarence Collins	2.00	.75
❑ 70 Willie Harper	2.00	.75
❑ 71 Jim LeClair	2.00	.75
❑ 72 Bobby Leopold XRC	2.00	.75
❑ 73 Brian Sipe	4.00	2.00
❑ 74 Herschel Walker XRC	25.00	12.50
❑ 75 Junior Ah You XRC	2.00	.75
❑ 76 Marcus Dupree XRC	6.00	2.50
❑ 77 Marcus Marek	2.00	.75
❑ 78 Tim Mazzetti	2.00	.75
❑ 79 Mike Robinson XRC	2.00	.75
❑ 80 Dan Ross	4.00	2.00
❑ 81 Mark Schellen	2.00	.75
❑ 82 Johnnie Walton	2.00	.75
❑ 83 Gordon Banks	2.00	.75
❑ 84 Fred Besana	2.00	.75
❑ 85 Dave Browning	2.00	.75
❑ 86 Eric Jordan	2.00	.75
❑ 87 Frank Manumaleuga	2.00	.75
❑ 88 Gary Plummer XRC	4.00	2.00
❑ 89 Stan Talley	2.00	.75
❑ 90 Arthur Whittington	2.00	.75
❑ 91 Terry Beeson	2.00	.75
❑ 92 Mel Gray	4.00	2.00
❑ 93 Mike Katolin	2.00	.75
❑ 94 Dewey McClain	2.00	.75
❑ 95 Sidney Thornton	2.00	.75
❑ 96 Doug Williams	4.00	2.00
❑ 97 Kelvin Bryant XRC	4.00	2.00
❑ 98 John Bunting	2.00	.75
❑ 99 Irv Eatman XRC	2.50	1.25
❑ 100 Scott Fitzkee	2.00	.75
❑ 101 Chuck Fusina	2.00	.75
❑ 102 Sean Landeta XRC	2.50	1.25
❑ 103 David Trout	2.00	.75
❑ 104 Scott Woerner	2.00	.75
❑ 105 Glenn Carano	2.00	.75
❑ 106 Ron Crosby	2.00	.75
❑ 107 Jerry Holmes	2.00	.75
❑ 108 Bruce Huther	2.00	.75
❑ 109 Mike Rozier XRC	4.00	2.00
❑ 110 Larry Swider	2.00	.75
❑ 111 Danny Buggs	2.00	.75
❑ 112 Putt Choate	2.00	.75
❑ 113 Rich Garza	2.00	.75
❑ 114 Joey Hackett	2.00	.75
❑ 115 Rick Neuheisel XRC	4.00	2.00
❑ 116 Mike St. Clair	2.00	.75
❑ 117 Gary Anderson XRC RB	4.00	2.00
❑ 118 Zenon Andrusyshyn	2.00	.75
❑ 119 Doug Beaudoin	2.00	.75
❑ 120 Mike Butler	2.00	.75
❑ 121 Willie Gillespie	2.00	.75
❑ 122 Fred Nordgren	2.00	.75
❑ 123 John Reaves	2.00	.75
❑ 124 Eric Truvillion	2.00	.75
❑ 125 Reggie Collier	2.00	.75
❑ 126 Mike Guess	2.00	.75
❑ 127 Mike Hohensee	2.00	.75
❑ 128 Craig James XRC	8.00	3.00
❑ 129 Eric Robinson	2.00	.75
❑ 130 Billy Taylor	2.00	.75
❑ 131 Joey Walters	2.00	.75
❑ 132 Checklist 1-132	2.50	1.25

1985 Topps

Card		
❑ COMPLETE SET (396)	60.00	35.00
❑ COMP.FACT.SET (396)	75.00	40.00
❑ 1 Mark Clayton RB	.50	.20
❑ 2 Eric Dickerson RB	.50	.20
❑ 3 Charlie Joiner RB	.50	.20
❑ 4 Dan Marino RB	6.00	3.00
❑ 5 Art Monk RB	.50	.20
❑ 6 Walter Payton RB	1.00	.40
❑ 7 NFC Champs/Suhey	.25	.08
❑ 8 AFC Championship	.25	.08
❑ 9 Super Bowl XIX	.25	.08
❑ 10 Atlanta Falcons TL	.10	.02
❑ 11 William Andrews	.25	.08
❑ 12 Stacey Bailey	.10	.02
❑ 13 Steve Bartkowski	.50	.20
❑ 14 Rick Bryan RC	.10	.02
❑ 15 Alfred Jackson	.10	.02
❑ 16 Kenny Johnson	.10	.02
❑ 17 Mike Kenn	.10	.02
❑ 18 Mike Pitts RC	.10	.02
❑ 19 Gerald Riggs	.25	.08
❑ 20 Sylvester Stamps	.10	.02
❑ 21 R.C. Thielemann	.10	.02
❑ 22 Bears TL/W.Payton	.75	.30
❑ 23 Todd Bell RC	.10	.02
❑ 24 Richard Dent RC	4.00	1.50
❑ 25 Gary Fencik	.25	.08
❑ 26 Dave Finzer	.10	.02
❑ 27 Leslie Frazier	.10	.02
❑ 28 Steve Fuller	.25	.08
❑ 29 Willie Gault	.50	.20
❑ 30 Dan Hampton	.50	.20
❑ 31 Jim McMahon	.75	.30
❑ 32 Steve McMichael RC	.50	.20
❑ 33 Walter Payton	4.00	1.50
❑ 34 Mike Singletary	.75	.30
❑ 35 Matt Suhey	.10	.02
❑ 36 Bob Thomas	.10	.02
❑ 37 Cowboys TL/Dorsett	.50	.20
❑ 38 Bill Bates RC	1.00	.40
❑ 39 Doug Cosbie	.25	.08
❑ 40 Tony Dorsett	.75	.30
❑ 41 Michael Downs	.10	.02
❑ 42 Mike Hegman RC UER	.10	.02
❑ 43 Tony Hill	.25	.08
❑ 44 Gary Hogeboom RC	.10	.02
❑ 45 Jim Jeffcoat RC	.50	.20
❑ 46 Ed Too Tall Jones	.50	.20
❑ 47 Mike Renfro	.10	.02
❑ 48 Rafael Septien	.10	.02
❑ 49 Dennis Thurman	.10	.02
❑ 50 Everson Walls	.25	.08
❑ 51 Danny White	.50	.20
❑ 52 Randy White	.50	.20
❑ 53 Detroit Lions TL	.10	.02
❑ 54 Jeff Chadwick	.10	.02
❑ 55 Michael Cofer RC	.10	.02
❑ 56 Gary Danielson	.10	.02
❑ 57 Keith Dorney	.10	.02
❑ 58 Doug English	.25	.08
❑ 59 William Gay	.10	.02
❑ 60 Ken Jenkins	.10	.02
❑ 61 James Jones FB	.25	.08
❑ 62 Eddie Murray	.25	.08
❑ 63 Billy Sims	.50	.20
❑ 64 Leonard Thompson	.10	.02
❑ 65 Bobby Watkins	.10	.02
❑ 66 Green Bay Packers TL	.25	.08
❑ 67 Paul Coffman	.10	.02
❑ 68 Lynn Dickey	.25	.08
❑ 69 Mike Douglass	.10	.02
❑ 70 Tom Flynn RC	.10	.02
❑ 71 Eddie Lee Ivery	.10	.02
❑ 72 Ezra Johnson	.10	.02
❑ 73 Mark Lee	.10	.02
❑ 74 Tim Lewis	.10	.02
❑ 75 James Lofton	.50	.20
❑ 76 Bucky Scribner	.10	.02
❑ 77 Rams TL/Dickerson	.50	.20
❑ 78 Nolan Cromwell	.25	.08
❑ 79 Eric Dickerson	1.25	.50
❑ 80 Henry Ellard RC	2.50	1.00
❑ 81 Kent Hill	.10	.02
❑ 82 LeRoy Irvin	.25	.08
❑ 83 Jeff Kemp RC	.25	.08
❑ 84 Mike Lansford	.10	.02
❑ 85 Barry Redden	.10	.02
❑ 86 Jackie Slater	.50	.20
❑ 87 Doug Smith C RC	.25	.08
❑ 88 Jack Youngblood	.25	.08
❑ 89 Minnesota Vikings TL	.10	.02
❑ 90 Alfred Anderson RC	.10	.02
❑ 91 Ted Brown	.25	.08
❑ 92 Greg Coleman	.10	.02
❑ 93 Tommy Hannon	.10	.02
❑ 94 Tommy Kramer	.25	.08
❑ 95 Leo Lewis RC	.25	.08
❑ 96 Doug Martin	.10	.02
❑ 97 Darrin Nelson	.25	.08
❑ 98 Jan Stenerud	.25	.08
❑ 99 Sammie White	.25	.08
❑ 100 New Orleans Saints TL	.10	.02
❑ 101 Morten Andersen	.50	.20
❑ 102 Hoby Brenner RC	.25	.08
❑ 103 Bruce Clark	.10	.02
❑ 104 Hokie Gajan	.10	.02
❑ 105 Brian Hansen RC	.10	.02
❑ 106 Rickey Jackson	.50	.20
❑ 107 George Rogers	.25	.08
❑ 108 Dave Wilson	.10	.02
❑ 109 Tyrone Young	.10	.02
❑ 110 New York Giants TL	.10	.02
❑ 111 Carl Banks RC	.50	.20
❑ 112 Jim Burt RC	.50	.20
❑ 113 Rob Carpenter	.10	.02
❑ 114 Harry Carson	.25	.08
❑ 115 Earnest Gray	.10	.02
❑ 116 Ali Haji-Sheikh	.10	.02
❑ 117 Mark Haynes	.25	.08
❑ 118 Bobby Johnson	.10	.02
❑ 119 Lionel Manuel RC	.25	.08
❑ 120 Joe Morris RC	.50	.20
❑ 121 Zeke Mowatt RC	.25	.08
❑ 122 Jeff Rutledge RC	.10	.02
❑ 123 Phil Simms	.50	.20
❑ 124 Lawrence Taylor	1.50	.60
❑ 125 Philadelphia Eagles TL	.10	.02
❑ 126 Greg Brown	.10	.02
❑ 127 Ray Ellis	.10	.02
❑ 128 Dennis Harrison	.10	.02
❑ 129 Wes Hopkins RC	.25	.08
❑ 130 Mike Horan RC	.10	.02
❑ 131 Kenny Jackson RC	.10	.02
❑ 132 Ron Jaworski	.25	.08
❑ 133 Paul McFadden	.10	.02
❑ 134 Wilbert Montgomery	.25	.08
❑ 135 Mike Quick	.50	.20
❑ 136 John Spagnola	.10	.02
❑ 137 St.Louis Cardinals TL	.10	.02
❑ 138 Ottis Anderson	.50	.20
❑ 139 Al(Bubba) Baker	.25	.08
❑ 140 Roy Green	.25	.08
❑ 141 Curtis Greer	.10	.02
❑ 142 E.J.Junior	.10	.02
❑ 143 Neil Lomax	.25	.08

❑	144 Stump Mitchell	.25	.08
❑	145 Neil O'Donoghue	.10	.02
❑	146 Pat Tilley	.10	.02
❑	147 Lionel Washington	.10	.02
❑	148 49ers TL/J.Montana	1.25	.50
❑	149 Dwaine Board	.10	.02
❑	150 Dwight Clark	.50	.20
❑	151 Roger Craig	1.00	.40
❑	152 Randy Cross	.25	.08
❑	153 Fred Dean	.25	.08
❑	154 Keith Fahnhorst RC	.10	.02
❑	155 Dwight Hicks	.10	.02
❑	156 Ronnie Lott	.50	.20
❑	157 Joe Montana	10.00	4.00
❑	158 Renaldo Nehemiah	.25	.08
❑	159 Fred Quillan	.10	.02
❑	160 Jack Reynolds	.10	.02
❑	161 Freddie Solomon	.10	.02
❑	162 Keena Turner RC	.10	.02
❑	163 Wendell Tyler	.10	.02
❑	164 Ray Wersching	.10	.02
❑	165 Carlton Williamson	.10	.02
❑	166 Tampa Bay Bucs TL	.25	.08
❑	167 Gerald Carter	.10	.02
❑	168 Mark Cotney	.10	.02
❑	169 Steve DeBerg	.50	.20
❑	170 Sean Farrell RC	.10	.02
❑	171 Hugh Green	.25	.08
❑	172 Kevin House	.25	.08
❑	173 David Logan	.10	.02
❑	174 Michael Morton	.10	.02
❑	175 Lee Roy Selmon	.50	.20
❑	176 James Wilder	.10	.02
❑	177 Redskins TL/J.Riggins	.50	.20
❑	178 Charlie Brown	.10	.02
❑	179 Monte Coleman RC	.25	.08
❑	180 Vernon Dean	.10	.02
❑	181 Darrell Green	.50	.20
❑	182 Russ Grimm	.25	.08
❑	183 Joe Jacoby	.25	.08
❑	184 Dexter Manley	.25	.08
❑	185 Art Monk	.50	.20
❑	186 Mark Moseley	.25	.08
❑	187 Calvin Muhammad	.10	.02
❑	188 Mike Nelms	.10	.02
❑	189 John Riggins	.50	.20
❑	190 Joe Theismann	.50	.20
❑	191 Joe Washington	.25	.08
❑	192 D.Marino/Montana LL	10.00	4.00
❑	193 Art Monk/O.Newsome LL	.25	.08
❑	194 E.Dickerson/Jackson LL	.50	.20
❑	195 Scoring Leaders	.10	.02
❑	196 Interception Leaders	.10	.02
❑	197 Punting Leaders	.10	.02
❑	198 Bills TL/Greg Bell	.10	.02
❑	199 Greg Bell RC	.25	.08
❑	200 Preston Dennard	.10	.02
❑	201 Joe Ferguson	.25	.08
❑	202 Byron Franklin	.10	.02
❑	203 Steve Freeman	.10	.02
❑	204 Jim Haslett	.25	.08
❑	205 Charles Romes	.10	.02
❑	206 Fred Smerlas	.10	.02
❑	207 Darryl Talley RC	.50	.20
❑	208 Van Williams	.10	.02
❑	209 Cincinnati Bengals TL	.25	.08
❑	210 Ken Anderson	.50	.20
❑	211 Jim Breech	.10	.02
❑	212 Louis Breeden	.10	.02
❑	213 James Brooks	.25	.08
❑	214 Ross Browner	.25	.08
❑	215 Eddie Edwards	.10	.02
❑	216 M.L. Harris	.10	.02
❑	217 Bobby Kemp	.10	.02
❑	218 Larry Kinnebrew RC	.10	.02
❑	219 Anthony Munoz	.50	.20
❑	220 Reggie Williams	.25	.08
❑	221 Cleveland Browns TL	.10	.02
❑	222 Matt Bahr	.25	.08
❑	223 Chip Banks	.10	.02
❑	224 Reggie Camp	.10	.02
❑	225 Tom Cousineau	.10	.02
❑	226 Joe DeLamielleure	.50	.20
❑	227 Ricky Feacher	.10	.02
❑	228 Boyce Green RC	.10	.02
❑	229 Al Gross	.10	.02
❑	230 Clay Matthews	.50	.20
❑	231 Paul McDonald	.10	.02
❑	232 Ozzie Newsome	.50	.20
❑	233 Mike Pruitt	.25	.08
❑	234 Don Rogers DB	.10	.02
❑	235 Broncos TL/J.Elway	2.50	1.00
❑	236 Rubin Carter	.10	.02
❑	237 Barney Chavous	.10	.02
❑	238 John Elway	12.00	5.00
❑	239 Steve Foley	.10	.02
❑	240 Mike Harden RC	.10	.02
❑	241 Tom Jackson	.50	.20
❑	242 Butch Johnson	.10	.02
❑	243 Rulon Jones	.10	.02
❑	244 Rich Karlis	.10	.02
❑	245 Steve Watson	.25	.08
❑	246 Gerald Willhite	.10	.02
❑	247 Sammy Winder	.25	.08
❑	248 Houston Oilers TL	.10	.02
❑	249 Jesse Baker	.10	.02
❑	250 Carter Hartwig	.10	.02
❑	251 Warren Moon RC	15.00	6.00
❑	252 Larry Moriarty RC	.10	.02
❑	253 Mike Munchak RC	1.50	.60
❑	254 Carl Roaches	.10	.02
❑	255 Tim Smith	.25	.08
❑	256 Willie Tullis	.10	.02
❑	257 Jamie Williams RC	.10	.02
❑	258 Indianapolis Colts TL	.10	.02
❑	259 Raymond Butler	.10	.02
❑	260 Johnie Cooks	.10	.02
❑	261 Eugene Daniel RC	.10	.02
❑	262 Curtis Dickey	.25	.08
❑	263 Chris Hinton	.25	.08
❑	264 Vernon Maxwell	.10	.02
❑	265 Randy McMillan	.10	.02
❑	266 Art Schlichter RC	.50	.20
❑	267 Rohn Stark	.25	.08
❑	268 Leo Wisniewski	.10	.02
❑	269 Kansas City Chiefs TL	.10	.02
❑	270 Jim Arnold	.10	.02
❑	271 Mike Bell	.10	.02
❑	272 Todd Blackledge RC	.25	.08
❑	273 Carlos Carson	.25	.08
❑	274 Deron Cherry	.25	.08
❑	275 Herman Heard RC	.10	.02
❑	276 Bill Kenney	.25	.08
❑	277 Nick Lowery	.50	.20
❑	278 Bill Maas RC	.10	.02
❑	279 Henry Marshall	.10	.02
❑	280 Art Still	.10	.02
❑	281 Raiders TL/M.Allen	.50	.20
❑	282 Marcus Allen	2.50	1.00
❑	283 Lyle Alzado	.25	.08
❑	284 Chris Bahr	.10	.02
❑	285 Malcolm Barnwell	.10	.02
❑	286 Cliff Branch	.50	.20
❑	287 Todd Christensen	.50	.20
❑	288 Ray Guy	.50	.20
❑	289 Lester Hayes	.25	.08
❑	290 Mike Haynes	.25	.08
❑	291 Henry Lawrence	.10	.02
❑	292 Howie Long	2.00	.75
❑	293 Rod Martin	.25	.08
❑	294 Vann McElroy	.10	.02
❑	295 Matt Millen	.25	.08
❑	296 Bill Pickel RC	.10	.02
❑	297 Jim Plunkett	.50	.20
❑	298 Dokie Williams RC	.10	.02
❑	299 Marc Wilson	.25	.08
❑	300 Dolphins TL/Duper	.25	.08
❑	301 Bob Baumhower	.10	.02
❑	302 Doug Betters	.10	.02
❑	303 Glenn Blackwood	.25	.08
❑	304 Lyle Blackwood	.25	.08
❑	305 Kim Bokamper	.10	.02
❑	306 Charles Bowser RC	.10	.02
❑	307 Jimmy Cefalo	.10	.02
❑	308 Mark Clayton RC	.75	.30
❑	309 A.J. Duhe	.10	.02
❑	310 Mark Duper	.50	.20
❑	311 Andra Franklin	.10	.02
❑	312 Bruce Hardy	.10	.02
❑	313 Pete Johnson	.25	.08
❑	314 Dan Marino	12.00	5.00
❑	315 Tony Nathan	.25	.08
❑	316 Ed Newman	.10	.02
❑	317 Reggie Roby	.50	.20
❑	318 Dwight Stephenson	1.00	.40
❑	319 Uwe Von Schamann	.10	.02
❑	320 New England Pats TL	.10	.02
❑	321 Raymond Clayborn	.25	.08
❑	322 Tony Collins	.25	.08
❑	323 Tony Eason RC	.50	.20
❑	324 Tony Franklin	.10	.02
❑	325 Irving Fryar RC	5.00	2.00
❑	326 John Hannah	.50	.20
❑	327 Brian Holloway	.10	.02
❑	328 Craig James RC	.75	.30
❑	329 Stanley Morgan	.25	.08
❑	330 Steve Nelson	.10	.02
❑	331 Derrick Ramsey	.10	.02
❑	332 Stephen Starring RC	.25	.08
❑	333 Mosi Tatupu	.10	.02
❑	334 Andre Tippett	.50	.20
❑	335 New York Jets TL	.25	.08
❑	336 Russell Carter RC	.10	.02
❑	337 Mark Gastineau	.25	.08
❑	338 Bruce Harper	.10	.02
❑	339 Bobby Humphery RC	.10	.02
❑	340 Johnny Lam Jones	.10	.02
❑	341 Joe Klecko	.25	.08
❑	342 Pat Leahy	.10	.02
❑	343 Marty Lyons	.25	.08
❑	344 Freeman McNeil	.25	.08
❑	345 Lance Mehl	.10	.02
❑	346 Ken O'Brien RC	.50	.20
❑	347 Marvin Powell	.10	.02
❑	348 Pat Ryan	.10	.02
❑	349 Mickey Shuler RC	.10	.02
❑	350 Wesley Walker	.25	.08
❑	351 Pittsburgh Steelers TL	.25	.08
❑	352 Walter Abercrombie	.10	.02
❑	353 Gary Anderson K	.25	.08
❑	354 Robin Cole	.10	.02
❑	355 Bennie Cunningham	.10	.02
❑	356 Rich Erenberg	.10	.02
❑	357 Jack Lambert	.50	.20
❑	358 Louis Lipps RC	.50	.20
❑	359 Mark Malone	.25	.08
❑	360 Mike Merriweather RC	.10	.02
❑	361 Frank Pollard	.10	.02
❑	362 Donnie Shell	.25	.08
❑	363 John Stallworth	.50	.20
❑	364 Sam Washington	.10	.02
❑	365 Mike Webster	.25	.08
❑	366 Dwayne Woodruff	.10	.02
❑	367 San Diego Chargers TL	.10	.02
❑	368 Rolf Benirschke	.10	.02
❑	369 Gill Byrd RC	.50	.20
❑	370 Wes Chandler	.25	.08
❑	371 Bobby Duckworth	.10	.02
❑	372 Dan Fouts	.50	.20
❑	373 Mike Green	.10	.02
❑	374 Pete Holohan RC	.10	.02
❑	375 Earnest Jackson RC	.25	.08
❑	376 Lionel James RC	.25	.08
❑	377 Charlie Joiner	.50	.20
❑	378 Billy Ray Smith	.25	.08
❑	379 Kellen Winslow	.50	.20
❑	380 Seattle Seahawks TL	.25	.08
❑	381 Dave Brown DB	.10	.02
❑	382 Jeff Bryant	.10	.02
❑	383 Dan Doornink	.10	.02
❑	384 Kenny Easley	.25	.08
❑	385 Jacob Green	.25	.08
❑	386 David Hughes	.10	.02
❑	387 Norm Johnson	.10	.02
❑	388 Dave Krieg	.50	.20
❑	389 Steve Largent	1.00	.40
❑	390 Joe Nash RC	.10	.02
❑	391 Daryl Turner RC	.10	.02
❑	392 Curt Warner	.50	.20
❑	393 Fredd Young RC	.25	.08
❑	394 Checklist 1-132	.25	.08
❑	395 Checklist 133-264	.25	.08
❑	396 Checklist 265-396	.25	.08

1985 Topps USFL

❑	COMP.FACT.SET (132)	120.00	60.00
❑	COMPLETE SET (132)	120.00	60.00
❑	1 Case DeBruijn	.50	.20
❑	2 Mike Katolin	.50	.20
❑	3 Bruce Laird	.50	.20
❑	4 Kit Lathrop	.50	.20

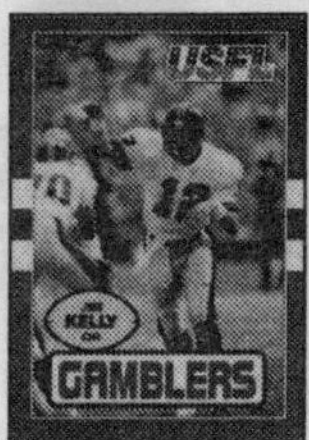

- ❑ 5 Kevin Long .50 .20
- ❑ 6 Karl Lorch .50 .20
- ❑ 7 Dave Tipton DT .50 .20
- ❑ 8 Doug Williams 2.00 .75
- ❑ 9 Luis Zendejas XRC .50 .20
- ❑ 10 Kelvin Bryant 1.00 .40
- ❑ 11 Willie Collier .50 .20
- ❑ 12 Irv Eatman .50 .20
- ❑ 13 Scott Fitzkee .50 .20
- ❑ 14 William Fuller XRC 3.00 1.25
- ❑ 15 Chuck Fusina .50 .20
- ❑ 16 Pete Kugler .50 .20
- ❑ 17 Garcia Lane .50 .20
- ❑ 18 Mike Lush .50 .20
- ❑ 19 Sam Mills XRC 5.00 2.00
- ❑ 20 Buddy Aydelette .50 .20
- ❑ 21 Joe Cribbs 2.00 .75
- ❑ 22 David Dumars .50 .20
- ❑ 23 Robin Earl .50 .20
- ❑ 24 Joey Jones .50 .20
- ❑ 25 Leon Perry RB .50 .20
- ❑ 26 Dave Pureifory .50 .20
- ❑ 27 Bill Roe .50 .20
- ❑ 28 Doug Smith DT XRC 2.00 .75
- ❑ 29 Cliff Stoudt 1.00 .40
- ❑ 30 Jeff Delaney .50 .20
- ❑ 31 Vince Evans 1.00 .40
- ❑ 32 Leonard Harris XRC .50 .20
- ❑ 33 Bill Johnson RB .50 .20
- ❑ 34 Marc Lewis XRC .50 .20
- ❑ 35 David Martin .50 .20
- ❑ 36 Bruce Thornton .50 .20
- ❑ 37 Craig Walls .50 .20
- ❑ 38 Vincent White .50 .20
- ❑ 39 Luther Bradley .50 .20
- ❑ 40 Pete Catan .50 .20
- ❑ 41 Kiki DeAyala .50 .20
- ❑ 42 Toni Fritsch .50 .20
- ❑ 43 Sam Harrell .50 .20
- ❑ 44 Richard Johnson WR XRC 1.00 .40
- ❑ 45 Jim Kelly 20.00 10.00
- ❑ 46 Gerald McNeil XRC .50 .20
- ❑ 47 Clarence Verdin XRC 2.00 .75
- ❑ 48 Dale Walters .50 .20
- ❑ 49 Gary Clark XRC 6.00 2.50
- ❑ 50 Tom Dinkel .50 .20
- ❑ 51 Mike Edwards LB .50 .20
- ❑ 52 Brian Franco .50 .20
- ❑ 53 Bob Gruber .50 .20
- ❑ 54 Robbie Mahfouz .50 .20
- ❑ 55 Mike Rozier 2.00 .75
- ❑ 56 Brian Sipe 1.00 .40
- ❑ 57 J.T. Turner .50 .20
- ❑ 58 Howard Carson .50 .20
- ❑ 59 Wymon Henderson XRC .50 .20
- ❑ 60 Kevin Nelson .50 .20
- ❑ 61 Jeff Partridge .50 .20
- ❑ 62 Ben Rudolph .50 .20
- ❑ 63 Jo Jo Townsell 1.00 .40
- ❑ 64 Eddie Weaver .50 .20
- ❑ 65 Steve Young 30.00 15.00
- ❑ 66 Tony Zendejas XRC 1.00 .40
- ❑ 67 Mossy Cade .50 .20
- ❑ 68 Leonard Coleman XRC .50 .20
- ❑ 69 John Corker .50 .20
- ❑ 70 Derrick Crawford .50 .20
- ❑ 71 Art Kuehn .50 .20
- ❑ 72 Walter Lewis .50 .20
- ❑ 73 Tyrone McGriff .50 .20
- ❑ 74 Tim Spencer 1.00 .40
- ❑ 75 Reggie White 25.00 12.50
- ❑ 76 Gizmo Williams XRC 2.00 .75
- ❑ 77 Sam Bowers .50 .20
- ❑ 78 Maurice Carthon XRC 2.00 .75
- ❑ 79 Clarence Collins .50 .20
- ❑ 80 Doug Flutie XRC 30.00 12.50
- ❑ 81 Freddie Gilbert DE .50 .20
- ❑ 82 Kerry Justin .50 .20
- ❑ 83 Dave Lapham .50 .20
- ❑ 84 Rick Partridge .50 .20
- ❑ 85 Roger Ruzek XRC 1.00 .40
- ❑ 86 Herschel Walker 8.00 3.00
- ❑ 87 Gordon Banks .50 .20
- ❑ 88 Monte Bennett .50 .20
- ❑ 89 Albert Bentley XRC 1.00 .40
- ❑ 90 Novo Bojovic .50 .20
- ❑ 91 Dave Browning .50 .20
- ❑ 92 Anthony Carter 2.00 .75
- ❑ 93 Bobby Hebert 2.00 .75
- ❑ 94 Ray Pinney .50 .20
- ❑ 95 Stan Talley .50 .20
- ❑ 96 Ruben Vaughan .50 .20
- ❑ 97 Curtis Bledsoe .50 .20
- ❑ 98 Reggie Collier .50 .20
- ❑ 99 Jerry Doerger .50 .20
- ❑ 100 Jerry Golsteyn .50 .20
- ❑ 101 Bob Niziolek .50 .20
- ❑ 102 Joel Patten .50 .20
- ❑ 103 Ricky Simmons .50 .20
- ❑ 104 Joey Walters .50 .20
- ❑ 105 Marcus Dupree 1.00 .40
- ❑ 106 Jeff Gossett 1.00 .40
- ❑ 107 Frank Lockett .50 .20
- ❑ 108 Marcus Marek .50 .20
- ❑ 109 Kenny Neil .50 .20
- ❑ 110 Robert Pennywell .50 .20
- ❑ 111 Matt Robinson .50 .20
- ❑ 112 Dan Ross 1.00 .40
- ❑ 113 Doug Woodward .50 .20
- ❑ 114 Danny Buggs .50 .20
- ❑ 115 Putt Choate .50 .20
- ❑ 116 Greg Fields .50 .20
- ❑ 117 Ken Hartley .50 .20
- ❑ 118 Nick Mike-Mayer .50 .20
- ❑ 119 Rick Neuheisel 2.00 .75
- ❑ 120 Peter Raeford .50 .20
- ❑ 121 Gary Worthy .50 .20
- ❑ 122 Gary Anderson RB 1.00 .40
- ❑ 123 Zenon Andrusyshyn .50 .20
- ❑ 124 Greg Boone .50 .20
- ❑ 125 Mike Butler .50 .20
- ❑ 126 Mike Clark .50 .20
- ❑ 127 Willie Gillespie .50 .20
- ❑ 128 James Harrell .50 .20
- ❑ 129 Marvin Harvey .50 .20
- ❑ 130 John Reaves 1.00 .40
- ❑ 131 Eric Truvillion .50 .20
- ❑ 132 Checklist 1-132 1.00 .40

1986 Topps

- ❑ COMPLETE SET (396) 120.00 60.00
- ❑ COMP.FACT.SET (396) 225.00 150.00
- ❑ 1 Marcus Allen RB .75 .30
- ❑ 2 Eric Dickerson RB .50 .20
- ❑ 3 Lionel James RB .10 .02
- ❑ 4 Steve Largent RB .50 .20
- ❑ 5 George Martin RB .10 .02
- ❑ 6 Stephone Paige RB .10 .02
- ❑ 7 Walter Payton RB .75 .30
- ❑ 8 Super Bowl XX .25 .08
- ❑ 9 Bears TL/W.Payton .60 .25
- ❑ 10 Jim McMahon .50 .20
- ❑ 11 Walter Payton 3.00 1.25
- ❑ 12 Matt Suhey .10 .02
- ❑ 13 Willie Gault .25 .08
- ❑ 14 Dennis McKinnon RC .10 .02
- ❑ 15 Emery Moorehead .10 .02
- ❑ 16 Jim Covert .25 .08
- ❑ 17 Jay Hilgenberg RC .50 .20
- ❑ 18 Kevin Butler RC .25 .08
- ❑ 19 Richard Dent .75 .30
- ❑ 20 William Perry RC .50 .20
- ❑ 21 Steve McMichael .50 .20
- ❑ 22 Dan Hampton .50 .20
- ❑ 23 Otis Wilson .10 .02
- ❑ 24 Mike Singletary .60 .25
- ❑ 25 Wilber Marshall RC .50 .20
- ❑ 26 Leslie Frazier .10 .02
- ❑ 27 Dave Duerson RC .10 .02
- ❑ 28 Gary Fencik .10 .02
- ❑ 29 Patriots TL .50 .20
- ❑ 30 Tony Eason .10 .02
- ❑ 31 Steve Grogan .25 .08
- ❑ 32 Craig James .50 .20
- ❑ 33 Tony Collins .10 .02
- ❑ 34 Irving Fryar 1.25 .50
- ❑ 35 Brian Holloway .10 .02
- ❑ 36 John Hannah .50 .20
- ❑ 37 Tony Franklin .10 .02
- ❑ 38 Garin Veris RC .10 .02
- ❑ 39 Andre Tippett .25 .08
- ❑ 40 Steve Nelson .10 .02
- ❑ 41 Raymond Clayborn .10 .02
- ❑ 42 Fred Marion RC .10 .02
- ❑ 43 Rich Camarillo .10 .02
- ❑ 44 Dolphins TL/D.Marino 2.00 .75
- ❑ 45 Dan Marino 8.00 4.00
- ❑ 46 Tony Nathan .25 .08
- ❑ 47 Ron Davenport RC .10 .02
- ❑ 48 Mark Duper .50 .20
- ❑ 49 Mark Clayton .50 .20
- ❑ 50 Nat Moore .25 .08
- ❑ 51 Bruce Hardy .10 .02
- ❑ 52 Roy Foster .10 .02
- ❑ 53 Dwight Stephenson .75 .30
- ❑ 54 Fuad Reveiz RC .25 .08
- ❑ 55 Bob Baumhower .10 .02
- ❑ 56 Mike Charles .10 .02
- ❑ 57 Hugh Green .25 .08
- ❑ 58 Glenn Blackwood .10 .02
- ❑ 59 Reggie Roby .25 .08
- ❑ 60 Raiders TL/M.Allen .50 .20
- ❑ 61 Marc Wilson .10 .02
- ❑ 62 Marcus Allen 1.50 .60
- ❑ 63 Dokie Williams .10 .02
- ❑ 64 Todd Christensen .50 .20
- ❑ 65 Chris Bahr .10 .02
- ❑ 66 Fulton Walker .10 .02
- ❑ 67 Howie Long 1.25 .50
- ❑ 68 Bill Pickel .10 .02
- ❑ 69 Ray Guy .50 .20
- ❑ 70 Greg Townsend RC .50 .20
- ❑ 71 Rod Martin .25 .08
- ❑ 72 Matt Millen .25 .08
- ❑ 73 Mike Haynes .25 .08
- ❑ 74 Lester Hayes .25 .08
- ❑ 75 Vann McElroy .10 .02
- ❑ 76 Rams TL/ Dickerson .50 .20
- ❑ 77 Dieter Brock RC .25 .08
- ❑ 78 Eric Dickerson .75 .30
- ❑ 79 Henry Ellard 1.00 .40
- ❑ 80 Ron Brown RC .25 .08
- ❑ 81 Tony Hunter RC .10 .02
- ❑ 82 Kent Hill AP .10 .02
- ❑ 83 Doug Smith .10 .02
- ❑ 84 Dennis Harrah .10 .02
- ❑ 85 Jackie Slater .50 .20
- ❑ 86 Mike Lansford .10 .02
- ❑ 87 Gary Jeter .10 .02
- ❑ 88 Mike Wilcher .10 .02
- ❑ 89 Jim Collins .10 .02
- ❑ 90 LeRoy Irvin .25 .08
- ❑ 91 Gary Green .10 .02
- ❑ 92 Nolan Cromwell .25 .08
- ❑ 93 Dale Hatcher RC .10 .02
- ❑ 94 Jets TL .25 .08

❑ 95 Ken O'Brien .50 .20
❑ 96 Freeman McNeil .25 .08
❑ 97 Tony Paige RC .10 .02
❑ 98 Johnny Lam Jones .10 .02
❑ 99 Wesley Walker .25 .08
❑ 100 Kurt Sohn .10 .02
❑ 101 Al Toon RC .50 .20
❑ 102 Mickey Shuler .10 .02
❑ 103 Marvin Powell .10 .02
❑ 104 Pat Leahy .10 .02
❑ 105 Mark Gastineau .25 .08
❑ 106 Joe Klecko .25 .08
❑ 107 Marty Lyons .10 .02
❑ 108 Lance Mehl .10 .02
❑ 109 Bobby Jackson .10 .02
❑ 110 Dave Jennings .10 .02
❑ 111 Broncos TL .25 .08
❑ 112 John Elway 8.00 4.00
❑ 113 Sammy Winder .25 .08
❑ 114 Gerald Willhite .10 .02
❑ 115 Steve Watson .10 .02
❑ 116 Vance Johnson RC .50 .20
❑ 117 Rich Karlis .10 .02
❑ 118 Rulon Jones .10 .02
❑ 119 Karl Mecklenburg RC .50 .20
❑ 120 Louis Wright .10 .02
❑ 121 Mike Harden .10 .02
❑ 122 Dennis Smith RC .50 .20
❑ 123 Steve Foley .10 .02
❑ 124 Cowboys TL .25 .08
❑ 125 Danny White .50 .20
❑ 126 Tony Dorsett .60 .25
❑ 127 Timmy Newsome .10 .02
❑ 128 Mike Renfro .10 .02
❑ 129 Tony Hill .25 .08
❑ 130 Doug Cosbie .25 .08
❑ 131 Rafael Septien .10 .02
❑ 132 Ed Too Tall Jones .50 .20
❑ 133 Randy White .50 .20
❑ 134 Jim Jeffcoat .50 .20
❑ 135 Everson Walls .25 .08
❑ 136 Dennis Thurman .10 .02
❑ 137 Giants TL .25 .08
❑ 138 Phil Simms .50 .20
❑ 139 Joe Morris .50 .20
❑ 140 George Adams RC .10 .02
❑ 141 Lionel Manuel .25 .08
❑ 142 Bobby Johnson .10 .02
❑ 143 Phil McConkey RC .25 .08
❑ 144 Mark Bavaro RC .50 .20
❑ 145 Zeke Mowatt .10 .02
❑ 146 Brad Benson RC .10 .02
❑ 147 Bart Oates RC .25 .08
❑ 148 Leonard Marshall RC .50 .20
❑ 149 Jim Burt .25 .08
❑ 150 George Martin .10 .02
❑ 151 Lawrence Taylor 1.25 .50
❑ 152 Harry Carson .25 .08
❑ 153 Elvis Patterson RC .10 .02
❑ 154 Sean Landeta RC .25 .08
❑ 155 49ers TL/Roger Craig .50 .20
❑ 156 Joe Montana 8.00 4.00
❑ 157 Roger Craig .50 .20
❑ 158 Wendell Tyler .10 .02
❑ 159 Carl Monroe .10 .02
❑ 160 Dwight Clark .25 .08
❑ 161 Jerry Rice RC ! 80.00 40.00
❑ 162 Randy Cross .25 .08
❑ 163 Keith Fahnhorst .10 .02
❑ 164 Jeff Stover .10 .02
❑ 165 Michael Carter RC .10 .02
❑ 166 Dwaine Board .10 .02
❑ 167 Eric Wright .25 .08
❑ 168 Ronnie Lott .75 .30
❑ 169 Carlton Williamson .10 .02
❑ 170 Redskins TL .25 .08
❑ 171 Joe Theismann .50 .20
❑ 172 Jay Schroeder RC .50 .20
❑ 173 George Rogers .25 .08
❑ 174 Ken Jenkins .10 .02
❑ 175 Art Monk .50 .20
❑ 176 Gary Clark RC 2.00 .75
❑ 177 Joe Jacoby .25 .08
❑ 178 Russ Grimm .25 .08
❑ 179 Mark Moseley .10 .02
❑ 180 Dexter Manley .25 .08
❑ 181 Charles Mann RC .50 .20
❑ 182 Vernon Dean .10 .02
❑ 183 Raphel Cherry RC .10 .02
❑ 184 Curtis Jordan .10 .02
❑ 185 Browns TL/Kosar .50 .20
❑ 186 Gary Danielson .25 .08
❑ 187 Bernie Kosar RC 3.00 1.25
❑ 188 Kevin Mack RC .50 .20
❑ 189 Earnest Byner RC .75 .30
❑ 190 Glen Young .10 .02
❑ 191 Ozzie Newsome .50 .20
❑ 192 Mike Baab .10 .02
❑ 193 Cody Risien .25 .08
❑ 194 Bob Golic .25 .08
❑ 195 Reggie Camp .10 .02
❑ 196 Chip Banks .25 .08
❑ 197 Tom Cousineau .10 .02
❑ 198 Frank Minnifield RC .10 .02
❑ 199 Al Gross .10 .02
❑ 200 Seahawks TL .25 .08
❑ 201 Dave Krieg .50 .20
❑ 202 Curt Warner .25 .08
❑ 203 Steve Largent .60 .25
❑ 204 Norm Johnson .10 .02
❑ 205 Daryl Turner .10 .02
❑ 206 Jacob Green .10 .02
❑ 207 Joe Nash .10 .02
❑ 208 Jeff Bryant .10 .02
❑ 209 Randy Edwards .10 .02
❑ 210 Fredd Young .10 .02
❑ 211 Kenny Easley .10 .02
❑ 212 John Harris .10 .02
❑ 213 Packers TL .10 .02
❑ 214 Lynn Dickey .25 .08
❑ 215 Gerry Ellis .10 .02
❑ 216 Eddie Lee Ivery .10 .02
❑ 217 Jessie Clark .10 .02
❑ 218 James Lofton .50 .20
❑ 219 Paul Coffman .10 .02
❑ 220 Alphonso Carreker .10 .02
❑ 221 Ezra Johnson .10 .02
❑ 222 Mike Douglass .10 .02
❑ 223 Tim Lewis .10 .02
❑ 224 Mark Murphy RC CB .10 .02
❑ 225 Joe Montana/K.O'Brien LL 1.00 .40
❑ 226 Receiving Leaders .25 .08
❑ 227 Marcus Allen/G.Riggs LL .50 .20
❑ 228 Scoring Leaders .25 .08
❑ 229 Interception Leaders .10 .02
❑ 230 Chargers TL/Dan Fouts .50 .20
❑ 231 Dan Fouts .50 .20
❑ 232 Lionel James .10 .02
❑ 233 Gary Anderson RB RC .50 .20
❑ 234 Tim Spencer RC .25 .08
❑ 235 Wes Chandler .25 .08
❑ 236 Charlie Joiner .50 .20
❑ 237 Kellen Winslow .50 .20
❑ 238 Jim Lachey RC .50 .20
❑ 239 Bob Thomas .10 .02
❑ 240 Jeffery Dale .10 .02
❑ 241 Ralf Mojsiejenko .10 .02
❑ 242 Lions TL .10 .02
❑ 243 Eric Hipple .10 .02
❑ 244 Billy Sims .25 .08
❑ 245 James Jones FB .10 .02
❑ 246 Pete Mandley RC .10 .02
❑ 247 Leonard Thompson .10 .02
❑ 248 Lomas Brown RC .25 .08
❑ 249 Eddie Murray .25 .08
❑ 250 Curtis Green .10 .02
❑ 251 William Gay .10 .02
❑ 252 Jimmy Williams .10 .02
❑ 253 Bobby Watkins .10 .02
❑ 254 Bengals TL/B.Esiason .50 .20
❑ 255 Boomer Esiason RC 5.00 2.00
❑ 256 James Brooks .25 .08
❑ 257 Larry Kinnebrew .10 .02
❑ 258 Cris Collinsworth .25 .08
❑ 259 Mike Martin .10 .02
❑ 260 Eddie Brown RC .50 .20
❑ 261 Anthony Munoz .50 .20
❑ 262 Jim Breech .10 .02
❑ 263 Ross Browner .25 .08
❑ 264 Carl Zander .10 .02
❑ 265 James Griffin .10 .02
❑ 266 Robert Jackson .10 .02
❑ 267 Pat McInally .10 .02
❑ 268 Eagles TL .50 .20
❑ 269 Ron Jaworski .25 .08
❑ 270 Earnest Jackson .25 .08
❑ 271 Mike Quick .25 .08
❑ 272 John Spagnola .10 .02
❑ 273 Mark Dennard .10 .02
❑ 274 Paul McFadden .10 .02
❑ 275 Reggie White RC 20.00 7.50
❑ 276 Greg Brown .10 .02
❑ 277 Herman Edwards .10 .02
❑ 278 Roynell Young .10 .02
❑ 279 Wes Hopkins .10 .02
❑ 280 Steelers TL .25 .08
❑ 281 Mark Malone .25 .08
❑ 282 Frank Pollard .10 .02
❑ 283 Walter Abercrombie .10 .02
❑ 284 Louis Lipps .50 .20
❑ 285 John Stallworth .50 .20
❑ 286 Mike Webster .25 .08
❑ 287 Gary Anderson K .25 .08
❑ 288 Keith Willis .10 .02
❑ 289 Mike Merriweather .10 .02
❑ 290 Dwayne Woodruff .10 .02
❑ 291 Donnie Shell .25 .08
❑ 292 Vikings TL .25 .08
❑ 293 Tommy Kramer .25 .08
❑ 294 Darrin Nelson .10 .02
❑ 295 Ted Brown .25 .08
❑ 296 Buster Rhymes .10 .02
❑ 297 Anthony Carter RC 1.00 .40
❑ 298 Steve Jordan RC .50 .20
❑ 299 Keith Millard RC .50 .20
❑ 300 Joey Browner RC .50 .20
❑ 301 John Turner .10 .02
❑ 302 Greg Coleman .10 .02
❑ 303 Chiefs TL .10 .02
❑ 304 Bill Kenney .10 .02
❑ 305 Herman Heard .10 .02
❑ 306 Stephone Paige RC .50 .20
❑ 307 Carlos Carson .25 .08
❑ 308 Nick Lowery .25 .08
❑ 309 Mike Bell .10 .02
❑ 310 Bill Maas .10 .02
❑ 311 Art Still .10 .02
❑ 312 Albert Lewis RC .50 .20
❑ 313 Deron Cherry .25 .08
❑ 314 Colts TL .10 .02
❑ 315 Mike Pagel .10 .02
❑ 316 Randy McMillan .10 .02
❑ 317 Albert Bentley RC .25 .08
❑ 318 George Wonsley RC .10 .02
❑ 319 Robbie Martin .10 .02
❑ 320 Pat Beach .10 .02
❑ 321 Chris Hinton .25 .08
❑ 322 Duane Bickett RC .50 .20
❑ 323 Eugene Daniel .10 .02
❑ 324 Cliff Odom RC .10 .02
❑ 325 Rohn Stark .25 .08
❑ 326 Cardinals TL .10 .02
❑ 327 Neil Lomax .25 .08
❑ 328 Stump Mitchell .25 .08
❑ 329 Ottis Anderson .50 .20
❑ 330 J.T.Smith .25 .08
❑ 331 Pat Tilley .10 .02
❑ 332 Roy Green .25 .08
❑ 333 Lance Smith RC .10 .02
❑ 334 Curtis Greer .10 .02
❑ 335 Freddie Joe Nunn RC .25 .08
❑ 336 E.J. Junior .25 .08
❑ 337 Lonnie Young RC .10 .02
❑ 338 Saints TL .10 .02
❑ 339 Bobby Hebert RC .50 .20
❑ 340 Dave Wilson .10 .02
❑ 341 Wayne Wilson .10 .02
❑ 342 Hoby Brenner .10 .02
❑ 343 Stan Brock .25 .08
❑ 344 Morten Andersen .50 .20
❑ 345 Bruce Clark .10 .02
❑ 346 Rickey Jackson .50 .20
❑ 347 Dave Waymer .10 .02
❑ 348 Brian Hansen .10 .02
❑ 349 Oilers TL/W.Moon .50 .20
❑ 350 Warren Moon 3.00 1.50
❑ 351 Mike Rozier RC .50 .20
❑ 352 Butch Woolfolk .10 .02
❑ 353 Drew Hill .50 .20
❑ 354 Willie Drewrey RC .10 .02
❑ 355 Tim Smith .25 .08

Card	Nrmt	Exc
❑ 356 Mike Munchak	.50	.20
❑ 357 Ray Childress RC	.50	.20
❑ 358 Frank Bush	.10	.02
❑ 359 Steve Brown	.10	.02
❑ 360 Falcons TL	.10	.02
❑ 361 David Archer RC	.50	.20
❑ 362 Gerald Riggs	.25	.08
❑ 363 William Andrews	.25	.08
❑ 364 Billy Johnson	.25	.08
❑ 365 Arthur Cox	.10	.02
❑ 366 Mike Kenn	.10	.02
❑ 367 Bill Fralic RC	.25	.08
❑ 368 Mick Luckhurst	.10	.02
❑ 369 Rick Bryan	.10	.02
❑ 370 Bobby Butler	.10	.02
❑ 371 Rick Donnelly RC	.10	.02
❑ 372 Buccaneers TL	.10	.02
❑ 373 Steve DeBerg	.50	.20
■ 374 Steve Young RC	20.00	10.00
❑ 375 James Wilder	.10	.02
❑ 376 Kevin House	.10	.02
❑ 377 Gerald Carter	.10	.02
❑ 378 Jimmie Giles	.25	.08
❑ 379 Sean Farrell	.10	.02
❑ 380 Donald Igwebuike	.10	.02
❑ 381 David Logan	.10	.02
❑ 382 Jeremiah Castille RC	.10	.02
❑ 383 Bills TL	.10	.02
❑ 384 Bruce Mathison RC	.10	.02
❑ 385 Joe Cribbs	.25	.08
❑ 386 Greg Bell	.25	.08
❑ 387 Jerry Butler	.10	.02
❑ 388 Andre Reed RC	6.00	2.50
❑ 389 Bruce Smith RC	5.00	2.00
❑ 390 Fred Smerlas	.10	.02
❑ 391 Darryl Talley	.50	.20
❑ 392 Jim Haslett	.25	.08
❑ 393 Charles Romes	.10	.02
❑ 394 Checklist 1-132	.20	.07
❑ 395 Checklist 133-264	.20	.07
❑ 396 Checklist 265-396	.20	.07

1987 Topps

Card	Nrmt	Exc
❑ COMPLETE SET (396)	30.00	15.00
❑ COMP.FACT.SET (396)	80.00	50.00
❑ 1 Super Bowl XXI	.50	.20
❑ 2 Todd Christensen RB	.25	.08
❑ 3 Dave Jennings RB	.10	.02
❑ 4 Charlie Joiner RB	.50	.20
❑ 5 Steve Largent RB	.50	.20
❑ 6 Dan Marino RB	2.00	.75
❑ 7 Donnie Shell RB	.25	.08
❑ 8 Phil Simms RB	.50	.20
❑ 9 New York Giants TL	.25	.08
❑ 10 Phil Simms	.50	.20
❑ 11 Joe Morris	.25	.08
❑ 12 Maurice Carthon RC	.50	.20
❑ 13 Lee Rouson	.10	.02
❑ 14 Bobby Johnson	.10	.02
❑ 15 Lionel Manuel	.10	.02
❑ 16 Phil McConkey	.10	.02
❑ 17 Mark Bavaro	.50	.20
❑ 18 Zeke Mowatt	.10	.02
❑ 19 Raul Allegre	.10	.02
❑ 20 Sean Landeta	.10	.02
❑ 21 Brad Benson	.10	.02
❑ 22 Jim Burt	.10	.02
❑ 23 Leonard Marshall	.50	.20
❑ 24 Carl Banks	.50	.20
❑ 25 Harry Carson	.10	.02
❑ 26 Lawrence Taylor	.75	.30
❑ 27 Terry Kinard RC	.10	.02
❑ 28 Pepper Johnson RC	.50	.20
❑ 29 Erik Howard RC	.10	.02
❑ 30 Broncos TL	.10	.02
❑ 31 John Elway	6.00	2.50
❑ 32 Gerald Willhite	.10	.02
❑ 33 Sammy Winder	.25	.08
❑ 34 Ken Bell	.10	.02
❑ 35 Steve Watson	.10	.02
❑ 36 Rich Karlis	.10	.02
❑ 37 Keith Bishop	.10	.02
❑ 38 Rulon Jones	.10	.02
❑ 39 Karl Mecklenburg	.50	.20
❑ 40 Louis Wright	.10	.02
❑ 41 Mike Harden	.10	.02
❑ 42 Dennis Smith	.25	.08
❑ 43 Bears TL/W.Payton	.50	.20
❑ 44 Jim McMahon	.50	.20
❑ 45 Doug Flutie RC	8.00	3.00
❑ 46 Walter Payton	2.00	.75
❑ 47 Matt Suhey	.10	.02
❑ 48 Willie Gault	.25	.08
❑ 49 Dennis Gentry RC	.10	.02
❑ 50 Kevin Butler	.10	.02
❑ 51 Jim Covert	.10	.02
❑ 52 Jay Hilgenberg	.25	.08
❑ 53 Dan Hampton	.50	.20
❑ 54 Steve McMichael	.50	.20
❑ 55 William Perry	.50	.20
❑ 56 Richard Dent	.50	.20
❑ 57 Otis Wilson	.10	.02
❑ 58 Mike Singletary	.50	.20
❑ 59 Wilber Marshall	.50	.20
❑ 60 Mike Richardson	.10	.02
❑ 61 Dave Duerson	.10	.02
❑ 62 Gary Fencik	.10	.02
❑ 63 Redskins TL	.25	.08
❑ 64 Jay Schroeder	.25	.08
❑ 65 George Rogers	.25	.08
❑ 66 Kelvin Bryant RC	.25	.08
❑ 67 Ken Jenkins	.10	.02
❑ 68 Gary Clark	.50	.20
❑ 69 Art Monk	.50	.20
❑ 70 Clint Didier RC	.10	.02
❑ 71 Steve Cox	.10	.02
❑ 72 Joe Jacoby	.10	.02
❑ 73 Russ Grimm	.10	.02
❑ 74 Charles Mann	.25	.08
❑ 75 Dave Butz	.10	.02
❑ 76 Dexter Manley	.25	.08
❑ 77 Darrell Green	.50	.20
❑ 78 Curtis Jordan	.10	.02
❑ 79 Browns TL	.10	.02
❑ 80 Bernie Kosar	.50	.20
❑ 81 Curtis Dickey	.10	.02
❑ 82 Kevin Mack	.25	.08
❑ 83 Herman Fontenot	.10	.02
❑ 84 Brian Brennan RC	.10	.02
❑ 85 Ozzie Newsome	.50	.20
❑ 86 Jeff Gossett	.25	.08
❑ 87 Cody Risien	.10	.02
❑ 88 Reggie Camp	.10	.02
❑ 89 Bob Golic	.10	.02
❑ 90 Carl Hairston	.10	.02
❑ 91 Chip Banks	.10	.02
❑ 92 Frank Minnifield	.10	.02
❑ 93 Hanford Dixon	.10	.02
❑ 94 Gerald McNeil RC	.10	.02
❑ 95 Dave Puzzuoli	.10	.02
❑ 96 Patriots TL	.10	.02
❑ 97 Tony Eason	.25	.08
❑ 98 Craig James	.25	.08
❑ 99 Tony Collins	.25	.08
❑ 100 Mosi Tatupu	.10	.02
❑ 101 Stanley Morgan	.25	.08
❑ 102 Irving Fryar	.50	.20
❑ 103 Stephen Starring	.10	.02
❑ 104 Tony Franklin	.10	.02
❑ 105 Rich Camarillo	.10	.02
❑ 106 Garin Veris	.10	.02
❑ 107 Andre Tippett	.25	.08
❑ 108 Don Blackmon	.10	.02
❑ 109 Ronnie Lippett RC	.10	.02
❑ 110 Raymond Clayborn	.10	.02
❑ 111 49ers TL/R.Craig	.25	.08
❑ 112 Joe Montana	6.00	2.50
❑ 113 Roger Craig	.50	.20
❑ 114 Joe Cribbs	.25	.08
❑ 115 Jerry Rice	6.00	2.50
❑ 116 Dwight Clark	.25	.08
❑ 117 Ray Wersching	.10	.02
❑ 118 Max Runager	.10	.02
❑ 119 Jeff Stover	.10	.02
❑ 120 Dwaine Board	.10	.02
❑ 121 Tim McKyer RC	.25	.08
❑ 122 Don Griffin RC	.25	.08
❑ 123 Ronnie Lott	.50	.20
❑ 124 Tom Holmoe	.10	.02
❑ 125 Charles Haley RC	1.25	.50
❑ 126 Jets TL	.10	.02
❑ 127 Ken O'Brien	.25	.08
❑ 128 Pat Ryan	.10	.02
❑ 129 Freeman McNeil	.25	.08
❑ 130 Johnny Hector RC	.10	.02
❑ 131 Al Toon	.50	.20
❑ 132 Wesley Walker	.25	.08
❑ 133 Mickey Shuler	.10	.02
❑ 134 Pat Leahy	.10	.02
❑ 135 Mark Gastineau	.25	.08
❑ 136 Joe Klecko	.25	.08
❑ 137 Marty Lyons	.10	.02
❑ 138 Bob Crable	.10	.02
❑ 139 Lance Mehl	.10	.02
❑ 140 Dave Jennings	.10	.02
❑ 141 Harry Hamilton RC	.10	.02
❑ 142 Lester Lyles	.10	.02
❑ 143 Bobby Humphery UER	.10	.02
❑ 144 Rams TL/E.Dickerson	.50	.20
❑ 145 Jim Everett RC	2.00	.75
❑ 146 Eric Dickerson	.50	.20
❑ 147 Barry Redden	.10	.02
❑ 148 Ron Brown	.25	.08
❑ 149 Kevin House	.10	.02
❑ 150 Henry Ellard	.50	.20
❑ 151 Doug Smith	.10	.02
❑ 152 Dennis Harrah	.10	.02
❑ 153 Jackie Slater	.25	.08
❑ 154 Gary Jeter	.10	.02
❑ 155 Carl Ekern	.10	.02
❑ 156 Mike Wilcher	.10	.02
❑ 157 Jerry Gray RC	.10	.02
❑ 158 LeRoy Irvin	.10	.02
❑ 159 Nolan Cromwell	.25	.08
❑ 160 Chiefs TL	.10	.02
❑ 161 Bill Kenney	.10	.02
❑ 162 Stephone Paige	.25	.08
❑ 163 Henry Marshall	.10	.02
❑ 164 Carlos Carson	.10	.02
❑ 165 Nick Lowery	.25	.08
❑ 166 Irv Eatman RC	.10	.02
❑ 167 Brad Budde	.10	.02
❑ 168 Art Still	.10	.02
❑ 169 Bill Maas	.10	.02
❑ 170 Lloyd Burruss RC	.10	.02
❑ 171 Deron Cherry	.10	.02
❑ 172 Seahawks TL	.25	.08
❑ 173 Dave Krieg	.50	.20
❑ 174 Curt Warner	.25	.08
❑ 175 John L.Williams RC	.50	.20
❑ 176 Bobby Joe Edmonds RC	.25	.08
❑ 177 Steve Largent	.60	.25
❑ 178 Bruce Scholtz	.10	.02
❑ 179 Norm Johnson	.10	.02
❑ 180 Jacob Green	.10	.02
❑ 181 Fredd Young	.10	.02
❑ 182 Dave Brown DB	.10	.02
❑ 183 Kenny Easley	.10	.02
❑ 184 Bengals TL	.25	.08
❑ 185 Boomer Esiason	.50	.20
❑ 186 James Brooks	.25	.08
❑ 187 Larry Kinnebrew	.10	.02
❑ 188 Cris Collinsworth	.25	.08
❑ 189 Eddie Brown	.50	.20
❑ 190 Tim McGee RC	.50	.20
❑ 191 Jim Breech	.10	.02
❑ 192 Anthony Munoz	.50	.20
❑ 193 Max Montoya	.10	.02
❑ 194 Eddie Edwards	.10	.02
❑ 195 Ross Browner	.25	.08
❑ 196 Emanuel King	.10	.02
❑ 197 Louis Breeden	.10	.02
❑ 198 Vikings TL	.10	.02

❑ 199 Tommy Kramer	.25	.08
❑ 200 Darrin Nelson	.10	.02
❑ 201 Allen Rice	.10	.02
❑ 202 Anthony Carter	.50	.20
❑ 203 Leo Lewis	.10	.02
❑ 204 Steve Jordan	.50	.20
❑ 205 Chuck Nelson RC	.10	.02
❑ 206 Greg Coleman	.10	.02
❑ 207 Gary Zimmerman RC	.50	.20
❑ 208 Doug Martin	.10	.02
❑ 209 Keith Millard	.10	.02
❑ 210 Issiac Holt RC	.10	.02
❑ 211 Joey Browner	.25	.08
❑ 212 Rufus Bess	.10	.02
❑ 213 Raiders TL/M.Allen	.50	.20
❑ 214 Jim Plunkett	.50	.20
❑ 215 Marcus Allen	1.00	.40
❑ 216 Napoleon McCallum RC	.25	.08
❑ 217 Dokie Williams	.10	.02
❑ 218 Todd Christensen	.50	.20
❑ 219 Chris Bahr	.10	.02
❑ 220 Howie Long	.60	.25
❑ 221 Bill Pickel	.10	.02
❑ 222 Sean Jones RC	.75	.30
❑ 223 Lester Hayes	.25	.08
❑ 224 Mike Haynes	.25	.08
❑ 225 Vann McElroy	.10	.02
❑ 226 Fulton Walker	.10	.02
❑ 227 Dan Marino/T.Kramer LL	1.25	.50
❑ 228 J.Rice/Christensen LL	1.25	.50
❑ 229 Eric Dickerson/Warner LL	.50	.20
❑ 230 Scoring Leaders	.10	.02
❑ 231 Interception Leaders	.50	.20
❑ 232 Dolphins TL	.25	.08
❑ 233 Dan Marino	6.00	2.50
❑ 234 Lorenzo Hampton RC	.10	.02
❑ 235 Tony Nathan	.25	.08
❑ 236 Mark Duper	.50	.20
❑ 237 Mark Clayton	.50	.20
❑ 238 Nat Moore	.25	.08
❑ 239 Bruce Hardy	.10	.02
❑ 240 Reggie Roby	.25	.08
❑ 241 Roy Foster	.10	.02
❑ 242 Dwight Stephenson	.50	.20
❑ 243 Hugh Green	.10	.02
❑ 244 John Offerdahl RC	.50	.20
❑ 245 Mark Brown	.10	.02
❑ 246 Doug Betters	.10	.02
❑ 247 Bob Baumhower	.10	.02
❑ 248 Falcons TL	.10	.02
❑ 249 David Archer	.50	.20
❑ 250 Gerald Riggs	.25	.08
❑ 251 William Andrews	.25	.08
❑ 252 Charlie Brown	.10	.02
❑ 253 Arthur Cox	.10	.02
❑ 254 Rick Donnelly	.10	.02
❑ 255 Bill Fralic	.10	.02
❑ 256 Mike Gann RC	.10	.02
❑ 257 Rick Bryan	.10	.02
❑ 258 Bret Clark	.10	.02
❑ 259 Mike Pitts	.10	.02
❑ 260 Cowboys TL/T.Dorsett	.50	.20
❑ 261 Danny White	.50	.20
❑ 262 Steve Pelluer RC	.10	.02
❑ 263 Tony Dorsett UER	.50	.20
❑ 264 Herschel Walker RC	2.50	1.00
❑ 265 Timmy Newsome	.10	.02
❑ 266 Tony Hill	.25	.08
❑ 267 Mike Sherrard RC	.50	.20
❑ 268 Jim Jeffcoat	.50	.20
❑ 269 Ron Fellows	.10	.02
❑ 270 Bill Bates	.50	.20
❑ 271 Michael Downs	.10	.02
❑ 272 Saints TL/B.Hebert	.25	.08
❑ 273 Dave Wilson	.10	.02
❑ 274 Rueben Mayes RC UER	.10	.02
❑ 275 Hoby Brenner	.10	.02
❑ 276 Eric Martin RC	.50	.20
❑ 277 Morten Andersen	.25	.08
❑ 278 Brian Hansen	.10	.02
❑ 279 Rickey Jackson	.50	.20
❑ 280 Dave Waymer	.10	.02
❑ 281 Bruce Clark	.10	.02
❑ 282 Jumpy Geathers RC	.25	.08
❑ 283 Steelers TL	.25	.08
❑ 284 Mark Malone	.25	.08
❑ 285 Earnest Jackson	.10	.02
❑ 286 Walter Abercrombie	.10	.02
❑ 287 Louis Lipps	.25	.08
❑ 288 John Stallworth UER	.50	.20
❑ 289 Gary Anderson K	.10	.02
❑ 290 Keith Willis	.10	.02
❑ 291 Mike Merriweather	.10	.02
❑ 292 Lupe Sanchez	.10	.02
❑ 293 Donnie Shell	.25	.08
❑ 294 Eagles TL/K.Byars	.50	.20
❑ 295 Mike Reichenbach	.10	.02
❑ 296 Randall Cunningham RC	6.00	3.00
❑ 297 Keith Byars RC	.75	.30
❑ 298 Mike Quick	.25	.08
❑ 299 Kenny Jackson	.10	.02
❑ 300 John Teltschik RC	.10	.02
❑ 301 Reggie White	3.00	1.50
❑ 302 Ken Clarke	.10	.02
❑ 303 Greg Brown	.10	.02
❑ 304 Roynell Young	.10	.02
❑ 305 Andre Waters RC	.50	.20
❑ 306 Oilers TL/W.Moon	.50	.20
❑ 307 Warren Moon	1.50	.60
❑ 308 Mike Rozier	.25	.08
❑ 309 Drew Hill	.25	.08
❑ 310 Ernest Givins RC	.50	.20
❑ 311 Lee Johnson RC	.10	.02
❑ 312 Kent Hill	.10	.02
❑ 313 Dean Steinkuhler RC	.25	.08
❑ 314 Ray Childress	.50	.20
❑ 315 John Grimsley RC	.10	.02
❑ 316 Jesse Baker	.10	.02
❑ 317 Lions TL	.10	.02
❑ 318 Chuck Long RC	.25	.08
❑ 319 James Jones FB	.10	.02
❑ 320 Garry James	.10	.02
❑ 321 Jeff Chadwick	.10	.02
❑ 322 Leonard Thompson	.10	.02
❑ 323 Pete Mandley	.10	.02
❑ 324 Jimmie Giles	.25	.08
❑ 325 Herman Hunter	.10	.02
❑ 326 Keith Ferguson	.10	.02
❑ 327 Devon Mitchell	.10	.02
❑ 328 Cardinals TL	.10	.02
❑ 329 Neil Lomax	.25	.08
❑ 330 Stump Mitchell	.10	.02
❑ 331 Earl Ferrell	.10	.02
❑ 332 Vai Sikahema RC	.25	.08
❑ 333 Ron Wolfley RC	.10	.02
❑ 334 J.T.Smith	.25	.08
❑ 335 Roy Green	.25	.08
❑ 336 Al(Bubba) Baker	.10	.02
❑ 337 Freddie Joe Nunn	.10	.02
❑ 338 Cedric Mack	.10	.02
❑ 339 Chargers TL	.25	.08
❑ 340 Dan Fouts	.50	.20
❑ 341 Gary Anderson RB UER	.50	.20
❑ 342 Wes Chandler	.25	.08
❑ 343 Kellen Winslow	.50	.20
❑ 344 Ralf Mojsiejenko	.10	.02
❑ 345 Rolf Benirschke	.10	.02
❑ 346 Lee Williams RC	.25	.08
❑ 347 Leslie O'Neal RC	1.00	.40
❑ 348 Billy Ray Smith	.25	.08
❑ 349 Gill Byrd	.25	.08
❑ 350 Packers TL	.10	.02
❑ 351 Randy Wright	.10	.02
❑ 352 Kenneth Davis RC	.50	.20
❑ 353 Gerry Ellis	.10	.02
❑ 354 James Lofton	.50	.20
❑ 355 Phillip Epps RC	.10	.02
❑ 356 Walter Stanley RC	.10	.02
❑ 357 Eddie Lee Ivery	.10	.02
❑ 358 Tim Harris RC	.50	.20
❑ 359 Mark Lee UER	.10	.02
❑ 360 Mossy Cade	.10	.02
❑ 361 Bills TL/J.Kelly	1.00	.40
❑ 362 Jim Kelly RC	10.00	4.00
❑ 363 Robb Riddick RC	.10	.02
❑ 364 Greg Bell	.10	.02
❑ 365 Andre Reed	1.25	.50
❑ 366 Pete Metzelaars RC	.50	.20
❑ 367 Sean McNanie	.10	.02
❑ 368 Fred Smerlas	.10	.02
❑ 369 Bruce Smith	2.00	.75
❑ 370 Darryl Talley	.25	.08
❑ 371 Charles Romes	.10	.02
❑ 372 Colts TL	.10	.02
❑ 373 Jack Trudeau RC	.25	.08
❑ 374 Gary Hogeboom	.10	.02
❑ 375 Randy McMillan	.10	.02
❑ 376 Albert Bentley	.10	.02
❑ 377 Matt Bouza	.10	.02
❑ 378 Bill Brooks RC	1.00	.40
❑ 379 Rohn Stark	.10	.02
❑ 380 Chris Hinton	.10	.02
❑ 381 Ray Donaldson	.10	.02
❑ 382 Jon Hand RC	.10	.02
❑ 383 Buccaneers TL	.10	.02
❑ 384 Steve Young	5.00	2.00
❑ 385 James Wilder	.10	.02
❑ 386 Frank Garcia	.10	.02
❑ 387 Gerald Carter	.10	.02
❑ 388 Phil Freeman	.10	.02
❑ 389 Calvin Magee	.10	.02
❑ 390 Donald Igwebuike	.10	.02
❑ 391 David Logan	.10	.02
❑ 392 Jeff Davis	.10	.02
❑ 393 Chris Washington	.10	.02
❑ 394 Checklist 1-132	.10	.02
❑ 395 Checklist 133-264	.10	.02
❑ 396 Checklist 265-396	.10	.02

1988 Topps

❑ COMPLETE SET (396)	20.00	7.50
❑ COMP.FACT.SET (396)	30.00	15.00
❑ 1 Super Bowl XXII	.20	.07
❑ 2 Vencie Glenn RB	.05	.01
❑ 3 Steve Largent RB	.40	.15
❑ 4 Joe Montana RB	.75	.30
❑ 5 Walter Payton RB	.40	.15
❑ 6 Jerry Rice RB	.75	.30
❑ 7 Redskins TL	.20	.07
❑ 8 Doug Williams	.20	.07
❑ 9 George Rogers	.20	.07
❑ 10 Kelvin Bryant	.20	.07
❑ 11 Timmy Smith SR	.20	.07
❑ 12 Art Monk	.40	.15
❑ 13 Gary Clark	.40	.15
❑ 14 Ricky Sanders RC	.40	.15
❑ 15 Steve Cox	.05	.01
❑ 16 Joe Jacoby	.05	.01
❑ 17 Charles Mann	.20	.07
❑ 18 Dave Butz	.05	.01
❑ 19 Darrell Green	.20	.07
❑ 20 Dexter Manley	.05	.01
❑ 21 Barry Wilburn	.05	.01
❑ 22 Broncos TL	.05	.01
❑ 23 John Elway	2.00	.75
❑ 24 Sammy Winder	.05	.01
❑ 25 Vance Johnson	.20	.07
❑ 26 Mark Jackson RC	.40	.15
❑ 27 Ricky Nattiel RC	.05	.01
❑ 28 Clarence Kay	.05	.01
❑ 29 Rich Karlis	.05	.01
❑ 30 Keith Bishop	.05	.01
❑ 31 Mike Horan	.05	.01
❑ 32 Rulon Jones	.05	.01
❑ 33 Karl Mecklenburg	.20	.07
❑ 34 Jim Ryan	.05	.01
❑ 35 Mark Haynes	.20	.07
❑ 36 Mike Harden	.05	.01
❑ 37 49ers TL	.40	.15
❑ 38 Joe Montana	2.00	.75
❑ 39 Steve Young	1.00	.40
❑ 40 Roger Craig	.20	.07
❑ 41 Tom Rathman RC	.40	.15

Card		
42 Joe Cribbs	.20	.07
43 Jerry Rice	2.00	.75
44 Mike Wilson RC	.05	.01
45 Ron Heller TE RC	.05	.01
46 Ray Wersching	.05	.01
47 Michael Carter	.05	.01
48 Dwaine Board	.05	.01
49 Michael Walter	.05	.01
50 Don Griffin	.05	.01
51 Ronnie Lott	.40	.15
52 Charles Haley	.40	.15
53 Dana McLemore	.05	.01
54 Saints TL	.20	.07
55 Bobby Hebert	.20	.07
56 Rueben Mayes	.05	.01
57 Dalton Hilliard RC	.05	.01
58 Eric Martin	.20	.07
59 John Tice RC	.05	.01
60 Brad Edelman	.05	.01
61 Morten Andersen	.20	.07
62 Brian Hansen	.05	.01
63 Mel Gray RC	.40	.15
64 Rickey Jackson	.20	.07
65 Sam Mills RC	.75	.30
66 Pat Swilling RC	.40	.15
67 Dave Waymer	.05	.01
68 Bears TL	.20	.07
69 Jim McMahon	.40	.15
70 Mike Tomczak RC	.05	.01
71 Neal Anderson RC	.40	.15
72 Willie Gault	.20	.07
73 Dennis Gentry	.05	.01
74 Dennis McKinnon	.05	.01
75 Kevin Butler	.05	.01
76 Jim Covert	.05	.01
77 Jay Hilgenberg	.05	.01
78 Steve McMichael	.20	.07
79 William Perry	.20	.07
80 Richard Dent	.40	.15
81 Ron Rivera RC	.05	.01
82 Mike Singletary	.40	.15
83 Dan Hampton	.40	.15
84 Dave Duerson	.05	.01
85 Browns TL	.20	.07
86 Bernie Kosar	.40	.15
87 Earnest Byner	.40	.15
88 Kevin Mack	.20	.07
89 Webster Slaughter RC	.40	.15
90 Gerald McNeil	.05	.01
91 Brian Brennan	.05	.01
92 Ozzie Newsome	.40	.15
93 Cody Risien	.05	.01
94 Bob Golic	.05	.01
95 Carl Hairston	.05	.01
96 Mike Johnson RC	.05	.01
97 Clay Matthews	.20	.07
98 Frank Minnifield	.05	.01
99 Hanford Dixon	.05	.01
100 Dave Puzzuoli	.05	.01
101 Felix Wright RC	.05	.01
102 Oilers TL/Moon	.40	.15
103 Warren Moon	.50	.20
104 Mike Rozier	.05	.01
105 Alonzo Highsmith RC	.20	.07
106 Drew Hill	.20	.07
107 Ernest Givins	.40	.15
108 Curtis Duncan RC	.40	.15
109 Tony Zendejas RC	.05	.01
110 Mike Munchak	.40	.15
111 Kent Hill	.05	.01
112 Ray Childress	.20	.07
113 Al Smith RC	.20	.07
114 Keith Bostic RC	.05	.01
115 Jeff Donaldson	.05	.01
116 Colts TL/Dickerson	.40	.15
117 Jack Trudeau	.05	.01
118 Eric Dickerson	.40	.15
119 Albert Bentley	.05	.01
120 Matt Bouza	.05	.01
121 Bill Brooks	.40	.15
122 Dean Biasucci RC	.05	.01
123 Chris Hinton	.05	.01
124 Ray Donaldson	.05	.01
125 Ron Solt RC	.05	.01
126 Donnell Thompson	.05	.01
127 Barry Krauss RC	.05	.01
128 Duane Bickett	.05	.01
129 Mike Prior RC	.05	.01
130 Seahawks TL	.20	.07
131 Dave Krieg	.20	.07
132 Curt Warner	.20	.07
133 John L.Williams	.40	.15
134 Bobby Joe Edmonds	.05	.01
135 Steve Largent	.40	.15
136 Raymond Butler	.05	.01
137 Norm Johnson	.05	.01
138 Ruben Rodriguez	.05	.01
139 Blair Bush	.05	.01
140 Jacob Green	.05	.01
141 Joe Nash	.05	.01
142 Jeff Bryant	.05	.01
143 Fredd Young	.05	.01
144 Brian Bosworth RC	1.50	.60
145 Kenny Easley	.05	.01
146 Vikings TL	.20	.07
147 Wade Wilson RC	.40	.15
148 Tommy Kramer	.20	.07
149 Darrin Nelson	.05	.01
150 D.J.Dozier RC	.20	.07
151 Anthony Carter	.20	.07
152 Leo Lewis	.05	.01
153 Steve Jordan	.20	.07
154 Gary Zimmerman	.05	.01
155 Chuck Nelson	.05	.01
156 Henry Thomas RC	.40	.15
157 Chris Doleman RC	.40	.15
158 Scott Studwell RC	.05	.01
159 Jesse Solomon RC	.05	.01
160 Joey Browner	.05	.01
161 Neal Guggemos	.05	.01
162 Steelers TL	.20	.07
163 Mark Malone	.05	.01
164 Walter Abercrombie	.05	.01
165 Earnest Jackson	.05	.01
166 Frank Pollard	.05	.01
167 Dwight Stone RC	.20	.07
168 Gary Anderson K	.05	.01
169 Harry Newsome RC	.05	.01
170 Keith Willis	.05	.01
171 Keith Gary	.05	.01
172 David Little RC	.20	.07
173 Mike Merriweather	.05	.01
174 Dwayne Woodruff	.05	.01
175 Patriots TL	.40	.15
176 Steve Grogan	.20	.07
177 Tony Eason	.20	.07
178 Tony Collins	.20	.07
179 Mosi Tatupu	.05	.01
180 Stanley Morgan	.20	.07
181 Irving Fryar	.40	.15
182 Stephen Starring	.05	.01
183 Tony Franklin	.05	.01
184 Rich Camarillo	.05	.01
185 Garin Veris	.05	.01
186 Andre Tippett	.20	.07
187 Ronnie Lippett	.05	.01
188 Fred Marion	.05	.01
189 Dolphins TL/D.Marino	.75	.30
190 Dan Marino	2.00	.75
191 Troy Stradford RC	.20	.07
192 Lorenzo Hampton	.05	.01
193 Mark Duper	.20	.07
194 Mark Clayton	.20	.07
195 Reggie Roby	.20	.07
196 Dwight Stephenson	.40	.15
197 T.J. Turner RC	.05	.01
198 John Bosa RC	.05	.01
199 Jackie Shipp	.05	.01
200 John Offerdahl	.20	.07
201 Mark Brown	.05	.01
202 Paul Lankford	.05	.01
203 Chargers TL	.40	.15
204 Tim Spencer	.05	.01
205 Gary Anderson RB	.20	.07
206 Curtis Adams	.05	.01
207 Lionel James	.05	.01
208 Chip Banks	.05	.01
209 Kellen Winslow	.40	.15
210 Ralf Mojsiejenko	.05	.01
211 Jim Lachey	.20	.07
212 Lee Williams	.05	.01
213 Billy Ray Smith	.05	.01
214 Vencie Glenn RC	.20	.07
215 J.Montana/B.Kosar LL	.50	.20
216 Receiving Leaders	.20	.07
217 Eric Dickerson/C.White L	.20	.07
218 Jerry Rice/J.Breech LL	.40	.15
219 Interception Leaders	.05	.01
220 Bills TL/Jim Kelly	.40	.15
221 Jim Kelly	.75	.30
222 Ronnie Harmon RC	.40	.15
223 Robb Riddick	.05	.01
224 Andre Reed	.40	.15
225 Chris Burkett RC	.05	.01
226 Pete Metzelaars	.40	.15
227 Bruce Smith	.50	.20
228 Darryl Talley	.20	.07
229 Eugene Marve	.05	.01
230 Cornelius Bennett RC	.75	.30
231 Mark Kelso RC	.05	.01
232 Shane Conlan RC	.40	.15
233 Eagles TL/R.Cunningham	.40	.15
234 Randall Cunningham	1.00	.40
235 Keith Byars	.40	.15
236 Anthony Toney RC	.05	.01
237 Mike Quick	.20	.07
238 Kenny Jackson	.05	.01
239 John Spagnola	.05	.01
240 Paul McFadden	.05	.01
241 Reggie White	.60	.25
242 Ken Clarke	.05	.01
243 Mike Pitts	.05	.01
244 Clyde Simmons RC	.40	.15
245 Seth Joyner RC	.40	.15
246 Andre Waters	.40	.15
247 Jerome Brown RC	.40	.15
248 Cardinals TL	.05	.01
249 Neil Lomax	.20	.07
250 Stump Mitchell	.05	.01
251 Earl Ferrell	.05	.01
252 Vai Sikahema	.05	.01
253 J.T. Smith	.20	.07
254 Roy Green	.20	.07
255 Robert Awalt RC	.20	.07
256 Freddie Joe Nunn	.05	.01
257 Leonard Smith RC	.05	.01
258 Travis Curtis	.05	.01
259 Cowboys TL/H.Walker	.40	.15
260 Danny White	.40	.15
261 Herschel Walker	.40	.15
262 Tony Dorsett	.40	.15
263 Doug Cosbie	.05	.01
264 Roger Ruzek RC	.20	.07
265 Darryl Clack	.05	.01
266 Ed Too Tall Jones	.40	.15
267 Jim Jeffcoat	.05	.01
268 Everson Walls	.05	.01
269 Bill Bates	.20	.07
270 Michael Downs	.05	.01
271 Giants TL	.20	.07
272 Phil Simms	.40	.15
273 Joe Morris	.20	.07
274 Lee Rouson	.05	.01
275 George Adams	.05	.01
276 Lionel Manuel	.05	.01
277 Mark Bavaro	.20	.07
278 Raul Allegre	.05	.01
279 Sean Landeta	.05	.01
280 Erik Howard	.05	.01
281 Leonard Marshall	.20	.07
282 Carl Banks	.20	.07
283 Pepper Johnson	.20	.07
284 Harry Carson	.20	.07
285 Lawrence Taylor	.40	.15
286 Terry Kinard	.05	.01
287 Rams TL/Everett	.40	.15
288 Jim Everett	.40	.15
289 Charles White	.20	.07
290 Ron Brown	.20	.07
291 Henry Ellard	.40	.15
292 Mike Lansford	.05	.01
293 Dale Hatcher	.05	.01
294 Doug Smith	.05	.01
295 Jackie Slater	.20	.07
296 Jim Collins	.05	.01
297 Jerry Gray	.05	.01
298 LeRoy Irvin	.05	.01
299 Nolan Cromwell	.20	.07
300 Kevin Greene RC	1.25	.50
301 Jets TL	.20	.07
302 Ken O'Brien	.20	.07

Card		
❑ 303 Freeman McNeil	.20	.07
❑ 304 Johnny Hector	.05	.01
❑ 305 Al Toon	.20	.07
❑ 306 JoJo Townsell RC	.20	.07
❑ 307 Mickey Shuler	.05	.01
❑ 308 Pat Leahy	.05	.01
❑ 309 Roger Vick	.05	.01
❑ 310 Alex Gordon RC	.05	.01
❑ 311 Troy Benson	.05	.01
❑ 312 Bob Crable	.05	.01
❑ 313 Harry Hamilton	.05	.01
❑ 314 Packers TL	.05	.01
❑ 315 Randy Wright	.05	.01
❑ 316 Kenneth Davis	.20	.07
❑ 317 Phillip Epps	.05	.01
❑ 318 Walter Stanley	.05	.01
❑ 319 Frankie Neal	.05	.01
❑ 320 Don Bracken	.05	.01
❑ 321 Brian Noble RC	.20	.07
❑ 322 Johnny Holland RC	.20	.07
❑ 323 Tim Harris	.20	.07
❑ 324 Mark Murphy	.05	.01
❑ 325 Raiders TL/B.Jackson	.50	.20
❑ 326 Marc Wilson	.05	.01
❑ 327 Bo Jackson RC	5.00	2.00
❑ 328 Marcus Allen	.40	.15
❑ 329 James Lofton	.40	.15
❑ 330 Todd Christensen	.20	.07
❑ 331 Chris Bahr	.05	.01
❑ 332 Stan Talley	.05	.01
❑ 333 Howie Long	.40	.15
❑ 334 Sean Jones	.40	.15
❑ 335 Matt Millen	.20	.07
❑ 336 Stacey Toran	.05	.01
❑ 337 Vann McElroy	.05	.01
❑ 338 Greg Townsend	.20	.07
❑ 339 Bengals TL/Esiason	.40	.15
❑ 340 Boomer Esiason	.40	.15
❑ 341 Larry Kinnebrew	.05	.01
❑ 342 Stanford Jennings RC	.05	.01
❑ 343 Eddie Brown	.20	.07
❑ 344 Jim Breech	.05	.01
❑ 345 Anthony Munoz	.40	.15
❑ 346 Scott Fulhage RC	.05	.01
❑ 347 Tim Krumrie RC	.05	.01
❑ 348 Reggie Williams	.20	.07
❑ 349 David Fulcher RC	.05	.01
❑ 350 Buccaneers TL	.05	.01
❑ 351 Frank Garcia	.05	.01
❑ 352 Vinny Testaverde RC	4.00	1.50
❑ 353 James Wilder	.05	.01
❑ 354 Jeff Smith RBK	.05	.01
❑ 355 Gerald Carter	.05	.01
❑ 356 Calvin Magee	.05	.01
❑ 357 Donald Igwebuike	.05	.01
❑ 358 Ron Holmes RC	.05	.01
❑ 359 Chris Washington	.05	.01
❑ 360 Ervin Randle	.05	.01
❑ 361 Chiefs TL	.05	.01
❑ 362 Bill Kenney	.05	.01
❑ 363 Christian Okoye RC	.40	.15
❑ 364 Paul Palmer	.05	.01
❑ 365 Stephone Paige	.20	.07
❑ 366 Carlos Carson	.05	.01
❑ 367 Kelly Goodburn RC	.05	.01
❑ 368 Bill Maas	.05	.01
❑ 369 Mike Bell	.05	.01
❑ 370 Dino Hackett RC	.05	.01
❑ 371 Deron Cherry	.05	.01
❑ 372 Lions TL	.05	.01
❑ 373 Chuck Long	.20	.07
❑ 374 Garry James	.05	.01
❑ 375 James Jones FB	.05	.01
❑ 376 Pete Mandley	.05	.01
❑ 377 Gary Lee RC	.05	.01
❑ 378 Eddie Murray	.05	.01
❑ 379 Jim Arnold	.05	.01
❑ 380 Dennis Gibson RC	.05	.01
❑ 381 Michael Cofer LB	.05	.01
❑ 382 James Griffin	.05	.01
❑ 383 Falcons TL	.05	.01
❑ 384 Scott Campbell	.05	.01
❑ 385 Gerald Riggs	.20	.07
❑ 386 Floyd Dixon RC	.05	.01
❑ 387 Rick Donnelly	.05	.01
❑ 388 Bill Fralic	.20	.07
❑ 389 Major Everett	.05	.01
❑ 390 Mike Gann	.05	.01
❑ 391 Tony Casillas RC	.20	.07
❑ 392 Rick Bryan	.05	.01
❑ 393 John Rade RC	.05	.01
❑ 394 Checklist 1-132	.05	.01
❑ 395 Checklist 133-264	.05	.01
❑ 396 Checklist 265-396	.05	.01

1989 Topps

Card		
❑ COMPLETE SET (396)	20.00	7.50
❑ COMP.FACT.SET (396)	25.00	10.00
❑ 1 Super Bowl XXIII/Montana	.50	.20
❑ 2 Tim Brown RB	.50	.20
❑ 3 Eric Dickerson RB	.10	.02
❑ 4 Steve Largent RB	.25	.08
❑ 5 Dan Marino RB	.75	.30
❑ 6 49ers TL/Montana	.50	.20
❑ 7 Jerry Rice	1.50	.60
❑ 8 Roger Craig	.25	.08
❑ 9 Ronnie Lott	.10	.02
❑ 10 Michael Carter	.05	.01
❑ 11 Charles Haley	.25	.08
❑ 12 Joe Montana	2.00	.75
❑ 13 John Taylor RC	.10	.02
❑ 14 Michael Walter	.05	.01
❑ 15 Mike Cofer K RC	.05	.01
❑ 16 Tom Rathman	.05	.01
❑ 17 Daniel Stubbs RC	.05	.01
❑ 18 Keena Turner	.05	.01
❑ 19 Tim McKyer	.05	.01
❑ 20 Larry Roberts	.05	.01
❑ 21 Jeff Fuller	.05	.01
❑ 22 Bubba Paris	.05	.01
❑ 23 Bengals Team UER	.10	.02
❑ 24 Eddie Brown	.05	.01
❑ 25 Boomer Esiason	.10	.02
❑ 26 Tim Krumrie	.05	.01
❑ 27 Ickey Woods RC	.10	.02
❑ 28 Anthony Munoz	.10	.02
❑ 29 Tim McGee	.05	.01
❑ 30 Max Montoya	.05	.01
❑ 31 David Grant	.05	.01
❑ 32 Rodney Holman RC	.05	.01
❑ 33 David Fulcher	.10	.02
❑ 34 Jim Skow	.05	.01
❑ 35 James Brooks	.10	.02
❑ 36 Reggie Williams	.05	.01
❑ 37 Eric Thomas RC	.05	.01
❑ 38 Stanford Jennings	.05	.01
❑ 39 Jim Breech	.05	.01
❑ 40 Bills TL/Jim Kelly	.25	.08
❑ 41 Shane Conlan	.05	.01
❑ 42 Scott Norwood RC	.05	.01
❑ 43 Cornelius Bennett	.10	.02
❑ 44 Bruce Smith	.25	.08
❑ 45 Thurman Thomas RC	1.25	.50
❑ 46 Jim Kelly	.50	.20
❑ 47 John Kidd	.05	.01
❑ 48 Kent Hull RC	.05	.01
❑ 49 Art Still	.05	.01
❑ 50 Fred Smerlas	.05	.01
❑ 51A Derrick Burroughs	.05	.01
❑ 51B Derrick Burroughs	.05	.01
❑ 52 Andre Reed	.25	.08
❑ 53 Robb Riddick	.05	.01
❑ 54 Chris Burkett	.05	.01
❑ 55 Ronnie Harmon	.10	.02
❑ 56 Mark Kelso UER	.05	.01
❑ 57 Bears Team	.05	.01
❑ 58 Mike Singletary	.10	.02
❑ 59 Jay Hilgenberg UER	.05	.01
❑ 60 Richard Dent	.10	.02
❑ 61 Ron Rivera	.05	.01
❑ 62 Jim McMahon	.10	.02
❑ 63 Mike Tomczak	.10	.02
❑ 64 Neal Anderson	.10	.02
❑ 65 Dennis Gentry	.05	.01
❑ 66 Dan Hampton	.10	.02
❑ 67 David Tate	.05	.01
❑ 68 Thomas Sanders RC	.05	.01
❑ 69 Steve McMichael	.10	.02
❑ 70 Dennis McKinnon	.05	.01
❑ 71 Brad Muster RC	.05	.01
❑ 72 Vestee Jackson RC	.05	.01
❑ 73 Dave Duerson	.05	.01
❑ 74 Vikings Team	.05	.01
❑ 75 Joey Browner	.05	.01
❑ 76 Carl Lee RC	.05	.01
❑ 77 Gary Zimmerman	.05	.01
❑ 78 Hassan Jones RC	.05	.01
❑ 79 Anthony Carter	.10	.02
❑ 80 Ray Berry	.05	.01
❑ 81 Steve Jordan	.05	.01
❑ 82 Issiac Holt	.05	.01
❑ 83 Wade Wilson	.10	.02
❑ 84 Chris Doleman	.10	.02
❑ 85 Alfred Anderson	.05	.01
❑ 86 Keith Millard	.05	.01
❑ 87 Darrin Nelson	.05	.01
❑ 88 D.J. Dozier	.05	.01
❑ 89 Scott Studwell	.05	.01
❑ 90 Oilers Team	.05	.01
❑ 91 Bruce Matthews RC	.75	.30
❑ 92 Curtis Duncan	.05	.01
❑ 93 Warren Moon	.25	.08
❑ 94 Johnny Meads RC	.05	.01
❑ 95 Drew Hill	.05	.01
❑ 96 Alonzo Highsmith	.05	.01
❑ 97 Mike Munchak	.10	.02
❑ 98 Mike Rozier	.05	.01
❑ 99 Tony Zendejas	.05	.01
❑ 100 Jeff Donaldson	.05	.01
❑ 101 Ray Childress	.05	.01
❑ 102 Sean Jones	.10	.02
❑ 103 Ernest Givins	.10	.02
❑ 104 William Fuller RC	.25	.08
❑ 105 Allen Pinkett RC	.05	.01
❑ 106 Eagles TL/R.Cunningham	.10	.02
❑ 107 Keith Jackson RC	.25	.08
❑ 108 Reggie White	.25	.08
❑ 109 Clyde Simmons	.10	.02
❑ 110 John Teltschik	.05	.01
❑ 111 Wes Hopkins	.05	.01
❑ 112 Keith Byars	.10	.02
❑ 113 Jerome Brown	.10	.02
❑ 114 Mike Quick	.05	.01
❑ 115 Randall Cunningham	.40	.15
❑ 116 Anthony Toney	.05	.01
❑ 117 Ron Johnson WR	.05	.01
❑ 118 Terry Hoage	.05	.01
❑ 119 Seth Joyner	.10	.02
❑ 120 Eric Allen RC	.25	.08
❑ 121 Cris Carter RC	1.50	.60
❑ 122 Rams Team	.05	.01
❑ 123 Tom Newberry RC	.05	.01
❑ 124 Pete Holohan	.05	.01
❑ 125 Robert Delpino RC UER	.05	.01
❑ 126 Carl Ekern	.05	.01
❑ 127 Greg Bell	.05	.01
❑ 128 Mike Lansford	.05	.01
❑ 129 Jim Everett	.10	.02
❑ 130 Mike Wilcher	.05	.01
❑ 131 Jerry Gray	.05	.01
❑ 132 Dale Hatcher	.05	.01
❑ 133 Doug Smith	.05	.01
❑ 134 Kevin Greene	.25	.08
❑ 135 Jackie Slater	.05	.01
❑ 136 Aaron Cox RC	.05	.01
❑ 137 Henry Ellard	.25	.08
❑ 138 Browns Team	.10	.02
❑ 139 Frank Minnifield	.05	.01
❑ 140 Webster Slaughter	.10	.02
❑ 141 Bernie Kosar	.10	.02
❑ 142 Charles Buchanan	.05	.01
❑ 143 Clay Matthews	.10	.02
❑ 144 Reggie Langhorne RC	.05	.01

❑ 145 Hanford Dixon	.05	.01
❑ 146 Brian Brennan	.05	.01
❑ 147 Earnest Byner	.05	.01
❑ 148 Michael Dean Perry RC	.10	.02
❑ 149 Kevin Mack	.05	.01
❑ 150 Matt Bahr	.05	.01
❑ 151 Ozzie Newsome	.10	.02
❑ 152 Saints Team	.10	.02
❑ 153 Morten Andersen	.05	.01
❑ 154 Pat Swilling	.10	.02
❑ 155 Sam Mills	.10	.02
❑ 156 Lonzell Hill	.05	.01
❑ 157 Dalton Hilliard	.05	.01
❑ 158 Craig Heyward RC	.10	.02
❑ 159 Vaughan Johnson RC	.05	.01
❑ 160 Rueben Mayes	.05	.01
❑ 161 Gene Atkins RC	.05	.01
❑ 162 Bobby Hebert	.10	.02
❑ 163 Rickey Jackson	.10	.02
❑ 164 Eric Martin	.05	.01
❑ 165 Giants Team	.05	.01
❑ 166 Lawrence Taylor	.25	.08
❑ 167 Bart Oates	.05	.01
❑ 168 Carl Banks	.05	.01
❑ 169 Eric Moore RC	.05	.01
❑ 170 Sheldon White RC	.05	.01
❑ 171 Mark Collins RC	.05	.01
❑ 172 Phil Simms	.10	.02
❑ 173 Jim Burt	.05	.01
❑ 174 Stephen Baker RC	.10	.02
❑ 175 Mark Bavaro	.10	.02
❑ 176 Pepper Johnson	.05	.01
❑ 177 Lionel Manuel	.05	.01
❑ 178 Joe Morris	.05	.01
❑ 179 Jumbo Elliott RC	.05	.01
❑ 180 Gary Reasons RC	.05	.01
❑ 181 Seahawks Team	.10	.02
❑ 182 Brian Blades RC	.25	.08
❑ 183 Steve Largent	.25	.08
❑ 184 Rufus Porter RC	.05	.01
❑ 185 Ruben Rodriguez	.05	.01
❑ 186 Curt Warner	.05	.01
❑ 187 Paul Moyer	.05	.01
❑ 188 Dave Krieg	.10	.02
❑ 189 Jacob Green	.05	.01
❑ 190 John L.Williams	.05	.01
❑ 191 Eugene Robinson RC	.05	.01
❑ 192 Brian Bosworth	.10	.02
❑ 193 Patriots Team	.05	.01
❑ 194 John Stephens RC	.05	.01
❑ 195 Robert Perryman RC	.05	.01
❑ 196 Andre Tippett	.05	.01
❑ 197 Fred Marion	.05	.01
❑ 198 Doug Flutie	1.00	.40
❑ 199 Stanley Morgan	.05	.01
❑ 200 Johnny Rembert RC	.05	.01
❑ 201 Tony Eason	.05	.01
❑ 202 Marvin Allen	.05	.01
❑ 203 Raymond Clayborn	.05	.01
❑ 204 Irving Fryar	.25	.08
❑ 205 Colts Team	.05	.01
❑ 206 Eric Dickerson	.10	.02
❑ 207 Chris Hinton	.05	.01
❑ 208 Duane Bickett	.05	.01
❑ 209 Chris Chandler RC	1.00	.40
❑ 210 Jon Hand	.05	.01
❑ 211 Ray Donaldson	.05	.01
❑ 212 Dean Biasucci	.05	.01
❑ 213 Bill Brooks	.10	.02
❑ 214 Chris Goode RC	.05	.01
❑ 215 Clarence Verdin RC	.05	.01
❑ 216 Albert Bentley	.05	.01
❑ 217 Passing Leaders	.10	.02
❑ 218 Receiving Leaders	.10	.02
❑ 219 Eric Dickerson/Walker LL	.10	.02
❑ 220 Scoring Leaders	.05	.01
❑ 221 Interception Leaders	.05	.01
❑ 222 Jets Team	.05	.01
❑ 223 Erik McMillan RC	.05	.01
❑ 224 James Hasty RC	.05	.01
❑ 225 Al Toon	.10	.02
❑ 226 John Booty RC	.05	.01
❑ 227 Johnny Hector	.05	.01
❑ 228 Ken O'Brien	.05	.01
❑ 229 Marty Lyons	.05	.01
❑ 230 Mickey Shuler	.05	.01
❑ 231 Robin Cole	.05	.01
❑ 232 Freeman McNeil	.05	.01
❑ 233 Marion Barber RC	.05	.01
❑ 234 Jo Jo Townsell	.05	.01
❑ 235 Wesley Walker	.05	.01
❑ 236 Roger Vick	.05	.01
❑ 237 Pat Leahy	.05	.01
❑ 238 Broncos TL/Elway	.50	.20
❑ 239 Mike Horan	.05	.01
❑ 240 Tony Dorsett	.25	.08
❑ 241 John Elway	2.00	.75
❑ 242 Mark Jackson	.05	.01
❑ 243 Sammy Winder	.05	.01
❑ 244 Rich Karlis	.05	.01
❑ 245 Vance Johnson	.10	.02
❑ 246 Steve Sewell RC	.05	.01
❑ 247 Karl Mecklenburg UER	.05	.01
❑ 248 Rulon Jones	.05	.01
❑ 249 Simon Fletcher RC	.05	.01
❑ 250 Redskins Team	.10	.02
❑ 251 Chip Lohmiller RC	.05	.01
❑ 252 Jamie Morris	.05	.01
❑ 253 Mark Rypien RC UER	.10	.02
❑ 254 Barry Wilburn	.05	.01
❑ 255 Mark May RC	.05	.01
❑ 256 Wilber Marshall	.05	.01
❑ 257 Charles Mann	.05	.01
❑ 258 Gary Clark	.25	.08
❑ 259 Doug Williams	.10	.02
❑ 260 Art Monk	.10	.02
❑ 261 Kelvin Bryant	.05	.01
❑ 262 Dexter Manley	.05	.01
❑ 263 Ricky Sanders	.05	.01
❑ 264 Raiders Team	.25	.08
❑ 265 Tim Brown RC	1.50	.60
❑ 266 Jay Schroeder	.05	.01
❑ 267 Marcus Allen	.25	.08
❑ 268 Mike Haynes	.10	.02
❑ 269 Bo Jackson	.30	.10
❑ 270 Steve Beuerlein RC	.60	.25
❑ 271 Vann McElroy	.05	.01
❑ 272 Willie Gault	.10	.02
❑ 273 Howie Long	.25	.08
❑ 274 Greg Townsend	.05	.01
❑ 275 Mike Wise DE	.05	.01
❑ 276 Cardinals Team	.05	.01
❑ 277 Luis Sharpe	.05	.01
❑ 278 Scott Dill	.05	.01
❑ 279 Vai Sikahema	.05	.01
❑ 280 Ron Wolfley	.05	.01
❑ 281 David Galloway	.05	.01
❑ 282 Jay Novacek RC	.25	.08
❑ 283 Neil Lomax	.05	.01
❑ 284 Robert Awalt	.05	.01
❑ 285 Cedric Mack	.05	.01
❑ 286 Freddie Joe Nunn	.05	.01
❑ 287 J.T. Smith	.05	.01
❑ 288 Stump Mitchell	.05	.01
❑ 289 Roy Green	.10	.02
❑ 290 Dolphins TL/Marino	.50	.20
❑ 291 Jarvis Williams RC	.05	.01
❑ 292 Troy Stradford	.05	.01
❑ 293 Dan Marino	2.00	.75
❑ 294 T.J. Turner	.05	.01
❑ 295 John Offerdahl	.05	.01
❑ 296 Ferrell Edmunds RC	.05	.01
❑ 297 Scott Schwedes	.05	.01
❑ 298 Lorenzo Hampton	.05	.01
❑ 299 Jim C.Jensen RC	.05	.01
❑ 300 Brian Sochia	.05	.01
❑ 301 Reggie Roby	.05	.01
❑ 302 Mark Clayton	.10	.02
❑ 303 Chargers Team	.05	.01
❑ 304 Lee Williams	.05	.01
❑ 305 Gary Plummer RC	.05	.01
❑ 306 Gary Anderson RB	.05	.01
❑ 307 Gill Byrd	.05	.01
❑ 308 Jamie Holland RC	.05	.01
❑ 309 Billy Ray Smith	.05	.01
❑ 310 Lionel James	.05	.01
❑ 311 Mark Vlasic RC	.05	.01
❑ 312 Curtis Adams	.05	.01
❑ 313 Anthony Miller RC	.25	.08
❑ 314 Steelers Team	.05	.01
❑ 315 Bubby Brister RC	.25	.08
❑ 316 David Little	.05	.01
❑ 317 Tunch Ilkin RC	.05	.01
❑ 318 Louis Lipps	.10	.02
❑ 319 Warren Williams RC	.05	.01
❑ 320 Dwight Stone	.10	.02
❑ 321 Merril Hoge RC	.05	.01
❑ 322 Thomas Everett RC	.05	.01
❑ 323 Rod Woodson RC	.50	.20
❑ 324 Gary Anderson K	.05	.01
❑ 325 Buccaneers Team	.05	.01
❑ 326 Donnie Elder	.05	.01
❑ 327 Vinny Testaverde	.30	.10
❑ 328 Harry Hamilton	.05	.01
❑ 329 James Wilder	.05	.01
❑ 330 Lars Tate	.05	.01
❑ 331 Mark Carrier RC WR	.25	.08
❑ 332 Bruce Hill RC	.05	.01
❑ 333 Paul Gruber RC	.05	.01
❑ 334 Ricky Reynolds	.05	.01
❑ 335 Eugene Marve	.05	.01
❑ 336 Falcons Team	.05	.01
❑ 337 Aundray Bruce RC	.05	.01
❑ 338 John Rade	.05	.01
❑ 339 Scott Case RC	.05	.01
❑ 340 Robert Moore	.05	.01
❑ 341 Chris Miller RC	.25	.08
❑ 342 Gerald Riggs	.10	.02
❑ 343 Gene Lang	.05	.01
❑ 344 Marcus Cotton	.05	.01
❑ 345 Rick Donnelly	.05	.01
❑ 346 John Settle RC	.05	.01
❑ 347 Bill Fralic	.05	.01
❑ 348 Chiefs Team	.05	.01
❑ 349 Steve DeBerg	.05	.01
❑ 350 Mike Stensrud	.05	.01
❑ 351 Dino Hackett	.05	.01
❑ 352 Deron Cherry	.10	.02
❑ 353 Christian Okoye	.05	.01
❑ 354 Bill Maas	.05	.01
❑ 355 Carlos Carson	.05	.01
❑ 356 Albert Lewis	.05	.01
❑ 357 Paul Palmer	.05	.01
❑ 358 Nick Lowery	.05	.01
❑ 359 Stephone Paige	.05	.01
❑ 360 Lions Team	.05	.01
❑ 361 Chris Spielman RC	.25	.08
❑ 362 Jim Arnold	.05	.01
❑ 363 Devon Mitchell	.05	.01
❑ 364 Mike Cofer	.05	.01
❑ 365 Bennie Blades RC	.05	.01
❑ 366 James Jones FB	.05	.01
❑ 367 Garry James	.05	.01
❑ 368 Pete Mandley	.05	.01
❑ 369 Keith Ferguson	.05	.01
❑ 370 Dennis Gibson	.05	.01
❑ 371 Packers Team UER	.05	.01
❑ 372 Brent Fullwood RC	.05	.01
❑ 373 Don Majkowski RC	.10	.02
❑ 374 Tim Harris	.05	.01
❑ 375 Keith Woodside RC	.05	.01
❑ 376 Mark Murphy	.05	.01
❑ 377 Dave Brown DB	.05	.01
❑ 378 Perry Kemp RC	.05	.01
❑ 379 Sterling Sharpe RC	.75	.30
❑ 380 Chuck Cecil RC	.05	.01
❑ 381 Walter Stanley	.05	.01
❑ 382 Cowboys Team	.05	.01
❑ 383 Michael Irvin RC	1.50	.60
❑ 384 Bill Bates	.10	.02
❑ 385 Herschel Walker	.25	.08
❑ 386 Darryl Clack	.05	.01
❑ 387 Danny Noonan	.05	.01
❑ 388 Eugene Lockhart RC	.05	.01
❑ 389 Ed Too Tall Jones	.10	.02
❑ 390 Steve Pelluer	.05	.01
❑ 391 Ray Alexander	.05	.01
❑ 392 Nate Newton RC	.10	.02
❑ 393 Garry Cobb	.05	.01
❑ 394 Checklist 1-132	.05	.01
❑ 395 Checklist 133-264	.05	.01
❑ 396 Checklist 265-396	.05	.01

1989 Topps Traded

❑ COMP.FACT.SET (132)	15.00	6.00
❑ 1T Eric Ball RC	.05	.01
❑ 2T Tony Mandarich RC	.05	.01
❑ 3T Shawn Collins RC	.05	.01
❑ 4T Ray Bentley RC	.05	.01
❑ 5T Tony Casillas	.05	.01
❑ 6T Al Del Greco RC	.05	.01

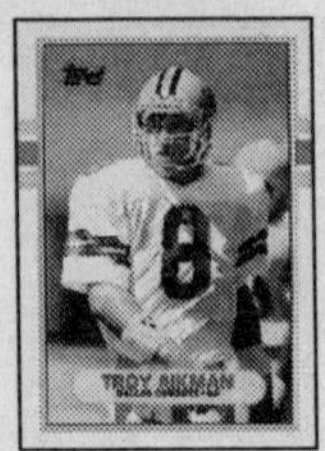

❑ 7T Dan Saleaumua RC .10 .02
❑ 8T Keith Bishop .05 .01
❑ 9T Rodney Peete RC .60 .25
❑ 10T Lorenzo White RC .25 .08
❑ 11T Steve Smith RC .10 .02
❑ 12T Pete Mandley .05 .01
❑ 13T Mervyn Fernandez RC**/C .05 .01
❑ 14T Flipper Anderson RC .25 .08
❑ 15T Louis Oliver RC .10 .02
❑ 16T Rick Fenney .05 .01
❑ 17T Gary Jeter .05 .01
❑ 18T Greg Cox .05 .01
❑ 19T Bubba McDowell RC .10 .02
❑ 20T Ron Heller .05 .01
❑ 21T Tim McDonald RC .05 .01
❑ 22T Jerrol Williams RC .05 .01
❑ 23T Marion Butts RC .10 .02
❑ 24T Steve Young .75 .30
❑ 25T Mike Merriweather .05 .01
❑ 26T Richard Johnson .05 .01
❑ 27T Gerald Riggs .10 .02
❑ 28T Dave Waymer .05 .01
❑ 29T Issiac Holt .05 .01
❑ 30T Deion Sanders RC 1.50 .60
❑ 31T Todd Blackledge .05 .01
❑ 32T Jeff Cross RC .05 .01
❑ 33T Steve Wisniewski RC .10 .02
❑ 34T Ron Brown .10 .02
❑ 35T Rod Bernstine RC .05 .01
❑ 36T Jeff Uhlenhake RC .05 .01
❑ 37T Donnell Woolford RC .25 .08
❑ 38T Bob Gagliano RC .05 .01
❑ 39T Ezra Johnson .05 .01
❑ 40T Ron Jaworski .05 .01
❑ 41T Lawyer Tillman RC .05 .01
❑ 42T Lorenzo Lynch RC .05 .01
❑ 43T Mike Alexander .05 .01
❑ 44T Tim Worley RC .05 .01
❑ 45T Guy Bingham .05 .01
❑ 46T Cleveland Gary RC .05 .01
❑ 47T Danny Peebles .05 .01
❑ 48T Clarence Weathers RC .05 .01
❑ 49T Jeff Lageman RC .25 .08
❑ 50T Eric Metcalf RC .25 .08
❑ 51T Myron Guyton RC .05 .01
❑ 52T Steve Atwater RC .05 .01
❑ 53T John Fourcade RC .05 .01
❑ 54T Randall McDaniel RC .25 .08
❑ 55T Al Noga RC .05 .01
❑ 56T Sammie Smith RC .10 .02
❑ 57T Jesse Solomon .05 .01
❑ 58T Greg Kragen RC .05 .01
❑ 59T Don Beebe RC .25 .08
❑ 60T Hart Lee Dykes RC .10 .02
❑ 61T Trace Armstrong RC .10 .02
❑ 62T Steve Pelluer .05 .01
❑ 63T Barry Krauss .05 .01
❑ 64T Kevin Murphy RC .05 .01
❑ 65T Steve Tasker RC .25 .08
❑ 66T Jessie Small RC .05 .01
❑ 67T Dave Meggett RC .25 .08
❑ 68T Dean Hamel .05 .01
❑ 69T Jim Covert .05 .01
❑ 70T Troy Aikman RC 5.00 2.00
❑ 71T Raul Allegre .05 .01
❑ 72T Chris Jacke RC .10 .02
❑ 73T Leslie O'Neal .10 .02
❑ 74T Keith Taylor RC .05 .01
❑ 75T Steve Walsh RC .25 .08
❑ 76T Tracy Rocker .05 .01
❑ 77T Robert Massey RC .10 .02
❑ 78T Bryan Wagner .05 .01
❑ 79T Steve DeOssie .05 .01
❑ 80T Carnell Lake RC .25 .08
❑ 81T Frank Reich RC .25 .08
❑ 82T Tyrone Braxton RC .05 .01
❑ 83T Barry Sanders RC 6.00 2.50
❑ 84T Pete Stoyanovich RC .10 .02
❑ 85T Paul Palmer .05 .01
❑ 86T Billy Joe Tolliver RC .05 .01
❑ 87T Eric Hill RC .10 .02
❑ 88T Gerald McNeil .05 .01
❑ 89T Bill Hawkins RC .05 .01
❑ 90T Derrick Thomas RC 1.25 .50
❑ 91T Jim Harbaugh RC .75 .30
❑ 92T Brian Williams OL RC .05 .01
❑ 93T Jack Trudeau .05 .01
❑ 94T Leonard Smith .05 .01
❑ 95T Gary Hogeboom .05 .01
❑ 96T A.J.Johnson RC .05 .01
❑ 97T Jim McMahon .10 .02
❑ 98T David Williams RC .05 .01
❑ 99T Rohn Stark .05 .01
❑ 100T Sean Landeta .05 .01
❑ 101T Tim Johnson RC .05 .01
❑ 102T Andre Rison RC .75 .30
❑ 103T Earnest Byner .10 .02
❑ 104T Don McPherson RC .05 .01
❑ 105T Zefross Moss RC .05 .01
❑ 106T Frank Stams RC .05 .01
❑ 107T Courtney Hall RC .10 .02
❑ 108T Marc Logan RC .05 .01
❑ 109T James Lofton .25 .08
❑ 110T Lewis Tillman RC .10 .02
❑ 111T Irv Pankey RC .05 .01
❑ 112T Ralf Mojsiejenko .05 .01
❑ 113T Bobby Humphrey RC .05 .01
❑ 114T Chris Burkett .05 .01
❑ 115T Greg Lloyd RC .25 .08
❑ 116T Matt Millen .10 .02
❑ 117T Carl Zander .05 .01
❑ 118T Wayne Martin RC .25 .08
❑ 119T Mike Saxon .05 .01
❑ 120T Herschel Walker .10 .02
❑ 121T Andy Heck RC .05 .01
❑ 122T Mark Robinson .05 .01
❑ 123T Keith Van Horne RC .05 .01
❑ 124T Ricky Hunley .05 .01
❑ 125T Timm Rosenbach RC .10 .02
❑ 126T Steve Grogan .10 .02
❑ 127T Stephen Braggs RC .05 .01
❑ 128T Terry Long .05 .01
❑ 129T Evan Cooper .05 .01
❑ 130T Robert Lyles .05 .01
❑ 131T Mike Webster .10 .02
❑ 132T Checklist 1-132 .05 .01

1990 Topps

❑ COMPLETE SET (528) 25.00 10.00
❑ COMP.FACT.SET (528) 30.00 12.50
❑ 1 Joe Montana RB .50 .20
❑ 2 Flipper Anderson RB .05 .01
❑ 3 Troy Aikman RB .40 .15
❑ 4 Kevin Butler RB .05 .01
❑ 5 Super Bowl XXIV .05 .01
❑ 6 Dexter Carter RC .05 .01
❑ 7 Matt Millen .10 .02
❑ 8 Jerry Rice .75 .30
❑ 9 Ronnie Lott .10 .02
❑ 10 John Taylor .10 .02
❑ 11 Guy McIntyre .05 .01
❑ 12 Roger Craig .10 .02
❑ 13 Joe Montana 1.25 .50
❑ 14 Brent Jones RC .25 .08
❑ 15 Tom Rathman .05 .01
❑ 16 Harris Barton .05 .01
❑ 17 Charles Haley .10 .02
❑ 18 Pierce Holt RC .05 .01
❑ 19 Michael Carter .05 .01
❑ 20 Chet Brooks .05 .01
❑ 21 Eric Wright .05 .01
❑ 22 Mike Cofer .05 .01
❑ 23 Jim Fahnhorst .05 .01
❑ 24 Keena Turner .05 .01
❑ 25 Don Griffin .05 .01
❑ 26 Kevin Fagan RC .05 .01
❑ 27 Bubba Paris .05 .01
❑ 28 Barry Sanders/C.Okoye LL .50 .20
❑ 29 Steve Atwater .05 .01
❑ 30 Tyrone Braxton .05 .01
❑ 31 Ron Holmes .05 .01
❑ 32 Bobby Humphrey .05 .01
❑ 33 Greg Kragen .05 .01
❑ 34 David Treadwell .05 .01
❑ 35 Karl Mecklenburg .05 .01
❑ 36 Dennis Smith .05 .01
❑ 37 John Elway 1.25 .50
❑ 38 Vance Johnson .05 .01
❑ 39 Simon Fletcher UER .05 .01
❑ 40 Jim Juriga .05 .01
❑ 41 Mark Jackson .05 .01
❑ 42 Melvin Bratton RC .05 .01
❑ 43 Wymon Henderson RC .05 .01
❑ 44 Ken Bell .05 .01
❑ 45 Sammy Winder .05 .01
❑ 46 Alphonso Carreker .05 .01
❑ 47 Orson Mobley RC .05 .01
❑ 48 Rodney Hampton RC .25 .08
❑ 49 Dave Meggett .10 .02
❑ 50 Myron Guyton .05 .01
❑ 51 Phil Simms .10 .02
❑ 52 Lawrence Taylor .25 .08
❑ 53 Carl Banks .05 .01
❑ 54 Pepper Johnson .05 .01
❑ 55 Leonard Marshall .05 .01
❑ 56 Mark Collins .05 .01
❑ 57 Erik Howard .05 .01
❑ 58 Eric Dorsey RC .05 .01
❑ 59 Ottis Anderson .10 .02
❑ 60 Mark Bavaro .05 .01
❑ 61 Odessa Turner RC .05 .01
❑ 62 Gary Reasons .05 .01
❑ 63 Maurice Carthon .05 .01
❑ 64 Lionel Manuel .05 .01
❑ 65 Sean Landeta .05 .01
❑ 66 Perry Williams .05 .01
❑ 67 Pat Terrell RC .05 .01
❑ 68 Flipper Anderson .05 .01
❑ 69 Jackie Slater .05 .01
❑ 70 Tom Newberry .05 .01
❑ 71 Jerry Gray .05 .01
❑ 72 Henry Ellard .10 .02
❑ 73 Doug Smith .05 .01
❑ 74 Kevin Greene .10 .02
❑ 75 Jim Everett .10 .02
❑ 76 Mike Lansford .05 .01
❑ 77 Greg Bell .05 .01
❑ 78 Pete Holohan .05 .01
❑ 79 Robert Delpino .05 .01
❑ 80 Mike Wilcher .05 .01
❑ 81 Mike Piel .05 .01
❑ 82 Mel Owens .05 .01
❑ 83 Michael Stewart RC .05 .01
❑ 84 Ben Smith RC .05 .01
❑ 85 Keith Jackson .10 .02
❑ 86 Reggie White .25 .08
❑ 87 Eric Allen .05 .01
❑ 88 Jerome Brown .05 .01
❑ 89 Robert Drummond .05 .01
❑ 90 Anthony Toney .05 .01
❑ 91 Keith Byars .05 .01
❑ 92 Cris Carter .50 .20
❑ 93 Randall Cunningham .25 .08
❑ 94 Ron Johnson WR .05 .01
❑ 95 Mike Quick .05 .01
❑ 96 Clyde Simmons .05 .01

❑ 97 Mike Pitts .05 .01
❑ 98 Izel Jenkins RC .05 .01
❑ 99 Seth Joyner .10 .02
❑ 100 Mike Schad .05 .01
❑ 101 Wes Hopkins .05 .01
❑ 102 Kirk Lowdermilk .05 .01
❑ 103 Rick Fenney .05 .01
❑ 104 Randall McDaniel .10 .02
❑ 105 Herschel Walker .10 .02
❑ 106 Al Noga .05 .01
❑ 107 Gary Zimmerman .05 .01
❑ 108 Chris Doleman .05 .01
❑ 109 Keith Millard .05 .01
❑ 110 Carl Lee .05 .01
❑ 111 Joey Browner .05 .01
❑ 112 Steve Jordan .05 .01
❑ 113 Reggie Rutland RC .05 .01
❑ 114 Wade Wilson .10 .02
❑ 115 Anthony Carter .10 .02
❑ 116 Rich Karlis .05 .01
❑ 117 Hassan Jones .05 .01
❑ 118 Henry Thomas .05 .01
❑ 119 Scott Studwell .05 .01
❑ 120 Ralf Mojsiejenko .05 .01
❑ 121 Earnest Byner .05 .01
❑ 122 Gerald Riggs .10 .02
❑ 123 Tracy Rocker .05 .01
❑ 124 A.J. Johnson .05 .01
❑ 125 Charles Mann .05 .01
❑ 126 Art Monk .10 .02
❑ 127 Ricky Sanders .05 .01
❑ 128 Gary Clark .25 .08
❑ 129 Jim Lachey .05 .01
❑ 130 Martin Mayhew RC .05 .01
❑ 131 Ravin Caldwell .05 .01
❑ 132 Don Warren .05 .01
❑ 133 Mark Rypien .10 .02
❑ 134 Ed Simmons RC .05 .01
❑ 135 Darryl Grant .05 .01
❑ 136 Darrell Green .10 .02
❑ 137 Chip Lohmiller .05 .01
❑ 138 Tony Bennett RC .25 .08
❑ 139 Tony Mandarich .05 .01
❑ 140 Sterling Sharpe .25 .08
❑ 141 Tim Harris .05 .01
❑ 142 Don Majkowski .05 .01
❑ 143 Rich Moran RC .05 .01
❑ 144 Jeff Query .05 .01
❑ 145 Brent Fullwood .05 .01
❑ 146 Chris Jacke .05 .01
❑ 147 Keith Woodside .05 .01
❑ 148 Perry Kemp .05 .01
❑ 149 Herman Fontenot .05 .01
❑ 150 Dave Brown DB .05 .01
❑ 151 Brian Noble .05 .01
❑ 152 Johnny Holland .05 .01
❑ 153 Mark Murphy .05 .01
❑ 154 Bob Nelson NT .05 .01
❑ 155 Darrell Thompson RC .05 .01
❑ 156 Lawyer Tillman .05 .01
❑ 157 Eric Metcalf .25 .08
❑ 158 Webster Slaughter .10 .02
❑ 159 Frank Minnifield .05 .01
❑ 160 Brian Brennan .05 .01
❑ 161 Thane Gash RC .05 .01
❑ 162 Robert Banks DE .05 .01
❑ 163 Bernie Kosar .10 .02
❑ 164 David Grayson .05 .01
❑ 165 Kevin Mack .05 .01
❑ 166 Mike Johnson .05 .01
❑ 167 Tim Manoa .05 .01
❑ 168 Ozzie Newsome .10 .02
❑ 169 Felix Wright .05 .01
❑ 170A Al Baker Orng. .10 .02
❑ 170B Al Baker Wht. .10 .02
❑ 171 Reggie Langhorne .05 .01
❑ 172 Clay Matthews .10 .02
❑ 173 Andrew Stewart .05 .01
❑ 174 Barry Foster RC .25 .08
❑ 175 Tim Worley .05 .01
❑ 176 Tim Johnson .05 .01
❑ 177 Carnell Lake .05 .01
❑ 178 Greg Lloyd .25 .08
❑ 179 Rod Woodson .25 .08
❑ 180 Tunch Ilkin .05 .01
❑ 181 Dermontti Dawson .10 .02
❑ 182 Gary Anderson K .05 .01
❑ 183 Bubby Brister .05 .01
❑ 184 Louis Lipps .10 .02
❑ 185 Merril Hoge .05 .01
❑ 186 Mike Mularkey .05 .01
❑ 187 Derek Hill .05 .01
❑ 188 Rodney Carter .05 .01
❑ 189 Dwayne Woodruff .05 .01
❑ 190 Keith Willis .05 .01
❑ 191 Jerry Olsavsky .05 .01
❑ 192 Mark Stock .05 .01
❑ 193 Sacks Leaders .05 .01
❑ 194 Leonard Smith .05 .01
❑ 195 Darryl Talley .05 .01
❑ 196 Mark Kelso .05 .01
❑ 197 Kent Hull .05 .01
❑ 198 Nate Odomes RC .10 .02
❑ 199 Pete Metzelaars .05 .01
❑ 200 Don Beebe .10 .02
❑ 201 Ray Bentley .05 .01
❑ 202 Steve Tasker .10 .02
❑ 203 Scott Norwood .05 .01
❑ 204 Andre Reed .25 .08
❑ 205 Bruce Smith .25 .08
❑ 206 Thurman Thomas .25 .08
❑ 207 Jim Kelly .25 .08
❑ 208 Cornelius Bennett .10 .02
❑ 209 Shane Conlan .05 .01
❑ 210 Larry Kinnebrew .05 .01
❑ 211 Jeff Alm RC .05 .01
❑ 212 Robert Lyles .05 .01
❑ 213 Bubba McDowell .05 .01
❑ 214 Mike Munchak .10 .02
❑ 215 Bruce Matthews .10 .02
❑ 216 Warren Moon .25 .08
❑ 217 Drew Hill .05 .01
❑ 218 Ray Childress .05 .01
❑ 219 Steve Brown .05 .01
❑ 220 Alonzo Highsmith .05 .01
❑ 221 Allen Pinkett .05 .01
❑ 222 Sean Jones .10 .02
❑ 223 Johnny Meads .05 .01
❑ 224 John Grimsley .05 .01
❑ 225 Haywood Jeffires RC .25 .08
❑ 226 Curtis Duncan .05 .01
❑ 227 Greg Montgomery RC .05 .01
❑ 228 Ernest Givins .10 .02
❑ 229 Joe Montana/B.Esiason LL .30 .10
❑ 230 Robert Massey .05 .01
❑ 231 John Fourcade .05 .01
❑ 232 Dalton Hilliard .05 .01
❑ 233 Vaughan Johnson .05 .01
❑ 234 Hoby Brenner .05 .01
❑ 235 Pat Swilling .10 .02
❑ 236 Kevin Haverdink .05 .01
❑ 237 Bobby Hebert .05 .01
❑ 238 Sam Mills .10 .02
❑ 239 Eric Martin .05 .01
❑ 240 Lonzell Hill .05 .01
❑ 241 Steve Trapilo .05 .01
❑ 242 Rickey Jackson .10 .02
❑ 243 Craig Heyward .10 .02
❑ 244 Rueben Mayes .05 .01
❑ 245 Morten Andersen .05 .01
❑ 246 Percy Snow RC .05 .01
❑ 247 Pete Mandley .05 .01
❑ 248 Derrick Thomas .25 .08
❑ 249 Dan Saleaumua .05 .01
❑ 250 Todd McNair RC .05 .01
❑ 251 Leonard Griffin .05 .01
❑ 252 Jonathan Hayes .05 .01
❑ 253 Christian Okoye .05 .01
❑ 254 Albert Lewis .05 .01
❑ 255 Nick Lowery .05 .01
❑ 256 Kevin Ross .05 .01
❑ 257 Steve DeBerg UER .05 .01
❑ 258 Stephone Paige .05 .01
❑ 259 James Saxon RC .05 .01
❑ 260 Herman Heard .05 .01
❑ 261 Deron Cherry .05 .01
❑ 262 Dino Hackett .05 .01
❑ 263 Neil Smith .25 .08
❑ 264 Steve Pelluer .05 .01
❑ 265 Eric Thomas .05 .01
❑ 266 Eric Ball .05 .01
❑ 267 Leon White .05 .01
❑ 268 Tim Krumrie .05 .01
❑ 269 Jason Buck .05 .01
❑ 270 Boomer Esiason .10 .02
❑ 271 Carl Zander .05 .01
❑ 272 Eddie Brown .05 .01
❑ 273 David Fulcher .05 .01
❑ 274 Tim McGee .05 .01
❑ 275 James Brooks .10 .02
❑ 276 Rickey Dixon RC .05 .01
❑ 277 Ickey Woods .05 .01
❑ 278 Anthony Munoz .10 .02
❑ 279 Rodney Holman .05 .01
❑ 280 Mike Alexander .05 .01
❑ 281 Mervyn Fernandez .05 .01
❑ 282 Steve Wisniewski .10 .02
❑ 283 Steve Smith .05 .01
❑ 284 Howie Long .25 .08
❑ 285 Bo Jackson .30 .10
❑ 286 Mike Dyal .05 .01
❑ 287 Thomas Benson .05 .01
❑ 288 Willie Gault .10 .02
❑ 289 Marcus Allen .25 .08
❑ 290 Greg Townsend .05 .01
❑ 291 Steve Beuerlein .10 .02
❑ 292 Scott Davis .05 .01
❑ 293 Eddie Anderson RC .05 .01
❑ 294 Terry McDaniel .05 .01
❑ 295 Tim Brown .25 .08
❑ 296 Bob Golic .05 .01
❑ 297 Jeff Jaeger RC .05 .01
❑ 298 Jeff George RC .50 .20
❑ 299 Chip Banks .05 .01
❑ 300 Andre Rison UER .25 .08
❑ 301 Rohn Stark .05 .01
❑ 302 Keith Taylor .05 .01
❑ 303 Jack Trudeau .05 .01
❑ 304 Chris Hinton .05 .01
❑ 305 Ray Donaldson .05 .01
❑ 306 Jeff Herrod RC .05 .01
❑ 307 Clarence Verdin .05 .01
❑ 308 Jon Hand .05 .01
❑ 309 Bill Brooks .05 .01
❑ 310 Albert Bentley .05 .01
❑ 311 Mike Prior .05 .01
❑ 312 Pat Beach .05 .01
❑ 313 Eugene Daniel .05 .01
❑ 314 Duane Bickett .05 .01
❑ 315 Dean Biasucci .05 .01
❑ 316 Richmond Webb RC .05 .01
❑ 317 Jeff Cross .05 .01
❑ 318 Louis Oliver .05 .01
❑ 319 Sammie Smith .05 .01
❑ 320 Pete Stoyanovich .05 .01
❑ 321 John Offerdahl .05 .01
❑ 322 Ferrell Edmunds .05 .01
❑ 323 Dan Marino 1.25 .50
❑ 324 Andre Brown .05 .01
❑ 325 Reggie Roby .05 .01
❑ 326 Jarvis Williams .05 .01
❑ 327 Roy Foster .05 .01
❑ 328 Mark Clayton .10 .02
❑ 329 Brian Sochia .05 .01
❑ 330 Mark Duper .10 .02
❑ 331 T.J. Turner .05 .01
❑ 332 Jeff Uhlenhake .05 .01
❑ 333 Jim C.Jensen .05 .01
❑ 334 Cortez Kennedy RC .25 .08
❑ 335 Andy Heck .05 .01
❑ 336 Rufus Porter .05 .01
❑ 337 Brian Blades .10 .02
❑ 338 Dave Krieg .10 .02
❑ 339 John L. Williams .05 .01
❑ 340 David Wyman .05 .01
❑ 341 Paul Skansi RC .05 .01
❑ 342 Eugene Robinson .05 .01
❑ 343 Joe Nash .05 .01
❑ 344 Jacob Green .05 .01
❑ 345 Jeff Bryant .05 .01
❑ 346 Ruben Rodriguez .05 .01
❑ 347 Norm Johnson .05 .01
❑ 348 Darren Comeaux .05 .01
❑ 349 Andre Ware RC .10 .02
❑ 350 Richard Johnson .05 .01
❑ 351 Rodney Peete .10 .02
❑ 352 Barry Sanders 1.25 .50
❑ 353 Chris Spielman .25 .08
❑ 354 Eddie Murray .05 .01
❑ 355 Jerry Ball .05 .01
❑ 356 Mel Gray .10 .02

Card	Price 1	Price 2
❑ 357 Eric Williams RC	.05	.01
❑ 358 Robert Clark RC	.05	.01
❑ 359 Jason Phillips	.05	.01
❑ 360 Terry Taylor RC	.05	.01
❑ 361 Bennie Blades	.05	.01
❑ 362 Michael Cofer	.05	.01
❑ 363 Jim Arnold	.05	.01
❑ 364 Marc Spindler RC	.05	.01
❑ 365 Jim Covert	.05	.01
❑ 366 Jim Harbaugh	.25	.08
❑ 367 Neal Anderson	.10	.02
❑ 368 Mike Singletary	.10	.02
❑ 369 John Roper	.05	.01
❑ 370 Steve McMichael	.10	.02
❑ 371 Dennis Gentry	.05	.01
❑ 372 Brad Muster	.05	.01
❑ 373 Ron Morris	.05	.01
❑ 374 James Thornton	.05	.01
❑ 375 Kevin Butler	.05	.01
❑ 376 Richard Dent	.10	.02
❑ 377 Dan Hampton	.10	.02
❑ 378 Jay Hilgenberg	.05	.01
❑ 379 Donnell Woolford	.05	.01
❑ 380 Trace Armstrong	.05	.01
❑ 381 Junior Seau RC	1.25	.50
❑ 382 Rod Bernstine	.05	.01
❑ 383 Marion Butts	.10	.02
❑ 384 Burt Grossman	.05	.01
❑ 385 Darrin Nelson	.05	.01
❑ 386 Leslie O'Neal	.10	.02
❑ 387 Billy Joe Tolliver	.05	.01
❑ 388 Courtney Hall	.05	.01
❑ 389 Lee Williams	.05	.01
❑ 390 Anthony Miller	.25	.08
❑ 391 Gill Byrd	.05	.01
❑ 392 Wayne Walker WR	.05	.01
❑ 393 Billy Ray Smith	.05	.01
❑ 394 Vencie Glenn	.05	.01
❑ 395 Tim Spencer	.05	.01
❑ 396 Gary Plummer	.05	.01
❑ 397 Arthur Cox	.05	.01
❑ 398 Jamie Holland	.05	.01
❑ 399 Keith McCants RC	.05	.01
❑ 400 Kevin Murphy	.05	.01
❑ 401 Danny Peebles	.05	.01
❑ 402 Mark Robinson	.05	.01
❑ 403 Broderick Thomas	.05	.01
❑ 404 Ron Hall	.05	.01
❑ 405 Mark Carrier WR	.25	.08
❑ 406 Paul Gruber	.05	.01
❑ 407 Vinny Testaverde	.10	.02
❑ 408 Bruce Hill	.05	.01
❑ 409 Lars Tate	.05	.01
❑ 410 Harry Hamilton	.05	.01
❑ 411 Ricky Reynolds	.05	.01
❑ 412 Donald Igwebuike	.05	.01
❑ 413 Reuben Davis	.05	.01
❑ 414 William Howard	.05	.01
❑ 415 Winston Moss RC	.05	.01
❑ 416 Chris Singleton RC	.05	.01
❑ 417 Hart Lee Dykes	.05	.01
❑ 418 Steve Grogan	.10	.02
❑ 419 Bruce Armstrong	.05	.01
❑ 420 Robert Perryman	.05	.01
❑ 421 Andre Tippett	.05	.01
❑ 422 Sammy Martin	.05	.01
❑ 423 Stanley Morgan	.05	.01
❑ 424 Cedric Jones	.05	.01
❑ 425 Sean Farrell	.05	.01
❑ 426 Marc Wilson	.05	.01
❑ 427 John Stephens	.05	.01
❑ 428 Eric Sievers RC	.05	.01
❑ 429 Maurice Hurst RC	.05	.01
❑ 430 Johnny Rembert	.05	.01
❑ 431 Jerry Rice/Andre Reed LL	.30	.10
❑ 432 Eric Hill	.05	.01
❑ 433 Gary Hogeboom	.05	.01
❑ 434 Timm Rosenbach UER	.05	.01
❑ 435 Tim McDonald	.05	.01
❑ 436 Rich Camarillo	.05	.01
❑ 437 Luis Sharpe	.05	.01
❑ 438 J.T. Smith	.05	.01
❑ 439 Roy Green	.10	.02
❑ 440 Ernie Jones RC	.05	.01
❑ 441 Robert Awalt	.05	.01
❑ 442 Vai Sikahema	.05	.01
❑ 443 Joe Wolf	.05	.01
❑ 444 Stump Mitchell	.05	.01
❑ 445 David Galloway	.05	.01
❑ 446 Ron Wolfley	.05	.01
❑ 447 Freddie Joe Nunn	.05	.01
❑ 448 Blair Thomas RC	.10	.02
❑ 449 Jeff Lageman	.05	.01
❑ 450 Tony Eason	.05	.01
❑ 451 Erik McMillan	.05	.01
❑ 452 Jim Sweeney	.05	.01
❑ 453 Ken O'Brien	.05	.01
❑ 454 Johnny Hector	.05	.01
❑ 455 Jo Jo Townsell	.05	.01
❑ 456 Roger Vick	.05	.01
❑ 457 James Hasty	.05	.01
❑ 458 Dennis Byrd RC	.10	.02
❑ 459 Ron Stallworth	.05	.01
❑ 460 Mickey Shuler	.05	.01
❑ 461 Bobby Humphery	.05	.01
❑ 462 Kyle Clifton	.05	.01
❑ 463 Al Toon	.10	.02
❑ 464 Freeman McNeil	.05	.01
❑ 465 Pat Leahy	.05	.01
❑ 466 Scott Case	.05	.01
❑ 467 Shawn Collins	.05	.01
❑ 468 Floyd Dixon	.05	.01
❑ 469 Deion Sanders	.50	.20
❑ 470 Tony Casillas	.05	.01
❑ 471 Michael Haynes RC	.25	.08
❑ 472 Chris Miller	.25	.08
❑ 473 John Settle	.05	.01
❑ 474 Aundray Bruce	.05	.01
❑ 475 Gene Lang	.05	.01
❑ 476 Tim Gordon RC	.05	.01
❑ 477 Scott Fulhage	.05	.01
❑ 478 Bill Fralic	.05	.01
❑ 479 Jessie Tuggle RC	.05	.01
❑ 480 Marcus Cotton	.05	.01
❑ 481 Steve Walsh	.10	.02
❑ 482 Troy Aikman	.75	.30
❑ 483 Ray Horton	.05	.01
❑ 484 Tony Tolbert RC	.10	.02
❑ 485 Steve Folsom	.05	.01
❑ 486 Ken Norton Jr. RC	.25	.08
❑ 487 Kelvin Martin RC	.05	.01
❑ 488 Jack Del Rio	.10	.02
❑ 489 Daryl Johnston RC	1.00	.40
❑ 490 Bill Bates	.10	.02
❑ 491 Jim Jeffcoat	.05	.01
❑ 492 Vince Albritton	.05	.01
❑ 493 Eugene Lockhart	.05	.01
❑ 494 Mike Saxon	.05	.01
❑ 495 James Dixon	.05	.01
❑ 496 Willie Broughton	.05	.01
❑ 497 Checklist 1-132	.05	.01
❑ 498 Checklist 133-264	.05	.01
❑ 499 Checklist 265-396	.05	.01
❑ 500 Checklist 397-528	.05	.01
❑ 501 Bears Team	.10	.02
❑ 502 Bengals Team	.05	.01
❑ 503 Bills Team	.05	.01
❑ 504 Broncos Team	.05	.01
❑ 505 Browns Team	.05	.01
❑ 506 Buccaneers Team	.05	.01
❑ 507 Cardinals Team	.05	.01
❑ 508 Chargers Team	.05	.01
❑ 509 Chiefs Team	.05	.01
❑ 510 Colts Team	.05	.01
❑ 511 Cowboys TL/Aikman	.30	.10
❑ 512 Dolphins Team	.05	.01
❑ 513 Eagles Team	.05	.01
❑ 514 Falcons Team	.05	.01
❑ 515 49ers TL/Montana/Craig	.30	.10
❑ 516 Giants Team	.05	.01
❑ 517 Jets Team	.05	.01
❑ 518 Lions Team	.05	.01
❑ 519 Oilers TL/Moon	.10	.02
❑ 520 Packers Team	.05	.01
❑ 521 Patriots Team	.05	.01
❑ 522 Raiders TL/Bo Jackson	.10	.02
❑ 523 Rams Team	.05	.01
❑ 524 Redskins Team	.05	.01
❑ 525 Saints Team	.05	.01
❑ 526 Seahawks Team	.05	.01
❑ 527 Steelers Team	.05	.01
❑ 528 Vikings Team	.05	.01

1990 Topps Traded

Card	Price 1	Price 2
❑ COMP.FACT.SET (132)	15.00	6.00
❑ 1T Gerald McNeil	.05	.01
❑ 2T Andre Rison	.25	.08
❑ 3T Steve Walsh	.25	.08
❑ 4T Lorenzo White	.10	.02
❑ 5T Max Montoya	.05	.01
❑ 6T William Roberts RC	.05	.01
❑ 7T Alonzo Highsmith	.05	.01
❑ 8T Chris Hinton	.10	.02
❑ 9T Stanley Morgan	.10	.02
❑ 10T Mickey Shuler	.05	.01
❑ 11T Bobby Humphery	.05	.01
❑ 12T Gary Anderson RB	.05	.01
❑ 13T Mike Tomczak	.10	.02
❑ 14T Anthony Pleasant RC	.10	.02
❑ 15T Walter Stanley	.05	.01
❑ 16T Greg Bell	.05	.01
❑ 17T Tony Martin RC	.75	.30
❑ 18T Terry Kinard	.05	.01
❑ 19T Cris Carter	.50	.20
❑ 20T James Wilder	.05	.01
❑ 21T Jerry Kauric	.05	.01
❑ 22T Irving Fryar	.25	.08
❑ 23T Ken Harvey RC	.25	.08
❑ 24T James Williams DB RC	.05	.01
❑ 25T Ron Cox RC	.05	.01
❑ 26T Andre Ware	.25	.08
❑ 27T Emmitt Smith RC	12.00	5.00
❑ 28T Junior Seau	.75	.30
❑ 29T Mark Carrier RC DB	.25	.08
❑ 30T Rodney Hampton	.25	.08
❑ 31T Rob Moore RC	.50	.20
❑ 32T Bern Brostek RC	.05	.01
❑ 33T Dexter Carter	.10	.02
❑ 34T Blair Thomas	.10	.02
❑ 35T Harold Green RC	.25	.08
❑ 36T Darrell Thompson	.05	.01
❑ 37T Eric Green RC	.25	.08
❑ 38T Renaldo Turnbull RC	.25	.08
❑ 39T Leroy Hoard RC	.25	.08
❑ 40T Anthony Thompson RC	.10	.02
❑ 41T Jeff George	.25	.08
❑ 42T Alexander Wright RC	.05	.01
❑ 43T Richmond Webb	.05	.01
❑ 44T Cortez Kennedy	.25	.08
❑ 45T Ray Agnew RC	.05	.01
❑ 46T Percy Snow	.05	.01
❑ 47T Chris Singleton	.05	.01
❑ 48T James Francis RC	.10	.02
❑ 49T Tony Bennett	.10	.02
❑ 50T Reggie Cobb RC	.10	.02
❑ 51T Barry Foster	.25	.08
❑ 52T Ben Smith	.05	.01
❑ 53T Anthony Smith RC	.25	.08
❑ 54T Steve Christie RC	.05	.01
❑ 55T Johnny Bailey RC	.10	.02
❑ 56T Alan Grant RC	.05	.01
❑ 57T Eric Floyd RC	.05	.01
❑ 58T Robert Blackmon RC	.05	.01
❑ 59T Brent Williams	.05	.01
❑ 60T Raymond Clayborn	.05	.01
❑ 61T Dave Duerson	.05	.01
❑ 62T Derrick Fenner RC	.10	.02
❑ 63T Ken Willis	.05	.01
❑ 64T Brad Baxter RC	.10	.02
❑ 65T Tony Paige	.05	.01
❑ 66T Jay Schroeder	.05	.01
❑ 67T Jim Breech	.05	.01

Card	Player	Mint	Nr Mt
❑ 68T	Barry Word RC	.10	.02
❑ 69T	Anthony Dilweg FTC	.05	.01
❑ 70T	Rich Gannon RC	2.00	.75
❑ 71T	Stan Humphries RC	.25	.08
❑ 72T	Jay Novacek	.25	.08
❑ 73T	Tommy Kane RC	.05	.01
❑ 74T	Everson Walls	.05	.01
❑ 75T	Mike Rozier	.10	.02
❑ 76T	Robb Thomas	.05	.01
❑ 77T	Terance Mathis RC	.75	.30
❑ 78T	LeRoy Irvin	.05	.01
❑ 79T	Jeff Donaldson	.05	.01
❑ 80T	Ethan Horton RC	.10	.02
❑ 81T	J.B.Brown RC	.05	.01
❑ 82T	Joe Kelly	.05	.01
❑ 83T	John Carney RC	.05	.01
❑ 84T	Dan Stryzinski RC	.05	.01
❑ 85T	John Kidd	.05	.01
❑ 86T	Al Smith	.10	.02
❑ 87T	Travis McNeal	.05	.01
❑ 88T	Reyna Thompson RC	.05	.01
❑ 89T	Rick Donnelly	.05	.01
❑ 90T	Marv Cook RC	.10	.02
❑ 91T	Mike Farr RC	.05	.01
❑ 92T	Daniel Stubbs	.05	.01
❑ 93T	Jeff Campbell RC	.05	.01
❑ 94T	Tim McKyer	.05	.01
❑ 95T	Ian Beckles RC	.05	.01
❑ 96T	Lemuel Stinson	.05	.01
❑ 97T	Frank Cornish	.05	.01
❑ 98T	Riki Ellison	.05	.01
❑ 99T	Jamie Mueller RC	.05	.01
❑ 100T	Brian Hansen	.05	.01
❑ 101T	Warren Powers RC	.05	.01
❑ 102T	Howard Cross RC	.05	.01
❑ 103T	Tim Grunhard RC	.05	.01
❑ 104T	Johnny Johnson RC	.25	.08
❑ 105T	Calvin Williams RC	.25	.08
❑ 106T	Keith McCants	.05	.01
❑ 107T	Lamar Lathon RC	.10	.02
❑ 108T	Steve Broussard RC	.10	.02
❑ 109T	Glenn Parker RC	.05	.01
❑ 110T	Alton Montgomery RC	.05	.01
❑ 111T	Jim McMahon	.10	.02
❑ 112T	Aaron Wallace RC	.05	.01
❑ 113T	Keith Sims RC	.05	.01
❑ 114T	Ervin Randle	.05	.01
❑ 115T	Walter Wilson	.05	.01
❑ 116T	Terry Wooden RC	.05	.01
❑ 117T	Bernard Clark	.05	.01
❑ 118T	Tony Stargell RC	.05	.01
❑ 119T	Jimmie Jones RC	.05	.01
❑ 120T	Andre Collins RC	.10	.02
❑ 121T	Ricky Proehl RC	.25	.08
❑ 122T	Darion Conner RC	.10	.02
❑ 123T	Jeff Rutledge	.05	.01
❑ 124T	Heath Sherman RC	.10	.02
❑ 125T	Tommie Agee RC	.05	.01
❑ 126T	Tory Epps RC	.05	.01
❑ 127T	Tommy Hodson RC	.05	.01
❑ 128T	Jessie Hester RC	.05	.01
❑ 129T	Alfred Oglesby RC	.05	.01
❑ 130T	Chris Chandler	.25	.08
❑ 131T	Fred Barnett RC	.25	.08
❑ 132T	Checklist 1-132	.05	.01

1991 Topps

	Mint	Nr Mt
❑ COMPLETE SET (660)	20.00	10.00
❑ COMP.FACT.SET (660)	30.00	15.00

Card	Player	Mint	Nr Mt
❑ 1	Super Bowl XXV	.05	.01
❑ 2	Roger Craig HL	.10	.02
❑ 3	Derrick Thomas HL	.10	.02
❑ 4	Pete Stoyanovich HL	.05	.01
❑ 5	Ottis Anderson HL	.10	.02
❑ 6	Jerry Rice HL	.50	.20
❑ 7	Warren Moon HL	.10	.02
❑ 8	Warren Moon/J.Everett LL	.10	.02
❑ 9	B.Sanders/T.Thomas LL	.40	.15
❑ 10	J.Rice/H.Jeffires LL	.30	.10
❑ 11	M.Carrier DB/R.Johnson DB LL	.05	.01
❑ 12	Derrick Thomas/C.Haley L	.10	.02
❑ 13	Jumbo Elliott	.05	.01
❑ 14	Leonard Marshall	.05	.01
❑ 15	William Roberts	.05	.01
❑ 16	Lawrence Taylor	.25	.08
❑ 17	Mark Ingram	.10	.02
❑ 18	Rodney Hampton	.25	.08
❑ 19	Carl Banks	.05	.01
❑ 20	Ottis Anderson	.10	.02
❑ 21	Mark Collins	.05	.01
❑ 22	Pepper Johnson	.05	.01
❑ 23	Dave Meggett	.10	.02
❑ 24	Reyna Thompson	.05	.01
❑ 25	Stephen Baker	.05	.01
❑ 26	Mike Fox	.05	.01
❑ 27	Maurice Carthon UER	.05	.01
❑ 28	Jeff Hostetler	.25	.08
❑ 29	Greg Jackson RC	.05	.01
❑ 30	Sean Landeta	.05	.01
❑ 31	Bart Oates	.05	.01
❑ 32	Phil Simms	.10	.02
❑ 33	Erik Howard	.05	.01
❑ 34	Myron Guyton	.05	.01
❑ 35	Mark Bavaro	.05	.01
❑ 36	Jarrod Bunch RC	.05	.01
❑ 37	Will Wolford	.05	.01
❑ 38	Ray Bentley	.05	.01
❑ 39	Nate Odomes	.05	.01
❑ 40	Scott Norwood	.05	.01
❑ 41	Darryl Talley	.05	.01
❑ 42	Carwell Gardner	.05	.01
❑ 43	James Lofton	.10	.02
❑ 44	Shane Conlan	.05	.01
❑ 45	Steve Tasker	.10	.02
❑ 46	James Williams	.05	.01
❑ 47	Kent Hull	.05	.01
❑ 48	Al Edwards	.05	.01
❑ 49	Frank Reich	.10	.02
❑ 50	Leon Seals	.05	.01
❑ 51	Keith McKeller	.05	.01
❑ 52	Thurman Thomas	.25	.08
❑ 53	Leonard Smith	.05	.01
❑ 54	Andre Reed	.10	.02
❑ 55	Kenneth Davis	.05	.01
❑ 56	Jeff Wright RC	.05	.01
❑ 57	Jamie Mueller	.05	.01
❑ 58	Jim Ritcher	.05	.01
❑ 59	Bruce Smith	.25	.08
❑ 60	Ted Washington RC	.05	.01
❑ 61	Guy McIntyre	.05	.01
❑ 62	Michael Carter	.05	.01
❑ 63	Pierce Holt	.05	.01
❑ 64	Darryl Pollard	.05	.01
❑ 65	Mike Sherrard	.05	.01
❑ 66	Dexter Carter	.05	.01
❑ 67	Bubba Paris	.05	.01
❑ 68	Harry Sydney	.05	.01
❑ 69	Tom Rathman	.05	.01
❑ 70	Jesse Sapolu	.05	.01
❑ 71	Mike Cofer	.05	.01
❑ 72	Keith DeLong	.05	.01
❑ 73	Joe Montana	1.25	.50
❑ 74	Bill Romanowski	.05	.01
❑ 75	John Taylor	.10	.02
❑ 76	Brent Jones	.25	.08
❑ 77	Harris Barton	.05	.01
❑ 78	Charles Haley	.10	.02
❑ 79	Eric Davis	.05	.01
❑ 80	Kevin Fagan	.05	.01
❑ 81	Jerry Rice	.75	.30
❑ 82	Dave Waymer	.05	.01
❑ 83	Todd Marinovich RC	.05	.01
❑ 84	Steve Smith	.05	.01
❑ 85	Tim Brown	.25	.08
❑ 86	Ethan Horton	.05	.01
❑ 87	Marcus Allen	.25	.08
❑ 88	Terry McDaniel	.05	.01
❑ 89	Thomas Benson	.05	.01
❑ 90	Roger Craig	.10	.02
❑ 91	Don Mosebar	.05	.01
❑ 92	Aaron Wallace	.05	.01
❑ 93	Eddie Anderson	.05	.01
❑ 94	Willie Gault	.10	.02
❑ 95	Howie Long	.25	.08
❑ 96	Jay Schroeder	.05	.01
❑ 97	Ronnie Lott	.10	.02
❑ 98	Bob Golic	.05	.01
❑ 99	Bo Jackson	.30	.10
❑ 100	Max Montoya	.05	.01
❑ 101	Scott Davis	.05	.01
❑ 102	Greg Townsend	.05	.01
❑ 103	Garry Lewis	.05	.01
❑ 104	Mervyn Fernandez	.05	.01
❑ 105	Steve Wisniewski UER	.05	.01
❑ 106	Jeff Jaeger	.05	.01
❑ 107	Nick Bell RC	.05	.01
❑ 108	Mark Dennis RC	.05	.01
❑ 109	Jarvis Williams	.05	.01
❑ 110	Mark Clayton	.10	.02
❑ 111	Harry Galbreath	.05	.01
❑ 112	Dan Marino	1.25	.50
❑ 113	Louis Oliver	.05	.01
❑ 114	Pete Stoyanovich	.05	.01
❑ 115	Ferrell Edmunds	.05	.01
❑ 116	Jeff Cross	.05	.01
❑ 117	Richmond Webb	.05	.01
❑ 118	Jim C. Jensen	.05	.01
❑ 119	Keith Sims	.05	.01
❑ 120	Mark Duper	.10	.02
❑ 121	Shawn Lee RC	.05	.01
❑ 122	Reggie Roby	.05	.01
❑ 123	Jeff Uhlenhake	.05	.01
❑ 124	Sammie Smith	.05	.01
❑ 125	John Offerdahl	.05	.01
❑ 126	Hugh Green	.05	.01
❑ 127	Tony Paige	.05	.01
❑ 128	David Griggs	.05	.01
❑ 129	J.B. Brown	.05	.01
❑ 130	Harvey Williams RC	.25	.08
❑ 131	John Alt	.05	.01
❑ 132	Albert Lewis	.05	.01
❑ 133	Robb Thomas	.05	.01
❑ 134	Neil Smith	.25	.08
❑ 135	Stephone Paige	.05	.01
❑ 136	Nick Lowery	.05	.01
❑ 137	Steve DeBerg	.05	.01
❑ 138	Rich Baldinger RC	.05	.01
❑ 139	Percy Snow	.05	.01
❑ 140	Kevin Porter	.05	.01
❑ 141	Chris Martin	.05	.01
❑ 142	Deron Cherry	.05	.01
❑ 143	Derrick Thomas	.25	.08
❑ 144	Tim Grunhard	.05	.01
❑ 145	Todd McNair	.05	.01
❑ 146	David Szott	.05	.01
❑ 147	Dan Saleaumua	.05	.01
❑ 148	Jonathan Hayes	.05	.01
❑ 149	Christian Okoye	.05	.01
❑ 150	Dino Hackett	.05	.01
❑ 151	Bryan Barker RC	.05	.01
❑ 152	Kevin Ross	.05	.01
❑ 153	Barry Word	.05	.01
❑ 154	Stan Thomas	.05	.01
❑ 155	Brad Muster	.05	.01
❑ 156	Donnell Woolford	.05	.01
❑ 157	Neal Anderson	.10	.02
❑ 158	Jim Covert	.05	.01
❑ 159	Jim Harbaugh	.25	.08
❑ 160	Shaun Gayle	.05	.01
❑ 161	William Perry	.10	.02
❑ 162	Ron Morris	.05	.01
❑ 163	Mark Bortz	.05	.01
❑ 164	James Thornton	.05	.01
❑ 165	Ron Rivera	.05	.01
❑ 166	Kevin Butler	.05	.01
❑ 167	Jay Hilgenberg	.05	.01
❑ 168	Peter Tom Willis	.05	.01
❑ 169	Johnny Bailey	.05	.01
❑ 170	Ron Cox	.05	.01
❑ 171	Keith Van Horne	.05	.01
❑ 172	Mark Carrier DB	.10	.02
❑ 173	Richard Dent	.10	.02
❑ 174	Wendell Davis	.05	.01

❑ 175 Trace Armstrong .05 .01
❑ 176 Mike Singletary .10 .02
❑ 177 Chris Zorich RC .25 .08
❑ 178 Gerald Riggs .05 .01
❑ 179 Jeff Bostic .05 .01
❑ 180 Kurt Gouveia RC .05 .01
❑ 181 Stan Humphries .25 .08
❑ 182 Chip Lohmiller .05 .01
❑ 183 Raleigh McKenzie RC .05 .01
❑ 184 Alvin Walton .05 .01
❑ 185 Earnest Byner .05 .01
❑ 186 Markus Koch .05 .01
❑ 187 Art Monk .10 .02
❑ 188 Ed Simmons .05 .01
❑ 189 Bobby Wilson RC .05 .01
❑ 190 Charles Mann .05 .01
❑ 191 Darrell Green .05 .01
❑ 192 Mark Rypien .10 .02
❑ 193 Ricky Sanders .05 .01
❑ 194 Jim Lachey .05 .01
❑ 195 Martin Mayhew .05 .01
❑ 196 Gary Clark .25 .08
❑ 197 Wilber Marshall .05 .01
❑ 198 Darryl Grant .05 .01
❑ 199 Don Warren .05 .01
❑ 200 Ricky Ervins RC UER .10 .02
❑ 201 Eric Allen .05 .01
❑ 202 Anthony Toney .05 .01
❑ 203 Ben Smith UER .05 .01
❑ 204 David Alexander .05 .01
❑ 205 Jerome Brown .05 .01
❑ 206 Mike Golic .05 .01
❑ 207 Roger Ruzek .05 .01
❑ 208 Andre Waters .05 .01
❑ 209 Fred Barnett .25 .08
❑ 210 Randall Cunningham .25 .08
❑ 211 Mike Schad .05 .01
❑ 212 Reggie White .25 .08
❑ 213 Mike Bellamy .05 .01
❑ 214 Jeff Feagles RC .05 .01
❑ 215 Wes Hopkins .05 .01
❑ 216 Clyde Simmons .05 .01
❑ 217 Keith Byars .05 .01
❑ 218 Seth Joyner .10 .02
❑ 219 Byron Evans .05 .01
❑ 220 Keith Jackson .10 .02
❑ 221 Calvin Williams .10 .02
❑ 222 Mike Dumas RC .05 .01
❑ 223 Ray Childress .05 .01
❑ 224 Ernest Givins .10 .02
❑ 225 Lamar Lathon .05 .01
❑ 226 Greg Montgomery .05 .01
❑ 227 Mike Munchak .10 .02
❑ 228 Al Smith .05 .01
❑ 229 Bubba McDowell .05 .01
❑ 230 Haywood Jeffires .10 .02
❑ 231 Drew Hill .05 .01
❑ 232 William Fuller .10 .02
❑ 233 Warren Moon .25 .08
❑ 234 Doug Smith DT RC .10 .02
❑ 235 Cris Dishman RC .05 .01
❑ 236 Teddy Garcia RC .05 .01
❑ 237 Richard Johnson CB RC .05 .01
❑ 238 Bruce Matthews .10 .02
❑ 239 Gerald McNeil .05 .01
❑ 240 Johnny Meads .05 .01
❑ 241 Curtis Duncan .05 .01
❑ 242 Sean Jones .10 .02
❑ 243 Lorenzo White .05 .01
❑ 244 Rob Carpenter RC WR .05 .01
❑ 245 Bruce Reimers .05 .01
❑ 246 Ickey Woods .05 .01
❑ 247 Lewis Billups .05 .01
❑ 248 Boomer Esiason .10 .02
❑ 249 Tim Krumrie .05 .01
❑ 250 David Fulcher .05 .01
❑ 251 Jim Breech .05 .01
❑ 252 Mitchell Price RC .05 .01
❑ 253 Carl Zander .05 .01
❑ 254 Barney Bussey RC .05 .01
❑ 255 Leon White .05 .01
❑ 256 Eddie Brown .05 .01
❑ 257 James Francis .05 .01
❑ 258 Harold Green .10 .02
❑ 259 Anthony Munoz .10 .02
❑ 260 James Brooks .10 .02
❑ 261 Kevin Walker RC UER .05 .01
❑ 262 Bruce Kozerski .05 .01
❑ 263 David Grant .05 .01
❑ 264 Tim McGee .05 .01
❑ 265 Rodney Holman .05 .01
❑ 266 Dan McGwire RC .05 .01
❑ 267 Andy Heck .05 .01
❑ 268 Dave Krieg .10 .02
❑ 269 David Wyman .05 .01
❑ 270 Robert Blackmon .05 .01
❑ 271 Grant Feasel .05 .01
❑ 272 Patrick Hunter RC .05 .01
❑ 273 Travis McNeal .05 .01
❑ 274 John L. Williams .05 .01
❑ 275 Tony Woods .05 .01
❑ 276 Derrick Fenner .05 .01
❑ 277 Jacob Green .05 .01
❑ 278 Brian Blades .10 .02
❑ 279 Eugene Robinson .05 .01
❑ 280 Terry Wooden .05 .01
❑ 281 Jeff Bryant .05 .01
❑ 282 Norm Johnson .05 .01
❑ 283 Joe Nash UER .05 .01
❑ 284 Rick Donnelly .05 .01
❑ 285 Chris Warren .25 .08
❑ 286 Tommy Kane .05 .01
❑ 287 Cortez Kennedy .25 .08
❑ 288 Ernie Mills RC .10 .02
❑ 289 Dermontti Dawson .05 .01
❑ 290 Tunch Ilkin .05 .01
❑ 291 Tim Worley .05 .01
❑ 292 David Little .05 .01
❑ 293 Gary Anderson K .05 .01
❑ 294 Chris Calloway .05 .01
❑ 295 Carnell Lake .05 .01
❑ 296 Dan Stryzinski .05 .01
❑ 297 Rod Woodson .25 .08
❑ 298 John Jackson T RC .05 .01
❑ 299 Bubby Brister .05 .01
❑ 300 Thomas Everett .05 .01
❑ 301 Merril Hoge .05 .01
❑ 302 Eric Green .05 .01
❑ 303 Greg Lloyd .25 .08
❑ 304 Gerald Williams .05 .01
❑ 305 Bryan Hinkle .05 .01
❑ 306 Keith Willis .05 .01
❑ 307 Louis Lipps .05 .01
❑ 308 Donald Evans .05 .01
❑ 309 D.J. Johnson .05 .01
❑ 310 Wesley Carroll RC .05 .01
❑ 311 Eric Martin .05 .01
❑ 312 Brett Maxie .05 .01
❑ 313 Rickey Jackson .05 .01
❑ 314 Robert Massey .05 .01
❑ 315 Pat Swilling .10 .02
❑ 316 Morten Andersen .05 .01
❑ 317 Toi Cook RC .05 .01
❑ 318 Sam Mills .05 .01
❑ 319 Steve Walsh .05 .01
❑ 320 Tommy Barnhardt RC .05 .01
❑ 321 Vince Buck .05 .01
❑ 322 Joel Hilgenberg .05 .01
❑ 323 Rueben Mayes .05 .01
❑ 324 Renaldo Turnbull .05 .01
❑ 325 Brett Perriman .25 .08
❑ 326 Vaughan Johnson .05 .01
❑ 327 Gill Fenerty .05 .01
❑ 328 Stan Brock .05 .01
❑ 329 Dalton Hilliard .05 .01
❑ 330 Hoby Brenner .05 .01
❑ 331 Craig Heyward .10 .02
❑ 332 Jon Hand .05 .01
❑ 333 Duane Bickett .05 .01
❑ 334 Jessie Hester .05 .01
❑ 335 Rohn Stark .05 .01
❑ 336 Zefross Moss .05 .01
❑ 337 Bill Brooks .05 .01
❑ 338 Clarence Verdin .05 .01
❑ 339 Mike Prior .05 .01
❑ 340 Chip Banks .05 .01
❑ 341 Dean Biasucci .05 .01
❑ 342 Ray Donaldson .05 .01
❑ 343 Jeff Herrod .05 .01
❑ 344 Donnell Thompson .05 .01
❑ 345 Chris Goode .05 .01
❑ 346 Eugene Daniel .05 .01
❑ 347 Pat Beach .05 .01
❑ 348 Keith Taylor .05 .01
❑ 349 Jeff George .25 .08
❑ 350 Tony Siragusa RC .10 .02
❑ 351 Randy Dixon .05 .01
❑ 352 Albert Bentley .05 .01
❑ 353 Russell Maryland RC .25 .08
❑ 354 Mike Saxon .05 .01
❑ 355 Godfrey Myles RC UER .05 .01
❑ 356 Mark Stepnoski RC .10 .02
❑ 357 James Washington RC .05 .01
❑ 358 Jay Novacek .25 .08
❑ 359 Kelvin Martin .05 .01
❑ 360 Emmitt Smith UER 2.50 1.00
❑ 361 Jim Jeffcoat .05 .01
❑ 362 Alexander Wright .05 .01
❑ 363 James Dixon UER .05 .01
❑ 364 Alonzo Highsmith .05 .01
❑ 365 Daniel Stubbs .05 .01
❑ 366 Jack Del Rio .10 .02
❑ 367 Mark Tuinei RC .05 .01
❑ 368 Michael Irvin .25 .08
❑ 369 John Gesek RC .05 .01
❑ 370 Ken Willis .05 .01
❑ 371 Troy Aikman .75 .30
❑ 372 Jimmie Jones .05 .01
❑ 373 Nate Newton .10 .02
❑ 374 Issiac Holt .05 .01
❑ 375 Alvin Harper RC .25 .08
❑ 376 Todd Kalis .05 .01
❑ 377 Wade Wilson .10 .02
❑ 378 Joey Browner .05 .01
❑ 379 Chris Doleman .05 .01
❑ 380 Hassan Jones .05 .01
❑ 381 Henry Thomas .05 .01
❑ 382 Darrell Fullington .05 .01
❑ 383 Steve Jordan .05 .01
❑ 384 Gary Zimmerman .05 .01
❑ 385 Ray Berry .05 .01
❑ 386 Cris Carter .50 .20
❑ 387 Mike Merriweather .05 .01
❑ 388 Carl Lee .05 .01
❑ 389 Keith Millard .05 .01
❑ 390 Reggie Rutland .05 .01
❑ 391 Anthony Carter .10 .02
❑ 392 Mark Dusbabek .05 .01
❑ 393 Kirk Lowdermilk .05 .01
❑ 394 Al Noga UER .05 .01
❑ 395 Herschel Walker .10 .02
❑ 396 Randall McDaniel .05 .01
❑ 397 Herman Moore RC .25 .08
❑ 398 Eddie Murray .05 .01
❑ 399 Lomas Brown .05 .01
❑ 400 Marc Spindler .05 .01
❑ 401 Bennie Blades .05 .01
❑ 402 Kevin Glover .05 .01
❑ 403 Aubrey Matthews RC .05 .01
❑ 404 Michael Cofer .05 .01
❑ 405 Robert Clark .05 .01
❑ 406 Eric Andolsek .05 .01
❑ 407 William White .05 .01
❑ 408 Rodney Peete .10 .02
❑ 409 Mel Gray .10 .02
❑ 410 Jim Arnold .05 .01
❑ 411 Jeff Campbell .05 .01
❑ 412 Chris Spielman .10 .02
❑ 413 Jerry Ball .05 .01
❑ 414 Dan Owens .05 .01
❑ 415 Barry Sanders 1.25 .50
❑ 416 Andre Ware .10 .02
❑ 417 Stanley Richard RC .05 .01
❑ 418 Gill Byrd .05 .01
❑ 419 John Kidd .05 .01
❑ 420 Sam Seale .05 .01
❑ 421 Gary Plummer .05 .01
❑ 422 Anthony Miller .10 .02
❑ 423 Ronnie Harmon .05 .01
❑ 424 Frank Cornish .05 .01
❑ 425 Marion Butts .10 .02
❑ 426 Leo Goeas .05 .01
❑ 427 Junior Seau .25 .08
❑ 428 Courtney Hall .05 .01
❑ 429 Leslie O'Neal .10 .02
❑ 430 Martin Bayless .05 .01
❑ 431 John Carney .05 .01
❑ 432 Lee Williams .05 .01
❑ 433 Arthur Cox .05 .01
❑ 434 Burt Grossman .05 .01
❑ 435 Nate Lewis RC .05 .01

❑ 436	Rod Bernstine	.05	.01
❑ 437	Henry Rolling RC	.05	.01
❑ 438	Billy Joe Tolliver	.05	.01
❑ 439	Vinnie Clark RC	.05	.01
❑ 440	Brian Noble	.05	.01
❑ 441	Charles Wilson	.05	.01
❑ 442	Don Majkowski	.05	.01
❑ 443	Tim Harris	.05	.01
❑ 444	Scott Stephen RC	.05	.01
❑ 445	Perry Kemp	.05	.01
❑ 446	Darrell Thompson	.05	.01
❑ 447	Chris Jacke	.05	.01
❑ 448	Mark Murphy	.05	.01
❑ 449	Ed West	.05	.01
❑ 450	LeRoy Butler	.10	.02
❑ 451	Keith Woodside	.05	.01
❑ 452	Tony Bennett	.10	.02
❑ 453	Mark Lee	.05	.01
❑ 454	James Campen RC	.05	.01
❑ 455	Robert Brown	.05	.01
❑ 456	Sterling Sharpe	.25	.08
❑ 457A	T.Mandarich ERR Bronc.	2.50	1.25
❑ 457B	T.Mandarich COR Packers	.05	.01
❑ 458	Johnny Holland	.05	.01
❑ 459	Matt Brock RC	.05	.01
❑ 460A	Esera Tuaolo RC ERR	.05	.01
❑ 460B	Esera Tuaolo RC COR	.05	.01
❑ 461	Freeman McNeil	.05	.01
❑ 462	Terance Mathis UER 460	.25	.08
❑ 463	Rob Moore	.25	.08
❑ 464	Darrell Davis RC	.05	.01
❑ 465	Chris Burkett	.05	.01
❑ 466	Jeff Criswell	.05	.01
❑ 467	Tony Stargell	.05	.01
❑ 468	Ken O'Brien	.05	.01
❑ 469	Erik McMillan	.05	.01
❑ 470	Jeff Lageman UER	.05	.01
❑ 471	Pat Leahy	.05	.01
❑ 472	Dennis Byrd	.05	.01
❑ 473	Jim Sweeney	.05	.01
❑ 474	Brad Baxter	.05	.01
❑ 475	Joe Kelly	.05	.01
❑ 476	Al Toon	.10	.02
❑ 477	Joe Prokop	.05	.01
❑ 478	Mark Boyer	.05	.01
❑ 479	Kyle Clifton	.05	.01
❑ 480	James Hasty	.05	.01
❑ 481	Browning Nagle RC	.05	.01
❑ 482	Gary Anderson RB	.05	.01
❑ 483	Mark Carrier WR	.25	.08
❑ 484	Ricky Reynolds	.05	.01
❑ 485	Bruce Hill	.05	.01
❑ 486	Steve Christie	.05	.01
❑ 487	Paul Gruber	.05	.01
❑ 488	Jesse Anderson	.05	.01
❑ 489	Reggie Cobb	.05	.01
❑ 490	Harry Hamilton	.05	.01
❑ 491	Vinny Testaverde	.10	.02
❑ 492	Mark Royals RC	.05	.01
❑ 493	Keith McCants	.05	.01
❑ 494	Ron Hall	.05	.01
❑ 495	Ian Beckles	.05	.01
❑ 496	Mark Robinson	.05	.01
❑ 497	Reuben Davis	.05	.01
❑ 498	Wayne Haddix	.05	.01
❑ 499	Kevin Murphy	.05	.01
❑ 500	Eugene Marve	.05	.01
❑ 501	Broderick Thomas	.05	.01
❑ 502	Eric Swann RC UER	.25	.08
❑ 503	Ernie Jones	.05	.01
❑ 504	Rich Camarillo	.05	.01
❑ 505	Tim McDonald	.05	.01
❑ 506	Freddie Joe Nunn	.05	.01
❑ 507	Tim Jorden RC	.05	.01
❑ 508	Johnny Johnson	.05	.01
❑ 509	Eric Hill	.05	.01
❑ 510	Derek Kennard	.05	.01
❑ 511	Ricky Proehl	.05	.01
❑ 512	Bill Lewis	.05	.01
❑ 513	Roy Green	.05	.01
❑ 514	Anthony Bell	.05	.01
■ 515	Timm Rosenbach	.05	.01
❑ 516	Jim Wahler RC	.05	.01
❑ 517	Anthony Thompson	.05	.01
❑ 518	Ken Harvey	.10	.02
❑ 519	Luis Sharpe	.05	.01
❑ 520	Walter Reeves	.05	.01
❑ 521	Lonnie Young	.05	.01
❑ 522	Rod Saddler	.05	.01
❑ 523	Todd Lyght RC	.05	.01
❑ 524	Alvin Wright	.05	.01
❑ 525	Flipper Anderson	.05	.01
❑ 526	Jackie Slater	.05	.01
❑ 527	Damone Johnson RC	.05	.01
❑ 528	Cleveland Gary	.05	.01
❑ 529	Mike Piel	.05	.01
❑ 530	Buford McGee	.05	.01
❑ 531	Michael Stewart	.05	.01
❑ 532	Jim Everett	.10	.02
❑ 533	Mike Wilcher	.05	.01
❑ 534	Irv Pankey	.05	.01
❑ 535	Bern Brostek	.05	.01
❑ 536	Henry Ellard	.10	.02
❑ 537	Doug Smith	.05	.01
❑ 538	Larry Kelm	.05	.01
❑ 539	Pat Terrell	.05	.01
❑ 540	Tom Newberry	.05	.01
❑ 541	Jerry Gray	.05	.01
❑ 542	Kevin Greene	.10	.02
❑ 543	Duval Love RC	.05	.01
❑ 544	Frank Stams	.05	.01
❑ 545	Mike Croel RC	.05	.01
❑ 546	Mark Jackson	.05	.01
❑ 547	Greg Kragen	.05	.01
❑ 548	Karl Mecklenburg	.05	.01
❑ 549	Simon Fletcher	.05	.01
❑ 550	Bobby Humphrey	.05	.01
❑ 551	Ken Lanier	.05	.01
❑ 552	Vance Johnson	.05	.01
❑ 553	Ron Holmes	.05	.01
❑ 554	John Elway	1.25	.50
❑ 555	Melvin Bratton	.05	.01
❑ 556	Dennis Smith	.05	.01
❑ 557	Ricky Nattiel	.05	.01
❑ 558	Clarence Kay	.05	.01
❑ 559	Michael Brooks	.05	.01
❑ 560	Mike Horan	.05	.01
❑ 561	Warren Powers	.05	.01
❑ 562	Keith Kartz	.05	.01
❑ 563	Shannon Sharpe	.50	.20
❑ 564	Wymon Henderson	.05	.01
❑ 565	Steve Atwater	.05	.01
❑ 566	David Treadwell	.05	.01
❑ 567	Bruce Pickens RC	.05	.01
❑ 568	Jessie Tuggle	.05	.01
❑ 569	Chris Hinton	.05	.01
❑ 570	Keith Jones	.05	.01
❑ 571	Bill Fralic	.05	.01
❑ 572	Mike Rozier	.05	.01
❑ 573	Scott Fulhage	.05	.01
❑ 574	Floyd Dixon	.05	.01
❑ 575	Andre Rison	.10	.02
❑ 576	Darion Conner	.05	.01
❑ 577	Brian Jordan	.10	.02
❑ 578	Michael Haynes	.25	.08
❑ 579	Oliver Barnett	.05	.01
❑ 580	Shawn Collins	.05	.01
❑ 581	Tim Green	.05	.01
❑ 582	Deion Sanders	.40	.15
❑ 583	Mike Kenn	.05	.01
❑ 584	Mike Gann	.05	.01
❑ 585	Chris Miller	.10	.02
❑ 586	Tory Epps	.05	.01
❑ 587	Steve Broussard	.05	.01
❑ 588	Gary Wilkins	.05	.01
❑ 589	Eric Turner RC	.10	.02
❑ 590	Thane Gash	.05	.01
❑ 591	Clay Matthews	.10	.02
❑ 592	Mike Johnson	.05	.01
❑ 593	Raymond Clayborn	.05	.01
❑ 594	Leroy Hoard	.10	.02
❑ 595	Reggie Langhorne	.05	.01
❑ 596	Mike Baab	.05	.01
❑ 597	Anthony Pleasant	.05	.01
❑ 598	David Grayson	.05	.01
❑ 599	Rob Burnett RC	.10	.02
❑ 600	Frank Minnifield	.05	.01
❑ 601	Gregg Rakoczy	.05	.01
❑ 602	Eric Metcalf UER	.25	.08
❑ 603	Paul Farren	.05	.01
❑ 604	Brian Brennan	.05	.01
❑ 605	Tony Jones T.RC	.05	.01
❑ 606	Stephen Braggs	.05	.01
❑ 607	Kevin Mack	.05	.01
❑ 608	Pat Harlow RC	.05	.01
❑ 609	Marv Cook	.05	.01
❑ 610	John Stephens	.05	.01
❑ 611	Ed Reynolds	.05	.01
❑ 612	Tim Goad	.05	.01
❑ 613	Chris Singleton	.05	.01
❑ 614	Bruce Armstrong	.05	.01
❑ 615	Tommy Hodson	.05	.01
❑ 616	Sammy Martin	.05	.01
❑ 617	Andre Tippett	.05	.01
❑ 618	Johnny Rembert	.05	.01
❑ 619	Maurice Hurst	.05	.01
❑ 620	Vincent Brown	.05	.01
❑ 621	Ray Agnew	.05	.01
❑ 622	Ronnie Lippett	.05	.01
❑ 623	Greg McMurtry	.05	.01
❑ 624	Brent Williams	.05	.01
❑ 625	Jason Staurovsky	.05	.01
❑ 626	Marvin Allen	.05	.01
❑ 627	Hart Lee Dykes	.05	.01
❑ 628	Atlanta Falcons	.05	.01
❑ 629	Buffalo Bills	.05	.01
❑ 630	Chicago Bears	.10	.02
❑ 631	Cincinnati Bengals	.05	.01
❑ 632	Cleveland Browns	.05	.01
❑ 633	Dallas Cowboys	.05	.01
❑ 634	Denver Broncos	.05	.01
❑ 635	Detroit Lions	.05	.01
❑ 636	Green Bay Packers	.05	.01
❑ 637	Oilers TL/Warren Moon	.10	.02
❑ 638	Colts TL/Jeff George	.05	.01
❑ 639	Kansas City Chiefs	.05	.01
❑ 640	Los Angeles Raiders	.10	.02
❑ 641	Los Angeles Rams	.05	.01
❑ 642	Miami Dolphins	.05	.01
❑ 643	Minnesota Vikings	.10	.02
❑ 644	New Eng. Patriots	.05	.01
❑ 645	New Orleans Saints	.05	.01
❑ 646	New York Giants	.05	.01
❑ 647	New York Jets	.05	.01
❑ 648	Eagles TL/R.Cunningham	.05	.01
❑ 649	Phoenix Cardinals	.05	.01
❑ 650	Pittsburgh Steelers	.05	.01
❑ 651	San Diego Chargers	.05	.01
❑ 652	San Francisco 49ers	.05	.01
❑ 653	Seattle Seahawks	.05	.01
❑ 654	Tampa Bay Buccaneers	.05	.01
❑ 655	Washington Redskins	.05	.01
❑ 656	Checklist 1-132	.05	.01
❑ 657	Checklist 132-264	.05	.01
❑ 658	Checklist 265-396	.05	.01
❑ 659	Checklist 397-528	.05	.01
❑ 660	Checklist 529-660	.05	.01

1992 Topps

❑ COMPLETE SET (759)	50.00	25.00
❑ COMP.FACT.SET (680)	80.00	40.00
❑ COMP.SERIES 1 (330)	20.00	10.00
❑ COMP.SERIES 2 (330)	20.00	10.00
❑ COMP.HIGH SER.(99)	10.00	5.00
❑ COMP.FACT.HIGH SET (113)	12.00	5.00
❑ 1 Tim McGee	.05	.01
❑ 2 Rich Camarillo	.05	.01
❑ 3 Anthony Johnson	.10	.02
❑ 4 Larry Kelm	.05	.01
❑ 5 Irving Fryar	.10	.02
❑ 6 Joey Browner	.05	.01
❑ 7 Michael Walter	.05	.01
❑ 8 Cortez Kennedy	.10	.02

❑ 9 Reyna Thompson	.05	.01
❑ 10 John Friesz	.10	.02
❑ 11 Leroy Hoard	.10	.02
❑ 12 Steve McMichael	.10	.02
❑ 13 Marvin Washington	.05	.01
❑ 14 Clyde Simmons	.05	.01
❑ 15 Stephone Paige	.05	.01
❑ 16 Mike Utley	.10	.02
❑ 17 Tunch Ilkin	.05	.01
❑ 18 Lawrence Dawsey	.10	.02
❑ 19 Vance Johnson	.05	.01
❑ 20 Bryce Paup	.25	.08
❑ 21 Jeff Wright	.05	.01
❑ 22 Gill Fenerty	.05	.01
❑ 23 Lamar Lathon	.05	.01
❑ 24 Danny Copeland	.05	.01
❑ 25 Marcus Allen	.25	.08
❑ 26 Tim Green	.05	.01
❑ 27 Pete Stoyanovich	.05	.01
❑ 28 Alvin Harper	.10	.02
❑ 29 Roy Foster	.05	.01
❑ 30 Eugene Daniel	.05	.01
❑ 31 Luis Sharpe	.05	.01
❑ 32 Terry Wooden	.05	.01
❑ 33 Jim Breech	.05	.01
❑ 34 Randy Hilliard RC	.05	.01
❑ 35 Roman Phifer	.05	.01
❑ 36 Erik Howard	.05	.01
❑ 37 Chris Singleton	.05	.01
❑ 38 Matt Stover	.05	.01
❑ 39 Tim Irwin	.05	.01
❑ 40 Karl Mecklenburg	.05	.01
❑ 41 Joe Phillips	.05	.01
❑ 42 Bill Jones RC	.05	.01
❑ 43 Mark Carrier DB	.05	.01
❑ 44 George Jamison	.05	.01
❑ 45 Rob Taylor	.05	.01
❑ 46 Jeff Jaeger	.05	.01
❑ 47 Don Majkowski	.05	.01
❑ 48 Al Edwards	.05	.01
❑ 49 Curtis Duncan	.05	.01
❑ 50 Sam Mills	.05	.01
❑ 51 Terance Mathis	.10	.02
❑ 52 Brian Mitchell	.10	.02
❑ 53 Mike Pritchard	.10	.02
❑ 54 Calvin Williams	.10	.02
❑ 55 Hardy Nickerson	.10	.02
❑ 56 Nate Newton	.05	.01
❑ 57 Steve Wallace	.05	.01
❑ 58 John Offerdahl	.05	.01
❑ 59 Aeneas Williams	.10	.02
❑ 60 Lee Johnson	.05	.01
❑ 61 Ricardo McDonald RC	.05	.01
❑ 62 David Richards	.05	.01
❑ 63 Paul Gruber	.05	.01
❑ 64 Greg McMurtry	.05	.01
❑ 65 Jay Hilgenberg	.05	.01
❑ 66 Tim Grunhard	.05	.01
❑ 67 Dwayne White RC	.05	.01
❑ 68 Don Beebe	.05	.01
❑ 69 Simon Fletcher	.05	.01
❑ 70 Warren Moon	.25	.08
❑ 71 Chris Jacke	.05	.01
❑ 72 Steve Wisniewski UER	.05	.01
❑ 73 Mike Cofer	.05	.01
❑ 74 Tim Johnson UER	.05	.01
❑ 75 T.J. Turner	.05	.01
❑ 76 Scott Case	.05	.01
❑ 77 Michael Jackson	.10	.02
❑ 78 Jon Hand	.05	.01
❑ 79 Stan Brock	.05	.01
❑ 80 Robert Blackmon	.05	.01
❑ 81 D.J. Johnson	.05	.01
❑ 82 Damone Johnson	.05	.01
❑ 83 Marc Spindler	.05	.01
❑ 84 Larry Brown DB	.05	.01
❑ 85 Ray Berry	.05	.01
❑ 86 Andre Waters	.05	.01
❑ 87 Carlos Huerta	.05	.01
❑ 88 Brad Muster	.05	.01
❑ 89 Chuck Cecil	.05	.01
❑ 90 Nick Lowery	.05	.01
❑ 91 Cornelius Bennett	.10	.02
❑ 92 Jessie Tuggle	.05	.01
❑ 93 Mark Schlereth RC	.05	.01
❑ 94 Vestee Jackson	.05	.01
❑ 95 Eric Bieniemy	.05	.01
❑ 96 Jeff Hostetler	.10	.02
❑ 97 Ken Lanier	.05	.01
❑ 98 Wayne Haddix	.05	.01
❑ 99 Lorenzo White	.05	.01
❑ 100 Mervyn Fernandez	.05	.01
❑ 101 Brent Williams	.05	.01
❑ 102 Ian Beckles	.05	.01
❑ 103 Harris Barton	.05	.01
❑ 104 Edgar Bennett RC	.25	.08
❑ 105 Mike Pitts	.05	.01
❑ 106 Fuad Reveiz	.05	.01
❑ 107 Vernon Turner	.05	.01
❑ 108 Tracy Hayworth RC	.05	.01
❑ 109 Checklist 1-110	.05	.01
❑ 110 Tom Waddle	.05	.01
❑ 111 Fred Stokes	.05	.01
❑ 112 Howard Ballard	.05	.01
❑ 113 David Szott	.05	.01
❑ 114 Tim McKyer	.05	.01
❑ 115 Kyle Clifton	.05	.01
❑ 116 Tony Bennett	.05	.01
❑ 117 Joel Hilgenberg	.05	.01
❑ 118 Dwayne Harper	.05	.01
❑ 119 Mike Baab	.05	.01
❑ 120 Mark Clayton	.10	.02
❑ 121 Eric Swann	.10	.02
❑ 122 Neil O'Donnell	.10	.02
❑ 123 Mike Munchak	.10	.02
❑ 124 Howie Long	.25	.08
❑ 125 John Elway	1.25	.50
❑ 126 Joe Prokop	.05	.01
❑ 127 Pepper Johnson	.05	.01
❑ 128 Richard Dent	.10	.02
❑ 129 Robert Porcher RC	.25	.08
❑ 130 Earnest Byner	.05	.01
❑ 131 Kent Hull	.05	.01
❑ 132 Mike Merriweather	.05	.01
❑ 133 Scott Fulhage	.05	.01
❑ 134 Kevin Porter	.05	.01
❑ 135 Tony Casillas	.05	.01
❑ 136 Dean Biasucci	.05	.01
❑ 137 Ben Smith	.05	.01
❑ 138 Bruce Kozerski	.05	.01
❑ 139 Jeff Campbell	.05	.01
❑ 140 Kevin Greene	.10	.02
❑ 141 Gary Plummer	.05	.01
❑ 142 Vincent Brown	.05	.01
❑ 143 Ron Hall	.05	.01
❑ 144 Louie Aguiar RC	.05	.01
❑ 145 Mark Duper	.05	.01
❑ 146 Jesse Sapolu	.05	.01
❑ 147 Jeff Gossett	.05	.01
❑ 148 Brian Noble	.05	.01
❑ 149 Derek Russell	.05	.01
❑ 150 Carlton Bailey RC	.05	.01
❑ 151 Kelly Goodburn	.05	.01
❑ 152 Audray McMillian UER	.05	.01
❑ 153 Neal Anderson	.05	.01
❑ 154 Bill Maas	.05	.01
❑ 155 Rickey Jackson	.05	.01
❑ 156 Chris Miller	.10	.02
❑ 157 Darren Comeaux	.05	.01
❑ 158 David Williams	.05	.01
❑ 159 Rich Gannon	.25	.08
❑ 160 Kevin Mack	.05	.01
❑ 161 Jim Arnold	.05	.01
❑ 162 Reggie White	.25	.08
❑ 163 Leonard Russell	.10	.02
❑ 164 Doug Smith	.05	.01
❑ 165 Tony Mandarich	.05	.01
❑ 166 Greg Lloyd	.10	.02
❑ 167 Jumbo Elliott	.05	.01
❑ 168 Jonathan Hayes	.05	.01
❑ 169 Jim Ritcher	.05	.01
❑ 170 Mike Kenn	.05	.01
❑ 171 James Washington	.05	.01
❑ 172 Tim Harris	.05	.01
❑ 173 James Thornton	.05	.01
❑ 174 John Brandes RC	.05	.01
❑ 175 Fred McAfee RC	.05	.01
❑ 176 Henry Rolling	.05	.01
❑ 177 Tony Paige	.05	.01
❑ 178 Jay Schroeder	.05	.01
❑ 179 Jeff Herrod	.05	.01
❑ 180 Emmitt Smith	1.50	.60
❑ 181 Wymon Henderson	.05	.01
❑ 182 Rob Moore	.10	.02
❑ 183 Robert Wilson	.05	.01
❑ 184 Michael Zordich RC	.05	.01
❑ 185 Jim Harbaugh	.25	.08
❑ 186 Vince Workman	.05	.01
❑ 187 Ernest Givins	.10	.02
❑ 188 Herschel Walker	.10	.02
❑ 189 Dan Fike	.05	.01
❑ 190 Seth Joyner	.05	.01
❑ 191 Steve Young	.60	.25
❑ 192 Dennis Gibson	.05	.01
❑ 193 Darryl Talley	.05	.01
❑ 194 Emile Harry	.05	.01
❑ 195 Bill Fralic	.05	.01
❑ 196 Michael Stewart	.05	.01
❑ 197 James Francis	.05	.01
❑ 198 Jerome Henderson	.05	.01
❑ 199 John L. Williams	.05	.01
❑ 200 Rod Woodson	.25	.08
❑ 201 Mike Farr	.05	.01
❑ 202 Greg Montgomery	.05	.01
❑ 203 Andre Collins	.05	.01
❑ 204 Scott Miller	.05	.01
❑ 205 Clay Matthews	.10	.02
❑ 206 Ethan Horton	.05	.01
❑ 207 Rich Miano	.05	.01
❑ 208 Chris Mims RC	.05	.01
❑ 209 Anthony Morgan	.05	.01
❑ 210 Rodney Hampton	.10	.02
❑ 211 Chris Hinton	.05	.01
❑ 212 Esera Tuaolo	.05	.01
❑ 213 Shane Conlan	.05	.01
❑ 214 John Carney	.05	.01
❑ 215 Kenny Walker	.05	.01
❑ 216 Scott Radecic	.05	.01
❑ 217 Chris Martin	.05	.01
❑ 218 Checklist 111-220 UER	.05	.01
❑ 219 Wesley Carroll	.05	.01
❑ 220 Bill Romanowski	.05	.01
❑ 221 Reggie Cobb	.05	.01
❑ 222 Alfred Anderson	.05	.01
❑ 223 Cleveland Gary	.05	.01
❑ 224 Eddie Blake RC	.05	.01
❑ 225 Chris Spielman	.10	.02
❑ 226 John Roper	.05	.01
❑ 227 George Thomas RC	.05	.01
❑ 228 Jeff Faulkner	.05	.01
❑ 229 Chip Lohmiller UER	.05	.01
❑ 230 Hugh Millen	.05	.01
❑ 231 Ray Horton	.05	.01
❑ 232 James Campen	.05	.01
❑ 233 Howard Cross	.05	.01
❑ 234 Keith McKeller	.05	.01
❑ 235 Dino Hackett	.05	.01
❑ 236 Jerome Brown	.05	.01
❑ 237 Andy Heck	.05	.01
❑ 238 Rodney Holman	.05	.01
❑ 239 Bruce Matthews	.05	.01
❑ 240 Jeff Lageman	.05	.01
❑ 241 Bobby Hebert	.05	.01
❑ 242 Gary Anderson K	.05	.01
❑ 243 Mark Bortz	.05	.01
❑ 244 Rich Moran	.05	.01
❑ 245 Jeff Uhlenhake	.05	.01
❑ 246 Ricky Sanders	.05	.01
❑ 247 Clarence Kay	.05	.01
❑ 248 Ed King	.05	.01
❑ 249 Eddie Anderson	.05	.01
❑ 250 Amp Lee RC	.05	.01
❑ 251 Norm Johnson	.05	.01
❑ 252 Michael Carter	.05	.01
❑ 253 Felix Wright	.05	.01
❑ 254 Leon Seals	.05	.01
❑ 255 Nate Lewis	.05	.01
❑ 256 Kevin Call	.05	.01
❑ 257 Darryl Henley	.05	.01
❑ 258 Jon Vaughn	.05	.01
❑ 259 Matt Bahr	.05	.01
❑ 260 Johnny Johnson	.05	.01
❑ 261 Ken Norton	.10	.02
❑ 262 Wendell Davis	.05	.01
❑ 263 Eugene Robinson	.05	.01
❑ 264 David Treadwell	.05	.01
❑ 265 Michael Haynes	.10	.02
❑ 266 Robb Thomas	.05	.01
❑ 267 Nate Odomes	.05	.01
❑ 268 Martin Mayhew	.05	.01
❑ 269 Perry Kemp	.05	.01

- ❑ 270 Jerry Ball .05 .01
- ❑ 271 Tommy Vardell RC .05 .01
- ❑ 272 Ernie Mills .05 .01
- ❑ 273 Mo Lewis .05 .01
- ❑ 274 Roger Ruzek .05 .01
- ❑ 275 Steve Smith .05 .01
- ❑ 276 Bo Orlando RC .05 .01
- ❑ 277 Louis Oliver .05 .01
- ❑ 278 Toi Cook .05 .01
- ❑ 279 Eddie Brown .05 .01
- ❑ 280 Keith McCants .05 .01
- ❑ 281 Rob Burnett .05 .01
- ❑ 282 Keith DeLong .05 .01
- ❑ 283 Stan Thomas UER .05 .01
- ❑ 284 Robert Brown .05 .01
- ❑ 285 John Alt .05 .01
- ❑ 286 Randy Dixon .05 .01
- ❑ 287 Siran Stacy RC .05 .01
- ❑ 288 Ray Agnew .05 .01
- ❑ 289 Darion Conner .05 .01
- ❑ 290 Kirk Lowdermilk .05 .01
- ❑ 291 Greg Jackson .05 .01
- ❑ 292 Ken Harvey .05 .01
- ❑ 293 Jacob Green .05 .01
- ❑ 294 Mark Tuinei .05 .01
- ❑ 295 Mark Rypien .05 .01
- ❑ 296 Gerald Robinson RC .05 .01
- ❑ 297 Broderick Thompson .05 .01
- ❑ 298 Doug Widell .05 .01
- ❑ 299 Carwell Gardner .05 .01
- ❑ 300 Barry Sanders 1.25 .50
- ❑ 301 Eric Metcalf .10 .02
- ❑ 302 Eric Thomas .05 .01
- ❑ 303 Terrell Buckley RC .05 .01
- ❑ 304 Byron Evans .05 .01
- ❑ 305 Johnny Hector .05 .01
- ❑ 306 Steve Broussard .05 .01
- ❑ 307 Gene Atkins .05 .01
- ❑ 308 Terry McDaniel .05 .01
- ❑ 309 Charles McRae .05 .01
- ❑ 310 Jim Lachey .05 .01
- ❑ 311 Pat Harlow .05 .01
- ❑ 312 Kevin Butler .05 .01
- ❑ 313 Scott Stephen .05 .01
- ❑ 314 Dermontti Dawson .05 .01
- ❑ 315 Johnny Meads .05 .01
- ❑ 316 Checklist 221-330 .05 .01
- ❑ 317 Aaron Craver .05 .01
- ❑ 318 Michael Brooks .05 .01
- ❑ 319 Guy McIntyre .05 .01
- ❑ 320 Thurman Thomas .25 .08
- ❑ 321 Courtney Hall .05 .01
- ❑ 322 Dan Saleaumua .05 .01
- ❑ 323 Vinson Smith RC .05 .01
- ❑ 324 Steve Jordan .05 .01
- ❑ 325 Walter Reeves .05 .01
- ❑ 326 Erik Kramer .10 .02
- ❑ 327 Duane Bickett .05 .01
- ❑ 328 Tom Newberry .05 .01
- ❑ 329 John Kasay .05 .01
- ❑ 330 Dave Meggett .10 .02
- ❑ 331 Kevin Ross .05 .01
- ❑ 332 Keith Hamilton RC .10 .02
- ❑ 333 Dwight Stone .05 .01
- ❑ 334 Mel Gray .10 .02
- ❑ 335 Harry Galbreath .05 .01
- ❑ 336 William Perry .10 .02
- ❑ 337 Brian Blades .10 .02
- ❑ 338 Randall McDaniel .05 .01
- ❑ 339 Pat Coleman RC .05 .01
- ❑ 340 Michael Irvin .25 .08
- ❑ 341 Checklist 331-440 .05 .01
- ❑ 342 Chris Mohr .05 .01
- ❑ 343 Greg Davis .05 .01
- ❑ 344 Dave Cadigan .05 .01
- ❑ 345 Art Monk .10 .02
- ❑ 346 Tim Goad .05 .01
- ❑ 347 Vinnie Clark .05 .01
- ❑ 348 David Fulcher .05 .01
- ❑ 349 Craig Heyward .10 .02
- ❑ 350 Ronnie Lott .10 .02
- ❑ 351 Dexter Carter .05 .01
- ❑ 352 Mark Jackson .05 .01
- ❑ 353 Brian Jordan .10 .02
- ❑ 354 Ray Donaldson .05 .01
- ❑ 355 Jim Price .05 .01
- ❑ 356 Rod Bernstine .05 .01
- ❑ 357 Tony Mayberry RC .05 .01
- ❑ 358 Richard Brown RC .05 .01
- ❑ 359 David Alexander .05 .01
- ❑ 360 Haywood Jeffires .10 .02
- ❑ 361 Henry Thomas .05 .01
- ❑ 362 Jeff Graham .25 .08
- ❑ 363 Don Warren .05 .01
- ❑ 364 Scott Davis .05 .01
- ❑ 365 Harlon Barnett .05 .01
- ❑ 366 Mark Collins .05 .01
- ❑ 367 Rick Tuten .05 .01
- ❑ 368 Lonnie Marts RC .05 .01
- ❑ 369 Dennis Smith .05 .01
- ❑ 370 Steve Tasker .10 .02
- ❑ 371 Robert Massey .05 .01
- ❑ 372 Ricky Reynolds .05 .01
- ❑ 373 Alvin Wright .05 .01
- ❑ 374 Kelvin Martin .05 .01
- ❑ 375 Vince Buck .05 .01
- ❑ 376 John Kidd .05 .01
- ❑ 377 William White .05 .01
- ❑ 378 Bryan Cox .10 .02
- ❑ 379 Jamie Dukes RC .05 .01
- ❑ 380 Anthony Munoz .10 .02
- ❑ 381 Mark Gunn RC .05 .01
- ❑ 382 Keith Henderson .05 .01
- ❑ 383 Charles Wilson .05 .01
- ❑ 384 Shawn McCarthy RC .05 .01
- ❑ 385 Ernie Jones .05 .01
- ❑ 386 Nick Bell .05 .01
- ❑ 387 Derrick Walker .05 .01
- ❑ 388 Mark Stepnoski .10 .02
- ❑ 389 Broderick Thomas .05 .01
- ❑ 390 Reggie Roby .05 .01
- ❑ 391 Bubba McDowell .05 .01
- ❑ 392 Eric Martin .05 .01
- ❑ 393 Toby Caston RC .05 .01
- ❑ 394 Bern Brostek .05 .01
- ❑ 395 Christian Okoye .05 .01
- ❑ 396 Frank Minnifield .05 .01
- ❑ 397 Mike Golic .05 .01
- ❑ 398 Grant Feasel .05 .01
- ❑ 399 Michael Ball .05 .01
- ❑ 400 Mike Croel .05 .01
- ❑ 401 Maury Buford .05 .01
- ❑ 402 Jeff Bostic UER .05 .01
- ❑ 403 Sean Landeta .05 .01
- ❑ 404 Terry Allen .25 .08
- ❑ 405 Donald Evans .05 .01
- ❑ 406 Don Mosebar .05 .01
- ❑ 407 D.J. Dozier .05 .01
- ❑ 408 Bruce Pickens .05 .01
- ❑ 409 Jim Dombrowski .05 .01
- ❑ 410 Deron Cherry .05 .01
- ❑ 411 Richard Johnson CB .05 .01
- ❑ 412 Alexander Wright .05 .01
- ❑ 413 Tom Rathman .05 .01
- ❑ 414 Mark Dennis .05 .01
- ❑ 415 Phil Hansen .05 .01
- ❑ 416 Lonnie Young .05 .01
- ❑ 417 Burt Grossman .05 .01
- ❑ 418 Tony Covington .05 .01
- ❑ 419 John Stephens .05 .01
- ❑ 420 Jim Everett .10 .02
- ❑ 421 Johnny Holland .05 .01
- ❑ 422 Mike Barber RC WR .05 .01
- ❑ 423 Carl Lee .05 .01
- ❑ 424 Craig Patterson RC .05 .01
- ❑ 425 Greg Townsend .05 .01
- ❑ 426 Brett Perriman .25 .08
- ❑ 427 Morten Andersen .05 .01
- ❑ 428 John Gesek .05 .01
- ❑ 429 Bryan Barker .05 .01
- ❑ 430 John Taylor .10 .02
- ❑ 431 Donnell Woolford .05 .01
- ❑ 432 Ron Holmes .05 .01
- ❑ 433 Lee Williams .05 .01
- ❑ 434 Alfred Oglesby .05 .01
- ❑ 435 Jarrod Bunch .05 .01
- ❑ 436 Carlton Haselrig RC .05 .01
- ❑ 437 Rufus Porter .05 .01
- ❑ 438 Rohn Stark .05 .01
- ❑ 439 Tony Jones T .05 .01
- ❑ 440 Andre Rison .10 .02
- ❑ 441 Eric Hill .05 .01
- ❑ 442 Jesse Solomon .05 .01
- ❑ 443 Jackie Slater .05 .01
- ❑ 444 Donnie Elder .05 .01
- ❑ 445 Brett Maxie .05 .01
- ❑ 446 Max Montoya .05 .01
- ❑ 447 Will Wolford .05 .01
- ❑ 448 Craig Taylor .05 .01
- ❑ 449 Jimmie Jones .05 .01
- ❑ 450 Anthony Carter .10 .02
- ❑ 451 Brian Bollinger RC .05 .01
- ❑ 452 Checklist 441-550 .05 .01
- ❑ 453 Brad Edwards .05 .01
- ❑ 454 Gene Chilton RC .05 .01
- ❑ 455 Eric Allen .05 .01
- ❑ 456 William Roberts .05 .01
- ❑ 457 Eric Green .05 .01
- ❑ 458 Irv Eatman .05 .01
- ❑ 459 Derrick Thomas .25 .08
- ❑ 460 Tommy Kane .05 .01
- ❑ 461 LeRoy Butler .05 .01
- ❑ 462 Oliver Barnett .05 .01
- ❑ 463 Anthony Smith .05 .01
- ❑ 464 Cris Dishman .05 .01
- ❑ 465 Pat Terrell .05 .01
- ❑ 466 Greg Kragen .05 .01
- ❑ 467 Rodney Peete .10 .02
- ❑ 468 Willie Drewrey .05 .01
- ❑ 469 Jim Wilks .05 .01
- ❑ 470 Vince Newsome .05 .01
- ❑ 471 Chris Gardocki .05 .01
- ❑ 472 Chris Chandler .25 .08
- ❑ 473 George Thornton .05 .01
- ❑ 474 Albert Lewis .05 .01
- ❑ 475 Kevin Glover .05 .01
- ❑ 476 Joe Bowden RC .05 .01
- ❑ 477 Harry Sydney .05 .01
- ❑ 478 Bob Golic .05 .01
- ❑ 479 Tony Zendejas .05 .01
- ❑ 480 Brad Baxter .05 .01
- ❑ 481 Steve Beuerlein .10 .02
- ❑ 482 Mark Higgs .05 .01
- ❑ 483 Drew Hill .05 .01
- ❑ 484 Bryan Millard .05 .01
- ❑ 485 Mark Kelso .05 .01
- ❑ 486 David Grant .05 .01
- ❑ 487 Gary Zimmerman .05 .01
- ❑ 488 Leonard Marshall .05 .01
- ❑ 489 Keith Jackson .10 .02
- ❑ 490 Sterling Sharpe .25 .08
- ❑ 491 Ferrell Edmunds .05 .01
- ❑ 492 Wilber Marshall .05 .01
- ❑ 493 Charles Haley .10 .02
- ❑ 494 Riki Ellison .05 .01
- ❑ 495 Bill Brooks .05 .01
- ❑ 496 Bill Hawkins .05 .01
- ❑ 497 Erik Williams .05 .01
- ❑ 498 Leon Searcy RC .05 .01
- ❑ 499 Mike Horan .05 .01
- ❑ 500 Pat Swilling .05 .01
- ❑ 501 Maurice Hurst .05 .01
- ❑ 502 William Fuller .05 .01
- ❑ 503 Tim Newton .05 .01
- ❑ 504 Lorenzo Lynch .05 .01
- ❑ 505 Tim Barnett .05 .01
- ❑ 506 Tom Thayer .05 .01
- ❑ 507 Chris Burkett .05 .01
- ❑ 508 Ronnie Harmon .05 .01
- ❑ 509 James Brooks .10 .02
- ❑ 510 Bennie Blades .05 .01
- ❑ 511 Roger Craig .10 .02
- ❑ 512 Tony Woods .05 .01
- ❑ 513 Greg Lewis .05 .01
- ❑ 514 Erric Pegram .10 .02
- ❑ 515 Elvis Patterson .05 .01
- ❑ 516 Jeff Cross .05 .01
- ❑ 517 Myron Guyton .05 .01
- ❑ 518 Jay Novacek .10 .02
- ❑ 519 Leo Barker RC .05 .01
- ❑ 520 Keith Byars .05 .01
- ❑ 521 Dalton Hilliard .05 .01
- ❑ 522 Ted Washington .05 .01
- ❑ 523 Dexter McNabb RC .05 .01
- ❑ 524 Frank Reich .10 .02
- ❑ 525 Henry Ellard .10 .02
- ❑ 526 Barry Foster .10 .02
- ❑ 527 Barry Word .05 .01
- ❑ 528 Gary Anderson RB .05 .01
- ❑ 529 Reggie Rutland .05 .01
- ❑ 530 Stephen Baker .05 .01

❑ 531 John Flannery .05 .01
❑ 532 Steve Wright .05 .01
❑ 533 Eric Sanders .05 .01
❑ 534 Bob Whitfield RC .05 .01
❑ 535 Gaston Green .05 .01
❑ 536 Anthony Pleasant .05 .01
❑ 537 Jeff Bryant .05 .01
❑ 538 Jarvis Williams .05 .01
❑ 539 Jim Morrissey .05 .01
❑ 540 Andre Tippett .05 .01
❑ 541 Gill Byrd .05 .01
❑ 542 Raleigh McKenzie .05 .01
❑ 543 Jim Sweeney .05 .01
❑ 544 David Lutz .05 .01
❑ 545 Wayne Martin .05 .01
❑ 546 Karl Wilson .05 .01
❑ 547 Pierce Holt .05 .01
❑ 548 Doug Smith .05 .01
❑ 549 Nolan Harrison RC .05 .01
❑ 550 Freddie Joe Nunn .05 .01
❑ 551 Eric Moore .05 .01
❑ 552 Cris Carter .50 .20
❑ 553 Kevin Gogan .05 .01
❑ 554 Harold Green .05 .01
❑ 555 Kenneth Davis .05 .01
❑ 556 Travis McNeal .05 .01
❑ 557 Jim C. Jensen .05 .01
❑ 558 Willie Green .05 .01
❑ 559 Scott Galbraith RC .05 .01
❑ 560 Louis Lipps .05 .01
❑ 561 Matt Brock .05 .01
❑ 562 Mike Prior .05 .01
❑ 563 Checklist 551-660 .05 .01
❑ 564 Robert Delpino .05 .01
❑ 565 Vinny Testaverde .10 .02
❑ 566 Willie Gault .10 .02
❑ 567 Quinn Early .10 .02
❑ 568 Eric Moten .05 .01
❑ 569 Lance Smith .05 .01
❑ 570 Darrell Green .05 .01
❑ 571 Moe Gardner .05 .01
❑ 572 Steve Atwater .05 .01
❑ 573 Ray Childress .05 .01
❑ 574 Dave Krieg .10 .02
❑ 575 Bruce Armstrong .05 .01
❑ 576 Fred Barnett .25 .08
❑ 577 Don Griffin .05 .01
❑ 578 David Brandon RC .05 .01
❑ 579 Robert Young .05 .01
❑ 580 Keith Van Horne .05 .01
❑ 581 Jeff Criswell .05 .01
❑ 582 Lewis Tillman .05 .01
❑ 583 Bubby Brister .05 .01
❑ 584 Aaron Wallace .05 .01
❑ 585 Chris Doleman .05 .01
❑ 586 Marty Carter RC .05 .01
❑ 587 Chris Warren .25 .08
❑ 588 David Griggs .05 .01
❑ 589 Darrell Thompson .05 .01
❑ 590 Marion Butts .05 .01
❑ 591 Scott Norwood .05 .01
❑ 592 Lomas Brown .05 .01
❑ 593 Daryl Johnston .25 .08
❑ 594 Alonzo Mitz RC .05 .01
❑ 595 Tommy Barnhardt .05 .01
❑ 596 Tim Jorden .05 .01
❑ 597 Neil Smith .25 .08
❑ 598 Todd Marinovich .05 .01
❑ 599 Sean Jones .05 .01
❑ 600 Clarence Verdin .05 .01
❑ 601 Trace Armstrong .05 .01
❑ 602 Steve Bono RC .25 .08
❑ 603 Mark Ingram .05 .01
❑ 604 Flipper Anderson .05 .01
❑ 605 James Jones DT .05 .01
❑ 606 Al Noga .05 .01
❑ 607 Rick Bryan .05 .01
❑ 608 Eugene Lockhart .05 .01
❑ 609 Charles Mann .05 .01
❑ 610 James Hasty .05 .01
❑ 611 Jeff Feagles .05 .01
❑ 612 Tim Brown .25 .08
❑ 613 David Little .05 .01
❑ 614 Keith Sims .05 .01
❑ 615 Kevin Murphy .05 .01
❑ 616 Ray Crockett .05 .01
❑ 617 Jim Jeffcoat .05 .01
❑ 618 Patrick Hunter .05 .01
❑ 619 Keith Kartz .05 .01
❑ 620 Peter Tom Willis .05 .01
❑ 621 Vaughan Johnson .05 .01
❑ 622 Shawn Jefferson .05 .01
❑ 623 Anthony Thompson .05 .01
❑ 624 John Rienstra .05 .01
❑ 625 Don Maggs .05 .01
❑ 626 Todd Lyght .05 .01
❑ 627 Brent Jones .10 .02
❑ 628 Todd McNair .05 .01
❑ 629 Winston Moss .05 .01
❑ 630 Mark Carrier WR .10 .02
❑ 631 Dan Owens .05 .01
❑ 632 Sammie Smith UER .05 .01
❑ 633 James Lofton .10 .02
❑ 634 Paul McJulien RC .05 .01
❑ 635 Tony Tolbert .05 .01
❑ 636 Carnell Lake .05 .01
❑ 637 Gary Clark .25 .08
❑ 638 Brian Washington .05 .01
❑ 639 Jessie Hester .05 .01
❑ 640 Doug Riesenberg .05 .01
❑ 641 Joe Walter RC .05 .01
❑ 642 John Rade .05 .01
❑ 643 Wes Hopkins .05 .01
❑ 644 Kelly Stouffer .05 .01
❑ 645 Marv Cook .05 .01
❑ 646 Ken Clarke .05 .01
❑ 647 Bobby Humphrey UER .05 .01
❑ 648 Tim McDonald .05 .01
❑ 649 Donald Frank RC .05 .01
❑ 650 Richmond Webb .05 .01
❑ 651 Lemuel Stinson .05 .01
❑ 652 Merton Hanks .10 .02
❑ 653 Frank Warren .05 .01
❑ 654 Thomas Benson .05 .01
❑ 655 Al Smith .05 .01
❑ 656 Steve DeBerg .05 .01
❑ 657 Jayice Pearson RC .05 .01
❑ 658 Joe Morris .05 .01
❑ 659 Fred Strickland .05 .01
❑ 660 Kelvin Pritchett .05 .01
❑ 661 Lewis Billups .05 .01
❑ 662 Todd Collins RC .05 .01
❑ 663 Corey Miller RC .05 .01
❑ 664 Levon Kirkland RC .05 .01
❑ 665 Jerry Rice .75 .30
❑ 666 Mike Lodish RC .05 .01
❑ 667 Chuck Smith RC .05 .01
❑ 668 Lance Olberding RC .05 .01
❑ 669 Kevin Smith RC DB .05 .01
❑ 670 Dale Carter RC .10 .02
❑ 671 Sean Gilbert RC .10 .02
❑ 672 Ken O'Brien .05 .01
❑ 673 Ricky Proehl .05 .01
❑ 674 Junior Seau .25 .08
❑ 675 Courtney Hawkins RC .10 .02
❑ 676 Eddie Robinson RC .05 .01
❑ 677 Tommy Jeter RC .05 .01
❑ 678 Jeff George .25 .08
❑ 679 Cary Conklin .05 .01
❑ 680 Rueben Mayes .05 .01
❑ 681 Sean Lumpkin RC .05 .01
❑ 682 Dan Marino 1.25 .50
❑ 683 Ed McDaniel RC .05 .01
❑ 684 Greg Skrepenak RC .05 .01
❑ 685 Tracy Scroggins RC .05 .01
❑ 686 Tommy Maddox RC 2.00 .75
❑ 687 Mike Singletary .10 .02
❑ 688 Patrick Rowe RC .05 .01
❑ 689 Phillippi Sparks RC .05 .01
❑ 690 Joel Steed RC .05 .01
❑ 691 Kevin Fagan .05 .01
❑ 692 Deion Sanders .50 .20
❑ 693 Bruce Smith .25 .08
❑ 694 David Klingler RC .05 .01
❑ 695 Clayton Holmes RC .05 .01
❑ 696 Brett Favre 6.00 2.50
❑ 697 Marc Boutte RC .05 .01
❑ 698 Dwayne Sabb RC .05 .01
❑ 699 Ed McCaffrey .30 .10
❑ 700 Randall Cunningham .25 .08
❑ 701 Quentin Coryatt RC .05 .01
❑ 702 Bernie Kosar .10 .02
❑ 703 Vaughn Dunbar RC .05 .01
❑ 704 Browning Nagle .05 .01
❑ 705 Mark Wheeler RC .05 .01
❑ 706 Paul Siever RC .05 .01
❑ 707 Anthony Miller .10 .02
❑ 708 Corey Widmer RC .05 .01
❑ 709 Eric Dickerson .10 .02
❑ 710 Martin Bayless .05 .01
❑ 711 Jason Hanson RC .10 .02
❑ 712 Michael Dean Perry .10 .02
❑ 713 Billy Joe Tolliver UER .05 .01
❑ 714 Chad Hennings RC .10 .02
❑ 715 Bucky Richardson RC .05 .01
❑ 716 Steve Israel RC .05 .01
❑ 717 Robert Harris RC .05 .01
❑ 718 Timm Rosenbach .05 .01
❑ 719 Joe Montana 1.25 .50
❑ 720 Derek Brown TE RC .05 .01
❑ 721 Robert Brooks RC .75 .30
❑ 722 Boomer Esiason .10 .02
❑ 723 Troy Auzenne RC .05 .01
❑ 724 John Fina RC .05 .01
❑ 725 Chris Crooms RC .05 .01
❑ 726 Eugene Chung RC .05 .01
❑ 727 Darren Woodson RC .25 .08
❑ 728 Leslie O'Neal .10 .02
❑ 729 Dan McGwire .05 .01
❑ 730 Al Toon .10 .02
❑ 731 Michael Brandon RC .05 .01
❑ 732 Steve DeOssie .05 .01
❑ 733 Jim Kelly .25 .08
❑ 734 Webster Slaughter .05 .01
❑ 735 Tony Smith RBK RC .05 .01
❑ 736 Shane Collins RC .05 .01
❑ 737 Randal Hill .05 .01
❑ 738 Chris Holder RC .05 .01
❑ 739 Russell Maryland .05 .01
❑ 740 Carl Pickens RC .25 .08
❑ 741 Andre Reed .10 .02
❑ 742 Steve Emtman RC .05 .01
❑ 743 Carl Banks .05 .01
❑ 744 Troy Aikman .75 .30
❑ 745 Mark Royals .05 .01
❑ 746 J.J.Birden .05 .01
❑ 747 Michael Cofer .05 .01
❑ 748 Darryl Ashmore RC .05 .01
❑ 749 Dion Lambert RC .05 .01
❑ 750 Phil Simms .10 .02
❑ 751 Reggie E.White RC .05 .01
❑ 752 Harvey Williams .25 .08
❑ 753 Ty Detmer .25 .08
❑ 754 Tony Brooks RC .05 .01
❑ 755 Steve Christie .05 .01
❑ 756 Lawrence Taylor .25 .08
❑ 757 Merril Hoge .05 .01
❑ 758 Robert Jones RC .05 .01
❑ 759 Checklist 661-759 .05 .01

1993 Topps

❑ COMPLETE SET (660) 40.00 20.00
❑ COMP.FACT.SET (673) 100.00 60.00
❑ COMP.SERIES 1 (330) 15.00 6.00
❑ COMP.SERIES 2 (330) 10.00 5.00
❑ 1 Art Monk RB .05 .01
❑ 2 Jerry Rice RB .50 .20
❑ 3 Stanley Richard .05 .01
❑ 4 Ron Hall .05 .01
❑ 5 Daryl Johnston .25 .08
❑ 6 Wendell Davis .05 .01
❑ 7 Vaughn Dunbar .05 .01
❑ 8 Mike Jones .05 .01

Card		
❑ 9 Anthony Johnson	.10	.02
❑ 10 Chris Miller	.10	.02
❑ 11 Kyle Clifton	.05	.01
❑ 12 Curtis Conway RC	.40	.15
❑ 13 Lionel Washington	.05	.01
❑ 14 Reggie Johnson	.05	.01
❑ 15 David Little	.05	.01
❑ 16 Nick Lowery	.05	.01
❑ 17 Darryl Williams	.05	.01
❑ 18 Brent Jones	.10	.02
❑ 19 Bruce Matthews	.05	.01
❑ 20 Heath Sherman	.05	.01
❑ 21 John Kasay UER	.05	.01
❑ 22 Troy Drayton RC	.10	.02
❑ 23 Eric Metcalf	.10	.02
❑ 24 Andre Tippett	.05	.01
❑ 25 Rodney Hampton	.10	.02
❑ 26 Henry Jones	.05	.01
❑ 27 Jim Everett	.10	.02
❑ 28 Steve Jordan	.05	.01
❑ 29 LeRoy Butler	.05	.01
❑ 30 Troy Vincent	.05	.01
❑ 31 Nate Lewis	.05	.01
❑ 32 Rickey Jackson	.05	.01
❑ 33 Darion Conner	.05	.01
❑ 34 Tom Carter RC	.10	.02
❑ 35 Jeff George	.25	.08
❑ 36 Larry Centers RC	.25	.08
❑ 37 Reggie Cobb	.05	.01
❑ 38 Mike Saxon	.05	.01
❑ 39 Brad Baxter	.05	.01
❑ 40 Reggie White	.25	.08
❑ 41 Haywood Jeffires	.10	.02
❑ 42 Alfred Williams	.05	.01
❑ 43 Aaron Wallace	.05	.01
❑ 44 Tracy Simien	.05	.01
❑ 45 Pat Harlow	.05	.01
❑ 46 D.J. Johnson	.05	.01
❑ 47 Don Griffin	.05	.01
❑ 48 Flipper Anderson	.05	.01
❑ 49 Keith Kartz	.05	.01
❑ 50 Bernie Kosar	.10	.02
❑ 51 Kent Hull	.05	.01
❑ 52 Erik Howard	.05	.01
❑ 53 Pierce Holt	.05	.01
❑ 54 Dwayne Harper	.05	.01
❑ 55 Bennie Blades	.05	.01
❑ 56 Mark Duper	.05	.01
❑ 57 Brian Noble	.05	.01
❑ 58 Jeff Feagles	.05	.01
❑ 59 Michael Haynes	.10	.02
❑ 60 Junior Seau	.25	.08
❑ 61 Gary Anderson RB	.05	.01
❑ 62 Jon Hand	.05	.01
❑ 63 Lin Elliott RC	.05	.01
❑ 64 Dana Stubblefield RC	.25	.08
❑ 65 Vaughan Johnson	.05	.01
❑ 66 Mo Lewis	.05	.01
❑ 67 Aeneas Williams	.05	.01
❑ 68 David Fulcher	.05	.01
❑ 69 Chip Lohmiller	.05	.01
❑ 70 Greg Townsend	.05	.01
❑ 71 Simon Fletcher	.05	.01
❑ 72 Sean Salisbury	.05	.01
❑ 73 Christian Okoye	.05	.01
❑ 74 Jim Arnold	.05	.01
❑ 75 Bruce Smith	.25	.08
❑ 76 Fred Barnett	.10	.02
❑ 77 Bill Romanowski	.05	.01
❑ 78 Dermontti Dawson	.05	.01
❑ 79 Bern Brostek	.05	.01
❑ 80 Warren Moon	.25	.08
❑ 81 Bill Fralic	.05	.01
❑ 82 Lomas Brown FP	.05	.01
❑ 83 Duane Bickett FP	.05	.01
❑ 84 Neil Smith FP	.10	.02
❑ 85 Reggie White FP	.10	.02
❑ 86 Tim McDonald FP	.05	.01
❑ 87 Leslie O'Neal FP	.05	.01
❑ 88 Steve Young FP	.40	.15
❑ 89 Paul Gruber FP	.05	.01
❑ 90 Wilber Marshall FP	.05	.01
❑ 91 Trace Armstrong	.05	.01
❑ 92 Bobby Houston RC	.05	.01
❑ 93 George Thornton	.05	.01
❑ 94 Keith McCants	.05	.01
❑ 95 Ricky Sanders	.05	.01
❑ 96 Jackie Harris	.05	.01
❑ 97 Todd Marinovich	.05	.01
❑ 98 Henry Thomas	.05	.01
❑ 99 Jeff Wright	.05	.01
❑ 100 John Elway	1.50	.60
❑ 101 Garrison Hearst RC	.75	.30
❑ 102 Roy Foster	.05	.01
❑ 103 David Lang	.05	.01
❑ 104 Matt Stover	.05	.01
❑ 105 Lawrence Taylor	.25	.08
❑ 106 Pete Stoyanovich	.05	.01
❑ 107 Jessie Tuggle	.05	.01
❑ 108 William White	.05	.01
❑ 109 Andy Harmon RC	.10	.02
❑ 110 John L. Williams	.05	.01
❑ 111 Jon Vaughn	.05	.01
❑ 112 John Alt	.05	.01
❑ 113 Chris Jacke	.05	.01
❑ 114 Jim Breech	.05	.01
❑ 115 Eric Martin	.05	.01
❑ 116 Derrick Walker	.05	.01
❑ 117 Ricky Ervins	.05	.01
❑ 118 Roger Craig	.10	.02
❑ 119 Jeff Gossett	.05	.01
❑ 120 Emmitt Smith	1.50	.60
❑ 121 Bob Whitfield	.05	.01
❑ 122 Alonzo Spellman	.05	.01
❑ 123 David Klingler	.05	.01
❑ 124 Tommy Maddox	.25	.08
❑ 125 Robert Porcher	.05	.01
❑ 126 Edgar Bennett	.25	.08
❑ 127 Harvey Williams	.10	.02
❑ 128 Dave Brown RC	.25	.08
❑ 129 Johnny Mitchell	.05	.01
❑ 130 Drew Bledsoe RC	2.50	1.00
❑ 131 Zefross Moss	.05	.01
❑ 132 Nate Odomes	.05	.01
❑ 133 Rufus Porter	.05	.01
❑ 134 Jackie Slater	.05	.01
❑ 135 Steve Young	.75	.30
❑ 136 Chris Calloway	.10	.02
❑ 137 Steve Atwater	.05	.01
❑ 138 Mark Carrier DB	.05	.01
❑ 139 Marvin Washington	.05	.01
❑ 140 Barry Foster	.10	.02
❑ 141 Ricky Reynolds	.05	.01
❑ 142 Bubba McDowell	.05	.01
❑ 143 Dan Footman RC	.05	.01
❑ 144 Richmond Webb	.05	.01
❑ 145 Mike Pritchard	.10	.02
❑ 146 Chris Spielman	.10	.02
❑ 147 Dave Krieg	.10	.02
❑ 148 Nick Bell	.05	.01
❑ 149 Vincent Brown	.05	.01
❑ 150 Seth Joyner	.05	.01
❑ 151 Tommy Kane	.05	.01
❑ 152 Carlton Gray RC	.05	.01
❑ 153 Harry Newsome	.05	.01
❑ 154 Rohn Stark	.05	.01
❑ 155 Shannon Sharpe	.25	.08
❑ 156 Charles Haley	.10	.02
❑ 157 Cornelius Bennett	.10	.02
❑ 158 Doug Riesenberg	.05	.01
❑ 159 Amp Lee	.05	.01
❑ 160 Sterling Sharpe UER	.25	.08
❑ 161 Alonzo Mitz	.05	.01
❑ 162 Pat Terrell	.05	.01
❑ 163 Mark Schlereth	.05	.01
❑ 164 Gary Anderson K	.05	.01
❑ 165 Quinn Early	.10	.02
❑ 166 Jerome Bettis RC	5.00	2.50
❑ 167 Lawrence Dawsey	.05	.01
❑ 168 Derrick Thomas	.25	.08
❑ 169 Rodney Peete	.05	.01
❑ 170 Jim Kelly	.25	.08
❑ 171 Deion Sanders TL	.25	.08
❑ 172 Richard Dent TL	.05	.01
❑ 173 Emmitt Smith TL	.75	.30
❑ 174 Barry Sanders TL	.60	.25
❑ 175 Sterling Sharpe TL	.10	.02
❑ 176 Cleveland Gary TL	.05	.01
❑ 177 Terry Allen TL	.10	.02
❑ 178 Vaughan Johnson TL	.05	.01
❑ 179 Rodney Hampton TL	.05	.01
❑ 180 Randall Cunningham TL	.10	.02
❑ 181 Ricky Proehl TL	.05	.01
❑ 182 Jerry Rice TL	.50	.20
❑ 183 Reggie Cobb TL	.05	.01
❑ 184 Earnest Byner TL	.05	.01
❑ 185 Jeff Lageman	.05	.01
❑ 186 Carlos Jenkins	.05	.01
❑ 187 G.Hearst/Dye/Moore/Cole.	.40	.15
❑ 188 Todd Lyght	.05	.01
❑ 189 Carl Simpson RC	.05	.01
❑ 190 Barry Sanders	1.25	.50
❑ 191 Jim Harbaugh	.25	.08
❑ 192 Roger Ruzek	.05	.01
❑ 193 Brent Williams	.05	.01
❑ 194 Chip Banks	.05	.01
❑ 195 Mike Croel	.05	.01
❑ 196 Marion Butts	.05	.01
❑ 197 James Washington	.05	.01
❑ 198 John Offerdahl	.05	.01
❑ 199 Tom Rathman	.05	.01
❑ 200 Joe Montana	1.50	.60
❑ 201 Pepper Johnson	.05	.01
❑ 202 Cris Dishman	.05	.01
❑ 203 Adrian White RC	.05	.01
❑ 204 Reggie Brooks RC	.10	.02
❑ 205 Cortez Kennedy	.10	.02
❑ 206 Robert Massey	.05	.01
❑ 207 Toi Cook	.05	.01
❑ 208 Harry Sydney	.05	.01
❑ 209 Lincoln Kennedy RC	.05	.01
❑ 210 Randall McDaniel	.05	.01
❑ 211 Eugene Daniel	.05	.01
❑ 212 Rob Burnett	.05	.01
❑ 213 Steve Broussard	.05	.01
❑ 214 Brian Washington	.05	.01
❑ 215 Leonard Renfro RC	.05	.01
❑ 216 Audray McMillian LL	.05	.01
❑ 217 Sterling Sharpe/Miller L	.05	.01
❑ 218 Clyde Simmons LL	.05	.01
❑ 219 Emmitt Smith/B.Foster LL	.40	.15
❑ 220 Steve Young/W.Moon LL	.25	.08
❑ 221 Mel Gray	.10	.02
❑ 222 Luis Sharpe	.05	.01
❑ 223 Eric Moten	.05	.01
❑ 224 Albert Lewis	.05	.01
❑ 225 Alvin Harper	.10	.02
❑ 226 Steve Wallace	.05	.01
❑ 227 Mark Higgs	.05	.01
❑ 228 Eugene Lockhart	.05	.01
❑ 229 Sean Jones	.05	.01
❑ 230 J.Lynch RC/Thom/DuBose	.60	.25
❑ 231 Jimmy Williams	.05	.01
❑ 232 Demetrius DuBose RC	.05	.01
❑ 233 John Roper	.05	.01
❑ 234 Keith Hamilton	.05	.01
❑ 235 Donald Evans	.05	.01
❑ 236 Kenneth Davis	.05	.01
❑ 237 John Copeland RC	.10	.02
❑ 238 Leonard Russell	.10	.02
❑ 239 Ken Harvey	.05	.01
❑ 240 Dale Carter	.05	.01
❑ 241 Anthony Pleasant	.05	.01
❑ 242 Darrell Green	.05	.01
❑ 243 Natrone Means RC	.25	.08
❑ 244 Rob Moore	.10	.02
❑ 245 Chris Doleman	.05	.01
❑ 246 J.B. Brown	.05	.01
❑ 247 Ray Crockett	.05	.01
❑ 248 John Taylor	.10	.02
❑ 249 Russell Maryland	.05	.01
❑ 250 Brett Favre	2.00	.75
❑ 251 Carl Pickens	.10	.02
❑ 252 Andy Heck	.05	.01
❑ 253 Jerome Henderson	.05	.01
❑ 254 Deion Sanders	.50	.20
❑ 255 Steve Emtman	.05	.01
❑ 256 Calvin Williams	.10	.02
❑ 257 Sean Gilbert	.10	.02
❑ 258 Don Beebe	.05	.01
❑ 259 Robert Smith RC	1.25	.50
❑ 260 Robert Blackmon	.05	.01
❑ 261 Jim Kelly TL	.10	.02
❑ 262 Harold Green TL UER	.05	.01
❑ 263 Clay Matthews TL	.05	.01
❑ 264 John Elway TL	.75	.30
❑ 265 Warren Moon TL	.10	.02
❑ 266 Jeff George TL	.10	.02
❑ 267 Derrick Thomas TL	.10	.02
❑ 268 Howie Long TL	.05	.01
❑ 269 Dan Marino TL	.75	.30

❑ 270 Jon Vaughn TL	.05	.01
❑ 271 Chris Burkett TL	.05	.01
❑ 272 Barry Foster TL	.05	.01
❑ 273 Marion Butts TL	.05	.01
❑ 274 Chris Warren TL	.05	.01
❑ 275 M.Strahan RC/M.Buck.	1.00	.40
❑ 276 Tony Casillas	.05	.01
❑ 277 Jarrod Bunch	.05	.01
❑ 278 Eric Green	.05	.01
❑ 279 Stan Brock	.05	.01
❑ 280 Chester McGlockton	.10	.02
❑ 281 Ricky Watters	.25	.08
❑ 282 Dan Saleaumua	.05	.01
❑ 283 Rich Camarillo	.05	.01
❑ 284 Cris Carter	.25	.08
❑ 285 Rick Mirer RC	.25	.08
❑ 286 Matt Brock	.05	.01
❑ 287 Burt Grossman	.05	.01
❑ 288 Andre Collins	.05	.01
❑ 289 Mark Jackson	.05	.01
❑ 290 Dan Marino	1.50	.60
❑ 291 Cornelius Bennett FG	.05	.01
❑ 292 Steve Atwater FG	.05	.01
❑ 293 Bryan Cox FG	.05	.01
❑ 294 Sam Mills FG	.05	.01
❑ 295 Pepper Johnson FG	.05	.01
❑ 296 Seth Joyner FG	.05	.01
❑ 297 Chris Spielman FG	.05	.01
❑ 298 Junior Seau FG	.10	.02
❑ 299 Cortez Kennedy FG	.05	.01
❑ 300 Broderick Thomas FG	.05	.01
❑ 301 Todd McNair	.05	.01
❑ 302 Nate Newton	.10	.02
❑ 303 Michael Walter	.05	.01
❑ 304 Clyde Simmons	.05	.01
❑ 305 Ernie Mills	.05	.01
❑ 306 Steve Wisniewski	.05	.01
❑ 307 Coleman Rudolph RC	.05	.01
❑ 308 Thurman Thomas	.25	.08
❑ 309 Reggie Roby	.05	.01
❑ 310 Eric Swann	.10	.02
❑ 311 Mark Wheeler	.05	.01
❑ 312 Jeff Herrod	.05	.01
❑ 313 Leroy Hoard	.10	.02
❑ 314 Patrick Bates RC	.05	.01
❑ 315 Earnest Byner	.05	.01
❑ 316 Dave Meggett	.05	.01
❑ 317 George Teague RC	.10	.02
❑ 318 Ray Childress	.05	.01
❑ 319 Mike Kenn	.05	.01
❑ 320 Jason Hanson	.05	.01
❑ 321 Gary Clark	.10	.02
❑ 322 Chris Gardocki	.05	.01
❑ 323 Ken Norton	.10	.02
❑ 324 Eric Curry RC	.05	.01
❑ 325 Byron Evans	.05	.01
❑ 326 O.J.McDuffie RC	.25	.08
❑ 327 Dwight Stone	.05	.01
❑ 328 Tommy Barnhardt	.05	.01
❑ 329 Checklist 1-165	.05	.01
❑ 330 Checklist 166-329	.05	.01
❑ 331 Erik Williams	.05	.01
❑ 332 Phil Hansen	.05	.01
❑ 333 Martin Harrison RC	.05	.01
❑ 334 Mark Ingram	.05	.01
❑ 335 Mark Rypien	.05	.01
❑ 336 Anthony Miller	.10	.02
❑ 337 Antone Davis	.05	.01
❑ 338 Mike Munchak	.10	.02
❑ 339 Wayne Martin	.05	.01
❑ 340 Joe Montana	1.50	.60
❑ 341 Deon Figures RC	.05	.01
❑ 342 Ed McDaniel	.05	.01
❑ 343 Chris Burkett	.05	.01
❑ 344 Tony Smith RB	.05	.01
❑ 345 James Lofton	.10	.02
❑ 346 Courtney Hawkins	.05	.01
❑ 347 Dennis Smith	.05	.01
❑ 348 Anthony Morgan	.05	.01
❑ 349 Chris Goode	.05	.01
❑ 350 Phil Simms	.10	.02
❑ 351 Patrick Hunter	.05	.01
❑ 352 Brett Perriman	.25	.08
❑ 353 Corey Miller	.05	.01
❑ 354 Harry Galbreath	.05	.01
❑ 355 Mark Carrier WR	.10	.02
❑ 356 Troy Drayton	.10	.02
❑ 357 Greg Davis	.05	.01
❑ 358 Tim Krumrie	.05	.01
❑ 359 Tim McDonald	.05	.01
❑ 360 Webster Slaughter	.05	.01
❑ 361 Steve Christie	.05	.01
❑ 362 Courtney Hall	.05	.01
❑ 363 Charles Mann	.05	.01
❑ 364 Vestee Jackson	.05	.01
❑ 365 Robert Jones	.05	.01
❑ 366 Rich Miano	.05	.01
❑ 367 Morten Andersen	.05	.01
❑ 368 Jeff Graham	.10	.02
❑ 369 Martin Mayhew	.05	.01
❑ 370 Anthony Carter	.10	.02
❑ 371 Greg Kragen	.05	.01
❑ 372 Ron Cox	.05	.01
❑ 373 Perry Williams	.05	.01
❑ 374 Willie Gault	.05	.01
❑ 375 Chris Warren	.10	.02
❑ 376 Reyna Thompson	.05	.01
❑ 377 Bennie Thompson	.05	.01
❑ 378 Kevin Mack	.05	.01
❑ 379 Clarence Verdin	.05	.01
❑ 380 Marc Boutte	.05	.01
❑ 381 Marvin Jones RC	.05	.01
❑ 382 Greg Jackson	.05	.01
❑ 383 Steve Bono	.10	.02
❑ 384 Terrell Buckley	.05	.01
❑ 385 Garrison Hearst	.25	.08
❑ 386 Mike Brim	.05	.01
❑ 387 Jesse Sapolu	.05	.01
❑ 388 Carl Lee	.05	.01
❑ 389 Jeff Cross	.05	.01
❑ 390 Karl Mecklenburg	.05	.01
❑ 391 Chad Hennings	.05	.01
❑ 392 Oliver Barnett	.05	.01
❑ 393 Dalton Hilliard	.05	.01
❑ 394 Broderick Thompson	.05	.01
❑ 395 Rocket Ismail	.10	.02
❑ 396 John Kidd	.05	.01
❑ 397 Eddie Anderson	.05	.01
❑ 398 Lamar Lathon	.05	.01
❑ 399 Darren Perry	.05	.01
❑ 400 Drew Bledsoe	1.25	.50
❑ 401 Ferrell Edmunds	.05	.01
❑ 402 Lomas Brown	.05	.01
❑ 403 Drew Hill	.05	.01
❑ 404 David Whitmore	.05	.01
❑ 405 Mike Johnson	.05	.01
❑ 406 Paul Gruber	.05	.01
❑ 407 Kirk Lowdermilk	.05	.01
❑ 408 Curtis Conway	.25	.08
❑ 409 Bryce Paup	.10	.02
❑ 410 Boomer Esiason	.10	.02
❑ 411 Jay Schroeder	.05	.01
❑ 412 Anthony Newman	.05	.01
❑ 413 Ernie Jones	.05	.01
❑ 414 Carlton Bailey	.05	.01
❑ 415 Kenneth Gant	.05	.01
❑ 416 Todd Scott	.05	.01
❑ 417 Anthony Smith	.05	.01
❑ 418 Erik McMillan	.05	.01
❑ 419 Ronnie Harmon	.05	.01
❑ 420 Andre Reed	.10	.02
❑ 421 Wymon Henderson	.05	.01
❑ 422 Carnell Lake	.05	.01
❑ 423 Al Noga	.05	.01
❑ 424 Curtis Duncan	.05	.01
❑ 425 Mike Gann	.05	.01
❑ 426 Eugene Robinson	.05	.01
❑ 427 Scott Mersereau	.05	.01
❑ 428 Chris Singleton	.05	.01
❑ 429 Gerald Robinson	.05	.01
❑ 430 Pat Swilling	.05	.01
❑ 431 Ed McCaffrey	.25	.08
❑ 432 Neal Anderson	.05	.01
❑ 433 Joe Phillips	.05	.01
❑ 434 Jerry Ball	.05	.01
❑ 435 Tyronne Stowe	.05	.01
❑ 436 Dana Stubblefield	.25	.08
❑ 437 Eric Curry	.05	.01
❑ 438 Derrick Fenner	.05	.01
❑ 439 Mark Clayton	.05	.01
❑ 440 Quentin Coryatt	.10	.02
❑ 441 Willie Roaf RC	.10	.02
❑ 442 Ernest Dye	.05	.01
❑ 443 Jeff Jaeger	.05	.01
❑ 444 Stan Humphries	.10	.02
❑ 445 Johnny Johnson	.05	.01
❑ 446 Larry Brown DB	.05	.01
❑ 447 Kurt Gouveia	.05	.01
❑ 448 Qadry Ismail RC	.25	.08
❑ 449 Dan Footman	.05	.01
❑ 450 Tom Waddle	.05	.01
❑ 451 Kelvin Martin	.05	.01
❑ 452 Kanavis McGhee	.05	.01
❑ 453 Herman Moore	.25	.08
❑ 454 Jesse Solomon	.05	.01
❑ 455 Shane Conlan	.05	.01
❑ 456 Joel Steed	.05	.01
❑ 457 Charles Arbuckle	.05	.01
❑ 458 Shane Dronett	.05	.01
❑ 459 Steve Tasker	.10	.02
❑ 460 Herschel Walker	.10	.02
❑ 461 Willie Davis	.25	.08
❑ 462 Al Smith	.05	.01
❑ 463 O.J.McDuffie	.25	.08
❑ 464 Kevin Fagan	.05	.01
❑ 465 Hardy Nickerson	.10	.02
❑ 466 Leonard Marshall	.05	.01
❑ 467 John Baylor	.05	.01
❑ 468 Jay Novacek	.10	.02
❑ 469 Wayne Simmons RC	.05	.01
❑ 470 Tommy Vardell	.05	.01
❑ 471 Cleveland Gary	.05	.01
❑ 472 Mark Collins	.05	.01
❑ 473 Craig Heyward	.10	.02
❑ 474 John Copeland UER	.10	.02
❑ 475 Jeff Hostetler	.10	.02
❑ 476 Brian Mitchell	.10	.02
❑ 477 Natrone Means	.25	.08
❑ 478 Brad Muster	.05	.01
❑ 479 David Lutz	.05	.01
❑ 480 Andre Rison	.10	.02
❑ 481 Michael Zordich	.05	.01
❑ 482 Jim McMahon	.10	.02
❑ 483 Carlton Gray	.05	.01
❑ 484 Chris Mohr	.05	.01
❑ 485 Ernest Givins	.10	.02
❑ 486 Tony Tolbert	.05	.01
❑ 487 Vai Sikahema	.05	.01
❑ 488 Larry Webster	.05	.01
❑ 489 James Hasty	.05	.01
❑ 490 Reggie White	.25	.08
❑ 491 Reggie Rivers RC	.05	.01
❑ 492 Roman Phifer	.05	.01
❑ 493 Levon Kirkland	.05	.01
❑ 494 Demetrius DuBose	.05	.01
❑ 495 William Perry	.10	.02
❑ 496 Clay Matthews	.10	.02
❑ 497 Aaron Jones	.05	.01
❑ 498 Jack Trudeau	.05	.01
❑ 499 Michael Brooks	.05	.01
❑ 500 Jerry Rice	1.00	.40
❑ 501 Lonnie Marts	.05	.01
❑ 502 Tim McGee	.05	.01
❑ 503 Kelvin Pritchett	.05	.01
❑ 504 Bobby Hebert	.05	.01
❑ 505 Audray McMillian	.05	.01
❑ 506 Chuck Cecil	.05	.01
❑ 507 Leonard Renfro	.05	.01
❑ 508 Ethan Horton	.05	.01
❑ 509 Kevin Smith	.10	.02
❑ 510 Louis Oliver	.05	.01
❑ 511 John Stephens	.05	.01
❑ 512 Browning Nagle	.05	.01
❑ 513 Ricardo McDonald	.05	.01
❑ 514 Leslie O'Neal	.10	.02
❑ 515 Lorenzo White	.05	.01
❑ 516 Thomas Smith RC	.10	.02
❑ 517 Tony Woods	.05	.01
❑ 518 Darryl Henley	.05	.01
❑ 519 Robert Delpino	.05	.01
❑ 520 Rod Woodson	.25	.08
❑ 521 Phillippi Sparks	.05	.01
❑ 522 Jessie Hester	.05	.01
❑ 523 Shaun Gayle	.05	.01
❑ 524 Brad Edwards	.05	.01
❑ 525 Randall Cunningham	.25	.08
❑ 526 Marv Cook	.05	.01
❑ 527 Dennis Gibson	.05	.01
❑ 528 Erric Pegram	.10	.02
❑ 529 Terry McDaniel	.05	.01
❑ 530 Troy Aikman	.75	.30

❑ 531 Irving Fryar .10 .02
❑ 532 Blair Thomas .05 .01
❑ 533 Jim Wilks .05 .01
❑ 534 Michael Jackson .10 .02
❑ 535 Eric Davis .05 .01
❑ 536 James Campen .05 .01
❑ 537 Steve Beuerlein .10 .02
❑ 538 Robert Smith .50 .20
❑ 539 J.J. Birden .05 .01
❑ 540 Broderick Thomas .05 .01
❑ 541 Darryl Talley .05 .01
❑ 542 Russell Freeman RC .05 .01
❑ 543 David Alexander .05 .01
❑ 544 Chris Mims .05 .01
❑ 545 Coleman Rudolph .05 .01
❑ 546 Steve McMichael .10 .02
❑ 547 David Williams .05 .01
❑ 548 Chris Hinton .05 .01
❑ 549 Jim Jeffcoat .05 .01
❑ 550 Howie Long .25 .08
❑ 551 Roosevelt Potts RC .05 .01
❑ 552 Bryan Cox .05 .01
❑ 553 David Richards UER .05 .01
❑ 554 Reggie Brooks .10 .02
❑ 555 Neil O'Donnell .25 .08
❑ 556 Irv Smith RC .05 .01
❑ 557 Henry Ellard .10 .02
❑ 558 Steve DeBerg .05 .01
❑ 559 Jim Sweeney .05 .01
❑ 560 Harold Green .05 .01
❑ 561 Darrell Thompson .05 .01
❑ 562 Vinny Testaverde .10 .02
❑ 563 Bubby Brister .05 .01
❑ 564 Sean Landeta .05 .01
❑ 565 Neil Smith .25 .08
❑ 566 Craig Erickson .10 .02
❑ 567 Jim Ritcher .05 .01
❑ 568 Don Mosebar .05 .01
❑ 569 John Gesek .05 .01
❑ 570 Gary Plummer .05 .01
❑ 571 Norm Johnson .05 .01
❑ 572 Ron Heller .05 .01
❑ 573 Carl Simpson .05 .01
❑ 574 Greg Montgomery .05 .01
❑ 575 Dana Hall .05 .01
❑ 576 Vencie Glenn .05 .01
❑ 577 Dean Biasucci .05 .01
❑ 578 Rod Bernstine UER .05 .01
❑ 579 Randal Hill .05 .01
❑ 580 Sam Mills .05 .01
❑ 581 Santana Dotson .10 .02
❑ 582 Greg Lloyd .10 .02
❑ 583 Eric Thomas .05 .01
❑ 584 Henry Rolling .05 .01
❑ 585 Tony Bennett .05 .01
❑ 586 Sheldon White .05 .01
❑ 587 Mark Kelso .05 .01
❑ 588 Marc Spindler .05 .01
❑ 589 Greg McMurtry .05 .01
❑ 590 Art Monk .10 .02
❑ 591 Marco Coleman .05 .01
❑ 592 Tony Jones T .05 .01
❑ 593 Melvin Jenkins .05 .01
❑ 594 Kevin Ross .05 .01
❑ 595 William Fuller .05 .01
❑ 596 James Joseph .05 .01
❑ 597 Lamar McGriggs RC .05 .01
❑ 598 Gill Byrd .05 .01
❑ 599 Alexander Wright .05 .01
❑ 600 Rick Mirer .25 .08
❑ 601 Richard Dent .10 .02
❑ 602 Thomas Everett .05 .01
❑ 603 Jack Del Rio .05 .01
❑ 604 Jerome Bettis 2.50 1.00
❑ 605 Ronnie Lott .10 .02
❑ 606 Marty Carter .05 .01
❑ 607 Arthur Marshall RC .05 .01
❑ 608 Lee Johnson .05 .01
❑ 609 Bruce Armstrong .05 .01
❑ 610 Ricky Proehl .05 .01
❑ 611 Will Wolford .05 .01
❑ 612 Mike Prior .05 .01
❑ 613 George Jamison .05 .01
❑ 614 Gene Atkins .05 .01
❑ 615 Merril Hoge .05 .01
❑ 616 Desmond Howard .10 .02
❑ 617 Jarvis Williams .05 .01
❑ 618 Marcus Allen .25 .08
❑ 619 Gary Brown .05 .01
❑ 620 Bill Brooks .05 .01
❑ 621 Eric Allen .05 .01
❑ 622 Todd Kelly .05 .01
❑ 623 Michael Dean Perry .10 .02
❑ 624 David Braxton .05 .01
❑ 625 Mike Sherrard .05 .01
❑ 626 Jeff Bryant .05 .01
❑ 627 Eric Bieniemy .05 .01
❑ 628 Tim Brown .25 .08
❑ 629 Troy Auzenne .05 .01
❑ 630 Michael Irvin .25 .08
❑ 631 Maurice Hurst .05 .01
❑ 632 Duane Bickett .05 .01
❑ 633 George Teague .10 .02
❑ 634 Vince Workman .05 .01
❑ 635 Renaldo Turnbull .05 .01
❑ 636 Johnny Bailey .05 .01
❑ 637 Dan Williams RC .05 .01
❑ 638 James Thornton .05 .01
❑ 639 Terry Allen .25 .08
❑ 640 Kevin Greene .10 .02
❑ 641 Tony Zendejas .05 .01
❑ 642 Scott Kowalkowski RC .05 .01
❑ 643 Jeff Query UER .05 .01
❑ 644 Brian Blades .10 .02
❑ 645 Keith Jackson .10 .02
❑ 646 Monte Coleman .05 .01
❑ 647 Guy McIntyre .05 .01
❑ 648 Barry Word .05 .01
❑ 649 Steve Everitt RC .05 .01
❑ 650 Patrick Bates .05 .01
❑ 651 Marcus Robertson RC .05 .01
❑ 652 John Carney .05 .01
❑ 653 Derek Brown TE .05 .01
❑ 654 Carwell Gardner .05 .01
❑ 655 Moe Gardner .05 .01
❑ 656 Andre Ware .05 .01
❑ 657 Keith Van Horne .05 .01
❑ 658 Hugh Millen .05 .01
❑ 659 Checklist 330-495 .05 .01
❑ 660 Checklist 496-660 .05 .01

1994 Topps

❑ COMPLETE SET (660) 80.00 40.00
❑ COMP.FACT.SET 80.00 45.00
❑ COMP.SERIES 1 (330) 25.00 12.50
❑ COMP.SERIES 2 (330) 25.00 12.50
❑ 1 Emmitt Smith 1.50 .60
❑ 2 Russell Copeland .05 .01
❑ 3 Jesse Sapolu .05 .01
❑ 4 David Szott .05 .01
❑ 5 Rodney Hampton .10 .02
❑ 6 Bubba McDowell .05 .01
❑ 7 Bryce Paup .10 .02
❑ 8 Winston Moss .05 .01
❑ 9 Brett Perriman .10 .02
❑ 10 Rod Woodson .10 .02
❑ 11 John Randle .10 .02
❑ 12 David Wyman .05 .01
❑ 13 Jeff Cross .05 .01
❑ 14 Richard Cooper .05 .01
❑ 15 Johnny Mitchell .05 .01
❑ 16 David Alexander .05 .01
❑ 17 Ronnie Harmon .05 .01
❑ 18 Tyronne Stowe UER .05 .01
❑ 19 Chris Zorich .05 .01
❑ 20 Rob Burnett .05 .01
❑ 21 Harold Alexander .05 .01
❑ 22 Rod Stephens .05 .01
❑ 23 Mark Wheeler .05 .01
❑ 24 Dwayne Sabb .05 .01
❑ 25 Troy Drayton .05 .01
❑ 26 Kurt Gouveia .05 .01
❑ 27 Warren Moon .25 .08
❑ 28 Jeff Query .05 .01
❑ 29 Chuck Levy RC .05 .01
❑ 30 Bruce Smith .25 .08
❑ 31 Doug Riesenberg .05 .01
❑ 32 Willie Drewrey .05 .01
❑ 33 Nate Newton UER .05 .01
❑ 34 James Jett .05 .01
❑ 35 George Teague .05 .01
❑ 36 Marc Spindler .05 .01
❑ 37 Jack Del Rio .05 .01
❑ 38 Dale Carter .05 .01
❑ 39 Steve Atwater .05 .01
❑ 40 Herschel Walker .10 .02
❑ 41 James Hasty .05 .01
❑ 42 Seth Joyner .05 .01
❑ 43 Keith Jackson .05 .01
❑ 44 Tommy Vardell .05 .01
❑ 45 Antonio Langham RC .10 .02
❑ 46 Derek Brown RBK .05 .01
❑ 47 John Wojciechowski .05 .01
❑ 48 Horace Copeland .05 .01
❑ 49 Luis Sharpe .05 .01
❑ 50 Pat Harlow .05 .01
❑ 51 David Palmer RC .25 .08
❑ 52 Tony Smith RB .05 .01
❑ 53 Tim Johnson .05 .01
❑ 54 Anthony Newman .05 .01
❑ 55 Terry Wooden .05 .01
❑ 56 Derrick Fenner .05 .01
❑ 57 Mike Fox .05 .01
❑ 58 Brad Hopkins .05 .01
❑ 59 Daryl Johnston UER .10 .02
❑ 60 Steve Young .75 .30
❑ 61 Scottie Graham RC .10 .02
❑ 62 Nolan Harrison .05 .01
❑ 63 David Richards .05 .01
❑ 64 Chris Mohr .05 .01
❑ 65 Hardy Nickerson .10 .02
❑ 66 Heath Sherman .05 .01
❑ 67 Irving Fryar .10 .02
❑ 68 Ray Buchanan UER .05 .01
❑ 69 Jay Taylor .05 .01
❑ 70 Shannon Sharpe .10 .02
❑ 71 Vinny Testaverde .10 .02
❑ 72 Renaldo Turnbull .05 .01
❑ 73 Dwight Stone .05 .01
❑ 74 Willie McGinest RC .25 .08
❑ 75 Darrell Green .05 .01
❑ 76 Kyle Clifton .05 .01
❑ 77 Leo Goeas .05 .01
❑ 78 Ken Ruettgers .05 .01
❑ 79 Craig Heyward .10 .02
❑ 80 Andre Rison .10 .02
❑ 81 Chris Mims .05 .01
❑ 82 Gary Clark .10 .02
❑ 83 Ricardo McDonald .05 .01
❑ 84 Patrick Hunter .05 .01
❑ 85 Bruce Matthews .05 .01
❑ 86 Russell Maryland .05 .01
❑ 87 Gary Anderson K .05 .01
❑ 88 Brad Edwards .05 .01
❑ 89 Carlton Bailey .05 .01
❑ 90 Qadry Ismail .25 .08
❑ 91 Terry McDaniel .05 .01
❑ 92 Willie Green .05 .01
❑ 93 Cornelius Bennett .10 .02
❑ 94 Paul Gruber .05 .01
❑ 95 Pete Stoyanovich .05 .01
❑ 96 Merton Hanks .10 .02
❑ 97 Tre Johnson RC .05 .01
❑ 98 Jonathan Hayes .05 .01
❑ 99 Jason Elam .10 .02
❑ 100 Jerome Bettis .50 .20
❑ 101 Ronnie Lott .10 .02
❑ 102 Maurice Hurst .05 .01
❑ 103 Kirk Lowdermilk .05 .01
❑ 104 Tony Jones T .05 .01
❑ 105 Steve Beuerlein .10 .02
❑ 106 Isaac Davis RC .05 .01
❑ 107 Vaughan Johnson .05 .01

❑	108	Terrell Buckley	.05	.01
❑	109	Pierce Holt	.05	.01
❑	110	Alonzo Spellman	.05	.01
❑	111	Patrick Robinson	.05	.01
❑	112	Cortez Kennedy	.10	.02
❑	113	Kevin Williams WR	.10	.02
❑	114	Danny Copeland	.05	.01
❑	115	Chris Doleman	.05	.01
❑	116	Jerry Rice LL	.50	.20
❑	117	Neil Smith LL	.10	.02
❑	118	Emmitt Smith LL	.75	.30
❑	119	E.Robinson/Odomes LL	.05	.01
❑	120	Steve Young LL	.25	.08
❑	121	Carnell Lake	.05	.01
❑	122	Ernest Givins UER	.10	.02
❑	123	Henry Jones	.05	.01
❑	124	Michael Brooks	.05	.01
❑	125	Jason Hanson	.05	.01
❑	126	Andy Harmon	.05	.01
❑	127	Errict Rhett RC	.25	.08
❑	128	Harris Barton	.05	.01
❑	129	Greg Robinson	.05	.01
❑	130	Derrick Thomas	.25	.08
❑	131	Keith Kartz	.05	.01
❑	132	Lincoln Kennedy	.05	.01
❑	133	Leslie O'Neal	.05	.01
❑	134	Tim Goad	.05	.01
❑	135	Rohn Stark	.05	.01
❑	136	O.J.McDuffie	.25	.08
❑	137	Donnell Woolford	.05	.01
❑	138	Jamir Miller RC	.10	.02
❑	139	Eric Thomas UER	.05	.01
❑	140	Willie Roaf	.05	.01
❑	141	Wayne Gandy RC	.05	.01
❑	142	Mike Brim	.05	.01
❑	143	Kelvin Martin	.05	.01
❑	144	Edgar Bennett	.25	.08
❑	145	Michael Dean Perry	.10	.02
❑	146	Shante Carver RC	.05	.01
❑	147	Jessie Armstead UER	.05	.01
❑	148	Mo Elewonibi	.05	.01
❑	149	Dana Stubblefield	.10	.02
❑	150	Cody Carlson	.05	.01
❑	151	Vencie Glenn	.05	.01
❑	152	Levon Kirkland	.05	.01
❑	153	Derrick Moore	.05	.01
❑	154	John Fina	.05	.01
❑	155	Jeff Hostetler	.10	.02
❑	156	Courtney Hawkins	.05	.01
❑	157	Todd Collins	.05	.01
❑	158	Neil Smith	.10	.02
❑	159	Simon Fletcher	.05	.01
❑	160	Dan Marino	2.00	.75
❑	161	Sam Adams RC	.10	.02
❑	162	Marvin Washington	.05	.01
❑	163	John Copeland	.05	.01
❑	164	Eugene Robinson	.05	.01
❑	165	Mark Carrier DB	.05	.01
❑	166	Mike Kenn	.05	.01
❑	167	Tyrone Hughes	.10	.02
❑	168	Darren Carrington	.05	.01
❑	169	Shane Conlan	.05	.01
❑	170	Ricky Proehl	.05	.01
❑	171	Jeff Herrod	.05	.01
❑	172	Mark Carrier WR	.10	.02
❑	173	George Koonce	.05	.01
❑	174	Desmond Howard	.10	.02
❑	175	Dave Meggett	.05	.01
❑	176	Charles Haley	.10	.02
❑	177	Steve Wisniewski	.05	.01
❑	178	Dermontti Dawson	.05	.01
❑	179	Tim McDonald	.05	.01
❑	180	Broderick Thomas	.05	.01
❑	181	Bernard Dafney	.05	.01
❑	182	Bo Orlando	.05	.01
❑	183	Andre Reed	.10	.02
❑	184	Randall Cunningham	.25	.08
❑	185	Chris Spielman	.10	.02
❑	186	Keith Byars	.05	.01
❑	187	Ben Coates	.10	.02
❑	188	Tracy Simien	.05	.01
❑	189	Carl Pickens	.10	.02
❑	190	Reggie White	.25	.08
❑	191	Norm Johnson	.05	.01
❑	192	Brian Washington	.05	.01
❑	193	Stan Humphries	.10	.02
❑	194	Fred Stokes	.05	.01
❑	195	Dan Williams	.05	.01
❑	196	John Elway TOG	.75	.30
❑	197	Eric Allen TOG	.05	.01
❑	198	Hardy Nickerson TOG	.10	.02
❑	199	Jerome Bettis TOG	.25	.08
❑	200	Troy Aikman TOG	.50	.20
❑	201	Thurman Thomas TOG	.10	.02
❑	202	Cornelius Bennett TOG UER	.10	.02
❑	203	Michael Irvin TOG	.10	.02
❑	204	Jim Kelly TOG	.10	.02
❑	205	Junior Seau TOG	.10	.02
❑	206	Heath Shuler RC UER	.25	.08
❑	207	Howard Cross UER	.05	.01
❑	208	Pat Swilling	.05	.01
❑	209	Pete Metzelaars	.05	.01
❑	210	Tony McGee	.05	.01
❑	211	Neil O'Donnell	.25	.08
❑	212	Eugene Chung	.05	.01
❑	213	J.B. Brown	.05	.01
❑	214	Marcus Allen	.25	.08
❑	215	Harry Newsome	.05	.01
❑	216	Greg Hill RC	.25	.08
❑	217	Ryan Yarborough	.05	.01
❑	218	Marty Carter	.05	.01
❑	219	Bern Brostek	.05	.01
❑	220	Boomer Esiason	.10	.02
❑	221	Vince Buck	.05	.01
❑	222	Jim Jeffcoat	.05	.01
❑	223	Bob Dahl	.05	.01
❑	224	Marion Butts	.05	.01
❑	225	Ronald Moore	.05	.01
❑	226	Robert Blackmon	.05	.01
❑	227	Curtis Conway	.25	.08
❑	228	Jon Hand	.05	.01
❑	229	Shane Dronett	.05	.01
❑	230	Erik Williams UER	.05	.01
❑	231	Dennis Brown	.05	.01
❑	232	Ray Childress	.05	.01
❑	233	Johnnie Morton RC	.50	.20
❑	234	Kent Hull	.05	.01
❑	235	John Elliott	.05	.01
❑	236	Ron Heller	.05	.01
❑	237	J.J. Birden	.05	.01
❑	238	Thomas Randolph RC	.05	.01
❑	239	Chip Lohmiller	.05	.01
❑	240	Tim Brown	.25	.08
❑	241	Steve Tovar	.05	.01
❑	242	Moe Gardner	.05	.01
❑	243	Vincent Brown	.05	.01
❑	244	Tony Zendejas	.05	.01
❑	245	Eric Allen	.05	.01
❑	246	Joe King RC	.05	.01
❑	247	Mo Lewis	.05	.01
❑	248	Rod Bernstine	.05	.01
❑	249	Tom Waddle	.05	.01
❑	250	Junior Seau	.25	.08
❑	251	Eric Metcalf	.10	.02
❑	252	Cris Carter	.50	.20
❑	253	Bill Hitchcock	.05	.01
❑	254	Zefross Moss	.05	.01
❑	255	Morten Andersen	.05	.01
❑	256	Keith Rucker RC	.05	.01
❑	257	Chris Jacke	.05	.01
❑	258	Richmond Webb	.05	.01
❑	259	Herman Moore	.25	.08
❑	260	Phil Simms	.10	.02
❑	261	Mark Tuinei	.05	.01
❑	262	Don Beebe	.05	.01
❑	263	Marc Logan	.05	.01
❑	264	Willie Davis	.10	.02
❑	265	David Klingler	.05	.01
❑	266	Martin Mayhew UER	.05	.01
❑	267	Mark Bavaro	.05	.01
❑	268	Greg Lloyd	.10	.02
❑	269	Al Del Greco	.05	.01
❑	270	Reggie Brooks	.10	.02
❑	271	Greg Townsend	.05	.01
❑	272	Rohn Stark CAL	.05	.01
❑	273	Marcus Allen CAL	.10	.02
❑	274	Ronnie Lott CAL	.10	.02
❑	275	Dan Marino CAL	.75	.30
❑	276	Sean Gilbert	.05	.01
❑	277	LeRoy Butler	.05	.01
❑	278	Troy Auzenne	.05	.01
❑	279	Eric Swann	.10	.02
❑	280	Quentin Coryatt	.05	.01
❑	281	Anthony Pleasant	.05	.01
❑	282	Brad Baxter	.05	.01
❑	283	Carl Lee	.05	.01
❑	284	Courtney Hall	.05	.01
❑	285	Quinn Early	.10	.02
❑	286	Eddie Robinson	.05	.01
❑	287	Marco Coleman	.05	.01
❑	288	Harold Green	.05	.01
❑	289	Santana Dotson	.10	.02
❑	290	Robert Porcher	.05	.01
❑	291	Joe Phillips	.05	.01
❑	292	Mark McMillian	.05	.01
❑	293	Eric Davis	.05	.01
❑	294	Mark Jackson	.05	.01
❑	295	Darryl Talley	.05	.01
❑	296	Curtis Duncan	.05	.01
❑	297	Bruce Armstrong	.05	.01
❑	298	Eric Hill	.05	.01
❑	299	Andre Collins	.05	.01
❑	300	Jay Novacek	.10	.02
❑	301	Roosevelt Potts	.05	.01
❑	302	Eric Martin	.05	.01
❑	303	Chris Warren	.10	.02
❑	304	Deral Boykin RC	.05	.01
❑	305	Jessie Tuggle	.05	.01
❑	306	Glyn Milburn	.10	.02
❑	307	Terry Obee	.05	.01
❑	308	Eric Turner	.05	.01
❑	309	Dewayne Washington RC	.10	.02
❑	310	Sterling Sharpe	.10	.02
❑	311	Jeff Gossett	.05	.01
❑	312	John Carney	.05	.01
❑	313	Aaron Glenn RC	.25	.08
❑	314	Nick Lowery	.05	.01
❑	315	Thurman Thomas	.25	.08
❑	316	Troy Aikman MG	.50	.20
❑	317	Thurman Thomas MG	.10	.02
❑	318	Michael Irvin MG	.10	.02
❑	319	Steve Beuerlein MG	.10	.02
❑	320	Jerry Rice	1.00	.40
❑	321	Alexander Wright	.05	.01
❑	322	Michael Bates	.05	.01
❑	323	Greg Davis	.05	.01
❑	324	Mark Bortz	.05	.01
❑	325	Kevin Greene	.10	.02
❑	326	Wayne Simmons	.05	.01
❑	327	Wayne Martin	.05	.01
❑	328	Michael Irvin UER	.25	.08
❑	329	Checklist Card	.05	.01
❑	330	Checklist Card	.05	.01
❑	331	Doug Pelfrey	.05	.01
❑	332	Myron Guyton	.05	.01
❑	333	Howard Ballard	.05	.01
❑	334	Ricky Ervins	.05	.01
❑	335	Steve Emtman	.05	.01
❑	336	Eric Curry	.05	.01
❑	337	Bert Emanuel RC	.25	.08
❑	338	Darryl Ashmore	.05	.01
❑	339	Stevon Moore	.05	.01
❑	340	Garrison Hearst	.25	.08
❑	341	Vance Johnson	.05	.01
❑	342	Anthony Johnson	.10	.02
❑	343	Merril Hoge	.05	.01
❑	344	William Thomas	.05	.01
❑	345	Scott Mitchell	.10	.02
❑	346	Jim Everett	.10	.02
❑	347	Ray Crockett	.05	.01
❑	348	Bryan Cox	.05	.01
❑	349	Charles Johnson RC	.25	.08
❑	350	Randall McDaniel	.05	.01
❑	351	Micheal Barrow	.05	.01
❑	352	Darrell Thompson	.05	.01
❑	353	Kevin Gogan	.05	.01
❑	354	Brad Daluiso	.05	.01
❑	355	Mark Collins	.05	.01
❑	356	Bryant Young RC	.25	.08
❑	357	Steve Christie	.05	.01
❑	358	Derek Kennard	.05	.01
❑	359	Jon Vaughn	.05	.01
❑	360	Drew Bledsoe 3X	.75	.30
❑	361	Randy Baldwin	.05	.01
❑	362	Kevin Ross	.05	.01
❑	363	Reuben Davis	.05	.01
❑	364	Chris Miller	.05	.01
❑	365	Tim McGee	.05	.01
❑	366	Tony Woods	.05	.01
❑	367	Dean Biasucci	.05	.01
❑	368	George Jamison	.05	.01

❑ 369 Lorenzo Lynch .05 .01
❑ 370 Johnny Johnson .05 .01
❑ 371 Greg Kragen .05 .01
❑ 372 Vinson Smith .05 .01
❑ 373 Vince Workman .05 .01
❑ 374 Allen Aldridge .05 .01
❑ 375 Terry Kirby .25 .08
❑ 376 Mario Bates RC .25 .08
❑ 377 Dixon Edwards .05 .01
❑ 378 Leon Searcy .05 .01
❑ 379 Eric Guliford RC .05 .01
❑ 380 Gary Brown .05 .01
❑ 381 Phil Hansen .05 .01
❑ 382 Keith Hamilton .05 .01
❑ 383 John Alt .05 .01
❑ 384 John Taylor .10 .02
❑ 385 Reggie Cobb .05 .01
❑ 386 Rob Fredrickson RC .10 .02
❑ 387 Pepper Johnson .05 .01
❑ 388 Kevin Lee RC .05 .01
❑ 389 Stanley Richard .05 .01
❑ 390 Jackie Slater .05 .01
❑ 391 Darrick Brilz .05 .01
❑ 392 John Gesek .05 .01
❑ 393 Kelvin Pritchett .05 .01
❑ 394 Aeneas Williams .05 .01
❑ 395 Henry Ford .05 .01
❑ 396 Eric Mahlum .05 .01
❑ 397 Tom Rouen .05 .01
❑ 398 Vinnie Clark .05 .01
❑ 399 Jim Sweeney .05 .01
❑ 400 Troy Aikman 1.00 .40
❑ 401 Toi Cook .05 .01
❑ 402 Dan Saleaumua .05 .01
❑ 403 Andy Heck .05 .01
❑ 404 Deon Figures .05 .01
❑ 405 Henry Thomas .05 .01
❑ 406 Glenn Montgomery .05 .01
❑ 407 Trent Dilfer RC 1.00 .40
❑ 408 Eddie Murray .05 .01
❑ 409 Gene Atkins .05 .01
❑ 410 Mike Sherrard .05 .01
❑ 411 Don Mosebar .05 .01
❑ 412 Thomas Smith .05 .01
❑ 413 Ken Norton Jr. .10 .02
❑ 414 Robert Brooks .25 .08
❑ 415 Jeff Lageman .05 .01
❑ 416 Tony Siragusa .05 .01
❑ 417 Brian Blades .10 .02
❑ 418 Matt Stover .05 .01
❑ 419 Jesse Solomon .05 .01
❑ 420 Reggie Roby .05 .01
❑ 421 Shawn Jefferson .05 .01
❑ 422 Marc Boutte .05 .01
❑ 423 William White .05 .01
❑ 424 Clyde Simmons .05 .01
❑ 425 Anthony Miller .10 .02
❑ 426 Brent Jones .10 .02
❑ 427 Tim Grunhard .05 .01
❑ 428 Alfred Williams .05 .01
❑ 429 Roy Barker RC .05 .01
❑ 430 Dante Jones .05 .01
❑ 431 Leroy Thompson .05 .01
❑ 432 Marcus Robertson .05 .01
❑ 433 Thomas Lewis RC .10 .02
❑ 434 Sean Jones .05 .01
❑ 435 Michael Haynes .10 .02
❑ 436 Albert Lewis .05 .01
❑ 437 Tim Bowens RC .10 .02
❑ 438 Marvcus Patton .05 .01
❑ 439 Rich Miano .05 .01
❑ 440 Craig Erickson .05 .01
❑ 441 Larry Allen RC .25 .08
❑ 442 Fernando Smith .05 .01
❑ 443 D.J. Johnson .05 .01
❑ 444 Leonard Russell .05 .01
❑ 445 Marshall Faulk RC 5.00 2.00
❑ 446 Najee Mustafaa .05 .01
❑ 447 Brian Hansen .05 .01
❑ 448 Isaac Bruce RC 4.00 2.00
❑ 449 Kevin Scott .05 .01
❑ 450 Natrone Means UER .25 .08
❑ 451 Tracy Rogers RC .05 .01
❑ 452 Mike Croel .05 .01
❑ 453 Anthony Edwards .05 .01
❑ 454 Brentson Buckner RC .05 .01
❑ 455 Tom Carter .05 .01
❑ 456 Burt Grossman .05 .01
❑ 457 Jimmy Spencer RC .05 .01
❑ 458 Rocket Ismail .10 .02
❑ 459 Fred Strickland .05 .01
❑ 460 Jeff Burris RC .10 .02
❑ 461 Adrian Hardy .05 .01
❑ 462 Lamar McGriggs .05 .01
❑ 463 Webster Slaughter .05 .01
❑ 464 Demetrius DuBose .05 .01
❑ 465 Dave Brown .10 .02
❑ 466 Kenneth Gant .05 .01
❑ 467 Erik Kramer .10 .02
❑ 468 Mark Ingram .05 .01
❑ 469 Roman Phifer .05 .01
❑ 470 Steve Young .50 .20
❑ 471 Nick Lowery .05 .01
❑ 472 Irving Fryar .10 .02
❑ 473 Art Monk .10 .02
❑ 474 Mel Gray .05 .01
❑ 475 Reggie White .25 .08
❑ 476 Eric Ball .05 .01
❑ 477 Dwayne Harper .05 .01
❑ 478 Will Shields .05 .01
❑ 479 Roger Harper .05 .01
❑ 480 Rick Mirer .25 .08
❑ 481 Vincent Brisby .10 .02
❑ 482 John Jurkovic RC .10 .02
❑ 483 Michael Jackson .10 .02
❑ 484 Ed Cunningham .05 .01
❑ 485 Brad Ottis .05 .01
❑ 486 Sterling Palmer RC .05 .01
❑ 487 Tony Bennett .05 .01
❑ 488 Mike Pritchard .05 .01
❑ 489 Bucky Brooks RC .05 .01
❑ 490 Troy Vincent .05 .01
❑ 491 Eric Green .05 .01
❑ 492 Van Malone .05 .01
❑ 493 Marcus Spears RC .05 .01
❑ 494 Brian Williams OL .05 .01
❑ 495 Robert Smith .25 .08
❑ 496 Haywood Jeffires .10 .02
❑ 497 Darrin Smith .05 .01
❑ 498 Tommy Barnhardt .05 .01
❑ 499 Anthony Smith .05 .01
❑ 500 Ricky Watters .10 .02
❑ 501 Antone Davis .05 .01
❑ 502 David Braxton .05 .01
❑ 503 Donnell Bennett RC .25 .08
❑ 504 Donald Evans .05 .01
❑ 505 Lewis Tillman .05 .01
❑ 506 Lance Smith .05 .01
❑ 507 Aaron Taylor .05 .01
❑ 508 Ricky Sanders .05 .01
❑ 509 Dennis Smith .05 .01
❑ 510 Barry Foster .05 .01
❑ 511 Stan Brock .05 .01
❑ 512 Henry Rolling .05 .01
❑ 513 Walter Reeves .05 .01
❑ 514 John Booty .05 .01
❑ 515 Kenneth Davis .05 .01
❑ 516 Cris Dishman .05 .01
❑ 517 Bill Lewis .05 .01
❑ 518 Jeff Bryant .05 .01
❑ 519 Brian Mitchell .05 .01
❑ 520 Joe Montana 2.00 .75
❑ 521 Keith Sims .05 .01
❑ 522 Harry Colon .05 .01
❑ 523 Leon Lett .05 .01
❑ 524 Carlos Jenkins .05 .01
❑ 525 Victor Bailey .05 .01
❑ 526 Harvey Williams .10 .02
❑ 527 Irv Smith .05 .01
❑ 528 Jason Sehorn RC .40 .15
❑ 529 John Thierry RC .05 .01
❑ 530 Brett Favre 2.00 .75
❑ 531 Sean Dawkins RC .25 .08
❑ 532 Erric Pegram .05 .01
❑ 533 Jimmy Williams .05 .01
❑ 534 Michael Timpson .05 .01
❑ 535 Flipper Anderson .05 .01
❑ 536 John Parrella .05 .01
❑ 537 Freddie Joe Nunn .05 .01
❑ 538 Doug Dawson .05 .01
❑ 539 Michael Stewart .05 .01
❑ 540 John Elway 2.00 .75
❑ 541 Ronnie Lott .10 .02
❑ 542 Barry Sanders TOG .75 .30
❑ 543 Andre Reed TOG .10 .02
❑ 544 Deion Sanders TOG .25 .08
❑ 545 Dan Marino TOG .75 .30
❑ 546 Carlton Bailey TOG .05 .01
❑ 547 Emmitt Smith TOG .75 .30
❑ 548 Alvin Harper TOG .10 .02
❑ 549 Eric Metcalf TOG .10 .02
❑ 550 Jerry Rice TOG .50 .20
❑ 551 Derrick Thomas TOG .25 .08
❑ 552 Mark Collins TOG .05 .01
❑ 553 Eric Turner TOG .05 .01
❑ 554 Sterling Sharpe TOG .10 .02
❑ 555 Steve Young TOG .25 .08
❑ 556 Darnay Scott RC .50 .20
❑ 557 Joel Steed .05 .01
❑ 558 Dennis Gibson .05 .01
❑ 559 Charles Mincy .05 .01
❑ 560 Rickey Jackson .05 .01
❑ 561 Dave Cadigan .05 .01
❑ 562 Rick Tuten .05 .01
❑ 563 Mike Caldwell .05 .01
❑ 564 Todd Steussie RC .10 .02
❑ 565 Kevin Smith .05 .01
❑ 566 Arthur Marshall .05 .01
❑ 567 Aaron Wallace .05 .01
❑ 568 Calvin Williams .10 .02
❑ 569 Todd Kelly .05 .01
❑ 570 Barry Sanders 1.50 .60
❑ 571 Shaun Gayle .05 .01
❑ 572 Will Wolford .05 .01
❑ 573 Ethan Horton .05 .01
❑ 574 Chris Slade .05 .01
❑ 575 Jeff Wright .05 .01
❑ 576 Toby Wright .05 .01
❑ 577 Lamar Thomas .05 .01
❑ 578 Chris Singleton .05 .01
❑ 579 Ed West .05 .01
❑ 580 Jeff George .25 .08
❑ 581 Kevin Mitchell .05 .01
❑ 582 Chad Brown .05 .01
❑ 583 Rich Camarillo .05 .01
❑ 584 Gary Zimmerman .05 .01
❑ 585 Randal Hill .05 .01
❑ 586 Keith Cash .05 .01
❑ 587 Sam Mills .05 .01
❑ 588 Shawn Lee .05 .01
❑ 589 Kent Graham .10 .02
❑ 590 Steve Everitt .05 .01
❑ 591 Rob Moore .10 .02
❑ 592 Kevin Mawae RC .25 .08
❑ 593 Jerry Ball .05 .01
❑ 594 Larry Brown DB .05 .01
❑ 595 Tim Krumrie .05 .01
❑ 596 Aubrey Beavers RC .05 .01
❑ 597 Chris Hinton .05 .01
❑ 598 Greg Montgomery .05 .01
❑ 599 Jimmie Jones .05 .01
❑ 600 Jim Kelly .25 .08
❑ 601 Joe Johnson RC .05 .01
❑ 602 Tim Irwin .05 .01
❑ 603 Steve Jackson .05 .01
❑ 604 James Williams RC LB .05 .01
❑ 605 Blair Thomas .05 .01
❑ 606 Danan Hughes .05 .01
❑ 607 Russell Freeman .05 .01
❑ 608 Andre Hastings .10 .02
❑ 609 Ken Harvey .05 .01
❑ 610 Jim Harbaugh .25 .08
❑ 611 Emmitt Smith MG .75 .30
❑ 612 Andre Rison MG .10 .02
❑ 613 Steve Young MG .25 .08
❑ 614 Anthony Miller MG .05 .01
❑ 615 Barry Sanders MG .75 .30
❑ 616 Bernie Kosar .10 .02
❑ 617 Chris Gardocki .05 .01
❑ 618 William Floyd RC .25 .08
❑ 619 Matt Brock .05 .01
❑ 620 Dan Wilkinson RC .10 .02
❑ 621 Tony Meola RC .10 .02
❑ 622 Tony Tolbert .05 .01
❑ 623 Mike Zandofsky .05 .01
❑ 624 William Fuller .05 .01
❑ 625 Steve Jordan .05 .01
❑ 626 Mike Johnson .05 .01
❑ 627 Ferrell Edmunds .05 .01
❑ 628 Gene Williams .05 .01
❑ 629 Willie Beamon .05 .01

❑ 630 Gerald Perry .05 .01
❑ 631 John Baylor .05 .01
❑ 632 Carwell Gardner .05 .01
❑ 633 Thomas Everett .05 .01
❑ 634 Lamar Lathon .05 .01
❑ 635 Michael Bankston .05 .01
❑ 636 Ray Crittenden RC .05 .01
❑ 637 Kimble Anders .10 .02
❑ 638 Robert Delpino .05 .01
❑ 639 Darren Perry .05 .01
❑ 640 Byron Evans .05 .01
❑ 641 Mark Higgs .05 .01
❑ 642 Lorenzo Neal .05 .01
❑ 643 Henry Ellard .10 .02
❑ 644 Trace Armstrong .05 .01
❑ 645 Greg McMurtry .05 .01
❑ 646 Steve McMichael .10 .02
❑ 647 Terance Mathis .10 .02
❑ 648 Eric Bieniemy .05 .01
❑ 649 Bobby Houston .05 .01
❑ 650 Alvin Harper .10 .02
❑ 651 James Folston RC .05 .01
❑ 652 Mel Gray .05 .01
❑ 653 Adrian Cooper .05 .01
❑ 654 Dexter Carter .05 .01
❑ 655 Don Griffin .05 .01
❑ 656 Corey Widmer .05 .01
❑ 657 Lee Johnson .05 .01
❑ 658 Nate Odomes .05 .01
❑ 659 Checklist Card .05 .01
❑ 660 Checklist Card .05 .01
❑ P1 Promo Sheet 4.00 1.50
❑ P2 Promo Sheet Special Effects 4.00 1.50

1995 Topps

❑ COMPLETE SET (468) 40.00 15.00
❑ COMP.FACT.SET (478) 50.00 25.00
❑ COMP.SERIES 1 (248) 20.00 7.50
❑ COMP.SERIES 2 (220) 20.00 7.50
❑ 1 Barry Sanders TYC .75 .30
❑ 2 Chris Warren TYC .20 .07
❑ 3 Jerry Rice TYC .50 .20
❑ 4 Emmitt Smith TYC .75 .30
❑ 5 Henry Ellard TYC .20 .07
❑ 6 Natrone Means TYC .20 .07
❑ 7 Terance Mathis TYC .20 .07
❑ 8 Tim Brown TYC .20 .07
❑ 9 Andre Reed TYC .20 .07
❑ 10 Marshall Faulk TYC .60 .25
❑ 11 Irving Fryar TYC .20 .07
❑ 12 Cris Carter TYC .30 .10
❑ 13 Michael Irvin TYC .30 .10
❑ 14 Jake Reed TYC .20 .07
❑ 15 Ben Coates TYC .20 .07
❑ 16 Herman Moore TYC .30 .10
❑ 17 Carl Pickens TYC .20 .07
❑ 18 Fred Barnett TYC .20 .07
❑ 19 Sterling Sharpe TYC .20 .07
❑ 20 Anthony Miller TYC .20 .07
❑ 21 Thurman Thomas TYC .30 .10
❑ 22 Andre Rison TYC .20 .07
❑ 23 Brian Blades TYC .20 .07
❑ 24 Rodney Hampton TYC .20 .07
❑ 25 Terry Allen TYC .20 .07
❑ 26 Jerome Bettis TYC .30 .10
❑ 27 Errict Rhett TYC .20 .07
❑ 28 Rob Moore TYC .20 .07
❑ 29 Shannon Sharpe TYC .20 .07
❑ 30 Drew Bledsoe TYC .30 .10
❑ 31 Dan Marino TYC 1.00 .40
❑ 32 Warren Moon TYC .20 .07
❑ 33 Steve Young TYC .40 .15
❑ 34 Brett Favre TYC 1.00 .40
❑ 35 Jim Everett TYC .10 .02
❑ 36 Jeff George TYC .20 .07
❑ 37 John Elway TYC 1.00 .40
❑ 38 Jeff Hostetler TYC .20 .07
❑ 39 Randall Cunningham TYC .30 .10
❑ 40 Stan Humphries TYC .20 .07
❑ 41 Jim Kelly TYC .30 .10
❑ 42 Tommy Barnhardt .10 .02
❑ 43 Bob Whitfield .10 .02
❑ 44 William Thomas .10 .02
❑ 45 Glyn Milburn .10 .02
❑ 46 Steve Christie .10 .02
❑ 47 Kevin Mawae .10 .02
❑ 48 Vencie Glenn .10 .02
❑ 49 Eric Curry .10 .02
❑ 50 Jeff Hostetler .20 .07
❑ 51 Tyronne Stowe .10 .02
❑ 52 Steve Jackson .10 .02
❑ 53 Ben Coleman .10 .02
❑ 54 Brad Baxter .10 .02
❑ 55 Darryl Williams .10 .02
❑ 56 Troy Drayton .10 .02
❑ 57 George Teague .10 .02
❑ 58 Calvin Williams .20 .07
❑ 59 Jeff Cross .10 .02
❑ 60 Leroy Hoard .10 .02
❑ 61 John Carney .10 .02
❑ 62 Daryl Johnston .20 .07
❑ 63 Jim Jeffcoat .10 .02
❑ 64 Matt Stover .10 .02
❑ 65 LeRoy Butler .10 .02
❑ 66 Curtis Conway .30 .10
❑ 67 O.J. McDuffie .30 .10
❑ 68 Robert Massey .10 .02
❑ 69 Ed McDaniel .10 .02
❑ 70 William Floyd .20 .07
❑ 71 Willie Davis .20 .07
❑ 72 William Roberts .10 .02
❑ 73 Chester McGlockton .20 .07
❑ 74 D.J. Johnson .10 .02
❑ 75 Rondell Jones .10 .02
❑ 76 Morten Andersen .10 .02
❑ 77 Glenn Parker .10 .02
❑ 78 William Fuller .10 .02
❑ 79 Ray Buchanan .10 .02
❑ 80 Maurice Hurst .10 .02
❑ 81 Wayne Gandy .10 .02
❑ 82 Marcus Turner .10 .02
❑ 83 Greg Davis .10 .02
❑ 84 Terry Wooden .10 .02
❑ 85 Thomas Everett .10 .02
❑ 86 Steve Broussard .10 .02
❑ 87 Tom Carter .10 .02
❑ 88 Glenn Montgomery .10 .02
❑ 89 Larry Allen .20 .07
❑ 90 Donnell Woolford .10 .02
❑ 91 John Alt .10 .02
❑ 92 Phil Hansen .10 .02
❑ 93 Seth Joyner .10 .02
❑ 94 Michael Brooks .10 .02
❑ 95 Randall McDaniel .10 .02
❑ 96 Tydus Winans .10 .02
❑ 97 Rob Fredrickson .10 .02
❑ 98 Ray Crockett .10 .02
❑ 99 Courtney Hall .10 .02
❑ 100 Merton Hanks .10 .02
❑ 101 Aaron Glenn .10 .02
❑ 102 Roosevelt Potts .10 .02
❑ 103 Leon Lett .10 .02
❑ 104 Jessie Tuggle .10 .02
❑ 105 Martin Mayhew .10 .02
❑ 106 Willie Roaf .10 .02
❑ 107 Todd Lyght .10 .02
❑ 108 Ernest Givins .10 .02
❑ 109 Tony McGee .10 .02
❑ 110 Barry Sanders 1.50 .60
❑ 111 Dermontti Dawson .20 .07
❑ 112 Rick Tuten .10 .02
❑ 113 Vincent Brisby .10 .02
❑ 114 Charlie Garner .30 .10
❑ 115 Irving Fryar .20 .07
❑ 116 Stevon Moore .10 .02
❑ 117 Matt Darby .10 .02
❑ 118 Howard Cross .10 .02
❑ 119 John Gesek .10 .02
❑ 120 Jack Del Rio .10 .02
❑ 121 Marcus Allen .30 .10
❑ 122 Torrance Small .10 .02
❑ 123 Chris Mims .10 .02
❑ 124 Don Mosebar .10 .02
❑ 125 Carl Pickens .20 .07
❑ 126 Tom Rouen .10 .02
❑ 127 Garrison Hearst .30 .10
❑ 128 Charles Johnson .20 .07
❑ 129 Derek Brown RBK .10 .02
❑ 130 Troy Aikman 1.00 .40
❑ 131 Troy Vincent .10 .02
❑ 132 Ken Ruettgers .10 .02
❑ 133 Michael Jackson .20 .07
❑ 134 Dennis Gibson .10 .02
❑ 135 Brett Perriman .20 .07
❑ 136 Jeff Graham .10 .02
❑ 137 Chad Brown .20 .07
❑ 138 Ken Norton Jr. .20 .07
❑ 139 Chris Slade .10 .02
❑ 140 Dave Brown .20 .07
❑ 141 Bert Emanuel .30 .10
❑ 142 Renaldo Turnbull .10 .02
❑ 143 Jim Harbaugh .20 .07
❑ 144 Micheal Barrow .10 .02
❑ 145 Vincent Brown .10 .02
❑ 146 Bryant Young .20 .07
❑ 147 Boomer Esiason .20 .07
❑ 148 Sean Gilbert .20 .07
❑ 149 Greg Truitt .10 .02
❑ 150 Rod Woodson .20 .07
❑ 151 Robert Porcher .10 .02
❑ 152 Joe Phillips .10 .02
❑ 153 Gary Zimmerman .10 .02
❑ 154 Bruce Smith .30 .10
❑ 155 Randall Cunningham .30 .10
❑ 156 Fred Strickland .10 .02
❑ 157 Derrick Alexander WR .30 .10
❑ 158 James Williams LB .10 .02
❑ 159 Scott Dill .10 .02
❑ 160 Tim Bowens .10 .02
❑ 161 Floyd Turner .10 .02
❑ 162 Ronnie Harmon .10 .02
❑ 163 Wayne Martin .10 .02
❑ 164 John Randle .20 .07
❑ 165 Larry Centers .20 .07
❑ 166 Larry Brown DB .10 .02
❑ 167 Albert Lewis .10 .02
❑ 168 Michael Strahan .30 .10
❑ 169 Reggie Brooks .20 .07
❑ 170 Craig Heyward .20 .07
❑ 171 Pat Harlow .10 .02
❑ 172 Eugene Robinson .10 .02
❑ 173 Shane Conlan .10 .02
❑ 174 Bennie Blades .10 .02
❑ 175 Neil O'Donnell .20 .07
❑ 176 Steve Tovar .10 .02
❑ 177 Donald Evans .10 .02
❑ 178 Brent Jones .10 .02
❑ 179 Ray Childress .10 .02
❑ 180 Reggie White .30 .10
❑ 181 David Alexander .10 .02
❑ 182 Greg Hill .20 .07
❑ 183 Vinny Testaverde .20 .07
❑ 184 Jeff Burris .10 .02
❑ 185 Hardy Nickerson .10 .02
❑ 186 Terry Kirby .20 .07
❑ 187 Kirk Lowdermilk .10 .02
❑ 188 Eric Swann .20 .07
❑ 189 Chris Zorich .10 .02
❑ 190 Simon Fletcher .10 .02
❑ 191 Qadry Ismail .20 .07
❑ 192 Heath Shuler .20 .07
❑ 193 Michael Haynes .20 .07
❑ 194 Mike Sherrard .10 .02
❑ 195 Nolan Harrison .10 .02
❑ 196 Marcus Robertson .10 .02
❑ 197 Kevin Williams WR .20 .07
❑ 198 Moe Gardner .10 .02
❑ 199 Rick Mirer .20 .07
❑ 200 Junior Seau .30 .10
❑ 201 Byron Bam Morris .10 .02
❑ 202 Willie McGinest .20 .07
❑ 203 Chris Spielman .20 .07
❑ 204 Darnay Scott .20 .07

❑ 205 Jesse Sapolu .10 .02
❑ 206 Marvin Washington .10 .02
❑ 207 Anthony Newman .10 .02
❑ 208 Cortez Kennedy .20 .07
❑ 209 Quentin Coryatt .20 .07
❑ 210 Neil Smith .20 .07
❑ 211 Keith Sims .10 .02
❑ 212 Sean Jones .10 .02
❑ 213 Tony Jones T .10 .02
❑ 214 Lewis Tillman .10 .02
❑ 215 Darren Woodson .20 .07
❑ 216 Jason Hanson .10 .02
❑ 217 John Taylor .10 .02
❑ 218 Shawn Lee .10 .02
❑ 219 Kevin Greene .20 .07
❑ 220 Jerry Rice 1.00 .40
❑ 221 Ki-Jana Carter RC .30 .10
❑ 222 Tony Boselli RC .30 .10
❑ 223 Michael Westbrook RC .30 .10
❑ 224 Kerry Collins RC 1.25 .50
❑ 225 Kevin Carter RC .30 .10
❑ 226 Kyle Brady RC .30 .10
❑ 227 J.J. Stokes RC .30 .10
❑ 228 Derrick Alexander DE RC .10 .02
❑ 229 Warren Sapp RC 1.50 .60
❑ 230 Ruben Brown RC .30 .10
❑ 231 Hugh Douglas RC .30 .10
❑ 232 Luther Elliss RC .10 .02
❑ 233 Rashaan Salaam RC .20 .07
❑ 234 Tyrone Poole RC .30 .10
❑ 235 Korey Stringer RC .20 .07
❑ 236 Devin Bush RC .10 .02
❑ 237 Cory Raymer RC .10 .02
❑ 238 Zach Wiegert RC .10 .02
❑ 239 Ron Davis RC .10 .02
❑ 240 Todd Collins RC .20 .07
❑ 241 Bobby Taylor RC .30 .10
❑ 242 Patrick Riley RC .10 .02
❑ 243 Scott Gragg .10 .02
❑ 244 Marvcus Patton .10 .02
❑ 245 Alvin Harper .10 .02
❑ 246 Ricky Watters .20 .07
❑ 247 Checklist 1 .10 .02
❑ 248 Checklist 2 .10 .02
❑ 249 Terance Mathis .20 .07
❑ 250 Mark Carrier DB .10 .02
❑ 251 Elijah Alexander .10 .02
❑ 252 George Koonce .10 .02
❑ 253 Tony Bennett .10 .02
❑ 254 Steve Wisniewski .10 .02
❑ 255 Bernie Parmalee .20 .07
❑ 256 Dwayne Sabb .10 .02
❑ 257 Lorenzo Neal .10 .02
❑ 258 Corey Miller .10 .02
❑ 259 Fred Barnett .20 .07
❑ 260 Greg Lloyd .20 .07
❑ 261 Robert Blackmon .10 .02
❑ 262 Ken Harvey .10 .02
❑ 263 Eric Hill .10 .02
❑ 264 Russell Copeland .10 .02
❑ 265 Jeff Blake RC .75 .30
❑ 266 Carl Banks .10 .02
❑ 267 Jay Novacek .20 .07
❑ 268 Mel Gray .10 .02
❑ 269 Kimble Anders .20 .07
❑ 270 Cris Carter .30 .10
❑ 271 Johnny Mitchell .10 .02
❑ 272 Shawn Jefferson .10 .02
❑ 273 Doug Brien .10 .02
❑ 274 Sean Landeta .10 .02
❑ 275 Scott Mitchell .20 .07
❑ 276 Charles Wilson .10 .02
❑ 277 Anthony Smith .10 .02
❑ 278 Anthony Miller .20 .07
❑ 279 Steve Walsh .10 .02
❑ 280 Drew Bledsoe .60 .25
❑ 281 Jamir Miller .10 .02
❑ 282 Robert Brooks .30 .10
❑ 283 Sean Lumpkin .10 .02
❑ 284 Bryan Cox .10 .02
❑ 285 Byron Evans .10 .02
❑ 286 Chris Doleman .10 .02
❑ 287 Anthony Pleasant .10 .02
❑ 288 Stephen Grant RC .10 .02
❑ 289 Doug Riesenberg .10 .02
❑ 290 Natrone Means .20 .07
❑ 291 Henry Thomas .10 .02
❑ 292 Mike Pritchard .10 .02
❑ 293 Courtney Hawkins .10 .02
❑ 294 Bill Bates .20 .07
❑ 295 Jerome Bettis .30 .10
❑ 296 Russell Maryland .10 .02
❑ 297 Stanley Richard .10 .02
❑ 298 William White .10 .02
❑ 299 Dan Wilkinson .20 .07
❑ 300 Steve Young .75 .30
❑ 301 Gary Brown .10 .02
❑ 302 Jake Reed .20 .07
❑ 303 Carlton Gray .10 .02
❑ 304 Levon Kirkland .10 .02
❑ 305 Shannon Sharpe .20 .07
❑ 306 Luis Sharpe .10 .02
❑ 307 Marshall Faulk 1.25 .50
❑ 308 Stan Humphries .20 .07
❑ 309 Chris Calloway .10 .02
❑ 310 Tim Brown .30 .10
❑ 311 Steve Everitt .10 .02
❑ 312 Raymont Harris .10 .02
❑ 313 Tim McDonald .10 .02
❑ 314 Trent Dilfer .30 .10
❑ 315 Jim Everett .10 .02
❑ 316 Ray Crittenden .10 .02
❑ 317 Jim Kelly .30 .10
❑ 318 Andre Reed .20 .07
❑ 319 Chris Miller .10 .02
❑ 320 Bobby Houston .10 .02
❑ 321 Charles Haley .20 .07
❑ 322 James Francis .10 .02
❑ 323 Bernard Williams .10 .02
❑ 324 Michael Bates .10 .02
❑ 325 Brian Mitchell .10 .02
❑ 326 Mike Johnson .10 .02
❑ 327 Eric Bieniemy .10 .02
❑ 328 Aubrey Beavers .10 .02
❑ 329 Dale Carter .20 .07
❑ 330 Emmitt Smith 1.50 .60
❑ 331 Darren Perry .10 .02
❑ 332 Marquez Pope .10 .02
❑ 333 Clyde Simmons .10 .02
❑ 334 Corey Croom .10 .02
❑ 335 Thomas Randolph .10 .02
❑ 336 Harvey Williams .10 .02
❑ 337 Michael Timpson .10 .02
❑ 338 Eugene Daniel .10 .02
❑ 339 Shane Dronett .10 .02
❑ 340 Eric Turner .10 .02
❑ 341 Eric Metcalf .20 .07
❑ 342 Leslie O'Neal .20 .07
❑ 343 Mark Wheeler .10 .02
❑ 344 Mark Pike .10 .02
❑ 345 Brett Favre 2.00 .75
❑ 346 Johnny Bailey .10 .02
❑ 347 Henry Ellard .20 .07
❑ 348 Chris Gardocki .10 .02
❑ 349 Henry Jones .10 .02
❑ 350 Dan Marino 2.00 .75
❑ 351 Lake Dawson .20 .07
❑ 352 Mark McMillian .10 .02
❑ 353 Deion Sanders .60 .25
❑ 354 Antonio London .10 .02
❑ 355 Cris Dishman .10 .02
❑ 356 Ricardo McDonald .10 .02
❑ 357 Dexter Carter .10 .02
❑ 358 Kevin Smith .10 .02
❑ 359 Yancey Thigpen RC .20 .07
❑ 360 Chris Warren .20 .07
❑ 361 Quinn Early .20 .07
❑ 362 John Mangum .10 .02
❑ 363 Santana Dotson .10 .02
❑ 364 Rocket Ismail .20 .07
❑ 365 Aeneas Williams .10 .02
❑ 366 Dan Williams .10 .02
❑ 367 Sean Dawkins .20 .07
❑ 368 Pepper Johnson .10 .02
❑ 369 Roman Phifer .10 .02
❑ 370 Rodney Hampton .20 .07
❑ 371 Darrell Green .10 .02
❑ 372 Michael Zordich .10 .02
❑ 373 Andre Coleman .10 .02
❑ 374 Wayne Simmons .10 .02
❑ 375 Michael Irvin .30 .10
❑ 376 Clay Matthews .20 .07
❑ 377 Dewayne Washington .20 .07
❑ 378 Keith Byars .10 .02
❑ 379 Todd Collins LB .30 .10
❑ 380 Mark Collins .10 .02
❑ 381 Joel Steed .10 .02
❑ 382 Bart Oates .10 .02
❑ 383 Al Smith .10 .02
❑ 384 Rafael Robinson .10 .02
❑ 385 Mo Lewis .10 .02
❑ 386 Aubrey Matthews .10 .02
❑ 387 Corey Sawyer .10 .02
❑ 388 Bucky Brooks .10 .02
❑ 389 Erik Kramer .10 .02
❑ 390 Tyrone Hughes .20 .07
❑ 391 Terry McDaniel .10 .02
❑ 392 Craig Erickson .10 .02
❑ 393 Mike Flores .10 .02
❑ 394 Harry Swayne .10 .02
❑ 395 Irving Spikes .20 .07
❑ 396 Lorenzo Lynch .10 .02
❑ 397 Antonio Langham .10 .02
❑ 398 Edgar Bennett .20 .07
❑ 399 Thomas Lewis .20 .07
❑ 400 John Elway 2.00 .75
❑ 401 Jeff George .20 .07
❑ 402 Errict Rhett .20 .07
❑ 403 Bill Romanowski .10 .02
❑ 404 Alexander Wright .10 .02
❑ 405 Warren Moon .20 .07
❑ 406 Eddie Robinson .10 .02
❑ 407 John Copeland .10 .02
❑ 408 Robert Jones .10 .02
❑ 409 Steve Bono .20 .07
❑ 410 Cornelius Bennett .20 .07
❑ 411 Ben Coates .20 .07
❑ 412 Dana Stubblefield .20 .07
❑ 413 Darryl Talley .10 .02
❑ 414 Brian Blades .20 .07
❑ 415 Herman Moore .30 .10
❑ 416 Nick Lowery .10 .02
❑ 417 Donnell Bennett .20 .07
❑ 418 Van Malone .10 .02
❑ 419 Pete Stoyanovich .10 .02
❑ 420 Joe Montana 2.00 .75
❑ 421 Steve Young .50 .20
❑ 422 Steve Young .50 .20
❑ 423 Steve Young .50 .20
❑ 424 Steve Young .50 .20
❑ 425 Steve Young .50 .20
❑ 426 Rod Stephens .10 .02
❑ 427 Ellis Johnson RC UER .10 .02
❑ 428 Kordell Stewart RC 1.25 .50
❑ 429 James O. Stewart RC 1.00 .40
❑ 430 Steve McNair RC 2.50 1.00
❑ 431 Brian DeMarco .20 .07
❑ 432 Matt O'Dwyer .10 .02
❑ 433 Lorenzo Styles RC .10 .02
❑ 434 Anthony Cook RC .10 .02
❑ 435 Jesse James .10 .02
❑ 436 Darryl Pounds RC .10 .02
❑ 437 Derrick Graham .10 .02
❑ 438 Vernon Turner .10 .02
❑ 439 Carlton Bailey .10 .02
❑ 440 Darion Conner .10 .02
❑ 441 Randy Baldwin .10 .02
❑ 442 Tim McKyer .10 .02
❑ 443 Sam Mills .20 .07
❑ 444 Bob Christian .10 .02
❑ 445 Steve Lofton .10 .02
❑ 446 Lamar Lathon .10 .02
❑ 447 Tony Smith RB .10 .02
❑ 448 Don Beebe .10 .02
❑ 449 Barry Foster .20 .07
❑ 450 Frank Reich .10 .02
❑ 451 Pete Metzelaars .10 .02
❑ 452 Reggie Cobb .10 .02
❑ 453 Jeff Lageman .10 .02
❑ 454 Derek Brown TE .10 .02
❑ 455 Desmond Howard .20 .07
❑ 456 Vinnie Clark .10 .02
❑ 457 Keith Goganious .10 .02
❑ 458 Shawn Bouwens .10 .02
❑ 459 Rob Johnson RC .75 .30
❑ 460 Steve Beuerlein .20 .07
❑ 461 Mark Brunell .60 .25
❑ 462 Harry Colon .10 .02
❑ 463 Chris Hudson .10 .02
❑ 464 Darren Carrington .10 .02
❑ 465 Ernest Givins .10 .02

❑ 466	Kelvin Pritchett	.10	.02
❑ 467	Checklist (249-358)	.10	.02
❑ 468	Checklist (358-468)	.10	.02

1996 Topps

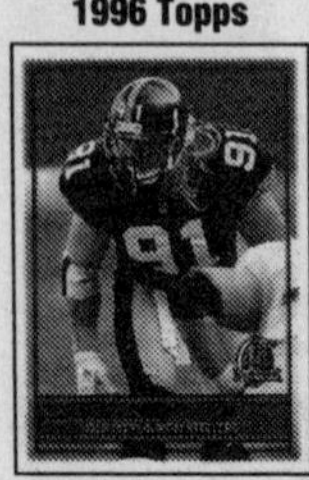

❑	COMPLETE SET (440)	40.00	20.00
❑	COMP.FACT.SET (448)	60.00	35.00
❑	COMP.CER.FACT.SET (445)	40.00	20.00
❑ 1	Troy Aikman	1.00	.40
❑ 2	Kevin Greene	.20	.07
❑ 3	Robert Brooks	.30	.10
❑ 4	Eugene Daniel	.10	.02
❑ 5	Rodney Peete	.10	.02
❑ 6	James Hasty	.10	.02
❑ 7	Tim McDonald	.10	.02
❑ 8	Darick Holmes	.10	.02
❑ 9	Morten Andersen	.10	.02
❑ 10	Junior Seau	.30	.10
❑ 11	Brett Perriman	.10	.02
❑ 12	Eric Green	.10	.02
❑ 13	Jim Flanigan	.10	.02
❑ 14	Cortez Kennedy	.10	.02
❑ 15	Orlando Thomas	.10	.02
❑ 16	Anthony Miller	.20	.07
❑ 17	Sean Gilbert	.10	.02
❑ 18	Rob Fredrickson	.10	.02
❑ 19	Willie Green	.10	.02
❑ 20	Jeff Blake	.30	.10
❑ 21	Trent Dilfer	.30	.10
❑ 22	Chris Chandler	.20	.07
❑ 23	Renaldo Turnbull	.10	.02
❑ 24	Dave Meggett	.10	.02
❑ 25	Heath Shuler	.20	.07
❑ 26	Michael Jackson	.20	.07
❑ 27	Thomas Randolph	.10	.02
❑ 28	Keith Goganious	.10	.02
❑ 29	Seth Joyner	.10	.02
❑ 30	Wayne Chrebet	.60	.25
❑ 31	Craig Newsome	.10	.02
❑ 32	William Fuller	.10	.02
❑ 33	Merton Hanks	.10	.02
❑ 34	Dale Carter	.10	.02
❑ 35	Quentin Coryatt	.10	.02
❑ 36	Robert Jones	.10	.02
❑ 37	Eric Metcalf	.10	.02
❑ 38	Byron Bam Morris	.10	.02
❑ 39	Bill Brooks	.10	.02
❑ 40	Barry Sanders	1.50	.60
❑ 41	Michael Haynes	.10	.02
❑ 42	Joey Galloway	.30	.10
❑ 43	Robert Smith	.20	.07
❑ 44	John Thierry	.10	.02
❑ 45	Bryan Cox	.10	.02
❑ 46	Anthony Parker	.10	.02
❑ 47	Harvey Williams	.10	.02
❑ 48	Terrell Davis	.75	.30
❑ 49	Darnay Scott	.20	.07
❑ 50	Kerry Collins	.30	.10
❑ 51	Cris Dishman	.10	.02
❑ 52	Dwayne Harper	.10	.02
❑ 53	Warren Sapp	.10	.02
❑ 54	Will Moore	.10	.02
❑ 55	Earnest Byner	.10	.02
❑ 56	Aaron Glenn	.10	.02
❑ 57	Michael Westbrook	.30	.10
❑ 58	Vencie Glenn	.10	.02
❑ 59	Rob Moore	.20	.07
❑ 60	Mark Brunell	.60	.25
❑ 61	Craig Heyward	.10	.02
❑ 62	Eric Allen	.10	.02
❑ 63	Bill Romanowski	.10	.02
❑ 64	Dana Stubblefield	.20	.07
❑ 65	Steve Bono	.10	.02
❑ 66	George Koonce	.10	.02
❑ 67	Larry Brown	.10	.02
❑ 68	Warren Moon	.20	.07
❑ 69	Erric Pegram	.10	.02
❑ 70	Jim Kelly	.30	.10
❑ 71	Jason Belser	.10	.02
❑ 72	Henry Thomas	.10	.02
❑ 73	Mark Carrier DB	.10	.02
❑ 74	Terry Wooden	.10	.02
❑ 75	Terry McDaniel	.10	.02
❑ 76	O.J. McDuffie	.20	.07
❑ 77	Dan Wilkinson	.10	.02
❑ 78	Blake Brockermeyer	.10	.02
❑ 79	Micheal Barrow	.10	.02
❑ 80	Dave Brown	.10	.02
❑ 81	Todd Lyght	.10	.02
❑ 82	Henry Ellard	.10	.02
❑ 83	Jeff Lageman	.10	.02
❑ 84	Anthony Pleasant	.10	.02
❑ 85	Aeneas Williams	.10	.02
❑ 86	Vincent Brisby	.10	.02
❑ 87	Terrell Fletcher	.10	.02
❑ 88	Brad Baxter	.10	.02
❑ 89	Shannon Sharpe	.20	.07
❑ 90	Errict Rhett	.20	.07
❑ 91	Michael Zordich	.10	.02
❑ 92	Dan Saleaumua	.10	.02
❑ 93	Devin Bush	.10	.02
❑ 94	Wayne Simmons	.10	.02
❑ 95	Tyrone Hughes	.10	.02
❑ 96	John Randle	.20	.07
❑ 97	Tony Tolbert	.10	.02
❑ 98	Yancey Thigpen	.20	.07
❑ 99	J.J. Stokes	.30	.10
❑ 100	Marshall Faulk	.40	.15
❑ 101	Barry Minter	.10	.02
❑ 102	Glenn Foley	.20	.07
❑ 103	Chester McGlockton	.10	.02
❑ 104	Carlton Gray	.10	.02
❑ 105	Terry Kirby	.20	.07
❑ 106	Darryll Lewis	.10	.02
❑ 107	Thomas Smith	.10	.02
❑ 108	Mike Fox	.10	.02
❑ 109	Antonio Langham	.10	.02
❑ 110	Drew Bledsoe	.60	.25
❑ 111	Troy Drayton	.10	.02
❑ 112	Marvcus Patton	.10	.02
❑ 113	Tyrone Wheatley	.20	.07
❑ 114	Desmond Howard	.20	.07
❑ 115	Johnny Mitchell	.10	.02
❑ 116	Dave Krieg	.10	.02
❑ 117	Natrone Means	.20	.07
❑ 118	Herman Moore	.20	.07
❑ 119	Darren Woodson	.20	.07
❑ 120	Ricky Watters	.20	.07
❑ 121	Emmitt Smith TYC	.75	.30
❑ 122	Barry Sanders TYC	.75	.30
❑ 123	Curtis Martin TYC	.30	.10
❑ 124	Chris Warren TYC	.20	.07
❑ 125	Terry Allen TYC	.20	.07
❑ 126	Ricky Watters TYC	.20	.07
❑ 127	Errict Rhett TYC	.20	.07
❑ 128	Rodney Hampton TYC	.10	.02
❑ 129	Terrell Davis TYC	.30	.10
❑ 130	Harvey Williams TYC	.10	.02
❑ 131	Craig Heyward TYC	.10	.02
❑ 132	Marshall Faulk TYC	.30	.10
❑ 133	Rashaan Salaam TYC	.20	.07
❑ 134	Garrison Hearst TYC	.20	.07
❑ 135	Edgar Bennett TYC	.20	.07
❑ 136	Thurman Thomas TYC	.20	.07
❑ 137	Brian Washington	.10	.02
❑ 138	Derek Loville	.10	.02
❑ 139	Curtis Conway	.30	.10
❑ 140	Isaac Bruce	.30	.10
❑ 141	Ricardo McDonald	.10	.02
❑ 142	Bruce Armstrong	.10	.02
❑ 143	Will Wolford	.10	.02
❑ 144	Thurman Thomas	.30	.10
❑ 145	Mel Gray	.10	.02
❑ 146	Napoleon Kaufman	.30	.10
❑ 147	Terry Allen	.20	.07
❑ 148	Chris Calloway	.10	.02
❑ 149	Harry Colon	.10	.02
❑ 150	Pepper Johnson	.10	.02
❑ 151	Marco Coleman	.10	.02
❑ 152	Shawn Jefferson	.10	.02
❑ 153	Larry Centers	.20	.07
❑ 154	Lamar Lathon	.10	.02
❑ 155	Mark Chmura	.20	.07
❑ 156	Dermontti Dawson	.10	.02
❑ 157	Alvin Harper	.10	.02
❑ 158	Randall McDaniel	.10	.02
❑ 159	Allen Aldridge	.10	.02
❑ 160	Chris Warren	.20	.07
❑ 161	Jessie Tuggle	.10	.02
❑ 162	Sean Lumpkin	.10	.02
❑ 163	Bobby Houston	.10	.02
❑ 164	Dexter Carter	.10	.02
❑ 165	Erik Kramer	.10	.02
❑ 166	Brock Marion	.10	.02
❑ 167	Toby Wright	.10	.02
❑ 168	John Copeland	.10	.02
❑ 169	Sean Dawkins	.10	.02
❑ 170	Tim Brown	.30	.10
❑ 171	Darion Conner	.10	.02
❑ 172	Aaron Hayden RC	.10	.02
❑ 173	Charlie Garner	.20	.07
❑ 174	Anthony Cook	.10	.02
❑ 175	Derrick Thomas	.30	.10
❑ 176	Willie McGinest	.10	.02
❑ 177	Thomas Lewis	.10	.02
❑ 178	Sherman Williams	.10	.02
❑ 179	Cornelius Bennett	.10	.02
❑ 180	Frank Sanders	.30	.10
❑ 181	Leroy Hoard	.10	.02
❑ 182	Bernie Parmalee	.10	.02
❑ 183	Sterling Palmer	.10	.02
❑ 184	Kelvin Pritchett	.10	.02
❑ 185	Kordell Stewart	.30	.10
❑ 186	Brent Jones	.10	.02
❑ 187	Robert Blackmon	.10	.02
❑ 188	Adrian Murrell	.20	.07
❑ 189	Edgar Bennett	.20	.07
❑ 190	Rashaan Salaam	.20	.07
❑ 191	Ellis Johnson	.10	.02
❑ 192	Andre Coleman	.10	.02
❑ 193	Will Shields	.10	.02
❑ 194	Derrick Brooks	.30	.10
❑ 195	Carl Pickens	.20	.07
❑ 196	Carlton Bailey	.10	.02
❑ 197	Terance Mathis	.20	.07
❑ 198	Carlos Jenkins	.10	.02
❑ 199	Derrick Alexander	.10	.02
❑ 200	Deion Sanders	.60	.25
❑ 201	Glyn Milburn	.10	.02
❑ 202	Chris Sanders	.20	.07
❑ 203	Rocket Ismail	.10	.02
❑ 204	Fred Barnett	.10	.02
❑ 205	Quinn Early	.10	.02
❑ 206	Henry Jones	.10	.02
❑ 207	Herschel Walker	.20	.07
❑ 208	James Washington	.10	.02
❑ 209	Lee Woodall	.10	.02
❑ 210	Neil Smith	.20	.07
❑ 211	Tony Bennett	.10	.02
❑ 212	Ernie Mills	.10	.02
❑ 213	Clyde Simmons	.10	.02
❑ 214	Chris Slade	.10	.02
❑ 215	Tony Boselli	.10	.02
❑ 216	Ryan McNeil	.10	.02
❑ 217	Rob Burnett	.10	.02
❑ 218	Stan Humphries	.20	.07
❑ 219	Rick Mirer	.20	.07
❑ 220	Troy Vincent	.10	.02
❑ 221	Sean Jones	.10	.02
❑ 222	Marty Carter	.10	.02
❑ 223	Boomer Esiason	.20	.07
❑ 224	Charles Haley	.20	.07
❑ 225	Sam Mills	.10	.02
❑ 226	Greg Biekert	.10	.02
❑ 227	Bryant Young	.20	.07
❑ 228	Ken Dilger	.20	.07
❑ 229	Levon Kirkland	.10	.02
❑ 230	Brian Mitchell	.10	.02
❑ 231	Hardy Nickerson	.10	.02
❑ 232	Elvis Grbac	.20	.07
❑ 233	Kurt Schulz	.10	.02
❑ 234	Chris Doleman	.10	.02
❑ 235	Tamarick Vanover	.20	.07

Card	Player	Price 1	Price 2
❑ 236	Jesse Campbell	.10	.02
❑ 237	William Thomas	.10	.02
❑ 238	Shane Conlan	.10	.02
❑ 239	Jason Elam	.20	.07
❑ 240	Steve McNair	.75	.30
❑ 241	Jerry Rice TYC	.50	.20
❑ 242	Isaac Bruce TYC	.30	.10
❑ 243	Herman Moore TYC	.20	.07
❑ 244	Michael Irvin TYC	.20	.07
❑ 245	Robert Brooks TYC	.30	.10
❑ 246	Brett Perriman TYC	.10	.02
❑ 247	Cris Carter TYC	.30	.10
❑ 248	Tim Brown TYC	.20	.07
❑ 249	Yancey Thigpen TYC	.20	.07
❑ 250	Jeff Graham TYC	.10	.02
❑ 251	Carl Pickens TYC	.20	.07
❑ 252	Tony Martin TYC	.10	.02
❑ 253	Eric Metcalf TYC	.10	.02
❑ 254	Jake Reed TYC	.20	.07
❑ 255	Quinn Early TYC	.10	.02
❑ 256	Anthony Miller TYC	.20	.07
❑ 257	Joey Galloway TYC	.30	.10
❑ 258	Bert Emanuel TYC	.20	.07
❑ 259	Terance Mathis TYC	.10	.02
❑ 260	Curtis Conway TYC	.20	.07
❑ 261	Henry Ellard TYC	.10	.02
❑ 262	Mark Carrier TYC	.10	.02
❑ 263	Brian Blades TYC	.10	.02
❑ 264	William Roaf	.10	.02
❑ 265	Ed McDaniel	.10	.02
❑ 266	Nate Newton	.10	.02
❑ 267	Brett Maxie	.10	.02
❑ 268	Anthony Smith	.10	.02
❑ 269	Mickey Washington	.10	.02
❑ 270	Jerry Rice	1.00	.40
❑ 271	Shaun Gayle	.10	.02
❑ 272	Gilbert Brown RC	.30	.10
❑ 273	Mark Bruener	.10	.02
❑ 274	Eugene Robinson	.10	.02
❑ 275	Marvin Washington	.10	.02
❑ 276	Keith Sims	.10	.02
❑ 277	Ashley Ambrose	.10	.02
❑ 278	Garrison Hearst	.20	.07
❑ 279	Donnell Woolford	.10	.02
❑ 280	Cris Carter	.30	.10
❑ 281	Curtis Martin	.75	.30
❑ 282	Scott Mitchell	.20	.07
❑ 283	Stevon Moore	.10	.02
❑ 284	Roman Phifer	.10	.02
❑ 285	Ken Harvey	.10	.02
❑ 286	Rodney Hampton	.20	.07
❑ 287	Willie Davis	.10	.02
❑ 288	Yonel Jourdain	.10	.02
❑ 289	Brian DeMarco	.10	.02
❑ 290	Reggie White	.30	.10
❑ 291	Kevin Williams	.10	.02
❑ 292	Gary Plummer	.10	.02
❑ 293	Terrance Shaw	.10	.02
❑ 294	Calvin Williams	.10	.02
❑ 295	Eddie Robinson	.10	.02
❑ 296	Tony McGee	.10	.02
❑ 297	Clay Matthews	.10	.02
❑ 298	Joe Cain	.10	.02
❑ 299	Tim McKyer	.10	.02
❑ 300	Greg Lloyd	.20	.07
❑ 301	Steve Wisniewski	.10	.02
❑ 302	Ray Buchanan	.10	.02
❑ 303	Lake Dawson	.10	.02
❑ 304	Kevin Carter	.10	.02
❑ 305	Phillippi Sparks	.10	.02
❑ 306	Emmitt Smith	1.50	.60
❑ 307	Ruben Brown	.10	.02
❑ 308	Tom Carter	.10	.02
❑ 309	William Floyd	.20	.07
❑ 310	Jim Everett	.10	.02
❑ 311	Vincent Brown	.10	.02
❑ 312	Dennis Gibson	.10	.02
❑ 313	Lorenzo Lynch	.10	.02
❑ 314	Corey Harris	.10	.02
❑ 315	James O.Stewart	.20	.07
❑ 316	Kyle Brady	.10	.02
❑ 317	Irving Fryar	.20	.07
❑ 318	Jake Reed	.20	.07
❑ 319	Vinny Testaverde	.20	.07
❑ 320	John Elway	2.00	.75
❑ 321	Tracy Scroggins	.10	.02
❑ 322	Chris Spielman	.10	.02
❑ 323	Horace Copeland	.10	.02
❑ 324	Chris Zorich	.10	.02
❑ 325	Mike Mamula	.10	.02
❑ 326	Henry Ford	.10	.02
❑ 327	Steve Walsh	.10	.02
❑ 328	Stanley Richard	.20	.07
❑ 329	Mike Jones	.10	.02
❑ 330	Jim Harbaugh	.20	.07
❑ 331	Darren Perry	.10	.02
❑ 332	Ken Norton	.10	.02
❑ 333	Kimble Anders	.20	.07
❑ 334	Harold Green	.10	.02
❑ 335	Tyrone Poole	.10	.02
❑ 336	Mark Fields	.10	.02
❑ 337	Darren Bennett	.10	.02
❑ 338	Mike Sherrard	.10	.02
❑ 339	Terry Ray RC	.10	.02
❑ 340	Bruce Smith	.20	.07
❑ 341	Daryl Johnston	.20	.07
❑ 342	Vinnie Clark	.10	.02
❑ 343	Mike Caldwell	.10	.02
❑ 344	Vinson Smith	.10	.02
❑ 345	Mo Lewis	.10	.02
❑ 346	Brian Blades	.10	.02
❑ 347	Rod Stephens	.10	.02
❑ 348	David Palmer	.10	.02
❑ 349	Blaine Bishop	.10	.02
❑ 350	Jeff George	.20	.07
❑ 351	George Teague	.10	.02
❑ 352	Jeff Hostetler	.10	.02
❑ 353	Michael Strahan	.20	.07
❑ 354	Eric Davis	.10	.02
❑ 355	Jerome Bettis	.30	.10
❑ 356	Irv Smith	.10	.02
❑ 357	Jeff Herrod	.10	.02
❑ 358	Jay Novacek	.10	.02
❑ 359	Bryce Paup	.10	.02
❑ 360	Neil O'Donnell	.20	.07
❑ 361	Eric Swann	.10	.02
❑ 362	Corey Sawyer	.10	.02
❑ 363	Ty Law	.30	.10
❑ 364	Bo Orlando	.10	.02
❑ 365	Marcus Allen	.30	.10
❑ 366	Mark McMillian	.10	.02
❑ 367	Mark Carrier WR	.10	.02
❑ 368	Jackie Harris	.10	.02
❑ 369	Steve Atwater	.10	.02
❑ 370	Steve Young	.75	.30
❑ 371	Brett Favre TYC	1.00	.40
❑ 372	Scott Mitchell TYC	.10	.02
❑ 373	Warren Moon TYC	.10	.02
❑ 374	Jeff George TYC	.20	.07
❑ 375	Jim Everett TYC	.10	.02
❑ 376	John Elway TYC	1.00	.40
❑ 377	Erik Kramer TYC	.10	.02
❑ 378	Jeff Blake TYC	.20	.07
❑ 379	Dan Marino TYC	1.00	.40
❑ 380	Dave Krieg TYC	.10	.02
❑ 381	Drew Bledsoe TYC	.30	.10
❑ 382	Stan Humphries TYC	.10	.02
❑ 383	Troy Aikman TYC	.50	.20
❑ 384	Steve Young TYC	.30	.10
❑ 385	Jim Kelly TYC	.30	.10
❑ 386	Steve Bono TYC	.10	.02
❑ 387	David Sloan	.10	.02
❑ 388	Jeff Graham	.10	.02
❑ 389	Hugh Douglas	.20	.07
❑ 390	Dan Marino	2.00	.75
❑ 391	Winston Moss	.10	.02
❑ 392	Darrell Green	.10	.02
❑ 393	Mark Stepnoski	.10	.02
❑ 394	Bert Emanuel	.20	.07
❑ 395	Eric Zeier	.10	.02
❑ 396	Willie Jackson	.20	.07
❑ 397	Qadry Ismail	.20	.07
❑ 398	Michael Brooks	.10	.02
❑ 399	D'Marco Farr	.10	.02
❑ 400	Brett Favre	2.00	.75
❑ 401	Carnell Lake	.10	.02
❑ 402	Pat Swilling	.10	.02
❑ 403	Stephen Grant	.10	.02
❑ 404	Steve Tasker	.10	.02
❑ 405	Ben Coates	.20	.07
❑ 406	Steve Tovar	.10	.02
❑ 407	Tony Martin	.20	.07
❑ 408	Greg Hill	.20	.07
❑ 409	Eric Guliford	.10	.02
❑ 410	Michael Irvin	.30	.10
❑ 411	Eric Hill	.10	.02
❑ 412	Mario Bates	.20	.07
❑ 413	Brian Stablein RC	.10	.02
❑ 414	Marcus Jones RC	.10	.02
❑ 415	Reggie Brown LB RC	.10	.02
❑ 416	Lawrence Phillips RC	.30	.10
❑ 417	Alex Van Dyke RC	.20	.07
❑ 418	Daryl Gardener RC	.10	.02
❑ 419	Mike Alstott RC	1.00	.40
❑ 420	Kevin Hardy RC	.30	.10
❑ 421	Rickey Dudley RC	.30	.10
❑ 422	Jerome Woods RC	.10	.02
❑ 423	Eric Moulds RC	1.25	.50
❑ 424	Cedric Jones RC	.10	.02
❑ 425	Simeon Rice RC	.75	.30
❑ 426	Marvin Harrison RC	2.50	1.00
❑ 427	Tim Biakabutuka RC	.30	.10
❑ 428	Duane Clemons RC	.10	.02
❑ 429	Alex Molden RC	.10	.02
❑ 430	Keyshawn Johnson RC	1.00	.40
❑ 431	Willie Anderson RC	.10	.02
❑ 432	John Mobley RC	.10	.02
❑ 433	Leeland McElroy RC	.20	.07
❑ 434	Regan Upshaw RC	.10	.02
❑ 435	Eddie George RC	1.25	.50
❑ 436	Jonathan Ogden RC	.30	.10
❑ 437	Eddie Kennison RC	.30	.10
❑ 438	Jermane Mayberry RC	.10	.02
❑ 439	Checklist 1 of 2	.10	.02
❑ 440	Checklist 2 of 2	.10	.02
❑ P1	Joe Namath/Steve Young Promo	15.00	7.50
❑ P1R	Joe Namath Promo Steve Young	20.00	10.00

1997 Topps

Card	Player	Price 1	Price 2
❑	COMPLETE SET (415)	40.00	20.00
❑	COMP.FACT.SET (424)	70.00	40.00
❑ 1	Brett Favre	2.00	.75
❑ 2	Lawyer Milloy	.30	.10
❑ 3	Tim Biakabutuka	.30	.10
❑ 4	Clyde Simmons	.20	.07
❑ 5	Deion Sanders	.50	.20
❑ 6	Anthony Miller	.20	.07
❑ 7	Marquez Pope	.20	.07
❑ 8	Mike Tomczak	.20	.07
❑ 9	William Thomas	.20	.07
❑ 10	Marshall Faulk	.60	.25
❑ 11	John Randle	.30	.10
❑ 12	Jim Kelly	.50	.20
❑ 13	Steve Bono	.30	.10
❑ 14	Rod Stephens	.20	.07
❑ 15	Stan Humphries	.20	.07
❑ 16	Terrell Buckley	.20	.07
❑ 17	Ki-Jana Carter	.20	.07
❑ 18	Marcus Robertson	.20	.07
❑ 19	Corey Harris	.20	.07
❑ 20	Rashaan Salaam	.20	.07
❑ 21	Rickey Dudley	.30	.10
❑ 22	Jamir Miller	.20	.07
❑ 23	Martin Mayhew	.20	.07
❑ 24	Jason Sehorn	.30	.10
❑ 25	Isaac Bruce	.50	.20
❑ 26	Johnnie Morton	.30	.10
❑ 27	Antonio Langham	.20	.07
❑ 28	Cornelius Bennett	.20	.07
❑ 29	Joe Johnson	.20	.07
❑ 30	Keyshawn Johnson	.50	.20
❑ 31	Willie Green	.20	.07
❑ 32	Craig Newsome	.20	.07

❑ 33	Brock Marion	.20	.07
❑ 34	Corey Fuller	.20	.07
❑ 35	Ben Coates	.30	.10
❑ 36	Ty Detmer	.30	.10
❑ 37	Charles Johnson	.30	.10
❑ 38	Willie Jackson	.20	.07
❑ 39	Tyronne Drakeford	.20	.07
❑ 40	Gus Frerotte	.20	.07
❑ 41	Robert Blackmon	.20	.07
❑ 42	Andre Coleman	.20	.07
❑ 43	Mario Bates	.20	.07
❑ 44	Chris Calloway	.20	.07
❑ 45	Terry McDaniel	.20	.07
❑ 46	Anthony Davis	.20	.07
❑ 47	Stanley Pritchett	.20	.07
❑ 48	Ray Buchanan	.20	.07
❑ 49	Chris Chandler	.30	.10
❑ 50	Ashley Ambrose	.20	.07
❑ 51	Tyrone Braxton	.20	.07
❑ 52	Pepper Johnson	.20	.07
❑ 53	Frank Sanders	.30	.10
❑ 54	Clay Matthews	.20	.07
❑ 55	Bruce Smith	.30	.10
❑ 56	Jermaine Lewis	.50	.20
❑ 57	Mark Carrier WR UER	.20	.07
❑ 58	Jeff Graham	.20	.07
❑ 59	Keith Lyle	.20	.07
❑ 60	Trent Dilfer	.50	.20
❑ 61	Trace Armstrong	.20	.07
❑ 62	Jeff Herrod	.20	.07
❑ 63	Tyrone Wheatley	.30	.10
❑ 64	Torrance Small	.20	.07
❑ 65	Chris Warren	.30	.10
❑ 66	Terry Kirby	.30	.10
❑ 67	Erric Pegram	.20	.07
❑ 68	Sean Gilbert	.20	.07
❑ 69	Greg Biekert	.20	.07
❑ 70	Ricky Watters	.30	.10
❑ 71	Chris Hudson	.20	.07
❑ 72	Tamarick Vanover	.30	.10
❑ 73	Orlando Thomas	.20	.07
❑ 74	Jimmy Spencer	.20	.07
❑ 75	John Mobley	.20	.07
❑ 76	Henry Thomas	.20	.07
❑ 77	Santana Dotson	.20	.07
❑ 78	Boomer Esiason	.30	.10
❑ 79	Bobby Hebert	.20	.07
❑ 80	Kerry Collins	.50	.20
❑ 81	Bobby Engram	.30	.10
❑ 82	Kevin Smith	.20	.07
❑ 83	Rick Mirer	.20	.07
❑ 84	Ted Johnson	.20	.07
❑ 85	Derrick Alexander WR	.30	.10
❑ 86	Hugh Douglas	.20	.07
❑ 87	Rodney Harrison RC	1.00	.40
❑ 88	Roman Phifer	.20	.07
❑ 89	Warren Moon	.50	.20
❑ 90	Thurman Thomas	.50	.20
❑ 91	Michael McCrary	.20	.07
❑ 92	Dana Stubblefield	.20	.07
❑ 93	Andre Hastings UER	.20	.07
❑ 94	William Fuller	.20	.07
❑ 95	Jeff Hostetler	.20	.07
❑ 96	Danny Kanell	.20	.07
❑ 97	Mark Fields	.20	.07
❑ 98	Eddie Robinson	.20	.07
❑ 99	Daryl Gardener	.20	.07
❑ 100	Drew Bledsoe	.60	.25
❑ 101	Winslow Oliver	.20	.07
❑ 102	Raymont Harris	.20	.07
❑ 103	LeShon Johnson	.20	.07
❑ 104	Byron Bam Morris	.20	.07
❑ 105	Herman Moore	.30	.10
❑ 106	Keith Jackson	.20	.07
❑ 107	Chris Penn	.20	.07
❑ 108	Robert Griffith RC	.20	.07
❑ 109	Jeff Burris	.20	.07
❑ 110	Troy Aikman	1.00	.40
❑ 111	Allen Aldridge	.20	.07
❑ 112	Mel Gray	.20	.07
❑ 113	Aaron Bailey	.20	.07
❑ 114	Michael Strahan	.30	.10
❑ 115	Adrian Murrell	.30	.10
❑ 116	Chris Mims	.20	.07
❑ 117	Robert Jones	.20	.07
❑ 118	Derrick Brooks	.50	.20
❑ 119	Tom Carter	.20	.07
❑ 120	Carl Pickens	.30	.10
❑ 121	Tony Brackens	.20	.07
❑ 122	O.J. McDuffie	.30	.10
❑ 123	Napoleon Kaufman	.50	.20
❑ 124	Chris T. Jones	.20	.07
❑ 125	Kordell Stewart	.50	.20
❑ 126	Ray Zellars	.20	.07
❑ 127	Jessie Tuggle	.20	.07
❑ 128	Greg Kragen	.20	.07
❑ 129	Brett Perriman	.20	.07
❑ 130	Steve Young	.60	.25
❑ 131	Willie Clay	.20	.07
❑ 132	Kimble Anders	.30	.10
❑ 133	Eugene Daniel	.20	.07
❑ 134	Jevon Langford	.20	.07
❑ 135	Shannon Sharpe	.30	.10
❑ 136	Wayne Simmons	.20	.07
❑ 137	Leeland McElroy	.20	.07
❑ 138	Mike Caldwell	.20	.07
❑ 139	Eric Moulds	.50	.20
❑ 140	Eddie George	.50	.20
❑ 141	Jamal Anderson	.50	.20
❑ 142	Michael Timpson	.20	.07
❑ 143	Tony Tolbert	.20	.07
❑ 144	Robert Smith	.30	.10
❑ 145	Mike Alstott	.50	.20
❑ 146	Gary Jones	.20	.07
❑ 147	Terrance Shaw	.20	.07
❑ 148	Carlton Gray	.20	.07
❑ 149	Kevin Carter	.20	.07
❑ 150	Darrell Green	.30	.10
❑ 151	David Dunn	.20	.07
❑ 152	Ken Norton	.20	.07
❑ 153	Chad Brown	.20	.07
❑ 154	Pat Swilling	.20	.07
❑ 155	Irving Fryar	.30	.10
❑ 156	Michael Haynes	.20	.07
❑ 157	Shawn Jefferson	.20	.07
❑ 158	Stephen Grant	.20	.07
❑ 159	James O.Stewart	.30	.10
❑ 160	Derrick Thomas	.50	.20
❑ 161	Tim Bowens	.20	.07
❑ 162	Dixon Edwards	.20	.07
❑ 163	Micheal Barrow	.20	.07
❑ 164	Antonio Freeman	.50	.20
❑ 165	Terrell Davis	.60	.25
❑ 166	Henry Ellard	.30	.10
❑ 167	Daryl Johnston	.30	.10
❑ 168	Bryan Cox	.20	.07
❑ 169	Chad Cota	.20	.07
❑ 170	Vinny Testaverde	.30	.10
❑ 171	Andre Reed	.30	.10
❑ 172	Larry Centers	.30	.10
❑ 173	Craig Heyward	.20	.07
❑ 174	Glyn Milburn	.20	.07
❑ 175	Hardy Nickerson	.20	.07
❑ 176	Corey Miller	.20	.07
❑ 177	Bobby Houston	.20	.07
❑ 178	Marco Coleman	.20	.07
❑ 179	Winston Moss	.20	.07
❑ 180	Tony Banks	.30	.10
❑ 181	Jeff Lageman	.20	.07
❑ 182	Jason Belser	.20	.07
❑ 183	James Jett	.30	.10
❑ 184	Wayne Martin	.20	.07
❑ 185	Dave Meggett	.20	.07
❑ 186	Terrell Owens	.60	.25
❑ 187	Willie Williams	.20	.07
❑ 188	Eric Turner	.20	.07
❑ 189	Chuck Smith	.20	.07
❑ 190	Simeon Rice	.30	.10
❑ 191	Kevin Greene	.30	.10
❑ 192	Lance Johnstone	.20	.07
❑ 193	Marty Carter	.20	.07
❑ 194	Ricardo McDonald	.20	.07
❑ 195	Michael Irvin	.50	.20
❑ 196	George Koonce	.20	.07
❑ 197	Robert Porcher	.20	.07
❑ 198	Mark Collins	.20	.07
❑ 199	Louis Oliver	.20	.07
❑ 200	John Elway	2.00	.75
❑ 201	Jake Reed	.30	.10
❑ 202	Rodney Hampton	.30	.10
❑ 203	Aaron Glenn	.20	.07
❑ 204	Mike Mamula	.20	.07
❑ 205	Terry Allen	.50	.20
❑ 206	John Lynch	.30	.10
❑ 207	Todd Lyght	.20	.07
❑ 208	Dean Wells	.20	.07
❑ 209	Aaron Hayden	.20	.07
❑ 210	Blaine Bishop	.20	.07
❑ 211	Bert Emanuel	.30	.10
❑ 212	Mark Carrier DB UER	.20	.07
❑ 213	Dale Carter	.20	.07
❑ 214	Jimmy Smith	.30	.10
❑ 215	Jim Harbaugh	.30	.10
❑ 216	Jeff George	.30	.10
❑ 217	Anthony Newman	.20	.07
❑ 218	Ty Law	.30	.10
❑ 219	Brent Jones	.20	.07
❑ 220	Emmitt Smith	1.50	.60
❑ 221	Bennie Blades	.20	.07
❑ 222	Alfred Williams	.20	.07
❑ 223	Eugene Robinson	.20	.07
❑ 224	Fred Barnett	.20	.07
❑ 225	Errict Rhett	.20	.07
❑ 226	Leslie O'Neal	.20	.07
❑ 227	Michael Sinclair	.20	.07
❑ 228	Marvcus Patton	.20	.07
❑ 229	Darrien Gordon	.20	.07
❑ 230	Jerome Bettis	.50	.20
❑ 231	Troy Vincent	.20	.07
❑ 232	Ray Mickens	.20	.07
❑ 233	Lonnie Johnson	.20	.07
❑ 234	Charles Way	.20	.07
❑ 235	Chris Sanders	.20	.07
❑ 236	Bracy Walker	.20	.07
❑ 237	Dave Krieg UER	.20	.07
❑ 238	Kent Graham	.20	.07
❑ 239	Ray Lewis	.75	.30
❑ 240	Cris Carter	.50	.20
❑ 241	Elvis Grbac	.30	.10
❑ 242	Eric Davis	.20	.07
❑ 243	Harvey Williams	.20	.07
❑ 244	Eric Allen	.20	.07
❑ 245	Bryant Young	.20	.07
❑ 246	Terrell Fletcher	.20	.07
❑ 247	Darren Perry	.20	.07
❑ 248	Ken Harvey	.20	.07
❑ 249	Marvin Washington	.20	.07
❑ 250	Marcus Allen	.50	.20
❑ 251	Darrin Smith	.20	.07
❑ 252	James Francis	.20	.07
❑ 253	Michael Jackson	.30	.10
❑ 254	Ryan McNeil	.20	.07
❑ 255	Mark Chmura	.30	.10
❑ 256	Keenan McCardell	.30	.10
❑ 257	Tony Bennett	.20	.07
❑ 258	Irving Spikes	.20	.07
❑ 259	Jason Dunn	.20	.07
❑ 260	Joey Galloway	.30	.10
❑ 261	Eddie Kennison	.30	.10
❑ 262	Lonnie Marts	.20	.07
❑ 263	Thomas Lewis	.20	.07
❑ 264	Tedy Bruschi	1.00	.40
❑ 265	Steve Atwater	.20	.07
❑ 266	Dorsey Levens	.50	.20
❑ 267	Kurt Schulz	.20	.07
❑ 268	Rob Moore	.30	.10
❑ 269	Walt Harris	.20	.07
❑ 270	Steve McNair	.60	.25
❑ 271	Bill Romanowski	.20	.07
❑ 272	Sean Dawkins	.20	.07
❑ 273	Don Beebe	.20	.07
❑ 274	Fernando Smith	.20	.07
❑ 275	Willie McGinest	.20	.07
❑ 276	Levon Kirkland	.20	.07
❑ 277	Tony Martin	.30	.10
❑ 278	Warren Sapp	.30	.10
❑ 279	Lamar Smith	.50	.20
❑ 280	Mark Brunell	.60	.25
❑ 281	Jim Everett	.20	.07
❑ 282	Victor Green	.20	.07
❑ 283	Mike Jones	.20	.07
❑ 284	Charlie Garner	.30	.10
❑ 285	Karim Abdul-Jabbar	.30	.10
❑ 286	Michael Westbrook	.30	.10
❑ 287	Lawrence Phillips	.20	.07
❑ 288	Amani Toomer	.30	.10
❑ 289	Neil Smith	.30	.10
❑ 290	Barry Sanders	1.50	.60
❑ 291	Willie Davis	.20	.07
❑ 292	Bo Orlando	.20	.07
❑ 293	Alonzo Spellman	.20	.07

❑ 294 Eric Hill .20 .07
❑ 295 Wesley Walls .30 .10
❑ 296 Todd Collins .20 .07
❑ 297 Stevon Moore .20 .07
❑ 298 Eric Metcalf .30 .10
❑ 299 Darren Woodson .20 .07
❑ 300 Jerry Rice 1.00 .40
❑ 301 Scott Mitchell .30 .10
❑ 302 Ray Crockett .20 .07
❑ 303 Jim Schwantz RC UER .20 .07
❑ 304 Steve Tovar .20 .07
❑ 305 Terance Mathis .30 .10
❑ 306 Earnest Byner .20 .07
❑ 307 Chris Spielman .20 .07
❑ 308 Curtis Conway .30 .10
❑ 309 Cris Dishman .20 .07
❑ 310 Marvin Harrison .50 .20
❑ 311 Sam Mills .20 .07
❑ 312 Brent Alexander RC .20 .07
❑ 313 Shawn Wooden RC .20 .07
❑ 314 Dewayne Washington .20 .07
❑ 315 Terry Glenn .50 .20
❑ 316 Winfred Tubbs .20 .07
❑ 317 Dave Brown .20 .07
❑ 318 Neil O'Donnell .30 .10
❑ 319 Anthony Parker .20 .07
❑ 320 Junior Seau .50 .20
❑ 321 Brian Mitchell .20 .07
❑ 322 Regan Upshaw .20 .07
❑ 323 Darryl Williams .20 .07
❑ 324 Chris Doleman .20 .07
❑ 325 Rod Woodson .30 .10
❑ 326 Derrick Witherspoon .20 .07
❑ 327 Chester McGlockton .20 .07
❑ 328 Mickey Washington .20 .07
❑ 329 Greg Hill .20 .07
❑ 330 Reggie White .50 .20
❑ 331 John Copeland .20 .07
❑ 332 Doug Evans .20 .07
❑ 333 Lamar Lathon .20 .07
❑ 334 Mark Maddox .20 .07
❑ 335 Natrone Means .30 .10
❑ 336 Corey Widmer .20 .07
❑ 337 Terry Wooden .20 .07
❑ 338 Merton Hanks .20 .07
❑ 339 Cortez Kennedy .20 .07
❑ 340 Tyrone Hughes .20 .07
❑ 341 Tim Brown .50 .20
❑ 342 John Jurkovic .20 .07
❑ 343 Carnell Lake .20 .07
❑ 344 Stanley Richard .20 .07
❑ 345 Darryll Lewis .20 .07
❑ 346 Dan Wilkinson .20 .07
❑ 347 Broderick Thomas .20 .07
❑ 348 Brian Williams .20 .07
❑ 349 Eric Swann .20 .07
❑ 350 Dan Marino 2.00 .75
❑ 351 Anthony Johnson .20 .07
❑ 352 Joe Cain .20 .07
❑ 353 Quinn Early .20 .07
❑ 354 Seth Joyner .20 .07
❑ 355 Garrison Hearst .30 .10
❑ 356 Edgar Bennett .30 .10
❑ 357 Brian Washington .20 .07
❑ 358 Kevin Hardy .20 .07
❑ 359 Quentin Coryatt .20 .07
❑ 360 Tim McDonald .20 .07
❑ 361 Brian Blades .20 .07
❑ 362 Courtney Hawkins .20 .07
❑ 363 Ray Farmer .20 .07
❑ 364 Jessie Armstead .20 .07
❑ 365 Curtis Martin .60 .25
❑ 366 Zach Thomas .50 .20
❑ 367 Frank Wycheck .30 .10
❑ 368 Darnay Scott .30 .10
❑ 369 Percy Ellsworth RC .20 .07
❑ 370 Desmond Howard .30 .10
❑ 371 Aeneas Williams .20 .07
❑ 372 Bryce Paup .20 .07
❑ 373 Michael Bates .20 .07
❑ 374 Brad Johnson .50 .20
❑ 375 Jeff Blake .30 .10
❑ 376 Donnell Woolford UER .20 .07
❑ 377 Mo Lewis .20 .07
❑ 378 Phillippi Sparks .20 .07
❑ 379 Michael Bankston .20 .07
❑ 380 LeRoy Butler .20 .07
❑ 381 Tyrone Poole .20 .07
❑ 382 Wayne Chrebet .50 .20
❑ 383 Chris Slade .20 .07
❑ 384 Checklist 1 (1-208) .20 .07
❑ 385 Checklist 2 (209-415) .20 .07
❑ 386 Will Blackwell RC SP .30 .10
❑ 387 Tom Knight RC SP .20 .07
❑ 388 Darnell Autry RC SP .50 .20
❑ 389 Bryant Westbrook RC SP .20 .07
❑ 390 David LaFleur RC SP .30 .10
❑ 391 Antowain Smith RC SP 2.50 1.00
❑ 392 Kevin Lockett RC SP .50 .20
❑ 393 Rae Carruth RC SP .30 .10
❑ 394 Renaldo Wynn RC SP .30 .10
❑ 395 Jim Druckenmiller RC SP .50 .20
❑ 396 Kenny Holmes RC SP .75 .30
❑ 397 Shawn Springs RC SP .50 .20
❑ 398 Troy Davis RC SP .50 .20
❑ 399 Dwayne Rudd RC SP .75 .30
❑ 400 Orlando Pace RC SP .75 .30
❑ 401 Byron Hanspard RC SP .50 .20
❑ 402 Corey Dillon RC SP 6.00 2.50
❑ 403 Walter Jones RC SP .75 .30
❑ 404 Reidel Anthony RC SP .75 .30
❑ 405 Peter Boulware RC SP .75 .30
❑ 406 Reinard Wilson RC SP .50 .20
❑ 407 Pat Barnes RC SP .75 .30
❑ 408 Yatil Green RC SP .75 .30
❑ 409 Joey Kent RC SP .75 .30
❑ 410 Ike Hilliard RC SP 1.50 .60
❑ 411 Jake Plummer SP RC 5.00 2.00
❑ 412 Darrell Russell RC SP .30 .10
❑ 413 James Farrior RC SP .75 .30
❑ 414 Tony Gonzalez RC SP 3.00 1.25
❑ 415 Warrick Dunn RC SP 3.00 1.25
❑ P40 Gus Frerotte PROMO .25 .10
❑ P170 Vinny Testaverde PROMO .25 .10
❑ P240 Cris Carter PROMO .40 .15
❑ P250 Marcus Allen PROMO .40 .15
❑ P285 Karim Abdul-Jabbar PROMO .25 .10
❑ P356 Edgar Bennett PROMO .25 .10

1998 Topps

❑ COMPLETE SET (360) 60.00 30.00
❑ COMP.FACT.SET (365) 80.00 40.00
❑ 1 Barry Sanders 1.50 .60
❑ 2 Derrick Rodgers .20 .07
❑ 3 Chris Calloway .20 .07
❑ 4 Bruce Armstrong .20 .07
❑ 5 Horace Copeland .20 .07
❑ 6 Chad Brown .20 .07
❑ 7 Ken Harvey .20 .07
❑ 8 Levon Kirkland .20 .07
❑ 9 Glenn Foley .30 .10
❑ 10 Corey Dillon .50 .20
❑ 11 Sean Dawkins .20 .07
❑ 12 Curtis Conway .30 .10
❑ 13 Chris Chandler .30 .10
❑ 14 Kerry Collins .30 .10
❑ 15 Jonathan Ogden .20 .07
❑ 16 Sam Shade .20 .07
❑ 17 Vaughn Hebron .20 .07
❑ 18 Quentin Coryatt .20 .07
❑ 19 Jerris McPhail .20 .07
❑ 20 Warrick Dunn .50 .20
❑ 21 Wayne Martin .20 .07
❑ 22 Chad Lewis .30 .10
❑ 23 Danny Kanell .30 .10
❑ 24 Shawn Springs .20 .07
❑ 25 Emmitt Smith 1.50 .60
❑ 26 Todd Lyght .20 .07
❑ 27 Donnie Edwards .20 .07
❑ 28 Charlie Jones .20 .07
❑ 29 Willie McGinest .20 .07
❑ 30 Steve Young .60 .25
❑ 31 Darrell Russell .20 .07
❑ 32 Gary Anderson .20 .07
❑ 33 Stanley Richard .20 .07
❑ 34 Leslie O'Neal .20 .07
❑ 35 Dermontti Dawson .20 .07
❑ 36 Jeff Brady .20 .07
❑ 37 Kimble Anders .30 .10
❑ 38 Glyn Milburn .20 .07
❑ 39 Greg Hill .20 .07
❑ 40 Freddie Jones .20 .07
❑ 41 Bobby Engram .30 .10
❑ 42 Aeneas Williams .20 .07
❑ 43 Antowain Smith .50 .20
❑ 44 Reggie White .50 .20
❑ 45 Rae Carruth .20 .07
❑ 46 Leon Johnson .20 .07
❑ 47 Bryant Young .20 .07
❑ 48 Jamie Asher .20 .07
❑ 49 Hardy Nickerson .20 .07
❑ 50 Jerome Bettis .50 .20
❑ 51 Michael Strahan .30 .10
❑ 52 John Randle .30 .10
❑ 53 Kevin Hardy .20 .07
❑ 54 Eric Bjornson .20 .07
❑ 55 Morten Andersen UER .20 .07
❑ 56 Larry Centers .20 .07
❑ 57 Bryce Paup .20 .07
❑ 58 John Mobley .20 .07
❑ 59 Michael Bates .20 .07
❑ 60 Tim Brown .50 .20
❑ 61 Doug Evans .20 .07
❑ 62 Will Shields .20 .07
❑ 63 Jeff Graham .20 .07
❑ 64 Henry Jones .20 .07
❑ 65 Steve Broussard .20 .07
❑ 66 Blaine Bishop .20 .07
❑ 67 Ernie Conwell .20 .07
❑ 68 Heath Shuler .20 .07
❑ 69 Eric Metcalf .20 .07
❑ 70 Terry Glenn .50 .20
❑ 71 James Hasty .20 .07
❑ 72 Robert Porcher .20 .07
❑ 73 Keenan McCardell .30 .10
❑ 74 Tyrone Hughes .20 .07
❑ 75 Troy Aikman 1.00 .40
❑ 76 Peter Boulware .20 .07
❑ 77 Rob Johnson .30 .10
❑ 78 Erik Kramer .20 .07
❑ 79 Kevin Smith .20 .07
❑ 80 Andre Rison .30 .10
❑ 81 Jim Harbaugh .30 .10
❑ 82 Chris Hudson .20 .07
❑ 83 Ray Zellars .20 .07
❑ 84 Jeff George .30 .10
❑ 85 Willie Davis .20 .07
❑ 86 Jason Gildon .20 .07
❑ 87 Robert Brooks .30 .10
❑ 88 Chad Cota .20 .07
❑ 89 Simeon Rice .30 .10
❑ 90 Mark Brunell .50 .20
❑ 91 Jay Graham .20 .07
❑ 92 Scott Greene .20 .07
❑ 93 Jeff Blake .30 .10
❑ 94 Jason Belser .20 .07
❑ 95 Derrick Alexander DE .20 .07
❑ 96 Ty Law .30 .10
❑ 97 Charles Johnson .20 .07
❑ 98 James Jett .30 .10
❑ 99 Darrell Green .30 .10
❑ 100 Brett Favre 2.00 .75
❑ 101 George Jones .20 .07
❑ 102 Derrick Mason .30 .10
❑ 103 Sam Adams .20 .07
❑ 104 Lawrence Phillips .20 .07
❑ 105 Randal Hill .20 .07
❑ 106 John Mangum .20 .07
❑ 107 Natrone Means .30 .10
❑ 108 Bill Romanowski .20 .07
❑ 109 Terance Mathis .30 .10
❑ 110 Bruce Smith .30 .10
❑ 111 Pete Mitchell .20 .07

❑ 112 Duane Clemons .20 .07
❑ 113 Willie Clay .20 .07
❑ 114 Eric Allen .20 .07
❑ 115 Troy Drayton .20 .07
❑ 116 Derrick Thomas .50 .20
❑ 117 Charles Way .20 .07
❑ 118 Wayne Chrebet .50 .20
❑ 119 Bobby Hoying .30 .10
❑ 120 Michael Jackson .20 .07
❑ 121 Gary Zimmerman .20 .07
❑ 122 Yancey Thigpen .20 .07
❑ 123 Dana Stubblefield .20 .07
❑ 124 Keith Lyle .20 .07
❑ 125 Marco Coleman .20 .07
❑ 126 Karl Williams .20 .07
❑ 127 Stephen Davis .20 .07
❑ 128 Chris Sanders .20 .07
❑ 129 Cris Dishman .20 .07
❑ 130 Jake Plummer .50 .20
❑ 131 Darryl Williams .20 .07
❑ 132 Merton Hanks .20 .07
❑ 133 Torrance Small .20 .07
❑ 134 Aaron Glenn .20 .07
❑ 135 Chester McGlockton .20 .07
❑ 136 William Thomas .20 .07
❑ 137 Kordell Stewart .50 .20
❑ 138 Jason Taylor .30 .10
❑ 139 Lake Dawson .20 .07
❑ 140 Carl Pickens .30 .10
❑ 141 Eugene Robinson .20 .07
❑ 142 Ed McCaffrey .30 .10
❑ 143 Lamar Lathon .20 .07
❑ 144 Ray Buchanan .20 .07
❑ 145 Thurman Thomas .50 .20
❑ 146 Andre Reed .30 .10
❑ 147 Wesley Walls .30 .10
❑ 148 Rob Moore .30 .10
❑ 149 Darren Woodson .20 .07
❑ 150 Eddie George .50 .20
❑ 151 Michael Irvin .50 .20
❑ 152 Johnnie Morton .30 .10
❑ 153 Ken Dilger .20 .07
❑ 154 Tony Boselli .20 .07
❑ 155 Randall McDaniel .20 .07
❑ 156 Mark Fields .20 .07
❑ 157 Phillippi Sparks .20 .07
❑ 158 Troy Davis .20 .07
❑ 159 Troy Vincent .20 .07
❑ 160 Cris Carter .50 .20
❑ 161 Amp Lee .20 .07
❑ 162 Will Blackwell .20 .07
❑ 163 Chad Scott .20 .07
❑ 164 Henry Ellard .30 .10
❑ 165 Robert Jones .20 .07
❑ 166 Garrison Hearst .50 .20
❑ 167 James McKnight .50 .20
❑ 168 Rodney Harrison .30 .10
❑ 169 Adrian Murrell .30 .10
❑ 170 Rod Smith WR .30 .10
❑ 171 Desmond Howard .30 .10
❑ 172 Ben Coates .30 .10
❑ 173 David Palmer .20 .07
❑ 174 Zach Thomas .50 .20
❑ 175 Dale Carter .20 .07
❑ 176 Mark Chmura .30 .10
❑ 177 Elvis Grbac .30 .10
❑ 178 Jason Hanson .20 .07
❑ 179 Walt Harris .20 .07
❑ 180 Ricky Watters .30 .10
❑ 181 Ray Lewis .50 .20
❑ 182 Lonnie Johnson .20 .07
❑ 183 Marvin Harrison .50 .20
❑ 184 Dorsey Levens .50 .20
❑ 185 Tony Gonzalez .50 .20
❑ 186 Andre Hastings .20 .07
❑ 187 Kevin Turner .20 .07
❑ 188 Mo Lewis .20 .07
❑ 189 Jason Sehorn .30 .10
❑ 190 Drew Bledsoe .75 .30
❑ 191 Michael Sinclair .20 .07
❑ 192 William Floyd .20 .07
❑ 193 Kenny Holmes .20 .07
❑ 194 Marvcus Patton .20 .07
❑ 195 Warren Sapp .30 .10
❑ 196 Junior Seau .50 .20
❑ 197 Ryan McNeil .20 .07
❑ 198 Tyrone Wheatley .30 .10
❑ 199 Robert Smith .50 .20
❑ 200 Terrell Davis .50 .20
❑ 201 Brett Perriman .20 .07
❑ 202 Tamarick Vanover .20 .07
❑ 203 Stephen Boyd .20 .07
❑ 204 Zack Crockett .20 .07
❑ 205 Sherman Williams .20 .07
❑ 206 Neil Smith .30 .10
❑ 207 Jermaine Lewis .30 .10
❑ 208 Kevin Williams .20 .07
❑ 209 Byron Hanspard .20 .07
❑ 210 Warren Moon .50 .20
❑ 211 Tony McGee .20 .07
❑ 212 Raymont Harris .20 .07
❑ 213 Eric Davis .20 .07
❑ 214 Darrien Gordon .20 .07
❑ 215 James Stewart .30 .10
❑ 216 Derrick Mayes .30 .10
❑ 217 Brad Johnson .50 .20
❑ 218 Karim Abdul-Jabbar UER .50 .20
❑ 219 Hugh Douglas .20 .07
❑ 220 Terry Allen .50 .20
❑ 221 Rhett Hall .20 .07
❑ 222 Terrell Fletcher .20 .07
❑ 223 Carnell Lake .20 .07
❑ 224 Darryll Lewis .20 .07
❑ 225 Chris Slade .20 .07
❑ 226 Michael Westbrook .30 .10
❑ 227 Willie Williams .20 .07
❑ 228 Tony Banks .30 .10
❑ 229 Keyshawn Johnson .50 .20
❑ 230 Mike Alstott .50 .20
❑ 231 Tiki Barber .50 .20
❑ 232 Jake Reed .30 .10
❑ 233 Eric Swann .20 .07
❑ 234 Eric Moulds .50 .20
❑ 235 Vinny Testaverde .30 .10
❑ 236 Jessie Tuggle .20 .07
❑ 237 Ryan Wetnight RC .20 .07
❑ 238 Tyrone Poole .20 .07
❑ 239 Bryant Westbrook .20 .07
❑ 240 Steve McNair .50 .20
❑ 241 Jimmy Smith .30 .10
❑ 242 Dewayne Washington .20 .07
❑ 243 Robert Harris .20 .07
❑ 244 Rod Woodson .30 .10
❑ 245 Reidel Anthony .30 .10
❑ 246 Jessie Armstead .20 .07
❑ 247 O.J. McDuffie .30 .10
❑ 248 Carlton Gray .20 .07
❑ 249 LeRoy Butler .20 .07
❑ 250 Jerry Rice 1.00 .40
❑ 251 Frank Sanders .30 .10
❑ 252 Todd Collins .20 .07
❑ 253 Fred Lane .20 .07
❑ 254 David Dunn .20 .07
❑ 255 Micheal Barrow .20 .07
❑ 256 Luther Elliss .20 .07
❑ 257 Scott Mitchell .30 .10
❑ 258 Dave Meggett .20 .07
❑ 259 Rickey Dudley .20 .07
❑ 260 Isaac Bruce .50 .20
❑ 261 Tony Martin .30 .10
❑ 262 Leslie Shepherd .20 .07
❑ 263 Derrick Brooks .50 .20
❑ 264 Greg Lloyd .20 .07
❑ 265 Terrell Buckley .20 .07
❑ 266 Antonio Freeman .50 .20
❑ 267 Tony Brackens .20 .07
❑ 268 Mark McMillian .20 .07
❑ 269 Dexter Coakley .20 .07
❑ 270 Dan Marino 2.00 .75
❑ 271 Bryan Cox .20 .07
❑ 272 Leeland McElroy .20 .07
❑ 273 Jeff Burris .20 .07
❑ 274 Eric Green .20 .07
❑ 275 Darnay Scott .30 .10
❑ 276 Greg Clark .20 .07
❑ 277 Mario Bates .30 .10
❑ 278 Eric Turner .20 .07
❑ 279 Neil O'Donnell .30 .10
❑ 280 Herman Moore .30 .10
❑ 281 Gary Brown .20 .07
❑ 282 Terrell Owens .50 .20
❑ 283 Frank Wycheck .20 .07
❑ 284 Trent Dilfer .50 .20
❑ 285 Curtis Martin .50 .20
❑ 286 Ricky Proehl .20 .07
❑ 287 Steve Atwater .20 .07
❑ 288 Aaron Bailey .20 .07
❑ 289 William Henderson .30 .10
❑ 290 Marcus Allen .50 .20
❑ 291 Tom Knight .20 .07
❑ 292 Quinn Early .20 .07
❑ 293 Michael McCrary .20 .07
❑ 294 Bert Emanuel .30 .10
❑ 295 Tom Carter .20 .07
❑ 296 Kevin Glover .20 .07
❑ 297 Marshall Faulk .60 .25
❑ 298 Harvey Williams .20 .07
❑ 299 Chris Warren .30 .10
❑ 300 John Elway 2.00 .75
❑ 301 Eddie Kennison .30 .10
❑ 302 Gus Frerotte .20 .07
❑ 303 Regan Upshaw .20 .07
❑ 304 Kevin Gogan .20 .07
❑ 305 Napoleon Kaufman .50 .20
❑ 306 Charlie Garner .30 .10
❑ 307 Shawn Jefferson .20 .07
❑ 308 Tommy Vardell .20 .07
❑ 309 Mike Hollis .20 .07
❑ 310 Irving Fryar .30 .10
❑ 311 Shannon Sharpe .30 .10
❑ 312 Byron Bam Morris .20 .07
❑ 313 Jamal Anderson .50 .20
❑ 314 Chris Gedney .20 .07
❑ 315 Chris Spielman .20 .07
❑ 316 Derrick Alexander WR .30 .10
❑ 317 O.J. Santiago .20 .07
❑ 318 Anthony Miller .20 .07
❑ 319 Ki-Jana Carter .20 .07
❑ 320 Deion Sanders .50 .20
❑ 321 Joey Galloway .30 .10
❑ 322 J.J. Stokes .30 .10
❑ 323 Rodney Thomas .20 .07
❑ 324 John Lynch .30 .10
❑ 325 Mike Pritchard .20 .07
❑ 326 Terrance Shaw .20 .07
❑ 327 Ted Johnson .20 .07
❑ 328 Ashley Ambrose .20 .07
❑ 329 Checklist 1 .20 .07
❑ 330 Checklist 2 .20 .07
❑ 331 Jerome Pathon RC 2.50 1.00
❑ 332 Ryan Leaf RC 2.50 1.00
❑ 333 Duane Starks RC 1.25 .50
❑ 334 Brian Simmons RC 2.00 .75
❑ 335 Keith Brooking RC 2.50 1.00
❑ 336 Robert Edwards RC 2.00 .75
❑ 337 Curtis Enis RC 1.25 .50
❑ 338 John Avery RC 2.00 .75
❑ 339 Fred Taylor RC 4.00 1.50
❑ 340 Germane Crowell RC 2.00 .75
❑ 341 Hines Ward RC 10.00 4.00
❑ 342 Marcus Nash RC 1.25 .50
❑ 343 Jacquez Green RC 2.00 .75
❑ 344 Joe Jurevicius RC 2.50 1.00
❑ 345 Greg Ellis RC 1.25 .50
❑ 346 Brian Griese RC 5.00 2.00
❑ 347 Tavian Banks RC 2.00 .75
❑ 348 Robert Holcombe RC 2.00 .75
❑ 349 Skip Hicks RC 2.00 .75
❑ 350 Ahman Green RC 12.00 5.00
❑ 351 Takeo Spikes RC 2.50 1.00
❑ 352 Randy Moss RC 12.00 6.00
❑ 353 Andre Wadsworth RC 2.00 .75
❑ 354 Jason Peter RC 1.25 .50
❑ 355 Grant Wistrom RC 2.00 .75
❑ 356 Charles Woodson RC 3.00 1.25
❑ 357 Kevin Dyson RC 2.50 1.00
❑ 358 Pat Johnson RC 2.00 .75
❑ 359 Tim Dwight RC 2.50 1.00
❑ 360 Peyton Manning RC 25.00 12.50
❑ P1 Robert Tisch 5.00 2.00

1999 Topps

❑ COMPLETE SET (357) 50.00 20.00
❑ COMP.SET w/o SP's (330) 20.00 10.00
❑ 1 Terrell Davis .60 .25
❑ 2 Adrian Murrell .40 .15
❑ 3 Ernie Mills .25 .08
❑ 4 Jimmy Hitchcock .25 .08
❑ 5 Charlie Garner .40 .15
❑ 6 Blaine Bishop .25 .08
❑ 7 Junior Seau .60 .25

❑	8	Andre Rison	.40	.15
❑	9	Jake Reed	.40	.15
❑	10	Cris Carter	.60	.25
❑	11	Torrance Small	.25	.08
❑	12	Ronald McKinnon	.25	.08
❑	13	Tyrone Davis	.25	.08
❑	14	Warren Moon	.60	.25
❑	15	Joe Johnson	.25	.08
❑	16	Bert Emanuel	.40	.15
❑	17	Brad Culpepper	.25	.08
❑	18	Henry Jones	.25	.08
❑	19	Jonathan Ogden	.25	.08
❑	20	Terrell Owens	.60	.25
❑	21	Derrick Mason	.40	.15
❑	22	Jon Ritchie	.25	.08
❑	23	Eric Metcalf	.25	.08
❑	24	Kevin Carter	.25	.08
❑	25	Fred Taylor	.60	.25
❑	26	DeWayne Washington	.25	.08
❑	27	William Thomas	.25	.08
❑	28	Rocket Ismail	.40	.15
❑	29	Jason Taylor	.25	.08
❑	30	Doug Flutie	.60	.25
❑	31	Michael Sinclair	.25	.08
❑	32	Yancey Thigpen	.25	.08
❑	33	Darnay Scott	.25	.08
❑	34	Amani Toomer	.25	.08
❑	35	Edgar Bennett	.25	.08
❑	36	LeRoy Butler	.25	.08
❑	37	Jessie Tuggle	.25	.08
❑	38	Andrew Glover	.25	.08
❑	39	Tim McDonald	.25	.08
❑	40	Marshall Faulk	.75	.30
❑	41	Ray Mickens	.25	.08
❑	42	Kimble Anders	.40	.15
❑	43	Trent Green	.60	.25
❑	44	Dermontti Dawson	.25	.08
❑	45	Greg Ellis	.25	.08
❑	46	Hugh Douglas	.25	.08
❑	47	Amp Lee	.25	.08
❑	48	Lamar Thomas	.25	.08
❑	49	Curtis Conway	.40	.15
❑	50	Emmitt Smith	1.25	.50
❑	51	Elvis Grbac	.40	.15
❑	52	Tony Simmons	.25	.08
❑	53	Darrin Smith	.25	.08
❑	54	Donovin Darius	.25	.08
❑	55	Corey Chavous	.25	.08
❑	56	Phillippi Sparks	.25	.08
❑	57	Luther Elliss	.25	.08
❑	58	Tim Dwight	.60	.25
❑	59	Andre Hastings	.25	.08
❑	60	Dan Marino	2.00	.75
❑	61	Micheal Barrow	.25	.08
❑	62	Corey Fuller	.25	.08
❑	63	Bill Romanowski	.25	.08
❑	64	Derrick Rodgers	.40	.15
❑	65	Natrone Means	.40	.15
❑	66	Peter Boulware	.25	.08
❑	67	Brian Mitchell	.25	.08
❑	68	Cornelius Bennett	.25	.08
❑	69	Dedric Ward	.25	.08
❑	70	Drew Bledsoe	.75	.30
❑	71	Freddie Jones	.25	.08
❑	72	Derrick Thomas	.60	.25
❑	73	Willie Davis	.25	.08
❑	74	Larry Centers	.25	.08
❑	75	Mark Brunell	.60	.25
❑	76	Chuck Smith	.25	.08
❑	77	Desmond Howard	.40	.15
❑	78	Sedrick Shaw	.25	.08
❑	79	Tiki Barber	.60	.25
❑	80	Curtis Martin	.60	.25
❑	81	Barry Minter	.25	.08
❑	82	Skip Hicks	.25	.08
❑	83	O.J. Santiago	.25	.08
❑	84	Ed McCaffrey	.40	.15
❑	85	Terrell Buckley	.25	.08
❑	86	Charlie Jones	.25	.08
❑	87	Pete Mitchell	.25	.08
❑	88	La'Roi Glover RC	.60	.25
❑	89	Eric Davis	.25	.08
❑	90	John Elway	2.00	.75
❑	91	Kavika Pittman	.25	.08
❑	92	Fred Lane	.25	.08
❑	93	Warren Sapp	.25	.08
❑	94	Lorenzo Bromell RC	.60	.25
❑	95	Lawyer Milloy	.40	.15
❑	96	Aeneas Williams	.25	.08
❑	97	Michael McCrary	.25	.08
❑	98	Rickey Dudley	.25	.08
❑	99	Bryce Paup	.25	.08
❑	100	Jamal Anderson	.60	.25
❑	101	D'Marco Farr	.25	.08
❑	102	Johnnie Morton	.40	.15
❑	103	Jeff Graham	.25	.08
❑	104	Sam Cowart	.25	.08
❑	105	Bryant Young	.25	.08
❑	106	Jermaine Lewis	.40	.15
❑	107	Chad Bratzke	.25	.08
❑	108	Jeff Burris	.25	.08
❑	109	Roell Preston	.25	.08
❑	110	Vinny Testaverde	.40	.15
❑	111	Ruben Brown	.25	.08
❑	112	Darryll Lewis	.25	.08
❑	113	Billy Davis	.25	.08
❑	114	Bryant Westbrook	.25	.08
❑	115	Stephen Alexander	.25	.08
❑	116	Terrell Fletcher	.25	.08
❑	117	Terry Glenn	.60	.25
❑	118	Rod Smith	.40	.15
❑	119	Carl Pickens	.40	.15
❑	120	Tim Brown	.60	.25
❑	121	Mikhael Ricks	.25	.08
❑	122	Jason Gildon	.25	.08
❑	123	Charles Way	.25	.08
❑	124	Rob Moore	.40	.15
❑	125	Jerome Bettis	.60	.25
❑	126	Kerry Collins	.40	.15
❑	127	Bruce Smith	.40	.15
❑	128	James Hasty	.25	.08
❑	129	Ken Norton Jr.	.25	.08
❑	130	Charles Woodson	.60	.25
❑	131	Tony McGee	.25	.08
❑	132	Kevin Turner	.25	.08
❑	133	Jerome Pathon	.25	.08
❑	134	Garrison Hearst	.40	.15
❑	135	Craig Newsome	.25	.08
❑	136	Hardy Nickerson	.25	.08
❑	137	Ray Lewis	.60	.25
❑	138	Derrick Alexander	.25	.08
❑	139	Phil Hansen	.25	.08
❑	140	Joey Galloway	.40	.15
❑	141	Oronde Gadsden	.40	.15
❑	142	Herman Moore	.40	.15
❑	143	Bobby Taylor	.25	.08
❑	144	Mario Bates	.25	.08
❑	145	Kevin Dyson	.40	.15
❑	146	Aaron Glenn	.25	.08
❑	147	Ed McDaniel	.25	.08
❑	148	Terry Allen	.40	.15
❑	149	Ike Hilliard	.25	.08
❑	150	Steve Young	.75	.30
❑	151	Eugene Robinson	.25	.08
❑	152	John Mobley	.25	.08
❑	153	Kevin Hardy	.25	.08
❑	154	Lance Johnstone	.25	.08
❑	155	Willie McGinest	.25	.08
❑	156	Gary Anderson	.25	.08
❑	157	Dexter Coakley	.25	.08
❑	158	Mark Fields	.25	.08
❑	159	Steve McNair	.60	.25
❑	160	Corey Dillon	.60	.25
❑	161	Zach Thomas	.60	.25
❑	162	Kent Graham	.25	.08
❑	163	Tony Parrish	.25	.08
❑	164	Sam Gash	.25	.08
❑	165	Kyle Brady	.25	.08
❑	166	Donnell Bennett	.25	.08
❑	167	Tony Martin	.40	.15
❑	168	Michael Bates	.25	.08
❑	169	Bobby Engram	.40	.15
❑	170	Jimmy Smith	.40	.15
❑	171	Vonnie Holliday	.25	.08
❑	172	Simeon Rice	.40	.15
❑	173	Kevin Greene	.25	.08
❑	174	Mike Alstott	.60	.25
❑	175	Eddie George	.60	.25
❑	176	Michael Jackson	.25	.08
❑	177	Neil O'Donnell	.40	.15
❑	178	Sean Dawkins	.25	.08
❑	179	Courtney Hawkins	.25	.08
❑	180	Michael Irvin	.40	.15
❑	181	Thurman Thomas	.40	.15
❑	182	Cam Cleeland	.25	.08
❑	183	Ellis Johnson	.25	.08
❑	184	Will Blackwell	.25	.08
❑	185	Ty Law	.40	.15
❑	186	Merton Hanks	.25	.08
❑	187	Dan Wilkinson	.25	.08
❑	188	Andre Wadsworth	.25	.08
❑	189	Troy Vincent	.25	.08
❑	190	Frank Sanders	.40	.15
❑	191	Stephen Boyd	.25	.08
❑	192	Jason Elam	.25	.08
❑	193	Kordell Stewart	.40	.15
❑	194	Ted Johnson	.25	.08
❑	195	Glyn Milburn	.25	.08
❑	196	Gary Brown	.25	.08
❑	197	Travis Hall	.25	.08
❑	198	John Randle	.40	.15
❑	199	Jay Riemersma	.25	.08
❑	200	Barry Sanders	2.00	.75
❑	201	Chris Spielman	.25	.08
❑	202	Rod Woodson	.40	.15
❑	203	Darrell Russell	.25	.08
❑	204	Tony Boselli	.25	.08
❑	205	Darren Woodson	.25	.08
❑	206	Muhsin Muhammad	.40	.15
❑	207	Jim Harbaugh	.40	.15
❑	208	Isaac Bruce	.60	.25
❑	209	Mo Lewis	.25	.08
❑	210	Dorsey Levens	.60	.25
❑	211	Frank Wycheck	.25	.08
❑	212	Napoleon Kaufman	.60	.25
❑	213	Walt Harris	.25	.08
❑	214	Leon Lett	.25	.08
❑	215	Karim Abdul-Jabbar	.40	.15
❑	216	Carnell Lake	.25	.08
❑	217	Byron Bam Morris	.25	.08
❑	218	John Avery	.25	.08
❑	219	Chris Slade	.25	.08
❑	220	Robert Smith	.60	.25
❑	221	Mike Pritchard	.25	.08
❑	222	Ty Detmer	.40	.15
❑	223	Randall Cunningham	.60	.25
❑	224	Alonzo Mayes	.25	.08
❑	225	Jake Plummer	.40	.15
❑	226	Derrick Mayes	.25	.08
❑	227	Jeff Brady	.25	.08
❑	228	John Lynch	.40	.15
❑	229	Steve Atwater	.25	.08
❑	230	Warrick Dunn	.60	.25
❑	231	Shawn Jefferson	.25	.08
❑	232	Erik Kramer	.25	.08
❑	233	Ken Dilger	.25	.08
❑	234	Ryan Leaf	.60	.25
❑	235	Ray Buchanan	.25	.08
❑	236	Kevin Williams	.25	.08
❑	237	Ricky Watters	.40	.15
❑	238	Dwayne Rudd	.25	.08
❑	239	Duce Staley	.60	.25
❑	240	Charlie Batch	.60	.25
❑	241	Tim Biakabutuka	.40	.15
❑	242	Tony Gonzalez	.60	.25
❑	243	Bryan Still	.25	.08
❑	244	Donnie Edwards	.25	.08
❑	245	Troy Aikman	1.25	.50
❑	246	Tony Banks	.40	.15
❑	247	Curtis Enis	.25	.08
❑	248	Chris Chandler	.40	.15
❑	249	James Jett	.40	.15
❑	250	Brett Favre	2.00	.75
❑	251	Keith Poole	.25	.08

❑ 252 Ricky Proehl	.25	.08
❑ 253 Shannon Sharpe	.40	.15
❑ 254 Robert Jones	.25	.08
❑ 255 Chad Brown	.25	.08
❑ 256 Ben Coates	.40	.15
❑ 257 Jacquez Green	.25	.08
❑ 258 Jessie Armstead	.25	.08
❑ 259 Dale Carter	.25	.08
❑ 260 Antowain Smith	.60	.25
❑ 261 Mark Chmura	.25	.08
❑ 262 Michael Westbrook	.40	.15
❑ 263 Marvin Harrison	.60	.25
❑ 264 Darrien Gordon	.25	.08
❑ 265 Rodney Harrison	.25	.08
❑ 266 Charles Johnson	.25	.08
❑ 267 Roman Phifer	.25	.08
❑ 268 Reidel Anthony	.40	.15
❑ 269 Jerry Rice	1.25	.50
❑ 270 Eric Moulds	.60	.25
❑ 271 Robert Porcher	.25	.08
❑ 272 Deion Sanders	.60	.25
❑ 273 Germane Crowell	.25	.08
❑ 274 Randy Moss	1.50	.60
❑ 275 Antonio Freeman	.60	.25
❑ 276 Trent Dilfer	.40	.15
❑ 277 Eric Turner	.25	.08
❑ 278 Jeff George	.40	.15
❑ 279 Levon Kirkland	.25	.08
❑ 280 O.J. McDuffie	.40	.15
❑ 281 Takeo Spikes	.25	.08
❑ 282 Jim Flanigan	.25	.08
❑ 283 Chris Warren	.25	.08
❑ 284 J.J. Stokes	.40	.15
❑ 285 Bryan Cox	.25	.08
❑ 286 Sam Madison	.25	.08
❑ 287 Priest Holmes	1.00	.40
❑ 288 Keenan McCardell	.40	.15
❑ 289 Michael Strahan	.40	.15
❑ 290 Robert Edwards	.25	.08
❑ 291 Tommy Vardell	.25	.08
❑ 292 Wayne Chrebet	.40	.15
❑ 293 Chris Calloway	.25	.08
❑ 294 Wesley Walls	.40	.15
❑ 295 Derrick Brooks	.60	.25
❑ 296 Trace Armstrong	.25	.08
❑ 297 Brian Simmons	.25	.08
❑ 298 Darrell Green	.25	.08
❑ 299 Robert Brooks	.40	.15
❑ 300 Peyton Manning	2.00	.75
❑ 301 Dana Stubblefield	.25	.08
❑ 302 Shawn Springs	.25	.08
❑ 303 Leslie Shepherd	.25	.08
❑ 304 Ken Harvey	.25	.08
❑ 305 Jon Kitna	.60	.25
❑ 306 Terance Mathis	.40	.15
❑ 307 Andre Reed	.40	.15
❑ 308 Jackie Harris	.25	.08
❑ 309 Rich Gannon	.60	.25
❑ 310 Keyshawn Johnson	.60	.25
❑ 311 Victor Green	.25	.08
❑ 312 Eric Allen	.25	.08
❑ 313 Terry Fair	.25	.08
❑ 314 Jason Elam SH	.25	.08
❑ 315 Garrison Hearst SH	.40	.15
❑ 316 Jake Plummer SH	.40	.15
❑ 317 Randall Cunningham SH	.60	.25
❑ 318 Randy Moss SH	.75	.30
❑ 319 Jamal Anderson SH	.60	.25
❑ 320 John Elway SH	1.00	.40
❑ 321 Doug Flutie SH	.40	.15
❑ 322 Emmitt Smith SH	.75	.30
❑ 323 Terrell Davis SH	.60	.25
❑ 324 Jerris McPhail	.25	.08
❑ 325 Damon Gibson	.25	.08
❑ 326 Jim Pyne	.25	.08
❑ 327 Antonio Langham	.25	.08
❑ 328 Freddie Solomon	.25	.08
❑ 329 Ricky Williams RC	4.00	1.50
❑ 330 Daunte Culpepper RC	8.00	3.00
❑ 331 Chris Claiborne RC	1.25	.50
❑ 332 Amos Zereoue RC	2.50	1.00
❑ 333 Chris McAlister RC	2.00	.75
❑ 334 Kevin Faulk RC	2.50	1.00
❑ 335 James Johnson RC	2.00	.75
❑ 336 Mike Cloud RC	2.00	.75
❑ 337 Jevon Kearse RC	4.00	1.50
❑ 338 Akili Smith RC	2.00	.75
❑ 339 Edgerrin James RC	8.00	3.00
❑ 340 Cecil Collins RC	1.25	.50
❑ 341 Donovan McNabb RC	10.00	4.00
❑ 342 Kevin Johnson RC	2.50	1.00
❑ 343 Torry Holt RC	5.00	2.00
❑ 344 Rob Konrad RC	1.25	.50
❑ 345 Tim Couch RC	2.50	1.00
❑ 346 David Boston RC	2.50	1.00
❑ 347 Karsten Bailey RC	2.00	.75
❑ 348 Troy Edwards RC	2.00	.75
❑ 349 Sedrick Irvin RC	1.25	.50
❑ 350 Shaun King RC	2.00	.75
❑ 351 Peerless Price RC	2.50	1.00
❑ 352 Brock Huard RC	2.50	1.00
❑ 353 Cade McNown RC	2.00	.75
❑ 354 Champ Bailey RC	3.00	1.25
❑ 355 D'Wayne Bates RC	2.00	.75
❑ 356 Checklist Card	.25	.08
❑ 357 Checklist Card	.25	.08

2000 Topps

❑ COMPLETE SET (400)	60.00	25.00
❑ COMP.SET w/o SP's (360)	20.00	7.50
❑ SBMVP STATED ODDS 1:1287 HTA		
❑ 1 Kurt Warner	1.25	.50
❑ 2 Darrell Russell	.25	.08
❑ 3 Tai Streets	.25	.08
❑ 4 Bryant Young	.25	.08
❑ 5 Kent Graham	.25	.08
❑ 6 Shawn Jefferson	.25	.08
❑ 7 Wesley Walls	.25	.08
❑ 8 Jessie Armstead	.25	.08
❑ 9 Dedric Ward	.25	.08
❑ 10 Emmitt Smith	1.25	.50
❑ 11 James Stewart	.40	.15
❑ 12 Frank Sanders	.25	.08
❑ 13 Ray Buchanan	.25	.08
❑ 14 Olindo Mare	.25	.08
❑ 15 Andre Reed	.40	.15
❑ 16 Curtis Conway	.40	.15
❑ 17 Patrick Jeffers	.60	.25
❑ 18 Greg Hill	.25	.08
❑ 19 John Unitas	.60	.25
❑ 20 Brett Favre	2.00	.75
❑ 21 Jerome Pathon	.40	.15
❑ 22 Jason Tucker	.25	.08
❑ 23 Charles Johnson	.40	.15
❑ 24 Brian Mitchell	.25	.08
❑ 25 Billy Miller	.25	.08
❑ 26 Jay Fiedler	.60	.25
❑ 27 Marcus Pollard	.25	.08
❑ 28 De'Mond Parker	.25	.08
❑ 29 Leslie Shepherd	.25	.08
❑ 30 Fred Taylor	.60	.25
❑ 31 Michael Pittman	.25	.08
❑ 32 Ricky Watters	.40	.15
❑ 33 Derrick Brooks	.60	.25
❑ 34 Junior Seau	.60	.25
❑ 35 Troy Vincent	.25	.08
❑ 36 Eric Allen	.25	.08
❑ 37 Pete Mitchell	.25	.08
❑ 38 Tony Simmons	.25	.08
❑ 39 Az-Zahir Hakim	.40	.15
❑ 40 Dan Marino	2.00	.75
❑ 41 Mac Cody	.25	.08
❑ 42 Scott Dreisbach	.25	.08
❑ 43 Al Wilson	.25	.08
❑ 44 Luther Broughton RC	.40	.15
❑ 45 Wane McGarity	.25	.08
❑ 46 Stephen Boyd	.25	.08
❑ 47 Michael Strahan	.40	.15
❑ 48 Chris Chandler	.40	.15
❑ 49 Tony Martin	.40	.15
❑ 50 Edgerrin James	1.00	.40
❑ 51 John Randle	.40	.15
❑ 52 Warrick Dunn	.60	.25
❑ 53 Elvis Grbac	.40	.15
❑ 54 Champ Bailey	.40	.15
❑ 55 Kyle Brady	.25	.08
❑ 56 John Lynch	.40	.15
❑ 57 Kevin Carter	.25	.08
❑ 58 Mike Pritchard	.25	.08
❑ 59 Deon Mitchell RC	.40	.15
❑ 60 Randy Moss	1.25	.50
❑ 61 Jermaine Fazande	.25	.08
❑ 62 Donovan McNabb	1.00	.40
❑ 63 Richard Huntley	.25	.08
❑ 64 Rich Gannon	.60	.25
❑ 65 Aaron Glenn	.25	.08
❑ 66 Amani Toomer	.25	.08
❑ 67 Andre Hastings	.25	.08
❑ 68 Ricky Williams	.60	.25
❑ 69 Sam Madison	.25	.08
❑ 70 Drew Bledsoe	.75	.30
❑ 71 Eric Moulds	.60	.25
❑ 72 Justin Armour	.25	.08
❑ 73 Jamal Anderson	.60	.25
❑ 74 Mario Bates	.25	.08
❑ 75 Sam Gash	.25	.08
❑ 76 Macey Brooks	.25	.08
❑ 77 Tremain Mack	.25	.08
❑ 78 David LaFleur	.25	.08
❑ 79 Dexter Coakley	.25	.08
❑ 80 Cris Carter	.60	.25
❑ 81 Byron Chamberlain	.25	.08
❑ 82 David Sloan	.25	.08
❑ 83 Mike Devlin RC	.25	.08
❑ 84 Jimmy Smith	.40	.15
❑ 85 Derrick Alexander	.40	.15
❑ 86 Damon Huard	.60	.25
❑ 87 Jake Reed	.40	.15
❑ 88 Darrell Green	.25	.08
❑ 89 Derrick Mason	.40	.15
❑ 90 Curtis Martin	.60	.25
❑ 91 Donnie Abraham	.25	.08
❑ 92 D'Marco Farr	.25	.08
❑ 93 Ahman Green	.60	.25
❑ 94 Shane Matthews	.40	.15
❑ 95 Torrance Small	.25	.08
❑ 96 Duce Staley	.60	.25
❑ 97 Jon Ritchie	.25	.08
❑ 98 Victor Green	.25	.08
❑ 99 Kerry Collins	.40	.15
❑ 100 Peyton Manning	1.50	.60
❑ 101 Ben Coates	.25	.08
❑ 102 Thurman Thomas	.40	.15
❑ 103 Cornelius Bennett	.25	.08
❑ 104 Terance Mathis	.40	.15
❑ 105 Adrian Murrell	.40	.15
❑ 106 Donald Hayes	.25	.08
❑ 107 Terry Kirby	.25	.08
❑ 108 James Allen	.40	.15
❑ 109 Ty Law	.40	.15
❑ 110 Tim Brown	.60	.25
❑ 111 Chad Bratzke	.25	.08
❑ 112 Deion Sanders	.60	.25
❑ 113 James Johnson	.25	.08
❑ 114 Tony Richardson RC	.40	.15
❑ 115 Tony Brackens	.25	.08
❑ 116 Ken Dilger	.25	.08
❑ 117 Albert Connell	.25	.08
❑ 118 Neil O'Donnell	.25	.08
❑ 119 Selucio Sanford EP RC	.60	.25
❑ 120 Steve Young	.75	.30
❑ 121 Tony Horne	.25	.08
❑ 122 Charlie Rogers	.25	.08
❑ 123 J.J. Stokes	.40	.15
❑ 124 Kenny Bynum	.25	.08
❑ 125 Jeff Graham	.25	.08
❑ 126 Ike Hilliard	.40	.15
❑ 127 Ray Lucas	.40	.15
❑ 128 Terry Glenn	.40	.15
❑ 129 Rickey Dudley	.25	.08
❑ 130 Joey Galloway	.40	.15
❑ 131 Brian Dawkins	.60	.25
❑ 132 Rob Moore	.40	.15

	No.	Player		
❑	133	Bob Christian	.25	.08
❑	134	Anthony Wright RC	2.00	.75
❑	135	Antowain Smith	.40	.15
❑	136	Kevin Johnson	.60	.25
❑	137	Scott Covington	.25	.08
❑	138	D'Wayne Bates	.25	.08
❑	139	Sam Cowart	.25	.08
❑	140	Isaac Bruce	.60	.25
❑	141	Tony McGee	.25	.08
❑	142	Dale Carter	.25	.08
❑	143	Matt Hasselbeck	.40	.15
❑	144	Torry Holt	.60	.25
❑	145	Daunte Culpepper	.75	.30
❑	146	Yatil Green	.25	.08
❑	147	Chris Howard	.25	.08
❑	148	Irving Fryar	.40	.15
❑	149	Derrick Mayes	.40	.15
❑	150	Warren Sapp	.40	.15
❑	151	Ricky Proehl	.25	.08
❑	152	Eric Kresser EP	.50	.20
❑	153	Jeff Garcia	.60	.25
❑	154	Freddie Jones	.25	.08
❑	155	Mike Cloud	.25	.08
❑	156	Wayne Chrebet	.40	.15
❑	157	Joe Montgomery	.25	.08
❑	158	Shannon Sharpe	.40	.15
❑	159	Eddie Kennison	.25	.08
❑	160	Eddie George	.60	.25
❑	161	Jay Riemersma	.25	.08
❑	162	Peter Boulware	.25	.08
❑	163	Aeneas Williams	.25	.08
❑	164	Jim Miller	.25	.08
❑	165	Jamir Miller	.25	.08
❑	166	Tim Biakabutuka	.40	.15
❑	167	Kordell Stewart	.40	.15
❑	168	Charlie Garner	.40	.15
❑	169	Germane Crowell	.25	.08
❑	170	Stephen Davis	.60	.25
❑	171	Jeff George	.40	.15
❑	172	Mark Brunell	.60	.25
❑	173	Stephen Alexander	.25	.08
❑	174	Mike Alstott	.60	.25
❑	175	Terry Allen	.40	.15
❑	176	Ed McCaffrey	.60	.25
❑	177	Bobby Engram	.25	.08
❑	178	Andre Cooper	.25	.08
❑	179	Kevin Faulk	.25	.08
❑	180	Errict Rhett	.40	.15
❑	181	Jammi German	.25	.08
❑	182	Oronde Gadsden	.40	.15
❑	183	Jevon Kearse	.60	.25
❑	184	Herman Moore	.40	.15
❑	185	Terrence Wilkins	.25	.08
❑	186	Rocket Ismail	.40	.15
❑	187	Patrick Johnson	.25	.08
❑	188	Simeon Rice	.40	.15
❑	189	Mo Lewis	.25	.08
❑	190	Qadry Ismail	.40	.15
❑	191	Terry Jackson	.25	.08
❑	192	Rashaan Shehee	.25	.08
❑	193	Charles Woodson	.40	.15
❑	194	Akili Smith	.25	.08
❑	195	Yancey Thigpen	.25	.08
❑	196	Michael Westbrook	.40	.15
❑	197	Donnell Bennett	.25	.08
❑	198	Sedrick Irvin	.25	.08
❑	199	Keenan McCardell	.40	.15
❑	200	Marshall Faulk	.75	.30
❑	201	Jeff Blake	.40	.15
❑	202	Rob Johnson	.40	.15
❑	203	Vinny Testaverde	.40	.15
❑	204	Andy Katzenmoyer	.25	.08
❑	205	Michael Basnight	.25	.08
❑	206	Lance Schulters	.25	.08
❑	207	Shaun King	.25	.08
❑	208	Bill Schroeder	.40	.15
❑	209	Skip Hicks	.25	.08
❑	210	Jake Plummer	.40	.15
❑	211	Leroy Hoard	.25	.08
❑	212	Reggie Barlow	.25	.08
❑	213	E.G. Green	.25	.08
❑	214	Fred Lane	.25	.08
❑	215	Antonio Freeman	.60	.25
❑	216	Grant Wistrom	.25	.08
❑	217	Kevin Dyson	.40	.15
❑	218	Mikhael Ricks	.25	.08
❑	219	Rod Woodson	.40	.15
❑	220	Tim Dwight	.60	.25
❑	221	Darnay Scott	.40	.15
❑	222	Curtis Enis	.25	.08
❑	223	Sean Bennett	.25	.08
❑	224	Napoleon Kaufman	.40	.15
❑	225	Jonathan Linton	.25	.08
❑	226	Jim Harbaugh	.40	.15
❑	227	Hardy Nickerson	.25	.08
❑	228	Todd Lyght	.25	.08
❑	229	Dorsey Levens	.40	.15
❑	230	Steve Beuerlein	.40	.15
❑	231	Marty Booker	.40	.15
❑	232	Andre Wadsworth	.25	.08
❑	233	James Hasty	.25	.08
❑	234	Shawn Bryson	.25	.08
❑	235	Larry Centers	.25	.08
❑	236	Charlie Batch	.60	.25
❑	237	Steve McNair	.60	.25
❑	238	Darrin Chiaverini	.25	.08
❑	239	Jerome Bettis	.60	.25
❑	240	Muhsin Muhammad	.40	.15
❑	241	Terrell Fletcher	.25	.08
❑	242	Jon Kitna	.60	.25
❑	243	Frank Wycheck	.25	.08
❑	244	Tony Gonzalez	.40	.15
❑	245	Ron Rivers	.25	.08
❑	246	Olandis Gary	.60	.25
❑	247	Jermaine Lewis	.25	.08
❑	248	Joe Jurevicius	.25	.08
❑	249	Richie Anderson	.40	.15
❑	250	Marcus Robinson	.60	.25
❑	251	Shawn Springs	.25	.08
❑	252	William Floyd	.25	.08
❑	253	Bobby Shaw RC	.60	.25
❑	254	Glyn Milburn	.25	.08
❑	255	Brian Griese	.60	.25
❑	256	Donnie Edwards	.25	.08
❑	257	Joe Horn	.40	.15
❑	258	Cameron Cleeland	.25	.08
❑	259	Glenn Foley	.25	.08
❑	260	Corey Dillon	.60	.25
❑	261	Troy Brown	.40	.15
❑	262	Stoney Case	.25	.08
❑	263	Kevin Williams	.25	.08
❑	264	London Fletcher RC	.40	.15
❑	265	O.J. McDuffie	.40	.15
❑	266	Jonathan Quinn	.25	.08
❑	267	Trent Dilfer	.40	.15
❑	268	Dameyune Craig	.25	.08
❑	269	Terrell Owens	.60	.25
❑	270	Tim Couch	.40	.15
❑	271	Dameane Douglas	.25	.08
❑	272	Moses Moreno	.25	.08
❑	273	Bruce Smith	.40	.15
❑	274	Peerless Price	.40	.15
❑	275	Sam Gamer	.25	.08
❑	276	Natrone Means	.25	.08
❑	277	Na Brown	.25	.08
❑	278	Dave Moore	.25	.08
❑	279	Chris Sanders	.25	.08
❑	280	Troy Aikman	1.25	.50
❑	281	Cecil Collins	.25	.08
❑	282	Matthew Hatchette	.25	.08
❑	283	Bill Romanowski	.25	.08
❑	284	Basil Mitchell	.25	.08
❑	285	Tony Banks	.40	.15
❑	286	Jake Delhomme RC	3.00	1.25
❑	287	Keyshawn Johnson	.60	.25
❑	288	Dexter McCleon RC	.60	.25
❑	289	Corey Bradford	.40	.15
❑	290	Terrell Davis	.60	.25
❑	291	Johnnie Morton	.40	.15
❑	292	Kevin Lockett	.25	.08
❑	293	Robert Smith	.60	.25
❑	294	Jeff Lewis	.25	.08
❑	295	Wali Rainer	.25	.08
❑	296	Troy Edwards	.25	.08
❑	297	Keith Poole	.25	.08
❑	298	Priest Holmes	.75	.30
❑	299	David Boston	.60	.25
❑	300	Marvin Harrison	.60	.25
❑	301	Levon Kirkland	.25	.08
❑	302	Robert Holcombe	.25	.08
❑	303	Autry Denson	.25	.08
❑	304	Kevin Hardy	.25	.08
❑	305	Rod Smith	.40	.15
❑	306	Robert Porcher	.25	.08
❑	307	Cade McNown	.25	.08
❑	308	Craig Yeast	.25	.08
❑	309	Doug Flutie	.60	.25
❑	310	Jerry Rice	1.25	.50
❑	311	Brad Johnson	.60	.25
❑	312	Tiki Barber	.60	.25
❑	313	Will Blackwell	.25	.08
❑	314	Sean Dawkins	.25	.08
❑	315	Jacquez Green	.25	.08
❑	316	Zach Thomas	.60	.25
❑	317	Gus Frerotte	.25	.08
❑	318	Chris Warren	.25	.08
❑	319	Carl Pickens	.40	.15
❑	320	Tyrone Wheatley HL	.25	.08
❑	321	Kurt Warner HL	.60	.25
❑	322	Dan Marino HL	1.00	.40
❑	323	Cris Carter HL	.40	.15
❑	324	Brett Favre HL	1.00	.40
❑	325	Marshall Faulk HL	.60	.25
❑	326	Jevon Kearse HL	.40	.15
❑	327	Edgerrin James HL	.60	.25
❑	328	Emmitt Smith HL	.60	.25
❑	329	Andre Reed HL	.25	.08
❑	330	K.Dyson/F.Wycheck HL	.25	.08
❑	331	Olindo Mare MM	.25	.08
❑	332	Marcus Coleman MM	.25	.08
❑	333	James Johnson MM	.25	.08
❑	334	Ray Lucas MM	.40	.15
❑	335	Dedric Ward MM	.25	.08
❑	336	Richie Cunningham MM	.25	.08
❑	337	James Hasty MM	.25	.08
❑	338	Sedrick Shaw MM	.25	.08
❑	339	Kurt Warner MM	.60	.25
❑	340	Marshall Faulk MM	.60	.25
❑	341	Brian Shay EP	.50	.20
❑	342	L.C. Stevens EP	.50	.20
❑	343	Corey Thomas EP	.50	.20
❑	344	Scott Milanovich EP	.60	.25
❑	345	Pat Barnes EP	.60	.25
❑	346	Danny Wuerffel EP	.60	.25
❑	347	Kevin Daft EP	.50	.20
❑	348	Ron Powlus EP RC	1.00	.40
❑	349	Tony Graziani EP	.60	.25
❑	350	Norman Miller EP RC	.50	.20
❑	351	Cory Sauter EP	.50	.20
❑	352	Marcus Crandell EP RC	.60	.25
❑	353	Sean Morey EP RC	.60	.25
❑	354	Jeff Ogden EP	.60	.25
❑	355	Ted White EP	.50	.20
❑	356	Jim Kubiak EP RC	.60	.25
❑	357	Aaron Stecker EP RC	1.00	.40
❑	358	Ronnie Powell EP	.50	.20
❑	359	Matt Lytle EP RC	.60	.25
❑	360	Kendrick Nord EP RC	.50	.20
❑	361	Tim Rattay RC	2.50	1.00
❑	362	Rob Morris RC	2.50	1.00
❑	363	Chris Samuels RC	2.00	.75
❑	364	Todd Husak RC	2.50	1.00
❑	365	Ahmed Plummer RC	2.50	1.00
❑	366	Frank Murphy RC	2.00	.75
❑	367	Michael Wiley RC	2.50	1.00
❑	368	Giovanni Carmazzi RC	2.00	.75
❑	369	Anthony Becht RC	2.50	1.00
❑	370	John Abraham RC	2.50	1.00
❑	371	Shaun Alexander RC	12.00	5.00
❑	372	Thomas Jones RC	4.00	1.50
❑	373	Courtney Brown RC	1.00	.40
❑	374	Curtis Keaton RC	2.00	.75
❑	375	Jerry Porter RC	3.00	1.25
❑	376	Corey Simon RC	1.00	.40
❑	377	Dez White RC	2.50	1.00
❑	378	Jamal Lewis RC	6.00	2.50
❑	379	Ron Dayne RC	2.50	1.00
❑	380	R.Jay Soward RC	2.50	1.00
❑	381	Tee Martin RC	2.50	1.00
❑	382	Shaun Ellis RC	2.50	1.00
❑	383	Brian Urlacher RC	10.00	4.00
❑	384	Reuben Droughns RC	4.00	1.50
❑	385	Travis Taylor RC	1.00	.40
❑	386	Plaxico Burress RC	5.00	2.00
❑	387	Chad Pennington RC	6.00	2.50
❑	388	Sylvester Morris RC	2.50	1.00
❑	389	Ron Dugans RC	2.00	.75
❑	390	Joe Hamilton RC	2.50	1.00
❑	391	Chris Redman RC	.60	.25
❑	392	Trung Canidate RC	2.50	1.00
❑	393	J.R. Redmond RC	2.50	1.00

	Card	Player	Price 1	Price 2
❑	394	Danny Farmer RC	2.50	1.00
❑	395	Todd Pinkston RC	2.50	1.00
❑	396	Dennis Northcutt RC	2.50	1.00
❑	397	Laveranues Coles RC	3.00	1.25
❑	398	Bubba Franks RC	2.50	1.00
❑	399	Travis Prentice RC	2.50	1.00
❑	400	Peter Warrick RC	2.50	1.00
❑	SBMVP	Kurt Warner FB AU	120.00	50.00

2001 Topps

	Card	Player	Price 1	Price 2
❑		COMPLETE SET (385)	75.00	45.00
❑	1	Marshall Faulk	.75	.30
❑	2	Lawyer Milloy	.40	.15
❑	3	Rich Gannon	.60	.25
❑	4	Rod Smith	.40	.15
❑	5	David Boston	.60	.25
❑	6	Jeremy McDaniel	.25	.08
❑	7	Joey Galloway	.40	.15
❑	8	Ron Dixon	.25	.08
❑	9	Terrell Fletcher	.25	.08
❑	10	Deion Sanders	.60	.25
❑	11	Jevon Kearse	.40	.15
❑	12	Charles Woodson	.40	.15
❑	13	Brian Walker	.25	.08
❑	14	Mike Peterson	.25	.08
❑	15	Marcus Robinson	.60	.25
❑	16	Duane Starks	.25	.08
❑	17	KaRon Coleman	.25	.08
❑	18	Randy Moss	1.25	.50
❑	19	Reggie Jones	.25	.08
❑	20	Derrick Brooks	.60	.25
❑	21	Eddie George	.60	.25
❑	22	Wayne Chrebet	.40	.15
❑	23	Kevin Hardy	.25	.08
❑	24	Bill Schroeder	.40	.15
❑	25	Doug Flutie	.60	.25
❑	26	Tim Dwight	.60	.25
❑	27	Eddie Kennison	.40	.15
❑	28	Reggie Kelly	.25	.08
❑	29	Ricky Watters	.40	.15
❑	30	Stephen Alexander	.25	.08
❑	31	Az-Zahir Hakim	.25	.08
❑	32	Henri Crockett	.25	.08
❑	33	Joe Horn	.40	.15
❑	34	Danny Farmer	.25	.08
❑	35	Shannon Sharpe	.40	.15
❑	36	Brad Hoover	.25	.08
❑	37	David Patten	.25	.08
❑	38	Kevin Faulk	.40	.15
❑	39	Freddie Jones	.25	.08
❑	40	Michael Westbrook	.40	.15
❑	41	Jacquez Green	.25	.08
❑	42	Torrance Small	.25	.08
❑	43	Terrence Wilkins	.25	.08
❑	44	Brett Favre	2.00	.75
❑	45	Tony Banks	.40	.15
❑	46	Johnnie Morton	.40	.15
❑	47	Jimmy Smith	.40	.15
❑	48	Jerry Rice	1.25	.50
❑	49	Jeff George	.40	.15
❑	50	Ray Lewis	.60	.25
❑	51	Joe Johnson	.25	.08
❑	52	Rocket Ismail	.40	.15
❑	53	Muhsin Muhammad	.40	.15
❑	54	Ken Dilger	.25	.08
❑	55	Ike Hilliard	.40	.15
❑	56	Joey Porter RC	12.00	5.00
❑	57	Shaun Alexander	.75	.30
❑	58	Jeff Garcia	.60	.25
❑	59	Jay Fiedler	.60	.25
❑	60	Wane McGarity	.25	.08
❑	61	Steve Beuerlein	.25	.08
❑	62	Tywan Mitchell	.25	.08
❑	63	Travis Prentice	.25	.08
❑	64	Robert Griffith	.25	.08
❑	65	Napoleon Kaufman	.25	.08
❑	66	Randall Godfrey	.25	.08
❑	67	Junior Seau	.60	.25
❑	68	Willie Jackson	.25	.08
❑	69	Larry Foster	.25	.08
❑	70	Brandon Stokley	.40	.15
❑	71	Hugh Douglas	.25	.08
❑	72	James Thrash	.40	.15
❑	73	Vinny Testaverde	.40	.15
❑	74	Leslie Shepherd	.25	.08
❑	75	Terrell Davis	.60	.25
❑	76	Jake Plummer	.40	.15
❑	77	Corey Dillon	.60	.25
❑	78	Ron Dayne	.60	.25
❑	79	Brock Huard	.25	.08
❑	80	Todd Husak	.25	.08
❑	81	Richard Huntley	.25	.08
❑	82	Shaun Ellis	.25	.08
❑	83	Kyle Brady	.25	.08
❑	84	Corey Bradford	.25	.08
❑	85	Eric Moulds	.40	.15
❑	86	Brian Finneran	.25	.08
❑	87	Antonio Freeman	.60	.25
❑	88	Terry Glenn	.25	.08
❑	89	Tai Streets	.25	.08
❑	90	Chris Sanders	.25	.08
❑	91	Sylvester Morris	.25	.08
❑	92	Peter Warrick	.60	.25
❑	93	Chris Greisen	.25	.08
❑	94	Cade McNown	.25	.08
❑	95	Jerome Pathon	.40	.15
❑	96	John Randle	.25	.08
❑	97	Curtis Conway	.40	.15
❑	98	Keyshawn Johnson	.60	.25
❑	99	Trent Green	.60	.25
❑	100	Mike Anderson	.60	.25
❑	101	Jeff Blake	.40	.15
❑	102	Tee Martin	.40	.15
❑	103	Darrell Jackson	.60	.25
❑	104	Mark Brunell	.60	.25
❑	105	Charlie Batch	.60	.25
❑	106	Wesley Walls	.25	.08
❑	107	Edgerrin James	.75	.30
❑	108	Robert Wilson	.25	.08
❑	109	Donovan McNabb	.75	.30
❑	110	Champ Bailey	.40	.15
❑	111	Isaac Bruce	.60	.25
❑	112	Michael Strahan	.40	.15
❑	113	Donnie Edwards	.25	.08
❑	114	Randall Cunningham	.60	.25
❑	115	Germane Crowell	.25	.08
❑	116	Jermaine Lewis	.25	.08
❑	117	Dennis McKinley	.25	.08
❑	118	Ryan Leaf	.40	.15
❑	119	Samari Rolle	.25	.08
❑	120	Daunte Culpepper	.60	.25
❑	121	Tim Couch	.40	.15
❑	122	Greg Biekert	.25	.08
❑	123	Warrick Dunn	.60	.25
❑	124	Richie Anderson	.25	.08
❑	125	Trace Armstrong	.25	.08
❑	126	Bernardo Harris	.25	.08
❑	127	Kwame Cavil	.25	.08
❑	128	James Allen	.40	.15
❑	129	Anthony Becht	.25	.08
❑	130	Tiki Barber	.60	.25
❑	131	Brad Johnson	.60	.25
❑	132	Tyrone Wheatley	.40	.15
❑	133	Kurt Warner	1.25	.50
❑	134	Desmond Howard	.25	.08
❑	135	Thomas Jones	.40	.15
❑	136	Peyton Manning	1.50	.60
❑	137	Tony Richardson	.25	.08
❑	138	Chris Chandler	.40	.15
❑	139	Plaxico Burress	.60	.25
❑	140	J.R. Redmond	.25	.08
❑	141	Fred Taylor	.60	.25
❑	142	Akili Smith	.25	.08
❑	143	Sammy Morris	.25	.08
❑	144	Jessie Armstead	.25	.08
❑	145	Charlie Garner	.40	.15
❑	146	Steve McNair	.60	.25
❑	147	Charles Johnson	.25	.08
❑	148	Troy Aikman	1.00	.40
❑	149	Kevin Johnson	.40	.15
❑	150	Brian Urlacher	1.00	.40
❑	151	Travis Taylor	.40	.15
❑	152	Aaron Shea	.25	.08
❑	153	Mike Cloud	.25	.08
❑	154	Donald Driver	.40	.15
❑	155	Chad Pennington	1.00	.40
❑	156	Troy Edwards	.25	.08
❑	157	Reidel Anthony	.25	.08
❑	158	Michael Bishop	.25	.08
❑	159	Mo Lewis	.25	.08
❑	160	Damon Huard	.25	.08
❑	161	James McKnight	.40	.15
❑	162	Craig Yeast	.25	.08
❑	163	Michael Pittman	.25	.08
❑	164	Robert Smith	.40	.15
❑	165	Terrelle Smith	.25	.08
❑	166	Jeremiah Trotter	.40	.15
❑	167	Amani Toomer	.25	.08
❑	168	JaJuan Dawson	.25	.08
❑	169	Tim Biakabutuka	.40	.15
❑	170	Oronde Gadsden	.40	.15
❑	171	Ray Lucas	.25	.08
❑	172	Jermaine Fazande	.25	.08
❑	173	Todd Bouman	.40	.15
❑	174	Frank Wycheck	.25	.08
❑	175	Hines Ward	.60	.25
❑	176	Ahman Green	.60	.25
❑	177	Kaseem Sinceno	.25	.08
❑	178	Jamal Anderson	.60	.25
❑	179	Jay Riemersma	.25	.08
❑	180	Jarious Jackson	.40	.15
❑	181	Andre Rison	.40	.15
❑	182	Jerome Bettis	.60	.25
❑	183	Blaine Bishop	.25	.08
❑	184	Dorsey Levens	.25	.08
❑	185	James Stewart	.40	.15
❑	186	Chad Lewis	.25	.08
❑	187	Justin Watson	.25	.08
❑	188	Warren Sapp	.40	.15
❑	189	Rod Woodson	.40	.15
❑	190	Ricky Williams	.60	.25
❑	191	Marty Booker	.25	.08
❑	192	MarTay Jenkins	.25	.08
❑	193	Peerless Price	.40	.15
❑	194	Tony Gonzalez	.40	.15
❑	195	Jon Kitna	.40	.15
❑	196	Stephen Davis	.60	.25
❑	197	Curtis Martin	.60	.25
❑	198	Matt Hasselbeck	.40	.15
❑	199	Pat Johnson	.25	.08
❑	200	Emmitt Smith	1.25	.50
❑	201	Doug Johnson	.25	.08
❑	202	Autry Denson	.25	.08
❑	203	Troy Brown	.40	.15
❑	204	Jeff Graham	.25	.08
❑	205	Corey Simon	.40	.15
❑	206	Jamel White	.25	.08
❑	207	Jeff Lewis	.25	.08
❑	208	Frank Sanders	.25	.08
❑	209	Al Wilson	.25	.08
❑	210	Jason Sehorn	.25	.08
❑	211	Shaun King	.25	.08
❑	212	Torry Holt	.60	.25
❑	213	Kordell Stewart	.40	.15
❑	214	Keenan McCardell	.25	.08
❑	215	Dedric Ward	.25	.08
❑	216	Michael Wiley	.25	.08
❑	217	Rob Johnson	.40	.15
❑	218	Jamal Lewis	1.00	.40
❑	219	Herman Moore	.40	.15
❑	220	Ron Dugans	.25	.08
❑	221	Jason Taylor	.25	.08
❑	222	Charles Lee	.25	.08
❑	223	J.J. Stokes	.40	.15
❑	224	Albert Connell	.25	.08
❑	225	Keith Poole	.25	.08
❑	226	Elvis Grbac	.40	.15
❑	227	Shawn Jefferson	.25	.08
❑	228	Jackie Harris	.25	.08
❑	229	Derrick Alexander	.40	.15
❑	230	Darnell Autry	.25	.08
❑	231	Bobby Shaw	.25	.08
❑	232	Aaron Brooks	.60	.25

❑ 233	Cris Carter	.60	.25
❑ 234	Desmond Clark	.25	.08
❑ 235	Spergon Wynn	.25	.08
❑ 236	Qadry Ismail	.40	.15
❑ 237	Sam Cowart	.25	.08
❑ 238	Zach Thomas	.60	.25
❑ 239	Drew Bledsoe	.75	.30
❑ 240	Ronney Jenkins	.25	.08
❑ 241	Keith Mitchell RC	.25	.08
❑ 242	Laveranues Coles	.60	.25
❑ 243	Marcus Pollard	.25	.08
❑ 244	Darren Sharper	.25	.08
❑ 245	Donald Hayes	.25	.08
❑ 246	Brian Griese	.60	.25
❑ 247	Frank Moreau	.25	.08
❑ 248	Bruce Smith	.25	.08
❑ 249	Fred Beasley	.25	.08
❑ 250	Mike Alstott	.60	.25
❑ 251	Trent Dilfer	.40	.15
❑ 252	Terance Mathis	.40	.15
❑ 253	Shawn Bryson	.25	.08
❑ 254	Dennis Northcutt	.40	.15
❑ 255	Brandon Bennett	.25	.08
❑ 256	Stacey Mack	.25	.08
❑ 257	Tim Brown	.60	.25
❑ 258	Duce Staley	.60	.25
❑ 259	Sean Dawkins	.25	.08
❑ 260	Ricky Proehl	.25	.08
❑ 261	Chris Fuamatu-ma'afala	.25	.08
❑ 262	La'Roi Glover	.25	.08
❑ 263	Bubba Franks	.40	.15
❑ 264	Kevin Lockett	.25	.08
❑ 265	Lamar Smith	.40	.15
❑ 266	Priest Holmes	.75	.30
❑ 267	Macey Brooks	.25	.08
❑ 268	Anthony Wright	.25	.08
❑ 269	Ed McCaffrey	.60	.25
❑ 270	Joe Jurevicius	.25	.08
❑ 271	Terrell Owens	.60	.25
❑ 272	Tony Simmons	.25	.08
❑ 273	Itula Mili	.25	.08
❑ 274	Chad Morton	.25	.08
❑ 275	Marvin Harrison	.60	.25
❑ 276	Jason Gildon	.25	.08
❑ 277	Derrick Mason	.40	.15
❑ 278	Greg Clark	.25	.08
❑ 279	Casey Crawford	.25	.08
❑ 280	Kerry Collins	.40	.15
❑ 281	Terrell Owens	.60	.25
❑ 282	Marshall Faulk	.60	.25
❑ 283	Mike Anderson	.40	.15
❑ 284	Cris Carter	.40	.15
❑ 285	Corey Dillon	.40	.15
❑ 286	Daunte Culpepper	.60	.25
❑ 287	Peyton Manning	.75	.30
❑ 288	Torry Holt	.60	.25
❑ 289	Marvin Harrison	.40	.15
❑ 290	Edgerrin James	.75	.30
❑ 291	Takeo Spikes	.25	.08
❑ 292	John Lynch	.40	.15
❑ 293	Sam Madison	.25	.08
❑ 294	Stephen Boyd	.25	.08
❑ 295	Tony Siragusa	.25	.08
❑ 296	Robert Porcher	.25	.08
❑ 297	Donnell Bennett	.25	.08
❑ 298	Hardy Nickerson	.25	.08
❑ 299	Jonathan Quinn	.25	.08
❑ 300	Rob Morris	.25	.08
❑ 301	E.G. Green	.25	.08
❑ 302	David Sloan	.25	.08
❑ 303	Jason Tucker	.25	.08
❑ 304	Darrin Chiaverini	.25	.08
❑ 305	Wali Rainer	.25	.08
❑ 306	Jerry Azumah	.25	.08
❑ 307	Jonathan Linton	.25	.08
❑ 308	Dameyune Craig	.25	.08
❑ 309	Courtney Brown	.25	.08
❑ 310	Jammi German	.25	.08
❑ 311	Michael Vick RC	8.00	3.00
❑ 312	Jamar Fletcher RC	.75	.30
❑ 313	Will Allen RC	.75	.30
❑ 314	Jamal Reynolds RC	1.25	.50
❑ 315	Quincy Morgan RC	1.25	.50
❑ 316	Eric Kelly RC	.50	.20
❑ 317	Michael Stone RC	.50	.20
❑ 318	Rod Gardner RC	1.25	.50
❑ 319	Ken-Yon Rambo RC	.75	.30
❑ 320	Eric Westmoreland RC	.75	.30
❑ 321	Steve Smith RC	3.00	1.50
❑ 322	George Layne RC	.75	.30
❑ 323	Justin McCareins RC	1.25	.50
❑ 324	Adam Archuleta RC	1.25	.50
❑ 325	Justin Smith RC	1.25	.50
❑ 326	David Terrell RC	1.25	.50
❑ 327	Correll Buckhalter RC	1.50	.60
❑ 328	Drew Brees RC	5.00	2.00
❑ 329	Chris Barnes RC	.75	.30
❑ 330	Santana Moss RC	2.00	.75
❑ 331	Josh Heupel RC	1.25	.50
❑ 332	Cedrick Wilson RC	1.25	.50
❑ 333	Gerard Warren RC	1.25	.50
❑ 334	Jamie Henderson RC	.75	.30
❑ 335	Onomo Ojo RC	.75	.30
❑ 336	Marcus Stroud RC	1.25	.50
❑ 337	Quincy Carter RC	1.25	.50
❑ 338	Koren Robinson RC	1.25	.50
❑ 339	Ryan Pickett RC	.50	.20
❑ 340	Chad Johnson RC	3.00	1.25
❑ 341	Nate Clements RC	1.25	.50
❑ 342	Jesse Palmer RC	1.25	.50
❑ 343	Snoop Minnis RC	.75	.30
❑ 344	Reggie Wayne RC	2.50	1.00
❑ 345	Kevin Kasper RC	1.25	.50
❑ 346	Will Peterson RC	.75	.30
❑ 347	Marques Tuiasosopo RC	1.25	.50
❑ 348	Sage Rosenfels RC	1.25	.50
❑ 349	Dan Alexander RC	1.25	.50
❑ 350	LaDainian Tomlinson RC	25.00	10.00
❑ 351	Dan Morgan RC	1.25	.50
❑ 352	Scotty Anderson RC	.75	.30
❑ 353	Deuce McAllister RC	2.50	1.00
❑ 354	Todd Heap RC	1.25	.50
❑ 355	Tony Dixon RC	.75	.30
❑ 356	Chris Chambers RC	2.00	.75
❑ 357	Eddie Berlin RC	.75	.30
❑ 358	Anthony Thomas RC	1.25	.50
❑ 359	James Jackson RC	1.25	.50
❑ 360	Richard Seymour RC	1.25	.50
❑ 361	Andre Carter RC	1.25	.50
❑ 362	Bobby Newcombe RC	.75	.30
❑ 363	Robert Ferguson RC	1.25	.50
❑ 364	Jonathan Carter RC	.75	.30
❑ 365	Damione Lewis RC	.75	.30
❑ 366	Damerien McCants RC	.75	.30
❑ 367	Tim Hasselbeck RC	1.25	.50
❑ 368	Derrick Gibson RC	.75	.30
❑ 369	Rudi Johnson RC	2.50	1.00
❑ 370	Alge Crumpler RC	1.50	.60
❑ 371	Derrick Blaylock RC	1.25	.50
❑ 372	Moran Norris RC	.50	.20
❑ 373	Travis Minor RC	.75	.30
❑ 374	LaMont Jordan RC	2.50	1.00
❑ 375	Kevan Barlow RC	1.25	.50
❑ 376	Freddie Mitchell RC	1.25	.50
❑ 377	Shaun Rogers RC	1.25	.50
❑ 378	Tay Cody RC	.50	.20
❑ 379	Travis Henry RC	2.00	.75
❑ 380	Chris Weinke RC	1.25	.50
❑ 381	Willie Middlebrooks RC	.75	.30
❑ 382	Rashard Casey RC	.75	.30
❑ 383	Mike McMahon RC	1.25	.50
❑ 384	Michael Bennett RC	1.25	.50
❑ 385	Jabari Holloway RC	.75	.30
❑ SBMVP	Ray Lewis FB AU	250.00	125.00

2002 Topps

❑	COMPLETE SET (385)	50.00	20.00
❑ 1	Kurt Warner	.60	.25
❑ 2	Jeff Graham	.25	.08
❑ 3	Todd Bouman	.25	.08
❑ 4	Duce Staley	.60	.25
❑ 5	Jon Kitna	.40	.15
❑ 6	Shannon Sharpe	.40	.15
❑ 7	Darrell Jackson	.40	.15
❑ 8	Michael Pittman	.25	.08
❑ 9	Tony Gonzalez	.40	.15
❑ 10	Wayne Chrebet	.40	.15
❑ 11	Jevon Kearse	.40	.15
❑ 12	Bill Schroeder	.40	.15
❑ 13	Jeremy McDaniel	.25	.08
❑ 14	Todd Pinkston	.40	.15
❑ 15	Maurice Smith	.40	.15
❑ 16	Charlie Batch	.40	.15
❑ 17	Olandis Gary	.40	.15
❑ 18	Ron Dugans	.25	.08
❑ 19	Brian Urlacher	1.00	.40
❑ 20	Amani Toomer	.40	.15
❑ 21	Tim Couch	.40	.15
❑ 22	Derrick Brooks	.60	.25
❑ 23	Frank Sanders	.25	.08
❑ 24	James Williams	.25	.08
❑ 25	Lamar Smith	.40	.15
❑ 26	Darrick Vaughn	.25	.08
❑ 27	Cris Carter	.60	.25
❑ 28	Roland Williams	.25	.08
❑ 29	Bobby Shaw	.25	.08
❑ 30	Jerome Pathon	.40	.15
❑ 31	Rod Woodson	.40	.15
❑ 32	Ronney Jenkins	.25	.08
❑ 33	Chris Chandler	.40	.15
❑ 34	Dez White	.25	.08
❑ 35	Rod Smith	.40	.15
❑ 36	Troy Brown	.40	.15
❑ 37	JaJuan Dawson	.25	.08
❑ 38	Reidel Anthony	.25	.08
❑ 39	Mike Green	.25	.08
❑ 40	Steve Smith	.60	.25
❑ 41	Willie Jackson	.25	.08
❑ 42	MarTay Jenkins	.25	.08
❑ 43	Reggie Germany	.25	.08
❑ 44	Desmond Howard	.25	.08
❑ 45	Fred Taylor	.60	.25
❑ 46	Scotty Anderson	.25	.08
❑ 47	John Lynch	.40	.15
❑ 48	Amos Zereoue	.60	.25
❑ 49	Darnay Scott	.25	.08
❑ 50	Anthony Thomas	.40	.15
❑ 51	Jeff Garcia	.60	.25
❑ 52	Charlie Garner	.40	.15
❑ 53	Drew Bledsoe	.60	.25
❑ 54	Donnie Edwards	.25	.08
❑ 55	Corey Bradford	.25	.08
❑ 56	Desmond Clark	.25	.08
❑ 57	Courtney Brown	.40	.15
❑ 58	Wesley Walls	.25	.08
❑ 59	Chad Brown	.25	.08
❑ 60	Shawn Jefferson	.25	.08
❑ 61	Corey Dillon	.40	.15
❑ 62	Johnnie Morton	.40	.15
❑ 63	Marcus Pollard	.25	.08
❑ 64	Jason Taylor	.25	.08
❑ 65	Kevin Faulk	.40	.15
❑ 66	Shane Matthews	.25	.08
❑ 67	Hines Ward	.60	.25
❑ 68	Garrison Hearst	.40	.15
❑ 69	Trung Canidate	.40	.15
❑ 70	Tony Banks	.25	.08
❑ 71	Matt Hasselbeck	.40	.15
❑ 72	Correll Buckhalter	.40	.15
❑ 73	Ron Dayne	.40	.15
❑ 74	Zach Thomas	.60	.25
❑ 75	Emmitt Smith	1.50	.60
❑ 76	Peter Warrick	.40	.15
❑ 77	Rob Johnson	.40	.15
❑ 78	Michael Strahan	.40	.15
❑ 79	Ray Lewis	.60	.25
❑ 80	Jamir Miller	.25	.08
❑ 81	Brian Griese	.60	.25
❑ 82	Stacey Mack	.25	.08
❑ 83	Michael Bennett	.40	.15
❑ 84	Ricky Williams	1.00	.40
❑ 85	Jamal Lewis	.60	.25
❑ 86	Doug Flutie	.60	.25

	No.	Player		
❑	87	Jonathan Quinn	.25	.08
❑	88	Mike Alstott	.60	.25
❑	89	Samari Rolle	.25	.08
❑	90	LaMont Jordan	.60	.25
❑	91	Dominic Rhodes	.40	.15
❑	92	Quincy Carter	.40	.15
❑	93	Marcus Robinson	.40	.15
❑	94	Travis Henry	.60	.25
❑	95	Jason Brookins	.25	.08
❑	96	Nick Goings	.25	.08
❑	97	Brian Finneran	.25	.08
❑	98	Dorsey Levens	.40	.15
❑	99	Reggie Swinton	.25	.08
❑	100	Chris Chambers	.60	.25
❑	101	Kordell Stewart	.40	.15
❑	102	Tai Streets	.25	.08
❑	103	Chris Redman	.25	.08
❑	104	Jacquez Green	.25	.08
❑	105	Rod Gardner	.40	.15
❑	106	Kevin Kasper	.25	.08
❑	107	Anthony Henry	.25	.08
❑	108	Dan Morgan	.25	.08
❑	109	Ronald McKinnon	.25	.08
❑	110	Qadry Ismail	.40	.15
❑	111	Chad Johnson	.60	.25
❑	112	James Stewart	.40	.15
❑	113	Terrence Wilkins	.25	.08
❑	114	Joey Galloway	.40	.15
❑	115	Deuce McAllister	.75	.30
❑	116	Joe Jurevicius	.25	.08
❑	117	Tyrone Wheatley	.40	.15
❑	118	Jason Gildon	.25	.08
❑	119	LaDainian Tomlinson	1.00	.40
❑	120	Grant Wistrom	.25	.08
❑	121	Eddie George	.60	.25
❑	122	Laveranues Coles	.40	.15
❑	123	Antowain Smith	.40	.15
❑	124	Larry Parker	.25	.08
❑	125	Bubba Franks	.40	.15
❑	126	Troy Hambrick	.25	.08
❑	127	Jamal Reynolds	.25	.08
❑	128	Doug Chapman	.25	.08
❑	129	Freddie Mitchell	.40	.15
❑	130	Tim Dwight	.40	.15
❑	131	Erron Kinney	.25	.08
❑	132	James Allen	.40	.15
❑	133	Eric Moulds	.40	.15
❑	134	Keenan McCardell	.25	.08
❑	135	David Sloan	.25	.08
❑	136	Dennis Northcutt	.40	.15
❑	137	Kevan Barlow	.40	.15
❑	138	Bobby Engram	.25	.08
❑	139	Champ Bailey	.40	.15
❑	140	Donald Hayes	.25	.08
❑	141	Brandon Bennett	.25	.08
❑	142	Deltha O'Neal	.25	.08
❑	143	James Jackson	.25	.08
❑	144	Shaun Rogers	.25	.08
❑	145	Joe Johnson	.25	.08
❑	146	Ricky Watters	.40	.15
❑	147	Warrick Dunn	.60	.25
❑	148	Steve McNair	.60	.25
❑	149	Marvin Harrison	.60	.25
❑	150	Kendrell Bell	.60	.25
❑	151	Jim Miller	.25	.08
❑	152	Terry Allen	.25	.08
❑	153	Jake Plummer	.40	.15
❑	154	James McKnight	.25	.08
❑	155	Curtis Martin	.60	.25
❑	156	Keyshawn Johnson	.60	.25
❑	157	Kevin Lockett	.25	.08
❑	158	Jeremiah Trotter	.25	.08
❑	159	Derrick Alexander	.40	.15
❑	160	Brandon Stokley	.40	.15
❑	161	J.J. Stokes	.40	.15
❑	162	Drew Bennett	.60	.25
❑	163	Drew Brees	.60	.25
❑	164	Tim Brown	.60	.25
❑	165	Daunte Culpepper	.60	.25
❑	166	Rocket Ismail	.40	.15
❑	167	Alex Van Pelt	.40	.15
❑	168	Arnold Jackson	.25	.08
❑	169	Oronde Gadsden	.40	.15
❑	170	Isaac Bruce	.60	.25
❑	171	Warren Sapp	.40	.15
❑	172	Michael Westbrook	.25	.08
❑	173	John Abraham	.40	.15
❑	174	Jessie Armstead	.25	.08
❑	175	Brock Marion	.25	.08
❑	176	Brett Favre	1.50	.60
❑	177	Benjamin Gay	.40	.15
❑	178	Muhsin Muhammad	.40	.15
❑	179	Reggie Wayne	.60	.25
❑	180	Kailee Wong	.25	.08
❑	181	Rich Gannon	.60	.25
❑	182	Chris Fuamatu-Ma'afala	.25	.08
❑	183	Shaun Alexander	.75	.30
❑	184	Kevin Dyson	.40	.15
❑	185	Kwamie Lassiter	.25	.08
❑	186	Elvis Joseph	.25	.08
❑	187	Trent Dilfer	.40	.15
❑	188	Marty Booker	.25	.08
❑	189	Travis Taylor	.40	.15
❑	190	Michael Vick	2.00	.75
❑	191	Mike McMahon	.60	.25
❑	192	Jay Fiedler	.40	.15
❑	193	Zack Bronson	.25	.08
❑	194	Derrick Mason	.40	.15
❑	195	Anthony Becht	.25	.08
❑	196	Ahman Green	.60	.25
❑	197	Alge Crumpler	.40	.15
❑	198	Thomas Jones	.40	.15
❑	199	Tiki Barber	.60	.25
❑	200	Donovan McNabb	.75	.30
❑	201	Andre Carter	.25	.08
❑	202	Stephen Davis	.40	.15
❑	203	Troy Edwards	.25	.08
❑	204	Lawyer Milloy	.40	.15
❑	205	Peyton Manning	1.25	.50
❑	206	James Farrior	.25	.08
❑	207	Gerard Warren	.25	.08
❑	208	Peerless Price	.40	.15
❑	209	Avion Black	.25	.08
❑	210	Marcellus Wiley	.25	.08
❑	211	Torry Holt	.60	.25
❑	212	A.J. Feeley	.60	.25
❑	213	Travis Minor	.25	.08
❑	214	Darren Sharper	.25	.08
❑	215	Jerry Porter	.25	.08
❑	216	Randall Cunningham	.25	.08
❑	217	Chris Weinke	.40	.15
❑	218	Mike Anderson	.60	.25
❑	219	Snoop Minnis	.25	.08
❑	220	David Martin	.25	.08
❑	221	Vinny Sutherland	.25	.08
❑	222	Ki-Jana Carter	.25	.08
❑	223	Kevin Swayne	.25	.08
❑	224	Mark Brunell	.60	.25
❑	225	Quincy Morgan	.25	.08
❑	226	David Terrell	.60	.25
❑	227	Terance Mathis	.25	.08
❑	228	Frank Wycheck	.25	.08
❑	229	Az-Zahir Hakim	.25	.08
❑	230	Freddie Jones	.25	.08
❑	231	Jerry Rice	1.25	.50
❑	232	Ike Hilliard	.40	.15
❑	233	Terrell Davis	.60	.25
❑	234	Shawn Bryson	.25	.08
❑	235	David Boston	.60	.25
❑	236	Edgerrin James	.75	.30
❑	237	Trent Green	.40	.15
❑	238	Charlie Rogers	.25	.08
❑	239	Vinny Testaverde	.40	.15
❑	240	Koren Robinson	.40	.15
❑	241	Ronde Barber	.25	.08
❑	242	Dwayne Carswell	.25	.08
❑	243	Dedric Ward	.25	.08
❑	244	Richard Huntley	.25	.08
❑	245	Jamal Anderson	.40	.15
❑	246	Ryan Leaf	.40	.15
❑	247	Priest Holmes	.75	.30
❑	248	Tom Brady	1.50	.60
❑	249	Charles Woodson	.40	.15
❑	250	Jerome Bettis	.60	.25
❑	251	Tommy Polley	.25	.08
❑	252	Anthony Wright	.25	.08
❑	253	Chad Pennington	.75	.30
❑	254	David Patten	.25	.08
❑	255	Antonio Freeman	.60	.25
❑	256	Jamel White	.25	.08
❑	257	Jermaine Lewis	.25	.08
❑	258	Aaron Brooks	.60	.25
❑	259	Ron Dixon	.25	.08
❑	260	James Thrash	.40	.15
❑	261	Junior Seau	.60	.25
❑	262	Byron Chamberlain	.25	.08
❑	263	Ed McCaffrey	.60	.25
❑	264	Nate Clements	.25	.08
❑	265	Tony Martin	.40	.15
❑	266	Germane Crowell	.25	.08
❑	267	Terrell Owens	.60	.25
❑	268	Marshall Faulk	.60	.25
❑	269	Dat Nguyen	.25	.08
❑	270	Elvis Grbac	.40	.15
❑	271	Dante Hall	.60	.25
❑	272	Sylvester Morris	.25	.08
❑	273	Mike Brown	.60	.25
❑	274	Kevin Johnson	.40	.15
❑	275	Jimmy Smith	.40	.15
❑	276	Randy Moss	1.25	.50
❑	277	Kerry Collins	.40	.15
❑	278	Santana Moss	.60	.25
❑	279	Plaxico Burress	.40	.15
❑	280	Brad Johnson	.40	.15
❑	281	Curtis Conway	.25	.08
❑	282	Eric Johnson	.40	.15
❑	283	Joe Horn	.40	.15
❑	284	Peter Boulware	.25	.08
❑	285	Larry Foster	.25	.08
❑	286	Nate Jacquet	.25	.08
❑	287	Terry Glenn	.40	.15
❑	288	Jarious Jackson	.25	.08
❑	289	Hugh Douglas	.25	.08
❑	290	Chad Lewis	.25	.08
❑	291	Ahman Green WW	.40	.15
❑	292	Peyton Manning WW	.60	.25
❑	293	Kurt Warner WW	.40	.15
❑	294	Daunte Culpepper WW	.60	.25
❑	295	Tom Brady WW	.75	.30
❑	296	Rod Gardner WW	.25	.08
❑	297	Corey Dillon WW	.40	.15
❑	298	Priest Holmes WW	.50	.20
❑	299	Shaun Alexander WW	.50	.20
❑	300	Randy Moss WW	.60	.25
❑	301	Eric Moulds WW	.25	.08
❑	302	Brett Favre WW	.75	.30
❑	303	Todd Bouman WW	.25	.08
❑	304	Dominic Rhodes WW	.40	.15
❑	305	Marvin Harrison WW	.40	.15
❑	306	Torry Holt WW	.60	.25
❑	307	Derrick Mason WW	.25	.08
❑	308	Jerry Rice WW	.60	.25
❑	309	Donovan McNabb WW	.40	.15
❑	310	Marshall Faulk WW	.40	.15
❑	311	David Carr RC	3.00	1.25
❑	312	Quentin Jammer RC	1.25	.50
❑	313	Mike Williams RC	1.00	.40
❑	314	Rocky Calmus RC	1.25	.50
❑	315	Travis Fisher RC	1.25	.50
❑	316	Dwight Freeney RC	2.00	.75
❑	317	Jeremy Shockey RC	4.00	1.50
❑	318	Marquise Walker RC	1.00	.40
❑	319	Eric Crouch RC	1.25	.50
❑	320	DeShaun Foster RC	1.25	.50
❑	321	Roy Williams RC	3.00	1.25
❑	322	Andre Davis RC	1.00	.40
❑	323	Alex Brown RC	1.25	.50
❑	324	Michael Lewis RC	1.25	.50
❑	325	Terry Charles RC	1.00	.40
❑	326	Clinton Portis RC	4.00	1.50
❑	327	Dennis Johnson RC	.60	.25
❑	328	Lito Sheppard RC	1.25	.50
❑	329	Ryan Sims RC	1.25	.50
❑	330	Raonall Smith RC	1.00	.40
❑	331	Albert Haynesworth RC	1.00	.40
❑	332	Eddie Freeman RC	.60	.25
❑	333	Levi Jones RC	1.00	.40
❑	334	Josh McCown RC	1.50	.60
❑	335	Cliff Russell RC	1.00	.40
❑	336	Maurice Morris RC	1.25	.50
❑	337	Antwaan Randle El RC	2.00	.75
❑	338	Ladell Betts RC	1.25	.50
❑	339	Daniel Graham RC	1.25	.50
❑	340	David Garrard RC	1.25	.50
❑	341	Antonio Bryant RC	1.25	.50
❑	342	Patrick Ramsey RC	1.50	.60
❑	343	Kelly Campbell RC	1.00	.40
❑	344	Will Overstreet RC	.60	.25
❑	345	Ryan Denney RC	1.00	.40
❑	346	John Henderson RC	1.25	.50
❑	347	Freddie Milons RC	1.00	.40

❑ 348 Tim Carter RC 1.00 .40
❑ 349 Kurt Kittner RC 1.00 .40
❑ 350 Joey Harrington RC 2.00 .75
❑ 351 Ricky Williams RC 1.25 .50
❑ 352 Bryant McKinnie RC 1.00 .40
❑ 353 Ed Reed RC 2.00 .75
❑ 354 Josh Reed RC 1.25 .50
❑ 355 Seth Burford RC 1.00 .40
❑ 356 Javon Walker RC 2.50 1.00
❑ 357 Jamar Martin RC 1.00 .40
❑ 358 Leonard Henry RC 1.00 .40
❑ 359 Julius Peppers RC 2.50 1.00
❑ 360 Jabar Gaffney RC 1.25 .50
❑ 361 Kalimba Edwards RC 1.25 .50
❑ 362 Napoleon Harris RC 1.25 .50
❑ 363 Ashley Lelie RC 2.50 1.00
❑ 364 Anthony Weaver RC 1.00 .40
❑ 365 Bryan Thomas RC 1.00 .40
❑ 366 Wendell Bryant RC .60 .25
❑ 367 Damien Anderson RC 1.00 .40
❑ 368 Travis Stephens RC 1.00 .40
❑ 369 Rohan Davey RC 1.25 .50
❑ 370 Mike Pearson RC .60 .25
❑ 371 Marc Colombo RC .60 .25
❑ 372 Phillip Buchanon RC 1.25 .50
❑ 373 T.J. Duckett RC 1.50 .60
❑ 374 Ron Johnson RC 1.00 .40
❑ 375 Larry Tripplett RC .60 .25
❑ 376 Randy Fasani RC 1.00 .40
❑ 377 Keyuo Craver RC 1.00 .40
❑ 378 Marquand Manuel RC .60 .25
❑ 379 Jonathan Wells RC 1.25 .50
❑ 380 Reche Caldwell RC 1.25 .50
❑ 381 Luke Staley RC 1.00 .40
❑ 382 Donte Stallworth RC 2.50 1.00
❑ 383 Levar Fisher RC .60 .25
❑ 384 Lamar Gordon RC 1.25 .50
❑ 385 William Green RC 1.25 .50
❑ SBMVP Tom Brady FB AU/150 500.00 300.00

2003 Topps

❑ COMPLETE SET (385) 60.00 25.00
❑ 1 Michael Vick 1.50 .60
❑ 2 Wesley Walls .25 .08
❑ 3 Josh Reed .40 .15
❑ 4 Josh McCown .40 .15
❑ 5 James Stewart .40 .15
❑ 6 Deltha O'Neal .25 .08
❑ 7 Quincy Morgan .40 .15
❑ 8 Tony Fisher .25 .08
❑ 9 Corey Bradford .25 .08
❑ 10 Byron Chamberlain .25 .08
❑ 11 James McKnight .25 .08
❑ 12 Fred Taylor .60 .25
❑ 13 David Patten .25 .08
❑ 14 Jerome Bettis .60 .25
❑ 15 Jerry Porter .40 .15
❑ 16 Anthony Becht .25 .08
❑ 17 Steve McNair .60 .25
❑ 18 Stephen Davis .40 .15
❑ 19 Terrence Wilkins .25 .08
❑ 20 Jamie Martin .25 .08
❑ 21 Tai Streets .25 .08
❑ 22 Frank Wycheck .25 .08
❑ 23 Sammy Knight .25 .08
❑ 24 Marcus Pollard .25 .08
❑ 25 Jamie Sharper .25 .08
❑ 26 T.J. Houshmandzadeh .25 .08
❑ 27 Javin Hunter .25 .08
❑ 28 Alge Crumpler .40 .15
❑ 29 Chris Weinke .40 .15
❑ 30 David Terrell .40 .15
❑ 31 Troy Hambrick .25 .08
❑ 32 Bubba Franks .40 .15
❑ 33 Todd Bouman .25 .08
❑ 34 Trent Green .40 .15
❑ 35 Mark Brunell .40 .15
❑ 36 James Thrash .25 .08
❑ 37 Donnie Edwards .25 .08
❑ 38 Mike Alstott .60 .25
❑ 39 Bobby Engram .25 .08
❑ 40 Deuce McAllister .60 .25
❑ 41 Santana Moss .40 .15
❑ 42 Kordell Stewart .40 .15
❑ 43 Jason Taylor .25 .08
❑ 44 Corey Dillon .40 .15
❑ 45 Damien Anderson .25 .08
❑ 46 Rodney Peete .25 .08
❑ 47 Jeff Blake .25 .08
❑ 48 Mike McMahon .40 .15
❑ 49 Ed McCaffrey .60 .25
❑ 50 Priest Holmes .75 .30
❑ 51 Moe Williams .25 .08
❑ 52 Brian Dawkins .40 .15
❑ 53 Tim Brown .60 .25
❑ 54 Curtis Martin .60 .25
❑ 55 Charles Stackhouse .25 .08
❑ 56 Derrius Thompson .25 .08
❑ 57 John Simon .25 .08
❑ 58 Joe Jurevicius .25 .08
❑ 59 Jonathan Wells .25 .08
❑ 60 William Green .40 .15
❑ 61 Ken-Yon Rambo .25 .08
❑ 62 Frank Sanders .25 .08
❑ 63 Chester Taylor .25 .08
❑ 64 Keith Brooking .25 .08
❑ 65 Bill Schroeder .40 .15
❑ 66 Travis Minor .25 .08
❑ 67 Eric Parker RC .60 .25
❑ 68 Phillip Buchanon .25 .08
❑ 69 Amos Zereoue .40 .15
❑ 70 Warren Sapp .40 .15
❑ 71 Ladell Betts .40 .15
❑ 72 Lamar Gordon .25 .08
❑ 73 Koren Robinson .25 .08
❑ 74 Ron Dayne .25 .08
❑ 75 Donovan McNabb .75 .30
❑ 76 Edgerrin James .60 .25
❑ 77 Stacey Mack .25 .08
❑ 78 Justin Smith .25 .08
❑ 79 Kelly Holcomb .40 .15
❑ 80 Thomas Jones .40 .15
❑ 81 Randy McMichael .40 .15
❑ 82 Daunte Culpepper .60 .25
❑ 83 Tommy Maddox .60 .25
❑ 84 Tyrone Wheatley .25 .08
❑ 85 Kevin Dyson .40 .15
❑ 86 Rod Gardner .40 .15
❑ 87 Wayne Chrebet .40 .15
❑ 88 Marc Boerigter .40 .15
❑ 89 Darnay Scott .25 .08
❑ 90 T.J. Duckett .40 .15
❑ 91 Marcel Shipp .40 .15
❑ 92 Ross Tucker .25 .08
❑ 93 Drew Bledsoe .60 .25
❑ 94 Scotty Anderson .25 .08
❑ 95 Rod Smith .40 .15
❑ 96 Jim Kleinsasser .25 .08
❑ 97 Peyton Manning 1.00 .40
❑ 98 Junior Seau .60 .25
❑ 99 Darrell Jackson .40 .15
❑ 100 Brett Favre 1.50 .60
❑ 101 Ashley Lelie .60 .25
❑ 102 Jajuan Dawson .25 .08
❑ 103 Kyle Brady .25 .08
❑ 104 Kevin Faulk .25 .08
❑ 105 Jeremy Shockey 1.00 .40
❑ 106 Hines Ward .60 .25
❑ 107 Jeff Garcia .60 .25
❑ 108 Shane Matthews .25 .08
❑ 109 Jevon Kearse .40 .15
❑ 110 Eddie Kennison .25 .08
❑ 111 Quincy Carter .40 .15
❑ 112 Brian Urlacher 1.00 .40
❑ 113 Charlie Rogers .25 .08
❑ 114 Robert Ferguson .25 .08
❑ 115 Christian Fauria .25 .08
❑ 116 Brian Westbrook .40 .15
❑ 117 Antwaan Randle El .60 .25
❑ 118 Eddie George .40 .15
❑ 119 Derrick Brooks .40 .15
❑ 120 Isaac Bruce .60 .25
❑ 121 Joe Horn .40 .15
❑ 122 Jermaine Lewis .25 .08
❑ 123 Jon Kitna .40 .15
❑ 124 David Boston .40 .15
❑ 125 Todd Heap .40 .15
❑ 126 Lamar Smith .25 .08
❑ 127 Marcus Robinson .40 .15
❑ 128 Germane Crowell .25 .08
❑ 129 Kevin Johnson .40 .15
❑ 130 Cris Carter .60 .25
❑ 131 Drew Brees .60 .25
❑ 132 Champ Bailey .40 .15
❑ 133 Brian Finneran .25 .08
❑ 134 Mike Anderson .60 .25
❑ 135 Derek Ross .25 .08
❑ 136 Javon Walker .40 .15
❑ 137 D'Wayne Bates .25 .08
❑ 138 Chad Lewis .25 .08
❑ 139 Charlie Garner .40 .15
❑ 140 Laveranues Coles .40 .15
❑ 141 Ron Dixon .25 .08
❑ 142 Rob Johnson .40 .15
❑ 143 Shaun Alexander .60 .25
❑ 144 Kevan Barlow .40 .15
❑ 145 Aaron Brooks .60 .25
❑ 146 Jay Foreman .25 .08
❑ 147 Mike Peterson .25 .08
❑ 148 Brandon Bennett .25 .08
❑ 149 Jake Plummer .40 .15
❑ 150 Emmitt Smith 1.50 .60
❑ 151 Mikhael Ricks .25 .08
❑ 152 Terry Glenn .25 .08
❑ 153 Michael Bennett .40 .15
❑ 154 Deion Branch .60 .25
❑ 155 Justin McCareins .25 .08
❑ 156 Keyshawn Johnson .60 .25
❑ 157 Marc Bulger .60 .25
❑ 158 Matt Hasselbeck .40 .15
❑ 159 Garrison Hearst .40 .15
❑ 160 Jamel White .25 .08
❑ 161 Doug Johnson .25 .08
❑ 162 Larry Centers .25 .08
❑ 163 Dee Brown .25 .08
❑ 164 Dez White .25 .08
❑ 165 Brian Griese .60 .25
❑ 166 Johnnie Morton .40 .15
❑ 167 Oronde Gadsden .25 .08
❑ 168 Chad Morton .25 .08
❑ 169 Rod Woodson .40 .15
❑ 170 Ricky Proehl .25 .08
❑ 171 Tim Dwight .40 .15
❑ 172 Patrick Ramsey .60 .25
❑ 173 Donald Driver .40 .15
❑ 174 Joey Harrington 1.00 .40
❑ 175 Ricky Williams .60 .25
❑ 176 David Givens .60 .25
❑ 177 Antonio Freeman .40 .15
❑ 178 Dwight Freeney .40 .15
❑ 179 Jabar Gaffney .40 .15
❑ 180 Leon Johnson .25 .08
❑ 181 Freddie Jones .25 .08
❑ 182 Ron Johnson .25 .08
❑ 183 Duce Staley .40 .15
❑ 184 Charles Woodson .40 .15
❑ 185 Trung Canidate .40 .15
❑ 186 Jerome Pathon .25 .08
❑ 187 Jimmy Smith .40 .15
❑ 188 Reggie Wayne .40 .15
❑ 189 Chad Johnson .60 .25
❑ 190 Steve Beuerlein .25 .08
❑ 191 Joey Galloway .40 .15
❑ 192 Chris Walsh .25 .08
❑ 193 Ty Law .40 .15
❑ 194 Ike Hilliard .25 .08
❑ 195 Curtis Conway .25 .08
❑ 196 Kenny Watson .25 .08
❑ 197 Brad Johnson .40 .15
❑ 198 Shawn Jefferson .25 .08
❑ 199 Jamal Lewis .60 .25
❑ 200 Terrell Owens .60 .25
❑ 201 Todd Pinkston .40 .15

❑ 202 Maurice Morris .25 .08
❑ 203 Dante Hall .60 .25
❑ 204 Jeremiah Trotter UER .25 .08
❑ 205 Keenan McCardell .25 .08
❑ 206 Antonio Bryant .40 .15
❑ 207 Trevor Gaylor .25 .08
❑ 208 Eric Moulds .40 .15
❑ 209 Jim Miller .25 .08
❑ 210 Kabeer Gbaja-Biamila .40 .15
❑ 211 James Mungro .25 .08
❑ 212 Troy Brown .40 .15
❑ 213 J.J. Stokes .40 .15
❑ 214 Rich Gannon .40 .15
❑ 215 Chad Pennington .75 .30
❑ 216 Michael Strahan .40 .15
❑ 217 David Garrard .25 .08
❑ 218 Chris Chambers .60 .25
❑ 219 Antowain Smith .40 .15
❑ 220 Olandis Gary .40 .15
❑ 221 Jason McAddley .25 .08
❑ 222 Brandon Stokley .40 .15
❑ 223 Derrick Alexander .25 .08
❑ 224 Hugh Douglas .25 .08
❑ 225 Danny Wuerffel .25 .08
❑ 226 Derrick Mason .40 .15
❑ 227 Michael Pittman .25 .08
❑ 228 Torry Holt .60 .25
❑ 229 Bobby Shaw .25 .08
❑ 230 Tony Gonzalez .40 .15
❑ 231 Ed Hartwell .25 .08
❑ 232 Kris Mangum RC .40 .15
❑ 233 Martay Jenkins .25 .08
❑ 234 Marty Booker .40 .15
❑ 235 London Fletcher .25 .08
❑ 236 Shannon Sharpe .40 .15
❑ 237 Zach Thomas .60 .25
❑ 238 Plaxico Burress .60 .25
❑ 239 Trent Dilfer .40 .15
❑ 240 Kurt Warner .60 .25
❑ 241 Vinny Testaverde .40 .15
❑ 242 Al Wilson .25 .08
❑ 243 Chris Redman .25 .08
❑ 244 Warrick Dunn .40 .15
❑ 245 Jay Fiedler .40 .15
❑ 246 A.J. Feeley .25 .08
❑ 247 LaMont Jordan .60 .25
❑ 248 Kerry Collins .40 .15
❑ 249 Michael Lewis .25 .08
❑ 250 Jerry Rice 1.25 .50
❑ 251 Simeon Rice .40 .15
❑ 252 Reche Caldwell .25 .08
❑ 253 Randy Moss 1.00 .40
❑ 254 Az-Zahir Hakim .25 .08
❑ 255 Nate Wayne .25 .08
❑ 256 James Allen .40 .15
❑ 257 Qadry Ismail .40 .15
❑ 258 Tom Brady 1.50 .60
❑ 259 Brian Kelly .25 .08
❑ 260 Ray Lucas .25 .08
❑ 261 Amani Toomer .40 .15
❑ 262 Travis Henry .40 .15
❑ 263 Chris Chandler .25 .08
❑ 264 Peter Warrick .40 .15
❑ 265 Ray Lewis .60 .25
❑ 266 Sam Cowart .25 .08
❑ 267 Donte Stallworth .60 .25
❑ 268 David Carr 1.00 .40
❑ 269 Andre Davis .25 .08
❑ 270 Jake Delhomme .60 .25
❑ 271 Travis Taylor .40 .15
❑ 272 Steve Smith .60 .25
❑ 273 Tiki Barber .60 .25
❑ 274 Chad Hutchinson .25 .08
❑ 275 Marshall Faulk .60 .25
❑ 276 Chris Claiborne .25 .08
❑ 277 Billy Miller .25 .08
❑ 278 Peerless Price .40 .15
❑ 279 Ed Reed .40 .15
❑ 280 Ahman Green .60 .25
❑ 281 Roy Williams .60 .25
❑ 282 Dennis Northcutt .25 .08
❑ 283 Julius Peppers .60 .25
❑ 284 John Davis .25 .08
❑ 285 LaDainian Tomlinson .60 .25
❑ 286 Muhsin Muhammad .40 .15
❑ 287 Tim Couch .25 .08
❑ 288 Clinton Portis 1.00 .40
❑ 289 Anthony Thomas .40 .15
❑ 290 Marvin Harrison .60 .25
❑ 291 Priest Holmes WW .40 .15
❑ 292 Drew Bledsoe WW .40 .15
❑ 293 Tom Brady WW .60 .25
❑ 294 Shaun Alexander WW .25 .08
❑ 295 Brett Favre WW .60 .25
❑ 296 Travis Henry WW .25 .08
❑ 297 Marshall Faulk WW .40 .15
❑ 298 Terrell Owens WW .25 .08
❑ 299 Jeff Garcia WW .25 .08
❑ 300 Plaxico Burress WW .25 .08
❑ 301 Donovan McNabb WW .40 .15
❑ 302 Ricky Williams WW .40 .15
❑ 303 Michael Vick WW .75 .30
❑ 304 Steve Smith WW .40 .15
❑ 305 Marvin Harrison WW .25 .08
❑ 306 Chad Pennington WW .40 .15
❑ 307 Jeremy Shockey WW .60 .25
❑ 308 Tommy Maddox WW .25 .08
❑ 309 Steve McNair WW .25 .08
❑ 310 Rich Gannon WW .25 .08
❑ 311 Carson Palmer RC 6.00 2.50
❑ 312 Keenan Howry RC 1.25 .50
❑ 313 Michael Haynes RC 1.25 .50
❑ 314 Terrell Suggs RC 2.00 .75
❑ 315 Rashean Mathis RC 1.00 .40
❑ 316 Chris Kelsay RC 1.25 .50
❑ 317 Brad Banks RC 1.00 .40
❑ 318 Jordan Gross RC 1.00 .40
❑ 319 Lee Suggs RC 1.25 .50
❑ 320 Kliff Kingsbury RC 1.00 .40
❑ 321 William Joseph RC 1.25 .50
❑ 322 Kelley Washington RC 1.25 .50
❑ 323 Jerome McDougle RC 1.25 .50
❑ 324 Osi Umenyiora RC 2.00 .75
❑ 325 Chris Simms RC 2.00 .75
❑ 326 Alonzo Jackson RC 1.00 .40
❑ 327 L.J. Smith RC 1.25 .50
❑ 328 Mike Doss RC 1.25 .50
❑ 329 Bobby Wade RC 1.25 .50
❑ 330 Ken Hamlin RC 1.25 .50
❑ 331 Brandon Lloyd RC 1.25 .50
❑ 332 Justin Fargas RC 1.25 .50
❑ 333 DeWayne Robertson RC 1.25 .50
❑ 334 Bryant Johnson RC 1.25 .50
❑ 335 Boss Bailey RC 1.25 .50
❑ 336 Onterrio Smith RC 1.25 .50
❑ 337 Doug Gabriel RC 1.25 .50
❑ 338 Jimmy Kennedy RC 1.25 .50
❑ 339 B.J. Askew RC 1.25 .50
❑ 340 Taylor Jacobs RC 1.00 .40
❑ 341 Dallas Clark RC 1.25 .50
❑ 342 DeWayne White RC 1.00 .40
❑ 343 Arnaz Battle RC 1.25 .50
❑ 344 Kareem Kelly RC 1.00 .40
❑ 345 Terry Pierce RC 1.00 .40
❑ 346 Billy McMullen RC 1.00 .40
❑ 347 Talman Gardner RC 1.25 .50
❑ 348 Anquan Boldin RC 3.00 1.25
❑ 349 Travis Anglin RC .60 .25
❑ 350 Byron Leftwich RC 4.00 1.50
❑ 351 Marcus Trufant RC 1.25 .50
❑ 352 Sam Aiken RC 1.00 .40
❑ 353 LaBrandon Toefield RC 1.25 .50
❑ 354 J.R. Tolver RC 1.00 .40
❑ 355 Charles Rogers RC 1.25 .50
❑ 356 Chaun Thompson RC .60 .25
❑ 357 Chris Brown RC 1.25 .50
❑ 358 Justin Gage RC 1.25 .50
❑ 359 Kevin Williams RC 1.25 .50
❑ 360 Willis McGahee RC 3.00 1.25
❑ 361 Victor Hobson RC 1.25 .50
❑ 362 Brian St.Pierre RC 1.25 .50
❑ 363 Nate Burleson RC 1.25 .50
❑ 364 Calvin Pace RC 1.00 .40
❑ 365 Larry Johnson RC 6.00 2.50
❑ 366 Andre Woolfolk RC 1.25 .50
❑ 367 Tyrone Calico RC 1.25 .50
❑ 368 Seneca Wallace RC 1.25 .50
❑ 369 Domanick Davis RC 1.25 .50
❑ 370 Rex Grossman RC 4.00 1.50
❑ 371 Artose Pinner RC 1.25 .50
❑ 372 Jason Witten RC 2.00 .75
❑ 373 Bennie Joppru RC 1.25 .50
❑ 374 Bethel Johnson RC 1.25 .50
❑ 375 Kyle Boller RC 1.25 .50
❑ 376 Shaun McDonald RC 1.25 .50
❑ 377 Musa Smith RC 1.25 .50
❑ 378 Ken Dorsey RC 1.25 .50
❑ 379 Johnathan Sullivan RC 1.00 .40
❑ 380 Andre Johnson RC 2.50 1.00
❑ 381 Nick Barnett RC 1.25 .50
❑ 382 Teyo Johnson RC 1.25 .50
❑ 383 Terence Newman RC 2.50 1.00
❑ 384 Kevin Curtis RC 1.25 .50
❑ 385 Dave Ragone RC 1.25 .50
❑ MVP Dex.Jackson FB AU/250 60.00 25.00

2004 Topps

❑ COMPLETE SET (385) 60.00 30.00
❑ RH38 STATED ODDS 1:36 H/HTA/R
❑ RH38A ODDS 1:13,494H, 1:3895HTA
❑ SBMVP ODDS
1:35,787H,1:10,710HTA,1:33,984R
❑ 1 Peyton Manning 1.00 .40
❑ 2 Curtis Conway .25 .08
❑ 3 Tim Brown .60 .25
❑ 4 David Givens .40 .15
❑ 5 Dorsey Levens .25 .08
❑ 6 Jamal Robertson .25 .08
❑ 7 Doug Flutie .60 .25
❑ 8 Lamar Gordon .25 .08
❑ 9 Leonard Little .25 .08
❑ 10 Patrick Ramsey .40 .15
❑ 11 Justin McCareins .25 .08
❑ 12 Charles Lee .25 .08
❑ 13 Matt Hasselbeck .40 .15
❑ 14 Chris Chambers .40 .15
❑ 15 Derrick Blaylock .40 .15
❑ 16 Shannon Sharpe .40 .15
❑ 17 Bubba Franks .40 .15
❑ 18 London Fletcher .25 .08
❑ 19 Eric Moulds .40 .15
❑ 20 Anquan Boldin .60 .25
❑ 21 Brian Urlacher .75 .30
❑ 22 Stephen Davis .40 .15
❑ 23 Mikhael Ricks .25 .08
❑ 24 Jason Taylor .25 .08
❑ 25 Michael Vick 1.25 .50
❑ 26 Dante Hall .60 .25
❑ 27 Marcus Pollard .25 .08
❑ 28 Rick Mirer .25 .08
❑ 29 David Tyree .25 .08
❑ 30 Chad Pennington .60 .25
❑ 31 Kevan Barlow .40 .15
❑ 32 James Farrior .25 .08
❑ 33 James Thrash .25 .08
❑ 34 Damerien McCants .25 .08
❑ 35 L.J. Smith .40 .15
❑ 36 Tommy Maddox .40 .15
❑ 37 Tedy Bruschi .40 .15
❑ 38 Moe Williams .25 .08
❑ 39 Todd Bouman .25 .08
❑ 40 Domanick Davis .60 .25
❑ 41 Dwight Freeney .40 .15
❑ 42 Kyle Brady .25 .08
❑ 43 LaVar Arrington 1.25 .50
❑ 44 Troy Hambrick .25 .08
❑ 45 Jake Plummer .40 .15
❑ 46 Freddie Jones .25 .08
❑ 47 Chester Taylor .25 .08
❑ 48 Willis McGahee .60 .25
❑ 49 Bobby Wade .25 .08
❑ 50 Steve McNair .60 .25
❑ 51 Joe Jurevicius .25 .08

❑ 52 Ladell Betts .25 .08
❑ 53 LaMont Jordan .60 .25
❑ 54 Kerry Collins .40 .15
❑ 55 Hines Ward .60 .25
❑ 56 Scott Fujita .25 .08
❑ 57 Kevin Johnson .25 .08
❑ 58 Troy Brown .40 .15
❑ 59 Jerome Pathon .25 .08
❑ 60 Andre Johnson .60 .25
❑ 61 DeShaun Foster .40 .15
❑ 62 Terrell Suggs .40 .15
❑ 63 Marcel Shipp .40 .15
❑ 64 Allen Rossum .25 .08
❑ 65 Kyle Boller .60 .25
❑ 66 Terence Newman .40 .15
❑ 67 Javon Walker .40 .15
❑ 68 Shawn Bryson .25 .08
❑ 69 Travis Minor .25 .08
❑ 70 Terrell Owens .60 .25
❑ 71 Kassim Osgood .25 .08
❑ 72 Bobby Engram .25 .08
❑ 73 Drew Bennett .40 .15
❑ 74 Rock Cartwright .25 .08
❑ 75 Ahman Green .60 .25
❑ 76 Steve Beuerlein .25 .08
❑ 77 Takeo Spikes .25 .08
❑ 78 Dez White .40 .15
❑ 79 Tim Couch .25 .08
❑ 80 Travis Henry .40 .15
❑ 81 T.J. Duckett .40 .15
❑ 82 LaBrandon Toefield .25 .08
❑ 83 Randy McMichael .25 .08
❑ 84 Jonathan Carter .25 .08
❑ 85 Jerry Rice 1.25 .50
❑ 86 Maurice Morris .25 .08
❑ 87 Kurt Warner .60 .25
❑ 88 Josh Scobey .25 .08
❑ 89 Travis Taylor .25 .08
❑ 90 Fred Taylor .40 .15
❑ 91 Zach Thomas .60 .25
❑ 92 Kelly Campbell .25 .08
❑ 93 Tim Carter .25 .08
❑ 94 Marques Tuiasosopo .40 .15
❑ 95 Laveranues Coles .40 .15
❑ 96 Chris Brown .60 .25
❑ 97 Thomas Jones .40 .15
❑ 98 Dane Looker .40 .15
❑ 99 Ross Tucker .25 .08
❑ 100 Priest Holmes .75 .30
❑ 101 Troy Walters .25 .08
❑ 102 Jamie Sharper .25 .08
❑ 103 Quincy Morgan .40 .15
❑ 104 Aveion Cason .25 .08
❑ 105 Joey Galloway .40 .15
❑ 106 Bill Schroeder .25 .08
❑ 107 Tony Fisher .25 .08
❑ 108 Adewale Ogunleye .40 .15
❑ 109 Justin Fargas .40 .15
❑ 110 Daunte Culpepper .60 .25
❑ 111 Donnie Edwards .25 .08
❑ 112 Jed Weaver .25 .08
❑ 113 Arlen Harris .25 .08
❑ 114 Keenan McCardell .25 .08
❑ 115 Chad Johnson .60 .25
❑ 116 Marty Booker .40 .15
❑ 117 Anthony Wright .25 .08
❑ 118 Brian Finneran .25 .08
❑ 119 Robert Ferguson .25 .08
❑ 120 Ricky Williams .60 .25
❑ 121 Shaun Ellis .25 .08
❑ 122 Brian Westbrook .40 .15
❑ 123 Sam Cowart .25 .08
❑ 124 Tim Rattay .25 .08
❑ 125 LaDainian Tomlinson .75 .30
❑ 126 Simeon Rice .40 .15
❑ 127 Jason Witten .40 .15
❑ 128 Lee Suggs .60 .25
❑ 129 Keith Brooking .25 .08
❑ 130 Rex Grossman .60 .25
❑ 131 Kelley Washington .25 .08
❑ 132 Antonio Bryant .40 .15
❑ 133 Dallas Clark .40 .15
❑ 134 Stacey Mack .25 .08
❑ 135 Charles Rogers .40 .15
❑ 136 Donte' Stallworth .40 .15
❑ 137 Deion Branch .60 .25
❑ 138 Nate Burleson .60 .25
❑ 139 Ike Hilliard .25 .08
❑ 140 Randy Moss .75 .30
❑ 141 Michael Strahan .40 .15
❑ 142 John Abraham .25 .08
❑ 143 Tim Dwight .40 .15
❑ 144 Isaac Bruce .40 .15
❑ 145 Brad Johnson .40 .15
❑ 146 Trung Canidate .25 .08
❑ 147 Warrick Dunn .40 .15
❑ 148 Josh McCown .40 .15
❑ 149 Muhsin Muhammad .40 .15
❑ 150 Donovan McNabb .75 .30
❑ 151 Tai Streets .25 .08
❑ 152 Antonio Gates .60 .25
❑ 153 Antwaan Randle El .60 .25
❑ 154 Doug Jolley .25 .08
❑ 155 Shaun Alexander .60 .25
❑ 156 William Green .40 .15
❑ 157 Carson Palmer .75 .30
❑ 158 Quentin Griffin .60 .25
❑ 159 Az-Zahir Hakim .25 .08
❑ 160 Edgerrin James .60 .25
❑ 161 Gus Frerotte .25 .08
❑ 162 Brandon Lloyd .40 .15
❑ 163 Brian Griese .40 .15
❑ 164 Boo Williams .25 .08
❑ 165 Santana Moss .40 .15
❑ 166 Tyrone Wheatley .25 .08
❑ 167 Eric Parker .25 .08
❑ 168 Amos Zereoue .25 .08
❑ 169 Itula Mili .25 .08
❑ 170 Marshall Faulk .60 .25
❑ 171 Tyrone Calico .40 .15
❑ 172 Tim Hasselbeck .25 .08
❑ 173 Anthony Becht .25 .08
❑ 174 Larry Johnson .75 .30
❑ 175 Marvin Harrison .60 .25
❑ 176 Tony Gonzalez .40 .15
❑ 177 Wayne Chrebet .40 .15
❑ 178 Mike Barrow .25 .08
❑ 179 Bethel Johnson .40 .15
❑ 180 Deuce McAllister .60 .25
❑ 181 Drew Brees .60 .25
❑ 182 Teyo Johnson .25 .08
❑ 183 Garrison Hearst .40 .15
❑ 184 Todd Pinkston .25 .08
❑ 185 Jeff Garcia .60 .25
❑ 186 Darrell Jackson .40 .15
❑ 187 Billy Volek .60 .25
❑ 188 Ray Lewis .60 .25
❑ 189 Ricky Proehl .25 .08
❑ 190 Rudi Johnson .40 .15
❑ 191 Emmitt Smith 1.25 .50
❑ 192 Cedrick Wilson .25 .08
❑ 193 Julius Peppers .60 .25
❑ 194 Peter Warrick .40 .15
❑ 195 Trent Green .40 .15
❑ 196 Derrius Thompson .25 .08
❑ 197 Onterrio Smith .40 .15
❑ 198 Jerome Bettis .60 .25
❑ 199 Keyshawn Johnson .40 .15
❑ 200 Jamal Lewis .60 .25
❑ 201 Alge Crumpler .40 .15
❑ 202 Justin Gage .40 .15
❑ 203 Mike Rucker .25 .08
❑ 204 Michael Bennett .40 .15
❑ 205 Jimmy Smith .40 .15
❑ 206 Ricky Williams TT .25 .08
❑ 207 Corey Bradford .25 .08
❑ 208 Jerry Porter .40 .15
❑ 209 Erron Kinney .25 .08
❑ 210 Marc Bulger .60 .25
❑ 211 Jeff Blake .25 .08
❑ 212 Terry Jones .25 .08
❑ 213 Kordell Stewart .40 .15
❑ 214 Andra Davis .25 .08
❑ 215 David Carr .60 .25
❑ 216 Nick Barnett .40 .15
❑ 217 Mark Brunell .40 .15
❑ 218 Daniel Graham .25 .08
❑ 219 Jim Kleinsasser .25 .08
❑ 220 Aaron Brooks .40 .15
❑ 221 Plaxico Burress .40 .15
❑ 222 Correll Buckhalter .40 .15
❑ 223 Jevon Kearse .40 .15
❑ 224 Michael Pittman .25 .08
❑ 225 Clinton Portis .60 .25
❑ 226 Corey Dillon .40 .15
❑ 227 Steve Smith .60 .25
❑ 228 David Thornton .25 .08
❑ 229 Eddie Kennison .25 .08
❑ 230 Amani Toomer .40 .15
❑ 231 Artose Pinner .25 .08
❑ 232 Kelly Holcomb .40 .15
❑ 233 Jay Fiedler .25 .08
❑ 234 Ernie Conwell .25 .08
❑ 235 Torry Holt .60 .25
❑ 236 Eddie George .40 .15
❑ 237 Jeremy Shockey .60 .25
❑ 238 Troy Edwards .25 .08
❑ 239 Antowain Smith .40 .15
❑ 240 Jon Kitna .40 .15
❑ 241 Bryant Johnson .25 .08
❑ 242 Todd Heap .40 .15
❑ 243 Doug Johnson .25 .08
❑ 244 Ashley Lelie .40 .15
❑ 245 Byron Leftwich .75 .30
❑ 246 Shawn Barber .25 .08
❑ 247 Duce Staley .40 .15
❑ 248 Rod Gardner .40 .15
❑ 249 Warren Sapp .40 .15
❑ 250 Brett Favre 1.50 .60
❑ 251 Olandis Gary .25 .08
❑ 252 Reggie Wayne .40 .15
❑ 253 Billy Miller .25 .08
❑ 254 Johnnie Morton .40 .15
❑ 255 Joe Horn .40 .15
❑ 256 Curtis Martin .60 .25
❑ 257 Freddie Mitchell .40 .15
❑ 258 Charlie Garner .40 .15
❑ 259 Marcus Robinson .40 .15
❑ 260 Derrick Mason .40 .15
❑ 261 Bobby Shaw .25 .08
❑ 262 Desmond Clark .25 .08
❑ 263 James Jackson .25 .08
❑ 264 Josh Reed .25 .08
❑ 265 David Boston .40 .15
❑ 266 Drew Bledsoe .60 .25
❑ 267 Brock Forsey .25 .08
❑ 268 Dat Nguyen .25 .08
❑ 269 Mike Anderson .40 .15
❑ 270 Anthony Thomas .40 .15
❑ 271 Najeh Davenport .25 .08
❑ 272 Jabar Gaffney .40 .15
❑ 273 Tiki Barber .60 .25
❑ 274 Rich Gannon .40 .15
❑ 275 Tom Brady 1.50 .60
❑ 276 Terry Glenn .25 .08
❑ 277 Dennis Northcutt .25 .08
❑ 278 A.J. Feeley .60 .25
❑ 279 Peerless Price .40 .15
❑ 280 Jake Delhomme .60 .25
❑ 281 Kevin Faulk .25 .08
❑ 282 Quincy Carter .40 .15
❑ 283 Andre' Davis .25 .08
❑ 284 Tony Hollings .25 .08
❑ 285 Joey Harrington .60 .25
❑ 286 Richie Anderson .25 .08
❑ 287 Donald Driver .40 .15
❑ 288 Koren Robinson .40 .15
❑ 289 Tony Banks .25 .08
❑ 290 Rod Smith .40 .15
❑ 291 Anquan Boldin WW .25 .08
❑ 292 Jamal Lewis WW .40 .15
❑ 293 Priest Holmes WW .60 .25
❑ 294 Peyton Manning WW .60 .25
❑ 295 Marvin Harrison WW .40 .15
❑ 296 Steve McNair WW .40 .15
❑ 297 Travis Henry WW .25 .08
❑ 298 Torry Holt WW .40 .15
❑ 299 Tom Brady WW .60 .25
❑ 300 Ahman Green WW .40 .15
❑ 301 Donovan McNabb WW .60 .25
❑ 302 Deuce McAllister WW .40 .15
❑ 303 Domanick Davis WW .40 .15
❑ 304 Clinton Portis WW .60 .25
❑ 305 Rudi Johnson WW .25 .08
❑ 306 Brett Favre WW .60 .25
❑ 307 LaDainian Tomlinson WW .50 .20
❑ 308 Steve Smith WW .40 .15
❑ 309 Edgerrin James WW .40 .15
❑ 310 Ty Law WW .25 .08
❑ 311 Ben Roethlisberger RC 15.00 6.00
❑ 312 Ahmad Carroll RC 1.50 .60

- ❑ 313 Johnnie Morant RC 1.50 .60
- ❑ 314 Greg Jones RC 1.50 .60
- ❑ 315 Michael Clayton RC 3.00 1.25
- ❑ 316 Josh Harris RC 1.50 .60
- ❑ 317 Tatum Bell RC 3.00 1.25
- ❑ 318 Robert Gallery RC 1.50 .60
- ❑ 319 B.J. Symons RC 1.50 .60
- ❑ 320 Roy Williams RC 4.00 1.50
- ❑ 321 DeAngelo Hall RC 2.00 .75
- ❑ 322 Jeff Smoker RC 1.50 .60
- ❑ 323 Lee Evans RC 2.00 .75
- ❑ 324 Michael Jenkins RC 1.50 .60
- ❑ 325 Steven Jackson RC 5.00 2.00
- ❑ 326 Will Smith RC 1.50 .60
- ❑ 327 Vince Wilfork RC 1.50 .60
- ❑ 328 Ben Troupe RC 1.50 .60
- ❑ 329 Chris Gamble RC 1.50 .60
- ❑ 330 Kevin Jones RC 4.00 1.50
- ❑ 331 Jonathan Vilma RC 1.50 .60
- ❑ 332 Dontarrious Thomas RC 1.50 .60
- ❑ 333 Michael Boulware RC 1.50 .60
- ❑ 334 Mewelde Moore RC 1.50 .60
- ❑ 335 Drew Henson RC 1.50 .60
- ❑ 336 D.J. Williams RC 1.50 .60
- ❑ 337 Ernest Wilford RC 1.50 .60
- ❑ 338 John Navarre RC 1.50 .60
- ❑ 339 Jerricho Cotchery RC 1.50 .60
- ❑ 340 Derrick Hamilton RC 1.25 .50
- ❑ 341 Carlos Francis RC 1.25 .50
- ❑ 342 Ben Watson RC 1.50 .60
- ❑ 343 Reggie Williams RC 2.00 .75
- ❑ 344 Devard Darling RC 1.50 .60
- ❑ 345 Chris Perry RC 2.50 1.00
- ❑ 346 Derrick Strait RC 1.50 .60
- ❑ 347 Sean Taylor RC 1.50 .60
- ❑ 348 Michael Turner RC 2.00 .75
- ❑ 349 Keary Colbert RC 2.00 .75
- ❑ 350 Eli Manning RC 10.00 4.00
- ❑ 351 Julius Jones RC 5.00 2.00
- ❑ 352 Jason Babin RC 1.50 .60
- ❑ 353 Cody Pickett RC 1.50 .60
- ❑ 354 Kenechi Udeze RC 1.50 .60
- ❑ 355 Rashaun Woods RC 1.50 .60
- ❑ 356 Matt Schaub RC 5.00 2.00
- ❑ 357 Tommie Harris RC 1.50 .60
- ❑ 358 Dwan Edwards RC .75 .30
- ❑ 359 Shawn Andrews RC 1.50 .60
- ❑ 360 Larry Fitzgerald RC 5.00 2.00
- ❑ 361 P.K. Sam RC 1.25 .50
- ❑ 362 Teddy Lehman RC 1.50 .60
- ❑ 363 Darius Watts RC 1.50 .60
- ❑ 364 D.J. Hackett RC 1.25 .50
- ❑ 365 Cedric Cobbs RC 1.50 .60
- ❑ 366 Antwan Odom RC 1.50 .60
- ❑ 367 Marquise Hill RC 1.25 .50
- ❑ 368 Luke McCown RC 1.50 .60
- ❑ 369 Triandos Luke RC 1.50 .60
- ❑ 370 Kellen Winslow RC 3.00 1.25
- ❑ 371 Derek Abney RC 1.50 .60
- ❑ 372 Chris Cooley RC 1.50 .60
- ❑ 373 Dunta Robinson RC 1.50 .60
- ❑ 374 Sean Jones RC 1.25 .50
- ❑ 375 Philip Rivers RC 5.00 2.00
- ❑ 376 Craig Krenzel RC 1.50 .60
- ❑ 377 Daryl Smith RC 1.50 .60
- ❑ 378 Samie Parker RC 1.50 .60
- ❑ 379 Ben Hartsock RC 1.50 .60
- ❑ 380 J.P. Losman RC 3.00 1.25
- ❑ 381 Karlos Dansby RC 1.50 .60
- ❑ 382 Ricardo Colclough RC 1.50 .60
- ❑ 383 Bernard Berrian RC 2.00 .75
- ❑ 384 Junior Siavii RC 1.50 .60
- ❑ 385 Devery Henderson RC 1.25 .50
- ❑ TB38 Tom Brady RH 6.00 2.50
- ❑ RHTBR2 Tom Brady RH AU 350.00 250.00
- ❑ SBMVP Tom Brady FB AU/99 500.00 300.00

2005 Topps

- ❑ COMP.COWBOYS SET (445) 50.00 25.00
- ❑ COMP.EAGLES SET (445) 50.00 25.00
- ❑ COMP.FACT.SET (445) 50.00 25.00
- ❑ COMP.PACKERS SET (445) 50.00 25.00
- ❑ COMP.RAIDERS SET (445) 50.00 25.00
- ❑ COMP.SB XL SET (445) 80.00 50.00
- ❑ COMPLETE SET (440) 50.00 25.00
- ❑ RH39 STATED ODDS 1:275 HOB/HTA/RET
- ❑ RH39A 1:62,233H, 1:15,547HTA, 1:51,346R

- ❑ SBMVP 1:27,629H, 1:7774HTA, 1:43,632R
- ❑ UNPRICED PLATINUM PRINT RUN 1 SET
- ❑ 1 Brian Westbrook .40 .15
- ❑ 2 Tim Rattay .30 .10
- ❑ 3 Domanick Davis .40 .15
- ❑ 4 Lee Suggs .40 .15
- ❑ 5 Keith Brooking .30 .10
- ❑ 6 Rex Grossman .40 .15
- ❑ 7 Chad Johnson .60 .25
- ❑ 8 Willis McGahee .60 .25
- ❑ 9 Eli Manning 1.25 .50
- ❑ 10 Tom Brady 1.50 .60
- ❑ 11 Ray Lewis .60 .25
- ❑ 12 Terence Newman .30 .10
- ❑ 13 Daunte Culpepper .60 .25
- ❑ 14 Marvin Harrison .60 .25
- ❑ 15 Greg Jones .30 .10
- ❑ 16 Anquan Boldin .40 .15
- ❑ 17 Julius Peppers .40 .15
- ❑ 18 Kevin Jones .60 .25
- ❑ 19 Javon Walker .40 .15
- ❑ 20 Michael Lewis .30 .10
- ❑ 21 Jamaar Taylor .30 .10
- ❑ 22 Hines Ward .60 .25
- ❑ 23 Drew Brees .60 .25
- ❑ 24 Marcus Trufant .30 .10
- ❑ 25 Derrick Brooks .40 .15
- ❑ 26 Sean Taylor .40 .15
- ❑ 27 Derrius Thompson .30 .10
- ❑ 28 Nick Barnett .30 .10
- ❑ 29 Dante Hall .40 .15
- ❑ 30 Mike Cloud .30 .10
- ❑ 31 Jake Plummer .40 .15
- ❑ 32 Donte Stallworth .40 .15
- ❑ 33 Shaun Ellis .30 .10
- ❑ 34 Jeremy Shockey .60 .25
- ❑ 35 Teyo Johnson .30 .10
- ❑ 36 Adam Archuleta .30 .10
- ❑ 37 Darius Watts .40 .15
- ❑ 38 Michael Pittman .30 .10
- ❑ 39 Drew Bennett .40 .15
- ❑ 40 Aaron Stecker .30 .10
- ❑ 41 Artose Pinner .30 .10
- ❑ 42 Dane Looker .30 .10
- ❑ 43 Jeff Garcia .40 .15
- ❑ 44 Travis Taylor .30 .10
- ❑ 45 Najeh Davenport .30 .10
- ❑ 46 Walter Jones .30 .10
- ❑ 47 Donnie Edwards .30 .10
- ❑ 48 Terrell Owens .60 .25
- ❑ 49 Matt Birk .30 .10
- ❑ 50 Chris Baker .30 .10
- ❑ 51 Brandon Lloyd .30 .10
- ❑ 52 Marshall Faulk .60 .25
- ❑ 53 Jonathan Vilma .40 .15
- ❑ 54 Dallas Clark .30 .10
- ❑ 55 David Carr .60 .25
- ❑ 56 Jerricho Cotchery .30 .10
- ❑ 57 Deuce McAllister .60 .25
- ❑ 58 Donald Driver .40 .15
- ❑ 59 Jeff Smoker .40 .15
- ❑ 60 Champ Bailey .40 .15
- ❑ 61 Jason Witten .40 .15
- ❑ 62 T.J. Houshmandzadeh .30 .10
- ❑ 63 Jay Fiedler .30 .10
- ❑ 64 Philip Rivers .60 .25
- ❑ 65 Jake Delhomme .60 .25
- ❑ 66 Terrence McGee RC .60 .25
- ❑ 67 Chester Taylor .40 .15
- ❑ 68 Tommy Maddox .30 .10
- ❑ 69 Bryant Johnson .30 .10
- ❑ 70 Justin Gage .30 .10
- ❑ 71 Troy Hambrick .30 .10
- ❑ 72 Kerry Collins .40 .15
- ❑ 73 Jeb Putzier .30 .10
- ❑ 74 Keary Colbert .40 .15
- ❑ 75 Jason Elam .30 .10
- ❑ 76 Jerramy Stevens .30 .10
- ❑ 77 Clinton Portis .60 .25
- ❑ 78 Sam Aiken .30 .10
- ❑ 79 Trent Green .40 .15
- ❑ 80 Dat Nguyen .30 .10
- ❑ 81 Ladell Betts .30 .10
- ❑ 82 Peter Warrick .30 .10
- ❑ 83 Dominic Rhodes .30 .10
- ❑ 84 Jason Taylor .30 .10
- ❑ 85 Antwaan Randle El .40 .15
- ❑ 86 Michael Jenkins .40 .15
- ❑ 87 Adam Vinatieri .60 .25
- ❑ 88 Mark Brunell .40 .15
- ❑ 89 Brian Finneran .30 .10
- ❑ 90 Ernie Conwell .30 .10
- ❑ 91 Chad Pennington .60 .25
- ❑ 92 Dan Morgan .30 .10
- ❑ 93 Kelly Holcomb .30 .10
- ❑ 94 Ronde Barber .30 .10
- ❑ 95 Torry Holt .60 .25
- ❑ 96 Bubba Franks .40 .15
- ❑ 97 Keyshawn Johnson .40 .15
- ❑ 98 J.P. Losman .60 .25
- ❑ 99 Ed Reed .40 .15
- ❑ 100 Chris McAlister .30 .10
- ❑ 101 Jamie Sharper .30 .10
- ❑ 102 Chad Lewis .30 .10
- ❑ 103 Chris Brown .40 .15
- ❑ 104 Marc Boerigter .40 .15
- ❑ 105 Zach Thomas .60 .25
- ❑ 106 Byron Leftwich .60 .25
- ❑ 107 Tatum Bell .40 .15
- ❑ 108 Tai Streets .30 .10
- ❑ 109 Tory James .30 .10
- ❑ 110 Cedrick Wilson .30 .10
- ❑ 111 Darrell Jackson .40 .15
- ❑ 112 Ben Roethlisberger 1.50 .60
- ❑ 113 Quentin Jammer .30 .10
- ❑ 114 Maurice Morris .30 .10
- ❑ 115 Simeon Rice .40 .15
- ❑ 116 Tyrone Calico .40 .15
- ❑ 117 Patrick Ramsey .40 .15
- ❑ 118 Marcus Robinson .40 .15
- ❑ 119 Reggie Wayne .40 .15
- ❑ 120 Kevin Faulk .30 .10
- ❑ 121 Nate Burleson .40 .15
- ❑ 122 Aaron Brooks .40 .15
- ❑ 123 Willie Roaf .30 .10
- ❑ 124 Fred Taylor .40 .15
- ❑ 125 Dwight Freeney .40 .15
- ❑ 126 Olin Kreutz .30 .10
- ❑ 127 Dunta Robinson .40 .15
- ❑ 128 Warren Sapp .40 .15
- ❑ 129 Chris Perry .40 .15
- ❑ 130 Desmond Clark .30 .10
- ❑ 131 Takeo Spikes .30 .10
- ❑ 132 B.J. Sams .30 .10
- ❑ 133 Bertrand Berry .30 .10
- ❑ 134 Drew Henson .40 .15
- ❑ 135 Robert Ferguson .30 .10
- ❑ 136 Julius Jones .75 .30
- ❑ 137 Jeremiah Trotter .30 .10
- ❑ 138 Chris Simms .40 .15
- ❑ 139 Damerien McCants .30 .10
- ❑ 140 Robert Gallery .40 .15
- ❑ 141 Michael Strahan .40 .15
- ❑ 142 Reggie Williams .40 .15
- ❑ 143 Tony Gonzalez .40 .15
- ❑ 144 Priest Holmes .60 .25
- ❑ 145 Luke McCown .30 .10
- ❑ 146 Allen Rossum .30 .10
- ❑ 147 Eric Moulds .40 .15
- ❑ 148 Jonathan Wells .30 .10
- ❑ 149 Randy McMichael .30 .10
- ❑ 150 John Abraham .30 .10
- ❑ 151 Doug Gabriel .30 .10
- ❑ 152 Tiki Barber .60 .25
- ❑ 153 Marcel Shipp .30 .10
- ❑ 154 LaDainian Tomlinson .75 .30
- ❑ 155 Richard Seymour .40 .15

❑ 156 Mike Vanderjagt .30 .10
❑ 157 Roy Williams WR .60 .25
❑ 158 William Green .30 .10
❑ 159 DeAngelo Hall .40 .15
❑ 160 Josh McCown .40 .15
❑ 161 Terrell Suggs .40 .15
❑ 162 Brian Dawkins .40 .15
❑ 163 Lee Evans .40 .15
❑ 164 Nick Goings .30 .10
❑ 165 Carson Palmer .60 .25
❑ 166 Charles Woodson .40 .15
❑ 167 Keenan McCardell .30 .10
❑ 168 Kevan Barlow .40 .15
❑ 169 Matt Hasselbeck .40 .15
❑ 170 Steven Jackson .75 .30
❑ 171 Ben Troupe .30 .10
❑ 172 Jamal Lewis .60 .25
❑ 173 Sammy Morris .30 .10
❑ 174 Troy Polamalu 1.00 .40
❑ 175 Donovan McNabb .75 .30
❑ 176 Curtis Martin .60 .25
❑ 177 David Givens .40 .15
❑ 178 Kenechi Udeze .30 .10
❑ 179 A.J. Feeley .40 .15
❑ 180 Eddie Kennison .30 .10
❑ 181 LaBrandon Toefield .30 .10
❑ 182 Jabar Gaffney .30 .10
❑ 183 Bethel Johnson .30 .10
❑ 184 Eddie Drummond .30 .10
❑ 185 Rod Smith .40 .15
❑ 186 La'Roi Glover .30 .10
❑ 187 Onterrio Smith .40 .15
❑ 188 Antonio Bryant .30 .10
❑ 189 Lee Mays .30 .10
❑ 190 Michael Vick 1.00 .40
❑ 191 Samie Parker .30 .10
❑ 192 London Fletcher .30 .10
❑ 193 DeShaun Foster .40 .15
❑ 194 Rashaun Woods .40 .15
❑ 195 Marc Bulger .60 .25
❑ 196 Adrian Peterson .30 .10
❑ 197 Justin McCareins .30 .10
❑ 198 Corey Dillon .40 .15
❑ 199 James Farrior .30 .10
❑ 200 Antonio Gates .60 .25
❑ 201 Todd Pinkston .30 .10
❑ 202 Randy Hymes .30 .10
❑ 203 Peyton Manning 1.00 .40
❑ 204 Ahman Green .60 .25
❑ 205 Charles Rogers .40 .15
❑ 206 John Lynch .40 .15
❑ 207 Larry Fitzgerald .60 .25
❑ 208 Jonathan Ogden .30 .10
❑ 209 Michael Bennett .40 .15
❑ 210 DeWayne Robertson .30 .10
❑ 211 Justin Fargas .30 .10
❑ 212 Duce Staley .40 .15
❑ 213 Koren Robinson .40 .15
❑ 214 Billy Volek .40 .15
❑ 215 Laveranues Coles .40 .15
❑ 216 Michael Clayton .60 .25
❑ 217 Amani Toomer .40 .15
❑ 218 Thomas Jones .40 .15
❑ 219 Todd Heap .40 .15
❑ 220 Ken Lucas .30 .10
❑ 221 Donovin Darius .30 .10
❑ 222 Ashley Lelie .40 .15
❑ 223 Warrick Dunn .40 .15
❑ 224 Doug Jolley .30 .10
❑ 225 Jimmy Smith .40 .15
❑ 226 Quentin Griffin .40 .15
❑ 227 Isaac Bruce .40 .15
❑ 228 Ronald Curry .40 .15
❑ 229 Corey Bradford .30 .10
❑ 230 LaVar Arrington .60 .25
❑ 231 William Henderson .30 .10
❑ 232 Brandon Stokley .40 .15
❑ 233 Alge Crumpler .40 .15
❑ 234 Joe Horn .40 .15
❑ 235 Bernard Berrian .30 .10
❑ 236 Michael Boulware .30 .10
❑ 237 Brett Favre 1.50 .60
❑ 238 Dennis Northcutt .30 .10
❑ 239 Muhsin Muhammad .40 .15
❑ 240 Shawn Springs .30 .10
❑ 241 Kelly Campbell .30 .10
❑ 242 Johnnie Morton .40 .15
❑ 243 Derrick Blaylock .30 .10
❑ 244 Chris Chambers .40 .15
❑ 245 Joey Harrington .60 .25
❑ 246 Brian Urlacher .60 .25
❑ 247 T.J. Duckett .40 .15
❑ 248 Quincy Morgan .30 .10
❑ 249 Darren Sharper .30 .10
❑ 250 L.J. Smith .30 .10
❑ 251 Steve McNair .60 .25
❑ 252 Eric Parker .30 .10
❑ 253 Jerome Bettis .60 .25
❑ 254 LaMont Jordan .60 .25
❑ 255 Tedy Bruschi .40 .15
❑ 256 Ernest Wilford .30 .10
❑ 257 Reuben Droughns .40 .15
❑ 258 Lito Sheppard .30 .10
❑ 259 Steve Smith .40 .15
❑ 260 Shaun Alexander .75 .30
❑ 261 Kevin Curtis .40 .15
❑ 262 Drew Bledsoe .60 .25
❑ 263 Derrick Mason .40 .15
❑ 264 Jevon Kearse .40 .15
❑ 265 Jerry Porter .40 .15
❑ 266 Edgerrin James .60 .25
❑ 267 Santana Moss .40 .15
❑ 268 Kyle Boller .40 .15
❑ 269 Travis Henry .40 .15
❑ 270 Stephen Davis .40 .15
❑ 271 Gibril Wilson .30 .10
❑ 272 Plaxico Burress .40 .15
❑ 273 Deion Branch .40 .15
❑ 274 Larry Johnson .60 .25
❑ 275 Rudi Johnson .40 .15
❑ 276 Andre Johnson .40 .15
❑ 277 David Akers .30 .10
❑ 278 Randy Moss .60 .25
❑ 279 Roy Williams S .40 .15
❑ 280 Antoine Winfield .30 .10
❑ 281 Antonio Pierce .30 .10
❑ 282 Keith Bulluck .30 .10
❑ 283 Correll Buckhalter .40 .15
❑ 284 Troy Vincent .30 .10
❑ 285 D.J. Williams .30 .10
❑ 286 Matt Schaub .40 .15
❑ 287 Clarence Moore .30 .10
❑ 288 Billy Miller .30 .10
❑ 289 Terrence Holt .30 .10
❑ 290 Tony Hollings .30 .10
❑ 291 E.J. Henderson .30 .10
❑ 292 Fred Smoot .30 .10
❑ 293 Patrick Crayton .30 .10
❑ 294 Mike Alstott .40 .15
❑ 295 Mewelde Moore .40 .15
❑ 296 Shawn Bryson .30 .10
❑ 297 David Garrard .30 .10
❑ 298 Kurt Warner .40 .15
❑ 299 Nate Clements .30 .10
❑ 300 Kellen Winslow .60 .25
❑ 301 Eric Johnson .40 .15
❑ 302 Peerless Price .30 .10
❑ 303 Joey Galloway .40 .15
❑ 304 Sebastian Janikowski .30 .10
❑ 305 Jason McAddley .30 .10
❑ 306 Chris Gamble .40 .15
❑ 307 Brian Griese .40 .15
❑ 308 Greg Lewis .60 .25
❑ 309 Wes Welker .30 .10
❑ 310 Jesse Chatman .30 .10
❑ 311 Curtis Martin LL .40 .15
❑ 312 Daunte Culpepper LL .40 .15
❑ 313 Muhsin Muhammad LL .30 .10
❑ 314 Shaun Alexander LL .60 .25
❑ 315 Trent Green LL .30 .10
❑ 316 Joe Horn LL .30 .10
❑ 317 Corey Dillon LL .30 .10
❑ 318 Peyton Manning LL .60 .25
❑ 319 Javon Walker LL .30 .10
❑ 320 Edgerrin James LL .40 .15
❑ 321 Jake Scott GM .30 .10
❑ 322 John Elway GM 1.00 .40
❑ 323 Dwight Clark GM .40 .15
❑ 324 Lawrence Taylor GM .60 .25
❑ 325 Joe Namath GM .75 .30
❑ 326 Richard Dent GM .40 .15
❑ 327 Peyton Manning GM .60 .25
❑ 328 Don Maynard GM .30 .10
❑ 329 Joe Greene GM .60 .25
❑ 330 Roger Staubach GM .75 .30
❑ 331 Daunte Culpepper AP .40 .15
❑ 332 Peyton Manning AP .60 .25
❑ 333 Tiki Barber AP .40 .15
❑ 334 Antonio Gates AP .40 .15
❑ 335 Marvin Harrison AP .40 .15
❑ 336 Lito Sheppard AP .30 .10
❑ 337 LaDainian Tomlinson AP .60 .25
❑ 338 Muhsin Muhammad AP .30 .10
❑ 339 Allen Rossum AP .30 .10
❑ 340 Dwight Freeney AP .40 .15
❑ 341 Jerome Bettis AP .40 .15
❑ 342 Alge Crumpler AP .30 .10
❑ 343 Ed Reed AP .30 .10
❑ 344 Ronde Barber AP .30 .10
❑ 345 Takeo Spikes AP .30 .10
❑ 346 Rudi Johnson AP .30 .10
❑ 347 Adam Vinatieri AP .40 .15
❑ 348 Torry Holt AP .40 .15
❑ 349 Chad Johnson AP .40 .15
❑ 350 Brian Westbrook AP .30 .10
❑ 351 Michael Vick AP .60 .25
❑ 352 Tom Brady AP .60 .25
❑ 353 Donovan McNabb AP .60 .25
❑ 354 Ahman Green AP .40 .15
❑ 355 Andre Johnson AP .30 .10
❑ 356 Drew Brees AP .40 .15
❑ 357 Hines Ward AP .40 .15
❑ 358 Deion Branch PH .30 .10
❑ 359 Philadelphia Eagles PH .60 .25
❑ 360 Tom Brady PH .60 .25
❑ 361 Taylor Stubblefield RC .75 .30
❑ 362 Dan Cody RC 1.50 .60
❑ 363 Ryan Claridge RC 1.25 .50
❑ 364 David Pollack RC 1.50 .60
❑ 365 Craig Bragg RC 1.25 .50
❑ 366 Alvin Pearman RC 1.50 .60
❑ 367 Marcus Maxwell RC 1.25 .50
❑ 368 Brock Berlin RC 1.25 .50
❑ 369 Khalif Barnes RC 1.25 .50
❑ 370 Eric King RC 1.25 .50
❑ 371 Alex Smith TE RC 1.50 .60
❑ 372 Dante Ridgeway RC 1.25 .50
❑ 373 Shaun Cody RC 1.50 .60
❑ 374 Donte Nicholson RC 1.50 .60
❑ 375 DeMarcus Ware RC 2.50 1.00
❑ 376 Lionel Gates RC 1.25 .50
❑ 377 Fabian Washington RC 1.50 .60
❑ 378 Brandon Jacobs RC 2.00 .75
❑ 379 Noah Herron RC 1.50 .60
❑ 380 Derrick Johnson RC 2.50 1.00
❑ 381 J.R. Russell RC 1.25 .50
❑ 382 Adrian McPherson RC 1.50 .60
❑ 383 Marcus Spears RC 1.50 .60
❑ 384 Justin Miller RC 1.25 .50
❑ 385 Marion Barber RC 2.50 1.00
❑ 386 Anthony Davis RC 1.25 .50
❑ 387 Chad Owens RC 1.50 .60
❑ 388 Craphonso Thorpe RC 1.25 .50
❑ 389 Travis Johnson RC 1.25 .50
❑ 390 Erasmus James RC 1.50 .60
❑ 391 Mike Patterson RC 1.50 .60
❑ 392 Alphonso Hodge RC .75 .30
❑ 393 Airese Currie RC 1.50 .60
❑ 394 Justin Tuck RC 1.50 .60
❑ 395 Dan Orlovsky RC 2.00 .75
❑ 396 Thomas Davis RC 1.50 .60
❑ 397 Derek Anderson RC 1.50 .60
❑ 398 Matt Roth RC 1.50 .60
❑ 399 Darryl Blackstock RC 1.25 .50
❑ 400 Chris Henry RC 1.50 .60
❑ 401 Rasheed Marshall RC 1.50 .60
❑ 402 Anttaj Hawthorne RC 1.25 .50
❑ 403 Bryant McFadden RC 1.50 .60
❑ 404 Darren Sproles RC 1.50 .60
❑ 405 Oshiomogho Atogwe RC 1.25 .50
❑ 406 Fred Gibson RC 1.25 .50
❑ 407 J.J. Arrington RC 2.00 .75
❑ 408 Cedric Benson RC 3.00 1.25
❑ 409 Mark Bradley RC 1.50 .60
❑ 410 Reggie Brown RC 1.50 .60
❑ 411 Ronnie Brown RC 6.00 2.50
❑ 412 Jason Campbell RC 2.50 1.00
❑ 413 Maurice Clarett 1.50 .60
❑ 414 Mark Clayton RC 2.00 .75
❑ 415 Braylon Edwards RC 5.00 2.00
❑ 416 Ciatrick Fason RC 1.50 .60

❑ 417 Charlie Frye RC	3.00	1.25
❑ 418 Frank Gore RC	3.00	1.25
❑ 419 David Greene RC	1.50	.60
❑ 420 Vincent Jackson RC	1.50	.60
❑ 421 Adam Jones RC	1.50	.60
❑ 422 Matt Jones RC	4.00	1.50
❑ 423 Stefan LeFors RC	1.50	.60
❑ 424 Heath Miller RC	4.00	1.50
❑ 425 Ryan Moats RC	1.50	.60
❑ 426 Vernand Morency RC	1.50	.60
❑ 427 Terrence Murphy RC	1.50	.60
❑ 428 Kyle Orton RC	2.50	1.00
❑ 429 Roscoe Parrish RC	1.50	.60
❑ 430 Courtney Roby RC	1.50	.60
❑ 431 Aaron Rodgers RC	5.00	2.00
❑ 432 Carlos Rogers RC	2.00	.75
❑ 433 Antrel Rolle RC	1.50	.60
❑ 434 Eric Shelton RC	1.50	.60
❑ 435 Alex Smith QB RC	6.00	2.50
❑ 436 Andrew Walter RC	2.50	1.00
❑ 437 Roddy White RC	1.50	.60
❑ 438 Cadillac Williams RC	8.00	3.00
❑ 439 Mike Williams	3.00	1.25
❑ 440 Troy Williamson RC	3.00	1.25
❑ RHDB Deion Branch RH	5.00	2.00
❑ RHDBA Deion Branch RH AU	350.00	200.00
❑ SBMVP D.Branch FB AU/200	150.00	60.00

1996 Topps Chrome

❑ COMPLETE SET (165)	100.00	40.00
❑ 1 Troy Aikman	2.50	1.00
❑ 2 Kevin Greene	.50	.20
❑ 3 Robert Brooks	1.00	.40
❑ 4 Junior Seau	1.00	.40
❑ 5 Brett Perriman	.20	.07
❑ 6 Cortez Kennedy	.20	.07
❑ 7 Orlando Thomas	.20	.07
❑ 8 Anthony Miller	.50	.20
❑ 9 Jeff Blake	1.00	.40
❑ 10 Trent Dilfer	1.00	.40
❑ 11 Heath Shuler	.50	.20
❑ 12 Michael Jackson	.50	.20
❑ 13 Merton Hanks	.20	.07
❑ 14 Dale Carter	.20	.07
❑ 15 Eric Metcalf	.20	.07
❑ 16 Barry Sanders	4.00	1.50
❑ 17 Joey Galloway	1.00	.40
❑ 18 Bryan Cox	.20	.07
❑ 19 Harvey Williams	.20	.07
❑ 20 Terrell Davis	1.50	.60
❑ 21 Darnay Scott	.50	.20
❑ 22 Kerry Collins	1.00	.40
❑ 23 Warren Sapp	.20	.07
❑ 24 Michael Westbrook	1.00	.40
❑ 25 Mark Brunell	1.50	.60
❑ 26 Craig Heyward	.20	.07
❑ 27 Eric Allen	.20	.07
❑ 28 Dana Stubblefield	.50	.20
❑ 29 Steve Bono	.20	.07
❑ 30 Larry Brown	.20	.07
❑ 31 Warren Moon	.50	.20
❑ 32 Jim Kelly	1.00	.40
❑ 33 Terry McDaniel	.20	.07
❑ 34 Dan Wilkinson	.20	.07
❑ 35 Dave Brown	.20	.07
❑ 36 Todd Lyght	.20	.07
❑ 37 Aeneas Williams	.20	.07
❑ 38 Shannon Sharpe	.50	.20
❑ 39 Errict Rhett	.50	.20
❑ 40 Yancey Thigpen	.50	.20
❑ 41 J.J. Stokes	1.00	.40
❑ 42 Marshall Faulk	1.25	.50
❑ 43 Chester McGlockton	.20	.07
❑ 44 Darryll Lewis	.20	.07
❑ 45 Drew Bledsoe	1.50	.60
❑ 46 Tyrone Wheatley	.50	.20
❑ 47 Herman Moore	.50	.20
❑ 48 Darren Woodson	.50	.20
❑ 49 Ricky Watters	.50	.20
❑ 50 Emmitt Smith TYC	1.50	.60
❑ 51 Barry Sanders TYC	1.50	.60
❑ 52 Curtis Martin TYC	1.00	.40
❑ 53 Chris Warren TYC	.50	.20
❑ 54 Errict Rhett TYC	.50	.20
❑ 55 Rodney Hampton TYC	.20	.07
❑ 56 Terrell Davis TYC	1.00	.40
❑ 57 Marshall Faulk TYC	1.00	.40
❑ 58 Rashaan Salaam TYC	.50	.20
❑ 59 Curtis Conway	1.00	.40
❑ 60 Isaac Bruce	1.00	.40
❑ 61 Thurman Thomas	1.00	.40
❑ 62 Terry Allen	.50	.20
❑ 63 Lamar Lathon	.20	.07
❑ 64 Mark Chmura	.50	.20
❑ 65 Chris Warren	.50	.20
❑ 66 Jessie Tuggle	.20	.07
❑ 67 Erik Kramer	.20	.07
❑ 68 Tim Brown	1.00	.40
❑ 69 Derrick Thomas	1.00	.40
❑ 70 Willie McGinest	.20	.07
❑ 71 Frank Sanders	.50	.20
❑ 72 Bernie Parmalee	.20	.07
❑ 73 Kordell Stewart	1.00	.40
❑ 74 Brent Jones	.20	.07
❑ 75 Edgar Bennett	.50	.20
❑ 76 Rashaan Salaam	.50	.20
❑ 77 Carl Pickens	.50	.20
❑ 78 Terance Mathis	.20	.07
❑ 79 Deion Sanders	1.25	.50
❑ 80 Glyn Milburn	.20	.07
❑ 81 Lee Woodall	.20	.07
❑ 82 Neil Smith	.50	.20
❑ 83 Stan Humphries	.50	.20
❑ 84 Rick Mirer	.50	.20
❑ 85 Troy Vincent	.20	.07
❑ 86 Sam Mills	.20	.07
❑ 87 Brian Mitchell	.20	.07
❑ 88 Hardy Nickerson	.20	.07
❑ 89 Tamarick Vanover	.50	.20
❑ 90 Steve McNair	1.50	.60
❑ 91 Jerry Rice TYC	1.00	.40
❑ 92 Isaac Bruce TYC	1.00	.40
❑ 93 Herman Moore TYC	.50	.20
❑ 94 Cris Carter TYC	1.00	.40
❑ 95 Tim Brown TYC	.50	.20
❑ 96 Carl Pickens TYC	.50	.20
❑ 97 Joey Galloway TYC	1.00	.40
❑ 98 Jerry Rice	2.50	1.00
❑ 99 Cris Carter	1.00	.40
❑ 100 Curtis Martin	1.50	.60
❑ 101 Scott Mitchell	.50	.20
❑ 102 Ken Harvey	.20	.07
❑ 103 Rodney Hampton	.50	.20
❑ 104 Reggie White	1.00	.40
❑ 105 Eddie Robinson	.20	.07
❑ 106 Greg Lloyd	.50	.20
❑ 107 Phillippi Sparks	.20	.07
❑ 108 Emmitt Smith	4.00	1.50
❑ 109 Tom Carter	.20	.07
❑ 110 Jim Everett	.20	.07
❑ 111 James O.Stewart	.50	.20
❑ 112 Kyle Brady	.20	.07
❑ 113 Irving Fryar	.50	.20
❑ 114 Vinny Testaverde	.50	.20
❑ 115 John Elway	5.00	2.00
❑ 116 Chris Spielman	.20	.07
❑ 117 Mike Mamula	.20	.07
❑ 118 Jim Harbaugh	.50	.20
❑ 119 Ken Norton	.20	.07
❑ 120 Bruce Smith	.50	.20
❑ 121 Daryl Johnston	.50	.20
❑ 122 Blaine Bishop	.20	.07
❑ 123 Jeff George	.50	.20
❑ 124 Jeff Hostetler	.20	.07
❑ 125 Jerome Bettis	1.00	.40
❑ 126 Jay Novacek	.20	.07
❑ 127 Bryce Paup	.20	.07
❑ 128 Neil O'Donnell	.50	.20
❑ 129 Marcus Allen	1.00	.40
❑ 130 Steve Young	1.50	.60
❑ 131 Brett Favre TYC	2.00	.75
❑ 132 Scott Mitchell TYC	.20	.07
❑ 133 John Elway TYC	2.00	.75
❑ 134 Jeff Blake TYC	.50	.20
❑ 135 Dan Marino TYC	2.00	.75
❑ 136 Drew Bledsoe TYC	1.00	.40
❑ 137 Troy Aikman TYC	1.00	.40
❑ 138 Steve Young TYC	1.00	.40
❑ 139 Jim Kelly TYC	1.00	.40
❑ 140 Jeff Graham	.20	.07
❑ 141 Hugh Douglas	.50	.20
❑ 142 Dan Marino	5.00	2.00
❑ 143 Darrell Green	.20	.07
❑ 144 Eric Zeier	.20	.07
❑ 145 Brett Favre	5.00	2.00
❑ 146 Carnell Lake	.20	.07
❑ 147 Ben Coates	.50	.20
❑ 148 Tony Martin	.50	.20
❑ 149 Michael Irvin	1.00	.40
❑ 150 Lawrence Phillips RC	1.00	.40
❑ 151 Alex Van Dyke RC	1.50	.60
❑ 152 Kevin Hardy RC	1.50	.60
❑ 153 Rickey Dudley RC	5.00	2.00
❑ 154 Eric Moulds RC	10.00	5.00
❑ 155 Simeon Rice RC	4.00	1.50
❑ 156 Marvin Harrison RC	30.00	15.00
❑ 157 Tim Biakabutuka RC	4.00	1.50
❑ 158 Duane Clemons RC	1.00	.40
❑ 159 Keyshawn Johnson RC	12.00	5.00
❑ 160 John Mobley RC	1.50	.60
❑ 161 Leeland McElroy RC	1.50	.60
❑ 162 Eddie George RC	12.00	6.00
❑ 163 Jonathan Ogden RC	2.00	.75
❑ 164 Eddie Kennison RC	5.00	2.00
❑ 165 Checklist	.20	.07

1997 Topps Chrome

❑ COMPLETE SET (165)	60.00	30.00
❑ 1 Brett Favre	6.00	2.50
❑ 2 Tim Biakabutuka	1.00	.40
❑ 3 Deion Sanders	1.50	.60
❑ 4 Marshall Faulk	2.00	.75
❑ 5 John Randle	1.00	.40
❑ 6 Stan Humphries	1.00	.40
❑ 7 Ki-Jana Carter	.60	.25
❑ 8 Rashaan Salaam	.60	.25
❑ 9 Rickey Dudley	1.00	.40
❑ 10 Isaac Bruce	1.50	.60
❑ 11 Keyshawn Johnson	1.50	.60
❑ 12 Ben Coates	1.00	.40
❑ 13 Ty Detmer	1.00	.40
❑ 14 Gus Frerotte	.60	.25
❑ 15 Mario Bates	.60	.25
❑ 16 Chris Calloway	.60	.25
❑ 17 Frank Sanders	1.00	.40
❑ 18 Bruce Smith	1.00	.40
❑ 19 Jeff Graham	.60	.25
❑ 20 Trent Dilfer	1.50	.60
❑ 21 Tyrone Wheatley	1.00	.40
❑ 22 Chris Warren	1.00	.40
❑ 23 Terry Kirby	1.00	.40
❑ 24 Tony Gonzalez RC	8.00	3.00
❑ 25 Ricky Watters	1.00	.40
❑ 26 Tamarick Vanover	1.00	.40
❑ 27 Kerry Collins	1.50	.60

❑ 28 Bobby Engram 1.00 .40
❑ 29 Derrick Alexander WR 1.00 .40
❑ 30 Hugh Douglas .60 .25
❑ 31 Thurman Thomas 1.50 .60
❑ 32 Drew Bledsoe 2.00 .75
❑ 33 LeShon Johnson .60 .25
❑ 34 Byron Bam Morris .60 .25
❑ 35 Herman Moore 1.00 .40
❑ 36 Troy Aikman 3.00 1.25
❑ 37 Mel Gray .60 .25
❑ 38 Adrian Murrell 1.00 .40
❑ 39 Carl Pickens 1.00 .40
❑ 40 Tony Brackens .60 .25
❑ 41 O.J. McDuffie 1.00 .40
❑ 42 Napoleon Kaufman 1.50 .60
❑ 43 Chris T. Jones .60 .25
❑ 44 Kordell Stewart 1.50 .60
❑ 45 Steve Young 2.00 .75
❑ 46 Shannon Sharpe 1.00 .40
❑ 47 Leeland McElroy .60 .25
❑ 48 Eric Moulds 1.50 .60
❑ 49 Eddie George 1.50 .60
❑ 50 Jamal Anderson 1.50 .60
❑ 51 Robert Smith 1.00 .40
❑ 52 Mike Alstott 1.50 .60
❑ 53 Darrell Green 1.00 .40
❑ 54 Irving Fryar 1.00 .40
❑ 55 Derrick Thomas 1.50 .60
❑ 56 Antonio Freeman 1.50 .60
❑ 57 Terrell Davis 2.00 .75
❑ 58 Henry Ellard .60 .25
❑ 59 Daryl Johnston 1.00 .40
❑ 60 Bryan Cox .60 .25
❑ 61 Vinny Testaverde 1.00 .40
❑ 62 Andre Reed 1.00 .40
❑ 63 Larry Centers 1.00 .40
❑ 64 Hardy Nickerson .60 .25
❑ 65 Tony Banks 1.00 .40
❑ 66 Dave Meggett .60 .25
❑ 67 Simeon Rice 1.00 .40
❑ 68 Warrick Dunn RC 8.00 3.00
❑ 69 Michael Irvin 1.50 .60
❑ 70 John Elway 6.00 2.50
❑ 71 Jake Reed 1.00 .40
❑ 72 Rodney Hampton 1.00 .40
❑ 73 Aaron Glenn .60 .25
❑ 74 Terry Allen 1.50 .60
❑ 75 Blaine Bishop .60 .25
❑ 76 Bert Emanuel 1.00 .40
❑ 77 Mark Carrier WR .60 .25
❑ 78 Jimmy Smith 1.00 .40
❑ 79 Jim Harbaugh 1.00 .40
❑ 80 Brent Jones 1.00 .40
❑ 81 Emmitt Smith 5.00 2.00
❑ 82 Fred Barnett .60 .25
❑ 83 Errict Rhett .60 .25
❑ 84 Michael Sinclair .60 .25
❑ 85 Jerome Bettis 1.50 .60
❑ 86 Chris Sanders .60 .25
❑ 87 Kent Graham .60 .25
❑ 88 Cris Carter 1.50 .60
❑ 89 Harvey Williams .60 .25
❑ 90 Eric Allen .60 .25
❑ 91 Bryant Young .60 .25
❑ 92 Marcus Allen 1.50 .60
❑ 93 Michael Jackson 1.00 .40
❑ 94 Mark Chmura 1.00 .40
❑ 95 Keenan McCardell 1.00 .40
❑ 96 Joey Galloway 1.00 .40
❑ 97 Eddie Kennison 1.00 .40
❑ 98 Steve Atwater .60 .25
❑ 99 Dorsey Levens 1.50 .60
❑ 100 Rob Moore 1.00 .40
❑ 101 Steve McNair 2.00 .75
❑ 102 Sean Dawkins .60 .25
❑ 103 Don Beebe .60 .25
❑ 104 Willie McGinest .60 .25
❑ 105 Tony Martin 1.00 .40
❑ 106 Mark Brunell 2.00 .75
❑ 107 Karim Abdul-Jabbar 1.50 .60
❑ 108 Michael Westbrook 1.00 .40
❑ 109 Lawrence Phillips .60 .25
❑ 110 Barry Sanders 5.00 2.00
❑ 111 Willie Davis .60 .25
❑ 112 Wesley Walls 1.00 .40
❑ 113 Todd Collins .60 .25
❑ 114 Jerry Rice 3.00 1.25
❑ 115 Scott Mitchell 1.00 .40
❑ 116 Terance Mathis 1.00 .40
❑ 117 Chris Spielman .60 .25
❑ 118 Curtis Conway 1.00 .40
❑ 119 Marvin Harrison 1.50 .60
❑ 120 Terry Glenn 1.50 .60
❑ 121 Dave Brown .60 .25
❑ 122 Neil O'Donnell 1.00 .40
❑ 123 Junior Seau 1.50 .60
❑ 124 Reggie White 1.50 .60
❑ 125 Lamar Lathon .60 .25
❑ 126 Natrone Means 1.00 .40
❑ 127 Tim Brown 1.50 .60
❑ 128 Eric Swann .60 .25
❑ 129 Dan Marino 6.00 2.50
❑ 130 Anthony Johnson .60 .25
❑ 131 Edgar Bennett 1.00 .40
❑ 132 Kevin Hardy .60 .25
❑ 133 Brian Blades .60 .25
❑ 134 Curtis Martin 2.00 .75
❑ 135 Zach Thomas 1.50 .60
❑ 136 Darnay Scott 1.00 .40
❑ 137 Desmond Howard 1.00 .40
❑ 138 Aeneas Williams .60 .25
❑ 139 Bryce Paup .60 .25
❑ 140 Brad Johnson 1.50 .60
❑ 141 Jeff Blake 1.00 .40
❑ 142 Wayne Chrebet 1.50 .60
❑ 143 Will Blackwell RC 1.25 .50
❑ 144 Tom Knight RC .60 .25
❑ 145 Darnell Autry RC 1.00 .40
❑ 146 Bryant Westbrook RC .60 .25
❑ 147 David LaFleur RC .75 .30
❑ 148 Antowain Smith RC 8.00 3.00
❑ 149 Rae Carruth RC .75 .30
❑ 150 Jim Druckenmiller RC 1.00 .40
❑ 151 Shawn Springs RC .75 .30
❑ 152 Troy Davis RC 1.25 .50
❑ 153 Orlando Pace RC 2.00 .75
❑ 154 Byron Hanspard RC 1.25 .50
❑ 155 Corey Dillon RC 20.00 7.50
❑ 156 Reidel Anthony RC 2.00 .75
❑ 157 Peter Boulware RC 2.00 .75
❑ 158 Reinard Wilson RC 1.25 .50
❑ 159 Pat Barnes RC 2.00 .75
❑ 160 Joey Kent RC 2.00 .75
❑ 161 Ike Hilliard RC 3.00 1.25
❑ 162 Jake Plummer RC 15.00 6.00
❑ 163 Darrell Russell RC .75 .30
❑ 164 Checklist Card .60 .25
❑ 165 Checklist Card .60 .25

1998 Topps Chrome

❑ COMPLETE SET (165) 120.00 50.00
❑ 1 Barry Sanders 4.00 1.50
❑ 2 Duane Starks RC 2.00 .75
❑ 3 J.J. Stokes .75 .30
❑ 4 Joey Galloway .75 .30
❑ 5 Deion Sanders 1.25 .50
❑ 6 Anthony Miller .50 .20
❑ 7 Jamal Anderson 1.25 .50
❑ 8 Shannon Sharpe .75 .30
❑ 9 Irving Fryar .75 .30
❑ 10 Curtis Martin 1.25 .50
❑ 11 Shawn Jefferson .50 .20
❑ 12 Charlie Garner .75 .30
❑ 13 Robert Edwards RC 3.00 1.25
❑ 14 Napoleon Kaufman 1.25 .50
❑ 15 Gus Frerotte .50 .20
❑ 16 John Elway 5.00 2.00
❑ 17 Jerome Pathon RC 4.00 1.50
❑ 18 Marshall Faulk 1.50 .60
❑ 19 Michael McCrary .50 .20
❑ 20 Marcus Allen 1.25 .50
❑ 21 Trent Dilfer 1.25 .50
❑ 22 Frank Wycheck .50 .20
❑ 23 Terrell Owens 1.25 .50
❑ 24 Herman Moore .75 .30
❑ 25 Neil O'Donnell .75 .30
❑ 26 Darnay Scott .75 .30
❑ 27 Keith Brooking RC 4.00 1.50
❑ 28 Eric Green .50 .20
❑ 29 Dan Marino 5.00 2.00
❑ 30 Antonio Freeman 1.25 .50
❑ 31 Tony Martin .75 .30
❑ 32 Isaac Bruce 1.25 .50
❑ 33 Rickey Dudley .50 .20
❑ 34 Scott Mitchell .75 .30
❑ 35 Randy Moss RC 20.00 10.00
❑ 36 Fred Lane .50 .20
❑ 37 Frank Sanders .75 .30
❑ 38 Jerry Rice 2.50 1.00
❑ 39 O.J. McDuffie .75 .30
❑ 40 Jessie Armstead .50 .20
❑ 41 Reidel Anthony .75 .30
❑ 42 Steve McNair 1.25 .50
❑ 43 Jake Reed .75 .30
❑ 44 Charles Woodson RC 5.00 2.00
❑ 45 Tiki Barber 1.25 .50
❑ 46 Mike Alstott 1.25 .50
❑ 47 Keyshawn Johnson 1.25 .50
❑ 48 Tony Banks .75 .30
❑ 49 Michael Westbrook .75 .30
❑ 50 Chris Slade .50 .20
❑ 51 Terry Allen 1.25 .50
❑ 52 Karim Abdul-Jabbar 1.25 .50
❑ 53 Brad Johnson 1.25 .50
❑ 54 Tony McGee .50 .20
❑ 55 Kevin Dyson RC 4.00 1.50
❑ 56 Warren Moon 1.25 .50
❑ 57 Byron Hanspard .50 .20
❑ 58 Jermaine Lewis .75 .30
❑ 59 Neil Smith .75 .30
❑ 60 Tamarick Vanover .50 .20
❑ 61 Terrell Davis 1.25 .50
❑ 62 Robert Smith 1.25 .50
❑ 63 Junior Seau 1.25 .50
❑ 64 Warren Sapp .75 .30
❑ 65 Michael Sinclair .50 .20
❑ 66 Ryan Leaf RC 4.00 1.50
❑ 67 Drew Bledsoe 2.00 .75
❑ 68 Jason Sehorn .75 .30
❑ 69 Andre Hastings .50 .20
❑ 70 Tony Gonzalez 1.25 .50
❑ 71 Dorsey Levens 1.25 .50
❑ 72 Ray Lewis 1.25 .50
❑ 73 Grant Wistrom RC 3.00 1.25
❑ 74 Elvis Grbac .75 .30
❑ 75 Mark Chmura .75 .30
❑ 76 Zach Thomas 1.25 .50
❑ 77 Ben Coates .75 .30
❑ 78 Rod Smith WR .75 .30
❑ 79 Andre Wadsworth RC 3.00 1.25
❑ 80 Garrison Hearst 1.25 .50
❑ 81 Will Blackwell .50 .20
❑ 82 Cris Carter 1.25 .50
❑ 83 Mark Fields .50 .20
❑ 84 Ken Dilger .50 .20
❑ 85 Johnnie Morton .75 .30
❑ 86 Michael Irvin 1.25 .50
❑ 87 Eddie George 1.25 .50
❑ 88 Rob Moore .75 .30
❑ 89 Takeo Spikes RC 4.00 1.50
❑ 90 Wesley Walls .75 .30
❑ 91 Andre Reed .75 .30
❑ 92 Thurman Thomas 1.25 .50
❑ 93 Ed McCaffrey .75 .30
❑ 94 Carl Pickens .75 .30
❑ 95 Jason Taylor .75 .30
❑ 96 Kordell Stewart 1.25 .50
❑ 97 Greg Ellis RC 2.00 .75
❑ 98 Aaron Glenn .50 .20
❑ 99 Jake Plummer 1.25 .50
❑ 100 Checklist .50 .20
❑ 101 Chris Sanders .50 .20
❑ 102 Michael Jackson .50 .20

❑ 103 Bobby Hoying	.75	.30
❑ 104 Wayne Chrebet	1.25	.50
❑ 105 Charles Way	.50	.20
❑ 106 Derrick Thomas	1.25	.50
❑ 107 Troy Drayton	.50	.20
❑ 108 Robert Holcombe RC	3.00	1.25
❑ 109 Pete Mitchell	.50	.20
❑ 110 Bruce Smith	.75	.30
❑ 111 Terance Mathis	.75	.30
❑ 112 Lawrence Phillips	.50	.20
❑ 113 Brett Favre	5.00	2.00
❑ 114 Darrell Green	.75	.30
❑ 115 Charles Johnson	.50	.20
❑ 116 Jeff Blake	.75	.30
❑ 117 Mark Brunell	1.25	.50
❑ 118 Simeon Rice	.75	.30
❑ 119 Robert Brooks	.75	.30
❑ 120 Jacquez Green RC	3.00	1.25
❑ 121 Willie Davis	.50	.20
❑ 122 Jeff George	.75	.30
❑ 123 Andre Rison	.75	.30
❑ 124 Erik Kramer	.50	.20
❑ 125 Peter Boulware	.50	.20
❑ 126 Marcus Nash RC	2.00	.75
❑ 127 Troy Aikman	2.50	1.00
❑ 128 Keenan McCardell	.75	.30
❑ 129 Bryant Westbrook	.50	.20
❑ 130 Terry Glenn	1.25	.50
❑ 131 Blaine Bishop	.50	.20
❑ 132 Tim Brown	1.25	.50
❑ 133 Brian Griese RC	8.00	3.00
❑ 134 John Mobley	.50	.20
❑ 135 Larry Centers	.50	.20
❑ 136 Eric Bjornson	.50	.20
❑ 137 Kevin Hardy	.50	.20
❑ 138 John Randle	.75	.30
❑ 139 Michael Strahan	.75	.30
❑ 140 Jerome Bettis	1.25	.50
❑ 141 Rae Carruth	.50	.20
❑ 142 Reggie White	1.25	.50
❑ 143 Antowain Smith	1.25	.50
❑ 144 Aeneas Williams	.50	.20
❑ 145 Bobby Engram	.75	.30
❑ 146 Germane Crowell RC	3.00	1.25
❑ 147 Freddie Jones	.50	.20
❑ 148 Kimble Anders	.75	.30
❑ 149 Steve Young	1.50	.60
❑ 150 Willie McGinest	.50	.20
❑ 151 Emmitt Smith	4.00	1.50
❑ 152 Fred Taylor RC	6.00	2.50
❑ 153 Danny Kanell	.75	.30
❑ 154 Warrick Dunn	1.25	.50
❑ 155 Kerry Collins	.75	.30
❑ 156 Chris Chandler	.75	.30
❑ 157 Curtis Conway	.75	.30
❑ 158 Curtis Enis RC	2.00	.75
❑ 159 Corey Dillon	1.25	.50
❑ 160 Glenn Foley	.75	.30
❑ 161 Marvin Harrison	1.25	.50
❑ 162 Chad Brown	.50	.20
❑ 163 Derrick Rodgers	.50	.20
❑ 164 Levon Kirkland	.50	.20
❑ 165 Peyton Manning RC	50.00	25.00

1999 Topps Chrome

❑ COMPLETE SET (165)	150.00	60.00
❑ COMP.SET w/o SP's (135)	50.00	25.00
❑ 1 Randy Moss	3.00	1.25
❑ 2 Keyshawn Johnson	1.25	.50
❑ 3 Priest Holmes	2.00	.75
❑ 4 Warren Moon	1.25	.50
❑ 5 Joey Galloway	.75	.30
❑ 6 Zach Thomas	1.25	.50
❑ 7 Cam Cleeland	.50	.20
❑ 8 Jim Harbaugh	.75	.30
❑ 9 Napoleon Kaufman	1.25	.50
❑ 10 Fred Taylor	1.25	.50
❑ 11 Mark Brunell	1.25	.50
❑ 12 Shannon Sharpe	.75	.30
❑ 13 Jacquez Green	.50	.20
❑ 14 Adrian Murrell	.75	.30
❑ 15 Cris Carter	1.25	.50
❑ 16 Jerome Pathon	.50	.20
❑ 17 Drew Bledsoe	1.50	.60
❑ 18 Curtis Martin	1.25	.50
❑ 19 Johnnie Morton	.75	.30
❑ 20 Doug Flutie	1.25	.50
❑ 21 Carl Pickens	.75	.30
❑ 22 Jerome Bettis	1.25	.50
❑ 23 Derrick Alexander	.50	.20
❑ 24 Antowain Smith	1.25	.50
❑ 25 Barry Sanders	4.00	1.50
❑ 26 Reidel Anthony	.75	.30
❑ 27 Wayne Chrebet	.75	.30
❑ 28 Terance Mathis	.75	.30
❑ 29 Shawn Springs	.50	.20
❑ 30 Emmitt Smith	2.50	1.00
❑ 31 Robert Smith	1.25	.50
❑ 32 Charles Johnson	.50	.20
❑ 33 Mike Alstott	1.25	.50
❑ 34 Ike Hilliard	.50	.20
❑ 35 Ricky Watters	.75	.30
❑ 36 Charles Woodson	1.25	.50
❑ 37 Rod Smith	.75	.30
❑ 38 Pete Mitchell	.50	.20
❑ 39 Derrick Thomas	1.25	.50
❑ 40 Dan Marino	4.00	1.50
❑ 41 Darnay Scott	.50	.20
❑ 42 Jake Reed	.75	.30
❑ 43 Chris Chandler	.75	.30
❑ 44 Dorsey Levens	1.25	.50
❑ 45 Kordell Stewart	.75	.30
❑ 46 Eddie George	1.25	.50
❑ 47 Corey Dillon	1.25	.50
❑ 48 Rich Gannon	1.25	.50
❑ 49 Chris Spielman	.50	.20
❑ 50 Jerry Rice	2.50	1.00
❑ 51 Trent Dilfer	.75	.30
❑ 52 Mark Chmura	.50	.20
❑ 53 Jimmy Smith	.75	.30
❑ 54 Isaac Bruce	1.25	.50
❑ 55 Karim Abdul-Jabbar	.75	.30
❑ 56 Sedrick Shaw	.50	.20
❑ 57 Jake Plummer	.75	.30
❑ 58 Tony Gonzalez	1.25	.50
❑ 59 Ben Coates	.75	.30
❑ 60 John Elway	4.00	1.50
❑ 61 Bruce Smith	.75	.30
❑ 62 Tim Brown	1.25	.50
❑ 63 Tim Dwight	1.25	.50
❑ 64 Yancey Thigpen	.50	.20
❑ 65 Terrell Owens	1.25	.50
❑ 66 Kyle Brady	.50	.20
❑ 67 Tony Martin	.75	.30
❑ 68 Michael Strahan	.75	.30
❑ 69 Deion Sanders	1.25	.50
❑ 70 Steve Young	1.50	.60
❑ 71 Dale Carter	.50	.20
❑ 72 Ty Law	.75	.30
❑ 73 Frank Wycheck	.50	.20
❑ 74 Marshall Faulk	1.50	.60
❑ 75 Vinny Testaverde	.75	.30
❑ 76 Chad Brown	.50	.20
❑ 77 Natrone Means	.75	.30
❑ 78 Bert Emanuel	.75	.30
❑ 79 Kerry Collins	.75	.30
❑ 80 Randall Cunningham	1.25	.50
❑ 81 Garrison Hearst	.75	.30
❑ 82 Curtis Enis	.50	.20
❑ 83 Steve Atwater	.50	.20
❑ 84 Kevin Greene	.50	.20
❑ 85 Steve McNair	1.25	.50
❑ 86 Andre Reed	.75	.30
❑ 87 J.J. Stokes	.75	.30
❑ 88 Eric Moulds	1.25	.50
❑ 89 Marvin Harrison	1.25	.50
❑ 90 Troy Aikman	2.50	1.00
❑ 91 Herman Moore	.75	.30
❑ 92 Michael Irvin	.75	.30
❑ 93 Frank Sanders	.75	.30
❑ 94 Duce Staley	1.25	.50
❑ 95 James Jett	.75	.30
❑ 96 Ricky Proehl	.50	.20
❑ 97 Andre Rison	.75	.30
❑ 98 Leslie Shepherd	.50	.20
❑ 99 Trent Green	1.25	.50
❑ 100 Terrell Davis	1.25	.50
❑ 101 Freddie Jones	.50	.20
❑ 102 Skip Hicks	.50	.20
❑ 103 Jeff Graham	.50	.20
❑ 104 Rob Moore	.75	.30
❑ 105 Torrance Small	.50	.20
❑ 106 Antonio Freeman	1.25	.50
❑ 107 Robert Brooks	.75	.30
❑ 108 Jon Kitna	1.25	.50
❑ 109 Curtis Conway	.75	.30
❑ 110 Brett Favre	4.00	1.50
❑ 111 Warrick Dunn	1.25	.50
❑ 112 Elvis Grbac	.75	.30
❑ 113 Corey Fuller	.50	.20
❑ 114 Rickey Dudley	.50	.20
❑ 115 Jamal Anderson	1.25	.50
❑ 116 Terry Glenn	1.25	.50
❑ 117 Rocket Ismail	.75	.30
❑ 118 John Randle	.75	.30
❑ 119 Chris Calloway	.50	.20
❑ 120 Peyton Manning	4.00	1.50
❑ 121 Keenan McCardell	.75	.30
❑ 122 O.J. McDuffie	.75	.30
❑ 123 Ed McCaffrey	.75	.30
❑ 124 Charlie Batch	1.25	.50
❑ 125 Jason Elam SH	.50	.20
❑ 126 Randy Moss SH	1.50	.60
❑ 127 John Elway SH	2.00	.75
❑ 128 Emmitt Smith SH	1.25	.50
❑ 129 Terrell Davis SH	1.25	.50
❑ 130 Jerris McPhail	.50	.20
❑ 131 Damon Gibson	.50	.20
❑ 132 Jim Pyne	.50	.20
❑ 133 Antonio Langham	.50	.20
❑ 134 Freddie Solomon	.50	.20
❑ 135 Ricky Williams RC	10.00	4.00
❑ 136 Daunte Culpepper RC	25.00	10.00
❑ 137 Chris Claiborne RC	2.00	.75
❑ 138 Amos Zereoue RC	5.00	2.00
❑ 139 Chris McAlister RC	4.00	1.50
❑ 140 Kevin Faulk RC	5.00	2.00
❑ 141 James Johnson RC	4.00	1.50
❑ 142 Mike Cloud RC	4.00	1.50
❑ 143 Jevon Kearse RC	10.00	4.00
❑ 144 Akili Smith RC	4.00	1.50
❑ 145 Edgerrin James RC	20.00	10.00
❑ 146 Cecil Collins RC	2.00	.75
❑ 147 Donovan McNabb RC	25.00	12.50
❑ 148 Kevin Johnson RC	5.00	2.00
❑ 149 Torry Holt RC	15.00	6.00
❑ 150 Rob Konrad RC	5.00	2.00
❑ 151 Tim Couch RC	5.00	2.00
❑ 152 David Boston RC	5.00	2.00
❑ 153 Karsten Bailey RC	4.00	1.50
❑ 154 Troy Edwards RC	4.00	1.50
❑ 155 Sedrick Irvin RC	2.00	.75
❑ 156 Shaun King RC	4.00	1.50
❑ 157 Peerless Price RC	5.00	2.00
❑ 158 Brock Huard RC	5.00	2.00
❑ 159 Cade McNown RC	4.00	1.50
❑ 160 Champ Bailey RC	8.00	3.00
❑ 161 D'Wayne Bates RC	4.00	1.50
❑ 162 Joe Germaine RC	4.00	1.50
❑ 163 Andy Katzenmoyer RC	4.00	1.50
❑ 164 Antoine Winfield RC	4.00	1.50
❑ 165 Checklist Card	.50	.20

2000 Topps Chrome

❑ COMPLETE SET (270)	800.00	400.00
❑ COMP.SET w/o SPs (180)	50.00	25.00
❑ 1 Daunte Culpepper	1.50	.60
❑ 2 Troy Edwards	.40	.15
❑ 3 Terrell Owens	1.25	.50
❑ 4 Ricky Proehl	.40	.15
❑ 5 Shaun King	.40	.15
❑ 6 Jeff George	.60	.25
❑ 7 Champ Bailey	.60	.25

8	Amani Toomer	.40	.15
9	Stephen Boyd	.40	.15
10	Thurman Thomas	.60	.25
11	Patrick Jeffers	1.25	.50
12	Jake Plummer	.60	.25
13	Peter Boulware	.40	.15
14	Darrin Chiaverini	.40	.15
15	Olandis Gary	1.25	.50
16	Peyton Manning	3.00	1.25
17	Joe Horn	.60	.25
18	Wayne Chrebet	.60	.25
19	Freddie Jones	.40	.15
20	Kurt Warner	2.50	1.00
21	Mike Alstott	1.25	.50
22	Stephen Davis	1.25	.50
23	Tim Brown	1.25	.50
24	Damon Huard	1.25	.50
25	Terry Glenn	.60	.25
26	Ricky Williams	1.25	.50
27	Tim Dwight	1.25	.50
28	Jay Riemersma	.40	.15
29	Carl Pickens	.60	.25
30	Brett Favre	4.00	1.50
31	Oronde Gadsden	.60	.25
32	Steve McNair	1.25	.50
33	Michael Pittman	.40	.15
34	Emmitt Smith	2.50	1.00
35	Mark Brunell	1.25	.50
36	Ed McCaffrey	1.25	.50
37	Tyrone Wheatley	.60	.25
38	Sean Dawkins	.40	.15
39	Jevon Kearse	1.25	.50
40	Tai Streets	.40	.15
41	Keyshawn Johnson	1.25	.50
42	Germane Crowell	.40	.15
43	Yatil Green	.40	.15
44	Anthony Wright RC	4.00	1.50
45	Jerry Rice	2.50	1.00
46	Az-Zahir Hakim	.60	.25
47	Stephen Alexander	.40	.15
48	Zach Thomas	1.25	.50
49	Tony Simmons	.40	.15
50	Jessie Armstead	.40	.15
51	Kordell Stewart	.60	.25
52	Cade McNown	.40	.15
53	Tony Gonzalez	.60	.25
54	John Randle	.60	.25
55	Donovan McNabb	2.00	.75
56	Warrick Dunn	1.25	.50
57	Dorsey Levens	.60	.25
58	Errict Rhett	.60	.25
59	Priest Holmes	1.50	.60
60	Terrell Davis	1.25	.50
61	Natrone Means	.40	.15
62	Brad Johnson	1.25	.50
63	Rickey Dudley	.40	.15
64	Moses Moreno	.40	.15
65	Randy Moss	2.50	1.00
66	Joe Montgomery	.40	.15
67	Johnnie Morton	.60	.25
68	Peerless Price	.60	.25
69	Rocket Ismail	.60	.25
70	David Boston	1.25	.50
71	Fred Taylor	1.25	.50
72	Jermaine Fazande	.40	.15
73	Elvis Grbac	.60	.25
74	Derrick Mayes	.60	.25
75	Yancey Thigpen	.40	.15
76	Ike Hilliard	.60	.25
77	Muhsin Muhammad	.60	.25
78	Shawn Jefferson	.40	.15
79	Rod Smith	.60	.25
80	Darnay Scott	.60	.25
81	Cam Cleeland	.40	.15
82	Steve Young	1.50	.60
83	E.G. Green	.40	.15
84	Robert Smith	1.25	.50
85	Jermaine Lewis	.60	.25
86	Tim Biakabutuka	.60	.25
87	Jerome Pathon	.60	.25
88	Kent Graham	.40	.15
89	Bruce Smith	.60	.25
90	Isaac Bruce	1.25	.50
91	Curtis Enis	.40	.15
92	Bert Emanuel	.40	.15
93	Keith Poole	.40	.15
94	Troy Aikman	2.50	1.00
95	Rich Gannon	1.25	.50
96	Michael Westbrook	.60	.25
97	Albert Connell	.40	.15
98	James Johnson	.40	.15
99	Jeff Blake	.60	.25
100	Joey Galloway	.60	.25
101	Rob Moore	.60	.25
102	Chris Chandler	.60	.25
103	Fred Lane	.40	.15
104	Eddie Kennison	.60	.25
105	Kevin Hardy	.40	.15
106	Napoleon Kaufman	.60	.25
107	Kevin Dyson	.60	.25
108	Keenan McCardell	.60	.25
109	Drew Bledsoe	1.50	.60
110	Kevin Johnson	1.25	.50
111	Terance Mathis	.60	.25
112	Gus Frerotte	.40	.15
113	Matthew Hatchette	.40	.15
114	Herman Moore	.60	.25
115	Curtis Martin	1.25	.50
116	Jacquez Green	.40	.15
117	Jake Reed	.60	.25
118	Antonio Freeman	1.25	.50
119	Jim Miller	.40	.15
120	Frank Sanders	.60	.25
121	Brian Griese	1.25	.50
122	Troy Brown	.60	.25
123	Jeff Graham	.40	.15
124	Marshall Faulk	1.50	.60
125	Vinny Testaverde	.60	.25
126	Frank Wycheck	.40	.15
127	Kerry Collins	.60	.25
128	Jay Fiedler	1.25	.50
129	Cris Carter	1.25	.50
130	Jason Tucker	.40	.15
131	Antowain Smith	.60	.25
132	Tony Banks	.60	.25
133	Terrence Wilkins	.40	.15
134	Tony Martin	.60	.25
135	Richard Huntley	.40	.15
136	J.J. Stokes	.60	.25
137	Ricky Watters	.60	.25
138	Pete Mitchell	.40	.15
139	Jimmy Smith	.60	.25
140	Doug Flutie	1.25	.50
141	Corey Bradford	.60	.25
142	Curtis Conway	.60	.25
143	Pete Mitchell	.40	.15
144	Torry Holt	1.25	.50
145	Warren Sapp	.60	.25
146	Duce Staley	1.25	.50
147	Mikhael Ricks	.40	.15
148	Edgerrin James	2.00	.75
149	Charlie Batch	1.25	.50
150	Rob Johnson	.60	.25
151	Jamal Anderson	1.25	.50
152	Tim Couch	.60	.25
153	O.J. McDuffie	.60	.25
154	Charles Woodson	.60	.25
155	Jake Delhomme RC	12.00	5.00
156	Eddie George	1.25	.50
157	Jim Harbaugh	.60	.25
158	Jon Kitna	1.25	.50
159	Derrick Alexander	.60	.25
160	Marvin Harrison	1.25	.50
161	James Stewart	.60	.25
162	Qadry Ismail	.60	.25
163	Wesley Walls	.40	.15
164	Steve Beuerlein	.60	.25
165	Marcus Robinson	1.25	.50
166	Bill Schroeder	.60	.25
167	Charles Johnson	.60	.25
168	Charlie Garner	.60	.25
169	Eric Moulds	1.25	.50
170	Jerome Bettis	1.25	.50
171	Tai Streets	.40	.15
172	Akili Smith	.40	.15
173	Jonathan Linton	.40	.15
174	Corey Dillon	1.25	.50
175	Junior Seau	1.25	.50
176	Jonathan Quinn	.40	.15
177	Bobby Engram	.40	.15
178	Shannon Sharpe	.60	.25
179	Michael Basnight	.40	.15
180	Sedrick Irvin	.40	.15
181	Sammy Morris RC	10.00	4.00
182	Ron Dixon RC	10.00	4.00
183	Trevor Gaylor RC	10.00	4.00
184	Chris Cole RC	8.00	3.00
185	Deltha O'Neal RC	15.00	6.00
186	Sebastian Janikowski RC	15.00	6.00
187	Kwame Cavil RC	8.00	3.00
188	Chad Morton RC	15.00	6.00
189	Terrelle Smith RC	10.00	4.00
190	Frank Moreau RC	10.00	4.00
191	Kurt Warner HL	1.50	.60
192	Dan Marino HL	2.50	1.00
193	Cris Carter HL	.60	.25
194	Brett Favre HL	2.50	1.00
195	Marshall Faulk HL	1.25	.50
196	Jevon Kearse HL	.60	.25
197	Edgerrin James HL	1.50	.60
198	Emmitt Smith HL	1.50	.60
199	Andre Reed HL	.40	.15
200	K.Dyson/F.Wycheck HL	.40	.15
201	Olindo Mare MM	.40	.15
202	Marcus Coleman MM	.40	.15
203	James Johnson MM	.40	.15
204	Ray Lucas MM	.60	.25
205	Dedric Ward MM	.40	.15
206	Richie Cunningham MM	.40	.15
207	James Hasty MM	.40	.15
208	Sedrick Shaw MM	.40	.15
209	Kurt Warner MM	1.50	.60
210	Marshall Faulk MM	1.25	.50
211	Brian Shay EP	1.00	.40
212	L.C. Stevens EP	1.00	.40
213	Corey Thomas EP	1.00	.40
214	Scott Milanovich EP	1.50	.60
215	Pat Barnes EP	1.50	.60
216	Danny Wuerffel EP	1.50	.60
217	Kevin Daft EP	1.00	.40
218	Ron Powlus EP RC	2.00	.75
219	Eric Kresser EP	1.00	.40
220	Norman Miller EP RC	1.00	.40
221	Cory Sauter EP	1.00	.40
222	Marcus Crandell EP RC	1.50	.60
223	Sean Morey EP RC	1.50	.60
224	Jeff Ogden EP	1.50	.60
225	Ted White EP	1.00	.40
226	Jim Kubiak EP RC	1.50	.60
227	Aaron Stecker EP RC	2.00	.75
228	Ronnie Powell EP	1.00	.40
229	Matt Lytle EP RC	1.50	.60
230	Kendrick Nord EP RC	1.00	.40
231	Tim Rattay RC	15.00	6.00
232	Rob Morris RC	10.00	4.00
233	Chris Samuels RC	10.00	4.00
234	Todd Husak RC	15.00	6.00
235	Ahmed Plummer RC	15.00	6.00
236	Frank Murphy RC	8.00	3.00
237	Michael Wiley RC	10.00	4.00
238	Giovanni Carmazzi RC	8.00	3.00
239	Anthony Becht RC	15.00	6.00
240	John Abraham RC	20.00	7.50
241	Shaun Alexander RC	60.00	25.00
242	Thomas Jones RC	30.00	12.50
243	Courtney Brown RC	15.00	6.00
244	Curtis Keaton RC	10.00	4.00
245	Jerry Porter RC	25.00	10.00
246	Corey Simon RC	15.00	6.00
247	Dez White RC	15.00	6.00
248	Jamal Lewis RC	30.00	12.50
249	Ron Dayne RC	15.00	6.00
250	R.Jay Soward RC	10.00	4.00
251	Tee Martin RC	15.00	6.00

❑ 252 Shaun Ellis RC 15.00 6.00
❑ 253 Brian Urlacher RC 50.00 20.00
❑ 254 Reuben Droughns RC 15.00 6.00
❑ 255 Travis Taylor RC 15.00 6.00
❑ 256 Plaxico Burress RC 30.00 12.50
❑ 257 Chad Pennington RC 30.00 12.50
❑ 258 Sylvester Morris RC 10.00 4.00
❑ 259 Ron Dugans RC 8.00 3.00
❑ 260 Joe Hamilton RC 10.00 4.00
❑ 261 Chris Redman RC 10.00 4.00
❑ 262 Trung Canidate RC 10.00 4.00
❑ 263 J.R. Redmond RC 10.00 4.00
❑ 264 Danny Farmer RC 10.00 4.00
❑ 265 Todd Pinkston RC 15.00 6.00
❑ 266 Dennis Northcutt RC 15.00 6.00
❑ 267 Laveranues Coles RC 20.00 7.50
❑ 268 Bubba Franks RC 15.00 6.00
❑ 269 Travis Prentice RC 10.00 4.00
❑ 270 Peter Warrick RC 15.00 6.00

2001 Topps Chrome

❑ COMP.SET w/o SP's (210) 50.00 20.00
❑ 1 Randy Moss 2.50 1.00
❑ 2 Desmond Howard .50 .20
❑ 3 Shawn Bryson .50 .20
❑ 4 Lamar Smith .75 .30
❑ 5 Peter Warrick 1.25 .50
❑ 6 Hines Ward 1.25 .50
❑ 7 J.R. Redmond .50 .20
❑ 8 Reidel Anthony .50 .20
❑ 9 Rich Gannon 1.25 .50
❑ 10 Ed McCaffrey 1.25 .50
❑ 11 Jamel White .50 .20
❑ 12 Michael Pittman .50 .20
❑ 13 Rob Johnson .75 .30
❑ 14 Tim Couch .75 .30
❑ 15 Stephen Alexander .50 .20
❑ 16 Ricky Watters .75 .30
❑ 17 Kerry Collins .75 .30
❑ 18 Ricky Williams 1.25 .50
❑ 19 Joey Galloway .75 .30
❑ 20 Chris Chandler .75 .30
❑ 21 Marty Booker .50 .20
❑ 22 Mark Brunell 1.25 .50
❑ 23 Antonio Freeman 1.25 .50
❑ 24 Richie Anderson .50 .20
❑ 25 Amani Toomer .75 .30
❑ 26 Trent Green 1.25 .50
❑ 27 Terrell Fletcher .50 .20
❑ 28 Kevin Lockett .50 .20
❑ 29 Ron Dixon .50 .20
❑ 30 Charlie Batch 1.25 .50
❑ 31 Oronde Gadsden .75 .30
❑ 32 Dorsey Levens .75 .30
❑ 33 Jamal Lewis 2.00 .75
❑ 34 Craig Yeast .50 .20
❑ 35 Muhsin Muhammad .75 .30
❑ 36 Willie Jackson .50 .20
❑ 37 Isaac Bruce 1.25 .50
❑ 38 Frank Wycheck .50 .20
❑ 39 Troy Brown .75 .30
❑ 40 Anthony Wright .50 .20
❑ 41 Zach Thomas 1.25 .50
❑ 42 Qadry Ismail .75 .30
❑ 43 Jake Plummer .75 .30
❑ 44 Keenan McCardell .50 .20
❑ 45 Charles Johnson .50 .20
❑ 46 Brett Favre 4.00 1.50
❑ 47 Jacquez Green .50 .20
❑ 48 Matt Hasselbeck .75 .30
❑ 49 Tiki Barber 1.25 .50
❑ 50 Jeff Garcia 1.25 .50
❑ 51 Shawn Jefferson .50 .20
❑ 52 Kevin Johnson .75 .30
❑ 53 Terrence Wilkins .50 .20
❑ 54 Mike Anderson 1.25 .50
❑ 55 Tim Brown 1.25 .50
❑ 56 Champ Bailey 1.25 .50
❑ 57 Jimmy Smith .75 .30
❑ 58 Trent Dilfer .75 .30
❑ 59 James Allen .75 .30
❑ 60 David Boston 1.25 .50
❑ 61 Jeremiah Trotter .75 .30
❑ 62 Freddie Jones .50 .20
❑ 63 Deion Sanders 1.25 .50
❑ 64 Darrell Jackson 1.25 .50
❑ 65 David Patten .50 .20
❑ 66 Jeremy McDaniel .50 .20
❑ 67 Jay Fiedler 1.25 .50
❑ 68 Chad Lewis .50 .20
❑ 69 Rocket Ismail .75 .30
❑ 70 Cade McNown .50 .20
❑ 71 Jevon Kearse .75 .30
❑ 72 Jermaine Fazande .50 .20
❑ 73 Junior Seau 1.25 .50
❑ 74 Rod Smith .75 .30
❑ 75 Jermaine Lewis .50 .20
❑ 76 Dennis Northcutt .75 .30
❑ 77 Charlie Garner .75 .30
❑ 78 Charles Woodson .75 .30
❑ 79 Wayne Chrebet .75 .30
❑ 80 Ahman Green 1.25 .50
❑ 81 Donald Hayes .50 .20
❑ 82 Terance Mathis .50 .20
❑ 83 Warrick Dunn 1.25 .50
❑ 84 Chris Sanders .50 .20
❑ 85 Albert Connell .50 .20
❑ 86 Robert Griffith .50 .20
❑ 87 Germane Crowell .50 .20
❑ 88 Tony Banks .75 .30
❑ 89 Travis Taylor .75 .30
❑ 90 Akili Smith .50 .20
❑ 91 Michael Westbrook .75 .30
❑ 92 Doug Flutie 1.25 .50
❑ 93 Ike Hilliard .75 .30
❑ 94 Terry Glenn .50 .20
❑ 95 Leslie Shepherd .50 .20
❑ 96 Az-Zahir Hakim .50 .20
❑ 97 La'Roi Glover .50 .20
❑ 98 Peyton Manning 3.00 1.25
❑ 99 Jackie Harris .50 .20
❑ 100 Edgerrin James 1.50 .60
❑ 101 Peerless Price .75 .30
❑ 102 Jamal Anderson 1.25 .50
❑ 103 Keyshawn Johnson 1.25 .50
❑ 104 Derrick Mason .75 .30
❑ 105 J.J. Stokes .75 .30
❑ 106 Kevin Faulk .75 .30
❑ 107 Tony Richardson .50 .20
❑ 108 James Stewart .75 .30
❑ 109 Tim Biakabutuka .75 .30
❑ 110 Jon Kitna 1.25 .50
❑ 111 Thomas Jones .75 .30
❑ 112 Steve McNair 1.25 .50
❑ 113 Sean Dawkins .50 .20
❑ 114 Jerome Bettis 1.25 .50
❑ 115 Donovan McNabb 1.50 .60
❑ 116 Bill Schroeder .75 .30
❑ 117 Rod Woodson .75 .30
❑ 118 James McKnight .75 .30
❑ 119 Daunte Culpepper 1.25 .50
❑ 120 Todd Husak .50 .20
❑ 121 Shaun King .50 .20
❑ 122 Tyrone Wheatley .75 .30
❑ 123 Curtis Martin 1.25 .50
❑ 124 Terrell Davis 1.25 .50
❑ 125 Steve Beuerlein .75 .30
❑ 126 Brad Johnson 1.25 .50
❑ 127 Joe Horn .75 .30
❑ 128 Fred Taylor 1.25 .50
❑ 129 Brian Urlacher 2.00 .75
❑ 130 Ray Lewis 1.25 .50
❑ 131 Marshall Faulk 1.50 .60
❑ 132 Curtis Conway .75 .30
❑ 133 Jason Sehorn .50 .20
❑ 134 Jerome Pathon .75 .30
❑ 135 Derrick Alexander .75 .30
❑ 136 Jerry Rice 2.50 1.00
❑ 137 Jeff George .75 .30
❑ 138 Johnnie Morton .75 .30
❑ 139 Eric Moulds .75 .30
❑ 140 Duce Staley 1.25 .50
❑ 141 Vinny Testaverde .75 .30
❑ 142 Eddie George 1.25 .50
❑ 143 Shaun Alexander 1.50 .60
❑ 144 Drew Bledsoe 1.50 .60
❑ 145 Emmitt Smith 2.50 1.00
❑ 146 Marvin Harrison 1.25 .50
❑ 147 Frank Sanders .50 .20
❑ 148 Aaron Shea .50 .20
❑ 149 Cris Carter 1.25 .50
❑ 150 Tony Gonzalez .75 .30
❑ 151 Marcus Robinson 1.25 .50
❑ 152 Danny Farmer .50 .20
❑ 153 Warren Sapp .75 .30
❑ 154 Kurt Warner 2.50 1.00
❑ 155 Jessie Armstead .50 .20
❑ 156 Lawyer Milloy .75 .30
❑ 157 Brian Griese 1.25 .50
❑ 158 Jason Taylor .50 .20
❑ 159 Jeff Lewis .50 .20
❑ 160 Travis Prentice .50 .20
❑ 161 Tim Dwight 1.25 .50
❑ 162 Kyle Brady .50 .20
❑ 163 Bubba Franks .75 .30
❑ 164 James Thrash .75 .30
❑ 165 Bobby Shaw .50 .20
❑ 166 Ron Dayne 1.25 .50
❑ 167 Mike Alstott 1.25 .50
❑ 168 Bruce Smith .50 .20
❑ 169 Jeff Graham .50 .20
❑ 170 Jeff Blake .75 .30
❑ 171 Laveranues Coles 1.25 .50
❑ 172 Herman Moore .75 .30
❑ 173 Shannon Sharpe .75 .30
❑ 174 Corey Dillon 1.25 .50
❑ 175 Ken Dilger .50 .20
❑ 176 Eddie Kennison .50 .20
❑ 177 Andre Rison .75 .30
❑ 178 Stephen Davis 1.25 .50
❑ 179 Torry Holt 1.25 .50
❑ 180 Samari Rolle .50 .20
❑ 181 Michael Strahan .75 .30
❑ 182 Plaxico Burress 1.25 .50
❑ 183 Darnell Autry .50 .20
❑ 184 Wesley Walls .50 .20
❑ 185 Elvis Grbac .75 .30
❑ 186 Marcus Pollard .50 .20
❑ 187 Keith Poole .50 .20
❑ 188 Ryan Leaf .75 .30
❑ 189 Terrell Owens 1.25 .50
❑ 190 Dedric Ward .50 .20
❑ 191 Donald Driver .75 .30
❑ 192 Larry Foster .50 .20
❑ 193 Priest Holmes 1.50 .60
❑ 194 Sammy Morris .50 .20
❑ 195 Reggie Jones .50 .20
❑ 196 Kordell Stewart .75 .30
❑ 197 Sylvester Morris .50 .20
❑ 198 Aaron Brooks 1.25 .50
❑ 199 Tai Streets .50 .20
❑ 200 Chad Pennington 2.00 .75
❑ 201 Terrell Owens SH 1.25 .50
❑ 202 Marshall Faulk SH 1.25 .50
❑ 203 Mike Anderson SH .75 .30
❑ 204 Cris Carter SH 1.25 .50
❑ 205 Corey Dillon SH 1.25 .50
❑ 206 Daunte Culpepper SH 1.25 .50
❑ 207 Peyton Manning SH 1.50 .60
❑ 208 Torry Holt SH 1.25 .50
❑ 209 Marvin Harrison SH 1.25 .50
❑ 210 Edgerrin James SH 1.25 .50
❑ 211 Sam Madison .50 .20
❑ 212 Jonathan Quinn .50 .20
❑ 213 Rob Morris .50 .20
❑ 214 E.G. Green .50 .20
❑ 215 David Sloan .50 .20
❑ 216 Jason Tucker .50 .20
❑ 217 Wali Rainer .50 .20
❑ 218 Jerry Azumah .50 .20
❑ 219 Dameyune Craig .50 .20
❑ 220 Jammi German .50 .20
❑ 221 LaDainian Tomlinson RC 300.00 175.00

❑	222 Quincy Morgan RC	20.00	7.50
❑	223 Steve Smith RC	40.00	20.00
❑	224 Santana Moss RC	30.00	12.50
❑	225 Koren Robinson RC	20.00	7.50
❑	226 Kevin Kasper RC	20.00	7.50
❑	227 Jamie Henderson RC	12.00	5.00
❑	228 Adam Archuleta RC	20.00	7.50
❑	229 Drew Brees RC	60.00	35.00
❑	230 Michael Stone RC	8.00	3.00
❑	231 Jamar Fletcher RC	12.00	5.00
❑	232 Eric Westmoreland RC	12.00	5.00
❑	233 Chris Barnes RC	12.00	5.00
❑	234 Gerard Warren RC	20.00	7.50
❑	235 Snoop Minnis RC	12.00	5.00
❑	236 Chris Chambers RC	25.00	12.50
❑	237 Damerien McCants RC	12.00	5.00
❑	238 Kevan Barlow RC	20.00	7.50
❑	239 Mike McMahon RC	20.00	7.50
❑	240 Jabari Holloway RC	12.00	5.00
❑	241 Travis Henry RC	30.00	12.50
❑	242 Derrick Blaylock RC	20.00	7.50
❑	243 Tim Hasselbeck RC	20.00	7.50
❑	244 Andre Carter RC	20.00	7.50
❑	245 Sage Rosenfels RC	20.00	7.50
❑	246 Cedrick Wilson RC	20.00	7.50
❑	247 Scotty Anderson RC	12.00	5.00
❑	248 Ken-Yon Rambo RC	12.00	5.00
❑	249 Marques Tuiasosopo RC	20.00	7.50
❑	250 Reggie Wayne RC	30.00	15.00
❑	251 Onomo Ojo RC	12.00	5.00
❑	252 James Jackson RC	20.00	7.50
❑	253 Moran Norris RC	8.00	3.00
❑	254 Rashard Casey RC	12.00	5.00
❑	255 Rudi Johnson RC	40.00	15.00
❑	256 Willie Middlebrooks RC	12.00	5.00
❑	257 Freddie Mitchell RC	20.00	7.50
❑	258 Deuce McAllister RC	40.00	20.00
❑	259 Chad Johnson RC	50.00	20.00
❑	260 David Terrell RC	20.00	7.50
❑	261 Jamal Reynolds RC	20.00	7.50
❑	262 Michael Vick RC	175.00	75.00
❑	263 Marcus Stroud RC	20.00	7.50
❑	264 Dan Alexander RC	20.00	7.50
❑	265 Jonathan Carter RC	12.00	5.00
❑	266 Bobby Newcombe RC	12.00	5.00
❑	267 Eddie Berlin RC	12.00	5.00
❑	268 LaMont Jordan RC	40.00	20.00
❑	269 Michael Bennett RC	20.00	7.50
❑	270 Shaun Rogers RC	20.00	7.50
❑	271 Travis Minor RC	12.00	5.00
❑	272 Jesse Palmer RC	20.00	7.50
❑	273 Derrick Gibson RC	12.00	5.00
❑	274 Chris Weinke RC	20.00	7.50
❑	275 Nate Clements RC	20.00	7.50
❑	276 Eric Kelly RC	8.00	3.00
❑	277 Justin Smith RC	20.00	7.50
❑	278 Ryan Pickett RC	8.00	3.00
❑	279 Anthony Thomas RC	20.00	7.50
❑	280 Will Allen RC	12.00	5.00
❑	281 Quincy Carter RC	20.00	7.50
❑	282 Richard Seymour RC	20.00	7.50
❑	283 Dan Morgan RC	20.00	7.50
❑	284 Tay Cody RC	8.00	3.00
❑	285 Alge Crumpler RC	25.00	10.00
❑	286 Robert Ferguson RC	20.00	7.50
❑	287 Will Peterson RC	12.00	5.00
❑	288 Tony Dixon RC	12.00	5.00
❑	289 Correll Buckhalter RC	20.00	7.50
❑	290 Rod Gardner RC	20.00	7.50
❑	291 Justin McCareins RC	20.00	7.50
❑	292 Josh Heupel RC	20.00	7.50
❑	293 Todd Heap RC	20.00	7.50
❑	294 Damione Lewis RC	12.00	5.00
❑	295 George Layne RC	12.00	5.00
❑	296 Jamie Winborn RC	12.00	5.00
❑	297 Billy Baber RC	8.00	3.00
❑	298 T.J. Houshmandzadeh RC	25.00	10.00
❑	299 Aaron Schobel RC	20.00	7.50
❑	300 Gary Baxter RC	12.00	5.00
❑	301 DeLawrence Grant RC	8.00	3.00
❑	302 Morlon Greenwood RC	12.00	5.00
❑	303 Shad Meier RC	12.00	5.00
❑	304 Torrance Marshall RC	20.00	7.50
❑	305 David Martin RC	12.00	5.00
❑	306 Anthony Henry RC	20.00	7.50
❑	307 Derrick Burgess RC	20.00	7.50
❑	308 Andre Dyson RC	8.00	3.00
❑	309 Ryan Helming RC	8.00	3.00
❑	310 Fred Smoot RC	20.00	7.50
❑	311 Arther Love RC	8.00	3.00
❑	312 John Capel RC	12.00	5.00
❑	313 Brandon Spoon RC	12.00	5.00
❑	314 Karon Riley RC	8.00	3.00
❑	315 Andre King RC	12.00	5.00
❑	316 Quentin McCord RC	12.00	5.00
❑	317 Zeke Moreno RC	20.00	7.50
❑	318 Francis St. Paul RC	12.00	5.00
❑	319 Richmond Flowers RC	12.00	5.00
❑	320 Derek Combs RC	12.00	5.00

2002 Topps Chrome

❑	COMP.SET w/o SP's (165)	50.00	20.00
❑	1 Anthony Thomas	.75	.30
❑	2 Jake Plummer	.75	.30
❑	3 Maurice Smith	.75	.30
❑	4 Jamal Lewis	1.25	.50
❑	5 Ray Lewis	1.25	.50
❑	6 Alex Van Pelt	.50	.20
❑	7 Chris Weinke	.75	.30
❑	8 Corey Dillon	.75	.30
❑	9 Quincy Morgan	.50	.20
❑	10 Rocket Ismail	.75	.30
❑	11 Brian Griese	1.25	.50
❑	12 Johnnie Morton	.75	.30
❑	13 Edgerrin James	1.50	.60
❑	14 Keenan McCardell	.50	.20
❑	15 Travis Minor	.75	.30
❑	16 Sylvester Morris	.50	.20
❑	17 Randy Moss	2.50	1.00
❑	18 Drew Bledsoe	1.50	.60
❑	19 Willie Jackson	.50	.20
❑	20 Michael Strahan	.75	.30
❑	21 Santana Moss	1.25	.50
❑	22 Duce Staley	1.25	.50
❑	23 Kendrell Bell	1.25	.50
❑	24 LaDainian Tomlinson	2.00	.75
❑	25 Terrell Owens	1.25	.50
❑	26 Shaun Alexander	1.50	.60
❑	27 Trung Canidate	.75	.30
❑	28 Mike Alstott	1.25	.50
❑	29 Kevin Dyson	.75	.30
❑	30 Rod Gardner	.75	.30
❑	31 David Boston	1.25	.50
❑	32 Michael Vick	4.00	1.50
❑	33 Qadry Ismail	.75	.30
❑	34 Peerless Price	.75	.30
❑	35 Rob Johnson	.75	.30
❑	36 Marcus Robinson	.75	.30
❑	37 Peter Warrick	.75	.30
❑	38 Kevin Johnson	.75	.30
❑	39 Ed McCaffrey	1.25	.50
❑	40 Shaun Rogers	.50	.20
❑	41 Marvin Harrison	1.25	.50
❑	42 Priest Holmes	1.50	.60
❑	43 Oronde Gadsden	.75	.30
❑	44 Terry Glenn	.75	.30
❑	45 Ike Hilliard	.75	.30
❑	46 Charles Woodson	.75	.30
❑	47 Freddie Mitchell	.75	.30
❑	48 Drew Brees	1.25	.50
❑	49 Jeff Garcia	1.25	.50
❑	50 Kurt Warner	1.25	.50
❑	51 Keyshawn Johnson	1.25	.50
❑	52 Jevon Kearse	.75	.30
❑	53 Stephen Davis	.75	.30
❑	54 Shannon Sharpe	.75	.30
❑	55 Eric Moulds	.75	.30
❑	56 Muhsin Muhammad	.75	.30
❑	57 Brian Urlacher	2.00	.75
❑	58 Chad Johnson	1.25	.50
❑	59 Tim Couch	.75	.30
❑	60 Mike Anderson	1.25	.50
❑	61 James Stewart	.75	.30
❑	62 Corey Bradford	.50	.20
❑	63 Reggie Wayne	1.25	.50
❑	64 Mark Brunell	1.25	.50
❑	65 Trent Green	.75	.30
❑	66 Zach Thomas	1.25	.50
❑	67 Michael Bennett	.75	.30
❑	68 Troy Brown	.75	.30
❑	69 Amani Toomer	.75	.30
❑	70 Curtis Martin	1.25	.50
❑	71 Tim Brown	1.25	.50
❑	72 Correll Buckhalter	.75	.30
❑	73 Kordell Stewart	.75	.30
❑	74 Junior Seau	1.25	.50
❑	75 Kevan Barlow	.75	.30
❑	76 Matt Hasselbeck	.75	.30
❑	77 Marshall Faulk	1.25	.50
❑	78 Warren Sapp	.75	.30
❑	79 Frank Wycheck	.50	.20
❑	80 Michael Westbrook	.50	.20
❑	81 Travis Henry	1.25	.50
❑	82 David Terrell	1.25	.50
❑	83 Jon Kitna	.75	.30
❑	84 James Jackson	.50	.20
❑	85 Joey Galloway	.75	.30
❑	86 Rod Smith	.75	.30
❑	87 Germane Crowell	.50	.20
❑	88 Bill Schroeder	.75	.30
❑	89 Dominic Rhodes	.75	.30
❑	90 Fred Taylor	1.25	.50
❑	91 Snoop Minnis	.50	.20
❑	92 Chris Chambers	1.25	.50
❑	93 Daunte Culpepper	1.25	.50
❑	94 Deuce McAllister	1.50	.60
❑	95 Kerry Collins	.75	.30
❑	96 John Abraham	.75	.30
❑	97 Rich Gannon	1.25	.50
❑	98 Tiki Barber	1.25	.50
❑	99 Hines Ward	1.25	.50
❑	100 Tom Brady	3.00	1.25
❑	101 Tim Dwight	.75	.30
❑	102 Garrison Hearst	.75	.30
❑	103 Darrell Jackson	.75	.30
❑	104 Isaac Bruce	1.25	.50
❑	105 Brad Johnson	.75	.30
❑	106 Steve McNair	1.25	.50
❑	107 Champ Bailey	.75	.30
❑	108 Emmitt Smith	3.00	1.25
❑	109 Mike McMahon	1.25	.50
❑	110 Terrell Davis	1.25	.50
❑	111 Antonio Freeman	1.25	.50
❑	112 Jimmy Smith	.75	.30
❑	113 Tony Gonzalez	.75	.30
❑	114 Jay Fiedler	.75	.30
❑	115 Cris Carter	1.25	.50
❑	116 David Patten	.50	.20
❑	117 Joe Horn	.75	.30
❑	118 Laveranues Coles	.75	.30
❑	119 Charlie Garner	.75	.30
❑	120 Donovan McNabb	1.50	.60
❑	121 Jerome Bettis	1.25	.50
❑	122 Curtis Conway	.50	.20
❑	123 Az-Zahir Hakim	.50	.20
❑	124 Warrick Dunn	1.25	.50
❑	125 Eddie George	1.25	.50
❑	126 Quincy Carter	.75	.30
❑	127 Ahman Green	1.25	.50
❑	128 Peyton Manning	2.50	1.00
❑	129 James McKnight	.50	.20
❑	130 Antowain Smith	.75	.30
❑	131 Ricky Williams	8.00	3.00
❑	132 Chad Pennington	1.50	.60
❑	133 Jerry Rice	2.50	1.00
❑	134 Todd Pinkston	.75	.30
❑	135 Plaxico Burress	.75	.30
❑	136 Doug Flutie	1.25	.50
❑	137 Koren Robinson	.75	.30
❑	138 Torry Holt	1.25	.50
❑	139 Aaron Brooks	1.25	.50
❑	140 Ron Dayne	.75	.30
❑	141 Vinny Testaverde	.75	.30

❑ 142 Brett Favre	3.00	1.25
❑ 143 James Thrash	.75	.30
❑ 144 Wayne Chrebet	.75	.30
❑ 145 Derrick Mason	.75	.30
❑ 146 Ahman Green WWU	.75	.30
❑ 147 Peyton Manning WWU	1.25	.50
❑ 148 Kurt Warner WWU	.75	.30
❑ 149 Daunte Culpepper WWU	.75	.30
❑ 150 Tom Brady WWU	1.50	.60
❑ 151 Rod Gardner WWU	.75	.30
❑ 152 Corey Dillon WWU	.75	.30
❑ 153 Priest Holmes WWU	1.00	.40
❑ 154 Shaun Alexander WWU	1.00	.40
❑ 155 Randy Moss WWU	1.25	.50
❑ 156 Eric Moulds WWU	.50	.20
❑ 157 Brett Favre WWU	1.50	.60
❑ 158 Todd Bouman WWU	.50	.20
❑ 159 Dominic Rhodes WWU	.50	.20
❑ 160 Marvin Harrison WWU	.75	.30
❑ 161 Torry Holt WWU	1.25	.50
❑ 162 Derrick Mason WWU	.50	.20
❑ 163 Jerry Rice WWU	1.25	.50
❑ 164 Donovan McNabb WWU	1.25	.50
❑ 165 Marshall Faulk WWU	1.25	.50
❑ 166 David Carr RC	30.00	12.50
❑ 167 Quentin Jammer RC	10.00	4.00
❑ 168 Mike Williams RC	8.00	3.00
❑ 169 Rocky Calmus RC	10.00	4.00
❑ 170 Travis Fisher RC	10.00	4.00
❑ 171 Dwight Freeney RC	15.00	6.00
❑ 172 Jeremy Shockey RC	40.00	15.00
❑ 173 Marquise Walker RC	8.00	3.00
❑ 174 Eric Crouch RC	10.00	4.00
❑ 175 DeShaun Foster RC	10.00	4.00
❑ 176 Roy Williams RC	25.00	12.50
❑ 177 Andre Davis RC	8.00	3.00
❑ 178 Alex Brown RC	10.00	4.00
❑ 179 Michael Lewis RC	10.00	4.00
❑ 180 Terry Charles RC	8.00	3.00
❑ 181 Clinton Portis RC	40.00	15.00
❑ 182 Dennis Johnson RC	5.00	2.00
❑ 183 Lito Sheppard RC	10.00	4.00
❑ 184 Ryan Sims RC	10.00	4.00
❑ 185 Raonall Smith RC	8.00	3.00
❑ 186 Albert Haynesworth RC	8.00	3.00
❑ 187 Eddie Freeman RC	5.00	2.00
❑ 188 Levi Jones RC	8.00	3.00
❑ 189 Josh McCown RC	12.00	5.00
❑ 190 Cliff Russell RC	8.00	3.00
❑ 191 Maurice Morris RC	10.00	4.00
❑ 192 Antwaan Randle El RC	15.00	6.00
❑ 193 Ladell Betts RC	10.00	4.00
❑ 194 Daniel Graham RC	10.00	4.00
❑ 195 David Garrard RC	10.00	4.00
❑ 196 Antonio Bryant RC	10.00	4.00
❑ 197 Patrick Ramsey RC	12.00	5.00
❑ 198 Kelly Campbell RC	8.00	3.00
❑ 199 Will Overstreet RC	5.00	2.00
❑ 200 Ryan Denney RC	8.00	3.00
❑ 201 John Henderson RC	10.00	4.00
❑ 202 Freddie Milons RC	8.00	3.00
❑ 203 Tim Carter RC	8.00	3.00
❑ 204 Kurt Kittner RC	8.00	3.00
❑ 205 Joey Harrington RC	15.00	6.00
❑ 206 Ricky Williams RC	8.00	3.00
❑ 207 Bryant McKinnie RC	8.00	3.00
❑ 208 Ed Reed RC	15.00	6.00
❑ 209 Josh Reed RC	10.00	4.00
❑ 210 Seth Burford RC	8.00	3.00
❑ 211 Javon Walker RC	20.00	7.50
❑ 212 Jamar Martin RC	8.00	3.00
❑ 213 Leonard Henry RC	8.00	3.00
❑ 214 Julius Peppers RC	20.00	7.50
❑ 215 Jabar Gaffney RC	10.00	4.00
❑ 216 Kalimba Edwards RC	10.00	4.00
❑ 217 Napoleon Harris RC	10.00	4.00
❑ 218 Ashley Lelie RC	20.00	7.50
❑ 219 Anthony Weaver RC	8.00	3.00
❑ 220 Bryan Thomas RC	8.00	3.00
❑ 221 Wendell Bryant RC	5.00	2.00
❑ 222 Damien Anderson RC	8.00	3.00
❑ 223 Travis Stephens RC	8.00	3.00
❑ 224 Rohan Davey RC	10.00	4.00
❑ 225 Mike Pearson RC	5.00	2.00
❑ 226 Marc Colombo RC	5.00	2.00
❑ 227 Phillip Buchanon RC	10.00	4.00
❑ 228 T.J. Duckett RC	12.00	5.00
❑ 229 Ron Johnson RC	8.00	3.00
❑ 230 Larry Tripplett RC	5.00	2.00
❑ 231 Randy Fasani RC	8.00	3.00
❑ 232 Keyuo Craver RC	8.00	3.00
❑ 233 Marquand Manuel RC	5.00	2.00
❑ 234 Jonathan Wells RC	10.00	4.00
❑ 235 Reche Caldwell RC	10.00	4.00
❑ 236 Luke Staley RC	8.00	3.00
❑ 237 Donte Stallworth RC	20.00	7.50
❑ 238 Levar Fisher RC	10.00	4.00
❑ 239 Lamar Gordon RC	10.00	4.00
❑ 240 William Green RC	10.00	4.00
❑ 241 Dusty Bonner RC	5.00	2.00
❑ 242 Craig Nall RC	10.00	4.00
❑ 243 Eric McCoo RC	5.00	2.00
❑ 244 David Thornton RC	5.00	2.00
❑ 245 Terry Jones RC	8.00	3.00
❑ 246 Lee Mays RC	10.00	4.00
❑ 247 Bryan Fletcher RC	5.00	2.00
❑ 248 Verron Haynes RC	10.00	4.00
❑ 249 Zak Kustok RC	10.00	4.00
❑ 250 Chad Hutchinson RC	8.00	3.00
❑ 251 Andra Davis RC	8.00	3.00
❑ 252 Wes Pate RC	5.00	2.00
❑ 253 Jon McGraw RC	5.00	2.00
❑ 254 Howard Green RC	5.00	2.00
❑ 255 Daryl Jones RC	8.00	3.00
❑ 256 David Priestley RC	8.00	3.00
❑ 257 Marques Anderson RC	10.00	4.00
❑ 258 Roosevelt Williams RC	5.00	2.00
❑ 259 Major Applewhite RC	10.00	4.00
❑ 260 Ronald Curry RC	10.00	4.00
❑ 261 Adrian Peterson RC	10.00	4.00
❑ 262 Tellis Redmon RC	8.00	3.00
❑ 263 Chester Taylor RC	20.00	7.50
❑ 264 Deion Branch RC	25.00	12.50
❑ 265 Tank Williams RC	5.00	2.00

2003 Topps Chrome

❑ COMP.SET w/o SP's (165)	40.00	15.00
❑ 1 Michael Vick	3.00	1.25
❑ 2 Josh Reed	.75	.30
❑ 3 James Stewart	.75	.30
❑ 4 Quincy Morgan	.75	.30
❑ 5 Corey Bradford	.50	.20
❑ 6 Fred Taylor	1.25	.50
❑ 7 David Patten	.50	.20
❑ 8 Jerome Bettis	1.25	.50
❑ 9 Jerry Porter	.75	.30
❑ 10 Steve McNair	1.25	.50
❑ 11 Stephen Davis	.75	.30
❑ 12 Frank Wycheck	.50	.20
❑ 13 Marcus Pollard	.50	.20
❑ 14 David Terrell	.75	.30
❑ 15 Bubba Franks	.75	.30
❑ 16 Trent Green	.75	.30
❑ 17 Mark Brunell	.75	.30
❑ 18 James Thrash	.50	.20
❑ 19 Mike Alstott	1.25	.50
❑ 20 Deuce McAllister	1.25	.50
❑ 21 Santana Moss	.75	.30
❑ 22 Jason Taylor	.50	.20
❑ 23 Corey Dillon	.75	.30
❑ 24 Jeff Blake	.50	.20
❑ 25 Ed McCaffrey	1.25	.50
❑ 26 Priest Holmes	1.50	.60
❑ 27 Tim Brown	1.25	.50
❑ 28 Curtis Martin	1.25	.50
❑ 29 Derrius Thompson	.50	.20
❑ 30 Jonathan Wells	.50	.20
❑ 31 William Green	.75	.30
❑ 32 Bill Schroeder	.75	.30
❑ 33 Amos Zereoue	.75	.30
❑ 34 Warren Sapp	.75	.30
❑ 35 Koren Robinson	.75	.30
❑ 36 Donovan McNabb	1.50	.60
❑ 37 Edgerrin James	1.25	.50
❑ 38 Kelly Holcomb	.75	.30
❑ 39 Daunte Culpepper	1.25	.50
❑ 40 Tommy Maddox	1.25	.50
❑ 41 Rod Gardner	.75	.30
❑ 42 T.J. Duckett	.75	.30
❑ 43 Drew Bledsoe	1.25	.50
❑ 44 Rod Smith	.75	.30
❑ 45 Peyton Manning	2.00	.75
❑ 46 Darrell Jackson	.75	.30
❑ 47 Brett Favre	3.00	1.25
❑ 48 Ashley Lelie	1.25	.50
❑ 49 Jeremy Shockey	2.00	.75
❑ 50 Hines Ward	1.25	.50
❑ 51 Jeff Garcia	1.25	.50
❑ 52 Eddie Kennison	.50	.20
❑ 53 Brian Urlacher	2.00	.75
❑ 54 Antwaan Randle El	1.25	.50
❑ 55 Eddie George	.75	.30
❑ 56 Derrick Brooks	.75	.30
❑ 57 Isaac Bruce	1.25	.50
❑ 58 Joe Horn	.75	.30
❑ 59 Jon Kitna	.75	.30
❑ 60 David Boston	.75	.30
❑ 61 Todd Heap	.75	.30
❑ 62 Lamar Smith	.50	.20
❑ 63 Germane Crowell	.50	.20
❑ 64 Kevin Johnson	.75	.30
❑ 65 Drew Brees	1.25	.50
❑ 66 Chad Lewis	.50	.20
❑ 67 Charlie Garner	.75	.30
❑ 68 Laveranues Coles	.75	.30
❑ 69 Shaun Alexander	1.25	.50
❑ 70 Kevan Barlow	.75	.30
❑ 71 Aaron Brooks	1.25	.50
❑ 72 Jake Plummer	.75	.30
❑ 73 Emmitt Smith	3.00	1.25
❑ 74 Terry Glenn	.50	.20
❑ 75 Michael Bennett	.75	.30
❑ 76 Deion Branch	1.25	.50
❑ 77 Keyshawn Johnson	1.25	.50
❑ 78 Marc Bulger	1.25	.50
❑ 79 Matt Hasselbeck	.75	.30
❑ 80 Garrison Hearst	.75	.30
❑ 81 Brian Griese	1.25	.50
❑ 82 Johnnie Morton	.75	.30
❑ 83 Patrick Ramsey	1.25	.50
❑ 84 Donald Driver	.75	.30
❑ 85 Joey Harrington	2.00	.75
❑ 86 Ricky Williams	1.25	.50
❑ 87 Jabar Gaffney	.75	.30
❑ 88 Duce Staley	.75	.30
❑ 89 Jimmy Smith	.75	.30
❑ 90 Reggie Wayne	.75	.30
❑ 91 Chad Johnson	1.25	.50
❑ 92 Steve Beuerlein	.50	.20
❑ 93 Joey Galloway	.75	.30
❑ 94 Curtis Conway	.50	.20
❑ 95 Brad Johnson	.75	.30
❑ 96 Jamal Lewis	1.25	.50
❑ 97 Terrell Owens	1.25	.50
❑ 98 Todd Pinkston	.75	.30
❑ 99 Keenan McCardell	.50	.20
❑ 100 Antonio Bryant	.75	.30
❑ 101 Eric Moulds	.75	.30
❑ 102 Jim Miller	.50	.20
❑ 103 Troy Brown	.75	.30
❑ 104 Rich Gannon	.75	.30
❑ 105 Chad Pennington	1.50	.60
❑ 106 Michael Strahan	.75	.30
❑ 107 Chris Chambers	1.25	.50
❑ 108 Antowain Smith	.75	.30
❑ 109 Derrick Mason	.75	.30
❑ 110 Michael Pittman	.50	.20
❑ 111 Torry Holt	1.25	.50
❑ 112 Tony Gonzalez	.75	.30
❑ 113 Marty Booker	.75	.30
❑ 114 Shannon Sharpe	.50	.20
❑ 115 Zach Thomas	1.25	.50
❑ 116 Plaxico Burress	.75	.30

❑ 117 Kurt Warner 1.25 .50
❑ 118 Warrick Dunn .75 .30
❑ 119 Jay Fiedler .75 .30
❑ 120 LaMont Jordan 1.25 .50
❑ 121 Kerry Collins .75 .30
❑ 122 Jerry Rice 2.50 1.00
❑ 123 Randy Moss 2.00 .75
❑ 124 Tom Brady 3.00 1.25
❑ 125 Amani Toomer .75 .30
❑ 126 Travis Henry .75 .30
❑ 127 Chris Chandler .50 .20
❑ 128 Ray Lewis 1.25 .50
❑ 129 Donte Stallworth 1.25 .50
❑ 130 David Carr 2.00 .75
❑ 131 Andre Davis .50 .20
❑ 132 Travis Taylor .75 .30
❑ 133 Steve Smith 1.25 .50
❑ 134 Tiki Barber 1.25 .50
❑ 135 Chad Hutchinson .50 .20
❑ 136 Marshall Faulk 1.25 .50
❑ 137 Peerless Price .75 .30
❑ 138 Ahman Green 1.25 .50
❑ 139 Julius Peppers 1.25 .50
❑ 140 LaDainian Tomlinson 1.25 .50
❑ 141 Muhsin Muhammad .75 .30
❑ 142 Tim Couch .50 .20
❑ 143 Clinton Portis 2.00 .75
❑ 144 Anthony Thomas .75 .30
❑ 145 Marvin Harrison 1.25 .50
❑ 146 Priest Holmes WW .75 .30
❑ 147 Drew Bledsoe WW .75 .30
❑ 148 Tom Brady WW 1.25 .50
❑ 149 Shaun Alexander WW .75 .30
❑ 150 Brett Favre WW 1.25 .50
❑ 151 Travis Henry WW .50 .20
❑ 152 Marshall Faulk WW .75 .30
❑ 153 Terrell Owens WW .50 .20
❑ 154 Jeff Garcia WW .50 .20
❑ 155 Plaxico Burress WW .50 .20
❑ 156 Donovan McNabb WW .75 .30
❑ 157 Ricky Williams WW .75 .30
❑ 158 Michael Vick WW 1.50 .60
❑ 159 Steve Smith WW .75 .30
❑ 160 Marvin Harrison WW .50 .20
❑ 161 Chad Pennington WW .75 .30
❑ 162 Jeremy Shockey WW .75 .30
❑ 163 Tommy Maddox WW .50 .20
❑ 164 Steve McNair WW .50 .20
❑ 165 Rich Gannon WW .50 .20
❑ 166 Carson Palmer RC 30.00 15.00
❑ 167 J.R. Tolver RC 6.00 2.50
❑ 168 Michael Haynes RC 8.00 3.00
❑ 169 Terrell Suggs RC 12.00 5.00
❑ 170 Rashean Mathis RC 6.00 2.50
❑ 171 Chris Kelsay RC 8.00 3.00
❑ 172 Brad Banks RC 6.00 2.50
❑ 173 Jordan Gross RC 6.00 2.50
❑ 174 Lee Suggs RC 8.00 3.00
❑ 175 Kliff Kingsbury RC 6.00 2.50
❑ 176 William Joseph RC 8.00 3.00
❑ 177 Kelley Washington RC 8.00 3.00
❑ 178 Jerome McDougle RC 8.00 3.00
❑ 179 Keenan Howry RC 8.00 3.00
❑ 180 Chris Simms RC 12.00 5.00
❑ 181 Alonzo Jackson RC 6.00 2.50
❑ 182 L.J. Smith RC 8.00 3.00
❑ 183 Mike Doss RC 8.00 3.00
❑ 184 Bobby Wade RC 8.00 3.00
❑ 185 Ken Hamlin RC 8.00 3.00
❑ 186 Brandon Lloyd RC 8.00 3.00
❑ 187 Justin Fargas RC 8.00 3.00
❑ 188 DeWayne Robertson RC 8.00 3.00
❑ 189 Bryant Johnson RC 8.00 3.00
❑ 190 Boss Bailey RC 8.00 3.00
❑ 191 Onterrio Smith RC 8.00 3.00
❑ 192 Doug Gabriel RC 8.00 3.00
❑ 193 Jimmy Kennedy RC 8.00 3.00
❑ 194 B.J. Askew RC 8.00 3.00
❑ 195 Taylor Jacobs RC 6.00 2.50
❑ 196 Dallas Clark RC 8.00 3.00
❑ 197 DeWayne White RC 6.00 2.50
❑ 198 Arnaz Battle RC 8.00 3.00
❑ 199 Kareem Kelly RC 6.00 2.50
❑ 200 Talman Gardner RC 8.00 3.00
❑ 201 Billy McMullen RC 6.00 2.50
❑ 202 Travis Anglin RC 4.00 1.50
❑ 203 Anquan Boldin RC 20.00 10.00
❑ 204 Osi Umenyiora RC 12.00 5.00
❑ 205 Byron Leftwich RC 25.00 10.00
❑ 206 Marcus Trufant RC 8.00 3.00
❑ 207 Sam Aiken RC 6.00 2.50
❑ 208 LaBrandon Toefield RC 8.00 3.00
❑ 209 Terry Pierce RC 6.00 2.50
❑ 210 Charles Rogers RC 8.00 3.00
❑ 211 Chaun Thompson RC 4.00 1.50
❑ 212 Chris Brown RC 8.00 3.00
❑ 213 Justin Gage RC 8.00 3.00
❑ 214 Kevin Williams RC 8.00 3.00
❑ 215 Willis McGahee RC 20.00 7.50
❑ 216 Victor Hobson RC 8.00 3.00
❑ 217 Brian St.Pierre RC 8.00 3.00
❑ 218 Nate Burleson RC 8.00 3.00
❑ 219 Calvin Pace RC 6.00 2.50
❑ 220 Larry Johnson RC 30.00 18.00
❑ 221 Andre Woolfolk RC 8.00 3.00
❑ 222 Tyrone Calico RC 8.00 3.00
❑ 223 Seneca Wallace RC 8.00 3.00
❑ 224 Domanick Davis RC 8.00 3.00
❑ 225 Rex Grossman RC 25.00 10.00
❑ 226 Artose Pinner RC 8.00 3.00
❑ 227 Jason Witten RC 12.00 5.00
❑ 228 Bennie Joppru RC 8.00 3.00
❑ 229 Bethel Johnson RC 8.00 3.00
❑ 230 Kyle Boller RC 8.00 3.00
❑ 231 Shaun McDonald RC 8.00 3.00
❑ 232 Musa Smith RC 8.00 3.00
❑ 233 Ken Dorsey RC 8.00 3.00
❑ 234 Johnathan Sullivan RC 6.00 2.50
❑ 235 Andre Johnson RC 15.00 6.00
❑ 236 Nick Barnett RC 8.00 3.00
❑ 237 Teyo Johnson RC 8.00 3.00
❑ 238 Terence Newman RC 15.00 6.00
❑ 239 Kevin Curtis RC 8.00 3.00
❑ 240 Dave Ragone RC 8.00 3.00
❑ 241 Ty Warren RC 8.00 3.00
❑ 242 Walter Young RC 4.00 1.50
❑ 243 Kevin Walter RC 6.00 2.50
❑ 244 Carl Ford RC 4.00 1.50
❑ 245 Cecil Sapp RC 6.00 2.50
❑ 246 Sultan McCullough RC 6.00 2.50
❑ 247 Eugene Wilson RC 8.00 3.00
❑ 248 Ricky Manning RC 8.00 3.00
❑ 249 Andrew Williams RC 6.00 2.50
❑ 250 Juston Wood RC 4.00 1.50
❑ 251 Cory Redding RC 6.00 2.50
❑ 252 Charles Tillman RC 10.00 4.00
❑ 253 Terrence Edwards RC 6.00 2.50
❑ 254 Adrian Madise RC 6.00 2.50
❑ 255 David Kircus RC 8.00 3.00
❑ 256 Zuriel Smith RC 4.00 1.50
❑ 257 Earnest Graham RC 6.00 2.50
❑ 258 Ronald Bellamy RC 6.00 2.50
❑ 259 John Anderson RC 4.00 1.50
❑ 260 David Tyree RC 6.00 2.50
❑ 261 Malaefou MacKenzie RC 4.00 1.50
❑ 262 Ahmaad Galloway RC 6.00 2.50
❑ 263 Brooks Bollinger RC 8.00 3.00
❑ 264 Gibran Hamdan RC 4.00 1.50
❑ 265 Taco Wallace RC 6.00 2.50
❑ 266 LaTarence Dunbar RC 6.00 2.50
❑ 267 Justin Griffith RC 6.00 2.50
❑ 268 Bradie James RC 8.00 3.00
❑ 269 Danny Curley RC 4.00 1.50
❑ 270 Kenny Peterson RC 6.00 2.50
❑ 271 DeAndrew Rubin RC 4.00 1.50
❑ 272 Ryan Hoag RC 4.00 1.50
❑ 273 Rien Long RC 4.00 1.50
❑ 274 Troy Polamalu RC 30.00 15.00
❑ 275 Terrence Holt RC 6.00 2.50

2004 Topps Chrome

❑ COMP.SET w/o SP's (165) 30.00 12.50
❑ 1 Peyton Manning 1.50 .60
❑ 2 Patrick Ramsey .60 .25
❑ 3 Justin McCareins .40 .15
❑ 4 Matt Hasselbeck .60 .25
❑ 5 Chris Chambers .60 .25
❑ 6 Bubba Franks .60 .25
❑ 7 Eric Moulds .60 .25
❑ 8 Anquan Boldin 1.00 .40
❑ 9 Brian Urlacher 1.25 .50
❑ 10 Stephen Davis .60 .25
❑ 11 Michael Vick 2.00 .75
❑ 12 Dante Hall 1.00 .40
❑ 13 Chad Pennington 1.00 .40
❑ 14 Kevan Barlow .60 .25
❑ 15 Tommy Maddox .60 .25
❑ 16 Domanick Davis 1.00 .40
❑ 17 Dwight Freeney .60 .25
❑ 18 LaVar Arrington 2.00 .75
❑ 19 Troy Hambrick .40 .15
❑ 20 Jake Plummer .60 .25
❑ 21 Willis McGahee 1.00 .40
❑ 22 Steve McNair 1.00 .40
❑ 23 Kerry Collins .60 .25
❑ 24 Hines Ward 1.00 .40
❑ 25 Terrell Owens 1.00 .40
❑ 26 Jerome Pathon .40 .15
❑ 27 Andre Johnson 1.00 .40
❑ 28 DeShaun Foster .60 .25
❑ 29 Terrell Suggs .60 .25
❑ 30 Marcel Shipp .60 .25
❑ 31 Kyle Boller 1.00 .40
❑ 32 Javon Walker .60 .25
❑ 33 Ahman Green 1.00 .40
❑ 34 Travis Henry .60 .25
❑ 35 Randy McMichael .40 .15
❑ 36 Jerry Rice 2.00 .75
❑ 37 Travis Taylor .40 .15
❑ 38 Fred Taylor .60 .25
❑ 39 Zach Thomas 1.00 .40
❑ 40 Marques Tuiasosopo .60 .25
❑ 41 Laveranues Coles .60 .25
❑ 42 Thomas Jones .60 .25
❑ 43 Jamie Sharper .40 .15
❑ 44 Quincy Morgan .60 .25
❑ 45 Troy Brown .60 .25
❑ 46 Joey Galloway .60 .25
❑ 47 Justin Fargas .60 .25
❑ 48 Daunte Culpepper 1.00 .40
❑ 49 Keenan McCardell .40 .15
❑ 50 Priest Holmes 1.25 .50
❑ 51 Chad Johnson 1.00 .40
❑ 52 Marty Booker .60 .25
❑ 53 Tim Rattay .40 .15
❑ 54 Brian Westbrook .60 .25
❑ 55 Ricky Williams 1.00 .40
❑ 56 Lee Suggs 1.00 .40
❑ 57 Keith Brooking .40 .15
❑ 58 Rex Grossman 1.00 .40
❑ 59 Dallas Clark .60 .25
❑ 60 Charles Rogers .60 .25
❑ 61 Donte' Stallworth .60 .25
❑ 62 Deion Branch 1.00 .40
❑ 63 Ike Hilliard .40 .15
❑ 64 Michael Strahan .60 .25
❑ 65 Randy Moss 1.25 .50
❑ 66 Isaac Bruce .60 .25
❑ 67 Brad Johnson .60 .25
❑ 68 Warrick Dunn .60 .25
❑ 69 Josh McCown .60 .25
❑ 70 Donovan McNabb 1.25 .50
❑ 71 Shaun Alexander 1.00 .40
❑ 72 William Green .60 .25
❑ 73 Carson Palmer 1.25 .50
❑ 74 Quentin Griffin 1.00 .40
❑ 75 LaDainian Tomlinson 1.25 .50
❑ 76 Edgerrin James 1.00 .40
❑ 77 Santana Moss .60 .25
❑ 78 Marshall Faulk 1.00 .40
❑ 79 Tyrone Calico .60 .25
❑ 80 Marvin Harrison 1.00 .40
❑ 81 Tony Gonzalez .60 .25
❑ 82 Deuce McAllister 1.00 .40

No.	Player		
83	Drew Brees	1.00	.40
84	Todd Pinkston	.40	.15
85	Jeff Garcia	1.00	.40
86	Darrell Jackson	.60	.25
87	Ray Lewis	1.00	.40
88	Billy Volek	1.00	.40
89	Rudi Johnson	.60	.25
90	Julius Peppers	1.00	.40
91	Peter Warrick	.60	.25
92	Trent Green	.60	.25
93	Onterrio Smith	.60	.25
94	Jerome Bettis	1.00	.40
95	Keyshawn Johnson	.60	.25
96	Jamal Lewis	1.00	.40
97	Alge Crumpler	.60	.25
98	Michael Bennett	.60	.25
99	Jimmy Smith	.60	.25
100	Brett Favre	2.50	1.00
101	Jerry Porter	.60	.25
102	Marc Bulger	1.00	.40
103	David Carr	1.00	.40
104	Mark Brunell	.60	.25
105	Aaron Brooks	.60	.25
106	Plaxico Burress	.60	.25
107	Correll Buckhalter	.60	.25
108	Jevon Kearse	.60	.25
109	Michael Pittman	.40	.15
110	Clinton Portis	1.00	.40
111	Corey Dillon	.60	.25
112	Steve Smith	1.00	.40
113	Eddie Kennison	.40	.15
114	Amani Toomer	.60	.25
115	Kelly Holcomb	.60	.25
116	Torry Holt	1.00	.40
117	Eddie George	.60	.25
118	Jeremy Shockey	1.00	.40
119	Jon Kitna	.60	.25
120	Todd Heap	.60	.25
121	Ashley Lelie	.60	.25
122	Byron Leftwich	1.25	.50
123	Duce Staley	.60	.25
124	Rod Gardner	.60	.25
125	Tom Brady	2.50	1.00
126	Reggie Wayne	.60	.25
127	Joe Horn	.60	.25
128	Curtis Martin	1.00	.40
129	Charlie Garner	.60	.25
130	Derrick Mason	.60	.25
131	Marcus Robinson	.60	.25
132	David Boston	.60	.25
133	Drew Bledsoe	1.00	.40
134	Anthony Thomas	.60	.25
135	Tiki Barber	1.00	.40
136	Terry Glenn	.40	.15
137	A.J. Feeley	1.00	.40
138	Peerless Price	.60	.25
139	Jake Delhomme	1.00	.40
140	Kevin Faulk	.40	.15
141	Quincy Carter	.60	.25
142	Joey Harrington	1.00	.40
143	Donald Driver	.60	.25
144	Koren Robinson	.60	.25
145	Rod Smith	.60	.25
146	Anquan Boldin WW	.40	.15
147	Jamal Lewis WW	.60	.25
148	Priest Holmes WW	1.00	.40
149	Peyton Manning WW	1.00	.40
150	Marvin Harrison WW	.60	.25
151	Steve McNair WW	.60	.25
152	Travis Henry WW	.40	.15
153	Torry Holt WW	.60	.25
154	Tom Brady WW	1.00	.40
155	Ahman Green WW	.60	.25
156	Donovan McNabb WW	1.00	.40
157	Deuce McAllister WW	.60	.25
158	Domanick Davis WW	.60	.25
159	Clinton Portis WW	1.00	.40
160	Rudi Johnson WW	.40	.15
161	Brett Favre WW	1.00	.40
162	LaDainian Tomlinson WW	.75	.30
163	Steve Smith WW	.60	.25
164	Edgerrin James WW	.60	.25
165	Ty Law WW	.40	.15
166	Ben Roethlisberger RC	40.00	20.00
167	Ahmad Carroll RC	5.00	2.00
168	Johnnie Morant RC	5.00	2.00
169	Greg Jones RC	5.00	2.00
170	Michael Clayton RC	10.00	4.00
171	Josh Harris RC	5.00	2.00
172	Tatum Bell RC	10.00	4.00
173	Robert Gallery RC	5.00	2.00
174	B.J. Symons RC	5.00	2.00
175	Roy Williams RC	12.00	5.00
176	DeAngelo Hall RC	6.00	2.50
177	Jeff Smoker RC	5.00	2.00
178	Lee Evans RC	6.00	2.50
179	Michael Jenkins RC	5.00	2.00
180	Steven Jackson RC	15.00	6.00
181	Will Smith RC	5.00	2.00
182	Vince Wilfork RC	5.00	2.00
183	Ben Troupe RC	5.00	2.00
184	Chris Gamble RC	5.00	2.00
185	Kevin Jones RC	12.00	5.00
186	Jonathan Vilma RC	5.00	2.00
187	Dontarrious Thomas RC	5.00	2.00
188	Michael Boulware RC	5.00	2.00
189	Mewelde Moore RC	5.00	2.00
190	Drew Henson RC	5.00	2.00
191	D.J. Williams RC	5.00	2.00
192	Ernest Wilford RC	5.00	2.00
193	John Navarre RC	5.00	2.00
194	Jerricho Cotchery RC	5.00	2.00
195	Derrick Hamilton RC	4.00	1.50
196	Carlos Francis RC	4.00	1.50
197	Ben Watson RC	5.00	2.00
198	Reggie Williams RC	6.00	2.50
199	Devard Darling RC	5.00	2.00
200	Chris Perry RC	8.00	3.00
201	Derrick Strait RC	5.00	2.00
202	Sean Taylor RC	5.00	2.00
203	Michael Turner RC	6.00	2.50
204	Keary Colbert RC	6.00	2.50
205	Eli Manning RC	30.00	15.00
206	Julius Jones RC	15.00	6.00
207	Jason Babin RC	5.00	2.00
208	Cody Pickett RC	5.00	2.00
209	Kenechi Udeze RC	5.00	2.00
210	Rashaun Woods RC	5.00	2.00
211	Matt Schaub RC	15.00	6.00
212	Tommie Harris RC	5.00	2.00
213	Dwan Edwards RC	2.50	1.00
214	Shawn Andrews RC	5.00	2.00
215	Larry Fitzgerald RC	15.00	6.00
216	P.K. Sam RC	4.00	1.50
217	Teddy Lehman RC	5.00	2.00
218	Darius Watts RC	5.00	2.00
219	D.J. Hackett RC	4.00	1.50
220	Cedric Cobbs RC	5.00	2.00
221	Antwan Odom RC	5.00	2.00
222	Marquise Hill RC	4.00	1.50
223	Luke McCown RC	5.00	2.00
224	Triandos Luke RC	5.00	2.00
225	Kellen Winslow RC	10.00	4.00
226	Derek Abney RC	5.00	2.00
227	Chris Cooley RC	5.00	2.00
228	Dunta Robinson RC	5.00	2.00
229	Sean Jones RC	4.00	1.50
230	Philip Rivers RC	20.00	8.00
231	Craig Krenzel RC	5.00	2.00
232	Daryl Smith RC	5.00	2.00
233	Samie Parker RC	5.00	2.00
234	Ben Hartsock RC	5.00	2.00
235	J.P. Losman RC	10.00	4.00
236	Karlos Dansby RC	5.00	2.00
237	Ricardo Colclough RC	5.00	2.00
238	Bernard Berrian RC	6.00	2.50
239	Junior Siavii RC	5.00	2.00
240	Devery Henderson RC	4.00	1.50
241	Adimchinobe Echemandu RC	4.00	1.50
242	Patrick Crayton RC	5.00	2.00
243	Marcus Tubbs RC	5.00	2.00
244	Jamaar Taylor RC	5.00	2.00
245	Andy Hall RC	4.00	1.50
246	Darnell Dockett RC	4.00	1.50
247	Darrion Scott RC	5.00	2.00
248	Jim Sorgi RC	5.00	2.00
249	Jeff Dugan RC	2.50	1.00
250	Ryan Krause RC	4.00	1.50
251	Nate Lawrie RC	4.00	1.50
252	Casey Bramlet RC	4.00	1.50
253	Donnell Washington RC	5.00	2.00
254	Jonathan Smith RC	4.00	1.50
255	Tank Johnson RC	4.00	1.50
256	Keith Smith RC	4.00	1.50
257	Brandon Miree RC	4.00	1.50
258	Michael Gaines RC	4.00	1.50
259	Keiwan Ratliff RC	4.00	1.50
260	Stuart Schweigert RC	5.00	2.00
261	Derrick Ward RC	2.50	1.00
262	Matt Ware RC	5.00	2.00
263	Tim Anderson RC	5.00	2.00
264	Bradlee Van Pelt RC	5.00	2.00
265	Shawntae Spencer RC	5.00	2.00
266	Joey Thomas RC	5.00	2.00
267	Maurice Mann RC	4.00	1.50
268	Tim Euhus RC	5.00	2.00
269	Matt Mauck RC	5.00	2.00
270	Sloan Thomas RC	4.00	1.50
271	Jeris McIntyre RC	4.00	1.50
272	Randy Starks RC	4.00	1.50
273	Clarence Moore RC	5.00	2.00
274	Drew Carter RC	5.00	2.00
275	Sean Ryan RC	4.00	1.50
RH38	Tom Brady RH	5.00	2.00

2005 Topps Chrome

COMPLETE SET (275)	150.00	75.00
COMP.SET w/o RC's (165)	30.00	12.50
ROOKIE STATED ODDS 1:2 HOB/RET		
RH STATED ODDS 1:288 HOB/RET		
RH REFRACT.ODDS 1:17,884 H, 1:22,080 R		

No.	Player		
1	Deuce McAllister	1.00	.40
2	Sean Taylor	.60	.25
3	Koren Robinson	.60	.25
4	Tiki Barber	1.00	.40
5	LaDainian Tomlinson	1.25	.50
6	Lee Evans	.60	.25
7	Aaron Brooks	.60	.25
8	LaMont Jordan	1.00	.40
9	Dante Hall	.60	.25
10	Daunte Culpepper	1.00	.40
11	Thomas Jones	.60	.25
12	Warrick Dunn	.60	.25
13	Willis McGahee	1.00	.40
14	Ed Reed	.60	.25
15	Derrick Mason	.60	.25
16	Jason Witten	.60	.25
17	Chad Johnson	1.00	.40
18	Amani Toomer	.60	.25
19	Joey Harrington	1.00	.40
20	Brian Urlacher	1.00	.40
21	Brian Westbrook	.60	.25
22	Matt Hasselbeck	.60	.25
23	Michael Vick	1.50	.60
24	Kevin Jones	1.00	.40
25	Julius Peppers	.60	.25
26	Michael Clayton	1.00	.40
27	Javon Walker	.60	.25
28	Santana Moss	.60	.25
29	Travis Henry	.60	.25
30	Stephen Davis	.60	.25
31	Larry Johnson	1.00	.40
32	Terrell Owens	1.00	.40
33	Ray Lewis	1.00	.40
34	Jake Plummer	.60	.25
35	Philip Rivers	1.00	.40
36	Eli Manning	2.00	.75
37	Tedy Bruschi	.60	.25
38	Adam Vinatieri	1.00	.40
39	J.P. Losman	1.00	.40
40	Zach Thomas	1.00	.40
41	Deion Branch	.60	.25
42	Andre Johnson	.60	.25

❑ 43 Marshall Faulk 1.00 .40
❑ 44 Bertrand Berry .50 .20
❑ 45 Terrell Suggs .60 .25
❑ 46 Tom Brady 2.50 1.00
❑ 47 Ashley Lelie .60 .25
❑ 48 Jonathan Wells .50 .20
❑ 49 Randy McMichael .50 .20
❑ 50 Charles Rogers .60 .25
❑ 51 Larry Fitzgerald 1.00 .40
❑ 52 Hines Ward 1.00 .40
❑ 53 Jason Taylor .50 .20
❑ 54 Ronde Barber .50 .20
❑ 55 T.J. Houshmandzadeh .50 .20
❑ 56 Keary Colbert .60 .25
❑ 57 DeAngelo Hall .60 .25
❑ 58 Chris Brown .60 .25
❑ 59 Chris Perry .60 .25
❑ 60 Steven Jackson 1.25 .50
❑ 61 Kyle Boller .60 .25
❑ 62 Rudi Johnson .60 .25
❑ 63 Roy Williams S .60 .25
❑ 64 Onterrio Smith .60 .25
❑ 65 Roy Williams WR 1.00 .40
❑ 66 Jerry Porter .60 .25
❑ 67 Edgerrin James 1.00 .40
❑ 68 Randy Moss 1.00 .40
❑ 69 Brian Griese .60 .25
❑ 70 Donovan McNabb 1.25 .50
❑ 71 Joe Horn .60 .25
❑ 72 Muhsin Muhammad .60 .25
❑ 73 Johnnie Morton .60 .25
❑ 74 Chad Pennington 1.00 .40
❑ 75 Torry Holt 1.00 .40
❑ 76 Marc Bulger 1.00 .40
❑ 77 Duce Staley .60 .25
❑ 78 Todd Heap .60 .25
❑ 79 Lee Suggs .60 .25
❑ 80 Patrick Ramsey .60 .25
❑ 81 Drew Bennett .60 .25
❑ 82 Michael Strahan .60 .25
❑ 83 Priest Holmes 1.00 .40
❑ 84 DeShaun Foster .60 .25
❑ 85 Corey Dillon .60 .25
❑ 86 Antonio Gates 1.00 .40
❑ 87 Trent Green .60 .25
❑ 88 Brandon Stokley .60 .25
❑ 89 Alge Crumpler .60 .25
❑ 90 Keyshawn Johnson .60 .25
❑ 91 Byron Leftwich 1.00 .40
❑ 92 Dunta Robinson .60 .25
❑ 93 Ben Roethlisberger 2.50 1.00
❑ 94 Rod Smith .60 .25
❑ 95 Robert Gallery .60 .25
❑ 96 Tony Gonzalez .60 .25
❑ 97 Steve McNair 1.00 .40
❑ 98 Jeremy Shockey 1.00 .40
❑ 99 Dominic Rhodes .50 .20
❑ 100 Michael Jenkins .60 .25
❑ 101 Jake Delhomme 1.00 .40
❑ 102 Jerome Bettis 1.00 .40
❑ 103 Jevon Kearse .60 .25
❑ 104 Plaxico Burress .60 .25
❑ 105 Dwight Freeney .60 .25
❑ 106 Marcus Robinson .60 .25
❑ 107 Rex Grossman .60 .25
❑ 108 Drew Henson .60 .25
❑ 109 Julius Jones 1.25 .50
❑ 110 Jamal Lewis 1.00 .40
❑ 111 Justin McCareins .50 .20
❑ 112 Billy Volek .60 .25
❑ 113 Curtis Martin 1.00 .40
❑ 114 Tatum Bell .60 .25
❑ 115 Domanick Davis .60 .25
❑ 116 Marvin Harrison 1.00 .40
❑ 117 Anquan Boldin .60 .25
❑ 118 Jimmy Smith .60 .25
❑ 119 Drew Brees 1.00 .40
❑ 120 Donte Stallworth .60 .25
❑ 121 Nate Burleson .60 .25
❑ 122 Fred Taylor .60 .25
❑ 123 Takeo Spikes .50 .20
❑ 124 Jonathan Ogden .50 .20
❑ 125 Michael Bennett .60 .25
❑ 126 Clinton Portis 1.00 .40
❑ 127 Ahman Green 1.00 .40
❑ 128 Drew Bledsoe 1.00 .40
❑ 129 Darrell Jackson .60 .25
❑ 130 Jonathan Vilma .60 .25
❑ 131 David Carr 1.00 .40
❑ 132 Champ Bailey .60 .25
❑ 133 Derrick Blaylock .50 .20
❑ 134 T.J. Duckett .60 .25
❑ 135 Shaun Alexander 1.25 .50
❑ 136 Peyton Manning 1.50 .60
❑ 137 Isaac Bruce .60 .25
❑ 138 LaVar Arrington 1.00 .40
❑ 139 Brett Favre 2.50 1.00
❑ 140 Allen Rossum .50 .20
❑ 141 Eric Moulds .60 .25
❑ 142 Carson Palmer 1.00 .40
❑ 143 Laveranues Coles .60 .25
❑ 144 Chester Taylor .60 .25
❑ 145 Reggie Wayne .60 .25
❑ 146 Curtis Martin LL .60 .25
❑ 147 Daunte Culpepper LL .60 .25
❑ 148 Muhsin Muhammad LL .50 .20
❑ 149 Shaun Alexander LL 1.00 .40
❑ 150 Trent Green LL .50 .20
❑ 151 Joe Horn LL .50 .20
❑ 152 Corey Dillon LL .50 .20
❑ 153 Peyton Manning LL 1.00 .40
❑ 154 Javon Walker LL .50 .20
❑ 155 Edgerrin James LL .60 .25
❑ 156 Jake Scott GM .50 .20
❑ 157 John Elway GM 2.00 .75
❑ 158 Dwight Clark GM .60 .25
❑ 159 Lawrence Taylor GM 1.00 .40
❑ 160 Joe Namath GM 1.25 .50
❑ 161 Richard Dent GM .60 .25
❑ 162 Peyton Manning GM 1.00 .40
❑ 163 Don Maynard GM .50 .20
❑ 164 Joe Greene GM 1.00 .40
❑ 165 Roger Staubach GM 1.25 .50
❑ 166 J.J. Arrington RC 8.00 3.00
❑ 167 Cedric Benson RC 10.00 4.00
❑ 168 Mark Bradley RC 5.00 2.00
❑ 169 Reggie Brown RC 5.00 2.00
❑ 170 Ronnie Brown RC 20.00 8.00
❑ 171 Jason Campbell RC 8.00 3.00
❑ 172 Maurice Clarett 5.00 2.00
❑ 173 Mark Clayton RC 6.00 2.50
❑ 174 Braylon Edwards RC 15.00 6.00
❑ 175 Ciatrick Fason RC 5.00 2.00
❑ 176 Charlie Frye RC 10.00 4.00
❑ 177 Frank Gore RC 12.00 5.00
❑ 178 David Greene RC 5.00 2.00
❑ 179 Vincent Jackson RC 5.00 2.00
❑ 180 Adam Jones RC 5.00 2.00
❑ 181 Matt Jones RC 12.00 5.00
❑ 182 Stefan LeFors RC 5.00 2.00
❑ 183 Heath Miller RC 12.00 5.00
❑ 184 Ryan Moats RC 5.00 2.00
❑ 185 Vernand Morency RC 5.00 2.00
❑ 186 Terrence Murphy RC 5.00 2.00
❑ 187 Kyle Orton RC 8.00 3.00
❑ 188 Roscoe Parrish RC 5.00 2.00
❑ 189 Courtney Roby RC 5.00 2.00
❑ 190 Aaron Rodgers RC 15.00 6.00
❑ 191 Carlos Rogers RC 6.00 2.50
❑ 192 Antrel Rolle RC 5.00 2.00
❑ 193 Eric Shelton RC 5.00 2.00
❑ 194 Alex Smith QB RC 20.00 8.00
❑ 195 Andrew Walter RC 8.00 3.00
❑ 196 Roddy White RC 5.00 2.00
❑ 197 Cadillac Williams RC 25.00 10.00
❑ 198 Mike Williams 10.00 4.00
❑ 199 Troy Williamson RC 10.00 4.00
❑ 200 Taylor Stubblefield RC 2.50 1.00
❑ 201 Dan Cody RC 5.00 2.00
❑ 202 David Pollack RC 5.00 2.00
❑ 203 Craig Bragg RC 4.00 1.50
❑ 204 Alvin Pearman RC 5.00 2.00
❑ 205 Marcus Maxwell RC 4.00 1.50
❑ 206 Brock Berlin RC 4.00 1.50
❑ 207 Khalif Barnes RC 4.00 1.50
❑ 208 Eric King RC 4.00 1.50
❑ 209 Alex Smith TE RC 5.00 2.00
❑ 210 Dante Ridgeway RC 4.00 1.50
❑ 211 Shaun Cody RC 5.00 2.00
❑ 212 Donte Nicholson RC 5.00 2.00
❑ 213 DeMarcus Ware RC 8.00 3.00
❑ 214 Lionel Gates RC 4.00 1.50
❑ 215 Fabian Washington RC 5.00 2.00
❑ 216 Brandon Jacobs RC 6.00 2.50
❑ 217 Noah Herron RC 5.00 2.00
❑ 218 Derrick Johnson RC 8.00 3.00
❑ 219 J.R. Russell RC 4.00 1.50
❑ 220 Adrian McPherson RC 5.00 2.00
❑ 221 Marcus Spears RC 5.00 2.00
❑ 222 Justin Miller RC 4.00 1.50
❑ 223 Marion Barber RC 8.00 3.00
❑ 224 Anthony Davis RC 4.00 1.50
❑ 225 Chad Owens RC 5.00 2.00
❑ 226 Craphonso Thorpe RC 4.00 1.50
❑ 227 Travis Johnson RC 4.00 1.50
❑ 228 Erasmus James RC 5.00 2.00
❑ 229 Mike Patterson RC 5.00 2.00
❑ 230 Airese Currie RC 5.00 2.00
❑ 231 Justin Tuck RC 5.00 2.00
❑ 232 Dan Orlovsky RC 6.00 2.50
❑ 233 Thomas Davis RC 5.00 2.00
❑ 234 Derek Anderson RC 5.00 2.00
❑ 235 Matt Roth RC 5.00 2.00
❑ 236 Chris Henry RC 5.00 2.00
❑ 237 Rasheed Marshall RC 5.00 2.00
❑ 238 Bryant McFadden RC 5.00 2.00
❑ 239 Darren Sproles RC 5.00 2.00
❑ 240 Fred Gibson RC 4.00 1.50
❑ 241 Barrett Ruud RC 5.00 2.00
❑ 242 Kelvin Hayden RC 4.00 1.50
❑ 243 Ryan Fitzpatrick RC 8.00 3.00
❑ 244 Patrick Estes RC 4.00 1.50
❑ 245 Zach Tuiasosopo RC 2.50 1.00
❑ 246 Luis Castillo RC 5.00 2.00
❑ 247 Lance Mitchell RC 4.00 1.50
❑ 248 Ronald Bartell RC 4.00 1.50
❑ 249 Jerome Mathis RC 5.00 2.00
❑ 250 Marlin Jackson RC 5.00 2.00
❑ 251 James Kilian RC 5.00 2.00
❑ 252 Roydell Williams RC 5.00 2.00
❑ 253 Joel Dreessen RC 4.00 1.50
❑ 254 Paris Warren RC 4.00 1.50
❑ 255 Dustin Fox RC 5.00 2.00
❑ 256 Ellis Hobbs RC 5.00 2.00
❑ 257 Mike Nugent RC 5.00 2.00
❑ 258 Channing Crowder RC 5.00 2.00
❑ 259 Kerry Rhodes RC 5.00 2.00
❑ 260 Jerome Collins RC 4.00 1.50
❑ 261 Stanford Routt RC 4.00 1.50
❑ 262 Madison Hedgecock RC 5.00 2.00
❑ 263 Rian Wallace RC 4.00 1.50
❑ 264 Larry Brackins RC 4.00 1.50
❑ 265 Manuel White RC 4.00 1.50
❑ 266 Corey Webster RC 5.00 2.00
❑ 267 Eric Moore RC 4.00 1.50
❑ 268 Kirk Morrison RC 5.00 2.00
❑ 269 Atiyyah Ellison RC 2.50 1.00
❑ 270 Travis Daniels RC 4.00 1.50
❑ 271 Boomer Grigsby RC 6.00 2.50
❑ 272 Alex Barron RC 2.50 1.00
❑ 273 Tab Perry RC 5.00 2.00
❑ 274 Cedric Houston RC 5.00 2.00
❑ 275 Kevin Burnett RC 5.00 2.00
❑ RH39 Deion Branch RH 5.00 2.00
❑ RH39R Deion Branch RHR/100 15.00 6.00

2006 Topps Chrome

❑ 1 Jonathan Vilma .60 .25
❑ 2 Chester Taylor .60 .25
❑ 3 Troy Polamalu 1.25 .50
❑ 4 Nathan Vasher .50 .20
❑ 5 Clinton Portis 1.00 .40
❑ 6 Willie Parker 1.25 .50

❑ 7 Lofa Tatupu .60 .25
❑ 8 Peyton Manning 1.50 .60
❑ 9 LaMont Jordan .60 .25
❑ 10 Jason Taylor .50 .20
❑ 11 Travis Taylor .50 .20
❑ 12 Derrick Johnson .60 .25
❑ 13 Jason Campbell .60 .25
❑ 14 Aaron Rodgers 1.00 .40
❑ 15 Deltha O'Neal .50 .20
❑ 16 LaDainian Tomlinson 1.25 .50
❑ 17 Keary Colbert .50 .20
❑ 18 Chris Chambers .60 .25
❑ 19 Chris Simms .60 .25
❑ 20 Troy Williamson .60 .25
❑ 21 Chad Johnson .60 .25
❑ 22 Jake Delhomme .60 .25
❑ 23 Willis McGahee 1.00 .40
❑ 24 Roddy White .60 .25
❑ 25 Rod Smith .60 .25
❑ 26 Zach Thomas 1.00 .40
❑ 27 Antonio Gates 1.00 .40
❑ 28 Michael Vick 1.25 .50
❑ 29 Antwaan Randle El .60 .25
❑ 30 Drew Bledsoe 1.00 .40
❑ 31 Randy McMichael .50 .20
❑ 32 Heath Miller 1.00 .40
❑ 33 Fred Taylor .60 .25
❑ 34 Alge Crumpler .60 .25
❑ 35 Roy Williams S .60 .25
❑ 36 Ryan Moats .50 .20
❑ 37 Dwight Freeney .60 .25
❑ 38 Jeremy Shockey 1.00 .40
❑ 39 Shawne Merriman .60 .25
❑ 40 Charlie Frye .60 .25
❑ 41 Reggie Wayne .60 .25
❑ 42 Alex Smith QB 1.25 .50
❑ 43 Jerome Bettis 1.00 .40
❑ 44 Chris Brown .60 .25
❑ 45 Michael Clayton .60 .25
❑ 46 Carlos Rogers .50 .20
❑ 47 DeAngelo Hall .60 .25
❑ 48 Drew Bennett .50 .20
❑ 49 Brandon Lloyd .60 .25
❑ 50 Corey Dillon .60 .25
❑ 51 Eli Manning 1.25 .50
❑ 52 Jerry Porter .60 .25
❑ 53 Carson Palmer 1.00 .40
❑ 54 Kevin Jones 1.00 .40
❑ 55 Andre Johnson .60 .25
❑ 56 Ray Lewis 1.00 .40
❑ 57 Kyle Orton .60 .25
❑ 58 Julius Jones 1.00 .40
❑ 59 Roy Williams WR 1.00 .40
❑ 60 Jonathan Ogden .50 .20
❑ 61 Antonio Pierce .50 .20
❑ 62 Larry Johnson 1.25 .50
❑ 63 Muhsin Muhammad .60 .25
❑ 64 Trent Green .60 .25
❑ 65 Tatum Bell .60 .25
❑ 66 Lee Evans .60 .25
❑ 67 Braylon Edwards 1.00 .40
❑ 68 Hines Ward 1.00 .40
❑ 69 Warrick Dunn .60 .25
❑ 70 Antonio Bryant .60 .25
❑ 71 Mewelde Moore .50 .20
❑ 72 Samkon Gado 1.00 .40
❑ 73 Mike Williams 1.00 .40
❑ 74 Marion Barber .60 .25
❑ 75 Samie Parker .50 .20
❑ 76 Julius Peppers .60 .25
❑ 77 Brian Westbrook .60 .25
❑ 78 Kevan Barlow .60 .25
❑ 79 Kyle Boller .50 .20
❑ 80 Donnie Edwards .50 .20
❑ 81 Courtney Roby .50 .20
❑ 82 Marc Bulger .60 .25
❑ 83 Steve Smith 1.00 .40
❑ 84 Ben Roethlisberger 1.50 .60
❑ 85 Byron Leftwich .60 .25
❑ 86 Isaac Bruce .60 .25
❑ 87 Kurt Warner .60 .25
❑ 88 Tiki Barber 1.00 .40
❑ 89 Derrick Mason .50 .20
❑ 90 Joe Horn .60 .25
❑ 91 Donovan McNabb 1.00 .40
❑ 92 DeShaun Foster .60 .25
❑ 93 Rex Grossman 1.00 .40
❑ 94 Randy Moss 1.00 .40
❑ 95 Tedy Bruschi 1.00 .40
❑ 96 Tony Gonzalez .60 .25
❑ 97 Cadillac Williams 1.00 .40
❑ 98 Torry Holt .60 .25
❑ 99 Philip Rivers 1.00 .40
❑ 100 Deuce McAllister .60 .25
❑ 101 Jason Witten .60 .25
❑ 102 Reggie Brown .60 .25
❑ 103 Ronnie Brown 1.00 .40
❑ 104 Deion Branch .60 .25
❑ 105 Terry Glenn .60 .25
❑ 106 Tom Brady 1.50 .60
❑ 107 Dallas Clark .50 .20
❑ 108 Mark Clayton .60 .25
❑ 109 D.J. Williams .50 .20
❑ 110 Matt Jones 1.00 .40
❑ 111 Ed Reed .60 .25
❑ 112 Reuben Droughns .60 .25
❑ 113 Matt Hasselbeck .60 .25
❑ 114 Anquan Boldin .60 .25
❑ 115 David Carr .60 .25
❑ 116 Domanick Davis .60 .25
❑ 117 Nate Burleson .60 .25
❑ 118 Shaun Alexander 1.00 .40
❑ 119 Dante Hall .60 .25
❑ 120 Santana Moss .60 .25
❑ 121 Brandon Stokley .60 .25
❑ 122 Larry Fitzgerald 1.00 .40
❑ 123 Marvin Harrison 1.00 .40
❑ 124 Steve McNair .60 .25
❑ 125 Osi Umenyiora .50 .20
❑ 126 Odell Thurman .50 .20
❑ 127 Josh McCown .60 .25
❑ 128 Curtis Martin 1.00 .40
❑ 129 Jake Plummer .60 .25
❑ 130 Cedric Benson 1.00 .40
❑ 131 J.P. Losman .60 .25
❑ 132 Joey Galloway .60 .25
❑ 133 Brian Griese .60 .25
❑ 134 Plaxico Burress .60 .25
❑ 135 Brian Urlacher 1.00 .40
❑ 136 T.J. Houshmandzadeh .60 .25
❑ 137 Todd Heap .60 .25
❑ 138 Champ Bailey .60 .25
❑ 139 Mark Brunell .60 .25
❑ 140 Chris Cooley .50 .20
❑ 141 Priest Holmes .60 .25
❑ 142 Aaron Brooks .60 .25
❑ 143 Steven Jackson 1.00 .40
❑ 144 Michael Strahan .60 .25
❑ 145 Rudi Johnson .60 .25
❑ 146 Terrell Owens 1.00 .40
❑ 147 John Abraham .50 .20
❑ 148 Jon Kitna .50 .20
❑ 149 LaVar Arrington 1.00 .40
❑ 150 Joe Jurevicius .60 .25
❑ 151 Dominic Rhodes .60 .25
❑ 152 Chad Pennington .60 .25
❑ 153 Charles Woodson .60 .25
❑ 154 Kerry Collins .60 .25
❑ 155 Drew Brees 1.00 .40
❑ 156 Keyshawn Johnson .60 .25
❑ 157 Mike Anderson .60 .25
❑ 158 Jimmy Smith .60 .25
❑ 159 Brett Favre 2.00 .75
❑ 160 Edgerrin James 1.00 .40
❑ 161 Jamal Lewis .60 .25
❑ 162 Daunte Culpepper 1.00 .40
❑ 163 Eric Moulds .60 .25
❑ 164 Patrick Ramsey .60 .25
❑ 165 Ahman Green .60 .25
❑ 166 Kamerion Wimbley RC 5.00 2.00
❑ 167 Bobby Carpenter RC 5.00 2.00
❑ 168 Abdul Hodge RC 5.00 2.00
❑ 169 P.J. Daniels RC 4.00 1.50
❑ 170 D'Qwell Jackson RC 4.00 1.50
❑ 171 Johnathan Joseph RC 4.00 1.50
❑ 172 Antonio Cromartie RC 5.00 2.00
❑ 173 Elvis Dumervil RC 2.50 1.00
❑ 174 Tamba Hali RC 5.00 2.00
❑ 175 Derek Hagan RC 5.00 2.00
❑ 176 Haloti Ngata RC 5.00 2.00
❑ 177 Manny Lawson RC 5.00 2.00
❑ 178 Kelly Jennings RC 5.00 2.00
❑ 179 Jason Allen RC 5.00 2.00
❑ 180 Mathias Kiwanuka RC 6.00 2.50
❑ 181 Marques Hagans RC 4.00 1.50
❑ 182 Devin Aromashodu RC 4.00 1.50
❑ 183 Brandon Johnson RC 4.00 1.50
❑ 184 Ingle Martin RC 5.00 2.00
❑ 185 Claude Wroten RC 2.50 1.00
❑ 186 Tye Hill RC 5.00 2.00
❑ 187 Ashton Youboty RC 5.00 2.00
❑ 188 DeMeco Ryans RC 6.00 2.50
❑ 189 Brodrick Bunkley RC 5.00 2.00
❑ 190 Thomas Howard RC 5.00 2.00
❑ 191 Ernie Sims RC 6.00 2.50
❑ 192 Rocky McIntosh RC 5.00 2.00
❑ 193 Donte Whitner RC 5.00 2.00
❑ 194 Anthony Schlegel RC 4.00 1.50
❑ 195 Jimmy Williams RC 5.00 2.00
❑ 196 Brett Basanez RC 5.00 2.00
❑ 197 Ben Obomanu RC 4.00 1.50
❑ 198 Jonathan Orr RC 4.00 1.50
❑ 199 Andre Hall RC 4.00 1.50
❑ 200 James Anderson RC 2.50 1.00
❑ 201 Darrell Bing RC 5.00 2.00
❑ 202 Jovon Bouknight RC 4.00 1.50
❑ 203 Gabe Watson RC 4.00 1.50
❑ 204 Garrett Mills RC 5.00 2.00
❑ 205 Jeff Webb RC 4.00 1.50
❑ 206 Kevin McMahan RC 4.00 1.50
❑ 207 D.J. Shockley RC 5.00 2.00
❑ 208 A.J. Nicholson RC 2.50 1.00
❑ 209 Cedric Humes RC 5.00 2.00
❑ 210 Winston Justice RC 5.00 2.00
❑ 211 Lawrence Vickers RC 4.00 1.50
❑ 212 Daniel Bullocks RC 5.00 2.00
❑ 213 Tim Day RC 4.00 1.50
❑ 214 Ko Simpson RC 4.00 1.50
❑ 215 Dusty Dvoracek RC 5.00 2.00
❑ 216 Davin Joseph RC 4.00 1.50
❑ 217 Dominique Byrd RC 4.00 1.50
❑ 218 Marcus Vick RC 4.00 1.50
❑ 219 John McCargo RC 4.00 1.50
❑ 220 Danieal Manning RC 5.00 2.00
❑ 221 Reggie Bush RC 40.00 20.00
❑ 222 A.J. Hawk RC 10.00 4.00
❑ 223 Vince Young RC 20.00 8.00
❑ 224 Matt Leinart RC 20.00 8.00
❑ 225 Kellen Clemens RC 6.00 2.50
❑ 226 Sinorice Moss RC 6.00 2.50
❑ 227 Laurence Maroney RC 12.00 5.00
❑ 228 DeAngelo Williams RC 12.00 5.00
❑ 229 Jay Cutler RC 20.00 8.00
❑ 230 LenDale White RC 10.00 4.00
❑ 231 Leonard Pope RC 5.00 2.00
❑ 232 Chad Greenway RC 5.00 2.00
❑ 233 Chad Jackson RC 8.00 3.00
❑ 234 Vernon Davis RC 10.00 4.00
❑ 235 Todd Watkins RC 4.00 1.50
❑ 236 David Thomas RC 5.00 2.00
❑ 237 Marcedes Lewis RC 5.00 2.00
❑ 238 Leon Washington RC 8.00 3.00
❑ 239 Will Blackmon RC 4.00 1.50
❑ 240 Michael Huff RC 6.00 2.50
❑ 241 Jerious Norwood RC 8.00 3.00
❑ 242 Reggie McNeal RC 4.00 1.50
❑ 243 Wali Lundy RC 5.00 2.00
❑ 244 Santonio Holmes RC 10.00 4.00
❑ 245 Jerome Harrison RC 5.00 2.00
❑ 246 Bruce Gradkowski RC 8.00 3.00
❑ 247 Maurice Drew RC 12.00 5.00
❑ 248 Brandon Williams RC 5.00 2.00
❑ 249 Anthony Fasano RC 5.00 2.00
❑ 250 Omar Jacobs RC 4.00 1.50
❑ 251 Domenik Hixon RC 4.00 1.50
❑ 252 Devin Hester RC 10.00 4.00
❑ 253 Maurice Stovall RC 5.00 2.00
❑ 254 Tarvaris Jackson RC 8.00 3.00
❑ 255 Michael Robinson RC 8.00 3.00
❑ 256 Mario Williams RC 8.00 3.00
❑ 257 Jason Avant RC 5.00 2.00
❑ 258 Brian Calhoun RC 5.00 2.00
❑ 259 Skyler Green RC 5.00 2.00
❑ 260 Greg Jennings RC 8.00 3.00
❑ 261 Charlie Whitehurst RC 6.00 2.50
❑ 262 Mike Hass RC 5.00 2.00
❑ 263 Brandon Marshall RC 5.00 2.00
❑ 264 Drew Olson RC 4.00 1.50
❑ 265 Demetrius Williams RC 6.00 2.50
❑ 266 Travis Wilson RC 5.00 2.00
❑ 267 Joe Klopfenstein RC 4.00 1.50

Card	Hi	Lo
❑ 268 Joseph Addai RC	15.00	6.00
❑ 269 Brad Smith RC	5.00	2.00
❑ 270 Willie Reid RC	5.00	2.00
❑ RH40 Hines Ward RH	6.00	2.50

2001 Topps Debut

Card	Hi	Lo
❑ COMP.SET w/o SP's (100)	20.00	7.50
❑ 1 Marshall Faulk	1.25	.50
❑ 2 Ricky Watters	.60	.25
❑ 3 Bill Schroeder	.60	.25
❑ 4 Muhsin Muhammad	.60	.25
❑ 5 Peter Warrick	1.00	.40
❑ 6 Marvin Harrison	1.00	.40
❑ 7 Stephen Davis	1.00	.40
❑ 8 Cris Carter	1.00	.40
❑ 9 Charlie Batch	1.00	.40
❑ 10 David Boston	1.00	.40
❑ 11 Ike Hilliard	.60	.25
❑ 12 Steve McNair	1.00	.40
❑ 13 Kordell Stewart	.60	.25
❑ 14 Travis Prentice	.40	.15
❑ 15 Sammy Morris	.40	.15
❑ 16 Vinny Testaverde	.60	.25
❑ 17 Tyrone Wheatley	.60	.25
❑ 18 Jeff Garcia	1.00	.40
❑ 19 Brett Favre	3.00	1.25
❑ 20 Jake Plummer	.60	.25
❑ 21 Cade McNown	.40	.15
❑ 22 Rob Johnson	.60	.25
❑ 23 Tim Couch	.60	.25
❑ 24 Jerome Bettis	1.00	.40
❑ 25 Ricky Williams	1.00	.40
❑ 26 Darrell Jackson	1.00	.40
❑ 27 Troy Brown	.60	.25
❑ 28 Jamal Lewis	1.50	.60
❑ 29 Isaac Bruce	1.00	.40
❑ 30 Lamar Smith	.60	.25
❑ 31 Qadry Ismail	.60	.25
❑ 32 Elvis Grbac	.60	.25
❑ 33 Shaun Alexander	1.25	.50
❑ 34 Peyton Manning	2.50	1.00
❑ 35 Curtis Martin	1.00	.40
❑ 36 Jamal Anderson	1.00	.40
❑ 37 Mark Brunell	1.00	.40
❑ 38 Emmitt Smith	2.00	.75
❑ 39 Chad Lewis	.40	.15
❑ 40 Randy Moss	2.00	.75
❑ 41 Kurt Warner	2.00	.75
❑ 42 Terrence Wilkins	.40	.15
❑ 43 Corey Dillon	1.00	.40
❑ 44 Brian Griese	1.00	.40
❑ 45 Jon Kitna	1.00	.40
❑ 46 Eric Moulds	.60	.25
❑ 47 Steve Beuerlein	.60	.25
❑ 48 James Allen	.60	.25
❑ 49 Amani Toomer	.40	.15
❑ 50 Daunte Culpepper	1.00	.40
❑ 51 Michael Pittman	.40	.15
❑ 52 Warrick Dunn	1.00	.40
❑ 53 Terrell Owens	1.00	.40
❑ 54 Donald Hayes	.40	.15
❑ 55 Keenan McCardell	.40	.15
❑ 56 Tony Gonzalez	.60	.25
❑ 57 Freddie Jones	.40	.15
❑ 58 Charlie Garner	.60	.25
❑ 59 Shawn Jefferson	.40	.15
❑ 60 Brian Urlacher	1.50	.60
❑ 61 Donovan McNabb	1.25	.50
❑ 62 Az-Zahir Hakim	.40	.15
❑ 63 James Thrash	.60	.25
❑ 64 Hines Ward	1.00	.40
❑ 65 Shawn Bryson	.40	.15
❑ 66 Wayne Chrebet	.60	.25
❑ 67 Kevin Johnson	.60	.25
❑ 68 Eddie George	1.00	.40
❑ 69 Derrick Alexander	.60	.25
❑ 70 Tim Brown	1.00	.40
❑ 71 Jay Fiedler	1.00	.40
❑ 72 Aaron Brooks	1.00	.40
❑ 73 Torry Holt	1.00	.40
❑ 74 Edgerrin James	1.25	.50
❑ 75 Shannon Sharpe	.60	.25
❑ 76 Oronde Gadsden	.60	.25
❑ 77 Rod Smith	.60	.25
❑ 78 Rich Gannon	1.00	.40
❑ 79 Fred Taylor	1.00	.40
❑ 80 Derrick Mason	.60	.25
❑ 81 Joe Horn	.60	.25
❑ 82 Robert Smith	.60	.25
❑ 83 James Stewart	.60	.25
❑ 84 Jeff George	.60	.25
❑ 85 Troy Aikman	1.50	.60
❑ 86 Charles Johnson	.40	.15
❑ 87 Ahman Green	1.00	.40
❑ 88 Shaun King	.40	.15
❑ 89 Ray Lewis	1.00	.40
❑ 90 Trent Dilfer	.60	.25
❑ 91 Drew Bledsoe	1.25	.50
❑ 92 Jimmy Smith	.60	.25
❑ 93 Ed McCaffrey	1.00	.40
❑ 94 Kerry Collins	.60	.25
❑ 95 Terry Glenn	.60	.25
❑ 96 Ron Dayne	1.00	.40
❑ 97 Keyshawn Johnson	1.00	.40
❑ 98 Antonio Freeman	1.00	.40
❑ 99 Tiki Barber	1.00	.40
❑ 100 Mike Anderson	1.00	.40
❑ 101 Drew Brees AU RC	100.00	50.00
❑ 102 Chris Weinke AU RC	20.00	7.50
❑ 103 LaDain.Tomlinson AU RC	250.00	150.00
❑ 104 Michael Bennett AU RC	20.00	7.50
❑ 105 Anthony Thomas AU RC	20.00	7.50
❑ 106 LaMont Jordan AU RC	25.00	10.00
❑ 107 David Terrell AU RC	20.00	7.50
❑ 108 Michael Vick AU RC	150.00	75.00
❑ 109 Deuce McAllister AU RC	40.00	20.00
❑ 110 James Jackson AU RC	15.00	6.00
❑ 111 Mike McMahon JSY RC	15.00	6.00
❑ 112 Cedrick Wilson JSY RC	15.00	6.00
❑ 113 Ken Lucas JSY RC	15.00	6.00
❑ 114 Fred Smoot JSY RC	15.00	6.00
❑ 115 Alge Crumpler JSY RC	20.00	10.00
❑ 116 Sage Rosenfels JSY RC	15.00	6.00
❑ 117 Rashard Casey JSY RC	10.00	4.00
❑ 118 David Allen JSY RC	10.00	4.00
❑ 119 Bobby Newcombe JSY RC	10.00	4.00
❑ 120 Jesse Palmer JSY RC	15.00	6.00
❑ 121 Tommy Polley JSY RC	15.00	6.00
❑ 122 Kevan Barlow JSY RC	15.00	6.00
❑ 123 Scotty Anderson JSY RC	10.00	4.00
❑ 124 Travis Minor JSY RC	10.00	4.00
❑ 125 Snoop Minnis JSY RC	10.00	4.00
❑ 126 Moran Norris JSY RC	8.00	3.00
❑ 127 Alex Lincoln JSY RC	10.00	4.00
❑ 128 Chad Johnson JSY RC	40.00	20.00
❑ 129 Boo Williams JSY RC	10.00	4.00
❑ 130 Brian Natkin JSY RC	8.00	3.00
❑ 131 Orlando Huff JSY RC	8.00	3.00
❑ 132 Derrick Gibson JSY RC	10.00	4.00
❑ 133 Tony Driver JSY RC	15.00	6.00
❑ 134 Torrance Marshall JSY RC	15.00	6.00
❑ 135 Alex Bannister JSY RC	10.00	4.00
❑ 136 Morlon Greenwood JSY RC	8.00	3.00
❑ 137 Ennis Davis JSY RC	8.00	3.00
❑ 138 Mike Cerimele JSY RC	8.00	3.00
❑ 139 David Rivers JSY RC	10.00	4.00
❑ 140 Dustin McClintock JSY RC	10.00	4.00
❑ 141 Tay Cody JSY RC	8.00	3.00
❑ 142 Arther Love JSY RC	8.00	3.00
❑ 143 Sly Johnson JSY RC	10.00	4.00
❑ 144 Dan Alexander JSY RC	15.00	6.00
❑ 145 Will Allen JSY RC	10.00	4.00
❑ 146 Andre Dyson JSY RC	8.00	3.00
❑ 147 Margin Hooks JSY RC	8.00	3.00
❑ 148 Adam Archuleta JSY RC	15.00	6.00
❑ 149 Sedrick Hodge JSY RC	8.00	3.00
❑ 150 Kendrell Bell JSY RC	20.00	7.50
❑ 151 Reggie Wayne RC	12.00	5.00
❑ 152 Rod Gardner RC	6.00	2.50
❑ 153 Chris Chambers RC	10.00	4.00
❑ 154 Jamal Reynolds RC	6.00	2.50
❑ 155 Ben Hamilton RC	6.00	2.50
❑ 156 Dan Morgan RC	20.00	7.50
❑ 157 Quincy Morgan RC	6.00	2.50
❑ 158 Travis Henry RC	10.00	4.00
❑ 159 Ken-Yon Rambo RC	4.00	1.50
❑ 160 Josh Heupel RC	6.00	2.50
❑ 161 Marcus Stroud RC	6.00	2.50
❑ 162 Marques Tuiasosopo RC	6.00	2.50
❑ 163 Reggie Germany RC	4.00	1.50
❑ 164 Robert Ferguson RC	6.00	2.50
❑ 165 Jabari Holloway RC	4.00	1.50
❑ 166 Ben Leard RC	6.00	2.50
❑ 167 Bhawoh Jue RC	8.00	3.00
❑ 168 Freddie Mitchell RC	6.00	2.50
❑ 169 Vinny Sutherland RC	4.00	1.50
❑ 170 Jeff Backus RC	4.00	1.50
❑ 171 Correll Buckhalter RC	8.00	3.00
❑ 172 Mario Fatefehi RC	4.00	1.50
❑ 173 Rudi Johnson RC	12.00	5.00
❑ 174 Koren Robinson RC	6.00	2.50
❑ 175 Santana Moss RC	10.00	4.00

2002 Topps Debut

Card	Hi	Lo
❑ COMP.SET w/o SP's (150)	25.00	10.00
❑ 1 Kurt Warner	1.00	.40
❑ 2 James Thrash	.60	.25
❑ 3 Aaron Brooks	1.00	.40
❑ 4 Mark Brunell	1.00	.40
❑ 5 Mike Anderson	1.00	.40
❑ 6 Benjamin Gay	.60	.25
❑ 7 Marvin Harrison	1.00	.40
❑ 8 Randy Moss	2.00	.75
❑ 9 Ron Dayne	.60	.25
❑ 10 Tim Brown	1.00	.40
❑ 11 Vinny Testaverde	.60	.25
❑ 12 Mike Alstott	1.00	.40
❑ 13 Tony Banks	.40	.15
❑ 14 Plaxico Burress	.60	.25
❑ 15 Chris Chambers	1.00	.40
❑ 16 Brett Favre	2.50	1.00
❑ 17 Quincy Carter	.60	.25
❑ 18 Brian Urlacher	1.50	.60
❑ 19 Byron Chamberlain	.40	.15
❑ 20 Tony Gonzalez	.60	.25
❑ 21 Troy Brown	.60	.25
❑ 22 Drew Brees	1.00	.40
❑ 23 Koren Robinson	.60	.25
❑ 24 Donald Hayes	.40	.15
❑ 25 Michael Vick	3.00	1.25
❑ 26 Travis Taylor	.60	.25
❑ 27 Peerless Price	.60	.25
❑ 28 Chad Johnson	1.00	.40
❑ 29 Tim Couch	.60	.25
❑ 30 Edgerrin James	1.25	.50
❑ 31 Willie Jackson	.40	.15
❑ 32 Hines Ward	1.00	.40
❑ 33 Terrell Owens	1.00	.40
❑ 34 Eddie George	1.00	.40
❑ 35 Michael Westbrook	.40	.15
❑ 36 Kerry Collins	.60	.25
❑ 37 Terrell Davis	1.00	.40
❑ 38 Marcus Robinson	.60	.25
❑ 39 Charlie Batch	.60	.25
❑ 40 Jake Plummer	.60	.25

❑ 41 Qadry Ismail .60 .25
❑ 42 Snoop Minnis .40 .15
❑ 43 Jimmy Smith .60 .25
❑ 44 Charlie Garner .60 .25
❑ 45 Jeff Graham .40 .15
❑ 46 Torry Holt 1.00 .40
❑ 47 Kevin Dyson .60 .25
❑ 48 Maurice Smith .60 .25
❑ 49 Muhsin Muhammad .60 .25
❑ 50 Curtis Martin 1.00 .40
❑ 51 Todd Pinkston .60 .25
❑ 52 Matt Hasselbeck .60 .25
❑ 53 Corey Dillon .60 .25
❑ 54 Michael Pittman .40 .15
❑ 55 Antonio Freeman 1.00 .40
❑ 56 Oronde Gadsden .60 .25
❑ 57 Tiki Barber 1.00 .40
❑ 58 Isaac Bruce 1.00 .40
❑ 59 Rod Gardner .60 .25
❑ 60 Derrick Mason .60 .25
❑ 61 Joe Horn .60 .25
❑ 62 Antowain Smith .60 .25
❑ 63 Johnnie Morton .60 .25
❑ 64 Kevin Johnson .60 .25
❑ 65 Nick Goings .40 .15
❑ 66 Jason Brookins .40 .15
❑ 67 Travis Henry 1.00 .40
❑ 68 Brian Griese 1.00 .40
❑ 69 Priest Holmes 1.25 .50
❑ 70 Daunte Culpepper 1.00 .40
❑ 71 Amani Toomer .60 .25
❑ 72 Rich Gannon 1.00 .40
❑ 73 Correll Buckhalter .60 .25
❑ 74 Kevan Barlow .60 .25
❑ 75 Stephen Davis .60 .25
❑ 76 Keenan McCardell .40 .15
❑ 77 Jon Kitna .60 .25
❑ 78 Eric Moulds .60 .25
❑ 79 Dez White .40 .15
❑ 80 Rocket Ismail .60 .25
❑ 81 Dominic Rhodes .60 .25
❑ 82 Lamar Smith .60 .25
❑ 83 David Patten .40 .15
❑ 84 Duce Staley 1.00 .40
❑ 85 Curtis Conway .40 .15
❑ 86 Kordell Stewart .60 .25
❑ 87 Brad Johnson .60 .25
❑ 88 Wayne Chrebet .60 .25
❑ 89 Michael Bennett .60 .25
❑ 90 Quincy Morgan .40 .15
❑ 91 Steve Smith 1.00 .40
❑ 92 David Boston 1.00 .40
❑ 93 Shannon Sharpe .60 .25
❑ 94 Mike McMahon 1.00 .40
❑ 95 Stacey Mack .40 .15
❑ 96 Santana Moss 1.00 .40
❑ 97 Jeff Garcia 1.00 .40
❑ 98 Keyshawn Johnson 1.00 .40
❑ 99 Rod Smith .60 .25
❑ 100 Jerome Bettis 1.00 .40
❑ 101 LaDainian Tomlinson 1.50 .60
❑ 102 Warrick Dunn 1.00 .40
❑ 103 Ray Lewis 1.00 .40
❑ 104 Chris Chandler .60 .25
❑ 105 Jim Miller .40 .15
❑ 106 Ahman Green 1.00 .40
❑ 107 Jay Fiedler .60 .25
❑ 108 Tom Brady 2.50 1.00
❑ 109 Michael Strahan .60 .25
❑ 110 James Jackson .40 .15
❑ 111 Rob Johnson .60 .25
❑ 112 Elvis Grbac .60 .25
❑ 113 Troy Hambrick .40 .15
❑ 114 Corey Bradford .40 .15
❑ 115 Trent Green .60 .25
❑ 116 Cris Carter 1.00 .40
❑ 117 Chris Fuamatu-Ma'afala .40 .15
❑ 118 Chris Weinke .60 .25
❑ 119 MarTay Jenkins .40 .15
❑ 120 Laveranues Coles .60 .25
❑ 121 Donovan McNabb 1.25 .50
❑ 122 Jerry Rice 2.00 .75
❑ 123 Garrison Hearst .60 .25
❑ 124 Steve McNair 1.00 .40
❑ 125 Trung Canidate .60 .25
❑ 126 Doug Flutie 1.00 .40
❑ 127 Ricky Williams
❑ 128 Peyton Manning 2.00 .75
❑ 129 Kevin Kasper .40 .15
❑ 130 Emmitt Smith 2.50 1.00
❑ 131 Peter Warrick .60 .25
❑ 132 Anthony Thomas .60 .25
❑ 133 Ike Hilliard .40 .15
❑ 134 Kendrell Bell 1.00 .40
❑ 135 Shaun Alexander 1.25 .50
❑ 136 Wesley Walls .40 .15
❑ 137 Gerard Warren .40 .15
❑ 138 James Stewart .60 .25
❑ 139 Drew Bledsoe 1.25 .50
❑ 140 Fred Taylor 1.00 .40
❑ 141 Marshall Faulk 1.00 .40
❑ 142 Marcus Pollard .40 .15
❑ 143 Bill Schroeder .60 .25
❑ 144 Marty Booker .40 .15
❑ 145 Amos Zereoue 1.00 .40
❑ 146 Darrell Jackson .60 .25
❑ 147 Brian Finneran .40 .15
❑ 148 Alex Van Pelt .60 .25
❑ 149 Andre Carter .40 .15
❑ 150 Joey Galloway .60 .25
❑ 151 Joey Harrington AU RC 25.00 10.00
❑ 152 Andre Davis AU RC 15.00 6.00
❑ 153 Eric Crouch AU RC 25.00 10.00
❑ 154 Kelly Campbell AU RC 15.00 6.00
❑ 155 Ron Johnson AU RC 15.00 6.00
❑ 156 David Carr JSY RC 25.00 10.00
❑ 157 Kurt Kittner JSY RC 12.00 5.00
❑ 158 Javon Walker JSY RC 25.00 12.50
❑ 159 DeShaun Foster JSY RC 12.00 5.00
❑ 160 Lamar Gordon JSY RC 12.00 5.00
❑ 161 Antwaan Randle El RC 5.00 2.00
❑ 162 Clinton Portis RC 12.00 5.00
❑ 163 Luke Staley RC 2.50 1.00
❑ 164 Daniel Graham RC 3.00 1.25
❑ 165 Ashley Lelie RC 6.00 2.50
❑ 166 Ladell Betts RC 3.00 1.25
❑ 167 Rocky Calmus RC 3.00 1.25
❑ 168 Ryan Sims RC 3.00 1.25
❑ 169 Jeremy Shockey RC 12.00 5.00
❑ 170 Damien Anderson RC 3.00 1.25
❑ 171 Bryant McKinnie RC 3.00 1.25
❑ 172 Kahlil Hill RC 2.50 1.00
❑ 173 John Henderson RC 3.00 1.25
❑ 174 Donte Stallworth RC 6.00 2.50
❑ 175 Kalimba Edwards RC 3.00 1.25
❑ 176 Freddie Milons RC 2.50 1.00
❑ 177 Antonio Bryant RC 3.00 1.25
❑ 178 Cliff Russell RC 2.50 1.00
❑ 179 T.J. Duckett RC 4.00 1.50
❑ 180 Roy Williams RC 8.00 3.00
❑ 181 Patrick Ramsey RC 4.00 1.50
❑ 182 Josh Reed RC 3.00 1.25
❑ 183 Wendell Bryant RC 1.50 .60
❑ 184 Jabar Gaffney RC 3.00 1.25
❑ 185 Napoleon Harris RC 3.00 1.25
❑ 186 Adrian Peterson RC 3.00 1.25
❑ 187 David Garrard RC 3.00 1.25
❑ 188 Levar Fisher RC 2.50 1.00
❑ 189 Quentin Jammer RC 3.00 1.25
❑ 190 Anthony Weaver RC 2.50 1.00
❑ 191 Dwight Freeney RC 5.00 2.00
❑ 192 Reche Caldwell RC 3.00 1.25
❑ 193 Larry Tripplett RC 2.50 1.00
❑ 194 Rohan Davey RC 3.00 1.25
❑ 195 Marquise Walker RC 2.50 1.00
❑ 196 William Green RC 3.00 1.25
❑ 197 Tracey Wistrom RC 2.50 1.00
❑ 198 Alan Harper RC 1.50 .60
❑ 199 Lito Sheppard RC 3.00 1.25
❑ 200 Albert Haynesworth RC 3.00 1.25

2003 Topps Draft Picks and Prospects

❑ COMPLETE SET (165) 50.00 25.00
❑ 1 Priest Holmes 1.25 .50
❑ 2 Tommy Maddox 1.00 .40
❑ 3 Donald Driver .60 .25
❑ 4 Drew Bledsoe 1.00 .40
❑ 5 Tiki Barber 1.00 .40
❑ 6 Terrell Owens 1.00 .40
❑ 7 Rich Gannon .60 .25
❑ 8 Isaac Bruce 1.00 .40
❑ 9 Stephen Davis .60 .25
❑ 10 Peyton Manning 1.50 .60
❑ 11 Tony Gonzalez .60 .25
❑ 12 Marty Booker .60 .25
❑ 13 Warrick Dunn .60 .25
❑ 14 Jimmy Smith .60 .25
❑ 15 Troy Brown .60 .25
❑ 16 Jerry Rice 2.00 .75
❑ 17 Curtis Conway .40 .15
❑ 18 Kurt Warner 1.00 .40
❑ 19 Steve McNair 1.00 .40
❑ 20 Edgerrin James 1.00 .40
❑ 21 Aaron Brooks 1.00 .40
❑ 22 Joey Galloway .60 .25
❑ 23 Peerless Price .60 .25
❑ 24 Torry Holt 1.00 .40
❑ 25 Derrick Mason .60 .25
❑ 26 Curtis Martin 1.00 .40
❑ 27 Daunte Culpepper 1.00 .40
❑ 28 Ahman Green 1.00 .40
❑ 29 Tim Couch .40 .15
❑ 30 Ricky Williams 1.00 .40
❑ 31 Darrell Jackson .60 .25
❑ 32 Keyshawn Johnson 1.00 .40
❑ 33 Jeff Garcia 1.00 .40
❑ 34 Charlie Garner .60 .25
❑ 35 Randy Moss 1.50 .60
❑ 36 Rod Smith .60 .25
❑ 37 Jamal Lewis 1.00 .40
❑ 38 Corey Dillon .60 .25
❑ 39 Marvin Harrison 1.00 .40
❑ 40 Joe Horn .60 .25
❑ 41 Laveranues Coles .60 .25
❑ 42 Hines Ward 1.00 .40
❑ 43 Brad Johnson .60 .25
❑ 44 Eddie George .60 .25
❑ 45 Donovan McNabb 1.25 .50
❑ 46 Marshall Faulk 1.00 .40
❑ 47 Amani Toomer .60 .25
❑ 48 Trent Green .60 .25
❑ 49 Emmitt Smith 2.50 1.00
❑ 50 Brett Favre 2.50 1.00
❑ 51 Brian Griese 1.00 .40
❑ 52 Eric Moulds .60 .25
❑ 53 Plaxico Burress .60 .25
❑ 54 Fred Taylor 1.00 .40
❑ 55 Tom Brady 2.50 1.00
❑ 56 Michael Vick 2.50 1.00
❑ 57 Andre Davis .40 .15
❑ 58 Chris Chambers 1.00 .40
❑ 59 Javon Walker .60 .25
❑ 60 Marc Bulger 1.00 .40
❑ 61 LaDainian Tomlinson 1.00 .40
❑ 62 Chad Pennington 1.25 .50
❑ 63 Marc Boerigter .60 .25
❑ 64 Rod Gardner .60 .25
❑ 65 DeShaun Foster .40 .15
❑ 66 Chris Redman .40 .15
❑ 67 Chad Hutchinson .40 .15
❑ 68 Deion Branch 1.00 .40
❑ 69 Jeremy Shockey 1.50 .60
❑ 70 Shaun Alexander 1.00 .40
❑ 71 Derrius Thompson .40 .15
❑ 72 A.J. Feeley .60 .25
❑ 73 Reggie Wayne .60 .25
❑ 74 William Green .60 .25
❑ 75 Julius Peppers 1.00 .40
❑ 76 Travis Henry .60 .25
❑ 77 Marcel Shipp .60 .25
❑ 78 Michael Bennett .60 .25
❑ 79 Maurice Morris .40 .15
❑ 80 Josh Reed .60 .25

❑ 81	David Terrell	.60	.25
❑ 82	Drew Brees	1.00	.40
❑ 83	Jonathan Wells	.40	.15
❑ 84	Anthony Thomas	.60	.25
❑ 85	Quincy Morgan	.60	.25
❑ 86	Jerry Porter	.60	.25
❑ 87	Ron Johnson	.40	.15
❑ 88	Najeh Davenport	.40	.15
❑ 89	Lamar Gordon	.40	.15
❑ 90	Joey Harrington	1.50	.60
❑ 91	Donte Stallworth	1.00	.40
❑ 92	Kenny Watson	.40	.15
❑ 93	LaMont Jordan	1.00	.40
❑ 94	Antonio Bryant	.60	.25
❑ 95	Steve Smith	1.00	.40
❑ 96	T.J. Duckett	.60	.25
❑ 97	Patrick Ramsey	1.00	.40
❑ 98	Santana Moss	.60	.25
❑ 99	Chad Johnson	1.00	.40
❑ 100	Clinton Portis	1.50	.60
❑ 101	Reche Caldwell	.40	.15
❑ 102	Kevan Barlow	.60	.25
❑ 103	Deuce McAllister	1.00	.40
❑ 104	Koren Robinson	.40	.15
❑ 105	Todd Heap	.60	.25
❑ 106	Jabar Gaffney	.60	.25
❑ 107	Randy McMichael	.60	.25
❑ 108	Dwight Freeney	.60	.25
❑ 109	Antwaan Randle El	1.00	.40
❑ 110	David Carr	1.50	.60
❑ 111	Carson Palmer RC	6.00	2.50
❑ 112	Dahrran Diedrick RC	1.50	.60
❑ 113	Kyle Boller RC	1.50	.60
❑ 114	Terrell Suggs RC	2.50	1.00
❑ 115	Rien Long RC	.75	.30
❑ 116	Justin Gage RC	1.50	.60
❑ 117	William Joseph RC	1.50	.60
❑ 118	Chris Simms RC	2.50	1.00
❑ 119	Avon Cobourne RC	.75	.30
❑ 120	Victor Hobson RC	1.50	.60
❑ 121	Jason Gesser RC	1.50	.60
❑ 122	Ronald Bellamy RC	1.25	.50
❑ 123	Terence Newman RC	3.00	1.25
❑ 124	Terrence Edwards RC	1.25	.50
❑ 125	Sultan McCullough RC	1.25	.50
❑ 126	Kareem Kelly RC	1.25	.50
❑ 127	Jason Witten RC	2.00	.75
❑ 128	Mike Doss RC	1.50	.60
❑ 129	Seneca Wallace RC	1.50	.60
❑ 130	Chris Brown RC	1.50	.60
❑ 131	Larry Johnson RC	6.00	3.00
❑ 132	Taylor Jacobs RC	1.25	.50
❑ 133	Jerome McDougle RC	1.50	.60
❑ 134	Kelley Washington RC	1.50	.60
❑ 135	Brad Banks RC	1.25	.50
❑ 136	DeWayne White RC	1.25	.50
❑ 137	LaBrandon Toefield RC	1.50	.60
❑ 138	Brian St.Pierre RC	1.50	.60
❑ 139	Kindal Moorehead RC	1.25	.50
❑ 140	Willis McGahee RC	4.00	1.50
❑ 141	Jimmy Kennedy RC	1.50	.60
❑ 142	Talman Gardner RC	1.50	.60
❑ 143	Chris Kelsay RC	1.50	.60
❑ 144	Cory Redding RC	1.25	.50
❑ 145	Dave Ragone RC	1.50	.60
❑ 146	Earnest Graham RC	1.25	.50
❑ 147	Andre Johnson RC	3.00	1.00
❑ 148	Boss Bailey RC	1.50	.60
❑ 149	Sam Aiken RC	1.25	.50
❑ 150	Byron Leftwich RC	5.00	2.00
❑ 151	Teyo Johnson RC	1.50	.60
❑ 152	Quentin Griffin RC	1.50	.60
❑ 153	Justin Fargas RC	1.50	.60
❑ 154	Bradie James RC	1.50	.60
❑ 155	Andre Woolfolk RC	1.50	.60
❑ 156	Marcus Trufant RC	1.50	.60
❑ 157	Ken Dorsey RC	1.50	.60
❑ 158	Onterrio Smith RC	1.50	.60
❑ 159	Bryant Johnson RC	1.50	.60
❑ 160	Charles Rogers RC	1.50	.60
❑ 161	Kliff Kingsbury RC	1.25	.50
❑ 162	Michael Haynes RC	1.50	.60
❑ 163	Bennie Joppru RC	1.50	.60
❑ 164	Brandon Lloyd RC	1.50	.60
❑ 165	Jarret Johnson RC	1.25	.50

2004 Topps Draft Picks and Prospects

❑	COMPLETE SET (165)	80.00	40.00
❑ 1	Steve McNair	1.00	.40
❑ 2	Stephen Davis	.60	.25
❑ 3	Chris Chambers	.60	.25
❑ 4	Curtis Martin	1.00	.40
❑ 5	Shaun Alexander	1.00	.40
❑ 6	Jon Kitna	.60	.25
❑ 7	Jimmy Smith	.60	.25
❑ 8	Travis Henry	.60	.25
❑ 9	Torry Holt	1.00	.40
❑ 10	Jamal Lewis	1.00	.40
❑ 11	Clinton Portis	1.00	.40
❑ 12	Aaron Brooks	.60	.25
❑ 13	Plaxico Burress	.60	.25
❑ 14	Trent Green	.60	.25
❑ 15	Chad Johnson	1.00	.40
❑ 16	Jake Delhomme	1.00	.40
❑ 17	David Boston	.60	.25
❑ 18	Joe Horn	.60	.25
❑ 19	Ahman Green	1.00	.40
❑ 20	Fred Taylor	.60	.25
❑ 21	Terrell Owens	1.00	.40
❑ 22	Brad Johnson	.60	.25
❑ 23	Laveranues Coles	.60	.25
❑ 24	Ricky Williams	1.00	.40
❑ 25	Peyton Manning	1.50	.60
❑ 26	Hines Ward	1.00	.40
❑ 27	Matt Hasselbeck	.60	.25
❑ 28	Marshall Faulk	1.00	.40
❑ 29	Tony Gonzalez	.60	.25
❑ 30	Marvin Harrison	1.00	.40
❑ 31	Eric Moulds	.60	.25
❑ 32	Chad Pennington	1.00	.40
❑ 33	Jerry Porter	.60	.25
❑ 34	Jeff Garcia	1.00	.40
❑ 35	Derrick Mason	.60	.25
❑ 36	Anthony Thomas	.60	.25
❑ 37	Drew Bledsoe	1.00	.40
❑ 38	Jake Plummer	.60	.25
❑ 39	Tiki Barber	1.00	.40
❑ 40	Brett Favre	2.50	1.00
❑ 41	Joey Harrington	1.00	.40
❑ 42	Daunte Culpepper	1.00	.40
❑ 43	LaVar Arrington	2.00	.75
❑ 44	Santana Moss	.60	.25
❑ 45	David Carr	1.00	.40
❑ 46	Randy Moss	1.25	.50
❑ 47	LaDainian Tomlinson	1.25	.50
❑ 48	Deuce McAllister	1.00	.40
❑ 49	Amani Toomer	.60	.25
❑ 50	Donovan McNabb	1.25	.50
❑ 51	Priest Holmes	1.25	.50
❑ 52	Corey Dillon	.60	.25
❑ 53	Tom Brady	2.50	1.00
❑ 54	Edgerrin James	1.00	.40
❑ 55	Michael Vick	2.00	.75
❑ 56	Anquan Boldin	1.00	.40
❑ 57	Robert Ferguson	.40	.15
❑ 58	Onterrio Smith	.60	.25
❑ 59	Marques Tuiasosopo	.60	.25
❑ 60	Rudi Johnson	.60	.25
❑ 61	Alge Crumpler	.60	.25
❑ 62	Antonio Bryant	.60	.25
❑ 63	LaMont Jordan	1.00	.40
❑ 64	Lamar Gordon	.40	.15
❑ 65	Tim Rattay	.40	.15
❑ 66	Antwaan Randle El	1.00	.40
❑ 67	Ladell Betts	.40	.15
❑ 68	LaBrandon Toefield	.40	.15
❑ 69	Ashley Lelie	.60	.25
❑ 70	Marc Bulger	1.00	.40
❑ 71	Reggie Wayne	.60	.25
❑ 72	William Green	.60	.25
❑ 73	Josh Reed	.40	.15
❑ 74	T.J. Duckett	.60	.25
❑ 75	Andre Johnson	1.00	.40
❑ 76	Deion Branch	1.00	.40
❑ 77	Tyrone Calico	.60	.25
❑ 78	Jeremy Shockey	1.00	.40
❑ 79	Najeh Davenport	.40	.15
❑ 80	Byron Leftwich	1.25	.50
❑ 81	Correll Buckhalter	.60	.25
❑ 82	Justin McCareins	.40	.15
❑ 83	Carson Palmer	1.25	.50
❑ 84	Bryant Johnson	.40	.15
❑ 85	Patrick Ramsey	.60	.25
❑ 86	Justin Fargas	.60	.25
❑ 87	Dallas Clark	.60	.25
❑ 88	Kelly Campbell	.40	.15
❑ 89	DeShaun Foster	.60	.25
❑ 90	Charles Rogers	.60	.25
❑ 91	Donte' Stallworth	.60	.25
❑ 92	Dante Hall	1.00	.40
❑ 93	Randy McMichael	.40	.15
❑ 94	Marcel Shipp	.60	.25
❑ 95	Kyle Boller	1.00	.40
❑ 96	Steve Smith	1.00	.40
❑ 97	Brian Westbrook	.60	.25
❑ 98	Kevan Barlow	.60	.25
❑ 99	Damerien McCants	.40	.15
❑ 100	Domanick Davis	1.00	.40
❑ 101	Andre' Davis	.40	.15
❑ 102	Nate Burleson	1.00	.40
❑ 103	Larry Johnson	1.25	.50
❑ 104	Drew Brees	1.00	.40
❑ 105	Koren Robinson	.60	.25
❑ 106	Quincy Carter	.60	.25
❑ 107	Javon Walker	.60	.25
❑ 108	Willis McGahee	1.00	.40
❑ 109	Chris Simms	.60	.25
❑ 110	Rex Grossman	1.00	.40
❑ 111	Steven Jackson RC	6.00	2.50
❑ 112	Greg Jones RC	2.00	.75
❑ 113	Brandon Everage RC	1.50	.60
❑ 114	DeAngelo Hall RC	2.50	1.00
❑ 115	Tatum Bell RC	4.00	1.50
❑ 116	B.J. Symons RC	2.00	.75
❑ 117	Michael Clayton RC	4.00	1.50
❑ 118	Jared Lorenzen RC	1.50	.60
❑ 119	Josh Harris RC	2.00	.75
❑ 120	Roy Williams RC	5.00	2.00
❑ 121	Mewelde Moore RC	2.00	.75
❑ 122	Jeff Smoker RC	2.00	.75
❑ 123	Lee Evans RC	2.50	1.00
❑ 124	Michael Jenkins RC	2.00	.75
❑ 125	Drew Henson RC	2.00	.75
❑ 126	Ben Watson RC	2.00	.75
❑ 127	Jerricho Cotchery RC	2.00	.75
❑ 128	Ben Troupe RC	2.00	.75
❑ 129	Chris Gamble RC	2.00	.75
❑ 130	Kevin Jones RC	5.00	2.00
❑ 131	Cody Pickett RC	2.00	.75
❑ 132	J.P. Losman RC	4.00	1.50
❑ 133	Michael Boulware RC	2.00	.75
❑ 134	Julius Jones RC	6.00	2.50
❑ 135	Keary Colbert RC	2.50	1.00
❑ 136	Vince Wilfork RC	2.00	.75
❑ 137	Ernest Wilford RC	2.00	.75
❑ 138	John Navarre RC	2.00	.75
❑ 139	D.J. Williams RC	2.00	.75
❑ 140	Larry Fitzgerald RC	6.00	2.50
❑ 141	Quincy Wilson RC	1.50	.60
❑ 142	James Newson RC	1.50	.60
❑ 143	Reggie Williams RC	2.50	1.00
❑ 144	Devard Darling RC	2.00	.75
❑ 145	Chris Perry RC	3.00	1.25
❑ 146	Derrick Strait RC	2.00	.75
❑ 147	Teddy Lehman RC	2.00	.75
❑ 148	Michael Turner RC	2.50	1.00
❑ 149	Will Smith RC	2.00	.75
❑ 150	Eli Manning RC	12.00	5.00
❑ 151	Cedric Cobbs RC	2.00	.75
❑ 152	Ell Roberson UER RC	2.00	.75

❑ 153 Matt Schaub RC 6.00 2.50
❑ 154 Derrick Knight RC 1.50 .60
❑ 155 Rashaun Woods RC 2.00 .75
❑ 156 Jonathan Vilma RC 2.00 .75
❑ 157 Tommie Harris RC 2.00 .75
❑ 158 Dwan Edwards RC 1.50 .60
❑ 159 Will Poole RC 2.00 .75
❑ 160 Mike Williams RC 15.00 6.00
❑ 161 Philip Rivers RC 6.00 2.50
❑ 162 Sean Taylor RC 2.00 .75
❑ 163 Darius Watts RC 2.00 .75
❑ 164 Casey Clausen RC 2.00 .75
❑ 165 Ben Roethlisberger RC 20.00 10.00

2005 Topps Draft Picks and Prospects

❑ COMP.SET w/o AU's (165) 40.00 15.00
❑ COMP.SET w/o RC's (110) 25.00 10.00
❑ ONE ROOKIE PER PACK
❑ DRAFT PICK AUTO ODDS 1:1179H, 1:1182R
❑ UNPRICED GOLD SUPERFRACTORS #'d TO 1
❑ UNPRICED PRINTING PLATES #'d TO 1
❑ 1 Marvin Harrison 1.00 .40
❑ 2 Rudi Johnson .60 .25
❑ 3 Matt Hasselbeck .60 .25
❑ 4 Plaxico Burress .60 .25
❑ 5 Chad Pennington 1.00 .40
❑ 6 Jamal Lewis 1.00 .40
❑ 7 Terrell Owens 1.00 .40
❑ 8 LaDainian Tomlinson 1.25 .50
❑ 9 Tiki Barber 1.00 .40
❑ 10 Dante Hall .60 .25
❑ 11 Peyton Manning 1.50 .60
❑ 12 Marshall Faulk 1.00 .40
❑ 13 Donovan McNabb 1.25 .50
❑ 14 Randy Moss 1.00 .40
❑ 15 Muhsin Muhammad .60 .25
❑ 16 Deuce McAllister 1.00 .40
❑ 17 Fred Taylor .60 .25
❑ 18 Jake Plummer .60 .25
❑ 19 Javon Walker .60 .25
❑ 20 Tony Gonzalez .60 .25
❑ 21 Michael Vick 1.50 .60
❑ 22 Brett Favre 2.50 1.00
❑ 23 Joe Horn .60 .25
❑ 24 Jeremy Shockey 1.00 .40
❑ 25 Laveranues Coles .60 .25
❑ 26 Trent Green .60 .25
❑ 27 Alge Crumpler .60 .25
❑ 28 Curtis Martin 1.00 .40
❑ 29 Torry Holt 1.00 .40
❑ 30 Daunte Culpepper 1.00 .40
❑ 31 Aaron Brooks .60 .25
❑ 32 Priest Holmes 1.00 .40
❑ 33 Eric Moulds .60 .25
❑ 34 Jerome Bettis 1.00 .40
❑ 35 David Carr 1.00 .40
❑ 36 Chad Johnson 1.00 .40
❑ 37 Ahman Green 1.00 .40
❑ 38 Clinton Portis 1.00 .40
❑ 39 Drew Brees 1.00 .40
❑ 40 Darrell Jackson .60 .25
❑ 41 Corey Dillon .60 .25
❑ 42 Reggie Wayne .60 .25
❑ 43 Shaun Alexander 1.25 .50
❑ 44 Hines Ward 1.00 .40
❑ 45 Tom Brady 2.50 1.00
❑ 46 Isaac Bruce .60 .25
❑ 47 Byron Leftwich 1.00 .40
❑ 48 Chris Chambers .60 .25
❑ 49 Marc Bulger 1.00 .40
❑ 50 Edgerrin James 1.00 .40
❑ 51 Jake Delhomme 1.00 .40
❑ 52 Koren Robinson .60 .25
❑ 53 Brian Westbrook .60 .25
❑ 54 Reuben Droughns .60 .25
❑ 55 Joey Harrington 1.00 .40
❑ 56 Eli Manning 2.00 .75
❑ 57 Julius Jones 1.25 .50
❑ 58 Nick Goings .50 .20
❑ 59 T.J. Houshmandzadeh .50 .20
❑ 60 Ben Roethlisberger 2.50 1.00
❑ 61 Charles Rogers .60 .25
❑ 62 Billy Volek .60 .25
❑ 63 Drew Henson .60 .25
❑ 64 Andre Johnson .60 .25
❑ 65 Carson Palmer 1.00 .40
❑ 66 Anquan Boldin .60 .25
❑ 67 Lee Suggs .60 .25
❑ 68 Jerry Porter .60 .25
❑ 69 J.P. Losman 1.00 .40
❑ 70 Nate Burleson .60 .25
❑ 71 Lee Evans .60 .25
❑ 72 Tatum Bell .60 .25
❑ 73 Chester Taylor .60 .25
❑ 74 Philip Rivers 1.00 .40
❑ 75 Rex Grossman .60 .25
❑ 76 Willis McGahee 1.00 .40
❑ 77 Antonio Gates 1.00 .40
❑ 78 Steven Jackson 1.25 .50
❑ 79 Roy Williams WR 1.00 .40
❑ 80 Chris Simms .60 .25
❑ 81 Najeh Davenport .50 .20
❑ 82 Kevin Jones 1.00 .40
❑ 83 Jason Witten .60 .25
❑ 84 Brandon Lloyd .50 .20
❑ 85 Larry Johnson 1.00 .40
❑ 86 Ronald Curry .60 .25
❑ 87 Chris Brown .60 .25
❑ 88 Kyle Boller .60 .25
❑ 89 Chris Perry .60 .25
❑ 90 Keary Colbert .60 .25
❑ 91 Sean Taylor .60 .25
❑ 92 Greg Jones .50 .20
❑ 93 Larry Fitzgerald 1.00 .40
❑ 94 Michael Clayton 1.00 .40
❑ 95 Mewelde Moore .60 .25
❑ 96 Drew Bennett .60 .25
❑ 97 Reggie Williams .60 .25
❑ 98 Quentin Griffin .60 .25
❑ 99 Josh McCown .60 .25
❑ 100 Santana Moss .60 .25
❑ 101 Kellen Winslow 1.00 .40
❑ 102 Michael Jenkins .60 .25
❑ 103 Dunta Robinson .60 .25
❑ 104 Luke McCown .50 .20
❑ 105 Brandon Stokley .60 .25
❑ 106 Derrick Blaylock .50 .20
❑ 107 Ernest Wilford .50 .20
❑ 108 Domanick Davis .60 .25
❑ 109 Jonathan Vilma .60 .25
❑ 110 Dwight Freeney .60 .25
❑ 111 Alex Smith QB AU RC 150.00 75.00
❑ 112 Derrick Johnson AU RC 120.00 60.00
❑ 113 Charlie Frye AU RC 100.00 50.00
❑ 114 Ronnie Brown AU RC 150.00 75.00
❑ 115 Mike Williams AU 100.00 40.00
❑ 116 Erasmus James RC 2.00 .75
❑ 117 Alex Smith TE RC 2.00 .75
❑ 118 Dan Orlovsky RC 2.50 1.00
❑ 119 Eric Shelton RC 2.00 .75
❑ 120 Reggie Brown RC 2.00 .75
❑ 121 Carlos Rogers RC 2.50 1.00
❑ 122 Dan Cody RC 2.00 .75
❑ 123 J.J. Arrington RC 2.50 1.00
❑ 124 Travis Johnson RC 1.50 .60
❑ 125 Antrel Rolle RC 2.00 .75
❑ 126 Andrew Walter RC 3.00 1.25
❑ 127 Craphonso Thorpe RC 1.50 .60
❑ 128 Bryan Randall RC 1.50 .60
❑ 129 Anttaj Hawthorne RC 1.50 .60
❑ 130 David Pollack RC 2.00 .75
❑ 131 Heath Miller RC 5.00 2.00
❑ 132 Charles Frederick RC 1.50 .60
❑ 133 Anthony Davis RC 1.50 .60
❑ 134 Chris Rix RC 1.50 .60
❑ 135 T.A. McLendon RC 1.50 .60
❑ 136 David Greene RC 2.00 .75
❑ 137 Timmy Chang RC 1.50 .60
❑ 138 Marcus Spears RC 2.00 .75
❑ 139 Airese Currie RC 2.00 .75
❑ 140 Chris Henry RC 2.00 .75
❑ 141 Josh Davis RC 1.50 .60
❑ 142 Jason Campbell RC 3.00 1.25
❑ 143 Barrett Ruud RC 2.00 .75
❑ 144 Courtney Roby RC 2.00 .75
❑ 145 Mike Patterson RC 2.00 .75
❑ 146 Jason White RC 2.00 .75
❑ 147 Fred Gibson RC 1.50 .60
❑ 148 Marion Barber RC 3.00 1.25
❑ 149 Braylon Edwards RC 6.00 2.50
❑ 150 Cadillac Williams RC 10.00 4.00
❑ 151 Kyle Orton RC 3.00 1.25
❑ 152 Aaron Rodgers RC 6.00 2.50
❑ 153 Alvin Pearman RC 2.00 .75
❑ 154 Stefan LeFors RC 2.00 .75
❑ 155 Marlin Jackson RC 2.00 .75
❑ 156 Taylor Stubblefield RC 1.50 .60
❑ 157 Ciatrick Fason RC 2.00 .75
❑ 158 Kay-Jay Harris RC 1.50 .60
❑ 159 Frank Gore RC 4.00 1.50
❑ 160 Vernand Morency RC 2.00 .75
❑ 161 Adam Jones RC 2.00 .75
❑ 162 Troy Williamson RC 4.00 1.50
❑ 163 Roddy White RC 2.00 .75
❑ 164 Thomas Davis RC 2.00 .75
❑ 165 Mark Clayton RC 2.50 1.00
❑ 166 Craig Bragg RC 1.50 .60
❑ 167 Noah Herron RC 2.00 .75
❑ 168 Darren Sproles RC 2.00 .75
❑ 169 Terrence Murphy RC 2.00 .75
❑ 170 Walter Reyes RC 1.50 .60

2006 Topps Draft Picks and Prospects

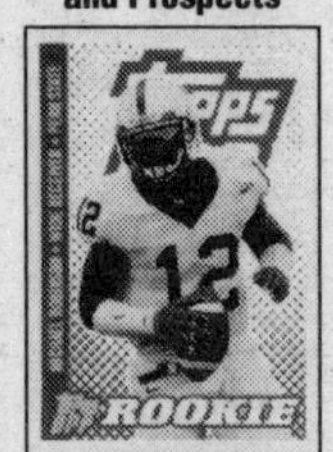

❑ COMP.SET w/o SP's (165) 30.00 12.50
❑ COMP.SET w/o RC's (110) 15.00 6.00
❑ ONE ROOKIE CARD PER PACK
❑ 166-175 ROOKIE AU/199 ODDS 1:1282
❑ 1 Plaxico Burress .60 .25
❑ 2 Ahman Green .60 .25
❑ 3 Domanick Davis .60 .25
❑ 4 Andre Johnson .60 .25
❑ 5 Donovan McNabb 1.00 .40
❑ 6 Marvin Harrison 1.00 .40
❑ 7 Michael Vick 1.25 .50
❑ 8 Priest Holmes .60 .25
❑ 9 Torry Holt .60 .25
❑ 10 Marc Bulger .60 .25
❑ 11 Ben Roethlisberger 1.50 .60
❑ 12 Larry Fitzgerald 1.00 .40
❑ 13 Peyton Manning 1.50 .60
❑ 14 Chris Perry .60 .25
❑ 15 Antonio Gates 1.00 .40
❑ 16 Eli Manning 1.25 .50
❑ 17 Brett Favre 2.00 .75
❑ 18 Reggie Brown .60 .25
❑ 19 Curtis Martin 1.00 .40
❑ 20 Charlie Frye .60 .25
❑ 21 Tom Brady 1.50 .60
❑ 22 Cadillac Williams 1.00 .40
❑ 23 Trent Green .60 .25
❑ 24 Matt Jones 1.00 .40
❑ 25 Anquan Boldin .60 .25
❑ 26 Larry Johnson 1.25 .50

	Card		
❑ 27	Rudi Johnson	.60	.25
❑ 28	Marion Barber	.60	.25
❑ 29	Jake Delhomme	.60	.25
❑ 30	Philip Rivers	1.00	.40
❑ 31	Fred Taylor	.60	.25
❑ 32	Frank Gore	1.00	.40
❑ 33	Shaun Alexander	1.00	.40
❑ 34	Chris Simms	.60	.25
❑ 35	LaDainian Tomlinson	1.25	.50
❑ 36	Troy Williamson	.60	.25
❑ 37	Clinton Portis	1.00	.40
❑ 38	Kyle Orton	.60	.25
❑ 39	Tony Gonzalez	.60	.25
❑ 40	Mark Clayton	.60	.25
❑ 41	Steve Smith	1.00	.40
❑ 42	Heath Miller	1.00	.40
❑ 43	Warrick Dunn	.60	.25
❑ 44	Alex Smith TE	.50	.20
❑ 45	Chris Brown	.60	.25
❑ 46	Billy Volek	.60	.25
❑ 47	Tiki Barber	1.00	.40
❑ 48	Julius Jones	1.00	.40
❑ 49	Drew Bledsoe	1.00	.40
❑ 50	Charles Rogers	.60	.25
❑ 51	Jake Plummer	.60	.25
❑ 52	Greg Jones	.50	.20
❑ 53	Chad Johnson	.60	.25
❑ 54	Braylon Edwards	1.00	.40
❑ 55	Carson Palmer	1.00	.40
❑ 56	Scottie Vines	.50	.20
❑ 57	Keary Colbert	.50	.20
❑ 58	Alex Smith QB	1.25	.50
❑ 59	Roy Williams WR	1.00	.40
❑ 60	Roddy White	.60	.25
❑ 61	Willis McGahee	1.00	.40
❑ 62	Michael Clayton	.60	.25
❑ 63	Edgerrin James	1.00	.40
❑ 64	Aaron Rodgers	1.00	.40
❑ 65	Byron Leftwich	.60	.25
❑ 66	Tatum Bell	.60	.25
❑ 67	Daunte Culpepper	1.00	.40
❑ 68	Chris Henry	.50	.20
❑ 69	Corey Dillon	.60	.25
❑ 70	Ronnie Brown	1.00	.40
❑ 71	Kevin Jones	1.00	.40
❑ 72	J.P. Losman	.60	.25
❑ 73	Steven Jackson	1.00	.40
❑ 74	Mike Williams	1.00	.40
❑ 75	Jeremy Shockey	1.00	.40
❑ 76	DeMarcus Ware	.60	.25
❑ 77	LaMont Jordan	.60	.25
❑ 78	Cedric Benson	1.00	.40
❑ 79	Ricky Williams	.60	.25
❑ 80	Brandon Jones	.50	.20
❑ 81	Brian Westbrook	.60	.25
❑ 82	Willie Parker	1.25	.50
❑ 83	Hines Ward	1.00	.40
❑ 84	Ernest Wilford	.50	.20
❑ 85	Matt Hasselbeck	.60	.25
❑ 86	Jason Campbell	.60	.25
❑ 87	Joey Galloway	.60	.25
❑ 88	Odell Thurman	.50	.20
❑ 89	Santana Moss	.60	.25
❑ 90	Courtney Roby	.50	.20
❑ 91	Deuce McAllister	.60	.25
❑ 92	Derrick Johnson	.60	.25
❑ 93	Drew Brees	1.00	.40
❑ 94	Michael Jenkins	.60	.25
❑ 95	Jerome Bettis	1.00	.40
❑ 96	Osi Umenyiora	.50	.20
❑ 97	Reggie Wayne	.60	.25
❑ 98	Ryan Moats	.50	.20
❑ 99	Randy Moss	1.00	.40
❑ 100	Samie Parker	.50	.20
❑ 101	Mark Bradley	.60	.25
❑ 102	Samkon Gado	1.00	.40
❑ 103	Matt Schaub	.60	.25
❑ 104	Shaun McDonald	.50	.20
❑ 105	D.J. Hackett	.50	.20
❑ 106	Mewelde Moore	.50	.20
❑ 107	Chester Taylor	.60	.25
❑ 108	Greg Lewis	.50	.20
❑ 109	Chris Cooley	.50	.20
❑ 110	Todd DeVoe RC	1.00	.40
❑ 111	Joel Klopfenstein RC	2.00	.75
❑ 112	Devin Hester RC	5.00	2.00
❑ 113	Brad Smith RC	2.50	1.00
❑ 114	Jason Avant RC	2.50	1.00
❑ 115	Michael Robinson RC	4.00	1.50
❑ 116	Kellen Clemens RC	3.00	1.25
❑ 117	Anthony Fasano RC	2.50	1.00
❑ 118	Leon Washington RC	4.00	1.50
❑ 119	Laurence Maroney RC	6.00	2.50
❑ 120	Martin Nance RC	2.00	.75
❑ 121	Demetrius Williams RC	3.00	1.25
❑ 122	A.J. Nicholson RC	1.25	.50
❑ 123	Jimmy Williams RC	2.50	1.00
❑ 124	Michael Huff RC	3.00	1.25
❑ 125	Chad Jackson RC	4.00	1.50
❑ 126	Mike Hass RC	2.50	1.00
❑ 127	Brodie Croyle RC	5.00	2.00
❑ 128	Jerome Harrison RC	2.50	1.00
❑ 129	Hank Baskett RC	2.50	1.00
❑ 130	Santonio Holmes RC	5.00	2.00
❑ 131	Chad Greenway RC	2.50	1.00
❑ 132	Mario Williams RC	4.00	1.50
❑ 133	Charlie Whitehurst RC	3.00	1.25
❑ 134	Darrell Hackney RC	2.00	.75
❑ 135	DeMeco Ryans RC	3.00	1.25
❑ 136	Mathias Kiwanuka RC	3.00	1.25
❑ 137	Omar Jacobs RC	2.00	.75
❑ 138	Bruce Gradkowski RC	4.00	1.50
❑ 139	Drew Olson RC	2.00	.75
❑ 140	Maurice Stovall RC	2.50	1.00
❑ 141	Greg Jennings RC	4.00	1.50
❑ 142	D'Brickashaw Ferguson RC	2.50	1.00
❑ 143	Manny Lawson RC	2.50	1.00
❑ 144	Tamba Hali RC	2.50	1.00
❑ 145	Vernon Davis RC	5.00	2.00
❑ 146	Greg Lee RC	2.00	.75
❑ 147	Dominique Byrd RC	2.00	.75
❑ 148	Leonard Pope RC	2.50	1.00
❑ 149	Bobby Carpenter RC	2.50	1.00
❑ 150	Haloti Ngata RC	2.50	1.00
❑ 151	Marcedes Lewis RC	2.50	1.00
❑ 152	Ernie Sims RC	3.00	1.25
❑ 153	Ashton Youboty RC	2.50	1.00
❑ 154	D.J. Shockley RC	2.50	1.00
❑ 155	Paul Pinegar RC	2.00	.75
❑ 156	Maurice Drew RC	6.00	2.50
❑ 157	Jeremy Bloom RC	2.00	.75
❑ 158	Cory Rodgers RC	2.50	1.00
❑ 159	Abdul Hodge RC	2.50	1.00
❑ 160	Tye Hill RC	2.50	1.00
❑ 161	D'Qwell Jackson RC	2.00	.75
❑ 162	Jonathan Orr RC	2.00	.75
❑ 163	Antonio Cromartie RC	2.50	1.00
❑ 164	Todd Watkins RC	2.00	.75
❑ 165	Gerald Riggs RC	2.50	1.00
❑ 166	Matt Leinart AU RC	200.00	100.00
❑ 167	Reggie Bush AU RC	400.00	200.00
❑ 168	DeAngelo Williams AU RC	120.00	60.00
❑ 169	A.J. Hawk AU RC	125.00	75.00
❑ 170	Vince Young AU RC	250.00	150.00
❑ 171	Derek Hagan AU RC	50.00	25.00
❑ 172	Joseph Addai AU RC	135.00	75.00
❑ 173	Jay Cutler AU RC	200.00	100.00
❑ 174	Sinorice Moss AU RC	80.00	30.00
❑ 175	LenDale White AU RC	80.00	40.00
❑ RBML	R.Bush/Leinart AU/25	550.00	350.00

2001 Topps Heritage

	Card		
❑	COMPLETE SET (146)	300.00	150.00
❑	COMP.SET w/o SP's (110)	25.00	10.00
❑ 1	Ray Lewis	1.25	.50
❑ 2	Peter Warrick	1.25	.50
❑ 3	James Stewart	.75	.30
❑ 4	Junior Seau	1.25	.50
❑ 5	Jeff George	.75	.30
❑ 6	Amani Toomer	.50	.20
❑ 7	Elvis Grbac	.75	.30
❑ 8	David Boston	1.25	.50
❑ 9	Jimmy Smith	.75	.30
❑ 10	Warrick Dunn	1.25	.50
❑ 11	Hines Ward	1.25	.50
❑ 12	Joe Horn	.75	.30
❑ 13	Stephen Davis	1.25	.50
❑ 14	Tyrone Wheatley	.75	.30
❑ 15	Brian Urlacher	2.00	.75
❑ 16	Fred Taylor	1.25	.50
❑ 17	Jerry Rice	2.50	1.00
❑ 18	Keyshawn Johnson	1.25	.50
❑ 19	Jay Fiedler	1.25	.50
❑ 20	Jamal Anderson	1.25	.50
❑ 21	Emmitt Smith	2.50	1.00
❑ 22	Tiki Barber	1.25	.50
❑ 23	Daunte Culpepper	1.25	.50
❑ 24	Torry Holt	1.25	.50
❑ 25	Peyton Manning	3.00	1.25
❑ 26	Eddie George	1.25	.50
❑ 27	Jamal Lewis	2.00	.75
❑ 28	Ricky Williams	1.25	.50
❑ 29	Ahman Green	1.25	.50
❑ 30	Ed McCaffrey	1.25	.50
❑ 31	Curtis Martin	1.25	.50
❑ 32	Isaac Bruce	1.25	.50
❑ 33	Doug Flutie	1.25	.50
❑ 34	Steve McNair	1.25	.50
❑ 35	Donovan McNabb	1.50	.60
❑ 36	Keenan McCardell	.50	.20
❑ 37	Charlie Batch	1.25	.50
❑ 38	Cade McNown	.50	.20
❑ 39	Terrell Owens	1.25	.50
❑ 40	Brad Johnson	1.25	.50
❑ 41	Robert Smith	1.25	.50
❑ 42	Muhsin Muhammad	.75	.30
❑ 43	Kurt Warner	2.50	1.00
❑ 44	Lamar Smith	.75	.30
❑ 45	Brian Griese	1.25	.50
❑ 46	Trent Dilfer	.75	.30
❑ 47	Jeff Garcia	1.25	.50
❑ 48	Derrick Mason	.75	.30
❑ 49	Drew Bledsoe	1.50	.60
❑ 50	Marshall Faulk	1.50	.60
❑ 51	Corey Dillon	1.25	.50
❑ 52	Tony Gonzalez	.75	.30
❑ 53	Chad Lewis	.50	.20
❑ 54	Shaun Alexander	1.50	.60
❑ 55	Edgerrin James	1.50	.60
❑ 56	Eric Moulds	.75	.30
❑ 57	Aaron Brooks	1.25	.50
❑ 58	Zach Thomas	1.25	.50
❑ 59	Jerome Bettis	1.25	.50
❑ 60	Shannon Sharpe	.75	.30
❑ 61	Kerry Collins	.75	.30
❑ 62	Ricky Watters	.75	.30
❑ 63	Tim Couch	.75	.30
❑ 64	Marvin Harrison	1.25	.50
❑ 65	Tim Brown	1.25	.50
❑ 66	Mark Brunell	1.25	.50
❑ 67	Wayne Chrebet	.75	.30
❑ 68	Terry Glenn	.75	.30
❑ 69	Mike Anderson	1.25	.50
❑ 70	Randy Moss	2.50	1.00
❑ 71	Freddie Jones	.50	.20
❑ 72	Ike Hilliard	.75	.30
❑ 73	Derrick Alexander	.75	.30
❑ 74	Travis Prentice	.50	.20
❑ 75	Brett Favre	4.00	1.50
❑ 76	Rod Smith	.75	.30
❑ 77	Troy Aikman	2.00	.75
❑ 78	Cris Carter	1.25	.50
❑ 79	Rich Gannon	1.25	.50
❑ 80	Charlie Garner	.75	.30
❑ 81	Michael Pittman	.50	.20
❑ 82	Jeff Graham	.50	.20
❑ 83	Albert Connell	.50	.20
❑ 84	Bill Schroeder	.75	.30
❑ 85	Jeff Blake	.75	.30
❑ 86	Jon Kitna	1.25	.50
❑ 87	Qadry Ismail	.75	.30
❑ 88	Joey Galloway	.75	.30
❑ 89	Charles Johnson	.50	.20

❑ 90 Troy Brown .75 .30
❑ 91 Johnnie Morton .75 .30
❑ 92 Chris Chandler .75 .30
❑ 93 Donald Hayes .50 .20
❑ 94 Shaun King .50 .20
❑ 95 Vinny Testaverde .75 .30
❑ 96 James Allen .75 .30
❑ 97 Jake Plummer .75 .30
❑ 98 Antonio Freeman 1.25 .50
❑ 99 Sean Dawkins .50 .20
❑ 100 Ron Dayne 1.25 .50
❑ 101 Rob Johnson .75 .30
❑ 102 Kordell Stewart .75 .30
❑ 103 Akili Smith .50 .20
❑ 104 Shawn Jefferson .50 .20
❑ 105 Germane Crowell .50 .20
❑ 106 Kevin Johnson .75 .30
❑ 107 Steve Beuerlein .75 .30
❑ 108 Marcus Robinson 1.25 .50
❑ 109 Peerless Price .75 .30
❑ 110 Jerome Pathon .75 .30
❑ 111 Sage Rosenfels RC 8.00 3.00
❑ 112 Quincy Morgan RC 8.00 3.00
❑ 113 Chad Johnson RC 20.00 7.50
❑ 114 Josh Heupel RC 8.00 3.00
❑ 115 Anthony Thomas RC 8.00 3.00
❑ 116 Drew Brees RC 25.00 10.00
❑ 117 Kevan Barlow RC 8.00 3.00
❑ 118 Chris Chambers RC 12.00 5.00
❑ 119 Mike McMahon RC 8.00 3.00
❑ 120 Todd Heap RC 8.00 3.00
❑ 121 Leonard Davis RC 5.00 2.00
❑ 122 Richard Seymour RC 8.00 3.00
❑ 123 Robert Ferguson RC 8.00 3.00
❑ 124 Andre Carter RC 8.00 3.00
❑ 125 Jesse Palmer RC 8.00 3.00
❑ 126 Travis Minor RC 5.00 2.00
❑ 127 Rudi Johnson RC 15.00 6.00
❑ 128 Rod Gardner RC 8.00 3.00
❑ 129 Snoop Minnis RC 5.00 2.00
❑ 130 Koren Robinson RC 8.00 3.00
❑ 131 Chris Weinke RC 8.00 3.00
❑ 132 James Jackson RC 8.00 3.00
❑ 133 Michael Vick RC 30.00 15.00
❑ 134 Marques Tuiasosopo RC 8.00 3.00
❑ 135 Michael Bennett RC 8.00 3.00
❑ 136 LaDainian Tomlinson RC 50.00 30.00
❑ 137 Freddie Mitchell RC 8.00 3.00
❑ 138 Deuce McAllister RC 15.00 6.00
❑ 139 Quincy Carter RC 8.00 3.00
❑ 140 Santana Moss RC 12.00 5.00
❑ 141 David Terrell RC 8.00 3.00
❑ 142 Reggie Wayne RC 15.00 6.00
❑ 143 Justin Smith RC 8.00 3.00
❑ 144 Gerard Warren RC 8.00 3.00
❑ 145 Travis Henry RC 12.00 5.00
❑ 146 Dan Morgan RC 8.00 3.00
❑ NNO Checklist CL .50 .20

2002 Topps Heritage

❑ COMPLETE SET (194) 250.00 125.00
❑ 1 Jerome Bettis 1.25 .50
❑ 2 Jeff Blake SP 1.00 .40
❑ 3 Rod Smith .75 .30
❑ 4 Eric Moulds .75 .30
❑ 5 Michael Vick 4.00 1.50
❑ 6 Randy Moss 2.50 1.00
❑ 7 Todd Pinkston .75 .30
❑ 8 Trung Canidate SP 1.50 .60
❑ 9 Steve McNair 1.25 .50
❑ 10 J.J. Stokes SP 1.50 .60
❑ 11 Ricky Williams 2.50 1.00
❑ 12 Germane Crowell SP 1.00 .40
❑ 13 Muhsin Muhammad SP 1.50 .60
❑ 14 Michael Pittman SP 1.00 .40
❑ 15 James Jackson SP 1.00 .40
❑ 16 Dominic Rhodes .75 .30
❑ 17 Jay Fiedler .75 .30
❑ 18 Marcus Robinson .75 .30
❑ 19 Qadry Ismail SP 1.50 .60
❑ 20 Michael Strahan .75 .30
❑ 21 Koren Robinson .75 .30
❑ 22 James Allen SP 1.50 .60
❑ 23 Chad Pennington 1.50 .60
❑ 24 Fred Taylor 1.25 .50
❑ 25 Corey Dillon .75 .30
❑ 26 Thomas Jones SP 1.50 .60
❑ 27 Anthony Thomas .75 .30
❑ 28 Priest Holmes 1.50 .60
❑ 29 Troy Brown .75 .30
❑ 30 Jerry Rice 2.50 1.00
❑ 31 Correll Buckhalter .75 .30
❑ 32 Drew Brees 1.25 .50
❑ 33 Isaac Bruce 1.25 .50
❑ 34 Warrick Dunn SP 2.50 1.00
❑ 35 Chris Chambers 1.25 .50
❑ 36 Antonio Freeman 1.25 .50
❑ 37 Joey Galloway SP 1.50 .60
❑ 38 Rob Johnson SP 1.50 .60
❑ 39 Reggie Wayne 1.25 .50
❑ 40 Santana Moss 1.25 .50
❑ 41 Plaxico Burress .75 .30
❑ 42 Frank Wycheck SP 1.00 .40
❑ 43 Johnnie Morton .75 .30
❑ 44 Chris Weinke .75 .30
❑ 45 Rocket Ismail SP 1.50 .60
❑ 46 Daunte Culpepper 1.25 .50
❑ 47 Deuce McAllister SP 3.00 1.25
❑ 48 Terrell Owens 1.25 .50
❑ 49 Michael Westbrook .50 .20
❑ 50 Tom Brady 3.00 1.25
❑ 51 Mike Anderson 1.25 .50
❑ 52 Jake Plummer .75 .30
❑ 53 Travis Taylor SP 1.50 .60
❑ 54 Marcus Pollard SP 1.00 .40
❑ 55 Zach Thomas 1.25 .50
❑ 56 Duce Staley 1.25 .50
❑ 57 Trent Dilfer .75 .30
❑ 58 Keyshawn Johnson 1.25 .50
❑ 59 Amani Toomer SP 1.50 .60
❑ 60 David Terrell 1.25 .50
❑ 61 Robert Ferguson SP 1.00 .40
❑ 62 Jeff Garcia 1.25 .50
❑ 63 Eddie George 1.25 .50
❑ 64 Marshall Faulk 1.25 .50
❑ 65 Travis Henry 1.25 .50
❑ 66 Tim Couch .75 .30
❑ 67 Mike McMahon 1.25 .50
❑ 68 John Abraham SP 1.50 .60
❑ 69 James Thrash .75 .30
❑ 70 Shaun Alexander 1.50 .60
❑ 71 Ike Hilliard SP 1.50 .60
❑ 72 Brian Griese 1.25 .50
❑ 73 Ray Lewis 1.25 .50
❑ 74 Jon Kitna .75 .30
❑ 75 Az-Zahir Hakim SP 1.00 .40
❑ 76 Oronde Gadsden SP 1.50 .60
❑ 77 Joe Horn .75 .30
❑ 78 Tim Brown 1.25 .50
❑ 79 Kendrell Bell 1.25 .50
❑ 80 LaDainian Tomlinson 2.00 .75
❑ 81 Brad Johnson .75 .30
❑ 82 Tony Gonzalez .75 .30
❑ 83 Bill Schroeder .75 .30
❑ 84 Quincy Carter .75 .30
❑ 85 Donald Hayes SP 1.00 .40
❑ 86 Peyton Manning 2.50 1.00
❑ 87 Drew Bledsoe 1.25 .50
❑ 88 Darrell Jackson .75 .30
❑ 89 Rod Gardner .75 .30
❑ 90 Derrick Mason .75 .30
❑ 91 Byron Chamberlain SP 1.00 .40
❑ 92 James Mcknight SP 1.00 .40
❑ 93 Kevin Johnson .75 .30
❑ 94 Terry Glenn .75 .30
❑ 95 Marty Booker SP 1.00 .40
❑ 96 Terrell Davis 1.25 .50
❑ 97 Vinny Testaverde .75 .30
❑ 98 Hines Ward 1.25 .50
❑ 99 Chad Lewis SP 1.00 .40
❑ 100 Kurt Warner 1.25 .50
❑ 101 Michael Bennett .75 .30
❑ 102 Edgerrin James 1.50 .60
❑ 103 Corey Bradford SP 1.00 .40
❑ 104 Chad Johnson SP 2.50 1.00
❑ 105 Alex Van Pelt .75 .30
❑ 106 Antowain Smith .75 .30
❑ 107 Rich Gannon 1.25 .50
❑ 108 Kevan Barlow SP 1.50 .60
❑ 109 Mike Alstott SP 2.50 1.00
❑ 110 Kerry Collins SP 1.50 .60
❑ 111 Jimmy Smith .75 .30
❑ 112 Jermaine Lewis SP 1.00 .40
❑ 113 Quincy Morgan SP 1.00 .40
❑ 114 Maurice Smith SP 1.50 .60
❑ 115 Willie Jackson .50 .20
❑ 116 Doug Flutie 1.25 .50
❑ 117 Matt Hasselbeck .75 .30
❑ 118 Amos Zereoue SP 2.50 1.00
❑ 119 Lamar Smith .75 .30
❑ 120 Snoop Minnis .50 .20
❑ 121 Troy Hambrick SP 1.00 .40
❑ 122 Shannon Sharpe SP 1.50 .60
❑ 123 Laveranues Coles .75 .30
❑ 124 Freddie Mitchell .75 .30
❑ 125 Kevin Dyson SP 1.50 .60
❑ 126 Torry Holt 1.25 .50
❑ 127 James Stewart SP 1.50 .60
❑ 128 Brian Urlacher 2.00 .75
❑ 129 David Boston 1.25 .50
❑ 130 Ron Dayne .75 .30
❑ 131 Garrison Hearst .75 .30
❑ 132 Stephen Davis .75 .30
❑ 133 Donovan McNabb 1.50 .60
❑ 134 David Patten .50 .20
❑ 135 Travis Minor SP 1.00 .40
❑ 136 Peerless Price SP 1.50 .60
❑ 137 Chris Redman SP 1.00 .40
❑ 138 Ahman Green 1.25 .50
❑ 139 Mark Brunell 1.25 .50
❑ 140 Charlie Garner .75 .30
❑ 141 Curtis Conway .50 .20
❑ 142 Wayne Chrebet .75 .30
❑ 143 Kordell Stewart .75 .30
❑ 144 Peter Warrick .75 .30
❑ 145 Emmitt Smith 3.00 1.25
❑ 146 Jim Miller SP 1.00 .40
❑ 147 Trent Green .75 .30
❑ 148 Cris Carter 1.25 .50
❑ 149 Aaron Brooks 1.25 .50
❑ 150 Curtis Martin 1.25 .50
❑ 151 Tiki Barber SP 2.50 1.00
❑ 152 Marvin Harrison 1.25 .50
❑ 153 Tyrone Wheatley SP 1.50 .60
❑ 154 Brett Favre 3.00 1.25
❑ 155 David Carr RC 8.00 3.00
❑ 156 Quentin Jammer RC 3.00 1.25
❑ 157 Julius Peppers RC 6.00 2.50
❑ 158 Mike Williams RC 2.50 1.00
❑ 159 Antwaan Randle El RC 5.00 2.00
❑ 160 Joey Harrington RC 5.00 2.00
❑ 161 Ashley Lelie RC 6.00 2.50
❑ 162 Marquise Walker RC 2.50 1.00
❑ 163 Rohan Davey RC 3.00 1.25
❑ 164 Patrick Ramsey RC 4.00 1.50
❑ 165 T.J. Duckett RC 4.00 1.50
❑ 166 DeShaun Foster RC 3.00 1.25
❑ 167 Donte Stallworth RC 6.00 2.50
❑ 168 William Green RC 3.00 1.25
❑ 169 Ron Johnson RC 2.50 1.00
❑ 170 Maurice Morris RC 3.00 1.25
❑ 171 Travis Stephens RC 2.50 1.00
❑ 172 Eric Crouch RC 3.00 1.25
❑ 173 David Garrard RC 3.00 1.25
❑ 174 Daniel Graham RC 3.00 1.25
❑ 175 Roy Williams RC 8.00 3.00
❑ 176 Jeremy Shockey RC 10.00 4.00
❑ 177 Josh McCown RC 4.00 1.50
❑ 178 Josh Reed RC 3.00 1.25
❑ 179 Andre Davis RC 2.50 1.00
❑ 180 Antonio Bryant RC 3.00 1.25
❑ 181 Clinton Portis RC 10.00 4.00
❑ 182 Javon Walker RC 6.00 2.50

❑ 183	Jabar Gaffney RC	3.00	1.25
❑ 184	Ladell Betts RC	3.00	1.25
❑ 185	Tim Carter RC	2.50	1.00
❑ 186	Reche Caldwell RC	3.00	1.25
❑ 187	Cliff Russell RC	2.50	1.00
❑ 188	Brian Westbrook SP RC	6.00	2.50
❑ 189	Freddie Milons RC	2.50	1.00
❑ 190	Phillip Buchanon RC	3.00	1.25
❑ 191	Lamar Gordon RC	3.00	1.25
❑ 192	Luke Staley RC	2.50	1.00
❑ 193	Albert Haynesworth RC	2.50	1.00
❑ 194	Kurt Kittner RC	2.50	1.00

2005 Topps Heritage

❑ COMPLETE SET (400) 150.00 75.00
❑ COMP.SET w/o SPs (300) 40.00 15.00
❑ 58T SP PRINTED WITH 1958 TOPPS DESIGN
❑ TBJ SP PRINTED W/THROWBACK JER.PHOTO

❑ 1	Curtis Martin	1.00	.40
❑ 2	Javon Walker	.60	.25
❑ 3	Derrick Mason	.60	.25
❑ 4	Julius Jones	1.25	.50
❑ 5	Marc Bulger	1.00	.40
❑ 6	Reggie Wayne	.60	.25
❑ 7	Isaac Bruce	.60	.25
❑ 8	Ray Lewis	1.00	.40
❑ 9	Drew Bledsoe	1.00	.40
❑ 10	Michael Vick	1.50	.60
❑ 11	Charles Rogers	.60	.25
❑ 12	Lee Evans	.60	.25
❑ 13	Jake Plummer	.60	.25
❑ 14	Edgerrin James	1.00	.40
❑ 15	Hines Ward	1.00	.40
❑ 16	Peyton Manning	1.50	.60
❑ 17	Andre Johnson	.60	.25
❑ 18	Trent Green	.60	.25
❑ 19	Brian Westbrook	.60	.25
❑ 20	Kevin Jones	1.00	.40
❑ 21	Deuce McAllister	1.00	.40
❑ 22	Marvin Harrison	1.00	.40
❑ 23	Dwight Freeney	.60	.25
❑ 24	Ahman Green	1.00	.40
❑ 25	Plaxico Burress	.60	.25
❑ 26	Daunte Culpepper	1.00	.40
❑ 27	Corey Dillon	.60	.25
❑ 28	Joe Horn	.60	.25
❑ 29	Torry Holt	1.00	.40
❑ 30	Randy Moss	1.00	.40
❑ 31	Drew Brees	1.00	.40
❑ 32	Jonathan Vilma	.60	.25
❑ 33	Jerome Bettis	1.00	.40
❑ 34	Byron Leftwich	1.00	.40
❑ 35	Marshall Faulk	1.00	.40
❑ 36	Brett Favre	2.50	1.00
❑ 37	Steve McNair	1.00	.40
❑ 38	Rudi Johnson	.60	.25
❑ 39	Tiki Barber	1.00	.40
❑ 40	Muhsin Muhammad	.60	.25
❑ 41	Tony Gonzalez	.60	.25
❑ 42	Chad Pennington	1.00	.40
❑ 43	Shaun Alexander	1.25	.50
❑ 44	Jamal Lewis	1.00	.40
❑ 45	Antonio Gates	1.00	.40
❑ 46	LaDainian Tomlinson	1.25	.50
❑ 47	Matt Hasselbeck	.60	.25
❑ 48	Jake Delhomme	1.00	.40
❑ 49	Chad Johnson	1.00	.40
❑ 50	Willis McGahee	1.00	.40
❑ 51	Jason Witten	.60	.25
❑ 52	J.P. Losman	1.00	.40
❑ 53	Donovan McNabb	1.25	.50
❑ 54A	Eric Shelton RC	2.50	1.00
❑ 54B	Eric Shelton 58T SP	3.00	1.25
❑ 55A	Alex Smith QB RC	10.00	4.00
❑ 55B	Alex Smith QB TBJ SP	12.00	5.00
❑ 56A	Kyle Orton RC	4.00	1.50
❑ 56B	Kyle Orton 58T SP	5.00	2.00
❑ 57A	Andrew Walter RC	4.00	1.50
❑ 57B	Andrew Walter TBJ SP	5.00	2.00
❑ 58A	Ryan Moats RC	2.50	1.00
❑ 58B	Ryan Moats 58T SP	3.00	1.25
❑ 59A	Ciatrick Fason RC	2.50	1.00
❑ 59B	Ciatrick Fason 58T SP	3.00	1.25
❑ 60A	Vincent Jackson RC	2.50	1.00
❑ 60B	Vincent Jackson 58T SP	3.00	1.25
❑ 61A	Heath Miller RC	6.00	2.50
❑ 61B	Heath Miller 58T SP	8.00	3.00
❑ 62A	Carlos Rogers RC	3.00	1.25
❑ 62B	Carlos Rogers TBJ SP	4.00	1.50
❑ 63A	Terrence Murphy RC	2.50	1.00
❑ 63B	Terrence Murphy 58T SP	3.00	1.25
❑ 64A	Mike Williams	5.00	2.00
❑ 64B	Mike Williams 58T SP	6.00	2.50
❑ 65A	Vernand Morency RC	2.50	1.00
❑ 65B	Vernand Morency 58T SP	3.00	1.25
❑ 66A	Maurice Clarett	2.50	1.00
❑ 66B	Maurice Clarett 58T SP	3.00	1.25
❑ 67A	Roscoe Parrish RC	2.50	1.00
❑ 67B	Roscoe Parrish 58T SP	3.00	1.25
❑ 68A	Courtney Roby RC	2.50	1.00
❑ 68B	Courtney Roby 58T SP	3.00	1.25
❑ 69	Tom Brady	2.50	1.00
❑ 70A	David Greene RC	2.50	1.00
❑ 70B	David Greene 58T SP	3.00	1.25
❑ 71A	Antrel Rolle RC	2.50	1.00
❑ 71B	Antrel Rolle 58T SP	3.00	1.25
❑ 72A	Mark Bradley RC	2.50	1.00
❑ 72B	Mark Bradley 58T SP	3.00	1.25
❑ 73A	Frank Gore RC	5.00	2.00
❑ 73B	Frank Gore 58T SP	6.00	2.50
❑ 74A	Cedric Benson RC	5.00	2.00
❑ 74B	Cedric Benson 58T SP	6.00	2.50
❑ 75A	Derrick Johnson 62T RC	4.00	1.50
❑ 75B	Derrick Johnson 58T SP	5.00	2.00
❑ 76A	Reggie Brown RC	2.50	1.00
❑ 76B	Reggie Brown 58T SP	3.00	1.25
❑ 77A	Ronnie Brown RC	10.00	4.00
❑ 77B	Ronnie Brown TBJ SP	12.00	5.00
❑ 78A	Jason Campbell RC	4.00	1.50
❑ 78B	Jason Campbell TBJ SP	5.00	2.00
❑ 79A	Charlie Frye RC	5.00	2.00
❑ 79B	Charlie Frye 58T SP	6.00	2.50
❑ 80	Jamie Sharper	.50	.20
❑ 81	Tony Romo	12.00	6.00
❑ 82	Rod Smith	.60	.25
❑ 83	Chester Taylor	.60	.25
❑ 84	Marcus Robinson	.60	.25
❑ 85	Terence Newman	.50	.20
❑ 86	Aaron Brooks	.60	.25
❑ 87	Kerry Collins	.60	.25
❑ 88	Brandon Lloyd	.50	.20
❑ 89	Michael Pittman	.50	.20
❑ 90	Sean Taylor	.60	.25
❑ 91	Michael Lewis	.50	.20
❑ 92	Jeremy Shockey	1.00	.40
❑ 93	Zach Thomas	1.00	.40
❑ 94	David Carr	1.00	.40
❑ 95	Champ Bailey	.60	.25
❑ 96	Julius Peppers	.60	.25
❑ 97	Brandon Stokley	.60	.25
❑ 98	Deion Branch	.60	.25
❑ 99	Charles Woodson	.60	.25
❑ 100	Darrell Jackson	.60	.25
❑ 101	Ronde Barber	.50	.20
❑ 102	Patrick Ramsey	.60	.25
❑ 103	Warrick Dunn	.60	.25
❑ 104	Takeo Spikes	.50	.20
❑ 105	Thomas Jones	.60	.25
❑ 106	T.J. Houshmandzadeh	.50	.20
❑ 107	Najeh Davenport	.50	.20
❑ 108	Nate Burleson	.60	.25
❑ 109	Kelly Campbell	.50	.20
❑ 110	LaVar Arrington	1.00	.40
❑ 111	Joey Harrington	1.00	.40
❑ 112	DeAngelo Hall	.60	.25
❑ 113	Derrick Blaylock	.50	.20
❑ 114	Michael Clayton	1.00	.40
❑ 115	Adam Archuleta	.50	.20
❑ 116	Jason Taylor	.50	.20
❑ 117	Donald Driver	.60	.25
❑ 118	Dan Morgan	.50	.20
❑ 119	Michael Jenkins	.60	.25
❑ 120	Drew Henson	.60	.25
❑ 121	Jay Fiedler	.50	.20
❑ 122	Ladell Betts	.50	.20
❑ 123	Jonathan Ogden	.50	.20
❑ 124	Domanick Davis	.60	.25
❑ 125	Sebastian Janikowski	.50	.20
❑ 126	Cedrick Wilson	.50	.20
❑ 127	Marcus Trufant	.50	.20
❑ 128	Santana Moss	.60	.25
❑ 129	Tatum Bell	.60	.25
❑ 130	Jonathan Wells	.50	.20
❑ 131	Laveranues Coles	.60	.25
❑ 132	Josh McCown	.60	.25
❑ 133	Antonio Bryant	.50	.20
❑ 134	John Lynch	.60	.25
❑ 135	Roy Williams WR	1.00	.40
❑ 136	Adam Vinatieri	1.00	.40
❑ 137	Dominic Rhodes	.50	.20
❑ 138	Tyrone Calico	.60	.25
❑ 139	Keenan McCardell	.50	.20
❑ 140	Antonio Pierce	.50	.20
❑ 141	Chris Chambers	.60	.25
❑ 142	Bubba Franks	.60	.25
❑ 143	Mike Vanderjagt	.50	.20
❑ 144	Ernest Wilford	.50	.20
❑ 145	Bertrand Berry	.50	.20
❑ 146	David Garrard	.50	.20
❑ 147	DeShaun Foster	.60	.25
❑ 148	Rashaun Woods	.60	.25
❑ 149	Wes Welker	.50	.20
❑ 150	Allen Rossum	.50	.20
❑ 151	Mike Anderson	.60	.25
❑ 152	Keyshawn Johnson	.60	.25
❑ 153	Alge Crumpler	.60	.25
❑ 154	Dunta Robinson	.60	.25
❑ 155	Kyle Boller	.60	.25
❑ 156	William Green	.50	.20
❑ 157	Peter Warrick	.50	.20
❑ 158	Doug Gabriel	.50	.20
❑ 159	Ashley Lelie	.60	.25
❑ 160	Ronald Curry	.60	.25
❑ 161	Keary Colbert	.60	.25
❑ 162	Shawn Bryson	.50	.20
❑ 163	Tim Rattay	.50	.20
❑ 164	Jabar Gaffney	.50	.20
❑ 165	Doug Jolley	.50	.20
❑ 166	Keith Brooking	.50	.20
❑ 167	Brian Urlacher	1.00	.40
❑ 168	Chris Gamble	.60	.25
❑ 169	Kurt Warner	.60	.25
❑ 170	Duce Staley	.60	.25
❑ 171	Steve Smith	.60	.25
❑ 172	Anquan Boldin	.60	.25
❑ 173	Fred Taylor	.60	.25
❑ 174	Donnie Edwards	.50	.20
❑ 175	Clarence Moore	.50	.20
❑ 176	Corey Bradford	.50	.20
❑ 177	Dante Hall	.60	.25
❑ 178	Warren Sapp	.60	.25
❑ 179	Todd Heap	.60	.25
❑ 180	Mewelde Moore	.60	.25
❑ 181	John Abraham	.50	.20
❑ 182	Rex Grossman	.60	.25
❑ 183	Stephen Davis	.60	.25
❑ 184	Greg Jones	.50	.20
❑ 185	Jeremiah Trotter	.50	.20
❑ 186	Carson Palmer	1.00	.40
❑ 187	Simeon Rice	.60	.25
❑ 188	A.J. Feeley	.60	.25
❑ 189	Matt Schaub	.60	.25
❑ 190	Jamaar Taylor	.50	.20
❑ 191	Joey Galloway	.60	.25
❑ 192	Quentin Griffin	.60	.25
❑ 193	Amani Toomer	.60	.25
❑ 194	Michael Strahan	.60	.25
❑ 195	Travis Henry	.60	.25
❑ 196	Billy Volek	.60	.25
❑ 197	Robert Ferguson	.50	.20
❑ 198	Reggie Williams	.60	.25
❑ 199	Jeff Garcia	.60	.25

❑ 200	Mark Brunell	.60	.25
❑ 201	Derrick Brooks	.60	.25
❑ 202	Tommy Maddox	.50	.20
❑ 203	William Henderson	.50	.20
❑ 204	Bryant Johnson	.50	.20
❑ 205	Philip Rivers	1.00	.40
❑ 206	James Farrior	.50	.20
❑ 207	Terrence McGee	.50	.20
❑ 208	Bernard Berrian	.50	.20
❑ 209	Gus Frerotte	.50	.20
❑ 210	Mike Alstott	.60	.25
❑ 211	Luke McCown	.50	.20
❑ 212	Michael Bennett	.60	.25
❑ 213	Kenechi Udeze	.50	.20
❑ 214	Chris Perry	.60	.25
❑ 215	Robert Gallery	.60	.25
❑ 216	Lito Sheppard	.50	.20
❑ 217	Brian Finneran	.50	.20
❑ 218	Brian Griese	.60	.25
❑ 219	Kevin Curtis	.60	.25
❑ 220	LaMont Jordan	1.00	.40
❑ 221	Jerry Porter	.60	.25
❑ 222	Reuben Droughns	.60	.25
❑ 223	Dallas Clark	.50	.20
❑ 224	Kevan Barlow	.60	.25
❑ 225	Ken Lucas	.50	.20
❑ 226	Lee Suggs	.60	.25
❑ 227	Marcus Pollard	.50	.20
❑ 228	David Givens	.60	.25
❑ 229	T.J. Duckett	.60	.25
❑ 230	Chris Simms	.60	.25
❑ 231	Maurice Morris	.50	.20
❑ 232	Chris McAllister	.50	.20
❑ 233	Justin Fargas	.50	.20
❑ 234	Jimmy Smith	.60	.25
❑ 235	Aaron Stecker	.50	.20
❑ 236	Donte Stallworth	.60	.25
❑ 237	Darren Sproles RC	2.50	1.00
❑ 238	Justin McCareins	.50	.20
❑ 239	Adrian McPherson RC	2.50	1.00
❑ 240	Brian Dawkins	.50	.20
❑ 241	Travis Taylor	.50	.20
❑ 242	Fabian Washington RC	2.50	1.00
❑ 243	Jerramy Stevens	.50	.20
❑ 244	Anthony Davis RC	2.00	.75
❑ 245	Alex Smith TE RC	2.50	1.00
❑ 246	Ricky Williams	.60	.25
❑ 247	Marion Barber RC	4.00	1.50
❑ 248	Marcus Spears RC	2.50	1.00
❑ 249	Mike Nugent RC	2.50	1.00
❑ 250	Dat Nguyen	.50	.20
❑ 251	Derek Anderson RC	2.50	1.00
❑ 252	Terrence Holt	.50	.20
❑ 253	Dane Looker	.50	.20
❑ 254	Randy McMichael	.50	.20
❑ 255	Craig Bragg RC	2.00	.75
❑ 256	James Kilian RC	2.50	1.00
❑ 257	Airese Currie RC	2.50	1.00
❑ 258	Noah Herron RC	2.50	1.00
❑ 259	Dan Cody RC	2.50	1.00
❑ 260	Willie Parker	10.00	4.00
❑ 261	Travis Johnson RC	2.00	.75
❑ 262	Dan Orlovsky RC	3.00	1.25
❑ 263	Chris Baker	.50	.20
❑ 264	Luis Castillo RC	2.50	1.00
❑ 265	Travis Daniels RC	2.00	.75
❑ 266	Justin Miller RC	2.00	.75
❑ 267	J.R. Russell RC	2.00	.75
❑ 268	Lance Mitchell RC	2.00	.75
❑ 269	T.A. McLendon RC	1.25	.50
❑ 270	Jerricho Cotchery	.50	.20
❑ 271	Chad Owens RC	2.50	1.00
❑ 272	Tab Perry RC	2.50	1.00
❑ 273	Corey Webster RC	2.50	1.00
❑ 274	Fred Gibson RC	2.00	.75
❑ 275	Brandon Jones RC	2.50	1.00
❑ 276	DeWayne Robertson	.50	.20
❑ 277	Brock Berlin RC	2.00	.75
❑ 278	Nehemiah Broughton RC	2.00	.75
❑ 279	Shaun Cody RC	2.50	1.00
❑ 280	Anthony Wright	.50	.20
❑ 281	Damien Nash RC	2.00	.75
❑ 282	Ryan Fitzpatrick RC	4.00	1.50
❑ 283	Paris Warren RC	2.00	.75
❑ 284	Justin Tuck RC	2.50	1.00
❑ 285	Cedric Houston RC	2.50	1.00
❑ 286	Odell Thurman RC	2.50	1.00
❑ 287	Kirk Morrison RC	2.50	1.00
❑ 288	Josh Davis RC	2.00	.75
❑ 289	Craphonso Thorpe RC	2.00	.75
❑ 290	Sam Aiken	.50	.20
❑ 291	Stanley Wilson RC	2.00	.75
❑ 292	Jonathan Babineaux RC	2.00	.75
❑ 293	Darryl Blackstock RC	2.00	.75
❑ 294	Roydell Williams RC	2.50	1.00
❑ 295	Channing Crowder RC	2.50	1.00
❑ 296	Deandra Cobb RC	2.00	.75
❑ 297	Larry Brackins RC	1.25	.50
❑ 298	Bryant McFadden RC	2.50	1.00
❑ 299	Kevin Burnett RC	2.50	1.00
❑ 300	Barrett Ruud RC	2.50	1.00
❑ 301	Terrell Owens SP	5.00	2.00
❑ 302	Ben Roethlisberger SP	12.00	5.00
❑ 303	Eric Moulds SP	3.00	1.25
❑ 304	Eli Manning SP	10.00	4.00
❑ 305	Ed Reed SP	3.00	1.25
❑ 306	Larry Fitzgerald SP	5.00	2.00
❑ 307	Clinton Portis SP	5.00	2.00
❑ 308	Priest Holmes SP	5.00	2.00
❑ 309	Drew Bennett SP	3.00	1.25
❑ 310	Steven Jackson SP	6.00	2.50
❑ 311	Roy Williams S SP	3.00	1.25
❑ 312	Marcel Shipp SP	2.50	1.00
❑ 313	Peerless Price SP	2.50	1.00
❑ 314	Troy Vincent SP	2.50	1.00
❑ 315	Justin Gage SP	2.50	1.00
❑ 316	Nick Goings SP	2.50	1.00
❑ 317	Dennis Northcutt SP	2.50	1.00
❑ 318	Quincy Morgan SP	2.50	1.00
❑ 319	Darius Watts SP	3.00	1.25
❑ 320	Jason Elam SP	2.50	1.00
❑ 321	Nick Barnett SP	2.50	1.00
❑ 322	Tony Hollings SP	2.50	1.00
❑ 323	Samie Parker SP	2.50	1.00
❑ 324	Kelly Campbell SP	2.50	1.00
❑ 325	Kelly Holcomb SP	2.50	1.00
❑ 326	Darren Sharper SP	2.50	1.00
❑ 327	Tedy Bruschi SP	3.00	1.25
❑ 328	Ernie Conwell SP	2.50	1.00
❑ 329	Shaun Ellis SP	2.50	1.00
❑ 330	Teyo Johnson SP	2.50	1.00
❑ 331	Chris Brown SP	3.00	1.25
❑ 332	Quentin Jammer SP	2.50	1.00
❑ 333	Fred Smoot SP	2.50	1.00
❑ 334	Eric Parker SP	2.50	1.00
❑ 335	Steve Heiden SP	2.50	1.00
❑ 336	Troy Polamalu SP	8.00	3.00
❑ 337	Todd Pinkston SP	2.50	1.00
❑ 338	L.J. Smith SP	2.50	1.00
❑ 339	London Fletcher SP	2.50	1.00
❑ 340	Devery Henderson SP	2.50	1.00
❑ 341A	Troy Williamson SP RC	6.00	2.50
❑ 341B	Troy Williamson TBJ SP	8.00	3.00
❑ 342A	J.J. Arrington SP RC	4.00	1.50
❑ 342B	J.J. Arrington 58T SP	5.00	2.00
❑ 343A	Cadillac Williams SP SP	12.00	5.00
❑ 343B	Cadillac Williams TBJ SP	15.00	6.00
❑ 344A	Aaron Rodgers SP RC	10.00	4.00
❑ 344B	Aaron Rodgers 58T SP	12.00	5.00
❑ 345A	Matt Jones SP RC	8.00	3.00
❑ 345B	Matt Jones 58T SP	10.00	4.00
❑ 346A	Roddy White SP RC	3.00	1.25
❑ 346B	Roddy White 58T SP	4.00	1.50
❑ 347A	Braylon Edwards SP RC	10.00	4.00
❑ 347B	Braylon Edwards TBJ SP	12.00	5.00
❑ 348A	Adam Jones SP RC	3.00	1.25
❑ 348B	Adam Jones TBJ SP	4.00	1.50
❑ 349A	Mark Clayton SP RC	4.00	1.50
❑ 349B	Mark Clayton TBJ SP	5.00	2.00
❑ 350A	Stefan LeFors SP RC	3.00	1.25
❑ 350B	Stefan LeFors 58T SP	4.00	1.50
❑ 351	Alvin Pearman SP RC	3.00	1.25
❑ 352	Erasmus James SP RC	3.00	1.25
❑ 353	David Pollack SP RC	3.00	1.25
❑ 354	Brandon Jacobs SP RC	4.00	1.50
❑ 355	Chris Henry SP RC	3.00	1.25
❑ 356	Thomas Davis SP RC	3.00	1.25
❑ 357	Rasheed Marshall SP RC	3.00	1.25
❑ 358	Matt Roth SP RC	3.00	1.25
❑ 359	DeMarcus Ware SP RC	5.00	2.00
❑ 360	Matt Cassell SP RC	5.00	2.00
❑ 361	Stanford Routt SP RC	2.50	1.00
❑ 362	Marlin Jackson SP RC	3.00	1.25
❑ 363	Der.Johnson 59T SP ERR	5.00	2.00
❑ 364	Jerome Mathis SP RC	3.00	1.25
❑ 365	Lionel Gates SP RC	2.50	1.00

2006 Topps Heritage

❑	COMPLETE SET (497)	250.00	125.00
❑	COMP.SET w/o SP's (207)	40.00	15.00
❑ 1	LaVar Arrington	1.50	.60
❑ 2	Justin McCareins	.75	.30
❑ 3	Simeon Rice	.75	.30
❑ 4	Dennis Northcutt	.75	.30
❑ 5	Jason Campbell	1.00	.40
❑ 6	Ricardo Colclough	.75	.30
❑ 7	Marion Barber	1.00	.40
❑ 8	Samie Parker	.75	.30
❑ 9	Nick Barnett	.75	.30
❑ 10	David Garrard	.75	.30
❑ 11	Roy Williams S	1.00	.40
❑ 12	Adrian Peterson	.75	.30
❑ 13	Marcus Robinson	1.00	.40
❑ 14	Andrew Walter	1.00	.40
❑ 15	Cedric Houston	.75	.30
❑ 16	John Abraham	.75	.30
❑ 17	Alex Smith TE	.75	.30
❑ 18	Travis Henry	.75	.30
❑ 19	Craig Krenzel	.75	.30
❑ 20	Brian Dawkins	.75	.30
❑ 21	Bryant Young	.75	.30
❑ 22	Al Wilson	.75	.30
❑ 23	Nick Goings	.75	.30
❑ 24	Shaun Ellis	.75	.30
❑ 25	Marty Booker	.75	.30
❑ 26	Daniel Graham	.75	.30
❑ 27	Jim Sorgi	.75	.30
❑ 28	Sebastian Janikowski	.75	.30
❑ 29	Allen Rossum	.75	.30
❑ 30	Jim Kleinsasser	.75	.30
❑ 31	Lee Evans	1.00	.40
❑ 32	Alex Brown	.75	.30
❑ 33	Steve Hutchinson	.75	.30
❑ 34	Sam Madison	.75	.30
❑ 35	Aaron Rodgers	1.50	.60
❑ 36	Justin Griffith	.75	.30
❑ 37	Terrence McGee	.75	.30
❑ 38	Odell Thurman	.75	.30
❑ 39	Marcus Trufant	.75	.30
❑ 40	Courtney Roby	.75	.30
❑ 41	Isaac Bruce	1.00	.40
❑ 42	Ben Watson	.75	.30
❑ 43	Brandon Stokley	1.00	.40
❑ 44	Koren Robinson	1.00	.40
❑ 45	Mark Clayton	1.00	.40
❑ 46	Darren Sproles	.75	.30
❑ 47	Matt Leinart RC	12.00	5.00
❑ 48	Terrell Owens	1.50	.60
❑ 49	Antonio Pierce	.75	.30
❑ 50	Mark Brunell	1.00	.40
❑ 51	T.J. Houshmandzadeh	1.00	.40
❑ 52	Chris Gamble	.75	.30
❑ 53	Jason Witten	1.00	.40
❑ 54	Michael Huff RC	4.00	1.50
❑ 55	Joey Porter	.75	.30
❑ 56	Eli Manning	2.00	.75
❑ 57	Ladell Betts	.75	.30
❑ 58	Kevin Curtis	.75	.30
❑ 59	Reggie Williams	1.00	.40
❑ 60	Alge Crumpler	1.00	.40
❑ 61	Joseph Addai RC	10.00	4.00
❑ 62	Todd Heap	1.00	.40
❑ 63	Trent Green	1.00	.40

❑	64	Muhsin Muhammad	1.00	.40
❑	65	Drew Bledsoe	1.50	.60
❑	66	LenDale White RC	6.00	2.50
❑	67	Kris Mangum	.75	.30
❑	68	Troy Vincent	.75	.30
❑	69	DeMarcus Ware	1.00	.40
❑	70	Brian Westbrook	1.00	.40
❑	71	Brandon Lloyd	1.00	.40
❑	72	Corey Dillon	1.00	.40
❑	73	Ernie Conwell	.75	.30
❑	74	Laveranues Coles	1.00	.40
❑	75	Santana Moss	1.00	.40
❑	76	Alvis Whitted	.75	.30
❑	77	Demorrio Williams RC	1.50	.60
❑	78	Matt Hasselbeck	1.00	.40
❑	79	Billy Volek	1.00	.40
❑	80	Sean Taylor	1.00	.40
❑	81	Plaxico Burress	1.00	.40
❑	82	Frank Gore	1.50	.60
❑	83	Chris McAlister	.75	.30
❑	84	Donnie Edwards	.75	.30
❑	85	Ed Reed	1.00	.40
❑	86	Tarvaris Jackson RC	5.00	2.00
❑	87	T.J. Duckett	1.00	.40
❑	88	Rex Grossman	1.50	.60
❑	89	Ronnie Brown	1.50	.60
❑	90	James Farrior	.75	.30
❑	91	Mike Alstott	.60	.25
❑	92	Eddie Kennison	.50	.20
❑	93	Charlie Frye	.60	.25
❑	94	Deion Branch	.60	.25
❑	95	Brandon Jacobs SP	1.00	.40
❑	96	Larry Fitzgerald	1.00	.40
❑	97	Domanick Davis	.60	.25
❑	98	Terrence Holt	.50	.20
❑	99	Dan Morgan	.50	.20
❑	100	Shaun Alexander SP	2.00	.75
❑	101	Shawne Merriman SP	1.25	.50
❑	102	Roddy White	.60	.25
❑	103	Ashley Lelie	.60	.25
❑	104	Jevon Kearse	.60	.25
❑	105	Andre Johnson	.60	.25
❑	106	Matt Mauck	.50	.20
❑	107	Dwight Freeney SP	1.25	.50
❑	108	Robert Gallery	.50	.20
❑	109	Chad Jackson SP RC	6.00	2.50
❑	110	Marques Tuiasosopo	.50	.20
❑	111	LaMont Jordan SP	1.25	.50
❑	112	Taylor Jacobs	.50	.20
❑	113	Byron Leftwich	.60	.25
❑	114	Fabian Washington	.50	.20
❑	115	Michael Jenkins	.60	.25
❑	116	Steven Jackson	1.00	.40
❑	117	Ronald Curry	.60	.25
❑	118	J.P. Losman	.60	.25
❑	119	Patrick Crayton	.50	.20
❑	120	Javon Walker	.60	.25
❑	121	Daunte Culpepper SP	2.00	.75
❑	122	Marc Bulger	.60	.25
❑	123	Kevin Jones SP	2.00	.75
❑	124	Tom Brady	1.50	.60
❑	125	Jay Cutler SP RC	15.00	6.00
❑	126	Tony Gonzalez	.60	.25
❑	127	Warrick Dunn SP	1.25	.50
❑	128	Michael Strahan	.60	.25
❑	129	Demetrius Williams SP RC	5.00	2.00
❑	130	Charles Woodson	.60	.25
❑	131	Tiki Barber SP	2.00	.75
❑	132	Hines Ward	1.00	.40
❑	133	Brian Calhoun SP RC	4.00	1.50
❑	134	Torry Holt	.60	.25
❑	135	Priest Holmes	.60	.25
❑	136	Philip Rivers	1.00	.40
❑	137	Joey Harrington	.60	.25
❑	138	Donte Stallworth	.60	.25
❑	139	Ken Lucas	.50	.20
❑	140	Chad Morton	.50	.20
❑	141	Osi Umenyiora	.50	.20
❑	142	Jamal Lewis	.60	.25
❑	143	Derek Hagan RC	2.50	1.00
❑	144	Deshaun Foster	.60	.25
❑	145	Michael Lewis	.50	.20
❑	146	Anquan Boldin	.60	.25
❑	147	Derrick Brooks	.60	.25
❑	148	Michael Turner	.50	.20
❑	149	Zach Thomas	1.00	.40
❑	150	Carson Palmer	1.00	.40
❑	151	Ryan Moats	.50	.20
❑	152	William Henderson	.50	.20
❑	153	Marcus Spears	.50	.20
❑	154	Travis Minor	.50	.20
❑	155	Scottie Vines	.50	.20
❑	156	Maurice Stovall RC	2.50	1.00
❑	157	Dante Hall	.60	.25
❑	158	Chris Simms	.60	.25
❑	159	Zack Crockett	.50	.20
❑	160	Thomas Jones	.60	.25
❑	161	Marcus Pollard	.50	.20
❑	162	Troy Polamalu	1.25	.50
❑	163	LeRon McCoy	.50	.20
❑	164	Najeh Davenport	.50	.20
❑	165	Keenan McCardell	.50	.20
❑	166	Chris Brown	.60	.25
❑	167	Derrick Johnson	.60	.25
❑	168	Chad Pennington	.60	.25
❑	169	Adam Jones	.50	.20
❑	170	Terry Glenn	.60	.25
❑	171	Antonio Bryant	.60	.25
❑	172	Jerramy Stevens	.60	.25
❑	173	Antrel Rolle	.50	.20
❑	174	Randy McMichael	.50	.20
❑	175	Orlando Pace	.50	.20
❑	176	Chris Perry	.60	.25
❑	177	Drew Bennett	.50	.20
❑	178	Cedric Benson	1.00	.40
❑	179	Ernest Wilford	.50	.20
❑	180	Dunta Robinson	.60	.25
❑	181	Reggie Wayne	.60	.25
❑	182	Lito Sheppard	.50	.20
❑	183	Maurice Drew RC	6.00	2.50
❑	184	Todd Bouman	.50	.20
❑	185	Martin Jackson	.50	.20
❑	186	D.J. Williams	.50	.20
❑	187	DeAngelo Hall	.60	.25
❑	188	Bubba Franks	.50	.20
❑	189	Greg Jones	.50	.20
❑	190	Dominic Rhodes	.60	.25
❑	191	Dallas Clark	.50	.20
❑	192	Dre Bly	.50	.20
❑	193	Charlie Whitehurst	1.25	.50
❑	194	Will Demps RC	1.00	.40
❑	195	Champ Bailey	.60	.25
❑	196	Sinorice Moss RC	3.00	1.25
❑	197	Jonathan Ogden	.50	.20
❑	198	Mike Peterson	.50	.20
❑	199	D.D. Lewis RC	1.25	.50
❑	200	Vincent Jackson	.50	.20
❑	201	Stefan Lefors	.50	.20
❑	202	Willie Parker	1.25	.50
❑	203	Antwaan Randle El	.60	.25
❑	204	Keary Colbert	.50	.20
❑	205	Tyrone Calico	.50	.20
❑	206	Mike Williams	1.00	.40
❑	207	David Carr	.60	.25
❑	208	Braylon Edwards	1.00	.40
❑	209	Michael Clayton	.60	.25
❑	210	Jerome Mathis	.50	.20
❑	211	Fred Taylor	.60	.25
❑	212	Jake Delhomme	.60	.25
❑	213	Roy Williams WR	1.00	.40
❑	214	Curtis Martin	1.00	.40
❑	215	Terrell Suggs	.60	.25
❑	216	Troy Williamson	.60	.25
❑	217	Marshall Faulk	.60	.25
❑	218	D'Brickashaw Ferguson RC	2.50	1.00
❑	219	Kelly Holcomb	.50	.20
❑	220	Matt Jones	1.00	.40
❑	221	Michael Vick	1.25	.50
❑	222	Deuce McAllister	.60	.25
❑	223	Eric Moulds	.60	.25
❑	224	Ike Taylor	.50	.20
❑	225	D.J. Hackett	.50	.20
❑	226	Keyshawn Johnson	.60	.25
❑	227	Josh McCown	.60	.25
❑	228	Joe Horn	.60	.25
❑	229	Jonathan Vilma	.60	.25
❑	230	Warren Sapp	.60	.25
❑	231	Reggie Brown	.60	.25
❑	232	Clinton Portis	1.00	.40
❑	233	Derrick Burgess	.50	.20
❑	234	Bob Sanders	.60	.25
❑	235	Lofa Tatupu	.60	.25
❑	236	Justin Fargas	.50	.20
❑	237	Kellen Clemens RC	3.00	1.25
❑	238	Richard Seymour	.50	.20
❑	239	Jeff Garcia	.60	.25
❑	240	Shaun Cody	.50	.20
❑	241	Brad Johnson	.60	.25
❑	242	Edgerrin James	1.00	.40
❑	243	Terence Newman	.50	.20
❑	244	Bernard Berrian	.50	.20
❑	245	Mike Anderson	.60	.25
❑	246	Ahman Green	.60	.25
❑	247	Erron Kinney	.50	.20
❑	248	David Pollack	.50	.20
❑	249	Kevin Faulk	.50	.20
❑	250	Laurence Maroney RC	6.00	2.50
❑	251	Chad Johnson	.60	.25
❑	252	Antonio Gates	1.00	.40
❑	253	Drew Brees	1.00	.40
❑	254	Jake Plummer	.60	.25
❑	255	Mario Williams RC	4.00	1.50
❑	256	Chester Taylor	.60	.25
❑	257	Shawn Bryson	.50	.20
❑	258	J.J. Arrington	.60	.25
❑	259	Robert Ferguson	.50	.20
❑	260	Reuben Droughns	.60	.25
❑	261	Tab Perry	.50	.20
❑	262	Troy Brown	.60	.25
❑	263	Luis Castillo	.50	.20
❑	264	Quincy Morgan	.50	.20
❑	265	Damon Huard	.50	.20
❑	266	Walter Jones	.50	.20
❑	267	Kyle Vanden Bosch	.50	.20
❑	268	Doug Gabriel	.50	.20
❑	269	Deltha O'Neal	.50	.20
❑	270	Randy Moss	1.00	.40
❑	271	Omar Jacobs RC	2.00	.75
❑	272	Kevan Barlow	.60	.25
❑	273	John Lynch	.60	.25
❑	274	Chris Cooley	.50	.20
❑	275	Zach Hilton	.50	.20
❑	276	Peter Warrick	.50	.20
❑	277	London Fletcher	.50	.20
❑	278	Nate Burleson	.60	.25
❑	279	Larry Foote	.50	.20
❑	280	Justin Miller	.50	.20
❑	281	Darius Watts	.50	.20
❑	282	Aaron Brooks	.60	.25
❑	283	Joey Galloway	.60	.25
❑	284	Darrell Jackson	.60	.25
❑	285	Alex Smith QB	1.25	.50
❑	286	Vonnie Holliday	.50	.20
❑	287	Nathan Vasher	.50	.20
❑	288	Tatum Bell	.60	.25
❑	289	Olin Kreutz	.50	.20
❑	290	Duce Staley	.60	.25
❑	291	Courtney Anderson	.50	.20
❑	292	Tory James	.50	.20
❑	293	Mike Vanderjagt	.50	.20
❑	294	Mark Bradley	.60	.25
❑	295	Kurt Warner	.60	.25
❑	296	Ray Lewis	1.00	.40
❑	297	Kassim Osgood	.50	.20
❑	298	Trent Dilfer	.60	.25
❑	299	Justin Gage	.50	.20
❑	300	DeAngelo Williams RC	6.00	2.50
❑	301	Luke McCown	.50	.20
❑	302	Charles Rogers	.60	.25
❑	303	Marcedes Lewis RC	2.50	1.00
❑	304	Samari Rolle	.50	.20
❑	305	Greg Lewis	.50	.20
❑	306	Peter Boulware	.50	.20
❑	307	Donald Driver	.60	.25
❑	308	Travis Taylor	.50	.20
❑	309	Quentin Jammer	.50	.20
❑	310	Carlos Rogers	.50	.20
❑	311	Peyton Manning	8.00	3.00
❑	312	Reggie Bush RC	20.00	8.00
❑	313	Vernon Davis RC	6.00	2.50
❑	314	Brett Favre	10.00	4.00
❑	315	Cadillac Williams	5.00	2.00
❑	316	Donovan McNabb	5.00	2.00
❑	317	Jason Avant RC	3.00	1.25
❑	318	Ben Roethlisberger	8.00	3.00
❑	319	Steve Smith	5.00	2.00
❑	320	Vince Young RC	12.00	5.00
❑	321	Willis McGahee	5.00	2.00
❑	322	Jeremy Shockey	5.00	2.00
❑	323	Rudi Johnson	3.00	1.25
❑	324	Brian Urlacher	5.00	2.00

❑ 325 Rod Smith 3.00 1.25
❑ 326 Santonio Holmes RC 6.00 2.50
❑ 327 Larry Johnson 6.00 2.50
❑ 328 Julius Jones 5.00 2.00
❑ 329 Marvin Harrison 5.00 2.00
❑ 330 Chris Chambers 3.00 1.25
❑ 331 Takeo Spikes 2.50 1.00
❑ 332 Brian Griese 3.00 1.25
❑ 333 Steve McNair 3.00 1.25
❑ 334 Willie McGinest 2.50 1.00
❑ 335 Tedy Bruschi 5.00 2.00
❑ 336 Roydell Williams 2.50 1.00
❑ 337 Patrick Ramsey 3.00 1.25
❑ 338 Kyle Boller 2.50 1.00
❑ 339 Bethel Johnson 2.50 1.00
❑ 340 Jerry Porter 3.00 1.25
❑ 341 Shawntae Spencer 2.50 1.00
❑ 342 Drew Carter 2.50 1.00
❑ 343 Jason Elam 2.50 1.00
❑ 344 Michael Pittman 2.50 1.00
❑ 345 Edell Shepherd RC 1.50 .60
❑ 346 Maurice Hicks 2.50 1.00
❑ 347 Ron Dayne 3.00 1.25
❑ 348 Josh Reed 2.50 1.00
❑ 349 Lorenzo Neal 2.50 1.00
❑ 350 LaDainian Tomlinson 6.00 2.50
❑ 351 David Tyree 2.50 1.00
❑ 352 Keith Brooking 2.50 1.00
❑ 353 Devery Henderson 2.50 1.00
❑ 354 Daylon McCutcheon 2.50 1.00
❑ 355 Derrick Mason 2.50 1.00
❑ 356 Fred Smoot 2.50 1.00
❑ 357 Ronde Barber 2.50 1.00
❑ 358 Dan Kreider 3.00 1.25
❑ 359 Shayne Graham 2.50 1.00
❑ 360 Vernand Morency 2.50 1.00
❑ 361 Shawn Springs 2.50 1.00
❑ 362 Amani Toomer 3.00 1.25
❑ 363 Eric Parker 2.50 1.00
❑ 364 Jason Taylor 2.50 1.00
❑ 365 Keith Bulluck 2.50 1.00
❑ 366 Sam Gado 5.00 2.00
❑ 367 Cedrick Wilson 2.50 1.00
❑ 368 Mewelde Moore 2.50 1.00
❑ 369 Travis Daniels 2.50 1.00
❑ 370 Arnaz Battle 2.50 1.00
❑ 371 Kyle Orton 3.00 1.25
❑ 372 Dane Looker 2.50 1.00
❑ 373 Kellen Winslow 5.00 2.00
❑ 374 Julius Peppers 3.00 1.25
❑ 375 Jeremiah Trotter 2.50 1.00
❑ 376 L.J. Smith 2.50 1.00
❑ 377 Gibril Wilson 2.50 1.00
❑ 378 Adam Archuleta 2.50 1.00
❑ 379 Darren Sharper 2.50 1.00
❑ 380 Joe Jurevicius 3.00 1.25
❑ 381 Patrick Pass 2.50 1.00
❑ 382 A.J. Feeley 2.50 1.00
❑ 383 Leroy Hill 2.50 1.00
❑ 384 Corey Webster 2.50 1.00
❑ 385 Heath Miller 5.00 2.00
❑ 386 Cato June 3.00 1.25
❑ 387 Brad Hoover 2.50 1.00
❑ 388 Michael Boulware 2.50 1.00
❑ 389 Matt Schaub 3.00 1.25
❑ 390 Kirk Morrison 2.50 1.00
❑ 391 Kevin Carter 2.50 1.00
❑ 392 David Givens 3.00 1.25
❑ 393 Alvin Pearman 2.50 1.00
❑ 394 Brian Finneran 2.50 1.00
❑ 395 Ike Hilliard 2.50 1.00
❑ 396 Angelo Crowell 2.50 1.00
❑ 397 Charlie Adams 2.50 1.00
❑ 398 Neil Rackers 2.50 1.00
❑ 399 Brandon Jones 2.50 1.00
❑ 400 B.J. Sams 2.50 1.00
❑ 401 Kyle Johnson 2.50 1.00
❑ 402 Adam Vinatieri 3.00 1.25
❑ 403 Bryant Johnson 2.50 1.00
❑ 404 Bryan Fletcher 2.50 1.00
❑ 405 Channing Crowder 2.50 1.00
❑ 406 Jerricho Cotchery 2.50 1.00
❑ 407 A.J. Hawk RC 6.00 2.50

2002 Topps Pristine

❑ COMP.SET w/o SP's (50) 50.00 20.00
❑ 1 Peyton Manning 5.00 2.00

❑ 2 Darrell Jackson 1.50 .60
❑ 3 Donovan McNabb 3.00 1.25
❑ 4 Rod Smith 1.50 .60
❑ 5 Daunte Culpepper 2.50 1.00
❑ 6 Drew Brees 2.50 1.00
❑ 7 Stephen Davis 1.50 .60
❑ 8 Kurt Warner 2.50 1.00
❑ 9 Eric Moulds 1.50 .60
❑ 10 Jake Plummer 1.50 .60
❑ 11 Chris Weinke 1.50 .60
❑ 12 Brian Griese 2.50 1.00
❑ 13 Corey Bradford 1.00 .40
❑ 14 Trent Green 1.50 .60
❑ 15 Tom Brady 6.00 2.50
❑ 16 Jeff Garcia 2.50 1.00
❑ 17 Tiki Barber 2.50 1.00
❑ 18 Eddie George 2.50 1.00
❑ 19 Jamal Lewis 2.50 1.00
❑ 20 Troy Brown 1.50 .60
❑ 21 Priest Holmes 3.00 1.25
❑ 22 Jimmy Smith 1.50 .60
❑ 23 Tim Brown 2.50 1.00
❑ 24 Plaxico Burress 2.50 1.00
❑ 25 Aaron Brooks 2.50 1.00
❑ 26 Marshall Faulk 2.50 1.00
❑ 27 Steve McNair 2.50 1.00
❑ 28 Curtis Martin 2.50 1.00
❑ 29 Corey Dillon 1.50 .60
❑ 30 Tim Couch 1.50 .60
❑ 31 Michael Vick 8.00 3.00
❑ 32 David Boston 2.50 1.00
❑ 33 Kordell Stewart 1.50 .60
❑ 34 Jerome Bettis 2.50 1.00
❑ 35 Keyshawn Johnson 2.50 1.00
❑ 36 Torry Holt 2.50 1.00
❑ 37 Shaun Alexander 3.00 1.25
❑ 38 Brett Favre 6.00 2.50
❑ 39 Marvin Harrison 2.50 1.00
❑ 40 Randy Moss 5.00 2.00
❑ 41 Jerry Rice 5.00 2.00
❑ 42 LaDainian Tomlinson 4.00 1.50
❑ 43 Terrell Owens 2.50 1.00
❑ 44 Edgerrin James 3.00 1.25
❑ 45 Anthony Thomas 1.50 .60
❑ 46 Drew Bledsoe 3.00 1.25
❑ 47 Ahman Green 2.50 1.00
❑ 48 Ricky Williams 2.50 1.00
❑ 49 Tony Gonzalez 1.50 .60
❑ 50 Emmitt Smith 6.00 2.50
❑ 51 Joey Harrington C RC 5.00 2.00
❑ 52 Joey Harrington U 6.00 2.50
❑ 53 Joey Harrington R 10.00 4.00
❑ 54 Josh McCown C RC 4.00 1.50
❑ 55 Josh McCown U 5.00 2.00
❑ 56 Josh McCown R 8.00 3.00
❑ 57 Antwaan Randle El C RC 5.00 2.00
❑ 58 Antwaan Randle El U 6.00 2.50
❑ 59 Antwaan Randle El R 10.00 4.00
❑ 60 Reche Caldwell C RC 3.00 1.25
❑ 61 Reche Caldwell U 4.00 1.50
❑ 62 Reche Caldwell R 6.00 2.50
❑ 63 Jason McAddley C RC 2.50 1.00
❑ 64 Jason McAddley U 3.00 1.25
❑ 65 Jason McAddley R 5.00 2.00
❑ 66 Ashley Lelie C RC 6.00 2.50
❑ 67 Ashley Lelie U 8.00 3.00
❑ 68 Ashley Lelie R 12.00 5.00
❑ 69 Travis Stephens C RC 2.50 1.00
❑ 70 Travis Stephens U 3.00 1.25
❑ 71 Travis Stephens R 5.00 2.00
❑ 72 Chad Hutchinson C RC 2.50 1.00
❑ 73 Chad Hutchinson U 3.00 1.25
❑ 74 Chad Hutchinson R 5.00 2.00
❑ 75 Quentin Jammer C RC 3.00 1.25
❑ 76 Quentin Jammer U 4.00 1.50
❑ 77 Quentin Jammer R 6.00 2.50
❑ 78 Tim Carter C RC 2.50 1.00
❑ 79 Tim Carter U 3.00 1.25
❑ 80 Tim Carter R 5.00 2.00
❑ 81 Antonio Bryant C RC 3.00 1.25
❑ 82 Antonio Bryant U 4.00 1.50
❑ 83 Antonio Bryant R 6.00 2.50
❑ 84 Cliff Russell C RC 2.50 1.00
❑ 85 Cliff Russell U 3.00 1.25
❑ 86 Cliff Russell R 5.00 2.00
❑ 87 Rohan Davey C RC 3.00 1.25
❑ 88 Rohan Davey U 4.00 1.50
❑ 89 Rohan Davey R 6.00 2.50
❑ 90 Javon Walker C RC 6.00 2.50
❑ 91 Javon Walker U 8.00 3.00
❑ 92 Javon Walker R 10.00 4.00
❑ 93 T.J. Duckett C RC 4.00 1.50
❑ 94 T.J. Duckett U 5.00 2.00
❑ 95 T.J. Duckett R 8.00 3.00
❑ 96 Donte Stallworth C RC 6.00 2.50
❑ 97 Donte Stallworth U 8.00 3.00
❑ 98 Donte Stallworth R 12.00 5.00
❑ 99 Andre Davis C RC 2.50 1.00
❑ 100 Andre Davis U 3.00 1.25
❑ 101 Andre Davis R 5.00 2.00
❑ 102 Mike Williams C RC 2.50 1.00
❑ 103 Mike Williams U 3.00 1.25
❑ 104 Mike Williams R 5.00 2.00
❑ 105 Freddie Milons C RC 2.50 1.00
❑ 106 Freddie Milons U 3.00 1.25
❑ 107 Freddie Milons R 5.00 2.00
❑ 108 John Henderson C RC 3.00 1.25
❑ 109 John Henderson U 3.00 1.25
❑ 110 John Henderson R 6.00 2.50
❑ 111 DeShaun Foster C RC 3.00 1.25
❑ 112 DeShaun Foster U 4.00 1.50
❑ 113 DeShaun Foster R 6.00 2.50
❑ 114 Josh Reed C RC 3.00 1.25
❑ 115 Josh Reed U 4.00 1.50
❑ 116 Josh Reed R 6.00 2.50
❑ 117 Jabar Gaffney C RC 3.00 1.25
❑ 118 Jabar Gaffney U 4.00 1.50
❑ 119 Jabar Gaffney R 6.00 2.50
❑ 120 Clinton Portis C RC 10.00 4.00
❑ 121 Clinton Portis U 12.00 5.00
❑ 122 Clinton Portis R 20.00 7.50
❑ 123 Jeremy Shockey C RC 10.00 4.00
❑ 124 Jeremy Shockey U 12.00 5.00
❑ 125 Jeremy Shockey R 20.00 7.50
❑ 126 Dwight Freeney C RC 5.00 2.00
❑ 127 Dwight Freeney U 6.00 2.50
❑ 128 Dwight Freeney R 10.00 4.00
❑ 129 Brian Westbrook C RC 5.00 2.00
❑ 130 Brian Westbrook U 6.00 2.50
❑ 131 Brian Westbrook R 10.00 4.00
❑ 132 Randy Fasani C RC 2.50 1.00
❑ 133 Randy Fasani U 3.00 1.25
❑ 134 Randy Fasani R 5.00 2.00
❑ 135 Julius Peppers C RC 6.00 2.50
❑ 136 Julius Peppers U 8.00 3.00
❑ 137 Julius Peppers R 12.00 5.00
❑ 138 Patrick Ramsey C RC 6.00 2.50
❑ 139 Patrick Ramsey U 5.00 2.00
❑ 140 Patrick Ramsey R 8.00 3.00
❑ 141 William Green C RC 3.00 1.25
❑ 142 William Green U 5.00 2.00
❑ 143 William Green R 8.00 3.00
❑ 144 Daniel Graham C RC 3.00 1.25
❑ 145 Daniel Graham U 4.00 1.50
❑ 146 Daniel Graham R 6.00 2.50
❑ 147 Ron Johnson C RC 2.50 1.00
❑ 148 Ron Johnson U 3.00 1.25
❑ 149 Ron Johnson R 5.00 2.00
❑ 150 Maurice Morris C RC 3.00 1.25
❑ 151 Maurice Morris U 4.00 1.50
❑ 152 Maurice Morris R 6.00 2.50
❑ 153 Eric Crouch C RC 3.00 1.25
❑ 154 Eric Crouch U 5.00 2.00
❑ 155 Eric Crouch R 8.00 3.00
❑ 156 Roy Williams C RC 8.00 3.00
❑ 157 Roy Williams U 10.00 4.00
❑ 158 Roy Williams R 15.00 6.00

❑ 159	Ladell Betts C RC	3.00	1.25
❑ 160	Ladell Betts U	5.00	2.00
❑ 161	Ladell Betts R	8.00	3.00
❑ 162	David Garrard C RC	3.00	1.25
❑ 163	David Garrard U	4.00	1.50
❑ 164	David Garrard R	6.00	2.50
❑ 165	Marquise Walker C RC	2.50	1.00
❑ 166	Marquise Walker U	3.00	1.25
❑ 167	Marquise Walker R	5.00	2.00
❑ 168	David Carr C RC	8.00	3.00
❑ 169	David Carr U	10.00	4.00
❑ 170	David Carr R	15.00	6.00
❑ ESA1	Emmitt Smith AU	300.00	175.00
❑ ESJ1	Emmitt Smith JSY	40.00	15.00

2003 Topps Pristine

❑	COMP.SET w/o SP's (50)	40.00	15.00
❑ 1	Brett Favre	6.00	2.50
❑ 2	Rich Gannon	1.50	.60
❑ 3	Randy Moss	4.00	1.50
❑ 4	Travis Henry	1.50	.60
❑ 5	Troy Brown	1.50	.60
❑ 6	Darrell Jackson	1.50	.60
❑ 7	Steve McNair	2.50	1.00
❑ 8	Plaxico Burress	1.50	.60
❑ 9	Jerry Rice	5.00	2.00
❑ 10	Donovan McNabb	3.00	1.25
❑ 11	Marty Booker	1.50	.60
❑ 12	Joey Galloway	1.50	.60
❑ 13	Peerless Price	1.50	.60
❑ 14	Emmitt Smith	6.00	2.50
❑ 15	David Carr	4.00	1.50
❑ 16	Priest Holmes	3.00	1.25
❑ 17	LaDainian Tomlinson	2.50	1.00
❑ 18	Hines Ward	2.50	1.00
❑ 19	Tiki Barber	2.50	1.00
❑ 20	Fred Taylor	2.50	1.00
❑ 21	Marvin Harrison	2.50	1.00
❑ 22	Marshall Faulk	2.50	1.00
❑ 23	Terrell Owens	2.50	1.00
❑ 24	Patrick Ramsey	2.50	1.00
❑ 25	Michael Vick	6.00	2.50
❑ 26	Tom Brady	6.00	2.50
❑ 27	Shaun Alexander	2.50	1.00
❑ 28	Derrick Mason	1.50	.60
❑ 29	Keyshawn Johnson	2.50	1.00
❑ 30	Ricky Williams	2.50	1.00
❑ 31	Ahman Green	2.50	1.00
❑ 32	Joey Harrington	4.00	1.50
❑ 33	Corey Dillon	1.50	.60
❑ 34	Jamal Lewis	2.50	1.00
❑ 35	Drew Bledsoe	2.50	1.00
❑ 36	Tommy Maddox	2.50	1.00
❑ 37	Kurt Warner	2.50	1.00
❑ 38	Deuce McAllister	2.50	1.00
❑ 39	Curtis Martin	2.50	1.00
❑ 40	Chad Pennington	3.00	1.25
❑ 41	Trent Green	1.50	.60
❑ 42	Edgerrin James	2.50	1.00
❑ 43	Clinton Portis	4.00	1.50
❑ 44	Eric Moulds	1.50	.60
❑ 45	Peyton Manning	4.00	1.50
❑ 46	Jeff Garcia	2.50	1.00
❑ 47	Daunte Culpepper	2.50	1.00
❑ 48	Tim Couch	1.00	.40
❑ 49	Drew Brees	2.50	1.00
❑ 50	Aaron Brooks	2.50	1.00
❑ 51	Anquan Boldin C RC	8.00	3.00
❑ 52	Anquan Boldin U	10.00	4.00
❑ 53	Anquan Boldin R	15.00	6.00
❑ 54	Andre Johnson C RC	6.00	2.50
❑ 55	Andre Johnson U	8.00	3.00
❑ 56	Andre Johnson R	12.00	5.00
❑ 57	Artose Pinner C RC	3.00	1.25
❑ 58	Artose Pinner U	4.00	1.50
❑ 59	Artose Pinner R	6.00	2.50
❑ 60	Bryant Johnson C RC	3.00	1.25
❑ 61	Bryant Johnson U	4.00	1.50
❑ 62	Bryant Johnson R	6.00	2.50
❑ 63	Bethel Johnson C RC	3.00	1.25
❑ 64	Bethel Johnson U	4.00	1.50
❑ 65	Bethel Johnson R	6.00	2.50
❑ 66	Byron Leftwich C RC	10.00	4.00
❑ 67	Byron Leftwich U	12.00	5.00
❑ 68	Byron Leftwich R	20.00	7.50
❑ 69	Brian St.Pierre C RC	3.00	1.25
❑ 70	Brian St.Pierre U	4.00	1.50
❑ 71	Brian St.Pierre R	6.00	2.50
❑ 72	Chris Brown C RC	3.00	1.25
❑ 73	Chris Brown U	4.00	1.50
❑ 74	Chris Brown R	5.00	2.00
❑ 75	Carson Palmer C RC	12.00	5.00
❑ 76	Carson Palmer U	15.00	6.00
❑ 77	Carson Palmer R	25.00	10.00
❑ 78	Charles Rogers C RC	3.00	1.25
❑ 79	Charles Rogers U	4.00	1.50
❑ 80	Charles Rogers R	5.00	2.00
❑ 81	Chris Simms C RC	5.00	2.00
❑ 82	Chris Simms U	6.00	2.50
❑ 83	Chris Simms R	10.00	4.00
❑ 84	Dallas Clark C RC	3.00	1.25
❑ 85	Dallas Clark U	4.00	1.50
❑ 86	Dallas Clark R	6.00	2.50
❑ 87	Dave Ragone C RC	3.00	1.25
❑ 88	Dave Ragone U	4.00	1.50
❑ 89	Dave Ragone R	5.00	2.00
❑ 90	DeWayne Robertson C RC	3.00	1.25
❑ 91	DeWayne Robertson U	4.00	1.50
❑ 92	DeWayne Robertson R	6.00	2.50
❑ 93	Justin Fargas C RC	3.00	1.25
❑ 94	Justin Fargas U	4.00	1.50
❑ 95	Justin Fargas R	6.00	2.50
❑ 96	Kyle Boller C RC	3.00	1.25
❑ 97	Kyle Boller U	4.00	1.50
❑ 98	Kyle Boller R	5.00	2.00
❑ 99	Kevin Curtis C RC	3.00	1.25
❑ 100	Kevin Curtis U	4.00	1.50
❑ 101	Kevin Curtis R	6.00	2.50
❑ 102	Ken Dorsey C RC	3.00	1.25
❑ 103	Ken Dorsey U	4.00	1.50
❑ 104	Ken Dorsey R	6.00	2.50
❑ 105	Kelley Washington C RC	3.00	1.25
❑ 106	Kelley Washington U	4.00	1.50
❑ 107	Kelley Washington R	6.00	2.50
❑ 108	Kliff Kingsbury C RC	2.50	1.00
❑ 109	Kliff Kingsbury U	3.00	1.25
❑ 110	Kliff Kingsbury R	5.00	2.00
❑ 111	Larry Johnson C RC	12.00	6.00
❑ 112	Larry Johnson U	15.00	7.50
❑ 113	Larry Johnson R	25.00	12.50
❑ 114	Musa Smith C RC	3.00	1.25
❑ 115	Musa Smith U	4.00	1.50
❑ 116	Musa Smith R	6.00	2.50
❑ 117	Marcus Trufant C RC	3.00	1.25
❑ 118	Marcus Trufant U	4.00	1.50
❑ 119	Marcus Trufant R	6.00	2.50
❑ 120	Nate Burleson C RC	3.00	1.25
❑ 121	Nate Burleson U	4.00	1.50
❑ 122	Nate Burleson R	5.00	2.00
❑ 123	Onterrio Smith C RC	3.00	1.25
❑ 124	Onterrio Smith U	4.00	1.50
❑ 125	Onterrio Smith R	6.00	2.50
❑ 126	Rex Grossman C RC	10.00	4.00
❑ 127	Rex Grossman U	12.00	5.00
❑ 128	Rex Grossman R	20.00	7.50
❑ 129	Seneca Wallace C RC	3.00	1.25
❑ 130	Seneca Wallace U	4.00	1.50
❑ 131	Seneca Wallace R	6.00	2.50
❑ 132	Tyrone Calico C RC	3.00	1.25
❑ 133	Tyrone Calico U	4.00	1.50
❑ 134	Tyrone Calico R	6.00	2.50
❑ 135	Taylor Jacobs C RC	2.50	1.00
❑ 136	Taylor Jacobs U	3.00	1.25
❑ 137	Taylor Jacobs R	5.00	2.00
❑ 138	Teyo Johnson C RC	3.00	1.25
❑ 139	Teyo Johnson U	4.00	1.50
❑ 140	Teyo Johnson R	6.00	2.50
❑ 141	Terence Newman C RC	6.00	2.50
❑ 142	Terence Newman U	8.00	3.00
❑ 143	Terence Newman R	12.00	5.00
❑ 144	Terrell Suggs C RC	5.00	2.00
❑ 145	Terrell Suggs U	6.00	2.50
❑ 146	Terrell Suggs R	10.00	4.00
❑ 147	Willis McGahee C RC	8.00	3.00
❑ 148	Willis McGahee U	10.00	4.00
❑ 149	Willis McGahee R	15.00	6.00

2004 Topps Pristine

❑	COMP.SET w/o SP's (50)	40.00	15.00
❑ 1	Michael Vick	5.00	2.00
❑ 2	Tony Gonzalez	1.50	.60
❑ 3	Terrell Owens	2.50	1.00
❑ 4	Brett Favre	6.00	2.50
❑ 5	Jamal Lewis	2.50	1.00
❑ 6	Tim Rattay	1.50	.60
❑ 7	Ricky Williams	2.50	1.00
❑ 8	Edgerrin James	2.50	1.00
❑ 9	Torry Holt	2.50	1.00
❑ 10	Randy Moss	3.00	1.25
❑ 11	Derrick Mason	1.50	.60
❑ 12	Joe Horn	1.50	.60
❑ 13	Marvin Harrison	2.50	1.00
❑ 14	Carson Palmer	3.00	1.25
❑ 15	Anquan Boldin	2.50	1.00
❑ 16	Quincy Carter	1.50	.60
❑ 17	Byron Leftwich	3.00	1.25
❑ 18	Eric Moulds	1.50	.60
❑ 19	Marc Bulger	2.50	1.00
❑ 20	Ahman Green	2.50	1.00
❑ 21	Jeff Garcia	2.50	1.00
❑ 22	Laveranues Coles	1.50	.60
❑ 23	Hines Ward	2.50	1.00
❑ 24	Santana Moss	1.50	.60
❑ 25	LaDainian Tomlinson	3.00	1.25
❑ 26	Domanick Davis	2.50	1.00
❑ 27	Stephen Davis	1.50	.60
❑ 28	Tiki Barber	2.50	1.00
❑ 29	Chris Chambers	1.50	.60
❑ 30	Priest Holmes	3.00	1.25
❑ 31	Chad Pennington	2.50	1.00
❑ 32	Shaun Alexander	2.50	1.00
❑ 33	Brad Johnson	1.50	.60
❑ 34	Marshall Faulk	2.50	1.00
❑ 35	Peyton Manning	4.00	1.50
❑ 36	Jake Plummer	1.50	.60
❑ 37	Clinton Portis	2.50	1.00
❑ 38	Matt Hasselbeck	1.50	.60
❑ 39	Amani Toomer	1.50	.60
❑ 40	Steve McNair	2.50	1.00
❑ 41	Daunte Culpepper	2.50	1.00
❑ 42	Fred Taylor	1.50	.60
❑ 43	Joey Harrington	2.50	1.00
❑ 44	Jake Delhomme	2.50	1.00
❑ 45	Deuce McAllister	2.50	1.00
❑ 46	Chad Johnson	2.50	1.00
❑ 47	Travis Henry	1.50	.60
❑ 48	Corey Dillon	1.50	.60
❑ 49	Tom Brady	6.00	2.50
❑ 50	Donovan McNabb	3.00	1.25
❑ 51	Ben Roethlisberger C RC	30.00	15.00
❑ 52	Ben Roethlisberger U	40.00	20.00
❑ 53	Ben Roethlisberger R	50.00	25.00
❑ 54	Ben Troupe C RC	3.00	1.25
❑ 55	Ben Troupe U	4.00	1.50
❑ 56	Ben Troupe R	5.00	2.00

❑ 57 Ben Watson C RC 3.00 1.25
❑ 58 Ben Watson U 4.00 1.50
❑ 59 Ben Watson R 5.00 2.00
❑ 60 Bernard Berrian C RC 4.00 1.50
❑ 61 Bernard Berrian U 5.00 2.00
❑ 62 Bernard Berrian R 6.00 2.50
❑ 63 Cedric Cobbs C RC 3.00 1.25
❑ 64 Cedric Cobbs U 4.00 1.50
❑ 65 Cedric Cobbs R 5.00 2.00
❑ 66 Chris Perry C RC 5.00 2.00
❑ 67 Chris Perry U 6.00 2.50
❑ 68 Chris Perry R 8.00 3.00
❑ 69 Darius Watts C RC 3.00 1.25
❑ 70 Darius Watts U 4.00 1.50
❑ 71 Darius Watts R 5.00 2.00
❑ 72 DeAngelo Hall C RC 4.00 1.50
❑ 73 DeAngelo Hall U 5.00 2.00
❑ 74 DeAngelo Hall R 6.00 2.50
❑ 75 Derrick Hamilton C RC 2.50 1.00
❑ 76 Derrick Hamilton U 3.00 1.25
❑ 77 Derrick Hamilton R 5.00 2.00
❑ 78 Devard Darling C RC 3.00 1.25
❑ 79 Devard Darling U 4.00 1.50
❑ 80 Devard Darling R 5.00 2.00
❑ 81 Devery Henderson C RC 2.50 1.00
❑ 82 Devery Henderson U 3.00 1.25
❑ 83 Devery Henderson R 4.00 1.50
❑ 84 Dunta Robinson C RC 3.00 1.25
❑ 85 Dunta Robinson U 4.00 1.50
❑ 86 Dunta Robinson R 5.00 2.00
❑ 87 Eli Manning C RC 15.00 7.50
❑ 88 Eli Manning U 20.00 7.50
❑ 89 Eli Manning R 25.00 10.00
❑ 90 Greg Jones C RC 3.00 1.25
❑ 91 Greg Jones U 4.00 1.50
❑ 92 Greg Jones R 5.00 2.00
❑ 93 J.P. Losman C RC 6.00 2.50
❑ 94 J.P. Losman U 8.00 3.00
❑ 95 J.P. Losman R 10.00 4.00
❑ 96 Julius Jones C RC 10.00 4.00
❑ 97 Julius Jones U 12.00 5.00
❑ 98 Julius Jones R 15.00 6.00
❑ 99 Keary Colbert C RC 4.00 1.50
❑ 100 Keary Colbert U 5.00 2.00
❑ 101 Keary Colbert R 6.00 2.50
❑ 102 Kellen Winslow C RC 6.00 2.50
❑ 103 Kellen Winslow U 8.00 3.00
❑ 104 Kellen Winslow R 10.00 4.00
❑ 105 Kevin Jones C RC 8.00 3.00
❑ 106 Kevin Jones U 10.00 4.00
❑ 107 Kevin Jones R 12.00 5.00
❑ 108 Larry Fitzgerald C RC 10.00 4.00
❑ 109 Larry Fitzgerald U 12.00 5.00
❑ 110 Larry Fitzgerald R 15.00 6.00
❑ 111 Lee Evans C RC 4.00 1.50
❑ 112 Lee Evans U 5.00 2.00
❑ 113 Lee Evans R 6.00 2.50
❑ 114 Luke McCown C RC 3.00 1.25
❑ 115 Luke McCown U 4.00 1.50
❑ 116 Luke McCown R 5.00 2.00
❑ 117 Matt Schaub C RC 8.00 3.00
❑ 118 Matt Schaub U 10.00 4.00
❑ 119 Matt Schaub R 12.00 5.00
❑ 120 Mewelde Moore C RC 3.00 1.25
❑ 121 Mewelde Moore U 4.00 1.50
❑ 122 Mewelde Moore R 5.00 2.00
❑ 123 Michael Clayton C RC 6.00 2.50
❑ 124 Michael Clayton U 8.00 3.00
❑ 125 Michael Clayton R 10.00 4.00
❑ 126 Michael Jenkins C RC 3.00 1.25
❑ 127 Michael Jenkins U 4.00 1.50
❑ 128 Michael Jenkins R 5.00 2.00
❑ 129 Philip Rivers C RC 10.00 4.00
❑ 130 Philip Rivers U 12.00 5.00
❑ 131 Philip Rivers R 15.00 6.00
❑ 132 Rashaun Woods C RC 3.00 1.25
❑ 133 Rashaun Woods U 4.00 1.50
❑ 134 Rashaun Woods R 5.00 2.00
❑ 135 Reggie Williams C RC 4.00 1.50
❑ 136 Reggie Williams U 5.00 2.00
❑ 137 Reggie Williams R 6.00 2.50
❑ 138 Robert Gallery C RC 3.00 1.25
❑ 139 Robert Gallery U 4.00 1.50
❑ 140 Robert Gallery R 5.00 2.00
❑ 141 Roy Williams C RC 8.00 3.00
❑ 142 Roy Williams U 10.00 4.00
❑ 143 Roy Williams R 12.00 5.00
❑ 144 Steven Jackson C RC 10.00 4.00
❑ 145 Steven Jackson U 12.00 5.00
❑ 146 Steven Jackson R 15.00 6.00
❑ 147 Tatum Bell C RC 6.00 2.50
❑ 148 Tatum Bell U 8.00 3.00
❑ 149 Tatum Bell R 10.00 4.00

2005 Topps Pristine

❑ COMP.SET w/o SP's (100) 60.00 25.00
❑ OVERALL JSY U STATED ODDS 1:6
❑ JSY U PRINT RUN 900 UNLESS NOTED
❑ AU R/100 STATED ODDS 1:37
❑ JSY AU S/25 STATED ODDS 1:675
❑ UNPRICED PRINT.PLATES PRINT RUN 1 SET
❑ 1 Tiki Barber C 2.50 1.00
❑ 2 LaDainian Tomlinson C 3.00 1.25
❑ 3 Drew Bennett C 1.50 .60
❑ 4 Jake Delhomme C 2.50 1.00
❑ 5 Deuce McAllister C 2.50 1.00
❑ 6 Jerome Bettis C 2.50 1.00
❑ 7 Javon Walker C 1.50 .60
❑ 8 Marshall Faulk C 2.50 1.00
❑ 9 Trent Green C 1.50 .60
❑ 10 Travis Henry C 1.50 .60
❑ 11 Eli Manning C 5.00 2.00
❑ 12 Donovan McNabb C 3.00 1.25
❑ 13 Priest Holmes C 2.50 1.00
❑ 14 Brandon Stokley C 1.50 .60
❑ 15 Curtis Martin C 2.50 1.00
❑ 16 Muhsin Muhammad C 1.50 .60
❑ 17 Corey Dillon C 1.50 .60
❑ 18 Fred Taylor C 1.50 .60
❑ 19 Michael Vick C 4.00 1.50
❑ 20 Michael Jenkins C 1.50 .60
❑ 21 Chris Brown C 1.50 .60
❑ 22 Willis McGahee C 2.50 1.00
❑ 23 Drew Bledsoe C 2.50 1.00
❑ 24 Michael Clayton C 2.50 1.00
❑ 25 Kerry Collins C 1.50 .60
❑ 26 Jason Witten C 1.50 .60
❑ 27 Clinton Portis C 2.50 1.00
❑ 28 Marc Bulger C 2.50 1.00
❑ 29 Julius Jones C 3.00 1.25
❑ 30 Chad Pennington C 2.50 1.00
❑ 31 Kevin Jones C 2.50 1.00
❑ 32 Domanick Davis C 1.50 .60
❑ 33 Reggie Wayne C 1.50 .60
❑ 34 Jimmy Smith C 1.50 .60
❑ 35 Byron Leftwich C 2.50 1.00
❑ 36 Randy Moss C 2.50 1.00
❑ 37 Isaac Bruce C 1.50 .60
❑ 38 LaMont Jordan C 2.50 1.00
❑ 39 Edgerrin James C 2.50 1.00
❑ 40 Aaron Brooks C 1.50 .60
❑ 41 Steven Jackson C 3.00 1.25
❑ 42 Cedric Benson C RC 8.00 3.00
❑ 43 Brian Westbrook C 1.50 .60
❑ 44 Andrew Walter C RC 6.00 2.50
❑ 45 Andre Johnson C 1.50 .60
❑ 46 David Greene C RC 4.00 1.50
❑ 47 David Carr C 2.50 1.00
❑ 48 Marion Barber C RC 6.00 2.50
❑ 49 Warrick Dunn C 1.50 .60
❑ 50 Terrence Murphy C RC 4.00 1.50
❑ 51 Dante Hall C 1.50 .60
❑ 52 Willie Parker C 12.00 5.00
❑ 53 Laveranues Coles C 1.50 .60
❑ 54 DeMarcus Ware C RC 6.00 2.50
❑ 55 Santana Moss C 1.50 .60
❑ 56 Alvin Pearman C RC 4.00 1.50
❑ 57 Keary Colbert C 1.50 .60
❑ 58 Carlos Rogers C RC 5.00 2.00
❑ 59 Jeremy Shockey C 2.50 1.00
❑ 60 Craig Bragg C RC 3.00 1.25
❑ 61 Daunte Culpepper C 2.50 1.00
❑ 62 Charlie Frye C RC 8.00 3.00
❑ 63 DeShaun Foster C 1.50 .60
❑ 64 Chad Owens C RC 4.00 1.50
❑ 65 Dunta Robinson C 1.50 .60
❑ 66 Mike Nugent C RC 4.00 1.50
❑ 67 Jonathan Vilma C 1.50 .60
❑ 68 Erasmus James C RC 4.00 1.50
❑ 69 Randy McMichael C 1.25 .50
❑ 70 Stefan LeFors C RC 4.00 1.50
❑ 71 Ben Roethlisberger C 6.00 2.50
❑ 72 Tab Perry C RC 4.00 1.50
❑ 73 Joey Harrington C 2.50 1.00
❑ 74 Adrian McPherson C RC 4.00 1.50
❑ 75 Roy Williams WR C 2.50 1.00
❑ 76 Vincent Jackson C RC 4.00 1.50
❑ 77 Lee Suggs C 1.50 .60
❑ 78 Ryan Moats C RC 4.00 1.50
❑ 79 Plaxico Burress C 1.50 .60
❑ 80 Chris Henry C RC 4.00 1.50
❑ 81 Larry Fitzgerald C 2.50 1.00
❑ 82 Travis Johnson C RC 3.00 1.25
❑ 83 Terrell Owens C 2.50 1.00
❑ 84 Fabian Washington C RC 4.00 1.50
❑ 85 Stephen Davis C 1.50 .60
❑ 86 Odell Thurman C RC 4.00 1.50
❑ 87 Tatum Bell C 1.50 .60
❑ 88 Roddy White C RC 4.00 1.50
❑ 89 J.P. Losman C 2.50 1.00
❑ 90 J.J. Arrington C RC 5.00 2.00
❑ 91 Thomas Jones C 1.50 .60
❑ 92 Eric Shelton C RC 4.00 1.50
❑ 93 Charles Rogers C 1.50 .60
❑ 94 Matt Jones C RC 10.00 4.00
❑ 95 Chris Chambers C 1.50 .60
❑ 96 Jerome Mathis C RC 4.00 1.50
❑ 97 Darrell Jackson C 1.50 .60
❑ 98 Justin Miller C RC 3.00 1.25
❑ 99 Donte Stallworth C 1.50 .60
❑ 100 Brandon Jacobs C RC 5.00 2.00
❑ 101 Alex Smith QB JSY U RC 20.00 8.00
❑ 102 Mark Clayton JSY U RC 10.00 4.00
❑ 103 Antrel Rolle JSY U RC 8.00 3.00
❑ 104 Kyle Orton JSY/500 U RC 12.00 5.00
❑ 105 Roscoe Parrish JSY U RC 8.00 3.00
❑ 106 Vernand Morency JSY U RC 8.003.00
❑ 107 Maurice Clarett JSY U 8.00 3.00
❑ 108 Mark Bradley JSY U RC 8.00 3.00
❑ 109 Reg.Brown JSY/500 U RC 10.00 4.00
❑ 110 Ronnie Brown JSY U RC 20.00 8.00
❑ 111 B.Edwards JSY/500 U RC 12.00 5.00
❑ 112 T.Williamson JSY/500 U RC 10.004.00
❑ 113 Cadillac Williams JSY U RC 20.007.50
❑ 114 Ricky Williams JSY/500 U 10.00 4.00
❑ 115 Jake Plummer JSY/500 U 10.00 4.00
❑ 116 Brian Urlacher JSY U 10.00 4.00
❑ 117 Joe Horn JSY/500 U 10.00 4.00
❑ 118 Anquan Boldin JSY/500 U 8.00 3.00
❑ 119 Carson Palmer JSY U 10.00 4.00
❑ 120 Rudi Johnson JSY/500 U 10.00 4.00
❑ 121 Matt Hasselbeck JSY/500 U 8.00 3.00
❑ 123 Steve McNair JSY/500 U 10.00 4.00
❑ 124 Shaun Alexander JSY U 12.00 5.00
❑ 125 Julius Peppers JSY/500 U 10.00 4.00
❑ 126 Dwight Freeney JSY/500 U 10.00 4.00
❑ 127 Patrick Kerney JSY U 8.00 3.00
❑ 128 Drew Brees JSY U 10.00 4.00
❑ 129 Tony Gonzalez JSY/500 U 8.00 3.00
❑ 130 Alge Crumpler JSY/500 U 8.00 3.00
❑ 131 Chad Johnson JSY/500 U 10.00 4.00
❑ 132 M.Muhammad JSY/500 U 8.00 3.00
❑ 133 Zach Thomas JSY/500 U 10.00 4.00
❑ 134 Marvin Harrison JSY U 10.00 4.00
❑ 135 LaVar Arrington JSY U 10.00 4.00
❑ 136 Eric Moulds JSY U 8.00 3.00
❑ 137 Michael Strahan JSY U 8.00 3.00
❑ 138 Jamal Lewis JSY/500 U 10.00 4.00
❑ 139 Ray Lewis JSY U 10.00 4.00
❑ 140 Hines Ward JSY/500 U 10.00 4.00
❑ 141 Peyton Manning JSY/500 U 15.006.00
❑ 142 Tom Brady JSY/500 U 15.00 6.00
❑ 143 Ahman Green JSY/500 U 10.00 4.00

❑ 144 Trent Green JSY/500 U 10.00 4.00
❑ 145 Brett Favre JSY/500 U 25.00 10.00
❑ 146 Aaron Rodgers AU R RC 80.00 30.00
❑ 147 Adam Jones AU R RC 20.00 7.50
❑ 148 Alex Smith QB AU R 100.00 50.00
❑ 149 Antrel Rolle AU R 25.00 10.00
❑ 150 Braylon Edwards AU R 60.00 30.00
❑ 151 Ciatrick Fason AU R RC 20.00 7.50
❑ 152 Courtney Roby AU R RC 20.00 7.50
❑ 153 Craphonso Thorpe AU R RC 20.00 7.50
❑ 154 Dan Cody AU R RC 20.00 7.50
❑ 155 Dan Orlovsky AU R RC 30.00 12.50
❑ 156 Darren Sproles AU R RC 20.00 7.50
❑ 157 David Pollack AU R RC 20.00 7.50
❑ 158 Derrick Johnson AU R RC 40.00 20.00
❑ 159 Frank Gore AU R RC 50.00 25.00
❑ 160 Heath Miller AU R RC 60.00 35.00
❑ 161 Jason Campbell AU R RC 40.00 20.00
❑ 162 Kyle Orton AU R 40.00 20.00
❑ 163 Mike Williams AU R 50.00 20.00
❑ 164 Ronnie Brown AU R 100.00 60.00
❑ 165 Troy Williamson AU R 40.00 20.00
❑ 166 Vernand Morency AU R 15.00 6.00
❑ 167 Deion Branch AU R 20.00 7.50
❑ 168 Brett Favre JSY AU S 300.00 175.00
❑ 169 Joe Montana JSY AU S 300.00 175.00
❑ 170 Barry Sanders JSY AU S 250.00 125.00
❑ 171 Tom Brady JSY AU S 250.00 125.00
❑ 172 Dan Marino JSY AU S 300.00 175.00

2003 Topps Total

❑ COMPLETE SET (550) 80.00 40.00
❑ 1 Rich Gannon .50 .20
❑ 2 Travis Henry .50 .20
❑ 3 Brian Finneran .30 .10
❑ 4 Ed Hartwell .30 .10
❑ 5 Az-Zahir Hakim .30 .10
❑ 6 Rodney Peete .30 .10
❑ 7 David Terrell .50 .20
❑ 8 Matt Schobel .30 .10
❑ 9 Andre Davis .30 .10
❑ 10 Dexter Coakley .30 .10
❑ 11 Rod Smith .50 .20
❑ 12 Damerien McCants .30 .10
❑ 13 Robert Ferguson .30 .10
❑ 14 Kailee Wong .30 .10
❑ 15 James Mungro .30 .10
❑ 16 Fred Taylor .75 .30
❑ 17 Tony Gonzalez .50 .20
❑ 18 Randall Godfrey .30 .10
❑ 19 Robert Thomas .30 .10
❑ 20 Rohan Davey .50 .20
❑ 21 Terrell Owens .75 .30
❑ 22 Ron Dayne .30 .10
❑ 23 Charlie Batch .30 .10
❑ 24 Brian Westbrook .50 .20
❑ 25 Plaxico Burress .50 .20
❑ 26 Reche Caldwell .30 .10
❑ 27 Fred Beasley .30 .10
❑ 28 Anthony Simmons .30 .10
❑ 29 Rod Woodson .50 .20
❑ 30 Derrick Brooks .50 .20
❑ 31 Shaun Ellis .30 .10
❑ 32 Ladell Betts .50 .20
❑ 33 Russell Davis .30 .10
❑ 34 Warrick Dunn .50 .20
❑ 35 Jeremy Shockey 1.25 .50
❑ 36 Alex Van Pelt .30 .10
❑ 37 Todd Bouman .30 .10
❑ 38 Kelly Campbell .30 .10
❑ 39 Justin Smith .30 .10
❑ 40 Jamel White .30 .10
❑ 41 La'Roi Glover .30 .10
❑ 42 Ian Gold .30 .10
❑ 43 Robert Porcher .30 .10
❑ 44 Jermaine Lewis .30 .10
❑ 45 Marvin Harrison .75 .30
❑ 46 Darren Sharper .30 .10
❑ 47 Jamie Sharper .30 .10
❑ 48 Tony Richardson .30 .10
❑ 49 Moe Williams .30 .10
❑ 50 Ricky Williams .75 .30
❑ 51 Ty Law .50 .20
❑ 52 Donte Stallworth .75 .30
❑ 53 Shannon Sharpe .50 .20
❑ 54 Santana Moss .50 .20
❑ 55 Charlie Garner .50 .20
❑ 56 Brian Dawkins .50 .20
❑ 57 Dan Campbell .30 .10
❑ 58 William Green .50 .20
❑ 59 Ron Dugans .30 .10
❑ 60 Darrell Jackson .50 .20
❑ 61 Marc Bulger .75 .30
❑ 62 Joe Jurevicius .30 .10
❑ 63 Erron Kinney .30 .10
❑ 64 Champ Bailey .50 .20
❑ 65 Peerless Price .50 .20
❑ 66 Gary Baxter .30 .10
❑ 67 Chris Redman .30 .10
❑ 68 London Fletcher .30 .10
❑ 69 Dee Brown .30 .10
❑ 70 Anthony Thomas .50 .20
❑ 71 Jake Delhomme .75 .30
❑ 72 Dorsey Levens .30 .10
❑ 73 Roy Williams .75 .30
❑ 74 Ashley Lelie .75 .30
❑ 75 Joey Harrington 1.25 .50
❑ 76 William Henderson .30 .10
❑ 77 Corey Bradford .30 .10
❑ 78 Reggie Wayne .50 .20
❑ 79 Kyle Brady .30 .10
❑ 80 Trent Green .50 .20
❑ 81 Bill Romanowski .30 .10
❑ 82 Chike Okeafor RC .75 .30
❑ 83 David Patten .30 .10
❑ 84 Terrelle Smith .30 .10
❑ 85 Kerry Collins .50 .20
❑ 86 Derrick Mason .50 .20
❑ 87 Trung Canidate .50 .20
❑ 88 A.J. Feeley .50 .20
❑ 89 Jason Gildon .30 .10
❑ 90 Doug Flutie .75 .30
❑ 91 Tai Streets .30 .10
❑ 92 Keith Newman .30 .10
❑ 93 Adam Archuleta .30 .10
❑ 94 Simeon Rice .50 .20
❑ 95 Eddie George .50 .20
❑ 96 Frank Sanders .30 .10
❑ 97 Freddie Jones .30 .10
❑ 98 Charles Johnson .30 .10
❑ 99 Keith Traylor .30 .10
❑ 100 Drew Bledsoe .75 .30
❑ 101 Muhsin Muhammad .50 .20
❑ 102 Marques Anderson .30 .10
❑ 103 Donald Hayes .30 .10
❑ 104 Quincy Morgan .50 .20
❑ 105 Chad Hutchinson .30 .10
❑ 106 Mike Anderson .50 .20
❑ 107 Randy McMichael .50 .20
❑ 108 Vonnie Holliday .30 .10
❑ 109 Marcus Coleman .30 .10
❑ 110 Edgerrin James .75 .30
❑ 111 Michael Lewis .30 .10
❑ 112 Wayne Chrebet .50 .20
❑ 113 Antwaan Randle El .75 .30
❑ 114 Byron Chamberlain .30 .10
❑ 115 Jeff Garcia .75 .30
❑ 116 Kim Herring .30 .10
❑ 117 Kenny Holmes .30 .10
❑ 118 John Lynch .50 .20
❑ 119 Doug Jolley .30 .10
❑ 120 Duce Staley .50 .20
❑ 121 Kordell Stewart .50 .20
❑ 122 Stephen Alexander .30 .10
❑ 123 Andre Carter .30 .10
❑ 124 Bobby Engram .30 .10
❑ 125 Marshall Faulk .75 .30
❑ 126 Peter Simon RC .50 .20
❑ 127 Alge Crumpler .50 .20
❑ 128 Kenny Watson .30 .10
❑ 129 Duane Starks .30 .10
❑ 130 Jeff Blake .30 .10
❑ 131 Todd Heap .50 .20
❑ 132 Bobby Shaw .30 .10
❑ 133 Ricky Proehl .30 .10
❑ 134 John Abraham .30 .10
❑ 135 T.J. Houshmandzadeh .30 .10
❑ 136 Brian Urlacher 1.25 .50
❑ 137 Darren Woodson .30 .10
❑ 138 Steve Beuerlein .30 .10
❑ 139 Cory Schlesinger .30 .10
❑ 140 Ahman Green .75 .30
❑ 141 Jabar Gaffney .50 .20
❑ 142 Eddie Drummond .30 .10
❑ 143 Stacey Mack .30 .10
❑ 144 Johnnie Morton .50 .20
❑ 145 Chris Chambers .75 .30
❑ 146 Jim Kleinsasser .30 .10
❑ 147 Tebucky Jones .30 .10
❑ 148 Marcus Pollard .30 .10
❑ 149 Tony Brackens .30 .10
❑ 150 Chad Pennington 1.00 .40
❑ 151 Kevin Faulk .30 .10
❑ 152 Michael Lewis .30 .10
❑ 153 Mark Bruener .30 .10
❑ 154 Tim Dwight .50 .20
❑ 155 Jerry Rice 1.50 .60
❑ 156 Trent Dilfer .50 .20
❑ 157 Jon Ritchie .30 .10
❑ 158 Michael Pittman .30 .10
❑ 159 Lamar Gordon .30 .10
❑ 160 Rod Gardner .50 .20
❑ 161 Ken Dilger .30 .10
❑ 162 Doug Johnson .30 .10
❑ 163 Peter Boulware .30 .10
❑ 164 Jevon Kearse .50 .20
❑ 165 Julius Peppers .75 .30
❑ 166 Chris Chandler .30 .10
❑ 167 Lorenzo Neal .30 .10
❑ 168 Kevin Johnson .50 .20
❑ 169 Kevin Hardy .30 .10
❑ 170 KaRon Coleman .30 .10
❑ 171 James Stewart .50 .20
❑ 172 Tony Fisher .30 .10
❑ 173 Billy Miller .30 .10
❑ 174 Phillip Crosby .30 .10
❑ 175 Priest Holmes 1.00 .40
❑ 176 Elvis Joseph .30 .10
❑ 177 Bryan Gilmore .30 .10
❑ 178 D'Wayne Bates .30 .10
❑ 179 Quincy Carter .50 .20
❑ 180 Joe Horn .50 .20
❑ 181 Anthony Henry .30 .10
❑ 182 Anthony Becht .30 .10
❑ 183 Mike Peterson .30 .10
❑ 184 James Thrash .30 .10
❑ 185 Jerome Bettis .75 .30
❑ 186 Marcellus Wiley .30 .10
❑ 187 Tim Rattay .50 .20
❑ 188 Maurice Morris .30 .10
❑ 189 Jason Taylor .30 .10
❑ 190 Keyshawn Johnson .75 .30
❑ 191 John Simon .30 .10
❑ 192 Fred Smoot .30 .10
❑ 193 Wendell Bryant .30 .10
❑ 194 Brandon Stokley .50 .20
❑ 195 Kurt Warner .75 .30
❑ 196 Steve Smith .75 .30
❑ 197 Dez White .30 .10
❑ 198 Jim Miller .30 .10
❑ 199 Robert Griffith .30 .10
❑ 200 Michael Vick 2.00 .75
❑ 201 Antonio Bryant .50 .20
❑ 202 Laveranues Coles .50 .20
❑ 203 Kalimba Edwards .30 .10
❑ 204 Bubba Franks .50 .20
❑ 205 David Carr 1.25 .50
❑ 206 Dwight Freeney .50 .20
❑ 207 Eric Johnson .50 .20
❑ 208 Reggie Tongue .30 .10
❑ 209 Cam Cleeland .30 .10
❑ 210 Michael Bennett .50 .20
❑ 211 Antowain Smith .50 .20

❑	212	Warren Sapp	.50	.20
❑	213	Ike Hilliard	.30	.10
❑	214	Olandis Gary	.50	.20
❑	215	Tim Brown	.75	.30
❑	216	Kevin Dyson	.50	.20
❑	217	Eddie Kennison	.30	.10
❑	218	Junior Seau	.75	.30
❑	219	Donnie Edwards	.30	.10
❑	220	Shaun Alexander	.75	.30
❑	221	Terrence Wilkins	.30	.10
❑	222	Garrison Hearst	.50	.20
❑	223	Keith Bulluck	.30	.10
❑	224	Zeron Flemister	.30	.10
❑	225	Jake Plummer	.50	.20
❑	226	Chad Johnson	.75	.30
❑	227	Travis Taylor	.50	.20
❑	228	Josh Reed	.50	.20
❑	229	James Farrior	.30	.10
❑	230	Marty Booker	.50	.20
❑	231	Todd Pinkston	.50	.20
❑	232	Dennis Northcutt	.50	.20
❑	233	Troy Hambrick	.30	.10
❑	234	Roland Williams	.30	.10
❑	235	Bill Schroeder	.50	.20
❑	236	Javon Walker	.50	.20
❑	237	Kevin Swayne	.30	.10
❑	238	Dominic Rhodes	.50	.20
❑	239	David Garrard	.30	.10
❑	240	Mike Maslowski RC	.50	.20
❑	241	Travis Minor	.30	.10
❑	242	Terry Glenn	.30	.10
❑	243	Deion Branch	.75	.30
❑	244	Adrian Peterson	.30	.10
❑	245	Tiki Barber	.75	.30
❑	246	Ray Lewis	.75	.30
❑	247	Marques Tuiasosopo	.50	.20
❑	248	Chad Lewis	.30	.10
❑	249	Takeo Spikes	.30	.10
❑	250	LaDainian Tomlinson	.75	.30
❑	251	Stephen Davis	.50	.20
❑	252	Koren Robinson	.50	.20
❑	253	Daylon McCutcheon	.30	.10
❑	254	Rob Johnson	.50	.20
❑	255	Donovan McNabb	1.00	.40
❑	256	Derrius Thompson	.30	.10
❑	257	Marcel Shipp	.50	.20
❑	258	Keith Brooking	.30	.10
❑	259	Chris McAlister	.30	.10
❑	260	Eric Moulds	.50	.20
❑	261	Amos Zereoue	.50	.20
❑	262	Drew Brees	.75	.30
❑	263	Jon Kitna	.50	.20
❑	264	Brad Johnson	.50	.20
❑	265	Emmitt Smith	2.00	.75
❑	266	Trevor Pryce	.30	.10
❑	267	Mike McMahon	.50	.20
❑	268	Patrick Ramsey	.75	.30
❑	269	Jonathan Wells	.30	.10
❑	270	Mark Brunell	.50	.20
❑	271	Marc Boerigter	.50	.20
❑	272	Rob Konrad	.30	.10
❑	273	Derrick Alexander	.30	.10
❑	274	Joey Galloway	.50	.20
❑	275	Peyton Manning	1.25	.50
❑	276	Najeh Davenport	.30	.10
❑	277	Jesse Palmer	.30	.10
❑	278	LaMont Jordan	.75	.30
❑	279	Ernie Conwell	.30	.10
❑	280	Hines Ward	.75	.30
❑	281	Freddie Mitchell	.50	.20
❑	282	Curtis Conway	.30	.10
❑	283	Cedrick Wilson	.30	.10
❑	284	Troy Brown	.50	.20
❑	285	Torry Holt	.75	.30
❑	286	Mike Alstott	.75	.30
❑	287	Frank Wycheck	.30	.10
❑	288	Jeremiah Trotter	.30	.10
❑	289	Tyrone Wheatley	.30	.10
❑	290	David Boston	.50	.20
❑	291	Jay Fiedler	.50	.20
❑	292	Troy Walters	.30	.10
❑	293	Warrick Holdman	.30	.10
❑	294	Peter Warrick	.50	.20
❑	295	Tim Couch	.30	.10
❑	296	Aaron Glenn	.30	.10
❑	297	Deuce McAllister	.75	.30
❑	298	Michael Strahan	.50	.20
❑	299	Tom Brady	2.00	.75
❑	300	Brett Favre	2.00	.75
❑	301	Isaac Bruce	.75	.30
❑	302	Jimmy Smith	.50	.20
❑	303	Dante Hall	.75	.30
❑	304	James McKnight	.30	.10
❑	305	Daunte Culpepper	.75	.30
❑	306	Lawyer Milloy	.50	.20
❑	307	Jerome Pathon	.30	.10
❑	308	Steve McNair	.75	.30
❑	309	Vinny Testaverde	.50	.20
❑	310	Tommy Maddox	.75	.30
❑	311	Amani Toomer	.50	.20
❑	312	Aaron Brooks	.75	.30
❑	313	Gus Frerotte	.30	.10
❑	314	Kevan Barlow	.50	.20
❑	315	Matt Hasselbeck	.50	.20
❑	316	Clinton Portis	1.25	.50
❑	317	Keenan McCardell	.30	.10
❑	318	Zach Thomas	.75	.30
❑	319	Curtis Martin	.75	.30
❑	320	Jamal Lewis	.75	.30
❑	321	T.J. Duckett	.50	.20
❑	322	Jerry Porter	.50	.20
❑	323	Randy Moss	1.25	.50
❑	324	Rosevelt Colvin	.30	.10
❑	325	Corey Dillon	.50	.20
❑	326	Kelly Holcomb	.50	.20
❑	327	Josh McCown	.50	.20
❑	328	Ed McCaffrey	.75	.30
❑	329	Mikhael Ricks	.30	.10
❑	330	Donald Driver	.50	.20
❑	331	Darling/Thompson/McKinnon	.30	.10
❑	332	Hall/Carpenter/Buchanon	.30	.10
❑	333	Thomas/Weaver/Gregg RC	1.00	.40
❑	334	Winfield/Wire/Clements	.30	.10
❑	335	Morgan/Fields/Witherspoon	.50	.20
❑	336	Brown/Robinson RC/Daniels	.50	.20
❑	337	Powell RC/Thornton/Williams RC	.50	.20
❑	338	Taylor RC/Little/Bentley	.75	.30
❑	339	Ekuban/Ellis/Myers	.30	.10
❑	340	Gard/Dalton RC/Berry RC	.75	.30
❑	341	Green/Curry RC/Holmes	.50	.20
❑	342	Hunt RC/KGB/Walker RC	.75	.30
❑	343	Walker/Deloach RC/Payne	.30	.10
❑	344	Bratzke/Washington/Morris	.30	.10
❑	345	Henderson/Coleman/Stroud	.50	.20
❑	346	Hicks/Browning RC/Sims	.50	.20
❑	347	A.Ogunleye RC/Chester RC	2.00	.75
❑	348	Robbins/Mixon/Johnstone	.30	.10
❑	349	Phifer/Johnson/Bruschi	.75	.30
❑	350	Grant/Chase RC/Howard	.50	.20
❑	351	Short/Jones RC/Barrow	.50	.20
❑	352	Jones/Lewis/Cowart	.30	.10
❑	353	Barton/Parrella/Harris	.30	.10
❑	354	Whiting/Simon/Walker	.30	.10
❑	355	Smith/Hamp/von Oel	1.00	.40
❑	356	Williams RC/Fisk/Johnson	.50	.20
❑	357	Smith/Ulbrich/Peterson	.30	.10
❑	358	Cochran RC/Eaton/Randle	.50	.20
❑	359	Lewis/Wistrom/Little	.30	.10
❑	360	Rudd/Spires/Quarles RC	.75	.30
❑	361	Haynesworth/Carter/Smith	.30	.10
❑	362	Smith/Armstead/Upshaw	.30	.10
❑	363	Ad.Wilson/Dex.Jackson RC	.75	.30
❑	364	F.Wakefield/K.Vanden	.30	.10
❑	365	K.Kasper/J.McAddley	.30	.10
❑	366	B.Smith/P.Kerney	.30	.10
❑	367	M.Jenkins/T.Gaylor	.30	.10
❑	368	C.Draft/M.Stewart	.30	.10
❑	369	J.Hunter/R.Johnson	.30	.10
❑	370	C.Fuller/E.Reed	.50	.20
❑	371	A.Schobel/J.Posey RC	.50	.20
❑	372	P.Williams/S.Adams	.30	.10
❑	373	D.Grant/M.Minter	.30	.10
❑	374	B.Buckner/K.Jenkins	.30	.10
❑	375	R.Howard RC/T.Cousin RC	.50	.20
❑	376	M.Brown/M.Green	.50	.20
❑	377	J.Azumah/R.W.McQuarters	.30	.10
❑	378	B.Simmons/S.Foley	.30	.10
❑	379	A.Hawkins/J.Burris	.30	.10
❑	380	Jo.Armour RC/M.Manuel	.30	.10
❑	381	G.Warren/O.Roye	.30	.10
❑	382	C.Brown/K.Lang	.30	.10
❑	383	D.Ross/M.Edwards	.30	.10
❑	384	A.Singleton RC/D.Nguyen	.50	.20
❑	385	A.Wilson/J.Mobley	.30	.10
❑	386	D.O'Neal/K.Kennedy	.30	.10
❑	387	L.Elliss/S.Rogers	.30	.10
❑	388	C.Cash/D.Bly	.30	.10
❑	389	B.Walker/C.Harris	.30	.10
❑	390	H.Navies RC/N.Diggs	.30	.10
❑	391	A.Harris/M.McKenzie	.30	.10
❑	392	C.Clemons/J.Foreman	.30	.10
❑	393	E.Brown/M.Stevens	.30	.10
❑	394	B.Scioli/L.Tripplett	.30	.10
❑	395	D.Macklin/W.Harris	.30	.10
❑	396	A.Ayodele/H.Douglas	.30	.10
❑	397	F.Bryant/J.Craft RC	.30	.10
❑	398	D.Darius/M.McCree	.30	.10
❑	399	S.Fujita/S.Barber	.50	.20
❑	400	E.Warfield RC/W.Bartee	.75	.30
❑	401	G.Wesley/J.Woods	.30	.10
❑	402	P.Surtain/S.Madison	.30	.10
❑	403	B.Marion/S.Knight	.30	.10
❑	404	G.Biekert/H.Crockett	.30	.10
❑	405	C.Claiborne/C.Hovan	.30	.10
❑	406	C.Chavous/K.Irvin	.30	.10
❑	407	C.Fauria/D.Graham	.30	.10
❑	408	O.Smith/R.Harrison	.30	.10
❑	409	A.Pleasant/R.Seymour	.30	.10
❑	410	D.Smith/S.Hodge	.30	.10
❑	411	A.Ambrose/D.Carter	.30	.10
❑	412	M.Mitchell/D.Rodgers	.30	.10
❑	413	W.Allen/W.Peterson	.30	.10
❑	414	C.Griffin/K.Hamilton	.30	.10
❑	415	O.Stoutmire/S.Williams	.30	.10
❑	416	A.Beasley/D.Abraham	.30	.10
❑	417	J.McGraw/S.Games	.30	.10
❑	418	C.Woodson/P.Buchanon	.50	.20
❑	419	T.Bryant/T.Armstrong	.30	.10
❑	420	B.Taylor/T.Vincent	.30	.10
❑	421	C.Emmons/N.Wayne	.30	.10
❑	422	B.Alexander/C.Hope	.50	.20
❑	423	J.Porter/K.Bell	.75	.30
❑	424	C.Scott/D.Washington	.30	.10
❑	425	B.Leber/R.McNeil	.30	.10
❑	426	Q.Jammer/T.Cody	.30	.10
❑	427	A.Plummer/J.Webster	.30	.10
❑	428	T.Parrish/Z.Bronson	.30	.10
❑	429	I.Mili/J.Stevens	.30	.10
❑	430	K.Lucas/S.Springs	.30	.10
❑	431	C.Brown/O.Huff	.30	.10
❑	432	J.Duncan/T.Polley	.30	.10
❑	433	A.Williams/T.Fisher	.30	.10
❑	434	B.Kelly/R.Barber	.30	.10
❑	435	A.Stecker/K.Williams	.30	.10
❑	436	D.Bennett/J.McCareins	.50	.20
❑	437	L.Schulters/T.Williams	.30	.10
❑	438	A.Dyson/S.Rolle	.30	.10
❑	439	I.Ohalete/M.Bowen	.30	.10
❑	440	B.Noble/D.Wilkinson	.30	.10
❑	441	Charles Rogers RC	1.25	.50
❑	442	Jimmy Kennedy RC	1.25	.50
❑	443	Kelley Washington RC	1.25	.50
❑	444	Trent Smith RC	1.00	.40
❑	445	Rashean Mathis RC	1.00	.40
❑	446	Brian St.Pierre RC	1.25	.50
❑	447	Bethel Johnson RC	1.25	.50
❑	448	Alonzo Jackson RC	1.00	.40
❑	449	Arnaz Battle RC	1.25	.50
❑	450	Carson Palmer RC	6.00	2.50
❑	451	Michael Haynes RC	1.25	.50
❑	452	LaBrandon Toefield RC	1.25	.50
❑	453	Earnest Graham RC	1.00	.40
❑	454	Walter Young RC	.60	.25
❑	455	Terry Pierce RC	1.00	.40
❑	456	Talman Gardner RC	1.25	.50
❑	457	J.T. Wall RC	.60	.25
❑	458	DeWayne Robertson RC	1.25	.50
❑	459	Bradie James RC	1.25	.50
❑	460	Andre Johnson RC	2.50	1.00
❑	461	Bobby Wade RC	1.25	.50
❑	462	Chris Davis RC	1.00	.40
❑	463	Kliff Kingsbury RC	1.00	.40
❑	464	Osi Umenyiora RC	2.00	.75
❑	465	Domanick Davis RC	1.25	.50
❑	466	Sam Aiken RC	1.00	.40
❑	467	Ty Warren RC	1.25	.50
❑	468	Terence Newman RC	2.50	1.00
❑	469	Zuriel Smith RC	.60	.25
❑	470	Willis McGahee RC	3.00	1.25
❑	471	David Kircus RC	1.25	.50
❑	472	Billy McMullen RC	1.00	.40

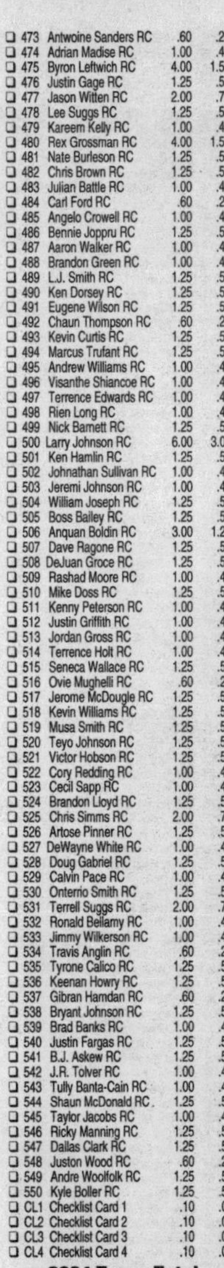

❑ 473 Antwoine Sanders RC .60 .25
❑ 474 Adrian Madise RC 1.00 .40
❑ 475 Byron Leftwich RC 4.00 1.50
❑ 476 Justin Gage RC 1.25 .50
❑ 477 Jason Witten RC 2.00 .75
❑ 478 Lee Suggs RC 1.25 .50
❑ 479 Kareem Kelly RC 1.00 .40
❑ 480 Rex Grossman RC 4.00 1.50
❑ 481 Nate Burleson RC 1.25 .50
❑ 482 Chris Brown RC 1.25 .50
❑ 483 Julian Battle RC 1.00 .40
❑ 484 Carl Ford RC .60 .25
❑ 485 Angelo Crowell RC 1.00 .40
❑ 486 Bennie Joppru RC 1.25 .50
❑ 487 Aaron Walker RC 1.00 .40
❑ 488 Brandon Green RC 1.00 .40
❑ 489 L.J. Smith RC 1.25 .50
❑ 490 Ken Dorsey RC 1.25 .50
❑ 491 Eugene Wilson RC 1.25 .50
❑ 492 Chaun Thompson RC .60 .25
❑ 493 Kevin Curtis RC 1.25 .50
❑ 494 Marcus Trufant RC 1.25 .50
❑ 495 Andrew Williams RC 1.00 .40
❑ 496 Visanthe Shiancoe RC 1.00 .40
❑ 497 Terrence Edwards RC 1.00 .40
❑ 498 Rien Long RC 1.00 .40
❑ 499 Nick Barnett RC 1.25 .50
❑ 500 Larry Johnson RC 6.00 3.00
❑ 501 Ken Hamlin RC 1.25 .50
❑ 502 Johnathan Sullivan RC 1.00 .40
❑ 503 Jeremi Johnson RC 1.00 .40
❑ 504 William Joseph RC 1.25 .50
❑ 505 Boss Bailey RC 1.25 .50
❑ 506 Anquan Boldin RC 3.00 1.25
❑ 507 Dave Ragone RC 1.25 .50
❑ 508 DeJuan Groce RC 1.25 .50
❑ 509 Rashad Moore RC 1.00 .40
❑ 510 Mike Doss RC 1.25 .50
❑ 511 Kenny Peterson RC 1.00 .40
❑ 512 Justin Griffith RC 1.00 .40
❑ 513 Jordan Gross RC 1.00 .40
❑ 514 Terrence Holt RC 1.00 .40
❑ 515 Seneca Wallace RC 1.25 .50
❑ 516 Ovie Mughelli RC .60 .25
❑ 517 Jerome McDougle RC 1.25 .50
❑ 518 Kevin Williams RC 1.25 .50
❑ 519 Musa Smith RC 1.25 .50
❑ 520 Teyo Johnson RC 1.25 .50
❑ 521 Victor Hobson RC 1.25 .50
❑ 522 Cory Redding RC 1.00 .40
❑ 523 Cecil Sapp RC 1.00 .40
❑ 524 Brandon Lloyd RC 1.25 .50
❑ 525 Chris Simms RC 2.00 .75
❑ 526 Artose Pinner RC 1.25 .50
❑ 527 DeWayne White RC 1.00 .40
❑ 528 Doug Gabriel RC 1.25 .50
❑ 529 Calvin Pace RC 1.00 .40
❑ 530 Onterrio Smith RC 1.25 .50
❑ 531 Terrell Suggs RC 2.00 .75
❑ 532 Ronald Bellamy RC 1.00 .40
❑ 533 Jimmy Wilkerson RC 1.00 .40
❑ 534 Travis Anglin RC .60 .25
❑ 535 Tyrone Calico RC 1.25 .50
❑ 536 Keenan Howry RC 1.25 .50
❑ 537 Gibran Hamdan RC .60 .25
❑ 538 Bryant Johnson RC 1.25 .50
❑ 539 Brad Banks RC 1.00 .40
❑ 540 Justin Fargas RC 1.25 .50
❑ 541 B.J. Askew RC 1.25 .50
❑ 542 J.R. Tolver RC 1.00 .40
❑ 543 Tully Banta-Cain RC 1.00 .40
❑ 544 Shaun McDonald RC 1.25 .50
❑ 545 Taylor Jacobs RC 1.00 .40
❑ 546 Ricky Manning RC 1.25 .50
❑ 547 Dallas Clark RC 1.25 .50
❑ 548 Juston Wood RC .60 .25
❑ 549 Andre Woolfolk RC 1.25 .50
❑ 550 Kyle Boller RC 1.25 .50
❑ CL1 Checklist Card 1 .10 .02
❑ CL2 Checklist Card 2 .10 .02
❑ CL3 Checklist Card 3 .10 .02
❑ CL4 Checklist Card 4 .10 .02

2004 Topps Total

❑ COMPLETE SET (440) 80.00 40.00
❑ 1 Donovan McNabb 1.00 .40
❑ 2 Zach Thomas .75 .30

❑ 3 Randy Moss 1.00 .40
❑ 4 Kerry Collins .50 .20
❑ 5 Hines Ward .75 .30
❑ 6 Tyrone Calico .50 .20
❑ 7 Patrick Ramsey .50 .20
❑ 8 Jeff Garcia .75 .30
❑ 9 Aveion Cason .30 .10
❑ 10 Stephen Davis .50 .20
❑ 11 Marcel Shipp .50 .20
❑ 12 T.J. Duckett .50 .20
❑ 13 Chris McAlister .30 .10
❑ 14 Peter Warrick .50 .20
❑ 15 Ahman Green .75 .30
❑ 16 Deion Branch .75 .30
❑ 17 David Boston .50 .20
❑ 18 Wayne Chrebet .50 .20
❑ 19 Michael Strahan .50 .20
❑ 20 Amaz Battle .50 .20
❑ 21 Darrell Jackson .50 .20
❑ 22 Chris Chandler .50 .20
❑ 23 Charlie Garner .50 .20
❑ 24 James Thrash .30 .10
❑ 25 LaDainian Tomlinson 1.00 .40
❑ 26 Jerry Porter .50 .20
❑ 27 Jerome Pathon .30 .10
❑ 28 Jerome Bettis .75 .30
❑ 29 Eddie George .50 .20
❑ 30 Jamal Lewis .75 .30
❑ 31 Ricky Proehl .30 .10
❑ 32 Josh Reed .30 .10
❑ 33 David Terrell .50 .20
❑ 34 Antonio Bryant .50 .20
❑ 35 Domanick Davis .75 .30
❑ 36 Artose Pinner .30 .10
❑ 37 Jed Weaver .30 .10
❑ 38 Johnnie Morton .50 .20
❑ 39 Troy Edwards .30 .10
❑ 40 Marvin Harrison .75 .30
❑ 41 Chris Hovan .30 .10
❑ 42 Boo Williams .30 .10
❑ 43 Ike Hilliard .30 .10
❑ 44 Sam Cowart .30 .10
❑ 45 Shaun Alexander .75 .30
❑ 46 Freddie Mitchell .50 .20
❑ 47 Garrison Hearst .50 .20
❑ 48 Joe Jurevicius .30 .10
❑ 49 Freddie Jones .30 .10
❑ 50 Michael Vick 1.50 .60
❑ 51 Mike Rucker .30 .10
❑ 52 Carson Palmer 1.00 .40
❑ 53 Az-Zahir Hakim .30 .10
❑ 54 Billy Miller .30 .10
❑ 55 Chad Pennington .75 .30
❑ 56 Charles Woodson .50 .20
❑ 57 Andre Carter .30 .10
❑ 58 Maurice Morris .30 .10
❑ 59 Leonard Little .30 .10
❑ 60 Travis Henry .50 .20
❑ 61 Thomas Jones .50 .20
❑ 62 Dennis Northcutt .30 .10
❑ 63 Quentin Griffin .75 .30
❑ 64 Joey Harrington .75 .30
❑ 65 Edgerrin James .75 .30
❑ 66 Cortez Hankton .30 .10
❑ 67 Jason Taylor .30 .10
❑ 68 Eddie Kennison .30 .10
❑ 69 Ty Law .50 .20
❑ 70 Aaron Brooks .50 .20
❑ 71 Antonio Gates .75 .30
❑ 72 Antwaan Randle El .75 .30
❑ 73 Kevan Barlow .50 .20
❑ 74 Chris Brown .75 .30
❑ 75 Clinton Portis .75 .30
❑ 76 Rod Gardner .50 .20
❑ 77 Isaac Bruce .50 .20
❑ 78 Mike Alstott .50 .20
❑ 79 Brian Westbrook .50 .20
❑ 80 Amani Toomer .50 .20
❑ 81 Justin Fargas .50 .20
❑ 82 Michael Bennett .50 .20
❑ 83 Dante Hall .75 .30
❑ 84 Marcus Pollard .30 .10
❑ 85 Fred Taylor .50 .20
❑ 86 Tai Streets .30 .10
❑ 87 Robert Ferguson .30 .10
❑ 88 Roy Williams S .50 .20
❑ 89 Lee Suggs .75 .30
❑ 90 Chad Johnson .75 .30
❑ 91 DeShaun Foster .50 .20
❑ 92 Alge Crumpler .50 .20
❑ 93 Travis Taylor .30 .10
❑ 94 London Fletcher .30 .10
❑ 95 Priest Holmes 1.00 .40
❑ 96 A.J. Feeley .75 .30
❑ 97 Kevin Faulk .30 .10
❑ 98 Shaun Ellis .30 .10
❑ 99 Tim Dwight .50 .20
❑ 100 Peyton Manning 1.25 .50
❑ 101 Dane Looker .50 .20
❑ 102 Mark Brunell .50 .20
❑ 103 Bryant Johnson .30 .10
❑ 104 Kelley Washington .30 .10
❑ 105 Rex Grossman .75 .30
❑ 106 William Green .50 .20
❑ 107 Keyshawn Johnson .50 .20
❑ 108 Trevor Pryce .30 .10
❑ 109 Donald Driver .50 .20
❑ 110 David Carr .75 .30
❑ 111 Marcus Robinson .50 .20
❑ 112 Justin McCareins .30 .10
❑ 113 Tim Brown .75 .30
❑ 114 James Farrior .30 .10
❑ 115 Deuce McAllister .75 .30
❑ 116 Simeon Rice .50 .20
❑ 117 Koren Robinson .50 .20
❑ 118 Kassim Osgood .30 .10
❑ 119 Tim Rattay .30 .10
❑ 120 Laveranues Coles .50 .20
❑ 121 Brian Finneran .30 .10
❑ 122 Todd Heap .50 .20
❑ 123 Bobby Shaw .30 .10
❑ 124 Anthony Thomas .50 .20
❑ 125 Brett Favre 2.00 .75
❑ 126 Dwight Freeney .50 .20
❑ 127 Randy McMichael .30 .10
❑ 128 David Givens .50 .20
❑ 129 Rich Gannon .50 .20
❑ 130 Tiki Barber .75 .30
❑ 131 Terrell Owens .75 .30
❑ 132 Drew Bennett .50 .20
❑ 133 Shawn Bryson .30 .10
❑ 134 Jabar Gaffney .50 .20
❑ 135 Jake Delhomme .75 .30
❑ 136 Warrick Dunn .50 .20
❑ 137 Brandon Lloyd .50 .20
❑ 138 Brad Johnson .50 .20
❑ 139 Jon Kitna .50 .20
❑ 140 Marshall Faulk .75 .30
❑ 141 Javon Walker .50 .20
❑ 142 Nate Burleson .75 .30
❑ 143 Jimmy Smith .50 .20
❑ 144 Adewale Ogunleye .50 .20
❑ 145 Trent Green .50 .20
❑ 146 Richard Seymour .30 .10
❑ 147 Donte' Stallworth .50 .20
❑ 148 Curtis Martin .75 .30
❑ 149 Todd Pinkston .30 .10
❑ 150 Steve McNair .75 .30
❑ 151 Josh McCown .50 .20
❑ 152 Ray Lewis .75 .30
❑ 153 Muhsin Muhammad .50 .20
❑ 154 Quincy Morgan .50 .20
❑ 155 Jake Plummer .50 .20
❑ 156 Jason Witten .50 .20
❑ 157 Dallas Clark .50 .20
❑ 158 Onterrio Smith .50 .20
❑ 159 Jeremy Shockey .75 .30

❑ 160 Ricky Williams .75 .30
❑ 161 Jevon Kearse .50 .20
❑ 162 Plaxico Burress .50 .20
❑ 163 Drew Brees .75 .30
❑ 164 Bobby Engram .30 .10
❑ 165 Torry Holt .75 .30
❑ 166 Ladell Betts .30 .10
❑ 167 Kelly Holcomb .50 .20
❑ 168 Vinny Testaverde .50 .20
❑ 169 Marty Booker .50 .20
❑ 170 Rudi Johnson .50 .20
❑ 171 Andra Davis .30 .10
❑ 172 Kurt Warner .75 .30
❑ 173 Troy Brown .50 .20
❑ 174 Jerry Rice 1.50 .60
❑ 175 Daunte Culpepper .75 .30
❑ 176 Darren Sharper .30 .10
❑ 177 Charles Rogers .50 .20
❑ 178 Ashley Lelie .50 .20
❑ 179 Correll Buckhalter .50 .20
❑ 180 Anquan Boldin .75 .30
❑ 181 Terrell Suggs .50 .20
❑ 182 Reggie Wayne .50 .20
❑ 183 Duce Staley .50 .20
❑ 184 Donnie Edwards .30 .10
❑ 185 Joe Horn .50 .20
❑ 186 LaVar Arrington 1.50 .60
❑ 187 Keenan McCardell .30 .10
❑ 188 Cedrick Wilson .30 .10
❑ 189 Bubba Franks .50 .20
❑ 190 Santana Moss .50 .20
❑ 191 Peerless Price .50 .20
❑ 192 Kyle Boller .75 .30
❑ 193 Julius Peppers .75 .30
❑ 194 Drew Bledsoe .75 .30
❑ 195 Marc Bulger .75 .30
❑ 196 Brian Urlacher 1.00 .40
❑ 197 Andre' Davis .30 .10
❑ 198 Terry Glenn .30 .10
❑ 199 Champ Bailey .50 .20
❑ 200 Tom Brady 2.00 .75
❑ 201 Chris Chambers .50 .20
❑ 202 Tommy Maddox .50 .20
❑ 203 Derrick Brooks .50 .20
❑ 204 Corey Dillon .50 .20
❑ 205 Matt Hasselbeck .50 .20
❑ 206 Keith Brooking .30 .10
❑ 207 Steve Smith .75 .30
❑ 208 Tony Gonzalez .50 .20
❑ 209 Joey Galloway .50 .20
❑ 210 Derrick Mason .50 .20
❑ 211 Quincy Carter .50 .20
❑ 212 Rod Smith .50 .20
❑ 213 Andre Johnson .75 .30
❑ 214 Rod Woodson .50 .20
❑ 215 Byron Leftwich 1.00 .40
❑ 216 Kevin Dyson .30 .10
❑ 217 Keith Bulluck .30 .10
❑ 218 Eric Moulds .50 .20
❑ 219 Jamie Sharper .30 .10
❑ 220 Takeo Spikes .30 .10
❑ 221 C.Pace/F.Wakefield .30 .10
❑ 222 B.Smith/P.Kerney .30 .10
❑ 223 E.Reed/G.Baxter .50 .20
❑ 224 A.Schobel/J.Posey .30 .10
❑ 225 K.Jenkins/B.Buckner .30 .10
❑ 226 J.Smith/D.Clemons .30 .10
❑ 227 M.Haynes/B.Robinson .30 .10
❑ 228 C.Brown/G.Warren .50 .20
❑ 229 T.Newman/D.Woodson .50 .20
❑ 230 R.Johnson/M.Fatafehi .30 .10
❑ 231 R.Porcher/J.Hall RC .75 .30
❑ 232 K.Gbaja-Biamila/C.Hunt .50 .20
❑ 233 A.Glenn/M.Coleman .30 .10
❑ 234 N.Harper RC/J.Jefferson .75 .30
❑ 235 H.Douglas/T.Brackens .30 .10
❑ 236 V.Holliday/E.Hicks .30 .10
❑ 237 S.Knight/A.Freeman .30 .10
❑ 238 S.Martin/N.Rogers .30 .10
❑ 239 R.Colvin/W.McGinest .30 .10
❑ 240 O.Stoutmire/S.Williams .30 .10
❑ 241 E.Barton/V.Hobson .30 .10
❑ 242 W.Sapp/T.Washington .50 .20
❑ 243 C.Simon/D.Walker .50 .20
❑ 244 T.Polamalu/M.Logan 2.00 .75
❑ 245 J.Williams/A.Dingle RC .30 .10
❑ 246 B.Young/B.Whiting .30 .10
❑ 247 K.Hamlin/D.Robinson RC .30 .10
❑ 248 D.Lewis/R.Pickett .30 .10
❑ 249 A.McFarland/G.Spires .30 .10
❑ 250 A.Haynesworth/R.Long .30 .10
❑ 251 I.Ohalete/M.Bowen .30 .10
❑ 252 B.Berry/K.King .30 .10
❑ 253 E.Johnson/E.Jasper .30 .10
❑ 254 C.Tillman/J.Azumah .50 .20
❑ 255 M.Wiley/L.Glover .30 .10
❑ 256 S.Rogers/D.Wilkinson .30 .10
❑ 257 G.Walker/R.Smith .30 .10
❑ 258 M.Doss/I.Bashir .30 .10
❑ 259 M.Stroud/J.Henderson .50 .20
❑ 260 R.Sims/J.Browning .30 .10
❑ 261 J.Seau/M.Greenwood .75 .30
❑ 262 K.Williams/K.Mixon .30 .10
❑ 263 T.Warren/K.Traylor .30 .10
❑ 264 W.Allen/W.Peterson .30 .10
❑ 265 D.Barrett/R.Tongue .30 .10
❑ 266 P.Buchanon/D.Gibson .30 .10
❑ 267 L.Sheppard/S.Brown .30 .10
❑ 268 B.Taylor/M.Trufant .50 .20
❑ 269 M.Washington/M.Barrow .30 .10
❑ 270 C.Draft/M.Stewart .30 .10
❑ 271 M.Brown/M.Green .50 .20
❑ 272 E.Brown/M.McCree .30 .10
❑ 273 P.Surtain/S.Madison .50 .20
❑ 274 B.Dawkins/M.Lewis .50 .20
❑ 275 S.Springs/F.Smoot .50 .20
❑ 276 McKinnon/Fisher/Thompson .30 .10
❑ 277 Webster/McBride RC/Scott .30 .10
❑ 278 Boulware/Hartwell/Thomas 1.00 .40
❑ 279 Vincent/Milloy/Clements .50 .20
❑ 280 Witherspoon/Morgan/Fields .50 .20
❑ 281 Simmons/Hardy/Webster .30 .10
❑ 282 Odom RC/Brown/Briggs 2.50 1.00
❑ 283 Holdman/Thompson/Lang .30 .10
❑ 284 Nguyen/Coakley/Singleton .30 .10
❑ 285 Wilson/Spragan RC/Holland .30 .10
❑ 286 Holmes/J.Davis RC/Bailey .75 .30
❑ 287 Barnett/Diggs/Navies .30 .10
❑ 288 Foreman/Peek/Wong .30 .10
❑ 289 Brock RC/Reagor/Tripplett .75 .30
❑ 290 Ayodele/Favors/Peterson .50 .20
❑ 291 Barber/Maslowsk/Fujita .50 .20
❑ 292 Claiborne/Henderson/Nattiel .50 .20
❑ 293 Bruschi/Phifer/Vrabel .75 .30
❑ 294 Grant/Howard/Sullivan .30 .10
❑ 295 Robbins/Joseph/Umenyiora .75 .30
❑ 296 Abra/Rober/Fergus.RC 1.25 .50
❑ 297 Harris/Rudd/Brayton .50 .20
❑ 298 Simoneau/Wayne/Jones .30 .10
❑ 299 Porter/Bell/Haggans RC 2.00 .75
❑ 300 Jammer/Davis/Florence .50 .20
❑ 301 Peterson/Ulbrich/Smith .30 .10
❑ 302 Simmons/Huff/Brown .30 .10
❑ 303 Tinoisamoa/Polley/Thomas .30 .10
❑ 304 Quarles/Wyms/Nece .30 .10
❑ 305 Carter/Hall/Simon .50 .20
❑ 306 Griffin/Daniels/Wynn .30 .10
❑ 307 Jackson/Wilson/Macklin .30 .10
❑ 308 Gregg/Douglas/Weaver .30 .10
❑ 309 Williams/Denney/Adams .30 .10
❑ 310 Hawkins/Minter/Manning .30 .10
❑ 311 James/Herring/Beckett .30 .10
❑ 312 Griffith/Little/Henry .30 .10
❑ 313 Lynch/Ferg.RC/Hern.RC .75 .30
❑ 314 Bly/Marion/Bryant .30 .10
❑ 315 Harris/Roman/McKenzie .30 .10
❑ 316 Thorn/Morris/Brackett RC 1.25 .50
❑ 317 Mathis/Darius/Bolden RC .50 .20
❑ 318 Warfield/Wesley/Woods .30 .10
❑ 319 Winfield/Russell RC/Chavous .50 .20
❑ 320 Harrison/Wilson/Poole .50 .20
❑ 321 Rodgers/Ruff/Hodge .30 .10
❑ 322 Green/Greisen/Emmons .30 .10
❑ 323 Von Oelhoffen/Smith/Hampton .75 .30
❑ 324 Godfrey/Foley/Leber .30 .10
❑ 325 Plummer/Parrish/Rumph .30 .10
❑ 326 Okeafor/Wistrom/Moore .30 .10
❑ 327 Archuleta/Williams/Butler .30 .10
❑ 328 Barber/Smith/Phillips .50 .20
❑ 329 Dyson/Schulters/Williams .30 .10
❑ 330 Thomas/Bellamy/Jones .30 .10
❑ 331 Philip Rivers RC 5.00 2.00
❑ 332 Dwan Edwards RC .75 .30
❑ 333 Ben Watson RC 1.50 .60
❑ 334 Karlos Dansby RC 1.50 .60
❑ 335 Cedric Cobbs RC 1.50 .60
❑ 336 Chris Perry RC 2.50 1.00
❑ 337 Darius Watts RC 1.50 .60
❑ 338 Ricardo Colclough RC 1.50 .60
❑ 339 Derrick Hamilton RC 1.25 .50
❑ 340 Devard Darling RC 1.50 .60
❑ 341 Daryl Smith RC 1.50 .60
❑ 342 Luke McCown RC 1.50 .60
❑ 343 Dunta Robinson RC 1.50 .60
❑ 344 Keith Smith RC 1.25 .50
❑ 345 Ben Hartsock RC 1.50 .60
❑ 346 J.P. Losman RC 3.00 1.25
❑ 347 Chris Cooley RC 1.50 .60
❑ 348 Keary Colbert RC 2.00 .75
❑ 349 Tommie Harris RC 1.50 .60
❑ 350 Eli Manning RC 8.00 4.00
❑ 351 Kevin Jones RC 4.00 1.50
❑ 352 Lee Evans RC 2.00 .75
❑ 353 D.J. Williams RC 1.50 .60
❑ 354 Ben Troupe RC 1.50 .60
❑ 355 Mewelde Moore RC 1.50 .60
❑ 356 Michael Clayton RC 3.00 1.25
❑ 357 Michael Jenkins RC 1.50 .60
❑ 358 Adimchinobe Echemandu RC 1.25 .50
❑ 359 Rashaun Woods RC 1.50 .60
❑ 360 Bernard Berrian RC 2.00 .75
❑ 361 Carlos Francis RC 1.25 .50
❑ 362 Roy Williams RC 4.00 1.50
❑ 363 Sean Taylor RC 1.50 .60
❑ 364 Steven Jackson RC 5.00 2.00
❑ 365 Tatum Bell RC 3.00 1.25
❑ 366 Jonathan Vilma RC 1.50 .60
❑ 367 Derrick Strait RC 2.00 .75
❑ 368 Andy Hall RC 1.25 .50
❑ 369 Jason Babin RC 1.50 .60
❑ 370 Will Smith RC 1.50 .60
❑ 371 Kenechi Udeze RC 1.50 .60
❑ 372 Vince Wilfork RC 1.50 .60
❑ 373 Ahmad Carroll RC 1.50 .60
❑ 374 Marquise Hill RC 1.25 .50
❑ 375 Ben Roethlisberger RC 15.00 7.50
❑ 376 Chris Gamble RC 1.50 .60
❑ 377 Junior Siavii RC 1.50 .60
❑ 378 Teddy Lehman RC 1.50 .60
❑ 379 Antwan Odom RC 1.50 .60
❑ 380 DeAngelo Hall RC 2.00 .75
❑ 381 Nathan Vasher RC 2.00 .75
❑ 382 B.J. Symons RC 1.50 .60
❑ 383 Reggie Williams RC 2.00 .75
❑ 384 Michael Boulware RC 1.50 .60
❑ 385 Matt Schaub RC 5.00 2.00
❑ 386 Sean Jones RC 1.25 .50
❑ 387 Courtney Watson RC 1.50 .60
❑ 388 Nathaniel Adibi RC 1.50 .60
❑ 389 Devery Henderson RC 1.25 .50
❑ 390 Greg Jones RC 1.50 .60
❑ 391 Joey Thomas RC 1.50 .60
❑ 392 Drew Carter RC 1.50 .60
❑ 393 Julius Jones RC 5.00 2.00
❑ 394 Keyaron Fox RC 1.25 .50
❑ 395 Darrion Scott RC 1.50 .60
❑ 396 Rich Gardner RC 1.25 .50
❑ 397 Jeff Smoker RC 1.50 .60
❑ 398 Will Poole RC 1.50 .60
❑ 399 Samie Parker RC 1.50 .60
❑ 400 Larry Fitzgerald RC 5.00 2.00
❑ 401 Jerricho Cotchery RC 1.50 .60
❑ 402 Ernest Wilford RC 1.50 .60
❑ 403 Johnnie Morant RC 1.50 .60
❑ 404 Craig Krenzel RC 1.50 .60
❑ 405 Michael Turner RC 2.00 .75
❑ 406 D.J. Hackett RC 1.25 .50
❑ 407 P.K. Sam RC 1.25 .50
❑ 408 Triandos Luke RC 1.50 .60
❑ 409 Josh Harris RC 1.50 .60
❑ 410 Drew Henson RC 1.50 .60
❑ 411 John Navarre RC 1.50 .60
❑ 412 Cody Pickett RC 1.50 .60
❑ 413 Clarence Moore RC 1.50 .60
❑ 414 Michael Gaines RC 1.25 .50
❑ 415 Derek Abney RC 1.50 .60
❑ 416 Dontarrious Thomas RC 1.50 .60
❑ 417 Reggie Torbor RC 1.25 .50
❑ 418 Ryan Krause RC 1.25 .50
❑ 419 Travis LaBoy RC 1.50 .60
❑ 420 Kellen Winslow RC 3.00 1.25

❑ 421 Keiwan Ratliff RC 1.25 .50
❑ 422 Gilbert Gardner RC 1.25 .50
❑ 423 Jamaar Taylor RC 1.50 .60
❑ 424 Matt Ware RC 1.50 .60
❑ 425 Stuart Schweigert RC 1.50 .60
❑ 426 Marcus Tubbs RC 1.50 .60
❑ 427 Brandon Chillar RC 1.25 .50
❑ 428 Shawntae Spencer RC 1.50 .60
❑ 429 Marquis Cooper RC 1.25 .50
❑ 430 Derrick Ward RC .75 .30
❑ 431 Tim Euhus RC 1.50 .60
❑ 432 Patrick Crayton RC 1.50 .60
❑ 433 Caleb Miller RC 1.25 .50
❑ 434 Donnell Washington RC 1.50 .60
❑ 435 Thomas Tapeh RC 1.25 .50
❑ 436 Randy Starks RC 1.25 .50
❑ 437 Sloan Thomas RC 1.25 .50
❑ 438 Maurice Mann RC 1.25 .50
❑ 439 Jim Sorgi RC 1.50 .60
❑ 440 Nate Lawrie RC 1.25 .50

2005 Topps Total

❑ COMPLETE SET (550) 80.00 30.00
❑ COMP.PACKERS TIN (20) 20.00 10.00
❑ COMP.STEELERS TIN (20) 20.00 10.00
❑ 1 Michael Vick 1.00 .40
❑ 2 O.Kreutz/Q.Mitchell RC .40 .15
❑ 3 Re.Williams/Garrard/T.Edwards .50 .20
❑ 4 Terence Newman .40 .15
❑ 5 D.Jolley/C.Baker .40 .15
❑ 6 D.Clark/S.Will.RC/B.Hamilton .40 .15
❑ 7 Terrell Owens .75 .30
❑ 8 I.Ohalete/A.Wilson .40 .15
❑ 9 G.Walker/Payne/Rob.Smith .40 .15
❑ 10 Quentin Jammer .40 .15
❑ 11 Ke.Smith/D.Bly .40 .15
❑ 12 C.Taylor/Ogden/B.Sams .50 .20
❑ 13 Torry Holt .75 .30
❑ 14 W.Henderson/N.Davenport .40 .15
❑ 15 J.Siavii/Hicks/J.Allen .50 .20
❑ 16 Keith Bulluck .40 .15
❑ 17 K.Irvin/C.Chavous .40 .15
❑ 18 F.Jackson/A.Bryant/A.Davis .75 .30
❑ 19 Michael Pittman .40 .15
❑ 20 Vanderjagt/H.Smith RC .40 .15
❑ 21 J.Winborn/Ulbrich/D.Smith .40 .15
❑ 22 Reggie Wayne .50 .20
❑ 23 S.Lechler/Janikowski .40 .15
❑ 24 K.Mathis RC/J.Webster/B.Scott .40 .15
❑ 25 Daunte Culpepper .75 .30
❑ 26 W.Peterson/W.Allen .40 .15
❑ 27 T.Walter/F.Adams/L.Allen .40 .15
❑ 28 Tauscher/M.Flanagan/Clifton RC .40 .15
❑ 29 Jerome Bettis .75 .30
❑ 30 M.Brown/R.McQuarters .40 .15
❑ 31 Andre Johnson .50 .20
❑ 32 Toefield/G.Jones/Fuamatu-Ma'Afala .40 .15
❑ 33 G.Lewis/B.McMullen .75 .30
❑ 34 Kyle Boller .50 .20
❑ 35 Kacyvenski/T.White RC/Bates .40 .15
❑ 36 Chris Brown .50 .20
❑ 37 J.Phillips/B.Kelly .40 .15
❑ 38 Saturday RC/Diem RC/Ta.Glenn 1.25 .50
❑ 39 Clinton Portis .75 .30
❑ 40 M.Scifres/N.Kaeding .40 .15
❑ 41 Ke.Williams/Udeze/Johnstone .40 .15
❑ 42 Tony Parrish .40 .15
❑ 43 D.Armstrong/J.Gaffney .40 .15
❑ 44 F.Bryant/C.Cash/Te.Holt .40 .15
❑ 45 Kerry Collins .50 .20
❑ 46 M.Strong/M.Morris .50 .20
❑ 47 Robertson/J.Abraham/S.Ellis .40 .15
❑ 48 Darrell Jackson .50 .20
❑ 49 P.Price/A.Rossum .40 .15
❑ 50 A.Henry/N.Jones RC/Frazier RC .40 .15
❑ 51 Steven Jackson 1.00 .40
❑ 52 R.Sims/J.Browning .40 .15
❑ 53 Robbins/Umenyiora/W.Joseph .75 .30
❑ 54 Billy Volek .50 .20
❑ 55 A.Ayodele/Da.Smith .40 .15
❑ 56 I.Scott RC/Odom/T.Johnson .40 .15
❑ 57 Onterrio Smith .50 .20
❑ 58 M.Stover/D.Zastudil RC .40 .15
❑ 59 Hunt/Gbaja-Biamila/Kampman RC .50 .20
❑ 60 Dante Hall .50 .20
❑ 61 J.Peterson/B.Young .40 .15
❑ 62 Hardwick/Olivea RC/Oben .40 .15
❑ 63 Chad Pennington .75 .30
❑ 64 D.Clark/A.Moorehead .40 .15
❑ 65 B.Taylor/K.Richard RC .40 .15
❑ 66 K.Walker/J.Wade RC .40 .15
❑ 67 Jeremy Shockey .75 .30
❑ 68 Daylon McCutcheon .40 .15
❑ 69 Coakley/Claiborne/Tinoisamoa .40 .15
❑ 70 Roy Williams WR .75 .30
❑ 71 L.Schulters/Ta.Williams .40 .15
❑ 72 S.Brown/Hood RC/Wynn .40 .15
❑ 73 Sean Taylor .50 .20
❑ 74 L.Little/B.Chillar .40 .15
❑ 75 Boiman/R.Starks/Clauss RC .40 .15
❑ 76 Lee Suggs .50 .20
❑ 77 P.Crayton/T.Glenn .40 .15
❑ 78 Dansby/Darling/G.Hayes .40 .15
❑ 79 Nick Barnett .40 .15
❑ 80 R.Coleman/A.Lake RC .40 .15
❑ 81 Berrian/J.Gage/D.Clark .40 .15
❑ 82 Dominic Rhodes .40 .15
❑ 83 C.Moore/R.Hymes .40 .15
❑ 84 Fraley RC/Runyan/T.Thomas .40 .15
❑ 85 Philip Rivers .75 .30
❑ 86 A.Harris/A.Carroll .40 .15
❑ 87 B.Sanders/Doss/J.Jefferson 1.25 .50
❑ 88 Cesaire RC/Ja.Will/Dingle .40 .15
❑ 89 Eric Moulds .50 .20
❑ 90 P.Zellner RC/R.Davis .40 .15
❑ 91 K.Wong/Babin/A.Peek .40 .15
❑ 92 Tony Richardson .40 .15
❑ 93 G.Wesley/J.Woods .40 .15
❑ 94 Fabini/Goodwin RC/K.Mawae .40 .15
❑ 95 Tatum Bell .50 .20
❑ 96 K.Lewis RC/C.Emmons .40 .15
❑ 97 J.Galloway/W.Heller .50 .20
❑ 98 Tom Brady 2.00 .75
❑ 99 R.Babers/B.Walker .40 .15
❑ 100 Mickens/McGraw/Buckley .40 .15
❑ 101 Zach Thomas .75 .30
❑ 102 Co.Brown RC/A.Weaver .40 .15
❑ 103 A.Will/J.Butler/K.Garrett .40 .15
❑ 104 Troy Polamalu 1.25 .50
❑ 105 W.Sapp/T.Washington .50 .20
❑ 106 T.Johnson/Crockett/Morant .40 .15
❑ 107 Chris McAlister .40 .15
❑ 108 C.Stanley RC/K.Brown .40 .15
❑ 109 Drew Henson .50 .20
❑ 110 James Hall .40 .15
❑ 111 S.Player/N.Rackers .40 .15
❑ 112 D.Watts/A.Lelie .50 .20
❑ 113 J.David/N.Harper .40 .15
❑ 114 R.Curry/D.Gabriel .50 .20
❑ 115 R.Colclough/W.Williams .50 .20
❑ 116 C.Tillman/J.Azumah .40 .15
❑ 117 M.Kemoeatu RC/Ad.Thomas 1.00 .40
❑ 118 M.Roman/J.Thomas .40 .15
❑ 119 D.Henderson/M.Lewis .40 .15
❑ 120 M.Furrey/Manumaleuna 1.00 .40
❑ 121 R.Mahe/C.Buckhalter .50 .20
❑ 122 E.Kinney/T.Fleming .40 .15
❑ 123 W.Dunn/T.Duckett .50 .20
❑ 124 T.Euhus/M.Campbell .40 .15
❑ 125 P.Hunter/A.Glenn .40 .15
❑ 126 R.Tongue/D.Barrett .40 .15
❑ 127 S.Morris/L.Gordon .40 .15
❑ 128 R.Clark RC/S.Springs .40 .15
❑ 129 J.Miller/A.Vinatieri .75 .30
❑ 130 E.Warfield/W.Bartee .40 .15
❑ 131 Me.Moore/M.Bennett .50 .20
❑ 132 N.Goings/B.Hoover .40 .15
❑ 133 Q.Harris/D.Macklin .40 .15
❑ 134 E.Drummond/R.Swinton .40 .15
❑ 135 J.Fargas/A.Whitted .40 .15
❑ 136 N.Clements/T.McGee RC .75 .30
❑ 137 T.Hollings/J.Wells .40 .15
❑ 138 D.Cooper RC/K.Thomas RC .40 .15
❑ 139 P.Dawson/D.Frost RC .40 .15
❑ 140 J.McCown/J.Navarre .50 .20
❑ 141 G.Ellis/K.Coleman .40 .15
❑ 142 G.Wilson/B.Alexander .40 .15
❑ 143 A.Woolfolk/L.Thompson .40 .15
❑ 144 E.Conwell/B.Williams .40 .15
❑ 145 D.Akers/Di.Johnson RC .40 .15
❑ 146 Hillenmeyer RC/L.Briggs 2.00 .75
❑ 147 R.Mathis RC/G.Brackett 1.50 .60
❑ 148 J.Rice/R.Alexander 1.25 .50
❑ 149 E.Coleman/D.Strait .40 .15
❑ 150 J.Hartwig RC/B.Troupe .40 .15
❑ 151 S.Davis/D.Florence .40 .15
❑ 152 P.Buchanon/M.Coleman .40 .15
❑ 153 S.Heiden/A.Shea .40 .15
❑ 154 T.Spikes/L.Fletcher .40 .15
❑ 155 T.Laboy/A.Odom .40 .15
❑ 156 A.Toomer/M.Cloud .50 .20
❑ 157 L.Tynes/C.Horn .50 .20
❑ 158 N.Diggs/P.Lenon RC .40 .15
❑ 159 R.Long/A.Haynesworth .40 .15
❑ 160 B.Askew/J.Sowell .40 .15
❑ 161 John CarneyMitch Berger .40 .15
❑ 162 K.Campbell/J.Wiggins .40 .15
❑ 163 Jerramy Stevens .40 .15
❑ 164 Willis McGahee .75 .30
❑ 165 Ed Reed .50 .20
❑ 166 Muhsin Muhammad .50 .20
❑ 167 Donovin Darius .40 .15
❑ 168 E.J. Henderson .40 .15
❑ 169 Tony Banks .40 .15
❑ 170 Fred Taylor .50 .20
❑ 171 Jeremiah Trotter .40 .15
❑ 172 Adam Archuleta .40 .15
❑ 173 Marcus Trufant .40 .15
❑ 174 Steve McNair .75 .30
❑ 175 Ben Roethlisberger 2.00 .75
❑ 176 Derrick Blaylock .40 .15
❑ 177 Michael Strahan .50 .20
❑ 178 Robert Gallery .50 .20
❑ 179 Drew Brees .75 .30
❑ 180 David Kircus .60 .25
❑ 181 Robert Ferguson .40 .15
❑ 182 Jim Sorgi .40 .15
❑ 183 Alge Crumpler .50 .20
❑ 184 DeShaun Foster .50 .20
❑ 185 Reuben Droughns .50 .20
❑ 186 Charles Grant .40 .15
❑ 187 Jason Taylor .40 .15
❑ 188 James Thrash .50 .20
❑ 189 LaDainian Tomlinson 1.00 .40
❑ 190 Tim Rattay .40 .15
❑ 191 Jeff Garcia .50 .20
❑ 192 Jerricho Cotchery .40 .15
❑ 193 Chris Simms .50 .20
❑ 194 Jevon Kearse .50 .20
❑ 195 Kyle Brady .40 .15
❑ 196 Trent Green .50 .20
❑ 197 Antoine Winfield .40 .15
❑ 198 Deion Branch .50 .20
❑ 199 Rudi Johnson .50 .20
❑ 200 Lee Evans .50 .20
❑ 201 Stephen Davis .50 .20
❑ 202 Darrell Dockett .40 .15
❑ 203 Kurt Warner .50 .20
❑ 204 Quincy Morgan .40 .15
❑ 205 Daimon Shelton .40 .15
❑ 206 Champ Bailey .50 .20
❑ 207 Jamal Lewis .75 .30
❑ 208 Brett Favre 2.00 .75
❑ 209 Charles Woodson .50 .20
❑ 210 Koren Robinson .50 .20
❑ 211 Chris Chambers .50 .20
❑ 212 Dave Ragone .40 .15
❑ 213 Travis Minor .40 .15
❑ 214 Simeon Rice .50 .20
❑ 215 Tommy Maddox .40 .15
❑ 216 Aaron Stecker .40 .15
❑ 217 Dwight Freeney .50 .20
❑ 218 Thomas Jones .50 .20

❑ 219 Patrick Ramsey .50 .20
❑ 220 Travis Taylor .40 .15
❑ 221 Chris Weinke .40 .15
❑ 222 Marc Bulger .75 .30
❑ 223 James Farrior .40 .15
❑ 224 Billy Miller .40 .15
❑ 225 Mike Peterson .40 .15
❑ 226 Eddie Kennison .40 .15
❑ 227 Aaron Brooks .50 .20
❑ 228 Plaxico Burress .50 .20
❑ 229 Jerry Porter .50 .20
❑ 230 Joey Harrington .75 .30
❑ 231 Bubba Franks .50 .20
❑ 232 Michael Jenkins .50 .20
❑ 233 Larry Fitzgerald .75 .30
❑ 234 Troy Vincent .40 .15
❑ 235 Chad Johnson .75 .30
❑ 236 Roy Williams S .50 .20
❑ 237 Corey Dillon .50 .20
❑ 238 Donovan McNabb 1.00 .40
❑ 239 Marcus Robinson .50 .20
❑ 240 Derrick Brooks .50 .20
❑ 241 David Bowens RC .50 .20
❑ 242 Renaldo Wynn .40 .15
❑ 243 Kevan Barlow .50 .20
❑ 244 Antonio Gates .75 .30
❑ 245 Duce Staley .50 .20
❑ 246 Ernest Wilford .40 .15
❑ 247 Kevin Jones .75 .30
❑ 248 Julius Peppers .50 .20
❑ 249 Terrell Suggs .50 .20
❑ 250 Bertrand Berry .40 .15
❑ 251 Brian Simmons .40 .15
❑ 252 Jake Plummer .50 .20
❑ 253 Brian Urlacher .75 .30
❑ 254 Justin McCareins .40 .15
❑ 255 L.J. Smith .40 .15
❑ 256 Matt Hasselbeck .50 .20
❑ 257 Rashaun Woods .50 .20
❑ 258 Rodney Harrison .50 .20
❑ 259 Brandon Stokley .50 .20
❑ 260 Tony Gonzalez .50 .20
❑ 261 J.P. Losman .75 .30
❑ 262 DeAngelo Hall .50 .20
❑ 263 Jake Delhomme .75 .30
❑ 264 Shaun Rogers .40 .15
❑ 265 Donald Driver .50 .20
❑ 266 Will Smith .40 .15
❑ 267 Brian Westbrook .50 .20
❑ 268 A.J. Feeley .50 .20
❑ 269 Marshall Faulk .75 .30
❑ 270 Marques Tuiasosopo .40 .15
❑ 271 Curtis Martin .75 .30
❑ 272 Jason Witten .50 .20
❑ 273 Kellen Winslow .75 .30
❑ 274 Corey Bradford .40 .15
❑ 275 Samari Rolle .40 .15
❑ 276 Anquan Boldin .50 .20
❑ 277 Adrian Peterson .40 .15
❑ 278 Javon Walker .50 .20
❑ 279 Fred Smoot .40 .15
❑ 280 Mike Alstott .50 .20
❑ 281 Randy McMichael .40 .15
❑ 282 Jay Fiedler .40 .15
❑ 283 Jamie Sharper .40 .15
❑ 284 Eli Manning 1.50 .60
❑ 285 Todd Pinkston .40 .15
❑ 286 La'Roi Glover .40 .15
❑ 287 Chris Perry .50 .20
❑ 288 David Carr .75 .30
❑ 289 Bryant Johnson .40 .15
❑ 290 Ray Lewis .75 .30
❑ 291 Tommie Harris .40 .15
❑ 292 Joe Horn .50 .20
❑ 293 Rod Smith .50 .20
❑ 294 Michael Clayton .75 .30
❑ 295 Tyrone Calico .50 .20
❑ 296 Santana Moss .50 .20
❑ 297 Hines Ward .75 .30
❑ 298 Jonathan Vilma .50 .20
❑ 299 Randy Moss .75 .30
❑ 300 Donte Stallworth .50 .20
❑ 301 Isaac Bruce .50 .20
❑ 302 Brian Griese .50 .20
❑ 303 Dennis Northcutt .40 .15
❑ 304 Michael Green .40 .15
❑ 305 Marvin Harrison .75 .30
❑ 306 Jimmy Smith .50 .20
❑ 307 Patrick Kerney .40 .15
❑ 308 Todd Heap .50 .20
❑ 309 Dan Morgan .40 .15
❑ 310 Charles Rogers .50 .20
❑ 311 Dunta Robinson .50 .20
❑ 312 Deuce McAllister .75 .30
❑ 313 Ronde Barber .40 .15
❑ 314 Brandon Lloyd .40 .15
❑ 315 Tiki Barber .75 .30
❑ 316 LaMont Jordan .75 .30
❑ 317 Lito Sheppard .40 .15
❑ 318 Laveranues Coles .50 .20
❑ 319 Drew Bennett .50 .20
❑ 320 Julius Jones 1.00 .40
❑ 321 Ahman Green .75 .30
❑ 322 Domanick Davis .50 .20
❑ 323 Byron Leftwich .75 .30
❑ 324 Nate Burleson .50 .20
❑ 325 David Givens .50 .20
❑ 326 Trent Dilfer .50 .20
❑ 327 T.J. Houshmandzadeh .40 .15
❑ 328 Keith Brooking .40 .15
❑ 329 Derrick Mason .50 .20
❑ 330 Ken Lucas .40 .15
❑ 331 Rex Grossman .50 .20
❑ 332 Edgerrin James .75 .30
❑ 333 Priest Holmes .75 .30
❑ 334 Donnie Edwards .40 .15
❑ 335 Pierson Prioleau RC .75 .30
❑ 336 Shaun Alexander 1.00 .40
❑ 337 D.J. Williams .40 .15
❑ 338 Peyton Manning 1.25 .50
❑ 339 Carson Palmer .75 .30
❑ 340 Keyshawn Johnson .50 .20
❑ 341 Tory James .40 .15
❑ 342 Drew Bledsoe .75 .30
❑ 343 Chris Gamble .50 .20
❑ 344 Mi.Lewis/B.Dawkins .50 .20
❑ 345 Forney/McClure RC/Weiner RC .40 .15
❑ 346 R.Smart/Kasay/J.Kyle .40 .15
❑ 347 J.Ferguson/Reeves/Nguyen .40 .15
❑ 348 Crocker/Lehan RC/M.Jameson .40 .15
❑ 349 Tyree/Ja.Taylor/T.Carter .40 .15
❑ 350 H.Thomas/D.Jones/Simoneau .40 .15
❑ 351 Royal/McCants/T.Jacobs .40 .15
❑ 352 Welker/D.Thompson/Gilmore .40 .15
❑ 353 D.Lewis/Pickett/Ty.Jackson .40 .15
❑ 354 F.Brown/F.Thomas/J.Bellamy .40 .15
❑ 355 Asomugha/M.Anderson/Schweigert .40 .15
❑ 356 M.Stroud/J.Hender/Favors .40 .15
❑ 357 W.Shields/Roaf/B.Waters RC .40 .15
❑ 358 Hamilton/Nalen/Lepsis .40 .15
❑ 359 J.Smith/Geathers/D.Clemons .40 .15
❑ 360 Wire/R.Baker/L.Milloy .40 .15
❑ 361 Ayanbadejo/J.Scobey/Hambrick .40 .15
❑ 362 St.Smith/Proehl/Colbert .50 .20
❑ 363 N.Harris/D.Thomas/Offord .40 .15
❑ 364 L.Neal/M.Turner/Pinnock .50 .20
❑ 365 Faneca/M.Smith RC/Hartings 1.25 .50
❑ 366 E.Moore/Pope/Ayanbadejo RC .75 .30
❑ 367 A.Plummer/Jo.Hanson RC/Spencer .40 .15
❑ 368 L.Betts/Brunell/C.Morton .50 .20
❑ 369 Pace/Timmerman/McCollum .40 .15
❑ 370 B.Thomas/Barton/Hobson .40 .15
❑ 371 S.Barber/K.Fox/K.Mitchell .40 .15
❑ 372 K.Edwards/Wilkinson/Redding .40 .15
❑ 373 Co.Jackson RC/Lang/McKinley .40 .15
❑ 374 Bannan/R.Edwards/S.Adams .40 .15
❑ 375 M.Schaub/D.White/Finneran .50 .20
❑ 376 Short/A.Wallace RC/K.Jenkins .40 .15
❑ 377 Leach/Carswell/Putzier .40 .15
❑ 378 Vrabel/T.Johnson/Bruschi .75 .30
❑ 379 Kiel/Je.Wilson RC/Fletcher .40 .15
❑ 380 Engelber/To.Brown RC/A.Adams .40 .15
❑ 381 Quarles/Gooch/D.White .40 .15
❑ 382 Madison/W.Poole/R.Howard .40 .15
❑ 383 Schneck RC/Gardocki/J.Reed .75 .30
❑ 384 J.Mitchell RC/Gross/Brzezinski RC .40 .15
❑ 385 Greisen/B.Green/A.Pierce .40 .15
❑ 386 C.Simon/D.Walker/McDougle .40 .15
❑ 387 D.Graham/Fauria/B.Watson .50 .20
❑ 388 E.Johnson/R.John/M.Coleman .40 .15
❑ 389 June/D.Thornton/Hutchins .50 .20
❑ 390 Teague/R.Tucker/M.Will.T .40 .15
❑ 391 M.Haynes/A.Brown/Ogunleye .75 .30
❑ 392 Ulmer RC/Br.Smith/De.Williams .40 .15
❑ 393 K.Faulk/Pass/Be.Johnson .50 .20
❑ 394 Tobeck RC/W.Jones/S.Hutchin .40 .15
❑ 395 V.Holliday/Y.Bell RC/K.Carter .40 .15
❑ 396 L.Foote/J.Porter/Al.Jackson .75 .30
❑ 397 Looker/K.Curtis/S.McDonald .50 .20
❑ 398 L.Marshall RC/C.Griffin/D.Evans .75 .30
❑ 399 D.Klecko/Izzo/R.Colvin .40 .15
❑ 400 M.Holland/Bentley/Gandy .40 .15
❑ 401 Petitgout/McKenzie RC/J.Whittle RC .40 .15
❑ 402 Sykes RC/Fatafehi/A.Wilson .40 .15
❑ 403 Meester RC/Ma.Will/Manuwai RC .40 .15
❑ 404 M.Schobel/K.Washing/Warrick .40 .15
❑ 405 M.Minter/R.Manning/C.Branch .40 .15
❑ 406 Jo.Reed/Jo.Smith/Aiken .40 .15
❑ 407 Birk/Liwienski/McKinnie .40 .15
❑ 408 Godfrey/Foley/Leber .40 .15
❑ 409 McFarland/Wyms/G.Spires .40 .15
❑ 410 E.Perry/Do.Lee/Booker .50 .20
❑ 411 Von Oelhoffen/Hoke RC/Aa.Smith .75 .30
❑ 412 B.Mitchell/Wistrom/Ra.Moore .40 .15
❑ 413 J.Green/Wilfork/T.Warren .50 .20
❑ 414 Middlebrooks/Lynch/N.Ferguson .40 .15
❑ 415 Reagor/R.Brock/Jo.Williams .40 .15
❑ 416 J.Dunn/S.Parker/La.Johnson .75 .30
❑ 417 La.Johnson/M.Wilkins RC/C.Miller .40 .15
❑ 418 Buckner/Moorehead/M.Rucker .40 .15
❑ 419 Denney/Kelsay/A.Schobel .40 .15
❑ 420 Singleton/B.James/K.O'Neil RC .40 .15
❑ 421 C.Thompson/Boyer/An.Davis .40 .15
❑ 422 D.Grant/Richardson RC/R.Mathis .40 .15
❑ 423 Schlesinger/Bryson/Pinner .40 .15
❑ 424 S.Johnson RC/R.Davis/Ru.Jones .40 .15
❑ 425 Phifer/Banta-Cain/McGinest .50 .20
❑ 426 McCardell/Osgood/E.Parker .40 .15
❑ 427 C.Woodard/Bernard/A.Cochran .40 .15
❑ 428 A.Battle/A.Walker/E.Johnson .40 .15
❑ 429 Salave'a RC/M.Wash/L.Arrington .75 .30
❑ 430 L.Mays/C.Wilson/Randle El .75 .30
❑ 431 D.Starks/E.Wilson/R.Gay .50 .20
❑ 432 Q.Griffin/M.Anderson/C.Sapp .50 .20
❑ 433 J.Thornton/L.Moore RC/Powell .40 .15
❑ 434 M.Gaines/Hankton/Seidman .40 .15
❑ 435 M.Haggan RC/Posey/A.Crowell .40 .15
❑ 436 O'Neal/M.Williams/K.Ratliff .40 .15
❑ 437 M.Light/Koppen RC/S.Neal RC .40 .15
❑ 438 C.Watson/D.Rodgers/J.Allen .50 .20
❑ 439 M.Boulware/Hamlin/Bierria RC .40 .15
❑ 440 T.Rogers RC/Unck RC/Roye .40 .15
❑ 441 Frank Gore RC 3.00 1.25
❑ 442 Mike Patterson RC 1.50 .60
❑ 443 DeMarcus Ware RC 2.50 1.00
❑ 444 Chris Henry RC 1.50 .60
❑ 445 Thomas Davis RC 1.50 .60
❑ 446 Justin Miller RC 1.25 .50
❑ 447 Shaun Cody RC 1.50 .60
❑ 448 Alex Barron RC .75 .30
❑ 449 Brock Berlin RC 1.25 .50
❑ 450 Travis Johnson RC 1.25 .50
❑ 451 Jerome Mathis RC 1.50 .60
❑ 452 Lance Mitchell RC 1.25 .50
❑ 453 Marlin Jackson RC 1.50 .60
❑ 454 Charlie Frye RC 3.00 1.25
❑ 455 Luis Castillo RC 1.50 .60
❑ 456 Fred Gibson RC 1.25 .50
❑ 457 Dustin Fox RC 1.50 .60
❑ 458 Ryan Fitzpatrick RC 2.50 1.00
❑ 459 Dan Orlovsky RC 2.00 .75
❑ 460 Justin Tuck RC 1.50 .60
❑ 461 Corey Webster RC 1.50 .60
❑ 462 Travis Daniels RC 1.25 .50
❑ 463 J.J. Arrington RC 2.00 .75
❑ 464 David Greene RC 1.50 .60
❑ 465 Alvin Pearman RC 1.50 .60
❑ 466 Manuel White RC 1.25 .50
❑ 467 Paris Warren RC 1.25 .50
❑ 468 Patrick Estes RC 1.25 .50
❑ 469 Cedric Houston RC 1.50 .60
❑ 470 David Pollack RC 1.50 .60
❑ 471 Craig Bragg RC 1.25 .50
❑ 472 Vincent Jackson RC 1.50 .60
❑ 473 Adam Jones RC 1.50 .60
❑ 474 Matt Jones RC 4.00 1.50
❑ 475 Stefan LeFors RC 1.50 .60
❑ 476 Heath Miller RC 4.00 1.50
❑ 477 Ryan Moats RC 1.50 .60
❑ 478 Vernand Morency RC 1.50 .60
❑ 479 Terrence Murphy RC 1.50 .60

No.	Card		
480	Kyle Orton RC	2.50	1.00
481	Roscoe Parrish RC	1.50	.60
482	Courtney Roby RC	1.50	.60
483	Aaron Rodgers RC	5.00	2.00
484	Carlos Rogers RC	2.00	.75
485	Antrel Rolle RC	1.50	.60
486	Eric Shelton RC	1.50	.60
487	Alex Smith QB RC	6.00	2.50
488	Andrew Walter RC	2.50	1.00
489	Roddy White RC	1.50	.60
490	Cadillac Williams RC	8.00	3.00
491	Mike Williams	3.00	1.25
492	Troy Williamson RC	3.00	1.25
493	Kirk Morrison RC	1.50	.60
494	Tab Perry RC	1.50	.60
495	Chad Owens RC	1.50	.60
496	Lofa Tatupu RC	2.00	.75
497	Craphonso Thorpe RC	1.25	.50
498	Ryan Riddle RC	.75	.30
499	Marcus Maxwell RC	1.25	.50
500	Barrett Ruud RC	1.50	.60
501	Stanley Wilson RC	1.25	.50
502	Mike Nugent RC	1.50	.60
503	Eric King RC	1.25	.50
504	Darryl Blackstock RC	1.25	.50
505	Attiyah Ellison RC	.75	.30
506	Donte Nicholson RC	1.50	.60
507	Airese Currie RC	1.50	.60
508	Larry Brackins RC	.75	.30
509	Joel Dreessen RC	1.25	.50
510	Cedric Benson RC	3.00	1.25
511	Mark Bradley RC	1.50	.60
512	Reggie Brown RC	1.50	.60
513	Ronnie Brown RC	6.00	2.50
514	Jason Campbell RC	2.50	1.00
515	Maurice Clarett	1.50	.60
516	Mark Clayton RC	2.00	.75
517	Braylon Edwards RC	5.00	2.00
518	Ciatrick Fason RC	1.50	.60
519	Dan Cody RC	1.50	.60
520	Taylor Stubblefield RC	.75	.30
521	J.R. Russell RC	1.25	.50
522	Rian Wallace RC	.40	.15
523	Anthony Davis RC	1.25	.50
524	Derek Anderson RC	1.50	.60
525	Boomer Grigsby RC	2.00	.75
526	Rasheed Marshall RC	1.50	.60
527	Adrian McPherson RC	1.50	.60
528	Noah Herron RC	1.50	.60
529	Bryant McFadden RC	1.50	.60
530	Lionel Gates RC	1.25	.50
531	Matt Roth RC	1.50	.60
532	Derrick Johnson RC	2.50	1.00
533	Stanford Routt RC	1.25	.50
534	Brandon Jacobs RC	2.00	.75
535	Kevin Burnett RC	1.50	.60
536	Ryan Claridge RC	1.25	.50
537	James Kilian RC	1.50	.60
538	Oshiomogho Atogwe RC	1.25	.50
539	Fabian Washington RC	1.50	.60
540	Marion Barber RC	2.50	1.00
541	Anttaj Hawthorne RC	1.25	.50
542	Zach Tuiasosopo RC	.75	.30
543	Ellis Hobbs RC	1.50	.60
544	Alex Smith TE RC	1.50	.60
545	Erasmus James RC	1.50	.60
546	Channing Crowder RC	1.50	.60
547	Kelvin Hayden RC	1.25	.50
548	Darren Sproles RC	1.50	.60
549	Marcus Spears RC	1.50	.60
550	Dante Ridgeway RC	1.25	.50
CL1	Checklist 1	.10	.02
CL2	Checklist 2	.10	.02
CL3	Checklist 3	.10	.02
CL4	Checklist 4	.10	.02
BR1	Ben Roethlisberger Jumbo	6.00	3.00
VL1	Vince Lombardi Jumbo	6.00	3.00

2006 Topps Triple Threads

No.	Card		
1	Shaun Alexander	4.00	1.50
2	Carson Palmer	4.00	1.50
3	Randy Moss	4.00	1.50
4	Dan Marino	10.00	4.00
5	Terrell Owens	4.00	1.50
6	Trent Green	2.50	1.00

No.	Card		
7	Brian Westbrook	2.50	1.00
8	Terry Bradshaw	8.00	3.00
9	Steven Jackson	4.00	1.50
10	Emmitt Smith	10.00	4.00
11	Ben Roethlisberger	6.00	2.50
12	Daunte Culpepper	4.00	1.50
13	Edgerrin James	4.00	1.50
14	Santana Moss	2.50	1.00
15	Larry Johnson	5.00	2.00
16	Johnny Unitas	8.00	3.00
17	Eric Moulds	2.50	1.00
18	LaDainian Tomlinson	5.00	2.00
19	Donovan McNabb	4.00	1.50
20	Fred Taylor	2.50	1.00
21	Hines Ward	4.00	1.50
22	Eli Manning	5.00	2.00
23	Tatum Bell	2.50	1.00
24	Donald Driver	2.50	1.00
25	Drew Bledsoe	4.00	1.50
26	Clinton Portis	4.00	1.50
27	Tony Gonzalez	2.50	1.00
28	Plaxico Burress	2.50	1.00
29	Shawne Merriman	2.50	1.00
30	Cadillac Williams	4.00	1.50
31	Larry Fitzgerald	4.00	1.50
32	Jake Plummer	2.50	1.00
33	Willis McGahee	4.00	1.50
34	Joe Namath	6.00	2.50
35	Ahman Green	2.50	1.00
36	Marvin Harrison	4.00	1.50
37	Ronnie Brown	4.00	1.50
38	Joe Montana	10.00	4.00
39	Deuce McAllister	2.50	1.00
40	Philip Rivers	4.00	1.50
41	Marion Barber	2.50	1.00
42	Chris Chambers	2.50	1.00
43	Jason Witten	2.50	1.00
44	Brett Favre	8.00	3.00
45	Anquan Boldin	2.50	1.00
46	Tiki Barber	4.00	1.50
47	Byron Leftwich	2.50	1.00
48	Steve Smith	4.00	1.50
49	Willie Parker	5.00	2.00
50	Darrell Jackson	2.50	1.00
51	David Carr	2.50	1.00
52	Chris Brown	2.50	1.00
53	Aaron Brooks	2.50	1.00
54	Donte Stallworth	2.50	1.00
55	Michael Vick	5.00	2.00
56	Curtis Martin	4.00	1.50
57	T.J. Houshmandzadeh	2.50	1.00
58	Steve McNair	2.50	1.00
59	Reggie Wayne	2.50	1.00
60	DeShaun Foster	2.50	1.00
61	Chad Johnson	2.50	1.00
62	Domanick Davis	2.50	1.00
63	Braylon Edwards	4.00	1.50
64	Drew Brees	4.00	1.50
65	Kevin Jones	4.00	1.50
66	Alge Crumpler	2.50	1.00
67	Lee Evans	2.50	1.00
68	Matt Hasselbeck	2.50	1.00
69	Jamal Lewis	2.50	1.00
70	Aaron Rodgers	4.00	1.50
71	Joey Galloway	2.50	1.00
72	LaMont Jordan	2.50	1.00
73	Mark Brunell	2.50	1.00
74	Torry Holt	2.50	1.00
75	Chester Taylor	2.50	1.00
76	Jake Delhomme	2.50	1.00
77	Doak Walker	5.00	2.00
78	Corey Dillon	2.50	1.00
79	Antonio Gates	4.00	1.50
80	Marc Bulger	2.50	1.00
81	Walter Payton	10.00	4.00
82	Mark Clayton	2.50	1.00
83	Brian Urlacher	4.00	1.50
84	Julius Jones	4.00	1.50
85	Tom Brady	6.00	2.50
86	Joe Horn	2.50	1.00
87	John Elway	8.00	3.00
88	Reggie Brown	2.50	1.00
89	Warrick Dunn	2.50	1.00
90	Charlie Frye	2.50	1.00
91	Isaac Bruce	2.50	1.00
92	Jim Thorpe	6.00	2.50
93	Drew Bennett	2.00	.75
94	Brad Johnson	2.50	1.00
95	Chad Pennington	2.50	1.00
96	Andre Johnson	2.50	1.00
97	Todd Heap	2.50	1.00
98	Rudi Johnson	2.50	1.00
99	Jeremy Shockey	4.00	1.50
100	Peyton Manning	6.00	2.50
102	A.J. Hawk JSY AU RC	80.00	30.00
103	Reggie Bush JSY AU RC	350.00	200.00
104	Matt Leinart JSY AU RC	200.00	100.00
105	Mario Williams JSY AU RC	50.00	20.00
106	S.Holmes JSY AU RC	80.00	30.00
107	DeA.Williams JSY AU RC	80.00	40.00
108	Jay Cutler JSY AU RC	200.00	100.00
109	J.Norwood JSY AU RC	60.00	30.00
110	Chad Jackson JSY AU RC	50.00	20.00
111	T.Jackson JSY AU RC	60.00	30.00
112	Brian Calhoun JSY AU RC	40.00	15.00
113	L.Maroney JSY AU RC	100.00	50.00
114	Maurice Stovall JSY AU RC	40.00	15.00
115	Travis Wilson JSY AU RC	40.00	15.00
116	Omar Jacobs JSY AU RC	30.00	12.00
117	Michael Huff JSY AU RC	50.00	20.00
118	Br.Williams JSY AU RC	30.00	12.00
119	Kellen Clemens JSY AU RC	50.00	20.00
120	Jason Avant JSY AU RC	40.00	15.00
121	M.Robinson JSY AU RC	50.00	20.00
122	M.Lewis JSY AU RC	30.00	12.00
123	B.Marshall JSY AU RC	50.00	20.00
124	Vernon Davis JSY AU RC	60.00	25.00
125	Dem.Williams JSY AU RC	40.00	15.00
126	C.Whitehurst JSY AU RC	40.00	15.00
127	Sinorice Moss JSY AU RC	50.00	20.00
128	Maurice Drew JSY AU RC	100.00	50.00
129	Derek Hagan JSY AU RC	30.00	12.00
130	L.Washington JSY AU RC	60.00	25.00
131	Joseph Addai JSY AU RC	120.00	60.00
132	Joe Klopfenstein JSY AU RC	25.00	10.00
133	LenDale White JSY AU RC	80.00	40.00
134	Anthony Fasano JSY AU RC	30.00	12.00
135	Mike Bell JSY AU RC	60.00	25.00
136	Will Blackmon JSY AU RC	30.00	12.00
137	B.Gradkowski JSY AU RC	50.00	20.00
138	Marques Hagans JSY AU RC	25.00	10.00
139	Jerome Harrison JSY AU RC	40.00	15.00
140	Devin Hester JSY AU RC	80.00	40.00
141	Greg Jennings JSY AU RC	50.00	20.00
142	M.Kiwanuka JSY AU RC	40.00	15.00
143	Ingle Martin JSY AU RC	40.00	15.00
144	Willie Reid JSY AU RC	40.00	15.00
145	Cory Rodgers JSY AU RC	30.00	12.00
146	Brad Smith JSY AU RC	40.00	15.00
147	Hank Baskett JSY AU RC	40.00	15.00
148	Kamerion Wimbley JSY AU RC	40.00	15.00
149	DeMeco Ryans JSY AU RC	50.00	20.00
150	David Anderson JSY AU RC	25.00	10.00

2005 Topps Turkey Red

No.	Card		
	COMPLETE SET (299)	250.00	125.00
	COMP.SET w/o SP's (249)	60.00	25.00
	COMMON CARD (1-245)	.50	.20
	SEMISTARS	.60	.25
	UNLISTED STARS	1.00	.40
	COMMON ROOKIE (181-230)	2.00	.75
	COMMON SP (246-285)	4.00	1.50
	SP UNL.STARS	5.00	2.00
	SP STATED ODDS 1:4		
	UNPRICED WOOD/1 ODDS 1:2072H, 1:2089R		
1A	Eli Manning	2.00	.75
1B	Eli Manning Ad Back	10.00	4.00

2	Clinton Portis	1.00	.40
3	Charles Woodson	.60	.25
4A	Ray Lewis	1.00	.40
4B	Ray Lewis Ad Back	5.00	2.00
5	Michael Clayton	1.00	.40
6	Eric Moulds	.60	.25
7	Derrick Blaylock	.50	.20
8	Carson Palmer	1.00	.40
9	Zach Thomas	1.00	.40
10	Dallas Clark	.50	.20
11	DeAngelo Hall	.60	.25
12	Terrell Owens	1.00	.40
13	Brian Griese	.60	.25
14	Dunta Robinson	.60	.25
15	Kevan Barlow	.60	.25
16	Jake Plummer	.60	.25
17	James Farrior	.50	.20
18A	Peyton Manning	1.50	.60
18B	Peyton Manning Ad Back	8.00	3.00
19	Michael Bennett	.60	.25
20	Brian Urlacher	1.00	.40
21	Dante Hall	.60	.25
22	Deion Branch	.60	.25
23	Billy Volek	.60	.25
24	Donald Driver	.60	.25
25	LaDainian Tomlinson CL	1.00	.40
26	Donte Stallworth CL	.50	.20
27	Joey Galloway	.60	.25
28	Joey Harrington	1.00	.40
29	T.J. Houshmandzadeh	.60	.25
30	LaDainian Tomlinson	1.25	.50
31	Darius Watts	.60	.25
32	Chris Gamble	.60	.25
33	Javon Walker	.60	.25
34	Kevin Curtis	.60	.25
35	Steven Jackson	1.25	.50
36	J.P. Losman	1.00	.40
37A	Champ Bailey	.60	.25
37B	Champ Bailey Ad Back	3.00	1.25
38	Tiki Barber	1.00	.40
39	LaVar Arrington	1.00	.40
40	Byron Leftwich	1.00	.40
41	Edgerrin James	1.00	.40
42	DeShaun Foster	.60	.25
43	Darrell Jackson	.60	.25
44	Julius Peppers	.60	.25
45	David Carr	1.00	.40
46	Drew Bennett	.50	.20
47	Antonio Gates	1.00	.40
48A	Deuce McAllister	1.00	.40
48B	Deuce McAllister Ad Back	5.00	2.00
49	Patrick Ramsey	.60	.25
50	Antonio Bryant	.60	.25
51	Quentin Jammer	.50	.20
52	Chris Brown	.60	.25
53	Eddie Kennison	.50	.20
54	Steve McNair	.60	.25
55	Corey Bradford	.50	.20
56	Chris Perry	.60	.25
57	Curtis Martin	1.00	.40
58	Mewelde Moore	.60	.25
59	Travis Taylor	.50	.20
60	Chad Pennington	1.00	.40
61	Chad Johnson	.60	.25
62	Kyle Boller	.60	.25
63	Tyrone Calico	.60	.25
64	Michael Pittman	.50	.20
65	Kerry Collins	.60	.25
66	Keary Colbert	.60	.25
67	LaMont Jordan CL	.50	.20
68	Robert Gallery	.60	.25
69	Derrick Mason	.60	.25
70	Brian Dawkins	.50	.20
71	Chris Simms	.60	.25
72	Marc Bulger	1.00	.40
73	Stephen Davis	.60	.25
74	Kurt Warner	.60	.25
75	Todd Heap	.60	.25
76	Domanick Davis CL	.50	.20
77	Shaun Alexander	1.00	.40
78	Jerry Porter	.60	.25
79	Chester Taylor	.60	.25
80A	Michael Vick	1.50	.60
80B	Michael Vick Ad Back	8.00	3.00
81	Justin McCareins	.50	.20
82	Fred Taylor	.60	.25
83	Laveranues Coles	.60	.25
84	Steve Smith	1.00	.40
85	Sean Taylor	.60	.25
86	Marvin Harrison	1.00	.40
87	Ashley Lelie	.60	.25
88	Willis McGahee	1.00	.40
89	Terence Newman	.50	.20
90	Joe Horn	.60	.25
91	Lee Suggs	.60	.25
92	Keyshawn Johnson	.60	.25
93	Desmond Clark	.50	.20
94	T.J. Duckett	.60	.25
95	Reggie Wayne	.60	.25
96	Donte Stallworth	.60	.25
97	Clarence Moore	.50	.20
98	Jason Witten	.60	.25
99	Jake Delhomme	1.00	.40
100	Julius Jones	1.25	.50
101	Ben Troupe	.50	.20
102	Hines Ward	1.00	.40
103	Domanick Davis	.60	.25
104	B.J. Sams	.50	.20
105	Marcus Robinson	.60	.25
106	Devery Henderson	.50	.20
107	Matt Hasselbeck	.60	.25
108	Antonio Pierce	.50	.20
109	Santana Moss	.60	.25
110	Adam Vinatieri	1.00	.40
111	Michael Strahan	.60	.25
112	Greg Jones	.50	.20
113	Drew Brees	1.00	.40
114	Marcus Robinson	.60	.25
115	Michael Jenkins	.60	.25
116	Randy McMichael	.50	.20
117	Jonathan Vilma	.60	.25
118	Greg Lewis	.50	.20
119	Ernest Wilford	.50	.20
120	Warrick Dunn	.60	.25
121	Shaun Alexander CL	.75	.30
122	Donnie Edwards	.50	.20
123	Antwaan Randle El	.60	.25
124	Rod Smith	.60	.25
125	Ed Reed	.60	.25
126	Muhsin Muhammad	.60	.25
127	L.J. Smith	.50	.20
128	Chris Chambers	.60	.25
129	Matt Schaub	.60	.25
130	Andre Johnson	.60	.25
131	Thomas Jones	.60	.25
132	Robert Ferguson	.50	.20
133	Jeremy Shockey	1.00	.40
134	William Green	.50	.20
135A	Ben Roethlisberger	2.50	1.00
135B	Ben Roethlisberger Ad Back	12.00	5.00
136A	Donovan McNabb	1.25	.50
136B	Donovan McNabb Ad Back	6.00	2.50
137	Duce Staley	.60	.25
138	Larry Fitzgerald	1.00	.40
139	Charles Rogers	.60	.25
140	Mark Brunell	.60	.25
141	Kevin Jones	1.25	.50
142	LaMont Jordan	.60	.25
143	Aaron Brooks	.60	.25
144	Brian Westbrook	.60	.25
145	Larry Johnson	1.25	.50
146	Tommy Maddox	.50	.20
147	Corey Dillon	.60	.25
148	William Henderson	.50	.20
149	Tony Hollings	.50	.20
150	Lee Evans	.60	.25
151	Kelly Holcomb	.50	.20
152	Reuben Droughns	.60	.25
153	Keenan McCardell	.50	.20
154	Ricky Williams	.60	.25
155	Rashaun Woods	.60	.25
156	D.J. Williams	.50	.20
157	Tom Brady	2.00	.75
158	Eric Parker	.50	.20
159	Mike Anderson	.60	.25
160	Roy Williams WR	1.00	.40
161	Mike Vanderjagt	.50	.20
162	Ronald Curry	.60	.25
163	Priest Holmes	1.00	.40
164	Bernard Berrian	.50	.20
165	Brian Finneran	.50	.20
166	Tony Gonzalez	.60	.25
167	Chris McAlister	.50	.20
168	Gus Frerotte	.50	.20
169	Bryant Johnson	.50	.20
170	Jay Fiedler	.50	.20
171	Bubba Franks	.50	.20
172	Tony Romo	10.00	5.00
173	Jamal Lewis	.60	.25
174	Torry Holt	.60	.25
175	Ladell Betts	.50	.20
176	Bertrand Berry	.50	.20
177	Josh McCown	.60	.25
178	Jonathan Wells	.50	.20
179	Plaxico Burress	.60	.25
180	Rudi Johnson	.60	.25
181	Cedric Benson RC	4.00	1.50
182	Carlos Rogers RC	2.50	1.00
183	Terrence Murphy RC	2.00	.75
184	Frank Gore RC	5.00	2.00
185	Vincent Jackson RC	2.00	.75
186	Ciatrick Fason RC	2.00	.75
187	Alex Smith QB RC	8.00	3.00
188	Mike Williams	2.50	1.00
189	Kyle Orton RC	3.00	1.25
190A	Ronnie Brown RC	8.00	3.00
190B	Ronnie Brown	10.00	4.00
191	Charlie Frye RC	4.00	1.50
192	Mark Bradley RC	2.00	.75
193	Antrel Rolle RC	2.00	.75
194	Roscoe Parrish RC	2.00	.75
195	Ryan Moats RC	2.00	.75
196	Andrew Walter RC	3.00	1.25
197	Troy Williamson RC	4.00	1.50
198	Cadillac Williams RC	8.00	3.00
199	Adam Jones RC	2.00	.75
200	Braylon Edwards RC	6.00	2.50
201	Vernand Morency RC	2.00	.75
202	Ryan Fitzpatrick RC	3.00	1.25
203	Heath Miller RC	5.00	2.00
204	Eric Shelton RC	2.00	.75
205	Jason Campbell RC	2.50	1.00
206	David Pollack RC	2.50	1.00
207	Stefan LeFors RC	2.00	.75
208	DeMarcus Ware RC	3.00	1.25
209	J.J. Arrington RC	2.50	1.00
210	Marion Barber RC	3.00	1.25
211	Samkon Gado RC	12.00	5.00
212	Roddy White RC	2.00	.75
213	Brandon Jacobs RC	2.50	1.00
214	Mark Clayton RC	2.50	1.00
215	Alex Smith TE RC	2.00	.75
216	Darren Sproles RC	2.00	.75
217	Fabian Washington RC	2.00	.75
218	Brandon Jones RC	2.00	.75
219	Derrick Johnson RC	3.00	1.25
220	Dan Orlovsky RC	2.50	1.00
221	Aaron Rodgers RC	6.00	2.50
222	Cedric Houston RC	2.00	.75
223	Reggie Brown RC	2.00	.75
224	Scottie Vines RC	2.00	.75
225	Willie Parker	8.00	3.00
226	Matt Jones RC	5.00	2.00
227	Odell Thurman RC	2.00	.75
228	Alvin Pearman RC	2.00	.75
229	Chris Henry RC	2.00	.75
230	Courtney Roby RC	2.00	.75
231	Isaac Bruce	.60	.25
232	Warrick Dunn CL	.50	.20
233	Willis McGahee CL	.75	.30
234	Marcus Pollard	.50	.20
235	Jason Taylor	.50	.20
236	Joe Namath	5.00	2.00
237	Joe Montana	10.00	4.00

Card	Player	Price 1	Price 2
❑ 238	Barry Sanders	6.00	2.50
❑ 239	Jim Brown	5.00	2.00
❑ 240	Terry Bradshaw	6.00	2.50
❑ 241	Ahman Green	1.00	.40
❑ 242	Tiki Barber CL	.75	.30
❑ 243	Julius Jones CL	1.00	.40
❑ 244	Daunte Culpepper	1.00	.40
❑ 245	Edgerrin James CL	.75	.30
❑ 246	Trent Green	5.00	2.00
❑ 247	Dwight Freeney	5.00	2.00
❑ 248A	Brett Favre	12.00	5.00
❑ 248B	Brett Favre Ad Back	15.00	6.00
❑ 249	Marshall Faulk	8.00	3.00
❑ 250	Jerome Bettis	8.00	3.00
❑ 251	Nate Burleson	5.00	2.00
❑ 252	Brandon Lloyd	5.00	2.00
❑ 253	Randy Moss	8.00	3.00
❑ 254	Drew Bledsoe	8.00	3.00
❑ 255	Brandon Stokley	5.00	2.00
❑ 256	Takeo Spikes	4.00	1.50
❑ 257	Philip Rivers	8.00	3.00
❑ 258	Lito Sheppard	4.00	1.50
❑ 259	Jimmy Smith	5.00	2.00
❑ 260	Tatum Bell	5.00	2.00
❑ 261	Allen Rossum	4.00	1.50
❑ 262	Amani Toomer	5.00	2.00
❑ 263	Jabar Gaffney	4.00	1.50
❑ 264	Jonathan Ogden	4.00	1.50
❑ 265	John Abraham	4.00	1.50
❑ 266	Aaron Stecker	4.00	1.50
❑ 267	Jason Elam	4.00	1.50
❑ 268	Najeh Davenport	4.00	1.50
❑ 269	Alge Crumpler	5.00	2.00
❑ 270	Roy Williams S	5.00	2.00
❑ 271	Trent Dilfer	5.00	2.00
❑ 272	Anquan Boldin	5.00	2.00
❑ 273	Artose Pinner	4.00	1.50
❑ 274	David Garrard	4.00	1.50
❑ 275	Terry Glenn	5.00	2.00
❑ 276	Adam Archuleta	4.00	1.50
❑ 277	Jeremiah Trotter	4.00	1.50
❑ 278	Travis Henry	5.00	2.00
❑ 279	Rex Grossman	8.00	3.00
❑ 280	Maurice Morris	4.00	1.50
❑ 281	Mike Alstott	5.00	2.00
❑ 282	Justin Gage	4.00	1.50
❑ 283	Dennis Northcutt	4.00	1.50
❑ 284	David Givens	5.00	2.00
❑ 285	Dominic Rhodes	5.00	2.00
❑ 286	Gerald Ford	5.00	2.00
❑ 287	Ronald Reagan	5.00	2.00
❑ 288	John F. Kennedy	5.00	2.00
❑ 289	Ulysses S. Grant	5.00	2.00
❑ CL1	Jumbo Checklist 1	1.00	.40
❑ CL2	Jumbo Checklist 2	1.00	.40

2006 Topps Turkey Red

Card	Player	Price 1	Price 2
❑ 1	LaVar Arrington	1.00	.40
❑ 2	Heath Miller	1.00	.40
❑ 3	Antwaan Randle El	.60	.25
❑ 4	Derrick Mason	.50	.20
❑ 5	Deshaun Foster	.60	.25
❑ 6	Andre Johnson	.60	.25
❑ 7	Jonathan Vilma	.60	.25
❑ 8	Trent Dilfer	.60	.25
❑ 9	Tatum Bell	.60	.25
❑ 10	Bubba Franks	.50	.20
❑ 11	T.J. Houshmandzadeh	.60	.25
❑ 12	Adam Vinatieri	.60	.25
❑ 13	Quentin Jammer	.50	.20
❑ 14	Jim Kleinsasser	.50	.20
❑ 15	Priest Holmes	.60	.25
❑ 16	Courtney Roby	.50	.20
❑ 17	Chris Simms	.60	.25
❑ 18	Terry Glenn	.60	.25
❑ 19	Jonathan Ogden	.50	.20
❑ 20	Andrew Walter	.60	.25
❑ 21	Lito Sheppard	.50	.20
❑ 22	Kevan Barlow	.60	.25
❑ 23	Santana Moss	.60	.25
❑ 24	Kelly Holcomb	.50	.20
❑ 25	Thomas Jones	.60	.25
❑ 26	Dennis Northcutt	.50	.20
❑ 27	Najeh Davenport	.50	.20
❑ 28	Edgerrin James	1.00	.40
❑ 29	Kevin Curtis	.50	.20
❑ 30	Brian Griese	.60	.25
❑ 31	Jason Taylor	.50	.20
❑ 32	T.J. Duckett	.60	.25
❑ 33	Antonio Bryant	.60	.25
❑ 34	Donald Driver	.60	.25
❑ 35	Brian Westbrook	.60	.25
❑ 36	Lofa Tatupu	.60	.25
❑ 37	Ben Troupe	.50	.20
❑ 38	Chris Cooley	.50	.20
❑ 39	Josh McCown	.60	.25
❑ 40	Chris Perry	.60	.25
❑ 41	Joe Horn	.60	.25
❑ 42	Kyle Boller	.50	.20
❑ 43	Keyshawn Johnson	.60	.25
❑ 44	Frank Gore	1.00	.40
❑ 45	Terence Newman	.50	.20
❑ 46	Devery Henderson	.50	.20
❑ 47	Michael Strahan	.60	.25
❑ 48	Ladell Betts	.50	.20
❑ 49	Patrick Ramsey	.60	.25
❑ 50	Anquan Boldin	.60	.25
❑ 51	Nathan Vasher	.50	.20
❑ 52	Dominic Rhodes	.60	.25
❑ 53	Travis Minor	.50	.20
❑ 54	Torry Holt	.60	.25
❑ 55	Sam Gado	1.00	.40
❑ 56	Fred Taylor	.60	.25
❑ 57	Braylon Edwards	1.00	.40
❑ 58	Tyrone Calico	.50	.20
❑ 59	Derrick Burgess	.50	.20
❑ 60	Chester Taylor	.60	.25
❑ 61	Julius Peppers	.60	.25
❑ 62	L.J. Smith	.50	.20
❑ 63	Keenan McCardell	.50	.20
❑ 64	Lee Evans	.60	.25
❑ 65	Champ Bailey	.60	.25
❑ 66	Alex Smith QB	1.25	.50
❑ 67	Tedy Bruschi	1.00	.40
❑ 68	Roddy White	.60	.25
❑ 69	Marty Booker	.50	.20
❑ 70	Fred Smoot	.50	.20
❑ 71	A.J. Feeley	.50	.20
❑ 72	Kellen Winslow	1.00	.40
❑ 73	Curtis Martin	1.00	.40
❑ 74	Ronald Curry	.60	.25
❑ 75	Sam Madison	.50	.20
❑ 76	Keary Colbert	.50	.20
❑ 77	Marcus Pollard	.50	.20
❑ 78	James Farrior	.50	.20
❑ 79	Travis Henry	.50	.20
❑ 80	Samari Rolle	.50	.20
❑ 81	Rodney Harrison	.50	.20
❑ 82	Matt Schaub	.60	.25
❑ 83	Philip Rivers	1.00	.40
❑ 84	DeMarcus Ware	.60	.25
❑ 85	Reggie Wayne	.60	.25
❑ 86	Derrick Johnson	.60	.25
❑ 87	Travis Taylor	.50	.20
❑ 88	Antonio Pierce	.50	.20
❑ 89	Jamal Lewis	.60	.25
❑ 90	Aaron Brooks	.60	.25
❑ 91	Michael Pittman	.50	.20
❑ 92	Jerricho Cotchery	.50	.20
❑ 93	Shayne Graham	.50	.20
❑ 94	Dante Hall	.60	.25
❑ 95	Warrick Dunn	.60	.25
❑ 96	Mewelde Moore	.50	.20
❑ 97	Brandon Lloyd	.60	.25
❑ 98	Chris Gamble	.50	.20
❑ 99	Odell Thurman	.50	.20
❑ 100	Osi Umenyiora	.50	.20
❑ 101	Jerry Porter	.60	.25
❑ 102	Brandon Stokley	.60	.25
❑ 103	Clinton Portis	1.00	.40
❑ 104	Quentin Jammer	.50	.20
❑ 105	Reuben Droughns	.60	.25
❑ 106	Jason Campbell	.60	.25
❑ 107	LaBrandon Toefield	.50	.20
❑ 108	Nate Burleson	.60	.25
❑ 109	Antrel Rolle	.50	.20
❑ 110A	Steve McNair PS	.60	.25
❑ 110B	Steve McNair YS	.60	.25
❑ 111A	Chad Johnson PBB	.60	.25
❑ 111B	Chad Johnson No PBB	.60	.25
❑ 112	Steven Jackson	1.00	.40
❑ 113	Ron Dayne	.60	.25
❑ 114	Deion Branch	.60	.25
❑ 115	Ed Reed	.60	.25
❑ 116	Ty Law	.60	.25
❑ 117	Drew Bledsoe	1.00	.40
❑ 118	Chris McAlister	.50	.20
❑ 119	Plaxico Burress	.60	.25
❑ 120	Aaron Rodgers	1.00	.40
❑ 121	Tony Gonzalez	.60	.25
❑ 122	David Givens	.60	.25
❑ 123	Michael Vick	1.25	.50
❑ 124	Antonio Gates	1.00	.40
❑ 125	Darrell Jackson	.60	.25
❑ 126	Adam Jones	.50	.20
❑ 127	LaDainian Tomlinson CL	1.00	.40
❑ 128	Chad Pennington	.60	.25
❑ 129	Kevin Faulk	.50	.20
❑ 130	Isaac Bruce	.60	.25
❑ 131	Tom Brady CL	1.25	.50
❑ 132	Deuce McAllister	.60	.25
❑ 133	Laveranues Coles	.60	.25
❑ 134	Donnie Edwards	.50	.20
❑ 135	Brian Urlacher CL	.75	.30
❑ 136	Dallas Clark	.50	.20
❑ 137	Drew Bennett	.50	.20
❑ 138	Domanick Davis	.60	.25
❑ 139	Cadillac Williams CL	.75	.30
❑ 140	David Garrard	.50	.20
❑ 141	Shaun Alexander CL	.75	.30
❑ 142	Troy Williamson	.60	.25
❑ 143	Steve Smith CL	.75	.30
❑ 144	Jake Plummer	.60	.25
❑ 145	Carson Palmer CL	.75	.30
❑ 146	DeAngelo Hall	.60	.25
❑ 147	Michael Vick CL	1.00	.40
❑ 148	Kyle Vanden Bosch	.50	.20
❑ 149	Larry Johnson CL	1.00	.40
❑ 150	LaDainian Tomlinson	1.25	.50
❑ 151	Dunta Robinson	.60	.25
❑ 152	Muhsin Muhammad	.60	.25
❑ 153	Steven Jackson CL	.75	.30
❑ 154	David Pollack	.50	.20
❑ 155	Mark Brunell	.60	.25
❑ 156	Donovan McNabb	1.00	.40
❑ 157	Jeremy Shockey	1.00	.40
❑ 158	Corey Dillon	.60	.25
❑ 159	Mark Clayton	.60	.25
❑ 160	Vincent Jackson	.50	.20
❑ 161	Kurt Warner	.60	.25
❑ 162	Marcus Robinson	.60	.25
❑ 163	Takeo Spikes	.50	.20
❑ 164	Charles Rogers	.60	.25
❑ 165	J.P. Losman	.60	.25
❑ 166	Matt Jones	1.00	.40
❑ 167	Rod Smith	.60	.25
❑ 168	Steve Smith	1.00	.40
❑ 169	Michael Vick	1.25	.50
❑ 170	Mike Vanderjagt	.50	.20
❑ 171	Amani Toomer	.60	.25
❑ 172	Deltha O'Neal	.50	.20
❑ 173	Michael Jenkins	.60	.25
❑ 174	David Carr	.60	.25
❑ 175	Chris Brown	.60	.25
❑ 176	Kevin Jones	1.00	.40
❑ 177	Roy Williams S	.60	.25
❑ 178	Marvin Harrison	1.00	.40
❑ 179	Drew Brees	1.00	.40
❑ 180	John Abraham	.50	.20
❑ 181	Joseph Addai RC SP	15.00	6.00
❑ 182	Sinorice Moss RC SP	6.00	2.50
❑ 183A	Vince Young PS RC	8.00	3.00
❑ 183B	Vince Young OS SP	20.00	8.00

❑ 184 Vernon Davis RC SP 10.00 4.00
❑ 185 Brandon Williams RC SP 5.00 2.00
❑ 186 Derek Hagan RC SP 5.00 2.00
❑ 187 Brian Calhoun RC SP 5.00 2.00
❑ 188 Mario Williams RC SP 8.00 3.00
❑ 189 DeAngelo Williams RC SP 12.00 5.00
❑ 190 Jay Cutler RC SP 20.00 8.00
❑ 191 A.J. Hawk RC SP 10.00 4.00
❑ 192 Reggie Bush RC 12.00 5.00
❑ 193 Laurence Maroney RC SP 12.00 5.00
❑ 194 D'Brickashaw Ferguson RC SP 5.00 2.00
❑ 195 Jason Avant RC SP 5.00 2.00
❑ 196 Brodie Croyle RC SP 10.00 4.00
❑ 197 Michael Huff RC SP 6.00 2.50
❑ 198 LenDale White RC SP 10.00 4.00
❑ 199 Marcedes Lewis RC SP 5.00 2.00
❑ 200 Travis Wilson RC SP 5.00 2.00
❑ 201 Haloti Ngata RC SP 5.00 2.00
❑ 202 Greg Jennings RC SP 8.00 3.00
❑ 203 Leon Washington RC SP 8.00 3.00
❑ 204 Tamba Hali RC SP 5.00 2.00
❑ 205 Santonio Holmes RC SP 10.00 4.00
❑ 206 Jerome Harrison RC SP 5.00 2.00
❑ 207 Tarvaris Jackson RC SP 8.00 3.00
❑ 208 Mathias Kiwanuka RC SP 6.00 2.50
❑ 209 Omar Jacobs RC SP 4.00 1.50
❑ 210 Alan Zemaitis RC SP 5.00 2.00
❑ 211 Demetrius Williams RC SP 6.00 2.50
❑ 212 Bobby Carpenter RC SP 5.00 2.00
❑ 213 Tye Hill RC SP 5.00 2.00
❑ 214 Chad Jackson RC SP 8.00 3.00
❑ 215 Joe Klopfenstein RC SP 4.00 1.50
❑ 216 Kamerion Wimbley RC SP 5.00 2.00
❑ 217 Michael Robinson RC SP 8.00 3.00
❑ 218 David Thomas RC SP 5.00 2.00
❑ 219 Charlie Whitehurst RC SP 6.00 2.50
❑ 220 Jerious Norwood RC SP 8.00 3.00
❑ 221 Bruce Gradkowski RC SP 8.00 3.00
❑ 222 Kellen Clemens RC SP 6.00 2.50
❑ 223 Thomas Howard RC SP 5.00 2.00
❑ 224 Anthony Fasano RC SP 5.00 2.00
❑ 225 Maurice Drew RC SP 12.00 5.00
❑ 226 Antonio Cromartie RC SP 5.00 2.00
❑ 227 Mike Bell RC SP 8.00 3.00
❑ 228 D'Qwell Jackson RC SP 4.00 1.50
❑ 229A Matt Leinart TIB RC 8.00 3.00
❑ 229B Matt Leinart SIB SP 20.00 8.00
❑ 230 Maurice Stovall RC SP 5.00 2.00
❑ 231A Carson Palmer BJ 1.00 .40
❑ 231A Carson Palmer WJ 1.00 .40
❑ 232 Courtney Anderson .50 .20
❑ 233 D.J. Williams .50 .20
❑ 234 Chris Chambers .60 .25
❑ 235 Zach Thomas 1.00 .40
❑ 236 Reggie Brown .60 .25
❑ 237 Cadillac Williams 1.00 .40
❑ 238 Randy McMichael .50 .20
❑ 239 Brian Urlacher 1.00 .40
❑ 240 Cedric Houston .50 .20
❑ 241 Marc Bulger .60 .25
❑ 242 Mike Anderson .60 .25
❑ 243 Allen Rossum .50 .20
❑ 244 William Henderson .50 .20
❑ 245 Eddie Kennison .50 .20
❑ 246 Adam Archuleta .50 .20
❑ 247 Ryan Moats .50 .20
❑ 248 D.J. Hackett .50 .20
❑ 249 Marion Barber .60 .25
❑ 250 Mike Alstott .60 .25
❑ 251 Shawne Merriman .60 .25
❑ 252 Byron Leftwich .60 .25
❑ 253 Dan Morgan .50 .20
❑ 254 Ronnie Brown 1.00 .40
❑ 255 Mark Bradley .60 .25
❑ 256 Mike Williams 1.00 .40
❑ 257 Ronde Barber .50 .20
❑ 258 Bernard Berrian .50 .20
❑ 259 Gibril Wilson .50 .20
❑ 260 Scottie Vines .50 .20
❑ 261 Rex Grossman 1.00 .40
❑ 262 Daniel Graham .50 .20
❑ 263 Ernest Wilford .50 .20
❑ 264 Javon Walker .60 .25
❑ 265 Corey Webster .50 .20
❑ 266 Jon Kitna .50 .20
❑ 267 Arnaz Battle .50 .20
❑ 268 Robert Ferguson SP 3.00 1.25
❑ 269 Cedric Benson 1.00 .40
❑ 270 Michael Clayton .60 .25
❑ 271 Brandon Jacobs .50 .20
❑ 272 Jason Witten SP 4.00 1.50
❑ 273A Randy Moss BS 1.00 .40
❑ 273B Randy Moss PS 1.00 .40
❑ 274 Daunte Culpepper SP 6.00 2.50
❑ 275 Ronnie Brown 1.00 .40
❑ 276 Dwight Freeney .60 .25
❑ 277 LaMont Jordan .60 .25
❑ 278 Jeremiah Trotter .50 .20
❑ 279A Hines Ward PO sky 1.00 .40
❑ 279B Hines Ward BY sky 1.00 .40
❑ 280A Tom Brady PBB 1.50 .60
❑ 280B Tom Brady No PBB 1.50 .60
❑ 281 Charles Woodson .60 .25
❑ 282A Shaun Alexander GJ 1.00 .40
❑ 282B Shaun Alexander WJ 1.00 .40
❑ 283 Eric Moulds .60 .25
❑ 284A Ben Roethlisberger BS 1.50 .60
❑ 284B Ben Roethlisberger PS 1.50 .60
❑ 285 Matt Hasselbeck .60 .25
❑ 286 Willis McGahee 1.00 .40
❑ 287 Carlos Rogers .50 .20
❑ 288 Brett Favre 2.00 .75
❑ 289 Larry Fitzgerald 1.00 .40
❑ 290 Billy Volek .60 .25
❑ 291 Julius Jones 1.00 .40
❑ 292 Trent Green .60 .25
❑ 293 Ashley Lelie .60 .25
❑ 294 Eli Manning 1.25 .50
❑ 295 Alge Crumpler .60 .25
❑ 296 Rudi Johnson .60 .25
❑ 297 Troy Polamalu 1.25 .50
❑ 298 Roy Williams WR 1.00 .40
❑ 299 Willie Parker 1.25 .50
❑ 300 Jake Delhomme .60 .25
❑ 301 Champ Bailey .60 .25
❑ 302 Ahman Green .60 .25
❑ 303 Robert Gallery .50 .20
❑ 304 Todd Heap .60 .25
❑ 305 Joey Harrington .60 .25
❑ 306 Terrell Owens 1.00 .40
❑ 307 Joey Galloway .60 .25
❑ 308A Larry Johnson OS 1.25 .50
❑ 308A Larry Johnson PS 1.25 .50
❑ 309 Brian Dawkins .50 .20
❑ 310 Ray Lewis 1.00 .40
❑ 311A Tiki Barber OS 1.00 .40
❑ 311B Tiki Barber BS SP 6.00 2.50
❑ 312 Donte Stallworth .60 .25
❑ 313 Eric Parker .50 .20
❑ 314 Charlie Frye .60 .25
❑ 315A Peyton Manning BYS 1.50 .60
❑ 315B Peyton Manning OS SP 40.00 15.00

2005 UD Mini Jersey Collection

❑ COMPLETE SET (100) 50.00 25.00
❑ 1 Kurt Warner .75 .30
❑ 2 Anquan Boldin .75 .30
❑ 3 Michael Vick 2.00 .75
❑ 4 Warrick Dunn .75 .30
❑ 5 Kyle Boller .75 .30
❑ 6 Ray Lewis 1.25 .50
❑ 7 Jake Delhomme 1.25 .50
❑ 8 DeShaun Foster .75 .30
❑ 9 Carson Palmer 1.25 .50
❑ 10 Chad Johnson 1.25 .50
❑ 11 Rudi Johnson .75 .30
❑ 12 Kellen Winslow 1.25 .50
❑ 13 Lee Suggs .75 .30
❑ 14 Julius Jones 1.50 .60
❑ 15 Drew Bledsoe 1.25 .50
❑ 16 Tatum Bell .75 .30
❑ 17 Jake Plummer .75 .30
❑ 18 Roy Williams WR 1.25 .50
❑ 19 Kevin Jones 1.25 .50
❑ 20 Brett Favre 3.00 1.25
❑ 21 Ahman Green 1.25 .50
❑ 22 David Carr 1.25 .50
❑ 23 Andre Johnson .75 .30
❑ 24 Peyton Manning 2.00 .75
❑ 25 Edgerrin James 1.25 .50
❑ 26 Marvin Harrison 1.25 .50
❑ 27 Byron Leftwich 1.25 .50
❑ 28 Fred Taylor .75 .30
❑ 29 Priest Holmes 1.25 .50
❑ 30 Trent Green .75 .30
❑ 31 Tony Gonzalez .75 .30
❑ 32 A.J. Feeley .75 .30
❑ 33 Randy McMichael .60 .25
❑ 34 Daunte Culpepper 1.25 .50
❑ 35 Nate Burleson .75 .30
❑ 36 Tom Brady 3.00 1.25
❑ 37 Corey Dillon .75 .30
❑ 38 Aaron Brooks .75 .30
❑ 39 Joe Horn .75 .30
❑ 40 Deuce McAllister 1.25 .50
❑ 41 Eli Manning 2.50 1.00
❑ 42 Tiki Barber 1.25 .50
❑ 43 Jeremy Shockey 1.25 .50
❑ 44 Chad Pennington 1.25 .50
❑ 45 Curtis Martin 1.25 .50
❑ 46 Santana Moss .75 .30
❑ 47 Randy Moss 1.25 .50
❑ 48 Kerry Collins .75 .30
❑ 49 Donovan McNabb 1.50 .60
❑ 50 Terrell Owens 1.25 .50
❑ 51 Brian Westbrook .75 .30
❑ 52 Ben Roethlisberger 3.00 1.25
❑ 53 Jerome Bettis 1.25 .50
❑ 54 Drew Brees 1.25 .50
❑ 55 LaDainian Tomlinson 1.50 .60
❑ 56 Kevan Barlow .75 .30
❑ 57 Tim Rattay .60 .25
❑ 58 Matt Hasselbeck .75 .30
❑ 59 Shaun Alexander 1.50 .60
❑ 60 Darrell Jackson .75 .30
❑ 61 Marc Bulger 1.25 .50
❑ 62 Steven Jackson 1.50 .60
❑ 63 Torry Holt 1.25 .50
❑ 64 Michael Pittman .60 .25
❑ 65 Brian Griese .75 .30
❑ 66 Michael Clayton 1.25 .50
❑ 67 Steve McNair 1.25 .50
❑ 68 Drew Bennett .75 .30
❑ 69 Clinton Portis 1.25 .50
❑ 70 Patrick Ramsey .75 .30
❑ 71 Alex Smith QB RC 8.00 3.00
❑ 72 Aaron Rodgers RC 6.00 2.50
❑ 73 Jason Campbell RC 3.00 1.25
❑ 74 Ronnie Brown RC 8.00 3.00
❑ 75 Cadillac Williams RC 10.00 4.00
❑ 76 Cedric Benson RC 4.00 1.50
❑ 77 J.J. Arrington RC 2.50 1.00
❑ 78 Braylon Edwards RC 6.00 2.50
❑ 79 Troy Williamson RC 4.00 1.50
❑ 80 Mike Williams 4.00 1.50
❑ 81 Matt Jones RC 5.00 2.00
❑ 82 Mark Clayton RC 2.50 1.00
❑ 83 Roddy White RC 2.00 .75
❑ 84 Reggie Brown RC 2.00 .75
❑ 85 Eric Shelton RC 2.00 .75
❑ 86 Peyton Manning SR 2.00 .75
❑ 87 Ben Roethlisberger SR 3.00 1.25
❑ 88 Julius Jones SR 1.50 .60
❑ 89 Michael Vick SR 2.00 .75
❑ 90 Tom Brady SR 3.00 1.25
❑ 91 Corey Dillon SR .75 .30
❑ 92 Terrell Owens SR 1.25 .50
❑ 93 Donovan McNabb SR 1.50 .60
❑ 94 Priest Holmes SR 1.25 .50
❑ 95 Kevin Jones SR 1.25 .50
❑ 96 Jerome Bettis SR 1.25 .50
❑ 97 Torry Holt SR 1.25 .50

98	Clinton Portis SR	1.25	.50
99	Drew Brees SR	1.25	.50
100	Tiki Barber SR	1.25	.50
NNO	Checklist Card	.15	.05

2005 UD Portraits

❑ DRAFT PICK PRINT RUN 425 SER.#'d SETS

1	Larry Fitzgerald	3.00	1.25
2	Anquan Boldin	2.00	.75
3	Josh McCown	2.00	.75
4	Michael Vick	5.00	2.00
5	Alge Crumpler	2.00	.75
6	Peerless Price	1.50	.60
7	Ray Lewis	3.00	1.25
8	Jamal Lewis	2.00	.75
9	Todd Heap	2.00	.75
10	Derrick Mason	2.00	.75
11	J.P. Losman	3.00	1.25
12	Willis McGahee	3.00	1.25
13	Eric Moulds	2.00	.75
14	Jake Delhomme	3.00	1.25
15	DeShaun Foster	2.00	.75
16	Steve Smith	3.00	1.25
17	Brian Urlacher	3.00	1.25
18	Rex Grossman	3.00	1.25
19	Muhsin Muhammad	2.00	.75
20	Carson Palmer	3.00	1.25
21	Rudi Johnson	2.00	.75
22	Chad Johnson	2.00	.75
23	Julius Jones	4.00	1.50
24	Keyshawn Johnson	2.00	.75
25	Drew Bledsoe	3.00	1.25
26	Tatum Bell	2.00	.75
27	Jake Plummer	2.00	.75
28	Ashley Lelie	2.00	.75
29	Roy Williams WR	3.00	1.25
30	Kevin Jones	4.00	1.50
31	Joey Harrington	3.00	1.25
32	Brett Favre	8.00	3.00
33	Ahman Green	3.00	1.25
34	Javon Walker	2.00	.75
35	David Carr	3.00	1.25
36	Andre Johnson	2.00	.75
37	Domanick Davis	2.00	.75
38	Peyton Manning	5.00	2.00
39	Reggie Wayne	2.00	.75
40	Edgerrin James	3.00	1.25
41	Marvin Harrison	3.00	1.25
42	Byron Leftwich	3.00	1.25
43	Fred Taylor	2.00	.75
44	Jimmy Smith	2.00	.75
45	Priest Holmes	3.00	1.25
46	Larry Johnson	4.00	1.50
47	Trent Green	2.00	.75
48	A.J. Feeley	2.00	.75
49	Chris Chambers	2.00	.75
50	Randy McMichael	1.50	.60
51	Daunte Culpepper	3.00	1.25
52	Onterrio Smith	2.00	.75
53	Nate Burleson	2.00	.75
54	Tom Brady	6.00	2.50
55	Corey Dillon	2.00	.75
56	Deion Branch	2.00	.75
57	David Givens	2.00	.75
58	Aaron Brooks	2.00	.75
59	Deuce McAllister	3.00	1.25
60	Joe Horn	2.00	.75
61	Eli Manning	6.00	2.50
62	Jeremy Shockey	3.00	1.25
63	Tiki Barber	3.00	1.25
64	Chad Pennington	3.00	1.25
65	Curtis Martin	3.00	1.25
66	Jonathan Vilma	2.00	.75
67	Kerry Collins	2.00	.75
68	Jerry Porter	2.00	.75
69	Randy Moss	3.00	1.25
70	Donovan McNabb	4.00	1.50
71	Terrell Owens	3.00	1.25
72	Brian Dawkins	1.50	.60
73	Brian Westbrook	2.00	.75
74	Ben Roethlisberger	8.00	3.00
75	Jerome Bettis	3.00	1.25
76	Hines Ward	3.00	1.25
77	Duce Staley	2.00	.75
78	Drew Brees	3.00	1.25
79	LaDainian Tomlinson	4.00	1.50
80	Antonio Gates	3.00	1.25
81	Eric Parker	1.50	.60
82	Tim Rattay	1.50	.60
83	Kevan Barlow	2.00	.75
84	Eric Johnson	2.00	.75
85	Shaun Alexander	3.00	1.25
86	Darrell Jackson	2.00	.75
87	Matt Hasselbeck	2.00	.75
88	Marc Bulger	3.00	1.25
89	Steven Jackson	4.00	1.50
90	Marshall Faulk	3.00	1.25
91	Torry Holt	2.00	.75
92	Michael Pittman	1.50	.60
93	Brian Griese	2.00	.75
94	Michael Clayton	3.00	1.25
95	Steve McNair	2.00	.75
96	Billy Volek	2.00	.75
97	Chris Brown	2.00	.75
98	Clinton Portis	3.00	1.25
99	Patrick Ramsey	2.00	.75
100	Santana Moss	2.00	.75
101	Aaron Rodgers RC	15.00	6.00
102	Alex Smith QB RC	20.00	8.00
103	Charlie Frye RC	10.00	4.00
104	Andrew Walter RC	8.00	3.00
105	Jason Campbell RC	8.00	3.00
106	Dan Orlovsky RC	6.00	2.50
107	Derek Anderson RC	5.00	2.00
108	Kyle Orton RC	8.00	3.00
109	David Greene RC	5.00	2.00
110	James Kilian RC	4.00	1.50
111	Matt Jones RC	12.00	5.00
112	Cedric Benson RC	10.00	4.00
113	Ronnie Brown RC	15.00	6.00
114	Cadillac Williams RC	25.00	10.00
115	Ciatrick Fason RC	5.00	2.00
116	Vernand Morency RC	5.00	2.00
117	Eric Shelton RC	5.00	2.00
118	Maurice Clarett	5.00	2.00
119	Marion Barber RC	8.00	3.00
120	Anthony Davis RC	4.00	1.50
121	J.J. Arrington RC	6.00	2.50
122	Ryan Moats RC	5.00	2.00
123	Frank Gore RC	10.00	4.00
124	Alvin Pearman RC	5.00	2.00
125	Darren Sproles RC	5.00	2.00
126	Cedric Houston RC	5.00	2.00
127	Braylon Edwards RC	15.00	6.00
128	Troy Williamson RC	10.00	4.00
129	Mark Clayton RC	6.00	2.50
130	Chris Henry RC	5.00	2.00
131	Roddy White RC	5.00	2.00
132	Fred Gibson RC	4.00	1.50
133	Craphonso Thorpe RC	4.00	1.50
134	Terrence Murphy RC	5.00	2.00
135	Roydell Williams RC	4.00	1.50
136	Roscoe Parrish RC	5.00	2.00
137	Reggie Brown RC	5.00	2.00
138	Craig Bragg RC	4.00	1.50
139	Larry Brackins RC	4.00	1.50
140	Rasheed Marshall RC	5.00	2.00
141	J.R. Russell RC	4.00	1.50
142	Vincent Jackson RC	5.00	2.00
143	Dante Ridgeway RC	4.00	1.50
144	Chad Owens RC	5.00	2.00
145	Airese Currie RC	4.00	1.50
146	Marcus Maxwell RC	4.00	1.50
147	Paris Warren RC	4.00	1.50
148	Tab Perry RC	5.00	2.00
149	Jerome Mathis RC	5.00	2.00
150	Courtney Roby RC	5.00	2.00
151	Heath Miller RC	12.00	5.00
152	Alex Smith TE RC	5.00	2.00
153	Kevin Everett RC	5.00	2.00
154	Travis Johnson RC	2.50	1.00
155	Mike Patterson RC	5.00	2.00
156	DeMarcus Ware RC	8.00	3.00
157	Erasmus James RC	4.00	1.50
158	Dan Cody RC	5.00	2.00
159	David Pollack RC	6.00	2.50
160	Shaun Cody RC	5.00	2.00
161	Matt Roth RC	5.00	2.00
162	Marcus Spears RC	5.00	2.00
163	Jonathan Babineaux RC	4.00	1.50
164	Justin Tuck RC	5.00	2.00
165	Channing Crowder RC	5.00	2.00
166	Odell Thurman RC	5.00	2.00
167	Barrett Ruud RC	5.00	2.00
168	Lance Mitchell RC	4.00	1.50
169	Derrick Johnson RC	5.00	2.00
170	Shawne Merriman RC	8.00	3.00
171	Kevin Burnett RC	5.00	2.00
172	Darryl Blackstock RC	4.00	1.50
173	Antrel Rolle RC	5.00	2.00
174	Adam Jones RC	5.00	2.00
175	Fabian Washington RC	5.00	2.00
176	Carlos Rogers RC	6.00	2.50
177	Corey Webster RC	4.00	1.50
178	Justin Miller RC	4.00	1.50
179	Eric Green RC	2.50	1.00
180	Marlin Jackson RC	5.00	2.00
181	Luis Castillo RC	5.00	2.00
182	Thomas Davis RC	4.00	1.50
183	Kirk Morrison RC	5.00	2.00
184	Vincent Fuller RC	4.00	1.50
185	Donte Nicholson RC	5.00	2.00
186	Brodney Pool RC	4.00	1.50
187	Mike Nugent RC	5.00	2.00
188	Timmy Chang RC	4.00	1.50
189	Matt Cassel RC	8.00	3.00
190	Adrian McPherson RC	5.00	2.00
191	Gino Guidugli RC	2.50	1.00
192	Stefan LeFors RC	5.00	2.00
193	Marcus Randall RC	4.00	1.50
194	Brandon Jacobs RC	6.00	2.50
195	Walter Reyes RC	2.50	1.00
196	Mark Bradley RC	5.00	2.00
197	Josh Bullocks RC	5.00	2.00
198	Chase Lyman RC	2.50	1.00
199	Harry Williams RC	4.00	1.50
200	Mike Williams	6.00	2.50

2003 Ultimate Collection

1	Peyton Manning	8.00	3.00
2	Aaron Brooks	5.00	2.00
3	Joey Harrington	8.00	3.00
4	Brett Favre	12.00	5.00
5	Donovan McNabb	6.00	2.50
6	Jeff Garcia	5.00	2.00
7	Michael Vick	12.00	5.00
8	David Carr	8.00	3.00
9	Drew Brees	5.00	2.00
10	Chad Pennington	6.00	2.50
11	Drew Bledsoe	5.00	2.00
12	Tom Brady	12.00	5.00
13	Kurt Warner	5.00	2.00
14	Brad Johnson	3.00	1.25
15	Jay Fiedler	3.00	1.25
16	Tim Couch	2.00	.75

❑ 17 Trent Green 3.00 1.25
❑ 18 Daunte Culpepper 5.00 2.00
❑ 19 Keyshawn Johnson 5.00 2.00
❑ 20 Garrison Hearst 3.00 1.25
❑ 21 LaDainian Tomlinson 5.00 2.00
❑ 22 Emmitt Smith 12.00 5.00
❑ 23 Steve McNair 5.00 2.00
❑ 24 Chris Redman 2.00 .75
❑ 25 Chad Hutchinson 2.00 .75
❑ 26 Deuce McAllister 5.00 2.00
❑ 27 Eddie George 3.00 1.25
❑ 28 Marshall Faulk 5.00 2.00
❑ 29 Ahman Green 5.00 2.00
❑ 30 Julius Peppers 5.00 2.00
❑ 31 Priest Holmes 6.00 2.50
❑ 32 Edgerrin James 5.00 2.00
❑ 33 Jerry Rice 10.00 4.00
❑ 34 Ricky Williams 5.00 2.00
❑ 35 Anthony Thomas 3.00 1.25
❑ 36 Jerome Bettis 5.00 2.00
❑ 37 Shaun Alexander 5.00 2.00
❑ 38 Randy Moss 8.00 3.00
❑ 39 Jeremy Shockey 8.00 3.00
❑ 40 Patrick Ramsey 5.00 2.00
❑ 41 Clinton Portis 8.00 3.00
❑ 42 Terrell Owens 5.00 2.00
❑ 43 Corey Dillon 3.00 1.25
❑ 44 Mark Brunell 3.00 1.25
❑ 45 Rich Gannon 3.00 1.25
❑ 46 Curtis Martin 5.00 2.00
❑ 47 Josh McCown 3.00 1.25
❑ 48 Kerry Collins 3.00 1.25
❑ 49 Peerless Price 3.00 1.25
❑ 50 David Boston 3.00 1.25
❑ 51 Plaxico Burress 3.00 1.25
❑ 52 Marvin Harrison 5.00 2.00
❑ 53 Travis Henry 3.00 1.25
❑ 54 Brian Urlacher 8.00 3.00
❑ 55 Jake Plummer 3.00 1.25
❑ 56 Dave Ragone/750 RC 10.00 4.00
❑ 57 Brian St.Pierre AU/250 RC 20.00 8.00
❑ 58 Tony Romo/750 RC 60.00 30.00
❑ 59 Dallas Clark/750 RC 10.00 4.00
❑ 60 Kirk Farmer/750 RC 8.00 3.00
❑ 61 Juston Wood/750 RC 8.00 3.00
❑ 62 Justin Gage/750 RC 10.00 4.00
❑ 63 Sam Aiken/750 RC 8.00 3.00
❑ 64 LaBrandon Toefield/750 RC 10.00 4.00
❑ 65 L.J. Smith/750 RC 10.00 4.00
❑ 66 Domanick Davis/750 RC 10.00 4.00
❑ 67 Artose Pinner/750 RC 10.00 4.00
❑ 68 Dahrran Diedrick/750 RC 10.00 4.00
❑ 69 Lee Suggs/750 RC 10.00 4.00
❑ 70 Bethel Johnson/750 RC 10.00 4.00
❑ 71 Tyrone Calico/750 RC 10.00 4.00
❑ 72 Kevin Curtis/750 RC 10.00 4.00
❑ 73 Bobby Wade/750 RC 10.00 4.00
❑ 74 Brandon Lloyd/750 RC 10.00 4.00
❑ 75 Bryant Johnson/750 RC 10.00 4.00
❑ 76 J.R. Tolver/750 RC 8.00 3.00
❑ 77 Billy McMullen/750 RC 8.00 3.00
❑ 78 Nate Burleson/750 RC 10.00 4.00
❑ 79 Jason Johnson AU/250 RC 20.00 8.00
❑ 80 Talman Gardner/250 RC 15.00 6.00
❑ 81 Anquan Boldin/250 RC 50.00 20.00
❑ 82 Musa Smith/250 RC 15.00 6.00
❑ 83 Teyo Johnson/250 RC 20.00 8.00
❑ 84 Kyle Boller AU/250 RC 30.00 12.50
❑ 85 Carson Palmer AU/250 RC 350.00 200.00
❑ 86 Byron Leftwich AU/250 RC 150.0075.00
❑ 87 Earnest Graham AU/250 RC 30.0012.50
❑ 88 Chris Brown AU/250 RC 30.00 12.50
❑ 89 Chris Simms AU/250 RC 120.00 60.00
❑ 90 Kliff Kingsbury AU/250 RC 30.00 12.50
❑ 91 Jason Gesser/750 RC 10.00 4.00
❑ 92 Brad Banks AU/250 RC 25.00 10.00
❑ 93 Ken Dorsey AU/250 RC 30.00 12.50
❑ 94 Rex Grossman AU/250 RC 150.0075.00
❑ 95 Willis McGahee AU/250 RC 200.00 100.00
❑ 96 Larry Johnson AU/250 RC 400.00200.00
❑ 97 Quentin Griffin AU/250 RC 30.00 12.50
❑ 98 Onterrio Smith AU/250 RC 30.00 12.50
❑ 99 Justin Fargas AU/250 RC 30.00 12.50
❑ 100 Kareem Kelly AU/250 RC 25.00 10.00
❑ 101 Arnaz Battle AU/250 RC 40.00 20.00
❑ 102 Kel Washington AU/250 RC 40.00 15.00
❑ 103 Seneca Wallace AU/250 RC 40.00 15.00
❑ 104 Taylor Jacobs AU/250 RC 25.00 10.00
❑ 105 Andre Johnson/750 RC 30.00 12.50
❑ 106 Charles Rogers/250 RC 15.00 6.00
❑ 107 Terrell Suggs AU/250 RC 40.00 15.00

2004 Ultimate Collection

❑ 1-65 PRINT RUN 750 SER.#'d SETS
❑ 66-91/99A/133-135 PRINT RUN 750 SETS
❑ 92-98 RC PRINT RUN 250 SER.#'d SETS
❑ 99B-124/131-132 AU RC PRINT RUN 250 SETS
❑ 125-130 AU RC PRINT RUN 150 SER.#'d SETS
❑ UNPRICED PLATINUM PRINT RUN 10 SETS
❑ 1 Emmitt Smith 10.00 4.00
❑ 2 Anquan Boldin 5.00 2.00
❑ 3 Michael Vick 10.00 4.00
❑ 4 Peerless Price 3.00 1.25
❑ 5 Kyle Boller 5.00 2.00
❑ 6 Jamal Lewis 5.00 2.00
❑ 7 Drew Bledsoe 5.00 2.00
❑ 8 Travis Henry 3.00 1.25
❑ 9 Stephen Davis 3.00 1.25
❑ 10 Jake Delhomme 5.00 2.00
❑ 11 Rex Grossman 5.00 2.00
❑ 12 Brian Urlacher 6.00 2.50
❑ 13 Carson Palmer 6.00 2.50
❑ 14 Chad Johnson 5.00 2.00
❑ 15 Jeff Garcia 5.00 2.00
❑ 16 Keyshawn Johnson 3.00 1.25
❑ 17 Roy Williams S 3.00 1.25
❑ 18 Jake Plummer 3.00 1.25
❑ 19 Joey Harrington 5.00 2.00
❑ 20 Charles Rogers 3.00 1.25
❑ 21 Ahman Green 5.00 2.00
❑ 22 Brett Favre 12.00 5.00
❑ 23 David Carr 5.00 2.00
❑ 24 Domanick Davis 5.00 2.00
❑ 25 Andre Johnson 5.00 2.00
❑ 26 Edgerrin James 5.00 2.00
❑ 27 Peyton Manning 8.00 3.00
❑ 28 Marvin Harrison 5.00 2.00
❑ 29 Byron Leftwich 6.00 2.50
❑ 30 Fred Taylor 3.00 1.25
❑ 31 Priest Holmes 6.00 2.50
❑ 32 Tony Gonzalez 3.00 1.25
❑ 33 Trent Green 3.00 1.25
❑ 34 Ricky Williams 5.00 2.00
❑ 35 Chris Chambers 3.00 1.25
❑ 36 Jay Fiedler 2.00 .75
❑ 37 Randy Moss 6.00 2.50
❑ 38 Daunte Culpepper 5.00 2.00
❑ 39 Tom Brady 12.00 5.00
❑ 40 Corey Dillon 3.00 1.25
❑ 41 Deuce McAllister 5.00 2.00
❑ 42 Aaron Brooks 3.00 1.25
❑ 43 Tiki Barber 5.00 2.00
❑ 44 Jeremy Shockey 5.00 2.00
❑ 45 Chad Pennington 5.00 2.00
❑ 46 Curtis Martin 5.00 2.00
❑ 47 Santana Moss 3.00 1.25
❑ 48 Jerry Rice 10.00 4.00
❑ 49 Rich Gannon 3.00 1.25
❑ 50 Donovan McNabb 6.00 2.50
❑ 51 Terrell Owens 5.00 2.00
❑ 52 Hines Ward 5.00 2.00
❑ 53 Plaxico Burress 3.00 1.25
❑ 54 LaDainian Tomlinson 6.00 2.50
❑ 55 Tim Rattay 2.00 .75
❑ 56 Matt Hasselbeck 3.00 1.25
❑ 57 Shaun Alexander 5.00 2.00
❑ 58 Marc Bulger 5.00 2.00
❑ 59 Marshall Faulk 5.00 2.00
❑ 60 Torry Holt 5.00 2.00
❑ 61 Brad Johnson 3.00 1.25
❑ 62 Steve McNair 5.00 2.00
❑ 63 Chris Brown 5.00 2.00
❑ 64 Mark Brunell 3.00 1.25
❑ 65 Clinton Portis 5.00 2.00
❑ 66 Michael Turner RC 15.00 6.00
❑ 67 Kris Wilson RC 10.00 4.00
❑ 68 Jeff Smoker RC 10.00 4.00
❑ 69 Adimchinobe Echemandu RC 8.00 3.00
❑ 71 Thomas Tapeh RC 8.00 3.00
❑ 72 Chris Cooley RC 10.00 4.00
❑ 73 Cody Pickett RC 10.00 4.00
❑ 74 P.K. Sam RC 8.00 3.00
❑ 75 Ben Hartsock RC 10.00 4.00
❑ 76 Tim Euhus RC 10.00 4.00
❑ 77 Jammal Lord RC 10.00 4.00
❑ 78 Ricardo Colclough RC 10.00 4.00
❑ 79 D.J. Hackett RC 8.00 3.00
❑ 80 Ahmad Carroll RC 10.00 4.00
❑ 81 Troy Fleming RC 8.00 3.00
❑ 82 John Navarre RC 10.00 4.00
❑ 83 Craig Krenzel RC 10.00 4.00
❑ 84 Johnnie Morant RC 10.00 4.00
❑ 85 D.J. Williams RC 10.00 4.00
❑ 86 Jarrett Payton RC 10.00 4.00
❑ 87 Quincy Wilson RC 8.00 3.00
❑ 88 B.J. Symons RC 10.00 4.00
❑ 89 Tommie Harris RC 10.00 4.00
❑ 90 Jonathan Vilma RC 10.00 4.00
❑ 91 Karlos Dansby RC 10.00 4.00
❑ 92 Jerricho Cotchery RC 12.00 5.00
❑ 93 Samie Parker RC 12.00 5.00
❑ 94 Carlos Francis RC 10.00 4.00
❑ 95 Jim Sorgi RC 12.00 5.00
❑ 96 Derrick Hamilton RC 10.00 4.00
❑ 97 Dunta Robinson RC 12.00 5.00
❑ 98 Chris Gamble RC 12.00 5.00
❑ 99A Josh Harris RC 10.00 4.00
❑ 99B Devery Henderson AU RC 25.0010.00
❑ 100 Julius Jones AU RC 120.00 60.00
❑ 101 Cedric Cobbs AU RC 25.00 10.00
❑ 102 Greg Jones AU RC 40.00 15.00
❑ 103 Tatum Bell AU RC 80.00 40.00
❑ 104 Michael Jenkins AU RC 25.00 10.00
❑ 105 Devard Darling AU RC 25.00 10.00
❑ 106 Lee Evans AU RC 40.00 20.00
❑ 107 Keary Colbert AU RC 40.00 15.00
❑ 108 Bernard Berrian AU RC 40.00 20.00
❑ 109 Ben Watson AU RC 30.00 15.00
❑ 110 Matt Schaub AU RC 135.00 75.00
❑ 111 Darius Watts AU RC 25.00 10.00
❑ 112 Kevin Jones AU RC 100.00 50.00
❑ 113 Luke McCown AU RC 30.00 12.50
❑ 114 DeAngelo Hall AU RC 40.00 20.00
❑ 115 Rashaun Woods AU RC 25.00 10.00
❑ 116 Michael Clayton AU RC 80.00 30.00
❑ 117 Ben Troupe AU RC 25.00 10.00
❑ 118 B.J. Sams AU RC EXCH 25.00 10.00
❑ 119 Reggie Williams AU RC 30.00 15.00
❑ 120 Chris Perry AU RC 50.00 20.00
❑ 121 Roy Williams AU RC 100.00 50.00
❑ 122 Robert Gallery AU RC 25.00 10.00
❑ 123 J.P. Losman AU RC 60.00 30.00
❑ 124 Steven Jackson AU RC 135.00 75.00
❑ 125 Drew Henson AU RC 30.00 15.00
❑ 126 Kellen Winslow AU RC 80.00 30.00
❑ 127 B.Roethlisberger AU RC 500.00250.00
❑ 128 Philip Rivers AU RC 250.00 150.00
❑ 129 Larry Fitzgerald AU RC 120.00 60.00
❑ 130 Eli Manning AU RC 400.00 200.00
❑ 131 Ernest Wilford AU RC 25.00 10.00
❑ 132 Mewelde Moore AU RC 25.00 10.00
❑ 133 Will Smith RC 10.00 4.00
❑ 134 Kenechi Udeze RC 10.00 4.00
❑ 135 Matt Mauck RC 10.00 4.00

2005 Ultimate Collection

❑ 1-100/270-289 PRINT RUN 550 SER.#'d SETS
❑ 101-200/250-269 PRINT RUN 235 SETS
❑ AUTO PRINT RUN 225 UNLESS NOTED
❑ 1 Larry Fitzgerald 5.00 2.00
❑ 2 Anquan Boldin 3.00 1.25
❑ 3 Kurt Warner 3.00 1.25
❑ 4 Michael Vick 8.00 3.00

❑ 5	Warrick Dunn	3.00	1.25
❑ 6	Alge Crumpler	3.00	1.25
❑ 7	Ray Lewis	5.00	2.00
❑ 8	Deion Sanders	5.00	2.00
❑ 9	Kyle Boller	3.00	1.25
❑ 10	Derrick Mason	3.00	1.25
❑ 11	J.P. Losman	5.00	2.00
❑ 12	Willis McGahee	5.00	2.00
❑ 13	Lee Evans	3.00	1.25
❑ 14	Eric Moulds	3.00	1.25
❑ 15	Jake Delhomme	5.00	2.00
❑ 16	Keary Colbert	3.00	1.25
❑ 17	DeShaun Foster	3.00	1.25
❑ 18	Brian Urlacher	5.00	2.00
❑ 19	Rex Grossman	3.00	1.25
❑ 20	Muhsin Muhammad	3.00	1.25
❑ 21	Carson Palmer	5.00	2.00
❑ 22	Rudi Johnson	3.00	1.25
❑ 23	Chad Johnson	5.00	2.00
❑ 24	Julius Jones	6.00	2.50
❑ 25	Keyshawn Johnson	3.00	1.25
❑ 26	Drew Bledsoe	5.00	2.00
❑ 27	Tatum Bell	3.00	1.25
❑ 28	Jake Plummer	3.00	1.25
❑ 29	Ashley Lelie	3.00	1.25
❑ 30	Roy Williams WR	5.00	2.00
❑ 31	Kevin Jones	5.00	2.00
❑ 32	Jeff Garcia	3.00	1.25
❑ 33	Brett Favre	12.00	5.00
❑ 34	Ahman Green	5.00	2.00
❑ 35	Javon Walker	3.00	1.25
❑ 36	David Carr	5.00	2.00
❑ 37	Andre Johnson	3.00	1.25
❑ 38	Domanick Davis	3.00	1.25
❑ 39	Peyton Manning	8.00	3.00
❑ 40	Reggie Wayne	3.00	1.25
❑ 41	Edgerrin James	5.00	2.00
❑ 42	Marvin Harrison	5.00	2.00
❑ 43	Byron Leftwich	5.00	2.00
❑ 44	Fred Taylor	3.00	1.25
❑ 45	Jimmy Smith	3.00	1.25
❑ 46	Priest Holmes	5.00	2.00
❑ 47	Larry Johnson	5.00	2.00
❑ 48	Trent Green	3.00	1.25
❑ 49	A.J. Feeley	3.00	1.25
❑ 50	Chris Chambers	3.00	1.25
❑ 51	Randy McMichael	2.50	1.00
❑ 52	Daunte Culpepper	5.00	2.00
❑ 53	Michael Bennett	3.00	1.25
❑ 54	Nate Burleson	3.00	1.25
❑ 55	Tom Brady	12.00	5.00
❑ 56	Corey Dillon	3.00	1.25
❑ 57	Deion Branch	3.00	1.25
❑ 58	David Givens	3.00	1.25
❑ 59	Aaron Brooks	3.00	1.25
❑ 60	Deuce McAllister	5.00	2.00
❑ 61	Joe Horn	3.00	1.25
❑ 62	Eli Manning	10.00	4.00
❑ 63	Jeremy Shockey	5.00	2.00
❑ 64	Tiki Barber	5.00	2.00
❑ 65	Chad Pennington	5.00	2.00
❑ 66	Curtis Martin	5.00	2.00
❑ 67	Laveranues Coles	3.00	1.25
❑ 68	Kerry Collins	3.00	1.25
❑ 69	LaMont Jordan	5.00	2.00
❑ 70	Randy Moss	5.00	2.00
❑ 71	Donovan McNabb	6.00	2.50
❑ 72	Terrell Owens	5.00	2.00
❑ 73	Brian Dawkins	2.50	1.00
❑ 74	Brian Westbrook	3.00	1.25
❑ 75	Ben Roethlisberger	12.00	5.00
❑ 76	Jerome Bettis	5.00	2.00
❑ 77	Hines Ward	5.00	2.00
❑ 78	Duce Staley	3.00	1.25
❑ 79	Drew Brees	5.00	2.00
❑ 80	LaDainian Tomlinson	6.00	2.50
❑ 81	Antonio Gates	5.00	2.00
❑ 82	Tim Rattay	2.50	1.00
❑ 83	Kevan Barlow	3.00	1.25
❑ 84	Eric Johnson	3.00	1.25
❑ 85	Shaun Alexander	6.00	2.50
❑ 86	Darrell Jackson	3.00	1.25
❑ 87	Matt Hasselbeck	3.00	1.25
❑ 88	Marc Bulger	5.00	2.00
❑ 89	Steven Jackson	6.00	2.50
❑ 90	Marshall Faulk	5.00	2.00
❑ 91	Torry Holt	5.00	2.00
❑ 92	Michael Pittman	2.50	1.00
❑ 93	Brian Griese	3.00	1.25
❑ 94	Michael Clayton	5.00	2.00
❑ 95	Steve McNair	5.00	2.00
❑ 96	Drew Bennett	3.00	1.25
❑ 97	Chris Brown	3.00	1.25
❑ 98	Clinton Portis	5.00	2.00
❑ 99	Patrick Ramsey	3.00	1.25
❑ 100	Santana Moss	3.00	1.25
❑ 101	James Kilian RC	10.00	4.00
❑ 102	Marlin Jackson RC	10.00	4.00
❑ 103	Corey Webster RC	10.00	4.00
❑ 104	Ryan Claridge RC	8.00	3.00
❑ 105	David Pollack RC	10.00	4.00
❑ 106	Deandra Cobb RC	8.00	3.00
❑ 107	Anttaj Hawthorne RC	8.00	3.00
❑ 108	Erasmus James RC	10.00	4.00
❑ 109	Dan Cody RC	10.00	4.00
❑ 110	Jerome Mathis RC	10.00	4.00
❑ 111	Barrett Ruud RC	10.00	4.00
❑ 112	Kevin Burnett RC	10.00	4.00
❑ 113	Jason White RC	10.00	4.00
❑ 114	Chase Lyman RC	8.00	3.00
❑ 115	Cedric Houston RC	10.00	4.00
❑ 116	Roydell Williams RC	10.00	4.00
❑ 117	Fred Gibson RC	8.00	3.00
❑ 118	Dustin Colquitt RC	8.00	3.00
❑ 119	Rasheed Marshall RC	10.00	4.00
❑ 120	Walter Reyes RC	8.00	3.00
❑ 121	Craig Bragg RC	8.00	3.00
❑ 122	Marcus Maxwell RC	8.00	3.00
❑ 123	LeRon McCoy RC	8.00	3.00
❑ 124	Harry Williams RC	8.00	3.00
❑ 125	Larry Brackins RC	8.00	3.00
❑ 126	J.R. Russell RC	8.00	3.00
❑ 127	Manuel White RC	8.00	3.00
❑ 128	Brandon Jones RC	10.00	4.00
❑ 129	Eric King RC	8.00	3.00
❑ 130	Travis Johnson RC	8.00	3.00
❑ 131	Mike Patterson RC	10.00	4.00
❑ 132	Marcus Spears RC	10.00	4.00
❑ 133	Darryl Blackstock RC	8.00	3.00
❑ 134	Michael Boley RC	8.00	3.00
❑ 135	Leroy Hill RC	10.00	4.00
❑ 136	Channing Crowder RC	10.00	4.00
❑ 137	Odell Thurman RC	10.00	4.00
❑ 138	Lance Mitchell RC	8.00	3.00
❑ 139	Jerome Collins RC	8.00	3.00
❑ 140	Stanford Routt RC	8.00	3.00
❑ 141	Justin Miller RC	8.00	3.00
❑ 142	Bryant McFadden RC	10.00	4.00
❑ 143	Eric Green RC	5.00	2.00
❑ 144	Fabian Washington RC	10.00	4.00
❑ 145	Antonio Perkins RC	8.00	3.00
❑ 146	Shaun Cody RC	10.00	4.00
❑ 147	Jonathan Babineaux RC	8.00	3.00
❑ 148	Ronald Bartell RC	8.00	3.00
❑ 149	Luis Castillo RC	10.00	4.00
❑ 150	Chris Carr RC	10.00	4.00
❑ 151	Justin Tuck RC	10.00	4.00
❑ 152	Brodney Pool RC	10.00	4.00
❑ 153	Matt Roth RC	10.00	4.00
❑ 154	DeMarcus Ware RC	15.00	6.00
❑ 155	Josh Bullocks RC	10.00	4.00
❑ 156	Vincent Fuller RC	8.00	3.00
❑ 157	Donte Nicholson RC	10.00	4.00
❑ 158	Rashied Davis RC	10.00	4.00
❑ 159	Nick Collins RC	10.00	4.00
❑ 160	Mike Nugent RC	10.00	4.00
❑ 161	Tyson Thompson RC	15.00	6.00
❑ 162	Darrent Williams RC	10.00	4.00
❑ 163	Kelvin Hayden RC	8.00	3.00
❑ 164	Oshiomogho Atogwe RC	8.00	3.00
❑ 165	Ryan Fitzpatrick RC	15.00	6.00
❑ 166	Stanley Wilson RC	8.00	3.00
❑ 167	Vonta Leach RC	10.00	4.00
❑ 168	Ellis Hobbs RC	10.00	4.00
❑ 169	Scott Starks RC	8.00	3.00
❑ 170	Lionel Gates RC	8.00	3.00
❑ 171	Alvin Pearman RC	10.00	4.00
❑ 172	Damien Nash RC	8.00	3.00
❑ 173	Noah Herron RC	10.00	4.00
❑ 174	Domonique Foxworth RC	10.00	4.00
❑ 175	Derrick Johnson CB RC	10.00	4.00
❑ 176	Lofa Tatupu RC	20.00	7.50
❑ 177	Daven Holly RC	10.00	4.00
❑ 178	Dante Ridgeway RC	8.00	3.00
❑ 179	Airese Currie RC	10.00	4.00
❑ 180	Adam Bergen RC	10.00	4.00
❑ 181	Kirk Morrison RC	10.00	4.00
❑ 182	Alfred Fincher RC	8.00	3.00
❑ 183	Jordan Beck RC	8.00	3.00
❑ 184	Sean Considine RC	10.00	4.00
❑ 185	Tab Perry RC	10.00	4.00
❑ 186	Travis Daniels RC	8.00	3.00
❑ 187	Paris Warren RC	8.00	3.00
❑ 188	Marviel Underwood RC	8.00	3.00
❑ 189	Jerome Carter RC	8.00	3.00
❑ 190	Kerry Rhodes RC	10.00	4.00
❑ 191	James Sanders RC	10.00	4.00
❑ 192	Stephen Spach RC	8.00	3.00
❑ 193	Bo Scaife RC	8.00	3.00
❑ 194	Andre Frazier RC	15.00	6.00
❑ 195	Alex Barron RC	5.00	2.00
❑ 196	Jammal Brown RC	10.00	4.00
❑ 197	Nehemiah Broughton RC	8.00	3.00
❑ 198	Elton Brown RC	5.00	2.00
❑ 199	David Baas RC	8.00	3.00
❑ 200	Joel Dreessen RC	8.00	3.00
❑ 201	Maurice Clarett AU/120	20.00	7.50
❑ 202	Craphonso Thorpe AU RC	15.00	6.00
❑ 203	Adam Jones AU RC	20.00	7.50
❑ 204	Mark Bradley AU RC	25.00	10.00
❑ 205	Vincent Jackson AU RC	25.00	10.00
❑ 206	Antrel Rolle AU RC	20.00	7.50
❑ 207	Heath Miller AU RC	80.00	30.00
❑ 208	Anthony Davis AU RC	15.00	6.00
❑ 209	Terrence Murphy AU RC	20.00	7.50
❑ 210	Chris Henry AU RC	25.00	12.50
❑ 211	Roscoe Parrish AU RC	20.00	7.50
❑ 212	Stefan LeFors AU RC	20.00	7.50
❑ 213	Derek Anderson AU RC	40.00	25.00
❑ 214	Darren Sproles AU RC	20.00	7.50
❑ 215	Adrian McPherson AU RC	20.00	7.50
❑ 216	Frank Gore AU RC	100.00	60.00
❑ 217	Marion Barber AU RC	60.00	35.00
❑ 218	Ryan Moats AU RC	25.00	12.50
❑ 219	Carlos Rogers AU RC	25.00	10.00
❑ 220	Vernand Morency AU RC	15.00	6.00
❑ 221	J.J. Arrington AU RC	25.00	10.00
❑ 222	Courtney Roby AU RC	20.00	7.50
❑ 223	Dan Orlovsky AU RC	25.00	10.00
❑ 224	Kyle Orton AU RC	40.00	15.00
❑ 225	David Greene AU RC	20.00	7.50
❑ 226	Roddy White AU/150 RC	30.00	12.50
❑ 227	Matt Jones AU/99 RC	100.00	50.00
❑ 228	Reggie Brown AU/150 RC	40.00	20.00
❑ 229	Mark Clayton AU/150 RC	40.00	20.00
❑ 230	Eric Shelton AU/150 RC	20.00	7.50
❑ 231	Ciatrick Fason AU/150 RC	20.00	7.50
❑ 232	Jason Campbell AU/150 RC	100.00	50.00
❑ 233	Charlie Frye AU/150 RC	80.00	30.00
❑ 234	Andrew Walter AU/150 RC	40.00	15.00
❑ 235	Troy Williamson AU/120 RC	50.00	30.00
❑ 236	Braylon Edwards AU/99 RC	120.00	60.00
❑ 237	Mike Williams AU/99	60.00	30.00
❑ 238	Cedric Benson AU/99 RC	150.00	75.00
❑ 239	Cadillac Williams AU/99 RC	175.00	90.00
❑ 240	Ronnie Brown AU/99 RC	175.00	90.00
❑ 241	Alex Smith QB AU/99 RC	175.00	100.00
❑ 242	Aaron Rodgers AU/99 RC	150.00	75.00
❑ 243	Matt Cassel AU RC	40.00	20.00
❑ 244	Brandon Jacobs AU RC	80.00	40.00
❑ 245	Alex Smith TE AU RC	20.00	7.50
❑ 246	Derrick Johnson AU RC	40.00	15.00
❑ 247	Chad Owens AU RC	30.00	15.00
❑ 248	Thomas Davis AU RC	20.00	7.50

❑ 249 Shawne Merriman AU RC 60.00 30.00
❑ 250 Gino Guidugli RC 5.00 2.00
❑ 251 Timmy Chang RC 8.00 3.00
❑ 252 Todd Mortensen RC 8.00 3.00
❑ 253 Bryan Randall RC 8.00 3.00
❑ 254 Brock Berlin RC 8.00 3.00
❑ 255 T.A. McLendon RC 5.00 2.00
❑ 256 Kay-Jay Harris RC 8.00 3.00
❑ 257 Bobby Purify RC 8.00 3.00
❑ 258 Steve Savoy RC 5.00 2.00
❑ 259 Keron Henry RC 5.00 2.00
❑ 260 Josh Davis RC 8.00 3.00
❑ 261 Chauncey Stovall RC 5.00 2.00
❑ 262 Efrem Hill RC 8.00 3.00
❑ 263 Sione Pouha RC 10.00 4.00
❑ 264 Jesse Lumsden RC 5.00 2.00
❑ 265 Vincent Burns RC 8.00 3.00
❑ 266 Brady Poppinga RC 10.00 4.00
❑ 267 Boomer Grigsby RC 15.00 6.00
❑ 268 Robert McCune RC 8.00 3.00
❑ 269 Fred Amey RC 8.00 3.00
❑ 270 T.J. Duckett 3.00 1.25
❑ 271 Jamal Lewis 5.00 2.00
❑ 272 Rod Gardner 3.00 1.25
❑ 273 Thomas Jones 3.00 1.25
❑ 274 Jason Witten 3.00 1.25
❑ 275 Roy Williams S 3.00 1.25
❑ 276 Mike Anderson 3.00 1.25
❑ 277 Joey Harrington 5.00 2.00
❑ 278 Charles Rogers 3.00 1.25
❑ 279 Donald Driver 3.00 1.25
❑ 280 Jabar Gaffney 2.50 1.00
❑ 281 Reggie Williams 3.00 1.25
❑ 282 Tony Gonzalez 3.00 1.25
❑ 283 Ricky Williams 3.00 1.25
❑ 284 Mewelde Moore 2.50 1.00
❑ 285 Plaxico Burress 3.00 1.25
❑ 286 Jerry Porter 3.00 1.25
❑ 287 Brandon Lloyd 2.50 1.00
❑ 288 Isaac Bruce 3.00 1.25
❑ 289 LaVar Arrington 5.00 2.00

1991 Ultra

❑ COMPLETE SET (300) 20.00 7.50
❑ 1 Don Beebe .05 .01
❑ 2 Shane Conlan .05 .01
❑ 3 Pete Metzelaars .05 .01
❑ 4 Jamie Mueller .05 .01
❑ 5 Scott Norwood .05 .01
❑ 6 Andre Reed .10 .02
❑ 7 Leon Seals .05 .01
❑ 8 Bruce Smith .25 .08
❑ 9 Leonard Smith .05 .01
❑ 10 Thurman Thomas .25 .08
❑ 11 Lewis Billups .05 .01
❑ 12 Jim Breech .05 .01
❑ 13 James Brooks .10 .02
❑ 14 Eddie Brown .05 .01
❑ 15 Boomer Esiason .10 .02
❑ 16 David Fulcher .05 .01
❑ 17 Rodney Holman .05 .01
❑ 18 Bruce Kozerski .05 .01
❑ 19 Tim Krumrie .05 .01
❑ 20 Tim McGee .05 .01
❑ 21 Anthony Munoz .10 .02
❑ 22 Leon White .05 .01
❑ 23 Ickey Woods .05 .01
❑ 24 Carl Zander .05 .01
❑ 25 Brian Brennan .05 .01
❑ 26 Thane Gash .05 .01
❑ 27 Leroy Hoard .10 .02
❑ 28 Mike Johnson .05 .01
❑ 29 Reggie Langhorne .05 .01
❑ 30 Kevin Mack .05 .01
❑ 31 Clay Matthews .10 .02
❑ 32 Eric Metcalf .10 .02
❑ 33 Steve Atwater .05 .01
❑ 34 Melvin Bratton .05 .01
❑ 35 John Elway 1.25 .50
❑ 36 Bobby Humphrey .05 .01
❑ 37 Mark Jackson .05 .01
❑ 38 Vance Johnson .05 .01
❑ 39 Ricky Nattiel .05 .01
❑ 40 Steve Sewell .05 .01
❑ 41 Dennis Smith .05 .01
❑ 42 David Treadwell .05 .01
❑ 43 Michael Young .05 .01
❑ 44 Ray Childress .05 .01
❑ 45 Cris Dishman RC .05 .01
❑ 46 William Fuller .10 .02
❑ 47 Ernest Givins .10 .02
❑ 48 John Grimsley UER .05 .01
❑ 49 Drew Hill .05 .01
❑ 50 Haywood Jeffires .10 .02
❑ 51 Sean Jones .10 .02
❑ 52 Johnny Meads .05 .01
❑ 53 Warren Moon .25 .08
❑ 54 Al Smith .05 .01
❑ 55 Lorenzo White .05 .01
❑ 56 Albert Bentley .05 .01
❑ 57 Duane Bickett .05 .01
❑ 58 Bill Brooks .05 .01
❑ 59 Jeff George .25 .08
❑ 60 Mike Prior .05 .01
❑ 61 Rohn Stark .05 .01
❑ 62 Jack Trudeau .05 .01
❑ 63 Clarence Verdin .05 .01
❑ 64 Steve DeBerg .05 .01
❑ 65 Emile Harry .05 .01
❑ 66 Albert Lewis .05 .01
❑ 67 Nick Lowery UER .05 .01
❑ 68 Todd McNair .05 .01
❑ 69 Christian Okoye .05 .01
❑ 70 Stephone Paige .05 .01
❑ 71 Kevin Porter UER .05 .01
❑ 72 Derrick Thomas .25 .08
❑ 73 Robb Thomas .05 .01
❑ 74 Barry Word .05 .01
❑ 75 Marcus Allen .25 .08
❑ 76 Eddie Anderson .05 .01
❑ 77 Tim Brown .25 .08
❑ 78 Mervyn Fernandez .05 .01
❑ 79 Willie Gault .10 .02
❑ 80 Ethan Horton .05 .01
❑ 81 Howie Long .25 .08
❑ 82 Vance Mueller .05 .01
❑ 83 Jay Schroeder .05 .01
❑ 84 Steve Smith .05 .01
❑ 85 Greg Townsend .05 .01
❑ 86 Mark Clayton .10 .02
❑ 87 Jim C. Jensen .05 .01
❑ 88 Dan Marino 1.25 .50
❑ 89 Tim McKyer UER .05 .01
❑ 90 John Offerdahl .05 .01
❑ 91 Louis Oliver .05 .01
❑ 92 Reggie Roby .05 .01
❑ 93 Sammie Smith .05 .01
❑ 94 Hart Lee Dykes .05 .01
❑ 95 Irving Fryar .10 .02
❑ 96 Tommy Hodson .05 .01
❑ 97 Maurice Hurst .05 .01
❑ 98 John Stephens .05 .01
❑ 99 Andre Tippett .05 .01
❑ 100 Mark Boyer .05 .01
❑ 101 Kyle Clifton .05 .01
❑ 102 James Hasty .05 .01
❑ 103 Erik McMillan .05 .01
❑ 104 Rob Moore .25 .08
❑ 105 Joe Mott .05 .01
❑ 106 Ken O'Brien .05 .01
❑ 107 Ron Stallworth UER .05 .01
❑ 108 Al Toon .10 .02
❑ 109 Gary Anderson K .05 .01
❑ 110 Bubby Brister .05 .01
❑ 111 Thomas Everett .05 .01
❑ 112 Merril Hoge .05 .01
❑ 113 Louis Lipps .05 .01
❑ 114 Greg Lloyd .25 .08
❑ 115 Hardy Nickerson .10 .02
❑ 116 Dwight Stone .05 .01
❑ 117 Rod Woodson .25 .08
❑ 118 Tim Worley .05 .01
❑ 119 Rod Bernstine .05 .01
❑ 120 Marion Butts .10 .02
❑ 121 Gill Byrd .05 .01
❑ 122 Arthur Cox .05 .01
❑ 123 Burt Grossman .05 .01
❑ 124 Ronnie Harmon .05 .01
❑ 125 Anthony Miller .10 .02
❑ 126 Leslie O'Neal .10 .02
❑ 127 Gary Plummer .05 .01
❑ 128 Sam Seale .05 .01
❑ 129 Junior Seau .25 .08
❑ 130 Broderick Thompson .05 .01
❑ 131 Billy Joe Tolliver .05 .01
❑ 132 Brian Blades .10 .02
❑ 133 Jeff Bryant .05 .01
❑ 134 Derrick Fenner .05 .01
❑ 135 Jacob Green .05 .01
❑ 136 Andy Heck .05 .01
❑ 137 Patrick Hunter RC UER .05 .01
❑ 138 Norm Johnson .05 .01
❑ 139 Tommy Kane .05 .01
❑ 140 Dave Krieg .10 .02
❑ 141 John L. Williams .05 .01
❑ 142 Terry Wooden .05 .01
❑ 143 Steve Broussard .05 .01
❑ 144 Keith Jones .05 .01
❑ 145 Brian Jordan .10 .02
❑ 146 Chris Miller .10 .02
❑ 147 John Rade .05 .01
❑ 148 Andre Rison .10 .02
❑ 149 Mike Rozier .05 .01
❑ 150 Deion Sanders .40 .15
❑ 151 Neal Anderson .10 .02
❑ 152 Trace Armstrong .05 .01
❑ 153 Kevin Butler .05 .01
❑ 154 Mark Carrier DB .10 .02
❑ 155 Richard Dent .10 .02
❑ 156 Dennis Gentry .05 .01
❑ 157 Jim Harbaugh .25 .08
❑ 158 Brad Muster .05 .01
❑ 159 William Perry .10 .02
❑ 160 Mike Singletary .10 .02
❑ 161 Lemuel Stinson .05 .01
❑ 162 Troy Aikman .75 .30
❑ 163 Michael Irvin .25 .08
❑ 164 Mike Saxon .05 .01
❑ 165 Emmitt Smith 2.50 1.00
❑ 166 Jerry Ball .05 .01
❑ 167 Michael Cofer .05 .01
❑ 168 Rodney Peete .10 .02
❑ 169 Barry Sanders 1.25 .50
❑ 170 Robert Brown .05 .01
❑ 171 Anthony Dilweg .05 .01
❑ 172 Tim Harris .05 .01
❑ 173 Johnny Holland .05 .01
❑ 174 Perry Kemp .05 .01
❑ 175 Don Majkowski .05 .01
❑ 176 Brian Noble .05 .01
❑ 177 Jeff Query .05 .01
❑ 178 Sterling Sharpe .25 .08
❑ 179 Charles Wilson .05 .01
❑ 180 Keith Woodside .05 .01
❑ 181 Flipper Anderson UER .05 .01
❑ 182 Bern Brostek .05 .01
❑ 183 Pat Carter RC .05 .01
❑ 184 Aaron Cox .05 .01
❑ 185 Henry Ellard .10 .02
❑ 186 Jim Everett .10 .02
❑ 187 Cleveland Gary .05 .01
❑ 188 Jerry Gray .05 .01
❑ 189 Kevin Greene .10 .02
❑ 190 Mike Wilcher .05 .01
❑ 191 Alfred Anderson .05 .01
❑ 192 Joey Browner .05 .01
❑ 193 Anthony Carter .10 .02
❑ 194 Chris Doleman .05 .01
❑ 195 Rick Fenney .05 .01
❑ 196 Darrell Fullington .05 .01
❑ 197 Rich Gannon .25 .08
❑ 198 Hassan Jones .05 .01
❑ 199 Steve Jordan .05 .01

❑ 200 Mike Merriweather .05 .01
❑ 201 Al Noga .05 .01
❑ 202 Herschel Walker .10 .02
❑ 203 Wade Wilson .10 .02
❑ 204 Morten Andersen .05 .01
❑ 205 Gene Atkins .05 .01
❑ 206 Toi Cook RC .05 .01
❑ 207 Craig Heyward .10 .02
❑ 208 Dalton Hilliard .05 .01
❑ 209 Vaughan Johnson .05 .01
❑ 210 Eric Martin .05 .01
❑ 211 Brett Perriman .25 .08
❑ 212 Pat Swilling .10 .02
❑ 213 Steve Walsh .05 .01
❑ 214 Ottis Anderson .10 .02
❑ 215 Carl Banks .05 .01
❑ 216 Maurice Carthon .05 .01
❑ 217 Mark Collins .05 .01
❑ 218 Rodney Hampton .25 .08
❑ 219 Erik Howard .05 .01
❑ 220 Mark Ingram .10 .02
❑ 221 Pepper Johnson .05 .01
❑ 222 Dave Meggett .10 .02
❑ 223 Phil Simms .10 .02
❑ 224 Lawrence Taylor .25 .08
❑ 225 Lewis Tillman .05 .01
❑ 226 Everson Walls .05 .01
❑ 227 Fred Barnett .25 .08
❑ 228 Jerome Brown .05 .01
❑ 229 Keith Byars .05 .01
❑ 230 Randall Cunningham .25 .08
❑ 231 Byron Evans .05 .01
❑ 232 Wes Hopkins .05 .01
❑ 233 Keith Jackson .10 .02
❑ 234 Heath Sherman .05 .01
❑ 235 Anthony Toney .05 .01
❑ 236 Reggie White .25 .08
❑ 237 Rich Camarillo .05 .01
❑ 238 Ken Harvey .10 .02
❑ 239 Eric Hill .05 .01
❑ 240 Johnny Johnson .05 .01
❑ 241 Ernie Jones .05 .01
❑ 242 Tim McDonald .05 .01
❑ 243 Timm Rosenbach .05 .01
❑ 244 Jay Taylor .05 .01
❑ 245 Dexter Carter .05 .01
❑ 246 Mike Cofer .05 .01
❑ 247 Kevin Fagan .05 .01
❑ 248 Don Griffin .05 .01
❑ 249 Charles Haley .10 .02
❑ 250 Brent Jones .25 .08
❑ 251 Joe Montana UER 1.25 .50
❑ 252 Darryl Pollard .05 .01
❑ 253 Tom Rathman .05 .01
❑ 254 Jerry Rice .75 .30
❑ 255 John Taylor .10 .02
❑ 256 Steve Young .75 .30
❑ 257 Gary Anderson RB .05 .01
❑ 258 Mark Carrier WR .25 .08
❑ 259 Chris Chandler .25 .08
❑ 260 Reggie Cobb .05 .01
❑ 261 Reuben Davis .05 .01
❑ 262 Willie Drewrey .05 .01
❑ 263 Ron Hall .05 .01
❑ 264 Eugene Marve .05 .01
❑ 265 Winston Moss UER .05 .01
❑ 266 Vinny Testaverde .10 .02
❑ 267 Broderick Thomas .05 .01
❑ 268 Jeff Bostic .05 .01
❑ 269 Earnest Byner .05 .01
❑ 270 Gary Clark .25 .08
❑ 271 Darrell Green .05 .01
❑ 272 Jim Lachey .05 .01
❑ 273 Wilber Marshall .05 .01
❑ 274 Art Monk .10 .02
❑ 275 Gerald Riggs .05 .01
❑ 276 Mark Rypien .10 .02
❑ 277 Ricky Sanders .05 .01
❑ 278 Alvin Walton .05 .01
❑ 279 Nick Bell RC .05 .01
❑ 280 Eric Bieniemy RC .05 .01
❑ 281 Jarrod Bunch RC .05 .01
❑ 282 Mike Croel RC .05 .01
❑ 283 Brett Favre RC 10.00 5.00
❑ 284 Moe Gardner RC .05 .01
❑ 285 Pat Harlow RC .05 .01
❑ 286 Randal Hill RC .10 .02
❑ 287 Todd Marinovich RC .05 .01
❑ 288 Russell Maryland RC .25 .08
❑ 289 Dan McGwire RC .05 .01
❑ 290 Ernie Mills RC UER .10 .02
❑ 291 Herman Moore RC .25 .08
❑ 292 Godfrey Myles RC .05 .01
❑ 293 Browning Nagle RC .05 .01
❑ 294 Mike Pritchard RC .25 .08
❑ 295 Esera Tuaolo RC .05 .01
❑ 296 Mark Vander Poel RC .05 .01
❑ 297 Ricky Watters RC 1.50 .60
❑ 298 Chris Zorich RC .25 .08
❑ 299 Checklist Card .10 .02
❑ 300 Checklist Card .10 .02

1991 Ultra Update

❑ COMP.FACT.SET (100) 25.00 10.00
❑ U1 Brett Favre 20.00 7.50
❑ U2 Moe Gardner .10 .02
❑ U3 Tim McKyer .10 .02
❑ U4 Bruce Pickens RC .10 .02
❑ U5 Mike Pritchard .40 .15
❑ U6 Cornelius Bennett .20 .07
❑ U7 Phil Hansen RC .10 .02
❑ U8 Henry Jones RC .20 .07
❑ U9 Mark Kelso .10 .02
❑ U10 James Lofton .20 .07
❑ U11 Anthony Morgan RC .10 .02
❑ U12 Stan Thomas .10 .02
❑ U13 Chris Zorich .20 .07
❑ U14 Reggie Rembert .10 .02
❑ U15 Alfred Williams RC .10 .02
❑ U16 Michael Jackson RC WR .40 .15
❑ U17 Ed King RC .10 .02
❑ U18 Joe Morris .10 .02
❑ U19 Vince Newsome .10 .02
❑ U20 Tony Casillas .10 .02
❑ U21 Russell Maryland .40 .15
❑ U22 Jay Novacek .40 .15
❑ U23 Mike Croel .10 .02
❑ U24 Gaston Green .10 .02
❑ U25 Kenny Walker RC .10 .02
❑ U26 Melvin Jenkins RC .10 .02
❑ U27 Herman Moore .40 .15
❑ U28 Kelvin Pritchett RC .20 .07
❑ U29 Chris Spielman .20 .07
❑ U30 Vinnie Clark RC .10 .02
❑ U31 Allen Rice .10 .02
❑ U32 Vai Sikahema .10 .02
❑ U33 Esera Tuaolo .10 .02
❑ U34 Mike Dumas RC .10 .02
❑ U35 John Flannery RC .10 .02
❑ U36 Allen Pinkett .10 .02
❑ U37 Tim Barnett RC .10 .02
❑ U38 Dan Saleaumua .10 .02
❑ U39 Harvey Williams RC .40 .15
❑ U40 Nick Bell .10 .02
❑ U41 Roger Craig .20 .07
❑ U42 Ronnie Lott .20 .07
❑ U43 Todd Marinovich .10 .02
❑ U44 Robert Delpino .10 .02
❑ U45 Todd Lyght RC .10 .02
❑ U46 Robert Young RC .20 .07
❑ U47 Aaron Craver RC .10 .02
❑ U48 Mark Higgs RC .10 .02
❑ U49 Vestee Jackson .10 .02
❑ U50 Carl Lee .10 .02
❑ U51 Felix Wright .10 .02
❑ U52 Darrell Fullington .10 .02
❑ U53 Pat Harlow .10 .02
❑ U54 Eugene Lockhart .10 .02
❑ U55 Hugh Millen RC .10 .02
❑ U56 Leonard Russell RC .40 .15
❑ U57 Jon Vaughn RC .10 .02
❑ U58 Quinn Early .20 .07
❑ U59 Bobby Hebert .10 .02
❑ U60 Rickey Jackson .10 .02
❑ U61 Sam Mills .20 .07
❑ U62 Jarrod Bunch .10 .02
❑ U63 John Elliott .10 .02
❑ U64 Jeff Hostetler .20 .07
❑ U65 Ed McCaffrey RC 6.00 2.50
❑ U66 Kanavis McGhee RC .10 .02
❑ U67 Mo Lewis RC .20 .07
❑ U68 Browning Nagle .10 .02
❑ U69 Blair Thomas .10 .02
❑ U70 Antone Davis RC .10 .02
❑ U71 Brad Goebel RC .10 .02
❑ U72 Jim McMahon .20 .07
❑ U73 Clyde Simmons .10 .02
❑ U74 Randal Hill UER U71 .20 .07
❑ U75 Eric Swann RC .40 .15
❑ U76 Tom Tupa .10 .02
❑ U77 Jeff Graham RC WR .40 .15
❑ U78 Eric Green .10 .02
❑ U79 Neil O'Donnell RC .40 .15
❑ U80 Huey Richardson RC .10 .02
❑ U81 Eric Bieniemy .10 .02
❑ U82 John Friesz .40 .15
❑ U83 Eric Moten RC .10 .02
❑ U84 Stanley Richard RC .10 .02
❑ U85 Todd Bowles .10 .02
❑ U86 Merton Hanks RC .40 .15
❑ U87 Tim Harris .10 .02
❑ U88 Pierce Holt .10 .02
❑ U89 Ted Washington RC .10 .02
❑ U90 John Kasay RC .20 .07
❑ U91 Dan McGwire .10 .02
❑ U92 Lawrence Dawsey RC .20 .07
❑ U93 Charles McRae RC .10 .02
❑ U94 Jesse Solomon .10 .02
❑ U95 Robert Wilson RC .10 .02
❑ U96 Ricky Ervins RC .20 .07
❑ U97 Charles Mann .10 .02
❑ U98 Bobby Wilson RC .10 .02
❑ U99 Jerry Rice PV 1.50 .60
❑ U100 Nick Bell/J.McMahon CL .10 .02

1992 Ultra

❑ COMPLETE SET (450) 15.00 6.00
❑ 1 Steve Broussard .10 .02
❑ 2 Rick Bryan .10 .02
❑ 3 Scott Case .10 .02
❑ 4 Darion Conner .10 .02
❑ 5 Bill Fralic .10 .02
❑ 6 Moe Gardner .10 .02
❑ 7 Tim Green .10 .02
❑ 8 Michael Haynes .20 .07
❑ 9 Chris Hinton .10 .02
❑ 10 Mike Kenn .10 .02
❑ 11 Tim McKyer .10 .02
❑ 12 Chris Miller .20 .07
❑ 13 Erric Pegram .20 .07
❑ 14 Mike Pritchard .20 .07
❑ 15 Andre Rison .20 .07
❑ 16 Jessie Tuggle .10 .02
❑ 17 Carlton Bailey RC .10 .02
❑ 18 Howard Ballard .10 .02

❑ 19 Cornelius Bennett	.20	.07
❑ 20 Shane Conlan	.10	.02
❑ 21 Kenneth Davis	.10	.02
❑ 22 Kent Hull	.10	.02
❑ 23 Mark Kelso	.10	.02
❑ 24 James Lofton	.20	.07
❑ 25 Keith McKeller	.10	.02
❑ 26 Nate Odomes	.10	.02
❑ 27 Jim Ritcher	.10	.02
❑ 28 Leon Seals	.10	.02
❑ 29 Darryl Talley	.10	.02
❑ 30 Steve Tasker	.20	.07
❑ 31 Thurman Thomas	.40	.15
❑ 32 Will Wolford	.10	.02
❑ 33 Jeff Wright	.10	.02
❑ 34 Neal Anderson	.10	.02
❑ 35 Trace Armstrong	.10	.02
❑ 36 Mark Carrier DB	.10	.02
❑ 37 Wendell Davis	.10	.02
❑ 38 Richard Dent	.20	.07
❑ 39 Shaun Gayle	.10	.02
❑ 40 Jim Harbaugh	.40	.15
❑ 41 Jay Hilgenberg	.10	.02
❑ 42 Darren Lewis	.10	.02
❑ 43 Steve McMichael	.20	.07
❑ 44 Anthony Morgan	.10	.02
❑ 45 Brad Muster	.10	.02
❑ 46 William Perry	.20	.07
❑ 47 John Roper	.10	.02
❑ 48 Lemuel Stinson	.10	.02
❑ 49 Tom Waddle	.10	.02
❑ 50 Donnell Woolford	.10	.02
❑ 51 Leo Barker RC	.10	.02
❑ 52 Eddie Brown	.10	.02
❑ 53 James Francis	.10	.02
❑ 54 David Fulcher UER	.10	.02
❑ 55 David Grant	.10	.02
❑ 56 Harold Green	.10	.02
❑ 57 Rodney Holman	.10	.02
❑ 58 Lee Johnson	.10	.02
❑ 59 Tim Krumrie	.10	.02
❑ 60 Tim McGee	.10	.02
❑ 61 Alonzo Mitz RC	.10	.02
❑ 62 Anthony Munoz	.20	.07
❑ 63 Alfred Williams	.10	.02
❑ 64 Stephen Braggs	.10	.02
❑ 65 Richard Brown RC	.10	.02
❑ 66 Randy Hilliard RC	.10	.02
❑ 67 Leroy Hoard	.20	.07
❑ 68 Michael Jackson	.20	.07
❑ 69 Mike Johnson	.10	.02
❑ 70 James Jones DT	.10	.02
❑ 71 Tony Jones T	.10	.02
❑ 72 Ed King	.10	.02
❑ 73 Kevin Mack	.10	.02
❑ 74 Clay Matthews	.20	.07
❑ 75 Eric Metcalf	.20	.07
❑ 76 Vince Newsome	.10	.02
❑ 77 Steve Beuerlein	.20	.07
❑ 78 Larry Brown DB	.10	.02
❑ 79 Tony Casillas	.10	.02
❑ 80 Alvin Harper	.20	.07
❑ 81 Issiac Holt	.10	.02
❑ 82 Ray Horton	.10	.02
❑ 83 Michael Irvin	.40	.15
❑ 84 Daryl Johnston	.40	.15
❑ 85 Kelvin Martin	.10	.02
❑ 86 Ken Norton	.20	.07
❑ 87 Jay Novacek	.20	.07
❑ 88 Emmitt Smith	3.00	1.50
❑ 89 Vinson Smith RC	.10	.02
❑ 90 Mark Stepnoski	.20	.07
❑ 91 Tony Tolbert	.10	.02
❑ 92 Alexander Wright	.10	.02
❑ 93 Steve Atwater	.10	.02
❑ 94 Tyrone Braxton	.10	.02
❑ 95 Michael Brooks	.10	.02
❑ 96 Mike Croel	.10	.02
❑ 97 John Elway	2.50	1.00
❑ 98 Simon Fletcher	.10	.02
❑ 99 Gaston Green	.10	.02
❑ 100 Mark Jackson	.10	.02
❑ 101 Keith Kartz	.10	.02
❑ 102 Greg Kragen	.10	.02
❑ 103 Greg Lewis	.10	.02
❑ 104 Karl Mecklenburg	.10	.02
❑ 105 Derek Russell	.10	.02
❑ 106 Steve Sewell	.10	.02
❑ 107 Dennis Smith	.10	.02
❑ 108 David Treadwell	.10	.02
❑ 109 Kenny Walker	.10	.02
❑ 110 Michael Young	.10	.02
❑ 111 Jerry Ball	.10	.02
❑ 112 Bennie Blades	.10	.02
❑ 113 Lomas Brown	.10	.02
❑ 114 Scott Conover RC	.10	.02
❑ 115 Ray Crockett	.10	.02
❑ 116 Mel Gray	.20	.07
❑ 117 Willie Green	.10	.02
❑ 118 Erik Kramer	.20	.07
❑ 119 Dan Owens	.10	.02
❑ 120 Rodney Peete	.20	.07
❑ 121 Brett Perriman	.40	.15
❑ 122 Barry Sanders	2.50	1.00
❑ 123 Chris Spielman	.20	.07
❑ 124 Marc Spindler	.10	.02
❑ 125 William White	.10	.02
❑ 126 Tony Bennett	.10	.02
❑ 127 Matt Brock	.10	.02
❑ 128 LeRoy Butler	.10	.02
❑ 129 Chuck Cecil	.10	.02
❑ 130 Johnny Holland	.10	.02
❑ 131 Perry Kemp	.10	.02
❑ 132 Don Majkowski	.10	.02
❑ 133 Tony Mandarich	.10	.02
❑ 134 Brian Noble	.10	.02
❑ 135 Bryce Paup	.40	.15
❑ 136 Sterling Sharpe	.40	.15
❑ 137 Darrell Thompson	.10	.02
❑ 138 Mike Tomczak	.10	.02
❑ 139 Vince Workman	.10	.02
❑ 140 Ray Childress	.10	.02
❑ 141 Cris Dishman	.10	.02
❑ 142 Curtis Duncan	.10	.02
❑ 143 William Fuller	.10	.02
❑ 144 Ernest Givins	.20	.07
❑ 145 Haywood Jeffires	.20	.07
❑ 146 Sean Jones	.10	.02
❑ 147 Lamar Lathon	.10	.02
❑ 148 Bruce Matthews	.10	.02
❑ 149 Bubba McDowell	.10	.02
❑ 150 Johnny Meads	.10	.02
❑ 151 Warren Moon	.40	.15
❑ 152 Mike Munchak	.20	.07
❑ 153 Bo Orlando RC	.10	.02
❑ 154 Al Smith	.10	.02
❑ 155 Doug Smith	.10	.02
❑ 156 Lorenzo White	.10	.02
❑ 157 Chip Banks	.10	.02
❑ 158 Duane Bickett	.10	.02
❑ 159 Bill Brooks	.10	.02
❑ 160 Eugene Daniel	.10	.02
❑ 161 Jon Hand	.10	.02
❑ 162 Jeff Herrod	.10	.02
❑ 163 Jessie Hester	.10	.02
❑ 164 Scott Radecic	.10	.02
❑ 165 Rohn Stark	.10	.02
❑ 166 Clarence Verdin	.10	.02
❑ 167 John Alt	.10	.02
❑ 168 Tim Barnett	.10	.02
❑ 169 Tim Grunhard	.10	.02
❑ 170 Dino Hackett	.10	.02
❑ 171 Jonathan Hayes	.10	.02
❑ 172 Bill Maas	.10	.02
❑ 173 Chris Martin	.10	.02
❑ 174 Christian Okoye	.10	.02
❑ 175 Stephone Paige	.10	.02
❑ 176 Jayice Pearson RC	.10	.02
❑ 177 Kevin Porter	.10	.02
❑ 178 Kevin Ross	.10	.02
❑ 179 Dan Saleaumua	.10	.02
❑ 180 Tracy Simien RC	.10	.02
❑ 181 Neil Smith	.40	.15
❑ 182 Derrick Thomas	.40	.15
❑ 183 Robb Thomas	.10	.02
❑ 184 Barry Word	.10	.02
❑ 185 Marcus Allen	.40	.15
❑ 186 Eddie Anderson	.10	.02
❑ 187 Nick Bell	.10	.02
❑ 188 Tim Brown	.40	.15
❑ 189 Mervyn Fernandez	.10	.02
❑ 190 Willie Gault	.20	.07
❑ 191 Jeff Gossett	.10	.02
❑ 192 Ethan Horton	.10	.02
❑ 193 Jeff Jaeger	.10	.02
❑ 194 Howie Long	.40	.15
❑ 195 Ronnie Lott	.20	.07
❑ 196 Todd Marinovich	.10	.02
❑ 197 Don Mosebar	.10	.02
❑ 198 Jay Schroeder	.10	.02
❑ 199 Anthony Smith	.10	.02
❑ 200 Greg Townsend	.10	.02
❑ 201 Lionel Washington	.10	.02
❑ 202 Steve Wisniewski	.10	.02
❑ 203 Flipper Anderson	.10	.02
❑ 204 Robert Delpino	.10	.02
❑ 205 Henry Ellard	.20	.07
❑ 206 Jim Everett	.20	.07
❑ 207 Kevin Greene	.20	.07
❑ 208 Darryl Henley	.10	.02
❑ 209 Damone Johnson	.10	.02
❑ 210 Larry Kelm	.10	.02
❑ 211 Todd Lyght	.10	.02
❑ 212 Jackie Slater	.10	.02
❑ 213 Michael Stewart	.10	.02
❑ 214 Pat Terrell	.10	.02
❑ 215 Robert Young	.10	.02
❑ 216 Mark Clayton	.20	.07
❑ 217 Bryan Cox	.20	.07
❑ 218 Jeff Cross	.10	.02
❑ 219 Mark Duper	.10	.02
❑ 220 Harry Galbreath	.10	.02
❑ 221 David Griggs	.10	.02
❑ 222 Mark Higgs	.10	.02
❑ 223 Vestee Jackson	.10	.02
❑ 224 John Offerdahl	.10	.02
❑ 225 Louis Oliver	.10	.02
❑ 226 Tony Paige	.10	.02
❑ 227 Reggie Roby	.10	.02
❑ 228 Pete Stoyanovich	.10	.02
❑ 229 Richmond Webb	.10	.02
❑ 230 Terry Allen	.40	.15
❑ 231 Ray Berry	.10	.02
❑ 232 Anthony Carter	.20	.07
❑ 233 Cris Carter	.75	.30
❑ 234 Chris Doleman	.10	.02
❑ 235 Rich Gannon	.40	.15
❑ 236 Steve Jordan	.10	.02
❑ 237 Carl Lee	.10	.02
❑ 238 Randall McDaniel	.10	.02
❑ 239 Mike Merriweather	.10	.02
❑ 240 Harry Newsome	.10	.02
❑ 241 John Randle	.20	.07
❑ 242 Henry Thomas	.10	.02
❑ 243 Bruce Armstrong	.10	.02
❑ 244 Vincent Brown	.10	.02
❑ 245 Marv Cook	.10	.02
❑ 246 Irving Fryar	.20	.07
❑ 247 Pat Harlow	.10	.02
❑ 248 Maurice Hurst	.10	.02
❑ 249 Eugene Lockhart	.10	.02
❑ 250 Greg McMurtry	.10	.02
❑ 251 Hugh Millen	.10	.02
❑ 252 Leonard Russell	.20	.07
❑ 253 Chris Singleton	.10	.02
❑ 254 Andre Tippett	.10	.02
❑ 255 Jon Vaughn	.10	.02
❑ 256 Morten Andersen	.10	.02
❑ 257 Gene Atkins	.10	.02
❑ 258 Wesley Carroll	.10	.02
❑ 259 Jim Dombrowski	.10	.02
❑ 260 Quinn Early	.20	.07
❑ 261 Bobby Hebert	.10	.02
❑ 262 Joel Hilgenberg	.10	.02
❑ 263 Rickey Jackson	.10	.02
❑ 264 Vaughan Johnson	.10	.02
❑ 265 Eric Martin	.10	.02
❑ 266 Brett Maxie	.10	.02
❑ 267 Fred McAfee RC	.10	.02
❑ 268 Sam Mills	.10	.02
❑ 269 Pat Swilling	.10	.02
❑ 270 Floyd Turner	.10	.02
❑ 271 Steve Walsh	.10	.02
❑ 272 Stephen Baker	.10	.02
❑ 273 Jarrod Bunch	.10	.02
❑ 274 Mark Collins	.10	.02
❑ 275 John Elliott	.10	.02
❑ 276 Myron Guyton	.10	.02
❑ 277 Rodney Hampton	.20	.07
❑ 278 Jeff Hostetler	.20	.07
❑ 279 Mark Ingram	.10	.02

❑ 280 Pepper Johnson .10 .02
❑ 281 Sean Landeta .10 .02
❑ 282 Leonard Marshall .10 .02
❑ 283 Kanavis McGhee .10 .02
❑ 284 Dave Meggett .20 .07
❑ 285 Bart Oates .10 .02
❑ 286 Phil Simms .20 .07
❑ 287 Reyna Thompson .10 .02
❑ 288 Lewis Tillman .10 .02
❑ 289 Brad Baxter .10 .02
❑ 290 Mike Brim RC .10 .02
❑ 291 Chris Burkett .10 .02
❑ 292 Kyle Clifton .10 .02
❑ 293 James Hasty .10 .02
❑ 294 Joe Kelly .10 .02
❑ 295 Jeff Lageman .10 .02
❑ 296 Mo Lewis .10 .02
❑ 297 Erik McMillan .10 .02
❑ 298 Scott Mersereau .10 .02
❑ 299 Rob Moore .20 .07
❑ 300 Tony Stargell .10 .02
❑ 301 Jim Sweeney .10 .02
❑ 302 Marvin Washington .10 .02
❑ 303 Lonnie Young .10 .02
❑ 304 Eric Allen .10 .02
❑ 305 Fred Barnett .40 .15
❑ 306 Keith Byars .10 .02
❑ 307 Byron Evans .10 .02
❑ 308 Wes Hopkins .10 .02
❑ 309 Keith Jackson .20 .07
❑ 310 James Joseph .10 .02
❑ 311 Seth Joyner .10 .02
❑ 312 Roger Ruzek .10 .02
❑ 313 Clyde Simmons .10 .02
❑ 314 William Thomas .10 .02
❑ 315 Reggie White .40 .15
❑ 316 Calvin Williams .20 .07
❑ 317 Rich Camarillo .10 .02
❑ 318 Jeff Faulkner .10 .02
❑ 319 Ken Harvey .10 .02
❑ 320 Eric Hill .10 .02
❑ 321 Johnny Johnson .10 .02
❑ 322 Ernie Jones .10 .02
❑ 323 Tim McDonald .10 .02
❑ 324 Freddie Joe Nunn .10 .02
❑ 325 Luis Sharpe .10 .02
❑ 326 Eric Swann .20 .07
❑ 327 Aeneas Williams .20 .07
❑ 328 Michael Zordich RC .10 .02
❑ 329 Gary Anderson K .10 .02
❑ 330 Bubby Brister .10 .02
❑ 331 Barry Foster .20 .07
❑ 332 Eric Green .10 .02
❑ 333 Bryan Hinkle .10 .02
❑ 334 Tunch Ilkin .10 .02
❑ 335 Carnell Lake .10 .02
❑ 336 Louis Lipps .10 .02
❑ 337 David Little .10 .02
❑ 338 Greg Lloyd .20 .07
❑ 339 Neil O'Donnell .20 .07
❑ 340 Rod Woodson .40 .15
❑ 341 Rod Bernstine .10 .02
❑ 342 Marion Butts .10 .02
❑ 343 Gill Byrd .10 .02
❑ 344 John Friesz .20 .07
❑ 345 Burt Grossman .10 .02
❑ 346 Courtney Hall .10 .02
❑ 347 Ronnie Harmon .10 .02
❑ 348 Shawn Jefferson .10 .02
❑ 349 Nate Lewis .10 .02
❑ 350 Craig McEwen RC .10 .02
❑ 351 Eric Moten .10 .02
❑ 352 Gary Plummer .10 .02
❑ 353 Henry Rolling .10 .02
❑ 354 Broderick Thompson .10 .02
❑ 355 Derrick Walker .10 .02
❑ 356 Harris Barton .10 .02
❑ 357 Steve Bono RC .40 .15
❑ 358 Todd Bowles .10 .02
❑ 359 Dexter Carter .10 .02
❑ 360 Michael Carter .10 .02
❑ 361 Keith DeLong .10 .02
❑ 362 Charles Haley .20 .07
❑ 363 Merton Hanks .20 .07
❑ 364 Tim Harris .10 .02
❑ 365 Brent Jones .20 .07
❑ 366 Guy McIntyre .10 .02
❑ 367 Tom Rathman .10 .02
❑ 368 Bill Romanowski .10 .02
❑ 369 Jesse Sapolu .10 .02
❑ 370 John Taylor .20 .07
❑ 371 Steve Young 1.50 .60
❑ 372 Robert Blackmon .10 .02
❑ 373 Brian Blades .20 .07
❑ 374 Jacob Green .10 .02
❑ 375 Dwayne Harper .10 .02
❑ 376 Andy Heck .10 .02
❑ 377 Tommy Kane .10 .02
❑ 378 John Kasay .10 .02
❑ 379 Cortez Kennedy .20 .07
❑ 380 Bryan Millard .10 .02
❑ 381 Rufus Porter .10 .02
❑ 382 Eugene Robinson .10 .02
❑ 383 John L. Williams .10 .02
❑ 384 Terry Wooden .10 .02
❑ 385 Gary Anderson RB .10 .02
❑ 386 Ian Beckles .10 .02
❑ 387 Mark Carrier WR .20 .07
❑ 388 Reggie Cobb .10 .02
❑ 389 Tony Covington .10 .02
❑ 390 Lawrence Dawsey .20 .07
❑ 391 Ron Hall .10 .02
❑ 392 Keith McCants .10 .02
❑ 393 Charles McRae .10 .02
❑ 394 Tim Newton .10 .02
❑ 395 Jesse Solomon .10 .02
❑ 396 Vinny Testaverde .20 .07
❑ 397 Broderick Thomas .10 .02
❑ 398 Robert Wilson .10 .02
❑ 399 Earnest Byner .10 .02
❑ 400 Gary Clark .40 .15
❑ 401 Andre Collins .10 .02
❑ 402 Brad Edwards .10 .02
❑ 403 Kurt Gouveia .10 .02
❑ 404 Darrell Green .10 .02
❑ 405 Joe Jacoby .10 .02
❑ 406 Jim Lachey .10 .02
❑ 407 Chip Lohmiller .10 .02
❑ 408 Charles Mann .10 .02
❑ 409 Wilber Marshall .10 .02
❑ 410 Brian Mitchell .20 .07
❑ 411 Art Monk .20 .07
❑ 412 Mark Rypien .10 .02
❑ 413 Ricky Sanders .10 .02
❑ 414 Mark Schlereth RC .10 .02
❑ 415 Fred Stokes .10 .02
❑ 416 Bobby Wilson .10 .02
❑ 417 Corey Barlow RC .10 .02
❑ 418 Edgar Bennett RC .40 .15
❑ 419 Eddie Blake RC .10 .02
❑ 420 Terrell Buckley RC .10 .02
❑ 421 Willie Clay RC .10 .02
❑ 422 Rodney Culver RC .10 .02
❑ 423 Ed Cunningham RC .10 .02
❑ 424 Mark D'Onofrio RC .10 .02
❑ 425 Matt Darby RC .10 .02
❑ 426 Charles Davenport RC .10 .02
❑ 427 Will Furrer RC .10 .02
❑ 428 Keith Goganious RC .10 .02
❑ 429 Mario Bailey RC .10 .02
❑ 430 Chris Hakel RC .10 .02
❑ 431 Keith Hamilton RC .20 .07
❑ 432 Aaron Pierce RC .10 .02
❑ 433 Amp Lee RC .10 .02
❑ 434 Scott Lockwood RC .10 .02
❑ 435 Ricardo McDonald RC .10 .02
❑ 436 Dexter McNabb RC .10 .02
❑ 437 Chris Mims RC .10 .02
❑ 438 Mike Mooney RC .10 .02
❑ 439 Ray Roberts RC .10 .02
❑ 440 Patrick Rowe RC .10 .02
❑ 441 Leon Searcy RC .10 .02
❑ 442 Siran Stacy RC .10 .02
❑ 443 Kevin Turner RC .10 .02
❑ 444 Tommy Vardell RC .10 .02
❑ 445 Bob Whitfield RC .10 .02
❑ 446 Darryl Williams RC .10 .02
❑ 447 Checklist 1-110 .10 .02
❑ 448 Checklist 111-224 .10 .02
❑ 449 Checklist 230-340 UER .10 .02
❑ 450 Checklist 341-450 .10 .02
❑ AD Super Bowl XXVII Strip 2.00 .75

1993 Ultra

❑ COMPLETE SET (500) 20.00 7.50
❑ 1 Vinnie Clark .10 .02
❑ 2 Darion Conner .10 .02
❑ 3 Eric Dickerson .20 .07
❑ 4 Moe Gardner .10 .02
❑ 5 Tim Green .10 .02
❑ 6 Roger Harper RC .10 .02
❑ 7 Michael Haynes .20 .07
❑ 8 Bobby Hebert .10 .02
❑ 9 Chris Hinton .10 .02
❑ 10 Pierce Holt .10 .02
❑ 11 Mike Kenn .10 .02
❑ 12 Lincoln Kennedy RC .10 .02
❑ 13 Chris Miller .20 .07
❑ 14 Mike Pritchard .20 .07
❑ 15 Andre Rison .20 .07
❑ 16 Deion Sanders .75 .30
❑ 17 Tony Smith RB .10 .02
❑ 18 Jessie Tuggle .10 .02
❑ 19 Howard Ballard .10 .02
❑ 20 Don Beebe .10 .02
❑ 21 Cornelius Bennett .20 .07
❑ 22 Bill Brooks .10 .02
❑ 23 Kenneth Davis .10 .02
❑ 24 Phil Hansen .10 .02
❑ 25 Henry Jones .10 .02
❑ 26 Jim Kelly .40 .15
❑ 27 Nate Odomes .10 .02
❑ 28 John Parrella RC .10 .02
❑ 29 Andre Reed .20 .07
❑ 30 Frank Reich .20 .07
❑ 31 Jim Ritcher .10 .02
❑ 32 Bruce Smith .40 .15
❑ 33 Thomas Smith RC .20 .07
❑ 34 Darryl Talley .10 .02
❑ 35 Steve Tasker .20 .07
❑ 36 Thurman Thomas .40 .15
❑ 37 Jeff Wright .10 .02
❑ 38 Neal Anderson .10 .02
❑ 39 Trace Armstrong .10 .02
❑ 40 Mark Carrier DB .10 .02
❑ 41 Curtis Conway RC .75 .30
❑ 42 Wendell Davis .10 .02
❑ 43 Richard Dent .20 .07
❑ 44 Shaun Gayle .10 .02
❑ 45 Jim Harbaugh .40 .15
❑ 46 Craig Heyward .20 .07
❑ 47 Darren Lewis .10 .02
❑ 48 Steve McMichael .20 .07
❑ 49 William Perry .20 .07
❑ 50 Carl Simpson RC .10 .02
❑ 51 Alonzo Spellman .10 .02
❑ 52 Keith Van Horne .10 .02
❑ 53 Tom Waddle .10 .02
❑ 54 Donnell Woolford .10 .02
❑ 55 John Copeland RC .20 .07
❑ 56 Derrick Fenner .10 .02
❑ 57 James Francis .10 .02
❑ 58 Harold Green .10 .02
❑ 59 David Klingler .10 .02
❑ 60 Tim Krumrie .10 .02
❑ 61 Ricardo McDonald .10 .02
❑ 62 Tony McGee RC .20 .07
❑ 63 Carl Pickens .20 .07
❑ 64 Lamar Rogers .10 .02
❑ 65 Jay Schroeder .10 .02
❑ 66 Daniel Stubbs .10 .02

❑ 67 Steve Tovar RC .10 .02
❑ 68 Alfred Williams .10 .02
❑ 69 Darryl Williams .10 .02
❑ 70 Jerry Ball .10 .02
❑ 71 David Brandon .10 .02
❑ 72 Rob Burnett .10 .02
❑ 73 Mark Carrier WR .20 .07
❑ 74 Steve Everitt RC .10 .02
❑ 75 Dan Footman RC .10 .02
❑ 76 Leroy Hoard .20 .07
❑ 77 Michael Jackson .20 .07
❑ 78 Mike Johnson .10 .02
❑ 79 Bernie Kosar .20 .07
❑ 80 Clay Matthews .20 .07
❑ 81 Eric Metcalf .20 .07
❑ 82 Michael Dean Perry .20 .07
❑ 83 Vinny Testaverde .20 .07
❑ 84 Tommy Vardell .10 .02
❑ 85 Troy Aikman 1.50 .60
❑ 86 Larry Brown DB .10 .02
❑ 87 Tony Casillas .10 .02
❑ 88 Thomas Everett .10 .02
❑ 89 Charles Haley .20 .07
❑ 90 Alvin Harper .20 .07
❑ 91 Michael Irvin .40 .15
❑ 92 Jim Jeffcoat .10 .02
❑ 93 Daryl Johnston .40 .15
❑ 94 Robert Jones .10 .02
❑ 95 Leon Lett RC .20 .07
❑ 96 Russell Maryland .10 .02
❑ 97 Nate Newton .20 .07
❑ 98 Ken Norton .20 .07
❑ 99 Jay Novacek .20 .07
❑ 100 Darrin Smith RC .20 .07
❑ 101 Emmitt Smith 3.00 1.25
❑ 102 Kevin Smith .20 .07
❑ 103 Mark Stepnoski .10 .02
❑ 104 Tony Tolbert .10 .02
❑ 105 Kevin Williams RC WR .40 .15
❑ 106 Steve Atwater .10 .02
❑ 107 Rod Bernstine .10 .02
❑ 108 Mike Croel .10 .02
❑ 109 Robert Delpino .10 .02
❑ 110 Shane Dronett .10 .02
❑ 111 John Elway 3.00 1.25
❑ 112 Simon Fletcher .10 .02
❑ 113 Greg Kragen .10 .02
❑ 114 Tommy Maddox .40 .15
❑ 115 Arthur Marshall RC .10 .02
❑ 116 Karl Mecklenburg .10 .02
❑ 117 Glyn Milburn RC .40 .15
❑ 118 Reggie Rivers RC .10 .02
❑ 119 Shannon Sharpe .40 .15
❑ 120 Dennis Smith .10 .02
❑ 121 Kenny Walker .10 .02
❑ 122 Dan Williams RC .10 .02
❑ 123 Bennie Blades .10 .02
❑ 124 Lomas Brown .10 .02
❑ 125 Bill Fralic .10 .02
❑ 126 Mel Gray .20 .07
❑ 127 Willie Green .10 .02
❑ 128 Jason Hanson .10 .02
❑ 129 Antonio London RC .10 .02
❑ 130 Ryan McNeil RC .40 .15
❑ 131 Herman Moore .40 .15
❑ 132 Rodney Peete .10 .02
❑ 133 Brett Perriman .40 .15
❑ 134 Kelvin Pritchett .10 .02
❑ 135 Barry Sanders 2.50 1.00
❑ 136 Tracy Scroggins .10 .02
❑ 137 Chris Spielman .20 .07
❑ 138 Pat Swilling .10 .02
❑ 139 Andre Ware .10 .02
❑ 140 Edgar Bennett .40 .15
❑ 141 Tony Bennett .10 .02
❑ 142 Matt Brock .10 .02
❑ 143 Terrell Buckley .10 .02
❑ 144 LeRoy Butler .10 .02
❑ 145 Mark Clayton .10 .02
❑ 146 Brett Favre 4.00 1.50
❑ 147 Jackie Harris .10 .02
❑ 148 Johnny Holland .10 .02
❑ 149 Bill Maas .10 .02
❑ 150 Brian Noble .10 .02
❑ 151 Bryce Paup .20 .07
❑ 152 Ken Ruettgers .10 .02
❑ 153 Sterling Sharpe .40 .15
❑ 154 Wayne Simmons RC .10 .02
❑ 155 John Stephens .10 .02
❑ 156 George Teague RC .20 .07
❑ 157 Reggie White .40 .15
❑ 158 Micheal Barrow RC .40 .15
❑ 159 Cody Carlson .10 .02
❑ 160 Ray Childress .10 .02
❑ 161 Cris Dishman .10 .02
❑ 162 Curtis Duncan .10 .02
❑ 163 William Fuller .10 .02
❑ 164 Ernest Givins .20 .07
❑ 165 Brad Hopkins RC .10 .02
❑ 166 Haywood Jeffires .20 .07
❑ 167 Lamar Lathon .10 .02
❑ 168 Wilber Marshall .10 .02
❑ 169 Bruce Matthews .10 .02
❑ 170 Bubba McDowell .10 .02
❑ 171 Warren Moon .40 .15
❑ 172 Mike Munchak .20 .07
❑ 173 Eddie Robinson .10 .02
❑ 174 Al Smith .10 .02
❑ 175 Lorenzo White .10 .02
❑ 176 Lee Williams .10 .02
❑ 177 Chip Banks .10 .02
❑ 178 John Baylor .10 .02
❑ 179 Duane Bickett .10 .02
❑ 180 Kerry Cash .10 .02
❑ 181 Quentin Coryatt .20 .07
❑ 182 Rodney Culver .10 .02
❑ 183 Steve Emtman .10 .02
❑ 184 Jeff George .40 .15
❑ 185 Jeff Herrod .10 .02
❑ 186 Jessie Hester .10 .02
❑ 187 Anthony Johnson .20 .07
❑ 188 Reggie Langhorne .10 .02
❑ 189 Roosevelt Potts RC .10 .02
❑ 190 Rohn Stark .10 .02
❑ 191 Clarence Verdin .10 .02
❑ 192 Will Wolford .10 .02
❑ 193 Marcus Allen .40 .15
❑ 194 John Alt .10 .02
❑ 195 Tim Barnett .10 .02
❑ 196 J.J.Birden .10 .02
❑ 197 Dale Carter .10 .02
❑ 198 Willie Davis .40 .15
❑ 199 Jaime Fields RC .10 .02
❑ 200 Dave Krieg .20 .07
❑ 201 Nick Lowery .10 .02
❑ 202 Charles Mincy RC .10 .02
❑ 203 Joe Montana 3.00 1.25
❑ 204 Christian Okoye .10 .02
❑ 205 Dan Saleaumua .10 .02
❑ 206 Will Shields RC .40 .15
❑ 207 Tracy Simien .10 .02
❑ 208 Neil Smith .40 .15
❑ 209 Derrick Thomas .40 .15
❑ 210 Harvey Williams .20 .07
❑ 211 Barry Word .10 .02
❑ 212 Eddie Anderson .10 .02
❑ 213 Patrick Bates RC .10 .02
❑ 214 Nick Bell .10 .02
❑ 215 Tim Brown .40 .15
❑ 216 Willie Gault .10 .02
❑ 217 Gaston Green .10 .02
❑ 218 Billy Joe Hobert RC .40 .15
❑ 219 Ethan Horton .10 .02
❑ 220 Jeff Hostetler .20 .07
❑ 221 James Lofton .20 .07
❑ 222 Howie Long .40 .15
❑ 223 Todd Marinovich .10 .02
❑ 224 Terry McDaniel .10 .02
❑ 225 Winston Moss .10 .02
❑ 226 Anthony Smith .10 .02
❑ 227 Greg Townsend .10 .02
❑ 228 Aaron Wallace .10 .02
❑ 229 Lionel Washington .10 .02
❑ 230 Steve Wisniewski .10 .02
❑ 231 Flipper Anderson .10 .02
❑ 232 Jerome Bettis RC 8.00 4.00
❑ 233 Marc Boutte .10 .02
❑ 234 Shane Conlan .10 .02
❑ 235 Troy Drayton RC .20 .07
❑ 236 Henry Ellard .20 .07
❑ 237 Jim Everett .20 .07
❑ 238 Cleveland Gary .10 .02
❑ 239 Sean Gilbert .20 .07
❑ 240 Darryl Henley .10 .02
❑ 241 David Lang .10 .02
❑ 242 Todd Lyght .10 .02
❑ 243 Anthony Newman .10 .02
❑ 244 Roman Phifer .10 .02
❑ 245 Gerald Robinson .10 .02
❑ 246 Henry Rolling .10 .02
❑ 247 Jackie Slater .10 .02
❑ 248 Keith Byars .10 .02
❑ 249 Marco Coleman .10 .02
❑ 250 Bryan Cox .10 .02
❑ 251 Jeff Cross .10 .02
❑ 252 Irving Fryar .20 .07
❑ 253 Mark Higgs .10 .02
❑ 254 Dwight Hollier RC .10 .02
❑ 255 Mark Ingram .10 .02
❑ 256 Keith Jackson .20 .07
❑ 257 Terry Kirby RC .40 .15
❑ 258 Dan Marino 3.00 1.25
❑ 259 O.J. McDuffie RC .40 .15
❑ 260 John Offerdahl .10 .02
❑ 261 Louis Oliver .10 .02
❑ 262 Pete Stoyanovich .10 .02
❑ 263 Troy Vincent .10 .02
❑ 264 Richmond Webb .10 .02
❑ 265 Jarvis Williams .10 .02
❑ 266 Terry Allen .40 .15
❑ 267 Anthony Carter .20 .07
❑ 268 Cris Carter .40 .15
❑ 269 Roger Craig .20 .07
❑ 270 Jack Del Rio .10 .02
❑ 271 Chris Doleman .10 .02
❑ 272 Qadry Ismail RC .40 .15
❑ 273 Steve Jordan .10 .02
❑ 274 Randall McDaniel .10 .02
❑ 275 Audray McMillian .10 .02
❑ 276 John Randle .20 .07
❑ 277 Sean Salisbury .10 .02
❑ 278 Todd Scott .10 .02
❑ 279 Robert Smith RC 2.50 1.00
❑ 280 Henry Thomas .10 .02
❑ 281 Ray Agnew .10 .02
❑ 282 Bruce Armstrong .10 .02
❑ 283 Drew Bledsoe RC 5.00 2.00
❑ 284 Vincent Brisby RC .40 .15
❑ 285 Vincent Brown .10 .02
❑ 286 Eugene Chung .10 .02
❑ 287 Marv Cook .10 .02
❑ 288 Pat Harlow .10 .02
❑ 289 Jerome Henderson .10 .02
❑ 290 Greg McMurtry .10 .02
❑ 291 Leonard Russell .20 .07
❑ 292 Chris Singleton .10 .02
❑ 293 Chris Slade RC .20 .07
❑ 294 Andre Tippett .10 .02
❑ 295 Brent Williams .10 .02
❑ 296 Scott Zolak .10 .02
❑ 297 Morten Andersen .10 .02
❑ 298 Gene Atkins .10 .02
❑ 299 Mike Buck .10 .02
❑ 300 Toi Cook .10 .02
❑ 301 Jim Dombrowski .10 .02
❑ 302 Vaughn Dunbar .10 .02
❑ 303 Quinn Early .20 .07
❑ 304 Joel Hilgenberg .10 .02
❑ 305 Dalton Hilliard .10 .02
❑ 306 Rickey Jackson .10 .02
❑ 307 Vaughan Johnson .10 .02
❑ 308 Reginald Jones .10 .02
❑ 309 Eric Martin .10 .02
❑ 310 Wayne Martin .10 .02
❑ 311 Sam Mills .10 .02
❑ 312 Brad Muster .10 .02
❑ 313 Willie Roaf RC .20 .07
❑ 314 Irv Smith RC .10 .02
❑ 315 Wade Wilson .10 .02
❑ 316 Carlton Bailey .10 .02
❑ 317 Michael Brooks .10 .02
❑ 318 Derek Brown TE .10 .02
❑ 319 Marcus Buckley RC .10 .02
❑ 320 Jarrod Bunch .10 .02
❑ 321 Mark Collins .10 .02
❑ 322 Eric Dorsey .10 .02
❑ 323 Rodney Hampton .20 .07
❑ 324 Mark Jackson .10 .02
❑ 325 Pepper Johnson .10 .02
❑ 326 Ed McCaffrey .40 .15
❑ 327 Dave Meggett .10 .02

Card	Price 1	Price 2
❑ 328 Bart Oates	.10	.02
❑ 329 Mike Sherrard	.10	.02
❑ 330 Phil Simms	.20	.07
❑ 331 Michael Strahan RC	2.00	.75
❑ 332 Lawrence Taylor	.40	.15
❑ 333 Brad Baxter	.10	.02
❑ 334 Chris Burkett	.10	.02
❑ 335 Kyle Clifton	.10	.02
❑ 336 Boomer Esiason	.20	.07
❑ 337 James Hasty	.10	.02
❑ 338 Johnny Johnson	.10	.02
❑ 339 Marvin Jones RC	.10	.02
❑ 340 Jeff Lageman	.10	.02
❑ 341 Mo Lewis	.10	.02
❑ 342 Ronnie Lott	.20	.07
❑ 343 Leonard Marshall	.10	.02
❑ 344 Johnny Mitchell	.10	.02
❑ 345 Rob Moore	.20	.07
❑ 346 Browning Nagle	.10	.02
❑ 347 Coleman Rudolph RC	.10	.02
❑ 348 Blair Thomas	.10	.02
❑ 349 Eric Thomas	.10	.02
❑ 350 Brian Washington	.10	.02
❑ 351 Marvin Washington	.10	.02
❑ 352 Eric Allen	.10	.02
❑ 353 Victor Bailey RC	.10	.02
❑ 354 Fred Barnett	.20	.07
❑ 355 Mark Bavaro	.10	.02
❑ 356 Randall Cunningham	.40	.15
❑ 357 Byron Evans	.10	.02
❑ 358 Andy Harmon RC	.20	.07
❑ 359 Tim Harris	.10	.02
❑ 360 Lester Holmes	.10	.02
❑ 361 Seth Joyner	.10	.02
❑ 362 Keith Millard	.10	.02
❑ 363 Leonard Renfro RC	.10	.02
❑ 364 Heath Sherman	.10	.02
❑ 365 Vai Sikahema	.10	.02
❑ 366 Clyde Simmons	.10	.02
❑ 367 William Thomas	.10	.02
❑ 368 Herschel Walker	.20	.07
❑ 369 Andre Waters	.10	.02
❑ 370 Calvin Williams	.20	.07
❑ 371 Johnny Bailey	.10	.02
❑ 372 Steve Beuerlein	.20	.07
❑ 373 Rich Camarillo	.10	.02
❑ 374 Chuck Cecil	.10	.02
❑ 375 Chris Chandler	.20	.07
❑ 376 Gary Clark	.20	.07
❑ 377 Ben Coleman RC	.10	.02
❑ 378 Ernest Dye RC	.10	.02
❑ 379 Ken Harvey	.10	.02
❑ 380 Garrison Hearst RC	1.50	.60
❑ 381 Randal Hill	.10	.02
❑ 382 Robert Massey	.10	.02
❑ 383 Freddie Joe Nunn	.10	.02
❑ 384 Ricky Proehl	.10	.02
❑ 385 Luis Sharpe	.10	.02
❑ 386 Tyronne Stowe	.10	.02
❑ 387 Eric Swann	.20	.07
❑ 388 Aeneas Williams	.10	.02
❑ 389 Chad Brown RC LB	.20	.07
❑ 390 Dermontti Dawson	.10	.02
❑ 391 Donald Evans	.10	.02
❑ 392 Deon Figures RC	.10	.02
❑ 393 Barry Foster	.20	.07
❑ 394 Jeff Graham	.20	.07
❑ 395 Eric Green	.10	.02
❑ 396 Kevin Greene	.20	.07
❑ 397 Carlton Haselrig	.10	.02
❑ 398 Andre Hastings RC	.20	.07
❑ 399 D.J. Johnson	.10	.02
❑ 400 Carnell Lake	.10	.02
❑ 401 Greg Lloyd	.20	.07
❑ 402 Neil O'Donnell	.40	.15
❑ 403 Darren Perry	.10	.02
❑ 404 Mike Tomczak	.10	.02
❑ 405 Rod Woodson	.40	.15
❑ 406 Eric Bieniemy	.10	.02
❑ 407 Marion Butts	.10	.02
❑ 408 Gill Byrd	.10	.02
❑ 409 Darren Carrington RC	.10	.02
❑ 410 Darrien Gordon RC	.10	.02
❑ 411 Burt Grossman	.10	.02
❑ 412 Courtney Hall	.10	.02
❑ 413 Ronnie Harmon	.10	.02
❑ 414 Stan Humphries	.20	.07

Card	Price 1	Price 2
❑ 415 Nate Lewis	.10	.02
❑ 416 Natrone Means RC	.40	.15
❑ 417 Anthony Miller	.20	.07
❑ 418 Chris Mims	.10	.02
❑ 419 Leslie O'Neal	.20	.07
❑ 420 Gary Plummer	.10	.02
❑ 421 Stanley Richard	.10	.02
❑ 422 Junior Seau	.40	.15
❑ 423 Harry Swayne	.10	.02
❑ 424 Jerrol Williams	.10	.02
❑ 425 Harris Barton	.10	.02
❑ 426 Steve Bono	.20	.07
❑ 427 Kevin Fagan	.10	.02
❑ 428 Don Griffin	.10	.02
❑ 429 Dana Hall	.10	.02
❑ 430 Adrian Hardy	.10	.02
❑ 431 Brent Jones	.20	.07
❑ 432 Todd Kelly RC	.10	.02
❑ 433 Amp Lee	.10	.02
❑ 434 Tim McDonald	.10	.02
❑ 435 Guy McIntyre	.10	.02
❑ 436 Tom Rathman	.10	.02
❑ 437 Jerry Rice	2.00	.75
❑ 438 Bill Romanowski	.10	.02
❑ 439 Dana Stubblefield RC	.40	.15
❑ 440 John Taylor	.20	.07
❑ 441 Steve Wallace	.10	.02
❑ 442 Michael Walter	.10	.02
❑ 443 Ricky Watters	.40	.15
❑ 444 Steve Young	1.50	.60
❑ 445 Robert Blackmon	.10	.02
❑ 446 Brian Blades	.20	.07
❑ 447 Jeff Bryant	.10	.02
❑ 448 Ferrell Edmunds	.10	.02
❑ 449 Carlton Gray RC	.10	.02
❑ 450 Dwayne Harper	.10	.02
❑ 451 Andy Heck	.10	.02
❑ 452 Tommy Kane	.10	.02
❑ 453 Cortez Kennedy	.20	.07
❑ 454 Kelvin Martin	.10	.02
❑ 455 Dan McGwire	.10	.02
❑ 456 Rick Mirer RC	.40	.15
❑ 457 Rufus Porter	.10	.02
❑ 458 Ray Roberts	.10	.02
❑ 459 Eugene Robinson	.10	.02
❑ 460 Chris Warren	.20	.07
❑ 461 John L. Williams	.10	.02
❑ 462 Gary Anderson RB	.10	.02
❑ 463 Tyji Armstrong	.10	.02
❑ 464 Reggie Cobb	.10	.02
❑ 465 Eric Curry RC	.10	.02
❑ 466 Lawrence Dawsey	.10	.02
❑ 467 Steve DeBerg	.10	.02
❑ 468 Santana Dotson	.20	.07
❑ 469 Demetrius DuBose RC	.10	.02
❑ 470 Paul Gruber	.10	.02
❑ 471 Ron Hall	.10	.02
❑ 472 Courtney Hawkins	.10	.02
❑ 473 Hardy Nickerson	.20	.07
❑ 474 Ricky Reynolds	.10	.02
❑ 475 Broderick Thomas	.10	.02
❑ 476 Mark Wheeler	.10	.02
❑ 477 Jimmy Williams	.10	.02
❑ 478 Carl Banks	.10	.02
❑ 479 Reggie Brooks RC	.20	.07
❑ 480 Earnest Byner	.10	.02
❑ 481 Tom Carter RC	.20	.07
❑ 482 Andre Collins	.10	.02
❑ 483 Brad Edwards	.10	.02
❑ 484 Ricky Ervins	.10	.02
❑ 485 Kurt Gouveia	.10	.02
❑ 486 Darrell Green	.10	.02
❑ 487 Desmond Howard	.20	.07
❑ 488 Jim Lachey	.10	.02
❑ 489 Chip Lohmiller	.10	.02
❑ 490 Charles Mann	.10	.02
❑ 491 Tim McGee	.10	.02
❑ 492 Brian Mitchell	.20	.07
❑ 493 Art Monk	.20	.07
❑ 494 Mark Rypien	.10	.02
❑ 495 Ricky Sanders	.10	.02
❑ 496 Checklist 1-126	.10	.02
❑ 497 Checklist 127-254	.10	.02
❑ 498 Checklist 255-382	.10	.02
❑ 499 Checklist 383-500	.10	.02
❑ 500 Inserts Checklist	.10	.02

1994 Ultra

Card	Price 1	Price 2
❑ COMPLETE SET (525)	25.00	10.00
❑ COMP.SERIES 1 (325)	12.00	5.00
❑ COMP.SERIES 2 (200)	12.00	5.00
❑ 1 Steve Beuerlein	.20	.07
❑ 2 Gary Clark	.20	.07
❑ 3 Randal Hill	.10	.02
❑ 4 Seth Joyner	.10	.02
❑ 5 Jamir Miller RC	.20	.07
❑ 6 Ronald Moore	.10	.02
❑ 7 Luis Sharpe	.10	.02
❑ 8 Clyde Simmons	.10	.02
❑ 9 Eric Swann	.20	.07
❑ 10 Aeneas Williams	.10	.02
❑ 11 Chris Doleman	.10	.02
❑ 12 Bert Emanuel RC	.40	.15
❑ 13 Moe Gardner	.10	.02
❑ 14 Jeff George	.40	.15
❑ 15 Roger Harper	.10	.02
❑ 16 Pierce Holt	.10	.02
❑ 17 Lincoln Kennedy	.10	.02
❑ 18 Erric Pegram	.10	.02
❑ 19 Andre Rison	.20	.07
❑ 20 Deion Sanders	.75	.30
❑ 21 Jessie Tuggle	.10	.02
❑ 22 Cornelius Bennett	.20	.07
❑ 23 Bill Brooks	.10	.02
❑ 24 Jeff Burris RC	.20	.07
❑ 25 Kent Hull	.10	.02
❑ 26 Henry Jones	.10	.02
❑ 27 Jim Kelly	.40	.15
❑ 28 Marvcus Patton	.10	.02
❑ 29 Andre Reed	.20	.07
❑ 30 Bruce Smith	.40	.15
❑ 31 Thomas Smith	.10	.02
❑ 32 Thurman Thomas	.40	.15
❑ 33 Jeff Wright	.10	.02
❑ 34 Trace Armstrong	.10	.02
❑ 35 Mark Carrier DB	.10	.02
❑ 36 Dante Jones	.10	.02
❑ 37 Erik Kramer	.20	.07
❑ 38 Terry Obee	.10	.02
❑ 39 Alonzo Spellman	.10	.02
❑ 40 John Thierry RC	.10	.02
❑ 41 Tom Waddle	.10	.02
❑ 42 Donnell Woolford	.10	.02
❑ 43 Tim Worley	.10	.02
❑ 44 Chris Zorich	.10	.02
❑ 45 John Copeland	.10	.02
❑ 46 Harold Green	.10	.02
❑ 47 David Klingler	.10	.02
❑ 48 Ricardo McDonald	.10	.02
❑ 49 Tony McGee	.10	.02
❑ 50 Louis Oliver	.10	.02
❑ 51 Carl Pickens	.20	.07
❑ 52 Darnay Scott RC	.75	.30
❑ 53 Steve Tovar	.10	.02
❑ 54 Dan Wilkinson RC	.20	.07
❑ 55 Darryl Williams	.10	.02
❑ 56 Derrick Alexander WR RC	.40	.15
❑ 57 Michael Jackson	.20	.07
❑ 58 Tony Jones T	.10	.02
❑ 59 Antonio Langham RC	.20	.07
❑ 60 Eric Metcalf	.20	.07
❑ 61 Stevon Moore	.10	.02
❑ 62 Michael Dean Perry	.20	.07
❑ 63 Anthony Pleasant	.10	.02
❑ 64 Vinny Testaverde	.20	.07

❑ 65 Eric Turner .10 .02
❑ 66 Tommy Vardell .10 .02
❑ 67 Troy Aikman 1.50 .60
❑ 68 Larry Brown DB .10 .02
❑ 69 Shante Carver RC .10 .02
❑ 70 Charles Haley .20 .07
❑ 71 Michael Irvin .40 .15
❑ 72 Leon Lett .10 .02
❑ 73 Nate Newton .10 .02
❑ 74 Jay Novacek .20 .07
❑ 75 Darrin Smith .10 .02
❑ 76 Emmitt Smith 2.50 1.00
❑ 77 Tony Tolbert .10 .02
❑ 78 Erik Williams .10 .02
❑ 79 Kevin Williams WR .20 .07
❑ 80 Steve Atwater .10 .02
❑ 81 Rod Bernstine .10 .02
❑ 82 Ray Crockett .10 .02
❑ 83 Mike Croel .10 .02
❑ 84 Shane Dronett .10 .02
❑ 85 Jason Elam .20 .07
❑ 86 John Elway 3.00 1.25
❑ 87 Simon Fletcher .10 .02
❑ 88 Glyn Milburn .20 .07
❑ 89 Anthony Miller .20 .07
❑ 90 Shannon Sharpe .20 .07
❑ 91 Gary Zimmerman .10 .02
❑ 92 Bennie Blades .10 .02
❑ 93 Lomas Brown .10 .02
❑ 94 Mel Gray .10 .02
❑ 95 Jason Hanson .10 .02
❑ 96 Ryan McNeil .10 .02
❑ 97 Scott Mitchell .20 .07
❑ 98 Herman Moore .40 .15
❑ 99 Johnnie Morton RC 1.50 .60
❑ 100 Robert Porcher .10 .02
❑ 101 Barry Sanders 2.50 1.00
❑ 102 Chris Spielman .20 .07
❑ 103 Pat Swilling .10 .02
❑ 104 Edgar Bennett .40 .15
❑ 105 Terrell Buckley .10 .02
❑ 106 Reggie Cobb .10 .02
❑ 107 Brett Favre 3.00 1.25
❑ 108 Sean Jones .10 .02
❑ 109 Ken Ruettgers .10 .02
❑ 110 Sterling Sharpe .20 .07
❑ 111 Wayne Simmons .10 .02
❑ 112 Aaron Taylor RC .10 .02
❑ 113 George Teague .10 .02
❑ 114 Reggie White .40 .15
❑ 115 Micheal Barrow .10 .02
❑ 116 Gary Brown .10 .02
❑ 117 Cody Carlson .10 .02
❑ 118 Ray Childress .10 .02
❑ 119 Cris Dishman .10 .02
❑ 120 Henry Ford RC .10 .02
❑ 121 Haywood Jeffires .20 .07
❑ 122 Bruce Matthews .10 .02
❑ 123 Bubba McDowell .10 .02
❑ 124 Marcus Robertson .10 .02
❑ 125 Eddie Robinson .10 .02
❑ 126 Webster Slaughter .10 .02
❑ 127 Trev Alberts RC .20 .07
❑ 128 Tony Bennett .10 .02
❑ 129 Ray Buchanan .10 .02
❑ 130 Quentin Coryatt .10 .02
❑ 131 Eugene Daniel .10 .02
❑ 132 Steve Emtman .10 .02
❑ 133 Marshall Faulk RC 6.00 2.50
❑ 134 Jim Harbaugh .40 .15
❑ 135 Roosevelt Potts .10 .02
❑ 136 Rohn Stark .10 .02
❑ 137 Marcus Allen .40 .15
❑ 138 Donnell Bennett RC .40 .15
❑ 139 Dale Carter .10 .02
❑ 140 Tony Casillas .10 .02
❑ 141 Mark Collins .10 .02
❑ 142 Willie Davis .20 .07
❑ 143 Tim Grunhard .10 .02
❑ 144 Greg Hill RC .40 .15
❑ 145 Joe Montana 3.00 1.25
❑ 146 Tracy Simien .10 .02
❑ 147 Neil Smith .20 .07
❑ 148 Derrick Thomas .40 .15
❑ 149 Tim Brown .40 .15
❑ 150 James Folston RC .10 .02
❑ 151 Rob Fredrickson RC .20 .07
❑ 152 Jeff Hostetler .20 .07
❑ 153 Rocket Ismail .20 .07
❑ 154 James Jett .10 .02
❑ 155 Terry McDaniel .10 .02
❑ 156 Winston Moss .10 .02
❑ 157 Greg Robinson .10 .02
❑ 158 Anthony Smith .10 .02
❑ 159 Steve Wisniewski .10 .02
❑ 160 Flipper Anderson .10 .02
❑ 161 Jerome Bettis .60 .25
❑ 162 Isaac Bruce RC 4.00 2.00
❑ 163 Shane Conlan .10 .02
❑ 164 Wayne Gandy RC .10 .02
❑ 165 Sean Gilbert .10 .02
❑ 166 Todd Lyght .10 .02
❑ 167 Chris Miller .10 .02
❑ 168 Anthony Newman .10 .02
❑ 169 Roman Phifer .10 .02
❑ 170 Jackie Slater .10 .02
❑ 171 Gene Atkins .10 .02
❑ 172 Aubrey Beavers RC .10 .02
❑ 173 Tim Bowens RC .20 .07
❑ 174 J.B. Brown .10 .02
❑ 175 Marco Coleman .10 .02
❑ 176 Bryan Cox .10 .02
❑ 177 Irving Fryar .20 .07
❑ 178 Terry Kirby .40 .15
❑ 179 Dan Marino 3.00 1.25
❑ 180 Troy Vincent .10 .02
❑ 181 Richmond Webb .10 .02
❑ 182 Terry Allen .20 .07
❑ 183 Cris Carter .75 .30
❑ 184 Jack Del Rio .10 .02
❑ 185 Vencie Glenn .10 .02
❑ 186 Randall McDaniel .10 .02
❑ 187 Warren Moon .40 .15
❑ 188 David Palmer RC .40 .15
❑ 189 John Randle .20 .07
❑ 190 Todd Scott .10 .02
❑ 191 Todd Steussie RC .20 .07
❑ 192 Henry Thomas .10 .02
❑ 193 Dewayne Washington RC .20 .07
❑ 194 Bruce Armstrong .10 .02
❑ 195 Harlon Barnett .10 .02
❑ 196 Drew Bledsoe 1.00 .40
❑ 197 Vincent Brisby .20 .07
❑ 198 Vincent Brown .10 .02
❑ 199 Marion Butts .10 .02
❑ 200 Ben Coates .20 .07
❑ 201 Todd Collins .10 .02
❑ 202 Maurice Hurst .10 .02
❑ 203 Willie McGinest RC .40 .15
❑ 204 Ricky Reynolds .10 .02
❑ 205 Chris Slade .10 .02
❑ 206 Mario Bates RC .40 .15
❑ 207 Derek Brown RBK .10 .02
❑ 208 Vince Buck .10 .02
❑ 209 Quinn Early .20 .07
❑ 210 Jim Everett .20 .07
❑ 211 Michael Haynes .20 .07
❑ 212 Tyrone Hughes .20 .07
❑ 213 Joe Johnson RC .10 .02
❑ 214 Vaughan Johnson .10 .02
❑ 215 Willie Roaf .10 .02
❑ 216 Renaldo Turnbull .10 .02
❑ 217 Michael Brooks .10 .02
❑ 218 Dave Brown .20 .07
❑ 219 Howard Cross .10 .02
❑ 220 Stacey Dillard .10 .02
❑ 221 Jumbo Elliott .10 .02
❑ 222 Keith Hamilton .10 .02
❑ 223 Rodney Hampton .20 .07
❑ 224 Thomas Lewis RC .20 .07
❑ 225 Dave Meggett .10 .02
❑ 226 Corey Miller .10 .02
❑ 227 Thomas Randolph RC .10 .02
❑ 228 Mike Sherrard .10 .02
❑ 229 Kyle Clifton .10 .02
❑ 230 Boomer Esiason .20 .07
❑ 231 Aaron Glenn RC .40 .15
❑ 232 James Hasty .10 .02
❑ 233 Bobby Houston .10 .02
❑ 234 Johnny Johnson .10 .02
❑ 235 Mo Lewis .10 .02
❑ 236 Ronnie Lott .20 .07
❑ 237 Rob Moore .20 .07
❑ 238 Marvin Washington .10 .02
❑ 239 Ryan Yarborough RC .10 .02
❑ 240 Eric Allen .10 .02
❑ 241 Victor Bailey .10 .02
❑ 242 Fred Barnett .20 .07
❑ 243 Mark Bavaro .10 .02
❑ 244 Randall Cunningham .40 .15
❑ 245 Byron Evans .10 .02
❑ 246 William Fuller .10 .02
❑ 247 Andy Harmon .10 .02
❑ 248 William Perry .20 .07
❑ 249 Herschel Walker .20 .07
❑ 250 Bernard Williams RC .10 .02
❑ 251 Dermontti Dawson .10 .02
❑ 252 Deon Figures .10 .02
❑ 253 Barry Foster .10 .02
❑ 254 Kevin Greene .20 .07
❑ 255 Charles Johnson RC .40 .15
❑ 256 Levon Kirkland .10 .02
❑ 257 Greg Lloyd .20 .07
❑ 258 Neil O'Donnell .40 .15
❑ 259 Darren Perry .10 .02
❑ 260 Dwight Stone .10 .02
❑ 261 Rod Woodson .20 .07
❑ 262 John Carney .10 .02
❑ 263 Isaac Davis RC .10 .02
❑ 264 Courtney Hall .10 .02
❑ 265 Ronnie Harmon .10 .02
❑ 266 Stan Humphries .20 .07
❑ 267 Vance Johnson .10 .02
❑ 268 Natrone Means .40 .15
❑ 269 Chris Mims .10 .02
❑ 270 Leslie O'Neal .10 .02
❑ 271 Stanley Richard .10 .02
❑ 272 Junior Seau .40 .15
❑ 273 Harris Barton .10 .02
❑ 274 Dennis Brown .10 .02
❑ 275 Eric Davis .10 .02
❑ 276 William Floyd RC .40 .15
❑ 277 John Johnson .10 .02
❑ 278 Tim McDonald .10 .02
❑ 279 Ken Norton Jr. .20 .07
❑ 280 Jerry Rice 1.50 .60
❑ 281 Jesse Sapolu .10 .02
❑ 282 Dana Stubblefield .20 .07
❑ 283 Ricky Watters .20 .07
❑ 284 Bryant Young RC .40 .15
❑ 285 Steve Young 1.00 .40
❑ 286 Sam Adams RC .20 .07
❑ 287 Brian Blades .20 .07
❑ 288 Ferrell Edmunds .10 .02
❑ 289 Patrick Hunter .10 .02
❑ 290 Cortez Kennedy .20 .07
❑ 291 Rick Mirer .40 .15
❑ 292 Nate Odomes .10 .02
❑ 293 Ray Roberts .10 .02
❑ 294 Eugene Robinson .10 .02
❑ 295 Rod Stephens .10 .02
❑ 296 Chris Warren .20 .07
❑ 297 Marty Carter .10 .02
❑ 298 Horace Copeland .10 .02
❑ 299 Eric Curry .10 .02
❑ 300 Santana Dotson .20 .07
❑ 301 Craig Erickson .10 .02
❑ 302 Paul Gruber .10 .02
❑ 303 Courtney Hawkins .10 .02
❑ 304 Martin Mayhew .10 .02
❑ 305 Hardy Nickerson .20 .07
❑ 306 Errict Rhett RC .40 .15
❑ 307 Vince Workman .10 .02
❑ 308 Reggie Brooks .20 .07
❑ 309 Tom Carter .10 .02
❑ 310 Andre Collins .10 .02
❑ 311 Brad Edwards .10 .02
❑ 312 Kurt Gouveia .10 .02
❑ 313 Darrell Green .10 .02
❑ 314 Ethan Horton .10 .02
❑ 315 Desmond Howard .20 .07
❑ 316 Tre Johnson RC .10 .02
❑ 317 Sterling Palmer RC .10 .02
❑ 318 Heath Shuler RC .40 .15
❑ 319 Tyronne Stowe .10 .02
❑ 320 NFL 75th Anniversary .10 .02
❑ 321 Checklist .10 .02
❑ 322 Checklist .10 .02
❑ 323 Checklist .10 .02
❑ 324 Checklist .10 .02
❑ 325 Checklist .10 .02

Card		
❑ 326 Garrison Hearst	.40	.15
❑ 327 Eric Hill	.10	.02
❑ 328 Seth Joyner	.10	.02
❑ 329 Jim McMahon	.20	.07
❑ 330 Jamir Miller	.10	.02
❑ 331 Ricky Proehl	.10	.02
❑ 332 Clyde Simmons	.10	.02
❑ 333 Chris Doleman	.10	.02
❑ 334 Bert Emanuel	.40	.15
❑ 335 Jeff George	.40	.15
❑ 336 D.J. Johnson	.10	.02
❑ 337 Terance Mathis	.20	.07
❑ 338 Clay Matthews	.10	.02
❑ 339 Tony Smith RB	.10	.02
❑ 340 Don Beebe	.10	.02
❑ 341 Bucky Brooks RC	.10	.02
❑ 342 Jeff Burris	.20	.07
❑ 343 Kenneth Davis	.10	.02
❑ 344 Phil Hansen	.10	.02
❑ 345 Pete Metzelaars	.10	.02
❑ 346 Darryl Talley	.10	.02
❑ 347 Joe Cain	.10	.02
❑ 348 Curtis Conway	.40	.15
❑ 349 Shaun Gayle	.10	.02
❑ 350 Chris Gedney	.10	.02
❑ 351 Erik Kramer	.20	.07
❑ 352 Vinson Smith	.10	.02
❑ 353 John Thierry	.10	.02
❑ 354 Lewis Tillman	.10	.02
❑ 355 Mike Brim	.10	.02
❑ 356 Derrick Fenner	.10	.02
❑ 357 James Francis	.10	.02
❑ 358 Louis Oliver	.10	.02
❑ 359 Darnay Scott	.40	.15
❑ 360 Dan Wilkinson	.20	.07
❑ 361 Alfred Williams	.10	.02
❑ 362 Derrick Alexander WR	.40	.15
❑ 363 Rob Burnett	.10	.02
❑ 364 Mark Carrier WR	.20	.07
❑ 365 Steve Everitt	.10	.02
❑ 366 Leroy Hoard	.10	.02
❑ 367 Pepper Johnson	.10	.02
❑ 368 Antonio Langham	.20	.07
❑ 369 Shante Carver	.10	.02
❑ 370 Alvin Harper	.20	.07
❑ 371 Daryl Johnston	.20	.07
❑ 372 Russell Maryland	.10	.02
❑ 373 Kevin Smith	.10	.02
❑ 374 Mark Stepnoski	.10	.02
❑ 375 Darren Woodson	.20	.07
❑ 376 Allen Aldridge RC	.10	.02
❑ 377 Ray Crockett	.10	.02
❑ 378 Karl Mecklenburg	.10	.02
❑ 379 Anthony Miller	.20	.07
❑ 380 Mike Pritchard	.10	.02
❑ 381 Leonard Russell	.10	.02
❑ 382 Dennis Smith	.10	.02
❑ 383 Anthony Carter	.20	.07
❑ 384 Van Malone RC	.10	.02
❑ 385 Robert Massey	.10	.02
❑ 386 Scott Mitchell	.20	.07
❑ 387 Johnnie Morton	.60	.25
❑ 388 Brett Perriman	.20	.07
❑ 389 Tracy Scroggins	.10	.02
❑ 390 Robert Brooks	.40	.15
❑ 391 LeRoy Butler	.10	.02
❑ 392 Reggie Cobb	.10	.02
❑ 393 Sean Jones	.10	.02
❑ 394 George Koonce	.10	.02
❑ 395 Steve McMichael	.20	.07
❑ 396 Bryce Paup	.20	.07
❑ 397 Aaron Taylor	.10	.02
❑ 398 Henry Ford	.10	.02
❑ 399 Ernest Givins	.20	.07
❑ 400 Jeremy Nunley RC	.10	.02
❑ 401 Bo Orlando	.10	.02
❑ 402 Al Smith	.10	.02
❑ 403 Barron Wortham RC	.10	.02
❑ 404 Trev Alberts	.20	.07
❑ 405 Tony Bennett	.10	.02
❑ 406 Kerry Cash	.10	.02
❑ 407 Sean Dawkins RC	.40	.15
❑ 408 Marshall Faulk	2.00	.75
❑ 409 Jim Harbaugh	.40	.15
❑ 410 Jeff Herrod	.10	.02
❑ 411 Kimble Anders	.20	.07
❑ 412 Donnell Bennett	.20	.07
❑ 413 J.J. Birden	.10	.02
❑ 414 Mark Collins	.10	.02
❑ 415 Lake Dawson RC	.20	.07
❑ 416 Greg Hill	.40	.15
❑ 417 Charles Mincy	.10	.02
❑ 418 Greg Biekert	.10	.02
❑ 419 Rob Fredrickson	.20	.07
❑ 420 Nolan Harrison	.10	.02
❑ 421 Jeff Jaeger	.10	.02
❑ 422 Albert Lewis	.10	.02
❑ 423 Chester McGlockton	.10	.02
❑ 424 Tom Rathman	.10	.02
❑ 425 Harvey Williams	.20	.07
❑ 426 Isaac Bruce	1.50	.60
❑ 427 Troy Drayton	.10	.02
❑ 428 Wayne Gandy	.10	.02
❑ 429 Fred Stokes	.10	.02
❑ 430 Robert Young	.10	.02
❑ 431 Gene Atkins	.10	.02
❑ 432 Aubrey Beavers	.10	.02
❑ 433 Tim Bowens	.20	.07
❑ 434 Keith Byars	.10	.02
❑ 435 Jeff Cross	.10	.02
❑ 436 Mark Ingram	.10	.02
❑ 437 Keith Jackson	.10	.02
❑ 438 Michael Stewart	.10	.02
❑ 439 Chris Hinton	.10	.02
❑ 440 Qadry Ismail	.40	.15
❑ 441 Carlos Jenkins	.10	.02
❑ 442 Warren Moon	.40	.15
❑ 443 David Palmer	.20	.07
❑ 444 Jake Reed	.20	.07
❑ 445 Robert Smith	.40	.15
❑ 446 Todd Steussie	.20	.07
❑ 447 Dewayne Washington	.20	.07
❑ 448 Marion Butts	.10	.02
❑ 449 Tim Goad	.10	.02
❑ 450 Myron Guyton	.10	.02
❑ 451 Kevin Lee RC	.10	.02
❑ 452 Willie McGinest	.40	.15
❑ 453 Ricky Reynolds	.10	.02
❑ 454 Michael Timpson	.10	.02
❑ 455 Morten Andersen	.10	.02
❑ 456 Jim Everett	.20	.07
❑ 457 Michael Haynes	.20	.07
❑ 458 Joe Johnson	.10	.02
❑ 459 Wayne Martin	.10	.02
❑ 460 Sam Mills	.10	.02
❑ 461 Irv Smith	.10	.02
❑ 462 Carlton Bailey	.10	.02
❑ 463 Chris Calloway	.10	.02
❑ 464 Mark Jackson	.10	.02
❑ 465 Thomas Lewis	.20	.07
❑ 466 Thomas Randolph	.10	.02
❑ 467 Stevie Anderson RC	.10	.02
❑ 468 Brad Baxter	.10	.02
❑ 469 Aaron Glenn	.20	.07
❑ 470 Jeff Lageman	.10	.02
❑ 471 Johnny Mitchell	.10	.02
❑ 472 Art Monk	.20	.07
❑ 473 William Fuller	.10	.02
❑ 474 Charlie Garner RC	1.25	.50
❑ 475 Vaughn Hebron	.10	.02
❑ 476 Bill Romanowski	.10	.02
❑ 477 William Thomas	.10	.02
❑ 478 Greg Townsend	.10	.02
❑ 479 Bernard Williams	.10	.02
❑ 480 Calvin Williams	.20	.07
❑ 481 Eric Green	.10	.02
❑ 482 Charles Johnson	.40	.15
❑ 483 Carnell Lake	.10	.02
❑ 484 Byron Bam Morris RC	.20	.07
❑ 485 John L. Williams	.10	.02
❑ 486 Darren Carrington	.10	.02
❑ 487 Andre Coleman RC	.10	.02
❑ 488 Isaac Davis	.10	.02
❑ 489 Dwayne Harper	.10	.02
❑ 490 Tony Martin	.40	.15
❑ 491 Mark Seay RC	.40	.15
❑ 492 Richard Dent	.20	.07
❑ 493 William Floyd	.40	.15
❑ 494 Rickey Jackson	.10	.02
❑ 495 Brent Jones	.20	.07
❑ 496 Ken Norton Jr.	.20	.07
❑ 497 Gary Plummer	.10	.02
❑ 498 Deion Sanders	.75	.30
❑ 499 John Taylor	.20	.07
❑ 500 Lee Woodall RC	.10	.02
❑ 501 Bryant Young	.40	.15
❑ 502 Sam Adams	.20	.07
❑ 503 Howard Ballard	.10	.02
❑ 504 Michael Bates	.10	.02
❑ 505 Robert Blackmon	.10	.02
❑ 506 John Kasay	.10	.02
❑ 507 Kelvin Martin	.10	.02
❑ 508 Kevin Mawae RC	.40	.15
❑ 509 Rufus Porter	.10	.02
❑ 510 Lawrence Dawsey	.10	.02
❑ 511 Trent Dilfer RC	1.25	.50
❑ 512 Thomas Everett	.10	.02
❑ 513 Jackie Harris	.10	.02
❑ 514 Errict Rhett	.20	.07
❑ 515 Henry Ellard	.20	.07
❑ 516 John Friesz	.20	.07
❑ 517 Ken Harvey	.10	.02
❑ 518 Ethan Horton	.10	.02
❑ 519 Tre Johnson	.10	.02
❑ 520 Jim Lachey	.10	.02
❑ 521 Heath Shuler	.40	.15
❑ 522 Tony Woods	.10	.02
❑ 523 Checklist	.10	.02
❑ 524 Checklist	.10	.02
❑ 525 Checklist	.10	.02

1995 Ultra

Card		
❑ COMPLETE SET (550)	50.00	20.00
❑ COMP.SERIES 1 (350)	25.00	10.00
❑ COMP.SERIES 2 (200)	25.00	10.00
❑ 1 Michael Bankston	.10	.02
❑ 2 Larry Centers	.20	.07
❑ 3 Garrison Hearst	.40	.15
❑ 4 Eric Hill	.10	.02
❑ 5 Seth Joyner	.10	.02
❑ 6 Lorenzo Lynch	.10	.02
❑ 7 Jamir Miller	.10	.02
❑ 8 Clyde Simmons	.10	.02
❑ 9 Eric Swann	.20	.07
❑ 10 Aeneas Williams	.10	.02
❑ 11 Devin Bush RC	.10	.02
❑ 12 Ron Davis RC	.10	.02
❑ 13 Chris Doleman	.10	.02
❑ 14 Bert Emanuel	.40	.15
❑ 15 Jeff George	.20	.07
❑ 16 Roger Harper	.10	.02
❑ 17 Craig Heyward	.20	.07
❑ 18 Pierce Holt	.10	.02
❑ 19 D.J. Johnson	.10	.02
❑ 20 Terance Mathis	.20	.07
❑ 21 Chuck Smith	.10	.02
❑ 22 Jessie Tuggle	.10	.02
❑ 23 Cornelius Bennett	.20	.07
❑ 24 Ruben Brown RC	.40	.15
❑ 25 Jeff Burris	.10	.02
❑ 26 Matt Darby	.10	.02
❑ 27 Phil Hansen	.10	.02
❑ 28 Henry Jones	.10	.02
❑ 29 Jim Kelly	.40	.15
❑ 30 Mark Maddox RC	.10	.02
❑ 31 Andre Reed	.20	.07
❑ 32 Bruce Smith	.40	.15
❑ 33 Don Beebe	.10	.02
❑ 34 Kerry Collins RC	1.50	.60
❑ 35 Darion Conner	.10	.02
❑ 36 Pete Metzelaars	.10	.02
❑ 37 Sam Mills	.20	.07
❑ 38 Tyrone Poole RC	.40	.15

❑ 39	Joe Cain	.10	.02
❑ 40	Mark Carrier DB	.10	.02
❑ 41	Curtis Conway	.40	.15
❑ 42	Jeff Graham	.10	.02
❑ 43	Raymont Harris	.10	.02
❑ 44	Erik Kramer	.10	.02
❑ 45	Rashaan Salaam RC	.20	.07
❑ 46	Lewis Tillman	.10	.02
❑ 47	Donnell Woolford	.10	.02
❑ 48	Chris Zorich	.10	.02
❑ 49	Jeff Blake RC	.75	.30
❑ 50	Mike Brim	.10	.02
❑ 51	Ki-Jana Carter RC	.40	.15
❑ 52	James Francis	.10	.02
❑ 53	Carl Pickens	.20	.07
❑ 54	Darnay Scott	.20	.07
❑ 55	Steve Tovar	.10	.02
❑ 56	Dan Wilkinson	.20	.07
❑ 57	Alfred Williams	.10	.02
❑ 58	Darryl Williams	.10	.02
❑ 59	Derrick Alexander WR	.40	.15
❑ 60	Rob Burnett	.10	.02
❑ 61	Steve Everitt	.10	.02
❑ 62	Leroy Hoard	.10	.02
❑ 63	Michael Jackson	.20	.07
❑ 64	Pepper Johnson	.10	.02
❑ 65	Tony Jones T	.10	.02
❑ 66	Antonio Langham	.10	.02
❑ 67	Anthony Pleasant	.10	.02
❑ 68	Craig Powell RC	.10	.02
❑ 69	Vinny Testaverde	.20	.07
❑ 70	Eric Turner	.10	.02
❑ 71	Troy Aikman	1.50	.60
❑ 72	Charles Haley	.20	.07
❑ 73	Michael Irvin	.40	.15
❑ 74	Daryl Johnston	.20	.07
❑ 75	Robert Jones	.10	.02
❑ 76	Leon Lett	.10	.02
❑ 77	Russell Maryland	.10	.02
❑ 78	Jay Novacek	.20	.07
❑ 79	Darrin Smith	.10	.02
❑ 80	Emmitt Smith	2.50	1.25
❑ 81	Kevin Smith	.10	.02
❑ 82	Erik Williams	.10	.02
❑ 83	Kevin Williams WR	.20	.07
❑ 84	Sherman Williams RC	.10	.02
❑ 85	Darren Woodson	.20	.07
❑ 86	Elijah Alexander RC	.10	.02
❑ 87	Steve Atwater	.10	.02
❑ 88	Ray Crockett	.10	.02
❑ 89	Shane Dronett	.10	.02
❑ 90	Jason Elam	.20	.07
❑ 91	John Elway	3.00	1.25
❑ 92	Simon Fletcher	.10	.02
❑ 93	Glyn Milburn	.10	.02
❑ 94	Anthony Miller	.20	.07
❑ 95	Leonard Russell	.10	.02
❑ 96	Shannon Sharpe	.20	.07
❑ 97	Bennie Blades	.10	.02
❑ 98	Lomas Brown	.10	.02
❑ 99	Willie Clay	.10	.02
❑ 100	Luther Elliss RC	.10	.02
❑ 101	Mike Johnson	.10	.02
❑ 102	Robert Massey	.10	.02
❑ 103	Scott Mitchell	.20	.07
❑ 104	Herman Moore	.40	.15
❑ 105	Brett Perriman	.20	.07
❑ 106	Robert Porcher	.10	.02
❑ 107	Barry Sanders	2.50	1.00
❑ 108	Chris Spielman	.20	.07
❑ 109	Edgar Bennett	.20	.07
❑ 110	Robert Brooks	.40	.15
❑ 111	LeRoy Butler	.10	.02
❑ 112	Brett Favre	3.00	1.50
❑ 113	Sean Jones	.10	.02
❑ 114	John Jurkovic	.10	.02
❑ 115	George Koonce	.10	.02
❑ 116	Wayne Simmons	.10	.02
❑ 117	George Teague	.10	.02
❑ 118	Reggie White	.40	.15
❑ 119	Micheal Barrow	.10	.02
❑ 120	Gary Brown	.10	.02
❑ 121	Cody Carlson	.10	.02
❑ 122	Ray Childress	.10	.02
❑ 123	Cris Dishman	.10	.02
❑ 124	Bruce Matthews	.10	.02
❑ 125	Steve McNair RC	3.00	1.25
❑ 126	Marcus Robertson	.10	.02
❑ 127	Webster Slaughter	.10	.02
❑ 128	Al Smith	.10	.02
❑ 129	Tony Bennett	.10	.02
❑ 130	Ray Buchanan	.10	.02
❑ 131	Quentin Coryatt	.20	.07
❑ 132	Sean Dawkins	.20	.07
❑ 133	Marshall Faulk	2.00	.75
❑ 134	Stephen Grant RC	.10	.02
❑ 135	Jim Harbaugh	.20	.07
❑ 136	Jeff Herrod	.10	.02
❑ 137	Ellis Johnson RC	.10	.02
❑ 138	Tony Siragusa	.10	.02
❑ 139	Steve Beuerlein	.20	.07
❑ 140	Tony Boselli RC	.40	.15
❑ 141	Darren Carrington	.10	.02
❑ 142	Reggie Cobb	.10	.02
❑ 143	Kelvin Martin	.10	.02
❑ 144	Kelvin Pritchett	.10	.02
❑ 145	Joel Smeenge	.10	.02
❑ 146	James O. Stewart RC	1.25	.50
❑ 147	Marcus Allen	.40	.15
❑ 148	Kimble Anders	.20	.07
❑ 149	Dale Carter	.20	.07
❑ 150	Mark Collins	.10	.02
❑ 151	Willie Davis	.20	.07
❑ 152	Lake Dawson	.20	.07
❑ 153	Greg Hill	.20	.07
❑ 154	Trezelle Jenkins RC	.10	.02
❑ 155	Darren Mickell	.10	.02
❑ 156	Tracy Simien	.10	.02
❑ 157	Neil Smith	.20	.07
❑ 158	William White	.10	.02
❑ 159	Joe Aska RC	.10	.02
❑ 160	Greg Biekert	.10	.02
❑ 161	Tim Brown	.40	.15
❑ 162	Rob Fredrickson	.10	.02
❑ 163	Andrew Glover RC	.10	.02
❑ 164	Jeff Hostetler	.20	.07
❑ 165	Rocket Ismail	.20	.07
❑ 166	Napoleon Kaufman RC	1.25	.50
❑ 167	Terry McDaniel	.10	.02
❑ 168	Chester McGlockton	.20	.07
❑ 169	Anthony Smith	.10	.02
❑ 170	Harvey Williams	.10	.02
❑ 171	Steve Wisniewski	.10	.02
❑ 172	Gene Atkins	.10	.02
❑ 173	Aubrey Beavers	.10	.02
❑ 174	Tim Bowens	.10	.02
❑ 175	Bryan Cox	.10	.02
❑ 176	Jeff Cross	.10	.02
❑ 177	Irving Fryar	.20	.07
❑ 178	Dan Marino	3.00	1.25
❑ 179	O.J. McDuffie	.40	.15
❑ 180	Billy Milner RC	.10	.02
❑ 181	Bernie Parmalee	.20	.07
❑ 182	Troy Vincent	.10	.02
❑ 183	Richmond Webb	.10	.02
❑ 184	Derrick Alexander DE RC	.10	.02
❑ 185	Cris Carter	.40	.15
❑ 186	Jack Del Rio	.10	.02
❑ 187	Qadry Ismail	.20	.07
❑ 188	Ed McDaniel	.10	.02
❑ 189	Randall McDaniel	.10	.02
❑ 190	Warren Moon	.20	.07
❑ 191	John Randle	.20	.07
❑ 192	Jake Reed	.20	.07
❑ 193	Fuad Reveiz	.10	.02
❑ 194	Korey Stringer RC	.20	.07
❑ 195	Dewayne Washington	.20	.07
❑ 196	Bruce Armstrong	.10	.02
❑ 197	Drew Bledsoe	1.00	.40
❑ 198	Vincent Brisby	.10	.02
❑ 199	Vincent Brown	.10	.02
❑ 200	Marion Butts	.10	.02
❑ 201	Ben Coates	.20	.07
❑ 202	Myron Guyton	.10	.02
❑ 203	Maurice Hurst	.10	.02
❑ 204	Mike Jones	.10	.02
❑ 205	Ty Law RC	1.50	.60
❑ 206	Willie McGinest	.20	.07
❑ 207	Chris Slade	.10	.02
❑ 208	Mario Bates	.20	.07
❑ 209	Quinn Early	.20	.07
❑ 210	Jim Everett	.10	.02
❑ 211	Mark Fields RC	.40	.15
❑ 212	Michael Haynes	.20	.07
❑ 213	Tyrone Hughes	.20	.07
❑ 214	Joe Johnson	.10	.02
❑ 215	Wayne Martin	.10	.02
❑ 216	Willie Roaf	.10	.02
❑ 217	Irv Smith	.10	.02
❑ 218	Jimmy Spencer	.10	.02
❑ 219	Winfred Tubbs	.10	.02
❑ 220	Renaldo Turnbull	.10	.02
❑ 221	Michael Brooks	.10	.02
❑ 222	Dave Brown	.20	.07
❑ 223	Chris Calloway	.10	.02
❑ 224	Howard Cross	.10	.02
❑ 225	John Elliott	.10	.02
❑ 226	Keith Hamilton	.10	.02
❑ 227	Rodney Hampton	.20	.07
❑ 228	Thomas Lewis	.20	.07
❑ 229	Thomas Randolph	.10	.02
❑ 230	Mike Sherrard	.10	.02
❑ 231	Michael Strahan	.40	.15
❑ 232	Tyrone Wheatley RC	1.25	.50
❑ 233	Brad Baxter	.10	.02
❑ 234	Kyle Brady RC	.40	.15
❑ 235	Kyle Clifton	.10	.02
❑ 236	Hugh Douglas RC	.40	.15
❑ 237	Boomer Esiason	.20	.07
❑ 238	Aaron Glenn	.10	.02
❑ 239	Bobby Houston	.10	.02
❑ 240	Johnny Johnson	.10	.02
❑ 241	Mo Lewis	.10	.02
❑ 242	Johnny Mitchell	.10	.02
❑ 243	Marvin Washington	.10	.02
❑ 244	Fred Barnett	.20	.07
❑ 245	Randall Cunningham	.40	.15
❑ 246	William Fuller	.10	.02
❑ 247	Charlie Garner	.40	.15
❑ 248	Andy Harmon	.10	.02
❑ 249	Greg Jackson	.10	.02
❑ 250	Mike Mamula RC	.10	.02
❑ 251	Bill Romanowski	.10	.02
❑ 252	Bobby Taylor RC	.40	.15
❑ 253	William Thomas	.10	.02
❑ 254	Calvin Williams	.20	.07
❑ 255	Michael Zordich	.10	.02
❑ 256	Chad Brown	.20	.07
❑ 257	Mark Bruener RC	.20	.07
❑ 258	Dermontti Dawson	.20	.07
❑ 259	Barry Foster	.20	.07
❑ 260	Kevin Greene	.20	.07
❑ 261	Charles Johnson	.20	.07
❑ 262	Carnell Lake	.10	.02
❑ 263	Greg Lloyd	.20	.07
❑ 264	Byron Bam Morris	.10	.02
❑ 265	Neil O'Donnell	.20	.07
❑ 266	Darren Perry	.10	.02
❑ 267	Ray Seals	.10	.02
❑ 268	Kordell Stewart RC	1.50	.60
❑ 269	John L. Williams	.10	.02
❑ 270	Rod Woodson	.20	.07
❑ 271	Jerome Bettis	.40	.15
❑ 272	Isaac Bruce	.75	.30
❑ 273	Kevin Carter RC	.40	.15
❑ 274	Shane Conlan	.10	.02
❑ 275	Troy Drayton	.10	.02
❑ 276	Sean Gilbert	.20	.07
❑ 277	Todd Lyght	.10	.02
❑ 278	Chris Miller	.10	.02
❑ 279	Anthony Newman	.10	.02
❑ 280	Roman Phifer	.10	.02
❑ 281	Robert Young	.10	.02
❑ 282	John Carney	.10	.02
❑ 283	Andre Coleman	.10	.02
❑ 284	Courtney Hall	.10	.02
❑ 285	Ronnie Harmon	.10	.02
❑ 286	Dwayne Harper	.10	.02
❑ 287	Stan Humphries	.20	.07
❑ 288	Shawn Jefferson	.10	.02
❑ 289	Tony Martin	.20	.07
❑ 290	Natrone Means	.20	.07
❑ 291	Chris Mims	.10	.02
❑ 292	Leslie O'Neal	.20	.07
❑ 293	Junior Seau	.40	.15
❑ 294	Mark Seay	.20	.07
❑ 295	Eric Davis	.10	.02
❑ 296	William Floyd	.20	.07
❑ 297	Merton Hanks	.10	.02
❑ 298	Brent Jones	.10	.02
❑ 299	Ken Norton Jr.	.20	.07

❑ 300 Gary Plummer .10 .02
❑ 301 Jerry Rice 1.50 .60
❑ 302 Deion Sanders 1.00 .40
❑ 303 Jesse Sapolu .10 .02
❑ 304 J.J. Stokes RC .40 .15
❑ 305 Dana Stubblefield .20 .07
❑ 306 John Taylor .10 .02
❑ 307 Steve Wallace .10 .02
❑ 308 Lee Woodall .10 .02
❑ 309 Bryant Young .20 .07
❑ 310 Steve Young 1.25 .50
❑ 311 Sam Adams .10 .02
❑ 312 Howard Ballard .10 .02
❑ 313 Robert Blackmon .10 .02
❑ 314 Brian Blades .20 .07
❑ 315 Joey Galloway RC 1.50 .60
❑ 316 Carlton Gray .10 .02
❑ 317 Cortez Kennedy .20 .07
❑ 318 Rick Mirer .20 .07
❑ 319 Eugene Robinson .10 .02
❑ 320 Chris Warren .20 .07
❑ 321 Terry Wooden .10 .02
❑ 322 Derrick Brooks RC 1.50 .60
❑ 323 Lawrence Dawsey .10 .02
❑ 324 Trent Dilfer .40 .15
❑ 325 Santana Dotson .10 .02
❑ 326 Thomas Everett .10 .02
❑ 327 Paul Gruber .10 .02
❑ 328 Jackie Harris .10 .02
❑ 329 Courtney Hawkins .10 .02
❑ 330 Martin Mayhew .10 .02
❑ 331 Hardy Nickerson .10 .02
❑ 332 Errict Rhett .20 .07
❑ 333 Warren Sapp RC 1.50 .60
❑ 334 Charles Wilson .10 .02
❑ 335 Reggie Brooks .20 .07
❑ 336 Tom Carter .10 .02
❑ 337 Henry Ellard .20 .07
❑ 338 Ricky Ervins .10 .02
❑ 339 Darrell Green .10 .02
❑ 340 Ken Harvey .10 .02
❑ 341 Brian Mitchell .10 .02
❑ 342 Cory Raymer RC .10 .02
❑ 343 Heath Shuler .20 .07
❑ 344 Michael Westbrook RC .40 .15
❑ 345 Tony Woods .10 .02
❑ 346 Checklist .10 .02
❑ 347 Checklist .10 .02
❑ 348 Checklist .10 .02
❑ 349 Checklist .10 .02
❑ 350 Checklist .10 .02
❑ 351 Checklist .10 .02
❑ 352 Checklist .10 .02
❑ 353 Dave Krieg .10 .02
❑ 354 Rob Moore .20 .07
❑ 355 J.J. Birden .10 .02
❑ 356 Eric Metcalf .20 .07
❑ 357 Bryce Paup .20 .07
❑ 358 Willie Green .20 .07
❑ 359 Derrick Moore .10 .02
❑ 360 Michael Timpson .10 .02
❑ 361 Eric Bieniemy .10 .02
❑ 362 Keenan McCardell .40 .15
❑ 363 Andre Rison .20 .07
❑ 364 Lorenzo White .10 .02
❑ 365 Deion Sanders 1.00 .40
❑ 366 Wade Wilson .10 .02
❑ 367 Aaron Craver .10 .02
❑ 368 Michael Dean Perry .10 .02
❑ 369 Rod Smith WR RC 12.00 5.00
❑ 370 Henry Thomas .10 .02
❑ 371 Mark Ingram .10 .02
❑ 372 Chris Chandler .20 .07
❑ 373 Mel Gray .10 .02
❑ 374 Flipper Anderson .10 .02
❑ 375 Craig Erickson .10 .02
❑ 376 Mark Brunell 1.00 .40
❑ 377 Ernest Givins .10 .02
❑ 378 Randy Jordan .10 .02
❑ 379 Webster Slaughter .10 .02
❑ 380 Tamarick Vanover RC .40 .15
❑ 381 Gary Clark .10 .02
❑ 382 Steve Emtman .10 .02
❑ 383 Eric Green .10 .02
❑ 384 Louis Oliver .10 .02
❑ 385 Robert Smith .40 .15
❑ 386 Dave Meggett .10 .02
❑ 387 Eric Allen .10 .02
❑ 388 Wesley Walls .20 .07
❑ 389 Herschel Walker .20 .07
❑ 390 Ronald Moore .10 .02
❑ 391 Adrian Murrell .20 .07
❑ 392 Charles Wilson .10 .02
❑ 393 Derrick Fenner .10 .02
❑ 394 Pat Swilling .10 .02
❑ 395 Kelvin Martin .10 .02
❑ 396 Rodney Peete .10 .02
❑ 397 Ricky Watters .20 .07
❑ 398 Erric Pegram .20 .07
❑ 399 Leonard Russell .10 .02
❑ 400 Alexander Wright .10 .02
❑ 401 Darrien Gordon .10 .02
❑ 402 Alfred Pupunu .10 .02
❑ 403 Elvis Grbac .40 .15
❑ 404 Derek Loville .10 .02
❑ 405 Steve Broussard .10 .02
❑ 406 Ricky Proehl .10 .02
❑ 407 Bobby Joe Edmonds .10 .02
❑ 408 Alvin Harper .10 .02
❑ 409 Dave Moore RC .10 .02
❑ 410 Terry Allen .20 .07
❑ 411 Gus Frerotte .20 .07
❑ 412 Leslie Shepherd RC .20 .07
❑ 413 Stoney Case RC .10 .02
❑ 414 Frank Sanders RC .40 .15
❑ 415 Roell Preston RC .20 .07
❑ 416 Lorenzo Styles RC .10 .02
❑ 417 Justin Armour RC .10 .02
❑ 418 Todd Collins RC .20 .07
❑ 419 Darick Holmes RC .20 .07
❑ 420 Kerry Collins .60 .25
❑ 421 Tyrone Poole .20 .07
❑ 422 Rashaan Salaam .20 .07
❑ 423 Todd Sauerbrun RC .10 .02
❑ 424 Ki-Jana Carter .40 .15
❑ 425 David Dunn RC .10 .02
❑ 426 Ernest Hunter RC .10 .02
❑ 427 Eric Zeier RC .40 .15
❑ 428 Eric Bjornson RC .10 .02
❑ 429 Sherman Williams .10 .02
❑ 430 Terrell Davis RC 2.50 1.00
❑ 431 Luther Elliss .10 .02
❑ 432 Kez McCorvey RC .10 .02
❑ 433 Antonio Freeman RC 1.25 .50
❑ 434 Craig Newsome RC .10 .02
❑ 435 Steve McNair 1.50 .60
❑ 436 Chris Sanders RC .20 .07
❑ 437 Zack Crockett RC .20 .07
❑ 438 Ellis Johnson .10 .02
❑ 439 Tony Boselli .40 .15
❑ 440 James O. Stewart .40 .15
❑ 441 Trezelle Jenkins .10 .02
❑ 442 Tamarick Vanover .40 .15
❑ 443 Derrick Alexander DE .10 .02
❑ 444 Chad May RC .10 .02
❑ 445 James A.Stewart RC .10 .02
❑ 446 Ty Law .40 .15
❑ 447 Curtis Martin RC 3.00 1.25
❑ 448 Will Moore RC .10 .02
❑ 449 Mark Fields .20 .07
❑ 450 Ray Zellars RC .20 .07
❑ 451 Charles Way RC .10 .02
❑ 452 Tyrone Wheatley .40 .15
❑ 453 Kyle Brady .40 .15
❑ 454 Wayne Chrebet RC 2.50 1.00
❑ 455 Hugh Douglas .20 .07
❑ 456 Chris T.Jones RC .10 .02
❑ 457 Mike Mamula .10 .02
❑ 458 Fred McCrary RC .10 .02
❑ 459 Bobby Taylor .40 .15
❑ 460 Mark Bruener .20 .07
❑ 461 Kordell Stewart .60 .25
❑ 462 Kevin Carter .20 .07
❑ 463 Lovell Pinkney RC .10 .02
❑ 464 Johnny Thomas WR RC .10 .02
❑ 465 Terrell Fletcher RC .10 .02
❑ 466 Jimmy Oliver RC .10 .02
❑ 467 J.J. Stokes .40 .15
❑ 468 Christian Fauria RC .20 .07
❑ 469 Joey Galloway .60 .25
❑ 470 Derrick Brooks .60 .25
❑ 471 Warren Sapp .40 .15
❑ 472 Michael Westbrook .40 .15
❑ 473 Garrison Hearst ES .40 .15
❑ 474 Jeff George ES .20 .07
❑ 475 Terance Mathis ES .20 .07
❑ 476 Andre Reed ES .20 .07
❑ 477 Bruce Smith ES .40 .15
❑ 478 Lamar Lathon ES .10 .02
❑ 479 Curtis Conway ES .40 .15
❑ 480 Jeff Blake ES .40 .15
❑ 481 Carl Pickens ES .20 .07
❑ 482 Eric Turner ES .10 .02
❑ 483 Troy Aikman ES .75 .30
❑ 484 Michael Irvin ES .40 .15
❑ 485 Emmitt Smith ES 1.25 .50
❑ 486 John Elway ES 1.50 .60
❑ 487 Shannon Sharpe ES .20 .07
❑ 488 Herman Moore ES .40 .15
❑ 489 Barry Sanders ES 1.25 .50
❑ 490 Brett Favre ES 1.50 .60
❑ 491 Reggie White ES .40 .15
❑ 492 Haywood Jeffires ES .10 .02
❑ 493 Sean Dawkins ES .10 .02
❑ 494 Marshall Faulk ES 1.00 .40
❑ 495 Desmond Howard ES .20 .07
❑ 496 Steve Bono ES .20 .07
❑ 497 Derrick Thomas ES .40 .15
❑ 498 Irving Fryar ES .20 .07
❑ 499 Terry Kirby ES .20 .07
❑ 500 Dan Marino ES 1.50 .60
❑ 501 O.J. McDuffie ES .40 .15
❑ 502 Cris Carter ES .40 .15
❑ 503 Warren Moon ES .20 .07
❑ 504 Jake Reed ES .20 .07
❑ 505 Drew Bledsoe ES .40 .15
❑ 506 Ben Coates ES .20 .07
❑ 507 Jim Everett ES .10 .02
❑ 508 Rodney Hampton ES .20 .07
❑ 509 Mo Lewis ES .10 .02
❑ 510 Tim Brown ES .40 .15
❑ 511 Jeff Hostetler ES .20 .07
❑ 512 Rocket Ismail ES .20 .07
❑ 513 Chester McGlockton ES .20 .07
❑ 514 Fred Barnett ES .20 .07
❑ 515 Greg Lloyd ES .20 .07
❑ 516 Byron Bam Morris ES .10 .02
❑ 517 Rod Woodson ES .20 .07
❑ 518 Jerome Bettis ES .40 .15
❑ 519 Isaac Bruce ES .40 .15
❑ 520 Stan Humphries ES .20 .07
❑ 521 Natrone Means ES .20 .07
❑ 522 Junior Seau ES .40 .15
❑ 523 William Floyd ES .20 .07
❑ 524 Jerry Rice ES .75 .30
❑ 525 Steve Young ES .60 .25
❑ 526 Cortez Kennedy ES .20 .07
❑ 527 Rick Mirer ES .20 .07
❑ 528 Chris Warren ES .20 .07
❑ 529 Trent Dilfer ES .40 .15
❑ 530 Errict Rhett ES .20 .07
❑ 531 Darrell Green ES .10 .02
❑ 532 Heath Shuler ES .20 .07
❑ 533 Stoney Case RO .10 .02
❑ 534 Eric Zeier RO .20 .07
❑ 535 Kerry Collins RO .20 .07
❑ 536 Steve McNair RO 1.25 .50
❑ 537 Kordell Stewart RO .60 .25
❑ 538 Rob Johnson RO RC 1.00 .40
❑ 539 Eric Ball EE .10 .02
❑ 540 Darrick Brownlow EE .10 .02
❑ 541 Paul Butcher EE .10 .02
❑ 542 Carlester Crumpler EE .10 .02
❑ 543 Maurice Douglas EE .10 .02
❑ 544 Keith Elias EE RC .10 .02
❑ 545 Kenneth Gant EE .10 .02
❑ 546 Corey Harris EE .10 .02
❑ 547 Andre Hastings EE .20 .07
❑ 548 Thomas Homco EE .10 .02
❑ 549 Lenny McGill EE .10 .02
❑ 550 Mark Pike EE .10 .02
❑ P1 Promo Sheet 2.00 .75
❑ P264 Byron Bam Morris Prototype 1.00 .40

1996 Ultra

❑ COMPLETE SET (200) 25.00 10.00
❑ 1 Larry Centers .25 .08
❑ 2 Garrison Hearst .25 .08
❑ 3 Rob Moore .25 .08
❑ 4 Eric Swann .10 .02
❑ 5 Aeneas Williams .10 .02

❑ 6 Bert Emanuel .25 .08
❑ 7 Jeff George .25 .08
❑ 8 Craig Heyward .10 .02
❑ 9 Terance Mathis .10 .02
❑ 10 Eric Metcalf .10 .02
❑ 11 Cornelius Bennett .10 .02
❑ 12 Darick Holmes .10 .02
❑ 13 Jim Kelly .50 .20
❑ 14 Bryce Paup .10 .02
❑ 15 Bruce Smith .25 .08
❑ 16 Mark Carrier WR .10 .02
❑ 17 Kerry Collins .50 .20
❑ 18 Lamar Lathon .10 .02
❑ 19 Derrick Moore .10 .02
❑ 20 Tyrone Poole .10 .02
❑ 21 Curtis Conway .50 .20
❑ 22 Jeff Graham .10 .02
❑ 23 Raymont Harris .25 .08
❑ 24 Erik Kramer .10 .02
❑ 25 Rashaan Salaam .25 .08
❑ 26 Jeff Blake .50 .20
❑ 27 Ki-Jana Carter .25 .08
❑ 28 Carl Pickens .25 .08
❑ 29 Darnay Scott .25 .08
❑ 30 Dan Wilkinson .10 .02
❑ 31 Leroy Hoard .10 .02
❑ 32 Michael Jackson .25 .08
❑ 33 Andre Rison .25 .08
❑ 34 Vinny Testaverde .25 .08
❑ 35 Eric Turner .10 .02
❑ 36 Troy Aikman 1.25 .50
❑ 37 Charles Haley .25 .08
❑ 38 Michael Irvin .50 .20
❑ 39 Daryl Johnston .25 .08
❑ 40 Jay Novacek .10 .02
❑ 41 Deion Sanders .75 .30
❑ 42 Emmitt Smith 2.00 .75
❑ 43 Steve Atwater .10 .02
❑ 44 Terrell Davis 1.00 .40
❑ 45 John Elway 2.50 1.00
❑ 46 Anthony Miller .25 .08
❑ 47 Shannon Sharpe .25 .08
❑ 48 Scott Mitchell .25 .08
❑ 49 Herman Moore .25 .08
❑ 50 Johnnie Morton .25 .08
❑ 51 Brett Perriman .10 .02
❑ 52 Barry Sanders 2.00 .75
❑ 53 Chris Spielman .10 .02
❑ 54 Edgar Bennett .25 .08
❑ 55 Robert Brooks .50 .20
❑ 56 Mark Chmura .25 .08
❑ 57 Brett Favre 2.50 1.00
❑ 58 Reggie White .50 .20
❑ 59 Mel Gray .10 .02
❑ 60 Haywood Jeffires .10 .02
❑ 61 Steve McNair 1.00 .40
❑ 62 Chris Sanders .25 .08
❑ 63 Rodney Thomas .10 .02
❑ 64 Quentin Coryatt .10 .02
❑ 65 Sean Dawkins .10 .02
❑ 66 Ken Dilger .25 .08
❑ 67 Marshall Faulk .60 .25
❑ 68 Jim Harbaugh .25 .08
❑ 69 Tony Boselli .10 .02
❑ 70 Mark Brunell .75 .30
❑ 71 Desmond Howard .25 .08
❑ 72 Jimmy Smith .50 .20
❑ 73 James O. Stewart .25 .08
❑ 74 Marcus Allen .50 .20
❑ 75 Steve Bono .10 .02
❑ 76 Lake Dawson .10 .02
❑ 77 Neil Smith .25 .08
❑ 78 Derrick Thomas .50 .20
❑ 79 Tamarick Vanover .25 .08
❑ 80 Bryan Cox .10 .02
❑ 81 Irving Fryar .25 .08
❑ 82 Eric Green .10 .02
❑ 83 Dan Marino 2.50 1.00
❑ 84 O.J. McDuffie .25 .08
❑ 85 Bernie Parmalee .10 .02
❑ 86 Cris Carter .50 .20
❑ 87 Qadry Ismail .25 .08
❑ 88 Warren Moon .25 .08
❑ 89 Jake Reed .25 .08
❑ 90 Robert Smith .25 .08
❑ 91 Drew Bledsoe .75 .30
❑ 92 Vincent Brisby .10 .02
❑ 93 Ben Coates .25 .08
❑ 94 Curtis Martin 1.00 .40
❑ 95 Willie McGinest .10 .02
❑ 96 Dave Meggett .10 .02
❑ 97 Mario Bates .25 .08
❑ 98 Quinn Early .10 .02
❑ 99 Jim Everett .10 .02
❑ 100 Michael Haynes .10 .02
❑ 101 Renaldo Turnbull .10 .02
❑ 102 Dave Brown .10 .02
❑ 103 Rodney Hampton .25 .08
❑ 104 Mike Sherrard .10 .02
❑ 105 Phillippi Sparks .10 .02
❑ 106 Tyrone Wheatley .25 .08
❑ 107 Hugh Douglas .25 .08
❑ 108 Boomer Esiason .25 .08
❑ 109 Aaron Glenn .10 .02
❑ 110 Mo Lewis .10 .02
❑ 111 Johnny Mitchell .10 .02
❑ 112 Tim Brown .50 .20
❑ 113 Jeff Hostetler .10 .02
❑ 114 Rocket Ismail .10 .02
❑ 115 Chester McGlockton .10 .02
❑ 116 Harvey Williams .10 .02
❑ 117 Fred Barnett .10 .02
❑ 118 William Fuller .10 .02
❑ 119 Charlie Garner .25 .08
❑ 120 Ricky Watters .25 .08
❑ 121 Calvin Williams .10 .02
❑ 122 Kevin Greene .25 .08
❑ 123 Greg Lloyd .25 .08
❑ 124 Byron Bam Morris .10 .02
❑ 125 Neil O'Donnell .25 .08
❑ 126 Erric Pegram .10 .02
❑ 127 Kordell Stewart .50 .20
❑ 128 Yancey Thigpen .25 .08
❑ 129 Rod Woodson .25 .08
❑ 130 Jerome Bettis .50 .20
❑ 131 Isaac Bruce .50 .20
❑ 132 Troy Drayton .10 .02
❑ 133 Sean Gilbert .10 .02
❑ 134 Chris Miller .10 .02
❑ 135 Andre Coleman .10 .02
❑ 136 Ronnie Harmon .10 .02
❑ 137 Aaron Hayden RC .10 .02
❑ 138 Stan Humphries .25 .08
❑ 139 Natrone Means .25 .08
❑ 140 Junior Seau .50 .20
❑ 141 William Floyd .25 .08
❑ 142 Merton Hanks .10 .02
❑ 143 Brent Jones .10 .02
❑ 144 Derek Loville .10 .02
❑ 145 Jerry Rice 1.25 .50
❑ 146 J.J. Stokes .50 .20
❑ 147 Steve Young 1.00 .40
❑ 148 Brian Blades .10 .02
❑ 149 Joey Galloway .50 .20
❑ 150 Cortez Kennedy .10 .02
❑ 151 Rick Mirer .25 .08
❑ 152 Chris Warren .25 .08
❑ 153 Derrick Brooks .50 .20
❑ 154 Trent Dilfer .50 .20
❑ 155 Alvin Harper .10 .02
❑ 156 Jackie Harris .10 .02
❑ 157 Hardy Nickerson .10 .02
❑ 158 Errict Rhett .25 .08
❑ 159 Terry Allen .25 .08
❑ 160 Henry Ellard .10 .02
❑ 161 Brian Mitchell .10 .02
❑ 162 Heath Shuler .25 .08
❑ 163 Michael Westbrook .50 .20
❑ 164 Tim Biakabutuka RC .50 .20
❑ 165 Tony Brackens RC .50 .20
❑ 166 Rickey Dudley RC .50 .20
❑ 167 Bobby Engram RC .50 .20
❑ 168 Daryl Gardener RC .10 .02
❑ 169 Eddie George RC 1.50 .60
❑ 170 Terry Glenn RC 1.25 .50
❑ 171 Kevin Hardy RC .50 .20
❑ 172 Keyshawn Johnson RC 1.25 .50
❑ 173 Cedric Jones RC .10 .02
❑ 174 Leeland McElroy RC .25 .08
❑ 175 Jonathan Ogden RC .50 .20
❑ 176 Lawrence Phillips RC .50 .20
❑ 177 Simeon Rice RC 1.25 .50
❑ 178 Regan Upshaw RC .10 .02
❑ 179 Justin Armour FI .10 .02
❑ 180 Kyle Brady FI .10 .02
❑ 181 Devin Bush FI .10 .02
❑ 182 Kevin Carter FI .10 .02
❑ 183 Wayne Chrebet FI .75 .30
❑ 184 Napoleon Kaufman FI .50 .20
❑ 185 Frank Sanders FI .25 .08
❑ 186 Warren Sapp FI .10 .02
❑ 187 Eric Zeier FI .10 .02
❑ 188 Ray Zellars FI .10 .02
❑ 189 Bill Brooks SW .10 .02
❑ 190 Chris Calloway SW .10 .02
❑ 191 Zack Crockett SW .10 .02
❑ 192 Antonio Freeman SW .50 .20
❑ 193 Tyrone Hughes SW .10 .02
❑ 194 Daryl Johnston SW .25 .08
❑ 195 Tony Martin SW .10 .02
❑ 196 Keenan McCardell SW .50 .20
❑ 197 Glyn Milburn SW .10 .02
❑ 198 David Palmer SW .10 .02
❑ 199 Checklist .10 .02
❑ 200 Checklist .10 .02
❑ P1 Promo Sheet 2.00 .75

1997 Ultra

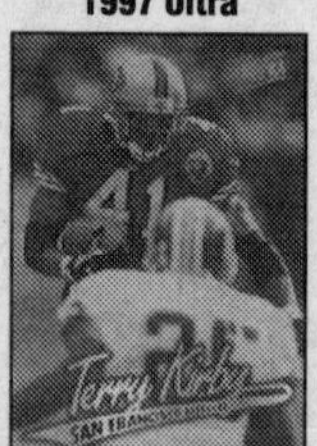

❑ COMPLETE SET (350) 80.00 40.00
❑ COMP.SERIES 1 (200) 30.00 15.00
❑ COMP.SERIES 2 (150) 50.00 25.00
❑ 1 Brett Favre 2.50 1.25
❑ 2 Ricky Watters .40 .15
❑ 3 Dan Marino 2.50 1.00
❑ 4 Bryan Still .25 .08
❑ 5 Chester McGlockton .25 .08
❑ 6 Tim Biakabutuka .40 .15
❑ 7 Dave Brown .25 .08
❑ 8 Mike Alstott .60 .25
❑ 9 O.J. McDuffie .40 .15
❑ 10 Mark Brunell .75 .30
❑ 11 Michael Bates .25 .08
❑ 12 Tyrone Wheatley .40 .15
❑ 13 Eddie George .60 .25
❑ 14 Kevin Greene .40 .15
❑ 15 Jerris McPhail .25 .08
❑ 16 Harvey Williams .25 .08
❑ 17 Eric Swann .25 .08
❑ 18 Carl Pickens .40 .15
❑ 19 Terrell Davis .75 .30
❑ 20 Charles Way .25 .08
❑ 21 Jamie Asher .25 .08
❑ 22 Qadry Ismail .40 .15
❑ 23 Lawrence Phillips .25 .08
❑ 24 John Friesz .25 .08
❑ 25 Dorsey Levens .60 .25

26	Willie McGinest	.25	.08
27	Chris T. Jones	.25	.08
28	Cortez Kennedy	.25	.08
29	Raymont Harris	.25	.08
30	William Roaf	.25	.08
31	Ted Johnson	.25	.08
32	Tony Martin	.40	.15
33	Jim Everett	.25	.08
34	Ray Zellars	.25	.08
35	Derrick Alexander WR	.40	.15
36	Leonard Russell	.25	.08
37	William Thomas	.25	.08
38	Karim Abdul-Jabbar	.40	.15
39	Kevin Turner	.25	.08
40	Robert Brooks	.40	.15
41	Kent Graham	.25	.08
42	Tony Brackens	.25	.08
43	Rodney Hampton	.40	.15
44	Drew Bledsoe	.75	.30
45	Barry Sanders	2.00	.75
46	Tim Brown	.60	.25
47	Reggie White	.60	.25
48	Terry Allen	.60	.25
49	Jim Harbaugh	.40	.15
50	John Elway	2.50	1.00
51	William Floyd	.40	.15
52	Michael Jackson	.40	.15
53	Larry Centers	.40	.15
54	Emmitt Smith	2.00	.75
55	Bruce Smith	.40	.15
56	Terrell Owens	.75	.30
57	Deion Sanders	.60	.25
58	Neil O'Donnell	.40	.15
59	Kordell Stewart	.60	.25
60	Bobby Engram	.40	.15
61	Keenan McCardell	.40	.15
62	Ben Coates	.40	.15
63	Curtis Martin	.75	.30
64	Hugh Douglas	.25	.08
65	Eric Moulds	.60	.25
66	Derrick Thomas	.60	.25
67	Byron Bam Morris	.25	.08
68	Bryan Cox	.25	.08
69	Rob Moore	.40	.15
70	Michael Haynes	.25	.08
71	Brian Mitchell	.25	.08
72	Alex Molden	.25	.08
73	Steve Young	.75	.30
74	Andre Reed	.40	.15
75	Michael Westbrook	.40	.15
76	Eric Metcalf	.40	.15
77	Tony Banks	.40	.15
78	Ken Dilger	.25	.08
79	John Henry Mills RC	.25	.08
80	Ashley Ambrose	.25	.08
81	Jason Dunn	.25	.08
82	Trent Dilfer	.60	.25
83	Wayne Chrebet	.60	.25
84	Ty Detmer	.40	.15
85	Aeneas Williams	.25	.08
86	Frank Wycheck	.25	.08
87	Jessie Tuggle	.25	.08
88	Steve McNair	.75	.30
89	Chris Slade	.25	.08
90	Anthony Johnson	.25	.08
91	Simeon Rice	.40	.15
92	Mike Tomczak	.25	.08
93	Sean Jones	.25	.08
94	Wesley Walls	.40	.15
95	Thurman Thomas	.60	.25
96	Scott Mitchell	.40	.15
97	Desmond Howard	.40	.15
98	Chris Warren	.40	.15
99	Glyn Milburn	.25	.08
100	Vinny Testaverde	.40	.15
101	James O.Stewart	.40	.15
102	Iheanyi Uwaezuoke	.25	.08
103	Stan Humphries	.40	.15
104	Terance Mathis	.40	.15
105	Thomas Lewis	.25	.08
106	Eddie Kennison	.40	.15
107	Rashaan Salaam	.25	.08
108	Curtis Conway	.40	.15
109	Chris Sanders	.25	.08
110	Marcus Allen	.60	.25
111	Gilbert Brown	.40	.15
112	Jason Sehorn	.40	.15
113	Zach Thomas	.60	.25
114	Bobby Hebert	.25	.08
115	Herman Moore	.40	.15
116	Ray Lewis	1.00	.40
117	Darnay Scott	.40	.15
118	Jamal Anderson	.60	.25
119	Keyshawn Johnson	.60	.25
120	Adrian Murrell	.40	.15
121	Sam Mills	.25	.08
122	Irving Fryar	.40	.15
123	Ki-Jana Carter	.25	.08
124	Gus Frerotte	.25	.08
125	Terry Glenn	.60	.25
126	Quentin Coryatt	.25	.08
127	Robert Smith	.40	.15
128	Jeff Blake	.40	.15
129	Natrone Means	.40	.15
130	Isaac Bruce	.60	.25
131	Lamar Lathon	.25	.08
132	Johnnie Morton	.40	.15
133	Jerry Rice	1.25	.50
134	Errict Rhett	.25	.08
135	Junior Seau	.60	.25
136	Joey Galloway	.40	.15
137	Napoleon Kaufman	.60	.25
138	Troy Aikman	1.25	.50
139	Kevin Hardy	.25	.08
140	Jimmy Smith	.40	.15
141	Edgar Bennett	.40	.15
142	Hardy Nickerson	.25	.08
143	Greg Lloyd	.25	.08
144	Dale Carter	.25	.08
145	Jake Reed	.40	.15
146	Cris Carter	.60	.25
147	Todd Collins	.25	.08
148	Mel Gray	.25	.08
149	Lawyer Milloy	.40	.15
150	Kimble Anders	.40	.15
151	Darick Holmes	.25	.08
152	Bert Emanuel	.40	.15
153	Marshall Faulk	.75	.30
154	Frank Sanders	.40	.15
155	Leeland McElroy	.25	.08
156	Rickey Dudley	.40	.15
157	Tamarick Vanover	.40	.15
158	Kerry Collins	.60	.25
159	Jeff Graham	.25	.08
160	Jerome Bettis	.60	.25
161	Greg Hill	.25	.08
162	John Mobley	.25	.08
163	Michael Irvin	.60	.25
164	Marvin Harrison	.60	.25
165	Jim Schwantz RC	.25	.08
166	Jermaine Lewis	.60	.25
167	Levon Kirkland	.25	.08
168	Nilo Silvan	.25	.08
169	Ken Norton	.25	.08
170	Yancey Thigpen	.40	.15
171	Antonio Freeman	.60	.25
172	Terry Kirby	.40	.15
173	Brad Johnson	.60	.25
174	Reidel Anthony RC	.60	.25
175	Tiki Barber RC	5.00	2.00
176	Pat Barnes RC	.60	.25
177	Michael Booker RC	.25	.08
178	Peter Boulware RC	.60	.25
179	Rae Carruth RC	.25	.08
180	Troy Davis RC	.40	.15
181	Corey Dillon RC	5.00	2.00
182	Jim Druckenmiller RC	.40	.15
183	Warrick Dunn RC	2.50	1.00
184	James Farrior RC	.60	.25
185	Yatil Green RC	.40	.15
186	Walter Jones RC	.60	.25
187	Tom Knight RC	.25	.08
188	Sam Madison RC	.60	.25
189	Tyrus McCloud RC	.25	.08
190	Orlando Pace RC	.60	.25
191	Jake Plummer RC	4.00	1.50
192	Dwayne Rudd RC	.60	.25
193	Darrell Russell RC	.25	.08
194	Sedrick Shaw RC	.40	.15
195	Shawn Springs RC	.40	.15
196	Bryant Westbrook RC	.25	.08
197	Danny Wuerffel RC	.60	.25
198	Reinard Wilson RC	.40	.15
199	Checklist	.25	.08
200	Checklist	.60	.25
201	Rick Mirer	.25	.08
202	Torrance Small	.25	.08
203	Ricky Proehl	.25	.08
204	Will Blackwell RC	.40	.15
205	Warrick Dunn	1.25	.50
206	Rob Johnson	.60	.25
207	Jim Schwantz	.25	.08
208	Ike Hilliard RC	1.25	.50
209	Chris Canty RC	.25	.08
210	Chris Boniol	.25	.08
211	Jim Druckenmiller	.25	.08
212	Tony Gonzalez RC	2.50	1.00
213	Scottie Graham	.25	.08
214	Byron Hanspard RC	.40	.15
215	Gary Brown	.25	.08
216	Darrell Russell	.25	.08
217	Sedrick Shaw	.40	.15
218	Boomer Esiason	.40	.15
219	Peter Boulware	.40	.15
220	Willie Green	.25	.08
221	Dietrich Jells	.25	.08
222	Freddie Jones RC	.40	.15
223	Eric Metcalf	.40	.15
224	John Henry Mills	.25	.08
225	Michael Timpson	.25	.08
226	Danny Wuerffel	.60	.25
227	Daimon Shelton RC	.25	.08
228	Henry Ellard	.25	.08
229	Flipper Anderson	.25	.08
230	Hunter Goodwin RC	.25	.08
231	Jay Graham RC	.40	.15
232	Duce Staley RC	6.00	2.50
233	Lamar Thomas	.25	.08
234	Rod Woodson	.40	.15
235	Zack Crockett	.25	.08
236	Ernie Mills	.25	.08
237	Kyle Brady	.25	.08
238	Jesse Campbell	.25	.08
239	Anthony Miller	.25	.08
240	Michael Haynes	.25	.08
241	Qadry Ismail	.40	.15
242	Tom Knight	.25	.08
243	Brian Manning RC	.25	.08
244	Derrick Mayes	.40	.15
245	Jamie Sharper RC	.40	.15
246	Sherman Williams	.25	.08
247	Yatil Green	.40	.15
248	Howard Griffith	.25	.08
249	Brian Blades	.25	.08
250	Mark Chmura	.40	.15
251	Chris Darkins	.25	.08
252	Willie Davis	.25	.08
253	Quinn Early	.25	.08
254	Marc Edwards RC	.25	.08
255	Charlie Jones	.25	.08
256	Jake Plummer	1.50	.60
257	Heath Shuler	.25	.08
258	Fred Barnett	.25	.08
259	William Henderson	.40	.15
260	Michael Booker	.25	.08
261	Chad Brown	.25	.08
262	Garrison Hearst	.40	.15
263	Leon Johnson RC	.40	.15
264	Antowain Smith RC	2.00	.75
265	Darnell Autry RC	.40	.15
266	Craig Heyward	.25	.08
267	Walter Jones	.25	.08
268	Dexter Coakley RC	.60	.25
269	Mercury Hayes	.25	.08
270	Brett Perriman	.25	.08
271	Chris Spielman	.25	.08
272	Kevin Greene	.40	.15
273	Kevin Lockett RC	.40	.15
274	Troy Davis	.40	.15
275	Brent Jones	.25	.08
276	Chris Chandler	.40	.15
277	Bryant Westbrook	.25	.08
278	Desmond Howard	.40	.15
279	Tyrone Hughes	.25	.08
280	Kez McCorvey	.25	.08
281	Stephen Davis	.60	.25
282	Steve Everitt	.25	.08
283	Andre Hastings	.25	.08
284	Marcus Robinson RC	5.00	2.00
285	Donnell Woolford	.25	.08
286	Mario Bates	.25	.08

❑ 287 Corey Dillon	2.00	.75
❑ 288 Jackie Harris	.25	.08
❑ 289 Lorenzo Neal	.25	.08
❑ 290 Anthony Pleasant	.25	.08
❑ 291 Andre Rison	.40	.15
❑ 292 Amani Toomer	.40	.15
❑ 293 Eric Turner	.25	.08
❑ 294 Elvis Grbac	.40	.15
❑ 295 Cris Dishman	.25	.08
❑ 296 Tom Carter	.25	.08
❑ 297 Mark Carrier DB	.25	.08
❑ 298 Orlando Pace	.40	.15
❑ 299 Jay Riemersma RC	.25	.08
❑ 300 Daryl Johnston	.40	.15
❑ 301 Joey Kent RC	.60	.25
❑ 302 Ronnie Harmon	.25	.08
❑ 303 Rocket Ismail	.40	.15
❑ 304 Terrell Davis	.75	.30
❑ 305 Sean Dawkins	.25	.08
❑ 306 Jeff George	.40	.15
❑ 307 David Palmer	.25	.08
❑ 308 Dwayne Rudd	.25	.08
❑ 309 J.J. Stokes	.40	.15
❑ 310 James Farrior	.40	.15
❑ 311 William Fuller	.25	.08
❑ 312 George Jones RC	.40	.15
❑ 313 John Allred RC	.25	.08
❑ 314 Tony Graziani RC	.60	.25
❑ 315 Jeff Hostetler	.25	.08
❑ 316 Keith Poole RC	.60	.25
❑ 317 Neil Smith	.40	.15
❑ 318 Steve Tasker	.25	.08
❑ 319 Mike Vrabel RC	10.00	4.00
❑ 320 Pat Barnes	.60	.25
❑ 321 James Hundon RC	.60	.25
❑ 322 O.J. Santiago RC	.40	.15
❑ 323 Billy Davis RC	.25	.08
❑ 324 Shawn Springs	.40	.15
❑ 325 Reinard Wilson	.25	.08
❑ 326 Charles Johnson	.40	.15
❑ 327 Micheal Barrow	.25	.08
❑ 328 Derrick Mason RC	3.00	1.25
❑ 329 Muhsin Muhammad	.40	.15
❑ 330 David LaFleur RC	.25	.08
❑ 331 Reidel Anthony	.40	.15
❑ 332 Tiki Barber	2.00	.75
❑ 333 Ray Buchanan	.25	.08
❑ 334 John Elway	2.50	1.00
❑ 335 Alvin Harper	.25	.08
❑ 336 Damon Jones RC	.25	.08
❑ 337 Dedric Ward RC	.40	.15
❑ 338 Jim Everett	.25	.08
❑ 339 Jon Harris	.25	.08
❑ 340 Warren Moon	.60	.25
❑ 341 Rae Carruth	.25	.08
❑ 342 John Mobley	.25	.08
❑ 343 Tyrone Poole	.25	.08
❑ 344 Mike Cherry RC	.25	.08
❑ 345 Horace Copeland	.25	.08
❑ 346 Deon Figures	.25	.08
❑ 347 Antwuan Wyatt RC	.25	.08
❑ 348 Tommy Vardell	.25	.08
❑ 349 Checklist (201-324)	.25	.08
❑ 350 Checklist (325-350/inserts)	.25	.08
❑ S1A T.Davis Sample AU	80.00	40.00
❑ AU3 Dan Marino AU	100.00	40.00
❑ S1 Terrell Davis Sample	3.00	1.25

1998 Ultra

❑ COMPLETE SET (425)	120.00	50.00
❑ COMP.SERIES 1 (225)	80.00	30.00
❑ COMP.SERIES 2 (200)	50.00	25.00
❑ 1 Barry Sanders	2.50	1.00
❑ 2 Brett Favre	3.00	1.50
❑ 3 Napoleon Kaufman	.75	.30
❑ 4 Robert Smith	.75	.30
❑ 5 Terry Allen	.75	.30
❑ 6 Vinny Testaverde	.50	.20
❑ 7 William Floyd	.30	.10
❑ 8 Carl Pickens	.50	.20
❑ 9 Antonio Freeman	.75	.30
❑ 10 Ben Coates	.50	.20
❑ 11 Elvis Grbac	.50	.20
❑ 12 Kerry Collins	.50	.20
❑ 13 Orlando Pace	.30	.10
❑ 14 Steve Broussard	.30	.10
❑ 15 Terance Mathis	.50	.20
❑ 16 Tiki Barber	.75	.30
❑ 17 Cris Carter	.75	.30
❑ 18 Eric Green	.30	.10
❑ 19 Eric Metcalf	.30	.10
❑ 20 Jeff George	.50	.20
❑ 21 Leslie Shepherd	.30	.10
❑ 22 Natrone Means	.50	.20
❑ 23 Scott Mitchell	.50	.20
❑ 24 Adrian Murrell	.50	.20
❑ 25 Gilbert Brown	.30	.10
❑ 26 Jimmy Smith	.50	.20
❑ 27 Mark Bruener	.30	.10
❑ 28 Troy Aikman	1.50	.60
❑ 29 Warrick Dunn	.75	.30
❑ 30 Jay Graham	.30	.10
❑ 31 Craig Whelihan RC	.30	.10
❑ 32 Ed McCaffrey	.50	.20
❑ 33 Jamie Asher	.30	.10
❑ 34 John Randle	.50	.20
❑ 35 Michael Jackson	.30	.10
❑ 36 Rickey Dudley	.30	.10
❑ 37 Sean Dawkins	.30	.10
❑ 38 Andre Rison	.50	.20
❑ 39 Bert Emanuel	.50	.20
❑ 40 Jeff Blake	.50	.20
❑ 41 Curtis Conway	.50	.20
❑ 42 Eddie Kennison	.50	.20
❑ 43 James McKnight	.75	.30
❑ 44 Rae Carruth	.30	.10
❑ 45 Tito Wooten RC	.30	.10
❑ 46 Cris Dishman	.30	.10
❑ 47 Ernie Conwell	.30	.10
❑ 48 Fred Lane	.30	.10
❑ 49 Jamal Anderson	.75	.30
❑ 50 Lake Dawson	.30	.10
❑ 51 Michael Strahan	.50	.20
❑ 52 Reggie White	.75	.30
❑ 53 Trent Dilfer	.75	.30
❑ 54 Troy Brown	.50	.20
❑ 55 Wesley Walls	.50	.20
❑ 56 Chidi Ahanotu	.30	.10
❑ 57 Dwayne Rudd	.30	.10
❑ 58 Jerry Rice	1.50	.60
❑ 59 Johnnie Morton	.50	.20
❑ 60 Sherman Williams	.30	.10
❑ 61 Steve McNair	.75	.30
❑ 62 Will Blackwell	.30	.10
❑ 63 Chris Chandler	.50	.20
❑ 64 Dexter Coakley	.30	.10
❑ 65 Horace Copeland	.30	.10
❑ 66 Jerald Moore	.30	.10
❑ 67 Leon Johnson	.30	.10
❑ 68 Mark Chmura	.50	.20
❑ 69 Micheal Barrow	.30	.10
❑ 70 Muhsin Muhammad	.50	.20
❑ 71 Terry Glenn	.75	.30
❑ 72 Tony Brackens	.30	.10
❑ 73 Chad Scott	.30	.10
❑ 74 Glenn Foley	.50	.20
❑ 75 Keenan McCardell	.50	.20
❑ 76 Peter Boulware	.30	.10
❑ 77 Reidel Anthony	.50	.20
❑ 78 William Henderson	.50	.20
❑ 79 Tony Martin	.50	.20
❑ 80 Tony Gonzalez	.75	.30
❑ 81 Charlie Jones	.30	.10
❑ 82 Chris Gedney	.30	.10
❑ 83 Chris Calloway	.30	.10
❑ 84 Dale Carter	.30	.10
❑ 85 Ki-Jana Carter	.30	.10
❑ 86 Shawn Springs	.30	.10
❑ 87 Antowain Smith	.75	.30
❑ 88 Eric Turner	.30	.10
❑ 89 John Mobley	.30	.10
❑ 90 Ken Dilger	.30	.10
❑ 91 Bobby Hoying	.50	.20
❑ 92 Curtis Martin	.75	.30
❑ 93 Drew Bledsoe	1.25	.50
❑ 94 Gary Brown	.30	.10
❑ 95 Marvin Harrison	.75	.30
❑ 96 Todd Collins	.30	.10
❑ 97 Chris Warren	.50	.20
❑ 98 Danny Kanell	.50	.20
❑ 99 Tony McGee	.30	.10
❑ 100 Rod Smith	.50	.20
❑ 101 Frank Sanders	.50	.20
❑ 102 Irving Fryar	.50	.20
❑ 103 Marcus Allen	.75	.30
❑ 104 Marshall Faulk	1.00	.40
❑ 105 Bruce Smith	.50	.20
❑ 106 Charlie Garner	.50	.20
❑ 107 Paul Justin	.30	.10
❑ 108 Randal Hill	.30	.10
❑ 109 Erik Kramer	.30	.10
❑ 110 Rob Moore	.50	.20
❑ 111 Shannon Sharpe	.50	.20
❑ 112 Warren Moon	.75	.30
❑ 113 Zach Thomas	.75	.30
❑ 114 Dan Marino	3.00	1.50
❑ 115 Duce Staley	1.00	.40
❑ 116 Eric Swann	.30	.10
❑ 117 Kenny Holmes	.30	.10
❑ 118 Merton Hanks	.30	.10
❑ 119 Raymont Harris	.30	.10
❑ 120 Terrell Davis	.75	.30
❑ 121 Thurman Thomas	.75	.30
❑ 122 Wayne Martin	.30	.10
❑ 123 Charles Way	.30	.10
❑ 124 Chuck Smith	.30	.10
❑ 125 Corey Dillon	.75	.30
❑ 126 Darnell Autry	.30	.10
❑ 127 Isaac Bruce	.75	.30
❑ 128 Joey Galloway	.50	.20
❑ 129 Kimble Anders	.50	.20
❑ 130 Aeneas Williams	.30	.10
❑ 131 Andre Hastings	.30	.10
❑ 132 Chad Lewis	.50	.20
❑ 133 J.J. Stokes	.50	.20
❑ 134 John Elway	3.00	1.25
❑ 135 Karim Abdul-Jabbar	.75	.30
❑ 136 Ken Harvey	.30	.10
❑ 137 Robert Brooks	.50	.20
❑ 138 Rodney Thomas	.30	.10
❑ 139 James Stewart	.50	.20
❑ 140 Billy Joe Hobert	.30	.10
❑ 141 Frank Wycheck	.30	.10
❑ 142 Jake Plummer	.75	.30
❑ 143 Jerris McPhail	.30	.10
❑ 144 Kordell Stewart	.75	.30
❑ 145 Terrell Owens	.75	.30
❑ 146 Willie Green	.30	.10
❑ 147 Anthony Miller	.30	.10
❑ 148 Courtney Hawkins	.30	.10
❑ 149 Larry Centers	.30	.10
❑ 150 Gus Frerotte	.30	.10
❑ 151 O.J. McDuffie	.50	.20
❑ 152 Ray Zellars	.30	.10
❑ 153 Terry Kirby	.30	.10
❑ 154 Tommy Vardell	.30	.10
❑ 155 Willie Davis	.30	.10
❑ 156 Chris Canty	.30	.10
❑ 157 Byron Hanspard	.30	.10
❑ 158 Chris Penn	.30	.10
❑ 159 Damon Jones	.30	.10
❑ 160 Derrick Mayes	.50	.20
❑ 161 Emmitt Smith	2.50	1.25
❑ 162 Keyshawn Johnson	.75	.30
❑ 163 Mike Alstott	.75	.30
❑ 164 Tom Carter	.30	.10
❑ 165 Tony Banks	.50	.20
❑ 166 Bryant Westbrook	.30	.10
❑ 167 Chris Sanders	.30	.10
❑ 168 Deion Sanders	.75	.30
❑ 169 Garrison Hearst	.75	.30
❑ 170 Jason Taylor	.50	.20
❑ 171 Jerome Bettis	.75	.30

❑ 172 John Lynch .50 .20
❑ 173 Troy Davis .30 .10
❑ 174 Freddie Jones .30 .10
❑ 175 Herman Moore .50 .20
❑ 176 Jake Reed .50 .20
❑ 177 Mark Brunell .75 .30
❑ 178 Ray Lewis .75 .30
❑ 179 Stephen Davis .30 .10
❑ 180 Tim Brown .75 .30
❑ 181 Willie McGinest .30 .10
❑ 182 Andre Reed .50 .20
❑ 183 Darrien Gordon .30 .10
❑ 184 David Palmer .30 .10
❑ 185 James Jett .50 .20
❑ 186 Junior Seau .75 .30
❑ 187 Zack Crockett .30 .10
❑ 188 Brad Johnson .75 .30
❑ 189 Charles Johnson .30 .10
❑ 190 Eddie George .75 .30
❑ 191 Jermaine Lewis .50 .20
❑ 192 Michael Irvin .75 .30
❑ 193 Reggie Brown LB .30 .10
❑ 194 Steve Young 1.00 .40
❑ 195 Warren Sapp .50 .20
❑ 196 Wayne Chrebet .75 .30
❑ 197 David Dunn .30 .10
❑ 198 Dorsey Levens CL .50 .20
❑ 199 Troy Aikman CL .75 .30
❑ 200 John Elway CL .75 .30
❑ 201 Peyton Manning RC 30.00 15.00
❑ 202 Ryan Leaf RC 3.00 1.25
❑ 203 Charles Woodson RC 4.00 1.50
❑ 204 Andre Wadsworth RC 2.50 1.00
❑ 205 Brian Simmons RC 2.50 1.00
❑ 206 Curtis Enis RC 1.50 .60
❑ 207 Randy Moss RC 15.00 7.50
❑ 208 Germane Crowell RC 2.50 1.00
❑ 209 Greg Ellis RC 1.50 .60
❑ 210 Kevin Dyson RC 3.00 1.25
❑ 211 Skip Hicks RC 2.50 1.00
❑ 212 Alonzo Mayes RC 1.50 .60
❑ 213 Robert Edwards RC 2.50 1.00
❑ 214 Fred Taylor RC 5.00 2.00
❑ 215 Robert Holcombe RC 2.50 1.00
❑ 216 John Dutton RC 1.50 .60
❑ 217 Vonnie Holliday RC 2.50 1.00
❑ 218 Tim Dwight RC 3.00 1.25
❑ 219 Tavian Banks RC 2.50 1.00
❑ 220 Marcus Nash RC 1.50 .60
❑ 221 Jason Peter RC 1.50 .60
❑ 222 Michael Myers RC 1.50 .60
❑ 223 Takeo Spikes RC 3.00 1.25
❑ 224 Kivuusama Mays RC 1.50 .60
❑ 225 Jacquez Green RC 2.50 1.00
❑ 226 Doug Flutie .75 .30
❑ 227 Ike Hilliard .50 .20
❑ 228 Craig Heyward .30 .10
❑ 229 Kevin Hardy .30 .10
❑ 230 Jason Dunn .30 .10
❑ 231 Billy Davis .30 .10
❑ 232 Chester McGlockton .30 .10
❑ 233 Sean Gilbert .30 .10
❑ 234 Bert Emanuel .50 .20
❑ 235 Keith Byars .30 .10
❑ 236 Tyrone Wheatley .50 .20
❑ 237 Ricky Proehl .30 .10
❑ 238 Michael Bates .30 .10
❑ 239 Derrick Alexander .50 .20
❑ 240 Harvey Williams .30 .10
❑ 241 Mike Pritchard .30 .10
❑ 242 Paul Justin .30 .10
❑ 243 Jeff Hostetler .30 .10
❑ 244 Eric Moulds .75 .30
❑ 245 Jeff Burris .30 .10
❑ 246 Gary Brown .30 .10
❑ 247 Anthony Johnson .30 .10
❑ 248 Dan Wilkinson .30 .10
❑ 249 Chris Warren .50 .20
❑ 250 Chris Darkins .30 .10
❑ 251 Eric Metcalf .30 .10
❑ 252 Pat Swilling .30 .10
❑ 253 Lamar Smith .50 .20
❑ 254 Quinn Early .30 .10
❑ 255 Carlester Crumpler .30 .10
❑ 256 Eric Bieniemy .30 .10
❑ 257 Aaron Bailey .30 .10
❑ 258 Neil O'Donnell .50 .20
❑ 259 Rod Woodson .50 .20
❑ 260 Ricky Whittle .30 .10
❑ 261 Iheanyi Uwaezuoke .30 .10
❑ 262 Heath Shuler .30 .10
❑ 263 Darren Sharper .50 .20
❑ 264 John Henry Mills .30 .10
❑ 265 Marco Battaglia .30 .10
❑ 266 Yancey Thigpen .30 .10
❑ 267 Irv Smith .30 .10
❑ 268 Jamie Sharper .30 .10
❑ 269 Marcus Robinson 5.00 2.00
❑ 270 Dorsey Levens .75 .30
❑ 271 Qadry Ismail .50 .20
❑ 272 Desmond Howard .50 .20
❑ 273 Webster Slaughter .30 .10
❑ 274 Eugene Robinson .30 .10
❑ 275 Bill Romanowski .30 .10
❑ 276 Vincent Brisby .30 .10
❑ 277 Errict Rhett .50 .20
❑ 278 Albert Connell .30 .10
❑ 279 Thomas Lewis .30 .10
❑ 280 John Farquhar RC .30 .10
❑ 281 Marc Edwards .30 .10
❑ 282 Tyrone Davis .30 .10
❑ 283 Eric Allen .30 .10
❑ 284 Aaron Glenn .30 .10
❑ 285 Roosevelt Potts .30 .10
❑ 286 Kez McCorvey .30 .10
❑ 287 Joey Kent .50 .20
❑ 288 Jim Druckenmiller .30 .10
❑ 289 Sean Dawkins .30 .10
❑ 290 Edgar Bennett .30 .10
❑ 291 Vinny Testaverde .50 .20
❑ 292 Chris Slade .30 .10
❑ 293 Lamar Lathon .30 .10
❑ 294 Jackie Harris .30 .10
❑ 295 Jim Harbaugh .50 .20
❑ 296 Rob Fredrickson .30 .10
❑ 297 Ty Detmer .50 .20
❑ 298 Karl Williams .30 .10
❑ 299 Troy Drayton .30 .10
❑ 300 Curtis Martin .75 .30
❑ 301 Tamarick Vanover .30 .10
❑ 302 Lorenzo Neal .30 .10
❑ 303 John Hall .30 .10
❑ 304 Kevin Greene .50 .20
❑ 305 Bryan Still .30 .10
❑ 306 Neil Smith .50 .20
❑ 307 Greg Lloyd .30 .10
❑ 308 Shawn Jefferson .30 .10
❑ 309 Aaron Taylor .30 .10
❑ 310 Sedrick Shaw .30 .10
❑ 311 O.J. Santiago .30 .10
❑ 312 Kevin Abrams .30 .10
❑ 313 Dana Stubblefield .30 .10
❑ 314 Daryl Johnston .50 .20
❑ 315 Bryan Cox .30 .10
❑ 316 Jeff Graham .30 .10
❑ 317 Mario Bates .50 .20
❑ 318 Adrian Murrell .50 .20
❑ 319 Greg Hill .30 .10
❑ 320 Jahine Arnold .30 .10
❑ 321 Justin Armour .30 .10
❑ 322 Ricky Watters .50 .20
❑ 323 Lamont Warren .30 .10
❑ 324 Mack Strong .75 .30
❑ 325 Darnay Scott .50 .20
❑ 326 Brian Mitchell .30 .10
❑ 327 Rob Johnson .50 .20
❑ 328 Kent Graham .30 .10
❑ 329 Hugh Douglas .30 .10
❑ 330 Simeon Rice .50 .20
❑ 331 Rick Mirer .30 .10
❑ 332 Randall Cunningham .75 .30
❑ 333 Steve Atwater .30 .10
❑ 334 Latario Rachal .30 .10
❑ 335 Tony Martin .50 .20
❑ 336 Leroy Hoard .30 .10
❑ 337 Howard Griffith .30 .10
❑ 338 Kevin Lockett .30 .10
❑ 339 William Floyd .30 .10
❑ 340 Jerry Ellison .30 .10
❑ 341 Kyle Brady .30 .10
❑ 342 Michael Westbrook .50 .20
❑ 343 Kevin Turner .30 .10
❑ 344 David LaFleur .30 .10
❑ 345 Robert Jones .30 .10
❑ 346 Dave Brown .30 .10
❑ 347 Kevin Williams .30 .10
❑ 348 Amani Toomer .50 .20
❑ 349 Amp Lee .30 .10
❑ 350 Bryce Paup .30 .10
❑ 351 Dewayne Washington .30 .10
❑ 352 Mercury Hayes .30 .10
❑ 353 Tim Biakabutuka .50 .20
❑ 354 Ray Crockett .30 .10
❑ 355 Ted Washington .30 .10
❑ 356 Pete Mitchell .30 .10
❑ 357 Billy Jenkins RC .30 .10
❑ 358 Troy Aikman CL .75 .30
❑ 359 Drew Bledsoe CL .75 .30
❑ 360 Steve Young CL .75 .30
❑ 361 Antonio Freeman NG .50 .20
❑ 362 Antowain Smith NG .50 .20
❑ 363 Barry Sanders NG 1.50 .60
❑ 364 Bobby Hoying NG .30 .10
❑ 365 Brett Favre NG 2.00 .75
❑ 366 Corey Dillon NG .50 .20
❑ 367 Dan Marino NG 2.00 .75
❑ 368 Drew Bledsoe NG .75 .30
❑ 369 Eddie George NG .50 .20
❑ 370 Emmitt Smith NG 1.50 .60
❑ 371 Herman Moore NG .50 .20
❑ 372 Jake Plummer NG .50 .20
❑ 373 Jerome Bettis NG .50 .20
❑ 374 Jerry Rice NG 1.00 .40
❑ 375 Joey Galloway NG .50 .20
❑ 376 John Elway NG 2.00 .75
❑ 377 Kordell Stewart NG .50 .20
❑ 378 Mark Brunell NG .75 .30
❑ 379 Keyshawn Johnson NG .50 .20
❑ 380 Steve Young NG .75 .30
❑ 381 Steve McNair NG .50 .20
❑ 382 Terrell Davis NG .75 .30
❑ 383 Tim Brown NG .50 .20
❑ 384 Troy Aikman NG 1.00 .40
❑ 385 Warrick Dunn NG .75 .30
❑ 386 Ryan Leaf 3.00 1.25
❑ 387 Tony Simmons RC 2.00 .75
❑ 388 Rodney Williams RC 1.25 .50
❑ 389 John Avery RC 2.00 .75
❑ 390 Shaun Williams RC 2.00 .75
❑ 391 Anthony Simmons RC 2.00 .75
❑ 392 Rashaan Shehee RC 2.00 .75
❑ 393 Robert Holcombe 2.00 .75
❑ 394 Larry Shannon RC 1.25 .50
❑ 395 Skip Hicks 2.00 .75
❑ 396 Rod Rutledge RC 1.25 .50
❑ 397 Donald Hayes RC 2.00 .75
❑ 398 Curtis Enis 1.25 .50
❑ 399 Mikhael Ricks RC 2.00 .75
❑ 400 Brian Griese RC 6.00 2.50
❑ 401 Michael Pittman RC 4.00 1.50
❑ 402 Jacquez Green 2.00 .75
❑ 403 Jerome Pathon RC 3.00 1.25
❑ 404 Ahman Green RC 15.00 6.00
❑ 405 Marcus Nash 1.25 .50
❑ 406 Randy Moss 15.00 6.00
❑ 407 Terry Fair RC 2.00 .75
❑ 408 Jammi German RC 1.25 .50
❑ 409 Stephen Alexander RC 2.00 .75
❑ 410 Grant Wistrom RC 2.00 .75
❑ 411 Charlie Batch RC 3.00 1.25
❑ 412 Fred Taylor 4.00 1.50
❑ 413 Pat Johnson RC 2.00 .75
❑ 414 Robert Edwards 2.00 .75
❑ 415 Keith Brooking RC 3.00 1.25
❑ 416 Peyton Manning 25.00 12.50
❑ 417 Duane Starks RC 1.25 .50
❑ 418 Andre Wadsworth 2.00 .75
❑ 419 Brian Alford RC 1.25 .50
❑ 420 Brian Kelly RC 2.00 .75
❑ 421 Joe Jurevicius RC 3.00 1.25
❑ 422 Tebucky Jones RC 1.25 .50
❑ 423 R.W. McQuarters RC 2.00 .75
❑ 424 Kevin Dyson 2.50 1.00
❑ 425 Charles Woodson 3.00 1.25
❑ R1 Reggie White COMM .60 .25
❑ P20 Jeff George Promo .75 .30

1999 Ultra

❑ COMPLETE SET (300) 100.00 40.00
❑ COMP.SET w/o SP's (250) 20.00 10.00
❑ 1 Terrell Davis .75 .30

❑	2	Courtney Hawkins	.30	.10
❑	3	Cris Carter	.75	.30
❑	4	Darnay Scott	.30	.10
❑	5	Darrell Green	.50	.20
❑	6	Jimmy Smith	.50	.20
❑	7	Doug Flutie	.75	.30
❑	8	Michael Jackson	.30	.10
❑	9	Warren Sapp	.50	.20
❑	10	Greg Hill	.30	.10
❑	11	Karim Abdul-Jabbar	.50	.20
❑	12	Greg Ellis	.30	.10
❑	13	Dan Marino	2.50	1.00
❑	14	Napoleon Kaufman	.75	.30
❑	15	Peyton Manning	2.50	1.00
❑	16	Simeon Rice	.50	.20
❑	17	Tony Simmons	.30	.10
❑	18	Carlester Crumpler	.30	.10
❑	19	Charles Johnson	.30	.10
❑	20	Derrick Alexander	.30	.10
❑	21	Kent Graham	.30	.10
❑	22	Randall Cunningham	.75	.30
❑	23	Trent Green	.75	.30
❑	24	Chris Spielman	.30	.10
❑	25	Carl Pickens	.50	.20
❑	26	Bill Romanowski	.30	.10
❑	27	Jermaine Lewis	.50	.20
❑	28	Ahman Green	.75	.30
❑	29	Bryan Still	.30	.10
❑	30	Dorsey Levens	.75	.30
❑	31	Frank Wycheck	.30	.10
❑	32	Jerome Bettis	.75	.30
❑	33	Reidel Anthony	.50	.20
❑	34	Robert Jones	.30	.10
❑	35	Terry Glenn	.75	.30
❑	36	Tim Brown	.75	.30
❑	37	Eric Metcalf	.30	.10
❑	38	Kevin Greene	.50	.20
❑	39	Takeo Spikes	.30	.10
❑	40	Brian Mitchell	.30	.10
❑	41	Duane Starks	.30	.10
❑	42	Eddie George	.75	.30
❑	43	Joe Jurevicius	.50	.20
❑	44	Kimble Anders	.50	.20
❑	45	Kordell Stewart	.50	.20
❑	46	Leroy Hoard	.30	.10
❑	47	Rod Smith	.50	.20
❑	48	Terrell Owens	.75	.30
❑	49	Ty Detmer	.50	.20
❑	50	Charles Woodson	.75	.30
❑	51	Andre Rison	.50	.20
❑	52	Chris Slade	.30	.10
❑	53	Frank Sanders	.50	.20
❑	54	Michael Irvin	.50	.20
❑	55	Jerome Pathon	.30	.10
❑	56	Desmond Howard	.50	.20
❑	57	Billy Davis	.30	.10
❑	58	Anthony Simmons	.30	.10
❑	59	James Jett	.50	.20
❑	60	Jake Plummer	.50	.20
❑	61	John Avery	.30	.10
❑	62	Marvin Harrison	.75	.30
❑	63	Merton Hanks	.30	.10
❑	64	Ricky Proehl	.30	.10
❑	65	Steve Beuerlein	.30	.10
❑	66	Willie McGinest	.30	.10
❑	67	Bryce Paup	.30	.10
❑	68	Brett Favre	2.50	1.00
❑	69	Brian Griese	.75	.30
❑	70	Curtis Martin	.75	.30
❑	71	Drew Bledsoe	1.00	.40
❑	72	Jim Harbaugh	.50	.20
❑	73	Joey Galloway	.50	.20
❑	74	Natrone Means	.50	.20
❑	75	O.J. McDuffie	.50	.20
❑	76	Tiki Barber	.75	.30
❑	77	Wesley Walls	.50	.20
❑	78	Will Blackwell	.30	.10
❑	79	Bert Emanuel	.50	.20
❑	80	J.J. Stokes	.50	.20
❑	81	Steve McNair	.75	.30
❑	82	Adrian Murrell	.50	.20
❑	83	Dexter Coakley	.30	.10
❑	84	Jeff George	.50	.20
❑	85	Marshall Faulk	1.00	.40
❑	86	Tim Biakabutuka	.50	.20
❑	87	Troy Drayton	.30	.10
❑	88	Ty Law	.50	.20
❑	89	Brian Simmons	.30	.10
❑	90	Eric Allen	.30	.10
❑	91	Jon Kitna	.75	.30
❑	92	Junior Seau	.75	.30
❑	93	Kevin Turner	.30	.10
❑	94	Larry Centers	.30	.10
❑	95	Robert Edwards	.30	.10
❑	96	Rocket Ismail	.50	.20
❑	97	Sam Madison	.30	.10
❑	98	Stephen Alexander	.30	.10
❑	99	Trent Dilfer	.50	.20
❑	100	Vonnie Holliday	.30	.10
❑	101	Charlie Garner	.50	.20
❑	102	Deion Sanders	.75	.30
❑	103	Jamal Anderson	.75	.30
❑	104	Mike Vanderjagt	.30	.10
❑	105	Aeneas Williams	.30	.10
❑	106	Daryl Johnston	.50	.20
❑	107	Hugh Douglas	.30	.10
❑	108	Torrance Small	.30	.10
❑	109	Amani Toomer	.30	.10
❑	110	Amp Lee	.30	.10
❑	111	Germane Crowell	.30	.10
❑	112	Marco Battaglia	.30	.10
❑	113	Michael Westbrook	.50	.20
❑	114	Randy Moss	2.00	.75
❑	115	Ricky Watters	.50	.20
❑	116	Rob Johnson	.50	.20
❑	117	Tony Gonzalez	.75	.30
❑	118	Charles Way	.30	.10
❑	119	Chris Penn	.30	.10
❑	120	Eddie Kennison	.50	.20
❑	121	Elvis Grbac	.50	.20
❑	122	Eric Moulds	.75	.30
❑	123	Terry Fair	.30	.10
❑	124	Tony Banks	.50	.20
❑	125	Chris Chandler	.50	.20
❑	126	Emmitt Smith	1.50	.60
❑	127	Herman Moore	.50	.20
❑	128	Irv Smith	.30	.10
❑	129	Kyle Brady	.30	.10
❑	130	Lamont Warren	.30	.10
❑	131	Troy Davis	.30	.10
❑	132	Andre Reed	.50	.20
❑	133	Justin Armour	.30	.10
❑	134	James Hasty	.30	.10
❑	135	Johnnie Morton	.50	.20
❑	136	Reggie Barlow	.30	.10
❑	137	Robert Holcombe	.30	.10
❑	138	Sean Dawkins	.30	.10
❑	139	Steve Atwater	.30	.10
❑	140	Tim Dwight	.75	.30
❑	141	Wayne Chrebet	.50	.20
❑	142	Alonzo Mayes	.30	.10
❑	143	Mark Brunell	.75	.30
❑	144	Antowain Smith	.75	.30
❑	145	Byron Bam Morris	.30	.10
❑	146	Isaac Bruce	.75	.30
❑	147	Bryan Cox	.30	.10
❑	148	Bryant Westbrook	.30	.10
❑	149	Duce Staley	.75	.30
❑	150	Barry Sanders	2.50	1.00
❑	151	La'Roi Glover RC	.75	.30
❑	152	Ray Crockett	.30	.10
❑	153	Tony Brackens	.30	.10
❑	154	Roy Barker	.30	.10
❑	155	Kerry Collins	.50	.20
❑	156	Andre Wadsworth	.30	.10
❑	157	Cameron Cleeland	.30	.10
❑	158	Koy Detmer	.30	.10
❑	159	Marcus Pollard	.30	.10
❑	160	Patrick Jeffers RC	6.00	2.50
❑	161	Aaron Glenn	.30	.10
❑	162	Andre Hastings	.30	.10
❑	163	Bruce Smith	.50	.20
❑	164	David Palmer	.30	.10
❑	165	Erik Kramer	.50	.20
❑	166	Orlando Pace	.30	.10
❑	167	Robert Brooks	.50	.20
❑	168	Shawn Springs	.30	.10
❑	169	Terance Mathis	.50	.20
❑	170	Chris Calloway	.30	.10
❑	171	Gilbert Brown	.30	.10
❑	172	Charlie Jones	.30	.10
❑	173	Curtis Enis	.30	.10
❑	174	Eugene Robinson	.30	.10
❑	175	Garrison Hearst	.50	.20
❑	176	Jason Elam	.30	.10
❑	177	John Randle	.50	.20
❑	178	Keith Poole	.30	.10
❑	179	Kevin Hardy	.30	.10
❑	180	Keyshawn Johnson	.75	.30
❑	181	O.J. Santiago	.30	.10
❑	182	Jacquez Green	.30	.10
❑	183	Bobby Engram	.50	.20
❑	184	Damon Jones	.30	.10
❑	185	Freddie Jones	.30	.10
❑	186	Jake Reed	.50	.20
❑	187	Jerry Rice	1.50	.60
❑	188	Joey Kent	.30	.10
❑	189	Lamar Smith	.50	.20
❑	190	John Elway	2.50	1.00
❑	191	Leon Johnson	.30	.10
❑	192	Mark Chmura	.50	.20
❑	193	Peter Boulware	.30	.10
❑	194	Zach Thomas	.75	.30
❑	195	Marc Edwards	.30	.10
❑	196	Mike Alstott	.75	.30
❑	197	Yancey Thigpen	.30	.10
❑	198	Oronde Gadsden	.50	.20
❑	199	Rae Carruth	.30	.10
❑	200	Troy Aikman	1.50	.60
❑	201	Shawn Jefferson	.30	.10
❑	202	Rob Moore	.50	.20
❑	203	Rickey Dudley	.30	.10
❑	204	Jason Taylor	.30	.10
❑	205	Curtis Conway	.50	.20
❑	206	Darrien Gordon	.30	.10
❑	207	Eric Green	.30	.10
❑	208	Jessie Armstead	.30	.10
❑	209	Keenan McCardell	.50	.20
❑	210	Robert Smith	.75	.30
❑	211	Mo Lewis	.30	.10
❑	212	Ryan Leaf	.75	.30
❑	213	Steve Young	1.00	.40
❑	214	Tyrone Davis	.30	.10
❑	215	Chad Brown	.30	.10
❑	216	Ike Hilliard	.30	.10
❑	217	Jimmy Hitchcock	.30	.10
❑	218	Kevin Dyson	.50	.20
❑	219	Levon Kirkland	.30	.10
❑	220	Neil O'Donnell	.50	.20
❑	221	Ray Lewis	.75	.30
❑	222	Shannon Sharpe	.50	.20
❑	223	Skip Hicks	.30	.10
❑	224	Brad Johnson	.75	.30
❑	225	Charlie Batch	.75	.30
❑	226	Corey Dillon	.75	.30
❑	227	Dale Carter	.30	.10
❑	228	John Mobley	.30	.10
❑	229	Hines Ward	.75	.30
❑	230	Leslie Shepherd	.30	.10
❑	231	Michael Strahan	.50	.20
❑	232	R.W. McQuarters	.30	.10
❑	233	Mike Pritchard	.30	.10
❑	234	Antonio Freeman	.75	.30
❑	235	Ben Coates	.50	.20
❑	236	Michael Bates	.30	.10
❑	237	Ed McCaffrey	.50	.20
❑	238	Gary Brown	.30	.10
❑	239	Mark Bruener	.30	.10
❑	240	Mikhael Ricks	.30	.10
❑	241	Muhsin Muhammad	.50	.20
❑	242	Priest Holmes	1.25	.50
❑	243	Stephen Davis	.75	.30
❑	244	Vinny Testaverde	.50	.20
❑	245	Warrick Dunn	.75	.30

No.	Player	Mint	Ex
❑ 246	Derrick Mayes	.30	.10
❑ 247	Fred Taylor	.75	.30
❑ 248	Drew Bledsoe CL	.50	.20
❑ 249	Eddie George CL	.50	.20
❑ 250	Steve Young CL	.50	.20
❑ 251	Jamal Anderson BB	.60	.25
❑ 252	D.Gordon/Romanowski BB	.30	.10
❑ 253	Shannon Sharpe BB	.30	.10
❑ 254	Terrell Davis BB	1.00	.40
❑ 255	Rod Smith BB	.30	.10
❑ 256	Rod Smith BB	.30	.10
❑ 257	John Elway BB	5.00	2.00
❑ 258	Tim Dwight BB	.60	.25
❑ 259	Elway/McC/Griff/Dav.BB	3.00	1.25
❑ 260	John Elway BB	5.00	2.00
❑ 261	Ricky Williams RC	6.00	2.50
❑ 262	Tim Couch RC	3.00	1.25
❑ 263	Chris Claiborne RC	1.50	.60
❑ 264	Champ Bailey RC	5.00	2.00
❑ 265	Torry Holt RC	8.00	3.00
❑ 266	Donovan McNabb RC	15.00	6.00
❑ 267	David Boston RC	3.00	1.25
❑ 268	Chris McAlister RC	2.50	1.00
❑ 269	Brock Huard RC	3.00	1.25
❑ 270	Daunte Culpepper RC	12.00	5.00
❑ 271	Matt Stinchcomb RC	1.50	.60
❑ 272	Edgerrin James RC	12.00	5.00
❑ 273	Jevon Kearse RC	6.00	2.50
❑ 274	Ebenezer Ekuban RC	2.50	1.00
❑ 275	Kris Farris RC	1.50	.60
❑ 276	Chris Terry RC	1.50	.60
❑ 277	Jerame Tuman RC	3.00	1.25
❑ 278	Akili Smith RC	2.50	1.00
❑ 279	Aaron Gibson RC	1.50	.60
❑ 280	Rahim Abdullah RC	2.50	1.00
❑ 281	Peerless Price RC	3.00	1.25
❑ 282	Antoine Winfield RC	2.50	1.00
❑ 283	Antuan Edwards RC	1.50	.60
❑ 284	Rob Konrad RC	3.00	1.25
❑ 285	Troy Edwards RC	2.50	1.00
❑ 286	John Thornton RC	1.50	.60
❑ 287	James Johnson RC	2.50	1.00
❑ 288	Gary Stills RC	1.50	.60
❑ 289	Mike Peterson RC	2.50	1.00
❑ 290	Kevin Faulk RC	3.00	1.25
❑ 291	Jared DeVries RC	1.50	.60
❑ 292	Martin Gramatica RC	1.50	.60
❑ 293	Montae Reagor RC	1.50	.60
❑ 294	Andy Katzenmoyer RC	2.50	1.00
❑ 295	Sedrick Irvin RC	1.50	.60
❑ 296	D'Wayne Bates RC	2.50	1.00
❑ 297	Amos Zereoue RC	3.00	1.25
❑ 298	Dre' Bly RC	3.00	1.25
❑ 299	Kevin Johnson RC	3.00	1.25
❑ 300	Cade McNown RC	2.50	1.00
❑ P247	Fred Taylor Promo	2.00	.75

2000 Ultra

No.	Player	Mint	Ex
❑	COMPLETE SET (249)	100.00	40.00
❑	COMP.SET w/o SP's (220)	20.00	7.50
❑ 1	Kurt Warner	1.50	.60
❑ 2	Derrick Alexander	.50	.20
❑ 3	Aaron Craver	.30	.10
❑ 4	Kevin Faulk	.50	.20
❑ 5	Marcus Robinson	.75	.30
❑ 6	Tony Banks	.50	.20
❑ 7	Jon Ritchie	.30	.10
❑ 8	Torry Holt	.75	.30
❑ 9	Joe Horn	.50	.20
❑ 10	Eddie George	.75	.30
❑ 11	Michael Westbrook	.50	.20
❑ 12	Gus Frerotte	.30	.10
❑ 13	Tim Brown	.75	.30
❑ 14	Tamarick Vanover	.30	.10
❑ 15	David Sloan	.30	.10
❑ 16	Darnay Scott	.30	.10
❑ 17	Junior Seau	.75	.30
❑ 18	Warren Sapp	.50	.20
❑ 19	Priest Holmes	1.00	.40
❑ 20	Jerry Rice	1.50	.60
❑ 21	Cade McNown	.30	.10
❑ 22	Johnnie Morton	.50	.20
❑ 23	Vinny Testaverde	.50	.20
❑ 24	James Jett	.30	.10
❑ 25	Tony Gonzalez	.50	.20
❑ 26	Charlie Batch	.75	.30
❑ 27	Tony Simmons	.30	.10
❑ 28	James Stewart	.50	.20
❑ 29	Corey Dillon	.75	.30
❑ 30	Ricky Williams	.75	.30
❑ 31	Ryan Leaf	.50	.20
❑ 32	Terry Allen	.50	.20
❑ 33	Freddie Jones	.30	.10
❑ 34	Terry Kirby	.30	.10
❑ 35	Charles Johnson	.50	.20
❑ 36	William Henderson	.50	.20
❑ 37	Stephen Alexander	.30	.10
❑ 38	Moe Williams	.50	.20
❑ 39	David Boston	.75	.30
❑ 40	Emmitt Smith	1.50	.60
❑ 41	Ken Oxendine	.30	.10
❑ 42	Byron Hanspard	.30	.10
❑ 43	Dwight Stone	.30	.10
❑ 44	Jim Harbaugh	.50	.20
❑ 45	Curtis Enis	.30	.10
❑ 46	Peerless Price	.50	.20
❑ 47	Terance Mathis	.50	.20
❑ 48	Mike Alstott	.75	.30
❑ 49	Rod Smith	.50	.20
❑ 50	Marshall Faulk	1.00	.40
❑ 51	Derrick Mayes	.50	.20
❑ 52	Keenan McCardell	.50	.20
❑ 53	Curtis Martin	.75	.30
❑ 54	Bobby Engram	.30	.10
❑ 55	Carl Pickens	.50	.20
❑ 56	Robert Smith	.75	.30
❑ 57	Ike Hilliard	.50	.20
❑ 58	Reidel Anthony	.50	.20
❑ 59	Jeff Graham	.30	.10
❑ 60	Mark Brunell	.75	.30
❑ 61	Joe Montgomery	.30	.10
❑ 62	Ed McCaffrey	.75	.30
❑ 63	Kenny Bynum	.30	.10
❑ 64	Curtis Conway	.50	.20
❑ 65	Trent Dilfer	.50	.20
❑ 66	Jake Reed	.50	.20
❑ 67	Jake Plummer	.50	.20
❑ 68	Tony Martin	.50	.20
❑ 69	Yatil Green	.30	.10
❑ 70	Keyshawn Johnson	.75	.30
❑ 71	Leroy Hoard	.30	.10
❑ 72	Skip Hicks	.30	.10
❑ 73	Marvin Harrison	.75	.30
❑ 74	Steve Beuerlein	.50	.20
❑ 75	Will Blackwell	.30	.10
❑ 76	Derek Loville	.30	.10
❑ 77	Warrick Dunn	.75	.30
❑ 78	Amos Zereoue	.75	.30
❑ 79	Ray Lucas	.50	.20
❑ 80	Randy Moss	1.50	.60
❑ 81	Wesley Walls	.30	.10
❑ 82	Jimmy Smith	.50	.20
❑ 83	Kordell Stewart	.50	.20
❑ 84	Brian Griese	.75	.30
❑ 85	Martin Gramatica	.30	.10
❑ 86	Chris Chandler	.50	.20
❑ 87	Reggie Barlow	.30	.10
❑ 88	Jeff George	.50	.20
❑ 89	Tavian Banks	.30	.10
❑ 90	Mushin Muhammad	.50	.20
❑ 91	Steve McNair	.75	.30
❑ 92	Hines Ward	.75	.30
❑ 93	Brian Mitchell	.30	.10
❑ 94	Daunte Culpepper	1.00	.40
❑ 95	Tim Dwight	.75	.30
❑ 96	Terrence Wilkins	.30	.10
❑ 97	Fred Lane	.30	.10
❑ 98	Brett Favre	2.50	1.00
❑ 99	Richie Anderson	.50	.20
❑ 100	Jamal Anderson	.75	.30
❑ 101	Doug Flutie	.75	.30
❑ 102	Charles Woodson	.50	.20
❑ 103	Jacquez Green	.30	.10
❑ 104	Olandis Gary	.75	.30
❑ 105	Steve Young	1.00	.40
❑ 106	Wayne Chrebet	.50	.20
❑ 107	Karim Abdul-Jabbar	.50	.20
❑ 108	Andre Rison	.50	.20
❑ 109	Eddie Kennison	.30	.10
❑ 110	Jevon Kearse	.75	.30
❑ 111	Tony Richardson RC	.50	.20
❑ 112	Jake Delhomme RC	3.00	1.25
❑ 113	Errict Rhett	.50	.20
❑ 114	Akili Smith	.30	.10
❑ 115	Tyrone Wheatley	.50	.20
❑ 116	Corey Bradford	.50	.20
❑ 117	J.J. Stokes	.50	.20
❑ 118	Simeon Rice	.50	.20
❑ 119	Brad Johnson	.75	.30
❑ 120	Edgerrin James	1.25	.50
❑ 121	Amani Toomer	.30	.10
❑ 122	O.J. McDuffie	.50	.20
❑ 123	Az-Zahir Hakim	.50	.20
❑ 124	Troy Edwards	.30	.10
❑ 125	Tim Biakabutuka	.50	.20
❑ 126	Jason Tucker	.30	.10
❑ 127	Charles Way	.30	.10
❑ 128	Terrell Davis	.75	.30
❑ 129	Garrison Hearst	.50	.20
❑ 130	Fred Taylor	.75	.30
❑ 131	Robert Holcombe	.30	.10
❑ 132	Frank Sanders	.50	.20
❑ 133	Morten Andersen	.30	.10
❑ 134	Cris Carter	.75	.30
❑ 135	Patrick Jeffers	.75	.30
❑ 136	Antonio Freeman	.75	.30
❑ 137	Jonathan Linton	.30	.10
❑ 138	Rashaan Shehee	.30	.10
❑ 139	Luther Broughton RC	.50	.20
❑ 140	Tim Couch	.50	.20
❑ 141	Keith Poole	.30	.10
❑ 142	Champ Bailey	.50	.20
❑ 143	Yancey Thigpen	.30	.10
❑ 144	Joey Galloway	.50	.20
❑ 145	Mac Cody	.30	.10
❑ 146	Damon Huard	.75	.30
❑ 147	Dorsey Levens	.50	.20
❑ 148	Donovan McNabb	1.25	.50
❑ 149	Jamie Asher	.30	.10
❑ 150	Peyton Manning	2.00	.75
❑ 151	Leslie Shepherd	.30	.10
❑ 152	Charlie Rogers	.30	.10
❑ 153	Tony Horne	.30	.10
❑ 154	Jim Miller	.30	.10
❑ 155	Richard Huntley	.30	.10
❑ 156	Germane Crowell	.30	.10
❑ 157	Natrone Means	.30	.10
❑ 158	Justin Armour	.30	.10
❑ 159	Drew Bledsoe	1.00	.40
❑ 160	Dedric Ward	.30	.10
❑ 161	Allen Rossum	.30	.10
❑ 162	Ricky Watters	.50	.20
❑ 163	Kerry Collins	.50	.20
❑ 164	James Johnson	.30	.10
❑ 165	Elvis Grbac	.50	.20
❑ 166	Larry Centers	.30	.10
❑ 167	Rob Moore	.50	.20
❑ 168	Jay Riemersma	.30	.10
❑ 169	Bill Schroeder	.50	.20
❑ 170	Deion Sanders	.75	.30
❑ 171	Jerome Bettis	.75	.30
❑ 172	Dan Marino	2.50	1.00
❑ 173	Terrell Owens	.75	.30
❑ 174	Kevin Carter	.30	.10
❑ 175	Lamar Smith	.50	.20
❑ 176	Ken Dilger	.30	.10
❑ 177	Napoleon Kaufman	.50	.20
❑ 178	Kevin Williams	.30	.10
❑ 179	Tremain Mack	.30	.10
❑ 180	Troy Aikman	1.50	.60
❑ 181	Glyn Milburn	.30	.10
❑ 182	Pete Mitchell	.30	.10
❑ 183	Cameron Cleeland	.30	.10

❑ 184 Qadry Ismail .50 .20
❑ 185 Michael Pittman .30 .10
❑ 186 Kevin Dyson .50 .20
❑ 187 Matt Hasselbeck .50 .20
❑ 188 Kevin Johnson .75 .30
❑ 189 Rich Gannon .75 .30
❑ 190 Stephen Davis .75 .30
❑ 191 Frank Wycheck .30 .10
❑ 192 Eric Moulds .75 .30
❑ 193 Jon Kitna .75 .30
❑ 194 Mario Bates .30 .10
❑ 195 Na Brown .30 .10
❑ 196 Jeff Blake .50 .20
❑ 197 Charles Evans .30 .10
❑ 198 Oronde Gadsden .50 .20
❑ 199 Donnell Bennett .30 .10
❑ 200 Isaac Bruce .75 .30
❑ 201 Olindo Mare .30 .10
❑ 202 Darnell McDonald .30 .10
❑ 203 Charlie Garner .50 .20
❑ 204 Shawn Jefferson .30 .10
❑ 205 Adrian Murrell .50 .20
❑ 206 Peter Boulware .30 .10
❑ 207 LeShon Johnson .30 .10
❑ 208 Herman Moore .50 .20
❑ 209 Duce Staley .75 .30
❑ 210 Sean Dawkins .30 .10
❑ 211 Antowain Smith .50 .20
❑ 212 Albert Connell .30 .10
❑ 213 Jeff Garcia .75 .30
❑ 214 Kimble Anders .30 .10
❑ 215 Shaun King .30 .10
❑ 216 Rocket Ismail .50 .20
❑ 217 Andrew Glover .30 .10
❑ 218 Rickey Dudley .30 .10
❑ 219 Michael Basnight .30 .10
❑ 220 Terry Glenn .50 .20
❑ 221 Peter Warrick RC 3.00 1.25
❑ 222 Ron Dayne RC 3.00 1.25
❑ 223 Thomas Jones RC 5.00 2.00
❑ 224 Joe Hamilton RC 2.50 1.00
❑ 225 Tim Rattay RC 3.00 1.25
❑ 226 Chad Pennington RC 8.00 3.00
❑ 227 Dennis Northcutt RC 3.00 1.25
❑ 228 Troy Walters RC 3.00 1.25
❑ 229 Travis Prentice RC 2.50 1.00
❑ 230 Shaun Alexander RC 15.00 6.00
❑ 231 J.R. Redmond RC 2.50 1.00
❑ 232 Chris Redman RC 2.50 1.00
❑ 233 Tee Martin RC 3.00 1.25
❑ 234 Tom Brady RC 30.00 15.00
❑ 235 Travis Taylor RC 3.00 1.25
❑ 236 R.Jay Soward RC 2.50 1.00
❑ 237 Jamal Lewis RC 8.00 3.00
❑ 238 Giovanni Carmazzi RC 2.00 .75
❑ 239 Dez White RC 3.00 1.25
❑ 240 LaVar Arrington RC SP 100.00 40.00
❑ 241 Laveranues Coles RC 4.00 1.50
❑ 242 Sherrod Gideon RC 2.00 .75
❑ 243 Trung Canidate RC 2.50 1.00
❑ 244 Michael Wiley RC 2.50 1.00
❑ 245 Anthony Lucas RC 2.00 .75
❑ 246 Darrell Jackson RC 6.00 2.50
❑ 247 Plaxico Burress RC 6.00 2.50
❑ 248 Reuben Droughns RC 4.00 1.50
❑ 249 Marc Bulger RC 6.00 2.50
❑ 250 Danny Farmer RC 2.50 1.00

2001 Ultra

❑ COMP.SET w/o SP's (250) 25.00 10.00
❑ 1 Daunte Culpepper .75 .30
❑ 2 Kurt Warner 1.50 .60
❑ 3 Emmitt Smith 1.50 .60
❑ 4 Eddie George .75 .30
❑ 5 Ron Dayne .75 .30
❑ 6 Zach Thomas .75 .30
❑ 7 Itula Mili .30 .10
❑ 8 Jake Reed .50 .20
❑ 9 James Stewart .50 .20
❑ 10 Terrence Wilkins .30 .10
❑ 11 Jeff Blake .50 .20
❑ 12 Kerry Collins .50 .20
❑ 13 Christian Fauria .30 .10
❑ 14 Jackie Harris .30 .10
❑ 15 Kevin Johnson .50 .20
❑ 16 Tony Martin .30 .10
❑ 17 Joey Galloway .50 .20
❑ 18 Junior Seau .75 .30
❑ 19 Jason Tucker .30 .10
❑ 20 Steve Beuerlein .30 .10
❑ 21 Mike Cloud .30 .10
❑ 22 Kevin Faulk .50 .20
❑ 23 Az-Zahir Hakim .30 .10
❑ 24 Charles Johnson .30 .10
❑ 25 Curtis Martin .75 .30
❑ 26 Eric Moulds .50 .20
❑ 27 Bill Schroeder .50 .20
❑ 28 Amani Toomer .30 .10
❑ 29 Obafemi Ayanbadejo .30 .10
❑ 30 Aaron Shea .30 .10
❑ 31 Ken Dilger .30 .10
❑ 32 Terry Glenn .30 .10
❑ 33 Rocket Ismail .50 .20
❑ 34 Dorsey Levens .30 .10
❑ 35 Brian Mitchell .30 .10
❑ 36 Tony Richardson .30 .10
❑ 37 Sam Madison .30 .10
❑ 38 Darren Sharper .30 .10
❑ 39 Derrick Alexander .50 .20
❑ 40 Aaron Brooks .75 .30
❑ 41 Casey Crawford .30 .10
❑ 42 Terrell Fletcher .30 .10
❑ 43 William Henderson .30 .10
❑ 44 Thomas Jones .50 .20
❑ 45 Keenan McCardell .30 .10
❑ 46 Chad Pennington 1.25 .50
❑ 47 Akili Smith .30 .10
❑ 48 Hines Ward .75 .30
❑ 49 Champ Bailey .50 .20
❑ 50 Cris Carter .75 .30
❑ 51 Corey Dillon .75 .30
❑ 52 Tony Gonzalez .50 .20
❑ 53 Darrell Jackson .75 .30
❑ 54 Chad Lewis .30 .10
❑ 55 Dave Moore .30 .10
❑ 56 Jay Riemersma .30 .10
❑ 57 J.J. Stokes .50 .20
❑ 58 Frank Wycheck .30 .10
❑ 59 Tiki Barber .75 .30
❑ 60 Tony Carter .30 .10
❑ 61 Rickey Dudley .30 .10
❑ 62 John Lynch .50 .20
❑ 63 Larry Foster .30 .10
❑ 64 Willie Jackson .30 .10
❑ 65 Jamal Lewis 1.25 .50
❑ 66 Herman Moore .50 .20
❑ 67 Andre Rison .50 .20
❑ 68 Michael Strahan .50 .20
❑ 69 Charlie Batch .75 .30
❑ 70 Larry Centers .30 .10
❑ 71 Ron Dugans .30 .10
❑ 72 Jeff Graham .30 .10
❑ 73 Edgerrin James 1.00 .40
❑ 74 Jermaine Lewis .30 .10
❑ 75 Charles Woodson .50 .20
❑ 76 Chris Redman .30 .10
❑ 77 Jon Ritchie .30 .10
❑ 78 Fred Taylor .75 .30
❑ 79 Jamal Anderson .75 .30
❑ 80 Isaac Bruce .75 .30
❑ 81 Terrell Davis .75 .30
❑ 82 Rich Gannon .75 .30
❑ 83 Joe Horn .50 .20
❑ 84 Eddie Kennison .50 .20
❑ 85 Steve McNair .75 .30
❑ 86 Travis Prentice .30 .10
❑ 87 Rod Smith .50 .20
❑ 88 Ricky Watters .50 .20
❑ 89 Michael Bates .30 .10
❑ 90 Byron Chamberlain .30 .10
❑ 91 Warrick Dunn .75 .30
❑ 92 Elvis Grbac .50 .20
❑ 93 Patrick Jeffers .50 .20
❑ 94 Ray Lewis .75 .30
❑ 95 Sammy Morris .30 .10
❑ 96 Marcus Robinson .75 .30
❑ 97 Travis Taylor .50 .20
❑ 98 Fred Beasley .30 .10
❑ 99 Chris Chandler .50 .20
❑ 100 Tim Dwight .75 .30
❑ 101 Ahman Green .75 .30
❑ 102 Shawn Jefferson .30 .10
❑ 103 Jeremy McDaniel .30 .10
❑ 104 Sylvester Morris .30 .10
❑ 105 John Randle .30 .10
❑ 106 Vinny Testaverde .50 .20
❑ 107 Anthony Becht .30 .10
❑ 108 Wayne Chrebet .50 .20
❑ 109 Stephen Boyd .30 .10
❑ 110 Jacquez Green .30 .10
❑ 111 MarTay Jenkins .30 .10
❑ 112 Jason Gildon .30 .10
❑ 113 Chad Morton .30 .10
❑ 114 Deion Sanders .75 .30
❑ 115 Yancey Thigpen .30 .10
❑ 116 Marty Booker .30 .10
❑ 117 Curtis Conway .50 .20
❑ 118 Jermaine Fazande .30 .10
❑ 119 Matthew Hatchette .30 .10
❑ 120 Pat Johnson .30 .10
❑ 121 Terance Mathis .50 .20
❑ 122 Terrell Owens .75 .30
❑ 123 Corey Simon .50 .20
❑ 124 Darrick Vaughn .30 .10
❑ 125 Drew Bledsoe 1.00 .40
❑ 126 Albert Connell .30 .10
❑ 127 Brett Favre 2.50 1.00
❑ 128 Marvin Harrison .75 .30
❑ 129 Keyshawn Johnson .75 .30
❑ 130 Derrick Mason .50 .20
❑ 131 Dennis Northcutt .50 .20
❑ 132 Shannon Sharpe .50 .20
❑ 133 Brian Urlacher 1.25 .50
❑ 134 Mike Anderson .75 .30
❑ 135 Mark Bruener .30 .10
❑ 136 Sean Dawkins .30 .10
❑ 137 Jeff Garcia .75 .30
❑ 138 Tony Horne .30 .10
❑ 139 Shaun King .30 .10
❑ 140 Cade McNown .30 .10
❑ 141 Peerless Price .50 .20
❑ 142 R.Jay Soward .30 .10
❑ 143 Tyrone Wheatley .50 .20
❑ 144 Richie Anderson .30 .10
❑ 145 Mark Brunell .75 .30
❑ 146 JaJuan Dawson .30 .10
❑ 147 Charlie Garner .50 .20
❑ 148 Desmond Howard .30 .10
❑ 149 Jon Kitna .50 .20
❑ 150 Duane Starks .30 .10
❑ 151 J.R. Redmond .30 .10
❑ 152 Duce Staley .75 .30
❑ 153 Dez White .30 .10
❑ 154 David Boston .75 .30
❑ 155 Tim Couch .50 .20
❑ 156 Jay Fiedler .75 .30
❑ 157 Jessie Armstead .30 .10
❑ 158 Rob Johnson .50 .20
❑ 159 Brad Johnson .75 .30
❑ 160 Derrick Mayes .30 .10
❑ 161 Jerome Pathon .50 .20
❑ 162 David Sloan .30 .10
❑ 163 Wesley Walls .30 .10
❑ 164 Shaun Alexander 1.00 .40
❑ 165 Derrick Brooks .75 .30
❑ 166 Germane Crowell .30 .10
❑ 167 Doug Flutie .75 .30
❑ 168 Ike Hilliard .50 .20
❑ 169 Hugh Douglas .30 .10
❑ 170 Wane McGarity .30 .10
❑ 171 Michael Pittman .30 .10
❑ 172 Shawn Bryson .30 .10
❑ 173 Richard Huntley .30 .10

❑ 174	Darnell Autry	.30	.10
❑ 175	Plaxico Burress	.75	.30
❑ 176	Trent Dilfer	.50	.20
❑ 177	Jeff George	.50	.20
❑ 178	Qadry Ismail	.50	.20
❑ 179	Ryan Leaf	.50	.20
❑ 180	Jim Miller	.30	.10
❑ 181	Jerry Rice	1.50	.60
❑ 182	Kordell Stewart	.50	.20
❑ 183	Ricky Williams	.75	.30
❑ 184	James Allen	.50	.20
❑ 185	Courtney Brown	.50	.20
❑ 186	Reidel Anthony	.30	.10
❑ 187	Bubba Franks	.50	.20
❑ 188	Priest Holmes	1.00	.40
❑ 189	Napoleon Kaufman	.30	.10
❑ 190	Trevor Pryce	.30	.10
❑ 191	Jake Plummer	.50	.20
❑ 192	Jimmy Smith	.50	.20
❑ 193	Michael Wiley	.30	.10
❑ 194	Brock Huard	.30	.10
❑ 195	Troy Brown	.50	.20
❑ 196	Stephen Davis	.75	.30
❑ 197	Oronde Gadsden	.50	.20
❑ 198	Brad Hoover	.30	.10
❑ 199	La'Roi Glover	.30	.10
❑ 200	Donovan McNabb	1.00	.40
❑ 201	Jerry Porter	.50	.20
❑ 202	Robert Smith	.50	.20
❑ 203	Justin Watson	.30	.10
❑ 204	Tim Biakabutuka	.50	.20
❑ 205	Laveranues Coles	.75	.30
❑ 206	Marshall Faulk	1.00	.40
❑ 207	Jim Harbaugh	.50	.20
❑ 208	Doug Johnson	.30	.10
❑ 209	Tee Martin	.50	.20
❑ 210	Muhsin Muhammad	.50	.20
❑ 211	Darnay Scott	.30	.10
❑ 212	Jeremiah Trotter	.50	.20
❑ 213	Troy Aikman	1.25	.50
❑ 214	Kyle Brady	.30	.10
❑ 215	Sam Cowart	.30	.10
❑ 216	Darren Howard	.30	.10
❑ 217	Donald Hayes	.30	.10
❑ 218	Freddie Jones	.30	.10
❑ 219	Ed McCaffrey	.75	.30
❑ 220	David Patten	.30	.10
❑ 221	Brian Griese	.75	.30
❑ 222	Dedric Ward	.30	.10
❑ 223	Jerome Bettis	.75	.30
❑ 224	Greg Clark	.30	.10
❑ 225	Bobby Engram	.30	.10
❑ 226	Matt Hasselbeck	.50	.20
❑ 227	James Jett	.30	.10
❑ 228	Peyton Manning	2.00	.75
❑ 229	Randy Moss	1.50	.60
❑ 230	Warren Sapp	.50	.20
❑ 231	James Thrash	.50	.20
❑ 232	Mike Alstott	.75	.30
❑ 233	Tim Brown	.75	.30
❑ 234	Randall Cunningham	.75	.30
❑ 235	Antonio Freeman	.75	.30
❑ 236	Torry Holt	.75	.30
❑ 237	Jevon Kearse	.50	.20
❑ 238	James McKnight	.50	.20
❑ 239	Marcus Pollard	.30	.10
❑ 240	Lamar Smith	.50	.20
❑ 241	Peter Warrick	.75	.30
❑ 242	Donnell Bennett	.30	.10
❑ 243	Joe Johnson	.30	.10
❑ 244	Troy Edwards	.30	.10
❑ 245	Trent Green	.75	.30
❑ 246	Jason Taylor	.30	.10
❑ 247	Aeneas Williams	.30	.10
❑ 248	Johnnie Morton	.50	.20
❑ 249	Frank Sanders	.30	.10
❑ 250	Jason Sehorn	.30	.10
❑ 251	Chris Weinke RC	6.00	2.50
❑ 252	Bobby Newcombe RC	4.00	1.50
❑ 253	LaDainian Tomlinson RC	50.00	20.00
❑ 254	Chad Johnson RC	15.00	6.00
❑ 255	Derrick Gibson RC	4.00	1.50
❑ 256	Sage Rosenfels RC	6.00	2.50
❑ 257	LaMont Jordan RC	12.00	5.00
❑ 258	Mike McMahon RC	6.00	2.50
❑ 259	Vinny Sutherland RC	4.00	1.50
❑ 260	Drew Brees RC	20.00	10.00
❑ 261	Deuce McAllister RC	12.00	5.00
❑ 262	Kevan Barlow RC	6.00	2.50
❑ 263	Jamar Fletcher RC	4.00	1.50
❑ 264	Gerard Warren RC	6.00	2.50
❑ 265	Todd Heap RC	6.00	2.50
❑ 266	Travis Henry RC	10.00	4.00
❑ 267	Quincy Morgan RC	6.00	2.50
❑ 268	Anthony Thomas RC	6.00	2.50
❑ 269	Andre Carter RC	6.00	2.50
❑ 270	Freddie Mitchell RC	6.00	2.50
❑ 271	Richard Seymour RC	6.00	2.50
❑ 272	Josh Booty RC	6.00	2.50
❑ 273	Robert Ferguson RC	6.00	2.50
❑ 274	Marques Tuiasosopo RC	6.00	2.50
❑ 275	Reggie Wayne RC	12.00	5.00
❑ 276	Jabari Holloway RC	4.00	1.50
❑ 277	Rudi Johnson RC	12.00	5.00
❑ 278	Michael Bennett RC	6.00	2.50
❑ 279	Snoop Minnis RC	4.00	1.50
❑ 280	Dan Morgan RC	6.00	2.50
❑ 281	Rod Gardner RC	6.00	2.50
❑ 282	Jesse Palmer RC	6.00	2.50
❑ 283	Michael Vick RC	30.00	15.00
❑ 284	Chris Chambers RC	10.00	4.00
❑ 285	James Jackson RC	6.00	2.50
❑ 286	David Terrell RC	6.00	2.50
❑ 287	Koren Robinson RC	6.00	2.50
❑ 288	Travis Minor RC	4.00	1.50
❑ 289	Santana Moss RC	10.00	4.00
❑ 290	Josh Heupel RC	6.00	2.50
❑ 291	Jamal Reynolds RC	6.00	2.50
❑ 292	Ken-Yon Rambo RC	4.00	1.50
❑ 293	Cedrick Wilson RC	6.00	2.50
❑ 294	Alge Crumpler RC	8.00	3.00
❑ 295	Fred Smoot RC	6.00	2.50
❑ 296	Dan Alexander RC	6.00	2.50
❑ 297	Tim Hasselbeck RC	6.00	2.50
❑ 298	Will Allen RC	4.00	1.50
❑ 299	Keith Adams RC	4.00	1.50
❑ 300	Heath Evans RC	4.00	1.50
❑ U301	Quincy Carter RC	6.00	2.50
❑ U302	Derrick Blaylock RC	6.00	2.50
❑ U303	Correll Buckhalter RC	6.00	2.50
❑ U304	A.J. Feeley RC	6.00	2.50
❑ U305	Milton Wynn RC	4.00	1.50
❑ U306	Kevin Kasper RC	6.00	2.50
❑ U307	Justin McCareins RC	6.00	2.50
❑ U308	Dave Dickenson RC	4.00	1.50
❑ U309	Steve Smith RC	15.00	7.50
❑ U310	Moran Norris RC	2.50	1.00

2002 Ultra

❑	COMP.SET w/o SP's (200)	25.00	10.00
❑ 1	Donovan McNabb	1.00	.40
❑ 2	Chad Pennington	1.00	.40
❑ 3	Shaun Alexander	1.00	.40
❑ 4	Corey Dillon	.50	.20
❑ 5	Kurt Warner	.75	.30
❑ 6	Ed McCaffrey	.75	.30
❑ 7	Hugh Douglas	.30	.10
❑ 8	Tony Gonzalez	.50	.20
❑ 9	Travis Taylor	.50	.20
❑ 10	Tony Boselli	.30	.10
❑ 11	Chad Scott	.30	.10
❑ 12	Ernie Conwell	.30	.10
❑ 13	Brad Johnson	.50	.20
❑ 14	Donald Hayes	.30	.10
❑ 15	Emmitt Smith	2.00	.75
❑ 16	Jimmy Smith	.50	.20
❑ 17	Anthony Becht	.30	.10
❑ 18	Rod Gardner	.50	.20
❑ 19	Muhsin Muhammad	.50	.20
❑ 20	Troy Hambrick	.30	.10
❑ 21	Keenan McCardell	.30	.10
❑ 22	Laveranues Coles	.50	.20
❑ 23	Kevin Dyson	.50	.20
❑ 24	Grant Wistrom	.30	.10
❑ 25	Eric Moulds	.50	.20
❑ 26	Nate Clements	.30	.10
❑ 27	Terrell Davis	.75	.30
❑ 28	Aaron Glenn	.30	.10
❑ 29	Eric Hicks	.30	.10
❑ 30	Tiki Barber	.75	.30
❑ 31	Jake Plummer	.50	.20
❑ 32	Junior Seau	.75	.30
❑ 33	Marshall Faulk	.75	.30
❑ 34	Warrick Dunn	.75	.30
❑ 35	Bill Gramatica	.30	.10
❑ 36	Tim Couch	.50	.20
❑ 37	Kabeer Gbaja-Biamila	.50	.20
❑ 38	Kailee Wong	.30	.10
❑ 39	David Patten	.30	.10
❑ 40	Correll Buckhalter	.50	.20
❑ 41	Troy Brown	.50	.20
❑ 42	Drew Bledsoe	1.00	.40
❑ 43	Travis Henry	.75	.30
❑ 44	Jim Miller	.30	.10
❑ 45	Rod Smith	.50	.20
❑ 46	Tai Streets	.30	.10
❑ 47	Snoop Minnis	.30	.10
❑ 48	Ron Dayne	.50	.20
❑ 49	Tyrone Wheatley	.50	.20
❑ 50	LaDainian Tomlinson	1.25	.50
❑ 51	Akili Smith	.30	.10
❑ 52	Warren Sapp	.50	.20
❑ 53	Adam Archuleta	.30	.10
❑ 54	Chris Fuamatu-Ma'afala	.30	.10
❑ 55	Marty Booker	.30	.10
❑ 56	Trevor Pryce	.30	.10
❑ 57	Peyton Manning	1.50	.60
❑ 58	Lamar Smith	.50	.20
❑ 59	Amani Toomer	.50	.20
❑ 60	Greg Biekert	.30	.10
❑ 61	Marcellus Wiley	.30	.10
❑ 62	Ahmed Plummer	.30	.10
❑ 63	Mike Alstott	.75	.30
❑ 64	Gary Walker	.30	.10
❑ 65	Champ Bailey	.50	.20
❑ 66	Chris Redman	.30	.10
❑ 67	David Terrell	.75	.30
❑ 68	Mike McMahon	.75	.30
❑ 69	Marvin Harrison	.75	.30
❑ 70	Jay Fiedler	.50	.20
❑ 71	JaJuan Dawson	.30	.10
❑ 72	Charlie Garner	.50	.20
❑ 73	Curtis Conway	.30	.10
❑ 74	J.J. Stokes	.50	.20
❑ 75	Ronde Barber	.30	.10
❑ 76	Alge Crumpler	.50	.20
❑ 77	Jamir Miller	.30	.10
❑ 78	Brett Favre	2.00	.75
❑ 79	Randy Moss	1.50	.60
❑ 80	Joe Horn	.50	.20
❑ 81	Hines Ward	.75	.30
❑ 82	Lawyer Milloy	.50	.20
❑ 83	Aeneas Williams	.30	.10
❑ 84	Chris McAlister	.30	.10
❑ 85	Anthony Thomas	.50	.20
❑ 86	Johnnie Morton	.50	.20
❑ 87	Edgerrin James	1.00	.40
❑ 88	Chris Chambers	.75	.30
❑ 89	Michael Strahan	.50	.20
❑ 90	Charles Woodson	.50	.20
❑ 91	Tim Dwight	.50	.20
❑ 92	Kevan Barlow	.50	.20
❑ 93	Donnie Abraham	.30	.10
❑ 94	Peter Boulware	.30	.10
❑ 95	Marcus Robinson	.50	.20
❑ 96	Shaun Rogers	.30	.10
❑ 97	Dominic Rhodes	.50	.20
❑ 98	Zach Thomas	.75	.30
❑ 99	Kerry Collins	.50	.20
❑ 100	Tim Brown	.75	.30
❑ 101	Garrison Hearst	.50	.20
❑ 102	Steve McNair	.75	.30
❑ 103	Fred Smoot	.30	.10

- ❑ 104 Isaac Bruce .75 .30
- ❑ 105 Jamal Lewis .75 .30
- ❑ 106 Brian Urlacher 1.25 .50
- ❑ 107 Takeo Spikes .30 .10
- ❑ 108 Marcus Pollard .30 .10
- ❑ 109 Jason Taylor .30 .10
- ❑ 110 Deuce McAllister 1.00 .40
- ❑ 111 Jerry Rice 1.50 .60
- ❑ 112 Terrell Owens .75 .30
- ❑ 113 Eddie George .75 .30
- ❑ 114 Rob Morris .30 .10
- ❑ 115 Mike Brown .75 .30
- ❑ 116 Joey Galloway .50 .20
- ❑ 117 Fred Taylor .75 .30
- ❑ 118 Rich Gannon .75 .30
- ❑ 119 Chris Chandler .50 .20
- ❑ 120 Koren Robinson .50 .20
- ❑ 121 Dan Morgan .30 .10
- ❑ 122 Rocket Ismail .50 .20
- ❑ 123 Mark Brunell .75 .30
- ❑ 124 John Abraham .50 .20
- ❑ 125 Stephen Davis .50 .20
- ❑ 126 Patrick Kerney .30 .10
- ❑ 127 Anthony Henry .30 .10
- ❑ 128 Scotty Anderson .30 .10
- ❑ 129 Oronde Gadsden .30 .10
- ❑ 130 Willie Jackson .30 .10
- ❑ 131 Kendrell Bell .75 .30
- ❑ 132 Ray Lewis .75 .30
- ❑ 133 Quincy Carter .50 .20
- ❑ 134 James Stewart .50 .20
- ❑ 135 Travis Minor .30 .10
- ❑ 136 Kyle Turley .30 .10
- ❑ 137 Jason Gildon .30 .10
- ❑ 138 David Boston .75 .30
- ❑ 139 Justin Smith .30 .10
- ❑ 140 Jamie Sharper .30 .10
- ❑ 141 Antowain Smith .50 .20
- ❑ 142 Freddie Mitchell .50 .20
- ❑ 143 Frank Sanders .30 .10
- ❑ 144 Kevin Johnson .50 .20
- ❑ 145 Darren Sharper .30 .10
- ❑ 146 Eric Johnson .30 .10
- ❑ 147 Ty Law .50 .20
- ❑ 148 James Thrash .50 .20
- ❑ 149 Matt Hasselbeck .50 .20
- ❑ 150 Peerless Price .50 .20
- ❑ 151 T.J. Houshmandzadeh .50 .20
- ❑ 152 Mike Anderson .75 .30
- ❑ 153 Jermaine Lewis .30 .10
- ❑ 154 Trent Green .50 .20
- ❑ 155 Ron Dixon .30 .10
- ❑ 156 Duce Staley .75 .30
- ❑ 157 Drew Brees .75 .30
- ❑ 158 Torry Holt .75 .30
- ❑ 159 Keyshawn Johnson .75 .30
- ❑ 160 Michael Vick 2.50 1.00
- ❑ 161 Benjamin Gay .30 .10
- ❑ 162 Bill Schroeder .50 .20
- ❑ 163 Byron Chamberlain .30 .10
- ❑ 164 Tedy Bruschi .75 .30
- ❑ 165 Kordell Stewart .50 .20
- ❑ 166 Deltha O'Neal .30 .10
- ❑ 167 Quincy Morgan .30 .10
- ❑ 168 Bubba Franks .50 .20
- ❑ 169 Daunte Culpepper .75 .30
- ❑ 170 Ricky Williams 4.00 1.50
- ❑ 171 Plaxico Burress .50 .20
- ❑ 172 Trent Dilfer .50 .20
- ❑ 173 Steve Smith .75 .30
- ❑ 174 Greg Ellis .30 .10
- ❑ 175 Tony Brackens .30 .10
- ❑ 176 Santana Moss .75 .30
- ❑ 177 Frank Wycheck .30 .10
- ❑ 178 Michael Pittman .30 .10
- ❑ 179 Peter Warrick .50 .20
- ❑ 180 Antonio Freeman .75 .30
- ❑ 181 Tom Brady 2.00 .75
- ❑ 182 Bobby Taylor .30 .10
- ❑ 183 Jeff Garcia .75 .30
- ❑ 184 Darrell Jackson .50 .20
- ❑ 185 Chris Weinke .50 .20
- ❑ 186 Darren Woodson .30 .10
- ❑ 187 Hardy Nickerson .30 .10
- ❑ 188 Wayne Chrebet .50 .20
- ❑ 189 Samari Rolle .30 .10
- ❑ 190 Jamal Anderson .50 .20
- ❑ 191 James Jackson .30 .10
- ❑ 192 Ahman Green .75 .30
- ❑ 193 Michael Bennett .50 .20
- ❑ 194 Aaron Brooks .75 .30
- ❑ 195 Jerome Bettis .75 .30
- ❑ 196 Jay Riemersma .30 .10
- ❑ 197 Brian Griese .75 .30
- ❑ 198 Priest Holmes 1.00 .40
- ❑ 199 Curtis Martin .75 .30
- ❑ 200 Derrick Mason .50 .20
- ❑ 201 Antonio Bryant RC 5.00 2.00
- ❑ 202 David Carr RC 12.00 5.00
- ❑ 203 Eric Crouch RC 5.00 2.00
- ❑ 204 Freddie Milons RC 4.00 1.50
- ❑ 205 Najeh Davenport RC 5.00 2.00
- ❑ 206 Rohan Davey RC 5.00 2.00
- ❑ 207 T.J. Duckett RC 6.00 2.50
- ❑ 208 DeShaun Foster RC 5.00 2.00
- ❑ 209 Jabar Gaffney RC 5.00 2.00
- ❑ 210 William Green RC 5.00 2.00
- ❑ 211 Joey Harrington RC 8.00 3.00
- ❑ 212 Travis Stephens RC 4.00 1.50
- ❑ 213 Julius Peppers RC 10.00 4.00
- ❑ 214 Adrian Peterson RC 5.00 2.00
- ❑ 215 Josh Reed RC 5.00 2.00
- ❑ 216 Mike Williams RC 5.00 2.00
- ❑ 217 Javon Walker RC 10.00 4.00
- ❑ 218 Marquise Walker RC 4.00 1.50
- ❑ 219 Patrick Ramsey RC 6.00 2.50
- ❑ 220 Lamar Gordon RC 5.00 2.00
- ❑ 221 David Garrard RC 5.00 2.00
- ❑ 222 Major Applewhite RC 5.00 2.00
- ❑ 223 Andre Davis RC 4.00 1.50
- ❑ 224 Roy Williams RC 12.00 5.00
- ❑ 225 Tim Carter RC 4.00 1.50
- ❑ 226 Ron Johnson RC 4.00 1.50
- ❑ 227 Randy Fasani RC 4.00 1.50
- ❑ 228 Ashley Lelie RC 10.00 4.00
- ❑ 229 Ladell Betts RC 5.00 2.00
- ❑ 230 Antwaan Randle El RC 8.00 3.00
- ❑ 231 Jonathan Wells RC 5.00 2.00
- ❑ 232 Brian Westbrook RC 8.00 3.00
- ❑ 233 Clinton Portis RC 15.00 6.00
- ❑ 234 Luke Staley RC 4.00 1.50
- ❑ 235 Cliff Russell RC 4.00 1.50
- ❑ 236 Jeremy Shockey RC 15.00 6.00
- ❑ 237 Donte Stallworth RC 10.00 4.00
- ❑ 238 Daniel Graham RC 5.00 2.00
- ❑ 239 Reche Caldwell RC 5.00 2.00
- ❑ 240 Ryan Sims RC 5.00 2.00

2003 Ultra

- ❑ COMP.SET w/o SP's (160) 30.00 12.50
- ❑ 1 Rich Gannon .50 .20
- ❑ 2 Warren Sapp .50 .20
- ❑ 3 Steve McNair .75 .30
- ❑ 4 Donovan McNabb 1.00 .40
- ❑ 5 Chad Pennington 1.00 .40
- ❑ 6 Michael Vick 2.00 .75
- ❑ 7 Hines Ward .75 .30
- ❑ 8 Terrell Owens .75 .30
- ❑ 9 Brett Favre 2.00 .75
- ❑ 10 Jeremy Shockey 1.25 .50
- ❑ 11 William Green .50 .20
- ❑ 12 Marvin Harrison .75 .30
- ❑ 13 Mark Brunell .50 .20
- ❑ 14 Todd Heap .50 .20
- ❑ 15 Tim Couch .30 .10
- ❑ 16 Javon Walker .50 .20
- ❑ 17 Zach Thomas .50 .20
- ❑ 18 Brian Westbrook .50 .20
- ❑ 19 Matt Hasselbeck .50 .20
- ❑ 20 Jevon Kearse .50 .20
- ❑ 21 David Boston .50 .20
- ❑ 22 Michael Bennett .50 .20
- ❑ 23 James Mungro .30 .10
- ❑ 24 Antowain Smith .50 .20
- ❑ 25 Laveranues Coles .50 .20
- ❑ 26 Curtis Conway .30 .10
- ❑ 27 Peerless Price .50 .20
- ❑ 28 Michael Strahan .50 .20
- ❑ 29 Tommy Maddox .75 .30
- ❑ 30 Dennis Northcutt .50 .20
- ❑ 31 Rod Gardner .50 .20
- ❑ 32 Marcel Shipp .50 .20
- ❑ 33 Quincy Morgan .50 .20
- ❑ 34 Reggie Wayne .50 .20
- ❑ 35 Troy Brown .50 .20
- ❑ 36 John Abraham .30 .10
- ❑ 37 Tim Dwight .50 .20
- ❑ 38 Jamal Lewis .75 .30
- ❑ 39 Chad Hutchinson .30 .10
- ❑ 40 Jerramy Stevens .30 .10
- ❑ 41 Deion Branch .75 .30
- ❑ 42 Jake Plummer .50 .20
- ❑ 43 Junior Seau .75 .30
- ❑ 44 T.J. Duckett .50 .20
- ❑ 45 Emmitt Smith 2.00 .75
- ❑ 46 Edgerrin James .75 .30
- ❑ 47 David Patten .30 .10
- ❑ 48 Charlie Garner .50 .20
- ❑ 49 Quentin Jammer .30 .10
- ❑ 50 Corey Dillon .50 .20
- ❑ 51 Rod Smith .50 .20
- ❑ 52 Marc Boerigter .50 .20
- ❑ 53 Michael Lewis .30 .10
- ❑ 54 Kendrell Bell .50 .20
- ❑ 55 Isaac Bruce .75 .30
- ❑ 56 Warrick Dunn .50 .20
- ❑ 57 Antonio Bryant .50 .20
- ❑ 58 Peyton Manning 1.25 .50
- ❑ 59 Ty Law .50 .20
- ❑ 60 Jerry Rice 1.50 .60
- ❑ 61 Jeff Garcia .75 .30
- ❑ 62 Joey Galloway .50 .20
- ❑ 63 Aaron Glenn .30 .10
- ❑ 64 Aaron Brooks .75 .30
- ❑ 65 Tim Brown .75 .30
- ❑ 66 David Terrell .50 .20
- ❑ 67 Fred Smoot .30 .10
- ❑ 68 Brian Finneran .30 .10
- ❑ 69 Roy Williams .75 .30
- ❑ 70 Corey Bradford .30 .10
- ❑ 71 Deuce McAllister .75 .30
- ❑ 72 Jerry Porter .50 .20
- ❑ 73 Kevan Barlow .50 .20
- ❑ 74 Keith Brooking .30 .10
- ❑ 75 Brian Urlacher 1.25 .50
- ❑ 76 Jabar Gaffney .50 .20
- ❑ 77 Randy Moss 1.25 .50
- ❑ 78 Charles Woodson .50 .20
- ❑ 79 Darrell Jackson .50 .20
- ❑ 80 John Lynch .50 .20
- ❑ 81 Chester Taylor .30 .10
- ❑ 82 Anthony Thomas .50 .20
- ❑ 83 Jonathan Wells .30 .10
- ❑ 84 Daunte Culpepper .75 .30
- ❑ 85 Phillip Buchanon .30 .10
- ❑ 86 Koren Robinson .30 .10
- ❑ 87 Ronde Barber .30 .10
- ❑ 88 Julius Peppers .75 .30
- ❑ 89 Clinton Portis 1.25 .50
- ❑ 90 Jay Fiedler .50 .20
- ❑ 91 Donte Stallworth .75 .30
- ❑ 92 Marc Bulger .75 .30
- ❑ 93 Joe Jurevicius .30 .10
- ❑ 94 Jon Kitna .50 .20
- ❑ 95 Ricky Williams .75 .30
- ❑ 96 Joe Horn .50 .20
- ❑ 97 Jerome Bettis .75 .30
- ❑ 98 Kurt Warner .75 .30
- ❑ 99 Travis Henry .50 .20
- ❑ 100 Ahman Green .75 .30
- ❑ 101 Jimmy Smith .50 .20
- ❑ 102 Curtis Martin .75 .30
- ❑ 103 Simeon Rice .50 .20

❑ 104 Patrick Ramsey .75 .30
❑ 105 Josh Reed .50 .20
❑ 106 James Stewart .50 .20
❑ 107 Trent Green .50 .20
❑ 108 Randy McMichael .50 .20
❑ 109 Amos Zereoue .50 .20
❑ 110 Keyshawn Johnson .75 .30
❑ 111 DeShaun Foster .30 .10
❑ 112 Kevin Johnson .50 .20
❑ 113 Dwight Freeney .50 .20
❑ 114 Tom Brady 2.00 .75
❑ 115 Santana Moss .50 .20
❑ 116 LaDainian Tomlinson .75 .30
❑ 117 Joey Harrington 1.25 .50
❑ 118 Priest Holmes 1.00 .40
❑ 119 Amani Toomer .50 .20
❑ 120 Plaxico Burress .50 .20
❑ 121 Brad Johnson .50 .20
❑ 122 Champ Bailey .50 .20
❑ 123 Muhsin Muhammad .50 .20
❑ 124 Ashley Lelie .75 .30
❑ 125 Tony Gonzalez .50 .20
❑ 126 Kerry Collins .50 .20
❑ 127 Antwaan Randle El .75 .30
❑ 128 Torry Holt .75 .30
❑ 129 Ladell Betts .50 .20
❑ 130 Travis Taylor .30 .10
❑ 131 Marty Booker .50 .20
❑ 132 Patrick Surtain .30 .10
❑ 133 Duce Staley .50 .20
❑ 134 Shaun Alexander .75 .30
❑ 135 Eddie George .50 .20
❑ 136 Eric Moulds .50 .20
❑ 137 David Carr 1.25 .50
❑ 138 Fred Taylor .75 .30
❑ 139 Wayne Chrebet .50 .20
❑ 140 Bobby Taylor .30 .10
❑ 141 Derrick Brooks .50 .20
❑ 142 Stephen Davis .50 .20
❑ 143 Ray Lewis .75 .30
❑ 144 Kelly Holcomb .50 .20
❑ 145 Terry Glenn .30 .10
❑ 146 Jason Taylor .30 .10
❑ 147 Todd Pinkston .50 .20
❑ 148 Derrick Mason .50 .20
❑ 149 Chad Johnson .75 .30
❑ 150 Ed McCaffrey .50 .20
❑ 151 Tiki Barber .75 .30
❑ 152 Drew Brees .75 .30
❑ 153 Marshall Faulk .75 .30
❑ 154 Drew Bledsoe .75 .30
❑ 155 Andre Davis .30 .10
❑ 156 Donald Driver .50 .20
❑ 157 Chris Chambers .75 .30
❑ 158 Brian Dawkins .50 .20
❑ 159 Garrison Hearst .50 .20
❑ 160 Frank Wycheck .30 .10
❑ 161 Carson Palmer RC 15.00 6.00
❑ 162 Byron Leftwich RC 12.00 5.00
❑ 163 Charles Rogers RC 4.00 1.50
❑ 164 Andre Johnson RC 8.00 3.00
❑ 165 Chris Simms RC 6.00 2.50
❑ 166 Rex Grossman RC 12.00 5.00
❑ 167 Brandon Lloyd RC 4.00 1.50
❑ 168 Lee Suggs RC 4.00 1.50
❑ 169 Larry Johnson RC 15.00 7.50
❑ 170 Onterrio Smith RC 4.00 1.50
❑ 171 Dave Ragone RC 4.00 1.50
❑ 172 Taylor Jacobs RC 3.00 1.25
❑ 173 Kelley Washington RC 4.00 1.50
❑ 174 Bryant Johnson RC 4.00 1.50
❑ 175 Kyle Boller RC 4.00 1.50
❑ 176 Ken Dorsey RC 4.00 1.50
❑ 177 Kliff Kingsbury RC 3.00 1.25
❑ 178 Jason Gesser RC 4.00 1.50
❑ 179 Brian St.Pierre RC 4.00 1.50
❑ 180 Brad Banks RC 3.00 1.25
❑ 181 Seneca Wallace RC 4.00 1.50
❑ 182 Tony Romo RC 25.00 12.50
❑ 183 Terrell Suggs RC 6.00 2.50
❑ 184 Terence Newman RC 8.00 3.00
❑ 185 Willis McGahee RC 10.00 4.00
❑ 186 Justin Fargas RC 4.00 1.50
❑ 187 Musa Smith RC 4.00 1.50
❑ 188 Earnest Graham RC 3.00 1.25
❑ 189 Chris Brown RC 4.00 1.50
❑ 190 LaBrandon Toefield RC 4.00 1.50
❑ 191 Bennie Joppru RC 4.00 1.50
❑ 192 Jason Witten RC 6.00 2.50
❑ 193 Anquan Boldin RC 10.00 4.00
❑ 194 Talman Gardner RC 4.00 1.50
❑ 195 Justin Gage RC 4.00 1.50
❑ 196 Sam Aiken RC 3.00 1.25
❑ 197 Kevin Curtis RC 4.00 1.50
❑ 198 Terrence Edwards RC 3.00 1.25
❑ U199 DeWayne Robertson RC 4.00 1.50
❑ U200 Kevin Williams RC 4.00 1.50
❑ U201 Marcus Trufant RC 4.00 1.50
❑ U202 Jimmy Kennedy RC 4.00 1.50
❑ U203 Ty Warren RC 4.00 1.50
❑ U204 Michael Haynes RC 4.00 1.50
❑ U205 Jerome McDougle RC 4.00 1.50
❑ U206 Dallas Clark RC 4.00 1.50
❑ U207 William Joseph RC 4.00 1.50
❑ U208 Andre Woolfolk RC 4.00 1.50
❑ U209 Bethel Johnson RC 4.00 1.50
❑ U210 Teyo Johnson RC 4.00 1.50
❑ U211 Tyrone Calico RC 4.00 1.50
❑ U212 L.J. Smith RC 4.00 1.50
❑ U213 Nate Burleson RC 4.00 1.50
❑ U214 B.J. Askew RC 4.00 1.50
❑ U215 Billy McMullen RC 4.00 1.50
❑ U216 Domanick Davis RC 4.00 1.50
❑ U217 Doug Gabriel RC 4.00 1.50
❑ U218 Quentin Griffin RC 4.00 1.50

2004 Ultra

❑ COMP.SET w/o L13's (218) 60.00 25.00
❑ COMP.SET w/o SP's (200) 30.00 12.50
❑ COMP.UPDATE SET (21) 40.00 15.00
❑ L13 201-213 ROOKIE ODDS 1:100H,1:530R
❑ L13 ROOKIE PRINT RUN 500 SER.#'d SETS
❑ 214-232 ROOKIE STATED ODDS 1:4H,1:6R
❑ U234-U254 ODDS 2:1 TRADITION HOT PACK
❑ 1 Michael Vick 1.50 .60
❑ 2 Kelley Washington .30 .10
❑ 3 Rex Grossman .75 .30
❑ 4 Boss Bailey .50 .20
❑ 5 Johnnie Morton .50 .20
❑ 6 Michael Strahan .50 .20
❑ 7 Joey Porter .50 .20
❑ 8 Keenan McCardell .30 .10
❑ 9 Quincy Carter .50 .20
❑ 10 Travis Henry .50 .20
❑ 11 Bertrand Berry .30 .10
❑ 12 Marvin Harrison .75 .30
❑ 13 Ty Law .50 .20
❑ 14 Phillip Buchanon .30 .10
❑ 15 Kevan Barlow .50 .20
❑ 16 Eddie George .50 .20
❑ 17 Drew Bledsoe .75 .30
❑ 18 Antonio Bryant .50 .20
❑ 19 Marcus Pollard .30 .10
❑ 20 Brian Russell RC .75 .30
❑ 21 Santana Moss .50 .20
❑ 22 Julian Peterson .30 .10
❑ 23 Justin McCareins .30 .10
❑ 24 Ed Reed .50 .20
❑ 25 Charles Tillman .50 .20
❑ 26 Dat Nguyen .30 .10
❑ 27 Ricky Manning .30 .10
❑ 28 Dwight Freeney .50 .20
❑ 29 Zach Thomas .75 .30
❑ 30 Tiki Barber .75 .30
❑ 31 Jay Riemersma .30 .10
❑ 32 Joe Jurevicius .30 .10
❑ 33 Marcel Shipp .50 .20
❑ 34 Justin Gage .50 .20
❑ 35 Charles Rogers .50 .20
❑ 36 Eddie Kennison .30 .10
❑ 37 Deion Branch .75 .30
❑ 38 Matt Hasselbeck .50 .20
❑ 39 L.J. Smith .50 .20
❑ 40 Jamal Lewis .75 .30
❑ 41 Muhsin Muhammad .50 .20
❑ 42 Terence Newman .50 .20
❑ 43 Jabar Gaffney .50 .20
❑ 44 Junior Seau .75 .30
❑ 45 Jeremy Shockey .75 .30
❑ 46 Hines Ward .75 .30
❑ 47 Brad Johnson .50 .20
❑ 48 Kyle Boller .75 .30
❑ 49 Steve Smith .75 .30
❑ 50 Quincy Morgan .50 .20
❑ 51 Corey Bradford .30 .10
❑ 52 Ricky Williams .75 .30
❑ 53 Amani Toomer .50 .20
❑ 54 Plaxico Burress .50 .20
❑ 55 Derrick Brooks .50 .20
❑ 56 Dre Bly .30 .10
❑ 57 Terrell Suggs .50 .20
❑ 58 DeShaun Foster .50 .20
❑ 59 Andre Davis .30 .10
❑ 60 Rod Smith .50 .20
❑ 61 Andre Johnson .75 .30
❑ 62 Randy McMichael .30 .10
❑ 63 Ike Hilliard .30 .10
❑ 64 Antwaan Randle El .75 .30
❑ 65 Warren Sapp .50 .20
❑ 66 LaBrandon Toefield .30 .10
❑ 67 Chad Johnson .75 .30
❑ 68 Javon Walker .50 .20
❑ 69 Jimmy Smith .50 .20
❑ 70 Donte Stallworth .50 .20
❑ 71 Brian Dawkins .50 .20
❑ 72 Leonard Little .30 .10
❑ 73 Ladell Betts .30 .10
❑ 74 Ray Lewis .75 .30
❑ 75 Stephen Davis .50 .20
❑ 76 Dennis Northcutt .30 .10
❑ 77 Ashley Lelie .50 .20
❑ 78 Billy Miller .30 .10
❑ 79 Chris Chambers .50 .20
❑ 80 John Abraham .30 .10
❑ 81 Quentin Jammer .30 .10
❑ 82 Isaac Bruce .50 .20
❑ 83 Peerless Price .50 .20
❑ 84 Jake Delhomme .75 .30
❑ 85 Lee Suggs .75 .30
❑ 86 Shannon Sharpe .50 .20
❑ 87 Domanick Davis .75 .30
❑ 88 Daunte Culpepper .75 .30
❑ 89 Shaun Ellis .30 .10
❑ 90 Drew Brees .75 .30
❑ 91 Torry Holt .75 .30
❑ 92 Alge Crumpler .50 .20
❑ 93 Mike Rucker .50 .20
❑ 94 Tim Couch .30 .10
❑ 95 Quentin Griffin .75 .30
❑ 96 David Carr .75 .30
❑ 97 Moe Williams .30 .10
❑ 98 Chad Pennington .75 .30
❑ 99 LaDainian Tomlinson 1.00 .40
❑ 100 Adam Archuleta .30 .10
❑ 101 Julius Peppers .75 .30
❑ 102 Clinton Portis .75 .30
❑ 103 Marcus Stroud .30 .10
❑ 104 Tom Brady 2.00 .75
❑ 105 Teyo Johnson .30 .10
❑ 106 Terrell Owens .75 .30
❑ 107 Keith Bulluck .30 .10
❑ 108 Eric Moulds .50 .20
❑ 109 Jake Plummer .50 .20
❑ 110 Reggie Wayne .50 .20
❑ 111 Tedy Bruschi .50 .20
❑ 112 Rich Gannon .50 .20
❑ 113 Tony Parrish .30 .10
❑ 114 Steve McNair .75 .30
❑ 115 T.J. Duckett .50 .20
❑ 116 Peter Warrick .50 .20
❑ 117 Donald Driver .50 .20
❑ 118 Fred Taylor .50 .20
❑ 119 Joe Horn .50 .20

❑ 120	Jerry Porter	.50	.20
❑ 121	Marc Bulger	.75	.30
❑ 122	Trung Canidate	.30	.10
❑ 123	Warrick Dunn	.50	.20
❑ 124	Kelly Holcomb	.50	.20
❑ 125	Robert Ferguson	.30	.10
❑ 126	Byron Leftwich	1.00	.40
❑ 127	Michael Lewis	.30	.10
❑ 128	Jerry Rice	1.50	.60
❑ 129	Marshall Faulk	.75	.30
❑ 130	Patrick Ramsey	.50	.20
❑ 131	Josh McCown	.50	.20
❑ 132	Anthony Thomas	.50	.20
❑ 133	Joey Harrington	.75	.30
❑ 134	Dante Hall	.75	.30
❑ 135	Daniel Graham	.30	.10
❑ 136	Richard Seymour	.30	.10
❑ 137	Brandon Lloyd	.50	.20
❑ 138	Anquan Boldin	.75	.30
❑ 139	Jon Kitna	.50	.20
❑ 140	Nick Barnett	.50	.20
❑ 141	Priest Holmes	1.00	.40
❑ 142	Bethel Johnson	.50	.20
❑ 143	Shaun Alexander	.75	.30
❑ 144	Todd Heap	.50	.20
❑ 145	Brian Urlacher	1.00	.40
❑ 146	Peyton Manning	1.25	.50
❑ 147	Jason Taylor	.30	.10
❑ 148	Kerry Collins	.50	.20
❑ 149	Tommy Maddox	.50	.20
❑ 150	Charles Lee	.30	.10
❑ 151	Tim Rattay	.30	.10
❑ 152	Carson Palmer	1.00	.40
❑ 153	Brett Favre	2.00	.75
❑ 154	Trent Green	.50	.20
❑ 155	Aaron Brooks	.50	.20
❑ 156	Brian Westbrook	.50	.20
❑ 157	Itula Mili	.30	.10
❑ 158	Keith Brooking	.30	.10
❑ 159	Rudi Johnson	.50	.20
❑ 160	Najeh Davenport	.30	.10
❑ 161	Kevin Johnson	.30	.10
❑ 162	Boo Williams	.30	.10
❑ 163	Corey Simon	.50	.20
❑ 164	Darrell Jackson	.50	.20
❑ 165	Damerien McCants	.30	.10
❑ 166	Willis McGahee	.75	.30
❑ 167	Terry Glenn	.30	.10
❑ 168	Dallas Clark	.50	.20
❑ 169	Randy Moss	1.00	.40
❑ 170	Charles Woodson	.50	.20
❑ 171	Jeff Garcia	.75	.30
❑ 172	Chris Brown	.75	.30
❑ 173	Emmitt Smith	1.50	.60
❑ 174	Marty Booker	.50	.20
❑ 175	Artose Pinner	.30	.10
❑ 176	Tony Gonzalez	.50	.20
❑ 177	Troy Brown	.50	.20
❑ 178	Freddie Mitchell	.50	.20
❑ 179	Marcus Trufant	.30	.10
❑ 180	London Fletcher	.30	.10
❑ 181	Roy Williams S	.50	.20
❑ 182	Edgerrin James	.75	.30
❑ 183	Michael Bennett	.50	.20
❑ 184	Jerald Sowell	.30	.10
❑ 185	David Boston	.50	.20
❑ 186	Derrick Mason	.50	.20
❑ 187	Bryant Johnson	.30	.10
❑ 188	Corey Dillon	.50	.20
❑ 189	Ahman Green	.75	.30
❑ 190	Vonnie Holliday	.30	.10
❑ 191	Deuce McAllister	.75	.30
❑ 192	Donovan McNabb	1.00	.40
❑ 193	Koren Robinson	.50	.20
❑ 194	Laveranues Coles	.50	.20
❑ 195	Takeo Spikes	.30	.10
❑ 196	Richie Anderson	.30	.10
❑ 197	Onterrio Smith	.50	.20
❑ 198	Curtis Martin	.75	.30
❑ 199	Antonio Gates	.75	.30
❑ 200	Champ Bailey	.50	.20
❑ 201	Eli Manning L13 RC	80.00	30.00
❑ 202	Philip Rivers L13 RC	50.00	25.00
❑ 203	Roy Williams L13 RC	50.00	20.00
❑ 204	Drew Henson L13 RC	20.00	7.50
❑ 205	Chris Perry L13 RC	25.00	10.00
❑ 206	Larry Fitzgerald L13 RC	50.00	20.00
❑ 207	Rashaun Woods L13 RC	20.00	7.50
❑ 208	Reggie Williams L13 RC	30.00	12.50
❑ 209	Mike Williams L13 RC	40.00	15.00
❑ 210	Kellen Winslow L13 RC	30.00	12.50
❑ 211	Steven Jackson L13 RC	50.00	20.00
❑ 212	Kevin Jones L13 RC	40.00	15.00
❑ 213	Ben Roethlisberger L13 RC	120.00	60.00
❑ 214	Michael Turner RC	6.00	2.50
❑ 215	Tatum Bell RC	8.00	3.00
❑ 216	Quincy Wilson RC	2.50	1.00
❑ 217	Devery Henderson RC	2.50	1.00
❑ 218	Ernest Wilford RC	4.00	1.50
❑ 219	Cody Pickett RC	4.00	1.50
❑ 220	Ryan Dinwiddie RC	2.50	1.00
❑ 221	J.P. Losman RC	8.00	3.00
❑ 222	Derrick Knight RC	2.50	1.00
❑ 223	Michael Jenkins RC	4.00	1.50
❑ 224	Greg Jones RC	4.00	1.50
❑ 225	Cedric Cobbs RC	4.00	1.50
❑ 226	Will Poole RC	4.00	1.50
❑ 227	Michael Clayton RC	8.00	3.00
❑ 228	Sean Taylor RC	4.00	1.50
❑ 229	Will Smith RC	4.00	1.50
❑ 230	Jonathan Vilma RC	4.00	1.50
❑ 231	Lee Evans RC	5.00	2.00
❑ 232	Julius Jones RC	12.00	5.00
❑ U234	D.J. Williams RC	5.00	2.00
❑ U235	Mewelde Moore RC	5.00	2.00
❑ U236	Ben Watson RC	5.00	2.00
❑ U237	Robert Gallery RC	5.00	2.00
❑ U238	DeAngelo Hall RC	6.00	2.50
❑ U239	Luke McCown RC	5.00	2.00
❑ U240	Ben Troupe RC	5.00	2.00
❑ U241	Keary Colbert RC	6.00	2.50
❑ U242	Matt Schaub RC	12.00	5.00
❑ U243	Kenechi Udeze RC	5.00	2.00
❑ U244	Jeff Smoker RC	5.00	2.00
❑ U245	Derrick Hamilton RC	4.00	1.50
❑ U246	Bernard Berrian RC	6.00	2.50
❑ U247	Devard Darling RC	5.00	2.00
❑ U248	Johnnie Morant RC	5.00	2.00
❑ U249	Vince Wilfork RC	5.00	2.00
❑ U250	Jerricho Cotchery RC	5.00	2.00
❑ U251	Darius Watts RC	5.00	2.00
❑ U252	Carlos Francis RC	4.00	1.50
❑ U253	P.K. Sam RC	4.00	1.50

2005 Ultra

❑ COMP.SET w/o RC's (200) 30.00 12.50
❑ 201-213 L13 PRINT RUN 599 SER.#'d SETS
❑ OVERALL ROOKIE ODDS 1:4 HOB, 1:5 RET

❑ 1	Peyton Manning	1.25	.50
❑ 2	Brian Westbrook	.50	.20
❑ 3	Daunte Culpepper	.75	.30
❑ 4	Marvin Harrison	.75	.30
❑ 5	Edgerrin James	.75	.30
❑ 6	Reggie Wayne	.50	.20
❑ 7	Michael Vick	1.25	.50
❑ 8	Donte Stallworth	.50	.20
❑ 9	Brian Urlacher	.75	.30
❑ 10	Hines Ward	.75	.30
❑ 11	Charles Rogers	.50	.20
❑ 12	Roy Williams WR	.75	.30
❑ 13	Julius Peppers	.50	.20
❑ 14	Eric Moulds	.50	.20
❑ 15	Ray Lewis	.75	.30
❑ 16	Byron Leftwich	.75	.30
❑ 17	Fred Taylor	.50	.20
❑ 18	Andre Johnson	.50	.20
❑ 19	Travis Henry	.50	.20
❑ 20	Tom Brady	2.00	.75
❑ 21	Drew Bledsoe	.75	.30
❑ 22	Tiki Barber	.75	.30
❑ 23	Larry Fitzgerald	.75	.30
❑ 24	Jeff Garcia	.50	.20
❑ 25	Rex Grossman	.50	.20
❑ 26	Larry Johnson	.75	.30
❑ 27	Curtis Martin	.75	.30
❑ 28	Chad Pennington	.75	.30
❑ 29	Dwight Freeney	.50	.20
❑ 30	Peerless Price	.40	.15
❑ 31	Rich Gannon	.50	.20
❑ 32	Matt Hasselbeck	.50	.20
❑ 33	Clinton Portis	.75	.30
❑ 34	Jerry Rice	1.25	.50
❑ 35	Jeremy Shockey	.75	.30
❑ 36	Tony Gonzalez	.50	.20
❑ 37	Deuce McAllister	.75	.30
❑ 38	Shaun Alexander	1.00	.40
❑ 39	Peter Warrick	.50	.20
❑ 40	Isaac Bruce	.50	.20
❑ 41	Antonio Bryant	.40	.15
❑ 42	Mike Alstott	.50	.20
❑ 43	Domanick Davis	.50	.20
❑ 44	Jake Delhomme	.75	.30
❑ 45	Santana Moss	.50	.20
❑ 46	Ahman Green	.75	.30
❑ 47	David Carr	.75	.30
❑ 48	Kyle Boller	.50	.20
❑ 49	Chris Chambers	.50	.20
❑ 50	Quentin Griffin	.40	.15
❑ 51	Donovan McNabb	1.00	.40
❑ 52	Eli Manning	1.50	.60
❑ 53	Julius Jones	1.00	.40
❑ 54	Sean Taylor	.50	.20
❑ 55	Javon Walker	.50	.20
❑ 56	Randy Moss	.75	.30
❑ 57	Thomas Jones	.50	.20
❑ 58	Joey Harrington	.75	.30
❑ 59	Michael Boulware	.40	.15
❑ 60	Marshall Faulk	.75	.30
❑ 61	Tony Parrish	.40	.15
❑ 62	Bertrand Berry	.40	.15
❑ 63	Alge Crumpler	.50	.20
❑ 64	Aaron Brooks	.50	.20
❑ 65	Muhsin Muhammad	.50	.20
❑ 66	Simeon Rice	.50	.20
❑ 67	Corey Dillon	.50	.20
❑ 68	Willis McGahee	.75	.30
❑ 69	Ben Roethlisberger	2.00	.75
❑ 70	Chad Johnson	.75	.30
❑ 71	Jamal Lewis	.75	.30
❑ 72	Drew Brees	.75	.30
❑ 73	LaDainian Tomlinson	1.00	.40
❑ 74	Reuben Droughns	.50	.20
❑ 75	Priest Holmes	.75	.30
❑ 76	Jerry Porter	.50	.20
❑ 77	Chris Brown	.50	.20
❑ 78	Steve McNair	.75	.30
❑ 79	Troy Brown	.50	.20
❑ 80	Jerome Bettis	.75	.30
❑ 81	Patrick Kerney	.40	.15
❑ 82	Terrell Owens	.75	.30
❑ 83	Brett Favre	2.00	.75
❑ 84	Carson Palmer	.75	.30
❑ 85	Jake Plummer	.50	.20
❑ 86	Tedy Bruschi	.50	.20
❑ 87	Plaxico Burress	.50	.20
❑ 88	Jonathan Vilma	.50	.20
❑ 89	Ed Reed	.50	.20
❑ 90	Brian Dawkins	.40	.15
❑ 91	Anquan Boldin	.50	.20
❑ 92	Vinny Testaverde	.50	.20
❑ 93	David Givens	.50	.20
❑ 94	Rudi Johnson	.50	.20
❑ 95	Philip Rivers	.75	.30
❑ 96	Jimmy Smith	.50	.20
❑ 97	Emmitt Smith	3.00	1.25
❑ 98	Eric Johnson	.50	.20
❑ 99	Jeremiah Trotter	.40	.15
❑ 100	Duce Staley	.50	.20
❑ 101	Warrick Dunn	.50	.20
❑ 102	Nate Burleson	.50	.20
❑ 103	Marc Bulger	.75	.30
❑ 104	Joe Horn	.50	.20
❑ 105	Rodney Harrison	.40	.15

106	Zach Thomas	.50	.20
107	Michael Clayton	.75	.30
108	Derrick Brooks	.50	.20
109	Michael Lewis	.40	.15
110	Kurt Warner	.50	.20
111	Jason Witten	.50	.20
112	Roy Williams S	.50	.20
113	Kabeer Gbaja-Biamila	.50	.20
114	Torry Holt	.75	.30
115	Tim Rattay	.40	.15
116	Josh McCown	.50	.20
117	Brian Griese	.50	.20
118	Patrick Ramsey	.50	.20
119	A.J. Feeley	.50	.20
120	Kerry Collins	.50	.20
121	Trent Green	.50	.20
122	Billy Volek	.50	.20
123	Travis Taylor	.40	.15
124	T.J. Houshmandzadeh	.40	.15
125	James Farrior	.40	.15
126	Bryan Scott	.40	.15
127	Lito Sheppard	.40	.15
128	David Patten	.40	.15
129	Antwaan Randle El	.50	.20
130	Antonio Gates	.75	.30
131	Brandon Stokley	.40	.15
132	Keyshawn Johnson	.50	.20
133	Amani Toomer	.50	.20
134	Shawn Springs	.40	.15
135	Eddie George	.50	.20
136	Kevin Jones	.75	.30
137	Darrell Jackson	.50	.20
138	Ricky Manning	.40	.15
139	Laveranues Coles	.50	.20
140	Champ Bailey	.50	.20
141	Rod Smith	.50	.20
142	Ashley Lelie	.50	.20
143	Charles Woodson	.50	.20
144	Drew Bennett	.50	.20
145	Derrick Mason	.50	.20
146	Donovin Darius	.40	.15
147	Dennis Northcutt	.40	.15
148	Jamie Sharper	.40	.15
149	Steven Jackson	1.00	.40
150	David Terrell	.40	.15
151	Onterrio Smith	.40	.15
152	Donald Driver	.50	.20
153	Antoine Winfield	.40	.15
154	Michael Pittman	.40	.15
155	Dan Morgan	.40	.15
156	Troy Polamalu	1.25	.50
157	Willie McGinest	.40	.15
158	Justin McCareins	.40	.15
159	Allen Rossum	.40	.15
160	Deion Branch	.50	.20
161	Deion Sanders	.75	.30
162	Josh Reed	.40	.15
163	Lee Evans	.50	.20
164	Lee Suggs	.50	.20
165	Dante Hall	.50	.20
166	Eddie Kennison	.40	.15
167	Ken Dorsey	.40	.15
168	Andre Dyson	.40	.15
169	Keith Bulluck	.40	.15
170	Todd Pinkston	.40	.15
171	Jevon Kearse	.50	.20
172	Dunta Robinson	.40	.15
173	Steve Smith	.50	.20
174	Koren Robinson	.40	.15
175	Freddie Mitchell	.40	.15
176	L.J. Smith	.40	.15
177	Kevin Curtis	.40	.15
178	Marcus Robinson	.40	.15
179	Kellen Winslow	.75	.30
180	Reggie Williams	.50	.20
181	Bubba Franks	.50	.20
182	J.P. Losman	.75	.30
183	Chris Perry	.50	.20
184	Michael Jenkins	.50	.20
185	T.J. Duckett	.50	.20
186	Rashaun Woods	.40	.15
187	Ben Watson	.50	.20
188	Bryant Johnson	.40	.15
189	Dallas Clark	.40	.15
190	William Green	.40	.15
191	Daniel Graham	.40	.15
192	Jerramy Stevens	.40	.15
193	DeShaun Foster	.50	.20
194	Nick Goings	.40	.15
195	Ronald Curry	.40	.15
196	Kevan Barlow	.50	.20
197	Kevin Faulk	.40	.15
198	Eric Parker	.40	.15
199	Keenan McCardell	.40	.15
200	LaMont Jordan	.75	.30
201	Alex Smith QB L13 RC	60.00	30.00
202	Aaron Rodgers L13 RC	60.00	25.00
203	Cedric Benson L13 RC	40.00	20.00
204	Braylon Edwards L13 RC	40.00	20.00
205	Ronnie Brown L13 RC	60.00	30.00
206	Cadillac Williams L13 RC	80.00	40.00
207	Troy Williamson L13 RC	25.00	12.50
208	Mark Clayton L13 RC	25.00	12.50
209	Charlie Frye L13 RC	30.00	15.00
210	Mike Williams L13	30.00	12.50
211	Marion Barber L13 RC	30.00	15.00
212	Eric Shelton L13 RC	20.00	7.50
213	Antrel Rolle L13 RC	20.00	7.50
214	Heath Miller RC	12.00	5.00
215	Dan Cody RC	5.00	2.00
216	Adam Jones RC	5.00	2.00
217	Derrick Johnson RC	8.00	3.00
218	Alex Smith TE RC	5.00	2.00
219	Kyle Orton RC	8.00	3.00
220	David Pollack RC	5.00	2.00
221	Erasmus James RC	5.00	2.00
222	Justin Tuck RC	5.00	2.00
223	Jason Campbell RC	8.00	3.00
224	Dan Orlovsky RC	6.00	2.50
225	Thomas Davis RC	5.00	2.00
226	J.J. Arrington RC	6.00	2.50
227	Roddy White RC	5.00	2.00
228	David Greene RC	5.00	2.00
229	Ciatrick Fason RC	5.00	2.00
230	Chris Henry RC	5.00	2.00
231	Reggie Brown RC	5.00	2.00
232	Vernand Morency RC	5.00	2.00
233	Carlos Rogers RC	6.00	2.50
234	Ryan Moats RC	5.00	2.00
235	Roscoe Parrish RC	5.00	2.00
236	Terrence Murphy RC	5.00	2.00
237	Shawne Merriman RC	8.00	3.00
238	Courtney Roby RC	5.00	2.00
239	Mark Bradley RC	5.00	2.00
240	Marcus Spears RC	5.00	2.00
241	Justin Miller RC	4.00	1.50
242	Matt Jones RC	12.00	5.00
243	DeMarcus Ware RC	8.00	3.00
244	Fabian Washington RC	5.00	2.00
245	Marlin Jackson RC	5.00	2.00
246	Corey Webster RC	5.00	2.00
247	Brandon Jacobs RC	6.00	2.50
248	Frank Gore RC	10.00	4.00

2006 Ultra

1	Larry Fitzgerald	.75	.30
2	Anquan Boldin	.50	.20
3	Kurt Warner	.50	.20
4	Bryant Johnson	.40	.15
5	Marcel Shipp	.40	.15
6	J.J. Arrington	.50	.20
7	Michael Vick	1.00	.40
8	Warrick Dunn	.50	.20
9	T.J. Duckett	.50	.20
10	Alge Crumpler	.50	.20
11	Michael Jenkins	.50	.20
12	DeAngelo Hall	.50	.20
13	Kyle Boller	.40	.15
14	Jamal Lewis	.50	.20
15	Todd Heap	.50	.20
16	Derrick Mason	.40	.15
17	Ray Lewis	.75	.30
18	Terrell Suggs	.50	.20
19	J.P. Losman	.50	.20
20	Willis McGahee	.75	.30
21	Eric Moulds	.50	.20
22	Lee Evans	.50	.20
23	Roscoe Parrish	.40	.15
24	Kelly Holcomb	.40	.15
25	Jake Delhomme	.50	.20
26	Steve Smith	.75	.30
27	Stephen Davis	.50	.20
28	Julius Peppers	.50	.20
29	DeShaun Foster	.50	.20
30	Keary Colbert	.40	.15
31	Chris Gamble	.40	.15
32	Kyle Orton	.50	.20
33	Thomas Jones	.50	.20
34	Rex Grossman	.75	.30
35	Muhsin Muhammad	.50	.20
36	Brian Urlacher	.75	.30
37	Adrian Peterson	.40	.15
38	Carson Palmer	.75	.30
39	Chad Johnson	.50	.20
40	Rudi Johnson	.50	.20
41	Chris Perry	.50	.20
42	T.J. Houshmandzadeh	.50	.20
43	Chris Henry	.40	.15
44	Deltha O'Neal	.40	.15
45	Trent Dilfer	.50	.20
46	Reuben Droughns	.50	.20
47	Antonio Bryant	.75	.30
48	Braylon Edwards	.75	.30
49	Charlie Frye	.50	.20
50	Dennis Northcutt	.40	.15
51	Drew Bledsoe	.75	.30
52	Julius Jones	.75	.30
53	Keyshawn Johnson	.50	.20
54	Jason Witten	.50	.20
55	Roy Williams S	.50	.20
56	Marion Barber	.50	.20
57	Terry Glenn	.50	.20
58	Jake Plummer	.50	.20
59	Mike Anderson	.50	.20
60	Champ Bailey	.50	.20
61	Tatum Bell	.50	.20
62	Rod Smith	.50	.20
63	Ashley Lelie	.50	.20
64	Joey Harrington	.50	.20
65	Kevin Jones	.75	.30
66	Roy Williams WR	.75	.30
67	Mike Williams	.75	.30
68	Marcus Pollard	.40	.15
69	Jeff Garcia	.50	.20
70	Brett Favre	1.50	.60
71	Javon Walker	.50	.20
72	Donald Driver	.50	.20
73	Samkon Gado	.75	.30
74	Najeh Davenport	.40	.15
75	Robert Ferguson	.40	.15
76	David Carr	.50	.20
77	Domanick Davis	.50	.20
78	Andre Johnson	.50	.20
79	Jabar Gaffney	.40	.15
80	Corey Bradford	.40	.15
81	Dunta Robinson	.50	.20
82	Peyton Manning	1.25	.50
83	Edgerrin James	.75	.30
84	Marvin Harrison	.75	.30
85	Reggie Wayne	.50	.20
86	Dallas Clark	.40	.15
87	Dwight Freeney	.50	.20
88	Cato June	.50	.20
89	Byron Leftwich	.50	.20
90	Fred Taylor	.50	.20
91	Jimmy Smith	.50	.20
92	Matt Jones	.75	.30
93	Ernest Wilford	.40	.15
94	Greg Jones	.40	.15
95	Trent Green	.50	.20
96	Priest Holmes	.50	.20
97	Larry Johnson	1.00	.40
98	Tony Gonzalez	.50	.20
99	Dante Hall	.50	.20
100	Eddie Kennison	.40	.15
101	Gus Frerotte	.40	.15
102	Chris Chambers	.50	.20
103	Ronnie Brown	.75	.30
104	Ricky Williams	.50	.20
105	Randy McMichael	.40	.15
106	Zach Thomas	.75	.30
107	Daunte Culpepper	.75	.30
108	Nate Burleson	.50	.20
109	Michael Bennett	.40	.15
110	Mewelde Moore	.40	.15
111	Troy Williamson	.50	.20
112	Travis Taylor	.40	.15
113	Jermaine Wiggins	.40	.15
114	Tom Brady	1.25	.50
115	Corey Dillon	.50	.20
116	Deion Branch	.50	.20

Card		
117 Tedy Bruschi	.75	.30
118 David Givens	.50	.20
119 Patrick Pass	.40	.15
120 Aaron Brooks	.50	.20
121 Deuce McAllister	.50	.20
122 Joe Horn	.50	.20
123 Donte Stallworth	.50	.20
124 Antowain Smith	.40	.15
125 Devery Henderson	.40	.15
126 Eli Manning	1.00	.40
127 Tiki Barber	.75	.30
128 Jeremy Shockey	.75	.30
129 Plaxico Burress	.50	.20
130 Amani Toomer	.50	.20
131 Michael Strahan	.50	.20
132 Chad Pennington	.50	.20
133 Curtis Martin	.75	.30
134 Jonathan Vilma	.50	.20
135 Laveranues Coles	.50	.20
136 Justin McCareins	.50	.20
137 Ty Law	.50	.20
138 Kerry Collins	.50	.20
139 LaMont Jordan	.50	.20
140 Randy Moss	.75	.30
141 Jerry Porter	.50	.20
142 Doug Gabriel	.40	.15
143 Zack Crockett	.40	.15
144 Donovan McNabb	.75	.30
145 Brian Westbrook	.50	.20
146 Terrell Owens	.75	.30
147 Jevon Kearse	.50	.20
148 L.J. Smith	.40	.15
149 Greg Lewis	.40	.15
150 Ben Roethlisberger	1.25	.50
151 Willie Parker	1.00	.40
152 Hines Ward	.75	.30
153 Jerome Bettis	.75	.30
154 Antwaan Randle El	.50	.20
155 Heath Miller	.75	.30
156 Joey Porter	.40	.15
157 Drew Brees	.75	.30
158 LaDainian Tomlinson	1.00	.40
159 Antonio Gates	.75	.30
160 Keenan McCardell	.40	.15
161 Donnie Edwards	.40	.15
162 Shawne Merriman	.50	.20
163 Eric Parker	.40	.15
164 Alex Smith	1.00	.40
165 Kevan Barlow	.50	.20
166 Frank Gore	.75	.30
167 Brandon Lloyd	.50	.20
168 Eric Johnson	.50	.20
169 Julian Peterson	.40	.15
170 Matt Hasselbeck	.50	.20
171 Shaun Alexander	.75	.30
172 Darrell Jackson	.50	.20
173 Joe Jurevicius	.50	.20
174 Jerramy Stevens	.50	.20
175 D.J. Hackett	.40	.15
176 Marc Bulger	.50	.20
177 Steven Jackson	.75	.30
178 Torry Holt	.50	.20
179 Isaac Bruce	.50	.20
180 Kevin Curtis	.40	.15
181 Marshall Faulk	.50	.20
182 Chris Simms	.50	.20
183 Cadillac Williams	.75	.30
184 Michael Pittman	.40	.15
185 Michael Clayton	.40	.15
186 Joey Galloway	.50	.20
187 Brian Griese	.50	.20
188 Steve McNair	.50	.20
189 Chris Brown	.50	.20
190 Drew Bennett	.40	.15
191 Travis Henry	.40	.15
192 Ben Troupe	.40	.15
193 Billy Volek	.50	.20
194 Erron Kinney	.40	.15
195 Mark Brunell	.40	.15
196 Santana Moss	.40	.15
197 Clinton Portis	.75	.30
198 Chris Cooley	.40	.15
199 Ladell Betts	.40	.15
200 Sean Taylor	.50	.20
201 Matt Leinart L13 RC	100.00	50.00
202 Vince Young L13 RC	120.00	60.00
203 Reggie Bush L13 RC	200.00	100.00
204 D'Brick Ferguson L13 RC	25.00	10.00
205 DeAngelo Williams L13 RC	80.00	40.00
206 Jay Cutler L13 RC	100.00	50.00
207 A.J. Hawk L13 RC	80.00	40.00
208 Mario Williams L13 RC	50.00	20.00
209 Santonio Holmes L13 RC	60.00	25.00
210 Chad Greenway L13 RC	40.00	20.00
211 Laurence Maroney L13 RC	80.00	30.00
212 LenDale White L13 RC	60.00	30.00
213 Sinorice Moss L13 RC	50.00	25.00
214 A.J. Nicholson RC	2.50	1.00
215 Abdul Hodge RC	5.00	2.00
216 Jeremy Bloom RC	4.00	1.50
217 Anthony Fasano RC	5.00	2.00
218 Bobby Carpenter RC	5.00	2.00
219 Brian Calhoun RC	5.00	2.00
220 Brodie Croyle RC	10.00	4.00
221 Chad Jackson RC	8.00	3.00
222 Charlie Whitehurst RC	6.00	2.50
223 Claude Wroten RC	2.50	1.00
224 Darnell Bing RC	5.00	2.00
225 Darrell Hackney RC	4.00	1.50
226 David Thomas RC	5.00	2.00
227 Demetrius Williams RC	6.00	2.50
228 Derek Hagan RC	5.00	2.00
229 Devin Hester RC	10.00	4.00
230 Dominique Byrd RC	4.00	1.50
231 D'Qwell Jackson RC	4.00	1.50
232 Elvis Dumervil RC	2.50	1.00
233 Haloti Ngata RC	5.00	2.00
234 Hank Baskett RC	5.00	2.00
235 Jason Avant RC	5.00	2.00
236 Jerome Harrison RC	5.00	2.00
237 Jimmy Williams RC	5.00	2.00
238 Joe Klopfenstein RC	4.00	1.50
239 Joseph Addai RC	15.00	6.00
240 Kellen Clemens RC	6.00	2.50
241 Cory Rodgers RC	5.00	2.00
242 Leon Washington RC	8.00	3.00
243 Leonard Pope RC	5.00	2.00
244 Marcedes Lewis RC	5.00	2.00
245 Martin Nance RC	4.00	1.50
246 Mathias Kiwanuka RC	6.00	2.50
247 Maurice Drew RC	12.00	5.00
248 Maurice Stovall RC	5.00	2.00
249 Michael Huff RC	6.00	2.50
250 Mike Hass RC	5.00	2.00
251 Omar Jacobs RC	4.00	1.50
252 Orien Harris RC	4.00	1.50
253 Owen Daniels RC	5.00	2.00
254 Reggie McNeal RC	4.00	1.50
255 DeMeco Ryans RC	6.00	2.50
256 Tamba Hali RC	5.00	2.00
257 Ernie Sims RC	6.00	2.50
258 Thomas Howard RC	5.00	2.00
259 Todd Watkins RC	4.00	1.50
260 Travis Wilson RC	5.00	2.00
261 Greg Lee RC	4.00	1.50
262 Tye Hill RC	5.00	2.00
263 Vernon Davis RC	10.00	4.00

1991 Upper Deck

Card		
COMPLETE SET (700)	15.00	6.00
COMP.FACT.SET (700)	25.00	10.00
COMP.SERIES 1 SET (500)	10.00	4.00
COMP.SERIES 2 SET (200)	5.00	2.00
COMP.FACT.SERIES 2 (200)	6.00	2.50
1 Dan McGwire CL	.05	.01
2 Eric Bieniemy RC	.05	.01
3 Mike Dumas RC	.05	.01
4 Mike Croel RC	.05	.01
5 Russell Maryland RC	.25	.08
6 Charles McRae RC	.05	.01
7 Dan McGwire RC	.05	.01
8 Mike Pritchard RC	.25	.08
9 Ricky Watters RC	1.50	.60
10 Chris Zorich RC	.25	.08
11 Browning Nagle RC	.05	.01
12 Wesley Carroll RC	.05	.01
13 Brett Favre RC	10.00	5.00
14 Rob Carpenter RC WR	.05	.01
15 Eric Swann RC	.25	.08
16 Stanley Richard RC	.05	.01
17 Herman Moore RC	.25	.08
18 Todd Marinovich RC	.05	.01
19 Aaron Craver RC	.05	.01
20 Chuck Webb RC	.05	.01
21 Todd Lyght RC	.05	.01
22 Greg Lewis RC	.05	.01
23 Eric Turner RC	.10	.02
24 Alvin Harper RC	.25	.08
25 Jarrod Bunch RC	.05	.01
26 Bruce Pickens RC	.05	.01
27 Harvey Williams RC	.25	.08
28 Randal Hill RC	.10	.02
29 Nick Bell RC	.05	.01
30 Jim Everett AT	.10	.02
31 R.Cunningham/Jackson AT	.05	.01
32 Steve DeBerg AT	.05	.01
33 Warren Moon/D.Hill AT	.10	.02
34 D.Marino/M.Clayton AT	.50	.20
35 J.Montana/J.Rice AT	.50	.20
36 Percy Snow	.05	.01
37 Kelvin Martin	.05	.01
38 Scott Case	.05	.01
39 John Gesek RC	.05	.01
40 Barry Word	.05	.01
41 Cornelius Bennett	.10	.02
42 Mike Kenn	.05	.01
43 Andre Reed	.10	.02
44 Bobby Hebert	.05	.01
45 William Perry	.10	.02
46 Dennis Byrd	.05	.01
47 Martin Mayhew	.05	.01
48 Issiac Holt	.05	.01
49 William White	.05	.01
50 JoJo Townsell	.05	.01
51 Jarvis Williams	.05	.01
52 Joey Browner	.05	.01
53 Pat Terrell	.05	.01
54 Joe Montana 3X UER	1.25	.50
55 Jeff Herrod	.05	.01
56 Cris Carter	.50	.20
57 Jerry Rice	.75	.30
58 Brett Perriman	.25	.08
59 Kevin Fagan	.05	.01
60 Wayne Haddix	.05	.01
61 Tommy Kane	.05	.01
62 Pat Beach	.05	.01
63 Jeff Lageman	.05	.01
64 Hassan Jones	.05	.01
65 Bennie Blades	.05	.01
66 Tim McGee	.05	.01
67 Robert Blackmon	.05	.01
68 Fred Stokes RC	.05	.01
69 Barney Bussey RC	.05	.01
70 Eric Metcalf	.10	.02
71 Mark Kelso	.05	.01
72 Neal Anderson TC	.05	.01
73 Boomer Esiason TC	.05	.01
74 Thurman Thomas TC	.25	.08
75 John Elway TC	.50	.20
76 Eric Metcalf TC	.10	.02
77 Vinny Testaverde TC	.10	.02
78 Johnny Johnson TC	.05	.01
79 Anthony Miller TC	.10	.02
80 Derrick Thomas TC	.10	.02
81 Jeff George TC	.10	.02
82 Troy Aikman TC	.40	.15
83 Dan Marino TC	.50	.20
84 Randall Cunningham TC	.10	.02
85 Deion Sanders TC	.05	.01
86 Jerry Rice TC	.40	.15
87 Lawrence Taylor TC	.10	.02
88 Al Toon TC	.05	.01
89 Barry Sanders TC	.50	.20

❑ 90 Warren Moon TC .10 .02
❑ 91 Don Majkowski TC .05 .01
❑ 92 Andre Tippett TC .05 .01
❑ 93 Bo Jackson TC .30 .10
❑ 94 Jim Everett TC .10 .02
❑ 95 Art Monk TC .10 .02
❑ 96 Morten Andersen TC .05 .01
❑ 97 John L. Williams TC .05 .01
❑ 98 Rod Woodson TC .10 .02
❑ 99 Herschel Walker TC .10 .02
❑ 100 Checklist 1-100 .05 .01
❑ 101 Steve Young .75 .30
❑ 102 Jim Lachey .05 .01
❑ 103 Tom Rathman .05 .01
❑ 104 Earnest Byner .05 .01
❑ 105 Karl Mecklenburg .05 .01
❑ 106 Wes Hopkins .05 .01
❑ 107 Michael Irvin .25 .08
❑ 108 Burt Grossman .05 .01
❑ 109 Jay Novacek UER .25 .08
❑ 110 Ben Smith .05 .01
❑ 111 Rod Woodson .25 .08
❑ 112 Ernie Jones .05 .01
❑ 113 Bryan Hinkle .05 .01
❑ 114 Vai Sikahema .05 .01
❑ 115 Bubby Brister .05 .01
❑ 116 Brian Blades .10 .02
❑ 117 Don Majkowski .05 .01
❑ 118 Rod Bernstine .05 .01
❑ 119 Brian Noble .05 .01
❑ 120 Eugene Robinson .05 .01
❑ 121 John Taylor .10 .02
❑ 122 Vance Johnson .05 .01
❑ 123 Art Monk .10 .02
❑ 124 John Elway 1.25 .50
❑ 125 Dexter Carter .05 .01
❑ 126 Anthony Miller .10 .02
❑ 127 Keith Jackson .10 .02
❑ 128 Albert Lewis .05 .01
❑ 129 Billy Ray Smith .05 .01
❑ 130 Clyde Simmons .05 .01
❑ 131 Merril Hoge .05 .01
❑ 132 Ricky Proehl .05 .01
❑ 133 Tim McDonald .05 .01
❑ 134 Louis Lipps .05 .01
❑ 135 Ken Harvey .10 .02
❑ 136 Sterling Sharpe .10 .02
❑ 137 Gill Byrd .05 .01
❑ 138 Tim Harris .05 .01
❑ 139 Derrick Fenner .05 .01
❑ 140 Johnny Holland .05 .01
❑ 141 Ricky Sanders .05 .01
❑ 142 Bobby Humphrey .05 .01
❑ 143 Roger Craig .10 .02
❑ 144 Steve Atwater .05 .01
❑ 145 Ickey Woods .05 .01
❑ 146 Randall Cunningham .25 .08
❑ 147 Marion Butts .10 .02
❑ 148 Reggie White .25 .08
❑ 149 Ronnie Harmon .05 .01
❑ 150 Mike Saxon .05 .01
❑ 151 Greg Townsend .05 .01
❑ 152 Troy Aikman .75 .30
❑ 153 Shane Conlan .05 .01
❑ 154 Deion Sanders .40 .15
❑ 155 Bo Jackson .30 .10
❑ 156 Jeff Hostetler .10 .02
❑ 157 Albert Bentley .05 .01
❑ 158 James Williams .05 .01
❑ 159 Bill Brooks .05 .01
❑ 160 Nick Lowery .05 .01
❑ 161 Ottis Anderson .10 .02
❑ 162 Kevin Greene .10 .02
❑ 163 Neil Smith .25 .08
❑ 164 Jim Everett .10 .02
❑ 165 Derrick Thomas .25 .08
❑ 166 John L. Williams .05 .01
❑ 167 Timm Rosenbach .05 .01
❑ 168 Leslie O'Neal .10 .02
❑ 169 Clarence Verdin .05 .01
❑ 170 Dave Krieg .10 .02
❑ 171 Steve Broussard .05 .01
❑ 172 Emmitt Smith 2.50 1.00
❑ 173 Andre Rison .10 .02
❑ 174 Bruce Smith .25 .08
❑ 175 Mark Clayton .10 .02
❑ 176 Christian Okoye .05 .01
❑ 177 Duane Bickett .05 .01
❑ 178 Stephone Paige .05 .01
❑ 179 Fredd Young .05 .01
❑ 180 Mervyn Fernandez .05 .01
❑ 181 Phil Simms .10 .02
❑ 182 Pete Holohan .05 .01
❑ 183 Pepper Johnson .05 .01
❑ 184 Jackie Slater .05 .01
❑ 185 Stephen Baker .05 .01
❑ 186 Frank Cornish .05 .01
❑ 187 Dave Waymer .05 .01
❑ 188 Terance Mathis .10 .02
❑ 189 Darryl Talley .05 .01
❑ 190 James Hasty .05 .01
❑ 191 Jay Schroeder .05 .01
❑ 192 Kenneth Davis .05 .01
❑ 193 Chris Miller .10 .02
❑ 194 Scott Davis .05 .01
❑ 195 Tim Green .05 .01
❑ 196 Dan Saleaumua .05 .01
❑ 197 Rohn Stark .05 .01
❑ 198 John Alt .05 .01
❑ 199 Steve Tasker .10 .02
❑ 200 Checklist 101-200 .05 .01
❑ 201 Freddie Joe Nunn .05 .01
❑ 202 Jim Breech .05 .01
❑ 203 Roy Green .05 .01
❑ 204 Gary Anderson RB .05 .01
❑ 205 Rich Camarillo .05 .01
❑ 206 Mark Bortz .05 .01
❑ 207 Eddie Brown .05 .01
❑ 208 Brad Muster .05 .01
❑ 209 Anthony Munoz .10 .02
❑ 210 Dalton Hilliard .05 .01
❑ 211 Erik McMillan .05 .01
❑ 212 Perry Kemp .05 .01
❑ 213 Jim Thornton .05 .01
❑ 214 Anthony Dilweg .05 .01
❑ 215 Cleveland Gary .05 .01
❑ 216 Leo Goeas .05 .01
❑ 217 Mike Merriweather .05 .01
❑ 218 Courtney Hall .05 .01
❑ 219 Wade Wilson .10 .02
❑ 220 Billy Joe Tolliver .05 .01
❑ 221 Harold Green .10 .02
❑ 222 Al(Bubba) Baker .10 .02
❑ 223 Carl Zander .05 .01
❑ 224 Thane Gash .05 .01
❑ 225 Kevin Mack .05 .01
❑ 226 Morten Andersen .05 .01
❑ 227 Dennis Gentry .05 .01
❑ 228 Vince Buck .05 .01
❑ 229 Mike Singletary .10 .02
❑ 230 Rueben Mayes .05 .01
❑ 231 Mark Carrier WR .25 .08
❑ 232 Tony Mandarich .05 .01
❑ 233 Al Toon .10 .02
❑ 234 Renaldo Turnbull .05 .01
❑ 235 Broderick Thomas .05 .01
❑ 236 Anthony Carter .10 .02
❑ 237 Flipper Anderson .05 .01
❑ 238 Jerry Robinson .05 .01
❑ 239 Vince Newsome .05 .01
❑ 240 Keith Millard .05 .01
❑ 241 Reggie Langhorne .05 .01
❑ 242 James Francis .05 .01
❑ 243 Felix Wright .05 .01
❑ 244 Neal Anderson .10 .02
❑ 245 Boomer Esiason .10 .02
❑ 246 Pat Swilling .10 .02
❑ 247 Richard Dent .10 .02
❑ 248 Craig Heyward .10 .02
❑ 249 Ron Morris .05 .01
❑ 250 Eric Martin .05 .01
❑ 251 Jim C. Jensen .05 .01
❑ 252 Anthony Toney .05 .01
❑ 253 Sammie Smith .05 .01
❑ 254 Calvin Williams .10 .02
❑ 255 Dan Marino 1.25 .50
❑ 256 Warren Moon .25 .08
❑ 257 Tommie Agee .05 .01
❑ 258 Haywood Jeffires .10 .02
❑ 259 Eugene Lockhart .05 .01
❑ 260 Drew Hill .05 .01
❑ 261 Vinny Testaverde .10 .02
❑ 262 Jim Arnold .05 .01
❑ 263 Steve Christie .05 .01
❑ 264 Chris Spielman .10 .02
❑ 265 Reggie Cobb .05 .01
❑ 266 John Stephens .05 .01
❑ 267 Jay Hilgenberg .05 .01
❑ 268 Brent Williams .05 .01
❑ 269 Rodney Hampton .25 .08
❑ 270 Irving Fryar .10 .02
❑ 271 Terry McDaniel .05 .01
❑ 272 Reggie Roby .05 .01
❑ 273 Allen Pinkett .05 .01
❑ 274 Tim McKyer .05 .01
❑ 275 Bob Golic .05 .01
❑ 276 Wilber Marshall .05 .01
❑ 277 Ray Childress .05 .01
❑ 278 Charles Mann .05 .01
❑ 279 Cris Dishman RC .05 .01
❑ 280 Mark Rypien .10 .02
❑ 281 Michael Cofer .05 .01
❑ 282 Keith Byars .05 .01
❑ 283 Mike Rozier .05 .01
❑ 284 Seth Joyner .10 .02
❑ 285 Jessie Tuggle .05 .01
❑ 286 Mark Bavaro .05 .01
❑ 287 Eddie Anderson .05 .01
❑ 288 Sean Landeta .05 .01
❑ 289 Howie Long/George Brett .25 .08
❑ 290 Reyna Thompson .05 .01
❑ 291 Ferrell Edmunds .05 .01
❑ 292 Willie Gault .10 .02
❑ 293 John Offerdahl .05 .01
❑ 294 Tim Brown .25 .08
❑ 295 Bruce Matthews .10 .02
❑ 296 Kevin Ross .05 .01
❑ 297 Lorenzo White .05 .01
❑ 298 Dino Hackett .05 .01
❑ 299 Curtis Duncan .05 .01
❑ 300 Checklist 201-300 .05 .01
❑ 301 Andre Ware .10 .02
❑ 302 David Little .05 .01
❑ 303 Jerry Ball .05 .01
❑ 304 Dwight Stone UER .05 .01
❑ 305 Rodney Peete .10 .02
❑ 306 Mike Baab .05 .01
❑ 307 Tim Worley .05 .01
❑ 308 Paul Farren .05 .01
❑ 309 Carnell Lake .05 .01
❑ 310 Clay Matthews .10 .02
❑ 311 Alton Montgomery .05 .01
❑ 312 Ernest Givins .10 .02
❑ 313 Mike Horan .05 .01
❑ 314 Sean Jones .10 .02
❑ 315 Leonard Smith .05 .01
❑ 316 Carl Banks .05 .01
❑ 317 Jerome Brown .05 .01
❑ 318 Everson Walls .05 .01
❑ 319 Ron Heller .05 .01
❑ 320 Mark Collins .05 .01
❑ 321 Eddie Murray .05 .01
❑ 322 Jim Harbaugh .25 .08
❑ 323 Mel Gray .10 .02
❑ 324 Keith Van Horne .05 .01
❑ 325 Lomas Brown .05 .01
❑ 326 Carl Lee .05 .01
❑ 327 Ken O'Brien .05 .01
❑ 328 Dermontti Dawson .05 .01
❑ 329 Brad Baxter .05 .01
❑ 330 Chris Doleman .05 .01
❑ 331 Louis Oliver .05 .01
❑ 332 Frank Stams .05 .01
❑ 333 Mike Munchak .10 .02
❑ 334 Fred Strickland .05 .01
❑ 335 Mark Duper .10 .02
❑ 336 Jacob Green .05 .01
❑ 337 Tony Paige .05 .01
❑ 338 Jeff Bryant .05 .01
❑ 339 Lemuel Stinson .05 .01
❑ 340 David Wyman .05 .01
❑ 341 Lee Williams .05 .01
❑ 342 Trace Armstrong .05 .01
❑ 343 Junior Seau .25 .08
❑ 344 John Roper .05 .01
❑ 345 Jeff George .25 .08
❑ 346 Herschel Walker .10 .02
❑ 347 Sam Clancy .05 .01
❑ 348 Steve Jordan .05 .01
❑ 349 Nate Odomes .05 .01
❑ 350 Martin Bayless .05 .01

❑ 351	Brent Jones	.25	.08
❑ 352	Ray Agnew	.05	.01
❑ 353	Charles Haley	.10	.02
❑ 354	Andre Tippett	.05	.01
❑ 355	Ronnie Lott	.10	.02
❑ 356	Thurman Thomas	.25	.08
❑ 357	Fred Barnett	.25	.08
❑ 358	James Lofton	.10	.02
❑ 359	William Frizzell RC	.05	.01
❑ 360	Keith McKeller	.05	.01
❑ 361	Rodney Holman	.05	.01
❑ 362	Henry Ellard	.10	.02
❑ 363	David Fulcher	.05	.01
❑ 364	Jerry Gray	.05	.01
❑ 365	James Brooks	.10	.02
❑ 366	Tony Stargell	.05	.01
❑ 367	Keith McCants	.05	.01
❑ 368	Lewis Billups	.05	.01
❑ 369	Ervin Randle	.05	.01
❑ 370	Pat Leahy	.05	.01
❑ 371	Bruce Armstrong	.05	.01
❑ 372	Steve DeBerg	.05	.01
❑ 373	Guy McIntyre	.05	.01
❑ 374	Deron Cherry	.05	.01
❑ 375	Fred Marion	.05	.01
❑ 376	Michael Haddix	.05	.01
❑ 377	Kent Hull	.05	.01
❑ 378	Jerry Holmes	.05	.01
❑ 379	Jim Ritcher	.05	.01
❑ 380	Ed West	.05	.01
❑ 381	Richmond Webb	.05	.01
❑ 382	Mark Jackson	.05	.01
❑ 383	Tom Newberry	.05	.01
❑ 384	Ricky Nattiel	.05	.01
❑ 385	Keith Sims	.05	.01
❑ 386	Ron Hall	.05	.01
❑ 387	Ken Norton	.10	.02
❑ 388	Paul Gruber	.05	.01
❑ 389	Daniel Stubbs	.05	.01
❑ 390	Ian Beckles	.05	.01
❑ 391	Hoby Brenner	.05	.01
❑ 392	Tory Epps	.05	.01
❑ 393	Sam Mills	.05	.01
❑ 394	Chris Hinton	.05	.01
❑ 395	Steve Walsh	.05	.01
❑ 396	Simon Fletcher	.05	.01
❑ 397	Tony Bennett	.10	.02
❑ 398	Aundray Bruce	.05	.01
❑ 399	Mark Murphy	.05	.01
❑ 400	Checklist 301-400	.05	.01
❑ 401	Barry Sanders SL	.50	.20
❑ 402	Jerry Rice SL	.40	.15
❑ 403	Warren Moon SL	.10	.02
❑ 404	Derrick Thomas SL	.10	.02
❑ 405	Nick Lowery LL	.05	.01
❑ 406	Mark Carrier DB LL	.10	.02
❑ 407	Michael Carter	.05	.01
❑ 408	Chris Singleton	.05	.01
❑ 409	Matt Millen	.10	.02
❑ 410	Ronnie Lippett	.05	.01
❑ 411	E.J. Junior	.05	.01
❑ 412	Ray Donaldson	.05	.01
❑ 413	Keith Willis	.05	.01
❑ 414	Jessie Hester	.05	.01
❑ 415	Jeff Cross	.05	.01
❑ 416	Greg Jackson RC	.05	.01
❑ 417	Alvin Walton	.05	.01
❑ 418	Bart Oates	.05	.01
❑ 419	Chip Lohmiller	.05	.01
❑ 420	John Elliott	.05	.01
❑ 421	Randall McDaniel	.05	.01
❑ 422	Richard Johnson CB RC	.05	.01
❑ 423	Al Noga	.05	.01
❑ 424	Lamar Lathon	.05	.01
❑ 425	Rick Fenney	.05	.01
❑ 426	Jack Del Rio	.10	.02
❑ 427	Don Mosebar	.05	.01
❑ 428	Luis Sharpe	.05	.01
❑ 429	Steve Wisniewski	.05	.01
❑ 430	Jimmie Jones	.05	.01
❑ 431	Freeman McNeil	.05	.01
❑ 432	Ron Rivera	.05	.01
❑ 433	Hart Lee Dykes	.05	.01
❑ 434	Mark Carrier DB	.10	.02
❑ 435	Rob Moore	.25	.08
❑ 436	Gary Clark	.25	.08
❑ 437	Heath Sherman	.05	.01
❑ 438	Darrell Green	.05	.01
❑ 439	Jessie Small	.05	.01
❑ 440	Monte Coleman	.05	.01
❑ 441	Leonard Marshall	.05	.01
❑ 442	Richard Johnson	.05	.01
❑ 443	Dave Meggett	.10	.02
❑ 444	Barry Sanders	1.25	.50
❑ 445	Lawrence Taylor	.25	.08
❑ 446	Marcus Allen	.25	.08
❑ 447	Johnny Johnson	.05	.01
❑ 448	Aaron Wallace	.05	.01
❑ 449	Anthony Thompson	.05	.01
❑ 450	D.Marino/S.DeBerg CL	.40	.15
❑ 451	Andre Rison TM	.10	.02
❑ 452	Thurman Thomas TM	.10	.02
❑ 453	Neal Anderson MVP	.05	.01
❑ 454	Boomer Esiason MVP	.05	.01
❑ 455	Eric Metcalf MVP	.10	.02
❑ 456	Emmitt Smith TM	1.25	.50
❑ 457	Bobby Humphrey MVP	.05	.01
❑ 458	Barry Sanders TM	.50	.20
❑ 459	Sterling Sharpe TM	.10	.02
❑ 460	Warren Moon TM	.10	.02
❑ 461	Albert Bentley MVP	.05	.01
❑ 462	Steve DeBerg MVP	.05	.01
❑ 463	Greg Townsend MVP	.05	.01
❑ 464	Henry Ellard MVP	.10	.02
❑ 465	Dan Marino TM	.50	.20
❑ 466	Anthony Carter MVP	.10	.02
❑ 467	John Stephens MVP	.05	.01
❑ 468	Pat Swilling MVP	.05	.01
❑ 469	Ottis Anderson MVP	.10	.02
❑ 470	Dennis Byrd MVP	.05	.01
❑ 471	Randall Cunningham TM	.10	.02
❑ 472	Johnny Johnson TM	.05	.01
❑ 473	Rod Woodson TM	.10	.02
❑ 474	Anthony Miller MVP	.10	.02
❑ 475	Jerry Rice TM	.40	.15
❑ 476	John L.Williams MVP	.05	.01
❑ 477	Wayne Haddix MVP	.05	.01
❑ 478	Earnest Byner MVP	.05	.01
❑ 479	Doug Widell	.05	.01
❑ 480	Tommy Hodson	.05	.01
❑ 481	Shawn Collins	.05	.01
❑ 482	Rickey Jackson	.05	.01
❑ 483	Tony Casillas	.05	.01
❑ 484	Vaughan Johnson	.05	.01
❑ 485	Floyd Dixon	.05	.01
❑ 486	Eric Green	.05	.01
❑ 487	Harry Hamilton	.05	.01
❑ 488	Gary Anderson K	.05	.01
❑ 489	Bruce Hill	.05	.01
❑ 490	Gerald Williams	.05	.01
❑ 491	Cortez Kennedy	.25	.08
❑ 492	Chet Brooks	.05	.01
❑ 493	Dwayne Harper RC	.05	.01
❑ 494	Don Griffin	.05	.01
❑ 495	Andy Heck	.05	.01
❑ 496	David Treadwell	.05	.01
❑ 497	Irv Pankey	.05	.01
❑ 498	Dennis Smith	.05	.01
❑ 499	Marcus Dupree	.05	.01
❑ 500	Checklist 401-500	.05	.01
❑ 501	Wendell Davis	.05	.01
❑ 502	Matt Bahr	.05	.01
❑ 503	Rob Burnett RC	.10	.02
❑ 504	Maurice Carthon	.05	.01
❑ 505	Donnell Woolford	.05	.01
❑ 506	Howard Ballard	.05	.01
❑ 507	Mark Boyer	.05	.01
❑ 508	Eugene Marve	.05	.01
❑ 509	Joe Kelly	.05	.01
❑ 510	Will Wolford	.05	.01
❑ 511	Robert Clark	.05	.01
❑ 512	Matt Brock RC	.05	.01
❑ 513	Chris Warren	.25	.08
❑ 514	Ken Willis	.05	.01
❑ 515	George Jamison RC	.05	.01
❑ 516	Rufus Porter	.05	.01
❑ 517	Mark Higgs RC	.05	.01
❑ 518	Thomas Everett	.05	.01
❑ 519	Robert Brown	.05	.01
❑ 520	Gene Atkins	.05	.01
❑ 521	Hardy Nickerson	.10	.02
❑ 522	Johnny Bailey	.05	.01
❑ 523	William Frizzell	.05	.01
❑ 524	Steve McMichael	.10	.02
❑ 525	Kevin Porter	.05	.01
❑ 526	Carwell Gardner	.05	.01
❑ 527	Eugene Daniel	.05	.01
❑ 528	Vestee Jackson	.05	.01
❑ 529	Chris Goode	.05	.01
❑ 530	Leon Seals	.05	.01
❑ 531	Darion Conner	.05	.01
❑ 532	Stan Brock	.05	.01
❑ 533	Kirby Jackson RC	.05	.01
❑ 534	Marv Cook	.05	.01
❑ 535	Bill Fralic	.05	.01
❑ 536	Keith Woodside	.05	.01
❑ 537	Hugh Green	.05	.01
❑ 538	Grant Feasel	.05	.01
❑ 539	Bubba McDowell	.05	.01
❑ 540	Vai Sikahema	.05	.01
❑ 541	Aaron Cox	.05	.01
❑ 542	Roger Craig	.10	.02
❑ 543	Robb Thomas	.05	.01
❑ 544	Ronnie Lott	.10	.02
❑ 545	Robert Delpino	.05	.01
❑ 546	Greg McMurtry	.05	.01
❑ 547	Jim Morrissey RC	.05	.01
❑ 548	Johnny Rembert	.05	.01
❑ 549	Markus Paul RC	.05	.01
❑ 550	Karl Wilson RC	.05	.01
❑ 551	Gaston Green	.05	.01
❑ 552	Willie Drewrey	.05	.01
❑ 553	Michael Young	.05	.01
❑ 554	Tom Tupa	.05	.01
❑ 555	John Friesz	.25	.08
❑ 556	Cody Carlson RC	.05	.01
❑ 557	Eric Allen	.05	.01
❑ 558	Thomas Benson	.05	.01
❑ 559	Scott Mersereau RC	.05	.01
❑ 560	Lionel Washington	.05	.01
❑ 561	Brian Brennan	.05	.01
❑ 562	Jim Jeffcoat	.05	.01
❑ 563	Jeff Jaeger	.05	.01
❑ 564	D.J. Johnson	.05	.01
❑ 565	Danny Villa	.05	.01
❑ 566	Don Beebe	.05	.01
❑ 567	Michael Haynes	.25	.08
❑ 568	Brett Faryniarz RC	.05	.01
❑ 569	Mike Prior	.05	.01
❑ 570	John Davis RC	.05	.01
❑ 571	Vernon Turner RC	.05	.01
❑ 572	Michael Brooks	.05	.01
❑ 573	Mike Gann	.05	.01
❑ 574	Ron Holmes	.05	.01
❑ 575	Gary Plummer	.05	.01
❑ 576	Bill Romanowski	.05	.01
❑ 577	Chris Jacke	.05	.01
❑ 578	Gary Reasons	.05	.01
❑ 579	Tim Jorden RC	.05	.01
❑ 580	Tim McKyer	.05	.01
❑ 581	Johnnie Jackson RC	.05	.01
❑ 582	Ethan Horton	.05	.01
❑ 583	Pete Stoyanovich	.05	.01
❑ 584	Jeff Query	.05	.01
❑ 585	Frank Reich	.10	.02
❑ 586	Riki Ellison	.05	.01
❑ 587	Eric Hill	.05	.01
❑ 588	Anthony Shelton RC	.05	.01
❑ 589	Steve Smith	.05	.01
❑ 590	Garth Jax RC	.05	.01
❑ 591	Greg Davis RC	.05	.01
❑ 592	Bill Maas	.05	.01
❑ 593	Henry Rolling RC	.05	.01
❑ 594	Keith Jones	.05	.01
❑ 595	Tootie Robbins	.05	.01
❑ 596	Brian Jordan	.10	.02
❑ 597	Derrick Walker RC	.05	.01
❑ 598	Jonathan Hayes	.05	.01
❑ 599	Nate Lewis RC	.05	.01
❑ 600	Checklist 501-600	.05	.01
❑ 601	Croel/Lewis/Tray/Walk CL	.05	.01
❑ 602	James Jones RC DT	.05	.01
❑ 603	Tim Barnett RC	.05	.01
❑ 604	Ed King RC	.05	.01
❑ 605	Shane Curry RF	.05	.01
❑ 606	Mike Croel	.05	.01
❑ 607	Bryan Cox RC	.25	.08
❑ 608	Shawn Jefferson RC	.10	.02
❑ 609	Kenny Walker RC	.05	.01
❑ 610	Michael Jackson RC WR	.25	.08
❑ 611	Jon Vaughn RC	.05	.01

❑ 612 Greg Lewis .05 .01
❑ 613 Joe Valerio RF .05 .01
❑ 614 Pat Harlow RC .05 .01
❑ 615 Henry Jones RC .10 .02
❑ 616 Jeff Graham RC WR .25 .08
❑ 617 Darryll Lewis RC .10 .02
❑ 618 Keith Traylor RC .05 .01
❑ 619 Scott Miller RF .05 .01
❑ 620 Nick Bell .05 .01
❑ 621 John Flannery RC .05 .01
❑ 622 Leonard Russell RC .10 .02
❑ 623 Alfred Williams RC .05 .01
❑ 624 Browning Nagle .05 .01
❑ 625 Harvey Williams .10 .02
❑ 626 Dan McGwire .05 .01
❑ 627 Favre/Pritchard/Pegram CL .50 .20
❑ 628 William Thomas RC .05 .01
❑ 629 Lawrence Dawsey RC .10 .02
❑ 630 Aeneas Williams RC .25 .08
❑ 631 Stan Thomas RF .05 .01
❑ 632 Randal Hill .05 .01
❑ 633 Moe Gardner RC .05 .01
❑ 634 Alvin Harper .10 .02
❑ 635 Esera Tuaolo RC .05 .01
❑ 636 Russell Maryland .10 .02
❑ 637 Anthony Morgan RC .05 .01
❑ 638 Erric Pegram RC .25 .08
❑ 639 Herman Moore .25 .08
❑ 640 Ricky Ervins RC .10 .02
❑ 641 Kelvin Pritchett RC .10 .02
❑ 642 Roman Phifer RC .05 .01
❑ 643 Antone Davis RC .05 .01
❑ 644 Mike Pritchard .10 .02
❑ 645 Vinnie Clark RC .05 .01
❑ 646 Jake Reed RC .50 .20
❑ 647 Brett Favre 4.00 1.50
❑ 648 Todd Lyght .05 .01
❑ 649 Bruce Pickens .05 .01
❑ 650 Darren Lewis RC .05 .01
❑ 651 Wesley Carroll .05 .01
❑ 652 James Joseph RC .10 .02
❑ 653 Robert Delpino AR .05 .01
❑ 654 Deion Sanders/V.Glenn AR .05 .01
❑ 655 J.Rice/T.McDaniels AR .30 .10
❑ 656 B.Sanders/D.Thomas AR .50 .20
❑ 657 Ken Tippins AR .05 .01
❑ 658 Christian Okoye AR .05 .01
❑ 659 Rich Gannon .25 .08
❑ 660 Johnny Meads .05 .01
❑ 661 J.J.Birden RC .10 .02
❑ 662 Bruce Kozerski .05 .01
❑ 663 Felix Wright .05 .01
❑ 664 Al Smith .05 .01
❑ 665 Stan Humphries .25 .08
❑ 666 Alfred Anderson .05 .01
❑ 667 Nate Newton .10 .02
❑ 668 Vince Workman RC .10 .02
❑ 669 Ricky Reynolds .05 .01
❑ 670 Bryce Paup RC .25 .08
❑ 671 Gill Fenerty .05 .01
❑ 672 Darrell Thompson .05 .01
❑ 673 Anthony Smith .05 .01
❑ 674 Darryl Henley RC .05 .01
❑ 675 Brett Maxie .05 .01
❑ 676 Craig Taylor RC .05 .01
❑ 677 Steve Wallace .10 .02
❑ 678 Jeff Feagles RC .05 .01
❑ 679 James Washington RC .05 .01
❑ 680 Tim Harris .05 .01
❑ 681 Dennis Gibson .05 .01
❑ 682 Toi Cook RC .05 .01
❑ 683 Lorenzo Lynch .05 .01
❑ 684 Brad Edwards RC .05 .01
❑ 685 Ray Crockett RC .05 .01
❑ 686 Harris Barton .05 .01
❑ 687 Byron Evans .05 .01
❑ 688 Eric Thomas .05 .01
❑ 689 Jeff Criswell .05 .01
❑ 690 Eric Ball .05 .01
❑ 691 Brian Mitchell .10 .02
❑ 692 Quinn Early .10 .02
❑ 693 Aaron Jones .05 .01
❑ 694 Jim Dombrowski .05 .01
❑ 695 Jeff Bostic .05 .01
❑ 696 Tony Casillas .05 .01
❑ 697 Ken Lanier .05 .01
❑ 698 Henry Thomas .05 .01
❑ 699 Steve Beuerlein .10 .02
❑ 700 Checklist 601-700 .05 .01
❑ P1 Joe Montana Promo 2.50 1.00
❑ P2 Barry Sanders Promo 2.00 .75
❑ SP1 Darrell Green Fastest .50 .20
❑ SP2 Don Shula 300th Win 2.00 .75

1992 Upper Deck

❑ COMPLETE SET (620) 15.00 6.00
❑ COMP.SERIES 1 (400) 10.00 4.00
❑ COMP.SERIES 2 (220) 5.00 2.50
❑ 1 Bennett/Buckley/McNabb C .10 .02
❑ 2 Edgar Bennett RC .25 .08
❑ 3 Eddie Blake RC .05 .01
❑ 4 Brian Bollinger RC .05 .01
❑ 5 Joe Bowden RC .05 .01
❑ 6 Terrell Buckley RC .05 .01
❑ 7 Willie Clay RC .05 .01
❑ 8 Ed Cunningham RC .05 .01
❑ 9 Matt Darby RC .05 .01
❑ 10 Will Furrer RC .05 .01
❑ 11 Chris Hakel RC .05 .01
❑ 12 Carlos Huerta .05 .01
❑ 13 Amp Lee RC .05 .01
❑ 14 Ricardo McDonald RC .05 .01
❑ 15 Dexter McNabb RC .05 .01
❑ 16 Chris Mims RC .05 .01
❑ 17 Derrick Moore RC .10 .02
❑ 18 Mark D'Onofrio RC .05 .01
❑ 19 Patrick Rowe RC .05 .01
❑ 20 Leon Searcy RC .05 .01
❑ 21 Torrance Small RC .10 .02
❑ 22 Jimmy Smith RC 3.00 1.25
❑ 23 Tony Smith RC WR .05 .01
❑ 24 Siran Stacy RC .05 .01
❑ 25 Kevin Turner RC .05 .01
❑ 26 Tommy Vardell RC .05 .01
❑ 27 Bob Whitfield RC .05 .01
❑ 28 Darryl Williams RC .05 .01
❑ 29 Jeff Sydner RC .05 .01
❑ 30 Mike Croel/L.Russell CL .05 .01
❑ 31 Todd Marinovich ART .05 .01
❑ 32 Leonard Russell ART .05 .01
❑ 33 Nick Bell ART .05 .01
❑ 34 Alvin Harper ART .05 .01
❑ 35 Mike Pritchard ART .05 .01
❑ 36 Lawrence Dawsey AR .05 .01
❑ 37 Tim Barnett AR .05 .01
❑ 38 John Flannery AR .05 .01
❑ 39 Stan Thomas AR .05 .01
❑ 40 Ed King AR .05 .01
❑ 41 Charles McRae AR .05 .01
❑ 42 Eric Moten AR .05 .01
❑ 43 Moe Gardner AR .05 .01
❑ 44 Kenny Walker AR .05 .01
❑ 45 Esera Tuaolo AR .05 .01
❑ 46 Alfred Williams AR .05 .01
❑ 47 Bryan Cox AR .05 .01
❑ 48 Mo Lewis AR .05 .01
❑ 49 Mike Croel ART .05 .01
❑ 50 Stanley Richard AR .05 .01
❑ 51 Tony Covington AR .05 .01
❑ 52 Larry Brown DB AR .05 .01
❑ 53 Aeneas Williams AR .05 .01
❑ 54 John Kasay AR .05 .01
❑ 55 Jon Vaughn ART .05 .01
❑ 56 David Fulcher .05 .01
❑ 57 Barry Foster .10 .02
❑ 58 Terry Wooden .05 .01
❑ 59 Gary Anderson K .05 .01
❑ 60 Alfred Williams .05 .01
❑ 61 Robert Blackmon .05 .01
❑ 62 Brian Noble .05 .01
❑ 63 Terry Allen .25 .08
❑ 64 Darrell Green .05 .01
❑ 65 Darren Comeaux .05 .01
❑ 66 Rob Burnett .05 .01
❑ 67 Jarrod Bunch .05 .01
❑ 68 Michael Jackson .10 .02
❑ 69 Greg Lloyd .10 .02
❑ 70 Richard Brown RC .05 .01
❑ 71 Harold Green .05 .01
❑ 72 William Fuller .05 .01
❑ 73 Mark Carrier DB TC .05 .01
❑ 74 David Fulcher TC .05 .01
❑ 75 Cornelius Bennett TC .05 .01
❑ 76 Steve Atwater TC .05 .01
❑ 77 Kevin Mack TC .05 .01
❑ 78 Mark Carrier WR TC .05 .01
❑ 79 Tim McDonald TC .05 .01
❑ 80 Marion Butts TC .05 .01
❑ 81 Christian Okoye TC .05 .01
❑ 82 Jeff Herrod TC .05 .01
❑ 83 Emmitt Smith TC .60 .25
❑ 84 Mark Duper TC .05 .01
❑ 85 Keith Jackson TC .05 .01
❑ 86 Andre Rison TC .10 .02
❑ 87 John Taylor TC .05 .01
❑ 88 Rodney Hampton TC .10 .02
❑ 89 Rob Moore TC .05 .01
❑ 90 Chris Spielman TC .05 .01
❑ 91 Haywood Jeffires TC .05 .01
❑ 92 Sterling Sharpe TC .10 .02
❑ 93 Irving Fryar TC .05 .01
❑ 94 Marcus Allen TC .10 .02
❑ 95 Henry Ellard TC .05 .01
❑ 96 Mark Rypien TC .05 .01
❑ 97 Pat Swilling TC .05 .01
❑ 98 Brian Blades TC .05 .01
❑ 99 Eric Green TC .05 .01
❑ 100 Anthony Carter TC .05 .01
❑ 101 Burt Grossman .05 .01
❑ 102 Gary Anderson RB .05 .01
❑ 103 Neil Smith .25 .08
❑ 104 Jeff Feagles .05 .01
❑ 105 Shane Conlan .05 .01
❑ 106 Jay Novacek .10 .02
❑ 107 Bill Brooks .05 .01
❑ 108 Mark Ingram .05 .01
❑ 109 Anthony Munoz .10 .02
❑ 110 Wendell Davis .05 .01
❑ 111 Jim Everett .10 .02
❑ 112 Bruce Matthews .05 .01
❑ 113 Mark Higgs .05 .01
❑ 114 Chris Warren .10 .02
❑ 115 Brad Baxter .05 .01
❑ 116 Greg Townsend .05 .01
❑ 117 Al Smith .05 .01
❑ 118 Jeff Cross .05 .01
❑ 119 Terry McDaniel .05 .01
❑ 120 Ernest Givins .10 .02
❑ 121 Fred Barnett .10 .02
❑ 122 Flipper Anderson .05 .01
❑ 123 Floyd Turner .05 .01
❑ 124 Stephen Baker .05 .01
❑ 125 Tim Johnson .05 .01
❑ 126 Brent Jones .10 .02
❑ 127 Leonard Marshall .05 .01
❑ 128 Jim Price .05 .01
❑ 129 Jessie Hester .05 .01
❑ 130 Mark Carrier WR .10 .02
❑ 131 Bubba McDowell .05 .01
❑ 132 Andre Tippett .05 .01
❑ 133 James Hasty .05 .01
❑ 134 Mel Gray .10 .02
❑ 135 Christian Okoye .05 .01
❑ 136 Earnest Byner .05 .01
❑ 137 Ferrell Edmunds .05 .01
❑ 138 Henry Ellard .10 .02
❑ 139 Rob Moore .10 .02
❑ 140 Brian Jordan .10 .02
❑ 141 Clarence Verdin .05 .01
❑ 142 Cornelius Bennett .10 .02
❑ 143 John Taylor .10 .02
❑ 144 Derrick Thomas .25 .08
❑ 145 Thurman Thomas .25 .08

❑ 146 Warren Moon .25 .08
❑ 147 Vinny Testaverde .10 .02
❑ 148 Steve Bono RC .25 .08
❑ 149 Robb Thomas .05 .01
❑ 150 John Friesz .10 .02
❑ 151 Richard Dent .10 .02
❑ 152 Eddie Anderson .05 .01
❑ 153 Kevin Greene .10 .02
❑ 154 Marion Butts .05 .01
❑ 155 Barry Sanders 1.25 .50
❑ 156 Andre Rison .10 .02
❑ 157 Ronnie Lott .10 .02
❑ 158 Eric Allen .05 .01
❑ 159 Mark Clayton .10 .02
❑ 160 Terance Mathis .10 .02
❑ 161 Darryl Talley .05 .01
❑ 162 Eric Metcalf .10 .02
❑ 163 Reggie Cobb .05 .01
❑ 164 Ernie Jones .05 .01
❑ 165 David Griggs .05 .01
❑ 166 Tom Rathman .05 .01
❑ 167 Bubby Brister .10 .02
❑ 168 Broderick Thomas .05 .01
❑ 169 Chris Doleman .05 .01
❑ 170 Charles Haley .10 .02
❑ 171 Michael Haynes .10 .02
❑ 172 Rodney Hampton .10 .02
❑ 173 Nick Bell .05 .01
❑ 174 Gene Atkins .05 .01
❑ 175 Mike Merriweather .05 .01
❑ 176 Reggie Roby .05 .01
❑ 177 Bennie Blades .05 .01
❑ 178 John L. Williams .05 .01
❑ 179 Rodney Peete .10 .02
❑ 180 Greg Montgomery .05 .01
❑ 181 Vince Newsome .05 .01
❑ 182 Andre Collins .05 .01
❑ 183 Erik Kramer .10 .02
❑ 184 Bryan Hinkle .05 .01
❑ 185 Reggie White .25 .08
❑ 186 Bruce Armstrong .05 .01
❑ 187 Anthony Carter .10 .02
❑ 188 Pat Swilling .05 .01
❑ 189 Robert Delpino .05 .01
❑ 190 Brent Williams .05 .01
❑ 191 Johnny Johnson .05 .01
❑ 192 Aaron Craver .05 .01
❑ 193 Vincent Brown .05 .01
❑ 194 Herschel Walker .10 .02
❑ 195 Tim McDonald .05 .01
❑ 196 Gaston Green .05 .01
❑ 197 Brian Blades .10 .02
❑ 198 Rod Bernstine .05 .01
❑ 199 Brett Perriman .10 .02
❑ 200 John Elway 1.25 .50
❑ 201 Michael Carter .05 .01
❑ 202 Mark Carrier DB .05 .01
❑ 203 Cris Carter .50 .20
❑ 204 Kyle Clifton .05 .01
❑ 205 Alvin Wright .05 .01
❑ 206 Andre Ware .05 .01
❑ 207 Dave Waymer .05 .01
❑ 208 Darren Lewis .05 .01
❑ 209 Joey Browner .05 .01
❑ 210 Rich Miano .05 .01
❑ 211 Marcus Allen .25 .08
❑ 212 Steve Broussard .05 .01
❑ 213 Joel Hilgenberg .05 .01
❑ 214 Bo Orlando RC .05 .01
❑ 215 Clay Matthews .10 .02
❑ 216 Chris Hinton .05 .01
❑ 217 Al Edwards .05 .01
❑ 218 Tim Brown .25 .08
❑ 219 Sam Mills .05 .01
❑ 220 Don Majkowski .05 .01
❑ 221 James Francis .05 .01
❑ 222 Steve Hendrickson RC .05 .01
❑ 223 James Thornton .05 .01
❑ 224 Byron Evans .05 .01
❑ 225 Pepper Johnson .05 .01
❑ 226 Darryl Henley .05 .01
❑ 227 Simon Fletcher .05 .01
❑ 228 Hugh Millen .05 .01
❑ 229 Tim McGee .05 .01
❑ 230 Richmond Webb .05 .01
❑ 231 Tony Bennett .05 .01
❑ 232 Nate Odomes .05 .01
❑ 233 Scott Case .05 .01
❑ 234 Dalton Hilliard .05 .01
❑ 235 Paul Gruber .05 .01
❑ 236 Jeff Lageman .05 .01
❑ 237 Tony Mandarich .05 .01
❑ 238 Cris Dishman .05 .01
❑ 239 Steve Walsh .05 .01
❑ 240 Moe Gardner .05 .01
❑ 241 Bill Romanowski .05 .01
❑ 242 Chris Zorich .10 .02
❑ 243 Stephone Paige .05 .01
❑ 244 Mike Croel .05 .01
❑ 245 Leonard Russell .10 .02
❑ 246 Mark Rypien .05 .01
❑ 247 Aeneas Williams .10 .02
❑ 248 Steve Atwater .05 .01
❑ 249 Michael Stewart .05 .01
❑ 250 Pierce Holt .05 .01
❑ 251 Kevin Mack .05 .01
❑ 252 Sterling Sharpe .25 .08
❑ 253 Lawrence Dawsey .10 .02
❑ 254 Emmitt Smith 1.50 .60
❑ 255 Todd Marinovich .05 .01
❑ 256 Neal Anderson .05 .01
❑ 257 Mo Lewis .05 .01
❑ 258 Vance Johnson .05 .01
❑ 259 Rickey Jackson .05 .01
❑ 260 Esera Tuaolo .05 .01
❑ 261 Wilber Marshall .05 .01
❑ 262 Keith Henderson .05 .01
❑ 263 William Thomas .05 .01
❑ 264 Rickey Dixon .05 .01
❑ 265 Dave Meggett .10 .02
❑ 266 Gerald Riggs .05 .01
❑ 267 Tim Harris .05 .01
❑ 268 Ken Harvey .05 .01
❑ 269 Clyde Simmons .05 .01
❑ 270 Irving Fryar .10 .02
❑ 271 Darion Conner .05 .01
❑ 272 Vince Workman .05 .01
❑ 273 Jim Harbaugh .25 .08
❑ 274 Lorenzo White .05 .01
❑ 275 Bobby Hebert .05 .01
❑ 276 Duane Bickett .05 .01
❑ 277 Jeff Bryant .05 .01
❑ 278 Scott Stephen .05 .01
❑ 279 Bob Golic .05 .01
❑ 280 Steve McMichael .10 .02
❑ 281 Jeff Graham .25 .08
❑ 282 Keith Jackson .10 .02
❑ 283 Howard Ballard .05 .01
❑ 284 Michael Brooks .05 .01
❑ 285 Freeman McNeil .10 .02
❑ 286 Rodney Holman .05 .01
❑ 287 Eric Bieniemy .05 .01
❑ 288 Seth Joyner .05 .01
❑ 289 Carwell Gardner .05 .01
❑ 290 Brian Mitchell .10 .02
❑ 291 Chris Miller .10 .02
❑ 292 Ray Berry .05 .01
❑ 293 Matt Brock .05 .01
❑ 294 Eric Thomas .05 .01
❑ 295 John Kasay .05 .01
❑ 296 Jay Hilgenberg .05 .01
❑ 297 Darrell Thompson .05 .01
❑ 298 Rich Gannon .25 .08
❑ 299 Steve Young .60 .25
❑ 300 Mike Kenn .05 .01
❑ 301 Emmitt Smith SL .60 .25
❑ 302 Haywood Jeffires SL .05 .01
❑ 303 Michael Irvin SL .25 .08
❑ 304 Warren Moon SL .10 .02
❑ 305 Chip Lohmiller SL .05 .01
❑ 306 Barry Sanders SL .50 .20
❑ 307 Ronnie Lott SL .10 .02
❑ 308 Pat Swilling SL .05 .01
❑ 309 Thurman Thomas SL .10 .02
❑ 310 Reggie Roby SL .05 .01
❑ 311 Moon/Irvin/T.Thomas CL .10 .02
❑ 312 Jacob Green .05 .01
❑ 313 Stephen Braggs .05 .01
❑ 314 Haywood Jeffires .10 .02
❑ 315 Freddie Joe Nunn .05 .01
❑ 316 Gary Clark .10 .02
❑ 317 Tim Barnett .05 .01
❑ 318 Mark Duper .05 .01
❑ 319 Eric Green .05 .01
❑ 320 Robert Wilson .05 .01
❑ 321 Michael Ball .05 .01
❑ 322 Eric Martin .05 .01
❑ 323 Alexander Wright .05 .01
❑ 324 Jessie Tuggle .05 .01
❑ 325 Ronnie Harmon .05 .01
❑ 326 Jeff Hostetler .10 .02
❑ 327 Eugene Daniel .05 .01
❑ 328 Ken Norton Jr. .10 .02
❑ 329 Reyna Thompson .05 .01
❑ 330 Jerry Ball .05 .01
❑ 331 Leroy Hoard .10 .02
❑ 332 Chris Martin .05 .01
❑ 333 Keith McKeller .05 .01
❑ 334 Brian Washington .05 .01
❑ 335 Eugene Robinson .05 .01
❑ 336 Maurice Hurst .05 .01
❑ 337 Dan Saleaumua .05 .01
❑ 338 Neil O'Donnell .10 .02
❑ 339 Dexter Davis .05 .01
❑ 340 Keith McCants .05 .01
❑ 341 Steve Beuerlein .10 .02
❑ 342 Roman Phifer .05 .01
❑ 343 Bryan Cox .10 .02
❑ 344 Art Monk .10 .02
❑ 345 Michael Irvin .25 .08
❑ 346 Vaughan Johnson .05 .01
❑ 347 Jeff Herrod .05 .01
❑ 348 Stanley Richard .05 .01
❑ 349 Michael Young .05 .01
❑ 350 Rod.Hampton/R.Cobb CL .10 .02
❑ 351 Jim Harbaugh MVP .10 .02
❑ 352 David Fulcher MVP .05 .01
❑ 353 Thurman Thomas MVP .10 .02
❑ 354 Gaston Green MVP .05 .01
❑ 355 Leroy Hoard MVP .05 .01
❑ 356 Reggie Cobb MVP .05 .01
❑ 357 Tim McDonald MVP .05 .01
❑ 358 Ronnie Harmon MVP UER .05 .01
❑ 359 Derrick Thomas MVP .10 .02
❑ 360 Jeff Herrod MVP .05 .01
❑ 361 Michael Irvin MVP .25 .08
❑ 362 Mark Higgs MVP .05 .01
❑ 363 Reggie White MVP .10 .02
❑ 364 Chris Miller MVP .05 .01
❑ 365 Steve Young MVP .30 .10
❑ 366 Rodney Hampton MVP .10 .02
❑ 367 Jeff Lageman MVP .05 .01
❑ 368 Barry Sanders MVP .50 .20
❑ 369 Haywood Jeffires MVP .05 .01
❑ 370 Tony Bennett MVP .05 .01
❑ 371 Leonard Russell MVP .05 .01
❑ 372 Jeff Jaeger MVP .05 .01
❑ 373 Robert Delpino MVP .05 .01
❑ 374 Mark Rypien MVP .05 .01
❑ 375 Pat Swilling MVP .05 .01
❑ 376 Cortez Kennedy MVP .10 .02
❑ 377 Eric Green MVP .05 .01
❑ 378 Cris Carter MVP .10 .02
❑ 379 John Roper .05 .01
❑ 380 Barry Word .05 .01
❑ 381 Shawn Jefferson .05 .01
❑ 382 Tony Casillas .05 .01
❑ 383 John Baylor RC .05 .01
❑ 384 Al Noga .05 .01
❑ 385 Charles Mann .05 .01
❑ 386 Gill Byrd .05 .01
❑ 387 Chris Singleton .05 .01
❑ 388 James Joseph .05 .01
❑ 389 Larry Brown DB .05 .01
❑ 390 Chris Spielman .10 .02
❑ 391 Anthony Thompson .05 .01
❑ 392 Karl Mecklenburg .05 .01
❑ 393 Joe Kelly .05 .01
❑ 394 Kanavis McGhee .05 .01
❑ 395 Bill Maas .05 .01
❑ 396 Marv Cook .05 .01
❑ 397 Louis Lipps .05 .01
❑ 398 Marty Carter RC .05 .01
❑ 399 Louis Oliver .05 .01
❑ 400 Eric Swann .10 .02
❑ 401 Troy Auzenne RC .05 .01
❑ 402 Kurt Barber .05 .01
❑ 403 Marc Boutte RC .05 .01
❑ 404 Dale Carter .10 .02
❑ 405 Marco Coleman .05 .01
❑ 406 Quentin Coryatt .05 .01

❑ 407 Shane Dronett RC .05 .01
❑ 408 Vaughn Dunbar .05 .01
❑ 409 Steve Emtman .05 .01
❑ 410 Dana Hall RC .05 .01
❑ 411 Jason Hanson RC .10 .02
❑ 412 Courtney Hawkins RC .10 .02
❑ 413 Terrell Buckley .05 .01
❑ 414 Robert Jones RC .05 .01
❑ 415 David Klingler .05 .01
❑ 416 Tommy Maddox 1.50 .60
❑ 417 Johnny Mitchell RC .05 .01
❑ 418 Carl Pickens .10 .02
❑ 419 Tracy Scroggins .05 .01
❑ 420 Tony Sacca RC .05 .01
❑ 421 Kevin Smith DB .05 .01
❑ 422 Alonzo Spellman .10 .02
❑ 423 Troy Vincent RC .05 .01
❑ 424 Sean Gilbert RC .10 .02
❑ 425 Larry Webster RC .05 .01
❑ 426 Carl Pickens/Klingler CL .10 .02
❑ 427 Bill Fralic .05 .01
❑ 428 Kevin Murphy .05 .01
❑ 429 Lemuel Stinson .05 .01
❑ 430 Harris Barton .05 .01
❑ 431 Dino Hackett .05 .01
❑ 432 John Stephens .05 .01
❑ 433 Keith Jennings RC .05 .01
❑ 434 Derrick Fenner .05 .01
❑ 435 Kenneth Gant RC .05 .01
❑ 436 Willie Gault .10 .02
❑ 437 Steve Jordan .05 .01
❑ 438 Charles Haley .10 .02
❑ 439 Keith Kartz .05 .01
❑ 440 Nate Lewis .05 .01
❑ 441 Doug Widell .05 .01
❑ 442 William White .05 .01
❑ 443 Eric Hill .05 .01
❑ 444 Melvin Jenkins .05 .01
❑ 445 David Wyman .05 .01
❑ 446 Ed West .05 .01
❑ 447 Brad Muster .05 .01
❑ 448 Ray Childress .05 .01
❑ 449 Kevin Ross .05 .01
❑ 450 Johnnie Jackson S .05 .01
❑ 451 Tracy Simien RC .05 .01
❑ 452 Don Mosebar .05 .01
❑ 453 Jay Hilgenberg .05 .01
❑ 454 Wes Hopkins .05 .01
❑ 455 Jay Schroeder .05 .01
❑ 456 Jeff Bostic .05 .01
❑ 457 Bryce Paup .25 .08
❑ 458 Dave Waymer .05 .01
❑ 459 Toi Cook .05 .01
❑ 460 Anthony Smith .05 .01
❑ 461 Don Griffin .05 .01
❑ 462 Bill Hawkins .05 .01
❑ 463 Courtney Hall .05 .01
❑ 464 Jeff Uhlenhake .05 .01
❑ 465 Mike Sherrard .05 .01
❑ 466 James Jones DT .05 .01
❑ 467 Jerrol Williams .05 .01
❑ 468 Eric Ball .05 .01
❑ 469 Randall McDaniel .05 .01
❑ 470 Alvin Harper .10 .02
❑ 471 Tom Waddle .05 .01
❑ 472 Tony Woods .05 .01
❑ 473 Kelvin Martin .05 .01
❑ 474 Jon Vaughn .05 .01
❑ 475 Gill Fenerty .05 .01
❑ 476 Aundray Bruce .05 .01
❑ 477 Morten Andersen .05 .01
❑ 478 Lamar Lathon .05 .01
❑ 479 Steve DeOssie .05 .01
❑ 480 Marvin Washington .05 .01
❑ 481 Herschel Walker .10 .02
❑ 482 Howie Long .25 .08
❑ 483 Calvin Williams .10 .02
❑ 484 Brett Favre 2.50 1.25
❑ 485 Johnny Bailey .05 .01
❑ 486 Jeff Gossett .05 .01
❑ 487 Carnell Lake .05 .01
❑ 488 Michael Zordich RC .05 .01
❑ 489 Henry Rolling .05 .01
❑ 490 Steve Smith .05 .01
❑ 491 Vestee Jackson .05 .01
❑ 492 Ray Crockett .05 .01
❑ 493 Dexter Carter .05 .01
❑ 494 Nick Lowery .05 .01
❑ 495 Cortez Kennedy .10 .02
❑ 496 Cleveland Gary .05 .01
❑ 497 Kelly Stouffer .05 .01
❑ 498 Carl Carter .05 .01
❑ 499 Shannon Sharpe .25 .08
❑ 500 Roger Craig .10 .02
❑ 501 Willie Drewrey .05 .01
❑ 502 Mark Schlereth RC .05 .01
❑ 503 Tony Martin .10 .02
❑ 504 Tom Newberry .05 .01
❑ 505 Ron Hall .05 .01
❑ 506 Scott Miller .05 .01
❑ 507 Donnell Woolford .05 .01
❑ 508 Dave Krieg .10 .02
❑ 509 Erric Pegram .10 .02
❑ 510 Checklist 401-510 .05 .01
❑ 511 Barry Sanders SBK .60 .25
❑ 512 Thurman Thomas SBK .10 .02
❑ 513 Warren Moon SBK .10 .02
❑ 514 John Elway SBK .50 .20
❑ 515 Ronnie Lott SBK .10 .02
❑ 516 Emmitt Smith SBK .60 .25
❑ 517 Andre Rison SBK .10 .02
❑ 518 Steve Atwater SBK .05 .01
❑ 519 Steve Young SBK .30 .10
❑ 520 Mark Rypien SBK .05 .01
❑ 521 Rich Camarillo .05 .01
❑ 522 Mark Bavaro .05 .01
❑ 523 Brad Edwards .05 .01
❑ 524 Chad Hennings RC .10 .02
❑ 525 Tony Paige .05 .01
❑ 526 Shawn Moore .05 .01
❑ 527 Sidney Johnson RC .05 .01
❑ 528 Sanjay Beach RC .05 .01
❑ 529 Kelvin Pritchett .05 .01
❑ 530 Jerry Holmes .05 .01
❑ 531 Al Del Greco .05 .01
❑ 532 Bob Gagliano .05 .01
❑ 533 Drew Hill .05 .01
❑ 534 Donald Frank RC .05 .01
❑ 535 Pio Sagapolutele RC .05 .01
❑ 536 Jackie Slater .05 .01
❑ 537 Vernon Turner .05 .01
❑ 538 Bobby Humphrey .05 .01
❑ 539 Audray McMillian .05 .01
❑ 540 Gary Brown RC .25 .08
❑ 541 Wesley Carroll .05 .01
❑ 542 Nate Newton .05 .01
❑ 543 Vai Sikahema .05 .01
❑ 544 Chris Chandler .25 .08
❑ 545 Nolan Harrison RC .05 .01
❑ 546 Mark Green .05 .01
❑ 547 Ricky Watters .25 .08
❑ 548 J.J. Birden .05 .01
❑ 549 Cody Carlson .05 .01
❑ 550 Tim Green .05 .01
❑ 551 Mark Jackson .05 .01
❑ 552 Vince Buck .05 .01
❑ 553 George Jamison .05 .01
❑ 554 Anthony Pleasant .05 .01
❑ 555 Reggie Johnson .05 .01
❑ 556 John Jackson WR .05 .01
❑ 557 Ian Beckles .05 .01
❑ 558 Buford McGee .05 .01
❑ 559 Fuad Reveiz UER .05 .01
❑ 560 Joe Montana 1.25 .50
❑ 561 Phil Simms .10 .02
❑ 562 Greg McMurtry .05 .01
❑ 563 Gerald Williams .05 .01
❑ 564 Dave Cadigan .05 .01
❑ 565 Rufus Porter .05 .01
❑ 566 Jim Kelly .25 .08
❑ 567 Deion Sanders .50 .20
❑ 568 Mike Singletary .10 .02
❑ 569 Boomer Esiason .10 .02
❑ 570 Andre Reed .10 .02
❑ 571 James Washington .05 .01
❑ 572 Jack Del Rio .05 .01
❑ 573 Gerald Perry .05 .01
❑ 574 Vinnie Clark .05 .01
❑ 575 Mike Piel .05 .01
❑ 576 Michael Dean Perry .10 .02
❑ 577 Ricky Proehl .05 .01
❑ 578 Leslie O'Neal .10 .02
❑ 579 Russell Maryland .05 .01
❑ 580 Eric Dickerson .10 .02
❑ 581 Fred Strickland .05 .01
❑ 582 Nick Lowery .05 .01
❑ 583 Joe Milinichik RC .05 .01
❑ 584 Mark Vlasic .05 .01
❑ 585 James Lofton .10 .02
❑ 586 Bruce Smith .25 .08
❑ 587 Harvey Williams .10 .02
❑ 588 Bernie Kosar .10 .02
❑ 589 Carl Banks .05 .01
❑ 590 Jeff George .25 .08
❑ 591 Fred Jones RC .05 .01
❑ 592 Todd Scott .05 .01
❑ 593 Keith Jones .05 .01
❑ 594A Tootie Robbins ERR .05 .01
❑ 594B Tootie Robbins COR .05 .01
❑ 595 Todd Philcox RC .05 .01
❑ 596 Browning Nagle .05 .01
❑ 597 Troy Aikman .75 .30
❑ 598 Dan Marino 1.25 .50
❑ 599 Lawrence Taylor .25 .08
❑ 600 Webster Slaughter .05 .01
❑ 601 Aaron Cox .05 .01
❑ 602 Matt Stover .05 .01
❑ 603 Keith Sims .05 .01
❑ 604 Dennis Smith .05 .01
❑ 605 Kevin Porter .05 .01
❑ 606 Anthony Miller .10 .02
❑ 607 Ken O'Brien .05 .01
❑ 608 Randall Cunningham .25 .08
❑ 609 Timm Rosenbach .05 .01
❑ 610 Junior Seau .25 .08
❑ 611 Johnny Rembert .05 .01
❑ 612 Rick Tuten .05 .01
❑ 613 Willie Green .05 .01
❑ 614 Sean Salisbury RC**/C .05 .01
❑ 615 Martin Bayless .05 .01
❑ 616 Jerry Rice .75 .30
❑ 617 Randal Hill .05 .01
❑ 618 Dan McGwire .05 .01
❑ 619 Merril Hoge .05 .01
❑ 620 Checklist 571-620 .05 .01
❑ A560 Joe Montana Blowup UDA 15.00 6.00
❑ A598 Dan Marino Blowup UDA 15.00 6.00
❑ SP3 James Lofton Yardage .75 .30
❑ SP4 Art Monk Catches .50 .20

1992 Upper Deck Gold

❑ COMPLETE SET (50) 12.00 5.00
❑ G1 Steve Emtman RC .10 .02
❑ G2 Carl Pickens RC .30 .10
❑ G3 Dale Carter RC .30 .10
❑ G4 Greg Skrepenak RC .10 .02
❑ G5 Kevin Smith RC DB .15 .05
❑ G6 Marco Coleman RC .15 .05
❑ G7 David Klingler RC .15 .05
❑ G8 Phillippi Sparks RC .10 .02
❑ G9 Tommy Maddox RC 1.50 .60
❑ G10 Quentin Coryatt RC .15 .05
❑ G11 Ty Detmer .30 .10
❑ G12 Vaughn Dunbar RC .10 .02
❑ G13 Ashley Ambrose RC .30 .10
❑ G14 Kurt Barber RC .10 .02
❑ G15 Chester McGlockton RC .30 .10
❑ G16 Todd Collins RC .10 .02
❑ G17 Steve Israel RC .10 .02
❑ G18 Marquez Pope RC .10 .02
❑ G19 Alonzo Spellman RC .15 .05
❑ G20 Tracy Scroggins RC .10 .02
❑ G21 Jim Kelly QC .30 .10

Card		
❑ G22 Troy Aikman QC	.60	.25
❑ G23 Randall Cunningham QC	.30	.10
❑ G24 Bernie Kosar QC	.15	.05
❑ G25 Dan Marino QC	1.00	.40
❑ G26 Andre Reed	.15	.05
❑ G27 Deion Sanders	.50	.20
❑ G28 Randal Hill	.10	.02
❑ G29 Eric Dickerson	.15	.05
❑ G30 Jim Kelly	.30	.10
❑ G31 Bernie Kosar	.15	.05
❑ G32 Mike Singletary	.15	.05
❑ G33 Anthony Miller	.15	.05
❑ G34 Harvey Williams	.30	.10
❑ G35 Randall Cunningham	.30	.10
❑ G36 Joe Montana	1.25	.50
❑ G37 Dan McGwire	.10	.02
❑ G38 Al Toon	.15	.05
❑ G39 Carl Banks	.10	.02
❑ G40 Troy Aikman	.75	.30
❑ G41 Junior Seau	.30	.10
❑ G42 Jeff George	.30	.10
❑ G43 Michael Dean Perry	.15	.05
❑ G44 Lawrence Taylor	.30	.10
❑ G45 Dan Marino	1.25	.50
❑ G46 Jerry Rice	.75	.30
❑ G47 Boomer Esiason	.15	.05
❑ G48 Bruce Smith	.30	.10
❑ G49 Leslie O'Neal	.15	.05
❑ G50 Checklist Card	.10	.02

1993 Upper Deck

Card		
❑ COMPLETE SET (530)	25.00	10.00
❑ 1 Mirer/Hearst/Con/Ken CL	.25	.08
❑ 2 Eric Curry RC	.05	.01
❑ 3 Rick Mirer RC	.25	.08
❑ 4 Dan Williams RC	.05	.01
❑ 5 Marvin Jones RC	.05	.01
❑ 6 Willie Roaf RC	.10	.02
❑ 7 Reggie Brooks RC	.10	.02
❑ 8 Horace Copeland RC	.10	.02
❑ 9 Lincoln Kennedy RC	.05	.01
❑ 10 Curtis Conway RC	.40	.15
❑ 11 Drew Bledsoe RC	2.50	1.00
❑ 12 Patrick Bates RC	.05	.01
❑ 13 Wayne Simmons RC	.05	.01
❑ 14 Irv Smith RC	.05	.01
❑ 15 Robert Smith RC	1.25	.50
❑ 16 O.J.McDuffie RC	.25	.08
❑ 17 Darrien Gordon RC	.05	.01
❑ 18 John Copeland RC	.10	.02
❑ 19 Derek Brown RC RBK	.05	.01
❑ 20 Jerome Bettis RC	5.00	2.50
❑ 21 Deon Figures RC	.05	.01
❑ 22 Glyn Milburn RC	.25	.08
❑ 23 Garrison Hearst RC	.75	.30
❑ 24 Qadry Ismail RC	.25	.08
❑ 25 Terry Kirby RC	.25	.08
❑ 26 Lamar Thomas RC	.05	.01
❑ 27 Tom Carter RC	.10	.02
❑ 28 Andre Hastings RC	.10	.02
❑ 29 George Teague RC	.10	.02
❑ 30 Tommy Maddox CL	.10	.02
❑ 31 David Klingler ART	.05	.01
❑ 32 Tommy Maddox ART	.10	.02
❑ 33 Vaughn Dunbar ART	.05	.01
❑ 34 Rodney Culver ART	.05	.01
❑ 35 Carl Pickens ART	.10	.02
❑ 36 Courtney Hawkins ART	.05	.01
❑ 37 Tyji Armstrong ART	.05	.01
❑ 38 Ray Roberts ART	.05	.01
❑ 39 Troy Auzenne ART	.05	.01
❑ 40 Shane Dronett ART	.05	.01
❑ 41 Chris Mims ART	.05	.01
❑ 42 Sean Gilbert ART	.05	.01
❑ 43 Steve Emtman ART	.05	.01
❑ 44 Robert Jones ART	.05	.01
❑ 45 Marco Coleman ART	.05	.01
❑ 46 Ricardo McDonald ART	.05	.01
❑ 47 Quentin Coryatt ART	.10	.02
❑ 48 Dana Hall ART	.05	.01
❑ 49 Darren Perry ART	.05	.01
❑ 50 Darryl Williams ART	.05	.01
❑ 51 Kevin Smith ART	.05	.01
❑ 52 Terrell Buckley ART	.05	.01
❑ 53 Troy Vincent ART	.05	.01
❑ 54 Lin Elliott ART	.05	.01
❑ 55 Dale Carter ART	.05	.01
❑ 56 Steve Atwater HIT	.05	.01
❑ 57 Junior Seau HIT	.10	.02
❑ 58 Ronnie Lott HIT	.05	.01
❑ 59 Louis Oliver HIT	.05	.01
❑ 60 Cortez Kennedy HIT	.05	.01
❑ 61 Pat Swilling HIT	.05	.01
❑ 62 Hitmen Checklist	.05	.01
❑ 63 Curtis Conway TC	.25	.08
❑ 64 Alfred Williams TC	.05	.01
❑ 65 Jim Kelly TC	.10	.02
❑ 66 Simon Fletcher TC	.05	.01
❑ 67 Eric Metcalf TC	.05	.01
❑ 68 Lawrence Dawsey TC	.05	.01
❑ 69 Garrison Hearst TC	.25	.08
❑ 70 Anthony Miller TC	.05	.01
❑ 71 Neil Smith TC	.05	.01
❑ 72 Jeff George TC	.10	.02
❑ 73 Emmitt Smith TC	.75	.30
❑ 74 Dan Marino TC	.75	.30
❑ 75 Clyde Simmons TC	.05	.01
❑ 76 Deion Sanders TC	.25	.08
❑ 77 Ricky Watters TC	.10	.02
❑ 78 Rodney Hampton TC	.10	.02
❑ 79 Brad Baxter TC	.05	.01
❑ 80 Barry Sanders TC	.60	.25
❑ 81 Warren Moon TC	.10	.02
❑ 82 Brett Favre TC	1.00	.40
❑ 83 Drew Bledsoe TC	1.25	.50
❑ 84 Eric Dickerson TC	.10	.02
❑ 85 Cleveland Gary TC	.05	.01
❑ 86 Earnest Byner TC	.05	.01
❑ 87 Wayne Martin TC	.05	.01
❑ 88 Rick Mirer TC	.25	.08
❑ 89 Barry Foster TC	.05	.01
❑ 90 Terry Allen TC	.10	.02
❑ 91 Vinnie Clark	.05	.01
❑ 92 Howard Ballard	.05	.01
❑ 93 Eric Ball	.05	.01
❑ 94 Marc Boutte	.05	.01
❑ 95 Larry Centers RC	.25	.08
❑ 96 Gary Brown	.05	.01
❑ 97 Hugh Millen	.05	.01
❑ 98 Anthony Newman RC	.05	.01
❑ 99 Darrell Thompson	.05	.01
❑ 100 George Jamison	.05	.01
❑ 101 James Francis	.05	.01
❑ 102 Leonard Harris	.05	.01
❑ 103 Lomas Brown	.05	.01
❑ 104 James Lofton	.10	.02
❑ 105 Jamie Dukes	.05	.01
❑ 106 Quinn Early	.10	.02
❑ 107 Ernie Jones	.05	.01
❑ 108 Torrance Small	.05	.01
❑ 109 Michael Carter	.05	.01
❑ 110 Aeneas Williams	.05	.01
❑ 111 Renaldo Turnbull	.05	.01
❑ 112 Al Smith	.05	.01
❑ 113 Troy Auzenne	.05	.01
❑ 114 Stephen Baker	.05	.01
❑ 115 Daniel Stubbs	.05	.01
❑ 116 Dana Hall	.05	.01
❑ 117 Lawrence Taylor	.25	.08
❑ 118 Ron Hall	.05	.01
❑ 119 Derrick Fenner	.05	.01
❑ 120 Martin Mayhew	.05	.01
❑ 121 Jay Schroeder	.05	.01
❑ 122 Michael Zordich	.05	.01
❑ 123 Ed McCaffrey	.25	.08
❑ 124 John Stephens	.05	.01
❑ 125 Brad Edwards	.05	.01
❑ 126 Don Griffin	.05	.01
❑ 127 Broderick Thomas	.05	.01
❑ 128 Ted Washington	.05	.01
❑ 129 Haywood Jeffires	.10	.02
❑ 130 Gary Plummer	.05	.01
❑ 131 Mark Wheeler	.05	.01
❑ 132 Ty Detmer	.25	.08
❑ 133 Derrick Walker	.05	.01
❑ 134 Henry Ellard	.10	.02
❑ 135 Neal Anderson	.05	.01
❑ 136 Bruce Smith	.25	.08
❑ 137 Cris Carter	.25	.08
❑ 138 Vaughn Dunbar	.05	.01
❑ 139 Dan Marino	1.50	.60
❑ 140 Troy Aikman	.75	.30
❑ 141 Randall Cunningham	.25	.08
❑ 142 Daryl Johnston	.25	.08
❑ 143 Mark Clayton	.05	.01
❑ 144 Rich Gannon	.25	.08
❑ 145 Nate Newton	.10	.02
❑ 146 Willie Gault	.05	.01
❑ 147 Brian Washington	.05	.01
❑ 148 Fred Barnett	.10	.02
❑ 149 Gill Byrd	.05	.01
❑ 150 Art Monk	.10	.02
❑ 151 Stan Humphries	.10	.02
❑ 152 Charles Mann	.05	.01
❑ 153 Greg Lloyd	.10	.02
❑ 154 Marvin Washington	.05	.01
❑ 155 Bernie Kosar	.10	.02
❑ 156 Pete Metzelaars	.05	.01
❑ 157 Chris Hinton	.05	.01
❑ 158 Jim Harbaugh	.25	.08
❑ 159 Willie Davis	.25	.08
❑ 160 Leroy Thompson	.05	.01
❑ 161 Scott Miller	.05	.01
❑ 162 Eugene Robinson	.05	.01
❑ 163 David Little	.05	.01
❑ 164 Pierce Holt	.05	.01
❑ 165 James Hasty	.05	.01
❑ 166 Dave Krieg	.10	.02
❑ 167 Gerald Williams	.05	.01
❑ 168 Kyle Clifton	.05	.01
❑ 169 Bill Brooks	.05	.01
❑ 170 Vance Johnson	.05	.01
❑ 171 Greg Townsend	.05	.01
❑ 172 Jason Belser	.05	.01
❑ 173 Brett Perriman	.25	.08
❑ 174 Steve Jordan	.05	.01
❑ 175 Kelvin Martin	.05	.01
❑ 176 Greg Kragen	.05	.01
❑ 177 Kerry Cash	.05	.01
❑ 178 Chester McGlockton	.10	.02
❑ 179 Jim Kelly	.25	.08
❑ 180 Todd McNair	.05	.01
❑ 181 Leroy Hoard	.10	.02
❑ 182 Seth Joyner	.05	.01
❑ 183 Sam Gash RC	.25	.08
❑ 184 Joe Nash	.05	.01
❑ 185 Lin Elliott RC	.05	.01
❑ 186 Robert Porcher	.05	.01
❑ 187 Tommy Hodson	.05	.01
❑ 188 Greg Lewis	.05	.01
❑ 189 Dan Saleaumua	.05	.01
❑ 190 Chris Goode	.05	.01
❑ 191 Henry Thomas	.05	.01
❑ 192 Bobby Hebert	.05	.01
❑ 193 Clay Matthews	.10	.02
❑ 194 Mark Carrier WR	.10	.02
❑ 195 Anthony Pleasant	.05	.01
❑ 196 Eric Dorsey	.05	.01
❑ 197 Clarence Verdin	.05	.01
❑ 198 Marc Spindler	.05	.01
❑ 199 Tommy Maddox	.25	.08
❑ 200 Wendell Davis	.05	.01
❑ 201 John Fina	.05	.01
❑ 202 Alonzo Spellman	.05	.01
❑ 203 Darryl Williams	.05	.01
❑ 204 Mike Croel	.05	.01
❑ 205 Ken Norton Jr.	.10	.02
❑ 206 Mel Gray	.10	.02
❑ 207 Chuck Cecil	.05	.01
❑ 208 John Flannery	.05	.01
❑ 209 Chip Banks	.05	.01
❑ 210 Chris Martin	.05	.01
❑ 211 Dennis Brown	.05	.01

❑	212	Vinny Testaverde	.10	.02
❑	213	Nick Bell	.05	.01
❑	214	Robert Delpino	.05	.01
❑	215	Mark Higgs	.05	.01
❑	216	Al Noga	.05	.01
❑	217	Andre Tippett	.05	.01
❑	218	Pat Swilling	.05	.01
❑	219	Phil Simms	.10	.02
❑	220	Ricky Proehl	.05	.01
❑	221	William Thomas	.05	.01
❑	222	Jeff Graham	.10	.02
❑	223	Darion Conner	.05	.01
❑	224	Mark Carrier DB	.05	.01
❑	225	Willie Green	.05	.01
❑	226	Reggie Rivers RC	.05	.01
❑	227	Andre Reed	.10	.02
❑	228	Deion Sanders	.50	.20
❑	229	Chris Doleman	.05	.01
❑	230	Jerry Ball	.05	.01
❑	231	Eric Dickerson	.10	.02
❑	232	Carlos Jenkins	.05	.01
❑	233	Mike Johnson	.05	.01
❑	234	Marco Coleman	.05	.01
❑	235	Leslie O'Neal	.10	.02
❑	236	Browning Nagle	.05	.01
❑	237	Carl Pickens	.10	.02
❑	238	Steve Emtman	.05	.01
❑	239	Alvin Harper	.10	.02
❑	240	Keith Jackson	.10	.02
❑	241	Jerry Rice	1.00	.40
❑	242	Cortez Kennedy	.10	.02
❑	243	Tyji Armstrong	.05	.01
❑	244	Troy Vincent	.05	.01
❑	245	Randal Hill	.05	.01
❑	246	Robert Blackmon	.05	.01
❑	247	Junior Seau	.25	.08
❑	248	Sterling Sharpe	.25	.08
❑	249	Thurman Thomas	.25	.08
❑	250	David Klingler	.05	.01
❑	251	Jeff George	.25	.08
❑	252	Anthony Miller	.10	.02
❑	253	Earnest Byner	.05	.01
❑	254	Eric Swann	.10	.02
❑	255	Jeff Herrod	.05	.01
❑	256	Eddie Robinson	.05	.01
❑	257	Eric Allen	.05	.01
❑	258	John Taylor	.10	.02
❑	259	Sean Gilbert	.10	.02
❑	260	Ray Childress	.05	.01
❑	261	Michael Haynes	.10	.02
❑	262	Greg McMurtry	.05	.01
❑	263	Bill Romanowski	.05	.01
❑	264	Todd Lyght	.05	.01
❑	265	Clyde Simmons	.05	.01
❑	266	Webster Slaughter	.05	.01
❑	267	J.J. Birden	.05	.01
❑	268	Aaron Wallace	.05	.01
❑	269	Carl Banks	.05	.01
❑	270	Ricardo McDonald	.05	.01
❑	271	Michael Brooks	.05	.01
❑	272	Dale Carter	.05	.01
❑	273	Mike Pritchard	.10	.02
❑	274	Derek Brown TE	.05	.01
❑	275	Burt Grossman	.05	.01
❑	276	Mark Schlereth	.05	.01
❑	277	Karl Mecklenburg	.05	.01
❑	278	Rickey Jackson	.05	.01
❑	279	Ricky Ervins	.05	.01
❑	280	Jeff Bryant	.05	.01
❑	281	Eric Martin	.05	.01
❑	282	Carlton Haselrig	.05	.01
❑	283	Kevin Mack	.05	.01
❑	284	Brad Muster	.05	.01
❑	285	Kelvin Pritchett	.05	.01
❑	286	Courtney Hawkins	.05	.01
❑	287	Levon Kirkland	.05	.01
❑	288	Steve DeBerg	.05	.01
❑	289	Edgar Bennett	.25	.08
❑	290	Michael Dean Perry	.10	.02
❑	291	Richard Dent	.10	.02
❑	292	Howie Long	.25	.08
❑	293	Chris Mims	.05	.01
❑	294	Kurt Barber	.05	.01
❑	295	Wilber Marshall	.05	.01
❑	296	Ethan Horton	.05	.01
❑	297	Tony Bennett	.05	.01
❑	298	Johnny Johnson	.05	.01
❑	299	Craig Heyward	.10	.02
❑	300	Steve Israel	.05	.01
❑	301	Kenneth Gant	.05	.01
❑	302	Eugene Chung	.05	.01
❑	303	Harvey Williams	.10	.02
❑	304	Jarrod Bunch	.05	.01
❑	305	Darren Perry	.05	.01
❑	306	Steve Christie	.05	.01
❑	307	John Randle	.10	.02
❑	308	Warren Moon	.25	.08
❑	309	Charles Haley	.10	.02
❑	310	Tony Smith RB	.05	.01
❑	311	Steve Broussard	.05	.01
❑	312	Alfred Williams	.05	.01
❑	313	Terrell Buckley	.05	.01
❑	314	Trace Armstrong	.05	.01
❑	315	Brian Mitchell	.10	.02
❑	316	Steve Atwater	.05	.01
❑	317	Nate Lewis	.05	.01
❑	318	Richard Brown	.05	.01
❑	319	Rufus Porter	.05	.01
❑	320	Pat Harlow	.05	.01
❑	321	Anthony Smith	.05	.01
❑	322	Jack Del Rio	.05	.01
❑	323	Darryl Talley	.05	.01
❑	324	Sam Mills	.05	.01
❑	325	Chris Miller	.10	.02
❑	326	Ken Harvey	.05	.01
❑	327	Rod Woodson	.25	.08
❑	328	Tony Tolbert	.05	.01
❑	329	Todd Kinchen	.05	.01
❑	330	Brian Noble	.05	.01
❑	331	Dave Meggett	.05	.01
❑	332	Chris Spielman	.10	.02
❑	333	Barry Word	.05	.01
❑	334	Jessie Hester	.05	.01
❑	335	Michael Jackson	.10	.02
❑	336	Mitchell Price	.05	.01
❑	337	Michael Irvin	.25	.08
❑	338	Simon Fletcher	.05	.01
❑	339	Keith Jennings	.05	.01
❑	340	Vai Sikahema	.05	.01
❑	341	Roger Craig	.10	.02
❑	342	Ricky Watters	.25	.08
❑	343	Reggie Cobb	.05	.01
❑	344	Kanavis McGhee	.05	.01
❑	345	Barry Foster	.10	.02
❑	346	Marion Butts	.05	.01
❑	347	Bryan Cox	.05	.01
❑	348	Wayne Martin	.05	.01
❑	349	Jim Everett	.10	.02
❑	350	Nate Odomes	.05	.01
❑	351	Anthony Johnson	.10	.02
❑	352	Rodney Hampton	.10	.02
❑	353	Terry Allen	.25	.08
❑	354	Derrick Thomas	.25	.08
❑	355	Calvin Williams	.10	.02
❑	356	Pepper Johnson	.05	.01
❑	357	John Elway	1.50	.60
❑	358	Steve Young	.75	.30
❑	359	Emmitt Smith	1.50	.60
❑	360	Brett Favre	2.00	.75
❑	361	Cody Carlson	.05	.01
❑	362	Vincent Brown	.05	.01
❑	363	Gary Anderson RB	.05	.01
❑	364	Jon Vaughn	.05	.01
❑	365	Todd Marinovich	.05	.01
❑	366	Carnell Lake	.05	.01
❑	367	Kurt Gouveia	.05	.01
❑	368	Lawrence Dawsey	.05	.01
❑	369	Neil O'Donnell	.25	.08
❑	370	Duane Bickett	.05	.01
❑	371	Ronnie Harmon	.05	.01
❑	372	Rodney Peete	.05	.01
❑	373	Cornelius Bennett	.10	.02
❑	374	Brad Baxter	.05	.01
❑	375	Ernest Givins	.10	.02
❑	376	Keith Byars	.05	.01
❑	377	Eric Bieniemy	.05	.01
❑	378	Mike Brim	.05	.01
❑	379	Darren Lewis	.05	.01
❑	380	Heath Sherman	.05	.01
❑	381	Leonard Russell	.10	.02
❑	382	Brent Jones	.10	.02
❑	383	David Whitmore	.05	.01
❑	384	Ray Roberts	.05	.01
❑	385	John Offerdahl	.05	.01
❑	386	Keith McCants	.05	.01
❑	387	John Baylor	.05	.01
❑	388	Amp Lee	.05	.01
❑	389	Chris Warren	.10	.02
❑	390	Herman Moore	.25	.08
❑	391	Johnny Bailey	.05	.01
❑	392	Tim Johnson	.05	.01
❑	393	Eric Metcalf	.10	.02
❑	394	Chris Chandler	.10	.02
❑	395	Mark Rypien	.05	.01
❑	396	Christian Okoye	.05	.01
❑	397	Shannon Sharpe	.25	.08
❑	398	Eric Hill	.05	.01
❑	399	David Lang	.05	.01
❑	400	Bruce Matthews	.05	.01
❑	401	Harold Green	.05	.01
❑	402	Mo Lewis	.05	.01
❑	403	Terry McDaniel	.05	.01
❑	404	Wesley Carroll	.05	.01
❑	405	Richmond Webb	.05	.01
❑	406	Andre Rison	.10	.02
❑	407	Lonnie Young	.05	.01
❑	408	Tommy Vardell	.05	.01
❑	409	Gene Atkins	.05	.01
❑	410	Sean Salisbury	.05	.01
❑	411	Kenneth Davis	.05	.01
❑	412	John L. Williams	.05	.01
❑	413	Roman Phifer	.05	.01
❑	414	Bennie Blades	.05	.01
❑	415	Tim Brown	.25	.08
❑	416	Lorenzo White	.05	.01
❑	417	Tony Casillas	.05	.01
❑	418	Tom Waddle	.05	.01
❑	419	David Fulcher	.05	.01
❑	420	Jessie Tuggle	.05	.01
❑	421	Emmitt Smith SL	.75	.30
❑	422	Clyde Simmons SL	.05	.01
❑	423	Sterling Sharpe SL	.10	.02
❑	424	Sterling Sharpe SL	.10	.02
❑	425	Emmitt Smith SL	.75	.30
❑	426	Dan Marino SL	.75	.30
❑	427	Henry Jones SL	.05	.01
❑	428	Thurman Thomas SL	.10	.02
❑	429	Greg Montgomery SL	.05	.01
❑	430	Pete Stoyanovich SL	.05	.01
❑	431	Emmitt Smith CL	.40	.15
❑	432	Steve Young BB	.40	.15
❑	433	Jerry Rice BB	.50	.20
❑	434	Ricky Watters BB	.10	.02
❑	435	Barry Foster BB	.05	.01
❑	436	Cortez Kennedy BB	.05	.01
❑	437	Warren Moon BB	.10	.02
❑	438	Thurman Thomas BB	.10	.02
❑	439	Brett Favre BB	1.00	.40
❑	440	Andre Rison BB	.10	.02
❑	441	Barry Sanders BB	.60	.25
❑	442	Chris Berman CL	.05	.01
❑	443	Moe Gardner	.05	.01
❑	444	Robert Jones	.05	.01
❑	445	Reggie Langhorne	.05	.01
❑	446	Flipper Anderson	.05	.01
❑	447	James Washington	.05	.01
❑	448	Aaron Craver	.05	.01
❑	449	Jack Trudeau	.05	.01
❑	450	Neil Smith	.25	.08
❑	451	Chris Burkett	.05	.01
❑	452	Russell Maryland	.05	.01
❑	453	Drew Hill	.05	.01
❑	454	Barry Sanders	1.25	.50
❑	455	Jeff Cross	.05	.01
❑	456	Bennie Thompson	.05	.01
❑	457	Marcus Allen	.25	.08
❑	458	Tracy Scroggins	.05	.01
❑	459	LeRoy Butler	.05	.01
❑	460	Joe Montana	1.50	.60
❑	461	Eddie Anderson	.05	.01
❑	462	Tim McDonald	.05	.01
❑	463	Ronnie Lott	.10	.02
❑	464	Gaston Green	.05	.01
❑	465	Shane Conlan	.05	.01
❑	466	Leonard Marshall	.05	.01
❑	467	Melvin Jenkins	.05	.01
❑	468	Don Beebe	.05	.01
❑	469	Johnny Mitchell	.05	.01
❑	470	Darryl Henley	.05	.01
❑	471	Boomer Esiason	.10	.02
❑	472	Mark Kelso	.05	.01

Card		
❑ 473 John Booty	.05	.01
❑ 474 Pete Stoyanovich	.05	.01
❑ 475 Thomas Smith RC	.10	.02
❑ 476 Carlton Gray RC	.05	.01
❑ 477 Dana Stubblefield RC	.25	.08
❑ 478 Ryan McNeil RC	.25	.08
❑ 479 Natrone Means RC	.25	.08
❑ 480 Carl Simpson RC	.05	.01
❑ 481 Robert O'Neal RC	.05	.01
❑ 482 Demetrius DuBose RC	.05	.01
❑ 483 Darrin Smith RC	.10	.02
❑ 484 Micheal Barrow RC	.25	.08
❑ 485 Chris Slade RC	.10	.02
❑ 486 Steve Tovar RC	.05	.01
❑ 487 Ron George RC	.05	.01
❑ 488 Steve Tasker	.10	.02
❑ 489 Will Furrer	.05	.01
❑ 490 Reggie White	.25	.08
❑ 491 Sean Jones	.05	.01
❑ 492 Gary Clark	.10	.02
❑ 493 Donnell Woolford	.05	.01
❑ 494 Steve Beuerlein	.10	.02
❑ 495 Anthony Carter	.10	.02
❑ 496 Louis Oliver	.05	.01
❑ 497 Chris Zorich	.05	.01
❑ 498 David Brandon	.05	.01
❑ 499 Bubba McDowell	.05	.01
❑ 500 Adrian Cooper	.05	.01
❑ 501 Bill Johnson	.05	.01
❑ 502 Shawn Jefferson	.05	.01
❑ 503 Siran Stacy	.05	.01
❑ 504 James Jones DT	.05	.01
❑ 505 Tom Rathman	.05	.01
❑ 506 Vince Buck	.05	.01
❑ 507 Kent Graham RC	.25	.08
❑ 508 Darren Carrington RC	.05	.01
❑ 509 Rickey Dixon	.05	.01
❑ 510 Toi Cook	.05	.01
❑ 511 Steve Smith	.05	.01
❑ 512 Eric Green	.05	.01
❑ 513 Phillippi Sparks	.05	.01
❑ 514 Lee Williams	.05	.01
❑ 515 Gary Reasons	.05	.01
❑ 516 Shane Dronett	.05	.01
❑ 517 Jay Novacek	.10	.02
❑ 518 Kevin Greene	.10	.02
❑ 519 Derek Russell	.05	.01
❑ 520 Quentin Coryatt	.10	.02
❑ 521 Santana Dotson	.10	.02
❑ 522 Donald Frank	.05	.01
❑ 523 Mike Prior	.05	.01
❑ 524 Dwight Hollier RC	.05	.01
❑ 525 Eric Davis	.05	.01
❑ 526 Dalton Hilliard	.05	.01
❑ 527 Rodney Culver	.05	.01
❑ 528 Jeff Hostetler	.10	.02
❑ 529 Ernie Mills	.05	.01
❑ 530 Craig Erickson	.10	.02
❑ P231 Eric Dickerson Promo	1.25	.50

1994 Upper Deck

Card		
❑ COMPLETE SET (330)	25.00	12.50
❑ 1 Dan Wilkinson RC	.20	.07
❑ 2 Antonio Langham RC	.20	.07
❑ 3 Derrick Alexander WR RC	.40	.15
❑ 4 Charles Johnson RC	.40	.15
❑ 5 Bucky Brooks RC	.10	.02
❑ 6 Trev Alberts RC	.20	.07
❑ 7 Marshall Faulk RC	6.00	2.50
❑ 8 Willie McGinest RC	.40	.15
❑ 9 Aaron Glenn RC	.40	.15
❑ 10 Ryan Yarborough RC	.10	.02
❑ 11 Greg Hill RC	.40	.15
❑ 12 Sam Adams RC	.20	.07
❑ 13 John Thierry RC	.10	.02
❑ 14 Johnnie Morton RC	.75	.30
❑ 15 LeShon Johnson RC	.20	.07
❑ 16 David Palmer RC	.40	.15
❑ 17 Trent Dilfer RC	1.25	.50
❑ 18 Jamir Miller RC	.20	.07
❑ 19 Thomas Lewis RC	.20	.07
❑ 20 Heath Shuler RC	.40	.15
❑ 21 Wayne Gandy	.10	.02
❑ 22 Isaac Bruce RC	4.00	2.00
❑ 23 Joe Johnson RC	.10	.02
❑ 24 Mario Bates RC	.40	.15
❑ 25 Bryant Young RC	.40	.15
❑ 26 William Floyd RC	.40	.15
❑ 27 Errict Rhett RC	.40	.15
❑ 28 Chuck Levy RC	.10	.02
❑ 29 Darnay Scott RC	.75	.30
❑ 30 Rob Fredrickson RC	.20	.07
❑ 31 Jamir Miller HW	.10	.02
❑ 32 Thomas Lewis HW	.10	.02
❑ 33 John Thierry HW	.10	.02
❑ 34 Sam Adams HW	.10	.02
❑ 35 Joe Johnson HW	.10	.02
❑ 36 Bryant Young HW	.20	.07
❑ 37 Wayne Gandy HW	.10	.02
❑ 38 LeShon Johnson HW	.10	.02
❑ 39 Mario Bates HW	.20	.07
❑ 40 Greg Hill HW	.20	.07
❑ 41 Andy Heck	.10	.02
❑ 42 Warren Moon	.40	.15
❑ 43 Jim Everett	.20	.07
❑ 44 Bill Romanowski	.10	.02
❑ 45 Michael Haynes	.20	.07
❑ 46 Chris Doleman	.10	.02
❑ 47 Merril Hoge	.10	.02
❑ 48 Chris Miller	.10	.02
❑ 49 Clyde Simmons	.10	.02
❑ 50 Jeff George	.40	.15
❑ 51 Jeff Burris RC	.20	.07
❑ 52 Ethan Horton	.10	.02
❑ 53 Scott Mitchell	.20	.07
❑ 54 Howard Ballard	.10	.02
❑ 55 Lewis Tillman	.10	.02
❑ 56 Marion Butts	.10	.02
❑ 57 Erik Kramer	.20	.07
❑ 58 Ken Norton Jr.	.20	.07
❑ 59 Anthony Miller	.20	.07
❑ 60 Chris Hinton	.10	.02
❑ 61 Ricky Proehl	.10	.02
❑ 62 Craig Heyward	.20	.07
❑ 63 Darryl Talley	.10	.02
❑ 64 Tim Worley	.10	.02
❑ 65 Derrick Fenner	.10	.02
❑ 66 Jerry Ball	.10	.02
❑ 67 Darrin Smith	.10	.02
❑ 68 Mike Croel	.10	.02
❑ 69 Ray Crockett	.10	.02
❑ 70 Tony Bennett	.10	.02
❑ 71 Webster Slaughter	.10	.02
❑ 72 Anthony Johnson	.20	.07
❑ 73 Charles Mincy	.10	.02
❑ 74 Calvin Jones RC	.10	.02
❑ 75 Henry Ellard	.20	.07
❑ 76 Troy Vincent	.10	.02
❑ 77 Sean Salisbury	.10	.02
❑ 78 Pat Harlow	.10	.02
❑ 79 James Williams RC LB	.10	.02
❑ 80 Dave Brown	.20	.07
❑ 81 Kent Graham	.20	.07
❑ 82 Seth Joyner	.10	.02
❑ 83 Deon Figures	.10	.02
❑ 84 Stanley Richard	.10	.02
❑ 85 Tom Rathman	.10	.02
❑ 86 Rod Stephens	.10	.02
❑ 87 Ray Seals	.10	.02
❑ 88 Andre Collins	.10	.02
❑ 89 Cornelius Bennett	.20	.07
❑ 90 Richard Dent	.20	.07
❑ 91 Louis Oliver	.10	.02
❑ 92 Rodney Peete	.10	.02
❑ 93 Jackie Harris	.10	.02
❑ 94 Tracy Simien	.10	.02
❑ 95 Greg Townsend	.10	.02
❑ 96 Michael Stewart	.10	.02
❑ 97 Irving Fryar	.20	.07
❑ 98 Todd Collins	.10	.02
❑ 99 Irv Smith	.10	.02
❑ 100 Chris Calloway	.10	.02
❑ 101 Kevin Greene	.20	.07
❑ 102 John Friesz	.20	.07
❑ 103 Steve Bono	.20	.07
❑ 104 Brian Blades	.20	.07
❑ 105 Reggie Cobb	.10	.02
❑ 106 Eric Swann	.20	.07
❑ 107 Mike Pritchard	.10	.02
❑ 108 Bill Brooks	.10	.02
❑ 109 Jim Harbaugh	.40	.15
❑ 110 David Whitmore	.10	.02
❑ 111 Eddie Anderson	.10	.02
❑ 112 Ray Crittenden RC	.10	.02
❑ 113 Mark Collins	.10	.02
❑ 114 Brian Washington	.10	.02
❑ 115 Barry Foster	.10	.02
❑ 116 Gary Plummer	.10	.02
❑ 117 Marc Logan	.10	.02
❑ 118 John L. Williams	.10	.02
❑ 119 Marty Carter	.10	.02
❑ 120 Kurt Gouveia	.10	.02
❑ 121 Ronald Moore	.10	.02
❑ 122 Pierce Holt	.10	.02
❑ 123 Henry Jones	.10	.02
❑ 124 Donnell Woolford	.10	.02
❑ 125 Steve Tovar	.10	.02
❑ 126 Anthony Pleasant	.10	.02
❑ 127 Jay Novacek	.20	.07
❑ 128 Dan Williams	.10	.02
❑ 129 Barry Sanders	2.50	1.00
❑ 130 Robert Brooks	.40	.15
❑ 131 Lorenzo White	.10	.02
❑ 132 Kerry Cash	.10	.02
❑ 133 Joe Montana	3.00	1.25
❑ 134 Jeff Hostetler	.20	.07
❑ 135 Jerome Bettis	.60	.25
❑ 136 Dan Marino	3.00	1.25
❑ 137 Vencie Glenn	.10	.02
❑ 138 Vincent Brown	.10	.02
❑ 139 Rickey Jackson	.10	.02
❑ 140 Carlton Bailey	.10	.02
❑ 141 Jeff Lageman	.10	.02
❑ 142 William Thomas	.10	.02
❑ 143 Neil O'Donnell	.40	.15
❑ 144 Shawn Jefferson	.10	.02
❑ 145 Steve Young	1.00	.40
❑ 146 Chris Warren	.20	.07
❑ 147 Courtney Hawkins	.10	.02
❑ 148 Brad Edwards	.10	.02
❑ 149 O.J.McDuffie	.40	.15
❑ 150 David Lang	.10	.02
❑ 151 Chuck Cecil	.10	.02
❑ 152 Norm Johnson	.10	.02
❑ 153 Pete Metzelaars	.10	.02
❑ 154 Shaun Gayle	.10	.02
❑ 155 Alfred Williams	.10	.02
❑ 156 Eric Turner	.10	.02
❑ 157A Emmitt Smith ERR 1900	2.50	1.00
❑ 157B Emmitt Smith COR	2.50	1.00
❑ 158 Steve Atwater	.10	.02
❑ 159 Robert Porcher	.10	.02
❑ 160 Edgar Bennett	.40	.15
❑ 161 Bubba McDowell	.10	.02
❑ 162 Jeff Herrod	.10	.02
❑ 163 Keith Cash	.10	.02
❑ 164 Patrick Bates	.10	.02
❑ 165 Todd Lyght	.10	.02
❑ 166 Mark Higgs	.10	.02
❑ 167 Carlos Jenkins	.10	.02
❑ 168 Drew Bledsoe	1.00	.40
❑ 169 Wayne Martin	.10	.02
❑ 170 Mike Sherrard	.10	.02
❑ 171 Ronnie Lott	.20	.07
❑ 172 Fred Barnett	.20	.07
❑ 173 Eric Green	.10	.02
❑ 174 Leslie O'Neal	.10	.02
❑ 175 Brent Jones	.20	.07
❑ 176 Jon Vaughn	.10	.02
❑ 177 Vince Workman	.10	.02
❑ 178 Ron Middleton	.10	.02

❑ 179 Terry McDaniel .10 .02
❑ 180 Willie Davis .20 .07
❑ 181 Gary Clark .20 .07
❑ 182 Bobby Hebert .10 .02
❑ 183 Russell Copeland .10 .02
❑ 184 Chris Gedney .10 .02
❑ 185 Tony McGee .10 .02
❑ 186 Rob Burnett .10 .02
❑ 187 Charles Haley .20 .07
❑ 188 Shannon Sharpe .20 .07
❑ 189 Mel Gray .10 .02
❑ 190 George Teague .10 .02
❑ 191 Ernest Givins .20 .07
❑ 192 Ray Buchanan .10 .02
❑ 193 J.J. Birden .10 .02
❑ 194 Tim Brown .40 .15
❑ 195 Tim Lester .10 .02
❑ 196 Marco Coleman .10 .02
❑ 197 Randall McDaniel .10 .02
❑ 198 Bruce Armstrong .10 .02
❑ 199 Willie Roaf .10 .02
❑ 200 Greg Jackson .10 .02
❑ 201 Johnny Mitchell .10 .02
❑ 202 Calvin Williams .20 .07
❑ 203 Jeff Graham .10 .02
❑ 204 Darren Carrington .10 .02
❑ 205 Jerry Rice 1.50 .60
❑ 206 Cortez Kennedy .20 .07
❑ 207 Charles Wilson .10 .02
❑ 208 James Jenkins TE RC .10 .02
❑ 209 Ray Childress .10 .02
❑ 210 LeRoy Butler .10 .02
❑ 211 Randal Hill .10 .02
❑ 212 Lincoln Kennedy .10 .02
❑ 213 Kenneth Davis .10 .02
❑ 214 Terry Obee .10 .02
❑ 215 Ricardo McDonald .10 .02
❑ 216 Pepper Johnson .10 .02
❑ 217 Alvin Harper .20 .07
❑ 218 John Elway 3.00 1.25
❑ 219 Derrick Moore .10 .02
❑ 220 Terrell Buckley .10 .02
❑ 221 Haywood Jeffires .20 .07
❑ 222 Jessie Hester .10 .02
❑ 223 Kimble Anders .20 .07
❑ 224 Rocket Ismail .20 .07
❑ 225 Roman Phifer .10 .02
❑ 226 Bryan Cox .10 .02
❑ 227 Cris Carter .75 .30
❑ 228 Sam Gash .10 .02
❑ 229 Renaldo Turnbull .10 .02
❑ 230 Rodney Hampton .20 .07
❑ 231 Johnny Johnson .10 .02
❑ 232 Tim Harris .10 .02
❑ 233 Leroy Thompson .10 .02
❑ 234 Junior Seau .40 .15
❑ 235 Tim McDonald .10 .02
❑ 236 Eugene Robinson .10 .02
❑ 237 Lawrence Dawsey .10 .02
❑ 238 Tim Johnson .10 .02
❑ 239 Jason Elam .20 .07
❑ 240 Willie Green .10 .02
❑ 241 Larry Centers .40 .15
❑ 242 Erric Pegram .10 .02
❑ 243 Bruce Smith .40 .15
❑ 244 Alonzo Spellman .10 .02
❑ 245 Carl Pickens .20 .07
❑ 246 Michael Jackson .20 .07
❑ 247 Kevin Williams WR .20 .07
❑ 248 Glyn Milburn .20 .07
❑ 249 Herman Moore .40 .15
❑ 250 Brett Favre 3.00 1.25
❑ 251 Al Smith .10 .02
❑ 252 Roosevelt Potts .10 .02
❑ 253 Marcus Allen .40 .15
❑ 254 Anthony Smith .10 .02
❑ 255 Sean Gilbert .10 .02
❑ 256 Keith Byars .10 .02
❑ 257 Scottie Graham RC .20 .07
❑ 258 Leonard Russell .10 .02
❑ 259 Eric Martin .10 .02
❑ 260 Jarrod Bunch .10 .02
❑ 261 Rob Moore .20 .07
❑ 262 Herschel Walker .20 .07
❑ 263 Levon Kirkland .10 .02
❑ 264 Chris Mims .10 .02
❑ 265 Ricky Watters .20 .07
❑ 266 Rick Mirer .40 .15
❑ 267 Santana Dotson .20 .07
❑ 268 Reggie Brooks .20 .07
❑ 269 Garrison Hearst .40 .15
❑ 270 Thurman Thomas .40 .15
❑ 271 Johnny Bailey .10 .02
❑ 272 Andre Rison .20 .07
❑ 273 Jim Kelly .40 .15
❑ 274 Mark Carrier DB .10 .02
❑ 275 David Klingler .10 .02
❑ 276 Eric Metcalf .20 .07
❑ 277 Troy Aikman UER 1.50 .60
❑ 278 Simon Fletcher .10 .02
❑ 279 Pat Swilling .10 .02
❑ 280 Sterling Sharpe .20 .07
❑ 281 Cody Carlson .10 .02
❑ 282 Steve Emtman .10 .02
❑ 283 Neil Smith .20 .07
❑ 284 James Jett .10 .02
❑ 285 Shane Conlan .10 .02
❑ 286 Keith Jackson .10 .02
❑ 287 Qadry Ismail .40 .15
❑ 288 Chris Slade .10 .02
❑ 289 Derek Brown RBK .10 .02
❑ 290 Phil Simms .20 .07
❑ 291 Boomer Esiason .20 .07
❑ 292 Eric Allen .10 .02
❑ 293 Rod Woodson .20 .07
❑ 294 Ronnie Harmon .10 .02
❑ 295 John Taylor .20 .07
❑ 296 Ferrell Edmunds .10 .02
❑ 297 Craig Erickson .10 .02
❑ 298 Brian Mitchell .10 .02
❑ 299 Dante Jones .10 .02
❑ 300 John Copeland .10 .02
❑ 301 Steve Beuerlein .20 .07
❑ 302 Deion Sanders .75 .30
❑ 303 Andre Reed .20 .07
❑ 304 Curtis Conway .40 .15
❑ 305 Harold Green .10 .02
❑ 306 Vinny Testaverde .20 .07
❑ 307 Michael Irvin .40 .15
❑ 308 Rod Bernstine .10 .02
❑ 309 Chris Spielman .20 .07
❑ 310 Reggie White .40 .15
❑ 311 Gary Brown .10 .02
❑ 312 Quentin Coryatt .10 .02
❑ 313 Derrick Thomas .40 .15
❑ 314 Greg Robinson .10 .02
❑ 315 Troy Drayton .10 .02
❑ 316 Terry Kirby .40 .15
❑ 317 John Randle .20 .07
❑ 318 Ben Coates .20 .07
❑ 319 Tyrone Hughes .20 .07
❑ 320 Corey Miller .10 .02
❑ 321 Brad Baxter .10 .02
❑ 322 Randall Cunningham .40 .15
❑ 323 Greg Lloyd .20 .07
❑ 324 Stan Humphries .20 .07
❑ 325 Dana Stubblefield .20 .07
❑ 326 Kelvin Martin .10 .02
❑ 327 Hardy Nickerson .20 .07
❑ 328 Desmond Howard .20 .07
❑ 329 Mark Carrier WR .20 .07
❑ 330 Daryl Johnston .20 .07
❑ P19 Joe Montana Promo 2.50 1.00

1995 Upper Deck

❑ COMPLETE SET (300) 30.00 12.50
❑ 1 Ki-Jana Carter RC .40 .15
❑ 2 Tony Boselli RC .40 .15
❑ 3 Steve McNair RC 4.00 1.50
❑ 4 Michael Westbrook RC .40 .15
❑ 5 Kerry Collins RC 2.00 .75
❑ 6 Kevin Carter RC .40 .15
❑ 7 James A.Stewart RC .10 .02
❑ 8 Joey Galloway RC 2.00 .75
❑ 9 Kyle Brady RC .40 .15
❑ 10 J.J. Stokes RC .40 .15
❑ 11 Derrick Alexander DE RC .10 .02
❑ 12 Warren Sapp RC 2.00 .75
❑ 13 Mark Fields RC .40 .15
❑ 14 Tyrone Wheatley RC 1.50 .60
❑ 15 Napoleon Kaufman RC 1.50 .60
❑ 16 James O. Stewart RC 1.50 .60
❑ 17 Luther Elliss RC .10 .02
❑ 18 Rashaan Salaam RC .20 .07
❑ 19 Jimmy Oliver RC .10 .02
❑ 20 Mark Bruener RC .20 .07
❑ 21 Derrick Brooks RC 2.00 .75
❑ 22 Christian Fauria RC .20 .07
❑ 23 Ray Zellars RC .20 .07
❑ 24 Todd Collins RC .20 .07
❑ 25 Sherman Williams RC .10 .02
❑ 26 Frank Sanders RC .40 .15
❑ 27 Rodney Thomas RC .20 .07
❑ 28 Rob Johnson RC 1.25 .50
❑ 29 Steve Stenstrom RC .10 .02
❑ 30 Curtis Martin RC 4.00 1.50
❑ 31 Gary Clark .10 .02
❑ 32 Troy Aikman 1.50 .60
❑ 33 Mike Sherrard .10 .02
❑ 34 Fred Barnett .20 .07
❑ 35 Henry Ellard .20 .07
❑ 36 Terry Allen .20 .07
❑ 37 Jeff Graham .10 .02
❑ 38 Herman Moore .40 .15
❑ 39 Brett Favre 3.00 1.25
❑ 40 Trent Dilfer .40 .15
❑ 41 Derek Brown RBK .10 .02
❑ 42 Andre Rison .20 .07
❑ 43 Flipper Anderson .10 .02
❑ 44 Jerry Rice 1.50 .60
❑ 45 Andre Reed .20 .07
❑ 46 Sean Dawkins .20 .07
❑ 47 Irving Fryar .20 .07
❑ 48 Vincent Brisby .10 .02
❑ 49 Rob Moore .20 .07
❑ 50 Carl Pickens .20 .07
❑ 51 Vinny Testaverde .20 .07
❑ 52 Ray Childress .10 .02
❑ 53 Eric Green .10 .02
❑ 54 Anthony Miller .20 .07
❑ 55 Lake Dawson .20 .07
❑ 56 Tim Brown .40 .15
❑ 57 Stan Humphries .20 .07
❑ 58 Rick Mirer .20 .07
❑ 59 Randal Hill .10 .02
❑ 60 Charles Haley .20 .07
❑ 61 Chris Calloway .10 .02
❑ 62 Calvin Williams .20 .07
❑ 63 Ethan Horton .10 .02
❑ 64 Cris Carter .40 .15
❑ 65 Curtis Conway .40 .15
❑ 66 Scott Mitchell .20 .07
❑ 67 Edgar Bennett .20 .07
❑ 68 Craig Erickson .10 .02
❑ 69 Jim Everett .10 .02
❑ 70 Terance Mathis .20 .07
❑ 71 Robert Young .10 .02
❑ 72 Brent Jones .10 .02
❑ 73 Bill Brooks .20 .07
❑ 74 Marshall Faulk 2.00 .75
❑ 75 O.J. McDuffie .40 .15
❑ 76 Ben Coates .20 .07
❑ 77 Johnny Mitchell .10 .02
❑ 78 Darnay Scott .20 .07
❑ 79 Derrick Alexander WR .40 .15
❑ 80 Lorenzo White .10 .02
❑ 81 Charles Johnson .20 .07
❑ 82 John Elway 3.00 1.25
❑ 83 Willie Davis .20 .07
❑ 84 James Jett .20 .07
❑ 85 Mark Seay .20 .07
❑ 86 Brian Blades .20 .07
❑ 87 Ronald Moore .10 .02
❑ 88 Alvin Harper .10 .02

❑ 89 Dave Brown .20 .07
❑ 90 Randall Cunningham .40 .15
❑ 91 Heath Shuler .20 .07
❑ 92 Jake Reed .20 .07
❑ 93 Donnell Woolford .10 .02
❑ 94 Barry Sanders 2.50 1.00
❑ 95 Reggie White .40 .15
❑ 96 Lawrence Dawsey .10 .02
❑ 97 Michael Haynes .20 .07
❑ 98 Bert Emanuel .40 .15
❑ 99 Troy Drayton .10 .02
❑ 100 Steve Young 1.25 .50
❑ 101 Bruce Smith .40 .15
❑ 102 Roosevelt Potts .10 .02
❑ 103 Dan Marino 3.00 1.25
❑ 104 Michael Timpson .10 .02
❑ 105 Boomer Esiason .20 .07
❑ 106 David Klingler .20 .07
❑ 107 Eric Metcalf .20 .07
❑ 108 Gary Brown .10 .02
❑ 109 Neil O'Donnell .20 .07
❑ 110 Shannon Sharpe .20 .07
❑ 111 Joe Montana 3.00 1.25
❑ 112 Jeff Hostetler .20 .07
❑ 113 Ronnie Harmon .10 .02
❑ 114 Chris Warren .20 .07
❑ 115 Larry Centers .20 .07
❑ 116 Michael Irvin .40 .15
❑ 117 Rodney Hampton .20 .07
❑ 118 Herschel Walker .20 .07
❑ 119 Reggie Brooks .20 .07
❑ 120 Qadry Ismail .20 .07
❑ 121 Chris Zorich .10 .02
❑ 122 Chris Spielman .20 .07
❑ 123 Sean Jones .10 .02
❑ 124 Errict Rhett .20 .07
❑ 125 Tyrone Hughes .20 .07
❑ 126 Jeff George .20 .07
❑ 127 Chris Miller .10 .02
❑ 128 Ricky Watters .20 .07
❑ 129 Jim Kelly .40 .15
❑ 130 Tony Bennett .10 .02
❑ 131 Terry Kirby .20 .07
❑ 132 Drew Bledsoe 1.00 .40
❑ 133 Johnny Johnson .10 .02
❑ 134 Dan Wilkinson .20 .07
❑ 135 Leroy Hoard .10 .02
❑ 136 Darryll Lewis .10 .02
❑ 137 Barry Foster .20 .07
❑ 138 Shane Dronett .10 .02
❑ 139 Marcus Allen .40 .15
❑ 140 Harvey Williams .10 .02
❑ 141 Tony Martin .20 .07
❑ 142 Rod Stephens .10 .02
❑ 143 Eric Swann .20 .07
❑ 144 Daryl Johnston .20 .07
❑ 145 Dave Meggett .10 .02
❑ 146 Charlie Garner .40 .15
❑ 147 Ken Harvey .10 .02
❑ 148 Warren Moon .20 .07
❑ 149 Steve Walsh .10 .02
❑ 150 Pat Swilling .10 .02
❑ 151 Terrell Buckley .10 .02
❑ 152 Courtney Hawkins .10 .02
❑ 153 Willie Roaf .10 .02
❑ 154 Chris Doleman .10 .02
❑ 155 Jerome Bettis .40 .15
❑ 156 Dana Stubblefield .20 .07
❑ 157 Cornelius Bennett .20 .07
❑ 158 Quentin Coryatt .20 .07
❑ 159 Bryan Cox .10 .02
❑ 160 Marion Butts .10 .02
❑ 161 Aaron Glenn .10 .02
❑ 162 Louis Oliver .10 .02
❑ 163 Eric Turner .10 .02
❑ 164 Cris Dishman .10 .02
❑ 165 John L. Williams .10 .02
❑ 166 Simon Fletcher .10 .02
❑ 167 Neil Smith .20 .07
❑ 168 Chester McGlockton .20 .07
❑ 169 Natrone Means .20 .07
❑ 170 Sam Adams .10 .02
❑ 171 Clyde Simmons .10 .02
❑ 172 Jay Novacek .20 .07
❑ 173 Keith Hamilton .10 .02
❑ 174 William Fuller .10 .02
❑ 175 Tom Carter .10 .02
❑ 176 John Randle .20 .07
❑ 177 Lewis Tillman .10 .02
❑ 178 Mel Gray .10 .02
❑ 179 George Teague .10 .02
❑ 180 Hardy Nickerson .10 .02
❑ 181 Mario Bates .20 .07
❑ 182 D.J. Johnson .10 .02
❑ 183 Sean Gilbert .20 .07
❑ 184 Bryant Young .20 .07
❑ 185 Jeff Burris .10 .02
❑ 186 Floyd Turner .10 .02
❑ 187 Troy Vincent .10 .02
❑ 188 Willie McGinest .20 .07
❑ 189 James Hasty .10 .02
❑ 190 Jeff Blake RC 1.00 .40
❑ 191 Stevon Moore .10 .02
❑ 192 Ernest Givins .10 .02
❑ 193 Byron Bam Morris .10 .02
❑ 194 Ray Crockett .10 .02
❑ 195 Dale Carter .20 .07
❑ 196 Terry McDaniel .10 .02
❑ 197 Leslie O'Neal .20 .07
❑ 198 Cortez Kennedy .20 .07
❑ 199 Seth Joyner .10 .02
❑ 200 Emmitt Smith 2.50 1.00
❑ 201 Thomas Lewis .20 .07
❑ 202 Andy Harmon .10 .02
❑ 203 Ricky Ervins .10 .02
❑ 204 Fuad Reveiz .10 .02
❑ 205 John Thierry .10 .02
❑ 206 Bennie Blades .10 .02
❑ 207 LeShon Johnson .20 .07
❑ 208 Charles Wilson .10 .02
❑ 209 Joe Johnson .10 .02
❑ 210 Chuck Smith .10 .02
❑ 211 Roman Phifer .10 .02
❑ 212 Ken Norton Jr. .20 .07
❑ 213 Bucky Brooks .10 .02
❑ 214 Ray Buchanan .10 .02
❑ 215 Tim Bowens .10 .02
❑ 216 Vincent Brown .10 .02
❑ 217 Marcus Turner .10 .02
❑ 218 Derrick Fenner .10 .02
❑ 219 Antonio Langham .10 .02
❑ 220 Cody Carlson .10 .02
❑ 221 Greg Lloyd .20 .07
❑ 222 Steve Atwater .10 .02
❑ 223 Donnell Bennett .20 .07
❑ 224 Rocket Ismail .20 .07
❑ 225 John Carney .10 .02
❑ 226 Eugene Robinson .10 .02
❑ 227 Aeneas Williams .10 .02
❑ 228 Darrin Smith .10 .02
❑ 229 Phillippi Sparks .10 .02
❑ 230 Eric Allen .10 .02
❑ 231 Brian Mitchell .10 .02
❑ 232 David Palmer .20 .07
❑ 233 Mark Carrier DB .10 .02
❑ 234 Dave Krieg .10 .02
❑ 235 Robert Brooks .40 .15
❑ 236 Eric Curry .10 .02
❑ 237 Wayne Martin .10 .02
❑ 238 Craig Heyward .20 .07
❑ 239 Isaac Bruce .75 .30
❑ 240 Deion Sanders 1.00 .40
❑ 241 Steve Tasker .20 .07
❑ 242 Jim Harbaugh .20 .07
❑ 243 Aubrey Beavers .10 .02
❑ 244 Chris Slade .10 .02
❑ 245 Mo Lewis .10 .02
❑ 246 Alfred Williams .10 .02
❑ 247 Michael Dean Perry .10 .02
❑ 248 Marcus Robertson .10 .02
❑ 249 Kevin Greene .20 .07
❑ 250 Leonard Russell .10 .02
❑ 251 Greg Hill .20 .07
❑ 252 Rob Fredrickson .10 .02
❑ 253 Junior Seau .40 .15
❑ 254 Rick Tuten .10 .02
❑ 255 Garrison Hearst .40 .15
❑ 256 Russell Maryland .10 .02
❑ 257 Michael Brooks .10 .02
❑ 258 Bernard Williams .10 .02
❑ 259 Reggie Roby .10 .02
❑ 260 Dewayne Washington .20 .07
❑ 261 Raymont Harris .10 .02
❑ 262 Brett Perriman .20 .07
❑ 263 LeRoy Butler .10 .02
❑ 264 Santana Dotson .10 .02
❑ 265 Irv Smith .10 .02
❑ 266 Ron George .10 .02
❑ 267 Marquez Pope .10 .02
❑ 268 William Floyd .20 .07
❑ 269 Matt Darby .10 .02
❑ 270 Jeff Herrod .10 .02
❑ 271 Bernie Parmalee .20 .07
❑ 272 Leroy Thompson .10 .02
❑ 273 Ronnie Lott .20 .07
❑ 274 Steve Tovar .10 .02
❑ 275 Michael Jackson .20 .07
❑ 276 Al Smith .10 .02
❑ 277 Rod Woodson .20 .07
❑ 278 Glyn Milburn .10 .02
❑ 279 Kimble Anders .20 .07
❑ 280 Anthony Smith .10 .02
❑ 281 Andre Coleman .10 .02
❑ 282 Terry Wooden .10 .02
❑ 283 Mickey Washington .10 .02
❑ 284 Steve Beuerlein .20 .07
❑ 285 Mark Brunell 1.00 .40
❑ 286 Keith Goganious .10 .02
❑ 287 Desmond Howard .20 .07
❑ 288 Darren Carrington .10 .02
❑ 289 Derek Brown TE .10 .02
❑ 290 Reggie Cobb .10 .02
❑ 291 Jeff Lageman .10 .02
❑ 292 Lamar Lathon .10 .02
❑ 293 Sam Mills .20 .07
❑ 294 Carlton Bailey .10 .02
❑ 295 Mark Carrier WR .20 .07
❑ 296 Willie Green .20 .07
❑ 297 Frank Reich .10 .02
❑ 298 Don Beebe .10 .02
❑ 299 Tim McKyer .10 .02
❑ 300 Pete Metzelaars .10 .02
❑ A19 Joe Montana 15.00 6.00
❑ A103 Dan Marino 15.00 6.00
❑ P1 Joe Montana Promo 2.00 .75
❑ P2 Joe Montana PromoNumbered 19 2.00 .75
❑ P3 Marshall Faulk Promo 1.00 .40

1996 Upper Deck

❑ COMPLETE SET (300) 30.00 12.50
❑ 1 Keyshawn Johnson RC 1.25 .50
❑ 2 Kevin Hardy RC .50 .20
❑ 3 Simeon Rice RC 1.25 .50
❑ 4 Jonathan Ogden RC .50 .20
❑ 5 Cedric Jones RC .10 .02
❑ 6 Lawrence Phillips RC .50 .20
❑ 7 Tim Biakabutuka RC .50 .20
❑ 8 Terry Glenn RC 1.25 .50
❑ 9 Rickey Dudley RC .50 .20
❑ 10 Willie Anderson RC .10 .02
❑ 11 Alex Molden RC .10 .02
❑ 12 Regan Upshaw RC .10 .02
❑ 13 Walt Harris RC .10 .02
❑ 14 Eddie George RC 1.50 .60
❑ 15 John Mobley RC .10 .02
❑ 16 Duane Clemons RC .10 .02
❑ 17 Eddie Kennison RC .50 .20
❑ 18 Marvin Harrison RC 3.00 1.25
❑ 19 Daryl Gardener RC .10 .02
❑ 20 Leeland McElroy RC .25 .08
❑ 21 Eric Moulds RC 1.50 .60
❑ 22 Alex Van Dyke RC .25 .08
❑ 23 Mike Alstott RC 1.25 .50

Card	Player	Mint	NrMt
❑ 24	Jeff Lewis RC	.25	.08
❑ 25	Bobby Engram RC	.50	.20
❑ 26	Derrick Mayes RC	.50	.20
❑ 27	Karim Abdul-Jabbar RC	.50	.20
❑ 28	Bobby Hoying RC	.50	.20
❑ 29	Stepfret Williams RC	.25	.08
❑ 30	Chris Darkins RC	.10	.02
❑ 31	Stephen Davis RC	2.00	.75
❑ 32	Danny Kanell RC	.50	.20
❑ 33	Tony Brackens RC	.50	.20
❑ 34	Leslie O'Neal	.10	.02
❑ 35	Chris Doleman	.10	.02
❑ 36	Larry Brown	.10	.02
❑ 37	Ronnie Harmon	.10	.02
❑ 38	Chris Spielman	.10	.02
❑ 39	John Jurkovic	.10	.02
❑ 40	Shawn Jefferson	.10	.02
❑ 41	William Floyd	.25	.08
❑ 42	Eric Davis	.10	.02
❑ 43	Willie Clay	.10	.02
❑ 44	Marco Coleman	.10	.02
❑ 45	Lorenzo White	.10	.02
❑ 46	Neil O'Donnell	.25	.08
❑ 47	Natrone Means	.25	.08
❑ 48	Cornelius Bennett	.10	.02
❑ 49	Steve Walsh	.10	.02
❑ 50	Jerome Bettis	.50	.20
❑ 51	Boomer Esiason	.25	.08
❑ 52	Glyn Milburn	.10	.02
❑ 53	Kevin Greene	.25	.08
❑ 54	Seth Joyner	.10	.02
❑ 55	Jeff Graham	.10	.02
❑ 56	Darren Woodson	.25	.08
❑ 57	Dale Carter	.10	.02
❑ 58	Lorenzo Lynch	.10	.02
❑ 59	Tim Brown	.50	.20
❑ 60	Jerry Rice	1.25	.50
❑ 61	Garrison Hearst	.25	.08
❑ 62	Eric Metcalf	.10	.02
❑ 63	Leroy Hoard	.10	.02
❑ 64	Thurman Thomas	.50	.20
❑ 65	Sam Mills	.10	.02
❑ 66	Curtis Conway	.50	.20
❑ 67	Carl Pickens	.25	.08
❑ 68	Deion Sanders	.75	.30
❑ 69	Shannon Sharpe	.25	.08
❑ 70	Herman Moore	.25	.08
❑ 71	Robert Brooks	.50	.20
❑ 72	Rodney Thomas	.10	.02
❑ 73	Ken Dilger	.25	.08
❑ 74	Mark Brunell	.75	.30
❑ 75	Marcus Allen	.50	.20
❑ 76	Dan Marino	2.50	1.00
❑ 77	Robert Smith	.25	.08
❑ 78	Drew Bledsoe	.75	.30
❑ 79	Jim Everett	.10	.02
❑ 80	Rodney Hampton	.25	.08
❑ 81	Adrian Murrell	.25	.08
❑ 82	Daryl Hobbs RC	.10	.02
❑ 83	Ricky Watters	.25	.08
❑ 84	Yancey Thigpen	.25	.08
❑ 85	Roman Phifer	.10	.02
❑ 86	Tony Martin	.25	.08
❑ 87	Dana Stubblefield	.25	.08
❑ 88	Joey Galloway	.50	.20
❑ 89	Errict Rhett	.25	.08
❑ 90	Terry Allen	.25	.08
❑ 91	Aeneas Williams	.10	.02
❑ 92	Craig Heyward	.10	.02
❑ 93	Vinny Testaverde	.25	.08
❑ 94	Bryce Paup	.10	.02
❑ 95	Kerry Collins	.50	.20
❑ 96	Rashaan Salaam	.25	.08
❑ 97	Dan Wilkinson	.10	.02
❑ 98	Jay Novacek	.10	.02
❑ 99	John Elway	2.50	1.00
❑ 100	Bennie Blades	.10	.02
❑ 101	Edgar Bennett	.25	.08
❑ 102	Darryll Lewis	.10	.02
❑ 103	Marshall Faulk	.60	.25
❑ 104	Bryan Schwartz	.10	.02
❑ 105	Tamarick Vanover	.25	.08
❑ 106	Terry Kirby	.25	.08
❑ 107	John Randle	.25	.08
❑ 108	Ted Johnson RC	.50	.20
❑ 109	Mario Bates	.25	.08
❑ 110	Phillippi Sparks	.10	.02
❑ 111	Marvin Washington	.10	.02
❑ 112	Terry McDaniel	.10	.02
❑ 113	Bobby Taylor	.10	.02
❑ 114	Carnell Lake	.10	.02
❑ 115	Troy Drayton	.10	.02
❑ 116	Darren Bennett	.10	.02
❑ 117	J.J. Stokes	.50	.20
❑ 118	Rick Mirer	.25	.08
❑ 119	Jackie Harris	.10	.02
❑ 120	Ken Harvey	.10	.02
❑ 121	Rob Moore	.25	.08
❑ 122	Jeff George	.25	.08
❑ 123	Andre Rison	.25	.08
❑ 124	Darick Holmes	.10	.02
❑ 125	Tim McKyer	.10	.02
❑ 126	Alonzo Spellman	.10	.02
❑ 127	Jeff Blake	.50	.20
❑ 128	Kevin Williams	.10	.02
❑ 129	Anthony Miller	.25	.08
❑ 130	Barry Sanders	2.00	.75
❑ 131	Brett Favre	2.50	1.25
❑ 132	Steve McNair	1.00	.40
❑ 133	Jim Harbaugh	.25	.08
❑ 134	Desmond Howard	.25	.08
❑ 135	Steve Bono	.10	.02
❑ 136	Bernie Parmalee	.10	.02
❑ 137	Warren Moon	.25	.08
❑ 138	Curtis Martin	1.00	.40
❑ 139	Irv Smith	.10	.02
❑ 140	Thomas Lewis	.10	.02
❑ 141	Kyle Brady	.10	.02
❑ 142	Napoleon Kaufman	.50	.20
❑ 143	Mike Mamula	.10	.02
❑ 144	Erric Pegram	.10	.02
❑ 145	Isaac Bruce	.50	.20
❑ 146	Andre Coleman	.10	.02
❑ 147	Merton Hanks	.10	.02
❑ 148	Brian Blades	.10	.02
❑ 149	Hardy Nickerson	.10	.02
❑ 150	Michael Westbrook	.50	.20
❑ 151	Larry Centers	.25	.08
❑ 152	Morten Andersen	.10	.02
❑ 153	Michael Jackson	.25	.08
❑ 154	Bruce Smith	.25	.08
❑ 155	Derrick Moore	.10	.02
❑ 156	Mark Carrier DB	.10	.02
❑ 157	John Copeland	.10	.02
❑ 158	Emmitt Smith	2.00	.75
❑ 159	Jason Elam	.25	.08
❑ 160	Scott Mitchell	.25	.08
❑ 161	Mark Chmura	.25	.08
❑ 162	Blaine Bishop	.10	.02
❑ 163	Tony Bennett	.10	.02
❑ 164	Pete Mitchell	.25	.08
❑ 165	Dan Saleaumua	.10	.02
❑ 166	Pete Stoyanovich	.10	.02
❑ 167	Cris Carter	.50	.20
❑ 168	Vince Brisby	.10	.02
❑ 169	Wayne Martin	.10	.02
❑ 170	Tyrone Wheatley	.25	.08
❑ 171	Mo Lewis	.10	.02
❑ 172	Harvey Williams	.10	.02
❑ 173	Calvin Williams	.10	.02
❑ 174	Norm Johnson	.10	.02
❑ 175	Mark Rypien	.10	.02
❑ 176	Stan Humphries	.25	.08
❑ 177	Derek Loville	.10	.02
❑ 178	Christian Fauria	.10	.02
❑ 179	Warren Sapp	.10	.02
❑ 180	Henry Ellard	.10	.02
❑ 181	Jamir Miller	.10	.02
❑ 182	Jessie Tuggle	.10	.02
❑ 183	Stevon Moore	.10	.02
❑ 184	Jim Kelly	.50	.20
❑ 185	Mark Carrier	.10	.02
❑ 186	Chris Zorich	.10	.02
❑ 187	Harold Green	.10	.02
❑ 188	Chris Boniol	.10	.02
❑ 189	Allen Aldridge	.10	.02
❑ 190	Brett Perriman	.10	.02
❑ 191	Chris Jacke	.10	.02
❑ 192	Todd McNair	.10	.02
❑ 193	Floyd Turner	.10	.02
❑ 194	Jeff Lageman	.10	.02
❑ 195	Derrick Thomas	.50	.20
❑ 196	Eric Green	.10	.02
❑ 197	Orlando Thomas	.10	.02
❑ 198	Ben Coates	.25	.08
❑ 199	Tyrone Hughes	.10	.02
❑ 200	Dave Brown	.10	.02
❑ 201	Brad Baxter	.10	.02
❑ 202	Chester McGlockton	.10	.02
❑ 203	Rodney Peete	.10	.02
❑ 204	Willie Williams	.10	.02
❑ 205	Kevin Carter	.10	.02
❑ 206	Aaron Hayden RC	.10	.02
❑ 207	Steve Young	1.00	.40
❑ 208	Chris Warren	.25	.08
❑ 209	Eric Curry	.10	.02
❑ 210	Brian Mitchell	.10	.02
❑ 211	Frank Sanders	.25	.08
❑ 212	Terance Mathis UER	.10	.02
❑ 213	Eric Turner	.10	.02
❑ 214	Bill Brooks	.10	.02
❑ 215	John Kasay	.10	.02
❑ 216	Erik Kramer	.10	.02
❑ 217	Darnay Scott	.25	.08
❑ 218	Charles Haley	.25	.08
❑ 219	Steve Atwater	.10	.02
❑ 220	Jason Hanson	.10	.02
❑ 221	LeRoy Butler	.10	.02
❑ 222	Cris Dishman	.10	.02
❑ 223	Sean Dawkins	.10	.02
❑ 224	James O. Stewart	.25	.08
❑ 225	Greg Hill	.25	.08
❑ 226	Jeff Cross	.10	.02
❑ 227	Qadry Ismail	.25	.08
❑ 228	Dave Meggett	.10	.02
❑ 229	Eric Allen	.10	.02
❑ 230	Chris Calloway	.10	.02
❑ 231	Wayne Chrebet	.75	.30
❑ 232	Jeff Hostetler	.10	.02
❑ 233	Andy Harmon	.10	.02
❑ 234	Greg Lloyd	.25	.08
❑ 235	Toby Wright	.10	.02
❑ 236	Junior Seau	.50	.20
❑ 237	Bryant Young	.25	.08
❑ 238	Robert Blackmon	.10	.02
❑ 239	Trent Dilfer	.50	.20
❑ 240	Leslie Shepherd	.10	.02
❑ 241	Eric Swann	.10	.02
❑ 242	Bert Emanuel	.25	.08
❑ 243	Antonio Langham	.10	.02
❑ 244	Steve Christie	.10	.02
❑ 245	Tyrone Poole	.10	.02
❑ 246	Jim Flanigan	.10	.02
❑ 247	Tony McGee	.10	.02
❑ 248	Michael Irvin	.50	.20
❑ 249	Byron Bam Morris	.10	.02
❑ 250	Terrell Davis	1.00	.40
❑ 251	Johnnie Morton	.25	.08
❑ 252	Sean Jones	.10	.02
❑ 253	Chris Sanders	.25	.08
❑ 254	Quentin Coryatt	.10	.02
❑ 255	Willie Jackson	.25	.08
❑ 256	Mark Collins	.10	.02
❑ 257	Randal Hill	.10	.02
❑ 258	David Palmer	.10	.02
❑ 259	Will Moore	.10	.02
❑ 260	Michael Haynes	.10	.02
❑ 261	Mike Sherrard	.10	.02
❑ 262	William Thomas	.10	.02
❑ 263	Kordell Stewart	.50	.20
❑ 264	D'Marco Farr	.10	.02
❑ 265	Terrell Fletcher	.10	.02
❑ 266	Lee Woodall	.10	.02
❑ 267	Eugene Robinson	.10	.02
❑ 268	Alvin Harper	.10	.02
❑ 269	Gus Frerotte	.25	.08
❑ 270	Antonio Freeman	.50	.20
❑ 271	Clyde Simmons	.10	.02
❑ 272	Chuck Smith	.10	.02
❑ 273	Steve Tasker	.10	.02
❑ 274	Kevin Butler	.10	.02
❑ 275	Steve Tovar	.10	.02
❑ 276	Troy Aikman	1.25	.50
❑ 277	Aaron Craver	.10	.02
❑ 278	Henry Thomas	.10	.02
❑ 279	Craig Newsome	.10	.02
❑ 280	Brent Jones	.10	.02
❑ 281	Micheal Barrow	.10	.02
❑ 282	Ray Buchanan	.10	.02
❑ 283	Jimmy Smith	.50	.20
❑ 284	Neil Smith	.25	.08

Card		
❑ 285 O.J. McDuffie	.25	.08
❑ 286 Jake Reed	.25	.08
❑ 287 Ty Law	.50	.20
❑ 288 Torrance Small	.10	.02
❑ 289 Hugh Douglas	.25	.08
❑ 290 Pat Swilling	.10	.02
❑ 291 Charlie Garner	.25	.08
❑ 292 Ernie Mills	.10	.02
❑ 293 John Carney	.10	.02
❑ 294 Ken Norton	.10	.02
❑ 295 Cortez Kennedy	.10	.02
❑ 296 Derrick Brooks	.50	.20
❑ 297 Heath Shuler	.25	.08
❑ 298 Reggie White	.50	.20
❑ 299 Kimble Anders	.25	.08
❑ 300 Willie McGinest	.10	.02
❑ P96 Dan Marino Promo	2.00	.75
❑ MS1 Dan Marino	5.00	2.00
❑ MS2 Dan Marino	5.00	2.00
❑ P13 Dan Marino Promo	2.50	1.00

1997 Upper Deck

Card		
❑ COMPLETE SET (300)	40.00	20.00
❑ 1 Orlando Pace RC	.60	.25
❑ 2 Darrell Russell RC	.25	.08
❑ 3 Shawn Springs RC	.40	.15
❑ 4 Bryant Westbrook RC	.25	.08
❑ 5 Ike Hilliard RC	1.25	.50
❑ 6 Peter Boulware RC	.60	.25
❑ 7 Tom Knight RC	.25	.08
❑ 8 Yatil Green RC	.40	.15
❑ 9 Tony Gonzalez RC	2.50	1.00
❑ 10 Reidel Anthony RC	.60	.25
❑ 11 Warrick Dunn RC	2.50	1.00
❑ 12 Kenny Holmes RC	.60	.25
❑ 13 Jim Druckenmiller RC	.40	.15
❑ 14 James Farrior RC	.60	.25
❑ 15 David LaFleur RC	.25	.08
❑ 16 Antowain Smith RC	2.00	.75
❑ 17 Rae Carruth RC	.25	.08
❑ 18 Dwayne Rudd RC	.60	.25
❑ 19 Jake Plummer RC	4.00	1.50
❑ 20 Reinard Wilson RC	.40	.15
❑ 21 Byron Hanspard RC	.40	.15
❑ 22 Will Blackwell RC	.40	.15
❑ 23 Troy Davis RC	.40	.15
❑ 24 Corey Dillon RC	5.00	2.00
❑ 25 Joey Kent RC	.60	.25
❑ 26 Renaldo Wynn RC	.25	.08
❑ 27 Pat Barnes RC	.60	.25
❑ 28 Kevin Lockett RC	.40	.15
❑ 29 Darnell Autry RC	.40	.15
❑ 30 Walter Jones RC	.60	.25
❑ 31 Trevor Pryce RC	.60	.25
❑ 32 Dan Marino SRF	1.25	.50
❑ 33 Steve Young SRF	.25	.08
❑ 34 John Elway SRF	1.25	.50
❑ 35 Jerry Rice SRF	.60	.25
❑ 36 Tim Brown SRF	.60	.25
❑ 37 Deion Sanders SRF	.60	.25
❑ 38 Troy Aikman SRF	.60	.25
❑ 39 Barry Sanders SRF	1.00	.40
❑ 40 Emmitt Smith SRF	1.00	.40
❑ 41 Junior Seau SRF	.60	.25
❑ 42 Neil Smith	.40	.15
❑ 43 Brett Perriman	.25	.08
❑ 44 Jim Everett	.25	.08
❑ 45 Qadry Ismail	.40	.15
❑ 46 Dana Stubblefield	.25	.08
❑ 47 Bryant Young	.25	.08
❑ 48 Ken Norton Jr.	.25	.08
❑ 49 Terrell Owens	.75	.30
❑ 50 Jerry Rice	1.25	.50
❑ 51 Steve Young	.75	.30
❑ 52 Terry Kirby	.40	.15
❑ 53 Chris Doleman	.25	.08
❑ 54 Lee Woodall	.25	.08
❑ 55 Merton Hanks	.25	.08
❑ 56 Garrison Hearst	.40	.15
❑ 57 Rashaan Salaam	.25	.08
❑ 58 Raymont Harris	.25	.08
❑ 59 Curtis Conway	.40	.15
❑ 60 Bobby Engram	.40	.15
❑ 61 Bryan Cox	.25	.08
❑ 62 Walt Harris	.25	.08
❑ 63 Tyrone Hughes	.25	.08
❑ 64 Rick Mirer	.25	.08
❑ 65 Jeff Blake	.40	.15
❑ 66 Carl Pickens	.40	.15
❑ 67 Darnay Scott	.40	.15
❑ 68 Tony McGee	.25	.08
❑ 69 Ki-Jana Carter	.25	.08
❑ 70 Ashley Ambrose	.25	.08
❑ 71 Dan Wilkinson	.25	.08
❑ 72 Chris Spielman	.25	.08
❑ 73 Todd Collins	.25	.08
❑ 74 Andre Reed	.40	.15
❑ 75 Quinn Early	.25	.08
❑ 76 Eric Moulds	.60	.25
❑ 77 Darick Holmes	.25	.08
❑ 78 Thurman Thomas	.60	.25
❑ 79 Bruce Smith	.40	.15
❑ 80 Bryce Paup	.25	.08
❑ 81 John Elway	2.50	1.00
❑ 82 Terrell Davis	.75	.30
❑ 83 Anthony Miller	.25	.08
❑ 84 Shannon Sharpe	.40	.15
❑ 85 Alfred Williams	.25	.08
❑ 86 John Mobley	.25	.08
❑ 87 Tory James	.25	.08
❑ 88 Steve Atwater	.25	.08
❑ 89 Darrien Gordon	.25	.08
❑ 90 Mike Alstott	.60	.25
❑ 91 Errict Rhett	.25	.08
❑ 92 Trent Dilfer	.60	.25
❑ 93 Courtney Hawkins	.25	.08
❑ 94 Warren Sapp	.40	.15
❑ 95 Regan Upshaw	.25	.08
❑ 96 Hardy Nickerson	.25	.08
❑ 97 Donnie Abraham RC	.60	.25
❑ 98 Larry Centers	.40	.15
❑ 99 Aeneas Williams	.25	.08
❑ 100 Kent Graham	.25	.08
❑ 101 Rob Moore	.40	.15
❑ 102 Frank Sanders	.40	.15
❑ 103 Leeland McElroy	.25	.08
❑ 104 Eric Swann	.25	.08
❑ 105 Simeon Rice	.40	.15
❑ 106 Seth Joyner	.25	.08
❑ 107 Stan Humphries	.40	.15
❑ 108 Tony Martin	.40	.15
❑ 109 Charlie Jones	.25	.08
❑ 110 Andre Coleman UER 103	.25	.08
❑ 111 Terrell Fletcher	.25	.08
❑ 112 Junior Seau	.60	.25
❑ 113 Eric Metcalf	.40	.15
❑ 114 Chris Penn	.25	.08
❑ 115 Marcus Allen	.60	.25
❑ 116 Greg Hill	.25	.08
❑ 117 Tamarick Vanover	.40	.15
❑ 118 Lake Dawson	.25	.08
❑ 119 Derrick Thomas	.60	.25
❑ 120 Dale Carter	.25	.08
❑ 121 Elvis Grbac	.40	.15
❑ 122 Aaron Bailey	.25	.08
❑ 123 Jim Harbaugh	.40	.15
❑ 124 Marshall Faulk	.75	.30
❑ 125 Sean Dawkins	.25	.08
❑ 126 Marvin Harrison	.60	.25
❑ 127 Ken Dilger	.25	.08
❑ 128 Tony Bennett	.25	.08
❑ 129 Jeff Herrod	.25	.08
❑ 130 Chris Gardocki	.25	.08
❑ 131 Cary Blanchard	.25	.08
❑ 132 Troy Aikman	1.25	.50
❑ 133 Emmitt Smith	2.00	.75
❑ 134 Sherman Williams	.25	.08
❑ 135 Michael Irvin	.60	.25
❑ 136 Eric Bjornson	.25	.08
❑ 137 Herschel Walker	.40	.15
❑ 138 Tony Tolbert	.25	.08
❑ 139 Deion Sanders	.60	.25
❑ 140 Daryl Johnston	.40	.15
❑ 141 Dan Marino	2.50	1.00
❑ 142 O.J. McDuffie	.40	.15
❑ 143 Troy Drayton	.25	.08
❑ 144 Karim Abdul-Jabbar	.40	.15
❑ 145 Stanley Pritchett	.25	.08
❑ 146 Fred Barnett	.25	.08
❑ 147 Zach Thomas	.60	.25
❑ 148 Shawn Wooden RC	.25	.08
❑ 149 Ty Detmer	.40	.15
❑ 150 Derrick Witherspoon	.25	.08
❑ 151 Ricky Watters	.40	.15
❑ 152 Charlie Garner	.40	.15
❑ 153 Chris T. Jones	.25	.08
❑ 154 Irving Fryar	.40	.15
❑ 155 Mike Mamula	.25	.08
❑ 156 Troy Vincent	.25	.08
❑ 157 Bobby Taylor	.25	.08
❑ 158 Chris Boniol	.25	.08
❑ 159 Devin Bush	.25	.08
❑ 160 Bert Emanuel	.40	.15
❑ 161 Jamal Anderson	.60	.25
❑ 162 Terance Mathis	.40	.15
❑ 163 Cornelius Bennett	.25	.08
❑ 164 Ray Buchanan	.25	.08
❑ 165 Chris Chandler	.40	.15
❑ 166 Dave Brown	.25	.08
❑ 167 Danny Kanell	.25	.08
❑ 168 Rodney Hampton	.40	.15
❑ 169 Tyrone Wheatley	.40	.15
❑ 170 Amani Toomer	.40	.15
❑ 171 Chris Calloway	.25	.08
❑ 172 Thomas Lewis	.25	.08
❑ 173 Phillippi Sparks	.25	.08
❑ 174 Mark Brunell	.75	.30
❑ 175 Keenan McCardell	.40	.15
❑ 176 Willie Jackson	.25	.08
❑ 177 Jimmy Smith	.40	.15
❑ 178 Pete Mitchell	.25	.08
❑ 179 Natrone Means	.40	.15
❑ 180 Kevin Hardy	.25	.08
❑ 181 Tony Brackens	.25	.08
❑ 182 James O. Stewart	.40	.15
❑ 183 Wayne Chrebet	.60	.25
❑ 184 Keyshawn Johnson	.60	.25
❑ 185 Adrian Murrell	.40	.15
❑ 186 Neil O'Donnell	.40	.15
❑ 187 Hugh Douglas	.25	.08
❑ 188 Mo Lewis	.25	.08
❑ 189 Marvin Washington	.25	.08
❑ 190 Aaron Glenn	.25	.08
❑ 191 Barry Sanders	2.00	.75
❑ 192 Scott Mitchell	.40	.15
❑ 193 Herman Moore	.40	.15
❑ 194 Johnnie Morton	.40	.15
❑ 195 Glyn Milburn	.25	.08
❑ 196 Reggie Brown LB	.40	.15
❑ 197 Jason Hanson	.25	.08
❑ 198 Steve McNair	.75	.30
❑ 199 Eddie George	.60	.25
❑ 200 Ronnie Harmon	.25	.08
❑ 201 Chris Sanders	.25	.08
❑ 202 Willie Davis	.25	.08
❑ 203 Frank Wycheck	.25	.08
❑ 204 Darryll Lewis	.25	.08
❑ 205 Blaine Bishop	.25	.08
❑ 206 Robert Brooks	.40	.15
❑ 207 Brett Favre	2.50	1.25
❑ 208 Edgar Bennett	.40	.15
❑ 209 Dorsey Levens	.60	.25
❑ 210 Derrick Mayes	.40	.15
❑ 211 Antonio Freeman	.60	.25
❑ 212 Mark Chmura	.40	.15
❑ 213 Reggie White	.60	.25
❑ 214 Gilbert Brown	.40	.15
❑ 215 LeRoy Butler	.25	.08
❑ 216 Craig Newsome	.25	.08
❑ 217 Kerry Collins	.60	.25
❑ 218 Wesley Walls	.40	.15
❑ 219 Muhsin Muhammad	.40	.15
❑ 220 Anthony Johnson	.25	.08

❑ 221 Tim Biakabutuka	.40	.15
❑ 222 Kevin Greene	.40	.15
❑ 223 Sam Mills	.25	.08
❑ 224 John Kasay	.25	.08
❑ 225 Micheal Barrow	.25	.08
❑ 226 Drew Bledsoe	.75	.30
❑ 227 Curtis Martin	.75	.30
❑ 228 Terry Glenn	.60	.25
❑ 229 Ben Coates	.40	.15
❑ 230 Shawn Jefferson	.25	.08
❑ 231 Willie McGinest	.25	.08
❑ 232 Ted Johnson	.25	.08
❑ 233 Lawyer Milloy	.40	.15
❑ 234 Ty Law	.40	.15
❑ 235 Willie Clay	.25	.08
❑ 236 Tim Brown	.60	.25
❑ 237 Rickey Dudley	.40	.15
❑ 238 Napoleon Kaufman	.60	.25
❑ 239 Chester McGlockton	.25	.08
❑ 240 Rob Fredrickson	.25	.08
❑ 241 Terry McDaniel	.25	.08
❑ 242 Desmond Howard	.40	.15
❑ 243 Jeff George	.40	.15
❑ 244 Isaac Bruce	.60	.25
❑ 245 Tony Banks	.40	.15
❑ 246 Lawrence Phillips UER 247	.25	.08
❑ 247 Kevin Carter	.25	.08
❑ 248 Roman Phifer	.25	.08
❑ 249 Keith Lyle	.25	.08
❑ 250 Eddie Kennison	.40	.15
❑ 251 Craig Heyward	.25	.08
❑ 252 Vinny Testaverde	.40	.15
❑ 253 Derrick Alexander WR	.40	.15
❑ 254 Michael Jackson	.40	.15
❑ 255 Byron Bam Morris	.25	.08
❑ 256 Eric Green	.25	.08
❑ 257 Ray Lewis	1.00	.40
❑ 258 Antonio Langham	.25	.08
❑ 259 Michael McCrary	.25	.08
❑ 260 Gus Frerotte	.25	.08
❑ 261 Terry Allen	.60	.25
❑ 262 Brian Mitchell	.25	.08
❑ 263 Michael Westbrook	.40	.15
❑ 264 Sean Gilbert	.25	.08
❑ 265 Rich Owens	.25	.08
❑ 266 Ken Harvey	.25	.08
❑ 267 Jeff Hostetler	.25	.08
❑ 268 Michael Haynes	.25	.08
❑ 269 Mario Bates	.25	.08
❑ 270 Renaldo Turnbull UER 273	.25	.08
❑ 271 Ray Zellars	.25	.08
❑ 272 Joe Johnson	.25	.08
❑ 273 Eric Allen	.25	.08
❑ 274 Heath Shuler	.25	.08
❑ 275 Daryl Hobbs	.25	.08
❑ 276 John Friesz	.25	.08
❑ 277 Brian Blades	.25	.08
❑ 278 Joey Galloway	.40	.15
❑ 279 Chris Warren	.40	.15
❑ 280 Lamar Smith	.60	.25
❑ 281 Cortez Kennedy	.25	.08
❑ 282 Chad Brown	.25	.08
❑ 283 Warren Moon	.60	.25
❑ 284 Jerome Bettis	.60	.25
❑ 285 Charles Johnson	.40	.15
❑ 286 Kordell Stewart	.60	.25
❑ 287 Erric Pegram	.25	.08
❑ 288 Norm Johnson	.25	.08
❑ 289 Levon Kirkland	.25	.08
❑ 290 Greg Lloyd	.25	.08
❑ 291 Carnell Lake	.25	.08
❑ 292 Brad Johnson	.60	.25
❑ 293 Cris Carter	.60	.25
❑ 294 Jake Reed	.40	.15
❑ 295 Robert Smith	.40	.15
❑ 296 Derrick Alexander DE	.25	.08
❑ 297 John Randle	.40	.15
❑ 298 Dixon Edwards	.25	.08
❑ 299 Orlanda Thomas	.25	.08
❑ 300 Dewayne Washington	.25	.08

1998 Upper Deck

❑ COMPLETE SET (255)	200.00	75.00
❑ COMP.SET w/o SP's (213)	25.00	12.50
❑ 1 Peyton Manning RC	50.00	25.00
❑ 2 Ryan Leaf RC	5.00	2.00
❑ 3 Andre Wadsworth RC	3.00	1.25
❑ 4 Charles Woodson RC	6.00	2.50
❑ 5 Curtis Enis RC	2.50	1.00
❑ 6 Grant Wistrom RC	3.00	1.25
❑ 7 Greg Ellis RC	2.50	1.00
❑ 8 Fred Taylor RC	8.00	3.00
❑ 9 Duane Starks RC	2.50	1.00
❑ 10 Keith Brooking RC	5.00	2.00
❑ 11 Takeo Spikes RC	5.00	2.00
❑ 12 Jason Peter RC	2.50	1.00
❑ 13 Anthony Simmons RC	3.00	1.25
❑ 14 Kevin Dyson RC	5.00	2.00
❑ 15 Brian Simmons RC	3.00	1.25
❑ 16 Robert Edwards RC	3.00	1.25
❑ 17 Randy Moss RC	25.00	12.50
❑ 18 John Avery RC	3.00	1.25
❑ 19 Marcus Nash RC	2.50	1.00
❑ 20 Jerome Pathon RC	5.00	2.00
❑ 21 Jacquez Green RC	3.00	1.25
❑ 22 Robert Holcombe RC	3.00	1.25
❑ 23 Pat Johnson RC	3.00	1.25
❑ 24 Germane Crowell RC	3.00	1.25
❑ 25 Joe Jurevicius RC	5.00	2.00
❑ 26 Skip Hicks RC	3.00	1.25
❑ 27 Ahman Green RC	25.00	10.00
❑ 28 Brian Griese RC	10.00	4.00
❑ 29 Hines Ward RC	20.00	10.00
❑ 30 Tavian Banks RC	3.00	1.25
❑ 31 Tony Simmons RC	3.00	1.25
❑ 32 Victor Riley RC	2.50	1.00
❑ 33 Rashaan Shehee RC	3.00	1.25
❑ 34 R.W. McQuarters RC	3.00	1.25
❑ 35 Flozell Adams RC	2.50	1.00
❑ 36 Tra Thomas RC	2.50	1.00
❑ 37 Greg Favors RC	3.00	1.25
❑ 38 Jon Ritchie RC	3.00	1.25
❑ 39 Jesse Haynes RC	2.50	1.00
❑ 40 Ryan Sutter RC	2.50	1.00
❑ 41 Mo Collins RC	2.50	1.00
❑ 42 Tim Dwight RC	5.00	2.00
❑ 43 Chris Chandler	.40	.15
❑ 44 Byron Hanspard	.25	.08
❑ 45 Jessie Tuggle	.25	.08
❑ 46 Jamal Anderson	.60	.25
❑ 47 Terance Mathis	.40	.15
❑ 48 Morten Andersen	.25	.08
❑ 49 Jake Plummer	.60	.25
❑ 50 Mario Bates	.40	.15
❑ 51 Frank Sanders	.40	.15
❑ 52 Adrian Murrell	.40	.15
❑ 53 Simeon Rice	.40	.15
❑ 54 Aeneas Williams	.25	.08
❑ 55 Eric Swann UER	.25	.08
❑ 56 Jim Harbaugh	.40	.15
❑ 57 Michael Jackson	.25	.08
❑ 58 Peter Boulware	.25	.08
❑ 59 Errict Rhett	.40	.15
❑ 60 Jermaine Lewis	.40	.15
❑ 61 Eric Zeier	.40	.15
❑ 62 Rod Woodson	.40	.15
❑ 63 Rob Johnson	.60	.25
❑ 64 Antowain Smith	.60	.25
❑ 65 Bruce Smith	.40	.15
❑ 66 Eric Moulds	.60	.25
❑ 67 Andre Reed	.40	.15
❑ 68 Thurman Thomas	.60	.25
❑ 69 Lonnie Johnson	.25	.08
❑ 70 Kerry Collins	.40	.15
❑ 71 Kevin Greene	.40	.15
❑ 72 Fred Lane	.25	.08
❑ 73 Rae Carruth	.25	.08
❑ 74 Michael Bates	.25	.08
❑ 75 William Floyd	.25	.08
❑ 76 Sean Gilbert	.25	.08
❑ 77 Erik Kramer	.25	.08
❑ 78 Edgar Bennett	.25	.08
❑ 79 Curtis Conway	.40	.15
❑ 80 Darnell Autry	.25	.08
❑ 81 Ryan Wetnight RC	.25	.08
❑ 82 Walt Harris	.25	.08
❑ 83 Bobby Engram	.40	.15
❑ 84 Jeff Blake	.40	.15
❑ 85 Carl Pickens	.40	.15
❑ 86 Darnay Scott	.40	.15
❑ 87 Corey Dillon	.60	.25
❑ 88 Reinard Wilson	.25	.08
❑ 89 Ashley Ambrose	.25	.08
❑ 90 Troy Aikman	1.25	.50
❑ 91 Michael Irvin	.60	.25
❑ 92 Emmitt Smith	2.00	.75
❑ 93 Deion Sanders	.60	.25
❑ 94 David LaFleur	.25	.08
❑ 95 Chris Warren	.40	.15
❑ 96 Darren Woodson	.25	.08
❑ 97 John Elway	2.50	1.00
❑ 98 Terrell Davis	.60	.25
❑ 99 Rod Smith	.40	.15
❑ 100 Shannon Sharpe	.40	.15
❑ 101 Ed McCaffrey	.40	.15
❑ 102 Steve Atwater	.25	.08
❑ 103 John Mobley	.25	.08
❑ 104 Darrien Gordon	.25	.08
❑ 105 Barry Sanders	2.00	.75
❑ 106 Scott Mitchell	.40	.15
❑ 107 Herman Moore	.40	.15
❑ 108 Johnnie Morton	.40	.15
❑ 109 Robert Porcher	.25	.08
❑ 110 Bryant Westbrook	.25	.08
❑ 111 Tommy Vardell	.25	.08
❑ 112 Brett Favre	2.50	1.00
❑ 113 Dorsey Levens	.60	.25
❑ 114 Reggie White	.60	.25
❑ 115 Antonio Freeman	.60	.25
❑ 116 Robert Brooks	.40	.15
❑ 117 Mark Chmura	.40	.15
❑ 118 Derrick Mayes	.40	.15
❑ 119 Gilbert Brown	.25	.08
❑ 120 Marshall Faulk	.75	.30
❑ 121 Jeff Burris	.25	.08
❑ 122 Marvin Harrison	.60	.25
❑ 123 Quentin Coryatt	.25	.08
❑ 124 Ken Dilger	.25	.08
❑ 125 Zack Crockett	.25	.08
❑ 126 Mark Brunell	.60	.25
❑ 127 Bryce Paup	.25	.08
❑ 128 Tony Brackens	.25	.08
❑ 129 Renaldo Wynn	.25	.08
❑ 130 Keenan McCardell	.40	.15
❑ 131 Jimmy Smith	.40	.15
❑ 132 Kevin Hardy	.25	.08
❑ 133 Elvis Grbac	.40	.15
❑ 134 Tamarick Vanover	.25	.08
❑ 135 Chester McGlockton	.25	.08
❑ 136 Andre Rison	.40	.15
❑ 137 Derrick Alexander	.40	.15
❑ 138 Tony Gonzalez	.60	.25
❑ 139 Derrick Thomas	.60	.25
❑ 140 Dan Marino	2.50	1.00
❑ 141 Karim Abdul-Jabbar	.60	.25
❑ 142 O.J. McDuffie	.40	.15
❑ 143 Yatil Green	.25	.08
❑ 144 Charles Jordan	.25	.08
❑ 145 Brock Marion	.25	.08
❑ 146 Zach Thomas	.60	.25
❑ 147 Brad Johnson	.60	.25
❑ 148 Cris Carter	.60	.25
❑ 149 Jake Reed	.40	.15
❑ 150 Robert Smith	.60	.25
❑ 151 John Randle	.40	.15
❑ 152 Dwayne Rudd	.25	.08
❑ 153 Randall Cunningham	.60	.25
❑ 154 Drew Bledsoe	1.00	.40
❑ 155 Terry Glenn	.60	.25
❑ 156 Ben Coates	.40	.15
❑ 157 Willie Clay	.25	.08
❑ 158 Chris Slade	.25	.08
❑ 159 Derrick Cullors RC	.25	.08
❑ 160 Ty Law	.40	.15

❑ 161 Danny Wuerffel .40 .15
❑ 162 Andre Hastings .25 .08
❑ 163 Troy Davis .25 .08
❑ 164 Billy Joe Hobert .25 .08
❑ 165 Eric Guliford .25 .08
❑ 166 Mark Fields .25 .08
❑ 167 Alex Molden .25 .08
❑ 168 Danny Kanell .40 .15
❑ 169 Tiki Barber .60 .25
❑ 170 Charles Way .25 .08
❑ 171 Amani Toomer .40 .15
❑ 172 Michael Strahan .40 .15
❑ 173 Jessie Armstead .25 .08
❑ 174 Jason Sehorn .40 .15
❑ 175 Glenn Foley .40 .15
❑ 176 Curtis Martin .60 .25
❑ 177 Aaron Glenn .25 .08
❑ 178 Keyshawn Johnson .60 .25
❑ 179 James Farrior .25 .08
❑ 180 Wayne Chrebet .60 .25
❑ 181 Keith Byars .25 .08
❑ 182 Jeff George .40 .15
❑ 183 Napoleon Kaufman .60 .25
❑ 184 Tim Brown .60 .25
❑ 185 Darrell Russell .25 .08
❑ 186 Rickey Dudley .25 .08
❑ 187 James Jett .40 .15
❑ 188 Desmond Howard .40 .15
❑ 189 Bobby Hoying .40 .15
❑ 190 Charlie Garner .40 .15
❑ 191 Irving Fryar .40 .15
❑ 192 Chris T. Jones .25 .08
❑ 193 Mike Mamula .25 .08
❑ 194 Troy Vincent .25 .08
❑ 195 Kordell Stewart .60 .25
❑ 196 Jerome Bettis .60 .25
❑ 197 Will Blackwell .25 .08
❑ 198 Levon Kirkland .25 .08
❑ 199 Carnell Lake .25 .08
❑ 200 Charles Johnson .25 .08
❑ 201 Greg Lloyd .25 .08
❑ 202 Donnell Woolford .25 .08
❑ 203 Tony Banks .40 .15
❑ 204 Amp Lee .25 .08
❑ 205 Isaac Bruce .60 .25
❑ 206 Eddie Kennison .40 .15
❑ 207 Ryan McNeil .25 .08
❑ 208 Mike Jones .25 .08
❑ 209 Ernie Conwell .25 .08
❑ 210 Natrone Means .40 .15
❑ 211 Junior Seau .60 .25
❑ 212 Tony Martin .40 .15
❑ 213 Freddie Jones .25 .08
❑ 214 Bryan Still .25 .08
❑ 215 Rodney Harrison .40 .15
❑ 216 Steve Young .75 .30
❑ 217 Jerry Rice 1.25 .50
❑ 218 Garrison Hearst .60 .25
❑ 219 J.J. Stokes .40 .15
❑ 220 Ken Norton .25 .08
❑ 221 Greg Clark .25 .08
❑ 222 Terrell Owens .60 .25
❑ 223 Bryant Young .25 .08
❑ 224 Warren Moon .60 .25
❑ 225 Jon Kitna .60 .25
❑ 226 Ricky Watters .40 .15
❑ 227 Chad Brown .25 .08
❑ 228 Joey Galloway .40 .15
❑ 229 Shawn Springs .25 .08
❑ 230 Cortez Kennedy .25 .08
❑ 231 Trent Dilfer .60 .25
❑ 232 Warrick Dunn .60 .25
❑ 233 Mike Alstott .60 .25
❑ 234 Warren Sapp .40 .15
❑ 235 Bert Emanuel .40 .15
❑ 236 Reidel Anthony .40 .15
❑ 237 Hardy Nickerson .25 .08
❑ 238 Derrick Brooks .60 .25
❑ 239 Steve McNair .60 .25
❑ 240 Yancey Thigpen .25 .08
❑ 241 Anthony Dorsett .25 .08
❑ 242 Blaine Bishop .25 .08
❑ 243 Kenny Holmes .25 .08
❑ 244 Eddie George .60 .25
❑ 245 Chris Sanders .25 .08
❑ 246 Gus Frerotte .25 .08
❑ 247 Terry Allen .60 .25
❑ 248 Dana Stubblefield .25 .08
❑ 249 Michael Westbrook .40 .15
❑ 250 Darrell Green .40 .15
❑ 251 Brian Mitchell .25 .08
❑ 252 Ken Harvey .25 .08
❑ CL1 Troy Aikman CL .60 .25
❑ CL2 Dan Marino CL .75 .30
❑ CL3 Herman Moore CL .40 .15

1999 Upper Deck

❑ COMPLETE SET (270) 100.00 50.00
❑ COMP.SET w/o SP's (225) 25.00 12.50
❑ 1 Jake Plummer .50 .20
❑ 2 Adrian Murrell .50 .20
❑ 3 Rob Moore .50 .20
❑ 4 Larry Centers .30 .10
❑ 5 Simeon Rice .50 .20
❑ 6 Andre Wadsworth .30 .10
❑ 7 Frank Sanders .50 .20
❑ 8 Tim Dwight .75 .30
❑ 9 Ray Buchanan .30 .10
❑ 10 Chris Chandler .50 .20
❑ 11 Jamal Anderson .75 .30
❑ 12 O.J. Santiago .30 .10
❑ 13 Danny Kanell .30 .10
❑ 14 Terance Mathis .50 .20
❑ 15 Priest Holmes 1.25 .50
❑ 16 Tony Banks .50 .20
❑ 17 Ray Lewis .75 .30
❑ 18 Patrick Johnson .30 .10
❑ 19 Michael Jackson .30 .10
❑ 20 Michael McCrary .30 .10
❑ 21 Jermaine Lewis .50 .20
❑ 22 Eric Moulds .75 .30
❑ 23 Doug Flutie .75 .30
❑ 24 Antowain Smith .75 .30
❑ 25 Rob Johnson .50 .20
❑ 26 Bruce Smith .50 .20
❑ 27 Andre Reed .50 .20
❑ 28 Thurman Thomas .50 .20
❑ 29 Fred Lane .30 .10
❑ 30 Wesley Walls .50 .20
❑ 31 Tim Biakabutuka .50 .20
❑ 32 Kevin Greene .30 .10
❑ 33 Steve Beuerlein .30 .10
❑ 34 Muhsin Muhammad .50 .20
❑ 35 Rae Carruth .30 .10
❑ 36 Bobby Engram .50 .20
❑ 37 Curtis Enis .30 .10
❑ 38 Edgar Bennett .30 .10
❑ 39 Erik Kramer .30 .10
❑ 40 Steve Stenstrom .30 .10
❑ 41 Alonzo Mayes .30 .10
❑ 42 Curtis Conway .50 .20
❑ 43 Tony McGee .30 .10
❑ 44 Darnay Scott .30 .10
❑ 45 Jeff Blake .50 .20
❑ 46 Corey Dillon .75 .30
❑ 47 Ki-Jana Carter .30 .10
❑ 48 Takeo Spikes .30 .10
❑ 49 Carl Pickens .50 .20
❑ 50 Ty Detmer .50 .20
❑ 51 Leslie Shepherd .30 .10
❑ 52 Terry Kirby .30 .10
❑ 53 Marquez Pope .30 .10
❑ 54 Antonio Langham .30 .10
❑ 55 Jamir Miller .30 .10
❑ 56 Derrick Alexander DT .30 .10
❑ 57 Troy Aikman 1.50 .60
❑ 58 Rocket Ismail .50 .20
❑ 59 Emmitt Smith 1.50 .60
❑ 60 Michael Irvin .50 .20
❑ 61 David LaFleur .30 .10
❑ 62 Chris Warren .30 .10
❑ 63 Deion Sanders .75 .30
❑ 64 Greg Ellis .30 .10
❑ 65 John Elway 2.50 1.00
❑ 66 Bubby Brister .30 .10
❑ 67 Terrell Davis .75 .30
❑ 68 Ed McCaffrey .50 .20
❑ 69 John Mobley .30 .10
❑ 70 Bill Romanowski .30 .10
❑ 71 Rod Smith .50 .20
❑ 72 Shannon Sharpe .50 .20
❑ 73 Charlie Batch .75 .30
❑ 74 Germane Crowell .30 .10
❑ 75 Johnnie Morton .30 .10
❑ 76 Barry Sanders 2.50 1.00
❑ 77 Robert Porcher .30 .10
❑ 78 Stephen Boyd .30 .10
❑ 79 Herman Moore .50 .20
❑ 80 Brett Favre 2.50 1.00
❑ 81 Mark Chmura .30 .10
❑ 82 Antonio Freeman .75 .30
❑ 83 Robert Brooks .50 .20
❑ 84 Vonnie Holliday .30 .10
❑ 85 Bill Schroeder .75 .30
❑ 86 Dorsey Levens .75 .30
❑ 87 Santana Dotson .30 .10
❑ 88 Peyton Manning 2.50 1.00
❑ 89 Jerome Pathon .30 .10
❑ 90 Marvin Harrison .75 .30
❑ 91 Ellis Johnson .30 .10
❑ 92 Ken Dilger .30 .10
❑ 93 E.G. Green .30 .10
❑ 94 Jeff Burris .30 .10
❑ 95 Mark Brunell .75 .30
❑ 96 Fred Taylor .75 .30
❑ 97 Jimmy Smith .50 .20
❑ 98 James Stewart .50 .20
❑ 99 Kyle Brady .30 .10
❑ 100 Dave Thomas RC .30 .10
❑ 101 Keenan McCardell .50 .20
❑ 102 Elvis Grbac .50 .20
❑ 103 Tony Gonzalez .75 .30
❑ 104 Andre Rison .50 .20
❑ 105 Donnell Bennett .30 .10
❑ 106 Derrick Thomas .75 .30
❑ 107 Warren Moon .75 .30
❑ 108 Derrick Alexander WR .50 .20
❑ 109 Dan Marino 2.50 1.00
❑ 110 O.J. McDuffie .50 .20
❑ 111 Karim Abdul-Jabbar .50 .20
❑ 112 John Avery .30 .10
❑ 113 Sam Madison .30 .10
❑ 114 Jason Taylor .30 .10
❑ 115 Zach Thomas .75 .30
❑ 116 Randall Cunningham .75 .30
❑ 117 Randy Moss 2.00 .75
❑ 118 Cris Carter .75 .30
❑ 119 Jake Reed .50 .20
❑ 120 Matthew Hatchette .30 .10
❑ 121 John Randle .50 .20
❑ 122 Robert Smith .75 .30
❑ 123 Drew Bledsoe 1.00 .40
❑ 124 Ben Coates .50 .20
❑ 125 Terry Glenn .75 .30
❑ 126 Ty Law .50 .20
❑ 127 Tony Simmons .30 .10
❑ 128 Ted Johnson .30 .10
❑ 129 Tony Carter .30 .10
❑ 130 Willie McGinest .30 .10
❑ 131 Danny Wuerffel .30 .10
❑ 132 Cameron Cleeland .30 .10
❑ 133 Eddie Kennison .50 .20
❑ 134 Joe Johnson .30 .10
❑ 135 Andre Hastings .30 .10
❑ 136 La'Roi Glover RC .75 .30
❑ 137 Kent Graham .30 .10
❑ 138 Tiki Barber .75 .30
❑ 139 Gary Brown .30 .10
❑ 140 Ike Hilliard .30 .10
❑ 141 Jason Sehorn .30 .10
❑ 142 Michael Strahan .50 .20
❑ 143 Amani Toomer .30 .10
❑ 144 Kerry Collins .50 .20

❑ 145	Vinny Testaverde	.50	.20
❑ 146	Wayne Chrebet	.50	.20
❑ 147	Curtis Martin	.75	.30
❑ 148	Mo Lewis	.30	.10
❑ 149	Aaron Glenn	.30	.10
❑ 150	Steve Atwater	.30	.10
❑ 151	Keyshawn Johnson	.75	.30
❑ 152	James Farrior	.30	.10
❑ 153	Rich Gannon	.75	.30
❑ 154	Tim Brown	.75	.30
❑ 155	Darrell Russell	.30	.10
❑ 156	Rickey Dudley	.30	.10
❑ 157	Charles Woodson	.75	.30
❑ 158	James Jett	.50	.20
❑ 159	Napoleon Kaufman	.75	.30
❑ 160	Duce Staley	.75	.30
❑ 161	Doug Pederson	.30	.10
❑ 162	Bobby Hoying	.50	.20
❑ 163	Koy Detmer	.30	.10
❑ 164	Kevin Turner	.30	.10
❑ 165	Charles Johnson	.30	.10
❑ 166	Mike Mamula	.30	.10
❑ 167	Jerome Bettis	.75	.30
❑ 168	Courtney Hawkins	.30	.10
❑ 169	Will Blackwell	.30	.10
❑ 170	Kordell Stewart	.50	.20
❑ 171	Richard Huntley	.50	.20
❑ 172	Levon Kirkland	.30	.10
❑ 173	Hines Ward	.75	.30
❑ 174	Trent Green	.75	.30
❑ 175	Marshall Faulk	1.00	.40
❑ 176	Az-Zahir Hakim	.30	.10
❑ 177	Amp Lee	.30	.10
❑ 178	Robert Holcombe	.30	.10
❑ 179	Isaac Bruce	.75	.30
❑ 180	Kevin Carter	.30	.10
❑ 181	Jim Harbaugh	.50	.20
❑ 182	Junior Seau	.75	.30
❑ 183	Natrone Means	.50	.20
❑ 184	Ryan Leaf	.75	.30
❑ 185	Charlie Jones	.30	.10
❑ 186	Rodney Harrison	.30	.10
❑ 187	Mikhael Ricks	.30	.10
❑ 188	Steve Young	1.00	.40
❑ 189	Terrell Owens	.75	.30
❑ 190	Jerry Rice	1.50	.60
❑ 191	J.J. Stokes	.50	.20
❑ 192	Irv Smith	.30	.10
❑ 193	Bryant Young	.30	.10
❑ 194	Garrison Hearst	.50	.20
❑ 195	Jon Kitna	.75	.30
❑ 196	Ahman Green	.75	.30
❑ 197	Joey Galloway	.50	.20
❑ 198	Ricky Watters	.50	.20
❑ 199	Chad Brown	.30	.10
❑ 200	Shawn Springs	.30	.10
❑ 201	Mike Pritchard	.30	.10
❑ 202	Trent Dilfer	.50	.20
❑ 203	Reidel Anthony	.50	.20
❑ 204	Bert Emanuel	.50	.20
❑ 205	Warrick Dunn	.75	.30
❑ 206	Jacquez Green	.30	.10
❑ 207	Hardy Nickerson	.30	.10
❑ 208	Mike Alstott	.75	.30
❑ 209	Eddie George	.75	.30
❑ 210	Steve McNair	.75	.30
❑ 211	Kevin Dyson	.50	.20
❑ 212	Frank Wycheck	.30	.10
❑ 213	Jackie Harris	.30	.10
❑ 214	Blaine Bishop	.30	.10
❑ 215	Yancey Thigpen	.30	.10
❑ 216	Brad Johnson	.75	.30
❑ 217	Rodney Peete	.30	.10
❑ 218	Michael Westbrook	.50	.20
❑ 219	Skip Hicks	.30	.10
❑ 220	Brian Mitchell	.30	.10
❑ 221	Dan Wilkinson	.30	.10
❑ 222	Dana Stubblefield	.30	.10
❑ 223	Kordell Stewart CL	.50	.20
❑ 224	Fred Taylor CL	.75	.30
❑ 225	Warrick Dunn CL	.50	.20
❑ 226	Champ Bailey RC	3.00	1.25
❑ 227	Chris McAlister RC	1.50	.60
❑ 228	Jevon Kearse RC	4.00	1.50
❑ 229	Ebenezer Ekuban RC	1.50	.60
❑ 230	Chris Claiborne RC	1.00	.40
❑ 231	Andy Katzenmoyer RC	1.50	.60
❑ 232	Tim Couch RC	2.00	.75
❑ 233	Daunte Culpepper RC	10.00	4.00
❑ 234	Akili Smith RC	1.50	.60
❑ 235	Donovan McNabb RC	12.00	5.00
❑ 236	Sean Bennett RC	1.00	.40
❑ 237	Brock Huard RC	2.00	.75
❑ 238	Cade McNown RC	1.50	.60
❑ 239	Shaun King RC	1.50	.60
❑ 240	Joe Germaine RC	1.50	.60
❑ 241	Ricky Williams RC	5.00	2.00
❑ 242	Edgerrin James RC	10.00	4.00
❑ 243	Sedrick Irvin RC	1.00	.40
❑ 244	Kevin Faulk RC	2.00	.75
❑ 245	Rob Konrad RC	2.00	.75
❑ 246	James Johnson RC	1.50	.60
❑ 247	Amos Zereoue RC	2.00	.75
❑ 248	Torry Holt RC	6.00	2.50
❑ 249	D'Wayne Bates RC	1.50	.60
❑ 250	David Boston RC	2.00	.75
❑ 251	Dameane Douglas RC	2.00	.75
❑ 252	Troy Edwards RC	1.50	.60
❑ 253	Kevin Johnson RC	2.00	.75
❑ 254	Peerless Price RC	2.00	.75
❑ 255	Antoine Winfield RC	1.50	.60
❑ 256	Mike Cloud RC	1.50	.60
❑ 257	Joe Montgomery RC	1.50	.60
❑ 258	Jermaine Fazande RC	1.50	.60
❑ 259	Scott Covington RC	2.00	.75
❑ 260	Aaron Brooks RC	5.00	2.00
❑ 261	Patrick Kerney RC	2.00	.75
❑ 262	Cecil Collins RC	1.00	.40
❑ 263	Chris Greisen RC	1.50	.60
❑ 264	Craig Yeast RC	1.50	.60
❑ 265	Karsten Bailey RC	1.50	.60
❑ 266	Reginald Kelly RC	1.00	.40
❑ 267	Al Wilson RC	1.50	.60
❑ 268	Jeff Paulk RC	1.00	.40
❑ 269	Jim Kleinsasser RC	2.00	.75
❑ 270	Darrin Chiaverini RC	1.50	.60

2000 Upper Deck

❑	COMPLETE SET (1-270)	120.00	60.00
❑	COMP.SET w/o SPs (222)	30.00	12.50
❑ 1	Jake Plummer	.50	.20
❑ 2	Michael Pittman	.30	.10
❑ 3	Rob Moore	.50	.20
❑ 4	David Boston	.75	.30
❑ 5	Frank Sanders	.50	.20
❑ 6	Aeneas Williams	.30	.10
❑ 7	Kwamie Lassiter	.30	.10
❑ 8	Rob Fredrickson	.30	.10
❑ 9	Tim Dwight	.75	.30
❑ 10	Chris Chandler	.50	.20
❑ 11	Jamal Anderson	.75	.30
❑ 12	Shawn Jefferson	.30	.10
❑ 13	Ken Oxendine	.30	.10
❑ 14	Terance Mathis	.50	.20
❑ 15	Bob Christian	.30	.10
❑ 16	Qadry Ismail	.50	.20
❑ 17	Jermaine Lewis	.50	.20
❑ 18	Rod Woodson	.50	.20
❑ 19	Michael McCrary	.30	.10
❑ 20	Tony Banks	.50	.20
❑ 21	Peter Boulware	.30	.10
❑ 22	Shannon Sharpe	.50	.20
❑ 23	Peerless Price	.50	.20
❑ 24	Rob Johnson	.50	.20
❑ 25	Eric Moulds	.75	.30
❑ 26	Doug Flutie	.75	.30
❑ 27	Jay Riemersma	.30	.10
❑ 28	Antowain Smith	.50	.20
❑ 29	Jonathan Linton	.30	.10
❑ 30	Muhsin Muhammad	.50	.20
❑ 31	Patrick Jeffers	.75	.30
❑ 32	Steve Beuerlein	.50	.20
❑ 33	Natrone Means	.30	.10
❑ 34	Tim Biakabutuka	.50	.20
❑ 35	Michael Bates	.30	.10
❑ 36	Chuck Smith	.30	.10
❑ 37	Wesley Walls	.30	.10
❑ 38	Cade McNown	.30	.10
❑ 39	Curtis Enis	.30	.10
❑ 40	Marcus Robinson	.75	.30
❑ 41	Eddie Kennison	.50	.20
❑ 42	Bobby Engram	.50	.20
❑ 43	Glyn Milburn	.30	.10
❑ 44	Marty Booker	.50	.20
❑ 45	Akili Smith	.30	.10
❑ 46	Corey Dillon	.75	.30
❑ 47	Darnay Scott	.50	.20
❑ 48	Tremain Mack	.30	.10
❑ 49	Damon Griffin	.30	.10
❑ 50	Takeo Spikes	.30	.10
❑ 51	Tony McGee	.30	.10
❑ 52	Tim Couch	.50	.20
❑ 53	Kevin Johnson	.75	.30
❑ 54	Darrin Chiaverini	.30	.10
❑ 55	Jamir Miller	.30	.10
❑ 56	Errict Rhett	.50	.20
❑ 57	Terry Kirby	.30	.10
❑ 58	Marc Edwards	.30	.10
❑ 59	Troy Aikman	1.50	.60
❑ 60	Emmitt Smith	1.50	.60
❑ 61	Rocket Ismail	.50	.20
❑ 62	Jason Tucker	.30	.10
❑ 63	Dexter Coakley	.30	.10
❑ 64	Joey Galloway	.50	.20
❑ 65	Wane McGarity	.30	.10
❑ 66	Terrell Davis	.75	.30
❑ 67	Olandis Gary	.75	.30
❑ 68	Brian Griese	.75	.30
❑ 69	Gus Frerotte	.30	.10
❑ 70	Byron Chamberlain	.30	.10
❑ 71	Ed McCaffrey	.75	.30
❑ 72	Rod Smith	.50	.20
❑ 73	Al Wilson	.30	.10
❑ 74	Charlie Batch	.75	.30
❑ 75	Germane Crowell	.30	.10
❑ 76	Sedrick Irvin	.30	.10
❑ 77	Johnnie Morton	.50	.20
❑ 78	Robert Porcher	.30	.10
❑ 79	Herman Moore	.50	.20
❑ 80	James Stewart	.50	.20
❑ 81	Brett Favre	2.50	1.00
❑ 82	Antonio Freeman	.75	.30
❑ 83	Bill Schroeder	.50	.20
❑ 84	Dorsey Levens	.50	.20
❑ 85	Corey Bradford	.50	.20
❑ 86	De'Mond Parker	.30	.10
❑ 87	Vonnie Holliday	.30	.10
❑ 88	Peyton Manning	2.00	.75
❑ 89	Edgerrin James	1.25	.50
❑ 90	Marvin Harrison	.75	.30
❑ 91	Ken Dilger	.30	.10
❑ 92	Terrence Wilkins	.30	.10
❑ 93	Marcus Pollard	.30	.10
❑ 94	Fred Lane	.30	.10
❑ 95	Mark Brunell	.75	.30
❑ 96	Fred Taylor	.75	.30
❑ 97	Jimmy Smith	.50	.20
❑ 98	Keenan McCardell	.50	.20
❑ 99	Carnell Lake	.30	.10
❑ 100	Tavian Banks	.30	.10
❑ 101	Kyle Brady	.30	.10
❑ 102	Hardy Nickerson	.30	.10
❑ 103	Elvis Grbac	.50	.20
❑ 104	Tony Gonzalez	.50	.20
❑ 105	Derrick Alexander WR	.50	.20
❑ 106	Donnell Bennett	.30	.10
❑ 107	Mike Cloud	.30	.10
❑ 108	Donnie Edwards	.30	.10
❑ 109	Jay Fiedler	.75	.30
❑ 110	James Johnson	.30	.10
❑ 111	Tony Martin	.50	.20
❑ 112	Damon Huard	.75	.30
❑ 113	O.J. McDuffie	.50	.20

❑ 114 Thurman Thomas .50 .20
❑ 115 Zach Thomas .75 .30
❑ 116 Oronde Gadsden .50 .20
❑ 117 Randy Moss 1.50 .60
❑ 118 Robert Smith .75 .30
❑ 119 Cris Carter .75 .30
❑ 120 Matthew Hatchette .30 .10
❑ 121 Daunte Culpepper 1.00 .40
❑ 122 Leroy Hoard .30 .10
❑ 123 Drew Bledsoe 1.00 .40
❑ 124 Terry Glenn .50 .20
❑ 125 Troy Brown .50 .20
❑ 126 Kevin Faulk .30 .10
❑ 127 Lawyer Milloy .50 .20
❑ 128 Ricky Williams .75 .30
❑ 129 Keith Poole .30 .10
❑ 130 Jake Reed .50 .20
❑ 131 Cam Cleeland .30 .10
❑ 132 Jeff Blake .50 .20
❑ 133 Andrew Glover .30 .10
❑ 134 Kerry Collins .50 .20
❑ 135 Amani Toomer .50 .20
❑ 136 Joe Montgomery .30 .10
❑ 137 Ike Hilliard .50 .20
❑ 138 Tiki Barber .75 .30
❑ 139 Pete Mitchell .30 .10
❑ 140 Ray Lucas .50 .20
❑ 141 Mo Lewis .30 .10
❑ 142 Curtis Martin .75 .30
❑ 143 Vinny Testaverde .50 .20
❑ 144 Wayne Chrebet .50 .20
❑ 145 Dedric Ward .30 .10
❑ 146 Tim Brown .75 .30
❑ 147 Rich Gannon .75 .30
❑ 148 Tyrone Wheatley .50 .20
❑ 149 Napoleon Kaufman .50 .20
❑ 150 Charles Woodson .50 .20
❑ 151 Darrell Russell .30 .10
❑ 152 James Jett .30 .10
❑ 153 Rickey Dudley .30 .10
❑ 154 Jon Ritchie .30 .10
❑ 155 Duce Staley .75 .30
❑ 156 Donovan McNabb 1.25 .50
❑ 157 Torrance Small .30 .10
❑ 158 Allen Rossum .30 .10
❑ 159 Mike Mamula .30 .10
❑ 160 Na Brown .30 .10
❑ 161 Charles Johnson .50 .20
❑ 162 Kent Graham .30 .10
❑ 163 Troy Edwards .30 .10
❑ 164 Jerome Bettis .75 .30
❑ 165 Hines Ward .75 .30
❑ 166 Kordell Stewart .50 .20
❑ 167 Levon Kirkland .30 .10
❑ 168 Richard Huntley .30 .10
❑ 169 Marshall Faulk 1.00 .40
❑ 170 Kurt Warner 1.50 .60
❑ 171 Torry Holt .75 .30
❑ 172 Isaac Bruce .75 .30
❑ 173 Kevin Carter .30 .10
❑ 174 Az-Zahir Hakim .50 .20
❑ 175 Ricky Proehl .30 .10
❑ 176 Jermaine Fazande .30 .10
❑ 177 Curtis Conway .50 .20
❑ 178 Freddie Jones .30 .10
❑ 179 Junior Seau .75 .30
❑ 180 Jeff Graham .30 .10
❑ 181 Jim Harbaugh .50 .20
❑ 182 Rodney Harrison .30 .10
❑ 183 Steve Young 1.00 .40
❑ 184 Jerry Rice 1.50 .60
❑ 185 Charlie Garner .50 .20
❑ 186 Terrell Owens .75 .30
❑ 187 Jeff Garcia .75 .30
❑ 188 Fred Beasley .30 .10
❑ 189 J.J. Stokes .50 .20
❑ 190 Ricky Watters .50 .20
❑ 191 Jon Kitna .75 .30
❑ 192 Derrick Mayes .50 .20
❑ 193 Sean Dawkins .30 .10
❑ 194 Charlie Rogers .30 .10
❑ 195 Mike Pritchard .30 .10
❑ 196 Cortez Kennedy .30 .10
❑ 197 Christian Fauria .30 .10
❑ 198 Warrick Dunn .75 .30
❑ 199 Shaun King .30 .10
❑ 200 Mike Alstott .75 .30
❑ 201 Warren Sapp .50 .20
❑ 202 Jacquez Green .30 .10
❑ 203 Reidel Anthony .30 .10
❑ 204 Dave Moore .30 .10
❑ 205 Keyshawn Johnson .75 .30
❑ 206 Eddie George .75 .30
❑ 207 Steve McNair .75 .30
❑ 208 Kevin Dyson .50 .20
❑ 209 Jevon Kearse .75 .30
❑ 210 Yancey Thigpen .30 .10
❑ 211 Frank Wycheck .30 .10
❑ 212 Isaac Byrd .30 .10
❑ 213 Neil O'Donnell .30 .10
❑ 214 Brad Johnson .75 .30
❑ 215 Stephen Davis .75 .30
❑ 216 Michael Westbrook .50 .20
❑ 217 Albert Connell .30 .10
❑ 218 Brian Mitchell .30 .10
❑ 219 Bruce Smith .50 .20
❑ 220 Stephen Alexander .30 .10
❑ 221 Jeff George .50 .20
❑ 222 Adrian Murrell .30 .10
❑ 223 Courtney Brown RC 4.00 1.50
❑ 224 John Engelberger RC 2.50 1.00
❑ 225 Deltha O'Neal RC 4.00 1.50
❑ 226 Corey Simon RC 4.00 1.50
❑ 227 R.Jay Soward RC 2.50 1.00
❑ 228 Marc Bulger RC 8.00 3.00
❑ 229 Raynoch Thompson RC 2.50 1.00
❑ 230 Deon Grant RC 2.50 1.00
❑ 231 Darrell Jackson RC 8.00 3.00
❑ 232 Chris Cole RC 2.50 1.00
❑ 233 Trevor Gaylor RC 2.50 1.00
❑ 234 John Abraham RC 4.00 1.50
❑ 235 Chris Redman RC 2.50 1.00
❑ 236 Joe Hamilton RC 2.50 1.00
❑ 237 Chad Pennington RC 10.00 4.00
❑ 238 Tee Martin RC 4.00 1.50
❑ 239 Giovanni Carmazzi RC 2.00 .75
❑ 240 Tim Rattay RC 4.00 1.50
❑ 241 Ron Dayne RC 4.00 1.50
❑ 242 Shaun Alexander RC 20.00 7.50
❑ 243 Thomas Jones RC 6.00 2.50
❑ 244 Reuben Droughns RC 4.00 1.50
❑ 245 Jamal Lewis RC 10.00 4.00
❑ 246 Michael Wiley RC 2.50 1.00
❑ 247 J.R. Redmond RC 2.50 1.00
❑ 248 Travis Prentice RC 2.50 1.00
❑ 249 Todd Husak RC 4.00 1.50
❑ 250 Trung Canidate RC 2.50 1.00
❑ 251 Brian Urlacher RC 15.00 6.00
❑ 252 Anthony Becht RC 4.00 1.50
❑ 253 Bubba Franks RC 4.00 1.50
❑ 254 Tom Brady RC 40.00 15.00
❑ 255 Peter Warrick RC 4.00 1.50
❑ 256 Plaxico Burress RC 8.00 3.00
❑ 257 Sylvester Morris RC 2.50 1.00
❑ 258 Dez White RC 4.00 1.50
❑ 259 Travis Taylor RC 4.00 1.50
❑ 260 Todd Pinkston RC 4.00 1.50
❑ 261 Dennis Northcutt RC 4.00 1.50
❑ 262 Jerry Porter RC 5.00 2.00
❑ 263 Laveranues Coles RC 5.00 2.00
❑ 264 Danny Farmer RC 2.50 1.00
❑ 265 Curtis Keaton RC 2.50 1.00
❑ 266 Sherrod Gideon RC 2.00 .75
❑ 267 Ron Dugans RC 2.00 .75
❑ 268 Steve McNair CL .50 .20
❑ 269 Jake Plummer CL .50 .20
❑ 270 Antonio Freeman CL .50 .20

2001 Upper Deck

❑ COMPLETE SET (280) 300.00 150.00
❑ COMP.SET w/o SP's (180) 25.00 10.00
❑ 1 Jake Plummer .50 .20
❑ 2 David Boston .75 .30
❑ 3 Thomas Jones .50 .20
❑ 4 Frank Sanders .30 .10
❑ 5 Eric Zeier .30 .10
❑ 6 Jamal Anderson .75 .30
❑ 7 Chris Chandler .50 .20
❑ 8 Shawn Jefferson .30 .10
❑ 9 Darrick Vaughn .30 .10
❑ 10 Terance Mathis .50 .20
❑ 11 Jamal Lewis 1.25 .50
❑ 12 Shannon Sharpe .50 .20
❑ 13 Elvis Grbac .50 .20 
❑ 14 Ray Lewis .75 .30
❑ 15 Qadry Ismail .50 .20
❑ 16 Chris Redman .30 .10
❑ 17 Rob Johnson .75 .30
❑ 18 Eric Moulds .50 .20
❑ 19 Sammy Morris .30 .10
❑ 20 Shawn Bryson .30 .10
❑ 21 Jeremy McDaniel .30 .10
❑ 22 Muhsin Muhammad .50 .20
❑ 23 Brad Hoover .30 .10
❑ 24 Tim Biakabutuka .50 .20
❑ 25 Steve Beuerlein .30 .10
❑ 26 Jeff Lewis .30 .10
❑ 27 Wesley Walls .30 .10
❑ 28 Cade McNown .30 .10
❑ 29 James Allen .50 .20
❑ 30 Marcus Robinson .75 .30
❑ 31 Brian Urlacher 1.25 .50
❑ 32 Bobby Engram .30 .10
❑ 33 Peter Warrick .75 .30
❑ 34 Corey Dillon .75 .30
❑ 35 Akili Smith .30 .10
❑ 36 Danny Farmer .30 .10
❑ 37 Ron Dugans .30 .10
❑ 38 Jon Kitna .75 .30
❑ 39 Tim Couch .50 .20
❑ 40 Kevin Johnson .50 .20
❑ 41 Travis Prentice .30 .10
❑ 42 Spergon Wynn .30 .10
❑ 43 Errict Rhett .30 .10
❑ 44 Dennis Northcutt .50 .20
❑ 45 Courtney Brown .50 .20
❑ 46 Tony Banks .30 .10
❑ 47 Emmitt Smith 1.50 .60
❑ 48 Joey Galloway .50 .20
❑ 49 Rocket Ismail .50 .20
❑ 50 Randall Cunningham .75 .30
❑ 51 James McKnight .50 .20
❑ 52 Terrell Davis .75 .30
❑ 53 Mike Anderson .75 .30
❑ 54 Brian Griese .75 .30
❑ 55 Rod Smith .50 .20
❑ 56 Ed McCaffrey .75 .30
❑ 57 Eddie Kennison .50 .20
❑ 58 Olandis Gary .50 .20
❑ 59 Charlie Batch .75 .30
❑ 60 Germane Crowell .30 .10
❑ 61 James O. Stewart .50 .20
❑ 62 Johnnie Morton .50 .20
❑ 63 Brett Favre 2.50 1.00
❑ 64 Antonio Freeman .75 .30
❑ 65 Dorsey Levens .50 .20
❑ 66 Ahman Green .75 .30
❑ 67 Bill Schroeder .50 .20
❑ 68 Peyton Manning 2.00 .75
❑ 69 Edgerrin James 1.00 .40
❑ 70 Marvin Harrison .75 .30
❑ 71 Jerome Pathon .50 .20
❑ 72 Ken Dilger .30 .10
❑ 73 Mark Brunell .75 .30
❑ 74 Fred Taylor .75 .30
❑ 75 Jimmy Smith .50 .20
❑ 76 Keenan McCardell .30 .10
❑ 77 R.Jay Soward .30 .10
❑ 78 Todd Collins .30 .10
❑ 79 Tony Gonzalez .50 .20
❑ 80 Derrick Alexander .50 .20
❑ 81 Tony Richardson .30 .10
❑ 82 Sylvester Morris .30 .10
❑ 83 Oronde Gadsden .50 .20

❑ 84	Lamar Smith	.50	.20
❑ 85	Jay Fiedler	.75	.30
❑ 86	Jason Taylor	.30	.10
❑ 87	Ray Lucas	.30	.10
❑ 88	O.J. McDuffie	.30	.10
❑ 89	Randy Moss	1.50	.60
❑ 90	Cris Carter	.75	.30
❑ 91	Daunte Culpepper	.75	.30
❑ 92	Moe Williams	.50	.20
❑ 93	Troy Walters	.30	.10
❑ 94	Drew Bledsoe	1.00	.40
❑ 95	Terry Glenn	.50	.20
❑ 96	Kevin Faulk	.50	.20
❑ 97	J.R. Redmond	.30	.10
❑ 98	Troy Brown	.50	.20
❑ 99	Ricky Williams	.75	.30
❑ 100	Jeff Blake	.50	.20
❑ 101	Joe Horn	.50	.20
❑ 102	Albert Connell	.30	.10
❑ 103	Aaron Brooks	.75	.30
❑ 104	Chad Morton	.30	.10
❑ 105	Kerry Collins	.50	.20
❑ 106	Amani Toomer	.50	.20
❑ 107	Ron Dayne	.75	.30
❑ 108	Tiki Barber	.75	.30
❑ 109	Ike Hilliard	.50	.20
❑ 110	Ron Dixon	.30	.10
❑ 111	Jason Sehorn	.30	.10
❑ 112	Vinny Testaverde	.50	.20
❑ 113	Wayne Chrebet	.50	.20
❑ 114	Curtis Martin	.75	.30
❑ 115	Dedric Ward	.30	.10
❑ 116	Laveranues Coles	.75	.30
❑ 117	Windrell Hayes	.30	.10
❑ 118	Tim Brown	.75	.30
❑ 119	Rich Gannon	.75	.30
❑ 120	Tyrone Wheatley	.50	.20
❑ 121	Charlie Garner	.50	.20
❑ 122	Andre Rison	.50	.20
❑ 123	Charles Woodson	.50	.20
❑ 124	Trace Armstrong	.30	.10
❑ 125	Duce Staley	.75	.30
❑ 126	Donovan McNabb	1.00	.40
❑ 127	Darnell Autry	.30	.10
❑ 128	Charles Johnson	.30	.10
❑ 129	Torrance Small	.30	.10
❑ 130	Kordell Stewart	.50	.20
❑ 131	Jerome Bettis	.75	.30
❑ 132	Plaxico Burress	.75	.30
❑ 133	Bobby Shaw	.30	.10
❑ 134	Troy Edwards	.30	.10
❑ 135	Marshall Faulk	1.00	.40
❑ 136	Kurt Warner	1.50	.60
❑ 137	Isaac Bruce	.75	.30
❑ 138	Torry Holt	.75	.30
❑ 139	Trent Green	.75	.30
❑ 140	Az-Zahir Hakim	.30	.10
❑ 141	Junior Seau	.75	.30
❑ 142	Curtis Conway	.50	.20
❑ 143	Doug Flutie	.75	.30
❑ 144	Jeff Graham	.30	.10
❑ 145	Freddie Jones	.30	.10
❑ 146	Marcellus Wiley	.30	.10
❑ 147	Jeff Garcia	.75	.30
❑ 148	Jerry Rice	1.50	.60
❑ 149	Fred Beasley	.30	.10
❑ 150	Terrell Owens	.75	.30
❑ 151	J.J. Stokes	.50	.20
❑ 152	Garrison Hearst	.50	.20
❑ 153	Ricky Watters	.30	.10
❑ 154	Shaun Alexander	1.00	.40
❑ 155	Matt Hasselbeck	.50	.20
❑ 156	Brock Huard	.30	.10
❑ 157	Darrell Jackson	.75	.30
❑ 158	John Randle	.30	.10
❑ 159	Warrick Dunn	.75	.30
❑ 160	Shaun King	.30	.10
❑ 161	Ryan Leaf	.50	.20
❑ 162	Mike Alstott	.75	.30
❑ 163	Jacquez Green	.30	.10
❑ 164	Brad Johnson	.75	.30
❑ 165	Keyshawn Johnson	.75	.30
❑ 166	Eddie George	.75	.30
❑ 167	Steve McNair	.75	.30
❑ 168	Neil O'Donnell	.30	.10
❑ 169	Derrick Mason	.50	.20
❑ 170	Frank Wycheck	.30	.10
❑ 171	Kevin Dyson	.50	.20
❑ 172	Jevon Kearse	.50	.20
❑ 173	Jeff George	.50	.20
❑ 174	Stephen Davis	.75	.30
❑ 175	Larry Centers	.30	.10
❑ 176	Michael Westbrook	.50	.20
❑ 177	Stephen Alexander	.50	.20
❑ 178	Ron Dayne	.75	.30
❑ 179	Donovan McNabb	1.00	.40
❑ 180	Jimmy Smith	.50	.20
❑ 181	Adam Archuleta RC	5.00	2.00
❑ 182	A.J. Feeley RC	5.00	2.00
❑ 183	Alex Bannister RC	3.00	1.25
❑ 184	Alge Crumpler RC	6.00	2.50
❑ 185	Andre Carter RC	5.00	2.00
❑ 186	Andre Dyson RC	2.00	.75
❑ 187	Anthony Thomas RC	5.00	2.00
❑ 188	Arther Love RC	2.00	.75
❑ 189	Bobby Newcombe RC	3.00	1.25
❑ 190	Brandon Spoon RC	5.00	2.00
❑ 191	Carlos Polk RC	2.00	.75
❑ 192	Casey Hampton RC	5.00	2.00
❑ 193	Cedrick Wilson RC	5.00	2.00
❑ 194	Chad Johnson RC	12.00	5.00
❑ 195	Chris Chambers RC	8.00	3.00
❑ 196	Chris Taylor RC	3.00	1.25
❑ 197	Chris Weinke RC	5.00	2.00
❑ 198	Correll Buckhalter RC	6.00	2.50
❑ 199	Damione Lewis RC	3.00	1.25
❑ 200	Dan Alexander RC	5.00	2.00
❑ 201	Dan Morgan RC	5.00	2.00
❑ 202	Willie Middlebrooks RC	3.00	1.25
❑ 203	David Terrell RC	5.00	2.00
❑ 204	Derrick Gibson RC	3.00	1.25
❑ 205	Deuce McAllister RC	10.00	4.00
❑ 206	Drew Brees RC	20.00	10.00
❑ 207	Edgerton Hartwell RC	2.00	.75
❑ 208	Fred Smoot RC	5.00	2.00
❑ 209	Freddie Mitchell RC	5.00	2.00
❑ 210	Gary Baxter RC	3.00	1.25
❑ 211	Gerard Warren RC	5.00	2.00
❑ 212	Hakim Akbar RC	2.00	.75
❑ 213	Heath Evans RC	3.00	1.25
❑ 214	Jabari Holloway RC	3.00	1.25
❑ 215	Jamal Reynolds RC	5.00	2.00
❑ 216	Jamar Fletcher RC	3.00	1.25
❑ 217	James Jackson RC	5.00	2.00
❑ 218	Jamie Winborn RC	3.00	1.25
❑ 219	Jesse Palmer RC	5.00	2.00
❑ 220	Josh Booty RC	5.00	2.00
❑ 221	Josh Heupel RC	5.00	2.00
❑ 222	Justin Smith RC	5.00	2.00
❑ 223	Karon Riley RC	2.00	.75
❑ 224	Ken Lucas RC	3.00	1.25
❑ 225	Kenyatta Walker RC	2.00	.75
❑ 226	Ken-Yon Rambo RC	3.00	1.25
❑ 227	Kevan Barlow RC	5.00	2.00
❑ 228	Kevin Kasper RC	5.00	2.00
❑ 229	Koren Robinson RC	5.00	2.00
❑ 230	LaDainian Tomlinson RC	60.00	30.00
❑ 231	LaMont Jordan RC	10.00	4.00
❑ 232	Leonard Davis RC	3.00	1.25
❑ 233	Marcus Stroud RC	5.00	2.00
❑ 234	Marques Tuiasosopo RC	5.00	2.00
❑ 235	Snoop Minnis RC	3.00	1.25
❑ 236	Michael Bennett RC	5.00	2.00
❑ 237	Michael Stone RC	2.00	.75
❑ 238	Mike McMahon RC	5.00	2.00
❑ 239	Michael Vick RC	25.00	12.50
❑ 240	Moran Norris RC	2.00	.75
❑ 241	Morlon Greenwood RC	3.00	1.25
❑ 242	Nate Clements RC	5.00	2.00
❑ 243	Orlando Huff RC	2.00	.75
❑ 244	Quincy Morgan RC	5.00	2.00
❑ 245	Reggie Wayne RC	10.00	4.00
❑ 246	Richard Seymour RC	5.00	2.00
❑ 247	Robert Ferguson RC	5.00	2.00
❑ 248	Rod Gardner RC	5.00	2.00
❑ 249	Rudi Johnson RC	10.00	4.00
❑ 250	Sage Rosenfels RC	5.00	2.00
❑ 251	Santana Moss RC	8.00	3.00
❑ 252	Scotty Anderson RC	3.00	1.25
❑ 253	Sedrick Hodge RC	2.00	.75
❑ 254	Shaun Rogers RC	5.00	2.00
❑ 255	Steve Hutchinson RC	3.00	1.25
❑ 256	T.J. Houshmandzadeh RC	6.00	2.50
❑ 257	Tay Cody RC	2.00	.75
❑ 258	George Layne RC	3.00	1.25
❑ 259	Todd Heap RC	5.00	2.00
❑ 260	Tommy Polley RC	5.00	2.00
❑ 261	Tony Dixon RC	3.00	1.25
❑ 262	Brian Allen RC	2.00	.75
❑ 263	Torrance Marshall RC	5.00	2.00
❑ 264	Travis Henry RC	8.00	3.00
❑ 265	Travis Minor RC	3.00	1.25
❑ 266	Vinny Sutherland RC	3.00	1.25
❑ 267	Will Allen RC	3.00	1.25
❑ 268	Derrick Blaylock RC	5.00	2.00
❑ 269	Zeke Moreno RC	5.00	2.00
❑ 270	Chris Barnes RC	3.00	1.25
❑ 271	Dee Brown RC	5.00	2.00
❑ 272	Reggie White RC	3.00	1.25
❑ 273	Derek Combs RC	3.00	1.25
❑ 274	Steve Smith RC	12.00	6.00
❑ 275	John Capel RC	3.00	1.25
❑ 276	Justin McCareins RC	5.00	2.00
❑ 277	Damerien McCants RC	3.00	1.25
❑ 278	Eddie Berlin RC	3.00	1.25
❑ 279	Francis St. Paul RC	3.00	1.25
❑ 280	Quincy Carter RC	5.00	2.00

2002 Upper Deck

❑	COMP.SET w/o SP's (180)	25.00	10.00
❑ 1	Jake Plummer	.50	.20
❑ 2	Marcel Shipp	.75	.30
❑ 3	David Boston	.75	.30
❑ 4	Arnold Jackson	.30	.10
❑ 5	Frank Sanders	.30	.10
❑ 6	Freddie Jones	.30	.10
❑ 7	Michael Vick	2.50	1.00
❑ 8	Jamal Anderson	.50	.20
❑ 9	Warrick Dunn	.75	.30
❑ 10	Maurice Smith	.30	.10
❑ 11	Shawn Jefferson	.30	.10
❑ 12	Chris Redman	.30	.10
❑ 13	Jeff Blake	.30	.10
❑ 14	Jamal Lewis	.75	.30
❑ 15	Travis Taylor	.50	.20
❑ 16	Ray Lewis	.75	.30
❑ 17	Chris McAlister	.30	.10
❑ 18	Drew Bledsoe	1.00	.40
❑ 19	Travis Henry	.75	.30
❑ 20	Larry Centers	.30	.10
❑ 21	Eric Moulds	.50	.20
❑ 22	Reggie Germany	.30	.10
❑ 23	Peerless Price	.50	.20
❑ 24	Chris Weinke	.50	.20
❑ 25	Lamar Smith	.50	.20
❑ 26	Nick Goings	.30	.10
❑ 27	Muhsin Muhammad	.50	.20
❑ 28	Isaac Byrd	.30	.10
❑ 29	Wesley Walls	.30	.10
❑ 30	Jim Miller	.30	.10
❑ 31	Anthony Thomas	.50	.20
❑ 32	Dez White	.30	.10
❑ 33	David Terrell	.75	.30
❑ 34	Marty Booker	.50	.20
❑ 35	Brian Urlacher	1.25	.50
❑ 36	Jon Kitna	.50	.20
❑ 37	Corey Dillon	.50	.20
❑ 38	Peter Warrick	.50	.20
❑ 39	Darnay Scott	.30	.10
❑ 40	Chad Johnson	.75	.30
❑ 41	Tim Couch	.50	.20
❑ 42	James Jackson	.30	.10
❑ 43	JaJuan Dawson	.30	.10

No.	Card		
44	Kevin Johnson	.50	.20
45	Quincy Morgan	.30	.10
46	Courtney Brown	.50	.20
47	Quincy Carter	.50	.20
48	Emmitt Smith	2.00	.75
49	Joey Galloway	.50	.20
50	Rocket Ismail	.50	.20
51	Ken-Yon Rambo	.30	.10
52	Brian Griese	.75	.30
53	Terrell Davis	.75	.30
54	Mike Anderson	.75	.30
55	Shannon Sharpe	.50	.20
56	Ed McCaffrey	.75	.30
57	Rod Smith	.50	.20
58	Mike McMahon	.75	.30
59	James Stewart	.50	.20
60	Az-Zahir Hakim	.30	.10
61	Desmond Howard	.30	.10
62	Germane Crowell	.30	.10
63	Brett Favre	2.00	.75
64	Ahman Green	.75	.30
65	Antonio Freeman	.75	.30
66	Terry Glenn	.50	.20
67	Kabeer Gbaja-Biamila	.50	.20
68	Kent Graham	.30	.10
69	James Allen	.50	.20
70	Corey Bradford	.30	.10
71	Jermaine Lewis	.30	.10
72	Jamie Sharper	.30	.10
73	Peyton Manning	1.50	.60
74	Edgerrin James	1.00	.40
75	Dominic Rhodes	.50	.20
76	Marvin Harrison	.75	.30
77	Qadry Ismail	.50	.20
78	Mark Brunell	.75	.30
79	Fred Taylor	.75	.30
80	Stacey Mack	.30	.10
81	Jimmy Smith	.50	.20
82	Keenan McCardell	.30	.10
83	Trent Green	.50	.20
84	Priest Holmes	1.00	.40
85	Derrick Alexander	.50	.20
86	Johnnie Morton	.50	.20
87	Snoop Minnis	.30	.10
88	Tony Gonzalez	.50	.20
89	Jay Fiedler	.50	.20
90	Ricky Williams	2.50	1.00
91	Chris Chambers	.75	.30
92	Oronde Gadsden	.30	.10
93	Zach Thomas	.75	.30
94	Daunte Culpepper	.75	.30
95	Michael Bennett	.50	.20
96	Randy Moss	1.50	.60
97	Sean Dawkins	.30	.10
98	Tom Brady	2.00	.75
99	Antowain Smith	.50	.20
100	David Patten	.30	.10
101	Troy Brown	.50	.20
102	Adam Vinatieri	.75	.30
103	Aaron Brooks	.75	.30
104	Deuce McAllister	1.00	.40
105	Jake Reed	.50	.20
106	Jerome Pathon	.50	.20
107	Joe Horn	.50	.20
108	Kyle Turley	.30	.10
109	Kerry Collins	.50	.20
110	Ron Dayne	.50	.20
111	Tiki Barber	.75	.30
112	Amani Toomer	.50	.20
113	Ike Hilliard	.50	.20
114	Michael Strahan	.50	.20
115	Vinny Testaverde	.50	.20
116	Chad Pennington	1.00	.40
117	Curtis Martin	.75	.30
118	Santana Moss	.75	.30
119	Laveranues Coles	.50	.20
120	Wayne Chrebet	.50	.20
121	Rich Gannon	.75	.30
122	Charlie Garner	.50	.20
123	Jerry Rice	1.50	.60
124	Tim Brown	.75	.30
125	Charles Woodson	.50	.20
126	Donovan McNabb	1.00	.40
127	Duce Staley	.75	.30
128	Correll Buckhalter	.50	.20
129	Freddie Mitchell	.50	.20
130	James Thrash	.50	.20
131	Todd Pinkston	.50	.20
132	Kordell Stewart	.50	.20
133	Jerome Bettis	.75	.30
134	Chris Fuamatu-Ma'afala	.30	.10
135	Hines Ward	.75	.30
136	Plaxico Burress	.50	.20
137	Kendrell Bell	.75	.30
138	Doug Flutie	.75	.30
139	Drew Brees	.75	.30
140	LaDainian Tomlinson	1.25	.50
141	Curtis Conway	.30	.10
142	Tim Dwight	.50	.20
143	Junior Seau	.75	.30
144	Jeff Garcia	.75	.30
145	Garrison Hearst	.50	.20
146	Kevan Barlow	.50	.20
147	Terrell Owens	.75	.30
148	J.J. Stokes	.50	.20
149	Trent Dilfer	.50	.20
150	Shaun Alexander	1.00	.40
151	Ricky Watters	.50	.20
152	Bobby Engram	.30	.10
153	Koren Robinson	.50	.20
154	Kurt Warner	.75	.30
155	Marshall Faulk	.75	.30
156	Isaac Bruce	.75	.30
157	Ricky Proehl	.30	.10
158	Terrence Wilkins	.30	.10
159	Torry Holt	.75	.30
160	Brad Johnson	.50	.20
161	Shaun King	.30	.10
162	Rob Johnson	.50	.20
163	Mike Alstott	.75	.30
164	Michael Pittman	.30	.10
165	Keyshawn Johnson	.75	.30
166	Steve McNair	.75	.30
167	Eddie George	.75	.30
168	Derrick Mason	.50	.20
169	Kevin Dyson	.50	.20
170	Frank Wycheck	.30	.10
171	Jevon Kearse	.50	.20
172	Danny Wuerffel	.50	.20
173	Stephen Davis	.50	.20
174	Michael Westbrook	.30	.10
175	Rod Gardner	.50	.20
176	Champ Bailey	.50	.20
177	Darrell Green	.30	.10
178	Kurt Warner CL	.50	.20
179	Brett Favre CL	1.00	.40
180	Randy Moss CL	.75	.30
181	David Boston SS	4.00	1.50
182	Jake Plummer SS	2.50	1.00
183	Michael Vick SS	12.00	5.00
184	Drew Bledsoe SS	5.00	2.00
185	Anthony Thomas SS	2.50	1.00
186	Tim Couch SS	2.50	1.00
187	Emmitt Smith SS	10.00	4.00
188	Ahman Green SS	4.00	1.50
189	Brett Favre SS	10.00	4.00
190	Edgerrin James SS	5.00	2.00
191	Peyton Manning SS	8.00	3.00
192	Mark Brunell SS	4.00	1.50
193	Daunte Culpepper SS	4.00	1.50
194	Randy Moss SS	8.00	3.00
195	Tom Brady SS	10.00	4.00
196	Aaron Brooks SS	4.00	1.50
197	Ricky Williams SS	4.00	1.50
198	Curtis Martin SS	4.00	1.50
199	Jerry Rice SS	8.00	3.00
200	Donovan McNabb SS	5.00	2.00
201	Jerome Bettis SS	4.00	1.50
202	Kordell Stewart SS	2.50	1.00
203	LaDainian Tomlinson SS	6.00	2.50
204	Jeff Garcia SS	4.00	1.50
205	Terrell Owens SS	4.00	1.50
206	Shaun Alexander SS	5.00	2.00
207	Kurt Warner SS	4.00	1.50
208	Marshall Faulk SS	4.00	1.50
209	Keyshawn Johnson SS	4.00	1.50
210	Steve McNair SS	4.00	1.50
211	Damien Anderson RC	5.00	2.00
212	Jason McAddley RC	5.00	2.00
213	Josh McCown RC	8.00	3.00
214	Josh Scobey RC	4.00	1.50
215	Preston Parsons RC	3.00	1.25
216	Dusty Bonner RC	3.00	1.25
217	Kahlil Hill RC	5.00	2.00
218	Kurt Kittner RC	5.00	2.00
219	T.J. Duckett RC	8.00	3.00
220	Chester Taylor RC	6.00	2.50
221	Kalimba Edwards RC	6.00	2.50
223	Ron Johnson RC	5.00	2.00
224	Tellis Redmon RC	5.00	2.00
225	Wes Pate RC	3.00	1.25
226	David Priestley RC	5.00	2.00
227	Josh Reed RC	6.00	2.50
228	Mike Williams RC	5.00	2.00
229	Ryan Denney RC	5.00	2.00
230	DeShaun Foster RC	6.00	2.50
231	Julius Peppers RC	12.00	5.00
232	Randy Fasani RC	5.00	2.00
233	Adrian Peterson RC	6.00	2.50
234	Alex Brown RC	6.00	2.50
235	Gavin Hoffman RC	3.00	1.25
236	Levi Jones RC	5.00	2.00
237	Andra Davis RC	5.00	2.00
238	Andre Davis RC	5.00	2.00
239	William Green RC	6.00	2.50
240	Antonio Bryant RC	6.00	2.50
241	Chad Hutchinson RC	5.00	2.00
242	Roy Williams RC	15.00	6.00
243	Woody Dantzler RC	5.00	2.00
244	Ashley Lelie RC	12.00	5.00
245	Clinton Portis RC	20.00	7.50
246	Lamont Thompson RC	5.00	2.00
247	James Mungro RC	6.00	2.50
248	Joey Harrington RC	10.00	4.00
249	Luke Staley RC	5.00	2.00
250	Craig Nall RC	6.00	2.50
251	Javon Walker RC	12.00	5.00
252	Najeh Davenport RC	6.00	2.50
253	David Carr RC	15.00	6.00
254	Saleem Rasheed RC	6.00	2.50
255	Mike Rumph RC	6.00	2.50
256	Jabar Gaffney RC	6.00	2.50
257	Jonathan Wells RC	6.00	2.50
258	Dwight Freeney RC	10.00	4.00
259	Larry Tripplett RC	3.00	1.25
260	David Garrard RC	6.00	2.50
261	John Henderson RC	6.00	2.50
262	Ryan Sims RC	6.00	2.50
263	Leonard Henry RC	5.00	2.00
264	Brian Allen RC	5.00	2.00
265	Atrews Bell RC	3.00	1.25
266	Bryant McKinnie RC	5.00	2.00
267	Kelly Campbell RC	5.00	2.00
268	Raonall Smith RC	5.00	2.00
269	Antwoine Womack RC	5.00	2.00
270	Daniel Graham RC	6.00	2.50
271	Deion Branch RC	12.00	5.00
272	Sam Simmons RC	3.00	1.25
273	Rohan Davey RC	6.00	2.50
274	Charles Grant RC	6.00	2.50
275	Derrick Lewis RC	3.00	1.25
276	Donte Stallworth RC	12.00	5.00
277	J.T. O'Sullivan RC	5.00	2.00
278	Keyuo Craver RC	5.00	2.00
279	Ricky Williams RC	5.00	2.00
280	Bryan Thomas RC	5.00	2.00
281	Jeremy Shockey RC	20.00	7.50
282	Tim Carter RC	5.00	2.00
283	Larry Ned RC	2.50	1.00
284	Napoleon Harris RC	4.00	1.50
285	Phillip Buchanon RC	6.00	2.50
286	Ronald Curry RC	6.00	2.50
287	Brian Westbrook RC	10.00	4.00
288	Freddie Milons RC	5.00	2.00
289	Lito Sheppard RC	6.00	2.50
290	Antwaan Randle El RC	10.00	4.00
291	Lee Mays RC	2.50	1.00
292	Daryl Jones RC	5.00	2.00
293	Justin Peelle RC	3.00	1.25
294	Quentin Jammer RC	4.00	1.50
295	Reche Caldwell RC	6.00	2.50
296	Seth Burford RC	5.00	2.00
297	Terry Charles RC	5.00	2.00
298	Brandon Doman RC	5.00	2.00
299	Maurice Morris RC	6.00	2.50
300	Eric Crouch RC	6.00	2.50
301	Lamar Gordon RC	6.00	2.50
302	Marquise Walker RC	5.00	2.00
303	Tracey Wistrom RC	5.00	2.00
304	Travis Stephens RC	5.00	2.00
305	Herb Haygood RC	3.00	1.25

	#	Player	Price 1	Price 2
❑	306	Albert Haynesworth RC	5.00	2.00
❑	307	Rocky Calmus RC	6.00	2.50
❑	308	Cliff Russell RC	5.00	2.00
❑	309	Ladell Betts RC	6.00	2.50
❑	310A	Patrick Ramsey RC	8.00	3.00
❑	310B	Ed Reed RC	10.00	4.00

2003 Upper Deck

	#	Player	Price 1	Price 2
❑		COMP.SET w/o SP's (180)	25.00	10.00
❑	1	Brad Johnson	.50	.20
❑	2	Derrick Brooks	.50	.20
❑	3	Simeon Rice	.50	.20
❑	4	Warren Sapp	.50	.20
❑	5	Thomas Jones	.50	.20
❑	6	Mike Alstott	.75	.30
❑	7	Michael Pittman	.30	.10
❑	8	Tim Brown	.75	.30
❑	9	Rich Gannon	.50	.20
❑	10	Charlie Garner	.50	.20
❑	11	Jerry Porter	.50	.20
❑	12	Phillip Buchanon	.30	.10
❑	13	Charles Woodson	.50	.20
❑	14	James Thrash	.30	.10
❑	15	Duce Staley	.50	.20
❑	16	Brian Westbrook	.50	.20
❑	17	Correll Buckhalter	.50	.20
❑	18	Koy Detmer	.30	.10
❑	19	Brian Dawkins	.50	.20
❑	20	Jon Ritchie	.30	.10
❑	21	Ahman Green	.75	.30
❑	22	Donald Driver	.50	.20
❑	23	Bubba Franks	.50	.20
❑	24	Javon Walker	.50	.20
❑	25	Kabeer Gbaja-Biamila	.50	.20
❑	26	Robert Ferguson	.30	.10
❑	27	Eddie George	.50	.20
❑	28	Jevon Kearse	.50	.20
❑	29	Billy Volek	.75	.30
❑	30	Frank Wycheck	.30	.10
❑	31	Derrick Mason	.50	.20
❑	32	Tommy Maddox	.75	.30
❑	33	Jerome Bettis	.75	.30
❑	34	Antwaan Randle El	.75	.30
❑	35	Amos Zereoue	.50	.20
❑	36	Hines Ward	.75	.30
❑	37	Jeff Garcia	.75	.30
❑	38	Terrell Owens	.75	.30
❑	39	Tim Rattay	.50	.20
❑	40	Brandon Doman	.30	.10
❑	41	Tai Streets	.30	.10
❑	42	Garrison Hearst	.50	.20
❑	43	Kerry Collins	.50	.20
❑	44	Tiki Barber	.75	.30
❑	45	Amani Toomer	.50	.20
❑	46	Jesse Palmer	.30	.10
❑	47	Tim Carter	.30	.10
❑	48	Michael Strahan	.50	.20
❑	49	Ike Hilliard	.30	.10
❑	50	Marvin Harrison	.75	.30
❑	51	Peyton Manning	1.25	.50
❑	52	Marcus Pollard	.30	.10
❑	53	James Mungro	.30	.10
❑	54	Reggie Wayne	.50	.20
❑	55	Peerless Price	.50	.20
❑	56	Warrick Dunn	.50	.20
❑	57	T.J. Duckett	.50	.20
❑	58	Keith Brooking	.30	.10
❑	59	Doug Johnson	.30	.10
❑	60	Brian Finneran	.30	.10
❑	61	Chad Pennington	1.00	.40
❑	62	Curtis Martin	.75	.30
❑	63	Marvin Jones	.30	.10
❑	64	Wayne Chrebet	.50	.20
❑	65	LaMont Jordan	.75	.30
❑	66	Curtis Conway	.30	.10
❑	67	Vinny Testaverde	.50	.20
❑	68	Tim Couch	.30	.10
❑	69	William Green	.50	.20
❑	70	Andre Davis	.30	.10
❑	71	Quincy Morgan	.50	.20
❑	72	Dennis Northcutt	.50	.20
❑	73	Kelly Holcomb	.50	.20
❑	74	Jake Plummer	.50	.20
❑	75	Mike Anderson	.75	.30
❑	76	Ashley Lelie	.75	.30
❑	77	Ed McCaffrey	.75	.30
❑	78	Shannon Sharpe	.30	.10
❑	79	Rod Smith	.50	.20
❑	80	Terrell Davis	.75	.30
❑	81	Antowain Smith	.50	.20
❑	82	Kevin Faulk	.30	.10
❑	83	David Patten	.30	.10
❑	84	Deion Branch	.75	.30
❑	85	Troy Brown	.50	.20
❑	86	Rohan Davey	.50	.20
❑	87	Jay Fiedler	.50	.20
❑	88	Randy McMichael	.50	.20
❑	89	Derrius Thompson	.30	.10
❑	90	Jason Taylor	.30	.10
❑	91	Zach Thomas	.75	.30
❑	92	Ricky Williams	.75	.30
❑	93	Deuce McAllister	.75	.30
❑	94	Donte Stallworth	.75	.30
❑	95	Jerome Pathon	.30	.10
❑	96	Michael Lewis	.30	.10
❑	97	Joe Horn	.50	.20
❑	98	Priest Holmes	1.00	.40
❑	99	Johnnie Morton	.50	.20
❑	100	Eddie Kennison	.30	.10
❑	101	Dante Hall	.75	.30
❑	102	Tony Gonzalez	.50	.20
❑	103	Marc Boerigter	.50	.20
❑	104	Drew Brees	.75	.30
❑	105	David Boston	.50	.20
❑	106	Reche Caldwell	.30	.10
❑	107	Tim Dwight	.50	.20
❑	108	Doug Flutie	.75	.30
❑	109	Drew Bledsoe	.75	.30
❑	110	Eric Moulds	.50	.20
❑	111	Alex Van Pelt	.30	.10
❑	112	Charles Johnson	.30	.10
❑	113	Takeo Spikes	.30	.10
❑	114	Josh Reed	.50	.20
❑	115	Ladell Betts	.50	.20
❑	116	Laveranues Coles	.50	.20
❑	117	Champ Bailey	.50	.20
❑	118	Trung Canidate	.50	.20
❑	119	Kenny Watson	.30	.10
❑	120	Rod Gardner	.50	.20
❑	121	Kurt Warner	.75	.30
❑	122	Lamar Gordon	.30	.10
❑	123	Shaun McDonald RC	.75	.30
❑	124	Marc Bulger	.75	.30
❑	125	Isaac Bruce	.75	.30
❑	126	Torry Holt	.75	.30
❑	127	Matt Hasselbeck	.50	.20
❑	128	Maurice Morris	.30	.10
❑	129	Bobby Engram	.30	.10
❑	130	Darrell Jackson	.50	.20
❑	131	Koren Robinson	.50	.20
❑	132	Chris Redman	.30	.10
❑	133	Todd Heap	.50	.20
❑	134	Travis Taylor	.50	.20
❑	135	Ron Johnson	.30	.10
❑	136	Ray Lewis	.75	.30
❑	137	Jake Delhomme	.75	.30
❑	138	Muhsin Muhammad	.50	.20
❑	139	Stephen Davis	.50	.20
❑	140	Julius Peppers	.75	.30
❑	141	Rodney Peete	.30	.10
❑	142	Mark Brunell	.50	.20
❑	143	Jimmy Smith	.50	.20
❑	144	Kyle Brady	.30	.10
❑	145	Kevin Lockett	.30	.10
❑	146	David Garrard	.30	.10
❑	147	Fred Taylor	.75	.30
❑	148	Michael Bennett	.50	.20
❑	149	Ronald Bellamy RC	1.00	.40
❑	150	Randy Moss	1.25	.50
❑	151	D'Wayne Bates	.30	.10
❑	152	Josh McCown	.50	.20
❑	153	Marquise Walker	.30	.10
❑	154	Jeff Blake	.30	.10
❑	155	Freddie Jones	.30	.10
❑	156	Marcel Shipp	.50	.20
❑	157	Troy Hambrick	.30	.10
❑	158	Joey Galloway	.50	.20
❑	159	Terry Glenn	.30	.10
❑	160	Roy Williams	.75	.30
❑	161	Antonio Bryant	.50	.20
❑	162	Quincy Carter	.50	.20
❑	163	Anthony Thomas	.50	.20
❑	164	Marty Booker	.50	.20
❑	165	Dez White	.30	.10
❑	166	Adrian Peterson	.30	.10
❑	167	Kordell Stewart	.50	.20
❑	168	David Terrell	.50	.20
❑	169	Jabar Gaffney	.50	.20
❑	170	Bennie Joppru RC	1.00	.40
❑	171	Corey Bradford	.30	.10
❑	172	David Carr	1.25	.50
❑	173	James Stewart	.50	.20
❑	174	Ty Detmer	.30	.10
❑	175	Az-Zahir Hakim	.30	.10
❑	176	Bill Schroeder	.50	.20
❑	177	Jon Kitna	.50	.20
❑	178	Chad Johnson	.75	.30
❑	179	Ron Dugans	.30	.10
❑	180	Peter Warrick	.50	.20
❑	181	Brett Favre SS	10.00	4.00
❑	182	Emmitt Smith SS	12.00	5.00
❑	183	LaDainian Tomlinson SS	5.00	2.00
❑	184	Joey Harrington SS	8.00	3.00
❑	185	Brian Urlacher SS	8.00	3.00
❑	186	Daunte Culpepper SS	5.00	2.00
❑	187	Jamal Lewis SS	5.00	2.00
❑	188	Shaun Alexander SS	5.00	2.00
❑	189	Marshall Faulk SS	5.00	2.00
❑	190	Travis Henry SS	4.00	1.50
❑	191	Trent Green SS	4.00	1.50
❑	192	Aaron Brooks SS	5.00	2.00
❑	193	Chris Chambers SS	5.00	2.00
❑	194	Tom Brady SS	10.00	4.00
❑	195	Clinton Portis SS	8.00	3.00
❑	196	Kevin Johnson SS	4.00	1.50
❑	197	Santana Moss SS	4.00	1.50
❑	198	Michael Vick SS	12.00	5.00
❑	199	Edgerrin James SS	.75	.30
❑	200	Jeremy Shockey SS	8.00	3.00
❑	201	Kevan Barlow SS	4.00	1.50
❑	202	Plaxico Burress SS	4.00	1.50
❑	203	Steve McNair SS	5.00	2.00
❑	204	Donovan McNabb SS	6.00	2.50
❑	205	Jerry Rice SS	10.00	4.00
❑	206	Keyshawn Johnson SS	5.00	2.00
❑	207	Patrick Ramsey SS	5.00	2.00
❑	208	Stephen Davis SS	4.00	1.50
❑	209	Corey Dillon SS	4.00	1.50
❑	210	Chad Hutchinson SS	4.00	1.50
❑	211	Brad Banks RC	4.00	1.50
❑	212	Kliff Kingsbury RC	4.00	1.50
❑	213	Jason Gesser RC	5.00	2.00
❑	214	Jason Johnson RC	3.00	1.25
❑	215	Brian St.Pierre RC	5.00	2.00
❑	216	Ken Dorsey RC	5.00	2.00
❑	217	Seneca Wallace RC	5.00	2.00
❑	218	Brooks Bollinger RC	5.00	2.00
❑	219	Chris Brown RC	6.00	2.00
❑	220	B.J Askew RC	5.00	2.00
❑	221	Earnest Graham RC	4.00	1.50
❑	222	Quentin Griffin RC	5.00	2.00
❑	223	Musa Smith RC	5.00	2.00
❑	224	Artose Pinner RC	5.00	2.00
❑	225	Domanick Davis RC	5.00	2.00
❑	226	Anquan Boldin RC	12.00	5.00
❑	227	Talman Gardner RC	5.00	2.00
❑	228	Brandon Lloyd RC	6.00	2.00
❑	229	Bryant Johnson RC	5.00	2.00
❑	230	Kareem Kelly RC	4.00	1.50
❑	231	Arnaz Battle RC	5.00	2.00
❑	232	Keenan Howry RC	5.00	2.00
❑	233	Justin Gage RC	5.00	2.00
❑	234	Tyrone Calico RC	5.00	2.00

❑ 235 Teyo Johnson RC 5.00 2.00
❑ 236 Malaefou MacKenzie RC 3.00 1.25
❑ 237 Terence Newman RC 10.00 5.00
❑ 238 Marcus Trufant RC 5.00 2.00
❑ 239 Mike Doss RC 5.00 2.00
❑ 240 Terrell Suggs RC 8.00 3.00
❑ 241 Carson Palmer RC 30.00 15.00
❑ 242 Byron Leftwich RC 25.00 10.00
❑ 243 Rex Grossman RC 25.00 10.00
❑ 244 Kyle Boller RC 8.00 3.00
❑ 245 Dave Ragone RC 8.00 3.00
❑ 246 Chris Simms RC 12.00 5.00
❑ 247 Larry Johnson RC 30.00 15.00
❑ 248 Lee Suggs RC 6.00 2.00
❑ 249 Justin Fargas RC 8.00 3.00
❑ 250 Onterrio Smith RC 8.00 3.00
❑ 251 Willis McGahee RC 20.00 7.50
❑ 252 Charles Rogers RC 5.00 2.00
❑ 253 Andre Johnson RC 15.00 6.00
❑ 254 Taylor Jacobs RC 8.00 3.00
❑ 255 Kelley Washington RC 8.00 3.00
❑ 256 Tony Romo RC 40.00 20.00
❑ 257 Jerel Myers RC 4.00 1.50
❑ 258 Kirk Farmer RC 4.00 1.50
❑ 259 Kevin Walter RC 5.00 2.00
❑ 260 Gibran Hamdan RC 4.00 1.50
❑ 261 Juston Wood RC 4.00 1.50
❑ 262 Travis Anglin RC 4.00 1.50
❑ 263 Marquel Blackwell RC 4.00 1.50
❑ 264 Jason Thomas RC 5.00 2.00
❑ 265 Carl Ford RC 4.00 1.50
❑ 266 Walter Young RC 4.00 1.50
❑ 267 Sultan McCullough RC 5.00 2.00
❑ 268 Dahrran Diedrick RC 6.00 2.50
❑ 269 Cecil Sapp RC 5.00 2.00
❑ 270 Doug Gabriel RC 6.00 2.50
❑ 271 LaBrandon Toefield RC 6.00 2.50
❑ 272 Adrian Madise RC 5.00 2.00
❑ 273 J.R. Tolver RC 5.00 2.00
❑ 274 Kevin Curtis RC 6.00 2.50
❑ 275 Bobby Wade RC 6.00 2.50
❑ 276 Sam Aiken RC 5.00 2.00
❑ 277 Mike Bush RC 4.00 1.50
❑ 278 Billy McMullen RC 5.00 2.00
❑ 279 Bethel Johnson RC 5.00 2.00
❑ 280 David Kircus RC 5.00 2.00
❑ 281 Zuriel Smith RC 4.00 1.50
❑ 282 LaTarence Dunbar RC 5.00 2.00
❑ 283 Nate Burleson RC 6.00 2.00
❑ 284 Antwone Savage RC 4.00 1.50
❑ 285 Terrence Edwards RC 5.00 2.00

2004 Upper Deck

❑ COMPLETE SET (275) 135.00 75.00
❑ COMP.SET w/o SP's (250) 60.00 30.00
❑ COMP.SET w/o RC's (200) 25.00 10.00
❑ 201-225 ROOKIE STATED ODDS 1:8
❑ 226-275 ROOKIE STATED ODDS 1:1
❑ UNPRICED PRINT PLATE PRINT RUN 1 SET
❑ 1 Anquan Boldin .75 .30
❑ 2 Josh McCown .50 .20
❑ 3 Emmitt Smith 1.50 .60
❑ 4 Freddie Jones .30 .10
❑ 5 Marcel Shipp .50 .20
❑ 6 Shaun King .30 .10
❑ 7 Michael Vick 1.50 .60
❑ 8 T.J. Duckett .50 .20
❑ 9 Peerless Price .50 .20
❑ 10 Warrick Dunn .50 .20
❑ 11 Keith Brooking .30 .10
❑ 12 Brian Finneran .30 .10
❑ 13 Anthony Wright .30 .10
❑ 14 Kyle Boller .75 .30
❑ 15 Jamal Lewis .75 .30
❑ 16 Todd Heap .50 .20
❑ 17 Ray Lewis .75 .30
❑ 18 Terrell Suggs .50 .20
❑ 19 Travis Taylor .30 .10
❑ 20 Drew Bledsoe .75 .30
❑ 21 Willis McGahee .75 .30
❑ 22 Eric Moulds .50 .20
❑ 23 Travis Henry .50 .20
❑ 24 Takeo Spikes .30 .10
❑ 25 Josh Reed .30 .10
❑ 26 Lawyer Milloy .50 .20
❑ 27 Stephen Davis .50 .20
❑ 28 Jake Delhomme .75 .30
❑ 29 Steve Smith .75 .30
❑ 30 DeShaun Foster .50 .20
❑ 31 Dan Morgan .30 .10
❑ 32 Julius Peppers .75 .30
❑ 33 Rod Smart .30 .10
❑ 34 Rex Grossman .75 .30
❑ 35 Thomas Jones .50 .20
❑ 36 Marty Booker .50 .20
❑ 37 Anthony Thomas .50 .20
❑ 38 Brian Urlacher 1.00 .40
❑ 39 Justin Gage .50 .20
❑ 40 Chad Johnson .75 .30
❑ 41 Carson Palmer 1.00 .40
❑ 42 Peter Warrick .50 .20
❑ 43 Jon Kitna .50 .20
❑ 44 Kelley Washington .30 .10
❑ 45 Rudi Johnson .50 .20
❑ 46 Jeff Garcia .75 .30
❑ 47 Dennis Northcutt .30 .10
❑ 48 Lee Suggs .75 .30
❑ 49 Andre Davis .30 .10
❑ 50 Quincy Morgan .50 .20
❑ 51 Kelly Holcomb .50 .20
❑ 52 Keyshawn Johnson .50 .20
❑ 53 Quincy Carter .50 .20
❑ 54 Antonio Bryant .50 .20
❑ 55 Terry Glenn .30 .10
❑ 56 Terence Newman .50 .20
❑ 57 Roy Williams S .50 .20
❑ 58 Champ Bailey .50 .20
❑ 59 Jake Plummer .50 .20
❑ 60 Quentin Griffin .75 .30
❑ 61 John Lynch .50 .20
❑ 62 Rod Smith .50 .20
❑ 63 Ashley Lelie .50 .20
❑ 64 Joey Harrington .75 .30
❑ 65 Az-Zahir Hakim .30 .10
❑ 66 Charles Rogers .50 .20
❑ 67 Tai Streets .30 .10
❑ 68 Shawn Bryson .30 .10
❑ 69 Artose Pinner .30 .10
❑ 70 Brett Favre 2.00 .75
❑ 71 Nick Barnett .50 .20
❑ 72 Ahman Green .75 .30
❑ 73 Kabeer Gbaja-Biamila .50 .20
❑ 74 Javon Walker .50 .20
❑ 75 Donald Driver .50 .20
❑ 76 Tim Couch .30 .10
❑ 77 David Carr .75 .30
❑ 78 Corey Bradford .30 .10
❑ 79 J.J. Moses .30 .10
❑ 80 Domanick Davis .75 .30
❑ 81 Jabar Gaffney .50 .20
❑ 82 Andre Johnson .75 .30
❑ 83 Marvin Harrison .75 .30
❑ 84 Peyton Manning 1.25 .50
❑ 85 Dallas Clark .50 .20
❑ 86 Edgerrin James .75 .30
❑ 87 Reggie Wayne .50 .20
❑ 88 Dwight Freeney .50 .20
❑ 89 Byron Leftwich 1.00 .40
❑ 90 LaBrandon Toefield .30 .10
❑ 91 Fred Taylor .50 .20
❑ 92 Troy Edwards .30 .10
❑ 93 Jimmy Smith .50 .20
❑ 94 Kyle Brady .30 .10
❑ 95 Trent Green .50 .20
❑ 96 Tony Gonzalez .50 .20
❑ 97 Dante Hall .75 .30
❑ 98 Priest Holmes 1.00 .40
❑ 99 Eddie Kennison .30 .10
❑ 100 Johnnie Morton .50 .20
❑ 101 Jay Fiedler .30 .10
❑ 102 Junior Seau .75 .30
❑ 103 Ricky Williams .75 .30
❑ 104 Chris Chambers .50 .20
❑ 105 Zach Thomas .75 .30
❑ 106 David Boston .50 .20
❑ 107 A.J. Feeley .75 .30
❑ 108 Daunte Culpepper .75 .30
❑ 109 Onterrio Smith .50 .20
❑ 110 Randy Moss 1.00 .40
❑ 111 Moe Williams .30 .10
❑ 112 Michael Bennett .50 .20
❑ 113 Jim Kleinsasser .30 .10
❑ 114 Tom Brady 2.00 .75
❑ 115 Kevin Faulk .30 .10
❑ 116 Deion Branch .75 .30
❑ 117 Corey Dillon .50 .20
❑ 118 Troy Brown .50 .20
❑ 119 Adam Vinatieri .75 .30
❑ 120 Tedy Bruschi .50 .20
❑ 121 Aaron Brooks .50 .20
❑ 122 Deuce McAllister .75 .30
❑ 123 Donte' Stallworth .50 .20
❑ 124 Joe Horn .50 .20
❑ 125 Jerome Pathon .30 .10
❑ 126 Boo Williams .30 .10
❑ 127 Jeremy Shockey .75 .30
❑ 128 Kurt Warner .75 .30
❑ 129 Amani Toomer .50 .20
❑ 130 Tiki Barber .75 .30
❑ 131 Ike Hilliard .30 .10
❑ 132 Michael Strahan .50 .20
❑ 133 Chad Pennington .75 .30
❑ 134 Santana Moss .50 .20
❑ 135 Wayne Chrebet .50 .20
❑ 136 Curtis Martin .75 .30
❑ 137 LaMont Jordan
❑ 138 Justin McCareins .30 .10
❑ 139 Jerry Rice 1.50 .60
❑ 140 Rich Gannon .50 .20
❑ 141 Tim Brown .75 .30
❑ 142 Jerry Porter .50 .20
❑ 143 Warren Sapp .50 .20
❑ 144 Charles Woodson .50 .20
❑ 145 Donovan McNabb 1.00 .40
❑ 146 Brian Westbrook .50 .20
❑ 147 Todd Pinkston .30 .10
❑ 148 Jevon Kearse .50 .20
❑ 149 Freddie Mitchell .50 .20
❑ 150 Correll Buckhalter .50 .20
❑ 151 Terrell Owens .75 .30
❑ 152 Tommy Maddox .50 .20
❑ 153 Duce Staley .50 .20
❑ 154 Plaxico Burress .50 .20
❑ 155 Hines Ward .75 .30
❑ 156 Antwaan Randle El .75 .30
❑ 157 Jerome Bettis .75 .30
❑ 158 Kendrell Bell .50 .20
❑ 159 LaDainian Tomlinson 1.00 .40
❑ 160 Doug Flutie .75 .30
❑ 161 Quentin Jammer .30 .10
❑ 162 Drew Brees .75 .30
❑ 163 Reche Caldwell .30 .10
❑ 164 Tim Dwight .50 .20
❑ 165 Tim Rattay .30 .10
❑ 166 Kevan Barlow .50 .20
❑ 167 Brandon Lloyd .50 .20
❑ 168 Cedrick Wilson .30 .10
❑ 169 Julian Peterson .30 .10
❑ 170 Ahmed Plummer .30 .10
❑ 171 Matt Hasselbeck .50 .20
❑ 172 Koren Robinson .50 .20
❑ 173 Shaun Alexander .75 .30
❑ 174 Darrell Jackson .50 .20
❑ 175 Marcus Trufant .30 .10
❑ 176 Bobby Engram .30 .10
❑ 177 Marc Bulger .75 .30
❑ 178 Torry Holt .75 .30
❑ 179 Marshall Faulk .75 .30
❑ 180 Orlando Pace .30 .10
❑ 181 Isaac Bruce .50 .20
❑ 182 Kyle Turley .30 .10
❑ 183 Brad Johnson .50 .20
❑ 184 Charlie Garner .50 .20

❑ 185	Keenan McCardell	.30	.10
❑ 186	Mike Alstott	.50	.20
❑ 187	Derrick Brooks	.50	.20
❑ 188	Brian Griese	.50	.20
❑ 189	Steve McNair	.75	.30
❑ 190	Chris Brown	.75	.30
❑ 191	Eddie George	.50	.20
❑ 192	Tyrone Calico	.50	.20
❑ 193	Derrick Mason	.50	.20
❑ 194	Drew Bennett	.50	.20
❑ 195	Mark Brunell	.50	.20
❑ 196	LaVar Arrington	1.50	.60
❑ 197	Clinton Portis	.75	.30
❑ 198	Laveranues Coles	.50	.20
❑ 199	Patrick Ramsey	.50	.20
❑ 200	Rod Gardner	.50	.20
❑ 201	Eli Manning RC	30.00	12.50
❑ 202	Larry Fitzgerald RC	15.00	6.00
❑ 203	Michael Jenkins RC	5.00	2.00
❑ 204	Ben Roethlisberger RC	40.00	20.00
❑ 025	Philip Rivers RC	15.00	7.50
❑ 206	Kellen Winslow RC	10.00	4.00
❑ 207	Kevin Jones RC	12.00	5.00
❑ 208	Steven Jackson RC	15.00	6.00
❑ 209	Reggie Williams RC	6.00	2.50
❑ 210	Chris Perry RC	8.00	3.00
❑ 211	Roy Williams RC	12.00	5.00
❑ 212	Rashaun Woods RC	5.00	2.00
❑ 213	Chris Gamble RC	5.00	2.00
❑ 214	Sean Taylor RC	5.00	2.00
❑ 215	Robert Gallery RC	5.00	2.00
❑ 216	Ben Troupe RC	5.00	2.00
❑ 217	Lee Evans RC	6.00	2.50
❑ 218	Michael Clayton RC	10.00	4.00
❑ 219	J.P. Losman RC	10.00	4.00
❑ 220	Devery Henderson RC	4.00	1.50
❑ 221	Drew Henson RC	5.00	2.00
❑ 222	DeAngelo Hall RC	6.00	2.50
❑ 223	Julius Jones RC	15.00	6.00
❑ 224	Ben Watson RC	5.00	2.00
❑ 225	Greg Jones RC	5.00	2.00
❑ 226	D.J. Williams RC	1.50	.60
❑ 227	Tommie Harris RC	1.50	.60
❑ 228	Shawn Andrews RC	1.50	.60
❑ 229	Vince Wilfork RC	2.00	.75
❑ 230	Dunta Robinson RC	1.50	.60
❑ 231	Will Smith RC	1.50	.60
❑ 232	Jonathan Vilma RC	1.50	.60
❑ 233	Ricardo Colclough RC	1.50	.60
❑ 234	Ahmad Carroll RC	1.50	.60
❑ 235	Karlos Dansby RC	1.50	.60
❑ 236	Matt Ware RC	1.50	.60
❑ 237	Jim Sorgi RC	1.50	.60
❑ 238	Will Poole RC	1.50	.60
❑ 239	Derrick Strait RC	1.50	.60
❑ 240	Andy Hall RC	1.25	.50
❑ 241	Nathan Vasher RC	2.00	.75
❑ 242	D.J. Hackett RC	1.25	.50
❑ 243	Jason Babin RC	1.50	.60
❑ 244	Derrick Hamilton RC	1.25	.50
❑ 245	Michael Boulware RC	1.50	.60
❑ 246	Michael Turner RC	2.00	.75
❑ 247	Sean Jones RC	1.25	.50
❑ 248	Ernest Wilford RC	1.50	.60
❑ 249	Cedric Cobbs RC	1.50	.60
❑ 250	Tatum Bell RC	4.00	1.50
❑ 251	Bernard Berrian RC	2.00	.75
❑ 252	Vernon Carey RC	1.25	.50
❑ 253	Kenechi Udeze RC	1.50	.60
❑ 254	P.K. Sam RC	1.25	.50
❑ 255	Ben Hartsock RC	1.50	.60
❑ 256	Chris Cooley RC	1.50	.60
❑ 257	Josh Harris RC	1.50	.60
❑ 258	Cody Pickett RC	1.50	.60
❑ 259	Carlos Francis RC	1.25	.50
❑ 260	Devard Darling RC	1.50	.60
❑ 261	Johnnie Morant RC	1.50	.60
❑ 262	John Navarre RC	1.50	.60
❑ 263	Kris Wilson RC	1.50	.60
❑ 264	Jerricho Cotchery RC	1.50	.60
❑ 265	Darius Watts RC	1.50	.60
❑ 266	Quincy Wilson RC	1.25	.50
❑ 267	Maurice Mann RC	1.25	.50
❑ 268	Samie Parker RC	1.50	.60
❑ 269	B.J. Symons RC	1.50	.60
❑ 270	Matt Schaub RC	6.00	2.50
❑ 271	Jeff Smoker RC	1.50	.60
❑ 272	Craig Krenzel RC	1.50	.60
❑ 273	Luke McCown RC	1.50	.60
❑ 274	Mewelde Moore RC	1.50	.60
❑ 275	Keary Colbert RC	2.50	1.00

2005 Upper Deck

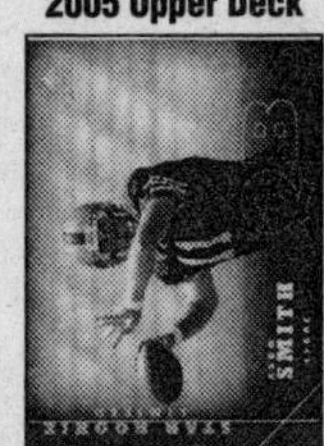

❑	COMPLETE SET (275)	250.00	125.00
❑	COMP.SET w/o SP's (250)	60.00	30.00
❑	COMP.SET w/o RC's (200)	30.00	12.50
❑	201-225 ROOKIE STATED ODDS 1:8		
❑	226-275 ROOKIE STATED ODDS 1:1		
❑ 1	Larry Fitzgerald	.75	.30
❑ 2	Anquan Boldin	.50	.20
❑ 3	Kurt Warner	.50	.20
❑ 4	Josh McCown	.50	.20
❑ 5	Bryant Johnson	.40	.15
❑ 6	Duane Starks	.40	.15
❑ 7	Michael Vick	1.25	.50
❑ 8	Warrick Dunn	.50	.20
❑ 9	T.J. Duckett	.50	.20
❑ 10	Peerless Price	.40	.15
❑ 11	Alge Crumpler	.50	.20
❑ 12	Patrick Kerney	.40	.15
❑ 13	Ed Reed	.50	.20
❑ 14	Ray Lewis	.75	.30
❑ 15	Kyle Boller	.50	.20
❑ 16	Ma'Ake Kemoeatu RC	.75	.30
❑ 17	Jamal Lewis	.75	.30
❑ 18	Derrick Mason	.50	.20
❑ 19	J.P. Losman	.75	.30
❑ 20	Willis McGahee	.75	.30
❑ 21	Lawyer Milloy	.40	.15
❑ 22	Lee Evans	.50	.20
❑ 23	Eric Moulds	.50	.20
❑ 24	Takeo Spikes	.40	.15
❑ 25	Jake Delhomme	.75	.30
❑ 26	DeShaun Foster	.50	.20
❑ 27	Keary Colbert	.50	.20
❑ 28	Stephen Davis	.50	.20
❑ 29	Nick Goings	.40	.15
❑ 30	Julius Peppers	.50	.20
❑ 31	Rex Grossman	.50	.20
❑ 32	Brian Urlacher	.75	.30
❑ 33	Thomas Jones	.50	.20
❑ 34	Muhsin Muhammad	.50	.20
❑ 35	Anthony Thomas	.50	.20
❑ 36	Bernard Berrian	.40	.15
❑ 37	Carson Palmer	.75	.30
❑ 38	Chad Johnson	.75	.30
❑ 39	Peter Warrick	.40	.15
❑ 40	T.J. Houshmandzadeh	.40	.15
❑ 41	Rudi Johnson	.50	.20
❑ 42	Justin Smith	.40	.15
❑ 43	Jeff Garcia	.50	.20
❑ 44	Lee Suggs	.50	.20
❑ 45	William Green	.40	.15
❑ 46	Kellen Winslow	.75	.30
❑ 47	Dennis Northcutt	.40	.15
❑ 48	Antonio Bryant	.40	.15
❑ 49	Julius Jones	1.00	.40
❑ 50	Drew Bledsoe	.75	.30
❑ 51	Keyshawn Johnson	.50	.20
❑ 52	Al Johnson	.40	.15
❑ 53	Jason Witten	.50	.20
❑ 54	Roy Williams S	.50	.20
❑ 55	Jake Plummer	.50	.20
❑ 56	Champ Bailey	.50	.20
❑ 57	Tatum Bell	.50	.20
❑ 58	Reuben Droughns	.50	.20
❑ 59	Ashley Lelie	.50	.20
❑ 60	Rod Smith	.50	.20
❑ 61	Kevin Jones	.75	.30
❑ 62	Roy Williams WR	.75	.30
❑ 63	Charles Rogers	.50	.20
❑ 64	Joey Harrington	.75	.30
❑ 65	Az-Zahir Hakim	.40	.15
❑ 66	Dre Bly	.40	.15
❑ 67	Brett Favre	2.00	.75
❑ 68	Javon Walker	.50	.20
❑ 69	Ahman Green	.75	.30
❑ 70	Donald Driver	.50	.20
❑ 71	Robert Ferguson	.40	.15
❑ 72	Nick Barnett	.40	.15
❑ 73	David Carr	.75	.30
❑ 74	Domanick Davis	.50	.20
❑ 75	Andre Johnson	.50	.20
❑ 76	Jabar Gaffney	.40	.15
❑ 77	Dunta Robinson	.50	.20
❑ 78	Jamie Sharper	.40	.15
❑ 79	Peyton Manning	1.25	.50
❑ 80	Edgerrin James	.75	.30
❑ 81	Marvin Harrison	.75	.30
❑ 82	Reggie Wayne	.50	.20
❑ 83	Brandon Stokley	.50	.20
❑ 84	Dwight Freeney	.50	.20
❑ 85	Byron Leftwich	.75	.30
❑ 86	Fred Taylor	.50	.20
❑ 87	Jimmy Smith	.50	.20
❑ 88	Greg Jones	.40	.15
❑ 89	Donovin Darius	.40	.15
❑ 90	Reggie Williams	.50	.20
❑ 91	Priest Holmes	.75	.30
❑ 92	Larry Johnson	.75	.30
❑ 93	Tony Gonzalez	.50	.20
❑ 94	Trent Green	.50	.20
❑ 95	Eddie Kennison	.40	.15
❑ 96	Johnnie Morton	.50	.20
❑ 97	Jason Taylor	.40	.15
❑ 98	A.J. Feeley	.50	.20
❑ 99	Sammy Morris	.40	.15
❑ 100	Chris Chambers	.50	.20
❑ 101	Randy McMichael	.40	.15
❑ 102	Zach Thomas	.75	.30
❑ 103	Antoine Winfield	.40	.15
❑ 104	Daunte Culpepper	.75	.30
❑ 105	Michael Bennett	.50	.20
❑ 106	Nate Burleson	.50	.20
❑ 107	Onterrio Smith	.50	.20
❑ 108	Marcus Robinson	.50	.20
❑ 109	Tom Brady	2.00	.75
❑ 110	Corey Dillon	.50	.20
❑ 111	David Givens	.50	.20
❑ 112	David Patten	.40	.15
❑ 113	Adam Vinatieri	.75	.30
❑ 114	Troy Brown	.50	.20
❑ 115	Aaron Brooks	.50	.20
❑ 116	Deuce McAllister	.75	.30
❑ 117	Joe Horn	.50	.20
❑ 118	Donte Stallworth	.50	.20
❑ 119	Charles Grant	.40	.15
❑ 120	Jerome Pathon	.40	.15
❑ 121	Eli Manning	1.50	.60
❑ 122	Tiki Barber	.75	.30
❑ 123	Amani Toomer	.50	.20
❑ 124	Jeremy Shockey	.75	.30
❑ 125	Michael Strahan	.50	.20
❑ 126	Plaxico Burress	.50	.20
❑ 127	Chad Pennington	.75	.30
❑ 128	Curtis Martin	.75	.30
❑ 129	Laveranues Coles	.50	.20
❑ 130	Wayne Chrebet	.50	.20
❑ 131	Jonathan Vilma	.50	.20
❑ 132	Justin McCareins	.40	.15
❑ 133	Kerry Collins	.50	.20
❑ 134	Jerry Porter	.50	.20
❑ 135	LaMont Jordan	.75	.30
❑ 136	Randy Moss	.75	.30
❑ 137	Barry Sims	.40	.15
❑ 138	Warren Sapp	.50	.20
❑ 139	Donovan McNabb	1.00	.40
❑ 140	Brian Westbrook	.50	.20
❑ 141	Terrell Owens	.75	.30
❑ 142	Jevon Kearse	.50	.20
❑ 143	Brian Dawkins	.50	.20
❑ 144	Ben Roethlisberger	2.00	.75
❑ 145	Jerome Bettis	.75	.30

146	Duce Staley	.50	.20
147	Cedrick Wilson	.40	.15
148	Hines Ward	.75	.30
149	Antwaan Randle El	.50	.20
150	Troy Polamalu	1.25	.50
151	Philip Rivers	.75	.30
152	Drew Brees	.75	.30
153	LaDainian Tomlinson	1.00	.40
154	Antonio Gates	.75	.30
155	Reche Caldwell	.40	.15
156	Eric Parker	.40	.15
157	Kevan Barlow	.50	.20
158	Tim Rattay	.40	.15
159	Eric Johnson	.50	.20
160	Rashaun Woods	.50	.20
161	Brandon Lloyd	.40	.15
162	Julian Peterson	.40	.15
163	Matt Hasselbeck	.50	.20
164	Shaun Alexander	1.00	.40
165	Michael Boulware	.40	.15
166	Darrell Jackson	.50	.20
167	Koren Robinson	.50	.20
168	Marcus Trufant	.40	.15
169	Marc Bulger	.75	.30
170	Steven Jackson	1.00	.40
171	Marshall Faulk	.75	.30
172	Issac Bruce	.50	.20
173	Torry Holt	.75	.30
174	Michael Clayton	.75	.30
175	Michael Pittman	.40	.15
176	Brian Griese	.50	.20
177	Joey Galloway	.50	.20
178	Derrick Brooks	.50	.20
179	Josh Savage RC	.50	.20
180	Steve McNair	.75	.30
181	Chris Brown	.50	.20
182	Billy Volek	.50	.20
183	Ben Troupe	.40	.15
184	Drew Bennett	.50	.20
185	Clinton Portis	.75	.30
186	Mark Brunell	.50	.20
187	Patrick Ramsey	.50	.20
188	Sean Taylor	.50	.20
189	LaVar Arrington	.75	.30
190	Santana Moss	.50	.20
191	David Terrell	.50	.20
192	Deion Branch	.50	.20
193	Chester Taylor	.50	.20
194	Derrick Blaylock	.40	.15
195	Shaun Ellis	.40	.15
196	Terrell Suggs	.50	.20
197	Charles Woodson	.50	.20
198	Jason Elam	.40	.15
199	Lawrence Tynes RC	.50	.20
200	David Akers	.40	.15
201	Alex Smith QB RC	25.00	10.00
202	Aaron Rodgers RC	20.00	7.50
203	Ronnie Brown RC	25.00	10.00
204	Cadillac Williams RC	25.00	12.50
205	Braylon Edwards RC	20.00	7.50
206	Antrel Rolle RC	6.00	2.50
207	Cedric Benson RC	12.00	5.00
208	Troy Williamson RC	12.00	5.00
209	Mark Clayton RC	8.00	3.00
210	Matt Jones RC	15.00	6.00
211	Reggie Brown RC	6.00	2.50
212	Charlie Frye RC	12.00	5.00
213	Heath Miller RC	15.00	6.00
214	Vincent Jackson RC	6.00	2.50
215	Andrew Walter RC	10.00	4.00
216	Roddy White RC	6.00	2.50
217	Adam Jones RC	6.00	2.50
218	J.J. Arrington RC	8.00	3.00
219	Eric Shelton RC	6.00	2.50
220	Terrence Murphy RC	6.00	2.50
221	Frank Gore RC	12.00	5.00
222	Roscoe Parrish RC	6.00	2.50
223	Jason Campbell RC	10.00	4.00
224	Carlos Rogers RC	8.00	3.00
225	Mike Williams	12.00	5.00
226	Erasmus James RC	6.00	2.50
227	Travis Johnson RC	1.50	.60
228	Dan Cody RC	2.00	.75
229	Thomas Davis RC	2.00	.75
230	David Pollack RC	2.00	.75
231	David Greene RC	2.00	.75
232	Alex Smith TE RC	2.00	.75
233	Ryan Moats RC	2.00	.75
234	Ciatrick Fason RC	2.00	.75
235	Vernand Morency RC	2.00	.75
236	Fred Gibson RC	6.00	2.50
237	Craphonso Thorpe RC	1.50	.60
238	Kevin Everett RC	2.00	.75
239	Kyle Orton RC	3.00	1.25
240	Derek Anderson RC	2.00	.75
241	Derrick Johnson RC	3.00	1.25
242	Mark Bradley RC	2.00	.75
243	Chris Henry RC	2.00	.75
244	DeMarcus Ware RC	3.00	1.25
245	Luis Castillo RC	2.00	.75
246	Mike Patterson RC	2.00	.75
247	Brodney Pool RC	2.00	.75
248	Barrett Ruud RC	2.00	.75
249	Darren Sproles RC	2.00	.75
250	Stefan LeFors RC	2.00	.75
251	Josh Bullocks RC	2.00	.75
252	Kevin Burnett RC	2.00	.75
253	Lofa Tatupu RC	2.50	1.00
254	Matt Roth RC	2.00	.75
255	Shaun Cody RC	2.00	.75
256	Shawne Merriman RC	3.00	1.25
257	Corey Webster RC	2.00	.75
258	Channing Crowder RC	2.00	.75
259	Justin Miller RC	1.50	.60
260	Eric Green RC	1.00	.40
261	Marcus Spears RC	2.00	.75
262	Marlin Jackson RC	2.00	.75
263	Odell Thurman RC	2.00	.75
264	Mike Nugent RC	2.00	.75
265	Marion Barber RC	3.00	1.25
266	Anttaj Hawthorne RC	1.50	.60
267	Dan Orlovsky RC	2.50	1.00
268	Fabian Washington RC	2.00	.75
269	Justin Tuck RC	2.00	.75
270	Jerome Mathis RC	2.00	.75
271	Ronald Bartell RC	1.50	.60
272	Kirk Morrison RC	2.00	.75
273	Adrian McPherson RC	2.00	.75
274	Matt Cassel RC	6.00	2.50
275	Maurice Clarett	2.00	.75

2006 Upper Deck

	COMP.SET w/o RC's (200)	30.00	12.00
1	Larry Fitzgerald	.75	.30
2	Anquan Boldin	.50	.20
3	J.J. Arrington	.50	.20
4	Kurt Warner	.50	.20
5	Neil Rackers	.40	.15
6	Edgerrin James	.75	.30
7	Michael Vick	1.00	.40
8	Alge Crumpler	.50	.20
9	Warrick Dunn	.50	.20
10	Michael Jenkins	.50	.20
11	Roddy White	.50	.20
12	DeAngelo Hall	.50	.20
13	Jamal Lewis	.50	.20
14	Derrick Mason	.40	.15
15	Todd Heap	.50	.20
16	Kyle Boller	.40	.15
17	Ray Lewis	.75	.30
18	Ed Reed	.50	.20
19	Willis McGahee	.75	.30
20	Lee Evans	.50	.20
21	J.P. Losman	.50	.20
22	Rashad Baker	.40	.15
23	Takeo Spikes	.40	.15
24	Aaron Schobel	.40	.15
25	Steve Smith	.75	.30
26	Jake Delhomme	.50	.20
27	DeShaun Foster	.50	.20
28	Keary Colbert	.40	.15
29	Julius Peppers	.50	.20
30	Ma'Ake Kemoeatu	.40	.15
31	Rex Grossman	.75	.30
32	Muhsin Muhammad	.50	.20
33	Brian Urlacher	.75	.30
34	Thomas Jones	.50	.20
35	Cedric Benson	.75	.30
36	Nathan Vasher	.40	.15
37	Rudi Johnson	.50	.20
38	Chad Johnson	.50	.20
39	T.J. Houshmandzadeh	.50	.20
40	Chris Henry	.40	.15
41	Deltha O'Neal	.40	.15
42	Odell Thurman	.40	.15
43	Carson Palmer	.75	.30
44	Charlie Frye	.50	.20
45	Reuben Droughns	.50	.20
46	Braylon Edwards	.75	.30
47	Kellen Winslow Jr.	.75	.30
48	Steve Heiden	.40	.15
49	Joe Jurevicius	.50	.20
50	Drew Bledsoe	.75	.30
51	Julius Jones	.75	.30
52	Terrell Owens	.75	.30
53	Terry Glenn	.50	.20
54	Jason Witten	.50	.20
55	DeMarcus Ware	.50	.20
56	Roy Williams S	.50	.20
57	Jake Plummer	.50	.20
58	Tatum Bell	.50	.20
59	Al Wilson	.40	.15
60	Rod Smith	.50	.20
61	Ashley Lelie	.50	.20
62	Champ Bailey	.50	.20
63	Javon Walker	.50	.20
64	Jon Kitna	.40	.15
65	Kevin Jones	.75	.30
66	Roy Williams WR	.75	.30
67	Mike Williams	.75	.30
68	Marcus Pollard	.40	.15
69	Dre Bly	.40	.15
70	Brett Favre	1.50	.60
71	Ahman Green	.50	.20
72	Donald Driver	.50	.20
73	Robert Ferguson	.40	.15
74	Bubba Franks	.40	.15
75	Kabeer Gbaja-Biamila	.50	.20
76	David Carr	.50	.20
77	Domanick Davis	.50	.20
78	Andre Johnson	.50	.20
79	Eric Moulds	.50	.20
80	Jeb Putzier	.40	.15
81	Dunta Robinson	.50	.20
82	Peyton Manning	1.25	.50
83	Dominic Rhodes	.50	.20
84	Reggie Wayne	.50	.20
85	Marvin Harrison	.75	.30
86	Dallas Clark	.40	.15
87	Dwight Freeney	.50	.20
88	Bob Sanders	.50	.20
89	Byron Leftwich	.50	.20
90	Fred Taylor	.50	.20
91	Greg Jones	.40	.15
92	Ernest Wilford	.40	.15
93	John Henderson	.40	.15
94	Matt Jones	.75	.30
95	Trent Green	.50	.20
96	Larry Johnson	1.00	.40
97	Priest Holmes	.50	.20
98	Eddie Kennison	.40	.15
99	Tony Gonzalez	.50	.20
100	Dante Hall	.50	.20
101	Daunte Culpepper	.75	.30
102	Ronnie Brown	.75	.30
103	Marty Booker	.40	.15
104	Chris Chambers	.50	.20
105	Randy McMichael	.40	.15
106	Zach Thomas	.75	.30
107	Brad Johnson	.50	.20
108	Chester Taylor	.50	.20
109	Antoine Winfield	.40	.15
110	Koren Robinson	.50	.20

❑ 111 Travis Taylor .40 .15
❑ 112 Darren Sharper .40 .15
❑ 113 Tom Brady 1.25 .50
❑ 114 Corey Dillon .50 .20
❑ 115 Deion Branch .50 .20
❑ 116 Reche Caldwell .40 .15
❑ 117 Ben Watson .40 .15
❑ 118 Tedy Bruschi .75 .30
❑ 119 Rodney Harrison .40 .15
❑ 120 Drew Brees .75 .30
❑ 121 Deuce McAllister .50 .20
❑ 122 Joe Horn .50 .20
❑ 123 Donte Stallworth .50 .20
❑ 124 Devery Henderson .40 .15
❑ 125 Will Smith .40 .15
❑ 126 Eli Manning 1.00 .40
❑ 127 Tiki Barber .75 .30
❑ 128 Plaxico Burress .50 .20
❑ 129 Amani Toomer .50 .20
❑ 130 Jeremy Shockey .75 .30
❑ 131 Michael Strahan .50 .20
❑ 132 Osi Umenyiora .40 .15
❑ 133 Chad Pennington .50 .20
❑ 134 Curtis Martin .75 .30
❑ 135 Justin McCareins .40 .15
❑ 136 Laveranues Coles .50 .20
❑ 137 Jonathan Vilma .50 .20
❑ 138 Shaun Ellis .40 .15
❑ 139 Aaron Brooks .50 .20
❑ 140 LaMont Jordan .50 .20
❑ 141 Randy Moss .75 .30
❑ 142 Jerry Porter .50 .20
❑ 143 Doug Gabriel .40 .15
❑ 144 Derrick Burgess .40 .15
❑ 145 Donovan McNabb .75 .30
❑ 146 Brian Westbrook .50 .20
❑ 147 Jevon Kearse .50 .20
❑ 148 Reggie Brown .50 .20
❑ 149 L.J. Smith .40 .15
❑ 150 Brian Dawkins .40 .15
❑ 151 Ben Roethlisberger 1.25 .50
❑ 152 Willie Parker 1.00 .40
❑ 153 Hines Ward .75 .30
❑ 154 Cedrick Wilson .40 .15
❑ 155 Heath Miller .75 .30
❑ 156 Joey Porter .40 .15
❑ 157 Troy Polamalu 1.00 .40
❑ 158 Philip Rivers .75 .30
❑ 159 LaDainian Tomlinson 1.00 .40
❑ 160 Keenan McCardell .40 .15
❑ 161 Eric Parker .40 .15
❑ 162 Antonio Gates .75 .30
❑ 163 Shawne Merriman .50 .20
❑ 164 Donnie Edwards .40 .15
❑ 165 Alex Smith QB 1.00 .40
❑ 166 Frank Gore .75 .30
❑ 167 Antonio Bryant .50 .20
❑ 168 Eric Johnson .50 .20
❑ 169 Arnaz Battle .40 .15
❑ 170 Bryant Young .40 .15
❑ 171 Matt Hasselbeck .50 .20
❑ 172 Shaun Alexander .75 .30
❑ 173 Darrell Jackson .50 .20
❑ 174 Etric Pruitt .50 .20
❑ 175 Julian Peterson .40 .15
❑ 176 Lofa Tatupu .50 .20
❑ 177 Marc Bulger .50 .20
❑ 178 Steven Jackson .75 .30
❑ 179 Torry Holt .50 .20
❑ 180 Kevin Curtis .40 .15
❑ 181 Isaac Bruce .50 .20
❑ 182 Leonard Little .40 .15
❑ 183 Chris Simms .50 .20
❑ 184 Cadillac Williams .75 .30
❑ 185 Joey Galloway .50 .20
❑ 186 Michael Clayton .50 .20
❑ 187 Derrick Brooks .50 .20
❑ 188 Ronde Barber .40 .15
❑ 189 Billy Volek .50 .20
❑ 190 Chris Brown .50 .20
❑ 191 Drew Bennett .40 .15
❑ 192 Ben Troupe .40 .15
❑ 193 David Givens .50 .20
❑ 194 Adam Jones .40 .15
❑ 195 Mark Brunell .50 .20
❑ 196 Clinton Portis .75 .30
❑ 197 Santana Moss .50 .20
❑ 198 Chris Cooley .40 .15
❑ 199 Antwaan Randle El .50 .20
❑ 200 Sean Taylor .50 .20
❑ 201 A.J. Hawk RC 12.00 5.00
❑ 202 Anthony Fasano RC 6.00 2.50
❑ 203 Brian Calhoun RC 6.00 2.50
❑ 204 Chad Greenway RC 6.00 2.50
❑ 205 Chad Jackson RC 10.00 4.00
❑ 206 DeAngelo Williams RC 15.00 6.00
❑ 207 D'Brickashaw Ferguson RC 6.00 2.50
❑ 208 Brodie Croyle RC 12.00 5.00
❑ 209 Haloti Ngata RC 6.00 2.50
❑ 210 Jay Cutler RC 25.00 10.00
❑ 211 Joseph Addai RC 20.00 8.00
❑ 212 Laurence Maroney RC 15.00 6.00
❑ 213 LenDale White RC 12.00 5.00
❑ 214 Maurice Drew RC 15.00 6.00
❑ 215 Mario Williams RC 10.00 4.00
❑ 216 Matt Leinart RC 25.00 10.00
❑ 217 Maurice Stovall RC 6.00 2.50
❑ 218 Michael Huff RC 8.00 3.00
❑ 219 Reggie Bush RC 40.00 15.00
❑ 220 Santonio Holmes RC 12.00 5.00
❑ 221 Sinorice Moss RC 8.00 3.00
❑ 222 Kellen Clemens RC 8.00 3.00
❑ 223 Tarvaris Jackson RC 10.00 4.00
❑ 224 Vernon Davis RC 12.00 5.00
❑ 225 Vince Young RC 25.00 10.00
❑ 226 Donte Whitner RC 2.50 1.00
❑ 227 Antonio Cromartie RC 2.50 1.00
❑ 228 Ashton Youboty RC 2.50 1.00
❑ 229 Bobby Carpenter RC 2.50 1.00
❑ 230 Brad Smith RC 2.50 1.00
❑ 231 Brandon Williams RC 2.50 1.00
❑ 232 Dominique Byrd RC 2.00 .75
❑ 233 Brodrick Bunkley RC 2.50 1.00
❑ 234 Charlie Whitehurst RC 3.00 1.25
❑ 235 Demetrius Williams RC 3.00 1.25
❑ 236 Cory Rodgers RC 2.50 1.00
❑ 237 Daniel Bullocks RC 2.50 1.00
❑ 238 Manny Lawson RC 2.50 1.00
❑ 239 Darrell Hackney RC 2.00 .75
❑ 240 Darryl Tapp RC 2.00 .75
❑ 241 David Thomas RC 2.50 1.00
❑ 242 DeMeco Ryans RC 3.00 1.25
❑ 243 Derek Hagan RC 2.50 1.00
❑ 244 Devin Hester RC 5.00 2.00
❑ 245 D'Qwell Jackson RC 2.00 .75
❑ 246 Brandon Marshall RC 2.50 1.00
❑ 247 Ernie Sims RC 3.00 1.25
❑ 248 Gabe Watson RC 2.00 .75
❑ 249 Jason Allen RC 2.50 1.00
❑ 250 Greg Jennings RC 4.00 1.50
❑ 251 Marcus Vick RC 2.00 .75
❑ 252 Jason Avant RC 2.50 1.00
❑ 253 Jeremy Bloom RC 2.00 .75
❑ 254 Jerome Harrison RC 2.50 1.00
❑ 255 Joe Klopfenstein RC 2.00 .75
❑ 256 Johnathan Joseph RC 2.00 .75
❑ 257 Jimmy Williams RC 2.50 1.00
❑ 258 Kamerion Wimbley RC 2.50 1.00
❑ 259 Leon Washington RC 4.00 1.50
❑ 260 Marcedes Lewis RC 2.50 1.00
❑ 261 Marcus McNeill RC 2.00 .75
❑ 262 Mathias Kiwanuka RC 3.00 1.25
❑ 263 Leonard Pope RC 2.50 1.00
❑ 264 Tamba Hali RC 2.50 1.00
❑ 265 Mike Hass RC 2.50 1.00
❑ 266 Omar Jacobs RC 2.00 .75
❑ 267 Jerious Norwood RC 4.00 1.50
❑ 268 Owen Daniels RC 2.50 1.00
❑ 269 P.J. Daniels RC 2.00 .75
❑ 270 Ray Edwards RC 2.00 .75
❑ 271 Michael Robinson RC 4.00 1.50
❑ 272 Rocky McIntosh RC 2.50 1.00
❑ 273 Travis Wilson RC 2.50 1.00
❑ 274 Tye Hill RC 2.50 1.00
❑ 275 Thomas Howard RC 2.50 1.00

2005 Upper Deck ESPN

❑ COMP.SET w/o RC's (100) 25.00 10.00
❑ DRAFT PICK STATED ODDS 1:4
❑ 1 Larry Fitzgerald .75 .30
❑ 2 Josh McCown .50 .20
❑ 3 Anquan Boldin .50 .20
❑ 4 Michael Vick 1.25 .50
❑ 5 Warrick Dunn .50 .20

❑ 6 Peerless Price .40 .15
❑ 7 Alge Crumpler .50 .20
❑ 8 Jamal Lewis .75 .30
❑ 9 Kyle Boller .50 .20
❑ 10 Derrick Mason .50 .20
❑ 11 Willis McGahee .75 .30
❑ 12 J.P. Losman .75 .30
❑ 13 Eric Moulds .50 .20
❑ 14 Jake Delhomme .75 .30
❑ 15 Steve Smith .50 .20
❑ 16 DeShaun Foster .50 .20
❑ 17 Muhsin Muhammad .50 .20
❑ 18 Thomas Jones .50 .20
❑ 19 Rex Grossman .50 .20
❑ 20 Chad Johnson .75 .30
❑ 21 Carson Palmer .75 .30
❑ 22 Rudi Johnson .50 .20
❑ 23 Lee Suggs .50 .20
❑ 24 Kellen Winslow .75 .30
❑ 25 Luke McCown .40 .15
❑ 26 Julius Jones 1.00 .40
❑ 27 Keyshawn Johnson .50 .20
❑ 28 Drew Bledsoe .75 .30
❑ 29 Tatum Bell .50 .20
❑ 30 Jake Plummer .50 .20
❑ 31 Rod Smith .50 .20
❑ 32 Roy Williams WR .75 .30
❑ 33 Kevin Jones .75 .30
❑ 34 Joey Harrington .75 .30
❑ 35 Jeff Garcia .50 .20
❑ 36 Brett Favre 2.00 .75
❑ 37 Javon Walker .50 .20
❑ 38 Ahman Green .75 .30
❑ 39 David Carr .75 .30
❑ 40 Andre Johnson .50 .20
❑ 41 Domanick Davis .50 .20
❑ 42 Peyton Manning 1.25 .50
❑ 43 Edgerrin James .75 .30
❑ 44 Marvin Harrison .75 .30
❑ 45 Byron Leftwich .75 .30
❑ 46 Fred Taylor .50 .20
❑ 47 Jimmy Smith .50 .20
❑ 48 Priest Holmes .75 .30
❑ 49 Trent Green .50 .20
❑ 50 Tony Gonzalez .50 .20
❑ 51 Larry Johnson .75 .30
❑ 52 Chris Chambers .50 .20
❑ 53 A.J. Feeley .50 .20
❑ 54 Randy McMichael .40 .15
❑ 55 Daunte Culpepper .75 .30
❑ 56 Nate Burleson .50 .20
❑ 57 Michael Bennett .50 .20
❑ 58 Tom Brady 2.00 .75
❑ 59 Deion Branch .50 .20
❑ 60 Corey Dillon .50 .20
❑ 61 Aaron Brooks .50 .20
❑ 62 Deuce McAllister .75 .30
❑ 63 Joe Horn .50 .20
❑ 64 Eli Manning 1.50 .60
❑ 65 Jeremy Shockey .75 .30
❑ 66 Tiki Barber .75 .30
❑ 67 Plaxico Burress .50 .20
❑ 68 Chad Pennington .75 .30
❑ 69 Curtis Martin .75 .30
❑ 70 Laveranues Coles .50 .20
❑ 71 Jerry Porter .50 .20
❑ 72 Randy Moss .75 .30
❑ 73 Kerry Collins .50 .20
❑ 74 Donovan McNabb 1.00 .40
❑ 75 Brian Westbrook .50 .20

❑ 76 Terrell Owens .75 .30
❑ 77 Ben Roethlisberger 2.00 .75
❑ 78 Jerome Bettis .75 .30
❑ 79 Hines Ward .75 .30
❑ 80 Drew Brees .75 .30
❑ 81 LaDainian Tomlinson 1.00 .40
❑ 82 Antonio Gates .75 .30
❑ 83 Tim Rattay .40 .15
❑ 84 Eric Johnson .50 .20
❑ 85 Rashaun Woods .50 .20
❑ 86 Matt Hasselbeck .50 .20
❑ 87 Shaun Alexander 1.00 .40
❑ 88 Darrell Jackson .50 .20
❑ 89 Marc Bulger .75 .30
❑ 90 Marshall Faulk .75 .30
❑ 91 Torry Holt .75 .30
❑ 92 Brian Griese .50 .20
❑ 93 Michael Pittman .40 .15
❑ 94 Michael Clayton .75 .30
❑ 95 Steve McNair .75 .30
❑ 96 Chris Brown .50 .20
❑ 97 Drew Bennett .50 .20
❑ 98 Clinton Portis .75 .30
❑ 99 Patrick Ramsey .50 .20
❑ 100 Santana Moss .50 .20
❑ 101 Aaron Rodgers RC 8.00 3.00
❑ 102 Alex Smith QB RC 10.00 4.00
❑ 103 Charlie Frye RC 5.00 2.00
❑ 104 Andrew Walter RC 4.00 1.50
❑ 105 David Greene RC 2.50 1.00
❑ 106 Dan Orlovsky RC 3.00 1.25
❑ 107 Derek Anderson RC 2.50 1.00
❑ 108 Cadillac Williams RC 12.00 5.00
❑ 109 Ronnie Brown RC 10.00 4.00
❑ 110 Ciatrick Fason RC 2.50 1.00
❑ 111 Cedric Benson RC 5.00 2.00
❑ 112 Vincent Jackson RC 2.50 1.00
❑ 113 Eric Shelton RC 2.50 1.00
❑ 114 Frank Gore RC 5.00 2.00
❑ 115 Braylon Edwards RC 8.00 3.00
❑ 116 Roddy White RC 2.50 1.00
❑ 117 Troy Williamson RC 5.00 2.00
❑ 118 Craphonso Thorpe RC 2.00 .75
❑ 119 Mark Clayton RC 3.00 1.25
❑ 120 Fred Gibson RC 2.00 .75
❑ 121 Reggie Brown RC 2.50 1.00
❑ 122 Matt Jones RC 6.00 2.50
❑ 123 David Pollack RC 2.50 1.00
❑ 124 Derrick Johnson RC 4.00 1.50
❑ 125 Erasmus James RC 2.50 1.00
❑ 126 Antrel Rolle RC 2.50 1.00
❑ 127 Thomas Davis RC 2.50 1.00
❑ 128 Adam Jones RC 2.50 1.00
❑ 129 Corey Webster RC 2.50 1.00
❑ 130 Marlin Jackson RC 2.50 1.00
❑ 131 Brodney Pool RC 2.50 1.00
❑ 132 Mark Bradley RC 2.50 1.00
❑ 133 Stefan LeFors RC 2.50 1.00
❑ 134 Alex Smith TE RC 2.50 1.00
❑ 135 Heath Miller RC 6.00 2.50
❑ 136 Jason Campbell RC 4.00 1.50
❑ 137 Kyle Orton RC 5.00 1.50
❑ 138 Vernand Morency RC 2.50 1.00
❑ 139 Carlos Rogers RC 3.00 1.25
❑ 140 J.J. Arrington RC 3.00 1.25
❑ 141 Ryan Moats RC 2.50 1.00
❑ 142 Chris Henry RC 2.50 1.00
❑ 143 Terrence Murphy RC 2.50 1.00
❑ 144 Fabian Washington RC 2.50 1.00
❑ 145 Roscoe Parrish RC 2.50 1.00
❑ 146 Kevin Everett RC 2.50 1.00
❑ 147 Travis Johnson RC 2.00 .75
❑ 148 Mike Williams 5.00 2.00
❑ 149 Maurice Clarett 2.50 1.00
❑ 150 Channing Crowder RC 2.50 1.00
❑ 151 Odell Thurman RC 2.00 .75
❑ 152 DeMarcus Ware RC 4.00 1.50
❑ 153 Shawne Merriman RC 4.00 1.50
❑ 154 Jerome Mathis RC 2.50 1.00
❑ 155 Marcus Spears RC 2.50 1.00
❑ 156 Luis Castillo RC 2.50 1.00
❑ 157 Darren Sproles RC 2.50 1.00
❑ 158 Marion Barber RC 4.00 1.50
❑ 159 Justin Tuck RC 2.50 1.00
❑ 160 Courtney Roby RC 2.50 1.00

2004 Upper Deck Foundations

❑ COMP.SET w/o SP's (100) 20.00 7.50
❑ 258-263 RC JSY PRINT RUN 499 SER.#'d SETS
❑ 1 Josh McCown .50 .20
❑ 2 Emmitt Smith 1.50 .60
❑ 3 Anquan Boldin .75 .30
❑ 4 T.J. Duckett .50 .20
❑ 5 Peerless Price .50 .20
❑ 6 Michael Vick 1.50 .60
❑ 7 Todd Heap .50 .20
❑ 8 Kyle Boller .75 .30
❑ 9 Jamal Lewis .75 .30
❑ 10 Travis Henry .50 .20
❑ 11 Eric Moulds .50 .20
❑ 12 Drew Bledsoe .75 .30
❑ 13 Steve Smith .75 .30
❑ 14 Stephen Davis .50 .20
❑ 15 Jake Delhomme .75 .30
❑ 16 Rex Grossman .75 .30
❑ 17 Brian Urlacher 1.00 .40
❑ 18 Anthony Thomas .50 .20
❑ 19 Rudi Johnson .50 .20
❑ 20 Chad Johnson .75 .30
❑ 21 Carson Palmer 1.00 .40
❑ 22 Quincy Morgan .50 .20
❑ 23 Jeff Garcia .75 .30
❑ 24 Andre Davis .30 .10
❑ 25 Roy Williams S .50 .20
❑ 26 Eddie George .50 .20
❑ 27 Keyshawn Johnson .50 .20
❑ 28 Jake Plummer .50 .20
❑ 29 Champ Bailey .50 .20
❑ 30 Ashley Lelie .50 .20
❑ 31 Joey Harrington .75 .30
❑ 32 Charles Rogers .50 .20
❑ 33 Az-Zahir Hakim .30 .10
❑ 34 Javon Walker .50 .20
❑ 35 Brett Favre 2.00 .75
❑ 36 Ahman Green .75 .30
❑ 37 Domanick Davis .75 .30
❑ 38 David Carr .75 .30
❑ 39 Andre Johnson .75 .30
❑ 40 Peyton Manning 1.25 .50
❑ 41 Marvin Harrison .75 .30
❑ 42 Edgerrin James .75 .30
❑ 43 Jimmy Smith .50 .20
❑ 44 Fred Taylor .50 .20
❑ 45 Byron Leftwich 1.00 .40
❑ 46 Trent Green .50 .20
❑ 47 Tony Gonzalez .50 .20
❑ 48 Priest Holmes 1.00 .40
❑ 49 Dante Hall .75 .30
❑ 50 Ricky Williams .75 .30
❑ 51 David Boston .50 .20
❑ 52 Chris Chambers .50 .20
❑ 53 A.J. Feeley .75 .30
❑ 54 Randy Moss 1.00 .40
❑ 55 Michael Bennett .50 .20
❑ 56 Daunte Culpepper .75 .30
❑ 57 Troy Brown .50 .20
❑ 58 Tom Brady 2.00 .75
❑ 59 Corey Dillon .50 .20
❑ 60 Donte' Stallworth .50 .20
❑ 61 Deuce McAllister .75 .30
❑ 62 Aaron Brooks .50 .20
❑ 63 Kurt Warner .75 .30
❑ 64 Jeremy Shockey .75 .30
❑ 65 Santana Moss .50 .20
❑ 66 Curtis Martin .75 .30
❑ 67 Chad Pennington .75 .30
❑ 68 Amani Toomer .50 .20
❑ 69 Tim Brown .75 .30
❑ 70 Rich Gannon .50 .20
❑ 71 Jerry Rice 1.50 .60
❑ 72 Jerry Porter .50 .20
❑ 73 Terrell Owens .75 .30
❑ 74 Jevon Kearse .50 .20
❑ 75 Donovan McNabb 1.00 .40
❑ 76 Tommy Maddox .50 .20
❑ 77 Plaxico Burress .50 .20
❑ 78 Hines Ward .75 .30
❑ 79 Duce Staley .50 .20
❑ 80 LaDainian Tomlinson 1.00 .40
❑ 81 Drew Brees .75 .30
❑ 82 Donnie Edwards .30 .10
❑ 83 Tim Rattay .30 .10
❑ 84 Kevan Barlow .50 .20
❑ 85 Brandon Lloyd .50 .20
❑ 86 Shaun Alexander .75 .30
❑ 87 Matt Hasselbeck .50 .20
❑ 88 Koren Robinson .50 .20
❑ 89 Torry Holt .75 .30
❑ 90 Marshall Faulk .75 .30
❑ 91 Marc Bulger .75 .30
❑ 92 Keenan McCardell .30 .10
❑ 93 Derrick Brooks .50 .20
❑ 94 Brad Johnson .50 .20
❑ 95 Steve McNair .75 .30
❑ 96 Derrick Mason .50 .20
❑ 97 Chris Brown .75 .30
❑ 98 Mark Brunell .50 .20
❑ 99 LaVar Arrington 1.50 .60
❑ 100 Clinton Portis .75 .30
❑ 101 Brandon Chillar RC 8.00 3.00
❑ 102 Mike Karney RC 8.00 3.00
❑ 103 Jamaar Taylor RC 10.00 4.00
❑ 104 Casey Clausen RC 10.00 4.00
❑ 105 Drew Carter RC 10.00 4.00
❑ 106 Travis LaBoy RC 10.00 4.00
❑ 107 Jonathan Vilma RC 10.00 4.00
❑ 108 Tramon Douglas RC 5.00 2.00
❑ 109 Bob Sanders RC 20.00 10.00
❑ 110 Mewelde Moore RC 10.00 4.00
❑ 111 Randy Starks RC 8.00 3.00
❑ 112 Tank Johnson RC 8.00 3.00
❑ 113 Triandos Luke RC 10.00 4.00
❑ 114 Dexter Reid RC 5.00 2.00
❑ 115 Cedric Cobbs RC 10.00 4.00
❑ 116 Darius Watts RC 10.00 4.00
❑ 117 Ryan Krause RC 8.00 3.00
❑ 118 Igor Olshansky RC 10.00 4.00
❑ 119 Adimchinobe Echemandu RC 8.003.00
❑ 120 Jason Fife RC 8.00 3.00
❑ 121 Justin Smiley RC 10.00 4.00
❑ 122 Marcus Tubbs RC 10.00 4.00
❑ 123 Nathan Vasher RC 12.00 5.00
❑ 124 Troy Fleming RC 8.00 3.00
❑ 125 Ben Troupe RC 10.00 4.00
❑ 126 Jammal Lord RC 10.00 4.00
❑ 127 Jared Lorenzen RC 8.00 3.00
❑ 128 Shawntae Spencer RC 10.00 4.00
❑ 129 Darnell Dockett RC 8.00 3.00
❑ 130 Derrick Strait RC 10.00 4.00
❑ 131 Clarence Moore RC 10.00 4.00
❑ 132 Jason Babin RC 10.00 4.00
❑ 133 Jerricho Cotchery RC 10.00 4.00
❑ 134 Karlos Dansby RC 10.00 4.00
❑ 135 Marquise Hill RC 8.00 3.00
❑ 136 Niko Koutouvides RC 8.00 3.00
❑ 137 Andy Hall RC 8.00 3.00
❑ 138 Teddy Lehman RC 10.00 4.00
❑ 139 Will Smith RC 10.00 4.00
❑ 140 Bernard Berrian RC 12.00 5.00
❑ 141 Chris Cooley RC 10.00 4.00
❑ 142 Landon Johnson RC 8.00 3.00
❑ 143 Devard Darling RC 10.00 4.00
❑ 144 Mark Jones RC 8.00 3.00
❑ 145 Jake Grove RC 5.00 2.00
❑ 146 John Navarre RC 10.00 4.00
❑ 147 Keary Colbert RC 12.00 5.00
❑ 148 Gilbert Gardner RC 8.00 3.00
❑ 149 P.K. Sam RC 8.00 3.00
❑ 150 Richard Seigler RC 8.00 3.00

❑ 151 Marquis Cooper RC 8.00 3.00
❑ 152 Tommie Harris RC 10.00 4.00
❑ 153 Thomas Tapeh RC 8.00 3.00
❑ 154 Ben Utecht RC 5.00 2.00
❑ 155 Chris Gamble RC 10.00 4.00
❑ 156 Daryl Smith RC 10.00 4.00
❑ 157 Sean Taylor RC 10.00 4.00
❑ 158 Caleb Miller RC 8.00 3.00
❑ 159 Johnnie Morant RC 10.00 4.00
❑ 160 Keith Smith RC 8.00 3.00
❑ 161 Matt Mauck RC 10.00 4.00
❑ 162 Matt Ware RC 10.00 4.00
❑ 163 Quincy Wilson RC 8.00 3.00
❑ 164 Samie Parker RC 10.00 4.00
❑ 165 Kendrick Starling RC 5.00 2.00
❑ 166 Antwan Odom RC 10.00 4.00
❑ 167 Brandon Miree RC 8.00 3.00
❑ 168 Casey Bramlet RC 8.00 3.00
❑ 169 Cody Pickett RC 10.00 4.00
❑ 170 Demorrio Williams RC 10.00 4.00
❑ 171 Dunta Robinson RC 10.00 4.00
❑ 172 D.J. Hackett RC 8.00 3.00
❑ 173 Josh Harris RC 10.00 4.00
❑ 174 Kenechi Udeze RC 10.00 4.00
❑ 175 Michael Boulware RC 10.00 4.00
❑ 176 Ricardo Colclough RC 10.00 4.00
❑ 177 Shawn Andrews RC 10.00 4.00
❑ 178 Jeris McIntyre RC 8.00 3.00
❑ 179 Jim Sorgi RC 10.00 4.00
❑ 180 Clarence Farmer RC 8.00 3.00
❑ 181 Courtney Watson RC 10.00 4.00
❑ 182 Derek Abney RC 10.00 4.00
❑ 183 Dwan Edwards RC 5.00 2.00
❑ 184 Ryan Dinwiddie RC 8.00 3.00
❑ 185 B.J. Johnson RC 8.00 3.00
❑ 186 Ben Watson RC 10.00 4.00
❑ 187 Kris Wilson RC 10.00 4.00
❑ 188 Michael Turner RC 12.00 5.00
❑ 189 Derrick Ward RC 5.00 2.00
❑ 190 Jonathan Smith RC 8.00 3.00
❑ 191 Vernon Carey RC 8.00 3.00
❑ 192 Ben Hartsock RC 10.00 4.00
❑ 193 Rich Gardner RC 8.00 3.00
❑ 194 D.J. Williams RC 10.00 4.00
❑ 195 Derrick Hamilton RC 8.00 3.00
❑ 196 Drew Henson RC 10.00 4.00
❑ 197 Jeff Smoker RC 10.00 4.00
❑ 198 Joey Thomas RC 10.00 4.00
❑ 199 Keyaron Fox RC 8.00 3.00
❑ 200 Nate Lawrie RC 8.00 3.00
❑ 201 Sloan Thomas RC 8.00 3.00
❑ 202 Justin Jenkins RC 8.00 3.00
❑ 203 Stuart Schweigert RC 10.00 4.00
❑ 204 Ran Carthon RC 8.00 3.00
❑ 205 Ahmad Carroll RC 10.00 4.00
❑ 206 Bradlee Van Pelt RC 10.00 4.00
❑ 207 Patrick Crayton RC 10.00 4.00
❑ 208 Chris Snee RC 8.00 3.00
❑ 209 Fred Russell RC 10.00 4.00
❑ 210 Dontarrious Thomas RC 10.00 4.00
❑ 211 Will Poole RC 10.00 4.00
❑ 212 Jarrett Payton RC 10.00 4.00
❑ 213 Keiwan Ratliff RC 8.00 3.00
❑ 214 Nate Kaeding RC 10.00 4.00
❑ 215 Tim Euhus RC 10.00 4.00
❑ 216 Sean Jones RC 8.00 3.00
❑ 217 Will Allen RC 10.00 4.00
❑ 218 B.J. Symons RC 10.00 4.00
❑ 219 Carlos Francis RC 8.00 3.00
❑ 220 Craig Krenzel RC 10.00 4.00
❑ 221 Andrae Thurman RC 5.00 2.00
❑ 222 Ernest Wilford RC 10.00 4.00
❑ 223 Glenn Earl RC 8.00 3.00
❑ 224 Jeremy LeSueur RC 8.00 3.00
❑ 225 Junior Siavii RC 10.00 4.00
❑ 226 Maurice Mann RC 8.00 3.00
❑ 227 Michael Waddell RC 5.00 2.00
❑ 228 Jason Wright RC 8.00 3.00
❑ 229 Sean Ryan RC 8.00 3.00
❑ 230 Vince Wilfork RC 10.00 4.00
❑ 231 Matt Kegel RC 10.00 4.00
❑ 232 Chris Collins RC 8.00 3.00
❑ 233 Jonathan Smith RC 8.00 3.00
❑ 234 Renaldo Works RC 10.00 4.00
❑ 235 Matt Kranchick RC 10.00 4.00
❑ 236 J.R. Reed RC 8.00 3.00
❑ 237 Jason Shivers RC 8.00 3.00
❑ 238 Donnell Washington RC 10.00 4.00
❑ 239 Jorge Cordova RC 5.00 2.00
❑ 240 Wes Welker RC 12.00 5.00
❑ 241 Robert Gallery JSY RC 8.00 3.00
❑ 242 Luke McCown JSY RC 6.00 2.50
❑ 243 Roy Williams JSY RC 15.00 6.00
❑ 244 Julius Jones JSY RC 20.00 7.50
❑ 245 Tatum Bell JSY RC 12.00 5.00
❑ 246 Steven Jackson JSY RC 20.00 7.50
❑ 247 Reggie Williams JSY RC 8.00 3.00
❑ 248 Devery Henderson JSY RC 5.00 2.00
❑ 249 DeAngelo Hall JSY RC 8.00 3.00
❑ 250 Rashaun Woods JSY RC 6.00 2.50
❑ 251 Chris Perry JSY RC 10.00 4.00
❑ 252 Matt Schaub JSY RC 20.00 7.50
❑ 253 Lee Evans JSY RC 12.00 5.00
❑ 254 Michael Jenkins JSY RC 6.00 2.50
❑ 255 J.P. Losman JSY RC 12.00 5.00
❑ 256 Kevin Jones JSY RC 15.00 6.00
❑ 257 Michael Clayton JSY RC 12.00 5.00
❑ 258 Eli Manning JSY RC 30.00 15.00
❑ 259 Roethlisberger JSY RC 60.00 30.00
❑ 260 Larry Fitzgerald JSY RC 20.00 7.50
❑ 261 Philip Rivers JSY RC 20.00 10.00
❑ 262 Greg Jones JSY RC 10.00 4.00
❑ 263 Kellen Winslow JSY RC 12.00 5.00

2005 Upper Deck Foundations

❑ COMP.SET w/o RCs (100) 20.00 7.50
❑ 101-200 RC PRINT RUN 399 SER.#'d SETS
❑ ROOKIE AU STATED ODDS 1:12
❑ UNPRICED ROOKIE FOUNDATIONS #'d TO 1
❑ CARD #233 WAS NOT RELEASED
❑ 1 Larry Fitzgerald .75 .30
❑ 2 Anquan Boldin .50 .20
❑ 3 Kurt Warner .50 .20
❑ 4 Michael Vick 1.25 .50
❑ 5 T.J. Duckett .50 .20
❑ 6 Peerless Price .40 .15
❑ 7 Todd Heap .50 .20
❑ 8 Jamal Lewis .75 .30
❑ 9 Kyle Boller .50 .20
❑ 10 Derrick Mason .50 .20
❑ 11 J.P. Losman .75 .30
❑ 12 Willis McGahee .75 .30
❑ 13 Lee Evans .50 .20
❑ 14 Eric Moulds .50 .20
❑ 15 Jake Delhomme .75 .30
❑ 16 Keary Colbert .50 .20
❑ 17 DeShaun Foster .50 .20
❑ 18 Brian Urlacher .75 .30
❑ 19 Rex Grossman .50 .20
❑ 20 Muhsin Muhammad .50 .20
❑ 21 Carson Palmer .75 .30
❑ 22 Rudi Johnson .50 .20
❑ 23 Chad Johnson .75 .30
❑ 24 Julius Jones 1.00 .40
❑ 25 Keyshawn Johnson .50 .20
❑ 26 Drew Bledsoe .75 .30
❑ 27 Tatum Bell .50 .20
❑ 28 Jake Plummer .50 .20
❑ 29 Ashley Lelie .50 .20
❑ 30 Roy Williams WR .75 .30
❑ 31 Kevin Jones .75 .30
❑ 32 Jeff Garcia .50 .20
❑ 33 Brett Favre 2.00 .75
❑ 34 Ahman Green .75 .30
❑ 35 Javon Walker .50 .20
❑ 36 David Carr .75 .30
❑ 37 Andre Johnson .50 .20
❑ 38 Domanick Davis .50 .20
❑ 39 Peyton Manning 1.25 .50
❑ 40 Reggie Wayne .50 .20
❑ 41 Edgerrin James .75 .30
❑ 42 Marvin Harrison .75 .30
❑ 43 Byron Leftwich .75 .30
❑ 44 Fred Taylor .50 .20
❑ 45 Jimmy Smith .50 .20
❑ 46 Priest Holmes .75 .30
❑ 47 Tony Gonzalez .50 .20
❑ 48 Trent Green .50 .20
❑ 49 A.J. Feeley .50 .20
❑ 50 Chris Chambers .50 .20
❑ 51 Randy McMichael .40 .15
❑ 52 Daunte Culpepper .75 .30
❑ 53 Michael Bennett .50 .20
❑ 54 Nate Burleson .50 .20
❑ 55 Tom Brady 2.00 .75
❑ 56 Corey Dillon .50 .20
❑ 57 Deion Branch .50 .20
❑ 58 Richard Seymour .50 .20
❑ 59 Aaron Brooks .50 .20
❑ 60 Deuce McAllister .75 .30
❑ 61 Joe Horn .50 .20
❑ 62 Eli Manning 1.50 .60
❑ 63 Jeremy Shockey .75 .30
❑ 64 Tiki Barber .75 .30
❑ 65 Chad Pennington .75 .30
❑ 66 Curtis Martin .75 .30
❑ 67 Laveranues Coles .50 .20
❑ 68 Kerry Collins .50 .20
❑ 69 LaMont Jordan .75 .30
❑ 70 Randy Moss .75 .30
❑ 71 Donovan McNabb 1.00 .40
❑ 72 Terrell Owens .75 .30
❑ 73 Jeremiah Trotter .40 .15
❑ 74 Brian Westbrook .50 .20
❑ 75 Ben Roethlisberger 2.00 .75
❑ 76 Jerome Bettis .75 .30
❑ 77 Hines Ward .75 .30
❑ 78 Antwaan Randle El .50 .20
❑ 79 Drew Brees .75 .30
❑ 80 LaDainian Tomlinson 1.00 .40
❑ 81 Antonio Gates .75 .30
❑ 82 Tim Rattay .40 .15
❑ 83 Brandon Lloyd .40 .15
❑ 84 Eric Johnson .50 .20
❑ 85 Shaun Alexander 1.00 .40
❑ 86 Darrell Jackson .50 .20
❑ 87 Matt Hasselbeck .50 .20
❑ 88 Marc Bulger .75 .30
❑ 89 Steven Jackson 1.00 .40
❑ 90 Marshall Faulk .75 .30
❑ 91 Torry Holt .75 .30
❑ 92 Joey Galloway .50 .20
❑ 93 Brian Griese .50 .20
❑ 94 Michael Clayton .75 .30
❑ 95 Steve McNair .75 .30
❑ 96 Drew Bennett .50 .20
❑ 97 Chris Brown .50 .20
❑ 98 Clinton Portis .75 .30
❑ 99 Patrick Ramsey .50 .20
❑ 100 Santana Moss .50 .20
❑ 101 Gino Guidugli RC 4.00 1.50
❑ 102 James Kilian RC 8.00 3.00
❑ 103 Matt Cassel RC 12.00 5.00
❑ 104 Adrian McPherson RC 8.00 3.00
❑ 105 Timmy Chang RC 6.00 2.50
❑ 106 Chris Rix RC 6.00 2.50
❑ 107 Lionel Gates RC 6.00 2.50
❑ 108 Alvin Pearman RC 8.00 3.00
❑ 109 Damien Nash RC 6.00 2.50
❑ 110 Noah Herron RC 8.00 3.00
❑ 111 Steve Savoy RC 4.00 1.50
❑ 112 Craig Bragg RC 6.00 2.50
❑ 113 Larry Brackins RC 6.00 2.50
❑ 114 Nick Collins RC 8.00 3.00
❑ 115 Josh Davis RC 6.00 2.50
❑ 116 Chad Owens RC 8.00 3.00
❑ 117 Dante Ridgeway RC 6.00 2.50
❑ 118 Airese Currie RC 8.00 3.00
❑ 119 Chauncey Stovall RC 4.00 1.50
❑ 120 Harry Williams RC 6.00 2.50
❑ 121 Alex Smith TE RC 8.00 3.00
❑ 122 Jerome Collins RC 6.00 2.50

❑	123	Rick Razzano RC	8.00	3.00
❑	124	Derrick Johnson RC	12.00	5.00
❑	125	Mike Patterson RC	8.00	3.00
❑	126	Jonathan Babineaux RC	6.00	2.50
❑	127	Matt Roth RC	8.00	3.00
❑	128	Shaun Cody RC	8.00	3.00
❑	129	Justin Tuck RC	8.00	3.00
❑	130	Vincent Burns RC	6.00	2.50
❑	131	DeMarcus Ware RC	12.00	5.00
❑	132	Jerome Mathis RC	8.00	3.00
❑	133	Darryl Blackstock RC	6.00	2.50
❑	134	Robert McCune RC	6.00	2.50
❑	135	Channing Crowder RC	8.00	3.00
❑	136	Odell Thurman RC	8.00	3.00
❑	137	Marcus Maxwell RC	6.00	2.50
❑	138	Lance Mitchell RC	6.00	2.50
❑	139	Jordan Beck RC	6.00	2.50
❑	140	Alfred Fincher RC	6.00	2.50
❑	141	Kirk Morrison RC	8.00	3.00
❑	142	Kelvin Hayden RC	6.00	2.50
❑	143	Justin Miller RC	6.00	2.50
❑	144	Bryant McFadden RC	8.00	3.00
❑	145	Eric Green RC	4.00	1.50
❑	146	Fabian Washington RC	8.00	3.00
❑	147	Ellis Hobbs RC	8.00	3.00
❑	148	Ronald Bartell RC	6.00	2.50
❑	149	Brodney Pool RC	8.00	3.00
❑	150	Josh Bullocks RC	8.00	3.00
❑	151	Vincent Fuller RC	6.00	2.50
❑	152	Donte Nicholson RC	8.00	3.00
❑	153	Sean Considine RC	8.00	3.00
❑	154	Oshiomogho Atogwe RC	6.00	2.50
❑	155	Dustin Fox RC	8.00	3.00
❑	156	Mike Nugent RC	8.00	3.00
❑	157	Shane Boyd RC	4.00	1.50
❑	158	Ryan Fitzpatrick RC	12.00	5.00
❑	159	Brock Berlin RC	6.00	2.50
❑	160	Bryan Randall RC	6.00	2.50
❑	161	Matt Jones RC	20.00	7.50
❑	162	Todd Mortensen RC	6.00	2.50
❑	163	Darian Durant RC	8.00	3.00
❑	164	Stanley Wilson RC	6.00	2.50
❑	165	Nehemiah Broughton RC	6.00	2.50
❑	166	Manuel White RC	6.00	2.50
❑	167	Zach Tuiasosopo RC	4.00	1.50
❑	168	Deandra Cobb RC	6.00	2.50
❑	169	Charles Frederick	6.00	2.50
❑	170	Efrem Hill RC	6.00	2.50
❑	171	Jason Anderson RC	6.00	2.50
❑	172	Rasheed Marshall RC	8.00	3.00
❑	173	Tab Perry RC	8.00	3.00
❑	174	Paris Warren RC	6.00	2.50
❑	175	Roydell Williams RC	8.00	3.00
❑	176	Fred Amey RC	6.00	2.50
❑	177	Kerry Wright RC	6.00	2.50
❑	178	Joel Dreessen RC	6.00	2.50
❑	179	Bo Scaife RC	6.00	2.50
❑	180	Alex Barron RC	4.00	1.50
❑	181	Jammal Brown RC	8.00	3.00
❑	182	Michael Roos RC	4.00	1.50
❑	183	Khalif Barnes RC	6.00	2.50
❑	184	Logan Mankins RC	10.00	4.00
❑	185	Elton Brown RC	4.00	1.50
❑	186	David Baas RC	6.00	2.50
❑	187	Chris Spencer RC	8.00	3.00
❑	188	Marcus Spears RC	8.00	3.00
❑	189	Trent Cole RC	8.00	3.00
❑	190	Luis Castillo RC	8.00	3.00
❑	191	Bill Swancutt RC	6.00	2.50
❑	192	Jesse Lumsden RC	4.00	1.50
❑	193	Lofa Tatupu RC	10.00	4.00
❑	194	Boomer Grigsby RC	10.00	4.00
❑	195	Domonique Foxworth RC	8.00	3.00
❑	196	Travis Daniels RC	6.00	2.50
❑	197	Darrent Williams RC	8.00	3.00
❑	198	Kerry Rhodes RC	8.00	3.00
❑	199	Mark Bradley RC	8.00	3.00
❑	200	Bobby Purify RC	6.00	2.50
❑	201	Dan Orlovsky AU/699 RC	12.00	5.00
❑	202	David Greene AU/699 RC	10.00	4.00
❑	203	Anthony Davis AU/699 RC	8.00	3.00
❑	204	Taylor Stubblefield AU/699 RC	8.00	3.00
❑	205	Walter Reyes AU/699 RC	8.00	3.00
❑	206	Darren Sproles AU/699 RC	10.00	4.00
❑	207	Courtney Roby AU/375 RC	12.00	5.00
❑	208	Marlin Jackson AU/699 RC	10.00	4.00
❑	209	Corey Webster AU/699 RC	10.00	4.00
❑	210	Ryan Moats AU/699 RC	15.00	6.00
❑	211	Marion Barber AU/375 RC	30.00	15.00
❑	212	Frank Gore AU/699 RC	40.00	20.00
❑	213	Kay-Jay Harris AU/699 RC	8.00	3.00
❑	214	Anttaj Hawthorne AU/699 RC	8.00	3.00
❑	215	Adam Jones AU/699 RC	10.00	4.00
❑	216	Stefan LeFors AU/375 RC	12.00	5.00
❑	217	Barrett Ruud AU/699 RC	10.00	4.00
❑	218	Kevin Burnett AU/699 RC	10.00	4.00
❑	219	T.A. McLendon AU/699 RC	8.00	3.00
❑	220	James Butler AU/699 RC	8.00	3.00
❑	221	J.R. Russell AU/699 RC	8.00	3.00
❑	222	Vincent Jackson AU/300 RC	12.00	5.00
❑	223	J.J. Arrington AU/699 RC	20.00	7.50
❑	224	Maurice Clarett AU/175	20.00	7.50
❑	225	Brandon Jacobs AU/699 RC	30.00	15.00
❑	226	Craphonso Thorpe AU/699 RC	8.00	3.00
❑	227	Fred Gibson AU/575 RC	8.00	3.00
❑	228	Travis Johnson AU/699 RC	8.00	3.00
❑	229	Kyle Orton AU/575 RC	30.00	12.50
❑	230	Jason White AU/575 RC	10.00	4.00
❑	231	Terrence Murphy AU/575 RC	10.00	4.00
❑	232	Mark Clayton AU/375 RC	20.00	7.50
❑	234	David Pollack AU/575 RC	12.00	5.00
❑	235	Erasmus James AU/575 RC	10.00	4.00
❑	236	Dan Cody AU/575 RC	10.00	4.00
❑	237	Thomas Davis AU/575 RC	10.00	4.00
❑	238	Carlos Rogers AU/575 RC	12.00	5.00
❑	239	Derek Anderson AU/699 RC	15.00	6.00
❑	240	Antrel Rolle AU/575 RC	10.00	4.00
❑	241	Shawne Merriman AU/575 RC	25.00	12.50
❑	242	Reggie Brown AU/699 RC	12.00	5.00
❑	243	Heath Miller AU/699 RC	40.00	15.00
❑	244	Roscoe Parrish AU/375 RC	12.00	5.00
❑	245	Roddy White AU/375 RC	12.00	5.00
❑	246	Eric Shelton AU/699 RC	10.00	4.00
❑	247	Vernand Morency AU/575 RC	10.00	4.00
❑	248	Ciatrick Fason AU/375 RC	12.00	5.00
❑	249	Andrew Walter AU/375 RC	20.00	7.50
❑	250	Jason Campbell AU/375 RC	40.00	25.00
❑	251	Charles Frederick AU/699 RC	8.00	3.00
❑	252	Troy Williamson AU/175 RC	30.00	12.50
❑	253	Braylon Edwards AU/175 RC	60.00	30.00
❑	254	Mike Williams AU/175	50.00	25.00
❑	255	Cedric Benson AU/50 RC	100.00	50.00
❑	256	Cadillac Williams AU/175 RC	100.00	50.00
❑	257	Ronnie Brown AU/175 RC	100.00	50.00
❑	258	Charlie Frye AU/175 RC	50.00	20.00
❑	259	Alex Smith QB AU/175 RC	100.00	50.00
❑	260	Aaron Rodgers AU/175 RC	80.00	40.00

1997 Upper Deck Legends

❑		COMPLETE SET (208)	80.00	30.00
❑	1	Bart Starr	2.50	1.00
❑	2	Jim Brown	2.50	1.00
❑	3	Joe Namath	3.00	1.25
❑	4	Walter Payton	5.00	2.00
❑	5	Terry Bradshaw	3.00	1.25
❑	6	Franco Harris	.60	.25
❑	7	Dan Fouts	.60	.25
❑	8	Steve Largent	.60	.25
❑	9	Johnny Unitas	2.50	1.00
❑	10	Gale Sayers	1.50	.60
❑	11	Roger Staubach	3.00	1.25
❑	12	Tony Dorsett	.60	.25
❑	13	Fran Tarkenton	1.50	.60
❑	14	Charley Taylor	.40	.15
❑	15	Ray Nitschke	.60	.25
❑	16	Jim Ringo	.40	.15
❑	17	Dick Butkus	1.50	.60
❑	18	Fred Biletnikoff	.60	.25
❑	19	Lenny Moore	.40	.15
❑	20	Len Dawson	.60	.25
❑	21	Lance Alworth	.40	.15
❑	22	Chuck Bednarik	.40	.15
❑	23	Raymond Berry	.40	.15
❑	24	Donnie Shell	.30	.10
❑	25	Mel Blount	.40	.15
❑	26	Willie Brown	.40	.15
❑	27	Ken Houston	.30	.10
❑	28	Larry Csonka	.60	.25
❑	29	Mike Ditka	1.25	.50
❑	30	Art Donovan	.40	.15
❑	31	Sam Huff	.40	.15
❑	32	Lem Barney	.30	.10
❑	33	Hugh McElhenny	.40	.15
❑	34	Otto Graham	.75	.30
❑	35	Joe Greene	.60	.25
❑	36	Mike Rozier	.30	.10
❑	37	Lou Groza	.40	.15
❑	38	Ted Hendricks	.30	.10
❑	39	Elroy Hirsch	.40	.15
❑	40	Paul Hornung	.75	.30
❑	41	Charlie Joiner	.40	.15
❑	42	Deacon Jones	.40	.15
❑	43	Bill Bradley	.30	.10
❑	44	Floyd Little	.30	.10
❑	45	Willie Lanier	.30	.10
❑	46	Bob Lilly	.40	.15
❑	47	Sid Luckman	.40	.15
❑	48	John Mackey	.30	.10
❑	49	Don Maynard	.40	.15
❑	50	Mike McCormack	.30	.10
❑	51	Bobby Mitchell	.40	.15
❑	52	Ron Mix	.40	.15
❑	53	Marion Motley	.30	.10
❑	54	Leo Nomellini	.40	.15
❑	55	Mark Duper	.30	.10
❑	56	Mel Renfro	.30	.10
❑	57	Jim Otto	.40	.15
❑	58	Alan Page	.40	.15
❑	59	Joe Perry	.40	.15
❑	60	Andy Robustelli	.30	.10
❑	61	Lee Roy Selmon	.40	.15
❑	62	Jackie Smith	.40	.15
❑	63	Art Shell	.40	.15
❑	64	Jan Stenerud	.30	.10
❑	65	Gene Upshaw	.40	.15
❑	66	Y.A. Tittle	.60	.25
❑	67	Paul Warfield	.60	.25
❑	68	Kellen Winslow	.40	.15
❑	69	Randy White	.40	.15
❑	70	Larry Wilson	.30	.10
❑	71	Willie Wood	.40	.15
❑	72	Jack Ham	.40	.15
❑	73	Jack Youngblood	.30	.10
❑	74	Dan Abramowicz	.30	.10
❑	75	Dick Anderson	.30	.10
❑	76	Ken Anderson	.40	.15
❑	77	Steve Bartkowski	.30	.10
❑	78	Bill Bergey	.30	.10
❑	79	Rocky Bleier	.40	.15
❑	80	Cliff Branch	.40	.15
❑	81	John Brodie	.30	.10
❑	82	Bobby Bell	.30	.10
❑	83	Billy Cannon	.30	.10
❑	84	Gino Cappelletti	.30	.10
❑	85	Harold Carmichael	.30	.10
❑	86	Dave Casper	.30	.10
❑	87	Wes Chandler	.30	.10
❑	88	Todd Christensen	.30	.10
❑	89	Dwight Clark	.40	.15
❑	90	Mark Clayton	.30	.10
❑	91	Cris Collinsworth	.30	.10
❑	92	Roger Craig	.40	.15
❑	93	Randy Cross	.30	.10
❑	94	Isaac Curtis	.30	.10
❑	95	Mike Curtis	.30	.10
❑	96	Ben Davidson	.30	.10
❑	97	Fred Dean	.30	.10
❑	98	Tom Dempsey	.30	.10
❑	99	Eric Dickerson	.40	.15
❑	100	Lynn Dickey	.30	.10
❑	101	John McKay LL	.30	.10
❑	102	Carl Eller	.30	.10
❑	103	Chuck Foreman	.30	.10

❑ 104 Russ Francis .30 .10
❑ 105 Joe Gibbs LL .40 .15
❑ 106 Gary Garrison .30 .10
❑ 107 Randy Gradishar .30 .10
❑ 108 L.C. Greenwood .40 .15
❑ 109 Rosey Grier .30 .10
❑ 110 Steve Grogan .30 .10
❑ 111 Ray Guy .30 .10
❑ 112 John Hadl .30 .10
❑ 113 Jim Hart .30 .10
❑ 114 George Halas LL .40 .15
❑ 115 Mike Haynes .30 .10
❑ 116 Charlie Hennigan .30 .10
❑ 117 Chuck Howley .30 .10
❑ 118 Harold Jackson .30 .10
❑ 119 Tom Jackson .30 .10
❑ 120 Ron Jaworski .30 .10
❑ 121 John Jefferson .30 .10
❑ 122 Billy Johnson .30 .10
❑ 123 Ed Too Tall Jones .40 .15
❑ 124 Jack Kemp 1.50 .60
❑ 125 Jim Kiick .30 .10
❑ 126 Billy Kilmer .40 .15
❑ 127 Jerry Kramer .40 .15
❑ 128 Paul Krause .30 .10
❑ 129 Daryle Lamonica .30 .10
❑ 130 Bill Walsh LL .40 .15
❑ 131 James Lofton .30 .10
❑ 132 Hank Stram LL .30 .10
❑ 133 Archie Manning .40 .15
❑ 134 Jim Marshall .30 .10
❑ 135 Harvey Martin .30 .10
❑ 136 Tommy McDonald .30 .10
❑ 137 Max McGee .40 .15
❑ 138 Reggie McKenzie .30 .10
❑ 139 Karl Mecklenburg .30 .10
❑ 140 Tom Landry LL .60 .25
❑ 141 Terry Metcalf .30 .10
❑ 142 Matt Millen .30 .10
❑ 143 Earl Morrall .30 .10
❑ 144 Mercury Morris .30 .10
❑ 145 Chuck Noll LL .40 .15
❑ 146 Joe Morris .30 .10
❑ 147 Mark Moseley .30 .10
❑ 148 Haven Moses .30 .10
❑ 149 Chuck Muncie .30 .10
❑ 150 Anthony Munoz .40 .15
❑ 151 Tommy Nobis .30 .10
❑ 152 Babe Parilli .30 .10
❑ 153 Drew Pearson .40 .15
❑ 154 Ozzie Newsome .30 .10
❑ 155 Jim Plunkett .40 .15
❑ 156 William Perry .30 .10
❑ 157 Johnny Robinson .30 .10
❑ 158 Ahmad Rashad .40 .15
❑ 159 George Rogers .30 .10
❑ 160 Sterling Sharpe .40 .15
❑ 161 Billy Sims .40 .15
❑ 162 Sid Gillman LL .30 .10
❑ 163 Mike Singletary .60 .25
❑ 164 Charlie Sanders .30 .10
❑ 165 Bubba Smith .30 .10
❑ 166 Ken Stabler 2.00 .75
❑ 167 Freddie Solomon .30 .10
❑ 168 John Stallworth .40 .15
❑ 169 Dwight Stephenson .40 .15
❑ 170 Vince Lombardi LL 1.00 .40
❑ 171 Weeb Ewbank LL .30 .10
❑ 172 Lionel Taylor .30 .10
❑ 173 Otis Taylor .30 .10
❑ 174 Joe Theismann .60 .25
❑ 175 Bob Trumpy .30 .10
❑ 176 Mike Webster .30 .10
❑ 177 Jim Zorn .30 .10
❑ 178 Joe Montana 5.00 2.00
❑ 179 Packers Superbowl SM .40 .15
❑ 180 Bart Starr SM 1.25 .50
❑ 181 Max McGee SM .40 .15
❑ 182 Joe Namath SM 1.50 .60
❑ 183 Johnny Unitas SM 1.25 .50
❑ 184 Len Dawson SM .40 .15
❑ 185 Chuck Howley SM .30 .10
❑ 186 Roger Staubach SM 1.50 .60
❑ 187 Paul Warfield SM .40 .15
❑ 188 Larry Csonka SM .40 .15
❑ 189 Fran Tarkenton SM .60 .25
❑ 190 Terry Bradshaw SM 1.50 .60
❑ 191 Ken Stabler SM .75 .30
❑ 192 Fred Biletnikoff SM .40 .15
❑ 193 Chuck Foreman SM .30 .10
❑ 194 Harvey Martin SM .30 .10
❑ 195 Tony Dorsett SM .40 .15
❑ 196 Terry Bradshaw SM 1.50 .60
❑ 197 John Stallworth SM .30 .10
❑ 198 Franco Harris SM .40 .15
❑ 199 Ken Anderson SM .30 .10
❑ 200 Joe Theismann SM .40 .15
❑ 201 Jim Plunkett SM .30 .10
❑ 202 Roger Craig SM .30 .10
❑ 203 William Perry SM .30 .10
❑ 204 Steve Grogan SM .30 .10
❑ 205 Joe Montana SM 2.50 1.00
❑ 206 Russ Francis SM .30 .10
❑ 207 Joe Montana SM 2.50 1.00
❑ 208 Joe Montana SM 2.50 1.00

2000 Upper Deck Legends

❑ COMPLETE SET (132) 400.00 200.00
❑ COMP.SET w/o SP's (90) 20.00 7.50
❑ 1 Jake Plummer .30 .10
❑ 2 Jamal Anderson .50 .20
❑ 3 Doug Flutie .50 .20
❑ 4 Jim Kelly .60 .25
❑ 5 Dick Butkus 1.00 .40
❑ 6 Mike Singletary .50 .20
❑ 7 Gale Sayers 1.00 .40
❑ 8 Boomer Esiason .30 .10
❑ 9 Anthony Munoz .30 .10
❑ 10 Otto Graham .30 .10
❑ 11 Jim Brown 1.25 .50
❑ 12 Ozzie Newsome .20 .07
❑ 13 Bob Lilly .30 .10
❑ 14 Troy Aikman 1.25 .50
❑ 15 Emmitt Smith 1.25 .50
❑ 16 Roger Staubach 1.25 .50
❑ 17 Deion Sanders .50 .20
❑ 18 Tony Dorsett .50 .20
❑ 19 Terrell Davis .50 .20
❑ 20 John Elway 2.00 .75
❑ 21 Charlie Batch .50 .20
❑ 22 Brett Favre 2.00 .75
❑ 23 Bart Starr 1.50 .60
❑ 24 Reggie White .50 .20
❑ 25 Earl Campbell .50 .20
❑ 26 Peyton Manning 1.50 .60
❑ 27 Edgerrin James 1.00 .40
❑ 28 Johnny Unitas 1.25 .50
❑ 29 Marvin Harrison .50 .20
❑ 30 Mark Brunell .50 .20
❑ 31 Fred Taylor .50 .20
❑ 32 Len Dawson .50 .20
❑ 33 Dan Marino 2.00 .75
❑ 34 Bob Griese .50 .20
❑ 35 Mark Duper .20 .07
❑ 36 Thurman Thomas .30 .10
❑ 37 Fran Tarkenton 1.00 .40
❑ 38 Randy Moss 1.25 .50
❑ 39 Cris Carter .50 .20
❑ 40 Gary Anderson .20 .07
❑ 41 John Randle .30 .10
❑ 42 Drew Bledsoe .75 .30
❑ 43 Archie Manning .30 .10
❑ 44 Ricky Williams .50 .20
❑ 45 Frank Gifford .50 .20
❑ 46 Kerry Collins .30 .10
❑ 47 Phil Simms .30 .10
❑ 48 Vinny Testaverde .30 .10
❑ 49 Curtis Martin .50 .20
❑ 50 Keyshawn Johnson .50 .20
❑ 51 Joe Namath 1.25 .50
❑ 52 Marcus Allen .60 .25
❑ 53 Bruce Smith .30 .10
❑ 54 Ken Stabler 1.25 .50
❑ 55 Fred Biletnikoff .50 .20
❑ 56 Howie Long .60 .25
❑ 57 Ron Jaworski .20 .07
❑ 58 Harold Carmichael .20 .07
❑ 59 Kordell Stewart .30 .10
❑ 60 Levon Kirkland .20 .07
❑ 61 Mel Blount .30 .10
❑ 62 Jerome Bettis .50 .20
❑ 63 John Stallworth .30 .10
❑ 64 Franco Harris .60 .25
❑ 65 Jim Harbaugh .30 .10
❑ 66 Kellen Winslow .30 .10
❑ 67 Charlie Joiner .20 .07
❑ 68 Junior Seau .50 .20
❑ 69 Jerry Rice 1.25 .50
❑ 70 Steve Young 1.00 .40
❑ 71 Joe Montana 2.50 1.00
❑ 72 Roger Craig .30 .10
❑ 73 Ronnie Lott .30 .10
❑ 74 Jon Kitna .50 .20
❑ 75 Steve Largent .50 .20
❑ 76 Ricky Watters .30 .10
❑ 77 Kurt Warner 1.25 .50
❑ 78 Marshall Faulk .75 .30
❑ 79 Isaac Bruce .50 .20
❑ 80 Merlin Olsen .30 .10
❑ 81 Lee Roy Selmon .20 .07
❑ 82 Tim Brown .50 .20
❑ 83 Tim Couch .30 .10
❑ 84 Mike Alstott .50 .20
❑ 85 Eddie George .50 .20
❑ 86 Steve McNair .50 .20
❑ 87 Brad Johnson .50 .20
❑ 88 Sonny Jurgensen .50 .20
❑ 89 Art Monk .30 .10
❑ 90 Joe Theismann .50 .20
❑ 91 Ray Nitschke TCL 10.00 4.00
❑ 92 Doak Walker TCL 10.00 4.00
❑ 93 Thurman Thomas TCL 10.00 4.00
❑ 94 Jim Brown TCL 12.00 5.00
❑ 95 Sammy Baugh TCL 15.00 6.00
❑ 96 Reggie White TCL 10.00 4.00
❑ 97 Eric Dickerson TCL 10.00 4.00
❑ 98 Paul Hornung TCL 10.00 4.00
❑ 99 Deion Sanders TCL 12.00 5.00
❑ 100 Bronko Nagurski TCL 10.00 4.00
❑ 101 Walter Payton TCL 25.00 12.50
❑ 102 Jim Thorpe TCL 12.00 5.00
❑ 103 Ron Dayne RC 6.00 2.50
❑ 104 Tim Rattay RC 6.00 2.50
❑ 105 Brian Urlacher RC 25.00 10.00
❑ 106 Bubba Franks RC 6.00 2.50
❑ 107 Chad Pennington RC 15.00 6.00
❑ 108 Chris Cole RC 5.00 2.00
❑ 109 Chris Redman RC 5.00 2.00
❑ 110 Courtney Brown RC 6.00 2.50
❑ 111 Curtis Keaton RC 5.00 2.00
❑ 112 Dennis Northcutt RC 10.00 4.00
❑ 113 Dez White RC 6.00 2.50
❑ 114 Giovanni Carmazzi RC 10.00 4.00
❑ 115 J.R. Redmond RC 5.00 2.00
❑ 116 JaJuan Dawson RC 10.00 4.00
❑ 117 Jamal Lewis RC 15.00 6.00
❑ 118 Jerry Porter RC 8.00 3.00
❑ 119 Laveranues Coles RC 8.00 3.00
❑ 120 Peter Warrick RC 6.00 2.50
❑ 121 Plaxico Burress RC 12.00 5.00
❑ 122 R.Jay Soward RC 5.00 2.00
❑ 123 Reuben Droughns RC 8.00 3.00
❑ 124 Ron Dixon RC 5.00 2.00
❑ 125 Ron Dugans RC 10.00 4.00
❑ 126 Shaun Alexander RC 30.00 12.50
❑ 127 Sylvester Morris RC 5.00 2.00
❑ 128 Thomas Jones RC 10.00 4.00
❑ 129 Todd Pinkston RC 6.00 2.50
❑ 130 Travis Prentice RC 5.00 2.00
❑ 131 Travis Taylor RC 10.00 4.00
❑ 132 Trung Canidate RC 5.00 2.00

2001 Upper Deck Legends

❑	COMP.SET w/o SP's (90)	30.00	12.50
❑ 1	Jake Plummer	.50	.20
❑ 2	Jamal Anderson	.75	.30
❑ 3	Ray Lewis	.75	.30
❑ 4	Johnny Unitas	1.50	.60
❑ 5	Jamal Lewis	1.50	.60
❑ 6	Andre Reed	.50	.20
❑ 7	Jim Kelly	1.25	.50
❑ 8	Thurman Thomas	.50	.20
❑ 9	Rob Johnson	.50	.20
❑ 10	Brian Urlacher	1.50	.60
❑ 11	Dick Butkus	1.50	.60
❑ 12	Gale Sayers	1.50	.60
❑ 13	James Allen	.50	.20
❑ 14	Corey Dillon	.75	.30
❑ 15	Jim Brown	1.50	.60
❑ 16	Tim Couch	.50	.20
❑ 17	Joey Galloway	.50	.20
❑ 18	Emmitt Smith	2.00	.75
❑ 19	Randy White	.50	.20
❑ 20	Roger Staubach	1.50	.60
❑ 21	Troy Aikman	1.50	.60
❑ 22	Tony Dorsett	.75	.30
❑ 23	Brian Griese	.75	.30
❑ 24	Floyd Little	.30	.10
❑ 25	John Elway	3.00	1.25
❑ 26	Mike Anderson	.75	.30
❑ 27	Terrell Davis	.75	.30
❑ 28	Barry Sanders	2.00	.75
❑ 29	Charlie Batch	.75	.30
❑ 30	Bart Starr	2.00	.75
❑ 31	Paul Hornung	.75	.30
❑ 32	Reggie White	.75	.30
❑ 33	Warren Moon	.75	.30
❑ 34	Edgerrin James	1.25	.50
❑ 35	Peyton Manning	2.50	1.00
❑ 36	Mark Brunell	.75	.30
❑ 37	Tony Gonzalez	.50	.20
❑ 38	Eric Dickerson	.50	.20
❑ 39	Jack Youngblood	.30	.10
❑ 40	Jay Fiedler	.75	.30
❑ 41	Lamar Smith	.50	.20
❑ 42	Dan Marino	3.00	1.25
❑ 43	Oronde Gadsden	.50	.20
❑ 44	Cris Carter	.75	.30
❑ 45	Fran Tarkenton	1.25	.50
❑ 46	Daunte Culpepper	.75	.30
❑ 47	Randy Moss	2.00	.75
❑ 48	Robert Smith	.30	.10
❑ 49	Drew Bledsoe	1.25	.50
❑ 50	Archie Manning	.50	.20
❑ 51	Jeff Blake	.50	.20
❑ 52	Ricky Williams	.75	.30
❑ 53	Kerry Collins	.50	.20
❑ 54	Ron Dayne	.75	.30
❑ 55	Lawrence Taylor	.75	.30
❑ 56	Wayne Chrebet	.50	.20
❑ 57	Vinny Testaverde	.50	.20
❑ 58	Joe Namath	1.50	.60
❑ 59	Jim Plunkett	.50	.20
❑ 60	George Blanda	.75	.30
❑ 61	Tim Brown	.75	.30
❑ 62	Jerry Rice	2.00	.75
❑ 63	Ken Stabler	1.50	.60
❑ 64	Marcus Allen	1.25	.50
❑ 65	Donovan McNabb	1.25	.50
❑ 66	Harold Carmichael	.30	.10
❑ 67	Franco Harris	1.25	.50
❑ 68	Jerome Bettis	.75	.30
❑ 69	Terry Bradshaw	1.50	.60
❑ 70	Doug Flutie	.75	.30
❑ 71	Lance Alworth	.50	.20
❑ 72	Junior Seau	.75	.30
❑ 73	Kellen Winslow	.50	.20
❑ 74	Dan Fouts	.75	.30
❑ 75	Joe Montana	5.00	2.00
❑ 76	Terrell Owens	.75	.30
❑ 77	Jeff Garcia	.75	.30
❑ 78	Steve Young	1.25	.50
❑ 79	Matt Hasselbeck	.50	.20
❑ 80	Kurt Warner	2.00	.75
❑ 81	Marshall Faulk	1.25	.50
❑ 82	Brad Johnson	.75	.30
❑ 83	Eddie George	.75	.30
❑ 84	Charley Taylor	.50	.20
❑ 85	Stephen Davis	.75	.30
❑ 86	Jeff George	.50	.20
❑ 87	John Riggins	1.25	.50
❑ 88	Joe Theismann	.75	.30
❑ 89	Michael Westbrook	.50	.20
❑ 90	Sonny Jurgensen	.75	.30
❑ 91	Andre Carter RC	8.00	3.00
❑ 92	Cedrick Wilson RC	8.00	3.00
❑ 93	Kevan Barlow RC	8.00	3.00
❑ 94	Anthony Thomas RC	8.00	3.00
❑ 95	David Terrell RC	8.00	3.00
❑ 96	Chad Johnson RC	20.00	7.50
❑ 97	Justin Smith RC	8.00	3.00
❑ 98	Rudi Johnson RC	15.00	6.00
❑ 99	T.J. Houshmandzadeh RC	10.00	4.00
❑ 100	Brandon Spoon RC	8.00	3.00
❑ 101	Nate Clements RC	8.00	3.00
❑ 102	Travis Henry RC	12.00	5.00
❑ 103	Kevin Kasper RC	8.00	3.00
❑ 104	Willie Middlebrooks RC	5.00	2.00
❑ 105	Gerard Warren RC	8.00	3.00
❑ 106	James Jackson RC	8.00	3.00
❑ 107	Quincy Morgan RC	8.00	3.00
❑ 108	Bobby Newcombe RC	5.00	2.00
❑ 109	Arnold Jackson RC	5.00	2.00
❑ 110	Carlos Polk RC	3.00	1.25
❑ 111	Drew Brees RC	25.00	10.00
❑ 112	LaDainian Tomlinson RC	60.00	30.00
❑ 113	Tay Cody RC	3.00	1.25
❑ 114	Zeke Moreno RC	8.00	3.00
❑ 115	Snoop Minnis RC	5.00	2.00
❑ 116	George Layne RC	5.00	2.00
❑ 117	Derrick Blaylock RC	8.00	3.00
❑ 118	Reggie Wayne RC	15.00	6.00
❑ 119	Tony Dixon RC	5.00	2.00
❑ 120	Quincy Carter RC	8.00	3.00
❑ 121	Chris Chambers RC	12.00	5.00
❑ 122	Jamar Fletcher RC	5.00	2.00
❑ 123	Josh Heupel RC	8.00	3.00
❑ 124	Travis Minor RC	5.00	2.00
❑ 125	A.J. Feeley RC	8.00	3.00
❑ 126	Correll Buckhalter RC	10.00	4.00
❑ 127	Freddie Mitchell RC	8.00	3.00
❑ 128	Alge Crumpler RC	10.00	4.00
❑ 129	Michael Vick RC	40.00	15.00
❑ 130	Vinny Sutherland RC	5.00	2.00
❑ 131	Marcus Stroud RC	8.00	3.00
❑ 132	Mike McMahon RC	8.00	3.00
❑ 133	Scotty Anderson RC	5.00	2.00
❑ 134	Shaun Rogers RC	8.00	3.00
❑ 135	Jesse Palmer RC	8.00	3.00
❑ 136	Will Allen RC	5.00	2.00
❑ 137	LaMont Jordan RC	15.00	6.00
❑ 138	Santana Moss RC	12.00	5.00
❑ 139	Reggie White RC	5.00	2.00
❑ 140	Jamal Reynolds RC	8.00	3.00
❑ 141	Robert Ferguson RC	8.00	3.00
❑ 142	Torrance Marshall RC	8.00	3.00
❑ 143	Chris Weinke RC	8.00	3.00
❑ 144	Dan Morgan RC	8.00	3.00
❑ 145	Steve Smith RC	20.00	7.50
❑ 146	Dee Brown RC	8.00	3.00
❑ 147	Arther Love RC	3.00	1.25
❑ 148	Hakim Akbar RC	3.00	1.25
❑ 149	Jabari Holloway RC	5.00	2.00
❑ 150	Derek Combs RC	5.00	2.00
❑ 151	Derrick Gibson RC	5.00	2.00
❑ 152	Ken-Yon Rambo RC	5.00	2.00
❑ 153	Marques Tuiasosopo RC	8.00	3.00
❑ 154	Adam Archuleta RC	8.00	3.00
❑ 155	Tommy Polley RC	8.00	3.00
❑ 156	Brian Allen RC	3.00	1.25
❑ 157	Milton Wynn RC	5.00	2.00
❑ 158	Francis St.Paul RC	5.00	2.00
❑ 159	Edgerton Hartwell RC	3.00	1.25
❑ 160	Gary Baxter RC	5.00	2.00
❑ 161	Todd Heap RC	8.00	3.00
❑ 162	Chris Barnes RC	5.00	2.00
❑ 163	Fred Smoot RC	8.00	3.00
❑ 164	Rod Gardner RC	8.00	3.00
❑ 165	Sage Rosenfels RC	8.00	3.00
❑ 166	Damerien McCants RC	5.00	2.00
❑ 167	Deuce McAllister RC	15.00	6.00
❑ 168	Moran Norris RC	3.00	1.25
❑ 169	Sedrick Hodge RC	3.00	1.25
❑ 170	Alex Bannister RC	5.00	2.00
❑ 171	Heath Evans RC	5.00	2.00
❑ 172	Josh Booty RC	8.00	3.00
❑ 173	Ken Lucas RC	5.00	2.00
❑ 174	Koren Robinson RC	8.00	3.00
❑ 175	Chris Taylor RC	5.00	2.00
❑ 176	Andre Dyson RC	3.00	1.25
❑ 177	Dan Alexander RC	8.00	3.00
❑ 178	Justin McCareins RC	8.00	3.00
❑ 179	Eddie Berlin RC	5.00	2.00
❑ 180	Michael Bennett RC	8.00	3.00

2004 Upper Deck Legends

❑	COMP.SET w/o SP's (90)	20.00	7.50
❑	91-110 LEGENDS/1250 ODDS 1:24		
❑	111-190 ROOKIE/650 ODDS 1:12		
❑ 1	Josh McCown	.50	.20
❑ 2	Emmitt Smith	1.50	.60
❑ 3	Michael Vick	1.50	.60
❑ 4	Peerless Price	.50	.20
❑ 5	Ray Lewis	.75	.30
❑ 6	Kyle Boller	.75	.30
❑ 7	Deion Sanders	.75	.30
❑ 8	Drew Bledsoe	.75	.30
❑ 9	Travis Henry	.50	.20
❑ 10	Eric Moulds	.50	.20
❑ 11	Steve Smith	.75	.30
❑ 12	Stephen Davis	.50	.20
❑ 13	Jake Delhomme	.75	.30
❑ 14	Rex Grossman	.75	.30
❑ 15	Brian Urlacher	1.00	.40
❑ 16	Thomas Jones	.50	.20
❑ 17	Chad Johnson	.75	.30
❑ 18	Rudi Johnson	.50	.20
❑ 19	Carson Palmer	1.00	.40
❑ 20	William Green	.50	.20
❑ 21	Andre Davis	.30	.10
❑ 22	Jeff Garcia	.75	.30
❑ 23	Roy Williams S	.50	.20
❑ 24	Eddie George	.50	.20
❑ 25	Keyshawn Johnson	.50	.20
❑ 26	Reuben Droughns	.50	.20
❑ 27	Jake Plummer	.50	.20
❑ 28	Champ Bailey	.50	.20
❑ 29	Charles Rogers	.50	.20
❑ 30	Joey Harrington	.75	.30
❑ 31	Ahman Green	.75	.30
❑ 32	Brett Favre	2.00	.75
❑ 33	Javon Walker	.50	.20
❑ 34	David Carr	.75	.30
❑ 35	Domanick Davis	.75	.30
❑ 36	Andre Johnson	.75	.30
❑ 37	Marvin Harrison	.75	.30

❑ 38 Edgerrin James .75 .30
❑ 39 Peyton Manning 1.25 .50
❑ 40 Byron Leftwich 1.00 .40
❑ 41 Fred Taylor .50 .20
❑ 42 Trent Green .50 .20
❑ 43 Tony Gonzalez .50 .20
❑ 44 Priest Holmes 1.00 .40
❑ 45 Zach Thomas .75 .30
❑ 46 Chris Chambers .50 .20
❑ 47 Jay Fiedler .30 .10
❑ 48 Daunte Culpepper .75 .30
❑ 49 Randy Moss 1.00 .40
❑ 50 Onterrio Smith .50 .20
❑ 51 Tom Brady 2.00 .75
❑ 52 Deion Branch .75 .30
❑ 53 Corey Dillon .50 .20
❑ 54 Deuce McAllister .75 .30
❑ 55 Aaron Brooks .50 .20
❑ 56 Joe Horn .50 .20
❑ 57 Tiki Barber .75 .30
❑ 58 Kurt Warner .75 .30
❑ 59 Jeremy Shockey .75 .30
❑ 60 Chad Pennington .75 .30
❑ 61 Santana Moss .50 .20
❑ 62 Curtis Martin .75 .30
❑ 63 Kerry Collins .50 .20
❑ 64 Jerry Rice 1.50 .60
❑ 65 Jerry Porter .50 .20
❑ 66 Terrell Owens .75 .30
❑ 67 Jevon Kearse .50 .20
❑ 68 Donovan McNabb 1.00 .40
❑ 69 Hines Ward .75 .30
❑ 70 Plaxico Burress .50 .20
❑ 71 Duce Staley .50 .20
❑ 72 Drew Brees .75 .30
❑ 73 LaDainian Tomlinson 1.00 .40
❑ 74 Tim Rattay .30 .10
❑ 75 Brandon Lloyd .50 .20
❑ 76 Kevan Barlow .50 .20
❑ 77 Shaun Alexander .75 .30
❑ 78 Koren Robinson .50 .20
❑ 79 Matt Hasselbeck .50 .20
❑ 80 Marshall Faulk .75 .30
❑ 81 Torry Holt .75 .30
❑ 82 Marc Bulger .75 .30
❑ 83 Brian Griese .50 .20
❑ 84 Derrick Brooks .50 .20
❑ 85 Steve McNair .75 .30
❑ 86 Derrick Mason .50 .20
❑ 87 Chris Brown .75 .30
❑ 88 Mark Brunell .50 .20
❑ 89 Laveranues Coles .50 .20
❑ 90 Clinton Portis .75 .30
❑ 91 Dick Butkus 8.00 3.00
❑ 92 Gale Sayers 6.00 2.50
❑ 93 Mike Ditka 5.00 2.00
❑ 94 Jim Brown 8.00 3.00
❑ 95 Roger Staubach 8.00 3.00
❑ 96 Troy Aikman 6.00 2.50
❑ 97 John Elway 8.00 3.00
❑ 98 Barry Sanders 8.00 3.00
❑ 99 Bart Starr 10.00 4.00
❑ 100 Paul Hornung 5.00 2.00
❑ 101 Len Dawson 5.00 2.00
❑ 102 Dan Marino 10.00 4.00
❑ 103 Fran Tarkenton 6.00 2.50
❑ 104 Archie Manning 5.00 2.00
❑ 105 Joe Namath 8.00 3.00
❑ 106 Ken Stabler 6.00 2.50
❑ 107 Lynn Swann 6.00 2.50
❑ 108 Terry Bradshaw 8.00 3.00
❑ 109 Joe Montana 12.00 5.00
❑ 110 Joe Theismann 5.00 2.00
❑ 111 Bernard Berrian RC 6.00 2.50
❑ 112 Ben Hartsock RC 5.00 2.00
❑ 113 Karlos Dansby RC 5.00 2.00
❑ 114 Thomas Tapeh RC 4.00 1.50
❑ 115 Keary Colbert RC 6.00 2.50
❑ 116 Ben Troupe RC 5.00 2.00
❑ 117 Jonathan Vilma RC 5.00 2.00
❑ 118 Jamaar Taylor RC 5.00 2.00
❑ 119 Ben Roethlisberger RC 50.00 25.00
❑ 120 Samie Parker RC 5.00 2.00
❑ 121 Dunta Robinson RC 5.00 2.00
❑ 122 Dontarrious Thomas RC 5.00 2.00
❑ 123 Adimchinobe Echemandu RC 4.00 1.50
❑ 124 Darius Watts RC 5.00 2.00
❑ 125 Ben Watson RC 5.00 2.00
❑ 126 Terry Johnson RC 4.00 1.50
❑ 127 D.J. Hackett RC 4.00 1.50
❑ 128 Devery Henderson RC 4.00 1.50
❑ 129 Kellen Winslow Jr. RC 10.00 4.00
❑ 130 Travis LaBoy RC 5.00 2.00
❑ 131 Maurice Mann RC 4.00 1.50
❑ 132 Rashaun Woods RC 5.00 2.00
❑ 133 Michael Turner RC 6.00 2.50
❑ 134 Junior Siavii RC 5.00 2.00
❑ 135 Johnnie Morant RC 5.00 2.00
❑ 136 Larry Fitzgerald RC 15.00 6.00
❑ 137 Kevin Jones RC 12.00 5.00
❑ 138 Will Smith RC 5.00 2.00
❑ 139 Robert Gallery RC 5.00 2.00
❑ 140 Michael Jenkins RC 5.00 2.00
❑ 141 Cedric Cobbs RC 5.00 2.00
❑ 142 Igor Olshansky RC 5.00 2.00
❑ 143 Josh Harris RC 5.00 2.00
❑ 144 Michael Clayton RC 10.00 4.00
❑ 145 Mewelde Moore RC 5.00 2.00
❑ 146 Jason Babin RC 5.00 2.00
❑ 147 Cody Pickett RC 5.00 2.00
❑ 148 Lee Evans RC 6.00 2.50
❑ 149 Greg Jones RC 5.00 2.00
❑ 150 Marcus Tubbs RC 5.00 2.00
❑ 151 Craig Krenzel RC 5.00 2.00
❑ 152 Roy Williams RC 12.00 5.00
❑ 153 Tatum Bell RC 10.00 4.00
❑ 154 Kenechi Udeze RC 5.00 2.00
❑ 155 Shawn Andrews RC 5.00 2.00
❑ 156 Reggie Williams RC 6.00 2.50
❑ 157 Julius Jones RC 15.00 6.00
❑ 158 Vince Wilfork RC 5.00 2.00
❑ 159 Vernon Carey RC 4.00 1.50
❑ 160 Eli Manning RC 25.00 12.50
❑ 161 Devard Darling RC 5.00 2.00
❑ 162 Sean Taylor RC 5.00 2.00
❑ 163 Teddy Lehman RC 5.00 2.00
❑ 164 Jammal Lord RC 5.00 2.00
❑ 165 J.P. Losman RC 10.00 4.00
❑ 166 Jerricho Cotchery RC 5.00 2.00
❑ 167 Ahmad Carroll RC 5.00 2.00
❑ 168 Michael Boulware RC 5.00 2.00
❑ 169 Quincy Wilson RC 4.00 1.50
❑ 170 Derrick Hamilton RC 4.00 1.50
❑ 171 Kris Wilson RC 5.00 2.00
❑ 172 D.J. Williams RC 5.00 2.00
❑ 173 P.K. Sam RC 4.00 1.50
❑ 174 Matt Schaub RC 15.00 6.00
❑ 175 Ernest Wilford RC 5.00 2.00
❑ 176 Chris Gamble RC 5.00 2.00
❑ 177 Courtney Watson RC 5.00 2.00
❑ 178 Drew Henson RC 5.00 2.00
❑ 179 Chris Perry RC 8.00 3.00
❑ 180 Tommie Harris RC 5.00 2.00
❑ 181 Marquis Cooper RC 4.00 1.50
❑ 182 Philip Rivers RC 15.00 6.00
❑ 183 Carlos Francis RC 4.00 1.50
❑ 184 DeAngelo Hall RC 6.00 2.50
❑ 185 Daryl Smith RC 5.00 2.00
❑ 186 Troy Fleming RC 4.00 1.50
❑ 187 Luke McCown RC 5.00 2.00
❑ 188 Steven Jackson RC 15.00 6.00
❑ 189 Ricardo Colclough RC 5.00 2.00
❑ 190 Gilbert Gardner RC 4.00 1.50

2005 Upper Deck Legends

❑ COMP.SET w/o SP's (100) 20.00 7.50
❑ ROOKIE PRINT RUN 725 SER.#'d SETS
❑ 166-195 LEG.PRINT RUN 1025 SER.#'d SETS
❑ 1 Charley Taylor .50 .20
❑ 2 Roger Craig .50 .20
❑ 3 Ozzie Newsome .50 .20
❑ 4 Rocky Bleier .75 .30
❑ 5 Russ Francis .40 .15
❑ 6 Jerry Rice 1.50 .60
❑ 7 Pat Haden .40 .15
❑ 8 Brett Favre 2.00 .75
❑ 9 Joe Ferguson .40 .15
❑ 10 Ed Jones .50 .20
❑ 11 Joe Washington .40 .15
❑ 12 John Brodie .40 .15
❑ 13 Peyton Manning 1.25 .50
❑ 14 Mark Van Eeghen .40 .15
❑ 15 William Perry .50 .20
❑ 16 Bob Brown .40 .15
❑ 17 Herb Adderley .40 .15
❑ 18 Deion Sanders 1.00 .40
❑ 19 Lenny Moore .50 .20
❑ 20 Tom Mack .40 .15
❑ 21 Jim McMahon .75 .30
❑ 22 Bobby Mitchell .50 .20
❑ 23 John Mackey .40 .15
❑ 24 Curtis Martin .75 .30
❑ 25 Junior Seau .50 .20
❑ 26 Harold Jackson .40 .15
❑ 27 Jim Zorn .40 .15
❑ 28 Chuck Foreman .40 .15
❑ 29 Willie Brown .40 .15
❑ 30 Cliff Branch .50 .20
❑ 31 Jerry Kramer .50 .20
❑ 32 Harry Carson .40 .15
❑ 33 Chuck Noll .50 .20
❑ 34 Len Hauss .40 .15
❑ 35 Jim Plunkett .50 .20
❑ 36 Ollie Matson .50 .20
❑ 37 Billy Kilmer .50 .20
❑ 38 Jim Marshall .40 .15
❑ 39 Dan Dierdorf .40 .15
❑ 40 Jim Kelly 1.00 .40
❑ 41 Vince Ferragamo .40 .15
❑ 42 Ottis Anderson .40 .15
❑ 43 Charlie Joiner .40 .15
❑ 44 George Blanda .75 .30
❑ 45 Drew Pearson .50 .20
❑ 46 Andre Reed .50 .20
❑ 47 Merlin Olsen .50 .20
❑ 48 Paul Warfield .50 .20
❑ 49 James Lofton .40 .15
❑ 50 Art Donovan .50 .20
❑ 51 Dwight Clark .50 .20
❑ 52 Raymond Berry .50 .20
❑ 53 L.C. Greenwood .50 .20
❑ 54 Dave Casper .40 .15
❑ 55 Don Maynard .50 .20
❑ 56 Bud Grant .40 .15
❑ 57 Roman Gabriel .50 .20
❑ 58 Cris Collinsworth .50 .20
❑ 59 Joe Theismann .75 .30
❑ 60 Paul Hornung .75 .30
❑ 61 Alan Page .50 .20
❑ 62 Deacon Jones .50 .20
❑ 63 Steve Largent .75 .30
❑ 64 Phil Simms .50 .20
❑ 65 Floyd Little .40 .15
❑ 66 Archie Manning .75 .30
❑ 67 Ken Stabler 1.00 .40
❑ 68 Fran Tarkenton 1.00 .40
❑ 69 Len Dawson .75 .30
❑ 70 Mike Ditka .75 .30
❑ 71 Conrad Dobler .40 .15
❑ 72 Jack Lambert .75 .30
❑ 73 Marcus Allen .75 .30
❑ 74 Bo Jackson 1.00 .40
❑ 75 Jerome Bettis .75 .30
❑ 76 Jack Ham .50 .20
❑ 77 Marshall Faulk .75 .30
❑ 78 Mike Singletary .75 .30
❑ 79 Bob Griese .75 .30
❑ 80 Dick Butkus 1.25 .50
❑ 81 Gale Sayers 1.00 .40
❑ 82 Earl Campbell .75 .30
❑ 83 Dan Fouts .75 .30
❑ 84 Franco Harris 1.00 .40
❑ 85 Steve Young 1.00 .40
❑ 86 Tony Dorsett .75 .30

❑ 87 Jim Brown 1.25 .50
❑ 88 Roger Staubach 1.25 .50
❑ 89 Troy Aikman 1.00 .40
❑ 90 Barry Sanders 1.25 .50
❑ 91 Bernie Kosar .50 .20
❑ 92 Dan Marino 2.00 .75
❑ 93 John Elway 1.25 .50
❑ 94 Randy Moss .75 .30
❑ 95 Joe Montana 2.50 1.00
❑ 96 Joe Montana CL 1.25 .50
❑ 97 Dan Marino CL 1.00 .40
❑ 98 John Elway CL .75 .30
❑ 99 Gale Sayers CL .50 .20
❑ 100 Paul Hornung CL .50 .20
❑ 101 Aaron Rodgers RC 15.00 6.00
❑ 102 Alex Smith QB RC 20.00 8.00
❑ 103 Cadillac Williams RC 25.00 10.00
❑ 104 Ronnie Brown RC 20.00 8.00
❑ 105 Ciatrick Fason RC 5.00 2.00
❑ 106 Charlie Frye RC 10.00 4.00
❑ 107 Derek Anderson RC 5.00 2.00
❑ 108 Braylon Edwards RC 15.00 6.00
❑ 109 Roddy White RC 5.00 2.00
❑ 110 Thomas Davis RC 5.00 2.00
❑ 111 Jason Campbell RC 8.00 3.00
❑ 112 Andrew Walter RC 8.00 3.00
❑ 113 Kyle Orton RC 8.00 3.00
❑ 114 David Greene RC 5.00 2.00
❑ 115 Cedric Benson RC 10.00 4.00
❑ 116 Vernand Morency RC 5.00 2.00
❑ 117 Eric Shelton RC 5.00 2.00
❑ 118 Maurice Clarett 5.00 2.00
❑ 119 Brandon Jacobs RC 6.00 2.50
❑ 120 Anthony Davis RC 4.00 1.50
❑ 121 Marion Barber RC 8.00 3.00
❑ 122 J.J. Arrington RC 6.00 2.50
❑ 123 Ryan Moats RC 5.00 2.00
❑ 124 Frank Gore RC 10.00 4.00
❑ 125 Stefan LeFors RC 5.00 2.00
❑ 126 Darren Sproles RC 5.00 2.00
❑ 127 Cedric Houston RC 5.00 2.00
❑ 128 Troy Williamson RC 10.00 4.00
❑ 129 Mark Clayton RC 6.00 2.50
❑ 130 Chris Henry RC 5.00 2.00
❑ 131 Fred Gibson RC 4.00 1.50
❑ 132 Craphonso Thorpe RC 4.00 1.50
❑ 133 Terrence Murphy RC 5.00 2.00
❑ 134 Dan Orlovsky RC 6.00 2.50
❑ 135 Roscoe Parrish RC 5.00 2.00
❑ 136 Reggie Brown RC 5.00 2.00
❑ 137 Craig Bragg RC 4.00 1.50
❑ 138 Larry Brackins RC 2.50 1.00
❑ 139 Adrian McPherson RC 5.00 2.00
❑ 140 Matt Jones RC 12.00 5.00
❑ 141 Heath Miller RC 12.00 5.00
❑ 142 Alex Smith TE RC 5.00 2.00
❑ 143 Kevin Everett RC 5.00 2.00
❑ 144 Jerome Mathis RC 5.00 2.00
❑ 145 Travis Johnson RC 4.00 1.50
❑ 146 Channing Crowder RC 5.00 2.00
❑ 147 Mike Williams 10.00 4.00
❑ 148 Barrett Ruud RC 5.00 2.00
❑ 149 Marcus Spears RC 5.00 2.00
❑ 150 Derrick Johnson RC 8.00 3.00
❑ 151 Shawne Merriman RC 8.00 3.00
❑ 152 Kevin Burnett RC 5.00 2.00
❑ 153 Erasmus James RC 5.00 2.00
❑ 154 Dan Cody RC 5.00 2.00
❑ 155 David Pollack RC 5.00 2.00
❑ 156 Antrel Rolle RC 5.00 2.00
❑ 157 Adam Jones RC 5.00 2.00
❑ 158 Mark Bradley RC 5.00 2.00
❑ 159 Carlos Rogers RC 6.00 2.50
❑ 160 Vincent Jackson RC 5.00 2.00
❑ 161 DeMarcus Ware RC 8.00 3.00
❑ 162 Corey Webster RC 5.00 2.00
❑ 163 Justin Miller RC 4.00 1.50
❑ 164 Eric Green RC 2.50 1.00
❑ 165 Marlin Jackson RC 5.00 2.00
❑ 166 Herb Adderley LH 3.00 1.25
❑ 167 Fran Tarkenton LH 6.00 2.50
❑ 168 Troy Aikman LH 6.00 2.50
❑ 169 Charlie Joiner LH 3.00 1.25
❑ 170 George Blanda LH 5.00 2.00
❑ 171 Jim Kelly LH 6.00 2.50
❑ 172 Joe Montana LH 12.00 5.00
❑ 173 Jack Ham LH 4.00 1.50
❑ 174 Marcus Allen LH 5.00 2.00
❑ 175 Tony Dorsett LH 5.00 2.00
❑ 176 Barry Sanders LH 8.00 3.00
❑ 177 Paul Warfield LH 4.00 1.50
❑ 178 Dan Marino LH 10.00 4.00
❑ 179 John Elway LH 8.00 3.00
❑ 180 Franco Harris LH 6.00 2.50
❑ 181 Mike Singletary LH 5.00 2.00
❑ 182 Gale Sayers LH 6.00 2.50
❑ 183 Bob Griese LH 5.00 2.00
❑ 184 Dan Fouts LH 5.00 2.00
❑ 185 Earl Campbell LH 5.00 2.00
❑ 186 Jim Brown LH 8.00 3.00
❑ 187 Dick Butkus LH 8.00 3.00
❑ 188 Paul Hornung LH 5.00 2.00
❑ 189 Roger Staubach LH 8.00 3.00
❑ 190 Steve Largent LH 5.00 2.00
❑ 191 Ryan Fitzpatrick RC 8.00 3.00
❑ 192 Alvin Pearman RC 5.00 2.00
❑ 193 Courtney Roby RC 5.00 2.00
❑ 194 Chase Lyman RC 4.00 1.50
❑ 195 Roydell Williams RC 5.00 2.00

2006 Upper Deck Legends

❑ COMP.SET w/o RC's (100) 20.00 8.00
❑ RC PRINT RUN 750 SER.#'d SETS
❑ 1 Marshall Faulk .50 .20
❑ 2 John Elway 1.25 .50
❑ 3 Barry Sanders 1.25 .50
❑ 4 Dan Marino 1.50 .60
❑ 5 Troy Aikman 1.00 .40
❑ 6 Roger Staubach 1.25 .50
❑ 7 Curtis Martin .75 .30
❑ 8 O.J. McDuffie .50 .20
❑ 9 Steve Young 1.00 .40
❑ 10 Jim Kelly 1.00 .40
❑ 11 Dan Fouts .75 .30
❑ 12 Franco Harris .75 .30
❑ 13 Christian Okoye .50 .20
❑ 14 Craig Morton .50 .20
❑ 15 Doug Flutie .50 .20
❑ 16 Gale Sayers 1.00 .40
❑ 17 Bob Griese .75 .30
❑ 18 Jim Plunkett .75 .30
❑ 19 Marvin Harrison .75 .30
❑ 20 L.C. Greenwood .50 .20
❑ 21 Len Dawson .75 .30
❑ 22 Ken Stabler 1.00 .40
❑ 23 Fran Tarkenton 1.00 .40
❑ 24 Herman Moore .40 .15
❑ 25 Joe Theismann .75 .30
❑ 26 Paul Hornung .75 .30
❑ 27 Herschel Walker .50 .20
❑ 28 Randy Moss .75 .30
❑ 29 Drew Pearson .50 .20
❑ 30 Don Maynard .50 .20
❑ 31 Dwight Clark .50 .20
❑ 32 Golden Richards .40 .15
❑ 33 Wesley Walker .50 .20
❑ 34 Greg Landry .40 .15
❑ 35 Mick Tingelhoff .40 .15
❑ 36 Ken O'Brien .40 .15
❑ 37 Emerson Boozer .40 .15
❑ 38 Reggie McKenzie .40 .15
❑ 39 Wally Hilgenberg .40 .15
❑ 40 Jan Stenerud .40 .15
❑ 41 Roger Craig .75 .30
❑ 42 Joe Cribbs .50 .20
❑ 43 Reggie Rucker .40 .15
❑ 44 Louis Lipps .40 .15
❑ 45 Rick Upchurch .40 .15
❑ 46 Ben Roethlisberger 1.50 .60
❑ 47 Rocket Ismail .50 .20
❑ 48 Gary Clark .50 .20
❑ 50 Dwight Stephenson .40 .15
❑ 51 Joe Klecko .40 .15
❑ 52 John Hannah .50 .20
❑ 53 John Cappelletti .50 .20
❑ 54 Tiki Barber .75 .30
❑ 55 Coy Bacon .40 .15
❑ 56 A.J. Duhe .40 .15
❑ 57 Brett Favre 2.00 .75
❑ 58 Jon Kolb .40 .15
❑ 59 Rich Saul .40 .15
❑ 60A Antonio Freeman .50 .20
❑ 60B Diron Talbert .40 .15
❑ 61 John Taylor .50 .20
❑ 62 Ron McDole .40 .15
❑ 63 Jethro Pugh .40 .15
❑ 64 Joe Jacoby .50 .20
❑ 65 Steve Smith .75 .30
❑ 66 Terrell Owens .75 .30
❑ 67 Charle Young .40 .15
❑ 68 Roy Jefferson .50 .20
❑ 69 Gary Fencik .40 .15
❑ 70 Terry Metcalf .50 .20
❑ 71 Johnny Rodgers .50 .20
❑ 72 Charles White .50 .20
❑ 73 Billy Sims .75 .30
❑ 74 Neal Anderson .50 .20
❑ 75 Marlin Briscoe .40 .15
❑ 76 Edgerrin James .75 .30
❑ 77 LaDainian Tomlinson 1.00 .40
❑ 78 Steve DeBerg .50 .20
❑ 79 Randy Grossman .50 .20
❑ 80 Ickey Woods .50 .20
❑ 81 Donovan McNabb .75 .30
❑ 82 Ron Mix .50 .20
❑ 83 Gerald Riggs Sr. .40 .15
❑ 84 Curt Warner .50 .20
❑ 85 Everson Walls .40 .15
❑ 86 Mike Quick .50 .20
❑ 87 Shaun Alexander .75 .30
❑ 88 Al Toon .50 .20
❑ 89 Nat Moore .50 .20
❑ 90 Michael Vick 1.00 .40
❑ 91 Carson Palmer .75 .30
❑ 92 Tom Brady 1.25 .50
❑ 93 Gary Garrison .40 .15
❑ 94 Fred Dean .40 .15
❑ 95 Bob Trumpy .50 .20
❑ 96 Doug Cosbie .50 .20
❑ 97 Tommy Kramer .50 .20
❑ 98 Peyton Manning 1.25 .50
❑ 99 John Brockington .50 .20
❑ 100 Stanley Morgan .50 .20
❑ 101 A.J. Hawk RC 12.00 5.00
❑ 102 Abdul Hodge RC 6.00 2.50
❑ 103 Antonio Cromartie RC 6.00 2.50
❑ 104 Anthony Fasano RC 6.00 2.50
❑ 105 Brandon Marshall RC 6.00 2.50
❑ 106 Ben Obomanu RC 5.00 2.00
❑ 107 Bobby Carpenter RC 6.00 2.50
❑ 108 Brad Smith RC 6.00 2.50
❑ 109 Erik Meyer RC 5.00 2.00
❑ 110 Brandon Williams RC 6.00 2.50
❑ 111 Brian Calhoun RC 6.00 2.50
❑ 112 Brodie Croyle RC 10.00 4.00
❑ 113 Frostee Rucker RC 5.00 2.00
❑ 114 Bruce Eugene RC 5.00 2.00
❑ 115 Bruce Gradkowski RC 10.00 4.00
❑ 116 Cedric Humes RC 6.00 2.50
❑ 117 Chad Greenway RC 6.00 2.50

❑	118 Chad Jackson RC	10.00	4.00
❑	119 Charles Davis RC	5.00	2.00
❑	120 Charlie Whitehurst RC	8.00	3.00
❑	121 Jason Allen RC	6.00	2.50
❑	122 Cory Rodgers RC	6.00	2.50
❑	123 Cory Ross RC	10.00	4.00
❑	124 D.J. Shockley RC	6.00	2.50
❑	125 Darnell Bing RC	6.00	2.50
❑	126 Darrell Hackney RC	5.00	2.00
❑	127 D'Brickashaw Ferguson RC	6.00	2.50
❑	128 DeAngelo Williams RC	15.00	6.00
❑	129 DeMeco Ryans RC	8.00	3.00
❑	130 Demetrius Williams RC	8.00	3.00
❑	131 Derek Hagan RC	6.00	2.50
❑	132 Devin Aromashodu RC	5.00	2.00
❑	133 Devin Hester RC	12.00	5.00
❑	134 Dominique Byrd RC	5.00	2.00
❑	135 Donte Whitner RC	6.00	2.50
❑	136 DonTrell Moore RC	5.00	2.00
❑	137 D'Qwell Jackson RC	5.00	2.00
❑	138 Ernie Sims RC	8.00	3.00
❑	139 John McCargo RC	5.00	2.00
❑	140 Gerald Riggs Jr. RC	6.00	2.50
❑	141 Greg Jennings RC	12.00	5.00
❑	142 Greg Lee RC	5.00	2.00
❑	143 Haloti Ngata RC	6.00	2.50
❑	144 Johnathan Joseph RC	5.00	2.00
❑	145 Jason Avant RC	6.00	2.50
❑	146 Jay Cutler RC	25.00	10.00
❑	147 Jeff King RC	5.00	2.00
❑	148 Jeff Webb RC	5.00	2.00
❑	149 Jeremy Bloom RC	5.00	2.00
❑	150 Jerious Norwood RC	10.00	4.00
❑	151 Jerome Harrison RC	6.00	2.50
❑	152 Jimmy Williams RC	6.00	2.50
❑	153 Joe Klopfenstein RC	5.00	2.00
❑	154 Jonathan Orr RC	5.00	2.00
❑	155 Joseph Addai RC	20.00	8.00
❑	156 Josh Betts RC	5.00	2.00
❑	157 Matt Baker RC	6.00	2.50
❑	158 Kamerion Wimbley RC	6.00	2.50
❑	159 Kellen Clemens RC	8.00	3.00
❑	160 Ko Simpson RC	5.00	2.00
❑	161 Laurence Maroney RC	20.00	8.00
❑	162 Lawrence Vickers RC	5.00	2.00
❑	163 LenDale White RC	12.00	5.00
❑	164 Leon Washington RC	10.00	4.00
❑	165 Leonard Pope RC	6.00	2.50
❑	166 Marcedes Lewis RC	6.00	2.50
❑	167 Marcus Vick RC	5.00	2.00
❑	168 Mario Williams RC	10.00	4.00
❑	169 Marques Hagans RC	5.00	2.00
❑	170 Martin Nance RC	5.00	2.00
❑	171 Mathias Kiwanuka RC	8.00	3.00
❑	172 Matt Bernstein RC	3.00	1.25
❑	173 Matt Leinart RC	25.00	10.00
❑	174 Maurice Drew RC	15.00	6.00
❑	175 Maurice Stovall RC	6.00	2.50
❑	176 Michael Huff RC	8.00	3.00
❑	177 Michael Robinson RC	10.00	4.00
❑	178 Mike Hass RC	6.00	2.50
❑	179 Miles Austin RC	5.00	2.00
❑	180 Omar Jacobs RC	5.00	2.00
❑	181 Owen Daniels RC	6.00	2.50
❑	182 P.J. Daniels RC	5.00	2.00
❑	183 Quinton Ganther RC	5.00	2.00
❑	184 Reggie Bush RC	50.00	25.00
❑	185 Reggie McNeal RC	5.00	2.00
❑	186 Santonio Holmes RC	12.00	5.00
❑	187 Sinorice Moss RC	8.00	3.00
❑	188 Skyler Green RC	6.00	2.50
❑	189 T.J. Williams RC	6.00	2.50
❑	190 Tamba Hali RC	6.00	2.50
❑	191 Manny Lawson RC	6.00	2.50
❑	192 Tarvaris Jackson RC	10.00	4.00
❑	193 Travis Wilson RC	6.00	2.50
❑	194 Tye Hill RC	6.00	2.50
❑	195 Vernon Davis RC	12.00	5.00
❑	196 Vince Young RC	25.00	10.00
❑	197 Wali Lundy RC	6.00	2.50
❑	198 Wendell Mathis RC	5.00	2.00
❑	199 Will Blackmon RC	5.00	2.00
❑	200 Willie Reid RC	6.00	2.50

1999 Upper Deck MVP

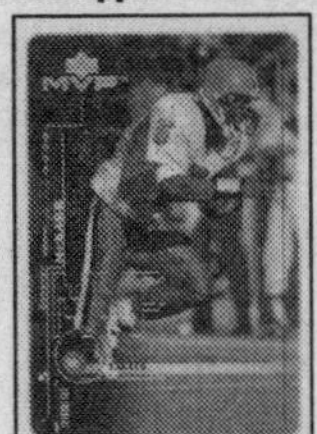

❑	COMPLETE SET (220)	25.00	10.00
❑	1 Jake Plummer	.30	.10
❑	2 Adrian Murrell	.30	.10
❑	3 Larry Centers	.20	.07
❑	4 Frank Sanders	.30	.10
❑	5 Andre Wadsworth	.20	.07
❑	6 Rob Moore	.30	.10
❑	7 Simeon Rice	.30	.10
❑	8 Jamal Anderson	.50	.20
❑	9 Chris Chandler	.30	.10
❑	10 Chuck Smith	.20	.07
❑	11 Terance Mathis	.30	.10
❑	12 Tim Dwight	.50	.20
❑	13 Ray Buchanan	.20	.07
❑	14 O.J. Santiago	.20	.07
❑	15 Eric Zeier	.30	.10
❑	16 Priest Holmes	.75	.30
❑	17 Michael Jackson	.20	.07
❑	18 Jermaine Lewis	.30	.10
❑	19 Michael McCrary	.20	.07
❑	20 Rob Johnson	.30	.10
❑	21 Antowain Smith	.50	.20
❑	22 Thurman Thomas	.30	.10
❑	23 Doug Flutie	.50	.20
❑	24 Eric Moulds	.50	.20
❑	25 Bruce Smith	.30	.10
❑	26 Andre Reed	.30	.10
❑	27 Fred Lane	.20	.07
❑	28 Tim Biakabutuka	.30	.10
❑	29 Rae Carruth	.20	.07
❑	30 Wesley Walls	.30	.10
❑	31 Steve Beuerlein	.20	.07
❑	32 Muhsin Muhammad	.30	.10
❑	33 Erik Kramer	.20	.07
❑	34 Edgar Bennett	.20	.07
❑	35 Curtis Conway	.30	.10
❑	36 Curtis Enis	.20	.07
❑	37 Bobby Engram	.30	.10
❑	38 Alonzo Mayes	.20	.07
❑	39 Corey Dillon	.50	.20
❑	40 Jeff Blake	.30	.10
❑	41 Carl Pickens	.30	.10
❑	42 Darnay Scott	.20	.07
❑	43 Tony McGee	.20	.07
❑	44 Ki-Jana Carter	.20	.07
❑	45 Ty Detmer	.30	.10
❑	46 Terry Kirby	.20	.07
❑	47 Justin Armour	.20	.07
❑	48 Freddie Solomon	.20	.07
❑	49 Marquez Pope	.20	.07
❑	50 Antonio Langham	.20	.07
❑	51 Troy Aikman	1.00	.40
❑	52 Emmitt Smith	1.00	.40
❑	53 Deion Sanders	.50	.20
❑	54 Rocket Ismail	.30	.10
❑	55 Michael Irvin	.30	.10
❑	56 Chris Warren	.20	.07
❑	57 Greg Ellis	.20	.07
❑	58 John Elway	1.50	.60
❑	59 Terrell Davis	.50	.20
❑	60 Rod Smith	.30	.10
❑	61 Shannon Sharpe	.30	.10
❑	62 Ed McCaffrey	.30	.10
❑	63 John Mobley	.20	.07
❑	64 Bill Romanowski	.20	.07
❑	65 Barry Sanders	1.50	.60
❑	66 Johnnie Morton	.30	.10
❑	67 Herman Moore	.30	.10
❑	68 Charlie Batch	.50	.20
❑	69 Germane Crowell	.20	.07
❑	70 Robert Porcher	.20	.07
❑	71 Brett Favre	1.50	.60
❑	72 Antonio Freeman	.50	.20
❑	73 Dorsey Levens	.50	.20
❑	74 Mark Chmura	.30	.10
❑	75 Vonnie Holliday	.20	.07
❑	76 Bill Schroeder	.50	.20
❑	77 Marshall Faulk	.60	.25
❑	78 Marvin Harrison	.50	.20
❑	79 Peyton Manning	1.50	.60
❑	80 Jerome Pathon	.20	.07
❑	81 E.G. Green	.20	.07
❑	82 Ellis Johnson	.20	.07
❑	83 Mark Brunell	.50	.20
❑	84 Jimmy Smith	.30	.10
❑	85 Keenan McCardell	.30	.10
❑	86 Fred Taylor	.50	.20
❑	87 James Stewart	.30	.10
❑	88 Kevin Hardy	.20	.07
❑	89 Elvis Grbac	.30	.10
❑	90 Andre Rison	.30	.10
❑	91 Derrick Alexander WR	.30	.10
❑	92 Tony Gonzalez	.50	.20
❑	93 Donnell Bennett	.20	.07
❑	94 Derrick Thomas	.50	.20
❑	95 Tamarick Vanover	.20	.07
❑	96 Dan Marino	1.50	.60
❑	97 Karim Abdul-Jabbar	.30	.10
❑	98 Zach Thomas	.50	.20
❑	99 O.J. McDuffie	.30	.10
❑	100 John Avery	.20	.07
❑	101 Sam Madison	.20	.07
❑	102 Randall Cunningham	.50	.20
❑	103 Cris Carter	.50	.20
❑	104 Robert Smith	.50	.20
❑	105 Randy Moss	1.25	.50
❑	106 Jake Reed	.30	.10
❑	107 Matthew Hatchette	.20	.07
❑	108 John Randle	.30	.10
❑	109 Drew Bledsoe	.60	.25
❑	110 Terry Glenn	.50	.20
❑	111 Ben Coates	.30	.10
❑	112 Ty Law	.30	.10
❑	113 Tony Simmons	.20	.07
❑	114 Ted Johnson	.20	.07
❑	115 Danny Wuerffel	.20	.07
❑	116 Lamar Smith	.30	.10
❑	117 Sean Dawkins	.20	.07
❑	118 Cameron Cleeland	.20	.07
❑	119 Joe Johnson	.20	.07
❑	120 Andre Hastings	.20	.07
❑	121 Kent Graham	.20	.07
❑	122 Gary Brown	.20	.07
❑	123 Amani Toomer	.20	.07
❑	124 Tiki Barber	.50	.20
❑	125 Ike Hilliard	.20	.07
❑	126 Jason Sehorn	.20	.07
❑	127 Vinny Testaverde	.30	.10
❑	128 Curtis Martin	.50	.20
❑	129 Keyshawn Johnson	.50	.20
❑	130 Wayne Chrebet	.30	.10
❑	131 Mo Lewis	.20	.07
❑	132 Steve Atwater	.20	.07
❑	133 Donald Hollas	.20	.07
❑	134 Napoleon Kaufman	.50	.20
❑	135 Tim Brown	.50	.20
❑	136 Darrell Russell	.20	.07
❑	137 Rickey Dudley	.20	.07
❑	138 Charles Woodson	.50	.20
❑	139 Koy Detmer	.20	.07
❑	140 Duce Staley	.50	.20
❑	141 Charlie Garner	.30	.10
❑	142 Doug Pederson	.20	.07
❑	143 Jeff Graham	.20	.07
❑	144 Charles Johnson	.20	.07

❑ 145 Kordell Stewart	.30	.10
❑ 146 Jerome Bettis	.50	.20
❑ 147 Hines Ward	.50	.20
❑ 148 Courtney Hawkins	.20	.07
❑ 149 Will Blackwell	.20	.07
❑ 150 Richard Huntley	.30	.10
❑ 151 Levon Kirkland	.20	.07
❑ 152 Trent Green	.50	.20
❑ 153 Tony Banks	.30	.10
❑ 154 Isaac Bruce	.50	.20
❑ 155 Eddie Kennison	.30	.10
❑ 156 Az-Zahir Hakim	.20	.07
❑ 157 Amp Lee	.20	.07
❑ 158 Robert Holcombe	.20	.07
❑ 159 Ryan Leaf	.50	.20
❑ 160 Natrone Means	.30	.10
❑ 161 Jim Harbaugh	.30	.10
❑ 162 Junior Seau	.50	.20
❑ 163 Charlie Jones	.20	.07
❑ 164 Rodney Harrison	.20	.07
❑ 165 Steve Young	.60	.25
❑ 166 Jerry Rice	1.00	.40
❑ 167 Garrison Hearst	.30	.10
❑ 168 Terrell Owens	.50	.20
❑ 169 J.J. Stokes	.30	.10
❑ 170 Bryant Young	.20	.07
❑ 171 Ricky Watters	.30	.10
❑ 172 Joey Galloway	.30	.10
❑ 173 Jon Kitna	.50	.20
❑ 174 Ahman Green	.50	.20
❑ 175 Mike Pritchard	.20	.07
❑ 176 Chad Brown	.20	.07
❑ 177 Warrick Dunn	.50	.20
❑ 178 Trent Dilfer	.30	.10
❑ 179 Mike Alstott	.50	.20
❑ 180 Reidel Anthony	.30	.10
❑ 181 Bert Emanuel	.30	.10
❑ 182 Jacquez Green	.20	.07
❑ 183 Hardy Nickerson	.20	.07
❑ 184 Steve McNair	.50	.20
❑ 185 Eddie George	.50	.20
❑ 186 Yancey Thigpen	.20	.07
❑ 187 Frank Wycheck	.20	.07
❑ 188 Kevin Dyson	.30	.10
❑ 189 Jackie Harris	.20	.07
❑ 190 Blaine Bishop	.20	.07
❑ 191 Skip Hicks	.20	.07
❑ 192 Michael Westbrook	.30	.10
❑ 193 Stephen Alexander	.20	.07
❑ 194 Leslie Shepherd	.20	.07
❑ 195 Jeff Hostetler	.20	.07
❑ 196 Brian Mitchell	.20	.07
❑ 197 Dan Wilkinson	.20	.07
❑ 198 Terrell Davis CL	.50	.20
❑ 199 Troy Aikman CL	.50	.20
❑ 200 Tim Couch CL	.50	.20
❑ 201 Ricky Williams RC	2.50	1.00
❑ 202 Tim Couch RC	1.00	.40
❑ 203 Akili Smith RC	.75	.30
❑ 204 Daunte Culpepper RC	5.00	2.00
❑ 205 Torry Holt RC	3.00	1.25
❑ 206 Edgerrin James RC	5.00	2.00
❑ 207 David Boston RC	1.00	.40
❑ 208 Peerless Price RC	1.00	.40
❑ 209 Chris Claiborne RC	.50	.20
❑ 210 Champ Bailey RC	1.25	.50
❑ 211 Cade McNown RC	.75	.30
❑ 212 Jevon Kearse RC	1.50	.60
❑ 213 Joe Germaine RC	.75	.30
❑ 214 D'Wayne Bates RC	.75	.30
❑ 215 Dameane Douglas RC	.50	.20
❑ 216 Troy Edwards RC	.75	.30
❑ 217 Sedrick Irvin RC	.50	.20
❑ 218 Brock Huard RC	1.00	.40
❑ 219 Amos Zereoue RC	1.00	.40
❑ 220 Donovan McNabb RC	6.00	2.50

2000 Upper Deck MVP

❑ COMPLETE SET (218)	25.00	10.00
❑ 1 Jake Plummer	.30	.10
❑ 2 Michael Pittman	.20	.07
❑ 3 Rob Moore	.30	.10
❑ 4 David Boston	.50	.20
❑ 5 Frank Sanders	.30	.10
❑ 6 Aeneas Williams	.20	.07
❑ 7 Kwamie Lassiter	.20	.07
❑ 8 Tim Dwight	.50	.20
❑ 9 Chris Chandler	.30	.10
❑ 10 Jamal Anderson	.50	.20
❑ 11 Shawn Jefferson	.20	.07
❑ 12 Qadry Ismail	.30	.10
❑ 13 Jermaine Lewis	.20	.07
❑ 14 Rod Woodson	.30	.10
❑ 15 Michael McCrary	.20	.07
❑ 16 Tony Banks	.30	.10
❑ 17 Peter Boulware	.20	.07
❑ 18 Shannon Sharpe	.30	.10
❑ 19 Peerless Price	.30	.10
❑ 20 Rob Johnson	.30	.10
❑ 21 Eric Moulds	.50	.20
❑ 22 Doug Flutie	.50	.20
❑ 23 Muhsin Muhammad	.30	.10
❑ 24 Patrick Jeffers	.50	.20
❑ 25 Steve Beuerlein	.30	.10
❑ 26 Tim Biakabutuka	.30	.10
❑ 27 Michael Bates	.20	.07
❑ 28 Cade McNown	.20	.07
❑ 29 Curtis Enis	.20	.07
❑ 30 Marcus Robinson	.50	.20
❑ 31 Shane Matthews	.30	.10
❑ 32 Bobby Engram	.30	.10
❑ 33 Glyn Milburn	.20	.07
❑ 34 Akili Smith	.20	.07
❑ 35 Corey Dillon	.50	.20
❑ 36 Darnay Scott	.30	.10
❑ 37 Tremain Mack	.20	.07
❑ 38 Tim Couch	.30	.10
❑ 39 Kevin Johnson	.50	.20
❑ 40 Darrin Chiaverini	.20	.07
❑ 41 Jamir Miller	.20	.07
❑ 42 Errict Rhett	.30	.10
❑ 43 Troy Aikman	1.00	.40
❑ 44 Emmitt Smith	1.00	.40
❑ 45 Rocket Ismail	.30	.10
❑ 46 Jason Tucker	.20	.07
❑ 47 Dexter Coakley	.20	.07
❑ 48 Joey Galloway	.30	.10
❑ 49 Greg Ellis	.20	.07
❑ 50 Terrell Davis	.50	.20
❑ 51 Olandis Gary	.50	.20
❑ 52 Brian Griese	.50	.20
❑ 53 Ed McCaffrey	.50	.20
❑ 54 Rod Smith	.30	.10
❑ 55 Trevor Pryce	.20	.07
❑ 56 Charlie Batch	.50	.20
❑ 57 Germane Crowell	.20	.07
❑ 58 Johnnie Morton	.30	.10
❑ 59 Robert Porcher	.20	.07
❑ 60 Luther Elliss	.20	.07
❑ 61 James Stewart	.30	.10
❑ 62 Brett Favre	1.50	.60
❑ 63 Antonio Freeman	.50	.20
❑ 64 Bill Schroeder	.30	.10
❑ 65 Dorsey Levens	.30	.10
❑ 66 Peyton Manning	1.25	.50
❑ 67 Edgerrin James	.75	.30
❑ 68 Marvin Harrison	.50	.20
❑ 69 Ken Dilger	.20	.07
❑ 70 Terrence Wilkins	.20	.07
❑ 71 Mark Brunell	.50	.20
❑ 72 Fred Taylor	.50	.20
❑ 73 Jimmy Smith	.30	.10
❑ 74 Keenan McCardell	.30	.10
❑ 75 Carnell Lake	.20	.07
❑ 76 Tony Brackens	.20	.07
❑ 77 Kevin Hardy	.20	.07
❑ 78 Hardy Nickerson	.20	.07
❑ 79 Elvis Grbac	.30	.10
❑ 80 Tony Gonzalez	.30	.10
❑ 81 Derrick Alexander	.30	.10
❑ 82 Donnell Bennett	.20	.07
❑ 83 James Hasty	.20	.07
❑ 84 Jay Fiedler	.50	.20
❑ 85 James Johnson	.20	.07
❑ 86 Tony Martin	.30	.10
❑ 87 Damon Huard	.50	.20
❑ 88 O.J. McDuffie	.30	.10
❑ 89 Oronde Gadsden	.30	.10
❑ 90 Zach Thomas	.50	.20
❑ 91 Sam Madison	.20	.07
❑ 92 Jeff George	.30	.10
❑ 93 Randy Moss	1.00	.40
❑ 94 Robert Smith	.50	.20
❑ 95 Cris Carter	.50	.20
❑ 96 Matthew Hatchette	.20	.07
❑ 97 Drew Bledsoe	.60	.25
❑ 98 Terry Glenn	.30	.10
❑ 99 Troy Brown	.30	.10
❑ 100 Kevin Faulk	.30	.10
❑ 101 Lawyer Milloy	.30	.10
❑ 102 Ricky Williams	.50	.20
❑ 103 Keith Poole	.20	.07
❑ 104 Jake Reed	.30	.10
❑ 105 Cam Cleeland	.20	.07
❑ 106 Jeff Blake	.30	.10
❑ 107 Andrew Glover	.20	.07
❑ 108 Kerry Collins	.30	.10
❑ 109 Amani Toomer	.20	.07
❑ 110 Joe Montgomery	.20	.07
❑ 111 Ike Hilliard	.30	.10
❑ 112 Michael Strahan	.30	.10
❑ 113 Jessie Armstead	.20	.07
❑ 114 Ray Lucas	.30	.10
❑ 115 Keyshawn Johnson	.50	.20
❑ 116 Curtis Martin	.50	.20
❑ 117 Vinny Testaverde	.30	.10
❑ 118 Wayne Chrebet	.30	.10
❑ 119 Dedric Ward	.20	.07
❑ 120 Tim Brown	.50	.20
❑ 121 Rich Gannon	.50	.20
❑ 122 Tyrone Wheatley	.30	.10
❑ 123 Napoleon Kaufman	.30	.10

❑ 124	Charles Woodson	.30	.10
❑ 125	Darrell Russell	.20	.07
❑ 126	Duce Staley	.50	.20
❑ 127	Donovan McNabb	.75	.30
❑ 128	Torrance Small	.20	.07
❑ 129	Allen Rossum	.20	.07
❑ 130	Brian Dawkins	.50	.20
❑ 131	Troy Vincent	.20	.07
❑ 132	Troy Edwards	.20	.07
❑ 133	Jerome Bettis	.50	.20
❑ 134	Hines Ward	.50	.20
❑ 135	Kordell Stewart	.30	.10
❑ 136	Levon Kirkland	.20	.07
❑ 137	Kent Graham	.20	.07
❑ 138	Marshall Faulk	.60	.25
❑ 139	Kurt Warner	1.00	.40
❑ 140	Torry Holt	.50	.20
❑ 141	Isaac Bruce	.50	.20
❑ 142	Kevin Carter	.20	.07
❑ 143	Az-Zahir Hakim	.30	.10
❑ 144	Todd Lyght	.20	.07
❑ 145	Jermaine Fazande	.20	.07
❑ 146	Curtis Conway	.30	.10
❑ 147	Freddie Jones	.20	.07
❑ 148	Junior Seau	.50	.20
❑ 149	Jeff Graham	.20	.07
❑ 150	Ryan Leaf	.30	.10
❑ 151	Rodney Harrison	.20	.07
❑ 152	Steve Young	.60	.25
❑ 153	Jerry Rice	1.00	.40
❑ 154	Charlie Garner	.30	.10
❑ 155	Terrell Owens	.50	.20
❑ 156	Jeff Garcia	.50	.20
❑ 157	Bryant Young	.20	.07
❑ 158	Lance Schulters	.20	.07
❑ 159	Ricky Watters	.30	.10
❑ 160	Jon Kitna	.50	.20
❑ 161	Derrick Mayes	.30	.10
❑ 162	Sean Dawkins	.20	.07
❑ 163	Cortez Kennedy	.20	.07
❑ 164	Chad Brown	.20	.07
❑ 165	Warrick Dunn	.50	.20
❑ 166	Shaun King	.20	.07
❑ 167	Mike Alstott	.50	.20
❑ 168	Warren Sapp	.30	.10
❑ 169	Jacquez Green	.20	.07
❑ 170	Derrick Brooks	.50	.20
❑ 171	John Lynch	.30	.10
❑ 172	Donnie Abraham	.20	.07
❑ 173	Eddie George	.50	.20
❑ 174	Steve McNair	.50	.20
❑ 175	Kevin Dyson	.30	.10
❑ 176	Jevon Kearse	.50	.20
❑ 177	Yancey Thigpen	.20	.07
❑ 178	Frank Wycheck	.20	.07
❑ 179	Eddie Robinson	.20	.07
❑ 180	Samari Rolle	.20	.07
❑ 181	Brad Johnson	.50	.20
❑ 182	Stephen Davis	.50	.20
❑ 183	Michael Westbrook	.30	.10
❑ 184	Albert Connell	.20	.07
❑ 185	Brian Mitchell	.20	.07
❑ 186	Bruce Smith	.30	.10
❑ 187	Stephen Alexander	.20	.07
❑ 188	Peter Warrick RC	.60	.25
❑ 189C	Cutout Card/Arrington	15.00	6.00
❑ 190	Chris Redman RC	.50	.20
❑ 191	Courtney Brown RC	.60	.25
❑ 192	Brian Urlacher RC	2.50	1.00
❑ 193	Plaxico Burress RC	1.25	.50
❑ 194	Corey Simon RC	.60	.25
❑ 195	Bubba Franks RC	.60	.25
❑ 196	Deon Grant RC	.50	.20
❑ 197	Michael Wiley RC	.50	.20
❑ 198	Tim Rattay RC	.60	.25
❑ 199	Ron Dayne RC	.60	.25
❑ 200	Sylvester Morris RC	.50	.20
❑ 201	Shaun Alexander RC	3.00	1.25
❑ 202	Dez White RC	.60	.25
❑ 203	Thomas Jones RC	1.00	.40
❑ 204	Reuben Droughns RC	.75	.30
❑ 205	Travis Taylor RC	.60	.25
❑ 206	Trevor Gaylor RC	.40	.15
❑ 207	Jamal Lewis RC	1.50	.60
❑ 208	Chad Pennington RC	1.50	.60
❑ 209	J.R. Redmond RC	.50	.20
❑ 210	Laveranues Coles RC	.75	.30
❑ 211	Travis Prentice RC	.50	.20
❑ 212	R.Jay Soward RC	.50	.20
❑ 213	Todd Pinkston RC	.60	.25
❑ 214	Dennis Northcutt RC	.60	.25
❑ 215	Shyrone Stith RC	.40	.15
❑ 216	Tee Martin RC	.60	.25
❑ 217	Giovanni Carmazzi RC	.40	.15
❑ 218	Drew Bledsoe CL	.30	.10
❑ 219	Steve Young CL	.30	.10
❑ 220A	Donovan McNabb CL SP	30.00	15.00
❑ 220B	D.McNabb CL SP Emb.	30.00	15.00

2001 Upper Deck MVP

❑	COMPLETE SET (330)	50.00	20.00
❑ 1	Jake Plummer	.30	.10
❑ 2	David Boston	.50	.20
❑ 3	Thomas Jones	.30	.10
❑ 4	Michael Pittman	.20	.07
❑ 5	Frank Sanders	.20	.07
❑ 6	MarTay Jenkins	.20	.07
❑ 7	Pat Tillman RC	20.00	10.00
❑ 8	Tywan Mitchell	.20	.07
❑ 9	Jamal Anderson	.50	.20
❑ 10	Doug Johnson	.20	.07
❑ 11	Ephraim Salaam RC	.50	.20
❑ 12	Chris Chandler	.30	.10
❑ 13	Shawn Jefferson	.20	.07
❑ 14	Tim Dwight	.50	.20
❑ 15	Terance Mathis	.30	.10
❑ 16	Jamal Lewis	.75	.30
❑ 17	Shannon Sharpe	.30	.10
❑ 18	Trent Dilfer	.30	.10
❑ 19	Ray Lewis	.50	.20
❑ 20	Qadry Ismail	.30	.10
❑ 21	Travis Taylor	.30	.10
❑ 22	Chris Redman	.20	.07
❑ 23	Priest Holmes	.60	.25
❑ 24	Rod Woodson	.30	.10
❑ 25	Jamie Sharper	.20	.07
❑ 26	Doug Flutie	.50	.20
❑ 27	Rob Johnson	.30	.10
❑ 28	Eric Moulds	.30	.10
❑ 29	Sammy Morris	.20	.07
❑ 30	Shawn Bryson	.20	.07
❑ 31	Antowain Smith	.30	.10
❑ 32	Jeremy McDaniel	.20	.07
❑ 33	Sam Cowart	.20	.07
❑ 34	Muhsin Muhammad	.30	.10
❑ 35	Brad Hoover	.20	.07
❑ 36	Tim Biakabutuka	.30	.10
❑ 37	Steve Beuerlein	.20	.07
❑ 38	Donald Hayes	.20	.07
❑ 39	Jeff Lewis	.20	.07
❑ 40	Dameyune Craig	.20	.07
❑ 41	Wesley Walls	.20	.07
❑ 42	Isaac Byrd	.20	.07
❑ 43	Cade McNown	.20	.07
❑ 44	James Allen	.30	.10
❑ 45	Marcus Robinson	.50	.20
❑ 46	Brian Urlacher	.75	.30
❑ 47	Jim Miller	.20	.07
❑ 48	Curtis Enis	.20	.07
❑ 49	Eddie Kennison	.30	.10
❑ 50	Marty Booker	.20	.07
❑ 51	Bobby Engram	.20	.07
❑ 52	Peter Warrick	.50	.20
❑ 53	Corey Dillon	.50	.20
❑ 54	Akili Smith	.20	.07
❑ 55	Danny Farmer	.20	.07
❑ 56	Brandon Bennett	.20	.07
❑ 57	Curtis Keaton	.20	.07
❑ 58	Ron Dugans	.20	.07
❑ 59	Takeo Spikes	.20	.07
❑ 60	Scott Mitchell	.20	.07
❑ 61	Tim Couch	.30	.10
❑ 62	Kevin Johnson	.30	.10
❑ 63	Travis Prentice	.20	.07
❑ 64	Spergon Wynn	.20	.07
❑ 65	Errict Rhett	.20	.07
❑ 66	David Patten	.20	.07
❑ 67	Dennis Northcutt	.30	.10
❑ 68	Aaron Shea	.20	.07
❑ 69	Courtney Brown	.30	.10
❑ 70	Troy Aikman	.75	.30
❑ 71	Emmitt Smith	1.00	.40
❑ 72	Joey Galloway	.30	.10
❑ 73	Rocket Ismail	.30	.10
❑ 74	Randall Cunningham	.50	.20
❑ 75	Anthony Wright	.20	.07
❑ 76	James McKnight	.30	.10
❑ 77	Dexter Coakley	.20	.07
❑ 78	Terrell Davis	.50	.20
❑ 79	Mike Anderson	.50	.20
❑ 80	Brian Griese	.50	.20
❑ 81	Rod Smith	.30	.10
❑ 82	Ed McCaffrey	.50	.20
❑ 83	Olandis Gary	.30	.10
❑ 84	Trevor Pryce	.20	.07
❑ 85	John Mobley	.20	.07
❑ 86	Charlie Batch	.50	.20
❑ 87	Germane Crowell	.20	.07
❑ 88	James O. Stewart	.30	.10
❑ 89	Johnnie Morton	.30	.10
❑ 90	Herman Moore	.30	.10
❑ 91	Mario Bates	.20	.07
❑ 92	Desmond Howard	.20	.07
❑ 93	Stephen Boyd	.20	.07
❑ 94	Chris Claiborne	.30	.10
❑ 95	Kurt Schulz	.20	.07
❑ 96	Brett Favre	1.50	.60
❑ 97	Antonio Freeman	.50	.20
❑ 98	Dorsey Levens	.20	.07

❑ 99	Ahman Green	.50	.20
❑ 100	Matt Hasselbeck	.30	.10
❑ 101	De'Mond Parker	.20	.07
❑ 102	Bill Schroeder	.30	.10
❑ 103	Bubba Franks	.30	.10
❑ 104	Donald Driver	.30	.10
❑ 105	Darren Sharper	.20	.07
❑ 106	Peyton Manning	1.25	.50
❑ 107	Edgerrin James	.60	.25
❑ 108	Marvin Harrison	.50	.20
❑ 109	Jerome Pathon	.30	.10
❑ 110	Terrence Wilkins	.20	.07
❑ 111	Ken Dilger	.20	.07
❑ 112	Marcus Pollard	.20	.07
❑ 113	Brad Scioli RC	.50	.20
❑ 114	Mark Brunell	.50	.20
❑ 115	Fred Taylor	.50	.20
❑ 116	Jimmy Smith	.30	.10
❑ 117	Jamie Martin	.30	.10
❑ 118	Keenan McCardell	.20	.07
❑ 119	Kyle Brady	.20	.07
❑ 120	R.Jay Soward	.20	.07
❑ 121	Alvis Whitted	.20	.07
❑ 122	Brant Boyer RC	.20	.07
❑ 123	Elvis Grbac	.30	.10
❑ 124	Tony Gonzalez	.30	.10
❑ 125	Derrick Alexander	.30	.10
❑ 126	Tony Richardson	.20	.07
❑ 127	Frank Moreau	.20	.07
❑ 128	Sylvester Morris	.20	.07
❑ 129	Kevin Lockett	.20	.07
❑ 130	Donnie Edwards	.20	.07
❑ 131	Oronde Gadsden	.30	.10
❑ 132	Lamar Smith	.30	.10
❑ 133	Jay Fiedler	.50	.20
❑ 134	James Johnson	.20	.07
❑ 135	Thurman Thomas	.20	.07
❑ 136	Leslie Shepherd	.20	.07
❑ 137	Tony Martin	.20	.07
❑ 138	O.J. McDuffie	.20	.07
❑ 139	Zach Thomas	.50	.20
❑ 140	Randy Moss	1.00	.40
❑ 141	Bubby Brister	.20	.07
❑ 142	Cris Carter	.50	.20
❑ 143	Daunte Culpepper	.50	.20
❑ 144	Moe Williams	.30	.10
❑ 145	Troy Walters	.20	.07
❑ 146	Chris Walsh RC	.20	.07
❑ 147	Matthew Hatchette	.20	.07
❑ 148	Kailee Wong	.20	.07
❑ 149	Robert Griffith	.20	.07
❑ 150	Drew Bledsoe	.60	.25
❑ 151	Terry Glenn	.20	.07
❑ 152	Kevin Faulk	.30	.10
❑ 153	J.R. Redmond	.20	.07
❑ 154	Tony Carter	.20	.07
❑ 155	Patrick Pass	.20	.07
❑ 156	Troy Brown	.30	.10
❑ 157	Tony Simmons	.20	.07
❑ 158	Michael Bishop	.20	.07
❑ 159	Lawyer Milloy	.30	.10
❑ 160	Ricky Williams	.50	.20
❑ 161	Jeff Blake	.30	.10
❑ 162	Joe Horn	.30	.10
❑ 163	Aaron Brooks	.50	.20
❑ 164	La'Roi Glover	.20	.07
❑ 165	Chad Morton	.20	.07
❑ 166	Keith Mitchell RC	.30	.10
❑ 167	Willie Jackson	.20	.07
❑ 168	Robert Wilson	.20	.07
❑ 169	Jake Reed	.30	.10
❑ 170	Kerry Collins	.30	.10
❑ 171	Amani Toomer	.20	.07
❑ 172	Ron Dayne	.50	.20
❑ 173	Tiki Barber	.50	.20
❑ 174	Greg Comella	.20	.07
❑ 175	Ike Hilliard	.30	.10
❑ 176	Joe Jurevicius	.20	.07
❑ 177	Ron Dixon	.20	.07
❑ 178	Jason Sehorn	.20	.07
❑ 179	Michael Strahan	.30	.10
❑ 180	Vinny Testaverde	.30	.10
❑ 181	Wayne Chrebet	.30	.10
❑ 182	Curtis Martin	.50	.20
❑ 183	Richie Anderson	.20	.07
❑ 184	Dedric Ward	.20	.07
❑ 185	Laveranues Coles	.50	.20
❑ 186	Windrell Hayes	.20	.07
❑ 187	Chad Pennington	.75	.30
❑ 188	Tim Brown	.50	.20
❑ 189	Rich Gannon	.50	.20
❑ 190	Tyrone Wheatley	.30	.10
❑ 191	Napoleon Kaufman	.20	.07
❑ 192	Jon Ritchie	.20	.07
❑ 193	James Jett	.20	.07
❑ 194	Rickey Dudley	.20	.07
❑ 195	Andre Rison	.30	.10
❑ 196	Eric Allen	.20	.07
❑ 197	Charles Woodson	.30	.10
❑ 198	Duce Staley	.50	.20
❑ 199	Donovan McNabb	.60	.25
❑ 200	Darnell Autry	.20	.07
❑ 201	Chad Lewis	.20	.07
❑ 202	Charles Johnson	.20	.07
❑ 203	Torrance Small	.20	.07
❑ 204	Todd Pinkston	.20	.07
❑ 205	Brian Mitchell	.20	.07
❑ 206	Hugh Douglas	.20	.07
❑ 207	David Akers RC	.30	.10
❑ 208	Kordell Stewart	.30	.10
❑ 209	Jerome Bettis	.50	.20
❑ 210	Bobby Shaw	.20	.07
❑ 211	Hines Ward	.50	.20
❑ 212	Plaxico Burress	.50	.20
❑ 213	Courtney Hawkins	.20	.07
❑ 214	Troy Edwards	.20	.07
❑ 215	Earl Holmes	.20	.07
❑ 216	Richard Huntley	.20	.07
❑ 217	Marshall Faulk	.60	.25
❑ 218	Kurt Warner	1.00	.40
❑ 219	Isaac Bruce	.50	.20
❑ 220	Torry Holt	.50	.20
❑ 221	Trent Green	.50	.20
❑ 222	Justin Watson	.20	.07
❑ 223	Trung Canidate	.30	.10
❑ 224	Az-Zahir Hakim	.20	.07
❑ 225	Ricky Proehl	.20	.07
❑ 226	Dexter McCleon	.20	.07
❑ 227	London Fletcher	.20	.07
❑ 228	Junior Seau	.50	.20
❑ 229	Curtis Conway	.30	.10
❑ 230	Rodney Harrison	.20	.07
❑ 231	Jeff Graham	.20	.07
❑ 232	Freddie Jones	.20	.07
❑ 233	Reggie Jones	.20	.07
❑ 234	Ronney Jenkins	.20	.07
❑ 235	Trevor Gaylor	.20	.07
❑ 236	Jeff Garcia	.50	.20
❑ 237	Jerry Rice	1.00	.40
❑ 238	Charlie Garner	.30	.10
❑ 239	Terrell Owens	.50	.20
❑ 240	J.J. Stokes	.30	.10
❑ 241	Fred Beasley	.20	.07
❑ 242	Tim Rattay	.30	.10
❑ 243	Garrison Hearst	.20	.07
❑ 244	Ricky Watters	.30	.10
❑ 245	Shaun Alexander	.60	.25
❑ 246	Jon Kitna	.30	.10
❑ 247	Brock Huard	.20	.07
❑ 248	Darrell Jackson	.50	.20
❑ 249	James Williams WR	.20	.07
❑ 250	Sean Dawkins	.20	.07
❑ 251	John Hilliard RC	.20	.07
❑ 252	Warrick Dunn	.50	.20
❑ 253	Shaun King	.20	.07
❑ 254	Ryan Leaf	.30	.10
❑ 255	Mike Alstott	.50	.20
❑ 256	Jacquez Green	.20	.07
❑ 257	Reidel Anthony	.20	.07
❑ 258	Derrick Brooks	.50	.20
❑ 259	John Lynch	.30	.10
❑ 260	Warren Sapp	.30	.10
❑ 261	Eddie George	.50	.20
❑ 262	Steve McNair	.50	.20
❑ 263	Rodney Thomas	.20	.07
❑ 264	Derrick Mason	.30	.10
❑ 265	Yancey Thigpen	.20	.07
❑ 266	Frank Wycheck	.20	.07
❑ 267	Chris Sanders	.20	.07
❑ 268	Carl Pickens	.20	.07
❑ 269	Kevin Dyson	.20	.07
❑ 270	Jevon Kearse	.30	.10
❑ 271	Jeff George	.30	.10
❑ 272	Stephen Davis	.50	.20
❑ 273	Brad Johnson	.50	.20
❑ 274	Albert Connell	.20	.07
❑ 275	James Thrash	.30	.10
❑ 276	Michael Westbrook	.30	.10
❑ 277	Stephen Alexander	.20	.07
❑ 278	Deion Sanders	.50	.20
❑ 279	Champ Bailey	.30	.10
❑ 280	Todd Husak	.20	.07
❑ 281	Dan Morgan RC	1.00	.40
❑ 282	Josh Booty RC	1.00	.40
❑ 283	Michael Vick RC	6.00	2.50
❑ 284	Mike McMahon RC	1.00	.40
❑ 285	Reggie White RC	.60	.25
❑ 286	Chris Weinke RC	1.00	.40
❑ 287	Drew Brees RC	4.00	1.50
❑ 288	Sage Rosenfels RC	1.00	.40
❑ 289	Marques Tuiasosopo RC	1.00	.40
❑ 290	Josh Heupel RC	1.00	.40
❑ 291	David Rivers RC	.60	.25
❑ 292	Kevin Kasper RC	1.00	.40
❑ 293	Jesse Palmer RC	1.00	.40
❑ 294	LaDainian Tomlinson RC	15.00	7.50
❑ 295	Deuce McAllister RC	2.00	.75
❑ 296	Kevan Barlow RC	1.00	.40
❑ 297	LaMont Jordan RC	2.00	.75
❑ 298	James Jackson RC	1.00	.40
❑ 299	Anthony Thomas RC	1.00	.40
❑ 300	Correll Buckhalter RC	1.25	.50
❑ 301	Travis Henry RC	1.50	.50
❑ 302	Dan Alexander RC	1.00	.40
❑ 303	Travis Minor RC	.60	.25
❑ 304	Derrick Gibson RC	.60	.25
❑ 305	Rudi Johnson RC	2.00	.75
❑ 306	Michael Bennett RC	1.00	.40
❑ 307	Alge Crumpler RC	1.25	.50
❑ 308	Todd Heap RC	1.00	.40
❑ 309	Snoop Minnis RC	.60	.25
❑ 310	Santana Moss RC	1.50	.60
❑ 311	Reggie Wayne RC	2.00	.75

❑ 312 Koren Robinson RC 1.00 .40
❑ 313 Chris Chambers RC 1.50 .60
❑ 314 David Terrell RC 1.00 .40
❑ 315 Rod Gardner RC 1.00 .40
❑ 316 Quincy Morgan RC 1.00 .40
❑ 317 Ken-Yon Rambo RC .60 .25
❑ 318 Vinny Sutherland RC .60 .25
❑ 319 David Allen RC .60 .25
❑ 320 Bobby Newcombe RC .60 .25
❑ 321 Ronney Daniels RC .40 .15
❑ 322 T.J. Houshmandzadeh RC 1.25 .50
❑ 323 Chad Johnson RC 2.50 1.00
❑ 324 Freddie Mitchell RC 1.00 .40
❑ 325 Moran Norris RC .40 .15
❑ 326 Ron Dayne CL .30 .10
❑ 327 Mike Anderson CL .20 .07
❑ 328 Jamal Lewis CL .40 .15
❑ 329 Brian Urlacher CL .40 .15
❑ 330 Darren Howard CL .20 .07

2002 Upper Deck MVP

❑ COMPLETE SET (300) 50.00 20.00
❑ 1 Arnold Jackson .20 .07
❑ 2 Dave Brown .20 .07
❑ 3 David Boston .50 .20
❑ 4 Frank Sanders .20 .07
❑ 5 Jake Plummer .30 .10
❑ 6 MarTay Jenkins .20 .07
❑ 7 Freddie Jones .20 .07
❑ 8 Jamal Anderson .30 .10
❑ 9 Keith Brooking .20 .07
❑ 10 Michael Vick 1.50 .60
❑ 11 Rodney Thomas .20 .07
❑ 12 Shawn Jefferson .20 .07
❑ 13 Tony Martin .20 .07
❑ 14 Warrick Dunn .50 .20
❑ 15 Brandon Stokley .30 .10
❑ 16 Chris McAlister .20 .07
❑ 17 Chris Redman .20 .07
❑ 18 Ray Lewis .50 .20
❑ 19 Sam Gash .20 .07
❑ 20 Travis Taylor .30 .10
❑ 21 Terry Allen .20 .07
❑ 22 Drew Bledsoe .60 .25
❑ 23 Alex Van Pelt .20 .07
❑ 24 Eric Moulds .30 .10
❑ 25 Kenyatta Wright .20 .07
❑ 26 Larry Centers .20 .07
❑ 27 Peerless Price .30 .10
❑ 28 Shawn Bryson .20 .07
❑ 29 Travis Henry .50 .20
❑ 30 Chris Weinke .30 .10
❑ 31 Lamar Smith .30 .10
❑ 32 Isaac Byrd .50 .20
❑ 33 Muhsin Muhammad .30 .10
❑ 34 Nick Goings .20 .07
❑ 35 Richard Huntley .20 .07
❑ 36 Tim Biakabutuka .20 .07
❑ 37 Wesley Walls .20 .07
❑ 38 Anthony Thomas .30 .10
❑ 39 Brian Urlacher .75 .30
❑ 40 David Terrell .50 .20
❑ 41 Dez White .20 .07
❑ 42 Jim Miller .20 .07
❑ 43 Larry Whigham .20 .07
❑ 44 Marty Booker .20 .07
❑ 45 Chris Chandler .30 .10
❑ 46 Corey Dillon .30 .10
❑ 47 Darnay Scott .20 .07
❑ 48 Jon Kitna .30 .10
❑ 49 Peter Warrick .30 .10
❑ 50 Ron Dugans .20 .07
❑ 51 Scott Mitchell .20 .07
❑ 52 Chad Johnson .50 .20
❑ 53 Courtney Brown .30 .10
❑ 54 JaJuan Dawson .20 .07
❑ 55 James Jackson .20 .07
❑ 56 Kevin Johnson .30 .10
❑ 57 Quincy Morgan .20 .07
❑ 58 Rickey Dudley .20 .07
❑ 59 Tim Couch .30 .10
❑ 60 Chris Sanders .20 .07
❑ 61 Emmitt Smith 1.25 .50
❑ 62 Joey Galloway .30 .10
❑ 63 Ken-Yon Rambo .20 .07
❑ 64 La'Roi Glover .20 .07
❑ 65 Quincy Carter .30 .10
❑ 66 Rocket Ismail .30 .10
❑ 67 Darren Woodson .20 .07
❑ 68 Ryan Leaf .30 .10
❑ 69 Chester McGlockton .20 .07
❑ 70 Brian Griese .50 .20
❑ 71 Shannon Sharpe .30 .10
❑ 72 Kevin Kasper .20 .07
❑ 73 Mike Anderson .50 .20
❑ 74 Olandis Gary .30 .10
❑ 75 Rod Smith .30 .10
❑ 76 Terrell Davis .50 .20
❑ 77 Anthony Carter .20 .07
❑ 78 Az-Zahir Hakim .20 .07
❑ 79 Charlie Batch .30 .10
❑ 80 Chris Claiborne .20 .07
❑ 81 Cory Schlesinger .20 .07
❑ 82 Desmond Howard .20 .07
❑ 83 Germane Crowell .20 .07
❑ 84 James Stewart .30 .10
❑ 85 Mike McMahon .50 .20
❑ 86 Bill Schroeder .30 .10
❑ 87 Ahman Green .50 .20
❑ 88 Brett Favre 1.25 .50
❑ 89 Bubba Franks .30 .10
❑ 90 Antonio Freeman .50 .20
❑ 91 Donald Driver .30 .10
❑ 92 Kabeer Gbaja-Biamila .30 .10
❑ 93 William Henderson .20 .07
❑ 94 Corey Bradford .20 .07
❑ 95 Jamie Sharper .20 .07
❑ 96 Jermaine Lewis .20 .07
❑ 97 Kailee Wong .20 .07
❑ 98 Matt Stevens .20 .07
❑ 99 Tony Boselli .20 .07
❑ 100 James Allen .30 .10
❑ 101 Aaron Glenn .20 .07
❑ 102 Edgerrin James .60 .25
❑ 103 Dominic Rhodes .30 .10
❑ 104 Marcus Pollard .20 .07
❑ 105 Marvin Harrison .50 .20
❑ 106 Peyton Manning 1.00 .40
❑ 107 Qadry Ismail .30 .10
❑ 108 Reggie Wayne .50 .20
❑ 109 Stacey Mack .20 .07
❑ 110 Elvis Joseph .20 .07
❑ 111 Fred Taylor .50 .20
❑ 112 Jimmy Smith .30 .10
❑ 113 Jonathan Quinn .20 .07
❑ 114 Keenan McCardell .20 .07
❑ 115 Mark Brunell .50 .20
❑ 116 Trent Green .30 .10
❑ 117 Derrick Alexander .30 .10
❑ 118 Johnnie Morton .30 .10
❑ 119 Snoop Minnis .20 .07
❑ 120 Mike Cloud .20 .07
❑ 121 Priest Holmes .60 .25
❑ 122 Tony Gonzalez .30 .10
❑ 123 Tony Richardson .20 .07
❑ 124 Ricky Williams 1.00 .40
❑ 125 Chris Chambers .50 .20
❑ 126 James McKnight .20 .07
❑ 127 Jay Fiedler .30 .10
❑ 128 Zach Thomas .50 .20
❑ 129 Oronde Gadsden .30 .10
❑ 130 Ray Lucas .20 .07
❑ 131 Randy Moss 1.00 .40
❑ 132 Spergon Wynn .20 .07
❑ 133 Cris Carter .50 .20
❑ 134 Daunte Culpepper .50 .20
❑ 135 Doug Chapman .20 .07
❑ 136 Michael Bennett .30 .10
❑ 137 Tom Brady 1.25 .50
❑ 138 Troy Brown .30 .10
❑ 139 Adam Vinatieri .50 .20
❑ 140 Antowain Smith .30 .10
❑ 141 David Patten .20 .07
❑ 142 Donald Hayes .20 .07
❑ 143 J.R. Redmond .20 .07
❑ 144 Willie Jackson .20 .07
❑ 145 Jerome Pathon .30 .10
❑ 146 Jake Reed .30 .10
❑ 147 Aaron Brooks .50 .20
❑ 148 John Carney .20 .07
❑ 149 Deuce McAllister .60 .25
❑ 150 Joe Horn .30 .10
❑ 151 Kyle Turley .20 .07
❑ 152 Robert Wilson .20 .07
❑ 153 Tiki Barber .50 .20
❑ 154 Amani Toomer .30 .10
❑ 155 Ike Hilliard .30 .10
❑ 156 Jason Sehorn .20 .07
❑ 157 Joe Jurevicius .20 .07
❑ 158 Kerry Collins .30 .10
❑ 159 Michael Strahan .30 .10
❑ 160 Ron Dayne .30 .10
❑ 161 Wayne Chrebet .30 .10
❑ 162 Chad Pennington .60 .25
❑ 163 Curtis Martin .50 .20
❑ 164 LaMont Jordan .50 .20
❑ 165 Laveranues Coles .30 .10
❑ 166 Marvin Jones .20 .07
❑ 167 Santana Moss .50 .20
❑ 168 Vinny Testaverde .30 .10
❑ 169 Tyrone Wheatley .30 .10
❑ 170 Charles Woodson .30 .10
❑ 171 Charlie Garner .30 .10
❑ 172 Jerry Rice 1.00 .40
❑ 173 John Parrella .20 .07
❑ 174 Jon Ritchie .20 .07
❑ 175 Rich Gannon .50 .20
❑ 176 Tim Brown .50 .20
❑ 177 Todd Pinkston .30 .10

❑	178	Correll Buckhalter	.30	.10
❑	179	Donovan McNabb	.60	.25
❑	180	Duce Staley	.50	.20
❑	181	Freddie Mitchell	.30	.10
❑	182	Hugh Douglas	.20	.07
❑	183	James Thrash	.30	.10
❑	184	Koy Detmer	.20	.07
❑	185	Troy Edwards	.20	.07
❑	186	Chris Fuamatu-Ma'afala	.20	.07
❑	187	Hines Ward	.50	.20
❑	188	Jerome Bettis	.50	.20
❑	189	Kendrell Bell	.50	.20
❑	190	Kordell Stewart	.30	.10
❑	191	Mark Bruener	.20	.07
❑	192	Plaxico Burress	.30	.10
❑	193	Tim Dwight	.30	.10
❑	194	Curtis Conway	.20	.07
❑	195	Doug Flutie	.50	.20
❑	196	Drew Brees	.50	.20
❑	197	Junior Seau	.50	.20
❑	198	LaDainian Tomlinson	.75	.30
❑	199	Marcellus Wiley	.20	.07
❑	200	Rodney Harrison	.20	.07
❑	201	Stephen Alexander	.20	.07
❑	202	Terrell Owens	.50	.20
❑	203	Andre Carter	.20	.07
❑	204	Cedrick Wilson	.20	.07
❑	205	Fred Beasley	.20	.07
❑	206	Garrison Hearst	.30	.10
❑	207	J.J. Stokes	.30	.10
❑	208	Jeff Garcia	.50	.20
❑	209	Kevan Barlow	.30	.10
❑	210	Tai Streets	.20	.07
❑	211	Doug Evans	.20	.07
❑	212	Bobby Engram	.20	.07
❑	213	Darrell Jackson	.30	.10
❑	214	James Williams	.20	.07
❑	215	John Randle	.20	.07
❑	216	Koren Robinson	.30	.10
❑	217	Matt Hasselbeck	.30	.10
❑	218	Shaun Alexander	.60	.25
❑	219	Trent Dilfer	.30	.10
❑	220	Aeneas Williams	.20	.07
❑	221	Isaac Bruce	.50	.20
❑	222	Kurt Warner	.50	.20
❑	223	Marshall Faulk	.50	.20
❑	224	Ricky Proehl	.20	.07
❑	225	Torry Holt	.50	.20
❑	226	Trung Canidate	.30	.10
❑	227	Terrence Wilkins	.20	.07
❑	228	John Lynch	.30	.10
❑	229	Keyshawn Johnson	.50	.20
❑	230	Michael Pittman	.20	.07
❑	231	Mike Alstott	.50	.20
❑	232	Rob Johnson	.30	.10
❑	233	Shaun King	.20	.07
❑	234	Warren Sapp	.30	.10
❑	235	Brad Johnson	.30	.10
❑	236	Derrick Mason	.30	.10
❑	237	Eddie George	.50	.20
❑	238	Frank Wycheck	.20	.07
❑	239	Jevon Kearse	.30	.10
❑	240	Kevin Dyson	.30	.10
❑	241	Steve McNair	.50	.20
❑	242	Chris Coleman	.20	.07
❑	243	Darrell Green	.20	.07
❑	244	Jacquez Green	.20	.07
❑	245	Ki-Jana Carter	.20	.07
❑	246	Michael Westbrook	.20	.07
❑	247	Rod Gardner	.30	.10
❑	248	Stephen Davis	.30	.10
❑	249	Tony Banks	.20	.07
❑	250	Champ Bailey	.30	.10
❑	251	David Carr RC	3.00	1.25
❑	252	DeShaun Foster RC	1.25	.50
❑	253	Antonio Bryant RC	1.25	.50
❑	254	Joey Harrington RC	2.00	.75
❑	255	William Green RC	1.25	.50
❑	256	Josh Reed RC	1.25	.50
❑	257	Patrick Ramsey RC	1.50	.60
❑	258	Clinton Portis RC	4.00	1.50
❑	259	Jabar Gaffney RC	1.25	.50
❑	260	Rohan Davey RC	1.25	.50
❑	261	T.J. Duckett RC	1.50	.60
❑	262	Ashley Lelie RC	2.50	1.00
❑	263	Kurt Kittner RC	1.00	.40
❑	264	Luke Staley RC	1.00	.40
❑	265	Ron Johnson RC	1.00	.40
❑	266	Antwaan Randle El RC	2.00	.75
❑	267	Travis Stephens RC	1.00	.40
❑	268	Marquise Walker RC	1.00	.40
❑	269	Julius Peppers RC	2.50	1.00
❑	270	Chad Hutchinson RC	1.00	.40
❑	271	Maurice Morris RC	1.25	.50
❑	272	Reche Caldwell RC	1.25	.50
❑	273	Randy Fasani RC	1.00	.40
❑	274	Lamar Gordon RC	1.25	.50
❑	275	Donte Stallworth RC	2.50	1.00
❑	276	Brandon Doman RC	1.00	.40
❑	277	Damien Anderson RC	1.00	.40
❑	278	Roy Williams RC	3.00	1.25
❑	279	J.T. O'Sullivan RC	1.00	.40
❑	280	Leonard Henry RC	1.00	.40
❑	281	Javon Walker RC	2.50	1.00
❑	282	David Garrard RC	1.25	.50
❑	283	Chester Taylor RC	2.50	1.00
❑	284	Andre Davis RC	1.00	.40
❑	285	Josh McCown RC	1.50	.60
❑	286	Adrian Peterson RC	1.25	.50
❑	287	Seth Burford RC	1.00	.40
❑	288	Deion Branch RC	2.50	1.00
❑	289	Jonathan Wells RC	1.25	.50
❑	290	Ladell Betts RC	1.25	.50
❑	291	Cliff Russell RC	1.00	.40
❑	292	Eric Crouch RC	1.25	.50
❑	293	Dusty Bonner RC	.60	.25
❑	294	Tim Carter RC	1.00	.40
❑	295	Brian Westbrook RC	2.00	.75
❑	296	Quentin Jammer RC	1.25	.50
❑	297	Brian Poli-Dixon RC	1.00	.40
❑	298	Donovan McNabb CL	.30	.10
❑	299	Curtis Martin CL	.20	.07
❑	300	Tom Brady CL	.60	.25

2003 Upper Deck MVP

❑		COMPLETE SET (440)	60.00	30.00
❑	1	Brad Johnson	.30	.10
❑	2	Dexter Jackson RC	.50	.20
❑	3	Derrick Brooks	.30	.10
❑	4	Simeon Rice	.30	.10
❑	5	Warren Sapp	.30	.10
❑	6	John Lynch	.30	.10
❑	7	Joe Jurevicius	.20	.07
❑	8	Ronde Barber	.20	.07
❑	9	Mike Alstott	.50	.20
❑	10	Michael Pittman	.20	.07
❑	11	Keyshawn Johnson	.50	.20
❑	12	Jerry Rice	1.00	.40
❑	13	Tim Brown	.50	.20
❑	14	Rich Gannon	.30	.10
❑	15	Charlie Garner	.30	.10
❑	16	Jerry Porter	.30	.10
❑	17	Sebastian Janikowski	.20	.07
❑	18	Zack Crockett	.20	.07
❑	19	Tyrone Wheatley	.20	.07
❑	20	Bill Romanowski	.20	.07
❑	21	Charles Woodson	.30	.10
❑	22	Rod Woodson	.30	.10
❑	23	Donovan McNabb	.60	.25
❑	24	James Thrash	.20	.07
❑	25	Duce Staley	.30	.10
❑	26	Brian Westbrook	.30	.10
❑	27	A.J. Feeley	.30	.10
❑	28	Koy Detmer	.20	.07
❑	29	Brian Dawkins	.30	.10
❑	30	Dorsey Levens	.20	.07
❑	31	Jon Ritchie	.20	.07
❑	32	Todd Pinkston	.30	.10
❑	33	Chad Lewis	.20	.07
❑	34	Brett Favre	1.25	.50
❑	35	Ahman Green	.50	.20
❑	36	Donald Driver	.30	.10
❑	37	Bubba Franks	.30	.10
❑	38	Javon Walker	.20	.07
❑	39	Kabeer Gbaja-Biamila	.30	.10
❑	40	Robert Ferguson	.20	.07
❑	41	Tony Fisher	.20	.07
❑	42	Marques Anderson	.20	.07
❑	43	Ryan Longwell	.20	.07
❑	44	Craig Nall	.20	.07
❑	45	Steve McNair	.50	.20
❑	46	Eddie George	.30	.10
❑	47	Jevon Kearse	.30	.10
❑	48	Kevin Carter	.20	.07
❑	49	Samari Rolle	.20	.07
❑	50	Keith Bulluck	.20	.07
❑	51	Joe Nedney	.20	.07
❑	52	Robert Holcombe	.20	.07
❑	53	Drew Bennett	.30	.10
❑	54	Frank Wycheck	.20	.07
❑	55	Derrick Mason	.30	.10
❑	56	Tommy Maddox	.50	.20
❑	57	Jerome Bettis	.50	.20
❑	58	Plaxico Burress	.30	.10
❑	59	Antwaan Randle El	.50	.20
❑	60	Amos Zereoue	.30	.10
❑	61	Chris Fuamatu-Ma'afala	.20	.07
❑	62	Jason Gildon	.20	.07
❑	63	Kendrell Bell	.30	.10
❑	64	Dewayne Washington	.20	.07
❑	65	Jeff Reed RC	2.50	1.00
❑	66	Hines Ward	.50	.20
❑	67	Jeff Garcia	.50	.20
❑	68	Terrell Owens	.50	.20
❑	69	Andre Carter	.20	.07
❑	70	Tai Streets	.20	.07
❑	71	Tim Rattay	.30	.10
❑	72	Eric Johnson	.30	.10
❑	73	Cedrick Wilson	.20	.07

❑ 74	Brandon Doman	.20	.07
❑ 75	Kevan Barlow	.30	.10
❑ 76	Bryant Young	.20	.07
❑ 77	Garrison Hearst	.30	.10
❑ 78	Kerry Collins	.30	.10
❑ 79	Daryl Jones	.20	.07
❑ 80	Tiki Barber	.50	.20
❑ 81	Amani Toomer	.30	.10
❑ 82	Tim Carter	.20	.07
❑ 83	Michael Strahan	.30	.10
❑ 84	Ike Hilliard	.20	.07
❑ 85	Brian Mitchell	.20	.07
❑ 86	Ron Dixon	.20	.07
❑ 87	Jeremy Shockey	.75	.30
❑ 88	Marvin Harrison	.50	.20
❑ 89	Peyton Manning	.75	.30
❑ 90	Edgerrin James	.50	.20
❑ 91	Dominic Rhodes	.30	.10
❑ 92	Brock Huard	.20	.07
❑ 93	Marcus Pollard	.20	.07
❑ 94	James Mungro	.20	.07
❑ 95	Dwight Freeney	.30	.10
❑ 96	Reggie Wayne	.30	.10
❑ 97	Rob Morris	.20	.07
❑ 98	Michael Vick	1.25	.50
❑ 99	Warrick Dunn	.30	.10
❑ 100	T.J. Duckett	.30	.10
❑ 101	Keith Brooking	.20	.07
❑ 102	Ray Buchanan	.20	.07
❑ 103	Alge Crumpler	.30	.10
❑ 104	Quentin McCord	.20	.07
❑ 105	Doug Johnson	.20	.07
❑ 106	Brian Finneran	.20	.07
❑ 107	Peerless Price	.30	.10
❑ 108	Chad Pennington	.60	.25
❑ 109	Curtis Martin	.50	.20
❑ 110	Laveranues Coles	.30	.10
❑ 111	Wayne Chrebet	.30	.10
❑ 112	LaMont Jordan	.50	.20
❑ 113	Anthony Becht	.20	.07
❑ 114	Marvin Jones	.20	.07
❑ 115	Mo Lewis	.20	.07
❑ 116	Sam Cowart	.20	.07
❑ 117	Vinnie Testaverde	.30	.10
❑ 118	Santana Moss	.30	.10
❑ 119	Tim Couch	.20	.07
❑ 120	William Green	.30	.10
❑ 121	Andre Davis	.20	.07
❑ 122	Quincy Morgan	.30	.10
❑ 123	Kevin Johnson	.30	.10
❑ 124	James Jackson	.20	.07
❑ 125	Jamel White	.20	.07
❑ 126	Robert Griffith	.20	.07
❑ 127	Dennis Northcutt	.30	.10
❑ 128	Josh Booty	.20	.07
❑ 129	Kelly Holcomb	.30	.10
❑ 130	Jake Plummer	.30	.10
❑ 131	Olandis Gary	.30	.10
❑ 132	Clinton Portis	.75	.30
❑ 133	Mike Anderson	.50	.20
❑ 134	Ashley Lelie	.50	.20
❑ 135	Ed McCaffrey	.50	.20
❑ 136	Shannon Sharpe	.30	.10
❑ 137	Rod Smith	.30	.10
❑ 138	John Mobley	.20	.07
❑ 139	Jason Elam	.20	.07
❑ 140	Terrell Davis	.50	.20
❑ 141	Tom Brady	1.25	.50
❑ 142	Christian Fauria	.20	.07
❑ 143	Antowain Smith	.30	.10
❑ 144	Kevin Faulk	.20	.07
❑ 145	Ty Law	.30	.10
❑ 146	Lawyer Milloy	.30	.10
❑ 147	David Patten	.20	.07
❑ 148	Deion Branch	.50	.20
❑ 149	Troy Brown	.30	.10
❑ 150	Rohan Davey	.30	.10
❑ 151	Adam Vinatieri	.50	.20
❑ 152	Jay Fiedler	.30	.10
❑ 153	Chris Chambers	.50	.20
❑ 154	Randy McMichael	.30	.10
❑ 155	Rob Konrad	.20	.07
❑ 156	Morlon Greenwood	.20	.07
❑ 157	Derrius Thompson	.20	.07
❑ 158	Travis Minor	.20	.07
❑ 159	Olindo Mare	.20	.07
❑ 160	Jason Taylor	.20	.07
❑ 161	Zach Thomas	.50	.20
❑ 162	Ricky Williams	.50	.20
❑ 163	Aaron Brooks	.50	.20
❑ 164	Deuce McAllister	.50	.20
❑ 165	Donte Stallworth	.50	.20
❑ 166	Jerome Pathon	.20	.07
❑ 167	J.T. O'Sullivan	.20	.07
❑ 168	Darrin Smith	.20	.07
❑ 169	Michael Lewis	.20	.07
❑ 170	John Carney	.20	.07
❑ 171	Kyle Turley	.20	.07
❑ 172	Joe Horn	.30	.10
❑ 173	Trent Green	.30	.10
❑ 174	Priest Holmes	.60	.25
❑ 175	Johnnie Morton	.30	.10
❑ 176	Eddie Kennison	.20	.07
❑ 177	Marvcus Patton	.20	.07
❑ 178	Omar Easy	.20	.07
❑ 179	Derrick Blaylock	.30	.10
❑ 180	Snoop Minnis	.20	.07
❑ 181	Dante Hall	.50	.20
❑ 182	Tony Gonzalez	.30	.10
❑ 183	Marc Boerigter	.30	.10
❑ 184	Drew Brees	.50	.20
❑ 185	David Boston	.30	.10
❑ 186	Stephen Alexander	.20	.07
❑ 187	Quentin Jammer	.20	.07
❑ 188	Donnie Edwards	.20	.07
❑ 189	LaDainian Tomlinson	.50	.20
❑ 190	Junior Seau	.50	.20
❑ 191	Reche Caldwell	.20	.07
❑ 192	Lorenzo Neal	.20	.07
❑ 193	Tim Dwight	.30	.10
❑ 194	Doug Flutie	.30	.10
❑ 195	Drew Bledsoe	.50	.20
❑ 196	Travis Henry	.30	.10
❑ 197	Eric Moulds	.30	.10
❑ 198	Alex Van Pelt	.20	.07
❑ 199	Charles Johnson	.20	.07
❑ 200	Nate Clements	.20	.07
❑ 201	Takeo Spikes	.20	.07
❑ 202	Bobby Shaw	.20	.07
❑ 203	London Fletcher	.20	.07
❑ 204	Sammy Morris	.20	.07
❑ 205	Josh Reed	.30	.10
❑ 206	Patrick Ramsey	.50	.20
❑ 207	Ladell Betts	.30	.10
❑ 208	Chad Morton	.20	.07
❑ 209	Trung Canidate	.30	.10
❑ 210	Kenny Watson	.20	.07
❑ 211	Jessie Armstead	.20	.07
❑ 212	Fred Smoot	.20	.07
❑ 213	Champ Bailey	.30	.10
❑ 214	Bruce Smith	.20	.07
❑ 215	Rod Gardner	.30	.10
❑ 216	Kurt Warner	.50	.20
❑ 217	Troy Edwards	.20	.07
❑ 218	Adam Archuleta	.20	.07
❑ 219	Grant Wistrom	.20	.07
❑ 220	Marshall Faulk	.50	.20
❑ 221	Jeff Wilkins	.20	.07
❑ 222	Aeneas Williams	.20	.07
❑ 223	Lamar Gordon	.20	.07
❑ 224	Marc Bulger	.50	.20
❑ 225	Isaac Bruce	.50	.20
❑ 226	Torry Holt	.50	.20
❑ 227	Matt Hasselbeck	.30	.10
❑ 228	Maurice Morris	.20	.07
❑ 229	Bobby Engram	.20	.07
❑ 230	Darrell Jackson	.30	.10
❑ 231	James Williams	.20	.07
❑ 232	Chad Brown	.20	.07
❑ 233	Anthony Simmons	.20	.07
❑ 234	Shaun Alexander	.50	.20
❑ 235	Koren Robinson	.30	.10
❑ 236	Chris Redman	.20	.07
❑ 237	Jamal Lewis	.50	.20
❑ 238	Brandon Stokley	.30	.10
❑ 239	Peter Boulware	.20	.07
❑ 240	Randy Hymes RC	.30	.10
❑ 241	Todd Heap	.30	.10
❑ 242	Travis Taylor	.30	.10
❑ 243	Ron Johnson	.20	.07
❑ 244	Ray Lewis	.50	.20
❑ 245	Jake Delhomme	.50	.20
❑ 246	DeShaun Foster	.20	.07
❑ 247	Dee Brown	.20	.07
❑ 248	Steve Smith	.50	.20
❑ 249	Kevin Dyson	.30	.10
❑ 250	Muhsin Muhammad	.30	.10
❑ 251	Stephen Davis	.30	.10
❑ 252	Julius Peppers	.50	.20
❑ 253	Rodney Peete	.20	.07
❑ 254	Mark Brunell	.30	.10
❑ 255	Jimmy Smith	.30	.10
❑ 256	Kyle Brady	.20	.07
❑ 257	Kevin Lockett	.20	.07
❑ 258	Quinn Gray	.20	.07
❑ 259	Tony Brackens	.20	.07
❑ 260	Marco Coleman	.20	.07
❑ 261	David Garrard	.20	.07
❑ 262	Fred Taylor	.50	.20
❑ 263	Daunte Culpepper	.50	.20
❑ 264	Michael Bennett	.30	.10
❑ 265	D'Wayne Bates	.20	.07
❑ 266	Cedric James	.20	.07
❑ 267	Kelly Campbell	.20	.07
❑ 268	Derrick Alexander	.20	.07
❑ 269	Byron Chamberlain	.20	.07
❑ 270	Shaun Hill	.20	.07
❑ 271	Randy Moss	.75	.30
❑ 272	Josh McCown	.30	.10
❑ 273	Thomas Jones	.30	.10
❑ 274	Wendell Bryant	.20	.07
❑ 275	Kevin Kasper	.20	.07
❑ 276	Jason McAddley	.20	.07
❑ 277	Emmitt Smith	1.25	.50
❑ 278	Preston Parsons	.20	.07
❑ 279	Freddie Jones	.20	.07
❑ 280	Marcel Shipp	.30	.10
❑ 281	Chad Hutchinson	.20	.07
❑ 282	Troy Hambrick	.20	.07
❑ 283	Dat Nguyen	.20	.07
❑ 284	Michael Wiley	.20	.07
❑ 285	Joey Galloway	.30	.10
❑ 286	Terry Glenn	.20	.07

❑ 287 La'Roi Glover	.20	.07
❑ 288 Roy Williams	.50	.20
❑ 289 Antonio Bryant	.50	.20
❑ 290 Quincy Carter	.30	.10
❑ 291 Anthony Thomas	.30	.10
❑ 292 Marty Booker	.30	.10
❑ 293 Dez White	.20	.07
❑ 294 Marcus Robinson	.30	.10
❑ 295 Kordell Stewart	.30	.10
❑ 296 David Terrell	.30	.10
❑ 297 John Davis	.20	.07
❑ 298 Mike Brown	.30	.10
❑ 299 Brian Urlacher	.75	.30
❑ 300 Jabar Gaffney	.30	.10
❑ 301 Jonathan Wells	.20	.07
❑ 302 JaJuan Dawson	.20	.07
❑ 303 Corey Bradford	.20	.07
❑ 304 Frank Murphy	.20	.07
❑ 305 Billy Miller	.20	.07
❑ 306 Aaron Glenn	.20	.07
❑ 307 Avion Black	.20	.07
❑ 308 David Carr	.75	.30
❑ 309 Joey Harrington	.75	.30
❑ 310 James Stewart	.30	.10
❑ 311 Ty Detmer	.20	.07
❑ 312 Jason Hanson	.20	.07
❑ 313 Bill Schroeder	.30	.10
❑ 314 Mikhael Ricks	.20	.07
❑ 315 Scotty Anderson	.20	.07
❑ 316 Robert Porcher	.20	.07
❑ 317 Az-Zahir Hakim	.20	.07
❑ 318 Jon Kitna	.30	.10
❑ 319 Ron Dugans	.20	.07
❑ 320 Chad Johnson	.50	.20
❑ 321 Brandon Bennett	.20	.07
❑ 322 T.J. Houshmandzadeh	.20	.07
❑ 323 Rudi Johnson	.50	.20
❑ 324 Kevin Hardy	.20	.07
❑ 325 Corey Dillon	.30	.10
❑ 326 Peter Warrick	.30	.10
❑ 327 Carson Palmer RC	5.00	2.00
❑ 328 Byron Leftwich RC	4.00	1.50
❑ 329 Rex Grossman RC	4.00	1.50
❑ 330 Kyle Boller RC	1.25	.50
❑ 331 Dave Ragone RC	1.25	.50
❑ 332 Chris Simms RC	2.00	.75
❑ 333 Brad Banks RC	1.00	.40
❑ 334 Kliff Kingsbury RC	1.00	.40
❑ 335 Jason Gesser RC	1.25	.50
❑ 336 Jason Johnson RC	.60	.25
❑ 337 Brian St.Pierre RC	1.25	.50
❑ 338 Ken Dorsey RC	1.25	.50
❑ 339 Seneca Wallace RC	1.25	.50
❑ 340 Seth Marler RC	1.00	.40
❑ 341 Tony Romo RC	20.00	10.00
❑ 342 J.T. Wall RC	.60	.25
❑ 343 Kirk Farmer RC	.60	.25
❑ 344 Ricky Manning RC	1.25	.50
❑ 345 B.J. Askew RC	1.25	.50
❑ 346 Juston Wood RC	.60	.25
❑ 347 Jeremi Johnson RC	1.00	.40
❑ 348 Tom Lopienski RC	1.00	.40
❑ 349 Justin Griffith RC	1.00	.40
❑ 350 Ovie Mughelli RC	.60	.25
❑ 351 Bradie James RC	1.25	.50
❑ 352 Larry Johnson RC	5.00	2.50
❑ 353 Lee Suggs RC	1.25	.50
❑ 354 Justin Fargas RC	1.25	.50
❑ 355 Chris Brown RC	1.25	.50
❑ 356 Onterrio Smith RC	1.25	.50
❑ 357 Willis McGahee RC	3.00	1.25
❑ 358 Claude Diggs RC	.60	.25
❑ 359 Lance Briggs RC	4.00	1.50
❑ 360 Earnest Graham RC	1.00	.40
❑ 361 Quentin Griffin RC	1.25	.50
❑ 362 Michael Haynes RC	1.25	.50
❑ 363 Musa Smith RC	1.25	.50
❑ 364 Artose Pinner RC	1.25	.50
❑ 365 Domanick Davis RC	1.25	.50
❑ 366 LaBrandon Toefield RC	1.25	.50
❑ 367 Bethel Johnson RC	1.25	.50
❑ 368 Sultan McCullough RC	1.00	.40
❑ 369 Dahrran Diedrick RC	1.25	.50
❑ 370 Soloman Bates RC	.60	.25
❑ 371 Andrew Pinnock RC	1.00	.40
❑ 372 Charles Rogers RC	1.25	.50
❑ 373 Andre Johnson RC	2.50	1.00
❑ 374 Taylor Jacobs RC	1.00	.40
❑ 375 Anquan Boldin RC	3.00	1.25
❑ 376 Talman Gardner RC	1.25	.50
❑ 377 Brandon Lloyd RC	1.25	.50
❑ 378 Bryant Johnson RC	1.25	.50
❑ 379 Kelley Washington RC	1.25	.50
❑ 380 Kareem Kelly RC	1.00	.40
❑ 381 Arnaz Battle RC	1.25	.50
❑ 382 Billy McMullen RC	1.00	.40
❑ 383 Kennan Howry RC	1.25	.50
❑ 384 Nate Burleson RC	1.25	.50
❑ 385 Doug Gabriel RC	1.25	.50
❑ 386 J.R. Tolver RC	1.00	.40
❑ 387 Wayne Hunter RC	.60	.25
❑ 388 Teyo Johnson RC	1.25	.50
❑ 389 Eric Steinbach RC	1.00	.40
❑ 390 Kevin Curtis RC	1.25	.50
❑ 391 Bobby Wade RC	1.25	.50
❑ 392 Sam Aiken RC	1.00	.40
❑ 393 Willie Pile RC	1.25	.50
❑ 394 Jerel Myers RC	.60	.25
❑ 395 Tyrone Calico RC	1.25	.50
❑ 396 Terrence Edwards RC	1.00	.40
❑ 397 Travis Anglin RC	.60	.25
❑ 398 Antwone Savage RC	.60	.25
❑ 399 Cato June RC	1.50	.60
❑ 400 Charles Drake RC	.60	.25
❑ 401 Ronald Bellamy RC	1.00	.40
❑ 402 Justin Gage RC	1.25	.50
❑ 403 Mat McBriar RC	.60	.25
❑ 404 Kevin Garrett RC	.60	.25
❑ 405 Kenny Peterson RC	1.00	.40
❑ 406 L.J. Smith RC	1.25	.50
❑ 407 Jason Witten RC	2.00	.75
❑ 408 Dallas Clark RC	1.25	.50
❑ 409 DeWayne White RC	1.00	.40
❑ 410 Mike Seidman RC	.60	.25
❑ 411 Aaron Walker RC	1.00	.40
❑ 412 Bennie Joppru RC	1.25	.50
❑ 413 Mike Pinkard RC	.60	.25
❑ 414 Danny Curley RC	.60	.25
❑ 415 Trent Smith RC	1.00	.40
❑ 416 George Wrighster RC	1.00	.40
❑ 417 Terrell Suggs RC	2.00	.75
❑ 418 Tully Banta-Cain RC	1.00	.40
❑ 419 Jerome McDougle RC	1.25	.50
❑ 420 William Joseph RC	1.25	.50
❑ 421 DeWayne Robertson RC	1.25	.50
❑ 422 Jimmy Kennedy RC	1.25	.50
❑ 423 Chris Kelsay RC	1.25	.50
❑ 424 Kevin Williams RC	1.25	.50
❑ 425 Boss Bailey RC	1.25	.50
❑ 426 Terry Pierce RC	1.00	.40
❑ 427 Terence Newman RC	2.50	1.00
❑ 428 Marcus Trufant RC	1.25	.50
❑ 429 Mike Doss RC	1.25	.50
❑ 430 Dennis Weathersby RC	.60	.25
❑ 431 Matt Wilhelm RC	1.25	.50
❑ 432 Andre Woolfolk RC	1.25	.50
❑ 433 Shane Walton RC	.60	.25
❑ 434 DeJuan Groce RC	1.25	.50
❑ 435 Antwoine Sanders RC	.60	.25
❑ 436 Julian Battle RC	1.00	.40
❑ 437 Brett Favre CL	.60	.25
❑ 438 Chad Pennington CL	.30	.10
❑ 439 David Carr CL	.50	.20
❑ 440 Drew Brees CL	.30	.10

2000 Upper Deck Pros and Prospects

Card		
❑ COMPLETE SET (126)	600.00	300.00
❑ COMP.SET w/o SP's (84)	20.00	7.50
❑ 1 Jake Plummer	.30	.10
❑ 2 Michael Pittman	.20	.07
❑ 3 Tim Dwight	.50	.20
❑ 4 Chris Chandler	.30	.10
❑ 5 Qadry Ismail	.30	.10
❑ 6 Shannon Sharpe	.30	.10
❑ 7 Peerless Price	.30	.10
❑ 8 Rob Johnson	.30	.10
❑ 9 Eric Moulds	.50	.20
❑ 10 Muhsin Muhammad	.30	.10
❑ 11 Patrick Jeffers	.50	.20
❑ 12 Steve Beuerlein	.30	.10
❑ 13 Cade McNown	.20	.07
❑ 14 Curtis Enis	.20	.07
❑ 15 Marcus Robinson	.50	.20
❑ 16 Akili Smith	.20	.07
❑ 17 Corey Dillon	.50	.20
❑ 18 Tim Couch	.30	.10
❑ 19 Kevin Johnson	.50	.20
❑ 20 Errict Rhett	.30	.10
❑ 21 Troy Aikman	1.00	.40
❑ 22 Emmitt Smith	1.00	.40
❑ 23 Rocket Ismail	.30	.10
❑ 24 Terrell Davis	.50	.20
❑ 25 Olandis Gary	.50	.20
❑ 26 Brian Griese	.50	.20
❑ 27 Ed McCaffrey	.50	.20
❑ 28 Charlie Batch	.50	.20
❑ 29 Germane Crowell	.20	.07
❑ 30 James O. Stewart	.30	.10
❑ 31 Brett Favre	1.50	.60
❑ 32 Antonio Freeman	.50	.20
❑ 33 Dorsey Levens	.30	.10
❑ 34 Peyton Manning	1.25	.50
❑ 35 Edgerrin James	.75	.30
❑ 36 Marvin Harrison	.50	.20
❑ 37 Mark Brunell	.50	.20
❑ 38 Fred Taylor	.50	.20
❑ 39 Jimmy Smith	.30	.10
❑ 40 Elvis Grbac	.30	.10

❑ 41 Tony Gonzalez .30 .10
❑ 42 Damon Huard .50 .20
❑ 43 James Johnson .20 .07
❑ 44 Jay Fiedler .50 .20
❑ 45 Randy Moss 1.00 .40
❑ 46 Robert Smith .50 .20
❑ 47 Cris Carter .50 .20
❑ 48 Drew Bledsoe .60 .25
❑ 49 Terry Glenn .30 .10
❑ 50 Ricky Williams .50 .20
❑ 51 Jeff Blake .30 .10
❑ 52 Keith Poole .20 .07
❑ 53 Kerry Collins .30 .10
❑ 54 Amani Toomer .20 .07
❑ 55 Vinny Testaverde .30 .10
❑ 56 Keyshawn Johnson .50 .20
❑ 57 Curtis Martin .50 .20
❑ 58 Tim Brown .50 .20
❑ 59 Rich Gannon .50 .20
❑ 60 Tyrone Wheatley .30 .10
❑ 61 Duce Staley .50 .20
❑ 62 Donovan McNabb .75 .30
❑ 63 Troy Edwards .20 .07
❑ 64 Jerome Bettis .50 .20
❑ 65 Marshall Faulk .60 .25
❑ 66 Kurt Warner 1.00 .40
❑ 67 Torry Holt .50 .20
❑ 68 Isaac Bruce .50 .20
❑ 69 Junior Seau .50 .20
❑ 70 Jeff Graham .20 .07
❑ 71 Steve Young .60 .25
❑ 72 Jerry Rice 1.00 .40
❑ 73 Charlie Garner .30 .10
❑ 74 Ricky Watters .30 .10
❑ 75 Jon Kitna .50 .20
❑ 76 Warrick Dunn .50 .20
❑ 77 Shaun King .20 .07
❑ 78 Mike Alstott .50 .20
❑ 79 Eddie George .50 .20
❑ 80 Steve McNair .50 .20
❑ 81 Kevin Dyson .30 .10
❑ 82 Brad Johnson .50 .20
❑ 83 Stephen Davis .50 .20
❑ 84 Michael Westbrook .30 .10
❑ 85 Peter Warrick RC 12.00 5.00
❑ 86 LaVar Arrington RC 50.00 20.00
❑ 87 Chris Redman RC 10.00 4.00
❑ 88 Courtney Brown RC 12.00 5.00
❑ 89 Plaxico Burress RC 25.00 10.00
❑ 90 Corey Simon RC 12.00 5.00
❑ 91 Bubba Franks RC 12.00 5.00
❑ 92 Deon Grant RC 10.00 4.00
❑ 93 Brian Urlacher RC 40.00 15.00
❑ 94 Ron Dayne RC 12.00 5.00
❑ 95 Sylvester Morris RC 10.00 4.00
❑ 96 Shaun Alexander RC 50.00 25.00
❑ 97 Dez White RC 12.00 5.00
❑ 98 Thomas Jones RC 20.00 7.50
❑ 99 Travis Taylor RC 12.00 5.00
❑ 100 Kwame Cavil RC 6.00 2.50
❑ 101 Jamal Lewis RC 25.00 10.00
❑ 102 Chad Pennington RC 25.00 10.00
❑ 103 J.R. Redmond RC 10.00 4.00
❑ 104 Sebastian Janikowski RC 12.00 5.00
❑ 105 Anthony Lucas RC 6.00 2.50
❑ 106 Travis Prentice RC 10.00 4.00
❑ 107 Danny Farmer RC 10.00 4.00
❑ 108 Sherrod Gideon RC 6.00 2.50
❑ 109 Todd Pinkston RC 12.00 5.00
❑ 110 Dennis Northcutt RC 12.00 5.00
❑ 111 Tim Rattay RC 12.00 5.00
❑ 112 Troy Walters RC 12.00 5.00
❑ 113 Michael Wiley RC 10.00 4.00
❑ 114 R.Jay Soward RC 10.00 4.00
❑ 115 Trung Canidate RC 10.00 4.00
❑ 116 Reuben Droughns RC 15.00 6.00
❑ 117 Rondell Mealey RC 6.00 2.50
❑ 118 Chris Coleman RC 12.00 5.00
❑ 119 Giovanni Carmazzi RC 10.00 4.00
❑ 120 Trevor Insley RC 10.00 4.00
❑ 121 Shyrone Stith RC 10.00 4.00
❑ 122 Gari Scott RC 6.00 2.50
❑ 123 Tee Martin RC 12.00 5.00
❑ 124 Tom Brady RC 120.00 60.00
❑ 125 Marcus Knight RC 10.00 4.00
❑ 126 Jerry Porter RC 25.00 10.00
❑ 127 Brad Hoover RC 5.00 2.00
❑ 128 Chad Morton RC 8.00 3.00
❑ 129 Charles Lee RC 5.00 2.00
❑ 130 Damon Hodge RC 5.00 2.00
❑ 131 Darrell Jackson RC 15.00 6.00
❑ 132 Doug Johnson RC 8.00 3.00
❑ 133 Frank Moreau RC 5.00 2.00
❑ 134 JaJuan Dawson RC 5.00 2.00
❑ 135 Jake Delhomme RC 30.00 15.00
❑ 136 Jarious Jackson RC 5.00 2.00
❑ 137 Joe Hamilton RC 5.00 2.00
❑ 138 Larry Foster RC 5.00 2.00
❑ 139 Laveranues Coles RC 10.00 4.00
❑ 140 Aaron Shea RC 8.00 3.00
❑ 141 Matt Lytle RC 5.00 2.00
❑ 142 Mike Anderson RC 15.00 6.00
❑ 143 Ron Dixon RC 5.00 2.00
❑ 144 Ronney Jenkins RC 5.00 2.00
❑ 145 Sammy Morris RC 5.00 2.00
❑ 146 Shockmain Davis RC 5.00 2.00
❑ 147 Spergon Wynn RC 5.00 2.00
❑ 148 Todd Husak RC 8.00 3.00
❑ 149 Trevor Gaylor RC 5.00 2.00
❑ 150 Tywan Mitchell RC 5.00 2.00
❑ 151 Windrell Hayes RC 5.00 2.00
❑ 152 Bobby Shaw RC 5.00 2.00

2001 Upper Deck Pros and Prospects

❑ COMP.SET w/o SP's (90) 15.00 6.00
❑ 1 Jake Plummer .30 .10
❑ 2 David Boston .50 .20
❑ 3 Jamal Anderson .50 .20
❑ 4 Doug Johnson .20 .07
❑ 5 Maurice Smith .30 .10
❑ 6 Jamal Lewis .75 .30
❑ 7 Shannon Sharpe .30 .10
❑ 8 Trent Dilfer .30 .10
❑ 9 Doug Flutie .50 .20
❑ 10 Rob Johnson .30 .10
❑ 11 Eric Moulds .50 .20
❑ 12 Muhsin Muhammad .30 .10
❑ 13 Brad Hoover .20 .07
❑ 14 Tim Biakabutuka .30 .10
❑ 15 Cade McNown .20 .07
❑ 16 James Allen .30 .10
❑ 17 Marcus Robinson .50 .20
❑ 18 Brian Urlacher .75 .30
❑ 19 Peter Warrick .50 .20
❑ 20 Corey Dillon .50 .20
❑ 21 Tim Couch .30 .10
❑ 22 Kevin Johnson .30 .10
❑ 23 Travis Prentice .20 .07
❑ 24 Troy Aikman .75 .30
❑ 25 Emmitt Smith 1.00 .40
❑ 26 Terrell Davis .50 .20
❑ 27 Mike Anderson .50 .20
❑ 28 Brian Griese .50 .20
❑ 29 Charlie Batch .50 .20
❑ 30 Germane Crowell .20 .07
❑ 31 James Stewart .30 .10
❑ 32 Brett Favre 1.50 .60
❑ 33 Antonio Freeman .50 .20
❑ 34 Dorsey Levens .30 .10
❑ 35 Ahman Green .50 .20
❑ 36 Peyton Manning 1.25 .50
❑ 37 Edgerrin James .60 .25
❑ 38 Marvin Harrison .50 .20
❑ 39 Mark Brunell .50 .20
❑ 40 Fred Taylor .50 .20
❑ 41 Jimmy Smith .30 .10
❑ 42 Elvis Grbac .30 .10
❑ 43 Tony Gonzalez .30 .10
❑ 44 Derrick Alexander .30 .10
❑ 45 Oronde Gadsden .30 .10
❑ 46 Lamar Smith .30 .10
❑ 47 Jay Fiedler .50 .20
❑ 48 Randy Moss 1.00 .40
❑ 49 Moe Williams .30 .10
❑ 50 Cris Carter .50 .20
❑ 51 Daunte Culpepper .50 .20
❑ 52 Drew Bledsoe .60 .25
❑ 53 Terry Glenn .30 .10
❑ 54 Ricky Williams .50 .20
❑ 55 Jeff Blake .30 .10
❑ 56 Joe Horn .30 .10
❑ 57 Aaron Brooks .50 .20
❑ 58 La'Roi Glover .20 .07
❑ 59 Kerry Collins .30 .10
❑ 60 Amani Toomer .30 .10
❑ 61 Ron Dayne .50 .20
❑ 62 Vinny Testaverde .30 .10
❑ 63 Wayne Chrebet .30 .10
❑ 64 Curtis Martin .50 .20
❑ 65 Tim Brown .50 .20
❑ 66 Rich Gannon .50 .20
❑ 67 Tyrone Wheatley .30 .10
❑ 68 Duce Staley .50 .20
❑ 69 Donovan McNabb .60 .25
❑ 70 Kordell Stewart .30 .10
❑ 71 Jerome Bettis .50 .20
❑ 72 Marshall Faulk .60 .25
❑ 73 Kurt Warner 1.00 .40
❑ 74 Isaac Bruce .50 .20
❑ 75 Junior Seau .50 .20
❑ 76 Curtis Conway .30 .10
❑ 77 Jeff Garcia .50 .20
❑ 78 Jerry Rice 1.00 .40
❑ 79 Charlie Garner .30 .10
❑ 80 Terrell Owens .50 .20
❑ 81 Ricky Watters .20 .07

- ❑ 82 Shaun Alexander .60 .25
- ❑ 83 Warrick Dunn .50 .20
- ❑ 84 Shaun King .20 .07
- ❑ 85 Derrick Brooks .50 .20
- ❑ 86 Eddie George .50 .20
- ❑ 87 Steve McNair .50 .20
- ❑ 88 Brad Johnson .50 .20
- ❑ 89 Jeff George .30 .10
- ❑ 90 Stephen Davis .50 .20
- ❑ 91 Jamal Reynolds RC 12.00 5.00
- ❑ 92 Justin Smith RC 12.00 5.00
- ❑ 93 Dan Morgan RC 12.00 5.00
- ❑ 94 Deuce McAllister RC 30.00 15.00
- ❑ 95 Drew Brees RC 50.00 20.00
- ❑ 96 Josh Booty RC 12.00 5.00
- ❑ 97 Mike McMahon RC 12.00 5.00
- ❑ 98 Sage Rosenfels RC 12.00 5.00
- ❑ 99 Marques Tuiasosopo RC 12.00 5.00
- ❑ 100 Josh Heupel RC 12.00 5.00
- ❑ 101 Heath Evans RC 8.00 3.00
- ❑ 102 Reggie White RC 8.00 3.00
- ❑ 103 Tim Hasselbeck RC 12.00 5.00
- ❑ 104 LaDainian Tomlinson RC 100.00 40.00
- ❑ 105 Kevan Barlow RC 12.00 5.00
- ❑ 106 LaMont Jordan RC 25.00 10.00
- ❑ 107 James Jackson RC 12.00 5.00
- ❑ 108 Anthony Thomas RC 12.00 5.00
- ❑ 109 Correll Buckhalter RC 15.00 6.00
- ❑ 110 Travis Henry RC 20.00 7.50
- ❑ 111 Dan Alexander RC 12.00 5.00
- ❑ 112 Travis Minor RC 8.00 3.00
- ❑ 113 Rudi Johnson RC 30.00 12.50
- ❑ 114 Michael Bennett RC 12.00 5.00
- ❑ 115 Todd Heap RC 12.00 5.00
- ❑ 116 Snoop Minnis RC 8.00 3.00
- ❑ 117 Santana Moss RC 20.00 7.50
- ❑ 118 Reggie Wayne RC 25.00 10.00
- ❑ 119 Koren Robinson RC 12.00 5.00
- ❑ 120 Chris Chambers RC 20.00 7.50
- ❑ 121 David Terrell RC 12.00 5.00
- ❑ 122 Rod Gardner RC 12.00 5.00
- ❑ 123 Quincy Morgan RC 12.00 5.00
- ❑ 124 Ken-Yon Rambo RC 8.00 3.00
- ❑ 125 Ronney Daniels RC 5.00 2.00
- ❑ 126 Ja'Mar Toombs RC 8.00 3.00
- ❑ 127 Bobby Newcombe RC 8.00 3.00
- ❑ 128 Cedrick Wilson RC 12.00 5.00
- ❑ 129 Chad Johnson RC 40.00 15.00
- ❑ 130 Shaun Rogers RC 12.00 5.00
- ❑ 131 Robert Ferguson RC 12.00 5.00
- ❑ 132 Kevin Kasper RC 12.00 5.00
- ❑ 133 Chris Weinke JSY RC 20.00 7.50
- ❑ 134 Freddie Mitchell JSY RC 15.00 6.00
- ❑ 135 Michael Vick JSY RC 60.00 30.00
- ❑ 136 Chris Taylor RC 8.00 3.00
- ❑ 137 Vinny Sutherland RC 8.00 3.00
- ❑ 138 Gerard Warren RC 12.00 5.00
- ❑ 139 Torrance Marshall RC 12.00 5.00
- ❑ 140 Jesse Palmer RC 12.00 5.00

2003 Upper Deck Pros and Prospects

- ❑ COMP.SET w/o SP's (90) 20.00 7.50
- ❑ 1 Jake Plummer .60 .25
- ❑ 2 David Boston .60 .25
- ❑ 3 Warrick Dunn .60 .25
- ❑ 4 T.J. Duckett .60 .25
- ❑ 5 Chris Redman .40 .15
- ❑ 6 Jamal Lewis 1.00 .40
- ❑ 7 Drew Bledsoe 1.00 .40
- ❑ 8 Travis Henry .60 .25

- ❑ 9 Eric Moulds .60 .25
- ❑ 10 Peerless Price .60 .25
- ❑ 11 Rodney Peete .60 .25
- ❑ 12 Julius Peppers 1.00 .40
- ❑ 13 Anthony Thomas .60 .25
- ❑ 14 Brian Urlacher 1.50 .60
- ❑ 15 Marty Booker .60 .25
- ❑ 16 David Terrell .60 .25
- ❑ 17 Corey Dillon .60 .25
- ❑ 18 Peter Warrick .60 .25
- ❑ 19 Jon Kitna .60 .25
- ❑ 20 Tim Couch .40 .15
- ❑ 21 Andre Davis .40 .15
- ❑ 22 Quincy Morgan .60 .25
- ❑ 23 Dennis Northcutt .60 .25
- ❑ 24 Roy Williams 1.00 .40
- ❑ 25 Emmitt Smith 2.50 1.00
- ❑ 26 Joey Galloway .60 .25
- ❑ 27 Antonio Bryant .60 .25
- ❑ 28 Brian Griese 1.00 .40
- ❑ 29 Clinton Portis 1.50 .60
- ❑ 30 Shannon Sharpe .60 .25
- ❑ 31 Joey Harrington 1.50 .60
- ❑ 32 Az-Zahir Hakim .40 .15
- ❑ 33 Brett Favre 2.50 1.00
- ❑ 34 Robert Ferguson .40 .15
- ❑ 35 Donald Driver .60 .25
- ❑ 36 David Carr 1.50 .60
- ❑ 37 Jabar Gaffney .60 .25
- ❑ 38 Edgerrin James 1.00 .40
- ❑ 39 Marvin Harrison 1.00 .40
- ❑ 40 Reggie Wayne .60 .25
- ❑ 41 Mark Brunell .60 .25
- ❑ 42 Fred Taylor 1.00 .40
- ❑ 43 Priest Holmes 1.25 .50
- ❑ 44 Trent Green .60 .25
- ❑ 45 Marc Boerigter .60 .25
- ❑ 46 Jay Fiedler .60 .25
- ❑ 47 Chris Chambers 1.00 .40
- ❑ 48 Randy McMichael .60 .25
- ❑ 49 Randy Moss 1.50 .60
- ❑ 50 Daunte Culpepper 1.00 .40
- ❑ 51 Michael Bennett .60 .25
- ❑ 52 Antowain Smith .60 .25
- ❑ 53 David Patten .40 .15
- ❑ 54 Troy Brown .60 .25
- ❑ 55 Aaron Brooks 1.00 .40
- ❑ 56 Joe Horn .60 .25
- ❑ 57 Donte Stallworth 1.00 .40
- ❑ 58 Amani Toomer .60 .25
- ❑ 59 Kerry Collins .60 .25
- ❑ 60 Tiki Barber 1.00 .40
- ❑ 61 Santana Moss .60 .25
- ❑ 62 Curtis Martin 1.00 .40
- ❑ 63 Wayne Chrebet .60 .25
- ❑ 64 Rich Gannon .60 .25
- ❑ 65 Charlie Garner .60 .25
- ❑ 66 Tim Brown 1.00 .40
- ❑ 67 Donovan McNabb 1.25 .50
- ❑ 68 Duce Staley .60 .25
- ❑ 69 Hines Ward 1.00 .40
- ❑ 70 Antwaan Randle El 1.00 .40
- ❑ 71 Plaxico Burress .60 .25
- ❑ 72 Jerome Bettis 1.00 .40
- ❑ 73 Junior Seau 1.00 .40
- ❑ 74 LaDainian Tomlinson 1.00 .40
- ❑ 75 Tai Streets .40 .15
- ❑ 76 Kevan Barlow .60 .25
- ❑ 77 Garrison Hearst .60 .25
- ❑ 78 Jeff Garcia 1.00 .40
- ❑ 79 Shaun Alexander 1.00 .40
- ❑ 80 Matt Hasselbeck .60 .25
- ❑ 81 Marshall Faulk 1.00 .40
- ❑ 82 Marc Bulger 1.00 .40
- ❑ 83 Torry Holt 1.00 .40
- ❑ 84 Isaac Bruce 1.00 .40
- ❑ 85 Brad Johnson .60 .25
- ❑ 86 Keyshawn Johnson 1.00 .40
- ❑ 87 Steve McNair 1.00 .40
- ❑ 88 Kevin Dyson .60 .25
- ❑ 89 Patrick Ramsey 1.00 .40
- ❑ 90 Ladell Betts .60 .25
- ❑ 91 Marcel Shipp SP 2.50 1.00
- ❑ 92 Michael Vick SP 8.00 3.00
- ❑ 93 Ray Lewis SP 3.00 1.25
- ❑ 94 Josh Reed SP 2.50 1.00
- ❑ 95 Josh McCown SP 2.50 1.00
- ❑ 96 Kelly Holcomb SP 2.50 1.00
- ❑ 97 William Green SP 2.50 1.00
- ❑ 98 Chad Hutchinson SP 1.50 .60
- ❑ 99 Rod Smith SP 2.50 1.00
- ❑ 100 James Stewart SP 2.50 1.00
- ❑ 101 Ahman Green SP 3.00 1.25
- ❑ 102 Peyton Manning SP 5.00 2.00
- ❑ 103 Jimmy Smith SP 2.50 1.00
- ❑ 104 Tony Gonzalez SP 2.50 1.00
- ❑ 105 Ricky Williams SP 3.00 1.25
- ❑ 106 Jason Taylor SP 1.50 .60
- ❑ 107 Tom Brady SP 6.00 2.50
- ❑ 108 Deuce McAllister SP 3.00 1.25
- ❑ 109 Jeremy Shockey SP 5.00 2.00
- ❑ 110 Chad Pennington SP 4.00 1.50
- ❑ 111 Jerry Rice SP 6.00 2.50
- ❑ 112 A.J. Feeley SP 2.50 1.00
- ❑ 113 Tommy Maddox SP 3.00 1.25
- ❑ 114 Drew Brees SP 3.00 1.25
- ❑ 115 Terrell Owens SP 3.00 1.25
- ❑ 116 Maurice Morris SP 1.50 .60
- ❑ 117 Kurt Warner SP 3.00 1.25
- ❑ 118 Derrick Brooks SP 2.50 1.00
- ❑ 119 Eddie George SP 2.50 1.00
- ❑ 120 Rod Gardner SP 2.50 1.00
- ❑ 121 Leftwich AU RC/Pnn.AU/250 80.00 30.00
- ❑ 122 Dorsey AU RC/Test/2000 20.00 7.50
- ❑ 123 Palmer AU RC/Mnn.AU/250 250.00 150.00
- ❑ 124 Simms AU RC/Bru.AU/250 50.00 30.00
- ❑ 125 A.Johnson RC/S.Moss 20.00 7.50
- ❑ 126 Banks AU RC/Brks.AU/250 30.00 12.50
- ❑ 127 J.R. Tolver RC/Hakim 4.00 1.50
- ❑ 128 J.Myers RC/J.Reed 2.50 1.00
- ❑ 129 R.Bellamy RC/A.Toomer 4.00 1.50
- ❑ 130 J.Gesser RC/D.Bledsoe 5.00 2.00
- ❑ 131 Kingsbury AU RC/S.Baugh 20.00 7.50
- ❑ 132 K.Boller RC/Brees AU/500 50.00 20.00
- ❑ 133 L.Johnson RC/Thomas AU 40.00 20.00
- ❑ 134 K.Kelly AU RC/Morton/2000 20.00 7.50
- ❑ 135 B.Johnson RC/Gard.AU/500 20.00 7.50
- ❑ 136 Johnson RC/Couch AU/500 25.00 10.00

- ❑ 137 T.Suggs AU RC/Nmll/2000 20.00 7.50
- ❑ 138 Ragone RC/Brnll AU/500 30.00 15.00
- ❑ 139 M.Smith RC/C.Trippi 5.00 2.00
- ❑ 140 J.Wood RC/J.Harrington 4.00 1.50
- ❑ 141 J.Thomas RC/Michael Vick 5.00 2.00
- ❑ 142 Graham AU RC/E.Smt/2000 30.00 12.50
- ❑ 143 McGahee AU RC/Jms/2000 50.00 20.00
- ❑ 144 R.Lee RC/Alexander AU/500 30.00 15.00
- ❑ 145 A.Boldin RC/J.Walker 12.00 5.00
- ❑ 146 Jacobs AU RC/Cald AU/250 30.00 12.50
- ❑ 147 T.Gardner RC/L.Coles 5.00 2.00
- ❑ 148 B.Wade RC/D.Northcutt 5.00 2.00
- ❑ 149 McMullen RC/Bruce AU/500 20.007.50
- ❑ 150 A.Cobourne RC/A.Zereoue 2.50 1.00
- ❑ 151 B.James RC/F.Kinard 5.00 2.00
- ❑ 152 Washing AU RC/Prc/2000 25.00 10.00
- ❑ 153 E.Steinbach RC/J.Parker 4.00 1.50
- ❑ 154 J.Kennedy RC/E.Stautner 5.00 2.00
- ❑ 155 R.Long RC/A.Weinmeister 2.50 1.00
- ❑ 156 C.Brown AU RC/Andr/2000 25.0010.00
- ❑ 157 T.Johnson RC/T.Gonzalez 5.00 2.00
- ❑ 158 O.Smith RC/M.Morris 8.00 3.00
- ❑ 159 Fargas AU RC/Portis/2000 20.00 7.50
- ❑ 160 S.Wallace RC/A.Randle El 5.00 2.00
- ❑ 161 St.Pierre RC/Mann AU/500 80.0040.00
- ❑ 162 Toefield RC/Tmln AU/500 80.00 40.00
- ❑ 163 M.Blackwell RC/Culpepper 2.50 1.00
- ❑ 164 K.Howry RC/A.J.Feeley 5.00 2.00
- ❑ 165 J.Gage RC/K.Farmer RC 5.00 2.00
- ❑ 166 S.Witten RC/A.Davis 2.50 1.00
- ❑ 167 Weathersby RC/A.Williams 2.50 1.00
- ❑ 168 B.Bailey RC/C.Bailey 6.00 2.50
- ❑ 169 B.Lloyd RC/K.Kittner 5.00 2.00
- ❑ 170 D.Gabriel RC/C.Chambers 5.00 2.00
- ❑ 171 A.Gbaja-Biamila RC/KGB 5.00 2.00
- ❑ 172 D.Diedrick RC/A.Green 5.00 2.00
- ❑ 173 K.Curtis RC/K.Dyson 5.00 2.00
- ❑ 174 McCull RC/McAll.AU/500 25.00 12.50
- ❑ 175 M.Bush RC/M.Trufant RC 5.00 2.00
- ❑ 176 Z.Hilton RC/S.Aiken RC 4.00 1.50
- ❑ 177 Newman RC/Woolfolk RC 12.00 6.00
- ❑ 178 T.Calico RC/K.Holcomb 6.00 2.50
- ❑ 179 J.T. Wall RC/T.Edwards RC 8.00 3.00
- ❑ 180 C.Paus RC/M.Seidman RC 8.00 3.00
- ❑ 181 L.J. Smith RC/M.Battaglia 5.00 2.00
- ❑ 182 Griffin AU RC/Sav.RC/2000 20.00 7.50
- ❑ 183 L.Suggs RC/M.Vick 15.00 6.00
- ❑ 184 B.Askew RC/B.Joppru RC 5.00 2.00
- ❑ 185 M.Pinkard RC/Todd Heap 2.50 1.00
- ❑ 186 A.Battle RC/Tim Brown 5.00 2.00
- ❑ 187 C.Rogers RC/P.Burress 5.00 2.00
- ❑ 188 A.Pinnock RC/D.Staley 4.00 1.50
- ❑ 189 Grossman RC/Mnn.AU/500 100.00 50.00
- ❑ 190 G.Wrighster RC/J.Peelle 4.00 1.50
- ❑ KBBF K.Boller/B.Favre AU/25 200.00 125.00
- ❑ RGBF Grossman/Favre AU/25 200.00 100.00

2005 Upper Deck Rookie Debut

- ❑ COMP.SET w/o SP's (100) 20.00 10.00
- ❑ ROOKIE STATED ODDS 1:3
- ❑ UNPRICED BLUE PRINT RUN 15 SETS
- ❑ 1 Larry Fitzgerald .75 .30
- ❑ 2 Kurt Warner .50 .20
- ❑ 3 Anquan Boldin .50 .20
- ❑ 4 Michael Vick 1.25 .50
- ❑ 5 Warrick Dunn .50 .20
- ❑ 6 Peerless Price .40 .15
- ❑ 7 Jamal Lewis .75 .30
- ❑ 8 Derrick Mason .50 .20
- ❑ 9 Kyle Boller .50 .20

- ❑ 10 Willis McGahee .75 .30
- ❑ 11 J.P. Losman .75 .30
- ❑ 12 Eric Moulds .50 .20
- ❑ 13 Stephen Davis .50 .20
- ❑ 14 Jake Delhomme .75 .30
- ❑ 15 Steve Smith .50 .20
- ❑ 16 Thomas Jones .50 .20
- ❑ 17 Brian Urlacher .75 .30
- ❑ 18 Rex Grossman .50 .20
- ❑ 19 Carson Palmer .75 .30
- ❑ 20 Rudi Johnson .50 .20
- ❑ 21 Chad Johnson .75 .30
- ❑ 22 Kellen Winslow .75 .30
- ❑ 23 Luke McCown .40 .15
- ❑ 24 Lee Suggs .50 .20
- ❑ 25 Drew Bledsoe .75 .30
- ❑ 26 Keyshawn Johnson .50 .20
- ❑ 27 Julius Jones 1.00 .40
- ❑ 28 Roy Williams S .50 .20
- ❑ 29 Jake Plummer .50 .20
- ❑ 30 Tatum Bell .50 .20
- ❑ 31 Rod Smith .50 .20
- ❑ 32 Roy Williams WR .75 .30
- ❑ 33 Joey Harrington .75 .30
- ❑ 34 Kevin Jones .75 .30
- ❑ 35 Brett Favre 2.00 .75
- ❑ 36 Javon Walker .50 .20
- ❑ 37 Ahman Green .75 .30
- ❑ 38 David Carr .75 .30
- ❑ 39 Andre Johnson .50 .20
- ❑ 40 Domanick Davis .50 .20
- ❑ 41 Peyton Manning 1.25 .50
- ❑ 42 Marvin Harrison .75 .30
- ❑ 43 Edgerrin James .75 .30
- ❑ 44 Reggie Wayne .50 .20
- ❑ 45 Byron Leftwich .75 .30
- ❑ 46 Jimmy Smith .50 .20
- ❑ 47 Fred Taylor .50 .20
- ❑ 48 Priest Holmes .75 .30
- ❑ 49 Trent Green .50 .20
- ❑ 50 Tony Gonzalez .50 .20
- ❑ 51 Chris Chambers .50 .20
- ❑ 52 Sammy Morris .40 .15
- ❑ 53 A.J. Feeley .50 .20
- ❑ 54 Daunte Culpepper .75 .30
- ❑ 55 Nate Burleson .50 .20
- ❑ 56 Michael Bennett .50 .20
- ❑ 57 Tom Brady 2.00 .75
- ❑ 58 David Givens .50 .20
- ❑ 59 Corey Dillon .50 .20
- ❑ 60 Ty Law .50 .20
- ❑ 61 Aaron Brooks .50 .20
- ❑ 62 Joe Horn .50 .20
- ❑ 63 Deuce McAllister .75 .30
- ❑ 64 Eli Manning 1.50 .60
- ❑ 65 Tiki Barber .75 .30
- ❑ 66 Amani Toomer .50 .20
- ❑ 67 Chad Pennington .75 .30
- ❑ 68 Curtis Martin .75 .30
- ❑ 69 Santana Moss .50 .20
- ❑ 70 Jerry Porter .50 .20
- ❑ 71 Randy Moss .75 .30
- ❑ 72 Kerry Collins .50 .20
- ❑ 73 Donovan McNabb 1.00 .40
- ❑ 74 Terrell Owens .75 .30
- ❑ 75 Brian Westbrook .50 .20
- ❑ 76 Ben Roethlisberger 2.00 .75
- ❑ 77 Hines Ward .75 .30
- ❑ 78 Jerome Bettis .75 .30
- ❑ 79 Duce Staley .50 .20
- ❑ 80 Drew Brees .75 .30
- ❑ 81 LaDainian Tomlinson 1.00 .40
- ❑ 82 Antonio Gates .75 .30
- ❑ 83 Tim Rattay .40 .15
- ❑ 84 Kevan Barlow .50 .20
- ❑ 85 Eric Johnson .50 .20
- ❑ 86 Matt Hasselbeck .50 .20
- ❑ 87 Shaun Alexander 1.00 .40
- ❑ 88 Darrell Jackson .50 .20
- ❑ 89 Marc Bulger .75 .30
- ❑ 90 Marshall Faulk .75 .30
- ❑ 91 Torry Holt .75 .30
- ❑ 92 Chris Simms .50 .20
- ❑ 93 Michael Clayton .75 .30
- ❑ 94 Michael Pittman .40 .15
- ❑ 95 Steve McNair .75 .30
- ❑ 96 Drew Bennett .50 .20
- ❑ 97 Chris Brown .50 .20
- ❑ 98 Clinton Portis .75 .30
- ❑ 99 Patrick Ramsey .50 .20
- ❑ 100 Laveranues Coles .50 .20
- ❑ 101 Gino Guidugli RC 1.50 .60
- ❑ 102 Kyle Orton RC 5.00 2.00
- ❑ 103 David Greene RC 3.00 1.25
- ❑ 104 Charlie Frye RC 6.00 2.50
- ❑ 105 Andrew Walter RC 5.00 2.00
- ❑ 106 Dan Orlovsky RC 4.00 1.50
- ❑ 107 Jason White RC 3.00 1.25
- ❑ 108 Sonny Cumbie RC 2.50 1.00
- ❑ 109 Ronnie Brown RC 12.00 5.00
- ❑ 110 Cadillac Williams RC 15.00 6.00
- ❑ 111 Anthony Davis RC 2.50 1.00
- ❑ 112 Kay-Jay Harris RC 2.50 1.00
- ❑ 113 Walter Reyes RC 2.50 1.00
- ❑ 114 Darren Sproles RC 3.00 1.25
- ❑ 115 Mark Clayton RC 4.00 1.50
- ❑ 116 Braylon Edwards RC 10.00 4.00
- ❑ 117 Charles Frederick RC 2.50 1.00
- ❑ 118 Fred Gibson RC 2.50 1.00
- ❑ 119 Craphonso Thorpe RC 2.50 1.00
- ❑ 120 Terrence Murphy RC 3.00 1.25
- ❑ 121 Antrel Rolle RC 3.00 1.25
- ❑ 122 Marlin Jackson RC 3.00 1.25
- ❑ 123 Corey Webster RC 3.00 1.25
- ❑ 124 Travis Johnson RC 2.50 1.00
- ❑ 125 Shawne Merriman RC 5.00 2.00
- ❑ 126 Aaron Rodgers RC 10.00 4.00
- ❑ 127 Alex Smith QB RC 12.00 5.00
- ❑ 128 T.A. McLendon RC 1.50 .60
- ❑ 129 Troy Williamson RC 6.00 2.50
- ❑ 130 Ryan Moats RC 3.00 1.25
- ❑ 131 Vernand Morency RC 3.00 1.25
- ❑ 132 Brock Berlin RC 2.50 1.00
- ❑ 133 J.J. Arrington RC 4.00 1.50
- ❑ 134 Frank Gore RC 6.00 2.50
- ❑ 135 Chris Henry RC 3.00 1.25
- ❑ 136 Roscoe Parrish RC 3.00 1.25
- ❑ 137 Alex Smith TE RC 3.00 1.25

❑ 138	Ciatrick Fason RC	3.00	1.25
❑ 139	Marion Barber RC	5.00	2.00
❑ 140	J.R. Russell RC	2.50	1.00
❑ 141	Heath Miller RC	8.00	3.00
❑ 142	Marcus Spears RC	3.00	1.25
❑ 143	Alvin Pearman RC	3.00	1.25
❑ 144	David Pollack RC	3.00	1.25
❑ 145	Erasmus James RC	3.00	1.25
❑ 146	Noah Herron RC	3.00	1.25
❑ 147	Dan Cody RC	3.00	1.25
❑ 148	Eric Shelton RC	3.00	1.25
❑ 149	Anttaj Hawthorne RC	2.50	1.00
❑ 150	Steve Savoy RC	1.50	.60
❑ 151	Mike Patterson RC	3.00	1.25
❑ 152	Kirk Morrison RC	3.00	1.25
❑ 153	Airese Currie RC	3.00	1.25
❑ 154	Derrick Johnson RC	5.00	2.00
❑ 155	Darryl Blackstock RC	2.50	1.00
❑ 156	Mike Williams	6.00	2.50
❑ 157	Ernest Shazor RC	3.00	1.25
❑ 158	James Butler RC	2.50	1.00
❑ 159	Thomas Davis RC	3.00	1.25
❑ 160	Carlos Rogers RC	4.00	1.50
❑ 161	Mark Bradley RC	3.00	1.25
❑ 162	Jerome Mathis RC	3.00	1.25
❑ 163	Justin Miller RC	2.50	1.00
❑ 164	Donte Nicholson RC	3.00	1.25
❑ 165	Derek Anderson RC	3.00	1.25
❑ 166	Brandon Browner RC	2.50	1.00
❑ 167	Domonique Foxworth RC	3.00	1.25
❑ 168	Kevin Burnett RC	3.00	1.25
❑ 169	Lorenzo Alexander RC	2.50	1.00
❑ 170	Oshiomogho Atogwe RC	2.50	1.00
❑ 171	Dustin Fox RC	3.00	1.25
❑ 172	Jamaal Brimmer RC	1.50	.60
❑ 173	Ryan Fitzpatrick RC	5.00	2.00
❑ 174	Bill Swancutt RC	2.50	1.00
❑ 175	Barrett Ruud RC	3.00	1.25
❑ 176	Channing Crowder RC	3.00	1.25
❑ 177	Timmy Chang RC	2.50	1.00
❑ 178	Chris Rix RC	2.50	1.00
❑ 179	Justin Tuck RC	3.00	1.25
❑ 180	Adam Jones RC	3.00	1.25
❑ 181	Bryant McFadden RC	3.00	1.25
❑ 182	Taylor Stubblefield RC	1.50	.60
❑ 183	Vincent Jackson RC	3.00	1.25
❑ 184	Craig Bragg RC	2.50	1.00
❑ 185	Reggie Brown RC	3.00	1.25
❑ 186	Roddy White RC	3.00	1.25
❑ 187	Jason Campbell RC	5.00	2.00
❑ 188	Derek Wake RC	3.00	1.25
❑ 189	Josh Davis RC	2.50	1.00
❑ 190	Mike Nugent RC	3.00	1.25
❑ 191	Maurice Clarett	3.00	1.25
❑ 192	Brandon Jacobs RC	4.00	1.50
❑ 193	Matt Jones RC	8.00	3.00
❑ 194	Chad Owens RC	3.00	1.25
❑ 195	Paris Warren RC	2.50	1.00
❑ 196	Tab Perry RC	3.00	1.25
❑ 197	Jovan Haye RC	2.50	1.00
❑ 198	Cedric Benson RC	6.00	2.50
❑ 199	Bobby Purify RC	2.50	1.00
❑ 200	Stefan LeFors RC	3.00	1.25

2006 Upper Deck Rookie Debut

❑	COMP.SET w/o RC's (100)	25.00	10.00
❑	101-200 ROOKIES ONE PER PACK		
❑	201-260 AU ROOKIE ODDS 1:28		
❑ 1	Anquan Boldin	.50	.20
❑ 2	Larry Fitzgerald	.75	.30
❑ 3	Edgerrin James	.75	.30
❑ 4	Warrick Dunn	.50	.20
❑ 5	Alge Crumpler	.50	.20
❑ 6	Michael Vick	1.00	.40
❑ 7	Jamal Lewis	.50	.20
❑ 8	Derrick Mason	.40	.15
❑ 9	Steve McNair	.50	.20
❑ 10	Willis McGahee	.75	.30
❑ 11	Lee Evans	.50	.20
❑ 12	J.P. Losman	.50	.20
❑ 13	Steve Smith	.75	.30
❑ 14	Jake Delhomme	.50	.20
❑ 15	DeShaun Foster	.50	.20
❑ 16	Rex Grossman	.75	.30
❑ 17	Brian Urlacher	.75	.30
❑ 18	Thomas Jones	.50	.20
❑ 19	Carson Palmer	.75	.30
❑ 20	Chad Johnson	.50	.20
❑ 21	T.J. Houshmandzadeh	.50	.20
❑ 22	Rudi Johnson	.50	.20
❑ 23	Charlie Frye	.50	.20
❑ 24	Reuben Droughns	.50	.20
❑ 25	Braylon Edwards	.75	.30
❑ 26	Terrell Owens	.75	.30
❑ 27	Julius Jones	.75	.30
❑ 28	Drew Bledsoe	.75	.30
❑ 29	Terry Glenn	.50	.20
❑ 30	Jake Plummer	.50	.20
❑ 31	Tatum Bell	.50	.20
❑ 32	Javon Walker	.50	.20
❑ 33	Kevin Jones	.75	.30
❑ 34	Roy Williams WR	.75	.30
❑ 35	Jon Kitna	.40	.15
❑ 36	Brett Favre	1.50	.60
❑ 37	Donald Driver	.50	.20
❑ 38	Ahman Green	.50	.20
❑ 39	David Carr	.50	.20
❑ 40	Domanick Davis	.50	.20
❑ 41	Andre Johnson	.50	.20
❑ 42	Peyton Manning	1.25	.50
❑ 43	Reggie Wayne	.50	.20
❑ 44	Marvin Harrison	.75	.30
❑ 45	Byron Leftwich	.50	.20
❑ 46	Greg Jones	.40	.15
❑ 47	Ernest Wilford	.40	.15
❑ 48	Trent Green	.50	.20
❑ 49	Larry Johnson	1.00	.40
❑ 50	Tony Gonzalez	.50	.20
❑ 51	Daunte Culpepper	.75	.30
❑ 52	Ronnie Brown	.75	.30
❑ 53	Chris Chambers	.50	.20
❑ 54	Brad Johnson	.50	.20
❑ 55	Chester Taylor	.50	.20
❑ 56	Troy Williamson	.50	.20
❑ 57	Tom Brady	1.25	.50
❑ 58	Deion Branch	.50	.20
❑ 59	Corey Dillon	.50	.20
❑ 60	Drew Brees	.75	.30
❑ 61	Deuce McAllister	.50	.20
❑ 62	Joe Horn	.50	.20
❑ 63	Eli Manning	1.00	.40
❑ 64	Tiki Barber	.75	.30
❑ 65	Plaxico Burress	.50	.20
❑ 66	Michael Strahan	.50	.20
❑ 67	Chad Pennington	.50	.20
❑ 68	Curtis Martin	.75	.30
❑ 69	Jonathan Vilma	.50	.20
❑ 70	Aaron Brooks	.50	.20
❑ 71	Randy Moss	.75	.30
❑ 72	LaMont Jordan	.50	.20
❑ 73	Donovan McNabb	.75	.30
❑ 74	Brian Westbrook	.50	.20
❑ 75	L.J. Smith	.40	.15
❑ 76	Ben Roethlisberger	1.25	.50
❑ 77	Hines Ward	.75	.30
❑ 78	Willie Parker	1.00	.40
❑ 79	LaDainian Tomlinson	1.00	.40
❑ 80	Philip Rivers	.75	.30
❑ 81	Antonio Gates	.75	.30
❑ 82	Alex Smith QB	1.00	.40
❑ 83	Antonio Bryant	.50	.20
❑ 84	Frank Gore	.75	.30
❑ 85	Matt Hasselbeck	.50	.20
❑ 86	Shaun Alexander	.75	.30
❑ 87	Nate Burleson	.50	.20
❑ 88	Julian Peterson	.40	.15
❑ 89	Torry Holt	.50	.20
❑ 90	Marc Bulger	.50	.20
❑ 91	Steven Jackson	.75	.30
❑ 92	Cadillac Williams	.75	.30
❑ 93	Chris Simms	.50	.20
❑ 94	Joey Galloway	.50	.20
❑ 95	Drew Bennett	.40	.15
❑ 96	David Givens	.50	.20
❑ 97	Chris Brown	.50	.20
❑ 98	Clinton Portis	.75	.30
❑ 99	Santana Moss	.50	.20
❑ 100	Antwaan Randle El	.50	.20
❑ 101	Todd Watkins RC	3.00	1.25
❑ 102	Damarius Bilbo RC	3.00	1.25
❑ 103	Troy Bergeron RC	3.00	1.25
❑ 104	Jerious Norwood RC	6.00	2.50
❑ 105	Adam Jennings RC	3.00	1.25
❑ 106	Haloti Ngata RC	4.00	1.50
❑ 107	Ed Hinkel RC	4.00	1.50
❑ 108	P.J. Daniels RC	3.00	1.25
❑ 109	Quinn Sypniewski RC	3.00	1.25
❑ 110	Donte Whitner RC	4.00	1.50
❑ 111	John McCargo RC	3.00	1.25
❑ 112	Chris Denney RC	2.00	.75
❑ 113	Richard Marshall RC	3.00	1.25
❑ 114	Brett Basanez RC	4.00	1.50
❑ 115	Nate Salley RC	3.00	1.25
❑ 116	Jeff King RC	3.00	1.25
❑ 117	Danieal Manning RC	4.00	1.50
❑ 118	Devin Hester RC	8.00	3.00
❑ 119	P.J. Pope RC	3.00	1.25
❑ 120	Johnathan Joseph RC	3.00	1.25
❑ 121	Andrew Whitworth RC	2.00	.75
❑ 122	Ethan Kilmer RC	4.00	1.50

❑ 123 Bennie Brazell RC	3.00	1.25
❑ 124 Erik Meyer RC	3.00	1.25
❑ 125 J.D. Runnels RC	3.00	1.25
❑ 126 Kamerion Wimbley RC	4.00	1.50
❑ 127 D'Qwell Jackson RC	3.00	1.25
❑ 128 Lawrence Vickers RC	3.00	1.25
❑ 129 Bobby Carpenter RC	4.00	1.50
❑ 130 Demetrius Summers RC	2.00	.75
❑ 131 Tony Scheffler RC	4.00	1.50
❑ 132 Domenik Hixon RC	3.00	1.25
❑ 133 Daniel Bullocks RC	4.00	1.50
❑ 134 Joe Klopfenstein RC	3.00	1.25
❑ 135 Joel Klatt RC	3.00	1.25
❑ 136 Daryn Colledge RC	4.00	1.50
❑ 137 Brandon Marshall RC	4.00	1.50
❑ 138 Brandon Williams RC	4.00	1.50
❑ 139 Ingle Martin RC	4.00	1.50
❑ 140 Matt Baker RC	4.00	1.50
❑ 141 David Anderson RC	3.00	1.25
❑ 142 Charles Spencer RC	2.00	.75
❑ 143 Wali Lundy RC	4.00	1.50
❑ 144 Mario Williams RC	6.00	2.50
❑ 145 David Kirtman RC	3.00	1.25
❑ 146 Tamba Hali RC	4.00	1.50
❑ 147 Bernard Pollard RC	3.00	1.25
❑ 148 Derrick Ross RC	3.00	1.25
❑ 149 Jeff Webb RC	3.00	1.25
❑ 150 De'Arrius Howard RC	4.00	1.50
❑ 151 Chris Hannon RC	3.00	1.25
❑ 152 Jason Allen RC	4.00	1.50
❑ 153 Devin Aromashodu RC	3.00	1.25
❑ 154 Cedric Griffin RC	3.00	1.25
❑ 155 Ryan Cook RC	3.00	1.25
❑ 156 Jason Carter RC	3.00	1.25
❑ 157 Barrick Nealy RC	3.00	1.25
❑ 158 Wendell Mathis RC	3.00	1.25
❑ 159 David Thomas RC	4.00	1.50
❑ 160 Garrett Mills RC	4.00	1.50
❑ 161 Roman Harper RC	3.00	1.25
❑ 162 Marques Colston RC	15.00	6.00
❑ 163 Travis Wilson RC	4.00	1.50
❑ 164 Anthony Mix RC	3.00	1.25
❑ 165 Nick Mangold RC	3.00	1.25
❑ 166 Brett Elliott RC	4.00	1.50
❑ 167 Antonio Cromartie RC	4.00	1.50
❑ 168 Kevin McMahan RC	3.00	1.25
❑ 169 Quadtrine Hill RC	3.00	1.25
❑ 170 Marcedes Lewis RC	4.00	1.50
❑ 171 Kent Smith RC	4.00	1.50
❑ 172 John Madsen RC	4.00	1.50
❑ 173 Charlie Whitehurst RC	5.00	2.00
❑ 174 Deuce Lutui RC	3.00	1.25
❑ 175 Jeremy Bloom RC	3.00	1.25
❑ 176 Cedric Humes RC	4.00	1.50
❑ 177 Jason Avant RC	4.00	1.50
❑ 178 Brodie Croyle RC	8.00	3.00
❑ 179 Marcus McNeill RC	3.00	1.25
❑ 180 Manny Lawson RC	4.00	1.50
❑ 181 Delanie Walker RC	3.00	1.25
❑ 182 Kelly Jennings RC	4.00	1.50
❑ 183 Darryl Tapp RC	3.00	1.25
❑ 184 Ben Obomanu RC	3.00	1.25
❑ 185 Travis Lulay RC	3.00	1.25
❑ 186 Matt Henshaw RC	3.00	1.25
❑ 187 Clinton Solomon RC	3.00	1.25
❑ 188 Marques Hagans RC	3.00	1.25
❑ 189 Davin Joseph RC	3.00	1.25
❑ 190 Jeremy Trueblood RC	3.00	1.25
❑ 191 T.J. Williams RC	4.00	1.50
❑ 192 Alan Zemaitis RC	4.00	1.50
❑ 193 Quinton Ganther RC	3.00	1.25
❑ 194 Cody Hodges RC	3.00	1.25
❑ 195 Jesse Mahelona RC	3.00	1.25
❑ 196 Rocky McIntosh RC	4.00	1.50
❑ 197 Mike Espy RC	4.00	1.50
❑ 198 Willie Reid RC	4.00	1.50
❑ 199 Jonathan Orr RC	3.00	1.25
❑ 200 Joe Rubin RC	3.00	1.25
❑ 201 A.J. Hawk AU/200* RC	60.00	30.00
❑ 202 Anthony Fasano AU RC	15.00	6.00
❑ 203 Ashton Youboty AU RC	10.00	4.00
❑ 204 Brad Smith AU RC	12.00	5.00
❑ 205 Thomas Howard AU RC	10.00	4.00
❑ 206 Will Blackmon AU RC	10.00	4.00
❑ 207 Brian Calhoun AU/200* RC	20.00	8.00
❑ 208 Terrence Whitehead AU RC	10.00	4.00
❑ 209 Brodrick Bunkley AU RC	10.00	4.00
❑ 210 Bruce Gradkowski AU RC	30.00	12.00
❑ 211 Chad Greenway AU RC	15.00	6.00
❑ 212 Chad Jackson AU/200* RC	25.00	10.00
❑ 213 Mike Bell AU RC	30.00	15.00
❑ 214 Clint Ingram AU RC	20.00	8.00
❑ 215 Josh Betts AU RC	10.00	4.00
❑ 216 D.J. Shockley AU RC	12.00	5.00
❑ 217 D.Ferguson AU RC	12.00	5.00
❑ 218 DeA.Williams AU/25* RC	250.00	150.00
❑ 219 DeMeco Ryans AU RC	12.00	5.00
❑ 220 Demetrius Williams AU RC	10.00	4.00
❑ 221 Martin Nance AU RC	10.00	4.00
❑ 222 Dominique Byrd AU RC	12.00	5.00
❑ 223 Drew Olson AU RC	10.00	4.00
❑ 224 Ernie Sims AU RC	12.00	5.00
❑ 225 Gerald Riggs AU RC	12.00	5.00
❑ 226 Greg Jennings AU RC	40.00	20.00
❑ 227 Greg Lee AU RC	10.00	4.00
❑ 228 Hank Baskett AU RC	12.00	5.00
❑ 229 Jay Cutler AU/50* RC	350.00	200.00
❑ 230 DonTrell Moore AU RC	10.00	4.00
❑ 231 Jerome Harrison AU RC	15.00	6.00
❑ 232 Jimmy Williams AU RC	12.00	5.00
❑ 233 Darnell Bing AU RC	10.00	4.00
❑ 234 Joseph Addai AU RC	100.00	50.00
❑ 235 Clemens AU/200* RC EXCH	20.00	8.00
❑ 236 Maroney AU/50* RC	200.00	100.00
❑ 237 LenDale White AU/200* RC	40.00	20.00
❑ 238 Leon Washington AU RC	25.00	10.00
❑ 239 Leonard Pope AU RC	12.00	5.00
❑ 240 Cory Rodgers AU RC	10.00	4.00
❑ 241 Darrell Hackney AU RC	10.00	4.00
❑ 242 Mathias Kiwanuka AU RC	15.00	6.00
❑ 243 Matt Leinart AU/50* RC	350.00	200.00
❑ 244 Maurice Drew AU/300* RC	60.00	30.00
❑ 245 Maurice Stovall AU/300* RC	20.00	8.00
❑ 246 Michael Huff AU/300* RC	20.00	8.00
❑ 247 Michael Robinson AU RC	20.00	8.00
❑ 248 Mike Hass AU RC	10.00	4.00
❑ 249 Omar Jacobs AU RC	10.00	4.00
❑ 250 Owen Daniels AU RC	20.00	8.00
❑ 251 Reggie Bush AU/25* RC	800.00	400.00
❑ 252 Reggie McNeal AU RC	10.00	4.00
❑ 253 S.Holmes AU/120* RC	50.00	25.00
❑ 254 Sinorice Moss AU/240* RC	30.00	15.00
❑ 255 Tarvaris Jackson AU/300* RC	50.00	25.00
❑ 256 Andre Hall AU RC	10.00	4.00
❑ 257 Tye Hill AU RC	12.00	5.00
❑ 258 V.Davis AU/100* RC EXCH	50.00	25.00
❑ 259 Vince Young AU/25* RC	500.00	300.00
❑ 260 Winston Justice AU RC	12.00	5.00

2006 Aspire

❑ COMPLETE SET (36)	25.00	10.00
❑ 1 Reggie Bush	6.00	2.50
❑ 2 Matt Leinart	4.00	1.50
❑ 3 Vince Young	4.00	1.50
❑ 4 Mario Williams	1.50	.60
❑ 5 Michael Huff	1.25	.50
❑ 6 Vernon Davis	2.00	.75
❑ 7 LenDale White	2.00	.75
❑ 8 Brodie Croyle	1.50	.60
❑ 9 Drew Olson	.75	.30
❑ 10 Maurice Drew	2.50	1.00
❑ 11 Tye Hill	1.00	.40
❑ 12 Michael Robinson	1.50	.60
❑ 13 Joseph Addai	3.00	1.25
❑ 14 Paul Pinegar	.75	.30
❑ 15 Jimmy Williams	1.00	.40
❑ 16 D.J. Shockley	1.00	.40
❑ 17 Mike Hass	1.00	.40
❑ 18 Demetrius Williams	1.25	.50
❑ 19 Reggie McNeal	.75	.30
❑ 20 Charlie Whitehurst	1.25	.50
❑ 21 Maurice Stovall	1.00	.40
❑ 22 Sinorice Moss	1.25	.50
❑ 23 Jason Avant	1.00	.40
❑ 24 Omar Jacobs	.75	.30
❑ 25 Laurence Maroney	3.00	1.25
❑ 26 Martin Nance	.75	.30
❑ 27 Leonard Pope	1.25	.50
❑ 28 Rodrique Wright	.50	.20
❑ 29 David Thomas	1.00	.40
❑ 30 Will Blackmon	.75	.30
❑ 31 Dominique Byrd	.75	.30
❑ 32 D'Brickashaw Ferguson	1.00	.40
❑ 33 Reggie Bush	6.00	2.50
❑ 34 Matt Leinart	4.00	1.50
❑ 35 Vince Young	4.00	1.50
❑ 36 Jay Cutler	4.00	1.50

1996 Press Pass

❑ COMPLETE SET (55)	20.00	7.50
❑ 1 Keyshawn Johnson	1.50	.60
❑ 2 Jonathan Ogden	.60	.25
❑ 3 Duane Clemons	.20	.07
❑ 4 Kevin Hardy	.20	.07
❑ 5 Eddie George	2.50	1.00
❑ 6 Karim Abdul-Jabbar	.60	.25
❑ 7 Terry Glenn	.60	.25
❑ 8 Leeland McElroy	.40	.15
❑ 9 Simeon Rice	.75	.30
❑ 10 Roman Oben	.20	.07
❑ 11 Daryl Gardener	.20	.07
❑ 12 Marcus Coleman	.20	.07
❑ 13 Christian Peter	.20	.07
❑ 14 Tim Biakabutuka	.60	.25
❑ 15 Eric Moulds	1.50	.60
❑ 16 Chris Darkins	.20	.07
❑ 17 Andre Johnson	.20	.07
❑ 18 Lawyer Milloy	.60	.25
❑ 19 Jon Runyan	.20	.07
❑ 20 Mike Alstott	1.50	.60
❑ 21 Jeff Hartings	.60	.25
❑ 22 Amani Toomer	1.25	.50
❑ 23 Danny Kanell	.60	.25
❑ 24 Marco Battaglia	.20	.07
❑ 25 Stephen Davis	1.50	.60
❑ 26 Johnny McWilliams	.20	.07
❑ 27 Israel Ifeanyi	.20	.07
❑ 28 Scott Slutzker	.20	.07
❑ 29 Bryant Mix	.20	.07
❑ 30 Brian Roche	.20	.07
❑ 31 Stanley Pritchett	.20	.07
❑ 32 Jerome Woods	.20	.07
❑ 33 Tommie Frazier	.40	.15
❑ 34 Stepfret Williams	.20	.07
❑ 35 Ray Mickens	.20	.07
❑ 36 Alex Van Dyke	.20	.07
❑ 37 Bobby Hoying	.60	.25
❑ 38 Tony Brackens	.60	.25
❑ 39 Dietrich Jells	.20	.07
❑ 40 Jason Odom	.20	.07
❑ 41 Randall Godfrey	.20	.07
❑ 42 Willie Anderson	.20	.07
❑ 43 Tony Banks	.60	.25
❑ 44 Michael Cheever	.20	.07
❑ 45 Je'Rod Cherry	.20	.07
❑ 46 Chris Doering	.20	.07
❑ 47 Steve Taneyhill	.20	.07
❑ 48 Kyle Wachholtz	.20	.07
❑ 49 Dusty Zeigler	.20	.07
❑ 50 Derrick Mayes	.40	.15
❑ 51 Orpheus Roye	.20	.07
❑ 52 Sedric Clark	.20	.07
❑ 53 Richard Huntley	.40	.15
❑ 54 Donnie Edwards	.60	.25
❑ 55 Zach Thomas CL	.60	.25
❑ RED Lawrence Phillips	6.00	2.50
❑ P1 Tim Biakabutuka Promo	1.00	.40

1996 Press Pass Paydirt

❑ COMPLETE SET (75)	25.00	12.50
❑ 1 Keyshawn Johnson	2.00	.75
❑ 2 Jonathan Ogden	.75	.30
❑ 3 Duane Clemons	.10	.02
❑ 4 Kevin Hardy	.30	.10
❑ 5 Eddie George	2.50	1.00
❑ 6 Karim Abdul-Jabbar	.75	.30
❑ 7 Terry Glenn	1.50	.60
❑ 8 Leeland McElroy	.30	.10
❑ 9 Simeon Rice	1.00	.40
❑ 10 Roman Oben	.10	.02
❑ 11 Daryl Gardener	.10	.02
❑ 12 Marcus Coleman	.10	.02
❑ 13 Christian Peter UER Chris Doering stamp on front	.10	.02
❑ 14 Tim Biakabutuka	.75	.30
❑ 15 Eric Moulds	.75	.30
❑ 16 Chris Darkins	.10	.02
❑ 17 Andre Johnson	.10	.02
❑ 18 Lawyer Milloy	.75	.30
❑ 19 Jon Runyan	.10	.02
❑ 20 Mike Alstott	1.50	.60
❑ 21 Jeff Hartings	.75	.30
❑ 22 Amani Toomer	1.25	.50
❑ 23 Danny Kanell	.75	.30
❑ 24 Marco Battaglia	.10	.02
❑ 25 Stephen Davis	1.50	.60
❑ 26 Johnny McWilliams	.10	.02
❑ 27 Israel Ifeanyi	.10	.02
❑ 28 Scott Slutzker	.10	.02
❑ 29 Bryant Mix	.10	.02
❑ 30 Brian Roche	.10	.02
❑ 31 Stanley Pritchett	.10	.02
❑ 32 Jerome Woods	.10	.02
❑ 33 Tommie Frazier	.30	.10
❑ 34 Stepfret Williams	.10	.02
❑ 35 Ray Mickens	.10	.02
❑ 36 Alex Van Dyke	.10	.02
❑ 37 Bobby Hoying	.75	.30
❑ 38 Tony Brackens	.75	.30
❑ 39 Dietrich Jells	.10	.02
❑ 40 Jason Odom	.10	.02
❑ 41 Randall Godfrey	.10	.02
❑ 42 Willie Anderson	.10	.02
❑ 43 Tony Banks	.75	.30
❑ 44 Michael Cheever	.10	.02
❑ 45 Je'Rod Cherry	.10	.02
❑ 46 Chris Doering	.10	.02
❑ 47 Steve Taneyhill	.10	.02
❑ 48 Kyle Wachholtz	.10	.02
❑ 49 Dusty Zeigler	.10	.02
❑ 50 Derrick Mayes	.30	.10
❑ 51 Orpheus Roye	.10	.02
❑ 52 Sedric Clark	.10	.02
❑ 53 Richard Huntley	.30	.10
❑ 54 Donnie Edwards	.75	.30
❑ 55 Zach Thomas	1.25	.50
❑ 56 Alex Molden	.10	.02
❑ 57 Jimmy Herndon	.10	.02
❑ 58 Mike Alstott	1.50	.60
❑ 59 Scott Greene	.10	.02
❑ 60 Danny Kanell	.75	.30
❑ 61 Jonathan Ogden	.75	.30
❑ 62 Simeon Rice	1.00	.40
❑ 63 Kevin Hardy	.30	.10
❑ 64 Jon Runyan	.10	.02
❑ 65 Stephen Davis	1.50	.60
❑ 66 Tim Biakabutuka	.75	.30
❑ 67 Terry Glenn	1.50	.60
❑ 68 Leeland McElroy	.30	.10
❑ 69 Eric Moulds	2.00	.75
❑ 70 Karim Abdul-Jabbar	.75	.30
❑ 71 Lawyer Milloy	.30	.10
❑ 72 Derrick Mayes	.75	.30
❑ 73 Tommie Frazier	.30	.10
❑ 74 Bobby Hoying	.75	.30
❑ 75 Kyle Wachholtz CL	.10	.02
❑ RED Lawrence Phillips	6.00	2.50

1997 Press Pass

❑ COMPLETE SET (49)	20.00	7.50
❑ 1 Orlando Pace	.50	.20
❑ 2 Warrick Dunn	1.25	.50
❑ 3 Danny Wuerffel	.50	.20
❑ 4 Darnell Autry	.20	.07
❑ 5 Troy Davis	.20	.07
❑ 6 Jake Plummer	2.00	.75
❑ 7 Corey Dillon	2.50	1.00
❑ 8 Reidel Anthony	.50	.20
❑ 9 Byron Hanspard	.30	.10
❑ 10 Tiki Barber	2.50	1.00
❑ 11 Ike Hilliard	.50	.20
❑ 12 Rae Carruth	.20	.07
❑ 13 Yatil Green	.30	.10
❑ 14 Peter Boulware	.50	.20
❑ 15 Jim Druckenmiller	.30	.10
❑ 16 Pat Barnes	.20	.07
❑ 17 Trevor Pryce	.50	.20
❑ 18 Kevin Lockett	.20	.07
❑ 19 Koy Detmer	.50	.20
❑ 20 Bryant Westbrook	.20	.07
❑ 21 Darrell Russell	.20	.07
❑ 22 Tony Gonzalez	1.25	.50
❑ 23 Shawn Springs	.30	.10
❑ 24 Chris Canty	.20	.07
❑ 25 David LaFleur	.20	.07
❑ 26 Dwayne Rudd	.20	.07
❑ 27 Bob Sapp	.50	.20
❑ 28 Mike Vrabel	2.00	.75
❑ 29 Antowain Smith	1.00	.40
❑ 30 Keith Poole	.20	.07
❑ 31 Sedrick Shaw	.30	.10
❑ 32 Tremain Mack	.20	.07
❑ 33 Matt Russell	.20	.07
❑ 34 Reinard Wilson	.30	.10
❑ 35 Marc Edwards	.30	.10
❑ 36 Greg Jones	.20	.07
❑ 37 Michael Booker	.20	.07
❑ 38 James Farrior	.50	.20
❑ 39 Danny Wuerffel HL	.30	.10
❑ 40 Troy Davis HL	.20	.07
❑ 41 Corey Dillon HL	1.00	.40
❑ 42 Jake Plummer HL	.75	.30
❑ 43 Peter Boulware HL	.30	.10
❑ 44 Eddie Robinson CO	.50	.20
❑ 45 Bobby Bowden CO	.75	.30
❑ 46 Steve Spurrier CO	1.25	.50

❑ 47 Gary Barnett CO .20 .07
❑ 48 Joe Paterno CO SP 50.00 20.00
❑ 49 Tom Osborne CO 1.25 .50
❑ 50 Jarrett Irons CL .20 .07

1998 Press Pass

❑ COMPLETE SET (50) 20.00 7.50
❑ 1 Peyton Manning 8.00 4.00
❑ 2 Ryan Leaf .50 .20
❑ 3 Charles Woodson .75 .30
❑ 4 Andre Wadsworth .30 .10
❑ 5 Randy Moss 4.00 1.50
❑ 6 Curtis Enis .25 .08
❑ 7 Tra Thomas .25 .08
❑ 8 Flozell Adams .25 .08
❑ 9 Jason Peter .25 .08
❑ 10 Brian Simmons .30 .10
❑ 11 Takeo Spikes .50 .20
❑ 12 Michael Myers .25 .08
❑ 13 Kevin Dyson .50 .20
❑ 14 Grant Wistrom .30 .10
❑ 15 Fred Taylor 1.25 .50
❑ 16 Germane Crowell .30 .10
❑ 17 Sam Cowart .30 .10
❑ 18 Anthony Simmons LB .30 .10
❑ 19 Robert Edwards .30 .10
❑ 20 Shaun Williams .30 .10
❑ 21 Phil Savoy .25 .08
❑ 22 Leonard Little .50 .20
❑ 23 Saladin McCullough .25 .08
❑ 24 Duane Starks .25 .08
❑ 25 John Avery .30 .10
❑ 26 Vonnie Holliday .50 .20
❑ 27 Tim Dwight .50 .20
❑ 28 Donovin Darius .30 .10
❑ 29 Alonzo Mayes .25 .08
❑ 30 Jerome Pathon .50 .20
❑ 31 Brian Kelly .30 .10
❑ 32 Hines Ward 2.50 1.25
❑ 33 Jacquez Green .30 .10
❑ 34 Marcus Nash .25 .08
❑ 35 Ahman Green 2.50 1.00
❑ 36 Joe Jurevicius .50 .20
❑ 37 Tavian Banks .30 .10
❑ 38 Donald Hayes .30 .10
❑ 39 Robert Holcombe .30 .10
❑ 40 E.G. Green .30 .10
❑ 41 John Dutton .25 .08
❑ 42 Skip Hicks .30 .10
❑ 43 Pat Johnson .30 .10
❑ 44 Keith Brooking .50 .20
❑ 45 Alan Faneca 1.00 .40
❑ 46 Steve Spurrier CO 1.00 .40
❑ 47 Mike Price CO .25 .08
❑ 48 Bobby Bowden CO .30 .10
❑ 49 Tom Osborne CO 1.00 .40
❑ 50 Peyton Manning CL 1.50 .60
❑ P1 Randy Moss Promo 3.00 1.25

1999 Press Pass

❑ COMPLETE SET (45) 20.00 7.50
❑ 1 Ricky Williams 1.25 .50

❑ 2 Tim Couch .60 .25
❑ 3 Champ Bailey 1.00 .40
❑ 4 Chris Claiborne .30 .10
❑ 5 Donovan McNabb 3.00 1.25
❑ 6 Edgerrin James 2.50 1.00
❑ 7 Akili Smith 1.00 .40
❑ 8 John Tait .30 .10
❑ 9 Jevon Kearse 1.50 .60
❑ 10 Torry Holt 1.50 .60
❑ 11 Troy Edwards .40 .15
❑ 12 Chris McAlister .40 .15
❑ 13 Daunte Culpepper 2.50 1.00
❑ 14 Andy Katzenmoyer .40 .15
❑ 15 David Boston .60 .25
❑ 16 Ebenezer Ekuban .40 .15
❑ 17 Peerless Price .60 .25
❑ 18 Shaun King .40 .15
❑ 19 Joe Germaine .40 .15
❑ 20 Brock Huard .60 .25
❑ 21 Michael Bishop .60 .25
❑ 22 Amos Zereoue .60 .25
❑ 23 Sedrick Irvin .30 .10
❑ 24 Autry Denson .40 .15
❑ 25 Kevin Faulk .60 .25
❑ 26 James Johnson .40 .15
❑ 27 D'Wayne Bates .40 .15
❑ 28 Kevin Johnson 1.00 .40
❑ 29 Tai Streets .60 .25
❑ 30 Craig Yeast .40 .15
❑ 31 Dre' Bly .60 .25
❑ 32 Anthony Poindexter .30 .10
❑ 33 Jared DeVries .30 .10
❑ 34 Rob Konrad .60 .25
❑ 35 Dat Nguyen .60 .25
❑ 36 Cade McNown .40 .15
❑ 37 Scott Covington .60 .25
❑ 38 Jon Jansen .30 .10
❑ 39 Rufus French .30 .10
❑ 40 Mike Rucker .60 .25
❑ 41 Aaron Gibson .30 .10
❑ 42 Kris Farris .30 .10
❑ 43 Anthony McFarland .30 .10
❑ 44 Matt Stinchcomb .40 .15
❑ 45 Dee Miller CL .30 .10

2000 Press Pass

❑ COMPLETE SET (45) 25.00 10.00
❑ 1 Peter Warrick .50 .20
❑ 2 Travis Claridge .25 .08
❑ 3 Courtney Brown .60 .25
❑ 4 Plaxico Burress 1.00 .40
❑ 5 Chad Pennington 1.00 .40
❑ 6 Thomas Jones .75 .30
❑ 7 Ron Dayne .50 .20
❑ 8 Brian Urlacher 2.00 .75
❑ 9 Corey Simon .60 .25
❑ 10 Chris Samuels .40 .15
❑ 11 Stockar McDougle .25 .08
❑ 12 Deon Grant .40 .15
❑ 13 Cosey Coleman .25 .08
❑ 14 Sylvester Morris .40 .15
❑ 15 Shyrone Stith .40 .15
❑ 16 Shaun Alexander 2.50 1.00
❑ 17 Dez White .50 .20
❑ 18 John Engelberger .40 .15
❑ 19 Tim Rattay .50 .20
❑ 20 Todd Pinkston .50 .20
❑ 21 John Abraham .50 .20
❑ 22 R.Jay Soward .40 .15
❑ 23 Shaun Ellis .50 .20
❑ 24 Keith Bulluck .50 .20
❑ 25 Jerry Porter .60 .25
❑ 26 Darren Howard .40 .15
❑ 27 Joe Hamilton .40 .15
❑ 28 Deltha O'Neal .50 .20
❑ 29 Chris Redman .40 .15
❑ 30 Deon Dyer .40 .15
❑ 31 Jamal Lewis 1.00 .40
❑ 32 Chris Hovan .40 .15
❑ 33 Raynoch Thompson .40 .15
❑ 34 Travis Taylor .50 .20
❑ 35 Sebastian Janikowski .50 .20
❑ 36 Travis Prentice .40 .15
❑ 37 Tom Brady 15.00 6.00
❑ 38 Tee Martin .50 .20
❑ 39 J.R. Redmond .40 .15
❑ 40 Dennis Northcutt .50 .20
❑ 41 Laveranues Coles .60 .25
❑ 42 Danny Farmer .40 .15
❑ 43 Darrell Jackson 1.00 .40
❑ 44 Chris McIntosh .25 .08
❑ 45 Peter Warrick CL .40 .15
❑ P1 Peter Warrick Promo 2.00 .75

2001 Press Pass

❑ COMPLETE SET (50) 25.00 10.00
❑ COMP.FACTORY SET (46) 25.00 10.00
❑ COMP.SET w/o SP's (45) 20.00 7.50
❑ 1 Michael Vick CL 2.00 .75
❑ 2 Drew Brees 3.00 1.25
❑ 3 Michael Vick 5.00 2.00
❑ 4 Chris Weinke .75 .30
❑ 5 Marques Tuiasosopo .75 .30
❑ 6 Josh Booty .75 .30
❑ 7 Josh Heupel .75 .30
❑ 8 Sage Rosenfels .75 .30
❑ 9 Mike McMahon .75 .30
❑ 10 Deuce McAllister 1.50 .60
❑ 11 LaDainian Tomlinson 12.00 5.00
❑ 12 LaMont Jordan 1.50 .60
❑ 13 James Jackson .75 .30
❑ 14 Travis Henry 1.50 .60
❑ 15 Anthony Thomas .75 .30

❑ 16	Travis Minor	.60	.25
❑ 17	Michael Bennett	.75	.30
❑ 18	Kevan Barlow	.75	.30
❑ 19	Rudi Johnson	1.50	.60
❑ 20	Santana Moss	1.50	.60
❑ 21	Quincy Morgan	.75	.30
❑ 22	Rod Gardner	.75	.30
❑ 23	David Terrell	.75	.30
❑ 24	Chris Chambers	1.50	.60
❑ 25	Reggie Wayne	2.00	.75
❑ 26	Ken-Yon Rambo	.60	.25
❑ 27	Chad Johnson	2.00	.75
❑ 28	Snoop Minnis	.60	.25
❑ 29	Freddie Mitchell	.75	.30
❑ 30	Koren Robinson	.75	.30
❑ 31	Bobby Newcombe	.60	.25
❑ 32	Robert Ferguson	.75	.30
❑ 33	Todd Heap	.75	.30
❑ 34	Steve Hutchinson	.60	.25
❑ 35	Leonard Davis	.60	.25
❑ 36	Kenyatta Walker	.40	.15
❑ 37	Justin Smith	.75	.30
❑ 38	Jamal Reynolds	.75	.30
❑ 39	Richard Seymour	.75	.30
❑ 40	Shaun Rogers	.75	.30
❑ 41	Gerard Warren	.75	.30
❑ 42	Jamar Fletcher	.60	.25
❑ 43	Gary Baxter	.60	.25
❑ 44	Nate Clements	.75	.30
❑ 45	Derrick Gibson	.60	.25
❑ 46	Drew Brees PP	6.00	2.50
❑ 47	Michael Vick PP	8.00	3.00
❑ 48	Deuce McAllister PP	4.00	1.50
❑ 49	LaDainian Tomlinson PP	15.00	6.00
❑ 50	David Terrell PP	1.00	.40

2002 Press Pass

❑	COMPLETE SET (50)	40.00	15.00
❑	COMP.SET w/o SP's (45)	25.00	10.00
❑ 1	David Carr	3.00	1.25
❑ 2	Eric Crouch	1.00	.40
❑ 3	Rohan Davey	1.00	.40
❑ 4	David Garrard	1.00	.40
❑ 5	Joey Harrington	2.00	.75
❑ 6	Kurt Kittner	.75	.30
❑ 7	David Neill	.75	.30
❑ 8	Patrick Ramsey	1.25	.50
❑ 9	Antwaan Randle El	1.50	.60
❑ 10	Damien Anderson	.75	.30
❑ 11	T.J. Duckett	1.25	.50
❑ 12	DeShaun Foster	1.00	.40
❑ 13	Lamar Gordon	1.00	.40
❑ 14	William Green	1.00	.40
❑ 15	Leonard Henry	.75	.30
❑ 16	Adrian Peterson	1.00	.40
❑ 17	Clinton Portis	4.00	1.50
❑ 18	Jonathan Wells	1.00	.40
❑ 19	Brian Westbrook	2.00	.75
❑ 20	Antonio Bryant	1.00	.40
❑ 21	Reche Caldwell	1.00	.40
❑ 22	Kelly Campbell	.75	.30
❑ 23	Andre Davis	.75	.30
❑ 24	Jabar Gaffney	1.00	.40
❑ 25	Ron Johnson	.75	.30
❑ 26	Ashley Lelie	2.00	.75
❑ 27	Josh Reed	1.00	.40
❑ 28	Cliff Russell	.75	.30
❑ 29	Donte Stallworth	2.00	.75
❑ 30	Javon Walker	2.00	.75
❑ 31	Marquise Walker	.75	.30
❑ 32	Daniel Graham	1.00	.40
❑ 33	Jeremy Shockey	4.00	1.50
❑ 34	Bryant McKinnie	.75	.30
❑ 35	Mike Pearson	.50	.20
❑ 36	Mike Williams	.75	.30
❑ 37	Phillip Buchanon	1.00	.40
❑ 38	Quentin Jammer	1.00	.40
❑ 39	Kalimba Edwards	1.00	.40
❑ 40	Julius Peppers	2.00	.75
❑ 41	Wendell Bryant	.50	.20
❑ 42	John Henderson	1.00	.40
❑ 43	Ryan Sims	1.00	.40
❑ 44	Roy Williams	2.50	1.00
❑ 45	David Carr CL	1.25	.50
❑ 46	David Carr PP	6.00	2.50
❑ 47	Joey Harrington PP	4.00	1.50
❑ 48	T.J. Duckett PP	3.00	1.25
❑ 49	Donte Stallworth PP	4.00	1.50
❑ 50	William Green PP	2.50	1.00

2003 Press Pass

❑	COMPLETE SET (50)	50.00	20.00
❑	COMP.SET w/o SP's (45)	25.00	10.00
❑ 1	Brad Banks	.75	.30
❑ 2	Kyle Boller	1.00	.40
❑ 3	Ken Dorsey	1.00	.40
❑ 4	Jason Gesser	1.00	.40
❑ 5	Rex Grossman	3.00	1.25
❑ 6	Kliff Kingsbury	.75	.30
❑ 7	Byron Leftwich	3.00	1.25
❑ 8	Carson Palmer	4.00	1.50
❑ 9	Dave Ragone	1.00	.40
❑ 10	Chris Simms	1.50	.60
❑ 11	Brian St.Pierre	1.00	.40
❑ 12	Chris Brown	1.00	.40
❑ 13	Avon Cobourne	.50	.20
❑ 14	Dahrran Diedrick	1.00	.40
❑ 15	Justin Fargas	1.00	.40
❑ 16	Earnest Graham	.75	.30
❑ 17	Larry Johnson	4.00	2.00
❑ 18	Willis McGahee	2.50	1.00
❑ 19	Musa Smith	1.00	.40
❑ 20	Onterrio Smith	1.00	.40
❑ 21	Lee Suggs	1.00	.40
❑ 22	Anquan Boldin	2.50	1.00
❑ 23	Talman Gardner	1.00	.40
❑ 24	Taylor Jacobs	.75	.30
❑ 25	Andre Johnson	2.00	.75
❑ 26	Bryant Johnson	1.00	.40
❑ 27	Brandon Lloyd	1.00	.40
❑ 28	Charles Rogers	1.00	.40
❑ 29	Kelley Washington	1.00	.40
❑ 30	Teyo Johnson	1.00	.40
❑ 31	Bennie Joppru	1.00	.40
❑ 32	Jason Witten	1.50	.60
❑ 33	Andrew Pinnock	.75	.30
❑ 34	Jordan Gross	.75	.30
❑ 35	Kwame Harris	.75	.30
❑ 36	Eric Steinbach	.75	.30
❑ 37	Brett Williams	.50	.20
❑ 38	Terence Newman	2.00	.75
❑ 39	Marcus Trufant	1.00	.40
❑ 40	Andre Woolfolk	1.00	.40
❑ 41	Terrell Suggs	1.50	.60
❑ 42	Jimmy Kennedy	1.00	.40
❑ 43	Boss Bailey	1.00	.40
❑ 44	Mike Doss	1.00	.40
❑ 45	Carson Palmer CL	1.50	.60
❑ 46	Carson Palmer PP	8.00	3.00
❑ 47	Byron Leftwich PP	6.00	2.50
❑ 48	Charles Rogers PP	2.00	.75
❑ 49	Kyle Boller PP	2.00	.75
❑ 50	Andre Johnson PP	4.00	1.50

2004 Press Pass

❑	COMPLETE SET (50)	50.00	20.00
❑	COMP.SET w/o SP's (45)	30.00	12.50
❑ 1	Casey Clausen	1.00	.40
❑ 2	Craig Krenzel	1.00	.40
❑ 3	J.P. Losman	2.00	.75
❑ 4	Eli Manning	5.00	2.00
❑ 5	Luke McCown	1.00	.40
❑ 6	John Navarre	1.00	.40
❑ 7	Cody Pickett	1.00	.40
❑ 8	Philip Rivers	3.00	1.25
❑ 9	Ben Roethlisberger	8.00	4.00
❑ 10	Matt Schaub	3.00	1.25
❑ 11	Cedric Cobbs	1.00	.40
❑ 12	Steven Jackson	3.00	1.25
❑ 13	Kevin Jones	2.50	1.00
❑ 14	Greg Jones	1.00	.40
❑ 15	Julius Jones	3.00	1.25
❑ 16	Jarrett Payton	1.00	.40
❑ 17	Chris Perry	1.50	.60
❑ 18	Michael Turner	1.25	.50
❑ 19	Quincy Wilson	.75	.30
❑ 20	Jason Wright	.50	.20
❑ 21	Bernard Berrian	1.25	.50
❑ 22	Michael Clayton	2.00	.75
❑ 23	Devard Darling	1.00	.40
❑ 24	Lee Evans	1.25	.50
❑ 25	Larry Fitzgerald	3.00	1.25
❑ 26	Devery Henderson	.75	.30
❑ 27	Michael Jenkins	1.00	.40
❑ 28	Darius Watts	1.00	.40
❑ 29	Mike Williams	2.50	1.00
❑ 30	Roy Williams WR	2.50	1.00
❑ 31	Rashaun Woods	1.00	.40
❑ 32	Ben Troupe	1.00	.40
❑ 33	Shawn Andrews	1.00	.40
❑ 34	Robert Gallery	1.00	.40
❑ 35	Tommie Harris	1.00	.40
❑ 36	Vince Wilfork	1.00	.40
❑ 37	Will Smith	1.00	.40
❑ 38	Teddy Lehman	1.00	.40
❑ 39	Jonathan Vilma	1.00	.40
❑ 40	D.J. Williams	1.00	.40
❑ 41	DeAngelo Hall	1.25	.50
❑ 42	Dunta Robinson	1.00	.40
❑ 43	Derrick Strait	1.00	.40
❑ 44	Keith Smith	.75	.30
❑ 45	Eli Manning CL	3.00	1.25
❑ 46	Eli Manning PP	10.00	4.00
❑ 47	Ben Roethlisberger PP	15.00	7.50
❑ 48	Larry Fitzgerald PP	6.00	2.50
❑ 49	Roy Williams PP	5.00	2.00
❑ 50	Philip Rivers PP	6.00	2.50

2005 Press Pass

❑ COMPLETE SET (50)	50.00	25.00
❑ COMP.SET w/o PP'S (45)	30.00	12.50
❑ POWER PICK STATED ODDS 1:14 H/R		
❑ UNPRICED HOBBY SOLO PRINT RUN 1 SET		
❑ 1 Derek Anderson	1.00	.40
❑ 2 Brock Berlin	.75	.30
❑ 3 Charlie Frye	2.00	.75
❑ 4 Gino Guidugli	.50	.20
❑ 5 David Greene	1.00	.40
❑ 6 Stefan LeFors	1.00	.40
❑ 7 Dan Orlovsky	1.25	.50
❑ 8 Kyle Orton	1.50	.60
❑ 9 Aaron Rodgers	3.00	1.25
❑ 10 Alex Smith QB	4.00	1.50
❑ 11 Andrew Walter	1.50	.60
❑ 12 Jason White	1.00	.40
❑ 13 J.J. Arrington	1.25	.50
❑ 14 Ronnie Brown	4.00	1.50
❑ 15 Anthony Davis	.75	.30
❑ 16 Kay-Jay Harris	.75	.30
❑ 17 T.A. McLendon	.50	.20
❑ 18 Ryan Moats	1.00	.40
❑ 19 Vernand Morency	1.00	.40
❑ 20 Cadillac Williams	5.00	2.00
❑ 21 Mark Bradley	1.00	.40
❑ 22 Reggie Brown	1.00	.40
❑ 23 Mark Clayton	1.25	.50
❑ 24 Braylon Edwards	3.00	1.25
❑ 25 Fred Gibson	.75	.30
❑ 26 Terrence Murphy	1.00	.40
❑ 27 J.R. Russell	.75	.30
❑ 28 Craphonso Thorpe	.75	.30
❑ 29 Roddy White	1.00	.40
❑ 30 Mike Williams	2.50	1.00
❑ 31 Troy Williamson	2.00	.75
❑ 32 Heath Miller	2.50	1.00
❑ 33 Alex Smith TE	1.00	.40
❑ 34 Khalif Barnes	.75	.30
❑ 35 Jammal Brown	1.00	.40
❑ 36 Brandon Browner	.75	.30
❑ 37 Marlin Jackson	1.00	.40
❑ 38 Carlos Rogers	1.25	.50
❑ 39 Antrel Rolle	1.00	.40
❑ 40 Dan Cody	1.00	.40
❑ 41 Erasmus James	1.00	.40
❑ 42 David Pollack	1.00	.40
❑ 43 Anttaj Hawthorne	.75	.30
❑ 44 Derrick Johnson	1.50	.60
❑ 45 Ronnie Brown CL	2.00	.75
❑ 46 Cadillac Williams PP	10.00	4.00
❑ 47 Aaron Rodgers PP	6.00	2.50
❑ 48 Alex Smith QB PP	8.00	3.00
❑ 49 Braylon Edwards PP	6.00	3.00
❑ 50 Mike Williams PP	5.00	2.00

2006 Press Pass

❑ COMPLETE SET (50)	50.00	20.00
❑ COMP.SET w/o SP's (45)	25.00	10.00
❑ POWER PICK ODDS 1:14		
❑ UNPRICED SOLO SER.#'d TO 1		
❑ 1 Brodie Croyle	1.50	.60
❑ 2 Jay Cutler	4.00	1.50
❑ 3 Omar Jacobs	.75	.30
❑ 4 Matt Leinart	4.00	1.50
❑ 5 Drew Olson	.75	.30
❑ 6 Michael Robinson	1.50	.60
❑ 7 D.J. Shockley	1.00	.40
❑ 8 Brad Smith	1.00	.40
❑ 9 Marcus Vick	.75	.30
❑ 10 Charlie Whitehurst	1.25	.50
❑ 11 Vince Young	4.00	1.50
❑ 12 Joseph Addai	3.00	1.25
❑ 13 Reggie Bush	6.00	2.50
❑ 14 Jerome Harrison	1.00	.40
❑ 15 Laurence Maroney	3.00	1.25
❑ 16 Leon Washington	1.50	.60
❑ 17 LenDale White	2.00	.75
❑ 18 DeAngelo Williams	2.50	1.00
❑ 19 Jason Avant	1.00	.40
❑ 20 Derek Hagan	1.00	.40
❑ 21 Chris Hannon	.75	.30
❑ 22 Santonio Holmes	2.00	.75
❑ 23 Chad Jackson	1.50	.60
❑ 24 Greg Lee	.75	.30
❑ 25 Sinorice Moss	1.25	.50
❑ 26 Martin Nance	.75	.30
❑ 27 Maurice Stovall	1.00	.40
❑ 28 Travis Wilson	1.00	.40
❑ 29 Dominique Byrd	.75	.30
❑ 30 Vernon Davis	2.00	.75
❑ 31 Marcedes Lewis	1.00	.40
❑ 32 Leonard Pope	1.25	.50
❑ 33 Jimmy Williams	1.00	.40
❑ 34 Darnell Bing	1.00	.40
❑ 35 Michael Huff	1.25	.50
❑ 36 Mathias Kiwanuka	1.25	.50
❑ 37 Mario Williams	1.50	.60
❑ 38 Haloti Ngata	1.00	.40
❑ 39 Gabe Watson	.75	.30
❑ 40 Rodrique Wright	.50	.20
❑ 41 D'Brickashaw Ferguson	1.00	.40
❑ 42 Chad Greenway	1.00	.40
❑ 43 A.J. Hawk	2.50	1.00
❑ 44 DeMeco Ryans	1.25	.50
❑ 45 Reggie Bush CL	3.00	1.25
❑ 46 Reggie Bush PP	12.00	5.00
❑ 47 Matt Leinart PP	8.00	3.00
❑ 48 Vince Young PP	8.00	3.00
❑ 49 A.J. Hawk PP	5.00	2.00
❑ 50 DeAngelo Williams PP	5.00	2.00

2002 Press Pass JE

❑ COMPLETE SET (45)	25.00	10.00
❑ 1 David Carr	3.00	1.25
❑ 2 Julius Peppers	2.00	.75
❑ 3 Joey Harrington	2.00	.75
❑ 4 Mike Williams	.75	.30
❑ 5 Quentin Jammer	1.00	.40
❑ 6 Ryan Sims	1.00	.40
❑ 7 Bryant McKinnie	.75	.30
❑ 8 Roy Williams	2.50	1.00
❑ 9 John Henderson	1.00	.40
❑ 10 Wendell Bryant	.50	.20
❑ 11 Donte Stallworth	2.00	.75
❑ 12 Jeremy Shockey	4.00	1.50
❑ 13 William Green	1.00	.40
❑ 14 Phillip Buchanon	1.00	.40
❑ 15 T.J. Duckett	1.25	.50
❑ 16 Ashley Lelie	2.00	.75
❑ 17 Javon Walker	2.00	.75
❑ 18 Daniel Graham	1.00	.40
❑ 19 Jerramy Stevens	1.00	.40
❑ 20 Patrick Ramsey	1.25	.50
❑ 21 Jabar Gaffney	1.00	.40
❑ 22 DeShaun Foster	1.00	.40
❑ 23 Kalimba Edwards	1.00	.40
❑ 24 Josh Reed	1.00	.40
❑ 25 Mike Pearson	.50	.20
❑ 26 Andre Davis	.75	.30
❑ 27 Reche Caldwell	1.00	.40
❑ 28 Clinton Portis	4.00	1.50
❑ 29 Maurice Morris	1.00	.40
❑ 30 Ladell Betts	1.00	.40
❑ 31 Antwaan Randle El	1.50	.60
❑ 32 Antonio Bryant	1.00	.40
❑ 33 Josh McCown	1.25	.50
❑ 34 Lamar Gordon	1.00	.40
❑ 35 Marquise Walker	.75	.30
❑ 36 Cliff Russell	.75	.30
❑ 37 Brian Westbrook	2.00	.75
❑ 38 Eric Crouch	1.00	.40
❑ 39 Jonathan Wells	1.00	.40
❑ 40 David Garrard	1.00	.40
❑ 41 Rohan Davey	1.00	.40
❑ 42 Ron Johnson	.75	.30
❑ 43 Kurt Kittner	.75	.30
❑ 44 Adrian Peterson	1.00	.40
❑ 45 David Carr CL	1.25	.50

2003 Press Pass JE

Card		
❑ COMPLETE SET (45)	25.00	10.00
❑ 1 Boss Bailey	1.00	.40
❑ 2 Brad Banks	.75	.30
❑ 3 Anquan Boldin	2.50	1.00
❑ 4 Kyle Boller	1.00	.40
❑ 5 Chris Brown	1.00	.40
❑ 6 Avon Cobourne	.50	.20
❑ 7 Ken Dorsey	1.00	.40
❑ 8 Justin Fargas	1.00	.40
❑ 9 Talman Gardner	1.00	.40
❑ 10 Jason Gesser	1.00	.40
❑ 11 Earnest Graham	.75	.30
❑ 12 Jordon Gross	.75	.30
❑ 13 Rex Grossman	3.00	1.25
❑ 14 Kwame Harris	.75	.30
❑ 15 Taylor Jacobs	.75	.30
❑ 16 Larry Johnson	4.00	2.00
❑ 17 Bryant Johnson	1.00	.40
❑ 18 Andre Johnson	2.00	.75
❑ 19 Teyo Johnson	1.00	.40
❑ 20 William Joseph	1.00	.40
❑ 21 Bennie Joppru	1.00	.40
❑ 22 Jimmy Kennedy	1.00	.40
❑ 23 Kliff Kingsbury	.75	.30
❑ 24 Byron Leftwich	3.00	1.25
❑ 25 Brandon Lloyd	1.25	.40
❑ 26 Jerome McDougle	1.00	.40
❑ 27 Willis McGahee	2.50	1.00
❑ 28 Terence Newman	2.00	.75
❑ 29 Carson Palmer	4.00	1.50
❑ 30 Terry Pierce	.75	.30
❑ 31 Dave Ragone	1.00	.40
❑ 32 DeWayne Robertson	1.00	.40
❑ 33 Charles Rogers	1.00	.40
❑ 34 Chris Simms	1.50	.60
❑ 35 Musa Smith	1.00	.40
❑ 36 Onterrio Smith	1.00	.40
❑ 37 Brian St.Pierre	1.00	.40
❑ 38 Lee Suggs	1.00	.40
❑ 39 Terrell Suggs	1.50	.60
❑ 40 Marcus Trufant	1.00	.40
❑ 41 Seneca Wallace	1.00	.40
❑ 42 Kelley Washington	1.00	.40
❑ 43 Jason Witten	1.50	.60
❑ 44 Andre Woolfolk	1.00	.40
❑ 45 Byron Leftwich CL	2.00	.75

2006 Press Pass Legends

Card		
❑ COMP.SET w/o SP's (90)	40.00	20.00
❑ UNPRICED PLATINUM PRINT RUN 1		
❑ UNPRICED PRINT PLATES SER.#'d TO 1		
❑ UNPRICED RED PRINT RUN 5		
❑ 1 Brodie Croyle	2.00	.75
❑ 2 Tarvaris Jackson	2.00	.75
❑ 3 Derek Hagan	1.25	.50
❑ 4 Devin Aromashodu	1.00	.40
❑ 5 Mathias Kiwanuka	1.50	.60
❑ 6 Omar Jacobs	1.00	.40
❑ 7 Tye Hill	1.25	.50
❑ 8 Charlie Whitehurst	1.50	.60
❑ 9 Joe Klopfenstein	1.00	.40
❑ 10 Chad Jackson	2.00	.75
❑ 11 Leon Washington	2.00	.75
❑ 12 Ernie Sims	1.50	.60
❑ 13 Leonard Pope	1.25	.50
❑ 14 D.J. Shockley	1.25	.50
❑ 15 Joseph Addai	4.00	1.50
❑ 16 Vernon Davis	2.50	1.00
❑ 17 DeAngelo Williams	3.00	1.25
❑ 18 Sinorice Moss	1.50	.60
❑ 19 Martin Nance	1.00	.40
❑ 20 Jason Avant	1.25	.50
❑ 21 Laurence Maroney	4.00	1.50
❑ 22 Brad Smith	1.25	.50
❑ 23 Mario Williams	2.00	.75
❑ 24 Brett Basanez	1.25	.50
❑ 25 Anthony Fasano	1.25	.50
❑ 26 Maurice Stovall	1.25	.50
❑ 27 Bobby Carpenter	1.25	.50
❑ 28 A.J. Hawk	3.00	1.25
❑ 29 Santonio Holmes	2.50	1.00
❑ 30 Ashton Youboty	1.25	.50
❑ 31 Travis Wilson	1.25	.50
❑ 32 Haloti Ngata	1.25	.50
❑ 33 Demetrius Williams	1.50	.60
❑ 34 Mike Hass	1.25	.50
❑ 35 Michael Robinson	2.00	.75
❑ 36 Greg Lee	1.00	.40
❑ 37 Cory Rodgers	1.25	.50
❑ 38 Michael Huff	1.50	.60
❑ 39A Vince Young Clr	5.00	2.00
❑ 39B Vince Young B&W	8.00	3.00
❑ 40 Reggie McNeal	1.00	.40
❑ 41 Bruce Gradkowski	2.00	.75
❑ 42 Darrell Hackney	1.00	.40
❑ 43 Maurice Drew	3.00	1.25
❑ 44 Marcedes Lewis	1.25	.50
❑ 45 Drew Olson	1.00	.40
❑ 46 Darnell Bing	1.25	.50
❑ 47A Reggie Bush Clr	8.00	3.00
❑ 47B Reggie Bush B&W	12.00	5.00
❑ 48 Dominique Byrd	1.00	.40
❑ 49A Matt Leinart Clr	5.00	2.00
❑ 49B Matt Leinart B&W	8.00	3.00
❑ 50 LenDale White	2.50	1.00
❑ 51A Jay Cutler Clr	5.00	2.00
❑ 51B Jay Cutler B&W	8.00	3.00
❑ 52 D'Brickashaw Ferguson	1.25	.50
❑ 53 Marcus Vick	1.00	.40
❑ 54 Jimmy Williams	1.25	.50
❑ 55 Jerome Harrison	1.25	.50
❑ 56 Ozzie Newsome	1.25	.50
❑ 57 Ken Stabler	2.00	.75
❑ 58A Bo Jackson B&W	2.00	.75
❑ 58B Bo Jackson Clr	3.00	1.25
❑ 59 Steve Spurrier	2.00	.75
❑ 60 Charlie Ward	1.25	.50
❑ 61 Fran Tarkenton	2.00	.75
❑ 62 Herschel Walker	1.25	.50
❑ 63 Billy Cannon	1.25	.50
❑ 64 Y.A. Tittle	1.50	.60
❑ 65 Roger Craig	1.50	.60
❑ 66 Tommie Frazier	1.25	.50
❑ 67 Rocky Bleier	1.50	.60
❑ 68A Tim Brown B&W	1.50	.60
❑ 68B Tim Brown Clr	2.50	1.00
❑ 69 Paul Hornung	1.50	.60
❑ 70 Joe Theismann	1.50	.60
❑ 71 Howard Cassady	1.25	.50
❑ 72 Archie Griffin	1.00	.40
❑ 73 Jack Tatum	1.00	.40
❑ 74 Paul Warfield	1.25	.50
❑ 75 Brian Bosworth	1.50	.60
❑ 76 Billy Sims	1.25	.50
❑ 77A Barry Sanders B&W	2.50	1.00
❑ 77B Barry Sanders Clr	4.00	1.50
❑ 78 Thurman Thomas	1.25	.50
❑ 79 Jack Ham	1.25	.50
❑ 80 Franco Harris	1.50	.60
❑ 81A Dan Marino B&W	3.00	1.25
❑ 81B Dan Marino Clr	5.00	2.00
❑ 82 Len Dawson	1.50	.60
❑ 83 Jim Plunkett	1.25	.50
❑ 84 Bob Lilly	1.25	.50
❑ 85 Steve Largent	1.50	.60
❑ 86 Ronnie Lott	1.25	.50
❑ 87 Bobby Bowden	1.50	.60
❑ 88 Bo Schembechler	1.00	.40
❑ 89 Darrell Royal	1.25	.50
❑ 90 Ara Parseghian	1.25	.50
❑ 91 Johnny Lattner SP	5.00	2.00
❑ 92 Desmond Howard SP	6.00	2.50

2001 Press Pass SE

Card		
❑ COMPLETE SET (45)	40.00	20.00
❑ 1 Michael Vick	5.00	2.00
❑ 2 Drew Brees	3.00	1.25
❑ 3 Quincy Carter	.75	.30
❑ 4 Marques Tuiasosopo	.75	.30
❑ 5 Chris Weinke	.75	.30
❑ 6 Sage Rosenfels	.75	.30
❑ 7 Jesse Palmer	.75	.30
❑ 8 Mike McMahon	.75	.30
❑ 9 Josh Booty	.75	.30
❑ 10 Josh Heupel	.75	.30
❑ 11 LaDainian Tomlinson	10.00	4.00
❑ 12 Deuce McAllister	1.50	.60
❑ 13 Michael Bennett	.75	.30
❑ 14 Anthony Thomas	.75	.30
❑ 15 LaMont Jordan	1.50	.60
❑ 16 Travis Henry	1.50	.60
❑ 17 James Jackson	.75	.30
❑ 18 Kevan Barlow	.75	.30
❑ 19 Travis Minor	.60	.25
❑ 20 Rudi Johnson	1.50	.60
❑ 21 David Terrell	.75	.30
❑ 22 Koren Robinson	.75	.30
❑ 23 Rod Gardner	.75	.30
❑ 24 Santana Moss	1.50	.60
❑ 25 Freddie Mitchell	.75	.30
❑ 26 Reggie Wayne	2.00	.75
❑ 27 Quincy Morgan	.75	.30
❑ 28 Chris Chambers	1.50	.60
❑ 29 Robert Ferguson	.75	.30
❑ 30 Chad Johnson	2.00	.75
❑ 31 Snoop Minnis	.60	.25
❑ 32 Todd Heap	.75	.30
❑ 33 Steve Hutchinson	.60	.25
❑ 34 Leonard Davis	.60	.25
❑ 35 Kenyatta Walker	.40	.15
❑ 36 Justin Smith	.75	.30
❑ 37 Andre Carter	.75	.30
❑ 38 Jamal Reynolds	.75	.30
❑ 39 Gerard Warren	.75	.30
❑ 40 Richard Seymour	.75	.30
❑ 41 Damione Lewis	.60	.25
❑ 42 Jamar Fletcher	.60	.25
❑ 43 Nate Clements	.75	.30

❑ 44 Derrick Gibson	.60	.25
❑ 45 David Terrell CL	.60	.25

2004 Press Pass SE

❑ COMPLETE SET (40)	30.00	15.00
❑ 1 Shawn Andrews	1.00	.40
❑ 2 Casey Clausen	1.00	.40
❑ 3 Michael Clayton	2.00	.75
❑ 4 Cedric Cobbs	1.00	.40
❑ 5 Devard Darling	1.00	.40
❑ 6 Lee Evans	1.25	.50
❑ 7 Larry Fitzgerald	3.00	1.25
❑ 8 Robert Gallery	1.00	.40
❑ 9 DeAngelo Hall	1.25	.50
❑ 10 Tommie Harris	1.00	.40
❑ 11 Ben Hartsock	1.00	.40
❑ 12 Devery Henderson	.75	.30
❑ 13 Steven Jackson	3.00	1.25
❑ 14 Michael Jenkins	1.00	.40
❑ 15 Greg Jones	1.00	.40
❑ 16 Kevin Jones	2.50	1.00
❑ 17 Teddy Lehman	1.00	.40
❑ 18 J.P. Losman	2.00	.75
❑ 19 Eli Manning	5.00	2.00
❑ 20 Mewelde Moore	1.00	.40
❑ 21 John Navarre	1.00	.40
❑ 22 Jarrett Payton	1.00	.40
❑ 23 Chris Perry	1.50	.60
❑ 24 Cody Pickett	1.00	.40
❑ 25 Philip Rivers	3.00	1.25
❑ 26 Ben Roethlisberger	8.00	4.00
❑ 27 Matt Schaub	3.00	1.25
❑ 28 Will Smith	1.00	.40
❑ 29 Ben Troupe	1.00	.40
❑ 30 Michael Turner	1.25	.50
❑ 31 Ben Watson	1.00	.40
❑ 32 Darius Watts	1.00	.40
❑ 33 Vince Wilfork	1.00	.40
❑ 34 Mike Williams	2.50	1.00
❑ 35 Reggie Williams	1.25	.50
❑ 36 Roy Williams WR	2.50	1.00
❑ 37 Quincy Wilson	.75	.30
❑ 38 Rashaun Woods	1.00	.40
❑ 39 Jason Wright	.75	.30
❑ 40 Eli Manning CL	3.00	1.25
❑ NNO Eli Manning Mini Helmet	120.00	60.00

2005 Press Pass SE

❑ COMPLETE SET (40)	25.00	10.00
❑ 1 Charlie Frye	2.00	.75
❑ 2 David Greene	1.00	.40
❑ 3 Gino Guidugli	.50	.20
❑ 4 Stefan LeFors	1.00	.40
❑ 5 Dan Orlovsky	1.25	.50
❑ 6 Kyle Orton	1.50	.60
❑ 7 Aaron Rodgers	3.00	1.25
❑ 8 Alex Smith QB	4.00	1.50
❑ 9 Andrew Walter	1.50	.60
❑ 10 Jason White	1.00	.40
❑ 11 J.J. Arrington	1.25	.50
❑ 12 Marion Barber	1.50	.60
❑ 13 Ronnie Brown	4.00	1.50
❑ 14 Anthony Davis	.75	.30
❑ 15 Ciatrick Fason	1.00	.40
❑ 16 T.A. McLendon	.50	.20
❑ 17 Vernand Morency	1.00	.40
❑ 18 Walter Reyes	.75	.30
❑ 19 Cadillac Williams	5.00	2.00
❑ 20 Mark Bradley	1.00	.40
❑ 21 Reggie Brown	1.00	.40
❑ 22 Mark Clayton	1.25	.50
❑ 23 Braylon Edwards	3.00	1.25
❑ 24 Fred Gibson	.75	.30
❑ 25 Chris Henry	1.00	.40
❑ 26 Terrence Murphy	1.00	.40
❑ 27 J.R. Russell	.75	.30
❑ 28 Craphonso Thorpe	.75	.30
❑ 29 Roddy White	1.00	.40
❑ 30 Mike Williams	2.50	1.00
❑ 31 Troy Williamson	2.00	.75
❑ 32 Heath Miller	2.50	1.00
❑ 33 Alex Smith TE	1.00	.40
❑ 34 Jammal Brown	1.00	.40
❑ 35 Marlin Jackson	1.00	.40
❑ 36 Antrel Rolle	1.00	.40
❑ 37 Dan Cody	1.00	.40
❑ 38 Derrick Johnson	1.50	.60
❑ 39 Thomas Davis	1.00	.40
❑ 40 Aaron Rodgers CL	2.00	.75

2006 Press Pass SE

❑ COMPLETE SET (40)	30.00	12.50
❑ 1 Joseph Addai	3.00	1.25
❑ 2 Jason Avant	1.00	.40
❑ 3 Reggie Bush	6.00	2.50
❑ 4 Dominique Byrd	.75	.30
❑ 5 Brodie Croyle	1.50	.60
❑ 6 Jay Cutler	4.00	1.50
❑ 7 Vernon Davis	2.00	.75
❑ 8 Maurice Drew	2.50	1.00
❑ 9 Anthony Fasano	1.00	.40
❑ 10 D'Brickashaw Ferguson	1.00	.40
❑ 11 Bruce Gradkowski	1.50	.60
❑ 12 Darrell Hackney	.75	.30
❑ 13 Derek Hagan	1.00	.40
❑ 14 Jerome Harrison	1.00	.40
❑ 15 A.J. Hawk	2.50	1.00
❑ 16 Santonio Holmes	2.00	.75
❑ 17 Michael Huff	1.25	.50
❑ 18 Chad Jackson	1.50	.60
❑ 19 Omar Jacobs	.75	.30
❑ 20 Matt Leinart	4.00	1.50
❑ 21 Marcedes Lewis	1.00	.40
❑ 22 Laurence Maroney	3.00	1.25
❑ 23 Reggie McNeal	.75	.30
❑ 24 Sinorice Moss	1.25	.50
❑ 25 Martin Nance	.75	.30
❑ 26 Haloti Ngata	1.00	.40
❑ 27 Leonard Pope	1.25	.50
❑ 28 Michael Robinson	1.50	.60
❑ 29 D.J. Shockley	1.00	.40
❑ 30 Maurice Stovall	1.00	.40
❑ 31 Marcus Vick	.75	.30
❑ 32 Leon Washington	1.50	.60
❑ 33 LenDale White	2.00	.75
❑ 34 Charlie Whitehurst	1.25	.50
❑ 35 Jimmy Williams	1.00	.40
❑ 36 Mario Williams	1.50	.60
❑ 37 DeAngelo Williams	2.50	1.00
❑ 38 Demetrius Williams	1.25	.50
❑ 39 Vince Young	4.00	1.50
❑ 40 Vince Young CL	2.00	.75

1999 SAGE

❑ COMPLETE SET (50)	30.00	15.00
❑ 1 Rahim Abdullah	.60	.25
❑ 2 Jerry Azumah	.60	.25
❑ 3 Champ Bailey	1.25	.50
❑ 4 D'Wayne Bates	.60	.25
❑ 5 Michael Bishop	1.00	.40
❑ 6 David Boston	1.00	.40
❑ 7 Fernando Bryant	.60	.25
❑ 8 Tony Bryant	.60	.25
❑ 9 Chris Claiborne	.40	.15
❑ 10 Mike Cloud	.60	.25
❑ 11 Cecil Collins	.40	.15
❑ 12 Tim Couch	1.00	.40
❑ 13 Daunte Culpepper	4.00	1.50
❑ 14 Jared DeVries	.60	.25
❑ 15 Adrian Dingle	.60	.25
❑ 16 Antuan Edwards	.60	.25
❑ 17 Troy Edwards	.60	.25
❑ 18 Kevin Faulk	1.00	.40
❑ 19 Rufus French	.40	.15
❑ 20 Martin Gramatica	.40	.15
❑ 21 Torry Holt	2.50	1.00
❑ 22 Sedrick Irvin	.40	.15
❑ 23 Edgerrin James	4.00	1.50
❑ 24 Jon Jansen	.40	.15
❑ 25 Andy Katzenmoyer	.60	.25
❑ 26 Jevon Kearse	2.50	1.00
❑ 27 Patrick Kerney	1.00	.40
❑ 28 Lamar King	.60	.25
❑ 29 Shaun King	.60	.25
❑ 30 Jim Kleinsasser	1.00	.40
❑ 31 Rob Konrad	1.00	.40
❑ 32 Brian Kuklick	.60	.25
❑ 33 Chris McAlister	.60	.25
❑ 34 Darnell McDonald	.60	.25
❑ 35 Reggie McGrew	.60	.25
❑ 36 Donovan McNabb	5.00	2.00
❑ 37 Cade McNown	.60	.25
❑ 38 Dat Nguyen	1.00	.40
❑ 39 Solomon Page	.40	.15
❑ 40 Mike Peterson	1.00	.40
❑ 41 Anthony Poindexter	.60	.25
❑ 42 Peerless Price	1.00	.40
❑ 43 Mike Rucker	1.00	.40
❑ 44 L.J. Shelton	.40	.15
❑ 45 Akili Smith	1.50	.60

❑ 46	John Tait	.40	.15
❑ 47	Fred Vinson	.60	.25
❑ 48	Al Wilson	1.00	.40
❑ 49	Antoine Winfield	.60	.25
❑ 50	Damien Woody	.60	.25

2000 SAGE

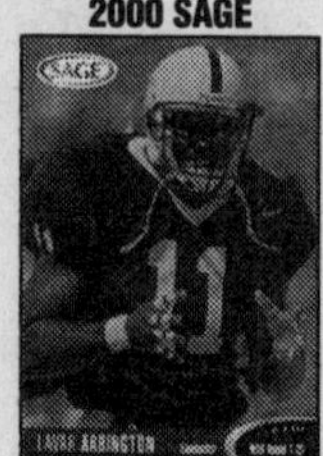

❑	COMPLETE SET (50)	15.00	6.00
❑ 1	John Abraham	.75	.30
❑ 2	Shaun Alexander	4.00	1.50
❑ 3	LaVar Arrington	3.00	1.25
❑ 4	Courtney Brown	1.00	.40
❑ 5	Keith Bulluck	.75	.30
❑ 6	Plaxico Burress	1.50	.60
❑ 7	Giovanni Carmazzi	.40	.15
❑ 8	Kwame Cavil	.40	.15
❑ 9	Cosey Coleman	.40	.15
❑ 10	Laveranues Coles	1.00	.40
❑ 11	Tim Couch	.75	.30
❑ 12	Ron Dayne	.75	.30
❑ 13	Reuben Droughns	1.00	.40
❑ 14	Shaun Ellis	.75	.30
❑ 15	John Engelberger	.60	.25
❑ 16	Danny Farmer	.60	.25
❑ 17	Dwayne Goodrich	.75	.30
❑ 18	Deon Grant	.60	.25
❑ 19	Chris Hovan	.60	.25
❑ 20	Darren Howard	.60	.25
❑ 21	Todd Husak	.75	.30
❑ 22	Thomas Jones	1.25	.50
❑ 23	Curtis Keaton	.60	.25
❑ 24	Jamal Lewis	1.50	.60
❑ 25	Anthony Lucas	.40	.15
❑ 26	Tee Martin	.75	.30
❑ 27	Stockar McDougle	.40	.15
❑ 28	Corey Moore	.40	.15
❑ 29	Rob Morris	.60	.25
❑ 30	Sammy Morris	.60	.25
❑ 31	Sylvester Morris	.60	.25
❑ 32	Chad Pennington	2.00	.75
❑ 33	Todd Pinkston	.75	.30
❑ 34	Ahmed Plummer	.75	.30
❑ 35	Jerry Porter	1.00	.40
❑ 36	Travis Prentice	.60	.25
❑ 37	Tim Rattay	.75	.30
❑ 38	Chris Redman	.60	.25
❑ 39	J.R. Redmond	.60	.25
❑ 40	Chris Samuels	.60	.25
❑ 41	Brandon Short	.60	.25
❑ 42	Corey Simon	1.00	.40
❑ 43	R.Jay Soward	.60	.25
❑ 44	Shyrone Stith	.60	.25
❑ 45	Raynoch Thompson	.60	.25
❑ 46	Brian Urlacher	3.00	1.25
❑ 47	Todd Wade	.40	.15
❑ 48	Troy Walters	.75	.30
❑ 49	Dez White	.75	.30
❑ 50	Michael Wiley	.60	.25

2001 SAGE

❑	COMPLETE SET (50)	20.00	7.50
❑ 1	Will Allen	.60	.25
❑ 2	Adam Archuleta	.75	.30
❑ 3	Jeff Backus	.60	.25
❑ 4	Alex Bannister	.60	.25
❑ 5	Gary Baxter	.60	.25
❑ 6	Michael Bennett	.60	.25
❑ 7	Josh Booty	.75	.30
❑ 8	Drew Brees	3.00	1.25
❑ 9	Correll Buckhalter	1.00	.40
❑ 10	Quincy Carter	.75	.30
❑ 11	Chris Chambers	1.50	.60
❑ 12	Alge Crumpler	1.00	.40
❑ 13	Andre Dyson	.40	.15
❑ 14	Robert Ferguson	.75	.30
❑ 15	Jamar Fletcher	.60	.25
❑ 16	Rod Gardner	.75	.30
❑ 17	Reggie Germany	.60	.25
❑ 18	Derrick Gibson	.60	.25
❑ 19	Casey Hampton	.75	.30
❑ 20	Tim Hasselbeck	.75	.30
❑ 21	Todd Heap	.75	.30
❑ 22	Travis Henry	1.50	.60
❑ 23	Josh Heupel	.75	.30
❑ 24	Willie Howard	.60	.25
❑ 25	Steve Hutchinson	.60	.25
❑ 26	James Jackson	.75	.30
❑ 27	Rudi Johnson	1.50	.60
❑ 28	LaMont Jordan	1.50	.60
❑ 29	Torrance Marshall	.75	.30
❑ 30	Deuce McAllister	1.50	.60
❑ 31	Willie Middlebrooks	.60	.25
❑ 32	Quincy Morgan	.75	.30
❑ 33	Santana Moss	1.50	.60
❑ 34	Jesse Palmer	.75	.30
❑ 35	Carlos Polk	.40	.15
❑ 36	Ken-Yon Rambo	.60	.25
❑ 37	Jamal Reynolds	.75	.30
❑ 38	Koren Robinson	.75	.30
❑ 39	Richard Seymour	.75	.30
❑ 40	Justin Smith	.75	.30
❑ 41	Fred Smoot	.75	.30
❑ 42	Marcus Stroud	.75	.30
❑ 43	David Terrell	.75	.30
❑ 44	LaDainian Tomlinson	10.00	4.00
❑ 45	Ja'Mar Toombs	.60	.25
❑ 46	Michael Vick	5.00	2.00
❑ 47	Kenyatta Walker	.40	.15
❑ 48	Gerard Warren	.75	.30
❑ 49	Reggie Wayne	2.00	.75
❑ 50	Jamie Winborn	.60	.25

2002 SAGE

❑	COMPLETE SET (45)	40.00	15.00
❑ 1	Ladell Betts	1.50	.60
❑ 2	Antonio Bryant	1.50	.60
❑ 3	Reche Caldwell	1.50	.60
❑ 4	Kelly Campbell	1.25	.50
❑ 5	David Carr	5.00	2.00
❑ 6	Tim Carter	1.25	.50
❑ 7	Eric Crouch	1.50	.60
❑ 8	Ronald Curr	1.50	.60
❑ 9	Rohan Davey	1.50	.60
❑ 10	Andre Davis	1.25	.50
❑ 11	T.J. Duckett	2.00	.75
❑ 12	Randy Fasani	1.25	.50
❑ 13	DeShaun Foster	1.50	.60
❑ 14	Dwight Freeney	2.50	1.00
❑ 15	Jabar Gaffney	1.50	.60
❑ 16	Lamar Gordon	1.50	.60
❑ 17	Daniel Graham	1.50	.60
❑ 18	Joey Harrington	3.00	1.25
❑ 19	Napoleon Harri	1.50	.60
❑ 20	Albert Haynesworth	1.25	.50
❑ 21	John Henderson	5.00	2.00
❑ 22	Chad Hutchinson	1.25	.50
❑ 23	Quentin Jammer	1.50	.60
❑ 24	Ron Johnson	1.25	.50
❑ 25	Kurt Kittner	1.25	.50
❑ 26	Ashley Lelie	3.00	1.25
❑ 27	Bryant McKinnie	1.25	.50
❑ 28	Maurice Morris	1.50	.60
❑ 29	David Neill	1.25	.50
❑ 30	J.T. O'Sullivan	1.25	.50
❑ 31	Brian Poli-Dixon	1.25	.50
❑ 32	Clinton Portis	6.00	2.50
❑ 33	Patrick Ramsey	2.00	.75
❑ 34	Josh Reed	1.50	.60
❑ 35	Cliff Russell	1.25	.50
❑ 36	Lito Sheppard	1.50	.60
❑ 37	Jeremy Shockey	6.00	2.50
❑ 38	Luke Staley	1.25	.50
❑ 39	Donte Stallworth	3.00	1.25
❑ 40	Travis Stephens	1.25	.50
❑ 41	Chester Taylor	2.50	1.00
❑ 42	Larry Tripplett	.75	.30
❑ 43	Javon Walker	3.00	1.25
❑ 44	Marquise Walker	1.25	.50
❑ 45	Jonathan Wells	1.50	.60

2003 SAGE

❑	COMPLETE SET (45)	25.00	10.00
❑ 1	Sam Aiken	1.25	.50
❑ 2	Boss Bailey	1.50	.60
❑ 3	Brad Banks	2.00	.75
❑ 4	Tully Banta-Cain	1.25	.50
❑ 5	Amaz Battle	1.50	.60
❑ 6	Ronald Bellamy	1.25	.50
❑ 7	Kyle Boller	1.50	.60
❑ 8	Chris Brown	1.50	.60
❑ 9	Tyrone Calico	1.50	.60
❑ 10	Dallas Clark	1.50	.60
❑ 11	Kevin Curtis	1.50	.60
❑ 12	Sammy Davis	1.50	.60
❑ 13	Dahrran Diedrick	1.50	.60
❑ 14	Ken Dorsey	1.50	.60
❑ 15	Justin Fargas	1.50	.60
❑ 16	Justin Gage	1.50	.60
❑ 17	Jason Gesser	1.50	.60
❑ 18	Cie Grant	1.50	.60
❑ 19	Rex Grossman	5.00	2.00
❑ 20	E.J. Henderson	1.50	.60
❑ 21	Taylor Jacobs	1.25	.50
❑ 22	Bryant Johnson	1.50	.60
❑ 23	Larry Johnson	6.00	3.00

❑ 24 Teyo Johnson 1.50 .60
❑ 25 Kliff Kingsbury 1.25 .50
❑ 26 Brandon Lloyd 1.50 .60
❑ 27 Rashean Mathis 1.25 .50
❑ 28 Jerome McDougle 1.50 .60
❑ 29 Willis McGahee 4.00 1.50
❑ 30 Billy McMullen 1.25 .50
❑ 31 Terence Newman 3.00 1.25
❑ 32 Donnie Nickey 1.25 .50
❑ 33 Terry Pierce 1.25 .50
❑ 34 Dave Ragone 1.50 .60
❑ 35 Charles Rogers 1.50 .60
❑ 36 Chris Simms 2.50 1.00
❑ 37 Musa Smith 1.50 .60
❑ 38 Lee Suggs 1.50 .60
❑ 39 Terrell Suggs 2.50 1.00
❑ 40 Marcus Trufant 1.50 .60
❑ 41 Seneca Wallace 1.50 .60
❑ 42 Kelley Washington 1.50 .60
❑ 43 Matt Wilhelm 1.50 .60
❑ 44 Jason Witten 2.50 1.00
❑ 45 George Wrighster 1.25 .50

2004 SAGE

❑ COMPLETE SET (46) 30.00 12.50
❑ STATED PRINT RUN 3200 SETS
❑ 1 Tatum Bell 2.50 1.00
❑ 2 Bernard Berrian 1.50 .60
❑ 3 Michael Boulware 1.25 .50
❑ 4 Drew Carter 1.25 .50
❑ 5 Maurice Clarett 1.50 .60
❑ 6 Casey Clausen 1.25 .50
❑ 7 Michael Clayton 2.50 1.00
❑ 8 Chris Collins 1.00 .40
❑ 9 Karlos Dansby 1.25 .50
❑ 10 Devard Darling 1.25 .50
❑ 11 Lee Evans 1.50 .60
❑ 12 Clarence Farmer 1.00 .40
❑ 13 Chris Gamble 1.25 .50
❑ 14 Jake Grove 1.00 .40
❑ 15 DeAngelo Hall 1.50 .60
❑ 16 Josh Harris 1.25 .50
❑ 17 Tommie Harris 1.25 .50
❑ 18 Devery Henderson 1.00 .40
❑ 19 Steven Jackson 4.00 1.50
❑ 20 Michael Jenkins 1.25 .50
❑ 21 Greg Jones 1.25 .50
❑ 22 Kevin Jones 3.00 1.25
❑ 23 Sean Jones 1.00 .40
❑ 24 Derrick Knight 1.00 .40
❑ 25 Craig Krenzel 1.25 .50
❑ 26 Jared Lorenzen 1.00 .40
❑ 27 Eli Manning 6.00 2.50
❑ 28 John Navarre 1.25 .50
❑ 29 Chris Perry 1.50 .60
❑ 30 Cody Pickett 1.25 .50
❑ 31 Will Poole 1.25 .50
❑ 32 Philip Rivers 4.00 1.50
❑ 33 Ell Roberson 1.25 .50
❑ 34 Dunta Robinson 1.25 .50
❑ 35 Ben Roethlisberger 10.00 5.00
❑ 36 Rod Rutherford 1.00 .40
❑ 37 P.K. Sam 1.00 .40
❑ 38 Matt Schaub 4.00 1.50
❑ 39 Will Smith 1.25 .50
❑ 40 Jeff Smoker 1.25 .50
❑ 41 Ben Troupe 1.25 .50
❑ 42 Ernest Wilford 1.25 .50
❑ 43 Reggie Williams 1.25 .50
❑ 44 Roy Williams WR 3.00 1.25
❑ 45 Quincy Wilson 1.00 .40
❑ 46 Rashaun Woods 1.25 .50

2005 SAGE

❑ COMPLETE SET (54) 30.00 12.50
❑ 1 Derek Anderson 1.25 .50
❑ 2 J.J. Arrington 1.50 .60
❑ 3 Marion Barber 2.00 .75
❑ 4 Brock Berlin 1.00 .40
❑ 5 Jammal Brown 1.25 .50
❑ 6 Reggie Brown 1.25 .50
❑ 7 Ronnie Brown 5.00 2.00
❑ 8 Jason Campbell 2.00 .75
❑ 9 Mark Clayton 1.50 .60
❑ 10 Channing Crowder 1.25 .50
❑ 11 Anthony Davis 1.00 .40
❑ 12 Josh Davis 1.00 .40
❑ 13 Thomas Davis 1.25 .50
❑ 14 Ciatrick Fason 1.25 .50
❑ 15 Ryan Fitzpatrick 1.25 .50
❑ 16 Charlie Frye 2.50 1.00
❑ 17 Fred Gibson 1.00 .40
❑ 18 Johnathan Goddard 1.00 .40
❑ 19 Frank Gore 2.50 1.00
❑ 20 David Greene 1.25 .50
❑ 21 Kay-Jay Harris 1.00 .40
❑ 22 Marlin Jackson 1.25 .50
❑ 23 Brandon Jacobs 1.50 .60
❑ 24 Derrick Johnson 1.50 .60
❑ 25 Matt Jones 3.00 1.25
❑ 26 T.A. McLendon 1.00 .40
❑ 27 Adrian McPherson 1.25 .50
❑ 28 Justin Miller 1.00 .40
❑ 29 Vernand Morency 1.25 .50
❑ 30 Terrence Murphy 1.25 .50
❑ 31 Dan Orlovsky 1.50 .60
❑ 32 Kyle Orton 2.00 .75
❑ 33 Roscoe Parrish 1.25 .50
❑ 34 Brodney Pool 1.25 .50
❑ 35 Dante Ridgeway 1.00 .40
❑ 36 Chris Rix 1.00 .40
❑ 37 Aaron Rodgers 4.00 1.50
❑ 38 Carlos Rogers 1.50 .60
❑ 39 J.R. Russell 1.00 .40
❑ 40 Alex Smith TE 1.25 .50
❑ 41 Alex Smith QB 5.00 2.00
❑ 42 Taylor Stubblefield 1.00 .40
❑ 43 Craphonso Thorpe 1.00 .40
❑ 44 Andrew Walter 2.00 .75
❑ 45 DeMarcus Ware 2.00 .75
❑ 46 Fabian Washington 1.25 .50
❑ 47 Corey Webster 1.25 .50
❑ 48 Jason White 1.25 .50
❑ 49 Roddy White 1.25 .50
❑ 50 Cadillac Williams 6.00 2.50
❑ 51 Troy Williamson 2.50 1.00
❑ 52 Maurice Clarett 1.25 .50
❑ 53 Ben Roethlisberger 4.00 1.50
❑ 54 Antrel Rolle 1.25 .50

2000 SAGE HIT

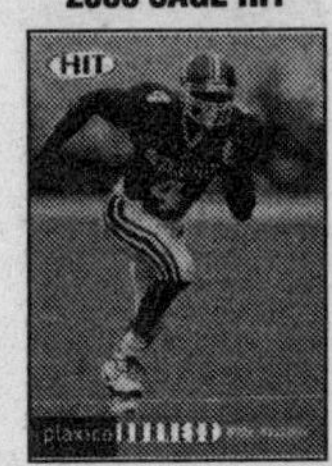

❑ COMPLETE SET (50) 25.00 10.00
❑ 1 Jerry Porter 1.00 .40
❑ 2 Tim Couch .75 .30
❑ 3 Chris Samuels .60 .25
❑ 4 Plaxico Burress 1.50 .60
❑ 5 Michael Wiley .60 .25
❑ 6 Thomas Jones 1.25 .50
❑ 7 Chris Redman .60 .25
❑ 8 Anthony Lucas .40 .15
❑ 9 Kwame Cavil .40 .15
❑ 10 Chad Pennington 2.00 .75
❑ 11 LaVar Arrington 4.00 1.50
❑ 12 Giovanni Carmazzi .40 .15
❑ 13 Tim Rattay .75 .30
❑ 14 Laveranues Coles 1.00 .40
❑ 15 Mario Edwards .60 .25
❑ 16 John Engelberger .60 .25
❑ 17 Tee Martin .75 .30
❑ 18 R.Jay Soward .60 .25
❑ 19 Ahmed Plummer .75 .30
❑ 20 Na'il Diggs .60 .25
❑ 21 J.R. Redmond .60 .25
❑ 22 Dez White .75 .30
❑ 23 Reuben Droughns 1.00 .40
❑ 24 Sylvester Morris .60 .25
❑ 25 Cosey Coleman .40 .15
❑ 26 Corey Moore .40 .15
❑ 27 Curtis Keaton .60 .25
❑ 28 Danny Farmer .60 .25
❑ 29 Travis Claridge .40 .15
❑ 30 Troy Walters .75 .30
❑ 31 Jamal Lewis 1.50 .60
❑ 32 Shaun King .40 .15
❑ 33 Ron Dayne .75 .30
❑ 34 Keith Bulluck .75 .30
❑ 35 Corey Simon 1.00 .40
❑ 36 Deon Dyer .60 .25
❑ 37 Shaun Alexander 4.00 1.50
❑ 38 Shyrone Stith .60 .25
❑ 39 Shaun Ellis .75 .30
❑ 40 Todd Pinkston .75 .30
❑ 41 Travis Prentice .60 .25
❑ 42 Chris Hovan .60 .25
❑ 43 Brandon Short .60 .25
❑ 44 Brian Urlacher 3.00 1.25
❑ 45 Rob Morris .75 .30
❑ 46 Raynoch Thompson .60 .25
❑ 47 Deon Grant .60 .25
❑ 48 Stockar McDougle .40 .15
❑ 49 Darren Howard .60 .25
❑ 50 Courtney Brown 1.00 .40

2001 SAGE HIT

❑ COMPLETE SET (50)	25.00	10.00
❑ 1 David Terrell	.75	.30
❑ 2 Jamar Fletcher	.60	.25
❑ 3 Koren Robinson	.75	.30
❑ 4 Ken-Yon Rambo	.60	.25
❑ 5 LaDainian Tomlinson	8.00	4.00
❑ 6 Santana Moss	1.50	.60
❑ 7 Michael Vick	5.00	2.00
❑ 8 Steve Hutchinson	.60	.25
❑ 9 Robert Ferguson	.75	.30
❑ 10 Torrance Marshall	.75	.30
❑ 11 Scotty Anderson	.75	.30
❑ 12 Derrick Gibson	.60	.25
❑ 13 Marcus Stroud	.75	.30
❑ 14 Josh Heupel	.75	.30
❑ 15 Drew Brees	3.00	1.25
❑ 16 Gerard Warren	.75	.30
❑ 17 Quincy Carter	.75	.30
❑ 18 Gary Baxter	.60	.25
❑ 19 Alex Bannister	.60	.25
❑ 20 Travis Henry	1.50	.60
❑ 21 Andre Dyson	.40	.15
❑ 22 Deuce McAllister	1.50	.60
❑ 23 Rod Gardner	.75	.30
❑ 24 Jamie Winborn	.60	.25
❑ 25 Will Allen	.60	.25
❑ 26 Kenyatta Walker	.40	.15
❑ 27 Tim Hasselbeck	.75	.30
❑ 28 Alge Crumpler	1.00	.40
❑ 30 LaMont Jordan	1.50	.60
❑ 31 Jeff Backus	.60	.25
❑ 32 Rudi Johnson	1.50	.60
❑ 33 Willie Howard	.60	.25
❑ 34 Josh Booty	.75	.30
❑ 35 Todd Heap	.75	.30
❑ 36 Correll Buckhalter	1.00	.40
❑ 37 Jesse Palmer	.75	.30
❑ 38 Carlos Polk	.40	.15
❑ 39 Richard Seymour	.75	.30
❑ 40 Adam Archuleta	.75	.30
❑ 41 James Jackson	.75	.30
❑ 42 Willie Middlebrooks	.60	.25
❑ 43 Ja'Mar Toombs	.60	.25
❑ 44 Chris Chambers	1.50	.60
❑ 45 Reggie Germany	.60	.25
❑ 46 Casey Hampton	.75	.30
❑ 47 Reggie Wayne	2.00	.75
❑ 48 Jamal Reynolds	.75	.30
❑ 49 Justin Smith	.75	.30
❑ 50 Quincy Morgan	.75	.30

2002 SAGE HIT

❑ COMPLETE SET (48)	30.00	12.50
❑ 1 John Henderson	1.25	.50
❑ 2 Tim Carter	1.00	.40
❑ 3 Joey Harrington	2.50	1.00
❑ 4 Marquise Walker	1.00	.40
❑ 5 Quentin Jammer	1.25	.50
❑ 6 Rohan Davey	1.25	.50
❑ 7A Eric Crouch QB	1.25	.50
❑ 7B Eric Crouch RB	1.25	.50
❑ 8 David Carr	4.00	1.50
❑ 9 Maurice Morris	1.25	.50
❑ 10 Jabar Gaffney	1.25	.50
❑ 11 David Neill	1.00	.40
❑ 12 Randy Fasani	1.00	.40
❑ 13 Alex Brown	1.25	.50
❑ 14 J.T. O'Sullivan	1.00	.40
❑ 15 Kurt Kittner	1.00	.40
❑ 16 Ashley Lelie	2.50	1.00
❑ 17 Reche Caldwell	1.25	.50
❑ 18 T.J. Duckett	1.50	.60
❑ 19 Chester Taylor	2.50	1.00
❑ 20 Jonathan Wells	1.25	.50
❑ 21 Kelly Campbell	1.00	.40
❑ 22 Bryant McKinnie	1.00	.40
❑ 23 Lito Sheppard	1.25	.50
❑ 24 Donte Stallworth	2.50	1.00
❑ 25 Josh Reed	1.25	.50
❑ 26 DeShaun Foster	1.25	.50
❑ 27 Patrick Ramsey	1.50	.60
❑ 28 Clinton Portis	5.00	2.00
❑ 29 Albert Haynesworth	1.00	.40
❑ 31 Cliff Russell	1.00	.40
❑ 32 Luke Staley	1.00	.40
❑ 33 Ron Johnson	1.00	.40
❑ 34 Travis Stephens	1.00	.40
❑ 35 Chad Hutchinson	1.00	.40
❑ 36 Lamar Gordon	1.25	.50
❑ 37 Larry Tripplett	.60	.25
❑ 38 Napoleon Harris	1.25	.50
❑ 39 Daniel Graham	1.25	.50
❑ 40 Antonio Bryant	1.25	.50
❑ 41 Javon Walker	2.50	1.00
❑ 42 Brian Poli-Dixon	1.00	.40
❑ 43 Jeremy Shockey	5.00	2.00
❑ 44 Andre Davis	1.00	.40
❑ 45 Ladell Betts	1.25	.50
❑ 46 Michael Vick	2.00	.75
❑ NNO David Carr CL	1.50	.60

2003 SAGE HIT

❑ COMPLETE SET (48)	25.00	10.00
❑ 1 Charles Rogers	1.00	.40
❑ 2 Willis McGahee	2.50	1.00
❑ 3 Arnaz Battle	1.00	.40
❑ 4 Terence Newman	2.00	.75
❑ 5 Larry Johnson	4.00	2.00

❑ 6 Taylor Jacobs	.75	.30
❑ 7 Kyle Boller	1.00	.40
❑ 8 Rex Grossman	3.00	1.25
❑ 9 Jerome McDougle	1.00	.40
❑ 10 Jason Witten	1.50	.60
❑ 11 Ken Dorsey	1.00	.40
❑ 12 Justin Gage	1.00	.40
❑ 13 Andy Groom	.75	.30
❑ 14 Seneca Wallace	1.00	.40
❑ 15 Dave Ragone	1.00	.40
❑ 16 Kliff Kingsbury	.75	.30
❑ 17 Jason Gesser	1.00	.40
❑ 18 George Wrighster	.75	.30
❑ 19 Ronald Bellamy	.75	.30
❑ 20 Donnie Nickey	.75	.30
❑ 21 Billy McMullen	.75	.30
❑ 22 Lee Suggs	1.00	.40
❑ 23 Chris Brown	1.00	.40
❑ 24 Bryant Johnson	1.00	.40
❑ 25 Justin Fargas	1.00	.40
❑ 26 Brandon Lloyd	1.00	.40
❑ 27 Tyrone Calico	1.00	.40
❑ 28 Sam Aiken	.75	.30
❑ 29 Cie Grant	1.00	.40
❑ 30 Dahrran Diedrick	1.00	.40
❑ 31 Kelley Washington	1.00	.40
❑ 32 Musa Smith	1.00	.40
❑ 33 Kevin Curtis	1.00	.40
❑ 34 Terry Pierce	.75	.30
❑ 35 Matt Wilhelm	1.00	.40
❑ 36 Rashean Mathis	.75	.30
❑ 37 Brad Banks	.75	.30
❑ 38 Tully Banta-Cain	.75	.30
❑ 39 Sammy Davis	1.00	.40
❑ 40 Teyo Johnson	1.00	.40
❑ 41 Chris Simms	1.50	.60
❑ 42 E.J. Henderson	1.00	.40
❑ 43 Terrell Suggs	1.50	.60
❑ 44 Dallas Clark	1.00	.40
❑ 45 Marcus Trufant	1.00	.40
❑ 46 Boss Bailey	1.00	.40
❑ 47 David Carr	1.50	.60
❑ NNO Charles Rogers CL	1.00	.40

2004 SAGE HIT

❑ COMPLETE SET (46)	30.00	12.50
❑ 1 Reggie Williams	1.25	.50
❑ 2 Bernard Berrian	1.25	.50
❑ 3 Lee Evans	1.25	.50
❑ 4 Roy Williams WR	2.50	1.00

❑ 5	Josh Harris	1.00	.40
❑ 6	Greg Jones	1.00	.40
❑ 7	Ben Roethlisberger	8.00	4.00
❑ 8	Drew Carter	1.00	.40
❑ 9	Devery Henderson	.75	.30
❑ 10	Eli Manning	5.00	2.00
❑ 11	Karlos Dansby	1.00	.40
❑ 12	Michael Jenkins	1.00	.40
❑ 13	Maurice Clarett	1.25	.50
❑ 14	Michael Clayton	2.00	.75
❑ 15	Casey Clausen	1.00	.40
❑ 16	John Navarre	1.00	.40
❑ 17	Philip Rivers	3.00	1.25
❑ 18	Jeff Smoker	1.00	.40
❑ 19	Ernest Wilford	1.00	.40
❑ 20	Derrick Knight	.75	.30
❑ 21	Chris Gamble	1.00	.40
❑ 22	Jared Lorenzen	.75	.30
❑ 23	Chris Perry	1.50	.60
❑ 24	Rod Rutherford	.75	.30
❑ 25	Kevin Jones	2.50	1.00
❑ 26	Michael Boulware	1.00	.40
❑ 27	Tatum Bell	2.00	.75
❑ 28	Will Poole	1.00	.40
❑ 29	Jake Grove	.75	.30
❑ 30	Ell Roberson	1.00	.40
❑ 31	Devard Darling	1.00	.40
❑ 32	Dunta Robinson	1.00	.40
❑ 33	Cody Pickett	1.00	.40
❑ 34	Steven Jackson	3.00	1.25
❑ 35	Matt Schaub	3.00	1.25
❑ 36	Sean Jones	.75	.30
❑ 37	Tommie Harris	1.00	.40
❑ 38	Chris Collins	.75	.30
❑ 39	Will Smith	1.00	.40
❑ 40	DeAngelo Hall	1.25	.50
❑ 41	Rashaun Woods	1.00	.40
❑ 42	Ben Troupe	1.00	.40
❑ 43	Quincy Wilson	.75	.30
❑ 44	P.K. Sam	.75	.30
❑ 45	Clarence Farmer	.75	.30
❑ NNO	Eli Manning CL	3.00	1.25
❑ EM	Eli Manning SEC/30	50.00	20.00

2005 SAGE HIT

❑	COMPLETE SET (50)	25.00	10.00
❑ 1	Craphonso Thorpe	.75	.30
❑ 2	Derrick Johnson	1.50	.60
❑ 3	Frank Gore SP	2.50	1.00
❑ 4	Ciatrick Fason	1.00	.40
❑ 5	Charlie Frye	2.00	.75
❑ 6	Antrel Rolle	1.00	.40
❑ 7	Dan Orlovsky	1.25	.50
❑ 8	Aaron Rodgers	3.00	1.25
❑ 9	Mark Clayton	1.25	.50
❑ 10	Thomas Davis	1.00	.40
❑ 11	Alex Smith QB	4.00	1.50
❑ 12	Fred Gibson SP	1.00	.40
❑ 13	Maurice Clarett SP	1.25	.50
❑ 14	David Greene	1.00	.40
❑ 15	Carlos Rogers	1.25	.50
❑ 16	Andrew Walter	1.50	.60
❑ 17	Jason Campbell	1.50	.60
❑ 18	Jason White	1.00	.40
❑ 19	Matt Jones	2.50	1.00
❑ 20	Marion Barber SP	2.00	.75
❑ 21	Taylor Stubblefield	.75	.30
❑ 22	Jammal Brown SP	1.25	.50
❑ 23	Ronnie Brown	4.00	1.50
❑ 24	Cadillac Williams	5.00	2.00
❑ 25	Kay-Jay Harris	.75	.30
❑ 26	Reggie Brown	1.00	.40
❑ 27	Troy Williamson	2.00	.75
❑ 28	Anthony Davis	.75	.30
❑ 29	Josh Davis SP	1.00	.40
❑ 30	J.J. Arrington	1.25	.50
❑ 31	Alex Smith TE	1.00	.40
❑ 32	Corey Webster SP	1.25	.50
❑ 33	Vernand Morency	1.00	.40
❑ 34	Derek Anderson	1.00	.40
❑ 35	DeMarcus Ware SP	2.00	.75
❑ 36	Kyle Orton	1.50	.60
❑ 37	Brock Berlin	.75	.30
❑ 38	Marlin Jackson	1.00	.40
❑ 39	Channing Crowder	1.00	.40
❑ 40	Roddy White	1.00	.40
❑ 41	Roscoe Parrish	1.00	.40
❑ 42	Adrian McPherson	1.00	.40
❑ 43	Brodney Pool	1.00	.40
❑ 44	T.A. McLendon	.75	.30
❑ 45	Terrence Murphy	1.00	.40
❑ 46	Chris Rix	.75	.30
❑ 47	Ben Roethlisberger SP	4.00	1.50
❑ 48	Dante Ridgeway SP	1.00	.40
❑ 49	Justin Miller	.75	.30
❑ 50	Johnathan Goddard SP	1.00	.40
❑ ROY	Roethlisberger ROY/100	20.00	7.50

2006 SAGE HIT

❑	COMPLETE SET (55)	25.00	10.00
❑	#56 ISSUED AT 2006 ANAHEIM NATIONAL		
❑ 1	Reggie McNeal	.75	.30
❑ 2	Jimmy Williams SP	1.00	.40
❑ 3	D.J. Shockley SP	1.00	.40
❑ 4	Omar Jacobs	.75	.30
❑ 5	Reggie Bush	6.00	2.50
❑ 6	Charlie Whitehurst	1.25	.50
❑ 7	Michael Huff	1.25	.50
❑ 8	Tye Hill	1.00	.40
❑ 9	Mario Williams	1.50	.60
❑ 10	Vince Young	4.00	1.50
❑ 11	Matt Leinart UER	4.00	1.50
❑ 12	Brodie Croyle	1.50	.60
❑ 13	Paul Pinegar	.75	.30
❑ 14	Drew Olson	.75	.30
❑ 15	Martin Nance	.75	.30
❑ 16	David Thomas	1.00	.40
❑ 17	Dwayne Slay SP	.75	.30
❑ 18	Vernon Davis	2.00	.75
❑ 19	Taurean Henderson SP	1.00	.40
❑ 20	Maurice Drew	2.50	1.00
❑ 21	LenDale White	2.00	.75
❑ 22	Laurence Maroney	3.00	1.25
❑ 23	Leon Washington	1.50	.60
❑ 24	Erik Meyer SP	.75	.30
❑ 25	Maurice Stovall	1.00	.40
❑ 26	Ashton Youboty	1.00	.40
❑ 27	Devin Aromashodu	.75	.30
❑ 28	Mike Hass	1.00	.40
❑ 29	Jonathan Orr	.75	.30
❑ 30	Joseph Addai	3.00	1.25
❑ 31	Leonard Pope	1.25	.50
❑ 32	Michael Robinson	1.50	.60
❑ 33	Mike Bell	1.50	.60
❑ 34	Ernie Sims SP	1.25	.50
❑ 35	Skyler Green	1.00	.40
❑ 36	Demetrius Williams	1.25	.50
❑ 37	Winston Justice	1.00	.40
❑ 38	Sinorice Moss	1.25	.50
❑ 39	Charles Gordon SP	.75	.30
❑ 40	Gerald Riggs	1.00	.40
❑ 41	Jerome Harrison	1.00	.40
❑ 42	Bobby Carpenter	1.00	.40
❑ 43	Dominique Byrd	.75	.30
❑ 44	Bruce Gradkowski	1.50	.60
❑ 45	Rodrique Wright	.50	.20
❑ 46	D'Brickashaw Ferguson	1.00	.40
❑ 47	Daniel Bullocks SP	1.00	.40
❑ 48	Jason Avant	1.00	.40
❑ 49	Will Blackmon	.75	.30
❑ 50	Devin Hester SP	2.00	.75
❑ 51	Alan Zemaitis SP	1.00	.40
❑ 52	Hank Baskett	1.00	.40
❑ 53	Cadillac Williams ROY SP	3.00	1.25
❑ 54	Bush/Leinart CL SP	3.00	1.25
❑ 55	Vince Young CL SP	2.00	.75
❑ 56	Jay Cutler	4.00	1.50

2004 SAGE Jersey Update

❑	PREMIUM SWATCH/10 NOT PRICED		
❑ 1	Tatum Bell	15.00	6.00
❑ 2	Maurice Clarett	12.00	5.00
❑ 3	Casey Clausen	10.00	4.00
❑ 4	Lee Evans	12.00	5.00
❑ 5	Josh Harris	10.00	4.00
❑ 6	Devery Henderson	8.00	3.00
❑ 7	Michael Jenkins	12.00	5.00
❑ 8	Greg Jones	10.00	4.00
❑ 9	Kevin Jones	15.00	6.00
❑ 10	Jared Lorenzen	8.00	3.00
❑ 11	Eli Manning	30.00	12.50
❑ 12	John Navarre	10.00	4.00
❑ 13	Chris Perry	12.00	5.00
❑ 14	Cody Pickett	12.00	5.00
❑ 15	Philip Rivers	20.00	7.50
❑ 16	Ell Roberson	10.00	4.00
❑ 17	Ben Roethlisberger	50.00	25.00
❑ 18	Rod Rutherford	8.00	3.00
❑ 19	Matt Schaub	20.00	7.50
❑ 20	Jeff Smoker	10.00	4.00
❑ 21	Reggie Williams	15.00	6.00
❑ 22	Roy Williams WR	20.00	7.50
❑ 23	Quincy Wilson	8.00	3.00
❑ 24	Rashaun Woods	10.00	4.00

Acknowledgments

Every year we make active solicitations for expert input. We are particularly appreciative of the help (however extensive or cursory) provided for this volume. We receive many inquiries, comments, and questions regarding material within this book. In fact, each and every one is read and digested. Time constraints, however, prevent us from personally replying. But keep sharing your knowledge. Even though we cannot respond to each letter, you are making significant contributions to the hobby through your interest and comments.

The effort to continually refine and improve our books also involves a growing number of people and types of expertise on our home team. Our company boasts a substantial Sports Data Publishing team, which strengthens our ability to provide comprehensive analysis of the marketplace.

Our football analysts played a major part in compiling this year s book, traveling thousands of miles during the past year to attend sportscard shows and visit card shops around the United States and Canada. The Beckett Football specialists are Brian Fleischer and Dan Hitt (Senior Manager of SDP).

Dave Lee s input as Beckett Football editor this past year helped immeasurably; Rich Klein as research analyst and primary proofer also added many hours of painstaking work.

The effort was ably assisted by the rest of the SDP Team: Matt Brumley, Keith Hower, Grant Sandground (Senior Price Guide Editor), and Tim Trout.

The price-gathering and analytical talents of this fine group of hobbyists have helped make our Beckett team stronger, while making this guide and its companion monthly Price Guide more widely recognized as the hobby s most reliable and relied-upon source of pricing information.

In addition, Bill Sutherland and Soma Madhdhipitla contributed many programming improvements to make this process smoother. Also, this book could not be produced without the fine work of our prepress team. Under the leadership of Pete Adauto, Gean Paul Figari was responsible for the layout and general presentation of this book.

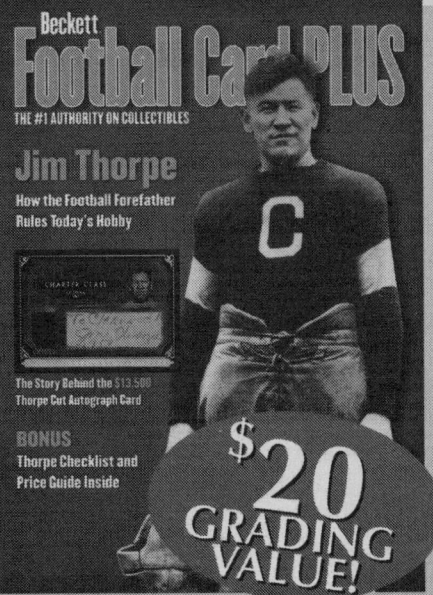

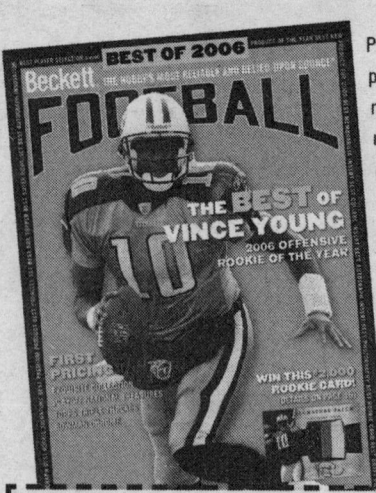